S0-AWT-179

Peterson's Graduate & Professional Programs

An Overview

2012

About Peterson's Publishing
To succeed on your lifelong educational journey, you will need accurate, dependable, and practical tools and resources. That is why Peterson's is everywhere education happens. Because whenever and however you need education content delivered, you can rely on Peterson's to provide the information, know-how, and guidance to help you reach your goals. Tools to match the right students with the right school. It's here. Personalized resources and expert guidance. It's here. Comprehensive and dependable education content—delivered whenever and however you need it. It's all here.

For more information, contact Peterson's, 2000 Lenox Drive, Lawrenceville, NJ 08648; 800-338-3282 Ext. 54229; or find us online at www.petersonspublishing.com.

Bernadette Webster, Director of Publishing; Jill C. Schwartz, Editor; Ken Britschge, Research Project Manager; Nicole Gallo, Amy L. Weber, Research Associates; Phyllis Johnson, Software Engineer; Ray Golaszewski, Publishing Operations Manager; Linda M. Williams, Composition Manager; Karen Mount, Fulfillment Coordinator; Danielle Vreeland, Shannon White, Client Relations Representatives

ISSN 1520-4359
ISBN-13: 978-0-7689-3280-5
ISBN-10: 0-7689-3280-7

Printed in the United States of America

10 9 8 7 6 5 4 3 2 1 14 13 12

Forty-sixth Edition

By producing this book on recycled paper (40% post consumer waste) 106 trees were saved.

Certified Chain of Custody

60% Certified Fiber Sourcing and
40% Post-Consumer Recycled

www.sfiprogram.org

*This label applies to the text stock.

Sustainability—Its Importance to Peterson's Publishing

What does sustainability mean to Peterson's Publishing? As a leading publisher, we are aware that our business has a direct impact on vital resources—most especially the trees that are used to make our books. Peterson's Publishing is proud that its products are certified by the Sustainable Forestry Initiative (SFI) and that all of its books are printed on paper that is 40 percent post-consumer waste using vegetable-based ink.

Being a part of the Sustainable Forestry Initiative (SFI) means that all of our vendors—from paper suppliers to printers—have undergone rigorous audits to demonstrate that they are maintaining a sustainable environment.

Peterson's Publishing continuously strives to find new ways to incorporate sustainability throughout all aspects of its business.

CONTENTS

A Note from the Peterson's Editors

The six volumes of Peterson's *Graduate and Professional Programs*, the only annually updated reference work of its kind, provide wide-ranging information on the graduate and professional programs offered by accredited colleges and universities in the United States, U.S. territories, and Canada and by those institutions outside the United States that are accredited by U.S. accrediting bodies. More than 37,000 individual academic and professional programs at nearly 2,400 institutions are listed. Peterson's *Graduate and Professional Programs* have been used for more than forty years by prospective graduate and professional students, placement counselors, faculty advisers, and all others interested in postbaccalaureate education.

Graduate & Professional Programs: An Overview contains information on institutions as a whole, while the other books in the series are devoted to specific academic and professional fields:

Graduate Programs in the Humanities, Arts & Social Sciences
Graduate Programs in the Biological Sciences
Graduate Programs in the Physical Sciences, Mathematics, Agricultural Sciences, the Environment & Natural Resources
Graduate Programs in Engineering & Applied Sciences
Graduate Programs in Business, Education, Health, Information Studies, Law & Social Work

The books may be used individually or as a set. For example, if you have chosen a field of study but do not know what institution you want to attend or if you have a college or university in mind but have not chosen an academic field of study, it is best to begin with the Overview guide.

Graduate & Professional Programs: An Overview presents several directories to help you identify programs of study that might interest you; you can then research those programs further in the other books in the series by using the Directory of Graduate and Professional Programs by Field, which lists 500 fields and gives the names of those institutions that offer graduate degree programs in each.

For geographical or financial reasons, you may be interested in attending a particular institution and will want to know what it has to offer. You should turn to the Directory of Institutions and Their Offerings, which lists the degree programs available at each institution. As in the Directory of Graduate and Professional Programs by Field, the level of degrees offered is also indicated.

All books in the series include advice on graduate education, including topics such as admissions tests, financial aid, and accreditation. **The Graduate Adviser** includes two essays and information about accreditation. The first essay, "The Admissions Process," discusses general admission requirements, admission tests, factors to consider when selecting a graduate school or program, when and how to apply, and how admission decisions are made. Special information for international students and tips for minority students are also included. The second essay, "Financial Support," is an overview of the broad range of support available at the graduate level. Fellowships, scholarships, and grants; assistantships and internships; federal and private loan programs, as well as Federal Work-Study; and the GI bill are detailed. This essay concludes with advice on applying for need-based financial aid. "Accreditation and Accrediting Agencies" gives information on accreditation and its purpose and lists institutional accrediting agencies first and then specialized accrediting agencies relevant to each volume's specific fields of study.

With information on more than 37,000 graduate programs in 500 disciplines, Peterson's *Graduate and Professional Programs* give you all the information you need about the programs that are of interest to you in three formats: **Profiles** (capsule summaries of basic information), **Displays** (information that an institution or program wants to emphasize), and **Close-Ups** (written by administrators, with more expansive information than the **Profiles**, emphasizing different aspects of the programs). By using these various formats of program information, coupled with **Appendixes** and **Indexes** covering directories and subject areas for all six books, you will find that these guides provide the most comprehensive, accurate, and up-to-date graduate study information available.

At the end of the book, you'll find a special section of ads placed by Peterson's preferred clients. Their financial support makes it possible for Peterson's Publishing to continue to provide you with the highest-quality educational exploration, test-prep, financial aid, and career-preparation resources you need to succeed on your educational journey.

Find Us on Facebook®

Join the grad school conversation on Facebook® at www.facebook.com/petersonspublishing. Peterson's expert resources are available to help you as you search for the right graduate program for you.

Peterson's publishes a full line of resources with information you need to guide you through the graduate admissions process. Peterson's publications can be found at college libraries and career centers and your local bookstore or library—or visit us on the Web at www.petersonspublishing.com. Peterson's books are now also available as eBooks.

Colleges and universities will be pleased to know that Peterson's helped you in your selection. Admissions staff members are more than happy to answer questions, address specific problems, and help in any way they can. The editors at Peterson's wish you great success in your graduate program search!

NOTICE: Certain portions of or information contained in this book have been submitted and paid for by the educational institution identified, and such institutions take full responsibility for the accuracy, timeliness, completeness, and functionality of such contents. Such portions or information include (i) each display ad that comprises a half page of information covering a single educational institution or program that appears in the section, "Profiles of Institutions Offering Graduate and Professional Work," and (ii) each two-page description or Close-Up of a graduate school or program that appears in the "Close-Ups of Institutions Offering Graduate and Professional Work" section of this guide.

THE GRADUATE ADVISER

The Admissions Process

Generalizations about graduate admissions practices are not always helpful because each institution has its own set of guidelines and procedures. Nevertheless, some broad statements can be made about the admissions process that may help you plan your strategy.

Factors Involved in Selecting a Graduate School or Program

Selecting a graduate school and a specific program of study is a complex matter. Quality of the faculty; program and course offerings; the nature, size, and location of the institution; admission requirements; cost; and the availability of financial assistance are among the many factors that affect one's choice of institution. Other considerations are job placement and achievements of the program's graduates and the institution's resources, such as libraries, laboratories, and computer facilities. If you are to make the best possible choice, you need to learn as much as you can about the schools and programs you are considering before you apply.

The following steps may help you narrow your choices.

- Talk to alumni of the programs or institutions you are considering to get their impressions of how well they were prepared for work in their fields of study.
- Remember that graduate school requirements change, so be sure to get the most up-to-date information possible.
- Talk to department faculty members and the graduate adviser at your undergraduate institution. They often have information about programs of study at other institutions.
- Visit the Web sites of the graduate schools in which you are interested to request a graduate catalog. Contact the department chair in your chosen field of study for additional information about the department and the field.
- Visit as many campuses as possible. Call ahead for an appointment with the graduate adviser in your field of interest and be sure to check out the facilities and talk to students.

General Requirements

Graduate schools and departments have requirements that applicants for admission must meet. Typically, these requirements include undergraduate transcripts (which provide information about undergraduate grade point average and course work applied toward a major), admission test scores, and letters of recommendation. Most graduate programs also ask for an essay or personal statement that describes your personal reasons for seeking graduate study. In some fields, such as art and music, portfolios or auditions may be required in addition to other evidence of talent. Some institutions require that the applicant have an undergraduate degree in the same subject as the intended graduate major.

Most institutions evaluate each applicant on the basis of the applicant's total record, and the weight accorded any given factor varies widely from institution to institution and from program to program.

The Application Process

You should begin the application process at least one year before you expect to begin your graduate study. Find out the application deadline for each institution (many are provided in the **Profile** section of this guide). Go to the institution's Web site and find out if you can apply online. If not, request a paper application form. Fill out this form thoroughly and neatly. Assume that the school needs all the information it is requesting and that the admissions officer will be sensitive to the neatness and overall quality of what you submit. Do not supply more information than the school requires.

The institution may ask at least one question that will require a three- or four-paragraph answer. Compose your response on the assumption that the admissions officer is interested in both what you think and how you express yourself. Keep your statement brief and to the point, but, at the same time, include all pertinent information about your past experiences and your educational goals. Individual statements vary greatly in style and content, which helps admissions officers differentiate among applicants. Many graduate departments give considerable weight to the statement in making their admissions decisions, so be sure to take the time to prepare a thoughtful and concise statement.

If recommendations are a part of the admissions requirements, carefully choose the individuals you ask to write them. It is generally best to ask current or former professors to write the recommendations, provided they are able to attest to your intellectual ability and motivation for doing the work required of a graduate student. It is advisable to provide stamped, preaddressed envelopes to people being asked to submit recommendations on your behalf.

Completed applications, including references, transcripts, and admission test scores, should be received at the institution by the specified date.

Be advised that institutions do not usually make admissions decisions until all materials have been received. Enclose a self-addressed postcard with your application, requesting confirmation of receipt. Allow at least ten days for the return of the postcard before making further inquiries.

If you plan to apply for financial support, it is imperative that you file your application early.

ADMISSION TESTS

The major testing program used in graduate admissions is the Graduate Record Examinations (GRE) testing program, sponsored by the GRE Board and administered by Educational Testing Service, Princeton, New Jersey.

The Graduate Record Examinations testing program consists of a General Test and eight Subject Tests. The General Test measures critical thinking, verbal reasoning, quantitative reasoning, and analytical writing skills. It is offered as an Internet-based test (iBT) in the United States, Canada, and many other countries.

The typical computer-based General Test consists of one 30-minute verbal reasoning section, one 45-minute quantitative reasoning sections, one 45-minute issue analysis (writing) section, and one 30-minute argument analysis (writing) section. In addition, an unidentified verbal or quantitative section that doesn't count toward a score may be included and an identified research section that is not scored may also be included.

The Subject Tests measure achievement and assume undergraduate majors or extensive background in the following eight disciplines:

- Biochemistry, Cell and Molecular Biology
- Biology
- Chemistry
- Computer Science
- Literature in English
- Mathematics
- Physics
- Psychology

The Subject Tests are available three times per year as paper-based administrations around the world. Testing time is approximately 2 hours and 50 minutes. You can obtain more information about the GRE by visiting the ETS Web site at www.ets.org or consulting the *GRE Information and Registration Bulletin*. The *Bulletin* can be obtained at many undergraduate colleges. You can also download it from the ETS Web site or obtain it by contacting Graduate Record Examinations, Educational Testing Service, P.O. Box 6000, Princeton, NJ 08541-6000; phone: 609-771-7670.

If you expect to apply for admission to a program that requires any of the GRE tests, you should select a test date well in advance of the application deadline. Scores on the computer-based General Test are reported within ten to fifteen days; scores on the paper-based Subject Tests are reported within six weeks.

Another testing program, the Miller Analogies Test (MAT), is administered at more than 500 Controlled Testing Centers, licensed by Harcourt Assessment, Inc., in the United States, Canada, and other countries. The MAT computer-based test is now available. Testing time is 60 minutes. The test consists of 120 partial analogies. You can obtain the *Candidate Information Booklet,* which contains a list of test centers and instructions for taking the test, from http://www.milleranalogies.com or by calling 800-622-3231 (toll-free).

Check the specific requirements of the programs to which you are applying.

How Admission Decisions Are Made

The program you apply to is directly involved in the admissions process. Although the final decision is usually made by the graduate dean (or an associate) or the faculty admissions committee, recommendations from faculty members in your intended field are important. At some institutions, an interview is incorporated into the decision process.

A Special Note for International Students

In addition to the steps already described, there are some special considerations for international students who intend to apply for graduate study in the United States. All graduate schools require an indication of competence in English. The purpose of the Test of English as a Foreign Language (TOEFL) is to evaluate the English proficiency of people who are nonnative speakers of English and want to study at colleges and universities where English is the language of instruction. The TOEFL is administered by Educational Testing Service (ETS) under the general direction of a policy board established by the College Board and the Graduate Record Examinations Board.

The TOEFL iBT assesses the four basic language skills: listening, reading, writing, and speaking. It was administered for the first time in September 2005, and ETS continues to introduce the TOEFL iBT in selected cities. The Internet-based test is administered at secure, official test centers. The testing time is approximately 4 hours. Because the TOEFL iBT includes a speaking section, the Test of Spoken English (TSE) is no longer needed.

The TOEFL is also offered in the paper-based format in areas of the world where Internet-based testing is not available. The paper-based TOEFL consists of three sections—listening comprehension, structure and written expression, and reading comprehension. The testing time is approximately 3 hours. The Test of Written English (TWE) is also given. The TWE is a 30-minute essay that measures the examinee's ability to compose in English. Examinees receive a TWE score separate from their TOEFL score. The *Information Bulletin* contains information on local fees and registration procedures.

Additional information and registration materials are available from TOEFL Services, Educational Testing Service, P.O. Box 6151, Princeton, New Jersey 08541-6151. Phone: 609-771-7100. Web site: www.toefl.org.

International students should apply especially early because of the number of steps required to complete the admissions process. Furthermore, many United States graduate schools have a limited number of spaces for international students, and many more students apply than the schools can accommodate.

International students may find financial assistance from institutions very limited. The U.S. government requires international applicants to submit a certification of support, which is a statement attesting to the applicant's financial resources. In addition, international students *must* have health insurance coverage.

Tips for Minority Students

Indicators of a university's values in terms of diversity are found both in its recruitment programs and its resources directed to student success. Important questions: Does the institution vigorously recruit minorities for its graduate programs? Is there funding available to help with the costs associated with visiting the school? Are minorities represented in the institution's brochures or Web site or on their faculty rolls? What campus-based resources or services (including assistance in locating housing or career counseling and placement) are available? Is funding available to members of underrepresented groups?

At the program level, it is particularly important for minority students to investigate the "climate" of a program under consideration. How many minority students are enrolled and how many have graduated? What opportunities are there to work with diverse faculty and mentors whose research interests match yours? How are conflicts resolved or concerns addressed? How interested are faculty in building strong and supportive relations with students? "Climate" concerns should be addressed by posing questions to various individuals, including faculty members, current students, and alumni.

Information is also available through various organizations, such as the Hispanic Association of Colleges & Universities (HACU), and publications such as *Diverse Issues in Higher Education* and *Hispanic Outlook* magazine. There are also books devoted to this topic, such as *The Multicultural Student's Guide to Colleges* by Robert Mitchell.

Financial Support

The range of financial support at the graduate level is very broad. The following descriptions will give you a general idea of what you might expect and what will be expected of you as a financial support recipient.

Fellowships, Scholarships, and Grants

These are usually outright awards of a few hundred to many thousands of dollars with no service to the institution required in return. Fellowships and scholarships are usually awarded on the basis of merit and are highly competitive. Grants are made on the basis of financial need or special talent in a field of study. Many fellowships, scholarships, and grants not only cover tuition, fees, and supplies but also include stipends for living expenses with allowances for dependents. However, the terms of each should be examined because some do not permit recipients to supplement their income with outside work. Fellowships, scholarships, and grants may vary in the number of years for which they are awarded.

In addition to the availability of these funds at the university or program level, many excellent fellowship programs are available at the national level and may be applied for before and during enrollment in a graduate program. A listing of many of these programs can be found at the Council of Graduate Schools' Web site: http://www.cgsnet.org. There is a wealth of information in the "Programs" and "Awards" sections.

Assistantships and Internships

Many graduate students receive financial support through assistantships, particularly involving teaching or research duties. It is important to recognize that such appointments should not be viewed simply as employment relationships but rather should constitute an integral and important part of a student's graduate education. As such, the appointments should be accompanied by strong faculty mentoring and increasingly responsible apprenticeship experiences. The specific nature of these appointments in a given program should be considered in selecting that graduate program.

TEACHING ASSISTANTSHIPS

These usually provide a salary and full or partial tuition remission and may also provide health benefits. Unlike fellowships, scholarships, and grants, which require no service to the institution, teaching assistantships require recipients to provide the institution with a specific amount of undergraduate teaching, ideally related to the student's field of study. Some teaching assistants are limited to grading papers, compiling bibliographies, taking notes, or monitoring laboratories. At some graduate schools, teaching assistants must carry lighter course loads than regular full-time students.

RESEARCH ASSISTANTSHIPS

These are very similar to teaching assistantships in the manner in which financial assistance is provided. The difference is that recipients are given basic research assignments in their disciplines rather than teaching responsibilities. The work required is normally related to the student's field of study; in most instances, the assistantship supports the student's thesis or dissertation research.

ADMINISTRATIVE INTERNSHIPS

These are similar to assistantships in application of financial assistance funds, but the student is given an assignment on a part-time basis, usually as a special assistant with one of the university's administrative offices. The assignment may not necessarily be directly related to the recipient's discipline.

RESIDENCE HALL AND COUNSELING ASSISTANTSHIPS

These assistantships are frequently assigned to graduate students in psychology, counseling, and social work, but they may be offered to students in other disciplines, especially if the student has worked in this capacity during his or her undergraduate years. Duties can vary from being available in a dean's office for a specific number of hours for consultation with undergraduates to living in campus residences and being responsible for both counseling and administrative tasks or advising student activity groups. Residence hall assistantships often include a room and board allowance and, in some cases, tuition assistance and stipends. Contact the Housing and Student Life Office for more information.

Health Insurance

The availability and affordability of health insurance is an important issue and one that should be considered in an applicant's choice of institution and program. While often included with assistantships and fellowships, this is not always the case and, even if provided, the benefits may be limited. It is important to note that the U.S. government requires international students to have health insurance.

The GI Bill

This provides financial assistance for students who are veterans of the United States armed forces. If you are a veteran, contact your local Veterans Administration office to determine your eligibility and to get full details about benefits. There are a number of programs that offer educational benefits to current military enlistees. Some states have tuition assistance programs for members of the National Guard. Contact the VA office at the college for more information.

Federal Work-Study Program (FWS)

Employment is another way some students finance their graduate studies. The federally funded Federal Work-Study Program provides eligible students with employment opportunities, usually in public and private nonprofit organizations. Federal funds pay up to 75 percent of the wages, with the remainder paid by the employing agency. FWS is available to graduate students who demonstrate financial need. Not all schools have these funds, and some only award them to undergraduates. Each school sets its application deadline and work-study earnings limits. Wages vary and are related to the type of work done. You must file the Free Application for Federal Student Aid (FAFSA) to be eligible for this program.

Loans

Many graduate students borrow to finance their graduate programs when other sources of assistance (which do not have to be repaid) prove insufficient. You should always read and understand the terms of any loan program before submitting your application.

FEDERAL DIRECT LOANS

Federal Direct Stafford Loans. The Federal Direct Stafford Loan Program offers low-interest loans to students with the Department of Education acting as the lender.

There are two components of the Federal Stafford Loan program. Under the *subsidized* component of the program, the federal government pays the interest on the loan while you are enrolled in graduate school on at least a half-time basis, during the six-month grace period after you drop below half-time enrollment, as well as during any period of deferment. Under the *unsubsidized* component of the program, you pay the interest on the loan from the day proceeds are issued. Eligibility for the federal subsidy is based on demonstrated financial need as determined by the financial aid office from the information you provide on the FAFSA. A cosigner is not required, since the loan is not based on creditworthiness.

Although *unsubsidized* Federal Direct Stafford Loans may not be as desirable as *subsidized* Federal Direct Stafford Loans from the student's perspective, they are a useful source of support for those who may not qualify for the subsidized loans or who need additional financial assistance.

Graduate students may borrow up to $20,500 per year through the Direct Stafford Loan Program, up to a cumulative maximum of $138,500, including undergraduate borrowing. This may include up to $8,500 in *subsidized* Direct Stafford Loans annually, depending on eligibility, up to a cumulative maximum of $65,500, including undergraduate borrowing. The amount of the loan borrowed through the *unsubsidized* Direct Stafford Loan Program equals the total amount of the loan (as much as $20,500) minus your eligibility for a *subsidized* Direct Loan (as much as $8,500). You may borrow up to the cost of attendance at the school in which you are enrolled or will attend, minus estimated financial assistance from other federal, state, and private sources, up to a maximum of $20,500.

Direct Stafford Loans made on or after July 1, 2006, carry a fixed interest rate of 6.8% both for in-school and in-repayment borrowers.

A fee is deducted from the loan proceeds upon disbursement. Loans with a first disbursement on or after July 1, 2010, have a borrower origination fee of 1 percent. The Department of Education offers a 0.5 percent origination fee rebate incentive. Borrowers must make their first twelve payments on time in order to retain the rebate.

Under the *subsidized* Federal Direct Stafford Loan Program, repayment begins six months after your last date of enrollment on at least a half-time basis. Under the *unsubsidized* program, repayment of interest begins within thirty days from disbursement of the loan proceeds, and repayment of the principal begins six months after your last enrollment on at least a half-time basis. Some borrowers may choose to defer interest payments while they are in school. The accrued interest is added to the loan balance when the borrower begins repayment. There are several repayment options.

Federal Perkins Loans. The Federal Perkins Loan is available to students demonstrating financial need and is administered directly by the school. Not all schools have these funds, and some may award them to undergraduates only. Eligibility is determined from the information you provide on the FAFSA. The school will notify you of your eligibility.

Eligible graduate students may borrow up to $6,000 per year, up to a maximum of $40,000, including undergraduate borrowing (even if your previous Perkins Loans have been repaid). The interest rate for Federal Perkins Loans is 5 percent, and no interest accrues while you remain in school at least half-time. There are no guarantee, loan, or disbursement fees. Repayment begins nine months after your last date of enrollment on at least a half-time basis and may extend over a maximum of ten years with no prepayment penalty.

Federal Direct Graduate PLUS Loans. Effective July 1, 2006, graduate and professional students are eligible for Graduate PLUS loans. This program allows students to borrow up to the cost of attendance, less any other aid received. These loans have a fixed interest rate of 7.9 percent, and interest begins to accrue at the time of disbursement. The PLUS loans do involve a credit check; a PLUS borrower may obtain a loan with a cosigner if his or her credit is not good enough. Grad PLUS loans may be deferred while a student in school and for the six months following a drop below half-time enrollment. For more information, contact your college financial aid office.

Deferring Your Federal Loan Repayments. If you borrowed under the Federal Direct Stafford Loan Program, Federal Direct PLUS Loan Program, or the Federal Perkins Loan Program for previous undergraduate or graduate study, your payments may be deferred when you return to graduate school, depending on when you borrowed and under which program.

There are other deferment options available if you are temporarily unable to repay your loan. Information about these deferments is provided at your entrance and exit interviews. If you believe you are eligible for a deferment of your loan payments, you must contact your lender or loan servicer to request a deferment. The deferment must be filed prior to the time your payment is due, and it must be refiled when it expires if you remain eligible for deferment at that time.

SUPPLEMENTAL (PRIVATE) LOANS

Many lending institutions offer supplemental loan programs and other financing plans, such as the ones described here, to students seeking additional assistance in meeting their education expenses. Some loan programs target all types of graduate students; others are designed specifically for business, law, or medical students. In addition, you can use private loans not specifically designed for education to help finance your graduate degree.

If you are considering borrowing through a supplemental or private loan program, you should carefully consider the terms and be sure to "read the fine print." Check with the program sponsor for the most current terms that will be applicable to the amounts you intend to borrow for graduate study. Most supplemental loan programs for graduate study offer unsubsidized, credit-based loans. In general, a credit-ready borrower is one who has a satisfactory credit history or no credit history at all. A creditworthy borrower generally must pass a credit test to be eligible to borrow or act as a cosigner for the loan funds.

Many supplemental loan programs have minimum and maximum annual loan limits. Some offer amounts equal to the cost of attendance minus any other aid you will receive for graduate study. If you are planning to borrow for several years of graduate study, consider whether there is a cumulative or aggregate limit on the amount you may borrow. Often this cumulative or aggregate limit will include any amounts you borrowed and have not repaid for undergraduate or previous graduate study.

The combination of the annual interest rate, loan fees, and the repayment terms you choose will determine how much you will repay over time. Compare these features in combination before you decide which loan program to use. Some loans offer interest rates that are adjusted monthly, some quarterly, some annually. Some offer interest rates that are lower during the in-school, grace, and deferment periods and then increase when you begin repayment. Some programs include a loan "origination" fee, which is usually deducted from the principal amount you receive when the loan is disbursed and must be repaid along with the interest and other principal when you graduate, withdraw from school, or drop below half-time study. Sometimes the loan fees are reduced if you borrow with a qualified cosigner. Some programs allow you to defer interest and/or principal payments while you are enrolled in graduate school. Many programs allow you to capitalize your interest payments; the interest due on your loan is added to the outstanding balance of your loan, so you don't have to repay immediately, but this increases the amount you owe. Other programs allow you to pay the interest as you go, which reduces the amount you later have to repay. The private loan market is very competitive, and your financial aid office can help you evaluate these programs.

Applying for Need-Based Financial Aid

Schools that award federal and institutional financial assistance based on need will require you to complete the FAFSA and, in some cases, an institutional financial aid application.

If you are applying for federal student assistance, you **must** complete the FAFSA. A service of the U.S. Department of Education, the FAFSA is free to all applicants. Most applicants apply online at www.fafsa.ed.gov. Paper applications are available at the financial aid office of your local college.

After your FAFSA information has been processed, you will receive a Student Aid Report (SAR). If you provided an e-mail address on the FAFSA, this will be sent to you electronically; otherwise, it will be mailed to your home address.

Follow the instructions on the SAR if you need to correct information reported on your original application. If your situation changes after you file your FAFSA, contact your financial aid officer to discuss amending your information. You can also appeal your financial aid award if you have extenuating circumstances.

If you would like more information on federal student financial aid, visit the FAFSA Web site or download the most recent version of *Funding Education Beyond High School: The Guide to Federal Student Aid* at http://studentaid.ed.gov/students/publications/student_guide/index.html. This guide is also available in Spanish.

The U.S. Department of Education also has a toll-free number for questions concerning federal student aid programs. The number is 1-800-4-FED AID (1-800-433-3243). If you are hearing impaired, call toll-free, 1-800-730-8913.

Summary

Remember that these are generalized statements about financial assistance at the graduate level. Because each institution allots its aid differently, you should communicate directly with the school and the specific department of interest to you. It is not unusual, for example, to find that an endowment vested within a specific department supports one or more fellowships. You may fit its requirements and specifications precisely.

Accreditation and Accrediting Agencies

Colleges and universities in the United States, and their individual academic and professional programs, are accredited by nongovernmental agencies concerned with monitoring the quality of education in this country. Agencies with both regional and national jurisdictions grant accreditation to institutions as a whole, while specialized bodies acting on a nationwide basis—often national professional associations—grant accreditation to departments and programs in specific fields.

Institutional and specialized accrediting agencies share the same basic concerns: the purpose an academic unit—whether university or program—has set for itself and how well it fulfills that purpose, the adequacy of its financial and other resources, the quality of its academic offerings, and the level of services it provides. Agencies that grant institutional accreditation take a broader view, of course, and examine university-wide or college-wide services with which a specialized agency may not concern itself.

Both types of agencies follow the same general procedures when considering an application for accreditation. The academic unit prepares a self-evaluation, focusing on the concerns mentioned above and usually including an assessment of both its strengths and weaknesses; a team of representatives of the accrediting body reviews this evaluation, visits the campus, and makes its own report; and finally, the accrediting body makes a decision on the application. Often, even when accreditation is granted, the agency makes a recommendation regarding how the institution or program can improve. All institutions and programs are also reviewed every few years to determine whether they continue to meet established standards; if they do not, they may lose their accreditation.

Accrediting agencies themselves are reviewed and evaluated periodically by the U.S. Department of Education and the Council for Higher Education Accreditation (CHEA). Recognized agencies adhere to certain standards and practices, and their authority in matters of accreditation is widely accepted in the educational community.

This does not mean, however, that accreditation is a simple matter, either for schools wishing to become accredited or for students deciding where to apply. Indeed, in certain fields the very meaning and methods of accreditation are the subject of a good deal of debate. For their part, those applying to graduate school should be aware of the safeguards provided by regional accreditation, especially in terms of degree acceptance and institutional longevity. Beyond this, applicants should understand the role that specialized accreditation plays in their field, as this varies considerably from one discipline to another. In certain professional fields, it is necessary to have graduated from a program that is accredited in order to be eligible for a license to practice, and in some fields the federal government also makes this a hiring requirement. In other disciplines, however, accreditation is not as essential, and there can be excellent programs that are not accredited. In fact, some programs choose not to seek accreditation, although most do.

Institutions and programs that present themselves for accreditation are sometimes granted the status of candidate for accreditation, or what is known as "preaccreditation." This may happen, for example, when an academic unit is too new to have met all the requirements for accreditation. Such status signifies initial recognition and indicates that the school or program in question is working to fulfill all requirements; it does not, however, guarantee that accreditation will be granted.

Institutional Accrediting Agencies—Regional

MIDDLE STATES ASSOCIATION OF COLLEGES AND SCHOOLS
Accredits institutions in Delaware, District of Columbia, Maryland, New Jersey, New York, Pennsylvania, Puerto Rico, and the Virgin Islands.
Dr. Elizabeth Sibolski, President
Middle States Commission on Higher Education
3624 Market Street, Second Floor West
Philadelphia, Pennsylvania 19104
Phone: 267-284-5000
Fax: 215-662-5501
E-mail: info@msche.org
Web: www.msche.org

NEW ENGLAND ASSOCIATION OF SCHOOLS AND COLLEGES
Accredits institutions in Connecticut, Maine, Massachusetts, New Hampshire, Rhode Island, and Vermont.
Barbara E. Brittingham, Director
Commission on Institutions of Higher Education
209 Burlington Road, Suite 201
Bedford, Massachusetts 01730-1433
Phone: 781-271-0022
Fax: 781-271-0950
E-mail: kwillis@neasc.org
Web: www.neasc.org

NORTH CENTRAL ASSOCIATION OF COLLEGES AND SCHOOLS
Accredits institutions in Arizona, Arkansas, Colorado, Illinois, Indiana, Iowa, Kansas, Michigan, Minnesota, Missouri, Nebraska, New Mexico, North Dakota, Ohio, Oklahoma, South Dakota, West Virginia, Wisconsin, and Wyoming.
Dr. Sylvia Manning, President
The Higher Learning Commission
230 South LaSalle Street, Suite 7-500
Chicago, Illinois 60604-1413
Phone: 312-263-0456
Fax: 312-263-7462
E-mail: smanning@hlcommission.org
Web: www.ncahlc.org

NORTHWEST COMMISSION ON COLLEGES AND UNIVERSITIES
Accredits institutions in Alaska, Idaho, Montana, Nevada, Oregon, Utah, and Washington.
Dr. Sandra E. Elman, President
8060 165th Avenue, NE, Suite 100
Redmond, Washington 98052
Phone: 425-558-4224
Fax: 425-376-0596
E-mail: selman@nwccu.org
Web: www.nwccu.org

SOUTHERN ASSOCIATION OF COLLEGES AND SCHOOLS
Accredits institutions in Alabama, Florida, Georgia, Kentucky, Louisiana, Mississippi, North Carolina, South Carolina, Tennessee, Texas, and Virginia.
Belle S. Wheelan, President
Commission on Colleges
1866 Southern Lane
Decatur, Georgia 30033-4097
Phone: 404-679-4500
Fax: 404-679-4558
E-mail: questions@sacscoc.org
Web: www.sacscoc.org

WESTERN ASSOCIATION OF SCHOOLS AND COLLEGES
Accredits institutions in California, Guam, and Hawaii.
Ralph A. Wolff, President and Executive Director
Accrediting Commission for Senior Colleges and Universities
985 Atlantic Avenue, Suite 100
Alameda, California 94501
Phone: 510-748-9001
Fax: 510-748-9797
E-mail: www.wascsenior.org/contact
Web: www.wascweb.org/contact

Institutional Accrediting Agencies—Other

ACCREDITING COUNCIL FOR INDEPENDENT COLLEGES AND SCHOOLS
Albert C. Gray, Ph.D., Executive Director and CEO
750 First Street, NE, Suite 980
Washington, DC 20002-4241
Phone: 202-336-6780
Fax: 202-842-2593
E-mail: info@acics.org
Web: www.acics.org

DISTANCE EDUCATION AND TRAINING COUNCIL (DETC)
Accrediting Commission
Michael P. Lambert, Executive Director
1601 18th Street, NW, Suite 2
Washington, DC 20009
Phone: 202-234-5100
Fax: 202-332-1386
E-mail: Brianna@detc.org
Web: www.detc.org

Specialized Accrediting Agencies

[Only *Graduate & Professional Programs: An Overview* of *Peterson's Graduate and Professional Programs* Series includes the complete list of specialized accrediting groups recognized by the U.S. Department of Education and the Council on Higher Education Accreditation (CHEA). The lists in all other five books are abridged.]

ACUPUNCTURE AND ORIENTAL MEDICINE
William W. Goding, M.Ed., RRT, Interim Executive Director
Accreditation Commission for Acupuncture and Oriental Medicine
14502 Greenview Drive, Suite 300B
Laurel, Maryland 20708
Phone: 301-313-0855
Fax: 301-313-0912
E-mail: info@acaom.org
Web: www.acaom.org

ART AND DESIGN
Samuel Hope, Executive Director
Karen P. Moynahan, Associate Director
National Association of Schools of Art and Design (NASAD)
Commission on Accreditation
11250 Roger Bacon Drive, Suite 21
Reston, Virginia 20190-5243
Phone: 703-437-0700
Fax: 703-437-6312
E-mail: info@arts-accredit.org
Web: www.arts-accredit.org

BUSINESS
Jerry Trapnell, Executive Vice President/Chief Accreditation Officer
AACSB International--The Association to Advance Collegiate Schools of Business
777 South Harbour Island Boulevard, Suite 750
Tampa, Florida 33602
Phone: 813-769-6500
Fax: 813-769-6559
E-mail: jerryt@aacsb.edu
Web: www.aacsb.edu

CHIROPRACTIC
Lee Van Dusen, President
Council on Chiropractic Education (CCE)
Commission on Accreditation
8049 North 85th Way
Scottsdale, Arizona 85258-4321
Phone: 480-443-8877
Fax: 480-483-7333
E-mail: cce@cce-usa.org
Web: www.cce-usa.org

CLINICAL LABORATORY SCIENCES
Dianne M. Cearlock, Ph.D., Chief Executive Officer
National Accrediting Agency for Clinical Laboratory Sciences
5600 N. River Road, Suite 720
Rosemont, Illinois 60018-5119
Phone: 773-714-8880
Fax: 773-714-8886
E-mail: info@naacls.org
Web: www.naacls.org

CLINICAL PASTORAL EDUCATION
Teresa E. Snorton, Executive Director
Accreditation Commission
Association for Clinical Pastoral Education, Inc.
1549 Claremont Road, Suite 103
Decatur, Georgia 30033-4611
Phone: 404-320-1472
Fax: 404-320-0849
E-mail: acpe@acpe.edu
Web: www.acpe.edu

DANCE
Samuel Hope, Executive Director
Karen P. Moynahan, Associate Director
National Association of Schools of Dance (NASD)
Commission on Accreditation
11250 Roger Bacon Drive, Suite 21
Reston, Virginia 20190-5248
Phone: 703-437-0700
Fax: 703-437-6312
E-mail: info@arts-accredit.org
Web: www.arts-accredit.org

DENTISTRY
Anthony Ziebert, Director
Commission on Dental Accreditation
American Dental Association
211 East Chicago Avenue, Suite 1900
Chicago, Illinois 60611
Phone: 312-440-4643
E-mail: accreditation@ada.org
Web: www.ada.org

DIETETICS
Ulric K. Chung, Ph.D., Executive Director
American Dietetic Association
Commission on Accreditation for Dietetics Education (CADE-ADA)
120 South Riverside Plaza, Suite 2000
Chicago, Illinois 60606-6995
Phone: 800-877-1600
Fax: 312-899-4817
E-mail: cade@eatright.org
Web: www.eatright.org/cade

ENGINEERING
Michael Milligan, Ph.D., PE, Executive Director
Accreditation Board for Engineering and Technology, Inc. (ABET)
111 Market Place, Suite 1050
Baltimore, Maryland 21202
Phone: 410-347-7700
Fax: 410-625-2238
E-mail: accreditation@abet.org
Web: www.abet.org

FORESTRY
Michael T. Goergen, Jr.
Executive Vice-President and CEO
Society of American Foresters (SAF)
5400 Grosvenor Lane
Bethesda, Maryland 20814-2198
Phone: 301-897-8720 Ext. 123
Fax: 301-897-3690
E-mail: goergenm@safnet.org
Web: www.safnet.org

HEALTH SERVICES ADMINISTRATION
Commission on Accreditation of Healthcare Management Education (CAHME)
John S. Lloyd, President and CEO
2111 Wilson Boulevard, Suite 700
Arlington, Virginia 22201
Phone: 703-351-5010
Fax: 703-991-5989
E-mail: info@cahme.org
Web: www.cahme.org

INTERIOR DESIGN
Holly Mattson, Executive Director
Council for Interior Design Accreditation
206 Grandview Avenue, Suite 350
Grand Rapids, Michigan 49503-4014
Phone: 616-458-0400
Fax: 616-458-0460
E-mail: info@accredit-id.org
Web: www.accredit-id.org

JOURNALISM AND MASS COMMUNICATIONS
Susanne Shaw, Executive Director
Accrediting Council on Education in Journalism and Mass Communications (ACEJMC)
School of Journalism
Stauffer-Flint Hall
University of Kansas
1435 Jayhawk Boulevard
Lawrence, Kansas 66045-7575
Phone: 785-864-3973
Fax: 785-864-5225
E-mail: sshaw@ku.edu
Web: www2.ku.edu/~acejmc

LANDSCAPE ARCHITECTURE
Ronald C. Leighton, Executive Director
Landscape Architectural Accreditation Board
American Society of Landscape Architects
636 Eye Street, NW
Washington, DC 20001-3736
Phone: 202-898-2444
Fax: 202-898-1185
E-mail: info@asla.org
Web: www.asla.org

LAW
Hulett H. Askew, Consultant on Legal Education
American Bar Association
321 North Clark Street, 21st Floor
Chicago, Illinois 60654
Phone: 312-988-6738
Fax: 312-988-5681
E-mail: legaled@americanbar.org
Web: www.abanet.org/legaled/

LIBRARY
Karen O'Brien, Director
Office for Accreditation
American Library Association
50 East Huron Street
Chicago, Illinois 60611
Phone: 800-545-2433 Ext. 2432
Fax: 312-280-2433
E-mail: accred@ala.org
Web: www.ala.org/accreditation/

MARRIAGE AND FAMILY THERAPY
Jeff S. Harmon, Director of Accreditation Services
Commission on Accreditation for Marriage and Family Therapy Education
American Association for Marriage and Family Therapy
112 South Alfred Street
Alexandria, Virginia 22314-3061
Phone: 703-838-9808
Fax: 703-838-9805
E-mail: coa@aamft.org
Web: www.aamft.org

MEDICAL ILLUSTRATION
Commission on Accreditation of Allied Health Education Programs (CAAHEP)
Kathleen Megivern, Executive Director
1361 Park Street
Clearwater, Florida 33756
Phone: 727-210-2350
Fax: 727-210-2354
E-mail: mail@caahep.org
Web: www.caahep.org

MEDICINE
Liaison Committee on Medical Education (LCME)

In odd-numbered years beginning each July 1, contact:
Barbara Barzansky, Ph.D., LCME Secretary
American Medical Association
Council on Medical Education
515 North State Street
Chicago, Illinois 60654
Phone: 312-464-4933
Fax: 312-464-5830
E-mail: cme@aamc.org
Web: www.ama-assn.org

In even-numbered years beginning each July 1, contact:
Dan Hunt, M.D., LCME Secretary
Association of American Medical Colleges
2450 N Street, NW
Washington, DC 20037
Phone: 202-828-0596
Fax: 202-828-1125
E-mail: dhunt@aamc.org
Web: www.lcme.org

MUSIC
Samuel Hope, Executive Director
Karen P. Moynahan, Associate Director
National Association of Schools of Music (NASM)
Commission on Accreditation
11250 Roger Bacon Drive, Suite 21
Reston, Virginia 20190-5248
Phone: 703-437-0700
Fax: 703-437-6312
E-mail: info@arts-accredit.org
Web: www.arts-accredit.org

NATUROPATHIC MEDICINE
Daniel Seitz, J.D., Ed.D., Executive Director
Council on Naturopathic Medical Education
P.O. Box 178
Great Barrington, Massachusetts 01230
Phone: 413-528-8877
Fax: 413-528-8880
E-mail: council@cnme.org
Web: www.cnme.org

NURSE ANESTHESIA
Francis R. Gerbasi, Executive Director
Council on Accreditation of Nurse Anesthesia Educational Programs
American Association of Nurse Anesthetists
222 South Prospect Avenue, Suite 304
Park Ridge, Illinois 60068
Phone: 847-692-7050 Ext. 1154
Fax: 847-692-6968
E-mail: fgerbasi@aana.com
Web: www.aana.com

NURSE EDUCATION
Jennifer L. Butlin, Director
Commission on Collegiate Nursing Education (CCNE)
One Dupont Circle, NW, Suite 530
Washington, DC 20036-1120
Phone: 202-887-6791
Fax: 202-887-8476
E-mail: jbutlin@aacn.nche.edu
Web: www.aacn.nche.edu/accreditation

NURSE MIDWIFERY
Mary Brucker, Chair
Accreditation Commission for Midwifery Education
American College of Nurse-Midwives
Nurse-Midwifery Program
8403 Colesville Road, Suite 1550
Silver Spring, Maryland 20910
Phone: 240-485-1800
Fax: 240-485-1818
E-mail: mary_brucker@baylor.edu
Web: www.midwife.org/acme.cfm

Jo Anne Myers-Ciecko, MPH, Executive Director
Midwifery Education Accreditation Council
P.O. Box 984
La Conner, Washington 98257
Phone: 360-466-2080
Fax: 480-907-2936
E-mail: info@meacschools.org
Web: www.meacschools.org

NURSE PRACTITIONER
Susan Wysocki, RNC, NP, President and CEO
National Association of Nurse Practitioners in Women's Health
Council on Accreditation
505 C Street, NE
Washington, DC 20002
Phone: 202-543-9693 Ext. 1
Fax: 202-543-9858
E-mail: info@npwh.org
Web: www.npwh.org

NURSING
Sharon J. Tanner, Ed.D., RN, Executive Director
National League for Nursing Accrediting Commission (NLNAC)
3343 Peachtree Road, NE, Suite 500
Atlanta, Georgia 30326
Phone: 404-975-5000
Fax: 404-975-5020
E-mail: nlnac@nlnac.org
Web: www.nlnac.org

OCCUPATIONAL THERAPY
Neil Harvison, Ph.D., OTR/L
Director of Accreditation and Academic Affairs
The American Occupational Therapy Association
4720 Montgomery Lane
P.O. Box 31220
Bethesda, Maryland 20824-1220
Phone: 301-652-2682 Ext. 2912
Fax: 301-652-7711
E-mail: accred@aota.org
Web: www.aota.org

OPTOMETRY
Joyce L. Urbeck, Administrative Director
Accreditation Council on Optometric Education
American Optometric Association (AOA)
243 North Lindbergh Boulevard
St. Louis, Missouri 63141
Phone: 314-991-4000 Ext. 246
Fax: 314-991-4101
E-mail: ACOE@aoa.org
Web: www.theacoe.org

OSTEOPATHIC MEDICINE
Konrad C. Miskowicz-Retz, Ph.D., CAE
Director, Department of Education
Commission on Osteopathic College Accreditation
American Osteopathic Association
142 East Ontario Street
Chicago, Illinois 60611
Phone: 312-202-8048
Fax: 312-202-8202
E-mail: kretz@osteopathic.org
Web: www.osteopathic.org

PHARMACY
Peter H. Vlasses, Executive Director
Accreditation Council for Pharmacy Education
20 North Clark Street, Suite 2500
Chicago, Illinois 60602-5109
Phone: 312-664-3575
Fax: 312-664-4652
E-mail: csinfo@acpe-accredit.org
Web: www.acpe-accredit.org

PHYSICAL THERAPY
Mary Jane Harris, Director
Commission on Accreditation in Physical Therapy Education (CAPTE)
American Physical Therapy Association (APTA)
1111 North Fairfax Street
Alexandria, Virginia 22314
Phone: 703-706-3245
Fax: 703-706-3387
E-mail: accreditation@apta.org
Web: www.capteonline.org

PHYSICIAN ASSISTANT STUDIES
John E. McCarty, Executive Director
Accreditation Review Commission on Education for the Physician Assistant, Inc. (ARC-PA)
12000 Findley Road, Suite 150
Johns Creek, Georgia 30097
Phone: 770-476-1224
Fax: 770-476-1738
E-mail: johnmccarty@arc-pa.org
Web: www.arc-pa.org

PLANNING
Shonagh Merits, Executive Director
American Institute of Certified Planners/Association of Collegiate Schools of Planning/American Planning Association
Planning Accreditation Board (PAB)
53 W. Jackson Boulevard, Suite 1315
Chicago, Illinois 60604
Phone: 312-334-1271
Fax: 312-334-1273
E-mail: pab@planning.org
Web: www.planningaccreditationboard.org

PODIATRIC MEDICINE
Alan R. Tinkleman, Executive Director
Council on Podiatric Medical Education (CPME)
American Podiatric Medical Association
9312 Old Georgetown Road
Bethesda, Maryland 20814-1621
Phone: 301-571-9200
Fax: 301-571-4903
E-mail: artinkleman@apma.org
Web: www.cpme.org

PSYCHOLOGY AND COUNSELING
Susan Zlotlow, Executive Director
Office of Program Consultation and Accreditation
American Psychological Association
750 First Street, NE
Washington, DC 20002-4242
Phone: 202-336-5979
Fax: 202-336-5978
E-mail: apaaccred@apa.org
Web: www.apa.org/ed/accreditation

Carol L. Bobby, Executive Director
Council for Accreditation of Counseling and Related Educational Programs (CACREP)
1001 North Fairfax Street, Suite 510
Alexandria, Virginia 22314
Phone: 703-535-5990
Fax: 703-739-6209
E-mail: cacrep@cacrep.org
Web: www.cacrep.org

PUBLIC AFFAIRS AND ADMINISTRATION
Crystal Calarusse, Executive Director
Commission on Peer Review and Accreditation
National Association of Schools of Public Affairs and Administration
1029 Vermont Avenue, NW, Suite 1100
Washington, DC 20005
Phone: 202-628-8965
Fax: 202-626-4978
E-mail: copra@naspaa.org
Web: www.naspaa.org

PUBLIC HEALTH
Laura Rasar King, M.P.H., CHES, Executive Director
Council on Education for Public Health
800 Eye Street, NW, Suite 202
Washington, DC 20001-3710
Phone: 202-789-1050
Fax: 202-789-1895
E-mail: Lking@ceph.org
Web: www.ceph.org

REHABILITATION EDUCATION
Dr. Tom Evenson, President
Council on Rehabilitation Education (CORE)
Commission on Standards and Accreditation
1699 Woodfield Road, Suite 300
Schaumburg, Illinois 60173
Phone: 847-944-1345
Fax: 847-944-1324
E-mail: evenson@unt.edu
Web: www.core-rehab.org

SOCIAL WORK
Stephen M. Holloway, Director of Accreditation
Commission on Accreditation
Council on Social Work Education
1701 Duke Street, Suite 200
Alexandria, Virginia 22314
Phone: 703-683-8080
Fax: 703-683-8099
E-mail: sholloway@cswe.org
Web: www.cswe.org

SPEECH-LANGUAGE PATHOLOGY AND AUDIOLOGY
Patrima L. Tice, Director of Credentialing
American Speech-Language-Hearing Association
Council on Academic Accreditation in Audiology and Speech-Language Pathology
2200 Research Boulevard
Rockville, Maryland 20850-3289
Phone: 301-296-5796
Fax: 301-296-8750
E-mail: ptice@asha.org
Web: www.asha.org/academic/accreditation/default.htm

TECHNOLOGY
Michale S. McComis, Ed.D., Executive Director
Accrediting Commission of Career Schools and Colleges
2101 Wilson Boulevard, Suite 302
Arlington, Virginia 22201
Phone: 703-247-4212
Fax: 703-247-4533
E-mail: mccomis@accsc.org
Web: www.accsc.org

TEACHER EDUCATION
James G. Cibulka, President
National Council for Accreditation of Teacher Education
2010 Massachusetts Avenue, NW, Suite 500
Washington, DC 20036-1023
Phone: 202-466-7496
Fax: 202-296-6620
E-mail: ncate@ncate.org
Web: www.ncate.org

Frank B. Murray, President
Teacher Education Accreditation Council (TEAC)
Accreditation Committee
One Dupont Circle, Suite 320
Washington, DC 20036-0110
Phone: 202-831-0400
Fax: 202-831-3013
E-mail: teac@teac.org
Web: www.teac.org

THEATER
Samuel Hope, Executive Director
Karen P. Moynahan, Associate Director
National Association of Schools of Theatre
Commission on Accreditation
11250 Roger Bacon Drive, Suite 21
Reston, Virginia 20190
Phone: 703-437-0700
Fax: 703-437-6312
E-mail: info@arts-accredit.org
Web: www.arts-accredit.org

THEOLOGY

Bernard Fryshman, Executive Vice President
Association of Advanced Rabbinical and Talmudic Schools (AARTS)
Accreditation Commission
11 Broadway, Suite 405
New York, New York 10004
Phone: 212-363-1991
Fax: 212-533-5335
E-mail: BFryshman@nyit.edu

Daniel O. Aleshire, Executive Director
Association of Theological Schools in the United States and Canada (ATS)
Commission on Accrediting
10 Summit Park Drive
Pittsburgh, Pennsylvania 15275-1110
Phone: 412-788-6505
Fax: 412-788-6510
E-mail: ats@ats.edu
Web: www.ats.edu

T. Paul Boatner, President
Transnational Association of Christian Colleges and Schools (TRACS)
Accreditation Commission
15935 Forest Road
Forest, Virginia 24551
Phone: 434-525-9539
Fax: 434-525-9538
E-mail: info@tracs.org
Web: www.tracs.org

VETERINARY MEDICINE

Elizabeth Sabin, Director
Education and Research Division
American Veterinary Medical Association (AVMA)
Council on Education
1931 North Meacham Road, Suite 100
Schaumburg, Illinois 60173
Phone: 847-925-8070 Ext. 6674
Fax: 847-925-9329
E-mail: info@avma.org
Web: www.avma.org

How to Use This Guide

As you identify the particular programs and institutions that interest you, you can use both the ***Graduate & Professional Programs: An Overview*** volume and the specialized volumes to obtain detailed information--***Graduate & Professional Programs: An Overview*** for information on the institutions overall and the specialized volumes for details about the individual graduate units and their degree programs.

Directory of Graduate and Professional Programs by Field

This directory lists the 500 fields covered in ***Peterson's Graduate and Professional Programs***, with an alphabetical listing of each of the institutions offering graduate or professional work in that field. Institutions in the United States and U.S. territories and those in Canada, Mexico, Europe, and Africa that are accredited by U.S. accrediting bodies are included. The directory enables readers who are interested in a particular academic area to quickly identify the colleges and universities that they might wish to attend. In each field, degree levels are given if an institution provided the information in response to *Peterson's Annual Survey of Graduate and Professional Institutions*. An *M* indicates that a master's degree program is offered; a *D* indicates that a doctoral program is offered; a *P* indicates that the first professional degree is offered; and an *O* signifies that other advanced degrees (e.g., certificates and specialist degrees) are offered. If no degree is listed, the school offers a degree in a subdiscipline of the field, not in the field itself.

All of the programs listed in this directory are profiled, and many are described in detail in **Close-Ups** or **Displays**in the specialized volumes. These **Displays** and **Close-Ups** are indicated in the directory listings by an asterisk, and their page numbers may be found by consulting the indexes of the specialized volumes. The **Profiles, Displays**, and **Close-Ups Index** at the back of this book indicate the institutions that chose to place a **Close-Up** or a **Display** in this volume.

Directory of Institutions and Their Offerings

This directory contains information identical to that in the **Directory of Graduate and Professional Programs by Field** but conversely presented. Accredited institutions in the United States and U.S. territories and those in Canada, Mexico, Europe, and Africa that are accredited by U.S. accrediting bodies are given here, with an alphabetical listing of which programs they offer out of the selected fields that are covered in the guides. The directory will be of value to readers who are interested in the range of programs at particular institutions, as well as those who wish to compare programs and degree levels. The degree levels are shown if the institution provided information in response to *Peterson's Annual Survey of Graduate and Professional Institutions*; the degree levels included are master's, doctorate, first professional, and other advanced degrees (e.g., certificates and specialist degrees), included as *M, D, P*, and *O*, respectively.

All of the programs listed in this directory are profiled, and many are described in detail in **Close-Ups** or outlined briefly in **Displays** in the specialized volumes. A note at the end of each institution's listing refers the reader to the specific page number if a **Display** or **Close-Up** appears in this book. If there is such information in the specialized volumes, an asterisk appears in the column that lists the degree level offered. The reader should then refer to the **Close-Ups and Displays Index** in the appropriate volume.

Profiles of Institutions Offering Graduate and Professional Work

This section presents profiles of accredited colleges and universities in the United States and U.S. territories and those in Canada, Mexico, Europe, and Africa that are accredited by U.S. accrediting bodies. Together with the other sections of this book, it is both a basic reference source and a foundation for the specialized volumes of ***Peterson's Graduate and Professional Programs***. (The specialized volumes provide descriptions of graduate programs in the humanities, arts, and social sciences; the biological sciences; the physical sciences, mathematics, agricultural sciences, the environment, and natural resources; engineering and applied sciences; and business, education, health, information studies, law, and social work, respectively.) The profiles in this section include the data on graduate and professional units that were submitted in 2011 by each institution in response to *Peterson's Annual Survey of Graduate and Professional Institutions*. If an institution provided all of the information requested, the profile includes all of the items listed below. A number of graduate school administrators have submitted **Displays**, which appear near their profiles. In these, readers will find information an institution wants to emphasize. In addition, bolded reference lines at the end of a profile indicate the page number on which the reader will find a **Display** and/or **Close-Up**, if the institution has chosen to submit one or both. The absence of a **Display** or **Close-Up** does not reflect any type of editorial judgment on the part of Peterson's.

General Information

Type. An institution's control is indicated as independent (private nonprofit), independent with religious affiliation, proprietary (private profit-making), or state-supported or state-related (public). Whether an institution is coeducational or primarily for men or women is indicated. A few schools are designated as undergraduate: women (or men) only; graduate: coed. Institutional type is given as university, comprehensive, graduate only, or upper level.

CGS Membership. Membership in the Council of Graduate Schools in the United States and in Canada is indicated here.

Enrollment. Enrollment figures include total matriculated students (graduate, professional, and undergraduate), total full- and part-time matriculated graduate and professional students, and the number of women in each category.

Enrollment by Degree Level. Figures include the total number of students enrolled at each degree level--master's, doctoral, first-professional, and other advanced degrees.

Graduate Faculty. The numbers of full-time and part-time/adjunct faculty members actively involved with graduate students through teaching or research are given, followed by numbers of women.

Graduate Expenses. Tuition and fees for the overall institution for 2010–11 are indicated on a full-time (per academic year, semester, quarter, etc.) and/or a part-time (per credit, semester hour, quarter hour, course, etc.) basis. In-state and out-of-state figures are supplied where applicable. For exact costs at any given time, contact the schools and programs directly. Keep in mind that the tuition of Canadian institutions is usually given in Canadian dollars.

Graduate Housing. Institutions were asked to indicate whether housing for single and married students is guaranteed or available on a first-come, first-served basis and whether that includes board and to indicate the typical cost per year.

Student Services. Each institution was asked which of the following services are available to graduate and professional students: campus employment opportunities, campus safety program, career counseling, child day-care facilities, disabled student services, exercise/

wellness program, free psychological counseling, grant writing training, international student services, low-cost health insurance, multicultural affairs office, teacher training, and writing training.

Library Facilities. The main library name and the number of additional on-campus libraries, if any, are provided. Also provided are online resources, such as library catalog, Web page, and other libraries' catalogs, and numbers of titles, current serial subscriptions, and audiovisual materials.

Research Affiliations. Institutions were asked to name up to six independent research centers, laboratories, or institutes with which they maintain formal arrangements providing extra research or study opportunities for graduate students.

Computer Facilities

Institutions were asked to provide the total number of PCs and/or terminals available for student use, whether a campuswide network is available, and whether Internet access and/or online class registration is available. The institution's Web site also appears here if that information was supplied.

General Application Contact

The name, title, phone number, fax number, and e-mail address of the person to contact for further information about applying to graduate and professional programs appear here.

Graduate Units

Each major graduate and professional unit within the institution (school, college, institute, center, etc.) is listed below the general information. These units are arranged to show the hierarchical structure of the institution. Those units offering advanced degree programs through the graduate school are listed immediately beneath it. Professional schools not connected with the graduate school are listed separately.

Enrollment. The number of full- and part-time matriculated students and the number of women, minority-group members, and international students are given. Average age is indicated, followed by the number of applicants, percentage accepted, and the number enrolled.

Faculty. Full-time and part-time/adjunct figures are given, and the number of women is indicated.

Expenses. For individual program expenses, readers are advised to contact the institution.

Financial Support. Information is given on the number of fellowships and assistantships awarded in 2010–11 and the availability of other types of aid. The financial aid application deadline is also indicated.

Degree Program Information. The number of degrees awarded in calendar year 2010 is given, broken down by degree level, followed by the availability of part-time and evening/weekend programs. Degree programs offered through the subunits and the specific degrees awarded are listed. Special degree information is also included, such as that a degree is offered jointly with another university.

Applying. The application deadline (for domestic and international students) and application fee are given, followed by a person to contact and a phone number, fax number, and e-mail address (if provided).

Head. The head of the unit and his or her title are indicated, along with a phone number, fax number, and e-mail address (if provided).

Close-Ups of Institutions Offering Graduate and Professional Work

The **Close-Ups** in this section present an overview of accredited graduate and professional schools in the United States and U.S. territories and institutions in Canada, Mexico, Europe, and Africa that are accredited by U.S. accrediting bodies. Critical information sought by all prospective graduate students--regardless of their intended field of study--has been supplied by the schools themselves.

In addition to listing the degree programs available, each entry gives valuable information on research facilities, financial aid opportunities, tuition rates, living and housing costs, students, the faculty, location, the university, and application criteria--in short, facts that all prospective graduate students need to know about an institution when selecting a graduate program.

After using the **Close-Ups** and the other sections of this volume to identify those universities that are appropriate to your needs, refer to the specialized volumes for specific program information. Graduate and professional schools and colleges within the institutions represented in this book are considered in detail in the specialized volumes, which cover the humanities, arts, and social sciences; the biological sciences; the physical sciences, mathematics, agricultural sciences, the environment, and natural resources; engineering and applied sciences; and business, education, health, information studies, law, and social work, respectively.

Appendixes

This section contains two appendixes. The first, *Institutional Changes Since the 2011 Edition,* lists institutions that have closed, moved, merged, or changed their name or status since the last edition of the guides. The second, *Abbreviations Used in the Guides,* gives abbreviations of degree names, along with what those abbreviations stand for. These appendixes are identical in all six volumes of *Peterson's Graduate and Professional Programs.*

Indexes

There are two indexes in this section. The first, **Profiles, Displays, and Close-Ups,** gives page references for all information on all graduate and professional schools in this volume. Location of the institution's **Profile** is indicated in normal type. An *italic* page number indicates that a **Display** follows the institution's **Profile**. A **boldface** page number indicates the location of an institution's **Close-Up**. The second, **Directories and Subject Areas in the Specialized Volumes**, gives references to the directories in other volumes of this set and also includes cross-references for subject area names not used in the directory structure, for example, "Arabic (*see* Near and Middle Eastern Languages)."

Data Collection Procedures

The information published in the directories and **Profiles** of all the books is collected through *Peterson's Annual Survey of Graduate and Professional Institutions.* The survey is sent each spring to nearly 2,400 institutions offering postbaccalaureate degree programs, including accredited institutions in the United States, U.S. territories, and Canada and those institutions outside the United States that are accredited by U.S. accrediting bodies. Deans and other administrators complete these surveys, providing information on programs in the 500 academic and professional fields covered in the guides as well as overall institutional information. While every effort has been made to ensure the accuracy and completeness of the data, information is sometimes unavailable or changes occur after publication deadlines. All usable information received in time for publication has been included. The omission of any particular item from a directory or **Profile** signifies either that the item is not applicable to the institution or program or that information was not available. **Profiles** of programs scheduled to begin during the 2011–12 academic year cannot, obviously, include statistics on enrollment or, in many cases, the number of faculty members. If no usable data were submitted by an institution, its name, address, and program name appear in order to indicate the availability of graduate work.

Criteria for Inclusion in This Guide

To be included in this guide, an institution must have full accreditation or be a candidate for accreditation (preaccreditation) status by an institutional or specialized accrediting body recognized by the U.S. Department of Education or the Council for Higher Education Accreditation (CHEA). Institutional accrediting bodies, which review each institution as a whole, include the six regional associations of schools and colleges (Middle States, New England, North Central, Northwest, Southern, and Western), each of which is responsible for a specified portion of the United States and its territories. Other institutional accrediting bodies are national in scope and accredit specific kinds of institutions (e.g., Bible colleges, independent colleges, and rabbinical and Talmudic schools). Program registration by the New York State Board of Regents is considered to be the equivalent of institutional accreditation, since the board requires that all programs offered by an institution meet its standards before recognition is granted. A Canadian institution must be chartered and authorized to grant degrees by the provincial government, affiliated with a chartered institution, or accredited by a recognized U.S. accrediting body. This guide also includes institutions outside the United States that are accredited by these U.S. accrediting bodies. There are recognized specialized or professional accrediting bodies in more than fifty different fields, each of which is authorized to accredit institutions or specific programs in its particular field. For specialized institutions that offer programs in one field only, we designate this to be the equivalent of institutional accreditation. A full explanation of the accrediting process and complete information on recognized institutional (regional and national) and specialized accrediting bodies can be found online at www.chea.org or at www.ed.gov/admins/finaid/accred/index.html.

NOTICE: Certain portions of or information contained in this book have been submitted and paid for by the educational institution identified, and such institutions take full responsibility for the accuracy, timeliness, completeness, and functionality of such contents. Such portions or information include (i) each display ad that comprises a half page of information covering a single educational institution or program that appears in the section, "Profiles of Institutions Offering Graduate and Professional Work," and (ii) each two-page description or Close-Up of a graduate school or program that appears in the "Close-Ups of Institutions Offering Graduate and Professional Work" section of this guide.

DIRECTORY OF GRADUATE AND PROFESSIONAL PROGRAMS BY FIELD

ACCOUNTING

Institution	Degrees
Abilene Christian University	M
Adelphi University	M*
Alabama State University	M
Albany State University	M
American InterContinental University Buckhead Campus	M
American InterContinental University Online	M
American InterContinental University South Florida	M
American International College	M
American Public University System	M
American University	M
Anderson University (IN)	M,D
Andrews University	M
Angelo State University	M
Appalachian State University	M
Argosy University, Atlanta	M,D*
Argosy University, Chicago	M,D*
Argosy University, Dallas	M,D,O*
Argosy University, Denver	M,D*
Argosy University, Hawai'i	M,D,O*
Argosy University, Inland Empire	M,D*
Argosy University, Los Angeles	M,D*
Argosy University, Nashville	M,D*
Argosy University, Orange County	M,D,O*
Argosy University, Phoenix	M,D*
Argosy University, Salt Lake City	M,D*
Argosy University, San Diego	M,D*
Argosy University, San Francisco Bay Area	M,D*
Argosy University, Sarasota	M,D,O*
Argosy University, Schaumburg	M,D,O*
Argosy University, Seattle	M,D*
Argosy University, Tampa	M,D*
Argosy University, Twin Cities	M,D*
Argosy University, Washington DC	M,D,O*
Arizona State University	M,D
Arkansas State University	M
Assumption College	M,O
Auburn University	M
Avila University	M
Babson College	M,O
Baker College Center for Graduate Studies—Online	M,D
Baldwin-Wallace College	M
Ball State University	M
Barry University	M*
Bayamón Central University	M
Baylor University	M*
Benedictine University	M
Bentley University	M,D
Bernard M. Baruch College of the City University of New York	M,D
Bob Jones University	P,M,D,O
Boise State University	M
Boston College	M*
Bowling Green State University	M*
Bradley University	M
Brenau University	M
Bridgewater State University	M
Brigham Young University	M*
Brock University	M
Brooklyn College of the City University of New York	M
Bryant University	M
Caldwell College	M
California Baptist University	M,D
California State Polytechnic University, Pomona	M
California State University, East Bay	M
California State University, Fresno	M
California State University, Fullerton	M
California State University, Los Angeles	M*
California State University, Sacramento	M
California Western School of Law	P,M
Canisius College	M
Capella University	M,D,O
Carnegie Mellon University	D*
Case Western Reserve University	M,D*
Centenary College	M
Central Michigan University	M
Central Washington University	M
Charleston Southern University	M
Chatham University	M
City University of Seattle	M,O
Clark Atlanta University	M
Clark University	M
Cleary University	M,O
Clemson University	M
Cleveland State University	M
Coastal Carolina University	M
The College at Brockport, State University of New York	M
College of Charleston	M
The College of Saint Rose	M
The College of William and Mary	M
Colorado State University	M
Colorado Technical University Colorado Springs	M,D
Colorado Technical University Denver	M
Columbia University	M,D*
Concordia University (Canada)	M,D,O
Cornell University	D*
Daemen College	M
Dallas Baptist University	M
Davenport University	M
Davenport University	M
Davenport University	M
Delaware Valley College	M
Delta State University	M
DePaul University	M
DeSales University	M
DeVry University	M
Dominican University	M
Drexel University	M,D,O*
Duquesne University	M
East Carolina University	M
Eastern Illinois University	M,O
Eastern Michigan University	M
East Tennessee State University	M
Edgewood College	M
Ellis University	M
Elmhurst College	M
Emory University	D*
Everest University	M
Everest University	M
Fairfield University	M,O
Fairleigh Dickinson University, College at Florham	M
Fairleigh Dickinson University, Metropolitan Campus	M,O
Fitchburg State University	M
Florida Agricultural and Mechanical University	M
Florida Atlantic University	M,D
Florida Gulf Coast University	M
Florida Institute of Technology	M
Florida International University	M
Florida State University	M,D
Fontbonne University	M
Fordham University	M
Freed-Hardeman University	M
Friends University	M
Gannon University	O
George Mason University	M*
The George Washington University	M,D
Georgia College & State University	M
Georgia Institute of Technology	M,D,O
Georgian Court University	M,O
Georgia Southern University	M
Georgia State University	M,D,O
Golden Gate University	M,D,O
Gonzaga University	M
Governors State University	M
Graduate School and University Center of the City University of New York	D
Grand Canyon University	M
Grand Valley State University	M
Harvard University	D*
Hawai'i Pacific University	M*
HEC Montreal	M,O
Hendrix College	M
Herzing University Online	M
Hofstra University	M,O
Hood College	M
Houston Baptist University	M
Howard University	M
Hunter College of the City University of New York	M
Illinois State University	M
Indiana Tech	M
Indiana University Northwest	M,O
Indiana University–Purdue University Indianapolis	M
Indiana University South Bend	M
Indiana Wesleyan University	M
Instituto Tecnologico de Santo Domingo	M,O
Inter American University of Puerto Rico, Aguadilla Campus	M
Inter American University of Puerto Rico, Arecibo Campus	M
Inter American University of Puerto Rico, Barranquitas Campus	M
Inter American University of Puerto Rico, Metropolitan Campus	M
Inter American University of Puerto Rico, Ponce Campus	M
Inter American University of Puerto Rico, San Germán Campus	M,D
Iona College	M,O
Iowa State University of Science and Technology	M*
Ithaca College	M
Jackson State University	M
James Madison University	M
John Carroll University	M
Johnson & Wales University	M
Jones International University	M
Kansas State University	M*
Kean University	M
Keiser University	M
Kennesaw State University	M
Kent State University	M,D*
Kentucky State University	M
Lakeland College	M
Lamar University	M
La Sierra University	M,O
Lehigh University	M
Lehman College of the City University of New York	M
Lenoir-Rhyne University	M
Lewis University	M
Lincoln University (MO)	M,O
Lindenwood University	M
Lipscomb University	M
Long Island University, Brooklyn Campus	M
Long Island University, C.W. Post Campus	M,O
Louisiana State University and Agricultural and Mechanical College	M,D
Louisiana Tech University	M,D
Loyola University Chicago	M
Loyola University Maryland	M
Maharishi University of Management	M,D
Marquette University	M
Maryville University of Saint Louis	M,O
McGill University	M,D,O
McNeese State University	M
Mercy College	M
Miami University	M
Michigan State University	M,D
Middle Tennessee State University	M
Millsaps College	M
Mississippi College	M,O
Mississippi State University	M,D
Missouri State University	M
Molloy College	M
Monmouth University	M,O
Montana State University	M
Montclair State University	M,O
Moravian College	M
Murray State University	M
National University	M
New England College	M
New Jersey City University	M
New Mexico State University	M
New York Institute of Technology	M,O
New York University	M,D
North Carolina State University	M*
Northeastern Illinois University	M
Northeastern State University	M
Northeastern University	M
Northern Illinois University	M
Northern Kentucky University	M,O
Northwestern University	D*
Northwest Missouri State University	M
Notre Dame College (OH)	M,O
Nova Southeastern University	M,D*
Oakland University	M,O
The Ohio State University	M,D
Oklahoma City University	M
Oklahoma State University	M,D*
Old Dominion University	M
Oral Roberts University	M
Our Lady of the Lake University of San Antonio	M
Pace University	M
Pacific States University	M,D
Pittsburg State University	M

Institution	Degrees
Polytechnic University of Puerto Rico, Miami Campus	M
Polytechnic University of Puerto Rico, Orlando Campus	M
Pontifical Catholic University of Puerto Rico	M,O
Prairie View A&M University	M
Providence College	M
Purdue University Calumet	M
Queens College of the City University of New York	M
Regis University	M,O
Rhode Island College	M,O
Rhodes College	M
Rider University	M
Robert Morris University Illinois	M
Rochester Institute of Technology	M
Rocky Mountain College	M
Roosevelt University	M
Rowan University	M
Rutgers, The State University of New Jersey, Newark	D*
Sacred Heart University	M
St. Ambrose University	M
St. Edward's University	M,O
St. Francis College	M
St. John's University (NY)	M,O
St. Joseph's College, Long Island Campus	M
St. Joseph's College, New York	M*
Saint Joseph's University	M
Saint Leo University	M
Saint Louis University	M
St. Mary's University (United States)	
Saint Peter's College	M
St. Thomas University	M,O
Salisbury University	M
Sam Houston State University	M
San Diego State University	M
San Francisco State University	M
San Jose State University	M
Santa Clara University	M
Seattle University	M
Seton Hall University	M,O
Shorter University	M
Southeastern Louisiana University	M
Southeast Missouri State University	M
Southern Adventist University	M
Southern Illinois University Carbondale	M,D
Southern Illinois University Edwardsville	M
Southern Methodist University	M
Southern New Hampshire University	M,D,O
Southern Polytechnic State University	M,O
Southern Utah University	M
Southwestern Adventist University	M
State University of New York at Binghamton	M,D
State University of New York at New Paltz	M
State University of New York College at Geneseo	M
State University of New York College at Old Westbury	M
State University of New York Institute of Technology	M
Stephen F. Austin State University	M
Stetson University	M
Stratford University	M
Strayer University	M
Suffolk University	M,O
Syracuse University	M,D*
Tabor College	M
Tarleton State University	M
Temple University	M,D*
Tennessee Technological University	M
Texas A&M International University	M
Texas A&M University	M,D
Texas A&M University–Corpus Christi	M
Texas A&M University–Texarkana	M
Texas Christian University	M
Texas State University–San Marcos	M
Texas Tech University	M,D*
Towson University	M
Trinity University	M
Troy University	M
Truman State University	M
Universidad del Este	M
Universidad del Turabo	M
Universidad Metropolitana	M
Université de Sherbrooke	M
Université du Québec à Montréal	M,O
Université du Québec à Trois-Rivières	M
Université du Québec en Outaouais	M,O
Université Laval	M,O
University at Albany, State University of New York	M
University at Buffalo, the State University of New York	M,D,O*
The University of Akron	M
The University of Alabama	M,D
The University of Alabama at Birmingham	M*
The University of Alabama in Huntsville	M
University of Alberta	D
The University of Arizona	M
University of Arkansas	M
University of Arkansas at Little Rock	M,O
University of Baltimore	M,O
The University of British Columbia	D
University of California, Berkeley	D,O*
University of California, Los Angeles	M,D*
University of Central Arkansas	M
University of Central Florida	M
University of Central Missouri	M
University of Charleston	M
University of Chicago	M
University of Cincinnati	M,D
University of Colorado Boulder	M,D*
University of Colorado Denver	M
University of Connecticut	M,D*
University of Dallas	M
University of Dayton	M
University of Delaware	M*
University of Denver	M
University of Florida	M,D*
University of Georgia	M
University of Hartford	M,O
University of Hawaii at Manoa	M,D
University of Houston	M,D
University of Houston–Clear Lake	M
University of Houston–Victoria	M
University of Idaho	M
University of Illinois at Chicago	M
University of Illinois at Springfield	M
University of Illinois at Urbana–Champaign	M,D
The University of Iowa	M,D*
The University of Kansas	M
University of Kentucky	M*
University of La Verne	M
University of Lethbridge	M,D
University of Louisville	M
University of Maine	M
The University of Manchester	M,D
University of Mary	M
University of Mary Hardin-Baylor	M
University of Maryland University College	M,O
University of Massachusetts Amherst	M*
University of Massachusetts Dartmouth	M,O
University of Memphis	M,D
University of Miami	M*
University of Michigan–Dearborn	M
University of Minnesota, Twin Cities Campus	M,D
University of Mississippi	M,D
University of Missouri	M,D*
University of Missouri–Kansas City	M,D*
University of Missouri–St. Louis	M,O
The University of Montana	M
University of Nebraska at Omaha	M
University of Nebraska–Lincoln	M,D*
University of Nevada, Las Vegas	M,O
University of Nevada, Reno	M*
University of New Hampshire	M
University of New Haven	M,O
University of New Mexico	M*
University of New Orleans	M
The University of North Carolina at Chapel Hill	M,D*
The University of North Carolina at Charlotte	M
The University of North Carolina at Greensboro	M,O
The University of North Carolina Wilmington	M
University of North Dakota	M
University of Northern Colorado	M
University of Northern Iowa	M
University of North Florida	M
University of North Texas	M,D
University of Notre Dame	M*
University of Oklahoma	M*
University of Oregon	M,D
University of Pennsylvania	M,D*
University of Phoenix	M
University of Phoenix–Atlanta Campus	M
University of Phoenix–Augusta Campus	M
University of Phoenix–Austin Campus	M
University of Phoenix–Birmingham Campus	M
University of Phoenix–Central Florida Campus	M
University of Phoenix–Central Valley Campus	M
University of Phoenix–Charlotte Campus	M
University of Phoenix–Chattanooga Campus	M
University of Phoenix–Cincinnati Campus	M
University of Phoenix–Cleveland Campus	M
University of Phoenix–Columbus Georgia Campus	M
University of Phoenix–Columbus Ohio Campus	M
University of Phoenix–Dallas Campus	M
University of Phoenix–Denver Campus	M
University of Phoenix–Des Moines Campus	M
University of Phoenix–Eastern Washington Campus	M
University of Phoenix–Harrisburg Campus	M
University of Phoenix–Hawaii Campus	M
University of Phoenix–Houston Campus	M
University of Phoenix–Idaho Campus	M
University of Phoenix–Indianapolis Campus	M
University of Phoenix–Jersey City Campus	M
University of Phoenix–Kansas City Campus	M
University of Phoenix–Las Vegas Campus	M
University of Phoenix–Louisiana Campus	M
University of Phoenix–Madison Campus	M
University of Phoenix–Maryland Campus	M
University of Phoenix–Memphis Campus	M
University of Phoenix–Milwaukee Campus	M,D
University of Phoenix–Minneapolis/St. Louis Park Campus	M
University of Phoenix–New Mexico Campus	M
University of Phoenix–Northern Nevada Campus	M
University of Phoenix–Northern Virginia Campus	M
University of Phoenix–North Florida Campus	M
University of Phoenix–Northwest Arkansas Campus	M
University of Phoenix–Oklahoma City Campus	M
University of Phoenix–Omaha Campus	M
University of Phoenix–Oregon Campus	M
University of Phoenix–Philadelphia Campus	M
University of Phoenix–Phoenix Campus	M
University of Phoenix–Pittsburgh Campus	M
University of Phoenix–Puerto Rico Campus	M
University of Phoenix–Raleigh Campus	M
University of Phoenix–Richmond Campus	M
University of Phoenix–Sacramento Valley Campus	M
University of Phoenix–St. Louis Campus	M
University of Phoenix–San Antonio Campus	M
University of Phoenix–San Diego Campus	M
University of Phoenix–Savannah Campus	M
University of Phoenix–Southern Arizona Campus	M

*M—master's degree; P—first professional degree; D—doctorate; O—other advanced degree; *—Close-Up and/or Display in one of the other books in this series*

University of Phoenix–Southern Colorado Campus M
University of Phoenix–South Florida Campus M
University of Phoenix–Springfield Campus M
University of Phoenix–Tulsa Campus M
University of Phoenix–Utah Campus M
University of Phoenix–Vancouver Campus M
University of Phoenix–Washington D.C. Campus M,D
University of Phoenix–West Florida Campus M
University of Pittsburgh M,D*
University of Puerto Rico, Río Piedras M,D
University of Rhode Island M,D
University of Rochester
University of St. Thomas (MN) M
University of San Diego M
University of Saskatchewan M
The University of Scranton M
University of South Africa M,D
University of South Alabama M
University of South Carolina M
The University of South Dakota M
University of Southern California M*
University of Southern Mississippi M
University of South Florida M,D*
The University of Tampa M
The University of Tennessee M,D
The University of Tennessee at Chattanooga M
The University of Texas at Arlington M,D
The University of Texas at Austin M,D
The University of Texas at Dallas M,D*
The University of Texas at El Paso M
The University of Texas at San Antonio M,D*
The University of Texas of the Permian Basin M
The University of Texas–Pan American M
University of the Incarnate Word M
University of the Sacred Heart M,O
The University of Toledo M
University of Toronto M,D
University of Tulsa M
University of Utah M,D*
University of Vermont M
University of Virginia M
University of Washington M,D*
University of Washington, Tacoma M
University of Waterloo M,D
University of West Florida M
University of West Georgia M
University of Wisconsin–Madison M,D*
University of Wisconsin–Whitewater M*
University of Wyoming M
Upper Iowa University M
Utah State University M
Utica College M
Vanderbilt University M*
Villanova University M
Virginia Commonwealth University M,D
Virginia International University M,O
Virginia Polytechnic Institute and State University M,D
Wagner College M
Wake Forest University M
Walden University M,D
Walsh College of Accountancy and Business Administration M
Washington State University M,D
Washington University in St. Louis M*
Wayne State University M,D*
Webber International University M
Weber State University M
Western Carolina University M
Western Connecticut State University M
Western Illinois University M
Western Michigan University M
Western New England University M
Westminster College (UT) M,O
West Texas A&M University M
West Virginia University M
Wheeling Jesuit University M
Wichita State University M
Widener University M
Wilfrid Laurier University M,D
Wilkes University M
Worcester State University M
Wright State University M
Yale University D*
Yeshiva University M*
York College of Pennsylvania M
Youngstown State University M

ACOUSTICS

Penn State University Park M,D
Rensselaer Polytechnic Institute M,D
University of Massachusetts Dartmouth M,D,O

ACTUARIAL SCIENCE

Ball State University M
Boston University M*
Central Connecticut State University M,O
Columbia University M*
DePaul University M,O
George Mason University M,D,O*
Georgia State University M
Maryville University of Saint Louis M
Roosevelt University M
St. John's University (NY) M
Simon Fraser University M,D
Temple University M*
Université du Québec à Montréal O
University of Central Florida M,O
University of Connecticut M,D*
University of Illinois at Urbana–Champaign M,D
The University of Iowa M,D*
The University of Manchester M,D
University of Nebraska–Lincoln M*
University of Northern Iowa M
The University of Texas at Austin M,D
University of Waterloo M,D
University of Wisconsin–Madison M*

ACUPUNCTURE AND ORIENTAL MEDICINE

Academy for Five Element Acupuncture M
Academy of Chinese Culture and Health Sciences M
Academy of Oriental Medicine at Austin M
Acupuncture & Integrative Medicine College, Berkeley M
Acupuncture and Massage College M
American College of Acupuncture and Oriental Medicine M
American College of Traditional Chinese Medicine M,D,O
Arizona School of Acupuncture and Oriental Medicine M
Atlantic Institute of Oriental Medicine M
Bastyr University M,D,O
Canadian Memorial Chiropractic College O
Colorado School of Traditional Chinese Medicine M
Dongguk University Los Angeles M
East West College of Natural Medicine M
Emperor's College of Traditional Oriental Medicine M,D
Five Branches University: Graduate School of Traditional Chinese Medicine M
Florida College of Integrative Medicine M
Institute of Clinical Acupuncture and Oriental Medicine M
Midwest College of Oriental Medicine M,O
National College of Natural Medicine M
National University of Health Sciences P,M,D
New England School of Acupuncture M
New York Chiropractic College M
New York College of Health Professions M
New York College of Traditional Chinese Medicine M
Northwestern Health Sciences University M
Oregon College of Oriental Medicine M,D
Pacific College of Oriental Medicine M,D
Pacific College of Oriental Medicine-Chicago M
Pacific College of Oriental Medicine-New York M
Samra University of Oriental Medicine M,D
Seattle Institute of Oriental Medicine M
South Baylo University M
Southern California University of Health Sciences M
Southwest Acupuncture College M
Swedish Institute, College of Health Sciences M
Tai Sophia Institute M,O
Texas College of Traditional Chinese Medicine M
Touro College M,D
Traditional Chinese Medical College of Hawaii M
Tri-State College of Acupuncture M,O
University of Bridgeport M
WON Institute of Graduate Studies M
World Medicine Institute of Acupuncture and Herbal Medicine M
Yo San University of Traditional Chinese Medicine M

ACUTE CARE/CRITICAL CARE NURSING

Allen College M,D,O
Barry University M,O*
Case Western Reserve University M,D*
The College of New Rochelle M,O
Columbia University M,O*
Duke University M,D,O*
East Tennessee State University M,D,O
Emory University M*
Georgetown University M
Grand Canyon University M,O
Indiana University–Purdue University Indianapolis M,D
Inter American University of Puerto Rico, Arecibo Campus M
The Johns Hopkins University M,O
Loyola University Chicago M,O
Marquette University M,D,O
New York University M,D,O
Northeastern University M,O
Purdue University Calumet M
Rush University M,D,O
Southern Adventist University M
Texas Tech University Health Sciences Center M,D,O
Texas Woman's University M,D
Universidad de Iberoamerica P,M,D
The University of Alabama in Huntsville M,D,O
University of Cincinnati M,D
University of Guelph M,D,O
University of Illinois at Chicago M
University of Massachusetts Worcester M,D,O
University of Miami M,D*
University of Michigan M*
University of Pennsylvania M*
University of Pittsburgh M,D*
University of Puerto Rico, Medical Sciences Campus M
University of Rochester M,D,O
University of South Africa M,D
University of South Carolina M,O
University of Virginia M,D
Vanderbilt University M,D*
Wayne State University M*
Wright State University M

ADDICTIONS/SUBSTANCE ABUSE COUNSELING

Adler School of Professional Psychology M,D,O
Alliant International University–Los Angeles M
Argosy University, Hawai'i O*
Cambridge College M,O
Capella University M,D,O

Cleveland State University M,O
The College of New Jersey M,O
College of St. Joseph M
The College of William and Mary M,D
Coppin State University M
East Carolina University M
Eastern Michigan University M
Governors State University M
Grand Canyon University M
Hazelden Graduate School of Addiction Studies M,O
Indiana University–Purdue University Indianapolis M,D
Indiana Wesleyan University M
The Johns Hopkins University M,D
Kean University M
Lewis & Clark College M
Long Island University, C.W. Post Campus M
Maryville University of Saint Louis M,O
McNeese State University M
Mercy College M,O
Montclair State University M,D,O
Northeastern State University M
Pace University M
Palm Beach Atlantic University M
St. Mary's University (United States) M,D,O
Shippensburg University of Pennsylvania M,O
Southeastern Louisiana University M
Southern New Hampshire University M,O
Springfield College M
Stony Brook University, State University of New York M
Syracuse University O*
Troy University M,O
United States International University M
Universidad Central del Caribe M
University of Arkansas at Pine Bluff M
University of California, Berkeley O*
University of Central Oklahoma M
University of Detroit Mercy M,O
University of Illinois at Springfield M
University of Lethbridge M,D
University of Louisiana at Monroe M
University of Louisville M,D,O
University of Mary M
University of New England M,O
University of Oklahoma M,O*
Waynesburg University M,D

ADULT EDUCATION

Alverno College M
Argosy University, Chicago M,D,O*
Argosy University, Hawai'i M,D*
Argosy University, Phoenix M,D,O*
Argosy University, Seattle M,D*
Armstrong Atlantic State University M
Athabasca University M
Auburn University M,D,O
Ball State University M,D
Boston University M,D,O*
Buffalo State College, State University of New York M,O
Capella University M,D,O
Central Michigan University M
Cheyney University of Pennsylvania M
Cleveland State University M,O
Colorado State University M,D
Concordia University (Canada) M,O
Coppin State University M
Cornell University M,D*
Defiance College M
Delaware State University M
DePaul University M
East Carolina University M,O
Eastern Washington University M
Florida Agricultural and Mechanical University M,D
Florida Atlantic University M,D,O
Florida International University M,D,O
Fordham University M,D,O
Grand Valley State University M,O
Indiana University of Pennsylvania M,D
Indiana University–Purdue University Indianapolis M
Instituto Tecnologico de Santo Domingo M,O
The Johns Hopkins University M,O
Jones International University M
Kansas State University M,D*
Kean University M
Marshall University M
Memorial University of Newfoundland M,D,O
Michigan State University M,D,O
Montana State University M,D,O
Montclair State University M,D,O
Morehead State University M,O
Mount Saint Vincent University M
National-Louis University M,D,O
North Carolina Agricultural and Technical State University M,D
North Carolina State University M,D*
North Dakota State University M,D,O
Northern Illinois University M,D
Northwestern State University of Louisiana M
Nova Southeastern University D*
Oregon State University M
Plymouth State University D
Portland State University M,D
Regis University M,O
St. Francis Xavier University M
Saint Joseph's University M,O
San Francisco State University M,O
Seattle University M,O
Suffolk University M,O
Teachers College, Columbia University M,D
Texas A&M University M,D
Texas A&M University–Kingsville M
Texas A&M University–Texarkana M
Texas State University–San Marcos M,D
Troy University M
TUI University M
Tusculum College M
Union Institute & University M,D,O
Universidad del Este M
Universidad Metropolitana M
Université du Québec en Outaouais O
University of Alaska Anchorage M
University of Alberta M,D,O
University of Arkansas at Little Rock M
The University of British Columbia M,D
University of Central Oklahoma M
University of Cincinnati M,D,O
University of Colorado Denver M
University of Connecticut M,D*
University of Denver M,D,O
University of Georgia M,D,O
University of Manitoba M
University of Memphis M,D
University of Minnesota, Twin Cities Campus M,D,O
University of Missouri M,D,O*
University of Missouri–St. Louis M,D,O
University of Nebraska–Lincoln M,D,O*
The University of North Carolina at Greensboro M,D,O
University of North Florida M
University of Oklahoma M,D*
University of Phoenix M
University of Phoenix–Omaha Campus M
University of Phoenix–Sacramento Valley Campus M,O
University of Phoenix–Southern Arizona Campus M,O
University of Phoenix–Southern California Campus M
University of Phoenix–Washington D.C. Campus M,D,O
University of Regina M
University of Rhode Island M,D
University of South Africa M,D
University of Southern Maine M,O
University of Southern Mississippi M,D,O
University of South Florida M,D,O*
The University of Tennessee M,D
The University of Texas at San Antonio M,D*
University of the Incarnate Word M,D,O
The University of West Alabama M
University of Wisconsin–Milwaukee D
University of Wisconsin–Platteville M
University of Wyoming M,D,O
Virginia Commonwealth University M
Walden University M,D,O
Wayne State University M,D,O*
Western Kentucky University M,D,O
Western Washington University M
Widener University M,D
Wright State University O

ADULT NURSING

Allen College M,D,O
American University of Beirut M
Angelo State University M
Bloomsburg University of Pennsylvania M
Boston College M,D*
Clarkson College M,O
College of Mount Saint Vincent M,O
College of Staten Island of the City University of New York M,O
Columbia University M,O*
Daemen College M,D,O
DePaul University M
DeSales University M,O
Duke University M,D,O*
Eastern Michigan University M,O
East Tennessee State University M,D,O
Emory University M*
Felician College M,O*
Florida Southern College M
The George Washington University M,D,O
Georgia College & State University M
Georgia State University M,D,O
Goldfarb School of Nursing at Barnes-Jewish College M,O
Grantham University M
Gwynedd-Mercy College M
Hampton University M
Hunter College of the City University of New York M
Indiana University–Purdue University Fort Wayne M,O
Indiana University–Purdue University Indianapolis M,D
The Johns Hopkins University M,O
Kent State University M,D*
Lehman College of the City University of New York M
Lewis University M
Loma Linda University M
Long Island University, Brooklyn Campus M,O
Louisiana State University Health Sciences Center M,D
Loyola University Chicago M,O
Loyola University New Orleans M,D
Madonna University M
Marian University (WI) M
Marquette University M,D,O
Maryville University of Saint Louis M,D
Medical University of South Carolina M
Molloy College M,O
Monmouth University M,D,O
Mount Carmel College of Nursing M
Mount Saint Mary College M,O
Mount St. Mary's College M
New Mexico State University M,D
New York University M,D,O
North Park University M
Oakland University M
Otterbein University M,O
Purdue University Calumet M
Quinnipiac University D
Rush University M,D,O
Rutgers, The State University of New Jersey, Newark M*
Sage Graduate School M,O
St. Catherine University M,D
Saint Peter's College M,D,O
Saint Xavier University M,O
Seattle Pacific University M,O
Seton Hall University M,D
Southeastern Louisiana University M
Southern Adventist University M
Spalding University M
State University of New York Institute of Technology M,O
Stony Brook University, State University of New York M,O
Texas Christian University M,D
Texas Woman's University M,D
Troy University M,D,O
Universidad del Turabo M
University at Buffalo, the State University of New York D,O*

*M—master's degree; P—first professional degree; D—doctorate; O—other advanced degree; *—Close-Up and/or Display in one of the other books in this series*

University of Central Florida M,D,O
University of Cincinnati M,D
University of Colorado at Colorado Springs M,D
University of Colorado Denver M,D
University of Delaware M,O*
University of Hawaii at Manoa M,D,O
University of Illinois at Chicago M
University of Louisville M,D
University of Massachusetts Dartmouth M,D,O
University of Massachusetts Worcester M,D,O
University of Medicine and Dentistry of New Jersey M,D,O
University of Miami M,D*
University of Michigan M,O*
University of Minnesota, Twin Cities Campus M
University of Missouri–Kansas City M,D*
University of Missouri–St. Louis M,D,O
The University of North Carolina at Chapel Hill M,D,O*
The University of North Carolina at Charlotte M,O
The University of North Carolina at Greensboro M,D,O
University of North Florida M,D,O
University of Pennsylvania M*
University of Pittsburgh M,D*
University of Puerto Rico, Medical Sciences Campus M
University of Rochester M,D,O
University of St. Francis (IL) M,D
University of San Diego M,D
The University of Scranton M,O
University of South Alabama M,D
University of South Carolina M
University of Southern Maine M,O
The University of Tampa M
The University of Texas–Pan American M
The University of Toledo M,O
University of Wisconsin–Eau Claire M,D
University of Wisconsin–Madison D*
University of Wisconsin–Oshkosh M
Vanderbilt University M,D*
Villanova University M,D,O
Virginia Commonwealth University M,D,O
Washburn University M
Wayne State University M*
Western Connecticut State University M
Wilmington University M
Winona State University M,D,O
Wright State University M

ADVERTISING AND PUBLIC RELATIONS

Academy of Art University M
Ball State University M
Boston University M*
California State University, Fullerton M
Central Connecticut State University M,O
Colorado State University M,D
DePaul University M
Emerson College M
George Mason University M,O*
Georgetown University M
Golden Gate University M,D,O
Immaculata University M
Iona College M
Lasell College M,O
La Sierra University M
Marquette University M,O
Michigan State University M,D
Mississippi College M
Monmouth University M,O
Montana State University Billings M
Montclair State University M
New York University M
Northern Kentucky University M,O
Northwestern University M*
Quinnipiac University M
Rowan University M
Royal Roads University O
San Diego State University M
Savannah College of Art and Design M
Seton Hall University M
Southern Methodist University M
Suffolk University M
Syracuse University M*
Texas Christian University M
Towson University O
Universidad Autonoma de Guadalajara M,D
Université Laval O
The University of Alabama M
University of Denver M,O
University of Florida M*
University of Houston M
University of Illinois at Urbana–Champaign M
University of Maryland, College Park M,D
University of Miami M,D*
University of Nebraska–Lincoln M,D*
The University of North Carolina at Charlotte M
University of Oklahoma M*
University of Southern California M*
University of Southern Mississippi M,D
The University of Tennessee M,D
The University of Texas at Austin M,D
University of the Sacred Heart M
University of Wisconsin–Stevens Point M
Virginia Commonwealth University M
Wayne State University M,D*
Webster University M

AEROSPACE/AERONAUTICAL ENGINEERING

Air Force Institute of Technology M,D
Arizona State University M,D
Auburn University M,D
California Institute of Technology M,D,O
California Polytechnic State University, San Luis Obispo M
California State Polytechnic University, Pomona M
California State University, Long Beach M
Carleton University M,D
Case Western Reserve University M,D*
Concordia University (Canada) M
Cornell University M,D*
École Polytechnique de Montréal M,D,O
Embry-Riddle Aeronautical University–Daytona M
Embry-Riddle Aeronautical University–Worldwide M
Florida Institute of Technology M,D
The George Washington University M,D,O
Georgia Institute of Technology M,D
Illinois Institute of Technology M,D
Iowa State University of Science and Technology M,D*
Massachusetts Institute of Technology M,D,O
McGill University M,D
Middle Tennessee State University M
Mississippi State University M,D
Missouri University of Science and Technology M,D
Naval Postgraduate School M
North Carolina State University M,D*
Old Dominion University M,D
Penn State University Park M,D
Polytechnic Institute of NYU, Long Island Graduate Center M
Princeton University M,D*
Purdue University M,D
Rensselaer Polytechnic Institute M,D
Rutgers, The State University of New Jersey, New Brunswick M,D*
San Diego State University M,D
San Jose State University M
Stanford University M,D,O
Stevens Institute of Technology M,O
Syracuse University M,D*
Texas A&M University M,D
Université Laval M
University at Buffalo, the State University of New York M,D*
The University of Alabama M,D
The University of Alabama in Huntsville M,D
The University of Arizona M,D
University of California, Davis M,D,O
University of California, Irvine M,D*
University of California, Los Angeles M,D*
University of California, San Diego M,D*
University of Central Florida M
University of Central Missouri M,D
University of Cincinnati M,D
University of Colorado at Colorado Springs M
University of Colorado Boulder M,D*
University of Dayton M,D
University of Florida M,D,O*
University of Illinois at Urbana–Champaign M,D
The University of Kansas M,D
The University of Manchester M,D
University of Maryland, College Park M,D
University of Miami M,D*
University of Michigan M,D*
University of Minnesota, Twin Cities Campus M,D
University of Missouri M,D*
University of Nevada, Las Vegas M,D
University of Notre Dame M,D*
University of Oklahoma M,D*
University of Ottawa M,D*
University of Southern California M,D,O*
The University of Tennessee M,D
The University of Tennessee Space Institute M,D
The University of Texas at Arlington M,D
The University of Texas at Austin M,D
University of Toronto M,D
University of Virginia M,D
University of Washington M,D*
Utah State University M,D
Virginia Polytechnic Institute and State University M,D,O
Washington University in St. Louis M,D*
Webster University M,D,O
West Virginia University M,D
Wichita State University M,D

AFRICAN-AMERICAN STUDIES

Arizona State University M,D,O
Boston University M*
Carnegie Mellon University M,D*
Clark Atlanta University M,D
Columbia University M*
Cornell University M,D*
Eastern Michigan University O
Florida Agricultural and Mechanical University M
Harvard University D*
Indiana University Bloomington M*
Michigan State University M,D
Morgan State University M,D
North Carolina Agricultural and Technical State University M
Northwestern University D*
The Ohio State University M
Rutgers, The State University of New Jersey, New Brunswick D*
Syracuse University M*
Temple University M,D*
University at Albany, State University of New York M
University of California, Berkeley D*
University of California, Los Angeles M*
The University of Iowa M*
The University of Kansas M,O
University of Louisville M
University of Massachusetts Amherst M,D*
University of Memphis M,D,O
University of Wisconsin–Madison M*
West Virginia University M,D
Yale University D*

AFRICAN STUDIES

Boston University M,O*
California State University, Long Beach M
Carnegie Mellon University M,D*
Claremont Graduate University M,D,O
Columbia University O*
Cornell University M,D*
Florida International University M
Harvard University D*
Howard University M,D
Indiana University Bloomington M*
Michigan State University M,D
New York University M,D,O
Northwestern University O*
The Ohio State University M

Ohio University M*
Rice University D
Rutgers, The State University of New Jersey, New Brunswick D*
St. John's University (NY) M,O
Stony Brook University, State University of New York M
Syracuse University M*
University at Albany, State University of New York M
University of California, Los Angeles M*
University of Connecticut M*
University of Florida M,D,O*
University of Illinois at Urbana–Champaign M
The University of Kansas M,O
University of Louisville M
University of Pennsylvania M,D*
University of Pittsburgh O*
University of South Florida M*
The University of Texas at Austin M,D
University of Wisconsin–Madison M,D*
University of Wisconsin–Milwaukee D
West Virginia University M,D
Yale University M*

AGRICULTURAL ECONOMICS AND AGRIBUSINESS

Alabama Agricultural and Mechanical University M
Alcorn State University M
American University of Beirut M
Arizona State University M,D
Auburn University M,D
California Polytechnic State University, San Luis Obispo M
Colorado State University M,D
Cornell University M*
Delaware Valley College M
Florida Agricultural and Mechanical University M
Illinois State University M
Instituto Centroamericano de Administración de Empresas M
Iowa State University of Science and Technology M,D*
Kansas State University M,D*
Louisiana State University and Agricultural and Mechanical College M,D
McGill University M
Michigan State University M,D
Mississippi State University M
New Mexico State University M,D
North Carolina Agricultural and Technical State University M
North Carolina State University M*
North Dakota State University M
Northwest Missouri State University M
The Ohio State University M,D
Oklahoma State University M,D*
Oregon State University M,D
Penn State University Park M,D
Prairie View A&M University M
Purdue University M,D
Rutgers, The State University of New Jersey, New Brunswick M*
Santa Clara University M
South Carolina State University M
Southern Illinois University Carbondale M
Texas A&M University M,D
Texas A&M University–Kingsville M
Texas Tech University M,D*
Tropical Agriculture Research and Higher Education Center M,D
Tuskegee University M
Universidad del Este M
Université Laval M
University of Alberta M,D
The University of Arizona M
University of Arkansas M
The University of British Columbia M
University of California, Berkeley D*
University of California, Davis M,D
University of California, Santa Barbara M,D
University of Connecticut M,D*
University of Delaware M*
University of Florida M,D*
University of Georgia M,D
University of Guelph M,D
University of Idaho M
University of Illinois at Urbana–Champaign M,D
University of Kentucky M,D*
University of Maine M
University of Manitoba M,D
University of Maryland, College Park M,D
University of Massachusetts Amherst M,D*
University of Missouri M,D*
University of Nebraska–Lincoln M,D*
University of Nevada, Reno M,D*
University of Puerto Rico, Mayagüez Campus M
University of Saskatchewan M,D,O
University of Vermont M
University of Wisconsin–Madison M,D*
University of Wyoming M
Virginia Polytechnic Institute and State University M,D
Washington State University M,D,O
West Texas A&M University M
West Virginia University M
William Woods University M,O

AGRICULTURAL EDUCATION

Alcorn State University M,O
Arkansas State University M,O
California Polytechnic State University, San Luis Obispo M
Clemson University M
Cornell University M,D*
Eastern Kentucky University M
Iowa State University of Science and Technology M,D*
Louisiana State University and Agricultural and Mechanical College M,D
Mississippi State University M,D
Missouri State University M
Montana State University M
Murray State University M
New Mexico State University M
North Carolina Agricultural and Technical State University M
North Carolina State University M,O*
North Dakota State University M
Northwest Missouri State University M
The Ohio State University M,D
Oklahoma State University M,D*
Oregon State University M
Penn State University Park M,D
Purdue University M,D,O
State University of New York at Oswego M
Stephen F. Austin State University M
Tarleton State University M
Texas A&M University M,D
Texas A&M University–Commerce M
Texas A&M University–Kingsville M
Texas State University–San Marcos M
Texas Tech University M,D*
The University of Arizona M
University of Arkansas M
University of Connecticut M,D,O*
University of Delaware M*
University of Florida M,D*
University of Georgia M
University of Idaho M
University of Illinois at Urbana–Champaign M,D
University of Minnesota, Twin Cities Campus M,D
University of Missouri M,D,O*
University of Nebraska–Lincoln M*
University of Puerto Rico, Mayagüez Campus M
The University of Tennessee M
University of Wisconsin–River Falls M
Utah State University M
Virginia Polytechnic Institute and State University M,D
West Virginia University M,D

AGRICULTURAL ENGINEERING

Cornell University M,D*
Dalhousie University M,D
Illinois Institute of Technology M,D
Instituto Tecnológico y de Estudios Superiores de Monterrey, Campus Monterrey M,D
Iowa State University of Science and Technology M,D*
Kansas State University M,D*
Louisiana State University and Agricultural and Mechanical College M,D
McGill University M,D
New York University M,D
North Carolina State University M,D,O*
North Dakota State University M,D
The Ohio State University M,D
Oklahoma State University M,D*
Penn State University Park M,D
Purdue University M,D
South Dakota State University M,D
Texas A&M University M,D
Université Laval M
The University of Arizona M,D
University of Arkansas M,D
University of Dayton M
University of Florida M,D,O*
University of Georgia M,D
University of Idaho M,D
University of Illinois at Urbana–Champaign M,D
University of Kentucky M,D*
University of Missouri M,D*
University of Nebraska–Lincoln M,D*
University of Saskatchewan M,D
The University of Tennessee M
University of Wisconsin–Madison M,D*
Utah State University M,D
Virginia Polytechnic Institute and State University M,D
Washington State University M,D

AGRICULTURAL SCIENCES—GENERAL

Alabama Agricultural and Mechanical University M,D
Alcorn State University M
Angelo State University M
Arkansas State University M,O
Auburn University M,D
Brigham Young University M,D*
California Polytechnic State University, San Luis Obispo M
California State Polytechnic University, Pomona M
Clemson University M,D
Colorado State University M,D
Dalhousie University M
Florida Agricultural and Mechanical University M
Illinois State University M
Instituto Tecnológico y de Estudios Superiores de Monterrey, Campus Monterrey M,D
Iowa State University of Science and Technology M,D*
Kansas State University M,D*
Louisiana State University and Agricultural and Mechanical College M,D
McGill University M,D,O
McNeese State University M
Michigan State University M,D
Mississippi State University M,D
Missouri State University M
Montana State University M,D
Morehead State University M
Murray State University M
New Mexico State University M
North Carolina Agricultural and Technical State University M
North Carolina State University M,D,O*
North Dakota State University M,D
Northwest Missouri State University M
Nova Scotia Agricultural College M
The Ohio State University M,D
Oklahoma State University M,D*
Oregon State University M,D
Penn State University Park M,D
Prairie View A&M University M
Purdue University M,D
Sam Houston State University M
South Dakota State University M,D
Southern Arkansas University–Magnolia M
Southern Illinois University Carbondale M
Southern University and Agricultural and Mechanical College M
Tarleton State University M

*M—master's degree; P—first professional degree; D—doctorate; O—other advanced degree; *—Close-Up and/or Display in one of the other books in this series*

Tennessee State University	M
Texas A&M University	M,D
Texas A&M University–Commerce	M
Texas A&M University–Kingsville	M,D
Texas Tech University	M,D*
Tropical Agriculture Research and Higher Education Center	M,D
Universidad Nacional Pedro Henriquez Urena	M
Université Laval	M,D,O
University of Alberta	M,D
The University of Arizona	M,D
University of Arkansas	M,D
The University of British Columbia	M,D
University of California, Davis	M
University of Connecticut	M,D*
University of Delaware	M,D*
University of Florida	M,D*
University of Georgia	M,D
University of Guelph	M,D,O
University of Hawaii at Manoa	M,D
University of Illinois at Urbana–Champaign	M
University of Kentucky	M,D*
University of Lethbridge	M,D
University of Maine	M,D,O
University of Manitoba	M,D
University of Maryland, College Park	P,M,D
University of Maryland Eastern Shore	M,D
University of Minnesota, Twin Cities Campus	M,D
University of Missouri	M,D,O*
University of Nebraska–Lincoln	M,D*
University of Nevada, Reno	M,D*
University of Puerto Rico, Mayagüez Campus	M
University of Saskatchewan	M,D,O
University of South Africa	M,D
The University of Tennessee	M,D
The University of Tennessee at Martin	M
University of Vermont	M,D
University of Wisconsin–Madison	M,D*
University of Wisconsin–River Falls	M
University of Wyoming	M,D
Utah State University	M,D
Virginia State University	M
Washington State University	M
Western Kentucky University	M
West Texas A&M University	M,D
West Virginia University	M,D

AGRONOMY AND SOIL SCIENCES

Alabama Agricultural and Mechanical University	M,D
Alcorn State University	M
American University of Beirut	M
Auburn University	M,D
Colorado State University	M,D
Cornell University	M,D*
Iowa State University of Science and Technology	M,D*
Kansas State University	M,D*
Louisiana State University and Agricultural and Mechanical College	M,D
McGill University	M,D
Michigan State University	M,D
Mississippi State University	M,D
North Carolina Agricultural and Technical State University	M
North Carolina State University	M,D*
North Dakota State University	M,D
Nova Scotia Agricultural College	M
The Ohio State University	M,D
Oklahoma State University	M,D*
Oregon State University	M,D
Penn State University Park	M,D
Prairie View A&M University	M
Purdue University	M,D
South Dakota State University	M,D
Southern Illinois University Carbondale	M
Texas A&M University	M,D
Texas A&M University–Kingsville	M,D
Texas Tech University	M,D*
Tuskegee University	M
Université Laval	M,D
University of Alberta	M,D
The University of Arizona	M,D
University of Arkansas	M,D
The University of British Columbia	M,D
University of California, Davis	M,D
University of California, Riverside	M,D
University of Connecticut	M,D*
University of Delaware	M,D*
University of Florida	M,D*
University of Georgia	M,D
University of Guelph	M,D
University of Idaho	M,D
University of Illinois at Urbana–Champaign	M,D
University of Kentucky	M,D*
University of Maine	M,D
University of Manitoba	M,D
University of Massachusetts Amherst	M,D*
University of Minnesota, Twin Cities Campus	M,D
University of Missouri	M,D*
University of Nebraska–Lincoln	M,D*
University of Puerto Rico, Mayagüez Campus	M
University of Saskatchewan	M,D,O
University of Vermont	M,D
University of Wisconsin–Madison	M,D*
University of Wyoming	M,D
Utah State University	M,D
Virginia Polytechnic Institute and State University	M,D
Washington State University	M,D
West Virginia University	D

ALLIED HEALTH—GENERAL

Alabama State University	D
American College of Healthcare Sciences	M
Andrews University	M
Athabasca University	M,O
A.T. Still University of Health Sciences	M,D
Baylor University	M,D*
Belmont University	P,M,D
Bennington College	O
Boston University	M,D,O*
Brock University	M,D
Cleveland State University	M
Creighton University	P,M,D
Dominican College	M,D
Drexel University	M,D,O*
Duquesne University	M,D
East Carolina University	M,D
Eastern Kentucky University	M
East Tennessee State University	M,D,O
Emory University	M,D*
Ferris State University	M
Florida Agricultural and Mechanical University	M
Florida Gulf Coast University	M,D
Georgia Health Sciences University	M
Georgia Southern University	M,D,O
Georgia State University	M,D,O
Grand Valley State University	M,D
Idaho State University	M,D,O
Ithaca College	M,D
Loma Linda University	M,D
Long Island University, C.W. Post Campus	M,O
Marymount University	M,D,O
Maryville University of Saint Louis	M,D,O
Medical University of South Carolina	M,D
Mercy College	M,D,O
Midwestern University, Downers Grove Campus	M,D
Midwestern University, Glendale Campus	P,M,D,O
Minnesota State University Mankato	M,D,O
Misericordia University	M,D
Moravian College	M
Mountain State University	M
New Jersey City University	M
Northeastern University	P,M,D,O
Northern Arizona University	M,D,O
Nova Southeastern University	M,D*
Oakland University	M,D,O
The Ohio State University	M,D
Old Dominion University	M,D
Quinnipiac University	M,D
Regis University	P,M,D,O
Rosalind Franklin University of Medicine and Science	M,D,O*
Saint Louis University	M,D,O
Seton Hall University	M,D
Shenandoah University	M,D,O
South Carolina State University	M
Southwestern Oklahoma State University	M
Temple University	M,D*
Tennessee State University	M,D
Texas Christian University	M,D
Texas State University–San Marcos	M,D
Texas Tech University Health Sciences Center	M,D
Texas Woman's University	M,D
Towson University	M
University at Buffalo, the State University of New York	M,D,O*
The University of Alabama at Birmingham	M,D*
University of Arkansas at Little Rock	M
University of Connecticut	M*
University of Detroit Mercy	M,O
University of Florida	M,D*
University of Illinois at Chicago	M,D
The University of Kansas	M,D,O
University of Kentucky	M,D*
University of Massachusetts Lowell	M,D,O
University of Medicine and Dentistry of New Jersey	M,D,O
University of Mississippi Medical Center	M
University of Nebraska Medical Center	M,D,O
University of Nevada, Las Vegas	M,D
The University of North Carolina at Chapel Hill	M,D*
University of North Florida	M,D,O
University of Oklahoma Health Sciences Center	M,D,O
University of Phoenix–Las Vegas Campus	M
University of Puerto Rico, Medical Sciences Campus	M,D,O
University of St. Francis (IL)	M,D
University of Saint Francis (IN)	M
University of South Alabama	M,D
The University of South Dakota	M,D
The University of Tennessee Health Science Center	M,D
The University of Texas at El Paso	D
The University of Texas Medical Branch	M,D
University of Vermont	M,D
University of Wisconsin–Milwaukee	M,D,O
Virginia Commonwealth University	D
Washington University in St. Louis	M,D,O*
Western University of Health Sciences	M,D
Wichita State University	M,D

ALLOPATHIC MEDICINE

Albany Medical College	P
Albert Einstein College of Medicine	P
American University of Beirut	P,M
Baylor College of Medicine	P*
Boston University	P*
Brown University	P
Case Western Reserve University	P*
Charles Drew University of Medicine and Science	P
Columbia University	P,M*
Creighton University	P
Dalhousie University	P,M,D
Dartmouth College	P
Drexel University	P*
Duke University	P*
East Carolina University	P
Eastern Virginia Medical School	P
East Tennessee State University	P
Emory University	P*
Florida International University	P
Georgetown University	P
The George Washington University	P
Georgia Health Sciences University	P
Harvard University	P,D*
Hofstra University	P,D
Howard University	P,D
Indiana University–Purdue University Indianapolis	P,M,D
Instituto Tecnologico de Santo Domingo	P,M
The Johns Hopkins University	P
Loma Linda University	P,M,D
Louisiana State University Health Sciences Center	P,M

- Louisiana State University Health Sciences Center at Shreveport P
- Loyola University Chicago P
- Marshall University P
- Mayo Medical School P
- McGill University M,D
- Medical College of Wisconsin P*
- Medical University of South Carolina P
- Meharry Medical College P
- Mercer University P,M
- Michigan State University P
- Morehouse School of Medicine P
- Mount Sinai School of Medicine P
- New York Medical College P*
- New York University P
- Northeastern Ohio Universities Colleges of Medicine and Pharmacy P
- Northwestern University *
- The Ohio State University P
- Oregon Health & Science University P*
- Penn State Hershey Medical Center P,M,D
- Ponce School of Medicine P
- Pontificia Universidad Catolica Madre y Maestra P
- Queen's University at Kingston P
- Rosalind Franklin University of Medicine and Science P*
- Rush University P
- Saint Louis University P
- San Juan Bautista School of Medicine P
- Stanford University P
- State University of New York Downstate Medical Center P,M
- State University of New York Upstate Medical University P
- Stony Brook University, State University of New York P
- Temple University P*
- Texas Tech University Health Sciences Center P
- Thomas Jefferson University P
- Tufts University P
- Tulane University P*
- Universidad Autonoma de Guadalajara P
- Universidad Central del Caribe P,M,D
- Universidad Central del Este P
- Universidad de Ciencias Medicas P,M,O
- Universidad de Iberoamerica P,M,D
- Universidad Iberoamericana P
- Universidad Nacional Pedro Henriquez Urena P
- Université de Montréal P
- Université de Sherbrooke P
- Université Laval P,O
- University at Buffalo, the State University of New York P*
- The University of Alabama at Birmingham P*
- The University of Arizona P
- University of Arkansas for Medical Sciences P
- The University of British Columbia P,M
- University of Calgary P
- University of California, Berkeley *
- University of California, Davis P
- University of California, Irvine P*
- University of California, Los Angeles P*
- University of California, San Diego P*
- University of California, San Francisco P,D
- University of Central Florida P,M
- University of Chicago P
- University of Cincinnati P,M
- University of Colorado Denver P
- University of Connecticut Health Center P*
- University of Florida P*
- University of Hawaii at Manoa P
- University of Illinois at Chicago P
- University of Illinois at Urbana–Champaign
- The University of Iowa P*
- The University of Kansas P
- University of Kentucky P*
- University of Louisville P
- University of Maryland, Baltimore P
- University of Massachusetts Worcester P
- University of Medicine and Dentistry of New Jersey P
- University of Miami P*
- University of Michigan P*
- University of Minnesota, Duluth P
- University of Minnesota, Twin Cities Campus P
- University of Mississippi Medical Center P
- University of Missouri P*
- University of Missouri–Kansas City P,M*
- University of Nebraska Medical Center P,O
- University of New Mexico P*
- The University of North Carolina at Chapel Hill P*
- University of North Dakota P
- University of Oklahoma Health Sciences Center P
- University of Ottawa P,M,D*
- University of Pennsylvania P,O*
- University of Pittsburgh P*
- University of Puerto Rico, Medical Sciences Campus P
- University of Rochester P
- University of Saskatchewan P
- University of South Alabama P
- University of South Carolina P
- The University of South Dakota P
- University of Southern California P*
- University of South Florida P,M,D*
- The University of Tennessee Health Science Center P,M,D
- The University of Texas Health Science Center at Houston P*
- The University of Texas Health Science Center at San Antonio P,M
- The University of Texas Medical Branch P
- The University of Texas Southwestern Medical Center at Dallas P
- University of Toronto P,M,D
- University of Utah P*
- University of Vermont P
- University of Virginia P,M,D
- University of Washington P*
- The University of Western Ontario P,M
- University of Wisconsin–Madison P*
- Vanderbilt University P,M,D*
- Virginia Commonwealth University P
- Wake Forest University P
- Washington University in St. Louis P*
- Wayne State University P*
- West Virginia University P
- Wright State University P
- Yale University P*

AMERICAN INDIAN/NATIVE AMERICAN STUDIES

- Central Michigan University M
- Montana State University M
- Trent University M,D
- The University of Arizona M,D
- University of California, Davis M,D
- University of California, Los Angeles M*
- University of Idaho P
- The University of Kansas M
- University of Lethbridge M,D
- University of Manitoba M
- University of Oklahoma M*
- University of Tulsa M

AMERICAN STUDIES

- American University M,D,O
- Appalachian State University M
- Baylor University M*
- Boston University D*
- Bowling Green State University M,D*
- Brown University M,D
- California State University, Fullerton M
- California State University, Long Beach M
- Central Michigan University M,D,O
- Claremont Graduate University M,D,O
- Clark University M,D
- The College at Brockport, State University of New York M
- The College of William and Mary M,D
- The Colorado College M
- Columbia University M*
- Cornell University M,D*
- East Carolina University M
- Eastern Michigan University M,O
- Emory & Henry College M
- Fairfield University M
- Georgetown University M,D
- The George Washington University M,D
- Harvard University D*
- Inter American University of Puerto Rico, Metropolitan Campus M,D
- Kennesaw State University M
- Lehigh University M,D
- Lindenwood University M
- Michigan State University M,D
- Mississippi State University M,D
- Monmouth University M
- New Mexico Highlands University M
- New York University M,D
- Northeastern State University M
- Northwestern University M*
- Norwich University M
- Penn State Harrisburg M,D
- Pepperdine University M
- Providence College M
- Purdue University M,D
- Regent University M
- Rice University D
- Rutgers, The State University of New Jersey, Newark M,D*
- Saint Louis University M,D
- State University of New York College at Cortland O
- Trinity College M
- Universidad de las Américas–Puebla M
- University at Buffalo, the State University of New York M,D*
- The University of Alabama M
- University of Central Oklahoma M
- University of Colorado Denver M
- University of Dallas M
- University of Delaware M*
- University of Florida M,D*
- University of Hawaii at Manoa M,D,O
- The University of Iowa M,D*
- The University of Kansas M,D
- University of Louisiana at Lafayette D*
- University of Maine M,D
- University of Maryland, College Park M,D
- University of Massachusetts Boston M
- University of Michigan M,D*
- University of Michigan–Flint M
- University of Minnesota, Twin Cities Campus D
- University of Mississippi M
- University of Missouri–St. Louis M,D
- University of New Mexico M,D*
- University of Southern California D*
- University of Southern Maine M
- University of South Florida M*
- The University of Texas at Austin M,D
- University of Utah M,D*
- University of Wisconsin–Madison M,D*
- University of Wyoming M
- Utah State University M
- Villanova University M,O
- Washington State University M,D
- West Virginia University M,D
- Wheaton College M
- Wilfrid Laurier University M,D
- Yale University D*
- Yorktown University M

ANALYTICAL CHEMISTRY

- Auburn University M,D
- Brigham Young University M,D*
- California State University, Los Angeles M*
- Cleveland State University M,D
- Cornell University D*
- Eastern New Mexico University M
- Florida State University M,D
- Georgetown University D
- The George Washington University M,D
- Governors State University M
- Howard University M,D
- Illinois Institute of Technology M,D
- Indiana University Bloomington M,D*
- Kansas State University M,D*
- Kent State University M,D*

*M—master's degree; P—first professional degree; D—doctorate; O—other advanced degree; *—Close-Up and/or Display in one of the other books in this series*

Laurentian University M
Marquette University M,D
McMaster University M,D
Northeastern University M,D
Old Dominion University M,D
Oregon State University M,D
Purdue University M,D
Rensselaer Polytechnic Institute M,D
Rutgers, The State University of New Jersey, Newark M,D*
Seton Hall University M,D
Southern University and Agricultural and Mechanical College M
State University of New York at Binghamton M,D
Stevens Institute of Technology M,D,O
Tufts University M,D
University of Calgary M,D
University of Cincinnati M,D
University of Georgia M,D
University of Louisville M,D
The University of Manchester M,D
University of Maryland, College Park M,D
University of Massachusetts Lowell M,D
University of Memphis M,D
University of Michigan D*
University of Missouri M,D*
University of Missouri–Kansas City M,D*
The University of Montana M,D
University of Nebraska–Lincoln M,D*
University of Regina M,D
University of Southern Mississippi M,D
University of South Florida M,D*
The University of Tennessee M,D
The University of Texas at Austin M,D
The University of Toledo M,D
Vanderbilt University M,D*
Virginia Commonwealth University M,D
Wake Forest University M,D
West Virginia University M,D
Youngstown State University M

ANATOMY

Albert Einstein College of Medicine D
Auburn University M,D
Barry University M*
Boston University M,D*
Case Western Reserve University M*
Columbia University M,D*
Cornell University M,D*
Creighton University M
Dalhousie University M,D
Des Moines University M
Duke University D*
East Carolina University D
East Tennessee State University D
Georgia Health Sciences University M,D
Howard University M,D
Indiana University–Purdue University Indianapolis M,D
The Johns Hopkins University D
Loma Linda University M,D
Louisiana State University Health Sciences Center M,D
Louisiana State University Health Sciences Center at Shreveport M,D
Loyola University Chicago M,D
McGill University M,D
New York Chiropractic College M
New York Medical College M,D*
The Ohio State University M,D
Palmer College of Chiropractic M
Penn State Hershey Medical Center M,D
Purdue University M,D
Queen's University at Kingston M,D
Rosalind Franklin University of Medicine and Science M,D*
Rush University M,D
Saint Louis University M,D
State University of New York Upstate Medical University M,D
Stony Brook University, State University of New York D
Temple University M,D*
Universidad Central del Caribe M,D
Universidad de Ciencias Medicas P,M,O
Université Laval M,D,O
University at Buffalo, the State University of New York M,D*
The University of Arizona D
University of Arkansas for Medical Sciences M,D
The University of British Columbia M,D
University of California, Irvine M,D*
University of California, Los Angeles D*
University of California, San Francisco D
University of Chicago D
University of Georgia M
University of Guelph M,D
University of Illinois at Chicago D
The University of Iowa D*
The University of Kansas M,D
University of Kentucky D*
University of Louisville M,D
University of Manitoba M,D
University of Mississippi Medical Center M,D
University of Missouri M*
University of Nebraska Medical Center M,D
University of North Dakota M,D
University of North Texas Health Science Center at Fort Worth M,D
University of Prince Edward Island M,D
University of Puerto Rico, Medical Sciences Campus M,D
University of Rochester M,D
University of Saskatchewan M,D
The University of Tennessee M,D
University of Utah D*
The University of Western Ontario M,D
Virginia Commonwealth University D,O
Wake Forest University D
Wayne State University M,D*
Wright State University M
Youngstown State University M

ANESTHESIOLOGIST ASSISTANT STUDIES

Case Western Reserve University M*
Emory University M*
South University (GA) M*
Université Laval O
University of Guelph M,D,O
University of Missouri–Kansas City P,M*

ANIMAL BEHAVIOR

Arizona State University M,D
Bucknell University M
Cornell University D*
Emory University D*
Hunter College of the City University of New York M,D
Illinois State University M,D
University of California, Davis D
University of Colorado Boulder M,D*
University of Massachusetts Amherst M,D*
University of Minnesota, Twin Cities Campus M,D
The University of Montana M,D,O
The University of Tennessee M,D
The University of Texas at Austin M,D
University of Washington D*
Wesleyan University D*

ANIMAL SCIENCES

Alabama Agricultural and Mechanical University M,D
Alcorn State University M
American University of Beirut M
Angelo State University M
Auburn University M,D
Boise State University M
Brigham Young University M,D*
California State University, Fresno M
Clemson University M,D
Colorado State University M,D
Cornell University M,D*
Florida Agricultural and Mechanical University M
Fort Valley State University M
Iowa State University of Science and Technology M,D*
Kansas State University M,D*
Louisiana State University and Agricultural and Mechanical College M,D
McGill University M,D
Michigan State University M,D
Mississippi State University M,D
Montana State University M,D
New Mexico State University M,D
North Carolina Agricultural and Technical State University M
North Carolina State University M,D*
North Dakota State University M,D
Nova Scotia Agricultural College M
The Ohio State University M,D
Oklahoma State University M,D*
Oregon State University M,D
Penn State University Park M,D
Prairie View A&M University M
Purdue University M,D
Rutgers, The State University of New Jersey, New Brunswick M,D*
South Dakota State University M,D
Southern Illinois University Carbondale M
Sul Ross State University M
Texas A&M University M,D
Texas A&M University–Kingsville M
Texas Tech University M,D*
Tufts University M
Tuskegee University M
Universidad Nacional Pedro Henriquez Urena M
Université Laval M,D
The University of Arizona M,D
University of Arkansas M,D
The University of British Columbia M,D
University of California, Davis M,D
University of Connecticut M,D*
University of Delaware M,D*
University of Florida M,D*
University of Georgia M,D
University of Guelph M,D
University of Hawaii at Manoa M
University of Idaho M,D
University of Illinois at Urbana–Champaign M,D
University of Kentucky M,D*
University of Maine M
University of Manitoba M,D
University of Maryland, College Park M,D
University of Massachusetts Amherst M,D*
University of Minnesota, Twin Cities Campus M,D
University of Missouri M,D*
University of Nebraska–Lincoln M,D*
University of Nevada, Reno M*
University of New Hampshire M,D
University of Puerto Rico, Mayagüez Campus M
University of Rhode Island M,D
University of Saskatchewan M,D
The University of Tennessee M,D
University of Vermont M,D
University of Wisconsin–Madison M,D*
University of Wyoming M,D
Utah State University M,D
Virginia Polytechnic Institute and State University M,D
Washington State University M,D
West Texas A&M University M
West Virginia University M,D

ANTHROPOLOGY

American University M,D,O
The American University in Cairo M
American University of Beirut M
Arizona State University M,D,O
Ball State University M
Biola University M,D,O
Boston University M,D*
Brandeis University M,D
Brigham Young University M*
Brown University M,D
California State University, Bakersfield M
California State University, Chico M
California State University, East Bay M
California State University, Fullerton M
California State University, Long Beach M
California State University, Los Angeles M*
California State University, Northridge M
California State University, Sacramento M
Carleton University M

Case Western Reserve University M,D*
The Catholic University of America M
Central European University M,D
The College of William and Mary M,D
Colorado State University M
Columbia University M,D*
Concordia University (Canada) M
Cornell University D*
Dalhousie University M,D
East Carolina University M
Eastern New Mexico University M
Emory University D*
Florida Atlantic University M
George Mason University M,D*
The George Washington University M,D
Georgia State University M
Graduate School and University Center of the City University of New York D
Harvard University M,D*
Hunter College of the City University of New York M
Idaho State University M
Indiana University Bloomington M,D*
Iowa State University of Science and Technology M*
The Johns Hopkins University D
Kent State University M*
Louisiana State University and Agricultural and Mechanical College M,D
McGill University M,D
McMaster University M,D
Memorial University of Newfoundland M,D
Michigan State University M,D
Minnesota State University Mankato M
Mississippi State University M
Missouri State University M
Montclair State University O
New Mexico Highlands University M
New Mexico State University M
The New School: A University M,D
New York University M,D
North Carolina State University M*
Northern Arizona University M
Northern Illinois University M
Northwestern University D*
The Ohio State University M,D
Oregon State University M
Penn State University Park M,D
Portland State University M,D,O
Princeton University D*
Purdue University M,D
Rice University M,D
Roosevelt University M
Rutgers, The State University of New Jersey, New Brunswick M,D*
San Diego State University M
San Francisco State University M
San Jose State University M
Simon Fraser University M,D
Sonoma State University M
Southern Illinois University Carbondale M,D
Southern Methodist University M,D
Stanford University M,D
State University of New York at Binghamton M,D
Stony Brook University, State University of New York M,D
Syracuse University M,D*
Teachers College, Columbia University M,D
Temple University D*
Texas A&M University M,D
Texas State University–San Marcos M
Texas Tech University M*
Trent University M
Tulane University M,D*
Universidad de las Américas–Puebla M
Université de Montréal M,D
Université Laval M,D
University at Albany, State University of New York M,D
University at Buffalo, the State University of New York M,D*
The University of Alabama M,D
The University of Alabama at Birmingham M*
University of Alaska Anchorage M
University of Alaska Fairbanks M,D
University of Alberta M,D
The University of Arizona M,D
University of Arkansas M,D
The University of British Columbia M,D
University of Calgary M,D
University of California, Berkeley D*
University of California, Davis M,D
University of California, Irvine M,D*
University of California, Los Angeles M,D*
University of California, Riverside M,D
University of California, San Diego D*
University of California, San Francisco D
University of California, Santa Barbara M,D
University of California, Santa Cruz D
University of Central Florida M
University of Chicago M,D
University of Cincinnati M
University of Colorado Boulder M,D*
University of Colorado Denver M
University of Connecticut M,D*
University of Denver M
University of Florida M,D*
University of Georgia M,D
University of Guelph M,D
University of Hawaii at Manoa M,D
University of Houston M
University of Idaho M
University of Illinois at Chicago M,D
University of Illinois at Urbana–Champaign M,D
University of Indianapolis M
The University of Iowa M,D*
The University of Kansas M,D
University of Kentucky M,D*
University of Lethbridge M,D
University of Louisville M
The University of Manchester M,D
University of Manitoba M,D
University of Maryland, College Park M
University of Massachusetts Amherst M,D*
University of Memphis M
University of Michigan D*
University of Minnesota, Duluth M
University of Minnesota, Twin Cities Campus M,D
University of Mississippi M
University of Missouri M,D*
The University of Montana M,D
University of Nebraska–Lincoln M*
University of Nevada, Las Vegas M,D
University of Nevada, Reno M,D*
University of New Brunswick Fredericton M
University of New Mexico M,D*
The University of North Carolina at Chapel Hill M,D*
University of North Texas M
University of Oklahoma M,D*
University of Oregon M,D
University of Ottawa M*
University of Pennsylvania M,D*
University of Pittsburgh M,D*
University of Regina M
University of Saskatchewan M
University of South Africa M,D
University of South Carolina M,D
University of Southern Mississippi M
University of South Florida M,D*
The University of Tennessee M,D
The University of Texas at Arlington M
The University of Texas at Austin M,D
The University of Texas at San Antonio M,D*
University of Toronto M,D
University of Tulsa M
University of Utah M,D*
University of Victoria M
University of Virginia M,D
University of Washington M,D*
University of Waterloo M
The University of Western Ontario M,D
University of West Florida M
University of Wisconsin–Madison D*
University of Wisconsin–Milwaukee M,D,O
University of Wyoming M,D
Vanderbilt University M,D*
Washington State University M,D
Washington University in St. Louis D*
Wayne State University M,D*
West Chester University of Pennsylvania M,O
Western Kentucky University M
Western Michigan University M
Western Washington University M
Wichita State University M
Yale University M,D*
York University M,D*

APPLIED ARTS AND DESIGN—GENERAL

Academy of Art University M
Alfred University M
Art Center College of Design M*
Bowling Green State University M*
Bradley University M
California College of the Arts M
California Institute of the Arts M,O
California State University, Fresno M
California State University, Fullerton M
California State University, Los Angeles M*
Cardinal Stritch University M
Carnegie Mellon University D*
Concordia University (Canada) O
Cranbrook Academy of Art M
Drexel University M*
Emily Carr University of Art + Design M
Fashion Institute of Technology M*
Ferris State University M
Florida Atlantic University M
Howard University M
Illinois Institute of Technology M,D
Indiana University–Purdue University Indianapolis M
Iowa State University of Science and Technology M*
Kansas State University M*
Lamar University M
Louisiana State University and Agricultural and Mechanical College M
Louisiana Tech University M
Maryland Institute College of Art M
Massachusetts College of Art and Design M
Memphis College of Art M*
Minneapolis College of Art and Design M
New Mexico State University M
The New School: A University M
New York University M
North Carolina State University M,D*
NSCAD University M
Oklahoma State University M,D*
Pacific Northwest College of Art M
Pratt Institute M,O*
Purdue University M
Rensselaer Polytechnic Institute M,D
Rhode Island School of Design M
Rutgers, The State University of New Jersey, New Brunswick M*
San Diego State University M
San Francisco Art Institute M,O
San Jose State University M
Savannah College of Art and Design M,O
School of the Art Institute of Chicago M
School of Visual Arts (NY) M
Southern Illinois University Carbondale M
Stephen F. Austin State University M
Suffolk University M
Sul Ross State University M
Syracuse University M*
University of Alberta M
University of Baltimore M
University of California, Berkeley M,O*
University of California, Los Angeles M*
University of Central Oklahoma M
University of Cincinnati M
University of Delaware M*
University of Illinois at Urbana–Champaign M,D
The University of Kansas M
University of Kentucky M*

*M—master's degree; P—first professional degree; D—doctorate; O—other advanced degree; *—Close-Up and/or Display in one of the other books in this series*

University of Massachusetts Amherst M*
University of Massachusetts Dartmouth M
University of Michigan M*
University of Minnesota, Twin Cities Campus M,D,O
University of North Texas M
University of Notre Dame M*
University of Oklahoma M*
The University of Texas at Austin M
University of Washington M*
University of Wisconsin–Madison M,D*
Virginia Commonwealth University M
Virginia Polytechnic Institute and State University M,D
Wayne State University M*
Western Carolina University M
Western Illinois University M
Western Michigan University M
Yale University M*
York University M*

APPLIED BEHAVIOR ANALYSIS

Auburn University M,D
Ball State University M,D,O
Caldwell College M,D
California State University, Stanislaus M
The Chicago School of Professional Psychology M,D
The Chicago School of Professional Psychology at Downtown Los Angeles M,D
Florida Institute of Technology M,D
Florida State University M
Johnson State College M
Long Island University at Riverhead M,O
McNeese State University M
Mercy College O
Northeastern University M
Oklahoma City University M
Oklahoma State University M,D,O*
Rowan University M
Sage Graduate School M,O
St. Cloud State University M
Saint Peter's College M,D,O
The School of Professional Psychology at Forest Institute M,D,O
Simmons College M,D,O
Spalding University M
Teachers College, Columbia University M,D
Temple University M,D*
Tennessee Technological University D
The University of Kansas M,D
University of Maryland, Baltimore County M,D
University of North Florida M
University of Southern Maine M,O
University of South Florida M*
Western New England University D,O
Westfield State University M
Wright State University M
Youngstown State University M

APPLIED ECONOMICS

American University M,D,O
Auburn University M,D
Buffalo State College, State University of New York M
Clemson University M,D
Cornell University M,D*
Eastern Michigan University M
Georgia Southern University M
HEC Montreal M
The Johns Hopkins University M
Mississippi State University M,D
New York University M,D,O
North Carolina Agricultural and Technical State University M
Northeastern University M,D
Ohio University M*
Old Dominion University M
Portland State University M,D
Roosevelt University M
St. Cloud State University M
San Jose State University M
Southern Methodist University M,D
Texas Tech University M,D*
University of California, Santa Cruz M
University of Georgia M,D
University of Houston M,D
University of Idaho M
University of Illinois at Urbana–Champaign M,D
University of Michigan M*
University of Minnesota, Twin Cities Campus M,D
University of Nevada, Reno M,D*
University of New Brunswick Fredericton M
The University of North Carolina at Greensboro M
University of North Dakota M
University of North Texas M
University of Oklahoma M,D*
University of Pennsylvania D*
University of Vermont M
University of Wisconsin–Madison M,D*
University of Wyoming M
Utah State University M
Virginia Polytechnic Institute and State University M,D
Washington State University M,D,O
Western Kentucky University M
Western Michigan University M,D
Wright State University M

APPLIED MATHEMATICS

Acadia University M
Air Force Institute of Technology M,D
Arizona State University M,D,O
Auburn University M,D
Bowie State University M
Brown University M,D
California Institute of Technology M,D
California State Polytechnic University, Pomona M
California State University, East Bay M
California State University, Fullerton M
California State University, Long Beach M,D
California State University, Los Angeles M*
California State University, Northridge M
Carnegie Mellon University M,D*
Case Western Reserve University M,D*
Central European University M,D
Claremont Graduate University M,D
Clemson University M,D
Columbia University M,D,O*
Cornell University M,D*
Dalhousie University M,D
Delaware State University M,D
DePaul University M,O
East Carolina University M
École Polytechnique de Montréal M,D,O
Florida Atlantic University M,D
Florida Institute of Technology M,D
Florida State University M,D
The George Washington University M,D
Georgia Institute of Technology M,D
Hampton University M
Harvard University M,D*
Howard University M,D
Hunter College of the City University of New York M
Illinois Institute of Technology M,D
Indiana University Bloomington M,D*
Indiana University of Pennsylvania M
Indiana University–Purdue University Fort Wayne M,O
Indiana University–Purdue University Indianapolis M,D
Indiana University South Bend M
Inter American University of Puerto Rico, San Germán Campus M
Iowa State University of Science and Technology M,D*
The Johns Hopkins University M,D,O
Kent State University M,D*
Lehigh University M,D
Long Island University, C.W. Post Campus M
McGill University M,D
Michigan State University M,D
Missouri University of Science and Technology M,D
Montclair State University M,D,O
Naval Postgraduate School M,D
New Jersey Institute of Technology M
New Mexico Institute of Mining and Technology M,D
North Carolina Central University M
North Carolina State University M,D*
North Dakota State University M,D
Northeastern University M,D
Northwestern University M,D*
Oakland University M,D
Oklahoma State University M,D*
Penn State University Park M,D
Princeton University D*
Rensselaer Polytechnic Institute M
Rice University M,D
Rochester Institute of Technology M
Rutgers, The State University of New Jersey, New Brunswick M,D*
St. John's University (NY) M
San Diego State University M
San Jose State University M
Santa Clara University M
Simon Fraser University M,D
Southern Methodist University M,D
Stevens Institute of Technology M
Stony Brook University, State University of New York M,D
Temple University M,D*
Texas A&M University–Corpus Christi M
Texas State University–San Marcos M
Towson University M
Tulane University M,D*
The University of Akron M,D
The University of Alabama M,D
The University of Alabama at Birmingham D*
The University of Alabama in Huntsville M,D
University of Alberta M,D,O
The University of Arizona M,D
University of Arkansas at Little Rock M,O
The University of British Columbia M,D
University of California, Berkeley D*
University of California, Davis M,D
University of California, Merced M,D
University of California, San Diego M,D*
University of California, Santa Barbara M,D
University of California, Santa Cruz M,D
University of Central Arkansas M
University of Central Florida M,D,O
University of Central Missouri M,D
University of Central Oklahoma M
University of Chicago M,D
University of Cincinnati M,D
University of Colorado at Colorado Springs M,D
University of Colorado Boulder M,D*
University of Colorado Denver M,D
University of Connecticut M*
University of Dayton M
University of Delaware M,D*
University of Georgia M,D
University of Guelph M,D
University of Houston M,D
University of Illinois at Chicago M,D
University of Illinois at Urbana–Champaign M,D
The University of Iowa D*
University of Kentucky M,D*
University of Louisville M,D
The University of Manchester M,D
University of Maryland, Baltimore County M,D
University of Maryland, College Park M,D
University of Massachusetts Amherst M*
University of Massachusetts Lowell M,D
University of Memphis M,D
University of Michigan–Dearborn M
University of Minnesota, Duluth M
University of Missouri M*
University of Missouri–St. Louis M,D
University of New Hampshire M,D,O
The University of North Carolina at Charlotte M,D
University of Northern Iowa M
University of Notre Dame M,D*
University of Pennsylvania D*
University of Pittsburgh M,D*

University of Puerto Rico, Mayagüez Campus M
University of Rhode Island M,D,O
University of Rochester
University of Southern California M,D*
The University of Tennessee M,D
The University of Tennessee Space Institute M
The University of Texas at Arlington M,D
The University of Texas at Austin M,D
The University of Texas at Dallas M,D*
The University of Texas at San Antonio M*
The University of Toledo M,D
University of Tulsa
University of Washington M,D*
University of Waterloo M,D
The University of Western Ontario M,D
University of West Georgia M
Utah State University M,D
Virginia Commonwealth University M
Washington State University M,D
Wayne State University M,D*
Western Illinois University M,O
Western Michigan University M
West Virginia University M,D
Wichita State University M,D
Worcester Polytechnic Institute M,D,O
Wright State University M
Yale University M,D*
York University M,D*
Youngstown State University M

APPLIED PHYSICS

Air Force Institute of Technology M,D
Alabama Agricultural and Mechanical University M,D
California Institute of Technology M,D
Carnegie Mellon University M,D*
Christopher Newport University M
Colorado School of Mines M,D
Columbia University M,D,O*
Cornell University M,D*
DePaul University M
George Mason University M,D*
Harvard University M,D*
Idaho State University M,D
Iowa State University of Science and Technology M,D*
The Johns Hopkins University M,O
Laurentian University M
Mississippi State University M,D
Naval Postgraduate School M,D
New Jersey Institute of Technology M,D
Northern Arizona University M
Oregon State University M,D
Pittsburg State University M
Polytechnic Institute of NYU M,D
Rice University M,D
Rutgers, The State University of New Jersey, Newark M,D*
Southern Illinois University Carbondale M,D
Stanford University M,D
State University of New York at Binghamton M,D
Texas A&M University M,D
Texas Tech University M,D*
Towson University M
The University of Arizona M
University of Arkansas M,D
University of California, San Diego M,D*
University of Denver M,D
University of Maryland, Baltimore County M,D
University of Massachusetts Boston M
University of Massachusetts Lowell M,D
University of Michigan D*
University of Missouri–St. Louis M,D
The University of North Carolina at Charlotte M,D
University of Northern Iowa M
University of South Florida M,D*
The University of Texas at Austin M,D
University of Washington M,D*
Virginia Commonwealth University M
West Virginia University M,D
Yale University M,D*

APPLIED PSYCHOLOGY

Angelo State University M
Antioch University New England M,D,O
Arizona State University M
Athabasca University M,O
Boston College M,D*
California State University, Chico M
California State University, Northridge M
The Catholic University of America M,D
Central Michigan University M,D
The Chicago School of Professional Psychology M,D
The Chicago School of Professional Psychology: Online M,O
Clemson University M
Coppin State University M
Eastern Washington University M
Fairfield University M,O
Fordham University D
Francis Marion University M,O
The George Washington University D
Hofstra University D
Hunter College of the City University of New York M,D
Indiana University South Bend M
Laurentian University M
Loras College M
Loyola University Chicago M,D
Lynn University M,O
Massachusetts School of Professional Psychology M,D,O
Memorial University of Newfoundland M,D
New York University M,D,O
Northeastern University M,D,O
Oklahoma State University M,D,O*
Old Dominion University D
Rowan University M
Rutgers, The State University of New Jersey, New Brunswick M,D*
Saint Mary's University (Canada) M,D
Shippensburg University of Pennsylvania M
Teachers College, Columbia University M,D
University of Arkansas at Little Rock M
University of Baltimore M
University of Calgary M,D
University of Central Florida M,D
University of Guelph M,D
University of Maryland, Baltimore County D
University of New Brunswick Saint John M,D
University of Pennsylvania M,D*
University of Pittsburgh M,D*
University of Regina M,D
University of South Carolina Aiken M
The University of Tennessee M,D
The University of Texas of the Permian Basin M
University of Windsor M,D
University of Wisconsin–Stout M

APPLIED SCIENCE AND TECHNOLOGY

American University M
The College of William and Mary M,D
Colorado State University–Pueblo M
Harvard University M,O*
James Madison University M
Louisiana State University and Agricultural and Mechanical College M
Missouri State University M
Naval Postgraduate School M
Oklahoma State University M,D,O*
Saint Mary's University (Canada) M
Southeastern Louisiana University M
Southern Methodist University M,D
Thomas Edison State College O
University of Arkansas at Little Rock M,D
University of California, Berkeley D*
University of California, Davis M,D
University of Colorado at Colorado Springs M,D
University of Colorado Denver M
University of Mississippi M,D

APPLIED SOCIAL RESEARCH

American University M,O
California State University, Dominguez Hills M,O*
Concordia University (CA) M
Hofstra University M
Hunter College of the City University of New York M
Laurentian University M
The New School: A University M,D
Portland State University M,D
University of California, Los Angeles M,D*
Virginia Commonwealth University M,O
West Virginia University M

APPLIED STATISTICS

American University M,O
Bowling Green State University M,D*
Brigham Young University M*
California State University, Long Beach M
Cornell University M,D*
DePaul University M,O
Eastern Michigan University M
Florida State University M,D
Indiana University–Purdue University Fort Wayne M,O
Indiana University–Purdue University Indianapolis M
Instituto Tecnológico y de Estudios Superiores de Monterrey, Campus Monterrey M,D
Kennesaw State University M
Louisiana State University and Agricultural and Mechanical College M
Loyola University Chicago M
McMaster University M
Michigan State University M,D
New Jersey Institute of Technology M
New Mexico State University M,D
North Dakota State University M,D,O
Northern Arizona University M,O
Oakland University M
Rochester Institute of Technology M,O
Rutgers, The State University of New Jersey, New Brunswick M,D*
St. Cloud State University M
Stevens Institute of Technology O
Syracuse University M*
The University of Alabama M,D
University of Arkansas at Little Rock M,O
University of California, Riverside M,D
University of California, Santa Barbara M,D
University of Guelph M,D
University of Illinois at Urbana–Champaign M,D
University of Memphis M,D
University of Michigan M,D*
University of Northern Colorado M,D
University of Pittsburgh M,D*
University of South Carolina M,D,O
The University of Texas at San Antonio M,D*
University of the District of Columbia M
University of West Florida M
Villanova University M
Washington State University M
West Chester University of Pennsylvania M,O
Worcester Polytechnic Institute M,D,O
Wright State University M

AQUACULTURE

American University of Beirut M,D
Auburn University M,D
Clemson University M,D
Kentucky State University M
Memorial University of Newfoundland M
Nova Scotia Agricultural College M
Purdue University M,D
Texas A&M University–Corpus Christi M
University of Arkansas at Pine Bluff M
University of Florida M,D*
University of Guelph M
University of Rhode Island M,D

*M—master's degree; P—first professional degree; D—doctorate; O—other advanced degree; *—Close-Up and/or Display in one of the other books in this series*

ARCHAEOLOGY

American University of Beirut	M
Arizona State University	M,D,O
Boston University	M,D*
Brown University	M,D
Bryn Mawr College	M,D*
California State University, Northridge	M
Columbia University	M,D*
Cornell University	M,D*
Florida State University	M,D
Gordon-Conwell Theological Seminary	P,M,D
Graduate School and University Center of the City University of New York	D
Harvard University	M,D*
Illinois State University	M
Indiana University of Pennsylvania	M
Massachusetts Institute of Technology	M,D,O
Memorial University of Newfoundland	M,D
Michigan Technological University	M,D
Midwestern Baptist Theological Seminary	P,M,D,O
New York University	M,D
Northern Arizona University	M
Northwestern State University of Louisiana	M
Princeton University	D*
Rice University	M,D
St. Cloud State University	M
San Francisco State University	M
Simon Fraser University	M,D
Temple Baptist Seminary	P,M,D
Trinity International University	P,M,D,O
Tufts University	M
Universidad de las Américas–Puebla	M
Université Laval	M,D
University of Alberta	M,D
The University of British Columbia	M,D
University of Calgary	M,D
University of California, Berkeley	M,D*
University of California, Los Angeles	M,D*
University of California, Santa Barbara	M,D
University of Chicago	M,D
University of Colorado Denver	M
University of Denver	M
University of Georgia	M,D
University of Lethbridge	M,D
The University of Manchester	M,D
University of Massachusetts Boston	M
University of Memphis	M,D,O
University of Michigan	D*
University of Minnesota, Twin Cities Campus	M,D
University of Missouri	M,D*
University of Nebraska–Lincoln	M,D*
The University of North Carolina at Chapel Hill	M,D*
University of Pennsylvania	M,D*
University of Saskatchewan	M,D
University of South Africa	M,D
The University of Tennessee	M,D
The University of Texas at Austin	M,D
University of West Florida	M
University of Wisconsin–Madison	D*
Washington State University	M,D
Washington University in St. Louis	M,D*
Wheaton College	M
Wilfrid Laurier University	M
Yale University	M,D*

ARCHITECTURAL ENGINEERING

Carnegie Mellon University	M,D*
Drexel University	M,D*
Illinois Institute of Technology	M,D
Kansas State University	M*
Lawrence Technological University	M,D
Penn State University Park	M,D
University of Colorado Boulder	M,D*
University of Detroit Mercy	M
The University of Kansas	M
University of Louisiana at Lafayette	M*
University of Massachusetts Amherst	M,D*
University of Miami	M,D*
University of Nebraska–Lincoln	M,D*
The University of Texas at Austin	M

ARCHITECTURAL HISTORY

Arizona State University	D
Cornell University	M,D*
Graduate School and University Center of the City University of New York	D
Harvard University	D*
Massachusetts Institute of Technology	M,D
Savannah College of Art and Design	M
University of California, Berkeley	M,D*
University of Colorado Denver	D
University of Pittsburgh	M,D*
The University of Texas at Austin	M,D
University of Virginia	M,D
Virginia Commonwealth University	M,D

ARCHITECTURE

Academy of Art University	M
Andrews University	M
Arizona State University	M,D
Auburn University	M
Ball State University	M
Boston Architectural College	M
California College of the Arts	M
California Polytechnic State University, San Luis Obispo	M
California State Polytechnic University, Pomona	M
Carleton University	M
Carnegie Mellon University	M,D*
The Catholic University of America	M
City College of the City University of New York	M
Clemson University	M
Columbia University	M,D*
Cooper Union for the Advancement of Science and Art	M
Cornell University	M,D*
Cranbrook Academy of Art	M
Dalhousie University	M
Drury University	M
Florida Agricultural and Mechanical University	M
Florida International University	M
Frank Lloyd Wright School of Architecture	M
Georgia Institute of Technology	M,D
Hampton University	M
Harvard University	M,D*
Illinois Institute of Technology	M,D
Instituto Tecnológico y de Estudios Superiores de Monterrey, Campus Estado de México	M,D
Instituto Tecnológico y de Estudios Superiores de Monterrey, Campus Irapuato	M,D
Iowa State University of Science and Technology	M*
Judson University	M
Kansas State University	M*
Kent State University	M,O*
Lawrence Technological University	M
Louisiana State University and Agricultural and Mechanical College	M
Marywood University	M
Massachusetts College of Art and Design	M
Massachusetts Institute of Technology	M,D
McGill University	M,D,O
Miami University	M
Mississippi State University	M
Montana State University	M
Morgan State University	M
New Jersey Institute of Technology	M
The New School: A University	M
Newschool of Architecture & Design	M
New York Institute of Technology	M
North Carolina State University	M*
Northeastern University	M
The Ohio State University	M,D
Penn State University Park	M,D
Philadelphia University	M
Pontificia Universidad Catolica Madre y Maestra	M
Prairie View A&M University	M
Pratt Institute	M*
Princeton University	M,D*
Rhode Island School of Design	M
Rice University	M,D
Rochester Institute of Technology	M
Roger Williams University	M
Savannah College of Art and Design	M
School of the Art Institute of Chicago	M
Southern California Institute of Architecture	M
Southern Illinois University Carbondale	M
Syracuse University	M*
Temple University	M*
Texas A&M University	M,D
Texas Tech University	M*
Tulane University	M*
Universidad Autonoma de Guadalajara	M,D
Universidad Nacional Pedro Henriquez Urena	M
Université Laval	M
University at Buffalo, the State University of New York	M*
The University of Arizona	M
The University of British Columbia	M
University of Calgary	M,D
University of California, Berkeley	M,D*
University of California, Los Angeles	M,D*
University of Cincinnati	M
University of Florida	M,D*
University of Hartford	M
University of Hawaii at Manoa	D
University of Houston	M
University of Idaho	M
University of Illinois at Chicago	M
University of Illinois at Urbana–Champaign	M,D
The University of Kansas	M,D,O
University of Kentucky	M*
The University of Manchester	M,D
University of Manitoba	M
University of Maryland, College Park	M
University of Massachusetts Amherst	M*
University of Memphis	M
University of Miami	M*
University of Michigan	M,D*
University of Minnesota, Twin Cities Campus	M
University of Missouri	M*
University of Nebraska–Lincoln	M,D*
University of Nevada, Las Vegas	M
University of New Mexico	M*
The University of North Carolina at Charlotte	M
The University of North Carolina at Greensboro	M,O
University of Notre Dame	M*
University of Oklahoma	M*
University of Oregon	M
University of Pennsylvania	M,D,O*
University of Puerto Rico, Río Piedras	M
University of Southern California	M,D*
University of South Florida	M*
The University of Tennessee	M
The University of Texas at Arlington	M
The University of Texas at Austin	M,D
The University of Texas at San Antonio	M*
University of Toronto	M
University of Utah	M*
University of Washington	M,D,O*
University of Waterloo	M
University of Wisconsin–Milwaukee	M,D,O
Virginia Polytechnic Institute and State University	M,D
Washington State University	M
Washington State University Spokane	M,D
Washington University in St. Louis	M*
Wentworth Institute of Technology	M*
Woodbury University	M
Yale University	M,D*

ARCHIVES/ARCHIVAL ADMINISTRATION

Claremont Graduate University	M,D,O
Columbia University	M*
Drexel University	M*
Duquesne University	M
East Tennessee State University	M,O

Institution	Degrees
Emporia State University	M,D,O
Long Island University, C.W. Post Campus	M,D,O
New York University	M,D,O
Pratt Institute	M,O*
Simmons College	O
The University of British Columbia	M,D
University of California, Los Angeles	M,D,O*
University of California, Riverside	M,D
University of Manitoba	M,D
University of Massachusetts Boston	M
University of Michigan	M,D*
University of South Carolina	M,O
University of Wisconsin–Milwaukee	M,D,O
Wayne State University	M,O*

ART/FINE ARTS

Institution	Degrees
Academy of Art University	M
Adams State College	M
Adelphi University	M*
Alfred University	M,D
American University	M
Anna Maria College	M,O
Antioch University Midwest	M
Arizona State University	M,D
Arkansas State University	M
Arkansas Tech University	M
Art Center College of Design	M*
The Art Institute of Boston at Lesley University	M
The Art Institute of California–San Francisco	M
Azusa Pacific University	M
Ball State University	M
Bard College	M
Barry University	M*
Bob Jones University	P,M,D,O
Boise State University	M
Boston University	M*
Bowling Green State University	M*
Bradley University	M
Brandeis University	O
Brigham Young University	M*
Brooklyn College of the City University of New York	M,D
California College of the Arts	M
California Institute of the Arts	M,O
California State University, Chico	M
California State University, Fresno	M
California State University, Fullerton	M
California State University, Long Beach	M
California State University, Los Angeles	M*
California State University, Northridge	M
California State University, Sacramento	M
California State University, San Bernardino	M
Carnegie Mellon University	M*
Central Washington University	M
City College of the City University of New York	M
Claremont Graduate University	M
Clemson University	M
Cleveland State University	M
The College at Brockport, State University of New York	M
The College of New Rochelle	M
Colorado State University	M
Columbia University	M*
Concordia University (Canada)	M
Cornell University	M*
Cranbrook Academy of Art	M
Drury University	M
Duke University	D*
East Carolina University	M
Eastern Illinois University	M
Eastern Michigan University	M
East Tennessee State University	M
Edinboro University of Pennsylvania	M
Emily Carr University of Art + Design	M
Fairleigh Dickinson University, Metropolitan Campus	M
Ferris State University	M
Florida Atlantic University	M
Florida International University	M
Florida State University	M
Fontbonne University	M
Fort Hays State University	M
Framingham State University	M
Full Sail University	M
The George Washington University	M
Georgia Southern University	M
Georgia State University	M
Governors State University	M
Hofstra University	M,O
Hollins University	M,O
Hood College	M,O
Howard University	M
Hunter College of the City University of New York	M
Idaho State University	M
Illinois State University	M
Indiana State University	M
Indiana University Bloomington	M,D*
Indiana University of Pennsylvania	M
Indiana University–Purdue University Indianapolis	M
Institute for Doctoral Studies in the Visual Arts	D
Inter American University of Puerto Rico, San Germán Campus	M
James Madison University	M
John F. Kennedy University	M
Johnson State College	M
Kansas State University	M*
Kean University	M
Kent State University	M*
Laguna College of Art & Design	M
Lamar University	M
Lehman College of the City University of New York	M
Lesley University	M
Lindenwood University	M
Long Island University, C.W. Post Campus	M
Louisiana State University and Agricultural and Mechanical College	M
Louisiana Tech University	M
Maine College of Art	M
Marshall University	M
Maryland Institute College of Art	M,O
Marywood University	M
Massachusetts College of Art and Design	M
Memphis College of Art	M*
Miami International University of Art & Design	M*
Miami University	M
Michigan State University	M
Mills College	M
Minneapolis College of Art and Design	M,O
Minnesota State University Mankato	M
Mississippi College	M
Missouri State University	M
Montana State University	M
Montclair State University	M,O
Moore College of Art & Design	M
Morehead State University	M
National University	M
New Jersey City University	M
New Mexico State University	M
The New School: A University	M
New York Academy of Art	M
New York Institute of Technology	M
New York Studio School of Drawing, Painting and Sculpture	M,O
New York University	M,D,O
Norfolk State University	M
Northeastern University	M
Northern Illinois University	M
Northwestern State University of Louisiana	M
Northwestern University	M*
NSCAD University	M
The Ohio State University	M
Ohio University	M*
Oklahoma City University	M
Otis College of Art and Design	M
Pacific Northwest College of Art	M
Penn State University Park	M,D
Pennsylvania Academy of the Fine Arts	M,O
Pittsburg State University	M
Pontifical Catholic University of Puerto Rico	M
Portland State University	M
Pratt Institute	M*
Purchase College, State University of New York	M
Purdue University	M
Queens College of the City University of New York	M
Radford University	M
Rensselaer Polytechnic Institute	M,D
Rhode Island College	M
Rhode Island School of Design	M
Rochester Institute of Technology	M
Rutgers, The State University of New Jersey, New Brunswick	M*
San Diego State University	M
San Francisco Art Institute	M,O
San Francisco State University	M
San Jose State University	M
Savannah College of Art and Design	M
School of the Art Institute of Chicago	M
School of the Museum of Fine Arts, Boston	M
School of Visual Arts (NY)	M
Seton Hall University	M
Sotheby's Institute of Art–London	M
Sotheby's Institute of Art–New York	M
Southern Illinois University Carbondale	M
Southern Illinois University Edwardsville	M
Southern Methodist University	M
Spring Hill College	M
Stanford University	M,D
State University of New York at New Paltz	M
State University of New York at Oswego	M
Stephen F. Austin State University	M
Stony Brook University, State University of New York	M
Sul Ross State University	M
Syracuse University	M*
Temple University	M*
Texas A&M University	M,D
Texas A&M University–Commerce	M
Texas A&M University–Corpus Christi	M
Texas A&M University–Kingsville	M
Texas Christian University	M
Texas Southern University	M
Texas Tech University	M,D*
Texas Woman's University	M
Towson University	M
Tufts University	M
Tulane University	M*
United Theological Seminary of the Twin Cities	P,M,D,O
Universidad del Turabo	M
Université du Québec à Chicoutimi	M
Université du Québec à Montréal	M
Université Laval	M
University at Albany, State University of New York	M
University at Buffalo, the State University of New York	M,O*
The University of Alabama	M
University of Alaska Fairbanks	M
University of Alberta	M
The University of Arizona	M
University of Arkansas	M
University of Arkansas at Little Rock	M
The University of British Columbia	M,D,O
University of Calgary	M
University of California, Berkeley	M,O*
University of California, Davis	M
University of California, Irvine	M,D*
University of California, Los Angeles	M*
University of California, Riverside	M
University of California, San Diego	M,D*
University of California, Santa Barbara	M,D
University of California, Santa Cruz	M,D
University of Central Florida	M
University of Chicago	M
University of Cincinnati	M
University of Colorado Boulder	M*
University of Connecticut	M*
University of Dallas	M
University of Delaware	M*
University of Denver	M,O
University of Florida	M,D*
University of Georgia	M
University of Guam	M
University of Guelph	M
University of Hartford	M

*M—master's degree; P—first professional degree; D—doctorate; O—other advanced degree; *—Close-Up and/or Display in one of the other books in this series*

University of Hawaii at Manoa M
University of Houston M
University of Idaho M
University of Illinois at Chicago M
University of Illinois at Urbana–Champaign M
University of Indianapolis M
The University of Iowa M*
The University of Kansas M
University of Kentucky M*
University of Lethbridge M,D
University of Louisville M,D
The University of Manchester M,D
University of Maryland, Baltimore County M
University of Maryland, College Park M
University of Massachusetts Amherst M*
University of Massachusetts Dartmouth M,O
University of Memphis M,O
University of Miami M*
University of Michigan M*
University of Minnesota, Duluth M
University of Minnesota, Twin Cities Campus M
University of Mississippi M
University of Missouri M*
University of Missouri–Kansas City M,D*
The University of Montana M
University of Nebraska–Lincoln M*
University of Nevada, Las Vegas M
University of Nevada, Reno M*
University of New Hampshire M
University of New Mexico M*
University of New Orleans M
The University of North Carolina at Chapel Hill M*
The University of North Carolina at Greensboro M
University of North Dakota M
University of Northern Colorado M
University of Northern Iowa M
University of North Texas M
University of Notre Dame M*
University of Oklahoma M*
University of Oregon M
University of Pennsylvania M*
University of Regina M
University of Rochester M,D
University of Saint Francis (IN) M
University of Saskatchewan M
University of South Carolina M
The University of South Dakota M
University of Southern California M,D,O*
University of South Florida M*
The University of Tennessee M
The University of Texas at Arlington M
The University of Texas at Austin M
The University of Texas at El Paso M
The University of Texas at San Antonio M*
The University of Texas at Tyler M
The University of Texas–Pan American M
The University of the Arts M*
University of Toronto M,D
University of Tulsa M
University of Utah M*
University of Victoria M
University of Washington M*
University of Waterloo M
University of Windsor M
University of Wisconsin–Madison M*
University of Wisconsin–Milwaukee M
University of Wisconsin–River Falls M
University of Wisconsin–Superior M
Utah State University M
Vermont College of Fine Arts M
Virginia Commonwealth University M,D
Virginia Polytechnic Institute and State University D,O
Washington State University M
Washington University in St. Louis M*
Wayne State University M*
Webster University M
Western Carolina University M
Western Connecticut State University M
Western Michigan University M
West Texas A&M University M
West Virginia University M
Wichita State University M
William Paterson University of New Jersey M
Winthrop University M
Yale University M*
York University M,D*

ART EDUCATION

Academy of Art University M
Adelphi University M*
American University of Puerto Rico M,O
Anna Maria College M
Arcadia University M,D,O*
Arizona State University M,D
Art Academy of Cincinnati M
Austin College M
Averett University M
Ball State University M
Bennington College M
Boise State University M
Boston University M*
Bowling Green State University M*
Bridgewater State University M
Brigham Young University M*
Brooklyn College of the City University of New York M,O
Buffalo State College, State University of New York M
California State University, Long Beach M
California State University, Los Angeles M*
California State University, Northridge M
Carlow University M
Carthage College M,O
Case Western Reserve University M*
Central Connecticut State University M,O
Chatham University M
Christopher Newport University M
Cleveland State University M
College of Mount St. Joseph M
The College of New Rochelle M
The College of Saint Rose M,O
The Colorado College M
Colorado State University–Pueblo M
Columbus State University M
Concordia University (Canada) M,D
Concordia University Wisconsin M
Converse College M,O
Corcoran College of Art and Design M
Delaware State University M
Eastern Illinois University M
Eastern Kentucky University M
Eastern Michigan University M
Endicott College M
Fitchburg State University M,O
Florida Atlantic University M
Florida International University M,D,O
Florida State University M,D,O
George Mason University M*
Georgia Southern University M
Georgia State University M,D,O
Harding University M,O
Harvard University M*
Hofstra University M,D,O
Indiana University Bloomington M,D,O*
Indiana University–Purdue University Indianapolis M
Indiana University South Bend M
James Madison University M
Kean University M
Kennesaw State University M
Kent State University M*
Kutztown University of Pennsylvania M,O
Lesley University M,D,O
Long Island University, C.W. Post Campus M
Manhattanville College M*
Mansfield University of Pennsylvania M
Maryland Institute College of Art M
Maryville University of Saint Louis M,D
Marywood University M
Massachusetts College of Art and Design M
Memphis College of Art M*
Messiah College M
Miami University M
Millersville University of Pennsylvania M
Mills College M,D
Minnesota State University Mankato M
Mississippi College M,D,O
Missouri State University M
Montclair State University M,O
Moore College of Art & Design M
Morehead State University M
Nazareth College of Rochester M
New Jersey City University M
New York University M
North Carolina Agricultural and Technical State University M
North Georgia College & State University M,O
Nova Southeastern University M,O*
The Ohio State University M,D
Pace University M,O
Pittsburg State University M
Pratt Institute M,O*
Purdue University M,D,O
Queens College of the City University of New York M,O
Rhode Island College M
Rhode Island School of Design M
Rochester Institute of Technology M
Sage Graduate School M
Saint Michael's College M,O
Salem State University M
School of the Art Institute of Chicago M
School of Visual Arts (NY) M
Simon Fraser University M,D
Southern Connecticut State University M
Southern Illinois University Edwardsville M
Southwestern Oklahoma State University M
Stanford University M,D
State University of New York at New Paltz M
State University of New York at Oswego M
Sul Ross State University M
Syracuse University M,O*
Teachers College, Columbia University M,D
Temple University M*
Texas Tech University M*
Towson University M,O
Troy University M
The University of Alabama at Birmingham M*
The University of Arizona M
University of Arkansas at Little Rock M
The University of British Columbia M,D
University of Central Florida M
University of Cincinnati M
University of Dayton M
University of Florida M,D*
University of Georgia M,D,O
University of Idaho M
University of Illinois at Urbana–Champaign M,D
University of Indianapolis M
The University of Iowa M,D*
The University of Kansas M
University of Kentucky M*
University of Louisville M,D
University of Maryland, Baltimore County M
University of Massachusetts Amherst M*
University of Massachusetts Dartmouth M
University of Minnesota, Twin Cities Campus M,D,O
University of Mississippi M
University of Missouri M,D,O*
University of Nebraska at Kearney M
University of New Mexico M*
The University of North Carolina at Charlotte M,D
The University of North Carolina at Pembroke M
University of Northern Iowa M
University of North Texas M,D,O
University of Rio Grande M
University of St. Francis (IL) M
University of South Carolina M,D
The University of Tennessee M,D,O
The University of Texas at Austin M
The University of Texas at El Paso M
The University of the Arts M*
The University of Toledo M,D,O
University of Utah M*

Institution	Degrees
University of Victoria	M,D
University of West Georgia	M,O
University of Wisconsin–Madison	M,D*
University of Wisconsin–Milwaukee	M
University of Wisconsin–Superior	M
Ursuline College	M
Virginia Commonwealth University	M
Wayne State University	M,D,O*
Western Kentucky University	M
Western Michigan University	M
West Virginia University	M
William Carey University	M,O
Winthrop University	M

ART HISTORY

Institution	Degrees
American University	M
American University of Puerto Rico	M,O
Arizona State University	M,D
Bard Graduate Center: Decorative Arts, Design History, Material Culture	M,D*
Boston University	M,D,O*
Bowling Green State University	M*
Brigham Young University	M*
Brooklyn College of the City University of New York	M,D
Brown University	M,D
Bryn Mawr College	M,D*
California State University, Chico	M
California State University, Fullerton	M
California State University, Long Beach	M
California State University, Los Angeles	M*
California State University, Northridge	M
Caribbean University	M,D
Carleton University	M
Case Western Reserve University	M,D*
Christie's Education	M
City College of the City University of New York	M
Cleveland State University	M
Columbia University	M,D*
Concordia University (Canada)	M,D
Cornell University	D*
Duke University	D*
Emory University	D*
Fashion Institute of Technology	M*
Florida State University	M,D,O
George Mason University	M*
The George Washington University	M
Georgia State University	M
Graduate School and University Center of the City University of New York	D
Graduate Theological Union	M,D,O
Harvard University	D*
Howard University	M
Hunter College of the City University of New York	M
Illinois State University	M
Indiana University Bloomington	M,D*
James Madison University	M
The Johns Hopkins University	M,D
Kent State University	M*
Lamar University	M
Lancaster Theological Seminary	P,M,D,O
Louisiana State University and Agricultural and Mechanical College	M
Massachusetts Institute of Technology	M,D
McGill University	M,D
Montana State University	M
New Mexico State University	M
New York University	M,D
Northwestern University	D*
The Ohio State University	M,D
Ohio University	M*
Penn State University Park	M,D
Pratt Institute	M*
Purchase College, State University of New York	M
Queens College of the City University of New York	M
Rice University	D
Richmond, The American International University in London	M
Rutgers, The State University of New Jersey, New Brunswick	M,D,O*
San Diego State University	M
San Francisco Art Institute	M
San Jose State University	M
Savannah College of Art and Design	M
School of the Art Institute of Chicago	M
Southern Methodist University	M
State University of New York at Binghamton	M,D
Stony Brook University, State University of New York	M,D
Sul Ross State University	M
Syracuse University	M*
Temple University	M,D*
Texas A&M University–Commerce	M
Texas Christian University	M
Texas Tech University	M*
Tufts University	M
Tulane University	M*
Université de Montréal	M,D
Université du Québec à Montréal	M,D
Université Laval	M,D
University at Buffalo, the State University of New York	M,O*
The University of Alabama	M
The University of Alabama at Birmingham	M*
University of Alberta	M
The University of Arizona	M,D
University of Arkansas at Little Rock	M
The University of British Columbia	M,D,O
University of California, Berkeley	D*
University of California, Davis	M
University of California, Irvine	M,D*
University of California, Los Angeles	M,D*
University of California, Riverside	M
University of California, Santa Barbara	D
University of Chicago	M,D
University of Cincinnati	M
University of Colorado Boulder	M*
University of Connecticut	M*
University of Delaware	M,D*
University of Denver	M
University of Florida	M,D*
University of Georgia	M
University of Hawaii at Manoa	M
University of Houston	M
University of Illinois at Chicago	M,D
University of Illinois at Urbana–Champaign	M,D
The University of Iowa	M,D*
The University of Kansas	M,D
University of Kentucky	M*
University of Louisville	M,D
The University of Manchester	D
University of Maryland, College Park	M,D
University of Massachusetts Amherst	M*
University of Memphis	M,O
University of Miami	M*
University of Michigan	D*
University of Minnesota, Twin Cities Campus	M,D
University of Mississippi	M
University of Missouri	M,D*
University of Missouri–Kansas City	M,D*
University of Nebraska–Lincoln	M*
University of New Mexico	M,D*
The University of North Carolina at Chapel Hill	M,D*
University of North Texas	M,D,O
University of Notre Dame	M*
University of Oklahoma	M,D*
University of Oregon	M,D
University of Pennsylvania	M,D*
University of Pittsburgh	M,D*
University of Rochester	M,D
University of St. Thomas (MN)	M
University of South Africa	M,D
University of South Carolina	M
University of Southern California	M,D,O*
University of South Florida	M*
The University of Texas at Austin	M,D
The University of Texas at San Antonio	M*
The University of Texas at Tyler	M
University of Toronto	M,D
University of Utah	M*
University of Victoria	M,D
University of Virginia	M,D
University of Washington	M,D*
University of Wisconsin–Madison	M,D*
University of Wisconsin–Milwaukee	M,O
University of Wisconsin–Superior	M
Virginia Commonwealth University	M,D
Washington University in St. Louis	M,D*
Wayne State University	M*
West Virginia University	M
Williams College	M
Yale University	D*
York University	M,D*

ARTIFICIAL INTELLIGENCE/ ROBOTICS

Institution	Degrees
California State University, Northridge	M
Carnegie Mellon University	M,D*
Cornell University	M,D*
Eastern Michigan University	M,O
Indiana University–Purdue University Indianapolis	M,D
Instituto Tecnológico y de Estudios Superiores de Monterrey, Campus Monterrey	M,D
Portland State University	M,D,O
South Dakota School of Mines and Technology	M
University of California, Riverside	M,D
University of California, San Diego	M,D*
University of Georgia	M
University of Pittsburgh	M,D*
University of Southern California	M,D*
Villanova University	M,O
Worcester Polytechnic Institute	M,D,O

ARTS ADMINISTRATION

Institution	Degrees
American University	M,O
Boston University	M,O*
Carnegie Mellon University	M*
Claremont Graduate University	M
The College at Brockport, State University of New York	M,O
College of Charleston	M,O
Columbia College Chicago	M
Drexel University	M*
Eastern Michigan University	M
Fashion Institute of Technology	M*
Florida State University	M,D
George Mason University	M,O*
Goucher College	M
HEC Montreal	O
Indiana University Bloomington	M*
Montclair State University	M
New York University	M
The Ohio State University	M
Pratt Institute	M*
Regis University	M,O
Rhode Island College	M
Ryerson University	M
Saint Mary's University of Minnesota	M
St. Thomas University	M
Savannah College of Art and Design	M
School of the Art Institute of Chicago	M
Shenandoah University	M,D,O
Sotheby's Institute of Art–London	M
Sotheby's Institute of Art–New York	M
Southern Methodist University	
Southern Utah University	M
Teachers College, Columbia University	M
Temple University	M,D*
Universidad del Turabo	M
The University of Akron	M
University of Cincinnati	M,D
University of Denver	M,O
University of Florida	M*
The University of Manchester	D
University of New Orleans	M
The University of North Carolina at Charlotte	M,D,O
University of North Carolina School of the Arts	M
University of Oregon	M
University of Southern California	M*
University of Wisconsin–Madison	M*
Valparaiso University	M
Webster University	M
Winthrop University	M

ARTS JOURNALISM

Institution	Degrees
School of the Art Institute of Chicago	M
Syracuse University	M*

*M—master's degree; P—first professional degree; D—doctorate; O—other advanced degree; *—Close-Up and/or Display in one of the other books in this series*

ART THERAPY

Adler Graduate School M,O
Adler School of Professional Psychology M,D,O
Albertus Magnus College M
Athabasca University M,O
Caldwell College M
California Institute of Integral Studies M,D
California State University, Los Angeles M*
The College of New Rochelle M
Concordia University (Canada) M
Drexel University M,O*
Eastern Virginia Medical School M
Emporia State University M
The George Washington University M
Hofstra University M,O
Lesley University M,D,O
Long Island University, C.W. Post Campus M
Marylhurst University M,O
Marywood University M,O
Mount Mary College M
Naropa University M
Nazareth College of Rochester M
New York University M
Notre Dame de Namur University M
Ottawa University M
Pratt Institute M*
Prescott College M
Saint Mary-of-the-Woods College M,O
Salve Regina University M,O
School of the Art Institute of Chicago M
School of Visual Arts (NY) M
Seton Hill University M
Southern Illinois University Edwardsville M
Southwestern College (NM) M
Springfield College M,O
University of Maryland, College Park M,D,O
University of Wisconsin–Superior M
Ursuline College M

ASIAN-AMERICAN STUDIES

California State University, Long Beach M
San Francisco State University M
University of California, Los Angeles M*

ASIAN LANGUAGES

Columbia University M,D*
Cornell University M,D*
Harvard University M,D*
Indiana University Bloomington M,D*
Naropa University M
The Ohio State University M,D
St. John's College (NM) M
Seton Hall University M
University of California, Berkeley M,D*
University of California, Irvine M,D*
University of California, Los Angeles M,D*
University of California, Santa Barbara M,D
University of Chicago M,D
University of Hawaii at Manoa M,D
University of Illinois at Urbana–Champaign M,D
The University of Kansas M
University of Michigan M,D*
University of Minnesota, Twin Cities Campus D
University of Oregon M,D
University of Southern California M,D*
The University of Texas at Austin M,D
University of Washington M,D*
University of Wisconsin–Madison M,D*
Washington University in St. Louis M,D*
Yale University D*

ASIAN STUDIES

California Institute of Integral Studies M,D
California State University, Long Beach M
Columbia University M,D,O*
Cornell University M,D*
Duke University M,O*
Florida International University M
Florida State University M
The George Washington University M
Harvard University M,D*
Indiana University Bloomington M,D*
The Johns Hopkins University M,D,O
Maharishi University of Management M,D
McGill University M,D
New York University M,D
Ohio University M*
Princeton University D*
Rutgers, The State University of New Jersey, New Brunswick D*
St. John's College (NM) M
St. John's University (NY) M,O
San Diego State University M
Seton Hall University M
Stanford University M
Texas A&M University M,O
United Theological Seminary of the Twin Cities P,M,D,O
University of Alberta M
The University of Arizona M,D
The University of British Columbia M,D
University of California, Berkeley M,D*
University of California, Los Angeles M,D*
University of California, Riverside M
University of California, Santa Barbara M,D
University of Chicago M,D
University of Colorado Boulder M,D*
University of Florida M,D*
University of Hawaii at Hilo M
University of Hawaii at Manoa O
University of Illinois at Urbana–Champaign M,D
The University of Iowa M*
The University of Kansas M
University of Maine M,D
The University of Manchester M,D
University of Michigan M,D,O*
University of Minnesota, Twin Cities Campus D
University of Oregon M
University of Pennsylvania M,D*
University of Pittsburgh M,O*
University of San Francisco M
University of Southern California M,D*
The University of Texas at Austin M,D
University of Toronto M,D
University of Utah M*
University of Victoria M
University of Virginia M
University of Washington M,D*
University of Wisconsin–Madison M,D*
Valparaiso University M
Washington State University M,D
Washington University in St. Louis M*
West Virginia University M,D
Yale University M*

ASTRONOMY

Boston University M,D*
Brigham Young University M,D*
California Institute of Technology D
Case Western Reserve University M,D*
Clemson University M,D
Columbia University M,D*
Cornell University D*
Dartmouth College M,D
Georgia State University D
Harvard University D*
Indiana University Bloomington M,D*
Iowa State University of Science and Technology M,D*
The Johns Hopkins University D
Louisiana State University and Agricultural and Mechanical College M,D
Michigan State University M,D
Minnesota State University Mankato M
New Mexico State University M,D
Northwestern University M,D*
The Ohio State University M,D
Ohio University M,D*
Penn State University Park M,D
Princeton University D*
Rice University M,D
Rutgers, The State University of New Jersey, New Brunswick M,D*
Saint Mary's University (Canada) M,D
San Diego State University M
Stony Brook University, State University of New York D
Université de Moncton M
The University of Arizona M,D
The University of British Columbia M,D
University of Calgary M,D
University of California, Los Angeles M,D*
University of California, Santa Cruz D
University of Chicago M,D
University of Delaware M,D*
University of Denver M,D
University of Florida M,D*
University of Hawaii at Manoa M,D
University of Illinois at Urbana–Champaign M,D
The University of Iowa M*
The University of Kansas M,D
University of Kentucky M,D*
University of Maine M
The University of Manchester M,D
University of Maryland, College Park M,D
University of Massachusetts Amherst M,D*
University of Michigan D*
University of Minnesota, Twin Cities Campus M,D
University of Missouri M,D*
University of Nebraska–Lincoln M,D*
University of Nevada, Las Vegas M,D
The University of North Carolina at Chapel Hill M,D*
University of Rochester
University of South Carolina M,D
The University of Texas at Austin M,D
University of Toronto M,D
University of Victoria M,D
University of Virginia M,D
University of Washington M,D*
The University of Western Ontario M,D
University of Wisconsin–Madison D*
Vanderbilt University M,D*
Wesleyan University M*
West Chester University of Pennsylvania M,O
Yale University M,D*
York University M,D*

ASTROPHYSICS

Air Force Institute of Technology M,D
Arizona State University M,D
Clemson University M,D
Cornell University D*
Harvard University D*
ICR Graduate School M
Indiana University Bloomington M,D*
Iowa State University of Science and Technology M,D*
Louisiana State University and Agricultural and Mechanical College M,D
McMaster University D
Michigan State University M,D
New Mexico Institute of Mining and Technology M,D
Northwestern University M,D*
Penn State University Park M,D
Princeton University D*
Rochester Institute of Technology M,D
Texas Christian University M,D
University of Alaska Fairbanks M,D
University of Alberta M,D
University of California, Berkeley D*
University of California, Los Angeles M,D*
University of California, Santa Cruz D
University of Chicago M,D
University of Colorado Boulder M,D*
The University of Manchester M,D
University of Maryland, Baltimore County M,D
University of Michigan D*
University of Minnesota, Twin Cities Campus M,D
University of Missouri–St. Louis M,D
The University of North Carolina at Chapel Hill M,D*
University of Pennsylvania M,D*
University of Toronto M,D
University of Victoria M,D
Yale University M,D*

ATHLETIC TRAINING AND SPORTS MEDICINE

Armstrong Atlantic State University M

A.T. Still University of Health Sciences M,D
Barry University M*
Bloomsburg University of Pennsylvania M
Boston University D*
Brigham Young University M,D*
California Baptist University M
California State University, Long Beach M
California University of Pennsylvania M
Eastern Michigan University M,O
East Tennessee State University M,D
Florida International University M
Georgia State University M
Humboldt State University M
Indiana State University M
Indiana University Bloomington M,D*
Inter American University of Puerto Rico, Metropolitan Campus M
Kent State University M*
Lenoir-Rhyne University M
Long Island University, Brooklyn Campus M
Manchester College M
Montana State University Billings M
Ohio University M*
Old Dominion University M
Plymouth State University M
Rocky Mountain University of Health Professions D
Saint Louis University M,D
Seton Hall University M
Shenandoah University M,O
Springfield College M,D
Stephen F. Austin State University M
Texas State University–San Marcos M
Texas Tech University Health Sciences Center M
United States Sports Academy M
Universidad del Turabo M
University of Arkansas M
University of Colorado at Colorado Springs M
The University of Findlay M
University of Florida M,D*
University of Miami M*
The University of North Carolina at Chapel Hill M*
University of Northern Iowa M,D
University of Pittsburgh M*
The University of Tennessee M,D
The University of Tennessee at Chattanooga M
The University of West Alabama M
University of Wisconsin–La Crosse M
Virginia Commonwealth University M
Weber State University M
West Chester University of Pennsylvania M,O
Western Michigan University M
West Virginia University M,D
West Virginia Wesleyan College M

ATMOSPHERIC SCIENCES

Arizona State University M,D,O
Bard College M,O
City College of the City University of New York M,D
Clemson University M,D
Colorado State University M,D
Columbia University M,D*
Cornell University M,D*
Creighton University M
George Mason University D*
Georgia Institute of Technology M,D
Hampton University M,D
Howard University M,D
Massachusetts Institute of Technology M,D
McGill University M,D
Michigan Technological University D
Mississippi State University M,D
New Mexico Institute of Mining and Technology M,D
North Carolina State University M,D*
Northern Arizona University M
The Ohio State University M,D
Oregon State University M,D
Princeton University D*
Purdue University M,D
Rutgers, The State University of New Jersey, New Brunswick M,D*
South Dakota School of Mines and Technology M,D
Stony Brook University, State University of New York M,D
Texas Tech University M,D*
Université du Québec à Montréal M,D,O
University at Albany, State University of New York M,D
The University of Alabama in Huntsville M,D
University of Alaska Fairbanks M,D
The University of Arizona M,D
The University of British Columbia M,D
University of California, Davis M,D
University of California, Los Angeles M,D*
University of Chicago M,D
University of Colorado Boulder M,D*
University of Guelph M,D
University of Houston M,D
University of Illinois at Urbana–Champaign M,D
The University of Kansas M,D
The University of Manchester M,D
University of Maryland, Baltimore County M,D
University of Massachusetts Lowell M,D
University of Michigan M,D*
University of Missouri M,D*
University of Nevada, Reno M,D*
The University of North Carolina at Chapel Hill M,D*
University of North Dakota M,D
University of Utah M,D*
University of Washington M,D*
University of Wisconsin–Madison M,D*
University of Wyoming M,D
Yale University D*

AUTOMOTIVE ENGINEERING

Central Michigan University M,O
Clemson University M,D
Lawrence Technological University M,D
Minnesota State University Mankato M
University of Michigan–Dearborn M,D
Wayne State University M,O*

AVIATION

Embry-Riddle Aeronautical University–Worldwide D
Everglades University M
Lewis University M
Southeastern Oklahoma State University M
University of Illinois at Urbana–Champaign M
University of North Dakota M
The University of Tennessee M
The University of Tennessee Space Institute M

AVIATION MANAGEMENT

Arizona State University M
Concordia University (Canada) M,D,O
Daniel Webster College M
Delta State University M
Dowling College M,O
Embry-Riddle Aeronautical University–Daytona M
Embry-Riddle Aeronautical University–Worldwide M,O
Lewis University M
Lynn University M
Middle Tennessee State University M
Southeastern Oklahoma State University M
Vaughn College of Aeronautics and Technology M

BACTERIOLOGY

Illinois State University M,D
The University of Iowa M,D*
University of Prince Edward Island M,D
The University of Texas Medical Branch D
University of Washington D*
University of Wisconsin–Madison M*

BIOCHEMICAL ENGINEERING

Cornell University M,D*
Dartmouth College M,D
Drexel University M*
Rutgers, The State University of New Jersey, New Brunswick M,D*
University of California, Irvine M,D*
University of Georgia M
The University of Iowa M,D*
The University of Manchester M,D
University of Maryland, Baltimore County M,D,O
The University of Western Ontario M,D
Villanova University M,O

BIOCHEMISTRY

Albert Einstein College of Medicine D
American University of Beirut P,M
Arizona State University M,D
Auburn University M,D
Baylor College of Medicine D*
Boston College D*
Boston University M,D*
Brandeis University D
Brigham Young University M,D*
Brown University M,D
California Institute of Technology M,D
California Polytechnic State University, San Luis Obispo M
California State University, East Bay M
California State University, Long Beach M
California State University, Los Angeles M*
California State University, Northridge M
Carnegie Mellon University M,D*
Case Western Reserve University M,D*
Central Connecticut State University M,O
City College of the City University of New York M,D
Clemson University D
Colorado State University M,D
Colorado State University–Pueblo M
Columbia University M,D*
Cornell University D*
Cornell University, Joan and Sanford I. Weill Medical College and Graduate School of Medical Sciences M,D
Dalhousie University M,D
Dartmouth College D
DePaul University M
Drexel University M,D*
Duke University D*
Duquesne University M,D
East Carolina University D
Eastern New Mexico University M
East Tennessee State University D
Emory University D*
Florida Institute of Technology M,D
Florida State University M,D
George Mason University M,D*
Georgetown University M,D
The George Washington University M,D
Georgia Health Sciences University M,D
Georgia Institute of Technology M,D
Georgia State University M,D
Graduate School and University Center of the City University of New York D
Harvard University D*
Howard University M,D
Hunter College of the City University of New York M,D
Illinois Institute of Technology M,D
Illinois State University M,D
Indiana University Bloomington M,D*
Indiana University–Purdue University Indianapolis M,D
Iowa State University of Science and Technology M,D*
The Johns Hopkins University M,D
Kansas State University M,D*
Kent State University M,D*
Laurentian University M
Lehigh University M,D
Loma Linda University M,D
Louisiana State University and Agricultural and Mechanical College M,D
Louisiana State University Health Sciences Center at Shreveport M,D
Loyola University Chicago M,D
Massachusetts Institute of Technology D
Mayo Graduate School D
McGill University M,D
McMaster University M,D
Medical College of Wisconsin D*

*M—master's degree; P—first professional degree; D—doctorate; O—other advanced degree; *—Close-Up and/or Display in one of the other books in this series*

Medical University of South Carolina	M,D
Memorial University of Newfoundland	M,D
Miami University	M,D
Michigan State University	M,D
Mississippi College	M
Mississippi State University	M,D
Montana State University	M,D
Montclair State University	M,O
New Mexico Institute of Mining and Technology	M,D
New York Medical College	M,D*
North Carolina State University	D*
North Dakota State University	M,D
Northeastern University	M,D
Northwestern University	D*
OGI School of Science & Engineering at Oregon Health & Science University	M,D
The Ohio State University	M,D
Ohio University	M,D*
Oklahoma State University	M,D*
Old Dominion University	M,D
Oregon Health & Science University	M,D*
Oregon State University	M,D
Penn State Hershey Medical Center	M,D
Penn State University Park	M,D
Purdue University	M,D
Queens College of the City University of New York	M
Queen's University at Kingston	M,D
Rensselaer Polytechnic Institute	M,D
Rice University	M,D
Rosalind Franklin University of Medicine and Science	M,D*
Rush University	D
Rutgers, The State University of New Jersey, Newark	M,D*
Rutgers, The State University of New Jersey, New Brunswick	M,D*
Saint Joseph College	M
Saint Louis University	D
San Francisco State University	M
Seton Hall University	M,D
Simon Fraser University	M,D
Southern Illinois University Carbondale	M,D
Southern University and Agricultural and Mechanical College	M
Stanford University	D
State University of New York College of Environmental Science and Forestry	M,D
State University of New York Upstate Medical University	M,D
Stevens Institute of Technology	M,D,O
Stony Brook University, State University of New York	D
Syracuse University	D*
Temple University	M,D*
Texas A&M University	M,D
Texas Christian University	M,D
Texas State University–San Marcos	M
Texas Tech University Health Sciences Center	M,D
Thomas Jefferson University	D
Tufts University	D
Tulane University	M,D*
Universidad Central del Caribe	M,D
Université de Moncton	M
Université de Montréal	M,D,O
Université de Sherbrooke	M,D
Université Laval	M,D,O
University at Albany, State University of New York	M,D
University at Buffalo, the State University of New York	M,D*
The University of Alabama at Birmingham	D*
University of Alaska Fairbanks	M,D
University of Alberta	M,D
The University of Arizona	D
University of Arkansas for Medical Sciences	M,D
The University of British Columbia	M,D
University of Calgary	M,D
University of California, Berkeley	D*
University of California, Davis	M,D
University of California, Irvine	M,D*
University of California, Los Angeles	M,D*
University of California, Riverside	M,D
University of California, San Diego	M,D*
University of California, San Francisco	D
University of California, Santa Barbara	D
University of California, Santa Cruz	M,D
University of Chicago	D
University of Cincinnati	M,D
University of Colorado Boulder	M,D*
University of Colorado Denver	D
University of Connecticut	M,D*
University of Connecticut Health Center	D*
University of Delaware	M,D*
University of Detroit Mercy	M
University of Florida	M,D*
University of Georgia	M,D
University of Guelph	M,D
University of Houston	M,D
University of Idaho	M,D
University of Illinois at Chicago	D
University of Illinois at Urbana–Champaign	M,D
The University of Iowa	M,D*
The University of Kansas	M,D
University of Kentucky	D*
University of Lethbridge	M,D
University of Louisville	M,D
University of Maine	M,D
The University of Manchester	M,D
University of Manitoba	M,D
University of Maryland, Baltimore	M,D
University of Maryland, Baltimore County	M,D
University of Maryland, College Park	M,D
University of Massachusetts Amherst	M,D*
University of Massachusetts Lowell	M,D
University of Massachusetts Worcester	M,D
University of Medicine and Dentistry of New Jersey	M,D
University of Miami	D*
University of Michigan	D*
University of Minnesota, Duluth	M,D
University of Minnesota, Twin Cities Campus	D
University of Mississippi Medical Center	M,D
University of Missouri	M,D*
University of Missouri–Kansas City	D*
University of Missouri–St. Louis	M,D
The University of Montana	M,D
University of Nebraska–Lincoln	M,D*
University of Nebraska Medical Center	M,D
University of Nevada, Las Vegas	M,D
University of Nevada, Reno	M,D*
University of New Hampshire	M,D
University of New Mexico	M,D,O*
The University of North Carolina at Chapel Hill	M,D*
The University of North Carolina at Greensboro	M
University of North Dakota	M,D
University of Northern Iowa	M
University of North Texas	M,D
University of North Texas Health Science Center at Fort Worth	M,D
University of Notre Dame	M,D*
University of Oklahoma	M,D*
University of Oklahoma Health Sciences Center	M,D
University of Oregon	M,D
University of Ottawa	M,D*
University of Pennsylvania	D*
University of Puerto Rico, Medical Sciences Campus	M,D
University of Regina	M,D
University of Rhode Island	M,D
University of Rochester	M,D
University of Saskatchewan	M,D
The University of Scranton	M
University of South Carolina	M,D
University of Southern California	M,D*
University of Southern Mississippi	M,D
University of South Florida	M,D*
The University of Tennessee	M,D
The University of Texas at Austin	M,D
The University of Texas Health Science Center at Houston	M,D*
The University of Texas Health Science Center at San Antonio	M,D
The University of Texas Medical Branch	D
The University of Texas Southwestern Medical Center at Dallas	D
University of the Sciences in Philadelphia	M,D
The University of Toledo	M,D
University of Toronto	M,D
University of Tulsa	M
University of Utah	M,D*
University of Vermont	M,D
University of Victoria	M,D
University of Virginia	D
University of Washington	D*
University of Waterloo	M,D
The University of Western Ontario	M,D
University of West Florida	M
University of Windsor	M,D
University of Wisconsin–Madison	M,D*
University of Wisconsin–Milwaukee	M,D
Utah State University	M,D
Vanderbilt University	M,D*
Virginia Commonwealth University	M,D,O
Virginia Polytechnic Institute and State University	M,D
Wake Forest University	D
Washington State University	M,D
Washington University in St. Louis	D*
Wayne State University	M,D*
Wesleyan University	M,D*
West Virginia University	M,D
Worcester Polytechnic Institute	M,D
Wright State University	M
Yale University	D*
Youngstown State University	M

BIOENGINEERING

Alfred University	M,D
Baylor College of Medicine	D*
California Institute of Technology	M,D
Carnegie Mellon University	M,D*
Clemson University	M,D
Cornell University	M,D*
Dalhousie University	M,D
Georgia Institute of Technology	M,D
Illinois Institute of Technology	M,D
Iowa State University of Science and Technology	M,D*
The Johns Hopkins University	M,D
Kansas State University	M,D*
Lehigh University	M,D
Louisiana State University and Agricultural and Mechanical College	M,D
Massachusetts Institute of Technology	M,D
McGill University	M,D
Mississippi State University	M,D
North Carolina Agricultural and Technical State University	M
North Carolina State University	M,D,O*
The Ohio State University	M,D
Oklahoma State University	M,D*
Oregon State University	M,D
Penn State Hershey Medical Center	M,D
Penn State University Park	M,D
Rensselaer Polytechnic Institute	M,D
Rice University	M,D
South Dakota School of Mines and Technology	D
Stanford University	M,D
Syracuse University	M,D*
Texas A&M University	M,D
Tufts University	M,D,O
University at Buffalo, the State University of New York	M,D*
University of Arkansas	M
University of California, Berkeley	D*
University of California, Davis	M,D
University of California, Merced	M,D
University of California, Riverside	M,D
University of California, San Diego	M,D*
University of California, San Francisco	D
University of California, Santa Barbara	D

University of Colorado Denver M,D
University of Dayton M
University of Denver M,D
University of Florida M,D,O*
University of Georgia M,D
University of Guelph M,D
University of Hawaii at Manoa M
University of Idaho M,D
University of Illinois at Chicago M,D
University of Illinois at Urbana–Champaign M,D
The University of Kansas M,D
University of Maine M
University of Maryland, College Park M,D
University of Missouri M,D*
University of Nebraska–Lincoln M,D*
University of Notre Dame M,D*
University of Oklahoma M,D*
University of Pennsylvania M,D*
University of Pittsburgh M,D*
The University of Texas at Arlington M,D
The University of Toledo M,D
University of Utah M,D*
University of Washington M,D*
University of Wisconsin–Madison M,D*
Virginia Commonwealth University M,D
Virginia Polytechnic Institute and State University M,D
Washington State University M,D

BIOETHICS

Albany Medical College M,O
Boston University M*
Case Western Reserve University M*
Cleveland State University M,O
Columbia University M*
Drew University M,D,O
Duquesne University M,D,O
Indiana University–Purdue University Indianapolis M,O
Instituto Tecnologico de Santo Domingo M,O
The Johns Hopkins University M,D
Kansas City University of Medicine and Biosciences M
Loma Linda University M,O
Loyola Marymount University M
McGill University M,D,O
Medical College of Wisconsin M,O*
Midwestern University, Glendale Campus M,O
Mount Sinai School of Medicine M
New York University M
Rush University M,O
Saint Louis University D,O
Trinity International University M
Union Graduate College M,O
Université de Montréal M,D,O
University of Pittsburgh M*
The University of Tennessee M,D
University of Toronto M,D
University of Virginia M
University of Washington M*

BIOINFORMATICS

Arizona State University M,D
Boston University M,D*
Brandeis University M,O
California State University Channel Islands M
California State University, Dominguez Hills M*
Dalhousie University M,D
Duke University D,O*
George Mason University M,D,O*
Georgetown University M
The George Washington University M
Georgia Institute of Technology M,D
Grand Valley State University M
Indiana University Bloomington M,D*
Iowa State University of Science and Technology M,D*
The Johns Hopkins University M,D,O
Marquette University M,D
McGill University M,D
Medical College of Wisconsin M*
Mississippi Valley State University M
Morgan State University M
New Jersey Institute of Technology M,D
New Mexico State University M,D
North Carolina State University M,D*
North Dakota State University M,D
Northeastern University M
Nova Southeastern University M,O*
Polytechnic Institute of NYU M
Polytechnic Institute of NYU, Long Island Graduate Center M
Polytechnic Institute of NYU, Westchester Graduate Center M
Rice University M,D
Rochester Institute of Technology M
Stevens Institute of Technology M,D,O
Université de Montréal M,D
University of Arkansas at Little Rock M,D
University of California, Los Angeles M,D*
University of California, Riverside D
University of California, San Diego D*
University of California, San Francisco D
University of California, Santa Cruz M,D
University of Cincinnati D
University of Colorado Denver D
University of Georgia M,D,O
University of Idaho M,D
University of Illinois at Urbana–Champaign M,D,O
The University of Manchester M,D
University of Massachusetts Worcester M,D
University of Medicine and Dentistry of New Jersey M,D
University of Michigan M,D*
University of Missouri D*
University of Missouri–Kansas City P,M,D*
University of Nebraska–Lincoln M,D*
The University of North Carolina at Chapel Hill D*
The University of North Carolina at Charlotte M,O
University of Oklahoma M,D*
University of Pittsburgh M,D,O*
University of Southern California D*
The University of Texas at El Paso M,D
The University of Texas Medical Branch D
University of the Sciences in Philadelphia M
The University of Toledo M,O
University of Utah M,D,O*
University of Washington M,D*
Vanderbilt University M,D*
Virginia Commonwealth University M,D
Virginia Polytechnic Institute and State University D
Wesleyan University D*
Yale University D*

BIOLOGICAL AND BIOMEDICAL SCIENCES—GENERAL

Acadia University M
Adelphi University M*
Alabama Agricultural and Mechanical University M
Alabama State University M
Albert Einstein College of Medicine D
Alcorn State University M
American University M
The American University of Athens M
American University of Beirut M
Andrews University M
Angelo State University M
Appalachian State University M
Arizona State University M,D
Arkansas State University M,O
A.T. Still University of Health Sciences P,M
Auburn University M,D
Austin Peay State University M
Ball State University M,D
Barry University M*
Baylor College of Medicine M,D*
Baylor University M,D*
Bemidji State University M
Bloomsburg University of Pennsylvania M
Boise State University M
Boston College D*
Boston University M,D,O*
Bowling Green State University M,D*
Bradley University M
Brandeis University O
Brigham Young University M,D*
Brock University M,D
Brooklyn College of the City University of New York M,D
Brown University M,D
Bucknell University M
Buffalo State College, State University of New York M
California Institute of Technology D
California Polytechnic State University, San Luis Obispo M
California State Polytechnic University, Pomona M
California State University, Bakersfield M
California State University, Chico M
California State University, Dominguez Hills M*
California State University, East Bay M
California State University, Fresno M
California State University, Fullerton M
California State University, Long Beach M
California State University, Los Angeles M*
California State University, Northridge M
California State University, Sacramento M
California State University, San Bernardino M
California State University, San Marcos M
Carleton University M,D
Carnegie Mellon University M,D*
Case Western Reserve University M,D*
The Catholic University of America M,D
Cedars-Sinai Medical Center D
Central Connecticut State University M,O
Central Michigan University M
Central Washington University M
Chatham University M
Chicago State University M
The Citadel, The Military College of South Carolina M
City College of the City University of New York M,D
City of Hope National Medical Center/Beckman Research Institute D*
Clarion University of Pennsylvania M
Clark Atlanta University M,D
Clark University M,D
Clemson University M,D
Cleveland State University M,D
Cold Spring Harbor Laboratory, Watson School of Biological Sciences D
The College at Brockport, State University of New York M
College of Staten Island of the City University of New York M
The College of William and Mary M
Colorado State University M,D
Colorado State University–Pueblo M
Columbia University P,M,D,O*
Concordia University (Canada) M,D,O
Cornell University M,D*
Cornell University, Joan and Sanford I. Weill Medical College and Graduate School of Medical Sciences M,D
Creighton University M,D
Dalhousie University M,D
Dartmouth College D
Delaware State University M
Delta State University M
DePaul University M
Des Moines University M
Dominican University of California M
Drew University M
Drexel University M,D,O*
Duke University D*
Duquesne University M,D
East Carolina University M,D
Eastern Illinois University M
Eastern Kentucky University M
Eastern Michigan University M
Eastern New Mexico University M
Eastern Virginia Medical School M,D

*M—master's degree; P—first professional degree; D—doctorate; O—other advanced degree; *—Close-Up and/or Display in one of the other books in this series*

Institution	Degrees
Eastern Washington University	M
East Stroudsburg University of Pennsylvania	M
East Tennessee State University	M,D
Edinboro University of Pennsylvania	M
Elizabeth City State University	M
Emory University	D*
Emporia State University	M
Fairleigh Dickinson University, College at Florham	M
Fairleigh Dickinson University, Metropolitan Campus	M
Fayetteville State University	M
Fisk University	M
Fitchburg State University	M,O
Florida Agricultural and Mechanical University	M
Florida Atlantic University	M,D
Florida Institute of Technology	M,D
Florida International University	M,D
Florida State University	M,D
Fordham University	M,D
Fort Hays State University	M
Frostburg State University	M
George Mason University	M,D,O*
Georgetown University	M,D
The George Washington University	M,D
Georgia Campus–Philadelphia College of Osteopathic Medicine	M,O
Georgia College & State University	M
Georgia Health Sciences University	M,D,O
Georgia Institute of Technology	M,D
Georgian Court University	M,O
Georgia Southern University	M
Georgia State University	M,D
Gerstner Sloan-Kettering Graduate School of Biomedical Sciences	D*
Goucher College	O
Graduate School and University Center of the City University of New York	D
Grand Valley State University	M
Hampton University	M
Harvard University	M,D,O*
Heritage University	M
Hofstra University	M,O
Hood College	M,O
Howard University	M,D
Humboldt State University	M
Hunter College of the City University of New York	M,D
ICR Graduate School	M
Idaho State University	M,D
Illinois Institute of Technology	M,D
Illinois State University	M,D
Indiana State University	M,D
Indiana University Bloomington	M,D*
Indiana University of Pennsylvania	M
Indiana University–Purdue University Fort Wayne	M
Indiana University–Purdue University Indianapolis	M,D
Iowa State University of Science and Technology	M,D*
Jackson State University	M,D
Jacksonville State University	M
James Madison University	M
John Carroll University	M
The Johns Hopkins University	M,D
Kansas City University of Medicine and Biosciences	M
Kansas State University	M,D*
Keck Graduate Institute of Applied Life Sciences	M,D,O
Kent State University	M,D*
Lake Erie College of Osteopathic Medicine	P,M,O
Lakehead University	M
Lamar University	M
Laurentian University	M,D
Lehigh University	M,D
Lehman College of the City University of New York	M
Loma Linda University	M,D
Long Island University, Brooklyn Campus	M
Long Island University, C.W. Post Campus	M
Louisiana State University and Agricultural and Mechanical College	M,D
Louisiana State University Health Sciences Center	M,D
Louisiana State University Health Sciences Center at Shreveport	M,D
Louisiana Tech University	M
Loyola University Chicago	M
Marquette University	M,D
Marshall University	M,D
Massachusetts Institute of Technology	P,M,D
Mayo Graduate School	D
McGill University	M,D
McMaster University	M,D
Medical College of Wisconsin	M,D,O*
Medical University of South Carolina	M,D
Meharry Medical College	D
Memorial University of Newfoundland	M,D,O
Michigan State University	M,D
Michigan Technological University	M,D
Middle Tennessee State University	M
Midwestern State University	M
Midwestern University, Downers Grove Campus	M
Midwestern University, Glendale Campus	M
Mills College	O
Minnesota State University Mankato	M
Mississippi College	M
Mississippi State University	M,D
Missouri State University	M
Missouri University of Science and Technology	M
Montana State University	M,D
Montclair State University	M,O
Morehead State University	M
Morehouse School of Medicine	M,D
Morgan State University	M,D
Mount Allison University	M
Mount Sinai School of Medicine	M,D
Murray State University	M,D
New Jersey Institute of Technology	M,D
New Mexico Institute of Mining and Technology	M
New Mexico State University	M,D
New York Medical College	M,D*
New York University	M,D
North Carolina Agricultural and Technical State University	M
North Carolina Central University	M
North Carolina State University	M,D,O*
North Dakota State University	M,D
Northeastern Illinois University	M
Northeastern University	M,D
Northern Arizona University	M,D
Northern Illinois University	M,D
Northern Michigan University	M
Northwestern University	D*
Northwest Missouri State University	M
Notre Dame de Namur University	O
Nova Southeastern University	M,D*
Oakland University	M,D
Occidental College	M
The Ohio State University	D
Ohio University	M,D*
Oklahoma State University Center for Health Sciences	M,D
Old Dominion University	M,D
Oregon Health & Science University	M,D,O*
Penn State Hershey Medical Center	M,D
Penn State University Park	M,D
Philadelphia College of Osteopathic Medicine	M,O*
Pittsburg State University	M
Point Loma Nazarene University	M
Ponce School of Medicine	D
Pontifical Catholic University of Puerto Rico	M
Portland State University	M,D
Prairie View A&M University	M
Purdue University	M,D
Purdue University Calumet	M
Queens College of the City University of New York	M
Queen's University at Kingston	M,D
Quinnipiac University	M
Rensselaer Polytechnic Institute	M,D
Rhode Island College	M,O
Rochester Institute of Technology	M
The Rockefeller University	M,D*
Rosalind Franklin University of Medicine and Science	M,D*
Rutgers, The State University of New Jersey, Camden	M
Rutgers, The State University of New Jersey, Newark	M,D*
Rutgers, The State University of New Jersey, New Brunswick	D*
St. Cloud State University	M
Saint Francis University	M
St. Francis Xavier University	M
St. John's University (NY)	M,D
Saint Joseph College	M
Saint Joseph's University	M
Saint Louis University	M,D
Sam Houston State University	M
San Diego State University	M,D
San Francisco State University	M
San Jose State University	M
The Scripps Research Institute	D
Seton Hall University	M,D
Shippensburg University of Pennsylvania	M
Simon Fraser University	M,D
Smith College	M
Sonoma State University	M
South Dakota State University	M,D
Southeastern Louisiana University	M
Southeast Missouri State University	M
Southern Connecticut State University	M
Southern Illinois University Carbondale	M,D
Southern Illinois University Edwardsville	M
Southern Methodist University	M,D
Southern University and Agricultural and Mechanical College	M
Stanford University	M,D
State University of New York at Binghamton	M,D
State University of New York at Fredonia	M
State University of New York at New Paltz	M
State University of New York College at Oneonta	M
State University of New York Downstate Medical Center	M,D
State University of New York Upstate Medical University	M,D
Stephen F. Austin State University	M
Stony Brook University, State University of New York	D
Sul Ross State University	M
Syracuse University	M,D*
Tarleton State University	M
Temple University	M,D*
Tennessee State University	M,D
Tennessee Technological University	M,D
Texas A&M Health Science Center	M,D
Texas A&M International University	M
Texas A&M University	M,D
Texas A&M University–Commerce	M
Texas A&M University–Corpus Christi	M
Texas A&M University–Kingsville	M
Texas Christian University	M
Texas Southern University	M
Texas State University–San Marcos	M
Texas Tech University	M,D*
Texas Tech University Health Sciences Center	M,D
Texas Woman's University	M,D
Thomas Jefferson University	M,D,O
Towson University	M
Trent University	M,D
Truman State University	M
Tufts University	P,M,D
Tulane University	M,D*
Tuskegee University	M,D
Uniformed Services University of the Health Sciences	M,D*
Universidad Central del Caribe	M,D
Universidad de Ciencias Medicas	P,M,O
Université de Moncton	M
Université de Montréal	M,D
Université de Sherbrooke	M,D,O
Université du Québec à Montréal	M,D

Institution	Degrees
Université du Québec en Abitibi-Témiscamingue	M,D
Université du Québec, Institut National de la Recherche Scientifique	M,D
Université Laval	M,D,O
University at Albany, State University of New York	M,D
University at Buffalo, the State University of New York	M,D*
The University of Akron	M,D
The University of Alabama	M,D
The University of Alabama at Birmingham	M,D*
The University of Alabama in Huntsville	M
University of Alaska Anchorage	M
University of Alaska Fairbanks	M,D
University of Alberta	P,M,D
The University of Arizona	M
University of Arkansas	M,D
University of Arkansas at Little Rock	M
University of Arkansas for Medical Sciences	M,D,O
University of Calgary	M,D
University of California, Berkeley	D*
University of California, Irvine	M,D*
University of California, Los Angeles	M,D*
University of California, Merced	M,D
University of California, Riverside	M,D
University of California, San Diego	M,D*
University of California, San Francisco	D
University of Central Arkansas	M
University of Central Florida	M,D,O
University of Central Missouri	M,D
University of Central Oklahoma	M
University of Chicago	D
University of Cincinnati	M,D
University of Colorado at Colorado Springs	M
University of Colorado Denver	M,D
University of Connecticut	D*
University of Connecticut Health Center	D*
University of Dayton	M,D
University of Delaware	M,D*
University of Denver	M,D
University of Florida	D*
University of Georgia	D
University of Guam	M
University of Guelph	M,D
University of Hartford	M
University of Hawaii at Manoa	M,D
University of Houston	M,D
University of Houston–Clear Lake	M
University of Idaho	M,D
University of Illinois at Chicago	M,D
University of Illinois at Springfield	M
University of Illinois at Urbana–Champaign	M,D
University of Indianapolis	M
The University of Iowa	M,D*
The University of Kansas	M,D
University of Kentucky	M,D*
University of Lethbridge	M,D
University of Louisiana at Lafayette	M,D*
University of Louisiana at Monroe	M
University of Louisville	M,D
University of Maine	D
The University of Manchester	M,D
University of Manitoba	M,D,O
University of Maryland, Baltimore	M,D
University of Maryland, Baltimore County	M,D
University of Maryland, College Park	M,D
University of Massachusetts Amherst	M,D*
University of Massachusetts Boston	M
University of Massachusetts Dartmouth	M
University of Massachusetts Lowell	M,D
University of Massachusetts Worcester	M,D
University of Medicine and Dentistry of New Jersey	M,D,O
University of Memphis	M,D
University of Miami	M,D*
University of Michigan	M,D*
University of Michigan–Flint	M
University of Minnesota, Duluth	M,D
University of Minnesota, Twin Cities Campus	M
University of Mississippi	M,D
University of Mississippi Medical Center	M,D
University of Missouri	M,D*
University of Missouri–Kansas City	M,D*
University of Missouri–St. Louis	M,D,O
The University of Montana	M,D
University of Nebraska at Kearney	M
University of Nebraska at Omaha	M
University of Nebraska–Lincoln	M,D*
University of Nebraska Medical Center	M,D
University of Nevada, Las Vegas	M,D
University of Nevada, Reno	M*
University of New Brunswick Fredericton	M,D
University of New Brunswick Saint John	M,D
University of New England	M
University of New Hampshire	M,D
University of New Mexico	M,D,O*
University of New Orleans	M,D
The University of North Carolina at Chapel Hill	M,D*
The University of North Carolina at Charlotte	M,D
The University of North Carolina at Greensboro	M
The University of North Carolina Wilmington	M,D
University of North Dakota	M,D
University of Northern Colorado	M
University of Northern Iowa	M
University of North Florida	M
University of North Texas	M,D
University of North Texas Health Science Center at Fort Worth	M,D
University of Notre Dame	M,D*
University of Oklahoma Health Sciences Center	M,D
University of Oregon	M,D
University of Ottawa	M,D*
University of Pennsylvania	M,D*
University of Pittsburgh	D*
University of Prince Edward Island	M
University of Puerto Rico, Mayagüez Campus	M
University of Puerto Rico, Medical Sciences Campus	M,D
University of Puerto Rico, Río Piedras	M,D
University of Regina	M,D
University of Rhode Island	M,D
University of Rochester	M,D
University of San Francisco	M
University of Saskatchewan	M,D
University of South Alabama	M,D
University of South Carolina	M,D,O
The University of South Dakota	M,D
University of Southern California	M,D*
University of Southern Maine	M
University of Southern Mississippi	M,D
University of South Florida	M,D*
The University of Tennessee	M,D
The University of Tennessee–Oak Ridge National Laboratory Graduate School of Genome Science and Technology	M,D
The University of Texas at Arlington	M,D
The University of Texas at Austin	M,D
The University of Texas at Brownsville	M
The University of Texas at Dallas	M,D*
The University of Texas at El Paso	M,D
The University of Texas at San Antonio	M,D*
The University of Texas at Tyler	M
The University of Texas Health Science Center at Houston	M,D*
The University of Texas Health Science Center at San Antonio	M,D
The University of Texas Medical Branch	M,D
The University of Texas of the Permian Basin	M
The University of Texas–Pan American	M
The University of Texas Southwestern Medical Center at Dallas	M,D
University of the Incarnate Word	M
University of the Pacific	M
The University of Toledo	M,D
University of Toronto	M,D
University of Tulsa	M,D
University of Utah	M,D,O*
University of Vermont	M,D
University of Victoria	M,D
University of Virginia	M,D
University of Washington	M,D*
University of Waterloo	M,D
University of West Florida	M
University of West Georgia	M
University of Windsor	M,D
University of Wisconsin–La Crosse	M
University of Wisconsin–Madison	M,D*
University of Wisconsin–Milwaukee	M,D
University of Wisconsin–Oshkosh	M
Utah State University	M,D
Vanderbilt University	M,D*
Villanova University	M
Virginia Commonwealth University	M,D,O
Virginia Polytechnic Institute and State University	M,D
Virginia State University	M
Wagner College	M
Wake Forest University	M,D
Walla Walla University	M
Washington State University	M
Washington State University Tri-Cities	M
Washington University in St. Louis	D*
Wayne State University	M,D*
Wesleyan University	D*
West Chester University of Pennsylvania	M,O
Western Carolina University	M
Western Connecticut State University	M
Western Illinois University	M,O
Western Kentucky University	M
Western Michigan University	M,D
Western University of Health Sciences	M
Western Washington University	M
West Texas A&M University	M
West Virginia University	M,D
Wichita State University	M
Wilfrid Laurier University	M
William Paterson University of New Jersey	M
Winthrop University	M
Worcester Polytechnic Institute	M,D
Wright State University	M,D
Yale University	D*
York University	M,D*
Youngstown State University	M

BIOLOGICAL ANTHROPOLOGY

Institution	Degrees
Duke University	D*
Kent State University	D*
Mercyhurst College	M

BIOMATHEMATICS

Institution	Degrees
North Carolina State University	M,D*
University of California, Los Angeles	M,D*
The University of Texas Health Science Center at Houston	M,D*

BIOMEDICAL ENGINEERING

Institution	Degrees
Arizona State University	M,D
Baylor College of Medicine	D*
Baylor University	M,D*
Boston University	M,D*
Brown University	M,D
Carleton University	M
Carnegie Mellon University	M,D*
Case Western Reserve University	M,D*
The Catholic University of America	M,D
City College of the City University of New York	M,D
Cleveland State University	D
Colorado State University	M,D
Columbia University	M,D*
Cornell University	M,D*
Dalhousie University	M,D
Dartmouth College	M,D
Drexel University	M,D*
Duke University	M,D*

*M—master's degree; P—first professional degree; D—doctorate; O—other advanced degree; *—Close-Up and/or Display in one of the other books in this series*

École Polytechnique de Montréal M,D,O
Florida Agricultural and Mechanical University M,D
Florida International University M,D
Florida State University M,D
Georgia Institute of Technology D
Graduate School and University Center of the City University of New York D
Harvard University M,D*
Illinois Institute of Technology D
Indiana University–Purdue University Indianapolis M,D,O
The Johns Hopkins University M,D,O
Louisiana Tech University M,D
Marquette University M,D
Massachusetts Institute of Technology M,D
Mayo Graduate School D
McGill University M,D
Mercer University M
Michigan Technological University D
Mississippi State University M,D
New Jersey Institute of Technology M,D
North Carolina State University M,D*
Northwestern University M,D*
OGI School of Science & Engineering at Oregon Health & Science University M,D
The Ohio State University M,D
Ohio University M,D*
Oregon Health & Science University M,D*
Polytechnic Institute of NYU M,D
Purdue University M,D
Rensselaer Polytechnic Institute M,D
Rice University M,D
Rose-Hulman Institute of Technology M
Rutgers, The State University of New Jersey, New Brunswick M,D*
St. Cloud State University M
Saint Louis University M,D
South Dakota School of Mines and Technology M,D
Southern Illinois University Carbondale M
Stanford University M
State University of New York at Binghamton M,D
State University of New York Downstate Medical Center M,D
Stevens Institute of Technology M,O
Stony Brook University, State University of New York M,D,O
Texas A&M University M,D
Thomas Jefferson University D
Tufts University M,D
Tulane University M,D*
Université de Montréal M,D,O
The University of Akron M,D
The University of Alabama at Birmingham M,D*
University of Alberta M,D
The University of Arizona M,D
University of Arkansas M
University of Calgary M,D
University of California, Davis M,D
University of California, Irvine M,D*
University of California, Los Angeles M,D*
University of Cincinnati D
University of Connecticut M,D*
University of Florida M,D,O*
University of Houston D
The University of Iowa M,D*
University of Kentucky M,D*
University of Maine D
University of Massachusetts Dartmouth D
University of Medicine and Dentistry of New Jersey M,D,O
University of Memphis M,D
University of Miami M,D*
University of Michigan M,D*
University of Minnesota, Twin Cities Campus M,D
University of Nevada, Las Vegas M,D
University of Nevada, Reno M,D*
University of New Mexico D*
The University of North Carolina at Chapel Hill M,D*
University of Ottawa M*
University of Rhode Island M,D,O
University of Rochester M,D
University of Saskatchewan M,D
University of Southern California M,D*
University of South Florida M,D*
The University of Tennessee M,D
The University of Texas at Austin M,D
The University of Texas at Dallas M,D*
The University of Texas at San Antonio M,D*
The University of Texas Southwestern Medical Center at Dallas M,D
The University of Toledo D
University of Toronto M,D
University of Vermont M
University of Virginia M,D
University of Washington M,D*
University of Wisconsin–Madison M,D*
Vanderbilt University M,D*
Virginia Commonwealth University M,D
Virginia Polytechnic Institute and State University M,D
Wake Forest University M,D
Washington University in St. Louis M,D*
Wayne State University M,D*
Worcester Polytechnic Institute M,D,O
Wright State University M
Yale University M,D*

BIOMETRY

Cornell University M,D*
San Diego State University M
University of California, Los Angeles M,D*
University of Wisconsin–Madison M*

BIOPHYSICS

Albert Einstein College of Medicine D
Baylor College of Medicine D*
Boston University D*
Brandeis University D
California Institute of Technology D
Carnegie Mellon University M,D*
Case Western Reserve University M,D*
Clemson University M,D
Columbia University M,D*
Cornell University D*
Cornell University, Joan and Sanford I. Weill Medical College and Graduate School of Medical Sciences M,D
Dalhousie University M,D
East Carolina University M,D
Emory University D*
Georgetown University M,D
Harvard University D*
Howard University D
Illinois State University M,D
Iowa State University of Science and Technology M,D*
The Johns Hopkins University D
Medical College of Wisconsin D*
Northwestern University D*
The Ohio State University M,D
Oregon State University M,D
Purdue University M,D
Rensselaer Polytechnic Institute M,D
Rosalind Franklin University of Medicine and Science M,D*
Simon Fraser University M,D
Stanford University D
Stony Brook University, State University of New York D
Syracuse University D*
Texas A&M University M,D
Thomas Jefferson University D
Université de Sherbrooke M,D
Université du Québec à Trois-Rivières M,D
University at Buffalo, the State University of New York M,D*
University of Arkansas for Medical Sciences M,D
University of California, Berkeley D*
University of California, Davis M,D
University of California, Irvine D*
University of California, San Diego M,D*
University of California, San Francisco D
University of California, Santa Barbara D
University of Chicago D
University of Cincinnati D
University of Connecticut M,D*
University of Guelph M,D
University of Illinois at Chicago M,D
University of Illinois at Urbana–Champaign M,D
The University of Iowa M,D*
The University of Kansas M,D
University of Louisville M,D
The University of Manchester M,D
University of Maryland, College Park D
University of Miami D*
University of Michigan D*
University of Minnesota, Duluth M,D
University of Minnesota, Twin Cities Campus M,D
University of Mississippi Medical Center M,D
University of Missouri–Kansas City D*
University of New Mexico M,D*
The University of North Carolina at Chapel Hill M,D*
University of Regina M,D
University of Rochester M,D
University of Southern California M,D*
The University of Texas Medical Branch D
University of Toronto M,D
University of Vermont M,D
University of Virginia M,D
University of Washington D*
The University of Western Ontario M,D
University of Wisconsin–Madison D*
Vanderbilt University M,D*
Washington State University M,D
Wright State University M
Yale University D*

BIOPSYCHOLOGY

Adler School of Professional Psychology M,D,O
American University M,D
Argosy University, Atlanta M,D,O*
Argosy University, Twin Cities M,D,O*
Brown University D
Carnegie Mellon University D*
Columbia University M,D*
Cornell University D*
Drexel University M,D*
Duke University D*
Graduate School and University Center of the City University of New York D
Harvard University D*
Howard University M,D
Hunter College of the City University of New York M,D
Indiana University–Purdue University Indianapolis M,D
Louisiana State University and Agricultural and Mechanical College M,D
Memorial University of Newfoundland M,D
Northwestern University D*
Oregon Health & Science University D*
Palo Alto University D
Penn State University Park D
Rutgers, The State University of New Jersey, Newark D*
Rutgers, The State University of New Jersey, New Brunswick D*
State University of New York at Binghamton M,D
Stony Brook University, State University of New York D
Texas A&M University D
University at Albany, State University of New York M,D,O
The University of British Columbia M,D
University of Connecticut M,D,O*
University of Michigan D*
University of Minnesota, Twin Cities Campus D
University of Nebraska at Omaha M,D,O
University of Nebraska–Lincoln M,D*
University of Oklahoma Health Sciences Center M,D
University of Oregon M,D
The University of Texas at Austin D
University of Windsor M,D
University of Wisconsin–Madison D*
Virginia Commonwealth University D
Wayne State University M,D*

BIOSTATISTICS

Institution	Degrees
American University of Beirut	M
Boston University	M,D*
Brown University	M,D
California State University, East Bay	M
Case Western Reserve University	M,D*
Columbia University	M,D*
Drexel University	M,D,O*
Duke University	M*
East Tennessee State University	M,D,O
Emory University	M,D*
Florida International University	M,D
Florida State University	M,D
George Mason University	M,D,O*
Georgetown University	M
The George Washington University	M,D
Georgia Health Sciences University	M,D
Georgia Southern University	M,D
Grand Valley State University	M
Harvard University	M,D*
Hunter College of the City University of New York	M
Iowa State University of Science and Technology	M,D*
The Johns Hopkins University	M,D
Loma Linda University	M,D,O
Louisiana State University Health Sciences Center	M,D
McGill University	M,D,O
Medical College of Wisconsin	D*
Medical University of South Carolina	M,D
Middle Tennessee State University	M
New Jersey Institute of Technology	M
The Ohio State University	M,D
Oregon Health & Science University	M*
Rice University	M,D
Rutgers, The State University of New Jersey, New Brunswick	M,D*
San Diego State University	M,D
Tufts University	M,D
Tulane University	M,D*
University at Albany, State University of New York	M,D
University at Buffalo, the State University of New York	M,D*
The University of Alabama at Birmingham	M,D*
University of Alberta	M,D,O
The University of Arizona	D
University of California, Berkeley	M,D*
University of California, Davis	M,D
University of California, Los Angeles	M,D*
University of Cincinnati	M,D
University of Colorado Denver	M,D
University of Florida	M*
University of Georgia	M
University of Illinois at Chicago	M,D
The University of Iowa	M,D*
The University of Kansas	M,D
University of Louisville	M,D
University of Maryland, Baltimore	M,D
University of Maryland, Baltimore County	M,D
University of Maryland, College Park	M,D
University of Massachusetts Amherst	M,D*
University of Medicine and Dentistry of New Jersey	M,D,O
University of Memphis	M
University of Michigan	M,D*
University of Minnesota, Twin Cities Campus	M,D
The University of North Carolina at Chapel Hill	M,D*
University of North Texas Health Science Center at Fort Worth	M,D
University of Oklahoma Health Sciences Center	M,D
University of Pennsylvania	M,D*
University of Pittsburgh	M,D*
University of Puerto Rico, Medical Sciences Campus	M
University of Rochester	M,D
University of South Carolina	M,D
University of Southern California	M,D*
University of Southern Mississippi	M
University of South Florida	M,D*
The University of Texas Health Science Center at Houston	M,D*
The University of Toledo	M,O
University of Utah	M,D*
University of Vermont	M
University of Washington	M,D*
University of Waterloo	M,D
The University of Western Ontario	M,D
Virginia Commonwealth University	M,D
Yale University	M,D,O*

BIOSYSTEMS ENGINEERING

Institution	Degrees
Clemson University	M,D
Iowa State University of Science and Technology	M,D*
Michigan State University	M,D
North Dakota State University	M,D
South Dakota State University	M,D
The University of Arizona	M,D
University of Dayton	M
University of Manitoba	M,D
University of Minnesota, Twin Cities Campus	M,D
The University of Tennessee	M,D

BIOTECHNOLOGY

Institution	Degrees
Albany College of Pharmacy and Health Sciences	P,M*
Arizona State University	P,M
Arkansas State University	D,O
Brandeis University	M
Brigham Young University	M,D*
Brock University	M,D
Brown University	M,D
California State Polytechnic University, Pomona	M
California State University Channel Islands	M
Carnegie Mellon University	M,D*
Claflin University	M
Concordia University (Canada)	M,D,O
Dartmouth College	M,D
Duquesne University	M
East Carolina University	M
Florida Institute of Technology	M,D
The George Washington University	M
Harvard University	M,O*
Hood College	M,O
Howard University	M,D
Illinois Institute of Technology	M,D
Illinois State University	M
Indiana University Bloomington	M,D*
Instituto Tecnológico y de Estudios Superiores de Monterrey, Campus Monterrey	M,D
Inter American University of Puerto Rico, Bayamón Campus	M
The Johns Hopkins University	M
Kean University	M
Marywood University	M
McGill University	M,D,O
New Mexico State University	M,D
North Carolina State University	M*
Northeastern University	M
Northwestern University	D*
Polytechnic Institute of NYU	M
Purdue University Calumet	M
Regis College (MA)	M
Roosevelt University	M
St. John's University (NY)	M
San Francisco State University	M
Simon Fraser University	M,D
Southeastern Oklahoma State University	M
Southern Illinois University Edwardsville	M
Stephen F. Austin State University	M
Texas Tech University	M*
Texas Tech University Health Sciences Center	M
Thomas Jefferson University	D
Tufts University	O
Universidad de las Américas–Puebla	M
Université de Sherbrooke	P,M,D,O
University at Buffalo, the State University of New York	M*
The University of Alabama in Huntsville	D
University of Alberta	M,D
University of Calgary	M
University of California, Irvine	M*
University of Central Florida	M
University of Delaware	M,D*
University of Guelph	M,D
University of Houston–Clear Lake	M
University of Illinois at Chicago	D
The University of Kansas	M
The University of Manchester	M,D
University of Maryland, Baltimore County	O
University of Maryland University College	M,O
University of Massachusetts Amherst	M,D*
University of Massachusetts Boston	M
University of Massachusetts Dartmouth	D
University of Massachusetts Lowell	M,D
University of Minnesota, Twin Cities Campus	M
University of Missouri–St. Louis	M,D,O
University of Nevada, Reno	M*
University of Northern Iowa	M
University of North Texas Health Science Center at Fort Worth	M,D
University of Pennsylvania	M*
University of Rhode Island	M,D
University of Saskatchewan	M
The University of Texas at Dallas	M,D*
The University of Texas at San Antonio	M,D*
University of the Sciences in Philadelphia	M,D
University of Toronto	M
University of Utah	M*
University of Washington	D*
University of West Florida	M
University of Wyoming	D
Virginia Polytechnic Institute and State University	M
West Virginia State University	M
William Paterson University of New Jersey	M
Worcester Polytechnic Institute	M,D
Worcester State University	M

BOTANY

Institution	Degrees
Auburn University	M,D
California State University, Chico	M
Claremont Graduate University	M,D
Colorado State University	M,D
Emporia State University	M
Illinois State University	M,D
Miami University	M,D
North Carolina State University	M,D*
North Dakota State University	M,D
Nova Scotia Agricultural College	M
Oklahoma State University	M,D*
Oregon State University	M,D
Purdue University	M,D
Texas A&M University	M,D
University of Alaska Fairbanks	M,D
The University of British Columbia	M,D
University of California, Riverside	M,D
University of Connecticut	M,D*
University of Florida	M,D*
University of Guelph	M,D
University of Hawaii at Manoa	M,D
The University of Kansas	M,D
University of Maine	M
University of Manitoba	M,D
The University of North Carolina at Chapel Hill	M,D*
University of North Dakota	M,D
University of Oklahoma	M,D*
University of Wisconsin–Madison	M,D*
University of Wisconsin–Oshkosh	M
University of Wyoming	M,D
Washington State University	M,D

BROADCAST JOURNALISM

Institution	Degrees
American University	M
The American University in Cairo	M
Boston University	M*
Emerson College	M
Northwestern University	M*
Syracuse University	M*
University of Maryland, College Park	M,D
University of Miami	M,D*
University of Oklahoma	M*

*M—master's degree; P—first professional degree; D—doctorate; O—other advanced degree; *—Close-Up and/or Display in one of the other books in this series*

University of Southern California M*
University of the Sacred Heart M,O

BUILDING SCIENCE

Arizona State University M,D
Auburn University M
Carnegie Mellon University M,D*
Cornell University M,D*
Georgia Institute of Technology M,D
Pontificia Universidad Catolica Madre y Maestra M
Rensselaer Polytechnic Institute M,D
University of California, Berkeley M,D*
University of Florida M,D*

BUSINESS ADMINISTRATION AND MANAGEMENT—GENERAL

Adelphi University M*
Alabama Agricultural and Mechanical University M
Alaska Pacific University M
Albany State University M
Albertus Magnus College M
Alcorn State University M
Alfred University M
Alliant International University–Los Angeles D
Alliant International University–México City M
Alliant International University–San Diego M,D
Alliant International University–San Francisco M
Alvernia University M
Alverno College M
Amberton University M
The American College M
American College of Thessaloniki M,O
American Graduate University M,O
American InterContinental University Buckhead Campus M
American InterContinental University Houston M
American InterContinental University London M
American InterContinental University Online M
American InterContinental University South Florida M
American International College M
American Jewish University M
American Public University System M
American Sentinel University M
American University M,D,O
The American University in Cairo M,O
The American University in Dubai M
The American University of Athens M
American University of Beirut M
The American University of Paris M
American University of Sharjah M
Anaheim University M,O
Anderson University (IN) M,D
Anderson University (SC) M
Andrew Jackson University M
Angelo State University M
Anna Maria College M,O
Antioch University Los Angeles M
Antioch University Midwest M
Antioch University New England M
Antioch University Seattle M
Appalachian State University M
Aquinas College M
Arcadia University M*
Argosy University, Atlanta M,D*
Argosy University, Chicago M,D*
Argosy University, Dallas M,D,O*
Argosy University, Denver M,D*
Argosy University, Hawai'i M,D,O*
Argosy University, Inland Empire M,D*
Argosy University, Los Angeles M,D*
Argosy University, Nashville M,D*
Argosy University, Orange County M,D,O*
Argosy University, Phoenix M,D*
Argosy University, Salt Lake City M,D*
Argosy University, San Diego M,D*
Argosy University, San Francisco Bay Area M,D*
Argosy University, Sarasota M,D,O*
Argosy University, Schaumburg M,D,O*
Argosy University, Seattle M,D*
Argosy University, Tampa M,D*
Argosy University, Twin Cities M,D*
Argosy University, Washington DC M,D,O*
Arizona State University M,D
Arkansas State University M,O
The Art Institute of Atlanta M
Ashland University M
Ashworth College M
Aspen University M,O
Assumption College M,O
Athabasca University M,O
Auburn University M,D
Auburn University Montgomery M
Augsburg College M
Augusta State University M
Aurora University M
Austin Peay State University M
Averett University M
Avila University M
Azusa Pacific University M
Babson College M,O
Baker College Center for Graduate Studies—Online M,D
Baker University M
Bakke Graduate University M,D
Baldwin-Wallace College M
Ball State University M
Barry University M,O*
Bayamón Central University M
Baylor University M*
Belhaven University (MS) M
Bellarmine University M
Bellevue University M,D
Belmont University M
Benedictine College M
Benedictine University M
Benedictine University at Springfield M
Bentley University M,D,O
Bernard M. Baruch College of the City University of New York M,D,O
Berry College M
Bethel College M
Bethel University (MN) M
Bethel University (TN) M
Biola University M
Black Hills State University M
Bloomsburg University of Pennsylvania M
Bluffton University M
Bob Jones University P,M,D,O
Boise State University M
Boston College M*
Boston University M,D*
Bowie State University M
Bowling Green State University M*
Bradley University M
Brandeis University M
Brenau University M
Brescia University M
Bridgewater State University M
Briercrest Seminary M
Brigham Young University M*
Broadview University M
Brock University M
Bryan College M
Bryant University M
Butler University M
Caldwell College M
California Baptist University M,D
California Coast University M
California Intercontinental University M,D
California International Business University M,D
California Lutheran University M,O
California Miramar University M
California National University for Advanced Studies M
California Polytechnic State University, San Luis Obispo M
California State Polytechnic University, Pomona M
California State University, Bakersfield M
California State University Channel Islands M
California State University, Chico M
California State University, Dominguez Hills M*
California State University, East Bay M
California State University, Fresno M
California State University, Fullerton M
California State University, Long Beach M
California State University, Los Angeles M*
California State University, Monterey Bay M
California State University, Northridge M
California State University, Sacramento M
California State University, San Bernardino M
California State University, San Marcos M
California State University, Stanislaus M
California University of Pennsylvania M
Cambridge College M
Cameron University M
Campbellsville University M
Campbell University M
Canisius College M
Cape Breton University M
Capella University M,D,O
Capital University M
Capitol College M
Cardinal Stritch University M
Carleton University M,D
Carlos Albizu University, Miami Campus M,D
Carlow University M
Carnegie Mellon University M,D*
Carroll University M
Carson-Newman College M
Case Western Reserve University M,D*
The Catholic University of America M
Centenary College M
Centenary College of Louisiana M
Central European University M
Central Michigan University M,O
Chadron State College M
Chaminade University of Honolulu M
Champlain College M
Chancellor University M
Chapman University M
Charleston Southern University M
Chatham University M
Christian Brothers University M,O
The Citadel, The Military College of South Carolina M
City University of Seattle M,O
Claflin University M
Claremont Graduate University M,D,O
Clarion University of Pennsylvania M
Clark Atlanta University M
Clarke University M
Clarkson University M*
Clark University M
Clayton State University M
Cleary University M,O
Clemson University M
Cleveland State University M,D
Coastal Carolina University M
College of Charleston M
College of Notre Dame of Maryland M
College of Saint Elizabeth M
College of St. Joseph M
The College of Saint Rose M
The College of St. Scholastica M,O
College of Staten Island of the City University of New York M
The College of William and Mary M
Colorado Christian University M
Colorado State University M
Colorado State University–Pueblo M
Colorado Technical University Colorado Springs M,D
Colorado Technical University Denver M
Colorado Technical University Sioux Falls M
Columbia College (MO) M
Columbia Southern University M,D
Columbia University M,D*
Columbus State University M,O
Concordia University (CA) M
Concordia University (OR) M
Concordia University (Canada) M,D,O
Concordia University Chicago M
Concordia University, St. Paul M
Concordia University Wisconsin M
Corban University M
Cornell University M,D*

Institution	Degrees
Cornerstone University	M,O
Creighton University	M
Cumberland University	M
Curry College	M,O
Daemen College	M
Dalhousie University	M,O
Dallas Baptist University	M
Daniel Webster College	M
Daniel Webster College–Portsmouth Campus	M
Dartmouth College	M
Davenport University	M
Davenport University	M
Davenport University	M
Defiance College	M
Delaware State University	M
Delaware Valley College	M
Delta State University	M
DePaul University	M
DeSales University	M
DeVry College of New York	M
DeVry University	M,O
DeVry University	M
DeVry University	M
DeVry University	M
DeVry University	M,O
DeVry University	M
DeVry University	M
DeVry University	M
DeVry University	M,O
DeVry University	M,O
DeVry University	M,O
DeVry University	M,O
DeVry University	M,O
DeVry University	M,O
DeVry University	M,O
DeVry University	M,O
DeVry University	M,O
DeVry University	M,O
DeVry University	M,O
DeVry University	M,O
DeVry University	M,O
DeVry University	M,O
DeVry University	M
DeVry University	M,O
DeVry University	M
DeVry University	M,O
DeVry University	M,O
DeVry University	M
DeVry University	M
DeVry University	M
DeVry University	M,O
DeVry University	M,O
DeVry University	M,O
DeVry University	M
DeVry University	M,O
DeVry University	M,O
DeVry University	M
DeVry University	M,O
DeVry University	M
DeVry University	M,O
DeVry University	M
DeVry University	M
DeVry University	M
DeVry University	M
DeVry University	M
DeVry University	M
DeVry University	M
DeVry University	M
DeVry University	M
DeVry University	M
DeVry University	M
DeVry University	M
DeVry University	M
DeVry University	M
DeVry University	M
DeVry University	M
DeVry University	M
DeVry University	M
DeVry University	M
DeVry University	M
DeVry University Online	M
Doane College	M
Dominican College	M
Dominican University	M
Dominican University of California	M
Dowling College	M,D,O
Drake University	M
Drexel University	M,D,O*
Drury University	M
Duke University	M,D*
Duquesne University	M
D'Youville College	M*
East Carolina University	M,D,O
Eastern Illinois University	M,O
Eastern Kentucky University	M
Eastern Mennonite University	M
Eastern Michigan University	M,O
Eastern Nazarene College	M
Eastern New Mexico University	M
Eastern Oregon University	M
Eastern University	M
Eastern Washington University	M
East Tennessee State University	M,O
Edgewood College	M
Ellis University	M
Elmhurst College	M
Elon University	M
Embry-Riddle Aeronautical University–Daytona	M
Embry-Riddle Aeronautical University–Worldwide	M
Emmanuel College (United States)	M,O
Emory University	M,D*
Emporia State University	M
Endicott College	M
Everest University (Tampa)	M
Everest University (Orlando)	M
Everest University (Jacksonville)	M
Everest University (Melbourne)	M
Everest University (Tampa)	M
Everest University (Orlando)	M
Everest University (Pompano Beach)	M
Everglades University	M
Excelsior College	M
Fairfield University	M,O
Fairleigh Dickinson University, College at Florham	M,O
Fairleigh Dickinson University, Metropolitan Campus	M,O
Fairmont State University	M
Fashion Institute of Technology	M*
Faulkner University	M
Fayetteville State University	M
Felician College	M*
Ferris State University	M
Fitchburg State University	M
Florida Agricultural and Mechanical University	M
Florida Atlantic University	M,D,O
Florida Gulf Coast University	M
Florida Institute of Technology	M
Florida International University	M,D
Florida Memorial University	M
Florida Southern College	M
Florida State University	M,D
Fontbonne University	M
Fordham University	M
Fort Hays State University	M
Framingham State University	M
Franciscan University of Steubenville	M
Francis Marion University	M
Franklin Pierce University	M,D,O
Franklin University	M
Freed-Hardeman University	M
Fresno Pacific University	M
Friends University	M
Frostburg State University	M
Full Sail University	M
Gannon University	M,O
Gardner-Webb University	M
Geneva College	M
George Fox University	M,D
George Mason University	M*
Georgetown University	M
The George Washington University	M,D,O
Georgia College & State University	M
Georgia Institute of Technology	M,D,O
Georgian Court University	M,O
Georgia Southern University	M
Georgia Southwestern State University	M
Georgia State University	M,D
Globe University	M
Goddard College	M
Golden Gate University	M,D,O
Goldey-Beacom College	M
Gonzaga University	M
Governors State University	M
Graduate School and University Center of the City University of New York	D
Grand Canyon University	M,D
Grand Valley State University	M
Grand View University	M
Grantham University	M
Green Mountain College	M
Gwynedd-Mercy College	M
Hamline University	M,D
Hampton University	M,D
Harding University	M
Hardin-Simmons University	M
Harvard University	M,D,O*
Hawai'i Pacific University	M*
HEC Montreal	M,D,O
Heidelberg University	M
Henderson State University	M
Herzing University Online	M
High Point University	M
Hodges University	M
Hofstra University	M,O
Holy Family University	M*
Holy Names University	M
Hood College	M
Hope International University	M
Houston Baptist University	M
Howard University	M
Hult International Business School (United States)	M
Hult International Business School (United States)	M
Humboldt State University	M
Husson University	M
Idaho State University	M,O
Illinois Institute of Technology	M,D
Illinois State University	M
IMCA–International Management Centres Association	M
Independence University	M
Indiana State University	M
Indiana Tech	M
Indiana University Bloomington	M,D*
Indiana University Kokomo	M
Indiana University Northwest	M,O
Indiana University of Pennsylvania	M
Indiana University–Purdue University Fort Wayne	M
Indiana University–Purdue University Indianapolis	M
Indiana University South Bend	M
Indiana University Southeast	M
Indiana Wesleyan University	M
Instituto Centroamericano de Administración de Empresas	M
Instituto Tecnologico de Santo Domingo	M,O
Instituto Tecnológico y de Estudios Superiores de Monterrey, Campus Central de Veracruz	M
Instituto Tecnológico y de Estudios Superiores de Monterrey, Campus Ciudad de México	M,D
Instituto Tecnológico y de Estudios Superiores de Monterrey, Campus Ciudad Juárez	M
Instituto Tecnológico y de Estudios Superiores de Monterrey, Campus Ciudad Obregón	M
Instituto Tecnológico y de Estudios Superiores de Monterrey, Campus Cuernavaca	M
Instituto Tecnológico y de Estudios Superiores de Monterrey, Campus Estado de México	M,D
Instituto Tecnológico y de Estudios Superiores de Monterrey, Campus Guadalajara	M
Instituto Tecnológico y de Estudios Superiores de Monterrey, Campus Irapuato	M,D
Instituto Tecnológico y de Estudios Superiores de Monterrey, Campus Laguna	M
Instituto Tecnológico y de Estudios Superiores de Monterrey, Campus León	M
Instituto Tecnológico y de Estudios Superiores de Monterrey, Campus Monterrey	M,D
Instituto Tecnológico y de Estudios Superiores de Monterrey, Campus Querétaro	M
Instituto Tecnológico y de Estudios Superiores de Monterrey, Campus Sonora Norte	M
Instituto Tecnológico y de Estudios Superiores de Monterrey, Campus Toluca	M
Inter American University of Puerto Rico, Aguadilla Campus	M
Inter American University of Puerto Rico, Arecibo Campus	M
Inter American University of Puerto Rico, Barranquitas Campus	M
Inter American University of Puerto Rico, Guayama Campus	M
Inter American University of Puerto Rico, Metropolitan Campus	M
Inter American University of Puerto Rico, San Germán Campus	M,D
International College of the Cayman Islands	M

*M—master's degree; P—first professional degree; D—doctorate; O—other advanced degree; *—Close-Up and/or Display in one of the other books in this series*

Institution	Degrees
International Technological University	M
The International University of Monaco	M
Iona College	M,O
Iowa State University of Science and Technology	M,D*
Ithaca College	M
ITT Technical Institute (IN)	M
Jackson State University	M,D
Jacksonville State University	M
Jacksonville University	M
James Madison University	M
John Brown University	M
John Carroll University	M
John F. Kennedy University	M,O
The Johns Hopkins University	M,O
Jones International University	M
Kansas State University	M*
Kansas Wesleyan University	M
Kaplan University, Davenport Campus	M
Kean University	M
Keiser University	M,D
Kennesaw State University	M,D
Kent State University	M*
Kent State University at Stark	M
Kentucky State University	M
Kettering University	M
Keuka College	M
King College	M
King's College	M
Kutztown University of Pennsylvania	M
Lake Erie College	M
Lake Forest Graduate School of Management	M
Lakeland College	M
Lamar University	M
La Salle University	M,O
Lasell College	M,O
La Sierra University	M,O
Laurel University	M
Laurentian University	M
Lawrence Technological University	M,D
Lebanese American University	M
Lebanon Valley College	M
Lehigh University	M,D,O
Le Moyne College	M
Lenoir-Rhyne University	M
LeTourneau University	M
Lewis University	M
Liberty University	M
LIM College	M
Lincoln Memorial University	M
Lincoln University (CA)	M,D
Lincoln University (MO)	M,O
Lincoln University (PA)	M
Lindenwood University	M,O
Lipscomb University	M
Long Island University, Brooklyn Campus	M
Long Island University, C.W. Post Campus	M,O
Long Island University, Rockland Graduate Campus	M,O
Long Island University, Westchester Graduate Campus	M
Longwood University	M
Louisiana State University and Agricultural and Mechanical College	M,D
Louisiana State University in Shreveport	M
Louisiana Tech University	M,D
Loyola Marymount University	M
Loyola University Chicago	M
Loyola University Maryland	M
Loyola University New Orleans	M
Lynchburg College	M
Lynn University	M
Madonna University	M
Maharishi University of Management	M,D
Malone University	M
Marian University (WI)	M
Marist College	M,O
Marlboro College	M
Marquette University	M
Marshall University	M,O
Maryland Institute College of Art	M
Marylhurst University	M
Marymount University	M,O
Maryville University of Saint Louis	M,O
Marywood University	M
Massachusetts Institute of Technology	M,D
McGill University	M,D,O
McKendree University	M
McMaster University	M,D
McNeese State University	M
Medaille College	M
Memorial University of Newfoundland	M
Mercer University	M
Mercy College	M
Meredith College	M
Mesa State College	M
Methodist University	M
Metropolitan College of New York	M
Metropolitan State University	M,D,O
Miami University	M
Michigan State University	M,D
Michigan Technological University	M
Mid-America Christian University	M
MidAmerica Nazarene University	M
Middle Tennessee State University	M
Midway College	M
Midwestern State University	M
Milligan College	M
Millikin University	M
Millsaps College	M
Mills College	M
Milwaukee School of Engineering	M
Minnesota State University Mankato	M
Minot State University	M
Misericordia University	M
Mississippi College	M,O
Mississippi State University	M,D
Missouri Baptist University	M,O
Missouri Southern State University	M
Missouri State University	M
Molloy College	M
Monmouth University	M,O
Monroe College	M
Montclair State University	M,O
Monterey Institute of International Studies	M
Montreat College	M
Moravian College	M
Morehead State University	M
Morgan State University	D
Morrison University	M
Mount Aloysius College	M
Mount Ida College	M
Mount Marty College	M
Mount Mary College	M
Mount Mercy University	M
Mount Saint Mary College	M
Mount St. Mary's College	M
Mount St. Mary's University	M
Mount Vernon Nazarene University	M
Murray State University	M
National American University	M
The National Graduate School of Quality Management	M
National-Louis University	M
National University	M
Naval Postgraduate School	M
Nazareth College of Rochester	M
New England College	M
New Jersey City University	M
New Jersey Institute of Technology	M
Newman University	M
New Mexico Highlands University	M
New Mexico State University	M,D
New York Institute of Technology	M,O
New York University	P,M,D,O
Niagara University	M
Nicholls State University	M
Nichols College	M
North Carolina Agricultural and Technical State University	M,D
North Carolina Central University	M
North Carolina State University	M*
North Central College	M
Northcentral University	M,D,O
North Dakota State University	M
Northeastern Illinois University	M
Northeastern State University	M
Northeastern University	M,O
Northern Arizona University	M
Northern Illinois University	M
Northern Kentucky University	M,O
North Park University	M
Northwest Christian University	M
Northwestern Polytechnic University	M
Northwestern University	M*
Northwest Missouri State University	M
Northwest Nazarene University	M
Northwest University	M
Northwood University	M
Norwich University	M
Notre Dame College (OH)	M,O
Notre Dame de Namur University	M
Nova Southeastern University	M,D*
Nyack College	M
Oakland City University	M
Oakland University	M,O
OGI School of Science & Engineering at Oregon Health & Science University	M,O
Oglala Lakota College	M
Ohio Dominican University	M
The Ohio State University	M,D
Ohio University	M*
Oklahoma City University	M
Oklahoma State University	M,D*
Old Dominion University	M,D
Olivet Nazarene University	M
Oral Roberts University	M
Oregon State University	M,O
Ottawa University	M
Otterbein University	M
Our Lady of the Lake University of San Antonio	M
Pace University	M,D,O
Pacific Lutheran University	M
Pacific States University	M,D
Palm Beach Atlantic University	M
Park University	M
Penn State Erie, The Behrend College	M
Penn State Great Valley	M
Penn State Harrisburg	M
Penn State University Park	M,D
Pepperdine University	M
Pfeiffer University	M
Philadelphia University	M
Phillips Theological Seminary	P,M,D
Piedmont College	M
Pittsburg State University	M
Plymouth State University	M
Point Loma Nazarene University	M
Point Park University	M
Polytechnic Institute of NYU	M,D,O
Polytechnic Institute of NYU, Westchester Graduate Center	M
Polytechnic University of Puerto Rico	M
Polytechnic University of Puerto Rico, Miami Campus	M
Polytechnic University of Puerto Rico, Orlando Campus	M
Pontifical Catholic University of Puerto Rico	M,D,O
Pontificia Universidad Catolica Madre y Maestra	M
Portland State University	M,D,O
Post University	M
Prairie View A&M University	M
Providence College	M
Purdue University	M,D
Purdue University Calumet	M
Queen's University at Kingston	M
Queens University of Charlotte	M
Quincy University	M
Quinnipiac University	M
Radford University	M
Regent's American College London	M
Regent University	M,D,O
Regis University	M,O
Reinhardt University	M
Rensselaer at Hartford	M
Rensselaer Polytechnic Institute	M,D
Rice University	M
The Richard Stockton College of New Jersey	M
Rider University	M
Rivier College	M
Robert Morris University	M
Robert Morris University Illinois	M
Roberts Wesleyan College	M,O
Rochester Institute of Technology	M
Rockford College	M
Rockhurst University	M
Rollins College	M
Roosevelt University	M
Roseman University of Health Sciences	M
Rosemont College	M
Rowan University	M
Royal Military College of Canada	M
Royal Roads University	M,O

Institution	Degrees
Rutgers, The State University of New Jersey, Camden	M
Rutgers, The State University of New Jersey, Newark	M,D*
Sacred Heart University	M
Sage Graduate School	M
Saginaw Valley State University	M
St. Ambrose University	M,D
St. Bonaventure University	M
St. Cloud State University	M
St. Edward's University	M,O
Saint Francis University	M
St. John Fisher College	M
St. John's University (NY)	M,O
Saint Joseph College	M
St. Joseph's College, Long Island Campus	M,O
St. Joseph's College, New York	M*
Saint Joseph's College of Maine	M
Saint Joseph's University	M,O
Saint Leo University	M
Saint Louis University	M
Saint Martin's University	M
Saint Mary's College of California	M
Saint Mary's University (Canada)	M,D
St. Mary's University (United States)	M
Saint Mary's University of Minnesota	M
Saint Michael's College	M,O
Saint Peter's College	M
St. Thomas Aquinas College	M
St. Thomas University	M,O
Saint Xavier University	M,O
Salem International University	M
Salem State University	M
Salisbury University	M
Salve Regina University	M,O
Samford University	M
Sam Houston State University	M
San Diego State University	M
San Francisco State University	M
San Jose State University	M
Santa Clara University	M
Savannah State University	M
Schiller International University (United States)	M
Schiller International University (Germany)	M
Schiller International University	M
Schiller International University (Spain)	M
Schiller International University	M
Seattle Pacific University	M
Seattle University	M,O
Seton Hall University	M,O
Seton Hill University	M,O
Shenandoah University	M,O
Shippensburg University of Pennsylvania	M,O
Shorter University	M
Silicon Valley University	M
Silver Lake College	M
Simmons College	M,O
Simon Fraser University	M,D
SIT Graduate Institute	M
Sonoma State University	M
Southeastern Louisiana University	M
Southeastern Oklahoma State University	M
Southeastern University (FL)	M
Southeast Missouri State University	M
Southern Adventist University	M
Southern Arkansas University–Magnolia	M
Southern Connecticut State University	M
Southern Illinois University Carbondale	M,D
Southern Illinois University Edwardsville	M
Southern Methodist University	M
Southern Nazarene University	M
Southern New Hampshire University	M,D,O
Southern Oregon University	M
Southern Polytechnic State University	M,O
Southern University and Agricultural and Mechanical College	M
Southern Utah University	M
Southern Wesleyan University	M
South University (VA)	M*
South University (FL)	M*
South University (TX)	M
South University (MI)	M*
South University (SC)	M*
South University (GA)	M*
South University (AL)	M*
South University	M*
Southwest Baptist University	M
Southwestern Adventist University	M
Southwestern College (KS)	M
Southwestern College (KS)	M
Southwestern Oklahoma State University	M
Southwest Minnesota State University	M
Southwest University	M
Spalding University	M
Spring Arbor University	M
Spring Hill College	M
Stanford University	M,D
State University of New York at Binghamton	M,D
State University of New York at New Paltz	M
State University of New York at Oswego	M
State University of New York College at Geneseo	M
State University of New York Empire State College	M
State University of New York Institute of Technology	M
Stephen F. Austin State University	M
Stephens College	M
Stetson University	M
Stevens Institute of Technology	M
Stony Brook University, State University of New York	M,O
Stratford University	M
Strayer University	M
Suffolk University	M,O
Sullivan University	P,M,D
Sul Ross State University	M
Syracuse University	M,D*
Tabor College	M
Tarleton State University	M
Taylor University	M
Temple University	M,D*
Tennessee State University	M
Tennessee Technological University	M
Texas A&M International University	M
Texas A&M University	M,D
Texas A&M University–Commerce	M
Texas A&M University–Corpus Christi	M
Texas A&M University–Kingsville	M
Texas A&M University–San Antonio	M
Texas A&M University–Texarkana	M
Texas Christian University	M,D
Texas Southern University	M
Texas State University–San Marcos	M
Texas Tech University	M,D*
Texas Wesleyan University	M
Texas Woman's University	M
Thomas College	M
Thomas Edison State College	M
Thomas More College	M
Thomas University	M
Thompson Rivers University	M
Thunderbird School of Global Management	M
Tiffin University	M
Trevecca Nazarene University	M
Trinity International University	P,M,D,O
Trinity University	M
Trinity (Washington) University	M
Trinity Western University	M
Troy University	M
TUI University	M,D
Tulane University	M,D*
Union Graduate College	M,O
Union University	M
United States International University	M
Universidad Autonoma de Guadalajara	M,D
Universidad de las Americas, A.C.	M
Universidad de las Américas–Puebla	M
Universidad del Este	M
Universidad del Turabo	M,D
Universidad Iberoamericana	P,M
Universidad Metropolitana	M
Université de Moncton	M
Université de Sherbrooke	P,M,D,O
Université du Québec à Chicoutimi	M
Université du Québec à Montréal	M,D,O
Université du Québec à Rimouski	M,O
Université du Québec à Trois-Rivières	M,D
Université du Québec en Abitibi-Témiscamingue	M
Université Laval	M,D,O
University at Albany, State University of New York	M
University at Buffalo, the State University of New York	M,D,O*
The University of Akron	M
The University of Alabama	M,D
The University of Alabama at Birmingham	M*
The University of Alabama in Huntsville	M
University of Alaska Anchorage	M
University of Alaska Fairbanks	M
University of Alaska Southeast	M
University of Alberta	M,D
The University of Arizona	M,D
University of Arkansas	M,D
University of Arkansas at Little Rock	M,O
University of Atlanta	P,M,D,O
University of Baltimore	M,O
University of Bridgeport	M
The University of British Columbia	M,D
University of Calgary	M,D
University of California, Berkeley	M,D,O*
University of California, Davis	M
University of California, Irvine	M,D*
University of California, Los Angeles	M,D*
University of California, Riverside	M
University of California, San Diego	M*
University of Central Arkansas	M
University of Central Florida	M,D,O
University of Central Missouri	M
University of Central Oklahoma	M
University of Charleston	M
University of Chicago	M,D
University of Cincinnati	M,D
University of Colorado at Colorado Springs	M
University of Colorado Boulder	M*
University of Colorado Denver	M
University of Connecticut	M,D*
University of Dallas	M
University of Dayton	M
University of Delaware	M,D*
University of Denver	M
University of Detroit Mercy	M,O
University of Dubuque	M
University of Evansville	M
The University of Findlay	M
University of Florida	M,D,O*
University of Georgia	M,D
University of Guam	M
University of Guelph	M,D
University of Hartford	M
University of Hawaii at Manoa	M
University of Houston	M,D
University of Houston–Clear Lake	M
University of Houston–Victoria	M
University of Idaho	M
University of Illinois at Chicago	M,D
University of Illinois at Springfield	M
University of Illinois at Urbana–Champaign	M,D
University of Indianapolis	M,O
The University of Iowa	M,D*
The University of Kansas	M,D
University of Kentucky	M,D*
University of La Verne	M,O
University of Lethbridge	M,D
University of Louisiana at Lafayette	M*
University of Louisiana at Monroe	M
University of Louisville	M
University of Maine	M
University of Management and Technology	M,D,O
The University of Manchester	M,D
University of Manitoba	M,D
University of Mary	M
University of Mary Hardin-Baylor	M
University of Maryland, College Park	M,D
University of Maryland University College	M,D,O
University of Mary Washington	M

*M—master's degree; P—first professional degree; D—doctorate; O—other advanced degree; *—Close-Up and/or Display in one of the other books in this series*

University of Massachusetts Amherst	M,D*
University of Massachusetts Boston	M
University of Massachusetts Dartmouth	M,O
University of Massachusetts Lowell	M,O
University of Memphis	M,D
University of Miami	M*
University of Michigan	D*
University of Michigan–Dearborn	M
University of Michigan–Flint	M
University of Minnesota, Duluth	M
University of Minnesota, Twin Cities Campus	M,D
University of Mississippi	M,D
University of Missouri	M,D*
University of Missouri–Kansas City	M,D*
University of Missouri–St. Louis	M,O
University of Mobile	M
The University of Montana	M
University of Montevallo	M
University of Nebraska at Kearney	M
University of Nebraska at Omaha	M
University of Nebraska–Lincoln	M,D*
University of Nevada, Las Vegas	M
University of Nevada, Reno	M*
University of New Brunswick Fredericton	M
University of New Brunswick Saint John	M
University of New Hampshire	M,O
University of New Haven	M,O
University of New Mexico	M*
University of New Orleans	M
University of North Alabama	M
The University of North Carolina at Chapel Hill	M,D*
The University of North Carolina at Charlotte	M,D,O
The University of North Carolina at Greensboro	M,O
The University of North Carolina at Pembroke	M
The University of North Carolina Wilmington	M
University of North Dakota	M
University of Northern Iowa	M
University of North Florida	M
University of North Texas	M,D
University of Notre Dame	M*
University of Oklahoma	M,D*
University of Oregon	M,D
University of Ottawa	M*
University of Pennsylvania	M,D*
University of Phoenix	M,D,O
University of Phoenix–Atlanta Campus	M
University of Phoenix–Augusta Campus	M
University of Phoenix–Austin Campus	M
University of Phoenix–Birmingham Campus	M
University of Phoenix–Boston Campus	M
University of Phoenix–Central Florida Campus	M
University of Phoenix–Central Massachusetts Campus	M
University of Phoenix–Central Valley Campus	M
University of Phoenix–Charlotte Campus	M
University of Phoenix–Chattanooga Campus	M
University of Phoenix–Cheyenne Campus	M
University of Phoenix–Chicago Campus	M
University of Phoenix–Cincinnati Campus	M
University of Phoenix–Cleveland Campus	M
University of Phoenix–Columbia Campus	M
University of Phoenix–Columbus Georgia Campus	M
University of Phoenix–Columbus Ohio Campus	M
University of Phoenix–Dallas Campus	M
University of Phoenix–Denver Campus	M
University of Phoenix–Des Moines Campus	M
University of Phoenix–Eastern Washington Campus	M
University of Phoenix–Fairfield County Campus	M
University of Phoenix–Harrisburg Campus	M
University of Phoenix–Hawaii Campus	M
University of Phoenix–Houston Campus	M
University of Phoenix–Idaho Campus	M
University of Phoenix–Indianapolis Campus	M
University of Phoenix–Jersey City Campus	M
University of Phoenix–Kansas City Campus	M
University of Phoenix–Las Vegas Campus	M
University of Phoenix–Little Rock Campus	M
University of Phoenix–Louisiana Campus	M
University of Phoenix–Louisville Campus	M
University of Phoenix–Madison Campus	M
University of Phoenix–Maryland Campus	M
University of Phoenix–Memphis Campus	M
University of Phoenix–Milwaukee Campus	M,D
University of Phoenix–Minneapolis/St. Louis Park Campus	M
University of Phoenix–Nashville Campus	M
University of Phoenix–New Mexico Campus	M
University of Phoenix–Northern Nevada Campus	M
University of Phoenix–Northern Virginia Campus	M
University of Phoenix–North Florida Campus	M
University of Phoenix–Northwest Arkansas Campus	M
University of Phoenix–Oklahoma City Campus	M
University of Phoenix–Omaha Campus	M
University of Phoenix–Oregon Campus	M
University of Phoenix–Philadelphia Campus	M
University of Phoenix–Phoenix Campus	M
University of Phoenix–Pittsburgh Campus	M
University of Phoenix–Puerto Rico Campus	M
University of Phoenix–Raleigh Campus	M
University of Phoenix–Richmond Campus	M
University of Phoenix–Sacramento Valley Campus	M
University of Phoenix–St. Louis Campus	M
University of Phoenix–San Antonio Campus	M
University of Phoenix–San Diego Campus	M
University of Phoenix–Savannah Campus	M
University of Phoenix–Southern Arizona Campus	M
University of Phoenix–Southern Colorado Campus	M
University of Phoenix–South Florida Campus	M
University of Phoenix–Springfield Campus	M
University of Phoenix–Tulsa Campus	M
University of Phoenix–Utah Campus	M
University of Phoenix–Vancouver Campus	M
University of Phoenix–Washington Campus	M
University of Phoenix–Washington D.C. Campus	M,D
University of Phoenix–West Florida Campus	M
University of Phoenix–West Michigan Campus	M
University of Phoenix–Wichita Campus	M
University of Pittsburgh	M,D,O*
University of Portland	M
University of Puerto Rico, Mayagüez Campus	M
University of Puerto Rico, Río Piedras	M,D
University of Redlands	M
University of Regina	M,O
University of Rhode Island	M,D
University of Richmond	M
University of Rochester	M,D
University of St. Francis (IL)	M
University of Saint Francis (IN)	M
University of Saint Mary	M
University of St. Thomas (TX)	M*
University of St. Thomas (MN)	M
University of San Diego	M,O
University of San Francisco	M
University of Saskatchewan	M
The University of Scranton	M
University of Sioux Falls	M
University of South Africa	M,D
University of South Alabama	M
University of South Carolina	M,D
The University of South Dakota	M
University of Southern California	M,D*
University of Southern Indiana	M
University of Southern Maine	M
University of Southern Mississippi	M
University of South Florida	M,D*
The University of Tampa	M
The University of Tennessee	M,D
The University of Tennessee at Chattanooga	M
The University of Tennessee at Martin	M
The University of Texas at Arlington	M,D
The University of Texas at Austin	M,D
The University of Texas at Brownsville	M
The University of Texas at Dallas	M,D*
The University of Texas at El Paso	M,D,O
The University of Texas at San Antonio	M,D*
The University of Texas at Tyler	M
The University of Texas of the Permian Basin	M
The University of Texas–Pan American	M,D
University of the Cumberlands	M
University of the District of Columbia	M
University of the Incarnate Word	M,O
University of the Pacific	M
University of the Sacred Heart	M,O
University of the Southwest	M
University of the Virgin Islands	M
University of the West	M
The University of Toledo	M,D,O
University of Toronto	M,D
University of Tulsa	M
University of Utah	M,D*
University of Vermont	M
University of Victoria	M
University of Virginia	M,D
University of Washington	M,D*
University of Washington, Bothell	M
University of Washington, Tacoma	M
University of Waterloo	M
The University of Western Ontario	M,D
University of West Florida	M
University of West Georgia	M
University of Windsor	M
University of Wisconsin–Eau Claire	M
University of Wisconsin–Green Bay	M
University of Wisconsin–La Crosse	M
University of Wisconsin–Madison	M*
University of Wisconsin–Milwaukee	M,D,O
University of Wisconsin–Oshkosh	M
University of Wisconsin–Parkside	M
University of Wisconsin–River Falls	M
University of Wisconsin–Stevens Point	M
University of Wisconsin–Whitewater	M*
University of Wyoming	M
Upper Iowa University	M
Urbana University	M
Ursuline College	M
Utah State University	M
Valdosta State University	M
Valparaiso University	M,O
Vancouver Island University	M
Vanderbilt University	M*
Vanguard University of Southern California	M
Villanova University	M

Virginia College at Birmingham M
Virginia Commonwealth University M,O
Virginia International University M,O
Virginia Polytechnic Institute and State University M,D
Viterbo University M
Wagner College M
Wake Forest University M
Walden University M,D
Walsh College of Accountancy and Business Administration M
Walsh University M
Warner Pacific College M
Warner University M
Washburn University M
Washington Adventist University M
Washington State University M,D
Washington State University Tri-Cities M
Washington State University Vancouver M
Washington University in St. Louis M,D*
Wayland Baptist University M
Waynesburg University M,D
Wayne State College M
Wayne State University M,D*
Webber International University M
Weber State University M
Webster University M,D,O
Wesleyan College M
Wesley College M
West Chester University of Pennsylvania M,O
Western Carolina University M
Western Connecticut State University M
Western Governors University M
Western Illinois University M
Western International University M
Western Kentucky University M
Western Michigan University M
Western New England University M
Western New Mexico University M
Western Washington University M
Westminster College (UT) M,O
West Texas A&M University M
West Virginia University M
West Virginia Wesleyan College M
Wheeling Jesuit University M
Wichita State University M
Widener University M
Wilfrid Laurier University M,D
Wilkes University M
Willamette University M
William Carey University M
William Paterson University of New Jersey M
Wilmington University M
Wingate University M
Winston-Salem State University M
Winthrop University M
Woodbury University M
Worcester Polytechnic Institute M,O
Worcester State University M
Wright State University M
Xavier University M
Yale University M,D*
York College of Pennsylvania M
Yorktown University M
York University M,D*
Youngstown State University M,O

BUSINESS EDUCATION

Arkansas State University M,O
Armstrong Atlantic State University M
Auburn University M,D,O
Ball State University M
Bloomsburg University of Pennsylvania M
Bowling Green State University M*
Buffalo State College, State University of New York M
Canisius College M
Chadron State College M,O
The College of Saint Rose M,O
Colorado Christian University M
Eastern Kentucky University M
Emporia State University M
Florida Agricultural and Mechanical University M
Georgia Southern University M
Hofstra University M,O
Inter American University of Puerto Rico, Metropolitan Campus M
Inter American University of Puerto Rico, San Germán Campus M
International College of the Cayman Islands M
Johnson & Wales University M
Lehman College of the City University of New York M
Louisiana State University and Agricultural and Mechanical College M,D
Louisiana Tech University M,D
Maryville University of Saint Louis M,O
Middle Tennessee State University M
Mississippi College M,D,O
Morehead State University M,O
Nazareth College of Rochester M
New York University M,O
North Carolina State University M*
Northwestern State University of Louisiana M
Old Dominion University M,D
Pontifical Catholic University of Puerto Rico M,D
Rider University O
Robert Morris University M,D,O
South Carolina State University M,D,O
Southern New Hampshire University M,O
State University of New York at Oswego M
Thomas College M
The University of British Columbia M,D
University of Delaware M,D*
University of Minnesota, Twin Cities Campus M,D
University of Missouri M,D,O*
University of St. Francis (IL) M
University of South Carolina M,D
University of the Cumberlands M,D,O
The University of Toledo M,D,O
University of Washington M,D*
University of West Georgia M,O
University of Wisconsin–Whitewater M*
Utah State University M,D
Wayne State College M
Wayne State University M,D,O*
Wright State University M

CANADIAN STUDIES

Carleton University M,D
Collège universitaire de Saint-Boniface M
Queen's University at Kingston M,D
Saint Mary's University (Canada) M,O
Trent University M,D
Université de Sherbrooke M,D
Université du Québec à Chicoutimi M
University of Lethbridge M,D
University of Maine M,D
University of Manitoba M
University of Ottawa D*
University of Regina M,D
University of Saskatchewan M,D
Wilfrid Laurier University M,D

CANCER BIOLOGY/ONCOLOGY

Baylor College of Medicine D*
Brown University M,D
Case Western Reserve University D*
Dartmouth College D
Duke University D*
Emory University D*
Gerstner Sloan-Kettering Graduate School of Biomedical Sciences D*
Mayo Graduate School D
McMaster University M,D
Medical University of South Carolina D
Meharry Medical College D
Memorial University of Newfoundland M,D
New York University P,M,D
Northwestern University D*
Oregon Health & Science University D*
Queen's University at Kingston M,D
Rutgers, The State University of New Jersey, New Brunswick M,D*
Stanford University D
State University of New York Upstate Medical University
Université Laval O
University at Buffalo, the State University of New York M,D*
University of Alberta M,D
The University of Arizona D
University of Calgary M,D
University of California, San Diego D*
University of Chicago D
University of Cincinnati D
University of Colorado Denver D
University of Delaware M,D*
The University of Manchester M,D
University of Manitoba M
University of Maryland, Baltimore M,D
University of Massachusetts Worcester M,D
University of Medicine and Dentistry of New Jersey D,O
University of Miami D*
University of Minnesota, Twin Cities Campus D
University of Nebraska Medical Center D
University of Pennsylvania D*
University of Regina M,D
University of South Florida D*
The University of Texas Health Science Center at Houston M,D*
The University of Texas Southwestern Medical Center at Dallas D
University of the District of Columbia M
The University of Toledo M,D
University of Utah M,D*
University of Wisconsin–La Crosse M
University of Wisconsin–Madison D*
Vanderbilt University M,D*
Wake Forest University D
Wayne State University M,D*
West Virginia University M,D
Yale University D*

CARDIOVASCULAR SCIENCES

Albany Medical College M,D
Baylor College of Medicine D*
Dartmouth College D
Geneva College M
Georgia Health Sciences University M,D
Long Island University, C.W. Post Campus M
Loyola University Chicago M,O
McMaster University M,D
Medical University of South Carolina D
Memorial University of Newfoundland M,D
Midwestern University, Glendale Campus M
Milwaukee School of Engineering M
Queen's University at Kingston M,D
Quinnipiac University M
State University of New York Upstate Medical University
Université Laval O
University of Calgary M,D
University of California, San Diego D*
University of Guelph M,D,O
University of Mary M
University of Medicine and Dentistry of New Jersey M,D
The University of South Dakota M,D
The University of Toledo M,D

CELL BIOLOGY

Albany College of Pharmacy and Health Sciences P,M*
Albany Medical College M,D
Albert Einstein College of Medicine D
Appalachian State University M
Arizona State University M,D
Auburn University M,D
Baylor College of Medicine D*
Boston University M,D*
Brandeis University M,D
Brown University M,D
California Institute of Technology D
Carnegie Mellon University M,D*
Case Western Reserve University M,D*
The Catholic University of America M,D
Colorado State University M,D

*M—master's degree; P—first professional degree; D—doctorate; O—other advanced degree; *—Close-Up and/or Display in one of the other books in this series*

Institution	Degrees
Columbia University	M,D*
Cornell University	M,D*
Cornell University, Joan and Sanford I. Weill Medical College and Graduate School of Medical Sciences	M,D
Dartmouth College	D
Drexel University	M,D*
Duke University	D,O*
East Carolina University	D
Eastern Michigan University	M
Eastern New Mexico University	M
Emory University	D*
Emporia State University	M
Florida Institute of Technology	M
Florida State University	M,D
Georgetown University	D
Georgia Health Sciences University	M,D
Georgia State University	M,D
Grand Valley State University	M
Harvard University	D*
Illinois Institute of Technology	M,D
Illinois State University	M,D
Indiana University Bloomington	M,D*
Indiana University–Purdue University Indianapolis	M,D
Iowa State University of Science and Technology	M,D*
The Johns Hopkins University	D
Kent State University	M,D*
Louisiana State University Health Sciences Center	M,D
Louisiana State University Health Sciences Center at Shreveport	M,D
Loyola University Chicago	M,D
Marquette University	M,D
Massachusetts Institute of Technology	D
Mayo Graduate School	D
McGill University	M,D
McMaster University	M,D
Medical University of South Carolina	D
Michigan State University	M,D
Missouri State University	M
New York Medical College	M,D*
New York University	P,M,D
North Carolina State University	M,D*
North Dakota State University	M,D
Northwestern University	D*
The Ohio State University	M,D
Ohio University	M,D*
Oregon Health & Science University	D*
Oregon State University	M,D
Penn State Hershey Medical Center	M,D
Purdue University	M,D
Queen's University at Kingston	M,D
Quinnipiac University	M
Rice University	M,D
Rosalind Franklin University of Medicine and Science	M,D*
Rush University	M,D
Rutgers, The State University of New Jersey, New Brunswick	M,D*
San Diego State University	M,D
San Francisco State University	M
State University of New York Downstate Medical Center	D
State University of New York Upstate Medical University	M,D
Stony Brook University, State University of New York	M,D
Temple University	M,D*
Texas A&M Health Science Center	D
Texas A&M University	M,D
Texas Tech University Health Sciences Center	M,D
Thomas Jefferson University	M,D
Tufts University	D
Tulane University	M,D*
Uniformed Services University of the Health Sciences	D*
Universidad Central del Caribe	M,D
Université de Montréal	M,D
Université de Sherbrooke	M,D
Université Laval	M,D
University at Albany, State University of New York	M,D
University at Buffalo, the State University of New York	D*
The University of Alabama at Birmingham	D*
University of Alberta	M,D
The University of Arizona	M,D
University of Arkansas	M,D
The University of British Columbia	M,D
University of California, Berkeley	D*
University of California, Davis	M,D
University of California, Irvine	M,D*
University of California, Los Angeles	D*
University of California, Riverside	M,D
University of California, San Diego	D*
University of California, San Francisco	D
University of California, Santa Barbara	M,D
University of California, Santa Cruz	M,D
University of Chicago	D
University of Cincinnati	D
University of Colorado Boulder	M,D*
University of Colorado Denver	D
University of Connecticut	M,D*
University of Connecticut Health Center	D*
University of Delaware	M,D*
University of Florida	M,D*
University of Georgia	M,D
University of Guelph	M,D
University of Illinois at Chicago	D
University of Illinois at Urbana–Champaign	D
The University of Iowa	M,D*
The University of Kansas	M,D
University of Maine	D
The University of Manchester	M,D
University of Maryland, Baltimore	M,D
University of Maryland, Baltimore County	D
University of Maryland, College Park	M,D
University of Massachusetts Amherst	M,D*
University of Massachusetts Boston	D
University of Massachusetts Worcester	M,D
University of Medicine and Dentistry of New Jersey	M,D
University of Miami	D*
University of Michigan	M,D*
University of Minnesota, Twin Cities Campus	M,D
University of Missouri	M,D*
University of Missouri–Kansas City	D*
University of Missouri–St. Louis	M,D,O
University of Nebraska Medical Center	M,D
University of Nevada, Reno	M,D*
University of New Haven	M,O
University of New Mexico	M,D,O*
The University of North Carolina at Chapel Hill	M,D*
University of North Dakota	M,D
University of Notre Dame	M,D*
University of Oklahoma Health Sciences Center	M,D
University of Ottawa	M,D*
University of Pennsylvania	D*
University of Pittsburgh	M,D*
University of Puerto Rico, Río Piedras	M,D
University of Rhode Island	M,D
University of Saskatchewan	M,D
University of South Carolina	M,D
The University of South Dakota	M,D
University of Southern California	M,D*
University of South Florida	M,D*
The University of Texas at Austin	D
The University of Texas at Dallas	M,D*
The University of Texas Health Science Center at Houston	M,D*
The University of Texas Health Science Center at San Antonio	M,D
The University of Texas Medical Branch	D
The University of Texas Southwestern Medical Center at Dallas	D
University of the Sciences in Philadelphia	M,D
The University of Toledo	M,D
University of Toronto	M,D
University of Vermont	M,D
University of Virginia	D
University of Washington	D*
The University of Western Ontario	M,D
University of Wisconsin–La Crosse	M
University of Wisconsin–Madison	D*
University of Wyoming	D
Vanderbilt University	M,D*
Washington State University	M,D
Washington University in St. Louis	D*
Wesleyan University	D*
West Virginia University	M,D
Yale University	D*

CELTIC LANGUAGES

Institution	Degrees
Harvard University	D*

CERAMIC SCIENCES AND ENGINEERING

Institution	Degrees
Alfred University	M,D
Missouri University of Science and Technology	M,D
Rensselaer Polytechnic Institute	M,D
University of Washington	M,D*

CHEMICAL ENGINEERING

Institution	Degrees
American University of Sharjah	M
Arizona State University	M,D
Auburn University	M,D
Brigham Young University	M,D*
Brown University	M,D
Bucknell University	M
California Institute of Technology	M,D
California State University, Long Beach	M
Carnegie Mellon University	M,D*
Case Western Reserve University	M,D*
City College of the City University of New York	M,D
Clarkson University	M,D*
Clemson University	M,D
Cleveland State University	M,D
Colorado School of Mines	M,D
Colorado State University	M,D
Columbia University	M,D*
Cooper Union for the Advancement of Science and Art	M
Cornell University	M,D*
Dalhousie University	M,D
Drexel University	M,D*
École Polytechnique de Montréal	M,D,O
Fairleigh Dickinson University, College at Florham	M,O
Florida Agricultural and Mechanical University	M,D
Florida Institute of Technology	M,D
Florida State University	M,D
Georgia Institute of Technology	M,D
Graduate School and University Center of the City University of New York	D
Howard University	M
Illinois Institute of Technology	M,D
Instituto Tecnológico y de Estudios Superiores de Monterrey, Campus Monterrey	M,D
Iowa State University of Science and Technology	M,D*
The Johns Hopkins University	M,D
Kansas State University	M,D*
Lamar University	M,D
Lehigh University	M,D
Louisiana State University and Agricultural and Mechanical College	M,D
Louisiana Tech University	M,D
Manhattan College	M
Massachusetts Institute of Technology	M,D
McGill University	M,D
McMaster University	M,D
McNeese State University	M
Michigan State University	M,D
Michigan Technological University	M,D
Mississippi State University	M,D
Missouri University of Science and Technology	M,D
Montana State University	M,D
New Jersey Institute of Technology	M,D
New Mexico State University	M,D
North Carolina Agricultural and Technical State University	M,D
North Carolina State University	M,D*
Northeastern University	M,D
Northwestern University	M,D*

The Ohio State University	M,D
Ohio University	M,D*
Oklahoma State University	M,D*
Oregon State University	M,D
Penn State University Park	M,D
Polytechnic Institute of NYU	M,D
Polytechnic Institute of NYU, Long Island Graduate Center	M
Princeton University	M,D*
Purdue University	M,D
Queen's University at Kingston	M,D
Rensselaer Polytechnic Institute	M,D
Rice University	M,D
Rose-Hulman Institute of Technology	M
Rowan University	M
Royal Military College of Canada	M,D
Rutgers, The State University of New Jersey, New Brunswick	M,D*
San Jose State University	M
South Dakota School of Mines and Technology	M,D
Stanford University	M,D,O
Stevens Institute of Technology	M,D,O
Syracuse University	M,D*
Tennessee Technological University	M,D
Texas A&M University	M,D
Texas A&M University–Kingsville	M
Texas Tech University	M,D*
Tufts University	M,D
Tulane University	D*
Universidad de las Américas–Puebla	M
Université de Sherbrooke	M,D
Université Laval	M,D
University at Buffalo, the State University of New York	M,D*
The University of Akron	M,D
The University of Alabama	M,D
The University of Alabama in Huntsville	M
University of Alberta	M,D
The University of Arizona	M,D
University of Arkansas	M,D
The University of British Columbia	M,D
University of Calgary	M,D
University of California, Berkeley	M,D*
University of California, Davis	M,D
University of California, Irvine	M,D*
University of California, Los Angeles	M,D*
University of California, Riverside	M,D
University of California, San Diego	M,D*
University of California, Santa Barbara	D
University of Cincinnati	M,D
University of Colorado Boulder	M,D*
University of Connecticut	M,D*
University of Dayton	M
University of Delaware	M,D*
University of Florida	M,D*
University of Houston	M,D
University of Idaho	M,D
University of Illinois at Chicago	M,D
University of Illinois at Urbana–Champaign	M,D
The University of Iowa	M,D*
The University of Kansas	M,D
University of Kentucky	M,D*
University of Louisiana at Lafayette	M*
University of Louisville	M,D
University of Maine	M,D
The University of Manchester	M,D
University of Maryland, Baltimore County	M,D
University of Maryland, College Park	M,D
University of Massachusetts Amherst	M,D*
University of Massachusetts Lowell	M,D
University of Michigan	M,D,O*
University of Minnesota, Twin Cities Campus	M,D
University of Missouri	M,D*
University of Nebraska–Lincoln	M,D*
University of Nevada, Reno	M,D*
University of New Brunswick Fredericton	M,D
University of New Hampshire	M,D
University of New Mexico	M,D*
University of North Dakota	M
University of Notre Dame	M,D*
University of Oklahoma	M,D*
University of Ottawa	M,D*
University of Pennsylvania	M,D*
University of Pittsburgh	M,D*
University of Puerto Rico, Mayagüez Campus	M,D
University of Rhode Island	M,D
University of Rochester	
University of Saskatchewan	M,D
University of South Africa	M
University of South Alabama	M
University of South Carolina	M,D
University of Southern California	M,D,O*
University of South Florida	M,D*
The University of Tennessee	M,D
The University of Tennessee at Chattanooga	M
The University of Texas at Austin	M,D
The University of Toledo	M,D
University of Toronto	M,D
University of Tulsa	M,D
University of Utah	M,D*
University of Virginia	M,D
University of Washington	M,D*
University of Waterloo	M,D
The University of Western Ontario	M,D
University of Wisconsin–Madison	M,D*
University of Wyoming	M,D
Vanderbilt University	M,D*
Villanova University	M,O
Virginia Commonwealth University	M,D
Virginia Polytechnic Institute and State University	M,D
Washington State University	M,D
Washington University in St. Louis	M,D*
Wayne State University	M,D*
Western Michigan University	M,D
West Virginia University	M,D
Widener University	M
Worcester Polytechnic Institute	M,D
Yale University	M,D*

CHEMICAL PHYSICS

Columbia University	M,D*
Cornell University	D*
Harvard University	D*
Kent State University	M,D*
Marquette University	M,D
McMaster University	M,D
Michigan State University	M,D
The Ohio State University	M,D
Simon Fraser University	M,D
University of Colorado Boulder	M,D*
University of Illinois at Urbana–Champaign	M,D
University of Louisville	M,D
University of Maryland, College Park	M,D
University of Nevada, Reno	D*
The University of Tennessee	M,D
University of Utah	M,D*
Virginia Commonwealth University	M,D
Wesleyan University	M,D*
West Virginia University	M,D

CHEMISTRY

Acadia University	M
American University	M,O
The American University in Cairo	M
American University of Beirut	M
Arizona State University	M,D
Arkansas State University	M,O
Auburn University	M,D
Ball State University	M
Baylor University	M,D*
Boston College	M,D*
Boston University	M,D,O*
Bowling Green State University	M,D*
Bradley University	M
Brandeis University	M,D
Brigham Young University	M,D*
Brock University	M,D
Brooklyn College of the City University of New York	M,D
Brown University	M,D
Bryn Mawr College	M,D*
Bucknell University	M
Buffalo State College, State University of New York	M
California Institute of Technology	M,D
California Polytechnic State University, San Luis Obispo	M
California State Polytechnic University, Pomona	M
California State University, East Bay	M
California State University, Fresno	M
California State University, Fullerton	M
California State University, Long Beach	M
California State University, Los Angeles	M*
California State University, Northridge	M
California State University, Sacramento	M
California State University, San Bernardino	M
Carleton University	M,D
Carnegie Mellon University	M,D*
Case Western Reserve University	M,D*
Central Connecticut State University	M,O
Central Michigan University	M
Central Washington University	M
Christopher Newport University	M
City College of the City University of New York	M,D
Clark Atlanta University	M,D
Clarkson University	M,D*
Clark University	M,D
Clemson University	M,D
Cleveland State University	M,D
The College of William and Mary	M
Colorado School of Mines	M,D
Colorado State University	M,D
Colorado State University–Pueblo	M
Columbia University	M,D*
Concordia University (Canada)	M,D
Cornell University	D*
Dalhousie University	M,D
Dartmouth College	D
Delaware State University	M
DePaul University	M
Drew University	M
Drexel University	M,D*
Duke University	D*
Duquesne University	M,D
East Carolina University	M
Eastern Illinois University	M
Eastern Kentucky University	M
Eastern Michigan University	M
Eastern New Mexico University	M
East Tennessee State University	M
Emory University	D*
Fairleigh Dickinson University, College at Florham	M
Fairleigh Dickinson University, Metropolitan Campus	M
Fisk University	M
Florida Agricultural and Mechanical University	M
Florida Atlantic University	M,D
Florida Institute of Technology	M,D
Florida International University	M,D
Florida State University	M,D
Furman University	M
George Mason University	M,D*
Georgetown University	D
The George Washington University	M,D
Georgia Institute of Technology	M,D
Georgia State University	M,D
Graduate School and University Center of the City University of New York	D
Hampton University	M
Harvard University	D*
Hofstra University	M,O
Howard University	M,D
Hunter College of the City University of New York	M,D
Idaho State University	M
Illinois Institute of Technology	M,D
Illinois State University	M
Indiana University Bloomington	M,D*
Indiana University of Pennsylvania	M
Indiana University–Purdue University Indianapolis	M,D
Instituto Tecnológico y de Estudios Superiores de Monterrey, Campus Monterrey	M,D
Iowa State University of Science and Technology	M,D*
Jackson State University	M,D
The Johns Hopkins University	D
Kansas State University	M,D*
Kent State University	M,D*

*M—master's degree; P—first professional degree; D—doctorate; O—other advanced degree; *—Close-Up and/or Display in one of the other books in this series*

Lakehead University	M
Lamar University	M
Laurentian University	M
Lehigh University	M,D
Long Island University, Brooklyn Campus	M
Louisiana State University and Agricultural and Mechanical College	M,D
Louisiana Tech University	M
Loyola University Chicago	M,D
Marquette University	M,D
Marshall University	M
Massachusetts College of Pharmacy and Health Sciences	M,D
Massachusetts Institute of Technology	D
McGill University	M,D
McMaster University	M,D
McNeese State University	M
Memorial University of Newfoundland	M,D
Miami University	M,D
Michigan State University	M,D
Michigan Technological University	M,D
Middle Tennessee State University	M,D
Mississippi College	M
Mississippi State University	M,D
Missouri State University	M
Missouri University of Science and Technology	M,D
Missouri Western State University	M
Montana State University	M,D
Montclair State University	M,O
Morgan State University	M
Mount Allison University	M
Murray State University	M
New Jersey Institute of Technology	M,D
New Mexico Highlands University	M
New Mexico Institute of Mining and Technology	M,D
New Mexico State University	M,D
New York University	M,D
North Carolina Agricultural and Technical State University	M
North Carolina Central University	M
North Carolina State University	M,D*
North Dakota State University	M,D
Northeastern Illinois University	M
Northeastern University	M,D
Northern Arizona University	M
Northern Illinois University	M,D
Northwestern University	D*
Oakland University	M,D
The Ohio State University	M,D
Oklahoma State University	M,D*
Old Dominion University	M,D
Oregon State University	M,D
Penn State University Park	M,D
Pittsburg State University	M
Polytechnic Institute of NYU	M,D
Polytechnic Institute of NYU, Long Island Graduate Center	M
Polytechnic Institute of NYU, Westchester Graduate Center	M
Pontifical Catholic University of Puerto Rico	M
Portland State University	M,D
Prairie View A&M University	M
Princeton University	M,D*
Purdue University	M,D
Queens College of the City University of New York	M
Queen's University at Kingston	M,D
Rensselaer Polytechnic Institute	M,D
Rice University	M,D
Rochester Institute of Technology	M
Roosevelt University	M
Royal Military College of Canada	M,D
Rutgers, The State University of New Jersey, Camden	M
Rutgers, The State University of New Jersey, Newark	M,D*
Rutgers, The State University of New Jersey, New Brunswick	M,D*
Sacred Heart University	M
St. Francis Xavier University	M
St. John's University (NY)	M
Saint Joseph College	M
Saint Louis University	M,D
Sam Houston State University	M
San Diego State University	M,D
San Francisco State University	M
San Jose State University	M
The Scripps Research Institute	D
Seton Hall University	M,D
Simon Fraser University	M,D
Smith College	M
South Dakota State University	M,D
Southeastern Louisiana University	M
Southeast Missouri State University	M
Southern Connecticut State University	M
Southern Illinois University Carbondale	M,D
Southern Illinois University Edwardsville	M
Southern Methodist University	M,D
Southern University and Agricultural and Mechanical College	M
Stanford University	D
State University of New York at Binghamton	M,D
State University of New York at Fredonia	M
State University of New York at New Paltz	M
State University of New York at Oswego	M
State University of New York College of Environmental Science and Forestry	M,D
Stephen F. Austin State University	M
Stevens Institute of Technology	M,D,O
Stony Brook University, State University of New York	M,D
Syracuse University	M,D*
Temple University	M,D*
Tennessee State University	M
Tennessee Technological University	M,D
Texas A&M University	M,D
Texas A&M University–Commerce	M
Texas A&M University–Kingsville	M
Texas Christian University	M,D
Texas Southern University	M
Texas State University–San Marcos	M
Texas Tech University	M,D*
Texas Woman's University	M
Trent University	M
Tufts University	M,D
Tulane University	M,D*
Tuskegee University	M
Universidad del Turabo	M,D
Université de Moncton	M
Université de Montréal	M,D
Université de Sherbrooke	M,D,O
Université du Québec à Montréal	M,D
Université du Québec à Trois-Rivières	M
Université Laval	M,D
University at Albany, State University of New York	M,D
University at Buffalo, the State University of New York	M,D*
The University of Akron	M,D
The University of Alabama at Birmingham	M,D*
The University of Alabama in Huntsville	M
University of Alaska Fairbanks	M,D
University of Alberta	M,D
The University of Arizona	D
University of Arkansas	M,D
University of Arkansas at Little Rock	M
The University of British Columbia	M,D
University of Calgary	M,D
University of California, Berkeley	D*
University of California, Davis	M,D
University of California, Irvine	M,D*
University of California, Los Angeles	M,D*
University of California, Merced	M,D
University of California, Riverside	M,D
University of California, San Diego	M,D*
University of California, San Francisco	D
University of California, Santa Barbara	M,D
University of California, Santa Cruz	M,D
University of Central Florida	M,D,O
University of Central Oklahoma	M
University of Chicago	D
University of Cincinnati	M,D
University of Colorado at Colorado Springs	M
University of Colorado Boulder	M,D*
University of Colorado Denver	M
University of Connecticut	M,D*
University of Dayton	M
University of Delaware	M,D*
University of Denver	M,D
University of Detroit Mercy	M
University of Florida	M,D*
University of Georgia	M,D
University of Guelph	M,D
University of Hawaii at Manoa	M,D
University of Houston	M,D
University of Houston–Clear Lake	M
University of Idaho	M,D
University of Illinois at Chicago	M,D
University of Illinois at Urbana–Champaign	M,D
The University of Iowa	M,D*
The University of Kansas	M,D
University of Kentucky	M,D*
University of Lethbridge	M,D
University of Louisville	M,D
University of Maine	M,D
The University of Manchester	M,D
University of Manitoba	M,D
University of Maryland, Baltimore County	M,D
University of Maryland, College Park	M,D
University of Massachusetts Amherst	M,D*
University of Massachusetts Boston	M
University of Massachusetts Dartmouth	M,D
University of Massachusetts Lowell	M,D
University of Memphis	M,D
University of Miami	M,D*
University of Michigan	D*
University of Minnesota, Duluth	M
University of Minnesota, Twin Cities Campus	M,D
University of Mississippi	M,D
University of Missouri	M,D*
University of Missouri–Kansas City	M,D*
University of Missouri–St. Louis	M,D
The University of Montana	M,D
University of Nebraska–Lincoln	M,D*
University of Nevada, Las Vegas	M,D
University of Nevada, Reno	M,D*
University of New Brunswick Fredericton	M,D
University of New Hampshire	M,D
University of New Mexico	M,D*
University of New Orleans	M,D
The University of North Carolina at Chapel Hill	M,D*
The University of North Carolina at Charlotte	M,D
The University of North Carolina at Greensboro	M
The University of North Carolina Wilmington	M
University of North Dakota	M,D
University of Northern Colorado	M,D
University of Northern Iowa	M
University of North Texas	M,D
University of Notre Dame	M,D*
University of Oklahoma	M,D*
University of Oregon	M,D
University of Ottawa	M,D*
University of Pennsylvania	M,D*
University of Pittsburgh	M,D*
University of Prince Edward Island	M
University of Puerto Rico, Mayagüez Campus	M,D
University of Puerto Rico, Río Piedras	M,D
University of Regina	M,D
University of Rhode Island	M,D
University of Rochester	M,D
University of San Francisco	M
University of Saskatchewan	M,D
The University of Scranton	M
University of South Carolina	M,D
The University of South Dakota	M,D
University of Southern California	D*
University of Southern Mississippi	M,D
University of South Florida	M,D*
The University of Tennessee	M,D

Institution	Degrees
The University of Texas at Arlington	M,D
The University of Texas at Austin	M,D
The University of Texas at Dallas	M,D*
The University of Texas at El Paso	M,D
The University of Texas at San Antonio	M,D*
The University of Texas–Pan American	M
University of the Sciences in Philadelphia	M,D
The University of Toledo	M,D
University of Toronto	M,D
University of Tulsa	M,D
University of Utah	M,D*
University of Vermont	M,D
University of Victoria	M,D
University of Virginia	M,D
University of Washington	M,D*
University of Waterloo	M,D
The University of Western Ontario	M,D
University of Windsor	M,D
University of Wisconsin–Madison	M,D*
University of Wisconsin–Milwaukee	M,D
University of Wyoming	M,D
Utah State University	M,D
Vanderbilt University	M,D*
Villanova University	M
Virginia Commonwealth University	M,D
Virginia Polytechnic Institute and State University	M,D
Wake Forest University	M,D
Washington State University	M,D
Washington State University Tri-Cities	M,D
Washington University in St. Louis	D*
Wayne State University	M,D*
Wesleyan University	M,D*
West Chester University of Pennsylvania	O
Western Carolina University	M
Western Illinois University	M
Western Kentucky University	M
Western Michigan University	M,D
Western Washington University	M
West Texas A&M University	M
West Virginia University	M,D
Wichita State University	M,D
Wilfrid Laurier University	M
Worcester Polytechnic Institute	M,D
Wright State University	M
Yale University	D*
York University	M,D*
Youngstown State University	M

CHILD AND FAMILY STUDIES

Institution	Degrees
Arizona State University	M,D
Asbury University	M
Assumption College	M,O
Auburn University	M,D
Bank Street College of Education	M
Bowling Green State University	M*
Brandeis University	M,D
Brigham Young University	M,D*
Brock University	M
California State University, Los Angeles	M*
Capella University	M,D,O
Central Michigan University	M,O
Central Washington University	M
Colorado State University	M,D
Concordia University (Canada)	M
Concordia University, St. Paul	M,O
Concordia University Wisconsin	M
Cornell University	D*
East Carolina University	M
Eastern Michigan University	M
Fairfield University	M
Florida State University	M,D
Indiana University Bloomington	M,D*
Indiana University–Purdue University Indianapolis	M
Iowa State University of Science and Technology	M,D*
Kansas State University	M,D*
Kent State University	M*
Loma Linda University	M,D,O
Miami University	M
Michigan State University	M,D
Middle Tennessee State University	M
Missouri State University	M
Mount Saint Vincent University	M
North Dakota State University	M,D
Northern Illinois University	M
Nova Southeastern University	M,D*
The Ohio State University	M,D
Ohio University	M*
Oklahoma State University	M,D*
Oregon State University	M,D
Oxford Graduate School	M,D
Penn State University Park	M,D
Purdue University	M,D
Purdue University Calumet	M
Roberts Wesleyan College	M
Sage Graduate School	M
St. Cloud State University	M
San Diego State University	M
San Jose State University	M
South Carolina State University	M
Spring Arbor University	M
Stanford University	D
State University of New York at Oswego	M
Syracuse University	M,D*
Texas State University–San Marcos	M
Texas Tech University	M,D*
Texas Woman's University	M,D
Towson University	M,O
Tufts University	M,D,O
The University of Akron	M
The University of Alabama	M
The University of Arizona	M
University of California, Santa Barbara	M,D
University of Central Florida	M,O
University of Connecticut	M,D,O*
University of Delaware	M,D*
University of Denver	M,D,O
University of Georgia	M,D,O
University of Guelph	M,D
University of Illinois at Springfield	M
University of Kentucky	M,D*
University of La Verne	M
University of Manitoba	M
University of Maryland, College Park	M,D
University of Massachusetts Amherst	M,D,O*
University of Minnesota, Twin Cities Campus	M,D
University of Missouri	M,D*
University of Nebraska–Lincoln	M,D*
University of Nevada, Reno	M*
University of New Hampshire	M
University of New Mexico	M,D*
The University of North Carolina at Greensboro	M,D
University of North Texas	M,O
University of Oklahoma	M,O*
University of Rhode Island	M
University of Southern California	M,D*
University of Southern Mississippi	M
The University of Tennessee	M,D
The University of Tennessee at Martin	M
The University of Texas at Austin	M,D
The University of Texas at Dallas	M,D*
University of Utah	M*
University of Victoria	M,D
University of Wisconsin–Madison	M,D*
University of Wisconsin–Stout	M
Utah State University	M,D
Vanderbilt University	M*
Walden University	M,D
West Virginia University	M
Wheelock College	M

CHILD DEVELOPMENT

Institution	Degrees
Arcadia University	M,D,O*
California State University, Los Angeles	M*
California State University, San Bernardino	M
East Carolina University	M
Erikson Institute	M
Lee University	M
Michigan State University	M,D
Middle Tennessee State University	M
North Dakota State University	M,D
Ohio University	M*
Purdue University	M,D
Purdue University Calumet	M
Rutgers, The State University of New Jersey, Camden	M,D
San Diego State University	M
Sarah Lawrence College	M
Southern New Hampshire University	M,O
Texas Woman's University	M,D
Tufts University	M,D,O
The University of Akron	M
University of California, Davis	M
University of La Verne	M
University of Minnesota, Twin Cities Campus	M,D
University of Nebraska–Lincoln	M,D*
The University of North Carolina at Charlotte	M,D
The University of Tennessee at Martin	M
The University of Texas at Austin	M,D
University of Wyoming	M
Whittier College	M

CHINESE

Institution	Degrees
Arizona State University	M,D
Cornell University	M,D*
Harvard University	D*
Indiana University Bloomington	M,D*
Middlebury College	M
The Ohio State University	M,D
San Francisco State University	M
Seton Hall University	M
Stanford University	M,D
Union Graduate College	M,O
University of Alberta	M
University of California, Berkeley	D*
University of California, Irvine	M,D*
University of Colorado Boulder	M,D*
University of Delaware	M*
University of Hawaii at Manoa	M,D,O
The University of Manchester	M,D
University of Massachusetts Amherst	M*
University of Oregon	M,D
University of Washington	M,D*
University of Wisconsin–Madison	M,D*
Washington University in St. Louis	M,D*

CHIROPRACTIC

Institution	Degrees
Canadian Memorial Chiropractic College	P,O
Cleveland Chiropractic College–Kansas City Campus	P
Cleveland Chiropractic College–Los Angeles Campus	P
D'Youville College	P*
Institut Franco-Européen de Chiropratique	P
Life Chiropractic College West	P
Life University	P
Logan University–College of Chiropractic	P,M
National University of Health Sciences	P,M,D
New York Chiropractic College	P
Northwestern Health Sciences University	P
Palmer College of Chiropractic	P
Parker College of Chiropractic	P
Sherman College of Chiropractic	P
Southern California University of Health Sciences	P
Texas Chiropractic College	P
Université du Québec à Trois-Rivières	P
University of Bridgeport	P
University of Western States	P

CIVIL ENGINEERING

Institution	Degrees
American University of Beirut	M,D
American University of Sharjah	M
Arizona State University	M,D
Auburn University	M,D
Boise State University	M
Bradley University	M
Brigham Young University	M,D*
Bucknell University	M
California Institute of Technology	M,D,O
California Polytechnic State University, San Luis Obispo	M
California State Polytechnic University, Pomona	M
California State University, Fresno	M
California State University, Fullerton	M
California State University, Long Beach	M

*M—master's degree; P—first professional degree; D—doctorate; O—other advanced degree; *—Close-Up and/or Display in one of the other books in this series*

California State University, Los Angeles	M*
California State University, Northridge	M
California State University, Sacramento	M
Carleton University	M,D
Carnegie Mellon University	M,D*
Case Western Reserve University	M,D*
The Catholic University of America	M,D
City College of the City University of New York	M,D
Clarkson University	M*
Clemson University	M,D
Cleveland State University	M,D
Colorado State University	M,D
Columbia University	M,D,O*
Concordia University (Canada)	M,D,O
Cooper Union for the Advancement of Science and Art	M
Cornell University	M,D*
Dalhousie University	M,D
Drexel University	M,D*
Duke University	M,D*
École Polytechnique de Montréal	M,D,O
Florida Agricultural and Mechanical University	M,D
Florida Atlantic University	M
Florida Institute of Technology	M,D
Florida International University	M,D
Florida State University	M,D
George Mason University	M,D,O*
The George Washington University	M,D,O
Georgia Institute of Technology	M,D
Graduate School and University Center of the City University of New York	D
Howard University	M
Idaho State University	M
Illinois Institute of Technology	M,D
Instituto Tecnológico y de Estudios Superiores de Monterrey, Campus Monterrey	M,D
Iowa State University of Science and Technology	M,D*
The Johns Hopkins University	M,D
Kansas State University	M,D*
Lamar University	M,D
Lawrence Technological University	M,D
Lehigh University	M,D
Louisiana State University and Agricultural and Mechanical College	M,D
Louisiana Tech University	M,D
Loyola Marymount University	M
Manhattan College	M
Marquette University	M,D,O
Massachusetts Institute of Technology	M,D,O
McGill University	M,D
McMaster University	M,D
McNeese State University	M
Memorial University of Newfoundland	M,D
Michigan State University	M,D
Michigan Technological University	M,D
Milwaukee School of Engineering	M
Mississippi State University	M,D
Missouri University of Science and Technology	M,D
Montana State University	M,D
Morgan State University	M,D
New Jersey Institute of Technology	M,D
New Mexico State University	M,D
North Carolina Agricultural and Technical State University	M
North Carolina State University	M,D*
North Dakota State University	M,D
Northeastern University	M,D
Northern Arizona University	M
Northwestern University	M,D*
Norwich University	M
The Ohio State University	M,D
Ohio University	M,D*
Oklahoma State University	M,D*
Old Dominion University	M,D
Oregon State University	M,D
Penn State University Park	M,D
Polytechnic Institute of NYU	M,D
Polytechnic Institute of NYU, Long Island Graduate Center	M
Polytechnic University of Puerto Rico	M
Portland State University	M,D,O
Princeton University	M,D*
Purdue University	M,D
Queen's University at Kingston	M,D
Rensselaer Polytechnic Institute	M,D
Rice University	M,D
Rose-Hulman Institute of Technology	M
Rowan University	M
Royal Military College of Canada	M,D
Rutgers, The State University of New Jersey, New Brunswick	M,D*
Saint Martin's University	M
San Diego State University	M
San Jose State University	M
Santa Clara University	M
South Carolina State University	M
South Dakota School of Mines and Technology	M
South Dakota State University	M
Southern Illinois University Carbondale	M
Southern Illinois University Edwardsville	M
Southern Methodist University	M,D
Stanford University	M,D,O
Stevens Institute of Technology	M,D,O
Syracuse University	M,D*
Temple University	M*
Tennessee Technological University	M,D
Texas A&M University	M,D
Texas A&M University–Kingsville	M
Texas Tech University	M,D*
Trine University	M
Tufts University	M,D
Université de Moncton	M
Université de Sherbrooke	M,D
Université Laval	M,D,O
University at Buffalo, the State University of New York	M,D*
The University of Akron	M,D
The University of Alabama	M,D
The University of Alabama at Birmingham	M,D*
The University of Alabama in Huntsville	M,D
University of Alaska Anchorage	M,O
University of Alaska Fairbanks	M,D
University of Alberta	M,D
The University of Arizona	M,D
University of Arkansas	M,D
The University of British Columbia	M,D
University of Calgary	M,D
University of California, Berkeley	M,D*
University of California, Davis	M,D,O
University of California, Irvine	M,D*
University of California, Los Angeles	M,D*
University of Central Florida	M,D,O
University of Cincinnati	M,D
University of Colorado Boulder	M,D*
University of Colorado Denver	M,D
University of Connecticut	M,D*
University of Dayton	M
University of Delaware	M,D*
University of Detroit Mercy	M,D
University of Florida	M,D,O*
University of Hawaii at Manoa	M,D
University of Houston	M,D
University of Idaho	M,D
University of Illinois at Chicago	M,D
University of Illinois at Urbana–Champaign	M,D
The University of Iowa	M,D*
The University of Kansas	M,D
University of Kentucky	M,D*
University of Louisiana at Lafayette	M*
University of Louisville	M,D
University of Maine	M,D
The University of Manchester	M,D
University of Manitoba	M,D
University of Maryland, Baltimore County	M,D
University of Maryland, College Park	M,D
University of Massachusetts Amherst	M,D*
University of Massachusetts Dartmouth	M
University of Massachusetts Lowell	M,D,O
University of Memphis	M,D
University of Miami	M,D*
University of Michigan	M,D,O*
University of Minnesota, Twin Cities Campus	M,D
University of Missouri	M,D*
University of Missouri–Kansas City	M,D*
University of Nebraska–Lincoln	M,D*
University of Nevada, Las Vegas	M,D
University of Nevada, Reno	M,D*
University of New Brunswick Fredericton	M,D
University of New Hampshire	M,D
University of New Mexico	M,D*
The University of North Carolina at Charlotte	M,D
University of North Dakota	M
University of North Florida	M
University of Notre Dame	M,D*
University of Oklahoma	M,D*
University of Ottawa	M,D*
University of Pittsburgh	M,D*
University of Puerto Rico, Mayagüez Campus	M,D
University of Rhode Island	M,D
University of Saskatchewan	M,D
University of South Alabama	M
University of South Carolina	M,D
University of Southern California	M,D,O*
University of South Florida	M,D*
The University of Tennessee	M,D
The University of Tennessee at Chattanooga	M
The University of Texas at Arlington	M,D
The University of Texas at Austin	M,D
The University of Texas at El Paso	M,D,O
The University of Texas at San Antonio	M,D*
The University of Texas at Tyler	M
The University of Toledo	M,D
University of Toronto	M,D
University of Utah	M,D*
University of Vermont	M,D
University of Virginia	M,D
University of Washington	M,D*
University of Waterloo	M,D
The University of Western Ontario	M,D
University of Windsor	M,D
University of Wisconsin–Madison	M,D*
University of Wisconsin–Milwaukee	M,D,O
University of Wyoming	M,D
Utah State University	M,D,O
Vanderbilt University	M,D*
Villanova University	M
Virginia Polytechnic Institute and State University	M,D,O
Washington State University	M,D
Wayne State University	M,D*
Western Michigan University	M
West Virginia University	M,D
Widener University	M
Worcester Polytechnic Institute	M,D,O
Youngstown State University	M

CLASSICS

Asbury University	M
Bethel Seminary	P,M,D,O
Boston College	M*
Boston University	M,D,O*
Brandeis University	M,O
Brock University	M
Brown University	M,D
Bryn Mawr College	M,D*
The Catholic University of America	M,D,O
Columbia University	M,D*
Cornell University	D*
Dalhousie University	M,D
Duke University	D*
Florida State University	M,D
Fordham University	M,D
Graduate School and University Center of the City University of New York	M,D
Harvard University	D*
Heritage Christian University	M
Hunter College of the City University of New York	M
Indiana University Bloomington	M,D*
The Johns Hopkins University	D
Kent State University	M,D*
Marshall University	M

McMaster University M,D
Memorial University of Newfoundland M
New York University M,D,O
The Ohio State University M,D
Princeton University D*
Queen's University at Kingston M
Rutgers, The State University of New Jersey, New Brunswick M,D*
San Francisco State University M
Stanford University M,D
Texas Tech University M*
Tufts University M
Tulane University M*
Union Graduate College M,O
Université de Montréal M
University at Buffalo, the State University of New York M,D,O*
University of Alberta M,D
The University of Arizona M
The University of British Columbia M,D
University of Calgary M,D
University of California, Berkeley M,D*
University of California, Irvine M,D*
University of California, Los Angeles M,D*
University of California, Riverside D
University of California, Santa Barbara M,D
University of Chicago M,D
University of Cincinnati M,D
University of Colorado Boulder M,D*
University of Florida M,D*
University of Georgia M
University of Illinois at Urbana–Champaign M,D
The University of Iowa M,D*
The University of Kansas M
University of Kentucky M*
The University of Manchester D
University of Manitoba M
University of Maryland, College Park M
University of Massachusetts Amherst M*
University of Michigan M,D,O*
University of Minnesota, Twin Cities Campus M,D
University of Missouri M,D*
University of Nebraska–Lincoln M*
University of New Brunswick Fredericton M
The University of North Carolina at Chapel Hill M,D*
The University of North Carolina at Greensboro M
University of Oregon M
University of Ottawa M,D*
University of Pennsylvania M,D*
University of Pittsburgh M,D*
University of South Africa M,D
University of Southern California M,D*
University of South Florida M*
The University of Texas at Austin M,D
University of Toronto M,D
University of Vermont M
University of Victoria M,D
University of Virginia M,D
University of Washington M,D*
The University of Western Ontario M
University of Wisconsin–Madison M,D*
University of Wisconsin–Milwaukee M,O
Vanderbilt University M*
Washington University in St. Louis M*
Wayne State University M*
Wilfrid Laurier University M
Yale University M,D*

CLINICAL LABORATORY SCIENCES/MEDICAL TECHNOLOGY

Austin Peay State University M
Baylor College of Medicine M,D*
The Catholic University of America M,D
Duke University M*
Fairleigh Dickinson University, Metropolitan Campus M
Inter American University of Puerto Rico, Metropolitan Campus M
Long Island University, C.W. Post Campus M
Medical College of Wisconsin M,D*
Michigan State University M
Milwaukee School of Engineering M
Pontifical Catholic University of Puerto Rico O
Quinnipiac University M
Rochester Institute of Technology M
Rush University M
State University of New York Upstate Medical University M
Thomas Jefferson University M
Universidad de las Américas–Puebla M
Université de Sherbrooke M,D
University at Buffalo, the State University of New York M*
University of Alberta M,D
University of Colorado Denver M,D
University of Kentucky M,D*
University of Maryland, Baltimore M
University of Massachusetts Lowell M,O
University of Medicine and Dentistry of New Jersey M,D
University of Mississippi Medical Center M,D
University of Nebraska Medical Center M,O
University of New Mexico M,O*
University of North Dakota M
University of Pennsylvania M*
University of Pittsburgh D*
University of Puerto Rico, Medical Sciences Campus M,O
University of Rhode Island M,D
University of Southern Mississippi M
The University of Texas Health Science Center at San Antonio M
The University of Texas Medical Branch M,D
University of Utah M*
University of Vermont M,D
University of Washington M*
Virginia Commonwealth University M,D

CLINICAL PSYCHOLOGY

Abilene Christian University M
Acadia University M
Adelphi University D*
Adler Graduate School M,O
Adler School of Professional Psychology M,D,O
Alabama Agricultural and Mechanical University M,O
Alliant International University–Fresno D
Alliant International University–Los Angeles D
Alliant International University–Sacramento D
Alliant International University–San Diego M,D
Alliant International University–San Francisco D,O
American International College M
American University M,D
Antioch University Los Angeles M
Antioch University New England M,D
Antioch University Santa Barbara D
Appalachian State University M,O
Argosy University, Atlanta M,D,O*
Argosy University, Chicago M,D*
Argosy University, Dallas M,D*
Argosy University, Denver M,D*
Argosy University, Hawai'i M,D,O*
Argosy University, Inland Empire M,D*
Argosy University, Los Angeles M,D*
Argosy University, Orange County M,D*
Argosy University, Phoenix M,D*
Argosy University, San Diego M,D*
Argosy University, San Francisco Bay Area M,D*
Argosy University, Schaumburg M,D,O*
Argosy University, Seattle M,D,O*
Argosy University, Tampa M,D*
Argosy University, Twin Cities M,D,O*
Argosy University, Washington DC M,D*
Arizona State University D
Azusa Pacific University M,D
Ball State University M
Barry University M,O*
Baylor University M,D*
Benedictine University M
Bethany University M
Bowling Green State University M,D*
Brigham Young University M,D*
California Institute of Integral Studies M,D
California Lutheran University M,D
California State University, Dominguez Hills M*
California State University, Fullerton M
California State University, Northridge M
California State University, San Bernardino M
Capella University M,D,O
Cardinal Stritch University M
Carlos Albizu University M,D
Carlos Albizu University, Miami Campus M,D
Case Western Reserve University D*
The Catholic University of America M,D
Central Michigan University D
Chestnut Hill College M,D,O*
The Chicago School of Professional Psychology M,D
The Chicago School of Professional Psychology at Downtown Los Angeles M,D
The Chicago School of Professional Psychology at Grayslake M
The Chicago School of Professional Psychology at Irvine D
The Chicago School of Professional Psychology at Westwood M
City College of the City University of New York M,D
Clark University D
Cleveland State University M,D,O
College of St. Joseph M
Concordia University (Canada) M,D,O
Dalhousie University M,D
DePaul University M,D
Drexel University D*
Duke University D*
Duquesne University D
East Carolina University M
Eastern Illinois University M,O
Eastern Kentucky University M,O
Eastern Michigan University M,D
Eastern Virginia Medical School D
Eastern Washington University M
East Tennessee State University M,D
Emory University D*
Emporia State University M
Evangel University M
Fairfield University M,O
Fairleigh Dickinson University, College at Florham M
Fairleigh Dickinson University, Metropolitan Campus M,D
Fielding Graduate University M,D,O
Fisk University M
Florida Institute of Technology M,D
Florida International University M,D,O
Florida State University D
Fordham University D
Francis Marion University M,O
Fuller Theological Seminary D
Gallaudet University M,D,O
George Fox University M,D,O
The George Washington University D
Georgian Court University M,O
Graduate School and University Center of the City University of New York D
Hawai'i Pacific University M*
Hofstra University D
Howard University M,D
Idaho State University D
Illinois Institute of Technology M,D
Illinois State University M,D,O
Immaculata University M,D,O
Indiana State University M,D
Indiana University of Pennsylvania D
Indiana University–Purdue University Indianapolis M,D
The Institute for the Psychological Sciences M,D
Institute of Transpersonal Psychology M,D
Jackson State University D
James Madison University M,D,O
The Johns Hopkins University M,D
Kean University M,D

*M—master's degree; P—first professional degree; D—doctorate; O—other advanced degree; *—Close-Up and/or Display in one of the other books in this series*

Kent State University M,D*
Lakehead University M,D
Lamar University M
La Salle University M,D
Lesley University M,D,O
Long Island University, Brooklyn Campus D
Long Island University, C.W. Post Campus D
Louisiana State University and Agricultural and Mechanical College M,D
Loyola University Chicago M,D
Loyola University Maryland M,D,O
Lynchburg College M
Madonna University M
Marquette University M,D,O
Marshall University M,D
Marywood University M,D
Massachusetts School of Professional Psychology M,D,O
McGill University M,D
Messiah College M,O
Michigan School of Professional Psychology M,D
Middle Tennessee State University M,O
Midwestern University, Downers Grove Campus M,D
Midwestern University, Glendale Campus D
Millersville University of Pennsylvania M
Minnesota State University Mankato M,D
Mississippi State University M,D
Missouri State University M
Montclair State University M,O
Morehead State University M
Murray State University M
Naropa University M
New Mexico Highlands University M
The New School: A University M,D
Norfolk State University M
North Dakota State University M,D
Northern Arizona University M
Northern Kentucky University M,O
Northwestern State University of Louisiana M
Northwestern University D*
Notre Dame de Namur University M
Nova Southeastern University D,O*
The Ohio State University M,D
Ohio University D*
Oklahoma State University M,D*
Old Dominion University D
Pace University M,D
Pacifica Graduate Institute M,D
Palo Alto University D
Pepperdine University M
Philadelphia College of Osteopathic Medicine M,D,O*
Ponce School of Medicine D
Pontifical Catholic University of Puerto Rico D
Pontificia Universidad Catolica Madre y Maestra M
Prairie View A&M University M,D
Queens College of the City University of New York M
Queen's University at Kingston M,D
Quincy University M
Radford University M
Regent University M,D,O
Rivier College M
Roosevelt University M
Rowan University M
Rutgers, The State University of New Jersey, New Brunswick M,D*
St. John's University (NY) M,D
Saint Louis University M,D
St. Mary's University (United States) M
Saint Michael's College M
Sam Houston State University M,D
San Diego State University M,D
San Francisco State University M
San Jose State University M
Saybrook University M,D
The School of Professional Psychology at Forest Institute M,D,O
Seattle Pacific University D
Shippensburg University of Pennsylvania M,O
Southeastern Oklahoma State University M
Southern Illinois University Carbondale M,D
Southern Illinois University Edwardsville M
Southern Methodist University D
Southern New Hampshire University M,O
Spalding University M,D
State University of New York at Binghamton M,D
Stony Brook University, State University of New York D
Suffolk University D
Syracuse University M,D*
Teachers College, Columbia University D
Temple University M,D*
Texas A&M University D
Texas Tech University M,D*
Towson University M
Troy University M,O
Uniformed Services University of the Health Sciences D*
Union College (KY) M
Union Institute & University M,D,O
Universidad de Iberoamerica P,M,D
Université Laval D
University at Albany, State University of New York M,D,O
University at Buffalo, the State University of New York M,D*
The University of Alabama D
University of Alaska Anchorage M,D
University of Alaska Fairbanks D
The University of British Columbia M,D
University of Calgary M,D
University of California, San Diego D*
University of California, Santa Barbara M,D
University of Central Florida M,D
University of Cincinnati D
University of Colorado Denver M,D
University of Connecticut M,D,O*
University of Dayton M
University of Delaware D*
University of Denver M,D
University of Detroit Mercy M,D
University of Florida D*
University of Guelph M,D
University of Hartford M,D
University of Hawaii at Manoa M,D,O
University of Houston M,D
University of Houston–Clear Lake M
University of Indianapolis M,D
The University of Kansas M,D
University of Kentucky M,D*
University of La Verne D
University of Louisville D
University of Maine M,D
The University of Manchester M,D
University of Manitoba M,D
University of Mary Hardin-Baylor M
University of Maryland, College Park M,D
University of Massachusetts Amherst M,D*
University of Massachusetts Boston D
University of Massachusetts Dartmouth M,O
University of Memphis M,D,O
University of Miami M,D*
University of Michigan D*
University of Michigan–Dearborn M
University of Minnesota, Twin Cities Campus D
University of Mississippi M,D
University of Missouri–Kansas City M,D*
University of Missouri–St. Louis M,D,O
The University of Montana M,D,O
University of Nebraska–Lincoln M,D*
University of Nevada, Las Vegas M,O
University of Nevada, Reno D*
University of New Brunswick Saint John M,D
University of New Mexico M,D*
The University of North Carolina at Chapel Hill D*
The University of North Carolina at Charlotte M,D,O
The University of North Carolina at Greensboro M,D
University of North Dakota M,D
University of North Texas M,D
University of Oregon D
University of Phoenix M
University of Puerto Rico, Río Piedras M,D
University of Regina M,D
University of Rhode Island M,D
University of Rochester
University of South Africa M,D
University of South Alabama M,D
University of South Carolina M,D
University of South Carolina Aiken M
The University of South Dakota M,D
University of Southern California M,D*
University of Southern Mississippi M,D
University of South Florida D*
The University of Tennessee M,D
The University of Texas at El Paso M,D
The University of Texas at Tyler M
The University of Texas of the Permian Basin M
The University of Texas–Pan American M
The University of Texas Southwestern Medical Center at Dallas D
University of the Cumberlands D
University of the District of Columbia M
The University of Toledo M,D
University of Tulsa M,D
University of Utah D*
University of Vermont D
University of Victoria M,D
University of Virginia D
University of Washington D*
University of Windsor M,D
University of Wisconsin–Madison D*
University of Wisconsin–Milwaukee M,D
Utah State University M,D
Valdosta State University M,O
Valparaiso University M,O
Vanguard University of Southern California M
Virginia Commonwealth University D
Virginia State University M,D
Walden University M,D,O
Washburn University M
Washington State University M,D
Washington University in St. Louis D*
Waynesburg University M,D
Wayne State University M,D,O*
West Chester University of Pennsylvania M,O
Western Illinois University M,O
Western Kentucky University M,O
Western Michigan University M,D
West Virginia University M,D
Wheaton College M,D
Wichita State University D
Widener University D
William Paterson University of New Jersey M
Wisconsin School of Professional Psychology M,D
Wright Institute D
Wright State University D
Xavier University M,D
Yale University D*
Yeshiva University D*

CLINICAL RESEARCH

Case Western Reserve University M*
Duke University M*
Eastern Michigan University M,O
Emory University M*
Georgia Health Sciences University M,O
The Johns Hopkins University M,D
Medical College of Wisconsin *
Medical University of South Carolina M
Memorial University of Newfoundland M
Morehouse School of Medicine M
Mount Sinai School of Medicine M,D
New York University P,M,D
Northwestern University M,O*
Oregon Health & Science University M,O*
Palmer College of Chiropractic M
Thomas Jefferson University O
Tufts University M,D
TUI University M,D,O
University of California, Berkeley O*
University of California, Davis M
University of California, Los Angeles M*
University of California, San Diego M*

University of Colorado Denver M,D
University of Connecticut M*
University of Connecticut Health Center M*
University of Florida M*
The University of Iowa M,D*
The University of Kansas M
University of Louisville M,D,O
University of Maryland, Baltimore M,D
University of Massachusetts Worcester M,D
University of Michigan M*
University of Minnesota, Twin Cities Campus M
University of Pittsburgh M,D,O*
University of Puerto Rico, Medical Sciences Campus M,O
University of Rochester M
University of Southern California M,D,O*
The University of Texas Health Science Center at San Antonio M
University of Virginia M
University of Washington M,D*
University of Wisconsin–Madison M,D*
Vanderbilt University M*
Walden University M,D,O
Washington University in St. Louis M*

CLOTHING AND TEXTILES

Academy of Art University M
Auburn University M
Central Michigan University M,O
Cornell University M,D*
Eastern Michigan University M
Fashion Institute of Technology M*
Iowa State University of Science and Technology M,D*
Kansas State University M,D*
North Carolina State University D*
The Ohio State University M,D
Ohio University M*
Oklahoma State University M,D*
Oregon State University M,D
Philadelphia University M
Purdue University M,D
Savannah College of Art and Design M,O
South Dakota State University M
The University of Akron M
The University of Alabama M
University of Alberta M,D
University of California, Davis M
University of Delaware M*
University of Georgia M,D
University of Kentucky M*
The University of Manchester M,D
University of Manitoba M
University of Minnesota, Twin Cities Campus M,D,O
University of Missouri M*
University of Nebraska–Lincoln M,D*
University of North Texas M
University of Rhode Island M
The University of Tennessee M,D
Virginia Polytechnic Institute and State University M,D
Washington State University M,D

COGNITIVE SCIENCES

Arizona State University M,D
Ball State University M
Boston University M,D*
Brandeis University M,D
Brown University M,D
Carleton University D
Carnegie Mellon University D*
Case Western Reserve University M*
Claremont Graduate University M,D,O
Cornell University D*
Dartmouth College D
Duke University D*
Emory University D*
Florida State University D
George Mason University M,D,O*
The George Washington University D
Graduate School and University Center of the City University of New York D
Grand Canyon University D
Harvard University M,D*
Hunter College of the City University of New York M,D
Indiana University Bloomington M,D*
Iowa State University of Science and Technology D*
The Johns Hopkins University D
Louisiana State University and Agricultural and Mechanical College M,D
Massachusetts Institute of Technology D
Mississippi State University M,D
The New School: A University M,D
New York University M,D,O
North Dakota State University M,D
Northwestern University D*
The Ohio State University M,D
Queen's University at Kingston M,D
Rensselaer Polytechnic Institute M,D
Rice University M,D
Rutgers, The State University of New Jersey, Newark D*
Rutgers, The State University of New Jersey, New Brunswick D*
State University of New York at Binghamton M,D
Temple University M,D*
Texas A&M University D
Texas A&M University–Commerce M,D
Texas Christian University M,D
University at Buffalo, the State University of New York M,D*
The University of British Columbia M,D
University of California, Merced M,D
University of California, San Diego D*
University of California, Santa Barbara M,D
University of Connecticut M,D,O*
University of Delaware D*
University of Florida M,D*
University of Guelph M,D
The University of Kansas M,D
University of Louisiana at Lafayette D*
University of Maryland, Baltimore County D
University of Maryland, College Park D
University of Massachusetts Amherst M,D*
University of Minnesota, Twin Cities Campus D
University of Nebraska–Lincoln M,D,O*
University of Nevada, Reno M,D*
The University of North Carolina at Chapel Hill D*
The University of North Carolina at Greensboro M,D
University of Notre Dame D*
University of Oregon M,D
University of Pittsburgh D*
University of Rochester M,D
University of Southern California M,D*
University of South Florida D*
The University of Texas at Austin M,D
The University of Texas at Dallas M,D*
University of Washington D*
University of Wisconsin–Madison D*
Virginia Polytechnic Institute and State University M,D,O
Wilfrid Laurier University M,D
Yale University D*

COMMUNICATION—GENERAL

Abilene Christian University M
American University M,D
The American University in Cairo M
The American University of Paris M
Andrews University M
Angelo State University M
Arizona State University M,D
Arkansas State University M,O
Arkansas Tech University M
Auburn University M
Austin Peay State University M
Ball State University M
Barry University M,O*
Baylor University M*
Bellarmine University M
Bethel University (MN) M,O
Boise State University M
Boston University M*
Bowling Green State University M,D*
Brandeis University M,O
Brigham Young University M*
California State University, Chico M
California State University, East Bay M
California State University, Fresno M
California State University, Fullerton M
California State University, Long Beach M
California State University, Los Angeles M*
California State University, Northridge M
California State University, Sacramento M
California State University, San Bernardino M
Carleton University M,D
Carnegie Mellon University M,D*
Central Connecticut State University M,O
Central Michigan University M
Clarion University of Pennsylvania M
Clark University M
Clemson University M,D
Cleveland State University M,O
The College at Brockport, State University of New York M
College of Charleston M
The College of New Rochelle M,O
College of Notre Dame of Maryland M
Columbia University M,D*
Concordia University (Canada) M,D,O
Cornell University M,D*
DePaul University M
DeVry University M
Drake University M
Drexel University M*
Drury University M
Duquesne University M,D
Eastern Michigan University M
Eastern New Mexico University M
Eastern Washington University M
East Tennessee State University M
Edinboro University of Pennsylvania M,O
Emerson College M
Fairfield University M
Fairleigh Dickinson University, Metropolitan Campus M
Fitchburg State University M,O
Florida Atlantic University M,O
Florida Institute of Technology M
Florida State University M,D
Fordham University M
Fort Hays State University M
George Mason University M,D*
Georgetown University M
The George Washington University M
Georgia State University M,D
Gonzaga University M
Governors State University M
Grand Valley State University M
Harvard University M,O*
Hawai'i Pacific University M*
Hofstra University M
Howard University M,D
Illinois Institute of Technology M,D
Illinois State University M
Immaculata University M
Indiana State University M
Indiana University Bloomington M,D*
Indiana University of Pennsylvania M,D
Indiana University–Purdue University Fort Wayne M
Instituto Tecnologico de Santo Domingo M,O
Instituto Tecnológico y de Estudios Superiores de Monterrey, Campus Ciudad Obregón M
Instituto Tecnológico y de Estudios Superiores de Monterrey, Campus Monterrey M,D
Ithaca College M
The Johns Hopkins University M
Kansas State University M*
Kean University M
Kent State University M,D*
Lasell College M,O
La Sierra University M
Liberty University M
Lindenwood University M,O
Louisiana State University and Agricultural and Mechanical College M,D
Marquette University M,O
Marshall University M

*M—master's degree; P—first professional degree; D—doctorate; O—other advanced degree; *—Close-Up and/or Display in one of the other books in this series*

Marywood University	M
McGill University	M,D
Michigan State University	M,D
Minnesota State University Mankato	M,O
Mississippi College	M
Missouri State University	M
Monmouth University	M,O
Montana State University Billings	M
Montclair State University	M
Morehead State University	M
National University	M
New Mexico State University	M
New York Institute of Technology	M
New York University	M,D
Norfolk State University	M
North Carolina State University	M*
North Dakota State University	M,D
Northeastern State University	M
Northeastern University	M
Northern Arizona University	M
Northern Illinois University	M
Northern Kentucky University	M,O
Northwestern University	M,D*
The Ohio State University	M,D
Ohio University	M,D*
Our Lady of the Lake University of San Antonio	M
Penn State University Park	M,D
Pepperdine University	M
Pittsburg State University	M
Point Park University	M
Polytechnic Institute of NYU	O
Purdue University	M,D
Purdue University Calumet	M
Queen's University at Kingston	M,D
Quinnipiac University	M
Regent University	M,D
Regis University	M,O
Rochester Institute of Technology	M
Roosevelt University	M
Rutgers, The State University of New Jersey, New Brunswick	D*
Saginaw Valley State University	M
Saint Louis University	M
St. Mary's University (United States)	M
St. Thomas University	M,D,O
San Diego State University	M
San Jose State University	M
Seton Hall University	M
Shippensburg University of Pennsylvania	M
Simon Fraser University	M,D
South Dakota State University	M
Southeastern Louisiana University	M
Southern Illinois University Carbondale	M,D
Southern Methodist University	M
Southern Polytechnic State University	M,O
Southern Utah University	M
Spalding University	M
Spring Arbor University	M
Stanford University	M,D
State University of New York College at Potsdam	M
State University of New York College of Environmental Science and Forestry	M,D
Stephen F. Austin State University	M
Stevens Institute of Technology	M,D,O
Suffolk University	M
Syracuse University	M,D*
Teachers College, Columbia University	M,D
Temple University	M,D*
Texas A&M University	M,D
Texas Southern University	M
Texas State University–San Marcos	M
Texas Tech University	M*
Towson University	M,O
Trinity International University	M
Trinity (Washington) University	M
Université de Montréal	M,D
Université du Québec à Montréal	M,D
Université du Québec à Trois-Rivières	M,O
University at Albany, State University of New York	M,D
University at Buffalo, the State University of New York	M,D*
The University of Akron	M
The University of Alabama	M,D
The University of Alabama at Birmingham	M*
University of Alaska Fairbanks	M
University of Alberta	M
The University of Arizona	M,D
University of Arkansas	M
University of Calgary	M,D
University of California, Davis	M
University of California, San Diego	M,D*
University of California, Santa Barbara	D
University of California, Santa Cruz	O
University of Central Florida	M
University of Cincinnati	M
University of Colorado at Colorado Springs	M
University of Colorado Boulder	M,D*
University of Colorado Denver	M
University of Connecticut	M*
University of Dayton	M
University of Delaware	M*
University of Dubuque	M
University of Florida	M,D*
University of Georgia	M,D
University of Hartford	M
University of Hawaii at Manoa	M,O
University of Houston	M
University of Illinois at Chicago	M,D
University of Illinois at Springfield	M
University of Illinois at Urbana–Champaign	M,D
The University of Iowa	M,D*
The University of Kansas	M,D
University of Kentucky	M,D*
University of Louisiana at Lafayette	M*
University of Louisiana at Monroe	M
University of Louisville	M
University of Maine	M,D
University of Maryland, Baltimore County	M
University of Maryland, College Park	M,D
University of Massachusetts Amherst	M,D*
University of Memphis	M,D
University of Miami	M,D*
University of Michigan	D*
University of Minnesota, Twin Cities Campus	M,D,O
University of Missouri	M,D*
University of Missouri–St. Louis	M
The University of Montana	M
University of Nebraska at Omaha	M
University of Nebraska–Lincoln	M,D*
University of Nevada, Las Vegas	M
University of New Mexico	M,D*
The University of North Carolina at Chapel Hill	D*
The University of North Carolina at Charlotte	M
The University of North Carolina at Greensboro	M
University of North Dakota	M,D
University of Northern Colorado	M
University of Northern Iowa	M
University of North Texas	M
University of Oklahoma	M,D*
University of Oregon	M,D
University of Ottawa	M*
University of Pennsylvania	D*
University of Pittsburgh	M,D*
University of Portland	M
University of Puerto Rico, Río Piedras	M
University of Rhode Island	M
University of South Africa	M,D
University of South Alabama	M
The University of South Dakota	M
University of Southern California	M,D*
University of Southern Indiana	M
University of South Florida	M,D*
The University of Tennessee	M,D
The University of Texas at Arlington	M
The University of Texas at Austin	M,D
The University of Texas at Dallas	M,D*
The University of Texas at El Paso	M
The University of Texas at San Antonio	M*
The University of Texas at Tyler	M
The University of Texas–Pan American	M
University of the Incarnate Word	M,O
University of the Pacific	M
University of the Sacred Heart	M,O
The University of Toledo	O
University of Utah	M,D*
University of Vermont	M
University of Washington	M,D*
University of West Florida	M
University of Windsor	M
University of Wisconsin–Madison	M,D*
University of Wisconsin–Milwaukee	M,D,O
University of Wisconsin–Stevens Point	M
University of Wisconsin–Superior	M
University of Wisconsin–Whitewater	M*
University of Wyoming	M
Utah State University	M
Valparaiso University	M,O
Villanova University	M
Virginia Commonwealth University	D
Virginia Polytechnic Institute and State University	M
Wake Forest University	M
Washington State University	M,D
Wayne State College	M
Wayne State University	M,D*
Webster University	M
West Chester University of Pennsylvania	M
Western Illinois University	M
Western Kentucky University	M,O
Western Michigan University	M
Westminster College (UT)	M
West Texas A&M University	M
West Virginia University	M,D
Wichita State University	M
Wilfrid Laurier University	M
William Paterson University of New Jersey	M
York University	M,D*

COMMUNICATION DISORDERS

Abilene Christian University	M
Adelphi University	M,D*
Alabama Agricultural and Mechanical University	M
Arizona State University	M,D
Arkansas State University	M
Armstrong Atlantic State University	M
A.T. Still University of Health Sciences	M,D
Auburn University	M,D
Ball State University	M,D
Barry University	M*
Baylor University	M*
Bloomsburg University of Pennsylvania	M,D
Boston University	M,D,O*
Bowling Green State University	M,D*
Brigham Young University	M*
Brooklyn College of the City University of New York	M,D
Buffalo State College, State University of New York	M
California State University, Chico	M
California State University, East Bay	M
California State University, Fresno	M
California State University, Fullerton	M
California State University, Long Beach	M
California State University, Los Angeles	M*
California State University, Northridge	M
California State University, Sacramento	M
California University of Pennsylvania	M
Canisius College	M,O
Carlos Albizu University	M,D
Case Western Reserve University	M,D*
Central Michigan University	M,D
Chapman University	M
Clarion University of Pennsylvania	M
Cleveland State University	M
The College of Saint Rose	M
Dalhousie University	M,D
Duquesne University	M,D
East Carolina University	M,D
Eastern Illinois University	M
Eastern Kentucky University	M
Eastern Michigan University	M

Eastern New Mexico University	M
Eastern Washington University	M
East Stroudsburg University of Pennsylvania	M
East Tennessee State University	M,D
Edinboro University of Pennsylvania	M
Elms College	M,O
Emerson College	M
Florida Atlantic University	M
Florida International University	M
Florida State University	M,D
Fontbonne University	M
Fort Hays State University	M
Gallaudet University	M,D,O
The George Washington University	M
Georgia State University	M
Governors State University	M
Graduate School and University Center of the City University of New York	D
Hampton University	M
Harding University	M
Harvard University	D*
Hofstra University	M,D,O
Howard University	M,D
Hunter College of the City University of New York	M
Idaho State University	M,D,O
Illinois State University	M
Indiana University Bloomington	M,D*
Indiana University of Pennsylvania	M
Indiana University–Purdue University Fort Wayne	M
Ithaca College	M
Jackson State University	M
James Madison University	M,D
Kansas State University	M*
Kean University	M
Kent State University	M,D*
Lamar University	M,D
La Salle University	M
Lehman College of the City University of New York	M
Lewis & Clark College	M
Loma Linda University	M
Long Island University, Brooklyn Campus	M
Long Island University, C.W. Post Campus	M
Longwood University	M
Louisiana State University and Agricultural and Mechanical College	M,D
Louisiana State University Health Sciences Center	M,D
Louisiana Tech University	M
Loyola University Maryland	M,O
Marquette University	M,O
Marshall University	M
Marywood University	M
Massachusetts Institute of Technology	D
McGill University	M,D
Mercy College	M
MGH Institute of Health Professions	M,O
Miami University	M
Michigan State University	M,D
Minnesota State University Mankato	M
Minnesota State University Moorhead	M
Minot State University	M
Misericordia University	M
Mississippi University for Women	M,O
Missouri State University	M,D
Montclair State University	M,D,O
Murray State University	M
National University	M
Nazareth College of Rochester	M
New Mexico State University	M,D
New York Medical College	M*
New York University	M,D
North Carolina Central University	M
Northeastern State University	M
Northeastern University	M,D
Northern Arizona University	M
Northern Illinois University	M,D
Northwestern University	M,D*
Nova Southeastern University	M,D*
The Ohio State University	M,D
Ohio University	M,D*
Oklahoma State University	M*
Old Dominion University	M
Our Lady of the Lake University of San Antonio	M
Penn State University Park	M,D
Portland State University	M
Purdue University	M,D
Queens College of the City University of New York	M
Radford University	M
Rockhurst University	M
Rush University	M,D
St. Ambrose University	M
St. Cloud State University	M
St. John's University (NY)	M,D
Saint Louis University	M
Saint Xavier University	M
Salus University	D
San Diego State University	M,D
San Francisco State University	M
San Jose State University	M
Seton Hall University	M
South Carolina State University	M
Southeastern Louisiana University	M
Southeast Missouri State University	M
Southern Connecticut State University	M
Southern Illinois University Carbondale	M
Southern Illinois University Edwardsville	M
State University of New York at Fredonia	M
State University of New York at New Paltz	M
State University of New York at Plattsburgh	M
Stephen F. Austin State University	M
Syracuse University	M,D*
Teachers College, Columbia University	M,D
Temple University	M,D*
Tennessee State University	M
Texas A&M University–Kingsville	M
Texas Christian University	M
Texas State University–San Marcos	M
Texas Tech University Health Sciences Center	M,D
Texas Woman's University	M
Touro College	M,D
Towson University	M,D
Truman State University	M
Universidad del Turabo	M
Université de Montréal	M,O
Université Laval	M
University at Buffalo, the State University of New York	M,D*
The University of Akron	M,D
The University of Alabama	M
University of Alberta	M,D
The University of Arizona	M,D
University of Arkansas	M
University of Arkansas for Medical Sciences	M,D
The University of British Columbia	M,D
University of California, San Diego	D*
University of Central Arkansas	M,D
University of Central Florida	M,D,O
University of Central Missouri	M
University of Central Oklahoma	M
University of Cincinnati	M,D,O
University of Colorado Boulder	M,D*
University of Connecticut	M,D*
University of Florida	M,D*
University of Georgia	M,D,O
University of Hawaii at Manoa	M
University of Houston	M
University of Illinois at Urbana–Champaign	M,D
The University of Iowa	M,D*
The University of Kansas	M,D
University of Kentucky	M*
University of Louisiana at Lafayette	M,D*
University of Louisiana at Monroe	M
University of Louisville	M,D
University of Maine	M
The University of Manchester	M,D
University of Maryland, College Park	M,D
University of Massachusetts Amherst	M,D*
University of Memphis	M,D
University of Minnesota, Duluth	M
University of Minnesota, Twin Cities Campus	M,D
University of Mississippi	M
University of Missouri	M*
University of Montevallo	M
University of Nebraska at Kearney	M
University of Nebraska at Omaha	M
University of Nebraska–Lincoln	M,D*
University of Nevada, Reno	M,D*
University of New Hampshire	M,O
University of New Mexico	M*
The University of North Carolina at Chapel Hill	M,D*
The University of North Carolina at Greensboro	M,D
University of North Dakota	M,D
University of Northern Colorado	M,D
University of Northern Iowa	M
University of North Florida	M
University of North Texas	M,D
University of Oklahoma Health Sciences Center	M,D,O
University of Ottawa	M*
University of Pittsburgh	M,D*
University of Puerto Rico, Medical Sciences Campus	M,D
University of Redlands	M
University of Rhode Island	M
University of San Diego	M
University of South Alabama	M,D
University of South Carolina	M,D
The University of South Dakota	M,D
University of Southern Mississippi	M,D
University of South Florida	M,D*
The University of Tennessee	M,D,O
The University of Texas at Austin	M,D
The University of Texas at Dallas	M,D*
The University of Texas at El Paso	M
The University of Texas Health Science Center at San Antonio	M
The University of Texas–Pan American	M
University of the District of Columbia	M
University of the Pacific	M
The University of Toledo	M,D
University of Toronto	M,D
University of Tulsa	M
University of Utah	M,D*
University of Virginia	M
University of Washington	M,D*
The University of Western Ontario	M
University of West Georgia	M,D,O
University of Wisconsin–Eau Claire	M
University of Wisconsin–Madison	M,D*
University of Wisconsin–Milwaukee	M,O
University of Wisconsin–River Falls	M
University of Wisconsin–Stevens Point	M,D
University of Wisconsin–Whitewater	M*
University of Wyoming	M
Utah State University	M,D,O
Vanderbilt University	M,D*
Washington State University Spokane	M
Washington University in St. Louis	M,D*
Wayne State University	M,D*
West Chester University of Pennsylvania	M,O
Western Carolina University	M
Western Illinois University	M
Western Kentucky University	M
Western Michigan University	M,D
Western Washington University	M
West Texas A&M University	M
West Virginia University	M,D
Wichita State University	M,D
William Paterson University of New Jersey	M
Worcester State University	M

COMMUNITY COLLEGE EDUCATION

Argosy University, Chicago	M,D,O*
Argosy University, Denver	M,D*
Argosy University, Inland Empire	M,D*
Argosy University, Los Angeles	M,D*
Argosy University, Orange County	M,D*
Argosy University, Phoenix	M,D,O*
Argosy University, San Diego	M,D*
Argosy University, San Francisco Bay Area	M,D*

*M—master's degree; P—first professional degree; D—doctorate; O—other advanced degree; *—Close-Up and/or Display in one of the other books in this series*

Argosy University, Schaumburg	M,D,O*
Argosy University, Seattle	M,D*
Argosy University, Tampa	M,D,O*
Argosy University, Washington DC	M,D,O*
Arkansas State University	M,D,O
California State University, Stanislaus	D
Central Michigan University	M
Colorado State University	M,D
Ferris State University	D
George Mason University	D,O*
Mississippi State University	M,D,O
Morgan State University	D
North Carolina State University	M,D*
Northern Arizona University	M,D,O
Old Dominion University	M,D
Pittsburg State University	O
University of Central Florida	M,D,O
University of Southern Mississippi	M,D,O
University of South Florida	M,D,O*
Walden University	M,D,O
Western Carolina University	M

COMMUNITY HEALTH

Adelphi University	M,O*
American University of Beirut	M
Arcadia University	M*
Arizona State University	M,D,O
Austin Peay State University	M
Bloomsburg University of Pennsylvania	M
Brooklyn College of the City University of New York	M
Brown University	M,D
Clemson University	M
The College at Brockport, State University of New York	M
Columbia University	M,D*
Dalhousie University	M
Duquesne University	M
Eastern Kentucky University	M
East Stroudsburg University of Pennsylvania	M
East Tennessee State University	M,D,O
George Mason University	M,O*
Georgetown University	M,D
Georgia Southern University	M,D
Hofstra University	M
Hunter College of the City University of New York	M
Idaho State University	O
Independence University	M
Indiana State University	M
The Johns Hopkins University	M,D
Long Island University, Brooklyn Campus	M
Louisiana State University Health Sciences Center	M,D
Massachusetts College of Pharmacy and Health Sciences	M
Massachusetts School of Professional Psychology	M,D,O
McGill University	M,D,O
Medical College of Wisconsin	M,D,O*
Meharry Medical College	M
Memorial University of Newfoundland	M,D,O
Minnesota State University Mankato	M,O
Montclair State University	M,O
Mount St. Mary's College	M
Mount Sinai School of Medicine	M,D
National University	M
New Jersey City University	M
New Mexico State University	M
New York University	D
Quinnipiac University	D
Sage Graduate School	M
Saint Louis University	M
Simon Fraser University	M
Southern Illinois University Carbondale	M
Southern New Hampshire University	M,O
State University of New York Downstate Medical Center	M
Stony Brook University, State University of New York	M,D
Syracuse University	M*
Universidad de Ciencias Medicas	P,M,O
Université de Montréal	M,D,O
Université Laval	M,D,O
The University of Alabama	M
University of Alberta	M,D
University of Calgary	M,D,O
University of California, Los Angeles	M,D*
University of Colorado Denver	M,D
University of Illinois at Chicago	M,D
University of Illinois at Urbana–Champaign	M,D
The University of Iowa	M,D*
University of Louisville	M
University of Manitoba	M,D,O
University of Massachusetts Amherst	M,D*
University of Minnesota, Twin Cities Campus	M
University of Nevada, Las Vegas	M,D,O
The University of North Carolina at Charlotte	M,D,O
The University of North Carolina at Greensboro	M,D
University of Northern British Columbia	M,D,O
University of Northern Iowa	M,D
University of North Florida	M,O
University of North Texas	M,D
University of North Texas Health Science Center at Fort Worth	M,D
University of Ottawa	M,D,O*
University of Phoenix–Birmingham Campus	M
University of Phoenix–Central Valley Campus	M
University of Phoenix–Chattanooga Campus	M
University of Phoenix–Hawaii Campus	M
University of Pittsburgh	M,D,O*
University of Saskatchewan	M,D
University of South Florida	M,D*
The University of Tennessee	M,D
The University of Texas Medical Branch	M,D
University of Virginia	M,D
University of Washington	M,D*
University of West Florida	M
University of Wisconsin–La Crosse	M
University of Wisconsin–Madison	M,D*
University of Wyoming	M,D
Virginia State University	M,D
Walden University	M,D,O
Wayne State University	M,O*
West Chester University of Pennsylvania	M,O
West Virginia University	M

COMMUNITY HEALTH NURSING

American University of Beirut	M
Arizona State University	M,D,O
Augsburg College	M
Boston College	M,D*
Case Western Reserve University	M,D*
Cleveland State University	M
D'Youville College	M,O*
Georgia Southern University	M,D,O
Hampton University	M
Hawai'i Pacific University	M*
Holy Family University	M*
Holy Names University	M,O
Hunter College of the City University of New York	M
Husson University	M,O
Independence University	M
Indiana University–Purdue University Indianapolis	M,D
Indiana Wesleyan University	M,O
The Johns Hopkins University	M
Kean University	M
Louisiana State University Health Sciences Center	M,D
Metropolitan State University	M,D
New Mexico State University	M,D
Oregon Health & Science University	M,O*
Rush University	M,D,O
Rutgers, The State University of New Jersey, Newark	M*
Sage Graduate School	M,O
Saint Xavier University	M,O
Seattle University	M
University of Cincinnati	M,D
University of Colorado at Colorado Springs	M,D
University of Hartford	M
University of Hawaii at Manoa	M,D,O
University of Illinois at Chicago	M
The University of Kansas	M,D,O
University of Maryland, Baltimore	M
University of Massachusetts Dartmouth	M,D,O
University of Michigan	M,O*
University of Minnesota, Twin Cities Campus	M
The University of North Carolina at Chapel Hill	M*
University of North Dakota	M,D
University of Puerto Rico, Medical Sciences Campus	M
University of South Alabama	M,D
University of South Carolina	M
The University of Texas at Brownsville	M
The University of Toledo	M,O
University of Washington, Tacoma	M
Wayne State University	M*
West Chester University of Pennsylvania	M,O
Worcester State University	M
Wright State University	M

COMPARATIVE AND INTERDISCIPLINARY ARTS

Bradley University	M
Brigham Young University	M*
Columbia College Chicago	M
Florida Atlantic University	D
Goddard College	M
John F. Kennedy University	M
Ohio University	D*
Simon Fraser University	M

COMPARATIVE LITERATURE

American University	M
The American University in Cairo	M
Antioch University Midwest	M
Arizona State University	M,D,O
Brigham Young University	M*
Brock University	M
Brown University	D
California State University, Fullerton	M
California State University, Northridge	M
Carleton University	D
Carnegie Mellon University	M,D*
Case Western Reserve University	M*
Claremont Graduate University	M,D
College of the Humanities and Sciences, Harrison Middleton University	M,D
Columbia University	M,D*
Cornell University	D*
Dartmouth College	M
Duke University	D*
Emory University	D,O*
Fairleigh Dickinson University, Metropolitan Campus	M
Florida Atlantic University	M
Georgetown University	M,D
Graduate School and University Center of the City University of New York	M,D
Harvard University	D*
Hofstra University	M
Indiana State University	M
Indiana University Bloomington	M,D*
The Johns Hopkins University	D
Kent State University	M,D*
Long Island University, Brooklyn Campus	M
Louisiana State University and Agricultural and Mechanical College	M,D
New York University	M,D
Northwestern University	M,D,O*
Oklahoma City University	M
Princeton University	D*
Purdue University	M,D
Rutgers, The State University of New Jersey, New Brunswick	M,D*
San Francisco State University	M
San Jose State University	M
Stanford University	D
State University of New York at Binghamton	M,D
Stony Brook University, State University of New York	M,D
Université de Montréal	M,D
Université de Sherbrooke	M,D
Université du Québec à Chicoutimi	M
Université du Québec à Montréal	M,D
Université du Québec à Rimouski	M,D
Université du Québec à Trois-Rivières	M
Université Laval	M,D

University at Buffalo, the State University of New York M,D*
University of Arkansas M,D
University of California, Berkeley D*
University of California, Davis D
University of California, Irvine M,D*
University of California, Los Angeles M,D*
University of California, Riverside M,D
University of California, San Diego M,D*
University of California, Santa Barbara D
University of California, Santa Cruz M,D
University of Chicago M,D
University of Colorado Boulder M,D*
University of Connecticut M,D*
University of Dallas D
University of Georgia M,D
University of Guelph D
University of Houston M
University of Illinois at Urbana–Champaign M,D
The University of Iowa M,D*
University of Maryland, College Park M,D
University of Massachusetts Amherst M,D*
University of Memphis M,D,O
University of Michigan D*
University of Minnesota, Twin Cities Campus D
University of Missouri M,D*
University of Nebraska–Lincoln M,D*
University of New Hampshire M,D
University of New Mexico M,D*
University of Notre Dame D*
University of Oregon M,D
University of Pennsylvania M,D*
University of Puerto Rico, Río Piedras M
University of Rochester
University of South Carolina M,D
University of Southern California D*
The University of Texas at Austin M,D
The University of Texas at Dallas M,D*
University of Toronto M,D
University of Utah M,D*
University of Washington M,D*
The University of Western Ontario M,D
University of Wisconsin–Madison M,D*
University of Wisconsin–Milwaukee M,D,O
Washington University in St. Louis M,D*
Wayne State University M*
Western Kentucky University M
Yale University D*

COMPUTATIONAL BIOLOGY

Arizona State University M,D
Baylor College of Medicine D*
Carnegie Mellon University M,D*
Claremont Graduate University M,D
Cornell University D*
Cornell University, Joan and Sanford I. Weill Medical College and Graduate School of Medical Sciences D
Florida State University D
George Mason University M,D,O*
Iowa State University of Science and Technology M,D*
Keck Graduate Institute of Applied Life Sciences M,D,O
Massachusetts Institute of Technology D
New Jersey Institute of Technology M
New York University D
Oregon Health & Science University M,D,O*
Princeton University D*
Rutgers, The State University of New Jersey, Newark M*
Rutgers, The State University of New Jersey, New Brunswick D*
University of California, Irvine D*
University of Colorado Denver D
University of Idaho M,D
University of Illinois at Urbana–Champaign M,D
The University of Iowa M,D,O*
University of Massachusetts Worcester M,D
The University of North Carolina at Chapel Hill D*
University of Pennsylvania D*
University of Pittsburgh D*
University of Rochester M,D
University of Southern California D*
The University of Texas Medical Branch D
University of Wyoming D
Virginia Polytechnic Institute and State University D
Washington University in St. Louis D*
Yale University D*

COMPUTATIONAL SCIENCES

American University of Beirut M
California Institute of Technology M,D
Carnegie Mellon University M,D*
Claremont Graduate University M,D
Clemson University M,D
The College at Brockport, State University of New York M
The College of William and Mary M
Cornell University M,D*
Florida State University M,D
George Mason University M,D,O*
Hampton University M
Lehigh University M,D
Marquette University M,D
Massachusetts Institute of Technology M
McGill University M,D
Memorial University of Newfoundland M
Miami University M
Michigan Technological University D
Princeton University D*
Rice University M,D
The Richard Stockton College of New Jersey M
Sam Houston State University M
San Diego State University M,D
Simon Fraser University M,D
South Dakota State University M,D
Southern Methodist University M,D
Stanford University M,D
Temple University M,D*
University of Alaska Fairbanks M,D
University of California, Santa Barbara M,D
The University of Iowa D*
The University of Kansas M,D
University of Lethbridge M,D
University of Manitoba M
University of Massachusetts Lowell M,D
University of Michigan–Dearborn M
University of Minnesota, Duluth M
University of Minnesota, Twin Cities Campus M,D
University of New Haven M,O
University of New Mexico O*
University of Pennsylvania D*
University of Puerto Rico, Mayagüez Campus M
The University of South Dakota M,D
University of Southern Mississippi M,D
The University of Tennessee at Chattanooga M,D
The University of Texas at Austin M,D
The University of Texas at El Paso M,D
University of Utah M*
University of Washington M,D*
Western Kentucky University M
Western Michigan University M

COMPUTER AND INFORMATION SYSTEMS SECURITY

American InterContinental University Online M
American InterContinental University South Florida M
Benedictine University M
Boston University M*
Brandeis University M,O
Capella University M,D,O
Capitol College M
Carnegie Mellon University M*
City University of Seattle M,O
Colorado Christian University M
Colorado Technical University Colorado Springs M,D
Colorado Technical University Denver M
Colorado Technical University Sioux Falls M
Concordia University (Canada) M,O
Concordia University College of Alberta M
Davenport University M
Davenport University M
Davenport University M
DePaul University M,D
Eastern Illinois University M,O
Eastern Michigan University M,O
Florida State University M,D
George Mason University M,D,O*
Georgia Institute of Technology M,D
Henley-Putnam University M
Hood College M,O
Inter American University of Puerto Rico, Guayama Campus M
The Johns Hopkins University M,O
Jones International University M
Kaplan University, Davenport Campus M
Kentucky State University M
Lewis University M
Marymount University M,O
Mercy College M
Metropolitan State University M,D,O
New York Institute of Technology M
Northern Kentucky University M,O
Northwestern University M*
Norwich University M
Nova Southeastern University M,D*
Our Lady of the Lake University of San Antonio M
Pace University M,D,O
Polytechnic Institute of NYU O
Purdue University M
Regis University M,O
Robert Morris University M,D
Rochester Institute of Technology M,O
Sacred Heart University M,O
St. Cloud State University M
Saint Leo University M
Salem International University M
Southern Polytechnic State University M,O
Stevens Institute of Technology M,D,O
Stratford University M
Strayer University M
Syracuse University O*
Texas A&M University–San Antonio M
Towson University M,D,O
TUI University M,D
Universidad del Este M
Université de Sherbrooke M
University of Advancing Technology M
The University of Alabama at Birmingham M*
University of Dayton M
University of Denver M,O
University of Houston M
University of Louisville M,D,O
University of Maryland University College M,O
University of Minnesota, Twin Cities Campus M
University of New Haven M,O
University of New Mexico M*
The University of North Carolina at Charlotte M,D,O
University of St. Thomas (MN) M,O
University of Southern California M,D*
The University of Texas at Dallas M*
The University of Texas at San Antonio M,D*
University of Wisconsin–Madison M*
Utica College M
Virginia Polytechnic Institute and State University M,D,O
Walden University M,D
West Chester University of Pennsylvania M,O
Western Governors University M
Wilmington University M

COMPUTER ART AND DESIGN

Academy of Art University M
Alfred University M
Art Center College of Design M*

*M—master's degree; P—first professional degree; D—doctorate; O—other advanced degree; *—Close-Up and/or Display in one of the other books in this series*

Bowling Green State University M*
Carnegie Mellon University M,D*
Chatham University M
Claremont Graduate University M
Clemson University M
Concordia University (Canada) O
Cornell University M,D*
DePaul University M,D
Digital Media Arts College M
Drexel University M*
East Tennessee State University M,O
Emily Carr University of Art + Design M
Florida Atlantic University M
Full Sail University M
Georgia Institute of Technology M,D
Goucher College M
Indiana University Bloomington M,D*
International Technological University M
Long Island University, Brooklyn Campus M
Long Island University, C.W. Post Campus M
Miami International University of Art & Design M*
Michigan State University M
Minneapolis College of Art and Design O
Mississippi State University M
National University M
The New School: A University M
New York Institute of Technology M
New York University M
North Carolina State University D*
Old Dominion University M
Philadelphia University M
Regent University M,D
Rensselaer Polytechnic Institute M,D
Rhode Island School of Design M
Rochester Institute of Technology M
St. Edward's University M
San Jose State University M
Savannah College of Art and Design M,O
School of Visual Arts (NY) M
Stevens Institute of Technology M,D,O
Syracuse University M*
Texas State University–San Marcos M
Universidad Autonoma de Guadalajara M,D
Universidad de las Américas–Puebla M
University of Alaska Fairbanks M
University of Baltimore M,D
University of California, Santa Cruz M,D
University of Central Arkansas M
University of Central Florida M
University of Denver M
University of Florida M,D*
The University of Kansas M
University of Massachusetts Dartmouth M
University of Missouri M*
University of Pennsylvania M*
University of Southern California M*
University of Victoria M
Washington State University M

COMPUTER EDUCATION

Arcadia University M,D,O*
California State University, Dominguez Hills M,O*
Cardinal Stritch University M
Christopher Newport University M
Eastern Washington University M
Florida Institute of Technology M,D,O
Fontbonne University M
Indiana University–Purdue University Indianapolis M,O
Jacksonville University M
Kent State University M*
Lesley University M,D,O
Long Island University, C.W. Post Campus M
Marlboro College M
Mississippi College M,D,O
Nova Southeastern University M,D,O*
Ohio University M,D*
Southern New Hampshire University M,O
Stanford University M,D
Stony Brook University, State University of New York M
Teachers College, Columbia University M
Thomas College M
Troy University M
University of Bridgeport M,O
University of Central Oklahoma M
University of Detroit Mercy M
University of Michigan M,D*
University of North Texas M,D
University of Phoenix–Central Florida Campus M
University of Phoenix–Central Valley Campus M
University of Phoenix–North Florida Campus M
University of Phoenix–Omaha Campus M
University of Phoenix–San Diego Campus M
University of Phoenix–Southern California Campus M
University of Phoenix–South Florida Campus M
University of Phoenix–Springfield Campus M
University of Phoenix–Vancouver Campus M
University of Phoenix–Washington D.C. Campus M,D,O
University of Phoenix–West Florida Campus M
Wilkes University M,D
Wright State University M

COMPUTER ENGINEERING

Air Force Institute of Technology M,D
American University of Beirut M,D
American University of Sharjah M
Auburn University M,D
Baylor University M,D*
Boise State University M,D
Boston University M,D*
Brigham Young University M,D*
Brown University M,D
California State University, Chico M
California State University, Long Beach M
Carnegie Mellon University M,D*
Case Western Reserve University M,D*
Clarkson University M,D*
Clemson University M,D
Colorado Technical University Colorado Springs M
Colorado Technical University Denver M
Columbia University M,D,O*
Concordia University (Canada) M,D
Cornell University M,D*
Dalhousie University M,D
Dartmouth College M,D
Drexel University M*
Duke University M,D*
École Polytechnique de Montréal M,D,O
Embry-Riddle Aeronautical University–Daytona M
Fairfield University M
Fairleigh Dickinson University, Metropolitan Campus M
Florida Atlantic University M,D
Florida Institute of Technology M,D
Florida International University M
George Mason University M,D,O*
The George Washington University M,D
Georgia Institute of Technology M,D
Grand Valley State University M
Illinois Institute of Technology M,D
Indiana State University M
Indiana University–Purdue University Fort Wayne M
Indiana University–Purdue University Indianapolis M,D
Instituto Tecnológico y de Estudios Superiores de Monterrey, Campus Chihuahua M,O
International Technological University M
Iowa State University of Science and Technology M,D*
The Johns Hopkins University M,D,O
Lakehead University M
Lawrence Technological University M,D
Lehigh University M,D
Louisiana State University and Agricultural and Mechanical College M,D
Manhattan College M
Marquette University M,D,O
Massachusetts Institute of Technology M,D,O
McGill University M,D
Memorial University of Newfoundland M,D
Mercer University M
Michigan Technological University D
Mississippi State University M,D
Missouri University of Science and Technology M,D
Montana State University M,D
Naval Postgraduate School M,D,O
New Jersey Institute of Technology M,D
New Mexico State University M,D
New York Institute of Technology M
Norfolk State University M
North Carolina Agricultural and Technical State University M,D
North Carolina State University M,D*
North Dakota State University M,D
Northeastern University M,D
Northwestern Polytechnic University M
Northwestern University M,D,O*
Oakland University M
OGI School of Science & Engineering at Oregon Health & Science University M,D
The Ohio State University M,D
Oklahoma State University M,D*
Old Dominion University M,D
Oregon Health & Science University M,D*
Oregon State University M,D
Penn State University Park M,D
Polytechnic Institute of NYU M,O
Polytechnic Institute of NYU, Long Island Graduate Center M
Polytechnic Institute of NYU, Westchester Graduate Center M
Polytechnic University of Puerto Rico M
Portland State University M,D
Purdue University M,D
Purdue University Calumet M
Queen's University at Kingston M,D
Rensselaer at Hartford M
Rensselaer Polytechnic Institute M,D
Rice University M,D
Rochester Institute of Technology M
Rose-Hulman Institute of Technology M
Royal Military College of Canada M,D
Rutgers, The State University of New Jersey, New Brunswick M,D*
St. Mary's University (United States) M
San Jose State University M
Santa Clara University M,D,O
Silicon Valley University M
Southern Illinois University Carbondale M,D
Southern Methodist University M,D
Southern Polytechnic State University M
Stevens Institute of Technology M,D,O
Stony Brook University, State University of New York M,D,O
Syracuse University M,D,O*
Temple University M*
Texas A&M University M,D
The University of Akron M,D
The University of Alabama M,D
The University of Alabama at Birmingham D*
The University of Alabama in Huntsville M,D
University of Alaska Fairbanks M,D
University of Alberta M,D
The University of Arizona M,D
University of Arkansas M,D
University of Bridgeport M,D
The University of British Columbia M,D
University of Calgary M,D
University of California, Davis M,D
University of California, Riverside M,D
University of California, San Diego M,D*

Institution	Degrees
University of California, Santa Barbara	M,D
University of California, Santa Cruz	M,D
University of Central Florida	M,D
University of Cincinnati	M,D
University of Colorado Boulder	M,D*
University of Dayton	M,D
University of Delaware	M,D*
University of Denver	M,D
University of Detroit Mercy	M,D
University of Florida	M,D,O*
University of Houston–Clear Lake	M
University of Idaho	M
University of Illinois at Chicago	M,D
University of Illinois at Urbana–Champaign	M,D
The University of Iowa	M,D*
The University of Kansas	M
University of Louisiana at Lafayette	M,D*
University of Louisville	M,D,O
University of Maine	M,D
University of Manitoba	M,D
University of Maryland, Baltimore County	M,D
University of Maryland, College Park	M,D
University of Massachusetts Amherst	M,D*
University of Massachusetts Dartmouth	M,D,O
University of Massachusetts Lowell	M
University of Memphis	M,D
University of Miami	M,D*
University of Michigan	M,D*
University of Michigan–Dearborn	M
University of Minnesota, Duluth	M
University of Minnesota, Twin Cities Campus	M,D
University of Missouri–Kansas City	M,D*
University of Nebraska–Lincoln	M,D*
University of Nevada, Las Vegas	M,D
University of Nevada, Reno	M,D*
University of New Brunswick Fredericton	M,D
University of New Haven	M
University of New Mexico	M,D,O*
The University of North Carolina at Charlotte	M,D
University of North Texas	M,D
University of Notre Dame	M,D*
University of Oklahoma	M,D*
University of Ottawa	M,D*
University of Pittsburgh	M,D*
University of Puerto Rico, Mayagüez Campus	M,D
University of Regina	M,D
University of Rhode Island	M,D,O
University of Rochester	M,D
University of South Carolina	M,D
University of Southern California	M,D,O*
University of South Florida	M,D*
The University of Tennessee	M,D
The University of Texas at Arlington	M,D
The University of Texas at Austin	M,D
The University of Texas at Dallas	M,D*
The University of Texas at El Paso	M,D
The University of Texas at San Antonio	M,D*
University of Toronto	M,D
University of Victoria	M,D
University of Virginia	M,D
University of Washington, Bothell	M
University of Washington, Tacoma	M
University of Waterloo	M,D
The University of Western Ontario	M,D
University of Wisconsin–Milwaukee	M,D,O
Villanova University	M,O
Virginia Polytechnic Institute and State University	M,D,O
Washington State University	M,D
Washington State University Tri-Cities	M,D
Washington University in St. Louis	M,D*
Wayne State University	M,D*
Western Michigan University	M,D
West Virginia University	D
Wichita State University	M,D
Widener University	M
Worcester Polytechnic Institute	M,D,O
Wright State University	M,D
Youngstown State University	M

COMPUTER SCIENCE

Institution	Degrees
Acadia University	M
Air Force Institute of Technology	M,D
Alabama Agricultural and Mechanical University	M
Alcorn State University	M
American Sentinel University	M
American University	M,O
The American University in Cairo	M
The American University of Athens	M
American University of Beirut	M
Appalachian State University	M
Arizona State University	M,D
Arkansas State University	M
Armstrong Atlantic State University	M
Auburn University	M,D
Ball State University	M
Baylor University	M*
Boise State University	M
Boston University	M,D*
Bowie State University	M,D
Bowling Green State University	M*
Bradley University	M
Brandeis University	M,D,O
Bridgewater State University	M
Brigham Young University	M,D*
Brock University	M
Brooklyn College of the City University of New York	M,D,O
Brown University	M,D
California Institute of Technology	M,D
California Polytechnic State University, San Luis Obispo	M
California State Polytechnic University, Pomona	M
California State University Channel Islands	M
California State University, Chico	M
California State University, Dominguez Hills	M*
California State University, East Bay	M
California State University, Fresno	M
California State University, Fullerton	M
California State University, Long Beach	M
California State University, Los Angeles	M*
California State University, Northridge	M
California State University, Sacramento	M
California State University, San Bernardino	M
California State University, San Marcos	M
Capitol College	M
Carleton University	M,D
Carnegie Mellon University	M,D*
Case Western Reserve University	M,D*
The Catholic University of America	M,D
Central Connecticut State University	M,O
Central Michigan University	M
Chicago State University	M
Christopher Newport University	M
The Citadel, The Military College of South Carolina	M
City College of the City University of New York	M,D
City University of Seattle	M,O
Clark Atlanta University	M
Clarkson University	M*
Clemson University	M,D
Cleveland State University	M,D
College of Charleston	M
The College of Saint Rose	M
College of Staten Island of the City University of New York	M
The College of William and Mary	M,D
Colorado School of Mines	M,D
Colorado State University	M,D
Colorado Technical University Colorado Springs	M,D
Colorado Technical University Denver	M
Colorado Technical University Sioux Falls	M
Columbia University	M,D,O*
Columbus State University	M,O
Concordia University (Canada)	M,D,O
Cornell University	M,D*
Dalhousie University	M,D
Dartmouth College	M,D
DePaul University	M,D
DigiPen Institute of Technology	M
Drexel University	M,D*
Duke University	M,D*
East Carolina University	M,D,O
Eastern Illinois University	M,O
Eastern Michigan University	M,O
Eastern Washington University	M
East Stroudsburg University of Pennsylvania	M
East Tennessee State University	M
École Polytechnique de Montréal	M,D,O
Elmhurst College	M
Emory University	M,D*
Fairleigh Dickinson University, College at Florham	M
Fairleigh Dickinson University, Metropolitan Campus	M
Ferris State University	M
Fitchburg State University	M
Florida Atlantic University	M,D
Florida Gulf Coast University	M
Florida Institute of Technology	M,D
Florida International University	M,D
Florida State University	M,D
Fordham University	M
Franklin University	M
Frostburg State University	M
Gannon University	M
George Mason University	M,D,O*
Georgetown University	M
The George Washington University	M,D
Georgia Institute of Technology	M,D
Georgia Southern University	M
Georgia Southwestern State University	M
Georgia State University	M,D
Governors State University	M
Graduate School and University Center of the City University of New York	D
Grand Valley State University	M
Hampton University	M
Harvard University	M,D*
Hofstra University	M
Hood College	M,O
Howard University	M
Illinois Institute of Technology	M,D
Indiana State University	M
Indiana University Bloomington	M,D*
Indiana University–Purdue University Fort Wayne	M
Indiana University–Purdue University Indianapolis	M,D
Indiana University South Bend	M
Instituto Tecnológico y de Estudios Superiores de Monterrey, Campus Central de Veracruz	M
Instituto Tecnológico y de Estudios Superiores de Monterrey, Campus Ciudad de México	M,D
Instituto Tecnológico y de Estudios Superiores de Monterrey, Campus Cuernavaca	M,D
Instituto Tecnológico y de Estudios Superiores de Monterrey, Campus Estado de México	M,D
Instituto Tecnológico y de Estudios Superiores de Monterrey, Campus Irapuato	M,D
Instituto Tecnológico y de Estudios Superiores de Monterrey, Campus Monterrey	M,D
Inter American University of Puerto Rico, Guayama Campus	M
Inter American University of Puerto Rico, Metropolitan Campus	M
International Technological University	M
Iona College	M
Iowa State University of Science and Technology	M,D*
Jackson State University	M
Jacksonville State University	M
James Madison University	M
The Johns Hopkins University	M,D,O

*M—master's degree; P—first professional degree; D—doctorate; O—other advanced degree; *—Close-Up and/or Display in one of the other books in this series*

Institution	Degrees
Kansas State University	M,D*
Kennesaw State University	M
Kent State University	M,D*
Kentucky State University	M
Knowledge Systems Institute	M
Kutztown University of Pennsylvania	M
Lakehead University	M
Lamar University	M
La Salle University	M
Lawrence Technological University	M
Lebanese American University	M
Lehigh University	M,D
Lehman College of the City University of New York	M
Long Island University, Brooklyn Campus	M
Long Island University, C.W. Post Campus	M
Louisiana State University and Agricultural and Mechanical College	M,D
Louisiana State University in Shreveport	M
Louisiana Tech University	M
Loyola Marymount University	M
Loyola University Chicago	M
Loyola University Maryland	M
Maharishi University of Management	M
Marist College	M,O
Marquette University	M,D
Massachusetts Institute of Technology	M,D,O
McGill University	M,D
McMaster University	M,D
McNeese State University	M
Memorial University of Newfoundland	M,D
Metropolitan State University	M
Michigan State University	M,D
Michigan Technological University	M,D
Middle Tennessee State University	M
Midwestern State University	M
Mills College	M,O
Mississippi College	M
Mississippi State University	M,D
Missouri State University	M
Missouri University of Science and Technology	M,D
Monmouth University	M,O
Montana State University	M,D
Montclair State University	M,O
National University	M
Naval Postgraduate School	M,D
New Jersey Institute of Technology	M,D
New Mexico Highlands University	M
New Mexico Institute of Mining and Technology	M,D
New Mexico State University	M,D
New York Institute of Technology	M
New York University	M,D
Nicholls State University	M
Norfolk State University	M
North Carolina Agricultural and Technical State University	M
North Carolina State University	M,D*
North Central College	M
North Dakota State University	M,D,O
Northeastern Illinois University	M
Northeastern University	M,D
Northern Arizona University	M
Northern Illinois University	M
Northern Kentucky University	M,O
Northwestern Polytechnic University	M
Northwestern University	M,D,O*
Northwest Missouri State University	M,O
Nova Southeastern University	M,D*
Oakland University	M
OGI School of Science & Engineering at Oregon Health & Science University	M,D
The Ohio State University	M,D
Ohio University	M,D*
Oklahoma City University	M
Oklahoma State University	M,D*
Old Dominion University	M,D
Oregon Health & Science University	M,D*
Oregon State University	M,D
Pace University	M,D,O
Pacific States University	M
Penn State University Park	M,D
Polytechnic Institute of NYU	M,D
Polytechnic Institute of NYU, Long Island Graduate Center	M
Polytechnic Institute of NYU, Westchester Graduate Center	M
Polytechnic University of Puerto Rico	M
Portland State University	M,D
Prairie View A&M University	M,D
Princeton University	M,D*
Purdue University	M,D
Purdue University Calumet	M
Queens College of the City University of New York	M
Queen's University at Kingston	M,D
Regis University	M,O
Rensselaer at Hartford	M
Rensselaer Polytechnic Institute	M,D
Rice University	M,D
Rivier College	M
Rochester Institute of Technology	M,D,O
Roosevelt University	M
Royal Military College of Canada	M
Rutgers, The State University of New Jersey, Camden	M
Rutgers, The State University of New Jersey, New Brunswick	M,D*
Sacred Heart University	M,O
St. Cloud State University	M
St. Francis Xavier University	M
St. John's University (NY)	M
Saint Joseph's University	M,O
St. Mary's University (United States)	M
Saint Xavier University	M
Sam Houston State University	M
San Diego State University	M
San Francisco State University	M
San Jose State University	M
Santa Clara University	M,D,O
Shippensburg University of Pennsylvania	M
Silicon Valley University	M
Simon Fraser University	M,D
Southeastern Louisiana University	M
Southern Arkansas University–Magnolia	M
Southern Connecticut State University	M
Southern Illinois University Carbondale	M,D
Southern Illinois University Edwardsville	M
Southern Methodist University	M,D
Southern Oregon University	M
Southern Polytechnic State University	M,O
Southern University and Agricultural and Mechanical College	M
Stanford University	M,D
State University of New York at Binghamton	M,D
State University of New York at New Paltz	M
State University of New York Institute of Technology	M
Stephen F. Austin State University	M
Stevens Institute of Technology	M,D,O
Stony Brook University, State University of New York	M,D,O
Suffolk University	M
Syracuse University	M*
Télé-université	M,D
Temple University	M,D*
Tennessee Technological University	M
Texas A&M University	M,D
Texas A&M University–Commerce	M
Texas A&M University–Corpus Christi	M
Texas A&M University–Kingsville	M
Texas Southern University	M
Texas State University–San Marcos	M
Texas Tech University	M,D*
Towson University	M
Toyota Technological Institute of Chicago	D
Trent University	M
Troy University	M
Tufts University	M,D,O
Union Graduate College	M
Universidad Autonoma de Guadalajara	M,D
Universidad de las Américas–Puebla	M,D
Université de Moncton	M,O
Université de Montréal	M,D
Université du Québec à Trois-Rivières	M
Université du Québec en Outaouais	M,D
Université Laval	M,D
University at Albany, State University of New York	M,D
University at Buffalo, the State University of New York	M,D*
University of Advancing Technology	M
The University of Akron	M
The University of Alabama	M,D
The University of Alabama at Birmingham	M,D*
The University of Alabama in Huntsville	M,D,O
University of Alaska Fairbanks	M
University of Alberta	M,D
The University of Arizona	M,D
University of Arkansas	M,D
University of Arkansas at Little Rock	M
University of Atlanta	P,M,D,O
University of Bridgeport	M,D
The University of British Columbia	M,D
University of Calgary	M,D
University of California, Berkeley	M,D*
University of California, Davis	M,D
University of California, Irvine	M,D*
University of California, Los Angeles	M,D*
University of California, Merced	M,D
University of California, Riverside	M,D
University of California, San Diego	M,D*
University of California, Santa Barbara	M,D
University of California, Santa Cruz	M,D
University of Central Arkansas	M
University of Central Florida	M,D
University of Central Missouri	M,D
University of Central Oklahoma	M
University of Chicago	M
University of Cincinnati	M,D
University of Colorado at Colorado Springs	M,D
University of Colorado Boulder	M,D*
University of Colorado Denver	M,D
University of Connecticut	M,D*
University of Dayton	M
University of Delaware	M,D*
University of Denver	M,D
University of Detroit Mercy	M
University of Evansville	M
University of Florida	M,D*
University of Georgia	M,D
University of Guelph	M,D
University of Hawaii at Manoa	M,D,O
University of Houston	M,D
University of Houston–Clear Lake	M
University of Houston–Victoria	M
University of Idaho	M,D
University of Illinois at Chicago	M,D
University of Illinois at Springfield	M
University of Illinois at Urbana–Champaign	M,D
The University of Iowa	M,D*
The University of Kansas	M,D
University of Kentucky	M,D*
University of Lethbridge	M,D
University of Louisiana at Lafayette	M,D*
University of Louisville	M,D,O
University of Maine	M,D
University of Management and Technology	M,O
The University of Manchester	M,D
University of Manitoba	M,D
University of Maryland, Baltimore County	M,D
University of Maryland, College Park	M,D
University of Maryland Eastern Shore	M
University of Massachusetts Amherst	M,D*
University of Massachusetts Boston	M,D
University of Massachusetts Dartmouth	M,O
University of Massachusetts Lowell	M,D

University of Memphis M,D
University of Miami M,D*
University of Michigan M,D*
University of Michigan–Dearborn M
University of Michigan–Flint M
University of Minnesota, Duluth M
University of Minnesota, Twin Cities Campus M,D
University of Missouri M,D*
University of Missouri–Kansas City M,D*
University of Missouri–St. Louis M,D
The University of Montana M
University of Nebraska at Omaha M
University of Nebraska–Lincoln M,D*
University of Nevada, Las Vegas M,D
University of Nevada, Reno M,D*
University of New Brunswick Fredericton M,D
University of New Hampshire M,D,O
University of New Haven M,D,O
University of New Mexico M,D*
University of New Orleans M
The University of North Carolina at Chapel Hill M,D*
The University of North Carolina at Charlotte M,O
The University of North Carolina at Greensboro M
The University of North Carolina Wilmington M
University of North Dakota M,D
University of Northern British Columbia M,D,O
University of Northern Iowa M
University of North Florida M
University of North Texas M,D
University of Notre Dame M,D*
University of Oklahoma M,D*
University of Oregon M,D
University of Ottawa M,D*
University of Pennsylvania M,D*
University of Pittsburgh M,D*
University of Puerto Rico, Mayagüez Campus M,D
University of Regina M,D
University of Rhode Island M,D,O
University of Rochester M,D
University of San Francisco M
University of Saskatchewan M,D
University of South Alabama M
University of South Carolina M,D
The University of South Dakota M,D
University of Southern California M,D*
University of Southern Maine M
University of Southern Mississippi M,D
University of South Florida M,D*
The University of Tennessee M,D
The University of Tennessee at Chattanooga M,O
The University of Tennessee Space Institute M,D
The University of Texas at Arlington M,D
The University of Texas at Austin M,D
The University of Texas at Dallas M,D*
The University of Texas at El Paso M,D
The University of Texas at San Antonio M,D*
The University of Texas at Tyler M
The University of Texas of the Permian Basin M
The University of Texas–Pan American M
University of the District of Columbia M
The University of Toledo M,D
University of Toronto M,D
University of Tulsa M,D
University of Utah M,D*
University of Vermont M,D
University of Victoria M,D
University of Virginia M,D
University of Washington M,D*
University of Waterloo M,D
The University of Western Ontario M,D
University of West Florida M
University of West Georgia M,O
University of Windsor M,D
University of Wisconsin–Madison M,D*
University of Wisconsin–Milwaukee M,D
University of Wisconsin–Parkside M
University of Wisconsin–Platteville M
University of Wyoming M,D
Utah State University M,D
Vanderbilt University M,D*
Villanova University M,O
Virginia Commonwealth University M,D
Virginia International University M
Virginia Polytechnic Institute and State University M,O
Virginia State University M
Wake Forest University M
Washington State University M,D
Washington State University Tri-Cities M,D
Washington State University Vancouver M
Washington University in St. Louis M,D*
Wayne State University M,D,O*
Webster University M,O
Wesleyan University M,D*
West Chester University of Pennsylvania M,O
Western Carolina University M
Western Illinois University M
Western Kentucky University M
Western Michigan University M,D
Western Washington University M
West Virginia University M,D
Wichita State University M,D
Winston-Salem State University M
Worcester Polytechnic Institute M,D,O
Wright State University M,D
Yale University M,D*
York University M,D*
Youngstown State University M

CONDENSED MATTER PHYSICS

Cleveland State University M
Emory University D*
Iowa State University of Science and Technology M,D*
Memorial University of Newfoundland M,D
Rutgers, The State University of New Jersey, New Brunswick M,D*
University of Alberta M,D
The University of Manchester M,D
University of Victoria M,D
West Virginia University M,D

CONFLICT RESOLUTION AND MEDIATION/PEACE STUDIES

Abilene Christian University M,O
American Public University System M
American University M,D,O
The American University of Paris M
Antioch University Midwest M
Arcadia University M*
Associated Mennonite Biblical Seminary P,M,O
Baker University M
Bethany Theological Seminary P,M,O
Bethel University (TN) M
California State University, Dominguez Hills M*
Cambridge College M
Carleton University M,O
Chaminade University of Honolulu M
Champlain College M
Colorado Technical University Colorado Springs M,D
Colorado Technical University Denver M
Columbia College (SC) M,O
Columbia University M*
Cornell University M,D*
Creighton University M,O
Dallas Baptist University M
Duquesne University M,O
Eastern Mennonite University M,O
Edinboro University of Pennsylvania M,O
Florida International University M,D,O
Fresno Pacific University M
George Mason University M,D,O*
Georgetown University M
Hult International Business School (United States) M
Jones International University M
Kennesaw State University M,D
Lipscomb University M,O
Marquette University M,O
Montclair State University M,O
National Defense University M
National University M
New York University M
Norwich University M
Nova Southeastern University M,D*
Pepperdine University M
Portland State University M
Regis University M,O
Royal Roads University M,O
St. Edward's University M,O
Saint Paul University M
Salisbury University M
SIT Graduate Institute M
Southern Methodist University M,O
Sullivan University P,M,D
Syracuse University O*
Tufts University M,D
TUI University M,D
United States International University M
United Theological Seminary of the Twin Cities P,M,D,O
Universidad del Turabo M
Université de Sherbrooke P,M,D,O
University of Arkansas at Little Rock O
University of Baltimore M
University of Bridgeport M
University of Denver M,O
University of Hawaii at Manoa O
University of Maine M
The University of Manchester D
University of Massachusetts Amherst M,D*
University of Massachusetts Boston M,O
University of Missouri M*
University of New Brunswick Fredericton M
University of New Haven M,O
The University of North Carolina at Greensboro M,O
University of Notre Dame M,D*
University of San Diego M
University of the Sacred Heart M
University of Victoria M,D
University of Wisconsin–Milwaukee M,D,O
Walden University M,D,O
Wayne State University M,O*
Wilfrid Laurier University D
Yeshiva University P,M*

CONSERVATION BIOLOGY

Antioch University New England M
California State University, Stanislaus M
Central Michigan University M
Colorado State University M,D
Columbia University M,D,O*
Frostburg State University M
Illinois State University M,D
North Dakota State University M,D
San Francisco State University M
State University of New York College of Environmental Science and Forestry M,D
Texas State University–San Marcos M
Tropical Agriculture Research and Higher Education Center M,D
University at Albany, State University of New York M
University of Alberta M,D
University of Central Florida M,D,O
University of Hawaii at Hilo M
University of Hawaii at Manoa M,D
University of Illinois at Urbana–Champaign M,D
University of Maryland, College Park M
University of Michigan M,D*
University of Minnesota, Twin Cities Campus M,D
University of Missouri–St. Louis M,D,O
University of Nevada, Reno D*
University of South Florida M,D*
University of Wisconsin–Madison M*

CONSTRUCTION ENGINEERING

The American University in Cairo M
Arizona State University M,D
Auburn University M,D
Bradley University M

*M—master's degree; P—first professional degree; D—doctorate; O—other advanced degree; *—Close-Up and/or Display in one of the other books in this series*

Columbia University M,D,O*
Concordia University (Canada) M,D,O
Illinois Institute of Technology M,D
Iowa State University of Science and Technology M,D*
Marquette University M,D,O
Massachusetts Institute of Technology M,D,O
Missouri University of Science and Technology M,D
Montana State University M,D
Ohio University M,D*
Oregon State University M,D
Pittsburg State University M
Stevens Institute of Technology M,O
Texas A&M University M,D
The University of Alabama M,D
The University of Alabama at Birmingham M*
University of Alberta M,D
University of Central Florida M,D,O
University of Colorado Boulder M,D*
University of Florida M,D*
University of Michigan M,D,O*
University of New Brunswick Fredericton M,D
University of Southern Mississippi M
University of Washington M,D*
Virginia Polytechnic Institute and State University M
Western Michigan University M

CONSTRUCTION MANAGEMENT

The American University in Dubai M
Arizona State University M,D
Auburn University M
Bowling Green State University M*
Brigham Young University M*
California State University, East Bay M
Carnegie Mellon University M,D*
Central Connecticut State University M,O
Clemson University M
Colorado State University M
Columbia University M,D,O*
Drexel University M*
Eastern Michigan University M
Florida International University M
Harrisburg University of Science and Technology M
Illinois Institute of Technology M,D
Indiana University–Purdue University Fort Wayne M
Instituto Tecnologico de Santo Domingo M,O
Marquette University M,D,O
Michigan State University M,D
Missouri State University M
New York University M,O
North Carolina Agricultural and Technical State University M
North Dakota State University M
Norwich University M
Philadelphia University M
Polytechnic Institute of NYU M,D,O
Polytechnic Institute of NYU, Long Island Graduate Center M
Polytechnic University of Puerto Rico, Miami Campus M
Polytechnic University of Puerto Rico, Orlando Campus M
Roger Williams University M
Rowan University M
South Dakota School of Mines and Technology M
Southern Polytechnic State University M
State University of New York College of Environmental Science and Forestry M,D
Stevens Institute of Technology M,O
Texas A&M University M,D
Universidad de las Américas–Puebla M
University of Arkansas at Little Rock M,O
University of California, Berkeley O*
University of Denver M
University of Houston M
The University of Kansas M
University of Nevada, Las Vegas M
University of New Mexico M*
University of North Florida M
University of Oklahoma M*
University of Southern California M,D,O*
The University of Texas at El Paso M,D,O
The University of Texas at San Antonio M*
University of Washington M*
Wentworth Institute of Technology M*
Western Carolina University M
Western Michigan University M
Worcester Polytechnic Institute M,D,O

CONSUMER ECONOMICS

California State University, Long Beach M
Colorado State University M
Cornell University M,D*
Eastern Illinois University M
Indiana State University M
Iowa State University of Science and Technology M,D*
Kansas State University D*
North Dakota State University M,D
The Ohio State University M,D
Oklahoma State University M,D*
Purdue University M,D
State University of New York at Oswego M
Texas Tech University M,D*
Université Laval O
The University of Alabama M
University of Georgia M,D
University of Guelph M
University of Idaho M
University of Illinois at Urbana–Champaign M,D
University of Missouri M*
University of Nebraska–Lincoln M,D*
University of South Carolina M
The University of Tennessee M,D
University of Utah M*
University of Wisconsin–Madison M,D*
University of Wyoming M
Utah State University M
Virginia Polytechnic Institute and State University M,D

CORPORATE AND ORGANIZATIONAL COMMUNICATION

American International College M
The American University of Athens M
Antioch University Seattle M
Argosy University, Schaumburg M,D,O*
Barry University M,O*
Bernard M. Baruch College of the City University of New York M
Boston University M*
Bowie State University M,O
California State University, San Bernardino M
Canisius College M
Carnegie Mellon University M*
Central Connecticut State University M,O
Central Michigan University M,O
Columbia University M*
Concordia University, St. Paul M
Concordia University Wisconsin M
Dallas Baptist University M
DePaul University M
Drexel University M*
Emerson College M
Fairleigh Dickinson University, College at Florham M
Florida Institute of Technology M
Florida State University M,D
Fordham University M
Franklin University M
HEC Montreal O
High Point University M
Howard University M,D
Illinois Institute of Technology M
Iowa State University of Science and Technology M,D*
John Carroll University M
Jones International University M
La Salle University M
Lasell College M,O
Lawrence Technological University M
Loyola University Chicago M
Marietta College M
Marist College M
Marywood University M,O
Metropolitan College of New York M
Minnesota State University Mankato M,O
Mississippi College M
Monmouth University M,O
Montclair State University M
Murray State University M
National University M
New Mexico State University M,D
New York University M
Northwestern University M*
Ohio University M,D*
Oklahoma City University M
Queens University of Charlotte M
Radford University M
Regis College (MA) M
Roosevelt University M
St. Bonaventure University M
Schiller International University (United Kingdom) M
Seton Hall University M
Simmons College M
Southern Illinois University Edwardsville M,O
Spalding University M
Stevens Institute of Technology O
Suffolk University M
Temple University M*
Towson University M
Universidad Autonoma de Guadalajara M,D
Université de Sherbrooke M
University of Alaska Fairbanks M
University of Colorado Denver M
University of Connecticut D*
University of Denver M,O
University of Nebraska–Lincoln M,D*
The University of North Carolina at Charlotte M
University of Portland M
University of St. Thomas (MN) M
University of Southern California M,D*
University of Wisconsin–Stevens Point M
University of Wisconsin–Whitewater M*
Walsh University M
Washington State University M,D
Wayne State University M,D*
Webster University M
Western Kentucky University M,O
Western Michigan University M
West Virginia University M,D,O

COUNSELING PSYCHOLOGY

Abilene Christian University M
Adelphi University M*
Adler Graduate School M,O
Adler School of Professional Psychology M,D,O
Alabama Agricultural and Mechanical University M,O
Alaska Pacific University M
Alliant International University–México City M
Amberton University M
Amridge University P,M,D
Andrews University D
Angelo State University M
Anna Maria College M
Antioch University Midwest M
Antioch University New England M
Appalachian State University M
Argosy University, Chicago D*
Argosy University, Denver M,D*
Argosy University, Hawai'i D*
Argosy University, Inland Empire M,D*
Argosy University, Los Angeles M,D*
Argosy University, Nashville M,D*
Argosy University, Orange County M,D*
Argosy University, Phoenix M*
Argosy University, Salt Lake City M,D*
Argosy University, San Diego M,D*
Argosy University, San Francisco Bay Area M,D*
Argosy University, Sarasota M,D*
Argosy University, Schaumburg M,D,O*
Argosy University, Seattle M,D*
Argosy University, Tampa M,D*
Argosy University, Washington DC M,D*
Arizona State University D

Institution	Degrees
Arkansas State University	M,O
Assumption College	M,O
Athabasca University	M,O
Avila University	M
Ball State University	M,D
Bemidji State University	M
Bethel University (MN)	M
Boston College	M,D*
Boston Graduate School of Psychoanalysis	M
Boston University	M,D,O*
Bowie State University	M
Bowling Green State University	M*
Brigham Young University	M,D,O*
Brooklyn College of the City University of New York	M,D,O
Caldwell College	M
California Baptist University	M
California Institute of Integral Studies	M,D
California State University, Bakersfield	M
California State University, Sacramento	M
California State University, San Bernardino	M
California State University, Stanislaus	M
Cambridge College	M,O
Capella University	M,D,O
Carlos Albizu University, Miami Campus	M,D
Carlow University	M,D
Centenary College	M
Central Michigan University	M,D,O
Central Washington University	M
Chaminade University of Honolulu	M
Chatham University	M,D
Chestnut Hill College	M,O*
The Chicago School of Professional Psychology at Grayslake	M
City College of the City University of New York	M
City University of Seattle	M
Clemson University	M
Cleveland State University	M,D,O
The College at Brockport, State University of New York	M,O
The College of New Rochelle	M,O
College of Saint Elizabeth	M,O
College of St. Joseph	M
College of Staten Island of the City University of New York	M
Colorado Christian University	M
Columbus State University	M,D,O
Concordia University Chicago	M
Concordia University Wisconsin	M
Dallas Baptist University	M
Dominican University of California	M
Eastern Nazarene College	M
Eastern University	M,O
Eastern Washington University	M
Emporia State University	M
Evangel University	M
Fairfield University	M,O
Fairleigh Dickinson University, College at Florham	M
Felician College	M*
Fitchburg State University	M
Florida Atlantic University	M,D,O
Florida International University	M,D,O
Florida State University	M,D,O
Fordham University	M,D,O
Fort Valley State University	M
Franciscan University of Steubenville	M
Francis Marion University	M,O
Frostburg State University	M
Gallaudet University	M,D,O
Gannon University	D
Gardner-Webb University	M
Geneva College	M
George Fox University	M,O
Georgian Court University	M,O
Georgia State University	M,D,O
Goddard College	M
Gonzaga University	M
Governors State University	M
Grace College	M
Grace University	M
Grand Canyon University	M
Harding University	M
Heidelberg University	M
Henderson State University	M
Hodges University	M
Hofstra University	M,O
Holy Family University	M*
Holy Names University	M,O
Houston Baptist University	M
Howard University	M,D
Humboldt State University	M
Husson University	M
Idaho State University	M,D,O
Illinois State University	M,D,O
Immaculata University	M,D,O
Indiana State University	M,D,O
Indiana Wesleyan University	M
Institute of Transpersonal Psychology	M,D
Instituto Tecnologico de Santo Domingo	M,O
Inter American University of Puerto Rico, Aguadilla Campus	M
Inter American University of Puerto Rico, Metropolitan Campus	M,D
Inter American University of Puerto Rico, San Germán Campus	M,D
Iona College	M
Iowa State University of Science and Technology	D*
James Madison University	M,O
John Carroll University	M,O
John F. Kennedy University	M
Kean University	M
Kent State University	M*
Kutztown University of Pennsylvania	M
Lancaster Bible College	M,D
La Salle University	M
Lee University	M
Lehigh University	M,D,O
Lesley University	M
Lewis & Clark College	M,O
Lewis University	M
Liberty University	M,D
Lindenwood University	M,D,O
Lindsey Wilson College	M
Lipscomb University	M,O
Long Island University, Brentwood Campus	M
Long Island University, Rockland Graduate Campus	M
Long Island University, Westchester Graduate Campus	M
Louisiana State University in Shreveport	M
Louisiana Tech University	M,D
Loyola University Chicago	D
Loyola University Maryland	M,O
Lynchburg College	M
Marist College	M,O
Marquette University	M,D,O
Mars Hill Graduate School	M
Marylhurst University	M,O
Marymount University	M,O
Marywood University	M
Massachusetts School of Professional Psychology	M,D,O
McGill University	M,D,O
McKendree University	M
McNeese State University	M
Medaille College	M
Mercy College	M,O
Messiah College	M,O
Michigan Theological Seminary	P,M,O
Mid-America Christian University	M
MidAmerica Nazarene University	M,O
Middle Tennessee State University	M,O
Minnesota State University Mankato	M,D,O
Mississippi College	M,O
Monmouth University	M,O
Montclair State University	M,D,O
Morehead State University	M
Mount St. Mary's College	M
Naropa University	M
National University	M
New England College	M
New Jersey City University	M
New Mexico State University	M,D,O
New York Institute of Technology	M
New York University	M,D,O
Nicholls State University	M,O
Northeastern State University	M
Northeastern University	M,D,O
Northern Arizona University	M,D,O
Northern Kentucky University	M,O
Northwestern Oklahoma State University	M
Northwestern University	M*
Northwest University	M,D
Nova Southeastern University	M*
Nyack College	M
Oakland University	M,D,O
Ottawa University	M
Our Lady of the Lake University of San Antonio	M,D
Pace University	M
Pacifica Graduate Institute	M,D
Palm Beach Atlantic University	M
Penn State University Park	M,D
Perelandra College	M
Philadelphia College of Osteopathic Medicine	M,D,O*
Phoenix Seminary	P,M,D,O
Prescott College	M
Providence College and Theological Seminary	P,M,D,O
Purdue University Calumet	M
Quincy University	M
Radford University	M,D
Regent University	M,D,O
Regis University	M,O
Rhode Island College	M,O
Richmont Graduate University	M
Rivier College	M,D,O
Rosemont College	M
Rowan University	M
Rutgers, The State University of New Jersey, New Brunswick	M*
Sage Graduate School	M
St. Bonaventure University	M,O
St. Edward's University	M
St. John Fisher College	M
Saint Joseph College	M
Saint Martin's University	M
St. Mary's University (United States)	M
Saint Mary's University of Minnesota	M,D,O
Saint Paul University	M
St. Thomas University	M
Saint Xavier University	M,O
Salem State University	M,O
Salve Regina University	M,O
San Francisco State University	M
Santa Clara University	M
Saybrook University	M
The School of Professional Psychology at Forest Institute	M,D,O
Seton Hall University	M,D
Shippensburg University of Pennsylvania	M,O
Simpson University	M
Sonoma State University	M
Southeastern Oklahoma State University	M
Southeastern University (FL)	M
Southeast Missouri State University	M,O
Southern Adventist University	M
Southern California Seminary	P,M,D
Southern Illinois University Carbondale	M,D
Southern Nazarene University	M
Southern Oregon University	M
South University (FL)	M*
South University (VA)	M*
South University (MI)	M*
South University (SC)	M*
South University (GA)	M*
South University (AL)	M*
South University (VA)	M*
Southwestern Assemblies of God University	M
Southwestern College (NM)	M,O
Spring Arbor University	M
Springfield College	M,O
Stanford University	D
State University of New York at New Paltz	M
State University of New York at Oswego	M,O
Stephens College	M
Suffolk University	M,O
Tarleton State University	M,O
Teachers College, Columbia University	M,D
Temple University	M,D*
Tennessee State University	M,D
Texas A&M International University	M
Texas A&M University	M,D
Texas A&M University–Commerce	M,D
Texas A&M University–Texarkana	M
Texas Tech University	M,D*
Texas Wesleyan University	M,D
Texas Woman's University	M,D,O
Towson University	O
Trevecca Nazarene University	M
Trinity International University	P,M,D,O
Trinity International University, South Florida Campus	M
Trinity Western University	M
Union College (KY)	M
Union Institute & University	M,D,O
United States International University	M
Universidad del Turabo	M,D,O
Universidad Metropolitana	M

*M—master's degree; P—first professional degree; D—doctorate; O—other advanced degree; *—Close-Up and/or Display in one of the other books in this series*

Institution	Degrees
University at Albany, State University of New York	M,D,O
University at Buffalo, the State University of New York	M,D,O*
The University of Akron	M,D
University of Alberta	M,D
University of Baltimore	M
The University of British Columbia	M,D,O
University of Calgary	M,D
University of California, Berkeley	O*
University of California, Santa Barbara	M,D
University of Central Arkansas	M
University of Central Missouri	M,D,O
University of Central Oklahoma	M
University of Colorado Denver	M
University of Connecticut	M,D,O*
University of Denver	M,D,O
University of Florida	M,D*
University of Great Falls	M
University of Hawaii at Hilo	M
University of Houston	M,D
University of Houston–Victoria	M
University of Indianapolis	M,D
The University of Iowa	M,D,O*
The University of Kansas	M,D
University of Kentucky	M,D,O*
University of La Verne	M
University of Lethbridge	M,D
The University of Manchester	M,D
University of Mary Hardin-Baylor	M
University of Maryland, College Park	M,D,O
University of Massachusetts Boston	M,O
University of Medicine and Dentistry of New Jersey	M,D,O
University of Memphis	M,D
University of Miami	D*
University of Minnesota, Twin Cities Campus	D
University of Missouri	M,D,O*
University of Missouri–Kansas City	M,D,O*
The University of Montana	M,D,O
University of Nebraska–Lincoln	M,D,O*
The University of North Carolina at Greensboro	M,D,O
University of North Dakota	M
University of Northern Iowa	M
University of North Florida	M
University of North Texas	M,D
University of Notre Dame	D*
University of Oklahoma	D*
University of Pennsylvania	M,D*
University of Phoenix	M
University of Phoenix–Las Vegas Campus	M
University of Phoenix–Phoenix Campus	M
University of Phoenix–Puerto Rico Campus	M
University of Phoenix–Southern California Campus	M
University of Puget Sound	M
University of Rhode Island	M
University of Saint Francis (IN)	M
University of St. Thomas (MN)	M,D,O
University of San Diego	M
University of San Francisco	M,D
The University of Scranton	M,O
University of South Africa	M,D
University of South Alabama	M,D
University of Southern Maine	M,O
University of Southern Mississippi	M,D
The University of Tennessee	M,D
The University of Texas at Austin	M,D
The University of Texas at Tyler	M
University of the Cumberlands	M
University of the District of Columbia	M
University of the Southwest	M
University of Utah	M,D*
University of Vermont	M
University of Victoria	M,D
The University of Western Ontario	M
University of West Florida	M
University of Wisconsin–Madison	D*
University of Wisconsin–Milwaukee	M,D
University of Wisconsin–Stout	M
Utah State University	M,D
Valdosta State University	M,O
Valparaiso University	M,O
Virginia Commonwealth University	M,D,O
Walden University	M,D,O
Walla Walla University	M
Walsh University	M
Washington Adventist University	M
Washington State University	M,D,O
Wayland Baptist University	M
Waynesburg University	M,D
Webster University	M
Western Kentucky University	M
Western Michigan University	M,D
Western Washington University	M
Westfield State University	M
Westminster College (UT)	M
West Virginia University	D
William Carey University	M
William Paterson University of New Jersey	M
Wright Institute	M
Yeshiva University	M*
Youngstown State University	M

COUNSELOR EDUCATION

Institution	Degrees
Acadia University	M
Adams State College	M
Adler Graduate School	M,O
Alabama Agricultural and Mechanical University	M,O
Alabama State University	M,O
Albany State University	M
Alcorn State University	M,O
Alfred University	M,D,O
American International College	M,D,O
American Public University System	M
Amridge University	P,M,D
Angelo State University	M
Appalachian State University	M
Argosy University, Atlanta	M,D,O*
Argosy University, Chicago	D*
Argosy University, Dallas	D*
Argosy University, Denver	M,D*
Argosy University, Nashville	D*
Argosy University, Salt Lake City	M,D*
Argosy University, Sarasota	M,D,O*
Argosy University, Schaumburg	M,D,O*
Argosy University, Tampa	M,D,O*
Argosy University, Washington DC	M,D*
Arizona State University	M
Arkansas State University	M,O
Ashland Theological Seminary	P,M,D,O
Athabasca University	M,O
Auburn University Montgomery	M,O
Augusta State University	M
Austin Peay State University	M,O
Azusa Pacific University	M
Baptist Bible College of Pennsylvania	M
Barry University	M,D,O*
Bayamón Central University	M,O
Bellevue University	M,D
Bloomsburg University of Pennsylvania	M
Bob Jones University	P,M,D,O
Boise State University	M
Boston University	M,D,O*
Bowie State University	M
Bowling Green State University	M*
Bradley University	M
Brandon University	M,O
Bridgewater State University	M,O
Brooklyn College of the City University of New York	M,O
Bucknell University	M
Buena Vista University	M
Butler University	M
Caldwell College	M
California Baptist University	M
California Lutheran University	M,D
California State University, Bakersfield	M
California State University, Dominguez Hills	M*
California State University, East Bay	M
California State University, Fresno	M
California State University, Fullerton	M
California State University, Long Beach	M
California State University, Los Angeles	M,D*
California State University, Northridge	M
California State University, Sacramento	M
California State University, San Bernardino	M
California State University, Stanislaus	M
California University of Pennsylvania	M
Cambridge College	M,D,O
Campbell University	M
Canisius College	M
Carlow University	M,D
Carson-Newman College	M
Carthage College	M,O
Central Connecticut State University	M,O
Central Methodist University	M
Central Michigan University	M
Central Washington University	M
Chadron State College	M,O
Chapman University	M,O
The Chicago School of Professional Psychology	M,D
Chicago State University	M
The Citadel, The Military College of South Carolina	M,O
Clark Atlanta University	M
Clemson University	M
Cleveland State University	M,D,O
The College at Brockport, State University of New York	M,O
The College of New Jersey	M
College of St. Joseph	M
The College of Saint Rose	M
The College of William and Mary	M,D
Colorado State University	M,D
Columbia International University	M,D,O
Columbus State University	M,D,O
Concordia University Chicago	M,O
Concordia University Wisconsin	M
Creighton University	M
Dallas Baptist University	M
Delta State University	M,D
DePaul University	M,D
Doane College	M
Duquesne University	M,D
East Carolina University	M,O
East Central University	M
Eastern Illinois University	M
Eastern Kentucky University	M
Eastern Michigan University	M,O
Eastern New Mexico University	M
Eastern University	M,O
Eastern Washington University	M
East Tennessee State University	M,D
Edinboro University of Pennsylvania	M,O
Emporia State University	M
Evangel University	M
Fairfield University	M,O
Faulkner University	M
Fitchburg State University	M
Florida Agricultural and Mechanical University	M,D
Florida Atlantic University	M,D,O
Florida Gulf Coast University	M
Florida International University	M,D,O
Florida State University	M,D,O
Fordham University	M,D,O
Fort Hays State University	M
Fort Valley State University	M,O
Freed-Hardeman University	M,O
Fresno Pacific University	M
Frostburg State University	M
Gallaudet University	M,D,O
Gannon University	M,O
Geneva College	M
George Fox University	M,O
George Mason University	M*
The George Washington University	M,D,O
Georgia Southern University	M,O
Georgia State University	M,D,O
Grambling State University	M,D
Grand Canyon University	M
Gwynedd-Mercy College	M
Hampton University	M
Harding University	M,O
Hardin-Simmons University	M
Henderson State University	M
Heritage University	M
Hofstra University	M,O
Houston Baptist University	M
Howard University	M

Institution	Degrees
Hunter College of the City University of New York	M
Husson University	M
Idaho State University	M,D,O
Immaculata University	M,D,O
Indiana State University	M,D,O
Indiana University Bloomington	M,D,O*
Indiana University of Pennsylvania	M
Indiana University–Purdue University Fort Wayne	M,O
Indiana University–Purdue University Indianapolis	M,O
Indiana University South Bend	M
Indiana University Southeast	M
Indiana Wesleyan University	M
Inter American University of Puerto Rico, Arecibo Campus	M
Inter American University of Puerto Rico, Metropolitan Campus	M,D
Inter American University of Puerto Rico, San Germán Campus	M,D
Iowa State University of Science and Technology	M,D*
Jackson State University	M
Jacksonville State University	M
John Brown University	M
John Carroll University	M,O
The Johns Hopkins University	M,O
Johnson State College	M
Kansas State University	M,D*
Kean University	M
Keene State College	M,O
Kent State University	M,D,O*
Kutztown University of Pennsylvania	M
Lakeland College	M
Lamar University	M,D,O
Lancaster Bible College	M,D
La Sierra University	M,O
Lee University	M
Lehigh University	M,D,O
Lehman College of the City University of New York	M
Lenoir-Rhyne University	M
LeTourneau University	M
Lewis University	M
Liberty University	M,D,O
Lincoln Memorial University	M,D,O
Lincoln University (MO)	M,O
Loma Linda University	M,D,O
Long Island University, Brentwood Campus	M
Long Island University, Brooklyn Campus	M,O
Long Island University, C.W. Post Campus	M
Long Island University, Rockland Graduate Campus	M
Long Island University, Westchester Graduate Campus	M
Longwood University	M
Louisiana State University and Agricultural and Mechanical College	M,D,O
Louisiana State University in Shreveport	M
Louisiana Tech University	M,D
Loyola Marymount University	M
Loyola University Chicago	M,O
Loyola University Maryland	M,O
Loyola University New Orleans	M
Lynchburg College	M
Lyndon State College	M
Malone University	M
Manhattan College	M,O
Marquette University	M,D,O
Marshall University	M,O
Marymount University	M
Marywood University	M,O
McDaniel College	M
McNeese State University	M,O
Mercy College	M,O
Messiah College	M,O
Michigan State University	M,D,O
Middle Tennessee State University	M,O
Midwestern State University	M
Minnesota State University Mankato	M,D,O
Minnesota State University Moorhead	M
Mississippi College	M,O
Mississippi State University	M,D,O
Missouri Baptist University	M,O
Missouri State University	M
Montana State University Billings	M
Montana State University–Northern	M
Montclair State University	M,D,O
Morehead State University	M,O
Mount Mary College	M
Multnomah University	M
Murray State University	M,O
Naropa University	M
National-Louis University	M,D,O
National University	M
New Mexico Highlands University	M
New Mexico State University	M,D,O
New York Institute of Technology	M
New York University	M,D,O
Niagara University	M,O
Nicholls State University	M
North Carolina Agricultural and Technical State University	M,D
North Carolina Central University	M
North Carolina State University	M,D*
North Dakota State University	M,D
Northeastern Illinois University	M
Northeastern State University	M
Northeastern University	M,O
Northern Arizona University	M,D,O
Northern Illinois University	M,D
Northern Kentucky University	M,O
Northern Michigan University	M
Northern State University	M
Northwest Christian University	M
Northwestern Oklahoma State University	M
Northwestern State University of Louisiana	M,O
Northwest Missouri State University	M
Northwest Nazarene University	M
Nova Southeastern University	M*
Nyack College	M
Ohio University	M,D*
Old Dominion University	M,D,O
Oregon State University	M,D
Ottawa University	M
Our Lady of Holy Cross College	M
Our Lady of the Lake University of San Antonio	M
Palm Beach Atlantic University	M
Penn State University Park	M,D
Phillips Graduate Institute	M
Pittsburg State University	M
Plymouth State University	M
Pontifical Catholic University of Puerto Rico	M
Portland State University	M,D
Prairie View A&M University	M,D
Prescott College	M,D
Providence College	M
Purdue University	M,D,O
Purdue University Calumet	M
Queens College of the City University of New York	M
Quincy University	M
Radford University	M
Regent University	M,D,O
Rhode Island College	M,O
Rider University	M,O
Rivier College	M,D,O
Roberts Wesleyan College	M
Rollins College	M
Roosevelt University	M
Rosemont College	M
Rowan University	M
Rutgers, The State University of New Jersey, New Brunswick	M*
Sage Graduate School	M,O
St. Bonaventure University	M,O
St. Cloud State University	M
St. John's University (NY)	M,O
Saint Joseph College	M
St. Lawrence University	M,O
Saint Louis University	M,D,O
Saint Martin's University	M
Saint Mary's College of California	M
St. Mary's University (United States)	D
Saint Peter's College	M,O
St. Thomas University	M,O
Saint Xavier University	M
Salem State University	M
Sam Houston State University	M,D
San Diego State University	M
San Jose State University	M
Santa Clara University	M
Seattle Pacific University	M,D,O
Seattle University	M,O
Shippensburg University of Pennsylvania	M,O
Simmons College	M,D,O
Simon Fraser University	M
Slippery Rock University of Pennsylvania	M
Sonoma State University	M
South Carolina State University	M,D,O
South Dakota State University	M
Southeastern Louisiana University	M
Southeastern Oklahoma State University	M
Southeastern University (FL)	M
Southeast Missouri State University	M,O
Southern Adventist University	M
Southern Arkansas University–Magnolia	M
Southern Connecticut State University	M,O
Southern Illinois University Carbondale	M,D
Southern Methodist University	M,O
Southern University and Agricultural and Mechanical College	M
Southwestern Oklahoma State University	M
Spalding University	M
Springfield College	M,O
State University of New York at New Paltz	M
State University of New York at Plattsburgh	M,O
State University of New York College at Oneonta	M,O
Stephen F. Austin State University	M
Stephens College	M
Stetson University	M
Suffolk University	M,O
Sul Ross State University	M
Syracuse University	M,D,O*
Tarleton State University	M,O
Teacher Education University	M
Teachers College, Columbia University	M
Tennessee State University	M,D
Texas A&M International University	M
Texas A&M University–Commerce	M,D
Texas A&M University–Corpus Christi	M,D
Texas A&M University–Kingsville	M
Texas A&M University–San Antonio	M
Texas Christian University	M,O
Texas Southern University	M,D
Texas State University–San Marcos	M
Texas Tech University	M,D*
Texas Wesleyan University	M,D
Texas Woman's University	M,D
Trevecca Nazarene University	M,D
Trinity (Washington) University	M
Troy University	M,O
Union Institute & University	M,D,O
Universidad del Turabo	M
Université de Moncton	M
Université Laval	M,D
University at Albany, State University of New York	M,D,O
University at Buffalo, the State University of New York	M,D,O*
The University of Akron	M,D
The University of Alabama	M,D,O
The University of Alabama at Birmingham	M*
University of Alaska Anchorage	M
University of Alaska Fairbanks	M
University of Alberta	M,D
The University of Arizona	M
University of Arkansas	M,D,O
University of Arkansas at Little Rock	M
University of Central Arkansas	M
University of Central Florida	M,D,O
University of Central Missouri	M,D,O
University of Central Oklahoma	M
University of Cincinnati	M,D,O
University of Colorado at Colorado Springs	M,D
University of Colorado Denver	M
University of Connecticut	M,D,O*
University of Dayton	M,O
University of Detroit Mercy	M
University of Florida	M,D,O*
University of Georgia	M,D,O
University of Guam	M
University of Hartford	M,O

*M—master's degree; P—first professional degree; D—doctorate; O—other advanced degree; *—Close-Up and/or Display in one of the other books in this series*

Institution	Degrees
University of Houston–Clear Lake	M
University of Houston–Victoria	M
University of Idaho	M
University of Illinois at Urbana–Champaign	M,D,O
The University of Iowa	M,D*
University of La Verne	M,O
University of Louisiana at Lafayette	M*
University of Louisiana at Monroe	M
University of Louisville	M,D
University of Maine	M,D,O
University of Manitoba	M
University of Mary Hardin-Baylor	M
University of Maryland, College Park	M,D,O
University of Maryland Eastern Shore	M
University of Massachusetts Amherst	M,D,O*
University of Massachusetts Boston	M,O
University of Memphis	M,D
University of Miami	M,O*
University of Minnesota, Twin Cities Campus	M,D,O
University of Mississippi	M,D,O
University of Missouri–St. Louis	M,D
The University of Montana	M,D,O
University of Montevallo	M
University of Nebraska at Kearney	M,O
University of Nebraska at Omaha	M
University of Nevada, Las Vegas	M,O
University of Nevada, Reno	M,D,O*
University of New Hampshire	M,O
University of New Mexico	M,D*
University of New Orleans	M,D,O
University of North Alabama	M
The University of North Carolina at Chapel Hill	M*
The University of North Carolina at Charlotte	M,D,O
The University of North Carolina at Greensboro	M,D,O
The University of North Carolina at Pembroke	M
University of Northern Colorado	M,D
University of Northern Iowa	M
University of North Florida	M,D
University of North Texas	M,D,O
University of Phoenix–Las Vegas Campus	M
University of Phoenix–New Mexico Campus	M
University of Phoenix–Southern Arizona Campus	M,O
University of Puerto Rico, Río Piedras	M,D
University of Puget Sound	M
University of Rochester	
University of Saint Francis (IN)	M
University of San Diego	M
University of San Francisco	M,D
The University of Scranton	M
University of South Africa	M,D
University of South Alabama	M,D
University of South Carolina	D,O
The University of South Dakota	M,D,O
University of Southern California	M*
University of Southern Maine	M,O
University of Southern Mississippi	M,D,O
University of South Florida	M,D,O*
The University of Tennessee	M,D,O
The University of Tennessee at Chattanooga	M
The University of Tennessee at Martin	M
The University of Texas at Austin	M,D
The University of Texas at Brownsville	M
The University of Texas at El Paso	M
The University of Texas at San Antonio	M,D*
The University of Texas of the Permian Basin	M
The University of Texas–Pan American	M
University of the Cumberlands	M,D,O
University of the District of Columbia	M
University of the Southwest	M
The University of Toledo	M,D,O
University of Utah	M,D*
University of Vermont	M
University of Victoria	M,D
University of Virginia	M,D,O
The University of West Alabama	M
University of West Florida	M,D,O
University of West Georgia	M,D,O
University of Wisconsin–Madison	M*
University of Wisconsin–Milwaukee	M,D
University of Wisconsin–Oshkosh	M
University of Wisconsin–Platteville	M
University of Wisconsin–River Falls	M,O
University of Wisconsin–Stevens Point	M
University of Wisconsin–Superior	M
University of Wisconsin–Whitewater	M*
University of Wyoming	M,D
Utah State University	M,D
Valdosta State University	M,O
Valparaiso University	
Vanderbilt University	M*
Villanova University	M
Virginia Commonwealth University	M
Virginia Polytechnic Institute and State University	M,D,O
Wake Forest University	M
Walden University	M,D
Walsh University	M
Washington State University Tri-Cities	M,D
Wayne State College	M
Wayne State University	M,D,O*
West Chester University of Pennsylvania	M,O
Western Carolina University	M
Western Connecticut State University	M
Western Illinois University	M
Western Kentucky University	M
Western Michigan University	M,D
Western New Mexico University	M
Western Washington University	M
Westfield State University	M
Westminster College (PA)	M,O
West Texas A&M University	M
West Virginia University	M
Whitworth University	M
Wichita State University	M,O
Widener University	M,D
William Paterson University of New Jersey	M
Wilmington University	M
Winona State University	M
Winthrop University	M
Wright State University	M
Xavier University	M
Xavier University of Louisiana	M
Youngstown State University	M

CRIMINAL JUSTICE AND CRIMINOLOGY

Institution	Degrees
Adler School of Professional Psychology	M,D,O
Albany State University	M
American Public University System	M
American University	M,D
American University of Puerto Rico	M
Anderson University (SC)	M
Andrew Jackson University	M
Anna Maria College	M
Appalachian State University	M
Arizona State University	M,D
Arkansas State University	M,O
Armstrong Atlantic State University	M
Ashworth College	M
Auburn University Montgomery	M
Aurora University	M,D
Ball State University	M
Bellevue University	M,D
Boise State University	M
Boston University	M*
Bowling Green State University	M*
Bridgewater State University	M
Buffalo State College, State University of New York	M
California Coast University	M
California State University, Fresno	M
California State University, Long Beach	M
California State University, Los Angeles	M*
California State University, Sacramento	M
California State University, San Bernardino	M
California State University, Stanislaus	M
California University of Pennsylvania	M
Calumet College of Saint Joseph	M
Capella University	M,D,O
Caribbean University	M,D
Carnegie Mellon University	M*
Central Connecticut State University	M
Chaminade University of Honolulu	M,O
Charleston Southern University	M
Chicago State University	M
Clark Atlanta University	M
College of Saint Elizabeth	M
Colorado Technical University Colorado Springs	M
Colorado Technical University Denver	M
Colorado Technical University Sioux Falls	M
Columbia College (MO)	M
Columbia Southern University	M
Columbus State University	M
Concordia University, St. Paul	M
Coppin State University	M
Curry College	M
Dallas Baptist University	M
Defiance College	M
Delta State University	M
DeSales University	M
Drury University	M
East Carolina University	M
East Central University	M
Eastern Kentucky University	M
Eastern Michigan University	M
East Tennessee State University	M,O
Everest University	M
Everest University	M
Everest University	M
Everest University	M
Fairleigh Dickinson University, Metropolitan Campus	M
Fairmont State University	M
Faulkner University	M
Fayetteville State University	M
Ferris State University	M
Florida Agricultural and Mechanical University	M
Florida Atlantic University	M
Florida Gulf Coast University	M
Florida International University	M
Florida State University	M,D
George Mason University	M,D*
The George Washington University	M
Georgia College & State University	M
Georgia State University	M,D,O
Graduate School and University Center of the City University of New York	D
Grambling State University	M
Grand Valley State University	M
Hodges University	M
Holy Family University	M*
Husson University	M
Illinois State University	M
Indiana State University	M
Indiana Tech	M
Indiana University Bloomington	M,D*
Indiana University Northwest	M,O
Indiana University of Pennsylvania	M,D
Indiana University–Purdue University Indianapolis	M,O
Inter American University of Puerto Rico, Aguadilla Campus	M
Inter American University of Puerto Rico, Metropolitan Campus	M
Inter American University of Puerto Rico, Ponce Campus	M
Iona College	M
Jackson State University	M
Jacksonville State University	M
John Jay College of Criminal Justice of the City University of New York	M,D
The Johns Hopkins University	M

Institution	Degrees
Kaplan University, Davenport Campus	M
Kean University	M
Keiser University	M
Kent State University	M*
Keuka College	M
Lamar University	M
Lewis University	M
Lincoln University (MO)	M,O
Lindenwood University	M,O
Long Island University, Brentwood Campus	M
Long Island University, C.W. Post Campus	M
Longwood University	M
Loyola University Chicago	M
Loyola University New Orleans	M
Lynn University	M,O
Madonna University	M
Marquette University	M,O
Marshall University	M
Marywood University	M
Mercyhurst College	M,O
Methodist University	M
Michigan State University	M,D
Middle Tennessee State University	M
Midwestern State University	M
Minot State University	M
Mississippi College	M,O
Mississippi Valley State University	M
Missouri Southern State University	M
Missouri State University	M
Molloy College	M
Monmouth University	M,O
Morehead State University	M
Mountain State University	M
Mount Aloysius College	M
National University	M
New Jersey City University	M
New Mexico State University	M
Niagara University	M
Nichols College	M
Norfolk State University	M
North Carolina Central University	M
North Dakota State University	M,D
Northeastern State University	M
Northeastern University	M,D
Northern Arizona University	M
Northern Michigan University	M
Norwich University	M
Nova Southeastern University	M*
Oklahoma City University	M
Old Dominion University	D
Point Park University	M
Polytechnic Institute of NYU	M,D,O
Polytechnic Institute of NYU, Westchester Graduate Center	M
Pontifical Catholic University of Puerto Rico	M
Pontificia Universidad Catolica Madre y Maestra	M
Portland State University	M,D
Radford University	M
Regis University	M
The Richard Stockton College of New Jersey	M
Rochester Institute of Technology	M
Roger Williams University	M
Rowan University	M
Rutgers, The State University of New Jersey, Camden	M
Rutgers, The State University of New Jersey, Newark	M,D*
Sacred Heart University	M
St. Ambrose University	M
St. Cloud State University	M
St. John's University (NY)	M
Saint Joseph's University	M,O
Saint Leo University	M
Saint Mary's University (Canada)	M
Saint Peter's College	M
St. Thomas University	M,O
Salem State University	M
Salve Regina University	M
Sam Houston State University	M,D
San Diego State University	M
San Jose State University	M
Seattle University	M
Shippensburg University of Pennsylvania	M
Simon Fraser University	M,D
Simpson College	M
Slippery Rock University of Pennsylvania	M
Southeastern Louisiana University	M
Southeast Missouri State University	M
Southern Illinois University Carbondale	M
Southern University and Agricultural and Mechanical College	M
South University (SC)	M*
South University (GA)	M*
Southwestern College (KS)	M
Southwest University	M
Suffolk University	M
Sul Ross State University	M
Tarleton State University	M
Temple University	M,D*
Tennessee State University	M
Texas A&M International University	M
Texas Southern University	M,D
Texas State University–San Marcos	M,D
Tiffin University	M
Trine University	M
Troy University	M,O
TUI University	M,D
Universidad del Este	M
Universidad del Turabo	M
Université de Montréal	M,D
University at Albany, State University of New York	M,D
The University of Alabama	M
The University of Alabama at Birmingham	M*
The University of Alabama in Huntsville	M,O
University of Alaska Fairbanks	M
University of Alberta	M,D
University of Arkansas at Little Rock	M,D
University of Baltimore	M
University of California, Irvine	M,D*
University of Central Florida	M,O
University of Central Missouri	M
University of Central Oklahoma	M
University of Cincinnati	M,D
University of Colorado at Colorado Springs	M
University of Colorado Denver	M,D
University of Delaware	M,D*
University of Denver	M,O
University of Detroit Mercy	M
University of Florida	M,D*
University of Great Falls	M
University of Guelph	M,D
University of Houston–Clear Lake	M
University of Houston–Downtown	M
University of Illinois at Chicago	M,D
University of Louisiana at Monroe	M
University of Louisville	M
University of Management and Technology	M
The University of Manchester	M,D
University of Maryland, College Park	M,D
University of Maryland Eastern Shore	M
University of Massachusetts Lowell	M
University of Memphis	M
University of Minnesota, Duluth	M
University of Missouri–Kansas City	M*
University of Missouri–St. Louis	M,D
The University of Montana	M
University of Nebraska at Omaha	M,D
University of Nevada, Las Vegas	M
University of Nevada, Reno	M*
University of New Haven	M,D,O
University of North Alabama	M
The University of North Carolina at Charlotte	M
The University of North Carolina at Greensboro	M
The University of North Carolina Wilmington	M
University of North Dakota	D
University of Northern Colorado	M
University of Northern Iowa	M
University of North Florida	M
University of North Texas	M
University of Ottawa	M,D*
University of Pennsylvania	M,D*
University of Phoenix	M
University of Phoenix–Augusta Campus	M
University of Phoenix–Austin Campus	M
University of Phoenix–Birmingham Campus	M
University of Phoenix–Cheyenne Campus	M
University of Phoenix–Dallas Campus	M
University of Phoenix–Des Moines Campus	M
University of Phoenix–Harrisburg Campus	M
University of Phoenix–Jersey City Campus	M
University of Phoenix–Kansas City Campus	M
University of Phoenix–Memphis Campus	M
University of Phoenix–Milwaukee Campus	M
University of Phoenix–Northern Nevada Campus	M
University of Phoenix–Northern Virginia Campus	M
University of Phoenix–Northwest Arkansas Campus	M
University of Phoenix–Omaha Campus	M
University of Phoenix–St. Louis Campus	M
University of Phoenix–San Antonio Campus	M
University of Phoenix–Savannah Campus	M
University of Phoenix–Southern California Campus	M
University of Phoenix–Springfield Campus	M
University of Phoenix–Washington Campus	M
University of Phoenix–Washington D.C. Campus	M
University of Pittsburgh	M,D*
University of Regina	M
University of South Africa	M,D
University of South Carolina	M,D
University of Southern Mississippi	M,D
University of South Florida	M,D*
The University of Tennessee	M,D
The University of Tennessee at Chattanooga	M
The University of Texas at Arlington	M
The University of Texas at Dallas	M,D*
The University of Texas at San Antonio	M*
The University of Texas at Tyler	M
The University of Texas of the Permian Basin	M
The University of Texas–Pan American	M
University of the Fraser Valley	M
University of the Pacific	P,M,D
The University of Toledo	M,O
University of Toronto	M,D
University of West Florida	M
University of West Georgia	M
University of Windsor	M,D
University of Wisconsin–Milwaukee	M
University of Wisconsin–Platteville	M
Upper Iowa University	M
Urbana University	M
Utica College	M
Valdosta State University	M
Virginia College at Birmingham	M
Virginia Commonwealth University	M,O
Walden University	M,D,O
Washburn University	M
Washington State University	M,D
Washington State University Spokane	M,D
Wayland Baptist University	M
Wayne State University	M*
Webber International University	M
Webster University	M,D,O
West Chester University of Pennsylvania	M
Western Connecticut State University	M
Western Illinois University	M,O
Western Kentucky University	M
Western Oregon University	M
Westfield State University	M
West Texas A&M University	M
Wichita State University	M
Widener University	M
Wilfrid Laurier University	M
Wilmington University	M
Wright State University	M
Xavier University	M
Youngstown State University	M

*M—master's degree; P—first professional degree; D—doctorate; O—other advanced degree; *—Close-Up and/or Display in one of the other books in this series*

CULTURAL ANTHROPOLOGY

Institution	Degrees
California Institute of Integral Studies	M,D
Concordia University (Canada)	M
Cornell University	D*
Duke University	D*
Graduate School and University Center of the City University of New York	D
Memorial University of Newfoundland	M,D
North Carolina State University	M*
Northern Arizona University	M
Rice University	M,D
San Francisco State University	M
Stanford University	M,D
University of California, Santa Barbara	M,D
University of California, Santa Cruz	D
University of Denver	M
The University of Tennessee	M,D
University of Wisconsin–Madison	D*
Washington State University	M,D

CULTURAL STUDIES

Institution	Degrees
Ambrose University College	P,M,O
American University	M,D,O
The American University of Paris	M
Appalachian State University	M
Arizona State University	M,D
Assemblies of God Theological Seminary	P,M,D
Athabasca University	M
Baptist Bible College	P,M
Biola University	M,D,O
Boston University	M*
Brock University	M
Carnegie Mellon University	M,D*
The Catholic University of America	M
Central Michigan University	M
Chapman University	D
Claremont Graduate University	M,D,O
Columbia International University	P,M,D,O
Concordia University (CA)	M
Cornell University	M,D*
Eastern Michigan University	M
George Mason University	M,D,O*
Goucher College	M
Grace Theological Seminary	P,M,D,O
Graduate Theological Union	M,D,O
Lewis & Clark College	M,O
Maranatha Baptist Bible College	M
McMaster University	M,D
New York University	M,D,O
Northeastern University	M
Northern Kentucky University	M,O
Northwest University	M
St. Francis Xavier University	M
San Francisco State University	M
Savannah College of Art and Design	M,O
Simmons College	M
Southern Illinois University Carbondale	M
State University of New York at Binghamton	M,D
Stony Brook University, State University of New York	M,D
Taylor College and Seminary	P,M,O
Texas A&M University	M,D
Trent University	D
Union Institute & University	M
Union University	M
University at Buffalo, the State University of New York	M*
University of Alaska Fairbanks	M
University of California, Davis	M,D
University of California, Irvine	D*
University of California, Santa Barbara	M
University of Denver	M,O
University of Hawaii at Hilo	M,D
University of Hawaii at Manoa	O
University of Houston	M
University of Houston–Clear Lake	M
The University of Manchester	M,D
University of Minnesota, Twin Cities Campus	D
University of Missouri–St. Louis	O
University of Pittsburgh	M,D,O*
University of Rochester	
University of Southern California	D*
The University of Texas at San Antonio	M,D*
University of the Sacred Heart	M
University of Washington, Bothell	M
Washington State University	M,D
Wheaton College	M,O
Wilfrid Laurier University	M,D

CURRICULUM AND INSTRUCTION

Institution	Degrees
Abilene Christian University	M
Acadia University	M
American College of Education	M
American InterContinental University Online	M
American University	M,O
Andrews University	M,D,O
Angelo State University	M
Appalachian State University	M
Arizona State University	M,D
Arkansas State University	M,D,O
Arkansas Tech University	M,O
Armstrong Atlantic State University	M
Ashland University	M
Auburn University	M,D,O
Augusta State University	M
Aurora University	M,D
Austin Peay State University	M,O
Averett University	M
Azusa Pacific University	M
Ball State University	M,O
Barry University	D,O*
Baylor University	M,D,O*
Benedictine University	M
Berry College	O
Black Hills State University	M
Bloomsburg University of Pennsylvania	M
Bob Jones University	P,M,D,O
Boise State University	D
Boston College	M,D,O*
Boston University	M,D,O*
Bowling Green State University	M*
Bradley University	M,O
Brandon University	M,O
Brescia University	M
Bucknell University	M
Buena Vista University	M
Caldwell College	M
California Baptist University	M
California Coast University	M,D
California State University, Bakersfield	M
California State University, Chico	M
California State University, Dominguez Hills	M*
California State University, Fresno	M
California State University, Northridge	M
California State University, Sacramento	M
California State University, San Bernardino	M
California State University, Stanislaus	M
Calvin College	M
Cambridge College	M,D,O
Campbellsville University	M
Capella University	M,D,O
Caribbean University	M,D
Carson-Newman College	M
Castleton State College	M
Centenary College of Louisiana	M
Central Michigan University	M,D,O
Chapman University	M,D
City University of Seattle	M,O
Clarion University of Pennsylvania	M
Clark Atlanta University	M
Clemson University	D
The College at Brockport, State University of New York	M
The College of Saint Rose	M,O
The College of William and Mary	M,D
Colorado Christian University	M
Columbia International University	M,D,O
Columbus State University	M,D,O
Concordia University (CA)	M
Concordia University (MI)	M
Concordia University (OR)	M
Concordia University Chicago	M
Concordia University, St. Paul	M,O
Concordia University Wisconsin	M
Converse College	O
Coppin State University	M
Cornell University	M,D*
Dakota Wesleyan University	M
Dallas Baptist University	M
Delaware State University	M
Delaware Valley College	M
DePaul University	M,D
Doane College	M
Dominican University	M
Drexel University	M*
Duquesne University	M,O
East Carolina University	M
Eastern Kentucky University	M
Eastern Michigan University	M
Eastern New Mexico University	M
Eastern Washington University	M
East Tennessee State University	M
Emporia State University	M
Fairleigh Dickinson University, Metropolitan Campus	M
Ferris State University	M
Fitchburg State University	M
Florida Atlantic University	M,D,O
Florida Gulf Coast University	M
Florida International University	M,D,O
Fordham University	M,D,O
Framingham State University	M
Franciscan University of Steubenville	M
Franklin Pierce University	M,D,O
Freed-Hardeman University	M,O
Fresno Pacific University	M
Frostburg State University	M
Furman University	M,O
Gannon University	M
Gardner-Webb University	D
George Fox University	M,D,O
George Mason University	M*
The George Washington University	M,D,O
Georgia College & State University	M,O
Georgia Southern University	D
Grambling State University	M,D
Grand Canyon University	M
Grand Valley State University	M
Harvard University	M*
Henderson State University	M
Hood College	M,O
Houston Baptist University	M
Idaho State University	M,O
Illinois State University	M,D
Indiana State University	M,D
Indiana University Bloomington	M,D,O*
Indiana University of Pennsylvania	M,D
Indiana University–Purdue University Indianapolis	M,O
Inter American University of Puerto Rico, Arecibo Campus	M
Inter American University of Puerto Rico, Barranquitas Campus	M
Inter American University of Puerto Rico, Metropolitan Campus	M,D
Inter American University of Puerto Rico, San Germán Campus	D
Iowa State University of Science and Technology	M,D*
The Johns Hopkins University	M,O
Johnson State College	M
Jones International University	M
Kansas State University	M,D*
Kean University	M
Keene State College	M,O
Kent State University	M,D,O*
Kutztown University of Pennsylvania	M,O
LaGrange College	M
Lake Erie College	M
Lander University	M
La Sierra University	M,D,O
Lehigh University	M,D,O
Lesley University	M,D,O
LeTourneau University	M
Lewis & Clark College	M
Lewis University	M
Liberty University	M,D,O
Lincoln Memorial University	M,D,O
Lipscomb University	M,D

Institution	Degrees
Louisiana State University in Shreveport	M
Louisiana Tech University	M,D
Loyola University Chicago	M,D
Loyola University Maryland	M,O
Lynchburg College	M
Lyndon State College	M
Malone University	M
Martin Luther College	M
Massachusetts College of Liberal Arts	M
McDaniel College	M
McGill University	M,D,O
McNeese State University	M
Medaille College	M
Memorial University of Newfoundland	M,D,O
Mercer University	M,D,O
Miami University	M,D
Michigan State University	M,D,O
Middle Tennessee State University	M,O
Midwestern State University	M
Mills College	M,D
Minnesota State University Mankato	M,O
Minnesota State University Moorhead	M
Misericordia University	M
Mississippi College	M,D,O
Mississippi State University	M,D,O
Mississippi University for Women	M
Missouri State University	M
Montana State University	M,D,O
Montana State University Billings	M
Montclair State University	M,D,O
Moravian College	M
Morehead State University	M,O
Mount Saint Vincent University	M
National-Louis University	M,D,O
Newman University	M
New Mexico Highlands University	M
New Mexico State University	M,D
New York University	M,D,O
Nicholls State University	M
North Carolina Central University	M
North Carolina State University	M,D*
North Central College	M
Northern Arizona University	M,D,O
Northern Illinois University	M,D
Northwestern Oklahoma State University	M
Northwestern State University of Louisiana	M
Northwest Nazarene University	M
Nova Southeastern University	M,O*
Ohio University	M,D*
Oklahoma State University	M,D*
Old Dominion University	M,D
Olivet Nazarene University	M
Oral Roberts University	M,D
Ottawa University	M
Our Lady of Holy Cross College	M
Our Lady of the Lake University of San Antonio	M
Pace University	M,O
Pacific Lutheran University	M
Penn State University Park	M,D
Peru State College	M
Philadelphia Biblical University	M
Point Park University	M
Pontifical Catholic University of Puerto Rico	M,D
Portland State University	M,D
Prairie View A&M University	M
Purdue University	M,D,O
Quincy University	M
Randolph College	M
Regis University	M,O
Rider University	M,O
Rivier College	M,D,O
Rosemont College	M
Rowan University	M
St. Catherine University	M
St. Cloud State University	M
St. Francis Xavier University	M
Saint Leo University	M,O
Saint Louis University	M,D
Saint Mary's College of California	M
Saint Michael's College	M,O
Saint Vincent College	M
Saint Xavier University	M,O
Salem International University	M
Sam Houston State University	M
San Diego State University	M
San Jose State University	M,O
Seattle Pacific University	M
Seattle University	M,O
Shawnee State University	M
Shaw University	M
Shepherd University	M
Shippensburg University of Pennsylvania	M
Shorter University	M
Simon Fraser University	M,D
Sonoma State University	M
South Dakota State University	M
Southeastern Louisiana University	M
Southern Arkansas University–Magnolia	M
Southern Illinois University Carbondale	M,D
Southern Illinois University Edwardsville	M
Southern Nazarene University	M
Southern New Hampshire University	M,O
Southwestern Adventist University	M
Southwestern Assemblies of God University	M
Southwestern College (KS)	M
Stanford University	M,D
State University of New York at Plattsburgh	M
State University of New York College at Potsdam	M
Stephens College	M
Syracuse University	M,D,O*
Tarleton State University	M
Teachers College, Columbia University	M,D
Tennessee State University	M,D
Tennessee Technological University	M,O
Tennessee Temple University	M
Texas A&M International University	M
Texas A&M University	M,D
Texas A&M University–Commerce	M,D
Texas A&M University–Corpus Christi	M,D
Texas A&M University–Texarkana	M
Texas Christian University	M
Texas Southern University	M,D
Texas Tech University	M,D*
Texas Woman's University	M,D
Trevecca Nazarene University	M
Trinity (Washington) University	M
Union Institute & University	M,D,O
Universidad Adventista de las Antillas	P,M
Universidad del Turabo	M,D
Universidad Metropolitana	M
Université de Montréal	M,D,O
Université Laval	M,D
University at Albany, State University of New York	M,D,O
University of Alaska Fairbanks	M,D,O
University of Arkansas	D
The University of British Columbia	M,D
University of Calgary	M,D,O
University of California, Davis	M,D
University of California, Riverside	M,D
University of Central Missouri	M,D,O
University of Cincinnati	M,D
University of Colorado at Colorado Springs	M,D
University of Colorado Boulder	M,D*
University of Delaware	M,D,O*
University of Denver	M,D,O
University of Detroit Mercy	M
University of Florida	M,D,O*
University of Hawaii at Manoa	M,D
University of Houston	M,D
University of Houston–Clear Lake	M
University of Houston–Downtown	M
University of Houston–Victoria	M
University of Idaho	M,O
University of Illinois at Chicago	M,D
University of Illinois at Urbana–Champaign	M,D,O
University of Indianapolis	M
The University of Iowa	M,D*
The University of Kansas	M,D
University of Kentucky	M,D*
University of Louisiana at Lafayette	M*
University of Louisiana at Monroe	M,D
University of Louisville	M,D
University of Maine	M
University of Manitoba	M
University of Mary	M
University of Mary Hardin-Baylor	M,D
University of Maryland, Baltimore County	M,D,O
University of Maryland, College Park	M,D,O
University of Massachusetts Boston	M
University of Massachusetts Lowell	M,D,O
University of Memphis	M,D
University of Michigan	M,D*
University of Michigan–Dearborn	D
University of Minnesota, Twin Cities Campus	M,D,O
University of Mississippi	M,D,O
University of Missouri	M,D,O*
University of Missouri–Kansas City	M,D,O*
University of Missouri–St. Louis	M,O
The University of Montana	M,D
University of Nebraska at Kearney	M
University of Nebraska–Lincoln	M,D,O*
University of Nevada, Las Vegas	M,D,O
University of Nevada, Reno	D*
University of New England	M,O
University of New Mexico	O*
University of New Orleans	M,D,O
The University of North Carolina at Chapel Hill	M,D*
The University of North Carolina at Charlotte	M,D
The University of North Carolina at Greensboro	M,D,O
The University of North Carolina Wilmington	M
University of Northern Iowa	D
University of North Texas	M,D
University of Oklahoma	M,D,O*
University of Phoenix	M,D,O
University of Phoenix–Austin Campus	M
University of Phoenix–Central Florida Campus	M
University of Phoenix–Central Valley Campus	M
University of Phoenix–Chattanooga Campus	M
University of Phoenix–Dallas Campus	M
University of Phoenix–Denver Campus	M
University of Phoenix–Hawaii Campus	M
University of Phoenix–Houston Campus	M
University of Phoenix–Idaho Campus	M
University of Phoenix–Las Vegas Campus	M
University of Phoenix–Louisiana Campus	M
University of Phoenix–Madison Campus	D,O
University of Phoenix–Memphis Campus	M
University of Phoenix–Milwaukee Campus	M,D,O
University of Phoenix–Nashville Campus	M
University of Phoenix–New Mexico Campus	M
University of Phoenix–Northern Nevada Campus	M
University of Phoenix–North Florida Campus	M
University of Phoenix–Omaha Campus	M
University of Phoenix–Oregon Campus	M
University of Phoenix–Phoenix Campus	M
University of Phoenix–Richmond Campus	M
University of Phoenix–Sacramento Valley Campus	M,O
University of Phoenix–San Antonio Campus	M
University of Phoenix–San Diego Campus	M
University of Phoenix–Southern Arizona Campus	M,O
University of Phoenix–Southern California Campus	M
University of Phoenix–Southern Colorado Campus	M,O
University of Phoenix–South Florida Campus	M
University of Phoenix–Springfield Campus	M
University of Phoenix–Utah Campus	M
University of Phoenix–Vancouver Campus	M
University of Phoenix–Washington D.C. Campus	M,D,O
University of Phoenix–West Florida Campus	M

*M—master's degree; P—first professional degree; D—doctorate; O—other advanced degree; *—Close-Up and/or Display in one of the other books in this series*

- University of Puerto Rico, Río Piedras M,D
- University of Regina M
- University of Rochester
- University of St. Francis (IL) M
- University of Saint Mary M
- University of St. Thomas (MN) M,O
- University of San Diego M
- University of San Francisco M,D
- University of Saskatchewan M,D,O
- The University of Scranton M
- University of South Africa M,D
- University of South Carolina D
- The University of South Dakota M,D,O
- University of Southern Mississippi M,D,O
- University of South Florida M,D,O*
- The University of Tampa M
- The University of Tennessee M,D,O
- The University of Texas at Arlington M
- The University of Texas at Austin M,D
- The University of Texas at Brownsville M
- The University of Texas at El Paso M,D
- The University of Texas at San Antonio M,D*
- University of the Pacific M,D
- University of the Southwest M
- The University of Toledo M,D,O
- University of Vermont M
- University of Victoria M,D
- University of Virginia M,D,O
- University of Washington M,D*
- The University of Western Ontario M
- University of West Florida M,D,O
- University of Wisconsin–Madison M,D*
- University of Wisconsin–Milwaukee M,D
- University of Wisconsin–Oshkosh M
- University of Wisconsin–Superior M
- University of Wisconsin–Whitewater M*
- University of Wyoming M,D
- Utah State University D
- Virginia Polytechnic Institute and State University M,D,O
- Walden University M,D,O
- Walla Walla University M
- Washburn University M
- Washington State University M,D
- Wayne State College M
- Wayne State University M,D,O*
- Weber State University M
- Western Connecticut State University M
- West Texas A&M University M
- West Virginia University M,D
- Wichita State University M
- Wilkes University M,D
- William Woods University M,O
- Wright State University M,O
- Xavier University of Louisiana M
- Youngstown State University M

DANCE

- Arizona State University M
- Bennington College M
- California Institute of the Arts M,O
- California State University, Fullerton M
- California State University, Long Beach M
- California State University, Sacramento M
- Case Western Reserve University M*
- The College at Brockport, State University of New York M
- Florida State University M
- George Mason University M*
- The George Washington University M
- Hollins University M
- Mills College M
- New York University M,D
- Northern Illinois University M
- The Ohio State University M,D
- Oklahoma City University M
- Purchase College, State University of New York M
- Sam Houston State University M
- Sarah Lawrence College M
- Smith College M
- Southern Methodist University M
- Temple University M,D*
- Texas Tech University D*
- Texas Woman's University M,D
- Tulane University M*
- Université du Québec à Montréal M
- The University of Arizona M
- University of California, Irvine M*
- University of California, Los Angeles M,D*
- University of California, Riverside M,D
- University of Colorado Boulder M,D*
- University of Hawaii at Manoa M,D
- University of Illinois at Urbana–Champaign M
- The University of Iowa M*
- University of Maryland, Baltimore County M
- University of Maryland, College Park M,D
- University of Michigan M*
- University of Minnesota, Twin Cities Campus M,D
- University of New Mexico M*
- The University of North Carolina at Charlotte M,D
- The University of North Carolina at Greensboro M
- University of Oklahoma M*
- University of Oregon M
- The University of Texas at Austin M,D
- University of Utah M*
- University of Washington M*
- University of Wisconsin–Milwaukee M
- York University M*

DATABASE SYSTEMS

- Boston University M*
- Colorado Technical University Colorado Springs M,D
- Colorado Technical University Denver M
- Ferris State University M
- George Mason University M,D,O*
- Minnesota State University Mankato M,O
- National University M
- New York University M,O
- Northwestern University M*
- Regis University M,O
- Rochester Institute of Technology M,O
- Sacred Heart University M,O
- Stevens Institute of Technology M,D,O
- Towson University M,D,O
- University of Denver M,O
- University of New Haven M,O
- The University of North Carolina at Charlotte M,O
- University of West Florida M

DECORATIVE ARTS

- Bard Graduate Center: Decorative Arts, Design History, Material Culture M,D*
- Corcoran College of Art and Design M
- The New School: A University M
- Sotheby's Institute of Art–London M
- Sotheby's Institute of Art–New York M

DEMOGRAPHY AND POPULATION STUDIES

- The American University in Cairo M,O
- Bowling Green State University M,D*
- Cornell University M,D*
- Emory University M*
- Florida State University M
- Harvard University M,D*
- The Johns Hopkins University M,D
- Princeton University D,O*
- Université de Montréal M,D
- Université du Québec, Institut National de la Recherche Scientifique M,D
- University at Albany, State University of New York M,D,O
- University of Alberta M,D
- University of California, Berkeley M,D*
- University of California, Irvine M*
- University of Guelph M,D
- University of Hawaii at Manoa O
- University of Pennsylvania M,D*
- University of Puerto Rico, Medical Sciences Campus M
- The University of Texas at San Antonio D*
- University of Washington M,D*
- Washington State University M,D

DENTAL HYGIENE

- Boston University P,M,D,O*
- Eastern Washington University M
- Georgia Health Sciences University M
- Idaho State University M
- Missouri Southern State University M
- Old Dominion University M
- Texas A&M Health Science Center M
- Université de Montréal O
- University of Alberta O
- University of Bridgeport M
- University of Maryland, Baltimore M
- University of Michigan M*
- University of Missouri–Kansas City P,M,D,O*
- University of New Mexico M*
- The University of North Carolina at Chapel Hill M,D*
- The University of Texas Health Science Center at San Antonio M

DENTISTRY

- Boston University P,M,D,O*
- Case Western Reserve University P*
- Columbia University P*
- Creighton University P
- Georgia Health Sciences University P
- Harvard University P,M,D,O*
- Howard University P,O
- Idaho State University O
- Indiana University–Purdue University Indianapolis P,M,D,O
- Loma Linda University P,M,O
- Louisiana State University Health Sciences Center P
- Marquette University P
- McGill University P,M,D,O
- Medical University of South Carolina P
- Meharry Medical College P
- Midwestern University, Glendale Campus P
- New York University P
- Nova Southeastern University P,M*
- The Ohio State University P,M,D
- Oregon Health & Science University P,O*
- Saint Louis University M
- Southern Illinois University Edwardsville P
- Stony Brook University, State University of New York P,O
- Temple University P*
- Texas A&M Health Science Center P
- Tufts University P
- Universidad Central del Este P
- Universidad Iberoamericana P,M
- Universidad Nacional Pedro Henriquez Urena P
- Université Laval P
- University at Buffalo, the State University of New York P,M,D,O*
- The University of Alabama at Birmingham P*
- University of Alberta P
- The University of British Columbia P
- University of California, Los Angeles P,O*
- University of California, San Francisco P
- University of Colorado Denver P
- University of Connecticut Health Center P,O*
- University of Detroit Mercy P
- University of Florida P,O*
- University of Illinois at Chicago P
- The University of Iowa P,M,D,O*
- University of Kentucky P*
- University of Louisville P,M
- The University of Manchester M,D
- University of Manitoba P
- University of Maryland, Baltimore P,O
- University of Medicine and Dentistry of New Jersey P,M,O
- University of Michigan P*
- University of Minnesota, Twin Cities Campus P
- University of Mississippi Medical Center P,M,D
- University of Missouri–Kansas City P,M,D,O*
- University of Nebraska Medical Center P,M,D,O
- The University of North Carolina at Chapel Hill P*
- University of Oklahoma Health Sciences Center P,O

University of Pennsylvania P*
University of Pittsburgh P,M,O*
University of Puerto Rico, Medical Sciences Campus P
University of Saskatchewan P
University of Southern California P*
The University of Tennessee Health Science Center P,M,O
The University of Texas Health Science Center at Houston P,M*
The University of Texas Health Science Center at San Antonio P,M,O
University of Toronto P
University of Washington P*
The University of Western Ontario P
Virginia Commonwealth University P,M
Western University of Health Sciences P
West Virginia University P

DEVELOPMENTAL BIOLOGY

Albert Einstein College of Medicine D
Baylor College of Medicine D*
Brigham Young University M,D*
Brown University M,D
California Institute of Technology D
Carnegie Mellon University M,D*
Columbia University M,D*
Cornell University M,D*
Duke University O*
Emory University D*
Illinois State University M,D
Iowa State University of Science and Technology M,D*
The Johns Hopkins University D
Louisiana State University Health Sciences Center M,D
Marquette University M,D
Massachusetts Institute of Technology D
Medical University of South Carolina D
New York University M,D
Northwestern University D*
The Ohio State University M,D
Oregon Health & Science University D*
Purdue University M,D
Rutgers, The State University of New Jersey, New Brunswick M,D*
San Francisco State University M
Stanford University D
Stony Brook University, State University of New York M,D
Thomas Jefferson University M,D
Tufts University D
University at Albany, State University of New York M,D
University of California, Davis M,D
University of California, Irvine M,D*
University of California, Los Angeles D*
University of California, Riverside M,D
University of California, San Diego D*
University of California, San Francisco D
University of California, Santa Barbara M,D
University of California, Santa Cruz M,D
University of Chicago D
University of Cincinnati D
University of Colorado Boulder M,D*
University of Colorado Denver D
University of Connecticut M,D*
University of Connecticut Health Center D*
University of Delaware M,D*
University of Hawaii at Manoa M,D
University of Illinois at Urbana–Champaign D
The University of Kansas M,D
The University of Manchester M,D
University of Massachusetts Amherst D*
University of Medicine and Dentistry of New Jersey D,O
University of Miami D*
University of Michigan M,D*
University of Minnesota, Twin Cities Campus M,D
The University of North Carolina at Chapel Hill M,D*
University of Pennsylvania D*
University of Pittsburgh M,D*
University of South Carolina M,D
The University of Texas Health Science Center at Houston M,D*
The University of Texas Southwestern Medical Center at Dallas D
Washington University in St. Louis D*
Wesleyan University D*
West Virginia University M,D
Yale University D*

DEVELOPMENTAL EDUCATION

Eastern Michigan University M,O
Ferris State University M
Grambling State University M,D
Instituto Tecnológico y de Estudios Superiores de Monterrey, Campus Ciudad Obregón M
National-Louis University M,D,O
North Carolina State University M,D,O*
Rutgers, The State University of New Jersey, New Brunswick M*
Texas State University–San Marcos M,D
The University of Iowa M,D*
Walden University M,D,O

DEVELOPMENTAL PSYCHOLOGY

Andrews University M,D
Arizona State University D
Bethel University (MN) M
Boston College M,D*
Bowling Green State University M,D*
Brandeis University M,D
Brown University D
Capella University M,D,O
Carnegie Mellon University D*
Chatham University M,D
Claremont Graduate University M,D,O
Clark University D
Cornell University D*
Duke University D*
Emory University D*
Erikson Institute M,O
Florida State University D
Fordham University D
Graduate School and University Center of the City University of New York D
Harvard University D*
Howard University M,D
Illinois State University M,D,O
Indiana University Bloomington M,D*
Louisiana State University and Agricultural and Mechanical College M,D
Loyola University Chicago M,D
McGill University M,D,O
The New School: A University M,D
New York University M,D
North Carolina State University D*
The Ohio State University M,D
Pontificia Universidad Catolica Madre y Maestra M
Queen's University at Kingston M,D
San Francisco State University M
Stanford University D
Teachers College, Columbia University M,D
Temple University M,D*
Texas A&M University D
Union Institute & University M,D,O
Université de Montréal M,D
The University of British Columbia M,D
University of California, Santa Barbara M,D
University of Connecticut M,D,O*
University of Denver D
University of Florida M,D*
University of Houston M,D
The University of Kansas M,D
University of Maine M,D
The University of Manchester M,D
University of Maryland, Baltimore County D
University of Maryland, College Park M,D
University of Massachusetts Amherst M,D*
University of Miami M,D*
University of Michigan D*
The University of Montana M,D,O
University of Nebraska at Omaha M,D,O
University of Nebraska–Lincoln M,D,O*
The University of North Carolina at Chapel Hill D*
The University of North Carolina at Greensboro M,D
University of Notre Dame D*
University of Oregon M,D
University of Pittsburgh M,D*
University of Rochester
University of Southern California M,D*
University of Victoria M,D
University of Washington D*
University of Wisconsin–Madison D*
University of Wisconsin–Milwaukee M,D
Virginia Commonwealth University D
Walden University M,D,O
West Virginia University M,D
Wilfrid Laurier University M,D
Yale University D*

DISABILITY STUDIES

Brandeis University D
Brock University M,O
Chapman University D
Syracuse University O*
University of Hawaii at Manoa O
University of Illinois at Chicago M,D
University of Manitoba M
University of Northern British Columbia M,D,O
Utah State University M,D,O
York University M,D*

DISTANCE EDUCATION DEVELOPMENT

Athabasca University M,O
Barry University O*
Colorado Christian University M
Endicott College M
Fairmont State University M
Florida State University M,D,O
Jones International University M
Liberty University M,D,O
New York Institute of Technology M,O
Nova Southeastern University M,D*
Saginaw Valley State University M
Télé-université M,D
Thomas Edison State College O
University of Central Florida M,O
University of Colorado Denver M
University of Maryland, Baltimore County M,O
University of Maryland University College M,O
University of Nebraska–Lincoln M*
University of Wyoming M,D,O
Virginia Polytechnic Institute and State University M,O
Walden University M,D,O
Western Illinois University M,O
Wilkes University M,D

EARLY CHILDHOOD EDUCATION

Adelphi University M,O*
Alabama Agricultural and Mechanical University M,O
Alabama State University M,O
Albany State University M
Albright College M
American International College M,D,O
American University M,O
Anna Maria College M,O
Antioch University New England M
Arcadia University M,D,O*
Arkansas State University M,O
Armstrong Atlantic State University M
Auburn University M,D,O
Auburn University Montgomery M,O
Aurora University M,D
Bank Street College of Education M
Barry University M,D,O*
Bayamón Central University M,O
Bellarmine University M,D,O
Belmont University M
Bennington College M
Berry College M
Bloomsburg University of Pennsylvania M
Boise State University M
Boston College M*
Boston University M,D,O*
Bowling Green State University M*
Brenau University M,O

*M—master's degree; P—first professional degree; D—doctorate; O—other advanced degree; *—Close-Up and/or Display in one of the other books in this series*

Institution	Degrees
Bridgewater State University	M
Brooklyn College of the City University of New York	M
Buffalo State College, State University of New York	M
California State University, Bakersfield	M
California State University, East Bay	M
California State University, Fresno	M
California State University, Northridge	M
California State University, Sacramento	M
Cambridge College	M,D,O
Canisius College	M,O
Caribbean University	M,D
Carlow University	M
Central Connecticut State University	M
Central Michigan University	M,O
Chatham University	M
Chestnut Hill College	M*
Cheyney University of Pennsylvania	O
Chicago State University	M
City College of the City University of New York	M
Clarion University of Pennsylvania	M
Clarke University	M
Clemson University	M
Cleveland State University	M
College of Charleston	M
College of Mount St. Joseph	M
The College of New Jersey	M
The College of New Rochelle	M
The College of Saint Rose	M,O
Colorado Christian University	M
Columbia International University	M,D,O
Columbus State University	M,O
Concordia University Chicago	M,D
Concordia University, Nebraska	M
Concordia University, St. Paul	M,O
Concordia University Wisconsin	M
Converse College	M,O
Daemen College	M
Dominican University	M
Dowling College	M,D,O
Duquesne University	M
Eastern Connecticut State University	M
Eastern Illinois University	M
Eastern Michigan University	M
Eastern Nazarene College	M,O
Eastern New Mexico University	M
Eastern Washington University	M
East Tennessee State University	M,D
Edinboro University of Pennsylvania	M,O
Ellis University	M
Elms College	M,O
Emporia State University	M
Endicott College	M
Erikson Institute	M
Fitchburg State University	M
Florida Agricultural and Mechanical University	M
Florida Atlantic University	M,D,O
Florida Gulf Coast University	M
Florida International University	M,D,O
Florida State University	M,D,O
Fordham University	M,D,O
Framingham State University	M
Francis Marion University	M
Furman University	M,O
Gallaudet University	M,D,O
Gannon University	M
The George Washington University	M
Georgia College & State University	M,O
Georgia Southern University	M,O
Georgia Southwestern State University	M,O
Georgia State University	M,D,O
Golden Gate Baptist Theological Seminary	P,M,D,O
Governors State University	M
Grand Valley State University	M,O
Hampton University	M
Harding University	M,O
Hebrew College	M,O
Henderson State University	M
Hofstra University	M,D,O
Hood College	M,O
Howard University	M
Hunter College of the City University of New York	M,O
Indiana State University	M
Indiana University–Purdue University Indianapolis	M,O
Inter American University of Puerto Rico, Guayama Campus	M
Jackson State University	M,D,O
Jacksonville State University	M
Jacksonville University	M,O
James Madison University	M
John Carroll University	M
The Johns Hopkins University	M,D,O
Kansas State University	M*
Kean University	M
Kennesaw State University	M
Kent State University	M*
Keuka College	M
Kutztown University of Pennsylvania	M,O
Lehman College of the City University of New York	M
Le Moyne College	M,O
Lenoir-Rhyne University	M
Lesley University	M,D,O
Lewis & Clark College	M
Liberty University	M,D,O
Lincoln University (PA)	M
Long Island University at Riverhead	M
Long Island University, Brentwood Campus	M
Long Island University, C.W. Post Campus	M
Long Island University, Rockland Graduate Campus	M
Long Island University, Westchester Graduate Campus	M,O
Loyola Marymount University	M
Loyola University Maryland	M,O
Manhattan College	M,O
Manhattanville College	M*
Marshall University	M
Maryville University of Saint Louis	M,D
Marywood University	M
McNeese State University	M
Mercer University	M,D,O
Mercy College	M
Merrimack College	M,O
Miami University	M
Middle Tennessee State University	M,O
Millersville University of Pennsylvania	M
Mills College	M,D
Minnesota State University Mankato	M,O
Minot State University	M
Missouri Southern State University	M
Missouri State University	M
Montana State University Billings	M
Montclair State University	M,O
Mount Saint Mary College	M,O
Murray State University	M
National-Louis University	M,D,O
Nazareth College of Rochester	M
New Jersey City University	M
New York University	M,D
Niagara University	M,O
Norfolk State University	M
Northeastern State University	M
Northern Arizona University	M
Northern Illinois University	M,D
North Georgia College & State University	M,O
Northwestern State University of Louisiana	M
Northwest Missouri State University	M
Nova Southeastern University	M,O*
Oakland University	M,D,O
Oberlin College	M
Oglethorpe University	M
The Ohio State University at Lima	M
The Ohio State University at Marion	M
The Ohio State University–Mansfield Campus	M
The Ohio State University–Newark Campus	M
Oklahoma City University	M
Old Dominion University	M,D
Ottawa University	M
Our Lady of the Lake University of San Antonio	M
Pace University	M,O
Pacific University	M
Piedmont College	M,D,O
Pittsburg State University	M
Pontificia Universidad Catolica Madre y Maestra	M
Portland State University	M,D
Prescott College	M,D
Queens College of the City University of New York	M,O
Radford University	M
Reinhardt University	M
Rhode Island College	M
Rivier College	M,D,O
Roberts Wesleyan College	M,O
Roosevelt University	M
Rutgers, The State University of New Jersey, New Brunswick	M,D*
Saginaw Valley State University	M
St. Bonaventure University	M
St. John's University (NY)	M
St. Joseph's College, Long Island Campus	M
St. Joseph's College, New York	M*
Saint Mary's College of California	M
Saint Xavier University	M,O
Salem College	M
Salem State University	M
Samford University	M,D,O
San Francisco State University	M,D,O
Shippensburg University of Pennsylvania	M
Siena Heights University	M
Sonoma State University	M
South Carolina State University	M,D,O
Southern Oregon University	M
Southwestern Oklahoma State University	M
Southwest Minnesota State University	M
Springfield College	M
Spring Hill College	M
State University of New York at Binghamton	M
State University of New York at New Paltz	M
State University of New York at Oswego	M
State University of New York College at Cortland	M
State University of New York College at Geneseo	M
State University of New York College at Potsdam	M
Stephen F. Austin State University	M
Syracuse University	M*
Teachers College, Columbia University	M,D
Temple University	M,D*
Tennessee Technological University	M,O
Texas A&M International University	M
Texas A&M University–Commerce	M,D
Texas A&M University–Corpus Christi	M,D
Texas A&M University–Kingsville	M
Texas A&M University–San Antonio	M
Texas State University–San Marcos	M
Texas Woman's University	M,D
Towson University	M,O
Trinity (Washington) University	M
Troy University	M,O
Tufts University	M,D,O
TUI University	M
Universidad del Turabo	M
University at Buffalo, the State University of New York	M,D,O*
The University of Alabama at Birmingham	M,D*
University of Alaska Anchorage	M,O
University of Alaska Southeast	M
University of Arkansas	M
University of Arkansas at Little Rock	M
University of Bridgeport	M,O
The University of British Columbia	M,D
University of Central Florida	M
University of Central Oklahoma	M
University of Cincinnati	M
University of Colorado Denver	M
University of Dayton	M
The University of Findlay	M
University of Florida	M,D,O*
University of Georgia	M,D,O
University of Hartford	M
University of Hawaii at Manoa	M

University of Houston–Clear Lake M
The University of Iowa M,D*
University of Kentucky M,D*
University of Louisville M,D
University of Maine at Farmington M
University of Mary M
University of Maryland, Baltimore County M
University of Maryland, College Park M,D
University of Massachusetts Amherst M,D,O*
University of Memphis M,D
University of Miami M,O*
University of Michigan M,D*
University of Minnesota, Twin Cities Campus M,D,O
University of Missouri M,D,O*
University of Missouri–St. Louis M,O
University of Nebraska–Lincoln M,D*
University of Nevada, Las Vegas M,D,O
University of New Hampshire M
University of New Mexico D*
The University of North Carolina at Chapel Hill M,D*
The University of North Carolina at Greensboro M,D,O
University of North Dakota M
University of Northern Colorado M,D
University of Northern Iowa M
University of North Texas M,D,O
University of Oklahoma M,D,O*
University of Phoenix M
University of Phoenix–Central Florida Campus M
University of Phoenix–Louisiana Campus M
University of Phoenix–North Florida Campus M
University of Phoenix–Oregon Campus M
University of Phoenix–Puerto Rico Campus M
University of Phoenix–Southern California Campus M
University of Phoenix–South Florida Campus M
University of Phoenix–Washington D.C. Campus M,D,O
University of Phoenix–West Florida Campus M
University of Pittsburgh M*
University of Puerto Rico, Río Piedras M
University of St. Thomas (MN) M,O
The University of Scranton M
University of South Alabama M,O
University of South Carolina M,D
University of South Carolina Upstate M
University of Southern Mississippi M,D,O
University of South Florida M,D,O*
The University of Tennessee M,D,O
The University of Texas at Brownsville M
The University of Texas at San Antonio M,D*
The University of Texas at Tyler M
The University of Texas of the Permian Basin M
The University of Texas–Pan American M
University of the District of Columbia M
University of the Incarnate Word M,D
University of the Sacred Heart M,O
University of the Southwest M
The University of Toledo M,D,O
University of Utah M,D*
University of Victoria M,D
University of Virginia M,D
The University of West Alabama M
University of West Florida M,D
University of West Georgia M,O
University of Wisconsin–Milwaukee M
University of Wisconsin–Oshkosh M
Ursuline College M
Virginia Commonwealth University M,O
Wagner College M
Walden University M,D,O
Wayne State College M
Wayne State University M,D,O*
Webster University M
Wesleyan College M
West Chester University of Pennsylvania M,O
Western Kentucky University M,O
Western Oregon University M
Westfield State University M
West Virginia University M,D
Wheelock College M
Wichita State University M
Widener University M,D
Wilkes University M,D
Worcester State University M
Wright State University M
Xavier University M
Youngstown State University M

EAST EUROPEAN AND RUSSIAN STUDIES

Boston College M*
Brown University M,D
Carleton University M,O
Columbia University M,O*
Cornell University M,D*
Florida State University M
Georgetown University M
The George Washington University M
Harvard University M*
Indiana University Bloomington M,O*
La Salle University M
The Ohio State University M,D
Stanford University M
University of Alberta M,D
The University of British Columbia M,D
University of Illinois at Urbana–Champaign M
The University of Kansas M
University of Michigan M,O*
The University of North Carolina at Chapel Hill M*
University of Pittsburgh O*
University of Saskatchewan M
The University of Texas at Austin M
University of Toronto M
University of Washington M*
Yale University M,D*

ECOLOGY

Baylor University D*
Brown University D
California State University, Stanislaus M
Clemson University M,D
Colorado State University M,D
Columbia University M,D,O*
Cornell University M,D*
Dartmouth College D
Duke University M,D,O*
Eastern Kentucky University M
Eastern Michigan University M
Eastern New Mexico University M
Emory University D*
Florida Institute of Technology M
Florida State University M,D
Frostburg State University M
Illinois State University M,D
Indiana State University M,D
Indiana University Bloomington M,D*
Inter American University of Puerto Rico, Bayamón Campus M
Iowa State University of Science and Technology M,D*
Kent State University M,D*
Laurentian University M,D
Lesley University M,D,O
Marquette University M,D
Michigan State University D
Michigan Technological University M
Montana State University M,D
Montclair State University M,O
North Dakota State University M,D
Nova Scotia Agricultural College M
The Ohio State University M,D
Ohio University M,D*
Old Dominion University D
Penn State University Park M,D
Princeton University D*
Purdue University M,D
Rice University M,D
Rutgers, The State University of New Jersey, New Brunswick M,D*
San Diego State University M,D
San Francisco State University M
San Jose State University M
State University of New York College of Environmental Science and Forestry M,D
Stony Brook University, State University of New York M,D
Tulane University M,D*
Universidad Nacional Pedro Henriquez Urena M
University at Albany, State University of New York M,D
University at Buffalo, the State University of New York M,D,O*
University of Alberta M,D
The University of Arizona M,D
University of California, Davis M,D
University of California, Irvine M,D*
University of California, Los Angeles M,D*
University of California, Riverside M,D
University of California, San Diego D*
University of California, Santa Barbara M,D
University of California, Santa Cruz M,D
University of Chicago D
University of Colorado Boulder M,D*
University of Colorado Denver M
University of Connecticut M,D,O*
University of Delaware M,D*
University of Florida M,D*
University of Georgia M,D
University of Guelph M,D
University of Hawaii at Manoa M,D
University of Illinois at Urbana–Champaign M,D
The University of Kansas M,D
University of Maine M,D
The University of Manchester M,D
University of Manitoba M,D
University of Maryland, College Park M,D
University of Massachusetts Amherst M,D*
University of Michigan M,D*
University of Minnesota, Twin Cities Campus M,D
University of Missouri M,D*
University of Missouri–St. Louis M,D,O
The University of Montana M,D
University of Nevada, Reno D*
University of New Haven M,O
The University of North Carolina at Chapel Hill M,D*
University of North Dakota M,D
University of Notre Dame M,D*
University of Oklahoma D*
University of Oregon M,D
University of Pittsburgh D*
University of Puerto Rico, Río Piedras M,D
University of South Carolina M,D
The University of Tennessee M,D
The University of Texas at Austin M,D
The University of Toledo M,D
University of Toronto M,D
University of Washington M,D*
University of Wisconsin–Madison M*
University of Wyoming M,D
Utah State University M,D
Washington University in St. Louis D*
Wesleyan University D*
Yale University D*

ECONOMIC DEVELOPMENT

Albany State University M
Boston University M*
Chicago State University M
Claremont Graduate University M,D,O
Cleveland State University M,D,O
Concordia University (Canada) O
Cornell University M,D*
Eastern Michigan University M
Eastern University M
Florida Atlantic University M,O
Fordham University M,O
Georgetown University D
Georgia Institute of Technology M,D
Georgia State University M,D,O
Indiana University Bloomington M,D,O*
New Mexico State University M,D
Southern New Hampshire University M,D
Troy University M
Université de Sherbrooke D
University of Central Arkansas M,O
University of Colorado Denver M
University of Houston–Victoria M
University of Massachusetts Lowell M,O

*M—master's degree; P—first professional degree; D—doctorate; O—other advanced degree; *—Close-Up and/or Display in one of the other books in this series*

Institution	Degrees
University of Miami	M,D*
University of Minnesota, Twin Cities Campus	M
The University of North Carolina at Greensboro	M,D,O
University of Puerto Rico, Río Piedras	M
University of Southern California	M,D*
University of Southern Mississippi	M,D
University of Waterloo	M
Vanderbilt University	M,D*
Virginia Polytechnic Institute and State University	M,D,O
Western Illinois University	M,O
West Virginia University	M,D
Yale University	M*

ECONOMICS

Institution	Degrees
Albany State University	M
American University	M,D,O
The American University in Cairo	M
American University of Beirut	M
Andrews University	M
Arizona State University	D
Assumption College	M,O
Auburn University	M
Baylor University	M*
Bernard M. Baruch College of the City University of New York	M
Boston College	D*
Boston University	M,D*
Bowling Green State University	M*
Brandeis University	M
Brock University	M
Brooklyn College of the City University of New York	M
Brown University	D
Buffalo State College, State University of New York	M
California Lutheran University	M,O
California State Polytechnic University, Pomona	M
California State University, East Bay	M
California State University, Fullerton	M
California State University, Long Beach	M
California State University, Los Angeles	M*
Carleton University	M,D
Carnegie Mellon University	D*
Case Western Reserve University	M*
The Catholic University of America	M
Central European University	M,D
Central Michigan University	M
Chapman University	P,M
City College of the City University of New York	M
Claremont Graduate University	M,D,O
Clark Atlanta University	M
Clark University	D
Clemson University	M,D
Cleveland State University	M,D,O
Colorado State University	M,D
Columbia University	M,D*
Concordia University (Canada)	M,D,O
Cornell University	M,D*
Dalhousie University	M,D
DePaul University	M
Drexel University	M,D,O*
Duke University	M,D*
East Carolina University	M
Eastern Illinois University	M
Eastern Michigan University	M
East Tennessee State University	M,O
Emory University	D*
Florida Agricultural and Mechanical University	M
Florida Atlantic University	M
Florida International University	M,D
Florida State University	M,D
Fordham University	M,D,O
George Mason University	M,D,O*
Georgetown University	D
The George Washington University	M,D
Georgia Institute of Technology	M
Georgia State University	M,D
Graduate School and University Center of the City University of New York	D
Harvard University	D*
Hawai'i Pacific University	M*
Howard University	M,D
Hunter College of the City University of New York	M
Illinois State University	M
Indiana University Bloomington	M,D*
Indiana University–Purdue University Indianapolis	M
Instituto Tecnologico de Santo Domingo	M,O
Instituto Tecnológico y de Estudios Superiores de Monterrey, Campus Ciudad de México	M,D
Iowa State University of Science and Technology	M,D*
The Johns Hopkins University	D
Kansas State University	M,D*
Kent State University	M*
Lakehead University	M
Lehigh University	M,D
Long Island University, Brooklyn Campus	M
Louisiana State University and Agricultural and Mechanical College	M,D
Louisiana Tech University	M,D
Marquette University	M
Massachusetts Institute of Technology	M,D
McGill University	M,D
McMaster University	M,D
Memorial University of Newfoundland	M
Miami University	M
Michigan State University	M,D
Middle Tennessee State University	M,D
Mississippi State University	M,D
Morgan State University	M
Murray State University	M
National University	M
New Mexico State University	M,D
The New School: A University	M,D
New York University	M,D,O
North Carolina State University	M,D*
Northeastern University	M,D
Northern Illinois University	M,D
Northwestern University	M,D*
Oakland University	O
The Ohio State University	M,D
Ohio University	M*
Oklahoma State University	M,D*
Old Dominion University	M
Oregon State University	M,D
Pace University	M
Penn State University Park	M,D
Pepperdine University	M
Peru State College	M
Portland State University	M,D,O
Princeton University	D,O*
Purdue University	D
Rice University	M,D
Roosevelt University	M
Rutgers, The State University of New Jersey, Newark	M,D*
Rutgers, The State University of New Jersey, New Brunswick	M,D*
St. Cloud State University	M
San Diego State University	M
San Francisco State University	M
San Jose State University	M
Simon Fraser University	M,D
South Dakota State University	M
Southern Illinois University Carbondale	M,D
Southern Illinois University Edwardsville	M
Southern Methodist University	M,D
Stanford University	D
State University of New York at Binghamton	M,D
Stony Brook University, State University of New York	M,D
Suffolk University	M,D
Syracuse University	M,D,O*
Tarleton State University	M
Teachers College, Columbia University	M,D
Temple University	M,D*
Texas A&M University	M,D
Texas A&M University–Commerce	M
Texas Tech University	M,D*
Trinity College	M
Tufts University	M
Tulane University	M,D*
Universidad de las Américas–Puebla	M
Université de Moncton	M
Université de Montréal	M,D,O
Université de Sherbrooke	M
Université du Québec à Montréal	M,D
Université Laval	M,D
University at Albany, State University of New York	M,D,O
University at Buffalo, the State University of New York	M,D,O*
The University of Akron	M
The University of Alabama	M,D
University of Alaska Fairbanks	M
University of Alberta	M,D
The University of Arizona	M,D
University of Arkansas	M,D
The University of British Columbia	M,D
University of Calgary	M,D
University of California, Berkeley	D*
University of California, Davis	M,D
University of California, Irvine	M,D*
University of California, Los Angeles	M,D*
University of California, Riverside	M,D
University of California, San Diego	M,D*
University of California, Santa Barbara	M,D
University of California, Santa Cruz	D
University of Central Arkansas	M
University of Chicago	M,D
University of Cincinnati	M
University of Colorado Boulder	M,D*
University of Colorado Denver	M
University of Connecticut	M,D*
University of Delaware	M,D*
University of Denver	M
University of Florida	M,D*
University of Georgia	M,D
University of Guelph	M,D
University of Hawaii at Manoa	M,D
University of Houston	M,D
University of Idaho	M
University of Illinois at Chicago	M,D
University of Illinois at Urbana–Champaign	M,D
The University of Iowa	D*
The University of Kansas	M,D
University of Kentucky	M,D*
University of Lethbridge	M,D
The University of Manchester	D
University of Manitoba	M,D
University of Maryland, Baltimore County	M,D
University of Maryland, College Park	M,D
University of Massachusetts Amherst	M,D*
University of Massachusetts Lowell	M,O
University of Memphis	M,D
University of Miami	M,D*
University of Michigan	M,D*
University of Minnesota, Twin Cities Campus	D
University of Mississippi	M,D
University of Missouri	M,D*
University of Missouri–Kansas City	M,D*
University of Missouri–St. Louis	M
The University of Montana	M
University of Nebraska at Omaha	M
University of Nebraska–Lincoln	M,D*
University of Nevada, Las Vegas	M
University of Nevada, Reno	M*
University of New Brunswick Fredericton	M
University of New Hampshire	M,D
University of New Mexico	M,D*
University of New Orleans	D
The University of North Carolina at Chapel Hill	M,D*
The University of North Carolina at Charlotte	M
The University of North Carolina at Greensboro	D
University of North Florida	M
University of North Texas	M
University of Notre Dame	M,D*
University of Oklahoma	M,D*
University of Oregon	M,D
University of Ottawa	M,D*
University of Pennsylvania	M,D*
University of Pittsburgh	M,D*
University of Puerto Rico, Río Piedras	M
University of Regina	M,D,O
University of Rhode Island	M,D
University of Rochester	M,D
University of San Francisco	M
University of Saskatchewan	M,O
University of South Africa	M,D
University of South Carolina	M,D
University of Southern California	M,D*

University of Southern Mississippi	M,D
University of South Florida	M,D*
The University of Tennessee	M,D
The University of Texas at Arlington	M
The University of Texas at Austin	M,D
The University of Texas at Dallas	M,D*
The University of Texas at El Paso	M
The University of Texas at San Antonio	M*
The University of Texas–Pan American	D
The University of Toledo	M,D,O
University of Toronto	M,D
University of Utah	M,D*
University of Victoria	M,D
University of Virginia	M,D
University of Washington	M,D*
University of Waterloo	M,D
The University of Western Ontario	M,D
University of Windsor	M
University of Wisconsin–Madison	D*
University of Wisconsin–Milwaukee	M,D
University of Wyoming	M,D
Utah State University	M,D
Vanderbilt University	P,M,D*
Virginia Commonwealth University	M
Virginia Polytechnic Institute and State University	D
Virginia State University	M
Washington State University	M,D,O
Washington University in St. Louis	D*
Wayne State University	M,D*
Western Illinois University	M,O
Western Michigan University	M,D
West Texas A&M University	M
West Virginia University	M,D
Wichita State University	M
Wilfrid Laurier University	M,D
Wright State University	M
Yale University	M,D*
Yorktown University	M
York University	M,D*
Youngstown State University	M

EDUCATION—GENERAL

Abilene Christian University	M,O
Acádia University	M
Adams State College	M
Adelphi University	M,D,O*
Alabama Agricultural and Mechanical University	M,O
Alaska Pacific University	M
Albany State University	M,O
Albertus Magnus College	M
Albright College	M
Alcorn State University	M,O
Alfred University	M
Alliant International University–Fresno	M
Alliant International University–Irvine	M,O
Alliant International University–Los Angeles	M
Alliant International University–México City	M
Alliant International University–Sacramento	M
Alliant International University–San Diego	M,O
Alliant International University–San Francisco	M,O
Alvernia University	M
Alverno College	M
American College of Education	M
American InterContinental University Online	M
American International College	M,D,O
American Jewish University	M
American Public University System	M
American University	M,O
American University of Beirut	M
American University of Puerto Rico	M,O
Anderson University (IN)	M
Anderson University (SC)	M
Andrews University	M,D,O
Angelo State University	M
Anna Maria College	M,O
Antioch University Los Angeles	M
Antioch University Midwest	M
Antioch University New England	M
Antioch University Santa Barbara	M
Antioch University Seattle	M
Aquinas College	M
Arcadia University	M,D,O*
Argosy University, Atlanta	M,D,O*
Argosy University, Chicago	M,D,O*
Argosy University, Dallas	M,D*
Argosy University, Denver	M,D*
Argosy University, Hawai'i	M,D*
Argosy University, Inland Empire	M,D*
Argosy University, Los Angeles	M,D*
Argosy University, Nashville	M,D,O*
Argosy University, Orange County	M,D*
Argosy University, Phoenix	M,D,O*
Argosy University, Salt Lake City	M,D*
Argosy University, San Diego	M,D*
Argosy University, San Francisco Bay Area	M,D*
Argosy University, Sarasota	M,D,O*
Argosy University, Schaumburg	M,D,O*
Argosy University, Seattle	M,D*
Argosy University, Tampa	M,D,O*
Argosy University, Twin Cities	M,D,O*
Argosy University, Washington DC	M,D,O*
Arizona State University	M,D,O
Arkansas State University	M,D,O
Arkansas Tech University	M,O
Armstrong Atlantic State University	M
Ashland University	M,D
Athabasca University	M,O
Atlantic Union College	M
Auburn University	M,D,O
Auburn University Montgomery	M,O
Augsburg College	M
Augustana College	M
Augusta State University	M,O
Aurora University	M,D
Austin College	M
Austin Peay State University	M,O
Averett University	M
Avila University	M,O
Azusa Pacific University	M,D,O
Baker University	M,D
Baldwin-Wallace College	M
Ball State University	M,D,O
Bank Street College of Education	M
Baptist Bible College of Pennsylvania	M
Bard College	M
Barry University	M,D,O*
Bayamón Central University	M,O
Baylor University	M,D,O*
Belhaven University (MS)	M
Bellarmine University	M,D,O
Belmont University	M
Bemidji State University	M
Benedictine University	M
Bennington College	M
Berry College	M,O
Bethany University	M
Bethel College	M
Bethel University (MN)	M,D,O
Bishop's University	M,O
Bloomsburg University of Pennsylvania	M
Bluffton University	M
Boise State University	M,D
Boston College	M,D,O*
Boston University	M,D,O*
Bowie State University	M
Bradley University	M,D,O
Brandon University	M,O
Brenau University	M,O
Bridgewater State University	M,O
Brigham Young University	M,D,O*
Brock University	M,D
Brooklyn College of the City University of New York	M,O
Brown University	M
Bucknell University	M
Buena Vista University	M
Butler University	M
Cabrini College	M
California Baptist University	M
California Coast University	M,D
California Lutheran University	M,D
California Polytechnic State University, San Luis Obispo	M
California State Polytechnic University, Pomona	M
California State University, Bakersfield	M,O
California State University, Chico	M
California State University, Dominguez Hills	M,O*
California State University, East Bay	M
California State University, Fresno	M,D
California State University, Long Beach	M,D
California State University, Los Angeles	M,D*
California State University, Monterey Bay	M
California State University, Northridge	M,D
California State University, Sacramento	M
California State University, San Bernardino	M,D
California State University, San Marcos	M
California State University, Stanislaus	M,D,O
California University of Pennsylvania	M
Calvin College	M
Cambridge College	M,D,O
Cameron University	M
Campbellsville University	M
Campbell University	M
Canisius College	M,O
Capella University	M,D,O
Cardinal Stritch University	M,D
Caribbean University	M,D
Carnegie Mellon University	M,D*
Carroll University	M
Carson-Newman College	M
Carthage College	M,O
Castleton State College	M,O
Catawba College	M
The Catholic University of America	M,D,O
Cedar Crest College	M
Cedarville University	M
Centenary College	M
Centenary College of Louisiana	M
Central Connecticut State University	M,D,O
Central Methodist University	M
Central Michigan University	M,D,O
Central State University	M
Central Washington University	M
Chadron State College	M,O
Chaminade University of Honolulu	M
Champlain College	M
Chapman University	M,D,O
Charleston Southern University	M
Chatham University	M
Chestnut Hill College	M*
Cheyney University of Pennsylvania	M,O
Chicago State University	M,D
Christian Brothers University	M
Christopher Newport University	M
The Citadel, The Military College of South Carolina	M,O
City College of the City University of New York	M,O
City University of Seattle	M,O
Claremont Graduate University	M,D,O
Clarion University of Pennsylvania	M,O
Clark Atlanta University	M,D,O
Clarke University	M
Clark University	M
Clayton State University	M
Clemson University	M,D,O
Cleveland State University	M,D,O
Coastal Carolina University	M
Coe College	M
The College at Brockport, State University of New York	M,O
College of Charleston	M,O
The College of Idaho	M
College of Mount St. Joseph	M
College of Mount Saint Vincent	M,O
The College of New Jersey	M,O
The College of New Rochelle	M,O
College of Notre Dame of Maryland	M
College of Saint Elizabeth	M,D,O
College of St. Joseph	M
College of Saint Mary	M
The College of Saint Rose	M,O
The College of St. Scholastica	M,O
College of Staten Island of the City University of New York	M,O
College of the Humanities and Sciences, Harrison Middleton University	M,D
The College of William and Mary	M,D,O
Collège universitaire de Saint-Boniface	M
Colorado Christian University	M
The Colorado College	M

*M—master's degree; P—first professional degree; D—doctorate; O—other advanced degree; *—Close-Up and/or Display in one of the other books in this series*

Colorado State University M,D
Colorado State University–Pueblo M
Columbia College (MO) M
Columbia College (SC) M
Columbia College Chicago M
Columbia International University M,D,O
Columbus State University M,D,O
Concordia College M
Concordia University (CA) M
Concordia University (OR) M
Concordia University (Canada) M,D,O
Concordia University Chicago M
Concordia University, Nebraska M
Concordia University, St. Paul M,O
Concordia University Texas M
Concordia University Wisconsin M
Converse College M,O
Coppin State University M
Corban University M
Cornell University M,D*
Cornerstone University M,O
Covenant College M
Creighton University M
Cumberland University M
Curry College M,O
Daemen College M
Dakota State University M*
Dakota Wesleyan University M
Dallas Baptist University M
Defiance College M
Delaware State University M,D
Delta State University M,D,O
DePaul University M,D
DeSales University M
Doane College M
Dominican College M
Dominican University M
Dominican University of California M,O
Dordt College M
Dowling College M,D,O
Drake University M,D,O
Drew University M
Drexel University M,D*
Drury University M
Duke University M*
Duquesne University M,D,O
D'Youville College M,O*
Earlham College M
East Carolina University M,D,O
East Central University M
Eastern Connecticut State University M
Eastern Illinois University M,O
Eastern Kentucky University M
Eastern Mennonite University M
Eastern Michigan University M,D,O
Eastern Nazarene College M,O
Eastern New Mexico University M
Eastern Oregon University M
Eastern University M,O
Eastern Washington University M
East Stroudsburg University of Pennsylvania M
East Tennessee State University M,D,O
Edgewood College M,D,O
Edinboro University of Pennsylvania M,O
Elizabeth City State University M
Ellis University M
Elms College M,O
Elon University M
Embry-Riddle Aeronautical University–Worldwide M
Emmanuel College (United States) M,O
Emory & Henry College M
Emory University M,D,O*
Emporia State University M,O
Evangel University M
The Evergreen State College M
Fairfield University M,O
Fairleigh Dickinson University, College at Florham M,O
Fairleigh Dickinson University, Metropolitan Campus M,O
Fairmont State University M
Faulkner University M
Felician College M,O*
Ferris State University M
Florida Agricultural and Mechanical University M,D
Florida Atlantic University M,D,O
Florida Gulf Coast University M
Florida International University M,D,O
Florida Memorial University M
Florida Southern College M
Florida State University M,D,O
Fontbonne University M
Fordham University M,D,O
Fort Hays State University M,O
Franciscan University of Steubenville M
Francis Marion University M
Freed-Hardeman University M,O
Fresno Pacific University M
Friends University M
Frostburg State University M
Furman University M,O
Gallaudet University M,D,O
Gannon University M,D,O
Gardner-Webb University M,D
Geneva College M
George Fox University M,D,O
George Mason University M,D*
Georgetown College M
The George Washington University M,D,O
Georgia College & State University M,O
Georgian Court University M
Georgia Southern University M,D,O
Georgia Southwestern State University M,O
Georgia State University M,D,O
Goddard College M
Gonzaga University M
Gordon College M
Goucher College M
Governors State University M
Graceland University (IA) M
Grambling State University M,D
Grand Canyon University M,D
Grand Valley State University M,O
Grand View University M
Gratz College M
Greensboro College M
Greenville College M
Gwynedd-Mercy College M
Hamline University M,D
Hampton University M
Hannibal-LaGrange University M
Harding University M,O
Hardin-Simmons University M
Harvard University M,D*
Hastings College M
Hebrew College M,O
Hebrew Union College–Jewish Institute of Religion (NY) M
Heidelberg University M
Henderson State University M,O
Heritage University M
High Point University M
Hodges University M
Hofstra University M,D,O
Hollins University M
Holy Family University M*
Holy Names University M,O
Hood College M,O
Hope International University M
Houston Baptist University M
Howard University M,D
Humboldt State University M
Hunter College of the City University of New York M,O
Huntington University M
Idaho State University M,D,O
Illinois State University M,D
Indiana State University M,D,O
Indiana University Bloomington M,D,O*
Indiana University East M
Indiana University Kokomo M
Indiana University Northwest M
Indiana University of Pennsylvania M,D,O
Indiana University–Purdue University Fort Wayne M,O
Indiana University–Purdue University Indianapolis M,O
Indiana University South Bend M
Indiana University Southeast M
Institute for Christian Studies M,D
Instituto Tecnologico de Santo Domingo M,O
Instituto Tecnológico y de Estudios Superiores de Monterrey, Campus Central de Veracruz M
Instituto Tecnológico y de Estudios Superiores de Monterrey, Campus Ciudad de México M,D
Instituto Tecnológico y de Estudios Superiores de Monterrey, Campus Ciudad Juárez M
Instituto Tecnológico y de Estudios Superiores de Monterrey, Campus Ciudad Obregón M
Instituto Tecnológico y de Estudios Superiores de Monterrey, Campus Estado de México M,D
Instituto Tecnológico y de Estudios Superiores de Monterrey, Campus Irapuato M,D
Instituto Tecnológico y de Estudios Superiores de Monterrey, Campus Sonora Norte M
Inter American University of Puerto Rico, Arecibo Campus M
Inter American University of Puerto Rico, Barranquitas Campus M
Inter American University of Puerto Rico, Metropolitan Campus M,D
International Baptist College M
Iona College M
Jackson State University M,D,O
Jacksonville State University M,O
Jacksonville University M,O
John Carroll University M
John F. Kennedy University M
The Johns Hopkins University M,D,O
Johnson & Wales University M
Johnson State College M,O
Johnson University M
Jones International University M
Judson University M
Kansas State University M,D*
Kaplan University, Davenport Campus M
Kean University M
Keene State College M,O
Keiser University M
Kennesaw State University M,D,O
Kent State University M,D,O*
Kutztown University of Pennsylvania M,O
LaGrange College M
Lake Erie College M
Lake Forest College M
Lakehead University M,D
Lakeland College M
Lamar University M,D,O
Lander University M
Langston University M
La Salle University M
Lasell College M
La Sierra University M,D,O
Lee University M,O
Lehigh University M,D,O
Lehman College of the City University of New York M
Le Moyne College M,O
Lenoir-Rhyne University M
Lesley University M,D,O
LeTourneau University M
Lewis University M,D,O
Liberty University M,D,O
Lincoln Memorial University M,D,O
Lindenwood University M,D,O
Lipscomb University M,D
Lock Haven University of Pennsylvania M
Long Island University at Riverhead M,O
Long Island University, Brentwood Campus M
Long Island University, Brooklyn Campus M,O
Long Island University, C.W. Post Campus M,D,O
Long Island University, Westchester Graduate Campus M,O
Longwood University M
Louisiana State University and Agricultural and Mechanical College M,D,O
Louisiana State University in Shreveport M
Louisiana Tech University M,D
Lourdes College M
Loyola Marymount University M,D
Loyola University Chicago M,D,O
Loyola University Maryland M,O
Lynchburg College M
Lyndon State College M
Lynn University M,D
Madonna University M
Maharishi University of Management M
Malone University M
Manchester College M
Manhattan College M,O
Manhattanville College M,D*
Mansfield University of Pennsylvania M
Marian University (IN) M
Marian University (WI) M,D
Marietta College M
Marist College M,O
Marlboro College M
Marquette University M,D,O

Marshall University M,D,O
Martin Luther College M
Mary Baldwin College M
Marygrove College M
Marylhurst University M
Marymount University M
Maryville University of Saint Louis M,D
Marywood University M
Massachusetts College of Art and Design M
Massachusetts College of Liberal Arts M
McGill University M,D,O
McKendree University M
Medaille College M
Memorial University of Newfoundland M,D,O
Mercer University M,D,O
Mercy College M,O
Meredith College M
Merrimack College M,O
Mesa State College M
Miami University M,D,O
Michigan State University M,D,O
MidAmerica Nazarene University M
Middle Tennessee State University M,D,O
Midwestern State University M
Millersville University of Pennsylvania M
Milligan College M
Mills College M,D
Minnesota State University Mankato M,D,O
Minnesota State University Moorhead M,O
Misericordia University M
Mississippi College M,D,O
Mississippi State University M,D,O
Mississippi University for Women M
Mississippi Valley State University M
Missouri Baptist University M,O
Missouri Southern State University M
Molloy College M,O
Monmouth University M,O
Montana State University M,D,O
Montana State University Billings M,O
Montana State University–Northern M
Montclair State University M,D,O
Montreat College M
Morehead State University M,O
Morgan State University M,D
Morningside College M
Mount Aloysius College M
Mount Mary College M
Mount Mercy University M
Mount Saint Mary College M,O
Mount St. Mary's College M
Mount St. Mary's University M
Mount Saint Vincent University M
Mount Vernon Nazarene University M
Multnomah University M
Murray State University M,D,O
Muskingum University M
Naropa University M
National-Louis University M,D,O
National University M
Nazareth College of Rochester M
Neumann University M
New England College M
Newman University M
New Mexico Highlands University M
New Mexico State University M,D,O
New York Institute of Technology M,O
New York University M,D,O
Niagara University M,O
Nicholls State University M
Nipissing University M,O
Norfolk State University M
North Carolina Agricultural and Technical State University M
North Carolina Central University M
North Carolina State University M,D,O*
North Central College M
Northcentral University M,D,O
North Dakota State University M,D,O
Northeastern Illinois University M
Northeastern State University M
Northern Arizona University M,D,O
Northern Illinois University M,D,O
Northern Kentucky University M,D,O
Northern Michigan University M,O
Northern State University M
North Georgia College & State University M,O
North Park University M
Northwest Christian University M
Northwestern Oklahoma State University M
Northwestern State University of Louisiana M,O
Northwestern University M,D*
Northwest Missouri State University M,O
Northwest Nazarene University M
Northwest University M
Notre Dame College (OH) M,O
Notre Dame de Namur University M,O
Nova Southeastern University M,D,O*
Nyack College M
Oakland City University M,D
Oakland University M,D,O
Oberlin College M
Occidental College M
Oglethorpe University M
Ohio Dominican University M
The Ohio State University M,D
The Ohio State University at Lima M
The Ohio State University at Marion M
The Ohio State University–Mansfield Campus M
The Ohio State University–Newark Campus M
Ohio University M,D*
Ohio Valley University M
Oklahoma City University M
Oklahoma State University M,D,O*
Old Dominion University M,D,O
Olivet College M
Olivet Nazarene University M
Oral Roberts University M,D
Oregon State University M,D
Oregon State University–Cascades M
Ottawa University M
Otterbein University M
Our Lady of Holy Cross College M
Our Lady of the Lake University of San Antonio M,D
Pace University M,O
Pacific Lutheran University M
Pacific Union College M
Pacific University M
Palm Beach Atlantic University M
Park University M
Penn State Great Valley M
Penn State Harrisburg M,D
Penn State University Park M,D
Pepperdine University M,D
Peru State College M
Philadelphia Biblical University M
Piedmont College M,D,O
Pittsburg State University M,O
Plymouth State University O
Point Loma Nazarene University M,O
Point Park University M
Pontifical Catholic University of Puerto Rico M,D
Portland State University M,D
Post University M
Prairie View A&M University M,D
Prescott College M,D
Providence College M
Purdue University M,D,O
Purdue University Calumet M
Purdue University North Central M
Queens College of the City University of New York M,O
Queen's University at Kingston M,D
Queens University of Charlotte M
Quincy University M
Quinnipiac University M
Radford University M
Randolph College M
Regent University M,D,O
Regis College (MA) M
Regis University M,O
Reinhardt University M
Rhode Island College D
Rice University M
The Richard Stockton College of New Jersey M
Rider University M,O
Rivier College M,D,O
Robert Morris University M,D,O
Roberts Wesleyan College M,O
Rockford College M,O
Rockhurst University M
Roger Williams University M
Rollins College M
Roosevelt University M,D
Rowan University M,D,O
Rutgers, The State University of New Jersey, New Brunswick M,D*
Sacred Heart University M,O
Sage Graduate School M,D,O
Saginaw Valley State University M,O
St. Ambrose University M
St. Bonaventure University M,O
St. Catherine University M
St. Cloud State University M,D,O
St. Edward's University M,O
Saint Francis University M
St. Francis Xavier University M
St. John Fisher College M,D,O
St. John's University (NY) M,D,O
Saint Joseph College M
St. Joseph's College, New York M*
Saint Joseph's College of Maine M
Saint Joseph's University M,D
St. Lawrence University M,O
Saint Leo University M,O
Saint Louis University M,D
Saint Martin's University M
Saint Mary's College of California M
St. Mary's College of Maryland M
St. Mary's University (United States) M,O
Saint Mary's University of Minnesota M,O
Saint Michael's College M,O
St. Norbert College M
Saint Peter's College M,D,O
St. Thomas Aquinas College M,O
St. Thomas University M,D,O
Saint Vincent College M
Saint Xavier University M,O
Salem College M
Salem International University M
Salisbury University M
Samford University M,D,O
Sam Houston State University M,D
San Diego State University M,D
San Francisco State University M,D,O
San Jose State University M,O
Santa Clara University M,O
Santa Fe University of Art and Design M
Sarah Lawrence College M
Savannah College of Art and Design M
Schreiner University M
Seattle University M,D,O
Seton Hall University M,D,O
Seton Hill University M
Shawnee State University M
Shenandoah University M,D,O
Shippensburg University of Pennsylvania M,O
Siena Heights University M
Sierra Nevada College M
Silver Lake College M
Simmons College M,D,O
Simon Fraser University M,D
Simpson College M
Simpson University M
Sinte Gleska University M
Slippery Rock University of Pennsylvania M
Smith College M
Sonoma State University M,D
South Carolina State University M,D,O
South Dakota State University M,D
Southeastern Louisiana University M,D
Southeastern Oklahoma State University M
Southeastern University (FL) M
Southern Adventist University M
Southern Arkansas University–Magnolia M
Southern Connecticut State University M,D,O
Southern Illinois University Carbondale M,D
Southern Illinois University Edwardsville M,D,O
Southern Methodist University M,D,O
Southern Nazarene University M
Southern New Hampshire University M,O
Southern Oregon University M
Southern University and Agricultural and Mechanical College M,D
Southern Utah University M
Southern Wesleyan University M
Southwest Baptist University M,O
Southwestern Adventist University M
Southwestern Assemblies of God University M
Southwestern College (KS) M

*M—master's degree; P—first professional degree; D—doctorate; O—other advanced degree; *—Close-Up and/or Display in one of the other books in this series*

Institution	Degrees
Southwestern Oklahoma State University	M
Southwest Minnesota State University	M
Spalding University	M,D
Spring Arbor University	M
Springfield College	M
Spring Hill College	M
Stanford University	M,D
State University of New York at Binghamton	M,D
State University of New York at Fredonia	M,O
State University of New York at New Paltz	M,O
State University of New York at Oswego	M,O
State University of New York College at Cortland	M,O
State University of New York College at Geneseo	M
State University of New York College at Oneonta	M,O
State University of New York Empire State College	M
Stephen F. Austin State University	M,D
Stetson University	M,O
Strayer University	M
Suffolk University	M,O
Sul Ross State University	M
Sweet Briar College	M
Syracuse University	M,D,O*
Tarleton State University	M,D,O
Teacher Education University	M
Teachers College, Columbia University	M,D,O
Temple University	M,D*
Tennessee State University	M,D,O
Tennessee Technological University	M,D,O
Tennessee Temple University	M
Texas A&M International University	M
Texas A&M University	M,D
Texas A&M University–Commerce	M,D
Texas A&M University–Corpus Christi	M,D
Texas A&M University–Kingsville	M,D
Texas A&M University–Texarkana	M
Texas Christian University	M,D,O
Texas Southern University	M,D
Texas State University–San Marcos	M,D,O
Texas Tech University	M,D*
Texas Wesleyan University	M,D
Texas Woman's University	M,D
Thomas More College	M
Thomas University	M
Thompson Rivers University	M
Touro University	P,M
Towson University	M
Trevecca Nazarene University	M,D
Trinity International University	M
Trinity University	M
Trinity (Washington) University	M
Troy University	M,O
Truman State University	M
Tufts University	M,D,O
TUI University	M,D
Tusculum College	M
Union College (KY)	M
Union Graduate College	M,O
Union Institute & University	M,D,O
Union University	M,D,O
Universidad Autonoma de Guadalajara	M,D
Universidad de las Americas, A.C.	M
Universidad de las Américas–Puebla	M
Universidad del Turabo	M,D,O
Universidad FLET	M
Universidad Metropolitana	M
Université de Moncton	M
Université de Montréal	M,D,O
Université de Sherbrooke	M,O
Université du Québec à Chicoutimi	M,D
Université du Québec à Montréal	M,D,O
Université du Québec à Rimouski	M,D,O
Université du Québec à Trois-Rivières	M,D
Université du Québec en Abitibi-Témiscamingue	M,D,O
Université du Québec en Outaouais	M,D,O
Université Laval	M,D,O
University at Albany, State University of New York	M,D,O
University at Buffalo, the State University of New York	M,D,O*
The University of Akron	M,D
The University of Alabama at Birmingham	M,D,O*
University of Alaska Anchorage	M,O
University of Alaska Fairbanks	M,D,O
University of Alaska Southeast	M
The University of Arizona	M,D,O
University of Arkansas	M,D,O
University of Arkansas at Little Rock	M,D,O
University of Arkansas at Monticello	M
University of Arkansas at Pine Bluff	M
University of Bridgeport	M,D,O
The University of British Columbia	M,D,O
University of California, Berkeley	M,D,O*
University of California, Davis	M,D
University of California, Irvine	M,D*
University of California, Los Angeles	M,D*
University of California, Riverside	M,D
University of California, San Diego	M,D*
University of California, Santa Barbara	M,D
University of California, Santa Cruz	M,D
University of Central Arkansas	M,O
University of Central Missouri	M,D,O
University of Central Oklahoma	M
University of Cincinnati	M,D,O
University of Colorado at Colorado Springs	M,D
University of Colorado Boulder	M,D*
University of Colorado Denver	M,D,O
University of Connecticut	M,D,O*
University of Dayton	M,D,O
University of Delaware	M,D,O*
University of Denver	M,D,O
University of Detroit Mercy	M
University of Evansville	M
The University of Findlay	M
University of Florida	M,D,O*
University of Georgia	M,D,O
University of Great Falls	M
University of Guam	M
University of Hartford	M,D,O
University of Hawaii at Hilo	M
University of Hawaii at Manoa	M,D,O
University of Houston	M,D
University of Houston–Clear Lake	M,D
University of Houston–Victoria	M
University of Idaho	M,D,O
University of Illinois at Chicago	M,D
University of Illinois at Springfield	M
University of Illinois at Urbana–Champaign	M,D,O
University of Indianapolis	M
The University of Iowa	M,D,O*
The University of Kansas	M,D,O
University of Kentucky	M,D,O*
University of La Verne	M,O
University of Lethbridge	M,D
University of Louisiana at Lafayette	M,D*
University of Louisiana at Monroe	M,D,O
University of Louisville	M,D,O
University of Maine	M,D,O
University of Maine at Farmington	M
The University of Manchester	M,D
University of Manitoba	M,D
University of Mary	M
University of Mary Hardin-Baylor	M,D
University of Maryland, Baltimore County	M,D,O
University of Maryland, College Park	M,D,O
University of Maryland Eastern Shore	M
University of Maryland University College	M
University of Mary Washington	M
University of Massachusetts Amherst	M,D,O*
University of Massachusetts Boston	M,D,O
University of Massachusetts Dartmouth	M,O
University of Massachusetts Lowell	M,D,O
University of Memphis	M,D,O
University of Miami	M,D,O*
University of Michigan	M,D*
University of Michigan–Dearborn	M,D
University of Michigan–Flint	M
University of Minnesota, Duluth	D
University of Minnesota, Twin Cities Campus	M,D,O
University of Mississippi	M,D,O
University of Missouri	M,D,O*
University of Missouri–Kansas City	M,D,O*
University of Missouri–St. Louis	M,D,O
University of Mobile	M
The University of Montana	M,D,O
University of Montevallo	M,O
University of Nebraska at Kearney	M,O
University of Nebraska at Omaha	M,D,O
University of Nevada, Las Vegas	M,D,O
University of Nevada, Reno	M,D,O*
University of New Brunswick Fredericton	M,D
University of New England	M,O
University of New Hampshire	M,D,O
University of New Haven	M
University of New Mexico	M,O*
University of New Orleans	M,D,O
University of North Alabama	M,O
The University of North Carolina at Chapel Hill	M,D*
The University of North Carolina at Greensboro	M,D,O
The University of North Carolina at Pembroke	M
The University of North Carolina Wilmington	M,D
University of North Dakota	M,D,O
University of Northern British Columbia	M,D,O
University of Northern Colorado	M,D,O
University of Northern Iowa	M,D,O
University of North Florida	M,D
University of North Texas	M,D,O
University of Notre Dame	M*
University of Oklahoma	M,D,O*
University of Oregon	M,D
University of Ottawa	M,D,O*
University of Pennsylvania	M,D*
University of Phoenix	M,D,O
University of Phoenix–Austin Campus	M
University of Phoenix–Central Florida Campus	M
University of Phoenix–Central Massachusetts Campus	M
University of Phoenix–Central Valley Campus	M
University of Phoenix–Chattanooga Campus	M
University of Phoenix–Dallas Campus	M
University of Phoenix–Denver Campus	M
University of Phoenix–Hawaii Campus	M
University of Phoenix–Houston Campus	M
University of Phoenix–Idaho Campus	M
University of Phoenix–Indianapolis Campus	M
University of Phoenix–Kansas City Campus	M
University of Phoenix–Las Vegas Campus	M
University of Phoenix–Louisiana Campus	M
University of Phoenix–Madison Campus	D,O
University of Phoenix–Memphis Campus	M
University of Phoenix–Metro Detroit Campus	M
University of Phoenix–Milwaukee Campus	M,D,O
University of Phoenix–Nashville Campus	M
University of Phoenix–New Mexico Campus	M
University of Phoenix–Northern Nevada Campus	M
University of Phoenix–Northern Virginia Campus	M
University of Phoenix–North Florida Campus	M
University of Phoenix–Omaha Campus	M
University of Phoenix–Oregon Campus	M
University of Phoenix–Phoenix Campus	M
University of Phoenix–Puerto Rico Campus	M
University of Phoenix–Richmond Campus	M
University of Phoenix–Sacramento Valley Campus	M,O
University of Phoenix–San Diego Campus	M

Institution	Degrees
University of Phoenix–Southern Arizona Campus	M,O
University of Phoenix–Southern California Campus	M
University of Phoenix–Southern Colorado Campus	M,O
University of Phoenix–South Florida Campus	M
University of Phoenix–Springfield Campus	M
University of Phoenix–Utah Campus	M
University of Phoenix–Vancouver Campus	M
University of Phoenix–Washington D.C. Campus	M,D,O
University of Phoenix–West Florida Campus	M
University of Pittsburgh	M,D*
University of Portland	M
University of Prince Edward Island	M
University of Puerto Rico, Río Piedras	M,D
University of Puget Sound	M
University of Redlands	M,D,O
University of Regina	M,D,O
University of Rhode Island	M,D
University of Rio Grande	M
University of Rochester	
University of St. Francis (IL)	M
University of Saint Francis (IN)	M
University of Saint Mary	M
University of St. Thomas (MN)	M,D,O
University of St. Thomas (TX)	M*
University of San Diego	M,D,O
University of San Francisco	M,D
University of Saskatchewan	M,D,O
The University of Scranton	M
University of Sioux Falls	M,O
University of South Africa	M,D
University of South Alabama	M,D,O
University of South Carolina	M,D,O
University of South Carolina Upstate	M
The University of South Dakota	M,D,O
University of Southern California	M,D*
University of Southern Indiana	M
University of Southern Maine	M,D,O
University of Southern Mississippi	M,D,O
University of South Florida	M,D,O*
The University of Tampa	M
The University of Tennessee	M,D,O
The University of Tennessee at Chattanooga	M,D,O
The University of Tennessee at Martin	M
The University of Texas at Arlington	M
The University of Texas at Austin	M,D
The University of Texas at Brownsville	M
The University of Texas at El Paso	M,D
The University of Texas of the Permian Basin	M
The University of Texas–Pan American	M,D
University of the Cumberlands	M,D,O
University of the District of Columbia	M
University of the Incarnate Word	M,D
University of the Pacific	M,D,O
University of the Sacred Heart	M,O
University of the Southwest	M
University of the Virgin Islands	M
The University of Toledo	M,D,O
University of Toronto	M,D
University of Tulsa	M
University of Utah	M,D*
University of Vermont	M,D
University of Victoria	M,D
University of Virginia	M,D,O
University of Washington	M,D,O*
University of Washington, Bothell	M
University of Washington, Tacoma	M
The University of West Alabama	M
The University of Western Ontario	M
University of West Georgia	M,D,O
University of Windsor	M,D
University of Wisconsin–Eau Claire	M
University of Wisconsin–Green Bay	M
University of Wisconsin–La Crosse	M
University of Wisconsin–Madison	M,D,O*
University of Wisconsin–Milwaukee	M,D,O
University of Wisconsin–Oshkosh	M
University of Wisconsin–Platteville	M
University of Wisconsin–River Falls	M
University of Wisconsin–Stevens Point	M
University of Wisconsin–Stout	M,O
University of Wisconsin–Superior	M
University of Wisconsin–Whitewater	M*
Upper Iowa University	M
Urbana University	M
Ursuline College	M
Utah State University	M,D,O
Utah Valley University	M
Utica College	M,O
Valley City State University	M
Valparaiso University	M
Vanderbilt University	M,D*
Vanguard University of Southern California	M
Villanova University	M
Virginia Commonwealth University	M,D,O
Virginia State University	M,O
Viterbo University	M
Wagner College	M
Wake Forest University	M
Walden University	M,D,O
Walla Walla University	M
Walsh University	M
Warner Pacific College	M
Warner University	M
Washburn University	M
Washington State University	M,D,O
Washington State University Spokane	M,O
Washington State University Tri-Cities	M,D
Washington State University Vancouver	M,D
Washington University in St. Louis	M,D*
Wayland Baptist University	M
Waynesburg University	M,D
Wayne State College	M,O
Wayne State University	M,D,O*
Weber State University	M
Webster University	M,O
Wesleyan College	M
Wesley College	M
West Chester University of Pennsylvania	M,O
Western Carolina University	M,D,O
Western Connecticut State University	M,D
Western Governors University	M,O
Western Illinois University	M,D,O
Western Michigan University	M,D,O
Western New Mexico University	M
Western Oregon University	M
Western State College of Colorado	M*
Western Washington University	M
Westfield State University	M,O
West Liberty University	M
Westminster College (PA)	M,O
Westminster College (UT)	M
West Texas A&M University	M
West Virginia University	M,D
West Virginia Wesleyan College	M
Wheaton College	M
Wheelock College	M
Whittier College	M
Whitworth University	M
Wichita State University	M,D,O
Widener University	M,D
Wilkes University	M,D
Willamette University	M
William Carey University	M,O
William Howard Taft University	M
William Paterson University of New Jersey	M
Wilmington College	M
Wilmington University	M
Wilson College	M
Wingate University	M
Winona State University	M
Winthrop University	M
Wittenberg University	M
Worcester State University	M,O
Wright State University	M,O
Xavier University	M
Xavier University of Louisiana	M
York College of Pennsylvania	M
York University	M,D*
Youngstown State University	M,D

EDUCATIONAL LEADERSHIP AND ADMINISTRATION

Institution	Degrees
Abilene Christian University	M,O
Acadia University	M
Adelphi University	M,O*
Alabama Agricultural and Mechanical University	M,O
Alabama State University	M,D,O
Albany State University	M,O
Alliant International University–Fresno	D
Alliant International University–Irvine	M,D,O
Alliant International University–Los Angeles	M,D,O
Alliant International University–San Diego	M,D,O
Alliant International University–San Francisco	M,D,O
Alverno College	M
American College of Education	M
American InterContinental University Online	M
American International College	M,D,O
American Public University System	M
Andrews University	M,D,O
Angelo State University	M,O
Antioch University New England	M
Appalachian State University	M,D,O
Arcadia University	M,D,O*
Argosy University, Atlanta	M,D,O*
Argosy University, Chicago	M,D,O*
Argosy University, Dallas	M,D*
Argosy University, Denver	M,D*
Argosy University, Hawai'i	M,D*
Argosy University, Inland Empire	M,D*
Argosy University, Los Angeles	M,D*
Argosy University, Nashville	M,D,O*
Argosy University, Orange County	M,D*
Argosy University, Phoenix	M,D,O*
Argosy University, Salt Lake City	M,D*
Argosy University, San Diego	M,D*
Argosy University, San Francisco Bay Area	M,D*
Argosy University, Sarasota	M,D,O*
Argosy University, Schaumburg	M,D,O*
Argosy University, Seattle	M,D*
Argosy University, Tampa	M,D,O*
Argosy University, Twin Cities	M,D,O*
Argosy University, Washington DC	M,D,O*
Arizona State University	M,D
Arkansas State University	M,D,O
Arkansas Tech University	M,O
Asbury University	M
Ashland University	M,D
Auburn University	M,D,O
Auburn University Montgomery	M,O
Augusta State University	M,O
Aurora University	M,D
Austin Peay State University	M,O
Azusa Pacific University	M,D
Baldwin-Wallace College	M
Ball State University	M,D,O
Bank Street College of Education	M
Barry University	M,D,O*
Bayamón Central University	M,O
Baylor University	M,O*
Bay Path College	M
Bellarmine University	M,D,O
Benedictine College	M
Benedictine University	M,D
Bernard M. Baruch College of the City University of New York	M,O
Berry College	O
Bethany University	M
Bethel University (MN)	M,D,O
Bethel University (TN)	M
Bob Jones University	P,M,D,O
Boise State University	M,D
Boston College	M,D,O*
Boston University	M,D,O*
Bowie State University	M,D
Bowling Green State University	M,D,O*
Bradley University	M
Brandon University	M,O
Bridgewater State University	M,O
Brigham Young University	M,D*

*M—master's degree; P—first professional degree; D—doctorate; O—other advanced degree; *—Close-Up and/or Display in one of the other books in this series*

Brooklyn College of the City University of New York M
Bucknell University M
Buffalo State College, State University of New York O
Butler University M
Caldwell College M
California Baptist University M
California Coast University M,D
California Lutheran University M,D
California State University, Bakersfield M
California State University Channel Islands M
California State University, Dominguez Hills M*
California State University, East Bay M,D
California State University, Fresno M,D
California State University, Fullerton M,D
California State University, Long Beach M,D
California State University, Northridge M,D
California State University, Sacramento M
California State University, San Bernardino M,D
California State University, Stanislaus M,D
California University of Pennsylvania M
Calumet College of Saint Joseph M
Calvin College M
Cambridge College M,D,O
Cameron University M
Campbell University M
Canisius College M,O
Capella University M,D,O
Cardinal Stritch University M,D
Caribbean University M,D
Carlow University M
Carson-Newman College M
Carthage College M,O
Castleton State College M,O
The Catholic University of America M,D,O
Centenary College M
Centenary College of Louisiana M
Central Connecticut State University M,D,O
Central Michigan University M,D,O
Chadron State College M,O
Chapman University M,O
Charleston Southern University M
Chestnut Hill College M*
Cheyney University of Pennsylvania M,O
Chicago State University M,D
Christian Brothers University M
The Citadel, The Military College of South Carolina M,O
City College of the City University of New York M,O
City University of Seattle M,O
Claremont Graduate University M,D,O
Clark Atlanta University M,D,O
Clarke University M
Clearwater Christian College M
Clemson University M,D,O
Cleveland State University M,D,O
Coastal Carolina University M
The College at Brockport, State University of New York O
College of Mount St. Joseph M
The College of New Jersey M,O
The College of New Rochelle M,O
College of Notre Dame of Maryland M,D
College of Saint Elizabeth M,D,O
College of Saint Mary M
The College of Saint Rose M,O
College of Staten Island of the City University of New York O
The College of William and Mary M,D
Colorado State University M,D
Columbia International University M,D,O
Columbus State University M,D,O
Concordia University (CA) M
Concordia University (MI) M
Concordia University (OR) M
Concordia University Chicago M,D,O
Concordia University, Nebraska M
Concordia University, St. Paul M,O
Concordia University Wisconsin M
Concord University M
Converse College M,O
Creighton University M
Dakota Wesleyan University M
Dallas Baptist University M
Delaware State University M,D
Delaware Valley College M
Delta State University M,D,O
DePaul University M,D
Doane College M
Dominican University M
Dowling College M,D,O
Drexel University M,D*
Duquesne University M,D,O
D'Youville College D*
East Carolina University M,D,O
Eastern Illinois University M,O
Eastern Kentucky University M
Eastern Michigan University M,D,O
Eastern Nazarene College M,O
Eastern New Mexico University M
Eastern Washington University M
East Tennessee State University M,D,O
Edgewood College M,D,O
Edinboro University of Pennsylvania M,O
Elizabeth City State University M
Ellis University M
Elmhurst College M
Emmanuel College (United States) M,O
Emporia State University M
Evangel University M
Fairleigh Dickinson University, College at Florham M
Fairleigh Dickinson University, Metropolitan Campus M
Fairmont State University M
Fayetteville State University M,D
Felician College M,O*
Ferris State University M,D
Fielding Graduate University M,D,O
Fitchburg State University M,O
Florida Agricultural and Mechanical University M,D
Florida Atlantic University M,D,O
Florida Gulf Coast University M
Florida International University M,D,O
Florida State University M,D,O
Fordham University M,D,O
Fort Hays State University M,O
Framingham State University M
Franciscan University of Steubenville M
Freed-Hardeman University M,O
Fresno Pacific University M
Frostburg State University M
Furman University M,O
Gallaudet University M,D,O
Gannon University M,D,O
Gardner-Webb University M,D
Geneva College M
George Fox University M,D,O
George Mason University M*
The George Washington University M,D,O
Georgia College & State University M,O
Georgian Court University M,O
Georgia Southern University M,D,O
Georgia State University M,D,O
Golden Gate Baptist Theological Seminary P,M,D,O
Gonzaga University M,D
Governors State University M
Graceland University (IA) M
Grambling State University M,D
Grand Canyon University M,D
Grand Valley State University M,O
Gwynedd-Mercy College M
Hampton University M,D
Harding University M,O
Harvard University M,D*
Henderson State University M,O
Heritage University M
High Point University M
Hofstra University M,D,O
Holy Family University M*
Hood College M,O
Hope International University M
Houston Baptist University M
Howard Payne University M
Howard University M,D,O
Hunter College of the City University of New York O
Idaho State University M,D,O
Illinois State University M,D
Immaculata University M,D,O
Indiana State University M,D,O
Indiana University Bloomington M,D,O*
Indiana University of Pennsylvania D,O
Indiana University–Purdue University Fort Wayne M,O
Indiana University–Purdue University Indianapolis M,O
Indiana Wesleyan University M,O
Instituto Tecnologico de Santo Domingo M,O
Instituto Tecnológico y de Estudios Superiores de Monterrey, Campus Central de Veracruz M
Instituto Tecnológico y de Estudios Superiores de Monterrey, Campus Ciudad Juárez M
Instituto Tecnológico y de Estudios Superiores de Monterrey, Campus Estado de México M,D
Instituto Tecnológico y de Estudios Superiores de Monterrey, Campus Irapuato M,D
Inter American University of Puerto Rico, Aguadilla Campus M
Inter American University of Puerto Rico, Arecibo Campus M
Inter American University of Puerto Rico, Barranquitas Campus M
Inter American University of Puerto Rico, Metropolitan Campus M,D
Inter American University of Puerto Rico, San Germán Campus M,D
Iona College M
Iowa State University of Science and Technology M,D*
Jackson State University M,D,O
Jacksonville State University M,O
James Madison University M
John Brown University M
John Carroll University M
The Johns Hopkins University M,D,O
Johnson & Wales University D
Jones International University M
Kansas State University M,D*
Kaplan University, Davenport Campus M
Kean University M,D
Keene State College M,O
Keiser University M,D
Kennesaw State University M,D,O
Kent State University M,D,O*
Kutztown University of Pennsylvania M
Lake Erie College M
Lamar University M,D,O
La Sierra University M,D,O
Lee University M,O
Lehigh University M,D,O
Le Moyne College M,O
LeTourneau University M
Lewis & Clark College D,O
Lewis University M,D,O
Liberty University M,D,O
Lincoln Memorial University M,D,O
Lincoln University (MO) M,O
Lindenwood University M,D,O
Lipscomb University M,D
Long Island University, Brooklyn Campus M
Long Island University, C.W. Post Campus M,D,O
Long Island University, Rockland Graduate Campus M,O
Longwood University M
Loras College M
Louisiana State University and Agricultural and Mechanical College M,D,O
Louisiana State University in Shreveport M
Louisiana Tech University M,D
Loyola Marymount University M,D
Loyola University Chicago M,D,O
Loyola University Maryland M,O
Lynchburg College M,D
Lynn University M,D
Madonna University M
Manhattan College M,O
Manhattanville College M,D*
Marian University (WI) M,D
Marquette University M,D,O
Marshall University M,D,O
Martin Luther College M
Marygrove College M
Marymount University M,O
Maryville University of Saint Louis M,D
Marywood University M,D

Massachusetts College of Liberal Arts	M
McDaniel College	M
McGill University	M,D,O
McKendree University	M
McNeese State University	M,O
Memorial University of Newfoundland	M,D,O
Mercer University	M,D,O
Mercy College	M,O
Mercyhurst College	M,O
Merrimack College	M,O
Mesa State College	M
Miami University	M,D
Michigan State University	M,D,O
Middle Tennessee State University	M,O
Midwestern State University	M
Mills College	M,D
Minnesota State University Mankato	M
Minnesota State University Moorhead	M,O
Mississippi College	M,D,O
Mississippi State University	M,D,O
Mississippi University for Women	M
Missouri Baptist University	M,O
Missouri State University	M,O
Monmouth University	M,O
Montana State University	M,D,O
Montclair State University	M,D,O
Morehead State University	M,O
Morgan State University	M,D
Mount St. Mary's College	M
Murray State University	M,O
National-Louis University	M,D,O
National University	M
Neumann University	D
New England College	M
New Jersey City University	M
Newman Theological College	M,O
Newman University	M
New Mexico Highlands University	M
New Mexico State University	M,D
New York Institute of Technology	O
New York University	M,D,O
Niagara University	M,O
Nicholls State University	M
Norfolk State University	M
North Carolina Agricultural and Technical State University	M,D
North Carolina Central University	M
North Carolina State University	M,D*
North Central College	M
North Dakota State University	M,O
Northeastern Illinois University	M
Northeastern State University	M
Northern Arizona University	M,D,O
Northern Illinois University	M,D,O
Northern Kentucky University	M,D,O
Northern Michigan University	M,O
Northern State University	M
North Georgia College & State University	M,O
Northwestern Oklahoma State University	M
Northwestern State University of Louisiana	M,O
Northwest Missouri State University	M,O
Northwest Nazarene University	M
Notre Dame de Namur University	M,O
Nova Southeastern University	M,D,O*
Oakland City University	M,D
Oakland University	M,D,O
Oglala Lakota College	M
The Ohio State University	M,D
Ohio University	M,D*
Oklahoma State University	M,D*
Old Dominion University	M,D,O
Olivet Nazarene University	M
Oral Roberts University	M,D
Oregon State University	M
Ottawa University	M
Our Lady of Holy Cross College	M
Our Lady of the Lake University of San Antonio	M
Pace University	M,O
Pacific Lutheran University	M
Park University	M
Pepperdine University	M,D
Philadelphia Biblical University	M
Piedmont College	M,D,O
Pittsburg State University	M,O
Plymouth State University	M
Point Park University	M
Pontifical Catholic University of Puerto Rico	D
Portland State University	M,D
Prairie View A&M University	M,D
Prescott College	M,D
Providence College	M
Purdue University	M,D,O
Purdue University Calumet	M
Queens College of the City University of New York	O
Queens University of Charlotte	M
Quincy University	M
Radford University	M
Regent University	M,D,O
Regis University	M,O
Rhode Island College	M,O
The Richard Stockton College of New Jersey	M
Rider University	M,O
Rivier College	M,D,O
Robert Morris University	M,D,O
Robert Morris University Illinois	M
Rocky Mountain College	M
Roosevelt University	M
Rowan University	M,D,O
Rutgers, The State University of New Jersey, Camden	M
Rutgers, The State University of New Jersey, New Brunswick	M,D*
Sacred Heart University	M,O
Sage Graduate School	D
Saginaw Valley State University	M,O
St. Ambrose University	M
St. Bonaventure University	M,O
St. Cloud State University	M,D
St. Edward's University	M,O
Saint Francis University	M
St. Francis Xavier University	M
St. John Fisher College	M,D
St. John's University (NY)	M,D,O
Saint Joseph's University	M,D
St. Lawrence University	M,O
Saint Leo University	M,O
Saint Louis University	M,D,O
Saint Martin's University	M
Saint Mary's College of California	M
St. Mary's University (United States)	M,O
Saint Mary's University of Minnesota	M,D,O
Saint Michael's College	M,O
Saint Peter's College	M,D
St. Thomas Aquinas College	M,O
St. Thomas University	M,D,O
Saint Vincent College	M
Saint Xavier University	M,O
Salem International University	M
Salem State University	M
Salisbury University	M
Samford University	M,D,O
Sam Houston State University	M,D
San Diego State University	M
San Francisco State University	M,D,O
San Jose State University	M
Santa Clara University	M,O
Seattle Pacific University	M,D,O
Seattle University	M,D,O
Seton Hall University	D,O
Shasta Bible College	M
Shenandoah University	M,D,O
Shippensburg University of Pennsylvania	M
Siena Heights University	M
Sierra Nevada College	M
Silver Lake College	M
Simmons College	M,D,O
Simon Fraser University	M,D
Simpson University	M
Slippery Rock University of Pennsylvania	M
Sonoma State University	M,D
South Carolina State University	M,D,O
South Dakota State University	M
Southeastern Louisiana University	M,D
Southeastern Oklahoma State University	M
Southeastern University (FL)	M
Southeast Missouri State University	M,O
Southern Adventist University	M
Southern Arkansas University–Magnolia	M
Southern Connecticut State University	M,D,O
Southern Illinois University Carbondale	M,D
Southern Illinois University Edwardsville	M,D,O
Southern Nazarene University	M
Southern New Hampshire University	M,O
Southern Oregon University	M
Southern University and Agricultural and Mechanical College	M
Southwest Baptist University	M,O
Southwestern Adventist University	M
Southwestern Assemblies of God University	M
Southwestern Oklahoma State University	M
Southwest Minnesota State University	M
Spalding University	M,D
Springfield College	M
Stanford University	M,D
State University of New York at Binghamton	M
State University of New York at Fredonia	O
State University of New York at New Paltz	M,O
State University of New York at Oswego	O
State University of New York at Plattsburgh	O
State University of New York College at Cortland	O
Stephen F. Austin State University	M,D
Stetson University	M,O
Stony Brook University, State University of New York	M,O
Suffolk University	M,O
Sul Ross State University	M
Syracuse University	M,D,O*
Tarleton State University	M,D,O
Teacher Education University	M
Teachers College, Columbia University	M,D
Temple University	M,D*
Tennessee State University	M,D,O
Tennessee Technological University	M,O
Tennessee Temple University	M
Texas A&M International University	M
Texas A&M University	M,D
Texas A&M University–Commerce	M,D
Texas A&M University–Corpus Christi	M,D
Texas A&M University–Kingsville	M,D
Texas A&M University–San Antonio	M
Texas A&M University–Texarkana	M
Texas Christian University	M,D,O
Texas Southern University	M,D
Texas State University–San Marcos	M
Texas Tech University	M,D*
Texas Woman's University	M,D
Thomas Edison State College	M
Trevecca Nazarene University	M,D
Trinity Baptist College	M
Trinity International University	M
Trinity University	M
Trinity (Washington) University	M
Trinity Western University	M,O
Troy University	M,O
TUI University	M,D
Union College (KY)	M
Union Graduate College	M,O
Union Institute & University	M,D,O
Union University	M,D,O
Universidad Adventista de las Antillas	P,M
Universidad del Turabo	M,D,O
Universidad Iberoamericana	P,M
Universidad Metropolitana	M
Université de Moncton	M
Université de Montréal	M,D,O
Université de Sherbrooke	M
Université du Québec à Trois-Rivières	O
Université Laval	M,D,O
University at Albany, State University of New York	M,D,O
University at Buffalo, the State University of New York	M,D,O*
The University of Akron	M,D
The University of Alabama	M,D,O
The University of Alabama at Birmingham	M,D,O*
University of Alaska Anchorage	M,O
University of Alberta	M,D,O
The University of Arizona	M,D,O
University of Arkansas	M,D,O
University of Arkansas at Little Rock	M,D,O
University of Arkansas at Monticello	M

*M—master's degree; P—first professional degree; D—doctorate; O—other advanced degree; *—Close-Up and/or Display in one of the other books in this series*

University of Atlanta P,M,D,O
University of Bridgeport D,O
The University of British Columbia M,D
University of Calgary M,D,O
University of California, Irvine M,D*
University of California, Los Angeles D*
University of California, Riverside M,D
University of California, Santa Barbara M,D
University of Central Arkansas M,O
University of Central Florida M,D
University of Central Missouri M,D,O
University of Central Oklahoma M
University of Cincinnati M,D,O
University of Colorado at Colorado Springs M,D
University of Colorado Denver M,D,O
University of Connecticut D,O*
University of Dayton M,D,O
University of Delaware M,D,O*
University of Denver M,D,O
University of Detroit Mercy M
The University of Findlay M
University of Florida M,D,O*
University of Georgia M,D,O
University of Guam M
University of Hartford D,O
University of Hawaii at Manoa M,D
University of Houston M,D
University of Houston–Clear Lake M,D
University of Houston–Victoria M
University of Idaho M,O
University of Illinois at Chicago M,D
University of Illinois at Springfield M
University of Illinois at Urbana–Champaign M,D,O
University of Indianapolis M
The University of Iowa M,D,O*
The University of Kansas M,D
University of Kentucky M,D,O*
University of La Verne M,D,O
University of Lethbridge M,D
University of Louisiana at Lafayette M,D*
University of Louisiana at Monroe M,D
University of Louisville M,D,O
University of Maine M,D,O
University of Maine at Farmington M
University of Manitoba M
University of Mary M
University of Mary Hardin-Baylor M,D
University of Maryland, College Park M,D,O
University of Maryland Eastern Shore D
University of Massachusetts Amherst M,D,O*
University of Massachusetts Boston M,D,O
University of Massachusetts Lowell M,D,O
University of Memphis M,D
University of Michigan M,D*
University of Michigan–Dearborn M,D
University of Minnesota, Twin Cities Campus M,D
University of Mississippi M,D,O
University of Missouri M,D,O*
University of Missouri–Kansas City M,D,O*
University of Missouri–St. Louis M,D,O
The University of Montana M,D,O
University of Montevallo M,O
University of Nebraska at Kearney M,O
University of Nebraska at Omaha M,D,O
University of Nebraska–Lincoln M,D,O*
University of Nevada, Las Vegas M,D
University of Nevada, Reno M,D,O*
University of New England M,O
University of New Hampshire M,O
University of New Mexico M,D,O*
University of New Orleans M,D,O
University of North Alabama O
The University of North Carolina at Chapel Hill M,D*
The University of North Carolina at Charlotte M,D
The University of North Carolina at Greensboro M,D,O
The University of North Carolina at Pembroke M
The University of North Carolina Wilmington M,D
University of North Dakota M,D,O
University of Northern Colorado M,D,O
University of Northern Iowa M,D
University of North Florida M,D
University of North Texas M,D
University of Oklahoma M,D,O*
University of Pennsylvania M,D*
University of Phoenix M,D,O
University of Phoenix–Central Florida Campus M
University of Phoenix–Chattanooga Campus M
University of Phoenix–Denver Campus M
University of Phoenix–Hawaii Campus M
University of Phoenix–Idaho Campus M
University of Phoenix–Kansas City Campus M
University of Phoenix–Las Vegas Campus M
University of Phoenix–Madison Campus D,O
University of Phoenix–Memphis Campus M
University of Phoenix–Metro Detroit Campus M
University of Phoenix–Milwaukee Campus M,D,O
University of Phoenix–Nashville Campus M
University of Phoenix–New Mexico Campus M
University of Phoenix–Northern Nevada Campus M
University of Phoenix–Northern Virginia Campus M
University of Phoenix–North Florida Campus M
University of Phoenix–Omaha Campus M
University of Phoenix–Phoenix Campus M
University of Phoenix–Puerto Rico Campus M
University of Phoenix–Richmond Campus M
University of Phoenix–Southern Arizona Campus M,O
University of Phoenix–Southern California Campus M
University of Phoenix–Southern Colorado Campus M,O
University of Phoenix–South Florida Campus M
University of Phoenix–Springfield Campus M
University of Phoenix–Utah Campus M
University of Phoenix–Vancouver Campus M
University of Phoenix–Washington D.C. Campus M,D,O
University of Phoenix–West Florida Campus M
University of Pittsburgh M,D*
University of Prince Edward Island M
University of Puerto Rico, Río Piedras M,D
University of Regina M
University of Rochester
University of St. Francis (IL) M
University of St. Thomas (MN) M,D,O
University of San Diego M,D,O
University of San Francisco M,D
University of Saskatchewan M,D,O
The University of Scranton M
University of Sioux Falls M,O
University of South Africa M,D
University of South Alabama M,O
University of South Carolina M,D,O
The University of South Dakota M,D,O
University of Southern California D*
University of Southern Maine M,O
University of Southern Mississippi M,D,O
University of South Florida M,D,O*
The University of Tampa M
The University of Tennessee M,D,O
The University of Tennessee at Chattanooga M,D,O
The University of Tennessee at Martin M
The University of Texas at Austin M,D
The University of Texas at Brownsville M
The University of Texas at El Paso M,D
The University of Texas at San Antonio M,D*
The University of Texas at Tyler M
The University of Texas of the Permian Basin M
The University of Texas–Pan American M,D
University of the Cumberlands M,D,O
University of the Incarnate Word M,D
University of the Pacific M,D
University of the Southwest M
The University of Toledo M,D,O
University of Utah M,D*
University of Vermont M,D
University of Victoria M,D
University of Virginia M,D,O
University of Washington M,D*
University of Washington, Bothell M
University of Washington, Tacoma M
The University of West Alabama M
University of West Florida M,D,O
University of West Georgia M,D,O
University of Wisconsin–Madison M,D,O*
University of Wisconsin–Milwaukee M,D,O
University of Wisconsin–Oshkosh M
University of Wisconsin–Stevens Point M
University of Wisconsin–Superior M,O
University of Wisconsin–Whitewater M*
University of Wyoming M,D,O
Upper Iowa University M
Ursuline College M
Valdosta State University M,D,O
Valparaiso University M
Vanderbilt University M,D*
Villanova University M
Virginia Commonwealth University D
Virginia Polytechnic Institute and State University M,D,O
Virginia State University M
Wagner College M
Walden University M,D,O
Walla Walla University M
Washburn University M
Washington State University M,D
Washington State University Spokane M,O
Washington State University Tri-Cities M,D
Wayland Baptist University M
Wayne State College M,O
Wayne State University M,D,O*
Webster University M,O
Western Carolina University M,D,O
Western Connecticut State University D
Western Governors University M,O
Western Illinois University M,D,O
Western Kentucky University M,D,O
Western Michigan University M,D,O
Western New Mexico University M
Western State College of Colorado M*
Western Washington University M
Westfield State University M,O
Westminster College (PA) M,O
West Texas A&M University M
West Virginia University M,D
Wheelock College M
Whittier College M
Whitworth University M
Wichita State University M,D,O
Widener University M,D
Wilkes University M,D
William Paterson University of New Jersey M
William Woods University M,O
Wilmington University M,D
Wingate University M
Winona State University M,O
Winthrop University M
Worcester State University M,O
Wright State University M,O
Xavier University M
Xavier University of Louisiana M
Yeshiva University M,D,O*
York College of Pennsylvania M
Youngstown State University M,D

EDUCATIONAL MEASUREMENT AND EVALUATION

American InterContinental University Online M

Angelo State University	M
Boston College	M,D*
Bucknell University	M
Cambridge College	M,D,O
Claremont Graduate University	M,D,O
College of Saint Mary	M
Eastern Michigan University	M,O
Florida State University	M,D,O
George Mason University	M*
Georgia State University	M,D
Harvard University	D*
Houston Baptist University	M
Indiana University Bloomington	M,D,O*
Iowa State University of Science and Technology	M,D*
Kent State University	M,D*
Louisiana State University and Agricultural and Mechanical College	M,D,O
Loyola University Chicago	M,D
McNeese State University	M,O
Michigan State University	M,D,O
Missouri Western State University	M
North Carolina State University	D*
Ohio University	M,D*
Rutgers, The State University of New Jersey, New Brunswick	M*
Seton Hall University	M,D,O
Southern Connecticut State University	M
Southern Illinois University Carbondale	M,D
Southwestern Oklahoma State University	M
Stanford University	M,D
Sul Ross State University	M
Syracuse University	M,D,O*
Teachers College, Columbia University	M,D
Tennessee Technological University	D
Texas A&M University	M,D
Texas A&M University–San Antonio	M
Université Laval	M,D,O
University at Albany, State University of New York	M,D,O
University of Arkansas	M,D
The University of British Columbia	M,D,O
University of Calgary	M,D,O
University of California, Santa Barbara	M,D
University of Colorado Boulder	D*
University of Colorado Denver	M,D,O
University of Connecticut	M,D,O*
University of Denver	M,D,O
University of Florida	M,D,O*
The University of Iowa	M,D,O*
The University of Kansas	M,D
University of Kentucky	M,D*
University of Louisiana at Monroe	M,D
University of Maryland, College Park	M,D
University of Massachusetts Amherst	M,D,O*
University of Memphis	M,D
University of Miami	M,D*
University of Michigan	M,D*
University of Michigan–Dearborn	M,O
University of Minnesota, Twin Cities Campus	M,D
University of Missouri–St. Louis	M,O
University of Nebraska–Lincoln	M,D,O*
University of New England	M,O
The University of North Carolina at Chapel Hill	M,D*
The University of North Carolina at Greensboro	D
University of North Dakota	D
University of Northern Colorado	M,D
University of North Texas	D
University of Oklahoma	M,D*
University of Pennsylvania	M,D*
University of Pittsburgh	M,D*
University of Puerto Rico, Río Piedras	M
University of South Carolina	M,D
University of Southern Mississippi	M,D,O
University of South Florida	M,D,O*
The University of Tennessee	M,D,O
The University of Texas at El Paso	M
The University of Texas–Pan American	M
University of the Southwest	M
The University of Toledo	M,D,O
University of Victoria	M,D
University of Virginia	M,D,O
University of Washington	M,D*
University of Wisconsin–Milwaukee	M,D
Utah State University	M,D
Vanderbilt University	M,D*
Virginia Commonwealth University	D
Virginia Polytechnic Institute and State University	M,D,O
Walden University	M,D,O
Washington University in St. Louis	D*
Wayne State University	M,D,O*
Western Governors University	M,O
Western Michigan University	M,D,O
West Texas A&M University	M
Wilkes University	M,D

EDUCATIONAL MEDIA/ INSTRUCTIONAL TECHNOLOGY

Acadia University	M
Adelphi University	M,O*
Alabama State University	M,O
Alliant International University–Irvine	M,O
Alverno College	M
American College of Education	M
American InterContinental University Online	M
American InterContinental University South Florida	M
Appalachian State University	M,O
Arcadia University	M,D,O*
Argosy University, Atlanta	M,D,O*
Argosy University, Denver	M,D*
Argosy University, Nashville	M,D,O*
Argosy University, Orange County	M,D*
Argosy University, Phoenix	M,D,O*
Argosy University, San Francisco Bay Area	M,D*
Argosy University, Sarasota	M,D,O*
Argosy University, Seattle	M,D*
Argosy University, Twin Cities	M,D,O*
Arizona State University	M,D,O
Ashland University	M
Auburn University	M,D,O
Aurora University	M,D
Azusa Pacific University	M
Baldwin-Wallace College	M
Barry University	M,D,O*
Bellevue University	M,D
Bloomsburg University of Pennsylvania	M
Boise State University	M
Boston University	M,D,O*
Bowling Green State University	M*
Bridgewater State University	M
Brigham Young University	M,D*
Buffalo State College, State University of New York	M
California Baptist University	M
California State University, Bakersfield	M
California State University, Dominguez Hills	M,O*
California State University, East Bay	M
California State University, Fullerton	M
California State University, Monterey Bay	M
California State University, Northridge	M
California State University, San Bernardino	M
California State University, Stanislaus	M
Cambridge College	M,D,O
Capella University	M,D,O
Cardinal Stritch University	M
Caribbean University	M,D
Carlow University	M
Central Connecticut State University	M
Central Michigan University	M,D,O
Chestnut Hill College	M,O*
Chicago State University	M
Clarke University	M
College of Mount Saint Vincent	M,O
College of Saint Elizabeth	M,D,O
The College of Saint Rose	M,O
The College of St. Scholastica	M
The College of William and Mary	M,D
Colorado Christian University	M
Colorado State University–Pueblo	M
Columbia International University	M,D,O
Concordia University (Canada)	M,D,O
Concordia University Chicago	M
Dakota State University	M*
Delaware Valley College	M
DeSales University	M
Dowling College	M,D,O
Drexel University	M,D*
Drury University	M
Duquesne University	M,D
East Carolina University	M,O
Eastern Connecticut State University	M
Eastern Michigan University	M,O
Eastern New Mexico University	M
Eastern Washington University	M
East Stroudsburg University of Pennsylvania	M
East Tennessee State University	M
Ellis University	M
Emporia State University	M
Fairfield University	M,O
Fairleigh Dickinson University, College at Florham	M,O
Fairleigh Dickinson University, Metropolitan Campus	M,O
Ferris State University	M
Fielding Graduate University	M,D,O
Fitchburg State University	M,O
Florida Gulf Coast University	M
Florida International University	M,D,O
Florida State University	M,D,O
Fort Hays State University	M
Framingham State University	M
Fresno Pacific University	M
Frostburg State University	M
Full Sail University	M
Gannon University	M
George Fox University	M,D,O
The George Washington University	M
Georgia College & State University	M,O
Georgia Southern University	M
Georgia State University	M,D,O
Governors State University	M
Graceland University (IA)	M
Grambling State University	M,D
Grand Valley State University	M,O
Harrisburg University of Science and Technology	M
Harvard University	M,O*
Idaho State University	M,D,O
Indiana State University	M,D
Indiana University Bloomington	M,D*
Indiana University of Pennsylvania	M,D
Instituto Tecnológico y de Estudios Superiores de Monterrey, Campus Central de Veracruz	M
Instituto Tecnológico y de Estudios Superiores de Monterrey, Campus Ciudad de México	M,D
Instituto Tecnológico y de Estudios Superiores de Monterrey, Campus Ciudad Juárez	M,D
Instituto Tecnológico y de Estudios Superiores de Monterrey, Campus Estado de México	M,D
Instituto Tecnológico y de Estudios Superiores de Monterrey, Campus Irapuato	M,D
Inter American University of Puerto Rico, Metropolitan Campus	M
Iowa State University of Science and Technology	M,D*
Jackson State University	M,D,O
Jacksonville State University	M
Jacksonville University	M
The Johns Hopkins University	M,D,O
Johnson University	M
Jones International University	M
Kaplan University, Davenport Campus	M
Keiser University	D
Kennesaw State University	M
Kent State University	M*
Kutztown University of Pennsylvania	M,O
Lamar University	M,D,O
La Salle University	M
Lawrence Technological University	M
Lehigh University	M,D,O
Lewis University	M
Liberty University	M,D,O
Lindenwood University	M,D,O
Lipscomb University	M,D

*M—master's degree; P—first professional degree; D—doctorate; O—other advanced degree; *—Close-Up and/or Display in one of the other books in this series*

Institution	Degrees
Long Island University, Brooklyn Campus	M
Long Island University, C.W. Post Campus	M
Longwood University	M
Louisiana State University and Agricultural and Mechanical College	M,D,O
Lourdes College	M
Loyola University Chicago	M,O
Loyola University Maryland	M
Marlboro College	M
Marywood University	M,O
McDaniel College	M
McNeese State University	M,O
Memorial University of Newfoundland	M,D,O
Miami University	M,O
Michigan State University	M,D,O
MidAmerica Nazarene University	M
Middle Tennessee State University	M,O
Midwestern State University	M
Minnesota State University Mankato	M,O
Mississippi State University	M,D,O
Missouri Southern State University	M
Missouri State University	M
Montana State University Billings	M
Montclair State University	M,O
Morehead State University	M,O
National-Louis University	M,D,O
National University	M
Nazareth College of Rochester	M
New Jersey City University	M
New York Institute of Technology	M,O
New York University	M,D,O
North Carolina Agricultural and Technical State University	M
North Carolina Central University	M
North Carolina State University	M,D*
Northeastern State University	M
Northern Arizona University	M,D,O
Northern Illinois University	M,D
Northern State University	M
Northwestern State University of Louisiana	M,O
Northwestern University	M,D*
Northwest Missouri State University	M
Nova Southeastern University	M,D,O*
Oakland University	O
Ohio University	M,D*
Old Dominion University	M,D
Ottawa University	M
Our Lady of the Lake University of San Antonio	M
Penn State University Park	M,D
Pepperdine University	M,D
Pittsburg State University	M
Portland State University	M,D
Post University	M
Purdue University	M,D,O
Purdue University Calumet	M
Ramapo College of New Jersey	M
Regis University	M,O
The Richard Stockton College of New Jersey	M
Sacred Heart University	M,O
Saginaw Valley State University	M
St. Cloud State University	M
St. Edward's University	M,O
Saint Joseph's University	M,D
Saint Leo University	M,O
Saint Michael's College	M,O
St. Thomas University	M,D,O
Saint Vincent College	M
Salem State University	M
Sam Houston State University	M
San Diego State University	M,D
San Francisco State University	O
Seton Hall University	M
Simmons College	M,D,O
Simon Fraser University	M,D
Southeastern Louisiana University	M,D
Southeast Missouri State University	M
Southern Illinois University Edwardsville	M,O
Southern Polytechnic State University	M,O
Southern University and Agricultural and Mechanical College	M
State University of New York College at Oneonta	M,O
State University of New York College at Potsdam	M
Stony Brook University, State University of New York	M,O
Strayer University	M
Syracuse University	M,O*
Teacher Education University	M
Teachers College, Columbia University	M,D
Texas A&M University	M,D
Texas A&M University–Commerce	M,D
Texas A&M University–Corpus Christi	M,D
Texas A&M University–Texarkana	M
Texas Tech University	M,D*
Thomas Edison State College	O
Towson University	M,D
Trevecca Nazarene University	M
Troy University	M
TUI University	M,D
Université Laval	M,D
University at Albany, State University of New York	M,D,O
University at Buffalo, the State University of New York	M,D,O*
University of Alaska Southeast	M
University of Alberta	M,D
University of Arkansas	M
University of Arkansas at Little Rock	M
University of Calgary	M,D,O
University of Central Arkansas	M
University of Central Florida	M,D,O
University of Central Missouri	M,D,O
University of Central Oklahoma	M
University of Colorado Denver	M
University of Connecticut	M,D,O*
University of Dayton	M
The University of Findlay	M
University of Georgia	M,D,O
University of Hartford	M
University of Hawaii at Manoa	M,D
University of Houston–Clear Lake	M
University of Kentucky	M,D*
University of Maine	M
University of Maryland, Baltimore County	M,O
University of Maryland, College Park	M,D,O
University of Massachusetts Amherst	M,D,O*
University of Memphis	M,D
University of Michigan	M,D*
University of Michigan–Flint	M
University of Minnesota, Twin Cities Campus	M,D,O
University of Missouri	M,D,O*
University of Nebraska at Kearney	M
University of Nebraska at Omaha	M,O
University of Nevada, Las Vegas	M,D,O
University of New Mexico	M,D,O*
The University of North Carolina at Charlotte	M,D
The University of North Carolina at Greensboro	M,D,O
The University of North Carolina Wilmington	M
University of North Dakota	M
University of Northern Colorado	M,D
University of Northern Iowa	M
University of North Florida	M,D
University of North Texas	M,D
University of Oklahoma	M,D*
University of Pennsylvania	M*
University of Phoenix	D,O
University of Phoenix–Washington D.C. Campus	M,D,O
University of Phoenix–West Florida Campus	M
University of St. Thomas (MN)	M,D,O
University of San Francisco	M,D
University of Sioux Falls	M,O
University of South Africa	M,D
University of South Alabama	M,D
University of South Carolina	M
University of South Carolina Aiken	M
The University of South Dakota	M,O
University of South Florida	M,D,O*
The University of Tennessee	M,D,O
The University of Tennessee at Chattanooga	O
The University of Texas at Brownsville	M
The University of Texas at San Antonio	M,D*
University of the Incarnate Word	M,D,O
University of the Sacred Heart	M
The University of Toledo	M,D,O
University of Utah	M,D*
University of Virginia	M,D,O
University of Washington	M,D*
The University of West Alabama	M
University of West Florida	M,D
University of West Georgia	M,O
University of Wisconsin–Milwaukee	D
University of Wyoming	M,D,O
Utah State University	M,D,O
Valley City State University	M
Virginia Commonwealth University	M
Virginia Polytechnic Institute and State University	M,O
Walden University	M,D,O
Wayland Baptist University	M
Waynesburg University	M,D
Wayne State University	M,D,O*
Webster University	M,O
West Chester University of Pennsylvania	M,O
Western Connecticut State University	M
Western Governors University	M,O
Western Illinois University	M,O
Western Kentucky University	M,O
Western Michigan University	M,D,O
Western Oregon University	M
Westfield State University	M
West Texas A&M University	M
West Virginia University	M,D
Widener University	M,D
Wilkes University	M,D
Wilmington University	M
Youngstown State University	M

EDUCATIONAL POLICY

Institution	Degrees
Alabama State University	M,D,O
Arizona State University	D
The Catholic University of America	M,D,O
The College of William and Mary	M,D
Florida State University	M,D,O
The George Washington University	M,D
Georgia State University	M,D,O
Harvard University	M*
Hofstra University	M,D,O
Illinois State University	M,D
Indiana University Bloomington	M,D,O*
Loyola University Chicago	M,D
Marquette University	M,D,O
Michigan State University	D
New York University	M,D
The Ohio State University	M,D
Penn State University Park	M,D
Portland State University	M,D
Rutgers, The State University of New Jersey, Camden	M
Rutgers, The State University of New Jersey, New Brunswick	D*
Teachers College, Columbia University	M,D
University of Alberta	M,D,O
University of Arkansas	D
The University of British Columbia	M,D
University of Colorado Boulder	M,D*
University of Colorado Denver	D
University of Georgia	M,D,O
University of Hawaii at Manoa	D
University of Illinois at Chicago	M,D
University of Illinois at Urbana–Champaign	M,D,O
The University of Iowa	M,D,O*
The University of Kansas	D
University of Kentucky	M,D*
University of Maryland, Baltimore County	M,D
University of Maryland, College Park	M,D
University of Massachusetts Amherst	M,D,O*
University of Minnesota, Twin Cities Campus	M,D,O
University of Pennsylvania	M,D*
University of Pittsburgh	D*
University of Rochester	

University of St. Thomas (MN) M,D,O
University of Southern California D*
University of Washington M,D*
The University of Western Ontario M
University of Wisconsin–Madison M,D,O*
Vanderbilt University M,D*
Virginia Commonwealth University D
Virginia Polytechnic Institute and State University M,D,O
Walden University M,D,O
Wayne State University M,D,O*

EDUCATIONAL PSYCHOLOGY

Alliant International University–Irvine M,D,O
Alliant International University–Los Angeles M,D,O
Alliant International University–San Diego M,D,O
Alliant International University–San Francisco M,D,O
American International College M,D
Andrews University M,D
Arcadia University M,D,O*
Auburn University M,D,O
Ball State University M,D,O
Baylor University M,D,O*
Boston College M,D*
Brigham Young University M,D*
California Coast University M,D
California State University, Long Beach M
California State University, Northridge M
Capella University M,D,O
The Catholic University of America M,D,O
Chapman University M,O
Clark Atlanta University M
The College of Saint Rose M,O
Dowling College M,D,O
Eastern Michigan University M,O
Edinboro University of Pennsylvania M,O
Florida State University M,D,O
Fordham University M,D,O
George Mason University M*
Georgia State University M,D
Graduate School and University Center of the City University of New York D
Harvard University M*
Holy Names University M,O
Howard University M,D
Illinois State University M,D,O
Indiana University Bloomington M,D,O*
Indiana University of Pennsylvania M,O
Instituto Tecnologico de Santo Domingo M,O
John Carroll University M
The Johns Hopkins University M,O
Kent State University M,D*
La Sierra University M,O
Long Island University, Westchester Graduate Campus M
Loyola University Chicago M
Marquette University M,D,O
McGill University M,D,O
Memorial University of Newfoundland M,D,O
Miami University M,O
Michigan School of Professional Psychology M,D
Michigan State University M,D,O
Mississippi State University M,D,O
Montclair State University M,O
Mount Saint Vincent University M
National-Louis University M,D,O
New Jersey City University M,O
New York University M,D
Northern Arizona University M,D,O
Northern Illinois University M,D,O
Oklahoma State University M,D,O*
Penn State University Park M,D
Pontifical Catholic University of Puerto Rico M
Purdue University M,D,O
Rhode Island College M,O
Rutgers, The State University of New Jersey, New Brunswick M,D*
Simon Fraser University M,D
Southern Illinois University Carbondale M,D
Stanford University D
State University of New York College at Oneonta M,O
Teachers College, Columbia University M,D
Temple University M,D*
Tennessee Technological University M,O
Texas A&M University M,D
Texas Christian University M,D,O
Texas Tech University M,D*
Union Institute & University M,D,O
Universidad de Iberoamerica P,M,D
Université de Moncton M
Université de Montréal M,D,O
Université du Québec à Trois-Rivières M,D
Université du Québec en Outaouais M
Université Laval M,D
University at Albany, State University of New York M,D,O
University at Buffalo, the State University of New York M,D,O*
University of Alberta M,D
The University of Arizona M,D,O
University of California, Davis M,D
University of California, Riverside M,D
University of Colorado Boulder M,D*
University of Colorado Denver M,O
University of Connecticut M,D,O*
University of Denver M,D,O
University of Florida M,D,O*
University of Georgia M,D,O
University of Hawaii at Manoa M,D
University of Houston M,D
University of Illinois at Chicago D
University of Illinois at Urbana–Champaign M,D,O
The University of Iowa M,D,O*
The University of Kansas M,D
University of Kentucky M,D,O*
University of Louisville M,D
The University of Manchester M,D
University of Manitoba M
University of Mary Hardin-Baylor M,D
University of Maryland, College Park M,D
University of Memphis M,D
University of Michigan–Dearborn D
University of Minnesota, Twin Cities Campus M,D,O
University of Missouri M,D,O*
University of Missouri–St. Louis D
University of Nebraska at Omaha M,D,O
University of Nebraska–Lincoln M,D,O*
University of Nevada, Las Vegas M,D,O
University of Nevada, Reno M,D,O*
University of New Mexico M,D*
The University of North Carolina at Chapel Hill M,D*
University of Northern Colorado M,D
University of Northern Iowa M,O
University of North Texas M
University of Oklahoma M,D*
University of Phoenix–Southern Arizona Campus M,O
University of Regina M
University of Saskatchewan M,D,O
University of South Africa M,D
University of South Carolina M,D
The University of South Dakota M,D,O
University of Southern California D*
University of Southern Maine M,O
The University of Tennessee M,D,O
The University of Texas at Austin M,D
The University of Texas at El Paso M
The University of Texas–Pan American M
University of the Pacific M,D,O
The University of Toledo M,D,O
University of Utah M,D*
University of Victoria M,D
University of Virginia M,D,O
University of Washington M,D*
The University of Western Ontario M
University of Wisconsin–Madison M,D*
University of Wisconsin–Milwaukee M,D
Virginia Commonwealth University D
Washington State University M,D,O
Wayne State University M,D,O*
West Virginia University M
Wichita State University M,O
Widener University M,D

EDUCATION OF STUDENTS WITH SEVERE/MULTIPLE DISABILITIES

Cleveland State University M
Fresno Pacific University M
Georgia State University M
Hunter College of the City University of New York M
Minot State University M
Montclair State University M,O
Norfolk State University M
Syracuse University M*
Teachers College, Columbia University M
University of Illinois at Urbana–Champaign M,D,O
West Virginia University M,D

EDUCATION OF THE GIFTED

Arkansas State University M,D,O
Ashland University M
Barry University M,D,O*
Bowling Green State University M*
Canisius College M,O
Carlos Albizu University, Miami Campus M,D
Carthage College M,O
The College of New Rochelle M,O
The College of William and Mary M
Converse College M
Dowling College M,D,O
Drury University M
Elon University M
Emporia State University M
Hampton University M
Hardin-Simmons University M
The Johns Hopkins University M,D,O
Johnson State College M
Kent State University M*
Liberty University M,D,O
Lynn University M,D
Maryville University of Saint Louis M,D
Millersville University of Pennsylvania M
Mississippi University for Women M
Morehead State University M,O
Northeastern Illinois University M
Nova Southeastern University M,O*
Purdue University M,D,O
Saint Leo University M,O
Saint Mary's University of Minnesota M,O
St. Thomas University M,D,O
Samford University M,D,O
Southern Methodist University M,D,O
Teachers College, Columbia University M,D
Tennessee Technological University D
Troy University M
University at Buffalo, the State University of New York M,D,O*
The University of Alabama M,D,O
University of Arkansas at Little Rock M
University of Calgary M,D,O
University of Central Florida M,O
University of Connecticut M,D,O*
University of Louisiana at Lafayette M*
University of Louisiana at Monroe M,D
University of Minnesota, Twin Cities Campus M,D,O
University of Missouri M,D*
The University of North Carolina at Charlotte M,D
University of Northern Iowa M
University of St. Thomas (MN) M,O
University of Southern Maine M,O
University of Southern Mississippi M,D,O
University of South Florida M,D*
The University of Texas–Pan American M
The University of Toledo M,D,O
University of Virginia M,D,O
Western Washington University M
West Virginia University M,D
Whitworth University M
Wichita State University M
William Carey University M,O
Wilmington University M
Wright State University M
Youngstown State University M

*M—master's degree; P—first professional degree; D—doctorate; O—other advanced degree; *—Close-Up and/or Display in one of the other books in this series*

ELECTRICAL ENGINEERING

Institution	Degrees
Air Force Institute of Technology	M,D
Alfred University	M,D
The American University in Cairo	M
American University of Beirut	M,D
American University of Sharjah	M
Arizona State University	M,D,O
Auburn University	M,D
Baylor University	M,D*
Boise State University	M,D
Boston University	M,D*
Bradley University	M
Brigham Young University	M,D*
Brown University	M,D
Bucknell University	M
California Institute of Technology	M,D,O
California Polytechnic State University, San Luis Obispo	M
California State Polytechnic University, Pomona	M
California State University, Chico	M
California State University, Fresno	M
California State University, Fullerton	M
California State University, Long Beach	M
California State University, Los Angeles	M*
California State University, Northridge	M
California State University, Sacramento	M
Capitol College	M
Carleton University	M,D
Carnegie Mellon University	M,D*
Case Western Reserve University	M,D*
The Catholic University of America	M,D
City College of the City University of New York	M,D
Clarkson University	M,D*
Clemson University	M,D
Cleveland State University	M,D
Colorado State University	M,D
Colorado Technical University Colorado Springs	M
Colorado Technical University Denver	M
Columbia University	M,D,O*
Concordia University (Canada)	M,D
Cooper Union for the Advancement of Science and Art	M
Cornell University	M,D*
Dalhousie University	M,D
Dartmouth College	M,D
Drexel University	M*
Duke University	M,D*
École Polytechnique de Montréal	M,D,O
Embry-Riddle Aeronautical University–Daytona	M
Fairfield University	M
Fairleigh Dickinson University, Metropolitan Campus	M
Florida Agricultural and Mechanical University	M,D
Florida Atlantic University	M,D
Florida Institute of Technology	M,D
Florida International University	M,D
Florida State University	M,D
Gannon University	M
George Mason University	M,D,O*
The George Washington University	M,D
Georgia Institute of Technology	M,D
Georgia Southern University	M,O
Graduate School and University Center of the City University of New York	D
Grand Valley State University	M
Howard University	M,D
Illinois Institute of Technology	M,D
Indiana University–Purdue University Fort Wayne	M
Indiana University–Purdue University Indianapolis	M,D
Instituto Tecnológico y de Estudios Superiores de Monterrey, Campus Chihuahua	M,O
Instituto Tecnológico y de Estudios Superiores de Monterrey, Campus Monterrey	M,D
International Technological University	M,D
Iowa State University of Science and Technology	M,D*
The Johns Hopkins University	M,D,O
Kansas State University	M,D*
Kettering University	M
Lakehead University	M
Lamar University	M,D
Lawrence Technological University	M,D
Lehigh University	M,D
Louisiana State University and Agricultural and Mechanical College	M,D
Louisiana Tech University	M,D
Loyola Marymount University	M
Manhattan College	M
Marquette University	M,D,O
Massachusetts Institute of Technology	M,D,O
McGill University	M,D
McMaster University	M,D
McNeese State University	M
Memorial University of Newfoundland	M,D
Mercer University	M
Michigan State University	M,D
Michigan Technological University	M,D
Minnesota State University Mankato	M
Mississippi State University	M,D
Missouri University of Science and Technology	M,D
Montana State University	M,D
Montana Tech of The University of Montana	M
Morgan State University	M,D
Naval Postgraduate School	M,D,O
New Jersey Institute of Technology	M,D
New Mexico Institute of Mining and Technology	M
New Mexico State University	M,D
New York Institute of Technology	M
Norfolk State University	M
North Carolina Agricultural and Technical State University	M,D
North Carolina State University	M,D*
North Dakota State University	M,D
Northeastern University	M,D
Northern Arizona University	M
Northern Illinois University	M
Northwestern Polytechnic University	M
Northwestern University	M,D,O*
Oakland University	M
OGI School of Science & Engineering at Oregon Health & Science University	M,D
The Ohio State University	M,D
Ohio University	M,D*
Oklahoma State University	M,D*
Old Dominion University	M,D
Oregon Health & Science University	M,D*
Oregon State University	M,D
Penn State University Park	M,D
Polytechnic Institute of NYU	M,D
Polytechnic Institute of NYU, Long Island Graduate Center	M
Polytechnic Institute of NYU, Westchester Graduate Center	M
Polytechnic University of Puerto Rico	M
Portland State University	M,D
Prairie View A&M University	M,D
Princeton University	M,D*
Purdue University	M,D
Purdue University Calumet	M
Queen's University at Kingston	M,D
Rensselaer at Hartford	M
Rensselaer Polytechnic Institute	M,D
Rice University	M,D
Rochester Institute of Technology	M
Rose-Hulman Institute of Technology	M
Rowan University	M
Royal Military College of Canada	M,D
Rutgers, The State University of New Jersey, New Brunswick	M,D*
St. Cloud State University	M
St. Mary's University (United States)	M
San Diego State University	M
San Jose State University	M
Santa Clara University	M,D,O
South Dakota School of Mines and Technology	M
South Dakota State University	M,D
Southern Illinois University Carbondale	M,D
Southern Illinois University Edwardsville	M
Southern Methodist University	M,D
Southern Polytechnic State University	M
Stanford University	M,D,O
State University of New York at Binghamton	M,D
State University of New York at New Paltz	M
Stevens Institute of Technology	M,D,O
Stony Brook University, State University of New York	M,D
Syracuse University	M,D,O*
Temple University	M*
Tennessee Technological University	M,D
Texas A&M University	M,D
Texas A&M University–Kingsville	M
Texas Tech University	M,D*
Tufts University	M,D,O
Tuskegee University	M
Union Graduate College	M
Universidad de las Américas–Puebla	M
Université de Moncton	M
Université de Sherbrooke	M,D
Université du Québec à Trois-Rivières	M,D
Université Laval	M,D
University at Buffalo, the State University of New York	M,D*
The University of Akron	M,D
The University of Alabama	M,D
The University of Alabama at Birmingham	M*
The University of Alabama in Huntsville	M,D
University of Alaska Fairbanks	M,D
University of Alberta	M,D
The University of Arizona	M,D
University of Arkansas	M,D
University of Bridgeport	M
The University of British Columbia	M,D
University of Calgary	M,D
University of California, Berkeley	M,D*
University of California, Davis	M,D
University of California, Irvine	M,D*
University of California, Los Angeles	M,D*
University of California, Merced	M,D
University of California, Riverside	M,D
University of California, San Diego	M,D*
University of California, Santa Barbara	M,D
University of California, Santa Cruz	M,D
University of Central Florida	M,D,O
University of Cincinnati	M,D
University of Colorado at Colorado Springs	M,D
University of Colorado Boulder	M,D*
University of Colorado Denver	M
University of Connecticut	M,D*
University of Dayton	M,D
University of Delaware	M,D*
University of Denver	M,D
University of Detroit Mercy	M,D
University of Evansville	M
University of Florida	M,D,O*
University of Hawaii at Manoa	M,D
University of Houston	M,D
University of Idaho	M,D
University of Illinois at Chicago	M,D
University of Illinois at Urbana–Champaign	M,D
The University of Iowa	M,D*
The University of Kansas	M,D
University of Kentucky	M,D*
University of Louisville	M,D
University of Maine	M,D
The University of Manchester	M,D
University of Manitoba	M,D
University of Maryland, Baltimore County	M,D
University of Maryland, College Park	M,D
University of Massachusetts Amherst	M,D*
University of Massachusetts Dartmouth	M,D,O
University of Massachusetts Lowell	M,D
University of Memphis	M,D
University of Miami	M,D*
University of Michigan	M,D*

University of Michigan–Dearborn M
University of Minnesota, Duluth M
University of Minnesota, Twin Cities Campus M,D
University of Missouri M,D*
University of Missouri–Kansas City M,D*
University of Nebraska–Lincoln M,D*
University of Nevada, Las Vegas M,D
University of Nevada, Reno M,D*
University of New Brunswick Fredericton M,D
University of New Hampshire M,D
University of New Haven M
University of New Mexico M,D,O*
The University of North Carolina at Charlotte M,D
University of North Dakota M
University of North Florida M
University of North Texas M
University of Notre Dame M,D*
University of Oklahoma M,D*
University of Ottawa M,D*
University of Pennsylvania M,D*
University of Pittsburgh M,D*
University of Puerto Rico, Mayagüez Campus M,D
University of Rhode Island M,D,O
University of Rochester
University of Saskatchewan M,D
University of South Alabama M
University of South Carolina M,D
University of Southern California M,D,O*
University of South Florida M,D*
The University of Tennessee M,D
The University of Tennessee at Chattanooga M
The University of Tennessee Space Institute M,D
The University of Texas at Arlington M,D
The University of Texas at Austin M,D
The University of Texas at Dallas M,D*
The University of Texas at El Paso M,D
The University of Texas at San Antonio M,D*
The University of Texas at Tyler M
The University of Texas–Pan American M
University of the District of Columbia M
The University of Toledo M,D
University of Toronto M,D
University of Tulsa M
University of Utah M,D*
University of Vermont M,D
University of Victoria M,D
University of Virginia M,D
University of Washington M,D*
University of Waterloo M,D
The University of Western Ontario M,D
University of Windsor M,D
University of Wisconsin–Madison M,D*
University of Wisconsin–Milwaukee M,D,O
University of Wyoming M,D
Utah State University M,D
Vanderbilt University M,D*
Villanova University M,O
Virginia Commonwealth University M,D
Virginia Polytechnic Institute and State University M,D,O
Washington State University M,D
Washington State University Tri-Cities M,D
Washington University in St. Louis M,D*
Wayne State University M,D*
Western Michigan University M,D
Western New England University M
West Virginia University M,D
Wichita State University M,D
Wilkes University M
Worcester Polytechnic Institute M,D,O
Wright State University M
Yale University M,D*
Youngstown State University M

ELECTRONIC COMMERCE

Adelphi University M*
Arkansas State University M,O
Boston University M*
California State University, Fullerton M
Carnegie Mellon University M*
Claremont Graduate University M,D,O
Columbia Southern University M
Dalhousie University M,D
Dallas Baptist University M
DePaul University M,D
Eastern Michigan University M,O
Ellis University M
Fairleigh Dickinson University, Metropolitan Campus M
Ferris State University M
Florida Institute of Technology M
George Mason University M,D,O*
Georgia Institute of Technology M,O
Hawai'i Pacific University M*
HEC Montreal M,O
Instituto Tecnológico y de Estudios Superiores de Monterrey, Campus Central de Veracruz M
Instituto Tecnológico y de Estudios Superiores de Monterrey, Campus Ciudad Juárez M
Instituto Tecnológico y de Estudios Superiores de Monterrey, Campus Estado de México M,D
Instituto Tecnológico y de Estudios Superiores de Monterrey, Campus Irapuato M,D
Inter American University of Puerto Rico, Bayamón Campus M
Lewis University M
Marywood University M,O
Mercy College M,O
The National Graduate School of Quality Management M
National University M
Northwestern University M*
Pace University M,D,O
Polytechnic Institute of NYU M,D,O
Regis University M,O
Saint Xavier University M,O
Stevens Institute of Technology M,O
Universidad del Este M
Université de Montréal M,D
Université de Sherbrooke M
Université Laval M,O
University at Buffalo, the State University of New York M,D,O*
The University of Akron M
University of Colorado Denver M
University of Dayton M
University of Denver M
University of Florida M*
University of Massachusetts Dartmouth M,O
University of New Brunswick Saint John M
University of North Florida M
University of Ottawa M,D,O*
University of Phoenix–Austin Campus M
University of Phoenix–Chicago Campus M
University of Phoenix–Cincinnati Campus M
University of Phoenix–Columbus Georgia Campus M
University of Phoenix–Dallas Campus M
University of Phoenix–Denver Campus M
University of Phoenix–Houston Campus M
University of Phoenix–Louisville Campus M
University of Phoenix–Madison Campus M
University of Phoenix–Maryland Campus M
University of Phoenix–Memphis Campus M
University of Phoenix–New Mexico Campus M
University of Phoenix–Oklahoma City Campus M
University of Phoenix–Pittsburgh Campus M
University of Phoenix–Raleigh Campus M
University of Phoenix–San Antonio Campus M
University of San Francisco M
The University of Texas at Dallas M*

ELECTRONIC MATERIALS

Colorado School of Mines M,D
Massachusetts Institute of Technology M,D,O
Northwestern University M,D,O*
Princeton University D*
University of Arkansas M,D

ELEMENTARY EDUCATION

Adelphi University M*
Alabama Agricultural and Mechanical University M,O
Alabama State University M,O
Alaska Pacific University M
Albright College M
Alcorn State University M,O
American International College M,D,O
American Public University System M
American University M,O
American University of Puerto Rico M,O
Andrews University M,D,O
Anna Maria College M,O
Antioch University New England M
Appalachian State University M
Arcadia University M,D,O*
Argosy University, Atlanta M,D,O*
Argosy University, Chicago M,D,O*
Argosy University, Denver M,D*
Argosy University, Hawai'i M,D*
Argosy University, Inland Empire M,D*
Argosy University, Los Angeles M,D*
Argosy University, Nashville M,D,O*
Argosy University, Orange County M,D*
Argosy University, Phoenix M,D,O*
Argosy University, San Diego M,D*
Argosy University, San Francisco Bay Area M,D*
Argosy University, Sarasota M,D,O*
Argosy University, Schaumburg M,D,O*
Argosy University, Seattle M,D*
Argosy University, Tampa M,D,O*
Argosy University, Twin Cities M,D,O*
Argosy University, Washington DC M,D,O*
Arizona State University M,D
Arkansas State University M,O
Armstrong Atlantic State University M
Auburn University M,D,O
Auburn University Montgomery M,O
Aurora University M,D
Austin College M
Austin Peay State University M,O
Averett University M
Ball State University M,D
Bank Street College of Education M
Barry University M,D,O*
Bayamón Central University M,O
Belhaven University (MS) M
Belmont University M
Benedictine University M
Benedictine University at Springfield M
Bennington College M
Bloomsburg University of Pennsylvania M
Blue Mountain College M
Bob Jones University P,M,D,O
Boston College M*
Boston University M,D,O*
Bowie State University M
Brandeis University M
Bridgewater State University M
Brooklyn College of the City University of New York M
Brown University M
Buffalo State College, State University of New York M
Butler University M
California Lutheran University M,D
California State University, Fullerton M
California State University, Long Beach M
California State University, Los Angeles M*
California State University, Northridge M
California State University, San Bernardino M
California State University, Stanislaus M
California University of Pennsylvania M
Cambridge College M,D,O
Campbell University M
Canisius College M,O
Capella University M,D,O
Caribbean University M,D

M—master's degree; P—first professional degree; D—doctorate; O—other advanced degree; *—Close-Up and/or Display in one of the other books in this series

Institution	Degrees
Carson-Newman College	M
Catawba College	M
Centenary College of Louisiana	M
Central Connecticut State University	M,O
Central Michigan University	M,O
Chadron State College	M,O
Chapman University	M,O
Charleston Southern University	M
Chatham University	M
Chestnut Hill College	M*
Cheyney University of Pennsylvania	M
Chicago State University	M
Christopher Newport University	M
The Citadel, The Military College of South Carolina	M
City University of Seattle	M,O
Clarion University of Pennsylvania	M
Clemson University	M
College of Charleston	M
The College of New Jersey	M
The College of New Rochelle	M
College of St. Joseph	M
The College of Saint Rose	M,O
College of Staten Island of the City University of New York	M
The College of William and Mary	M
Colorado Christian University	M
The Colorado College	M
Columbia College (SC)	M
Columbia College Chicago	M
Columbia International University	M,D,O
Concordia University (OR)	M
Concordia University Chicago	M
Concordia University, Nebraska	M
Converse College	M
Creighton University	M
Curry College	M,O
Dallas Baptist University	M
Delta State University	M,D,O
DePaul University	M,D
Dominican College	M
Dominican University	M
Drury University	M
Duquesne University	M
D'Youville College	M,O*
East Carolina University	M
Eastern Connecticut State University	M
Eastern Illinois University	M
Eastern Kentucky University	M
Eastern Michigan University	M
Eastern Nazarene College	M,O
Eastern New Mexico University	M
Eastern Oregon University	M
Eastern Washington University	M
East Stroudsburg University of Pennsylvania	M
East Tennessee State University	M,D
Edinboro University of Pennsylvania	M,O
Elizabeth City State University	M
Elms College	M,O
Elon University	M
Emmanuel College (United States)	M,O
Emporia State University	M
Endicott College	M
Fairfield University	M,O
Fayetteville State University	M
Ferris State University	M
Fitchburg State University	M
Florida Agricultural and Mechanical University	M
Florida Atlantic University	M
Florida Gulf Coast University	M
Florida Institute of Technology	M,D,O
Florida International University	M,D,O
Florida Memorial University	M
Florida State University	M,D,O
Fordham University	M,D,O
Framingham State University	M
Francis Marion University	M
Fresno Pacific University	M
Frostburg State University	M
Gallaudet University	M,D,O
Gardner-Webb University	M
The George Washington University	M
Grand Canyon University	M
Grand Valley State University	M,O
Greensboro College	M
Greenville College	M
Hampton University	M
Harding University	M,O
Hawai'i Pacific University	M*
High Point University	M
Hofstra University	M,O
Holy Family University	M*
Hood College	M,O
Howard University	M
Hunter College of the City University of New York	M
Idaho State University	M,O
Immaculata University	M,D,O
Indiana State University	M
Indiana University Bloomington	M,D,O*
Indiana University Kokomo	M
Indiana University Northwest	M
Indiana University of Pennsylvania	M
Indiana University–Purdue University Fort Wayne	M
Indiana University South Bend	M
Indiana University Southeast	M
Inter American University of Puerto Rico, Aguadilla Campus	M
Inter American University of Puerto Rico, Arecibo Campus	M
Inter American University of Puerto Rico, Barranquitas Campus	M
Inter American University of Puerto Rico, Guayama Campus	M
Inter American University of Puerto Rico, Metropolitan Campus	M
Inter American University of Puerto Rico, Ponce Campus	M
Inter American University of Puerto Rico, San Germán Campus	M
Iowa State University of Science and Technology	M,D*
Ithaca College	M
Jackson State University	M,D,O
Jacksonville State University	M
Jacksonville University	M
James Madison University	M
The Johns Hopkins University	M,O
Johnson & Wales University	M,D
Jones International University	M
Kennesaw State University	M
Kutztown University of Pennsylvania	M,O
Lancaster Bible College	M,D
Lander University	M
Langston University	M
Lasell College	M
Lee University	M,O
Lehigh University	M,D,O
Lehman College of the City University of New York	M
Le Moyne College	M,O
Lesley University	M,D,O
Lewis & Clark College	M
Lewis University	M
Liberty University	M,D,O
Lincoln University (MO)	M,O
Lincoln University (PA)	M
Lock Haven University of Pennsylvania	M
Long Island University at Riverhead	M
Long Island University, Brooklyn Campus	M
Long Island University, C.W. Post Campus	M
Long Island University, Rockland Graduate Campus	M
Long Island University, Westchester Graduate Campus	M,O
Longwood University	M
Louisiana State University and Agricultural and Mechanical College	M,D,O
Loyola Marymount University	M
Loyola University Chicago	M,O
Maharishi University of Management	M
Manhattanville College	M*
Mansfield University of Pennsylvania	M
Marquette University	M,D,O
Marshall University	M
Mary Baldwin College	M
Marygrove College	M
Marymount University	M
Maryville University of Saint Louis	M,D
Marywood University	M
McDaniel College	M
McNeese State University	M,O
Medaille College	M
Mercy College	M
Merrimack College	M,O
Metropolitan College of New York	M
Miami University	M
Middle Tennessee State University	M,O
Millersville University of Pennsylvania	M
Mills College	M,D
Minnesota State University Mankato	M,O
Minot State University	M
Mississippi College	M,D,O
Mississippi State University	M,D,O
Mississippi Valley State University	M
Missouri State University	M,O
Monmouth University	M,O
Montclair State University	M,O
Montreat College	M
Morehead State University	M,O
Morgan State University	M
Mount Saint Mary College	M,O
Mount St. Mary's College	M
Mount Saint Vincent University	M
Murray State University	M,O
National-Louis University	M,D,O
Nazareth College of Rochester	M
New Jersey City University	M
New York Institute of Technology	M
New York University	M,D
Niagara University	M,O
North Carolina Agricultural and Technical State University	M
North Carolina Central University	M
North Carolina State University	M*
Northern Arizona University	M
Northern Illinois University	M,D
Northern Michigan University	M
Northern State University	M
Northwestern Oklahoma State University	M
Northwestern State University of Louisiana	M,O
Northwestern University	M*
Northwest Missouri State University	M,O
Nova Southeastern University	M,O*
Nyack College	M
Occidental College	M
Oklahoma City University	M
Old Dominion University	M
Olivet Nazarene University	M
Oregon State University	M
Ottawa University	M
Our Lady of the Lake University of San Antonio	M
Pace University	M,O
Pacific University	M
Pfeiffer University	M
Pittsburg State University	M
Plymouth State University	M
Portland State University	M,D
Prescott College	M,D
Providence College	M
Purdue University	M,D,O
Purdue University North Central	M
Queens College of the City University of New York	M,O
Queens University of Charlotte	M
Quinnipiac University	M
Regent University	M,D,O
Regis College (MA)	M
Rhode Island College	M
Rider University	O
Rivier College	M,D,O
Rockford College	M
Roger Williams University	M
Rollins College	M
Roosevelt University	M
Rosemont College	M
Rowan University	M
Rutgers, The State University of New Jersey, New Brunswick	M,D*
Sacred Heart University	M,O
Sage Graduate School	M
Saginaw Valley State University	M
St. John Fisher College	M
St. John's University (NY)	M
Saint Joseph's University	M,D
Saint Mary's University of Minnesota	M,O
Saint Peter's College	M,O
St. Thomas Aquinas College	M,O
St. Thomas University	M,D,O
Saint Xavier University	M,O
Salem College	M
Salem State University	M
Samford University	M,D,O

Institution	Degrees
San Diego State University	M
San Francisco State University	M
San Jose State University	M,O
Seton Hill University	M,O
Shenandoah University	M,D,O
Shippensburg University of Pennsylvania	M
Siena Heights University	M
Sierra Nevada College	M
Simmons College	M,O
Sinte Gleska University	M
Slippery Rock University of Pennsylvania	M
Smith College	M
Sonoma State University	M
South Carolina State University	M,D,O
Southeastern Louisiana University	M
Southeastern University (FL)	M
Southeast Missouri State University	M,O
Southern Arkansas University–Magnolia	M
Southern Connecticut State University	M,O
Southern New Hampshire University	M,O
Southern Oregon University	M
Southern University and Agricultural and Mechanical College	M
Southwestern Oklahoma State University	M
Spalding University	M
Springfield College	M
Spring Hill College	M
State University of New York at Fredonia	M
State University of New York at New Paltz	M
State University of New York at Oswego	M
State University of New York at Plattsburgh	M
State University of New York College at Geneseo	M
State University of New York College at Oneonta	M
State University of New York College at Potsdam	M
Stephen F. Austin State University	M
Sul Ross State University	M
Teacher Education University	M
Teachers College, Columbia University	M,D,O
Temple University	M,D*
Tennessee State University	M,D
Tennessee Technological University	M,O
Texas A&M University–Commerce	M,D
Texas A&M University–Corpus Christi	M
Texas A&M University–Kingsville	M
Texas Christian University	M
Texas State University–San Marcos	M
Texas Tech University	M,D*
Towson University	M
Trevecca Nazarene University	M
Trinity (Washington) University	M
Troy University	M,O
Union College (KY)	M
Universidad del Este	M
Universidad Metropolitana	M
Université de Sherbrooke	M,O
University at Buffalo, the State University of New York	M,D,O*
The University of Akron	M,D
The University of Alabama	M,D,O
The University of Alabama at Birmingham	M*
University of Alaska Fairbanks	M,D,O
University of Alaska Southeast	M
University of Alberta	M,D
University of Arkansas	M,O
University of Arkansas at Pine Bluff	M
University of Bridgeport	M,O
University of California, Irvine	M,D*
University of Central Florida	M,D
University of Central Missouri	M,D,O
University of Central Oklahoma	M
University of Cincinnati	M
University of Colorado Denver	M
University of Connecticut	M,D,O*
The University of Findlay	M
University of Florida	M,D,O*
University of Georgia	M,D,O
University of Hartford	M
University of Houston–Downtown	M
University of Illinois at Chicago	M,D
University of Indianapolis	M
The University of Iowa	M,D*
University of Louisiana at Monroe	M,D
University of Louisville	M,D
University of Maine	M,O
University of Maryland, Baltimore County	M
University of Massachusetts Amherst	M,D,O*
University of Massachusetts Boston	M,D,O
University of Massachusetts Dartmouth	M,O
University of Memphis	M,D
University of Michigan–Flint	M
University of Minnesota, Twin Cities Campus	M,D,O
University of Missouri	M,D,O*
University of Missouri–St. Louis	M,O
University of Montevallo	M
University of Nebraska at Omaha	M
University of Nevada, Reno	M*
University of New Hampshire	M
University of New Mexico	M*
University of North Alabama	M
The University of North Carolina at Charlotte	M
The University of North Carolina at Greensboro	D
The University of North Carolina at Pembroke	M
The University of North Carolina Wilmington	M
University of North Dakota	M,D
University of Northern Iowa	M
University of North Florida	M
University of Oklahoma	M,D,O*
University of Pennsylvania	M*
University of Phoenix	M
University of Phoenix–Central Florida Campus	M
University of Phoenix–Central Valley Campus	M
University of Phoenix–Chattanooga Campus	M
University of Phoenix–Denver Campus	M
University of Phoenix–Hawaii Campus	M
University of Phoenix–Idaho Campus	M
University of Phoenix–Indianapolis Campus	M
University of Phoenix–Las Vegas Campus	M
University of Phoenix–Memphis Campus	M
University of Phoenix–Metro Detroit Campus	M
University of Phoenix–Nashville Campus	M
University of Phoenix–New Mexico Campus	M
University of Phoenix–Northern Nevada Campus	M
University of Phoenix–North Florida Campus	M
University of Phoenix–Omaha Campus	M
University of Phoenix–Oregon Campus	M
University of Phoenix–Phoenix Campus	M
University of Phoenix–Sacramento Valley Campus	M,O
University of Phoenix–San Diego Campus	M
University of Phoenix–Southern Arizona Campus	M,O
University of Phoenix–Southern Colorado Campus	M,O
University of Phoenix–South Florida Campus	M
University of Phoenix–Utah Campus	M
University of Phoenix–Washington D.C. Campus	M,D,O
University of Phoenix–West Florida Campus	M
University of Pittsburgh	M*
University of Puget Sound	M
University of Rhode Island	M,D
University of St. Francis (IL)	M
University of St. Thomas (MN)	M,O
The University of Scranton	M
University of South Alabama	M,O
University of South Carolina	M,D
University of South Carolina Upstate	M
The University of South Dakota	M
University of Southern Indiana	M
University of Southern Mississippi	M,D,O
University of South Florida	M,D,O*
The University of Tennessee	M,D,O
The University of Tennessee at Chattanooga	M,O
The University of Texas–Pan American	M
University of the Cumberlands	M,D,O
University of the Incarnate Word	M
The University of Toledo	M,D,O
University of Tulsa	M
University of Utah	M,D*
University of Virginia	M,D,O
University of Washington, Tacoma	M
The University of West Alabama	M
University of West Florida	M,D
University of Wisconsin–Eau Claire	M
University of Wisconsin–La Crosse	M
University of Wisconsin–Milwaukee	M
University of Wisconsin–Platteville	M
University of Wisconsin–River Falls	M
University of Wisconsin–Stevens Point	M
Utah State University	M
Vanderbilt University	M*
Villanova University	M
Virginia Commonwealth University	M,O
Wagner College	M
Walden University	M,D,O
Washington State University	M,D
Washington University in St. Louis	M*
Wayne State College	M
Wayne State University	M,D,O*
West Chester University of Pennsylvania	M,O
Western Illinois University	M
Western Kentucky University	M,O
Western New England University	M
Western New Mexico University	M
Western Washington University	M
Westfield State University	M
West Virginia University	M
Wheaton College	M
Wheelock College	M
Whittier College	M
Whitworth University	M
Widener University	M,D
William Carey University	M,O
William Woods University	M,O
Wilmington University	M
Wilson College	M
Wingate University	M
Winston-Salem State University	M
Worcester State University	M
Wright State University	M
Xavier University	M

EMERGENCY MANAGEMENT

Institution	Degrees
Adelphi University	O*
American Public University System	M
Anna Maria College	M,O
Arkansas Tech University	M
Benedictine University	M
Boston University	M*
California State University, Long Beach	M
Capella University	M,D
Drexel University	M*
Florida Institute of Technology	M
Fordham University	M
George Mason University	M,D,O*
The George Washington University	M,D,O
Georgia State University	M,D,O
Grand Canyon University	M
Indiana University of Pennsylvania	M
Jacksonville State University	M,D
The Johns Hopkins University	M,O
Lynn University	M,O
Massachusetts Maritime Academy	M
Millersville University of Pennsylvania	M
New Jersey Institute of Technology	M,D
New York Medical College	O*
North Dakota State University	M,D
Oklahoma State University	M,D*

*M—master's degree; P—first professional degree; D—doctorate; O—other advanced degree; *—Close-Up and/or Display in one of the other books in this series*

Park University M
Philadelphia University M
Royal Roads University M,O
San Diego State University M,D
TUI University M,D,O
Université de Montréal O
University of Central Florida M,O
University of Colorado Denver M,D
University of Denver M,O
University of Hawaii at Manoa O
University of Medicine and Dentistry of New Jersey M,D,O
University of Nevada, Las Vegas M,D,O
University of New Haven M,O
The University of North Carolina at Charlotte M,D,O
University of Rochester M,D,O
Virginia Commonwealth University M,O
Walden University M,D,O
West Chester University of Pennsylvania M,O
York University M*

EMERGENCY MEDICAL SERVICES

Baylor University D*
Drexel University M*
San Diego State University M,D
Université Laval O
University of Guelph M,D,O

ENERGY AND POWER ENGINEERING

Florida State University M,D
Instituto Tecnologico de Santo Domingo M,D,O
Lehigh University M
Marylhurst University M
New Jersey Institute of Technology M
New York Institute of Technology M,O
North Carolina Agricultural and Technical State University M,D
Northeastern University M
Santa Clara University M,D,O
Southern Illinois University Carbondale D
Universidad Autonoma de Guadalajara M,D
University of Alberta M,D
University of Massachusetts Lowell M,D
University of Memphis M,D
University of Rochester M,D*
The University of Tennessee at Chattanooga M,O
University of Wisconsin–Madison M,D*
Worcester Polytechnic Institute M,D

ENERGY MANAGEMENT AND POLICY

Franklin Pierce University M,D,O
Holy Names University M
Indiana University Bloomington M,D,O*
Instituto Tecnologico de Santo Domingo M,D,O
New York Institute of Technology M,O
Santa Clara University M,D,O
Université du Québec, Institut National de la Recherche Scientifique M,D
University of California, Berkeley M,D*
University of Colorado Denver M
University of Delaware M,D*
University of Denver M,O
University of Illinois at Urbana–Champaign M
University of Phoenix M
University of Phoenix–Puerto Rico Campus M
University of Tulsa M
University of Washington M,D*

ENGINEERING AND APPLIED SCIENCES—GENERAL

Air Force Institute of Technology M,D
Alabama Agricultural and Mechanical University M
Alfred University M,D
The American University in Cairo M,D,O
The American University of Athens M
American University of Beirut M,D
Andrews University M
Arizona State University M,D,O
Arkansas State University M
Arkansas Tech University M
Auburn University M,D
Baylor University M,D*
Boise State University M,D
Boston University M,D*
Bradley University M
Brigham Young University M,D*
Brown University M,D
Bucknell University M
California Institute of Technology M,D,O
California National University for Advanced Studies M
California Polytechnic State University, San Luis Obispo M
California State University, Chico M
California State University, East Bay M
California State University, Fresno M
California State University, Fullerton M
California State University, Los Angeles M*
California State University, Northridge M
California State University, Sacramento M
Carleton University M,D
Case Western Reserve University M,D*
The Catholic University of America M,D,O
Central Connecticut State University M,O
Central Michigan University M
Central Washington University M
Christian Brothers University M
City College of the City University of New York M,D
Clarkson University M,D*
Clemson University M,D
Cleveland State University M,D
Colorado School of Mines M,D,O
Colorado State University M,D
Colorado State University–Pueblo M
Columbia University M,D,O*
Concordia University (Canada) M,D,O
Cooper Union for the Advancement of Science and Art M
Cornell University M,D*
Dalhousie University M,D
Dartmouth College M,D
Drexel University M,D,O*
Duke University M*
Eastern Illinois University M,O
Eastern Michigan University M
École Polytechnique de Montréal M,D,O
Fairfield University M
Fairleigh Dickinson University, Metropolitan Campus M
Florida Agricultural and Mechanical University M,D
Florida Atlantic University M,D
Florida Institute of Technology M,D
Florida International University M,D
Florida State University M,D
George Mason University M,D,O*
The George Washington University M,D,O
Georgia Institute of Technology M,D
Graduate School and University Center of the City University of New York D
Grand Valley State University M
Harvard University M,D*
Howard University M,D
Idaho State University M,D,O
Illinois Institute of Technology M,D
Indiana State University M
Indiana University–Purdue University Fort Wayne M,O
Instituto Tecnologico de Santo Domingo M,O
Instituto Tecnológico y de Estudios Superiores de Monterrey, Campus Ciudad Obregón M
Instituto Tecnológico y de Estudios Superiores de Monterrey, Campus Monterrey M,D
Iowa State University of Science and Technology M,D*
The Johns Hopkins University M,D,O
Kansas State University M,D*
Kent State University M*
Lakehead University M
Lamar University M,D
Laurentian University M,D
Lawrence Technological University M,D
Lehigh University M,D
LeTourneau University M
Louisiana State University and Agricultural and Mechanical College M,D
Louisiana Tech University M,D
Manhattan College M
Marquette University M,D,O
Marshall University M
Massachusetts Institute of Technology M,D,O
McGill University M,D,O
McMaster University M,D
McNeese State University M
Memorial University of Newfoundland M,D
Mercer University M
Miami University M,O
Michigan State University M,D
Michigan Technological University M,D
Milwaukee School of Engineering M
Mississippi State University M,D
Missouri University of Science and Technology M,D
Missouri Western State University M
Montana State University M,D
Montana Tech of The University of Montana M
Morgan State University M,D
National University M
New Jersey Institute of Technology M,D,O
New Mexico State University M,D
New York Institute of Technology M,O
North Carolina Agricultural and Technical State University M,D
North Carolina State University M,D*
North Dakota State University M,D
Northeastern University M,D,O
Northern Arizona University M,D,O
Northern Illinois University M
Northwestern Polytechnic University M
Northwestern University M,D,O*
Oakland University M,D
The Ohio State University M,D
Ohio University M,D*
Oklahoma State University M,D*
Old Dominion University M,D
Oregon State University M,D
Penn State Erie, The Behrend College M
Penn State Great Valley M
Penn State Harrisburg M
Penn State University Park M,D
Pittsburg State University M
Pontificia Universidad Catolica Madre y Maestra M
Portland State University M,D,O
Prairie View A&M University M,D
Princeton University M,D*
Purdue University M,D,O
Purdue University Calumet M
Queen's University at Kingston M,D
Rensselaer at Hartford M
Rensselaer Polytechnic Institute M,D
Rice University M,D
Robert Morris University M
Rochester Institute of Technology M,D,O
Rose-Hulman Institute of Technology M
Rowan University M
Royal Military College of Canada M,D
St. Cloud State University M
St. Mary's University (United States) M
San Diego State University M,D
San Francisco State University M
San Jose State University M
Santa Clara University M,D,O
Seattle University M
Simon Fraser University M,D
South Dakota School of Mines and Technology M,D
South Dakota State University M,D
Southern Illinois University Carbondale M,D
Southern Illinois University Edwardsville M
Southern Methodist University M,D
Southern Polytechnic State University M,O
Southern University and Agricultural and Mechanical College M
Stanford University M,D,O
State University of New York at Binghamton M,D

State University of New York Institute of Technology	M
Stevens Institute of Technology	M,D,O
Stony Brook University, State University of New York	M,D,O
Syracuse University	M,D,O*
Temple University	M,D*
Tennessee State University	M,D
Tennessee Technological University	M,D
Texas A&M University	M,D
Texas A&M University–Kingsville	M,D
Texas Tech University	M,D*
Trine University	M
Tufts University	M,D
Tuskegee University	M,D
Union Graduate College	M
Universidad de las Américas–Puebla	M,D
Université de Moncton	M
Université de Sherbrooke	M,D,O
Université du Québec à Chicoutimi	M,D
Université du Québec à Rimouski	M
Université du Québec, École de technologie supérieure	M,D,O
Université du Québec en Abitibi-Témiscamingue	M,O
Université Laval	M,D,O
University at Buffalo, the State University of New York	M,D*
The University of Akron	M,D
The University of Alabama	M,D
The University of Alabama at Birmingham	M,D*
The University of Alabama in Huntsville	M,D
University of Alaska Anchorage	M,O
University of Alaska Fairbanks	M,D
The University of Arizona	M,D,O
University of Arkansas	M,D
University of Bridgeport	M,D
The University of British Columbia	M,D
University of Calgary	M,D
University of California, Berkeley	M,D,O*
University of California, Davis	M,D,O
University of California, Irvine	M,D*
University of California, Los Angeles	M,D*
University of California, Merced	M,D
University of California, Santa Barbara	M,D
University of California, Santa Cruz	M,D
University of Central Florida	M,D,O
University of Central Oklahoma	M
University of Cincinnati	M,D
University of Colorado at Colorado Springs	M,D
University of Colorado Boulder	M,D*
University of Colorado Denver	M,D
University of Connecticut	M,D*
University of Dayton	M,D
University of Delaware	M,D*
University of Denver	M,D
University of Detroit Mercy	M,D
University of Evansville	M
University of Florida	M,D,O*
University of Guelph	M,D
University of Hartford	M
University of Hawaii at Manoa	M,D
University of Houston	M,D
University of Idaho	M,D
University of Illinois at Chicago	M,D
University of Illinois at Urbana–Champaign	M,D
The University of Iowa	M,D*
The University of Kansas	M,D
University of Kentucky	M,D*
University of Louisville	M,D,O
University of Maine	M,D
University of Manitoba	M,D
University of Maryland, Baltimore County	M,D,O
University of Maryland, College Park	M
University of Massachusetts Amherst	M,D*
University of Massachusetts Dartmouth	M,D,O
University of Massachusetts Lowell	M,D,O
University of Memphis	M,D
University of Miami	M,D*
University of Michigan	M,D,O*
University of Michigan–Dearborn	M,D
University of Minnesota, Twin Cities Campus	M,D
University of Mississippi	M,D
University of Missouri	M,D*
University of Missouri–Kansas City	M,D*
University of Nebraska–Lincoln	M,D*
University of Nevada, Las Vegas	M,D
University of Nevada, Reno	M,D*
University of New Brunswick Fredericton	M,D,O
University of New Haven	M,O
University of New Mexico	M,D,O*
University of New Orleans	M,D,O
The University of North Carolina at Charlotte	M,D
University of North Dakota	D
University of North Texas	M
University of Notre Dame	M,D*
University of Oklahoma	M,D*
University of Ottawa	M,D,O*
University of Pennsylvania	M,D,O*
University of Pittsburgh	M,D*
University of Portland	M
University of Puerto Rico, Mayagüez Campus	M,D
University of Regina	M,D
University of Rhode Island	M,D,O
University of Rochester	M,D
University of St. Thomas (MN)	M,O
University of Saskatchewan	M,D,O
University of South Africa	M
University of South Alabama	M
University of South Carolina	M,D
University of Southern California	M,D,O*
University of Southern Indiana	M
University of South Florida	M,D*
The University of Tennessee	M,D
The University of Tennessee at Chattanooga	M,D,O
The University of Tennessee Space Institute	M,D
The University of Texas at Arlington	M,D
The University of Texas at Austin	M,D
The University of Texas at Dallas	M,D*
The University of Texas at El Paso	M,D,O
The University of Texas at San Antonio	M,D*
University of the District of Columbia	M
The University of Toledo	M
University of Toronto	M,D
University of Tulsa	M,D
University of Utah	M,D*
University of Vermont	M,D
University of Victoria	M,D
University of Virginia	M,D
University of Washington	M,D*
University of Waterloo	M,D
The University of Western Ontario	M,D
University of Windsor	M,D
University of Wisconsin–Madison	M,D*
University of Wisconsin–Milwaukee	M,D,O
University of Wisconsin–Platteville	M
University of Wyoming	M,D
Utah State University	M,D,O
Vanderbilt University	M,D*
Villanova University	M,D,O
Virginia Commonwealth University	M,D
Virginia Polytechnic Institute and State University	M,D,O
Washington State University	M,D
Washington State University Tri-Cities	M,D
Washington State University Vancouver	M
Washington University in St. Louis	M,D*
Wayne State University	M,D,O*
Western Michigan University	M,D
Western New England University	M,D
West Texas A&M University	M
West Virginia University	M,D
West Virginia University Institute of Technology	M
Wichita State University	M,D
Widener University	M
Wilkes University	M
Worcester Polytechnic Institute	M,D,O
Wright State University	M,D
Yale University	M,D*
Youngstown State University	M

ENGINEERING DESIGN

Northwestern University	M*
Polytechnic Institute of NYU, Long Island Graduate Center	M
Rochester Institute of Technology	M
San Diego State University	M,D
Santa Clara University	M,D,O
Stanford University	M
Stevens Institute of Technology	M
University of Central Florida	M,D,O
Worcester Polytechnic Institute	M,O

ENGINEERING MANAGEMENT

Air Force Institute of Technology	M
American University of Beirut	M,D
California National University for Advanced Studies	M
California State Polytechnic University, Pomona	M
California State University, East Bay	M
California State University, Long Beach	M,D
California State University, Northridge	M
Case Western Reserve University	M*
The Catholic University of America	M,O
Clarkson University	M*
Colorado School of Mines	M,D
Cornell University	M,D*
Dallas Baptist University	M
Dartmouth College	M
Drexel University	M,O*
Duke University	M*
Eastern Michigan University	M
Florida Institute of Technology	M,D
Gannon University	M
The George Washington University	M,D,O
Instituto Tecnológico y de Estudios Superiores de Monterrey, Campus Chihuahua	M,O
International Technological University	M
The Johns Hopkins University	M
Kansas State University	M,D*
Kettering University	M
Lamar University	M,D
Lawrence Technological University	M,D
Lehigh University	M,D
Long Island University, C.W. Post Campus	M
Loyola Marymount University	M
Marquette University	M,D,O
Marshall University	M
Massachusetts Institute of Technology	M,D
McNeese State University	M
Mercer University	M
Milwaukee School of Engineering	M
Missouri University of Science and Technology	M,D
National University	M
New Jersey Institute of Technology	M
New Mexico Institute of Mining and Technology	M
Northeastern University	M,D
Northwestern University	M*
Oakland University	M
Old Dominion University	M,D
Point Park University	M
Polytechnic University of Puerto Rico	M
Polytechnic University of Puerto Rico, Orlando Campus	M
Portland State University	M,D,O
Rensselaer Polytechnic Institute	M,D
Robert Morris University	M
Rochester Institute of Technology	M
Rose-Hulman Institute of Technology	M
Rowan University	M
St. Cloud State University	M
Saint Martin's University	M
St. Mary's University (United States)	M
Santa Clara University	M
South Dakota School of Mines and Technology	M
Southern Methodist University	M,D
Stanford University	M,D

*M—master's degree; P—first professional degree; D—doctorate; O—other advanced degree; *—Close-Up and/or Display in one of the other books in this series*

Stevens Institute of Technology	M,D
Syracuse University	M*
Texas Tech University	M,D*
Tufts University	M
Union Graduate College	M
Université de Sherbrooke	M,O
The University of Akron	M
The University of Alabama in Huntsville	M,D
University of Alaska Anchorage	M
University of Alaska Fairbanks	M,D
University of Alberta	M,D
University of California, Berkeley	M,D*
University of Colorado at Colorado Springs	M
University of Colorado Boulder	M*
University of Dayton	M
University of Detroit Mercy	M
University of Idaho	M
The University of Kansas	M
University of Louisiana at Lafayette	M*
University of Louisville	M,D,O
The University of Manchester	M,D
University of Maryland, Baltimore County	M,O
University of Massachusetts Amherst	*
University of Michigan–Dearborn	M,D
University of Minnesota, Duluth	M
University of Nebraska–Lincoln	M,D*
University of New Brunswick Fredericton	M
University of New Haven	M
University of New Orleans	M,O
The University of North Carolina at Charlotte	M
University of Oklahoma	M,D*
University of Ottawa	M,O*
University of St. Thomas (MN)	M,O
University of Southern California	M,D,O*
University of South Florida	M,D*
The University of Tennessee	M,D
The University of Tennessee at Chattanooga	M,O
The University of Tennessee Space Institute	M,D
The University of Texas at Arlington	M
University of Waterloo	M,D
University of Wisconsin–Madison	M*
University of Wisconsin–Milwaukee	M,D,O
Valparaiso University	M,O
Virginia Polytechnic Institute and State University	M,O
Walden University	M,D
Washington State University Spokane	M
Wayne State University	M*
Webster University	M
Western Michigan University	M
Western New England University	M,D
Widener University	M
Wilkes University	M

ENGINEERING PHYSICS

Air Force Institute of Technology	M,D
Appalachian State University	M
Cornell University	M,D*
Dartmouth College	M,D
École Polytechnique de Montréal	M,D,O
Embry-Riddle Aeronautical University–Daytona	D
George Mason University	M,D*
McMaster University	M,D
Michigan Technological University	D
Polytechnic Institute of NYU	M
Polytechnic Institute of NYU, Long Island Graduate Center	M
Rensselaer Polytechnic Institute	M,D
Stevens Institute of Technology	M,D,O
University of California, San Diego	M,D*
University of Maine	M
University of Oklahoma	M,D*
University of Saskatchewan	M,D
University of Tulsa	M
University of Virginia	M,D
University of Wisconsin–Madison	M,D*
Yale University	M,D*

ENGLISH

Abilene Christian University	M
Acadia University	M
The American University in Cairo	M
American University of Beirut	M
Andrews University	M
Angelo State University	M
Appalachian State University	M
Arcadia University	M*
Arizona State University	M,D,O
Arkansas State University	M,O
Arkansas Tech University	M
Asbury University	M
Auburn University	M,D
Austin Peay State University	M
Ball State University	M,D
Baylor University	M,D*
Belmont University	M
Bemidji State University	M
Bennington College	M
Bob Jones University	P,M,D,O
Boise State University	M
Boston College	M,D*
Boston University	M,D,O*
Bowie State University	M
Bowling Green State University	M,D*
Bradley University	M
Brandeis University	M,D
Bridgewater State University	M
Brigham Young University	M*
Brock University	M
Brooklyn College of the City University of New York	M,D
Brown University	M,D
Bucknell University	M
Buffalo State College, State University of New York	M
Butler University	M
California Baptist University	M
California Polytechnic State University, San Luis Obispo	M
California State Polytechnic University, Pomona	M
California State University, Bakersfield	M
California State University, Chico	M
California State University, Dominguez Hills	M,O*
California State University, East Bay	M
California State University, Fresno	M
California State University, Fullerton	M
California State University, Long Beach	M
California State University, Los Angeles	M*
California State University, Northridge	M
California State University, Sacramento	M
California State University, San Bernardino	M
California State University, San Marcos	M
California State University, Stanislaus	M,O
Carleton University	M,D
Carnegie Mellon University	M,D*
Case Western Reserve University	M,D*
The Catholic University of America	M,D,O
Central Connecticut State University	M,O
Central Michigan University	M
Central Washington University	M
Chapman University	M
Chicago State University	M
The Citadel, The Military College of South Carolina	M
City College of the City University of New York	M
Claremont Graduate University	M,D
Clarion University of Pennsylvania	M
Clark Atlanta University	M,D
Clark University	M
Clemson University	M
Cleveland State University	M
The College at Brockport, State University of New York	M
College of Charleston	M
The College of New Jersey	M
The College of Saint Rose	M
College of Staten Island of the City University of New York	M
Colorado State University	M
Columbia University	M,D*
Concordia University (Canada)	M
Converse College	M
Cornell University	M,D*
Creighton University	M
Dalhousie University	M,D
DePaul University	M
Drew University	M
Duke University	D*
Duquesne University	M,D
East Carolina University	M
Eastern Illinois University	M
Eastern Kentucky University	M
Eastern Michigan University	M,O
Eastern New Mexico University	M
Eastern Washington University	M
East Tennessee State University	M,O
Elmhurst College	M
Emory University	D,O*
Emporia State University	M
Fairleigh Dickinson University, Metropolitan Campus	M
Fayetteville State University	M
Fitchburg State University	M,O
Florida Atlantic University	M
Florida Gulf Coast University	M
Florida International University	M
Florida State University	M,D
Fordham University	M,D
Fort Hays State University	M
Gannon University	M
Gardner-Webb University	M
George Mason University	M,D,O*
Georgetown University	M
The George Washington University	M,D
Georgia College & State University	M
Georgia Southern University	M
Georgia State University	M,D
Governors State University	M
Graduate School and University Center of the City University of New York	D
Grambling State University	M,D
Grand Valley State University	M
Hardin-Simmons University	M
Harvard University	M,D,O*
Heritage University	M
Hofstra University	M
Hollins University	M
Howard University	M,D
Humboldt State University	M
Hunter College of the City University of New York	M
Idaho State University	M,D,O
Illinois State University	M,D
Indiana State University	M
Indiana University Bloomington	M,D*
Indiana University of Pennsylvania	M,D
Indiana University–Purdue University Fort Wayne	M,O
Indiana University–Purdue University Indianapolis	M
Indiana University South Bend	M
Inter American University of Puerto Rico, Metropolitan Campus	M
Iona College	M
Iowa State University of Science and Technology	M,D*
Jackson State University	M
Jacksonville State University	M
James Madison University	M
John Carroll University	M
The Johns Hopkins University	D
Kansas State University	M*
Kent State University	M,D*
Kutztown University of Pennsylvania	M
Lakehead University	M
Lamar University	M
La Sierra University	M
Lehigh University	M,D
Lehman College of the City University of New York	M
Long Island University, Brooklyn Campus	M
Long Island University, C.W. Post Campus	M
Longwood University	M
Louisiana State University and Agricultural and Mechanical College	M,D
Louisiana Tech University	M

Institution	Degrees
Loyola Marymount University	M
Loyola University Chicago	M,D
Lynchburg College	M
Marquette University	M,D
Marshall University	M
Mary Baldwin College	M
Marygrove College	M
Marymount University	M
McGill University	M,D
McMaster University	M,D
McNeese State University	M
Memorial University of Newfoundland	M,D
Mercy College	M
Miami University	M,D
Michigan State University	M,D
Middlebury College	M
Middle Tennessee State University	M,D
Midwestern State University	M
Millersville University of Pennsylvania	M
Mills College	M
Minnesota State University Mankato	M,O
Mississippi College	M
Mississippi State University	M
Missouri State University	M
Monmouth University	M
Montana State University	M
Montclair State University	M,O
Morehead State University	M
Morgan State University	M,D
Mount Mary College	M
Murray State University	M
National University	M
New Mexico Highlands University	M
New Mexico State University	M,D
New York University	M,D,O
North Carolina Agricultural and Technical State University	M
North Carolina Central University	M
North Carolina State University	M*
North Dakota State University	M
Northeastern Illinois University	M
Northeastern State University	M
Northeastern University	M,D
Northern Arizona University	M,D,O
Northern Illinois University	M,D
Northern Kentucky University	M,O
Northern Michigan University	M
Northwestern State University of Louisiana	M
Northwestern University	M,D*
Northwest Missouri State University	M
Notre Dame de Namur University	M,O
Oakland University	M
The Ohio State University	M,D
Ohio University	M,D*
Oklahoma State University	M,D*
Old Dominion University	M,D
Oregon State University	M
Our Lady of the Lake University of San Antonio	M
Penn State University Park	M,D
Pittsburg State University	M
Portland State University	M
Prairie View A&M University	M
Princeton University	D*
Purdue University	M,D
Purdue University Calumet	M
Queens College of the City University of New York	M
Queen's University at Kingston	M,D
Radford University	M
Rhode Island College	M,O
Rice University	M,D
Rivier College	M
Roosevelt University	M
Rosemont College	M
Rutgers, The State University of New Jersey, Camden	M
Rutgers, The State University of New Jersey, Newark	M*
Rutgers, The State University of New Jersey, New Brunswick	D*
St. Bonaventure University	M
St. Cloud State University	M
St. John's University (NY)	M,D
Saint Louis University	M,D
Saint Louis University–Madrid Campus	M
St. Mary's University (United States)	M
Saint Xavier University	M,O
Salem State University	M
Salisbury University	M
Sam Houston State University	M
San Diego State University	M
San Francisco State University	M
San Jose State University	M
Seton Hall University	M
Sewanee: The University of the South	M
Simmons College	M
Simon Fraser University	M,D
Sonoma State University	M
South Dakota State University	M
Southeastern Louisiana University	M
Southeast Missouri State University	M
Southern Connecticut State University	M
Southern Illinois University Carbondale	M,D
Southern Illinois University Edwardsville	M,O
Southern Methodist University	M,D
Spring Hill College	M
Stanford University	M,D
State University of New York at Binghamton	M,D
State University of New York at Fredonia	M
State University of New York at New Paltz	M
State University of New York at Oswego	M
State University of New York College at Cortland	M
State University of New York College at Potsdam	M
Stephen F. Austin State University	M
Stetson University	M
Stony Brook University, State University of New York	M,D,O
Sul Ross State University	M
Syracuse University	M,D*
Tarleton State University	M
Temple University	M,D*
Tennessee State University	M
Tennessee Technological University	M
Texas A&M International University	M,D
Texas A&M University	M,D
Texas A&M University–Commerce	M,D
Texas A&M University–Corpus Christi	M
Texas A&M University–Kingsville	M
Texas A&M University–San Antonio	M
Texas A&M University–Texarkana	M
Texas Christian University	M,D
Texas Southern University	M
Texas State University–San Marcos	M
Texas Tech University	M,D*
Texas Woman's University	M,D
Trinity College	M
Trinity Western University	M
Truman State University	M
Tufts University	M,D
Tulane University	M,D*
Universidad de las Américas–Puebla	M
Université de Montréal	M,D
Université Laval	M,D
University at Albany, State University of New York	M,D
University at Buffalo, the State University of New York	M,D*
The University of Akron	M
The University of Alabama	M,D
The University of Alabama at Birmingham	M*
The University of Alabama in Huntsville	M,O
University of Alaska Anchorage	M
University of Alaska Fairbanks	M
University of Alberta	M,D
The University of Arizona	M,D
University of Arkansas	M,D
The University of British Columbia	M,D
University of Calgary	M,D
University of California, Berkeley	D*
University of California, Davis	M,D
University of California, Irvine	M,D*
University of California, Los Angeles	M,D*
University of California, Riverside	M,D
University of California, San Diego	M*
University of California, Santa Barbara	D
University of California, Santa Cruz	M,D
University of Central Arkansas	M
University of Central Florida	M,O
University of Central Missouri	M
University of Central Oklahoma	M
University of Chicago	M,D
University of Cincinnati	M,D
University of Colorado Boulder	M,D*
University of Colorado Denver	M
University of Connecticut	M,D*
University of Dallas	M
University of Dayton	M
University of Delaware	M,D*
University of Denver	M,D
University of Florida	M,D*
University of Georgia	M,D
University of Guam	M
University of Guelph	M
University of Hawaii at Manoa	M,D
University of Houston–Clear Lake	M
University of Houston–Downtown	M
University of Idaho	M
University of Illinois at Chicago	M,D
University of Illinois at Springfield	M
University of Illinois at Urbana–Champaign	M,D
University of Indianapolis	M
The University of Iowa	M,D*
The University of Kansas	M,D
University of Kentucky	M,D*
University of Lethbridge	M,D
University of Louisiana at Lafayette	M,D*
University of Louisiana at Monroe	M
University of Louisville	M,D
University of Maine	M
The University of Manchester	D
University of Manitoba	M,D
University of Maryland, College Park	M,D
University of Massachusetts Amherst	M,D*
University of Massachusetts Boston	M
University of Memphis	M,D,O
University of Miami	M,D*
University of Michigan	M,D,O*
University of Michigan–Flint	M
University of Minnesota, Duluth	M
University of Minnesota, Twin Cities Campus	M,D
University of Mississippi	M,D
University of Missouri	M,D*
University of Missouri–Kansas City	M,D*
University of Missouri–St. Louis	M,O
The University of Montana	M
University of Montevallo	M
University of Nebraska at Kearney	M
University of Nebraska at Omaha	M,O
University of Nebraska–Lincoln	M,D*
University of Nevada, Las Vegas	M,D
University of Nevada, Reno	M,D*
University of New Brunswick Fredericton	M,D
University of New Hampshire	M,D
University of New Mexico	M,D*
University of New Orleans	M
University of North Alabama	M
The University of North Carolina at Chapel Hill	M,D*
The University of North Carolina at Charlotte	M,O
The University of North Carolina at Greensboro	M,D
The University of North Carolina Wilmington	M
University of North Dakota	M,D
University of Northern Colorado	M
University of Northern Iowa	M
University of North Florida	M
University of North Texas	M,D
University of Notre Dame	M,D*
University of Oklahoma	M,D*
University of Oregon	M,D
University of Ottawa	M,D*
University of Pennsylvania	M,D*
University of Pittsburgh	M,D*
University of Puerto Rico, Mayagüez Campus	M
University of Puerto Rico, Río Piedras	M,D
University of Regina	M

*M—master's degree; P—first professional degree; D—doctorate; O—other advanced degree; *—Close-Up and/or Display in one of the other books in this series*

University of Rhode Island M,D
University of Rochester
University of St. Thomas (MN) M
University of Saskatchewan M,D
University of South Africa M,D
University of South Alabama M
University of South Carolina M,D
The University of South Dakota M,D
University of Southern California M,D*
University of Southern Mississippi M,D
University of South Florida M,D*
The University of Tennessee M,D
The University of Tennessee at Chattanooga M,O
The University of Texas at Arlington M,D
The University of Texas at Austin M,D
The University of Texas at Brownsville M
The University of Texas at Dallas M,D*
The University of Texas at El Paso M,D,O
The University of Texas at San Antonio M,D*
The University of Texas at Tyler M
The University of Texas of the Permian Basin M
The University of Texas–Pan American M
University of the District of Columbia M
The University of Toledo M,O
University of Toronto M,D
University of Tulsa M,D
University of Utah M,D*
University of Vermont M
University of Victoria M,D
University of Virginia M,D,O
University of Washington M,D*
University of Waterloo M,D
The University of Western Ontario M,D
University of West Florida M
University of West Georgia M
University of Windsor M
University of Wisconsin–Eau Claire M
University of Wisconsin–Madison M,D*
University of Wisconsin–Milwaukee M,D,O
University of Wisconsin–Oshkosh M
University of Wisconsin–Stevens Point M
University of Wyoming M
Utah State University M
Valdosta State University M
Valparaiso University M,O
Vanderbilt University M,D*
Villanova University M
Virginia Commonwealth University M
Virginia Polytechnic Institute and State University M,D
Virginia State University M
Wake Forest University M
Washington College M
Washington State University M,D
Washington University in St. Louis M,D*
Wayne State University M,D*
Weber State University M
West Chester University of Pennsylvania M,O
Western Carolina University M
Western Connecticut State University M
Western Illinois University M,O
Western Kentucky University M
Western Michigan University M,D
Western Washington University M
Westfield State University M
West Texas A&M University M
West Virginia University M,D
Wichita State University M
Wilfrid Laurier University M,D
William Paterson University of New Jersey M
Winona State University M
Winthrop University M
Wright State University M
Xavier University M
Yale University M,D*
York University M,D*
Youngstown State University M

ENGLISH AS A SECOND LANGUAGE

Adelphi University M,O*
Albright College M
Alliant International University–Fresno M,D,O
Alliant International University–Irvine M,D
Alliant International University–San Diego M,D,O
American College of Education M
American University M,O
The American University in Cairo M,O
American University of Sharjah M
Anaheim University M,O
Andrews University M,D,O
Arizona State University M,D,O
Arkansas Tech University M
Asbury University M
Avila University M,O
Azusa Pacific University M
Ball State University M,D
Barry University M,D,O*
Biola University M,D,O
Bishop's University M,O
Boston University M,D,O*
Brigham Young University M,O*
Brock University M
Buena Vista University M
California Baptist University M
California State University, Dominguez Hills M,O*
California State University, Fresno M
California State University, Fullerton M
California State University, Long Beach M
California State University, Sacramento M
California State University, San Bernardino M,D
California State University, Stanislaus M,O
Cambridge College M,D,O
Cardinal Stritch University M
Carlos Albizu University, Miami Campus M,D
Carson-Newman College M
Central Connecticut State University M,O
Central Michigan University M
Central Washington University M
Christopher Newport University M
Cleveland State University M
College of Charleston O
The College of New Jersey M,O
The College of New Rochelle M,O
College of Notre Dame of Maryland M
College of Saint Mary M
Columbia International University M,D,O
Concordia University (Canada) M,O
Cornerstone University M,O
Dallas Baptist University M
DeSales University M
Dominican University M
Duquesne University M,D
Eastern Michigan University M,O
Eastern Nazarene College M,O
Eastern New Mexico University M
Eastern Washington University M
Elms College M,O
Emporia State University M
Erikson Institute M,O
Fairfield University M,O
Florida Atlantic University M,D,O
Florida International University M,D,O
Fordham University M,D,O
Framingham State University M
Fresno Pacific University M
Furman University M,O
Gannon University O
George Fox University M
George Mason University M,D,O*
Georgetown University M,D,O
Georgia State University M,D,O
Gonzaga University M
Grand Valley State University M,O
Greensboro College M
Hamline University M,D
Harding University M,O
Hawai'i Pacific University M*
Heritage University M
Hofstra University M,O
Holy Names University M,O
Houston Baptist University M
Hunter College of the City University of New York M
Idaho State University M,D,O
Indiana State University M,O
Indiana University Bloomington M,D*
Indiana University of Pennsylvania M,D
Indiana University–Purdue University Fort Wayne M,O
Indiana University–Purdue University Indianapolis M,O
Inter American University of Puerto Rico, Arecibo Campus M
Inter American University of Puerto Rico, Barranquitas Campus M
Inter American University of Puerto Rico, Metropolitan Campus M
Inter American University of Puerto Rico, Ponce Campus M
Inter American University of Puerto Rico, San Germán Campus M
The Johns Hopkins University M,D,O
Kean University M
Kennesaw State University M
Kent State University M,D*
Langston University M
Lehigh University M,O
Lehman College of the City University of New York M
Le Moyne College M,O
Lewis University M
Lipscomb University M,D
Long Island University, Brooklyn Campus M
Long Island University, C.W. Post Campus M
Long Island University, Westchester Graduate Campus M,O
Loyola Marymount University M
Loyola University Chicago M,O
Madonna University M
Manhattanville College M*
Marymount University M
Mercy College M,O
Merrimack College M,O
Mesa State College M
Michigan State University M,D
MidAmerica Nazarene University M
Middle Tennessee State University M,O
Midwest University P,M,D
Minnesota State University Mankato M,O
Mississippi College M
Missouri Western State University M
Monmouth University M,O
Montclair State University M,O
Monterey Institute of International Studies M
Mount Saint Vincent University M
Multnomah University M
Murray State University M
Nazareth College of Rochester M
New Jersey City University M
Newman University M
The New School: A University M
New York University M,D,O
Northeastern Illinois University M
Northern Arizona University M,D,O
Northwest Missouri State University M,O
Notre Dame de Namur University M,O
Nova Southeastern University M,O*
Oakland University M,O
Ohio Dominican University M
Ohio University M*
Oklahoma City University M
Our Lady of the Lake University of San Antonio M
Pontifical Catholic University of Puerto Rico M
Portland State University M
Providence College and Theological Seminary P,M,D,O
Queens College of the City University of New York M
Regent University M,D,O
Rhode Island College M
Rider University O
Rowan University O
Rutgers, The State University of New Jersey, New Brunswick M,D*
St. Cloud State University M
St. John's University (NY) M
Saint Martin's University M
Saint Michael's College M,O
St. Thomas University M,D,O
Salem College M
Salem State University M
Salisbury University M

San Diego State University	M,O
San Francisco State University	M
San Jose State University	M,O
Seattle Pacific University	M
Seattle University	M,O
Shenandoah University	M,D,O
Simmons College	M,O
Simon Fraser University	M
SIT Graduate Institute	M
Soka University of America	O
Southeast Missouri State University	M
Southern Arkansas University–Magnolia	M
Southern Connecticut State University	M
Southern Illinois University Carbondale	M
Southern Illinois University Edwardsville	M,O
Southern New Hampshire University	M,O
Southwest Minnesota State University	M
State University of New York at Fredonia	M
State University of New York at New Paltz	M
State University of New York College at Cortland	M
Stony Brook University, State University of New York	M
Syracuse University	M,O*
Taylor College and Seminary	P,M,O
Teachers College, Columbia University	M,D
Temple University	M,D*
Texas A&M University	M,D
Texas A&M University–Commerce	M,D
Texas A&M University–Kingsville	M
Trevecca Nazarene University	M
Trinity (Washington) University	M
Trinity Western University	M
Universidad del Este	M
Universidad del Turabo	M
University at Buffalo, the State University of New York	M,D,O*
The University of Alabama	M,D
The University of Alabama in Huntsville	M,O
University of Alberta	M,D
The University of Arizona	M,D
University of Arkansas at Little Rock	M
The University of British Columbia	M,D
University of Calgary	M,D,O
University of California, Berkeley	O*
University of California, Los Angeles	M,D,O*
University of Central Florida	M,D,O
University of Central Missouri	M
University of Central Oklahoma	M
University of Cincinnati	M,D,O
University of Delaware	M,D,O*
The University of Findlay	M
University of Florida	M,D,O*
University of Guam	M
University of Hawaii at Manoa	M,D,O
University of Idaho	M
University of Illinois at Chicago	M
University of Illinois at Urbana–Champaign	M,D
The University of Manchester	M,D
University of Manitoba	M
University of Maryland, Baltimore County	M,O
University of Maryland, College Park	M,D,O
University of Massachusetts Amherst	M,D,O*
University of Massachusetts Boston	M
University of Memphis	M,D,O
University of Michigan	M,D*
University of Minnesota, Twin Cities Campus	M
University of Missouri–St. Louis	M,O
University of Nebraska at Omaha	M,O
University of Nevada, Reno	M*
The University of North Carolina at Chapel Hill	M*
The University of North Carolina at Greensboro	M,D,O
University of Northern Iowa	M
University of North Florida	M
University of Pennsylvania	M,D*
University of Phoenix–Milwaukee Campus	M,D,O
University of Phoenix–Omaha Campus	M
University of Phoenix–San Diego Campus	M
University of Phoenix–Southern California Campus	M
University of Phoenix–Springfield Campus	M
University of Phoenix–Washington D.C. Campus	M,D,O
University of Pittsburgh	O*
University of Puerto Rico, Río Piedras	M
University of St. Thomas (MN)	M,O
University of San Diego	M
University of San Francisco	M,D
The University of Scranton	M
University of South Africa	M,D
University of South Carolina	M,D,O
University of Southern California	M*
University of Southern Maine	M,O
University of South Florida	M,D,O*
The University of Tennessee	M,D,O
The University of Texas at Arlington	M
The University of Texas at Brownsville	M
The University of Texas at El Paso	M,O
The University of Texas at San Antonio	M,D*
The University of Texas of the Permian Basin	M
The University of Texas–Pan American	M
The University of Toledo	M,D,O
University of Washington	M,D*
University of Wisconsin–River Falls	M
Valley City State University	M
Valparaiso University	M,O
Virginia International University	M,O
Walden University	M,D,O
Wayne State College	M
Webster University	M
West Chester University of Pennsylvania	M,O
Western Carolina University	M
Western Connecticut State University	M
Western Illinois University	M,O
Western Kentucky University	M
Western New Mexico University	M
West Virginia University	M
Wheaton College	M,O
Wilkes University	M,D
Wright State University	M

ENGLISH EDUCATION

Alabama State University	M,O
Andrews University	M,D,O
Anna Maria College	M,O
Appalachian State University	M
Arcadia University	M,D,O*
Arkansas State University	M,O
Arkansas Tech University	M,O
Armstrong Atlantic State University	M
Auburn University	M,D,O
Averett University	M
Belmont University	M
Bennington College	M
Bob Jones University	P,M,D,O
Boston University	M,D,O*
Brooklyn College of the City University of New York	M,O
Brown University	M
Buffalo State College, State University of New York	M
California Baptist University	M
California State University, Northridge	M
California State University, San Bernardino	M,D
Campbell University	M
Caribbean University	M,D
Carthage College	M,O
Chadron State College	M,O
Chatham University	M
Christopher Newport University	M
The Citadel, The Military College of South Carolina	M
City College of the City University of New York	M,O
Clarion University of Pennsylvania	M
Clayton State University	M
The College at Brockport, State University of New York	M
College of St. Joseph	M
The College of William and Mary	M
The Colorado College	M
Columbia College Chicago	M
Columbus State University	M,O
Converse College	M
Delta State University	M
Duquesne University	M
East Carolina University	M
Eastern Kentucky University	M
Eastern Michigan University	M,O
Elms College	M,O
Fitchburg State University	M,O
Florida Agricultural and Mechanical University	M
Florida Atlantic University	M
Florida Gulf Coast University	M
Florida International University	M,D,O
Florida State University	M,D,O
Framingham State University	M
Gardner-Webb University	M
Georgia Southern University	M
Georgia State University	M,D,O
Grand Valley State University	M
Harding University	M,O
Hofstra University	M,D,O
Humboldt State University	M
Hunter College of the City University of New York	M
Indiana State University	M
Indiana University of Pennsylvania	M,D
Indiana University–Purdue University Fort Wayne	M,O
Indiana University–Purdue University Indianapolis	M
Iona College	M
Ithaca College	M
Jackson State University	M
The Johns Hopkins University	M,O
Kennesaw State University	M
Kent State University	M,D*
Kutztown University of Pennsylvania	M,O
Lehman College of the City University of New York	M
Le Moyne College	M,O
Lincoln Memorial University	M,D,O
Long Island University, Brooklyn Campus	M
Long Island University, C.W. Post Campus	M
Longwood University	M
Louisiana Tech University	M,D
Manhattanville College	M*
Millersville University of Pennsylvania	M
Mills College	M,D
Minnesota State University Mankato	M,O
Mississippi College	M,D,O
Montclair State University	M,O
Morehead State University	M,O
National-Louis University	M,D,O
New York University	M,D,O
North Carolina Agricultural and Technical State University	M
North Carolina State University	M*
Northeastern Illinois University	M
Northern Arizona University	M,D,O
North Georgia College & State University	M,O
Northwestern State University of Louisiana	M
Northwest Missouri State University	M
Nova Southeastern University	M,O*
Occidental College	M
Our Lady of the Lake University of San Antonio	M
Plymouth State University	M
Purdue University	M,D,O
Queens College of the City University of New York	M,O
Quinnipiac University	M
Rhode Island College	M
Rider University	O
Rollins College	M
Rutgers, The State University of New Jersey, New Brunswick	M*
Sage Graduate School	M
St. John Fisher College	M
Salem State University	M
San Francisco State University	M,O
Shippensburg University of Pennsylvania	M
Slippery Rock University of Pennsylvania	M

*M—master's degree; P—first professional degree; D—doctorate; O—other advanced degree; *—Close-Up and/or Display in one of the other books in this series*

Institution	Degrees
Smith College	M
South Carolina State University	M,D,O
Southeastern Louisiana University	M
Southern Illinois University Edwardsville	M,O
Southwestern Oklahoma State University	M
Stanford University	M,D
State University of New York at Binghamton	M
State University of New York at New Paltz	M
State University of New York at Plattsburgh	M
State University of New York College at Cortland	M
Stony Brook University, State University of New York	M,D,O
Syracuse University	M,D*
Teachers College, Columbia University	M,D
Temple University	M,D*
Texas A&M University	M,D
Texas A&M University–Commerce	M,D
Texas Tech University	M,D*
Trinity (Washington) University	M
Troy University	M
Union Graduate College	M,O
University at Buffalo, the State University of New York	M,D,O*
University of Alaska Fairbanks	M,D,O
The University of Arizona	D
University of Central Florida	M
University of Colorado Denver	M
University of Connecticut	M,D,O*
University of Florida	M,D,O*
University of Georgia	M,D,O
University of Illinois at Chicago	M,D
University of Indianapolis	M
The University of Iowa	M,D*
University of Maine	M
University of Manitoba	M
University of Maryland, Baltimore County	M
University of Michigan	M,D*
University of Minnesota, Twin Cities Campus	M
University of Missouri	M,D,O*
The University of Montana	M
University of New Hampshire	M,D
The University of North Carolina at Chapel Hill	M*
The University of North Carolina at Charlotte	M,O
The University of North Carolina at Greensboro	M,D
The University of North Carolina at Pembroke	M
University of Northern Iowa	M
University of Oklahoma	M,D,O*
University of Phoenix–Omaha Campus	M
University of Phoenix–Southern California Campus	M
University of Phoenix–Springfield Campus	M
University of Phoenix–Washington D.C. Campus	M,D,O
University of Pittsburgh	M,D*
University of Puerto Rico, Mayagüez Campus	M
University of St. Francis (IL)	M
University of South Carolina	M,D
University of South Florida	M,D,O*
The University of Tennessee	M,D,O
The University of Texas at El Paso	M,D,O
University of the Sacred Heart	M,O
The University of Toledo	M,D,O
University of Tulsa	M
University of Victoria	M,D
University of Virginia	M,D,O
University of Washington	M,D*
The University of West Alabama	M
University of West Georgia	M,O
University of Wisconsin–Platteville	M
Vanderbilt University	M*
Washington State University	M,D
Wayne State College	M
Wayne State University	M,D,O*
Western Connecticut State University	M
Western Governors University	M,O
Western Kentucky University	M
Western Michigan University	M,D
Western New England University	M
Widener University	M,D
Wilkes University	M,D
William Carey University	M,O
Worcester State University	M

ENTERTAINMENT MANAGEMENT

Institution	Degrees
California Intercontinental University	M
Carnegie Mellon University	M*
Columbia College Chicago	M
Dowling College	M,O
Full Sail University	M
Hofstra University	M,O
Maryville University of Saint Louis	M,O
Universidad Autonoma de Guadalajara	M,D
University of Dallas	M
University of Massachusetts Amherst	*
University of South Carolina	M
Valparaiso University	M

ENTOMOLOGY

Institution	Degrees
Auburn University	M,D
Clemson University	M,D
Colorado State University	M,D
Cornell University	M,D*
Florida Agricultural and Mechanical University	M
Illinois State University	M,D
Iowa State University of Science and Technology	M,D*
Kansas State University	M,D*
Louisiana State University and Agricultural and Mechanical College	M,D
McGill University	M,D
Michigan State University	M,D
Mississippi State University	M,D
New Mexico State University	M
North Carolina State University	M,D*
North Dakota State University	M,D
The Ohio State University	M,D
Oklahoma State University	M,D*
Penn State University Park	M,D
Purdue University	M,D
Rutgers, The State University of New Jersey, New Brunswick	M,D*
Simon Fraser University	M,D
State University of New York College of Environmental Science and Forestry	M,D
Texas A&M University	M,D
The University of Arizona	M,D
University of Arkansas	M,D
University of California, Davis	M,D
University of California, Riverside	M,D
University of Connecticut	M,D*
University of Delaware	M,D*
University of Florida	M,D*
University of Georgia	M,D
University of Guelph	M,D
University of Hawaii at Manoa	M,D
University of Idaho	M,D
University of Illinois at Urbana–Champaign	M,D
The University of Kansas	M,D
University of Kentucky	M,D*
University of Maine	M
University of Manitoba	M,D
University of Maryland, College Park	M,D
University of Massachusetts Amherst	M,D*
University of Minnesota, Twin Cities Campus	M,D
University of Missouri	M,D*
University of Nebraska–Lincoln	M,D*
University of North Dakota	M,D
University of Rhode Island	M,D
The University of Tennessee	M,D
University of Wisconsin–Madison	M,D*
University of Wyoming	M,D
Virginia Polytechnic Institute and State University	M,D
Washington State University	M,D
West Virginia University	M,D

ENTREPRENEURSHIP

Institution	Degrees
American College of Thessaloniki	M,O
American Public University System	M
American University	M
Andrew Jackson University	M
Arizona State University	M
Azusa Pacific University	M
Babson College	M,O
Bakke Graduate University	M,D
Baldwin-Wallace College	M
Bay Path College	M
Benedictine University	M
Bernard M. Baruch College of the City University of New York	M,D
Brandeis University	M
California Intercontinental University	M,D
California Lutheran University	M,O
California State University, East Bay	M
California State University, Fullerton	M
Cambridge College	M
Cameron University	M
Carlos Albizu University, Miami Campus	M,D
Carnegie Mellon University	D*
Columbia University	M*
Dallas Baptist University	M
DePaul University	M
Eastern Michigan University	M,O
East Tennessee State University	M,O
Fairfield University	M,O
Fairleigh Dickinson University, College at Florham	M,O
Fairleigh Dickinson University, Metropolitan Campus	M,O
Felician College	M*
Florida Atlantic University	M,D
George Mason University	M,O*
Georgia Institute of Technology	M,O
Georgia State University	M,D
Grand Canyon University	M
Harrisburg University of Science and Technology	M
Hult International Business School (United States)	M
Inter American University of Puerto Rico, San Germán Campus	D
The International University of Monaco	M
Jones International University	M
Kaplan University, Davenport Campus	M
Lamar University	M
Lenoir-Rhyne University	M
LIM College	M
Lincoln University (MO)	M,O
Lindenwood University	M
Long Island University, Rockland Graduate Campus	M,O
Marquette University	O
McGill University	M,D,O
North Carolina State University	M*
Northeastern University	M
Oakland University	M,O
Oral Roberts University	M
Park University	M
Peru State College	M
Polytechnic Institute of NYU	M,D,O
Pontificia Universidad Catolica Madre y Maestra	M
Post University	M
Providence College	M
Queen's University at Kingston	M
Regent University	M,D,O
Rensselaer Polytechnic Institute	M,D
Rollins College	M
Rowan University	M
San Diego State University	M
Santa Clara University	M
Seton Hill University	M,O
South Carolina State University	M
Southeast Missouri State University	M
Southern Methodist University	M
South University (GA)	M*
Stevens Institute of Technology	M,O
Stratford University	M
Suffolk University	M,O
Syracuse University	M,O*
Temple University	D*
Texas Tech University	M*
United States International University	M
Université Laval	M,O
The University of Akron	M
University of Central Florida	M,O
University of Chicago	M
University of Colorado Boulder	M,D*

University of Colorado Denver	M,D
University of Dayton	M
University of Delaware	M,D*
University of Florida	M,D,O*
University of Hawaii at Manoa	M,O
University of Houston–Victoria	M
University of Louisville	M,D
University of Massachusetts Lowell	M,O
University of Missouri–Kansas City	M,D*
University of Nevada, Las Vegas	O
University of New Brunswick Fredericton	M
University of Phoenix–Puerto Rico Campus	M
University of Portland	M
University of Rochester	M
University of San Francisco	M
University of South Florida	M,O*
The University of Tampa	M
The University of Texas at Austin	M
The University of Texas at Dallas	M*
University of the Incarnate Word	M,D
The University of Toledo	M
University of Waterloo	M
The University of Western Ontario	M,D
University of Wisconsin–Madison	M*
Wake Forest University	M
Walden University	M,D
West Chester University of Pennsylvania	M,O
Western Carolina University	M
Wilkes University	M
Yorktown University	M

ENVIRONMENTAL AND OCCUPATIONAL HEALTH

American University of Beirut	M
Anna Maria College	M
Boston University	M,D*
California State University, Northridge	M
Capella University	M,D
Colorado State University	M,D
Columbia Southern University	M
Columbia University	M,D*
Duke University	M,D,O*
East Carolina University	M
Eastern Kentucky University	M
East Tennessee State University	M,D,O
Emory University	M*
Florida International University	M,D
Fort Valley State University	M
Gannon University	O
The George Washington University	M
Georgia Southern University	M,D
Harvard University	M,D*
Hunter College of the City University of New York	M
Indiana State University	M
Indiana University of Pennsylvania	M
The Johns Hopkins University	M,D
Lewis University	M
Loma Linda University	M
Louisiana State University Health Sciences Center	M,D
Loyola University Chicago	M,O
McGill University	M,D,O
Medical College of Wisconsin	M*
Meharry Medical College	M
Mississippi Valley State University	M
Murray State University	M
New York Medical College	M,O*
New York University	M,D
North Carolina Agricultural and Technical State University	M
Oakland University	M
OGI School of Science & Engineering at Oregon Health & Science University	M,D
Old Dominion University	M
Oregon State University	M
Saint Joseph's University	M,O
Saint Mary's University of Minnesota	M
San Diego State University	M,D
Stony Brook University, State University of New York	M,O
Temple University	M,D*
Texas A&M Health Science Center	M
Towson University	D
Tufts University	M,D
TUI University	M,D,O
Tulane University	M,D*
Uniformed Services University of the Health Sciences	M,D*
Universidad Autonoma de Guadalajara	M,D
Universidad de Ciencias Medicas	P,M,O
Université de Montréal	M
Université du Québec à Montréal	O
Université Laval	O
University at Albany, State University of New York	M,D
The University of Alabama at Birmingham	D*
University of Alberta	M,D
University of Arkansas for Medical Sciences	M,O
The University of British Columbia	M,D
University of California, Berkeley	M,D*
University of California, Los Angeles	M,D*
University of Central Missouri	M
University of Cincinnati	M,D
University of Colorado Denver	M,D
University of Connecticut	M*
University of Denver	M,O
University of Florida	M*
University of Georgia	M
University of Illinois at Chicago	M,D
The University of Iowa	M,D,O*
University of Louisville	M,D
University of Maryland, College Park	M,D
University of Massachusetts Amherst	M,D*
University of Medicine and Dentistry of New Jersey	M,D,O
University of Memphis	M
University of Miami	M*
University of Michigan	M,D*
University of Minnesota, Twin Cities Campus	M,D,O
University of Nevada, Reno	M,D*
University of New Haven	M,O
The University of North Carolina at Chapel Hill	M,D*
University of North Texas Health Science Center at Fort Worth	M,D
University of Oklahoma Health Sciences Center	M,D
University of Pennsylvania	M*
University of Pittsburgh	M,D,O*
University of Puerto Rico, Medical Sciences Campus	M,D
University of South Alabama	M
University of South Carolina	M,D
University of Southern Mississippi	M
University of South Florida	M,D*
The University of Texas at Tyler	M
University of the Sacred Heart	M
The University of Toledo	M,O
University of Washington	M,D*
University of West Florida	M
University of Wisconsin–Whitewater	M*
Wayne State University	M,O*
West Chester University of Pennsylvania	M,O
West Virginia University	D
Yale University	M,D,O*

ENVIRONMENTAL BIOLOGY

Baylor University	M,D*
Chatham University	M
Emporia State University	M
Georgia State University	M,D
Governors State University	M
Hampton University	M
Hood College	M
Inter American University of Puerto Rico, San Germán Campus	M
Massachusetts Institute of Technology	M,D,O
Missouri University of Science and Technology	M
Morgan State University	D
Nicholls State University	M
Nova Scotia Agricultural College	M
Ohio University	M,D*
Rutgers, The State University of New Jersey, New Brunswick	M,D*
Sonoma State University	M
State University of New York College of Environmental Science and Forestry	M,D
Universidad del Turabo	M,D
University of Alberta	M,D
University of California, Santa Cruz	M,D
University of Guelph	M,D
University of Louisiana at Lafayette	M,D*
University of Louisville	M,D
The University of Manchester	M,D
University of Massachusetts Amherst	M,D*
University of Massachusetts Boston	D
University of North Dakota	M,D
University of Southern California	M,D*
University of Southern Mississippi	M,D
University of West Florida	M
University of Wisconsin–Madison	M,D*
Washington University in St. Louis	D*
West Virginia University	M,D
Youngstown State University	M

ENVIRONMENTAL DESIGN

Arizona State University	D
Art Center College of Design	M*
Clemson University	D
Columbia University	M*
Cornell University	M*
Florida Atlantic University	M,O
Michigan State University	M,D
San Diego State University	M
Texas Tech University	M,D*
Université de Montréal	M,D,O
University of Calgary	M,D
University of California, Berkeley	M,D*
University of California, Irvine	D*
University of Georgia	M
The University of Manchester	M,D
University of Missouri	M*
Virginia Polytechnic Institute and State University	D
Yale University	M,D*

ENVIRONMENTAL EDUCATION

Alaska Pacific University	M
Antioch University New England	M
Arcadia University	M,D,O*
Brooklyn College of the City University of New York	M
California State University, San Bernardino	M
Chatham University	M
Concordia University Wisconsin	M
Florida Atlantic University	M
Florida Institute of Technology	M,D,O
Gannon University	M
Goshen College	M
Hamline University	M,D
Instituto Tecnologico de Santo Domingo	M,D,O
Lesley University	M,D,O
Montreat College	M
New York University	M
Nova Southeastern University	M,O*
Prescott College	M,D
Royal Roads University	M,O
Saint Vincent College	M
Slippery Rock University of Pennsylvania	M
Southern Connecticut State University	M,O
Southern Oregon University	M
Université du Québec à Montréal	M,D,O
University of Colorado Denver	M
University of Minnesota, Twin Cities Campus	M,D,O
University of New Hampshire	M
The University of North Carolina Wilmington	M
University of South Africa	M,D
University of Victoria	M,D
Western Washington University	M
West Virginia University	M,D

ENVIRONMENTAL ENGINEERING

Air Force Institute of Technology	M
Arizona State University	M,D
Auburn University	M,D
California Institute of Technology	M,D
California Polytechnic State University, San Luis Obispo	M
Carleton University	M,D

*M—master's degree; P—first professional degree; D—doctorate; O—other advanced degree; *—Close-Up and/or Display in one of the other books in this series*

Institution	Degrees
Carnegie Mellon University	M,D*
The Catholic University of America	M,D
Clarkson University	M,D*
Clemson University	M,D
Cleveland State University	M,D
Colorado School of Mines	M,D
Columbia University	M,D,O*
Concordia University (Canada)	M,D,O
Cornell University	M,D*
Dalhousie University	M,D
Dartmouth College	M,D
Drexel University	M,D*
Duke University	M,D*
École Polytechnique de Montréal	M,D,O
Florida Agricultural and Mechanical University	M,D
Florida International University	M
Florida State University	M,D
Gannon University	M
The George Washington University	M,D,O
Georgia Institute of Technology	M,D
Idaho State University	M
Illinois Institute of Technology	M,D
Instituto Tecnologico de Santo Domingo	M,O
Instituto Tecnológico y de Estudios Superiores de Monterrey, Campus Ciudad de México	M,D
Instituto Tecnológico y de Estudios Superiores de Monterrey, Campus Monterrey	M,D
Iowa State University of Science and Technology	M,D*
The Johns Hopkins University	M,D,O
Lakehead University	M
Lamar University	M,D
Lehigh University	M,D
Louisiana State University and Agricultural and Mechanical College	M,D
Manhattan College	M
Marquette University	M,D,O
Marshall University	M
Massachusetts Institute of Technology	M,D,O
McGill University	M,D
Memorial University of Newfoundland	M
Mercer University	M
Michigan State University	M,D
Michigan Technological University	M,D
Milwaukee School of Engineering	M
Missouri University of Science and Technology	M,D
Montana State University	M,D
Montana Tech of The University of Montana	M
National University	M
New Jersey Institute of Technology	M,D
New Mexico Institute of Mining and Technology	M
New Mexico State University	M,D
New York Institute of Technology	M
North Dakota State University	M,D
Northeastern University	M,D
Northern Arizona University	M
Northwestern University	M,D*
Norwich University	M
OGI School of Science & Engineering at Oregon Health & Science University	M,D
Ohio University	M,D*
Oklahoma State University	M,D*
Old Dominion University	M,D
Oregon Health & Science University	M,D*
Oregon State University	M,D
Penn State University Park	M,D
Polytechnic Institute of NYU	M
Polytechnic Institute of NYU, Long Island Graduate Center	M
Polytechnic University of Puerto Rico, Miami Campus	M
Polytechnic University of Puerto Rico, Orlando Campus	M
Portland State University	M,D
Rensselaer Polytechnic Institute	M,D
Rice University	M,D
Rose-Hulman Institute of Technology	M
Royal Military College of Canada	M,D
Rutgers, The State University of New Jersey, New Brunswick	M,D*
Southern Methodist University	M,D
Stanford University	M,D,O
State University of New York College of Environmental Science and Forestry	M,D
Stevens Institute of Technology	M,D,O
Syracuse University	M*
Texas A&M University	M,D
Texas A&M University–Kingsville	M,D
Texas Tech University	M,D*
Tufts University	M,D
Universidad Central del Este	M
Universidad Nacional Pedro Henriquez Urena	M
Université de Sherbrooke	M
Université Laval	M,D
University at Buffalo, the State University of New York	M,D*
The University of Alabama	M,D
The University of Alabama in Huntsville	M,D
University of Alaska Anchorage	M
University of Alaska Fairbanks	M,D
University of Alberta	M,D
The University of Arizona	M,D
University of Arkansas	M
University of California, Berkeley	M,D*
University of California, Davis	M,D,O
University of California, Irvine	M,D*
University of California, Los Angeles	M,D*
University of California, Riverside	M,D
University of Central Florida	M,D
University of Cincinnati	M,D
University of Colorado Boulder	M,D*
University of Colorado Denver	M,D
University of Connecticut	M,D*
University of Dayton	M
University of Delaware	M,D*
University of Detroit Mercy	M,D
University of Florida	M,D,O*
University of Georgia	M
University of Guelph	M,D
University of Hawaii at Manoa	M,D
University of Idaho	M
University of Illinois at Urbana–Champaign	M,D
The University of Iowa	M,D*
The University of Kansas	M,D
University of Louisville	M,D
The University of Manchester	M,D
University of Maryland, College Park	M,D
University of Massachusetts Amherst	M*
University of Massachusetts Dartmouth	M
University of Massachusetts Lowell	M,D,O
University of Memphis	M,D
University of Michigan	M,D,O*
University of Missouri	M,D*
University of Nebraska–Lincoln	M,D*
University of Nevada, Las Vegas	M,D
University of New Brunswick Fredericton	M,D
University of New Haven	M,O
The University of North Carolina at Chapel Hill	M,D*
The University of North Carolina at Charlotte	M,D
University of North Dakota	M
University of Notre Dame	M,D*
University of Oklahoma	M,D*
University of Pittsburgh	M,D*
University of Regina	M,D
University of Rhode Island	M,D
University of Saskatchewan	M,D,O
University of Southern California	M,D,O*
University of South Florida	M,D*
The University of Tennessee	M
The University of Texas at Austin	M,D
The University of Texas at El Paso	M,D,O
The University of Texas at San Antonio	M,D*
The University of Texas at Tyler	M
University of Utah	M,D*
University of Vermont	M,D
University of Washington	M,D*
University of Waterloo	M,D
The University of Western Ontario	M,D
University of Windsor	M,D
University of Wisconsin–Madison	M,D*
University of Wyoming	M
Utah State University	M,D,O
Vanderbilt University	M,D*
Villanova University	M,O
Virginia Polytechnic Institute and State University	M,D,O
Washington State University	M
Washington University in St. Louis	M,D*
West Virginia University	M,D
Worcester Polytechnic Institute	M,D,O
Yale University	M,D*
Youngstown State University	M

ENVIRONMENTAL LAW

Institution	Degrees
Chapman University	P,M
Florida State University	P,M
Golden Gate University	P,M,D
Lehigh University	M,O
Lewis & Clark College	P,M
Pace University	P,M,D
University of Calgary	M,O
University of Colorado Denver	M,D
University of Florida	P,M,D*
University of Houston	P,M
University of Idaho	P
University of Pittsburgh	M,O*
University of Tulsa	P,M,O
Vermont Law School	M,O

ENVIRONMENTAL MANAGEMENT AND POLICY

Institution	Degrees
Adelphi University	M*
Air Force Institute of Technology	M
American Public University System	M
American University	M,D,O
American University of Beirut	M
Antioch University New England	M,D
Antioch University Seattle	M
Appalachian State University	M
Arizona State University	M
Bard College	M,O
Baylor University	M*
Bemidji State University	M
Boise State University	M
Boston University	M,D,O*
Brown University	M
California State University, Fullerton	M
Central European University	M,D
Clark University	M
Clemson University	M,D
Cleveland State University	M,O
College of the Atlantic	M
Columbia University	M*
Concordia University (Canada)	M,O
Cornell University	M,D*
Dalhousie University	M
Drexel University	M*
Duke University	M,D*
Duquesne University	M,O
The Evergreen State College	M
Florida Atlantic University	M,O
Florida Gulf Coast University	M
Florida Institute of Technology	M,D
Florida International University	M
George Mason University	M,D,O*
The George Washington University	M
Georgia Institute of Technology	M,D
Goddard College	M
Green Mountain College	M
Hardin-Simmons University	M
Harvard University	M,O*
Humboldt State University	M
Idaho State University	M
Illinois Institute of Technology	M
Indiana University Bloomington	M,D,O*
Instituto Tecnologico de Santo Domingo	M,D,O
Instituto Tecnológico y de Estudios Superiores de Monterrey, Campus Estado de México	M,D
Instituto Tecnológico y de Estudios Superiores de Monterrey, Campus Irapuato	M,D
Inter American University of Puerto Rico, Metropolitan Campus	M
The Johns Hopkins University	M,O
Kean University	M
Lamar University	M,D
Lehigh University	M,O

Long Island University, C.W. Post Campus	M
Louisiana State University and Agricultural and Mechanical College	M
Marylhurst University	M
McGill University	M,D
Michigan Technological University	M,D
Missouri State University	M
Montclair State University	M,D
Monterey Institute of International Studies	M
Morehead State University	M
Naropa University	M
New Jersey Institute of Technology	M
The New School: A University	M
New York Institute of Technology	M,O
New York University	M
Northeastern Illinois University	M
Northern Arizona University	M
Nova Scotia Agricultural College	M
Ohio University	M*
Pace University	M
Penn State University Park	M
Plymouth State University	M
Point Park University	M
Polytechnic University of Puerto Rico	M
Polytechnic University of Puerto Rico, Miami Campus	M
Polytechnic University of Puerto Rico, Orlando Campus	M
Portland State University	M,D
Prescott College	M
Purdue University	M,D
Rensselaer Polytechnic Institute	D
Rice University	M
Rochester Institute of Technology	M
Royal Roads University	M,O
St. Cloud State University	M
Saint Mary-of-the-Woods College	M
Samford University	M
San Francisco State University	M
San Jose State University	M
Shippensburg University of Pennsylvania	M
Simon Fraser University	M,D
Slippery Rock University of Pennsylvania	M
Southeast Missouri State University	M
Southern Illinois University Edwardsville	M
Stanford University	M
State University of New York College of Environmental Science and Forestry	M,D
Stony Brook University, State University of New York	M,O
Texas Southern University	M,D
Texas State University–San Marcos	M
Texas Tech University	D*
Towson University	M
Trent University	M,D
Tropical Agriculture Research and Higher Education Center	M,D
Troy University	M
Tufts University	M,D,O
Universidad Autonoma de Guadalajara	M,D
Universidad del Turabo	M,D
Universidad Metropolitana	M
Université de Montréal	O
Université du Québec à Chicoutimi	M
Université du Québec, Institut National de la Recherche Scientifique	M,D
Université Laval	M,D,O
University at Albany, State University of New York	M
University of Alaska Fairbanks	M,D
University of Alberta	M,D
University of Calgary	M,D,O
University of California, Berkeley	M,D,O*
University of California, Santa Barbara	M,D
University of California, Santa Cruz	D
University of Central Missouri	M,D
University of Chicago	M,D
University of Colorado Boulder	M,D*
University of Colorado Denver	M,D
University of Dayton	M,D
University of Delaware	M,D*
University of Denver	M,O
The University of Findlay	M
University of Guelph	M,D
University of Hawaii at Manoa	M,D,O
University of Houston–Clear Lake	M
University of Illinois at Springfield	M
University of Maine	M,D
The University of Manchester	M,D
University of Maryland, Baltimore County	M,D
University of Maryland University College	M,O
University of Massachusetts Amherst	M,D*
University of Massachusetts Dartmouth	M,O
University of Massachusetts Lowell	M,D,O
University of Miami	M,D*
University of Michigan	M,D*
University of Minnesota, Twin Cities Campus	M
The University of Montana	M
University of Nevada, Reno	M*
University of New Brunswick Fredericton	M,D
University of New Hampshire	M
University of New Haven	M,O
University of New Mexico	M*
The University of North Carolina at Chapel Hill	M,D*
The University of North Carolina Wilmington	M
University of Northern British Columbia	M,D,O
University of Oregon	M,D
University of Pennsylvania	M*
University of Pittsburgh	M,O*
University of Puerto Rico, Río Piedras	M
University of Rhode Island	M,D
University of South Africa	M,D
University of South Carolina	M
University of South Florida	M*
The University of Tennessee	M,D
University of Washington	M,D*
University of Waterloo	M
University of Wisconsin–Green Bay	M
Utah State University	M,D
Vanderbilt University	M,D*
Vermont Law School	M,O
Virginia Commonwealth University	M
Virginia Polytechnic Institute and State University	M,D,O
Webster University	M,D,O
Wesley College	M
West Virginia University	M,D
Wilfrid Laurier University	M,D
Willamette University	M
Yale University	M,D*
York University	M,D*
Youngstown State University	M,O

ENVIRONMENTAL SCIENCES

Alabama Agricultural and Mechanical University	M,D
Alabama State University	M,D
Alaska Pacific University	M
American University	M,O
American University of Beirut	M,D
Antioch University New England	M,D
Arizona State University	M,D,O
Arkansas State University	M,D
Baylor University	D*
Brigham Young University	M,D*
California State Polytechnic University, Pomona	M
California State University, Chico	M
California State University, Dominguez Hills	M*
California State University, East Bay	M
California State University, Fullerton	M
California State University, Northridge	M
California State University, San Bernardino	M
Christopher Newport University	M
City College of the City University of New York	M,D
Clarkson University	M,D*
Clemson University	M,D
Cleveland State University	M,D
The College at Brockport, State University of New York	M
College of Charleston	M
College of Staten Island of the City University of New York	M
Colorado School of Mines	M,D
Columbia University	M*
Columbus State University	M
Cornell University	M,D*
Drexel University	M,D*
Duke University	M,D*
Duquesne University	M,O
Florida Agricultural and Mechanical University	M,D
Florida Atlantic University	M
Florida Gulf Coast University	M
Florida Institute of Technology	M,D
Florida International University	M
Florida State University	M,D
Gannon University	M,O
George Mason University	M,D,O*
Georgia Institute of Technology	M,D
Graduate School and University Center of the City University of New York	D
Harvard University	M*
Howard University	M,D
Humboldt State University	M
Hunter College of the City University of New York	M,O
Idaho State University	M,O
Indiana University Bloomington	M,D*
Indiana University Northwest	M,O
Instituto Tecnologico de Santo Domingo	M,D,O
Instituto Tecnológico y de Estudios Superiores de Monterrey, Campus Ciudad de México	M,D
Inter American University of Puerto Rico, San Germán Campus	M
Iowa State University of Science and Technology	M,D*
Jackson State University	M,D
The Johns Hopkins University	M
Kentucky State University	M
Laurentian University	M
Lehigh University	M,D
Louisiana State University and Agricultural and Mechanical College	M,D
Loyola Marymount University	M
Marshall University	M
Massachusetts Institute of Technology	M,D,O
McNeese State University	M
Memorial University of Newfoundland	M
Mercer University	M
Miami University	M
Michigan State University	M,D
Minnesota State University Mankato	M
Montana State University	M,D
Montclair State University	M,D,O
Murray State University	M
New Jersey Institute of Technology	M,D
New Mexico Institute of Mining and Technology	M,D
New Mexico State University	M,D
North Carolina Agricultural and Technical State University	M
North Dakota State University	M,D
Northern Arizona University	M
Nova Scotia Agricultural College	M
Nova Southeastern University	M*
Oakland University	M,D
OGI School of Science & Engineering at Oregon Health & Science University	M,D
The Ohio State University	M,D
Oklahoma State University	M,D,O*
Oregon Health & Science University	M,D*
Oregon State University	M,D
Pace University	M
Penn State Harrisburg	M
Penn State University Park	M
Polytechnic Institute of NYU	M
Pontifical Catholic University of Puerto Rico	M
Portland State University	M,D
Queens College of the City University of New York	M
Rice University	M,D
The Richard Stockton College of New Jersey	M
Rochester Institute of Technology	M
Royal Military College of Canada	M,D
Rutgers, The State University of New Jersey, Newark	M,D*

*M—master's degree; P—first professional degree; D—doctorate; O—other advanced degree; *—Close-Up and/or Display in one of the other books in this series*

Rutgers, The State University of New Jersey, New Brunswick M,D*
South Dakota School of Mines and Technology D
Southeast Missouri State University M
Southern Illinois University Carbondale D
Southern Illinois University Edwardsville M
Southern Methodist University M,D
Southern University and Agricultural and Mechanical College M
Stanford University M,D,O
State University of New York College of Environmental Science and Forestry M,D
Stephen F. Austin State University M
Tarleton State University M
Taylor University M
Tennessee Technological University D
Texas A&M University–Corpus Christi M
Texas Christian University M
Texas Tech University M,D*
Thompson Rivers University M
Towson University M,O
Tufts University M,D
Tuskegee University M
Universidad del Turabo M,D
Universidad Nacional Pedro Henriquez Urena M
Université de Sherbrooke M,O
Université du Québec à Montréal M,D,O
Université du Québec à Trois-Rivières M,D
Université du Québec en Abitibi-Témiscamingue M,D
Université Laval M,D
University at Albany, State University of New York M
University at Buffalo, the State University of New York M,D,O*
The University of Alabama in Huntsville M,D
University of Alaska Anchorage M
University of Alaska Fairbanks M,D
University of Alberta M,D
The University of Arizona M,D
University of California, Berkeley M,D*
University of California, Davis M,D
University of California, Los Angeles M,D*
University of California, Merced M,D
University of California, Riverside M,D
University of California, Santa Barbara M,D
University of Chicago M,D
University of Cincinnati M,D
University of Colorado at Colorado Springs M
University of Colorado Denver M
University of Guam M
University of Guelph M,D
University of Hawaii at Hilo M
University of Houston–Clear Lake M
University of Idaho M,D
University of Illinois at Springfield M
University of Illinois at Urbana–Champaign M,D
The University of Kansas M,D
University of Lethbridge M,D
University of Maine M,D
The University of Manchester M,D
University of Manitoba M,D
University of Maryland, Baltimore M,D
University of Maryland, Baltimore County M,D
University of Maryland, College Park M,D
University of Maryland Eastern Shore M,D
University of Massachusetts Boston D
University of Massachusetts Lowell M,D,O
University of Medicine and Dentistry of New Jersey D
University of Michigan M,D*
University of Michigan–Dearborn M
The University of Montana M
University of Nevada, Las Vegas M,D,O
University of Nevada, Reno M,D*
University of New Haven M,O
University of New Orleans M
The University of North Carolina at Chapel Hill M,D*
University of Northern Iowa M
University of North Texas M,D
University of Oklahoma M,D*
University of Pennsylvania M,D*
University of Puerto Rico, Río Piedras M,D
University of Rhode Island M,D
University of Saskatchewan M
University of South Africa M,D
University of South Florida M,D*
The University of Tennessee at Chattanooga M
The University of Texas at Arlington M,D
The University of Texas at El Paso M,D
The University of Texas at San Antonio M,D*
University of the Virgin Islands M
The University of Toledo M
University of Toronto M,D
University of Utah M*
University of Virginia M,D
The University of Western Ontario M,D
University of West Florida M
University of Windsor M,D
University of Wisconsin–Green Bay M
University of Wisconsin–Madison M,D*
Vanderbilt University M*
Virginia Polytechnic Institute and State University M,D,O
Washington State University M,D
Washington State University Tri-Cities M,D
Washington State University Vancouver M
Wesleyan University M*
Western Connecticut State University M
Western Washington University M
West Texas A&M University M
Wichita State University M
Wilfrid Laurier University M,D
Wright State University M,D
Yale University M,D*

EPIDEMIOLOGY

American University of Beirut M
Boston University M,D*
Brown University M,D
Case Western Reserve University M,D*
Columbia University M,D*
Cornell University M,D*
Cornell University, Joan and Sanford I. Weill Medical College and Graduate School of Medical Sciences M
Dalhousie University M
Drexel University M,D,O*
East Tennessee State University M,D,O
Emory University M,D*
Florida International University M,D
George Mason University M,O*
Georgetown University M
The George Washington University M,D
Georgia Southern University M,D
Harvard University M,D*
Hunter College of the City University of New York M
Indiana University–Purdue University Indianapolis M
The Johns Hopkins University M,D
Loma Linda University M,D,O
Louisiana State University Health Sciences Center M,D
McGill University M,D,O
Medical College of Wisconsin M*
Medical University of South Carolina M,D
Memorial University of Newfoundland M,D,O
Michigan State University M,D
Morehouse School of Medicine M
New York Medical College M*
New York University M,D
North Carolina State University M,D*
Oregon Health & Science University M*
Ponce School of Medicine M,D
Purdue University M,D
Queen's University at Kingston M,D
San Diego State University M,D
Stanford University M,D
Temple University M,D*
Texas A&M Health Science Center M
Texas A&M University M
Thomas Edison State College O
Thomas Jefferson University M,D,O
Tufts University M,D,O
Tulane University M,D*
Université Laval M,D
University at Albany, State University of New York M,D
University at Buffalo, the State University of New York M,D*
The University of Alabama at Birmingham D*
University of Alberta M,D
The University of Arizona M,D
The University of British Columbia M,D
University of Calgary M,D
University of California, Berkeley M,D*
University of California, Davis M,D
University of California, Irvine M,D*
University of California, Los Angeles M,D*
University of California, San Diego D*
University of California, San Francisco D
University of Cincinnati M,D
University of Colorado Denver M,D
University of Florida M*
University of Georgia M
University of Guelph M,D
University of Hawaii at Manoa D
University of Illinois at Chicago M,D
The University of Iowa M,D*
The University of Kansas M
University of Louisville M,D
University of Maryland, Baltimore M,D
University of Maryland, Baltimore County M,O
University of Maryland, College Park M,D
University of Massachusetts Amherst M,D*
University of Massachusetts Lowell M,D,O
University of Massachusetts Worcester M,D
University of Medicine and Dentistry of New Jersey M,D,O
University of Memphis M
University of Miami D*
University of Michigan M,D*
University of Minnesota, Twin Cities Campus M,D
The University of North Carolina at Chapel Hill M,D*
University of North Texas Health Science Center at Fort Worth M,D
University of Oklahoma Health Sciences Center M,D
University of Ottawa M*
University of Pennsylvania M,D*
University of Pittsburgh M,D*
University of Prince Edward Island M,D
University of Puerto Rico, Medical Sciences Campus M
University of Rochester M,D
University of Saskatchewan M,D
University of South Carolina M,D
University of Southern California M,D*
University of Southern Mississippi M
University of South Florida M,D*
The University of Toledo M,O
University of Washington M,D*
The University of Western Ontario M,D
University of Wisconsin–Madison M,D*
Walden University M,D,O
Yale University M,D,O*

ERGONOMICS AND HUMAN FACTORS

Arizona State University M
Bentley University M
California State University, Long Beach M
California State University, Northridge M
The Catholic University of America M,D
Clemson University D
Cornell University M*
Embry-Riddle Aeronautical University–Daytona M
Florida Institute of Technology M

Georgia Institute of Technology	M,D
Indiana University Bloomington	M,D*
Missouri Western State University	M
New York University	M,D
North Carolina State University	D*
Old Dominion University	D
Tufts University	M,D
Université de Montréal	O
Université du Québec à Montréal	O
The University of Alabama	M
University of Central Florida	M,D,O
University of Cincinnati	M,D
University of Illinois at Urbana–Champaign	M
The University of Iowa	M,D*
University of Massachusetts Lowell	M,D,O
University of Miami	M*
University of Wisconsin–Milwaukee	M,D,O
Wright State University	M,D

ETHICS

American University	M,D,O
Arizona State University	M,D
Azusa Pacific University	M
Biola University	P,M,D
Chicago Theological Seminary	P,M,D
Claremont Graduate University	M,D
Claremont School of Theology	M,D
Columbia University	M*
Duquesne University	M
Emory University	P,M,D*
Fordham University	M,O
Freed-Hardeman University	M
George Mason University	M,D,O*
Georgetown University	M,D
Graduate Theological Union	M,D,O
John Brown University	M
Lancaster Theological Seminary	P,M,D,O
Lutheran Theological Seminary	P,M,D
Marquette University	M,D
New England College of Business and Finance	M
Northwestern University	M*
Phillips Theological Seminary	P,M,D
St. Edward's University	M
Southeastern Baptist Theological Seminary	P,M,D
Spring Hill College	M
Suffolk University	M
Union Institute & University	D
Université de Sherbrooke	M,D,O
Université du Québec à Chicoutimi	O
Université du Québec à Rimouski	M,O
Université Laval	O
University of Baltimore	M
University of Nevada, Las Vegas	M
University of New England	M,O
The University of North Carolina at Charlotte	M,O
University of North Florida	M,O
University of Pennsylvania	M,D*
University of South Africa	M,D
Valparaiso University	M,O
Warner Pacific College	M
West Chester University of Pennsylvania	M,O

ETHNIC STUDIES

Cornell University	M,D*
Minnesota State University Mankato	M,O
Northern Arizona University	O
Norwich University	M
San Francisco State University	M
United Theological Seminary of the Twin Cities	P,M,D,O
Université Laval	M,D
University of California, Berkeley	D*
University of California, Riverside	D
University of California, San Diego	M,D*
University of Nevada, Las Vegas	M,D
The University of North Carolina at Charlotte	M
Washington State University	M,D

EVOLUTIONARY BIOLOGY

Arizona State University	M,D
Brown University	D
Clemson University	M,D
Columbia University	M,D,O*
Cornell University	D*
Dartmouth College	D
Emory University	D*
Florida State University	M,D
George Mason University	M,D*
Harvard University	D*
Illinois State University	M,D
Indiana University Bloomington	M,D*
Iowa State University of Science and Technology	M,D*
The Johns Hopkins University	D
Michigan State University	D
Montclair State University	M,O
Northwestern University	D*
The Ohio State University	M,D
Ohio University	M,D*
Princeton University	D*
Purdue University	M,D
Rice University	M,D
Rutgers, The State University of New Jersey, New Brunswick	M,D*
Stony Brook University, State University of New York	M,D
Tulane University	M,D*
University at Albany, State University of New York	M,D
University at Buffalo, the State University of New York	M,D,O*
University of Alberta	M,D
The University of Arizona	M,D
University of California, Davis	D
University of California, Irvine	M,D*
University of California, Los Angeles	M,D*
University of California, Riverside	M,D
University of California, San Diego	D*
University of California, Santa Barbara	M,D
University of California, Santa Cruz	M,D
University of Chicago	D
University of Colorado Boulder	M,D*
University of Delaware	M,D*
University of Guelph	M,D
University of Hawaii at Manoa	M,D
University of Illinois at Urbana–Champaign	M,D
The University of Iowa	M,D*
The University of Kansas	M,D
University of Louisiana at Lafayette	M,D*
The University of Manchester	M,D
University of Maryland, College Park	M,D
University of Massachusetts Amherst	M,D*
University of Miami	M,D*
University of Michigan	M,D*
University of Minnesota, Twin Cities Campus	M,D
University of Missouri	M,D*
University of Missouri–St. Louis	M,D,O
University of Nevada, Reno	D*
The University of North Carolina at Chapel Hill	M,D*
University of Notre Dame	M,D*
University of Oklahoma	D*
University of Oregon	M,D
University of Pittsburgh	D*
University of Puerto Rico, Río Piedras	M,D
University of South Carolina	M,D
University of Southern California	D*
The University of Tennessee	M,D
The University of Texas at Austin	M,D
University of Toronto	M,D
Washington University in St. Louis	D*
Wesleyan University	D*
West Virginia University	M,D
Yale University	D*

EXERCISE AND SPORTS SCIENCE

American University	M
Appalachian State University	M
Arizona State University	M,D,O
Arkansas State University	M,O
Armstrong Atlantic State University	M
Ashland University	M
Auburn University	M,D,O
Austin Peay State University	M
Ball State University	D
Barry University	M*
Baylor University	M,D*
Benedictine University	M
Bloomsburg University of Pennsylvania	M
Boise State University	M
Brigham Young University	M,D*
Brooklyn College of the City University of New York	M
California Baptist University	M
California State University, East Bay	M
California State University, Fresno	M
California State University, Long Beach	M
California University of Pennsylvania	M
Central Connecticut State University	M,O
Central Michigan University	M,D
Central Washington University	M
Cleveland State University	M
The College of St. Scholastica	M
Colorado State University	M,D
Concordia University (Canada)	M
Concordia University Chicago	M
Delaware State University	M
Delta State University	M
East Carolina University	M,D
Eastern Illinois University	M
Eastern Michigan University	M
Eastern New Mexico University	M
Eastern Washington University	M
East Stroudsburg University of Pennsylvania	M
East Tennessee State University	M,D
Florida Atlantic University	M
Florida State University	M,D
Gardner-Webb University	M
George Mason University	M*
The George Washington University	M
Georgia College & State University	M
Georgia State University	M
Hofstra University	M,O
Howard University	M
Humboldt State University	M
Indiana State University	M
Indiana University Bloomington	M,D*
Indiana University of Pennsylvania	M
Inter American University of Puerto Rico, Metropolitan Campus	M
Ithaca College	M
Kean University	M
Kennesaw State University	M
Kent State University	M,D*
Lakehead University	M
Life University	M
Lipscomb University	M
Logan University–College of Chiropractic	M
Long Island University, Brooklyn Campus	M
Louisiana Tech University	M
Manhattanville College	M*
Marshall University	M
Marywood University	M
McNeese State University	M
Memorial University of Newfoundland	M
Miami University	M
Middle Tennessee State University	M,D
Mississippi State University	M
Montclair State University	M,O
Morehead State University	M
Murray State University	M
New Mexico Highlands University	M
North Dakota State University	M
Northeastern University	M
Northern Michigan University	M
Oakland University	M,O
Ohio University	M,D*
Old Dominion University	M
Oregon State University	M,D
Purdue University	M,D
Queens College of the City University of New York	M
Queen's University at Kingston	M,D
Rocky Mountain University of Health Professions	D
Sacred Heart University	M,D
St. Cloud State University	M
Saint Mary's College of California	M
San Diego State University	M

*M—master's degree; P—first professional degree; D—doctorate; O—other advanced degree; *—Close-Up and/or Display in one of the other books in this series*

San Francisco State University M
Smith College M
Southeast Missouri State University M
Southern Connecticut State University M
Southern Utah University M
Springfield College M,D
State University of New York College at Cortland M
Syracuse University M*
Tennessee State University M
Texas A&M University–Commerce M,D
Texas Tech University M*
Texas Woman's University M,D
Troy University M
United States Sports Academy M
University at Buffalo, the State University of New York M,D*
The University of Akron M
The University of Alabama M,D
University of Alberta M,D
University of Calgary M,D
University of California, Davis M
University of Central Florida M,D,O
University of Central Missouri M
University of Connecticut M,D*
University of Dayton M,D
University of Delaware M*
University of Florida M,D*
University of Houston M,D
University of Houston–Clear Lake M
The University of Iowa M,D*
University of Kentucky M,D*
University of Lethbridge M,D
University of Louisiana at Monroe M
University of Louisville M
University of Maine M
University of Mary Hardin-Baylor M,D
University of Memphis M
University of Miami M,D*
University of Minnesota, Twin Cities Campus M,D,O
University of Mississippi M,D
University of Missouri M,D*
The University of Montana M
University of Nebraska at Kearney M
University of Nebraska–Lincoln M,D*
University of Nevada, Las Vegas M
University of New Brunswick Fredericton M
University of New Mexico D*
The University of North Carolina at Chapel Hill M*
The University of North Carolina at Charlotte M
The University of North Carolina at Greensboro M,D
University of Northern Colorado M,D
University of Oklahoma M,D*
University of Pittsburgh M,D*
University of Puerto Rico, Río Piedras M
University of Rhode Island M
University of South Alabama M
University of South Carolina M,D
University of Southern Mississippi M,D
University of South Florida M*
The University of Tennessee M,D,O
University of the Pacific M
The University of Toledo M,D
University of Utah M,D*
University of West Florida M
University of Wisconsin–La Crosse M
University of Wyoming M
Virginia Commonwealth University M
Wake Forest University M
Washington State University M,D
Washington State University Spokane M
Wayne State College M
West Chester University of Pennsylvania M,O
Western Michigan University M
Western Washington University M
West Texas A&M University M
West Virginia University M,D
Wichita State University M

EXPERIMENTAL PSYCHOLOGY

American University M,D
Appalachian State University M,O
Auburn University M,D
Bowling Green State University M,D*
Brooklyn College of the City University of New York M,D
California State University, Northridge M
California State University, San Bernardino M
Case Western Reserve University D*
The Catholic University of America M,D
Central Michigan University M,D
Central Washington University M
City College of the City University of New York M,D
Cleveland State University M,D,O
The College of William and Mary M
Columbia University M,D*
Cornell University D*
Dallas Baptist University M
DePaul University M,D
Duke University D*
Eastern Washington University M
Fairleigh Dickinson University, Metropolitan Campus M,O
Georgia Institute of Technology M,D
Graduate School and University Center of the City University of New York D
Harvard University D*
Howard University M,D
Illinois State University M,D,O
Iona College M
Kent State University M,D*
Lakehead University M,D
Laurentian University M
McGill University M,D
McNeese State University M
Memorial University of Newfoundland M,D
Middle Tennessee State University M,O
Mississippi State University M,D
Missouri State University M
Morehead State University M
North Carolina State University D*
Northeastern University M,D
Ohio University D*
Old Dominion University D
Radford University M
Rivier College M
St. John's University (NY) M
Saint Louis University M,D
San Jose State University M
Seton Hall University M
Southern Illinois University Carbondale M,D
Stony Brook University, State University of New York D
Syracuse University D*
Texas Christian University M,D
Texas Tech University M,D*
University at Albany, State University of New York M,D,O
The University of Alabama D
The University of Alabama in Huntsville M
University of Central Florida M,D
University of Cincinnati D
University of Connecticut M,D,O*
University of Hartford M
University of Kentucky M,D*
University of Louisiana at Monroe M
University of Louisville D
University of Maine M,D
University of Maryland, College Park M,D
University of Memphis M,D,O
University of Michigan D*
University of Mississippi M,D
The University of Montana M,D,O
University of New Brunswick Saint John M,D
The University of North Carolina at Chapel Hill D*
University of North Dakota M,D
University of North Texas M,D
University of Regina M,D
University of South Carolina M,D
University of Southern Mississippi M,D
The University of Tennessee M,D
The University of Tennessee at Chattanooga M
The University of Texas at Arlington M,D
The University of Texas at El Paso M,D
The University of Texas of the Permian Basin M
The University of Texas–Pan American M
The University of Toledo M,D
University of Victoria M,D
University of Wisconsin–Oshkosh M
Washington State University M,D
Washington University in St. Louis D*
Western Kentucky University M,O
Western Washington University M
Xavier University M,D

FACILITIES MANAGEMENT

Cornell University M*
Indiana University of Pennsylvania M
Indiana University–Purdue University Fort Wayne M
Massachusetts Maritime Academy M
Pratt Institute M*
Université Laval M,O
University of California, Berkeley O*
The University of Kansas M,D,O
University of New Haven M,O

FAMILY AND CONSUMER SCIENCES-GENERAL

Alabama Agricultural and Mechanical University M,D
Ball State University M
Bowling Green State University M*
California State University, Fresno M
California State University, Long Beach M
California State University, Northridge M
Central Michigan University M,O
Central Washington University M
Eastern Illinois University M
Florida State University M,D
Fontbonne University M
Hofstra University M,O
Illinois State University M
Indiana State University M
Iowa State University of Science and Technology M*
Kansas State University M,D*
Lamar University M,O
Louisiana State University and Agricultural and Mechanical College M,D
Louisiana Tech University M
Marshall University M
Missouri State University M
New Mexico State University M
North Carolina Central University M
North Dakota State University M
Ohio University M*
Oklahoma State University M,D*
Oregon State University M
Prairie View A&M University M
Purdue University M,D
Queens College of the City University of New York M
Sam Houston State University M
San Francisco State University M
South Carolina State University M
South Dakota State University M
State University of New York College at Oneonta M
Stephen F. Austin State University M
Tennessee State University M
Texas A&M University–Kingsville M
Texas Southern University M
Texas Tech University M,D*
Tufts University M,D,O
The University of Alabama M,D
University of Alberta M,D
The University of Arizona M,D
University of Arkansas M
University of Central Arkansas M
University of Central Oklahoma M
University of Florida M*
University of Georgia M,D
University of Houston M
University of Manitoba M
University of Maryland, College Park M,D
University of Memphis M
University of Mississippi M
University of Missouri M,D*
University of Nebraska–Lincoln M,D*
The University of North Carolina at Greensboro M,D,O

University of Puerto Rico, Río Piedras M
University of South Africa M,D
The University of Tennessee D
The University of Tennessee at Martin M
The University of Texas at Austin M,D
University of Wisconsin–Madison M,D*
University of Wisconsin–Stevens Point M
Utah State University M,D
Western Michigan University M

FAMILY NURSE PRACTITIONER STUDIES

Abilene Christian University M,O
Albany State University M
Allen College M,D,O
Arizona State University M,D,O
Barry University M,O*
Baylor University M*
Bellarmine University M,D
Belmont University M
Bloomsburg University of Pennsylvania M
Bowie State University M
Brenau University M
Brigham Young University M*
California State University, Fresno M
Carlow University M,D
Carson-Newman College M
Case Western Reserve University M,D*
Clarke University M,O
Clarkson College M,O
College of Mount Saint Vincent M,O
The College of New Rochelle M,O
Columbia University M,O*
Concordia University Wisconsin M
Coppin State University M,O
Cox College M
Delta State University M
DeSales University M,O
Dominican College M
Duke University M,D,O*
Duquesne University M,O
D'Youville College M,O*
Eastern Kentucky University M
East Tennessee State University M,D,O
Emory University M*
Fairfield University M,D
Felician College M,O*
Florida Southern College M
Florida State University M,D,O
Frontier School of Midwifery and Family Nursing M,O
Gannon University M,O
Georgetown University M
The George Washington University M,D,O
Georgia College & State University M
Georgia Health Sciences University M,O
Georgia Southern University M,O
Georgia State University M,D,O
Goshen College M
Graceland University (IA) M,O
Grambling State University M,O
Grand Canyon University M,O
Gwynedd-Mercy College M
Hardin-Simmons University M
Hawai'i Pacific University M*
Holy Names University M,O
Howard University M,O
Husson University M,O
Illinois State University M,D,O
Indiana University–Purdue University Indianapolis M,D
The Johns Hopkins University M,O
Kent State University M,D*
Lincoln Memorial University M
Long Island University, C.W. Post Campus M,O
Loyola University Chicago M,O
Loyola University New Orleans M,D
Malone University M
Marymount University M,D,O
Maryville University of Saint Louis M,D
McGill University M,D,O
McNeese State University M
Medical University of South Carolina M
Middle Tennessee State University M,O
Midwestern State University M
Minnesota State University Mankato M,D
Missouri State University M
Molloy College M,O
Monmouth University M,D,O
Montana State University M,O
Mountain State University M
Mount Carmel College of Nursing M
Mount Saint Mary College M,O
Murray State University M
Northern Arizona University M,O
North Georgia College & State University M
Oakland University M,O
Ohio University M*
Old Dominion University M
Oregon Health & Science University M,O*
Otterbein University M,O
Pace University M,D,O
Pacific Lutheran University M
Prairie View A&M University M
Purdue University Calumet M
Queen's University at Kingston M,D,O
Quinnipiac University D
Regis College (MA) M,D,O
Regis University P,M,D,O
Research College of Nursing M
Rivier College M
Rocky Mountain University of Health Professions D
Rush University M,D,O
Rutgers, The State University of New Jersey, Newark M*
Sacred Heart University M,D
Sage Graduate School M,O
Saginaw Valley State University M
St. John Fisher College M,O
Saint Xavier University M,O
Samford University M,D
Samuel Merritt University M,O
San Francisco State University M
Seattle Pacific University M,O
Shenandoah University M,D,O
Sonoma State University M
Southeastern Louisiana University M
Southern Adventist University M
Southern Illinois University Edwardsville M,D,O
Southern University and Agricultural and Mechanical College M,D,O
Spalding University M
State University of New York Downstate Medical Center M,O
State University of New York Institute of Technology M,O
State University of New York Upstate Medical University M,O
Stony Brook University, State University of New York M,O
Tennessee State University M
Tennessee Technological University M
Texas A&M International University M
Texas A&M University–Corpus Christi M
Texas Tech University Health Sciences Center M,D,O
Texas Woman's University M,D
Troy University M,D,O
Uniformed Services University of the Health Sciences M*
Union University M,D,O
United States University M
Universidad del Turabo M
University at Buffalo, the State University of New York D,O*
The University of Alabama in Huntsville M,D,O
University of Alaska Anchorage M,O
The University of Arizona M,D,O
University of Central Arkansas M
University of Central Florida M,D,O
University of Colorado at Colorado Springs M,D
University of Colorado Denver M,D
University of Delaware M,O*
University of Detroit Mercy M,O
University of Hawaii at Manoa M,D,O
University of Illinois at Chicago M
The University of Kansas M,D,O
University of Louisville M,D
University of Maine M,O
University of Mary M
University of Massachusetts Lowell M
University of Massachusetts Worcester M,D,O
University of Medicine and Dentistry of New Jersey M,D,O
University of Memphis M,O
University of Miami M,D*
University of Michigan M,O*
University of Minnesota, Twin Cities Campus M
University of Missouri–Kansas City M,D*
University of Missouri–St. Louis M,D,O
University of Nevada, Las Vegas M,D,O
University of New Hampshire M,O
The University of North Carolina at Chapel Hill M,D,O*
The University of North Carolina at Charlotte M,O
The University of North Carolina Wilmington M
University of North Dakota M,D
University of Northern Colorado M,D
University of Pennsylvania M,O*
University of Phoenix–Hawaii Campus M
University of Phoenix–Phoenix Campus M
University of Phoenix–Sacramento Valley Campus M
University of Phoenix–Southern California Campus M
University of Pittsburgh M,D*
University of Puerto Rico, Medical Sciences Campus M
University of Rhode Island M,D
University of Rochester M,D,O
University of St. Francis (IL) M,D
University of San Diego M,D
University of San Francisco D
The University of Scranton M,O
University of South Carolina M
University of Southern Maine M,O
University of Southern Mississippi M,D
The University of Tampa M
The University of Tennessee at Chattanooga M,D,O
The University of Texas at Arlington M,D
The University of Texas at El Paso M,D,O
The University of Texas at Tyler M,D
The University of Texas–Pan American M
The University of Toledo M,O
University of Victoria M,D
University of Wisconsin–Eau Claire M,D
University of Wisconsin–Milwaukee M,D,O
University of Wisconsin–Oshkosh M
Vanderbilt University M,D*
Villanova University M,D,O
Virginia Commonwealth University M,O
Wagner College O
Washburn University M
Western University of Health Sciences M,D
Westminster College (UT) M
Wichita State University M,D
Wilmington University M
Winona State University M,D,O
Wright State University M

FILM, TELEVISION, AND VIDEO PRODUCTION

Academy of Art University M
American Film Institute Conservatory M
American University M
Antioch University Midwest M
Arizona State University M
Art Center College of Design M*
The Art Institute of California–San Francisco M
Bob Jones University P,M,D,O
Boston University M*
Bowling Green State University M,D*
Brigham Young University M*
Brooklyn College of the City University of New York M
California College of the Arts M
California Institute of the Arts M,O
California State University, Fullerton M
California State University, Los Angeles M*
California State University, Northridge M

*M—master's degree; P—first professional degree; D—doctorate; O—other advanced degree; *—Close-Up and/or Display in one of the other books in this series*

Institution	Degrees
Carleton University	M
Carnegie Mellon University	M*
Central Michigan University	M
Chapman University	M
Chatham University	M
Columbia College Chicago	M
Columbia University	M*
Concordia University (Canada)	M
DePaul University	M,D
Drexel University	M*
Florida Atlantic University	M,O
Florida State University	M
Georgia State University	M,D
Hofstra University	M
Hollins University	M
Howard University	M
Humboldt State University	M
Loyola Marymount University	M
Marywood University	M
Massachusetts College of Art and Design	M
Miami International University of Art & Design	M*
Minneapolis College of Art and Design	M
Montana State University	M
New York Film Academy	M
New York University	M
Northwestern University	M,D*
Ohio University	M*
Pepperdine University	M
Polytechnic Institute of NYU	O
Regent University	M,D
Rochester Institute of Technology	M
St. Thomas University	M
San Diego State University	M
San Francisco Art Institute	M,O
San Francisco State University	M
San Jose State University	M
Savannah College of Art and Design	M
School of the Art Institute of Chicago	M
School of Visual Arts (NY)	M
Southern Methodist University	M
Syracuse University	M*
Temple University	M*
Universidad Autonoma de Guadalajara	M,D
The University of Alabama	M
The University of British Columbia	M,O
University of California, Los Angeles	M,D*
University of California, Santa Barbara	D
University of Central Arkansas	M
University of Central Florida	M
The University of Iowa	M*
University of Memphis	M,D
University of Miami	M,D*
University of Nevada, Las Vegas	M
University of New Orleans	M
The University of North Carolina at Greensboro	M
University of North Carolina School of the Arts	M
University of North Texas	M
University of Oklahoma	M*
University of Southern California	M*
The University of Texas at Arlington	M
The University of Texas at Austin	M,D
University of the Sacred Heart	M,O
University of Utah	M*
University of Victoria	M
University of Wisconsin–Milwaukee	M
Western State College of Colorado	M*
York University	M,D*

FILM, TELEVISION, AND VIDEO THEORY AND CRITICISM

Institution	Degrees
Boston University	M*
California College of the Arts	M
Central Michigan University	M
Claremont Graduate University	M,D
College of Staten Island of the City University of New York	M
Concordia University (Canada)	M
Emory University	M,D,O*
Florida Atlantic University	M,O
Hollins University	M
Indiana University Bloomington	M,D*
New York University	M,D
Ohio University	M*
San Francisco State University	M
Savannah College of Art and Design	M
Syracuse University	M*
Université de Montréal	M,D
Université Laval	M,D
The University of British Columbia	M,O
University of California, Santa Cruz	D
University of Chicago	M,D
The University of Iowa	M,D*
The University of Kansas	M,D
University of Miami	M,D*
University of Michigan	D,O*
University of Pittsburgh	O*
University of Southern California	M,D*
University of South Florida	M*
University of Toronto	M
University of Wisconsin–Madison	M,D*
Wilfrid Laurier University	M,D
Yale University	D*

FINANCE AND BANKING

Institution	Degrees
Adelphi University	M*
Alliant International University–San Diego	M,D
The American College	M
American College of Thessaloniki	M,O
American InterContinental University Buckhead Campus	M
American InterContinental University Online	M
American InterContinental University South Florida	M
American International College	M
American Public University System	M
American University	M,D,O
The American University in Dubai	M
Andrew Jackson University	M
Andrews University	M
Argosy University, Atlanta	M,D*
Argosy University, Chicago	M,D*
Argosy University, Dallas	M,D,O*
Argosy University, Denver	M,D*
Argosy University, Hawai'i	M,D,O*
Argosy University, Inland Empire	M,D*
Argosy University, Los Angeles	M,D*
Argosy University, Nashville	M,D*
Argosy University, Orange County	M,D,O*
Argosy University, Phoenix	M,D*
Argosy University, Salt Lake City	M,D*
Argosy University, San Diego	M,D*
Argosy University, San Francisco Bay Area	M,D*
Argosy University, Sarasota	M,D,O*
Argosy University, Schaumburg	M,D,O*
Argosy University, Seattle	M,D*
Argosy University, Tampa	M,D*
Argosy University, Twin Cities	M,D*
Argosy University, Washington DC	M,D,O*
Arizona State University	M,D
Aspen University	M,O
Assumption College	M,O
Auburn University	M
Avila University	M
Azusa Pacific University	M
Baker College Center for Graduate Studies—Online	M,D
Barry University	O*
Bayamón Central University	M
Benedictine University	M
Bentley University	M
Bernard M. Baruch College of the City University of New York	M,D
Boston College	M,D*
Boston University	P,M*
Brandeis University	M
Bridgewater State University	M
Brigham Young University	M*
Brooklyn College of the City University of New York	M
California College of the Arts	M
California Intercontinental University	M,D
California Lutheran University	M,O
California State University, East Bay	M
California State University, Fullerton	M
California State University, Los Angeles	M*
California State University, Stanislaus	M
Capella University	M,D,O
Carnegie Mellon University	D*
Case Western Reserve University	M,D*
Central European University	M
Central Michigan University	M
Charleston Southern University	M
Christian Brothers University	M,O
City University of Seattle	M,O
Claremont McKenna College	M
Clark University	M
Cleary University	M,O
Cleveland State University	M,D,O
College for Financial Planning	M
Colorado State University	M
Colorado Technical University Colorado Springs	M,D
Colorado Technical University Denver	M
Columbia Southern University	M
Columbia University	M,D*
Concordia University Wisconsin	M
Cornell University	D*
Curry College	M,O
Dalhousie University	M
Dallas Baptist University	M
Davenport University	M
Davenport University	M
Davenport University	M
DePaul University	M,O
DeSales University	M
DeVry University	M
Dowling College	M,O
Drexel University	M,D,O*
Eastern Michigan University	M,O
East Tennessee State University	M,O
Ellis University	M
Emory University	D*
Fairfield University	M,O
Fairleigh Dickinson University, College at Florham	M,O
Fairleigh Dickinson University, Metropolitan Campus	M,O
Florida Agricultural and Mechanical University	M
Florida Atlantic University	M,D
Florida Institute of Technology	M
Florida International University	M
Florida State University	M,D
Fordham University	M
Gannon University	O
George Fox University	M,D
Georgetown University	D
The George Washington University	M,D
Georgia Institute of Technology	M,D,O
Georgia State University	M,D,O
Golden Gate University	M,D,O
Goldey-Beacom College	M
Graduate School and University Center of the City University of New York	D
Grand Canyon University	M
Hawai'i Pacific University	M*
HEC Montreal	M,O
Hofstra University	M,O
Holy Family University	M*
Holy Names University	M
Hood College	M
Howard University	M
Hult International Business School (United States)	M
Hult International Business School (United States)	M
Hult International Business School (United States)	M
Illinois Institute of Technology	P,M
Indiana University Bloomington	M,D,O*
Indiana University Southeast	M
Instituto Centroamericano de Administración de Empresas	M
Instituto Tecnologico de Santo Domingo	M,O
Instituto Tecnológico y de Estudios Superiores de Monterrey, Campus Central de Veracruz	M
Instituto Tecnológico y de Estudios Superiores de Monterrey, Campus Ciudad de México	M,D
Instituto Tecnológico y de Estudios Superiores de	

Institution	Degrees
Monterrey, Campus Ciudad Obregón	M
Instituto Tecnológico y de Estudios Superiores de Monterrey, Campus Cuernavaca	M
Instituto Tecnológico y de Estudios Superiores de Monterrey, Campus Estado de México	M,D
Instituto Tecnológico y de Estudios Superiores de Monterrey, Campus Guadalajara	M
Instituto Tecnológico y de Estudios Superiores de Monterrey, Campus Irapuato	M,D
Instituto Tecnológico y de Estudios Superiores de Monterrey, Campus Monterrey	M
Inter American University of Puerto Rico, Aguadilla Campus	M
Inter American University of Puerto Rico, Arecibo Campus	M
Inter American University of Puerto Rico, Barranquitas Campus	M
Inter American University of Puerto Rico, Metropolitan Campus	M
Inter American University of Puerto Rico, Ponce Campus	M
Inter American University of Puerto Rico, San Germán Campus	M,D
The International University of Monaco	M
Iona College	M,O
The Johns Hopkins University	M,O
Jones International University	M
Kaplan University, Davenport Campus	M
Kent State University	D*
Kentucky State University	M
Lakeland College	M
Lamar University	M
La Sierra University	M,O
Lehigh University	M
Lewis University	M
Lincoln University (CA)	M,D
Lincoln University (PA)	M
Lindenwood University	M
Lipscomb University	M
Long Island University, C.W. Post Campus	M,O
Long Island University, Rockland Graduate Campus	M,O
Louisiana State University and Agricultural and Mechanical College	M,D
Louisiana Tech University	M,D
Loyola University Chicago	M
Loyola University Maryland	M
Manhattanville College	M*
Marquette University	M
Marylhurst University	M
Marywood University	M
McGill University	M,D,O
Michigan State University	M,D
MidAmerica Nazarene University	M
Mississippi College	M,O
Mississippi State University	M,D
Molloy College	M
Monmouth University	M,O
Montclair State University	M,O
Mount Saint Mary College	M
National University	M
New England College of Business and Finance	M
New Jersey City University	M
Newman University	M
The New School: A University	M,D
New York Institute of Technology	M,O
New York Law School	P,M
New York University	M,D,O
North Central College	M
Northeastern Illinois University	M
Northeastern State University	M
Northwestern University	D*
Norwich University	M
Notre Dame College (OH)	M,O
Notre Dame de Namur University	M
Nova Southeastern University	D*
Oakland University	M,O
Ohio University	M*
Oklahoma City University	M
Oklahoma State University	M,D*
Old Dominion University	M,D
Oral Roberts University	M
Ottawa University	M
Our Lady of the Lake University of San Antonio	M
Pace University	M
Pacific States University	M,D
Pepperdine University	M
Philadelphia University	M
Polytechnic Institute of NYU	M,O
Polytechnic Institute of NYU, Westchester Graduate Center	M,O
Polytechnic University of Puerto Rico, Miami Campus	M
Polytechnic University of Puerto Rico, Orlando Campus	M
Pontifical Catholic University of Puerto Rico	M
Pontificia Universidad Catolica Madre y Maestra	M
Portland State University	M
Post University	M
Princeton University	M*
Providence College	M
Purdue University	M
Queen's University at Kingston	M
Quinnipiac University	M
Regent's American College London	M
Regis University	M,O
Rhode Island College	M,O
Robert Morris University Illinois	M
Rochester Institute of Technology	M
Rollins College	M
Rowan University	M
Rutgers, The State University of New Jersey, Newark	D*
Sacred Heart University	M
Sage Graduate School	M
St. Edward's University	M,O
St. John's University (NY)	M,O
Saint Joseph's University	M
Saint Louis University	M
St. Mary's University (United States)	M
Saint Peter's College	M
St. Thomas Aquinas College	M
Saint Xavier University	M,O
Sam Houston State University	M
San Diego State University	M
Santa Clara University	M
Schiller International University (United States)	M
Seattle University	M,O
Seton Hall University	M
Simon Fraser University	M,D
Southeast Missouri State University	M
Southern Adventist University	M
Southern Illinois University Edwardsville	M
Southern Methodist University	M
Southern New Hampshire University	M,D,O
Southwestern Adventist University	M
State University of New York at Binghamton	M,D
Stevens Institute of Technology	M
Stony Brook University, State University of New York	M,O
Strayer University	M
Suffolk University	M,O
Syracuse University	M,D*
Tarleton State University	M
Télé-université	M,D
Temple University	M,D*
Tennessee Technological University	M
Texas A&M International University	M
Texas A&M University	M,D
Texas A&M University–San Antonio	M
Texas Tech University	M,D*
Thomas Jefferson School of Law	M
Tiffin University	M
Troy University	M
TUI University	M,D
Union Graduate College	M,O
United States International University	M
Universidad Central del Este	M
Universidad de las Americas, A.C.	M
Universidad de las Américas–Puebla	M
Universidad Metropolitana	M
Université de Sherbrooke	M
Université du Québec à Montréal	O
Université du Québec à Trois-Rivières	O
Université du Québec en Outaouais	M,O
Université Laval	M,O
University at Albany, State University of New York	M
University at Buffalo, the State University of New York	M,D,O*
The University of Akron	M
The University of Alabama	M,D
The University of Alabama in Huntsville	M
University of Alaska Fairbanks	M
University of Alberta	M,D
The University of Arizona	M,D
University of Baltimore	M
The University of British Columbia	D
University of California, Berkeley	D,O*
University of California, Los Angeles	M,D*
University of California, Santa Cruz	M
University of Central Missouri	M
University of Chicago	M
University of Cincinnati	D
University of Colorado Boulder	M,D*
University of Colorado Denver	M
University of Connecticut	M,D,O*
University of Dallas	M
University of Dayton	M
University of Delaware	M*
University of Denver	M
University of Florida	M,D,O*
University of Hawaii at Manoa	M,D
University of Houston	M
University of Houston–Clear Lake	M
University of Houston–Victoria	M
University of Illinois at Urbana–Champaign	M,D
The University of Iowa	M,D*
University of La Verne	M
University of Lethbridge	M,D
University of Maine	M
University of Maryland University College	M,O
University of Massachusetts Dartmouth	M,O
University of Memphis	M,D
University of Miami	M*
University of Michigan–Dearborn	M
University of Minnesota, Twin Cities Campus	M,D
University of Missouri–St. Louis	M,O
University of Nebraska–Lincoln	M,D*
University of Nevada, Las Vegas	O
University of Nevada, Reno	M*
University of New Haven	M,O
University of New Mexico	M,D*
University of New Orleans	M,D
The University of North Carolina at Chapel Hill	D*
The University of North Carolina at Charlotte	M,D,O
The University of North Carolina at Greensboro	M,O
University of North Florida	M
University of North Texas	M,D
University of Oregon	D
University of Ottawa	D,O*
University of Pennsylvania	M,D*
University of Pittsburgh	M,D,O*
University of Portland	M
University of Puerto Rico, Mayagüez Campus	M
University of Puerto Rico, Río Piedras	M,D
University of Rhode Island	M,D
University of San Francisco	M
University of Saskatchewan	M
The University of Scranton	M
University of Southern Maine	M
University of South Florida	M,D*
The University of Tampa	M
The University of Tennessee	M,D
The University of Texas at Arlington	M,D
The University of Texas at Austin	D
The University of Texas at Dallas	M,D*
The University of Texas at San Antonio	M,D*
The University of Texas–Pan American	D
University of the West	M
The University of Toledo	M
University of Toronto	M
University of Tulsa	M
University of Utah	M,D*
University of Virginia	M
University of Washington	M,D*

*M—master's degree; P—first professional degree; D—doctorate; O—other advanced degree; *—Close-Up and/or Display in one of the other books in this series*

University of Washington, Tacoma M
University of Waterloo M,D
The University of Western Ontario M,D
University of Wisconsin–Madison M,D*
University of Wisconsin–Whitewater M*
University of Wyoming M
Upper Iowa University M
Valparaiso University M
Vanderbilt University M*
Villanova University M
Virginia Commonwealth University M
Virginia International University M,O
Virginia Polytechnic Institute and State University M,D
Wagner College M
Wake Forest University M
Walden University M,D
Walsh College of Accountancy and Business Administration M
Washington State University M,D
Washington University in St. Louis M*
Waynesburg University M,D
Webster University M
Western International University M
Western Michigan University M
West Texas A&M University M
Wilfrid Laurier University M,D
Wilkes University M
Wilmington University M
Wright State University M
Xavier University M
Yale University D*
York College of Pennsylvania M
York University M,D*
Youngstown State University M

FINANCIAL ENGINEERING

Claremont Graduate University M
Columbia University M,D,O*
HEC Montreal M
The International University of Monaco M
Kent State University M*
North Carolina State University M*
Polytechnic Institute of NYU M,O
Polytechnic Institute of NYU, Long Island Graduate Center M,O
Polytechnic Institute of NYU, Westchester Graduate Center M,O
Princeton University M,D*
Rensselaer Polytechnic Institute M,D
Stevens Institute of Technology M
Temple University M*
University at Buffalo, the State University of New York M,D,O*
University of California, Berkeley M*
University of California, Los Angeles M,D*
University of Hawaii at Manoa M
University of Illinois at Urbana–Champaign M
The University of Texas at Dallas M*
University of Tulsa M

FIRE PROTECTION ENGINEERING

Anna Maria College M
Oklahoma State University M,D*
University of Maryland, College Park M
University of New Haven M,O
Worcester Polytechnic Institute M,D,O

FISH, GAME, AND WILDLIFE MANAGEMENT

Arkansas Tech University M
Auburn University M,D
Brigham Young University M,D*
Clemson University M,D
Colorado State University M,D
Cornell University M,D*
Frostburg State University M
Humboldt State University M
Iowa State University of Science and Technology M,D*
Louisiana State University and Agricultural and Mechanical College M,D
McGill University M,D
Memorial University of Newfoundland M,O
Michigan State University M,D
Mississippi State University M,D
Montana State University M,D
New Mexico Highlands University M
New Mexico State University M
North Carolina State University M,D*
Oregon State University M,D
Purdue University M,D
South Dakota State University M,D
State University of New York College of Environmental Science and Forestry M,D
Sul Ross State University M
Tennessee Technological University M
Texas A&M University M,D
Texas A&M University–Kingsville M,D
Texas State University–San Marcos M
Texas Tech University M,D*
Université du Québec à Rimouski M,D,O
University of Alaska Fairbanks M,D
The University of Arizona M,D
University of Arkansas at Pine Bluff M
University of Delaware M,D*
University of Florida M,D*
University of Idaho M,D
University of Maine M,D
University of Massachusetts Amherst M,D*
University of Miami M,D*
University of Missouri M,D*
The University of Montana M,D
University of New Hampshire M
University of North Dakota M,D
University of Rhode Island M,D
The University of Tennessee M
University of Washington M,D*
University of Wisconsin–Madison M,D*
Utah State University M,D
Virginia Polytechnic Institute and State University M,D
West Virginia University M

FOLKLORE

George Mason University M,D,O*
The George Washington University M,D
Indiana University Bloomington M,D*
Memorial University of Newfoundland M,D
University of Alberta M,D
University of California, Berkeley M*
University of Louisiana at Lafayette M,D*
The University of North Carolina at Chapel Hill M*
University of Oregon M
The University of Texas at Austin M,D
University of Wisconsin–Madison M,D*
Utah State University M

FOOD SCIENCE AND TECHNOLOGY

Alabama Agricultural and Mechanical University M,D
American University of Beirut M
Auburn University M,D
Boston University M*
Brigham Young University M*
California State University, Fresno M
California State University, Long Beach M
Chapman University M
Clemson University M,D
Colorado State University M,D
Cornell University M,D*
Dalhousie University M,D
Drexel University M*
Florida Agricultural and Mechanical University M
Florida State University M,D
Framingham State University M
Illinois Institute of Technology M
Iowa State University of Science and Technology M,D*
Kansas State University M,D*
Louisiana State University and Agricultural and Mechanical College M,D
McGill University M,D
Memorial University of Newfoundland M,D
Michigan State University M,D
Middle Tennessee State University M
Mississippi State University M,D
Montclair State University M,O
New York University M,D
North Carolina State University M,D*
North Dakota State University M,D
Nova Scotia Agricultural College M
The Ohio State University M,D
Oklahoma State University M,D*
Oregon State University M,D
Penn State University Park M,D
Purdue University M,D
Rutgers, The State University of New Jersey, New Brunswick M,D*
South Dakota State University M,D
Texas A&M University M,D
Texas Tech University M,D*
Texas Woman's University M,D
Tuskegee University M
Universidad de las Américas–Puebla M
Université de Moncton M
Université Laval M,D
University of Arkansas M,D
The University of British Columbia M,D
University of California, Davis M,D
University of Delaware M,D*
University of Florida M,D*
University of Georgia M,D
University of Guelph M,D
University of Hawaii at Manoa M
University of Idaho M,D
University of Illinois at Urbana–Champaign M,D
University of Maine M,D
University of Manitoba M,D
University of Maryland, College Park M,D
University of Maryland Eastern Shore M,D
University of Massachusetts Amherst M,D*
University of Minnesota, Twin Cities Campus M,D
University of Missouri M,D*
University of Nebraska–Lincoln M,D*
University of Puerto Rico, Mayagüez Campus M
University of Rhode Island M,D
University of Saskatchewan M,D
University of Southern California M,D,O*
The University of Tennessee M,D
The University of Tennessee at Martin M
University of Vermont D
University of Wisconsin–Madison M,D*
University of Wisconsin–Stout M
University of Wyoming M
Utah State University M,D
Virginia Polytechnic Institute and State University M,D,O
Washington State University M,D
Wayne State University M,D*
West Virginia University M,D

FOREIGN LANGUAGES EDUCATION

The American University in Cairo M
Andrews University M,D,O
Appalachian State University M
Arizona State University M,D
Auburn University M,D,O
Bennington College M
Boston University M,D,O*
Bowling Green State University M*
Brigham Young University M*
Brooklyn College of the City University of New York M,O
California State University, Chico M
California State University, Sacramento M
Caribbean University M,D
Central Connecticut State University M,O
Christopher Newport University M
Cleveland State University M
The College at Brockport, State University of New York M,O
College of Charleston M
The College of William and Mary M
The Colorado College M
Colorado State University M
Colorado State University–Pueblo M

Concordia College	M
Cornell University	M,D*
Delaware State University	M
Drew University	M
Duquesne University	M
Eastern Washington University	M
Elms College	M,O
Florida International University	M,D,O
Framingham State University	M
George Mason University	M*
Georgia Southern University	M
Harding University	M,O
Hofstra University	M,O
Hunter College of the City University of New York	M
Indiana University Bloomington	M,D*
Indiana University–Purdue University Indianapolis	M,O
Inter American University of Puerto Rico, Arecibo Campus	M
Inter American University of Puerto Rico, Barranquitas Campus	M
Inter American University of Puerto Rico, Metropolitan Campus	M
Iona College	M
Ithaca College	M
The Johns Hopkins University	M,O
Kean University	M
Kent State University	M,D*
Long Island University, C.W. Post Campus	M
Louisiana Tech University	M,D
Manhattanville College	M*
Marquette University	M
McGill University	M,D,O
Michigan State University	D
Middle Tennessee State University	M
Mills College	M,D
Mississippi State University	M
Missouri State University	M
Monterey Institute of International Studies	M
Morehead State University	M
New York University	M,D,O
Northern Arizona University	M
Occidental College	M
Portland State University	M
Purdue University	M,D,O
Queens College of the City University of New York	M,O
Quinnipiac University	M
Rhode Island College	M
Rider University	O
Rivier College	M
Rowan University	M
Rutgers, The State University of New Jersey, New Brunswick	M,D*
St. John Fisher College	M
Shippensburg University of Pennsylvania	M
Smith College	M
Soka University of America	O
Southern Illinois University Edwardsville	M
Southern Oregon University	M
Stanford University	M
State University of New York at Binghamton	M
State University of New York at Plattsburgh	M
State University of New York College at Cortland	M
Stony Brook University, State University of New York	M,O
Temple University	M,D*
Texas A&M International University	M,D
Texas A&M University–Kingsville	M
Union Graduate College	M,O
Universidad del Este	M
Université du Québec en Outaouais	O
University at Buffalo, the State University of New York	M,D,O*
University of Arkansas at Little Rock	M
University of Calgary	M,D,O
University of California, Irvine	M,D*
University of Central Arkansas	M
University of Connecticut	M,D,O*
University of Delaware	M*
University of Georgia	M,D,O
University of Hawaii at Hilo	M,D
University of Hawaii at Manoa	M,D,O
University of Illinois at Urbana–Champaign	M,D
University of Indianapolis	M
The University of Iowa	M,D*
University of Kentucky	M*
University of Maine	M
University of Maryland, Baltimore County	M
University of Maryland, College Park	D
University of Massachusetts Amherst	M*
University of Massachusetts Boston	M
University of Michigan	M,D*
University of Minnesota, Twin Cities Campus	M
University of Missouri	M,D,O*
University of Nebraska at Kearney	M
University of Nebraska at Omaha	M
University of Nevada, Reno	M*
The University of North Carolina at Chapel Hill	M*
The University of North Carolina at Greensboro	M,D,O
University of Northern Colorado	M
University of Pittsburgh	M,D*
University of Puerto Rico, Río Piedras	M,D
University of South Carolina	M,D
University of Southern Mississippi	M
University of South Florida	M,D,O*
The University of Tennessee	M,D,O
The University of Texas at Austin	M,D
University of the Sacred Heart	M,O
The University of Toledo	M,D,O
University of Utah	M,D*
University of Vermont	M
University of Victoria	M
University of Virginia	M,D,O
University of West Georgia	M,O
University of Wisconsin–Madison	M,D*
Vanderbilt University	M,D*
Virginia Polytechnic Institute and State University	M
Washington State University	M
Wayne State University	M,D,O*
West Chester University of Pennsylvania	M,O
Western Kentucky University	M
Worcester State University	M

FORENSIC NURSING

Boston College	M,D*
Cleveland State University	M
Duquesne University	M,O
Fitchburg State University	M,O
George Mason University	M,D,O*
Monmouth University	M,D,O
University of Colorado at Colorado Springs	M,D

FORENSIC PSYCHOLOGY

Adler School of Professional Psychology	M,D,O
Alliant International University–Fresno	D
Alliant International University–Irvine	D
Alliant International University–Los Angeles	D
American International College	M
Argosy University, Atlanta	M,D,O*
Argosy University, Chicago	D*
Argosy University, Dallas	M*
Argosy University, Denver	M,D*
Argosy University, Hawai'i	M*
Argosy University, Inland Empire	M,D*
Argosy University, Los Angeles	M,D*
Argosy University, Orange County	M*
Argosy University, Phoenix	M*
Argosy University, Salt Lake City	M,D*
Argosy University, San Diego	M,D*
Argosy University, San Francisco Bay Area	M*
Argosy University, Sarasota	M,D*
Argosy University, Schaumburg	M,D,O*
Argosy University, Twin Cities	M,D,O*
Argosy University, Washington DC	M,D*
California Baptist University	M
Cambridge College	M,O
Castleton State College	M
The Chicago School of Professional Psychology	M,D
The Chicago School of Professional Psychology at Downtown Los Angeles	D
The Chicago School of Professional Psychology at Irvine	D
The Chicago School of Professional Psychology: Online	M,O
College of Saint Elizabeth	M,O
Drexel University	D*
Fairleigh Dickinson University, Metropolitan Campus	M
Holy Names University	M,O
John Jay College of Criminal Justice of the City University of New York	M,D
Marymount University	M
Massachusetts School of Professional Psychology	M,D,O
Oklahoma State University Center for Health Sciences	M,O
Pontificia Universidad Catolica Madre y Maestra	M
Prairie View A&M University	M,D
Roger Williams University	M
Sage Graduate School	M,O
Tiffin University	M
Universidad de Iberoamerica	P,M,D
University of Denver	M,D
University of Massachusetts Boston	M,O
University of New Haven	M,D,O
University of North Dakota	M,D
Walden University	M,D,O

FORENSIC SCIENCES

Albany State University	M
Alliant International University–Irvine	D
Arcadia University	M*
Boston University	M*
Cedar Crest College	M
Chaminade University of Honolulu	M
Champlain College	M
DeSales University	M
Duquesne University	M
Florida Gulf Coast University	M
Florida International University	M
George Mason University	M,D,O*
The George Washington University	M
Golden Gate University	M,O
John Jay College of Criminal Justice of the City University of New York	M,D
Long Island University, C.W. Post Campus	M
McGill University	M,D,O
Mercyhurst College	M
Michigan State University	M,D
Missouri Western State University	M
National University	M
Nebraska Wesleyan University	M
Oklahoma State University Center for Health Sciences	M,O
Pace University	M
Philadelphia College of Osteopathic Medicine	M*
Saint Leo University	M
Sam Houston State University	M,D
Southern Utah University	M
Stevenson University	M
Syracuse University	M*
Towson University	M
Universidad del Turabo	M
University at Albany, State University of New York	M,D
The University of Alabama at Birmingham	M*
University of California, Davis	M
University of Central Florida	M,D,O
University of Colorado Denver	M
University of Florida	M,O*
University of Illinois at Chicago	M
University of Nevada, Las Vegas	M,O
University of New Haven	M,D,O
University of North Texas Health Science Center at Fort Worth	M,D
University of Rhode Island	M,D,O
University of Southern Mississippi	M,D
Utica College	M

*M—master's degree; P—first professional degree; D—doctorate; O—other advanced degree; *—Close-Up and/or Display in one of the other books in this series*

Virginia Commonwealth University M
West Virginia University M,D

FORESTRY

Auburn University M,D
California Polytechnic State University, San Luis Obispo M
Clemson University M,D
Colorado State University M,D
Cornell University M,D*
Duke University M*
Harvard University M*
Humboldt State University M
Iowa State University of Science and Technology M,D*
Lakehead University M,D
Louisiana State University and Agricultural and Mechanical College M,D
McGill University M,D
Michigan State University M,D
Michigan Technological University M,D
Mississippi State University M,D
North Carolina State University M,D*
Northern Arizona University M,D
Oklahoma State University M,D*
Oregon State University M,D
Penn State University Park M,D
Purdue University M,D
Southern Illinois University Carbondale M
Southern University and Agricultural and Mechanical College M
State University of New York College of Environmental Science and Forestry M,D
Stephen F. Austin State University M,D
Texas A&M University M,D
Tropical Agriculture Research and Higher Education Center M,D
Université du Québec en Abitibi-Témiscamingue M,D
Université Laval M,D
University of Alberta M,D
The University of Arizona M,D
University of Arkansas at Monticello M
The University of British Columbia M,D
University of California, Berkeley M,D*
University of Florida M,D*
University of Georgia M,D
University of Kentucky M*
University of Maine M,D
University of Massachusetts Amherst M,D*
University of Missouri M,D*
The University of Montana M,D
University of New Brunswick Fredericton M,D
University of New Hampshire M
The University of Tennessee M
University of Toronto M,D
University of Vermont M,D
University of Washington M,D*
University of Wisconsin–Madison M,D*
Utah State University M,D
Virginia Polytechnic Institute and State University M,D,O
West Virginia University M,D
Yale University M,D*

FOUNDATIONS AND PHILOSOPHY OF EDUCATION

Antioch University New England M
Arizona State University M
Arkansas State University M,D,O
Ashland University M
Azusa Pacific University M
Ball State University D
Bank Street College of Education M
Brigham Young University M,D*
Central Connecticut State University M
Chicago State University M
Curry College M,O
Duquesne University M
Eastern Michigan University M
Eastern Washington University M
Fairfield University M,O
Fairleigh Dickinson University, Metropolitan Campus M
Florida Atlantic University M
Florida State University M,D,O
Georgia State University M,D
Harvard University M,O*
Hofstra University M,D,O
Indiana University Bloomington M,D,O*
Iowa State University of Science and Technology M,D*
Kent State University M,D*
Marquette University M,D,O
McGill University M,D,O
Millersville University of Pennsylvania M
Montclair State University O
Mount Saint Vincent University M
New York University M,D
Niagara University M
Northeastern State University M
Northern Arizona University M,D,O
Northern Illinois University M,D,O
Oakland University M
Purdue University M,D,O
Regis University M,O
Rutgers, The State University of New Jersey, New Brunswick M,D*
Saint Louis University M,D
Simon Fraser University M,D
Southeast Missouri State University M
Southern Connecticut State University M,D,O
Southern Illinois University Edwardsville M
Spring Hill College M
Stanford University M,D
State University of New York at Binghamton D
Suffolk University M,O
Syracuse University M,D*
Teachers College, Columbia University M,D
Troy University M
The University of British Columbia M,D
University of Calgary M,D,O
University of Central Missouri M,D,O
University of Cincinnati M,D
University of Connecticut D*
University of Florida M,D,O*
University of Georgia M,D,O
University of Hawaii at Manoa M,D
University of Houston M,D
University of Houston–Clear Lake M
The University of Iowa M,D,O*
The University of Kansas D
University of Manitoba M
University of Maryland, College Park M,D,O
University of Michigan M,D*
University of Minnesota, Twin Cities Campus M,D,O
University of New Mexico M,D*
University of Pittsburgh M,D*
University of Saskatchewan M,D,O
University of South Africa M,D
University of South Carolina D
The University of Tennessee M,D,O
The University of Texas of the Permian Basin M
The University of Toledo M,D,O
University of Utah M,D*
University of Victoria M,D
University of Washington M,D*
The University of West Alabama M
University of Wisconsin–Milwaukee M,D
Wayne State University M,D,O*
Western Illinois University M,O
Widener University M,D
Youngstown State University M,D

FRENCH

American University M,O
Arizona State University M
Asbury University M
Bennington College M
Boston College M,D*
Boston University M,D,O*
Bowling Green State University M*
Brigham Young University M*
Brooklyn College of the City University of New York M,D
Brown University D
Bryn Mawr College M,D*
California State University, Fullerton M
California State University, Long Beach M
California State University, Los Angeles M*
California State University, Sacramento M
Carleton University M
Case Western Reserve University M*
Central Connecticut State University M,O
Cleveland State University M
Columbia University M,D*
Concordia University (Canada) M,O
Cornell University D*
Dalhousie University M,D
Drew University M
Duke University D*
Eastern Michigan University M,O
Emory University D,O*
Florida Atlantic University M
Florida State University M,D
Georgia State University M,O
Graduate School and University Center of the City University of New York D
Harvard University M,D*
Hofstra University M,O
Howard University M
Hunter College of the City University of New York M
Illinois State University M
Indiana University Bloomington M,D*
The Johns Hopkins University D
Kansas State University M*
Kent State University M,D*
Louisiana State University and Agricultural and Mechanical College M,D
McGill University M,D
McMaster University M
Memorial University of Newfoundland M
Miami University M
Michigan State University M,D
Middlebury College M,D
Millersville University of Pennsylvania M
Minnesota State University Mankato M
Mississippi State University M
Montclair State University M,O
New York University M,D,O
North Carolina State University M*
Northern Illinois University M
Northwestern University D,O*
The Ohio State University M,D
Ohio University M*
Penn State University Park M,D
Portland State University M
Princeton University D*
Purdue University M,D
Queens College of the City University of New York M
Queen's University at Kingston M,D
Rider University O
Rutgers, The State University of New Jersey, New Brunswick M,D*
Saint Louis University M
San Francisco State University M
San Jose State University M
Simon Fraser University M
Smith College M
Stanford University M,D
State University of New York at Binghamton M
State University of New York at New Paltz M
Stony Brook University, State University of New York M
Syracuse University M*
Texas Tech University M*
Tufts University M
Tulane University M,D*
Université de Moncton M,D
Université de Montréal M,D
Université de Sherbrooke M,D
Université du Québec à Chicoutimi O
University at Albany, State University of New York M,D
University at Buffalo, the State University of New York M,D,O*
The University of Alabama M,D
University of Alberta M,D
The University of Arizona M
University of Arkansas M
The University of British Columbia M,D
University of California, Berkeley D*
University of California, Davis D
University of California, Irvine M,D*
University of California, Los Angeles M,D*
University of California, San Diego M*
University of California, Santa Barbara D
University of Chicago M,D
University of Cincinnati M,D
University of Colorado Boulder M,D*
University of Connecticut M,D*
University of Delaware M*

- University of Florida M,D*
- University of Georgia M
- University of Guelph M
- University of Hawaii at Manoa M
- University of Illinois at Chicago M
- University of Illinois at Urbana–Champaign M,D
- The University of Iowa M,D*
- The University of Kansas M,D
- University of Kentucky M*
- University of Lethbridge M,D
- University of Louisiana at Lafayette M,D*
- University of Louisville M
- University of Maine M
- The University of Manchester M,D
- University of Manitoba M,D
- University of Maryland, College Park M,D
- University of Massachusetts Amherst M*
- University of Memphis M
- University of Miami D*
- University of Michigan D*
- University of Minnesota, Twin Cities Campus M,D
- University of Mississippi M
- University of Missouri M,D*
- The University of Montana M
- University of Nebraska–Lincoln M,D*
- University of Nevada, Reno M*
- University of New Mexico M,D*
- The University of North Carolina at Chapel Hill M,D*
- The University of North Carolina at Greensboro M
- University of Northern Iowa M
- University of North Texas M
- University of Notre Dame M*
- University of Oklahoma M,D*
- University of Oregon M
- University of Ottawa M,D*
- University of Pennsylvania M,D*
- University of Pittsburgh M,D*
- University of Regina M
- University of Rochester
- University of Saskatchewan M
- University of South Africa M,D
- University of South Carolina M,D
- University of South Florida M*
- The University of Tennessee M,D
- The University of Texas at Arlington M
- The University of Texas at Austin M,D
- The University of Toledo M
- University of Toronto M,D
- University of Utah M,D*
- University of Vermont M
- University of Victoria M
- University of Virginia M,D
- University of Washington M,D*
- University of Waterloo M,D
- The University of Western Ontario M,D
- University of West Georgia M,O
- University of Wisconsin–Madison M,D,O*
- University of Wisconsin–Milwaukee M,O
- University of Wyoming M
- Vanderbilt University M,D*
- Washington University in St. Louis M,D*
- Wayne State University M,D*
- West Chester University of Pennsylvania M,O
- Western Kentucky University M
- West Virginia University M
- Yale University M,D*
- York University M*

GAME DESIGN AND DEVELOPMENT

- Academy of Art University M
- Concordia University (Canada) M,O
- DePaul University M,D
- Full Sail University M
- George Mason University M,D,O*
- Michigan State University M
- National University M
- Rochester Institute of Technology M
- Savannah College of Art and Design M,O
- University of Advancing Technology M
- University of Central Florida M
- The University of North Carolina at Charlotte M,D,O
- University of Southern California M,D*

GENDER STUDIES

- The American University in Cairo M,O
- Arizona State University M,D,O
- Brandeis University M,D
- Carnegie Mellon University M,D*
- Central European University M,D
- Central Michigan University M
- Cornell University M,D*
- Eastern Michigan University M,O
- Indiana University Bloomington D*
- Indiana University–Purdue University Indianapolis M
- Instituto Tecnologico de Santo Domingo M,O
- Memorial University of Newfoundland M,D
- Minnesota State University Mankato M,O
- Northern Arizona University O
- Northwestern University *
- Norwich University M
- Queen's University at Kingston M,D
- Roosevelt University M,O
- Rutgers, The State University of New Jersey, New Brunswick M,D*
- Saint Mary's University (Canada) M
- Simmons College M
- Syracuse University O*
- The University of Arizona M,D
- University of Colorado Denver M
- University of Florida M,O*
- University of Maine M
- University of Missouri–St. Louis O
- The University of North Carolina at Charlotte M
- The University of North Carolina at Greensboro M,O
- University of Northern British Columbia M,D,O
- University of Northern Iowa M
- University of Oklahoma O*
- University of Saskatchewan M,D
- The University of Texas at El Paso O
- University of Toronto M
- Virginia Polytechnic Institute and State University M,D,O
- Wilfrid Laurier University M,D

GENETIC COUNSELING

- Arcadia University M*
- Brandeis University M
- California State University, Stanislaus M
- Case Western Reserve University M*
- The Johns Hopkins University M,D
- Long Island University, C.W. Post Campus M
- McGill University M,D
- Mount Sinai School of Medicine M,D
- Northwestern University M*
- Sarah Lawrence College M
- Université de Montréal O
- The University of Alabama at Birmingham M*
- University of Arkansas for Medical Sciences M
- The University of British Columbia M
- University of California, Irvine M*
- University of Cincinnati M
- University of Colorado Denver M
- University of Maryland, Baltimore M
- University of Michigan M,D*
- University of Minnesota, Twin Cities Campus M,D
- The University of North Carolina at Greensboro M
- University of Oklahoma Health Sciences Center M
- University of Pittsburgh M,D,O*
- University of South Carolina M
- The University of Texas Health Science Center at Houston M*
- University of Toronto M,D
- University of Wisconsin–Madison M*
- Wayne State University M*

GENETICS

- Albert Einstein College of Medicine D
- Baylor College of Medicine D*
- Brandeis University M,D
- California Institute of Technology D
- Carnegie Mellon University M,D*
- Case Western Reserve University D*
- Clemson University M,D
- Columbia University M,D*
- Cornell University D*
- Dartmouth College D
- Drexel University M,D*
- Duke University D*
- Emory University D*
- Florida State University M,D
- The George Washington University D
- Harvard University D*
- Illinois State University M,D
- Indiana University Bloomington M,D*
- Iowa State University of Science and Technology M,D*
- The Johns Hopkins University M,D
- Kansas State University M,D*
- Marquette University M,D
- Massachusetts Institute of Technology D
- Mayo Graduate School D
- McMaster University M,D
- Medical University of South Carolina D
- Michigan State University M,D
- Mississippi State University M,D
- New York University M,D
- North Carolina State University M,D*
- Northwestern University D*
- The Ohio State University M,D
- Oregon Health & Science University D*
- Oregon State University M,D
- Penn State Hershey Medical Center M,D
- Penn State University Park M,D
- Purdue University M,D
- Rutgers, The State University of New Jersey, New Brunswick M,D*
- Stanford University D
- Stony Brook University, State University of New York D
- Temple University M,D*
- Texas A&M University M,D
- Thomas Jefferson University D
- Tufts University D
- Université de Montréal O
- Université du Québec à Chicoutimi M
- University at Albany, State University of New York M,D
- The University of Alabama at Birmingham D*
- University of Alberta M,D
- The University of Arizona M,D
- The University of British Columbia M,D
- University of California, Davis M,D
- University of California, Irvine D*
- University of California, Riverside D
- University of California, San Diego D*
- University of California, San Francisco D
- University of Chicago D
- University of Colorado Boulder M,D*
- University of Colorado Denver D
- University of Connecticut M,D*
- University of Connecticut Health Center D*
- University of Delaware M,D*
- University of Florida D*
- University of Georgia M,D
- University of Hawaii at Manoa M,D
- University of Illinois at Chicago D
- The University of Iowa M,D*
- The University of Manchester M,D
- University of Massachusetts Amherst M,D*
- University of Miami M,D*
- University of Minnesota, Twin Cities Campus M,D
- University of Missouri M,D*
- University of Nebraska Medical Center M,D
- University of New Hampshire M,D
- University of New Mexico M,D,O*
- The University of North Carolina at Chapel Hill M,D*
- University of North Dakota M,D
- University of North Texas Health Science Center at Fort Worth M,D
- University of Notre Dame M,D*
- University of Oregon M,D
- University of Pennsylvania D*

*M—master's degree; P—first professional degree; D—doctorate; O—other advanced degree; *—Close-Up and/or Display in one of the other books in this series*

Institution	Degrees
University of Puerto Rico, Río Piedras	M,D
University of Rochester	M,D
University of Southern California	M,D*
The University of Tennessee	M,D
The University of Texas Health Science Center at Houston	M,D*
The University of Texas Medical Branch	D
The University of Texas Southwestern Medical Center at Dallas	D
University of Toronto	M,D
University of Washington	M,D*
University of Wisconsin–Madison	M,D*
University of Wyoming	D
Virginia Commonwealth University	M,D
Virginia Polytechnic Institute and State University	D
Washington State University	M,D
Washington University in St. Louis	M,D,O*
Wayne State University	M,D*
Wesleyan University	D*
West Virginia University	M,D
Yale University	D*

GENOMIC SCIENCES

Institution	Degrees
Albert Einstein College of Medicine	D
Black Hills State University	M
Case Western Reserve University	D*
Concordia University (Canada)	M,D,O
Georgia Health Sciences University	M,D
Harvard University	D*
North Carolina State University	M,D*
North Dakota State University	M,D
University of California, Riverside	D
University of California, San Francisco	D
University of Chicago	D
University of Cincinnati	M,D
University of Connecticut	M*
University of Florida	D*
University of Georgia	M,D
University of Maine	D
University of Maryland, Baltimore	M,D
University of Pennsylvania	D*
The University of Tennessee	M,D
The University of Tennessee–Oak Ridge National Laboratory Graduate School of Genome Science and Technology	M,D
The University of Toledo	M,O
University of Washington	D*
Wake Forest University	D
Washington University in St. Louis	M*
Wesleyan University	D*
West Virginia University	M,D
Yale University	D*

GEOCHEMISTRY

Institution	Degrees
California Institute of Technology	M,D
California State University, Fullerton	M
Colorado School of Mines	M,D
Columbia University	M,D*
Cornell University	M,D*
Georgia Institute of Technology	M,D
Indiana University Bloomington	M,D*
Massachusetts Institute of Technology	M,D
McMaster University	M,D
Missouri University of Science and Technology	M,D
Montana Tech of The University of Montana	M
New Mexico Institute of Mining and Technology	M,D
Ohio University	M*
University of California, Los Angeles	M,D*
University of Hawaii at Manoa	M,D
The University of Manchester	M,D
University of Nevada, Reno	M,D*
University of New Hampshire	M
The University of Texas at Dallas	M,D*
University of Wisconsin–Milwaukee	M,D
Yale University	D*

GEODETIC SCIENCES

Institution	Degrees
Columbia University	M,D*
The Ohio State University	M,D
State University of New York College of Environmental Science and Forestry	M,D
Université Laval	M,D
University of New Brunswick Fredericton	M,D,O

GEOGRAPHIC INFORMATION SYSTEMS

Institution	Degrees
Acadia University	M
Appalachian State University	M
Arizona State University	M,D,O
Boston University	M,D*
Clark University	M
Cleveland State University	M,D,O
Eastern Michigan University	M,O
Florida State University	M,D
George Mason University	M,D,O*
Georgia Institute of Technology	M,D
Georgia State University	O
Hunter College of the City University of New York	M,O
Idaho State University	M,O
Indiana University–Purdue University Indianapolis	M,O
Minnesota State University Mankato	M,O
Montclair State University	M,D,O
North Carolina State University	M,D*
Northern Arizona University	M,O
Northern Kentucky University	M,O
Northwest Missouri State University	M,O
Saint Louis University	M,D,O
Saint Mary's University of Minnesota	M,O
Salisbury University	M
San Francisco State University	M
San Jose State University	M,O
State University of New York College of Environmental Science and Forestry	M,D
Texas State University–San Marcos	M,D
Université du Québec à Montréal	O
Université Laval	M,O
University at Albany, State University of New York	M,O
University at Buffalo, the State University of New York	M,D,O*
The University of Akron	M
University of Central Arkansas	M,O
University of Colorado Denver	M,D
University of Connecticut	M,D,O*
University of Denver	M,D,O
University of Lethbridge	M,D
University of Maryland, Baltimore County	M,O
University of Memphis	M,D,O
University of Minnesota, Twin Cities Campus	M
The University of Montana	M
University of New Haven	M,O
The University of North Carolina at Charlotte	M,D
The University of North Carolina at Greensboro	M,D,O
University of Pittsburgh	M,D*
University of Redlands	M
University of Southern California	M,O*
The University of Texas at Dallas	M,D*
The University of Toledo	M,D,O
University of Wisconsin–Madison	M,D,O*
University of Wisconsin–Milwaukee	M,O
Virginia Commonwealth University	O
Virginia Polytechnic Institute and State University	D,O
West Chester University of Pennsylvania	M,O
Western Illinois University	M,O
Western Michigan University	M,O
West Virginia University	M,D

GEOGRAPHY

Institution	Degrees
Appalachian State University	M
Arizona State University	M,D,O
Auburn University	M
Ball State University	M
Boston University	M,D*
Brigham Young University	M*
Brock University	M
California State University, Chico	M
California State University, East Bay	M
California State University, Fullerton	M
California State University, Long Beach	M
California State University, Los Angeles	M*
California State University, Northridge	M
Carleton University	M,D
Central Connecticut State University	M
Chicago State University	M
Clark University	M,D
Concordia University (Canada)	M,D,O
Concord University	M
East Carolina University	M
Eastern Michigan University	M,O
Florida Atlantic University	M,D
Florida State University	M,D
Fort Hays State University	M
George Mason University	M,D,O*
The George Washington University	M
Georgia State University	M
Hunter College of the City University of New York	M,O
Indiana State University	M,D
Indiana University Bloomington	M,D*
Indiana University of Pennsylvania	M
The Johns Hopkins University	M,D
Kansas State University	M,D*
Kent State University	M,D*
Louisiana State University and Agricultural and Mechanical College	M,D
Marshall University	M
McGill University	M,D
McMaster University	M,D
Memorial University of Newfoundland	M,D
Miami University	M
Michigan State University	M,D
Minnesota State University Mankato	M,O
Missouri State University	M
New Mexico State University	M
Northeastern Illinois University	M
Northern Arizona University	M,O
Northern Illinois University	M,D
Northwest Missouri State University	M,O
The Ohio State University	M,D
Ohio University	M*
Oklahoma State University	M,D*
Oregon State University	M,D
Penn State University Park	M,D
Portland State University	M,D
Queen's University at Kingston	M,D
Rutgers, The State University of New Jersey, New Brunswick	M,D*
St. Cloud State University	M
Salem State University	M
San Diego State University	M,D
San Francisco State University	M
San Jose State University	M,O
Shippensburg University of Pennsylvania	M
Simon Fraser University	M,D
South Dakota State University	M
Southern Illinois University Carbondale	M,D
Southern Illinois University Edwardsville	M
State University of New York at Binghamton	M
Syracuse University	M,D*
Temple University	M,D*
Texas A&M University	M,D
Texas State University–San Marcos	M,D
Towson University	M
Trent University	M,D
Université de Montréal	M,D,O
Université de Sherbrooke	M,D
Université du Québec à Montréal	M
Université Laval	M,D
University at Albany, State University of New York	M,O
University at Buffalo, the State University of New York	M,D,O*
The University of Akron	M
The University of Alabama	M
University of Alaska Fairbanks	M,D
The University of Arizona	M,D
University of Arkansas	M
The University of British Columbia	M,D
University of Calgary	M,D
University of California, Berkeley	D*

University of California, Davis	M,D
University of California, Los Angeles	M,D*
University of California, Santa Barbara	M,D
University of Central Arkansas	M,O
University of Cincinnati	M,D
University of Colorado at Colorado Springs	M
University of Colorado Boulder	M,D*
University of Connecticut	M,D,O*
University of Delaware	M,D*
University of Denver	M,D
University of Florida	M,D*
University of Georgia	M,D
University of Guelph	M,D
University of Hawaii at Manoa	M,D,O
University of Idaho	M,D
University of Illinois at Chicago	M
University of Illinois at Urbana–Champaign	M,D
The University of Iowa	M,D*
The University of Kansas	M,D
University of Kentucky	M,D*
University of Lethbridge	M,D
University of Louisville	M
The University of Manchester	M,D
University of Manitoba	M,D
University of Maryland, Baltimore County	M,D
University of Maryland, College Park	M,D
University of Massachusetts Amherst	M*
University of Memphis	M,D,O
University of Miami	M*
University of Missouri	M*
The University of Montana	M
University of Nebraska at Omaha	M,O
University of Nebraska–Lincoln	M,D*
University of Nevada, Reno	M,D*
University of New Mexico	M*
University of New Orleans	M
The University of North Carolina at Chapel Hill	M,D*
The University of North Carolina at Charlotte	M,D
The University of North Carolina at Greensboro	M,D,O
University of North Dakota	M
University of Northern Iowa	M
University of North Texas	M
University of Oklahoma	M,D*
University of Oregon	M,D
University of Ottawa	M,D*
University of Prince Edward Island	M
University of Regina	M
University of Saskatchewan	M,D
University of South Africa	M,D
University of South Carolina	M,D
University of Southern California	M,O*
University of Southern Mississippi	M,D
University of South Florida	M,D*
The University of Tennessee	M,D
The University of Texas at Austin	M,D
The University of Toledo	M,D,O
University of Toronto	M,D
University of Utah	M,D*
University of Victoria	M,D
University of Washington	M,D*
University of Waterloo	M,D
The University of Western Ontario	M,D
University of Wisconsin–Madison	M,D,O*
University of Wisconsin–Milwaukee	M,D
University of Wyoming	M
Utah State University	M,D
Virginia Polytechnic Institute and State University	M,D
Wayne State University	M*
West Chester University of Pennsylvania	M,O
Western Illinois University	M,O
Western Michigan University	M,O
Western Washington University	M
West Virginia University	M,D
Wilfrid Laurier University	M,D
York University	M,D*

GEOLOGICAL ENGINEERING

Arizona State University	M,D
Colorado School of Mines	M,D
Michigan Technological University	M,D
Missouri University of Science and Technology	M,D
Montana Tech of The University of Montana	M
South Dakota School of Mines and Technology	M,D
University of Alaska Anchorage	M
University of Alaska Fairbanks	M,D
The University of Arizona	M,D,O
The University of British Columbia	M,D
University of Hawaii at Manoa	M,D
University of Idaho	M
University of Minnesota, Twin Cities Campus	M,D
University of Nevada, Reno	M,D*
University of North Dakota	M
University of Oklahoma	M,D*
University of Utah	M,D*
University of Wisconsin–Madison	M,D*

GEOLOGY

Acadia University	M
Alabama State University	M,D
American University of Beirut	M
Arizona State University	M,D
Auburn University	M
Ball State University	M
Baylor University	M,D*
Boise State University	M,D
Boston College	M*
Bowling Green State University	M*
Brigham Young University	M*
Brooklyn College of the City University of New York	M,D
California Institute of Technology	M,D
California State University, Bakersfield	M
California State University, Chico	M
California State University, East Bay	M
California State University, Fresno	M
California State University, Fullerton	M
California State University, Long Beach	M
California State University, Los Angeles	M*
California State University, Northridge	M
Case Western Reserve University	M,D*
Central Washington University	M
Colorado School of Mines	M,D
Cornell University	M,D*
Duke University	M,D*
East Carolina University	M
Eastern Kentucky University	M,D
Florida Atlantic University	M,D
Florida State University	M,D
Fort Hays State University	M
Georgia State University	M
Hofstra University	M,O
Humboldt State University	M
ICR Graduate School	M
Idaho State University	M,O
Indiana University Bloomington	M,D*
Indiana University–Purdue University Indianapolis	M,D
Iowa State University of Science and Technology	M,D*
Kansas State University	M*
Kent State University	M,D*
Lakehead University	M
Laurentian University	M,D
Lehigh University	M,D
Louisiana State University and Agricultural and Mechanical College	M,D
Massachusetts Institute of Technology	M,D
McMaster University	M,D
Memorial University of Newfoundland	M,D
Miami University	M,D
Michigan Technological University	M,D
Missouri State University	M
Missouri University of Science and Technology	M,D
Montana Tech of The University of Montana	M
New Mexico Institute of Mining and Technology	M,D
New Mexico State University	M
Northern Arizona University	M
Northern Illinois University	M,D
Northwestern University	M,D*
The Ohio State University	M,D
Ohio University	M*
Oklahoma State University	M,D*
Oregon State University	M,D
Portland State University	M,D
Queens College of the City University of New York	M
Queen's University at Kingston	M,D
Rensselaer Polytechnic Institute	M,D
Rutgers, The State University of New Jersey, Newark	M*
Rutgers, The State University of New Jersey, New Brunswick	M,D*
St. Francis Xavier University	M
San Diego State University	M
San Jose State University	M
South Dakota School of Mines and Technology	M,D
Southern Illinois University Carbondale	M,D
Southern Methodist University	M,D
State University of New York at Binghamton	M,D
Stephen F. Austin State University	M
Sul Ross State University	M
Syracuse University	M,D*
Temple University	M*
Texas A&M University	M,D
Texas A&M University–Kingsville	M
Texas Christian University	M
Université du Québec à Montréal	M,D,O
Université Laval	M,D
University at Albany, State University of New York	M,D
University at Buffalo, the State University of New York	M,D*
The University of Akron	M
The University of Alabama	M,D
University of Alaska Fairbanks	M,D
University of Arkansas	M
The University of British Columbia	M,D
University of Calgary	M,D
University of California, Berkeley	M,D*
University of California, Davis	M,D
University of California, Los Angeles	M,D*
University of California, Riverside	M,D
University of California, Santa Barbara	M,D
University of Cincinnati	M,D
University of Colorado Boulder	M,D*
University of Connecticut	M,D*
University of Delaware	M,D*
University of Florida	M,D*
University of Georgia	M,D
University of Hawaii at Manoa	M,D
University of Houston	M,D
University of Idaho	M,D
University of Illinois at Chicago	M,D
University of Illinois at Urbana–Champaign	M,D
The University of Kansas	M,D
University of Kentucky	M,D*
University of Louisiana at Lafayette	M*
University of Maine	M,D
University of Manitoba	M,D
University of Maryland, College Park	M,D
University of Memphis	M,D,O
University of Michigan	M,D*
University of Minnesota, Duluth	M,D
University of Minnesota, Twin Cities Campus	M,D
University of Missouri	M,D*
University of Missouri–Kansas City	M,D*
The University of Montana	M,D
University of Nevada, Reno	M,D*
University of New Brunswick Fredericton	M,D
University of New Hampshire	M
The University of North Carolina at Chapel Hill	M,D*
The University of North Carolina Wilmington	M
University of North Dakota	M,D
University of Oklahoma	M,D*
University of Oregon	M,D
University of Pittsburgh	M,D*
University of Puerto Rico, Mayagüez Campus	M
University of Regina	M,D
University of Rochester	M,D
University of Saskatchewan	M,D,O
University of South Carolina	M,D
University of Southern Mississippi	M,D
University of South Florida	M,D*
The University of Tennessee	M,D

*M—master's degree; P—first professional degree; D—doctorate; O—other advanced degree; *—Close-Up and/or Display in one of the other books in this series*

The University of Texas at Arlington M,D
The University of Texas at Austin M,D
The University of Texas at El Paso M,D
The University of Texas at San Antonio M*
The University of Texas of the Permian Basin M
The University of Toledo M
University of Toronto M,D
University of Utah M,D*
University of Vermont M
University of Washington M,D*
The University of Western Ontario M,D
University of Wisconsin–Madison M,D*
University of Wisconsin–Milwaukee M,D
University of Wyoming M,D
Utah State University M
Washington State University M,D
Wayne State University M*
West Chester University of Pennsylvania M,O
Western Kentucky University M
Western Washington University M
West Virginia University M,D
Wichita State University M
Wright State University M
Yale University D*

GEOPHYSICS

Boise State University M,D
Boston College M*
Bowling Green State University M*
California Institute of Technology M,D
California State University, Long Beach M
Colorado School of Mines M,D
Columbia University M,D*
Cornell University M,D*
Florida State University D
Georgia Institute of Technology M,D
ICR Graduate School M
Idaho State University M,O
Indiana University Bloomington M,D*
Louisiana State University and Agricultural and Mechanical College M,D
Massachusetts Institute of Technology M,D
Memorial University of Newfoundland M,D
Michigan Technological University M
Missouri University of Science and Technology M,D
New Mexico Institute of Mining and Technology M,D
Ohio University M*
Oregon State University M,D
Rice University M
Saint Louis University M,D
Southern Methodist University M,D
Stanford University M,D
Texas A&M University M,D
The University of Akron M
University of Alaska Fairbanks M,D
University of Alberta M,D
The University of British Columbia M,D
University of Calgary M,D
University of California, Berkeley M,D*
University of California, Los Angeles M,D*
University of California, Santa Barbara M,D
University of Chicago M,D
University of Colorado Boulder M,D*
University of Hawaii at Manoa M,D
University of Houston M,D
University of Manitoba M,D
University of Memphis M,D,O
University of Miami M,D*
University of Minnesota, Twin Cities Campus M,D
University of Nevada, Reno M,D*
University of Oklahoma M,D*
The University of Texas at Dallas M,D*
The University of Texas at El Paso M
University of Utah M,D*
University of Victoria M,D
University of Washington M,D*
The University of Western Ontario M,D
University of Wisconsin–Madison M,D*
University of Wyoming M,D
West Virginia University M,D
Wright State University M
Yale University D*

GEOSCIENCES

Alabama State University M,D
Arizona State University M,D
Baylor University M,D*
Boise State University M
Boston University M,D,O*
Brock University M
Brooklyn College of the City University of New York M,O
Brown University M,D
California State University, Chico M
Carleton University M,D
Case Western Reserve University M,D*
Central Connecticut State University M,O
City College of the City University of New York M,D
Colorado State University M,D
Columbia University M,D*
Cornell University M,D*
Dalhousie University M,D
Dartmouth College M,D
Eastern Michigan University M
Emporia State University M,O
Florida Atlantic University M,D
Florida International University M,D
Fort Hays State University M
George Mason University M,D,O*
Georgia Institute of Technology M,D
Georgia State University M,O
Graduate School and University Center of the City University of New York D
Harvard University M,D*
Hofstra University M,O
Hunter College of the City University of New York M,O
Idaho State University M,O
Indiana University Bloomington M,D*
Indiana University–Purdue University Indianapolis M,D
Iowa State University of Science and Technology M,D*
The Johns Hopkins University M,D
Lehigh University M,D
Loma Linda University M,D
Long Island University, C.W. Post Campus M
Massachusetts Institute of Technology M,D
McGill University M,D
McMaster University M,D
Memorial University of Newfoundland M,D
Michigan State University M,D
Middle Tennessee State University O
Mississippi State University M,D
Missouri State University M
Montana State University M,D
Montana Tech of The University of Montana M
Montclair State University M,D,O
Murray State University M
New Mexico Institute of Mining and Technology M,D
North Carolina Central University M
North Carolina State University M,D*
Northwestern University M,D*
Oregon State University M,D
Penn State University Park M,D
Princeton University D*
Purdue University M,D
Rice University M,D
St. Francis Xavier University M
Saint Louis University M,D
St. Thomas University M,D,O
San Francisco State University M
Simon Fraser University M,D
South Dakota State University D
Stanford University M,D,O
State University of New York at New Paltz M
State University of New York College at Oneonta M
Stony Brook University, State University of New York M,D
Texas A&M University–Commerce M
Texas Tech University M,D*
Université du Québec à Chicoutimi M
Université du Québec à Montréal M,D,O
Université du Québec, Institut National de la Recherche Scientifique M,D
Université Laval M,D
University at Albany, State University of New York M,D
University at Buffalo, the State University of New York M,D,O*
The University of Akron M
University of Alberta M,D
The University of Arizona M,D
University of Arkansas at Little Rock O
University of California, Irvine M,D*
University of California, Los Angeles M,D*
University of California, San Diego D*
University of California, Santa Barbara M,D
University of California, Santa Cruz M,D
University of Chicago M,D
University of Florida M,D*
University of Illinois at Chicago M,D
University of Illinois at Urbana–Champaign M,D
The University of Iowa M,D*
University of Maine M,D
The University of Manchester M,D
University of Massachusetts Amherst M,D*
University of Missouri–Kansas City M,D*
The University of Montana M,D
University of Nebraska–Lincoln M,D*
University of Nevada, Las Vegas M,D
University of New Hampshire M
University of New Haven M,O
University of New Mexico M,D*
University of New Orleans M
The University of North Carolina at Charlotte M,D
The University of North Carolina Wilmington M
University of North Dakota M,D
University of Northern Colorado M
University of Northern Iowa M
University of Notre Dame M,D*
University of Ottawa M,D*
University of Pennsylvania M,D*
University of Rhode Island M,D
University of Rochester M,D
University of South Carolina M,D
University of Southern California M,D*
The University of Texas at Austin M,D
The University of Texas at Dallas M,D*
The University of Toledo M
University of Tulsa M,D
University of Victoria M,D
University of Waterloo M,D
The University of Western Ontario M,D
University of Windsor M,D
Virginia Polytechnic Institute and State University M,D
Washington State University M,D
Washington University in St. Louis M,D*
Wesleyan University M*
West Chester University of Pennsylvania M,O
Western Connecticut State University M
Western Kentucky University M
Western Michigan University M,D
Yale University D*
York University M,D*

GEOTECHNICAL ENGINEERING

Auburn University M,D
Cornell University M,D*
Drexel University M,D*
École Polytechnique de Montréal M,D,O
Illinois Institute of Technology M,D
Iowa State University of Science and Technology M,D*
Louisiana State University and Agricultural and Mechanical College M,D
Marquette University M,D,O
Massachusetts Institute of Technology M,D,O
McGill University M,D
Missouri University of Science and Technology M,D
Northwestern University M,D*
Norwich University M
Ohio University M,D*
Oregon State University M,D
Penn State University Park M,D
Rensselaer Polytechnic Institute M,D
Texas A&M University M,D
Tufts University M,D

Institution	Degrees
The University of Alabama in Huntsville	M,D
University of Alberta	M,D
University of Calgary	M,D
University of California, Berkeley	M,D*
University of Colorado Boulder	M,D*
University of Colorado Denver	M,D
University of Delaware	M,D*
University of Missouri	M,D*
University of New Brunswick Fredericton	M,D
The University of Texas at Austin	M,D
University of Washington	M,D*

GERMAN

Institution	Degrees
Arizona State University	M
Bowling Green State University	M*
Brown University	D
California State University, Fullerton	M
California State University, Long Beach	M
California State University, Sacramento	M
Central Connecticut State University	M,O
Columbia University	M,D*
Cornell University	M,D*
Dalhousie University	M
Duke University	D*
Eastern Michigan University	M,O
Florida State University	M
Georgetown University	M,D
Georgia State University	M,O
Graduate School and University Center of the City University of New York	M,D
Harvard University	D*
Hofstra University	M,O
Illinois State University	M
Indiana University Bloomington	M,D*
The Johns Hopkins University	D
Kansas State University	M*
Kent State University	M,D*
McGill University	M,D
Memorial University of Newfoundland	M
Michigan State University	M,D
Middlebury College	M,D
Millersville University of Pennsylvania	M
Mississippi State University	M
New York University	M,D
Northwestern University	D*
The Ohio State University	M,D
Penn State University Park	M,D
Portland State University	M
Princeton University	D*
Purdue University	M,D
Queen's University at Kingston	M,D
Rider University	O
Rutgers, The State University of New Jersey, New Brunswick	M,D*
San Francisco State University	M
Stanford University	M,D
Texas Tech University	M*
Tufts University	M
Université de Montréal	M
University at Buffalo, the State University of New York	M,D,O*
The University of Alabama	M,D
University of Alberta	M,D
The University of Arizona	M
University of Arkansas	M
The University of British Columbia	M,D
University of Calgary	M
University of California, Berkeley	D*
University of California, Davis	M,D
University of California, Irvine	M,D*
University of California, Los Angeles	M,D*
University of California, San Diego	M*
University of Chicago	M,D
University of Cincinnati	M,D
University of Colorado Boulder	M*
University of Connecticut	M,D*
University of Delaware	M*
University of Florida	M,D*
University of Georgia	M
University of Illinois at Chicago	M,D
University of Illinois at Urbana–Champaign	M,D
The University of Iowa	M,D*
The University of Kansas	M,D
University of Kentucky	M*
University of Lethbridge	M,D
The University of Manchester	M,D
University of Manitoba	M
University of Maryland, College Park	M,D
University of Massachusetts Amherst	M,D*
University of Michigan	M,D*
University of Minnesota, Twin Cities Campus	M,D
University of Mississippi	M
University of Missouri	M*
The University of Montana	M
University of Nebraska–Lincoln	M,D*
University of Nevada, Reno	M*
University of New Mexico	M,D*
The University of North Carolina at Chapel Hill	M,D*
University of Northern Iowa	M
University of Oklahoma	M*
University of Oregon	M,D
University of Pennsylvania	M,D*
University of Pittsburgh	M,D*
University of Rochester	
University of Saskatchewan	M
University of South Africa	M,D
University of South Carolina	M,D
The University of Tennessee	M,D
The University of Texas at Austin	M,D
The University of Toledo	M
University of Toronto	M,D
University of Utah	M,D*
University of Vermont	M
University of Victoria	M
University of Virginia	M,D
University of Washington	M,D*
University of Waterloo	M,D
University of Wisconsin–Madison	M,D*
University of Wisconsin–Milwaukee	M,O
University of Wyoming	M
Vanderbilt University	M,D*
Washington University in St. Louis	M,D*
Wayne State University	M,D*
Western Kentucky University	M
Yale University	D*

GERONTOLOGICAL NURSING

Institution	Degrees
Allen College	M,D,O
Boston College	M,D*
California State University, Stanislaus	M
Caribbean University	M,D
Case Western Reserve University	M,D*
College of Mount Saint Vincent	M,O
College of Staten Island of the City University of New York	M,O
Columbia University	M,O*
Concordia University Wisconsin	M
Duke University	M,D,O*
East Tennessee State University	M,D,O
Emory University	M*
Gwynedd-Mercy College	M
Hampton University	M
Hunter College of the City University of New York	M
Independence University	M
Kent State University	M,D*
Lehman College of the City University of New York	M
Loma Linda University	M
Marquette University	M,D,O
Maryville University of Saint Louis	M,D
MGH Institute of Health Professions	M,D,O
Nazareth College of Rochester	M
New York University	M,D,O
Oakland University	M,O
Oregon Health & Science University	O*
Rush University	M,D,O
Rutgers, The State University of New Jersey, Newark	M*
Sage Graduate School	M,D,O
St. Catherine University	M,D
San Jose State University	M,O
Seattle Pacific University	M,O
Seton Hall University	M,D
Southern University and Agricultural and Mechanical College	M,D,O
State University of New York Institute of Technology	M,O
Texas Christian University	M,D
Texas Tech University Health Sciences Center	M,D,O
University of Central Florida	M,D,O
University of Delaware	M,O*
University of Illinois at Chicago	M
University of Maryland, Baltimore	M
University of Massachusetts Lowell	M,O
University of Massachusetts Worcester	M,D,O
University of Michigan	M*
University of Minnesota, Twin Cities Campus	M
The University of North Carolina at Greensboro	M,D,O
University of North Dakota	M,D
University of Puerto Rico, Medical Sciences Campus	M
University of Rhode Island	M,D
University of Rochester	M,D,O
University of San Diego	M,D
University of Utah	M,O*
University of Wisconsin–Eau Claire	M,D
University of Wisconsin–Madison	D*
Vanderbilt University	M,D*
Virginia Polytechnic Institute and State University	M,D,O

GERONTOLOGY

Institution	Degrees
Adelphi University	M,O*
Adler School of Professional Psychology	M,D,O
Alliant International University–Los Angeles	M
Arizona State University	M,D,O
Arkansas State University	M,O
A.T. Still University of Health Sciences	M,D
Ball State University	M
Bethel University (MN)	M
California State University, Fullerton	M
California State University, Long Beach	M
Capella University	M,D
Central Michigan University	M,O
Cleveland State University	M,D,O
The College of New Rochelle	M,O
Concordia University Chicago	M
Eastern Illinois University	M
Eastern Michigan University	M,O
East Tennessee State University	M,D,O
Emory University	M*
Gannon University	O
George Mason University	M,O*
Georgia State University	M
Hofstra University	M,O
Kent State University	M*
Lakehead University	M,D
Lindenwood University	M,O
Long Island University, C.W. Post Campus	M,O
Long Island University, Rockland Graduate Campus	M,O
Marywood University	M
Miami University	M,D
Middle Tennessee State University	O
Minnesota State University Mankato	M,O
Morehead State University	M
Mount Saint Vincent University	M
New York University	D
North Dakota State University	M,D
Northeastern Illinois University	M
Oregon Health & Science University	M,O*
Oregon State University	M
Portland State University	O
Rochester Institute of Technology	M,O
Sacred Heart University	M
Sage Graduate School	M,O
St. Cloud State University	M
Saint Joseph College	M,O
Saint Joseph's University	M,O
San Diego State University	M
San Francisco State University	M
San Jose State University	M,O
Shippensburg University of Pennsylvania	M,O
Simon Fraser University	M,D
Texas A&M University–Kingsville	M
Texas Tech University	M,D*
Towson University	M,O
Université de Sherbrooke	M
Université Laval	O
University of Arkansas at Little Rock	O
University of Central Florida	M,O
University of Central Missouri	M
University of Central Oklahoma	M

*M—master's degree; P—first professional degree; D—doctorate; O—other advanced degree; *—Close-Up and/or Display in one of the other books in this series*

University of Georgia O
University of Illinois at Springfield M
University of Indianapolis M,O
The University of Kansas M,D,O
University of Kentucky D*
University of La Verne M,O
University of Louisiana at Monroe M,O
University of Louisville M,D,O
University of Maryland, Baltimore M,D
University of Maryland, Baltimore County M,D
University of Massachusetts Boston M,D,O
University of Missouri–St. Louis M,O
University of Nebraska at Omaha M,O
University of Nebraska–Lincoln M,D*
University of New England M,O
The University of North Carolina at Charlotte M,O
The University of North Carolina at Greensboro M,O
The University of North Carolina Wilmington M
University of Northern Colorado M
University of North Florida M,O
University of North Texas M,D,O
University of Phoenix M
University of Phoenix–Birmingham Campus M
University of Phoenix–Central Valley Campus M
University of Phoenix–Charlotte Campus M
University of Phoenix–Chattanooga Campus M
University of Phoenix–Des Moines Campus M,D
University of Phoenix–Hawaii Campus M
University of Phoenix–Louisville Campus M
University of Phoenix–Milwaukee Campus M,D
University of Phoenix–Raleigh Campus M,D
University of Phoenix–Southern Colorado Campus M
University of Phoenix–Washington D.C. Campus M,D
University of Pittsburgh M,D,O*
University of Puerto Rico, Medical Sciences Campus M,O
University of Regina M
University of Rhode Island M,D
University of South Alabama O
University of South Carolina O
University of Southern California M,D,O*
University of South Florida M,D*
The University of Tennessee M
The University of Toledo M,O
University of Utah M,O*
University of West Florida M
University of Wisconsin–Milwaukee M,D,O
Valparaiso University M,O
Virginia Commonwealth University M,D,O
Webster University M
West Chester University of Pennsylvania M,O
Wichita State University M
Wilmington University M

GRAPHIC DESIGN

Academy of Art University M
Atlantic College M
Bob Jones University P,M,D,O
Boston University M*
Bowling Green State University M*
California Institute of the Arts M,O
California State University, Los Angeles M*
Cardinal Stritch University M
City College of the City University of New York M
The College of New Rochelle M
Cranbrook Academy of Art M
Digital Media Arts College M
Florida Atlantic University M
Full Sail University M
George Mason University M*
Illinois State University M
Indiana State University M
Iowa State University of Science and Technology M*
Kent State University M*
Louisiana State University and Agricultural and Mechanical College M
Louisiana Tech University M
Maryland Institute College of Art M
Marywood University M
Miami International University of Art & Design M*
Minneapolis College of Art and Design M,O
Morehead State University M
New York Institute of Technology M
New York University M
North Carolina State University M*
Ohio University M*
Otis College of Art and Design M
Pittsburg State University M
Pratt Institute M*
Rhode Island School of Design M
Rochester Institute of Technology M
San Diego State University M
Savannah College of Art and Design M
School of the Art Institute of Chicago M
Southern Polytechnic State University M,O
Suffolk University M
Temple University M*
Texas State University–San Marcos M
Université Laval M
University of Baltimore M,D
University of Cincinnati M
University of Florida M,D*
University of Guam M
University of Idaho M
University of Illinois at Chicago M
University of Illinois at Urbana–Champaign M
University of Massachusetts Dartmouth M
University of Memphis M,O
University of Miami M*
University of Minnesota, Duluth M
University of Notre Dame M*
The University of Tennessee M
University of Utah M*
Vermont College of Fine Arts M
Western Illinois University M,O
West Virginia University M
Yale University M*

HAZARDOUS MATERIALS MANAGEMENT

Humboldt State University M
Idaho State University M
Marquette University M,D,O
New Mexico Institute of Mining and Technology M
Rutgers, The State University of New Jersey, New Brunswick M,D*
Stony Brook University, State University of New York M,O
Tufts University M,D
University of Colorado Denver M
The University of Manchester M,D
University of New Haven M,O
University of South Carolina M,D
University of Southern California M,D,O*
Virginia Polytechnic Institute and State University M,D,O

HEALTH COMMUNICATION

Arkansas State University M,O
Chapman University M
Cleveland State University M,O
East Carolina University M
Emerson College M
Fitchburg State University M,O
The Johns Hopkins University M,D
Marquette University M,O
Marywood University M,O
Michigan State University M
Ohio University M,D*
Southern Illinois University Edwardsville M
Tufts University M
Tulane University M*
University of Florida M,D,O*
University of Houston M
The University of North Carolina at Charlotte M
University of Southern California M,D*
Washington State University M,D

HEALTH EDUCATION

Adelphi University M,O*
Alabama State University M
Albany State University M
Alcorn State University M,O
Allen College M,D,O
American University M,O
Arcadia University M*
Arizona State University D
Arkansas State University M,O
A.T. Still University of Health Sciences M,D
Auburn University M,D,O
Augusta State University M
Austin Peay State University M
Averett University M
Baylor University M,D*
Benedictine University M
Boston University M,D,O*
Brandeis University D
Brigham Young University M*
Brooklyn College of the City University of New York M,O
California State University, Long Beach M
California State University, Los Angeles M*
California State University, San Bernardino M
Cambridge College M,D,O
The Citadel, The Military College of South Carolina M
Cleveland State University M
The College at Brockport, State University of New York M
The College of New Jersey M
College of Saint Mary D
Colorado State University–Pueblo M
Dalhousie University M
Delta State University M
D'Youville College D*
East Carolina University M
Eastern Kentucky University M
Eastern Michigan University M
Eastern University M
East Stroudsburg University of Pennsylvania M
Emory University M*
Florida Agricultural and Mechanical University M
Florida State University M,D
Fort Hays State University M
Framingham State University M
Georgia College & State University M
Georgia Southern University M,D
Georgia Southwestern State University M,O
Georgia State University M
Grand Canyon University D
Harding University M,O
Hofstra University M,O
Howard University M
Idaho State University M
Illinois State University M
Indiana State University M
Indiana University Bloomington M,D*
Indiana University of Pennsylvania M
Indiana University–Purdue University Indianapolis M,D
Inter American University of Puerto Rico, Metropolitan Campus M
Ithaca College M
Jackson State University M
James Madison University M
John F. Kennedy University M
The Johns Hopkins University M,D
Kent State University M,D*
Lake Erie College of Osteopathic Medicine P,M,O
Lehman College of the City University of New York M
Loma Linda University M,D
Long Island University, Brooklyn Campus M
Louisiana Tech University M,D
Marshall University M
Marywood University D
Middle Tennessee State University M
Midwestern University, Glendale Campus M
Mills College M,D
Minnesota State University Mankato M,O
Mississippi University for Women M
Montana State University M
Montclair State University M,O
Morehead State University M
Morehouse School of Medicine M
Mount Mary College M
New Jersey City University M
New Mexico Highlands University M

New Mexico State University M
New York Medical College O*
North Carolina Agricultural and Technical State University M
Northeastern State University M
Northern State University M
Northwestern State University of Louisiana M
Northwest Missouri State University M
Nova Southeastern University M,D*
Oklahoma State University M,D,O*
Plymouth State University M
Portland State University M,O
Prairie View A&M University M
Regis University P,M,D,O
Rhode Island College M,O
Rosalind Franklin University of Medicine and Science M*
Sage Graduate School M
Saint Francis University M
Saint Joseph's University M,O
San Francisco State University M
San Jose State University M,O
Simmons College M,D,O
South Dakota State University M
Southeastern Louisiana University M
Southern Connecticut State University M
Southern Illinois University Carbondale M,D
Southern Illinois University Edwardsville M
Springfield College M,D,O
State University of New York College at Cortland M
Suffolk University M
Teachers College, Columbia University M,D
Temple University M,D*
Tennessee Technological University M
Texas A&M Health Science Center M
Texas A&M University M,D
Texas A&M University–Commerce M,D
Texas A&M University–Kingsville M
Texas Southern University M
Texas State University–San Marcos M
Texas Woman's University M,D
Thomas Jefferson University M,D,O
TUI University M,D,O
Tulane University M*
Union College (KY) M
Universidad Adventista de las Antillas P,M
The University of Alabama M,D
The University of Alabama at Birmingham M,D*
University of Arkansas M,D
University of Calgary M,D
University of Central Arkansas M
University of Central Oklahoma M
University of Cincinnati M,D
University of Colorado Denver M,D
University of Florida M,D,O*
University of Georgia M,D
University of Houston M,D
University of Illinois at Chicago M
The University of Kansas M,D,O
University of Louisville M,D
University of Maryland, Baltimore County M,O
University of Maryland, College Park M,D
University of Massachusetts Amherst M,D*
University of Medicine and Dentistry of New Jersey M,D,O
University of Michigan M,D*
University of Michigan–Flint M
University of Missouri M,D,O*
The University of Montana M
University of Nebraska at Omaha M
University of Nebraska–Lincoln M*
University of New England P,M
University of New Mexico M*
The University of North Carolina at Chapel Hill M,D*
University of Northern Colorado M
University of Northern Iowa M,D
University of Oklahoma Health Sciences Center D
University of Phoenix M
University of Phoenix–Charlotte Campus M
University of Phoenix–Des Moines Campus M,D
University of Phoenix–Louisville Campus M
University of Phoenix–Milwaukee Campus M,D
University of Phoenix–Raleigh Campus M,D
University of Phoenix–Southern Colorado Campus M
University of Phoenix–Washington D.C. Campus M,D
University of Pittsburgh M,D,O*
University of Puerto Rico, Medical Sciences Campus M
University of Rhode Island M
University of Rochester M,D,O
University of South Africa M,D
University of South Alabama M
University of South Carolina M,D,O
The University of South Dakota M
University of Southern Mississippi M
The University of Tennessee M
The University of Texas at Austin M,D
The University of Texas at El Paso M
The University of Texas at San Antonio M*
The University of Texas at Tyler M
The University of Toledo M,D,O
University of Utah M,D*
University of Virginia M,D
University of Waterloo M,D
University of West Florida M
University of Wisconsin–La Crosse M
University of Wisconsin–Milwaukee M,D,O
University of Wyoming M
Utah State University M
Virginia Commonwealth University M,O
Virginia State University M,D
Wayne State University M,D,O*
West Chester University of Pennsylvania M,O
Western Illinois University M,O
Western Michigan University D
Western Oregon University M
Western University of Health Sciences M
West Virginia University M,D
Widener University M,D
Worcester State University M
Wright State University M

HEALTH INFORMATICS

American Sentinel University M
Arkansas Tech University M
Barry University O*
Benedictine University M
Boston University M*
Brandeis University M,O
Claremont Graduate University M,D,O
The College of St. Scholastica M,O
Emory University M,D*
George Mason University M,O*
Georgia Health Sciences University M
Golden Gate University M,D,O
Grand Canyon University M
Indiana University Bloomington M,D*
The Johns Hopkins University M
National University M
Northeastern University M,D
Northern Kentucky University M,O
Nova Southeastern University M,O*
Oregon Health & Science University M,D,O*
Saint Joseph's University M,O
Stephens College M,O
Stevens Institute of Technology M,D,O
Temple University M*
TUI University M,D,O
The University of Alabama at Birmingham M*
University of Central Florida M,O
University of Illinois at Chicago M
University of Illinois at Urbana–Champaign M,D,O
The University of Iowa M,D,O*
The University of Kansas M
University of La Verne M
University of Maryland University College M,O
University of Massachusetts Lowell M,O
University of Michigan M,D*
University of Minnesota, Twin Cities Campus M,D
University of Missouri M*
The University of North Carolina at Charlotte M,D,O
University of Phoenix M
University of Phoenix–Birmingham Campus M
University of Phoenix–Charlotte Campus M
University of Phoenix–Des Moines Campus M,D
University of Phoenix–Louisville Campus M
University of Phoenix–Milwaukee Campus M,D
University of Phoenix–Raleigh Campus M,D
University of Phoenix–Washington D.C. Campus M,D
University of Pittsburgh M*
University of Puerto Rico, Medical Sciences Campus M
University of San Diego M,D
The University of Texas Health Science Center at Houston M,D,O*
University of Toronto M
University of Victoria M
University of Virginia M
University of Washington M,D*
University of Wisconsin–Milwaukee M,O
Walden University M,D,O

HEALTH LAW

Boston University M*
DePaul University P,M,O
Georgetown University P,M,D
Loyola University Chicago P,M,D
Nova Southeastern University M*
Quinnipiac University P,M
Seton Hall University P,M
Southern Illinois University Carbondale M
Suffolk University P,M
Union Graduate College M,O
Université de Sherbrooke P,M,D,O
University of California, San Diego M*
University of Denver M,O
University of Houston P,M
The University of Manchester M,D
University of Pittsburgh M,O*
University of Tulsa P,M,O
Widener University P,M,D
Xavier University M

HEALTH PHYSICS/ RADIOLOGICAL HEALTH

Bloomsburg University of Pennsylvania M
Emory University D*
Georgetown University M
Georgia Institute of Technology M,D
Idaho State University M,D
Illinois Institute of Technology M,D
McMaster University M,D
Midwestern State University M
New York Chiropractic College M
Oregon State University M,D
Quinnipiac University M
San Diego State University M
Texas A&M University M,D
Université Laval O
University of Alberta M,D
University of Cincinnati M
University of Kentucky M*
University of Massachusetts Lowell M
University of Medicine and Dentistry of New Jersey M
University of Michigan M,D,O*
University of Missouri M,D*
University of Nevada, Las Vegas M
University of Oklahoma Health Sciences Center M,D
Virginia Commonwealth University D
Wayne State University M,D*

HEALTH PROMOTION

American University of Beirut M
Auburn University M,D,O
Ball State University M
Benedictine University M
Boston University D*
Bridgewater State University M
Brigham Young University M,D*
California State University, Fresno M
Canisius College M
Claremont Graduate University M,D

*M—master's degree; P—first professional degree; D—doctorate; O—other advanced degree; *—Close-Up and/or Display in one of the other books in this series*

Cleveland Chiropractic College–Kansas City Campus M
Cleveland Chiropractic College–Los Angeles Campus M
Concord University M
Eastern Kentucky University M
Eastern Michigan University M,O
East Tennessee State University M,D
Emory University M*
Florida Atlantic University M
Florida International University M,D
George Mason University M*
Georgetown University M,D
Georgia College & State University M
Georgia State University M,D,O
Goddard College M
Harvard University M,D*
Independence University M
Indiana State University M
Indiana University Bloomington M,D*
Instituto Tecnologico de Santo Domingo M,O
Kent State University M,D*
Lehman College of the City University of New York M
Loma Linda University M,D
Louisiana State University in Shreveport M
Marymount University M
McNeese State University M
Mississippi State University M,D
Missouri State University M
Morehouse School of Medicine M
Nebraska Methodist College M
New York Medical College M*
New York University M,D,O
Oakland University O
Old Dominion University M
Oregon State University M,D
Portland State University M,O
Purdue University M,D
Rocky Mountain University of Health Professions D
Rowan University M
San Diego State University M,D
Simmons College M,O
Springfield College M,D
Texas A&M University–Commerce M,D
Union Institute & University M,D,O
Universidad del Turabo M
The University of Alabama M,D
The University of Alabama at Birmingham D*
University of Alberta M,O
University of Arkansas for Medical Sciences D
University of Central Florida M,O
University of Chicago M,D
University of Colorado at Colorado Springs M
University of Delaware M*
University of Georgia M,D
University of Kentucky M,D*
University of Louisville D
University of Massachusetts Lowell D
University of Memphis M
University of Michigan M,D*
The University of Montana M
University of Nebraska–Lincoln M,D*
University of Nevada, Las Vegas M
The University of North Carolina at Chapel Hill M*
University of Oklahoma M,D*
University of Oklahoma Health Sciences Center M,D
University of Pittsburgh M,D,O*
University of Puerto Rico, Medical Sciences Campus O
University of Rochester M,D,O
University of South Carolina M,D,O
University of Southern California M*
The University of Tennessee M
The University of Texas at El Paso M
University of the Incarnate Word M
The University of Toledo M,D,O
University of Utah M,D*
University of Wisconsin–Stevens Point M
University of Wyoming M
Walden University M,D,O
West Virginia University M,D
Wilfrid Laurier University M
Wright State University M

HEALTH PSYCHOLOGY

Adler School of Professional Psychology M,D,O
Appalachian State University M,O
Argosy University, Atlanta M,D,O*
Argosy University, Chicago D*
Argosy University, Schaumburg M,D,O*
Argosy University, Twin Cities M,D,O*
Argosy University, Washington DC M,D*
Bastyr University M
California Institute of Integral Studies M,D
Central Connecticut State University M
Central Michigan University M,D
Chatham University M,D
Claremont Graduate University M,D,O
Drexel University D*
Duke University D*
East Carolina University D
Georgian Court University M,O
John F. Kennedy University M
Lesley University M
North Dakota State University M,D
Northern Kentucky University M,O
Philadelphia College of Osteopathic Medicine M,D,O*
Prescott College M
Rhode Island College M,O
Rutgers, The State University of New Jersey, New Brunswick D*
San Diego State University M,D
Saybrook University M,D
Southwestern College (NM) O
Stony Brook University, State University of New York D
Texas State University–San Marcos M
United States International University M
The University of British Columbia M,D
University of Connecticut M,D,O*
University of Florida D*
University of Michigan–Dearborn M
University of Missouri–Kansas City M,D*
The University of North Carolina at Charlotte M,D,O
University of North Texas M,D
The University of Texas at Arlington M,D
University of the Sciences in Philadelphia M
Virginia Commonwealth University D
Virginia State University M,D
Walden University M,D,O
West Chester University of Pennsylvania M,O
Yeshiva University D*

HEALTH SERVICES MANAGEMENT AND HOSPITAL ADMINISTRATION

Alaska Pacific University M
Albany State University M
American InterContinental University Online M
American Sentinel University M
The American University in Dubai M
American University of Beirut M
Andrew Jackson University M
Aquinas Institute of Theology P,M,D,O
Argosy University, Atlanta M,D*
Argosy University, Chicago M,D*
Argosy University, Dallas M,D,O*
Argosy University, Denver M,D*
Argosy University, Hawai'i M,D,O*
Argosy University, Inland Empire M,D*
Argosy University, Los Angeles M,D*
Argosy University, Nashville M,D*
Argosy University, Orange County M,D,O*
Argosy University, Phoenix M,D*
Argosy University, Salt Lake City M,D*
Argosy University, San Francisco Bay Area M,D*
Argosy University, Sarasota M,D,O*
Argosy University, Schaumburg M,D,O*
Argosy University, Seattle M,D*
Argosy University, Tampa M,D*
Argosy University, Twin Cities M,D*
Argosy University, Washington DC M,D,O*
Arkansas State University M,O
Armstrong Atlantic State University M
Ashworth College M
A.T. Still University of Health Sciences M,D
Avila University M
Baker College Center for Graduate Studies—Online M,D
Baldwin-Wallace College M
Barry University M,O*
Baylor University M*
Bellevue University M
Benedictine University M
Benedictine University at Springfield M
Bernard M. Baruch College of the City University of New York M
Boston University M,D*
Brandeis University M
Brenau University M
Broadview University M
Brooklyn College of the City University of New York M
California Coast University M
California Intercontinental University M,D
California State University, Bakersfield M
California State University, Chico M
California State University, East Bay M
California State University, Fresno M
California State University, Long Beach M
California State University, Los Angeles M*
California State University, Northridge M
California State University, San Bernardino M
Cambridge College M
Capella University M,D,O
Carnegie Mellon University M*
Central Michigan University M,D,O
Champlain College M
Charleston Southern University M
Clark University M
Clayton State University M
Cleveland State University M
The College at Brockport, State University of New York M,O
College of Saint Elizabeth M
Colorado Technical University Sioux Falls M
Columbia Southern University M
Columbia University M*
Columbus State University M,O
Concordia University (Canada) M,D,O
Concordia University, St. Paul M
Concordia University Wisconsin M
Cornell University M,D*
Daemen College M
Dalhousie University M,D
Dallas Baptist University M
Dartmouth College M,D
Davenport University M
Davenport University M
Davenport University M
Defiance College M
Delta State University M
DePaul University M,O
DeSales University M
Des Moines University M
Dowling College M,O
Duke University O*
Duquesne University M
D'Youville College M,D,O*
Eastern Kentucky University M
Eastern Michigan University M,O
Eastern University M
East Tennessee State University M,D,O
Ellis University M
Emory University M,D*
Fairfield University M,D
Fairleigh Dickinson University, College at Florham M
Fairleigh Dickinson University, Metropolitan Campus M
Felician College M*
Florida Institute of Technology M
Florida International University M,D
Florida State University M,D,O

Institution	Degrees
Framingham State University	M
Francis Marion University	M
Franklin Pierce University	M,D,O
Friends University	M
George Mason University	M,D,O*
The George Washington University	M,D,O
Georgia College & State University	M
Georgia Institute of Technology	M
Georgia Southern University	M,D
Georgia State University	M
Globe University	M
Goldfarb School of Nursing at Barnes-Jewish College	M,O
Governors State University	M
Grambling State University	M
Grand Canyon University	M,O
Grand Valley State University	M,D
Grantham University	M
Hampton University	M,D
Harding University	M
Harrisburg University of Science and Technology	M
Harvard University	M,D*
Herzing University Online	M
Hofstra University	M,O
Holy Family University	M*
Houston Baptist University	M
Hunter College of the City University of New York	M
Husson University	M
Independence University	M
Indiana Tech	M
Indiana University Northwest	M,O
Indiana University of Pennsylvania	M,D
Indiana University–Purdue University Indianapolis	M
Indiana University South Bend	M,O
Institute of Public Administration	M,O
Iona College	M,O
The Johns Hopkins University	M,D,O
Jones International University	M
Kaplan University, Davenport Campus	M,O
Kean University	M
Keiser University	M
Kennesaw State University	M
King's College	M
Lake Erie College	M
Lake Forest Graduate School of Management	M
Lakeland College	M
Lamar University	M
Lewis University	M
Lindenwood University	M,O
Lipscomb University	M
Loma Linda University	M
Long Island University, Brooklyn Campus	M
Long Island University, C.W. Post Campus	M,O
Long Island University, Rockland Graduate Campus	M,O
Louisiana State University Health Sciences Center	M,D
Louisiana State University in Shreveport	M
Loyola University Chicago	M
Loyola University New Orleans	M,D
Madonna University	M
Marlboro College	M
Marquette University	M,O
Marshall University	M,D
Marylhurst University	M
Marymount University	M,O
Marywood University	M
Massachusetts College of Pharmacy and Health Sciences	M
McGill University	M,D,O
Medical University of South Carolina	M,D
Meharry Medical College	M
Mercy College	M
Middle Tennessee State University	O
Midwestern State University	M
Mississippi College	M
Missouri State University	M
Monmouth University	M,O
Montana State University Billings	M
Morehouse School of Medicine	M
National University	M
National University of Health Sciences	M
Nebraska Methodist College	M
New England College	M
New Jersey City University	M
New York Medical College	M,D,O*
New York University	M,O
Northeastern University	M,D,O
Northern Arizona University	O
OGI School of Science & Engineering at Oregon Health & Science University	M,O
The Ohio State University	M,D
Ohio University	M*
Oklahoma City University	M
Oklahoma State University Center for Health Sciences	M
Oregon Health & Science University	M*
Oregon State University	M,D
Our Lady of the Lake University of San Antonio	M
Pace University	M
Pacific University	M
Park University	M
Penn State University Park	M,D
Pfeiffer University	M
Philadelphia University	M
Portland State University	M
Queen's University at Kingston	M,D
Quinnipiac University	M
Regis College (MA)	M,D,O
Regis University	P,M,D,O
Rice University	M
Robert Morris University Illinois	M
Roberts Wesleyan College	M
Rochester Institute of Technology	M,O
Rosalind Franklin University of Medicine and Science	M,O*
Royal Roads University	O
Rush University	M,D
Rutgers, The State University of New Jersey, Newark	M,D*
Sacred Heart University	M,D
Sage Graduate School	M,D,O
Saginaw Valley State University	M
St. Ambrose University	M,D
St. Joseph's College, Long Island Campus	M,O
St. Joseph's College, New York	M*
Saint Joseph's College of Maine	M
Saint Joseph's University	M,O
Saint Leo University	M
Saint Louis University	M,D
Saint Mary's University of Minnesota	M
Saint Peter's College	M
St. Thomas University	M,O
Saint Xavier University	M,O
Salve Regina University	M,O
San Diego State University	M,D
Seton Hall University	M,D,O
Simmons College	M,O
Southeast Missouri State University	M
Southern Adventist University	M
Southern Illinois University Carbondale	M
South University	M*
South University (SC)	M*
South University (AL)	M*
South University	M*
Southwest Baptist University	M
Springfield College	M
State University of New York at Binghamton	M,D
State University of New York Institute of Technology	M
Stony Brook University, State University of New York	M,D,O
Strayer University	M
Suffolk University	M,O
Syracuse University	O*
Temple University	M*
Texas A&M Health Science Center	M
Texas A&M University–Corpus Christi	M
Texas A&M University–San Antonio	M
Texas State University–San Marcos	M
Texas Tech University	M,D*
Texas Tech University Health Sciences Center	M
Texas Wesleyan University	M
Texas Woman's University	M,D
Thomas Jefferson University	M,D,O
Tiffin University	M
Towson University	O
Trinity University	M
Trinity Western University	M,O
Troy University	M
TUI University	M,D,O
Tulane University	M,D*
Union Graduate College	M,O
Universidad de Ciencias Medicas	P,M,O
Universidad de Iberoamerica	P,M,D
Université de Montréal	M,O
University at Albany, State University of New York	M
The University of Akron	M
The University of Alabama at Birmingham	M,D*
The University of Alabama in Huntsville	M,D,O
University of Alberta	M,D
University of Atlanta	P,M,D,O
University of Baltimore	M
The University of British Columbia	M,D
University of California, Berkeley	D*
University of California, Irvine	M*
University of California, Los Angeles	M,D*
University of California, San Diego	M*
University of Central Florida	M,O
University of Colorado Denver	M,D
University of Connecticut	M,D*
University of Dallas	M
University of Denver	M,O
University of Detroit Mercy	M
University of Evansville	M
The University of Findlay	M
University of Florida	M,D*
University of Georgia	M
University of Houston–Clear Lake	M
University of Illinois at Chicago	M,D
The University of Iowa	M,D*
The University of Kansas	M,D
University of Kentucky	M*
University of La Verne	M,O
University of Louisville	D
University of Mary	M
University of Maryland, Baltimore County	M,D,O
University of Maryland, College Park	M,D
University of Maryland University College	M,O
University of Massachusetts Amherst	M,D*
University of Massachusetts Boston	M,D,O
University of Massachusetts Lowell	M,O
University of Medicine and Dentistry of New Jersey	M,D,O
University of Memphis	M
University of Michigan	M,D*
University of Minnesota, Twin Cities Campus	M,D
University of Missouri	M*
University of Missouri–St. Louis	M,O
University of Nevada, Las Vegas	M
University of New Haven	M,O
University of New Orleans	M
The University of North Carolina at Chapel Hill	M,D*
The University of North Carolina at Charlotte	M,D,O
University of North Florida	M,O
University of North Texas Health Science Center at Fort Worth	M,D
University of Oklahoma	M*
University of Oklahoma Health Sciences Center	M,D
University of Ottawa	M*
University of Pennsylvania	M,D*
University of Phoenix	M,D,O
University of Phoenix–Atlanta Campus	M
University of Phoenix–Augusta Campus	M
University of Phoenix–Austin Campus	M
University of Phoenix–Birmingham Campus	M
University of Phoenix–Central Florida Campus	M
University of Phoenix–Central Valley Campus	M
University of Phoenix–Charlotte Campus	M
University of Phoenix–Chattanooga Campus	M
University of Phoenix–Cheyenne Campus	M
University of Phoenix–Denver Campus	M
University of Phoenix–Des Moines Campus	M,D
University of Phoenix–Harrisburg Campus	M
University of Phoenix–Hawaii Campus	M
University of Phoenix–Houston Campus	M
University of Phoenix–Indianapolis Campus	M
University of Phoenix–Louisville Campus	M
University of Phoenix–Maryland Campus	M

*M—master's degree; P—first professional degree; D—doctorate; O—other advanced degree; *—Close-Up and/or Display in one of the other books in this series*

University of Phoenix–Memphis Campus M,D
University of Phoenix–Milwaukee Campus M,D
University of Phoenix–Nashville Campus M
University of Phoenix–New Mexico Campus M
University of Phoenix–Northern Nevada Campus M
University of Phoenix–Northern Virginia Campus M
University of Phoenix–North Florida Campus M
University of Phoenix–Northwest Arkansas Campus M
University of Phoenix–Omaha Campus M
University of Phoenix–Oregon Campus M
University of Phoenix–Phoenix Campus M
University of Phoenix–Pittsburgh Campus M
University of Phoenix–Raleigh Campus M,D
University of Phoenix–Richmond Campus M
University of Phoenix–Sacramento Valley Campus M
University of Phoenix–San Antonio Campus M
University of Phoenix–Savannah Campus M
University of Phoenix–Southern Colorado Campus M
University of Phoenix–South Florida Campus M
University of Phoenix–Springfield Campus M
University of Phoenix–Vancouver Campus M
University of Phoenix–Washington D.C. Campus M,D
University of Phoenix–West Florida Campus M
University of Pittsburgh M,D,O*
University of Portland M
University of Puerto Rico, Medical Sciences Campus M
University of Regina M,D,O
University of Rochester M,D,O
University of St. Francis (IL) M
University of St. Thomas (MN) M
University of San Francisco M
University of Saskatchewan M
The University of Scranton M
University of South Africa M,D
University of South Carolina M,D
University of Southern California M,O*
University of Southern Indiana M
University of Southern Maine M,O
University of Southern Mississippi M
University of South Florida M,D*
The University of Tennessee M
The University of Texas at Arlington M
The University of Texas at Dallas M*
The University of Texas at El Paso M,D,O
The University of Texas at Tyler M
University of the Incarnate Word M,O
University of the Sciences in Philadelphia M,D
The University of Toledo M,O
University of Toronto M,D
University of Utah M*
University of Virginia M
University of Washington M*
The University of Western Ontario M,D
University of West Georgia M,O
University of Wisconsin–Oshkosh M
Utica College M
Villanova University M,D,O
Virginia Commonwealth University M,D
Virginia International University M,O
Wagner College M
Wake Forest University M
Walden University M,D,O
Walsh University M
Washington State University M
Washington State University Spokane M
Wayland Baptist University M
Waynesburg University M,D
Weber State University M
Webster University M,D,O
West Chester University of Pennsylvania M,O
Western Carolina University M
Western Connecticut State University M
Western Illinois University M,O
Western Kentucky University M
Western Michigan University M,D,O
Widener University M
Wilkes University M
William Woods University M,O
Wilmington University M
Worcester State University M
Wright State University M
Xavier University M
Yale University M,D,O*
Youngstown State University M

HEALTH SERVICES RESEARCH

Albany College of Pharmacy and Health Sciences P,M*
Brown University M,D
Case Western Reserve University M,D*
Clarkson University M*
Cornell University, Joan and Sanford I. Weill Medical College and Graduate School of Medical Sciences M
Dartmouth College M,D
Emory University M,D*
The George Washington University M,D,O
The Johns Hopkins University M,D
Lakehead University M
McMaster University M,D
Medical University of South Carolina M
Old Dominion University D
Penn State Hershey Medical Center M
Stanford University M
Texas State University–San Marcos M
Thomas Jefferson University M,D,O
University of Alberta M,D
University of Arkansas for Medical Sciences D
University of Central Florida M,O
University of Colorado Denver M,D
University of Florida M,D*
University of Illinois at Chicago M,D
University of La Verne M
University of Maryland, Baltimore M,D
University of Massachusetts Worcester M,D
University of Minnesota, Twin Cities Campus M,D
University of New Brunswick Fredericton M
The University of North Carolina at Charlotte M,D,O
University of Ottawa D,O*
University of Pennsylvania M*
University of Puerto Rico, Medical Sciences Campus M
University of Regina M,D,O
University of Rochester M,D,O
University of Southern California D*
University of Virginia M
University of Washington M,D*
University of Wisconsin–Madison M,D*
Virginia Commonwealth University D
Wake Forest University M

HIGHER EDUCATION

Abilene Christian University M
Alliant International University–Irvine M,D,O
Alliant International University–Los Angeles M,D,O
Alliant International University–San Diego M,D,O
Alliant International University–San Francisco M,D,O
Angelo State University M
Appalachian State University M,O
Argosy University, Atlanta M,D,O*
Argosy University, Chicago M,D,O*
Argosy University, Dallas M,D*
Argosy University, Denver M,D*
Argosy University, Hawai'i M,D*
Argosy University, Inland Empire M,D*
Argosy University, Los Angeles M,D*
Argosy University, Nashville M,D,O*
Argosy University, Orange County M,D*
Argosy University, Phoenix M,D,O*
Argosy University, San Diego M,D*
Argosy University, San Francisco Bay Area M,D*
Argosy University, Sarasota M,D,O*
Argosy University, Schaumburg M,D,O*
Argosy University, Seattle M,D*
Argosy University, Tampa M,D,O*
Argosy University, Twin Cities M,D,O*
Argosy University, Washington DC M,D,O*
Arizona State University M
Auburn University M,D,O
Azusa Pacific University M,D
Ball State University M,D
Barry University M,D*
Bay Path College M
Benedictine University D
Bernard M. Baruch College of the City University of New York M
Bethel University (MN) M,O
Boston College M,D*
Boston University M,D,O*
Bowling Green State University D*
California Lutheran University M,D
California State University, Long Beach M
Capella University M,D,O
Central Michigan University M,D,O
Chicago State University M,D
Claremont Graduate University M,D,O
Clemson University D
College of Saint Elizabeth M,O
Columbia International University M,D,O
Dallas Baptist University M
Delta State University D
Drexel University M*
Eastern Kentucky University M
Fitchburg State University M,O
Florida Atlantic University M,D,O
Florida International University M,D,O
Florida State University M,D,O
Geneva College M
George Fox University M,D,O
George Mason University D,O*
The George Washington University M,D,O
Georgia Southern University M
Grambling State University M,D
Grand Canyon University D
Grand Valley State University M,O
Harvard University D*
Hofstra University M,D,O
Illinois State University M,D
Indiana State University M,D,O
Indiana University Bloomington M,D,O*
Indiana University of Pennsylvania M
Indiana University–Purdue University Indianapolis M,O
Indiana Wesleyan University M
Inter American University of Puerto Rico, Metropolitan Campus M
Iowa State University of Science and Technology M,D*
John Brown University M
Johnson & Wales University D
Jones International University M
Kansas State University M,D*
Kaplan University, Davenport Campus M
Kent State University M,D,O*
Lincoln Memorial University M,D,O
Louisiana State University and Agricultural and Mechanical College M,D,O
Loyola University Chicago M,D
Maryville University of Saint Louis M,D
Marywood University M,D
McKendree University M
Merrimack College M,O
Miami University M,D
Michigan State University M,D,O
Minnesota State University Mankato M
Mississippi College M,D,O
Montana State University M,D,O
Morehead State University M,O
Morgan State University D
New England College M
New York University M,D

North Carolina State University M,D*
Northeastern State University M
Northern Arizona University M,D,O
Northern Illinois University M,D
Northwestern University M*
Northwest Missouri State University M,O
Nova Southeastern University D*
Oakland University M,D,O
Ohio University M,D*
Oklahoma State University M,D*
Old Dominion University M,D,O
Oral Roberts University M,D
Phillips Theological Seminary P,M,D
Pittsburg State University M,O
Portland State University M,D
Purdue University M,D,O
Rowan University M
St. Cloud State University M,D
Saint Leo University M,O
Saint Louis University M,D,O
Salem State University M
San Diego State University M
San Jose State University M
Seton Hall University D
Shippensburg University of Pennsylvania M
Southeast Missouri State University M,O
Southern Baptist Theological Seminary P,M,D
Southern Illinois University Carbondale M
Stanford University M,D
Syracuse University M,D*
Taylor University M
Teachers College, Columbia University M,D
Texas A&M University M,D
Texas A&M University–Commerce M,D
Texas A&M University–Kingsville D
Texas Southern University M,D
Texas Tech University M,D*
Troy University M
TUI University M,D
Union Institute & University M,D,O
Union University M,D,O
Universidad Central del Este M
Université de Sherbrooke M,O
University at Buffalo, the State University of New York M,D,O*
The University of Akron M
The University of Alabama M,D
The University of Arizona M,D
University of Arkansas M,D,O
University of Arkansas at Little Rock D
The University of British Columbia M,D
University of Calgary M,D,O
University of California, Riverside M,D
University of Central Florida M,D
University of Central Oklahoma M
University of Connecticut M*
University of Delaware M,D,O*
University of Denver M,D,O
University of Florida M,D,O*
University of Georgia D
University of Houston M,D
The University of Iowa M,D,O*
The University of Kansas M,D
University of Kentucky M,D*
University of Louisville M,D,O
University of Maine M,D,O
University of Manitoba M
University of Mary M
University of Maryland, College Park M,D
University of Massachusetts Amherst M,D,O*
University of Massachusetts Boston M,D,O
University of Memphis M,D
University of Miami M,D,O*
University of Michigan M,D*
University of Minnesota, Twin Cities Campus M,D
University of Mississippi M,D,O
University of Missouri M,D,O*
University of Missouri–St. Louis M,D,O
University of New Hampshire M
University of New Mexico O*
The University of North Carolina at Greensboro D
University of Northern Colorado D
University of Northern Iowa M
University of North Texas M,D,O
University of Oklahoma M,D,O*
University of Phoenix D,O
University of Phoenix–Madison Campus D,O
University of Phoenix–Milwaukee Campus M,D,O
University of Phoenix–Washington D.C. Campus M,D,O
University of Pittsburgh M,D*
University of Rochester
University of San Diego M,D,O
University of South Carolina M
University of Southern California D*
University of Southern Maine M,O
University of Southern Mississippi M,D,O
University of South Florida M,D,O*
University of the Incarnate Word M,D
The University of Toledo M,D,O
University of Virginia M,D,O
University of Washington M,D*
University of Wisconsin–Milwaukee M,O
University of Wisconsin–Whitewater M*
Upper Iowa University M
Vanderbilt University M,D*
Villanova University M
Virginia Polytechnic Institute and State University M,D,O
Walden University M,D,O
Washington State University M,D,O
Wayland Baptist University M
Wayne State University M,D,O*
Western Carolina University M
Western Governors University M,O
Western Kentucky University M
Western Washington University M
West Virginia University M,D
Wilkes University M,D
Wright State University M,O

HISPANIC AND LATIN AMERICAN LANGUAGES

Boston University M,D*
Brigham Young University M*
Central Connecticut State University M,O
Cornell University D*
Eastern Michigan University M,O
Graduate School and University Center of the City University of New York D
Indiana University Bloomington M,D*
Michigan State University M,D
Queens College of the City University of New York M
Stony Brook University, State University of New York M,D
Université de Montréal M,D
University of California, Berkeley D*
University of California, Los Angeles D*
University of California, Santa Barbara M,D
University of Colorado Boulder M,D*
University of Illinois at Chicago M,D
University of Massachusetts Amherst M,D*
University of Minnesota, Twin Cities Campus M,D
The University of North Carolina at Greensboro M,O
University of Pittsburgh M,D*
The University of Texas at Austin M,D
University of Washington M*

HISPANIC STUDIES

Brown University M,D
California State University, Los Angeles M*
California State University, Northridge M
Eastern Michigan University M,O
La Salle University M
Louisiana State University and Agricultural and Mechanical College M
McGill University M,D
Michigan State University M,D
New York University M,D
Pontifical Catholic University of Puerto Rico M,O
Queen's University at Kingston M
St. Thomas University M,O
San Jose State University M
Texas A&M International University M,D
University of Alberta M,D
The University of British Columbia M,D
University of California, Riverside M,D
University of California, Santa Barbara M,D
University of Houston M,D
University of Illinois at Chicago M,D
University of Kentucky M,D*
The University of Manchester M,D
University of Nevada, Las Vegas M
The University of North Carolina at Greensboro M,O
The University of North Carolina Wilmington M,O
University of Puerto Rico, Mayagüez Campus M
University of Puerto Rico, Río Piedras M,D
The University of Texas at Austin M
University of Victoria M
University of Washington M,D*
Villanova University M

HISTORIC PRESERVATION

Arkansas State University M,D
Ball State University M
Boston University M*
Buffalo State College, State University of New York M,O
Clemson University M
College of Charleston M
Columbia University M,O*
Cornell University M,D*
Delaware State University M
Eastern Michigan University M,O
The George Washington University M,D
Georgia State University M,O
Goucher College M
Kent State University M,O*
Michigan Technological University D
New York University M
Northwestern State University of Louisiana M
Pratt Institute M*
Rutgers, The State University of New Jersey, New Brunswick M,D,O*
St. Cloud State University M
Savannah College of Art and Design M,O
School of the Art Institute of Chicago M
Southeast Missouri State University M,O
Syracuse University O*
Texas Tech University M*
Universidad Nacional Pedro Henriquez Urena M
University of California, Los Angeles M*
University of California, Riverside M,D
University of Colorado Denver M
University of Delaware M,D*
University of Florida D*
University of Georgia M
University of Hawaii at Manoa O
University of Kentucky M*
University of Maryland, College Park M,O
University of Massachusetts Amherst M*
University of New Mexico O*
The University of North Carolina at Greensboro M,O
University of Oregon M
University of Pennsylvania M,O*
University of South Carolina M,O
The University of Texas at Austin M,D
University of Vermont M
University of Washington O*
University of Wisconsin–Milwaukee M,D,O
Ursuline College M
Virginia Commonwealth University O

HISTORY

Adams State College M
American Public University System M
American University M,D
American University of Beirut M
Andrews University M
Angelo State University M
Appalachian State University M
Arizona State University M,D,O
Arkansas State University M,O
Arkansas Tech University M
Armstrong Atlantic State University M

*M—master's degree; P—first professional degree; D—doctorate; O—other advanced degree; *—Close-Up and/or Display in one of the other books in this series*

Ashland Theological Seminary	P,M,D,O
Ashland University	M
Auburn University	M,D
Ball State University	M
Baylor University	M*
Bob Jones University	P,M,D,O
Boise State University	M
Boston College	M,D*
Boston University	M,D,O*
Bowling Green State University	M,D*
Brandeis University	M,D
Brock University	M
Brooklyn College of the City University of New York	M,D
Brown University	M,D
Buffalo State College, State University of New York	M
Butler University	M
California Polytechnic State University, San Luis Obispo	M
California State Polytechnic University, Pomona	M
California State University, Bakersfield	M
California State University, Chico	M
California State University, East Bay	M
California State University, Fresno	M
California State University, Fullerton	M
California State University, Long Beach	M
California State University, Los Angeles	M*
California State University, Northridge	M
California State University, Stanislaus	M
Cardinal Stritch University	M
Carleton University	M,D
Carnegie Mellon University	M,D*
Case Western Reserve University	M,D*
The Catholic University of America	M,D
Central Connecticut State University	M,O
Central European University	M,D
Central Michigan University	M,D,O
Central Washington University	M
Centro de Estudios Avanzados de Puerto Rico y el Caribe	M,D
Chicago State University	M
The Citadel, The Military College of South Carolina	M
City College of the City University of New York	M
Claremont Graduate University	M,D,O
Clark Atlanta University	M,D
Clark University	M,D,O
Clemson University	M
Cleveland State University	M
The College at Brockport, State University of New York	M
College of Charleston	M
The College of Saint Rose	M
College of Staten Island of the City University of New York	M
The College of William and Mary	M,D
Colorado State University	M
Columbia University	M,D*
Concordia University (Canada)	M,D
Converse College	M
Cornell University	M,D*
Dalhousie University	M,D
DePaul University	M
Drew University	M,D
Duke University	M,D*
Duquesne University	M
East Carolina University	M
Eastern Illinois University	M
Eastern Kentucky University	M
Eastern Michigan University	M,O
Eastern Washington University	M
East Stroudsburg University of Pennsylvania	M
East Tennessee State University	M
Emory & Henry College	M
Emory University	D*
Emporia State University	M
Fairleigh Dickinson University, Metropolitan Campus	M
Faulkner University	M
Fayetteville State University	M
Fitchburg State University	M,O
Florida Agricultural and Mechanical University	M
Florida Atlantic University	M,O
Florida Gulf Coast University	M
Florida International University	M,D
Florida State University	M,D
Fordham University	M,D
Fort Hays State University	M
George Mason University	M,D*
Georgetown University	M,D
The George Washington University	M,D
Georgia College & State University	M
Georgia Southern University	M
Georgia State University	M,D
Graduate School and University Center of the City University of New York	D
Hardin-Simmons University	M
Harvard University	D*
High Point University	M
Howard University	M,D
Hunter College of the City University of New York	M
Idaho State University	M
Illinois State University	M
Indiana State University	M
Indiana University Bloomington	M,D*
Indiana University of Pennsylvania	M
Indiana University–Purdue University Indianapolis	M
Inter American University of Puerto Rico, Metropolitan Campus	M,D
Iona College	M
Iowa State University of Science and Technology	M,D*
Jackson State University	M
Jacksonville State University	M
James Madison University	M
John Carroll University	M
The Johns Hopkins University	D
Kansas State University	M,D*
Kent State University	M,D*
Lakehead University	M
Lamar University	M
La Salle University	M
Laurentian University	M
Lehigh University	M,D
Lehman College of the City University of New York	M
Lincoln University (MO)	M,O
Long Island University, Brooklyn Campus	M,O
Long Island University, C.W. Post Campus	M
Louisiana State University and Agricultural and Mechanical College	M,D
Louisiana Tech University	M
Loyola University Chicago	M,D
Lynchburg College	M
Marquette University	M,D
Marshall University	M
McGill University	M,D
McMaster University	M,D
Memorial University of Newfoundland	M,D
Miami University	M
Michigan State University	M,D
Middle Tennessee State University	M
Midwestern State University	M
Millersville University of Pennsylvania	M
Minnesota State University Mankato	M
Mississippi College	M,O
Mississippi State University	M,D
Missouri State University	M
Monmouth University	M
Montana State University	M,D
Montclair State University	M,O
Morgan State University	M,D
Murray State University	M
National University	M
Nebraska Wesleyan University	M
New Jersey Institute of Technology	M
New Mexico State University	M
The New School: A University	M,D
New York University	M,D,O
North Carolina Central University	M
North Carolina State University	M*
North Dakota State University	M,D
Northeastern Illinois University	M
Northeastern University	M,D
Northern Arizona University	M,D
Northern Illinois University	M,D
Northwestern University	M,D*
Northwest Missouri State University	M
Oakland University	M
The Ohio State University	M,D
Ohio University	M,D*
Oklahoma State University	M,D*
Old Dominion University	M
Oregon State University	M,D
Penn State University Park	M,D
Pepperdine University	M
Pittsburg State University	M
Pontifical Catholic University of Puerto Rico	M
Portland State University	M
Princeton University	D*
Providence College	M
Purdue University	M,D
Purdue University Calumet	M
Queens College of the City University of New York	M
Rhode Island College	M
Rice University	M,D
Roosevelt University	M
Rutgers, The State University of New Jersey, Camden	M
Rutgers, The State University of New Jersey, Newark	M*
Rutgers, The State University of New Jersey, New Brunswick	D*
St. Cloud State University	M
St. John's University (NY)	M,D
Saint Louis University	M,D
Saint Mary's University (Canada)	M
Salem State University	M
Salisbury University	M
Sam Houston State University	M
San Diego State University	M
San Francisco State University	M
San Jose State University	M
Sarah Lawrence College	M
Seton Hall University	M
Shippensburg University of Pennsylvania	M,O
Simmons College	M
Simon Fraser University	M,D
Slippery Rock University of Pennsylvania	M
Smith College	M
Sonoma State University	M
Southeastern Louisiana University	M
Southeast Missouri State University	M,O
Southern Connecticut State University	M
Southern Illinois University Carbondale	M,D
Southern Illinois University Edwardsville	M
Southern Methodist University	M,D
Southern University and Agricultural and Mechanical College	M
Southwestern Assemblies of God University	M
Spring Hill College	M
Stanford University	M,D
State University of New York at Binghamton	M,D
State University of New York at Oswego	M
State University of New York College at Cortland	M
Stephen F. Austin State University	M
Stony Brook University, State University of New York	M,D
Sul Ross State University	M
Syracuse University	M,D*
Tarleton State University	M
Teachers College, Columbia University	M,D
Temple University	M,D*
Texas A&M International University	M
Texas A&M University	M,D
Texas A&M University–Commerce	M
Texas A&M University–Corpus Christi	M
Texas A&M University–Kingsville	M
Texas Christian University	M,D
Texas Southern University	M
Texas State University–San Marcos	M
Texas Tech University	M,D*
Texas Woman's University	M
Trinity Western University	M
Troy University	M
Tufts University	M,D
Tulane University	M,D*
Union Institute & University	M

Université de Moncton M
Université de Montréal M,D
Université de Sherbrooke M
Université du Québec à Montréal M,D
Université Laval M,D
University at Albany, State University of New York M,D,O
University at Buffalo, the State University of New York M,D*
The University of Akron M,D
The University of Alabama M,D
The University of Alabama at Birmingham M*
The University of Alabama in Huntsville M
University of Alaska Fairbanks M
University of Alberta M,D
The University of Arizona M,D.
University of Arkansas M,D
The University of British Columbia M,D
University of Calgary M,D
University of California, Berkeley M,D*
University of California, Davis M,D
University of California, Irvine M,D*
University of California, Los Angeles M,D*
University of California, Riverside M,D
University of California, San Diego M,D*
University of California, Santa Barbara D
University of California, Santa Cruz M,D
University of Central Arkansas M
University of Central Florida M
University of Central Missouri M
University of Central Oklahoma M
University of Chicago D
University of Cincinnati M,D
University of Colorado at Colorado Springs M
University of Colorado Boulder M,D*
University of Colorado Denver M
University of Connecticut M,D*
University of Delaware M,D*
University of Denver M,O
University of Florida M,D*
University of Georgia M,D
University of Guelph M,D
University of Hawaii at Manoa M,D
University of Houston M,D
University of Houston–Clear Lake M
University of Idaho M,D
University of Illinois at Chicago M,D
University of Illinois at Springfield M
University of Illinois at Urbana–Champaign M,D
University of Indianapolis M
The University of Iowa M,D*
The University of Kansas M,D
University of Kentucky M,D*
University of Lethbridge M,D
University of Louisiana at Lafayette M*
University of Louisiana at Monroe M
University of Louisville M,O
University of Maine M,D
The University of Manchester D
University of Manitoba M,D
University of Maryland, Baltimore County M
University of Maryland, College Park M,D
University of Massachusetts Amherst M,D*
University of Massachusetts Boston M
University of Memphis M,D
University of Miami M,D*
University of Michigan D,O*
University of Minnesota, Twin Cities Campus M,D
University of Mississippi M,D
University of Missouri M,D*
University of Missouri–Kansas City M,D*
The University of Montana M,D
University of Nebraska at Kearney M
University of Nebraska at Omaha M
University of Nebraska–Lincoln M,D*
University of Nevada, Las Vegas M,D
University of Nevada, Reno M,D*
University of New Brunswick Fredericton M,D
University of New Hampshire M,D
University of New Mexico M,D*
University of New Orleans M
University of North Alabama M
The University of North Carolina at Chapel Hill M,D*
The University of North Carolina at Charlotte M
The University of North Carolina at Greensboro M,D,O
The University of North Carolina Wilmington M
University of North Dakota M,D
University of Northern British Columbia M,D,O
University of Northern Colorado M
University of Northern Iowa M
University of North Florida M
University of North Texas M,D
University of Notre Dame M,D*
University of Oklahoma M,D*
University of Oregon M,D
University of Ottawa M,D*
University of Pennsylvania M,D*
University of Pittsburgh M,D*
University of Puerto Rico, Río Piedras M,D
University of Regina M
University of Rhode Island M
University of Rochester M,D
University of San Diego M
University of Saskatchewan M,D
The University of Scranton M
University of South Africa M,D
University of South Alabama M
University of South Carolina M,D,O
The University of South Dakota M
University of Southern California D*
University of Southern Mississippi M,D
University of South Florida M,D*
The University of Tennessee M,D
The University of Texas at Arlington M,D
The University of Texas at Austin M,D
The University of Texas at Brownsville M
The University of Texas at Dallas M,D*
The University of Texas at El Paso M,D
The University of Texas at San Antonio M*
The University of Texas at Tyler M
The University of Texas of the Permian Basin M
The University of Texas–Pan American M
The University of Toledo M,D
University of Toronto M,D
University of Tulsa M
University of Utah M,D*
University of Vermont M
University of Victoria M,D
University of Virginia M,D
University of Washington M,D*
University of Waterloo M,D
The University of Western Ontario M,D
University of West Florida M
University of West Georgia M,O
University of Windsor M
The University of Winnipeg M
University of Wisconsin–Eau Claire M
University of Wisconsin–Madison M,D*
University of Wisconsin–Milwaukee M,D
University of Wisconsin–Stevens Point M
University of Wyoming M
Utah State University M
Valdosta State University M
Valparaiso University M,O
Vanderbilt University M,D*
Villanova University M
Virginia Commonwealth University M,D
Virginia Polytechnic Institute and State University M
Virginia State University M
Washington College M
Washington State University M,D
Washington State University Vancouver M
Washington University in St. Louis M,D*
Wayne State University M,D*
West Chester University of Pennsylvania M,O
Western Carolina University M
Western Connecticut State University M
Western Illinois University M
Western Kentucky University M
Western Michigan University M,D
Western Washington University M
Westfield State University M
West Texas A&M University M
West Virginia University M,D
Wichita State University M
Wilfrid Laurier University M,D*
William Paterson University of New Jersey M
Winthrop University M
Worcester State University M
Wright State University M
Yale University M,D*
York University M,D*
Youngstown State University M

HISTORY OF MEDICINE

McGill University M,D
Rutgers, The State University of New Jersey, New Brunswick D*
The University of Manchester M,D
University of Minnesota, Twin Cities Campus M,D
Yale University M,D*

HISTORY OF SCIENCE AND TECHNOLOGY

Arizona State University D
Carnegie Mellon University M,D*
Cornell University M,D*
Drexel University M*
Georgia Institute of Technology M,D
Harvard University M,D*
Indiana University Bloomington M,D*
Iowa State University of Science and Technology M,D*
The Johns Hopkins University M,D
Massachusetts Institute of Technology D
Oregon State University M,D
Polytechnic Institute of NYU M
Princeton University D*
Rensselaer Polytechnic Institute M,D
Rutgers, The State University of New Jersey, New Brunswick D*
University of California, Berkeley D*
University of California, San Diego M,D*
University of California, San Francisco M,D
University of Delaware M,D*
University of Maine M,D
The University of Manchester M,D
University of Massachusetts Amherst M,D*
University of Minnesota, Twin Cities Campus M,D
University of Notre Dame M,D*
University of Oklahoma M,D*
University of Pennsylvania M,D*
University of Pittsburgh M,D*
University of Toronto M,D
University of Wisconsin–Madison M,D*
Virginia Polytechnic Institute and State University M,D,O
West Virginia University M,D
Yale University M,D*

HIV/AIDS NURSING

University of Delaware M,O*

HOLOCAUST AND GENOCIDE STUDIES

Clark University D
Drew University M,D,O
Gratz College M,O
Kean University M
Laura and Alvin Siegal College of Judaic Studies M
The Richard Stockton College of New Jersey M
Seton Hall University M
Seton Hill University O
West Chester University of Pennsylvania M,O

HOME ECONOMICS EDUCATION

Cambridge College M,D,O
Central Washington University M
Eastern Kentucky University M
Indiana State University M

*M—master's degree; P—first professional degree; D—doctorate; O—other advanced degree; *—Close-Up and/or Display in one of the other books in this series*

Iowa State University of Science and Technology M,D*
Louisiana State University and Agricultural and Mechanical College M,D
Montana State University M
Montclair State University M,O
Northwestern State University of Louisiana M
Purdue University M,D,O
Queens College of the City University of New York M
South Carolina State University M,D,O
State University of New York College at Oneonta M
Texas Tech University M,D*
The University of British Columbia M,D
University of Central Oklahoma M
University of Nebraska–Lincoln M,D*
Utah State University M
Wayne State College M

HOMELAND SECURITY

American Public University System M
Chaminade University of Honolulu M,O
Drexel University M*
Fairleigh Dickinson University, Metropolitan Campus M
George Mason University M,D,O*
Henley-Putnam University M
The Johns Hopkins University M,O
Long Island University at Riverhead M,O
Monmouth University M,O
National Defense University M
National University M
Notre Dame College (OH) M,O
Pace University M
Penn State University Park M,D
Saint Joseph's University M,O
Salve Regina University M,O
Texas A&M University M,O
Thomas Edison State College O
Tiffin University M
Towson University M,O
University of Central Florida M,O
University of Colorado Denver M,D
University of Connecticut M*
University of Denver M,D,O
University of New Haven M,O
University of Southern California M,O*
The University of Texas at El Paso M,O
The University of Toledo M,O
Upper Iowa University M
Virginia Commonwealth University M,O
Virginia Polytechnic Institute and State University M,D,O
Walden University M,D,O
Wayland Baptist University M
Western Kentucky University M
Wilmington University M

HORTICULTURE

Auburn University M,D
Colorado State University M,D
Cornell University M,D*
Iowa State University of Science and Technology M,D*
Kansas State University M,D*
Louisiana State University and Agricultural and Mechanical College M,D
Michigan State University M,D
Mississippi State University M,D
New Mexico State University M,D
North Carolina State University M,D,O*
Nova Scotia Agricultural College M
The Ohio State University M,D
Oklahoma State University M,D*
Oregon State University M,D
Penn State University Park M,D
Purdue University M,D
Rutgers, The State University of New Jersey, New Brunswick M,D*
Southern Illinois University Carbondale M
Texas A&M University M,D
Texas Tech University M,D*
Universidad Nacional Pedro Henriquez Urena M
University of Arkansas M
University of California, Davis M
University of Delaware M*
University of Florida M,D*
University of Georgia M,D
University of Guelph M,D
University of Hawaii at Manoa M,D
University of Maine M
University of Manitoba M,D
University of Maryland, College Park M,D
University of Missouri M,D*
University of Nebraska–Lincoln M,D*
University of Puerto Rico, Mayagüez Campus M
University of South Africa M,D
University of Vermont M,D
University of Washington M,D*
University of Wisconsin–Madison M,D*
Virginia Polytechnic Institute and State University M,D
Washington State University M,D
West Virginia University M,D

HOSPICE NURSING

Madonna University M

HOSPITALITY MANAGEMENT

American International College M
Andrew Jackson University M
Baltimore International College M
California State University, Long Beach M
California State University, Northridge M
Columbia Southern University M
Cornell University M,D*
Drexel University M*
Eastern Michigan University M,O
East Stroudsburg University of Pennsylvania M
Ecole Hôtelière de Lausanne M
Endicott College M
Fairleigh Dickinson University, College at Florham M
Fairleigh Dickinson University, Metropolitan Campus M
Florida International University M
The George Washington University M,O
Glion Institute of Higher Education M
Iowa State University of Science and Technology M,D*
Johnson & Wales University M
Kansas State University M,D*
Kent State University M*
Lasell College M,O
Lynn University M
Michigan State University M
New York University M,D,O
The Ohio State University M,D
Oklahoma State University M,D*
Penn State University Park M,D
Pontificia Universidad Catolica Madre y Maestra M
Purdue University M,D
Rochester Institute of Technology M
Roosevelt University M
Royal Roads University M,O
Schiller International University (United States) M
Schiller International University (United Kingdom) M
South Dakota State University M,D
Southern New Hampshire University M,D,O
South University (GA) M*
Strayer University M
Temple University M,D*
Texas Tech University M,D*
Troy University M
The University of Alabama M
University of Central Florida M,O
University of Delaware M*
The University of Findlay M
University of Guelph M
University of Houston M
University of Kentucky M*
University of Massachusetts Amherst M*
University of Missouri M,D*
University of Nevada, Las Vegas M,D
University of New Orleans M
University of North Texas M
University of South Carolina M
The University of Tennessee M
Virginia Polytechnic Institute and State University M,D

HUMAN-COMPUTER INTERACTION

Carnegie Mellon University M,D*
Cornell University D*
Dalhousie University M
DePaul University M,D
Georgia Institute of Technology M
Indiana University Bloomington M,D*
Iowa State University of Science and Technology M,D*
Old Dominion University M,D
Rensselaer Polytechnic Institute M
Rochester Institute of Technology M
State University of New York at Oswego M
Tufts University O
University of Baltimore M,D
University of Illinois at Urbana–Champaign M,D,O
University of Michigan M,D*
Virginia Polytechnic Institute and State University M,D,O

HUMAN DEVELOPMENT

Argosy University, Chicago D*
Arizona State University M,D
Auburn University M,D
Boston University M,D,O*
Bowling Green State University M*
Bradley University M
Brigham Young University M,D*
Brock University M,D
California State University, San Bernardino M
Central Michigan University M,O
Claremont Graduate University M,D,O
Clemson University M
Colorado State University M,D
Cornell University D*
DePaul University M,D
Duke University D*
East Tennessee State University M,D
Erikson Institute M,O
Fielding Graduate University M,D,O
The George Washington University M
Harvard University M,D*
Hofstra University D
Hood College M,O
Indiana University Bloomington M,D*
Iowa State University of Science and Technology M,D*
Kansas State University M,D*
Kent State University M,D*
Laurentian University M
Lehigh University M,D
Lindsey Wilson College M
Marywood University D
Montana State University M
National-Louis University M,D,O
New York University M,D,O
North Dakota State University D
Northern Arizona University O
Northwestern University D*
The Ohio State University M,D
Oklahoma State University M,D*
Oregon State University M,D
Our Lady of the Lake University of San Antonio M
Pacific Oaks College M
Penn State University Park M,D
Purdue University M,D
Saint Joseph College M,O
St. Lawrence University M,O
Saint Louis University M,D,O
Saint Mary's University of Minnesota M
South Dakota State University M
Southern Illinois University Carbondale M,D
Texas A&M University M,D
Texas Tech University M,D*
Union Institute & University M,D,O
The University of Alabama M
The University of Arizona M
The University of British Columbia M,D,O
University of Calgary M,D
University of California, Berkeley M,D*

University of California, Davis D
University of Central Oklahoma M
University of Chicago D
University of Colorado Denver M,O
University of Connecticut M,D,O*
University of Dayton M,O
University of Delaware M,D*
University of Guelph M,D
University of Illinois at Chicago M,D
University of Illinois at Springfield M
University of Illinois at Urbana–Champaign M,D
University of Maine M
University of Maryland, College Park M,D
University of Missouri M,D*
University of Nebraska–Lincoln M,D,O*
University of Nevada, Reno M*
The University of North Carolina at Greensboro M,D
University of North Texas M,O
University of Pennsylvania M,D*
University of Rochester
University of St. Thomas (MN) M,D,O
University of South Africa M,D
The University of Texas at Austin M,D
University of Utah M*
University of Victoria M,D
University of Washington M,D*
University of Wisconsin–Madison M,D*
University of Wisconsin–Stevens Point M
University of Wisconsin–Stout M
Utah State University M,D
Vanderbilt University M*
Washington State University M
West Virginia University M,D
Wheelock College M

HUMAN GENETICS

Baylor College of Medicine D*
Case Western Reserve University D*
The Johns Hopkins University D
Louisiana State University Health Sciences Center M,D
McGill University M,D
Memorial University of Newfoundland M,D
Sarah Lawrence College M
Tulane University M,D*
University of California, Los Angeles M,D*
University of Chicago D
University of Manitoba M,D
University of Maryland, Baltimore M,D
University of Michigan M,D*
University of Pittsburgh M,D,O*
The University of Texas Health Science Center at Houston M,D*
University of Utah M,D*
Vanderbilt University D*
Virginia Commonwealth University M,D,O
Wake Forest University D
West Virginia University M,D

HUMANITIES

American Public University System M
Arcadia University M*
Brigham Young University M*
California Institute of Integral Studies M,D
California State University, Dominguez Hills M*
California State University, East Bay M
Carlow University M
Central European University M,D
Central Michigan University M
Claremont Graduate University M,D,O
Clemson University D
College of the Humanities and Sciences, Harrison Middleton University M,D
The Colorado College M
Concordia University (Canada) D
Dominican University of California M
Drew University M,D,O
Duke University M*
Georgetown University M,D
Hofstra University D
Hollins University M,O
Hood College M
Instituto Tecnologico de Santo Domingo M,O
Instituto Tecnológico y de Estudios Superiores de Monterrey, Campus Central de Veracruz M
Instituto Tecnológico y de Estudios Superiores de Monterrey, Campus Ciudad de México M,D
Instituto Tecnológico y de Estudios Superiores de Monterrey, Campus Ciudad Juárez M
Instituto Tecnológico y de Estudios Superiores de Monterrey, Campus Estado de México M,D
Instituto Tecnológico y de Estudios Superiores de Monterrey, Campus Irapuato M,D
John Carroll University M
Laura and Alvin Siegal College of Judaic Studies M
Laurentian University M
Marshall University M
Marymount University M
Memorial University of Newfoundland M
Mount St. Mary's College M
National University M
New York University M,O
Nova Southeastern University M,O*
Old Dominion University M
Penn State Harrisburg M,D
Pepperdine University M
Polytechnic Institute of NYU M,O
Prescott College M
St. Edward's University M,O
Salve Regina University M,D,O
Sam Houston State University M,D
San Francisco State University M
Stanford University M
Texas Tech University M,D*
Tiffin University M
Towson University M
Trinity Western University M
Union Institute & University D
United Theological Seminary of the Twin Cities P,M,D,O
University of California, Santa Cruz D
University of Chicago M
University of Colorado Denver M
University of Dallas M
University of Houston–Clear Lake M
University of Louisville M,D
University of South Florida M*
The University of Texas at Dallas M,D*
The University of Texas Medical Branch M,D
University of Utah M*
Villanova University M
Virginia Commonwealth University M,D,O
Virginia Polytechnic Institute and State University D,O
Wright State University M
York University M,D*

HUMAN RESOURCES DEVELOPMENT

Abilene Christian University M
Amberton University M
American International College M
Antioch University Los Angeles M
Azusa Pacific University M
Barry University M,D*
Bowie State University M
California State University, Sacramento M
Claremont Graduate University M,D,O
Clemson University M
The College of New Rochelle M
Drexel University M*
Florida International University M,D,O
Florida State University M,D,O
Friends University M
The George Washington University M,D,O
Grantham University M
Illinois Institute of Technology M,D
Indiana State University M
Indiana Tech M
Indiana University of Pennsylvania M
Inter American University of Puerto Rico, Metropolitan Campus M
Inter American University of Puerto Rico, San Germán Campus M,D
Iowa State University of Science and Technology M,D*
John F. Kennedy University M,O
The Johns Hopkins University M,O
Kentucky State University M
Lincoln Memorial University M,D,O
Louisiana State University and Agricultural and Mechanical College M,D
Manhattanville College M*
Marquette University M
McDaniel College M
Midwestern State University M
Mississippi State University M,D,O
Moravian College M
National-Louis University M
Naval Postgraduate School M
New York University M,O
North Carolina Agricultural and Technical State University M,D
North Carolina State University M*
Northeastern Illinois University M
Oakland University M
Ottawa University M
Penn State University Park M
Pittsburg State University M
Rochester Institute of Technology M
Rollins College M
Roosevelt University M
St. John Fisher College M
Salve Regina University M,O
Southern New Hampshire University M,O
Suffolk University M,O
Syracuse University D*
Texas A&M University M,D
Towson University M
Universidad Central del Este M
Universidad Iberoamericana P,M
University of Bridgeport M
University of California, Los Angeles M,D*
University of Connecticut M*
University of Denver M,O
University of Houston M
University of Illinois at Urbana–Champaign M,D,O
University of Louisville M,D,O
University of Minnesota, Twin Cities Campus M,D,O
University of Missouri–St. Louis M,O
University of Oklahoma M,O*
University of Regina M
University of St. Thomas (MN) M,D,O
The University of Scranton M
University of South Africa M,D
The University of Tennessee M
The University of Texas at Tyler M,D
University of Wisconsin–Milwaukee M,O
University of Wisconsin–Stout M
Villanova University M
Virginia Commonwealth University M
Walden University M,D,O
Webster University M,D,O
Western Carolina University M
Western Michigan University M,D
Western Seminary M
William Woods University M,O
Xavier University M

HUMAN RESOURCES MANAGEMENT

Adelphi University M,O*
Alabama Agricultural and Mechanical University M,O
Albany State University M
Amberton University M
American InterContinental University Online M
American InterContinental University South Florida M
American Public University System M
Andrew Jackson University M
Ashworth College M
Assumption College M,O
Auburn University M,D
Azusa Pacific University M
Baker College Center for Graduate Studies—Online M,D
Baldwin-Wallace College M
Barry University O*
Benedictine University M

*M—master's degree; P—first professional degree; D—doctorate; O—other advanced degree; *—Close-Up and/or Display in one of the other books in this series*

Institution	Degrees
Bernard M. Baruch College of the City University of New York	M,D
Briar Cliff University	M
Brigham Young University	M*
Buffalo State College, State University of New York	M,O
California Coast University	M
California Intercontinental University	M,D
California State University, East Bay	M
California State University, Sacramento	M
Capella University	M,D,O
Caribbean University	M,D
Case Western Reserve University	M*
The Catholic University of America	M
Central Michigan University	M,O
City University of Seattle	M,O
Claremont Graduate University	M
Clemson University	M
Cleveland State University	M
Colorado Technical University Colorado Springs	M,D
Colorado Technical University Denver	M
Colorado Technical University Sioux Falls	M
Columbia Southern University	M
Columbia University	M*
Concordia University, St. Paul	M
Concordia University Wisconsin	M
Cornell University	M,D*
Dallas Baptist University	M
Davenport University	M
Davenport University	M
Davenport University	M
DePaul University	M
DeSales University	M
DeVry University	M
Dowling College	M,O
East Central University	M
Eastern Michigan University	M,O
Emmanuel College (United States)	M,O
Everest University	M
Everest University	M
Fairfield University	M,O
Fairleigh Dickinson University, College at Florham	M
Fairleigh Dickinson University, Metropolitan Campus	M,O
Fitchburg State University	M
Florida Institute of Technology	M
Florida International University	M
Fordham University	M,D,O
Framingham State University	M
Franklin Pierce University	M,D,O
Gannon University	O
George Fox University	M,D
George Mason University	M*
Georgetown University	M,D
The George Washington University	M,D
Georgia State University	M,D
Golden Gate University	M,D,O
Goldey-Beacom College	M
Grambling State University	M
Grand Canyon University	M
Hawai'i Pacific University	M*
HEC Montreal	M
Herzing University Online	M
Hofstra University	M,O
Holy Family University	M*
Hood College	M
Houston Baptist University	M
Howard University	M
Indiana Tech	M
Indiana Wesleyan University	M
Instituto Tecnologico de Santo Domingo	M,O
Instituto Tecnológico y de Estudios Superiores de Monterrey, Campus Cuernavaca	M
Inter American University of Puerto Rico, Aguadilla Campus	M
Inter American University of Puerto Rico, Arecibo Campus	M
Inter American University of Puerto Rico, Bayamón Campus	M
Inter American University of Puerto Rico, Metropolitan Campus	M
Inter American University of Puerto Rico, Ponce Campus	M
Inter American University of Puerto Rico, San Germán Campus	M,D
International College of the Cayman Islands	M
Iona College	M,O
Kaplan University, Davenport Campus	M
La Roche College	M,O
Lasell College	M,O
La Sierra University	M,O
Lewis University	M
Lincoln University (CA)	M,D
Lincoln University (PA)	M
Lindenwood University	M,O
Long Island University, Brooklyn Campus	M
Loyola University Chicago	M
Marquette University	M
Marshall University	M
Marygrove College	M
Marymount University	M,O
McKendree University	M
McMaster University	M,D
Mercy College	M,O
Michigan State University	M,D
Moravian College	M
National-Louis University	M
National University	M
Nazareth College of Rochester	M
New Mexico Highlands University	M
New York Institute of Technology	M,O
New York University	M,D,O
North Central College	M
North Greenville University	M
Notre Dame de Namur University	M
Nova Southeastern University	M,D*
Oakland University	M,O
The Ohio State University	M,D
Ottawa University	M
Penn State University Park	M
Polytechnic Institute of NYU	M,D,O
Polytechnic University of Puerto Rico, Miami Campus	M
Polytechnic University of Puerto Rico, Orlando Campus	M
Pontifical Catholic University of Puerto Rico	M,O
Pontificia Universidad Catolica Madre y Maestra	M
Purdue University	M,D
Quincy University	M
Regent's American College London	M
Regis University	M,O
Robert Morris University	M
Robert Morris University Illinois	M
Rollins College	M
Roosevelt University	M
Royal Roads University	M,O
Rutgers, The State University of New Jersey, Newark	M,D*
Rutgers, The State University of New Jersey, New Brunswick	M,D*
Sage Graduate School	M
St. Ambrose University	M,D
St. Edward's University	M,O
Saint Francis University	M
St. Joseph's College, Long Island Campus	M,O
Saint Joseph's University	M
Saint Leo University	M
Saint Mary's University of Minnesota	M
Saint Peter's College	M
St. Thomas University	M,O
Salve Regina University	M,O
San Diego State University	M
Southern New Hampshire University	M,D,O
Stevens Institute of Technology	M
Stony Brook University, State University of New York	M,O
Strayer University	M
Tarleton State University	M
Temple University	M*
Tennessee Technological University	M
Texas A&M University	M,D
Texas A&M University–San Antonio	M
Thomas College	M
Thomas Edison State College	M,O
Tiffin University	M
Trinity (Washington) University	M
Troy University	M
TUI University	M,D
Union Graduate College	M,O
United States International University	M
Universidad del Este	M
Universidad del Turabo	M
Universidad Metropolitana	M
University at Albany, State University of New York	M
University at Buffalo, the State University of New York	M,D,O*
The University of Akron	M
The University of Alabama in Huntsville	M
University of California, Berkeley	O*
University of Chicago	M
University of Colorado Denver	M
University of Connecticut	M*
University of Dallas	M
University of Denver	M,O
University of Florida	M*
University of Georgia	M,D,O
University of Hawaii at Manoa	M
University of Houston–Clear Lake	M
University of Illinois at Urbana–Champaign	M,D,O
University of Lethbridge	M,D
University of Louisville	M,D
University of Mary	M
University of Minnesota, Twin Cities Campus	M,D
University of Missouri–St. Louis	M,O
University of New Haven	M,O
University of New Mexico	M,D*
University of North Florida	M
University of Oklahoma	M*
University of Phoenix	M
University of Phoenix–Atlanta Campus	M
University of Phoenix–Augusta Campus	M
University of Phoenix–Austin Campus	M
University of Phoenix–Birmingham Campus	M
University of Phoenix–Central Florida Campus	M
University of Phoenix–Central Valley Campus	M
University of Phoenix–Chattanooga Campus	M
University of Phoenix–Cheyenne Campus	M
University of Phoenix–Chicago Campus	M
University of Phoenix–Cincinnati Campus	M
University of Phoenix–Cleveland Campus	M
University of Phoenix–Columbus Georgia Campus	M
University of Phoenix–Columbus Ohio Campus	M
University of Phoenix–Dallas Campus	M
University of Phoenix–Denver Campus	M
University of Phoenix–Des Moines Campus	M
University of Phoenix–Eastern Washington Campus	M
University of Phoenix–Harrisburg Campus	M
University of Phoenix–Hawaii Campus	M
University of Phoenix–Houston Campus	M
University of Phoenix–Idaho Campus	M
University of Phoenix–Indianapolis Campus	M
University of Phoenix–Jersey City Campus	M
University of Phoenix–Kansas City Campus	M
University of Phoenix–Las Vegas Campus	M
University of Phoenix–Louisiana Campus	M
University of Phoenix–Madison Campus	M
University of Phoenix–Maryland Campus	M
University of Phoenix–Memphis Campus	M
University of Phoenix–Milwaukee Campus	M,D
University of Phoenix–Minneapolis/St. Louis Park Campus	M
University of Phoenix–Nashville Campus	M
University of Phoenix–New Mexico Campus	M
University of Phoenix–Northern Nevada Campus	M
University of Phoenix–North Florida Campus	M
University of Phoenix–Northwest Arkansas Campus	M
University of Phoenix–Oklahoma City Campus	M
University of Phoenix–Omaha Campus	M
University of Phoenix–Oregon Campus	M
University of Phoenix–Philadelphia Campus	M

University of Phoenix–Pittsburgh Campus M
University of Phoenix–Puerto Rico Campus M
University of Phoenix–Raleigh Campus M
University of Phoenix–Richmond Campus M
University of Phoenix–Sacramento Valley Campus M
University of Phoenix–St. Louis Campus M
University of Phoenix–San Antonio Campus M
University of Phoenix–San Diego Campus M
University of Phoenix–Savannah Campus M
University of Phoenix–Southern Arizona Campus M
University of Phoenix–Southern Colorado Campus M
University of Phoenix–South Florida Campus M
University of Phoenix–Springfield Campus M
University of Phoenix–Tulsa Campus M
University of Phoenix–Utah Campus M
University of Phoenix–Vancouver Campus M
University of Phoenix–Washington D.C. Campus M,D
University of Phoenix–West Florida Campus M
University of Pittsburgh M,D,O*
University of Puerto Rico, Mayagüez Campus M
University of Puerto Rico, Río Piedras M,D
University of Regina M,O
University of Rhode Island M
University of St. Thomas (MN) M,D,O
The University of Scranton M
University of South Carolina M
The University of Texas at Arlington M
University of the Sacred Heart M
University of Toronto M,D
University of Wisconsin–Madison M,D*
University of Wisconsin–Whitewater M*
Upper Iowa University M
Utah State University M
Virginia International University M,O
Walden University M,D
Wayland Baptist University M
Waynesburg University M,D
Webster University M,D,O
West Chester University of Pennsylvania M,O
Widener University M
Wilfrid Laurier University M,D
Wilkes University M
Wilmington University M
York University M,D*

HUMAN SERVICES

Abilene Christian University M,O
Albertus Magnus College M
Andrews University M
Bellevue University M
Boricua College M
Brandeis University M
California State University, Sacramento M
Capella University M,D,O
Chestnut Hill College M*
Concordia University Chicago M
Concordia University Wisconsin M,D
Coppin State University M
DePaul University M,D
Drury University M
Eastern Michigan University O
Eastern New Mexico University M
Fairfield University M,O
Fairmont State University M
Ferris State University M
Georgia State University M
Indiana University Northwest M,O
Kansas State University M*
Kent State University M,D,O*
Lehigh University M,D,O
Liberty University M,D
Lincoln University (PA) M
Lindenwood University M
Louisiana State University in Shreveport M
McDaniel College M
Minnesota State University Mankato M
Minnesota State University Moorhead M,O
Montana State University Billings M
Murray State University M
National-Louis University M,D,O
National University M
New England College M
Nova Southeastern University M,D*
Pontifical Catholic University of Puerto Rico M,D
Post University M
Purdue University Calumet M
Roberts Wesleyan College M
Rosemont College M
St. Joseph's College, New York M*
Saint Joseph's University M,O
St. Mary's University (United States) M,D,O
Sojourner-Douglass College M
South Carolina State University M
Southeastern University (FL) M
Springfield College M
Syracuse University O*
Texas Southern University M
Thomas University M
Universidad del Turabo M
Université de Montréal D
University of Baltimore M
University of Bridgeport M
University of Central Missouri M,D,O
University of Colorado at Colorado Springs M,D
University of Great Falls M
University of Illinois at Springfield M
University of Maryland, Baltimore County M,D
University of Massachusetts Boston M
University of Northern Iowa M,D
University of Oklahoma M,O*
University of Phoenix–Minneapolis/St. Louis Park Campus M
University of Phoenix–Puerto Rico Campus M
Upper Iowa University M
Walden University M,D
West Virginia University M
Wichita State University M
Wilmington University M
Youngstown State University M

HYDRAULICS

Auburn University M,D
Drexel University M,D*
École Polytechnique de Montréal M,D,O
McGill University M,D
Missouri University of Science and Technology M,D
University of Colorado Denver M,D

HYDROGEOLOGY

California State University, Chico M
Clemson University M
Georgia State University M,O
Illinois State University M
Indiana University Bloomington M,D*
Montana Tech of The University of Montana M
Ohio University M*
University of Hawaii at Manoa M,D
University of Nevada, Reno M,D*
The University of Texas at Dallas M,D*
West Virginia University M,D

HYDROLOGY

Auburn University M,D
California State University, Bakersfield M
California State University, Chico M
Colorado State University M,D
Cornell University M,D*
Drexel University M,D*
Idaho State University M,O
Illinois State University M
Massachusetts Institute of Technology M,D,O
Missouri University of Science and Technology M,D
Murray State University M
New Mexico Institute of Mining and Technology M,D
Stevens Institute of Technology M,D,O
Université du Québec, Institut National de la Recherche Scientifique M,D
The University of Arizona M,D
University of California, Davis M,D
University of Colorado Boulder M,D*
University of Colorado Denver M,D
University of Idaho M
University of Nevada, Reno M,D*
University of New Brunswick Fredericton M,D
University of New Hampshire M
University of Southern Mississippi M,D
University of Washington M,D*
Virginia Polytechnic Institute and State University M,D,O

ILLUSTRATION

Academy of Art University M
Bob Jones University P,M,D,O
Bradley University M
Fashion Institute of Technology M*
Kent State University M*
Maryland Institute College of Art M
Marywood University M
Mills College M
Minneapolis College of Art and Design M
San Jose State University M
Savannah College of Art and Design M
School of Visual Arts (NY) M
Syracuse University M*
University of Massachusetts Dartmouth M
Western Connecticut State University M

IMMUNOLOGY

Albany Medical College M,D
Albert Einstein College of Medicine D
Baylor College of Medicine D*
Boston University M,D*
Brown University M,D
California Institute of Technology D
Case Western Reserve University M,D*
Colorado State University M,D
Cornell University M,D*
Cornell University, Joan and Sanford I. Weill Medical College and Graduate School of Medical Sciences M,D
Creighton University M,D
Dalhousie University M,D
Dartmouth College
Drexel University M,D*
Duke University D*
East Carolina University D
Emory University D*
Georgetown University M,D
The George Washington University D
Harvard University D*
Hood College M,O
Illinois State University M,D
Indiana University–Purdue University Indianapolis M,D
Iowa State University of Science and Technology M,D*
The Johns Hopkins University M,D
Long Island University, C.W. Post Campus M
Louisiana State University Health Sciences Center M,D
Louisiana State University Health Sciences Center at Shreveport M,D
Loyola University Chicago M,D
Massachusetts Institute of Technology D
Mayo Graduate School D
McGill University M,D
McMaster University M,D
Medical University of South Carolina M,D
Meharry Medical College D
Memorial University of Newfoundland M,D
Montana State University M,D
New York Medical College M,D*
New York University P,M,D
North Carolina State University M,D*
Northwestern University D*
The Ohio State University D
Oregon Health & Science University D*
Penn State Hershey Medical Center M,D
Purdue University M,D
Queen's University at Kingston M,D
Rosalind Franklin University of Medicine and Science M,D*
Rush University M,D
Rutgers, The State University of New Jersey, New Brunswick M,D*
Saint Louis University D

*M—master's degree; P—first professional degree; D—doctorate; O—other advanced degree; *—Close-Up and/or Display in one of the other books in this series*

- Stanford University D
- State University of New York Upstate Medical University M,D
- Stony Brook University, State University of New York M,D
- Temple University M,D*
- Texas A&M Health Science Center D
- Thomas Jefferson University D
- Tufts University D
- Tulane University M,D*
- Uniformed Services University of the Health Sciences D*
- Universidad Central del Caribe M,D
- Université de Montréal M,D
- Université de Sherbrooke M,D
- Université du Québec, Institut National de la Recherche Scientifique M,D
- Université Laval M,D
- University at Albany, State University of New York M,D
- University at Buffalo, the State University of New York M,D*
- University of Alberta M,D
- The University of Arizona M,D
- University of Arkansas for Medical Sciences M,D
- The University of British Columbia M,D
- University of Calgary M,D
- University of California, Berkeley D*
- University of California, Davis M,D
- University of California, Los Angeles M,D*
- University of California, San Diego D*
- University of California, San Francisco D
- University of Chicago D
- University of Cincinnati M,D
- University of Colorado Denver D
- University of Connecticut Health Center D*
- University of Florida D*
- University of Guelph M,D,O
- University of Illinois at Chicago D
- The University of Iowa M,D*
- University of Louisville M,D
- The University of Manchester M,D
- University of Manitoba M,D
- University of Maryland, Baltimore D
- University of Massachusetts Worcester M,D
- University of Medicine and Dentistry of New Jersey M,D,O
- University of Miami D*
- University of Michigan D*
- University of Minnesota, Duluth M,D
- University of Minnesota, Twin Cities Campus D
- University of Missouri M,D*
- The University of North Carolina at Chapel Hill M,D*
- University of North Dakota M,D
- University of North Texas Health Science Center at Fort Worth M,D
- University of Oklahoma Health Sciences Center M,D
- University of Ottawa M,D*
- University of Pennsylvania D*
- University of Pittsburgh M,D*
- University of Prince Edward Island M,D
- University of Rochester University of Saskatchewan M,D
- The University of South Dakota M,D
- University of Southern California M,D*
- University of Southern Maine M
- The University of Texas Health Science Center at Houston M,D*
- The University of Texas Health Science Center at San Antonio D
- The University of Texas Medical Branch M,D
- The University of Texas Southwestern Medical Center at Dallas D
- The University of Toledo M,D
- University of Toronto M,D
- University of Washington D*
- The University of Western Ontario M,D
- Vanderbilt University M,D*
- Virginia Commonwealth University M,D
- Wake Forest University D
- Washington University in St. Louis D*
- Wayne State University M,D*
- West Virginia University M,D
- Wright State University M
- Yale University D*

INDUSTRIAL/MANAGEMENT ENGINEERING

- Arizona State University M,D
- Auburn University M,D
- Bradley University M
- Buffalo State College, State University of New York M
- California Polytechnic State University, San Luis Obispo M
- California State University, Fresno M
- California State University, Northridge M
- Central Washington University M
- Clemson University M,D
- Cleveland State University M,D
- Colorado State University–Pueblo M
- Columbia University M,D,O*
- Concordia University (Canada) M,D,O
- Cornell University M,D*
- Dalhousie University M,D
- East Carolina University M,D,O
- Eastern Kentucky University M
- École Polytechnique de Montréal M,D,O
- Florida Agricultural and Mechanical University M,D
- Florida State University M,D
- Georgia Institute of Technology M,D
- Illinois State University M
- Indiana State University M
- Indiana University–Purdue University Fort Wayne M
- Instituto Tecnologico de Santo Domingo M,O
- Instituto Tecnológico y de Estudios Superiores de Monterrey, Campus Chihuahua M,O
- Instituto Tecnológico y de Estudios Superiores de Monterrey, Campus Ciudad de México M,D
- Instituto Tecnológico y de Estudios Superiores de Monterrey, Campus Laguna M
- Instituto Tecnológico y de Estudios Superiores de Monterrey, Campus Monterrey M,D
- Iowa State University of Science and Technology M,D*
- Kansas State University M,D*
- Lamar University M,D
- Lawrence Technological University M,D
- Lehigh University M,D
- Louisiana State University and Agricultural and Mechanical College M,D
- Louisiana Tech University M
- Mississippi State University M,D
- Montana State University M,D
- Montana Tech of The University of Montana M
- Morehead State University M
- Morgan State University M,D
- New Jersey Institute of Technology M,D
- New Mexico State University M,D
- North Carolina Agricultural and Technical State University M,D
- North Carolina State University M,D*
- North Dakota State University M,D
- Northeastern University M,D
- Northern Illinois University M
- Northwestern University M,D*
- The Ohio State University M,D
- Ohio University M,D*
- Oklahoma State University M,D*
- Oregon State University M,D
- Penn State University Park M,D
- Polytechnic Institute of NYU M
- Polytechnic Institute of NYU, Long Island Graduate Center M
- Polytechnic Institute of NYU, Westchester Graduate Center M
- Purdue University M,D
- Rensselaer Polytechnic Institute M,D
- Rochester Institute of Technology M
- Rutgers, The State University of New Jersey, New Brunswick M,D*
- St. Mary's University (United States) M
- Sam Houston State University M
- San Jose State University M
- South Dakota State University M
- Southern Illinois University Edwardsville M
- Southern Polytechnic State University M,O
- Stanford University M,D
- State University of New York at Binghamton M,D
- Texas A&M University M,D
- Texas A&M University–Commerce M
- Texas A&M University–Kingsville M
- Texas Southern University M
- Texas State University–San Marcos M
- Texas Tech University M,D*
- Universidad de las Américas–Puebla M
- Université de Moncton M
- Université du Québec à Trois-Rivières M,O
- Université Laval O
- University at Buffalo, the State University of New York M,D*
- The University of Alabama in Huntsville M,D
- The University of Arizona M,D
- University of Arkansas M,D
- University of California, Berkeley M,D*
- University of Central Florida M,D,O
- University of Cincinnati M,D
- University of Florida M,D,O*
- University of Houston M,D
- University of Illinois at Chicago M,D
- University of Illinois at Urbana–Champaign M,D
- The University of Iowa M,D*
- University of Louisville M,D,O
- University of Manitoba M,D
- University of Massachusetts Amherst M,D*
- University of Massachusetts Lowell M,D,O
- University of Memphis M,D
- University of Miami M,D*
- University of Michigan M,D*
- University of Michigan–Dearborn M,D
- University of Minnesota, Twin Cities Campus M,D
- University of Missouri M,D*
- University of Nebraska–Lincoln M,D*
- University of New Haven M,O
- University of Oklahoma M,D*
- University of Pittsburgh M,D*
- University of Puerto Rico, Mayagüez Campus M
- University of Regina M,D
- University of Southern California M,D,O*
- University of South Florida M,D*
- The University of Tennessee M,D
- The University of Tennessee at Chattanooga M
- The University of Texas at Arlington M,D
- The University of Texas at Austin M,D
- The University of Texas at El Paso M,O
- The University of Toledo M,D
- University of Toronto M,D
- University of Washington M,D*
- University of Windsor M,D
- University of Wisconsin–Madison M,D*
- University of Wisconsin–Milwaukee M,D,O
- University of Wisconsin–Stout M
- Virginia Polytechnic Institute and State University M,D,O
- Wayne State University M,D*
- Western Carolina University M
- Western Michigan University M,D
- Western New England University M
- West Virginia University M,D
- Wichita State University M,D
- Youngstown State University M

INDUSTRIAL AND LABOR RELATIONS

- Bernard M. Baruch College of the City University of New York M
- Carnegie Mellon University M,D*
- Case Western Reserve University M*
- Cleveland State University P,M,O
- Cornell University M,D*
- Georgetown University D

- Indiana University of Pennsylvania M
- Inter American University of Puerto Rico, Metropolitan Campus M,D
- Loyola University Chicago M
- McMaster University M
- Memorial University of Newfoundland M
- Michigan State University M,D
- New York Institute of Technology M,O
- The Ohio State University M,D
- Penn State University Park M
- Queen's University at Kingston M
- Rutgers, The State University of New Jersey, New Brunswick M,D*
- State University of New York Empire State College M
- Université de Montréal M,D,O
- Université du Québec à Trois-Rivières O
- Université du Québec en Outaouais M,D,O
- Université Laval M,D
- University of Alberta D
- University of California, Berkeley D*
- University of Cincinnati M
- University of Illinois at Urbana–Champaign M,D
- University of Massachusetts Amherst M*
- University of Minnesota, Twin Cities Campus M,D
- University of New Haven M,O
- University of New Mexico M,D*
- University of North Texas M
- University of Rhode Island M
- University of Saskatchewan M
- University of Toronto M,D
- University of Wisconsin–Milwaukee M,O
- West Virginia University M

INDUSTRIAL AND MANUFACTURING MANAGEMENT

- American InterContinental University Online M
- The American University in Cairo M
- California Polytechnic State University, San Luis Obispo M
- California State University, East Bay M
- Carnegie Mellon University M,D*
- Case Western Reserve University M,D*
- Central Connecticut State University M,O
- Central Michigan University M
- Cleveland State University D
- Colorado Technical University Colorado Springs M,D
- Colorado Technical University Denver M
- DePaul University M
- Friends University M
- Georgetown University D
- Harvard University D*
- HEC Montreal M
- Illinois Institute of Technology M
- Instituto Tecnologico de Santo Domingo M,O
- Instituto Tecnológico y de Estudios Superiores de Monterrey, Campus Estado de México M,D
- Instituto Tecnológico y de Estudios Superiores de Monterrey, Campus Irapuato M,D
- Inter American University of Puerto Rico, Metropolitan Campus M
- Inter American University of Puerto Rico, San Germán Campus M,D
- International Technological University M
- Kansas State University M*
- Lawrence Technological University M,D
- Marist College M,O
- Marquette University M
- McGill University M,D,O
- Milwaukee School of Engineering M
- Northeastern State University M
- Northern Illinois University M
- Oakland University M,O
- Penn State University Park M
- Polytechnic University of Puerto Rico M
- Polytechnic University of Puerto Rico, Miami Campus M
- Polytechnic University of Puerto Rico, Orlando Campus M
- Portland State University M,D
- Purdue University M
- Regis University M,O
- Rochester Institute of Technology M
- San Diego State University M
- San Jose State University M
- Southeast Missouri State University M
- Stevens Institute of Technology M
- Syracuse University D*
- Texas A&M University M,D
- Texas Tech University M,D*
- Universidad de las Américas–Puebla M
- University of Arkansas M
- University of California, Berkeley D*
- University of California, Los Angeles M,D*
- University of Central Missouri M,D
- University of Cincinnati D
- University of Dayton M
- The University of Manchester M,D
- University of Minnesota, Twin Cities Campus D
- University of Missouri–St. Louis M,O
- University of New Haven M
- University of Pittsburgh M,O*
- University of Puerto Rico, Mayagüez Campus M
- University of Puerto Rico, Río Piedras M,D
- University of Rhode Island M,D
- University of Southern Indiana M
- The University of Tennessee M,D
- The University of Texas at Arlington M,D
- The University of Texas at Austin D
- The University of Texas at Tyler M,D
- The University of Toledo M,D,O
- Wake Forest University M
- Washington State University M,D
- Wilkes University M

INDUSTRIAL AND ORGANIZATIONAL PSYCHOLOGY

- Adler School of Professional Psychology M,D,O
- Alliant International University–Fresno M,D
- Alliant International University–Los Angeles M,D
- Alliant International University–Sacramento D
- Alliant International University–San Diego M,D
- Alliant International University–San Francisco M,D
- American InterContinental University Online M
- Angelo State University M
- Antioch University Seattle M
- Appalachian State University M,O
- Argosy University, Atlanta M,D,O*
- Argosy University, Chicago M,D*
- Argosy University, Dallas M*
- Argosy University, Denver M,D*
- Argosy University, Inland Empire M,D*
- Argosy University, Phoenix M*
- Argosy University, Schaumburg M,D,O*
- Argosy University, Tampa M,D*
- Argosy University, Twin Cities M,D,O*
- Auburn University M,D
- Bayamón Central University M
- Bernard M. Baruch College of the City University of New York M,D,O
- Bowling Green State University M,D*
- Brooklyn College of the City University of New York M
- California State University, Long Beach M
- California State University, San Bernardino M
- Capella University M,D,O
- Carlos Albizu University M,D
- Carlos Albizu University, Miami Campus M,D
- Central Michigan University M,D
- Chatham University M,D
- The Chicago School of Professional Psychology M,D
- The Chicago School of Professional Psychology at Downtown Los Angeles M
- The Chicago School of Professional Psychology: Online M,D,O
- Claremont Graduate University M,D,O
- Clemson University D
- Cleveland State University M,D,O
- DePaul University M,D
- Eastern Kentucky University M,O
- Elmhurst College M
- Emporia State University M
- Fairfield University M,O
- Fairleigh Dickinson University, College at Florham M
- Florida Institute of Technology M,D
- The George Washington University M,D
- Georgia Institute of Technology M,D
- Goddard College M
- Graduate School and University Center of the City University of New York D
- Grand Canyon University D
- Hofstra University M,D
- Illinois Institute of Technology M,D
- Illinois State University M,D,O
- Indiana University–Purdue University Indianapolis M
- Inter American University of Puerto Rico, Metropolitan Campus M,D
- Iona College M
- John F. Kennedy University M,O
- Kean University M
- Lamar University M
- Louisiana State University and Agricultural and Mechanical College M,D
- Louisiana Tech University M,D
- Marshall University M,D
- Massachusetts School of Professional Psychology M,D,O
- Middle Tennessee State University M,O
- Minnesota State University Mankato M,D
- Missouri State University M
- Montclair State University M,O
- New York University M,D,O
- North Carolina State University D*
- Northern Kentucky University M,O
- Ohio University D*
- Old Dominion University D
- Philadelphia College of Osteopathic Medicine M,D,O*
- Pontifical Catholic University of Puerto Rico D
- Radford University M
- Rice University M,D
- Roosevelt University M,D
- St. Cloud State University M
- Saint Joseph's University M,O
- Saint Louis University M,D
- Saint Mary's University (Canada) M,D
- St. Mary's University (United States) M
- San Diego State University M,D
- San Francisco State University M
- San Jose State University M
- Seattle Pacific University M,D
- Southern Illinois University Edwardsville M
- Springfield College M,O
- Teachers College, Columbia University M
- Temple University M*
- Texas A&M University D
- Union Institute & University M,D,O
- University at Albany, State University of New York M,D,O
- The University of Akron M,D
- The University of Alabama in Huntsville M
- University of Baltimore M
- University of Central Florida M,D
- University of Connecticut M,D,O*
- University of Detroit Mercy M
- University of Guelph M,D
- University of Houston M,D
- University of Maryland, Baltimore County M
- University of Maryland, College Park M,D
- University of Minnesota, Twin Cities Campus D
- University of Missouri–St. Louis M,D,O
- University of Nebraska at Omaha M,D,O

*M—master's degree; P—first professional degree; D—doctorate; O—other advanced degree; *—Close-Up and/or Display in one of the other books in this series*

University of New Haven M,O
The University of North Carolina at Charlotte M,D,O
University of Oklahoma M,D*
University of Phoenix D,O
University of Phoenix–Chattanooga Campus M,D
University of Phoenix–Milwaukee Campus M,D
University of Phoenix–Washington D.C. Campus M,D
University of Puerto Rico, Río Piedras M,D
University of South Africa M,D
University of South Florida D*
The University of Tennessee D
The University of Tennessee at Chattanooga M
The University of Texas at Arlington M,D
University of Tulsa M,D
University of West Florida M
University of Wisconsin–Oshkosh M
Valdosta State University M,O
Walden University M,D,O
Wayne State University M,D*
West Chester University of Pennsylvania M,O
Western Kentucky University M,O
Western Michigan University M,D
Wright State University M,D
Xavier University M,D

INDUSTRIAL DESIGN

Academy of Art University M
Art Center College of Design M*
Auburn University M
Brigham Young University M*
Carleton University M
North Carolina State University M*
The Ohio State University M
Pratt Institute M*
Rhode Island School of Design M
Rochester Institute of Technology M
San Francisco State University M
Savannah College of Art and Design M
University of Cincinnati M
University of Illinois at Chicago M
University of Illinois at Urbana–Champaign M
University of Notre Dame M*
The University of the Arts M*
University of Washington M*

INDUSTRIAL HYGIENE

California State University, Northridge M
Montana Tech of The University of Montana M
Murray State University M
New York Medical College O*
University of Central Missouri M
University of Cincinnati M,D
University of Massachusetts Lowell M,D,O
University of Michigan M,D*
University of Minnesota, Twin Cities Campus M,D
The University of North Carolina at Chapel Hill M,D*
University of Puerto Rico, Medical Sciences Campus M
University of South Carolina M,D
University of Wisconsin–Stout M
West Virginia University M

INFECTIOUS DISEASES

Cornell University M,D*
George Mason University M,D*
Georgetown University M,D
The George Washington University M
Harvard University D*
The Johns Hopkins University M,D
Loyola University Chicago M,O
Montana State University M,D
North Carolina State University M,D*
State University of New York Upstate Medical University
Tulane University M,D,O*
Uniformed Services University of the Health Sciences D*
Université Laval O
University of Calgary M,D
University of California, Berkeley M,D*
University of Georgia M,D
University of Guelph M,D,O
University of Medicine and Dentistry of New Jersey D,O
University of Minnesota, Twin Cities Campus M,D
The University of Montana D
University of Pittsburgh M,D,O*
The University of Texas Medical Branch D
Yale University D*

INFORMATION SCIENCE

Alcorn State University M
American InterContinental University Atlanta M
American InterContinental University Online M
American InterContinental University South Florida M
Arizona State University M
Arkansas Tech University M
Aspen University M,O
Athabasca University M
Ball State University M
Barry University M*
Bellevue University M
Bentley University M
Bradley University M
Brigham Young University M*
Brooklyn College of the City University of New York M,D,O
California State University, Fullerton M
Capitol College M
Carleton University M,D
Carnegie Mellon University M,D*
Case Western Reserve University M,D*
The Citadel, The Military College of South Carolina M
Claremont Graduate University M,D,O
Clark Atlanta University M
Clarkson University M*
Clark University M
Cleveland State University M,D
Coleman University M
The College of Saint Rose M
Cornell University D*
Dakota State University M,D*
DePaul University M,D
DeSales University M
Drexel University M,D*
East Carolina University M
East Tennessee State University M
Everglades University M
Florida Gulf Coast University M
Florida International University M,D
Gannon University M
George Mason University M,D,O*
Georgia Southwestern State University M
Georgia State University M
Grand Valley State University M
Harvard University M,D,O*
Hood College M,O
Indiana University Bloomington M,D,O*
Indiana University–Purdue University Fort Wayne M
Indiana University–Purdue University Indianapolis M,D
Instituto Tecnologico de Santo Domingo M,O
Instituto Tecnológico y de Estudios Superiores de Monterrey, Campus Cuernavaca M,D
Instituto Tecnológico y de Estudios Superiores de Monterrey, Campus Estado de México M,D
Instituto Tecnológico y de Estudios Superiores de Monterrey, Campus Irapuato M,D
Instituto Tecnológico y de Estudios Superiores de Monterrey, Campus Monterrey M,D
Instituto Tecnológico y de Estudios Superiores de Monterrey, Campus Sonora Norte M
Iowa State University of Science and Technology M*
The Johns Hopkins University M
Kansas State University M,D*
Kennesaw State University M
Kent State University M*
Kentucky State University M
Knowledge Systems Institute M
Lamar University M
Lehigh University M
Long Island University, C.W. Post Campus M
Loyola University Chicago M
Marlboro College M,O
Marshall University M
Marywood University M,O
Massachusetts Institute of Technology M,D,O
Missouri University of Science and Technology M
Montclair State University M,O
National University M
Naval Postgraduate School M,O
New Jersey Institute of Technology M,D
Northeastern University M,D,O
Northern Kentucky University M,O
Northwestern University M*
Nova Southeastern University M,D*
The Ohio State University M,D
Oklahoma State University M,D*
Old Dominion University D
Pace University M,D,O
Penn State University Park M,D
Polytechnic Institute of NYU, Westchester Graduate Center M
Regis University M,O
Rensselaer at Hartford M
Rensselaer Polytechnic Institute M
Robert Morris University M,D
Rochester Institute of Technology M,D
Sacred Heart University M,O
St. Mary's University (United States) M
Saint Xavier University M
Sam Houston State University M
Simon Fraser University M,D
Southern Methodist University M,D
Southern Polytechnic State University M,O
State University of New York Institute of Technology M
Stevens Institute of Technology M,O
Strayer University M
Syracuse University D,O*
Temple University M,D*
Towson University M,D,O
Trevecca Nazarene University M
Université de Sherbrooke M,D
University at Albany, State University of New York M,D,O
The University of Alabama at Birmingham M,D*
University of Arkansas at Little Rock M
University of Baltimore M,D
University of California, Irvine M,D*
University of Central Missouri M,D,O
University of Colorado at Colorado Springs M
University of Colorado Denver M,D
University of Delaware M,D*
University of Detroit Mercy M
University of Florida M,D*
University of Hawaii at Manoa M,D
University of Houston M,D
University of Houston–Clear Lake M
University of Illinois at Urbana–Champaign M,D,O
The University of Iowa M,D,O*
University of Management and Technology M,O
University of Maryland, Baltimore County M,D
University of Maryland University College M,O
University of Michigan M,D*
University of Michigan–Dearborn M,D
University of Michigan–Flint M
University of Minnesota, Twin Cities Campus M,D
University of Nebraska at Omaha M,D,O
University of Nebraska–Lincoln M,D*
University of Nevada, Las Vegas M,D
University of New Haven M,O
The University of North Carolina at Charlotte M,D,O
University of Oregon M,D
University of Ottawa M,O*
University of Pennsylvania M,D*
University of Phoenix–Cincinnati Campus M
University of Pittsburgh M,D,O*
University of Puerto Rico, Mayagüez Campus M,D
University of Puerto Rico, Río Piedras M,O
University of South Africa M,D
University of South Alabama M

The University of Tennessee M,D
The University of Texas at El Paso M,D
The University of Texas at San Antonio M*
University of the Sacred Heart O
University of Washington M,D*
University of Waterloo M,D
University of Wisconsin–Parkside M
University of Wisconsin–Stout M
Youngstown State University M

INFORMATION STUDIES

The Catholic University of America M
Central Connecticut State University M
Columbia University M*
Cornell University D*
Dalhousie University M
Dominican University M,D,O
Drexel University M*
Emporia State University M,D,O
Florida State University M,D,O
Indiana University Bloomington M,D,O*
Long Island University, C.W. Post Campus M,D,O
Long Island University, Westchester Graduate Campus M
Louisiana State University and Agricultural and Mechanical College M
Mansfield University of Pennsylvania M
McGill University M,D,O
Metropolitan State University M,D,O
North Carolina Central University M
Pratt Institute M,O*
Queens College of the City University of New York M,O
Queen's University at Kingston M,D
Rutgers, The State University of New Jersey, New Brunswick M,D*
St. Catherine University M
St. John's University (NY) M,O
San Jose State University M,D
Simmons College M,D
Southern Connecticut State University M,O
Syracuse University M,D*
Universidad del Turabo M
Université de Montréal M,D
University at Albany, State University of New York M,O
University at Buffalo, the State University of New York M,O*
The University of Alabama M,D
University of Alberta M
The University of Arizona M,D
The University of British Columbia M,D
University of California, Berkeley M,D*
University of California, Los Angeles M,D,O*
University of Hawaii at Manoa M,O
University of Illinois at Urbana–Champaign M,D,O
The University of Iowa M*
University of Maryland, College Park M,D
University of Michigan M,D*
University of Missouri M,D,O*
The University of North Carolina at Chapel Hill M,D,O*
The University of North Carolina at Greensboro M
University of North Texas M,D
University of Oklahoma M,O*
University of Pittsburgh M,D,O*
University of Puerto Rico, Río Piedras M,O
University of Rhode Island M
University of South Carolina M,D,O
University of South Florida M*
The University of Texas at Austin M,D
University of Toronto M,D,O
The University of Western Ontario M,D
University of Wisconsin–Madison M,D*
University of Wisconsin–Milwaukee M,D,O
Valdosta State University M
Wayne State University M,O*

INORGANIC CHEMISTRY

Auburn University M,D
Boston College M,D*
Brandeis University M,D
California State University, Los Angeles M*
Carnegie Mellon University M,D*
Cleveland State University M,D
Columbia University M,D*
Cornell University D*
Eastern New Mexico University M
Florida State University M,D
Georgetown University D
The George Washington University M,D
Harvard University D*
Howard University M,D
Indiana University Bloomington M,D*
Kansas State University M,D*
Kent State University M,D*
Marquette University M,D
Massachusetts Institute of Technology D
McMaster University M,D
Northeastern University M,D
Oregon State University M,D
Purdue University M,D
Rensselaer Polytechnic Institute M,D
Rice University M,D
Rutgers, The State University of New Jersey, Newark M,D*
Rutgers, The State University of New Jersey, New Brunswick M,D*
Seton Hall University M,D
Southern University and Agricultural and Mechanical College M
State University of New York at Binghamton M,D
Texas Christian University M,D
Tufts University M,D
University of Calgary M,D
University of Cincinnati M,D
University of Georgia M,D
University of Louisville M,D
The University of Manchester M,D
University of Maryland, College Park M,D
University of Massachusetts Lowell M,D
University of Memphis M,D
University of Miami M,D*
University of Michigan D*
University of Missouri M,D*
University of Missouri–Kansas City M,D*
University of Missouri–St. Louis M,D
The University of Montana M,D
University of Nebraska–Lincoln M,D*
University of Notre Dame M,D*
University of Regina M,D
University of Southern Mississippi M,D
University of South Florida M,D*
The University of Tennessee M,D
The University of Texas at Austin M,D
The University of Toledo M,D
Vanderbilt University M,D*
Virginia Commonwealth University M,D
Wake Forest University M,D
Wesleyan University M,D*
West Virginia University M,D
Yale University D*
Youngstown State University M

INSURANCE

Florida State University M,D
Georgia State University M,D,O
Pontificia Universidad Catolica Madre y Maestra M
St. John's University (NY) M
Temple University D*
Tennessee Technological University M
Thomas M. Cooley Law School P,M
University of Pennsylvania M,D*
University of Wisconsin–Madison M,D*
Virginia Commonwealth University M

INTELLECTUAL PROPERTY LAW

Boston University P,M*
Case Western Reserve University P,M*
DePaul University P,M
Fordham University P,M
Golden Gate University P,M,D
Montclair State University M,O
Santa Clara University P,M,O
Suffolk University P,M
University of Houston P,M
University of Pittsburgh M,O*
University of San Francisco M
University of Washington P,M,D*
Webster University M,O
Yeshiva University P,M*

INTERDISCIPLINARY STUDIES

Alaska Pacific University M
Amberton University M
American University M
Angelo State University M
Antioch University New England M
Arizona State University M
Athabasca University M
Baylor University M,D*
Boise State University M
Bowling Green State University M,D*
Buffalo State College, State University of New York M
California Institute of Integral Studies M,D
California State University, Bakersfield M
California State University, Chico M
California State University, East Bay M
California State University, Long Beach M
California State University, Monterey Bay M
California State University, Northridge M
California State University, San Bernardino M
California State University, Stanislaus M
Cambridge College M,D,O
Campbell University M
Central Washington University M
College of the Humanities and Sciences, Harrison Middleton University M,D
Columbia University M*
Concordia University (Canada) M,D
Dalhousie University D
Dallas Baptist University M
DePaul University M
Drew University M,D,O
Eastern Washington University M
Embry-Riddle Aeronautical University–Daytona M
Emory University D*
Fitchburg State University O
Florida Gulf Coast University M
Florida Institute of Technology M,D
Franklin Pierce University M,D,O
Fresno Pacific University M
Frostburg State University M
George Mason University M*
Georgetown University M,D
Goddard College M
Graduate School and University Center of the City University of New York M,D
Hiram College M
Hodges University M
Hollins University M,O
Idaho State University M
Iowa State University of Science and Technology M*
John F. Kennedy University M
Lehigh University M,D
Lesley University M
Long Island University, C.W. Post Campus M
Marquette University M,D
Marylhurst University M
Marywood University M
Mills College M,O
Minnesota State University Mankato M
Mississippi State University M,D
Montana State University Billings M
Montana Tech of The University of Montana M
Mountain State University M
New Mexico State University M,D
New York University M
Niagara University M
Northeastern University D
Nova Southeastern University M*
The Ohio State University M,D
Oregon State University M
Polytechnic Institute of NYU M
Polytechnic Institute of NYU, Long Island Graduate Center M
Polytechnic Institute of NYU, Westchester Graduate Center M
Quinnipiac University D
Regis University M,O
Rensselaer Polytechnic Institute M,D
Rochester Institute of Technology M
Rosalind Franklin University of Medicine and Science D*

*M—master's degree; P—first professional degree; D—doctorate; O—other advanced degree; *—Close-Up and/or Display in one of the other books in this series*

Rutgers, The State University of New Jersey, New Brunswick	D*
San Diego State University	M
San Jose State University	M
Sarah Lawrence College	M
Sonoma State University	M
Southern Oregon University	M
Stanford University	M,D
State University of New York at Fredonia	M
Stephen F. Austin State University	M
Teachers College, Columbia University	M,D
Texas A&M University–Texarkana	M
Texas State University–San Marcos	M
Texas Tech University	M*
Trinity Western University	M
Tulane University	D*
Union Institute & University	M,D
The University of Alabama	D
The University of Alabama at Birmingham	D*
The University of Alabama in Huntsville	M,D,O
University of Alaska Anchorage	M
University of Alaska Fairbanks	M,D
The University of Arizona	M,D
University of Arkansas	M,D
The University of British Columbia	M
University of California, Santa Cruz	M,D
University of Central Florida	M
University of Chicago	D
University of Cincinnati	D
University of Denver	M,D
University of Houston–Victoria	M
University of Idaho	M
University of Illinois at Springfield	M
The University of Kansas	M,D
University of Louisville	M,D
University of Maine	M,D
University of Manitoba	M,D
University of Massachusetts Worcester	M,D
University of Medicine and Dentistry of New Jersey	M,D
University of Memphis	M,D,O
University of Minnesota, Twin Cities Campus	D
University of Missouri–Kansas City	D*
University of Missouri–St. Louis	O
The University of Montana	M,D
University of New Brunswick Fredericton	M,D
The University of North Carolina at Charlotte	M,O
University of Northern British Columbia	M,D,O
University of North Texas	M
University of Oklahoma	M,D*
University of Oregon	M
University of Ottawa	D,O*
University of Pittsburgh	D*
The University of South Dakota	M
University of South Florida	M,D*
The University of Texas at Arlington	M
The University of Texas at Brownsville	M
The University of Texas at Dallas	M*
The University of Texas at El Paso	M
The University of Texas at San Antonio	M,D*
The University of Texas at Tyler	M
The University of Texas–Pan American	M
University of the Incarnate Word	M
University of Vermont	M
University of Virginia	M,D
University of Washington, Tacoma	M
The University of Western Ontario	M,D
University of Wisconsin–Milwaukee	D
Virginia Commonwealth University	M
Virginia Polytechnic Institute and State University	M,D,O
Virginia State University	M
Washington State University	D
Wayland Baptist University	M
Western Kentucky University	M,O
Western New Mexico University	M
West Texas A&M University	M
Worcester Polytechnic Institute	M,D,O
Wright State University	M
York University	M*

INTERIOR DESIGN

Academy of Art University	M
Arizona State University	M,D
Boston Architectural College	M
Brenau University	M
Chatham University	M
Corcoran College of Art and Design	M
Cornell University	M*
Drexel University	M*
Eastern Michigan University	M
Endicott College	M
Fashion Institute of Technology	M*
Florida International University	M
Florida State University	M
The George Washington University	M
Harrington College of Design	M
Interior Designers Institute	M
Iowa State University of Science and Technology	M*
Lawrence Technological University	M
Louisiana Tech University	M
Marymount University	M
Marywood University	M
Miami International University of Art & Design	M*
Michigan State University	M,D
Missouri State University	M
Moore College of Art & Design	M
Mount Ida College	M
The New School: A University	M
New York School of Interior Design	M
The Ohio State University	M
Pontificia Universidad Catolica Madre y Maestra	M
Pratt Institute	M*
Rhode Island School of Design	M
San Diego State University	M
Savannah College of Art and Design	M
School of the Art Institute of Chicago	M
South Dakota State University	M
Suffolk University	M
Texas Tech University	M,D*
The University of Alabama	M
University of California, Berkeley	O*
University of Central Oklahoma	M
University of Cincinnati	M
University of Florida	M,D*
University of Georgia	M,D
University of Kentucky	M*
University of Manitoba	M
University of Massachusetts Amherst	M*
University of Memphis	M,O
University of Minnesota, Twin Cities Campus	M,D,O
University of Nebraska–Lincoln	M,D*
The University of North Carolina at Greensboro	M,O
University of Oregon	M
Utah State University	M
Virginia Commonwealth University	M
Virginia Polytechnic Institute and State University	M,D
Washington State University	M,D
Washington State University Spokane	M,D

INTERNATIONAL AFFAIRS

Alliant International University–México City	M
Alliant International University–San Diego	M
American Graduate School in Paris	M,D
American Public University System	M
American University	M,D,O
The American University of Paris	M
Appalachian State University	M
Azusa Pacific University	M
Baylor University	M,D*
Boston University	M,D,O*
Brandeis University	M,D
Brock University	M
Brooklyn College of the City University of New York	M,D
California State University, Fresno	M
California State University, Sacramento	M
California State University, Stanislaus	M
Carleton University	M,D
The Catholic University of America	M,D
Central Connecticut State University	M
Central European University	M,D
Central Michigan University	M,O
Chapman University	M
City College of the City University of New York	M
Claremont Graduate University	M,D
Colorado School of Mines	M,O
Columbia University	M*
Concordia University (CA)	M
Cornell University	D*
Creighton University	M
East Carolina University	M
Fairleigh Dickinson University, Metropolitan Campus	M
Florida Agricultural and Mechanical University	M
Florida International University	M,D
Florida State University	M
Fordham University	M,O
George Mason University	M*
Georgetown University	P,M,D
The George Washington University	M
Georgia Institute of Technology	M,D
Harvard University	P,D*
Hult International Business School (United States)	M
Hult International Business School (United States)	M
Indiana University Bloomington	M,D,O*
Instituto Tecnologico de Santo Domingo	M,O
Instituto Tecnológico y de Estudios Superiores de Monterrey, Campus Ciudad Obregón	M
The Johns Hopkins University	M,D,O
Kansas State University	M*
Kennesaw State University	M
Kentucky State University	M
Lebanese American University	M
Lesley University	M,O
Lindenwood University	M
Long Island University, Brooklyn Campus	M,O
Long Island University, C.W. Post Campus	M
Marquette University	M,D
McMaster University	M,D
Missouri State University	M
Monterey Institute of International Studies	M
Morgan State University	M
Naval Postgraduate School	M
New England College	M
The New School: A University	M
New York University	M,D,O
North Carolina State University	M*
Northeastern University	M,D,O
Northwestern University	P,M,O*
Norwich University	M
Ohio University	M*
Oklahoma State University	M,D,O*
Old Dominion University	M,D
Pepperdine University	M
Pontificia Universidad Catolica Madre y Maestra	M
Princeton University	M,D*
Queen's University at Kingston	M,D
Regent's American College London	M
Richmond, The American International University in London	M
Rutgers, The State University of New Jersey, Camden	M
Rutgers, The State University of New Jersey, Newark	M,D*
Rutgers, The State University of New Jersey, New Brunswick	D*
St. John Fisher College	M
St. John's University (NY)	M
St. Mary's University (United States)	M
Salve Regina University	M,O
San Francisco State University	M

Schiller International University (United Kingdom)	M
Schiller International University	M
Seton Hall University	M
SIT Graduate Institute	M
Stanford University	M
Syracuse University	M*
Texas A&M University	M,O
Texas State University–San Marcos	M
Troy University	M
Tufts University	M,D
United States International University	M
Universidad de las Americas, A.C.	M
Universidad Nacional Pedro Henriquez Urena	M
Université de Montréal	M,O
Université Laval	M,D
University of Bridgeport	M
The University of British Columbia	M
University of California, Berkeley	M,D*
University of California, San Diego	M,D*
University of California, Santa Barbara	M,D
University of California, Santa Cruz	D
University of Central Oklahoma	M
University of Chicago	M
University of Colorado Boulder	M,D*
University of Colorado Denver	M
University of Connecticut	M*
University of Delaware	M,D*
University of Denver	M,D,O
University of Florida	M*
University of Hawaii at Manoa	O
University of Indianapolis	M
The University of Kansas	M
University of Kentucky	M*
The University of Manchester	D
University of Miami	M,D*
University of Northern British Columbia	M,D,O
University of Oklahoma	M,O*
University of Oregon	M
University of Pennsylvania	M*
University of Pittsburgh	M,D,O*
University of Rhode Island	M
University of San Diego	M
University of San Francisco	M
University of South Carolina	M,D
University of Southern California	M,D*
University of Southern Mississippi	M,D
University of South Florida	M,D*
University of the Pacific	P,M,D
University of Toronto	M
University of Utah	M*
University of Virginia	M,D
University of Washington	M*
University of Waterloo	M,D
University of Wyoming	M
Virginia Polytechnic Institute and State University	M,D,O
Walden University	M,D,O
Washington State University	M,D
Webster University	M
Western Michigan University	M
West Virginia University	M,D
Wilfrid Laurier University	M,D
Yale University	M*
York University	M*

INTERNATIONAL AND COMPARATIVE EDUCATION

American University	M
The American University in Cairo	M
Bowling Green State University	M*
California Baptist University	M
California State University, Dominguez Hills	M*
The College of New Jersey	M,O
Drexel University	M*
Florida International University	M,D,O
Florida State University	M,D,O
Gallaudet University	M,D,O
The George Washington University	M
Harvard University	M*
Indiana University Bloomington	M,D,O*
Lehigh University	M,O
Louisiana State University and Agricultural and Mechanical College	M,D
Morehead State University	M,O
New York University	M,D,O
SIT Graduate Institute	M
Stanford University	M,D
Teachers College, Columbia University	M,D
University of Bridgeport	M,O
University of California, Santa Barbara	M,D
University of Central Florida	M,O
University of Maryland, College Park	M,D
University of Massachusetts Amherst	M,D,O*
University of Minnesota, Twin Cities Campus	M,D
University of North Texas	M,D
University of Pennsylvania	M,D*
University of Pittsburgh	M,D*
University of San Francisco	M,D
University of South Africa	M,D
Vanderbilt University	M,D*
Walden University	M,D,O
Wright State University	M

INTERNATIONAL BUSINESS

Alliant International University–México City	M
Alliant International University–San Diego	M,D
American InterContinental University Atlanta	M
American InterContinental University London	M
American InterContinental University Online	M
American InterContinental University South Florida	M
American International College	M
American Public University System	M
American University	M,O
The American University in Dubai	M
The American University of Paris	M
Andrew Jackson University	M
Argosy University, Atlanta	M,D*
Argosy University, Chicago	M,D*
Argosy University, Dallas	M,D,O*
Argosy University, Denver	M,D*
Argosy University, Hawai'i	M,D,O*
Argosy University, Inland Empire	M,D*
Argosy University, Los Angeles	M,D*
Argosy University, Nashville	M,D*
Argosy University, Orange County	M,D,O*
Argosy University, Phoenix	M,D*
Argosy University, Salt Lake City	M,D*
Argosy University, San Diego	M,D*
Argosy University, San Francisco Bay Area	M,D*
Argosy University, Sarasota	M,D,O*
Argosy University, Schaumburg	M,D,O*
Argosy University, Seattle	M,D*
Argosy University, Tampa	M,D*
Argosy University, Twin Cities	M,D*
Argosy University, Washington DC	M,D,O*
Ashworth College	M
Assumption College	M,O
Avila University	M
Azusa Pacific University	M
Baldwin-Wallace College	M
Barry University	O*
Benedictine University	M
Bernard M. Baruch College of the City University of New York	M
Boston University	M*
Brandeis University	M,D
Brooklyn College of the City University of New York	M
California Intercontinental University	M,D
California Lutheran University	M,O
California State University, East Bay	M
California State University, Fullerton	M
California State University, Los Angeles	M*
California State University, Stanislaus	M
Canisius College	M
Central European University	M,D
Central Michigan University	M,O
City University of Seattle	M,O
Clark University	M
Cleveland State University	M,D,O
Columbia Southern University	M
Columbia University	M*
Concordia University Wisconsin	M
Daemen College	M
Dallas Baptist University	M
Delaware Valley College	M
DePaul University	M
Dominican University of California	M
Duquesne University	M
D'Youville College	M*
Eastern Michigan University	M,O
Ellis University	M
Emerson College	M
Everest University	M
Everest University	M
Fairfield University	M,O
Fairleigh Dickinson University, College at Florham	M,O
Fairleigh Dickinson University, Metropolitan Campus	M
Florida Atlantic University	M,D
Florida International University	M
Friends University	M
Georgetown University	P,M,D
The George Washington University	M,D
Georgia Institute of Technology	M,O
Georgia State University	M
Golden Gate University	M,D,O
Goldey-Beacom College	M
Harding University	M
Hawai'i Pacific University	M*
HEC Montreal	M
Hofstra University	M,O
Hope International University	M
Howard University	M
Hult International Business School (United States)	M
Hult International Business School (United States)	M
Hult International Business School (United States)	M
Hult International Business School (United States)	M
Indiana Tech	D
Instituto Tecnologico de Santo Domingo	M,O
Instituto Tecnológico y de Estudios Superiores de Monterrey, Campus Central de Veracruz	M
Instituto Tecnológico y de Estudios Superiores de Monterrey, Campus Chihuahua	M,O
Instituto Tecnológico y de Estudios Superiores de Monterrey, Campus Ciudad de México	M,D
Instituto Tecnológico y de Estudios Superiores de Monterrey, Campus Cuernavaca	M
Instituto Tecnológico y de Estudios Superiores de Monterrey, Campus Irapuato	M,D
Instituto Tecnológico y de Estudios Superiores de Monterrey, Campus Monterrey	M
Inter American University of Puerto Rico, Metropolitan Campus	M,D
Inter American University of Puerto Rico, San Germán Campus	D
The International University of Monaco	M
Iona College	M,O
John Brown University	M
John Marshall Law School	P,M
Johnson & Wales University	M
Kaplan University, Davenport Campus	M
Kean University	M
Keiser University	M,D
Lake Forest Graduate School of Management	M
Lawrence Technological University	M,D
Lewis University	M
Lincoln University (CA)	M,D
Lindenwood University	M
Long Island University, C.W. Post Campus	M,O
Loyola University Maryland	M
Lynn University	M
Madonna University	M
Maine Maritime Academy	M,O
Manhattanville College	M*
Marquette University	M
McGill University	M,D,O
McKendree University	M
MidAmerica Nazarene University	M
Milwaukee School of Engineering	M
Montclair State University	M,O
Monterey Institute of International Studies	M
National University	M

*M—master's degree; P—first professional degree; D—doctorate; O—other advanced degree; *—Close-Up and/or Display in one of the other books in this series*

Newman University M
New Mexico Highlands University M
New York Institute of Technology M,O
New York University M,D,O
Norwich University M
Nova Southeastern University M,D*
Oakland University M,O
Oklahoma City University M
Old Dominion University M
Oral Roberts University M
Pace University M
Pacific States University M,D
Park University M
Pepperdine University M
Philadelphia University M
Polytechnic University of Puerto Rico M
Polytechnic University of Puerto Rico, Miami Campus M
Polytechnic University of Puerto Rico, Orlando Campus M
Pontifical Catholic University of Puerto Rico M
Pontificia Universidad Catolica Madre y Maestra M
Portland State University M
Providence College M
Purdue University M
Regent's American College London M
Regis University M,O
Rochester Institute of Technology M
Rollins College M
Roosevelt University M
Rutgers, The State University of New Jersey, Newark D*
St. Edward's University M,O
St. John's University (NY) M,O
Saint Joseph's University M
Saint Louis University M,D
St. Mary's University (United States) M
Saint Mary's University of Minnesota M
Saint Peter's College M
St. Thomas University M,O
Salem International University M
San Diego State University M
Santa Clara University M
Schiller International University (United States) M
Schiller International University (Germany) M
Schiller International University (United Kingdom) M
Schiller International University M
Schiller International University (Spain) M
Schiller International University M
Seton Hall University M,O
Simon Fraser University M,D
SIT Graduate Institute M
Southeast Missouri State University M
Southern New Hampshire University M,D,O
Stevens Institute of Technology M
Suffolk University M,D,O
Taylor University M
Temple University M,D*
Tennessee Technological University M
Texas A&M International University M
Texas A&M University–Corpus Christi M
Texas A&M University–San Antonio M
Texas Christian University M
Texas Tech University M*
Thomas Jefferson School of Law M
Thunderbird School of Global Management M
Tiffin University M
Trinity Western University M
Troy University M
Tufts University M,D
TUI University M,D
United States International University M
Universidad Autonoma de Guadalajara M,D
Universidad Metropolitana M
Université de Sherbrooke M
Université du Québec, École nationale d'administration publique M,O
Université Laval M,O
University at Buffalo, the State University of New York M,D,O*
The University of Akron M
University of Alberta M
The University of British Columbia D
University of California, Berkeley O*
University of California, Los Angeles M,D*
University of Chicago M
University of Colorado Denver M
University of Dallas M
University of Dayton M
University of Denver M,D,O
University of Florida P,M,D*
University of Hawaii at Manoa M,D
University of Houston–Victoria M
University of Kentucky M*
University of La Verne M
University of Lethbridge M,D
University of Louisville M
University of Maryland University College M,O
University of Memphis M,D
University of Miami M*
University of Michigan–Dearborn M
University of New Brunswick Saint John M
University of New Haven M,O
University of New Mexico M*
University of North Florida M
University of Pennsylvania M*
University of Phoenix M
University of Phoenix–Atlanta Campus M
University of Phoenix–Augusta Campus M
University of Phoenix–Austin Campus M
University of Phoenix–Birmingham Campus M
University of Phoenix–Boston Campus M
University of Phoenix–Central Florida Campus M
University of Phoenix–Central Valley Campus M
University of Phoenix–Charlotte Campus M
University of Phoenix–Chattanooga Campus M
University of Phoenix–Cheyenne Campus M
University of Phoenix–Chicago Campus M
University of Phoenix–Cincinnati Campus M
University of Phoenix–Cleveland Campus M
University of Phoenix–Columbus Georgia Campus M
University of Phoenix–Columbus Ohio Campus M
University of Phoenix–Dallas Campus M
University of Phoenix–Denver Campus M
University of Phoenix–Des Moines Campus M
University of Phoenix–Harrisburg Campus M
University of Phoenix–Hawaii Campus M
University of Phoenix–Houston Campus M
University of Phoenix–Idaho Campus M
University of Phoenix–Indianapolis Campus M
University of Phoenix–Jersey City Campus M
University of Phoenix–Kansas City Campus M
University of Phoenix–Las Vegas Campus M
University of Phoenix–Louisiana Campus M
University of Phoenix–Madison Campus M
University of Phoenix–Maryland Campus M
University of Phoenix–Memphis Campus M
University of Phoenix–Minneapolis/St. Louis Park Campus M
University of Phoenix–New Mexico Campus M
University of Phoenix–Northern Nevada Campus M
University of Phoenix–North Florida Campus M
University of Phoenix–Northwest Arkansas Campus M
University of Phoenix–Oklahoma City Campus M
University of Phoenix–Omaha Campus M
University of Phoenix–Oregon Campus M
University of Phoenix–Philadelphia Campus M
University of Phoenix–Pittsburgh Campus M
University of Phoenix–Puerto Rico Campus M
University of Phoenix–Raleigh Campus M
University of Phoenix–Richmond Campus M
University of Phoenix–Sacramento Valley Campus M
University of Phoenix–St. Louis Campus M
University of Phoenix–San Antonio Campus M
University of Phoenix–San Diego Campus M
University of Phoenix–Savannah Campus M
University of Phoenix–Southern Arizona Campus M
University of Phoenix–Southern Colorado Campus M
University of Phoenix–South Florida Campus M
University of Phoenix–Springfield Campus M
University of Phoenix–Tulsa Campus M
University of Phoenix–Utah Campus M
University of Phoenix–Vancouver Campus M
University of Phoenix–West Florida Campus M
University of Pittsburgh M*
University of Puerto Rico, Río Piedras M,D
University of Regina M,O
University of San Diego M
University of San Francisco M
University of Saskatchewan M,D
The University of Scranton M
University of South Carolina M
The University of Tampa M
The University of Texas at Dallas M,D*
The University of Texas at El Paso M,D,O
The University of Texas at San Antonio M,D*
The University of Texas–Pan American D
University of the Incarnate Word M,O
University of the West M
University of Tulsa M
University of Washington M,D,O*
The University of Western Ontario M,D
University of Wisconsin–Milwaukee M,O
University of Wisconsin–Oshkosh M
University of Wisconsin–Whitewater M*
Upper Iowa University M
Valparaiso University M
Villanova University M
Virginia International University M,O
Wagner College M
Walden University M,D
Washington State University M,D,O
Wayland Baptist University M
Webster University M
Western International University M
Whitworth University M
Wilkes University M
Wright State University M
Xavier University M
York University M,D*

INTERNATIONAL DEVELOPMENT

American University M,D,O
Andrews University M
Athabasca University M
Brandeis University M
Clark University M
Cornell University M*
Dalhousie University M
Duke University M,O*
Eastern University M
Fordham University M,O
The George Washington University M
Harvard University M*
Hope International University M
John Brown University M
The Johns Hopkins University M,D,O
Lehigh University M,O
McGill University M,D,O
Ohio University M*
Rutgers, The State University of New Jersey, Camden M
Saint Mary's University (Canada) M,O
Tufts University M,D
Tulane University M,D*
University of Denver M,D,O
University of Florida M,D,O*

University of Guelph	M,D
The University of Manchester	M,D
University of Minnesota, Twin Cities Campus	M
University of New Hampshire	M,D,O
University of New Mexico	M,D*
University of Ottawa	M*
University of Pittsburgh	M,O*
University of San Francisco	M
University of Southern Mississippi	M,D
Walden University	M,D,O

INTERNATIONAL ECONOMICS

Claremont Graduate University	M,D,O
Eastern Michigan University	M
Fordham University	M,O
The Johns Hopkins University	M,D,O
The New School: A University	M,D
University of Denver	M,D,O
University of Miami	M,D*
University of New Mexico	M,D*
Valparaiso University	M
West Virginia University	M,D
Wilfrid Laurier University	M
Yale University	M*

INTERNATIONAL HEALTH

Arizona State University	M,D,O
Boston University	M,D*
Brandeis University	M,D
Central Michigan University	M,D,O
Duke University	M*
Emory University	M*
George Mason University	M,O*
Georgetown University	P,M,D
The George Washington University	M
Harvard University	M,D*
The Johns Hopkins University	M,D
Loma Linda University	M
Massachusetts School of Professional Psychology	M,D,O
Medical University of South Carolina	M
Morehouse School of Medicine	M
New York Medical College	O*
San Diego State University	M,D
Tufts University	M,D
TUI University	M,D,O
Tulane University	M,D*
Uniformed Services University of the Health Sciences	M,D*
University of Alberta	M,D
University of Colorado Denver	M
University of Denver	M,D,O
University of Michigan	M,D*
University of Minnesota, Twin Cities Campus	M,D
University of Pennsylvania	M*
University of Southern California	M*
University of South Florida	M,D*
University of Washington	M,D*
Yale University	M,D,O*

INTERNATIONAL TRADE POLICY

The George Washington University	M
Monterey Institute of International Studies	M

INTERNET AND INTERACTIVE MULTIMEDIA

Academy of Art University	M
Alfred University	M
Brooklyn College of the City University of New York	M,O
California State University, East Bay	M
Concordia University (Canada)	M,O
DePaul University	M,D
Duquesne University	M,O
Elon University	M
Full Sail University	M
George Mason University	M,D,O*
Georgetown University	M
Georgia Institute of Technology	M,D
Indiana University–Purdue University Indianapolis	M,D
Long Island University, C.W. Post Campus	M
Marlboro College	M
Mercy College	M,O
National University	M
New Mexico Highlands University	M
New York University	M
North Central College	M
Northwestern University	M*
Pace University	M,D,O
Polytechnic Institute of NYU	M,O
Pratt Institute	M*
Quinnipiac University	M
Robert Morris University	M,D
Rochester Institute of Technology	M,O
Sacred Heart University	M,O
San Diego State University	M
Savannah College of Art and Design	M,O
School of Visual Arts (NY)	M
Simon Fraser University	M,D
Southern Polytechnic State University	M,O
Stevens Institute of Technology	M,D,O
Towson University	M,D,O
Universidad Autonoma de Guadalajara	M,D
University of Advancing Technology	M
University of Denver	M,O
University of Florida	M,D*
University of Georgia	M
University of Miami	M*
University of Phoenix–Madison Campus	M
University of San Francisco	M
University of Southern California	M,D,O*
The University of Texas at Dallas	M,D*
University of the Sacred Heart	M,O
Virginia Commonwealth University	M
Virginia Polytechnic Institute and State University	M
Western Illinois University	M,O
Wilmington University	M

INTERNET ENGINEERING

New Jersey Institute of Technology	M
University of Denver	M,O
University of Georgia	M
University of San Francisco	M
Wilmington University	M

INVESTMENT MANAGEMENT

Alaska Pacific University	M,O
Boston University	M,D*
Concordia University (Canada)	M,D,O
Gannon University	O
The George Washington University	M,D
Hofstra University	M,O
The Johns Hopkins University	M,O
Lincoln University (CA)	M,D
Lynn University	M
Marywood University	M
Pace University	M
Quinnipiac University	M
St. John's University (NY)	M,O
Thomas Jefferson School of Law	M
The University of Iowa	M*
University of San Francisco	M
The University of Texas at Dallas	M*
University of Tulsa	M
University of Wisconsin–Madison	D*
University of Wisconsin–Milwaukee	M,D,O

ITALIAN

Boston College	M,D*
Brown University	D
Central Connecticut State University	M,O
Columbia University	M,D*
Cornell University	D*
Drew University	M
Florida State University	M
Graduate School and University Center of the City University of New York	M,D
Harvard University	M,D*
Hunter College of the City University of New York	M
Indiana University Bloomington	M,D*
Iona College	M
The Johns Hopkins University	D
McGill University	M,D
Middlebury College	M,D
Montclair State University	M,O
New York University	M,D
Northwestern University	D,O*
The Ohio State University	M,D
Queens College of the City University of New York	M
Rutgers, The State University of New Jersey, New Brunswick	M,D*
San Francisco State University	M
Stanford University	M,D
State University of New York at Binghamton	M
Stony Brook University, State University of New York	M
University at Albany, State University of New York	M
University of Alberta	M,D
University of California, Berkeley	D*
University of California, Los Angeles	M,D*
University of Chicago	M,D
University of Connecticut	M,D*
University of Illinois at Urbana–Champaign	M,D
The University of Manchester	M,D
University of Massachusetts Amherst	M*
University of Michigan	D*
The University of North Carolina at Chapel Hill	M,D*
University of Notre Dame	M*
University of Oregon	M
University of Pennsylvania	M,D*
University of Pittsburgh	M*
University of South Africa	M,D
The University of Tennessee	D
The University of Texas at Austin	M,D
University of Toronto	M,D
University of Victoria	M
University of Virginia	M
University of Washington	M,D*
University of Wisconsin–Madison	M,D*
University of Wisconsin–Milwaukee	M,O
Wayne State University	M*
Yale University	D*

JAPANESE

Arizona State University	M
Cornell University	M,D*
Eastern Michigan University	M,O
Harvard University	D*
Indiana University Bloomington	M,D*
Kent State University	M,D*
The Ohio State University	M,D
Portland State University	M
San Francisco State University	M
Soka University of America	O
Stanford University	M,D
University of Alberta	M
University of California, Berkeley	D*
University of California, Irvine	M,D*
University of Colorado Boulder	M,D*
University of Hawaii at Manoa	M,D,O
The University of Manchester	M,D
University of Massachusetts Amherst	M*
University of Oregon	M,D
University of Washington	M,D*
University of Wisconsin–Madison	M,D*
Washington University in St. Louis	M,D*

JEWISH STUDIES

American Jewish University	M
Brandeis University	M,D
Brooklyn College of the City University of New York	M
Brown University	D
Central Yeshiva Tomchei Tmimim-Lubavitch	M
Columbia University	M,D*
Concordia University (Canada)	M
Cornell University	M,D*
The Criswell College	P,M
Emory University	M*
Graduate Theological Union	M,D,O
Gratz College	M,O
Harvard University	M,D*
Hebrew College	M,O
Hebrew Union College–Jewish Institute of Religion (NY)	M
The Jewish Theological Seminary	M,D
Jewish University of America	P,D
Laura and Alvin Siegal College of Judaic Studies	M
Marquette University	M,D
McGill University	M
New York University	M,D,O

*M—master's degree; P—first professional degree; D—doctorate; O—other advanced degree; *—Close-Up and/or Display in one of the other books in this series*

Reconstructionist Rabbinical College	P,M,D,O
Rice University	D
Seton Hall University	M
Southern Evangelical Seminary	P,M,D,O
Spertus Institute of Jewish Studies	M,D
Telshe Yeshiva–Chicago	O
Touro College	M
Towson University	M,D,O
University of California, Berkeley	D*
University of California, San Diego	M,D*
University of Connecticut	M*
University of Maryland, College Park	M
University of Michigan	M,D,O*
The University of Montana	M
University of St. Michael's College	P,M,D,O
University of Wisconsin–Madison	M,D*
University of Wisconsin–Milwaukee	M,O
Yeshiva University	M,D*

JOURNALISM

American University	M
The American University in Cairo	M
Angelo State University	M
Arizona State University	M,D
Arkansas State University	M
Arkansas Tech University	M
Ball State University	M
Baylor University	M*
Bob Jones University	P,M,D,O
Boston University	M*
California State University, Fresno	M
California State University, Fullerton	M
California State University, Northridge	M
Carleton University	M,D
Columbia College Chicago	M
Columbia University	M,D,O*
Concordia University (Canada)	O
CUNY Graduate School of Journalism	M
DePaul University	M
Drexel University	M*
Emerson College	M
Florida Agricultural and Mechanical University	M
Florida Atlantic University	M,O
Full Sail University	M
Georgetown University	M,D
Harvard University	M,O*
Hofstra University	M
Indiana University Bloomington	M,D*
Iona College	M
Iowa State University of Science and Technology	M*
Kent State University	M*
Marquette University	M,O
Marshall University	M
Michigan State University	M
New York University	M,D,O
Northwestern University	M*
Ohio University	M,D*
Point Park University	M
Polytechnic Institute of NYU	M
Quinnipiac University	M
Regent University	M,D
Roosevelt University	M
School of the Art Institute of Chicago	M
South Dakota State University	M
Southern Illinois University Carbondale	D
Stanford University	M,D
Syracuse University	M*
Temple University	M*
Texas A&M University	M
Texas Christian University	M
Université Laval	O
The University of Alabama	M
University of Arkansas	M
University of Arkansas at Little Rock	M
The University of British Columbia	M
University of California, Berkeley	M*
University of Colorado Boulder	M,D*
University of Florida	M*
University of Georgia	M,D
University of Illinois at Springfield	M
University of Illinois at Urbana–Champaign	M
The University of Iowa	M*
The University of Kansas	M
University of Maryland, College Park	M,D
University of Memphis	M
University of Miami	M,D*
University of Mississippi	M
University of Missouri	M,D*
The University of Montana	M
University of Nebraska–Lincoln	M*
University of Nevada, Las Vegas	M
University of Nevada, Reno	M*
University of North Texas	M,O
University of Oklahoma	M*
University of Oregon	M,D
University of Puerto Rico, Río Piedras	M
University of South Carolina	M,D
University of Southern California	M*
The University of Tennessee	M,D
The University of Texas at Austin	M,D
The University of Western Ontario	M
University of Wisconsin–Madison	M,D*
Virginia Commonwealth University	M
West Virginia University	M,O

KINESIOLOGY AND MOVEMENT STUDIES

Acadia University	M
Arizona State University	M,D,O
A.T. Still University of Health Sciences	M,D
Auburn University	M,D,O
Barry University	M*
Bowling Green State University	M*
California Baptist University	M
California Polytechnic State University, San Luis Obispo	M
California State Polytechnic University, Pomona	M
California State University, Chico	M
California State University, Fresno	M
California State University, Long Beach	M
California State University, Los Angeles	M*
California State University, Northridge	M
California State University, San Bernardino	M
Canisius College	M
Columbia University	M,D*
Dalhousie University	M
Dallas Baptist University	M
Eastern Illinois University	M
Eastern Michigan University	M
Fresno Pacific University	M
Georgia College & State University	M
Georgia Southern University	M
Georgia State University	D
Hardin-Simmons University	M
Humboldt State University	M
Indiana University Bloomington	M,D*
Inter American University of Puerto Rico, San Germán Campus	M
Iowa State University of Science and Technology	M,D*
James Madison University	M
Kansas State University	M*
Lakehead University	M
Lamar University	M
Louisiana State University and Agricultural and Mechanical College	M,D
Louisiana State University in Shreveport	M
Marywood University	M
McGill University	M,D,O
McMaster University	M,D
Memorial University of Newfoundland	M
Michigan State University	M,D
Midwestern State University	M
Mississippi College	M
Mississippi State University	M
New York University	M,D,O
Northwestern University	D*
Old Dominion University	D
Oregon State University	M
Penn State University Park	M,D
Saint Mary's College of California	M
Sam Houston State University	M
San Diego State University	M
San Francisco State University	M
San Jose State University	M
Simon Fraser University	M,D
Sonoma State University	M
Southeastern Louisiana University	M
Southern Arkansas University–Magnolia	M
Southern Illinois University Edwardsville	M
Southwestern Oklahoma State University	M
Stephen F. Austin State University	M
Teachers College, Columbia University	M,D
Temple University	M,D*
Tennessee Technological University	M
Texas A&M University	M,D
Texas A&M University–Commerce	M,D
Texas A&M University–Corpus Christi	M,D
Texas A&M University–Kingsville	M
Texas A&M University–San Antonio	M
Texas Christian University	M
Texas Woman's University	M,D
Towson University	M
Université de Montréal	M,D,O
Université de Sherbrooke	M,O
Université du Québec à Montréal	M
Université Laval	M,D
The University of Alabama	M,D
University of Arkansas	M,D
The University of British Columbia	M,D
University of Calgary	M,D
University of Central Arkansas	M
University of Colorado Boulder	M,D*
University of Delaware	M,D*
University of Florida	M,D*
University of Georgia	M,D
University of Hawaii at Manoa	M,D
University of Houston	M,D
University of Illinois at Chicago	M,D
University of Illinois at Urbana–Champaign	M,D
University of Kentucky	M,D*
University of Lethbridge	M,D
University of Maine	M
University of Manitoba	M
University of Maryland, College Park	M,D
University of Massachusetts Amherst	M,D*
University of Medicine and Dentistry of New Jersey	M,D
University of Michigan	M,D*
University of Minnesota, Twin Cities Campus	M,D
University of Nevada, Las Vegas	M
University of New Hampshire	M
The University of North Carolina at Chapel Hill	M,D*
The University of North Carolina at Charlotte	M
University of North Dakota	M
University of Northern Iowa	M
University of North Texas	M
University of Ottawa	M*
University of Regina	M,D
University of Saskatchewan	M,D,O
University of Southern California	M,D*
The University of Tennessee	M,D
The University of Texas at Austin	M,D
The University of Texas at El Paso	M
The University of Texas at San Antonio	M*
The University of Texas at Tyler	M
The University of Texas of the Permian Basin	M
The University of Texas–Pan American	M
University of the Incarnate Word	M,D
University of Victoria	M
University of Virginia	M,D
University of Waterloo	M,D
The University of Western Ontario	M,D
University of Windsor	M
University of Wisconsin–Madison	M,D*
University of Wisconsin–Milwaukee	M
University of Wyoming	M
Washington University in St. Louis	D*
Wayne State University	M*
West Chester University of Pennsylvania	M,O
Western Illinois University	M
Wilfrid Laurier University	M
York University	M,D*

LANDSCAPE ARCHITECTURE

Arizona State University	M,D
Auburn University	M
Ball State University	M

California State Polytechnic University, Pomona M
Chatham University M
City College of the City University of New York M
Clemson University M
Colorado State University M,D
Columbia University M*
Conway School of Landscape Design M
Cornell University M*
Florida Agricultural and Mechanical University M
Florida International University M
Harvard University M,D*
Illinois Institute of Technology M,D
Iowa State University of Science and Technology M*
Kansas State University M*
Louisiana State University and Agricultural and Mechanical College M
Mississippi State University M
Morgan State University M
North Carolina State University M*
The Ohio State University M,D
Oklahoma State University M,D*
Penn State University Park M
Polytechnic University of Puerto Rico M
Pontificia Universidad Catolica Madre y Maestra M
Rhode Island School of Design M
State University of New York College of Environmental Science and Forestry M
Temple University M*
Texas A&M University M,D
Texas Tech University M*
The University of Arizona M
The University of British Columbia M
University of California, Berkeley M,D,O*
University of Colorado Denver M
University of Florida M*
University of Georgia M
University of Guelph M
University of Idaho M
University of Illinois at Urbana–Champaign M,D
The University of Manchester M,D
University of Manitoba M
University of Maryland, College Park M
University of Massachusetts Amherst M*
University of Michigan M,D*
University of Minnesota, Twin Cities Campus M
University of New Mexico M*
University of Oklahoma M*
University of Oregon M
University of Pennsylvania M,O*
The University of Tennessee M
The University of Texas at Arlington M
The University of Texas at Austin M,D
University of Virginia M
University of Washington M*
University of Wisconsin–Madison M*
Utah State University M
Virginia Polytechnic Institute and State University M,D,O
Washington State University M,D
Washington State University Spokane M,D

LATIN AMERICAN STUDIES

American University M,O
Arizona State University M,D,O
Boricua College M
Brown University M,D
California State University, Long Beach M
California State University, Los Angeles M*
Centro de Estudios Avanzados de Puerto Rico y el Caribe M,D
Cleveland State University M
Columbia University M,O*
Cornell University M,D*
Duke University M,D*
Florida International University M
Fordham University M,O
Georgetown University M
The George Washington University M
Georgia State University M,D,O
Indiana University Bloomington M*
La Salle University M
Michigan State University D
New York University M,D,O
Ohio University M*
San Diego State University M
Simon Fraser University M
Syracuse University O*
Tulane University M,D*
University at Albany, State University of New York M,O
University at Buffalo, the State University of New York M*
The University of Arizona M
University of California, Berkeley M*
University of California, Los Angeles M*
University of California, San Diego M*
University of California, Santa Barbara M
University of Central Florida M,D,O
University of Chicago M
University of Connecticut M*
University of Florida M,D,O*
University of Illinois at Urbana–Champaign M
The University of Kansas M,O
The University of Manchester M,D
University of Massachusetts Dartmouth M,D
University of Miami M*
University of New Mexico M,D*
The University of North Carolina at Chapel Hill M,D,O*
The University of North Carolina at Charlotte M,O
University of Notre Dame M*
University of Pittsburgh O*
University of Southern California D*
University of South Florida M,D*
The University of Texas at Austin M,D
The University of Texas at Dallas M,D*
The University of Texas at El Paso M,O
University of Wisconsin–Madison M,D*
Vanderbilt University M*
West Virginia University M,D
Yale University D*

LAW

Albany Law School P,M
American University P,M,O
The American University in Cairo M
The American University of Paris M
Appalachian School of Law P
Arizona State University P,M
Atlanta's John Marshall Law School P,M
Ave Maria School of Law P
Barry University P*
Baylor University P*
Boston College P*
Boston University P,M*
Brigham Young University P,M*
Brooklyn Law School P
California Western School of Law P,M
Campbell University P
Capital University P,M
Case Western Reserve University P,M*
The Catholic University of America P
Central European University M,D
Champlain College M
Chapman University P,M
Charlotte School of Law P
City University of New York School of Law at Queens College P
Cleveland State University P,M,O
The College of William and Mary P,M
Columbia University P,M,D*
Concord Law School P
Cornell University P,M,D*
Creighton University P,M,O
Dalhousie University M,D
DePaul University P,M
Drake University P
Duke University P,M,D*
Duquesne University P,M
Elon University P
Emory University P,M,O*
Facultad de derecho Eugenio María de Hostos P
Faulkner University P
Florida Agricultural and Mechanical University P
Florida Coastal School of Law P
Florida International University P
Florida State University P,M
Fordham University P,M
Franklin Pierce Law Center P,M,O
Friends University M
George Mason University P,M*
Georgetown University P,M,D
The George Washington University P,M,D
Georgia State University P
Golden Gate University P,M,D
Gonzaga University P
Hamline University P,M
Harvard University P,M,D*
Hofstra University P,M
Howard University P,M
Humphreys College P
Illinois Institute of Technology P,M
Indiana University Bloomington P,M,D,O*
Indiana University–Purdue University Indianapolis P,M,D
Instituto Tecnológico y de Estudios Superiores de Monterrey, Campus Ciudad de México P
Inter American University of Puerto Rico School of Law P
John F. Kennedy University P
John Marshall Law School P,M
The Judge Advocate General's School, U.S. Army M
Kaplan University, Davenport Campus M
Lewis & Clark College P,M
Liberty University P
Lincoln Memorial University P
Louisiana State University and Agricultural and Mechanical College M,O
Loyola Marymount University P,M
Loyola University Chicago P,M,D
Loyola University New Orleans P,M
Marquette University P
Massachusetts School of Law at Andover P
McGill University P,M,D,O
Mercer University P
Michigan State University College of Law P,M
Mississippi College P,O
Montclair State University M,O
New England LawûBoston P,M
New York Law School P,M
New York University P,M,D,O
North Carolina Central University P
Northeastern University P
Northern Illinois University P
Northern Kentucky University P
Northwestern University P,M,O*
Nova Southeastern University P,M,O*
Ohio Northern University P,M
The Ohio State University P,M
Oklahoma City University P
Pace University P,M,D
Park University M
Penn State Dickinson School of Law P,M
Pepperdine University P
Pontifical Catholic University of Puerto Rico P
Pontificia Universidad Católica Madre y Maestra M
Queen's University at Kingston P,M
Quinnipiac University P,M
Regent University P,M
Roger Williams University P
Rutgers, The State University of New Jersey, Camden P
Rutgers, The State University of New Jersey, Newark P*
St. John's University (NY) P
Saint Joseph's University M,O
Saint Louis University P,M
St. Mary's University (United States) P
St. Thomas University P,M
Samford University P,M
San Joaquin College of Law P
Santa Clara University P,M,O
Seattle University P,O
Seton Hall University P,M
Southern Illinois University Carbondale P,M
Southern Methodist University P,M,D
Southern University and Agricultural and Mechanical College P
South Texas College of Law P
Southwestern Law School P,M
Stanford University P,M,D
Stetson University P,M
Suffolk University P,M

*M—master's degree; P—first professional degree; D—doctorate; O—other advanced degree; *—Close-Up and/or Display in one of the other books in this series*

Institution	Degrees
Syracuse University	P*
Taft Law School	P,M
Temple University	P,M,D*
Texas Southern University	P
Texas Tech University	P*
Texas Wesleyan University	P
Thomas Jefferson School of Law	P,M
Thomas M. Cooley Law School	P,M
Touro College	P,M
Trinity International University	P
Tufts University	M,D
Tulane University	P,M,D*
Universidad Autonoma de Guadalajara	M,D
Universidad Central del Este	P
Universidad Iberoamericana	P,M
Université de Montréal	P,M,D,O
Université de Sherbrooke	P,M,D,O
Université du Québec à Montréal	O
Université Laval	M,D,O
University at Buffalo, the State University of New York	P,M*
The University of Akron	P,M
The University of Alabama	P,M
University of Alberta	P,M
The University of Arizona	P,M
University of Arkansas	P,M
University of Arkansas at Little Rock	P
University of Atlanta	P,M,D,O
University of Baltimore	M
The University of British Columbia	M,D
University of Calgary	P,M,O
University of California, Berkeley	P,M,D*
University of California, Davis	P,M
University of California, Hastings College of the Law	P,M
University of California, Irvine	P*
University of California, Los Angeles	P,M,D*
University of California, San Diego	M*
University of Chicago	P,M,D
University of Cincinnati	P
University of Colorado Boulder	P*
University of Connecticut	P*
University of Dayton	P,M
University of Denver	P,M
University of Detroit Mercy	P
University of Florida	P,M,D*
University of Georgia	P,M
University of Hawaii at Manoa	P,M,O
University of Houston	P,M
University of Idaho	P
University of Illinois at Urbana–Champaign	P,M,D
The University of Iowa	P,M*
The University of Kansas	P
University of Kentucky	P*
University of La Verne	P
University of Louisville	P
The University of Manchester	M,D
University of Manitoba	M
University of Maryland, Baltimore	P,M
University of Maryland, College Park	
University of Massachusetts Dartmouth	P
University of Memphis	P
University of Miami	P,M*
University of Michigan	P,M,D*
University of Minnesota, Twin Cities Campus	P,M
University of Mississippi	P
University of Missouri	P,M*
University of Missouri–Kansas City	P,M*
The University of Montana	P
University of Nebraska–Lincoln	P,M*
University of Nevada, Las Vegas	P
University of New Brunswick Fredericton	P
University of New Mexico	P*
The University of North Carolina at Chapel Hill	P*
University of North Dakota	P
University of Notre Dame	P,M,D*
University of Oklahoma	P,M*
University of Oregon	P,M
University of Ottawa	M,D*
University of Pennsylvania	P,M,D*
University of Pittsburgh	P,M,O*
University of Puerto Rico, Río Piedras	P,M
University of Richmond	P
University of St. Thomas (MN)	P
University of San Diego	P,M,O
University of San Francisco	P,M
University of Saskatchewan	P,M
University of South Africa	M,D
University of South Carolina	P
The University of South Dakota	P
University of Southern California	P,M*
University of Southern Maine	P
The University of Tennessee	P
The University of Texas at Austin	P,M,O
The University of Texas at Dallas	M,D*
University of the District of Columbia	P,M
University of the Pacific	P,M,D
The University of Toledo	P
University of Toronto	P,M,D
University of Tulsa	P,M,O
University of Utah	P,M*
University of Victoria	P,M,D
University of Virginia	P,M,D,O
University of Washington	P,M,D*
The University of Western Ontario	P,M,O
University of Wisconsin–Madison	P,M,D*
University of Wyoming	P
Valparaiso University	P,M
Vanderbilt University	P,M,D*
Vermont Law School	P,O
Villanova University	P
Wake Forest University	P,M,D
Walden University	M,D,O
Washburn University	P
Washington and Lee University	P,M
Washington University in St. Louis	P,M,D*
Wayne State University	P,M,D*
Western New England University	P,M
Western State University College of Law	P
West Virginia University	P
Whittier College	P,M
Widener University	P,M,D
Willamette University	P,M
William Mitchell College of Law	P,M
Yale University	P,M,D*
Yeshiva University	P,M*
York University	P,M,D*

LEGAL AND JUSTICE STUDIES

Institution	Degrees
American Public University System	M
American University	M,D,O
Arizona State University	P,M,D,O
Boston University	M*
Brock University	M
California University of Pennsylvania	M
Capital University	M
Carleton University	M,O
Case Western Reserve University	P,M*
The Catholic University of America	D,O
Central European University	M,D
College of the Humanities and Sciences, Harrison Middleton University	M,D
Georgetown University	P,M,D
The George Washington University	M,O
Golden Gate University	P,M,D
Governors State University	M
Harvard University	P*
Hodges University	M
Hofstra University	P,M
Hollins University	M,O
John Jay College of Criminal Justice of the City University of New York	M,D
John Marshall Law School	P,M
Kaplan University, Davenport Campus	M,O
Loyola University Chicago	M,O
Marlboro College	M
Marygrove College	M
Marymount University	M,O
Michigan State University College of Law	P,M
Mississippi College	M,O
Montclair State University	O
New York University	M,D
Northeastern University	M,D
Nova Southeastern University	M,O*
Pace University	P,M,D
Prairie View A&M University	M,D
Queen's University at Kingston	M,D
Regent University	P,M
Rutgers, The State University of New Jersey, New Brunswick	D*
St. John's University (NY)	M
Salve Regina University	M
San Francisco State University	M
Southern Illinois University Carbondale	M
State University of New York at Binghamton	M,D
Taft Law School	P,M
Temple University	P,M,D*
Texas State University–San Marcos	M
Thomas Jefferson School of Law	M
TUI University	M,D,O
Universidad Autonoma de Guadalajara	M,D
Université Laval	O
University of Baltimore	M
University of Calgary	M,O
University of California, Berkeley	D*
University of California, San Diego	M*
University of Charleston	M
University of Denver	M,O
University of Illinois at Springfield	M
University of Mississippi	M
University of Nebraska–Lincoln	M*
University of Nevada, Reno	M,D*
University of New Hampshire	M
University of Oklahoma	M,O*
University of Pennsylvania	M,D*
University of Pittsburgh	M,O*
University of San Diego	P,M,O
University of the District of Columbia	P,M
University of the Pacific	P,M,D
University of the Sacred Heart	M
University of Washington	P,M,D*
University of Windsor	M
University of Wisconsin–Madison	M,D*
Valparaiso University	O
Vermont Law School	M,O
Weber State University	M
Webster University	M
West Virginia University	M
Whittier College	P,M
Wilfrid Laurier University	D

LEISURE STUDIES

Institution	Degrees
Bowling Green State University	M*
California State University, Long Beach	M
Central Michigan University	M
The College at Brockport, State University of New York	M
Dalhousie University	M
East Carolina University	M
Gallaudet University	M,D,O
Howard University	M
Indiana University Bloomington	M,D,O*
Murray State University	M
Penn State University Park	M,D
Prescott College	M
San Francisco State University	M
Southeast Missouri State University	M
Southern Connecticut State University	M
Temple University	M*
Texas State University–San Marcos	M
Universidad Metropolitana	M
Université du Québec à Trois-Rivières	M,O
University of Connecticut	M,D*
University of Georgia	M,D,O
University of Illinois at Urbana–Champaign	M,D
The University of Iowa	M*
University of Memphis	M
University of Minnesota, Twin Cities Campus	M,D
University of Mississippi	M,D
University of Nevada, Las Vegas	M
University of Northern Iowa	M,D
University of North Texas	M,O
University of South Alabama	M
University of Southern Mississippi	M,D
The University of Tennessee	M,D
University of Utah	M,D*
University of Victoria	M
University of Waterloo	M,D
University of West Florida	M

LIBERAL STUDIES

Institution	Degrees
Abilene Christian University	M
Alaska Pacific University	M
Albertus Magnus College	M
Alvernia University	M

Antioch University Midwest M
Arizona State University M
Armstrong Atlantic State University M
Auburn University Montgomery M
Baker University M
Barry University M*
Bradley University M
Brooklyn College of the City University of New York M
California State University, Sacramento M
Cardinal Stritch University M
Clark University M
Clayton State University M
The College at Brockport, State University of New York M
College of Notre Dame of Maryland M
College of Staten Island of the City University of New York M
The Colorado College M
Columbia University M*
Concordia University Chicago M
Converse College M
Creighton University M
Dallas Baptist University M
Dartmouth College M
Dowling College M
Duke University M*
Duquesne University M
East Tennessee State University M,O
Excelsior College M
Faulkner University M
Florida Atlantic University M
Florida International University M
Fordham University M
Fort Hays State University M
Georgetown University M,D
Graduate School and University Center of the City University of New York M
Hamline University M,O
Harvard University M,O*
Henderson State University M
Hollins University M,O
Houston Baptist University M
Indiana University Kokomo M
Indiana University–Purdue University Fort Wayne M
Indiana University–Purdue University Indianapolis M,D,O
Indiana University South Bend M
Indiana University Southeast M
Jacksonville State University M
The Johns Hopkins University M,O
Kean University M
Kent State University M*
Lake Forest College M
Lock Haven University of Pennsylvania M
Louisiana State University and Agricultural and Mechanical College M
Louisiana State University in Shreveport M
Loyola University Maryland M
Madonna University M
Manhattanville College M*
McDaniel College M
Metropolitan State University M
Minnesota State University Moorhead M
Mississippi College M
Monmouth University M
Nazareth College of Rochester M
The New School: A University M
North Carolina State University M*
North Central College M
Northern Arizona University M
Northern Kentucky University M,O
Northwestern University M*
Oakland University M
Occidental College M
Ohio Dominican University M
Oklahoma City University M
Queens College of the City University of New York M
Ramapo College of New Jersey M
Reed College M
Rice University M
Rollins College M
Rutgers, The State University of New Jersey, Camden M
St. Edward's University M,O
St. John's College (MD) M
St. John's College (NM) M
St. John's University (NY) M
St. Norbert College M
San Diego State University M
Simon Fraser University M
Skidmore College M
Southern Methodist University M
Spring Hill College M
State University of New York at Plattsburgh M
State University of New York Empire State College M
Stony Brook University, State University of New York M,O
Tarleton State University M
Temple University M*
Texas Christian University M
Thomas Edison State College M
Towson University M
Tulane University M*
University at Albany, State University of New York M
University of Arkansas at Little Rock M
University of Delaware M*
University of Detroit Mercy M
University of Maine M
University of Memphis M
University of Miami M*
University of Michigan–Dearborn M
University of Minnesota, Duluth M
University of New Hampshire M
The University of North Carolina at Asheville M
The University of North Carolina at Charlotte M,O
The University of North Carolina at Greensboro M
The University of North Carolina Wilmington M
University of Oklahoma M*
University of Pennsylvania M*
University of St. Thomas (TX) M*
University of Southern Indiana M
The University of Texas at El Paso M
The University of Toledo M
University of Wisconsin–Milwaukee M
Ursuline College M
Utica College M
Valparaiso University M,O
Vanderbilt University M*
Villanova University M,O
Virginia Polytechnic Institute and State University M,O
Wake Forest University M
Washburn University M
Wesleyan University M,O*
Western Illinois University M
West Virginia University M
Wichita State University M
Widener University M
Winthrop University M

LIBRARY SCIENCE

Appalachian State University M,O
Azusa Pacific University M,O
The Catholic University of America M
Chicago State University M
Clarion University of Pennsylvania M,O
Dalhousie University M
Dominican University M,D,O
Drexel University M,D,O*
East Carolina University M,O
Eastern Kentucky University M
Emporia State University M,D,O
Florida State University M,D,O
Georgia College & State University M,O
Indiana University Bloomington M,D,O*
Indiana University–Purdue University Indianapolis M
Instituto Tecnológico y de Estudios Superiores de Monterrey, Campus Irapuato M,D
Inter American University of Puerto Rico, Barranquitas Campus M
Inter American University of Puerto Rico, San Germán Campus M
Kent State University M*
Kutztown University of Pennsylvania M,O
Long Island University, C.W. Post Campus M,D,O
Long Island University, Westchester Graduate Campus M
Louisiana State University and Agricultural and Mechanical College M
Mansfield University of Pennsylvania M
Marywood University M,O
McDaniel College M
McGill University M,D,O
McNeese State University M,O
North Carolina Central University M
Old Dominion University M
Olivet Nazarene University M
Pratt Institute M,O*
Queens College of the City University of New York M,O
Rowan University M
Rutgers, The State University of New Jersey, New Brunswick M,D*
St. Catherine University M
St. John's University (NY) M,O
Sam Houston State University M
San Jose State University M,D
Simmons College M,D
Southern Arkansas University–Magnolia M
Southern Connecticut State University M,O
Syracuse University M,O*
Tennessee Technological University M
Texas Woman's University M,D
Trevecca Nazarene University M
Universidad del Turabo M,O
Université de Montréal M,D
University at Buffalo, the State University of New York M,O*
The University of Alabama M,D
University of Alberta M
The University of Arizona M,D
The University of British Columbia M,D
University of California, Los Angeles M,D,O*
University of Central Arkansas M
University of Central Missouri M,D,O
University of Denver M,D,O
University of Hawaii at Manoa M,O
University of Houston–Clear Lake M
University of Illinois at Urbana–Champaign M,D,O
The University of Iowa M*
University of Kentucky M*
University of Maryland, College Park
University of Michigan M,D*
University of Missouri M,D,O*
The University of North Carolina at Chapel Hill M,D,O*
The University of North Carolina at Greensboro M
University of Northern Colorado M
University of North Texas M,D
University of Oklahoma M,O*
University of Pittsburgh M,D,O*
University of Puerto Rico, Río Piedras M,O
University of Rhode Island M
University of South Carolina M,D,O
University of Southern Mississippi M
University of South Florida M*
University of Toronto M,D,O
University of Washington M,D*
The University of Western Ontario M,D
University of Wisconsin–Eau Claire M
University of Wisconsin–Madison M,D*
University of Wisconsin–Milwaukee M,D,O
Valdosta State University M
Valley City State University M
Wayne State University M,O*
Wright State University M

LIGHTING DESIGN

The New School: A University M
New York School of Interior Design M
Rensselaer Polytechnic Institute M,D
University of Washington M,D,O*

LIMNOLOGY

Baylor University M,D*
Cornell University D*
University of Alaska Fairbanks M,D
University of Florida M,D*
University of Wisconsin–Madison M,D*

LINGUISTICS

Arizona State University M,D,O
Ball State University M,D

*M—master's degree; P—first professional degree; D—doctorate; O—other advanced degree; *—Close-Up and/or Display in one of the other books in this series*

Biola University	M,D,O
Boston College	M*
Boston University	M,D*
Brandeis University	M
Brigham Young University	M,O*
Brown University	M,D
California State University, Fresno	M
California State University, Fullerton	M
California State University, Long Beach	M
California State University, Northridge	M
Carleton University	M
Carnegie Mellon University	D*
Case Western Reserve University	M*
Cleveland State University	M
Concordia University (Canada)	M,O
Cornell University	M,D*
Eastern Michigan University	M
Florida Atlantic University	M
Florida International University	M
Gallaudet University	M,D,O
George Mason University	M,D,O*
Georgetown University	M,D,O
Georgia State University	M,D
Graduate Institute of Applied Linguistics	M,O
Graduate School and University Center of the City University of New York	M,D
Harvard University	D*
Hofstra University	M,D
Indiana State University	M,O
Indiana University Bloomington	M,D*
Indiana University of Pennsylvania	M,D
Instituto Tecnologico de Santo Domingo	M,O
Louisiana State University and Agricultural and Mechanical College	M,D
Massachusetts Institute of Technology	D
McGill University	M,D
Memorial University of Newfoundland	M,D
Michigan State University	M,D
Midwestern Baptist Theological Seminary	P,M,D,O
Montclair State University	M,O
New York University	M,D,O
Northeastern Illinois University	M
Northern Arizona University	M,D,O
Northwestern University	M,D*
Oakland University	M,O
The Ohio State University	M,D
Ohio University	M*
Old Dominion University	M
Penn State University Park	M,D
Purdue University	M,D
Queens College of the City University of New York	M
Rice University	M,D
Rutgers, The State University of New Jersey, New Brunswick	D*
San Diego State University	M,O
San Francisco State University	M
San Jose State University	M,O
Simon Fraser University	M,D
Southern Illinois University Carbondale	M
Stanford University	M,D
Stony Brook University, State University of New York	M,D
Syracuse University	M*
Teachers College, Columbia University	M,D
Temple University	M,D*
Texas Tech University	M*
Trinity Western University	M
Universidad de las Américas–Puebla	M
Université de Montréal	M,D,O
Université de Sherbrooke	M,D
Université du Québec à Chicoutimi	M
Université du Québec à Montréal	M,D
Université Laval	M,D
University at Buffalo, the State University of New York	M,D*
University of Alaska Fairbanks	M
University of Alberta	M,D
The University of Arizona	M,D
The University of British Columbia	M,D
University of Calgary	M,D
University of California, Berkeley	D*
University of California, Davis	M,D
University of California, Los Angeles	M,D*
University of California, San Diego	D*
University of California, Santa Barbara	M,D
University of California, Santa Cruz	M,D
University of Chicago	M,D
University of Colorado Boulder	M,D*
University of Colorado Denver	M
University of Connecticut	M,D*
University of Delaware	M,D*
University of Florida	M,D,O*
University of Georgia	M,D
University of Hawaii at Manoa	M,D
University of Houston	M,D
University of Illinois at Chicago	M
University of Illinois at Urbana–Champaign	M,D
The University of Iowa	M,D*
The University of Kansas	M,D
The University of Manchester	M,D
University of Manitoba	M,D
University of Maryland, Baltimore County	M
University of Maryland, College Park	M,D
University of Massachusetts Amherst	M,D*
University of Massachusetts Boston	M
University of Memphis	M,D,O
University of Michigan	D*
University of Minnesota, Twin Cities Campus	M,D
University of Missouri–St. Louis	M,O
The University of Montana	M,D
University of New Hampshire	M,D
University of New Mexico	M,D*
The University of North Carolina at Chapel Hill	M,D*
University of North Dakota	M
University of Oregon	M,D
University of Ottawa	M,D*
University of Pennsylvania	M,D*
University of Pittsburgh	M,D*
University of Puerto Rico, Río Piedras	M,D
University of Regina	M
University of Rochester	
University of South Africa	M,D
University of South Carolina	M,D,O
University of Southern California	M,D*
University of South Florida	M*
The University of Tennessee	D
The University of Texas at Arlington	M,D
The University of Texas at Austin	M,D
The University of Texas at El Paso	M,O
University of Toronto	M,D
University of Utah	M,D*
University of Victoria	M,D
University of Virginia	M
University of Washington	M,D*
University of Wisconsin–Madison	M,D*
University of Wisconsin–Milwaukee	M,D,O
Wayne State University	M*
West Virginia University	M
Yale University	D*
York University	M,D*

LOGISTICS

Air Force Institute of Technology	M,D
American Public University System	M
Benedictine University	M
California State University, Long Beach	M
Case Western Reserve University	M,D*
Central Connecticut State University	M,O
Central Michigan University	M,O
Colorado Technical University Colorado Springs	M,D
East Carolina University	M,D,O
Embry-Riddle Aeronautical University–Worldwide	M
Florida Institute of Technology	M
George Mason University	M*
Georgia College & State University	M
Georgia Southern University	D
HEC Montreal	M
Kaplan University, Davenport Campus	M
Maine Maritime Academy	M,O
Massachusetts Institute of Technology	M,D
North Dakota State University	M,D
The Ohio State University	M
Polytechnic University of Puerto Rico, Miami Campus	M
Pontifical Catholic University of Puerto Rico	O
Pontificia Universidad Catolica Madre y Maestra	M
Stevens Institute of Technology	M,D,O
TUI University	M,D
Universidad del Turabo	M
University at Buffalo, the State University of New York	M,D,O*
The University of Alabama in Huntsville	M
University of Alaska Anchorage	M,O
University of Dallas	M
University of Houston	M
University of Louisville	M,D,O
University of Minnesota, Twin Cities Campus	D
University of Missouri–St. Louis	M,D,O
University of New Hampshire	M,D
University of North Florida	M
University of South Africa	M,D
The University of Tennessee	M,D
The University of Texas at Arlington	M
University of Washington	O*
Virginia International University	M,O
Wilmington University	M
Wright State University	M

MANAGEMENT INFORMATION SYSTEMS

Adelphi University	M*
Air Force Institute of Technology	M
Alliant International University–San Diego	M,D
American InterContinental University Atlanta	M
American InterContinental University London	M
American International College	M
American Public University System	M
American Sentinel University	M
American University	M
The American University in Cairo	M
Argosy University, Atlanta	M,D*
Argosy University, Chicago	M,D*
Argosy University, Dallas	M,D,O*
Argosy University, Denver	M,D*
Argosy University, Hawai'i	M,D,O*
Argosy University, Inland Empire	M,D*
Argosy University, Los Angeles	M,D*
Argosy University, Nashville	M,D*
Argosy University, Orange County	M,D,O*
Argosy University, Phoenix	M,D*
Argosy University, Salt Lake City	M,D*
Argosy University, San Diego	M,D*
Argosy University, San Francisco Bay Area	M,D*
Argosy University, Sarasota	M,D,O*
Argosy University, Schaumburg	M,D,O*
Argosy University, Seattle	M,D*
Argosy University, Tampa	M,D*
Argosy University, Twin Cities	M,D*
Argosy University, Washington DC	M,D,O*
Arizona State University	M,D
Arkansas State University	M,O
Aspen University	M,O
Auburn University	M,D
Avila University	M
Baker College Center for Graduate Studies—Online	M,D
Barry University	O*
Baylor University	M*
Bay Path College	M
Bellarmine University	M
Bellevue University	M
Benedictine University	M
Bernard M. Baruch College of the City University of New York	M,D
Boise State University	M
Boston University	M*
Bowie State University	M,O
Brandeis University	M,O
Brigham Young University	M*

Institution	Degrees
Broadview University	M
California Intercontinental University	M,D
California Lutheran University	M,O
California State Polytechnic University, Pomona	M
California State University, East Bay	M
California State University, Fullerton	M
California State University, Los Angeles	M*
California State University, Monterey Bay	M
California State University, Sacramento	M
Capella University	M,D,O
Capitol College	M
Carnegie Mellon University	M,D*
Case Western Reserve University	M,D*
Central European University	M
Central Michigan University	M,O
Charleston Southern University	M
City University of Seattle	M,O
Claremont Graduate University	M,D,O
Clark University	M
Cleveland State University	M,D
College of Charleston	M
The College of St. Scholastica	M,O
Colorado State University	M
Colorado Technical University Sioux Falls	M
Concordia University Wisconsin	M
Creighton University	M
Daemen College	M
Dalhousie University	M
Dallas Baptist University	M
DePaul University	M,D
DeSales University	M
DeVry University	M
Dowling College	M,O
Duquesne University	M
East Carolina University	M,D,O
Eastern Michigan University	M,O
East Tennessee State University	M
Ellis University	M
Emory University	D*
Endicott College	M
Fairfield University	M,O
Fairleigh Dickinson University, Metropolitan Campus	M,O
Ferris State University	M
Florida Agricultural and Mechanical University	M
Florida Atlantic University	M
Florida Institute of Technology	M
Florida International University	M
Florida State University	M,D
Fordham University	M
Franklin Pierce University	M,D,O
Friends University	M
George Mason University	M,D,O*
The George Washington University	M,D
Georgia College & State University	M
Georgia Institute of Technology	M,D,O
Georgia State University	M,D
Globe University	M
Golden Gate University	M,D,O
Goldey-Beacom College	M
Governors State University	M
Graduate School and University Center of the City University of New York	D
Grand Canyon University	M
Grand Valley State University	M
Grantham University	M
Harrisburg University of Science and Technology	M
Hawai'i Pacific University	M*
HEC Montreal	M
Hodges University	M
Hofstra University	M,O
Holy Family University	M*
Hood College	M
Howard University	M
Idaho State University	M,O
Illinois Institute of Technology	M,D
Illinois State University	M
Indiana University Bloomington	M,D,O*
Indiana University South Bend	M
Instituto Tecnológico y de Estudios Superiores de Monterrey, Campus Central de Veracruz	M
Instituto Tecnológico y de Estudios Superiores de Monterrey, Campus Ciudad de México	M,D
Instituto Tecnológico y de Estudios Superiores de Monterrey, Campus Ciudad Juárez	M
Instituto Tecnológico y de Estudios Superiores de Monterrey, Campus Ciudad Obregón	M
Instituto Tecnológico y de Estudios Superiores de Monterrey, Campus Estado de México	M,D
Instituto Tecnológico y de Estudios Superiores de Monterrey, Campus Irapuato	M,D
Instituto Tecnológico y de Estudios Superiores de Monterrey, Campus Laguna	M
Inter American University of Puerto Rico, Aguadilla Campus	M
Inter American University of Puerto Rico, Metropolitan Campus	M
Inter American University of Puerto Rico, San Germán Campus	M,D
Iowa State University of Science and Technology	M*
John Marshall Law School	P,M
The Johns Hopkins University	M,O
Kaplan University, Davenport Campus	M
Kent State University	D*
Kentucky State University	M
Lawrence Technological University	M,D
Lewis University	M
Lincoln University (CA)	M,D
Lindenwood University	M,O
Long Island University, C.W. Post Campus	M,O
Louisiana State University and Agricultural and Mechanical College	M,D
Loyola University Chicago	M
Loyola University Maryland	M
Marist College	M,O
Marquette University	M
Marymount University	M,O
Marywood University	M
McGill University	M,D,O
McMaster University	D
Metropolitan State University	M,D,O
Michigan State University	M,D
Middle Tennessee State University	M
Minnesota State University Mankato	M,O
Minot State University	M
Mississippi State University	M,D
Missouri State University	M
Missouri Western State University	M
Montclair State University	M,O
Morehead State University	M
National University	M
Naval Postgraduate School	M,O
New Jersey Institute of Technology	M,D
Newman University	M
New Mexico Highlands University	M
New York Institute of Technology	M,O
New York University	M,D,O
North Central College	M
Northeastern University	M,D
Northern Illinois University	M
Northwestern University	M*
Northwest Missouri State University	M
Norwich University	M
Notre Dame College (OH)	M,O
Nova Southeastern University	M,D*
Oakland University	M,O
The Ohio State University	M,D
Oklahoma City University	M
Oklahoma State University	M,D*
Old Dominion University	M
Our Lady of the Lake University of San Antonio	M
Pace University	M
Pacific States University	M,D
Park University	M
Polytechnic Institute of NYU	M,D,O
Polytechnic Institute of NYU, Westchester Graduate Center	M,O
Polytechnic University of Puerto Rico	M
Pontifical Catholic University of Puerto Rico	M,O
Prairie View A&M University	M,D
Quinnipiac University	M
Regent's American College London	M
Regis University	M,O
Rivier College	M
Robert Morris University	M,D
Robert Morris University Illinois	M
Rochester Institute of Technology	M
Roosevelt University	M
Rowan University	M
Rutgers, The State University of New Jersey, Newark	D*
Sacred Heart University	M,O
St. Edward's University	M,O
St. John's University (NY)	M,O
Saint Joseph's University	M
Saint Peter's College	M
San Diego State University	M
San Jose State University	M
Santa Clara University	M
Schiller International University (United States)	M
Schiller International University (Germany)	M
Schiller International University (United Kingdom)	M
Seattle Pacific University	M
Southeastern Louisiana University	M
Southeastern Oklahoma State University	M
Southern Illinois University Edwardsville	M
Southern Methodist University	M
Southern New Hampshire University	M,D,O
Stevens Institute of Technology	M,D,O
Stony Brook University, State University of New York	M,D,O
Stratford University	M
Strayer University	M
Sullivan University	P,M,D
Syracuse University	M,D,O*
Tarleton State University	M
Temple University	D*
Tennessee Technological University	M
Texas A&M International University	M
Texas A&M University	M,D
Texas A&M University–San Antonio	M
Texas Southern University	M
Texas State University–San Marcos	M
Texas Tech University	M,D*
Towson University	M,D,O
Troy University	M
TUI University	M,D,O
United States International University	M
Universidad del Este	M
Universidad del Turabo	M,D
Universidad Metropolitana	M
Université de Sherbrooke	M,O
Université du Québec à Montréal	M
Université Laval	M,O
University at Buffalo, the State University of New York	M,D,O*
The University of Akron	M
The University of Alabama in Huntsville	M,O
The University of Arizona	M
University of Arkansas	M
University of Arkansas at Little Rock	M,O
University of Atlanta	P,M,D,O
University of Baltimore	M,O
The University of British Columbia	D
University of California, Berkeley	O*
University of California, Los Angeles	M,D*
University of California, Santa Cruz	M,D
University of Central Missouri	M
University of Cincinnati	M,D
University of Colorado Boulder	M,D*
University of Colorado Denver	M,D
University of Dallas	M
University of Dayton	M
University of Delaware	M*
University of Denver	M,O
University of Detroit Mercy	M
University of Florida	M,D*
University of Georgia	D
University of Hawaii at Manoa	M,D,O
University of Houston–Clear Lake	M
University of Illinois at Chicago	M,D
University of Illinois at Springfield	M
The University of Kansas	M
University of La Verne	M
University of Lethbridge	M,D

*M—master's degree; P—first professional degree; D—doctorate; O—other advanced degree; *—Close-Up and/or Display in one of the other books in this series*

University of Maine M
University of Management and Technology M,O
University of Mary Hardin-Baylor M
University of Maryland University College M,O
University of Mary Washington M
University of Memphis M,D
University of Miami M*
University of Michigan–Dearborn M
University of Minnesota, Twin Cities Campus M,D
University of Mississippi M,D
University of Missouri–St. Louis M,D,O
University of Nebraska at Omaha M,D,O
University of Nebraska–Lincoln M*
University of Nevada, Las Vegas M,O
University of Nevada, Reno M*
University of New Mexico M*
The University of North Carolina at Chapel Hill D*
The University of North Carolina at Greensboro M,D,O
University of North Florida M
University of North Texas M,D
University of Oklahoma M,D,O*
University of Oregon M
University of Pennsylvania M,D*
University of Phoenix M
University of Phoenix–Atlanta Campus M
University of Phoenix–Augusta Campus M
University of Phoenix–Austin Campus M
University of Phoenix–Birmingham Campus M
University of Phoenix–Boston Campus M
University of Phoenix–Central Florida Campus M
University of Phoenix–Central Valley Campus M
University of Phoenix–Charlotte Campus M
University of Phoenix–Chattanooga Campus M
University of Phoenix–Cheyenne Campus M
University of Phoenix–Chicago Campus M
University of Phoenix–Cincinnati Campus M
University of Phoenix–Cleveland Campus M
University of Phoenix–Columbus Georgia Campus M
University of Phoenix–Columbus Ohio Campus M
University of Phoenix–Dallas Campus M
University of Phoenix–Denver Campus M
University of Phoenix–Des Moines Campus M
University of Phoenix–Eastern Washington Campus M
University of Phoenix–Harrisburg Campus M
University of Phoenix–Hawaii Campus M
University of Phoenix–Houston Campus M
University of Phoenix–Idaho Campus M
University of Phoenix–Indianapolis Campus M
University of Phoenix–Jersey City Campus M
University of Phoenix–Las Vegas Campus M
University of Phoenix–Louisiana Campus M
University of Phoenix–Madison Campus M
University of Phoenix–Maryland Campus M
University of Phoenix–Memphis Campus M
University of Phoenix–Metro Detroit Campus M
University of Phoenix–Milwaukee Campus M,D
University of Phoenix–Nashville Campus M
University of Phoenix–New Mexico Campus M
University of Phoenix–Northern Nevada Campus M
University of Phoenix–Northern Virginia Campus M
University of Phoenix–North Florida Campus M
University of Phoenix–Northwest Arkansas Campus M
University of Phoenix–Oklahoma City Campus M
University of Phoenix–Omaha Campus M
University of Phoenix–Oregon Campus M
University of Phoenix–Philadelphia Campus M
University of Phoenix–Pittsburgh Campus M
University of Phoenix–Raleigh Campus M
University of Phoenix–Richmond Campus M
University of Phoenix–Sacramento Valley Campus M
University of Phoenix–St. Louis Campus M
University of Phoenix–San Antonio Campus M
University of Phoenix–San Diego Campus M
University of Phoenix–Savannah Campus M
University of Phoenix–Southern Arizona Campus M
University of Phoenix–Southern Colorado Campus M
University of Phoenix–South Florida Campus M
University of Phoenix–Springfield Campus M
University of Phoenix–Tulsa Campus M
University of Phoenix–Utah Campus M
University of Phoenix–Vancouver Campus M
University of Phoenix–Washington D.C. Campus M,D
University of Phoenix–West Florida Campus M
University of Pittsburgh M,D,O*
University of Redlands M
University of St. Thomas (MN) M,O
University of San Francisco M
The University of Scranton M
University of South Africa M
University of South Alabama M
University of Southern Mississippi M
University of South Florida M,D*
The University of Tampa M
The University of Texas at Arlington M,D
The University of Texas at Austin D
The University of Texas at Dallas M,D*
The University of Texas at San Antonio M,D*
The University of Texas–Pan American D
University of the Sacred Heart M
University of the West M
The University of Toledo M,D,O
University of Tulsa M
University of Utah M*
University of Virginia M
University of Wisconsin–Madison D*
Utah State University M,D
Valparaiso University M
Villanova University M
Virginia Commonwealth University M,D
Virginia International University M
Virginia Polytechnic Institute and State University M,D,O
Walden University M,D
Walsh College of Accountancy and Business Administration M
Washington State University M,D
Wayland Baptist University M
Webster University M,D,O
West Chester University of Pennsylvania M,O
Western Governors University M
Western International University M
Wilmington University M
Winston-Salem State University M
Worcester Polytechnic Institute M,O
Wright State University M
Xavier University M

MANAGEMENT OF TECHNOLOGY

Air Force Institute of Technology M,D
Alliant International University–San Diego M,D
The American University in Cairo M
Arizona State University M
Athabasca University M,O
Boston University M*
California Lutheran University M,O
California State University, Los Angeles M*
Cambridge College M
Capella University M,D,O
Carleton University M
Carnegie Mellon University M,D*
Central Connecticut State University M,O
Champlain College M
City University of Seattle M,O
Coleman University M
Colorado School of Mines M,D
Colorado Technical University Colorado Springs M,D
Colorado Technical University Denver M
Colorado Technical University Sioux Falls M
Columbia University M*
Dallas Baptist University M
DePaul University M,D
East Carolina University M,D,O
Eastern Michigan University D
École Polytechnique de Montréal M,D,O
Embry-Riddle Aeronautical University–Worldwide M
Fairfield University M
Fairleigh Dickinson University, College at Florham M,O
Florida Institute of Technology M
George Mason University M,D*
The George Washington University M,D
Georgia Institute of Technology M,O
Golden Gate University M,D,O
Harding University M
Harrisburg University of Science and Technology M
Harvard University D*
Herzing University Online M
Hodges University M
Idaho State University M
Illinois State University M
Indiana State University D
Instituto Centroamericano de Administración de Empresas M
Instituto Tecnológico y de Estudios Superiores de Monterrey, Campus Central de Veracruz M
Instituto Tecnológico y de Estudios Superiores de Monterrey, Campus Cuernavaca M,D
Instituto Tecnológico y de Estudios Superiores de Monterrey, Campus Irapuato M,D
Iona College M,O
The Johns Hopkins University M,O
Jones International University M
La Salle University M
Lawrence Technological University M,D
Lewis University M
Marist College M,O
Marquette University M,D
Marshall University M
Mercer University M
Murray State University M
National University M
New Jersey Institute of Technology M
North Carolina Agricultural and Technical State University M,D
North Carolina State University D*
Northern Kentucky University M
OGI School of Science & Engineering at Oregon Health & Science University M,O
Old Dominion University M
Oregon Health & Science University M*
Pacific Lutheran University M
Pacific States University M,D
Polytechnic Institute of NYU M,D,O
Polytechnic Institute of NYU, Long Island Graduate Center M
Polytechnic Institute of NYU, Westchester Graduate Center M
Polytechnic University of Puerto Rico M
Polytechnic University of Puerto Rico, Orlando Campus M
Portland State University M,D
Regis University M,O

Institution	Degree
Rollins College	M
Rutgers, The State University of New Jersey, Newark	D*
St. Ambrose University	M
Santa Clara University	M
Seton Hall University	M
Simon Fraser University	M,D
South Dakota School of Mines and Technology	M
Southeast Missouri State University	M
State University of New York Institute of Technology	M
Stevens Institute of Technology	M,D,O
Stevenson University	M
Stony Brook University, State University of New York	M
Sullivan University	P,M,D
Teachers College, Columbia University	M
Texas A&M University–Commerce	M
Texas State University–San Marcos	M
Trevecca Nazarene University	M
University at Albany, State University of New York	M
University of Advancing Technology	M
The University of Akron	M
University of Arkansas at Little Rock	M,O
University of Bridgeport	M
University of California, Santa Cruz	M,D
University of Central Missouri	M,D
University of Colorado Denver	M,D
University of Dallas	M
University of Delaware	M*
University of Denver	M,O
University of Illinois at Urbana–Champaign	M,D
University of Maryland University College	M,O
University of Miami	M,D*
University of Minnesota, Twin Cities Campus	M
University of New Hampshire	M,O
University of New Mexico	M*
University of North Dakota	M
University of Pennsylvania	M*
University of Phoenix	M
University of Phoenix–Atlanta Campus	M
University of Phoenix–Augusta Campus	M
University of Phoenix–Austin Campus	M
University of Phoenix–Birmingham Campus	M
University of Phoenix–Boston Campus	M
University of Phoenix–Central Florida Campus	M
University of Phoenix–Central Massachusetts Campus	M
University of Phoenix–Central Valley Campus	M
University of Phoenix–Charlotte Campus	M
University of Phoenix–Chattanooga Campus	M
University of Phoenix–Cheyenne Campus	M
University of Phoenix–Chicago Campus	M
University of Phoenix–Cincinnati Campus	M
University of Phoenix–Cleveland Campus	M
University of Phoenix–Columbia Campus	M
University of Phoenix–Columbus Georgia Campus	M
University of Phoenix–Columbus Ohio Campus	M
University of Phoenix–Dallas Campus	M
University of Phoenix–Denver Campus	M
University of Phoenix–Des Moines Campus	M
University of Phoenix–Eastern Washington Campus	M
University of Phoenix–Harrisburg Campus	M
University of Phoenix–Hawaii Campus	M
University of Phoenix–Houston Campus	M
University of Phoenix–Idaho Campus	M
University of Phoenix–Indianapolis Campus	M
University of Phoenix–Jersey City Campus	M
University of Phoenix–Kansas City Campus	M
University of Phoenix–Las Vegas Campus	M
University of Phoenix–Louisiana Campus	M
University of Phoenix–Louisville Campus	M
University of Phoenix–Madison Campus	M
University of Phoenix–Maryland Campus	M
University of Phoenix–Memphis Campus	M
University of Phoenix–Minneapolis/St. Louis Park Campus	M
University of Phoenix–Nashville Campus	M
University of Phoenix–New Mexico Campus	M
University of Phoenix–Northern Nevada Campus	M
University of Phoenix–Northwest Arkansas Campus	M
University of Phoenix–Oklahoma City Campus	M
University of Phoenix–Omaha Campus	M
University of Phoenix–Oregon Campus	M
University of Phoenix–Philadelphia Campus	M
University of Phoenix–Pittsburgh Campus	M
University of Phoenix–Puerto Rico Campus	M
University of Phoenix–Raleigh Campus	M
University of Phoenix–Richmond Campus	M
University of Phoenix–Sacramento Valley Campus	M
University of Phoenix–San Antonio Campus	M
University of Phoenix–San Diego Campus	M
University of Phoenix–Savannah Campus	M
University of Phoenix–Southern Arizona Campus	M
University of Phoenix–Southern Colorado Campus	M
University of Phoenix–Springfield Campus	M
University of Phoenix–Tulsa Campus	M
University of Phoenix–Utah Campus	M
University of Phoenix–Vancouver Campus	M
University of Phoenix–West Florida Campus	M
University of Portland	M
University of St. Thomas (MN)	M,O
The University of Texas at San Antonio	M,D*
University of Toronto	M
University of Washington	M,D*
University of Waterloo	M,D
University of Wisconsin–Madison	M*
University of Wisconsin–Stout	M
University of Wisconsin–Whitewater	M*
Walden University	M,D
Western Kentucky University	M
Westminster College (UT)	M,O
Wilfrid Laurier University	M,D

MANAGEMENT STRATEGY AND POLICY

Institution	Degree
Alliant International University–San Diego	M,D
American Public University System	M
Azusa Pacific University	M
Bernard M. Baruch College of the City University of New York	M,D
Black Hills State University	M
Boston University	M*
California Miramar University	M
California State University, East Bay	M
Case Western Reserve University	M*
Claremont Graduate University	M,D,O
Davenport University	M
Davenport University	M
Defiance College	M
DePaul University	M
Dominican University of California	M
Drexel University	M,D,O*
Duquesne University	M
East Tennessee State University	M,O
Florida State University	M,D
Franklin Pierce University	M,D,O
Freed-Hardeman University	M
The George Washington University	M,D
Georgia Institute of Technology	M,D,O
Georgia State University	M,D
Grantham University	M
Harvard University	D*
HEC Montreal	M
Lamar University	M
LeTourneau University	M
Manhattanville College	M*
McGill University	M,D,O
Middle Tennessee State University	M,O
Mountain State University	M
Neumann University	M
New England College	M
New York University	M,D,O
North Central College	M
Northwestern University	M,D*
Pace University	M
Pontificia Universidad Catolica Madre y Maestra	M
Regent University	M,D,O
Regis University	M,O
Roberts Wesleyan College	M,O
Sage Graduate School	M
Saint Joseph's University	M
Saint Mary-of-the-Woods College	M
Southern Methodist University	M
Stevens Institute of Technology	M
Suffolk University	M,O
Syracuse University	D*
Taylor University	M
Temple University	D*
Tennessee Technological University	M
Towson University	O
Tufts University	O
United States International University	M
Universidad del Este	M
The University of Arizona	D
The University of British Columbia	D
University of Calgary	M,D
University of California, Los Angeles	M,D*
University of Central Missouri	M
University of Chicago	M
University of Colorado Denver	M
University of Dallas	M
University of Dayton	M
University of Denver	M
University of Florida	M*
University of Illinois at Urbana–Champaign	M,D,O
The University of Iowa	M*
University of Lethbridge	M,D
University of Mary	M
University of Minnesota, Twin Cities Campus	D
University of New Haven	M,O
University of New Mexico	M*
The University of North Carolina at Chapel Hill	D*
University of Pittsburgh	M,O*
The University of Texas at Dallas	M,D*
The University of Western Ontario	M,D
University of West Florida	M
University of Wisconsin–Madison	M*
Villanova University	M
Walden University	M,D
Western Governors University	M
Western International University	M
Xavier University	M

MANUFACTURING ENGINEERING

Institution	Degree
Arizona State University	M
Boston University	M,D*
Bowling Green State University	M*
Bradley University	M
California State University, Northridge	M
Clemson University	M
Cornell University	M,D*
Dartmouth College	M,D
East Carolina University	M,D,O
Eastern Kentucky University	M
East Tennessee State University	M,O
Florida State University	M,D
Grand Valley State University	M
Illinois Institute of Technology	M,D
Instituto Tecnológico y de Estudios Superiores de Monterrey, Campus Monterrey	M,D
Kansas State University	M,D*
Kettering University	M

*M—master's degree; P—first professional degree; D—doctorate; O—other advanced degree; *—Close-Up and/or Display in one of the other books in this series*

Lawrence Technological University M,D
Lehigh University M
Massachusetts Institute of Technology M,D,O
Michigan State University M,D
Minnesota State University Mankato M
Missouri University of Science and Technology M,D
New Jersey Institute of Technology M
North Carolina State University M*
North Dakota State University M,D
Northeastern University M,D
Oregon State University M,D
Penn State University Park M,D
Polytechnic Institute of NYU M
Polytechnic Institute of NYU, Long Island Graduate Center M
Polytechnic Institute of NYU, Westchester Graduate Center M
Polytechnic University of Puerto Rico M
Portland State University M,D
Rochester Institute of Technology M
Southern Illinois University Carbondale M
Southern Methodist University M,D
Stevens Institute of Technology M
Texas A&M University M
Texas Tech University M,D*
Tufts University O
Universidad Autonoma de Guadalajara M,D
Universidad de las Américas–Puebla M
University of Calgary M,D
University of California, Los Angeles M*
University of Colorado at Colorado Springs M
The University of Iowa M,D*
University of Kentucky M*
University of Manitoba M,D
University of Maryland, College Park M,D
University of Memphis M
University of Michigan–Dearborn M
University of Missouri M,D*
University of Nebraska–Lincoln M,D*
University of New Mexico M*
University of St. Thomas (MN) M,O
University of Southern California M,D,O*
University of Southern Maine M
The University of Texas at El Paso M,O
The University of Texas at San Antonio M*
The University of Texas–Pan American M
University of Toronto M
University of Windsor M,D
University of Wisconsin–Madison M*
University of Wisconsin–Milwaukee M,D,O
University of Wisconsin–Stout M
Villanova University M,O
Wayne State University M*
Western Illinois University M
Western Michigan University M
Western New England University M
Wichita State University M,D
Worcester Polytechnic Institute M,D

MARINE AFFAIRS

Dalhousie University M
Duke University M*
East Carolina University D
Louisiana State University and Agricultural and Mechanical College M,D
Memorial University of Newfoundland M,D,O
Nova Southeastern University M*
Old Dominion University M
Oregon State University M
Stevens Institute of Technology M
Stony Brook University, State University of New York M
Université du Québec à Rimouski M,O
University of Delaware M,D*
University of Maine M
University of Miami M*
University of Rhode Island M,D
University of San Diego M
University of Washington M,O*
University of West Florida M

MARINE BIOLOGY

College of Charleston M
Florida Institute of Technology M
Memorial University of Newfoundland M,D
Nicholls State University M
Northeastern University M,D
Nova Southeastern University M,D*
Princeton University D*
Rutgers, The State University of New Jersey, New Brunswick M,D*
San Francisco State University M
Texas A&M University at Galveston M,D
Texas State University–San Marcos M,D
University of Alaska Fairbanks M,D
University of California, San Diego D*
University of California, Santa Barbara M,D
University of Colorado Boulder M,D*
University of Guam M
University of Hawaii at Hilo M
University of Hawaii at Manoa M,D
University of Maine M,D
University of Massachusetts Dartmouth M
University of Miami M,D*
The University of North Carolina Wilmington M,D
University of Oregon M,D
University of Southern California M,D*
University of Southern Mississippi M,D
University of South Florida M,D*
Western Illinois University M,O
Woods Hole Oceanographic Institution D

MARINE GEOLOGY

Cornell University M,D*
Massachusetts Institute of Technology M,D
University of Delaware M,D*
University of Hawaii at Manoa M,D
University of Miami M,D*
University of Washington M,D*
Woods Hole Oceanographic Institution D

MARINE SCIENCES

American University M
California State University, East Bay M
California State University, Fresno M
California State University, Monterey Bay M
California State University, Sacramento M
Coastal Carolina University M
College of Charleston M
The College of William and Mary M,D
Cornell University M,D*
Duke University M*
Florida State University M,D
Georgia Institute of Technology M,D
Hawai'i Pacific University M*
Instituto Tecnologico de Santo Domingo M,D,O
Medical University of South Carolina D
Memorial University of Newfoundland M,O
North Carolina State University M,D*
Nova Southeastern University M*
Oregon State University M
San Francisco State University M
San Jose State University M
Savannah State University M
Stony Brook University, State University of New York M,D
Texas A&M University at Galveston M
Texas A&M University–Corpus Christi D
University of Alaska Fairbanks M,D
The University of British Columbia M,D
University of California, San Diego M*
University of California, Santa Barbara M,D
University of California, Santa Cruz M,D
University of Connecticut M,D*
University of Delaware M,D*
University of Florida M,D*
University of Georgia M,D
University of Hawaii at Manoa O
University of Maine M,D
University of Maryland, Baltimore M,D
University of Maryland, Baltimore County M,D
University of Maryland, College Park M,D
University of Maryland Eastern Shore M,D
University of Massachusetts Amherst M,D*
University of Massachusetts Boston D
University of Miami M,D*
University of Michigan M,D*
University of New England M
University of New Hampshire M
The University of North Carolina at Chapel Hill M,D*
The University of North Carolina Wilmington M,D
University of Puerto Rico, Mayagüez Campus M,D
University of Rhode Island M,D
University of San Diego M
University of South Alabama M,D
University of South Carolina M,D
University of Southern California M,D*
University of Southern Mississippi M,D
University of South Florida M,D*
The University of Texas at Austin M,D
University of the Virgin Islands M
University of Wisconsin–La Crosse M
University of Wisconsin–Madison M,D*
Western Washington University M

MARKETING

Adelphi University M*
Alabama Agricultural and Mechanical University M
Alliant International University–San Diego M,D
American College of Thessaloniki M,O
American InterContinental University Buckhead Campus M
American InterContinental University Online M
American InterContinental University South Florida M
American International College M
American Public University System M
American University M
The American University in Dubai M
Andrew Jackson University M
Argosy University, Atlanta M,D*
Argosy University, Chicago M,D*
Argosy University, Dallas M,D,O*
Argosy University, Denver M,D*
Argosy University, Hawai'i M,D,O*
Argosy University, Inland Empire M,D*
Argosy University, Los Angeles M,D*
Argosy University, Nashville M,D*
Argosy University, Orange County M,D,O*
Argosy University, Phoenix M,D*
Argosy University, Salt Lake City M,D*
Argosy University, San Diego M,D*
Argosy University, San Francisco Bay Area M,D*
Argosy University, Sarasota M,D,O*
Argosy University, Schaumburg M,D,O*
Argosy University, Seattle M,D*
Argosy University, Tampa M,D*
Argosy University, Twin Cities M,D*
Argosy University, Washington DC M,D,O*
Arizona State University M,D
Ashworth College M
Assumption College M,O
Avila University M
Azusa Pacific University M
Baker College Center for Graduate Studies—Online M,D
Barry University O*

Institution	Degrees
Bayamón Central University	M
Benedictine University	M
Bentley University	M
Bernard M. Baruch College of the City University of New York	M,D
California Coast University	M
California Intercontinental University	M,D
California Lutheran University	M,O
California State University, East Bay	M
California State University, Fullerton	M
California State University, Los Angeles	M*
Canisius College	M
Capella University	M,D,O
Carnegie Mellon University	D*
Case Western Reserve University	M,D*
Central European University	M
Central Michigan University	M
City University of Seattle	M,O
Clark University	M
Clemson University	M
Cleveland State University	M,D,O
Colorado Technical University Colorado Springs	M,D
Colorado Technical University Denver	M
Columbia Southern University	M
Columbia University	M,D*
Concordia University Wisconsin	M
Cornell University	D*
Daemen College	M
Dallas Baptist University	M
Davenport University	M
DePaul University	M
DeSales University	M
Dowling College	M,O
Drexel University	M,D,O*
Eastern Michigan University	M,O
Ellis University	M
Emerson College	M
Emory University	D*
Fairfield University	M,O
Fairleigh Dickinson University, College at Florham	M,O
Fairleigh Dickinson University, Metropolitan Campus	M,O
Fashion Institute of Technology	M*
Florida Agricultural and Mechanical University	M
Florida Institute of Technology	M
Florida State University	M,D
Fordham University	M
Franklin University	M
Full Sail University	M
Gannon University	O
George Fox University	M,D
The George Washington University	M,D
Georgia Institute of Technology	M,D,O
Georgia State University	M,D
Golden Gate University	M,D,O
Goldey-Beacom College	M
Grand Canyon University	M
Harvard University	D*
Hawai'i Pacific University	M*
HEC Montreal	M
Herzing University Online	M
Hofstra University	M,O
Holy Names University	M
Hood College	M
Howard University	M
Hult International Business School (United States)	M
Illinois Institute of Technology	M
Indiana Tech	M
Instituto Tecnologico de Santo Domingo	M,O
Instituto Tecnológico y de Estudios Superiores de Monterrey, Campus Central de Veracruz	M
Instituto Tecnológico y de Estudios Superiores de Monterrey, Campus Ciudad Obregón	M
Instituto Tecnológico y de Estudios Superiores de Monterrey, Campus Cuernavaca	M
Instituto Tecnológico y de Estudios Superiores de Monterrey, Campus Estado de México	M,D
Instituto Tecnológico y de Estudios Superiores de Monterrey, Campus Monterrey	M
Inter American University of Puerto Rico, Aguadilla Campus	M
Inter American University of Puerto Rico, Guayama Campus	M
Inter American University of Puerto Rico, Metropolitan Campus	M
Inter American University of Puerto Rico, Ponce Campus	M
Inter American University of Puerto Rico, San Germán Campus	M,D
The International University of Monaco	M
Iona College	M,O
The Johns Hopkins University	M
Kansas State University	M*
Kaplan University, Davenport Campus	M
Keiser University	M,D
Kent State University	D*
Kentucky State University	M
Lake Forest Graduate School of Management	M
Lasell College	M,O
La Sierra University	M,O
Lewis University	M
Lindenwood University	M
Long Island University, C.W. Post Campus	M,O
Louisiana State University and Agricultural and Mechanical College	D
Louisiana Tech University	M,D
Loyola University Chicago	M
Loyola University Maryland	M
Lynn University	M
Manhattanville College	M*
Marquette University	M
Marylhurst University	M
Maryville University of Saint Louis	M,O
McGill University	M,D,O
Michigan State University	M,D
Middle Tennessee State University	M
Milwaukee School of Engineering	M
Mississippi State University	M,D
Montclair State University	M,O
National University	M
New England College	M
New Mexico State University	D
New York Institute of Technology	M,O
New York University	M,D,O
North Central College	M
Northeastern Illinois University	M
Northwestern University	M,D*
Notre Dame de Namur University	M
Nova Southeastern University	D*
Oakland University	M,O
The Ohio State University	M,D
Oklahoma City University	M
Oklahoma State University	M,D*
Old Dominion University	D
Oral Roberts University	M
Ottawa University	M
Pace University	M
Philadelphia University	M
Polytechnic University of Puerto Rico, Miami Campus	M
Pontifical Catholic University of Puerto Rico	M
Pontificia Universidad Catolica Madre y Maestra	M
Post University	M
Providence College	M
Queen's University at Kingston	M
Quinnipiac University	M
Regent's American College London	M
Regis University	M,O
Roberts Wesleyan College	M,O
Rollins College	M
Rowan University	M
Rutgers, The State University of New Jersey, Newark	D*
Sacred Heart University	M
Sage Graduate School	M
St. Edward's University	M,O
St. John's University (NY)	M,O
Saint Joseph's University	M,O
Saint Leo University	M
Saint Peter's College	M
St. Thomas Aquinas College	M
Saint Xavier University	M,O
San Diego State University	M
Santa Clara University	M
Seton Hall University	M
Southern Adventist University	M
Southern Methodist University	M
Southern New Hampshire University	M,D,O
Southwest Minnesota State University	M
Stephen F. Austin State University	M
Stony Brook University, State University of New York	M,O
Strayer University	M
Suffolk University	M,O
Syracuse University	M,D*
Temple University	M,D*
Texas A&M University	M,D
Texas Tech University	M,D*
Tiffin University	M
TUI University	M,D
United States International University	M
Universidad del Turabo	M
Universidad Iberoamericana	P,M
Universidad Metropolitana	M
Université de Sherbrooke	M
Université Laval	M,O
University at Albany, State University of New York	M
The University of Akron	M
The University of Alabama	M,D
The University of Alabama in Huntsville	M
University of Alberta	D
The University of Arizona	M,D
University of Baltimore	M
The University of British Columbia	D
University of California, Berkeley	D,O*
University of California, Los Angeles	M,D*
University of Central Missouri	M
University of Chicago	M
University of Cincinnati	M,D
University of Colorado Boulder	M,D*
University of Colorado Denver	M
University of Connecticut	M,D*
University of Dallas	M
University of Dayton	M
University of Denver	M
University of Florida	M,D*
University of Hawaii at Manoa	M,D
University of Houston	D
University of Houston–Victoria	M
The University of Iowa	M,D*
University of La Verne	M
University of Massachusetts Dartmouth	M,O
University of Memphis	M,D
University of Miami	M*
University of Michigan–Dearborn	M
University of Minnesota, Twin Cities Campus	M,D
University of Missouri–St. Louis	M,O
University of Nebraska–Lincoln	M,D*
University of New Brunswick Fredericton	M,D
University of New Haven	M,O
University of New Mexico	M*
The University of North Carolina at Chapel Hill	D*
The University of North Carolina at Charlotte	M,D,O
The University of North Carolina at Greensboro	M,D
University of North Texas	D
University of Oregon	D
University of Pennsylvania	M,D*
University of Phoenix	M
University of Phoenix–Atlanta Campus	M
University of Phoenix–Augusta Campus	M
University of Phoenix–Austin Campus	M
University of Phoenix–Birmingham Campus	M
University of Phoenix–Central Florida Campus	M
University of Phoenix–Central Valley Campus	M
University of Phoenix–Chattanooga Campus	M
University of Phoenix–Cheyenne Campus	M
University of Phoenix–Cincinnati Campus	M
University of Phoenix–Cleveland Campus	M
University of Phoenix–Columbus Georgia Campus	M
University of Phoenix–Columbus Ohio Campus	M
University of Phoenix–Dallas Campus	M
University of Phoenix–Denver Campus	M
University of Phoenix–Des Moines Campus	M
University of Phoenix–Eastern Washington Campus	M
University of Phoenix–Harrisburg Campus	M

*M—master's degree; P—first professional degree; D—doctorate; O—other advanced degree; *—Close-Up and/or Display in one of the other books in this series*

University of Phoenix–Hawaii Campus M
University of Phoenix–Houston Campus M
University of Phoenix–Idaho Campus M
University of Phoenix–Indianapolis Campus M
University of Phoenix–Jersey City Campus M
University of Phoenix–Kansas City Campus M
University of Phoenix–Las Vegas Campus M
University of Phoenix–Louisiana Campus M
University of Phoenix–Madison Campus M
University of Phoenix–Maryland Campus M
University of Phoenix–Memphis Campus M
University of Phoenix–Minneapolis/St. Louis Park Campus M
University of Phoenix–New Mexico Campus M
University of Phoenix–Northern Nevada Campus M
University of Phoenix–North Florida Campus M
University of Phoenix–Northwest Arkansas Campus M
University of Phoenix–Oklahoma City Campus M
University of Phoenix–Omaha Campus M
University of Phoenix–Oregon Campus M
University of Phoenix–Philadelphia Campus M
University of Phoenix–Pittsburgh Campus M
University of Phoenix–Puerto Rico Campus M
University of Phoenix–Raleigh Campus M
University of Phoenix–Richmond Campus M
University of Phoenix–Sacramento Valley Campus M
University of Phoenix–St. Louis Campus M
University of Phoenix–San Antonio Campus M
University of Phoenix–San Diego Campus M
University of Phoenix–Savannah Campus M
University of Phoenix–Southern Arizona Campus M
University of Phoenix–Southern Colorado Campus M
University of Phoenix–South Florida Campus M
University of Phoenix–Springfield Campus M
University of Phoenix–Tulsa Campus M
University of Phoenix–Utah Campus M
University of Phoenix–Vancouver Campus M
University of Phoenix–West Florida Campus M
University of Pittsburgh M,D,O*
University of Portland M
University of Puerto Rico, Río Piedras M,D
University of Rhode Island M,D
University of San Francisco M
University of Saskatchewan M
The University of Scranton M
University of South Africa M,D
University of South Florida M,D*
The University of Tampa M
The University of Tennessee M,D
The University of Texas at Arlington M,D
The University of Texas at Austin D
The University of Texas at Dallas M,D*
The University of Texas at San Antonio M,D*
The University of Texas–Pan American D
University of the Cumberlands M,D,O
University of the Sacred Heart M
University of Virginia M
The University of Western Ontario M,D
University of Wisconsin–Madison D*
University of Wisconsin–Whitewater M*
Villanova University M
Virginia Commonwealth University M
Virginia International University M,O
Virginia Polytechnic Institute and State University M,D
Wagner College M
Wake Forest University M
Walden University M,D
Walsh University M
Washington State University M,D
Webster University M,D,O
West Chester University of Pennsylvania M
Western International University M
West Virginia University M
Wilfrid Laurier University M,D
Wilkes University M
Worcester Polytechnic Institute M,O
Wright State University M
Xavier University M
Yale University D*
York College of Pennsylvania M
Youngstown State University M

MARKETING RESEARCH

American University M
Hofstra University M,O
Instituto Tecnológico y de Estudios Superiores de Monterrey, Campus Irapuato M,D
Marquette University M
Pace University M
Southern Illinois University Edwardsville M
Universidad Autonoma de Guadalajara M,D
Universidad de las Americas, A.C. M
University of Colorado Denver M
University of Georgia M
The University of Texas at Arlington M,D
University of Wisconsin–Madison M*

MARRIAGE AND FAMILY THERAPY

Abilene Christian University M
Adler Graduate School M,O
Adler School of Professional Psychology M,D,O
Alliant International University–Irvine M,D
Alliant International University–Los Angeles M
Alliant International University–Sacramento M
Alliant International University–San Diego M,D
Amridge University P,M,D
Antioch University New England M,D
Appalachian State University M
Argosy University, Atlanta M,D,O*
Argosy University, Chicago D*
Argosy University, Denver M,D*
Argosy University, Hawai'i M*
Argosy University, Inland Empire M,D*
Argosy University, Los Angeles M,D*
Argosy University, Orange County M,D*
Argosy University, Salt Lake City M,D*
Argosy University, San Diego M,D*
Argosy University, Sarasota M,D*
Argosy University, Schaumburg M,D,O*
Argosy University, Tampa M,D*
Argosy University, Twin Cities M,D,O*
Argosy University, Washington DC M,D*
Arizona State University M,D
Azusa Pacific University M,D
Barry University M,O*
Bayamón Central University M,O
Bethel Seminary P,M,D,O
Briercrest Seminary M
Brigham Young University M,D*
California Lutheran University M,D
California State University, Chico M
California State University, Dominguez Hills M*
California State University, Fresno M
California State University, Long Beach M
California State University, Northridge M
Cambridge College M,O
Capella University M,D,O
Carlos Albizu University, Miami Campus M,D
Central Connecticut State University M,O
Chapman University M
Chatham University M,D
The Chicago School of Professional Psychology at Downtown Los Angeles M,D
The Chicago School of Professional Psychology at Irvine M,D
The Chicago School of Professional Psychology at Westwood M,D
Christian Theological Seminary P,M,D
The College of New Jersey O
The College of William and Mary M,D
Converse College O
Denver Seminary P,M,D,O
Dominican University of California M
Drexel University M,D*
East Carolina University M
Eastern Nazarene College M
Eastern University D
East Tennessee State University M,D
Edgewood College M
Evangelical Theological Seminary P,M
Fairfield University M
Florida Atlantic University M,D,O
Florida State University M,D
Fresno Pacific University M,O
Friends University M
Fuller Theological Seminary M,O
Geneva College M
George Fox University M,O
Grand Canyon University M
Harding University M
Hardin-Simmons University M
Hofstra University M,O
Hope International University M
Idaho State University M,D,O
Indiana University–Purdue University Fort Wayne M,O
Indiana Wesleyan University M
Instituto Tecnologico de Santo Domingo M,O
Iona College M,O
John Brown University M
Johnson University M
Kansas State University M,D*
Kean University O
Kutztown University of Pennsylvania M
Lancaster Bible College M,D
La Salle University D
Lee University M
Lewis & Clark College M
Loyola Marymount University M
Maryville University of Saint Louis M,O
Mercy College M,O
Messiah College M,O
Michigan State University M,D
Mid-America Christian University M
Minnesota State University Mankato M,D,O
Mississippi College M,O
Montclair State University M,O
Mount St. Mary's College M
Northcentral University M,D,O
North Dakota State University M,D
Northern Kentucky University M,O
Northwestern University M*
Northwest Nazarene University M
Notre Dame de Namur University M
Nova Southeastern University M,D,O*
Nyack College M
Oklahoma State University M,D*
Oral Roberts University P,M,D
Ottawa University M
Our Lady of Holy Cross College M
Our Lady of the Lake University of San Antonio M,D
Pacific Lutheran University M
Pacific Oaks College M
Palm Beach Atlantic University M
Pepperdine University M
Phillips Graduate Institute M
Purdue University M,D
Purdue University Calumet M
Reformed Theological Seminary–Jackson Campus P,M,D,O
Regis University M,O
Richmont Graduate University M
St. Cloud State University M
Saint Joseph College M

Saint Louis University	M,D,O
Saint Mary's College of California	M
St. Mary's University (United States)	M,D
Saint Mary's University of Minnesota	M,O
Saint Paul University	M
St. Thomas University	M,O
San Francisco State University	M
Saybrook University	M,D
The School of Professional Psychology at Forest Institute	M,D,O
Seattle Pacific University	M,O
Seton Hall University	M,D,O
Seton Hill University	M
Shippensburg University of Pennsylvania	M,O
Sioux Falls Seminary	M
Sonoma State University	M
Southeastern Louisiana University	M
Southern California Seminary	P,M,D
Southern Nazarene University	M
Springfield College	M,O
Stephens College	M
Stetson University	M
Syracuse University	M*
Texas Tech University	M,D*
Texas Wesleyan University	M,D
Texas Woman's University	M,D
Thomas Jefferson University	M
Trevecca Nazarene University	M
Universidad de las Americas, A.C.	M
The University of Akron	M
University of Arkansas at Little Rock	O
University of Central Florida	M,O
University of Florida	M,D,O*
University of Guelph	M,D
University of Houston–Clear Lake	M
University of La Verne	M
University of Louisiana at Monroe	M,D
University of Louisville	M,D,O
University of Mary Hardin-Baylor	M
University of Maryland, College Park	M,D
University of Massachusetts Boston	M,O
University of Miami	M,O*
University of Minnesota, Twin Cities Campus	M,D
University of Mobile	M
University of Montevallo	M
University of Nebraska–Lincoln	M,D*
University of Nevada, Las Vegas	M
University of New Hampshire	M
The University of North Carolina at Greensboro	M,D,O
University of Phoenix–Central Valley Campus	M
University of Phoenix–Las Vegas Campus	M
University of Phoenix–Puerto Rico Campus	M
University of Phoenix–Southern California Campus	M
University of Rochester	M
University of St. Thomas (MN)	M,D,O
University of San Diego	M
University of San Francisco	M,D
University of Southern California	M*
University of Southern Mississippi	M
The University of Texas at Tyler	M
The University of Winnipeg	P,M,O
University of Wisconsin–Milwaukee	M,D,O
University of Wisconsin–Stout	M
Utah State University	M,D
Valdosta State University	M
Virginia Polytechnic Institute and State University	M,D,O
Walden University	M,D
Wesley Biblical Seminary	P,M
Western Kentucky University	M
Western Seminary–Sacramento Campus	M
Western Seminary–San Jose Campus	P,M,O

MASS COMMUNICATION

American University	M,D,O
The American University in Cairo	M
Arizona State University	M,D
Auburn University	M
Boston University	M*
Brigham Young University	M*
California State University, Fresno	M
California State University, Northridge	M
Central Michigan University	M
The College of Saint Rose	M
Colorado State University	M,D
Drexel University	M*
Florida International University	M
Florida State University	M,D
Fordham University	M
The George Washington University	M
Georgia State University	M,D
Grambling State University	M
Howard University	M,D
Indiana University Bloomington	M,D*
Iona College	M
Iowa State University of Science and Technology	M*
Jackson State University	M
Kansas State University	M*
Kent State University	M*
Louisiana State University and Agricultural and Mechanical College	M,D
Lynn University	M
Marquette University	M,O
Marshall University	M
Middle Tennessee State University	M
Murray State University	M
North Dakota State University	M,D
Oklahoma City University	M
Oklahoma State University	M*
Point Park University	M
St. Cloud State University	M
San Jose State University	M
Southern Illinois University Carbondale	M
Southern Illinois University Edwardsville	M
Southern University and Agricultural and Mechanical College	M
Stephen F. Austin State University	M
Syracuse University	M,D*
Temple University	D*
Texas State University–San Marcos	M
Texas Tech University	M,D*
Université Laval	M,D
The University of Alabama	D
University of Arkansas at Little Rock	M
University of Central Missouri	M
University of Colorado Boulder	M,D*
University of Denver	M
University of Florida	M,D*
University of Georgia	M,D
University of Houston	M
The University of Iowa	M,D*
University of Louisiana at Lafayette	M*
University of Maine	M,D
University of Michigan	D*
University of Minnesota, Twin Cities Campus	M,D
University of Nebraska–Lincoln	M*
The University of North Carolina at Chapel Hill	M,D*
University of Oklahoma	M*
University of Puerto Rico, Río Piedras	M
University of Southern California	M,D*
University of Southern Mississippi	M,D
University of South Florida	M*
University of Wisconsin–Madison	M,D*
University of Wisconsin–Stevens Point	M
University of Wisconsin–Superior	M
University of Wisconsin–Whitewater	M*
Virginia Commonwealth University	M

MATERIALS ENGINEERING

Arizona State University	M,D
Auburn University	M,D
Boise State University	M
Boston University	M,D*
California State University, Northridge	M
Carleton University	M,D
Carnegie Mellon University	M,D*
Case Western Reserve University	M,D*
The Catholic University of America	M
Clemson University	M,D
Colorado School of Mines	M,D
Columbia University	M,D,O*
Cornell University	M,D*
Dalhousie University	M,D
Dartmouth College	M,D
Drexel University	M,D*
Duke University	M*
Florida International University	M,D
Georgia Institute of Technology	M,D
Illinois Institute of Technology	M,D
Instituto Tecnológico y de Estudios Superiores de Monterrey, Campus Estado de México	M,D
Iowa State University of Science and Technology	M,D*
The Johns Hopkins University	M,D
Lehigh University	M,D
Massachusetts Institute of Technology	M,D,O
McGill University	M,D,O
McMaster University	M,D
Michigan State University	M,D
Michigan Technological University	M,D
New Jersey Institute of Technology	M,D
New Mexico Institute of Mining and Technology	M,D
North Carolina State University	M,D*
Northwestern University	M,D,O*
The Ohio State University	M,D
Penn State University Park	M,D
Purdue University	M,D
Rensselaer Polytechnic Institute	M,D
Rochester Institute of Technology	M
Rutgers, The State University of New Jersey, New Brunswick	M,D*
San Jose State University	M
Santa Clara University	M,D,O
South Dakota School of Mines and Technology	M,D
Stanford University	M,D,O
State University of New York at Binghamton	M,D
Stevens Institute of Technology	M,D
Stony Brook University, State University of New York	M,D
Texas A&M University	M,D
Tuskegee University	D
The University of Alabama	M,D
The University of Alabama at Birmingham	M,D*
University of Alberta	M,D
The University of Arizona	M,D
The University of British Columbia	M,D
University of California, Berkeley	M,D*
University of California, Davis	M,D
University of California, Irvine	M,D*
University of California, Los Angeles	M,D*
University of California, Riverside	M,D
University of California, Santa Barbara	M,D
University of Central Florida	M,D
University of Cincinnati	M,D
University of Connecticut	M,D*
University of Dayton	M,D
University of Delaware	M,D*
University of Denver	M,D
University of Florida	M,D,O*
University of Illinois at Chicago	M,D
University of Illinois at Urbana–Champaign	M,D
University of Maryland, College Park	M,D
University of Massachusetts Lowell	M,D,O
University of Michigan	M,D*
University of Minnesota, Twin Cities Campus	M,D
University of Nebraska–Lincoln	M,D*
University of Nevada, Las Vegas	M,D
University of Nevada, Reno	M,D*
University of Pennsylvania	M,D*
University of Southern California	M,D,O*
The University of Tennessee	M,D
The University of Tennessee Space Institute	M
The University of Texas at Arlington	M,D
The University of Texas at Austin	M,D
The University of Texas at Dallas	M,D*
The University of Texas at El Paso	M,D

*M—master's degree; P—first professional degree; D—doctorate; O—other advanced degree; *—Close-Up and/or Display in one of the other books in this series*

University of Toronto M,D
University of Utah M,D*
University of Washington M,D*
The University of Western Ontario M,D
University of Windsor M,D
University of Wisconsin–Madison M,D*
University of Wisconsin–Milwaukee M,D,O
Virginia Polytechnic Institute and State University M,D
Washington State University M
Wayne State University M,D,O*
Worcester Polytechnic Institute M,D
Wright State University M

MATERIALS SCIENCES

Air Force Institute of Technology M,D
Alabama Agricultural and Mechanical University M,D
Alfred University M,D
Arizona State University M,D
Boston University M,D*
Brown University M,D
California Institute of Technology M,D
Carnegie Mellon University M,D*
Case Western Reserve University M,D*
The Catholic University of America M
Central Michigan University D
Clemson University M,D
Colorado School of Mines M,D
Columbia University M,D,O*
Cornell University M,D*
Dartmouth College M,D
Duke University M,D*
Florida International University M,D
Florida State University M,D
Georgetown University D
The George Washington University M,D
Illinois Institute of Technology M,D
Indiana University Bloomington M,D*
Instituto Tecnológico y de Estudios Superiores de Monterrey, Campus Estado de México M,D
Iowa State University of Science and Technology M,D*
Jackson State University M
The Johns Hopkins University M,D
Lehigh University M,D
Massachusetts Institute of Technology M,D,O
McMaster University M,D
Michigan State University M,D
Missouri State University M
New Jersey Institute of Technology M,D
Norfolk State University M
North Carolina State University M,D*
North Dakota State University D
Northwestern University M,D,O*
The Ohio State University M,D
Oregon State University M,D
Penn State University Park M,D
Princeton University D*
Rensselaer Polytechnic Institute M,D
Rice University M,D
Rochester Institute of Technology M
Royal Military College of Canada M,D
Rutgers, The State University of New Jersey, New Brunswick M,D*
School of the Art Institute of Chicago M
South Dakota School of Mines and Technology M,D
Stanford University M,D,O
State University of New York at Binghamton M,D
Stony Brook University, State University of New York M,D
Texas A&M Health Science Center M
Texas State University–San Marcos D
Trent University M
Université du Québec, Institut National de la Recherche Scientifique M,D
University at Buffalo, the State University of New York M*
The University of Alabama D
The University of Alabama at Birmingham D*
The University of Alabama in Huntsville M,D
The University of Arizona M,D
The University of British Columbia M,D
University of California, Berkeley M,D*
University of California, Davis M,D
University of California, Irvine M,D*
University of California, Los Angeles M,D*
University of California, Riverside M,D
University of California, San Diego M,D*
University of California, Santa Barbara M,D
University of Central Florida M,D
University of Cincinnati M,D
University of Connecticut M,D*
University of Delaware M,D*
University of Denver M,D
University of Florida M,D,O*
University of Idaho M,D
University of Illinois at Urbana–Champaign M,D
University of Kentucky M,D*
The University of Manchester M,D
University of Maryland, College Park M,D
University of Michigan M,D*
University of Minnesota, Twin Cities Campus M,D
University of Nebraska–Lincoln M,D*
University of New Brunswick Fredericton M,D
University of New Hampshire M,D
The University of North Carolina at Chapel Hill M,D*
University of North Texas M,D
University of Pennsylvania M,D*
University of Pittsburgh M,D*
University of Rochester M,D
University of Southern California M,D,O*
The University of Tennessee M,D
The University of Tennessee Space Institute M
The University of Texas at Arlington M,D
The University of Texas at Austin M,D
The University of Texas at Dallas M,D*
The University of Texas at El Paso M,D
University of Toronto M,D
University of Utah M,D*
University of Vermont M,D
University of Virginia M,D
University of Washington M,D*
University of Wisconsin–Madison M,D*
Vanderbilt University M,D*
Virginia Polytechnic Institute and State University M,D
Washington State University M,D
Wayne State University M,D,O*
Worcester Polytechnic Institute M,D
Wright State University M

MATERNAL AND CHILD/ NEONATAL NURSING

Baylor University M*
Boston College M,D*
Case Western Reserve University M,D*
Columbia University M,O*
Duke University M,D,O*
Hardin-Simmons University M
Indiana University–Purdue University Indianapolis M,D
Lehman College of the City University of New York M
Marquette University M,D,O
Medical University of South Carolina M
Northeastern University M,O
Regis University P,M,D,O
Rush University M,D,O
Rutgers, The State University of New Jersey, Newark M*
St. Catherine University M,D
Saint Francis Medical Center College of Nursing M,D,O
Stony Brook University, State University of New York M,O
University of Alberta P
University of Cincinnati M,D
University of Colorado at Colorado Springs M,D
University of Delaware M,O*
University of Illinois at Chicago M
University of Louisville M,D
University of Maryland, Baltimore M
University of Missouri–Kansas City M,D*
University of Missouri–St. Louis M,D,O
University of Pennsylvania M,O*
University of Pittsburgh M,D*
University of Puerto Rico, Medical Sciences Campus M
University of Rochester M,D,O
University of South Africa M,D
University of South Alabama M,D
University of Southern Mississippi M,D
Vanderbilt University M,D*
Wayne State University M,O*

MATERNAL AND CHILD HEALTH

Bank Street College of Education M
Boston University M,D*
Columbia University M*
Future Generations Graduate School M
Instituto Tecnologico de Santo Domingo M,O
Oakland University M,D,O
Syracuse University M*
Troy University M,D,O
Tulane University M,D*
University of California, Davis M
University of Maryland, College Park M,D
University of Minnesota, Twin Cities Campus M
University of Mississippi Medical Center M
The University of North Carolina at Chapel Hill M,D*
University of Puerto Rico, Medical Sciences Campus M
University of Washington M,D*

MATHEMATICAL AND COMPUTATIONAL FINANCE

Bernard M. Baruch College of the City University of New York M
Boston University M,D*
Carnegie Mellon University M,D*
DePaul University M,D
Florida State University M,D
Georgia Institute of Technology M,D
Illinois Institute of Technology M
The Johns Hopkins University M,D
Monmouth University M
New York University M,D
North Carolina State University M*
Polytechnic Institute of NYU M,O
Polytechnic Institute of NYU, Westchester Graduate Center M,O
Rice University M,D
Santa Clara University M
Stanford University M,D
Université de Montréal M,D,O
University of Alberta M,D,O
University of California, Santa Barbara M,D
University of Chicago M
University of Connecticut M*
University of Dayton M
University of Illinois at Chicago M,D
The University of Manchester M,D
The University of North Carolina at Charlotte M
University of Southern California M,D*
University of Toronto M

MATHEMATICAL PHYSICS

New Mexico Institute of Mining and Technology M,D
University of Alberta M,D,O
University of Colorado Boulder M,D*

MATHEMATICS

Alabama State University M,O
American University M,O
American University of Beirut M
Andrews University M
Appalachian State University M
Arizona State University M,D
Arkansas State University M
Auburn University M,D
Aurora University M
Ball State University M
Baylor University M,D*
Bemidji State University M

Institution	Degree
Boston College	D*
Boston University	M,D*
Bowling Green State University	M,D*
Brandeis University	M,D,O
Brigham Young University	M,D*
Brock University	M
Brooklyn College of the City University of New York	M,D
Brown University	M,D
Bryn Mawr College	M,D*
Bucknell University	M
California Institute of Technology	D
California Polytechnic State University, San Luis Obispo	M
California State Polytechnic University, Pomona	M
California State University Channel Islands	M
California State University, East Bay	M
California State University, Fresno	M
California State University, Fullerton	M
California State University, Long Beach	M
California State University, Los Angeles	M*
California State University, Northridge	M
California State University, Sacramento	M
California State University, San Bernardino	M
California State University, San Marcos	M
Carleton University	M,D
Carnegie Mellon University	M,D*
Case Western Reserve University	M,D*
Central Connecticut State University	M,O
Central Michigan University	M,D
Central Washington University	M
Chicago State University	M
City College of the City University of New York	M
Claremont Graduate University	M,D
Clark Atlanta University	M
Clarkson University	M,D*
Clemson University	M,D
Cleveland State University	M
The College at Brockport, State University of New York	M
College of Charleston	M,O
Colorado School of Mines	M,D
Colorado State University	M,D
Columbia University	M,D*
Concordia University (Canada)	M,D
Cornell University	D*
Dalhousie University	M,D
Dartmouth College	D
Delaware State University	M
DePaul University	M,O
Dowling College	M
Drexel University	M,D*
Duke University	D*
Duquesne University	M
East Carolina University	M
Eastern Illinois University	M
Eastern Kentucky University	M
Eastern Michigan University	M
Eastern New Mexico University	M
Eastern Washington University	M
East Tennessee State University	M
Elizabeth City State University	M
Emory University	M,D*
Emporia State University	M
Fairfield University	M
Fairleigh Dickinson University, Metropolitan Campus	M
Fayetteville State University	M
Florida Atlantic University	M,D
Florida International University	M
Florida State University	M,D
George Mason University	M,D,O*
Georgetown University	M
The George Washington University	M,D
Georgia Institute of Technology	M,D
Georgian Court University	M,O
Georgia Southern University	M
Georgia State University	M,D
Graduate School and University Center of the City University of New York	D
Hardin-Simmons University	M,D
Harvard University	D*
Howard University	M,D
Hunter College of the City University of New York	M
Idaho State University	M,D
Illinois State University	M
Indiana State University	M
Indiana University Bloomington	M,D*
Indiana University of Pennsylvania	M
Indiana University–Purdue University Fort Wayne	M,O
Indiana University–Purdue University Indianapolis	M,D
Instituto Tecnologico de Santo Domingo	M,D,O
Iowa State University of Science and Technology	M,D*
Jackson State University	M
Jacksonville State University	M
James Madison University	M
John Carroll University	M
The Johns Hopkins University	D
Kansas State University	M,D*
Kent State University	M,D*
Lakehead University	M
Lamar University	M
Lehigh University	M,D
Lehman College of the City University of New York	M
Long Island University, C.W. Post Campus	M
Louisiana State University and Agricultural and Mechanical College	M,D
Louisiana Tech University	M
Loyola University Chicago	M
Marquette University	M,D
Marshall University	M
Massachusetts Institute of Technology	D
McGill University	M,D
McMaster University	M,D
McNeese State University	M
Memorial University of Newfoundland	M,D
Miami University	M
Michigan State University	M,D
Michigan Technological University	M,D
Middle Tennessee State University	M,D
Minnesota State University Mankato	M
Mississippi College	M
Mississippi State University	M,D
Missouri State University	M
Missouri University of Science and Technology	M,D
Montana State University	M,D
Morgan State University	M
Murray State University	M
Naval Postgraduate School	M,D
New Jersey Institute of Technology	D
New Mexico Institute of Mining and Technology	M,D
New Mexico State University	M,D
New York University	M,D
Nicholls State University	M
North Carolina Central University	M
North Carolina State University	M,D*
North Dakota State University	M,D
Northeastern Illinois University	M
Northeastern University	M,D
Northern Arizona University	M,O
Northern Illinois University	M,D
Northwestern University	D*
Oakland University	M
The Ohio State University	M,D
Ohio University	M,D*
Oklahoma State University	M,D*
Old Dominion University	M,D
Oregon State University	M,D
Penn State University Park	M,D
Pittsburg State University	M
Polytechnic Institute of NYU	M,D
Portland State University	M,D,O
Prairie View A&M University	M
Princeton University	D*
Purdue University	M,D
Purdue University Calumet	M
Queens College of the City University of New York	M
Queen's University at Kingston	M,D
Rensselaer Polytechnic Institute	M,D
Rhode Island College	M,O
Rice University	D
Rivier College	M
Roosevelt University	M
Rowan University	M
Royal Military College of Canada	M
Rutgers, The State University of New Jersey, Camden	M
Rutgers, The State University of New Jersey, Newark	D*
Rutgers, The State University of New Jersey, New Brunswick	M,D*
St. Cloud State University	M
St. John's University (NY)	M
Saint Joseph's University	M,O
Saint Louis University	M,D
Saint Xavier University	M
Salem State University	M
Sam Houston State University	M
San Diego State University	M,D
San Francisco State University	M
San Jose State University	M
Simon Fraser University	M,D
Smith College	O
South Dakota State University	M,D
Southeastern Louisiana University	M
Southeast Missouri State University	M
Southern Connecticut State University	M
Southern Illinois University Carbondale	M,D
Southern Illinois University Edwardsville	M
Southern Methodist University	M,D
Southern University and Agricultural and Mechanical College	M
Stanford University	M,D
State University of New York at Binghamton	M,D
State University of New York at Fredonia	M
State University of New York College at Cortland	M
State University of New York College at Potsdam	M
Stephen F. Austin State University	M
Stevens Institute of Technology	M,D
Stony Brook University, State University of New York	M,D
Syracuse University	M,D*
Tarleton State University	M
Temple University	M,D*
Tennessee State University	M
Tennessee Technological University	M
Texas A&M International University	M
Texas A&M University	M,D
Texas A&M University–Commerce	M
Texas A&M University–Corpus Christi	M
Texas A&M University–Kingsville	M
Texas Christian University	M,D
Texas Southern University	M
Texas State University–San Marcos	M,D
Texas Tech University	M,D*
Texas Woman's University	M
Tufts University	M,D
Tulane University	M,D*
Université de Moncton	M
Université de Montréal	M,D,O
Université de Sherbrooke	M,D
Université du Québec à Montréal	M,D
Université du Québec à Trois-Rivières	M
Université Laval	M,D
University at Albany, State University of New York	M,D
University at Buffalo, the State University of New York	M,D*
The University of Akron	M
The University of Alabama	M,D
The University of Alabama at Birmingham	M*
The University of Alabama in Huntsville	M,D
University of Alaska Fairbanks	M,D
University of Alberta	M,D,O
The University of Arizona	M,D
University of Arkansas	M,D
University of Arkansas at Little Rock	M,O
The University of British Columbia	M,D
University of Calgary	M,D
University of California, Berkeley	M,D*
University of California, Davis	M,D
University of California, Irvine	M,D*

*M—master's degree; P—first professional degree; D—doctorate; O—other advanced degree; *—Close-Up and/or Display in one of the other books in this series*

University of California, Los Angeles M,D*
University of California, Riverside M,D
University of California, San Diego M,D*
University of California, Santa Barbara M,D
University of California, Santa Cruz M,D
University of Central Arkansas M
University of Central Florida M,D,O
University of Central Missouri M,D
University of Central Oklahoma M
University of Chicago M,D
University of Cincinnati M,D
University of Colorado at Colorado Springs M,D
University of Colorado Boulder M,D*
University of Colorado Denver M
University of Connecticut M,D*
University of Delaware M,D*
University of Denver M,D
University of Florida M,D*
University of Georgia M,D
University of Guelph M,D
University of Hawaii at Manoa M,D
University of Houston M,D
University of Houston–Clear Lake M
University of Idaho M,D
University of Illinois at Chicago M,D
University of Illinois at Urbana–Champaign M,D
The University of Iowa M,D*
The University of Kansas M,D
University of Kentucky M,D*
University of Lethbridge M,D
University of Louisiana at Lafayette M,D*
University of Louisville M,D
University of Maine M
The University of Manchester M,D
University of Manitoba M,D
University of Maryland, College Park M,D
University of Massachusetts Amherst M,D*
University of Massachusetts Lowell M,D
University of Memphis M,D
University of Miami M,D*
University of Michigan M,D*
University of Minnesota, Twin Cities Campus M,D
University of Mississippi M,D
University of Missouri M,D*
University of Missouri–Kansas City M,D*
University of Missouri–St. Louis M,D
The University of Montana M,D
University of Nebraska at Omaha M
University of Nebraska–Lincoln M,D*
University of Nevada, Las Vegas M,D
University of Nevada, Reno M*
University of New Brunswick Fredericton M,D
University of New Hampshire M,D,O
University of New Mexico M,D*
University of New Orleans M
The University of North Carolina at Chapel Hill M,D*
The University of North Carolina at Charlotte M,D
The University of North Carolina at Greensboro M,D
The University of North Carolina Wilmington M
University of North Dakota M
University of Northern British Columbia M,D,O
University of Northern Colorado M,D
University of Northern Iowa M
University of North Florida M
University of North Texas M,D
University of Notre Dame M,D*
University of Oklahoma M,D*
University of Oregon M,D
University of Ottawa M,D*
University of Pennsylvania M,D*
University of Pittsburgh M,D*
University of Puerto Rico, Mayagüez Campus M
University of Puerto Rico, Río Piedras M,D
University of Regina M,D
University of Rhode Island M,D
University of Rochester
University of Saskatchewan M,D
University of South Alabama M
University of South Carolina M,D
The University of South Dakota M
University of Southern California M,D*
University of Southern Mississippi M,D
University of South Florida M,D*
The University of Tennessee M,D
The University of Texas at Arlington M,D
The University of Texas at Austin M,D
The University of Texas at Brownsville M
The University of Texas at Dallas M,D*
The University of Texas at El Paso M
The University of Texas at San Antonio M*
The University of Texas at Tyler M
The University of Texas–Pan American M
University of the Incarnate Word M
The University of Toledo M,D
University of Toronto M,D
University of Tulsa M
University of Utah M,D*
University of Vermont M,D
University of Victoria M,D
University of Virginia M,D
University of Washington M,D*
University of Waterloo M,D
The University of Western Ontario M,D
University of West Florida M
University of West Georgia M
University of Windsor M,D
University of Wisconsin–Madison D*
University of Wisconsin–Milwaukee M,D
University of Wyoming M,D
Utah State University M,D
Vanderbilt University M,D*
Villanova University M
Virginia Commonwealth University M
Virginia Polytechnic Institute and State University M,D
Virginia State University M
Wake Forest University M
Washington State University M,D
Washington University in St. Louis M,D*
Wayne State University M,D*
Wesleyan University M,D*
West Chester University of Pennsylvania M,O
Western Carolina University M
Western Connecticut State University M
Western Illinois University M,O
Western Kentucky University M
Western Michigan University M,D
Western Washington University M
West Texas A&M University M
West Virginia University M,D
Wichita State University M,D
Wilfrid Laurier University M
Wilkes University M
Worcester Polytechnic Institute M,D,O
Wright State University M
Yale University M,D*
York University M,D*
Youngstown State University M

MATHEMATICS EDUCATION

Acadia University M
Alabama State University M,O
Albany State University M
Alfred University M
Appalachian State University M
Arcadia University M,D,O*
Arizona State University M,D
Arkansas State University M
Armstrong Atlantic State University M
Asbury University M
Auburn University M,D,O
Aurora University M
Averett University M
Ball State University M
Bank Street College of Education M
Belmont University M
Bemidji State University M
Bennington College M
Bob Jones University P,M,D,O
Boston University M,D,O*
Bowling Green State University M,D*
Bridgewater State University M
Brigham Young University M*
Brooklyn College of the City University of New York M,O
Buffalo State College, State University of New York M
California State University, Bakersfield M
California State University, Chico M
California State University, Dominguez Hills M*
California State University, East Bay M
California State University, Fresno M
California State University, Fullerton M
California State University, Long Beach M
California State University, Northridge M
California State University, San Bernardino M
Cambridge College M,D,O
Campbell University M
Caribbean University M,D
Central Michigan University M,D
Chatham University M
Christopher Newport University M
The Citadel, The Military College of South Carolina M
City College of the City University of New York M,O
Clark Atlanta University M
Clayton State University M
Clemson University M
Cleveland State University M
The College at Brockport, State University of New York M
College of Charleston M
The College of William and Mary M
The Colorado College M
Columbus State University M,O
Concordia University (Canada) M,D
Converse College M
Cornell University M,D*
Delaware State University M
DePaul University M,O
Drew University M
Drexel University M*
Drury University M
Duquesne University M
East Carolina University M
Eastern Illinois University M
Eastern Kentucky University M
Eastern Michigan University M
Eastern Washington University M
Florida Agricultural and Mechanical University M
Florida Institute of Technology M,D,O
Florida International University M,D,O
Florida State University M,D,O
Framingham State University M
Fresno Pacific University M
Georgia Southern University M
Georgia State University M,D,O
Grambling State University M,D
Harding University M,O
Harvard University M,O*
High Point University M
Hofstra University M,D,O
Hood College M,O
Hunter College of the City University of New York M
Idaho State University M,D
Illinois Institute of Technology M,D
Illinois State University D
Indiana State University M
Indiana University Bloomington M,D,O*
Indiana University of Pennsylvania M
Indiana University–Purdue University Fort Wayne M,O
Indiana University–Purdue University Indianapolis M,D
Instituto Tecnológico y de Estudios Superiores de Monterrey, Campus Ciudad Obregón M
Inter American University of Puerto Rico, Arecibo Campus M
Inter American University of Puerto Rico, Barranquitas Campus M
Inter American University of Puerto Rico, Metropolitan Campus M
Inter American University of Puerto Rico, Ponce Campus M

Institution	Degrees
Iona College	M
Iowa State University of Science and Technology	M,D*
Ithaca College	M
Jackson State University	M
Jacksonville University	M
The Johns Hopkins University	M,O
Kaplan University, Davenport Campus	M
Kean University	M
Kennesaw State University	M
Kutztown University of Pennsylvania	M,O
Lehman College of the City University of New York	M
Lewis University	M
Lipscomb University	M,D
Long Island University, Brooklyn Campus	M
Long Island University, C.W. Post Campus	M
Louisiana Tech University	M,D
Loyola Marymount University	M
Loyola University Chicago	M,O
Manhattanville College	M*
Marquette University	M,D
Miami University	M
Michigan State University	M,D
Middle Tennessee State University	M,D
Millersville University of Pennsylvania	M
Mills College	M,D
Minnesota State University Mankato	M
Minot State University	M
Mississippi College	M,D,O
Missouri University of Science and Technology	M,D
Montana State University	M,D
Montclair State University	M,D,O
Morehead State University	M
Morgan State University	M,D
National-Louis University	M,D,O
New Jersey City University	M
New York University	M
Nicholls State University	M
North Carolina Agricultural and Technical State University	M
North Carolina Central University	M
North Carolina State University	M,D*
North Dakota State University	M,D,O
Northeastern Illinois University	M
Northeastern State University	M
Northern Arizona University	M,O
North Georgia College & State University	M,O
Northwestern State University of Louisiana	M
Northwest Missouri State University	M
Nova Southeastern University	M,O*
Oakland University	M,D,O
Occidental College	M
Ohio University	M,D*
Oklahoma State University	M,D*
Oregon State University	M,D
Our Lady of the Lake University of San Antonio	M
Plymouth State University	M
Portland State University	M,D
Providence College	M
Purdue University	M,D,O
Purdue University Calumet	M
Queens College of the City University of New York	M,O
Quinnipiac University	M
Regent University	M,D,O
Rhode Island College	M
Rider University	O
Rollins College	M
Rutgers, The State University of New Jersey, New Brunswick	M,D*
Sage Graduate School	M
St. John Fisher College	M
Saint Peter's College	M,D,O
Salem State University	M
Salisbury University	M
San Diego State University	M,D
San Francisco State University	M
San Jose State University	M
Shippensburg University of Pennsylvania	M
Siena Heights University	M
Simon Fraser University	M,D
Slippery Rock University of Pennsylvania	M
Smith College	M
South Carolina State University	M,D,O
Southeastern Oklahoma State University	M
Southern Illinois University Edwardsville	M
Southern University and Agricultural and Mechanical College	D
Southwestern Oklahoma State University	M
Southwest Minnesota State University	M
Stanford University	M,D
State University of New York at Binghamton	M
State University of New York at Plattsburgh	M
State University of New York College at Cortland	M
State University of New York College at Potsdam	M
Stephen F. Austin State University	M
Stony Brook University, State University of New York	M,O
Syracuse University	M,D*
Teachers College, Columbia University	M,D
Temple University	M,D*
Texas A&M University	M,D
Texas A&M University–Corpus Christi	M
Texas State University–San Marcos	M,D
Texas Woman's University	M
Towson University	M
Troy University	M
Union Graduate College	M,O
Universidad Autonoma de Guadalajara	M,D
University at Albany, State University of New York	M,D
University at Buffalo, the State University of New York	M,D,O*
University of Arkansas	M
The University of British Columbia	M,D
University of California, Berkeley	M,D*
University of California, San Diego	D*
University of Central Arkansas	M
University of Central Florida	M,D,O
University of Central Oklahoma	M
University of Cincinnati	M,D
University of Colorado Denver	M,D
University of Connecticut	M,D,O*
University of Dayton	M
University of Detroit Mercy	M
University of Florida	M,D,O*
University of Georgia	M,D,O
University of Illinois at Chicago	M
University of Illinois at Urbana–Champaign	M,D
University of Indianapolis	M
The University of Iowa	M,D*
University of Maine	M
University of Maryland, Baltimore County	M
University of Massachusetts Dartmouth	D
University of Massachusetts Lowell	M,D,O
University of Miami	D*
University of Michigan	M,D*
University of Minnesota, Twin Cities Campus	M
University of Missouri	M,D,O*
The University of Montana	M,D
University of Nevada, Reno	M*
University of New Hampshire	M,D,O
The University of North Carolina at Chapel Hill	M*
The University of North Carolina at Charlotte	M,D
The University of North Carolina at Greensboro	M,D,O
The University of North Carolina at Pembroke	M
University of Northern Colorado	M,D
University of Northern Iowa	M
University of Oklahoma	M,D,O*
University of Phoenix–Central Florida Campus	M
University of Phoenix–North Florida Campus	M
University of Phoenix–Omaha Campus	M
University of Phoenix–Southern California Campus	M
University of Phoenix–South Florida Campus	M
University of Phoenix–Springfield Campus	M
University of Phoenix–Washington D.C. Campus	M,D,O
University of Phoenix–West Florida Campus	M
University of Pittsburgh	M,D*
University of Puerto Rico, Río Piedras	M,D
University of Rio Grande	M
University of St. Francis (IL)	M
University of St. Thomas (MN)	M,O
University of South Africa	M,D
University of South Carolina	M,D
University of Southern Mississippi	M,D
University of South Florida	M,D,O*
The University of Tennessee	M,D,O
The University of Texas at Arlington	M,D
The University of Texas at Austin	M,D
The University of Texas at Dallas	M*
The University of Texas at El Paso	M
The University of Texas at San Antonio	M*
The University of Texas–Pan American	M
University of the District of Columbia	M
University of the Sacred Heart	M,O
University of the Virgin Islands	M
The University of Toledo	M,D,O
University of Tulsa	M
University of Vermont	M,D
University of Victoria	M,D
University of Virginia	M,D,O
University of Washington	M,D*
University of Washington, Tacoma	M
The University of West Alabama	M
University of West Georgia	M,O
University of Wisconsin–Madison	M,D*
University of Wisconsin–Oshkosh	M
University of Wisconsin–River Falls	M
University of Wyoming	M,D
Ursuline College	M
Virginia Polytechnic Institute and State University	D,O
Virginia State University	M
Walden University	M,D,O
Washington State University	M,D
Wayne State College	M
Wayne State University	M,D,O*
Webster University	M,O
Western Connecticut State University	M
Western Governors University	M,O
Western Michigan University	M,D
Western New England University	M
Western Oregon University	M
West Virginia University	M,D
Widener University	M,D
Wilkes University	M,D
Wright State University	M
Youngstown State University	M

MECHANICAL ENGINEERING

Institution	Degrees
Alfred University	M,D
The American University in Cairo	M
American University of Beirut	M,D
American University of Sharjah	M
Arizona State University	M,D
Auburn University	M,D
Baylor University	M,D*
Boise State University	M
Boston University	M,D*
Bradley University	M
Brigham Young University	M,D*
Brown University	M,D
Bucknell University	M
California Institute of Technology	M,D,O
California Polytechnic State University, San Luis Obispo	M
California State Polytechnic University, Pomona	M
California State University, Fresno	M
California State University, Fullerton	M
California State University, Long Beach	M,D
California State University, Los Angeles	M*
California State University, Northridge	M

*M—master's degree; P—first professional degree; D—doctorate; O—other advanced degree; *—Close-Up and/or Display in one of the other books in this series*

Institution	Degrees
California State University, Sacramento	M
Carleton University	M,D
Carnegie Mellon University	M,D*
Case Western Reserve University	M,D*
The Catholic University of America	M,D
City College of the City University of New York	M,D
Clarkson University	M,D*
Clemson University	M,D
Cleveland State University	M,D
Colorado State University	M,D
Columbia University	M,D,O*
Concordia University (Canada)	M,D,O
Cooper Union for the Advancement of Science and Art	M
Cornell University	M,D*
Dalhousie University	M,D
Dartmouth College	M,D
Drexel University	M,D*
Duke University	M,D*
École Polytechnique de Montréal	M,D,O
Embry-Riddle Aeronautical University–Daytona	M
Fairfield University	M
Florida Agricultural and Mechanical University	M,D
Florida Atlantic University	M,D
Florida Institute of Technology	M,D
Florida International University	M,D
Florida State University	M,D
Gannon University	M
The George Washington University	M,D,O
Georgia Institute of Technology	M,D
Georgia Southern University	M,O
Graduate School and University Center of the City University of New York	D
Grand Valley State University	M
Howard University	M,D
Idaho State University	M
Illinois Institute of Technology	M,D
Indiana University–Purdue University Fort Wayne	M
Indiana University–Purdue University Indianapolis	M,D,O
Instituto Tecnológico y de Estudios Superiores de Monterrey, Campus Chihuahua	M,O
Instituto Tecnológico y de Estudios Superiores de Monterrey, Campus Monterrey	M,D
Iowa State University of Science and Technology	M,D*
The Johns Hopkins University	M,D
Kansas State University	M,D*
Kettering University	M
Lamar University	M,D
Lawrence Technological University	M,D
Lehigh University	M,D
Louisiana State University and Agricultural and Mechanical College	M,D
Louisiana Tech University	M,D
Loyola Marymount University	M
Manhattan College	M
Marquette University	M,D,O
Massachusetts Institute of Technology	M,D,O
McGill University	M,D
McMaster University	M,D
McNeese State University	M
Memorial University of Newfoundland	M,D
Mercer University	M
Michigan State University	M,D
Michigan Technological University	M,D
Mississippi State University	M,D
Missouri University of Science and Technology	M,D
Montana State University	M,D
Naval Postgraduate School	M,D,O
New Jersey Institute of Technology	M,D,O
New Mexico State University	M,D
North Carolina Agricultural and Technical State University	M,D
North Carolina State University	M,D*
North Dakota State University	M,D
Northeastern University	M,D
Northern Arizona University	M
Northern Illinois University	M
Northwestern University	M,D*
Oakland University	M,D
The Ohio State University	M,D
Ohio University	M,D*
Oklahoma State University	M,D*
Old Dominion University	M,D
Oregon State University	M,D
Penn State University Park	M,D
Polytechnic Institute of NYU	M,D
Polytechnic Institute of NYU, Long Island Graduate Center	M
Polytechnic University of Puerto Rico	M
Portland State University	M,D,O
Princeton University	M,D*
Purdue University	M,D,O
Purdue University Calumet	M
Queen's University at Kingston	M,D
Rensselaer at Hartford	M
Rensselaer Polytechnic Institute	M,D
Rice University	M,D
Rochester Institute of Technology	M
Rose-Hulman Institute of Technology	M
Rowan University	M
Royal Military College of Canada	M,D
Rutgers, The State University of New Jersey, New Brunswick	M,D*
St. Cloud State University	M
San Diego State University	M,D
San Jose State University	M
Santa Clara University	M,D,O
South Carolina State University	M
South Dakota School of Mines and Technology	M,D
South Dakota State University	M
Southern Illinois University Carbondale	M
Southern Illinois University Edwardsville	M
Southern Methodist University	M,D
Stanford University	M,D,O
State University of New York at Binghamton	M,D
Stevens Institute of Technology	M,D,O
Stony Brook University, State University of New York	M,D
Syracuse University	M,D*
Temple University	M*
Tennessee Technological University	M,D
Texas A&M University	M,D
Texas A&M University–Kingsville	M
Texas Tech University	M,D*
Trine University	M
Tufts University	M,D
Tuskegee University	M
Union Graduate College	M
Université de Moncton	M
Université de Sherbrooke	M,D
Université Laval	M,D
University at Buffalo, the State University of New York	M,D*
The University of Akron	M,D
The University of Alabama	M,D
The University of Alabama at Birmingham	M*
The University of Alabama in Huntsville	M,D
University of Alaska Fairbanks	M,D
University of Alberta	M,D
The University of Arizona	M,D
University of Arkansas	M,D
University of Bridgeport	M
The University of British Columbia	M,D
University of Calgary	M,D
University of California, Berkeley	M,D*
University of California, Davis	M,D,O
University of California, Irvine	M,D*
University of California, Los Angeles	M,D*
University of California, Merced	M,D
University of California, Riverside	M,D
University of California, San Diego	M,D*
University of California, Santa Barbara	M,D
University of Central Florida	M,D,O
University of Cincinnati	M,D
University of Colorado at Colorado Springs	M
University of Colorado Boulder	M,D*
University of Colorado Denver	M,D
University of Connecticut	M,D*
University of Dayton	M,D
University of Delaware	M,D*
University of Denver	M,D
University of Detroit Mercy	M,D
University of Florida	M,D,O*
University of Hawaii at Manoa	M,D
University of Houston	M,D
University of Illinois at Chicago	M,D
University of Illinois at Urbana–Champaign	M,D
The University of Iowa	M,D*
The University of Kansas	M,D
University of Kentucky	M,D*
University of Louisiana at Lafayette	M*
University of Louisville	M,D
University of Maine	M,D
The University of Manchester	M,D
University of Manitoba	M,D
University of Maryland, Baltimore County	M,D,O
University of Maryland, College Park	M,D
University of Massachusetts Amherst	M,D*
University of Massachusetts Dartmouth	M
University of Massachusetts Lowell	M,D
University of Memphis	M,D
University of Miami	M,D*
University of Michigan	M,D*
University of Michigan–Dearborn	M
University of Minnesota, Twin Cities Campus	M,D
University of Missouri	M,D*
University of Missouri–Kansas City	M,D*
University of Nebraska–Lincoln	M,D*
University of Nevada, Las Vegas	M,D
University of Nevada, Reno	M,D*
University of New Brunswick Fredericton	M,D
University of New Hampshire	M,D
University of New Haven	M
University of New Mexico	M,D*
University of New Orleans	M
The University of North Carolina at Charlotte	M,D
University of North Dakota	M
University of North Florida	M
University of Notre Dame	M,D*
University of Oklahoma	M,D*
University of Ottawa	M,D*
University of Pennsylvania	M,D*
University of Pittsburgh	M,D*
University of Puerto Rico, Mayagüez Campus	M
University of Rochester	M,D
University of St. Thomas (MN)	M,O
University of Saskatchewan	M,D
University of South Alabama	M
University of South Carolina	M,D
University of Southern California	M,D,O*
University of South Florida	M,D*
The University of Tennessee	M,D
The University of Tennessee at Chattanooga	M
The University of Tennessee Space Institute	M,D
The University of Texas at Arlington	M,D
The University of Texas at Austin	M,D
The University of Texas at Dallas	M*
The University of Texas at El Paso	M
The University of Texas at San Antonio	M*
The University of Texas at Tyler	M
The University of Texas–Pan American	M
The University of Toledo	M,D
University of Toronto	M,D
University of Tulsa	M,D
University of Utah	M,D*
University of Vermont	M,D
University of Victoria	M,D
University of Virginia	M,D
University of Washington	M,D*
University of Waterloo	M,D
The University of Western Ontario	M,D
University of Windsor	M,D
University of Wisconsin–Madison	M,D*
University of Wisconsin–Milwaukee	M,D,O
University of Wyoming	M,D
Utah State University	M,D
Vanderbilt University	M,D*
Villanova University	M,O

Virginia Commonwealth University M,D
Virginia Polytechnic Institute and State University M,D
Washington State University M,D
Washington State University Tri-Cities M,D
Washington State University Vancouver M
Washington University in St. Louis M,D*
Wayne State University M,D*
Western Michigan University M,D
Western New England University M
West Virginia University M,D
Wichita State University M,D
Widener University M
Wilkes University M
Worcester Polytechnic Institute M,D,O
Wright State University M
Yale University M,D*
Youngstown State University M

MECHANICS

Brown University M,D
California Institute of Technology M,D
California State University, Fullerton M
Carnegie Mellon University M,D*
Columbia University M,D,O*
Cornell University M,D*
Drexel University M,D*
École Polytechnique de Montréal M,D,O
Georgia Institute of Technology M,D
Iowa State University of Science and Technology M,D*
The Johns Hopkins University M
Lehigh University M,D
Louisiana State University and Agricultural and Mechanical College M,D
McGill University M,D
Michigan State University M,D
Michigan Technological University M
Missouri University of Science and Technology M,D
Montana State University M,D
New Mexico Institute of Mining and Technology M
North Dakota State University M,D
Northwestern University M,D*
Ohio University M,D*
Penn State University Park M,D
Rutgers, The State University of New Jersey, New Brunswick M,D*
San Diego State University M,D
Southern Illinois University Carbondale M,D
The University of Alabama M,D
The University of Arizona M,D
University of California, Berkeley M,D*
University of California, Merced M,D
University of California, San Diego M,D*
University of Cincinnati M,D
University of Dayton M
University of Illinois at Urbana–Champaign M,D
University of Maryland, College Park M,D
University of Massachusetts Lowell M,D
University of Minnesota, Twin Cities Campus M,D
University of Nebraska–Lincoln M,D*
University of New Brunswick Fredericton M,D
University of Pennsylvania M,D*
University of Southern California M,D,O*
The University of Tennessee Space Institute M,D
The University of Texas at Austin M,D
University of Wisconsin–Madison M,D*
University of Wisconsin–Milwaukee M,D,O
Virginia Polytechnic Institute and State University M,D,O

MEDIA STUDIES

American University M,D
Arizona State University M,D
Arkansas State University M
Bob Jones University P,M,D,O
Boston University M*
Brooklyn College of the City University of New York M
California State University, Fullerton M
Carnegie Mellon University M*
Central Michigan University M
City College of the City University of New York M
Claremont Graduate University M,D,O
College of Staten Island of the City University of New York M
Columbia College Chicago M
Concordia University (Canada) M,D,O
Dallas Theological Seminary M,D,O
DePaul University M
Digital Media Arts College M
Duke University M*
Emerson College M
Fairleigh Dickinson University, Metropolitan Campus M
Florida State University M,D
Fordham University M
Full Sail University M
Georgetown University M,D
Governors State University M
Howard University M,D
Hunter College of the City University of New York M
Indiana State University M
Indiana University Bloomington M,D*
Indiana University of Pennsylvania M,D
Kutztown University of Pennsylvania M
Louisiana State University and Agricultural and Mechanical College M,D
Lynn University M
Marquette University M,O
Marywood University M
Massachusetts Institute of Technology M,D
Metropolitan College of New York M
Michigan State University M,D
Missouri Western State University M
National University M
New Mexico Highlands University M
The New School: A University M,O
New York University M,D
Norfolk State University M
Northeastern University M
Northern Kentucky University M,O
Northwestern University M,D*
Ohio University M,D*
Rochester Institute of Technology M
Rutgers, The State University of New Jersey, New Brunswick D*
Saginaw Valley State University M
St. Edward's University M
San Diego State University M
San Francisco State University M
Savannah College of Art and Design M
Southern Illinois University Carbondale M
Southern Illinois University Edwardsville O
Syracuse University M*
Temple University M,D*
University at Buffalo, the State University of New York M,D,O*
The University of Alabama M
The University of Arizona M
University of California, Santa Barbara M,D
University of Chicago M,D
University of Colorado Boulder D*
University of Denver M
University of Florida M*
University of Illinois at Urbana–Champaign M,D
The University of Iowa M,D*
The University of Kansas M,D
University of Lethbridge M,D
University of Maine M
University of Maryland, College Park M,D
University of Michigan M*
University of Missouri–Kansas City M,D*
University of Nevada, Las Vegas M
The University of North Carolina at Charlotte M
The University of North Carolina at Greensboro M
University of Oregon M
University of Regina M
University of South Carolina M
University of Southern California M,D*
The University of Tennessee M,D
The University of Texas at Austin M,D
The University of Western Ontario M,D
University of Wisconsin–Madison M,D*
University of Wisconsin–Milwaukee M,O
Valparaiso University M,O
Virginia Commonwealth University M,D
Washington State University M,D
Wayne State University M,D*
Webster University M
West Virginia State University M
Wilfrid Laurier University M,D

MEDICAL/SURGICAL NURSING

Angelo State University M
Boston College M,D*
Columbia University M,O*
Daemen College M,D,O
Eastern Virginia Medical School O
Gannon University M,O
Inter American University of Puerto Rico, Arecibo Campus M
New Mexico State University M,D
Pontifical Catholic University of Puerto Rico M
Rush University M,D,O
Saint Francis Medical Center College of Nursing M,D,O
State University of New York Downstate Medical Center M,O
Uniformed Services University of the Health Sciences M*
Universidad Adventista de las Antillas P,M
University of Maryland, Baltimore M
University of Massachusetts Lowell M,D,O
University of Michigan M*
University of South Africa M,D
University of South Carolina M
University of Southern Maine M,O
Ursuline College M,D
Vanderbilt University M,D*
Waynesburg University M,D

MEDICAL ILLUSTRATION

Georgia Health Sciences University M
The Johns Hopkins University M
Rochester Institute of Technology M
University of Illinois at Chicago M
The University of Texas Southwestern Medical Center at Dallas M

MEDICAL IMAGING

Boston University M*
Cleveland State University M
Illinois Institute of Technology M,D
Medical College of Wisconsin D*
Medical University of South Carolina D
MGH Institute of Health Professions O
National University of Health Sciences M
New York University P,M,D
University of Cincinnati D
University of Colorado Denver M,D
University of Florida M,D*
University of Guelph M,D,O
University of Medicine and Dentistry of New Jersey M
University of Southern California M,D*

MEDICAL INFORMATICS

Arizona State University M,D
Cambridge College M
Columbia University M,D,O*
Dalhousie University M,D
Drexel University M,D,O*
Excelsior College O
Grand Valley State University M
Harvard University M*
Marymount University M,O

*M—master's degree; P—first professional degree; D—doctorate; O—other advanced degree; *—Close-Up and/or Display in one of the other books in this series*

Massachusetts Institute of Technology M
Medical College of Wisconsin M*
Middle Tennessee State University M
Milwaukee School of Engineering M
Northwestern University M*
Nova Southeastern University M,O*
Oregon Health & Science University M,D,O*
Rochester Institute of Technology M
Stanford University M,D
The University of Arizona M,D,O
University of California, Davis M
University of California, San Francisco D
University of Colorado Denver M,D
University of Illinois at Urbana–Champaign M,D,O
The University of Kansas M,D,O
University of Medicine and Dentistry of New Jersey M,D,O
The University of Tennessee at Chattanooga M,D,O
University of Washington M,D*
University of Wisconsin–Milwaukee D

MEDICAL MICROBIOLOGY

Creighton University M,D
Idaho State University M,D
Rutgers, The State University of New Jersey, New Brunswick M,D*
Texas Tech University Health Sciences Center M,D
Université du Québec, Institut National de la Recherche Scientifique M,D
University of Alberta M,D
University of Hawaii at Manoa M,D
University of Manitoba M,D
University of Minnesota, Duluth M,D
University of Wisconsin–La Crosse M
University of Wisconsin–Madison D*

MEDICAL PHYSICS

Cleveland State University M
Columbia University M,D,O*
East Carolina University M,D
Georgia Institute of Technology M,D
Hampton University M,D
Harvard University D*
Louisiana State University and Agricultural and Mechanical College M,D
Massachusetts Institute of Technology D
McGill University M,D
McMaster University M,D
Oakland University M,D
Rosalind Franklin University of Medicine and Science M*
Rush University M,D
Stony Brook University, State University of New York M,D
University of Alberta M,D
University of California, Los Angeles M,D*
University of Central Arkansas M
University of Chicago D
University of Cincinnati M
University of Colorado Boulder M,D*
University of Kentucky M*
University of Minnesota, Twin Cities Campus M,D
University of Missouri M,D*
University of Oklahoma Health Sciences Center M,D
University of Pennsylvania M,D*
The University of Texas Health Science Center at Houston M,D*
The University of Texas Health Science Center at San Antonio M,D
The University of Toledo M
University of Utah M,D*
University of Victoria M,D
University of Wisconsin–Madison M,D*
Vanderbilt University M*
Virginia Commonwealth University M,D
Wayne State University M,D*
Wright State University M

MEDICINAL AND PHARMACEUTICAL CHEMISTRY

Cleveland State University M,D
Duquesne University M,D
Florida Agricultural and Mechanical University M,D
Idaho State University M,D
Long Island University, C.W. Post Campus M
Medical University of South Carolina D
Purdue University M,D
Rutgers, The State University of New Jersey, New Brunswick M,D*
Temple University M,D*
University at Buffalo, the State University of New York M,D*
University of California, Irvine D*
University of California, San Francisco D
University of Connecticut M,D*
University of Florida M,D*
The University of Kansas M,D
University of Michigan D*
University of Minnesota, Twin Cities Campus M,D
University of Mississippi M,D
University of Rhode Island M,D
University of the Sciences in Philadelphia M,D
The University of Toledo M,D
University of Utah M,D*
University of Washington D*
Virginia Commonwealth University M,D
Wayne State University P,M,D*
West Virginia University M,D

MEDIEVAL AND RENAISSANCE STUDIES

Arizona State University M,D,O
California State University, Long Beach M
The Catholic University of America M,D,O
Central European University M,D
Columbia University M*
Cornell University M,D*
Fordham University M,O
Georgetown University M,D
Graduate School and University Center of the City University of New York M,D
Harvard University D*
Indiana University Bloomington M,D*
Rutgers, The State University of New Jersey, New Brunswick D*
Southern Methodist University M
University of California, Santa Barbara M,D
University of Connecticut M,D*
University of Guelph D
University of Michigan O*
University of Minnesota, Twin Cities Campus M,D
University of Notre Dame M,D*
University of Pittsburgh O*
University of Toronto M,D
Western Michigan University M
Yale University M,D*

METALLURGICAL ENGINEERING AND METALLURGY

Colorado School of Mines M,D
Columbia University M,D,O*
Massachusetts Institute of Technology M,D,O
Michigan Technological University M,D
Missouri University of Science and Technology M,D
Montana Tech of The University of Montana M
The Ohio State University M,D
Rensselaer Polytechnic Institute M,D
Université Laval M,D
The University of Alabama M,D
The University of British Columbia M,D
University of Connecticut M,D*
University of Idaho M,D
The University of Manchester M,D
University of Nebraska–Lincoln M,D*
University of Nevada, Reno M,D*
The University of Texas at El Paso M,D
University of Utah M,D*
Wayne State University M,D,O*

METEOROLOGY

Columbia University M*
Florida Institute of Technology M,D
Florida State University M,D
Georgia Institute of Technology M,D
Iowa State University of Science and Technology M,D*
McGill University M,D
Naval Postgraduate School M,D
North Carolina State University M,D*
Northern Arizona University M
Penn State University Park M,D
Plymouth State University M
Saint Louis University M,D
San Jose State University M
Texas A&M University M,D
Université du Québec à Montréal M,D,O
University of Hawaii at Manoa M,D
University of Maryland, College Park M,D
University of Miami M,D*
University of Oklahoma M,D*
Utah State University M,D
Yale University D*

MICROBIOLOGY

Albany Medical College M,D
Albert Einstein College of Medicine D
American University of Beirut P,M
Arizona State University M,D
Auburn University M,D
Baylor College of Medicine D*
Boston University M,D*
Brandeis University M,D
Brigham Young University M,D*
Brown University M,D
California State University, Long Beach M
Case Western Reserve University D*
The Catholic University of America M,D
Clemson University M,D
Colorado State University M,D
Columbia University M,D*
Cornell University D*
Dalhousie University M,D
Dartmouth College D
Drexel University M,D*
Duke University D*
East Carolina University D
Eastern New Mexico University M
East Tennessee State University M,D
Emory University D*
Emporia State University M
George Mason University M,D*
Georgetown University M,D
The George Washington University M,D,O
Georgia State University M,D
Harvard University D*
Hood College M,O
Howard University D
Idaho State University M,D
Illinois Institute of Technology M,D
Illinois State University M,D
Indiana State University M,D
Indiana University Bloomington M,D*
Indiana University–Purdue University Indianapolis M,D
Inter American University of Puerto Rico, Metropolitan Campus M
Iowa State University of Science and Technology M,D*
The Johns Hopkins University M,D
Kansas State University M,D*
Loma Linda University M,D
Long Island University, C.W. Post Campus M
Louisiana State University Health Sciences Center M,D
Louisiana State University Health Sciences Center at Shreveport M,D
Loyola University Chicago M,D
Marquette University M,D
Massachusetts Institute of Technology D
McGill University M,D
Medical College of Wisconsin M,D*
Medical University of South Carolina M,D
Meharry Medical College D
Miami University M,D
Michigan State University M,D
Montana State University M,D
New York Medical College M,D*
New York University P,M,D
North Carolina State University M,D*
North Dakota State University M,D
Northwestern University D*
The Ohio State University M,D
Ohio University M,D*
Oklahoma State University M,D*
Oregon Health & Science University D*
Oregon State University M,D

Institution	Degrees
Penn State Hershey Medical Center	M,D
Penn State University Park	M,D
Purdue University	M,D
Queen's University at Kingston	M,D
Quinnipiac University	M
Rosalind Franklin University of Medicine and Science	M,D*
Rush University	M,D
Rutgers, The State University of New Jersey, New Brunswick	M,D*
Saint Louis University	D
San Diego State University	M
San Francisco State University	M
San Jose State University	M
Seton Hall University	M,D
South Dakota State University	M,D
Southern Illinois University Carbondale	M,D
Southwestern Oklahoma State University	M
Stanford University	D
State University of New York Upstate Medical University	M,D
Stony Brook University, State University of New York	D
Temple University	M,D*
Texas A&M Health Science Center	D
Texas A&M University	M,D
Texas Tech University	M,D*
Thomas Jefferson University	M,D
Tufts University	D
Tulane University	M,D*
Universidad Central del Caribe	M,D
Université de Montréal	M,D
Université de Sherbrooke	M,D
Université du Québec, Institut National de la Recherche Scientifique	M,D
Université Laval	M,D
University at Buffalo, the State University of New York	M,D*
The University of Alabama at Birmingham	D*
University of Alberta	M,D
The University of Arizona	M,D
University of Arkansas for Medical Sciences	M,D
The University of British Columbia	M,D
University of Calgary	M,D
University of California, Berkeley	D*
University of California, Davis	M,D
University of California, Irvine	M,D*
University of California, Los Angeles	M,D*
University of California, Riverside	M,D
University of California, San Diego	D*
University of California, San Francisco	D
University of Chicago	D
University of Cincinnati	M,D
University of Colorado Boulder	M,D*
University of Colorado Denver	D
University of Connecticut	M,D*
University of Delaware	M,D*
University of Florida	M,D*
University of Georgia	M,D
University of Guelph	M,D
University of Hawaii at Manoa	M,D
University of Idaho	M,D
University of Illinois at Chicago	D
University of Illinois at Urbana–Champaign	M,D
The University of Iowa	M,D*
The University of Kansas	M,D
University of Kentucky	D*
University of Louisville	M,D
University of Maine	M,D
The University of Manchester	M,D
University of Manitoba	M,D
University of Maryland, Baltimore	D
University of Massachusetts Amherst	M,D*
University of Massachusetts Worcester	M,D
University of Medicine and Dentistry of New Jersey	M,D
University of Miami	D*
University of Michigan	D*
University of Minnesota, Twin Cities Campus	D
University of Mississippi Medical Center	M,D
University of Missouri	M,D*
The University of Montana	M,D
University of Nebraska Medical Center	M,D
University of New Hampshire	M,D
University of New Mexico	M,D,O*
The University of North Carolina at Chapel Hill	M,D*
University of North Dakota	M,D
University of North Texas Health Science Center at Fort Worth	M,D
University of Oklahoma	M,D*
University of Oklahoma Health Sciences Center	M,D
University of Ottawa	M,D*
University of Pennsylvania	D*
University of Pittsburgh	M,D,O*
University of Puerto Rico, Medical Sciences Campus	M,D
University of Rhode Island	M,D
University of Rochester	
University of Saskatchewan	M,D
The University of South Dakota	M,D
University of Southern California	M,D*
University of Southern Mississippi	M,D
The University of Tennessee	M,D
The University of Texas at Austin	D
The University of Texas Health Science Center at Houston	M,D*
The University of Texas Health Science Center at San Antonio	D
The University of Texas Medical Branch	M,D
The University of Texas Southwestern Medical Center at Dallas	D
University of Vermont	M,D
University of Victoria	M,D
University of Virginia	D
University of Washington	D*
The University of Western Ontario	M,D
University of Wisconsin–La Crosse	M
University of Wisconsin–Madison	D*
University of Wisconsin–Oshkosh	M
University of Wyoming	D
Utah State University	M,D
Vanderbilt University	M,D*
Virginia Commonwealth University	M,D,O
Virginia Polytechnic Institute and State University	D
Wagner College	M
Wake Forest University	D
Washington State University	M,D
Washington University in St. Louis	D*
Wayne State University	M,D*
West Virginia University	M,D
Wright State University	M
Yale University	D*
Youngstown State University	M

MIDDLE SCHOOL EDUCATION

Institution	Degrees
Alaska Pacific University	M
Albany State University	M
American International College	M,D,O
Appalachian State University	M
Arkansas State University	M,O
Armstrong Atlantic State University	M
Austin College	M
Bellarmine University	M,D,O
Belmont University	M
Berry College	M
Brenau University	M,O
Brooklyn College of the City University of New York	M
California Lutheran University	M,D
California State University, Bakersfield	M
California State University, Fullerton	M
Cambridge College	M,D,O
Campbell University	M
Canisius College	M,O
Capella University	M,D,O
Carlow University	M
Central Michigan University	M
Chicago State University	M
City College of the City University of New York	M,O
Clemson University	M
Cleveland State University	M
The College at Brockport, State University of New York	M
College of Mount St. Joseph	M
College of Mount Saint Vincent	M,O
Columbus State University	M,O
Daemen College	M
Dowling College	M,D,O
Drury University	M
East Carolina University	M
Eastern Illinois University	M
Eastern Michigan University	M
Eastern Nazarene College	M,O
Edinboro University of Pennsylvania	M
Emory University	M,D,O*
Fayetteville State University	M
Fitchburg State University	M
Fresno Pacific University	M
Gardner-Webb University	M
Georgia College & State University	M,O
Georgia Southern University	M
Georgia Southwestern State University	M,O
Georgia State University	M,O
Grand Valley State University	M,O
Hampton University	M
Hebrew College	M,O
Henderson State University	M
Hofstra University	M,O
Hood College	M,O
James Madison University	M
John Carroll University	M
Kennesaw State University	M
Kent State University	M*
LaGrange College	M
Le Moyne College	M,O
Lesley University	M,D,O
Lewis & Clark College	M
Long Island University, C.W. Post Campus	M
Manhattanville College	M*
Mary Baldwin College	M
Maryville University of Saint Louis	M,D
McNeese State University	M,O
Mercer University	M,D,O
Mercy College	M
Merrimack College	M,O
Middle Tennessee State University	M,O
Montclair State University	M,D,O
Morehead State University	M,O
Morgan State University	M
Mount Saint Mary College	M,O
Mount Saint Vincent University	M
Murray State University	M,O
Nazareth College of Rochester	M
Niagara University	M,O
North Carolina Central University	M
North Carolina State University	M*
North Georgia College & State University	M,O
Northwestern State University of Louisiana	M
Northwest Missouri State University	M
Oberlin College	M
The Ohio State University at Lima	M
The Ohio State University at Marion	M
The Ohio State University–Mansfield Campus	M
The Ohio State University–Newark Campus	M
Ohio University	M,D*
Old Dominion University	M
Our Lady of the Lake University of San Antonio	M
Pacific University	M
Park University	M
Piedmont College	M,D,O
Plymouth State University	M
Quinnipiac University	M
Roberts Wesleyan College	M,O
Saginaw Valley State University	M
St. Bonaventure University	M
St. John Fisher College	M
St. John's University (NY)	M,O
Saint Peter's College	M,O
St. Thomas Aquinas College	M,O
Salem College	M
Salem State University	M
Shenandoah University	M,D,O
Shippensburg University of Pennsylvania	M
Siena Heights University	M
Simmons College	M,O
Smith College	M
Southeast Missouri State University	M
Southern Arkansas University–Magnolia	M
Spalding University	M

*M—master's degree; P—first professional degree; D—doctorate; O—other advanced degree; *—Close-Up and/or Display in one of the other books in this series*

State University of New York at Oswego M
State University of New York College at Oneonta M
State University of New York College at Potsdam M
Suffolk University M,O
Texas Christian University M
Tufts University M,D
Union College (KY) M
Union Graduate College M,O
University of Arkansas M,D,O
University of Arkansas at Little Rock M
University of Central Florida M
University of Dayton M
University of Georgia M,D,O
University of Kentucky M,D*
University of Louisiana at Monroe M
University of Louisville M,D
University of Massachusetts Dartmouth M,O
University of Memphis M,D
University of Missouri–St. Louis M,O
The University of North Carolina at Charlotte M,D
The University of North Carolina at Greensboro M,D,O
The University of North Carolina at Pembroke M
The University of North Carolina Wilmington M
University of Northern Iowa M
University of Phoenix–Oregon Campus M
University of Southern Maine M,O
University of the Cumberlands M,D,O
The University of Toledo M,D,O
University of Washington, Bothell M
University of West Florida M,D,O
University of West Georgia M,O
University of Wisconsin–Milwaukee M
University of Wisconsin–Platteville M
Ursuline College M
Valdosta State University M,O
Wagner College M
Walden University M,D,O
Western Kentucky University M,O
Widener University M,D
Winthrop University M
Worcester State University M
Wright State University M
Youngstown State University M

MILITARY AND DEFENSE STUDIES

American Public University System M
Austin Peay State University M
Columbia College (MO) M
The George Washington University M
Hawai'i Pacific University M*
Henley-Putnam University M
The Institute of World Politics M,O
The Johns Hopkins University M
The Judge Advocate General's School, U.S. Army M
Missouri State University M
National Defense Intelligence College M
National Defense University M
Naval Postgraduate School M,D
Norwich University M
Royal Military College of Canada M,D
School of Advanced Air and Space Studies M
United States Army Command and General Staff College M
University of Calgary M,D
University of Colorado Denver M,D
University of Detroit Mercy M
University of Pittsburgh M*
The University of Texas at El Paso M,O
University of West Florida M

MINERAL/MINING ENGINEERING

Colorado School of Mines M,D
Columbia University M,D,O*
Dalhousie University M,D
Laurentian University M,D
McGill University M,D,O
Michigan Technological University M,D
Missouri University of Science and Technology M,D
Montana Tech of The University of Montana M
New Mexico Institute of Mining and Technology M
Penn State University Park M,D
Queen's University at Kingston M,D
Southern Illinois University Carbondale M
Université du Québec en Abitibi-Témiscamingue M,O
Université Laval M,D
University of Alaska Fairbanks M
University of Alberta M,D
The University of Arizona M,O
The University of British Columbia M,D
University of Idaho M,D
University of Kentucky M,D*
University of Nevada, Reno M*
University of North Dakota M
The University of Texas at Austin M
University of Utah M,D*
Virginia Polytechnic Institute and State University M,D
West Virginia University M,D

MINERAL ECONOMICS

Colorado School of Mines M,D
Michigan Technological University M
The University of Texas at Austin M

MINERALOGY

Cornell University M,D*
Indiana University Bloomington M,D*
Université du Québec à Chicoutimi D
Université du Québec à Montréal M,D,O

MISSIONS AND MISSIOLOGY

Abilene Christian University M
Ambrose University College P,M,O
Anderson University (IN) P,M,D
Asbury Theological Seminary M,D,O
Assemblies of God Theological Seminary P,M,D
Associated Mennonite Biblical Seminary P,M,O
Baptist Bible College of Pennsylvania P,M,D
Bethel Seminary P,M,D,O
Biblical Theological Seminary P,M,D,O
Biola University M,D,O
Briercrest Seminary M
Calvin Theological Seminary P,M,D
Catholic Theological Union at Chicago P,M,D,O
Central Baptist Theological Seminary P,M,O
Columbia International University P,M,D,O
Dallas Baptist University M
Dallas Theological Seminary M,D,O
Eastern University D
Emmanuel Christian Seminary P,M,D
Evangelical Theological Seminary P,M
Faulkner University M
Fresno Pacific University M
Fuller Theological Seminary P,M,D
Gardner-Webb University P,D
George Fox University P,M,D,O
Global University P,M
Gordon-Conwell Theological Seminary P,M,D
Grace Theological Seminary P,M,D,O
Grand Rapids Theological Seminary of Cornerstone University P,M
Hope International University M
Knox Theological Seminary M
Luther Rice University P,M,D
Midwestern Baptist Theological Seminary P,M,D,O
Nazarene Theological Seminary P,M,D
Northwest Nazarene University P,M
Northwest University M
Oral Roberts University P,M,D
Phillips Theological Seminary P,M,D
Providence College and Theological Seminary P,M,D,O
Reformed Theological Seminary–Jackson Campus P,M,D,O
Regent University P,M,D
Rochester College M
Saint Paul University M
Simpson University P,M
Southeastern Baptist Theological Seminary P,M,D
Southern Adventist University M
Southern Baptist Theological Seminary P,M,D
Southern Evangelical Seminary P,M,D,O
Southwestern Assemblies of God University P,M
Southwestern Christian University M
Taylor College and Seminary P,M,O
Trinity International University P,M,D,O
Trinity School for Ministry P,M,D,O
Tyndale University College & Seminary P,M,O
University of South Africa M,D
Villanova University M
Wesley Biblical Seminary P,M
Westminster Theological Seminary P,M,D,O
Wheaton College M,O

MODELING AND SIMULATION

Academy of Art University M
Arizona State University M,D
California State University, Chico M
Columbus State University M,O
George Mason University M,D,O*
Louisiana Tech University M,D
Naval Postgraduate School M,D
Old Dominion University M,D
Portland State University M,D,O
Stevens Institute of Technology M,D,O
Trent University M,D
Université Laval M,O
University at Buffalo, the State University of New York M,D,O*
The University of Alabama in Huntsville M,D,O
University of California, San Diego M,D*
University of Central Florida M,D,O
The University of Manchester M,D
University of Northern Iowa M
University of Southern California M,D*
Worcester Polytechnic Institute M,D

MOLECULAR BIOLOGY

Albany Medical College M,D
Albert Einstein College of Medicine D
Appalachian State University M
Arizona State University M,D
Arkansas State University D,O
Auburn University M,D
Baylor College of Medicine D*
Boston University M,D*
Brandeis University M,D
Brigham Young University M,D*
Brown University M,D
California Institute of Technology D
Carnegie Mellon University M,D*
Case Western Reserve University D*
Central Connecticut State University M
Clemson University D
Colorado State University M,D
Columbia University D*
Cornell University D*
Cornell University, Joan and Sanford I. Weill Medical College and Graduate School of Medical Sciences M,D
Dartmouth College D
Drexel University M,D*
Duke University D,O*
East Carolina University M,D
Eastern Michigan University M
Eastern New Mexico University M
Emory University D*
Florida Institute of Technology M
Florida State University M,D
George Mason University M,D*
Georgetown University M,D
The George Washington University M,D
Georgia Health Sciences University M,D
Georgia State University M,D
Grand Valley State University M
Harvard University D*
Hood College M,O

Howard University M,D
Illinois Institute of Technology M,D
Illinois State University M,D
Indiana University Bloomington M,D*
Indiana University–Purdue University Indianapolis D
Inter American University of Puerto Rico, Metropolitan Campus M
Iowa State University of Science and Technology M,D*
The Johns Hopkins University M,D
Kent State University M,D*
Lehigh University M,D
Louisiana State University Health Sciences Center at Shreveport M,D
Loyola University Chicago M,D
Marquette University M,D
Massachusetts Institute of Technology D
Mayo Graduate School D
McMaster University M,D
Medical University of South Carolina M,D
Michigan State University M,D
Mississippi State University M,D
Missouri State University M
Montclair State University M,O
New Mexico State University M,D
New York Medical College M,D*
New York University P,M,D
North Dakota State University M,D
Northwestern University D*
OGI School of Science & Engineering at Oregon Health & Science University M,D
The Ohio State University M,D
Ohio University M,D*
Oklahoma State University M,D*
Oklahoma State University Center for Health Sciences M,O
Oregon Health & Science University M,D*
Oregon State University M,D
Penn State Hershey Medical Center M,D
Penn State University Park M,D
Princeton University D*
Purdue University M,D
Queen's University at Kingston M,D
Quinnipiac University M
Rosalind Franklin University of Medicine and Science M,D*
Rutgers, The State University of New Jersey, New Brunswick M,D*
Saint Louis University D
San Diego State University M,D
San Francisco State University M
San Jose State University M
Seton Hall University M,D
Simon Fraser University M,D
Southern Illinois University Carbondale M,D
State University of New York Downstate Medical Center D
State University of New York Upstate Medical University M,D
Stony Brook University, State University of New York M,D
Temple University M,D*
Texas A&M Health Science Center D
Texas Woman's University M,D
Thomas Jefferson University D
Tufts University D
Tulane University M,D*
Uniformed Services University of the Health Sciences D*
Universidad Central del Caribe M,D
Université de Montréal M,D
Université Laval M,D
University at Albany, State University of New York M,D
University at Buffalo, the State University of New York D*
The University of Alabama at Birmingham D*
University of Alberta M,D
The University of Arizona M,D
University of Arkansas M,D
University of Arkansas for Medical Sciences M,D
The University of British Columbia M,D
University of Calgary M,D
University of California, Berkeley D*
University of California, Davis M,D
University of California, Irvine M,D*
University of California, Los Angeles M,D*
University of California, Riverside M,D
University of California, San Diego D*
University of California, San Francisco D
University of California, Santa Barbara M,D
University of California, Santa Cruz M,D
University of Chicago D
University of Cincinnati M,D
University of Colorado Boulder M,D*
University of Colorado Denver D
University of Connecticut M*
University of Connecticut Health Center D*
University of Delaware M,D*
University of Florida M,D*
University of Georgia M,D
University of Guelph M,D
University of Hawaii at Manoa M,D
University of Idaho M,D
University of Illinois at Chicago D
The University of Iowa D*
The University of Kansas M,D
University of Lethbridge M,D
University of Louisville M,D
University of Maine M,D
The University of Manchester M,D
University of Maryland, Baltimore M,D
University of Maryland, Baltimore County M,D
University of Maryland, College Park D
University of Massachusetts Boston D
University of Medicine and Dentistry of New Jersey M,D
University of Miami D*
University of Michigan M,D*
University of Minnesota, Duluth M,D
University of Minnesota, Twin Cities Campus M,D
University of Missouri–Kansas City D*
University of Missouri–St. Louis M,D,O
University of Nebraska Medical Center M,D
University of Nevada, Reno M,D*
University of New Haven M,O
University of New Mexico M,D,O*
The University of North Carolina at Chapel Hill M,D*
University of North Dakota M,D
University of North Texas M,D
University of North Texas Health Science Center at Fort Worth M,D
University of Notre Dame M,D*
University of Oklahoma Health Sciences Center M,D
University of Oregon M,D
University of Ottawa M,D*
University of Pennsylvania D*
University of Pittsburgh D*
University of Puerto Rico, Río Piedras M,D
University of Rhode Island M,D
University of South Carolina M,D
The University of South Dakota M,D
University of Southern California M,D*
University of Southern Maine M
University of Southern Mississippi M,D
University of South Florida M,D*
The University of Texas at Austin D
The University of Texas at Dallas M,D*
The University of Texas Health Science Center at Houston M,D*
University of the Sciences in Philadelphia D
University of Utah D*
University of Vermont M,D
University of Washington D*
The University of Western Ontario M,D
University of Wisconsin–La Crosse M
University of Wisconsin–Madison D*
University of Wisconsin–Parkside M
University of Wyoming M,D
Utah State University M,D
Vanderbilt University M,D*
Virginia Commonwealth University M,D
Virginia Polytechnic Institute and State University D
Wake Forest University D
Washington State University M,D
Washington University in St. Louis D*
Wayne State University M,D*
Wesleyan University D*
West Virginia University M,D
Wright State University M
Yale University D*
Youngstown State University M

MOLECULAR BIOPHYSICS

Baylor College of Medicine D*
California Institute of Technology M,D
Carnegie Mellon University D*
Duke University O*
Florida State University D
Illinois Institute of Technology M,D
The Johns Hopkins University M,D
Rutgers, The State University of New Jersey, New Brunswick D*
Texas Tech University Health Sciences Center M,D
University of Massachusetts Amherst D*
University of Pennsylvania D*
University of Pittsburgh D*
The University of Texas Medical Branch M,D
The University of Texas Southwestern Medical Center at Dallas D
Washington University in St. Louis D*
Yale University D*

MOLECULAR GENETICS

Albert Einstein College of Medicine D
Duke University D*
Emory University D*
The George Washington University M,D
Georgia State University M,D
Harvard University D*
Illinois State University M,D
Indiana University–Purdue University Indianapolis M,D
Medical College of Wisconsin M,D*
Michigan State University M,D
New York University M,D
The Ohio State University M,D
Oklahoma State University M,D*
Rutgers, The State University of New Jersey, New Brunswick M,D*
Stony Brook University, State University of New York D
Texas Tech University Health Sciences Center M,D
The University of Alabama at Birmingham D*
University of California, Irvine M,D*
University of California, Los Angeles M,D*
University of California, Riverside D
University of Cincinnati M,D
University of Florida M,D*
University of Guelph M,D
University of Illinois at Chicago D
The University of Manchester M,D
University of Maryland, College Park M,D
University of Massachusetts Worcester M,D
University of Medicine and Dentistry of New Jersey M,D
University of Pittsburgh M,D*
University of Rhode Island M,D
The University of Texas Health Science Center at Houston M,D*
University of Vermont M,D
University of Virginia D
Wake Forest University D
Washington University in St. Louis D*

MOLECULAR MEDICINE

Baylor College of Medicine D*
Boston University D*
Case Western Reserve University D*
Cleveland State University M,D
Cornell University M,D*
Dartmouth College D
Drexel University M*

*M—master's degree; P—first professional degree; D—doctorate; O—other advanced degree; *—Close-Up and/or Display in one of the other books in this series*

- The George Washington University D
- Georgia Health Sciences University M,D
- Hofstra University P,D
- The Johns Hopkins University D
- North Shore–LIJ Graduate School of Molecular Medicine D
- Penn State Hershey Medical Center M,D
- Queen's University at Kingston M,D
- Texas A&M Health Science Center D
- University of Chicago D
- University of Cincinnati D
- University of Maryland, Baltimore M,D
- University of Medicine and Dentistry of New Jersey D
- The University of Texas Health Science Center at San Antonio M,D
- University of Washington D*
- Wake Forest University M,D
- Yale University D*

MOLECULAR PATHOGENESIS

- Dartmouth College D
- Emory University D*
- North Dakota State University M,D
- Texas A&M Health Science Center D
- University at Albany, State University of New York M,D
- University of Chicago D
- Washington University in St. Louis D*

MOLECULAR PATHOLOGY

- Texas Tech University Health Sciences Center M
- University of California, San Diego D*
- University of Medicine and Dentistry of New Jersey M,D,O
- University of Michigan D*
- University of Pittsburgh M,D*
- The University of Texas Health Science Center at Houston M,D*
- Yale University D*

MOLECULAR PHARMACOLOGY

- Albert Einstein College of Medicine D
- Brown University M,D
- Dartmouth College D
- Harvard University D*
- Mayo Graduate School D
- Medical University of South Carolina M,D
- New York University D
- Purdue University M,D
- Rosalind Franklin University of Medicine and Science M,D*
- Rutgers, The State University of New Jersey, New Brunswick D*
- Stanford University D
- Thomas Jefferson University D
- University at Buffalo, the State University of New York D*
- University of Massachusetts Worcester M,D
- University of Medicine and Dentistry of New Jersey M,D
- University of Nevada, Reno D*
- University of Pittsburgh M,D*
- University of Southern California M,D*

MOLECULAR PHYSIOLOGY

- Baylor College of Medicine D*
- Case Western Reserve University M,D*
- Loyola University Chicago M,D
- Rutgers, The State University of New Jersey, New Brunswick M,D*
- Stony Brook University, State University of New York D
- Texas Tech University Health Sciences Center M,D
- Thomas Jefferson University D
- Tufts University D
- The University of Alabama at Birmingham D*
- University of Chicago D
- University of Illinois at Urbana–Champaign M,D
- The University of North Carolina at Chapel Hill D*
- University of Pittsburgh M,D*
- University of Vermont M,D
- University of Virginia M,D
- Vanderbilt University M,D*
- Yale University D*

MOLECULAR TOXICOLOGY

- Massachusetts Institute of Technology D
- New York University M,D
- North Carolina State University M,D*
- Oregon State University M,D
- Penn State Hershey Medical Center M,D
- University of California, Berkeley D*
- University of California, Los Angeles D*
- University of Cincinnati M,D

MULTILINGUAL AND MULTICULTURAL EDUCATION

- Alliant International University–Irvine M,O
- Alliant International University–San Francisco M,O
- American College of Education M
- Azusa Pacific University M
- Bank Street College of Education M
- Belhaven University (MS) M
- Bennington College M
- Brooklyn College of the City University of New York M
- Brown University M,D
- Buffalo State College, State University of New York M
- California State University, Bakersfield M
- California State University, Chico M
- California State University, Dominguez Hills M*
- California State University, Fullerton M
- California State University, Northridge M
- California State University, Sacramento M
- California State University, San Bernardino M
- California State University, Stanislaus M
- Capella University M,D,O
- Chicago State University M
- City College of the City University of New York M
- The College at Brockport, State University of New York M,O
- College of Mount St. Joseph M
- College of Mount Saint Vincent M,O
- The College of New Rochelle M,O
- The College of Saint Rose M,O
- Columbia College Chicago M
- Columbia International University M,D,O
- DePaul University M,D
- Eastern Michigan University M,D,O
- Eastern New Mexico University M
- Eastern University M
- Fairfield University M,O
- Fairleigh Dickinson University, Metropolitan Campus M
- Florida Atlantic University M,D,O
- Florida International University M,D,O
- Fordham University M,D,O
- Fresno Pacific University M
- George Fox University M
- Georgetown University M,D,O
- Graduate Institute of Applied Linguistics M,O
- Harvard University D*
- Heritage University M
- Hofstra University M,D,O
- Howard University M,D
- Hunter College of the City University of New York M
- Immaculata University M
- Indiana State University M,O
- Indiana University Bloomington M,D*
- Kean University M
- Langston University M
- Lehman College of the City University of New York M
- Long Island University, Brooklyn Campus M
- Long Island University, C.W. Post Campus M
- Long Island University, Westchester Graduate Campus M,O
- Loyola Marymount University M
- Manhattan College M,O
- Mercy College M,O
- Mercyhurst College M,O
- Minnesota State University Mankato M,O
- National University M
- New Jersey City University M
- New Mexico State University M,D
- New York University M,D,O
- Northeastern Illinois University M
- Northern Arizona University M,D,O
- Nova Southeastern University M,O*
- Ohio University M,D*
- Our Lady of the Lake University of San Antonio M
- Park University M
- Queens College of the City University of New York M,O
- Rowan University O
- Rutgers, The State University of New Jersey, New Brunswick M,D*
- St. John's University (NY) M
- San Diego State University M,D
- Seton Hall University O
- Southern Connecticut State University M
- Southern Methodist University M,D,O
- State University of New York at New Paltz M
- State University of New York College at Geneseo M
- Sul Ross State University M
- Teachers College, Columbia University M
- Texas A&M University M,D
- Texas A&M University–Commerce M,D
- Texas A&M University–Kingsville M,D
- Texas A&M University–San Antonio M
- Texas Southern University M,D
- Texas State University–San Marcos M
- Texas Tech University M,D*
- University at Buffalo, the State University of New York M,D,O*
- University of Alaska Fairbanks M,D,O
- University of Alberta M
- The University of Arizona M,D,O
- University of California, Riverside M,D
- University of Colorado Boulder M,D*
- University of Colorado Denver M
- University of Connecticut M,D,O*
- University of Delaware M,D,O*
- The University of Findlay M
- University of Florida M,D,O*
- University of Houston–Clear Lake M
- University of Houston–Downtown M
- University of Illinois at Chicago M,D
- University of La Verne O
- University of Maryland, Baltimore County M,D
- University of Massachusetts Amherst M,D,O*
- University of Massachusetts Boston M
- University of Miami D*
- University of Michigan M,D*
- University of Minnesota, Twin Cities Campus M
- University of New Mexico D*
- The University of North Carolina at Greensboro M,D,O
- University of Oklahoma M,D,O*
- University of Pennsylvania M,D*
- University of St. Thomas (MN) M,O
- University of San Francisco M,D
- University of Southern California D*
- The University of Tennessee M,D,O
- The University of Texas at Brownsville M
- The University of Texas at El Paso M,D,O
- The University of Texas at San Antonio M,D*
- The University of Texas–Pan American M
- University of the Incarnate Word M,D
- University of Washington M,D*
- University of Wisconsin–Milwaukee D
- Utah State University M
- Vanderbilt University M,D*
- Walden University M,D,O
- Washington State University M,D
- Wayne State University M,D,O*

Western New Mexico University M
Western Oregon University M
Xavier University M

MUSEUM EDUCATION

Bank Street College of Education M
The George Washington University M
Seton Hall University M
The University of the Arts M*

MUSEUM STUDIES

Arizona State University M,D,O
Bard College M
Baylor University M*
Boston University M,D,O*
Brown University M,D
California College of the Arts M
California State University, Chico M
Caribbean University M,D
Case Western Reserve University M,D*
Christie's Education M
City College of the City University of New York M
Claremont Graduate University M,D,O
Cleveland State University M,D
Duquesne University M
Fashion Institute of Technology M*
Florida State University M,D,O
The George Washington University M,O
Harvard University M,O*
Indiana University–Purdue University Indianapolis M,O
John F. Kennedy University M,O
The Johns Hopkins University M
Maryland Institute College of Art M
Montclair State University M,O
New York University M,O
San Francisco Art Institute M
San Francisco State University M
Seton Hall University M
Southern Illinois University Edwardsville O
State University of New York College at Oneonta M
Syracuse University M*
Texas Tech University M*
Tufts University O
Université de Montréal M
Université du Québec à Montréal M
Université Laval O
University at Buffalo, the State University of New York M,O*
The University of British Columbia M,D,O
University of California, Riverside M,D
University of Central Oklahoma M
University of Colorado Boulder M*
University of Denver M
University of Florida M,D*
University of Hawaii at Manoa O
The University of Kansas M
University of Louisville M,D
The University of Manchester D
University of Missouri–St. Louis M,O
University of New Hampshire M,D
The University of North Carolina at Greensboro M,D,O
University of North Texas M,D,O
University of Oklahoma M*
University of South Carolina M,O
The University of the Arts M*
University of Toronto M,D
University of Tulsa M
University of Washington M*
University of West Georgia M,O
University of Wisconsin–Milwaukee M,D,O
Virginia Commonwealth University M,D
Western Illinois University M,O

MUSIC

Academy of Art University M
Alabama Agricultural and Mechanical University M
Alabama State University M
Andrews University M
Appalachian State University M
Arizona State University M,D
Arkansas State University M,O
Austin Peay State University M
Azusa Pacific University M
Bard College M
Baylor University M*
Belmont University M
Bennington College M
Bethesda Christian University P,M
Bob Jones University P,M,D,O
Boise State University M
The Boston Conservatory M,O
Boston University M,D,O*
Bowling Green State University M,D*
Brandeis University M,D
Brandon University M
Brigham Young University M*
Brooklyn College of the City University of New York M,D,O
Brown University D
Butler University M
California Baptist University M
California Institute of the Arts M,O
California State University, Chico M
California State University, East Bay M
California State University, Fresno M
California State University, Fullerton M
California State University, Long Beach M
California State University, Los Angeles M*
California State University, Northridge M
California State University, Sacramento M
Campbellsville University M
Capital University M
Cardinal Stritch University M
Carleton University M
Carnegie Mellon University M*
Case Western Reserve University M,D*
The Catholic University of America M,D,O
Central Michigan University M
Central Washington University M
City College of the City University of New York M
Claremont Graduate University M,D
Cleveland Institute of Music M,D,O
Cleveland State University M
The College of Saint Rose M
Colorado State University M
Columbia College Chicago M
Columbia University M,D*
Concordia University (Canada) O
Concordia University Chicago M
Concordia University Wisconsin M
Conservatorio de Musica O
Converse College M
Cornell University M,D*
Curtis Institute of Music M
Dalhousie University M
Dartmouth College M
DePaul University M,O
Duke University M,D*
Duquesne University M,O
East Carolina University M
Eastern Illinois University M
Eastern Kentucky University M
Eastern Michigan University M
Eastern Washington University M
Edinboro University of Pennsylvania M,O
Emory University M*
Emporia State University M
Five Towns College M,D
Florida Atlantic University M
Florida International University M
Florida State University M,D
Fuller Theological Seminary P,M,D
Garrett-Evangelical Theological Seminary P,M,D
George Mason University M,D,O*
Georgia Southern University M
Georgia State University M
Graduate School and University Center of the City University of New York D
Gratz College M,O
Hardin-Simmons University M
Harvard University M,D*
Hebrew College M,O
Hebrew Union College–Jewish Institute of Religion (NY) M
Hofstra University M,O
Hollins University M,O
Holy Names University M,O
Hope International University M
Houghton College M
Howard University M
Hunter College of the City University of New York M
Illinois State University M
Indiana State University M
Indiana University Bloomington M,D,O*
Indiana University of Pennsylvania M
Indiana University–Purdue University Indianapolis M
Indiana University South Bend M
Ithaca College M
Jacksonville State University M
James Madison University D
The Jewish Theological Seminary M
The Johns Hopkins University M,D,O
The Juilliard School M,D,O
Kansas State University M*
Kent State University M,D*
Lamar University M
Lee University M
Long Island University, C.W. Post Campus M
Longy School of Music M,O
Louisiana State University and Agricultural and Mechanical College M,D
Loyola University New Orleans M
Lynchburg College M
Lynn University M,O
Manhattan School of Music M,D,O
Mansfield University of Pennsylvania M
Marshall University M
McGill University M,D
Memorial University of Newfoundland M,D
Mercer University P,M
Messiah College M
Miami University M
Michigan State University M,D
Middle Tennessee State University M
Midwestern Baptist Theological Seminary P,M,D,O
Mills College M
Minnesota State University Mankato M
Mississippi College M
Missouri State University M
Montclair State University M,O
Morehead State University M
Morgan State University M
Murray State University M
New England Conservatory of Music M,D,O
New Jersey City University M
New Mexico State University M
New Orleans Baptist Theological Seminary P,M,D
The New School: A University M
New York University M,D,O
The Nigerian Baptist Theological Seminary P,M,D,O
Norfolk State University M
North Carolina Central University M
North Dakota State University M,D
Northeastern Illinois University M
Northern Arizona University M,O
Northern Illinois University M,O
Northern Kentucky University M,O
North Park University M
Northwestern State University of Louisiana M
Northwestern University M,D,O*
Notre Dame de Namur University M,O
Oakland University M,D
Oberlin College M,O
The Ohio State University M,D
Ohio University M,O*
Oklahoma City University M
Oklahoma State University M*
Penn State University Park M,D
Phillips Theological Seminary P,M,D
Pittsburg State University M
Point Park University M
Portland State University M
Princeton University D*
Purchase College, State University of New York M
Queens College of the City University of New York M
Radford University M
Reinhardt University M
Rice University M,D
Rider University M

*M—master's degree; P—first professional degree; D—doctorate; O—other advanced degree; *—Close-Up and/or Display in one of the other books in this series*

Institution	Degrees
Roosevelt University	M,O
Rowan University	M
Rutgers, The State University of New Jersey, Newark	M*
Rutgers, The State University of New Jersey, New Brunswick	M,D,O*
St. Cloud State University	M
Saint John's University (MN)	P,M
Saint Joseph's College	M,O
St. Vladimir's Orthodox Theological Seminary	P,M,D
Samford University	M
Sam Houston State University	M
San Diego State University	M
San Francisco Conservatory of Music	M
San Francisco State University	M
San Jose State University	M
Savannah College of Art and Design	M,O
School of the Art Institute of Chicago	M
Seabury-Western Theological Seminary	P,M,D,O
Shenandoah University	M,D,O
Southeastern Baptist Theological Seminary	P,M,D
Southeastern Louisiana University	M
Southern Baptist Theological Seminary	P,M,D
Southern Illinois University Carbondale	M
Southern Illinois University Edwardsville	M
Southern Methodist University	M,O
Southwestern Baptist Theological Seminary	M,D,O
Southwestern College (KS)	M
Southwestern Oklahoma State University	M
Stanford University	M,D
State University of New York at Binghamton	M
State University of New York at Fredonia	M
State University of New York at New Paltz	M
State University of New York College at Potsdam	M
Stephen F. Austin State University	M
Stony Brook University, State University of New York	M,D
Syracuse University	M*
Temple University	M,D*
Texas A&M University–Commerce	M
Texas Christian University	M,D,O
Texas Southern University	M
Texas State University–San Marcos	M
Texas Tech University	M,D*
Texas Woman's University	M
Towson University	M
Trinity Lutheran Seminary	P,M
Troy University	M
Truman State University	M
Tufts University	M
Tulane University	M*
Université de Montréal	M,D,O
Université Laval	M,D
University at Buffalo, the State University of New York	M,D*
The University of Akron	M
The University of Alabama	M,D
University of Alaska Fairbanks	M
University of Alberta	M,D
The University of Arizona	M,D
University of Arkansas	M
The University of British Columbia	M,D
University of Calgary	M,D
University of California, Berkeley	D*
University of California, Davis	M,D
University of California, Irvine	M*
University of California, Los Angeles	M,D*
University of California, Riverside	M,D
University of California, San Diego	M,D*
University of California, Santa Barbara	M,D
University of California, Santa Cruz	M,D
University of Central Arkansas	M
University of Central Florida	M
University of Central Missouri	M
University of Central Oklahoma	M
University of Chicago	M,D
University of Cincinnati	M,D,O
University of Colorado Boulder	M,D*
University of Colorado Denver	M
University of Connecticut	M,D,O*
University of Delaware	M*
University of Denver	M,O
University of Florida	M,D*
University of Georgia	M,D
University of Hartford	M,D,O
University of Hawaii at Manoa	M,D
University of Houston	M,D
University of Idaho	M
University of Illinois at Urbana–Champaign	M,D,O
The University of Iowa	M,D*
The University of Kansas	M,D
University of Kentucky	M,D*
University of Lethbridge	M,D
University of Louisiana at Lafayette	M*
University of Louisiana at Monroe	M
University of Louisville	M
University of Maine	M
The University of Manchester	D
University of Manitoba	M
University of Maryland, Baltimore County	O
University of Maryland, College Park	M,D
University of Massachusetts Amherst	M,D*
University of Massachusetts Lowell	M
University of Memphis	M,D
University of Miami	M,D,O*
University of Michigan	M,D,O*
University of Minnesota, Duluth	M
University of Minnesota, Twin Cities Campus	M,D
University of Mississippi	M,D
University of Missouri	M*
University of Missouri–Kansas City	M,D*
The University of Montana	M
University of Nebraska at Omaha	M
University of Nebraska–Lincoln	M,D*
University of Nevada, Las Vegas	M,D
University of Nevada, Reno	M*
University of New Hampshire	M
University of New Mexico	M*
University of New Orleans	M
The University of North Carolina at Chapel Hill	M,D*
The University of North Carolina at Greensboro	M,D
University of North Carolina School of the Arts	M
University of North Dakota	M,D
University of Northern Colorado	M,D
University of Northern Iowa	M
University of North Texas	M,D
University of Oklahoma	M,D*
University of Oregon	M,D
University of Ottawa	M,O*
University of Pennsylvania	M,D*
University of Pittsburgh	M,D*
University of Redlands	M
University of Regina	M
University of Rhode Island	M
University of Rochester	
University of St. Thomas (MN)	M
University of Saskatchewan	M
University of South Africa	M,D
University of South Carolina	M,D,O
The University of South Dakota	M
University of Southern California	M,D,O*
University of Southern Maine	M
University of Southern Mississippi	M,D
University of South Florida	M,D*
The University of Tennessee	M
The University of Tennessee at Chattanooga	M
The University of Texas at Arlington	M
The University of Texas at Austin	M,D
The University of Texas at El Paso	M
The University of Texas at San Antonio	M,O*
The University of Texas–Pan American	M
The University of the Arts	M*
University of the Pacific	M
The University of Toledo	M
University of Toronto	M,D
University of Trinity College	P,M,D,O
University of Utah	M,D*
University of Victoria	M,D
University of Virginia	M,D
University of Washington	M,D*
The University of Western Ontario	M,D
University of West Georgia	M
University of Wisconsin–Madison	M,D*
University of Wisconsin–Milwaukee	M,O
University of Wyoming	M
Valley Forge Christian College	M
Vermont College of Fine Arts	M
Virginia Commonwealth University	M
Washington State University	M
Washington University in St. Louis	M,D*
Wayne State University	M,O*
Webster University	M
Wesleyan University	M,D*
West Chester University of Pennsylvania	M,O
Western Carolina University	M
Western Illinois University	M
Western Michigan University	M
Western Oregon University	M
Western Washington University	M
West Texas A&M University	M
West Virginia University	M,D
Wichita State University	M
William Paterson University of New Jersey	M
Winthrop University	M
Wright State University	M
Yale University	M,D,O*
York University	M,D*
Youngstown State University	M

MUSIC EDUCATION

Institution	Degrees
Alabama Agricultural and Mechanical University	M
Appalachian State University	M
Arcadia University	M,D,O*
Arizona State University	M,D
Arkansas State University	M,O
Auburn University	M,D,O
Austin College	M
Austin Peay State University	M
Azusa Pacific University	M
Ball State University	M,D
Belmont University	M
Bennington College	M
Bob Jones University	P,M,D,O
Boise State University	M
The Boston Conservatory	M,O
Boston University	M,D*
Bowling Green State University	M,D*
Brandon University	M
Brigham Young University	M*
Brooklyn College of the City University of New York	M,D,O
Butler University	M
California Baptist University	M
California State University, Fresno	M
California State University, Fullerton	M
California State University, Los Angeles	M*
California State University, Northridge	M
Campbellsville University	M
Capital University	M
Carnegie Mellon University	M*
Case Western Reserve University	M,D*
Central Connecticut State University	M,O
Central Michigan University	M
Christopher Newport University	M
Cleveland State University	M
College of Charleston	M
College of Mount St. Joseph	M
The College of Saint Rose	M,O
The Colorado College	M
Colorado State University–Pueblo	M
Columbus State University	M,O
Conservatorio de Musica	M
Converse College	M
DePaul University	M,O
Duquesne University	M,O
East Carolina University	M
Eastern Kentucky University	M
Eastern Michigan University	M

Institution	Degrees
Eastern Washington University	M
Emporia State University	M
Five Towns College	M,D
Florida International University	M
Florida State University	M,D
George Mason University	M,D,O*
Georgia College & State University	M
Georgia State University	M,D,O
Gordon College	M
Hampton University	M
Hardin-Simmons University	M
Hebrew College	M,O
Heidelberg University	M
Hofstra University	M,O
Holy Names University	M,O
Howard University	M
Hunter College of the City University of New York	M
Indiana University of Pennsylvania	M
Inter American University of Puerto Rico, Metropolitan Campus	M
Inter American University of Puerto Rico, San Germán Campus	M
Ithaca College	M
Jackson State University	M
Jacksonville University	M
James Madison University	M,D
Kansas State University	M*
Kent State University	M,D*
Lamar University	M
Lebanon Valley College	M
Lee University	M
Lehman College of the City University of New York	M
Long Island University, C.W. Post Campus	M
Louisiana State University and Agricultural and Mechanical College	M,D
Manhattanville College	M*
Marywood University	M
McGill University	M,D
McKendree University	M
McNeese State University	M,O
Miami University	M
Michigan State University	M,D
Minot State University	M
Mississippi College	M
Missouri State University	M
Montclair State University	M,O
Morehead State University	M
Murray State University	M
Nazareth College of Rochester	M
New Jersey City University	M
New Mexico State University	M
New York University	M,D,O
Norfolk State University	M
North Dakota State University	M,D,O
Northwestern University	M,D*
Northwest Missouri State University	M
Oakland University	M,D
Ohio University	M,O*
Oklahoma State University	M*
Old Dominion University	M
Oregon State University	M
Pittsburg State University	M
Portland State University	M
Queens College of the City University of New York	M,O
Radford University	M
Reinhardt University	M
Rhode Island College	M
Rider University	M
Rollins College	M
Roosevelt University	M,O
Rutgers, The State University of New Jersey, New Brunswick	M,D,O*
St. Cloud State University	M
Samford University	M
Sam Houston State University	M
San Diego State University	M
San Francisco State University	M
Shenandoah University	M,D,O
Silver Lake College	M
Southern Illinois University Carbondale	M
Southern Illinois University Edwardsville	M,O
Southern Methodist University	M,O
Southwestern College (KS)	M
Southwestern Oklahoma State University	M
State University of New York at Fredonia	M
State University of New York College at Potsdam	M
Syracuse University	M*
Tarleton State University	M
Teachers College, Columbia University	M,D
Temple University	M,D*
Tennessee State University	M
Texas A&M University–Commerce	M
Texas A&M University–Kingsville	M
Texas Christian University	M,D,O
Texas State University–San Marcos	M
Texas Tech University	M,D*
Towson University	M,O
Troy University	M
Union College (KY)	M
Université Laval	M,D
University at Buffalo, the State University of New York	M,D,O*
The University of Akron	M
The University of Alabama	M,D,O
University of Alaska Fairbanks	M
The University of Arizona	M,D
The University of British Columbia	M,D
University of Central Arkansas	M
University of Central Oklahoma	M
University of Cincinnati	M
University of Colorado Boulder	M,D*
University of Connecticut	M,D,O*
University of Dayton	M
University of Delaware	M*
University of Denver	M,O
University of Florida	M,D*
University of Georgia	M,D,O
University of Hartford	M,D,O
University of Houston	M,D
University of Illinois at Urbana–Champaign	M,D,O
The University of Kansas	M,D
University of Kentucky	M,D*
University of Louisiana at Lafayette	M*
University of Louisville	M,D
University of Maryland, Baltimore County	M
University of Maryland, College Park	M,D
University of Massachusetts Lowell	M
University of Memphis	M,D
University of Miami	M,D,O*
University of Michigan	M,D,O*
University of Minnesota, Duluth	M
University of Missouri	M,D,O*
University of Missouri–Kansas City	M,D*
University of Missouri–St. Louis	M
The University of Montana	M
University of Nebraska at Kearney	M
University of Nebraska–Lincoln	M,D*
University of New Hampshire	M
University of New Mexico	M*
The University of North Carolina at Chapel Hill	M*
The University of North Carolina at Charlotte	M,D
The University of North Carolina at Greensboro	M,D
The University of North Carolina at Pembroke	M
University of North Dakota	M,D
University of Northern Colorado	M,D
University of Northern Iowa	M
University of North Texas	M,D
University of Oklahoma	M,D*
University of Oregon	M,D
University of Ottawa	M,O*
University of Rhode Island	M,D
University of Rochester	
University of St. Thomas (MN)	M
University of South Carolina	M,D,O
University of Southern California	M,D,O*
University of Southern Mississippi	M,D
University of South Florida	M,D*
The University of Tennessee	M
The University of Tennessee at Chattanooga	M
The University of Texas at Arlington	M
The University of Texas at El Paso	M
The University of Texas–Pan American	M
The University of the Arts	M*
University of the Pacific	M
The University of Toledo	M,D,O
University of Toronto	M,D
University of Victoria	M,D
University of Washington	M,D*
University of West Georgia	M
University of Wisconsin–Madison	M,D*
University of Wisconsin–Milwaukee	M,O
University of Wisconsin–Stevens Point	M
University of Wyoming	M
VanderCook College of Music	M
Virginia Commonwealth University	M
Washington State University	M
Wayne State College	M
Wayne State University	M,O*
Webster University	M
West Chester University of Pennsylvania	M,O
Western Carolina University	M
Western Connecticut State University	M
Western Kentucky University	M
Western Michigan University	M
West Virginia University	M,D
Wichita State University	M
Winthrop University	M
Wright State University	M
Youngstown State University	M

NANOTECHNOLOGY

Institution	Degrees
Arizona State University	M,D
The Johns Hopkins University	M
North Dakota State University	D
Oregon State University	M,D
South Dakota School of Mines and Technology	D
University at Albany, State University of New York	M,D
University of Alberta	M,D
University of California, Riverside	M,D
University of New Mexico	M,D*
University of Washington	M,D*
Virginia Commonwealth University	M,D

NATIONAL SECURITY

Institution	Degrees
American Public University System	M
California State University, San Bernardino	M
George Mason University	M,D,O*
Henley-Putnam University	D
Hult International Business School (United States)	M
The Institute of World Politics	M,O
Kansas State University	M,D*
National Defense University	M
Naval Postgraduate School	M
Naval War College	M
New York University	M
Nova Southeastern University	M,O*
Texas A&M University	M,O
Trinity (Washington) University	M
Troy University	M
University of Denver	M,D,O
University of New Haven	M,O
University of Pittsburgh	M*
The University of Texas at El Paso	M,O
Virginia Polytechnic Institute and State University	M,O

NATURAL RESOURCES

Institution	Degrees
American University	M,D,O
Auburn University	M,D
Ball State University	M
California Polytechnic State University, San Luis Obispo	M
Central Washington University	M
Colorado State University	M,D
Cornell University	M,D*
Dalhousie University	M
Delaware State University	M
Duke University	M,D*
East Carolina University	D
Georgia Institute of Technology	M,D
Humboldt State University	M
Instituto Tecnologico de Santo Domingo	M,D,O
Iowa State University of Science and Technology	M,D*
Laurentian University	M,D
Louisiana State University and Agricultural and Mechanical College	M,D
Marylhurst University	M
McGill University	M,D
Michigan State University	M,D
Missouri State University	M
Montana State University	M
North Carolina State University	M,D*

*M—master's degree; P—first professional degree; D—doctorate; O—other advanced degree; *—Close-Up and/or Display in one of the other books in this series*

Institution	Degrees
North Dakota State University	M,D
The Ohio State University	M,D
Oklahoma State University	M,D*
Purdue University	M,D
San Francisco State University	M
State University of New York College of Environmental Science and Forestry	M,D
Texas A&M University	M,D
Texas Tech University	M,D*
Universidad Metropolitana	M
Universidad Nacional Pedro Henriquez Urena	M
Université du Québec à Montréal	M,D,O
Université du Québec en Abitibi-Témiscamingue	M,D
University of Alaska Fairbanks	M,D
University of Alberta	M,D
University of Arkansas at Monticello	M
The University of British Columbia	M,D
University of California, Berkeley	M,D*
University of Connecticut	M,D*
University of Delaware	M*
University of Denver	M,O
University of Florida	M,D*
University of Georgia	M,D
University of Guelph	M,D
University of Hawaii at Manoa	M,D
University of Idaho	M,D
University of Illinois at Urbana–Champaign	M,D
University of Maine	M,D
The University of Manchester	M,D
University of Manitoba	M,D
University of Maryland, College Park	M,D
University of Michigan	M,D*
University of Minnesota, Twin Cities Campus	M,D
University of Missouri	M*
The University of Montana	M,D
University of Nebraska–Lincoln	M,D*
University of New Brunswick Saint John	M
University of New Hampshire	M,D
University of New Mexico	M,D*
University of Northern British Columbia	M,D,O
University of Northern Iowa	M
University of Oklahoma	M,D*
University of Rhode Island	M,D
University of San Francisco	M
University of South Africa	M,D
The University of Texas at Austin	M
University of Vermont	M,D
University of Washington	M,D*
University of Wisconsin–Madison	M,D*
University of Wisconsin–Stevens Point	M
University of Wyoming	M,D
Utah State University	M
Virginia Polytechnic Institute and State University	M,O
Washington State University	M,D
West Virginia University	M,D

NATUROPATHIC MEDICINE

Institution	Degrees
Bastyr University	D
Canadian College of Naturopathic Medicine	D*
National College of Natural Medicine	M,D
National University of Health Sciences	P,M,D
Southwest College of Naturopathic Medicine and Health Sciences	D
Universidad del Turabo	D
University of Bridgeport	D

NEAR AND MIDDLE EASTERN LANGUAGES

Institution	Degrees
The American University in Cairo	M,O
American University of Beirut	M
Bethel Seminary	P,M,D,O
Brandeis University	M,D
The Catholic University of America	M,D
Columbia University	M,D*
Georgetown University	M,D
Harvard University	M,D*
Hebrew Union College–Jewish Institute of Religion (NY)	D
Indiana University Bloomington	M,D*
The Ohio State University	M,D
Oral Roberts University	P,M,D
University of California, Los Angeles	M,D*
University of Chicago	M,D
The University of Manchester	M,D
University of Maryland, College Park	M,O
University of Michigan	M,D*
University of South Africa	M,D
The University of Texas at Austin	M,D
University of Utah	M,D*
University of Wisconsin–Madison	M,D*
Wayne State University	M*
Yale University	M,D*

NEAR AND MIDDLE EASTERN STUDIES

Institution	Degrees
The American University in Cairo	M,O
American University of Beirut	M
The American University of Paris	M
Brandeis University	M,D
California State University, Long Beach	M
The Catholic University of America	M,D
Columbia University	M,D,O*
Cornell University	M,D*
Emory University	D,O*
Georgetown University	M,D,O
The George Washington University	M
Harvard University	M,D*
The Johns Hopkins University	D
McGill University	M,D,O
New York University	M,D,O
Princeton University	M,D*
Rice University	D
Southern Evangelical Seminary	P,M,D,O
Syracuse University	O*
The University of Arizona	M,D
University of California, Berkeley	M,D*
University of California, Los Angeles	M,D*
University of Chicago	M,D
The University of Kansas	M
The University of Manchester	M,D
University of Memphis	M,D
University of Michigan	M,D*
University of Pennsylvania	M,D*
University of South Africa	M,D
The University of Texas at Austin	M,D
University of Toronto	M,D
University of Utah	M,D*
University of Virginia	M
University of Washington	M,D*
University of Waterloo	M
University of Wisconsin–Madison	M,D*
Wayne State University	M*
Wilfrid Laurier University	M
Yale University	M,D*

NEUROBIOLOGY

Institution	Degrees
Albert Einstein College of Medicine	D
Brandeis University	M,D
California Institute of Technology	D
Carnegie Mellon University	M,D*
Case Western Reserve University	D*
Columbia University	D*
Cornell University	D*
Dalhousie University	M,D
Duke University	D*
Georgia State University	M,D
Harvard University	D*
Illinois State University	M,D
Louisiana State University Health Sciences Center	M,D
Loyola University Chicago	M,D
Massachusetts Institute of Technology	D
New York University	M,D
Northwestern University	M,D*
Purdue University	M,D
Queen's University at Kingston	M,D
Université Laval	M,D
University at Albany, State University of New York	M,D
The University of Alabama at Birmingham	D*
University of Arkansas for Medical Sciences	M,D
University of California, Irvine	M,D*
University of California, Los Angeles	D*
University of California, San Diego	D*
University of Chicago	D
University of Colorado Boulder	M,D*
University of Connecticut	M,D*
University of Illinois at Chicago	D
The University of Iowa	M,D*
University of Kentucky	D*
University of Louisville	M,D
The University of Manchester	M,D
University of Maryland, Baltimore	D
University of Minnesota, Twin Cities Campus	M,D
University of Missouri	M,D*
The University of North Carolina at Chapel Hill	D*
University of Oklahoma	M,D*
University of Rochester	M,D
University of Southern California	M,D*
The University of Texas at Austin	D
The University of Texas at San Antonio	M,D*
University of Utah	D*
University of Washington	D*
University of Wisconsin–Madison	D*
Virginia Commonwealth University	D
Wake Forest University	D
Wesleyan University	D*
West Virginia University	M,D
Yale University	D*

NEUROSCIENCE

Institution	Degrees
Albany Medical College	M,D
American University	M,D
American University of Beirut	P,M
Argosy University, Chicago	D*
Argosy University, Phoenix	M,D*
Argosy University, Schaumburg	M,D,O*
Argosy University, Tampa	M,D*
Arizona State University	M,D
Baylor College of Medicine	D*
Boston University	M,D*
Brandeis University	M,D
Brigham Young University	M,D*
Brock University	M,D
Brown University	D
California Institute of Technology	M,D
Carleton University	M,D
Carnegie Mellon University	D*
Case Western Reserve University	D*
Central Michigan University	M,D
College of Staten Island of the City University of New York	M
Colorado State University	D
Cornell University, Joan and Sanford I. Weill Medical College and Graduate School of Medical Sciences	M,D
Dalhousie University	M,D
Dartmouth College	D
Delaware State University	M,D
Drexel University	M,D*
Duke University	D,O*
Emory University	D*
Florida Atlantic University	D
Florida State University	M,D
George Mason University	M,D,O*
Georgetown University	D
Georgia Health Sciences University	M,D
Graduate School and University Center of the City University of New York	D
Harvard University	D*
Hunter College of the City University of New York	M,D
Illinois State University	M,D
Indiana University Bloomington	D*
Iowa State University of Science and Technology	M,D*
The Johns Hopkins University	D
Kent State University	M,D*
Lehigh University	M,D
Louisiana State University Health Sciences Center	M,D
Loyola University Chicago	M,D
Marquette University	M,D
Massachusetts Institute of Technology	D
Mayo Graduate School	D
McGill University	M,D
McMaster University	M,D
Medical College of Wisconsin	D*
Medical University of South Carolina	M,D
Meharry Medical College	D
Memorial University of Newfoundland	M,D
Michigan State University	M,D
Montana State University	M,D
Mount Sinai School of Medicine	M,D
New York Medical College	M,D*

Institution	Degree
New York University	P,M,D
Northwestern University	D*
The Ohio State University	M,D
Ohio University	M,D*
Oregon Health & Science University	D*
Penn State Hershey Medical Center	M,D
Princeton University	D*
Queen's University at Kingston	M,D
Rosalind Franklin University of Medicine and Science	D*
Rush University	M,D
Rutgers, The State University of New Jersey, Newark	D*
Rutgers, The State University of New Jersey, New Brunswick	M,D*
Seton Hall University	M,D
Stanford University	D
State University of New York Downstate Medical Center	D
State University of New York Upstate Medical University	D
Stony Brook University, State University of New York	D
Teachers College, Columbia University	M
Temple University	M,D*
Texas A&M Health Science Center	D
Texas A&M University	M,D
Texas Christian University	M,D
Texas Tech University Health Sciences Center	M,D
Thomas Jefferson University	D
Tufts University	D
Tulane University	M,D*
Uniformed Services University of the Health Sciences	D*
Universidad de Iberoamerica	P,M,D
Université de Montréal	M,D
University at Albany, State University of New York	M,D
University at Buffalo, the State University of New York	M,D*
University of Alberta	M,D
The University of Arizona	D
The University of British Columbia	M,D
University of Calgary	M,D
University of California, Berkeley	D*
University of California, Davis	D
University of California, Irvine	D*
University of California, Los Angeles	D*
University of California, Riverside	D
University of California, San Diego	D*
University of California, San Francisco	D
University of Chicago	D
University of Cincinnati	D
University of Colorado Denver	D
University of Connecticut	M,D,O*
University of Connecticut Health Center	D*
University of Delaware	D*
University of Denver	D
University of Florida	M,D*
University of Georgia	D
University of Guelph	M,D,O
University of Hartford	M
University of Idaho	M,D
University of Illinois at Chicago	D
University of Illinois at Urbana–Champaign	D
The University of Iowa	D*
The University of Kansas	M,D
University of Lethbridge	M,D
University of Maine	D
The University of Manchester	M,D
University of Maryland, Baltimore	D
University of Maryland, Baltimore County	D
University of Maryland, College Park	M,D
University of Massachusetts Amherst	M,D*
University of Massachusetts Worcester	M,D
University of Medicine and Dentistry of New Jersey	M,D
University of Miami	M,D*
University of Michigan	D*
University of Minnesota, Twin Cities Campus	M,D
University of Missouri	M,D*
University of Missouri–St. Louis	M,D,O
The University of Montana	M,D
University of Nebraska Medical Center	M,D
University of New Mexico	M,D,O*
University of Oklahoma Health Sciences Center	M,D
University of Oregon	M,D
University of Pennsylvania	D*
University of Pittsburgh	D*
University of Puerto Rico, Río Piedras	M,D
University of Rochester	M,D
The University of South Dakota	M,D
University of Southern California	M,D*
University of South Florida	D*
The University of Texas at Austin	D
The University of Texas at Dallas	M,D*
The University of Texas Health Science Center at Houston	M,D*
The University of Texas Health Science Center at San Antonio	D
The University of Texas Medical Branch	D
The University of Texas Southwestern Medical Center at Dallas	D
The University of Toledo	M,D
University of Utah	D*
University of Vermont	D
University of Virginia	D
The University of Western Ontario	M,D
University of Wisconsin–Madison	D*
Virginia Commonwealth University	M,D,O
Wake Forest University	D
Washington State University	M,D
Washington University in St. Louis	D*
Wayne State University	M,D*
West Virginia University	D
Wilfrid Laurier University	M,D
Yale University	D*

NONPROFIT MANAGEMENT

Institution	Degree
American International College	M
American Jewish University	M
American Public University System	M
American University	M,D,O
Arizona State University	M,D,O
Assumption College	M,O
Avila University	M,O
Azusa Pacific University	M
Bay Path College	M
Bernard M. Baruch College of the City University of New York	M
Brandeis University	M
Brigham Young University	M*
California Lutheran University	M,O
Cambridge College	M
Capella University	M,D,O
Carlos Albizu University, Miami Campus	M,D
Case Western Reserve University	M,O*
Cleary University	M,O
Cleveland State University	M,D,O
The College at Brockport, State University of New York	M,O
College of Notre Dame of Maryland	M
The College of Saint Rose	O
Columbia University	M*
Corban University	M
Daemen College	M
Dallas Baptist University	M
DePaul University	M,O
Eastern Michigan University	M,O
Eastern University	M
East Tennessee State University	M,O
Fairleigh Dickinson University, Metropolitan Campus	M,O
Florida Atlantic University	M
George Mason University	M,D,O*
Georgia State University	M,D,O
Hamline University	M,D
Hebrew Union College–Jewish Institute of Religion (NY)	M
High Point University	M
Hope International University	M
Husson University	M
Indiana University Bloomington	M,D,O*
Indiana University Northwest	M,O
Indiana University–Purdue University Indianapolis	M,O
Indiana University South Bend	M,O
John Carroll University	M
Kean University	M
Kentucky State University	M
Lasell College	M,O
Lindenwood University	M
Lipscomb University	M
Long Island University, C.W. Post Campus	M,O
Marquette University	M,O
Marylhurst University	M
Marywood University	M
Metropolitan State University	M,D,O
MidAmerica Nazarene University	M
New England College	M
New Mexico Highlands University	M
The New School: A University	M
New York University	M,D,O
North Carolina State University	M,D,O*
North Central College	M
Northern Kentucky University	M,O
North Park University	M
Oklahoma City University	M
Oral Roberts University	M
Our Lady of the Lake University of San Antonio	M
Pace University	M
Park University	M
Providence College	M
Regis University	M,O
Robert Morris University	M
Roberts Wesleyan College	M,O
St. Cloud State University	M
Saint Xavier University	M,O
San Francisco State University	M
Seattle University	M
Seton Hall University	M,O
Southern Adventist University	M
Southern New Hampshire University	M,D,O
Spertus Institute of Jewish Studies	M
Suffolk University	M,O
Texas A&M University	M,O
Trinity (Washington) University	M
Trinity Western University	M,O
Troy University	M
Tufts University	O
University of Arkansas at Little Rock	O
University of Central Florida	M,O
University of Colorado Denver	M,D
University of Connecticut	M,O*
University of Delaware	M,D*
University of Georgia	M,O
University of La Verne	M,O
University of Louisville	M,D
University of Maryland, Baltimore County	M,O
University of Memphis	M
University of Michigan–Dearborn	M,O
University of Missouri–St. Louis	M,O
University of Nevada, Las Vegas	M,D,O
The University of North Carolina at Charlotte	M,D,O
The University of North Carolina at Greensboro	M,O
University of Northern Iowa	M
University of North Florida	M,O
University of Notre Dame	M*
University of Pittsburgh	M*
University of Portland	M
University of San Diego	M,D,O
University of San Francisco	M
University of Southern California	M,O*
University of Southern Maine	M,O
The University of Tampa	M
The University of Tennessee at Chattanooga	M,O
University of the Sacred Heart	M
University of the West	M
The University of Toledo	M,O
University of Wisconsin–Milwaukee	M,D,O
Virginia Commonwealth University	O
Virginia Polytechnic Institute and State University	M,D,O
Walden University	M,D,O
Webster University	M,D,O
West Chester University of Pennsylvania	M,O
Western Michigan University	M,D,O
Worcester State University	M

*M—master's degree; P—first professional degree; D—doctorate; O—other advanced degree; *—Close-Up and/or Display in one of the other books in this series*

NORTHERN STUDIES

Institution	Degrees
University of Alaska Fairbanks	M
University of Manitoba	M

NUCLEAR ENGINEERING

Institution	Degrees
Air Force Institute of Technology	M,D
Arizona State University	M,D,O
Colorado School of Mines	M,D
École Polytechnique de Montréal	M,D,O
Georgia Institute of Technology	M,D
Idaho State University	M,D,O
Kansas State University	M,D*
Massachusetts Institute of Technology	M,D,O
McMaster University	M,D
Missouri University of Science and Technology	M,D
North Carolina State University	M,D*
The Ohio State University	M,D
Oregon State University	M,D
Penn State University Park	M,D
Purdue University	M,D
Rensselaer Polytechnic Institute	M,D
Royal Military College of Canada	M,D
Texas A&M University	M,D
University of California, Berkeley	M,D*
University of Cincinnati	M,D
University of Florida	M,D,O*
University of Idaho	M,D
University of Illinois at Urbana–Champaign	M,D
The University of Manchester	M,D
University of Maryland, College Park	M,D
University of Massachusetts Lowell	M,D
University of Michigan	M,D,O*
University of Missouri	M,D*
University of Nevada, Las Vegas	M,D
University of New Mexico	M,D*
University of South Carolina	M,D
The University of Tennessee	M,D
University of Utah	M,D*
University of Wisconsin–Madison	M,D*

NURSE ANESTHESIA

Institution	Degrees
Albany Medical College	M
Arkansas State University	M,O
Barry University	M*
Baylor College of Medicine	M,D*
Boston College	M,D*
Bradley University	M
BryanLGH College of Health Sciences	M
Case Western Reserve University	M*
Central Connecticut State University	M,O
Columbia University	M,O*
DePaul University	M
Drexel University	M*
Duke University	M,D,O*
Fairfield University	M,D
Florida Hospital College of Health Sciences	M
Gannon University	M,O
Georgetown University	M
Georgia Health Sciences University	M
Goldfarb School of Nursing at Barnes-Jewish College	M,O
Gonzaga University	M
Gooding Institute of Nurse Anesthesia	M
Inter American University of Puerto Rico, Arecibo Campus	M
La Roche College	M
Lincoln Memorial University	M
Louisiana State University Health Sciences Center	M,D
Mayo School of Health Sciences	M
Medical University of South Carolina	M
Middle Tennessee School of Anesthesia	M
Midwestern University, Glendale Campus	M
Millikin University	M
Missouri State University	M
Mount Marty College	M
Murray State University	M
Newman University	M
Northeastern University	M,O
Oakland University	M,O
Old Dominion University	M
Oregon Health & Science University	M*
Our Lady of the Lake College	M
Rosalind Franklin University of Medicine and Science	M*
Rush University	M,D,O
Saint Joseph's University	M,O
Saint Mary's University of Minnesota	M
Saint Vincent College	M
Samford University	M,D
Samuel Merritt University	M,O
Southern Illinois University Edwardsville	M,O
State University of New York Downstate Medical Center	M
Texas Christian University	M,D
Texas Wesleyan University	M,D
Uniformed Services University of the Health Sciences	M*
Union University	M,D,O
The University of Alabama at Birmingham	M*
The University of British Columbia	M,D
University of Cincinnati	M,D
University of Detroit Mercy	M
The University of Kansas	M
University of Medicine and Dentistry of New Jersey	M,D,O
University of Miami	M,D*
University of Michigan–Flint	M
University of Minnesota, Twin Cities Campus	M
University of New England	M
The University of North Carolina at Charlotte	M,O
The University of North Carolina at Greensboro	M,D,O
University of North Dakota	M,D
University of North Florida	M,D,O
University of Pennsylvania	M*
University of Pittsburgh	M,D*
The University of Scranton	M,O
University of South Carolina	M
The University of Tennessee at Chattanooga	M,D,O
University of Wisconsin–La Crosse	M
Villanova University	M,D,O
Virginia Commonwealth University	M,D
Wayne State University	M,O*
Webster University	M
Westminster College (UT)	M

NURSE MIDWIFERY

Institution	Degrees
Case Western Reserve University	M,D*
Columbia University	M*
DeSales University	M,O
Emory University	M*
Frontier School of Midwifery and Family Nursing	M,O
Georgetown University	M
Marquette University	M,D,O
Midwives College of Utah	M
National College of Midwifery	M,D
New York University	M,D,O
Old Dominion University	M
Oregon Health & Science University	M,O*
Philadelphia University	M,O
Shenandoah University	M,D,O
State University of New York Downstate Medical Center	M,O
Stony Brook University, State University of New York	M,O
University of Cincinnati	M,D
University of Colorado Denver	M,D
University of Illinois at Chicago	M
University of Indianapolis	M
The University of Kansas	M,D,O
The University of Manchester	M,D
University of Maryland, Baltimore	M
University of Medicine and Dentistry of New Jersey	M,O
University of Miami	M,D*
University of Michigan	M,O*
University of Minnesota, Twin Cities Campus	M
University of Pennsylvania	M*
University of Puerto Rico, Medical Sciences Campus	M,O
University of South Africa	M,D
Vanderbilt University	M,D*
Wichita State University	M,D

NURSING—GENERAL

Institution	Degrees
Abilene Christian University	M,O
Adelphi University	M,D,O*
Albany State University	M
Alcorn State University	M
Allen College	M,D,O
Alverno College	M
American International College	M
American Sentinel University	M
American University of Beirut	M
Andrews University	M
Arizona State University	M,D,O
Arkansas State University	M,O
Arkansas Tech University	M
Armstrong Atlantic State University	M
Athabasca University	M,O
Auburn University	M
Augsburg College	M
Aurora University	M,D
Austin Peay State University	M
Azusa Pacific University	M,D
Ball State University	M,D
Barry University	M,D,O*
Baylor University	M*
Bellarmine University	M,D
Bellin College	M
Belmont University	M
Benedictine University	M
Bethel College	M
Bethel University (MN)	M,O
Blessing-Rieman College of Nursing	M
Bloomsburg University of Pennsylvania	M
Boston College	M,D*
Bowie State University	M
Bradley University	M
Briar Cliff University	M
Brigham Young University	M*
California Baptist University	M
California State University, Bakersfield	M
California State University, Chico	M
California State University, Dominguez Hills	M*
California State University, Fresno	M
California State University, Fullerton	M
California State University, Long Beach	M
California State University, Los Angeles	M*
California State University, Sacramento	M
California State University, San Bernardino	M
California State University, Stanislaus	M
Capital University	M
Cardinal Stritch University	M
Carlow University	M,D
Carson-Newman College	M
Case Western Reserve University	M,D*
The Catholic University of America	M,D,O
Central Methodist University	M
Chatham University	M,D
Clarion University of Pennsylvania	M
Clarke University	M,O
Clarkson College	M,O
Clayton State University	M
Clemson University	M,D
Cleveland State University	M
College of Mount St. Joseph	M
College of Mount Saint Vincent	M,O
The College of New Jersey	M,O
The College of New Rochelle	M,O
College of Saint Elizabeth	M
College of Saint Mary	M
The College of St. Scholastica	M,O
College of Staten Island of the City University of New York	M,O
Colorado State University–Pueblo	M
Columbia University	M,D,O*
Concordia University Wisconsin	M
Coppin State University	M,O
Cox College	M
Creighton University	M,D
Curry College	M
Daemen College	M,D,O
Dalhousie University	M,D
Delaware State University	M
Delta State University	M
DePaul University	M
DeSales University	M,O
Dominican College	M
Dominican University of California	M
Drexel University	M*
Duke University	D*
Duquesne University	M,D,O
D'Youville College	M,O*
East Carolina University	M,D
Eastern Kentucky University	M
East Tennessee State University	M,D,O
Edgewood College	M

Institution	Degrees
Edinboro University of Pennsylvania	M,O
Elmhurst College	M
Elms College	M
Emory University	M,D*
Endicott College	M
Excelsior College	M
Fairfield University	M,D
Fairleigh Dickinson University, Metropolitan Campus	M,D,O
Fairmont State University	M
Felician College	M,D,O*
Ferris State University	M
Florida Agricultural and Mechanical University	M
Florida Atlantic University	M,D,O
Florida Gulf Coast University	M
Florida International University	M,D
Florida Southern College	M
Florida State University	M,D,O
Fort Hays State University	M
Framingham State University	M
Franciscan University of Steubenville	M
Franklin Pierce University	M,D,O
Frontier School of Midwifery and Family Nursing	M,O
Gannon University	M,O
Gardner-Webb University	M,D,O
George Mason University	M,D,O*
Georgetown University	M
The George Washington University	M,D,O
Georgia College & State University	M
Georgia Health Sciences University	D
Georgia Southern University	M,D,O
Georgia State University	M,D,O
Goldfarb School of Nursing at Barnes-Jewish College	M,O
Gonzaga University	M
Goshen College	M
Governors State University	M
Graceland University (IA)	M,O
Graduate School and University Center of the City University of New York	D
Grambling State University	M,O
Grand Canyon University	M,O
Grand Valley State University	M,D
Grand View University	M
Gwynedd-Mercy College	M
Hampton University	M,D
Hardin-Simmons University	M
Hawai'i Pacific University	M*
Herzing University Online	M
Holy Family University	M*
Holy Names University	M,O
Howard University	M,O
Hunter College of the City University of New York	M,O
Husson University	M,O
Idaho State University	M,O
Illinois State University	M,D,O
Immaculata University	M
Independence University	M
Indiana State University	M
Indiana University of Pennsylvania	D
Indiana University–Purdue University Fort Wayne	M,O
Indiana University–Purdue University Indianapolis	M,D
Indiana Wesleyan University	M,O
Inter American University of Puerto Rico, Arecibo Campus	M
Jacksonville State University	M
Jacksonville University	M
James Madison University	M
Jefferson College of Health Sciences	M
The Johns Hopkins University	M,D,O
Kaplan University, Davenport Campus	M
Kean University	M
Keiser University	M
Kennesaw State University	M,D
Kent State University	M,D*
Keuka College	M
Lamar University	M
La Roche College	M
La Salle University	M,O
Laurentian University	M
Lehman College of the City University of New York	M
Le Moyne College	M,O
Lewis University	M
Liberty University	M,D
Lincoln Memorial University	M
Loma Linda University	M
Long Island University, Brooklyn Campus	M,O
Long Island University, C.W. Post Campus	M,O
Louisiana State University Health Sciences Center	M,D
Loyola University Chicago	M,D
Loyola University New Orleans	M,D
Lynchburg College	M
Madonna University	M
Malone University	M
Mansfield University of Pennsylvania	M
Marian University (WI)	M
Marquette University	M,D,O
Marshall University	M
Marymount University	M,D,O
Maryville University of Saint Louis	M,D
Massachusetts College of Pharmacy and Health Sciences	M
McGill University	M,D,O
McKendree University	M
McMaster University	M,D
McNeese State University	M
Medical University of South Carolina	D
Memorial University of Newfoundland	M,O
Mercer University	M,D,O
Mercy College	M,O
Metropolitan State University	M,D
MGH Institute of Health Professions	M,D,O
Michigan State University	M,D
Middle Tennessee State University	M,O
Midwestern State University	M
Millersville University of Pennsylvania	M
Millikin University	M
Minnesota State University Mankato	M,D
Minnesota State University Moorhead	M,O
Misericordia University	M
Mississippi University for Women	M,O
Missouri Southern State University	M
Missouri State University	M
Missouri Western State University	M
Molloy College	M,O
Monmouth University	M,D,O
Moravian College	M
Morgan State University	M,D
Mountain State University	M
Mount Carmel College of Nursing	M
Mount Marty College	M
Mount Saint Mary College	M,O
Mount St. Mary's College	M
Murray State University	M
Nazareth College of Rochester	M
Nebraska Methodist College	M
Nebraska Wesleyan University	M
Neumann University	M
New Mexico State University	M,D
New York University	M,D,O
North Dakota State University	M,D
Northeastern University	M,O
Northern Arizona University	M,O
Northern Illinois University	M
Northern Kentucky University	M,O
Northern Michigan University	M
North Park University	M
Northwestern State University of Louisiana	M
Nova Southeastern University	M,D*
Oakland University	M,D,O
The Ohio State University	M,D
Ohio University	M*
Oklahoma City University	M,D
Old Dominion University	M,D
Oregon Health & Science University	M,D,O*
Otterbein University	M,O
Our Lady of the Lake College	M
Pace University	M,D,O
Pacific Lutheran University	M
Penn State University Park	M,D
Pittsburg State University	M
Point Loma Nazarene University	M,O
Pontifical Catholic University of Puerto Rico	M
Prairie View A&M University	M
Purdue University Calumet	M
Queen's University at Kingston	M,D,O
Queens University of Charlotte	M
Quinnipiac University	D
Radford University	M,D
Ramapo College of New Jersey	M
Regis College (MA)	M,D,O
Regis University	P,M,D,O
Research College of Nursing	M
Resurrection University	M
Rhode Island College	M
The Richard Stockton College of New Jersey	M
Rivier College	M
Robert Morris University	M,D
Roberts Wesleyan College	M
Rocky Mountain University of Health Professions	M,D
Rush University	M,D,O
Rutgers, The State University of New Jersey, Newark	M*
Sacred Heart University	M,D
Sage Graduate School	M,D,O
Saginaw Valley State University	M
St. Ambrose University	M
Saint Anthony College of Nursing	M
St. Catherine University	M,D
Saint Francis Medical Center College of Nursing	M,D,O
St. John Fisher College	M,D,O
Saint Joseph College	M
St. Joseph's College, Long Island Campus	M
St. Joseph's College, New York	M*
Saint Joseph's College of Maine	M,O
Saint Louis University	M,D,O
Saint Peter's College	M,D,O
Saint Xavier University	M,O
Salem State University	M
Salisbury University	M
Samford University	M,D
Samuel Merritt University	M,O
San Diego State University	M
San Francisco State University	M
San Jose State University	M,O
Seattle Pacific University	M,O
Seattle University	M
Seton Hall University	M,D
Shenandoah University	M,D,O
Simmons College	M,D,O
South Dakota State University	M,D
Southeastern Louisiana University	M
Southeast Missouri State University	M
Southern Adventist University	M
Southern Connecticut State University	M
Southern Illinois University Edwardsville	M,D,O
Southern Nazarene University	M
Southern University and Agricultural and Mechanical College	M,D,O
Spalding University	M
Spring Arbor University	M
Spring Hill College	M
State University of New York at Binghamton	M,D,O
State University of New York Downstate Medical Center	M,O
State University of New York Institute of Technology	M,O
State University of New York Upstate Medical University	M,O
Stevenson University	M
Stony Brook University, State University of New York	M,D,O
Temple University	M*
Tennessee State University	M
Tennessee Technological University	M
Texas A&M International University	M
Texas A&M University–Corpus Christi	M
Texas Christian University	M,D
Texas Tech University Health Sciences Center	M,D,O
Texas Woman's University	M,D
Thomas Edison State College	M
Thomas Jefferson University	M
Thomas University	M
Towson University	M,O
Trinity Western University	M
Troy University	M,D,O
Uniformed Services University of the Health Sciences	M*
Union University	M,D,O
Universidad del Turabo	M
Universidad Metropolitana	M,O
Université de Montréal	M,D,O
Université du Québec à Rimouski	M,O

*M—master's degree; P—first professional degree; D—doctorate; O—other advanced degree; *—Close-Up and/or Display in one of the other books in this series*

Institution	Degrees
Université du Québec à Trois-Rivières	M,O
Université du Québec en Outaouais	M,O
Université Laval	M,D,O
University at Buffalo, the State University of New York	D,O*
The University of Akron	M,D
The University of Alabama	M,D
The University of Alabama at Birmingham	M,D*
The University of Alabama in Huntsville	M,D,O
University of Alaska Anchorage	M,O
University of Alberta	M,D
The University of Arizona	M,D,O
University of Arkansas	M
University of Arkansas for Medical Sciences	D
The University of British Columbia	M,D
University of Calgary	M,D,O
University of California, Irvine	M*
University of California, Los Angeles	M,D*
University of California, San Francisco	M,D
University of Central Arkansas	M
University of Central Florida	M,D,O
University of Central Missouri	M
University of Cincinnati	M,D
University of Colorado at Colorado Springs	M,D
University of Colorado Denver	M,D
University of Connecticut	M,D,O*
University of Delaware	M,O*
University of Evansville	M
University of Florida	M,D*
University of Hartford	M
University of Hawaii at Manoa	M,D,O
University of Houston–Victoria	M
University of Illinois at Chicago	M,D
University of Indianapolis	M
The University of Iowa	M,D*
The University of Kansas	M,D,O
University of Kentucky	M,D*
University of Lethbridge	M,D
University of Louisiana at Lafayette	M*
University of Louisville	M,D
University of Maine	M,O
The University of Manchester	M,D
University of Manitoba	M
University of Mary	M
University of Mary Hardin-Baylor	M
University of Maryland, Baltimore	M,D
University of Massachusetts Amherst	M,D*
University of Massachusetts Boston	M,D
University of Massachusetts Dartmouth	M,D,O
University of Massachusetts Lowell	M,D,O
University of Massachusetts Worcester	M,D,O
University of Medicine and Dentistry of New Jersey	M,O
University of Memphis	M,O
University of Miami	M,D*
University of Michigan	M,D,O*
University of Michigan–Flint	D
University of Minnesota, Twin Cities Campus	M,D
University of Mississippi Medical Center	M,D
University of Missouri	M,D*
University of Missouri–Kansas City	M,D*
University of Missouri–St. Louis	M,D,O
University of Mobile	M
University of Nebraska Medical Center	M,D
University of Nevada, Las Vegas	M,D,O
University of Nevada, Reno	M,D*
University of New Brunswick Fredericton	M
University of New Hampshire	M,O
University of New Mexico	M,D*
University of North Alabama	M
The University of North Carolina at Chapel Hill	M,D,O*
The University of North Carolina at Charlotte	M,O
The University of North Carolina at Greensboro	M,D,O
The University of North Carolina Wilmington	M
University of North Dakota	M,D
University of Northern Colorado	M,D
University of North Florida	M,D,O
University of Oklahoma Health Sciences Center	M
University of Ottawa	M,D,O*
University of Pennsylvania	M,D,O*
University of Phoenix	M,D,O
University of Phoenix–Atlanta Campus	M
University of Phoenix–Augusta Campus	M
University of Phoenix–Austin Campus	M
University of Phoenix–Birmingham Campus	M
University of Phoenix–Central Florida Campus	M
University of Phoenix–Central Valley Campus	M
University of Phoenix–Charlotte Campus	M
University of Phoenix–Chattanooga Campus	M
University of Phoenix–Cheyenne Campus	M
University of Phoenix–Cleveland Campus	M,D
University of Phoenix–Columbus Georgia Campus	M
University of Phoenix–Columbus Ohio Campus	M,D
University of Phoenix–Denver Campus	M
University of Phoenix–Des Moines Campus	M,D
University of Phoenix–Harrisburg Campus	M
University of Phoenix–Hawaii Campus	M
University of Phoenix–Houston Campus	M
University of Phoenix–Idaho Campus	M
University of Phoenix–Indianapolis Campus	M
University of Phoenix–Louisiana Campus	M
University of Phoenix–Louisville Campus	M
University of Phoenix–Maryland Campus	M
University of Phoenix–Memphis Campus	M,D
University of Phoenix–Metro Detroit Campus	M
University of Phoenix–Milwaukee Campus	M,D
University of Phoenix–Nashville Campus	M
University of Phoenix–New Mexico Campus	M
University of Phoenix–Northern Nevada Campus	M
University of Phoenix–Northern Virginia Campus	M
University of Phoenix–North Florida Campus	M
University of Phoenix–Northwest Arkansas Campus	M
University of Phoenix–Oklahoma City Campus	M
University of Phoenix–Omaha Campus	M
University of Phoenix–Oregon Campus	M
University of Phoenix–Phoenix Campus	M
University of Phoenix–Pittsburgh Campus	M
University of Phoenix–Raleigh Campus	M,D
University of Phoenix–Richmond Campus	M
University of Phoenix–Sacramento Valley Campus	M
University of Phoenix–San Antonio Campus	M
University of Phoenix–San Diego Campus	M
University of Phoenix–Savannah Campus	M
University of Phoenix–Southern California Campus	M
University of Phoenix–Southern Colorado Campus	M
University of Phoenix–South Florida Campus	M
University of Phoenix–Springfield Campus	M
University of Phoenix–Tulsa Campus	M
University of Phoenix–Utah Campus	M
University of Phoenix–Vancouver Campus	M
University of Phoenix–Washington D.C. Campus	M,D
University of Phoenix–West Florida Campus	M
University of Pittsburgh	M,D*
University of Portland	M,D
University of Puerto Rico, Medical Sciences Campus	M
University of Rhode Island	M,D
University of Rochester	M,D,O
University of St. Francis (IL)	M,D
University of Saint Francis (IN)	M
University of San Diego	M,D
University of San Francisco	M,D
University of Saskatchewan	M
The University of Scranton	M,O
University of South Alabama	M,D
University of South Carolina	M,O
University of Southern Indiana	M,D
University of Southern Maine	M,O
University of Southern Mississippi	M,D
University of South Florida	M,D*
The University of Tampa	M
The University of Tennessee	M,D
The University of Tennessee at Chattanooga	M,D,O
The University of Tennessee Health Science Center	M,D
The University of Texas at Arlington	M,D
The University of Texas at Austin	M,D
The University of Texas at El Paso	M,D,O
The University of Texas at Tyler	M,D
The University of Texas Health Science Center at Houston	M,D*
The University of Texas Health Science Center at San Antonio	M,D
The University of Texas Medical Branch	M,D
The University of Texas–Pan American	M
University of the Incarnate Word	M
The University of Toledo	M,D,O
University of Toronto	M,D
University of Utah	M,D*
University of Vermont	M
University of Victoria	M,D
University of Virginia	M,D
University of Washington	M,D,O*
University of Washington, Bothell	M
University of Washington, Tacoma	M
The University of Western Ontario	M,D
University of West Georgia	M,O
University of Windsor	M
University of Wisconsin–Eau Claire	M,D
University of Wisconsin–Madison	D*
University of Wisconsin–Milwaukee	M,D,O
University of Wisconsin–Oshkosh	M
University of Wyoming	M
Urbana University	M
Ursuline College	M,D
Utah Valley University	M
Valparaiso University	M,O
Vanderbilt University	M,D*
Villanova University	M,D,O
Virginia Commonwealth University	M,D,O
Viterbo University	M
Wagner College	M
Walden University	M,O
Washburn University	M
Washington Adventist University	M
Washington State University Spokane	M
Washington State University Tri-Cities	M
Washington State University Vancouver	M
Waynesburg University	M,D
Wayne State University	D*
Webster University	M,O
Wesley College	M
West Chester University of Pennsylvania	M,O
Western Carolina University	M,O
Western Connecticut State University	M
Western Kentucky University	M
Western Michigan University	M
Western University of Health Sciences	M,D
Westminster College (UT)	M
West Texas A&M University	M

West Virginia University	M,D,O
West Virginia Wesleyan College	M
Wheeling Jesuit University	M
Wichita State University	M,D
Widener University	M,D,O
Wilkes University	M,D
William Carey University	M
William Paterson University of New Jersey	M
Wilmington University	M
Winona State University	M,D,O
Winston-Salem State University	M
Wright State University	M
Xavier University	M
Yale University	M,D,O*
York College of Pennsylvania	M
York University	M*
Youngstown State University	M

NURSING AND HEALTHCARE ADMINISTRATION

Abilene Christian University	M,O
Allen College	M,D,O
American International College	M
American University of Beirut	M
Arizona State University	M,D,O
Athabasca University	M,O
Austin Peay State University	M
Barry University	M,D,O*
Baylor University	M*
Bellarmine University	M,D
Bellin College	M
Bloomsburg University of Pennsylvania	M
Bowie State University	M
Bradley University	M
Brenau University	M
Capital University	M
Carlow University	M,D
Case Western Reserve University	D*
Central Methodist University	M
Chatham University	M,D
Clarke University	M,O
Clarkson College	M,O
College of Mount Saint Vincent	M,O
The College of New Rochelle	M,O
Cox College	M
Daemen College	M,D,O
Dominican University of California	M
Duke University	M,D,O*
D'Youville College	M,O*
Eastern Michigan University	M,O
East Tennessee State University	M,D,O
Elms College	M
Emory University	M*
Excelsior College	O
Fairfield University	M,D
Fairmont State University	M
Ferris State University	M
Florida Agricultural and Mechanical University	M
Framingham State University	M
Gannon University	M,O
George Mason University	M,D,O*
The George Washington University	M,D,O
Georgia College & State University	M
Georgia Health Sciences University	M
Goshen College	M
Grand Valley State University	M,D
Grantham University	M
Herzing University Online	M
Holy Family University	M*
Holy Names University	M,O
Independence University	M
Indiana University of Pennsylvania	M
Indiana University–Purdue University Fort Wayne	M,O
Indiana Wesleyan University	M,O
Jefferson College of Health Sciences	M
The Johns Hopkins University	M,O
Kaplan University, Davenport Campus	M
Kean University	M
Kent State University	M,D*
Lamar University	M
La Roche College	M
Le Moyne College	M,O
Lewis University	M
Loma Linda University	M
Long Island University, Brooklyn Campus	M
Loyola University Chicago	M
Madonna University	M
Marquette University	M,D,O
Marywood University	M
McKendree University	M
McNeese State University	M
Medical University of South Carolina	M
Mercy College	M,O
Metropolitan State University	M,D
Millikin University	M
Missouri Western State University	M
Molloy College	M,O
Monmouth University	M,D,O
Montana State University	M,O
Moravian College	M
Mountain State University	M
Mount Carmel College of Nursing	M
Mount Saint Mary College	M,O
Mount St. Mary's College	M
Nebraska Methodist College	M
New Mexico State University	M,D
New York University	M
Northeastern University	M
North Park University	M
Northwest Nazarene University	M
Norwich University	M
Ohio University	M*
Old Dominion University	M
Otterbein University	M,O
Our Lady of the Lake College	M
Pace University	M,D,O
Pacific Lutheran University	M
Prairie View A&M University	M
Purdue University Calumet	M
Queens University of Charlotte	M
Regis University	P,M,D,O
Research College of Nursing	M
Roberts Wesleyan College	M
Sacred Heart University	M,D
Sage Graduate School	M,D,O
Saginaw Valley State University	M
Saint Joseph's College of Maine	M,O
Saint Peter's College	M,D,O
Saint Vincent College	M
Saint Xavier University	M,O
Samford University	M,D
Samuel Merritt University	M,O
San Francisco State University	M
San Jose State University	M,O
Seattle Pacific University	M,O
Seattle University	M
Seton Hall University	M,D
Southeastern Louisiana University	M
Southern Adventist University	M
Southern Connecticut State University	M
Southern Illinois University Edwardsville	M,O
Southern Nazarene University	M
Southern University and Agricultural and Mechanical College	M,D,O
Spalding University	M
State University of New York Institute of Technology	M,O
Teachers College, Columbia University	M,D
Tennessee Technological University	M
Texas A&M University–Corpus Christi	M
Texas Christian University	M,D
Texas Tech University Health Sciences Center	M,D,O
Texas Woman's University	M,D
TUI University	M,D,O
Union University	M,D,O
Universidad Metropolitana	M,O
University of Central Florida	M,D,O
University of Cincinnati	M,D
University of Colorado at Colorado Springs	M,D
University of Colorado Denver	M,D
University of Delaware	M,O*
University of Hawaii at Manoa	M,D,O
University of Illinois at Chicago	M
University of Indianapolis	M
The University of Kansas	M,D,O
University of Mary	M
University of Maryland, Baltimore	M
University of Massachusetts Lowell	D
University of Massachusetts Worcester	M,D,O
University of Memphis	M,O
University of Michigan	M*
University of Minnesota, Twin Cities Campus	M
University of Missouri–Kansas City	M,D*
University of Missouri–St. Louis	M,D,O
The University of North Carolina at Chapel Hill	M,D,O*
The University of North Carolina at Greensboro	M,D,O
University of North Florida	M,D,O
University of Pennsylvania	M,D*
University of Pittsburgh	M,D*
University of Rhode Island	M,D
University of Rochester	M,D,O
University of San Diego	M,D
University of San Francisco	D
University of South Carolina	M
University of Southern Maine	M,O
University of Southern Mississippi	M,D
The University of Tennessee at Chattanooga	M,D,O
The University of Texas at Arlington	M,D
The University of Texas at El Paso	M,D,O
The University of Texas at Tyler	M,D
The University of Toledo	M,O
University of Victoria	M,D
University of Virginia	M,D
University of Washington, Tacoma	M
University of West Florida	M
University of Wisconsin–Eau Claire	M,D
Ursuline College	M,D
Vanderbilt University	M,D*
Villanova University	M,D,O
Virginia Commonwealth University	M,D,O
Walden University	M,O
Washburn University	M
Washington Adventist University	M
Waynesburg University	M,D
West Chester University of Pennsylvania	M,O
Wichita State University	M,D
Winona State University	M,D,O
Wright State University	M
Xavier University	M

NURSING EDUCATION

Abilene Christian University	M,O
Albany State University	M
American International College	M
Angelo State University	M
Austin Peay State University	M
Azusa Pacific University	M,D
Barry University	M,O*
Bellarmine University	M,D
Bellin College	M
Bethel University (MN)	M,O
Bowie State University	M
Brenau University	M
California State University, Fresno	M
California State University, Stanislaus	M
Capella University	M,D
Carlow University	M,D
Carson-Newman College	M
Case Western Reserve University	D*
Chatham University	M,D
Clarke University	M,O
Clarkson College	M,O
Cleveland State University	M
College of Mount Saint Vincent	M,O
The College of New Rochelle	M,O
College of Staten Island of the City University of New York	O
Concordia University Wisconsin	M
Cox College	M
Daemen College	M,D,O
Delta State University	M
DeSales University	M,O
Duke University	M,D,O*
Duquesne University	M
D'Youville College	M,O*
Eastern Michigan University	M,O
East Tennessee State University	M,D,O
Edinboro University of Pennsylvania	M,O
Elms College	M
Fairmont State University	M
Felician College	M,O*
Ferris State University	M
Florida Southern College	M
Florida State University	M,D,O
Framingham State University	M
George Mason University	M,D,O*
Georgetown University	M
Goldfarb School of Nursing at Barnes-Jewish College	M,O
Graceland University (IA)	M,O

*M—master's degree; P—first professional degree; D—doctorate; O—other advanced degree; *—Close-Up and/or Display in one of the other books in this series*

Grambling State University M,O
Grand Canyon University M,O
Grand Valley State University M,D
Grantham University M
Herzing University Online M
Holy Family University M*
Holy Names University M,O
Indiana University of Pennsylvania M
Indiana University–Purdue University Fort Wayne M,O
Indiana Wesleyan University M,O
Jefferson College of Health Sciences M
Kaplan University, Davenport Campus M
Lamar University M
La Roche College M
Le Moyne College M,O
Lewis University M
Marian University (WI) M
Marymount University M,D,O
Maryville University of Saint Louis M,D
McKendree University M
McNeese State University M
Medical University of South Carolina M
Mercy College M,O
Metropolitan State University M,D
MGH Institute of Health Professions M,D,O
Midwestern State University M
Millikin University M
Minnesota State University Moorhead M
Missouri State University M
Molloy College M,O
Monmouth University M,D,O
Montana State University M,O
Moravian College M
Mountain State University M
Mount Carmel College of Nursing M
Mount Saint Mary College M,O
Mount St. Mary's College M
Nebraska Methodist College M
New York University M,O
Northeastern State University M
Northern Arizona University M,O
North Georgia College & State University M
Norwich University M
Oakland University M,O
Ohio University M*
Old Dominion University M
Oregon Health & Science University M,O*
Our Lady of the Lake College M
Pace University M,D,O
Prairie View A&M University M
Ramapo College of New Jersey M
Regis College (MA) M,D,O
Research College of Nursing M
Rivier College M
Roberts Wesleyan College M
Sage Graduate School D
St. Catherine University M,D
Saint Francis Medical Center College of Nursing M,D,O
St. John Fisher College M,O
Saint Joseph's College of Maine M,O
Samford University M,D
San Francisco State University M
San Jose State University M,O
Seattle Pacific University M,O
Seton Hall University M,D
Shenandoah University M,D,O
Southeastern Louisiana University M
Southern Connecticut State University M
Southern Illinois University Edwardsville M,O
Southern Nazarene University M
Southern University and Agricultural and Mechanical College M,D,O
State University of New York Institute of Technology M,O
Teachers College, Columbia University M,D
Tennessee Technological University M
Texas Christian University M,D
Texas Tech University Health Sciences Center M,D,O
Texas Woman's University M,D
Thomas Edison State College O
Towson University M,O
Union University M,D,O
The University of Alabama in Huntsville M,D,O
University of Alaska Anchorage M,O
University of Central Florida M,D,O
University of Hartford M
University of Indianapolis M
University of Mary M
University of Maryland, Baltimore M
University of Massachusetts Lowell M,D,O
University of Massachusetts Worcester M,D,O
University of Memphis M,O
University of Missouri–Kansas City M,D*
University of Missouri–St. Louis M,D,O
University of Nevada, Las Vegas M,D,O
University of New Brunswick Fredericton M
The University of North Carolina at Charlotte M,O
The University of North Carolina at Greensboro M,D,O
The University of North Carolina Wilmington M
University of North Dakota M,D
University of Northern Colorado M,D
University of Phoenix M
University of Phoenix–Atlanta Campus M
University of Phoenix–Augusta Campus M
University of Phoenix–Birmingham Campus M
University of Phoenix–Central Florida Campus M
University of Phoenix–Charlotte Campus M
University of Phoenix–Cheyenne Campus M
University of Phoenix–Des Moines Campus M,D
University of Phoenix–Harrisburg Campus M
University of Phoenix–Hawaii Campus M
University of Phoenix–Idaho Campus M
University of Phoenix–Indianapolis Campus M
University of Phoenix–Louisville Campus M
University of Phoenix–Maryland Campus M
University of Phoenix–Metro Detroit Campus M
University of Phoenix–Milwaukee Campus M,D
University of Phoenix–New Mexico Campus M
University of Phoenix–Northern Nevada Campus M
University of Phoenix–North Florida Campus M
University of Phoenix–Northwest Arkansas Campus M
University of Phoenix–Phoenix Campus M
University of Phoenix–Pittsburgh Campus M
University of Phoenix–Raleigh Campus M,D
University of Phoenix–Richmond Campus M
University of Phoenix–Sacramento Valley Campus M
University of Phoenix–San Diego Campus M
University of Phoenix–Savannah Campus M
University of Phoenix–Southern California Campus M
University of Phoenix–South Florida Campus M
University of Phoenix–Utah Campus M
University of Phoenix–Washington D.C. Campus M,D
University of Phoenix–West Florida Campus M
University of Rhode Island M,D
University of Southern Maine M,O
The University of Tennessee at Chattanooga M,D,O
The University of Texas at Arlington M,D
The University of Texas at Tyler M,D
The University of Toledo M,O
University of Victoria M,D
University of Washington, Tacoma M
University of West Georgia M,O
University of Wisconsin–Eau Claire M,D
Ursuline College M,D
Valparaiso University M,O
Villanova University M,D,O
Virginia Commonwealth University M,D,O
Walden University M,O
Waynesburg University M,D
Wayne State University M,O*
West Chester University of Pennsylvania M,O
Western Carolina University M,O
Westminster College (UT) M
Winona State University M,D,O
Worcester State University M
Xavier University M

NURSING INFORMATICS

Austin Peay State University M
Case Western Reserve University M*
Duke University M,D,O*
East Tennessee State University M,D,O
Ferris State University M
Grantham University M
Loyola University Chicago M,O
Molloy College M,O
New York University M,O
Seattle Pacific University M,O
Tennessee State University M
Tennessee Technological University M
Troy University M,D,O
University of Medicine and Dentistry of New Jersey M
University of Memphis M,O
University of Phoenix M
University of Phoenix–Charlotte Campus M
University of Phoenix–Des Moines Campus M,D
University of Phoenix–Louisville Campus M
University of Phoenix–Milwaukee Campus M,D
University of Phoenix–Phoenix Campus M
University of Phoenix–Raleigh Campus M,D
University of Phoenix–Washington D.C. Campus M,D
Vanderbilt University M,D*
Walden University M,O
Waynesburg University M,D
Xavier University M

NUTRITION

American University of Beirut M
Andrews University M
Appalachian State University M
Arizona State University M,D,O
Auburn University M,D
Bastyr University M
Baylor University M,D*
Benedictine University M
Boston University M*
Bowling Green State University M*
Brigham Young University M*
Brooklyn College of the City University of New York M
California State University, Chico M
California State University, Long Beach M
California State University, Los Angeles M*
Case Western Reserve University M,D*
Central Michigan University M,D,O
Central Washington University M
Chapman University M
Clemson University M
College of Saint Elizabeth M,O
Colorado State University M,D
Columbia University M,D*
Cornell University M,D*
Drexel University M*
D'Youville College M*
East Carolina University M
Eastern Illinois University M
Eastern Kentucky University M
Eastern Michigan University M
East Tennessee State University M
Emory University M,D*
Florida International University M,D
Florida State University M,D
Framingham State University M
George Mason University M,O*
Georgia State University M
Harvard University D*
Howard University M,D
Hunter College of the City University of New York M

Huntington College of Health Sciences M
Idaho State University M,O
Immaculata University M
Indiana State University M
Indiana University Bloomington M,D*
Indiana University of Pennsylvania M
Indiana University–Purdue University Indianapolis M,D
Instituto Tecnologico de Santo Domingo M,O
Iowa State University of Science and Technology M,D*
The Johns Hopkins University M,D
Kansas State University M,D*
Kent State University M*
Lehman College of the City University of New York M
Lipscomb University M
Logan University–College of Chiropractic M
Loma Linda University M,D
Long Island University, C.W. Post Campus M,O
Louisiana Tech University M
Loyola University Chicago M,O
Marshall University M
Marywood University M,O
McGill University M,D,O
McMaster University M,D
McNeese State University M
Meredith College M,O
Michigan State University M,D
Middle Tennessee State University M
Mississippi State University M,D
Montclair State University M,O
Mount Mary College M
Mount Saint Vincent University M
New York Chiropractic College M
New York Institute of Technology M
New York University M,D
North Carolina Agricultural and Technical State University M
North Carolina State University M,D*
North Dakota State University M
Northern Illinois University M
The Ohio State University M,D
Ohio University M*
Oklahoma State University M,D*
Oregon Health & Science University M,O*
Oregon State University M,D
Penn State University Park M,D
Purdue University M,D
Rosalind Franklin University of Medicine and Science M*
Rush University M
Rutgers, The State University of New Jersey, New Brunswick M,D*
Sacred Heart University M,D
Sage Graduate School M,O
Saint Joseph College M
Saint Louis University M
Sam Houston State University M
San Diego State University M
San Jose State University M
Saybrook University M,D,O
Simmons College M,O
South Carolina State University M
South Dakota State University M,D
Southeast Missouri State University M
Southern Illinois University Carbondale M
State University of New York College at Oneonta M
Syracuse University M*
Teachers College, Columbia University M,D
Texas A&M University M,D
Texas State University–San Marcos M
Texas Tech University M,D*
Texas Woman's University M,D
Tufts University M,D
Tulane University M*
Tuskegee University M
Université de Moncton M
Université de Montréal M,D,O
Université Laval M,D
University at Buffalo, the State University of New York M,D*
The University of Akron M
The University of Alabama M
The University of Alabama at Birmingham M,D*
University of Alaska Fairbanks M,D
The University of Arizona M,D
University of Arkansas for Medical Sciences M
University of Bridgeport M
The University of British Columbia M,D
University of California, Berkeley D*
University of California, Davis M,D
University of Central Oklahoma M
University of Chicago D
University of Cincinnati M
University of Colorado at Colorado Springs M
University of Connecticut M,D*
University of Delaware M*
University of Florida M,D*
University of Georgia M,D
University of Guelph M,D
University of Hawaii at Manoa M,D
University of Houston M,D
University of Illinois at Chicago M,D
University of Illinois at Urbana–Champaign M,D
The University of Kansas M,D,O
University of Kentucky M,D*
University of Maine M,D
University of Manitoba M,D
University of Maryland, College Park M,D
University of Massachusetts Amherst M,D*
University of Massachusetts Lowell M,O
University of Medicine and Dentistry of New Jersey M,D,O
University of Memphis M
University of Michigan M,D*
University of Minnesota, Twin Cities Campus M,D
University of Missouri M,D*
University of Nebraska–Lincoln M,D*
University of Nebraska Medical Center O
University of Nevada, Reno M*
University of New Hampshire M,D
University of New Haven M
University of New Mexico M*
The University of North Carolina at Chapel Hill M,D*
The University of North Carolina at Greensboro M,D
University of North Florida M
University of Oklahoma Health Sciences Center M
University of Pittsburgh M*
University of Puerto Rico, Medical Sciences Campus M,D,O
University of Puerto Rico, Río Piedras M
University of Rhode Island M,D
University of Southern Mississippi M,D
The University of Tennessee M
The University of Tennessee at Martin M
The University of Texas at Austin M,D
The University of Texas Southwestern Medical Center at Dallas M
University of the District of Columbia M
University of the Incarnate Word M,O
The University of Toledo M,O
University of Toronto M,D
University of Utah M*
University of Vermont M,D
University of Washington M,D*
University of Wisconsin–Madison M,D*
University of Wisconsin–Stevens Point M
University of Wisconsin–Stout M
University of Wyoming M
Utah State University M,D
Vanderbilt University M,D*
Virginia Polytechnic Institute and State University M,D
Washington State University M,D
Wayne State University M,D*
West Chester University of Pennsylvania M,O
West Virginia University M
Winthrop University M

OCCUPATIONAL HEALTH NURSING

University of Cincinnati M,D
University of Illinois at Chicago M
University of Medicine and Dentistry of New Jersey M,D,O
University of Michigan M,O*
University of Minnesota, Twin Cities Campus M,D
The University of North Carolina at Chapel Hill M*
University of Pennsylvania M*
University of the Sacred Heart M

OCCUPATIONAL THERAPY

Alvernia University M
American International College M
A.T. Still University of Health Sciences M,D
Barry University M*
Bay Path College M
Belmont University M,D
Boston University M,D*
Brenau University M
California State University, Dominguez Hills M*
Canisius College M
Chatham University M,D
Cleveland State University M
College of Saint Mary M
The College of St. Scholastica M
Colorado State University M
Columbia University M,D*
Concordia University Wisconsin M
Creighton University D
Dalhousie University M
Dominican College M
Dominican University of California M
Duquesne University M,D
D'Youville College M*
East Carolina University M
Eastern Kentucky University M
Eastern Michigan University M
Eastern Washington University M
Elizabethtown College M
Florida Agricultural and Mechanical University M
Florida Gulf Coast University M
Florida International University M
Gannon University M
Governors State University M
Grand Valley State University M
Husson University M
Idaho State University M
Indiana University–Purdue University Indianapolis M,D
Ithaca College M
James Madison University M
Jefferson College of Health Sciences M
Kean University M
Keuka College M
Lenoir-Rhyne University M
Loma Linda University M,D
Louisiana State University Health Sciences Center M
Maryville University of Saint Louis M
McMaster University M
Medical University of South Carolina M
Mercy College M
Midwestern University, Downers Grove Campus M
Midwestern University, Glendale Campus M
Milligan College M
Misericordia University M,D
Mount Mary College M
New York Institute of Technology M
New York University M,D
Nova Southeastern University M,D*
The Ohio State University M
Pacific University M
Philadelphia University M
Queen's University at Kingston M,D
Quinnipiac University M
Radford University M
The Richard Stockton College of New Jersey M
Rockhurst University M
Rocky Mountain University of Health Professions D
Rush University M
Sacred Heart University M
Sage Graduate School M
Saginaw Valley State University M
St. Ambrose University M
St. Catherine University M
Saint Francis University M
Saint Louis University M
Salem State University M
Samuel Merritt University M
San Jose State University M
Seton Hall University M
Shawnee State University M
Shenandoah University M
Spalding University M
Springfield College M,O
Stony Brook University, State University of New York M,D,O

*M—master's degree; P—first professional degree; D—doctorate; O—other advanced degree; *—Close-Up and/or Display in one of the other books in this series*

Institution	Degrees
Temple University	M,D*
Texas Tech University Health Sciences Center	M
Texas Woman's University	M,D
Thomas Jefferson University	M
Touro College	M
Towson University	M
Tufts University	M,D,O
Université de Montréal	O
University at Buffalo, the State University of New York	M*
The University of Alabama at Birmingham	M*
University of Alberta	M,D
The University of British Columbia	M
University of Central Arkansas	M
The University of Findlay	M
University of Florida	M*
University of Illinois at Chicago	M,D
University of Indianapolis	M,D
The University of Kansas	M,D
University of Manitoba	M,D
University of Mary	M
University of Mississippi Medical Center	M
University of Missouri	M*
University of New England	M
University of New Hampshire	M,O
University of New Mexico	M*
The University of North Carolina at Chapel Hill	M,D*
University of North Dakota	M
University of Oklahoma Health Sciences Center	M
University of Pittsburgh	M*
University of Puerto Rico, Medical Sciences Campus	M
University of Puget Sound	M
University of St. Augustine for Health Sciences	M,D
The University of Scranton	M
University of South Alabama	M
The University of South Dakota	M
University of Southern California	M,D*
University of Southern Indiana	M
University of Southern Maine	M
The University of Texas at El Paso	M
The University of Texas Health Science Center at San Antonio	M
The University of Texas Medical Branch	M
The University of Texas–Pan American	M
The University of Toledo	M,D
University of Toronto	M
University of Utah	M,D*
University of Washington	M,D*
The University of Western Ontario	M
University of Wisconsin–La Crosse	M
University of Wisconsin–Madison	M,D*
University of Wisconsin–Milwaukee	M,O
Utica College	M
Virginia Commonwealth University	M,D
Washington University in St. Louis	M,D*
Wayne State University	M*
Western Michigan University	M
Western New Mexico University	M
West Virginia University	M
Winston-Salem State University	M
Worcester State University	M
Xavier University	M

OCEAN ENGINEERING

Institution	Degrees
Florida Atlantic University	M,D
Florida Institute of Technology	M,D
Massachusetts Institute of Technology	M,D,O
Memorial University of Newfoundland	M,D
OGI School of Science & Engineering at Oregon Health & Science University	M,D
Oregon State University	M,D
Princeton University	D*
Stevens Institute of Technology	M,D
Texas A&M University	M,D
University of Alaska Anchorage	M,O
University of California, San Diego	M,D*
University of Delaware	M,D*
University of Florida	M,D,O*
University of Hawaii at Manoa	M,D
University of Maine	D
University of Michigan	M,D,O*
University of New Hampshire	M,D,O
University of Rhode Island	M,D
Virginia Polytechnic Institute and State University	M,O
Woods Hole Oceanographic Institution	D

OCEANOGRAPHY

Institution	Degrees
Columbia University	M,D*
Cornell University	D*
Dalhousie University	M,D
Florida Institute of Technology	M,D
Florida State University	M,D
Georgia Institute of Technology	M,D
Louisiana State University and Agricultural and Mechanical College	M,D
Massachusetts Institute of Technology	M,D,O
McGill University	M,D
Memorial University of Newfoundland	M,D
Naval Postgraduate School	M,D
North Carolina State University	M,D*
Nova Southeastern University	M,D*
Old Dominion University	M,D
Oregon State University	M,D
Princeton University	D*
Rutgers, The State University of New Jersey, New Brunswick	M,D*
Texas A&M University	M,D
Université du Québec à Rimouski	M,D
Université Laval	D
University of Alaska Fairbanks	M,D
The University of British Columbia	M,D
University of California, San Diego	D*
University of Colorado Boulder	M,D*
University of Connecticut	M,D*
University of Delaware	M,D*
University of Hawaii at Manoa	M,D
University of Maine	M,D
University of Maryland, College Park	M,D
University of Miami	M,D*
University of New Hampshire	M,D,O
University of Rhode Island	M,D,O
University of Southern California	M,D*
University of South Florida	M,D*
University of Victoria	M,D
University of Washington	M,D*
University of Wisconsin–Madison	M,D*
Woods Hole Oceanographic Institution	D
Yale University	D*

ONCOLOGY NURSING

Institution	Degrees
Columbia University	M,O*
Duke University	M,D,O*
Goldfarb School of Nursing at Barnes-Jewish College	M,O
Gwynedd-Mercy College	M
Loyola University Chicago	M,O
Universidad Metropolitana	M,O
University of Delaware	M,O*
University of Pennsylvania	M*

OPERATIONS RESEARCH

Institution	Degrees
Air Force Institute of Technology	M,D
Bowling Green State University	M*
California State University, East Bay	M
Carnegie Mellon University	D*
Case Western Reserve University	M*
Claremont Graduate University	M,D
Clemson University	M,D
The College of William and Mary	M
Columbia University	M,D,O*
Cornell University	M,D*
École Polytechnique de Montréal	M,D,O
Florida Institute of Technology	M,D
George Mason University	M,D,O*
Georgia Institute of Technology	M,D
Georgia State University	M,D
HEC Montreal	M
Idaho State University	M
Indiana University–Purdue University Fort Wayne	M,O
Iowa State University of Science and Technology	M,D*
The Johns Hopkins University	M,D
Kansas State University	M,D*
Massachusetts Institute of Technology	M,D
Naval Postgraduate School	M,D
New Mexico Institute of Mining and Technology	M,D
North Carolina State University	M,D*
North Dakota State University	M,D,O
Northeastern University	M,D
The Ohio State University	M
Oregon State University	M,D
Princeton University	M,D*
Rutgers, The State University of New Jersey, New Brunswick	D*
St. Mary's University (United States)	M
Southern Methodist University	M,D
The University of Alabama in Huntsville	M
University of Arkansas	M,D
The University of British Columbia	M
University of California, Berkeley	M,D*
University of Central Florida	M,D,O
University of Colorado Boulder	M*
University of Delaware	M,D*
University of Illinois at Chicago	D
The University of Iowa	M,D*
University of Massachusetts Amherst	M,D*
University of Michigan	M,D*
The University of North Carolina at Chapel Hill	M,D*
University of Southern California	M,D,O*
The University of Texas at Austin	M,D
University of Waterloo	M,D
Virginia Commonwealth University	M

OPTICAL SCIENCES

Institution	Degrees
Air Force Institute of Technology	M,D
Alabama Agricultural and Mechanical University	M,D
Cleveland State University	M
Delaware State University	M,D
Duke University	M*
École Polytechnique de Montréal	M,D,O
Norfolk State University	M
North Carolina Agricultural and Technical State University	M,D
The Ohio State University	P,M,D
Rochester Institute of Technology	M,D
Rose-Hulman Institute of Technology	M
The University of Alabama in Huntsville	M,D
The University of Arizona	M,D
University of Central Florida	M,D
University of Colorado Boulder	M,D*
University of Dayton	M,D
University of Maryland, Baltimore County	M,D
University of Massachusetts Lowell	M,D
University of New Mexico	M,D*
The University of North Carolina at Charlotte	M,D
University of Rochester	M,D,O

OPTOMETRY

Institution	Degrees
Ferris State University	P
Illinois College of Optometry	P
Indiana University Bloomington	P,M,D*
Inter American University of Puerto Rico School of Optometry	P
Midwestern University, Glendale Campus	P
The New England College of Optometry	P,M
Northeastern State University	P
Nova Southeastern University	P,M*
The Ohio State University	P,M,D
Salus University	P
Southern California College of Optometry	P
Southern College of Optometry	P
State University of New York College of Optometry	P

Université de Montréal P
The University of Alabama at Birmingham P*
University of California, Berkeley P,O*
University of Houston P
The University of Manchester M,D
University of Missouri–St. Louis P
University of the Incarnate Word P
University of Waterloo M,D
Western University of Health Sciences P

ORAL AND DENTAL SCIENCES

A.T. Still University of Health Sciences P,M,D,O
Boston University P,M,D,O*
Case Western Reserve University M,O*
Columbia University M,D,O*
Dalhousie University
Georgia Health Sciences University M,D
Harvard University M,D,O*
Howard University P,O
Idaho State University O
Jacksonville University O
Loma Linda University M,O
Marquette University M
Massachusetts College of Pharmacy and Health Sciences M
McGill University M,D,O
New York University M,D,O
The Ohio State University P,M,D
Oregon Health & Science University P,M,O*
Roseman University of Health Sciences M
Saint Louis University M
Seton Hill University O
Stony Brook University, State University of New York P,M,D,O
Temple University M,O*
Texas A&M Health Science Center P,M,D,O
Tufts University M,O
Université de Montréal M,O
Université Laval M,O
University at Buffalo, the State University of New York M,D*
The University of Alabama at Birmingham M*
University of Alberta M,D
The University of British Columbia M,D,O
University of California, Los Angeles M,D*
University of California, San Francisco M,D
University of Connecticut M*
University of Connecticut Health Center M,D*
University of Detroit Mercy M,O
University of Florida M,D,O*
University of Illinois at Chicago M,D
The University of Iowa M,D,O*
University of Kentucky M*
University of Louisville P,M
The University of Manchester M,D
University of Manitoba M,D
University of Maryland, Baltimore P,M,D,O
University of Medicine and Dentistry of New Jersey P,M,O
University of Michigan M,D*
University of Minnesota, Twin Cities Campus M,D,O
University of Mississippi Medical Center M,D
University of Missouri–Kansas City P,M,D,O*
The University of North Carolina at Chapel Hill M,D*
University of Oklahoma Health Sciences Center M
University of Pittsburgh M,O*
University of Puerto Rico, Medical Sciences Campus O
University of Rochester M
University of Southern California M,D,O*
The University of Tennessee Health Science Center P,M,O
The University of Texas Health Science Center at San Antonio M,O
The University of Toledo M
University of Toronto M,D
University of Washington P,M,O*
The University of Western Ontario M
West Virginia University M

ORGANIC CHEMISTRY

Auburn University M,D
Boston College M,D*
Brandeis University M,D
California State University, Los Angeles M*
Carnegie Mellon University M,D*
Cleveland State University M,D
Columbia University M,D*
Cornell University D*
Eastern New Mexico University M
Florida State University M,D
Georgetown University D
The George Washington University M,D
Harvard University D*
Howard University M,D
Indiana University Bloomington M,D*
Instituto Tecnológico y de Estudios Superiores de Monterrey, Campus Monterrey M,D
Kansas State University M,D*
Kent State University M,D*
Laurentian University M
Marquette University M,D
Massachusetts College of Pharmacy and Health Sciences M
Massachusetts Institute of Technology M,D,O
McMaster University M,D
Northeastern University M,D
Old Dominion University M,D
Oregon State University M,D
Purdue University M,D
Rensselaer Polytechnic Institute M,D
Rice University M,D
Rutgers, The State University of New Jersey, Newark M,D*
Rutgers, The State University of New Jersey, New Brunswick M,D*
Seton Hall University M,D
Southern University and Agricultural and Mechanical College M
State University of New York at Binghamton M,D
State University of New York College of Environmental Science and Forestry M,D
Stevens Institute of Technology M,D,O
Texas Christian University M,D
Tufts University M,D
University of Calgary M,D
University of Cincinnati M,D
University of Georgia M,D
University of Louisville M,D
The University of Manchester M,D
University of Maryland, College Park M,D
University of Massachusetts Lowell M,D
University of Memphis M,D
University of Miami M,D*
University of Michigan D*
University of Missouri M,D*
University of Missouri–Kansas City M,D*
University of Missouri–St. Louis M,D
The University of Montana M,D
University of Nebraska–Lincoln M,D*
University of Notre Dame M,D*
University of Regina M,D
University of Southern Mississippi M,D
University of South Florida M,D*
The University of Tennessee M,D
The University of Texas at Austin M,D
The University of Toledo M,D
Vanderbilt University M,D*
Virginia Commonwealth University M,D
Wake Forest University M,D
Wesleyan University M,D*
West Virginia University M,D
Yale University D*
Youngstown State University M

ORGANIZATIONAL BEHAVIOR

Amridge University P,M,D
Argosy University, Chicago D*
Benedictine University M
Benedictine University at Springfield M
Bernard M. Baruch College of the City University of New York M,D
Boston College D*
Brooklyn College of the City University of New York M
California Lutheran University M,O
Carnegie Mellon University D*
Case Western Reserve University M*
Columbia College (SC) M,O
Cornell University M,D*
Drexel University M,D,O*
Fairleigh Dickinson University, College at Florham M,O
Florida Institute of Technology M,D
Florida State University M,D
Georgia Institute of Technology M,D,O
Graduate School and University Center of the City University of New York D
Harvard University D*
John Jay College of Criminal Justice of the City University of New York M,D
Lake Forest Graduate School of Management M
Marylhurst University M
New York University M,D
Northwestern University M,D*
Phillips Graduate Institute D
Polytechnic Institute of NYU M,O
Purdue University D
Saybrook University M,D
Silver Lake College M
Suffolk University M,O
Syracuse University D*
Towson University O
Universidad de las Americas, A.C. M
Université de Sherbrooke M
The University of British Columbia D
University of California, Berkeley D*
University of California, Los Angeles M,D*
University of Chicago M
University of Hartford M
University of Hawaii at Manoa M
The University of North Carolina at Chapel Hill D*
University of Oklahoma M*
University of Pennsylvania M*
University of Pittsburgh M,D,O*
University of Saskatchewan M
Western International University M
Wilfrid Laurier University M,D

ORGANIZATIONAL MANAGEMENT

Adler Graduate School M,O
Alvernia University D
The American College M
American International College M
American Public University System M
American University M
Amridge University P,M,D
Antioch University Los Angeles M
Antioch University New England M,O
Antioch University Santa Barbara M
Antioch University Seattle M
Argosy University, Chicago D*
Argosy University, Denver M,D*
Argosy University, Hawai'i D*
Argosy University, Inland Empire M,D*
Argosy University, Los Angeles M,D*
Argosy University, Orange County D*
Argosy University, San Diego M,D*
Argosy University, San Francisco Bay Area M,D*
Argosy University, Sarasota M,D,O*
Argosy University, Seattle M,D*
Argosy University, Tampa M,D*
Argosy University, Twin Cities M,D*
Argosy University, Washington DC M,D,O*
Athabasca University M
Augsburg College M
Avila University M,O
Azusa Pacific University M
Benedictine University M,D
Benedictine University at Springfield M,D
Bernard M. Baruch College of the City University of New York M,D
Bethel University (MN) M
Biola University M
Bluffton University M
Boston College D*
Bowling Green State University M*
Brenau University M
Briercrest Seminary M
Cabrini College M
California Coast University M,D
California College of the Arts M

*M—master's degree; P—first professional degree; D—doctorate; O—other advanced degree; *—Close-Up and/or Display in one of the other books in this series*

California Intercontinental University M,D
California State University, East Bay M
Cambridge College M
Capella University M,D,O
Carlos Albizu University, Miami Campus M,D
Carlow University M,D
Charleston Southern University M
City University of Seattle M,O
Cleary University M,O
College of Mount St. Joseph M
College of Saint Mary M
Colorado State University M
Colorado Technical University Sioux Falls M
Columbus State University M,O
Concordia University (MI) M
Concordia University (Canada) M
Concordia University, St. Paul M
Dominican University M
Duquesne University M
Eastern Connecticut State University M
Eastern Michigan University M,O
Eastern University M,D
Emory & Henry College M
Emory University D*
Endicott College M
Evangel University M
Fairleigh Dickinson University, College at Florham M,O
Fielding Graduate University M,D,O
Gannon University D
Geneva College M
George Fox University M,D
George Mason University M*
The George Washington University M,D
Georgia State University M,D
Gonzaga University M
Grand Canyon University D
Grand View University M
Grantham University M
Harding University M
Hawai'i Pacific University M*
HEC Montreal M
Immaculata University M
Indiana Tech M
Indiana University–Purdue University Fort Wayne M,O
Indiana Wesleyan University D
Instituto Tecnologico de Santo Domingo M,O
John F. Kennedy University M,O
Jones International University M
Judson University M
Kaplan University, Davenport Campus M
Keiser University D
LaGrange College M
Lewis University M
Lourdes College M
Malone University M
Manhattanville College M*
Mansfield University of Pennsylvania M
Marian University (WI) M
Marymount University M,O
Maryville University of Saint Louis M
Medaille College M
Mercy College M
Mercyhurst College M,O
Mid-America Christian University M
MidAmerica Nazarene University M
Midway College M
Misericordia University M
Mountain State University D
National University M
Newman University M
The New School: A University M
New York University M,D
North Carolina Agricultural and Technical State University M,D
North Central College M
Northern Kentucky University M
Northwestern College M
Northwestern University M,D*
Northwest University M
Norwich University M
Nova Southeastern University D*
Nyack College M
Olivet Nazarene University M
Our Lady of the Lake University of San Antonio M,D
Oxford Graduate School M,D
Palm Beach Atlantic University M
Pepperdine University M
Peru State College M
Pfeiffer University M
Philadelphia Biblical University M
Point Park University M
Quinnipiac University M
Regent University M,D,O
Regis University M,O
Rider University M
Robert Morris University M,D
Roosevelt University M,D
Rutgers, The State University of New Jersey, Newark D*
Sage Graduate School M
St. Ambrose University M
St. Catherine University M
St. Edward's University M
St. Joseph's College, Long Island Campus M,O
Saint Joseph's University M,D,O
Saint Louis University M,D,O
Saint Mary's University of Minnesota M
Santa Clara University M
Saybrook University M,D
Seattle University M,O
Shenandoah University M,D,O
Shippensburg University of Pennsylvania M
Southern New Hampshire University M,D,O
Southwestern College (KS) M
Southwest University M
Spring Arbor University M
Springfield College M
State University of New York at Plattsburgh M
State University of New York College at Potsdam M
Suffolk University M,O
Syracuse University O*
Teachers College, Columbia University M
Thomas Edison State College O
Trevecca Nazarene University M
Trinity (Washington) University M
Trinity Western University M,O
Troy University M
Tusculum College M
United States International University M
Université Laval M,O
University of Alberta D
University of Cincinnati M
University of Colorado Boulder M,D*
University of Dallas M
University of Denver M,O
The University of Findlay M
University of Guelph M
University of Hawaii at Manoa M,D
The University of Kansas M,D,O
University of La Verne M,O
University of Maryland Eastern Shore D
University of Massachusetts Dartmouth M,O
University of New Haven M,O
University of New Mexico M*
University of Pennsylvania M*
University of Phoenix D,O
University of Phoenix–Milwaukee Campus M,D
University of Phoenix–Washington D.C. Campus M,D
University of Regina M,O
University of St. Thomas (MN) M,D,O
University of San Francisco M
The University of Scranton M
University of Southern California M*
The University of Texas at Dallas M*
The University of Texas at San Antonio M,D*
University of the Incarnate Word M,D,O
Upper Iowa University M
Vanderbilt University M,D*
Walden University M,D,O
Warner Pacific College M
Wayland Baptist University M
Waynesburg University M,D
Wayne State College M
Webster University M
Western International University M
Wheeling Jesuit University M
Wilfrid Laurier University M,D
Wilkes University M
Wilmington University M
Woodbury University M
Worcester Polytechnic Institute M,O
Worcester State University M
Yale University D*

OSTEOPATHIC MEDICINE

A.T. Still University of Health Sciences P,M
Des Moines University P,M
East Tennessee State University M,D,O
Edward Via Virginia College of Osteopathic Medicine P
Georgia Campus–Philadelphia College of Osteopathic Medicine P
Kansas City University of Medicine and Biosciences P
Lake Erie College of Osteopathic Medicine P,M,O
Lincoln Memorial University P
Michigan State University P
Midwestern University, Downers Grove Campus P
Midwestern University, Glendale Campus P
New York Institute of Technology P
Nova Southeastern University P,M,O*
Ohio University P*
Oklahoma State University Center for Health Sciences P
Philadelphia College of Osteopathic Medicine P*
Pikeville College P
Touro University P,M
University of Medicine and Dentistry of New Jersey P
University of New England P
University of North Texas Health Science Center at Fort Worth P,M
Western University of Health Sciences P
West Virginia School of Osteopathic Medicine P

PACIFIC AREA/PACIFIC RIM STUDIES

University of California, San Diego M,D*
University of Guam M
University of Hawaii at Manoa M,O
University of San Francisco M
University of Victoria M

PALEONTOLOGY

Cornell University M,D*
Duke University D*
East Tennessee State University M
South Dakota School of Mines and Technology M,D
University of Chicago M,D
The University of Manchester M,D
The University of Texas at Dallas M,D*
West Virginia University M,D
Yale University D*

PAPER AND PULP ENGINEERING

Miami University M
North Carolina State University M,D*
Oregon State University M,D
State University of New York College of Environmental Science and Forestry M,D
The University of Manchester M,D
Western Michigan University M,D

PARASITOLOGY

Illinois State University M,D
Louisiana State University Health Sciences Center M,D
McGill University M,D,O
New York University P,M,D
Texas A&M University M,D
Tulane University M,D,O*
University of Notre Dame M,D*
University of Prince Edward Island M,D
University of Washington D*

PASTORAL MINISTRY AND COUNSELING

Abilene Christian University M,D
American Baptist Seminary of the West P,M
Amridge University P,M,D
Anderson University (SC) M
Andrews University P,M,D,O
Anna Maria College M
Appalachian Bible College M
Aquinas Institute of Theology P,M,D,O
Argosy University, Sarasota M,D*
Asbury Theological Seminary M,D,O
Ashland Theological Seminary P,M,D,O

Assemblies of God Theological Seminary	P,M,D
The Athenaeum of Ohio	P,M,O
Atlantic School of Theology	P,M,O
Austin Presbyterian Theological Seminary	P,M,D
Ave Maria University	M,D
Azusa Pacific University	P,M
Bakke Graduate University	M,D
Baptist Bible College	P,M
Baptist Bible College of Pennsylvania	P,M,D
Baptist Theological Seminary at Richmond	P,M,D
Barry University	M,D*
Bethany Theological Seminary	P,M,O
Bethel College	M
Bethel Seminary	P,M,D,O
Biblical Theological Seminary	P,M,D,O
Bob Jones University	P,M,D,O
Boston College	P,M,D,O*
Briercrest Seminary	P,M
Caldwell College	M
California Baptist University	M
Calvary Bible College and Theological Seminary	P,M
Calvin Theological Seminary	P,M,D
Capital Bible Seminary	P,M,O
Cardinal Stritch University	M
Carolina Evangelical Divinity School	D
Catholic Theological Union at Chicago	P,M,D,O
The Catholic University of America	P,M,D,O
Chaminade University of Honolulu	M
Chicago Theological Seminary	P,M,D
Christian Theological Seminary	P,M,D
Christ the King Seminary	P,M
Cincinnati Christian University	M
Claremont School of Theology	M,D
College of Mount St. Joseph	M,O
Columbia International University	P,M,D,O
Concordia University, Nebraska	M
Concordia University, St. Paul	M,O
Corban University	M
The Criswell College	P,M
Dallas Baptist University	M
Dallas Theological Seminary	M,D,O
Denver Seminary	P,M,D,O
Dominican University	M
Eastern Mennonite University	P,M,O
Eastern University	D
Ecumenical Theological Seminary	D
Emmanuel Christian Seminary	P,M,D
Emory University	P,M,D*
Evangelical Theological Seminary	P,M
Faith Baptist Bible College and Theological Seminary	P,M
Faulkner University	M
Fordham University	M,D,O
Freed-Hardeman University	M
Fresno Pacific University	M
Fuller Theological Seminary	P,M,D
Gannon University	M,O
Gardner-Webb University	P,D
Garrett-Evangelical Theological Seminary	P,M,D
General Theological Seminary	P,M,D,O
George Fox University	P,M,D,O
Georgian Court University	M,O
Golden Gate Baptist Theological Seminary	P,M,D,O
Gonzaga University	M
Gordon-Conwell Theological Seminary	P,M,D
Graceland University (IA)	M
Grace Theological Seminary	P,M,D,O
Grace University	M
Grand Rapids Theological Seminary of Cornerstone University	P,M
Greenville College	M
Hampton University	M
Harding University	M
Harding University Graduate School of Religion	P,M,D
Hardin-Simmons University	M,D
Hartford Seminary	M,D,O
Heritage Baptist College and Heritage Theological Seminary	P,M,D,O
Heritage Christian University	M
Hillsdale Free Will Baptist College	M
Holmes Institute	M
Holy Names University	M,O
Houston Baptist University	M
Houston Graduate School of Theology	P,M,D
Howard Payne University	M
Huntington University	M
Iliff School of Theology	P,M,D
Indiana Wesleyan University	M
Institute of Transpersonal Psychology	M
Inter American University of Puerto Rico, Metropolitan Campus	D
International Baptist College	M,D
Iona College	M,O
Jewish University of America	M,D
John Brown University	M
Knox Theological Seminary	D
Lancaster Bible College	M,D
La Salle University	M
La Sierra University	P,M
Lee University	M
Liberty University	M,D
Lincoln Christian Seminary	P,M,D
Loma Linda University	M,O
Loras College	M
Loyola Marymount University	M
Loyola University Chicago	M,O
Loyola University Maryland	M,D,O
Lutheran School of Theology at Chicago	P,M,D
Lutheran Theological Seminary	P,M,D
Lutheran Theological Seminary at Gettysburg	P,M,D
The Lutheran Theological Seminary at Philadelphia	P,M,D,O
Luther Rice University	P,M,D
Madonna University	M
Maple Springs Baptist Bible College and Seminary	P,M,D,O
Maranatha Baptist Bible College	M
Martin University	M
Marymount University	M,O
The Master's College and Seminary	P,M,D
McCormick Theological Seminary	P,M,D,O
McMaster University	P,M,D,O
Meadville Lombard Theological School	P,M,D
Messiah College	M
Mid-America Christian University	M
Midwestern Baptist Theological Seminary	P,M,D,O
Missouri Baptist University	M,O
Moody Bible Institute	P,M,O
Moravian Theological Seminary	P,M
Mount Marty College	M
Mount Mary College	M
Neumann University	M,O
New Brunswick Theological Seminary	D
New Orleans Baptist Theological Seminary	P,M,D
The Nigerian Baptist Theological Seminary	P,M,D,O
Northern Baptist Theological Seminary	P,M,D
North Greenville University	M
North Park Theological Seminary	M,O
Northwest Nazarene University	P,M
Northwest University	M
Notre Dame College (OH)	M,O
Nyack College	P,M,D
Oakwood University	M
Oblate School of Theology	P,M,D,O
Oklahoma Christian University	P,M
Oral Roberts University	P,M,D
Ottawa University	M
Pentecostal Theological Seminary	P,M,D
Pepperdine University	M
Philadelphia Biblical University	M
Phillips Theological Seminary	D
Phoenix Seminary	P,M,D,O
Providence College and Theological Seminary	P,M,D,O
Reformed Theological Seminary–Charlotte Campus	P,M,D
Reformed Theological Seminary–Jackson Campus	P,M,D,O
Reformed Theological Seminary–Orlando Campus	P,M,D
Regent University	P,M,D
Regis College (Canada)	P,M,D,O
Roberts Wesleyan College	M
Sacred Heart Major Seminary	P,M
St. Ambrose University	M
St. Augustine's Seminary of Toronto	P,M,O
Saint Bernard's School of Theology and Ministry	P,M,O
St. Catherine University	M,O
Saint Francis Seminary	P,M
St. John's Seminary (CA)	P,M
Saint John's University (MN)	P,M
St. John's University (NY)	P,M,O
Saint Leo University	M
Saint Mary-of-the-Woods College	M,O
St. Mary's University (United States)	M
Saint Mary's University of Minnesota	M,O
Saint Paul University	M,D,O
Saints Cyril and Methodius Seminary	P,M
St. Stephen's College	M,D
St. Thomas University	M,D,O
Santa Clara University	M
Seattle University	M
Seminary of the Immaculate Conception	P,M,D,O
Seminary of the Southwest	P,M,O
Seton Hall University	P,M,O
Shasta Bible College	M
Simpson University	P,M
Sioux Falls Seminary	P,M
Southeastern University (FL)	M
Southern Baptist Theological Seminary	P,M,D
Southern Evangelical Seminary	P,M,D,O
Southern Wesleyan University	M
Southwestern Assemblies of God University	P,M
Southwestern Christian University	M
Spring Arbor University	M
Spring Hill College	M
Trinity Baptist College	M
Trinity International University	P,M,D,O
Trinity Lutheran Seminary	P,M
Trinity School for Ministry	P,M,D,O
Trinity Western University	P,M,D
Tyndale University College & Seminary	P,M,O
Unification Theological Seminary	P,M,D
Union University	M,D
United Theological Seminary of the Twin Cities	P,M,D,O
Universidad Adventista de las Antillas	P,M
University of Dallas	M
University of Dayton	M,D
University of Portland	M
University of Puget Sound	M
University of Saint Francis (IN)	M
University of St. Michael's College	P,M,D,O
University of St. Thomas (MN)	P,M
University of South Africa	M,D
University of Trinity College	P,M,D,O
Warner Pacific College	M
Wayland Baptist University	M
Wesley Biblical Seminary	P,M
Western Seminary	P,M,D,O
Western Seminary–Sacramento Campus	M,O
Western Seminary–San Jose Campus	P,M,O
Westminster Theological Seminary	P,M,D,O
Wheaton College	M,D
Wilfrid Laurier University	P,M,D,O
Xavier University	M
Xavier University of Louisiana	M

PATHOBIOLOGY

Auburn University	M,D
Brown University	M,D
Columbia University	M,D*
Drexel University	M,D*
The Johns Hopkins University	D
Kansas State University	M,D*
Medical University of South Carolina	D
Michigan State University	M,D
New York University	P,M,D
The Ohio State University	M,D
Penn State University Park	D
Purdue University	M,D
Texas A&M University	M,D
The University of Arizona	M,D
University of Cincinnati	D
University of Connecticut	M,D*
University of Illinois at Urbana–Champaign	M,D
University of Missouri	M,D*
University of Southern California	M,D*
University of Toronto	M,D
University of Washington	D*

*M—master's degree; P—first professional degree; D—doctorate; O—other advanced degree; *—Close-Up and/or Display in one of the other books in this series*

- University of Wyoming M
- Wake Forest University M,D
- Yale University D*

PATHOLOGY

- Albert Einstein College of Medicine D
- Baylor College of Medicine D*
- Brown University M,D
- Case Western Reserve University M,D*
- Colorado State University M,D
- Columbia University M,D*
- Dalhousie University M,D
- Duke University M,D*
- East Carolina University D
- Georgetown University M,D
- Harvard University D*
- Indiana University–Purdue University Indianapolis M,D
- Iowa State University of Science and Technology M,D*
- The Johns Hopkins University D
- Loma Linda University M,D
- Louisiana State University Health Sciences Center M,D
- McGill University M,D
- Medical University of South Carolina M,D
- Michigan State University M,D
- New York Medical College M,D*
- North Carolina State University M,D*
- North Dakota State University M,D
- The Ohio State University M
- Purdue University M,D
- Queen's University at Kingston M,D
- Quinnipiac University M
- Rosalind Franklin University of Medicine and Science M*
- Saint Louis University D
- Stony Brook University, State University of New York M,D
- Temple University D*
- Texas A&M University M,D
- Université de Montréal M,D
- Université Laval O
- University at Buffalo, the State University of New York M,D*
- The University of Alabama at Birmingham D*
- University of Alberta M,D
- University of Arkansas for Medical Sciences M
- The University of British Columbia M,D
- University of California, Davis M,D
- University of California, Irvine D*
- University of California, Los Angeles M,D*
- University of California, San Francisco D
- University of Chicago D
- University of Cincinnati D
- University of Florida D*
- University of Georgia M,D
- University of Guelph M,D,O
- The University of Iowa M*
- The University of Kansas M,D
- University of Manitoba M
- University of Maryland, Baltimore M
- University of Massachusetts Lowell M,O
- University of Medicine and Dentistry of New Jersey D
- University of Michigan D*
- University of Mississippi Medical Center M,D
- University of Missouri M*
- University of Nebraska Medical Center M,D
- University of New Mexico M,D,O*
- The University of North Carolina at Chapel Hill D*
- University of Oklahoma Health Sciences Center D
- University of Pittsburgh M,D*
- University of Prince Edward Island M,D
- University of Rochester M,D
- University of Saskatchewan M,D
- University of Southern California M,D*
- The University of Texas Medical Branch D
- The University of Toledo O
- University of Utah M,D*
- University of Vermont M
- University of Virginia D
- University of Washington D*
- The University of Western Ontario M,D
- University of Wisconsin–Madison D*
- Vanderbilt University D*
- Virginia Commonwealth University D
- Wayne State University M,D*
- Yale University M,D*

PEDIATRIC NURSING

- Boston College M,D*
- Caribbean University M,D
- Case Western Reserve University M,D*
- Columbia University M,O*
- Duke University M,D,O*
- Emory University M*
- Georgia Health Sciences University M,O
- Georgia State University M,D,O
- Gwynedd-Mercy College M
- Hampton University M
- Indiana University–Purdue University Indianapolis M,D
- The Johns Hopkins University M,O
- Kent State University M,D*
- Lehman College of the City University of New York M
- Loma Linda University M
- Marquette University M,D,O
- MGH Institute of Health Professions M,D,O
- Molloy College M,O
- New York University M,D,O
- Northeastern University M,O
- Queen's University at Kingston M,D,O
- Rocky Mountain University of Health Professions D
- Rush University M,D,O
- St. Catherine University M,D
- Seton Hall University M,D
- Spalding University M
- Stony Brook University, State University of New York M,O
- Texas Christian University M,D
- Texas Tech University Health Sciences Center M,D,O
- Texas Woman's University M,D
- University of Cincinnati M,D
- University of Colorado Denver M,D
- University of Delaware M,O*
- University of Illinois at Chicago M
- University of Maryland, Baltimore M
- University of Michigan M,O*
- University of Minnesota, Twin Cities Campus M
- University of Missouri–Kansas City M,D*
- University of Missouri–St. Louis M,D,O
- University of Nevada, Las Vegas M,D,O
- The University of North Carolina at Chapel Hill M,D,O*
- University of Pennsylvania M*
- University of Pittsburgh M,D*
- University of Puerto Rico, Medical Sciences Campus M
- University of Rochester M,D,O
- University of San Diego M,D
- University of South Carolina M
- The University of Texas–Pan American M
- The University of Toledo M,O
- University of Wisconsin–Madison D*
- Vanderbilt University M,D*
- Villanova University M,D,O
- Virginia Commonwealth University M,D,O
- Wayne State University M,O*
- Wright State University M

PERFUSION

- Long Island University, C.W. Post Campus M
- Milwaukee School of Engineering M
- Quinnipiac University M
- The University of Arizona M,D
- University of Nebraska Medical Center M

PETROLEUM ENGINEERING

- Colorado School of Mines M,D
- Louisiana State University and Agricultural and Mechanical College M,D
- Missouri University of Science and Technology M,D
- Montana Tech of The University of Montana M
- New Mexico Institute of Mining and Technology M,D
- Stanford University M,D,O
- Texas A&M University M,D
- Texas A&M University–Kingsville M
- Texas Tech University M,D*
- University of Alaska Fairbanks M,D
- University of Alberta M,D
- University of Calgary M,D
- University of Houston M,D
- The University of Kansas M,D
- University of Louisiana at Lafayette M*
- University of Oklahoma M,D*
- University of Pittsburgh M,D*
- University of Regina M,D
- University of Southern California M,D,O*
- The University of Texas at Austin M,D
- University of Tulsa M,D
- University of Wyoming M,D
- West Virginia University M,D

PHARMACEUTICAL ADMINISTRATION

- Columbia University M*
- Duquesne University M
- Emmanuel College (United States) M,O
- Fairleigh Dickinson University, Metropolitan Campus M,O
- Florida Agricultural and Mechanical University M,D
- Idaho State University P,M,D
- Long Island University, Brooklyn Campus M
- The Ohio State University P,M,D
- Purdue University M,D,O
- St. John's University (NY) M
- San Diego State University M
- Temple University M*
- University of Arkansas for Medical Sciences M
- University of Florida M,D*
- University of Houston P,M,D
- University of Illinois at Chicago M,D
- University of Maryland, Baltimore M,D
- University of Michigan D*
- University of Minnesota, Twin Cities Campus M,D
- University of Mississippi M,D
- University of Pittsburgh M*
- University of the Sciences in Philadelphia M
- The University of Toledo M
- University of West Florida M
- University of Wisconsin–Madison M,D*
- Virginia Commonwealth University M,D
- Wayne State University P,M,D,O*
- West Virginia University M,D

PHARMACEUTICAL ENGINEERING

- New Jersey Institute of Technology M

PHARMACEUTICAL SCIENCES

- Auburn University M,D
- Boston University M,D*
- Butler University P,M
- Campbell University P,M
- Creighton University M,D
- Dartmouth College D
- Duquesne University M,D
- Florida Agricultural and Mechanical University M,D
- Idaho State University M,D
- The Johns Hopkins University M
- Long Island University, Brooklyn Campus M,D
- Long Island University, Rockland Graduate Campus M
- Massachusetts College of Pharmacy and Health Sciences M,D
- Memorial University of Newfoundland M,D
- Mercer University P,M,D
- North Dakota State University M,D
- Northeastern University P,M,D
- Oregon State University P,M,D
- Purdue University M,D
- Queen's University at Kingston M,D
- Rush University M,D
- Rutgers, The State University of New Jersey, New Brunswick M,D*
- St. John's University (NY) M,D
- South Dakota State University M,D
- Stevens Institute of Technology M,O
- Temple University M*
- Texas Tech University Health Sciences Center M,D
- Université de Montréal M,D,O
- Université Laval M,D,O
- University at Buffalo, the State University of New York M,D*
- University of Alberta M,D
- The University of Arizona M,D
- University of Arkansas for Medical Sciences M
- The University of British Columbia P,M,D

University of California, San Francisco	D
University of Cincinnati	M,D
University of Colorado Denver	P,D
University of Connecticut	M,D*
University of Florida	M,D*
University of Georgia	M,D,O
University of Houston	P,M,D
University of Illinois at Chicago	M,D
The University of Kansas	M
University of Kentucky	M,D*
University of Louisiana at Monroe	M
The University of Manchester	M,D
University of Manitoba	M,D
University of Maryland, Baltimore	D
University of Michigan	D*
University of Minnesota, Twin Cities Campus	M,D
University of Mississippi	M,D
University of Missouri–Kansas City	P,D*
The University of Montana	M,D
University of Nebraska Medical Center	M,D
University of New Mexico	M,D*
The University of North Carolina at Chapel Hill	M,D*
University of Oklahoma Health Sciences Center	M,D
University of Pittsburgh	M,D*
University of Puerto Rico, Medical Sciences Campus	P,M
University of Rhode Island	M,D
University of Saskatchewan	M,D
University of South Carolina	M,D
University of Southern California	M,D,O*
The University of Texas at Austin	M,D
University of the Pacific	M,D
University of the Sciences in Philadelphia	M,D
The University of Toledo	M
University of Toronto	M,D
University of Utah	M*
University of Washington	M,D*
University of Wisconsin–Madison	M,D*
Virginia Commonwealth University	M,D
Wayne State University	P,M,D,O*
Western University of Health Sciences	M
West Virginia University	M,D

PHARMACOLOGY

Albany Medical College	M,D
Alliant International University–San Francisco	M
American University of Beirut	P,M
Argosy University, Hawai'i	M,O*
Auburn University	M,D
Baylor College of Medicine	D*
Boston University	M,D*
Case Western Reserve University	D*
Columbia University	M,D*
Cornell University	M,D*
Cornell University, Joan and Sanford I. Weill Medical College and Graduate School of Medical Sciences	M,D
Creighton University	M,D
Dalhousie University	M,D
Dartmouth College	D
Drexel University	M,D*
Duke University	D*
Duquesne University	M,D
East Carolina University	D
East Tennessee State University	D
Emory University	D*
Fairleigh Dickinson University, College at Florham	M,O
Florida Agricultural and Mechanical University	M,D
Georgetown University	M,D
Georgia Health Sciences University	M,D
Howard University	M,D
Idaho State University	M,D
Indiana University–Purdue University Indianapolis	M,D
The Johns Hopkins University	D
Kent State University	M,D*
Loma Linda University	M,D
Long Island University, Brooklyn Campus	M,D
Louisiana State University Health Sciences Center	M,D
Louisiana State University Health Sciences Center at Shreveport	D
Loyola University Chicago	M,D
Massachusetts College of Pharmacy and Health Sciences	M,D
McGill University	M,D
McMaster University	M,D
Medical College of Wisconsin	D*
Meharry Medical College	D
Michigan State University	M,D
New York Medical College	M,D*
New York University	P,M,D
North Carolina State University	M,D*
Northwestern University	D*
Nova Southeastern University	M*
The Ohio State University	P,M,D
Oregon Health & Science University	D*
Penn State Hershey Medical Center	M,D
Purdue University	M,D
Queen's University at Kingston	M,D
Rush University	M,D
Saint Louis University	D
Southern Illinois University Carbondale	M,D
State University of New York Upstate Medical University	D
Stony Brook University, State University of New York	D
Temple University	D*
Texas Tech University Health Sciences Center	M,D
Thomas Jefferson University	M
Tufts University	D
Tulane University	M,D*
Universidad Central del Caribe	M,D
Université de Montréal	M,D
Université de Sherbrooke	M,D
University at Buffalo, the State University of New York	M,D*
The University of Alabama at Birmingham	D*
University of Alberta	M,D
The University of Arizona	M,D
University of Arkansas for Medical Sciences	M,D
The University of British Columbia	M,D
University of California, Davis	M,D
University of California, Irvine	M,D*
University of California, Los Angeles	D*
University of California, San Diego	D*
University of California, San Francisco	D
University of Chicago	D
University of Cincinnati	D
University of Colorado Denver	D
University of Connecticut	M,D*
University of Florida	M,D*
University of Georgia	M,D
University of Guelph	M,D
University of Houston	P,M,D
University of Illinois at Chicago	D
The University of Iowa	M,D*
The University of Kansas	M,D
University of Kentucky	D*
University of Louisville	M,D
The University of Manchester	M,D
University of Manitoba	M,D
University of Maryland, Baltimore	M,D
University of Medicine and Dentistry of New Jersey	D
University of Miami	D*
University of Michigan	M,D*
University of Minnesota, Duluth	M,D
University of Minnesota, Twin Cities Campus	M,D
University of Mississippi	M,D
University of Mississippi Medical Center	M,D
University of Missouri	M,D*
University of Nebraska Medical Center	M,D
The University of North Carolina at Chapel Hill	D*
University of North Dakota	M,D
University of North Texas Health Science Center at Fort Worth	M,D
University of Pennsylvania	D*
University of Prince Edward Island	M,D
University of Puerto Rico, Medical Sciences Campus	M,D
University of Rhode Island	M,D
University of Rochester	M,D
University of Saskatchewan	M,D
The University of South Dakota	M,D
The University of Texas Health Science Center at San Antonio	D
The University of Texas Medical Branch	M,D
University of the Sciences in Philadelphia	M,D
The University of Toledo	M
University of Toronto	M,D
University of Utah	D*
University of Vermont	M,D
University of Virginia	D
University of Washington	D*
University of Wisconsin–Madison	D*
Vanderbilt University	D*
Virginia Commonwealth University	M,D,O
Wake Forest University	D
Wayne State University	P,M,D*
West Virginia University	M,D
Wright State University	M
Yale University	D*

PHARMACY

Albany College of Pharmacy and Health Sciences	P,M*
Auburn University	P
Belmont University	P
Butler University	P,M
Campbell University	P,M
Creighton University	P
Duquesne University	P
D'Youville College	P*
East Tennessee State University	P
Ferris State University	P
Florida Agricultural and Mechanical University	P,D
Hampton University	P
Harding University	P
Howard University	P
Idaho State University	P,M,D
Lake Erie College of Osteopathic Medicine	P,M,O
Lebanese American University	P
Lipscomb University	P
Loma Linda University	P
Massachusetts College of Pharmacy and Health Sciences	P
Medical University of South Carolina	P
Mercer University	P,M,D
Midwestern University, Downers Grove Campus	P
Midwestern University, Glendale Campus	P
Northeastern Ohio Universities Colleges of Medicine and Pharmacy	P
Nova Southeastern University	P,D*
Ohio Northern University	P
The Ohio State University	P,M,D
Oregon State University	P,M,D
Pacific University	P
Palm Beach Atlantic University	P
Purdue University	P
Regis University	P,M,D,O
Roosevelt University	P
Roseman University of Health Sciences	P
Rutgers, The State University of New Jersey, New Brunswick	P,M,D*
St. John Fisher College	P
St. John's University (NY)	P
St. Louis College of Pharmacy	P
Samford University	P
Shenandoah University	P
South Dakota State University	P
Southern Illinois University Edwardsville	P
South University (SC)	P*
South University (GA)	P*
Southwestern Oklahoma State University	P
Temple University	P*
Texas Southern University	P,M,D
Thomas Jefferson University	P
Touro University	P,M
Universidad de Ciencias Medicas	P,M,O
University at Buffalo, the State University of New York	P*
University of Alberta	M,D
The University of Arizona	P
University of Arkansas for Medical Sciences	P,M
The University of British Columbia	P,M,D
University of California, San Diego	P*
University of California, San Francisco	P
University of Charleston	P
University of Cincinnati	P
University of Connecticut	P*
The University of Findlay	P
University of Florida	P*
University of Georgia	P
University of Houston	P,M,D

*M—master's degree; P—first professional degree; D—doctorate; O—other advanced degree; *—Close-Up and/or Display in one of the other books in this series*

Institution	Degrees
University of Illinois at Chicago	P,D
The University of Iowa	M,D*
University of Kentucky	P*
University of Louisiana at Monroe	D
The University of Manchester	M,D
University of Maryland, Baltimore	P,M,D
University of Michigan	P*
University of Minnesota, Duluth	M,D
University of Minnesota, Twin Cities Campus	P,M,D
University of Mississippi	P
University of Missouri–Kansas City	P,D*
The University of Montana	P,M,D
University of Nebraska Medical Center	P
University of New England	P
University of New Mexico	P*
University of Oklahoma Health Sciences Center	P
University of Pittsburgh	P*
University of Puerto Rico, Medical Sciences Campus	P,M
University of Rhode Island	M,D
University of South Carolina	P
University of Southern California	P*
The University of Tennessee Health Science Center	P,M,D
The University of Texas at Austin	P
University of the Incarnate Word	P
University of the Pacific	P
University of Utah	P*
University of Washington	P,M,D*
University of Wisconsin–Madison	P*
University of Wyoming	P
Virginia Commonwealth University	P
Washington State University	P,D
Washington State University Spokane	P
Wayne State University	P,M,D,O*
Western University of Health Sciences	P
West Virginia University	P,M,D
Wilkes University	P
Wingate University	P
Xavier University of Louisiana	P

PHILANTHROPIC STUDIES

Institution	Degrees
Indiana University–Purdue University Indianapolis	M,D
Saint Mary's University of Minnesota	M

PHILOSOPHY

Institution	Degrees
American University	M
American University of Beirut	M
Arizona State University	M,D,O
Baylor University	M,D*
Boston College	M,D*
Boston University	M,D*
Bowling Green State University	M,D*
Brandeis University	M
Brock University	M
Brown University	M,D
California Institute of Integral Studies	M,D
California State University, Long Beach	M
California State University, Los Angeles	M*
Carleton University	M
Carnegie Mellon University	M,D*
The Catholic University of America	M,D,O
Central European University	M,D
Claremont Graduate University	M,D
Cleveland State University	M,O
Collège Dominicain de Philosophie et de Théologie	M,D
College of the Humanities and Sciences, Harrison Middleton University	M,D
Colorado State University	M
Columbia University	M,D*
Concordia University (Canada)	M
Cornell University	D*
Dalhousie University	M,D
DePaul University	M,D
Dominican School of Philosophy and Theology	M
Duke University	M,D*
Duquesne University	M,D
Emory University	D,O*
Florida State University	M,D
Fordham University	M,D
Franciscan University of Steubenville	M
George Mason University	M*
Georgetown University	M,D
The George Washington University	M
Georgia State University	M
Gonzaga University	M
Graduate School and University Center of the City University of New York	M,D
Harvard University	M,D*
Howard University	M
Indiana University Bloomington	M,D*
Indiana University–Purdue University Indianapolis	M,O
Institute for Christian Studies	M,D
Institute for Doctoral Studies in the Visual Arts	D
The Johns Hopkins University	M,D
Kent State University	M*
Louisiana State University and Agricultural and Mechanical College	M
Loyola Marymount University	M
Loyola University Chicago	M,D
Marquette University	M,D
Massachusetts Institute of Technology	D
McGill University	M,D
McMaster University	M,D
Memorial University of Newfoundland	M
Miami University	M
Michigan State University	M,D
Montclair State University	D,O
Mount St. Mary's University	M
The New School: A University	M,D
New York University	M,D
Northern Illinois University	M
Northwestern University	D*
The Ohio State University	M,D
Ohio University	M*
Oklahoma City University	M
Oklahoma State University	M*
Penn State University Park	M,D
Princeton University	D*
Purdue University	M,D
Queen's University at Kingston	M,D
Regis College (Canada)	P,M,D,O
Rice University	M,D
Rutgers, The State University of New Jersey, New Brunswick	D*
St. John's University (NY)	M
Saint Louis University	M,D
Saint Mary's University (Canada)	M
San Diego State University	M
San Francisco State University	M,O
San Jose State University	M
Simon Fraser University	M,D
Southeastern Baptist Theological Seminary	P,M,D
Southern Baptist Theological Seminary	P,M,D
Southern Evangelical Seminary	P,M,D,O
Southern Illinois University Carbondale	M,D
Stanford University	M,D
State University of New York at Binghamton	M,D
Stony Brook University, State University of New York	M,D
Syracuse University	M,D*
Temple University	M,D*
Texas A&M University	M,D
Texas Tech University	M*
Trinity Western University	M
Tufts University	M
Tulane University	M,D*
Universidad Autonoma de Guadalajara	M,D
Université de Montréal	M,D
Université de Sherbrooke	M,D,O
Université du Québec à Montréal	M,D
Université du Québec à Trois-Rivières	M,D
Université Laval	M,D
University at Albany, State University of New York	M,D
University at Buffalo, the State University of New York	M,D*
University of Alberta	M,D
The University of Arizona	M,D
University of Arkansas	M,D
The University of British Columbia	M,D
University of Calgary	M,D
University of California, Berkeley	D*
University of California, Davis	M,D
University of California, Irvine	M,D*
University of California, Los Angeles	M,D*
University of California, Riverside	M,D
University of California, San Diego	D*
University of California, Santa Barbara	D
University of California, Santa Cruz	M,D
University of Chicago	M,D
University of Cincinnati	M,D
University of Colorado Boulder	M,D*
University of Connecticut	M,D*
University of Dallas	M,D
University of Florida	M,D*
University of Georgia	M,D
University of Guelph	M,D
University of Hawaii at Manoa	M,D
University of Houston	M
University of Illinois at Chicago	M,D
University of Illinois at Urbana–Champaign	M,D
The University of Iowa	M,D*
The University of Kansas	M,D
University of Kentucky	M,D*
University of Lethbridge	M,D
University of Louisville	M
The University of Manchester	M,D
University of Manitoba	M
University of Maryland, College Park	M,D
University of Massachusetts Amherst	M,D*
University of Memphis	M,D
University of Miami	M,D*
University of Michigan	M,D*
University of Minnesota, Twin Cities Campus	M,D
University of Mississippi	M
University of Missouri	M,D*
University of Missouri–St. Louis	M
The University of Montana	M
University of Nebraska–Lincoln	M,D*
University of Nevada, Reno	M*
University of New Brunswick Fredericton	M
University of New Mexico	M,D*
The University of North Carolina at Chapel Hill	M,D*
The University of North Carolina at Charlotte	M,O
University of North Florida	M,O
University of North Texas	M,D
University of Notre Dame	D*
University of Oklahoma	M,D*
University of Oregon	M,D
University of Ottawa	M,D*
University of Pennsylvania	M,D*
University of Pittsburgh	M,D*
University of Puerto Rico, Río Piedras	M
University of Regina	M
University of Rochester	M,D
University of St. Thomas (TX)	M,D*
University of Saskatchewan	M
University of South Africa	M,D
University of South Carolina	M,D
University of Southern California	M,D*
University of South Florida	M,D*
The University of Tennessee	M,D
The University of Texas at Austin	D
The University of Texas at Dallas	M,D*
The University of Texas at El Paso	M
The University of Toledo	M
University of Toronto	M,D
University of Utah	M,D*
University of Victoria	M
University of Virginia	M,D
University of Washington	M,D*
University of Waterloo	M,D
The University of Western Ontario	M,D
University of Windsor	M
University of Wisconsin–Madison	M,D*
University of Wisconsin–Milwaukee	M
University of Wyoming	M
Vanderbilt University	M,D*
Villanova University	D
Virginia Polytechnic Institute and State University	M
Washington State University	M
Washington University in St. Louis	M,D*
Wayne State University	M,D*
West Chester University of Pennsylvania	M,O
Western Michigan University	M
Wilfrid Laurier University	M

Yale University	D*
York University	M,D*

PHOTOGRAPHY

Academy of Art University	M
Bard College	M
Barry University	M*
Bradley University	M
Brooklyn College of the City University of New York	M,D
Brooks Institute	M
California College of the Arts	M
California Institute of the Arts	M,O
California State University, Fullerton	M
California State University, Los Angeles	M*
Claremont Graduate University	M
Columbia College Chicago	M
Columbia University	M*
Cornell University	M*
Cranbrook Academy of Art	M
The George Washington University	M
Georgia State University	M,D
Howard University	M
Illinois State University	M
Indiana State University	M
Inter American University of Puerto Rico, San Germán Campus	M
James Madison University	M
Lamar University	M
Louisiana State University and Agricultural and Mechanical College	M
Louisiana Tech University	M
Maryland Institute College of Art	M
Marywood University	M
Massachusetts College of Art and Design	M
Mills College	M
Minneapolis College of Art and Design	M
New Mexico State University	M
The New School: A University	M
New York Film Academy	M
Ohio University	M*
Otis College of Art and Design	M
Pratt Institute	M*
Rhode Island School of Design	M
Rochester Institute of Technology	M
San Francisco Art Institute	M,O
San Jose State University	M
Savannah College of Art and Design	M
School of the Art Institute of Chicago	M
School of Visual Arts (NY)	M
Sotheby's Institute of Art–London	M
Southern Methodist University	M
Syracuse University	M*
Temple University	M*
The University of Alabama	M
University of Alaska Fairbanks	M
University of Colorado Boulder	M*
University of Florida	M,D*
University of Illinois at Chicago	M
University of Illinois at Urbana–Champaign	M
University of Massachusetts Dartmouth	M
University of Memphis	M,O
University of Miami	M*
University of Notre Dame	M*
University of Oklahoma	M*
University of Southern California	M*
The University of Tennessee	M
University of Utah	M*
University of Victoria	M
University of Washington	M*
Virginia Commonwealth University	M,D
Washington State University	M
Yale University	M*

PHOTONICS

Boston University	M,D*
Duke University	M*
Lehigh University	M,D
Oklahoma State University	M,D,O*
Princeton University	D*
Stevens Institute of Technology	M,D,O
The University of Alabama in Huntsville	M,D
University of Arkansas	M,D
University of California, San Diego	M,D*
University of California, Santa Barbara	M,D
University of Central Florida	M,D

PHYSICAL CHEMISTRY

Auburn University	M,D
Boston College	M,D*
Brandeis University	M,D
California State University, Los Angeles	M*
Cleveland State University	M,D
Cornell University	D*
Eastern New Mexico University	M
Florida State University	M,D
Georgetown University	D
The George Washington University	M,D
Harvard University	D*
Howard University	M,D
Indiana University Bloomington	M,D*
Kansas State University	M,D*
Kent State University	M,D*
Laurentian University	M
Marquette University	M,D
Massachusetts Institute of Technology	D
McMaster University	M,D
Northeastern University	M,D
Old Dominion University	M,D
Oregon State University	M,D
Purdue University	M,D
Rensselaer Polytechnic Institute	M,D
Rice University	M,D
Rutgers, The State University of New Jersey, Newark	M,D*
Rutgers, The State University of New Jersey, New Brunswick	M,D*
Seton Hall University	M,D
Southern University and Agricultural and Mechanical College	M
State University of New York at Binghamton	M,D
Stevens Institute of Technology	M,D,O
Texas Christian University	M,D
Tufts University	M,D
University of Calgary	M,D
University of Cincinnati	M,D
University of Georgia	M,D
University of Louisville	M,D
The University of Manchester	M,D
University of Maryland, College Park	M,D
University of Memphis	M,D
University of Miami	M,D*
University of Michigan	D*
University of Missouri	M,D*
University of Missouri–Kansas City	M,D*
University of Missouri–St. Louis	M,D
The University of Montana	M,D
University of Nebraska–Lincoln	M,D*
University of Notre Dame	M,D*
University of Southern California	D*
University of Southern Mississippi	M,D
University of South Florida	M,D*
The University of Tennessee	M,D
The University of Texas at Austin	M,D
The University of Toledo	M,D
Vanderbilt University	M,D*
Virginia Commonwealth University	M,D
Wake Forest University	M,D
West Virginia University	M,D
Yale University	D*
Youngstown State University	M

PHYSICAL EDUCATION

Adams State College	M
Adelphi University	M,O*
Alabama Agricultural and Mechanical University	M
Alabama State University	M
Albany State University	M
Alcorn State University	M,O
American University of Puerto Rico	M,O
Arizona State University	M,D
Arkansas State University	M,O
Ashland University	M
Auburn University	M,D,O
Auburn University Montgomery	M,O
Augusta State University	M
Austin College	M
Averett University	M
Azusa Pacific University	M
Ball State University	M,D
Baylor University	M,D*
Boise State University	M
Boston University	M,D,O*
Bridgewater State University	M
Brooklyn College of the City University of New York	M,O
California Baptist University	M
California State University, Dominguez Hills	M*
California State University, East Bay	M
California State University, Fullerton	M
California State University, Long Beach	M
California State University, Los Angeles	M*
California State University, Sacramento	M
California State University, Stanislaus	M
Campbell University	M
Canisius College	M
Caribbean University	M,D
Central Connecticut State University	M,O
Central Michigan University	M
Chicago State University	M
The Citadel, The Military College of South Carolina	M
Cleveland State University	M
The College at Brockport, State University of New York	M
The College of New Jersey	M
Colorado State University–Pueblo	M
Columbus State University	M,O
Concordia University (CA)	M
Defiance College	M
Delta State University	M
DePaul University	M,D
Eastern Kentucky University	M
Eastern Michigan University	M
Eastern New Mexico University	M
Eastern Washington University	M
East Stroudsburg University of Pennsylvania	M
East Tennessee State University	M,D
Emporia State University	M
Florida Agricultural and Mechanical University	M
Florida International University	M,D,O
Florida State University	M,D
Fort Hays State University	M
Gardner-Webb University	M
Georgia College & State University	M
Georgia Southwestern State University	M,O
Georgia State University	M
Henderson State University	M
Hofstra University	M,D,O
Howard University	M
Humboldt State University	M
Idaho State University	M
Illinois State University	M
Indiana State University	M
Indiana University Bloomington	M,D*
Indiana University of Pennsylvania	M
Indiana University–Purdue University Indianapolis	M
Inter American University of Puerto Rico, Metropolitan Campus	M
Inter American University of Puerto Rico, San Germán Campus	M
Ithaca College	M
Jackson State University	M
Jacksonville State University	M,O
Long Island University, Brooklyn Campus	M
Louisiana Tech University	M,D
McDaniel College	M
McGill University	M,D,O
Memorial University of Newfoundland	M
Middle Tennessee State University	M
Minnesota State University Mankato	M
Mississippi State University	M
Missouri State University	M
Montana State University Billings	M
Montclair State University	M,O
Morehead State University	M
Murray State University	M,O
North Carolina Agricultural and Technical State University	M
North Carolina Central University	M
North Dakota State University	M
Northern Illinois University	M

*M—master's degree; P—first professional degree; D—doctorate; O—other advanced degree; *—Close-Up and/or Display in one of the other books in this series*

Northern State University M
North Georgia College & State University M,O
Northwest Missouri State University M
The Ohio State University M,D
Ohio University M*
Old Dominion University M
Pittsburg State University M
Prairie View A&M University M
Purdue University M,D
Rhode Island College M,O
Saginaw Valley State University M
St. Cloud State University M
Salem State University M
San Diego State University M
Slippery Rock University of Pennsylvania M
South Dakota State University M
Southern Connecticut State University M
Southern Illinois University Carbondale M
Springfield College M,D,O
State University of New York College at Cortland M
Stony Brook University, State University of New York M,O
Sul Ross State University M
Tarleton State University M
Teachers College, Columbia University M,D
Temple University M,D*
Tennessee State University M
Tennessee Technological University M
Texas A&M University M,D
Texas A&M University–Commerce M,D
Texas Southern University M
Texas State University–San Marcos M
Texas Woman's University M,D
Troy University M
Union College (KY) M
United States Sports Academy M
Universidad del Turabo M
Universidad Metropolitana M
Université de Montréal M,D,O
Université de Sherbrooke M,O
Université du Québec à Trois-Rivières M
The University of Akron M
The University of Alabama M,D
The University of Alabama at Birmingham M*
University of Alberta M,D
University of Arkansas M
University of Arkansas at Pine Bluff M
The University of British Columbia M,D
University of Central Florida M,O
University of Central Missouri M
University of Dayton M,D
University of Florida M,D*
University of Georgia M,D
University of Houston M,D
University of Idaho M
University of Indianapolis M
The University of Iowa M,D*
The University of Kansas M,D
University of Louisville M
University of Maine M
University of Manitoba M
University of Memphis M
University of Minnesota, Twin Cities Campus M,D,O
The University of Montana M
University of Nebraska at Kearney M
University of Nebraska at Omaha M
University of Nevada, Las Vegas M,D
University of New Brunswick Fredericton M
University of New Mexico M,D*
The University of North Carolina at Chapel Hill M*
The University of North Carolina at Pembroke M
University of Northern Colorado M,D
University of Northern Iowa M
University of Puerto Rico, Mayagüez Campus M
University of Rhode Island M
University of South Alabama M
University of South Carolina M,D
The University of South Dakota M
University of Southern Mississippi M,D
University of South Florida M*
The University of Tennessee at Chattanooga M
University of the Incarnate Word M,O
The University of Toledo M
University of Toronto M,D
University of Victoria M
University of Virginia M,D
University of Washington M,D*
The University of West Alabama M
University of West Florida M
University of West Georgia M,O
University of Wisconsin–La Crosse M
University of Wyoming M
Utah State University M
Virginia Commonwealth University M,D,O
Wayne State College M
Wayne State University M*
West Chester University of Pennsylvania M,O
Western Carolina University M
Western Kentucky University M
Western Michigan University M
Western Washington University M
Westfield State University M
West Virginia University M,D
Wilfrid Laurier University M
William Woods University M,O
Wingate University M
Winthrop University M
Wright State University M

PHYSICAL THERAPY

Alabama State University D
American International College D
Andrews University D
Angelo State University D
Arcadia University D*
Arkansas State University M,D
Armstrong Atlantic State University D
A.T. Still University of Health Sciences M,D
Azusa Pacific University D
Baylor University M,D*
Bellarmine University M,D
Belmont University D
Boston University D*
Bradley University D
California State University, Fresno M,D
California State University, Long Beach M
California State University, Northridge M
Carroll University M,D
Central Michigan University M,D
Chapman University D
Chatham University D
Clarke University D
Clarkson University D*
Cleveland State University D
College of Mount St. Joseph D
The College of St. Scholastica D
Columbia University D*
Concordia University Wisconsin M,D
Creighton University D
Daemen College D,O
Dalhousie University M
Des Moines University D
Dominican College M,D
Drexel University M,D,O*
Duke University D*
Duquesne University M,D
D'Youville College M,D,O*
East Carolina University M,D
Eastern Washington University D
East Tennessee State University D
Elon University D
Emory University D*
Florida Agricultural and Mechanical University M
Florida Gulf Coast University M,D
Florida International University D
Franklin Pierce University M,D,O
Gannon University D
George Fox University D
The George Washington University D
Georgia State University D
Governors State University M,D
Graduate School and University Center of the City University of New York D
Grand Valley State University D
Hampton University D
Hardin-Simmons University D
Humboldt State University M
Husson University D
Idaho State University D
Indiana University–Purdue University Indianapolis M,D
Ithaca College M,D
Langston University D
Lebanon Valley College D
Loma Linda University M,D
Long Island University, Brooklyn Campus D
Louisiana State University Health Sciences Center D
Lynchburg College D
Marquette University D
Marymount University D
Maryville University of Saint Louis D
Mayo School of Health Sciences D
McMaster University M
Medical University of South Carolina D
Mercy College D
MGH Institute of Health Professions M,D,O
Midwestern University, Downers Grove Campus D
Midwestern University, Glendale Campus D
Misericordia University M,D
Missouri State University D
Mount St. Mary's College D
Nazareth College of Rochester M,D
Neumann University D
New York Institute of Technology D
New York Medical College D*
New York University M,D,O
Northeastern University D
Northern Arizona University D,O
Northern Illinois University M
North Georgia College & State University D
Northwestern University D*
Nova Southeastern University D*
Oakland University M,D,O
The Ohio State University D
Ohio University D*
Old Dominion University D
Pacific University D
Queen's University at Kingston M,D
Quinnipiac University M,D
Regis University P,M,D,O
The Richard Stockton College of New Jersey D
Rockhurst University D
Rocky Mountain University of Health Professions D
Rosalind Franklin University of Medicine and Science M,D*
Rutgers, The State University of New Jersey, Camden D
Sacred Heart University M,D
Sage Graduate School D
St. Ambrose University D
St. Catherine University D
Saint Francis University D
Saint Louis University M,D
Samuel Merritt University D
San Francisco State University M,D
Seton Hall University D
Shenandoah University D
Simmons College D
Slippery Rock University of Pennsylvania D
Southwest Baptist University D
Springfield College D
State University of New York Upstate Medical University D
Stony Brook University, State University of New York M,D,O
Temple University D*
Tennessee State University M,D
Texas State University–San Marcos D
Texas Tech University Health Sciences Center D
Texas Woman's University D
Thomas Jefferson University M,D
Touro College M,D
University at Buffalo, the State University of New York D*
The University of Alabama at Birmingham D*
University of Alberta M,D
University of California, San Francisco M,D
University of Central Arkansas D
University of Central Florida D
University of Colorado Denver D
University of Connecticut D*
University of Dayton M,D
University of Delaware D*
University of Evansville D
The University of Findlay D

University of Florida	D*
University of Hartford	M,D
University of Illinois at Chicago	M,D
University of Indianapolis	M,D
The University of Iowa	D*
The University of Kansas	D
University of Kentucky	M*
University of Manitoba	M,D
University of Mary	D
University of Maryland, Baltimore	D
University of Maryland Eastern Shore	D
University of Massachusetts Lowell	D
University of Medicine and Dentistry of New Jersey	M,D
University of Miami	D*
University of Michigan–Flint	D
University of Minnesota, Twin Cities Campus	D
University of Mississippi Medical Center	M
University of Missouri	M*
The University of Montana	D
University of Nebraska Medical Center	D
University of Nevada, Las Vegas	D
University of New England	D
University of New Mexico	D*
The University of North Carolina at Chapel Hill	M,D*
University of North Dakota	M,D
University of North Florida	D
University of Oklahoma Health Sciences Center	M
University of Pittsburgh	M,D*
University of Puerto Rico, Medical Sciences Campus	M
University of Puget Sound	D
University of Rhode Island	D
University of St. Augustine for Health Sciences	M,D,O
The University of Scranton	M,D
University of South Alabama	D
The University of South Dakota	D
University of Southern California	M,D*
University of South Florida	M,D*
The University of Tennessee at Chattanooga	D
The University of Tennessee Health Science Center	M,D
The University of Texas at El Paso	M
The University of Texas Health Science Center at San Antonio	M
The University of Texas Medical Branch	M,D
The University of Texas Southwestern Medical Center at Dallas	D
University of the Pacific	M,D
The University of Toledo	M,D
University of Toronto	M
University of Utah	D,O*
University of Vermont	D
University of Washington	M,D*
The University of Western Ontario	M,O
University of Wisconsin–La Crosse	M,D
University of Wisconsin–Milwaukee	D
Utica College	D
Virginia Commonwealth University	M,D
Walsh University	D
Washington University in St. Louis	D,O*
Wayne State University	D*
Western Carolina University	M
Western University of Health Sciences	D
West Virginia University	D
Wheeling Jesuit University	D
Wichita State University	D
Widener University	M,D
Winston-Salem State University	M
Youngstown State University	D

PHYSICIAN ASSISTANT STUDIES

Albany Medical College	M
Alderson-Broaddus College	M
A.T. Still University of Health Sciences	M,D
Augsburg College	M
Barry University	M*
Baylor College of Medicine	M*
Bethel University (TN)	M
Butler University	P,M
Carroll University	M
Central Michigan University	M,D
Chatham University	M
Cleveland State University	M,D
Cornell University, Joan and Sanford I. Weill Medical College and Graduate School of Medical Sciences	M
Daemen College	M
DeSales University	M
Des Moines University	M
Drexel University	M*
Duke University	M*
Duquesne University	M,D
D'Youville College	M*
East Carolina University	M
Eastern Virginia Medical School	M
Emory University	M*
Franklin Pierce University	M,D,O
Gannon University	M
The George Washington University	M
Grand Valley State University	M
Harding University	M
Idaho State University	M
James Madison University	M
Jefferson College of Health Sciences	M
Keiser University	M
King's College	M
Le Moyne College	M
Lock Haven University of Pennsylvania	M
Loma Linda University	M
Marietta College	M
Marquette University	M
Marywood University	M
Massachusetts College of Pharmacy and Health Sciences	M
Medical University of South Carolina	M
Mercy College	M
Methodist University	M
Midwestern University, Downers Grove Campus	M
Midwestern University, Glendale Campus	M
Missouri State University	M
Mountain State University	M
New York Institute of Technology	M
Northeastern University	M
Nova Southeastern University	M*
Oregon Health & Science University	M*
Our Lady of the Lake College	M
Pace University	M
Pacific University	M
Philadelphia College of Osteopathic Medicine	M*
Philadelphia University	M
Quinnipiac University	M
Rocky Mountain College	M
Rosalind Franklin University of Medicine and Science	M*
Rush University	M
Saint Francis University	M
Saint Louis University	M
Salus University	M
Samuel Merritt University	M
Seton Hall University	M
Seton Hill University	M
Shenandoah University	M
South College	M
Southern Illinois University Carbondale	M
South University	M*
South University (GA)	M*
Springfield College	M
Stony Brook University, State University of New York	M,D,O
Texas Tech University Health Sciences Center	M
Touro University	P,M
Towson University	M
Trevecca Nazarene University	M
Union College (NE)	M
The University of Alabama at Birmingham	M*
University of Colorado Denver	M
University of Detroit Mercy	M
The University of Findlay	M
University of Florida	M*
The University of Iowa	M*
University of Kentucky	M*
University of Medicine and Dentistry of New Jersey	M
University of Nebraska Medical Center	M
University of New England	M
University of New Mexico	M*
University of North Dakota	M
University of North Texas Health Science Center at Fort Worth	M
University of Pittsburgh	M*
University of St. Francis (IL)	M
University of Saint Francis (IN)	M
University of South Alabama	M
The University of South Dakota	M
University of Southern California	M*
The University of Texas Health Science Center at San Antonio	M
The University of Texas Medical Branch	M
The University of Texas Southwestern Medical Center at Dallas	M
University of the Cumberlands	M
The University of Toledo	M
University of Utah	M*
University of Wisconsin–La Crosse	M
Wagner College	M
Wayne State University	M*
Western Michigan University	M
Western University of Health Sciences	M
Wichita State University	M
Yale University	M,O*

PHYSICS

Alabama Agricultural and Mechanical University	M,D
American University of Beirut	M
Arizona State University	M,D
Auburn University	M,D
Ball State University	M
Baylor University	M,D*
Boston College	M,D*
Boston University	M,D,O*
Bowling Green State University	M*
Brandeis University	M,D
Brigham Young University	M,D*
Brock University	M
Brooklyn College of the City University of New York	M,D
Brown University	M,D
Bryn Mawr College	M,D*
California Institute of Technology	D
California State University, Fresno	M
California State University, Fullerton	M
California State University, Long Beach	M
California State University, Los Angeles	M*
California State University, Northridge	M
Carleton University	M,D
Carnegie Mellon University	M,D*
Case Western Reserve University	M,D*
The Catholic University of America	M,D
Central Connecticut State University	M,O
Central Michigan University	M,D
Christopher Newport University	M
City College of the City University of New York	M,D
Clark Atlanta University	M
Clarkson University	M,D*
Clark University	M,D
Clemson University	M,D
Cleveland State University	M
The College of William and Mary	M,D
Colorado School of Mines	M,D
Colorado State University	M,D
Columbia University	M,D*
Concordia University (Canada)	M,D
Cornell University	M,D*
Creighton University	M
Dalhousie University	M,D
Dartmouth College	M,D
Delaware State University	M,D
DePaul University	M
Drew University	M
Drexel University	M,D*
Duke University	M,D*
East Carolina University	M,D
Eastern Michigan University	M
Emory University	D*
Fisk University	M
Florida Agricultural and Mechanical University	M,D
Florida Atlantic University	M,D
Florida Institute of Technology	M,D
Florida International University	M,D
Florida State University	M,D
George Mason University	M,D*
The George Washington University	M,D
Georgia Institute of Technology	M,D
Georgia State University	M,D

*M—master's degree; P—first professional degree; D—doctorate; O—other advanced degree; *—Close-Up and/or Display in one of the other books in this series*

Graduate School and University Center of the City University of New York	D
Hampton University	M,D
Harvard University	D*
Hofstra University	M,O
Howard University	M,D
Hunter College of the City University of New York	M,D
Idaho State University	M,D
Illinois Institute of Technology	M,D
Indiana University Bloomington	M,D*
Indiana University of Pennsylvania	M
Indiana University–Purdue University Indianapolis	M,D
Iowa State University of Science and Technology	M,D*
The Johns Hopkins University	D
Kent State University	M,D*
Lakehead University	M
Lehigh University	M,D
Louisiana State University and Agricultural and Mechanical College	M,D
Louisiana Tech University	M,D
Marshall University	M
Massachusetts Institute of Technology	M,D
McGill University	M,D
McMaster University	D
Memorial University of Newfoundland	M,D
Miami University	M
Michigan State University	M,D
Michigan Technological University	M,D
Minnesota State University Mankato	M
Mississippi State University	M,D
Missouri University of Science and Technology	M,D
Montana State University	M,D
Naval Postgraduate School	M,D
New Mexico Institute of Mining and Technology	M,D
New Mexico State University	M,D
New York University	M,D
North Carolina Central University	M
North Carolina State University	M,D*
North Dakota State University	M,D
Northeastern University	M,D
Northern Arizona University	M
Northern Illinois University	M,D
Northwestern University	M,D*
Oakland University	M,D
The Ohio State University	M,D
Ohio University	M,D*
Oklahoma State University	M,D*
Old Dominion University	M,D
Oregon State University	M,D
Penn State University Park	M,D
Pittsburg State University	M
Portland State University	M,D
Princeton University	D*
Purdue University	M,D
Queens College of the City University of New York	M,D
Queen's University at Kingston	M,D
Rensselaer Polytechnic Institute	M,D
Rice University	M,D
Royal Military College of Canada	M
Rutgers, The State University of New Jersey, New Brunswick	M,D*
St. Francis Xavier University	M
San Diego State University	M
San Francisco State University	M
San Jose State University	M
Simon Fraser University	M,D
South Dakota School of Mines and Technology	M,D
South Dakota State University	M
Southeastern Louisiana University	M
Southern Illinois University Carbondale	M,D
Southern Methodist University	M,D
Southern University and Agricultural and Mechanical College	M
Stanford University	D
State University of New York at Binghamton	M,D
Stephen F. Austin State University	M
Stevens Institute of Technology	M,D,O
Stony Brook University, State University of New York	M,D
Syracuse University	M,D*
Temple University	M,D*
Texas A&M University	M,D
Texas A&M University–Commerce	M
Texas Christian University	M,D
Texas State University–San Marcos	M
Texas Tech University	M,D*
Trent University	M
Tufts University	M,D
Tulane University	D*
Université de Moncton	M
Université de Montréal	M,D
Université de Sherbrooke	M,D
Université du Québec à Trois-Rivières	M,D
Université Laval	M,D
University at Albany, State University of New York	M,D
University at Buffalo, the State University of New York	M,D*
The University of Akron	M
The University of Alabama	M,D
The University of Alabama at Birmingham	M,D*
The University of Alabama in Huntsville	M,D
University of Alaska Fairbanks	M,D
University of Alberta	M,D
The University of Arizona	M,D
University of Arkansas	M,D
The University of British Columbia	M,D
University of Calgary	M,D
University of California, Berkeley	D*
University of California, Davis	M,D
University of California, Irvine	M,D*
University of California, Los Angeles	M,D*
University of California, Merced	M,D
University of California, Riverside	M,D
University of California, San Diego	M,D*
University of California, Santa Barbara	D
University of California, Santa Cruz	M,D
University of Central Florida	M,D
University of Central Oklahoma	M
University of Chicago	M,D
University of Cincinnati	M,D
University of Colorado at Colorado Springs	M
University of Colorado Boulder	M,D*
University of Connecticut	M,D*
University of Delaware	M,D*
University of Denver	M,D
University of Florida	M,D*
University of Georgia	M,D
University of Guelph	M,D
University of Hawaii at Manoa	M,D
University of Houston	M,D
University of Houston–Clear Lake	M
University of Idaho	M,D
University of Illinois at Chicago	M,D
University of Illinois at Urbana–Champaign	M,D
The University of Iowa	M,D*
The University of Kansas	M,D
University of Kentucky	M,D*
University of Lethbridge	M,D
University of Louisiana at Lafayette	M*
University of Louisville	M,D
University of Maine	M,D
The University of Manchester	M,D
University of Manitoba	M,D
University of Maryland, Baltimore County	M,D
University of Maryland, College Park	M,D
University of Massachusetts Amherst	M,D*
University of Massachusetts Dartmouth	M
University of Massachusetts Lowell	M,D
University of Memphis	M
University of Miami	M,D*
University of Michigan	M,D*
University of Minnesota, Duluth	M
University of Minnesota, Twin Cities Campus	M,D
University of Mississippi	M,D
University of Missouri	M,D*
University of Missouri–Kansas City	M,D*
University of Missouri–St. Louis	M,D
University of Nebraska–Lincoln	M,D*
University of Nevada, Las Vegas	M,D
University of Nevada, Reno	M,D*
University of New Brunswick Fredericton	M,D
University of New Hampshire	M,D
University of New Mexico	M,D*
University of New Orleans	M,D
The University of North Carolina at Chapel Hill	M,D*
University of North Dakota	M,D
University of Northern Iowa	M
University of North Texas	M,D
University of Notre Dame	M,D*
University of Oklahoma	M,D*
University of Oregon	M,D
University of Ottawa	M,D*
University of Pennsylvania	M,D*
University of Pittsburgh	M,D*
University of Puerto Rico, Mayagüez Campus	M
University of Puerto Rico, Río Piedras	M,D
University of Regina	M,D
University of Rhode Island	M,D
University of Rochester	
University of Saskatchewan	M,D
University of South Carolina	M,D
The University of South Dakota	M,D
University of Southern California	M,D*
University of Southern Mississippi	M,D
University of South Florida	M,D*
The University of Tennessee	M,D
The University of Tennessee Space Institute	M,D
The University of Texas at Arlington	M,D
The University of Texas at Austin	M,D
The University of Texas at Brownsville	M
The University of Texas at Dallas	M,D*
The University of Texas at El Paso	M
The University of Texas at San Antonio	M,D*
The University of Toledo	M,D
University of Toronto	M,D
University of Tulsa	M
University of Utah	M,D*
University of Vermont	M
University of Victoria	M,D
University of Virginia	M,D
University of Washington	M,D*
University of Waterloo	M,D
The University of Western Ontario	M,D
University of Windsor	M,D
University of Wisconsin–Madison	M,D*
University of Wisconsin–Milwaukee	M,D
Utah State University	M,D
Vanderbilt University	M,D*
Virginia Commonwealth University	M
Virginia Polytechnic Institute and State University	M,D
Virginia State University	M
Wake Forest University	M,D
Washington State University	M,D
Washington University in St. Louis	D*
Wayne State University	M,D*
Wesleyan University	M,D*
Western Illinois University	M
Western Kentucky University	M
Western Michigan University	M,D
West Virginia University	M,D
Worcester Polytechnic Institute	M,D
Wright State University	M
Yale University	D*
York University	M,D*

PHYSIOLOGY

Albert Einstein College of Medicine	D
American University of Beirut	P,M
Ball State University	M
Boston University	M,D*
Brigham Young University	M,D*
Brown University	M,D
Case Western Reserve University	M,D*
Columbia University	M,D*
Cornell University	M,D*

Cornell University, Joan and Sanford I. Weill Medical College and Graduate School of Medical Sciences	M,D
Dalhousie University	M,D
Dartmouth College	D
East Carolina University	D
Eastern Michigan University	M
East Tennessee State University	D
Georgetown University	M,D
Georgia Health Sciences University	M,D
Georgia Institute of Technology	M
Georgia State University	M,D
Harvard University	M,D*
Howard University	D
Illinois State University	M,D
Indiana State University	M,D
The Johns Hopkins University	M,D
Kansas State University	D*
Kent State University	M,D*
Loma Linda University	M,D
Louisiana State University Health Sciences Center	M,D
Louisiana State University Health Sciences Center at Shreveport	M,D
Loyola University Chicago	M,D
Marquette University	M,D
McGill University	M,D
McMaster University	M,D
Medical College of Wisconsin	D*
Michigan State University	M,D
Montclair State University	M,O
New York Medical College	M,D*
New York University	P,M,D
North Carolina State University	M,D*
Northwestern University	M*
Nova Scotia Agricultural College	M
The Ohio State University	M,D
Ohio University	M,D*
Oregon Health & Science University	D*
Penn State Hershey Medical Center	M,D
Penn State University Park	M,D
Purdue University	M,D
Queen's University at Kingston	M,D
Rocky Mountain University of Health Professions	D
Rosalind Franklin University of Medicine and Science	M,D*
Rush University	D
Rutgers, The State University of New Jersey, New Brunswick	M,D*
Saint Louis University	D
Salisbury University	M
San Francisco State University	M
San Jose State University	M
Southern Illinois University Carbondale	M,D
Stanford University	D
State University of New York Upstate Medical University	M,D
Stony Brook University, State University of New York	D
Teachers College, Columbia University	M,D
Temple University	D*
Texas A&M University	M,D
Tufts University	D
Tulane University	M,D*
Universidad Central del Caribe	M,D
Université de Montréal	M,D
Université de Sherbrooke	M,D
Université Laval	M,D
University at Buffalo, the State University of New York	M,D*
University of Alberta	M,D
The University of Arizona	M,D
University of Arkansas for Medical Sciences	M,D
The University of British Columbia	M,D
University of California, Berkeley	M,D*
University of California, Davis	M,D
University of California, Irvine	D*
University of California, Los Angeles	M,D*
University of California, San Diego	D*
University of California, San Francisco	D
University of Chicago	D
University of Cincinnati	D
University of Colorado Boulder	M,D*
University of Colorado Denver	D
University of Connecticut	M,D*
University of Delaware	M,D*
University of Florida	M,D*
University of Georgia	M,D
University of Guelph	M,D
University of Hawaii at Manoa	M,D
University of Illinois at Chicago	M,D
University of Illinois at Urbana–Champaign	M,D
The University of Iowa	M,D*
The University of Kansas	M,D
University of Kentucky	M,D*
University of Louisville	M,D
The University of Manchester	M,D
University of Manitoba	M,D
University of Massachusetts Amherst	M,D*
University of Medicine and Dentistry of New Jersey	M,D
University of Miami	D*
University of Michigan	D*
University of Minnesota, Duluth	M,D
University of Minnesota, Twin Cities Campus	D
University of Mississippi Medical Center	M,D
University of Missouri	M,D*
University of Nebraska Medical Center	M,D
University of Nevada, Reno	D*
University of New Mexico	M,D,O*
University of North Dakota	M,D
University of North Texas Health Science Center at Fort Worth	M,D
University of Notre Dame	M,D*
University of Oklahoma Health Sciences Center	M,D
University of Oregon	M,D
University of Pennsylvania	D*
University of Prince Edward Island	M,D
University of Puerto Rico, Medical Sciences Campus	M,D
University of Rochester	M,D
University of Saskatchewan	M,D
The University of South Dakota	M,D
University of Southern California	M,D*
The University of Tennessee	M,D
The University of Texas Health Science Center at San Antonio	M,D
The University of Texas Medical Branch	M,D
University of Toronto	M,D
University of Utah	D*
University of Virginia	D
University of Washington	D*
The University of Western Ontario	M,D
University of Wisconsin–La Crosse	M
University of Wisconsin–Madison	M,D*
University of Wyoming	M,D
Virginia Commonwealth University	M,D,O
Wake Forest University	D
Wayne State University	M,D*
Western Michigan University	M
West Virginia University	M,D
Wright State University	M
Yale University	D*
Youngstown State University	M

PLANETARY AND SPACE SCIENCES

Air Force Institute of Technology	M,D
Arizona State University	M,D
California Institute of Technology	M,D
Columbia University	M,D*
Cornell University	D*
Florida Institute of Technology	M,D
Georgia Institute of Technology	M,D
Hampton University	M,D
Harvard University	M,D*
Massachusetts Institute of Technology	M,D
McGill University	M,D
St. Thomas University	M,D,O
The University of Arizona	M,D
University of Arkansas	M,D
University of California, Los Angeles	M,D*
University of California, Santa Cruz	M,D
University of Chicago	M,D
University of Hawaii at Manoa	M,D
University of Houston	M,D
University of Maryland, Baltimore County	M
University of Michigan	M,D*
University of New Mexico	M,D*
University of North Dakota	M
University of Pittsburgh	M,D*
Washington University in St. Louis	M,D*
West Chester University of Pennsylvania	M,O
Western Connecticut State University	M
Yale University	M,D*
York University	M,D*

PLANT BIOLOGY

Clemson University	M,D
Cornell University	M,D*
Eastern New Mexico University	M
Florida State University	M,D
Illinois State University	M,D
Indiana University Bloomington	M,D*
Iowa State University of Science and Technology	M,D*
Miami University	M,D
Michigan State University	M,D
New York University	M,D
North Carolina State University	M,D*
Ohio University	M,D*
Rutgers, The State University of New Jersey, New Brunswick	M,D*
Southern Illinois University Carbondale	M,D
Texas A&M University	M,D
Université Laval	M,D
University of Alberta	M,D
University of California, Berkeley	D*
University of California, Davis	M,D
University of California, Riverside	M,D
University of California, San Diego	D*
University of Connecticut	M,D*
University of Florida	M,D*
University of Georgia	M,D
University of Illinois at Urbana–Champaign	M,D
University of Maine	M,D
University of Maryland, College Park	M,D
University of Massachusetts Amherst	M,D*
University of Minnesota, Twin Cities Campus	M,D
University of Missouri	M,D*
University of New Hampshire	M,D
The University of Texas at Austin	M,D
University of Vermont	M,D
The University of Western Ontario	M,D
Washington University in St. Louis	D*
Yale University	D*

PLANT MOLECULAR BIOLOGY

Cornell University	M,D*
Illinois State University	M,D
Michigan Technological University	M,D
Rutgers, The State University of New Jersey, New Brunswick	M,D*
University of California, San Diego	D*
University of Connecticut	M,D*
University of Florida	M,D*
University of Massachusetts Amherst	M,D*
Washington State University	M,D

PLANT PATHOLOGY

Auburn University	M,D
Colorado State University	M,D
Cornell University	M,D*
Iowa State University of Science and Technology	M,D*
Kansas State University	M,D*
Louisiana State University and Agricultural and Mechanical College	M,D
Michigan State University	M,D
Mississippi State University	M,D
Montana State University	M,D
New Mexico State University	M
North Carolina State University	M,D*
North Dakota State University	M,D
Nova Scotia Agricultural College	M
The Ohio State University	M,D
Oklahoma State University	M,D*
Oregon State University	M,D
Penn State University Park	M,D
Purdue University	M,D

*M—master's degree; P—first professional degree; D—doctorate; O—other advanced degree; *—Close-Up and/or Display in one of the other books in this series*

Rutgers, The State University of New Jersey, New Brunswick M,D*
State University of New York College of Environmental Science and Forestry M,D
Texas A&M University M,D
The University of Arizona M,D
University of Arkansas M
University of California, Davis M,D
University of California, Riverside M,D
University of Florida M,D*
University of Georgia M,D
University of Guelph M,D
University of Hawaii at Manoa M,D
University of Kentucky M,D*
University of Maine M
University of Minnesota, Twin Cities Campus M,D
The University of Tennessee M,D
University of Wisconsin–Madison M,D*
Virginia Polytechnic Institute and State University M,D
Washington State University M,D
West Virginia University M,D

PLANT PHYSIOLOGY

Cornell University M,D*
Nova Scotia Agricultural College M
Oregon State University M,D
Penn State University Park M,D
Purdue University M,D
University of Kentucky D*
University of Manitoba M,D
University of Massachusetts Amherst M,D*
The University of Tennessee M,D
Virginia Polytechnic Institute and State University M,D

PLANT SCIENCES

Alabama Agricultural and Mechanical University M,D
American University of Beirut M
Brigham Young University M,D*
California State University, Fresno M
Clemson University M,D
Colorado State University M,D
Cornell University M,D*
Delaware State University M
Florida Agricultural and Mechanical University M
Illinois State University M,D
Lehman College of the City University of New York D
McGill University M,D,O
Miami University M,D
Michigan State University M,D
Mississippi State University M,D
Missouri State University M
Montana State University M,D
New Mexico State University M,D
North Carolina Agricultural and Technical State University M
North Dakota State University M,D
Oklahoma State University M,D,O*
South Dakota State University M,D
Southern Illinois University Carbondale M
State University of New York College of Environmental Science and Forestry M,D
Texas A&M University M,D
Texas A&M University–Kingsville M,D
Texas Tech University M,D*
Tuskegee University M
The University of Arizona M,D
University of Arkansas D
The University of British Columbia M,D
University of California, Riverside M,D
University of Connecticut M,D*
University of Delaware M,D*
University of Florida D*
University of Georgia M,D
University of Hawaii at Manoa M,D
University of Idaho M,D
University of Kentucky M*
University of Maine M,D
The University of Manchester M,D
University of Manitoba M,D
University of Massachusetts Amherst M,D*
University of Minnesota, Twin Cities Campus M,D
University of Missouri M,D*
University of Rhode Island M,D
University of Saskatchewan M,D
The University of Tennessee M
University of Vermont M,D
The University of Western Ontario M,D
University of Wisconsin–Madison M,D*
Utah State University M,D
Virginia State University M
West Texas A&M University M
West Virginia University D

PLASMA PHYSICS

Princeton University D*
University of Colorado Boulder M,D*
West Virginia University M,D

PODIATRIC MEDICINE

Barry University P*
California School of Podiatric Medicine at Samuel Merritt University P
Des Moines University P
Midwestern University, Glendale Campus P
New York College of Podiatric Medicine P
Ohio College of Podiatric Medicine P
Rosalind Franklin University of Medicine and Science P*
Temple University P*

POLITICAL SCIENCE

Acadia University M
American Public University System M
American University M,D,O
The American University in Cairo M
The American University of Athens M
American University of Beirut M
Appalachian State University M
Arizona State University M,D
Arkansas State University M,O
Ashland University M
Auburn University M,D
Auburn University Montgomery M,D
Augusta State University M
Ball State University M
Baylor University M,D*
Boston College M,D*
Boston University M,D,O*
Bowling Green State University *
Brandeis University M,D
Brigham Young University M*
Brock University M
Brooklyn College of the City University of New York M,D
Brown University D
California Polytechnic State University, San Luis Obispo M
California State University, Chico M
California State University, Fullerton M
California State University, Long Beach M
California State University, Los Angeles M*
California State University, Northridge M
California State University, Sacramento M
Carleton University M,D
Case Western Reserve University M,D*
The Catholic University of America M,D
Central European University M,D
Central Michigan University M,O
Claremont Graduate University M,D
Clark Atlanta University M,D
The College of Saint Rose M
Colorado State University M,D
Columbia University M,D*
Concordia University (Canada) M,D
Converse College M
Cornell University D*
Dalhousie University M,D
Duke University M,D*
East Carolina University M
Eastern Illinois University M
Eastern Kentucky University M
East Stroudsburg University of Pennsylvania M
East Tennessee State University M
Emory University D*
Fairleigh Dickinson University, Metropolitan Campus M
Fayetteville State University M
Florida Agricultural and Mechanical University M
Florida Atlantic University M
Florida International University M,D
Florida State University M,D
Fordham University M
George Mason University M,D,O*
Georgetown University M,D
The George Washington University M,D
Georgia State University M,D
Governors State University M
Graduate School and University Center of the City University of New York M,D
Grambling State University M
Harvard University M,D*
Howard University M,D
Hult International Business School (United States) M
Idaho State University M,D
Illinois State University M
Indiana State University M
Indiana University Bloomington M,D*
Indiana University–Purdue University Indianapolis M,O
Institute for Christian Studies M,D
The Institute of World Politics M,O
Iowa State University of Science and Technology M*
Jackson State University M
Jacksonville State University M
James Madison University M
The Johns Hopkins University M,D,O
Kansas State University M*
Kaplan University, Davenport Campus M,O
Kean University M
Kent State University M,D*
Lamar University M
Lehigh University M
Lincoln University (MO) M,O
Long Island University, Brooklyn Campus M
Long Island University, C.W. Post Campus M
Louisiana State University and Agricultural and Mechanical College M,D
Loyola University Chicago M,D
Marquette University M
Marshall University M
Massachusetts Institute of Technology M,D
McGill University M,D
McMaster University M,D
Memorial University of Newfoundland M
Miami University M
Michigan State University M,D
Midwestern State University M
Mississippi College M,O
Mississippi State University M,D
Missouri State University M
Montclair State University M,O
Naval Postgraduate School M
New Mexico State University M
The New School: A University M,D
New York University M,D
Northeastern Illinois University M
Northeastern University M,D,O
Northern Arizona University M,D,O
Northern Illinois University M,D
Northwestern University M,D*
The Ohio State University M,D
Ohio University M*
Oklahoma State University M,D*
Penn State University Park M,D
Pepperdine University M
Portland State University M,D
Princeton University D*
Purdue University M,D
Queen's University at Kingston M,D
Regent University M
Rice University D
Roosevelt University M
Rutgers, The State University of New Jersey, Newark M*
Rutgers, The State University of New Jersey, New Brunswick D*
St. John's University (NY) M
Saint Louis University M

- St. Mary's University (United States) M
- Sam Houston State University M
- San Diego State University M
- San Francisco State University M
- Simon Fraser University M,D
- Sonoma State University M
- Southern Connecticut State University M
- Southern Illinois University Carbondale M,D
- Southern University and Agricultural and Mechanical College M
- Stanford University M,D
- State University of New York at Binghamton M,D
- Stony Brook University, State University of New York M,D
- Suffolk University M,O
- Sul Ross State University M
- Syracuse University M,D,O*
- Tarleton State University M
- Teachers College, Columbia University M,D
- Temple University M,D*
- Texas A&M International University M
- Texas A&M University D
- Texas A&M University–Kingsville M
- Texas State University–San Marcos M
- Texas Tech University M,D*
- Texas Woman's University M
- Troy University M
- Tulane University M,D*
- Universidad Nacional Pedro Henriquez Urena M
- Université de Montréal M,D
- Université du Québec à Montréal M,D
- Université Laval M,D
- University at Albany, State University of New York M,D
- University at Buffalo, the State University of New York M,D*
- The University of Akron M
- The University of Alabama M,D
- University of Alberta M,D
- The University of Arizona M,D
- University of Arkansas M
- The University of British Columbia M,D
- University of Calgary M,D
- University of California, Berkeley D*
- University of California, Davis M,D
- University of California, Irvine D*
- University of California, Los Angeles M,D*
- University of California, Riverside M,D
- University of California, San Diego M,D*
- University of California, Santa Barbara M,D
- University of California, Santa Cruz D
- University of Central Florida M
- University of Central Oklahoma M
- University of Chicago D
- University of Cincinnati M,D
- University of Colorado Boulder M,D*
- University of Colorado Denver M,D
- University of Connecticut M,D*
- University of Dallas M,D
- University of Delaware M,D*
- University of Florida M,D,O*
- University of Georgia M,D
- University of Guelph M
- University of Hawaii at Manoa M,D
- University of Houston M,D
- University of Idaho M,D
- University of Illinois at Chicago M,D
- University of Illinois at Springfield M
- University of Illinois at Urbana–Champaign M,D
- The University of Iowa M,D*
- The University of Kansas M,D
- University of Kentucky M,D*
- University of Lethbridge M,D
- University of Louisville M
- The University of Manchester M,D
- University of Manitoba M
- University of Maryland, College Park D
- University of Massachusetts Amherst M,D*
- University of Massachusetts Boston M,D,O
- University of Memphis M
- University of Miami M*
- University of Michigan M,D*
- University of Minnesota, Twin Cities Campus D
- University of Mississippi M,D
- University of Missouri M,D*
- University of Missouri–Kansas City M,D*
- University of Missouri–St. Louis M,D,O
- The University of Montana M
- University of Nebraska at Omaha M
- University of Nebraska–Lincoln M,D,O*
- University of Nevada, Las Vegas M,D
- University of Nevada, Reno M,D*
- University of New Brunswick Fredericton M
- University of New Hampshire M
- University of New Mexico M,D*
- University of New Orleans M,D
- The University of North Carolina at Chapel Hill M,D,O*
- The University of North Carolina at Charlotte M
- The University of North Carolina at Greensboro M,O
- University of Northern British Columbia M,D,O
- University of Northern Iowa M
- University of North Texas M,D
- University of Notre Dame D*
- University of Oklahoma M,D*
- University of Oregon M,D
- University of Ottawa M,D*
- University of Pennsylvania M,D*
- University of Pittsburgh M,D*
- University of Regina M
- University of Rhode Island M
- University of Rochester M,D
- University of Saskatchewan M
- University of South Africa M,D
- University of South Carolina M,D
- The University of South Dakota M,D
- University of Southern California M,D*
- University of Southern Mississippi M,D
- University of South Florida M,D*
- The University of Tennessee M,D
- The University of Texas at Arlington M
- The University of Texas at Austin D
- The University of Texas at Brownsville M
- The University of Texas at Dallas M,D*
- The University of Texas at El Paso M
- The University of Texas at San Antonio M*
- The University of Texas at Tyler M
- The University of Texas of the Permian Basin M
- The University of Toledo M,O
- University of Toronto M,D
- University of Utah M,D*
- University of Victoria M,D
- University of Virginia M,D
- University of Washington M,D*
- University of Waterloo M,D
- The University of Western Ontario M,D
- University of West Florida M
- University of West Georgia M,O
- University of Windsor M
- University of Wisconsin–Madison D*
- University of Wisconsin–Milwaukee M,D
- University of Wyoming M
- Utah State University M
- Vanderbilt University M,D*
- Villanova University M
- Virginia Commonwealth University M,D,O
- Virginia Polytechnic Institute and State University M,D,O
- Washington State University M,D
- Washington University in St. Louis M,D*
- Wayne State University M,D*
- West Chester University of Pennsylvania M,O
- Western Illinois University M
- Western Kentucky University M
- Western Michigan University M,D
- Western Washington University M
- West Texas A&M University M
- West Virginia University M,D
- Wilfrid Laurier University M,D
- Yale University D*
- Yorktown University M
- York University M,D*

POLYMER SCIENCE AND ENGINEERING

- California Polytechnic State University, San Luis Obispo M
- Carnegie Mellon University M,D*
- Case Western Reserve University M,D*
- Cornell University M,D*
- DePaul University M
- Eastern Michigan University M
- Florida State University M
- Georgia Institute of Technology M,D
- Lehigh University M,D
- Massachusetts Institute of Technology M,D,O
- North Carolina State University D*
- North Dakota State University M,D
- Polytechnic Institute of NYU M
- Rensselaer Polytechnic Institute M,D
- Stevens Institute of Technology M,D,O
- The University of Akron M,D
- University of Connecticut M,D*
- The University of Manchester M,D
- University of Massachusetts Amherst M,D*
- University of Massachusetts Lowell M,D,O
- University of Missouri–Kansas City M,D*
- University of Southern Mississippi M,D
- University of South Florida M,D*
- The University of Tennessee M,D
- University of Wisconsin–Madison M,D*
- Wayne State University M,D,O*

PORTUGUESE

- Brigham Young University M*
- Emory University D,O*
- Harvard University M,D*
- Indiana University Bloomington M,D*
- Michigan State University M,D
- New York University M,D
- The Ohio State University M,D
- Princeton University D*
- Tulane University M,D*
- University of California, Los Angeles M*
- University of California, Santa Barbara M,D
- University of Illinois at Urbana–Champaign M,D
- University of Maryland, College Park M,D
- University of Massachusetts Amherst M,D*
- University of Massachusetts Dartmouth M,D
- University of Minnesota, Twin Cities Campus M,D
- University of New Mexico M,D*
- The University of North Carolina at Chapel Hill M,D*
- University of South Africa M,D
- The University of Tennessee D
- The University of Texas at Austin M,D
- University of Toronto M,D
- University of Washington M*
- University of Wisconsin–Madison M,D*
- Vanderbilt University M,D*
- Yale University D*

PROJECT MANAGEMENT

- American Graduate University M,O
- American InterContinental University Online M
- Aspen University M,O
- Athabasca University M,O
- Avila University M,O
- Boston University M*
- Brandeis University M,O
- Brenau University M
- California Intercontinental University M,D
- Capella University M,D,O
- Christian Brothers University M,O
- City University of Seattle M,O
- Colorado Christian University M
- Colorado Technical University Colorado Springs M,D
- Colorado Technical University Denver M
- Colorado Technical University Sioux Falls M
- Dallas Baptist University M
- DeSales University M

*M—master's degree; P—first professional degree; D—doctorate; O—other advanced degree; *—Close-Up and/or Display in one of the other books in this series*

DeVry University M
Dowling College M,O
Drexel University M*
Ellis University M
Embry-Riddle Aeronautical University–Worldwide M
Florida Institute of Technology M
The George Washington University M,D
Granite State College M
Grantham University M
Harrisburg University of Science and Technology M
Herzing University Online M
Jones International University M
Kaplan University, Davenport Campus M
Lakeland College M
Lasell College M,O
Lawrence Technological University M,D
Lehigh University M,D,O
Lewis University M
Marlboro College M,O
Marymount University M,O
Maryville University of Saint Louis M,O
Metropolitan State University M,D,O
Mississippi State University M
Missouri State University M
Montana Tech of The University of Montana M
New England College M
Northwestern University M*
Norwich University M
Polytechnic Institute of NYU M,D,O
Polytechnic University of Puerto Rico, Miami Campus M
Queen's University at Kingston M
Regis University M,O
Robert Morris University M,D
Rowan University M
Royal Roads University O
St. Edward's University M
Saint Mary's University of Minnesota M,O
Southern Illinois University Edwardsville M
Southern New Hampshire University M,D,O
Stevens Institute of Technology M,O
Texas A&M University–San Antonio M
TUI University M,D
Universidad del Turabo M
Universidad Nacional Pedro Henriquez Urena M
Université du Québec à Chicoutimi M
Université du Québec à Montréal M,O
Université du Québec à Rimouski M,O
Université du Québec en Abitibi-Témiscamingue M,O
Université du Québec en Outaouais M,O
The University of Alabama in Huntsville M
University of Alaska Anchorage M
University of Atlanta P,M,D,O
University of California, Berkeley O*
University of Dallas M
University of Denver M,O
University of Houston M
University of Management and Technology M,D,O
University of Mary M
University of Michigan–Dearborn M,D
University of Oklahoma M*
University of Ottawa M,O*
University of Phoenix M
University of Phoenix–Puerto Rico Campus M
University of Regina M,O
University of San Francisco M
The University of Tennessee at Chattanooga M,O
The University of Texas at Dallas M*
University of the Incarnate Word M,O
University of Wisconsin–Platteville M
Walden University M,D
Western Carolina University M
Winthrop University M,O
Wright State University M

PSYCHIATRIC NURSING

Allen College M,D,O
American University of Beirut M
Arizona State University M,D,O
Boston College M,D*
Case Western Reserve University D*
Columbia University M,O*
East Tennessee State University M,D,O
Fairfield University M,D
Georgia State University M,D,O
Hampton University M
Hunter College of the City University of New York M,O
Husson University M,O
Indiana University–Purdue University Indianapolis M,D
Kent State University M,D*
Lincoln Memorial University M
MGH Institute of Health Professions M,D,O
Midwestern State University M
Molloy College M,O
Monmouth University M,D,O
Montana State University M,O
New Mexico State University M,D
New York University M,D,O
Northeastern University M,O
Oregon Health & Science University M,O*
Pontifical Catholic University of Puerto Rico M
Rivier College M
Rush University M,D,O
Rutgers, The State University of New Jersey, Newark M*
Sage Graduate School M,O
Saint Xavier University M,O
Seattle University M
Shenandoah University M,D,O
Southeastern Louisiana University M
Southern Arkansas University–Magnolia M
Stony Brook University, State University of New York M,O
Uniformed Services University of the Health Sciences M*
University of Alaska Anchorage M,O
University of Cincinnati M,D
University of Colorado Denver M,D
University of Delaware M,O*
University of Illinois at Chicago M
The University of Kansas M,D,O
University of Louisville M,D
University of Maryland, Baltimore M
University of Massachusetts Lowell M,O
University of Michigan M*
University of Minnesota, Twin Cities Campus M
University of Missouri–St. Louis M,D,O
The University of North Carolina at Chapel Hill M,D,O*
The University of North Carolina at Charlotte M,O
University of North Dakota M,D
University of Pennsylvania M*
University of Pittsburgh M,D*
University of Puerto Rico, Medical Sciences Campus M
University of Rhode Island M,D
University of Rochester M,D,O
University of San Diego M,D
University of South Carolina M,O
University of Southern Maine M,O
University of Southern Mississippi M,D
The University of Toledo M,O
University of Virginia M,D
University of Wisconsin–Madison D*
Vanderbilt University M,D*
Virginia Commonwealth University M,D,O
Wayne State University M,O*

PSYCHOANALYSIS AND PSYCHOTHERAPY

Adler Graduate School M,O
Adler School of Professional Psychology M,D,O
Argosy University, Chicago D*
Boston Graduate School of Psychoanalysis M,D,O
Naropa University M
New York University M,D,O
Prescott College M
Regent University M,D

PSYCHOLOGY—GENERAL

Abilene Christian University M
Acadia University M
Adelphi University M,D*
Adler School of Professional Psychology M,D,O
Alabama Agricultural and Mechanical University M,O
Alliant International University–Fresno D
Alliant International University–Los Angeles M,D
Alliant International University–Sacramento M,D
Alliant International University–San Diego M,D
Alliant International University–San Francisco M,D,O
American International College M,D
American Public University System M
American University M,D
American University of Beirut M
Andrews University M,D,O
Angelo State University M
Antioch University Los Angeles M
Antioch University Midwest M
Antioch University Santa Barbara M
Antioch University Seattle M,D
Appalachian State University M,O
Arcadia University M,D,O*
Argosy University, Atlanta M,D,O*
Argosy University, Chicago M,D*
Argosy University, Dallas M,D*
Argosy University, Denver M,D*
Argosy University, Hawai'i M,D,O*
Argosy University, Inland Empire M,D*
Argosy University, Los Angeles M,D*
Argosy University, Nashville M,D*
Argosy University, Orange County M,D*
Argosy University, Phoenix M,D*
Argosy University, Salt Lake City M,D*
Argosy University, San Diego M,D*
Argosy University, San Francisco Bay Area M,D*
Argosy University, Sarasota M,D*
Argosy University, Schaumburg M,D,O*
Argosy University, Seattle M,D,O*
Argosy University, Tampa M,D*
Argosy University, Twin Cities M,D,O*
Argosy University, Washington DC M,D*
Arizona State University M,D
Arkansas Tech University M
Assumption College M,O
Auburn University M,D
Auburn University Montgomery M
Augusta State University M
Austin Peay State University M,O
Avila University M
Azusa Pacific University M,D
Ball State University M
Barry University M,O*
Baylor University M,D*
Biola University D
Boston College M,D*
Boston Graduate School of Psychoanalysis M
Boston University M,D*
Bowling Green State University M,D*
Brandeis University M,D
Brenau University M
Bridgewater State University M
Brigham Young University M,D*
Brock University M,D
Brooklyn College of the City University of New York M,D
Brown University D
Bucknell University M
California Coast University M
California Institute of Integral Studies M,D
California Lutheran University M,D
California Polytechnic State University, San Luis Obispo M
California State Polytechnic University, Pomona M
California State University, Bakersfield M
California State University, Chico M
California State University, Dominguez Hills M*
California State University, Fresno M
California State University, Fullerton M
California State University, Long Beach M

Institution	Degrees
California State University, Los Angeles	M*
California State University, Northridge	M
California State University, Sacramento	M
California State University, San Bernardino	M
California State University, San Marcos	M
California State University, Stanislaus	M
Cambridge College	M,O
Cameron University	M
Capella University	M,D,O
Cardinal Stritch University	M
Carleton University	M,D
Carlos Albizu University	M,D
Carlos Albizu University, Miami Campus	M,D
Carnegie Mellon University	D*
Case Western Reserve University	D*
Castleton State College	M
The Catholic University of America	M,D
Central Connecticut State University	M
Central Michigan University	M,D,O
Central Washington University	M
Chestnut Hill College	M,D,O*
The Chicago School of Professional Psychology	D
The Chicago School of Professional Psychology at Irvine	D
The Chicago School of Professional Psychology at Westwood	D
The Chicago School of Professional Psychology: Online	M,D
The Citadel, The Military College of South Carolina	M,O
City College of the City University of New York	M,D
Claremont Graduate University	M,D,O
Clemson University	D
Cleveland State University	M,D,O
The College at Brockport, State University of New York	M
College of Saint Elizabeth	M,O
College of St. Joseph	M
Colorado State University	M,D
Columbia University	M,D*
Concordia University (Canada)	M,D
Concordia University Chicago	M
Concordia University Wisconsin	M
Connecticut College	M
Cornell University	D*
Dalhousie University	M,D
Dartmouth College	D
DePaul University	M,D
Drexel University	M,D*
Duke University	D*
Duquesne University	D
East Carolina University	M
East Central University	M
Eastern Illinois University	M,O
Eastern Kentucky University	M,O
Eastern Michigan University	M,D
Eastern Washington University	M
East Tennessee State University	M,D
Emory University	D*
Emporia State University	M
Evangel University	M
Fairleigh Dickinson University, College at Florham	M,O
Fairleigh Dickinson University, Metropolitan Campus	M,D,O
Fayetteville State University	M
Fielding Graduate University	M,D,O
Fisk University	M
Florida Agricultural and Mechanical University	M
Florida Atlantic University	M,D
Florida Institute of Technology	M,D
Florida International University	M,D
Florida State University	M,D
Fordham University	D
Fort Hays State University	M,O
Framingham State University	M
Francis Marion University	M,O
Frostburg State University	M
Fuller Theological Seminary	M,D,O
Gardner-Webb University	M
Geneva College	M
George Mason University	M,D,O*
Georgetown University	D
The George Washington University	D
Georgia Institute of Technology	M,D
Georgia Southern University	M,D
Georgia State University	M,D
Golden Gate University	M,D,O
Governors State University	M
Graduate School and University Center of the City University of New York	D
Grand Canyon University	D
Hardin-Simmons University	M
Harvard University	D*
Hodges University	M
Hood College	M,O
Houston Baptist University	M
Howard University	M,D
Humboldt State University	M
Hunter College of the City University of New York	M,D
Idaho State University	M,D
Illinois Institute of Technology	M,D
Illinois State University	M,D,O
Immaculata University	M,D,O
Indiana State University	M,D
Indiana University Bloomington	M,D*
Indiana University of Pennsylvania	M,D
Indiana University–Purdue University Indianapolis	M,D
Institute of Transpersonal Psychology	M,D,O
Inter American University of Puerto Rico, Metropolitan Campus	M,D
Inter American University of Puerto Rico, San Germán Campus	M,D
Iona College	M
Iowa State University of Science and Technology	D*
Jackson State University	D
Jacksonville State University	M
James Madison University	M,D,O
John F. Kennedy University	M,D,O
The Johns Hopkins University	D
Kansas State University	M,D*
Kean University	M
Kent State University	M,D*
Lakehead University	M,D
Lamar University	M
La Salle University	D
Laurentian University	M
Lehigh University	M,D
Lesley University	M,D,O
LeTourneau University	M
Lewis & Clark College	M,O
Lipscomb University	M,O
Loma Linda University	D
Long Island University, Brooklyn Campus	M,D
Long Island University, C.W. Post Campus	M,D
Louisiana State University and Agricultural and Mechanical College	M,D
Louisiana Tech University	M,D
Loyola University Chicago	M,D
Loyola University Maryland	M,D,O
Madonna University	M
Mansfield University of Pennsylvania	M
Marietta College	M
Marist College	M,O
Marquette University	D
Marshall University	M,D
Martin University	M
Marywood University	M
Massachusetts School of Professional Psychology	M,D,O
McGill University	M,D
McMaster University	M,D
McNeese State University	M
Medaille College	M
Memorial University of Newfoundland	M,D
Mercy College	M
Metropolitan State University	M,O
Miami University	D
Michigan School of Professional Psychology	M,D
Michigan State University	M,D
Middle Tennessee State University	M
Midwestern State University	M
Millersville University of Pennsylvania	M
Minnesota State University Mankato	M,D
Mississippi State University	M,D
Missouri State University	M
Monmouth University	M,O
Montana State University	M
Montana State University Billings	M
Montclair State University	M,O
Morehead State University	M
Morgan State University	M,D
Mountain State University	M,O
Mount Aloysius College	M
Mount Holyoke College	M
Mount St. Mary's College	M
Murray State University	M
National-Louis University	M,D,O
National University	M
New Mexico Highlands University	M
New Mexico State University	M,D
The New School: A University	M,D
New York University	M,D,O
Norfolk State University	M,D
North Carolina Central University	M
North Carolina State University	D*
Northcentral University	M,D,O
North Dakota State University	M,D
Northeastern State University	M
Northern Arizona University	M
Northern Illinois University	M,D
Northern Michigan University	M
Northwestern State University of Louisiana	M
Northwestern University	D*
Northwest Missouri State University	M
Northwest University	M,D
Notre Dame de Namur University	M
Nova Southeastern University	M,D,O*
The Ohio State University	M,D
Ohio University	D*
Oklahoma State University	M,D*
Old Dominion University	M,D
Our Lady of the Lake University of San Antonio	M,D
Pace University	M
Pacifica Graduate Institute	M,D
Pacific University	M,D
Palo Alto University	M,D
Penn State Harrisburg	M,D
Penn State University Park	M,D
Pepperdine University	D
Philadelphia College of Osteopathic Medicine	M,D,O*
Pittsburg State University	M
Polytechnic Institute of NYU	M,O
Pontifical Catholic University of Puerto Rico	M,D
Pontificia Universidad Catolica Madre y Maestra	M
Portland State University	M,D,O
Princeton University	D*
Purdue University	D
Queens College of the City University of New York	M
Queen's University at Kingston	M,D
Radford University	M
Regis University	M,O
Rhode Island College	M,O
Rice University	M,D
Richmont Graduate University	M
Rivier College	M
Rochester Institute of Technology	M
Roosevelt University	M,D
Rosalind Franklin University of Medicine and Science	M,D*
Rowan University	M
Rutgers, The State University of New Jersey, Camden	M
Rutgers, The State University of New Jersey, Newark	D*
Rutgers, The State University of New Jersey, New Brunswick	D*
Sage Graduate School	M
St. Cloud State University	M,D
St. John's University (NY)	M,D
Saint Joseph's University	M,O
Saint Louis University	M,D
Saint Mary's University (Canada)	M,D
St. Mary's University (United States)	M
Saint Xavier University	M,O
Salem State University	M,O
Sam Houston State University	M,D
San Diego State University	M,D
San Francisco State University	M
San Jose State University	M
Saybrook University	M,D
The School of Professional Psychology at Forest Institute	M,D,O

*M—master's degree; P—first professional degree; D—doctorate; O—other advanced degree; *—Close-Up and/or Display in one of the other books in this series*

Institution	Degrees
Seattle University	M
Seton Hall University	M,D,O
Shippensburg University of Pennsylvania	M
Simmons College	M,D
Simon Fraser University	M,D
Southeastern Baptist Theological Seminary	P,M,D
Southeastern Louisiana University	M
Southern Adventist University	M
Southern California Seminary	P,M,D
Southern Connecticut State University	M
Southern Illinois University Carbondale	M,D
Southern Illinois University Edwardsville	M,O
Southern Methodist University	D
Southern Nazarene University	M
Southern New Hampshire University	M,O
Southern Oregon University	M
Southern University and Agricultural and Mechanical College	M
Southwestern College (NM)	O
Spalding University	M,D
Stanford University	D
State University of New York at Binghamton	M,D
State University of New York at New Paltz	M
State University of New York at Plattsburgh	M,O
Stephen F. Austin State University	M
Stony Brook University, State University of New York	D
Suffolk University	D
Sul Ross State University	M
Temple University	M,D*
Tennessee State University	M,D
Texas A&M International University	M
Texas A&M University	D
Texas A&M University–Commerce	M,D
Texas A&M University–Corpus Christi	M
Texas A&M University–Kingsville	M
Texas A&M University–Texarkana	M
Texas Christian University	M,D
Texas Southern University	M
Texas State University–San Marcos	M
Texas Tech University	M,D*
Texas Woman's University	M,D,O
Trevecca Nazarene University	M,D
Tufts University	M,D
Tulane University	M,D*
Uniformed Services University of the Health Sciences	D*
Union College (KY)	M
Union Institute & University	M,D,O
Universidad de las Americas, A.C.	M
Universidad de las Américas–Puebla	M
Université de Montréal	M,D
Université de Sherbrooke	M
Université du Québec à Montréal	D
Université du Québec à Trois-Rivières	D,O
Université Laval	D
University at Albany, State University of New York	M,D,O
University at Buffalo, the State University of New York	M,D*
The University of Akron	M,D
The University of Alabama	D
The University of Alabama at Birmingham	M,D*
The University of Alabama in Huntsville	M
University of Alaska Anchorage	M,D
University of Alaska Fairbanks	D
University of Alberta	M,D
The University of Arizona	M,D
University of Arkansas	M,D
University of Arkansas at Little Rock	M
The University of British Columbia	M,D
University of Calgary	M,D
University of California, Berkeley	D*
University of California, Davis	D
University of California, Irvine	D*
University of California, Los Angeles	M,D*
University of California, Riverside	M,D
University of California, San Diego	D*
University of California, Santa Barbara	D
University of California, Santa Cruz	D
University of Central Arkansas	M,D
University of Central Florida	M,D
University of Central Missouri	M
University of Central Oklahoma	M
University of Chicago	D
University of Cincinnati	D
University of Colorado at Colorado Springs	M,D
University of Colorado Boulder	M,D*
University of Connecticut	M,D,O*
University of Dallas	M
University of Dayton	M
University of Delaware	D*
University of Denver	M,D
University of Detroit Mercy	M,D,O
University of Florida	M,D*
University of Georgia	M,D
University of Guelph	M,D
University of Hartford	M,D
University of Hawaii at Manoa	M,D,O
University of Houston	M,D
University of Houston–Clear Lake	M
University of Houston–Victoria	M
University of Idaho	M
University of Illinois at Chicago	D
University of Illinois at Urbana–Champaign	M,D
University of Indianapolis	M,D
The University of Iowa	M,D,O*
The University of Kansas	M,D
University of Kentucky	M,D*
University of La Verne	M,D
University of Lethbridge	M,D
University of Louisiana at Lafayette	M*
University of Louisiana at Monroe	M,O
University of Louisville	D
University of Maine	M,D
The University of Manchester	M,D
University of Manitoba	M,D
University of Mary Hardin-Baylor	M
University of Maryland, Baltimore County	M,D
University of Maryland, College Park	M,D
University of Massachusetts Amherst	M,D*
University of Massachusetts Dartmouth	M,O
University of Massachusetts Lowell	M
University of Memphis	M,D,O
University of Miami	M,D*
University of Michigan	D,O*
University of Minnesota, Twin Cities Campus	D
University of Mississippi	M,D
University of Missouri	M,D*
University of Missouri–Kansas City	M,D*
University of Missouri–St. Louis	M,D,O
The University of Montana	M,D,O
University of Nebraska at Omaha	M,D,O
University of Nebraska–Lincoln	M,D*
University of Nevada, Las Vegas	M,D
University of Nevada, Reno	M,D*
University of New Brunswick Saint John	M,D
University of New Hampshire	D
University of New Mexico	M,D*
University of New Orleans	M,D
The University of North Carolina at Chapel Hill	D*
The University of North Carolina at Charlotte	M,D,O
The University of North Carolina at Greensboro	M,D
The University of North Carolina Wilmington	M
University of North Dakota	M,D
University of Northern British Columbia	M,D,O
University of Northern Colorado	M,D
University of Northern Iowa	M
University of North Florida	M
University of North Texas	M,D
University of Notre Dame	D*
University of Oklahoma	M,D*
University of Oregon	M,D
University of Ottawa	D*
University of Pennsylvania	D*
University of Philosophical Research	M
University of Phoenix	M
University of Phoenix–Birmingham Campus	M
University of Phoenix–Chattanooga Campus	M,D
University of Phoenix–Cincinnati Campus	M
University of Phoenix–Jersey City Campus	M
University of Phoenix–Milwaukee Campus	M,D
University of Phoenix–Philadelphia Campus	M
University of Phoenix–Phoenix Campus	M
University of Phoenix–Southern Arizona Campus	M
University of Phoenix–Southern California Campus	M
University of Phoenix–Washington D.C. Campus	M,D
University of Pittsburgh	M,D*
University of Puerto Rico, Río Piedras	M,D
University of Regina	M,D
University of Rhode Island	M,D
University of Rochester	
University of Saint Francis (IN)	M
University of Saint Mary	M
University of St. Thomas (MN)	M,D,O
University of Saskatchewan	M,D
University of South Africa	M,D
University of South Alabama	M,D
University of South Carolina	M,D
The University of South Dakota	M,D
University of Southern California	M,D*
University of Southern Mississippi	M,D
University of South Florida	D*
The University of Tennessee	M,D
The University of Tennessee at Chattanooga	M
The University of Texas at Arlington	M,D
The University of Texas at Austin	D
The University of Texas at Brownsville	M
The University of Texas at Dallas	M,D*
The University of Texas at El Paso	M,D
The University of Texas at San Antonio	M*
The University of Texas at Tyler	M
The University of Texas of the Permian Basin	M
The University of Texas–Pan American	M
University of the Pacific	M
University of the Rockies	M,D
University of the West	M
The University of Toledo	M,D
University of Toronto	M,D
University of Tulsa	M,D
University of Utah	D*
University of Vermont	D
University of Victoria	M,D
University of Virginia	M,D
University of Washington	D*
University of Waterloo	M,D
The University of Western Ontario	M,D
University of West Florida	M
University of West Georgia	M,D
University of Windsor	M,D
University of Wisconsin–Eau Claire	M,O
University of Wisconsin–La Crosse	M,O
University of Wisconsin–Madison	D*
University of Wisconsin–Milwaukee	M,D
University of Wisconsin–Oshkosh	M
University of Wisconsin–Whitewater	M,O*
University of Wyoming	M,D
Utah State University	M,D
Valdosta State University	M,O
Valparaiso University	M,O
Vanderbilt University	M,D*
Villanova University	M
Virginia Commonwealth University	D
Virginia Polytechnic Institute and State University	M,D
Virginia State University	M,D
Wake Forest University	M
Walden University	M,D,O
Washburn University	M

Washington College M
Washington State University M,D
Washington University in St. Louis D*
Wayne State University M,D*
West Chester University of Pennsylvania M,O
Western Carolina University M
Western Illinois University M,O
Western Kentucky University M,O
Western Michigan University M,D
Western Washington University M
Westfield State University M
West Texas A&M University M
West Virginia University M,D
Wheaton College M,D
Wichita State University D
Widener University
Wilfrid Laurier University M,D
William Carey University M
Winthrop University M,O
Wisconsin School of Professional Psychology M,D
Wright Institute D
Wright State University M,D
Xavier University M,D
Yale University D*
Yeshiva University M,D*
York University M,D*
Youngstown State University M

PUBLIC ADMINISTRATION

Adelphi University O*
Albany State University M
American International College M
American Public University System M
American University M,D,O
The American University in Cairo M,O
American University of Beirut M
American University of Sharjah M
Andrew Jackson University M
Angelo State University M
Anna Maria College M
Appalachian State University M
Argosy University, Chicago M,D*
Argosy University, Dallas M,D,O*
Argosy University, Denver M,D*
Argosy University, Inland Empire M,D*
Argosy University, Los Angeles M,D*
Argosy University, Orange County M,D,O*
Argosy University, Phoenix M,D*
Argosy University, Salt Lake City M,D*
Argosy University, San Diego M,D*
Argosy University, San Francisco Bay Area M,D*
Argosy University, Sarasota M,D,O*
Argosy University, Schaumburg M,D,O*
Argosy University, Seattle M,D*
Argosy University, Tampa M,D*
Argosy University, Twin Cities M,D*
Argosy University, Washington DC M,D,O*
Arkansas State University M,O
Auburn University M,D
Auburn University Montgomery M,D
Azusa Pacific University M
Ball State University M
Barry University M*
Baylor University M,D*
Belhaven University (MS) M
Bellevue University M,D
Bernard M. Baruch College of the City University of New York M
Boise State University M
Boston University M,D,O*
Bowie State University M
Bowling Green State University M*
Bridgewater State University M
Brigham Young University M*
California Baptist University M
California Lutheran University M
California State Polytechnic University, Pomona M
California State University, Bakersfield M
California State University, Chico M
California State University, Dominguez Hills M*
California State University, East Bay M
California State University, Fresno M
California State University, Fullerton M
California State University, Long Beach M
California State University, Los Angeles M*
California State University, Northridge M
California State University, Sacramento M
California State University, San Bernardino M
California State University, Stanislaus M
Capella University M,D
Carleton University M,D
Carnegie Mellon University M*
Central Michigan University M,O
Cheyney University of Pennsylvania M
City College of the City University of New York M,D
Clark Atlanta University M
Clark University M,O
Clemson University M
Cleveland State University M,O
The College at Brockport, State University of New York M,O
College of Charleston M
College of Saint Elizabeth M
Columbia University M*
Columbus State University M
Concordia University (Canada) M,D
Concordia University Wisconsin M
Cumberland University M
Dalhousie University M,O
DePaul University M,O
DeVry University M
Drake University M
Duquesne University M,O
East Carolina University M
Eastern Kentucky University M
Eastern Michigan University M,O
Eastern Washington University M
The Evergreen State College M
Fairleigh Dickinson University, College at Florham M
Fairleigh Dickinson University, Metropolitan Campus M,O
Florida Agricultural and Mechanical University M
Florida Atlantic University M,D
Florida Gulf Coast University M
Florida Institute of Technology M
Florida International University M,D
Florida State University M,D,O
Framingham State University M
Gannon University M,O
George Mason University M,D,O*
The George Washington University M
Georgia College & State University M
Georgia Southern University M
Georgia State University M,D,O
Golden Gate University M,D,O
Governors State University M
Grambling State University M
Grand Canyon University M
Grand Valley State University M
Hamline University M,D
Harrisburg University of Science and Technology M
Harvard University M*
Hodges University M
Hood College M
Howard University M
Idaho State University M
Illinois Institute of Technology M
Indiana State University M
Indiana University Bloomington M,D,O*
Indiana University Kokomo M,O
Indiana University Northwest M,O
Indiana University–Purdue University Indianapolis M,O
Indiana University South Bend M,O
Institute of Public Administration M,O
Instituto Tecnológico y de Estudios Superiores de Monterrey, Campus Ciudad Juárez M
Iowa State University of Science and Technology M*
Jackson State University M,D
James Madison University M
John Jay College of Criminal Justice of the City University of New York M
Kansas State University M*
Kean University M
Kennesaw State University M
Kent State University M*
Kentucky State University M
Kutztown University of Pennsylvania M
Lamar University M
Lewis University M
Lincoln University (MO) M,O
Lindenwood University M
Long Island University, Brooklyn Campus M
Long Island University, C.W. Post Campus M,O
Long Island University, Rockland Graduate Campus M,O
Louisiana State University and Agricultural and Mechanical College M,D
Marist College M
Marquette University M,O
Marylhurst University M
Marywood University M
McMaster University M,D
Metropolitan College of New York M
Metropolitan State University M,D,O
Mid-America Christian University M
Midwestern State University M
Minnesota State University Mankato M
Minnesota State University Moorhead M
Mississippi State University M,D
Missouri State University M
Montana State University M
Montana State University Billings M
Monterey Institute of International Studies M
Morehead State University M
National University M
National University of Singapore M,D
New York University M,D,O
North Carolina Central University M
North Carolina State University M,D*
Northeastern University M,D,O
Northern Arizona University M,D,O
Northern Illinois University M
Northern Kentucky University M,O
Northern Michigan University M
North Georgia College & State University M
Northwestern University M*
Norwich University M
Notre Dame de Namur University M
Nova Southeastern University M*
Oakland University M
The Ohio State University M,D
Ohio University M*
Old Dominion University M,D
Pace University M
Park University M
Pepperdine University M
Pontifical Catholic University of Puerto Rico M
Portland State University M,D
Regent University M
Rhode Island College M
Roger Williams University M
Roosevelt University M
Rutgers, The State University of New Jersey, Camden M
Rutgers, The State University of New Jersey, Newark M,D*
Sage Graduate School M
Saginaw Valley State University M
Saint Louis University M,D,O
St. Mary's University (United States) M
St. Thomas University M,O
Sam Houston State University M
San Diego State University M
San Francisco State University M
San Jose State University M
Savannah State University M
Seattle University M
Seton Hall University M,O
Shenandoah University M,D,O
Shippensburg University of Pennsylvania M

*M—master's degree; P—first professional degree; D—doctorate; O—other advanced degree; *—Close-Up and/or Display in one of the other books in this series*

Institution	Degrees
Sojourner-Douglass College	M
Sonoma State University	M
Southeast Missouri State University	M
Southern Arkansas University–Magnolia	M
Southern Illinois University Carbondale	M
Southern Illinois University Edwardsville	M
Southern University and Agricultural and Mechanical College	M
Southern Utah University	M
State University of New York at Binghamton	M
Stephen F. Austin State University	M
Strayer University	M
Suffolk University	M,O
Sul Ross State University	M
Syracuse University	M,D,O*
Tennessee State University	M,D
Texas A&M International University	M
Texas A&M University	M,O
Texas A&M University–Corpus Christi	M
Texas Southern University	M
Texas State University–San Marcos	M
Thomas Edison State College	O
Troy University	M
Tufts University	O
TUI University	M,D
Université de Moncton	M
Université de Sherbrooke	M
Université du Québec à Montréal	M
Université du Québec, École nationale d'administration publique	D,O
University at Albany, State University of New York	M,D,O
The University of Akron	M
The University of Alabama	M,D
The University of Alabama at Birmingham	M*
University of Alaska Anchorage	M
University of Alaska Southeast	M
The University of Arizona	M,D
University of Arkansas	M
University of Arkansas at Little Rock	M
University of Baltimore	M,D
University of Central Florida	M,O
University of Colorado at Colorado Springs	M
University of Colorado Denver	M,D
University of Connecticut	M,O*
University of Dayton	M
University of Delaware	M*
University of Evansville	M
The University of Findlay	M
University of Georgia	M,D
University of Guam	M
University of Guelph	M
University of Hawaii at Manoa	M,O
University of Houston	M,D
University of Idaho	M
University of Illinois at Chicago	M,D
University of Illinois at Springfield	M,D
The University of Kansas	M,D
University of Kentucky	M,D*
University of La Verne	M,D
University of Louisville	M,D
University of Maine	M,D
University of Management and Technology	M,O
University of Manitoba	M
University of Maryland, College Park	M
University of Massachusetts Amherst	M*
University of Memphis	M
University of Michigan–Dearborn	M,O
University of Michigan–Flint	M
University of Missouri–Kansas City	M,D*
University of Missouri–St. Louis	M,D,O
The University of Montana	M
University of Nebraska at Omaha	M,D,O
University of Nevada, Las Vegas	M,D,O
University of Nevada, Reno	M*
University of New Brunswick Fredericton	M
University of New Hampshire	M,O
University of New Haven	M,O
University of New Mexico	M*
University of New Orleans	M
The University of North Carolina at Chapel Hill	M*
The University of North Carolina at Charlotte	M,D,O
The University of North Carolina at Pembroke	M
The University of North Carolina Wilmington	M
University of North Dakota	M
University of North Florida	M,O
University of North Texas	M,D
University of Oklahoma	M*
University of Ottawa	D,O*
University of Pennsylvania	M*
University of Phoenix	M
University of Phoenix–Atlanta Campus	M
University of Phoenix–Augusta Campus	M
University of Phoenix–Austin Campus	M
University of Phoenix–Birmingham Campus	M
University of Phoenix–Central Florida Campus	M
University of Phoenix–Central Valley Campus	M
University of Phoenix–Chattanooga Campus	M
University of Phoenix–Cheyenne Campus	M
University of Phoenix–Cincinnati Campus	M
University of Phoenix–Cleveland Campus	M
University of Phoenix–Columbus Georgia Campus	M
University of Phoenix–Columbus Ohio Campus	M
University of Phoenix–Dallas Campus	M
University of Phoenix–Denver Campus	M
University of Phoenix–Des Moines Campus	M
University of Phoenix–Eastern Washington Campus	M
University of Phoenix–Harrisburg Campus	M
University of Phoenix–Hawaii Campus	M
University of Phoenix–Houston Campus	M
University of Phoenix–Idaho Campus	M
University of Phoenix–Indianapolis Campus	M
University of Phoenix–Jersey City Campus	M
University of Phoenix–Kansas City Campus	M
University of Phoenix–Las Vegas Campus	M
University of Phoenix–Louisiana Campus	M
University of Phoenix–Madison Campus	M
University of Phoenix–Maryland Campus	M
University of Phoenix–Memphis Campus	M
University of Phoenix–Milwaukee Campus	M,D
University of Phoenix–Minneapolis/St. Louis Park Campus	M
University of Phoenix–Northern Nevada Campus	M
University of Phoenix–Northern Virginia Campus	M
University of Phoenix–North Florida Campus	M
University of Phoenix–Northwest Arkansas Campus	M
University of Phoenix–Omaha Campus	M
University of Phoenix–Oregon Campus	M
University of Phoenix–Philadelphia Campus	M
University of Phoenix–Pittsburgh Campus	M
University of Phoenix–Richmond Campus	M
University of Phoenix–Sacramento Valley Campus	M
University of Phoenix–St. Louis Campus	M
University of Phoenix–San Antonio Campus	M
University of Phoenix–San Diego Campus	M
University of Phoenix–Savannah Campus	M
University of Phoenix–Southern Colorado Campus	M
University of Phoenix–South Florida Campus	M
University of Phoenix–Springfield Campus	M
University of Phoenix–Washington D.C. Campus	M,D
University of Phoenix–West Florida Campus	M
University of Pittsburgh	M,D,O*
University of Puerto Rico, Río Piedras	M
University of Regina	M,D,O
University of Rhode Island	M
University of San Francisco	M
University of South Africa	M,D
University of South Alabama	M
University of South Carolina	M
The University of South Dakota	M,D
University of Southern California	M,O*
University of Southern Indiana	M
University of South Florida	M,D*
The University of Tennessee	M
The University of Tennessee at Chattanooga	M,O
The University of Texas at Arlington	M
The University of Texas at Brownsville	M
The University of Texas at El Paso	M,O
The University of Texas at San Antonio	M*
The University of Texas at Tyler	M
The University of Texas–Pan American	M
University of the District of Columbia	M
University of the Virgin Islands	M
The University of Toledo	M,O
University of Utah	M*
University of Vermont	M
University of Victoria	M,D
University of Washington	M,D*
University of West Florida	M
University of West Georgia	M,O
The University of Winnipeg	M
University of Wisconsin–Milwaukee	M
University of Wisconsin–Oshkosh	M
University of Wyoming	M
Upper Iowa University	M
Villanova University	M
Virginia Commonwealth University	M,O
Virginia Polytechnic Institute and State University	M,D,O
Walden University	M,D,O
Washington Adventist University	M
Wayland Baptist University	M
Wayne State University	M*
Webster University	M,D,O
West Chester University of Pennsylvania	M,O
Western International University	M
Western Kentucky University	M
Western Michigan University	M,D,O
West Virginia University	M
Wichita State University	M
Widener University	M
Wilmington University	M
Wright State University	M
York University	M,D*

PUBLIC AFFAIRS

Institution	Degrees
American University	M
Arizona State University	M,D
Clemson University	D
Concordia University (Canada)	O
Cornell University	M*
DePaul University	M,O
George Mason University	M,D,O*
The George Washington University	M
Indiana University Bloomington	M,D,O*
Indiana University Northwest	M,O
Indiana University of Pennsylvania	M
Indiana University–Purdue University Fort Wayne	M,O
Indiana University–Purdue University Indianapolis	M,O
Indiana University South Bend	M,O
The Institute of World Politics	M,O
Jackson State University	M,D
McMaster University	M,D
Murray State University	M
National University of Singapore	M,D
New Mexico Highlands University	M
Northeastern University	M,D,O
Notre Dame de Namur University	M
The Ohio State University	M,D

Institution	Degrees
Park University	M
Penn State Harrisburg	M,D
Princeton University	M,D,O*
Texas A&M University	M,O
The University of Alabama in Huntsville	M
University of Arkansas at Little Rock	M,O
University of Central Florida	D
University of Colorado at Colorado Springs	M
University of Colorado Denver	M,D
University of Florida	M,D,O*
University of Idaho	M,D
University of Louisville	M,D
University of Massachusetts Boston	M
University of Minnesota, Twin Cities Campus	M
University of Missouri	M*
University of Missouri–Kansas City	M,D*
University of Nevada, Las Vegas	M,D,O
The University of North Carolina at Greensboro	M,O
University of San Francisco	M
University of Saskatchewan	M,D
The University of Texas at Arlington	D
The University of Texas at Austin	M,D
The University of Texas at Dallas	M,D*
University of Washington	M,D*
University of Waterloo	M
University of Wisconsin–Madison	M*
Virginia Commonwealth University	M,D,O
Virginia Polytechnic Institute and State University	M,D,O
Washington State University Vancouver	M
West Chester University of Pennsylvania	M,O
Western Carolina University	M
Western Michigan University	M,D,O
York University	M*

PUBLIC HEALTH—GENERAL

Institution	Degrees
Adelphi University	O*
American Public University System	M
American University of Beirut	M
Argosy University, Atlanta	M*
Argosy University, Chicago	M*
Argosy University, Dallas	M*
Argosy University, Denver	M*
Argosy University, Inland Empire	M*
Argosy University, Los Angeles	M*
Argosy University, Nashville	M*
Argosy University, Orange County	M*
Argosy University, Phoenix	M*
Argosy University, Salt Lake City	M*
Argosy University, San Diego	M*
Argosy University, San Francisco Bay Area	M*
Argosy University, Seattle	M*
Argosy University, Twin Cities	M*
Argosy University, Washington DC	M*
Arizona State University	M,D,O
Armstrong Atlantic State University	M
A.T. Still University of Health Sciences	M,D
Austin Peay State University	M
Barry University	M*
Bellevue University	M,D
Benedictine University	M
Boise State University	M
Boston University	P,M,D,O*
Bowling Green State University	M*
Brooklyn College of the City University of New York	M
Brown University	M
California State University, Fresno	M
California State University, Fullerton	M
California State University, Northridge	M
California State University, San Bernardino	M
Case Western Reserve University	M*
Charles Drew University of Medicine and Science	M
Claremont Graduate University	M,D
Cleveland State University	M
Columbia University	M,D*
Dartmouth College	M
Davenport University	M
Davenport University	M
Davenport University	M
Des Moines University	M
Drexel University	M,D,O*
East Carolina University	M
Eastern Virginia Medical School	M
East Stroudsburg University of Pennsylvania	M
East Tennessee State University	M,D,O
Emory University	M,D,O*
Florida Agricultural and Mechanical University	M
Florida International University	M,D
Florida State University	M
Fort Valley State University	M
George Mason University	M,O*
Georgetown University	M,D
The George Washington University	M,O
Georgia Southern University	M,D
Georgia State University	M,D,O
Graduate School and University Center of the City University of New York	D
Grand Canyon University	M
Harvard University	M,D*
Howard University	M
Hunter College of the City University of New York	M
Idaho State University	M,O
Independence University	M
Indiana University Bloomington	M,D*
Indiana University–Purdue University Indianapolis	M
The Johns Hopkins University	M,D
Laurentian University	D
Loma Linda University	M,D,O
Louisiana State University Health Sciences Center	M,D
Louisiana State University in Shreveport	M
Loyola University Chicago	M
Medical College of Wisconsin	M,D,O*
Michigan State University	M
Missouri State University	M
Montclair State University	M,O
Morehouse School of Medicine	M
Morgan State University	M,D
National University	M
New Mexico State University	M
New York Medical College	M,D,O*
New York University	D
Northeastern University	M
Northern Arizona University	O
Northern Illinois University	M
Northwestern University	M*
Nova Southeastern University	M*
The Ohio State University	M,D
Ohio University	M*
Old Dominion University	M
Oregon State University	M,D
Penn State Hershey Medical Center	M
Ponce School of Medicine	M,D
Portland State University	M,O
Purdue University	M,D
Queen's University at Kingston	M,D
Rutgers, The State University of New Jersey, New Brunswick	M,D*
St. Catherine University	M
Saint Louis University	M,D
Saint Xavier University	M,O
San Diego State University	M,D
San Francisco State University	M
San Jose State University	M,O
Sarah Lawrence College	M
Simon Fraser University	M
Southern Connecticut State University	M
State University of New York Downstate Medical Center	M
Stony Brook University, State University of New York	M
Teachers College, Columbia University	M,D
Temple University	M,D*
Texas A&M Health Science Center	M
Texas A&M University	M
Thomas Jefferson University	M,O
Touro College	M,D
Touro University	P,M
Trinity (Washington) University	M
Tufts University	M
TUI University	M,D,O
Tulane University	M,D,O*
Uniformed Services University of the Health Sciences	M,D*
Université de Montréal	M,D,O
University at Albany, State University of New York	M,D
University at Buffalo, the State University of New York	M,D*
The University of Akron	M,D
The University of Alabama at Birmingham	M,D*
University of Alaska Anchorage	M
University of Alberta	M,D
The University of Arizona	M,D
The University of British Columbia	M,D
University of California, Berkeley	M,D*
University of California, Irvine	M,D*
University of California, Los Angeles	M,D*
University of California, San Diego	D*
University of Colorado Denver	M,D
University of Connecticut	M*
University of Connecticut Health Center	M*
University of Florida	M*
University of Hawaii at Manoa	M,D,O
University of Illinois at Chicago	M,D
University of Illinois at Springfield	M
University of Illinois at Urbana–Champaign	M,D
The University of Iowa	M,D,O*
The University of Kansas	M
University of Kentucky	M*
University of Louisville	M,D
The University of Manchester	M,D
University of Maryland, College Park	M,D
University of Massachusetts Amherst	M,D*
University of Massachusetts Lowell	M,O
University of Medicine and Dentistry of New Jersey	M,D,O
University of Memphis	M
University of Miami	M*
University of Michigan	M,D*
University of Minnesota, Twin Cities Campus	M,D,O
University of Missouri	M*
The University of Montana	M,O
University of Nebraska Medical Center	M
University of Nevada, Las Vegas	M,D
University of Nevada, Reno	M,D*
University of New England	M,O
University of New Hampshire	M,O
University of New Mexico	M*
The University of North Carolina at Chapel Hill	M,D*
The University of North Carolina at Charlotte	M,D,O
University of Northern Colorado	M
University of North Florida	M,O
University of North Texas Health Science Center at Fort Worth	M,D
University of Oklahoma Health Sciences Center	M,D
University of Ottawa	D*
University of Pennsylvania	M*
University of Pittsburgh	M,D,O*
University of Rochester	M
University of South Africa	M,D
University of South Carolina	M
University of Southern California	M*
University of Southern Mississippi	M
University of South Florida	M,D*
The University of Tennessee	M
The University of Texas at El Paso	M
The University of Texas Health Science Center at Houston	M,D,O*
The University of Texas Medical Branch	M
University of the Sciences in Philadelphia	M,D
University of Toronto	M,D
University of Utah	M,D*
University of Virginia	M,D
University of Waterloo	M
University of West Florida	M
University of Wisconsin–La Crosse	M
University of Wisconsin–Milwaukee	M,D,O
Vanderbilt University	M*

*M—master's degree; P—first professional degree; D—doctorate; O—other advanced degree; *—Close-Up and/or Display in one of the other books in this series*

Virginia Commonwealth University M,D
Virginia Polytechnic Institute and State University M
Walden University M,D,O
Washington University in St. Louis M,D*
Wayne State University M,O*
West Chester University of Pennsylvania M,O
Western Kentucky University M
Westminster College (UT) M
West Virginia University M
Wright State University M
Yale University M,D,O*

PUBLIC HISTORY

Appalachian State University M
Arizona State University M,D,O
California State University, Sacramento M
Eastern Illinois University M
Florida State University M,D
Georgia College & State University M
Indiana University–Purdue University Indianapolis M
Loyola University Chicago M,D
Middle Tennessee State University M,D
New York University M,D,O
North Carolina State University M*
Northeastern University M,D
Northern Kentucky University M,O
Rutgers, The State University of New Jersey, Camden M
Shippensburg University of Pennsylvania M,O
Simmons College O
Sonoma State University M
Southeast Missouri State University M,O
University at Albany, State University of New York M,D,O
University of Arkansas at Little Rock M
University of Colorado Denver M
University of Illinois at Springfield M
University of Louisville M,O
University of Maryland, Baltimore County M,D
University of Massachusetts Amherst M,D*
University of Northern Iowa M
University of South Carolina M,O
The University of Texas at Austin M,D
University of West Florida M
University of West Georgia M,O
Washington State University M,D

PUBLIC POLICY

Albany State University M
American University M
The American University in Cairo M,O
The American University of Paris M
Arizona State University P,M,D
Baylor University M,D*
Bernard M. Baruch College of the City University of New York M
Boise State University M
Boston University M,D,O*
Brandeis University M
Brigham Young University M*
Brock University M
Brooklyn College of the City University of New York M,D
Brown University M
California Lutheran University M
California State University, Long Beach M
California State University, Monterey Bay M
California State University, Sacramento M
Carleton University M,D
Carnegie Mellon University M,D*
Central European University M,D
Claremont Graduate University M,D,O
Clemson University D,O
The College of William and Mary M
Columbia University M*
Concordia University (Canada) M,D
Cornell University M,D*
DePaul University M,O
Duke University M,D,O*
Duquesne University M,O
Eastern Michigan University M,O
Florida State University M,D,O
Frederick S. Pardee RAND Graduate School D
George Mason University M,D*
Georgetown University M,D
The George Washington University M,D
Georgia Institute of Technology M,D
Georgia State University M,D,O
Graduate School and University Center of the City University of New York M,D
Harvard University M,D*
Indiana University Bloomington M,D,O*
Indiana University–Purdue University Indianapolis M,O
The Institute of World Politics M,O
Jackson State University M,D
John Jay College of Criminal Justice of the City University of New York M,D
The Johns Hopkins University M
Kent State University M,D*
Lincoln University (MO) M,O
Marylhurst University M
McMaster University M,D
Mills College M
Mississippi State University M,D
Monmouth University M
Morehead State University M
National-Louis University M,D,O
National University of Singapore M,D
New England College M
The New School: A University D
Northeastern University M,D
Northwestern University M,D*
The Ohio State University M,D
Pepperdine University M
Princeton University M,D*
Queen's University at Kingston M
Rochester Institute of Technology M
Rutgers, The State University of New Jersey, Camden M
Rutgers, The State University of New Jersey, Newark M,D*
Rutgers, The State University of New Jersey, New Brunswick M,D*
Saint Louis University M,D,O
San Francisco State University M
Seton Hall University M,O
Simon Fraser University M
Southeastern Louisiana University M
Southern New Hampshire University M,D
Southern University and Agricultural and Mechanical College D
State University of New York at Binghamton M,D
State University of New York Empire State College M
Stony Brook University, State University of New York M
Suffolk University M
Syracuse University O*
Trinity College M
Tufts University M
Union Institute & University M,D
Universidad Autonoma de Guadalajara M,D
Universidad del Este M
Université de Montréal O
University at Albany, State University of New York M,D,O
The University of Arizona M,D
University of Arkansas D
University of California, Berkeley M,D*
University of California, Los Angeles M*
University of Chicago M,D
University of Colorado Boulder M,D*
University of Delaware M,D*
University of Denver M
University of Georgia M,D
University of Guelph M
University of Hawaii at Manoa O
University of Louisville M,D
University of Maryland, Baltimore County M,D
University of Maryland, College Park M,D
University of Massachusetts Amherst M*
University of Massachusetts Boston D
University of Massachusetts Dartmouth M,O
University of Medicine and Dentistry of New Jersey M,O
University of Memphis M
University of Michigan M,D*
University of Michigan–Dearborn M
University of Minnesota, Twin Cities Campus M
University of Missouri–St. Louis M,D,O
University of Nebraska–Lincoln M,D,O*
University of Nevada, Las Vegas M
University of New Brunswick Fredericton M
The University of North Carolina at Chapel Hill D*
The University of North Carolina at Charlotte M,D,O
University of Northern Iowa M
University of Oregon M
University of Pennsylvania M,D*
University of Pittsburgh M,D,O*
University of Puerto Rico, Río Piedras M
University of Regina M,D,O
University of Rhode Island M
University of Saskatchewan M,D
University of Southern California M,D,O*
University of Southern Maine M,D,O
The University of Texas at Austin M,D
The University of Texas at Brownsville M
The University of Texas at Dallas M,D*
The University of Texas at El Paso M,O
University of the Pacific P,M,D
University of Tulsa P,M,O
University of Virginia M
University of Washington M,D*
University of Washington, Bothell M
Vanderbilt University M,D*
Virginia Commonwealth University D
Virginia Polytechnic Institute and State University M,O
Walden University M,D,O
Washington State University M,D
Washington University in St. Louis M*
West Virginia University M,D
Wilfrid Laurier University M
William Paterson University of New Jersey M
York University M*

PUBLISHING

Arizona State University M,D,O
Carnegie Mellon University M*
DePaul University M
Drexel University M*
Emerson College M
The George Washington University M
New York University M
Northwestern University M*
Pace University M,O
Rosemont College M
Simon Fraser University M
University of Baltimore M
University of Houston–Victoria M

QUALITY MANAGEMENT

California Intercontinental University M,D
California State University, Dominguez Hills M*
Calumet College of Saint Joseph M
Case Western Reserve University M,D*
Eastern Michigan University M,O
Ferris State University M
Florida Institute of Technology M
Hofstra University M,O
Instituto Tecnologico de Santo Domingo M,O
Instituto Tecnológico y de Estudios Superiores de Monterrey, Campus Ciudad de México M,D
Instituto Tecnológico y de Estudios Superiores de Monterrey, Campus Ciudad Juárez M
Instituto Tecnológico y de Estudios Superiores de Monterrey, Campus Estado de México M,D

Institution	Degrees
Instituto Tecnológico y de Estudios Superiores de Monterrey, Campus Irapuato	M,D
Madonna University	M
Marian University (WI)	M
The National Graduate School of Quality Management	M
Northwestern University	M*
Penn State University Park	M
Regis College (MA)	M
Rutgers, The State University of New Jersey, New Brunswick	M,D*
Saint Joseph's College of Maine	M
San Jose State University	M
Southern Polytechnic State University	M,O
Stevens Institute of Technology	M,O
TUI University	M,D,O
Universidad de las Americas, A.C.	M
Universidad del Turabo	M
The University of Alabama	M
The University of Tennessee at Chattanooga	M,O
Upper Iowa University	M
Webster University	M,D,O

QUANTITATIVE ANALYSIS

Institution	Degrees
Bernard M. Baruch College of the City University of New York	M
Drexel University	M,D,O*
Georgia State University	M,D
Instituto Tecnologico de Santo Domingo	M,O
Lehigh University	M
New York University	M,D,O
Oklahoma State University	M,D*
St. John's University (NY)	M,O
Syracuse University	D*
Texas Tech University	M,D*
The University of British Columbia	M,D
University of California, Santa Barbara	M,D
University of Cincinnati	M,D
University of Colorado Denver	M
University of Connecticut	M,O*
University of Florida	M*
University of Illinois at Chicago	M,D
University of Medicine and Dentistry of New Jersey	M,O
University of North Texas	M,D
University of Oregon	M
University of Pittsburgh	D*
University of Puerto Rico, Río Piedras	M,D
University of South Africa	M,D
University of Southern California	M,D*
The University of Texas at Arlington	M,D
Virginia Commonwealth University	M
Virginia Polytechnic Institute and State University	M,O
Walden University	M,D

RADIATION BIOLOGY

Institution	Degrees
Auburn University	M,D
Austin Peay State University	M
Colorado State University	M,D
Georgetown University	M
Université de Sherbrooke	M,D
The University of Iowa	M,D*
University of Oklahoma Health Sciences Center	M,D

RANGE SCIENCE

Institution	Degrees
Colorado State University	M,D
Kansas State University	M,D*
Montana State University	M,D
New Mexico State University	M,D
North Dakota State University	M,D
Oregon State University	M,D
Sul Ross State University	M
Texas A&M University	M,D
Texas A&M University–Kingsville	M
Texas Tech University	M,D*
The University of Arizona	M,D
University of California, Berkeley	M*
University of Wyoming	M,D
Utah State University	M,D

READING EDUCATION

Institution	Degrees
Adelphi University	M*
Alfred University	M
Alverno College	M
American International College	M,D,O
Andrews University	M
Angelo State University	M
Appalachian State University	M
Arcadia University	M,D,O*
Arkansas State University	M,O
Asbury University	M
Ashland University	M
Auburn University	M,D,O
Auburn University Montgomery	M,O
Aurora University	M,D
Austin Peay State University	M
Averett University	M
Baldwin-Wallace College	M
Bank Street College of Education	M
Barry University	M,D,O*
Bellarmine University	M,D,O
Benedictine University	M
Benedictine University at Springfield	M
Berry College	M
Bethel University (MN)	M,D,O
Bloomsburg University of Pennsylvania	M
Boise State University	M
Boston College	M,O*
Boston University	M,D,O*
Bowie State University	M
Bowling Green State University	M,O*
Bridgewater State University	M,O
Brigham Young University	M*
Bucknell University	M
Buffalo State College, State University of New York	M
Butler University	M
California Baptist University	M
California State University, Bakersfield	M,O
California State University, East Bay	M
California State University, Fresno	M
California State University, Fullerton	M
California State University, Los Angeles	M*
California State University, Northridge	M
California State University, Sacramento	M
California State University, San Bernardino	M
California State University, Stanislaus	M
California University of Pennsylvania	M
Calvin College	M
Cambridge College	M,D,O
Canisius College	M
Capella University	M,D,O
Cardinal Stritch University	M
Carthage College	M,O
Castleton State College	M,O
Central Connecticut State University	M,O
Central Michigan University	M,O
Central Washington University	M
Chapman University	M,O
Chicago State University	M
The Citadel, The Military College of South Carolina	M
City College of the City University of New York	M
City University of Seattle	M,O
Clarion University of Pennsylvania	M
Clarke University	M
Clemson University	M
The College at Brockport, State University of New York	M
College of Mount St. Joseph	M
The College of New Jersey	M,O
The College of New Rochelle	M
College of St. Joseph	M
The College of Saint Rose	M,O
The College of William and Mary	M
Concordia University Chicago	M
Concordia University, Nebraska	M
Concordia University, St. Paul	M,O
Concordia University Wisconsin	M
Concord University	M
Coppin State University	M
Curry College	M,O
Dallas Baptist University	M
Delaware State University	M
DePaul University	M,D
Dominican University	M
Dowling College	M,D,O
Drury University	M
Duquesne University	M
East Carolina University	M
Eastern Connecticut State University	M
Eastern Michigan University	M
Eastern Nazarene College	M,O
Eastern New Mexico University	M
Eastern Washington University	M
East Stroudsburg University of Pennsylvania	M
East Tennessee State University	M
Edinboro University of Pennsylvania	M,O
Elms College	M,O
Emory & Henry College	M
Emporia State University	M
Endicott College	M
Evangel University	M
Fairleigh Dickinson University, College at Florham	M,O
Fairleigh Dickinson University, Metropolitan Campus	M,O
Fairmont State University	M
Fayetteville State University	M
Ferris State University	M
Florida Atlantic University	M
Florida Gulf Coast University	M
Florida International University	M,D,O
Florida Memorial University	M
Florida State University	M,D,O
Fordham University	M,D,O
Framingham State University	M
Fresno Pacific University	M
Frostburg State University	M
Furman University	M,O
Gannon University	M,O
Geneva College	M
George Fox University	M,D,O
Georgetown College	M
Georgia Southern University	M
Georgia Southwestern State University	M,O
Georgia State University	M,D,O
Gonzaga University	M
Governors State University	M
Grambling State University	M,D
Grand Valley State University	M
Gwynedd-Mercy College	M
Hamline University	M,D
Hannibal-LaGrange University	M
Harding University	M,O
Hardin-Simmons University	M
Harvard University	M*
Henderson State University	M
Heritage University	M
Hofstra University	M,D,O
Holy Family University	M*
Hood College	M,O
Houston Baptist University	M
Hunter College of the City University of New York	M,O
Idaho State University	M,O
Illinois State University	M
Indiana University Bloomington	M,D,O*
Indiana University of Pennsylvania	M
Indiana University–Purdue University Indianapolis	M,O
Iona College	M
Jacksonville State University	M
Jacksonville University	M
James Madison University	M
The Johns Hopkins University	M,D,O
Johnson State College	M
Judson University	M
Kaplan University, Davenport Campus	M
Kean University	M
Kent State University	M*
King's College	M
Kutztown University of Pennsylvania	M
Lake Erie College	M
Lehman College of the City University of New York	M
Le Moyne College	M,O
Lesley University	M,D,O
Lewis University	M
Liberty University	M,D,O
Lincoln University (PA)	M
Long Island University at Riverhead	M
Long Island University, Brentwood Campus	M
Long Island University, Brooklyn Campus	M
Long Island University, C.W. Post Campus	M
Long Island University, Rockland Graduate Campus	M

*M—master's degree; P—first professional degree; D—doctorate; O—other advanced degree; *—Close-Up and/or Display in one of the other books in this series*

Long Island University, Westchester Graduate Campus	M,O
Longwood University	M
Loyola Marymount University	M
Loyola University Chicago	M,O
Loyola University Maryland	M,O
Lynchburg College	M
Lyndon State College	M
Madonna University	M
Malone University	M
Manhattanville College	M*
Marquette University	M,D,O
Marshall University	M,O
Marygrove College	M
Maryville University of Saint Louis	M,D
Marywood University	M
Massachusetts College of Liberal Arts	M
McDaniel College	M
McNeese State University	M
Medaille College	M
Mercer University	M,D,O
Mercy College	M
Merrimack College	M,O
MGH Institute of Health Professions	M,O
Miami University	M
Michigan State University	M
Middle Tennessee State University	M,D
Midwestern State University	M
Millersville University of Pennsylvania	M
Minnesota State University Moorhead	M
Mississippi University for Women	M
Missouri State University	M
Monmouth University	M,O
Montana State University Billings	M
Montclair State University	M,O
Morehead State University	M,O
Mount Mercy University	M
Mount Saint Mary College	M,O
Mount Saint Vincent University	M
Murray State University	M,O
National-Louis University	M,D,O
Nazareth College of Rochester	M
New Jersey City University	M
Newman University	M
New York University	M
Niagara University	M
North Carolina Agricultural and Technical State University	M
Northeastern Illinois University	M
Northeastern State University	M
Northern Illinois University	M,D
Northern Michigan University	M,O
Northwestern Oklahoma State University	M
Northwestern State University of Louisiana	M,O
Northwest Missouri State University	M
Northwest Nazarene University	M
Notre Dame College (OH)	M,O
Notre Dame de Namur University	M,O
Nova Southeastern University	M,O*
Oakland University	M,D,O
Ohio University	M,D*
Old Dominion University	M,D
Olivet Nazarene University	M
Oregon State University	M
Our Lady of the Lake University of San Antonio	M
Pace University	M,O
Pittsburg State University	M
Plymouth State University	M
Portland State University	M,D
Providence College	M
Purdue University	M,D,O
Queens College of the City University of New York	M
Queens University of Charlotte	M
Quincy University	M
Radford University	M
Regis College (MA)	M
Regis University	M,O
Rhode Island College	M
Rider University	M,O
Rivier College	M,D,O
Roberts Wesleyan College	M,O
Rockford College	M
Roger Williams University	M
Roosevelt University	M
Rowan University	M
Rutgers, The State University of New Jersey, New Brunswick	M,D*
Sacred Heart University	M,O
Sage Graduate School	M
Saginaw Valley State University	M
St. Bonaventure University	M
Saint Francis University	M
St. John Fisher College	M
St. John's University (NY)	M,D,O
St. Joseph's College, Long Island Campus	M
St. Joseph's College, New York	M*
Saint Joseph's University	M,D
Saint Leo University	M,O
Saint Martin's University	M
Saint Mary's College of California	M
St. Mary's University (United States)	M
Saint Mary's University of Minnesota	M,O
Saint Michael's College	M,O
Saint Peter's College	M,O
St. Thomas Aquinas College	M,O
St. Thomas University	M,D,O
Saint Xavier University	M,O
Salem College	M
Salem State University	M
Salisbury University	M
Sam Houston State University	M,D
San Diego State University	M
San Francisco State University	M,O
San Jose State University	M,O
Seattle Pacific University	M
Seattle University	M,O
Shenandoah University	M,D,O
Shippensburg University of Pennsylvania	M
Siena Heights University	M
Slippery Rock University of Pennsylvania	M
Sojourner-Douglass College	M
Sonoma State University	M
Southeastern Louisiana University	M
Southeastern Oklahoma State University	M
Southern Adventist University	M
Southern Arkansas University–Magnolia	M
Southern Connecticut State University	M,O
Southern Illinois University Edwardsville	M,O
Southern Oregon University	M
Southwestern Adventist University	M
Southwest Minnesota State University	M
State University of New York at Binghamton	M
State University of New York at Fredonia	M
State University of New York at New Paltz	M
State University of New York at Oswego	M
State University of New York at Plattsburgh	M
State University of New York College at Cortland	M
State University of New York College at Geneseo	M
State University of New York College at Oneonta	M
State University of New York College at Potsdam	M
Stetson University	M
Sul Ross State University	M
Syracuse University	M,D*
Teachers College, Columbia University	M
Temple University	M,D*
Tennessee Technological University	M,D,O
Texas A&M International University	M
Texas A&M University	M,D
Texas A&M University–Commerce	M,D
Texas A&M University–Corpus Christi	M,D
Texas A&M University–Kingsville	M
Texas A&M University–San Antonio	M
Texas State University–San Marcos	M
Texas Tech University	M,D*
Texas Woman's University	M,D
Towson University	M,O
Trevecca Nazarene University	M
Trinity (Washington) University	M
Troy University	M
TUI University	M
Union College (KY)	M
Union Institute & University	M,D,O
University at Albany, State University of New York	M,D,O
University at Buffalo, the State University of New York	M,D,O*
University of Alaska Fairbanks	M,D,O
The University of Arizona	M,D,O
University of Arkansas at Little Rock	M,O
University of Bridgeport	M,O
The University of British Columbia	M,D
University of California, Riverside	M,D
University of Central Arkansas	M
University of Central Florida	M,D,O
University of Central Missouri	M,D,O
University of Central Oklahoma	M
University of Cincinnati	M,D
University of Colorado Denver	M
University of Connecticut	M,D,O*
University of Dayton	M
University of Florida	M,D,O*
University of Georgia	M,D,O
University of Guam	M
University of Houston–Clear Lake	M
University of Illinois at Chicago	M,D
University of La Verne	M,O
University of Louisiana at Monroe	M,D
University of Louisville	M,D
University of Maine	M,D,O
University of Mary	M
University of Mary Hardin-Baylor	M,D
University of Maryland, Baltimore County	M,D,O
University of Maryland, College Park	M,D,O
University of Massachusetts Amherst	M,D,O*
University of Massachusetts Lowell	M,D,O
University of Memphis	M,D
University of Miami	D*
University of Michigan	M,D*
University of Michigan–Flint	M
University of Minnesota, Twin Cities Campus	M,D,O
University of Missouri	M,D,O*
University of Missouri–Kansas City	M,D,O*
University of Missouri–St. Louis	M,O
University of Nebraska at Kearney	M
University of Nebraska at Omaha	M
University of Nevada, Reno	M,D*
University of New England	M,O
University of New Hampshire	M
The University of North Carolina at Chapel Hill	M,D*
The University of North Carolina at Charlotte	M
The University of North Carolina at Greensboro	M,D,O
The University of North Carolina at Pembroke	M
The University of North Carolina Wilmington	M
University of North Dakota	M
University of Northern Colorado	M
University of Northern Iowa	M
University of North Florida	M
University of North Texas	M,D
University of Oklahoma	M,D,O*
University of Oklahoma Health Sciences Center	M,D,O
University of Pennsylvania	M,D*
University of Pittsburgh	M,D*
University of Rhode Island	M,D
University of Rio Grande	M
University of St. Francis (IL)	M
University of St. Thomas (MN)	M,O
University of San Diego	M
University of San Francisco	M,D
The University of Scranton	M
University of Sioux Falls	M,O
University of South Alabama	M,O
University of South Carolina	M,D
University of Southern Maine	M,O
University of Southern Mississippi	M,D,O
University of South Florida	M,D,O*
The University of Tennessee	M,D,O
The University of Texas at Brownsville	M
The University of Texas at El Paso	M,D
The University of Texas at San Antonio	M,D*

The University of Texas at Tyler M
The University of Texas of the Permian Basin M
The University of Texas–Pan American M
University of the Cumberlands M,D,O
University of the Incarnate Word M,D
University of the Southwest M
University of Utah M,D*
University of Vermont M
University of Victoria M,D
University of Virginia M,D,O
University of Washington M,D*
University of West Florida M
University of West Georgia M,D,O
University of Wisconsin–Eau Claire M
University of Wisconsin–Milwaukee M
University of Wisconsin–Oshkosh M
University of Wisconsin–River Falls M
University of Wisconsin–Stevens Point M
University of Wisconsin–Superior M
University of Wisconsin–Whitewater M*
Ursuline College M
Vanderbilt University M*
Virginia Commonwealth University M,O
Wagner College M
Walden University M,D,O
Walla Walla University M
Washburn University M
Washington State University M,D
Washington State University Tri-Cities M,D
Wayne State University M,D,O*
West Chester University of Pennsylvania M,O
Western Connecticut State University M
Western Illinois University M
Western Kentucky University M,O
Western Michigan University M,D
Western New Mexico University M
Western State College of Colorado M*
Westfield State University M
Westminster College (PA) M,O
West Texas A&M University M
West Virginia University M
Wheelock College M
Widener University M,D
Wilkes University M,D
Willamette University M
William Paterson University of New Jersey M
Wilmington College M
Wilmington University M
Winthrop University M
Worcester State University M,O
Xavier University M
York College of Pennsylvania M
Youngstown State University M

REAL ESTATE

American University M
Arizona State University M,D
California State University, Sacramento M
Central European University M
Clemson University M
Cleveland State University M,D,O
Columbia University M*
Cornell University M*
DePaul University M
Drexel University M*
Florida International University M
George Mason University M*
Georgetown University M,D
The George Washington University M,D
Georgia State University M,D,O
Hofstra University M,O
Instituto Centroamericano de Administración de Empresas M
John Marshall Law School P,M
The Johns Hopkins University M
Marquette University M
Marylhurst University M
Massachusetts Institute of Technology M
Monmouth University M,O
New York University M,O
Nova Southeastern University M*
Pacific States University M,D
Pontificia Universidad Catolica Madre y Maestra M
Roosevelt University M,O
Southern Methodist University M
Texas A&M University M
Texas Tech University M*
Universidad Iberoamericana P,M
University of California, Berkeley D*
University of Central Florida M
University of Denver M
University of Florida M,D,O*
University of Hawaii at Manoa M
University of Illinois at Chicago M
University of Maryland, College Park M
University of Memphis M,D
University of Michigan M,O*
The University of North Carolina at Charlotte M,D,O
University of North Texas M,D
University of Pennsylvania M,D*
University of St. Thomas (MN) M
University of San Diego M,O
University of South Africa M,D
University of Southern California M,O*
University of South Florida M,D*
The University of Texas at Arlington M,D
The University of Texas at Dallas M*
The University of Texas at San Antonio M*
University of Utah M*
University of Wisconsin–Madison M,D*
University of Wisconsin–Milwaukee M,O
Villanova University M
Virginia Commonwealth University M,O

RECREATION AND PARK MANAGEMENT

Acadia University M
Arizona State University M,D,O
Aurora University M
Bowling Green State University M*
Brigham Young University M*
California State University, Chico M
California State University, East Bay M
California State University, Long Beach M
California State University, Northridge M
California State University, Sacramento M
Central Michigan University M,O
Clemson University M,D
The College at Brockport, State University of New York M
Colorado State University M,D
Delta State University M
East Carolina University M
Eastern Kentucky University M
Florida Agricultural and Mechanical University M
Florida International University M,D,O
Florida State University M,D
Frostburg State University M
George Mason University M*
Georgia College & State University M
Hardin-Simmons University M
Indiana University Bloomington M,D,O*
Kent State University M*
Lehman College of the City University of New York M
Michigan State University M,D
Middle Tennessee State University M
Naropa University M
New England College M
North Carolina Central University M
North Carolina State University M,D*
Northwest Missouri State University M
Ohio University M*
Old Dominion University M
Penn State University Park M,D
San Francisco State University M
San Jose State University M
South Dakota State University M
Southern Adventist University M
Southern Connecticut State University M
Southern Illinois University Carbondale M
Southern University and Agricultural and Mechanical College M
Southwestern Oklahoma State University M
Springfield College M
State University of New York College at Cortland M
Temple University M*
Texas A&M University M,D
Texas State University–San Marcos M
Universidad Metropolitana M
University of Alberta M,D
University of Arkansas M,D
University of Florida M,D*
University of Idaho M
The University of Iowa M*
University of Manitoba M
University of Minnesota, Twin Cities Campus M,D
University of Mississippi M,D
University of Missouri M*
The University of Montana M,D
University of Nebraska at Omaha M
University of New Brunswick Fredericton M
University of New Hampshire M
The University of North Carolina at Greensboro M
University of North Texas M,O
University of Rhode Island M
University of South Alabama M
University of Southern Mississippi M,D
The University of Tennessee M,D
University of Utah M,D*
University of Waterloo M,D
University of Wisconsin–La Crosse M
University of Wisconsin–Milwaukee M,O
Utah State University M,D
Virginia Commonwealth University M
Wayne State University M*
Western Illinois University M
Western Kentucky University M
West Virginia University M
Winona State University M,O
Wright State University M

REHABILITATION COUNSELING

Adler School of Professional Psychology M,D,O
Arkansas State University M,O
Assumption College M,O
Auburn University M,D
Barry University M,O*
Bayamón Central University M,O
Bowling Green State University M*
California State University, Fresno M
California State University, Los Angeles M,D*
California State University, San Bernardino M
Central Connecticut State University M,O
Coppin State University M
East Carolina University M
East Central University M
Edinboro University of Pennsylvania M,O
Emporia State University M
Florida Atlantic University M,D,O
Florida International University M,D,O
Florida State University M,D,O
Fort Valley State University M
The George Washington University M
Georgia State University M
Hofstra University M,O
Hunter College of the City University of New York M
Illinois Institute of Technology M,D
Indiana University–Purdue University Indianapolis M,D
Jackson State University M
Kent State University M,O*
Langston University M
La Salle University D
Louisiana State University Health Sciences Center M
Maryville University of Saint Louis M,O
Michigan State University M,D,O
Minnesota State University Mankato M
Montana State University Billings M
North Carolina Agricultural and Technical State University M,D
Northeastern Illinois University M
Ohio University M,D*

*M—master's degree; P—first professional degree; D—doctorate; O—other advanced degree; *—Close-Up and/or Display in one of the other books in this series*

Pontifical Catholic University of Puerto Rico	M
St. Cloud State University	M
St. John's University (NY)	M,D,O
Salve Regina University	M,O
San Diego State University	M
San Francisco State University	M
South Carolina State University	M
Southern Illinois University Carbondale	M,D
Southern University and Agricultural and Mechanical College	M
Springfield College	M
Teachers College, Columbia University	M
Texas Tech University Health Sciences Center	M
Thomas University	M
Troy University	M,O
University at Albany, State University of New York	M
University at Buffalo, the State University of New York	M,D,O*
The University of Arizona	M,D
University of Arkansas	M,D
University of Arkansas at Little Rock	M,O
The University of Iowa	M,D*
The University of Kansas	M,D
University of Kentucky	M,D*
University of Louisiana at Lafayette	M*
University of Maryland, College Park	M,D,O
University of Maryland Eastern Shore	M
University of Massachusetts Boston	M,O
University of Medicine and Dentistry of New Jersey	M,D
University of Memphis	M,D
University of Nevada, Las Vegas	M,O
The University of North Carolina at Chapel Hill	M,D*
University of Northern Colorado	M,D
University of North Florida	M,O
University of North Texas	M
University of Pittsburgh	M*
University of Puerto Rico, Río Piedras	M
The University of Scranton	M
University of South Alabama	M,D
University of South Carolina	M,O
University of Southern Maine	M,O
University of South Florida	M*
The University of Tennessee	M,D
The University of Texas at El Paso	M
The University of Texas–Pan American	M,D
The University of Texas Southwestern Medical Center at Dallas	M
University of Wisconsin–Madison	M,D*
University of Wisconsin–Stout	M
Utah State University	M
Virginia Commonwealth University	M,O
Wayne State University	M,D,O*
Western Michigan University	M
Western Oregon University	M
Western Washington University	M
West Virginia University	M
Wilberforce University	M
Winston-Salem State University	M
Wright State University	M

REHABILITATION SCIENCES

Appalachian State University	M
Boston University	D*
California University of Pennsylvania	M
Central Michigan University	M,D
Clarion University of Pennsylvania	M
Concordia University Wisconsin	M
Duquesne University	M,D
East Carolina University	M
East Stroudsburg University of Pennsylvania	M
George Mason University	M,O*
Indiana University–Purdue University Indianapolis	M,D
Logan University–College of Chiropractic	M
McGill University	M,D,O
McMaster University	M,D
Medical University of South Carolina	D
Northwestern Health Sciences University	O
Northwestern University	D*
The Ohio State University	M,D
Queen's University at Kingston	M,D
Salus University	M,O
Texas Tech University Health Sciences Center	D
Université de Montréal	O
University at Buffalo, the State University of New York	M,D,O*
The University of Alabama at Birmingham	D*
University of Alberta	D
The University of British Columbia	M,D
University of Cincinnati	D
University of Florida	D*
University of Illinois at Urbana–Champaign	M,D
The University of Iowa	D*
The University of Kansas	M,D
University of Kentucky	D*
University of Manitoba	M,D
University of Maryland, Baltimore	D
University of Maryland Eastern Shore	M
University of Northern Iowa	M,D
University of North Texas	M
University of Oklahoma Health Sciences Center	M
University of Ottawa	M*
University of Pittsburgh	M,D*
University of South Carolina	M,O
University of Toronto	M,D
University of Utah	D,O*
University of Washington	M,D*
University of Wisconsin–La Crosse	M
University of Wisconsin–Madison	M*
Virginia Commonwealth University	D
Western Michigan University	M

RELIABILITY ENGINEERING

Arizona State University	M
The University of Arizona	M
University of Maryland, College Park	M,D
The University of Tennessee	M,D

RELIGION

Ambrose University College	P,M,O
Amridge University	P,M,D
Arizona State University	M,D,O
Baptist Bible College of Pennsylvania	P,M,D
Baptist Theological Seminary at Richmond	P,M,D
Baylor University	M,D*
Bellarmine University	M
Bethany Theological Seminary	P,M,O
Bethel Seminary	P,M,D,O
Bethesda Christian University	P,M
Beulah Heights University	M
Biola University	P,M,D
Bob Jones University	P,M,D,O
Boston University	M,D*
Briercrest Seminary	P,M
Brown University	D
Bryn Athyn College of the New Church	P,M
California Institute of Integral Studies	M,D
California State University, Long Beach	M
Calvin Theological Seminary	P,M,D
Cardinal Stritch University	M
The Catholic University of America	P,M,D,O
Chestnut Hill College	M,O*
Chicago Theological Seminary	P,M,D
Christian Brothers University	M
Christian Theological Seminary	P,M,D
Cincinnati Christian University	P,M
Claremont Graduate University	M,D
Claremont School of Theology	M,D
College of the Humanities and Sciences, Harrison Middleton University	M,D
Columbia University	M,D*
Concordia University (CA)	M
Concordia University (Canada)	M,D
Concordia University Chicago	M
Concordia University College of Alberta	M
Cornell University	D*
Denver Seminary	P,M,D,O
Duke University	M,D*
Earlham School of Religion	P,M
Eastern Mennonite University	P,M,O
Edgewood College	M
Elms College	M
Emmanuel Christian Seminary	P,M,D
Emory University	D,O*
Faith Baptist Bible College and Theological Seminary	P,M
Florida International University	M
Florida State University	M,D
Fordham University	M,D,O
Gardner-Webb University	M
General Theological Seminary	P,M,D,O
Georgetown University	M,D
The George Washington University	M
Georgia State University	M
Gonzaga University	M
Gordon-Conwell Theological Seminary	P,M,D
Graceland University (IA)	M
Graduate Theological Union	M,D,O
Grand Rapids Theological Seminary of Cornerstone University	P,M
Harding University Graduate School of Religion	P,M,D
Hardin-Simmons University	M
Hartford Seminary	M,D,O
Harvard University	D*
Heritage Christian University	M
Holy Names University	M,O
Hope International University	M
Iliff School of Theology	P,M,D
Indiana University Bloomington	M,D*
The Jewish Theological Seminary	M,D
John Carroll University	M
Kentucky Christian University	M
Knox Theological Seminary	M
Lancaster Theological Seminary	P,M,D,O
La Salle University	M
La Sierra University	P,M
Lee University	M
Liberty University	P,M,D
Lipscomb University	P,M
Loma Linda University	M
Louisville Presbyterian Theological Seminary	P,M,D
Lutheran Theological Seminary	P,M,D
Lutheran Theological Seminary at Gettysburg	P,M,D
The Lutheran Theological Seminary at Philadelphia	P,M,D,O
Maranatha Baptist Bible College	M
Marquette University	M,D
Mars Hill Graduate School	M
McGill University	M,D
McMaster University	M,D
Memorial University of Newfoundland	M
Miami University	M
Michigan Theological Seminary	P,M,O
Midwestern Baptist Theological Seminary	P,M,D,O
Missouri State University	M
Mount St. Mary's College	M
Naropa University	M
New Life Theological Seminary	M
New Saint Andrews College	M,O
New York University	M,O
Northwestern University	M*
Northwest Nazarene University	P,M
Oblate School of Theology	P,M,D,O
Oklahoma City University	M
Olivet Nazarene University	M
Oxford Graduate School	M,D
Pacific School of Religion	P,M,D,O
Pepperdine University	P,M
Point Loma Nazarene University	M
Princeton Theological Seminary	P,M,D
Princeton University	D*
Providence College	M
Queen's University at Kingston	M
Reformed Theological Seminary–Charlotte Campus	P,M,D
Reformed Theological Seminary–Washington D.C.	P,M
Rice University	D
The Robert E. Webber Institute for Worship Studies	M,D
Sacred Heart University	M

St. Bonaventure University M
St. Charles Borromeo Seminary, Overbrook M
Saint John's Seminary (MA) P,M
Saint Mary's University (Canada) M
Seminary of the Southwest P,M,O
Seton Hall University P,M,O
Sioux Falls Seminary M
Southern Adventist University M
Southern Baptist Theological Seminary P,M,D
Southern California Seminary P,M,D
Southern Evangelical Seminary P,M,D,O
Southern Methodist University M,D
Southern Nazarene University M
Southwestern Assemblies of God University P,M
Stanford University M,D
Syracuse University M,D*
Taylor University M
Temple Baptist Seminary P,M,D
Temple University M,D*
Trevecca Nazarene University M
Trinity International University, South Florida Campus M,O
Trinity School for Ministry P,M,D,O
Unification Theological Seminary P,M,D
Union University M,D
United Theological Seminary of the Twin Cities P,M,D,O
Université de Montréal M,D,O
Université de Sherbrooke M,D,O
Université du Québec à Montréal M,D
Université Laval M,D
The University of British Columbia M,D
University of Calgary M,D
University of California, Berkeley D*
University of California, Santa Barbara M,D
University of Chicago P,M,D
University of Colorado Boulder M*
University of Denver M,D
University of Detroit Mercy M
University of Florida M,D*
University of Georgia M
University of Hawaii at Manoa M
The University of Iowa M,D*
The University of Kansas M
University of Lethbridge M,D
The University of Manchester D
University of Manitoba M,D
University of Michigan M,D*
University of Minnesota, Twin Cities Campus M,D
University of Missouri M*
University of Mobile M
The University of North Carolina at Chapel Hill M,D*
The University of North Carolina at Charlotte M
University of North Texas M,D
University of Notre Dame M*
University of Ottawa M,D*
University of Pennsylvania D*
University of Pittsburgh M,D*
University of Regina M
University of St. Thomas (MN) M
University of St. Thomas (TX) M*
University of Saskatchewan M
University of South Africa M,D
University of South Carolina M
University of South Florida M*
The University of Tennessee M,D
University of the Cumberlands M
University of the Incarnate Word M
University of the West M,D
University of Toronto M,D
University of Virginia M,D
University of Washington M,D*
University of Waterloo D
The University of Winnipeg M
Valley Forge Christian College M
Vanderbilt University M,D*
Vanguard University of Southern California M
Virginia Polytechnic Institute and State University O
Virginia University of Lynchburg P
Wake Forest University M
Warner Pacific College M
Washington Adventist University M
Wayland Baptist University M
Wesley Biblical Seminary P,M
Western Michigan University M
Western Seminary M,O
Westminster Seminary California P,M
Westminster Theological Seminary P,M,D,O
Wheaton College M
Wilfrid Laurier University M,D
WON Institute of Graduate Studies M
Wycliffe College P,M,D,O
Yale University D*
Yeshiva Derech Chaim D

RELIGIOUS EDUCATION

Andover Newton Theological School P,M,D
Andrews University M,D,O
Asbury Theological Seminary M,D,O
Azusa Pacific University M
Baptist Bible College of Pennsylvania P,M,D
Baptist Theological Seminary at Richmond P,M,D
Bethel Seminary P,M,D,O
Biola University P,M,D
Boston College P,M,D,O*
Brandeis University M
Brigham Young University M*
Calvin Theological Seminary P,M,D
Campbell University P,M,D
Canadian Southern Baptist Seminary P,M
Claremont School of Theology M,D
College of Mount St. Joseph M,O
Columbia International University P,M,D,O
Concordia University Chicago M
Concordia University, Nebraska M
Concordia University, St. Paul M,O
Dallas Baptist University M
Dallas Theological Seminary M,D,O
Emmanuel Christian Seminary P,M,D
Felician College M,O*
Fordham University M,D,O
Gardner-Webb University P,D
Garrett-Evangelical Theological Seminary P,M,D
George Fox University P,M,D,O
Georgian Court University M,O
Global University P,M
Grand Rapids Theological Seminary of Cornerstone University P,M
Gratz College M,D,O
Hebrew College M,O
Hebrew Union College–Jewish Institute of Religion (NY) M
Inter American University of Puerto Rico, Metropolitan Campus D
The Jewish Theological Seminary M,D
Jewish University of America M,D
Lancaster Theological Seminary P,M,D,O
La Sierra University P,M
Laura and Alvin Siegal College of Judaic Studies M
Lincoln Christian Seminary P,M,D
Loyola Marymount University M
Loyola University Chicago M,O
Luther Rice University P,M,D
Maple Springs Baptist Bible College and Seminary P,M,D,O
Michigan Theological Seminary P,M,O
Midwestern Baptist Theological Seminary P,M,D,O
Nazarene Theological Seminary P,M,D
Newman Theological College M,O
New Orleans Baptist Theological Seminary P,M,D
The Nigerian Baptist Theological Seminary P,M,D,O
Oral Roberts University P,M,D
Pfeiffer University M
Phillips Theological Seminary P,M,D
Pontifical Catholic University of Puerto Rico M
Providence College and Theological Seminary P,M,D,O
Reformed Theological Seminary–Jackson Campus P,M,D,O
Regent University M,D,O
Rochester College M
St. Augustine's Seminary of Toronto P,M,O
Saint Mary's University of Minnesota M
Saints Cyril and Methodius Seminary P,M
St. Vladimir's Orthodox Theological Seminary P,M,D
Shasta Bible College M
Southeastern Baptist Theological Seminary P,M,D
Southern Adventist University M
Southern Baptist Theological Seminary P,M,D
Southern Evangelical Seminary P,M,D,O
Southwestern Assemblies of God University M
Southwestern Baptist Theological Seminary M,D,O
Spertus Institute of Jewish Studies M
Temple Baptist Seminary P,M,D
Towson University M,D,O
Trinity International University P,M,D,O
Trinity Lutheran Seminary P,M
Unification Theological Seminary P,M,D
Union Presbyterian Seminary P,M,D
University of St. Michael's College P,M,D,O
University of St. Thomas (MN) P,M
University of San Francisco M,D
Wesley Biblical Seminary P,M
Wheaton College M
Xavier University M
Yeshiva University M,D,O*

REPRODUCTIVE BIOLOGY

Cornell University M,D*
Eastern Virginia Medical School M
Northwestern University D*
Queen's University at Kingston M,D
Rutgers, The State University of New Jersey, New Brunswick M,D*
The University of British Columbia M,D
University of Hawaii at Manoa M,D
University of Saskatchewan M,D
University of Wyoming M,D
West Virginia University M,D

RHETORIC

Abilene Christian University M
Ball State University M
Bob Jones University P,M,D,O
Bowling Green State University M,D*
Brigham Young University M*
California State University, Dominguez Hills M,O*
California State University, Northridge M
California State University, Stanislaus M,O
Carnegie Mellon University M,D*
The Catholic University of America M,D,O
Clemson University D
Duquesne University M,D
Eastern Washington University M
Florida State University M,D
Georgia State University M,D
Idaho State University M
Indiana University Bloomington M,D*
Indiana University of Pennsylvania M,D
Iowa State University of Science and Technology M,D*
Kansas State University M*
Kent State University M,D*
Michigan State University M,D
Michigan Technological University M,D
Missouri Western State University M
Monmouth University M
New Mexico Highlands University M
New Mexico State University M,D
North Carolina State University D*
Northern Kentucky University M,O
Ohio University M,D*
Rensselaer Polytechnic Institute M,D
San Diego State University M
Southern Illinois University Carbondale M,D
Syracuse University M,D*
Texas Christian University M,D

*M—master's degree; P—first professional degree; D—doctorate; O—other advanced degree; *—Close-Up and/or Display in one of the other books in this series*

Institution	Degrees
Texas State University–San Marcos	M
Texas Tech University	M,D*
Texas Woman's University	M,D
The University of Alabama	M,D
The University of Arizona	D
University of Arkansas at Little Rock	M
University of California, Berkeley	D*
University of Colorado Denver	M
University of Denver	M,D
The University of Iowa	M,D*
University of Louisiana at Lafayette	M,D*
University of Louisville	M,D
University of Nebraska–Lincoln	M,D*
The University of North Carolina at Charlotte	M
The University of North Carolina at Greensboro	M,D
The University of Tennessee at Chattanooga	M,O
The University of Texas at El Paso	M,D,O
University of Utah	M,D*
University of Wisconsin–Madison	M,D*
University of Wisconsin–Milwaukee	M,D,O
Virginia Commonwealth University	M
Wright State University	M

ROMANCE LANGUAGES

Institution	Degrees
Appalachian State University	M
Boston University	M,D*
Clark Atlanta University	M,D
Columbia University	M,D*
Cornell University	M,D*
Hunter College of the City University of New York	M
The Johns Hopkins University	D
Michigan State University	M,D
New York University	M,D
Northern Illinois University	M
Queens College of the City University of New York	M
San Diego State University	M
Stony Brook University, State University of New York	M
Texas Tech University	M,D*
University at Buffalo, the State University of New York	M,D*
The University of Alabama	M,D
University of California, Berkeley	D*
University of Chicago	M,D
University of Cincinnati	M,D
University of Georgia	M,D
University of Miami	D*
University of Michigan	D*
University of Missouri	M,D*
University of Missouri–Kansas City	M*
University of New Orleans	M
The University of North Carolina at Chapel Hill	M,D*
University of Notre Dame	M*
University of Oregon	M,D
University of Pennsylvania	M,D*
University of Rochester	
University of South Africa	M,D
The University of Texas at Austin	M,D
University of Virginia	M,D
University of Washington	M,D*
Washington University in St. Louis	M,D*

RURAL PLANNING AND STUDIES

Institution	Degrees
Brandon University	M,O
California State University, Chico	M
Concordia University (Canada)	M,D,O
Cornell University	M*
Dalhousie University	M
George Mason University	M,O*
Iowa State University of Science and Technology	M,D*
Université Laval	O
University of Alaska Fairbanks	M
University of Guelph	M,D
The University of Montana	M
University of West Georgia	M,O
University of Wyoming	M

RURAL SOCIOLOGY

Institution	Degrees
Auburn University	M
Cornell University	M,D*
Iowa State University of Science and Technology	M,D*
The Ohio State University	M,D
Penn State University Park	M,D
South Dakota State University	M,D
University of Alberta	M,D
University of Missouri	M,D*
The University of Montana	M
University of Wisconsin–Madison	M,D*

RUSSIAN

Institution	Degrees
American University	M,O
Boston College	M*
Brown University	M,D
Columbia University	M,D*
Harvard University	D*
Hofstra University	M,O
Kent State University	M,D*
McGill University	M,D
Middlebury College	M,D
New York University	M
The Ohio State University	M,D
Princeton University	D*
Stanford University	M,D
University at Albany, State University of New York	M,O
The University of Arizona	M
University of California, Berkeley	D*
The University of Manchester	M,D
University of Michigan	M,D*
The University of North Carolina at Chapel Hill	M,D*
University of Oregon	M
University of South Africa	M,D
The University of Tennessee	D
University of Washington	M,D*
University of Waterloo	M,D
Wayne State University	M,D*
Yale University	D*

SAFETY ENGINEERING

Institution	Degrees
Embry-Riddle Aeronautical University–Prescott	M
Indiana University Bloomington	M,D*
Murray State University	M
National University	M
New Jersey Institute of Technology	M
The University of Alabama at Birmingham	M*
University of Minnesota, Duluth	M
University of Southern California	M,D,O*
West Virginia University	M

SCANDINAVIAN LANGUAGES

Institution	Degrees
Cornell University	M,D*
Harvard University	D*
University of California, Berkeley	D*
University of California, Los Angeles	M*
University of Massachusetts Amherst	M,D*
University of Minnesota, Twin Cities Campus	M,D
University of Washington	M,D*
University of Wisconsin–Madison	M,D*

SCHOOL NURSING

Institution	Degrees
Cambridge College	M,D,O
Eastern University	M,O
Felician College	M,O*
Kean University	M
Kutztown University of Pennsylvania	M,O
Monmouth University	M,D,O
Saint Joseph's University	M,O
Seton Hall University	M,D
University of Illinois at Chicago	M
West Chester University of Pennsylvania	M,O
Wright State University	M

SCHOOL PSYCHOLOGY

Institution	Degrees
Abilene Christian University	O
Adelphi University	M*
Alabama Agricultural and Mechanical University	M,O
Alfred University	M,D,O
Alliant International University–Irvine	M,D,O
Alliant International University–Los Angeles	M,D,O
Alliant International University–San Diego	M,D,O
Alliant International University–San Francisco	M,D,O
Andrews University	M,O
Appalachian State University	M
Arcadia University	M*
Argosy University, Dallas	M,D*
Argosy University, Hawai'i	M*
Argosy University, Phoenix	M,D*
Argosy University, Sarasota	M,D,O*
Arkansas State University	M,O
Assumption College	M,O
Azusa Pacific University	M
Ball State University	M,D,O
Barry University	M,O*
Boston University	M,D,O*
Bowling Green State University	M,O*
Brigham Young University	M,D,O*
Brooklyn College of the City University of New York	M,O
Bucknell University	M
California Baptist University	M
California State University, Los Angeles	M,D*
California State University, Northridge	M
California State University, Sacramento	M
California University of Pennsylvania	M
Cambridge College	M,D,O
Canisius College	M
Capella University	M,D,O
Carlos Albizu University, Miami Campus	M,D
Central Connecticut State University	M,O
Central Michigan University	D,O
Central Washington University	M
Chapman University	M,D,O
The Chicago School of Professional Psychology	O
The Chicago School of Professional Psychology at Grayslake	O
The Citadel, The Military College of South Carolina	O
City University of Seattle	M,O
Cleveland State University	M,D,O
The College of New Rochelle	M
College of St. Joseph	M
The College of Saint Rose	M,O
The College of William and Mary	M,O
Duquesne University	M,D,O
East Carolina University	
Eastern Illinois University	M,O
Eastern Kentucky University	M,O
Eastern University	M,O
Eastern Washington University	M
Edinboro University of Pennsylvania	M,O
Emporia State University	M,O
Evangel University	M
Fairfield University	M,O
Fairleigh Dickinson University, Metropolitan Campus	M,D
Florida Agricultural and Mechanical University	M
Florida International University	M,D,O
Florida State University	M,O
Fordham University	M,D,O
Fort Hays State University	O
Francis Marion University	M,O
Fresno Pacific University	M
Gallaudet University	M,D,O
Gardner-Webb University	M
George Fox University	M,O
George Mason University	O*
Georgian Court University	M,O
Georgia Southern University	M,O
Georgia State University	M,D,O
Grand Valley State University	M
Hofstra University	D
Howard University	M,D
Humboldt State University	M
Idaho State University	M,D,O
Illinois State University	D,O
Immaculata University	M,D,O
Indiana State University	M,D,O
Indiana University Bloomington	M,D,O*
Indiana University of Pennsylvania	D,O
Inter American University of Puerto Rico, Metropolitan Campus	M,D
Inter American University of Puerto Rico, San Germán Campus	M,D
Iona College	M
James Madison University	M,D,O
The Johns Hopkins University	M,O
Kean University	D,O
Keene State College	M,O
Kent State University	M,D,O*
La Sierra University	M,O
Lehigh University	D,O
Lenoir-Rhyne University	M
Lesley University	M
Lewis & Clark College	M,O
Lindenwood University	M,D,O
Long Island University, Brooklyn Campus	M
Long Island University, Westchester Graduate Campus	M

Louisiana State University and Agricultural and Mechanical College	M,D
Louisiana State University in Shreveport	O
Loyola Marymount University	M
Loyola University Chicago	D,O
Lynchburg College	M
Marist College	M,O
Marshall University	O
Marywood University	O
Massachusetts School of Professional Psychology	M,D,O
McGill University	M,D,O
McNeese State University	M,O
Mercy College	M
Miami University	M,O
Michigan State University	M,D,O
Middle Tennessee State University	M,O
Millersville University of Pennsylvania	M
Minnesota State University Mankato	M,D
Minnesota State University Moorhead	M,O
Minot State University	O
Mississippi State University	M,D,O
Montana State University	M,D,O
Montclair State University	M,O
Mount Saint Vincent University	M
National-Louis University	M,D,O
National University	M
New Jersey City University	M,O
New Mexico Highlands University	M
New Mexico State University	M,D,O
Niagara University	M,O
Nicholls State University	M,O
North Carolina State University	D*
Northeastern University	M,D,O
Northern Arizona University	M,D,O
Northwest Nazarene University	M
Nova Southeastern University	O*
Oregon State University–Cascades	M
Ottawa University	M
Our Lady of the Lake University of San Antonio	M,D
Pace University	M,D
Penn State University Park	M,D
Philadelphia College of Osteopathic Medicine	M,D,O*
Phillips Graduate Institute	M
Pittsburg State University	O
Purdue University Calumet	M
Queens College of the City University of New York	M,O
Quincy University	M
Radford University	M,O
Rhode Island College	M,O
Rider University	O
Roberts Wesleyan College	M
Rowan University	M,O
Rutgers, The State University of New Jersey, New Brunswick	M,D*
St. John's University (NY)	M,D
San Diego State University	M
San Francisco State University	M
Seattle University	M,O
Seton Hall University	O
Southeast Missouri State University	M,O
Southern Connecticut State University	M,O
Southern Illinois University Edwardsville	O
Southwestern Oklahoma State University	M
State University of New York at Oswego	M,O
State University of New York at Plattsburgh	M,O
Stephen F. Austin State University	M
Syracuse University	M,D,O*
Tarleton State University	M,O
Teachers College, Columbia University	M,D
Temple University	M,D*
Tennessee State University	M,D
Texas A&M University	M,D
Texas State University–San Marcos	O
Texas Woman's University	M,D,O
Towson University	O
Trinity University	M
Troy University	M,O
Tufts University	M,O
Union College (KY)	M
University at Albany, State University of New York	M,D,O
The University of Akron	M
University of Alberta	M,D
The University of Arizona	D,O
The University of British Columbia	M,D,O
University of Calgary	M,D
University of California, Riverside	M,D
University of California, Santa Barbara	M,D
University of Central Arkansas	M,D
University of Central Florida	O
University of Cincinnati	D,O
University of Colorado Denver	M,O
University of Connecticut	M,D,O*
University of Dayton	M,O
University of Delaware	M,D,O*
University of Denver	M,D,O
University of Detroit Mercy	O
University of Florida	M,D,O*
University of Hartford	M
University of Houston–Clear Lake	M
University of Houston–Victoria	M
University of Idaho	O
The University of Iowa	M,D,O*
The University of Kansas	D,O
University of Kentucky	M,D,O*
University of Louisiana at Monroe	M,O
University of Manitoba	M,D
University of Mary	M
University of Mary Hardin-Baylor	M
University of Maryland, College Park	M,D,O
University of Massachusetts Amherst	M,D,O*
University of Massachusetts Boston	M,O
University of Memphis	M,D,O
University of Minnesota, Twin Cities Campus	M,D,O
University of Missouri	M,D,O*
University of Missouri–St. Louis	O
The University of Montana	M,D,O
University of Nebraska at Kearney	M,O
University of Nebraska at Omaha	M,D,O
University of Nebraska–Lincoln	M,D,O*
The University of North Carolina at Chapel Hill	M,D*
The University of North Carolina at Greensboro	M,D,O
University of Northern Colorado	D,O
University of Northern Iowa	M,O
University of North Texas	M
University of Phoenix–Denver Campus	M
University of Phoenix–Las Vegas Campus	M
University of Phoenix–Puerto Rico Campus	M
University of Phoenix–Southern California Campus	M
University of Phoenix–Southern Colorado Campus	M,O
University of Phoenix–Utah Campus	M
University of Rhode Island	M,D
University of South Alabama	M,D
University of South Carolina	D
University of Southern Maine	M,D
University of Southern Mississippi	M,D
University of South Florida	M,D,O*
The University of Tennessee	M,D,O
The University of Tennessee at Chattanooga	O
The University of Texas at Austin	M,D
The University of Texas at San Antonio	M*
The University of Texas at Tyler	M
The University of Texas–Pan American	M
University of the Pacific	M,D,O
The University of Toledo	M,D,O
University of Utah	M,D*
University of Virginia	M,D
University of Washington	M,D*
University of Wisconsin–Eau Claire	M,O
University of Wisconsin–La Crosse	M,O
University of Wisconsin–Milwaukee	D,O
University of Wisconsin–River Falls	M,O
University of Wisconsin–Stout	M,O
University of Wisconsin–Superior	M
University of Wisconsin–Whitewater	M,O*
Utah State University	M,D
Valdosta State University	M,O
Valparaiso University	
Washington State University	M,D,O
Wayne State University	M,D,O*
Western Carolina University	M
Western Illinois University	M,O
Western Kentucky University	M,O
Western New Mexico University	M
Wichita State University	M,O
Worcester State University	M,O
Yeshiva University	D*
Youngstown State University	M

SCIENCE EDUCATION

Acadia University	M
Alabama State University	M,O
Albany State University	M
Alverno College	M
American University of Puerto Rico	M,O
Andrews University	M,D,O
Antioch University New England	M
Appalachian State University	M
Arcadia University	M,D,O*
Arkansas State University	M,O
Armstrong Atlantic State University	M
Asbury University	M
Auburn University	M,D,O
Aurora University	M
Averett University	M
Ball State University	M,D
Belmont University	M
Benedictine University	M
Bennington College	M
Biola University	M
Bloomsburg University of Pennsylvania	M
Boise State University	M,D
Boston College	M,D*
Boston University	M,D,O*
Bowling Green State University	M*
Bridgewater State University	M
Brigham Young University	M,D*
Brooklyn College of the City University of New York	M,O
Brown University	M
Buffalo State College, State University of New York	M
California State University, Chico	M
California State University, Fullerton	M
California State University, Long Beach	M
California State University, Northridge	M
California State University, San Bernardino	M
Cambridge College	M,D,O
Caribbean University	M,D
Carthage College	M,O
Central Connecticut State University	M,O
Central Michigan University	M
Chatham University	M
Christopher Newport University	M
The Citadel, The Military College of South Carolina	M
City College of the City University of New York	M
Clarion University of Pennsylvania	M
Clark Atlanta University	M
Clemson University	M
Cleveland State University	M
The College at Brockport, State University of New York	M
College of Charleston	M
College of the Humanities and Sciences, Harrison Middleton University	M,D
The College of William and Mary	M
The Colorado College	M
Columbia University	M,D,O*
Columbus State University	M,O
Converse College	M
Cornell University	M,D*
Delaware State University	M,D
Drew University	M
Duquesne University	M
East Carolina University	M
Eastern Connecticut State University	M
Eastern Kentucky University	M
Eastern Michigan University	M
Eastern New Mexico University	M

*M—master's degree; P—first professional degree; D—doctorate; O—other advanced degree; *—Close-Up and/or Display in one of the other books in this series*

East Stroudsburg University of Pennsylvania	M
Elms College	M,O
Fairleigh Dickinson University, Metropolitan Campus	M
Fitchburg State University	M,O
Florida Agricultural and Mechanical University	M
Florida Institute of Technology	M,D,O
Florida International University	M,D,O
Florida State University	M,D,O
Fresno Pacific University	M
Gannon University	M
Georgia Southern University	M
Georgia State University	M,D,O
Grambling State University	M,D
Hamline University	M,D
Hardin-Simmons University	M,D
Harvard University	M*
Heritage University	M
Hofstra University	M,D,O
Hood College	M,O
Hunter College of the City University of New York	M,O
ICR Graduate School	M
Illinois Institute of Technology	M,D
Indiana State University	M,D
Indiana Tech	M
Indiana University Bloomington	M,D,O*
Instituto Tecnológico y de Estudios Superiores de Monterrey, Campus Monterrey	M,D
Inter American University of Puerto Rico, Arecibo Campus	M
Inter American University of Puerto Rico, Barranquitas Campus	M
Inter American University of Puerto Rico, Metropolitan Campus	M
Inter American University of Puerto Rico, Ponce Campus	M
Inter American University of Puerto Rico, San Germán Campus	M
Iona College	M
Ithaca College	M
Jackson State University	M
John Carroll University	M
The Johns Hopkins University	M,O
Johnson State College	M
Kaplan University, Davenport Campus	M
Kean University	M
Kennesaw State University	M
Kutztown University of Pennsylvania	M,O
Laurentian University	O
Lawrence Technological University	M
Lebanon Valley College	M
Lehman College of the City University of New York	M
Lesley University	M,D,O
Lewis University	M
Long Island University, C.W. Post Campus	M
Louisiana Tech University	M,D
Loyola University Chicago	M,O
Lynchburg College	M
Lyndon State College	M
Manhattanville College	M*
McNeese State University	M
Michigan State University	M,D
Michigan Technological University	M
Middle Tennessee State University	M
Mills College	M,D
Minnesota State University Mankato	M
Minot State University	M
Mississippi College	M,D,O
Missouri State University	M
Montclair State University	M,D,O
Morehead State University	M
Morgan State University	M,D
National-Louis University	M,D,O
New Mexico Institute of Mining and Technology	M
New York University	M
North Carolina Agricultural and Technical State University	M
North Carolina State University	M,D*
North Dakota State University	M,D,O
Northeastern State University	M
Northern Arizona University	M,O
Northern Michigan University	M
North Georgia College & State University	M,O
Northwestern State University of Louisiana	M
Northwest Missouri State University	M
Norwich University	M
Nova Southeastern University	M,O*
Occidental College	M
Ohio University	M*
Old Dominion University	M
Oregon State University	M,D
Our Lady of the Lake University of San Antonio	M
Plymouth State University	M
Portland State University	M,D
Purdue University	M,D,O
Purdue University Calumet	M
Queens College of the City University of New York	M,O
Quinnipiac University	M
Regis University	M,O
Rice University	M,D
Rider University	O
Rutgers, The State University of New Jersey, New Brunswick	M,D*
Saginaw Valley State University	M
St. John Fisher College	M
Salem State University	M
San Diego State University	M,D
San Jose State University	M
Shippensburg University of Pennsylvania	M
Slippery Rock University of Pennsylvania	M
Smith College	M
South Carolina State University	M,D,O
Southeast Missouri State University	M
Southern Connecticut State University	M,O
Southern Illinois University Edwardsville	M
Southern University and Agricultural and Mechanical College	D
Southwestern Oklahoma State University	M
Stanford University	M,D
State University of New York at Binghamton	M
State University of New York at Fredonia	M
State University of New York at New Paltz	M
State University of New York at Plattsburgh	M
State University of New York College at Cortland	M
State University of New York College at Potsdam	M
Stony Brook University, State University of New York	M,D,O
Syracuse University	M,D*
Teachers College, Columbia University	M,D
Temple University	M,D*
Texas A&M University	M,D
Texas Christian University	M
Texas State University–San Marcos	M
Towson University	M
Troy University	M
Union Graduate College	M,O
Universidad Nacional Pedro Henriquez Urena	M
University at Albany, State University of New York	M,D
University at Buffalo, the State University of New York	M,D,O*
University of Arkansas at Pine Bluff	M
The University of British Columbia	M,D
University of California, Berkeley	M,D*
University of California, Los Angeles	M,D*
University of California, San Diego	D*
University of Central Florida	M,D,O
University of Chicago	D
University of Cincinnati	M,D,O
University of Colorado Denver	M,D
University of Connecticut	M,D*
University of Florida	M,D,O*
University of Georgia	M,D,O
University of Illinois at Urbana–Champaign	M,D
University of Indianapolis	M
The University of Iowa	M,D*
University of Maine	M,O
University of Maryland, Baltimore County	M
University of Massachusetts Amherst	M,D,O*
University of Massachusetts Lowell	M,D,O
University of Miami	D*
University of Michigan	M,D*
University of Michigan–Dearborn	M
University of Minnesota, Twin Cities Campus	M
University of Missouri	M,D,O*
University of Nebraska at Kearney	M
University of New Hampshire	M,D
University of New Mexico	O*
The University of North Carolina at Chapel Hill	M*
The University of North Carolina at Greensboro	M,D,O
The University of North Carolina at Pembroke	M
University of Northern Colorado	M,D
University of Northern Iowa	M
University of North Texas Health Science Center at Fort Worth	M,D
University of Oklahoma	M,D,O*
University of Pittsburgh	M,D*
University of Puerto Rico, Río Piedras	M,D
University of St. Francis (IL)	M
University of South Africa	M,D
University of South Alabama	M,O
University of South Carolina	M,D
University of Southern Mississippi	M,D
University of South Florida	M,D,O*
The University of Tennessee	M,D,O
The University of Texas at Austin	M,D
The University of Texas at Dallas	M*
The University of Texas at El Paso	M
University of the Incarnate Word	M
The University of Toledo	M,D,O
University of Tulsa	M
University of Utah	M,D*
University of Vermont	M,D
University of Victoria	M,D
University of Virginia	M,D,O
University of Washington	M,D*
University of Washington, Tacoma	M
The University of West Alabama	M
University of West Florida	M
University of West Georgia	M,O
University of Wisconsin–Madison	M,D*
University of Wisconsin–River Falls	M
University of Wisconsin–Stevens Point	M
University of Wyoming	M
Ursuline College	M
Vanderbilt University	M,D*
Walden University	M,D,O
Wayne State College	M
Wayne State University	M,D,O*
West Chester University of Pennsylvania	M,O
Western Connecticut State University	M
Western Governors University	M,O
Western Michigan University	M,D
Western Oregon University	M
Western Washington University	M
Widener University	M,D
Wilkes University	M,D
Wright State University	M
Youngstown State University	M

SECONDARY EDUCATION

Adelphi University	M*
Alabama Agricultural and Mechanical University	M,O
Alabama State University	M,O
Alcorn State University	M,O
American International College	M,D,O
American Public University System	M
American University	M,O
Andrews University	M,D,O
Arcadia University	M,D,O*
Argosy University, Atlanta	M,D,O*
Argosy University, Chicago	M,D,O*
Argosy University, Hawai'i	M,D*
Argosy University, Inland Empire	M,D*
Argosy University, Los Angeles	M,D*
Argosy University, Nashville	M,D,O*
Argosy University, Orange County	M,D*
Argosy University, Phoenix	M,D,O*
Argosy University, San Diego	M,D*

Institution	Degrees
Argosy University, San Francisco Bay Area	M,D*
Argosy University, Sarasota	M,D,O*
Argosy University, Schaumburg	M,D,O*
Argosy University, Seattle	M,D*
Argosy University, Tampa	M,D,O*
Argosy University, Twin Cities	M,D,O*
Argosy University, Washington DC	M,D,O*
Arizona State University	M,D
Arkansas Tech University	M,O
Armstrong Atlantic State University	M
Auburn University	M,D,O
Auburn University Montgomery	M,O
Augusta State University	M,O
Austin College	M
Austin Peay State University	M,O
Ball State University	M
Belhaven University (MS)	M
Bellarmine University	M,D,O
Belmont University	M
Benedictine University	M
Bennington College	M
Berry College	M
Bethel University (MN)	M,D,O
Bob Jones University	P,M,D,O
Boston College	M*
Bowie State University	M
Brandeis University	M
Brenau University	M,O
Bridgewater State University	M
Brooklyn College of the City University of New York	M,O
Brown University	M
Butler University	M
California State University, Bakersfield	M
California State University, Fullerton	M
California State University, Long Beach	M
California State University, Los Angeles	M*
California State University, Northridge	M
California State University, San Bernardino	M
California State University, Stanislaus	M
California University of Pennsylvania	M
Campbell University	M
Canisius College	M,O
Carlow University	M
Carson-Newman College	M
The Catholic University of America	M,D,O
Centenary College of Louisiana	M
Central Connecticut State University	M
Central Michigan University	M,O
Chadron State College	M,O
Chapman University	M,O
Charleston Southern University	M
Chatham University	M
Chestnut Hill College	M*
Chicago State University	M
Christopher Newport University	M
The Citadel, The Military College of South Carolina	M
City College of the City University of New York	M,O
Clemson University	M
Coastal Carolina University	M
Colgate University	M
College of Mount St. Joseph	M
The College of New Jersey	M
College of St. Joseph	M
The College of Saint Rose	M,O
College of Staten Island of the City University of New York	M
The College of William and Mary	M
The Colorado College	M
Columbus State University	M,O
Concordia University (OR)	M
Concordia University Chicago	M
Concordia University, Nebraska	M
Converse College	M
Creighton University	M
Dakota Wesleyan University	M
Dallas Baptist University	M
Defiance College	M
Delta State University	M
DePaul University	M,D
Drury University	M
Duquesne University	M
D'Youville College	M,O*
Eastern Connecticut State University	M
Eastern Kentucky University	M
Eastern Michigan University	M
Eastern Nazarene College	M,O
Eastern New Mexico University	M
Eastern Oregon University	M
East Stroudsburg University of Pennsylvania	M
East Tennessee State University	M,D
Edinboro University of Pennsylvania	M
Elms College	M,O
Emmanuel College (United States)	M,O
Emory University	M,D,O*
Emporia State University	M
Evangel University	M
Fairfield University	M,O
Fayetteville State University	M
Fitchburg State University	M
Florida Agricultural and Mechanical University	M
Fordham University	M,D,O
Francis Marion University	M
Fresno Pacific University	M
Frostburg State University	M
Gallaudet University	M,D,O
George Fox University	M,D,O
The George Washington University	M
Georgia College & State University	M,O
Georgia Southwestern State University	M,O
Georgia State University	M,D,O
Grand Canyon University	M
Grand Valley State University	M,O
Greenville College	M
Hampton University	M
Harding University	M,O
Hawai'i Pacific University	M*
High Point University	M
Hofstra University	M,O
Holy Family University	M*
Hood College	M,O
Howard University	M
Hunter College of the City University of New York	M
Idaho State University	M,O
Immaculata University	M,D,O
Indiana University Bloomington	M,D,O*
Indiana University Northwest	M
Indiana University–Purdue University Fort Wayne	M
Indiana University South Bend	M
Indiana University Southeast	M
Instituto Tecnologico de Santo Domingo	M,O
Ithaca College	M
Jackson State University	M,D,O
Jacksonville State University	M
James Madison University	M
John Carroll University	M
The Johns Hopkins University	M,O
Johnson & Wales University	M,D
Johnson State College	M,O
Jones International University	M
Kaplan University, Davenport Campus	M
Kennesaw State University	M
Kent State University	M*
Kutztown University of Pennsylvania	M,O
LaGrange College	M
Lancaster Bible College	M,D
Lee University	M,O
Le Moyne College	M,O
Lewis & Clark College	M
Lewis University	M
Liberty University	M,D,O
Lincoln University (MO)	M,O
Long Island University, C.W. Post Campus	M
Long Island University, Rockland Graduate Campus	M
Long Island University, Westchester Graduate Campus	M,O
Longwood University	M
Louisiana State University and Agricultural and Mechanical College	M,D,O
Louisiana Tech University	M,D
Loyola Marymount University	M
Loyola University Chicago	M,O
Maharishi University of Management	M
Manhattanville College	M*
Mansfield University of Pennsylvania	M
Marquette University	M,D,O
Marshall University	M
Marygrove College	M
Marymount University	M
Maryville University of Saint Louis	M,D
Marywood University	M
McDaniel College	M
McNeese State University	M,O
Medaille College	M
Mercer University	M,D,O
Mercy College	M
Merrimack College	M,O
Metropolitan State University	M,O
Miami University	M
Middle Tennessee State University	M,O
Mills College	M,D
Minnesota State University Mankato	M,O
Mississippi College	M,D,O
Mississippi State University	M,D,O
Missouri State University	M,O
Monmouth University	M,O
Montana State University Billings	M
Morehead State University	M,O
Morgan State University	M
Mount Saint Mary College	M,O
Mount St. Mary's College	M
Murray State University	M,O
National-Louis University	M,D,O
New Jersey City University	M
New York University	M,D,O
Niagara University	M,O
Norfolk State University	M
North Carolina State University	M*
Northern Arizona University	M
Northern Illinois University	M,D
Northern Michigan University	M
Northern State University	M
North Georgia College & State University	M,O
Northwestern Oklahoma State University	M
Northwestern State University of Louisiana	M,O
Northwestern University	M*
Northwest Missouri State University	M,O
Nova Southeastern University	M,O*
Oakland University	M
Occidental College	M
Ohio University	M,D*
Old Dominion University	M
Olivet Nazarene University	M
Our Lady of the Lake University of San Antonio	M
Pacific University	M
Park University	M
Piedmont College	M,D,O
Pittsburg State University	M
Plymouth State University	M
Portland State University	M,D
Prescott College	M,D
Providence College	M
Queens College of the City University of New York	M,O
Quinnipiac University	M
Rhode Island College	M
Roberts Wesleyan College	M,O
Rochester Institute of Technology	M
Rockford College	M,O
Rollins College	M
Roosevelt University	M
Rowan University	M
Sacred Heart University	M,O
Saginaw Valley State University	M
St. Bonaventure University	M
St. John's University (NY)	M
Saint Joseph's University	M,D
Saint Mary's University of Minnesota	M,O
Saint Peter's College	M,O
St. Thomas Aquinas College	M,O
Saint Xavier University	M,O
Salem College	M
Salem State University	M
Samford University	M,D,O
San Diego State University	M
San Francisco State University	M
San Jose State University	O
Seattle Pacific University	M,O
Shenandoah University	M,D,O
Siena Heights University	M
Sierra Nevada College	M
Simmons College	M,O
Simpson College	M
Slippery Rock University of Pennsylvania	M
Smith College	M
South Carolina State University	M,D,O
Southeast Missouri State University	M,O
Southern Arkansas University–Magnolia	M

*M—master's degree; P—first professional degree; D—doctorate; O—other advanced degree; *—Close-Up and/or Display in one of the other books in this series*

Southern Illinois University Edwardsville M
Southern New Hampshire University M,O
Southern Oregon University M
Southern University and Agricultural and Mechanical College M
Southwestern Assemblies of God University M
Southwestern Oklahoma State University M
Spalding University M
Springfield College M
Spring Hill College M
State University of New York at Binghamton M
State University of New York at Fredonia M
State University of New York at New Paltz M
State University of New York at Oswego M
State University of New York at Plattsburgh M
State University of New York College at Cortland M
State University of New York College at Geneseo M
State University of New York College at Oneonta M
State University of New York College at Potsdam M
Stephen F. Austin State University M,D
Suffolk University M,O
Sul Ross State University M
Tarleton State University M,O
Tennessee Technological University M,O
Texas A&M University–Commerce M,D
Texas A&M University–Corpus Christi M
Texas A&M University–Kingsville M
Texas Christian University M
Texas Southern University M,D
Texas State University–San Marcos M
Texas Tech University M,D*
Towson University M
Trevecca Nazarene University M
Trinity (Washington) University M
Troy University M
Tufts University M,D
Union College (KY) M
Universidad Metropolitana M
The University of Akron M,D
The University of Alabama M,D,O
The University of Alabama at Birmingham M*
University of Alaska Fairbanks M,D,O
University of Alaska Southeast M
University of Alberta M,D
University of Arkansas M,O
University of Arkansas at Little Rock M
University of Arkansas at Pine Bluff M
University of Bridgeport M,O
University of California, Irvine M,D*
University of Central Missouri M,D,O
University of Central Oklahoma M
University of Cincinnati M
University of Colorado Denver M
University of Connecticut M,D,O*
University of Dayton M
University of Great Falls M
University of Guam M
University of Houston–Downtown M
University of Illinois at Chicago M,D
University of Indianapolis M
The University of Iowa M,D*
University of Louisiana at Monroe M
University of Louisville M,D
University of Maine M,O
University of Maryland, Baltimore County M
University of Maryland, College Park M,D,O
University of Massachusetts Amherst M,D,O*
University of Massachusetts Boston M,D,O
University of Massachusetts Dartmouth M,O
University of Memphis M,D
University of Missouri–St. Louis M,O
University of Montevallo M
University of Nebraska at Omaha M
University of Nevada, Reno M*
University of New Hampshire M
University of New Mexico M*
University of North Alabama M
The University of North Carolina at Chapel Hill M*
The University of North Carolina at Charlotte M,D
The University of North Carolina Wilmington M
University of North Dakota D
University of Northern Iowa M
University of North Florida M
University of North Texas M,O
University of Oklahoma M,D,O*
University of Pennsylvania M*
University of Phoenix M
University of Phoenix–Central Florida Campus M
University of Phoenix–Central Valley Campus M
University of Phoenix–Chattanooga Campus M
University of Phoenix–Denver Campus M
University of Phoenix–Hawaii Campus M
University of Phoenix–Idaho Campus M
University of Phoenix–Indianapolis Campus M
University of Phoenix–Memphis Campus M
University of Phoenix–Metro Detroit Campus M
University of Phoenix–Nashville Campus M
University of Phoenix–New Mexico Campus M
University of Phoenix–Northern Nevada Campus M
University of Phoenix–North Florida Campus M
University of Phoenix–Omaha Campus M
University of Phoenix–Oregon Campus M
University of Phoenix–Phoenix Campus M
University of Phoenix–Sacramento Valley Campus M,O
University of Phoenix–San Diego Campus M
University of Phoenix–Southern Arizona Campus M,O
University of Phoenix–Southern Colorado Campus M,O
University of Phoenix–South Florida Campus M
University of Phoenix–Utah Campus M
University of Phoenix–Washington D.C. Campus M,D,O
University of Phoenix–West Florida Campus M
University of Pittsburgh M,D*
University of Puget Sound M
University of Rhode Island M,D
University of St. Francis (IL) M
University of St. Thomas (MN) M,O
The University of Scranton M
University of South Alabama M,O
University of South Carolina M,D
The University of South Dakota M
University of Southern Indiana M
University of Southern Mississippi M,D,O
University of South Florida M,D,O*
The University of Tennessee M,D,O
The University of Tennessee at Chattanooga M,O
The University of Texas–Pan American M
University of the Cumberlands M,D,O
University of the Incarnate Word M
The University of Toledo M,D,O
University of Tulsa M
University of Utah M,D*
University of Washington, Bothell M
The University of West Alabama M
University of West Florida M,D,O
University of West Georgia M,O
University of Wisconsin–Eau Claire M
University of Wisconsin–La Crosse M
University of Wisconsin–Milwaukee M
University of Wisconsin–Platteville M
University of Wisconsin–Whitewater M*
Utah State University M
Valdosta State University M,O
Vanderbilt University M*
Villanova University M
Virginia Commonwealth University M,O
Wagner College M
Wake Forest University M
Walden University M,D,O
Washington State University M,D
Washington State University Tri-Cities M,D
Washington University in St. Louis M*
Wayne State University M,D,O*
West Chester University of Pennsylvania M,O
Western Connecticut State University M
Western Kentucky University M,O
Western New Mexico University M
Western Oregon University M
Western Washington University M
Westfield State University M
West Virginia University M,D
Wheaton College M
Whittier College M
Whitworth University M
Wilkes University M,D
William Carey University M,O
William Woods University M,O
Wilmington University M
Wilson College M
Winthrop University M
Worcester State University M
Wright State University M
Xavier University M
Youngstown State University M

SLAVIC LANGUAGES

Boston College M*
Brown University M,D
Columbia University M,D*
Cornell University M,D*
Duke University M,O*
Florida State University M
Harvard University D*
Indiana University Bloomington M,D*
New York University M
Northwestern University D*
The Ohio State University M,D
Princeton University D*
Stanford University M,D
University of Alberta M,D
University of California, Berkeley D*
University of California, Los Angeles M,D*
University of Chicago M,D
University of Illinois at Urbana–Champaign M,D
The University of Kansas M,D
The University of Manchester M,D
University of Manitoba M
University of Michigan M,D*
The University of North Carolina at Chapel Hill M,D*
University of Pittsburgh M,D*
University of Southern California M,D*
The University of Texas at Austin M,D
University of Toronto M,D
University of Virginia M,D
University of Washington M,D*
University of Wisconsin–Madison M,D*
University of Wisconsin–Milwaukee M,O
Yale University D*

SOCIAL PSYCHOLOGY

Adler School of Professional Psychology M,D,O
Alvernia University M
American University M,D
Andrews University M
Arcadia University M*
Argosy University, Atlanta M,D,O*
Argosy University, Chicago M,D*
Argosy University, Dallas M*
Argosy University, Sarasota M,D*
Argosy University, Schaumburg M,D,O*
Argosy University, Washington DC M,D*
Arizona State University D
Ball State University M
Bethel University (MN) M
Boston University M,D,O*
Bowling Green State University M,D*
Brandeis University M,D
Brigham Young University M,D*
Brock University M,D

Institution	Degree
Brooklyn College of the City University of New York	M
Brown University	D
California Institute of Integral Studies	M,D
California State University, Fullerton	M
Canisius College	M
Carnegie Mellon University	D*
Central Connecticut State University	M
Claremont Graduate University	M,D,O
Clark University	D
The College of New Rochelle	M
College of St. Joseph	M
Columbia University	M,D*
Cornell University	M,D*
Creighton University	M
DePaul University	M,D
Eastern Michigan University	M,O
Eastern University	M,O
Florida Agricultural and Mechanical University	M
Florida State University	D
Future Generations Graduate School	M
The George Washington University	M,D
Graduate School and University Center of the City University of New York	D
Harvard University	D*
Hofstra University	D
Howard University	M,D
Hunter College of the City University of New York	M,D
Indiana University Bloomington	M,D*
Indiana Wesleyan University	M
Iowa State University of Science and Technology	D*
Lamar University	M
Lenoir-Rhyne University	M
Lesley University	M,D,O
Lewis & Clark College	M
Loyola University Chicago	M,D
Lynchburg College	M
Martin University	M
Memorial University of Newfoundland	M,D
Missouri State University	M
Montclair State University	M,D,O
Mount Aloysius College	M
Mount Mary College	M
Naropa University	M
New York University	M,D,O
Norfolk State University	M
North Carolina Central University	M
North Carolina State University	M*
North Dakota State University	M,D
Northern Kentucky University	M,O
North Georgia College & State University	M
Northwestern University	D*
Northwest Nazarene University	M
The Ohio State University	M,D
Oregon State University–Cascades	M
Pittsburg State University	M
Queen's University at Kingston	M,D
Regent University	M,D,O
Regis University	M,O
Rutgers, The State University of New Jersey, Newark	D*
Rutgers, The State University of New Jersey, New Brunswick	D*
Sage Graduate School	M
St. Bonaventure University	M,O
St. Cloud State University	M
Saint Joseph College	M
Saint Martin's University	M
St. Mary's University (United States)	M
San Francisco State University	M
Southeastern Louisiana University	M
Southeast Missouri State University	M,O
Southwestern College (NM)	O
Springfield College	M
Stony Brook University, State University of New York	D
Syracuse University	D*
Teachers College, Columbia University	M
Temple University	M,D*
Texas A&M University	D
Texas Christian University	M,D
Thomas University	M
Troy University	M,O
Université du Québec à Rimouski	M
Université Laval	D
University at Albany, State University of New York	M,D,O
University at Buffalo, the State University of New York	M,D*
The University of Akron	M
University of Alaska Anchorage	M,D
University of Alaska Fairbanks	M,D
The University of British Columbia	M,D
University of Central Arkansas	M
University of Connecticut	M,D,O*
University of Dayton	M,O
University of Delaware	D*
University of Denver	D
University of Florida	M,D*
University of Guelph	M,D
University of Hawaii at Manoa	M,D,O
University of Houston	M,D
The University of Iowa	M,D*
The University of Kansas	M,D
University of La Verne	D
University of Mary	M
University of Maryland, College Park	M,D
University of Massachusetts Amherst	M,D*
University of Massachusetts Lowell	M
University of Michigan	D*
University of Minnesota, Twin Cities Campus	D
University of Missouri–Kansas City	M,D*
University of Missouri–St. Louis	M,D,O
University of Montevallo	M
University of Nebraska–Lincoln	M,D*
University of Nevada, Reno	D*
University of New Haven	M,O
The University of North Carolina at Chapel Hill	D*
The University of North Carolina at Charlotte	M,D,O
The University of North Carolina at Greensboro	M,D
University of Oklahoma	M*
University of Oregon	M,D
University of Phoenix	M
University of Phoenix–Minneapolis/St. Louis Park Campus	M
University of Phoenix–Phoenix Campus	M
University of Phoenix–Southern California Campus	M
University of Puerto Rico, Río Piedras	M,D
University of Rochester	M,D
The University of Scranton	M
University of South Carolina	M,D
University of Southern California	M,D*
The University of Tennessee at Chattanooga	M
The University of Tennessee at Martin	M
The University of Toledo	M,D,O
University of Victoria	M,D
University of Washington	D*
University of Windsor	M,D
University of Wisconsin–Madison	D*
University of Wisconsin–Milwaukee	M,D
University of Wisconsin–Superior	M
University of Wisconsin–Whitewater	M*
Virginia Commonwealth University	D
Walden University	M,D,O
Washington State University	M,D
Washington University in St. Louis	D*
Western Carolina University	M
Western Connecticut State University	M
Western Illinois University	M,O
Wichita State University	D
Wilfrid Laurier University	M,D
Wilmington University	M
Yale University	D*

SOCIAL SCIENCES

Institution	Degree
Arkansas Tech University	M
California Institute of Technology	M,D
California State University, Chico	M
California State University, San Bernardino	M
California University of Pennsylvania	M
Campbellsville University	M
Carnegie Mellon University	D*
Central European University	M,D
The Citadel, The Military College of South Carolina	M
Clemson University	D
College of the Humanities and Sciences, Harrison Middleton University	M,D
Columbia University	M*
Eastern Michigan University	M,O
Edinboro University of Pennsylvania	M
Florida Agricultural and Mechanical University	M
Graduate Theological Union	M,D,O
Hollins University	M,O
Humboldt State University	M
Indiana University Bloomington	P,M,D,O*
The Johns Hopkins University	M,D
Lincoln University (MO)	M,O
Long Island University, Brooklyn Campus	M,O
Long Island University, C.W. Post Campus	M
Massachusetts Institute of Technology	D
Middle Tennessee State University	M,O
Mississippi College	M,O
Montclair State University	M,O
The New School: A University	M,D
New York University	M,O
North Dakota State University	M,D
Northwestern University	M,O*
Nova Southeastern University	M,O*
Ohio University	M*
Queens College of the City University of New York	M
St. Edward's University	M,O
Southern University and Agricultural and Mechanical College	M
Stony Brook University, State University of New York	M,O
Syracuse University	M,D*
Texas A&M International University	M
Texas A&M University–Commerce	M
Towson University	M
University of Atlanta	P,M,D,O
University of California, Irvine	M,D*
University of California, Merced	M,D
University of California, Santa Barbara	D
University of California, Santa Cruz	D
University of Chicago	M,D
University of Colorado Denver	M
University of Florida	M*
University of Idaho	M,D
University of Illinois at Springfield	M
University of Lethbridge	M,D
The University of Manchester	M,D
University of Maryland, Baltimore County	D
University of Memphis	M
University of Michigan	D*
University of Michigan–Flint	M
The University of North Carolina at Charlotte	M
University of Northern Iowa	M
University of Regina	M
The University of Texas at Tyler	M
University of Washington	M,D*
University of Wisconsin–Madison	D*
Wilfrid Laurier University	M
Worcester Polytechnic Institute	M,D,O
Yale University	M,D,O*
York University	M*

SOCIAL SCIENCES EDUCATION

Institution	Degree
Acadia University	M
Alabama State University	M,O
American Public University System	M
Andrews University	M,D,O
Appalachian State University	M
Arcadia University	M,D,O*
Arkansas State University	M,O
Armstrong Atlantic State University	M
Asbury University	M

*M—master's degree; P—first professional degree; D—doctorate; O—other advanced degree; *—Close-Up and/or Display in one of the other books in this series*

Auburn University M,D,O
Averett University M
Belmont University M
Bennington College M
Bob Jones University P,M,D,O
Boston University M,D,O*
Bridgewater State University M
Brooklyn College of the City University of New York M,O
Brown University M
Buffalo State College, State University of New York M
California State University, Chico M
California State University, Fresno M
California State University, San Bernardino M,D
Cambridge College M,D,O
Campbell University M
Caribbean University M,D
Carthage College M,O
Chadron State College M,O
Chaminade University of Honolulu M
Chatham University M
Christopher Newport University M
The Citadel, The Military College of South Carolina M
City College of the City University of New York M,O
Clarion University of Pennsylvania M
Clemson University M
The College at Brockport, State University of New York M
College of St. Joseph M
The College of William and Mary M
The Colorado College M
Columbus State University M,O
Concord University M
Converse College M
Delta State University M
Drew University M
Duquesne University M
East Carolina University M
Eastern Kentucky University M
East Stroudsburg University of Pennsylvania M
Emporia State University M
Fayetteville State University M
Fitchburg State University M,O
Florida Agricultural and Mechanical University M
Florida International University M,D,O
Florida State University M
Framingham State University M
Georgia Southern University M
Georgia State University M,D,O
Grambling State University M
Harding University M,O
Hofstra University M,D,O
Hunter College of the City University of New York M
Indiana University Bloomington M,D,O*
Instituto Tecnologico de Santo Domingo M,O
Inter American University of Puerto Rico, Arecibo Campus M
Inter American University of Puerto Rico, Barranquitas Campus M
Inter American University of Puerto Rico, Metropolitan Campus M
Inter American University of Puerto Rico, Ponce Campus M
Iona College M
Ithaca College M
The Johns Hopkins University M,O
Kutztown University of Pennsylvania M,O
Lehman College of the City University of New York M
Le Moyne College M,O
Lewis University M
Louisiana Tech University M,D
Manhattanville College M*
Michigan State University M,D
Mills College M,D
Minnesota State University Mankato M
Mississippi College M,D,O
Missouri State University M
Montclair State University M,O
Morehead State University M,O
New York University M,D,O
North Carolina Agricultural and Technical State University M
North Carolina State University M*
North Dakota State University M,D,O
North Georgia College & State University M,O
Northwestern State University of Louisiana M
Northwest Missouri State University M
Nova Southeastern University M,O*
Occidental College M
Ohio University M,D*
Portland State University M
Purdue University M,D,O
Queens College of the City University of New York M,O
Quinnipiac University M
Rhode Island College M
Rider University O
Rivier College M
Rutgers, The State University of New Jersey, New Brunswick M,D*
Sage Graduate School M
St. John Fisher College M
Smith College M
South Carolina State University M,D,O
Southern Illinois University Edwardsville M
Southwestern Oklahoma State University M
Spring Hill College M
Stanford University M,D
State University of New York at Binghamton M
State University of New York at New Paltz M
State University of New York at Plattsburgh M
State University of New York College at Cortland M
State University of New York College at Potsdam M
Stony Brook University, State University of New York M,O
Syracuse University M*
Teachers College, Columbia University M,D
Texas A&M University–Commerce M
Texas State University–San Marcos D
Trinity (Washington) University M
Troy University M
Union Graduate College M,O
University at Buffalo, the State University of New York M,D,O*
University of Arkansas at Pine Bluff M
The University of British Columbia M,D
University of California, Santa Cruz M
University of Central Florida M,D
University of Cincinnati M,D,O
University of Connecticut M,D,O*
University of Florida M,D,O*
University of Georgia M,D,O
University of Indianapolis M
The University of Iowa M,D*
University of Maine M,O
University of Maryland, Baltimore County M
University of Michigan M,D*
University of Minnesota, Twin Cities Campus M
University of Missouri M,D,O*
The University of North Carolina at Chapel Hill M*
The University of North Carolina at Charlotte M
The University of North Carolina at Greensboro M,D,O
The University of North Carolina at Pembroke M
University of Oklahoma M,D,O*
University of Pittsburgh M,D*
University of Puerto Rico, Río Piedras M,D
University of St. Francis (IL) M
University of South Carolina M,D
University of Southern Mississippi M,D,O
University of South Florida M,D,O*
The University of Tennessee M,D,O
The University of Toledo M,D,O
University of Victoria M,D
University of Virginia M,D,O
University of Washington M,D*
The University of West Alabama M
University of West Georgia M,O
University of Wisconsin–River Falls M
Ursuline College M
Virginia Polytechnic Institute and State University D,O
Wayne State College M
Wayne State University M,D,O*
Webster University M,O
Western Oregon University M
Widener University M,D
Wilkes University M,D
William Carey University M,O
Worcester State University M

SOCIAL WORK

Abilene Christian University M
Adelphi University M,D*
Alabama Agricultural and Mechanical University M
Albany State University M
American Jewish University M
Andrews University M
Appalachian State University M
Arizona State University M,D,O
Arkansas State University M,O
Asbury University M
Augsburg College M
Aurora University M,D
Austin Peay State University M
Azusa Pacific University M
Barry University M,D*
Baylor University M*
Boise State University M
Boston College M,D*
Boston University M,D*
Bridgewater State University M
Brigham Young University M*
Bryn Mawr College M,D*
California State University, Bakersfield M
California State University, Chico M
California State University, Dominguez Hills M*
California State University, East Bay M
California State University, Fresno M
California State University, Fullerton M
California State University, Long Beach M
California State University, Los Angeles M*
California State University, Monterey Bay M
California State University, Northridge M
California State University, Sacramento M
California State University, San Bernardino M
California State University, Stanislaus M
California University of Pennsylvania M
Campbellsville University
Carleton University M
Case Western Reserve University M,D*
The Catholic University of America M,D
Chicago State University M
Clark Atlanta University M,D
Cleveland State University M
The College at Brockport, State University of New York M
Colorado State University M
Columbia University M,D*
Cornell University M,D*
Dalhousie University M
Delaware State University M
Dominican University M
East Carolina University M
Eastern Michigan University M
Eastern Washington University M
East Tennessee State University M
Edinboro University of Pennsylvania M
Fayetteville State University M
Florida Agricultural and Mechanical University M
Florida Atlantic University M
Florida Gulf Coast University M
Florida International University M,D
Florida State University M,D
Fordham University M,D
Gallaudet University M,D,O
George Mason University M*
Georgia State University M
Governors State University M
Graduate School and University Center of the City University of New York D
Grambling State University M
Grand Valley State University M
Gratz College M,O
Hawai'i Pacific University M*
Howard University M,D

Institution	Degrees
Humboldt State University	M
Hunter College of the City University of New York	M,D
Illinois State University	M
Indiana University East	M
Indiana University Northwest	M
Indiana University–Purdue University Indianapolis	M,D,O
Indiana University South Bend	M
Institute for Clinical Social Work	D
Inter American University of Puerto Rico, Metropolitan Campus	M
Jackson State University	M,D
Kean University	M
Kennesaw State University	M
Kutztown University of Pennsylvania	M
Lakehead University	M
Laurentian University	M
Loma Linda University	M,D
Long Island University, C.W. Post Campus	M
Louisiana State University and Agricultural and Mechanical College	M,D
Loyola University Chicago	M,D,O
Marywood University	M,D
McGill University	M,D,O
McMaster University	M
Memorial University of Newfoundland	M
Michigan State University	M,D
Middle Tennessee State University	M
Millersville University of Pennsylvania	M
Minnesota State University Mankato	M
Missouri State University	M
Molloy College	M
Monmouth University	M,O
Morgan State University	M,D
Nazareth College of Rochester	M
Newman University	M
New Mexico Highlands University	M
New Mexico State University	M
New York University	M,D
Norfolk State University	M,D
North Carolina Agricultural and Technical State University	M
North Carolina State University	M*
Northern Kentucky University	M
Northwest Nazarene University	M
The Ohio State University	M,D
The Ohio State University at Lima	M
The Ohio State University–Mansfield Campus	M
The Ohio State University–Newark Campus	M
Ohio University	M*
Our Lady of the Lake University of San Antonio	M
Phillips Theological Seminary	P,M,D
Pontifical Catholic University of Puerto Rico	M
Portland State University	M,D
Radford University	M
Rhode Island College	M
The Richard Stockton College of New Jersey	M
Roberts Wesleyan College	M
Rutgers, The State University of New Jersey, New Brunswick	M,D*
St. Ambrose University	M
St. Catherine University	M
St. Cloud State University	M
Saint Leo University	M
Saint Louis University	M
Salem State University	M
Salisbury University	M
San Diego State University	M
San Francisco State University	M
San Jose State University	M,O
Savannah State University	M
Shippensburg University of Pennsylvania	M,O
Simmons College	M,D,O
Smith College	M,D
Southern Adventist University	M
Southern Connecticut State University	M
Southern Illinois University Carbondale	M
Southern Illinois University Edwardsville	M
Southern University at New Orleans	M
Spalding University	M
Springfield College	M
State University of New York at Binghamton	M
Stephen F. Austin State University	M
Stony Brook University, State University of New York	M,D
Syracuse University	M*
Temple University	M*
Texas A&M University–Commerce	M
Texas State University–San Marcos	M
Thompson Rivers University	M
Troy University	M,O
Tulane University	M*
Universidad del Este	M
Université de Moncton	M
Université de Montréal	O
Université de Sherbrooke	M
Université du Québec à Montréal	M
Université du Québec en Abitibi-Témiscamingue	M
Université du Québec en Outaouais	M
Université Laval	M,D
University at Albany, State University of New York	M,D
University at Buffalo, the State University of New York	M,D*
The University of Akron	M
The University of Alabama	M,D
University of Alaska Anchorage	M,O
University of Arkansas	M
University of Arkansas at Little Rock	M
The University of British Columbia	M,D
University of Calgary	M,D,O
University of California, Berkeley	M,D*
University of California, Los Angeles	M,D*
University of Central Florida	M,O
University of Chicago	M,D
University of Cincinnati	M
University of Denver	M,D,O
University of Georgia	M,D,O
University of Guam	M
University of Hawaii at Manoa	M,D
University of Houston	M,D
University of Illinois at Chicago	M,D
University of Illinois at Urbana–Champaign	M,D
The University of Iowa	M,D*
The University of Kansas	M,D
University of Kentucky	M,D*
University of Louisville	M,D,O
University of Maine	M
The University of Manchester	M,D
University of Manitoba	M,D
University of Maryland, Baltimore	M,D
University of Maryland, College Park	
University of Michigan	M,D*
University of Minnesota, Duluth	M
University of Minnesota, Twin Cities Campus	M,D
University of Mississippi	M
University of Missouri	M*
University of Missouri–Kansas City	M*
University of Missouri–St. Louis	M,O
The University of Montana	M
University of Nebraska at Omaha	M
University of Nevada, Las Vegas	M,O
University of Nevada, Reno	M*
University of New England	M,O
University of New Hampshire	M,O
The University of North Carolina at Chapel Hill	M,D*
The University of North Carolina at Charlotte	M
The University of North Carolina at Greensboro	M
The University of North Carolina Wilmington	M
University of North Dakota	M
University of Northern British Columbia	M,D,O
University of Northern Iowa	M
University of Oklahoma	M*
University of Ottawa	M*
University of Pennsylvania	M,D*
University of Pittsburgh	M,D,O*
University of Puerto Rico, Río Piedras	M,D
University of Regina	M
University of St. Francis (IL)	M
University of St. Thomas (MN)	M
University of South Africa	M,D
University of South Carolina	M,D
University of Southern California	M,D*
University of Southern Indiana	M
University of Southern Maine	M
University of Southern Mississippi	M
University of South Florida	M,D*
The University of Tennessee	M,D
The University of Texas at Arlington	M,D
The University of Texas at Austin	M,D
The University of Texas at El Paso	M
The University of Texas at San Antonio	M*
The University of Texas–Pan American	M
The University of Toledo	M,O
University of Toronto	M,D
University of Utah	M,D*
University of Vermont	M
University of Victoria	M
University of Washington	M,D*
University of Washington, Tacoma	M
University of West Florida	M
University of Windsor	M
University of Wisconsin–Green Bay	M
University of Wisconsin–Madison	M,D*
University of Wisconsin–Milwaukee	M,D,O
University of Wisconsin–Oshkosh	M
University of Wyoming	M
Valdosta State University	M
Virginia Commonwealth University	M,D
Walden University	M,D
Walla Walla University	M
Washburn University	M
Washington University in St. Louis	M,D*
Wayne State University	M,D,O*
West Chester University of Pennsylvania	M
Western Carolina University	M
Western Kentucky University	M
Western Michigan University	M
Western New Mexico University	M
West Virginia University	M
Wheelock College	M
Wichita State University	M
Widener University	M,D
Wilfrid Laurier University	M,D
Winthrop University	M
Yeshiva University	M,D*
York University	M,D*

SOCIOLOGY

Institution	Degrees
Acadia University	M
American University	M,O
The American University in Cairo	M
American University of Beirut	M
Arizona State University	M,D
Arkansas State University	M,O
Auburn University	M
Ball State University	M
Baylor University	M,D*
Boston College	M,D*
Boston University	M,D*
Bowling Green State University	M,D*
Brandeis University	M,D
Brigham Young University	M*
Brock University	M
Brooklyn College of the City University of New York	M,D
Brown University	M,D
California State University, Bakersfield	M
California State University, Dominguez Hills	M,O*
California State University, Fullerton	M
California State University, Los Angeles	M*
California State University, Northridge	M
California State University, Sacramento	M
California State University, San Marcos	M
Carleton University	M,D
Case Western Reserve University	M,D*
The Catholic University of America	M
Central European University	M,D
City College of the City University of New York	M
Clark Atlanta University	M

*M—master's degree; P—first professional degree; D—doctorate; O—other advanced degree; *—Close-Up and/or Display in one of the other books in this series*

Institution	Degrees
Clemson University	M
Cleveland State University	M
Colorado State University	M,D
Columbia University	M,D*
Concordia University (Canada)	M
Cornell University	M,D*
Dalhousie University	M,D
DePaul University	M
Duke University	M,D*
East Carolina University	M
Eastern Michigan University	M
East Tennessee State University	M
Emory University	M,D*
Fayetteville State University	M
Florida Agricultural and Mechanical University	M
Florida Atlantic University	M
Florida International University	M,D
Florida State University	M,D
Fordham University	M
George Mason University	M,D*
The George Washington University	M
Georgia Southern University	M
Georgia State University	M,D
Graduate School and University Center of the City University of New York	D
Harvard University	D*
Hofstra University	M
Howard University	M,D
Humboldt State University	M
Hunter College of the City University of New York	M
Idaho State University	M
Illinois State University	M
Indiana University Bloomington	M,D*
Indiana University of Pennsylvania	M
Indiana University–Purdue University Fort Wayne	M
Indiana University–Purdue University Indianapolis	M
Iowa State University of Science and Technology	M,D*
Jackson State University	M
The Johns Hopkins University	M,D
Kansas State University	M,D*
Kean University	M
Kent State University	M,D*
Lakehead University	M
Laurentian University	M
Lehigh University	M
Lincoln University (MO)	M,O
Louisiana State University and Agricultural and Mechanical College	M,D
Loyola University Chicago	M,D
Marshall University	M
McGill University	M,D,O
McMaster University	M,D
Memorial University of Newfoundland	M,D
Michigan State University	M,D
Middle Tennessee State University	M
Minnesota State University Mankato	M
Mississippi State University	M,D
Montclair State University	M
Morehead State University	M
Morgan State University	M
The New School: A University	M,D
New York University	M,D
Norfolk State University	M
North Carolina Central University	M
North Carolina State University	M,D*
North Dakota State University	M,D
Northeastern University	M,D
Northern Arizona University	M
Northern Illinois University	M
Northwestern University	D*
The Ohio State University	M,D
Ohio University	M*
Oklahoma City University	M
Oklahoma State University	M,D*
Old Dominion University	M
Oxford Graduate School	M,D
Penn State University Park	M,D
Portland State University	M,D,O
Prairie View A&M University	M
Princeton University	D,O*
Purdue University	M,D
Queens College of the City University of New York	M
Queen's University at Kingston	M,D
Rice University	D
Roosevelt University	M
Rutgers, The State University of New Jersey, New Brunswick	M,D*
St. John's University (NY)	M
Sam Houston State University	M
San Diego State University	M
San Jose State University	M
Shippensburg University of Pennsylvania	M
Simon Fraser University	M,D
Southeastern Louisiana University	M
Southern Connecticut State University	M
Southern Illinois University Carbondale	M,D
Southern Illinois University Edwardsville	M
Stanford University	D
State University of New York at Binghamton	M,D
State University of New York Institute of Technology	M
Stony Brook University, State University of New York	M,D
Syracuse University	M,D*
Teachers College, Columbia University	M,D
Temple University	M,D*
Texas A&M International University	M
Texas A&M University	M,D
Texas A&M University–Commerce	M
Texas A&M University–Kingsville	M
Texas Southern University	M
Texas State University–San Marcos	M
Texas Tech University	M*
Texas Woman's University	M,D
Tulane University	M,D*
Université de Montréal	M,D
Université du Québec à Montréal	M,D
Université Laval	M,D
University at Albany, State University of New York	M,D,O
University at Buffalo, the State University of New York	M,D*
The University of Akron	M,D
The University of Alabama at Birmingham	M,D*
University of Alberta	M,D
The University of Arizona	D
University of Arkansas	M
The University of British Columbia	M,D
University of Calgary	M,D
University of California, Berkeley	D*
University of California, Davis	M,D
University of California, Irvine	M,D*
University of California, Los Angeles	M,D*
University of California, Riverside	M,D
University of California, San Diego	D*
University of California, San Francisco	D
University of California, Santa Barbara	M,D
University of California, Santa Cruz	D
University of Central Florida	M,D,O
University of Central Missouri	M
University of Chicago	D
University of Cincinnati	M,D
University of Colorado at Colorado Springs	M
University of Colorado Boulder	D*
University of Colorado Denver	M
University of Connecticut	M,D*
University of Delaware	M,D*
University of Florida	M,D*
University of Georgia	M,D
University of Guelph	M,D
University of Hawaii at Manoa	M,D
University of Houston	M
University of Houston–Clear Lake	M
University of Illinois at Chicago	M,D
University of Illinois at Urbana–Champaign	M,D
University of Indianapolis	M
The University of Iowa	M,D*
The University of Kansas	M,D
University of Kentucky	M,D*
University of Lethbridge	M,D
University of Louisville	M
The University of Manchester	M,D
University of Manitoba	M,D
University of Maryland, Baltimore County	M,O
University of Maryland, College Park	M,D
University of Massachusetts Amherst	M,D*
University of Massachusetts Boston	M
University of Massachusetts Lowell	M,O
University of Memphis	M
University of Miami	M,D*
University of Michigan	D,O*
University of Minnesota, Duluth	M
University of Minnesota, Twin Cities Campus	M,D
University of Mississippi	M
University of Missouri	M,D*
University of Missouri–Kansas City	M,D*
The University of Montana	M
University of Nebraska–Lincoln	M,D*
University of Nevada, Las Vegas	M,D
University of Nevada, Reno	M*
University of New Brunswick Fredericton	M,D
University of New Hampshire	M,D
University of New Mexico	M,D*
University of New Orleans	M
The University of North Carolina at Chapel Hill	M,D*
The University of North Carolina at Charlotte	M
The University of North Carolina at Greensboro	M
The University of North Carolina Wilmington	M
University of North Dakota	M
University of Northern Colorado	M
University of Northern Iowa	M
University of North Texas	M,D
University of Notre Dame	D*
University of Oklahoma	M,D*
University of Oregon	M,D
University of Ottawa	M*
University of Pennsylvania	M,D*
University of Pittsburgh	M,D*
University of Puerto Rico, Río Piedras	M
University of Regina	M
University of Saskatchewan	M,D
University of South Africa	M,D
University of South Alabama	M
University of South Carolina	M,D
University of Southern California	D*
University of South Florida	M,D*
The University of Tennessee	M,D
The University of Texas at Arlington	M
The University of Texas at Austin	M,D
The University of Texas at Dallas	M*
The University of Texas at El Paso	M,O
The University of Texas at San Antonio	M*
The University of Texas at Tyler	M
The University of Texas–Pan American	M
The University of Toledo	M
University of Toronto	M,D
University of Utah	M,D*
University of Victoria	M,D
University of Virginia	M,D
University of Washington	M,D*
University of Waterloo	M,D
The University of Western Ontario	M,D
University of West Florida	M
University of West Georgia	M
University of Windsor	M,D
University of Wisconsin–Madison	M,D*
University of Wisconsin–Milwaukee	M
University of Wyoming	M
Utah State University	M,D
Valdosta State University	M
Vanderbilt University	M,D*
Virginia Commonwealth University	M,O
Virginia Polytechnic Institute and State University	M,D,O
Washington State University	M,D
Wayne State University	M,D*
West Chester University of Pennsylvania	M,O
Western Illinois University	M
Western Kentucky University	M
Western Michigan University	M,D
West Virginia University	M
Wichita State University	M
Wilfrid Laurier University	M
William Paterson University of New Jersey	M
Yale University	D*
York University	M,D*

SOFTWARE ENGINEERING

Institution	Degrees
Andrews University	M
Arizona State University	M
Auburn University	M,D
Bowling Green State University	M*
Brandeis University	M,O
California State University, Fullerton	M
California State University, Northridge	M
California State University, Sacramento	M
Carnegie Mellon University	M,D*
Carroll University	M
Cleveland State University	M,D
Colorado Technical University Colorado Springs	M,D
Colorado Technical University Denver	M
Colorado Technical University Sioux Falls	M
Concordia University (Canada)	M,D,O
DePaul University	M,D
Drexel University	M,D,O*
Embry-Riddle Aeronautical University–Daytona	M
Fairfield University	M
Florida Agricultural and Mechanical University	M
Florida Institute of Technology	M,D
Gannon University	M
George Mason University	M,D,O*
Grand Valley State University	M
Hawai'i Pacific University	M*
Illinois Institute of Technology	M,D
Instituto Tecnologico de Santo Domingo	M,O
International Technological University	M,D
Jacksonville State University	M
Kansas State University	M,D*
Loyola University Chicago	M
Loyola University Maryland	M
Marist College	M,O
McMaster University	M,D
Mercer University	M
Miami University	M,O
Monmouth University	M,O
National University	M
Naval Postgraduate School	M,D
New Jersey Institute of Technology	M,D
North Dakota State University	M,D,O
Northern Kentucky University	M,O
Northwestern University	M*
Oakland University	M
Pace University	M,D,O
Polytechnic Institute of NYU	O
Portland State University	M,D
Regis University	M,O
Rochester Institute of Technology	M
Rose-Hulman Institute of Technology	M
Royal Military College of Canada	M,D
St. Mary's University (United States)	M
San Francisco State University	M
San Jose State University	M
Santa Clara University	M,D,O
Seattle University	M
Southern Methodist University	M,D
Southern Polytechnic State University	M,O
Stevens Institute of Technology	M,D,O
Stony Brook University, State University of New York	M,D,O
Stratford University	M
Strayer University	M
Texas State University–San Marcos	M
Texas Tech University	M,D*
Towson University	M,D,O
Université du Québec en Outaouais	O
Université Laval	O
The University of Alabama in Huntsville	M,D,O
University of Alaska Fairbanks	M
The University of British Columbia	M
University of Calgary	M,D
University of Colorado at Colorado Springs	M
University of Connecticut	M,D*
University of Denver	M,O
University of Detroit Mercy	M
University of Houston–Clear Lake	M
University of Management and Technology	M,O
University of Massachusetts Dartmouth	M,O
University of Michigan–Dearborn	M
University of Missouri–Kansas City	M,D*
University of New Hampshire	M,D,O
University of New Haven	M,O
University of North Florida	M
University of Regina	M,D
University of St. Thomas (MN)	M,O
University of St. Thomas (MN)	M,O
The University of Scranton	M
University of South Carolina	M,D
University of Southern California	M,D*
The University of Texas at Arlington	M,D
The University of Texas at Dallas	M,D*
The University of Texas at San Antonio	M,D*
University of Washington, Bothell	M
University of Washington, Tacoma	M
University of Waterloo	M,D
University of West Florida	M
University of West Georgia	M,O
University of Wisconsin–La Crosse	M
Villanova University	M
Virginia Polytechnic Institute and State University	M,O
Walden University	M,D
West Virginia University	M
Widener University	M
Winthrop University	M,O

SPANISH

Institution	Degrees
American University	M,O
Arizona State University	M,D
Arkansas Tech University	M
Asbury University	M
Auburn University	M
Baylor University	M*
Bennington College	M
Boston College	M,D*
Boston University	M,D,O*
Bowling Green State University	M*
Brigham Young University	M*
Brooklyn College of the City University of New York	M,D
California State University, Bakersfield	M
California State University, Fresno	M
California State University, Fullerton	M
California State University, Long Beach	M
California State University, Los Angeles	M*
California State University, Northridge	M
California State University, Sacramento	M
California State University, San Bernardino	M
California State University, San Marcos	M
The Catholic University of America	M,D
Central Connecticut State University	M,O
Central Michigan University	M
City College of the City University of New York	M
Cleveland State University	M
Columbia University	M,D*
Cornell University	D*
Drew University	M
Duke University	D*
Eastern Michigan University	M,O
Emory University	D,O*
Florida Atlantic University	M
Florida International University	M,D
Florida State University	M,D
Framingham State University	M
Georgetown University	M,D
Georgia Southern University	M
Georgia State University	M,O
Harvard University	M,D*
Hofstra University	M,O
Howard University	M
Hunter College of the City University of New York	M
Illinois State University	M
Indiana University Bloomington	M,D*
Inter American University of Puerto Rico, Metropolitan Campus	M
Inter American University of Puerto Rico, Ponce Campus	M
Iona College	M
The Johns Hopkins University	D
Kansas State University	M*
Kean University	M
Kent State University	M,D*
Lehman College of the City University of New York	M
Long Island University, C.W. Post Campus	M
Loyola University Chicago	M
Marquette University	M
Marshall University	M
Michigan State University	M,D
Middlebury College	M,D
Millersville University of Pennsylvania	M
Minnesota State University Mankato	M
Mississippi State University	M
Missouri State University	M
Montclair State University	M,O
New Mexico State University	M
New York University	M,D
North Carolina State University	M*
Northern Arizona University	M
Northern Illinois University	M
Nova Southeastern University	M,O*
The Ohio State University	M,D
Ohio University	M*
Penn State University Park	M,D
Pontifical Catholic University of Puerto Rico	M,O
Portland State University	M
Princeton University	D*
Purdue University	M,D
Queens College of the City University of New York	M
Queen's University at Kingston	M
Rider University	O
Roosevelt University	M
Rutgers, The State University of New Jersey, New Brunswick	M,D*
St. John's University (NY)	M
Saint Louis University	M
Saint Louis University–Madrid Campus	M
Salem State University	M
San Diego State University	M
San Francisco State University	M
San Jose State University	M
Simmons College	M
Stanford University	M,D
State University of New York at Binghamton	M,O
State University of New York at New Paltz	M
Syracuse University	M*
Temple University	M,D*
Texas A&M International University	M,D
Texas A&M University	M,D
Texas A&M University–Commerce	M,D
Texas A&M University–Kingsville	M
Texas State University–San Marcos	M
Texas Tech University	M,D*
Tulane University	M,D*
Universidad Autonoma de Guadalajara	M,D
Université de Montréal	M
Université Laval	M,D
University at Albany, State University of New York	M,D
University at Buffalo, the State University of New York	M,D,O*
The University of Akron	M
The University of Alabama	M,D
The University of Arizona	M,D
University of Arkansas	M
University of California, Berkeley	D*
University of California, Davis	M,D
University of California, Irvine	M,D*
University of California, Los Angeles	M*
University of California, Riverside	M,D
University of California, San Diego	M*
University of California, Santa Barbara	M,D
University of Central Florida	M
University of Chicago	M,D
University of Cincinnati	M,D
University of Colorado Boulder	M,D*

*M—master's degree; P—first professional degree; D—doctorate; O—other advanced degree; *—Close-Up and/or Display in one of the other books in this series*

University of Colorado Denver M
University of Connecticut M,D*
University of Delaware M*
University of Florida M,D*
University of Georgia M
University of Hawaii at Manoa M
University of Houston M,D
University of Illinois at Chicago M,D
University of Illinois at Urbana–Champaign M,D
The University of Iowa M,D*
The University of Kansas M,D
University of Lethbridge M,D
University of Louisville M
The University of Manchester M,D
University of Maryland, College Park M,D
University of Massachusetts Amherst M,D*
University of Memphis M
University of Miami M,D*
University of Michigan D*
University of Minnesota, Twin Cities Campus M,D
University of Mississippi M
University of Missouri M,D*
The University of Montana M
University of Nebraska–Lincoln M,D*
University of Nevada, Reno M*
University of New Hampshire M
University of New Mexico M,D*
The University of North Carolina at Chapel Hill M,D*
The University of North Carolina at Charlotte M
The University of North Carolina at Greensboro M,O
The University of North Carolina Wilmington M,O
University of Northern Colorado M
University of Northern Iowa M
University of North Texas M
University of Notre Dame M*
University of Oklahoma M,D*
University of Oregon M
University of Ottawa M,D*
University of Pennsylvania M,D*
University of Pittsburgh M,D*
University of Rhode Island M
University of Rochester M
University of South Africa M,D
University of South Carolina M,D
University of Southern California D*
University of South Florida M*
The University of Tennessee M,D
The University of Texas at Arlington M
The University of Texas at Austin M,D
The University of Texas at Brownsville M
The University of Texas at El Paso M,O
The University of Texas at San Antonio M*
The University of Texas of the Permian Basin M
The University of Texas–Pan American M
The University of Toledo M
University of Toronto M,D
University of Utah M,D*
University of Virginia M,D
University of Washington M*
The University of Western Ontario M,D
University of West Georgia M,O
University of Wisconsin–Madison M,D*
University of Wisconsin–Milwaukee M,O
University of Wyoming M
Vanderbilt University M,D*
Washington State University M
Washington University in St. Louis M,D*
Wayne State University M,D*
West Chester University of Pennsylvania M,O
Western Kentucky University M
Western Michigan University M,D
West Virginia University M
Wichita State University M
Winthrop University M
Worcester State University M
Yale University D*

SPECIAL EDUCATION

Acadia University M
Adams State College M
Adelphi University M,O*
Alabama Agricultural and Mechanical University M,O
Alabama State University M
Albany State University M
Albright College M
Alcorn State University M,O
Alliant International University–Irvine M,O
Alliant International University–San Francisco M,O
American International College M,D,O
American University M
American University of Puerto Rico M,O
Andrews University M,D,O
Angelo State University M
Appalachian State University M
Arcadia University M,D,O*
Arizona State University M,O
Arkansas State University M,D,O
Armstrong Atlantic State University M
Asbury University M
Ashland University M
Assumption College M,O
Auburn University M,D
Auburn University Montgomery M,O
Augusta State University M,O
Aurora University M,D
Austin Peay State University M,O
Averett University M
Azusa Pacific University M
Baldwin-Wallace College M
Ball State University M,D,O
Bank Street College of Education M
Barry University M,D,O*
Bayamón Central University M,O
Bellarmine University M,D,O
Belmont University M
Bemidji State University M
Benedictine University M
Bethel University (MN) M,D,O
Bloomsburg University of Pennsylvania M
Bob Jones University P,M,D,O
Boise State University M
Boston College M,O*
Boston University M,D,O*
Bowie State University M
Bowling Green State University M*
Brandon University M,O
Brenau University M,O
Bridgewater State University M
Brigham Young University M,D,O*
Brooklyn College of the City University of New York M
Buffalo State College, State University of New York M
Butler University M
Caldwell College M
California Baptist University M
California Lutheran University M,D
California State University, Bakersfield M
California State University, Chico M
California State University, Dominguez Hills M*
California State University, East Bay M
California State University, Fresno M
California State University, Fullerton M
California State University, Long Beach M
California State University, Los Angeles M,D*
California State University, Northridge M
California State University, Sacramento M
California State University, San Bernardino M
California State University, Stanislaus M
California University of Pennsylvania M
Calvin College M
Cambridge College M,D,O
Campbellsville University M
Canisius College M,O
Cardinal Stritch University M
Caribbean University M,D
Carlos Albizu University, Miami Campus M,D
Carlow University M
Castleton State College M,O
The Catholic University of America M,D,O
Centenary College M
Central Connecticut State University M,O
Central Michigan University M,O
Central Washington University M
Chapman University M,O
Chatham University M
Cheyney University of Pennsylvania M
Chicago State University M
City College of the City University of New York M,O
City University of Seattle M,O
Claremont Graduate University M,D,O
Clarion University of Pennsylvania M
Clark Atlanta University M
Clarke University M
Clemson University M
Cleveland State University M
College of Charleston M
The College of New Jersey M,O
The College of New Rochelle M
College of St. Joseph M
The College of Saint Rose M,O
College of Staten Island of the City University of New York M
The College of William and Mary M
Colorado Christian University M
Colorado State University–Pueblo M
Columbia International University M,D,O
Columbus State University M,O
Concordia University, St. Paul M,O
Concordia University Wisconsin M
Converse College M
Coppin State University M
Creighton University M
Curry College M,O
Daemen College M
Defiance College M
Delaware State University M
Delta State University M
DePaul University M,D
Dominican College M
Dominican University M
Dominican University of California O
Dowling College M,D,O
Drexel University M*
Drury University M
Duquesne University M
D'Youville College M,O*
East Carolina University M
Eastern Illinois University M
Eastern Kentucky University M
Eastern Michigan University M,O
Eastern Nazarene College M,O
Eastern New Mexico University M
Eastern Washington University M
East Stroudsburg University of Pennsylvania M
East Tennessee State University M,D
Edgewood College M,D,O
Edinboro University of Pennsylvania M,O
Elmhurst College M
Elms College M,O
Elon University M
Emporia State University M
Endicott College M
Fairfield University M,O
Fairleigh Dickinson University, Metropolitan Campus M
Fairmont State University M
Ferris State University M
Fitchburg State University M
Florida Atlantic University M,D
Florida Gulf Coast University M
Florida International University M,D,O
Florida Memorial University M
Florida State University M,D,O
Fontbonne University M
Fordham University M,D,O
Fort Hays State University M
Framingham State University M
Francis Marion University M
Franklin Pierce University M,D,O
Freed-Hardeman University M,O
Fresno Pacific University M
Frostburg State University M
Furman University M,O
Gallaudet University M,D,O
Geneva College M
George Mason University M*
Georgetown College M
The George Washington University M,D,O
Georgia College & State University M,O
Georgia Southern University M
Georgia Southwestern State University M,O
Georgia State University M,D
Gonzaga University M

Institution	Degrees
Governors State University	M
Graceland University (IA)	M
Grand Canyon University	M
Grand Valley State University	M
Greensboro College	M
Gwynedd-Mercy College	M
Hampton University	M
Harding University	M,O
Hebrew College	M,O
Henderson State University	M
Heritage University	M
High Point University	M
Hofstra University	M,D,O
Holy Family University	M*
Holy Names University	M,O
Hood College	M,O
Howard University	M
Hunter College of the City University of New York	M
Idaho State University	M,D,O
Illinois State University	M,D
Immaculata University	M,D,O
Indiana University Bloomington	M,D,O*
Indiana University of Pennsylvania	M
Indiana University–Purdue University Fort Wayne	M,O
Indiana University–Purdue University Indianapolis	M,O
Indiana University South Bend	M
Inter American University of Puerto Rico, Barranquitas Campus	M
Inter American University of Puerto Rico, Metropolitan Campus	M
Inter American University of Puerto Rico, San Germán Campus	M
Iowa State University of Science and Technology	M,D*
Jackson State University	M,O
Jacksonville State University	M
James Madison University	M
The Johns Hopkins University	M,D,O
Johnson & Wales University	M
Johnson State College	M
Kansas State University	M,D*
Kaplan University, Davenport Campus	M
Kean University	M
Keene State College	M,O
Kennesaw State University	M
Kent State University	M,D,O*
Kentucky State University	M
Kutztown University of Pennsylvania	M,O
Lamar University	M,D
Lancaster Bible College	M,D
Lasell College	M
Lee University	M,O
Lehigh University	M,D,O
Lehman College of the City University of New York	M
Le Moyne College	M,O
Lesley University	M,D,O
Lewis & Clark College	M
Lewis University	M
Liberty University	M,D,O
Lincoln University (MO)	M,O
Lipscomb University	M,D
Long Island University at Riverhead	M
Long Island University, Brentwood Campus	M
Long Island University, Brooklyn Campus	M
Long Island University, C.W. Post Campus	M
Long Island University, Rockland Graduate Campus	M
Long Island University, Westchester Graduate Campus	M,O
Longwood University	M
Loras College	M
Louisiana Tech University	M,D
Loyola Marymount University	M
Loyola University Chicago	M,O
Loyola University Maryland	M,O
Lynchburg College	M
Lyndon State College	M
Lynn University	M,D
Madonna University	M
Malone University	M
Manhattan College	M,O
Manhattanville College	M*
Marshall University	M
Martin Luther College	M
Marymount University	M
Marywood University	M
Massachusetts College of Liberal Arts	M
McDaniel College	M
McKendree University	M
McNeese State University	M,O
Medaille College	M
Mercy College	M,O
Mercyhurst College	M,O
Merrimack College	M,O
Miami University	M,O
Michigan State University	M,D,O
MidAmerica Nazarene University	M
Middle Tennessee State University	M,O
Midwestern State University	M
Millersville University of Pennsylvania	M
Minnesota State University Mankato	M,O
Minnesota State University Moorhead	M
Minot State University	M
Mississippi College	M,D,O
Mississippi State University	M,D,O
Missouri State University	M,D
Missouri Western State University	M
Monmouth University	M,O
Montana State University Billings	M
Montclair State University	M,O
Morehead State University	M,O
Morningside College	M
Mount Mercy University	M
Mount Saint Mary College	M,O
Mount St. Mary's College	M
Mount Saint Vincent University	M
Murray State University	M
National-Louis University	M,D,O
National University	M
New England College	M
New Jersey City University	M
New Mexico Highlands University	M
New Mexico State University	M,D
New York University	M,D
Niagara University	M,O
Norfolk State University	M
North Carolina Central University	M
North Carolina State University	M*
Northeastern Illinois University	M
Northern Arizona University	M,D,O
Northern Illinois University	M,D
Northern Kentucky University	M,O
Northern Michigan University	M
North Georgia College & State University	M,O
Northwestern State University of Louisiana	M,O
Northwestern University	M,D*
Northwest Missouri State University	M
Northwest Nazarene University	M
Notre Dame College (OH)	M,O
Notre Dame de Namur University	M,O
Nova Southeastern University	M,D,O*
Nyack College	M
Oakland University	M,O
Ohio University	M,D*
Old Dominion University	M,D
Ottawa University	M
Our Lady of the Lake University of San Antonio	M
Pace University	M,O
Pacific University	M
Park University	M
Penn State University Park	M,D
Piedmont College	M,D,O
Pittsburg State University	M
Plymouth State University	M,D,O
Portland State University	M,D
Prairie View A&M University	M
Pratt Institute	M*
Prescott College	M,D
Providence College	M
Purdue University	M,D,O
Purdue University Calumet	M
Queens College of the City University of New York	M
Quincy University	M
Radford University	M
Randolph College	M
Regent University	M,D,O
Regis College (MA)	M
Regis University	M,O
Rhode Island College	M,O
Rider University	M,O
Rivier College	M,D,O
Roberts Wesleyan College	M,O
Rochester Institute of Technology	M
Rockford College	M,O
Roosevelt University	M
Rowan University	M
Rutgers, The State University of New Jersey, New Brunswick	M,D*
Sage Graduate School	M
Saginaw Valley State University	M
St. Ambrose University	M
St. Bonaventure University	M
St. Cloud State University	M
St. Edward's University	M,O
St. John Fisher College	M,O
St. John's University (NY)	M
Saint Joseph College	M
St. Joseph's College, Long Island Campus	M
St. Joseph's College, New York	M*
Saint Joseph's University	M,D
Saint Louis University	M,D
Saint Martin's University	M
Saint Mary's College of California	M
Saint Mary's University of Minnesota	M,O
Saint Michael's College	M,O
Saint Peter's College	M,O
St. Thomas Aquinas College	M,O
St. Thomas University	M,D,O
Saint Vincent College	M
Saint Xavier University	M,O
Salem College	M
Salem State University	M
Salus University	M,O
Sam Houston State University	M,D
San Diego State University	M
San Francisco State University	M,D,O
San Jose State University	M
Seattle University	M,O
Seton Hill University	M,O
Shenandoah University	M,D,O
Shippensburg University of Pennsylvania	M
Silver Lake College	M
Simmons College	M,D,O
Slippery Rock University of Pennsylvania	M
Smith College	M
Sonoma State University	M,D
South Carolina State University	M,D,O
Southeastern Louisiana University	M
Southeastern Oklahoma State University	M
Southeast Missouri State University	M
Southern Connecticut State University	M,O
Southern Illinois University Carbondale	M
Southern Illinois University Edwardsville	M,O
Southern New Hampshire University	M,O
Southern Oregon University	M
Southern University and Agricultural and Mechanical College	M,D
Southwestern College (KS)	M
Southwestern Oklahoma State University	M
Southwest Minnesota State University	M
Spalding University	M
Spring Arbor University	M
Springfield College	M
State University of New York at Binghamton	M
State University of New York at New Paltz	M
State University of New York at Oswego	M
State University of New York at Plattsburgh	M
State University of New York College at Cortland	M
State University of New York College at Oneonta	M,O
State University of New York College at Potsdam	M
Stephen F. Austin State University	M
Syracuse University	M,D*
Tarleton State University	M,O
Teachers College, Columbia University	M,D,O
Temple University	M,D*
Tennessee State University	M,D
Tennessee Technological University	M,O
Texas A&M International University	M
Texas A&M University	M,D
Texas A&M University–Commerce	M,D
Texas A&M University–Corpus Christi	M
Texas A&M University–Kingsville	M
Texas A&M University–San Antonio	M
Texas A&M University–Texarkana	M
Texas Christian University	M

*M—master's degree; P—first professional degree; D—doctorate; O—other advanced degree; *—Close-Up and/or Display in one of the other books in this series*

Texas State University–San Marcos	M
Texas Tech University	M,D*
Texas Woman's University	M,D
Towson University	M,O
Trinity Baptist College	M
Trinity (Washington) University	M
Union College (KY)	M
Universidad del Este	M
Universidad del Turabo	M
Universidad Iberoamericana	P,M
Universidad Metropolitana	M
Université de Sherbrooke	M,O
University at Albany, State University of New York	M
University at Buffalo, the State University of New York	M,D,O*
The University of Akron	M
The University of Alabama	M,D,O
The University of Alabama at Birmingham	M*
University of Alaska Anchorage	M,O
University of Alaska Fairbanks	M,D,O
University of Alberta	M,D
The University of Arizona	M,D,O
University of Arkansas	M
University of Arkansas at Little Rock	M,O
The University of British Columbia	M,D,O
University of Calgary	M,D
University of California, Berkeley	M,D*
University of California, Los Angeles	D*
University of California, Riverside	M,D
University of California, Santa Barbara	M,D
University of Central Arkansas	M
University of Central Florida	M,D,O
University of Central Missouri	M,D,O
University of Central Oklahoma	M
University of Cincinnati	M,D
University of Colorado at Colorado Springs	M,D
University of Colorado Denver	M
University of Connecticut	M,D,O*
University of Dayton	M
University of Detroit Mercy	M
The University of Findlay	M
University of Florida	M,D,O*
University of Georgia	M,D,O
University of Guam	M
University of Hawaii at Manoa	M,D
University of Houston	M,D
University of Houston–Victoria	M
University of Idaho	M
University of Illinois at Chicago	M,D
University of Illinois at Urbana–Champaign	M,D,O
The University of Iowa	M,D*
The University of Kansas	M,D
University of Kentucky	M,D*
University of La Verne	M
University of Louisville	M,D
University of Maine	M,O
University of Manitoba	M
University of Mary	M
University of Maryland, College Park	M,D,O
University of Maryland Eastern Shore	M
University of Massachusetts Amherst	M,D,O*
University of Massachusetts Boston	M
University of Memphis	M,D
University of Miami	M,D,O*
University of Michigan–Dearborn	M,D
University of Michigan–Flint	M
University of Minnesota, Twin Cities Campus	M,D,O
University of Missouri	M,D*
University of Missouri–Kansas City	M,D,O*
University of Missouri–St. Louis	M,O
University of Nebraska at Kearney	M
University of Nebraska at Omaha	M
University of Nebraska–Lincoln	M,D,O*
University of Nevada, Las Vegas	M,D,O
University of Nevada, Reno	M,D*
University of New England	M,O
University of New Hampshire	M,O
University of New Mexico	M,D,O*
University of New Orleans	M,D,O
University of North Alabama	M
The University of North Carolina at Charlotte	M,D
The University of North Carolina at Greensboro	M,D,O
University of North Dakota	M,D
University of Northern Colorado	M,D
University of Northern Iowa	M,D
University of North Florida	M
University of North Texas	M,D,O
University of Oklahoma	M,D*
University of Oklahoma Health Sciences Center	M,D,O
University of Phoenix	M
University of Phoenix–Hawaii Campus	M
University of Phoenix–Metro Detroit Campus	M
University of Phoenix–Omaha Campus	M
University of Phoenix–Phoenix Campus	M
University of Phoenix–Southern Arizona Campus	M,O
University of Phoenix–Southern California Campus	M
University of Phoenix–Utah Campus	M
University of Phoenix–Washington D.C. Campus	M,D,O
University of Pittsburgh	M,D*
University of Puerto Rico, Medical Sciences Campus	O
University of Puerto Rico, Río Piedras	M
University of Rhode Island	M,D
University of Rio Grande	M
University of St. Francis (IL)	M
University of Saint Francis (IN)	M
University of Saint Mary	M
University of St. Thomas (MN)	M,O
University of San Diego	M
University of Saskatchewan	M,D,O
The University of Scranton	M
University of South Alabama	M,O
University of South Carolina	M,D
University of South Carolina Upstate	M
The University of South Dakota	M
University of Southern Maine	M,O
University of Southern Mississippi	M,D,O
University of South Florida	M,D*
The University of Tennessee	M,D,O
The University of Tennessee at Chattanooga	M,O
The University of Texas at Austin	M,D
The University of Texas at Brownsville	M
The University of Texas at El Paso	M
The University of Texas at San Antonio	M,D*
The University of Texas at Tyler	M
The University of Texas of the Permian Basin	M
The University of Texas–Pan American	M
University of the Cumberlands	M,D,O
University of the District of Columbia	M
University of the Incarnate Word	M,D
University of the Pacific	M,D
University of the Southwest	M
The University of Toledo	M,D,O
University of Utah	M,D*
University of Vermont	M
University of Victoria	M,D
University of Virginia	M,D,O
University of Washington	M,D*
University of Washington, Tacoma	M
The University of West Alabama	M
The University of Western Ontario	M
University of West Florida	M,D
University of West Georgia	M,D,O
University of Wisconsin–Eau Claire	M
University of Wisconsin–La Crosse	M
University of Wisconsin–Madison	M,D*
University of Wisconsin–Milwaukee	M,D,O
University of Wisconsin–Oshkosh	M
University of Wisconsin–Stevens Point	M
University of Wisconsin–Superior	M
University of Wisconsin–Whitewater	M*
University of Wyoming	M,D,O
Ursuline College	M
Utah State University	M,D,O
Valdosta State University	M,O
Vanderbilt University	M,D*
Virginia Commonwealth University	M,D,O
Walden University	M,D,O
Walla Walla University	M
Washburn University	M
Washington University in St. Louis	M,D*
Wayland Baptist University	M
Waynesburg University	M,D
Wayne State College	M
Wayne State University	M,D,O*
Webster University	M,O
West Chester University of Pennsylvania	M,O
Western Connecticut State University	M
Western Illinois University	M
Western Kentucky University	M,O
Western Michigan University	M,D
Western New Mexico University	M
Western Oregon University	M
Westfield State University	M
West Texas A&M University	M
West Virginia University	M,D
Wheelock College	M
Whitworth University	M
Wichita State University	M
Widener University	M,D
Wilkes University	M,D
Willamette University	M
William Carey University	M,O
William Paterson University of New Jersey	M
William Woods University	M,O
Wilmington College	M
Wilmington University	M
Winona State University	M
Winthrop University	M
Worcester State University	M
Wright State University	M
Xavier University	M
Youngstown State University	M

SPEECH AND INTERPERSONAL COMMUNICATION

Arkansas State University	M,O
Ball State University	M
Bob Jones University	P,M,D,O
Bowling Green State University	M,D*
Brooklyn College of the City University of New York	M,D
California State University, Fullerton	M
California State University, Los Angeles	M*
California State University, Northridge	M
Central Michigan University	M
Colorado State University	M
Eastern Illinois University	M
Florida State University	M,D
Georgia State University	M,D
Hofstra University	M
Idaho State University	M
Indiana University Bloomington	M,D*
Kansas State University	M*
Louisiana Tech University	M
Marquette University	M,O
New York University	M,D
North Dakota State University	M,D
Northeastern Illinois University	M
Northeastern University	D
Northwestern University	M,D*
Ohio University	M,D*
Old Dominion University	M
Portland State University	M,O
Rensselaer Polytechnic Institute	M,D
Sam Houston State University	M,D
San Francisco State University	M
San Jose State University	M
Seton Hall University	M
Southern Illinois University Carbondale	M,D
Southern Illinois University Edwardsville	M
Texas A&M University–Commerce	M
Texas Christian University	M
The University of Alabama	M
University of Arkansas at Little Rock	M
University of California, Santa Barbara	D

University of Central Missouri M
University of Denver M,D
University of Georgia M,D
University of Hawaii at Manoa M
University of Houston M
University of Maryland, College Park M,D
University of Nebraska–Lincoln M,D*
University of Nevada, Reno M*
University of South Carolina M,D
University of Southern California M,D*
University of Southern Mississippi M,D
The University of Tennessee M,D
University of Wisconsin–Madison M,D*
University of Wisconsin–Stevens Point M
University of Wisconsin–Superior M
Wake Forest University M
Washington University in St. Louis M,D*
Wayne State University M,D*

SPORT PSYCHOLOGY

Adler School of Professional Psychology M,D,O
Argosy University, Atlanta M,D,O*
Argosy University, Inland Empire M,D*
Argosy University, Orange County M*
Argosy University, Phoenix M,D*
Argosy University, San Francisco Bay Area M,D*
Barry University M*
Boston University M,D,O*
California State University, East Bay M
California State University, Fresno M
California State University, Long Beach M
California University of Pennsylvania M
Capella University M,D,O
Chatham University M,D
Cleveland State University M
Eastern Washington University M
Florida State University M,D,O
John F. Kennedy University M
Memorial University of Newfoundland M
Purdue University M,D
Queen's University at Kingston M,D
Southern Connecticut State University M
Springfield College M,D,O
University of Denver M,D
The University of Iowa M,D*
University of Rhode Island M
The University of Texas at Austin M,D
West Virginia University M,D

SPORTS MANAGEMENT

American Public University System M
Angelo State University M
Arkansas State University M,O
Ashland University M
Augustana College M
Barry University M*
Belmont University M
Bowling Green State University M*
Brooklyn College of the City University of New York M
California Baptist University M
California State University, Long Beach M
California University of Pennsylvania M
Canisius College M
Cardinal Stritch University M
Central Michigan University M,O
Cleveland State University M
The College at Brockport, State University of New York M
Columbia University M*
Concordia University (CA) M
Concordia University (Canada) M,D,O
Concordia University, St. Paul M,O
Dowling College M,O
Drexel University M*
Duquesne University M
Eastern Kentucky University M
Eastern Michigan University M
Eastern New Mexico University M
Eastern Washington University M
East Stroudsburg University of Pennsylvania M
East Tennessee State University M,D
Endicott College M
Fairleigh Dickinson University, College at Florham M
Fairleigh Dickinson University, Metropolitan Campus M
Florida International University M,D,O
Florida State University M,D
Franklin Pierce University M,D,O
George Mason University M*
Georgetown University M,D
The George Washington University M,O
Georgia Southern University M
Georgia State University M
Gonzaga University M
Grambling State University M
Henderson State University M
Hofstra University M,O
Holy Names University M
Howard University M
Indiana State University M
Indiana University Bloomington M,D,O*
Indiana University of Pennsylvania M
Ithaca College M
Kansas Wesleyan University M
Kent State University M*
Lasell College M,O
Liberty University M,D,O
Lindenwood University M
Lipscomb University M
Lynn University M
Manhattanville College M*
Marquette University M,O
Marshall University M
Maryville University of Saint Louis M,O
Millersville University of Pennsylvania M
Mississippi State University M
Missouri State University M
Montana State University Billings M
Montclair State University M,O
Morehead State University M
Neumann University M
New England College M
New Mexico Highlands University M
New York University M,O
Nichols College M
North Carolina Central University M
North Carolina State University M,D*
North Central College M
North Dakota State University M
Northern Illinois University M
Northwestern University M*
Nova Southeastern University M,O*
Ohio University M*
Old Dominion University M
St. Cloud State University M
St. Edward's University M,O
St. John's University (NY) M
Saint Leo University M
Saint Mary's College of California M
St. Thomas University M,O
San Diego State University M
Seattle University M
Seton Hall University M
Southeast Missouri State University M
Southern New Hampshire University M,D,O
Springfield College M,D,O
State University of New York College at Cortland M
Temple University M,D*
Texas A&M University M,D
Texas Woman's University M,D
Tiffin University M
Troy University M
United States Sports Academy M,D
The University of Alabama M,D
University of Alberta M
University of Central Florida M
University of Dallas M
University of Florida M,D*
The University of Iowa M*
University of Louisville M
University of Massachusetts Amherst M,D*
University of Miami M*
University of Michigan M,D*
University of Minnesota, Twin Cities Campus M,D,O
University of Nevada, Las Vegas M,D
University of New Brunswick Fredericton M
University of New Haven M,O
The University of North Carolina at Chapel Hill M*
The University of North Carolina at Charlotte M,D,O
University of Northern Colorado M,D
University of North Florida M,D
University of San Francisco M
University of South Carolina M
University of Southern Maine M,O
University of Southern Mississippi M,D
The University of Tennessee M,D
University of the Incarnate Word M,O
University of the Southwest M
University of West Georgia M,O
Valparaiso University M
Washington State University M,D,O
Wayne State College M
Wayne State University M*
Webber International University M
West Chester University of Pennsylvania M,O
Western Illinois University M
Western Kentucky University M
Western Michigan University M
Western New England University M
West Virginia University M,D
Wichita State University M
Wingate University M
Winona State University M,O
Xavier University M
Yorktown University M

STATISTICS

Acadia University M
American University M,O
American University of Beirut M
Arizona State University M,D,O
Auburn University M,D
Ball State University M
Baylor University M,D*
Bernard M. Baruch College of the City University of New York M
Bowling Green State University M,D*
Brigham Young University M*
Brock University M
California State University, East Bay M
California State University, Sacramento M
Carnegie Mellon University M,D*
Case Western Reserve University M,D*
Central Connecticut State University M,O
Claremont Graduate University M,D
Clemson University M,D
Colorado State University M,D
Columbia University M,D*
Cornell University M,D*
Dalhousie University M,D
Duke University D*
Florida Atlantic University M,D
Florida International University M
Florida State University M,D,O
George Mason University M,D,O*
Georgetown University M
The George Washington University M,D,O
Georgia Institute of Technology M,D
Georgia State University M,D
Hampton University M
Harvard University M,D*
Indiana University Bloomington M,D*
Iowa State University of Science and Technology M,D*
James Madison University M
The Johns Hopkins University M,D
Kansas State University M,D*
Lehigh University M,D
Louisiana State University and Agricultural and Mechanical College M
Louisiana Tech University M
Loyola University Chicago M
McGill University M,D,O
McMaster University M
McNeese State University M
Memorial University of Newfoundland M,D
Miami University M

*M—master's degree; P—first professional degree; D—doctorate; O—other advanced degree; *—Close-Up and/or Display in one of the other books in this series*

Michigan State University M,D
Minnesota State University Mankato M
Mississippi State University M,D
Missouri University of Science and Technology M,D
Montana State University M,D
Montclair State University M,D,O
Murray State University M
New York University M,D
North Carolina State University M,D*
North Dakota State University M,D,O
Northern Arizona University M,O
Northern Illinois University M
Northwestern University M,D*
Oakland University O
The Ohio State University M,D
Oklahoma State University M,D*
Oregon State University M,D
Penn State University Park M,D
Portland State University M,D
Purdue University M,D,O
Queen's University at Kingston M,D
Rice University M,D
Rochester Institute of Technology M,O
Rutgers, The State University of New Jersey, New Brunswick M,D*
St. John's University (NY) M
Sam Houston State University M
San Diego State University M
San Jose State University M
Simon Fraser University M,D
South Dakota State University M,D
Southern Illinois University Carbondale M,D
Southern Methodist University M,D
Stanford University M,D
State University of New York at Binghamton M,D
Stephen F. Austin State University M
Stevens Institute of Technology M,O
Stony Brook University, State University of New York M,D
Temple University M,D*
Texas A&M University M,D
Texas Tech University M,D*
Tulane University M,D*
Université de Montréal M,D,O
Université Laval M
University at Albany, State University of New York M,D,O
The University of Akron M
University of Alaska Fairbanks M,D
University of Alberta M,D,O
The University of Arizona M,D
University of Arkansas M
The University of British Columbia M,D
University of Calgary M,D
University of California, Berkeley M,D*
University of California, Davis M,D
University of California, Irvine M,D*
University of California, Los Angeles M,D*
University of California, Riverside M,D
University of California, San Diego M,D*
University of California, Santa Barbara M,D
University of California, Santa Cruz M,D
University of Central Florida M,O
University of Central Oklahoma M
University of Chicago M,D
University of Cincinnati M,D
University of Connecticut M,D*
University of Delaware M*
University of Denver M
University of Florida M,D*
University of Georgia M,D
University of Guelph M,D
University of Houston–Clear Lake M
University of Idaho M
University of Illinois at Chicago M,D
University of Illinois at Urbana–Champaign M,D
The University of Iowa M,D,O*
University of Kentucky M,D*
The University of Manchester M,D
University of Manitoba M,D
University of Maryland, Baltimore County M,D
University of Maryland, College Park M,D
University of Massachusetts Amherst M,D*
University of Memphis M,D
University of Michigan M,D*
University of Minnesota, Twin Cities Campus M,D
University of Missouri M,D*
University of Missouri–Kansas City M,D*
University of Nebraska–Lincoln M,D*
University of New Brunswick Fredericton M,D
University of New Hampshire M,D,O
University of New Mexico M,D*
The University of North Carolina at Chapel Hill M,D*
University of North Florida M
University of Ottawa M,D*
University of Pennsylvania M,D*
University of Pittsburgh M,D*
University of Puerto Rico, Mayagüez Campus M
University of Regina M,D
University of Rhode Island M,D,O
University of Rochester M,D
University of Saskatchewan M,D
University of South Africa M,D
University of South Carolina M,D,O
The University of South Dakota M,D
University of Southern California M,D*
University of Southern Maine M
University of South Florida M,D*
The University of Tennessee M,D
The University of Texas at Austin M
The University of Texas at Dallas M,D*
The University of Texas at El Paso M
The University of Texas at San Antonio M,D*
University of the Incarnate Word M
The University of Toledo M,D
University of Toronto M,D
University of Utah M,D*
University of Vermont M
University of Victoria M,D
University of Virginia M,D
University of Washington M,D*
University of Waterloo M,D
The University of Western Ontario M,D
University of Windsor M,D
University of Wisconsin–Madison M,D*
University of Wyoming M,D
Utah State University M,D
Virginia Commonwealth University M
Virginia Polytechnic Institute and State University M,D
Washington State University M
Washington University in St. Louis M,D*
Wayne State University M,D*
Western Michigan University M,D
West Virginia University M,D
Yale University M,D*
York University M,D*
Youngstown State University M

STRUCTURAL BIOLOGY

Baylor College of Medicine D*
Carnegie Mellon University D*
Columbia University D*
Cornell University M,D*
Cornell University, Joan and Sanford I. Weill Medical College and Graduate School of Medical Sciences M,D
Duke University O*
Florida State University M,D
Harvard University D*
Illinois State University M,D
Iowa State University of Science and Technology M,D*
Massachusetts Institute of Technology D
Mayo Graduate School D
Michigan State University D
New York University P,M,D
Northwestern University D*
Stanford University D
Stony Brook University, State University of New York D
Syracuse University D*
Thomas Jefferson University D
Tulane University M,D*
University at Albany, State University of New York M,D
University at Buffalo, the State University of New York M,D*
University of California, San Diego D*
University of Connecticut M,D*
The University of Manchester M,D
University of Minnesota, Twin Cities Campus D
University of Pittsburgh D*
The University of Texas Health Science Center at San Antonio M,D
The University of Texas Medical Branch D
University of Washington D*

STRUCTURAL ENGINEERING

Auburn University M,D
California State University, Northridge M
Cornell University M,D*
Drexel University M,D*
École Polytechnique de Montréal M,D,O
Illinois Institute of Technology M,D
Instituto Tecnologico de Santo Domingo M,O
Iowa State University of Science and Technology M,D*
Lehigh University M,D
Louisiana State University and Agricultural and Mechanical College M,D
Marquette University M,D,O
Massachusetts Institute of Technology M,D,O
McGill University M,D
Milwaukee School of Engineering M
Northwestern University M,D*
Norwich University M
Ohio University M,D*
Oregon State University M,D
Pontificia Universidad Catolica Madre y Maestra M
Rensselaer Polytechnic Institute M,D
Stevens Institute of Technology M,D,O
Texas A&M University M,D
Tufts University M,D
University at Buffalo, the State University of New York M,D*
The University of Alabama in Huntsville M,D
University of Alberta M,D
University of California, Berkeley M,D*
University of California, San Diego M,D*
University of Central Florida M,D,O
University of Colorado Boulder M,D*
University of Colorado Denver M,D
University of Dayton M
University of Delaware M,D*
The University of Manchester M,D
University of Memphis M,D
University of Michigan M,D,O*
University of Missouri M,D*
University of New Brunswick Fredericton M,D
University of North Dakota M
The University of Texas at Tyler M
University of Washington M,D*
Washington University in St. Louis M,D*
Western Michigan University M

STUDENT AFFAIRS

Alliant International University–Los Angeles M,D,O
Alliant International University–San Diego M,D,O
Appalachian State University M
Arkansas State University M,O
Arkansas Tech University M,O
Ashland University M
Azusa Pacific University M
Bloomsburg University of Pennsylvania M
Bob Jones University P,M,D,O
Bowling Green State University M*
Bucknell University M
Buffalo State College, State University of New York M
California State University, Bakersfield M
California State University, Long Beach M
Canisius College M,O
Central Michigan University M,D,O

The Citadel, The Military College of South Carolina	M
Claremont Graduate University	M,D,O
Clemson University	M
Cleveland State University	M,O
College of Saint Elizabeth	M,O
The College of Saint Rose	M,O
Colorado State University	M,D
Concordia University Wisconsin	M
Creighton University	M
Eastern Illinois University	M
Fresno Pacific University	M
Grambling State University	M,D
Hampton University	M
Illinois State University	M
Indiana State University	M,D,O
Indiana University of Pennsylvania	M
Indiana University–Purdue University Indianapolis	M,O
Kansas State University	M,D*
Kaplan University, Davenport Campus	M
Kent State University	M*
Lee University	M
Lehigh University	M,D,O
Lewis University	M
Manhattan College	M,O
Marquette University	M,D,O
Massachusetts School of Professional Psychology	M,D,O
Miami University	M,D
Minnesota State University Mankato	M,D,O
Mississippi State University	M,D,O
Missouri State University	M
New York University	M,D
Northeastern University	M,O
Northern Arizona University	M,D,O
Northern Kentucky University	M,O
Northwestern State University of Louisiana	M,O
Nova Southeastern University	M*
Ohio University	M,D*
Oregon State University	M
Providence College and Theological Seminary	P,M,D,O
Radford University	M
Regent University	M,D,O
Rutgers, The State University of New Jersey, New Brunswick	M*
St. Cloud State University	M
St. Edward's University	M
Saint Louis University	M,D,O
San Jose State University	M
Seton Hall University	M
Shippensburg University of Pennsylvania	M,O
Slippery Rock University of Pennsylvania	M
Springfield College	M,O
State University of New York at Binghamton	M
Syracuse University	M*
Teachers College, Columbia University	M,D
Tennessee Technological University	M,O
University at Buffalo, the State University of New York	M,D,O*
University of Bridgeport	M
University of Central Arkansas	M
University of Central Florida	M,D
University of Central Missouri	M,D,O
University of Dayton	M,O
University of Florida	M,D,O*
University of Georgia	M,D,O
The University of Iowa	M,D*
University of La Verne	M
University of Louisville	M,D
University of Mary	M
University of Maryland, College Park	M,D,O
University of Minnesota, Twin Cities Campus	M,D,O
University of Mississippi	M,D,O
University of Northern Colorado	D
University of Northern Iowa	M
University of Rhode Island	M
University of St. Thomas (MN)	M,D,O
University of South Carolina	M
University of Southern California	M*
University of Southern Mississippi	M,D,O
University of South Florida	M,D,O*
The University of Tennessee	M
University of the Cumberlands	M,D,O
University of Virginia	M,D,O
University of West Florida	M,D,O
University of Wisconsin–La Crosse	M
University of Wyoming	M,D
Virginia Commonwealth University	M
Washington State University	M,D,O
Western Illinois University	M
Western Kentucky University	M

SUPPLY CHAIN MANAGEMENT

American University	M
Arizona State University	M,D
California State University, East Bay	M
Case Western Reserve University	M*
Central Connecticut State University	M,O
Eastern Michigan University	M,O
Elmhurst College	M
Embry-Riddle Aeronautical University–Worldwide	M
Florida Institute of Technology	M
Georgia Southern University	D
Golden Gate University	M,D,O
HEC Montreal	O
Howard University	M
Kaplan University, Davenport Campus	M
Lehigh University	M,D,O
Maine Maritime Academy	M,O
Marquette University	M
Michigan State University	M,D
Moravian College	M
North Carolina State University	M*
Polytechnic University of Puerto Rico, Miami Campus	M
Quinnipiac University	M
Rutgers, The State University of New Jersey, Newark	D*
Santa Clara University	M
Seton Hall University	M
Southeastern Louisiana University	M
Strayer University	M
Syracuse University	M,D*
Texas A&M University–San Antonio	M
The University of Akron	M
The University of Alabama in Huntsville	M
University of Dallas	M
University of Florida	M,D*
University of Houston	M
University of Louisville	M,D,O
University of Massachusetts Dartmouth	M,O
University of Memphis	M,D
University of Michigan–Dearborn	M
University of Minnesota, Twin Cities Campus	M
University of Missouri–St. Louis	M,D,O
The University of North Carolina at Greensboro	M,D,O
University of Rhode Island	M,D
University of San Diego	M,O
University of Southern California	M,D,O*
The University of Texas at Austin	D
The University of Texas at Dallas	M*
The University of Toledo	M,D,O
University of Wisconsin–Madison	M*
University of Wisconsin–Whitewater	M*
Walden University	M,D
Washington University in St. Louis	M*
Wilfrid Laurier University	M,D
Wright State University	M

SURVEYING SCIENCE AND ENGINEERING

The Ohio State University	M,D
University of New Brunswick Fredericton	M,D,O

SURVEY METHODOLOGY

University of Maryland, College Park	M,D
University of Michigan	M,D,O*
University of Nebraska–Lincoln	M,D*

SUSTAINABILITY MANAGEMENT

Alliant International University–San Diego	M,D
Alliant International University–San Francisco	M
Anaheim University	M,O
Antioch University New England	M
Argosy University, Chicago	M,D*
Argosy University, Dallas	M,D,O*
Argosy University, Denver	M,D*
Argosy University, Hawai'i	M,D,O*
Argosy University, Inland Empire	M,D*
Argosy University, Los Angeles	M,D*
Argosy University, Orange County	M,D,O*
Argosy University, Phoenix	M,D*
Argosy University, Salt Lake City	M,D*
Argosy University, San Francisco Bay Area	M,D*
Argosy University, Sarasota	M,D,O*
Argosy University, Schaumburg	M,D,O*
Argosy University, Seattle	M,D*
Argosy University, Tampa	M,D*
Argosy University, Twin Cities	M,D*
Argosy University, Washington DC	M,D,O*
Baldwin-Wallace College	M
Bard College	M,O
City University of Seattle	M,O
Cleary University	M,O
Colorado State University	M
Columbia University	M*
Dominican University of California	M
Duquesne University	M
Fairleigh Dickinson University, College at Florham	O
Franklin Pierce University	M,D,O
Goddard College	M
Illinois Institute of Technology	M
Indiana University Bloomington	M,D,O*
Lipscomb University	M
Maharishi University of Management	M,D
Marlboro College	M
Michigan Technological University	O
The New School: A University	M
Rochester Institute of Technology	M,D
South University (GA)	M*
Syracuse University	O*
University of California, Berkeley	O*
University of Colorado Denver	M
University of Maine	M
University of Portland	M
University of Saskatchewan	M
Walden University	M,D

SUSTAINABLE DEVELOPMENT

American University	M,D,O
Appalachian State University	M
Arizona State University	M,D,O
Brandeis University	M
California State University, Stanislaus	M
The Catholic University of America	M
City College of the City University of New York	M
Clarkson University	M,D*
Clark University	M
Columbia University	M,D*
Dominican University of California	M
Emory University	M*
Fashion Institute of Technology	M*
Florida Atlantic University	M,O
George Mason University	M,D,O*
Hawai'i Pacific University	M*
HEC Montreal	O
Instituto Centroamericano de Administración de Empresas	M
Instituto Tecnologico de Santo Domingo	M,O
Iowa State University of Science and Technology	M,D*
Lesley University	M
Lipscomb University	M
Marylhurst University	M
Michigan Technological University	O
Minneapolis College of Art and Design	O
New York School of Interior Design	M
New York University	M,O
Northern Arizona University	M
Pace University	P,M,D
Philadelphia University	M
Pratt Institute	M*
Ramapo College of New Jersey	M
Rensselaer Polytechnic Institute	M,D
Rochester Institute of Technology	M,D
Rollins College	M
Saybrook University	M,D
SIT Graduate Institute	M

*M—master's degree; P—first professional degree; D—doctorate; O—other advanced degree; *—Close-Up and/or Display in one of the other books in this series*

Slippery Rock University of Pennsylvania	M
University of Alaska Fairbanks	M,D
University of California, Berkeley	O*
University of California, Santa Barbara	M
University of Colorado Denver	M,D
University of Connecticut	M*
University of Georgia	M,D
University of Maryland, College Park	M
University of Massachusetts Lowell	M,D,O
University of Michigan	M,D*
University of New Brunswick Fredericton	M
University of Southern California	M,D,O*
University of Washington	P,M,D*
The University of Western Ontario	M,D
University of Wisconsin–Madison	M*
Walden University	M,D,O
Wayne State University	O*
West Chester University of Pennsylvania	M,O
Western Illinois University	M,O
West Virginia University	D

SYSTEMS BIOLOGY

Cornell University, Joan and Sanford I. Weill Medical College and Graduate School of Medical Sciences	M,D
Dartmouth College	D
Harvard University	D*
Massachusetts Institute of Technology	D
Michigan State University	D
Rutgers, The State University of New Jersey, New Brunswick	D*
Texas A&M Health Science Center	D
University of California, Irvine	D*
University of California, Merced	M,D
University of California, San Diego	D*
University of Chicago	D
University of Pittsburgh	D*
University of Southern California	D*
University of Toronto	M,D
Virginia Commonwealth University	D

SYSTEMS ENGINEERING

Air Force Institute of Technology	M,D
The American University of Athens	M
Arizona State University	M
Auburn University	M,D
Boston University	M,D*
California Institute of Technology	M,D
California State University, Fullerton	M
California State University, Northridge	M
Carleton University	M,D
Carnegie Mellon University	M*
Case Western Reserve University	M,D*
Colorado School of Mines	M,D
Colorado State University–Pueblo	M
Colorado Technical University Colorado Springs	M
Colorado Technical University Denver	M
Concordia University (Canada)	M,O
Cornell University	M*
Embry-Riddle Aeronautical University–Daytona	M
Florida Institute of Technology	M,D
George Mason University	M,D,O*
The George Washington University	M,D,O
Georgia Institute of Technology	M,D
Harrisburg University of Science and Technology	M
Indiana University–Purdue University Fort Wayne	M
Instituto Tecnológico y de Estudios Superiores de Monterrey, Campus Chihuahua	M,O
Instituto Tecnológico y de Estudios Superiores de Monterrey, Campus Monterrey	M,D
Iowa State University of Science and Technology	M*
The Johns Hopkins University	M,O
Lehigh University	M,D
Loyola Marymount University	M
Massachusetts Institute of Technology	M,D
Mississippi State University	M,D
Missouri University of Science and Technology	M,D
National University	M
Naval Postgraduate School	M,D,O
North Carolina Agricultural and Technical State University	M,D
Oakland University	M,D
The Ohio State University	M,D
Ohio University	M*
Old Dominion University	M,D
Oregon State University	M,D
Polytechnic Institute of NYU	M
Polytechnic Institute of NYU, Long Island Graduate Center	M
Portland State University	M,O
Regis University	M,O
Rensselaer Polytechnic Institute	M,D
Rochester Institute of Technology	M,D
Rutgers, The State University of New Jersey, New Brunswick	M,D*
San Jose State University	M
Southern Methodist University	M,D
Southern Polytechnic State University	M,O
Stevens Institute of Technology	M,D,O
Stony Brook University, State University of New York	M
Texas Tech University	M,D*
The University of Alabama in Huntsville	M,D
University of Alberta	M,D
The University of Arizona	M,D
University of Arkansas at Little Rock	O
University of Central Florida	M,D,O
University of Denver	M,D
University of Florida	M,D,O*
University of Houston–Clear Lake	M
University of Illinois at Urbana–Champaign	M,D
University of Maryland, Baltimore County	M,O
University of Maryland, College Park	M
University of Michigan–Dearborn	M,D
University of Minnesota, Twin Cities Campus	M
University of New Haven	M,O
The University of North Carolina at Charlotte	M,D
University of Pennsylvania	M,D*
University of Regina	M,D
University of St. Thomas (MN)	M,O
University of Southern California	M,D,O*
The University of Texas at Arlington	M
The University of Texas at Dallas	M*
The University of Texas at El Paso	M,O
University of Virginia	M,D
University of Waterloo	M,D
University of Wisconsin–Madison	M,D*
Virginia Polytechnic Institute and State University	M,D,O
Western International University	M
West Virginia University Institute of Technology	M

SYSTEMS SCIENCE

Arizona State University	M
Carleton University	M,D
Claremont Graduate University	M,D,O
Eastern Illinois University	M,O
Fairleigh Dickinson University, Metropolitan Campus	M
Hood College	M
Louisiana State University and Agricultural and Mechanical College	M,D
Louisiana State University in Shreveport	M
Miami University	M
Oakland University	M
Portland State University	M,D,O
Rensselaer at Hartford	M
Southern Methodist University	M,D
State University of New York at Binghamton	M,D
Stevens Institute of Technology	M,D
Strayer University	M
Universidad Autonoma de Guadalajara	M,D
University of Michigan–Dearborn	M,D
The University of North Carolina Wilmington	M
University of Ottawa	M,D,O*
Washington University in St. Louis	M,D*
Worcester Polytechnic Institute	M,D,O

TAXATION

American International College	M
American University	M,O
Bentley University	M
Bernard M. Baruch College of the City University of New York	M
Boise State University	M
Boston University	P,M*
Bryant University	M
California Miramar University	M
California Polytechnic State University, San Luis Obispo	M
California State University, East Bay	M
California State University, Fullerton	M
California State University, Los Angeles	M*
California State University, Northridge	M
Capital University	M
Chapman University	P,M
Cleveland State University	M
DePaul University	M
Fairfield University	M,O
Fairleigh Dickinson University, College at Florham	M,O
Fairleigh Dickinson University, Metropolitan Campus	M
Florida Atlantic University	M
Florida Gulf Coast University	M
Florida International University	M
Florida State University	M,D
Fontbonne University	M
Fordham University	M
George Mason University	M*
Georgetown University	P,M,D
Georgia State University	M
Golden Gate University	P,M,D,O
Goldey-Beacom College	M
Grand Valley State University	M
HEC Montreal	O
Hofstra University	M,O
Illinois Institute of Technology	P,M
Instituto Tecnologico de Santo Domingo	M,O
John Marshall Law School	P,M
Long Island University, Brooklyn Campus	M
Long Island University, C.W. Post Campus	M,O
Loyola Marymount University	P,M
Mississippi State University	M,D
New York Law School	P,M
New York University	P,M,D,O
Northern Illinois University	M
Northern Kentucky University	M,O
Northwestern University	P,M*
Nova Southeastern University	M*
Pace University	M
Philadelphia University	M
Robert Morris University	M
St. John's University (NY)	M,O
St. Thomas University	P,M
San Jose State University	M
Seton Hall University	M,O
Southern Illinois University Edwardsville	M
Southern Methodist University	P,M,D
Southern New Hampshire University	M,D,O
Strayer University	M
Suffolk University	M,O
Taft Law School	P,M
Temple University	P,M,D*
Texas Tech University	M,D*
Thomas Jefferson School of Law	M
Thomas M. Cooley Law School	P,M
Troy University	M,O
Université de Montréal	P,M,D,O
Université de Sherbrooke	M,O
University at Albany, State University of New York	M
The University of Akron	M
The University of Alabama	M,D

The University of Alabama in Huntsville M
University of Arkansas at Little Rock M,O
University of Baltimore M
University of Central Florida M
University of Denver M
University of Florida P,M,D*
University of Hartford M,O
University of Hawaii at Manoa M
University of Houston P,M
University of Illinois at Urbana–Champaign M,D
University of Memphis M
University of Miami M*
University of Michigan P,M,D*
University of Minnesota, Twin Cities Campus M
University of Mississippi M,D
University of Missouri–Kansas City P,M*
University of New Haven M
University of New Mexico M*
University of New Orleans M
The University of North Carolina at Greensboro M,O
University of North Texas M,D
University of Notre Dame M*
University of San Diego P,M,O
University of Southern California M*
University of Southern Maine M
The University of Texas at Arlington M,D
The University of Texas at Dallas M*
The University of Texas at San Antonio M,D*
University of the Pacific P,M,D
University of the Sacred Heart M
University of Tulsa M
University of Washington P,M,D*
University of Waterloo M,D
University of Wisconsin–Madison M*
University of Wisconsin–Milwaukee M,D,O
Villanova University M
Virginia Commonwealth University M
Wake Forest University M
Walsh College of Accountancy and Business Administration M
Washington State University M
Wayne State University M,D*
Weber State University M
Widener University M
William Howard Taft University M

TECHNICAL COMMUNICATION

Boise State University M
Bowling Green State University M,D*
Colorado State University M,D
Drexel University M*
Eastern Michigan University M,O
Eastern Washington University M
Florida Institute of Technology M
Harvard University M*
Lawrence Technological University M
Michigan Technological University M,D
Minnesota State University Mankato M,O
Missouri Western State University M
Montana Tech of The University of Montana M
New Jersey Institute of Technology M
North Carolina State University M*
North Central College M
Rensselaer Polytechnic Institute M
Rochester Institute of Technology O
Southern Polytechnic State University M,O
Texas State University–San Marcos M
University of Colorado Denver M
University of Houston–Downtown M
University of Nebraska at Omaha M,O
University of Washington M,D*
University of Wisconsin–Milwaukee M,D,O

TECHNICAL WRITING

Carnegie Mellon University M*
Colorado State University M,D
Drexel University M*
Fitchburg State University M,O
Illinois Institute of Technology M,D
James Madison University M
The Johns Hopkins University M
Laurentian University O
Massachusetts Institute of Technology M
Metropolitan State University M
Northern Arizona University M,D,O
Polytechnic Institute of NYU M
Texas Tech University M,D*
The University of Alabama in Huntsville M,O
University of Arkansas at Little Rock M
The University of North Carolina at Greensboro M,D,O
University of the Sciences in Philadelphia M,O
University of Waterloo M,D

TECHNOLOGY AND PUBLIC POLICY

Arizona State University M
Carnegie Mellon University M,D*
Eastern Michigan University M
The George Washington University M
Massachusetts Institute of Technology M,D
Rensselaer Polytechnic Institute M,D
Rochester Institute of Technology M
St. Cloud State University M
Stony Brook University, State University of New York D
University of Minnesota, Twin Cities Campus M
University of South Africa M,D
The University of Texas at Austin M
Western Illinois University M

TELECOMMUNICATIONS

The American University of Athens M
Ball State University M
Boston University M*
California Miramar University M
Claremont Graduate University M,D,O
Drexel University M*
Florida International University M,D
Franklin Pierce University M,D,O
George Mason University M,D,O*
The George Washington University M,D
Illinois Institute of Technology M,D
Indiana University Bloomington M*
Instituto Tecnologico de Santo Domingo M,O
Iona College M
The Johns Hopkins University M,O
Michigan State University M
National University M
Ohio University M*
Pace University M,D,O
Polytechnic Institute of NYU M
Polytechnic Institute of NYU, Long Island Graduate Center M
Polytechnic Institute of NYU, Westchester Graduate Center M
Rochester Institute of Technology M
Roosevelt University M
Saint Mary's University of Minnesota M
Southern Methodist University M,D
State University of New York Institute of Technology M
Stevens Institute of Technology M,D,O
Stratford University M
Syracuse University M*
Universidad del Turabo M
Université du Québec, Institut National de la Recherche Scientifique M,D
University of Alberta M,D
University of Arkansas M,D
University of California, San Diego M,D*
University of California, Santa Cruz M,D
University of Colorado Boulder M*
University of Denver M,O
University of Hawaii at Manoa O
University of Houston M
University of Louisiana at Lafayette M*
University of Maryland, College Park M
University of Massachusetts Dartmouth M,D,O
University of Missouri–Kansas City M,D*
University of Oklahoma M*
University of Oklahoma—Tulsa M
University of Pennsylvania M*
University of Pittsburgh M,D,O*
University of Southern California M,D,O*
The University of Texas at Dallas M,D*
Widener University M

TELECOMMUNICATIONS MANAGEMENT

Alaska Pacific University M
Boston University M*
California Miramar University M
Capitol College M
Carnegie Mellon University M*
Concordia University (Canada) M,O
George Mason University M,D,O*
Hawai'i Pacific University M*
Instituto Tecnológico y de Estudios Superiores de Monterrey, Campus Ciudad de México M
Instituto Tecnológico y de Estudios Superiores de Monterrey, Campus Ciudad Obregón M
Instituto Tecnológico y de Estudios Superiores de Monterrey, Campus Estado de México M,D
Instituto Tecnológico y de Estudios Superiores de Monterrey, Campus Irapuato M,D
Morgan State University M
Murray State University M
Northeastern University M
Oklahoma State University M,D*
Polytechnic Institute of NYU M
San Diego State University M
Stevens Institute of Technology M,D,O
Strayer University M
Syracuse University M,O*
University of Colorado Boulder M*
University of New Haven M,O
University of Pennsylvania M*
University of San Francisco M
University of South Africa M,D
University of Wisconsin–Stout M
Webster University M,D,O

TERATOLOGY

West Virginia University M,D

TEXTILE DESIGN

Academy of Art University M
California College of the Arts M
California State University, Los Angeles M*
Cornell University M,D*
Cranbrook Academy of Art M
Drexel University M*
Illinois State University M
James Madison University M
Kent State University M*
LIM College M
Marywood University M
Massachusetts College of Art and Design M
Missouri State University M
The New School: A University M
Philadelphia University M
Rhode Island School of Design M
Savannah College of Art and Design M
School of the Art Institute of Chicago M,O
Sul Ross State University M
Temple University M*
University of California, Davis M
University of Cincinnati M
The University of Manchester M,D
University of Massachusetts Dartmouth M,O
University of Minnesota, Twin Cities Campus M,D,O
The University of North Carolina at Greensboro M,D

*M—master's degree; P—first professional degree; D—doctorate; O—other advanced degree; *—Close-Up and/or Display in one of the other books in this series*

TEXTILE SCIENCES AND ENGINEERING

Auburn University D
Cornell University M,D*
Georgia Institute of Technology M,D
North Carolina State University M,D*
Philadelphia University M,D
University of Massachusetts Dartmouth M
The University of Texas at Austin M

THANATOLOGY

Brooklyn College of the City University of New York M
Hood College M,O
Southwestern College (NM) M,O

THEATER

American Conservatory Theater M,O
Antioch University Midwest M
Arcadia University M,D,O*
Arizona State University M,D
Arkansas State University M,O
Austin College M
Baylor University M*
Bennington College M
Bob Jones University P,M,D,O
The Boston Conservatory M
Boston University M,O*
Bowling Green State University M,D*
Brandeis University M
Brigham Young University M*
Brooklyn College of the City University of New York M,D
Brown University M,D
California Institute of the Arts M,O
California State University, Fullerton M
California State University, Long Beach M
California State University, Los Angeles M*
California State University, Northridge M
California State University, Sacramento M
California State University, San Bernardino M
Carnegie Mellon University M*
Case Western Reserve University M*
The Catholic University of America M
Central Washington University M
Columbia University M,D*
Cornell University D*
Dell'Arte International School of Physical Theatre M
DePaul University M
Drew University M
Eastern Michigan University M
Emerson College M
Florida Atlantic University M
Florida State University M,D
Fontbonne University M
The George Washington University M
Graduate School and University Center of the City University of New York D
Hollins University M
Humboldt State University M
Hunter College of the City University of New York M
Idaho State University M
Illinois State University M
Indiana University Bloomington M,D*
Kansas State University M*
Kent State University M*
Lamar University M
Lindenwood University M
Long Island University, C.W. Post Campus M
Louisiana State University and Agricultural and Mechanical College M,D
Mary Baldwin College M
Massachusetts College of Art and Design M
Miami University M
Michigan State University M
Minnesota State University Mankato M
Missouri State University M
Montclair State University M
Naropa University M
National Theatre Conservatory M,O
The New School: A University M
New York University M,D,O
Northern Illinois University M
Northwestern University M,D*
The Ohio State University M,D
Ohio University M*
Oklahoma City University M
Oklahoma State University M*
Pace University M
Penn State University Park M
Pittsburg State University M
Point Park University M
Portland State University M
Purchase College, State University of New York M
Purdue University M
Regent University M,D
Roosevelt University M
Rowan University M
Rutgers, The State University of New Jersey, New Brunswick M*
San Diego State University M
San Francisco State University M
San Jose State University M
Sarah Lawrence College M
Savannah College of Art and Design M
Smith College M
Southern Illinois University Carbondale M,D
Southern Methodist University M
Stanford University D
State University of New York at Binghamton M
Stony Brook University, State University of New York M
Temple University M*
Texas A&M University–Commerce M
Texas State University–San Marcos M
Texas Tech University M,D*
Texas Woman's University M
Towson University M
Tufts University M,D
Tulane University M*
Université de Sherbrooke M,D
Université Laval M,D
University at Albany, State University of New York M
The University of Akron M
The University of Alabama M
University of Alberta M
The University of Arizona M
University of Arkansas M
The University of British Columbia M,D
University of Calgary M
University of California, Berkeley D*
University of California, Davis M,D
University of California, Irvine M,D*
University of California, Los Angeles M,D*
University of California, San Diego M,D*
University of California, Santa Barbara M,D
University of California, Santa Cruz O
University of Central Florida M
University of Central Missouri M
University of Cincinnati M,D
University of Colorado Boulder M,D*
University of Connecticut M*
University of Delaware M*
University of Florida M*
University of Georgia M,D
University of Guelph M
University of Hawaii at Manoa M,D
University of Houston M
University of Idaho M
University of Illinois at Urbana–Champaign M,D
The University of Iowa M*
The University of Kansas M,D
University of Kentucky M*
University of Lethbridge M,D
University of Louisville M
The University of Manchester D
University of Maryland, Baltimore County M
University of Maryland, College Park M
University of Massachusetts Amherst M*
University of Memphis M
University of Michigan M,D*
University of Minnesota, Twin Cities Campus M,D
University of Missouri M,D*
University of Missouri–Kansas City M*
The University of Montana M
University of Nebraska at Omaha M
University of Nebraska–Lincoln M*
University of Nevada, Las Vegas M
University of New Mexico M*
University of New Orleans M
The University of North Carolina at Chapel Hill M*
The University of North Carolina at Charlotte M,D
The University of North Carolina at Greensboro M
University of North Carolina School of the Arts M
University of North Dakota M
University of Oklahoma M*
University of Oregon M,D
University of Ottawa M*
University of Pittsburgh M,D*
University of Portland M
University of San Diego M
University of Saskatchewan M
University of South Carolina M,D
The University of South Dakota M
University of Southern California M*
University of Southern Mississippi M
The University of Tennessee M
The University of Texas at Austin M,D
The University of Texas–Pan American M
University of the Cumberlands M,D,O
University of Toronto M,D
University of Tulsa M
University of Victoria M
University of Virginia M
University of Washington M,D*
University of Wisconsin–Madison M,D*
University of Wisconsin–Milwaukee M
University of Wisconsin–Superior M
Utah State University M
Villanova University M
Virginia Commonwealth University M
Virginia Polytechnic Institute and State University M
Wayne State University M,D*
Western Illinois University M
West Virginia University M
Yale University M,D,O*
York University M,D*

THEOLOGY

Abilene Christian University P,M
Acadia University P,M,D
Ambrose University College P,M,O
American Baptist Seminary of the West P,M
American Jewish University M
Amridge University P,M,D
Anderson University (IN) P,M,D
Andover Newton Theological School P,M,D
Andrews University P,M,D,O
Apex School of Theology P,M,D
Aquinas Institute of Theology P,M,D,O
Asbury Theological Seminary M,D,O
Ashland Theological Seminary P,M,D,O
Assemblies of God Theological Seminary P,M,D
Associated Mennonite Biblical Seminary P,M,O
The Athenaeum of Ohio P,M,O
Atlantic School of Theology P,M,O
Austin Graduate School of Theology M
Austin Presbyterian Theological Seminary P,M,D
Ave Maria University M,D
Azusa Pacific University M,D
Bangor Theological Seminary P,M,D
Baptist Bible College P,M
Baptist Bible College of Pennsylvania P,M,D
Baptist Missionary Association Theological Seminary P,M
Baptist Theological Seminary at Richmond P,M,D
Barry University M,D*
Baylor University P,M,D*
Bethany Theological Seminary P,M,O
Bethel College M
Bethel Seminary P,M,D,O
Bethesda Christian University P,M
Beth HaMedrash Shaarei Yosher Institute
Beth Hatalmud Rabbinical College

Institution	Degrees
Beth Medrash Govoha	
Bethune-Cookman University	M
Bexley Hall Episcopal Seminary	P,M
Biblical Theological Seminary	P,M,D,O
Biola University	P,M,D
Blessed John XXIII National Seminary	P
Bob Jones University	P,M,D,O
Boston College	P,M,D,O*
Boston University	P,M,D*
Briercrest Seminary	P,M
Bryn Athyn College of the New Church	P,M
California Institute of Integral Studies	M,D
Calvary Baptist Theological Seminary	P,M,D
Calvary Bible College and Theological Seminary	P,M
Calvin Theological Seminary	P,M,D
Campbellsville University	M
Campbell University	P,M,D
Canadian Southern Baptist Seminary	P,M
Capital Bible Seminary	P,M,O
Carey Theological College	P,M,D
Carolina Evangelical Divinity School	P,M
Carson-Newman College	M
The Catholic Distance University	M
Catholic Theological Union at Chicago	P,M,D,O
The Catholic University of America	P,M,D,O
Central Baptist Theological Seminary	P,M,O
Central Baptist Theological Seminary of Virginia Beach	P,M
Central Yeshiva Tomchei Tmimim-Lubavitch	M
Chaminade University of Honolulu	M
Chicago Theological Seminary	P,M,D
Christendom College	M
Christian Theological Seminary	P,M,D
Christ the King Seminary	P,M
Church Divinity School of the Pacific	P,M,D,O
Cincinnati Christian University	P,M
Claremont Graduate University	M,D
Claremont School of Theology	P,M,D
Colgate Rochester Crozer Divinity School	P,M,D,O
Collège Dominicain de Philosophie et de Théologie	M,D,O
College of Emmanuel and St. Chad	P,M
College of Mount St. Joseph	M,O
College of Saint Elizabeth	M
Columbia International University	P,M,D,O
Columbia Theological Seminary	P,M,D
Concordia Lutheran Seminary	P,O
Concordia Seminary	P,M,D,O
Concordia Theological Seminary	P,M,D
Concordia University (CA)	M
Concordia University (Canada)	M
Concordia University College of Alberta	M
Concordia University, St. Paul	M,O
Covenant Theological Seminary	P,M,D,O
Creighton University	M
The Criswell College	P,M
Crown College	M
Dallas Theological Seminary	M,D,O
Darkei Noam Rabbinical College	
Denver Seminary	P,M,D,O
Dominican House of Studies, Pontifical Faculty of the Immaculate Conception	P,M,O
Dominican School of Philosophy and Theology	P,M,O
Drew University	P,M,D,O
Duke University	P,M,D*
Duquesne University	M,D
Earlham School of Religion	P,M
Eastern Mennonite University	P,M,O
Eastern University	P,M,D
Ecumenical Theological Seminary	P
Eden Theological Seminary	P,M,D
Emmanuel Christian Seminary	P,M,D
Emory University	P,M,D*
Episcopal Divinity School	P,M,D,O
Erskine Theological Seminary	P,M,D
Evangelical Seminary of Puerto Rico	P,M,D
Evangelical Theological Seminary	P,M
Faith Baptist Bible College and Theological Seminary	P,M
Faith Evangelical Lutheran Seminary	P,M,D
Faith Theological Seminary	P,D
Faulkner University	M
Fordham University	M,D
Franciscan School of Theology	P,M
Franciscan University of Steubenville	M
Freed-Hardeman University	P,M
Fresno Pacific University	P,M
Friends University	M
Fuller Theological Seminary	P,M,D
Gardner-Webb University	P,D
Garrett-Evangelical Theological Seminary	P,M,D
General Theological Seminary	P,M,D,O
George Fox University	P,M,D,O
Georgetown University	D
Georgian Court University	M,O
Global University	P,M
Golden Gate Baptist Theological Seminary	P,M,D,O
Gordon-Conwell Theological Seminary	P,M,D
Graceland University (IA)	M
Grace Theological Seminary	P,M,D,O
Grace University	M
Graduate Theological Union	M,D,O
Grand Rapids Theological Seminary of Cornerstone University	P,M
Harding University Graduate School of Religion	P,M,D
Hardin-Simmons University	P,M,D
Hartford Seminary	M,D,O
Harvard University	P,M,D*
Hebrew College	M
Hebrew Union College–Jewish Institute of Religion (NY)	P,D
Heritage Baptist College and Heritage Theological Seminary	P,M,D,O
Holy Apostles College and Seminary	P,M,O
Holy Cross Greek Orthodox School of Theology	P,M
Hood Theological Seminary	P,M,D
Houston Baptist University	M
Houston Graduate School of Theology	P,M,D
Howard University	P,M,D
Iliff School of Theology	P,M,D
Indiana Wesleyan University	P
Institute for Christian Studies	M,D
Inter American University of Puerto Rico, Metropolitan Campus	D
Interdenominational Theological Center	P,M,D
International Baptist College	M
The Jewish Theological Seminary	M,D,O
Johnson University	M
Kehilath Yakov Rabbinical Seminary	
Kenrick-Glennon Seminary	P,M
Kentucky Christian University	M
Knox College	P,M,D
Knox Theological Seminary	P,M,O
Kol Yaakov Torah Center	O
Lakeland College	M
Lancaster Bible College	M,D
Lancaster Theological Seminary	P,M,D,O
La Salle University	M
Lee University	M
Lexington Theological Seminary	P,M,D
Liberty University	P,M,D
Lincoln Christian Seminary	P,M,D
Lipscomb University	P,M
Logos Evangelical Seminary	P,M,D
Loras College	M
Louisville Presbyterian Theological Seminary	P,M,D
Loyola Marymount University	M
Loyola University Chicago	P,M,D,O
Loyola University New Orleans	M,O
Lubbock Christian University	M
Lutheran School of Theology at Chicago	P,M,D
Lutheran Theological Seminary	P,M,D
Lutheran Theological Seminary at Gettysburg	P,M,D
The Lutheran Theological Seminary at Philadelphia	P,M,D,O
Lutheran Theological Southern Seminary	P,M,D
Luther Rice University	P,M,D
Luther Seminary	P,M,D
Machzikei Hadath Rabbinical College	O
Madonna University	M
Malone University	M
Maple Springs Baptist Bible College and Seminary	P,M,D,O
Maranatha Baptist Bible College	P,M
Marquette University	M,D
Mars Hill Graduate School	M
Marylhurst University	P,M
The Master's College and Seminary	P,M,D
McCormick Theological Seminary	P,M,D,O
McGill University	M,D
McMaster University	P,M,D,O
Meadville Lombard Theological School	P,M,D
Memphis Theological Seminary	P,M,D
Mercer University	P,M,D
Mesivta of Eastern Parkway–Yeshiva Zichron Meilech	
Mesivta Tifereth Jerusalem of America	
Mesivta Torah Vodaath Rabbinical Seminary	
Methodist Theological School in Ohio	P,M,D
Michigan Theological Seminary	P,M,O
Mid-America Baptist Theological Seminary	P,M,D
Mid-America Baptist Theological Seminary Northeast Branch	P
Mid-America Reformed Seminary	P,M
Midwestern Baptist Theological Seminary	P,M,D,O
Midwest University	P,M,D
Mirrer Yeshiva	
Moody Bible Institute	P,M,O
Moravian Theological Seminary	P,M
Mount Angel Seminary	P,M
Mount St. Mary's University	P,M
Mount Vernon Nazarene University	M
Naropa University	P
Nashotah House	P,M,O
Nazarene Theological Seminary	P,M,D
Ner Israel Rabbinical College	M,D,O
Ner Israel Yeshiva College of Toronto	
New Brunswick Theological Seminary	P,M,D
Newman Theological College	P,M
Newman University	M
New Orleans Baptist Theological Seminary	P,M,D
New Saint Andrews College	M,O
New York Theological Seminary	P,M,D
The Nigerian Baptist Theological Seminary	P,M,D,O
Northeastern Seminary at Roberts Wesleyan College	P,M,D
Northern Baptist Theological Seminary	P,M,D
North Park Theological Seminary	P,M,D
Northwest Baptist Seminary	P,M,D,O
Northwestern College	M
Northwest University	M
Notre Dame Seminary	P,M
Nyack College	P,M,D
Oakland City University	P,D
Oblate School of Theology	P,M,D,O
Ohio Dominican University	M
Ohr Hameir Theological Seminary	
Oklahoma Christian University	P,M
Olivet Nazarene University	M
Oral Roberts University	P,M,D
Pacific Lutheran Theological Seminary	P,M,D,O
Pacific School of Religion	P,M,D,O
Payne Theological Seminary	P
Pentecostal Theological Seminary	P,M,D
Pepperdine University	P
Pfeiffer University	M
Philadelphia Biblical University	P,M

*M—master's degree; P—first professional degree; D—doctorate; O—other advanced degree; *—Close-Up and/or Display in one of the other books in this series*

- Phillips Theological Seminary P,M,D
- Phoenix Seminary P,M,D,O
- Piedmont Baptist College and Graduate School M,D
- Pittsburgh Theological Seminary P,M,D
- Pontifical Catholic University of Puerto Rico P
- Pontifical College Josephinum P,M
- Princeton Theological Seminary P,M,D
- Providence College M
- Providence College and Theological Seminary P,M,D,O
- Queen's University at Kingston P,M,O
- Quincy University M
- Rabbi Isaac Elchanan Theological Seminary O
- Rabbinical Academy Mesivta Rabbi Chaim Berlin O
- Rabbinical College Beth Shraga
- Rabbinical College Bobover Yeshiva B'nei Zion
- Rabbinical College Ch'san Sofer
- Rabbinical College of Long Island
- Rabbinical Seminary M'kor Chaim
- Rabbinical Seminary of America
- Reconstructionist Rabbinical College P,M,D,O
- Reformed Presbyterian Theological Seminary P,M,D
- Reformed Theological Seminary–Atlanta Campus P,M,D,O
- Reformed Theological Seminary–Charlotte Campus P,M,D
- Reformed Theological Seminary–Jackson Campus P,M,D,O
- Reformed Theological Seminary–Orlando Campus P,M,D
- Reformed Theological Seminary–Washington D.C. P,M
- Regent College P,M,O
- Regent University P,M,D
- Regis College (Canada) P,M,D,O
- Sacred Heart Major Seminary P,M
- Sacred Heart School of Theology P,M
- St. Andrew's College P,M
- St. Andrew's College in Winnipeg P
- St. Augustine's Seminary of Toronto P,M,O
- Saint Bernard's School of Theology and Ministry P,M,O
- St. Catherine University M,O
- St. Charles Borromeo Seminary, Overbrook P,M
- Saint Francis Seminary P,M
- St. John's Seminary (CA) P,M
- Saint John's Seminary (MA) P,M
- Saint John's University (MN) P,M
- St. John's University (NY) P,M,O
- St. Joseph's Seminary P,M
- Saint Leo University M
- Saint Louis University M,D
- Saint Mary-of-the-Woods College M,O
- Saint Mary Seminary and Graduate School of Theology P,M,D
- St. Mary's Seminary and University P,M,D,O
- Saint Mary's University (Canada) M
- St. Mary's University (United States) M
- Saint Meinrad School of Theology P,M
- Saint Michael's College M,O
- St. Norbert College M
- St. Patrick's Seminary & University P,M
- Saint Paul School of Theology P,M,D
- Saint Paul University M,D,O
- St. Peter's Seminary P,M
- Saints Cyril and Methodius Seminary P,M
- St. Stephen's College M,D
- St. Thomas University M,D,O
- St. Tikhon's Orthodox Theological Seminary P
- Saint Vincent de Paul Regional Seminary P,M
- Saint Vincent Seminary P,M
- St. Vladimir's Orthodox Theological Seminary P,M,D
- Samford University P,M,D
- San Francisco Theological Seminary P,M,D
- Santa Clara University P,M,D,O
- Seabury-Western Theological Seminary P,M,D,O
- Seattle Pacific University P,M
- Seattle University P,M,O
- Seminary of the Immaculate Conception P,M,D,O
- Seminary of the Southwest P,M,O
- Seton Hall University P,M,O
- Sewanee: The University of the South P,M,D
- Shaw University P,M
- Sh'or Yoshuv Rabbinical College
- Sioux Falls Seminary M,D,O
- Southeastern Baptist Theological Seminary P,M,D
- Southern Adventist University M
- Southern Baptist Theological Seminary P,M,D
- Southern California Seminary P,M,D
- Southern Evangelical Seminary P,M,D,O
- Southern Methodist University P,M,D
- Southern Nazarene University M
- Southwestern Assemblies of God University P,M
- Southwestern Baptist Theological Seminary P,M,D,O
- Southwestern College (KS) M
- Spring Arbor University M
- Spring Hill College M
- Starr King School for the Ministry P
- Talmudic College of Florida M
- Taylor College and Seminary P,M,O
- Temple Baptist Seminary P,M,D
- Toronto School of Theology P,M,D
- Trevecca Nazarene University M
- Trinity International University P,M,D,O
- Trinity Lutheran Seminary P,M
- Trinity School for Ministry P,M,D,O
- Trinity Western University P,M,D
- Tyndale University College & Seminary P,M,O
- Unification Theological Seminary P,M,D
- Union Theological Seminary in the City of New York P,M,D
- United Talmudical Seminary
- United Theological Seminary P,M,D
- United Theological Seminary of the Twin Cities P,M,D,O
- Universidad FLET M
- Université de Montréal M,D,O
- Université de Sherbrooke M,D,O
- Université du Québec à Chicoutimi M,D
- Université Laval M,D
- University of Chicago P,M,D
- University of Dallas M
- University of Dayton M,D
- University of Denver D
- University of Dubuque P,M,D
- The University of Manchester D
- University of Mobile M
- University of Notre Dame P,M,D*
- University of Philosophical Research M
- University of Saint Mary of the Lake–Mundelein Seminary P,M,D
- University of St. Michael's College P,M,D,O
- University of St. Thomas (TX) P,M*
- University of St. Thomas (MN) P,M
- The University of Scranton M
- University of South Africa M,D
- University of Trinity College P,M,D,O
- The University of Winnipeg P,M,O
- Ursuline College M
- Valley Forge Christian College M
- Valparaiso University M,O
- Vancouver School of Theology P,M,O
- Vanderbilt University P,M*
- Vanguard University of Southern California M
- Victoria University P,M,D,O
- Villanova University M
- Virginia Theological Seminary P,M,D
- Virginia Union University P,D
- Walsh University M
- Warner Pacific College M
- Wartburg Theological Seminary P,M
- Washington Theological Union P,M,D
- Wesley Biblical Seminary P,M
- Wesley Theological Seminary P,M,D
- Western Seminary P,M,O
- Western Seminary–Sacramento Campus P,M,O
- Western Seminary–San Jose Campus P,M,O
- Western Theological Seminary P,M,D
- Westminster Seminary California P,M
- Westminster Theological Seminary P,M,D,O
- Wheaton College M,D
- Whitworth University M
- Wilfrid Laurier University P,M,D,O
- Winebrenner Theological Seminary P,M,D
- Wycliffe College P,M,D,O
- Xavier University M
- Xavier University of Louisiana M
- Yale University P,M*
- Yeshiva Beth Moshe O
- Yeshiva Karlin Stolin Rabbinical Institute O
- Yeshiva of Nitra Rabbinical College
- Yeshiva Shaar Hatorah Talmudic Research Institute
- Yeshivath Zichron Moshe O
- Yeshiva Toras Chaim Talmudical Seminary

THEORETICAL CHEMISTRY

- Carnegie Mellon University M,D*
- Cornell University D*
- Georgetown University D
- Laurentian University M
- University of Calgary M,D
- The University of Manchester M,D
- University of Regina M,D
- The University of Tennessee M,D
- Vanderbilt University M,D*
- Wesleyan University M,D*
- West Virginia University M,D
- Yale University D*

THEORETICAL PHYSICS

- Cornell University M,D*
- Delaware State University D
- Harvard University D*
- Rutgers, The State University of New Jersey, New Brunswick M,D*
- The University of Manchester M,D
- University of Victoria M,D
- West Virginia University M,D

THERAPIES—DANCE, DRAMA, AND MUSIC

- Antioch University New England M
- Appalachian State University M
- Arizona State University M,D
- California Institute of Integral Studies M,D
- Columbia College Chicago M,O
- Drexel University M,O*
- East Carolina University M
- Florida State University M,D
- Georgia College & State University M
- Immaculata University M
- Lesley University M,D,O
- Loyola University New Orleans M
- Maryville University of Saint Louis M
- Marywood University M,O
- Michigan State University M,D
- Molloy College M
- Montclair State University M,O
- Naropa University M
- Nazareth College of Rochester M
- New York University M
- Ohio University M,O*
- Pratt Institute M*
- Radford University M
- Saint Mary-of-the-Woods College M
- Shenandoah University M,D,O
- State University of New York at New Paltz M
- Temple University M,D*
- The University of Kansas M
- University of Miami M,D,O*
- University of the Pacific M
- Western Michigan University M
- Wilfrid Laurier University M

TOXICOLOGY

- American University M,O
- Brown University M,D
- Columbia University M,D*
- Cornell University M,D*
- Dartmouth College D

Duke University D,O*
Florida Agricultural and Mechanical University M,D
The George Washington University M
Indiana University Bloomington M,D*
Indiana University–Purdue University Indianapolis M,D
Iowa State University of Science and Technology M,D*
The Johns Hopkins University M,D
Long Island University, Brooklyn Campus M,D
Louisiana State University and Agricultural and Mechanical College M
Massachusetts Institute of Technology M,D
Medical College of Wisconsin D*
Medical University of South Carolina D
Michigan State University M,D
New York University M,D
North Carolina State University M,D*
Northwestern University D*
The Ohio State University M,D
Oklahoma State University Center for Health Sciences M,O
Oregon State University M,D
Prairie View A&M University M
Purdue University M,D
Queen's University at Kingston M,D
Rutgers, The State University of New Jersey, New Brunswick M,D*
St. John's University (NY) M
San Diego State University M,D
Simon Fraser University M,D
Texas A&M University M,D
Texas Southern University M,D
Texas Tech University M,D*
Université de Montréal O
University at Albany, State University of New York M,D
University at Buffalo, the State University of New York M,D*
The University of Alabama at Birmingham D*
University of Arkansas for Medical Sciences M,D
University of California, Davis M,D
University of California, Irvine M,D*
University of California, Los Angeles D*
University of California, Riverside M,D
University of California, Santa Cruz M,D
University of Colorado Denver D
University of Connecticut M,D*
University of Florida M,D,O*
University of Georgia M,D
University of Guelph M,D
The University of Iowa M,D*
The University of Kansas M,D
University of Kentucky M,D*
University of Louisville M,D
University of Maine D
The University of Manchester M,D
University of Maryland, Baltimore M,D
University of Maryland Eastern Shore M,D
University of Medicine and Dentistry of New Jersey M,D
University of Michigan M,D*
University of Minnesota, Duluth M,D
University of Minnesota, Twin Cities Campus M,D
University of Mississippi Medical Center M,D
The University of Montana M,D
University of Nebraska–Lincoln M,D*
University of Nebraska Medical Center M,D
University of New Mexico M,D,O*
The University of North Carolina at Chapel Hill M,D*
University of Prince Edward Island M,D
University of Puerto Rico, Medical Sciences Campus M,D
University of Rhode Island M,D
University of Rochester M,D
University of Saskatchewan M,D,O
University of South Alabama M
University of Southern California M,D*
The University of Texas Medical Branch M,D
University of the Sciences in Philadelphia M,D
University of Toronto M,D
University of Utah D*
University of Washington M,D*
University of Wisconsin–Madison M,D*
Utah State University M,D
Virginia Commonwealth University M,D,O
Wayne State University M,D*
West Virginia University M,D
Wright State University M

TRANSCULTURAL NURSING

Augsburg College M
University of Medicine and Dentistry of New Jersey D

TRANSLATIONAL BIOLOGY

Baylor College of Medicine D*
Cedars-Sinai Medical Center D
Texas A&M Health Science Center D
The University of Iowa M,D*
Washington University in St. Louis M*

TRANSLATION AND INTERPRETATION

American University M,O
American University of Sharjah M
Babel University School of Translation M
Concordia University (Canada) M,O
Drew University M
Gallaudet University M,D,O
Georgia State University O
Kent State University M,D*
Marygrove College O
Montclair State University M,O
Monterey Institute of International Studies M
New York University M,D
Rutgers, The State University of New Jersey, New Brunswick M,D*
State University of New York at Binghamton M,O
Universidad Autonoma de Guadalajara M,D
Université de Montréal M,D,O
Université Laval M,O
University at Albany, State University of New York M,O
University of Arkansas M
University of California, Santa Barbara M,D
University of Delaware M*
University of Denver M,O
The University of Iowa M*
The University of Manchester M,D
University of North Florida M
University of Ottawa M,D*
University of Puerto Rico, Río Piedras M,O
University of Rochester
University of Wisconsin–Milwaukee M,O
York University M*

TRANSPERSONAL AND HUMANISTIC PSYCHOLOGY

Atlantic University M
Institute of Transpersonal Psychology M,D,O
John F. Kennedy University M
Kona University M
Michigan School of Professional Psychology M,D
Naropa University M
Saybrook University M,D
Seattle University M

TRANSPORTATION AND HIGHWAY ENGINEERING

Arizona State University M,D,O
Auburn University M,D
Cornell University M,D*
École Polytechnique de Montréal M,D,O
Illinois Institute of Technology M,D
Iowa State University of Science and Technology M,D*
Louisiana State University and Agricultural and Mechanical College M,D
Marquette University M,D,O
Massachusetts Institute of Technology M,D,O
Morgan State University M
New Jersey Institute of Technology M,D
Northwestern University M,D*
Ohio University M,D*
Oregon State University M,D
Polytechnic Institute of NYU M,D
Polytechnic Institute of NYU, Long Island Graduate Center M
Rensselaer Polytechnic Institute M,D
South Carolina State University M
Texas A&M University M,D
Texas Southern University M
The University of Alabama in Huntsville M,D
University of Arkansas M
University of California, Berkeley M,D*
University of California, Davis M,D
University of California, Irvine M,D*
University of Central Florida M,D,O
University of Colorado Denver M,D
University of Dayton M
University of Delaware M,D*
University of Memphis M,D
University of Missouri M,D*
University of Nevada, Las Vegas M,D
University of New Brunswick Fredericton M,D
University of Southern California M,D,O*
The University of Texas at Tyler M
University of Washington M,D*
Virginia Polytechnic Institute and State University M,D,O
Western Michigan University M

TRANSPORTATION MANAGEMENT

American Public University System M
Concordia University (Canada) M,D,O
Florida Institute of Technology M
George Mason University M*
Instituto Tecnologico de Santo Domingo M,O
Iowa State University of Science and Technology M*
Maine Maritime Academy M,O
McGill University M,D
Morgan State University M
New Jersey Institute of Technology M,D
North Dakota State University M,D
Polytechnic Institute of NYU M
Pontifical Catholic University of Puerto Rico O
San Jose State University M
State University of New York Maritime College M
Texas Southern University M
The University of British Columbia D
University of California, Davis M,D
University of California, Santa Barbara M,D
The University of Tennessee M,D
University of Washington O*
Wilmington University M

TRAVEL AND TOURISM

Arizona State University M,D,O
Boston University M*
California State University, East Bay M
California State University, Fullerton M
California State University, Northridge M
Clemson University M,D
Eastern Michigan University M,O
East Stroudsburg University of Pennsylvania M
Florida Atlantic University M,O
The George Washington University M,O
Hawai'i Pacific University M*
Indiana University Bloomington M,D,O*
Kent State University M*
New York University M,O
North Carolina State University M,D*
Old Dominion University M
Penn State University Park M,D
Pontificia Universidad Catolica Madre y Maestra M
Purdue University M,D
Rochester Institute of Technology M
Royal Roads University M,O
Saint Xavier University M,O
Schiller International University (United States) M

*M—master's degree; P—first professional degree; D—doctorate; O—other advanced degree; *—Close-Up and/or Display in one of the other books in this series*

Schiller International University (United Kingdom)	M
Strayer University	M
Temple University	M*
Tropical Agriculture Research and Higher Education Center	M,D
Université du Québec à Trois-Rivières	M,O
University of Central Florida	M,O
University of Hawaii at Manoa	M
University of Massachusetts Amherst	M*
University of New Orleans	M
University of South Africa	M,D
University of South Carolina	M
The University of Tennessee	M
University of Waterloo	M
Virginia Polytechnic Institute and State University	M,D
Western Illinois University	M

URBAN AND REGIONAL PLANNING

Alabama Agricultural and Mechanical University	M
American University of Beirut	M,D
American University of Sharjah	M
Arizona State University	M,D,O
Auburn University	M
Ball State University	M
Boston University	M*
California Polytechnic State University, San Luis Obispo	M
California State Polytechnic University, Pomona	M
California State University, Chico	M
The Catholic University of America	M
Clark University	M
Clemson University	M
Cleveland State University	M,O
College of Charleston	O
Columbia University	M,D*
Concordia University (Canada)	O
Cornell University	M,D*
Dalhousie University	M
Delta State University	M
DePaul University	M,O
Eastern Kentucky University	M
Eastern Michigan University	M,O
Eastern University	M
Eastern Washington University	M
East Tennessee State University	M,O
Florida Atlantic University	M,O
Florida State University	M,D
Georgia Institute of Technology	M,D
Georgia State University	M,D,O
Harvard University	M,D*
Hunter College of the City University of New York	M
Iowa State University of Science and Technology	M*
Jackson State University	M,D
John Brown University	M
Kansas State University	M*
Lesley University	M
Loyola University Chicago	M,O
Massachusetts Institute of Technology	M,D
McGill University	M,D
Michigan State University	M,D
Minnesota State University Mankato	M,O
Missouri State University	M
Montclair State University	O
Morgan State University	M
New York University	M,O
Northeastern University	M,D,O
The Ohio State University	M,D
Polytechnic Institute of NYU	M
Portland State University	M
Pratt Institute	M*
Queen's University at Kingston	M
Rutgers, The State University of New Jersey, New Brunswick	M,D*
San Diego State University	M
San Jose State University	M,O
State University of New York College of Environmental Science and Forestry	M,D
Temple University	M*
Texas A&M University	M,D
Texas Southern University	M,D
Tufts University	M
Université de Montréal	M,D,O
Université du Québec à Rimouski	M,D,O
Université du Québec en Outaouais	M
Université Laval	M,D
University at Albany, State University of New York	M
University at Buffalo, the State University of New York	M*
The University of Akron	M
The University of Arizona	M
The University of British Columbia	M,D
University of California, Berkeley	M,D*
University of California, Davis	M
University of California, Irvine	M,D*
University of California, Los Angeles	M,D*
University of Central Arkansas	M,O
University of Central Florida	M,O
University of Cincinnati	M
University of Colorado Denver	M,D
University of Florida	M*
University of Hawaii at Manoa	M,D,O
University of Idaho	M
University of Illinois at Chicago	M,D
University of Illinois at Urbana–Champaign	M,D
The University of Iowa	M*
The University of Kansas	M
University of Louisville	M,D
University of Manitoba	M
University of Maryland, College Park	M,D
University of Massachusetts Amherst	M,D*
University of Memphis	M
University of Michigan	M,D,O*
University of Minnesota, Twin Cities Campus	M
University of Nebraska–Lincoln	M,D*
University of New Haven	M,O
University of New Mexico	M*
University of New Orleans	M
The University of North Carolina at Chapel Hill	M,D*
The University of North Carolina at Charlotte	M,D,O
University of Oklahoma	M*
University of Oregon	M
University of Pennsylvania	M,D,O*
University of Pittsburgh	M,O*
University of Puerto Rico, Río Piedras	M
University of Southern California	M,D,O*
University of Southern Maine	M,O
The University of Texas at Arlington	M
The University of Texas at Austin	M,D
The University of Toledo	M,D,O
University of Toronto	M,D
University of Utah	M,D*
University of Virginia	M,O
University of Washington	M,D*
University of Waterloo	M,D
University of Wisconsin–Madison	M,D*
University of Wisconsin–Milwaukee	M,O
Utah State University	M,D
Vanderbilt University	M*
Virginia Commonwealth University	M
Virginia Polytechnic Institute and State University	M,D,O
Wayne State University	M*
West Chester University of Pennsylvania	M,O
West Virginia University	M,D

URBAN DESIGN

American University of Beirut	M,D
Arizona State University	M,D
Ball State University	M
Carnegie Mellon University	M,D*
City College of the City University of New York	M
Cleveland State University	M,O
Cornell University	M,D*
Georgia Institute of Technology	M,D
Harvard University	M*
Kent State University	M,O*
Lawrence Technological University	M
The New School: A University	M
New York Institute of Technology	M
Prairie View A&M University	M
Pratt Institute	M*
Rice University	M,D
Rollins College	M
Savannah College of Art and Design	M
State University of New York College of Environmental Science and Forestry	M
Temple University	M,D*
University at Buffalo, the State University of New York	M*
University of California, Berkeley	M,D*
University of California, Los Angeles	M,D*
University of Colorado Denver	M,D
University of Idaho	M
University of Miami	M*
University of Michigan	M*
University of New Mexico	O*
The University of North Carolina at Charlotte	M
University of Pennsylvania	D*
The University of Texas at Austin	M,D
University of Toronto	M,D
University of Washington	M,D,O*
Washington University in St. Louis	M*
Woodbury University	M

URBAN EDUCATION

Alvernia University	M
Bakke Graduate University	M,D
Brown University	M
Cardinal Stritch University	M,D
Claremont Graduate University	M,D,O
Cleveland State University	D
College of Mount Saint Vincent	M,O
Columbia College Chicago	M
DePaul University	M,D
Florida International University	M,D,O
Graduate School and University Center of the City University of New York	D
Holy Names University	M,O
The Johns Hopkins University	M,O
Kean University	D
Langston University	M
Loyola Marymount University	M
Marygrove College	M
Mercy College	M
Metropolitan State University	M,O
Morgan State University	M,D
New Jersey City University	M
Norfolk State University	M
Northeastern Illinois University	M
Nova Southeastern University	M,O*
Roberts Wesleyan College	M,O
Simmons College	M,O
Sojourner-Douglass College	M
Teachers College, Columbia University	D
Temple University	M,D*
Texas A&M University	M,D
University of Central Florida	M,O
University of Houston–Downtown	M
University of Illinois at Chicago	M,D
University of Massachusetts Boston	M,D,O
University of Michigan–Dearborn	D
University of Nebraska at Omaha	M,O
University of Southern California	D*
University of Wisconsin–Milwaukee	M,D
Vanderbilt University	M*
Virginia Commonwealth University	D

URBAN STUDIES

Azusa Pacific University	M
Boston University	M*
Brooklyn College of the City University of New York	M,D
Cleveland State University	M,D,O
Concordia University (Canada)	M,O
Eastern University	M
East Tennessee State University	M,O
Fordham University	M
Graduate School and University Center of the City University of New York	M,D
Hunter College of the City University of New York	M
Le Moyne College	M,O
Long Island University, Brooklyn Campus	M
Loyola University Chicago	M,D

Massachusetts Institute of Technology M,D
Minnesota State University Mankato M,O
Moody Bible Institute P,M,O
New Jersey City University M
New Jersey Institute of Technology D
The New School: A University M
Norfolk State University M
Northeastern University M,D,O
Old Dominion University D
Polytechnic Institute of NYU M
Portland State University M,D
Queens College of the City University of New York M
Rutgers, The State University of New Jersey, Newark M,D*
Saint Louis University M,D,O
San Francisco Art Institute M
Savannah State University M
Simon Fraser University M,O
Southern Connecticut State University M
Temple University M,D*
Tufts University M
Université du Québec à Montréal M,D
Université du Québec, École nationale d'administration publique M
Université du Québec, Institut National de la Recherche Scientifique M,D
University at Albany, State University of New York M,D,O
The University of Akron M,D
University of California, Irvine M,D*
University of Central Oklahoma M
University of Delaware M,D*
University of Lethbridge M,D
University of Louisville M,D
University of Maryland, Baltimore County M,D
University of New Orleans M,D
University of Wisconsin–Milwaukee M,D
Wright State University M

VETERINARY MEDICINE

Auburn University P
Colorado State University P
Cornell University P*
Iowa State University of Science and Technology P,M*
Louisiana State University and Agricultural and Mechanical College P
Michigan State University P
Mississippi State University P
North Carolina State University P,M*
Oklahoma State University P*
Oregon State University P
Purdue University P
Texas A&M University P,M
Tufts University P,M,D
Tuskegee University P,M
Université de Montréal D
University of California, Davis P
University of Florida P*
University of Georgia P,M
University of Guelph M,D,O
University of Illinois at Urbana–Champaign P
University of Maryland, College Park P
University of Minnesota, Twin Cities Campus P
University of Missouri P*
University of Pennsylvania P*
University of Prince Edward Island P
University of Saskatchewan P,M,D
The University of Tennessee P
University of Wisconsin–Madison P*
Virginia Polytechnic Institute and State University P
Washington State University P
Western University of Health Sciences P

VETERINARY SCIENCES

Auburn University M,D
Clemson University M,D
Colorado State University M,D
Drexel University M*
Iowa State University of Science and Technology M,D*
Kansas State University M*
Louisiana State University and Agricultural and Mechanical College M,D
Michigan State University M,D
Mississippi State University M,D
North Carolina State University M,D*
North Dakota State University M,D
The Ohio State University M,D
Oklahoma State University M,D*
Oregon State University D
Penn State Hershey Medical Center M
Penn State University Park D
Purdue University M,D
South Dakota State University M,D
Texas A&M University M
Tuskegee University P,M
Université de Montréal M,D
University of California, Davis M,O
University of Florida M,D,O*
University of Georgia M,D
University of Guelph M,D,O
University of Idaho M,D
University of Illinois at Urbana–Champaign M,D
University of Kentucky M,D*
University of Maryland, College Park M,D
University of Minnesota, Twin Cities Campus M,D
University of Missouri M,D*
University of Nebraska–Lincoln M,D*
University of Prince Edward Island M,D
University of Saskatchewan M,D
University of Washington M*
University of Wisconsin–Madison M,D*
Utah State University M,D
Virginia Polytechnic Institute and State University M,D
Washington State University M,D

VIROLOGY

Baylor College of Medicine D*
Case Western Reserve University D*
Mayo Graduate School D
McMaster University M,D
The Ohio State University D
Penn State Hershey Medical Center M,D
Purdue University M,D
Rush University M,D
Rutgers, The State University of New Jersey, New Brunswick M,D*
Texas A&M Health Science Center D
Université de Montréal D
Université du Québec, Institut National de la Recherche Scientifique M,D
University of California, San Diego D*
The University of Iowa M,D*
University of Massachusetts Worcester M,D
University of Minnesota, Twin Cities Campus D
University of Pennsylvania D*
University of Pittsburgh M,D*
University of Prince Edward Island M,D
The University of Texas Health Science Center at Houston M,D*
The University of Texas Medical Branch D
Yale University D*

VISION SCIENCES

Eastern Virginia Medical School O
The New England College of Optometry P,M
Nova Southeastern University P,M*
Salus University M,O
State University of New York College of Optometry D
Université de Montréal M,O
The University of Alabama at Birmingham M,D*
The University of Alabama in Huntsville M,D
University of Alberta M,D
University of California, Berkeley M,D*
University of Chicago D
University of Guelph M,D,O
University of Houston M,D
The University of Manchester M,D
University of Missouri–St. Louis M,D
University of Waterloo M,D

VITICULTURE AND ENOLOGY

California State University, Fresno M
University of California, Davis M,D

VOCATIONAL AND TECHNICAL EDUCATION

Alabama Agricultural and Mechanical University M
Alcorn State University M,O
Appalachian State University M
Ball State University M
Bowling Green State University M*
Buffalo State College, State University of New York M
California Baptist University M
California State University, Sacramento M
California State University, San Bernardino M
California University of Pennsylvania M
Central Connecticut State University M,O
Chicago State University M
Clarion University of Pennsylvania M
Colorado State University M,D
East Carolina University M
Eastern Kentucky University M
Eastern Michigan University M
Eastern New Mexico University M
Fitchburg State University M
Florida Agricultural and Mechanical University M
Idaho State University M
Indiana State University M
Inter American University of Puerto Rico, Metropolitan Campus M
Iowa State University of Science and Technology M,D*
Jackson State University M
James Madison University M
Kansas State University M,D*
Kent State University M*
Louisiana State University and Agricultural and Mechanical College M,D
Marshall University M
Middle Tennessee State University M
Millersville University of Pennsylvania M
Mississippi State University M,D,O
Montana State University M,D,O
Morehead State University M
Murray State University M
North Carolina Agricultural and Technical State University M,D
North Dakota State University M,D,O
Northern Arizona University M,D,O
Nova Southeastern University D*
Old Dominion University M,D
Our Lady of the Lake University of San Antonio M
Penn State University Park M,D
Pittsburg State University M,O
Purdue University M,D,O
Rhode Island College M
Saint Martin's University M
South Carolina State University M,D,O
Southern Illinois University Carbondale M,D
Southern New Hampshire University M,O
State University of New York at Oswego M
Temple University M,D*
Texas State University–San Marcos M
Trevecca Nazarene University M
The University of Akron M
University of Arkansas M,D
The University of British Columbia M,D
University of Calgary M,D,O
University of Central Florida M
University of Central Missouri M,D,O
University of Georgia M,D,O
University of Illinois at Urbana–Champaign M,D,O
University of Kentucky M*
University of Maryland Eastern Shore M
University of Minnesota, Twin Cities Campus M,D,O
University of Missouri M,D,O*
University of Nebraska–Lincoln M,D,O*

*M—master's degree; P—first professional degree; D—doctorate; O—other advanced degree; *—Close-Up and/or Display in one of the other books in this series*

University of Northern Iowa M,D
University of North Texas M,D
University of Phoenix–Phoenix Campus M
University of South Africa M,D
University of Southern Mississippi M
University of South Florida M,D,O*
The University of Texas at Tyler M,D
The University of Toledo M,D,O
University of Victoria M,D
University of West Florida M
University of Wisconsin–Stout M,O
Utah State University M
Valley City State University M
Virginia Polytechnic Institute and State University M,D,O
Virginia State University M,O
Wayne State College M
Wayne State University M,D,O*
Western Michigan University M
Westfield State University M,O
Wilmington University M
Wright State University M

WATER RESOURCES

Albany State University M
California State University, Monterey Bay M
Colorado State University M,D
Duke University M*
Eastern Michigan University M,O
Humboldt State University M
Inter American University of Puerto Rico, San Germán Campus M
Marquette University M,D,O
Missouri University of Science and Technology M,D
Nova Scotia Agricultural College M
Rutgers, The State University of New Jersey, New Brunswick M,D*
State University of New York College of Environmental Science and Forestry M,D
Tropical Agriculture Research and Higher Education Center M,D
University of Alaska Fairbanks M,D
The University of Arizona M,D
University of California, Riverside M,D
University of Colorado Denver M
University of Florida M,D*
University of Idaho M,D
University of Maine M,D
University of Massachusetts Amherst M,D*
University of Minnesota, Twin Cities Campus M,D
University of Nevada, Las Vegas M
University of New Brunswick Fredericton M,D
University of New Hampshire M
University of New Mexico M*
University of Southern California M,D,O*
University of the Pacific P,M,D
University of Wisconsin–Madison M*
University of Wisconsin–Milwaukee M,D
University of Wyoming M,D
Utah State University M,D
Virginia Polytechnic Institute and State University M,D,O

WATER RESOURCES ENGINEERING

American University of Beirut M,D
Cornell University M,D*
George Mason University M,D,O*
Indiana University Bloomington M,D*
Louisiana State University and Agricultural and Mechanical College M,D
Marquette University M,D,O
McGill University M,D
New Mexico Institute of Mining and Technology M
Norwich University M
Ohio University M,D*
Oregon State University M,D
State University of New York College of Environmental Science and Forestry M,D
Stevens Institute of Technology M,D,O
Texas A&M University M,D
Tufts University M,D
The University of Alabama in Huntsville M,D
University of Alberta M,D
University of California, Berkeley M,D*
University of Colorado Boulder M,D*
University of Dayton M
University of Delaware M,D*
University of Guelph M,D
University of Maine M,D
University of Memphis M,D
University of Missouri M,D*
University of New Haven M,O
The University of Texas at Austin M,D
The University of Texas at Tyler M
University of Washington M,D*
Utah State University M,D
Villanova University M,O
Virginia Polytechnic Institute and State University M,D,O

WESTERN EUROPEAN STUDIES

American University M,D,O
Boston College M,D*
Brown University M,D
California State University, Long Beach M
Carleton University M,O
The Catholic University of America M,D
Central Michigan University M,D,O
Claremont Graduate University M,D,O
Columbia University M,O*
Cornell University M,D*
East Carolina University M
Georgetown University M
The George Washington University M
Indiana University Bloomington M*
Mississippi State University M,D
Monmouth University M
New York University M
San Diego State University M
Syracuse University O*
University of Colorado Denver M
University of Connecticut M*
University of Florida M,D*
University of Guelph M
University of Illinois at Urbana–Champaign M
University of Maine M,D
University of Nevada, Reno D*
University of Pittsburgh O*
Washington State University M,D

WOMEN'S HEALTH NURSING

Case Western Reserve University M,D*
Columbia University O*
Emory University M*
Frontier School of Midwifery and Family Nursing M,O
Georgia Southern University M,D,O
Georgia State University M,D,O
Hampton University M
Indiana University–Purdue University Fort Wayne M,O
Indiana University–Purdue University Indianapolis M,D
The Johns Hopkins University M,O
Kent State University M,D*
Loyola University Chicago M
Metropolitan State University M,D
MGH Institute of Health Professions M,D,O
Old Dominion University M
Queen's University at Kingston M,D,O
Quinnipiac University D
Rosalind Franklin University of Medicine and Science M,O*
Stony Brook University, State University of New York M,O
Texas Woman's University M,D
University of Cincinnati M,D
University of Colorado at Colorado Springs M,D
University of Colorado Denver M,D
University of Delaware M,O*
University of Illinois at Chicago M
University of Medicine and Dentistry of New Jersey M,D,O
University of Minnesota, Twin Cities Campus M
University of Missouri–Kansas City M,D*
University of Missouri–St. Louis M,D,O
The University of North Carolina at Chapel Hill M,D,O*
University of Pennsylvania M*
University of South Carolina M
Vanderbilt University M,D*
Virginia Commonwealth University M,D,O
Wilmington University M

WOMEN'S STUDIES

The American University in Cairo M,O
Brandeis University M,D
California Institute of Integral Studies M,D
Claremont Graduate University M,D
Clark Atlanta University M,D
Cornell University M,D*
Eastern Michigan University M,O
Emory University D,O*
Florida Atlantic University M,O
The George Washington University M,O
Georgia State University M,O
Graduate School and University Center of the City University of New York M,D
Institute of Transpersonal Psychology M
Inter American University of Puerto Rico, Metropolitan Campus M
The Jewish Theological Seminary M,D
Lakehead University M,D
Lesley University M
Memorial University of Newfoundland M
Minnesota State University Mankato M,O
Mount Saint Vincent University M
Northern Arizona University O
The Ohio State University M,D
Old Dominion University M,D
Queen's University at Kingston M,D
Reconstructionist Rabbinical College P,M,D,O
Roosevelt University M,O
Rutgers, The State University of New Jersey, New Brunswick M,D*
Saint Mary's University (Canada) M
San Diego State University M
San Francisco State University M
Sarah Lawrence College M
Simon Fraser University M,D
Smith College O
Southeastern Baptist Theological Seminary P,M,D
Southern Connecticut State University M
Stony Brook University, State University of New York O
Suffolk University M
Syracuse University O*
Texas Woman's University M,D
Towson University M,O
United Theological Seminary of the Twin Cities P,M,D,O
Université Laval O
University at Albany, State University of New York M,D
The University of Alabama M
The University of Arizona M,D
University of California, Los Angeles M,D*
University of California, Santa Barbara M,D
University of Cincinnati M,O
University of Colorado Denver M
University of Florida M,O*
University of Georgia O
University of Hawaii at Manoa O
The University of Iowa D*
University of Lethbridge M,D
University of Louisville M,O
University of Maryland, Baltimore County O
University of Maryland, College Park M,D
University of Massachusetts Boston M,D,O
University of Michigan D,O*
University of Minnesota, Twin Cities Campus D
University of Nevada, Las Vegas O
University of New Mexico O*
The University of North Carolina at Charlotte M,O
The University of North Carolina at Greensboro M,D,O

Institution	Degrees
University of Northern Iowa	M
University of Oklahoma	O*
University of Ottawa	M*
University of Pittsburgh	O*
University of Regina	M
University of Saskatchewan	M,D
University of South Carolina	O
University of South Florida	M*
The University of Texas at El Paso	O
University of Toronto	M
University of Washington	D*
University of Wisconsin–Madison	M,D*
University of Wisconsin–Milwaukee	M
Virginia Polytechnic Institute and State University	M,D,O
Washington State University	M,D
Western Seminary	M
Western Seminary–Sacramento Campus	O
York University	M,D*

WRITING

Institution	Degrees
Abilene Christian University	M
Adelphi University	M*
Albertus Magnus College	M
American University	M
Antioch University Los Angeles	M,O
Antioch University Midwest	M
Arizona State University	M
Asbury University	M
Ashland University	M
Ball State University	M,D
Belmont University	M
Bennington College	M
Boise State University	M
Boston University	M,D*
Bowling Green State University	M,D*
Brigham Young University	M*
Brooklyn College of the City University of New York	M
Brown University	M
California College of the Arts	M
California Institute of Integral Studies	M,D
California Institute of the Arts	M,O
California State University, Fresno	M
California State University, Long Beach	M
California State University, Northridge	M
California State University, Sacramento	M
California State University, San Bernardino	M
California State University, San Marcos	M
California State University, Stanislaus	M,O
Carlow University	M
Carnegie Mellon University	M*
Central Michigan University	M
Chapman University	M
Chatham University	M
Chicago State University	M
City College of the City University of New York	M
Claremont Graduate University	M,D
Clemson University	M
Cleveland State University	M
Coastal Carolina University	M
The College at Brockport, State University of New York	M
Colorado State University	M
Columbia College Chicago	M
Columbia University	M*
Concordia University (Canada)	M
Cornell University	M,D*
Creighton University	M
DePaul University	M
Drew University	M
Eastern Kentucky University	M
Eastern Michigan University	M,O
Eastern Washington University	M
Emerson College	M
Fairfield University	M
Fairleigh Dickinson University, College at Florham	M
Florida Atlantic University	M
Florida International University	M
Florida State University	M,D
Full Sail University	M
George Mason University	M*
Georgia College & State University	M
Georgia State University	M,D
Goddard College	M
Goucher College	M
Hamline University	M,O
Hofstra University	M,D,O
Hollins University	M
Holy Names University	M
Hunter College of the City University of New York	M
Illinois State University	M
Indiana State University	M
Indiana University Bloomington	M,D*
Indiana University of Pennsylvania	M,D
Iowa State University of Science and Technology	M,D*
The Johns Hopkins University	M
Kean University	M
Kennesaw State University	M
Kent State University	M,D*
La Sierra University	M
Lesley University	M
Lindenwood University	M,O
Long Island University, Brooklyn Campus	M
Longwood University	M
Louisiana State University and Agricultural and Mechanical College	M,D
Loyola Marymount University	M
Manhattanville College	M*
Massachusetts Institute of Technology	M
McNeese State University	M
Michigan State University	M,D
Mills College	M
Minnesota State University Mankato	M,O
Minnesota State University Moorhead	M
Missouri Western State University	M
Monmouth University	M
Montclair State University	M,O
Murray State University	M
Naropa University	M
National-Louis University	M,D,O
National University	M
New England College	M
New Mexico Highlands University	M
New Mexico State University	M,D
The New School: A University	M
New York University	M,D
North Carolina State University	M*
Northeastern Illinois University	M
Northern Arizona University	M,D,O
Northern Kentucky University	M,O
Northern Michigan University	M
Northwestern University	M*
Oklahoma City University	M
Oklahoma State University	M,D*
Old Dominion University	M
Otis College of Art and Design	M
Our Lady of the Lake University of San Antonio	M
Pacific Lutheran University	M
Pacific University	M
Penn State University Park	M,D
Pepperdine University	M
Perelandra College	M
Purdue University	M,D
Queens College of the City University of New York	M
Queens University of Charlotte	M
Rhode Island College	M,O
Rivier College	M
Roosevelt University	M
Rosemont College	M
Rowan University	M
Rutgers, The State University of New Jersey, Camden	M
Rutgers, The State University of New Jersey, Newark	M*
Rutgers, The State University of New Jersey, New Brunswick	M*
Saint Joseph's University	M
Saint Mary's College of California	M
Saint Xavier University	M,O
Salisbury University	M
San Diego State University	M
San Francisco State University	M
Sarah Lawrence College	M
Savannah College of Art and Design	M
School of the Art Institute of Chicago	M,O
Seattle Pacific University	M
Seton Hall University	M
Seton Hill University	M,O
Sewanee: The University of the South	M
Sonoma State University	M
Southeastern Louisiana University	M
Southern Illinois University Carbondale	M
Southern Illinois University Edwardsville	M
Southern New Hampshire University	M,O
Spalding University	M
Stony Brook University, State University of New York	M,O
Syracuse University	M,D*
Temple University	M*
Texas State University–San Marcos	M
Towson University	M
Union Institute & University	M
The University of Akron	M
The University of Alabama	M,D
University of Alaska Anchorage	M
University of Alaska Fairbanks	M
The University of Arizona	M
University of Arkansas	M
University of Arkansas at Little Rock	M
University of Baltimore	M
The University of British Columbia	M,O
University of California, Berkeley	O*
University of California, Davis	M,D
University of California, Irvine	M*
University of California, Riverside	M
University of California, Santa Cruz	M
University of Central Florida	M,O
University of Central Oklahoma	M
University of Colorado Boulder	M,D*
University of Colorado Denver	M
University of Denver	M,D,O
University of Florida	M,D*
University of Georgia	M,D
University of Houston	M,D
University of Houston–Downtown	M
University of Idaho	M
University of Illinois at Chicago	M,D
University of Illinois at Urbana–Champaign	M,D
The University of Iowa	M,D*
The University of Kansas	M,D
University of Louisiana at Lafayette	M,D*
University of Louisville	M,D
University of Maine	M
The University of Manchester	D
University of Maryland, College Park	M,D
University of Massachusetts Amherst	M,D*
University of Massachusetts Dartmouth	M,O
University of Memphis	M,D,O
University of Miami	M,D*
University of Michigan	M*
University of Missouri–Kansas City	M,D*
University of Missouri–St. Louis	M,O
The University of Montana	M
University of Nebraska at Kearney	M
University of Nebraska at Omaha	M,O
University of Nebraska–Lincoln	M,D*
University of Nevada, Las Vegas	M,D
University of New Hampshire	M,D
University of New Mexico	M,D*
The University of North Carolina at Charlotte	M,O
The University of North Carolina at Greensboro	M
The University of North Carolina Wilmington	M
University of Northern Iowa	M
University of North Florida	M
University of North Texas	M,D
University of Notre Dame	M*
University of Oklahoma	M,D*
University of Oregon	M
University of Pennsylvania	M,D*
University of Pittsburgh	M,D*

*M—master's degree; P—first professional degree; D—doctorate; O—other advanced degree; *—Close-Up and/or Display in one of the other books in this series*

University of San Francisco M
University of South Carolina M,D
University of Southern California M,D*
University of Southern Maine M
University of Southern Mississippi M,D
The University of Tennessee at Chattanooga M,O
The University of Texas at Austin M,D
The University of Texas at El Paso M,D,O
University of the Sacred Heart M,O
The University of Toledo M,O
University of Utah M,D*
University of Victoria M
University of Virginia M
University of Washington M*
University of West Florida M
University of Windsor M
University of Wisconsin–Eau Claire M
University of Wisconsin–Madison M,D*
University of Wisconsin–Milwaukee M,D,O
University of Wyoming M
Utah State University M
Vanderbilt University M*
Vermont College of Fine Arts M
Virginia Commonwealth University M
Warren Wilson College M
Washington University in St. Louis M*
Wayne State University M,D*
Western Connecticut State University M
Western Illinois University M,O
Western Kentucky University M
Western Michigan University M,D
Western State College of Colorado M*
Westminster College (UT) M
West Virginia University M
Wichita State University M
Wilkes University M
Wright State University M

ZOOLOGY

Auburn University M,D
Colorado State University M,D
Cornell University M,D*
Eastern New Mexico University M
Emporia State University M
Illinois State University M,D
Indiana University Bloomington M,D*
Miami University M,D
Michigan State University M,D
North Carolina State University M,D*
North Dakota State University M,D
Oklahoma State University M,D*
Oregon State University M,D
Southern Illinois University Carbondale M,D
Texas A&M University M,D
Texas Tech University M,D*
Uniformed Services University of the Health Sciences M,D*
University of Alaska Fairbanks M,D
The University of British Columbia M,D
University of California, Davis M
University of Chicago D
University of Connecticut M,D*
University of Florida M,D*
University of Guelph M,D
University of Hawaii at Manoa M,D
University of Illinois at Urbana–Champaign M,D
University of Maine M,D
University of Manitoba M,D
The University of Montana M,D
University of New Hampshire M,D
University of North Dakota M,D
University of Oklahoma M,D*
The University of Western Ontario M,D
University of Wisconsin–Madison M,D*
University of Wisconsin–Oshkosh M
University of Wyoming M,D
Washington State University M,D
Western Illinois University M,O

DIRECTORY OF INSTITUTIONS AND THEIR OFFERINGS

ABILENE CHRISTIAN UNIVERSITY

Accounting M
Clinical Psychology M
Communication Disorders M
Communication—General M
Conflict Resolution and Mediation/Peace Studies M,O
Counseling Psychology M
Curriculum and Instruction M
Education—General M,O
Educational Leadership and Administration M,O
English M
Family Nurse Practitioner Studies M,O
Higher Education M
Human Resources Development M
Human Services M,O
Liberal Studies M
Marriage and Family Therapy M
Missions and Missiology M
Nursing and Healthcare Administration M,O
Nursing Education M,O
Nursing—General M,O
Pastoral Ministry and Counseling M,D
Psychology—General M
Rhetoric M
School Psychology O
Social Work M
Theology P,M
Writing M

ACADEMY FOR FIVE ELEMENT ACUPUNCTURE

Acupuncture and Oriental Medicine M

ACADEMY OF ART UNIVERSITY

Advertising and Public Relations M
Applied Arts and Design—General M
Architecture M
Art Education M
Art/Fine Arts M
Clothing and Textiles M
Computer Art and Design M
Film, Television, and Video Production M
Game Design and Development M
Graphic Design M
Illustration M
Industrial Design M
Interior Design M
Internet and Interactive Multimedia M
Modeling and Simulation M
Music M
Photography M
Textile Design M

ACADEMY OF CHINESE CULTURE AND HEALTH SCIENCES

Acupuncture and Oriental Medicine M

ACADEMY OF ORIENTAL MEDICINE AT AUSTIN

Acupuncture and Oriental Medicine M

ACADIA UNIVERSITY

Applied Mathematics M
Biological and Biomedical Sciences—General M
Chemistry M
Clinical Psychology M
Computer Science M
Counselor Education M
Curriculum and Instruction M
Education—General M
Educational Leadership and Administration M
Educational Media/ Instructional Technology M
English M
Geographic Information Systems M
Geology M
Kinesiology and Movement Studies M
Mathematics Education M
Political Science M
Psychology—General M
Recreation and Park Management M
Science Education M
Social Sciences Education M
Sociology M
Special Education M
Statistics M
Theology P,M,D

ACUPUNCTURE & INTEGRATIVE MEDICINE COLLEGE, BERKELEY

Acupuncture and Oriental Medicine M

ACUPUNCTURE AND MASSAGE COLLEGE

Acupuncture and Oriental Medicine M

ADAMS STATE COLLEGE

Art/Fine Arts M
Counselor Education M
Education—General M
History M
Physical Education M
Special Education M

ADELPHI UNIVERSITY

Accounting M
Art Education M
Art/Fine Arts M*
Biological and Biomedical Sciences—General M*
Business Administration and Management—General M*
Clinical Psychology D
Communication Disorders M,D
Community Health M,O
Counseling Psychology M
Early Childhood Education M,O
Education—General M,D,O*
Educational Leadership and Administration M,O
Educational Media/ Instructional Technology M,O
Electronic Commerce M
Elementary Education M
Emergency Management O
English as a Second Language M,O
Environmental Management and Policy M*
Finance and Banking M
Gerontology M,O
Health Education M,O
Human Resources Management M,O
Management Information Systems M
Marketing M
Nursing—General M,D,O*
Physical Education M,O
Psychology—General M,D*
Public Administration O
Public Health—General O
Reading Education M
School Psychology M
Secondary Education M
Social Work M,D*
Special Education M,O
Writing M*

ADLER GRADUATE SCHOOL

Art Therapy M,O
Clinical Psychology M,O
Counseling Psychology M,O
Counselor Education M,O
Marriage and Family Therapy M,O
Organizational Management M,O
Psychoanalysis and Psychotherapy M,O

ADLER SCHOOL OF PROFESSIONAL PSYCHOLOGY

Addictions/Substance Abuse Counseling M,D,O
Art Therapy M,D,O
Biopsychology M,D,O
Clinical Psychology M,D,O
Counseling Psychology M,D,O
Criminal Justice and Criminology M,D,O
Forensic Psychology M,D,O
Gerontology M,D,O
Health Psychology M,D,O
Industrial and Organizational Psychology M,D,O
Marriage and Family Therapy M,D,O
Psychoanalysis and Psychotherapy M,D,O
Psychology—General M,D,O*
Rehabilitation Counseling M,D,O
Social Psychology M,D,O
Sport Psychology M,D,O

AIR FORCE INSTITUTE OF TECHNOLOGY

Aerospace/Aeronautical Engineering M,D
Applied Mathematics M,D
Applied Physics M,D
Astrophysics M,D
Computer Engineering M,D
Computer Science M,D
Electrical Engineering M,D
Engineering and Applied Sciences—General M,D
Engineering Management M
Engineering Physics M,D
Environmental Engineering M
Environmental Management and Policy M
Logistics M,D
Management Information Systems M
Management of Technology M,D
Materials Sciences M,D
Nuclear Engineering M,D
Operations Research M,D
Optical Sciences M,D
Planetary and Space Sciences M,D
Systems Engineering M,D

ALABAMA AGRICULTURAL AND MECHANICAL UNIVERSITY

Agricultural Economics and Agribusiness M
Agricultural Sciences—General M,D
Agronomy and Soil Sciences M,D
Animal Sciences M,D
Applied Physics M,D
Biological and Biomedical Sciences—General M
Business Administration and Management—General M
Clinical Psychology M,O
Communication Disorders M
Computer Science M
Counseling Psychology M,O
Counselor Education M,O
Early Childhood Education M,O
Education—General M,O
Educational Leadership and Administration M,O
Elementary Education M,O
Engineering and Applied Sciences—General M
Environmental Sciences M,D
Family and Consumer Sciences-General M,D
Food Science and Technology M,D
Human Resources Management M,O
Marketing M
Materials Sciences M,D
Music Education M
Music M
Optical Sciences M,D
Physical Education M
Physics M,D
Plant Sciences M,D
Psychology—General M,O
School Psychology M,O
Secondary Education M,O
Social Work M
Special Education M,O
Urban and Regional Planning M
Vocational and Technical Education M

ALABAMA STATE UNIVERSITY

Accounting M
Allied Health—General D
Biological and Biomedical Sciences—General M
Counselor Education M,O
Early Childhood Education M,O
Educational Leadership and Administration M,D,O
Educational Media/ Instructional Technology M,O
Educational Policy M,D,O
Elementary Education M,O
English Education M,O
Environmental Sciences M,D
Geology M,D
Geosciences M,D
Health Education M
Mathematics Education M,O
Mathematics M,O
Music M
Physical Education M
Physical Therapy D
Science Education M,O
Secondary Education M,O
Social Sciences Education M,O
Special Education M

ALASKA PACIFIC UNIVERSITY

Business Administration and Management—General M
Counseling Psychology M
Education—General M
Elementary Education M
Environmental Education M
Environmental Sciences M
Health Services Management and Hospital Administration M
Interdisciplinary Studies M
Investment Management M,O
Liberal Studies M
Middle School Education M
Telecommunications Management M

ALBANY COLLEGE OF PHARMACY AND HEALTH SCIENCES

Biotechnology P,M

Cell Biology P,M
Health Services Research P,M
Pharmacy P,M*

ALBANY LAW SCHOOL

Law P,M

ALBANY MEDICAL COLLEGE

Allopathic Medicine P
Bioethics M,O
Cardiovascular Sciences M,D
Cell Biology M,D
Immunology M,D
Microbiology M,D
Molecular Biology M,D
Neuroscience M,D
Nurse Anesthesia M
Pharmacology M,D
Physician Assistant Studies M

ALBANY STATE UNIVERSITY

Accounting M
Business Administration and Management—General M
Counselor Education M
Criminal Justice and Criminology M
Early Childhood Education M
Economic Development M
Economics M
Education—General M,O
Educational Leadership and Administration M,O
Family Nurse Practitioner Studies M
Forensic Sciences M
Health Education M
Health Services Management and Hospital Administration M
Human Resources Management M
Mathematics Education M
Middle School Education M
Nursing Education M
Nursing—General M
Physical Education M
Public Administration M
Public Policy M
Science Education M
Social Work M
Special Education M
Water Resources M

ALBERT EINSTEIN COLLEGE OF MEDICINE

Allopathic Medicine P
Anatomy D
Biochemistry D
Biological and Biomedical Sciences—General D
Biophysics D
Cell Biology D
Developmental Biology D
Genetics D
Genomic Sciences D
Immunology D
Microbiology D
Molecular Biology D
Molecular Genetics D
Molecular Pharmacology D
Neurobiology D
Pathology D
Physiology D

ALBERTUS MAGNUS COLLEGE

Art Therapy M
Business Administration and Management—General M
Education—General M
Human Services M
Liberal Studies M
Writing M

ALBRIGHT COLLEGE

Early Childhood Education M
Education—General M
Elementary Education M
English as a Second Language M
Special Education M

ALCORN STATE UNIVERSITY

Agricultural Economics and Agribusiness M
Agricultural Education M,O
Agricultural Sciences—General M
Agronomy and Soil Sciences M
Animal Sciences M
Biological and Biomedical Sciences—General M
Business Administration and Management—General M
Computer Science M
Counselor Education M,O
Education—General M,O
Elementary Education M,O
Health Education M,O
Information Science M
Nursing—General M
Physical Education M,O
Secondary Education M,O
Special Education M,O
Vocational and Technical Education M,O

ALDERSON-BROADDUS COLLEGE

Physician Assistant Studies M

ALFRED UNIVERSITY

Applied Arts and Design—General M
Art/Fine Arts M,D
Bioengineering M,D
Business Administration and Management—General M
Ceramic Sciences and Engineering M,D
Computer Art and Design M
Counselor Education M,D,O
Education—General M
Electrical Engineering M,D
Engineering and Applied Sciences—General M,D
Internet and Interactive Multimedia M
Materials Sciences M,D
Mathematics Education M
Mechanical Engineering M,D
Reading Education M
School Psychology M,D,O

ALLEN COLLEGE

Acute Care/Critical Care Nursing M,D,O
Adult Nursing M,D,O
Family Nurse Practitioner Studies M,D,O
Gerontological Nursing M,D,O
Health Education M,D,O
Nursing and Healthcare Administration M,D,O
Nursing—General M,D,O
Psychiatric Nursing M,D,O

ALLIANT INTERNATIONAL UNIVERSITY–FRESNO

Clinical Psychology D
Education—General M
Educational Leadership and Administration D
English as a Second Language M,D,O
Forensic Psychology D
Industrial and Organizational Psychology M,D
Psychology—General D

ALLIANT INTERNATIONAL UNIVERSITY–IRVINE

Education—General M,O
Educational Leadership and Administration M,D,O
Educational Media/Instructional Technology M,O
Educational Psychology M,D,O
English as a Second Language M,D
Forensic Psychology D
Forensic Sciences D
Higher Education M,D,O
Marriage and Family Therapy M,D
Multilingual and Multicultural Education M,O
School Psychology M,D,O
Special Education M,O

ALLIANT INTERNATIONAL UNIVERSITY–LOS ANGELES

Addictions/Substance Abuse Counseling M
Business Administration and Management—General D
Clinical Psychology D
Education—General M
Educational Leadership and Administration M,D,O
Educational Psychology M,D,O
Forensic Psychology D
Gerontology M
Higher Education M,D,O
Industrial and Organizational Psychology M,D
Marriage and Family Therapy M
Psychology—General M,D
School Psychology M,D,O
Student Affairs M,D,O

ALLIANT INTERNATIONAL UNIVERSITY–MÉXICO CITY

Business Administration and Management—General M
Counseling Psychology M
Education—General M
International Affairs M
International Business M

ALLIANT INTERNATIONAL UNIVERSITY–SACRAMENTO

Clinical Psychology D
Education—General M
Industrial and Organizational Psychology D
Marriage and Family Therapy M
Psychology—General M,D

ALLIANT INTERNATIONAL UNIVERSITY–SAN DIEGO

Business Administration and Management—General M,D
Clinical Psychology M,D
Education—General M,O
Educational Leadership and Administration M,D,O
Educational Psychology M,D,O
English as a Second Language M,D,O
Finance and Banking M,D
Higher Education M,D,O
Industrial and Organizational Psychology M,D
International Affairs M
International Business M,D
Management Information Systems M,D
Management of Technology M,D
Management Strategy and Policy M,D
Marketing M,D
Marriage and Family Therapy M,D
Psychology—General M,D
School Psychology M,D,O
Student Affairs M,D,O
Sustainability Management M,D

ALLIANT INTERNATIONAL UNIVERSITY–SAN FRANCISCO

Business Administration and Management—General M
Clinical Psychology D,O
Education—General M,O
Educational Leadership and Administration M,D,O
Educational Psychology M,D,O
Higher Education M,D,O
Industrial and Organizational Psychology M,D
Multilingual and Multicultural Education M,O
Pharmacology M
Psychology—General M,D,O
School Psychology M,D,O
Special Education M,O
Sustainability Management M

ALVERNIA UNIVERSITY

Business Administration and Management—General M
Education—General M
Liberal Studies M
Occupational Therapy M
Organizational Management D
Social Psychology M
Urban Education M

ALVERNO COLLEGE

Adult Education M
Business Administration and Management—General M
Education—General M
Educational Leadership and Administration M
Educational Media/Instructional Technology M
Nursing—General M
Reading Education M
Science Education M

AMBERTON UNIVERSITY

Business Administration and Management—General M
Counseling Psychology M
Human Resources Development M
Human Resources Management M
Interdisciplinary Studies M

AMBROSE UNIVERSITY COLLEGE

Cultural Studies P,M,O
Missions and Missiology P,M,O
Religion P,M,O
Theology P,M,O

*M—master's degree; P—first professional degree; D—doctorate; O—other advanced degree; *—Close-Up and/or Display in one of the other books in this series*

AMERICAN BAPTIST SEMINARY OF THE WEST

Pastoral Ministry and Counseling P,M
Theology P,M

THE AMERICAN COLLEGE

Business Administration and Management—General M
Finance and Banking M
Organizational Management M

AMERICAN COLLEGE OF ACUPUNCTURE AND ORIENTAL MEDICINE

Acupuncture and Oriental Medicine M

AMERICAN COLLEGE OF EDUCATION

Curriculum and Instruction M
Education—General M
Educational Leadership and Administration M
Educational Media/Instructional Technology M
English as a Second Language M
Multilingual and Multicultural Education M

AMERICAN COLLEGE OF HEALTHCARE SCIENCES

Allied Health—General M

AMERICAN COLLEGE OF THESSALONIKI

Business Administration and Management—General M,O
Entrepreneurship M,O
Finance and Banking M,O
Marketing M,O

AMERICAN COLLEGE OF TRADITIONAL CHINESE MEDICINE

Acupuncture and Oriental Medicine M,D,O

AMERICAN CONSERVATORY THEATER

Theater M,O

AMERICAN FILM INSTITUTE CONSERVATORY

Film, Television, and Video Production M

AMERICAN GRADUATE SCHOOL IN PARIS

International Affairs M,D

AMERICAN GRADUATE UNIVERSITY

Business Administration and Management—General M,O
Project Management M,O

AMERICAN INTERCONTINENTAL UNIVERSITY ATLANTA

Information Science M
International Business M
Management Information Systems M

AMERICAN INTERCONTINENTAL UNIVERSITY BUCKHEAD CAMPUS

Accounting M
Business Administration and Management—General M
Finance and Banking M
Marketing M

AMERICAN INTERCONTINENTAL UNIVERSITY HOUSTON

Business Administration and Management—General M

AMERICAN INTERCONTINENTAL UNIVERSITY LONDON

Business Administration and Management—General M
International Business M
Management Information Systems M

AMERICAN INTERCONTINENTAL UNIVERSITY ONLINE

Accounting M
Business Administration and Management—General M
Computer and Information Systems Security M
Curriculum and Instruction M
Education—General M
Educational Leadership and Administration M
Educational Measurement and Evaluation M
Educational Media/Instructional Technology M
Finance and Banking M
Health Services Management and Hospital Administration M
Human Resources Management M
Industrial and Manufacturing Management M
Industrial and Organizational Psychology M
Information Science M
International Business M
Marketing M
Project Management M

AMERICAN INTERCONTINENTAL UNIVERSITY SOUTH FLORIDA

Accounting M
Business Administration and Management—General M
Computer and Information Systems Security M
Educational Media/Instructional Technology M
Finance and Banking M
Human Resources Management M
Information Science M
International Business M
Marketing M

AMERICAN INTERNATIONAL COLLEGE

Accounting M
Business Administration and Management—General M
Clinical Psychology M
Corporate and Organizational Communication M
Counselor Education M,D,O
Early Childhood Education M,D,O
Education—General M,D,O
Educational Leadership and Administration M,D,O
Educational Psychology M,D
Elementary Education M,D,O
Finance and Banking M
Forensic Psychology M
Hospitality Management M
Human Resources Development M
International Business M
Management Information Systems M
Marketing M
Middle School Education M,D,O
Nonprofit Management M
Nursing and Healthcare Administration M
Nursing Education M
Nursing—General M
Occupational Therapy M
Organizational Management M
Physical Therapy D
Psychology—General M,D
Public Administration M
Reading Education M,D,O
Secondary Education M,D,O
Special Education M,D,O
Taxation M

AMERICAN JEWISH UNIVERSITY

Business Administration and Management—General M
Education—General M
Jewish Studies M
Nonprofit Management M
Social Work M
Theology M

AMERICAN PUBLIC UNIVERSITY SYSTEM

Accounting M
Business Administration and Management—General M
Conflict Resolution and Mediation/Peace Studies M
Counselor Education M
Criminal Justice and Criminology M
Education—General M
Educational Leadership and Administration M
Elementary Education M
Emergency Management M
Entrepreneurship M
Environmental Management and Policy M
Finance and Banking M
History M
Homeland Security M
Human Resources Management M
Humanities M
International Affairs M
International Business M
Legal and Justice Studies M
Logistics M
Management Information Systems M
Management Strategy and Policy M
Marketing M
Military and Defense Studies M
National Security M
Nonprofit Management M
Organizational Management M
Political Science M
Psychology—General M
Public Administration M
Public Health—General M
Secondary Education M
Social Sciences Education M
Sports Management M
Transportation Management M

AMERICAN SENTINEL UNIVERSITY

Business Administration and Management—General M
Computer Science M
Health Informatics M
Health Services Management and Hospital Administration M
Management Information Systems M
Nursing—General M

AMERICAN UNIVERSITY

Accounting M
American Studies M,D,O
Anthropology M,D,O
Applied Economics M,D,O
Applied Science and Technology M
Applied Social Research M,O
Applied Statistics M,O
Art History M
Art/Fine Arts M
Arts Administration M,O
Biological and Biomedical Sciences—General M
Biopsychology M,D
Broadcast Journalism M
Business Administration and Management—General M,D,O
Chemistry M,O
Clinical Psychology M,D
Communication—General M,D
Comparative Literature M
Computer Science M,O
Conflict Resolution and Mediation/Peace Studies M,D,O
Criminal Justice and Criminology M,D
Cultural Studies M,D,O
Curriculum and Instruction M,O
Early Childhood Education M,O
Economics M,D,O
Education—General M,O
Elementary Education M,O
English as a Second Language M,O
Entrepreneurship M
Environmental Management and Policy M,D,O
Environmental Sciences M,O
Ethics M,D,O
Exercise and Sports Science M
Experimental Psychology M,D
Film, Television, and Video Production M
Finance and Banking M,D,O
French M,O
Health Education M,O
History M,D
Interdisciplinary Studies M
International Affairs M,D,O
International and Comparative Education M
International Business M,O
International Development M,D,O
Journalism M
Latin American Studies M,O
Law P,M,O
Legal and Justice Studies M,D,O
Management Information Systems M
Marine Sciences M
Marketing Research M
Marketing M
Mass Communication M,D,O
Mathematics M,O
Media Studies M,D
Natural Resources M,D,O

Neuroscience	M,D
Nonprofit Management	M,D,O
Organizational Management	M
Philosophy	M
Political Science	M,D,O
Psychology—General	M,D
Public Administration	M,D,O
Public Affairs	M
Public Policy	M
Real Estate	M
Russian	M,O
Secondary Education	M,O
Social Psychology	M,D
Sociology	M,O
Spanish	M,O
Special Education	M
Statistics	M,O
Supply Chain Management	M
Sustainable Development	M,D,O
Taxation	M,O
Toxicology	M,O
Translation and Interpretation	M,O
Western European Studies	M,D,O
Writing	M

THE AMERICAN UNIVERSITY IN CAIRO

Anthropology	M
Broadcast Journalism	M
Business Administration and Management—General	M,O
Chemistry	M
Communication—General	M
Comparative Literature	M
Computer Science	M
Construction Engineering	M
Demography and Population Studies	M,O
Economics	M
Electrical Engineering	M
Engineering and Applied Sciences—General	M,D,O
English as a Second Language	M,O
English	M
Foreign Languages Education	M
Gender Studies	M,O
Industrial and Manufacturing Management	M
International and Comparative Education	M
Journalism	M
Law	M
Management Information Systems	M
Management of Technology	M
Mass Communication	M
Mechanical Engineering	M
Near and Middle Eastern Languages	M,O
Near and Middle Eastern Studies	M,O
Political Science	M
Public Administration	M,O
Public Policy	M,O
Sociology	M
Women's Studies	M,O

THE AMERICAN UNIVERSITY IN DUBAI

Business Administration and Management—General	M
Construction Management	M
Finance and Banking	M
Health Services Management and Hospital Administration	M
International Business	M
Marketing	M

THE AMERICAN UNIVERSITY OF ATHENS

Biological and Biomedical Sciences—General	M
Business Administration and Management—General	M
Computer Science	M
Corporate and Organizational Communication	M
Engineering and Applied Sciences—General	M
Political Science	M
Systems Engineering	M
Telecommunications	M

AMERICAN UNIVERSITY OF BEIRUT

Adult Nursing	M
Agricultural Economics and Agribusiness	M
Agronomy and Soil Sciences	M
Allopathic Medicine	P,M
Animal Sciences	M
Anthropology	M
Aquaculture	M
Archaeology	M
Biochemistry	P,M
Biological and Biomedical Sciences—General	M
Biostatistics	M
Business Administration and Management—General	M
Chemistry	M
Civil Engineering	M,D
Community Health Nursing	M
Community Health	M
Computational Sciences	M
Computer Engineering	M,D
Computer Science	M
Economics	M
Education—General	M
Electrical Engineering	M,D
Engineering and Applied Sciences—General	M,D
Engineering Management	M,D
English	M
Environmental and Occupational Health	M
Environmental Management and Policy	M
Environmental Sciences	M,D
Epidemiology	M
Food Science and Technology	M
Geology	M
Health Promotion	M
Health Services Management and Hospital Administration	M
History	M
Mathematics	M
Mechanical Engineering	M,D
Microbiology	P,M
Near and Middle Eastern Languages	M
Near and Middle Eastern Studies	M
Neuroscience	P,M
Nursing and Healthcare Administration	M
Nursing—General	M
Nutrition	M
Pharmacology	P,M
Philosophy	M
Physics	M
Physiology	P,M
Plant Sciences	M
Political Science	M
Psychiatric Nursing	M
Psychology—General	M
Public Administration	M
Public Health—General	M
Sociology	M
Statistics	M
Urban and Regional Planning	M,D
Urban Design	M,D
Water Resources Engineering	M,D

THE AMERICAN UNIVERSITY OF PARIS

Business Administration and Management—General	M
Communication—General	M
Conflict Resolution and Mediation/Peace Studies	M
Cultural Studies	M
International Affairs	M
International Business	M
Law	M
Near and Middle Eastern Studies	M
Public Policy	M

AMERICAN UNIVERSITY OF PUERTO RICO

Art Education	M,O
Art History	M,O
Criminal Justice and Criminology	M
Education—General	M,O
Elementary Education	M,O
Physical Education	M,O
Science Education	M,O
Special Education	M,O

AMERICAN UNIVERSITY OF SHARJAH

Business Administration and Management—General	M
Chemical Engineering	M
Civil Engineering	M
Computer Engineering	M
Electrical Engineering	M
English as a Second Language	M
Mechanical Engineering	M
Public Administration	M
Translation and Interpretation	M
Urban and Regional Planning	M

AMRIDGE UNIVERSITY

Counseling Psychology	P,M,D
Counselor Education	P,M,D
Marriage and Family Therapy	P,M,D
Organizational Behavior	P,M,D
Organizational Management	P,M,D
Pastoral Ministry and Counseling	P,M,D
Religion	P,M,D
Theology	P,M,D

ANAHEIM UNIVERSITY

Business Administration and Management—General	M,O
English as a Second Language	M,O
Sustainability Management	M,O

ANDERSON UNIVERSITY (IN)

Accounting	M,D
Business Administration and Management—General	M,D
Education—General	M
Missions and Missiology	P,M,D
Theology	P,M,D

ANDERSON UNIVERSITY (SC)

Business Administration and Management—General	M
Criminal Justice and Criminology	M
Education—General	M
Pastoral Ministry and Counseling	M

ANDOVER NEWTON THEOLOGICAL SCHOOL

Religious Education	P,M,D
Theology	P,M,D

ANDREW JACKSON UNIVERSITY

Business Administration and Management—General	M
Criminal Justice and Criminology	M
Entrepreneurship	M
Finance and Banking	M
Health Services Management and Hospital Administration	M
Hospitality Management	M
Human Resources Management	M
International Business	M
Marketing	M
Public Administration	M

ANDREWS UNIVERSITY

Accounting	M
Allied Health—General	M
Architecture	M
Biological and Biomedical Sciences—General	M
Communication—General	M
Counseling Psychology	D
Curriculum and Instruction	M,D,O
Developmental Psychology	M,D
Economics	M
Education—General	M,D,O
Educational Leadership and Administration	M,D,O
Educational Psychology	M,D
Elementary Education	M,D,O
Engineering and Applied Sciences—General	M
English as a Second Language	M,D,O
English Education	M,D,O
English	M
Finance and Banking	M
Foreign Languages Education	M,D,O
History	M
Human Services	M
International Development	M
Mathematics	M
Music	M
Nursing—General	M
Nutrition	M
Pastoral Ministry and Counseling	P,M,D,O
Physical Therapy	D
Psychology—General	M,D,O
Reading Education	M
Religious Education	M,D,O
School Psychology	M,O
Science Education	M,D,O
Secondary Education	M,D,O
Social Psychology	M
Social Sciences Education	M,D,O
Social Work	M
Software Engineering	M
Special Education	M,D,O
Theology	P,M,D,O

ANGELO STATE UNIVERSITY

Accounting	M
Adult Nursing	M

*M—master's degree; P—first professional degree; D—doctorate; O—other advanced degree; *—Close-Up and/or Display in one of the other books in this series*

- Agricultural Sciences—General M
- Animal Sciences M
- Applied Psychology M
- Biological and Biomedical Sciences—General M
- Business Administration and Management—General M
- Communication—General M
- Counseling Psychology M
- Counselor Education M
- Curriculum and Instruction M
- Education—General M
- Educational Leadership and Administration M,O
- Educational Measurement and Evaluation M
- English M
- Higher Education M
- History M
- Industrial and Organizational Psychology M
- Interdisciplinary Studies M
- Journalism M
- Medical/Surgical Nursing M
- Nursing Education M
- Physical Therapy D
- Psychology—General M
- Public Administration M
- Reading Education M
- Special Education M
- Sports Management M

ANNA MARIA COLLEGE

- Art Education M
- Art/Fine Arts M,O
- Business Administration and Management—General M,O
- Counseling Psychology M
- Criminal Justice and Criminology M
- Early Childhood Education M,O
- Education—General M,O
- Elementary Education M,O
- Emergency Management M,O
- English Education M,O
- Environmental and Occupational Health M
- Fire Protection Engineering M
- Pastoral Ministry and Counseling M
- Public Administration M

ANTIOCH UNIVERSITY LOS ANGELES

- Business Administration and Management—General M
- Clinical Psychology M
- Education—General M
- Human Resources Development M
- Organizational Management M
- Psychology—General M
- Writing M,O

ANTIOCH UNIVERSITY MIDWEST

- Art/Fine Arts M
- Business Administration and Management—General M
- Comparative Literature M
- Conflict Resolution and Mediation/Peace Studies M
- Counseling Psychology M
- Education—General M
- Film, Television, and Video Production M
- Liberal Studies M
- Psychology—General M
- Theater M
- Writing M

ANTIOCH UNIVERSITY NEW ENGLAND

- Applied Psychology M,D,O
- Business Administration and Management—General M
- Clinical Psychology M,D
- Conservation Biology M
- Counseling Psychology M
- Early Childhood Education M
- Education—General M
- Educational Leadership and Administration M
- Elementary Education M
- Environmental Education M
- Environmental Management and Policy M,D
- Environmental Sciences M,D
- Foundations and Philosophy of Education M
- Interdisciplinary Studies M
- Marriage and Family Therapy M,D
- Organizational Management M,O
- Science Education M
- Sustainability Management M
- Therapies—Dance, Drama, and Music M

ANTIOCH UNIVERSITY SANTA BARBARA

- Clinical Psychology D
- Education—General M
- Organizational Management M
- Psychology—General M

ANTIOCH UNIVERSITY SEATTLE

- Business Administration and Management—General M
- Corporate and Organizational Communication M
- Education—General M
- Environmental Management and Policy M
- Industrial and Organizational Psychology M
- Organizational Management M
- Psychology—General M,D

APEX SCHOOL OF THEOLOGY

- Theology P,M,D

APPALACHIAN BIBLE COLLEGE

- Pastoral Ministry and Counseling M

APPALACHIAN SCHOOL OF LAW

- Law P

APPALACHIAN STATE UNIVERSITY

- Accounting M
- American Studies M
- Biological and Biomedical Sciences—General M
- Business Administration and Management—General M
- Cell Biology M
- Clinical Psychology M,O
- Computer Science M
- Counseling Psychology M
- Counselor Education M
- Criminal Justice and Criminology M
- Cultural Studies M
- Curriculum and Instruction M
- Educational Leadership and Administration M,D,O
- Educational Media/Instructional Technology M,O
- Elementary Education M
- Engineering Physics M
- English Education M
- English M
- Environmental Management and Policy M
- Exercise and Sports Science M
- Experimental Psychology M,O
- Foreign Languages Education M
- Geographic Information Systems M
- Geography M
- Health Psychology M,O
- Higher Education M,O
- History M
- Industrial and Organizational Psychology M,O
- International Affairs M
- Library Science M,O
- Marriage and Family Therapy M
- Mathematics Education M
- Mathematics M
- Middle School Education M
- Molecular Biology M
- Music Education M
- Music M
- Nutrition M
- Political Science M
- Psychology—General M,O
- Public Administration M
- Public History M
- Reading Education M
- Rehabilitation Sciences M
- Romance Languages M
- School Psychology M
- Science Education M
- Social Sciences Education M
- Social Work M
- Special Education M
- Student Affairs M
- Sustainable Development M
- Therapies—Dance, Drama, and Music M
- Vocational and Technical Education M

AQUINAS COLLEGE

- Business Administration and Management—General M
- Education—General M

AQUINAS INSTITUTE OF THEOLOGY

- Health Services Management and Hospital Administration P,M,D,O
- Pastoral Ministry and Counseling P,M,D,O
- Theology P,M,D,O

ARCADIA UNIVERSITY

- Art Education M,D,O
- Business Administration and Management—General M
- Child Development M,D,O
- Community Health M
- Computer Education M,D,O
- Conflict Resolution and Mediation/Peace Studies M*
- Early Childhood Education M,D,O
- Education—General M,D,O
- Educational Leadership and Administration M,D,O
- Educational Media/Instructional Technology M,D,O
- Educational Psychology M,D,O
- Elementary Education M,D,O
- English Education M,D,O
- English M
- Environmental Education M,D,O
- Forensic Sciences M*
- Genetic Counseling M
- Health Education M
- Humanities M
- Mathematics Education M,D,O
- Music Education M,D,O
- Physical Therapy D
- Psychology—General M,D,O
- Reading Education M,D,O
- School Psychology M
- Science Education M,D,O
- Secondary Education M,D,O
- Social Psychology M
- Social Sciences Education M,D,O
- Special Education M,D,O
- Theater M,D,O

ARGOSY UNIVERSITY, ATLANTA

- Accounting M,D
- Biopsychology M,D,O
- Business Administration and Management—General M,D*
- Clinical Psychology M,D,O
- Counselor Education M,D,O
- Education—General M,D,O
- Educational Leadership and Administration M,D,O*
- Educational Media/Instructional Technology M,D,O
- Elementary Education M,D,O
- Finance and Banking M,D
- Forensic Psychology M,D,O
- Health Psychology M,D,O
- Health Services Management and Hospital Administration M,D
- Higher Education M,D,O
- Industrial and Organizational Psychology M,D,O
- International Business M,D
- Management Information Systems M,D
- Marketing M,D
- Marriage and Family Therapy M,D,O
- Psychology—General M,D,O*
- Public Health—General M
- Secondary Education M,D,O
- Social Psychology M,D,O
- Sport Psychology M,D,O

ARGOSY UNIVERSITY, CHICAGO

- Accounting M,D
- Adult Education M,D,O
- Business Administration and Management—General M,D*
- Clinical Psychology M,D*
- Community College Education M,D,O
- Counseling Psychology D
- Counselor Education D
- Education—General M,D,O*
- Educational Leadership and Administration M,D,O
- Elementary Education M,D,O
- Finance and Banking M,D
- Forensic Psychology D
- Health Psychology D
- Health Services Management and Hospital Administration M,D
- Higher Education M,D,O
- Human Development D
- Industrial and Organizational Psychology M,D
- International Business M,D
- Management Information Systems M,D
- Marketing M,D
- Marriage and Family Therapy D
- Neuroscience D

Organizational Behavior D
Organizational Management D
Psychoanalysis and Psychotherapy D
Psychology—General M,D
Public Administration M,D
Public Health—General M
Secondary Education M,D,O
Social Psychology M,D
Sustainability Management M,D

ARGOSY UNIVERSITY, DALLAS

Accounting M,D,O
Business Administration and Management—General M,D,O*
Clinical Psychology M,D*
Counselor Education D
Education—General M,D*
Educational Leadership and Administration M,D
Finance and Banking M,D,O
Forensic Psychology M
Health Services Management and Hospital Administration M,D,O
Higher Education M,D
Industrial and Organizational Psychology M
International Business M,D,O
Management Information Systems M,D,O
Marketing M,D,O
Psychology—General M,D
Public Administration M,D,O
Public Health—General M
School Psychology M,D
Social Psychology M
Sustainability Management M,D,O

ARGOSY UNIVERSITY, DENVER

Accounting M,D
Business Administration and Management—General M,D*
Clinical Psychology M,D
Community College Education M,D
Counseling Psychology M,D
Counselor Education M,D
Education—General M,D*
Educational Leadership and Administration M,D
Educational Media/Instructional Technology M,D
Elementary Education M,D
Finance and Banking M,D
Forensic Psychology M,D
Health Services Management and Hospital Administration M,D
Higher Education M,D
Industrial and Organizational Psychology M,D
International Business M,D
Management Information Systems M,D
Marketing M,D
Marriage and Family Therapy M,D
Organizational Management M,D
Psychology—General M,D
Public Administration M,D
Public Health—General M
Sustainability Management M,D

ARGOSY UNIVERSITY, HAWAI'I

Accounting M,D,O
Addictions/Substance Abuse Counseling O
Adult Education M,D
Business Administration and Management—General M,D,O*
Clinical Psychology M,D,O
Counseling Psychology D
Education—General M,D*
Educational Leadership and Administration M,D
Elementary Education M,D
Finance and Banking M,D,O
Forensic Psychology M
Health Services Management and Hospital Administration M,D,O
Higher Education M,D
International Business M,D,O
Management Information Systems M,D,O
Marketing M,D,O
Marriage and Family Therapy M
Organizational Management D
Pharmacology M,O
Psychology—General M,D,O*
School Psychology M
Secondary Education M,D
Sustainability Management M,D,O

ARGOSY UNIVERSITY, INLAND EMPIRE

Accounting M,D
Business Administration and Management—General M,D*
Clinical Psychology M,D
Community College Education M,D
Counseling Psychology M,D
Education—General M,D
Educational Leadership and Administration M,D*
Elementary Education M,D
Finance and Banking M,D
Forensic Psychology M,D
Health Services Management and Hospital Administration M,D
Higher Education M,D
Industrial and Organizational Psychology M,D
International Business M,D
Management Information Systems M,D
Marketing M,D
Marriage and Family Therapy M,D
Organizational Management M,D
Psychology—General M,D*
Public Administration M,D
Public Health—General M
Secondary Education M,D
Sport Psychology M,D
Sustainability Management M,D

ARGOSY UNIVERSITY, LOS ANGELES

Accounting M,D
Business Administration and Management—General M,D*
Clinical Psychology M,D*
Community College Education M,D
Counseling Psychology M,D
Education—General M,D*
Educational Leadership and Administration M,D
Elementary Education M,D
Finance and Banking M,D
Forensic Psychology M,D
Health Services Management and Hospital Administration M,D
Higher Education M,D
International Business M,D
Management Information Systems M,D
Marketing M,D
Marriage and Family Therapy M,D
Organizational Management M,D
Psychology—General M,D
Public Administration M,D
Public Health—General M
Secondary Education M,D
Sustainability Management M,D

ARGOSY UNIVERSITY, NASHVILLE

Accounting M,D
Business Administration and Management—General M,D
Counseling Psychology M,D*
Counselor Education D
Education—General M,D,O
Educational Leadership and Administration M,D,O*
Educational Media/Instructional Technology M,D,O
Elementary Education M,D,O
Finance and Banking M,D
Health Services Management and Hospital Administration M,D
Higher Education M,D,O
International Business M,D
Management Information Systems M,D
Marketing M,D
Psychology—General M,D
Public Health—General M
Secondary Education M,D,O

ARGOSY UNIVERSITY, ORANGE COUNTY

Accounting M,D,O
Business Administration and Management—General M,D,O*
Clinical Psychology M,D
Community College Education M,D
Counseling Psychology M,D
Education—General M,D*
Educational Leadership and Administration M,D
Educational Media/Instructional Technology M,D
Elementary Education M,D
Finance and Banking M,D,O
Forensic Psychology M
Health Services Management and Hospital Administration M,D,O
Higher Education M,D
International Business M,D,O
Management Information Systems M,D,O
Marketing M,D,O
Marriage and Family Therapy M,D
Organizational Management D
Psychology—General M,D*
Public Administration M,D,O
Public Health—General M
Secondary Education M,D
Sport Psychology M
Sustainability Management M,D,O

ARGOSY UNIVERSITY, PHOENIX

Accounting M,D
Adult Education M,D,O
Business Administration and Management—General M,D*
Clinical Psychology M,D
Community College Education M,D,O
Counseling Psychology M
Education—General M,D,O*
Educational Leadership and Administration M,D,O
Educational Media/Instructional Technology M,D,O
Elementary Education M,D,O
Finance and Banking M,D
Forensic Psychology M
Health Services Management and Hospital Administration M,D
Higher Education M,D,O
Industrial and Organizational Psychology M
International Business M,D
Management Information Systems M,D
Marketing M,D
Neuroscience M,D
Psychology—General M,D*
Public Administration M,D
Public Health—General M
School Psychology M,D
Secondary Education M,D,O
Sport Psychology M,D
Sustainability Management M,D

ARGOSY UNIVERSITY, SALT LAKE CITY

Accounting M,D
Business Administration and Management—General M,D*
Counseling Psychology M,D
Counselor Education M,D
Education—General M,D*
Educational Leadership and Administration M,D
Finance and Banking M,D
Forensic Psychology M,D
Health Services Management and Hospital Administration M,D
International Business M,D
Management Information Systems M,D
Marketing M,D
Marriage and Family Therapy M,D
Psychology—General M,D*
Public Administration M,D
Public Health—General M
Sustainability Management M,D

ARGOSY UNIVERSITY, SAN DIEGO

Accounting M,D
Business Administration and Management—General M,D*
Clinical Psychology M,D
Community College Education M,D
Counseling Psychology M,D*
Education—General M,D*
Educational Leadership and Administration M,D
Elementary Education M,D
Finance and Banking M,D
Forensic Psychology M,D
Higher Education M,D
International Business M,D
Management Information Systems M,D
Marketing M,D
Marriage and Family Therapy M,D
Organizational Management M,D
Psychology—General M,D
Public Administration M,D

*M—master's degree; P—first professional degree; D—doctorate; O—other advanced degree; *—Close-Up and/or Display in one of the other books in this series*

Public Health—General M
Secondary Education M,D

ARGOSY UNIVERSITY, SAN FRANCISCO BAY AREA

Accounting M,D
Business Administration and Management—General M,D*
Clinical Psychology M,D
Community College Education M,D
Counseling Psychology M,D
Education—General M,D*
Educational Leadership and Administration M,D
Educational Media/Instructional Technology M,D
Elementary Education M,D
Finance and Banking M,D
Forensic Psychology M
Health Services Management and Hospital Administration M,D
Higher Education M,D
International Business M,D
Management Information Systems M,D
Marketing M,D
Organizational Management M,D
Psychology—General M,D*
Public Administration M,D
Public Health—General M
Secondary Education M,D
Sport Psychology M,D
Sustainability Management M,D

ARGOSY UNIVERSITY, SARASOTA

Accounting M,D,O
Business Administration and Management—General M,D,O*
Counseling Psychology M,D
Counselor Education M,D,O
Education—General M,D,O*
Educational Leadership and Administration M,D,O
Educational Media/Instructional Technology M,D,O
Elementary Education M,D,O
Finance and Banking M,D,O
Forensic Psychology M,D
Health Services Management and Hospital Administration M,D,O
Higher Education M,D,O
International Business M,D,O
Management Information Systems M,D,O
Marketing M,D,O
Marriage and Family Therapy M,D
Organizational Management M,D,O
Pastoral Ministry and Counseling M,D
Psychology—General M,D*
Public Administration M,D,O
School Psychology M,D,O
Secondary Education M,D,O
Social Psychology M,D
Sustainability Management M,D,O

ARGOSY UNIVERSITY, SCHAUMBURG

Accounting M,D,O
Business Administration and Management—General M,D,O*
Clinical Psychology M,D,O*
Community College Education M,D,O
Corporate and Organizational Communication M,D,O
Counseling Psychology M,D,O
Counselor Education M,D,O
Education—General M,D,O*
Educational Leadership and Administration M,D,O
Elementary Education M,D,O
Finance and Banking M,D,O
Forensic Psychology M,D,O
Health Psychology M,D,O
Health Services Management and Hospital Administration M,D,O
Higher Education M,D,O
Industrial and Organizational Psychology M,D,O
International Business M,D,O
Management Information Systems M,D,O
Marketing M,D,O
Marriage and Family Therapy M,D,O
Neuroscience M,D,O
Psychology—General M,D,O
Public Administration M,D,O
Secondary Education M,D,O
Social Psychology M,D,O
Sustainability Management M,D,O

ARGOSY UNIVERSITY, SEATTLE

Accounting M,D
Adult Education M,D
Business Administration and Management—General M,D*
Clinical Psychology M,D,O*
Community College Education M,D
Counseling Psychology M,D
Education—General M,D*
Educational Leadership and Administration M,D
Educational Media/Instructional Technology M,D
Elementary Education M,D
Finance and Banking M,D
Health Services Management and Hospital Administration M,D
Higher Education M,D
International Business M,D
Management Information Systems M,D
Marketing M,D
Organizational Management M,D
Psychology—General M,D,O
Public Administration M,D
Public Health—General M
Secondary Education M,D
Sustainability Management M,D

ARGOSY UNIVERSITY, TAMPA

Accounting M,D
Business Administration and Management—General M,D
Clinical Psychology M,D
Community College Education M,D,O
Counseling Psychology M,D
Counselor Education M,D,O
Education—General M,D,O*
Educational Leadership and Administration M,D,O
Elementary Education M,D,O
Finance and Banking M,D
Health Services Management and Hospital Administration M,D
Higher Education M,D,O
Industrial and Organizational Psychology M,D
International Business M,D
Management Information Systems M,D
Marketing M,D
Marriage and Family Therapy M,D
Neuroscience M,D
Organizational Management M,D
Psychology—General M,D*
Public Administration M,D
Secondary Education M,D,O
Sustainability Management M,D

ARGOSY UNIVERSITY, TWIN CITIES

Accounting M,D
Biopsychology M,D,O
Business Administration and Management—General M,D*
Clinical Psychology M,D,O
Education—General M,D,O*
Educational Leadership and Administration M,D,O
Educational Media/Instructional Technology M,D,O
Elementary Education M,D,O
Finance and Banking M,D
Forensic Psychology M,D,O
Health Psychology M,D,O
Health Services Management and Hospital Administration M,D
Higher Education M,D,O
Industrial and Organizational Psychology M,D,O
International Business M,D
Management Information Systems M,D
Marketing M,D
Marriage and Family Therapy M,D,O
Organizational Management M,D
Psychology—General M,D,O*
Public Administration M,D
Public Health—General M
Secondary Education M,D,O
Sustainability Management M,D

ARGOSY UNIVERSITY, WASHINGTON DC

Accounting M,D,O
Business Administration and Management—General M,D,O*
Clinical Psychology M,D*
Community College Education M,D,O
Counseling Psychology M,D
Counselor Education M,D
Education—General M,D,O*
Educational Leadership and Administration M,D,O
Elementary Education M,D,O
Finance and Banking M,D,O
Forensic Psychology M,D
Health Psychology M,D
Health Services Management and Hospital Administration M,D,O
Higher Education M,D,O
International Business M,D,O
Management Information Systems M,D,O
Marketing M,D,O
Marriage and Family Therapy M,D
Organizational Management M,D,O
Psychology—General M,D
Public Administration M,D,O
Public Health—General M
Secondary Education M,D,O
Social Psychology M,D
Sustainability Management M,D,O

ARIZONA SCHOOL OF ACUPUNCTURE AND ORIENTAL MEDICINE

Acupuncture and Oriental Medicine M

ARIZONA STATE UNIVERSITY

Accounting M,D
Aerospace/Aeronautical Engineering M,D
African-American Studies M,D,O
Agricultural Economics and Agribusiness M,D
Animal Behavior M,D
Anthropology M,D,O
Applied Mathematics M,D,O
Applied Psychology M
Archaeology M,D,O
Architectural History D
Architecture M,D
Art Education M,D
Art History M,D
Art/Fine Arts M,D
Astrophysics M,D
Atmospheric Sciences M,D,O
Aviation Management M
Biochemistry M,D
Bioinformatics M,D
Biological and Biomedical Sciences—General M,D
Biomedical Engineering M,D
Biotechnology P,M
Building Science M,D
Business Administration and Management—General M,D
Cell Biology M,D
Chemical Engineering M,D
Chemistry M,D
Child and Family Studies M,D
Chinese M,D
Civil Engineering M,D
Clinical Psychology D
Cognitive Sciences M,D
Communication Disorders M,D
Communication—General M,D
Community Health Nursing M,D,O
Community Health M,D,O
Comparative Literature M,D,O
Computational Biology M,D
Computer Science M,D
Construction Engineering M,D
Construction Management M,D
Counseling Psychology D
Counselor Education M
Criminal Justice and Criminology M,D
Cultural Studies M,D
Curriculum and Instruction M,D
Dance M
Developmental Psychology D
Economics D
Education—General M,D,O
Educational Leadership and Administration M,D
Educational Media/Instructional Technology M,D,O
Educational Policy D
Electrical Engineering M,D,O
Elementary Education M,D
Engineering and Applied Sciences—General M,D,O
English as a Second Language M,D,O
English M,D,O
Entrepreneurship M
Environmental Design D
Environmental Engineering M,D

Program	Degrees
Environmental Management and Policy	M
Environmental Sciences	M,D,O
Ergonomics and Human Factors	M
Ethics	M,D
Evolutionary Biology	M,D
Exercise and Sports Science	M,D,O
Family Nurse Practitioner Studies	M,D,O
Film, Television, and Video Production	M
Finance and Banking	M,D
Foreign Languages Education	M,D
Foundations and Philosophy of Education	M
French	M
Gender Studies	M,D,O
Geographic Information Systems	M,D,O
Geography	M,D,O
Geological Engineering	M,D
Geology	M,D
Geosciences	M,D
German	M
Gerontology	M,D,O
Health Education	D
Higher Education	M
History of Science and Technology	D
History	M,D,O
Human Development	M,D
Industrial/Management Engineering	M,D
Information Science	M
Interdisciplinary Studies	M
Interior Design	M,D
International Health	M,D,O
Japanese	M
Journalism	M,D
Kinesiology and Movement Studies	M,D,O
Landscape Architecture	M,D
Latin American Studies	M,D,O
Law	P,M
Legal and Justice Studies	P,M,D,O
Liberal Studies	M
Linguistics	M,D,O
Management Information Systems	M,D
Management of Technology	M
Manufacturing Engineering	M
Marketing	M,D
Marriage and Family Therapy	M,D
Mass Communication	M,D
Materials Engineering	M,D
Materials Sciences	M,D
Mathematics Education	M,D
Mathematics	M,D
Mechanical Engineering	M,D
Media Studies	M,D
Medical Informatics	M,D
Medieval and Renaissance Studies	M,D,O
Microbiology	M,D
Modeling and Simulation	M,D
Molecular Biology	M,D
Museum Studies	M,D,O
Music Education	M,D
Music	M,D
Nanotechnology	M,D
Neuroscience	M,D
Nonprofit Management	M,D,O
Nuclear Engineering	M,D,O
Nursing and Healthcare Administration	M,D,O
Nursing—General	M,D,O
Nutrition	M,D,O
Philosophy	M,D,O
Physical Education	M,D
Physics	M,D
Planetary and Space Sciences	M,D
Political Science	M,D
Psychiatric Nursing	M,D,O
Psychology—General	M,D
Public Affairs	M,D
Public Health—General	M,D,O
Public History	M,D,O
Public Policy	P,M,D
Publishing	M,D,O
Real Estate	M,D
Recreation and Park Management	M,D,O
Reliability Engineering	M
Religion	M,D,O
Secondary Education	M,D
Social Psychology	D
Social Work	M,D,O
Sociology	M,D
Software Engineering	M
Spanish	M,D
Special Education	M,O
Statistics	M,D,O
Supply Chain Management	M,D
Sustainable Development	M,D,O
Systems Engineering	M
Systems Science	M
Technology and Public Policy	M
Theater	M,D
Therapies—Dance, Drama, and Music	M,D
Transportation and Highway Engineering	M,D,O
Travel and Tourism	M,D,O
Urban and Regional Planning	M,D,O
Urban Design	M,D
Writing	M

ARKANSAS STATE UNIVERSITY

Program	Degrees
Accounting	M
Agricultural Education	M,O
Agricultural Sciences—General	M,O
Art/Fine Arts	M
Biological and Biomedical Sciences—General	M,O
Biotechnology	D,O
Business Administration and Management—General	M,O
Business Education	M,O
Chemistry	M,O
Communication Disorders	M
Communication—General	M,O
Community College Education	M,D,O
Computer Science	M
Counseling Psychology	M,O
Counselor Education	M,O
Criminal Justice and Criminology	M,O
Curriculum and Instruction	M,D,O
Early Childhood Education	M,O
Education of the Gifted	M,D,O
Education—General	M,D,O
Educational Leadership and Administration	M,D,O
Electronic Commerce	M,O
Elementary Education	M,O
Engineering and Applied Sciences—General	M
English Education	M,O
English	M,O
Environmental Sciences	M,D
Exercise and Sports Science	M,O
Foundations and Philosophy of Education	M,D,O
Gerontology	M,O
Health Communication	M,O
Health Education	M,O
Health Services Management and Hospital Administration	M,O
Historic Preservation	M,D
History	M,O
Journalism	M
Management Information Systems	M,O
Mathematics Education	M
Mathematics	M
Media Studies	M
Middle School Education	M,O
Molecular Biology	D,O
Music Education	M,O
Music	M,O
Nurse Anesthesia	M,O
Nursing—General	M,O
Physical Education	M,O
Physical Therapy	M,D
Political Science	M,O
Public Administration	M,O
Reading Education	M,O
Rehabilitation Counseling	M,O
School Psychology	M,O
Science Education	M,O
Social Sciences Education	M,O
Social Work	M,O
Sociology	M,O
Special Education	M,D,O
Speech and Interpersonal Communication	M,O
Sports Management	M,O
Student Affairs	M,O
Theater	M,O

ARKANSAS TECH UNIVERSITY

Program	Degrees
Art/Fine Arts	M
Communication—General	M
Curriculum and Instruction	M,O
Education—General	M,O
Educational Leadership and Administration	M,O
Emergency Management	M
Engineering and Applied Sciences—General	M
English as a Second Language	M
English Education	M,O
English	M
Fish, Game, and Wildlife Management	M
Health Informatics	M
History	M
Information Science	M
Journalism	M
Nursing—General	M
Psychology—General	M
Secondary Education	M,O
Social Sciences	M
Spanish	M
Student Affairs	M,O

ARMSTRONG ATLANTIC STATE UNIVERSITY

Program	Degrees
Adult Education	M
Athletic Training and Sports Medicine	M
Business Education	M
Communication Disorders	M
Computer Science	M
Criminal Justice and Criminology	M
Curriculum and Instruction	M
Early Childhood Education	M
Education—General	M
Elementary Education	M
English Education	M
Exercise and Sports Science	M
Health Services Management and Hospital Administration	M
History	M
Liberal Studies	M
Mathematics Education	M
Middle School Education	M
Nursing—General	M
Physical Therapy	D
Public Health—General	M
Science Education	M
Secondary Education	M
Social Sciences Education	M
Special Education	M

ART ACADEMY OF CINCINNATI

Program	Degrees
Art Education	M

ART CENTER COLLEGE OF DESIGN

Program	Degrees
Applied Arts and Design—General	M*
Art/Fine Arts	M
Computer Art and Design	M
Environmental Design	M
Film, Television, and Video Production	M
Industrial Design	M

THE ART INSTITUTE OF ATLANTA

Program	Degrees
Business Administration and Management—General	M

THE ART INSTITUTE OF BOSTON AT LESLEY UNIVERSITY

Program	Degrees
Art/Fine Arts	M

THE ART INSTITUTE OF CALIFORNIA–SAN FRANCISCO

Program	Degrees
Art/Fine Arts	M
Film, Television, and Video Production	M

ASBURY THEOLOGICAL SEMINARY

Program	Degrees
Missions and Missiology	M,D,O
Pastoral Ministry and Counseling	M,D,O
Religious Education	M,D,O
Theology	M,D,O

ASBURY UNIVERSITY

Program	Degrees
Child and Family Studies	M
Classics	M
Educational Leadership and Administration	M
English as a Second Language	M
English	M
French	M
Mathematics Education	M
Reading Education	M
Science Education	M
Social Sciences Education	M
Social Work	M
Spanish	M
Special Education	M
Writing	M

ASHLAND THEOLOGICAL SEMINARY

Program	Degrees
Counselor Education	P,M,D,O
History	P,M,D,O
Pastoral Ministry and Counseling	P,M,D,O
Theology	P,M,D,O

ASHLAND UNIVERSITY

Program	Degrees
Business Administration and Management—General	M
Curriculum and Instruction	M
Education of the Gifted	M
Education—General	M,D
Educational Leadership and Administration	M,D
Educational Media/Instructional Technology	M
Exercise and Sports Science	M
Foundations and Philosophy of Education	M
History	M
Physical Education	M
Political Science	M
Reading Education	M
Special Education	M
Sports Management	M

*M—master's degree; P—first professional degree; D—doctorate; O—other advanced degree; *—Close-Up and/or Display in one of the other books in this series*

Student Affairs M
Writing M

ASHWORTH COLLEGE

Business Administration and Management—General M
Criminal Justice and Criminology M
Health Services Management and Hospital Administration M
Human Resources Management M
International Business M
Marketing M

ASPEN UNIVERSITY

Business Administration and Management—General M,O
Finance and Banking M,O
Information Science M,O
Management Information Systems M,O
Project Management M,O

ASSEMBLIES OF GOD THEOLOGICAL SEMINARY

Cultural Studies P,M,D
Missions and Missiology P,M,D
Pastoral Ministry and Counseling P,M,D
Theology P,M,D

ASSOCIATED MENNONITE BIBLICAL SEMINARY

Conflict Resolution and Mediation/Peace Studies P,M,O
Missions and Missiology P,M,O
Theology P,M,O

ASSUMPTION COLLEGE

Accounting M,O
Business Administration and Management—General M,O
Child and Family Studies M,O
Counseling Psychology M,O
Economics M,O
Finance and Banking M,O
Human Resources Management M,O
International Business M,O
Marketing M,O
Nonprofit Management M,O
Psychology—General M,O
Rehabilitation Counseling M,O
School Psychology M,O
Special Education M,O

ATHABASCA UNIVERSITY

Adult Education M
Allied Health—General M,O
Applied Psychology M,O
Art Therapy M,O
Business Administration and Management—General M,O
Counseling Psychology M,O
Counselor Education M,O
Cultural Studies M
Distance Education Development M,O
Education—General M,O
Information Science M
Interdisciplinary Studies M
International Development M
Management of Technology M,O
Nursing and Healthcare Administration M,O
Nursing—General M,O
Organizational Management M
Project Management M,O

THE ATHENAEUM OF OHIO

Pastoral Ministry and Counseling P,M,O
Theology P,M,O

ATLANTA'S JOHN MARSHALL LAW SCHOOL

Law P,M

ATLANTIC COLLEGE

Graphic Design M

ATLANTIC INSTITUTE OF ORIENTAL MEDICINE

Acupuncture and Oriental Medicine M

ATLANTIC SCHOOL OF THEOLOGY

Pastoral Ministry and Counseling P,M,O
Theology P,M,O

ATLANTIC UNION COLLEGE

Education—General M

ATLANTIC UNIVERSITY

Transpersonal and Humanistic Psychology M

A.T. STILL UNIVERSITY OF HEALTH SCIENCES

Allied Health—General M,D
Athletic Training and Sports Medicine M,D
Biological and Biomedical Sciences—General P,M
Communication Disorders M,D
Gerontology M,D
Health Education M,D
Health Services Management and Hospital Administration M,D
Kinesiology and Movement Studies M,D
Occupational Therapy M,D
Oral and Dental Sciences P,M,D,O
Osteopathic Medicine P,M
Physical Therapy M,D
Physician Assistant Studies M,D
Public Health—General M,D

AUBURN UNIVERSITY

Accounting M
Adult Education M,D,O
Aerospace/Aeronautical Engineering M,D
Agricultural Economics and Agribusiness M,D
Agricultural Sciences—General M,D
Agronomy and Soil Sciences M,D
Analytical Chemistry M,D
Anatomy M,D
Animal Sciences M,D
Applied Behavior Analysis M,D
Applied Economics M,D
Applied Mathematics M,D
Aquaculture M,D
Architecture M
Biochemistry M,D
Biological and Biomedical Sciences—General M,D
Botany M,D
Building Science M
Business Administration and Management—General M,D
Business Education M,D,O
Cell Biology M,D
Chemical Engineering M,D
Chemistry M,D
Child and Family Studies M,D
Civil Engineering M,D
Clothing and Textiles M
Communication Disorders M,D
Communication—General M
Computer Engineering M,D
Computer Science M,D
Construction Engineering M,D
Construction Management M
Curriculum and Instruction M,D,O
Early Childhood Education M,D,O
Economics M
Education—General M,D,O
Educational Leadership and Administration M,D,O
Educational Media/Instructional Technology M,D,O
Educational Psychology M,D,O
Electrical Engineering M,D
Elementary Education M,D,O
Engineering and Applied Sciences—General M,D
English Education M,D,O
English M,D
Entomology M,D
Environmental Engineering M,D
Exercise and Sports Science M,D,O
Experimental Psychology M,D
Finance and Banking M
Fish, Game, and Wildlife Management M,D
Food Science and Technology M,D
Foreign Languages Education M,D,O
Forestry M,D
Geography M
Geology M
Geotechnical Engineering M,D
Health Education M,D,O
Health Promotion M,D,O
Higher Education M,D,O
History M,D
Horticulture M,D
Human Development M,D
Human Resources Management M,D
Hydraulics M,D
Hydrology M,D
Industrial and Organizational Psychology M,D
Industrial Design M
Industrial/Management Engineering M,D
Inorganic Chemistry M,D
Kinesiology and Movement Studies M,D,O
Landscape Architecture M
Management Information Systems M,D
Mass Communication M
Materials Engineering M,D
Mathematics Education M,D,O
Mathematics M,D
Mechanical Engineering M,D
Microbiology M,D
Molecular Biology M,D
Music Education M,D,O
Natural Resources M,D
Nursing—General M
Nutrition M,D
Organic Chemistry M,D
Pathobiology M,D
Pharmaceutical Sciences M,D
Pharmacology M,D
Pharmacy P
Physical Chemistry M,D
Physical Education M,D,O
Physics M,D
Plant Pathology M,D
Political Science M,D
Psychology—General M,D
Public Administration M,D
Radiation Biology M,D
Reading Education M,D,O
Rehabilitation Counseling M,D
Rural Sociology M
Science Education M,D,O
Secondary Education M,D,O
Social Sciences Education M,D,O
Sociology M
Software Engineering M,D
Spanish M
Special Education M,D
Statistics M,D
Structural Engineering M,D
Systems Engineering M,D
Textile Sciences and Engineering D
Transportation and Highway Engineering M,D
Urban and Regional Planning M
Veterinary Medicine P
Veterinary Sciences M,D
Zoology M,D

AUBURN UNIVERSITY MONTGOMERY

Business Administration and Management—General M
Counselor Education M,O
Criminal Justice and Criminology M
Early Childhood Education M,O
Education—General M,O
Educational Leadership and Administration M,O
Elementary Education M,O
Liberal Studies M
Physical Education M,O
Political Science M,D
Psychology—General M
Public Administration M,D
Reading Education M,O
Secondary Education M,O
Special Education M,O

AUGSBURG COLLEGE

Business Administration and Management—General M
Community Health Nursing M
Education—General M
Nursing—General M
Organizational Management M
Physician Assistant Studies M
Social Work M
Transcultural Nursing M

AUGUSTANA COLLEGE

Education—General M
Sports Management M

AUGUSTA STATE UNIVERSITY

Business Administration and Management—General M
Counselor Education M
Curriculum and Instruction M
Education—General M,O
Educational Leadership and Administration M,O
Health Education M
Physical Education M
Political Science M
Psychology—General M
Secondary Education M,O
Special Education M,O

AURORA UNIVERSITY

Business Administration and Management—General M
Criminal Justice and Criminology M,D
Curriculum and Instruction M,D
Early Childhood Education M,D
Education—General M,D

Educational Leadership and Administration M,D
Educational Media/ Instructional Technology M,D
Elementary Education M,D
Mathematics Education M
Mathematics M
Nursing—General M,D
Reading Education M,D
Recreation and Park Management M
Science Education M
Social Work M,D
Special Education M,D

AUSTIN COLLEGE

Art Education M
Education—General M
Elementary Education M
Middle School Education M
Music Education M
Physical Education M
Secondary Education M
Theater M

AUSTIN GRADUATE SCHOOL OF THEOLOGY

Theology M

AUSTIN PEAY STATE UNIVERSITY

Biological and Biomedical Sciences—General M
Business Administration and Management—General M
Clinical Laboratory Sciences/Medical Technology M
Communication—General M
Community Health M
Counselor Education M,O
Curriculum and Instruction M,O
Education—General M,O
Educational Leadership and Administration M,O
Elementary Education M,O
English M
Exercise and Sports Science M
Health Education M
Military and Defense Studies M
Music Education M
Music M
Nursing and Healthcare Administration M
Nursing Education M
Nursing Informatics M
Nursing—General M
Psychology—General M,O
Public Health—General M
Radiation Biology M
Reading Education M
Secondary Education M,O
Social Work M
Special Education M,O

AUSTIN PRESBYTERIAN THEOLOGICAL SEMINARY

Pastoral Ministry and Counseling P,M,D
Theology P,M,D

AVE MARIA SCHOOL OF LAW

Law P

AVE MARIA UNIVERSITY

Pastoral Ministry and Counseling M,D
Theology M,D

AVERETT UNIVERSITY

Art Education M
Business Administration and Management—General M
Curriculum and Instruction M
Education—General M
Elementary Education M
English Education M
Health Education M
Mathematics Education M
Physical Education M
Reading Education M
Science Education M
Social Sciences Education M
Special Education M

AVILA UNIVERSITY

Accounting M
Business Administration and Management—General M
Counseling Psychology M
Education—General M,O
English as a Second Language M,O
Finance and Banking M
Health Services Management and Hospital Administration M
International Business M
Management Information Systems M
Marketing M
Nonprofit Management M,O
Organizational Management M,O
Project Management M,O
Psychology—General M

AZUSA PACIFIC UNIVERSITY

Art/Fine Arts M
Business Administration and Management—General M
Clinical Psychology M,D
Counselor Education M
Curriculum and Instruction M
Education—General M,D,O
Educational Leadership and Administration M,D
Educational Media/ Instructional Technology M
English as a Second Language M
Entrepreneurship M
Ethics M
Finance and Banking M
Foundations and Philosophy of Education M
Higher Education M,D
Human Resources Development M
Human Resources Management M
International Affairs M
International Business M
Library Science M,O
Management Strategy and Policy M
Marketing M
Marriage and Family Therapy M,D
Multilingual and Multicultural Education M
Music Education M
Music M
Nonprofit Management M
Nursing Education M,D
Nursing—General M,D
Organizational Management M
Pastoral Ministry and Counseling P,M
Physical Education M
Physical Therapy D
Psychology—General M,D
Public Administration M
Religious Education M
School Psychology M
Social Work M
Special Education M
Student Affairs M
Theology M,D
Urban Studies M

BABEL UNIVERSITY SCHOOL OF TRANSLATION

Translation and Interpretation M

BABSON COLLEGE

Accounting M,O
Business Administration and Management—General M,O
Entrepreneurship M,O

BAKER COLLEGE CENTER FOR GRADUATE STUDIES—ONLINE

Accounting M,D
Business Administration and Management—General M,D
Finance and Banking M,D
Health Services Management and Hospital Administration M,D
Human Resources Management M,D
Management Information Systems M,D
Marketing M,D

BAKER UNIVERSITY

Business Administration and Management—General M
Conflict Resolution and Mediation/Peace Studies M
Education—General M,D
Liberal Studies M

BAKKE GRADUATE UNIVERSITY

Business Administration and Management—General M,D
Entrepreneurship M,D
Pastoral Ministry and Counseling M,D
Urban Education M,D

BALDWIN-WALLACE COLLEGE

Accounting M
Business Administration and Management—General M
Education—General M
Educational Leadership and Administration M
Educational Media/ Instructional Technology M
Entrepreneurship M
Health Services Management and Hospital Administration M
Human Resources Management M
International Business M
Reading Education M
Special Education M
Sustainability Management M

BALL STATE UNIVERSITY

Accounting M
Actuarial Science M
Adult Education M,D
Advertising and Public Relations M
Anthropology M
Applied Behavior Analysis M,D,O
Architecture M
Art Education M
Art/Fine Arts M
Biological and Biomedical Sciences—General M,D
Business Administration and Management—General M
Business Education M
Chemistry M
Clinical Psychology M
Cognitive Sciences M
Communication Disorders M,D
Communication—General M
Computer Science M
Counseling Psychology M,D
Criminal Justice and Criminology M
Curriculum and Instruction M,O
Education—General M,D,O
Educational Leadership and Administration M,D,O
Educational Psychology M,D,O
Elementary Education M,D
English as a Second Language M,D
English M,D
Exercise and Sports Science D
Family and Consumer Sciences-General M
Foundations and Philosophy of Education D
Geography M
Geology M
Gerontology M
Health Promotion M
Higher Education M,D
Historic Preservation M
History M
Information Science M
Journalism M
Landscape Architecture M
Linguistics M,D
Mathematics Education M
Mathematics M
Music Education M,D
Natural Resources M
Nursing—General M,D
Physical Education M,D
Physics M
Physiology M
Political Science M
Psychology—General M
Public Administration M
Rhetoric M
School Psychology M,D,O
Science Education M,D
Secondary Education M
Social Psychology M
Sociology M
Special Education M,D,O
Speech and Interpersonal Communication M
Statistics M
Telecommunications M
Urban and Regional Planning M
Urban Design M
Vocational and Technical Education M
Writing M,D

BALTIMORE INTERNATIONAL COLLEGE

Hospitality Management M

BANGOR THEOLOGICAL SEMINARY

Theology P,M,D

BANK STREET COLLEGE OF EDUCATION

Child and Family Studies M
Early Childhood Education M
Education—General M
Educational Leadership and Administration M
Elementary Education M

*M—master's degree; P—first professional degree; D—doctorate; O—other advanced degree; *—Close-Up and/or Display in one of the other books in this series*

Foundations and Philosophy of Education M
Maternal and Child Health M
Mathematics Education M
Multilingual and Multicultural Education M
Museum Education M
Reading Education M
Special Education M

BAPTIST BIBLE COLLEGE

Cultural Studies P,M
Pastoral Ministry and Counseling P,M
Theology P,M

BAPTIST BIBLE COLLEGE OF PENNSYLVANIA

Counselor Education M
Education—General M
Missions and Missiology P,M,D
Pastoral Ministry and Counseling P,M,D
Religion P,M,D
Religious Education P,M,D
Theology P,M,D

BAPTIST MISSIONARY ASSOCIATION THEOLOGICAL SEMINARY

Theology P,M

BAPTIST THEOLOGICAL SEMINARY AT RICHMOND

Pastoral Ministry and Counseling P,M,D
Religion P,M,D
Religious Education P,M,D
Theology P,M,D

BARD COLLEGE

Art/Fine Arts M
Atmospheric Sciences M,O
Education—General M
Environmental Management and Policy M,O
Museum Studies M
Music M
Photography M
Sustainability Management M,O

BARD GRADUATE CENTER: DECORATIVE ARTS, DESIGN HISTORY, MATERIAL CULTURE

Art History M,D*
Decorative Arts M,D

BARRY UNIVERSITY

Accounting M
Acute Care/Critical Care Nursing M,O
Anatomy M
Art/Fine Arts M
Athletic Training and Sports Medicine M
Biological and Biomedical Sciences—General M
Business Administration and Management—General M,O
Clinical Psychology M,O
Communication Disorders M
Communication—General M,O
Corporate and Organizational Communication M,O
Counselor Education M,D,O
Curriculum and Instruction D,O
Distance Education Development O
Early Childhood Education M,D,O
Education of the Gifted M,D,O
Education—General M,D,O
Educational Leadership and Administration M,D,O
Educational Media/Instructional Technology M,D,O
Elementary Education M,D,O
English as a Second Language M,D,O
Exercise and Sports Science M
Family Nurse Practitioner Studies M,O
Finance and Banking O
Health Informatics O
Health Services Management and Hospital Administration M,O
Higher Education M,D
Human Resources Development M,D
Human Resources Management O
Information Science M
International Business O
Kinesiology and Movement Studies M
Law P
Liberal Studies M
Management Information Systems O
Marketing O
Marriage and Family Therapy M,O
Nurse Anesthesia M
Nursing and Healthcare Administration M,D,O
Nursing Education M,O
Nursing—General M,D,O
Occupational Therapy M
Pastoral Ministry and Counseling M,D
Photography M
Physician Assistant Studies M
Podiatric Medicine P
Psychology—General M,O*
Public Administration M
Public Health—General M
Reading Education M,D,O
Rehabilitation Counseling M,O
School Psychology M,O
Social Work M,D
Special Education M,D,O
Sport Psychology M
Sports Management M
Theology M,D

BASTYR UNIVERSITY

Acupuncture and Oriental Medicine M,D,O
Health Psychology M
Naturopathic Medicine D
Nutrition M

BAYAMÓN CENTRAL UNIVERSITY

Accounting M
Business Administration and Management—General M
Counselor Education M,O
Early Childhood Education M,O
Education—General M,O
Educational Leadership and Administration M,O
Elementary Education M,O
Finance and Banking M
Industrial and Organizational Psychology M
Marketing M
Marriage and Family Therapy M,O
Rehabilitation Counseling M,O
Special Education M,O

BAYLOR COLLEGE OF MEDICINE

Allopathic Medicine P
Biochemistry D
Bioengineering D
Biological and Biomedical Sciences—General M,D
Biomedical Engineering D
Biophysics D
Cancer Biology/Oncology D
Cardiovascular Sciences D
Cell Biology D
Clinical Laboratory Sciences/Medical Technology M,D
Computational Biology D*
Developmental Biology D*
Genetics D
Human Genetics D
Immunology D
Microbiology D
Molecular Biology D
Molecular Biophysics D
Molecular Medicine D
Molecular Physiology D
Neuroscience D
Nurse Anesthesia M,D
Pathology D
Pharmacology D
Physician Assistant Studies M
Structural Biology D
Translational Biology D
Virology D

BAYLOR UNIVERSITY

Accounting M
Allied Health—General M,D
American Studies M
Biological and Biomedical Sciences—General M,D
Biomedical Engineering M,D
Business Administration and Management—General M
Chemistry M,D
Clinical Psychology M,D
Communication Disorders M
Communication—General M
Computer Engineering M,D
Computer Science M
Curriculum and Instruction M,D,O
Ecology D
Economics M
Education—General M,D,O
Educational Leadership and Administration M,O
Educational Psychology M,D,O
Electrical Engineering M,D
Emergency Medical Services D
Engineering and Applied Sciences—General M,D
English M,D
Environmental Biology M,D
Environmental Management and Policy M
Environmental Sciences D
Exercise and Sports Science M,D
Family Nurse Practitioner Studies M
Geology M,D
Geosciences M,D
Health Education M,D
Health Services Management and Hospital Administration M
History M
Interdisciplinary Studies M,D
International Affairs M,D
Journalism M
Law P
Limnology M,D
Management Information Systems M
Maternal and Child/Neonatal Nursing M
Mathematics M,D
Mechanical Engineering M,D
Museum Studies M
Music M
Nursing and Healthcare Administration M
Nursing—General M
Nutrition M,D
Philosophy M,D
Physical Education M,D
Physical Therapy M,D
Physics M,D
Political Science M,D
Psychology—General M,D*
Public Administration M,D
Public Policy M,D
Religion M,D
Social Work M
Sociology M,D
Spanish M
Statistics M,D
Theater M
Theology P,M,D

BAY PATH COLLEGE

Educational Leadership and Administration M
Entrepreneurship M
Higher Education M
Management Information Systems M
Nonprofit Management M
Occupational Therapy M

BELHAVEN UNIVERSITY (MS)

Business Administration and Management—General M
Education—General M
Elementary Education M
Multilingual and Multicultural Education M
Public Administration M
Secondary Education M

BELLARMINE UNIVERSITY

Business Administration and Management—General M
Communication—General M
Early Childhood Education M,D,O
Education—General M,D,O
Educational Leadership and Administration M,D,O
Family Nurse Practitioner Studies M,D
Management Information Systems M
Middle School Education M,D,O
Nursing and Healthcare Administration M,D
Nursing Education M,D
Nursing—General M,D
Physical Therapy M,D
Reading Education M,D,O
Religion M
Secondary Education M,D,O
Special Education M,D,O

BELLEVUE UNIVERSITY

Business Administration and Management—General M,D
Counselor Education M,D
Criminal Justice and Criminology M,D
Educational Media/Instructional Technology M,D
Health Services Management and Hospital Administration M
Human Services M
Information Science M
Management Information Systems M
Public Administration M,D
Public Health—General M,D

BELLIN COLLEGE

Nursing and Healthcare Administration M
Nursing Education M
Nursing—General M

BELMONT UNIVERSITY

Allied Health—General P,M,D
Business Administration and Management—General M
Early Childhood Education M
Education—General M
Elementary Education M
English Education M
English M
Family Nurse Practitioner Studies M
Mathematics Education M
Middle School Education M
Music Education M
Music M
Nursing—General M
Occupational Therapy M,D
Pharmacy P
Physical Therapy D
Science Education M
Secondary Education M
Social Sciences Education M
Special Education M
Sports Management M
Writing M

BEMIDJI STATE UNIVERSITY

Biological and Biomedical Sciences—General M
Counseling Psychology M
Education—General M
English M
Environmental Management and Policy M
Mathematics Education M
Mathematics M
Special Education M

BENEDICTINE COLLEGE

Business Administration and Management—General M
Educational Leadership and Administration M

BENEDICTINE UNIVERSITY

Accounting M
Business Administration and Management—General M
Clinical Psychology M
Computer and Information Systems Security M
Curriculum and Instruction M
Education—General M
Educational Leadership and Administration M,D
Elementary Education M
Emergency Management M
Entrepreneurship M
Exercise and Sports Science M
Finance and Banking M
Health Education M
Health Informatics M
Health Promotion M
Health Services Management and Hospital Administration M
Higher Education D
Human Resources Management M
International Business M
Logistics M
Management Information Systems M
Marketing M
Nursing—General M
Nutrition M
Organizational Behavior M
Organizational Management M,D
Public Health—General M
Reading Education M
Science Education M
Secondary Education M
Special Education M

BENEDICTINE UNIVERSITY AT SPRINGFIELD

Business Administration and Management—General M
Elementary Education M
Health Services Management and Hospital Administration M
Organizational Behavior M
Organizational Management M,D
Reading Education M

BENNINGTON COLLEGE

Allied Health—General O
Art Education M
Dance M
Early Childhood Education M
Education—General M
Elementary Education M
English Education M
English M
Foreign Languages Education M
French M
Mathematics Education M
Multilingual and Multicultural Education M
Music Education M
Music M
Science Education M
Secondary Education M
Social Sciences Education M
Spanish M
Theater M
Writing M

BENTLEY UNIVERSITY

Accounting M,D
Business Administration and Management—General M,D,O
Ergonomics and Human Factors M
Finance and Banking M
Information Science M
Marketing M
Taxation M

BERNARD M. BARUCH COLLEGE OF THE CITY UNIVERSITY OF NEW YORK

Accounting M,D
Business Administration and Management—General M,D,O
Corporate and Organizational Communication M
Economics M
Educational Leadership and Administration M,O
Entrepreneurship M,D
Finance and Banking M,D
Health Services Management and Hospital Administration M
Higher Education M
Human Resources Management M,D
Industrial and Labor Relations M
Industrial and Organizational Psychology M,D,O
International Business M
Management Information Systems M,D
Management Strategy and Policy M,D
Marketing M,D
Mathematical and Computational Finance M
Nonprofit Management M
Organizational Behavior M,D
Organizational Management M,D
Public Administration M
Public Policy M
Quantitative Analysis M
Statistics M
Taxation M

BERRY COLLEGE

Business Administration and Management—General M
Curriculum and Instruction O
Early Childhood Education M
Education—General M,O
Educational Leadership and Administration O
Middle School Education M
Reading Education M
Secondary Education M

BETHANY THEOLOGICAL SEMINARY

Conflict Resolution and Mediation/Peace Studies P,M,O
Pastoral Ministry and Counseling P,M,O
Religion P,M,O
Theology P,M,O

BETHANY UNIVERSITY

Clinical Psychology M
Education—General M
Educational Leadership and Administration M

BETHEL COLLEGE

Business Administration and Management—General M
Education—General M
Nursing—General M
Pastoral Ministry and Counseling M
Theology M

BETHEL SEMINARY

Classics P,M,D,O
Marriage and Family Therapy P,M,D,O
Missions and Missiology P,M,D,O
Near and Middle Eastern Languages P,M,D,O
Pastoral Ministry and Counseling P,M,D,O
Religion P,M,D,O
Religious Education P,M,D,O
Theology P,M,D,O

BETHEL UNIVERSITY (MN)

Business Administration and Management—General M
Communication—General M,O
Counseling Psychology M
Developmental Psychology M
Education—General M,D,O
Educational Leadership and Administration M,D,O
Gerontology M
Higher Education M,O
Nursing Education M,O
Nursing—General M,O
Organizational Management M
Reading Education M,D,O
Secondary Education M,D,O
Social Psychology M
Special Education M,D,O

BETHEL UNIVERSITY (TN)

Business Administration and Management—General M
Conflict Resolution and Mediation/Peace Studies M
Educational Leadership and Administration M
Physician Assistant Studies M

BETHESDA CHRISTIAN UNIVERSITY

Music P,M
Religion P,M
Theology P,M

BETH HAMEDRASH SHAAREI YOSHER INSTITUTE

Theology

BETH HATALMUD RABBINICAL COLLEGE

Theology

BETH MEDRASH GOVOHA

Theology

BETHUNE-COOKMAN UNIVERSITY

Theology M

BEULAH HEIGHTS UNIVERSITY

Religion M

BEXLEY HALL EPISCOPAL SEMINARY

Theology P,M

BIBLICAL THEOLOGICAL SEMINARY

Missions and Missiology P,M,D,O
Pastoral Ministry and Counseling P,M,D,O
Theology P,M,D,O

BIOLA UNIVERSITY

Anthropology M,D,O
Business Administration and Management—General M
Cultural Studies M,D,O
English as a Second Language M,D,O
Ethics P,M,D
Linguistics M,D,O
Missions and Missiology M,D,O
Organizational Management M
Psychology—General D
Religion P,M,D
Religious Education P,M,D
Science Education M
Theology P,M,D

BISHOP'S UNIVERSITY

Education—General M,O
English as a Second Language M,O

BLACK HILLS STATE UNIVERSITY

Business Administration and Management—General M
Curriculum and Instruction M
Genomic Sciences M

*M—master's degree; P—first professional degree; D—doctorate; O—other advanced degree; *—Close-Up and/or Display in one of the other books in this series*

Management Strategy and Policy M

BLESSED JOHN XXIII NATIONAL SEMINARY

Theology P

BLESSING-RIEMAN COLLEGE OF NURSING

Nursing—General M

BLOOMSBURG UNIVERSITY OF PENNSYLVANIA

Adult Nursing M
Athletic Training and Sports Medicine M
Biological and Biomedical Sciences—General M
Business Administration and Management—General M
Business Education M
Communication Disorders M,D
Community Health M
Counselor Education M
Curriculum and Instruction M
Early Childhood Education M
Education—General M
Educational Media/Instructional Technology M
Elementary Education M
Exercise and Sports Science M
Family Nurse Practitioner Studies M
Health Physics/Radiological Health M
Nursing and Healthcare Administration M
Nursing—General M
Reading Education M
Science Education M
Special Education M
Student Affairs M

BLUE MOUNTAIN COLLEGE

Elementary Education M

BLUFFTON UNIVERSITY

Business Administration and Management—General M
Education—General M
Organizational Management M

BOB JONES UNIVERSITY

Accounting P,M,D,O
Art/Fine Arts P,M,D,O
Business Administration and Management—General P,M,D,O
Counselor Education P,M,D,O
Curriculum and Instruction P,M,D,O
Educational Leadership and Administration P,M,D,O
Elementary Education P,M,D,O
English Education P,M,D,O
English P,M,D,O
Film, Television, and Video Production P,M,D,O
Graphic Design P,M,D,O
History P,M,D,O
Illustration P,M,D,O
Journalism P,M,D,O
Mathematics Education P,M,D,O
Media Studies P,M,D,O
Music Education P,M,D,O
Music P,M,D,O
Pastoral Ministry and Counseling P,M,D,O
Religion P,M,D,O
Rhetoric P,M,D,O
Secondary Education P,M,D,O
Social Sciences Education P,M,D,O
Special Education P,M,D,O
Speech and Interpersonal Communication P,M,D,O
Student Affairs P,M,D,O
Theater P,M,D,O
Theology P,M,D,O

BOISE STATE UNIVERSITY

Accounting M
Animal Sciences M
Art Education M
Art/Fine Arts M
Biological and Biomedical Sciences—General M
Business Administration and Management—General M
Civil Engineering M
Communication—General M
Computer Engineering M,D
Computer Science M
Counselor Education M
Criminal Justice and Criminology M
Curriculum and Instruction D
Early Childhood Education M
Education—General M,D
Educational Leadership and Administration M,D
Educational Media/Instructional Technology M
Electrical Engineering M,D
Engineering and Applied Sciences—General M,D
English M
Environmental Management and Policy M
Exercise and Sports Science M
Geology M,D
Geophysics M,D
Geosciences M
History M
Interdisciplinary Studies M
Management Information Systems M
Materials Engineering M
Mechanical Engineering M
Music Education M
Music M
Physical Education M
Public Administration M
Public Health—General M
Public Policy M
Reading Education M
Science Education M,D
Social Work M
Special Education M
Taxation M
Technical Communication M
Writing M

BORICUA COLLEGE

Human Services M
Latin American Studies M

BOSTON ARCHITECTURAL COLLEGE

Architecture M
Interior Design M

BOSTON COLLEGE

Accounting M
Adult Nursing M,D
Applied Psychology M,D
Biochemistry D
Biological and Biomedical Sciences—General D*
Business Administration and Management—General M
Chemistry M,D
Classics M
Community Health Nursing M,D
Counseling Psychology M,D
Curriculum and Instruction M,D,O
Developmental Psychology M,D
Early Childhood Education M
East European and Russian Studies M
Economics D
Education—General M,D,O
Educational Leadership and Administration M,D,O
Educational Measurement and Evaluation M,D
Educational Psychology M,D
Elementary Education M
English M,D
Finance and Banking M,D
Forensic Nursing M,D
French M,D
Geology M
Geophysics M
Gerontological Nursing M,D
Higher Education M,D
History M,D
Inorganic Chemistry M,D
Italian M,D
Law P
Linguistics M
Maternal and Child/Neonatal Nursing M,D
Mathematics D
Medical/Surgical Nursing M,D
Nurse Anesthesia M,D
Nursing—General M,D
Organic Chemistry M,D
Organizational Behavior D
Organizational Management D
Pastoral Ministry and Counseling P,M,D,O
Pediatric Nursing M,D
Philosophy M,D
Physical Chemistry M,D
Physics M,D
Political Science M,D
Psychiatric Nursing M,D
Psychology—General M,D
Reading Education M,O
Religious Education P,M,D,O
Russian M
Science Education M,D
Secondary Education M
Slavic Languages M
Social Work M,D
Sociology M,D
Spanish M,D
Special Education M,O
Theology P,M,D,O
Western European Studies M,D

THE BOSTON CONSERVATORY

Music Education M,O
Music M,O
Theater M

BOSTON GRADUATE SCHOOL OF PSYCHOANALYSIS

Counseling Psychology M
Psychoanalysis and Psychotherapy M,D,O
Psychology—General M

BOSTON UNIVERSITY

Actuarial Science M
Adult Education M,D,O
Advertising and Public Relations M
African Studies M,O
African-American Studies M
Allied Health—General M,D,O
Allopathic Medicine P
American Studies D
Anatomy M,D
Anthropology M,D
Archaeology M,D
Art Education M
Art History M,D,O
Art/Fine Arts M
Arts Administration M,O
Astronomy M,D
Athletic Training and Sports Medicine D
Biochemistry M,D
Bioethics M
Bioinformatics M,D
Biological and Biomedical Sciences—General M,D,O
Biomedical Engineering M,D
Biophysics D
Biostatistics M,D
Broadcast Journalism M
Business Administration and Management—General M,D
Cell Biology M,D
Chemistry M,D,O
Classics M,D,O
Cognitive Sciences M,D
Communication Disorders M,D,O
Communication—General M
Computer and Information Systems Security M
Computer Engineering M,D
Computer Science M,D
Corporate and Organizational Communication M
Counseling Psychology M,D,O
Counselor Education M,D,O
Criminal Justice and Criminology M
Cultural Studies M
Curriculum and Instruction M,D,O
Database Systems M
Dental Hygiene P,M,D,O
Dentistry P,M,D,O
Early Childhood Education M,D,O
Economic Development M
Economics M,D
Education—General M,D,O
Educational Leadership and Administration M,D,O
Educational Media/Instructional Technology M,D,O
Electrical Engineering M,D
Electronic Commerce M
Elementary Education M,D,O
Emergency Management M
Engineering and Applied Sciences—General M,D
English as a Second Language M,D,O
English Education M,D,O
English M,D,O
Environmental and Occupational Health M,D
Environmental Management and Policy M,D,O
Epidemiology M,D
Film, Television, and Video Production M
Film, Television, and Video Theory and Criticism M
Finance and Banking P,M
Food Science and Technology M
Foreign Languages Education M,D,O
Forensic Sciences M
French M,D,O
Geographic Information Systems M,D
Geography M,D
Geosciences M,D,O
Graphic Design M
Health Education M,D,O
Health Informatics M
Health Law M
Health Promotion D
Health Services Management and Hospital Administration M,D
Higher Education M,D,O
Hispanic and Latin American Languages M,D
Historic Preservation M
History M,D,O
Human Development M,D,O

Immunology M,D
Intellectual Property Law P,M
International Affairs M,D,O
International Business M
International Health M,D
Investment Management M,D
Journalism M
Law P,M
Legal and Justice Studies M
Linguistics M,D
Management Information Systems M
Management of Technology M
Management Strategy and Policy M
Manufacturing Engineering M,D
Mass Communication M
Materials Engineering M,D
Materials Sciences M,D
Maternal and Child Health M,D
Mathematical and Computational Finance M,D
Mathematics Education M,D,O
Mathematics M,D
Mechanical Engineering M,D
Media Studies M
Medical Imaging M
Microbiology M,D
Molecular Biology M,D
Molecular Medicine D
Museum Studies M,D,O
Music Education M,D
Music M,D,O
Neuroscience M,D
Nutrition M
Occupational Therapy M,D
Oral and Dental Sciences P,M,D,O
Pharmaceutical Sciences M,D
Pharmacology M,D
Philosophy M,D
Photonics M,D
Physical Education M,D,O
Physical Therapy D
Physics M,D,O*
Physiology M,D
Political Science M,D,O
Project Management M
Psychology—General M,D
Public Administration M,D,O
Public Health—General P,M,D,O
Public Policy M,D,O
Reading Education M,D,O
Rehabilitation Sciences D
Religion M,D
Romance Languages M,D
School Psychology M,D,O
Science Education M,D,O
Social Psychology M,D,O
Social Sciences Education M,D,O
Social Work M,D
Sociology M,D
Spanish M,D,O
Special Education M,D,O
Sport Psychology M,D,O
Systems Engineering M,D
Taxation P,M
Telecommunications Management M
Telecommunications M
Theater M,O
Theology P,M,D
Travel and Tourism M
Urban and Regional Planning M
Urban Studies M
Writing M,D

BOWIE STATE UNIVERSITY

Applied Mathematics M
Business Administration and Management—General M
Computer Science M,D
Corporate and Organizational Communication M,O
Counseling Psychology M
Counselor Education M
Education—General M
Educational Leadership and Administration M,D
Elementary Education M
English M
Family Nurse Practitioner Studies M
Human Resources Development M
Management Information Systems M,O
Nursing and Healthcare Administration M
Nursing Education M
Nursing—General M
Public Administration M
Reading Education M
Secondary Education M
Special Education M

BOWLING GREEN STATE UNIVERSITY

Accounting M
American Studies M,D
Applied Arts and Design—General M
Applied Statistics M,D
Art Education M
Art History M
Art/Fine Arts M
Biological and Biomedical Sciences—General M,D*
Business Administration and Management—General M
Business Education M
Chemistry M,D
Child and Family Studies M
Clinical Psychology M,D
Communication Disorders M,D
Communication—General M,D
Computer Art and Design M
Computer Science M
Construction Management M
Counseling Psychology M
Counselor Education M
Criminal Justice and Criminology M
Curriculum and Instruction M
Demography and Population Studies M,D
Developmental Psychology M,D
Early Childhood Education M
Economics M
Education of the Gifted M
Educational Leadership and Administration M,D,O
Educational Media/ Instructional Technology M
English M,D
Experimental Psychology M,D
Family and Consumer Sciences-General M
Film, Television, and Video Production M,D
Foreign Languages Education M
French M
Geology M
Geophysics M
German M
Graphic Design M
Higher Education D
History M,D
Human Development M
Industrial and Organizational Psychology M,D
Interdisciplinary Studies M,D
International and Comparative Education M
Kinesiology and Movement Studies M
Leisure Studies M
Manufacturing Engineering M
Mathematics Education M,D
Mathematics M,D
Music Education M,D
Music M,D
Nutrition M
Operations Research M
Organizational Management M
Philosophy M,D
Physics M
Political Science
Psychology—General M,D
Public Administration M
Public Health—General M
Reading Education M,O
Recreation and Park Management M
Rehabilitation Counseling M
Rhetoric M,D
School Psychology M,O
Science Education M
Social Psychology M,D
Sociology M,D
Software Engineering M
Spanish M
Special Education M
Speech and Interpersonal Communication M,D
Sports Management M
Statistics M,D
Student Affairs M
Technical Communication M,D
Theater M,D
Vocational and Technical Education M
Writing M,D

BRADLEY UNIVERSITY

Accounting M
Applied Arts and Design—General M
Art/Fine Arts M
Biological and Biomedical Sciences—General M
Business Administration and Management—General M
Chemistry M
Civil Engineering M
Comparative and Interdisciplinary Arts M
Computer Science M
Construction Engineering M
Counselor Education M
Curriculum and Instruction M,O
Education—General M,D,O
Educational Leadership and Administration M
Electrical Engineering M
Engineering and Applied Sciences—General M
English M
Human Development M
Illustration M
Industrial/Management Engineering M
Information Science M
Liberal Studies M
Manufacturing Engineering M
Mechanical Engineering M
Nurse Anesthesia M
Nursing and Healthcare Administration M
Nursing—General M
Photography M
Physical Therapy D

BRANDEIS UNIVERSITY

Anthropology M,D
Art/Fine Arts O
Biochemistry D
Bioinformatics M,O
Biological and Biomedical Sciences—General O
Biophysics D
Biotechnology M
Business Administration and Management—General M
Cell Biology M,D
Chemistry M,D
Child and Family Studies M,D
Classics M,O
Cognitive Sciences M,D
Communication—General M,O
Computer and Information Systems Security M,O
Computer Science M,D,O
Developmental Psychology M,D
Disability Studies D
Economics M
Elementary Education M
English M,D
Entrepreneurship M
Finance and Banking M
Gender Studies M,D
Genetic Counseling M
Genetics M,D
Health Education D
Health Informatics M,O
Health Services Management and Hospital Administration M
History M,D
Human Services M
Inorganic Chemistry M,D
International Affairs M,D
International Business M,D
International Development M
International Health M,D
Jewish Studies M,D
Linguistics M
Management Information Systems M,O
Mathematics M,D,O
Microbiology M,D
Molecular Biology M,D
Music M,D
Near and Middle Eastern Languages M,D
Near and Middle Eastern Studies M,D
Neurobiology M,D
Neuroscience M,D
Nonprofit Management M
Organic Chemistry M,D
Philosophy M
Physical Chemistry M,D
Physics M,D
Political Science M,D
Project Management M,O
Psychology—General M,D
Public Policy M
Religious Education M
Secondary Education M
Social Psychology M,D
Sociology M,D
Software Engineering M,O
Sustainable Development M
Theater M
Women's Studies M,D

BRANDON UNIVERSITY

Counselor Education M,O
Curriculum and Instruction M,O
Education—General M,O
Educational Leadership and Administration M,O
Music Education M
Music M
Rural Planning and Studies M,O
Special Education M,O

BRENAU UNIVERSITY

Accounting M
Business Administration and Management—General M
Early Childhood Education M,O
Education—General M,O
Family Nurse Practitioner Studies M
Health Services Management and Hospital Administration M
Interior Design M
Middle School Education M,O

*M—master's degree; P—first professional degree; D—doctorate; O—other advanced degree; *—Close-Up and/or Display in one of the other books in this series*

- Nursing and Healthcare Administration — M
- Nursing Education — M
- Occupational Therapy — M
- Organizational Management — M
- Project Management — M
- Psychology—General — M
- Secondary Education — M,O
- Special Education — M,O

BRESCIA UNIVERSITY

- Business Administration and Management—General — M
- Curriculum and Instruction — M

BRIAR CLIFF UNIVERSITY

- Human Resources Management — M
- Nursing—General — M

BRIDGEWATER STATE UNIVERSITY

- Accounting — M
- Art Education — M
- Business Administration and Management—General — M
- Computer Science — M
- Counselor Education — M,O
- Criminal Justice and Criminology — M
- Early Childhood Education — M
- Education—General — M,O
- Educational Leadership and Administration — M,O
- Educational Media/Instructional Technology — M
- Elementary Education — M
- English — M
- Finance and Banking — M
- Health Promotion — M
- Mathematics Education — M
- Physical Education — M
- Psychology—General — M
- Public Administration — M
- Reading Education — M,O
- Science Education — M
- Secondary Education — M
- Social Sciences Education — M
- Social Work — M
- Special Education — M

BRIERCREST SEMINARY

- Business Administration and Management—General — M
- Marriage and Family Therapy — M
- Missions and Missiology — M
- Organizational Management — M
- Pastoral Ministry and Counseling — P,M
- Religion — P,M
- Theology — P,M

BRIGHAM YOUNG UNIVERSITY

- Accounting — M
- Agricultural Sciences—General — M,D
- Analytical Chemistry — M,D
- Animal Sciences — M,D
- Anthropology — M
- Applied Statistics — M
- Art Education — M
- Art History — M
- Art/Fine Arts — M
- Astronomy — M,D
- Athletic Training and Sports Medicine — M,D
- Biochemistry — M,D
- Biological and Biomedical Sciences—General — M,D
- Biotechnology — M,D
- Business Administration and Management—General — M
- Chemical Engineering — M,D
- Chemistry — M,D
- Child and Family Studies — M,D
- Civil Engineering — M,D
- Clinical Psychology — M,D
- Communication Disorders — M
- Communication—General — M
- Comparative and Interdisciplinary Arts — M
- Comparative Literature — M
- Computer Engineering — M,D
- Computer Science — M,D
- Construction Management — M
- Counseling Psychology — M,D,O
- Developmental Biology — M,D
- Education—General — M,D,O
- Educational Leadership and Administration — M,D
- Educational Media/Instructional Technology — M,D
- Educational Psychology — M,D
- Electrical Engineering — M,D
- Engineering and Applied Sciences—General — M,D
- English as a Second Language — M,O
- English — M
- Environmental Sciences — M,D
- Exercise and Sports Science — M,D
- Family Nurse Practitioner Studies — M
- Film, Television, and Video Production — M
- Finance and Banking — M
- Fish, Game, and Wildlife Management — M,D
- Food Science and Technology — M
- Foreign Languages Education — M
- Foundations and Philosophy of Education — M,D
- French — M
- Geography — M
- Geology — M
- Health Education — M
- Health Promotion — M,D
- Hispanic and Latin American Languages — M
- Human Development — M,D
- Human Resources Management — M
- Humanities — M
- Industrial Design — M
- Information Science — M
- Law — P,M
- Linguistics — M,O
- Management Information Systems — M
- Marriage and Family Therapy — M,D
- Mass Communication — M
- Mathematics Education — M
- Mathematics — M,D
- Mechanical Engineering — M,D
- Microbiology — M,D
- Molecular Biology — M,D
- Music Education — M
- Music — M
- Neuroscience — M,D
- Nonprofit Management — M
- Nursing—General — M
- Nutrition — M
- Physics — M,D
- Physiology — M,D
- Plant Sciences — M,D
- Political Science — M
- Portuguese — M
- Psychology—General — M,D
- Public Administration — M
- Public Policy — M
- Reading Education — M
- Recreation and Park Management — M
- Religious Education — M
- Rhetoric — M
- School Psychology — M,D,O
- Science Education — M,D
- Social Psychology — M,D
- Social Work — M
- Sociology — M
- Spanish — M
- Special Education — M,D,O
- Statistics — M
- Theater — M
- Writing — M

BROADVIEW UNIVERSITY

- Business Administration and Management—General — M
- Health Services Management and Hospital Administration — M
- Management Information Systems — M

BROCK UNIVERSITY

- Accounting — M
- Allied Health—General — M,D
- Biological and Biomedical Sciences—General — M,D
- Biotechnology — M,D
- Business Administration and Management—General — M
- Chemistry — M,D
- Child and Family Studies — M
- Classics — M
- Comparative Literature — M
- Computer Science — M
- Cultural Studies — M
- Disability Studies — M,O
- Economics — M
- Education—General — M,D
- English as a Second Language — M
- English — M
- Geography — M
- Geosciences — M
- History — M
- Human Development — M,D
- International Affairs — M
- Legal and Justice Studies — M
- Mathematics — M
- Neuroscience — M,D
- Philosophy — M
- Physics — M
- Political Science — M
- Psychology—General — M,D
- Public Policy — M
- Social Psychology — M,D
- Sociology — M
- Statistics — M

BROOKLYN COLLEGE OF THE CITY UNIVERSITY OF NEW YORK

- Accounting — M
- Art Education — M,O
- Art History — M,D
- Art/Fine Arts — M,D
- Biological and Biomedical Sciences—General — M,D
- Chemistry — M,D
- Communication Disorders — M,D
- Community Health — M
- Computer Science — M,D,O
- Counseling Psychology — M,D,O
- Counselor Education — M,O
- Early Childhood Education — M
- Economics — M
- Education—General — M,O
- Educational Leadership and Administration — M
- Elementary Education — M
- English Education — M,O
- English — M,D
- Environmental Education — M
- Exercise and Sports Science — M
- Experimental Psychology — M,D
- Film, Television, and Video Production — M
- Finance and Banking — M
- Foreign Languages Education — M,O
- French — M,D
- Geology — M,D
- Geosciences — M,O
- Health Education — M,O
- Health Services Management and Hospital Administration — M
- History — M,D
- Industrial and Organizational Psychology — M
- Information Science — M,D,O
- International Affairs — M,D
- International Business — M
- Internet and Interactive Multimedia — M,O
- Jewish Studies — M
- Liberal Studies — M
- Mathematics Education — M,O
- Mathematics — M,D
- Media Studies — M
- Middle School Education — M
- Multilingual and Multicultural Education — M
- Music Education — M,D,O
- Music — M,D,O
- Nutrition — M
- Organizational Behavior — M
- Photography — M,D
- Physical Education — M,O
- Physics — M,D
- Political Science — M,D
- Psychology—General — M,D
- Public Health—General — M
- Public Policy — M,D
- School Psychology — M,O
- Science Education — M,O
- Secondary Education — M,O
- Social Psychology — M
- Social Sciences Education — M,O
- Sociology — M,D
- Spanish — M,D
- Special Education — M
- Speech and Interpersonal Communication — M,D
- Sports Management — M
- Thanatology — M
- Theater — M,D
- Urban Studies — M,D
- Writing — M

BROOKLYN LAW SCHOOL

- Law — P

BROOKS INSTITUTE

- Photography — M

BROWN UNIVERSITY

- Allopathic Medicine — P
- American Studies — M,D
- Anthropology — M,D
- Applied Mathematics — M,D
- Archaeology — M,D
- Art History — M,D
- Biochemistry — M,D
- Biological and Biomedical Sciences—General — M,D
- Biomedical Engineering — M,D
- Biopsychology — D
- Biostatistics — M,D
- Biotechnology — M,D
- Cancer Biology/Oncology — M,D
- Cell Biology — M,D
- Chemical Engineering — M,D
- Chemistry — M,D
- Classics — M,D
- Cognitive Sciences — M,D
- Community Health — M,D
- Comparative Literature — D
- Computer Engineering — M,D
- Computer Science — M,D
- Developmental Biology — M,D

Developmental Psychology D
East European and Russian Studies M,D
Ecology D
Economics D
Education—General M
Electrical Engineering M,D
Elementary Education M
Engineering and Applied Sciences—General M,D
English Education M
English M,D
Environmental Management and Policy M
Epidemiology M,D
Evolutionary Biology D
French D
Geosciences M,D
German D
Health Services Research M,D
Hispanic Studies M,D
History M,D
Immunology M,D
Italian D
Jewish Studies D
Latin American Studies M,D
Linguistics M,D
Materials Sciences M,D
Mathematics M,D
Mechanical Engineering M,D
Mechanics M,D
Microbiology M,D
Molecular Biology M,D
Molecular Pharmacology M,D
Multilingual and Multicultural Education M,D
Museum Studies M,D
Music D
Neuroscience D
Pathobiology M,D
Pathology M,D
Philosophy M,D
Physics M,D
Physiology M,D
Political Science D
Psychology—General D
Public Health—General M
Public Policy M
Religion D
Russian M,D
Science Education M
Secondary Education M
Slavic Languages M,D
Social Psychology D
Social Sciences Education M
Sociology M,D
Theater M,D
Toxicology M,D
Urban Education M
Western European Studies M,D
Writing M

BRYAN COLLEGE

Business Administration and Management—General M

BRYANLGH COLLEGE OF HEALTH SCIENCES

Nurse Anesthesia M

BRYANT UNIVERSITY

Accounting M
Business Administration and Management—General M
Taxation M

BRYN ATHYN COLLEGE OF THE NEW CHURCH

Religion P,M
Theology P,M

BRYN MAWR COLLEGE

Archaeology M,D*
Art History M,D
Chemistry M,D*
Classics M,D
French M,D
Mathematics M,D*
Physics M,D*
Social Work M,D*

BUCKNELL UNIVERSITY

Animal Behavior M
Biological and Biomedical Sciences—General M
Chemical Engineering M
Chemistry M
Civil Engineering M
Counselor Education M
Curriculum and Instruction M
Education—General M
Educational Leadership and Administration M
Educational Measurement and Evaluation M
Electrical Engineering M
Engineering and Applied Sciences—General M
English M
Mathematics M
Mechanical Engineering M
Psychology—General M
Reading Education M
School Psychology M
Student Affairs M

BUENA VISTA UNIVERSITY

Counselor Education M
Curriculum and Instruction M
Education—General M
English as a Second Language M

BUFFALO STATE COLLEGE, STATE UNIVERSITY OF NEW YORK

Adult Education M,O
Applied Economics M
Art Education M
Biological and Biomedical Sciences—General M
Business Education M
Chemistry M
Communication Disorders M
Criminal Justice and Criminology M
Early Childhood Education M
Economics M
Educational Leadership and Administration O
Educational Media/Instructional Technology M
Elementary Education M
English Education M
English M
Historic Preservation M,O
History M
Human Resources Management M,O
Industrial/Management Engineering M
Interdisciplinary Studies M
Mathematics Education M
Multilingual and Multicultural Education M
Reading Education M
Science Education M
Social Sciences Education M
Special Education M
Student Affairs M
Vocational and Technical Education M

BUTLER UNIVERSITY

Business Administration and Management—General M
Counselor Education M
Education—General M
Educational Leadership and Administration M
Elementary Education M
English M
History M
Music Education M
Music M
Pharmaceutical Sciences P,M
Pharmacy P,M
Physician Assistant Studies P,M
Reading Education M
Secondary Education M
Special Education M

CABRINI COLLEGE

Education—General M
Organizational Management M

CALDWELL COLLEGE

Accounting M
Applied Behavior Analysis M,D
Art Therapy M
Business Administration and Management—General M
Counseling Psychology M
Counselor Education M
Curriculum and Instruction M
Educational Leadership and Administration M
Pastoral Ministry and Counseling M
Special Education M

CALIFORNIA BAPTIST UNIVERSITY

Accounting M,D
Athletic Training and Sports Medicine M
Business Administration and Management—General M,D
Counseling Psychology M
Counselor Education M
Curriculum and Instruction M
Education—General M
Educational Leadership and Administration M
Educational Media/Instructional Technology M
English as a Second Language M
English Education M
English M
Exercise and Sports Science M
Forensic Psychology M
International and Comparative Education M
Kinesiology and Movement Studies M
Music Education M
Music M
Nursing—General M
Pastoral Ministry and Counseling M
Physical Education M
Public Administration M
Reading Education M
School Psychology M
Special Education M
Sports Management M
Vocational and Technical Education M

CALIFORNIA COAST UNIVERSITY

Business Administration and Management—General M
Criminal Justice and Criminology M
Curriculum and Instruction M,D
Education—General M,D
Educational Leadership and Administration M,D
Educational Psychology M,D
Health Services Management and Hospital Administration M
Human Resources Management M
Marketing M
Organizational Management M,D
Psychology—General M

CALIFORNIA COLLEGE OF THE ARTS

Applied Arts and Design—General M
Architecture M
Art/Fine Arts M
Film, Television, and Video Production M
Film, Television, and Video Theory and Criticism M
Finance and Banking M
Museum Studies M
Organizational Management M
Photography M
Textile Design M
Writing M

CALIFORNIA INSTITUTE OF INTEGRAL STUDIES

Art Therapy M,D
Asian Studies M,D
Clinical Psychology M,D
Counseling Psychology M,D
Cultural Anthropology M,D
Health Psychology M,D
Humanities M,D
Interdisciplinary Studies M,D
Philosophy M,D
Psychology—General M,D
Religion M,D
Social Psychology M,D
Theology M,D
Therapies—Dance, Drama, and Music M,D
Women's Studies M,D
Writing M,D

CALIFORNIA INSTITUTE OF TECHNOLOGY

Aerospace/Aeronautical Engineering M,D,O
Applied Mathematics M,D
Applied Physics M,D
Astronomy D
Biochemistry M,D
Bioengineering M,D
Biological and Biomedical Sciences—General D*
Biophysics D
Cell Biology D
Chemical Engineering M,D
Chemistry M,D
Civil Engineering M,D,O
Computational Sciences M,D
Computer Science M,D
Developmental Biology D
Electrical Engineering M,D,O
Engineering and Applied Sciences—General M,D,O
Environmental Engineering M,D
Genetics D
Geochemistry M,D
Geology M,D
Geophysics M,D
Immunology D
Materials Sciences M,D
Mathematics D
Mechanical Engineering M,D,O
Mechanics M,D
Molecular Biology D

*M—master's degree; P—first professional degree; D—doctorate; O—other advanced degree; *—Close-Up and/or Display in one of the other books in this series*

Molecular Biophysics M,D
Neurobiology D
Neuroscience M,D
Physics D
Planetary and Space Sciences M,D
Social Sciences M,D
Systems Engineering M,D

CALIFORNIA INSTITUTE OF THE ARTS

Applied Arts and Design—General M,O
Art/Fine Arts M,O
Dance M,O
Film, Television, and Video Production M,O
Graphic Design M,O
Music M,O
Photography M,O
Theater M,O
Writing M,O

CALIFORNIA INTERCONTINENTAL UNIVERSITY

Business Administration and Management—General M,D
Entertainment Management M
Entrepreneurship M,D
Finance and Banking M,D
Health Services Management and Hospital Administration M,D
Human Resources Management M,D
International Business M,D
Management Information Systems M,D
Marketing M,D
Organizational Management M,D
Project Management M,D
Quality Management M,D

CALIFORNIA INTERNATIONAL BUSINESS UNIVERSITY

Business Administration and Management—General M,D

CALIFORNIA LUTHERAN UNIVERSITY

Business Administration and Management—General M,O
Clinical Psychology M,D
Counselor Education M,O
Economics M,O
Education—General M,D
Educational Leadership and Administration M,D
Elementary Education M,D
Entrepreneurship M,O
Finance and Banking M,O
Higher Education M,D
International Business M,O
Management Information Systems M,O
Management of Technology M,O
Marketing M,O
Marriage and Family Therapy M,D
Middle School Education M,D
Nonprofit Management M,O
Organizational Behavior M,O
Psychology—General M,D
Public Administration M
Public Policy M
Special Education M,D

CALIFORNIA MIRAMAR UNIVERSITY

Business Administration and Management—General M
Management Strategy and Policy M
Taxation M
Telecommunications Management M
Telecommunications M

CALIFORNIA NATIONAL UNIVERSITY FOR ADVANCED STUDIES

Business Administration and Management—General M
Engineering and Applied Sciences—General M
Engineering Management M

CALIFORNIA POLYTECHNIC STATE UNIVERSITY, SAN LUIS OBISPO

Aerospace/Aeronautical Engineering M
Agricultural Economics and Agribusiness M
Agricultural Education M
Agricultural Sciences—General M
Architecture M
Biochemistry M
Biological and Biomedical Sciences—General M
Business Administration and Management—General M
Chemistry M
Civil Engineering M
Computer Science M
Education—General M
Electrical Engineering M
Engineering and Applied Sciences—General M
English M
Environmental Engineering M
Forestry M
History M
Industrial and Manufacturing Management M
Industrial/Management Engineering M
Kinesiology and Movement Studies M
Mathematics M
Mechanical Engineering M
Natural Resources M
Political Science M
Polymer Science and Engineering M
Psychology—General M
Taxation M
Urban and Regional Planning M

CALIFORNIA SCHOOL OF PODIATRIC MEDICINE AT SAMUEL MERRITT UNIVERSITY

Podiatric Medicine P

CALIFORNIA STATE POLYTECHNIC UNIVERSITY, POMONA

Accounting M
Aerospace/Aeronautical Engineering M
Agricultural Sciences—General M
Applied Mathematics M
Architecture M
Biological and Biomedical Sciences—General M
Biotechnology M
Business Administration and Management—General M
Chemistry M
Civil Engineering M
Computer Science M
Economics M
Education—General M
Electrical Engineering M
Engineering Management M
English M
Environmental Sciences M
History M
Kinesiology and Movement Studies M
Landscape Architecture M
Management Information Systems M
Mathematics M
Mechanical Engineering M
Psychology—General M
Public Administration M
Urban and Regional Planning M

CALIFORNIA STATE UNIVERSITY, BAKERSFIELD

Anthropology M
Biological and Biomedical Sciences—General M
Business Administration and Management—General M
Counseling Psychology M
Counselor Education M
Curriculum and Instruction M
Early Childhood Education M
Education—General M,O
Educational Leadership and Administration M
Educational Media/Instructional Technology M
English M
Geology M
Health Services Management and Hospital Administration M
History M
Hydrology M
Interdisciplinary Studies M
Mathematics Education M
Middle School Education M
Multilingual and Multicultural Education M
Nursing—General M
Psychology—General M
Public Administration M
Reading Education M,O
Secondary Education M
Social Work M
Sociology M
Spanish M
Special Education M
Student Affairs M

CALIFORNIA STATE UNIVERSITY CHANNEL ISLANDS

Bioinformatics M
Biotechnology M
Business Administration and Management—General M
Computer Science M
Educational Leadership and Administration M
Mathematics M

CALIFORNIA STATE UNIVERSITY, CHICO

Anthropology M
Applied Psychology M
Art History M
Art/Fine Arts M
Biological and Biomedical Sciences—General M
Botany M
Business Administration and Management—General M
Communication Disorders M
Communication—General M
Computer Engineering M
Computer Science M
Curriculum and Instruction M
Education—General M
Electrical Engineering M
Engineering and Applied Sciences—General M
English M
Environmental Sciences M
Foreign Languages Education M
Geography M
Geology M
Geosciences M
Health Services Management and Hospital Administration M
History M
Hydrogeology M
Hydrology M
Interdisciplinary Studies M
Kinesiology and Movement Studies M
Marriage and Family Therapy M
Mathematics Education M
Modeling and Simulation M
Multilingual and Multicultural Education M
Museum Studies M
Music M
Nursing—General M
Nutrition M
Political Science M
Psychology—General M
Public Administration M
Recreation and Park Management M
Rural Planning and Studies M
Science Education M
Social Sciences Education M
Social Sciences M
Social Work M
Special Education M
Urban and Regional Planning M

CALIFORNIA STATE UNIVERSITY, DOMINGUEZ HILLS

Applied Social Research M,O
Bioinformatics M
Biological and Biomedical Sciences—General M
Business Administration and Management—General M
Clinical Psychology M
Computer Education M,O
Computer Science M
Conflict Resolution and Mediation/Peace Studies M
Counselor Education M
Curriculum and Instruction M
Education—General M,O
Educational Leadership and Administration M
Educational Media/Instructional Technology M,O
English as a Second Language M,O
English M,O
Environmental Sciences M
Humanities M*
International and Comparative Education M
Marriage and Family Therapy M
Mathematics Education M
Multilingual and Multicultural Education M
Nursing—General M
Occupational Therapy M
Physical Education M

Psychology—General	M
Public Administration	M
Quality Management	M
Rhetoric	M,O
Social Work	M
Sociology	M,O
Special Education	M

CALIFORNIA STATE UNIVERSITY, EAST BAY

Accounting	M
Anthropology	M
Applied Mathematics	M
Biochemistry	M
Biological and Biomedical Sciences—General	M
Biostatistics	M
Business Administration and Management—General	M
Chemistry	M
Communication Disorders	M
Communication—General	M
Computer Science	M
Construction Management	M
Counselor Education	M
Early Childhood Education	M
Economics	M
Education—General	M
Educational Leadership and Administration	M,D
Educational Media/Instructional Technology	M
Engineering and Applied Sciences—General	M
Engineering Management	M
English	M
Entrepreneurship	M
Environmental Sciences	M
Exercise and Sports Science	M
Finance and Banking	M
Geography	M
Geology	M
Health Services Management and Hospital Administration	M
History	M
Human Resources Management	M
Humanities	M
Industrial and Manufacturing Management	M
Interdisciplinary Studies	M
International Business	M
Internet and Interactive Multimedia	M
Management Information Systems	M
Management Strategy and Policy	M
Marine Sciences	M
Marketing	M
Mathematics Education	M
Mathematics	M
Music	M
Operations Research	M
Organizational Management	M
Physical Education	M
Public Administration	M
Reading Education	M
Recreation and Park Management	M
Social Work	M
Special Education	M
Sport Psychology	M
Statistics	M
Supply Chain Management	M
Taxation	M
Travel and Tourism	M

CALIFORNIA STATE UNIVERSITY, FRESNO

Accounting	M
Animal Sciences	M
Applied Arts and Design—General	M
Art/Fine Arts	M
Biological and Biomedical Sciences—General	M
Business Administration and Management—General	M
Chemistry	M
Civil Engineering	M
Communication Disorders	M
Communication—General	M
Computer Science	M
Counselor Education	M
Criminal Justice and Criminology	M
Curriculum and Instruction	M
Early Childhood Education	M
Education—General	M,D
Educational Leadership and Administration	M,D
Electrical Engineering	M
Engineering and Applied Sciences—General	M
English as a Second Language	M
English	M
Exercise and Sports Science	M
Family and Consumer Sciences-General	M
Family Nurse Practitioner Studies	M
Food Science and Technology	M
Geology	M
Health Promotion	M
Health Services Management and Hospital Administration	M
History	M
Industrial/Management Engineering	M
International Affairs	M
Journalism	M
Kinesiology and Movement Studies	M
Linguistics	M
Marine Sciences	M
Marriage and Family Therapy	M
Mass Communication	M
Mathematics Education	M
Mathematics	M
Mechanical Engineering	M
Music Education	M
Music	M
Nursing Education	M
Nursing—General	M
Physical Therapy	M,D
Physics	M
Plant Sciences	M
Psychology—General	M
Public Administration	M
Public Health—General	M
Reading Education	M
Rehabilitation Counseling	M
Social Sciences Education	M
Social Work	M
Spanish	M
Special Education	M
Sport Psychology	M
Viticulture and Enology	M
Writing	M

CALIFORNIA STATE UNIVERSITY, FULLERTON

Accounting	M
Advertising and Public Relations	M
American Studies	M
Anthropology	M
Applied Arts and Design—General	M
Applied Mathematics	M
Art History	M
Art/Fine Arts	M
Biological and Biomedical Sciences—General	M
Business Administration and Management—General	M
Chemistry	M
Civil Engineering	M
Clinical Psychology	M
Communication Disorders	M
Communication—General	M
Comparative Literature	M
Computer Science	M
Counselor Education	M
Dance	M
Economics	M
Educational Leadership and Administration	M,D
Educational Media/Instructional Technology	M
Electrical Engineering	M
Electronic Commerce	M
Elementary Education	M
Engineering and Applied Sciences—General	M
English as a Second Language	M
English	M
Entrepreneurship	M
Environmental Management and Policy	M
Environmental Sciences	M
Film, Television, and Video Production	M
Finance and Banking	M
French	M
Geochemistry	M
Geography	M
Geology	M
German	M
Gerontology	M
History	M
Information Science	M
International Business	M
Journalism	M
Linguistics	M
Management Information Systems	M
Marketing	M
Mathematics Education	M
Mathematics	M
Mechanical Engineering	M
Mechanics	M
Media Studies	M
Middle School Education	M
Multilingual and Multicultural Education	M
Music Education	M
Music	M
Nursing—General	M
Photography	M
Physical Education	M
Physics	M
Political Science	M
Psychology—General	M
Public Administration	M
Public Health—General	M
Reading Education	M
Science Education	M
Secondary Education	M
Social Psychology	M
Social Work	M
Sociology	M
Software Engineering	M
Spanish	M
Special Education	M
Speech and Interpersonal Communication	M
Systems Engineering	M
Taxation	M
Theater	M
Travel and Tourism	M

CALIFORNIA STATE UNIVERSITY, LONG BEACH

Aerospace/Aeronautical Engineering	M
African Studies	M
American Studies	M
Anthropology	M
Applied Mathematics	M,D
Applied Statistics	M
Art Education	M
Art History	M
Art/Fine Arts	M
Asian Studies	M
Asian-American Studies	M
Athletic Training and Sports Medicine	M
Biochemistry	M
Biological and Biomedical Sciences—General	M
Business Administration and Management—General	M
Chemical Engineering	M
Chemistry	M
Civil Engineering	M
Communication Disorders	M
Communication—General	M
Computer Engineering	M
Computer Science	M
Consumer Economics	M
Counselor Education	M
Criminal Justice and Criminology	M
Dance	M
Economics	M
Education—General	M,D
Educational Leadership and Administration	M,D
Educational Psychology	M
Electrical Engineering	M
Elementary Education	M
Emergency Management	M
Engineering Management	M,D
English as a Second Language	M
English	M
Ergonomics and Human Factors	M
Exercise and Sports Science	M
Family and Consumer Sciences-General	M
Food Science and Technology	M
French	M
Geography	M
Geology	M
Geophysics	M
German	M
Gerontology	M
Health Education	M
Health Services Management and Hospital Administration	M
Higher Education	M
History	M
Hospitality Management	M
Industrial and Organizational Psychology	M
Interdisciplinary Studies	M
Kinesiology and Movement Studies	M
Latin American Studies	M
Leisure Studies	M
Linguistics	M
Logistics	M
Marriage and Family Therapy	M
Mathematics Education	M
Mathematics	M
Mechanical Engineering	M,D
Medieval and Renaissance Studies	M
Microbiology	M
Music	M
Near and Middle Eastern Studies	M
Nursing—General	M
Nutrition	M
Philosophy	M
Physical Education	M
Physical Therapy	M
Physics	M
Political Science	M
Psychology—General	M
Public Administration	M
Public Policy	M

*M—master's degree; P—first professional degree; D—doctorate; O—other advanced degree; *—Close-Up and/or Display in one of the other books in this series*

Recreation and Park Management	M
Religion	M
Science Education	M
Secondary Education	M
Social Work	M
Spanish	M
Special Education	M
Sport Psychology	M
Sports Management	M
Student Affairs	M
Theater	M
Western European Studies	M
Writing	M

CALIFORNIA STATE UNIVERSITY, LOS ANGELES

Accounting	M
Analytical Chemistry	M
Anthropology	M
Applied Arts and Design—General	M
Applied Mathematics	M
Art Education	M
Art History	M
Art Therapy	M
Art/Fine Arts	M
Biochemistry	M
Biological and Biomedical Sciences—General	M
Business Administration and Management—General	M
Chemistry	M
Child and Family Studies	M
Child Development	M
Civil Engineering	M
Communication Disorders	M
Communication—General	M
Computer Science	M
Counselor Education	M,D
Criminal Justice and Criminology	M
Economics	M
Education—General	M,D
Electrical Engineering	M
Elementary Education	M
Engineering and Applied Sciences—General	M*
English	M
Film, Television, and Video Production	M
Finance and Banking	M
French	M
Geography	M
Geology	M
Graphic Design	M
Health Education	M
Health Services Management and Hospital Administration	M
Hispanic Studies	M
History	M
Inorganic Chemistry	M
International Business	M
Kinesiology and Movement Studies	M
Latin American Studies	M
Management Information Systems	M
Management of Technology	M
Marketing	M
Mathematics	M
Mechanical Engineering	M
Music Education	M
Music	M
Nursing—General	M
Nutrition	M
Organic Chemistry	M
Philosophy	M
Photography	M
Physical Chemistry	M
Physical Education	M
Physics	M
Political Science	M
Psychology—General	M
Public Administration	M
Reading Education	M
Rehabilitation Counseling	M,D
School Psychology	M,D
Secondary Education	M
Social Work	M
Sociology	M
Spanish	M
Special Education	M,D
Speech and Interpersonal Communication	M
Taxation	M
Textile Design	M
Theater	M

CALIFORNIA STATE UNIVERSITY, MONTEREY BAY

Business Administration and Management—General	M
Education—General	M
Educational Media/Instructional Technology	M
Interdisciplinary Studies	M
Management Information Systems	M
Marine Sciences	M
Public Policy	M
Social Work	M
Water Resources	M

CALIFORNIA STATE UNIVERSITY, NORTHRIDGE

Anthropology	M
Applied Mathematics	M
Applied Psychology	M
Archaeology	M
Art Education	M
Art History	M
Art/Fine Arts	M
Artificial Intelligence/Robotics	M
Biochemistry	M
Biological and Biomedical Sciences—General	M
Business Administration and Management—General	M
Chemistry	M
Civil Engineering	M
Clinical Psychology	M
Communication Disorders	M
Communication—General	M
Comparative Literature	M
Computer Science	M
Counselor Education	M
Curriculum and Instruction	M
Early Childhood Education	M
Education—General	M,D
Educational Leadership and Administration	M,D
Educational Media/Instructional Technology	M
Educational Psychology	M
Electrical Engineering	M
Elementary Education	M
Engineering and Applied Sciences—General	M
Engineering Management	M
English Education	M
English	M
Environmental and Occupational Health	M
Environmental Sciences	M
Ergonomics and Human Factors	M
Experimental Psychology	M
Family and Consumer Sciences-General	M
Film, Television, and Video Production	M
Geography	M
Geology	M
Health Services Management and Hospital Administration	M
Hispanic Studies	M
History	M
Hospitality Management	M
Industrial Hygiene	M
Industrial/Management Engineering	M
Interdisciplinary Studies	M
Journalism	M
Kinesiology and Movement Studies	M
Linguistics	M
Manufacturing Engineering	M
Marriage and Family Therapy	M
Mass Communication	M
Materials Engineering	M
Mathematics Education	M
Mathematics	M
Mechanical Engineering	M
Multilingual and Multicultural Education	M
Music Education	M
Music	M
Physical Therapy	M
Physics	M
Political Science	M
Psychology—General	M
Public Administration	M
Public Health—General	M
Reading Education	M
Recreation and Park Management	M
Rhetoric	M
School Psychology	M
Science Education	M
Secondary Education	M
Social Work	M
Sociology	M
Software Engineering	M
Spanish	M
Special Education	M
Speech and Interpersonal Communication	M
Structural Engineering	M
Systems Engineering	M
Taxation	M
Theater	M
Travel and Tourism	M
Writing	M

CALIFORNIA STATE UNIVERSITY, SACRAMENTO

Accounting	M
Anthropology	M
Art/Fine Arts	M
Biological and Biomedical Sciences—General	M
Business Administration and Management—General	M
Chemistry	M
Civil Engineering	M
Communication Disorders	M
Communication—General	M
Computer Science	M
Counseling Psychology	M
Counselor Education	M
Criminal Justice and Criminology	M
Curriculum and Instruction	M
Dance	M
Early Childhood Education	M
Education—General	M
Educational Leadership and Administration	M
Electrical Engineering	M
Engineering and Applied Sciences—General	M
English as a Second Language	M
English	M
Foreign Languages Education	M
French	M
German	M
Human Resources Development	M
Human Resources Management	M
Human Services	M
International Affairs	M
Liberal Studies	M
Management Information Systems	M
Marine Sciences	M
Mathematics	M
Mechanical Engineering	M
Multilingual and Multicultural Education	M
Music	M
Nursing—General	M
Physical Education	M
Political Science	M
Psychology—General	M
Public Administration	M
Public History	M
Public Policy	M
Reading Education	M
Real Estate	M
Recreation and Park Management	M
School Psychology	M
Social Work	M
Sociology	M
Software Engineering	M
Spanish	M
Special Education	M
Statistics	M
Theater	M
Vocational and Technical Education	M
Writing	M

CALIFORNIA STATE UNIVERSITY, SAN BERNARDINO

Art/Fine Arts	M
Biological and Biomedical Sciences—General	M
Business Administration and Management—General	M
Chemistry	M
Child Development	M
Clinical Psychology	M
Communication—General	M
Computer Science	M
Corporate and Organizational Communication	M
Counseling Psychology	M
Counselor Education	M
Criminal Justice and Criminology	M
Curriculum and Instruction	M
Education—General	M,D
Educational Leadership and Administration	M,D
Educational Media/Instructional Technology	M
Elementary Education	M
English as a Second Language	M,D
English Education	M,D
English	M
Environmental Education	M
Environmental Sciences	M
Experimental Psychology	M
Health Education	M
Health Services Management and Hospital Administration	M
Human Development	M
Industrial and Organizational Psychology	M
Interdisciplinary Studies	M
Kinesiology and Movement Studies	M
Mathematics Education	M
Mathematics	M
Multilingual and Multicultural Education	M
National Security	M
Nursing—General	M
Psychology—General	M
Public Administration	M
Public Health—General	M
Reading Education	M
Rehabilitation Counseling	M
Science Education	M
Secondary Education	M

Social Sciences Education M,D
Social Sciences M
Social Work M
Spanish M
Special Education M
Theater M
Vocational and Technical Education M
Writing M

CALIFORNIA STATE UNIVERSITY, SAN MARCOS

Biological and Biomedical Sciences—General M
Business Administration and Management—General M
Computer Science M
Education—General M
English M
Mathematics M
Psychology—General M
Sociology M
Spanish M
Writing M

CALIFORNIA STATE UNIVERSITY, STANISLAUS

Applied Behavior Analysis M
Business Administration and Management—General M
Community College Education D
Conservation Biology M
Counseling Psychology M
Counselor Education M
Criminal Justice and Criminology M
Curriculum and Instruction M
Ecology M
Education—General M,D,O
Educational Leadership and Administration M,D
Educational Media/Instructional Technology M
Elementary Education M
English as a Second Language M,O
English M,O
Finance and Banking M
Genetic Counseling M
Gerontological Nursing M
History M
Interdisciplinary Studies M
International Affairs M
International Business M
Multilingual and Multicultural Education M
Nursing Education M
Nursing—General M
Physical Education M
Psychology—General M
Public Administration M
Reading Education M
Rhetoric M,O
Secondary Education M
Social Work M
Special Education M
Sustainable Development M
Writing M,O

CALIFORNIA UNIVERSITY OF PENNSYLVANIA

Athletic Training and Sports Medicine M
Business Administration and Management—General M
Communication Disorders M
Counselor Education M
Criminal Justice and Criminology M
Education—General M
Educational Leadership and Administration M
Elementary Education M
Exercise and Sports Science M
Legal and Justice Studies M
Reading Education M
Rehabilitation Sciences M
School Psychology M
Secondary Education M
Social Sciences M
Social Work M
Special Education M
Sport Psychology M
Sports Management M
Vocational and Technical Education M

CALIFORNIA WESTERN SCHOOL OF LAW

Accounting P,M
Law P,M

CALUMET COLLEGE OF SAINT JOSEPH

Criminal Justice and Criminology M
Educational Leadership and Administration M
Quality Management M

CALVARY BAPTIST THEOLOGICAL SEMINARY

Theology P,M,D

CALVARY BIBLE COLLEGE AND THEOLOGICAL SEMINARY

Pastoral Ministry and Counseling P,M
Theology P,M

CALVIN COLLEGE

Curriculum and Instruction M
Education—General M
Educational Leadership and Administration M
Reading Education M
Special Education M

CALVIN THEOLOGICAL SEMINARY

Missions and Missiology P,M,D
Pastoral Ministry and Counseling P,M,D
Religion P,M,D
Religious Education P,M,D
Theology P,M,D

CAMBRIDGE COLLEGE

Addictions/Substance Abuse Counseling M,O
Business Administration and Management—General M
Conflict Resolution and Mediation/Peace Studies M
Counseling Psychology M,O
Counselor Education M,D,O
Curriculum and Instruction M,D,O
Early Childhood Education M,D,O
Education—General M,D,O
Educational Leadership and Administration M,D,O
Educational Measurement and Evaluation M,D,O
Educational Media/Instructional Technology M,D,O
Elementary Education M,D,O
English as a Second Language M,D,O
Entrepreneurship M
Forensic Psychology M,O
Health Education M,D,O
Health Services Management and Hospital Administration M
Home Economics Education M,D,O
Interdisciplinary Studies M,D,O
Management of Technology M
Marriage and Family Therapy M,O
Mathematics Education M,D,O
Medical Informatics M
Middle School Education M,D,O
Nonprofit Management M
Organizational Management M
Psychology—General M,O
Reading Education M,D,O
School Nursing M,D,O
School Psychology M,D,O
Science Education M,D,O
Social Sciences Education M,D,O
Special Education M,D,O

CAMERON UNIVERSITY

Business Administration and Management—General M
Education—General M
Educational Leadership and Administration M
Entrepreneurship M
Psychology—General M

CAMPBELLSVILLE UNIVERSITY

Business Administration and Management—General M
Curriculum and Instruction M
Education—General M
Music Education M
Music M
Social Sciences M
Social Work
Special Education M
Theology M

CAMPBELL UNIVERSITY

Business Administration and Management—General M
Counselor Education M
Education—General M
Educational Leadership and Administration M
Elementary Education M
English Education M
Interdisciplinary Studies M
Law P
Mathematics Education M
Middle School Education M
Pharmaceutical Sciences P,M
Pharmacy P,M
Physical Education M
Religious Education P,M,D
Secondary Education M
Social Sciences Education M
Theology P,M,D

CANADIAN COLLEGE OF NATUROPATHIC MEDICINE

Naturopathic Medicine D*

CANADIAN MEMORIAL CHIROPRACTIC COLLEGE

Acupuncture and Oriental Medicine O
Chiropractic P,O

CANADIAN SOUTHERN BAPTIST SEMINARY

Religious Education P,M
Theology P,M

CANISIUS COLLEGE

Accounting M
Business Administration and Management—General M
Business Education M
Communication Disorders M,O
Corporate and Organizational Communication M
Counselor Education M
Early Childhood Education M,O
Education of the Gifted M,O
Education—General M,O
Educational Leadership and Administration M,O
Elementary Education M,O
Health Promotion M
International Business M
Kinesiology and Movement Studies M
Marketing M
Middle School Education M,O
Occupational Therapy M
Physical Education M
Reading Education M
School Psychology M
Secondary Education M,O
Social Psychology M
Special Education M,O
Sports Management M
Student Affairs M,O

CAPE BRETON UNIVERSITY

Business Administration and Management—General M

CAPELLA UNIVERSITY

Accounting M,D,O
Addictions/Substance Abuse Counseling M,D,O
Adult Education M,D,O
Business Administration and Management—General M,D,O
Child and Family Studies M,D,O
Clinical Psychology M,D,O
Computer and Information Systems Security M,D,O
Counseling Psychology M,D,O
Criminal Justice and Criminology M,D,O
Curriculum and Instruction M,D,O
Developmental Psychology M,D,O
Education—General M,D,O
Educational Leadership and Administration M,D,O
Educational Media/Instructional Technology M,D,O
Educational Psychology M,D,O
Elementary Education M,D,O
Emergency Management M,D
Environmental and Occupational Health M,D
Finance and Banking M,D,O
Gerontology M,D
Health Services Management and Hospital Administration M,D,O
Higher Education M,D,O
Human Resources Management M,D,O
Human Services M,D,O
Industrial and Organizational Psychology M,D,O
Management Information Systems M,D,O
Management of Technology M,D,O
Marketing M,D,O
Marriage and Family Therapy M,D,O
Middle School Education M,D,O
Multilingual and Multicultural Education M,D,O
Nonprofit Management M,D,O
Nursing Education M,D
Organizational Management M,D,O
Project Management M,D,O
Psychology—General M,D,O

*M—master's degree; P—first professional degree; D—doctorate; O—other advanced degree; *—Close-Up and/or Display in one of the other books in this series*

Public Administration M,D
Reading Education M,D,O
School Psychology M,D,O
Sport Psychology M,D,O

CAPITAL BIBLE SEMINARY

Pastoral Ministry and Counseling P,M,O
Theology P,M,O

CAPITAL UNIVERSITY

Business Administration and Management—General M
Law P,M
Legal and Justice Studies M
Music Education M
Music M
Nursing and Healthcare Administration M
Nursing—General M
Taxation M

CAPITOL COLLEGE

Business Administration and Management—General M
Computer and Information Systems Security M
Computer Science M
Electrical Engineering M
Information Science M
Management Information Systems M
Telecommunications Management M

CARDINAL STRITCH UNIVERSITY

Applied Arts and Design—General M
Business Administration and Management—General M
Clinical Psychology M
Computer Education M
Education—General M,D
Educational Leadership and Administration M,D
Educational Media/Instructional Technology M
English as a Second Language M
Graphic Design M
History M
Liberal Studies M
Music M
Nursing—General M
Pastoral Ministry and Counseling M
Psychology—General M
Reading Education M
Religion M
Special Education M
Sports Management M
Urban Education M,D

CAREY THEOLOGICAL COLLEGE

Theology P,M,D

CARIBBEAN UNIVERSITY

Art History M,D
Criminal Justice and Criminology M,D
Curriculum and Instruction M,D
Early Childhood Education M,D
Education—General M,D
Educational Leadership and Administration M,D
Educational Media/Instructional Technology M,D
Elementary Education M,D
English Education M,D
Foreign Languages Education M,D
Gerontological Nursing M,D
Human Resources Management M,D
Mathematics Education M,D
Museum Studies M,D
Pediatric Nursing M,D
Physical Education M,D
Science Education M,D
Social Sciences Education M,D
Special Education M,D

CARLETON UNIVERSITY

Aerospace/Aeronautical Engineering M,D
Anthropology M
Architecture M
Art History M
Biological and Biomedical Sciences—General M,D
Biomedical Engineering M
Business Administration and Management—General M,D
Canadian Studies M,D
Chemistry M,D
Civil Engineering M,D
Cognitive Sciences D
Communication—General M,D
Comparative Literature D
Computer Science M,D
Conflict Resolution and Mediation/Peace Studies M,O
East European and Russian Studies M,O
Economics M,D
Electrical Engineering M,D
Engineering and Applied Sciences—General M,D
English M,D
Environmental Engineering M,D
Film, Television, and Video Production M
French M
Geography M,D
Geosciences M,D
History M,D
Industrial Design M
Information Science M,D
International Affairs M,D
Journalism M,D
Legal and Justice Studies M,O
Linguistics M
Management of Technology M
Materials Engineering M,D
Mathematics M,D
Mechanical Engineering M,D
Music M
Neuroscience M,D
Philosophy M
Physics M,D
Political Science M,D
Psychology—General M,D
Public Administration M,D
Public Policy M,D
Social Work M
Sociology M,D
Systems Engineering M,D
Systems Science M,D
Western European Studies M,O

CARLOS ALBIZU UNIVERSITY

Clinical Psychology M,D
Communication Disorders M,D
Industrial and Organizational Psychology M,D
Psychology—General M,D

CARLOS ALBIZU UNIVERSITY, MIAMI CAMPUS

Business Administration and Management—General M,D
Clinical Psychology M,D
Counseling Psychology M,D
Education of the Gifted M,D
English as a Second Language M,D
Entrepreneurship M,D
Industrial and Organizational Psychology M,D
Marriage and Family Therapy M,D
Nonprofit Management M,D
Organizational Management M,D
Psychology—General M,D
School Psychology M,D
Special Education M,D

CARLOW UNIVERSITY

Art Education M
Business Administration and Management—General M
Counseling Psychology M,D
Counselor Education M,D
Early Childhood Education M
Educational Leadership and Administration M
Educational Media/Instructional Technology M
Family Nurse Practitioner Studies M,D
Humanities M
Middle School Education M
Nursing and Healthcare Administration M,D
Nursing Education M,D
Nursing—General M,D
Organizational Management M,D
Secondary Education M
Special Education M
Writing M

CARNEGIE MELLON UNIVERSITY

Accounting D
African Studies M,D
African-American Studies M,D
Applied Arts and Design—General D
Applied Mathematics M,D
Applied Physics M,D
Architectural Engineering M,D
Architecture M,D
Art/Fine Arts M
Artificial Intelligence/Robotics M,D
Arts Administration M
Biochemistry M,D
Bioengineering M,D
Biological and Biomedical Sciences—General M,D
Biomedical Engineering M,D
Biophysics M,D
Biopsychology D
Biotechnology M,D
Building Science M,D
Business Administration and Management—General M,D
Cell Biology M,D
Chemical Engineering M,D
Chemistry M,D
Civil Engineering M,D
Cognitive Sciences D
Communication—General M,D
Comparative Literature M,D
Computational Biology M,D
Computational Sciences M,D
Computer and Information Systems Security M
Computer Art and Design M,D
Computer Engineering M,D*
Computer Science M,D
Construction Management M,D
Corporate and Organizational Communication M
Criminal Justice and Criminology M
Cultural Studies M,D
Developmental Biology M,D
Developmental Psychology D
Economics D
Education—General M,D
Electrical Engineering M,D
Electronic Commerce M
English M,D
Entertainment Management M
Entrepreneurship D
Environmental Engineering M,D
Film, Television, and Video Production M
Finance and Banking D
Gender Studies M,D
Genetics M,D
Health Services Management and Hospital Administration M
History of Science and Technology M,D
History M,D
Human-Computer Interaction M,D
Industrial and Labor Relations M,D
Industrial and Manufacturing Management M,D
Information Science M,D
Inorganic Chemistry M,D
Linguistics D
Management Information Systems M,D
Management of Technology M,D
Marketing D
Materials Engineering M,D
Materials Sciences M,D
Mathematical and Computational Finance M,D
Mathematics M,D
Mechanical Engineering M,D
Mechanics M,D
Media Studies M
Molecular Biology M,D
Molecular Biophysics D
Music Education M
Music M
Neurobiology M,D
Neuroscience D
Operations Research D
Organic Chemistry M,D
Organizational Behavior D
Philosophy M,D
Physics M,D
Polymer Science and Engineering M,D
Psychology—General D
Public Administration M
Public Policy M,D
Publishing M
Rhetoric M,D
Social Psychology D
Social Sciences D
Software Engineering M,D
Statistics M,D
Structural Biology D
Systems Engineering M
Technical Writing M
Technology and Public Policy M,D*
Telecommunications Management M
Theater M
Theoretical Chemistry M,D
Urban Design M,D
Writing M

CAROLINA EVANGELICAL DIVINITY SCHOOL

Pastoral Ministry and Counseling D
Theology P,M

CARROLL UNIVERSITY

Business Administration and Management—General M
Education—General M
Physical Therapy M,D
Physician Assistant Studies M
Software Engineering M

CARSON-NEWMAN COLLEGE

Business Administration and Management—General M
Counselor Education M
Curriculum and Instruction M
Education—General M
Educational Leadership and Administration M
Elementary Education M
English as a Second Language M
Family Nurse Practitioner Studies M
Nursing Education M
Nursing—General M
Secondary Education M
Theology M

CARTHAGE COLLEGE

Art Education M,O
Counselor Education M,O
Education of the Gifted M,O
Education—General M,O
Educational Leadership and Administration M,O
English Education M,O
Reading Education M,O
Science Education M,O
Social Sciences Education M,O

CASE WESTERN RESERVE UNIVERSITY

Accounting M,D
Acute Care/Critical Care Nursing M,D
Aerospace/Aeronautical Engineering M,D
Allopathic Medicine P
Anatomy M
Anesthesiologist Assistant Studies M
Anthropology M,D
Applied Mathematics M,D
Art Education M
Art History M,D
Astronomy M,D
Biochemistry M,D
Bioethics M
Biological and Biomedical Sciences—General M,D
Biomedical Engineering M,D*
Biophysics M,D
Biostatistics M,D
Business Administration and Management—General M,D
Cancer Biology/Oncology D
Cell Biology M,D
Chemical Engineering M,D
Chemistry M,D
Civil Engineering M,D
Clinical Psychology D
Clinical Research M
Cognitive Sciences M
Communication Disorders M,D
Community Health Nursing M,D
Comparative Literature M
Computer Engineering M,D
Computer Science M,D
Dance M
Dentistry P
Economics M
Electrical Engineering M,D
Engineering and Applied Sciences—General M,D
Engineering Management M
English M,D
Epidemiology M,D
Experimental Psychology D
Family Nurse Practitioner Studies M,D
Finance and Banking M,D
French M
Genetic Counseling M
Genetics D
Genomic Sciences D
Geology M,D
Geosciences M,D
Gerontological Nursing M,D
Health Services Research M,D
History M,D
Human Genetics D
Human Resources Management M
Immunology M,D
Industrial and Labor Relations M
Industrial and Manufacturing Management M,D
Information Science M,D
Intellectual Property Law P,M
Law P,M
Legal and Justice Studies P,M
Linguistics M
Logistics M,D
Management Information Systems M,D
Management Strategy and Policy M
Marketing M,D
Materials Engineering M,D
Materials Sciences M,D
Maternal and Child/Neonatal Nursing M,D
Mathematics M,D
Mechanical Engineering M,D
Microbiology D
Molecular Biology D
Molecular Medicine D
Molecular Physiology M,D
Museum Studies M,D
Music Education M,D
Music M,D
Neurobiology D
Neuroscience D
Nonprofit Management M,O
Nurse Anesthesia M
Nurse Midwifery M,D
Nursing and Healthcare Administration D
Nursing Education D
Nursing Informatics M
Nursing—General M,D
Nutrition M,D*
Operations Research M
Oral and Dental Sciences M,O
Organizational Behavior M
Pathology M,D
Pediatric Nursing M,D
Pharmacology D
Physics M,D
Physiology M,D*
Political Science M,D
Polymer Science and Engineering M,D
Psychiatric Nursing D
Psychology—General D
Public Health—General M
Quality Management M,D
Social Work M,D
Sociology M,D
Statistics M,D
Supply Chain Management M
Systems Engineering M,D
Theater M
Virology D
Women's Health Nursing M,D

CASTLETON STATE COLLEGE

Curriculum and Instruction M
Education—General M,O
Educational Leadership and Administration M,O
Forensic Psychology M
Psychology—General M
Reading Education M,O
Special Education M,O

CATAWBA COLLEGE

Education—General M
Elementary Education M

THE CATHOLIC DISTANCE UNIVERSITY

Theology M

CATHOLIC THEOLOGICAL UNION AT CHICAGO

Missions and Missiology P,M,D,O
Pastoral Ministry and Counseling P,M,D,O
Theology P,M,D,O

THE CATHOLIC UNIVERSITY OF AMERICA

Anthropology M
Applied Psychology M,D
Architecture M
Biological and Biomedical Sciences—General M,D
Biomedical Engineering M,D
Business Administration and Management—General M
Cell Biology M,D
Civil Engineering M,D
Classics M,D,O
Clinical Laboratory Sciences/Medical Technology M,D
Clinical Psychology M,D
Computer Science M,D
Cultural Studies M
Economics M
Education—General M,D,O
Educational Leadership and Administration M,D,O
Educational Policy M,D,O
Educational Psychology M,D,O
Electrical Engineering M,D
Engineering and Applied Sciences—General M,D,O
Engineering Management M,O
English M,D,O
Environmental Engineering M,D
Ergonomics and Human Factors M,D
Experimental Psychology M,D
History M,D
Human Resources Management M
Information Studies M
International Affairs M,D
Law P
Legal and Justice Studies D,O
Library Science M
Materials Engineering M
Materials Sciences M
Mechanical Engineering M,D
Medieval and Renaissance Studies M,D,O
Microbiology M,D
Music M,D,O
Near and Middle Eastern Languages M,D
Near and Middle Eastern Studies M,D
Nursing—General M,D,O
Pastoral Ministry and Counseling P,M,D,O
Philosophy M,D,O
Physics M,D
Political Science M,D
Psychology—General M,D
Religion P,M,D,O
Rhetoric M,D,O
Secondary Education M,D,O
Social Work M,D
Sociology M
Spanish M,D
Special Education M,D,O
Sustainable Development M
Theater M
Theology P,M,D,O
Urban and Regional Planning M
Western European Studies M,D

CEDAR CREST COLLEGE

Education—General M
Forensic Sciences M

CEDARS-SINAI MEDICAL CENTER

Biological and Biomedical Sciences—General D
Translational Biology D

CEDARVILLE UNIVERSITY

Education—General M

CENTENARY COLLEGE

Accounting M
Business Administration and Management—General M
Counseling Psychology M
Education—General M
Educational Leadership and Administration M
Special Education M

CENTENARY COLLEGE OF LOUISIANA

Business Administration and Management—General M
Curriculum and Instruction M
Education—General M
Educational Leadership and Administration M
Elementary Education M
Secondary Education M

CENTRAL BAPTIST THEOLOGICAL SEMINARY

Missions and Missiology P,M,O
Theology P,M,O

CENTRAL BAPTIST THEOLOGICAL SEMINARY OF VIRGINIA BEACH

Theology P,M

CENTRAL CONNECTICUT STATE UNIVERSITY

Actuarial Science M,O
Advertising and Public Relations M,O
Art Education M,O
Biochemistry M,O
Biological and Biomedical Sciences—General M,O
Chemistry M,O
Communication—General M,O
Computer Science M,O
Construction Management M,O
Corporate and Organizational Communication M,O
Counselor Education M,O
Criminal Justice and Criminology M
Early Childhood Education M
Education—General M,D,O
Educational Leadership and Administration M,D,O
Educational Media/Instructional Technology M
Elementary Education M,O

*M—master's degree; P—first professional degree; D—doctorate; O—other advanced degree; *—Close-Up and/or Display in one of the other books in this series*

Engineering and Applied Sciences—General M,O
English as a Second Language M,O
English M,O
Exercise and Sports Science M,O
Foreign Languages Education M,O
Foundations and Philosophy of Education M
French M,O
Geography M
Geosciences M,O
German M,O
Health Psychology M
Hispanic and Latin American Languages M,O
History M,O
Industrial and Manufacturing Management M,O
Information Studies M
International Affairs M
Italian M,O
Logistics M,O
Management of Technology M,O
Marriage and Family Therapy M,O
Mathematics M,O
Molecular Biology M
Music Education M,O
Nurse Anesthesia M,O
Physical Education M,O
Physics M,O
Psychology—General M
Reading Education M,O
Rehabilitation Counseling M,O
School Psychology M,O
Science Education M,O
Secondary Education M
Social Psychology M
Spanish M,O
Special Education M,O
Statistics M,O
Supply Chain Management M,O
Vocational and Technical Education M,O

CENTRAL EUROPEAN UNIVERSITY

Anthropology M,D
Applied Mathematics M,D
Business Administration and Management—General M
Economics M,D
Environmental Management and Policy M,D
Finance and Banking M
Gender Studies M,D
History M,D
Humanities M,D
International Affairs M,D
International Business M,D
Law M,D
Legal and Justice Studies M,D
Management Information Systems M
Marketing M
Medieval and Renaissance Studies M,D
Philosophy M,D
Political Science M,D
Public Policy M,D
Real Estate M
Social Sciences M,D
Sociology M,D

CENTRAL METHODIST UNIVERSITY

Counselor Education M
Education—General M
Nursing and Healthcare Administration M
Nursing—General M

CENTRAL MICHIGAN UNIVERSITY

Accounting M
Adult Education M
American Indian/Native American Studies M
American Studies M,D,O
Applied Psychology M,D
Automotive Engineering M,O
Biological and Biomedical Sciences—General M
Business Administration and Management—General M,O
Chemistry M
Child and Family Studies M,O
Clinical Psychology D
Clothing and Textiles M,O
Communication Disorders M,D
Communication—General M
Community College Education M
Computer Science M
Conservation Biology M
Corporate and Organizational Communication M,O
Counseling Psychology M,D,O
Counselor Education M
Cultural Studies M
Curriculum and Instruction M,D,O
Early Childhood Education M,O
Economics M
Education—General M,D,O
Educational Leadership and Administration M,D,O
Educational Media/Instructional Technology M,D,O
Elementary Education M,O
Engineering and Applied Sciences—General M
English as a Second Language M
English M
Exercise and Sports Science M,D
Experimental Psychology M,D
Family and Consumer Sciences-General M,O
Film, Television, and Video Production M
Film, Television, and Video Theory and Criticism M
Finance and Banking M
Gender Studies M
Gerontology M,O
Health Psychology M,D
Health Services Management and Hospital Administration M,D,O
Higher Education M,D,O
History M,D,O
Human Development M,O
Human Resources Management M,O
Humanities M
Industrial and Manufacturing Management M
Industrial and Organizational Psychology M,D
International Affairs M,O
International Business M,O
International Health M,D,O
Leisure Studies M
Logistics M,O
Management Information Systems M,O
Marketing M
Mass Communication M
Materials Sciences D
Mathematics Education M,D
Mathematics M,D
Media Studies M
Middle School Education M
Music Education M
Music M
Neuroscience M,D
Nutrition M,D,O
Physical Education M
Physical Therapy M,D
Physician Assistant Studies M,D
Physics M,D
Political Science M,O
Psychology—General M,D,O
Public Administration M,O
Reading Education M,O
Recreation and Park Management M,O
Rehabilitation Sciences M,D
School Psychology D,O
Science Education M
Secondary Education M,O
Spanish M
Special Education M,O
Speech and Interpersonal Communication M
Sports Management M,O
Student Affairs M,D,O
Western European Studies M,D,O
Writing M

CENTRAL STATE UNIVERSITY

Education—General M

CENTRAL WASHINGTON UNIVERSITY

Accounting M
Art/Fine Arts M
Biological and Biomedical Sciences—General M
Chemistry M
Child and Family Studies M
Counseling Psychology M
Counselor Education M
Education—General M
Engineering and Applied Sciences—General M
English as a Second Language M
English M
Exercise and Sports Science M
Experimental Psychology M
Family and Consumer Sciences-General M
Geology M
History M
Home Economics Education M
Industrial/Management Engineering M
Interdisciplinary Studies M
Mathematics M
Music M
Natural Resources M
Nutrition M
Psychology—General M
Reading Education M
School Psychology M
Special Education M
Theater M

CENTRAL YESHIVA TOMCHEI TMIMIM-LUBAVITCH

Jewish Studies M
Theology M

CENTRO DE ESTUDIOS AVANZADOS DE PUERTO RICO Y EL CARIBE

History M,D
Latin American Studies M,D

CHADRON STATE COLLEGE

Business Administration and Management—General M
Business Education M,O
Counselor Education M,O
Education—General M,O
Educational Leadership and Administration M,O
Elementary Education M,O
English Education M,O
Secondary Education M,O
Social Sciences Education M,O

CHAMINADE UNIVERSITY OF HONOLULU

Business Administration and Management—General M
Conflict Resolution and Mediation/Peace Studies M
Counseling Psychology M
Criminal Justice and Criminology M,O
Education—General M
Forensic Sciences M
Homeland Security M,O
Pastoral Ministry and Counseling M
Social Sciences Education M
Theology M

CHAMPLAIN COLLEGE

Business Administration and Management—General M
Conflict Resolution and Mediation/Peace Studies M
Education—General M
Forensic Sciences M
Health Services Management and Hospital Administration M
Law M
Management of Technology M

CHANCELLOR UNIVERSITY

Business Administration and Management—General M

CHAPMAN UNIVERSITY

Business Administration and Management—General M
Communication Disorders M
Counselor Education M,O
Cultural Studies D
Curriculum and Instruction M,D
Disability Studies D
Economics P,M
Education—General M,D,O
Educational Leadership and Administration M,O
Educational Psychology M,O
Elementary Education M,O
English M
Environmental Law P,M
Film, Television, and Video Production M
Food Science and Technology M
Health Communication M
International Affairs M
Law P,M
Marriage and Family Therapy M
Nutrition M
Physical Therapy D
Reading Education M,O
School Psychology M,D,O
Secondary Education M,O
Special Education M,O
Taxation P,M
Writing M

CHARLES DREW UNIVERSITY OF MEDICINE AND SCIENCE

Allopathic Medicine P
Public Health—General M

CHARLESTON SOUTHERN UNIVERSITY

Accounting M
Business Administration and Management—General M
Criminal Justice and Criminology M
Education—General M
Educational Leadership and Administration M
Elementary Education M
Finance and Banking M
Health Services Management and Hospital Administration M
Management Information Systems M
Organizational Management M
Secondary Education M

CHARLOTTE SCHOOL OF LAW

Law P

CHATHAM UNIVERSITY

Accounting M
Art Education M
Biological and Biomedical Sciences—General M
Business Administration and Management—General M
Computer Art and Design M
Counseling Psychology M,D
Developmental Psychology M,D
Early Childhood Education M
Education—General M
Elementary Education M
English Education M
Environmental Biology M
Environmental Education M
Film, Television, and Video Production M
Health Psychology M,D
Industrial and Organizational Psychology M,D
Interior Design M
Landscape Architecture M
Marriage and Family Therapy M,D
Mathematics Education M
Nursing and Healthcare Administration M,D
Nursing Education M,D
Nursing—General M,D
Occupational Therapy M,D
Physical Therapy D
Physician Assistant Studies M
Science Education M
Secondary Education M
Social Sciences Education M
Special Education M
Sport Psychology M,D
Writing M

CHESTNUT HILL COLLEGE

Clinical Psychology M,D,O
Counseling Psychology M,O
Early Childhood Education M
Education—General M*
Educational Leadership and Administration M
Educational Media/Instructional Technology M,O
Elementary Education M
Human Services M
Psychology—General M,D,O
Religion M,O
Secondary Education M

CHEYNEY UNIVERSITY OF PENNSYLVANIA

Adult Education M
Early Childhood Education O
Education—General M,O
Educational Leadership and Administration M,O
Elementary Education M
Public Administration M
Special Education M

THE CHICAGO SCHOOL OF PROFESSIONAL PSYCHOLOGY

Applied Behavior Analysis M,D
Applied Psychology M,D
Clinical Psychology M,D
Counselor Education M,D
Forensic Psychology M,D
Industrial and Organizational Psychology M,D
Psychology—General D
School Psychology O

THE CHICAGO SCHOOL OF PROFESSIONAL PSYCHOLOGY AT DOWNTOWN LOS ANGELES

Applied Behavior Analysis M,D
Clinical Psychology M,D
Forensic Psychology D
Industrial and Organizational Psychology M
Marriage and Family Therapy M,D

THE CHICAGO SCHOOL OF PROFESSIONAL PSYCHOLOGY AT GRAYSLAKE

Clinical Psychology M
Counseling Psychology M
School Psychology O

THE CHICAGO SCHOOL OF PROFESSIONAL PSYCHOLOGY AT IRVINE

Clinical Psychology D
Forensic Psychology D
Marriage and Family Therapy M,D
Psychology—General D

THE CHICAGO SCHOOL OF PROFESSIONAL PSYCHOLOGY AT WESTWOOD

Clinical Psychology M
Marriage and Family Therapy M,D
Psychology—General D

THE CHICAGO SCHOOL OF PROFESSIONAL PSYCHOLOGY: ONLINE

Applied Psychology M,O
Forensic Psychology M,O
Industrial and Organizational Psychology M,D,O
Psychology—General M,D

CHICAGO STATE UNIVERSITY

Biological and Biomedical Sciences—General M
Computer Science M
Counselor Education M
Criminal Justice and Criminology M
Early Childhood Education M
Economic Development M
Education—General M,D
Educational Leadership and Administration M,D
Educational Media/Instructional Technology M
Elementary Education M
English M
Foundations and Philosophy of Education M
Geography M
Higher Education M,D
History M
Library Science M
Mathematics M
Middle School Education M
Multilingual and Multicultural Education M
Physical Education M
Reading Education M
Secondary Education M
Social Work M
Special Education M
Vocational and Technical Education M
Writing M

CHICAGO THEOLOGICAL SEMINARY

Ethics P,M,D
Pastoral Ministry and Counseling P,M,D
Religion P,M,D
Theology P,M,D

CHRISTENDOM COLLEGE

Theology M

CHRISTIAN BROTHERS UNIVERSITY

Business Administration and Management—General M,O
Education—General M
Educational Leadership and Administration M
Engineering and Applied Sciences—General M
Finance and Banking M,O
Project Management M,O
Religion M

CHRISTIAN THEOLOGICAL SEMINARY

Marriage and Family Therapy P,M,D
Pastoral Ministry and Counseling P,M,D
Religion P,M,D
Theology P,M,D

CHRISTIE'S EDUCATION

Art History M
Museum Studies M

CHRISTOPHER NEWPORT UNIVERSITY

Applied Physics M
Art Education M
Chemistry M
Computer Education M
Computer Science M
Education—General M
Elementary Education M
English as a Second Language M
English Education M
Environmental Sciences M
Foreign Languages Education M
Mathematics Education M
Music Education M
Physics M
Science Education M
Secondary Education M
Social Sciences Education M

CHRIST THE KING SEMINARY

Pastoral Ministry and Counseling P,M
Theology P,M

CHURCH DIVINITY SCHOOL OF THE PACIFIC

Theology P,M,D,O

CINCINNATI CHRISTIAN UNIVERSITY

Pastoral Ministry and Counseling M
Religion P,M
Theology P,M

THE CITADEL, THE MILITARY COLLEGE OF SOUTH CAROLINA

Biological and Biomedical Sciences—General M
Business Administration and Management—General M
Computer Science M
Counselor Education M,O
Education—General M,O
Educational Leadership and Administration M,O
Elementary Education M
English Education M
English M
Health Education M
History M
Information Science M
Mathematics Education M
Physical Education M
Psychology—General M,O
Reading Education M
School Psychology O
Science Education M
Secondary Education M
Social Sciences Education M
Social Sciences M
Student Affairs M

CITY COLLEGE OF THE CITY UNIVERSITY OF NEW YORK

Architecture M
Art History M
Art/Fine Arts M
Atmospheric Sciences M,D
Biochemistry M,D
Biological and Biomedical Sciences—General M,D
Biomedical Engineering M,D
Chemical Engineering M,D
Chemistry M,D
Civil Engineering M,D
Clinical Psychology M,D
Computer Science M,D
Counseling Psychology M
Early Childhood Education M
Economics M
Education—General M,O
Educational Leadership and Administration M,O
Electrical Engineering M,D
Engineering and Applied Sciences—General M,D
English Education M,O
English M
Environmental Sciences M,D
Experimental Psychology M,D
Geosciences M,D
Graphic Design M
History M
International Affairs M
Landscape Architecture M
Mathematics Education M,O
Mathematics M
Mechanical Engineering M,D
Media Studies M
Middle School Education M,O
Multilingual and Multicultural Education M
Museum Studies M

*M—master's degree; P—first professional degree; D—doctorate; O—other advanced degree; *—Close-Up and/or Display in one of the other books in this series*

Music	M
Physics	M,D
Psychology—General	M,D
Public Administration	M,D
Reading Education	M
Science Education	M
Secondary Education	M,O
Social Sciences Education	M,O
Sociology	M
Spanish	M
Special Education	M,O
Sustainable Development	M
Urban Design	M
Writing	M

CITY OF HOPE NATIONAL MEDICAL CENTER/BECKMAN RESEARCH INSTITUTE

Biological and Biomedical Sciences—General	D*

CITY UNIVERSITY OF NEW YORK SCHOOL OF LAW AT QUEENS COLLEGE

Law	P

CITY UNIVERSITY OF SEATTLE

Accounting	M,O
Business Administration and Management—General	M,O
Computer and Information Systems Security	M,O
Computer Science	M,O
Counseling Psychology	M
Curriculum and Instruction	M,O
Education—General	M,O
Educational Leadership and Administration	M,O
Elementary Education	M,O
Finance and Banking	M,O
Human Resources Management	M,O
International Business	M,O
Management Information Systems	M,O
Management of Technology	M,O
Marketing	M,O
Organizational Management	M,O
Project Management	M,O
Reading Education	M,O
School Psychology	M,O
Special Education	M,O
Sustainability Management	M,O

CLAFLIN UNIVERSITY

Biotechnology	M
Business Administration and Management—General	M

CLAREMONT GRADUATE UNIVERSITY

African Studies	M,D,O
American Studies	M,D,O
Applied Mathematics	M,D
Archives/Archival Administration	M,D,O
Art/Fine Arts	M
Arts Administration	M
Botany	M,D
Business Administration and Management—General	M,D,O
Cognitive Sciences	M,D,O
Comparative Literature	M,D
Computational Biology	M,D
Computational Sciences	M,D
Computer Art and Design	M
Cultural Studies	M,D,O
Developmental Psychology	M,D,O
Economic Development	M,D,O
Economics	M,D,O
Education—General	M,D,O
Educational Leadership and Administration	M,D,O
Educational Measurement and Evaluation	M,D,O
Electronic Commerce	M,D,O
English	M,D
Ethics	M,D
Film, Television, and Video Theory and Criticism	M,D
Financial Engineering	M
Health Informatics	M,D,O
Health Promotion	M,D
Health Psychology	M,D,O
Higher Education	M,D,O
History	M,D,O
Human Development	M,D,O
Human Resources Development	M,D,O
Human Resources Management	M
Humanities	M,D,O
Industrial and Organizational Psychology	M,D,O
Information Science	M,D,O
International Affairs	M,D
International Economics	M,D,O
Management Information Systems	M,D,O
Management Strategy and Policy	M,D,O
Mathematics	M,D
Media Studies	M,D,O
Museum Studies	M,D,O
Music	M,D
Operations Research	M,D
Philosophy	M,D
Photography	M
Political Science	M,D
Psychology—General	M,D,O
Public Health—General	M,D
Public Policy	M,D,O
Religion	M,D
Social Psychology	M,D,O
Special Education	M,D,O
Statistics	M,D
Student Affairs	M,D,O
Systems Science	M,D,O
Telecommunications	M,D,O
Theology	M,D
Urban Education	M,D,O
Western European Studies	M,D,O
Women's Studies	M,D
Writing	M,D

CLAREMONT MCKENNA COLLEGE

Finance and Banking	M

CLAREMONT SCHOOL OF THEOLOGY

Ethics	M,D
Pastoral Ministry and Counseling	M,D
Religion	M,D
Religious Education	M,D
Theology	P,M,D

CLARION UNIVERSITY OF PENNSYLVANIA

Biological and Biomedical Sciences—General	M
Business Administration and Management—General	M
Communication Disorders	M
Communication—General	M
Curriculum and Instruction	M
Early Childhood Education	M
Education—General	M,O
Elementary Education	M
English Education	M
English	M
Library Science	M,O
Nursing—General	M
Reading Education	M
Rehabilitation Sciences	M
Science Education	M
Social Sciences Education	M
Special Education	M
Vocational and Technical Education	M

CLARK ATLANTA UNIVERSITY

Accounting	M
African-American Studies	M,D
Biological and Biomedical Sciences—General	M,D
Business Administration and Management—General	M
Chemistry	M,D
Computer Science	M
Counselor Education	M
Criminal Justice and Criminology	M
Curriculum and Instruction	M
Economics	M
Education—General	M,D,O
Educational Leadership and Administration	M,D,O
Educational Psychology	M
English	M,D
History	M,D
Information Science	M
Mathematics Education	M
Mathematics	M
Physics	M
Political Science	M,D
Public Administration	M
Romance Languages	M,D
Science Education	M
Social Work	M,D
Sociology	M
Special Education	M
Women's Studies	M,D

CLARKE UNIVERSITY

Business Administration and Management—General	M
Early Childhood Education	M
Education—General	M
Educational Leadership and Administration	M
Educational Media/Instructional Technology	M
Family Nurse Practitioner Studies	M,O
Nursing and Healthcare Administration	M,O
Nursing Education	M,O
Nursing—General	M,O
Physical Therapy	D
Reading Education	M
Special Education	M

CLARKSON COLLEGE

Adult Nursing	M,O
Family Nurse Practitioner Studies	M,O
Nursing and Healthcare Administration	M,O
Nursing Education	M,O
Nursing—General	M,O

CLARKSON UNIVERSITY

Business Administration and Management—General	M
Chemical Engineering	M,D
Chemistry	M,D
Civil Engineering	M
Computer Engineering	M,D
Computer Science	M
Electrical Engineering	M,D
Engineering and Applied Sciences—General	M,D
Engineering Management	M
Environmental Engineering	M,D
Environmental Sciences	M,D
Health Services Research	M
Information Science	M
Mathematics	M,D
Mechanical Engineering	M,D
Physical Therapy	D
Physics	M,D
Sustainable Development	M,D

CLARK UNIVERSITY

Accounting	M
American Studies	M,D
Biological and Biomedical Sciences—General	M,D
Business Administration and Management—General	M
Chemistry	M,D
Clinical Psychology	D
Communication—General	M
Developmental Psychology	D
Economics	D
Education—General	M
English	M
Environmental Management and Policy	M
Finance and Banking	M
Geographic Information Systems	M
Geography	M,D
Health Services Management and Hospital Administration	M
History	M,D,O
Holocaust and Genocide Studies	D
Information Science	M
International Business	M
International Development	M
Liberal Studies	M
Management Information Systems	M
Marketing	M
Physics	M,D
Public Administration	M,O
Social Psychology	D
Sustainable Development	M
Urban and Regional Planning	M

CLAYTON STATE UNIVERSITY

Business Administration and Management—General	M
Education—General	M
English Education	M
Health Services Management and Hospital Administration	M
Liberal Studies	M
Mathematics Education	M
Nursing—General	M

CLEARWATER CHRISTIAN COLLEGE

Educational Leadership and Administration	M

CLEARY UNIVERSITY

Accounting	M,O
Business Administration and Management—General	M,O
Finance and Banking	M,O
Nonprofit Management	M,O
Organizational Management	M,O
Sustainability Management	M,O

CLEMSON UNIVERSITY

Accounting	M
Agricultural Education	M

Program	Degrees
Agricultural Sciences—General	M,D
Animal Sciences	M,D
Applied Economics	M,D
Applied Mathematics	M,D
Applied Psychology	M
Aquaculture	M,D
Architecture	M
Art/Fine Arts	M
Astronomy	M,D
Astrophysics	M,D
Atmospheric Sciences	M,D
Automotive Engineering	M,D
Biochemistry	D
Bioengineering	M,D
Biological and Biomedical Sciences—General	M,D
Biophysics	M,D
Biosystems Engineering	M,D
Business Administration and Management—General	M
Chemical Engineering	M,D
Chemistry	M,D
Civil Engineering	M,D
Communication—General	M,D
Community Health	M
Computational Sciences	M,D
Computer Art and Design	M
Computer Engineering	M,D
Computer Science	M,D
Construction Management	M
Counseling Psychology	M
Counselor Education	M
Curriculum and Instruction	D
Early Childhood Education	M
Ecology	M,D
Economics	M,D
Education—General	M,D,O
Educational Leadership and Administration	M,D,O
Electrical Engineering	M,D
Elementary Education	M
Engineering and Applied Sciences—General	M,D
English	M
Entomology	M,D
Environmental Design	D
Environmental Engineering	M,D
Environmental Management and Policy	M,D
Environmental Sciences	M,D
Ergonomics and Human Factors	D
Evolutionary Biology	M,D
Fish, Game, and Wildlife Management	M,D
Food Science and Technology	M,D
Forestry	M,D
Genetics	M,D
Higher Education	D
Historic Preservation	M
History	M
Human Development	M
Human Resources Development	M
Human Resources Management	M
Humanities	D
Hydrogeology	M
Industrial and Organizational Psychology	D
Industrial/Management Engineering	M,D
Landscape Architecture	M
Manufacturing Engineering	M
Marketing	M
Materials Engineering	M,D
Materials Sciences	M,D
Mathematics Education	M
Mathematics	M,D
Mechanical Engineering	M,D
Microbiology	M,D
Middle School Education	M
Molecular Biology	D
Nursing—General	M,D
Nutrition	M
Operations Research	M,D
Physics	M,D
Plant Biology	M,D
Plant Sciences	M,D
Psychology—General	D
Public Administration	M
Public Affairs	D
Public Policy	D,O
Reading Education	M
Real Estate	M
Recreation and Park Management	M,D
Rhetoric	D
Science Education	M
Secondary Education	M
Social Sciences Education	M
Social Sciences	D
Sociology	M
Special Education	M
Statistics	M,D
Student Affairs	M
Travel and Tourism	M,D
Urban and Regional Planning	M
Veterinary Sciences	M,D
Writing	M

CLEVELAND CHIROPRACTIC COLLEGE–KANSAS CITY CAMPUS

Program	Degrees
Chiropractic	P
Health Promotion	M

CLEVELAND CHIROPRACTIC COLLEGE–LOS ANGELES CAMPUS

Program	Degrees
Chiropractic	P
Health Promotion	M

CLEVELAND INSTITUTE OF MUSIC

Program	Degrees
Music	M,D,O

CLEVELAND STATE UNIVERSITY

Program	Degrees
Accounting	M
Addictions/Substance Abuse Counseling	M,O
Adult Education	M,O
Allied Health—General	M
Analytical Chemistry	M,D
Art Education	M
Art History	M
Art/Fine Arts	M
Bioethics	M,O
Biological and Biomedical Sciences—General	M,D
Biomedical Engineering	D
Business Administration and Management—General	M,D
Chemical Engineering	M,D
Chemistry	M,D
Civil Engineering	M,D
Clinical Psychology	M,D,O
Communication Disorders	M
Communication—General	M,O
Community Health Nursing	M
Computer Science	M,D
Condensed Matter Physics	M
Counseling Psychology	M,D,O
Counselor Education	M,D,O
Early Childhood Education	M
Economic Development	M,D,O
Economics	M,D,O
Education of Students with Severe/Multiple Disabilities	M
Education—General	M,D,O
Educational Leadership and Administration	M,D,O
Electrical Engineering	M,D
Engineering and Applied Sciences—General	M,D
English as a Second Language	M
English	M
Environmental Engineering	M,D
Environmental Management and Policy	M,O
Environmental Sciences	M,D
Exercise and Sports Science	M
Experimental Psychology	M,D,O
Finance and Banking	M,D,O
Foreign Languages Education	M
Forensic Nursing	M
French	M
Geographic Information Systems	M,D,O
Gerontology	M,D,O
Health Communication	M,O
Health Education	M
Health Services Management and Hospital Administration	M
History	M
Human Resources Management	M
Industrial and Labor Relations	P,M,O
Industrial and Manufacturing Management	D
Industrial and Organizational Psychology	M,D,O
Industrial/Management Engineering	M,D
Information Science	M,D
Inorganic Chemistry	M,D
International Business	M,D,O
Latin American Studies	M
Law	P,M,O
Linguistics	M
Management Information Systems	M,D
Marketing	M,D,O
Mathematics Education	M
Mathematics	M
Mechanical Engineering	M,D
Medical Imaging	M
Medical Physics	M
Medicinal and Pharmaceutical Chemistry	M,D
Middle School Education	M
Molecular Medicine	M,D
Museum Studies	M,D
Music Education	M
Music	M
Nonprofit Management	M,D,O
Nursing Education	M
Nursing—General	M
Occupational Therapy	M
Optical Sciences	M
Organic Chemistry	M,D
Philosophy	M,O
Physical Chemistry	M,D
Physical Education	M
Physical Therapy	D
Physician Assistant Studies	M,D
Physics	M
Psychology—General	M,D,O
Public Administration	M,O
Public Health—General	M
Real Estate	M,D,O
School Psychology	M,D,O
Science Education	M
Social Work	M
Sociology	M
Software Engineering	M,D
Spanish	M
Special Education	M
Sport Psychology	M
Sports Management	M
Student Affairs	M,O
Taxation	M
Urban and Regional Planning	M,O
Urban Design	M,O
Urban Education	D
Urban Studies	M,D,O
Writing	M

COASTAL CAROLINA UNIVERSITY

Program	Degrees
Accounting	M
Business Administration and Management—General	M
Education—General	M
Educational Leadership and Administration	M
Marine Sciences	M
Secondary Education	M
Writing	M

COE COLLEGE

Program	Degrees
Education—General	M

COLD SPRING HARBOR LABORATORY, WATSON SCHOOL OF BIOLOGICAL SCIENCES

Program	Degrees
Biological and Biomedical Sciences—General	D*

COLEMAN UNIVERSITY

Program	Degrees
Information Science	M
Management of Technology	M

COLGATE ROCHESTER CROZER DIVINITY SCHOOL

Program	Degrees
Theology	P,M,D,O

COLGATE UNIVERSITY

Program	Degrees
Secondary Education	M

THE COLLEGE AT BROCKPORT, STATE UNIVERSITY OF NEW YORK

Program	Degrees
Accounting	M
American Studies	M
Art/Fine Arts	M
Arts Administration	M,O
Biological and Biomedical Sciences—General	M
Communication—General	M
Community Health	M
Computational Sciences	M
Counseling Psychology	M,O
Counselor Education	M,O
Curriculum and Instruction	M
Dance	M
Education—General	M,O
Educational Leadership and Administration	O
English Education	M
English	M
Environmental Sciences	M
Foreign Languages Education	M,O
Health Education	M
Health Services Management and Hospital Administration	M,O
History	M
Leisure Studies	M
Liberal Studies	M
Mathematics Education	M
Mathematics	M
Middle School Education	M
Multilingual and Multicultural Education	M,O
Nonprofit Management	M,O
Physical Education	M
Psychology—General	M
Public Administration	M,O
Reading Education	M
Recreation and Park Management	M
Science Education	M
Social Sciences Education	M

*M—master's degree; P—first professional degree; D—doctorate; O—other advanced degree; *—Close-Up and/or Display in one of the other books in this series*

Social Work M
Sports Management M
Writing M

COLLÈGE DOMINICAIN DE PHILOSOPHIE ET DE THÉOLOGIE

Philosophy M,D
Theology M,D,O

COLLEGE FOR FINANCIAL PLANNING

Finance and Banking M

COLLEGE OF CHARLESTON

Accounting M
Arts Administration M,O
Business Administration and Management—General M
Communication—General M
Computer Science M
Early Childhood Education M
Education—General M,O
Elementary Education M
English as a Second Language O
English M
Environmental Sciences M
Foreign Languages Education M
Historic Preservation M
History M
Management Information Systems M
Marine Biology M
Marine Sciences M
Mathematics Education M
Mathematics M,O
Music Education M
Public Administration M
Science Education M
Special Education M
Urban and Regional Planning O

COLLEGE OF EMMANUEL AND ST. CHAD

Theology P,M

THE COLLEGE OF IDAHO

Education—General M

COLLEGE OF MOUNT ST. JOSEPH

Art Education M
Early Childhood Education M
Education—General M
Educational Leadership and Administration M
Middle School Education M
Multilingual and Multicultural Education M
Music Education M
Nursing—General M
Organizational Management M
Pastoral Ministry and Counseling M,O
Physical Therapy D
Reading Education M
Religious Education M,O
Secondary Education M
Theology M,O

COLLEGE OF MOUNT SAINT VINCENT

Adult Nursing M,O
Education—General M,O
Educational Media/Instructional Technology M,O
Family Nurse Practitioner Studies M,O
Gerontological Nursing M,O
Middle School Education M,O
Multilingual and Multicultural Education M,O
Nursing and Healthcare Administration M,O
Nursing Education M,O
Nursing—General M,O
Urban Education M,O

THE COLLEGE OF NEW JERSEY

Addictions/Substance Abuse Counseling M,O
Counselor Education M
Early Childhood Education M
Education—General M,O
Educational Leadership and Administration M,O
Elementary Education M
English as a Second Language M,O
English M
Health Education M
International and Comparative Education M,O
Marriage and Family Therapy O
Nursing—General M,O
Physical Education M
Reading Education M,O
Secondary Education M
Special Education M,O

THE COLLEGE OF NEW ROCHELLE

Acute Care/Critical Care Nursing M,O
Art Education M
Art Therapy M
Art/Fine Arts M
Communication—General M,O
Counseling Psychology M,O
Early Childhood Education M
Education of the Gifted M,O
Education—General M,O
Educational Leadership and Administration M,O
Elementary Education M
English as a Second Language M,O
Family Nurse Practitioner Studies M,O
Gerontology M,O
Graphic Design M
Human Resources Development M
Multilingual and Multicultural Education M,O
Nursing and Healthcare Administration M,O
Nursing Education M,O
Nursing—General M,O
Reading Education M
School Psychology M
Social Psychology M
Special Education M

COLLEGE OF NOTRE DAME OF MARYLAND

Business Administration and Management—General M
Communication—General M
Education—General M
Educational Leadership and Administration M,D
English as a Second Language M
Liberal Studies M
Nonprofit Management M

COLLEGE OF SAINT ELIZABETH

Business Administration and Management—General M
Counseling Psychology M,O
Criminal Justice and Criminology M
Education—General M,D,O
Educational Leadership and Administration M,D,O
Educational Media/Instructional Technology M,D,O
Forensic Psychology M,O
Health Services Management and Hospital Administration M
Higher Education M,O
Nursing—General M
Nutrition M,O
Psychology—General M,O
Public Administration M
Student Affairs M,O
Theology M

COLLEGE OF ST. JOSEPH

Addictions/Substance Abuse Counseling M
Business Administration and Management—General M
Clinical Psychology M
Counseling Psychology M
Counselor Education M
Education—General M
Elementary Education M
English Education M
Psychology—General M
Reading Education M
School Psychology M
Secondary Education M
Social Psychology M
Social Sciences Education M
Special Education M

COLLEGE OF SAINT MARY

Education—General M
Educational Leadership and Administration M
Educational Measurement and Evaluation M
English as a Second Language M
Health Education D
Nursing—General M
Occupational Therapy M
Organizational Management M

THE COLLEGE OF SAINT ROSE

Accounting M
Art Education M,O
Business Administration and Management—General M
Business Education M,O
Communication Disorders M
Computer Science M
Counselor Education M
Curriculum and Instruction M,O
Early Childhood Education M,O
Education—General M,O
Educational Leadership and Administration M,O
Educational Media/Instructional Technology M,O
Educational Psychology M,O
Elementary Education M,O
English M
History M
Information Science M
Mass Communication M
Multilingual and Multicultural Education M,O
Music Education M,O
Music M
Nonprofit Management O
Political Science M
Reading Education M,O
School Psychology M,O
Secondary Education M,O
Special Education M,O
Student Affairs M,O

THE COLLEGE OF ST. SCHOLASTICA

Business Administration and Management—General M,O
Education—General M,O
Educational Media/Instructional Technology M
Exercise and Sports Science M
Health Informatics M,O
Management Information Systems M,O
Nursing—General M,O
Occupational Therapy M
Physical Therapy D

COLLEGE OF STATEN ISLAND OF THE CITY UNIVERSITY OF NEW YORK

Adult Nursing M,O
Biological and Biomedical Sciences—General M
Business Administration and Management—General M
Computer Science M
Counseling Psychology M
Education—General M,O
Educational Leadership and Administration O
Elementary Education M
English M
Environmental Sciences M
Film, Television, and Video Theory and Criticism M
Gerontological Nursing M,O
History M
Liberal Studies M
Media Studies M
Neuroscience M
Nursing Education O
Nursing—General M,O
Secondary Education M
Special Education M

COLLEGE OF THE ATLANTIC

Environmental Management and Policy M

COLLEGE OF THE HUMANITIES AND SCIENCES, HARRISON MIDDLETON UNIVERSITY

Comparative Literature M,D
Education—General M,D
Humanities M,D
Interdisciplinary Studies M,D
Legal and Justice Studies M,D
Philosophy M,D
Religion M,D
Science Education M,D
Social Sciences M,D

THE COLLEGE OF WILLIAM AND MARY

Accounting M
Addictions/Substance Abuse Counseling M,D
American Studies M,D
Anthropology M,D
Applied Science and Technology M,D
Biological and Biomedical Sciences—General M
Business Administration and Management—General M
Chemistry M
Computational Sciences M
Computer Science M,D
Counselor Education M,D
Curriculum and Instruction M,D
Education of the Gifted M
Education—General M,D,O

Educational Leadership and Administration M,D
Educational Media/ Instructional Technology M,D
Educational Policy M,D
Elementary Education M
English Education M
Experimental Psychology M
Foreign Languages Education M
History M,D
Law P,M
Marine Sciences M,D
Marriage and Family Therapy M,D
Mathematics Education M
Operations Research M
Physics M,D
Public Policy M
Reading Education M
School Psychology M,O
Science Education M
Secondary Education M
Social Sciences Education M
Special Education M

COLLÈGE UNIVERSITAIRE DE SAINT-BONIFACE

Canadian Studies M
Education—General M

COLORADO CHRISTIAN UNIVERSITY

Business Administration and Management—General M
Business Education M
Computer and Information Systems Security M
Counseling Psychology M
Curriculum and Instruction M
Distance Education Development M
Early Childhood Education M
Education—General M
Educational Media/ Instructional Technology M
Elementary Education M
Project Management M
Special Education M

THE COLORADO COLLEGE

American Studies M
Art Education M
Education—General M
Elementary Education M
English Education M
Foreign Languages Education M
Humanities M
Liberal Studies M
Mathematics Education M
Music Education M
Science Education M
Secondary Education M
Social Sciences Education M

COLORADO SCHOOL OF MINES

Applied Physics M,D
Chemical Engineering M,D
Chemistry M,D
Computer Science M,D
Electronic Materials M,D
Engineering and Applied Sciences—General M,D,O
Engineering Management M,D
Environmental Engineering M,D
Environmental Sciences M,D
Geochemistry M,D
Geological Engineering M,D
Geology M,D
Geophysics M,D
International Affairs M,O
Management of Technology M,D
Materials Engineering M,D
Materials Sciences M,D
Mathematics M,D
Metallurgical Engineering and Metallurgy M,D
Mineral Economics M,D
Mineral/Mining Engineering M,D
Nuclear Engineering M,D
Petroleum Engineering M,D
Physics M,D
Systems Engineering M,D

COLORADO SCHOOL OF TRADITIONAL CHINESE MEDICINE

Acupuncture and Oriental Medicine M

COLORADO STATE UNIVERSITY

Accounting M
Adult Education M,D
Advertising and Public Relations M,D
Agricultural Economics and Agribusiness M,D
Agricultural Sciences—General M,D
Agronomy and Soil Sciences M,D
Animal Sciences M,D
Anthropology M
Art/Fine Arts M
Atmospheric Sciences M,D
Biochemistry M,D
Biological and Biomedical Sciences—General M,D
Biomedical Engineering M,D
Botany M,D
Business Administration and Management—General M
Cell Biology M,D
Chemical Engineering M,D
Chemistry M,D
Child and Family Studies M,D
Civil Engineering M,D
Community College Education M,D
Computer Science M,D
Conservation Biology M,D
Construction Management M
Consumer Economics M
Counselor Education M,D
Ecology M,D
Economics M,D
Education—General M,D
Educational Leadership and Administration M,D
Electrical Engineering M,D
Engineering and Applied Sciences—General M,D
English M
Entomology M,D
Environmental and Occupational Health M,D
Exercise and Sports Science M,D
Finance and Banking M
Fish, Game, and Wildlife Management M,D
Food Science and Technology M,D
Foreign Languages Education M
Forestry M,D
Geosciences M,D
History M
Horticulture M,D
Human Development M,D
Hydrology M,D
Immunology M,D
Landscape Architecture M,D
Management Information Systems M
Mass Communication M,D
Mathematics M,D
Mechanical Engineering M,D
Microbiology M,D
Molecular Biology M,D
Music M
Natural Resources M,D
Neuroscience D
Nutrition M,D
Occupational Therapy M
Organizational Management M
Pathology M,D
Philosophy M
Physics M,D
Plant Pathology M,D
Plant Sciences M,D
Political Science M,D
Psychology—General M,D
Radiation Biology M,D
Range Science M,D
Recreation and Park Management M,D
Social Work M
Sociology M,D
Speech and Interpersonal Communication M
Statistics M,D
Student Affairs M,D
Sustainability Management M
Technical Communication M,D
Technical Writing M,D
Veterinary Medicine P
Veterinary Sciences M,D
Vocational and Technical Education M,D
Water Resources M,D
Writing M
Zoology M,D

COLORADO STATE UNIVERSITY–PUEBLO

Applied Science and Technology M
Art Education M
Biochemistry M
Biological and Biomedical Sciences—General M
Business Administration and Management—General M
Chemistry M
Education—General M
Educational Media/ Instructional Technology M
Engineering and Applied Sciences—General M
Foreign Languages Education M
Health Education M
Industrial/Management Engineering M
Music Education M
Nursing—General M
Physical Education M
Special Education M
Systems Engineering M

COLORADO TECHNICAL UNIVERSITY COLORADO SPRINGS

Accounting M,D
Business Administration and Management—General M,D
Computer and Information Systems Security M,D
Computer Engineering M
Computer Science M,D
Conflict Resolution and Mediation/Peace Studies M,D
Criminal Justice and Criminology M
Database Systems M,D
Electrical Engineering M
Finance and Banking M,D
Human Resources Management M,D
Industrial and Manufacturing Management M,D
Logistics M,D
Management of Technology M,D
Marketing M,D
Project Management M,D
Software Engineering M,D
Systems Engineering M

COLORADO TECHNICAL UNIVERSITY DENVER

Accounting M
Business Administration and Management—General M
Computer and Information Systems Security M
Computer Engineering M
Computer Science M
Conflict Resolution and Mediation/Peace Studies M
Criminal Justice and Criminology M
Database Systems M
Electrical Engineering M
Finance and Banking M
Human Resources Management M
Industrial and Manufacturing Management M
Management of Technology M
Marketing M
Project Management M
Software Engineering M
Systems Engineering M

COLORADO TECHNICAL UNIVERSITY SIOUX FALLS

Business Administration and Management—General M
Computer and Information Systems Security M
Computer Science M
Criminal Justice and Criminology M
Health Services Management and Hospital Administration M
Human Resources Management M
Management Information Systems M
Management of Technology M
Organizational Management M
Project Management M
Software Engineering M

COLUMBIA COLLEGE (MO)

Business Administration and Management—General M
Criminal Justice and Criminology M
Education—General M
Military and Defense Studies M

COLUMBIA COLLEGE (SC)

Conflict Resolution and Mediation/Peace Studies M,O
Education—General M
Elementary Education M
Organizational Behavior M,O

COLUMBIA COLLEGE CHICAGO

Arts Administration M
Comparative and Interdisciplinary Arts M
Education—General M
Elementary Education M
English Education M

*M—master's degree; P—first professional degree; D—doctorate; O—other advanced degree; *—Close-Up and/or Display in one of the other books in this series*

Entertainment Management M
Film, Television, and Video Production M
Journalism M
Media Studies M
Multilingual and Multicultural Education M
Music M
Photography M
Therapies—Dance, Drama, and Music M,O
Urban Education M
Writing M

COLUMBIA INTERNATIONAL UNIVERSITY

Counselor Education M,D,O
Cultural Studies P,M,D,O
Curriculum and Instruction M,D,O
Early Childhood Education M,D,O
Education—General M,D,O
Educational Leadership and Administration M,D,O
Educational Media/Instructional Technology M,D,O
Elementary Education M,D,O
English as a Second Language M,D,O
Higher Education M,D,O
Missions and Missiology P,M,D,O
Multilingual and Multicultural Education M,D,O
Pastoral Ministry and Counseling P,M,D,O
Religious Education P,M,D,O
Special Education M,D,O
Theology P,M,D,O

COLUMBIA SOUTHERN UNIVERSITY

Business Administration and Management—General M,D
Criminal Justice and Criminology M
Electronic Commerce M
Environmental and Occupational Health M
Finance and Banking M
Health Services Management and Hospital Administration M
Hospitality Management M
Human Resources Management M
International Business M
Marketing M

COLUMBIA THEOLOGICAL SEMINARY

Theology P,M,D

COLUMBIA UNIVERSITY

Accounting M,D
Actuarial Science M
Acute Care/Critical Care Nursing M,O
Adult Nursing M,O
African Studies O
African-American Studies M
Allopathic Medicine P,M
American Studies M
Anatomy M,D
Anthropology M,D
Applied Mathematics M,D,O
Applied Physics M,D,O*
Archaeology M,D
Architecture M,D
Archives/Archival Administration M
Art History M,D
Art/Fine Arts M
Asian Languages M,D
Asian Studies M,D,O
Astronomy M,D
Atmospheric Sciences M,D
Biochemistry M,D
Bioethics M
Biological and Biomedical Sciences—General P,M,D,O
Biomedical Engineering M,D
Biophysics M,D
Biopsychology M,D
Biostatistics M,D
Business Administration and Management—General M,D
Cell Biology M,D
Chemical Engineering M,D
Chemical Physics M,D
Chemistry M,D
Civil Engineering M,D,O
Classics M,D
Communication—General M,D
Community Health M,D
Comparative Literature M,D
Computer Engineering M,D,O
Computer Science M,D,O*
Conflict Resolution and Mediation/Peace Studies M
Conservation Biology M,D,O
Construction Engineering M,D,O
Construction Management M,D,O
Corporate and Organizational Communication M
Dentistry P
Developmental Biology M,D
East European and Russian Studies M,O
Ecology M,D,O
Economics M,D
Electrical Engineering M,D,O*
Engineering and Applied Sciences—General M,D,O
English M,D
Entrepreneurship M
Environmental and Occupational Health M,D
Environmental Design M
Environmental Engineering M,D,O
Environmental Management and Policy M
Environmental Sciences M*
Epidemiology M,D
Ethics M
Evolutionary Biology M,D,O
Experimental Psychology M,D
Family Nurse Practitioner Studies M,O
Film, Television, and Video Production M
Finance and Banking M,D
Financial Engineering M,D,O
French M,D
Genetics M,D
Geochemistry M,D
Geodetic Sciences M,D
Geophysics M,D
Geosciences M,D
German M,D
Gerontological Nursing M,O
Health Services Management and Hospital Administration M
Historic Preservation M,O
History M,D
Human Resources Management M
Industrial/Management Engineering M,D,O
Information Studies M
Inorganic Chemistry M,D
Interdisciplinary Studies M
International Affairs M
International Business M
Italian M,D
Jewish Studies M,D
Journalism M,D,O
Kinesiology and Movement Studies M,D
Landscape Architecture M
Latin American Studies M,O
Law P,M,D
Liberal Studies M
Management of Technology M
Marketing M,D
Materials Engineering M,D,O
Materials Sciences M,D,O
Maternal and Child Health M
Maternal and Child/Neonatal Nursing M,O
Mathematics M,D
Mechanical Engineering M,D,O
Mechanics M,D,O
Medical Informatics M,D,O
Medical Physics M,D,O
Medical/Surgical Nursing M,O
Medieval and Renaissance Studies M
Metallurgical Engineering and Metallurgy M,D,O
Meteorology M
Microbiology M,D
Mineral/Mining Engineering M,D,O
Molecular Biology D
Music M,D
Near and Middle Eastern Languages M,D
Near and Middle Eastern Studies M,D,O
Neurobiology D
Nonprofit Management M
Nurse Anesthesia M,O
Nurse Midwifery M
Nursing—General M,D,O
Nutrition M,D
Occupational Therapy M,D
Oceanography M,D
Oncology Nursing M,O
Operations Research M,D,O
Oral and Dental Sciences M,D,O
Organic Chemistry M,D
Pathobiology M,D
Pathology M,D
Pediatric Nursing M,O
Pharmaceutical Administration M
Pharmacology M,D
Philosophy M,D
Photography M
Physical Therapy D
Physics M,D
Physiology M,D
Planetary and Space Sciences M,D
Political Science M,D
Psychiatric Nursing M,O
Psychology—General M,D
Public Administration M
Public Health—General M,D
Public Policy M
Real Estate M
Religion M,D
Romance Languages M,D
Russian M,D
Science Education M,D,O
Slavic Languages M,D
Social Psychology M,D
Social Sciences M
Social Work M,D
Sociology M,D
Spanish M,D
Sports Management M
Statistics M,D
Structural Biology D
Sustainability Management M*
Sustainable Development M,D
Theater M,D*
Toxicology M,D
Urban and Regional Planning M,D
Western European Studies M,O
Women's Health Nursing O
Writing M

COLUMBUS STATE UNIVERSITY

Art Education M
Business Administration and Management—General M,O
Computer Science M,O
Counseling Psychology M,D,O
Counselor Education M,D,O
Criminal Justice and Criminology M
Curriculum and Instruction M,D,O
Early Childhood Education M,O
Education—General M,D,O
Educational Leadership and Administration M,D,O
English Education M,O
Environmental Sciences M
Health Services Management and Hospital Administration M,O
Mathematics Education M,O
Middle School Education M,O
Modeling and Simulation M,O
Music Education M,O
Organizational Management M,O
Physical Education M,O
Public Administration M
Science Education M,O
Secondary Education M,O
Social Sciences Education M,O
Special Education M,O

CONCORDIA COLLEGE

Education—General M
Foreign Languages Education M

CONCORDIA LUTHERAN SEMINARY

Theology P,O

CONCORDIA SEMINARY

Theology P,M,D,O

CONCORDIA THEOLOGICAL SEMINARY

Theology P,M,D

CONCORDIA UNIVERSITY (CA)

Applied Social Research M
Business Administration and Management—General M
Cultural Studies M
Curriculum and Instruction M
Education—General M
Educational Leadership and Administration M
International Affairs M
Physical Education M
Religion M
Sports Management M
Theology M

CONCORDIA UNIVERSITY (CANADA)

Accounting M,D,O
Adult Education M,O
Aerospace/Aeronautical Engineering M
Anthropology M
Applied Arts and Design—General O
Art Education M,D
Art History M,D
Art Therapy M
Art/Fine Arts M
Aviation Management M,D,O
Biological and Biomedical Sciences—General M,D,O
Biotechnology M,D,O
Business Administration and Management—General M,D,O
Chemistry M,D
Child and Family Studies M
Civil Engineering M,D,O

Clinical Psychology M,D,O
Communication—General M,D,O
Computer and Information Systems Security M,O
Computer Art and Design O
Computer Engineering M,D
Computer Science M,D,O
Construction Engineering M,D,O
Cultural Anthropology M
Economic Development O
Economics M,D,O
Education—General M,D,O
Educational Media/ Instructional Technology M,D,O
Electrical Engineering M,D
Engineering and Applied Sciences—General M,D,O
English as a Second Language M,O
English M
Environmental Engineering M,D,O
Environmental Management and Policy M,O
Exercise and Sports Science M
Film, Television, and Video Production M
Film, Television, and Video Theory and Criticism M
French M,O
Game Design and Development M,O
Genomic Sciences M,D,O
Geography M,D,O
Health Services Management and Hospital Administration M,D,O
History M,D
Humanities D
Industrial/Management Engineering M,D,O
Interdisciplinary Studies M,D
Internet and Interactive Multimedia M,O
Investment Management M,D,O
Jewish Studies M
Journalism O
Linguistics M,O
Mathematics Education M,D
Mathematics M,D
Mechanical Engineering M,D,O
Media Studies M,D,O
Music O
Organizational Management M
Philosophy M
Physics M,D
Political Science M,D
Psychology—General M,D
Public Administration M,D
Public Affairs O
Public Policy M,D
Religion M,D
Rural Planning and Studies M,D,O
Sociology M
Software Engineering M,D,O
Sports Management M,D,O
Systems Engineering M,O
Telecommunications Management M,O
Theology M
Translation and Interpretation M,O
Transportation Management M,D,O
Urban and Regional Planning O
Urban Studies M,O
Writing M

CONCORDIA UNIVERSITY (MI)

Curriculum and Instruction M
Educational Leadership and Administration M
Organizational Management M

CONCORDIA UNIVERSITY (OR)

Business Administration and Management—General M
Curriculum and Instruction M
Education—General M
Educational Leadership and Administration M
Elementary Education M
Secondary Education M

CONCORDIA UNIVERSITY CHICAGO

Business Administration and Management—General M
Counseling Psychology M
Counselor Education M,O
Curriculum and Instruction M
Early Childhood Education M,D
Education—General M
Educational Leadership and Administration M,D,O
Educational Media/ Instructional Technology M
Elementary Education M
Exercise and Sports Science M
Gerontology M
Human Services M
Liberal Studies M
Music M
Psychology—General M
Reading Education M
Religion M
Religious Education M
Secondary Education M

CONCORDIA UNIVERSITY COLLEGE OF ALBERTA

Computer and Information Systems Security M
Religion M
Theology M

CONCORDIA UNIVERSITY, NEBRASKA

Early Childhood Education M
Education—General M
Educational Leadership and Administration M
Elementary Education M
Pastoral Ministry and Counseling M
Reading Education M
Religious Education M
Secondary Education M

CONCORDIA UNIVERSITY, ST. PAUL

Business Administration and Management—General M
Child and Family Studies M,O
Corporate and Organizational Communication M
Criminal Justice and Criminology M
Curriculum and Instruction M,O
Early Childhood Education M,O
Education—General M,O
Educational Leadership and Administration M,O
Health Services Management and Hospital Administration M
Human Resources Management M
Organizational Management M
Pastoral Ministry and Counseling M,O
Reading Education M,O
Religious Education M,O
Special Education M,O
Sports Management M,O
Theology M,O

CONCORDIA UNIVERSITY TEXAS

Education—General M

CONCORDIA UNIVERSITY WISCONSIN

Art Education M
Business Administration and Management—General M
Child and Family Studies M
Corporate and Organizational Communication M
Counseling Psychology M
Counselor Education M
Curriculum and Instruction M
Early Childhood Education M
Education—General M
Educational Leadership and Administration M
Environmental Education M
Family Nurse Practitioner Studies M
Finance and Banking M
Gerontological Nursing M
Health Services Management and Hospital Administration M
Human Resources Management M
Human Services M,D
International Business M
Management Information Systems M
Marketing M
Music M
Nursing Education M
Nursing—General M
Occupational Therapy M
Physical Therapy M,D
Psychology—General M
Public Administration M
Reading Education M
Rehabilitation Sciences M
Special Education M
Student Affairs M

CONCORD LAW SCHOOL

Law P

CONCORD UNIVERSITY

Educational Leadership and Administration M
Geography M
Health Promotion M
Reading Education M
Social Sciences Education M

CONNECTICUT COLLEGE

Psychology—General M

CONSERVATORIO DE MUSICA

Music Education M
Music O

CONVERSE COLLEGE

Art Education M,O
Curriculum and Instruction O
Early Childhood Education M,O
Education of the Gifted M
Education—General M,O
Educational Leadership and Administration M,O
Elementary Education M
English Education M
English M
History M
Liberal Studies M
Marriage and Family Therapy O
Mathematics Education M
Music Education M
Music M
Political Science M
Science Education M
Secondary Education M
Social Sciences Education M
Special Education M

CONWAY SCHOOL OF LANDSCAPE DESIGN

Landscape Architecture M

COOPER UNION FOR THE ADVANCEMENT OF SCIENCE AND ART

Architecture M
Chemical Engineering M
Civil Engineering M
Electrical Engineering M
Engineering and Applied Sciences—General M
Mechanical Engineering M

COPPIN STATE UNIVERSITY

Addictions/Substance Abuse Counseling M
Adult Education M
Applied Psychology M
Criminal Justice and Criminology M
Curriculum and Instruction M
Education—General M
Family Nurse Practitioner Studies M,O
Human Services M
Nursing—General M,O
Reading Education M
Rehabilitation Counseling M
Special Education M

CORBAN UNIVERSITY

Business Administration and Management—General M
Education—General M
Nonprofit Management M
Pastoral Ministry and Counseling M

CORCORAN COLLEGE OF ART AND DESIGN

Art Education M
Decorative Arts M
Interior Design M

CORNELL UNIVERSITY

Accounting D
Adult Education M,D
Aerospace/Aeronautical Engineering M,D
African Studies M,D
African-American Studies M,D
Agricultural Economics and Agribusiness M
Agricultural Education M,D
Agricultural Engineering M,D
Agronomy and Soil Sciences M,D
American Studies M,D
Analytical Chemistry D
Anatomy M,D
Animal Behavior D
Animal Sciences M,D
Anthropology D
Applied Economics M,D
Applied Mathematics M,D
Applied Physics M,D
Applied Statistics M,D
Archaeology M,D
Architectural History M,D
Architecture M,D
Art History D
Art/Fine Arts M
Artificial Intelligence/ Robotics M,D

*M—master's degree; P—first professional degree; D—doctorate; O—other advanced degree; *—Close-Up and/or Display in one of the other books in this series*

Asian Languages	M,D
Asian Studies	M,D
Astronomy	D
Astrophysics	D
Atmospheric Sciences	M,D
Biochemical Engineering	M,D
Biochemistry	D
Bioengineering	M,D
Biological and Biomedical Sciences—General	M,D
Biomedical Engineering	M,D
Biometry	M,D
Biophysics	D
Biopsychology	D
Building Science	M,D
Business Administration and Management—General	M,D
Cell Biology	M,D
Chemical Engineering	M,D
Chemical Physics	D
Chemistry	D
Child and Family Studies	D
Chinese	M,D
Civil Engineering	M,D
Classics	D
Clothing and Textiles	M,D
Cognitive Sciences	D
Communication—General	M,D
Comparative Literature	D
Computational Biology	D
Computational Sciences	M,D
Computer Art and Design	M,D
Computer Engineering	M,D
Computer Science	M,D
Conflict Resolution and Mediation/Peace Studies	M,D
Consumer Economics	M,D
Cultural Anthropology	D
Cultural Studies	M,D
Curriculum and Instruction	M,D
Demography and Population Studies	M,D
Developmental Biology	M,D
Developmental Psychology	D
East European and Russian Studies	M,D
Ecology	M,D
Economic Development	M,D
Economics	M,D
Education—General	M,D
Electrical Engineering	M,D
Engineering and Applied Sciences—General	M,D
Engineering Management	M,D
Engineering Physics	M,D
English	M,D
Entomology	M,D
Environmental Design	M
Environmental Engineering	M,D
Environmental Management and Policy	M,D
Environmental Sciences	M,D
Epidemiology	M,D
Ergonomics and Human Factors	M
Ethnic Studies	M,D
Evolutionary Biology	D
Experimental Psychology	D
Facilities Management	M
Finance and Banking	D
Fish, Game, and Wildlife Management	M,D
Food Science and Technology	M,D
Foreign Languages Education	M,D
Forestry	M,D
French	D
Gender Studies	M,D
Genetics	D
Geochemistry	M,D
Geology	M,D
Geophysics	M,D
Geosciences	M,D
Geotechnical Engineering	M,D
German	M,D
Health Services Management and Hospital Administration	M,D
Hispanic and Latin American Languages	D
Historic Preservation	M,D
History of Science and Technology	M,D
History	M,D
Horticulture	M,D
Hospitality Management	M,D
Human Development	D
Human Resources Management	M,D
Human-Computer Interaction	D
Hydrology	M,D
Immunology	M,D
Industrial and Labor Relations	M,D*
Industrial/Management Engineering	M,D
Infectious Diseases	M,D
Information Science	D
Information Studies	D
Inorganic Chemistry	D
Interior Design	M
International Affairs	D
International Development	M
Italian	D
Japanese	M,D
Jewish Studies	M,D
Landscape Architecture	M
Latin American Studies	M,D
Law	P,M,D
Limnology	D
Linguistics	M,D
Manufacturing Engineering	M,D
Marine Geology	M,D
Marine Sciences	M,D
Marketing	D
Materials Engineering	M,D
Materials Sciences	M,D
Mathematics Education	M,D
Mathematics	D
Mechanical Engineering	M,D
Mechanics	M,D
Medieval and Renaissance Studies	M,D
Microbiology	D
Mineralogy	M,D
Molecular Biology	D
Molecular Medicine	M,D
Music	M,D
Natural Resources	M,D
Near and Middle Eastern Studies	M,D
Neurobiology	D
Nutrition	M,D
Oceanography	D
Operations Research	M,D
Organic Chemistry	D
Organizational Behavior	M,D
Paleontology	M,D
Pharmacology	M,D
Philosophy	D
Photography	M
Physical Chemistry	D
Physics	M,D
Physiology	M,D
Planetary and Space Sciences	D
Plant Biology	M,D
Plant Molecular Biology	M,D
Plant Pathology	M,D
Plant Physiology	M,D
Plant Sciences	M,D
Political Science	D
Polymer Science and Engineering	M,D
Psychology—General	D
Public Affairs	M
Public Policy	M,D
Real Estate	M
Religion	D
Reproductive Biology	M,D
Romance Languages	M,D
Rural Planning and Studies	M
Rural Sociology	M,D
Scandinavian Languages	M,D
Science Education	M,D
Slavic Languages	M,D
Social Psychology	M,D
Social Work	M,D
Sociology	M,D
Spanish	D
Statistics	M,D
Structural Biology	M,D
Structural Engineering	M,D
Systems Engineering	M
Textile Design	M,D
Textile Sciences and Engineering	M,D
Theater	D
Theoretical Chemistry	D
Theoretical Physics	M,D
Toxicology	M,D
Transportation and Highway Engineering	M,D
Urban and Regional Planning	M,D
Urban Design	M,D
Veterinary Medicine	P
Water Resources Engineering	M,D
Western European Studies	M,D
Women's Studies	M,D
Writing	M,D
Zoology	M,D

CORNELL UNIVERSITY, JOAN AND SANFORD I. WEILL MEDICAL COLLEGE AND GRADUATE SCHOOL OF MEDICAL SCIENCES

Biochemistry	M,D
Biological and Biomedical Sciences—General	M,D
Biophysics	M,D
Cell Biology	M,D
Computational Biology	D
Epidemiology	M
Health Services Research	M
Immunology	M,D
Molecular Biology	M,D
Neuroscience	M,D
Pharmacology	M,D
Physician Assistant Studies	M
Physiology	M,D
Structural Biology	M,D
Systems Biology	M,D

CORNERSTONE UNIVERSITY

Business Administration and Management—General	M,O
Education—General	M,O
English as a Second Language	M,O

COVENANT COLLEGE

Education—General	M

COVENANT THEOLOGICAL SEMINARY

Theology	P,M,D,O

COX COLLEGE

Family Nurse Practitioner Studies	M
Nursing and Healthcare Administration	M
Nursing Education	M
Nursing—General	M

CRANBROOK ACADEMY OF ART

Applied Arts and Design—General	M
Architecture	M
Art/Fine Arts	M
Graphic Design	M
Photography	M
Textile Design	M

CREIGHTON UNIVERSITY

Allied Health—General	P,M,D
Allopathic Medicine	P
Anatomy	M
Atmospheric Sciences	M
Biological and Biomedical Sciences—General	M,D
Business Administration and Management—General	M
Conflict Resolution and Mediation/Peace Studies	M,O
Counselor Education	M
Dentistry	P
Education—General	M
Educational Leadership and Administration	M
Elementary Education	M
English	M
Immunology	M,D
International Affairs	M
Law	P,M,O
Liberal Studies	M
Management Information Systems	M
Medical Microbiology	M,D
Nursing—General	M,D
Occupational Therapy	D
Pharmaceutical Sciences	M,D
Pharmacology	M,D
Pharmacy	P
Physical Therapy	D
Physics	M
Secondary Education	M
Social Psychology	M
Special Education	M
Student Affairs	M
Theology	M
Writing	M

THE CRISWELL COLLEGE

Jewish Studies	P,M
Pastoral Ministry and Counseling	P,M
Theology	P,M

CROWN COLLEGE

Theology	M

CUMBERLAND UNIVERSITY

Business Administration and Management—General	M
Education—General	M
Public Administration	M

CUNY GRADUATE SCHOOL OF JOURNALISM

Journalism	M

CURRY COLLEGE

Business Administration and Management—General	M,O
Criminal Justice and Criminology	M
Education—General	M,O
Elementary Education	M,O
Finance and Banking	M,O
Foundations and Philosophy of Education	M,O
Nursing—General	M
Reading Education	M,O
Special Education	M,O

CURTIS INSTITUTE OF MUSIC

Music	M

DAEMEN COLLEGE

Accounting	M
Adult Nursing	M,D,O

Program	Degree
Business Administration and Management—General	M
Early Childhood Education	M
Education—General	M
Health Services Management and Hospital Administration	M
International Business	M
Management Information Systems	M
Marketing	M
Medical/Surgical Nursing	M,D,O
Middle School Education	M
Nonprofit Management	M
Nursing and Healthcare Administration	M,D,O
Nursing Education	M,D,O
Nursing—General	M,D,O
Physical Therapy	D,O
Physician Assistant Studies	M
Special Education	M

DAKOTA STATE UNIVERSITY

Program	Degree
Education—General	M
Educational Media/Instructional Technology	M
Information Science	M,D

DAKOTA WESLEYAN UNIVERSITY

Program	Degree
Curriculum and Instruction	M
Education—General	M
Educational Leadership and Administration	M
Secondary Education	M

DALHOUSIE UNIVERSITY

Program	Degree
Agricultural Engineering	M,D
Agricultural Sciences—General	M
Allopathic Medicine	P,M,D
Anatomy	M,D
Anthropology	M,D
Applied Mathematics	M,D
Architecture	M
Biochemistry	M,D
Bioengineering	M,D
Bioinformatics	M,D
Biological and Biomedical Sciences—General	M,D
Biomedical Engineering	M,D
Biophysics	M,D
Business Administration and Management—General	M,O
Chemical Engineering	M,D
Chemistry	M,D
Civil Engineering	M,D
Classics	M,D
Clinical Psychology	M,D
Communication Disorders	M,D
Community Health	M
Computer Engineering	M,D
Computer Science	M,D
Economics	M,D
Electrical Engineering	M,D
Electronic Commerce	M,D
Engineering and Applied Sciences—General	M,D
English	M,D
Environmental Engineering	M,D
Environmental Management and Policy	M
Epidemiology	M
Finance and Banking	M
Food Science and Technology	M,D
French	M,D
Geosciences	M,D
German	M
Health Education	M
Health Services Management and Hospital Administration	M,D
History	M,D
Human-Computer Interaction	M
Immunology	M,D
Industrial/Management Engineering	M,D
Information Studies	M
Interdisciplinary Studies	D
International Development	M
Kinesiology and Movement Studies	M
Law	M,D
Leisure Studies	M
Library Science	M
Management Information Systems	M
Marine Affairs	M
Materials Engineering	M,D
Mathematics	M,D
Mechanical Engineering	M,D
Medical Informatics	M,D
Microbiology	M,D
Mineral/Mining Engineering	M,D
Music	M
Natural Resources	M
Neurobiology	M,D
Neuroscience	M,D
Nursing—General	M,D
Occupational Therapy	M
Oceanography	M,D
Oral and Dental Sciences	
Pathology	M,D
Pharmacology	M,D
Philosophy	M,D
Physical Therapy	M
Physics	M,D
Physiology	M,D
Political Science	M,D
Psychology—General	M,D
Public Administration	M,O
Rural Planning and Studies	M
Social Work	M
Sociology	M,D
Statistics	M,D
Urban and Regional Planning	M

DALLAS BAPTIST UNIVERSITY

Program	Degree
Accounting	M
Business Administration and Management—General	M
Conflict Resolution and Mediation/Peace Studies	M
Corporate and Organizational Communication	M
Counseling Psychology	M
Counselor Education	M
Criminal Justice and Criminology	M
Curriculum and Instruction	M
Education—General	M
Educational Leadership and Administration	M
Electronic Commerce	M
Elementary Education	M
Engineering Management	M
English as a Second Language	M
Entrepreneurship	M
Experimental Psychology	M
Finance and Banking	M
Health Services Management and Hospital Administration	M
Higher Education	M
Human Resources Management	M
Interdisciplinary Studies	M
International Business	M
Kinesiology and Movement Studies	M
Liberal Studies	M
Management Information Systems	M
Management of Technology	M
Marketing	M
Missions and Missiology	M
Nonprofit Management	M
Pastoral Ministry and Counseling	M
Project Management	M
Reading Education	M
Religious Education	M
Secondary Education	M

DALLAS THEOLOGICAL SEMINARY

Program	Degree
Media Studies	M,D,O
Missions and Missiology	M,D,O
Pastoral Ministry and Counseling	M,D,O
Religious Education	M,D,O
Theology	M,D,O

DANIEL WEBSTER COLLEGE

Program	Degree
Aviation Management	M
Business Administration and Management—General	M

DANIEL WEBSTER COLLEGE–PORTSMOUTH CAMPUS

Program	Degree
Business Administration and Management—General	M

DARKEI NOAM RABBINICAL COLLEGE

Program	Degree
Theology	

DARTMOUTH COLLEGE

Program	Degree
Allopathic Medicine	P
Astronomy	M,D
Biochemical Engineering	M,D
Biochemistry	D
Biological and Biomedical Sciences—General	D
Biomedical Engineering	M,D
Biotechnology	M,D
Business Administration and Management—General	M
Cancer Biology/Oncology	D
Cardiovascular Sciences	D
Cell Biology	D
Chemistry	D
Cognitive Sciences	D
Comparative Literature	M
Computer Engineering	M,D
Computer Science	M,D
Ecology	D
Electrical Engineering	M,D
Engineering and Applied Sciences—General	M,D
Engineering Management	M
Engineering Physics	M,D
Environmental Engineering	M,D
Evolutionary Biology	D
Genetics	D
Geosciences	M,D
Health Services Management and Hospital Administration	M,D
Health Services Research	M,D
Immunology	
Liberal Studies	M
Manufacturing Engineering	M,D
Materials Engineering	M,D
Materials Sciences	M,D
Mathematics	D
Mechanical Engineering	M,D
Microbiology	D
Molecular Biology	D
Molecular Medicine	D
Molecular Pathogenesis	D
Molecular Pharmacology	D
Music	M
Neuroscience	D
Pharmaceutical Sciences	D
Pharmacology	D
Physics	M,D
Physiology	D
Psychology—General	D
Public Health—General	M
Systems Biology	D
Toxicology	D

DAVENPORT UNIVERSITY

Program	Degree
Accounting	M
Business Administration and Management—General	M
Computer and Information Systems Security	M
Finance and Banking	M
Health Services Management and Hospital Administration	M
Human Resources Management	M
Management Strategy and Policy	M
Marketing	M
Public Health—General	M

DAVENPORT UNIVERSITY

Program	Degree
Accounting	M
Business Administration and Management—General	M
Computer and Information Systems Security	M
Finance and Banking	M
Health Services Management and Hospital Administration	M
Human Resources Management	M
Management Strategy and Policy	M
Public Health—General	M

DAVENPORT UNIVERSITY

Program	Degree
Accounting	M
Business Administration and Management—General	M
Computer and Information Systems Security	M
Finance and Banking	M
Health Services Management and Hospital Administration	M
Human Resources Management	M
Public Health—General	M

DEFIANCE COLLEGE

Program	Degree
Adult Education	M
Business Administration and Management—General	M
Criminal Justice and Criminology	M
Education—General	M
Health Services Management and Hospital Administration	M
Management Strategy and Policy	M
Physical Education	M
Secondary Education	M
Special Education	M

DELAWARE STATE UNIVERSITY

Program	Degree
Adult Education	M
Applied Mathematics	M,D
Art Education	M
Biological and Biomedical Sciences—General	M
Business Administration and Management—General	M
Chemistry	M
Curriculum and Instruction	M
Education—General	M,D

*M—master's degree; P—first professional degree; D—doctorate; O—other advanced degree; *—Close-Up and/or Display in one of the other books in this series*

Educational Leadership and Administration M,D
Exercise and Sports Science M
Foreign Languages Education M
Historic Preservation M
Mathematics Education M
Mathematics M
Natural Resources M
Neuroscience M,D
Nursing—General M
Optical Sciences M,D
Physics M,D
Plant Sciences M
Reading Education M
Science Education M,D
Social Work M
Special Education M
Theoretical Physics D

DELAWARE VALLEY COLLEGE

Accounting M
Agricultural Economics and Agribusiness M
Business Administration and Management—General M
Curriculum and Instruction M
Educational Leadership and Administration M
Educational Media/Instructional Technology M
International Business M

DELL'ARTE INTERNATIONAL SCHOOL OF PHYSICAL THEATRE

Theater M

DELTA STATE UNIVERSITY

Accounting M
Aviation Management M
Biological and Biomedical Sciences—General M
Business Administration and Management—General M
Counselor Education M,D
Criminal Justice and Criminology M
Education—General M,D,O
Educational Leadership and Administration M,D,O
Elementary Education M,D,O
English Education M
Exercise and Sports Science M
Family Nurse Practitioner Studies M
Health Education M
Health Services Management and Hospital Administration M
Higher Education D
Nursing Education M
Nursing—General M
Physical Education M
Recreation and Park Management M
Secondary Education M
Social Sciences Education M
Special Education M
Urban and Regional Planning M

DENVER SEMINARY

Marriage and Family Therapy P,M,D,O
Pastoral Ministry and Counseling P,M,D,O
Religion P,M,D,O
Theology P,M,D,O

DEPAUL UNIVERSITY

Accounting M
Actuarial Science M,O
Adult Education M
Adult Nursing M
Advertising and Public Relations M
Applied Mathematics M,O
Applied Physics M
Applied Statistics M,O
Biochemistry M
Biological and Biomedical Sciences—General M
Business Administration and Management—General M
Chemistry M
Clinical Psychology M,D
Communication—General M
Computer and Information Systems Security M,D
Computer Art and Design M,D
Computer Science M,D
Corporate and Organizational Communication M
Counselor Education M,D
Curriculum and Instruction M,D
Economics M
Education—General M,D
Educational Leadership and Administration M,D
Electronic Commerce M,D
Elementary Education M,D
English M
Entrepreneurship M
Experimental Psychology M,D
Film, Television, and Video Production M,D
Finance and Banking M,O
Game Design and Development M,D
Health Law P,M,O
Health Services Management and Hospital Administration M,O
History M
Human Development M,D
Human Resources Management M
Human Services M,D
Human-Computer Interaction M,D
Industrial and Manufacturing Management M
Industrial and Organizational Psychology M,D
Information Science M,D
Intellectual Property Law P,M
Interdisciplinary Studies M
International Business M
Internet and Interactive Multimedia M,D
Journalism M
Law P,M
Management Information Systems M,D
Management of Technology M,D
Management Strategy and Policy M
Marketing M
Mathematical and Computational Finance M,D
Mathematics Education M,O
Mathematics M,O
Media Studies M
Multilingual and Multicultural Education M,D
Music Education M,O
Music M,O
Nonprofit Management M,O
Nurse Anesthesia M
Nursing—General M
Philosophy M,D
Physical Education M,D
Physics M
Polymer Science and Engineering M
Psychology—General M,D
Public Administration M,O
Public Affairs M,O
Public Policy M,O
Publishing M
Reading Education M,D
Real Estate M
Secondary Education M,D
Social Psychology M,D
Sociology M
Software Engineering M,D
Special Education M,D
Taxation M
Theater M
Urban and Regional Planning M,O
Urban Education M,D
Writing M

DESALES UNIVERSITY

Accounting M
Adult Nursing M,O
Business Administration and Management—General M
Criminal Justice and Criminology M
Education—General M
Educational Media/Instructional Technology M
English as a Second Language M
Family Nurse Practitioner Studies M,O
Finance and Banking M
Forensic Sciences M
Health Services Management and Hospital Administration M
Human Resources Management M
Information Science M
Management Information Systems M
Marketing M
Nurse Midwifery M,O
Nursing Education M,O
Nursing—General M,O
Physician Assistant Studies M
Project Management M

DES MOINES UNIVERSITY

Anatomy M
Biological and Biomedical Sciences—General M
Health Services Management and Hospital Administration M
Osteopathic Medicine P,M
Physical Therapy D
Physician Assistant Studies M
Podiatric Medicine P
Public Health—General M

DEVRY COLLEGE OF NEW YORK

Business Administration and Management—General M

DEVRY UNIVERSITY

Business Administration and Management—General M

DEVRY UNIVERSITY

Business Administration and Management—General M

DEVRY UNIVERSITY

Business Administration and Management—General M

DEVRY UNIVERSITY

Business Administration and Management—General M,O

DEVRY UNIVERSITY

Business Administration and Management—General M

DEVRY UNIVERSITY

Business Administration and Management—General M,O

DEVRY UNIVERSITY

Business Administration and Management—General M

DEVRY UNIVERSITY

Business Administration and Management—General M,O

DEVRY UNIVERSITY

Business Administration and Management—General M

DEVRY UNIVERSITY

Business Administration and Management—General M

DEVRY UNIVERSITY

Business Administration and Management—General M

DEVRY UNIVERSITY

Business Administration and Management—General M

DEVRY UNIVERSITY

Business Administration and Management—General M,O

DEVRY UNIVERSITY

Business Administration and Management—General M

DEVRY UNIVERSITY

Business Administration and Management—General M,O

DEVRY UNIVERSITY

Business Administration and Management—General M

DEVRY UNIVERSITY

Business Administration and Management—General M

DEVRY UNIVERSITY

Business Administration and Management—General M,O

DEVRY UNIVERSITY

Business Administration and Management—General M

DEVRY UNIVERSITY

Business Administration and Management—General M,O

DEVRY UNIVERSITY
Business Administration and Management—General M,O

DEVRY UNIVERSITY
Business Administration and Management—General M,O

DEVRY UNIVERSITY
Business Administration and Management—General M,O

DEVRY UNIVERSITY
Business Administration and Management—General M

DEVRY UNIVERSITY
Business Administration and Management—General M,O

DEVRY UNIVERSITY
Business Administration and Management—General M

DEVRY UNIVERSITY
Business Administration and Management—General M

DEVRY UNIVERSITY
Business Administration and Management—General M

DEVRY UNIVERSITY
Business Administration and Management—General M,O

DEVRY UNIVERSITY
Accounting M
Business Administration and Management—General M
Communication—General M
Finance and Banking M
Human Resources Management M
Management Information Systems M
Project Management M
Public Administration M

DEVRY UNIVERSITY
Business Administration and Management—General M,O

DEVRY UNIVERSITY
Business Administration and Management—General M,O

DEVRY UNIVERSITY
Business Administration and Management—General M,O

DEVRY UNIVERSITY
Business Administration and Management—General M,O

DEVRY UNIVERSITY
Business Administration and Management—General M,O

DEVRY UNIVERSITY
Business Administration and Management—General M

DEVRY UNIVERSITY
Business Administration and Management—General M

DEVRY UNIVERSITY
Business Administration and Management—General M,O

DEVRY UNIVERSITY (MD)
Business Administration and Management—General M

DEVRY UNIVERSITY
Business Administration and Management—General M,O

DEVRY UNIVERSITY (NV)
Business Administration and Management—General M

DEVRY UNIVERSITY
Business Administration and Management—General M

DEVRY UNIVERSITY
Business Administration and Management—General M

DEVRY UNIVERSITY
Business Administration and Management—General M

DEVRY UNIVERSITY
Business Administration and Management—General M,O

DEVRY UNIVERSITY
Business Administration and Management—General M,O

DEVRY UNIVERSITY (OR)
Business Administration and Management—General M

DEVRY UNIVERSITY
Business Administration and Management—General M

DEVRY UNIVERSITY
Business Administration and Management—General M,O

DEVRY UNIVERSITY
Business Administration and Management—General M,O

DEVRY UNIVERSITY
Business Administration and Management—General M

DEVRY UNIVERSITY
Business Administration and Management—General M

DEVRY UNIVERSITY
Business Administration and Management—General M

DEVRY UNIVERSITY
Business Administration and Management—General M,O

DEVRY UNIVERSITY (UT)
Business Administration and Management—General M

DEVRY UNIVERSITY
Business Administration and Management—General M

DEVRY UNIVERSITY
Business Administration and Management—General M

DEVRY UNIVERSITY
Business Administration and Management—General M,O

DEVRY UNIVERSITY
Business Administration and Management—General M

DEVRY UNIVERSITY
Business Administration and Management—General M

DEVRY UNIVERSITY
Business Administration and Management—General M,O

DEVRY UNIVERSITY ONLINE
Business Administration and Management—General M

DIGIPEN INSTITUTE OF TECHNOLOGY
Computer Science M

DIGITAL MEDIA ARTS COLLEGE
Computer Art and Design M
Graphic Design M
Media Studies M

DOANE COLLEGE
Business Administration and Management—General M
Counselor Education M
Curriculum and Instruction M
Education—General M
Educational Leadership and Administration M

DOMINICAN COLLEGE
Allied Health—General M,D
Business Administration and Management—General M
Education—General M
Elementary Education M
Family Nurse Practitioner Studies M
Nursing—General M
Occupational Therapy M
Physical Therapy M,D
Special Education M

DOMINICAN HOUSE OF STUDIES, PONTIFICAL FACULTY OF THE IMMACULATE CONCEPTION
Theology P,M,O

DOMINICAN SCHOOL OF PHILOSOPHY AND THEOLOGY
Philosophy M
Theology P,M,O

DOMINICAN UNIVERSITY
Accounting M
Business Administration and Management—General M
Curriculum and Instruction M
Early Childhood Education M
Education—General M
Educational Leadership and Administration M
Elementary Education M
English as a Second Language M
Information Studies M,D,O
Library Science M,D,O
Organizational Management M
Pastoral Ministry and Counseling M
Reading Education M
Social Work M
Special Education M

DOMINICAN UNIVERSITY OF CALIFORNIA
Biological and Biomedical Sciences—General M
Business Administration and Management—General M
Counseling Psychology M
Education—General M,O
Humanities M
International Business M
Management Strategy and Policy M
Marriage and Family Therapy M
Nursing and Healthcare Administration M
Nursing—General M
Occupational Therapy M
Special Education O
Sustainability Management M
Sustainable Development M

DONGGUK UNIVERSITY LOS ANGELES
Acupuncture and Oriental Medicine M

DORDT COLLEGE
Education—General M

DOWLING COLLEGE
Aviation Management M,O

*M—master's degree; P—first professional degree; D—doctorate; O—other advanced degree; *—Close-Up and/or Display in one of the other books in this series*

Business Administration and Management—General	M,D,O
Early Childhood Education	M,D,O
Education of the Gifted	M,D,O
Education—General	M,D,O
Educational Leadership and Administration	M,D,O
Educational Media/Instructional Technology	M,D,O
Educational Psychology	M,D,O
Entertainment Management	M,O
Finance and Banking	M,O
Health Services Management and Hospital Administration	M,O
Human Resources Management	M,O
Liberal Studies	M
Management Information Systems	M,O
Marketing	M,O
Mathematics	M
Middle School Education	M,D,O
Project Management	M,O
Reading Education	M,D,O
Special Education	M,D,O
Sports Management	M,O

DRAKE UNIVERSITY

Business Administration and Management—General	M
Communication—General	M
Education—General	M,D,O
Law	P
Public Administration	M

DREW UNIVERSITY

Bioethics	M,D,O
Biological and Biomedical Sciences—General	M
Chemistry	M
Education—General	M
English	M
Foreign Languages Education	M
French	M
History	M,D
Holocaust and Genocide Studies	M,D,O
Humanities	M,D,O
Interdisciplinary Studies	M,D,O
Italian	M
Mathematics Education	M
Physics	M
Science Education	M
Social Sciences Education	M
Spanish	M
Theater	M
Theology	P,M,D,O
Translation and Interpretation	M
Writing	M

DREXEL UNIVERSITY

Accounting	M,D,O
Allied Health—General	M,D,O
Allopathic Medicine	P
Applied Arts and Design—General	M
Architectural Engineering	M,D
Archives/Archival Administration	M
Art Therapy	M,O
Arts Administration	M
Biochemical Engineering	M
Biochemistry	M,D
Biological and Biomedical Sciences—General	M,D,O
Biomedical Engineering	M,D
Biopsychology	M,D
Biostatistics	M,D,O
Business Administration and Management—General	M,D,O
Cell Biology	M,D
Chemical Engineering	M,D
Chemistry	M,D
Civil Engineering	M,D
Clinical Psychology	D
Communication—General	M
Computer Art and Design	M
Computer Engineering	M
Computer Science	M,D
Construction Management	M
Corporate and Organizational Communication	M
Curriculum and Instruction	M
Economics	M,D,O
Education—General	M,D
Educational Leadership and Administration	M,D
Educational Media/Instructional Technology	M,D
Electrical Engineering	M
Emergency Management	M
Emergency Medical Services	M
Engineering and Applied Sciences—General	M,D,O
Engineering Management	M,O
Environmental Engineering	M,D
Environmental Management and Policy	M
Environmental Sciences	M,D
Epidemiology	M,D,O
Film, Television, and Video Production	M
Finance and Banking	M,D,O
Food Science and Technology	M
Forensic Psychology	D
Genetics	M,D
Geotechnical Engineering	M,D
Health Psychology	D
Higher Education	M
History of Science and Technology	M
Homeland Security	M
Hospitality Management	M
Human Resources Development	M
Hydraulics	M,D
Hydrology	M,D
Immunology	M,D
Information Science	M,D
Information Studies	M
Interior Design	M
International and Comparative Education	M
Journalism	M
Library Science	M,D,O*
Management Strategy and Policy	M,D,O
Marketing	M,D,O
Marriage and Family Therapy	M,D
Mass Communication	M
Materials Engineering	M,D
Mathematics Education	M
Mathematics	M,D
Mechanical Engineering	M,D
Mechanics	M,D
Medical Informatics	M,D,O
Microbiology	M,D
Molecular Biology	M,D
Molecular Medicine	M
Neuroscience	M,D
Nurse Anesthesia	M
Nursing—General	M
Nutrition	M
Organizational Behavior	M,D,O
Pathobiology	M,D
Pharmacology	M,D
Physical Therapy	M,D,O
Physician Assistant Studies	M
Physics	M,D
Project Management	M
Psychology—General	M,D
Public Health—General	M,D,O
Publishing	M
Quantitative Analysis	M,D,O
Real Estate	M
Software Engineering	M,D,O
Special Education	M
Sports Management	M
Structural Engineering	M,D
Technical Communication	M
Technical Writing	M
Telecommunications	M
Textile Design	M
Therapies—Dance, Drama, and Music	M,O
Veterinary Sciences	M

DRURY UNIVERSITY

Architecture	M
Art/Fine Arts	M
Business Administration and Management—General	M
Communication—General	M
Criminal Justice and Criminology	M
Education of the Gifted	M
Education—General	M
Educational Media/Instructional Technology	M
Elementary Education	M
Human Services	M
Mathematics Education	M
Middle School Education	M
Reading Education	M
Secondary Education	M
Special Education	M

DUKE UNIVERSITY

Acute Care/Critical Care Nursing	M,D,O
Adult Nursing	M,D,O
Allopathic Medicine	P
Anatomy	D
Art History	D
Art/Fine Arts	D
Asian Studies	M,O
Biochemistry	D
Bioinformatics	D,O
Biological and Biomedical Sciences—General	D
Biological Anthropology	D
Biomedical Engineering	M,D
Biopsychology	D
Biostatistics	M
Business Administration and Management—General	M,D
Cancer Biology/Oncology	D
Cell Biology	D,O
Chemistry	D
Civil Engineering	M,D
Classics	D
Clinical Laboratory Sciences/Medical Technology	M
Clinical Psychology	D
Clinical Research	M
Cognitive Sciences	D
Comparative Literature	D
Computer Engineering	M,D
Computer Science	M,D
Cultural Anthropology	D
Developmental Biology	O
Developmental Psychology	D
Ecology	M,D,O
Economics	M,D
Education—General	M
Electrical Engineering	M,D*
Engineering and Applied Sciences—General	M
Engineering Management	M
English	D
Environmental and Occupational Health	M,D,O
Environmental Engineering	M,D
Environmental Management and Policy	M,D
Environmental Sciences	M,D
Experimental Psychology	D
Family Nurse Practitioner Studies	M,D,O
Forestry	M
French	D
Genetics	D
Geology	M,D
German	D
Gerontological Nursing	M,D,O
Health Psychology	D
Health Services Management and Hospital Administration	O
History	M,D
Human Development	D
Humanities	M
Immunology	D
International Development	M,O
International Health	M
Latin American Studies	M,D
Law	P,M,D
Liberal Studies	M
Marine Affairs	M
Marine Sciences	M
Materials Engineering	M
Materials Sciences	M,D
Maternal and Child/Neonatal Nursing	M,D,O
Mathematics	D
Mechanical Engineering	M,D
Media Studies	M
Microbiology	D
Molecular Biology	D,O
Molecular Biophysics	O
Molecular Genetics	D
Music	M,D
Natural Resources	M,D
Neurobiology	D
Neuroscience	D,O
Nurse Anesthesia	M,D,O
Nursing and Healthcare Administration	M,D,O
Nursing Education	M,D,O
Nursing Informatics	M,D,O
Nursing—General	D
Oncology Nursing	M,D,O
Optical Sciences	M
Paleontology	D
Pathology	M,D
Pediatric Nursing	M,D,O
Pharmacology	D
Philosophy	M,D
Photonics	M
Physical Therapy	D
Physician Assistant Studies	M
Physics	M,D
Political Science	M,D
Psychology—General	D
Public Policy	M,D,O
Religion	M,D
Slavic Languages	M,O
Sociology	M,D
Spanish	D
Statistics	D
Structural Biology	O
Theology	P,M,D
Toxicology	D,O
Water Resources	M

DUQUESNE UNIVERSITY

Accounting	M
Allied Health—General	M,D
Archives/Archival Administration	M
Biochemistry	M,D
Bioethics	M,D,O
Biological and Biomedical Sciences—General	M,D
Biotechnology	M
Business Administration and Management—General	M
Chemistry	M,D
Clinical Psychology	D
Communication Disorders	M,D
Communication—General	M,D
Community Health	M
Conflict Resolution and Mediation/Peace Studies	M,O

Counselor Education M,D
Curriculum and Instruction M,O
Early Childhood Education M
Education—General M,D,O
Educational Leadership and Administration M,D,O
Educational Media/Instructional Technology M,D
Elementary Education M
English as a Second Language M,D
English Education M
English M,D
Environmental Management and Policy M,O
Environmental Sciences M,O
Ethics M
Family Nurse Practitioner Studies M,O
Foreign Languages Education M
Forensic Nursing M,O
Forensic Sciences M
Foundations and Philosophy of Education M
Health Services Management and Hospital Administration M,D
History M
International Business M
Internet and Interactive Multimedia M,O
Law P,M
Liberal Studies M
Management Information Systems M
Management Strategy and Policy M
Mathematics Education M
Mathematics M
Medicinal and Pharmaceutical Chemistry M,D
Museum Studies M
Music Education M,O
Music M,O
Nursing Education M
Nursing—General M,D,O
Occupational Therapy M,D
Organizational Management M
Pharmaceutical Administration M
Pharmaceutical Sciences M,D
Pharmacology M,D
Pharmacy P
Philosophy M,D
Physical Therapy M,D
Physician Assistant Studies M,D
Psychology—General D
Public Administration M,O
Public Policy M,O
Reading Education M
Rehabilitation Sciences M,D
Rhetoric M,D
School Psychology M,D,O
Science Education M
Secondary Education M
Social Sciences Education M
Special Education M
Sports Management M
Sustainability Management M
Theology M,D

D'YOUVILLE COLLEGE

Business Administration and Management—General M
Chiropractic P
Community Health Nursing M,O
Education—General M,O
Educational Leadership and Administration D
Elementary Education M,O
Family Nurse Practitioner Studies M,O
Health Education D
Health Services Management and Hospital Administration M,D,O
International Business M
Nursing and Healthcare Administration M,O
Nursing Education M,O
Nursing—General M,O*
Nutrition M
Occupational Therapy M
Pharmacy P
Physical Therapy M,D,O
Physician Assistant Studies M
Secondary Education M,O
Special Education M,O

EARLHAM COLLEGE

Education—General M

EARLHAM SCHOOL OF RELIGION

Religion P,M
Theology P,M

EAST CAROLINA UNIVERSITY

Accounting M
Addictions/Substance Abuse Counseling M
Adult Education M,O
Allied Health—General M,D
Allopathic Medicine P
American Studies M
Anatomy D
Anthropology M
Applied Mathematics M
Art/Fine Arts M
Biochemistry D
Biological and Biomedical Sciences—General M,D
Biophysics M,D
Biotechnology M
Business Administration and Management—General M,D,O
Cell Biology D
Chemistry M
Child and Family Studies M
Child Development M
Clinical Psychology M
Communication Disorders M,D
Computer Science M,D,O
Counselor Education M,O
Criminal Justice and Criminology M
Curriculum and Instruction M
Economics M
Education—General M,D,O
Educational Leadership and Administration M,D,O
Educational Media/Instructional Technology M,O
Elementary Education M
English Education M
English M
Environmental and Occupational Health M
Exercise and Sports Science M,D
Geography M
Geology M
Health Communication M
Health Education M
Health Psychology D
History M
Immunology D
Industrial/Management Engineering M,D,O
Information Science M
International Affairs M
Leisure Studies M
Library Science M,O
Logistics M,D,O
Management Information Systems M,D,O
Management of Technology M,D,O
Manufacturing Engineering M,D,O
Marine Affairs D
Marriage and Family Therapy M
Mathematics Education M
Mathematics M
Medical Physics M,D
Microbiology D
Middle School Education M
Molecular Biology M,D
Music Education M
Music M
Natural Resources D
Nursing—General M,D
Nutrition M
Occupational Therapy M
Pathology D
Pharmacology D
Physical Therapy M,D
Physician Assistant Studies M
Physics M,D
Physiology D
Political Science M
Psychology—General M
Public Administration M
Public Health—General M
Reading Education M
Recreation and Park Management M
Rehabilitation Counseling M
Rehabilitation Sciences M
School Psychology
Science Education M
Social Sciences Education M
Social Work M
Sociology M
Special Education M
Therapies—Dance, Drama, and Music M
Vocational and Technical Education M
Western European Studies M

EAST CENTRAL UNIVERSITY

Counselor Education M
Criminal Justice and Criminology M
Education—General M
Human Resources Management M
Psychology—General M
Rehabilitation Counseling M

EASTERN CONNECTICUT STATE UNIVERSITY

Early Childhood Education M
Education—General M
Educational Media/Instructional Technology M
Elementary Education M
Organizational Management M
Reading Education M
Science Education M
Secondary Education M

EASTERN ILLINOIS UNIVERSITY

Accounting M,O
Art Education M
Art/Fine Arts M
Biological and Biomedical Sciences—General M
Business Administration and Management—General M,O
Chemistry M
Clinical Psychology M,O
Communication Disorders M
Computer and Information Systems Security M,O
Computer Science M,O
Consumer Economics M
Counselor Education M
Early Childhood Education M
Economics M
Education—General M,O
Educational Leadership and Administration M,O
Elementary Education M
Engineering and Applied Sciences—General M,O
English M
Exercise and Sports Science M
Family and Consumer Sciences-General M
Gerontology M
History M
Kinesiology and Movement Studies M
Mathematics Education M
Mathematics M
Middle School Education M
Music M
Nutrition M
Political Science M
Psychology—General M,O
Public History M
School Psychology M,O
Special Education M
Speech and Interpersonal Communication M
Student Affairs M
Systems Science M,O

EASTERN KENTUCKY UNIVERSITY

Agricultural Education M
Allied Health—General M
Art Education M
Biological and Biomedical Sciences—General M
Business Administration and Management—General M
Business Education M
Chemistry M
Clinical Psychology M,O
Communication Disorders M
Community Health M
Counselor Education M
Criminal Justice and Criminology M
Curriculum and Instruction M
Ecology M
Education—General M
Educational Leadership and Administration M
Elementary Education M
English Education M
English M
Environmental and Occupational Health M
Family Nurse Practitioner Studies M
Geology M,D
Health Education M
Health Promotion M
Health Services Management and Hospital Administration M
Higher Education M
History M
Home Economics Education M
Industrial and Organizational Psychology M,O
Industrial/Management Engineering M
Library Science M
Manufacturing Engineering M
Mathematics Education M
Mathematics M
Music Education M
Music M
Nursing—General M
Nutrition M
Occupational Therapy M
Physical Education M
Political Science M
Psychology—General M,O
Public Administration M
Recreation and Park Management M

*M—master's degree; P—first professional degree; D—doctorate; O—other advanced degree; *—Close-Up and/or Display in one of the other books in this series*

School Psychology M,O
Science Education M
Secondary Education M
Social Sciences Education M
Special Education M
Sports Management M
Urban and Regional Planning M
Vocational and Technical Education M
Writing M

EASTERN MENNONITE UNIVERSITY

Business Administration and Management—General M
Conflict Resolution and Mediation/Peace Studies M,O
Education—General M
Pastoral Ministry and Counseling P,M,O
Religion P,M,O
Theology P,M,O

EASTERN MICHIGAN UNIVERSITY

Accounting M
Addictions/Substance Abuse Counseling M
Adult Nursing M,O
African-American Studies O
American Studies M,O
Applied Economics M
Applied Statistics M
Art Education M
Art/Fine Arts M
Artificial Intelligence/Robotics M,O
Arts Administration M
Athletic Training and Sports Medicine M,O
Biological and Biomedical Sciences—General M
Business Administration and Management—General M,O
Cell Biology M
Chemistry M
Child and Family Studies M
Clinical Psychology M,D
Clinical Research M,O
Clothing and Textiles M
Communication Disorders M
Communication—General M
Computer and Information Systems Security M,O
Computer Science M,O
Construction Management M
Counselor Education M,O
Criminal Justice and Criminology M
Cultural Studies M
Curriculum and Instruction M
Developmental Education M,O
Early Childhood Education M
Ecology M
Economic Development M
Economics M
Education—General M,D,O
Educational Leadership and Administration M,D,O
Educational Measurement and Evaluation M,O
Educational Media/Instructional Technology M,O
Educational Psychology M,O
Electronic Commerce M,O
Elementary Education M
Engineering and Applied Sciences—General M
Engineering Management M
English as a Second Language M,O
English Education M,O
English M,O
Entrepreneurship M,O
Exercise and Sports Science M
Finance and Banking M,O
Foundations and Philosophy of Education M
French M,O
Gender Studies M,O
Geographic Information Systems M,O
Geography M,O
Geosciences M
German M,O
Gerontology M,O
Health Education M
Health Promotion M,O
Health Services Management and Hospital Administration M,O
Hispanic and Latin American Languages M,O
Hispanic Studies M,O
Historic Preservation M,O
History M,O
Hospitality Management M,O
Human Resources Management M,O
Human Services O
Interior Design M
International Business M,O
International Economics M
Japanese M,O
Kinesiology and Movement Studies M
Linguistics M
Management Information Systems M,O
Management of Technology D
Marketing M,O
Mathematics Education M
Mathematics M
Middle School Education M
Molecular Biology M
Multilingual and Multicultural Education M,D,O
Music Education M
Music M
Nonprofit Management M,O
Nursing and Healthcare Administration M,O
Nursing Education M,O
Nutrition M
Occupational Therapy M
Organizational Management M,O
Physical Education M
Physics M
Physiology M
Polymer Science and Engineering M
Psychology—General M,D
Public Administration M,O
Public Policy M,O
Quality Management M,O
Reading Education M
Science Education M
Secondary Education M
Social Psychology M,O
Social Sciences M,O
Social Work M
Sociology M
Spanish M,O
Special Education M,O
Sports Management M
Supply Chain Management M,O
Technical Communication M,O
Technology and Public Policy M
Theater M
Travel and Tourism M,O
Urban and Regional Planning M,O
Vocational and Technical Education M
Water Resources M,O
Women's Studies M,O
Writing M,O

EASTERN NAZARENE COLLEGE

Business Administration and Management—General M
Counseling Psychology M
Early Childhood Education M,O
Education—General M,O
Educational Leadership and Administration M,O
Elementary Education M,O
English as a Second Language M,O
Marriage and Family Therapy M
Middle School Education M,O
Reading Education M,O
Secondary Education M,O
Special Education M,O

EASTERN NEW MEXICO UNIVERSITY

Analytical Chemistry M
Anthropology M
Biochemistry M
Biological and Biomedical Sciences—General M
Business Administration and Management—General M
Cell Biology M
Chemistry M
Communication Disorders M
Communication—General M
Counselor Education M
Curriculum and Instruction M
Early Childhood Education M
Ecology M
Education—General M
Educational Leadership and Administration M
Educational Media/Instructional Technology M
Elementary Education M
English as a Second Language M
English M
Exercise and Sports Science M
Human Services M
Inorganic Chemistry M
Mathematics M
Microbiology M
Molecular Biology M
Multilingual and Multicultural Education M
Organic Chemistry M
Physical Chemistry M
Physical Education M
Plant Biology M
Reading Education M
Science Education M
Secondary Education M
Special Education M
Sports Management M
Vocational and Technical Education M
Zoology M

EASTERN OREGON UNIVERSITY

Business Administration and Management—General M
Education—General M
Elementary Education M
Secondary Education M

EASTERN UNIVERSITY

Business Administration and Management—General M
Counseling Psychology M,O
Counselor Education M,O
Economic Development M
Education—General M,O
Health Education M
Health Services Management and Hospital Administration M
International Development M
Marriage and Family Therapy D
Missions and Missiology D
Multilingual and Multicultural Education M
Nonprofit Management M
Organizational Management M,D
Pastoral Ministry and Counseling D
School Nursing M,O
School Psychology M,O
Social Psychology M,O
Theology P,M,D
Urban and Regional Planning M
Urban Studies M

EASTERN VIRGINIA MEDICAL SCHOOL

Allopathic Medicine P
Art Therapy M
Biological and Biomedical Sciences—General M,D
Clinical Psychology D
Medical/Surgical Nursing O
Physician Assistant Studies M
Public Health—General M
Reproductive Biology M
Vision Sciences O

EASTERN WASHINGTON UNIVERSITY

Adult Education M
Applied Psychology M
Biological and Biomedical Sciences—General M
Business Administration and Management—General M
Clinical Psychology M
Communication Disorders M
Communication—General M
Computer Education M
Computer Science M
Counseling Psychology M
Counselor Education M
Curriculum and Instruction M
Dental Hygiene M
Early Childhood Education M
Education—General M
Educational Leadership and Administration M
Educational Media/Instructional Technology M
Elementary Education M
English as a Second Language M
English M
Exercise and Sports Science M
Experimental Psychology M
Foreign Languages Education M
Foundations and Philosophy of Education M
History M
Interdisciplinary Studies M
Mathematics Education M
Mathematics M
Music Education M
Music M
Occupational Therapy M
Physical Education M
Physical Therapy D
Psychology—General M
Public Administration M
Reading Education M
Rhetoric M
School Psychology M
Social Work M
Special Education M
Sport Psychology M

Sports Management M
Technical Communication M
Urban and Regional Planning M
Writing M

EAST STROUDSBURG UNIVERSITY OF PENNSYLVANIA

Biological and Biomedical Sciences—General M
Communication Disorders M
Community Health M
Computer Science M
Education—General M
Educational Media/Instructional Technology M
Elementary Education M
Exercise and Sports Science M
Health Education M
History M
Hospitality Management M
Physical Education M
Political Science M
Public Health—General M
Reading Education M
Rehabilitation Sciences M
Science Education M
Secondary Education M
Social Sciences Education M
Special Education M
Sports Management M
Travel and Tourism M

EAST TENNESSEE STATE UNIVERSITY

Accounting M
Acute Care/Critical Care Nursing M,D,O
Adult Nursing M,D,O
Allied Health—General M,D,O
Allopathic Medicine P
Anatomy D
Archives/Archival Administration M,O
Art/Fine Arts M
Athletic Training and Sports Medicine M,D
Biochemistry D
Biological and Biomedical Sciences—General M,D
Biostatistics M,D,O
Business Administration and Management—General M,O
Chemistry M
Clinical Psychology M,D
Communication Disorders M,D
Communication—General M
Community Health M,D,O
Computer Art and Design M,O
Computer Science M
Counselor Education M,D
Criminal Justice and Criminology M,O
Curriculum and Instruction M
Early Childhood Education M,D
Economics M,O
Education—General M,D,O
Educational Leadership and Administration M,D,O
Educational Media/Instructional Technology M
Elementary Education M,D
English M,O
Entrepreneurship M,O
Environmental and Occupational Health M,D,O
Epidemiology M,D,O
Exercise and Sports Science M,D
Family Nurse Practitioner Studies M,D,O
Finance and Banking M,O
Gerontological Nursing M,D,O
Gerontology M,D,O
Health Promotion M,D
Health Services Management and Hospital Administration M,D,O
History M
Human Development M,D
Information Science M
Liberal Studies M,O
Management Information Systems M
Management Strategy and Policy M,O
Manufacturing Engineering M,O
Marriage and Family Therapy M,D
Mathematics M
Microbiology M,D
Nonprofit Management M,O
Nursing and Healthcare Administration M,D,O
Nursing Education M,D,O
Nursing Informatics M,D,O
Nursing—General M,D,O
Nutrition M
Osteopathic Medicine M,D,O
Paleontology M
Pharmacology D
Pharmacy P
Physical Education M,D
Physical Therapy D
Physiology D
Political Science M
Psychiatric Nursing M,D,O
Psychology—General M,D
Public Health—General M,D,O
Reading Education M
Secondary Education M,D
Social Work M
Sociology M
Special Education M,D
Sports Management M,D
Urban and Regional Planning M,O
Urban Studies M,O

EAST WEST COLLEGE OF NATURAL MEDICINE

Acupuncture and Oriental Medicine M

ECOLE HÔTELIÈRE DE LAUSANNE

Hospitality Management M

ÉCOLE POLYTECHNIQUE DE MONTRÉAL

Aerospace/Aeronautical Engineering M,D,O
Applied Mathematics M,D,O
Biomedical Engineering M,D,O
Chemical Engineering M,D,O
Civil Engineering M,D,O
Computer Engineering M,D,O
Computer Science M,D,O
Electrical Engineering M,D,O
Engineering and Applied Sciences—General M,D,O
Engineering Physics M,D,O
Environmental Engineering M,D,O
Geotechnical Engineering M,D,O
Hydraulics M,D,O
Industrial/Management Engineering M,D,O
Management of Technology M,D,O
Mechanical Engineering M,D,O
Mechanics M,D,O
Nuclear Engineering M,D,O
Operations Research M,D,O
Optical Sciences M,D,O
Structural Engineering M,D,O
Transportation and Highway Engineering M,D,O

ECUMENICAL THEOLOGICAL SEMINARY

Pastoral Ministry and Counseling D
Theology P

EDEN THEOLOGICAL SEMINARY

Theology P,M,D

EDGEWOOD COLLEGE

Accounting M
Business Administration and Management—General M
Education—General M,D,O
Educational Leadership and Administration M,D,O
Marriage and Family Therapy M
Nursing—General M
Religion M
Special Education M,D,O

EDINBORO UNIVERSITY OF PENNSYLVANIA

Art/Fine Arts M
Biological and Biomedical Sciences—General M
Communication Disorders M
Communication—General M,O
Conflict Resolution and Mediation/Peace Studies M,O
Counselor Education M,O
Early Childhood Education M,O
Education—General M,O
Educational Leadership and Administration M,O
Educational Psychology M,O
Elementary Education M,O
Middle School Education M
Music M,O
Nursing Education M,O
Nursing—General M,O
Reading Education M,O
Rehabilitation Counseling M,O
School Psychology M,O
Secondary Education M
Social Sciences M
Social Work M
Special Education M,O

EDWARD VIA VIRGINIA COLLEGE OF OSTEOPATHIC MEDICINE

Osteopathic Medicine P

ELIZABETH CITY STATE UNIVERSITY

Biological and Biomedical Sciences—General M
Education—General M
Educational Leadership and Administration M
Elementary Education M
Mathematics M

ELIZABETHTOWN COLLEGE

Occupational Therapy M

ELLIS UNIVERSITY

Accounting M
Business Administration and Management—General M
Early Childhood Education M
Education—General M
Educational Leadership and Administration M
Educational Media/Instructional Technology M
Electronic Commerce M
Finance and Banking M
Health Services Management and Hospital Administration M
International Business M
Management Information Systems M
Marketing M
Project Management M

ELMHURST COLLEGE

Accounting M
Business Administration and Management—General M
Computer Science M
Educational Leadership and Administration M
English M
Industrial and Organizational Psychology M
Nursing—General M
Special Education M
Supply Chain Management M

ELMS COLLEGE

Communication Disorders M,O
Early Childhood Education M,O
Education—General M,O
Elementary Education M,O
English as a Second Language M,O
English Education M,O
Foreign Languages Education M,O
Nursing and Healthcare Administration M
Nursing Education M
Nursing—General M
Reading Education M,O
Religion M
Science Education M,O
Secondary Education M,O
Special Education M,O

ELON UNIVERSITY

Business Administration and Management—General M
Education of the Gifted M
Education—General M
Elementary Education M
Internet and Interactive Multimedia M
Law P
Physical Therapy D
Special Education M

EMBRY-RIDDLE AERONAUTICAL UNIVERSITY–DAYTONA

Aerospace/Aeronautical Engineering M
Aviation Management M*
Business Administration and Management—General M
Computer Engineering M
Electrical Engineering M
Engineering Physics D
Ergonomics and Human Factors M
Interdisciplinary Studies M
Mechanical Engineering M
Software Engineering M
Systems Engineering M

EMBRY-RIDDLE AERONAUTICAL UNIVERSITY–PRESCOTT

Safety Engineering M

EMBRY-RIDDLE AERONAUTICAL UNIVERSITY–WORLDWIDE

Aerospace/Aeronautical Engineering M
Aviation Management M,O

*M—master's degree; P—first professional degree; D—doctorate; O—other advanced degree; *—Close-Up and/or Display in one of the other books in this series*

Aviation	D
Business Administration and Management—General	M
Education—General	M
Logistics	M
Management of Technology	M
Project Management	M
Supply Chain Management	M

EMERSON COLLEGE

Advertising and Public Relations	M
Broadcast Journalism	M
Communication Disorders	M
Communication—General	M
Corporate and Organizational Communication	M
Health Communication	M
International Business	M
Journalism	M
Marketing	M
Media Studies	M
Publishing	M
Theater	M
Writing	M

EMILY CARR UNIVERSITY OF ART + DESIGN

Applied Arts and Design—General	M
Art/Fine Arts	M
Computer Art and Design	M

EMMANUEL CHRISTIAN SEMINARY

Missions and Missiology	P,M,D
Pastoral Ministry and Counseling	P,M,D
Religion	P,M,D
Religious Education	P,M,D
Theology	P,M,D

EMMANUEL COLLEGE (UNITED STATES)

Business Administration and Management—General	M,O
Education—General	M,O
Educational Leadership and Administration	M,O
Elementary Education	M,O
Human Resources Management	M,O
Pharmaceutical Administration	M,O
Secondary Education	M,O

EMORY & HENRY COLLEGE

American Studies	M
Education—General	M
History	M
Organizational Management	M
Reading Education	M

EMORY UNIVERSITY

Accounting	D
Acute Care/Critical Care Nursing	M
Adult Nursing	M
Allied Health—General	M,D
Allopathic Medicine	P
Anesthesiologist Assistant Studies	M
Animal Behavior	D
Anthropology	D
Art History	D
Biochemistry	D
Biological and Biomedical Sciences—General	D
Biophysics	D
Biostatistics	M,D
Business Administration and Management—General	M,D
Cancer Biology/Oncology	D
Cell Biology	D
Chemistry	D
Clinical Psychology	D
Clinical Research	M
Cognitive Sciences	D
Comparative Literature	D,O
Computer Science	M,D
Condensed Matter Physics	D
Demography and Population Studies	M
Developmental Biology	D
Developmental Psychology	D
Ecology	D
Economics	D
Education—General	M,D,O
English	D,O
Environmental and Occupational Health	M
Epidemiology	M,D
Ethics	P,M,D
Evolutionary Biology	D
Family Nurse Practitioner Studies	M
Film, Television, and Video Theory and Criticism	M,D,O
Finance and Banking	D
French	D,O
Genetics	D
Gerontological Nursing	M
Gerontology	M
Health Education	M
Health Informatics	M,D
Health Physics/Radiological Health	D
Health Promotion	M
Health Services Management and Hospital Administration	M,D
Health Services Research	M,D
History	D
Immunology	D
Interdisciplinary Studies	D
International Health	M
Jewish Studies	M
Law	P,M,O
Management Information Systems	D
Marketing	D
Mathematics	M,D
Microbiology	D
Middle School Education	M,D,O
Molecular Biology	D
Molecular Genetics	D
Molecular Pathogenesis	D
Music	M
Near and Middle Eastern Studies	D,O
Neuroscience	D
Nurse Midwifery	M
Nursing and Healthcare Administration	M
Nursing—General	M,D*
Nutrition	M,D
Organizational Management	D
Pastoral Ministry and Counseling	P,M,D
Pediatric Nursing	M
Pharmacology	D
Philosophy	D,O
Physical Therapy	D
Physician Assistant Studies	M
Physics	D
Political Science	D
Portuguese	D,O
Psychology—General	D
Public Health—General	M,D,O
Religion	D,O
Secondary Education	M,D,O
Sociology	M,D
Spanish	D,O
Sustainable Development	M
Theology	P,M,D
Women's Health Nursing	M
Women's Studies	D,O

EMPEROR'S COLLEGE OF TRADITIONAL ORIENTAL MEDICINE

Acupuncture and Oriental Medicine	M,D

EMPORIA STATE UNIVERSITY

Archives/Archival Administration	M,D,O
Art Therapy	M
Biological and Biomedical Sciences—General	M
Botany	M
Business Administration and Management—General	M
Business Education	M
Cell Biology	M
Clinical Psychology	M
Counseling Psychology	M
Counselor Education	M
Curriculum and Instruction	M
Early Childhood Education	M
Education of the Gifted	M
Education—General	M,O
Educational Leadership and Administration	M
Educational Media/Instructional Technology	M
Elementary Education	M
English as a Second Language	M
English	M
Environmental Biology	M
Geosciences	M,O
History	M
Industrial and Organizational Psychology	M
Information Studies	M,D,O
Library Science	M,D,O
Mathematics	M
Microbiology	M
Music Education	M
Music	M
Physical Education	M
Psychology—General	M
Reading Education	M
Rehabilitation Counseling	M
School Psychology	M,O
Secondary Education	M
Social Sciences Education	M
Special Education	M
Zoology	M

ENDICOTT COLLEGE

Art Education	M
Business Administration and Management—General	M
Distance Education Development	M
Early Childhood Education	M
Elementary Education	M
Hospitality Management	M
Interior Design	M
Management Information Systems	M
Nursing—General	M
Organizational Management	M
Reading Education	M
Special Education	M
Sports Management	M

EPISCOPAL DIVINITY SCHOOL

Theology	P,M,D,O

ERIKSON INSTITUTE

Child Development	M
Developmental Psychology	M,O
Early Childhood Education	M
English as a Second Language	M,O
Human Development	M,O

ERSKINE THEOLOGICAL SEMINARY

Theology	P,M,D

EVANGELICAL SEMINARY OF PUERTO RICO

Theology	P,M,D

EVANGELICAL THEOLOGICAL SEMINARY

Marriage and Family Therapy	P,M
Missions and Missiology	P,M
Pastoral Ministry and Counseling	P,M
Theology	P,M

EVANGEL UNIVERSITY

Clinical Psychology	M
Counseling Psychology	M
Counselor Education	M
Education—General	M
Educational Leadership and Administration	M
Organizational Management	M
Psychology—General	M
Reading Education	M
School Psychology	M
Secondary Education	M

EVEREST UNIVERSITY

Accounting	M
Business Administration and Management—General	M
Human Resources Management	M
International Business	M

EVEREST UNIVERSITY

Business Administration and Management—General	M
Criminal Justice and Criminology	M

EVEREST UNIVERSITY

Business Administration and Management—General	M

EVEREST UNIVERSITY

Accounting	M
Business Administration and Management—General	M
Human Resources Management	M
International Business	M

EVEREST UNIVERSITY

Business Administration and Management—General	M
Criminal Justice and Criminology	M

EVEREST UNIVERSITY

Criminal Justice and Criminology	M

EVEREST UNIVERSITY

Business Administration and Management—General	M

EVEREST UNIVERSITY

Business Administration and Management—General M
Criminal Justice and Criminology M

EVERGLADES UNIVERSITY

Aviation M
Business Administration and Management—General M
Information Science M

THE EVERGREEN STATE COLLEGE

Education—General M
Environmental Management and Policy M
Public Administration M

EXCELSIOR COLLEGE

Business Administration and Management—General M
Liberal Studies M
Medical Informatics O
Nursing and Healthcare Administration O
Nursing—General M

FACULTAD DE DERECHO EUGENIO MARÍA DE HOSTOS

Law P

FAIRFIELD UNIVERSITY

Accounting M,O
American Studies M
Applied Psychology M,O
Business Administration and Management—General M,O
Child and Family Studies M
Clinical Psychology M,O
Communication—General M
Computer Engineering M
Counseling Psychology M,O
Counselor Education M,O
Education—General M,O
Educational Media/Instructional Technology M,O
Electrical Engineering M
Elementary Education M,O
Engineering and Applied Sciences—General M
English as a Second Language M,O
Entrepreneurship M,O
Family Nurse Practitioner Studies M,D
Finance and Banking M,O
Foundations and Philosophy of Education M,O
Health Services Management and Hospital Administration M,D
Human Resources Management M,O
Human Services M,O
Industrial and Organizational Psychology M,O
International Business M,O
Management Information Systems M,O
Management of Technology M
Marketing M,O
Marriage and Family Therapy M
Mathematics M
Mechanical Engineering M
Multilingual and Multicultural Education M,O
Nurse Anesthesia M,D
Nursing and Healthcare Administration M,D
Nursing—General M,D
Psychiatric Nursing M,D
School Psychology M,O
Secondary Education M,O
Software Engineering M
Special Education M,O
Taxation M,O
Writing M

FAIRLEIGH DICKINSON UNIVERSITY, COLLEGE AT FLORHAM

Accounting M
Biological and Biomedical Sciences—General M
Business Administration and Management—General M,O
Chemical Engineering M,O
Chemistry M
Clinical Psychology M
Computer Science M
Corporate and Organizational Communication M
Counseling Psychology M
Education—General M,O
Educational Leadership and Administration M
Educational Media/Instructional Technology M,O
Entrepreneurship M,O
Finance and Banking M,O
Health Services Management and Hospital Administration M
Hospitality Management M
Human Resources Management M
Industrial and Organizational Psychology M
International Business M,O
Management of Technology M,O
Marketing M,O
Organizational Behavior M,O
Organizational Management M,O
Pharmacology M,O
Psychology—General M,O
Public Administration M
Reading Education M,O
Sports Management M
Sustainability Management O
Taxation M,O
Writing M

FAIRLEIGH DICKINSON UNIVERSITY, METROPOLITAN CAMPUS

Accounting M,O
Art/Fine Arts M
Biological and Biomedical Sciences—General M
Business Administration and Management—General M,O
Chemistry M
Clinical Laboratory Sciences/Medical Technology M
Clinical Psychology M,D
Communication—General M
Comparative Literature M
Computer Engineering M
Computer Science M
Criminal Justice and Criminology M
Curriculum and Instruction M
Education—General M,O
Educational Leadership and Administration M
Educational Media/Instructional Technology M,O
Electrical Engineering M
Electronic Commerce M
Engineering and Applied Sciences—General M
English M
Entrepreneurship M,O
Experimental Psychology M,O
Finance and Banking M,O
Forensic Psychology M
Foundations and Philosophy of Education M
Health Services Management and Hospital Administration M
History M
Homeland Security M
Hospitality Management M
Human Resources Management M,O
International Affairs M
International Business M
Management Information Systems M,O
Marketing M,O
Mathematics M
Media Studies M
Multilingual and Multicultural Education M
Nonprofit Management M,O
Nursing—General M,D,O
Pharmaceutical Administration M,O
Political Science M
Psychology—General M,D,O
Public Administration M,O
Reading Education M,O
School Psychology M,D
Science Education M
Special Education M
Sports Management M
Systems Science M
Taxation M

FAIRMONT STATE UNIVERSITY

Business Administration and Management—General M
Criminal Justice and Criminology M
Distance Education Development M
Education—General M
Educational Leadership and Administration M
Human Services M
Nursing and Healthcare Administration M
Nursing Education M
Nursing—General M
Reading Education M
Special Education M

FAITH BAPTIST BIBLE COLLEGE AND THEOLOGICAL SEMINARY

Pastoral Ministry and Counseling P,M
Religion P,M
Theology P,M

FAITH EVANGELICAL LUTHERAN SEMINARY

Theology P,M,D

FAITH THEOLOGICAL SEMINARY

Theology P,D

FASHION INSTITUTE OF TECHNOLOGY

Applied Arts and Design—General M*
Art History M
Arts Administration M*
Business Administration and Management—General M*
Clothing and Textiles M
Illustration M*
Interior Design M*
Marketing M*
Museum Studies M*
Sustainable Development M

FAULKNER UNIVERSITY

Business Administration and Management—General M
Counselor Education M
Criminal Justice and Criminology M
Education—General M
History M
Law P
Liberal Studies M
Missions and Missiology M
Pastoral Ministry and Counseling M
Theology M

FAYETTEVILLE STATE UNIVERSITY

Biological and Biomedical Sciences—General M
Business Administration and Management—General M
Criminal Justice and Criminology M
Educational Leadership and Administration M,D
Elementary Education M
English M
History M
Mathematics M
Middle School Education M
Political Science M
Psychology—General M
Reading Education M
Secondary Education M
Social Sciences Education M
Social Work M
Sociology M

FELICIAN COLLEGE

Adult Nursing M,O
Business Administration and Management—General M*
Counseling Psychology M*
Education—General M,O*
Educational Leadership and Administration M,O
Entrepreneurship M
Family Nurse Practitioner Studies M,O
Health Services Management and Hospital Administration M
Nursing Education M,O
Nursing—General M,D,O*
Religious Education M,O
School Nursing M,O

FERRIS STATE UNIVERSITY

Allied Health—General M
Applied Arts and Design—General M
Art/Fine Arts M
Business Administration and Management—General M
Community College Education D
Computer Science M
Criminal Justice and Criminology M
Curriculum and Instruction M
Database Systems M
Developmental Education M
Education—General M

*M—master's degree; P—first professional degree; D—doctorate; O—other advanced degree; *—Close-Up and/or Display in one of the other books in this series*

Educational Leadership and Administration M,D
Educational Media/ Instructional Technology M
Electronic Commerce M
Elementary Education M
Human Services M
Management Information Systems M
Nursing and Healthcare Administration M
Nursing Education M
Nursing Informatics M
Nursing—General M
Optometry P
Pharmacy P
Quality Management M
Reading Education M
Special Education M

FIELDING GRADUATE UNIVERSITY

Clinical Psychology M,D,O
Educational Leadership and Administration M,D,O
Educational Media/ Instructional Technology M,D,O
Human Development M,D,O
Organizational Management M,D,O
Psychology—General M,D,O

FISK UNIVERSITY

Biological and Biomedical Sciences—General M
Chemistry M
Clinical Psychology M
Physics M
Psychology—General M

FITCHBURG STATE UNIVERSITY

Accounting M
Art Education M,O
Biological and Biomedical Sciences—General M,O
Business Administration and Management—General M
Communication—General M,O
Computer Science M
Counseling Psychology M
Counselor Education M
Curriculum and Instruction M
Early Childhood Education M
Educational Leadership and Administration M,O
Educational Media/ Instructional Technology M,O
Elementary Education M
English Education M,O
English M,O
Forensic Nursing M,O
Health Communication M,O
Higher Education M,O
History M,O
Human Resources Management M
Interdisciplinary Studies O
Middle School Education M
Science Education M,O
Secondary Education M
Social Sciences Education M,O
Special Education M
Technical Writing M,O
Vocational and Technical Education M

FIVE BRANCHES UNIVERSITY: GRADUATE SCHOOL OF TRADITIONAL CHINESE MEDICINE

Acupuncture and Oriental Medicine M

FIVE TOWNS COLLEGE

Music Education M,D
Music M,D

FLORIDA AGRICULTURAL AND MECHANICAL UNIVERSITY

Accounting M
Adult Education M,D
African-American Studies M
Agricultural Economics and Agribusiness M
Agricultural Sciences—General M
Allied Health—General M
Animal Sciences M
Architecture M
Biological and Biomedical Sciences—General M
Biomedical Engineering M,D
Business Administration and Management—General M
Business Education M
Chemical Engineering M,D
Chemistry M
Civil Engineering M,D
Counselor Education M,D
Criminal Justice and Criminology M
Early Childhood Education M
Economics M
Education—General M,D
Educational Leadership and Administration M,D
Electrical Engineering M,D
Elementary Education M
Engineering and Applied Sciences—General M,D
English Education M
Entomology M
Environmental Engineering M,D
Environmental Sciences M,D
Finance and Banking M
Food Science and Technology M
Health Education M
History M
Industrial/Management Engineering M,D
International Affairs M
Journalism M
Landscape Architecture M
Law P
Management Information Systems M
Marketing M
Mathematics Education M
Mechanical Engineering M,D
Medicinal and Pharmaceutical Chemistry M,D
Nursing and Healthcare Administration M
Nursing—General M
Occupational Therapy M
Pharmaceutical Administration M,D
Pharmaceutical Sciences M,D
Pharmacology M,D
Pharmacy P,D
Physical Education M
Physical Therapy M
Physics M,D
Plant Sciences M
Political Science M
Psychology—General M
Public Administration M
Public Health—General M
Recreation and Park Management M
School Psychology M
Science Education M
Secondary Education M
Social Psychology M
Social Sciences Education M
Social Sciences M
Social Work M
Sociology M
Software Engineering M
Toxicology M,D
Vocational and Technical Education M

FLORIDA ATLANTIC UNIVERSITY

Accounting M,D
Adult Education M,D,O
Anthropology M
Applied Arts and Design—General M
Applied Mathematics M,D
Art Education M
Art/Fine Arts M
Biological and Biomedical Sciences—General M,D
Business Administration and Management—General M,D,O
Chemistry M,D
Civil Engineering M
Communication Disorders M
Communication—General M,O
Comparative and Interdisciplinary Arts D
Comparative Literature M
Computer Art and Design M
Computer Engineering M,D
Computer Science M,D
Counseling Psychology M,D,O
Counselor Education M,D,O
Criminal Justice and Criminology M
Curriculum and Instruction M,D,O
Early Childhood Education M,D,O
Economic Development M,O
Economics M
Education—General M,D,O
Educational Leadership and Administration M,D,O
Electrical Engineering M,D
Elementary Education M
Engineering and Applied Sciences—General M,D
English as a Second Language M,D,O
English Education M
English M
Entrepreneurship M,D
Environmental Design M,O
Environmental Education M
Environmental Management and Policy M,O
Environmental Sciences M
Exercise and Sports Science M
Film, Television, and Video Production M,O
Film, Television, and Video Theory and Criticism M,O
Finance and Banking M,D
Foundations and Philosophy of Education M
French M
Geography M,D
Geology M,D
Geosciences M,D
Graphic Design M
Health Promotion M
Higher Education M,D,O
History M,O
International Business M,D
Journalism M,O
Liberal Studies M
Linguistics M
Management Information Systems M
Marriage and Family Therapy M,D,O
Mathematics M,D
Mechanical Engineering M,D
Multilingual and Multicultural Education M,D,O
Music M
Neuroscience D
Nonprofit Management M
Nursing—General M,D,O
Ocean Engineering M,D
Physics M,D
Political Science M
Psychology—General M,D
Public Administration M,D
Reading Education M
Rehabilitation Counseling M,D,O
Social Work M
Sociology M
Spanish M
Special Education M,D
Statistics M,D
Sustainable Development M,O
Taxation M
Theater M
Travel and Tourism M,O
Urban and Regional Planning M,O
Women's Studies M,O
Writing M

FLORIDA COASTAL SCHOOL OF LAW

Law P

FLORIDA COLLEGE OF INTEGRATIVE MEDICINE

Acupuncture and Oriental Medicine M

FLORIDA GULF COAST UNIVERSITY

Accounting M
Allied Health—General M,D
Business Administration and Management—General M
Computer Science M
Counselor Education M
Criminal Justice and Criminology M
Curriculum and Instruction M
Early Childhood Education M
Education—General M
Educational Leadership and Administration M
Educational Media/ Instructional Technology M
Elementary Education M
English Education M
English M
Environmental Management and Policy M
Environmental Sciences M
Forensic Sciences M
History M
Information Science M
Interdisciplinary Studies M
Nursing—General M
Occupational Therapy M
Physical Therapy M,D
Public Administration M
Reading Education M
Social Work M
Special Education M
Taxation M

FLORIDA HOSPITAL COLLEGE OF HEALTH SCIENCES

Nurse Anesthesia M

FLORIDA INSTITUTE OF TECHNOLOGY

Accounting M
Aerospace/Aeronautical Engineering M,D
Applied Behavior Analysis M,D
Applied Mathematics M,D
Biochemistry M,D
Biological and Biomedical Sciences—General M,D
Biotechnology M,D
Business Administration and Management—General M

Cell Biology	M
Chemical Engineering	M,D
Chemistry	M,D
Civil Engineering	M,D
Clinical Psychology	M,D
Communication—General	M
Computer Education	M,D,O
Computer Engineering	M,D
Computer Science	M,D
Corporate and Organizational Communication	M
Ecology	M
Electrical Engineering	M,D
Electronic Commerce	M
Elementary Education	M,D,O
Emergency Management	M
Engineering and Applied Sciences—General	M,D
Engineering Management	M,D
Environmental Education	M,D,O
Environmental Management and Policy	M,D
Environmental Sciences	M,D
Ergonomics and Human Factors	M
Finance and Banking	M
Health Services Management and Hospital Administration	M
Human Resources Management	M
Industrial and Organizational Psychology	M,D
Interdisciplinary Studies	M,D
Logistics	M
Management Information Systems	M
Management of Technology	M
Marine Biology	M
Marketing	M
Mathematics Education	M,D,O
Mechanical Engineering	M,D
Meteorology	M,D
Molecular Biology	M
Ocean Engineering	M,D
Oceanography	M,D
Operations Research	M,D
Organizational Behavior	M,D
Physics	M,D
Planetary and Space Sciences	M,D
Project Management	M
Psychology—General	M,D
Public Administration	M
Quality Management	M
Science Education	M,D,O
Software Engineering	M,D
Supply Chain Management	M
Systems Engineering	M,D
Technical Communication	M
Transportation Management	M

FLORIDA INTERNATIONAL UNIVERSITY

Accounting	M
Adult Education	M,D,O
African Studies	M
Allopathic Medicine	P
Architecture	M
Art Education	M,D,O
Art/Fine Arts	M
Asian Studies	M
Athletic Training and Sports Medicine	M
Biological and Biomedical Sciences—General	M,D
Biomedical Engineering	M,D
Biostatistics	M,D
Business Administration and Management—General	M,D
Chemistry	M,D
Civil Engineering	M,D
Clinical Psychology	M,D,O
Communication Disorders	M
Computer Engineering	M
Computer Science	M,D
Conflict Resolution and Mediation/Peace Studies	M,D,O
Construction Management	M
Counseling Psychology	M,D,O
Counselor Education	M,D,O
Criminal Justice and Criminology	M
Curriculum and Instruction	M,D,O
Early Childhood Education	M,D,O
Economics	M,D
Education—General	M,D,O
Educational Leadership and Administration	M,D,O
Educational Media/Instructional Technology	M,D,O
Electrical Engineering	M,D
Elementary Education	M,D,O
Engineering and Applied Sciences—General	M,D*
English as a Second Language	M,D,O
English Education	M,D,O
English	M
Environmental and Occupational Health	M,D
Environmental Engineering	M
Environmental Management and Policy	M
Environmental Sciences	M
Epidemiology	M,D
Finance and Banking	M
Foreign Languages Education	M,D,O
Forensic Sciences	M
Geosciences	M,D
Health Promotion	M,D
Health Services Management and Hospital Administration	M,D
Higher Education	M,D,O
History	M,D
Hospitality Management	M
Human Resources Development	M,D,O
Human Resources Management	M
Information Science	M,D
Interior Design	M
International Affairs	M,D
International and Comparative Education	M,D,O
International Business	M
Landscape Architecture	M
Latin American Studies	M
Law	P
Liberal Studies	M
Linguistics	M
Management Information Systems	M
Mass Communication	M
Materials Engineering	M,D
Materials Sciences	M,D
Mathematics Education	M,D,O
Mathematics	M
Mechanical Engineering	M,D
Multilingual and Multicultural Education	M,D,O
Music Education	M
Music	M
Nursing—General	M,D
Nutrition	M,D
Occupational Therapy	M
Physical Education	M,D,O
Physical Therapy	D
Physics	M,D
Political Science	M,D
Psychology—General	M,D
Public Administration	M,D
Public Health—General	M,D
Reading Education	M,D,O
Real Estate	M
Recreation and Park Management	M,D,O
Rehabilitation Counseling	M,D,O
Religion	M
School Psychology	M,D,O
Science Education	M,D,O
Social Sciences Education	M,D,O
Social Work	M,D
Sociology	M,D
Spanish	M,D
Special Education	M,D,O
Sports Management	M,D,O
Statistics	M
Taxation	M
Telecommunications	M,D
Urban Education	M,D,O
Writing	M

FLORIDA MEMORIAL UNIVERSITY

Business Administration and Management—General	M
Education—General	M
Elementary Education	M
Reading Education	M
Special Education	M

FLORIDA SOUTHERN COLLEGE

Adult Nursing	M
Business Administration and Management—General	M*
Education—General	M
Family Nurse Practitioner Studies	M
Nursing Education	M
Nursing—General	M

FLORIDA STATE UNIVERSITY

Accounting	M,D
Analytical Chemistry	M,D
Applied Behavior Analysis	M
Applied Mathematics	M,D
Applied Statistics	M,D
Archaeology	M,D
Art Education	M,D,O
Art History	M,D,O
Art/Fine Arts	M
Arts Administration	M,D
Asian Studies	M
Biochemistry	M,D
Biological and Biomedical Sciences—General	M,D
Biomedical Engineering	M,D
Biostatistics	M,D
Business Administration and Management—General	M,D
Cell Biology	M,D
Chemical Engineering	M,D
Chemistry	M,D
Child and Family Studies	M,D
Civil Engineering	M,D
Classics	M,D
Clinical Psychology	D
Cognitive Sciences	D
Communication Disorders	M,D
Communication—General	M,D
Computational Biology	D
Computational Sciences	M,D
Computer and Information Systems Security	M,D
Computer Science	M,D
Corporate and Organizational Communication	M,D
Counseling Psychology	M,D,O
Counselor Education	M,D,O
Criminal Justice and Criminology	M,D
Dance	M
Demography and Population Studies	M
Developmental Psychology	D
Distance Education Development	M,D,O
Early Childhood Education	M,D,O
East European and Russian Studies	M
Ecology	M,D
Economics	M,D
Education—General	M,D,O
Educational Leadership and Administration	M,D,O
Educational Measurement and Evaluation	M,D,O
Educational Media/Instructional Technology	M,D,O
Educational Policy	M,D,O
Educational Psychology	M,D,O
Electrical Engineering	M,D
Elementary Education	M,D,O
Energy and Power Engineering	M,D
Engineering and Applied Sciences—General	M,D
English Education	M,D,O
English	M,D
Environmental Engineering	M,D
Environmental Law	P,M
Environmental Sciences	M,D
Evolutionary Biology	M,D
Exercise and Sports Science	M,D
Family and Consumer Sciences-General	M,D
Family Nurse Practitioner Studies	M,D,O
Film, Television, and Video Production	M
Finance and Banking	M,D
Food Science and Technology	M,D
Foundations and Philosophy of Education	M,D,O
French	M,D
Genetics	M,D
Geographic Information Systems	M,D
Geography	M,D
Geology	M,D
Geophysics	D
German	M
Health Education	M,D
Health Services Management and Hospital Administration	M,D,O
Higher Education	M,D,O
History	M,D
Human Resources Development	M,D,O
Industrial/Management Engineering	M,D
Information Studies	M,D,O
Inorganic Chemistry	M,D
Insurance	M,D
Interior Design	M
International Affairs	M
International and Comparative Education	M,D,O
Italian	M
Law	P,M
Library Science	M,D,O
Management Information Systems	M,D
Management Strategy and Policy	M,D
Manufacturing Engineering	M,D
Marine Sciences	M,D
Marketing	M,D
Marriage and Family Therapy	M,D
Mass Communication	M,D
Materials Sciences	M,D
Mathematical and Computational Finance	M,D
Mathematics Education	M,D,O
Mathematics	M,D
Mechanical Engineering	M,D
Media Studies	M,D
Meteorology	M,D
Molecular Biology	M,D
Molecular Biophysics	D
Museum Studies	M,D,O
Music Education	M,D
Music	M,D
Neuroscience	M,D
Nursing Education	M,D,O
Nursing—General	M,D,O
Nutrition	M,D

*M—master's degree; P—first professional degree; D—doctorate; O—other advanced degree; *—Close-Up and/or Display in one of the other books in this series*

Oceanography M,D
Organic Chemistry M,D
Organizational Behavior M,D
Philosophy M,D
Physical Chemistry M,D
Physical Education M,D
Physics M,D*
Plant Biology M,D
Political Science M,D
Polymer Science and Engineering M
Psychology—General M,D
Public Administration M,D,O
Public Health—General M
Public History M,D
Public Policy M,D,O
Reading Education M,D,O
Recreation and Park Management M,D
Rehabilitation Counseling M,D,O
Religion M,D
Rhetoric M,D
School Psychology M,O
Science Education M,D,O
Slavic Languages M
Social Psychology D
Social Sciences Education M
Social Work M,D
Sociology M,D
Spanish M,D
Special Education M,D,O
Speech and Interpersonal Communication M,D
Sport Psychology M,D,O
Sports Management M,D
Statistics M,D,O
Structural Biology M,D
Taxation M,D
Theater M,D
Therapies—Dance, Drama, and Music M,D
Urban and Regional Planning M,D
Writing M,D

FONTBONNE UNIVERSITY

Accounting M
Art/Fine Arts M
Business Administration and Management—General M
Communication Disorders M
Computer Education M
Education—General M
Family and Consumer Sciences-General M
Special Education M
Taxation M
Theater M

FORDHAM UNIVERSITY

Accounting M
Adult Education M,D,O
Applied Psychology D
Biological and Biomedical Sciences—General M,D
Business Administration and Management—General M
Classics M,D
Clinical Psychology D
Communication—General M
Computer Science M
Corporate and Organizational Communication M
Counseling Psychology M,D,O
Counselor Education M,D,O
Curriculum and Instruction M,D,O
Developmental Psychology D
Early Childhood Education M,D,O
Economic Development M,O
Economics M,D,O
Education—General M,D,O
Educational Leadership and Administration M,D,O
Educational Psychology M,D,O
Elementary Education M,D,O
Emergency Management M
English as a Second Language M,D,O
English M,D
Ethics M,O
Finance and Banking M
History M,D
Human Resources Management M,D,O
Intellectual Property Law P,M
International Affairs M,O
International Development M,O
International Economics M,O
Latin American Studies M,O
Law P,M
Liberal Studies M
Management Information Systems M
Marketing M
Mass Communication M
Media Studies M
Medieval and Renaissance Studies M,O
Multilingual and Multicultural Education M,D,O
Pastoral Ministry and Counseling M,D,O
Philosophy M,D
Political Science M
Psychology—General D
Reading Education M,D,O
Religion M,D,O
Religious Education M,D,O
School Psychology M,D,O
Secondary Education M,D,O
Social Work M,D
Sociology M
Special Education M,D,O
Taxation M
Theology M,D
Urban Studies M

FORT HAYS STATE UNIVERSITY

Art/Fine Arts M
Biological and Biomedical Sciences—General M
Business Administration and Management—General M
Communication Disorders M
Communication—General M
Counselor Education M
Education—General M,O
Educational Leadership and Administration M,O
Educational Media/ Instructional Technology M
English M
Geography M
Geology M
Geosciences M
Health Education M
History M
Liberal Studies M
Nursing—General M
Physical Education M
Psychology—General M,O
School Psychology O
Special Education M

FORT VALLEY STATE UNIVERSITY

Animal Sciences M
Counseling Psychology M
Counselor Education M,O
Environmental and Occupational Health M
Public Health—General M
Rehabilitation Counseling M

FRAMINGHAM STATE UNIVERSITY

Art/Fine Arts M
Business Administration and Management—General M
Curriculum and Instruction M
Early Childhood Education M
Educational Leadership and Administration M
Educational Media/ Instructional Technology M
Elementary Education M
English as a Second Language M
English Education M
Food Science and Technology M
Foreign Languages Education M
Health Education M
Health Services Management and Hospital Administration M
Human Resources Management M
Mathematics Education M
Nursing and Healthcare Administration M
Nursing Education M
Nursing—General M
Nutrition M
Psychology—General M
Public Administration M
Reading Education M
Social Sciences Education M
Spanish M
Special Education M

FRANCISCAN SCHOOL OF THEOLOGY

Theology P,M

FRANCISCAN UNIVERSITY OF STEUBENVILLE

Business Administration and Management—General M
Counseling Psychology M
Curriculum and Instruction M
Education—General M
Educational Leadership and Administration M
Nursing—General M
Philosophy M
Theology M

FRANCIS MARION UNIVERSITY

Applied Psychology M,O
Business Administration and Management—General M
Clinical Psychology M,O
Counseling Psychology M,O
Early Childhood Education M
Education—General M
Elementary Education M
Health Services Management and Hospital Administration M
Psychology—General M,O
School Psychology M,O
Secondary Education M
Special Education M

FRANKLIN PIERCE LAW CENTER

Law P,M,O

FRANKLIN PIERCE UNIVERSITY

Business Administration and Management—General M,D,O
Curriculum and Instruction M,D,O
Energy Management and Policy M,D,O
Health Services Management and Hospital Administration M,D,O
Human Resources Management M,D,O
Interdisciplinary Studies M,D,O
Management Information Systems M,D,O
Management Strategy and Policy M,D,O
Nursing—General M,D,O
Physical Therapy M,D,O
Physician Assistant Studies M,D,O
Special Education M,D,O
Sports Management M,D,O
Sustainability Management M,D,O
Telecommunications M,D,O

FRANKLIN UNIVERSITY

Business Administration and Management—General M
Computer Science M
Corporate and Organizational Communication M
Marketing M

FRANK LLOYD WRIGHT SCHOOL OF ARCHITECTURE

Architecture M

FREDERICK S. PARDEE RAND GRADUATE SCHOOL

Public Policy D

FREED-HARDEMAN UNIVERSITY

Accounting M
Business Administration and Management—General M
Counselor Education M,O
Curriculum and Instruction M,O
Education—General M,O
Educational Leadership and Administration M,O
Ethics M
Management Strategy and Policy M
Pastoral Ministry and Counseling M
Special Education M,O
Theology P,M

FRESNO PACIFIC UNIVERSITY

Business Administration and Management—General M
Conflict Resolution and Mediation/Peace Studies M
Counselor Education M
Curriculum and Instruction M
Education of Students with Severe/Multiple Disabilities M
Education—General M
Educational Leadership and Administration M
Educational Media/ Instructional Technology M
Elementary Education M
English as a Second Language M
Interdisciplinary Studies M
Kinesiology and Movement Studies M
Marriage and Family Therapy M,O
Mathematics Education M
Middle School Education M
Missions and Missiology M
Multilingual and Multicultural Education M
Pastoral Ministry and Counseling M
Reading Education M
School Psychology M
Science Education M
Secondary Education M
Special Education M

Student Affairs M
Theology P,M

FRIENDS UNIVERSITY

Accounting M
Business Administration and Management—General M
Education—General M
Health Services Management and Hospital Administration M
Human Resources Development M
Industrial and Manufacturing Management M
International Business M
Law M
Management Information Systems M
Marriage and Family Therapy M
Theology M

FRONTIER SCHOOL OF MIDWIFERY AND FAMILY NURSING

Family Nurse Practitioner Studies M,O
Nurse Midwifery M,O
Nursing—General M,O
Women's Health Nursing M,O

FROSTBURG STATE UNIVERSITY

Biological and Biomedical Sciences—General M
Business Administration and Management—General M
Computer Science M
Conservation Biology M
Counseling Psychology M
Counselor Education M
Curriculum and Instruction M
Ecology M
Education—General M
Educational Leadership and Administration M
Educational Media/Instructional Technology M
Elementary Education M
Fish, Game, and Wildlife Management M
Interdisciplinary Studies M
Psychology—General M
Reading Education M
Recreation and Park Management M
Secondary Education M
Special Education M

FULLER THEOLOGICAL SEMINARY

Clinical Psychology D
Marriage and Family Therapy M,O
Missions and Missiology P,M,D
Music P,M,D
Pastoral Ministry and Counseling P,M,D
Psychology—General M,D,O
Theology P,M,D

FULL SAIL UNIVERSITY

Art/Fine Arts M
Business Administration and Management—General M
Computer Art and Design M
Educational Media/Instructional Technology M
Entertainment Management M
Game Design and Development M
Graphic Design M
Internet and Interactive Multimedia M
Journalism M
Marketing M
Media Studies M
Writing M

FURMAN UNIVERSITY

Chemistry M
Curriculum and Instruction M,O
Early Childhood Education M,O
Education—General M,O
Educational Leadership and Administration M,O
English as a Second Language M,O
Reading Education M,O
Special Education M,O

FUTURE GENERATIONS GRADUATE SCHOOL

Maternal and Child Health M
Social Psychology M

GALLAUDET UNIVERSITY

Clinical Psychology M,D,O
Communication Disorders M,D,O
Counseling Psychology M,D,O
Counselor Education M,D,O
Early Childhood Education M,D,O
Education—General M,D,O
Educational Leadership and Administration M,D,O
Elementary Education M,D,O
International and Comparative Education M,D,O
Leisure Studies M,D,O
Linguistics M,D,O
School Psychology M,D,O
Secondary Education M,D,O
Social Work M,D,O
Special Education M,D,O
Translation and Interpretation M,D,O

GANNON UNIVERSITY

Accounting O
Business Administration and Management—General M,O
Computer Science M
Counseling Psychology D
Counselor Education M,O
Curriculum and Instruction M
Early Childhood Education M
Education—General M,D,O
Educational Leadership and Administration M,D,O
Educational Media/Instructional Technology M
Electrical Engineering M
Engineering Management M
English as a Second Language O
English M
Environmental and Occupational Health O
Environmental Education M
Environmental Engineering M
Environmental Sciences M,O
Family Nurse Practitioner Studies M,O
Finance and Banking O
Gerontology O
Human Resources Management O
Information Science M
Investment Management O
Marketing O
Mechanical Engineering M
Medical/Surgical Nursing M,O
Nurse Anesthesia M,O
Nursing and Healthcare Administration M,O
Nursing—General M,O
Occupational Therapy M
Organizational Management D
Pastoral Ministry and Counseling M,O
Physical Therapy D
Physician Assistant Studies M
Public Administration M,O
Reading Education M,O
Science Education M
Software Engineering M

GARDNER-WEBB UNIVERSITY

Business Administration and Management—General M
Counseling Psychology M
Curriculum and Instruction D
Education—General M,D
Educational Leadership and Administration M,D
Elementary Education M
English Education M
English M
Exercise and Sports Science M
Middle School Education M
Missions and Missiology P,D
Nursing—General M,D,O
Pastoral Ministry and Counseling P,D
Physical Education M
Psychology—General M
Religion M
Religious Education P,D
School Psychology M
Theology P,D

GARRETT-EVANGELICAL THEOLOGICAL SEMINARY

Music P,M,D
Pastoral Ministry and Counseling P,M,D
Religious Education P,M,D
Theology P,M,D

GENERAL THEOLOGICAL SEMINARY

Pastoral Ministry and Counseling P,M,D,O
Religion P,M,D,O
Theology P,M,D,O

GENEVA COLLEGE

Business Administration and Management—General M
Cardiovascular Sciences M
Counseling Psychology M
Counselor Education M
Education—General M
Educational Leadership and Administration M
Higher Education M
Marriage and Family Therapy M
Organizational Management M
Psychology—General M
Reading Education M
Special Education M

GEORGE FOX UNIVERSITY

Business Administration and Management—General M,D
Clinical Psychology M,D,O
Counseling Psychology M,O
Counselor Education M,O
Curriculum and Instruction M,D,O
Education—General M,D,O
Educational Leadership and Administration M,D,O
Educational Media/Instructional Technology M,D,O
English as a Second Language M
Finance and Banking M,D
Higher Education M,D,O
Human Resources Management M,D
Marketing M,D
Marriage and Family Therapy M,O
Missions and Missiology P,M,D,O
Multilingual and Multicultural Education M
Organizational Management M,D
Pastoral Ministry and Counseling P,M,D,O
Physical Therapy D
Reading Education M,D,O
Religious Education P,M,D,O
School Psychology M,O
Secondary Education M,D,O
Theology P,M,D,O

GEORGE MASON UNIVERSITY

Accounting M
Actuarial Science M,D,O
Advertising and Public Relations M,O
Anthropology M,D
Applied Physics M,D
Art Education M
Art History M
Arts Administration M,O
Atmospheric Sciences D
Biochemistry M,D
Bioinformatics M,D,O
Biological and Biomedical Sciences—General M,D,O
Biostatistics M,D,O
Business Administration and Management—General M
Chemistry M,D
Civil Engineering M,D,O
Cognitive Sciences M,D,O
Communication—General M,D
Community College Education D,O
Community Health M,O
Computational Biology M,D,O
Computational Sciences M,D,O
Computer and Information Systems Security M,D,O
Computer Engineering M,D,O
Computer Science M,D,O
Conflict Resolution and Mediation/Peace Studies M,D,O
Counselor Education M
Criminal Justice and Criminology M,D
Cultural Studies M,D,O
Curriculum and Instruction M
Dance M
Database Systems M,D,O
Economics M,D,O
Education—General M,D
Educational Leadership and Administration M
Educational Measurement and Evaluation M
Educational Psychology M
Electrical Engineering M,D,O
Electronic Commerce M,D,O
Emergency Management M,D,O
Engineering and Applied Sciences—General M,D,O
Engineering Physics M,D
English as a Second Language M,D,O
English M,D,O
Entrepreneurship M,O
Environmental Management and Policy M,D,O
Environmental Sciences M,D,O
Epidemiology M,O

*M—master's degree; P—first professional degree; D—doctorate; O—other advanced degree; *—Close-Up and/or Display in one of the other books in this series*

Ethics M,D,O
Evolutionary Biology M,D
Exercise and Sports Science M
Folklore M,D,O
Foreign Languages Education M
Forensic Nursing M,D,O
Forensic Sciences M,D,O
Game Design and Development M,D,O
Geographic Information Systems M,D,O
Geography M,D,O
Geosciences M,D,O
Gerontology M,O
Graphic Design M
Health Informatics M,O
Health Promotion M
Health Services Management and Hospital Administration M,D,O
Higher Education D,O
History M,D
Homeland Security M,D,O
Human Resources Management M
Infectious Diseases M,D
Information Science M,D,O
Interdisciplinary Studies M
International Affairs M
International Health M,O
Internet and Interactive Multimedia M,D,O
Law P,M
Linguistics M,D,O
Logistics M
Management Information Systems M,D,O
Management of Technology M,D
Mathematics M,D,O
Microbiology M,D
Modeling and Simulation M,D,O
Molecular Biology M,D
Music Education M,D,O
Music M,D,O
National Security M,D,O
Neuroscience M,D,O
Nonprofit Management M,D,O
Nursing and Healthcare Administration M,D,O
Nursing Education M,D,O
Nursing—General M,D,O
Nutrition M,O
Operations Research M,D,O
Organizational Management M
Philosophy M
Physics M,D
Political Science M,D,O
Psychology—General M,D,O
Public Administration M,D,O
Public Affairs M,D,O
Public Health—General M,O
Public Policy M,D
Real Estate M
Recreation and Park Management M
Rehabilitation Sciences M,O
Rural Planning and Studies M,O
School Psychology O
Social Work M
Sociology M,D
Software Engineering M,D,O
Special Education M
Sports Management M
Statistics M,D,O
Sustainable Development M,D,O
Systems Engineering M,D,O
Taxation M
Telecommunications Management M,D,O
Telecommunications M,D,O
Transportation Management M
Water Resources Engineering M,D,O
Writing M

GEORGETOWN COLLEGE

Education—General M
Reading Education M
Special Education M

GEORGETOWN UNIVERSITY

Acute Care/Critical Care Nursing M
Advertising and Public Relations M
Allopathic Medicine P
American Studies M,D
Analytical Chemistry D
Biochemistry M,D
Bioinformatics M
Biological and Biomedical Sciences—General M,D
Biophysics M,D
Biostatistics M
Business Administration and Management—General M
Cell Biology D
Chemistry D
Communication—General M
Community Health M,D
Comparative Literature M,D
Computer Science M
Conflict Resolution and Mediation/Peace Studies M
East European and Russian Studies M
Economic Development D
Economics D
English as a Second Language M,D,O
English M
Epidemiology M
Ethics M,D
Family Nurse Practitioner Studies M
Finance and Banking D
German M,D
Health Law P,M,D
Health Physics/Radiological Health M
Health Promotion M,D
History M,D
Human Resources Management M,D
Humanities M,D
Immunology M,D
Industrial and Labor Relations D
Industrial and Manufacturing Management D
Infectious Diseases M,D
Inorganic Chemistry D
Interdisciplinary Studies M,D
International Affairs P,M,D
International Business P,M,D
International Health P,M,D
Internet and Interactive Multimedia M
Journalism M,D
Latin American Studies M
Law P,M,D
Legal and Justice Studies P,M,D
Liberal Studies M,D
Linguistics M,D,O
Materials Sciences D
Mathematics M
Media Studies M,D
Medieval and Renaissance Studies M,D
Microbiology M,D
Molecular Biology M,D
Multilingual and Multicultural Education M,D,O
Near and Middle Eastern Languages M,D
Near and Middle Eastern Studies M,D,O
Neuroscience D
Nurse Anesthesia M
Nurse Midwifery M
Nursing Education M
Nursing—General M
Organic Chemistry D
Pathology M,D
Pharmacology M,D
Philosophy M,D
Physical Chemistry D
Physiology M,D
Political Science M,D
Psychology—General D
Public Health—General M,D
Public Policy M,D
Radiation Biology M
Real Estate M,D
Religion M,D
Spanish M,D
Sports Management M,D
Statistics M
Taxation P,M,D
Theology D
Theoretical Chemistry D
Western European Studies M

THE GEORGE WASHINGTON UNIVERSITY

Accounting M,D
Adult Nursing M,D,O
Aerospace/Aeronautical Engineering M,D,O
Allopathic Medicine P
American Studies M,D
Analytical Chemistry M,D
Anthropology M,D
Applied Mathematics M,D
Applied Psychology D
Art History M
Art Therapy M
Art/Fine Arts M
Asian Studies M
Biochemistry M,D
Bioinformatics M
Biological and Biomedical Sciences—General M,D
Biostatistics M,D
Biotechnology M
Business Administration and Management—General M,D,O
Chemistry M,D
Civil Engineering M,D,O
Clinical Psychology D
Cognitive Sciences D
Communication Disorders M
Communication—General M
Computer Engineering M,D
Computer Science M,D
Counselor Education M,D,O
Criminal Justice and Criminology M
Curriculum and Instruction M,D,O
Dance M
Early Childhood Education M
East European and Russian Studies M
Economics M,D
Education—General M,D,O
Educational Leadership and Administration M,D,O
Educational Media/Instructional Technology M
Educational Policy M,D
Electrical Engineering M,D
Elementary Education M
Emergency Management M,D,O
Engineering and Applied Sciences—General M,D,O
Engineering Management M,D,O
English M,D
Environmental and Occupational Health M
Environmental Engineering M,D,O
Environmental Management and Policy M
Epidemiology M,D
Exercise and Sports Science M
Family Nurse Practitioner Studies M,D,O
Finance and Banking M,D
Folklore M,D
Forensic Sciences M
Genetics D
Geography M
Health Services Management and Hospital Administration M,D,O
Health Services Research M,D,O
Higher Education M,D,O
Historic Preservation M,D
History M,D
Hospitality Management M,O
Human Development M
Human Resources Development M,D,O
Human Resources Management M,D
Immunology D
Industrial and Organizational Psychology M,D
Infectious Diseases M
Inorganic Chemistry M,D
Interior Design M
International Affairs M
International and Comparative Education M
International Business M,D
International Development M
International Health M
International Trade Policy M
Investment Management M,D
Latin American Studies M
Law P,M,D
Legal and Justice Studies M,O
Management Information Systems M,D
Management of Technology M,D
Management Strategy and Policy M,D
Marketing M,D
Mass Communication M
Materials Sciences M,D
Mathematics M,D
Mechanical Engineering M,D,O
Microbiology M,D,O
Military and Defense Studies M
Molecular Biology M,D
Molecular Genetics M,D
Molecular Medicine D
Museum Education M
Museum Studies M,O
Near and Middle Eastern Studies M
Nursing and Healthcare Administration M,D,O
Nursing—General M,D,O
Organic Chemistry M,D
Organizational Management M,D
Philosophy M
Photography M
Physical Chemistry M,D
Physical Therapy D
Physician Assistant Studies M
Physics M,D
Political Science M,D
Project Management M,D
Psychology—General D
Public Administration M
Public Affairs M
Public Health—General M,O
Public Policy M,D
Publishing M
Real Estate M,D
Rehabilitation Counseling M
Religion M
Secondary Education M
Social Psychology M,D
Sociology M
Special Education M,D,O
Sports Management M,O
Statistics M,D,O
Systems Engineering M,D,O
Technology and Public Policy M
Telecommunications M,D

Theater	M
Toxicology	M
Travel and Tourism	M,O
Western European Studies	M
Women's Studies	M,O

GEORGIA CAMPUS–PHILADELPHIA COLLEGE OF OSTEOPATHIC MEDICINE

Biological and Biomedical Sciences—General	M,O
Osteopathic Medicine	P

GEORGIA COLLEGE & STATE UNIVERSITY

Accounting	M
Adult Nursing	M
Biological and Biomedical Sciences—General	M
Business Administration and Management—General	M
Criminal Justice and Criminology	M
Curriculum and Instruction	M,O
Early Childhood Education	M,O
Education—General	M,O
Educational Leadership and Administration	M,O
Educational Media/Instructional Technology	M,O
English	M
Exercise and Sports Science	M
Family Nurse Practitioner Studies	M
Health Education	M
Health Promotion	M
Health Services Management and Hospital Administration	M
History	M
Kinesiology and Movement Studies	M
Library Science	M,O
Logistics	M
Management Information Systems	M
Middle School Education	M,O
Music Education	M
Nursing and Healthcare Administration	M
Nursing—General	M
Physical Education	M
Public Administration	M
Public History	M
Recreation and Park Management	M
Secondary Education	M,O
Special Education	M,O
Therapies—Dance, Drama, and Music	M
Writing	M

GEORGIA HEALTH SCIENCES UNIVERSITY

Allied Health—General	M
Allopathic Medicine	P
Anatomy	M,D
Biochemistry	M,D
Biological and Biomedical Sciences—General	M,D,O
Biostatistics	M,D
Cardiovascular Sciences	M,D
Cell Biology	M,D
Clinical Research	M,O
Dental Hygiene	M
Dentistry	P
Family Nurse Practitioner Studies	M,O
Genomic Sciences	M,D
Health Informatics	M
Medical Illustration	M
Molecular Biology	M,D
Molecular Medicine	M,D
Neuroscience	M,D
Nurse Anesthesia	M
Nursing and Healthcare Administration	M
Nursing—General	D
Oral and Dental Sciences	M,D
Pediatric Nursing	M,O
Pharmacology	M,D
Physiology	M,D

GEORGIA INSTITUTE OF TECHNOLOGY

Accounting	M,D,O
Aerospace/Aeronautical Engineering	M,D
Applied Mathematics	M,D
Architecture	M,D
Atmospheric Sciences	M,D
Biochemistry	M,D
Bioengineering	M,D
Bioinformatics	M,D
Biological and Biomedical Sciences—General	M,D
Biomedical Engineering	D
Building Science	M,D
Business Administration and Management—General	M,D,O
Chemical Engineering	M,D
Chemistry	M,D
Civil Engineering	M,D
Computer and Information Systems Security	M,D
Computer Art and Design	M,D
Computer Engineering	M,D
Computer Science	M,D
Economic Development	M,D
Economics	M
Electrical Engineering	M,D
Electronic Commerce	M,O
Engineering and Applied Sciences—General	M,D
Entrepreneurship	M,O
Environmental Engineering	M,D
Environmental Management and Policy	M,D
Environmental Sciences	M,D
Ergonomics and Human Factors	M,D
Experimental Psychology	M,D
Finance and Banking	M,D,O
Geochemistry	M,D
Geographic Information Systems	M,D
Geophysics	M,D
Geosciences	M,D
Health Physics/Radiological Health	M,D
Health Services Management and Hospital Administration	M
History of Science and Technology	M,D
Human-Computer Interaction	M
Industrial and Organizational Psychology	M,D
Industrial/Management Engineering	M,D
International Affairs	M,D
International Business	M,O
Internet and Interactive Multimedia	M,D
Management Information Systems	M,D,O
Management of Technology	M,O
Management Strategy and Policy	M,D,O
Marine Sciences	M,D
Marketing	M,D,O
Materials Engineering	M,D
Mathematical and Computational Finance	M,D
Mathematics	M,D
Mechanical Engineering	M,D
Mechanics	M,D
Medical Physics	M,D
Meteorology	M,D
Natural Resources	M,D
Nuclear Engineering	M,D
Oceanography	M,D
Operations Research	M,D
Organizational Behavior	M,D,O
Physics	M,D
Physiology	M
Planetary and Space Sciences	M,D
Polymer Science and Engineering	M,D
Psychology—General	M,D
Public Policy	M,D
Statistics	M,D
Systems Engineering	M,D
Textile Sciences and Engineering	M,D
Urban and Regional Planning	M,D
Urban Design	M,D

GEORGIAN COURT UNIVERSITY

Accounting	M,O
Biological and Biomedical Sciences—General	M,O
Business Administration and Management—General	M,O
Clinical Psychology	M,O
Counseling Psychology	M,O
Education—General	M
Educational Leadership and Administration	M,O
Health Psychology	M,O
Mathematics	M,O
Pastoral Ministry and Counseling	M,O
Religious Education	M,O
School Psychology	M,O
Theology	M,O

GEORGIA SOUTHERN UNIVERSITY

Accounting	M
Allied Health—General	M,D,O
Applied Economics	M
Art Education	M
Art/Fine Arts	M
Biological and Biomedical Sciences—General	M
Biostatistics	M,D
Business Administration and Management—General	M
Business Education	M
Community Health Nursing	M,D,O
Community Health	M,D
Computer Science	M
Counselor Education	M,O
Curriculum and Instruction	D
Early Childhood Education	M,O
Education—General	M,D,O
Educational Leadership and Administration	M,D,O
Educational Media/Instructional Technology	M
Electrical Engineering	M,O
English Education	M
English	M
Environmental and Occupational Health	M,D
Epidemiology	M,D
Family Nurse Practitioner Studies	M,O
Foreign Languages Education	M
Health Education	M,D
Health Services Management and Hospital Administration	M,D
Higher Education	M
History	M
Kinesiology and Movement Studies	M
Logistics	D
Mathematics Education	M
Mathematics	M
Mechanical Engineering	M,O
Middle School Education	M
Music	M
Nursing—General	M,D,O
Psychology—General	M,D
Public Administration	M
Public Health—General	M,D
Reading Education	M
School Psychology	M,O
Science Education	M
Social Sciences Education	M
Sociology	M
Spanish	M
Special Education	M
Sports Management	M
Supply Chain Management	D
Women's Health Nursing	M,D,O

GEORGIA SOUTHWESTERN STATE UNIVERSITY

Business Administration and Management—General	M
Computer Science	M
Early Childhood Education	M,O
Education—General	M,O
Health Education	M,O
Information Science	M
Middle School Education	M,O
Physical Education	M,O
Reading Education	M,O
Secondary Education	M,O
Special Education	M,O

GEORGIA STATE UNIVERSITY

Accounting	M,D,O
Actuarial Science	M
Adult Nursing	M,D,O
Allied Health—General	M,D,O
Anthropology	M
Art Education	M,D,O
Art History	M
Art/Fine Arts	M
Astronomy	D
Athletic Training and Sports Medicine	M
Biochemistry	M,D
Biological and Biomedical Sciences—General	M,D
Business Administration and Management—General	M,D
Cell Biology	M,D
Chemistry	M,D
Communication Disorders	M
Communication—General	M,D
Computer Science	M,D
Counseling Psychology	M,D,O
Counselor Education	M,D,O
Criminal Justice and Criminology	M,D,O
Early Childhood Education	M,D,O
Economic Development	M,D,O
Economics	M,D
Education of Students with Severe/Multiple Disabilities	M
Education—General	M,D,O
Educational Leadership and Administration	M,D,O
Educational Measurement and Evaluation	M,D
Educational Media/Instructional Technology	M,D,O
Educational Policy	M,D,O
Educational Psychology	M,D
Emergency Management	M,D,O
English as a Second Language	M,D,O
English Education	M,D,O
English	M,D
Entrepreneurship	M,D
Environmental Biology	M,D
Exercise and Sports Science	M

*M—master's degree; P—first professional degree; D—doctorate; O—other advanced degree; *—Close-Up and/or Display in one of the other books in this series*

Family Nurse Practitioner Studies	M,D,O
Film, Television, and Video Production	M,D
Finance and Banking	M,D,O
Foundations and Philosophy of Education	M,D
French	M,O
Geographic Information Systems	O
Geography	M
Geology	M
Geosciences	M,O
German	M,O
Gerontology	M
Health Education	M
Health Promotion	M,D,O
Health Services Management and Hospital Administration	M
Historic Preservation	M,O
History	M,D
Human Resources Management	M,D
Human Services	M
Hydrogeology	M,O
Information Science	M
Insurance	M,D,O
International Business	M
Kinesiology and Movement Studies	D
Latin American Studies	M,D,O
Law	P
Linguistics	M,D
Management Information Systems	M,D
Management Strategy and Policy	M,D
Marketing	M,D
Mass Communication	M,D
Mathematics Education	M,D,O
Mathematics	M,D
Microbiology	M,D
Middle School Education	M,O
Molecular Biology	M,D
Molecular Genetics	M,D
Music Education	M,D,O
Music	M
Neurobiology	M,D
Nonprofit Management	M,D,O
Nursing—General	M,D,O
Nutrition	M
Operations Research	M,D
Organizational Management	M,D
Pediatric Nursing	M,D,O
Philosophy	M
Photography	M,D
Physical Education	M
Physical Therapy	D
Physics	M,D
Physiology	M,D
Political Science	M,D
Psychiatric Nursing	M,D,O
Psychology—General	M,D
Public Administration	M,D,O
Public Health—General	M,D,O
Public Policy	M,D,O
Quantitative Analysis	M,D
Reading Education	M,D,O
Real Estate	M,D,O
Rehabilitation Counseling	M
Religion	M
Rhetoric	M,D
School Psychology	M,D,O
Science Education	M,D,O
Secondary Education	M,D,O
Social Sciences Education	M,D,O
Social Work	M
Sociology	M,D
Spanish	M,O
Special Education	M,D
Speech and Interpersonal Communication	M,D
Sports Management	M
Statistics	M,D
Taxation	M
Translation and Interpretation	O
Urban and Regional Planning	M,D,O
Women's Health Nursing	M,D,O
Women's Studies	M,O
Writing	M,D

GERSTNER SLOAN-KETTERING GRADUATE SCHOOL OF BIOMEDICAL SCIENCES

Biological and Biomedical Sciences—General	D
Cancer Biology/Oncology	D*

GLION INSTITUTE OF HIGHER EDUCATION

Hospitality Management	M

GLOBAL UNIVERSITY

Missions and Missiology	P,M
Religious Education	P,M
Theology	P,M

GLOBE UNIVERSITY

Business Administration and Management—General	M
Health Services Management and Hospital Administration	M
Management Information Systems	M

GODDARD COLLEGE

Business Administration and Management—General	M
Comparative and Interdisciplinary Arts	M
Counseling Psychology	M
Education—General	M
Environmental Management and Policy	M
Health Promotion	M
Industrial and Organizational Psychology	M
Interdisciplinary Studies	M
Sustainability Management	M
Writing	M

GOLDEN GATE BAPTIST THEOLOGICAL SEMINARY

Early Childhood Education	P,M,D,O
Educational Leadership and Administration	P,M,D,O
Pastoral Ministry and Counseling	P,M,D,O
Theology	P,M,D,O

GOLDEN GATE UNIVERSITY

Accounting	M,D,O
Advertising and Public Relations	M,D,O
Business Administration and Management—General	M,D,O
Environmental Law	P,M,D
Finance and Banking	M,D,O
Forensic Sciences	M,O
Health Informatics	M,D,O
Human Resources Management	M,D,O
Intellectual Property Law	P,M,D
International Business	M,D,O
Law	P,M,D
Legal and Justice Studies	P,M,D
Management Information Systems	M,D,O
Management of Technology	M,D,O
Marketing	M,D,O
Psychology—General	M,D,O
Public Administration	M,D,O
Supply Chain Management	M,D,O
Taxation	P,M,D,O

GOLDEY-BEACOM COLLEGE

Business Administration and Management—General	M
Finance and Banking	M
Human Resources Management	M
International Business	M
Management Information Systems	M
Marketing	M
Taxation	M

GOLDFARB SCHOOL OF NURSING AT BARNES-JEWISH COLLEGE

Adult Nursing	M,O
Health Services Management and Hospital Administration	M,O
Nurse Anesthesia	M,O
Nursing Education	M,O
Nursing—General	M,O
Oncology Nursing	M,O

GONZAGA UNIVERSITY

Accounting	M
Business Administration and Management—General	M
Communication—General	M
Counseling Psychology	M
Education—General	M
Educational Leadership and Administration	M,D
English as a Second Language	M
Law	P
Nurse Anesthesia	M
Nursing—General	M
Organizational Management	M
Pastoral Ministry and Counseling	M
Philosophy	M
Reading Education	M
Religion	M
Special Education	M
Sports Management	M

GOODING INSTITUTE OF NURSE ANESTHESIA

Nurse Anesthesia	M

GORDON COLLEGE

Education—General	M
Music Education	M

GORDON-CONWELL THEOLOGICAL SEMINARY

Archaeology	P,M,D
Missions and Missiology	P,M,D
Pastoral Ministry and Counseling	P,M,D
Religion	P,M,D
Theology	P,M,D

GOSHEN COLLEGE

Environmental Education	M
Family Nurse Practitioner Studies	M
Nursing and Healthcare Administration	M
Nursing—General	M

GOUCHER COLLEGE

Arts Administration	M
Biological and Biomedical Sciences—General	O
Computer Art and Design	M
Cultural Studies	M
Education—General	M
Historic Preservation	M
Writing	M

GOVERNORS STATE UNIVERSITY

Accounting	M
Addictions/Substance Abuse Counseling	M
Analytical Chemistry	M
Art/Fine Arts	M
Business Administration and Management—General	M
Communication Disorders	M
Communication—General	M
Computer Science	M
Counseling Psychology	M
Early Childhood Education	M
Education—General	M
Educational Leadership and Administration	M
Educational Media/Instructional Technology	M
English	M
Environmental Biology	M
Health Services Management and Hospital Administration	M
Legal and Justice Studies	M
Management Information Systems	M
Media Studies	M
Nursing—General	M
Occupational Therapy	M
Physical Therapy	M,D
Political Science	M
Psychology—General	M
Public Administration	M
Reading Education	M
Social Work	M
Special Education	M

GRACE COLLEGE

Counseling Psychology	M

GRACELAND UNIVERSITY (IA)

Education—General	M
Educational Leadership and Administration	M
Educational Media/Instructional Technology	M
Family Nurse Practitioner Studies	M,O
Nursing Education	M,O
Nursing—General	M,O
Pastoral Ministry and Counseling	M
Religion	M
Special Education	M
Theology	M

GRACE THEOLOGICAL SEMINARY

Cultural Studies	P,M,D,O
Missions and Missiology	P,M,D,O
Pastoral Ministry and Counseling	P,M,D,O
Theology	P,M,D,O

GRACE UNIVERSITY

Counseling Psychology	M
Pastoral Ministry and Counseling	M
Theology	M

GRADUATE INSTITUTE OF APPLIED LINGUISTICS

Linguistics	M,O
Multilingual and Multicultural Education	M,O

GRADUATE SCHOOL AND UNIVERSITY CENTER OF THE CITY UNIVERSITY OF NEW YORK

- Accounting D
- Anthropology D
- Archaeology D
- Architectural History D
- Art History D
- Biochemistry D
- Biological and Biomedical Sciences—General D
- Biomedical Engineering D
- Biopsychology D
- Business Administration and Management—General D
- Chemical Engineering D
- Chemistry D
- Civil Engineering D
- Classics M,D
- Clinical Psychology D
- Cognitive Sciences D
- Communication Disorders D
- Comparative Literature M,D
- Computer Science D
- Criminal Justice and Criminology D
- Cultural Anthropology D
- Developmental Psychology D
- Economics D
- Educational Psychology D
- Electrical Engineering D
- Engineering and Applied Sciences—General D
- English D
- Environmental Sciences D
- Experimental Psychology D
- Finance and Banking D
- French D
- Geosciences D
- German M,D
- Hispanic and Latin American Languages D
- History D
- Industrial and Organizational Psychology D
- Interdisciplinary Studies M,D
- Italian M,D
- Liberal Studies M
- Linguistics M,D
- Management Information Systems D
- Mathematics D
- Mechanical Engineering D
- Medieval and Renaissance Studies M,D
- Music D
- Neuroscience D
- Nursing—General D
- Organizational Behavior D
- Philosophy M,D
- Physical Therapy D
- Physics D
- Political Science M,D
- Psychology—General D
- Public Health—General D
- Public Policy M,D
- Social Psychology D
- Social Work D
- Sociology D
- Theater D
- Urban Education D
- Urban Studies M,D
- Women's Studies M,D

GRADUATE THEOLOGICAL UNION

- Art History M,D,O
- Cultural Studies M,D,O
- Ethics M,D,O
- Jewish Studies M,D,O
- Religion M,D,O
- Social Sciences M,D,O
- Theology M,D,O

GRAMBLING STATE UNIVERSITY

- Counselor Education M,D
- Criminal Justice and Criminology M
- Curriculum and Instruction M,D
- Developmental Education M,D
- Education—General M,D
- Educational Leadership and Administration M,D
- Educational Media/Instructional Technology M,D
- English M,D
- Family Nurse Practitioner Studies M,O
- Health Services Management and Hospital Administration M
- Higher Education M,D
- Human Resources Management M
- Mass Communication M
- Mathematics Education M,D
- Nursing Education M,O
- Nursing—General M,O
- Political Science M
- Public Administration M
- Reading Education M,D
- Science Education M,D
- Social Sciences Education M
- Social Work M
- Sports Management M
- Student Affairs M,D

GRAND CANYON UNIVERSITY

- Accounting M
- Acute Care/Critical Care Nursing M,O
- Addictions/Substance Abuse Counseling M
- Business Administration and Management—General M,D
- Cognitive Sciences D
- Counseling Psychology M
- Counselor Education M
- Curriculum and Instruction M
- Education—General M,D
- Educational Leadership and Administration M,D
- Elementary Education M
- Emergency Management M
- Entrepreneurship M
- Family Nurse Practitioner Studies M,O
- Finance and Banking M
- Health Education D
- Health Informatics M
- Health Services Management and Hospital Administration M,O
- Higher Education D
- Human Resources Management M
- Industrial and Organizational Psychology D
- Management Information Systems M
- Marketing M
- Marriage and Family Therapy M
- Nursing Education M,O
- Nursing—General M,O
- Organizational Management D
- Psychology—General D
- Public Administration M
- Public Health—General M
- Secondary Education M
- Special Education M

GRAND RAPIDS THEOLOGICAL SEMINARY OF CORNERSTONE UNIVERSITY

- Missions and Missiology P,M
- Pastoral Ministry and Counseling P,M
- Religion P,M
- Religious Education P,M
- Theology P,M

GRAND VALLEY STATE UNIVERSITY

- Accounting M
- Adult Education M,O
- Allied Health—General M,D
- Bioinformatics M
- Biological and Biomedical Sciences—General M
- Biostatistics M
- Business Administration and Management—General M
- Cell Biology M
- Communication—General M
- Computer Engineering M
- Computer Science M
- Criminal Justice and Criminology M
- Curriculum and Instruction M
- Early Childhood Education M,O
- Education—General M,O
- Educational Leadership and Administration M,O
- Educational Media/Instructional Technology M,O
- Electrical Engineering M
- Elementary Education M,O
- Engineering and Applied Sciences—General M
- English as a Second Language M,O
- English Education M
- English M
- Health Services Management and Hospital Administration M,D
- Higher Education M,O
- Information Science M
- Management Information Systems M
- Manufacturing Engineering M
- Mechanical Engineering M
- Medical Informatics M
- Middle School Education M,O
- Molecular Biology M
- Nursing and Healthcare Administration M,D
- Nursing Education M,D
- Nursing—General M,D
- Occupational Therapy M
- Physical Therapy D
- Physician Assistant Studies M
- Public Administration M
- Reading Education M
- School Psychology M
- Secondary Education M,O
- Social Work M
- Software Engineering M
- Special Education M
- Taxation M

GRAND VIEW UNIVERSITY

- Business Administration and Management—General M
- Education—General M
- Nursing—General M
- Organizational Management M

GRANITE STATE COLLEGE

- Project Management M

GRANTHAM UNIVERSITY

- Adult Nursing M
- Business Administration and Management—General M
- Health Services Management and Hospital Administration M
- Human Resources Development M
- Management Information Systems M
- Management Strategy and Policy M
- Nursing and Healthcare Administration M
- Nursing Education M
- Nursing Informatics M
- Organizational Management M
- Project Management M

GRATZ COLLEGE

- Education—General M
- Holocaust and Genocide Studies M,O
- Jewish Studies M,O
- Music M,O
- Religious Education M,D,O
- Social Work M,O

GREEN MOUNTAIN COLLEGE

- Business Administration and Management—General M
- Environmental Management and Policy M

GREENSBORO COLLEGE

- Education—General M
- Elementary Education M
- English as a Second Language M
- Special Education M

GREENVILLE COLLEGE

- Education—General M
- Elementary Education M
- Pastoral Ministry and Counseling M
- Secondary Education M

GWYNEDD-MERCY COLLEGE

- Adult Nursing M
- Business Administration and Management—General M
- Counselor Education M
- Education—General M
- Educational Leadership and Administration M
- Family Nurse Practitioner Studies M
- Gerontological Nursing M
- Nursing—General M
- Oncology Nursing M
- Pediatric Nursing M
- Reading Education M
- Special Education M

HAMLINE UNIVERSITY

- Business Administration and Management—General M,D
- Education—General M,D
- English as a Second Language M,D
- Environmental Education M,D
- Law P,M
- Liberal Studies M,O
- Nonprofit Management M,D
- Public Administration M,D
- Reading Education M,D
- Science Education M,D
- Writing M,O

HAMPTON UNIVERSITY

- Adult Nursing M
- Applied Mathematics M
- Architecture M
- Atmospheric Sciences M,D
- Biological and Biomedical Sciences—General M

*M—master's degree; P—first professional degree; D—doctorate; O—other advanced degree; *—Close-Up and/or Display in one of the other books in this series*

Business Administration and Management—General M,D
Chemistry M
Communication Disorders M
Community Health Nursing M
Computational Sciences M
Computer Science M
Counselor Education M
Early Childhood Education M
Education of the Gifted M
Education—General M
Educational Leadership and Administration M,D
Elementary Education M
Environmental Biology M
Gerontological Nursing M
Health Services Management and Hospital Administration M,D
Medical Physics M,D
Middle School Education M
Music Education M
Nursing—General M,D
Pastoral Ministry and Counseling M
Pediatric Nursing M
Pharmacy P
Physical Therapy D
Physics M,D
Planetary and Space Sciences M,D
Psychiatric Nursing M
Secondary Education M
Special Education M
Statistics M
Student Affairs M
Women's Health Nursing M

HANNIBAL-LAGRANGE UNIVERSITY

Education—General M
Reading Education M

HARDING UNIVERSITY

Art Education M,O
Business Administration and Management—General M
Communication Disorders M
Counseling Psychology M
Counselor Education M,O
Early Childhood Education M,O
Education—General M,O
Educational Leadership and Administration M,O
Elementary Education M,O
English as a Second Language M,O
English Education M,O
Foreign Languages Education M,O
Health Education M,O
Health Services Management and Hospital Administration M
International Business M
Management of Technology M
Marriage and Family Therapy M
Mathematics Education M,O
Organizational Management M
Pastoral Ministry and Counseling M
Pharmacy P
Physician Assistant Studies M
Reading Education M,O
Secondary Education M,O
Social Sciences Education M,O
Special Education M,O

HARDING UNIVERSITY GRADUATE SCHOOL OF RELIGION

Pastoral Ministry and Counseling P,M,D
Religion P,M,D
Theology P,M,D

HARDIN-SIMMONS UNIVERSITY

Business Administration and Management—General M
Counselor Education M
Education of the Gifted M
Education—General M
English M
Environmental Management and Policy M
Family Nurse Practitioner Studies M
History M
Kinesiology and Movement Studies M
Marriage and Family Therapy M
Maternal and Child/Neonatal Nursing M
Mathematics M,D
Music Education M
Music M
Nursing—General M
Pastoral Ministry and Counseling M,D
Physical Therapy D
Psychology—General M
Reading Education M
Recreation and Park Management M
Religion M
Science Education M,D
Theology P,M,D

HARRINGTON COLLEGE OF DESIGN

Interior Design M

HARRISBURG UNIVERSITY OF SCIENCE AND TECHNOLOGY

Construction Management M
Educational Media/Instructional Technology M
Entrepreneurship M
Health Services Management and Hospital Administration M
Management Information Systems M
Management of Technology M
Project Management M
Public Administration M
Systems Engineering M

HARTFORD SEMINARY

Pastoral Ministry and Counseling M,D,O
Religion M,D,O
Theology M,D,O

HARVARD UNIVERSITY

Accounting D
African Studies D
African-American Studies D
Allopathic Medicine P,D
American Studies D
Anthropology M,D
Applied Mathematics M,D
Applied Physics M,D
Applied Science and Technology M,O
Archaeology M,D
Architectural History D
Architecture M,D
Art Education M
Art History D
Asian Languages M,D
Asian Studies M,D
Astronomy D
Astrophysics D
Biochemistry D
Biological and Biomedical Sciences—General M,D,O
Biomedical Engineering M,D
Biophysics D*
Biopsychology D
Biostatistics M,D
Biotechnology M,O
Business Administration and Management—General M,D,O
Cell Biology D
Celtic Languages D
Chemical Physics D
Chemistry D*
Chinese D
Classics D
Cognitive Sciences M,D
Communication Disorders D
Communication—General M,O
Comparative Literature D
Computer Science M,D
Curriculum and Instruction M
Demography and Population Studies M,D
Dentistry P,M,D,O
Developmental Psychology D
East European and Russian Studies M
Economics D
Education—General M,D
Educational Leadership and Administration M,D
Educational Measurement and Evaluation D
Educational Media/Instructional Technology M,O
Educational Policy M
Educational Psychology M
Engineering and Applied Sciences—General M,D
English M,D,O
Environmental and Occupational Health M,D
Environmental Management and Policy M,O
Environmental Sciences M
Epidemiology M,D
Evolutionary Biology D
Experimental Psychology D
Forestry M
Foundations and Philosophy of Education M,O
French M,D
Genetics D
Genomic Sciences D
Geosciences M,D
German D
Health Promotion M,D
Health Services Management and Hospital Administration M,D
Higher Education D
History of Science and Technology M,D
History D
Human Development M,D
Immunology D
Industrial and Manufacturing Management D
Infectious Diseases D
Information Science M,D,O
Inorganic Chemistry D
International Affairs P,D
International and Comparative Education M
International Development M
International Health M,D
Italian M,D
Japanese D
Jewish Studies M,D
Journalism M,O
Landscape Architecture M,D
Law P,M,D
Legal and Justice Studies P
Liberal Studies M,O
Linguistics D
Management of Technology D
Management Strategy and Policy D
Marketing D
Mathematics Education M,O
Mathematics D
Medical Informatics M
Medical Physics D
Medieval and Renaissance Studies D
Microbiology D
Molecular Biology D
Molecular Genetics D
Molecular Pharmacology D
Multilingual and Multicultural Education D
Museum Studies M,O
Music M,D
Near and Middle Eastern Languages M,D
Near and Middle Eastern Studies M,D
Neurobiology D
Neuroscience D
Nutrition D
Oral and Dental Sciences M,D,O
Organic Chemistry D
Organizational Behavior D
Pathology D
Philosophy M,D
Physical Chemistry D
Physics D
Physiology M,D
Planetary and Space Sciences M,D
Political Science M,D
Portuguese M,D
Psychology—General D
Public Administration M
Public Health—General M,D
Public Policy M,D
Reading Education M
Religion D
Russian D
Scandinavian Languages D
Science Education M
Slavic Languages D
Social Psychology D
Sociology D
Spanish M,D
Statistics M,D
Structural Biology D
Systems Biology D
Technical Communication M
Theology P,M,D
Theoretical Physics D
Urban and Regional Planning M,D
Urban Design M

HASTINGS COLLEGE

Education—General M

HAWAI'I PACIFIC UNIVERSITY

Accounting M
Business Administration and Management—General M*
Clinical Psychology M
Communication—General M*
Community Health Nursing M
Economics M
Electronic Commerce M
Elementary Education M
English as a Second Language M*
Family Nurse Practitioner Studies M
Finance and Banking M
Human Resources Management M*
International Business M
Management Information Systems M*

Program	Degrees
Marine Sciences	M*
Marketing	M
Military and Defense Studies	M*
Nursing—General	M*
Organizational Management	M*
Secondary Education	M*
Social Work	M*
Software Engineering	M
Sustainable Development	M*
Telecommunications Management	M
Travel and Tourism	M

HAZELDEN GRADUATE SCHOOL OF ADDICTION STUDIES

Program	Degrees
Addictions/Substance Abuse Counseling	M,O

HEBREW COLLEGE

Program	Degrees
Early Childhood Education	M,O
Education—General	M,O
Jewish Studies	M,O
Middle School Education	M,O
Music Education	M,O
Music	M,O
Religious Education	M,O
Special Education	M,O
Theology	M

HEBREW UNION COLLEGE–JEWISH INSTITUTE OF RELIGION (NY)

Program	Degrees
Education—General	M
Jewish Studies	M
Music	M
Near and Middle Eastern Languages	D
Nonprofit Management	M
Religious Education	M
Theology	P,D

HEC MONTREAL

Program	Degrees
Accounting	M,O
Applied Economics	M
Arts Administration	O
Business Administration and Management—General	M,D,O
Corporate and Organizational Communication	O
Electronic Commerce	M,O
Finance and Banking	M,O
Financial Engineering	M
Human Resources Management	M
Industrial and Manufacturing Management	M
International Business	M
Logistics	M
Management Information Systems	M
Management Strategy and Policy	M
Marketing	M
Operations Research	M
Organizational Management	M
Supply Chain Management	O
Sustainable Development	O
Taxation	O

HEIDELBERG UNIVERSITY

Program	Degrees
Business Administration and Management—General	M
Counseling Psychology	M
Education—General	M
Music Education	M

HENDERSON STATE UNIVERSITY

Program	Degrees
Business Administration and Management—General	M
Counseling Psychology	M
Counselor Education	M
Curriculum and Instruction	M
Early Childhood Education	M
Education—General	M,O
Educational Leadership and Administration	M,O
Liberal Studies	M
Middle School Education	M
Physical Education	M
Reading Education	M
Special Education	M
Sports Management	M

HENDRIX COLLEGE

Program	Degrees
Accounting	M

HENLEY-PUTNAM UNIVERSITY

Program	Degrees
Computer and Information Systems Security	M
Homeland Security	M
Military and Defense Studies	M
National Security	D

HERITAGE BAPTIST COLLEGE AND HERITAGE THEOLOGICAL SEMINARY

Program	Degrees
Pastoral Ministry and Counseling	P,M,D,O
Theology	P,M,D,O

HERITAGE CHRISTIAN UNIVERSITY

Program	Degrees
Classics	M
Pastoral Ministry and Counseling	M
Religion	M

HERITAGE UNIVERSITY

Program	Degrees
Biological and Biomedical Sciences—General	M
Counselor Education	M
Education—General	M
Educational Leadership and Administration	M
English as a Second Language	M
English	M
Multilingual and Multicultural Education	M
Reading Education	M
Science Education	M
Special Education	M

HERZING UNIVERSITY ONLINE

Program	Degrees
Accounting	M
Business Administration and Management—General	M
Health Services Management and Hospital Administration	M
Human Resources Management	M
Management of Technology	M
Marketing	M
Nursing and Healthcare Administration	M
Nursing Education	M
Nursing—General	M
Project Management	M

HIGH POINT UNIVERSITY

Program	Degrees
Business Administration and Management—General	M
Corporate and Organizational Communication	M
Education—General	M
Educational Leadership and Administration	M
Elementary Education	M
History	M
Mathematics Education	M
Nonprofit Management	M
Secondary Education	M
Special Education	M

HILLSDALE FREE WILL BAPTIST COLLEGE

Program	Degrees
Pastoral Ministry and Counseling	M

HIRAM COLLEGE

Program	Degrees
Interdisciplinary Studies	M

HODGES UNIVERSITY

Program	Degrees
Business Administration and Management—General	M
Counseling Psychology	M
Criminal Justice and Criminology	M
Education—General	M
Interdisciplinary Studies	M
Legal and Justice Studies	M
Management Information Systems	M
Management of Technology	M
Psychology—General	M
Public Administration	M

HOFSTRA UNIVERSITY

Program	Degrees
Accounting	M,O
Allopathic Medicine	P,D
Applied Psychology	D
Applied Social Research	M
Art Education	M,D,O
Art Therapy	M,O
Art/Fine Arts	M,O
Biological and Biomedical Sciences—General	M,O
Business Administration and Management—General	M,O
Business Education	M,O
Chemistry	M,O
Clinical Psychology	D
Communication Disorders	M,D,O
Communication—General	M
Community Health	M
Comparative Literature	M
Computer Science	M
Counseling Psychology	M,O
Counselor Education	M,O
Early Childhood Education	M,D,O
Education—General	M,D,O
Educational Leadership and Administration	M,D,O
Educational Policy	M,D,O
Elementary Education	M,O
English as a Second Language	M,O
English Education	M,D,O
English	M
Entertainment Management	M,O
Exercise and Sports Science	M,O
Family and Consumer Sciences-General	M,O
Film, Television, and Video Production	M
Finance and Banking	M,O
Foreign Languages Education	M,O
Foundations and Philosophy of Education	M,D,O
French	M,O
Geology	M,O
Geosciences	M,O
German	M,O
Gerontology	M,O
Health Education	M,O
Health Services Management and Hospital Administration	M,O
Higher Education	M,D,O
Human Development	D
Human Resources Management	M,O
Humanities	D
Industrial and Organizational Psychology	M,D
International Business	M,O
Investment Management	M,O
Journalism	M
Law	P,M
Legal and Justice Studies	P,M
Linguistics	M,D
Management Information Systems	M,O
Marketing Research	M,O
Marketing	M,O
Marriage and Family Therapy	M,O
Mathematics Education	M,D,O
Middle School Education	M,O
Molecular Medicine	P,D
Multilingual and Multicultural Education	M,D,O
Music Education	M,O
Music	M,O
Physical Education	M,D,O
Physics	M,O
Quality Management	M,O
Reading Education	M,D,O
Real Estate	M,O
Rehabilitation Counseling	M,O
Russian	M,O
School Psychology	D
Science Education	M,D,O
Secondary Education	M,O
Social Psychology	D
Social Sciences Education	M,D,O
Sociology	M
Spanish	M,O
Special Education	M,D,O
Speech and Interpersonal Communication	M
Sports Management	M,O
Taxation	M,O
Writing	M,D,O

HOLLINS UNIVERSITY

Program	Degrees
Art/Fine Arts	M,O
Dance	M
Education—General	M
English	M
Film, Television, and Video Production	M
Film, Television, and Video Theory and Criticism	M
Humanities	M,O
Interdisciplinary Studies	M,O
Legal and Justice Studies	M,O
Liberal Studies	M,O
Music	M,O
Social Sciences	M,O
Theater	M
Writing	M

HOLMES INSTITUTE

Program	Degrees
Pastoral Ministry and Counseling	M

HOLY APOSTLES COLLEGE AND SEMINARY

Program	Degrees
Theology	P,M,O

HOLY CROSS GREEK ORTHODOX SCHOOL OF THEOLOGY

Program	Degrees
Theology	P,M

*M—master's degree; P—first professional degree; D—doctorate; O—other advanced degree; *—Close-Up and/or Display in one of the other books in this series*

HOLY FAMILY UNIVERSITY

Business Administration and Management—General M*
Community Health Nursing M
Counseling Psychology M*
Criminal Justice and Criminology M*
Education—General M*
Educational Leadership and Administration M
Elementary Education M
Finance and Banking M
Health Services Management and Hospital Administration M
Human Resources Management M*
Management Information Systems M*
Nursing and Healthcare Administration M
Nursing Education M
Nursing—General M*
Reading Education M
Secondary Education M
Special Education M

HOLY NAMES UNIVERSITY

Business Administration and Management—General M
Community Health Nursing M,O
Counseling Psychology M,O
Education—General M,O
Educational Psychology M,O
Energy Management and Policy M
English as a Second Language M,O
Family Nurse Practitioner Studies M,O
Finance and Banking M
Forensic Psychology M,O
Marketing M
Music Education M,O
Music M,O
Nursing and Healthcare Administration M,O
Nursing Education M,O
Nursing—General M,O
Pastoral Ministry and Counseling M,O
Religion M,O
Special Education M,O
Sports Management M
Urban Education M,O
Writing M

HOOD COLLEGE

Accounting M
Art/Fine Arts M,O
Biological and Biomedical Sciences—General M,O
Biotechnology M,O
Business Administration and Management—General M
Computer and Information Systems Security M,O
Computer Science M,O
Curriculum and Instruction M,O
Early Childhood Education M,O
Education—General M,O
Educational Leadership and Administration M,O
Elementary Education M,O
Environmental Biology M
Finance and Banking M
Human Development M,O
Human Resources Management M
Humanities M
Immunology M,O
Information Science M,O
Management Information Systems M
Marketing M
Mathematics Education M,O
Microbiology M,O
Middle School Education M,O
Molecular Biology M,O
Psychology—General M,O
Public Administration M
Reading Education M,O
Science Education M,O
Secondary Education M,O
Special Education M,O
Systems Science M
Thanatology M,O

HOOD THEOLOGICAL SEMINARY

Theology P,M,D

HOPE INTERNATIONAL UNIVERSITY

Business Administration and Management—General M
Education—General M
Educational Leadership and Administration M
International Business M
International Development M
Marriage and Family Therapy M
Missions and Missiology M
Music M
Nonprofit Management M
Religion M

HOUGHTON COLLEGE

Music M

HOUSTON BAPTIST UNIVERSITY

Accounting M
Business Administration and Management—General M
Counseling Psychology M
Counselor Education M
Curriculum and Instruction M
Education—General M
Educational Leadership and Administration M
Educational Measurement and Evaluation M
English as a Second Language M
Health Services Management and Hospital Administration M
Human Resources Management M
Liberal Studies M
Pastoral Ministry and Counseling M
Psychology—General M
Reading Education M
Theology M

HOUSTON GRADUATE SCHOOL OF THEOLOGY

Pastoral Ministry and Counseling P,M,D
Theology P,M,D

HOWARD PAYNE UNIVERSITY

Educational Leadership and Administration M
Pastoral Ministry and Counseling M

HOWARD UNIVERSITY

Accounting M
African Studies M,D
Allopathic Medicine P,D
Analytical Chemistry M,D
Anatomy M,D
Applied Arts and Design—General M
Applied Mathematics M,D
Art History M
Art/Fine Arts M
Atmospheric Sciences M,D
Biochemistry M,D
Biological and Biomedical Sciences—General M,D
Biophysics D
Biopsychology M,D
Biotechnology M,D
Business Administration and Management—General M
Chemical Engineering M
Chemistry M,D
Civil Engineering M
Clinical Psychology M,D
Communication Disorders M,D
Communication—General M,D
Computer Science M
Corporate and Organizational Communication M,D
Counseling Psychology M,D
Counselor Education M
Dentistry P,O
Developmental Psychology M,D
Early Childhood Education M
Economics M,D
Education—General M,D
Educational Leadership and Administration M,D,O
Educational Psychology M,D
Electrical Engineering M,D
Elementary Education M
Engineering and Applied Sciences—General M,D
English M,D
Environmental Sciences M,D
Exercise and Sports Science M
Experimental Psychology M,D
Family Nurse Practitioner Studies M,O
Film, Television, and Video Production M
Finance and Banking M
French M
Health Education M
History M,D
Human Resources Management M
Inorganic Chemistry M,D
International Business M
Law P,M
Leisure Studies M
Management Information Systems M
Marketing M
Mass Communication M,D
Mathematics M,D
Mechanical Engineering M,D
Media Studies M,D
Microbiology D
Molecular Biology M,D
Multilingual and Multicultural Education M,D
Music Education M
Music M
Nursing—General M,O
Nutrition M,D
Oral and Dental Sciences P,O
Organic Chemistry M,D
Pharmacology M,D
Pharmacy P
Philosophy M
Photography M
Physical Chemistry M,D
Physical Education M
Physics M,D
Physiology D
Political Science M,D
Psychology—General M,D
Public Administration M
Public Health—General M
School Psychology M,D
Secondary Education M
Social Psychology M,D
Social Work M,D
Sociology M,D
Spanish M
Special Education M
Sports Management M
Supply Chain Management M
Theology P,M,D

HULT INTERNATIONAL BUSINESS SCHOOL (UNITED STATES)

Business Administration and Management—General M
Conflict Resolution and Mediation/Peace Studies M
Entrepreneurship M
Finance and Banking M
International Affairs M
International Business M
Marketing M
National Security M
Political Science M

HUMBOLDT STATE UNIVERSITY

Athletic Training and Sports Medicine M
Biological and Biomedical Sciences—General M
Business Administration and Management—General M
Counseling Psychology M
Education—General M
English Education M
English M
Environmental Management and Policy M
Environmental Sciences M
Exercise and Sports Science M
Film, Television, and Video Production M
Fish, Game, and Wildlife Management M
Forestry M
Geology M
Hazardous Materials Management M
Kinesiology and Movement Studies M
Natural Resources M
Physical Education M
Physical Therapy M
Psychology—General M
School Psychology M
Social Sciences M
Social Work M
Sociology M
Theater M
Water Resources M

HUMPHREYS COLLEGE

Law P

HUNTER COLLEGE OF THE CITY UNIVERSITY OF NEW YORK

Accounting M
Adult Nursing M
Animal Behavior M,D
Anthropology M
Applied Mathematics M
Applied Psychology M,D
Applied Social Research M
Art History M
Art/Fine Arts M
Biochemistry M,D
Biological and Biomedical Sciences—General M,D
Biopsychology M,D
Biostatistics M
Chemistry M,D
Classics M
Cognitive Sciences M,D
Communication Disorders M

- Community Health Nursing M
- Community Health M
- Counselor Education M
- Early Childhood Education M,O
- Economics M
- Education of Students with Severe/Multiple Disabilities M
- Education—General M,O
- Educational Leadership and Administration O
- Elementary Education M
- English as a Second Language M
- English Education M
- English M
- Environmental and Occupational Health M
- Environmental Sciences M,O
- Epidemiology M
- Foreign Languages Education M
- French M
- Geographic Information Systems M,O
- Geography M,O
- Geosciences M,O
- Gerontological Nursing M
- Health Services Management and Hospital Administration M
- History M
- Italian M
- Mathematics Education M
- Mathematics M
- Media Studies M
- Multilingual and Multicultural Education M
- Music Education M
- Music M
- Neuroscience M,D
- Nursing—General M,O
- Nutrition M
- Physics M,D
- Psychiatric Nursing M,O
- Psychology—General M,D
- Public Health—General M
- Reading Education M,O
- Rehabilitation Counseling M
- Romance Languages M
- Science Education M,O
- Secondary Education M
- Social Psychology M,D
- Social Sciences Education M
- Social Work M,D
- Sociology M
- Spanish M
- Special Education M
- Theater M
- Urban and Regional Planning M
- Urban Studies M
- Writing M

HUNTINGTON COLLEGE OF HEALTH SCIENCES

- Nutrition M

HUNTINGTON UNIVERSITY

- Education—General M
- Pastoral Ministry and Counseling M

HUSSON UNIVERSITY

- Business Administration and Management—General M
- Community Health Nursing M,O
- Counseling Psychology M
- Counselor Education M
- Criminal Justice and Criminology M
- Family Nurse Practitioner Studies M,O
- Health Services Management and Hospital Administration M
- Nonprofit Management M
- Nursing—General M,O
- Occupational Therapy M
- Physical Therapy D
- Psychiatric Nursing M,O

ICR GRADUATE SCHOOL

- Astrophysics M
- Biological and Biomedical Sciences—General M
- Geology M
- Geophysics M
- Science Education M

IDAHO STATE UNIVERSITY

- Allied Health—General M,D,O
- Anthropology M
- Applied Physics M,D
- Art/Fine Arts M
- Biological and Biomedical Sciences—General M,D
- Business Administration and Management—General M,O
- Chemistry M
- Civil Engineering M
- Clinical Psychology D
- Communication Disorders M,D,O
- Community Health O
- Counseling Psychology M,D,O
- Counselor Education M,D,O
- Curriculum and Instruction M,O
- Dental Hygiene M
- Dentistry O
- Education—General M,D,O
- Educational Leadership and Administration M,D,O
- Educational Media/Instructional Technology M,D,O
- Elementary Education M,O
- Engineering and Applied Sciences—General M,D,O
- English as a Second Language M,D,O
- English M,D,O
- Environmental Engineering M
- Environmental Management and Policy M
- Environmental Sciences M,O
- Geographic Information Systems M,O
- Geology M,O
- Geophysics M,O
- Geosciences M,O
- Hazardous Materials Management M
- Health Education M
- Health Physics/Radiological Health M,D
- History M
- Hydrology M,O
- Interdisciplinary Studies M
- Management Information Systems M,O
- Management of Technology M
- Marriage and Family Therapy M,D,O
- Mathematics Education M,D
- Mathematics M,D
- Mechanical Engineering M
- Medical Microbiology M,D
- Medicinal and Pharmaceutical Chemistry M,D
- Microbiology M,D
- Nuclear Engineering M,D,O
- Nursing—General M,O
- Nutrition M,O
- Occupational Therapy M
- Operations Research M
- Oral and Dental Sciences O
- Pharmaceutical Administration P,M,D
- Pharmaceutical Sciences M,D
- Pharmacology M,D
- Pharmacy P,M,D
- Physical Education M
- Physical Therapy D
- Physician Assistant Studies M
- Physics M,D
- Political Science M,D
- Psychology—General M,D
- Public Administration M
- Public Health—General M,O
- Reading Education M,O
- Rhetoric M
- School Psychology M,D,O
- Secondary Education M,O
- Sociology M
- Special Education M,D,O
- Speech and Interpersonal Communication M
- Theater M
- Vocational and Technical Education M

ILIFF SCHOOL OF THEOLOGY

- Pastoral Ministry and Counseling P,M,D
- Religion P,M,D
- Theology P,M,D

ILLINOIS COLLEGE OF OPTOMETRY

- Optometry P

ILLINOIS INSTITUTE OF TECHNOLOGY

- Aerospace/Aeronautical Engineering M,D
- Agricultural Engineering M,D
- Analytical Chemistry M,D
- Applied Arts and Design—General M,D
- Applied Mathematics M,D
- Architectural Engineering M,D
- Architecture M,D
- Biochemistry M,D
- Bioengineering M,D
- Biological and Biomedical Sciences—General M,D
- Biomedical Engineering D
- Biotechnology M,D
- Business Administration and Management—General M,D
- Cell Biology M,D
- Chemical Engineering M,D
- Chemistry M,D
- Civil Engineering M,D
- Clinical Psychology M,D
- Communication—General M,D
- Computer Engineering M,D
- Computer Science M,D
- Construction Engineering M,D
- Construction Management M,D
- Corporate and Organizational Communication M
- Electrical Engineering M,D
- Engineering and Applied Sciences—General M,D
- Environmental Engineering M,D
- Environmental Management and Policy M
- Finance and Banking P,M
- Food Science and Technology M
- Geotechnical Engineering M,D
- Health Physics/Radiological Health M,D
- Human Resources Development M,D
- Industrial and Manufacturing Management M
- Industrial and Organizational Psychology M,D
- Landscape Architecture M,D
- Law P,M
- Management Information Systems M,D
- Manufacturing Engineering M,D
- Marketing M
- Materials Engineering M,D
- Materials Sciences M,D
- Mathematical and Computational Finance M
- Mathematics Education M,D
- Mechanical Engineering M,D
- Medical Imaging M,D
- Microbiology M,D
- Molecular Biology M,D
- Molecular Biophysics M,D
- Physics M,D
- Psychology—General M,D
- Public Administration M
- Rehabilitation Counseling M,D
- Science Education M,D
- Software Engineering M,D
- Structural Engineering M,D
- Sustainability Management M
- Taxation P,M
- Technical Writing M,D
- Telecommunications M,D
- Transportation and Highway Engineering M,D

ILLINOIS STATE UNIVERSITY

- Accounting M
- Agricultural Economics and Agribusiness M
- Agricultural Sciences—General M
- Animal Behavior M,D
- Archaeology M
- Art History M
- Art/Fine Arts M
- Bacteriology M,D
- Biochemistry M,D
- Biological and Biomedical Sciences—General M,D
- Biophysics M,D
- Biotechnology M
- Botany M,D
- Business Administration and Management—General M
- Cell Biology M,D
- Chemistry M
- Clinical Psychology M,D,O
- Communication Disorders M
- Communication—General M
- Conservation Biology M,D
- Counseling Psychology M,D,O
- Criminal Justice and Criminology M
- Curriculum and Instruction M,D
- Developmental Biology M,D
- Developmental Psychology M,D,O
- Ecology M,D
- Economics M
- Education—General M,D
- Educational Leadership and Administration M,D
- Educational Policy M,D
- Educational Psychology M,D,O
- English M,D
- Entomology M,D
- Evolutionary Biology M,D
- Experimental Psychology M,D,O
- Family and Consumer Sciences-General M
- Family Nurse Practitioner Studies M,D,O
- French M
- Genetics M,D
- German M
- Graphic Design M
- Health Education M
- Higher Education M,D
- History M

*M—master's degree; P—first professional degree; D—doctorate; O—other advanced degree; *—Close-Up and/or Display in one of the other books in this series*

Hydrogeology M
Hydrology M
Immunology M,D
Industrial and Organizational Psychology M,D,O
Industrial/Management Engineering M
Management Information Systems M
Management of Technology M
Mathematics Education D
Mathematics M
Microbiology M,D
Molecular Biology M,D
Molecular Genetics M,D
Music M
Neurobiology M,D
Neuroscience M,D
Nursing—General M,D,O
Parasitology M,D
Photography M
Physical Education M
Physiology M,D
Plant Biology M,D
Plant Molecular Biology M,D
Plant Sciences M,D
Political Science M
Psychology—General M,D,O
Reading Education M
School Psychology D,O
Social Work M
Sociology M
Spanish M
Special Education M,D
Structural Biology M,D
Student Affairs M
Textile Design M
Theater M
Writing M
Zoology M,D

IMCA–INTERNATIONAL MANAGEMENT CENTRES ASSOCIATION

Business Administration and Management—General M

IMMACULATA UNIVERSITY

Advertising and Public Relations M
Clinical Psychology M,D,O
Communication—General M
Counseling Psychology M,D,O
Counselor Education M,D,O
Educational Leadership and Administration M,D,O
Elementary Education M,D,O
Multilingual and Multicultural Education M
Nursing—General M
Nutrition M
Organizational Management M
Psychology—General M,D,O
School Psychology M,D,O
Secondary Education M,D,O
Special Education M,D,O
Therapies—Dance, Drama, and Music M

INDEPENDENCE UNIVERSITY

Business Administration and Management—General M
Community Health Nursing M
Community Health M
Gerontological Nursing M
Health Promotion M
Health Services Management and Hospital Administration M
Nursing and Healthcare Administration M
Nursing—General M
Public Health—General M

INDIANA STATE UNIVERSITY

Art/Fine Arts M
Athletic Training and Sports Medicine M
Biological and Biomedical Sciences—General M,D
Business Administration and Management—General M
Clinical Psychology M,D
Communication—General M
Community Health M
Comparative Literature M
Computer Engineering M
Computer Science M
Consumer Economics M
Counseling Psychology M,D,O
Counselor Education M,D,O
Criminal Justice and Criminology M
Curriculum and Instruction M,D
Early Childhood Education M
Ecology M,D
Education—General M,D,O
Educational Leadership and Administration M,D,O
Educational Media/Instructional Technology M,D
Elementary Education M
Engineering and Applied Sciences—General M
English as a Second Language M,O
English Education M
English M
Environmental and Occupational Health M
Exercise and Sports Science M
Family and Consumer Sciences-General M
Geography M,D
Graphic Design M
Health Education M
Health Promotion M
Higher Education M,D,O
History M
Home Economics Education M
Human Resources Development M
Industrial/Management Engineering M
Linguistics M,O
Management of Technology D
Mathematics Education M
Mathematics M
Media Studies M
Microbiology M,D
Multilingual and Multicultural Education M,O
Music M
Nursing—General M
Nutrition M
Photography M
Physical Education M
Physiology M,D
Political Science M
Psychology—General M,D
Public Administration M
School Psychology M,D,O
Science Education M,D
Sports Management M
Student Affairs M,D,O
Vocational and Technical Education M
Writing M

INDIANA TECH

Accounting M
Business Administration and Management—General M
Criminal Justice and Criminology M
Health Services Management and Hospital Administration M
Human Resources Development M
Human Resources Management M
International Business D
Marketing M
Organizational Management M
Science Education M

INDIANA UNIVERSITY BLOOMINGTON

African Studies M
African-American Studies M
Analytical Chemistry M,D
Anthropology M,D
Applied Mathematics M,D
Art Education M,D,O
Art History M,D
Art/Fine Arts M,D
Arts Administration M
Asian Languages M,D
Asian Studies M,D
Astronomy M,D
Astrophysics M,D
Athletic Training and Sports Medicine M,D
Biochemistry M,D
Bioinformatics M,D
Biological and Biomedical Sciences—General M,D
Biotechnology M,D
Business Administration and Management—General M,D
Cell Biology M,D
Chemistry M,D
Child and Family Studies M,D
Chinese M,D
Classics M,D
Cognitive Sciences M,D
Communication Disorders M,D
Communication—General M,D
Comparative Literature M,D
Computer Art and Design M,D
Computer Science M,D
Counselor Education M,D,O
Criminal Justice and Criminology M,D
Curriculum and Instruction M,D,O
Developmental Psychology M,D
East European and Russian Studies M,O
Ecology M,D
Economic Development M,D,O
Economics M,D
Education—General M,D,O
Educational Leadership and Administration M,D,O
Educational Measurement and Evaluation M,D,O
Educational Media/Instructional Technology M,D
Educational Policy M,D,O
Educational Psychology M,D,O
Elementary Education M,D,O
Energy Management and Policy M,D,O
English as a Second Language M,D
English M,D
Environmental Management and Policy M,D,O
Environmental Sciences M,D
Ergonomics and Human Factors M,D
Evolutionary Biology M,D
Exercise and Sports Science M,D
Film, Television, and Video Theory and Criticism M,D
Finance and Banking M,D,O
Folklore M,D
Foreign Languages Education M,D
Foundations and Philosophy of Education M,D,O
French M,D
Gender Studies D
Genetics M,D
Geochemistry M,D
Geography M,D
Geology M,D
Geophysics M,D
Geosciences M,D
German M,D
Health Education M,D
Health Informatics M,D
Health Promotion M,D
Higher Education M,D,O
Hispanic and Latin American Languages M,D
History of Science and Technology M,D
History M,D
Human Development M,D
Human-Computer Interaction M,D
Hydrogeology M,D
Information Science M,D,O
Information Studies M,D,O
Inorganic Chemistry M,D
International Affairs M,D,O
International and Comparative Education M,D,O
Italian M,D
Japanese M,D
Journalism M,D
Kinesiology and Movement Studies M,D
Latin American Studies M
Law P,M,D,O
Leisure Studies M,D,O
Library Science M,D,O
Linguistics M,D
Management Information Systems M,D,O
Mass Communication M,D
Materials Sciences M,D
Mathematics Education M,D,O
Mathematics M,D
Media Studies M,D
Medieval and Renaissance Studies M,D
Microbiology M,D
Mineralogy M,D
Molecular Biology M,D
Multilingual and Multicultural Education M,D
Music M,D,O
Near and Middle Eastern Languages M,D
Neuroscience D
Nonprofit Management M,D,O
Nutrition M,D
Optometry P,M,D
Organic Chemistry M,D
Philosophy M,D
Physical Chemistry M,D
Physical Education M,D
Physics M,D
Plant Biology M,D
Political Science M,D
Portuguese M,D
Psychology—General M,D
Public Administration M,D,O
Public Affairs M,D,O
Public Health—General M,D
Public Policy M,D,O
Reading Education M,D,O
Recreation and Park Management M,D,O
Religion M,D
Rhetoric M,D
Safety Engineering M,D
School Psychology M,D,O
Science Education M,D,O
Secondary Education M,D,O
Slavic Languages M,D
Social Psychology M,D
Social Sciences Education M,D,O
Social Sciences P,M,D,O

Program	Degrees
Sociology	M,D
Spanish	M,D
Special Education	M,D,O
Speech and Interpersonal Communication	M,D
Sports Management	M,D,O
Statistics	M,D
Sustainability Management	M,D,O
Telecommunications	M
Theater	M,D
Toxicology	M,D
Travel and Tourism	M,D,O
Water Resources Engineering	M,D
Western European Studies	M
Writing	M,D
Zoology	M,D

INDIANA UNIVERSITY EAST

Program	Degrees
Education—General	M
Social Work	M

INDIANA UNIVERSITY KOKOMO

Program	Degrees
Business Administration and Management—General	M
Education—General	M
Elementary Education	M
Liberal Studies	M
Public Administration	M,O

INDIANA UNIVERSITY NORTHWEST

Program	Degrees
Accounting	M,O
Business Administration and Management—General	M,O
Criminal Justice and Criminology	M,O
Education—General	M
Elementary Education	M
Environmental Sciences	M,O
Health Services Management and Hospital Administration	M,O
Human Services	M,O
Nonprofit Management	M,O
Public Administration	M,O
Public Affairs	M,O
Secondary Education	M
Social Work	M

INDIANA UNIVERSITY OF PENNSYLVANIA

Program	Degrees
Adult Education	M,D
Applied Mathematics	M
Archaeology	M
Art/Fine Arts	M
Biological and Biomedical Sciences—General	M
Business Administration and Management—General	M
Chemistry	M
Clinical Psychology	D
Communication Disorders	M
Communication—General	M,D
Counselor Education	M
Criminal Justice and Criminology	M,D
Curriculum and Instruction	M,D
Education—General	M,D,O
Educational Leadership and Administration	D,O
Educational Media/Instructional Technology	M,D
Educational Psychology	M,O
Elementary Education	M
Emergency Management	M
English as a Second Language	M,D
English Education	M,D
English	M,D
Environmental and Occupational Health	M
Exercise and Sports Science	M
Facilities Management	M
Geography	M
Health Education	M
Health Services Management and Hospital Administration	M,D
Higher Education	M
History	M
Human Resources Development	M
Industrial and Labor Relations	M
Linguistics	M,D
Mathematics Education	M
Mathematics	M
Media Studies	M,D
Music Education	M
Music	M
Nursing and Healthcare Administration	M
Nursing Education	M
Nursing—General	D
Nutrition	M
Physical Education	M
Physics	M
Psychology—General	M,D
Public Affairs	M
Reading Education	M
Rhetoric	M,D
School Psychology	D,O
Sociology	M
Special Education	M
Sports Management	M
Student Affairs	M
Writing	M,D

INDIANA UNIVERSITY–PURDUE UNIVERSITY FORT WAYNE

Program	Degrees
Adult Nursing	M,O
Applied Mathematics	M,O
Applied Statistics	M,O
Biological and Biomedical Sciences—General	M
Business Administration and Management—General	M
Communication Disorders	M
Communication—General	M
Computer Engineering	M
Computer Science	M
Construction Management	M
Counselor Education	M,O
Education—General	M,O
Educational Leadership and Administration	M,O
Electrical Engineering	M
Elementary Education	M
Engineering and Applied Sciences—General	M,O
English as a Second Language	M,O
English Education	M,O
English	M,O
Facilities Management	M
Industrial/Management Engineering	M
Information Science	M
Liberal Studies	M
Marriage and Family Therapy	M,O
Mathematics Education	M,O
Mathematics	M,O
Mechanical Engineering	M
Nursing and Healthcare Administration	M,O
Nursing Education	M,O
Nursing—General	M,O
Operations Research	M,O
Organizational Management	M,O
Public Affairs	M,O
Secondary Education	M
Sociology	M
Special Education	M,O
Systems Engineering	M
Women's Health Nursing	M,O

INDIANA UNIVERSITY–PURDUE UNIVERSITY INDIANAPOLIS

Program	Degrees
Accounting	M
Acute Care/Critical Care Nursing	M,D
Addictions/Substance Abuse Counseling	M,D
Adult Education	M
Adult Nursing	M,D
Allopathic Medicine	P,M,D
Anatomy	M,D
Applied Arts and Design—General	M
Applied Mathematics	M,D
Applied Statistics	M
Art Education	M
Art/Fine Arts	M
Artificial Intelligence/Robotics	M,D
Biochemistry	M,D
Bioethics	M,O
Biological and Biomedical Sciences—General	M,D
Biomedical Engineering	M,D,O
Biopsychology	M,D
Business Administration and Management—General	M
Cell Biology	M,D
Chemistry	M,D
Child and Family Studies	M
Clinical Psychology	M,D
Community Health Nursing	M,D
Computer Education	M,O
Computer Engineering	M,D
Computer Science	M,D
Counselor Education	M,O
Criminal Justice and Criminology	M,O
Curriculum and Instruction	M,O
Dentistry	P,M,D,O
Early Childhood Education	M,O
Economics	M
Education—General	M,O
Educational Leadership and Administration	M,O
Electrical Engineering	M,D
English as a Second Language	M,O
English Education	M
English	M
Epidemiology	M
Family Nurse Practitioner Studies	M,D
Foreign Languages Education	M,O
Gender Studies	M
Geographic Information Systems	M,O
Geology	M,D
Geosciences	M,D
Health Education	M,D
Health Services Management and Hospital Administration	M
Higher Education	M,O
History	M
Immunology	M,D
Industrial and Organizational Psychology	M
Information Science	M,D
Internet and Interactive Multimedia	M,D
Law	P,M,D
Liberal Studies	M,D,O
Library Science	M
Maternal and Child/Neonatal Nursing	M,D
Mathematics Education	M,D
Mathematics	M,D
Mechanical Engineering	M,D,O
Microbiology	M,D
Molecular Biology	D
Molecular Genetics	M,D
Museum Studies	M,O
Music	M
Nonprofit Management	M,O
Nursing—General	M,D
Nutrition	M,D
Occupational Therapy	M,D
Pathology	M,D
Pediatric Nursing	M,D
Pharmacology	M,D
Philanthropic Studies	M,D
Philosophy	M,O
Physical Education	M
Physical Therapy	M,D
Physics	M,D
Political Science	M,O
Psychiatric Nursing	M,D
Psychology—General	M,D
Public Administration	M,O
Public Affairs	M,O
Public Health—General	M
Public History	M
Public Policy	M,O
Reading Education	M,O
Rehabilitation Counseling	M,D
Rehabilitation Sciences	M,D
Social Work	M,D,O
Sociology	M
Special Education	M,O
Student Affairs	M,O
Toxicology	M,D
Women's Health Nursing	M,D

INDIANA UNIVERSITY SOUTH BEND

Program	Degrees
Accounting	M
Applied Mathematics	M
Applied Psychology	M
Art Education	M
Business Administration and Management—General	M
Computer Science	M
Counselor Education	M
Education—General	M
Elementary Education	M
English	M
Health Services Management and Hospital Administration	M,O
Liberal Studies	M
Management Information Systems	M
Music	M
Nonprofit Management	M,O
Public Administration	M,O
Public Affairs	M,O
Secondary Education	M
Social Work	M
Special Education	M

INDIANA UNIVERSITY SOUTHEAST

Program	Degrees
Business Administration and Management—General	M
Counselor Education	M
Education—General	M
Elementary Education	M
Finance and Banking	M
Liberal Studies	M
Secondary Education	M

INDIANA WESLEYAN UNIVERSITY

Program	Degrees
Accounting	M
Addictions/Substance Abuse Counseling	M
Business Administration and Management—General	M
Community Health Nursing	M,O
Counseling Psychology	M
Counselor Education	M
Educational Leadership and Administration	M,O
Higher Education	M
Human Resources Management	M

*M—master's degree; P—first professional degree; D—doctorate; O—other advanced degree; *—Close-Up and/or Display in one of the other books in this series*

Marriage and Family Therapy M
Nursing and Healthcare Administration M,O
Nursing Education M,O
Nursing—General M,O
Organizational Management D
Pastoral Ministry and Counseling M
Social Psychology M
Theology P

INSTITUTE FOR CHRISTIAN STUDIES

Education—General M,D
Philosophy M,D
Political Science M,D
Theology M,D

INSTITUTE FOR CLINICAL SOCIAL WORK

Social Work D

INSTITUTE FOR DOCTORAL STUDIES IN THE VISUAL ARTS

Art/Fine Arts D
Philosophy D

THE INSTITUTE FOR THE PSYCHOLOGICAL SCIENCES

Clinical Psychology M,D

INSTITUTE OF CLINICAL ACUPUNCTURE AND ORIENTAL MEDICINE

Acupuncture and Oriental Medicine M

INSTITUTE OF PUBLIC ADMINISTRATION

Health Services Management and Hospital Administration M,O
Public Administration M,O

INSTITUTE OF TRANSPERSONAL PSYCHOLOGY

Clinical Psychology M,D
Counseling Psychology M,D
Pastoral Ministry and Counseling M
Psychology—General M,D,O
Transpersonal and Humanistic Psychology M,D,O
Women's Studies M

THE INSTITUTE OF WORLD POLITICS

Military and Defense Studies M,O
National Security M,O
Political Science M,O
Public Affairs M,O
Public Policy M,O

INSTITUT FRANCO-EUROPÉEN DE CHIROPRATIQUE

Chiropractic P

INSTITUTO CENTROAMERICANO DE ADMINISTRACIÓN DE EMPRESAS

Agricultural Economics and Agribusiness M
Business Administration and Management—General M
Finance and Banking M
Management of Technology M
Real Estate M
Sustainable Development M

INSTITUTO TECNOLOGICO DE SANTO DOMINGO

Accounting M,O
Adult Education M,O
Allopathic Medicine P,M
Bioethics M,O
Business Administration and Management—General M,O
Communication—General M,O
Construction Management M,O
Counseling Psychology M,O
Economics M,O
Education—General M,O
Educational Leadership and Administration M,O
Educational Psychology M,O
Energy and Power Engineering M,D,O
Energy Management and Policy M,D,O
Engineering and Applied Sciences—General M,O
Environmental Education M,D,O
Environmental Engineering M,O
Environmental Management and Policy M,D,O
Environmental Sciences M,D,O
Finance and Banking M,O
Gender Studies M,O
Health Promotion M,O
Human Resources Management M,O
Humanities M,O
Industrial and Manufacturing Management M,O
Industrial/Management Engineering M,O
Information Science M,O
International Affairs M,O
International Business M,O
Linguistics M,O
Marine Sciences M,D,O
Marketing M,O
Marriage and Family Therapy M,O
Maternal and Child Health M,O
Mathematics M,D,O
Natural Resources M,D,O
Nutrition M,O
Organizational Management M,O
Quality Management M,O
Quantitative Analysis M,O
Secondary Education M,O
Social Sciences Education M,O
Software Engineering M,O
Structural Engineering M,O
Sustainable Development M,O
Taxation M,O
Telecommunications M,O
Transportation Management M,O

INSTITUTO TECNOLÓGICO Y DE ESTUDIOS SUPERIORES DE MONTERREY, CAMPUS CENTRAL DE VERACRUZ

Business Administration and Management—General M
Computer Science M
Education—General M
Educational Leadership and Administration M
Educational Media/Instructional Technology M
Electronic Commerce M
Finance and Banking M
Humanities M
International Business M
Management Information Systems M
Management of Technology M
Marketing M

INSTITUTO TECNOLÓGICO Y DE ESTUDIOS SUPERIORES DE MONTERREY, CAMPUS CHIHUAHUA

Computer Engineering M,O
Electrical Engineering M,O
Engineering Management M,O
Industrial/Management Engineering M,O
International Business M,O
Mechanical Engineering M,O
Systems Engineering M,O

INSTITUTO TECNOLÓGICO Y DE ESTUDIOS SUPERIORES DE MONTERREY, CAMPUS CIUDAD DE MÉXICO

Business Administration and Management—General M,D
Computer Science M,D
Economics M,D
Education—General M,D
Educational Media/Instructional Technology M,D
Environmental Engineering M,D
Environmental Sciences M,D
Finance and Banking M,D
Humanities M,D
Industrial/Management Engineering M,D
International Business M,D
Law P
Management Information Systems M,D
Quality Management M,D
Telecommunications Management M

INSTITUTO TECNOLÓGICO Y DE ESTUDIOS SUPERIORES DE MONTERREY, CAMPUS CIUDAD JUÁREZ

Business Administration and Management—General M
Education—General M
Educational Leadership and Administration M
Educational Media/Instructional Technology M,D
Electronic Commerce M
Humanities M
Management Information Systems M
Public Administration M
Quality Management M

INSTITUTO TECNOLÓGICO Y DE ESTUDIOS SUPERIORES DE MONTERREY, CAMPUS CIUDAD OBREGÓN

Business Administration and Management—General M
Communication—General M
Developmental Education M
Education—General M
Engineering and Applied Sciences—General M
Finance and Banking M
International Affairs M
Management Information Systems M
Marketing M
Mathematics Education M
Telecommunications Management M

INSTITUTO TECNOLÓGICO Y DE ESTUDIOS SUPERIORES DE MONTERREY, CAMPUS CUERNAVACA

Business Administration and Management—General M
Computer Science M,D
Finance and Banking M
Human Resources Management M
Information Science M,D
International Business M
Management of Technology M,D
Marketing M

INSTITUTO TECNOLÓGICO Y DE ESTUDIOS SUPERIORES DE MONTERREY, CAMPUS ESTADO DE MÉXICO

Architecture M,D
Business Administration and Management—General M,D
Computer Science M,D
Education—General M,D
Educational Leadership and Administration M,D
Educational Media/Instructional Technology M,D
Electronic Commerce M,D
Environmental Management and Policy M,D
Finance and Banking M,D
Humanities M,D
Industrial and Manufacturing Management M,D
Information Science M,D
Management Information Systems M,D
Marketing M,D
Materials Engineering M,D
Materials Sciences M,D
Quality Management M,D
Telecommunications Management M,D

INSTITUTO TECNOLÓGICO Y DE ESTUDIOS SUPERIORES DE MONTERREY, CAMPUS GUADALAJARA

Business Administration and Management—General M
Finance and Banking M

INSTITUTO TECNOLÓGICO Y DE ESTUDIOS SUPERIORES DE MONTERREY, CAMPUS IRAPUATO

Architecture M,D
Business Administration and Management—General M,D
Computer Science M,D
Education—General M,D
Educational Leadership and Administration M,D
Educational Media/Instructional Technology M,D
Electronic Commerce M,D
Environmental Management and Policy M,D
Finance and Banking M,D
Humanities M,D
Industrial and Manufacturing Management M,D
Information Science M,D
International Business M,D
Library Science M,D
Management Information Systems M,D

Management of Technology M,D
Marketing Research M,D
Quality Management M,D
Telecommunications Management M,D

INSTITUTO TECNOLÓGICO Y DE ESTUDIOS SUPERIORES DE MONTERREY, CAMPUS LAGUNA

Business Administration and Management—General M
Industrial/Management Engineering M
Management Information Systems M

INSTITUTO TECNOLÓGICO Y DE ESTUDIOS SUPERIORES DE MONTERREY, CAMPUS LEÓN

Business Administration and Management—General M

INSTITUTO TECNOLÓGICO Y DE ESTUDIOS SUPERIORES DE MONTERREY, CAMPUS MONTERREY

Agricultural Engineering M,D
Agricultural Sciences—General M,D
Applied Statistics M,D
Artificial Intelligence/Robotics M,D
Biotechnology M,D
Business Administration and Management—General M,D
Chemical Engineering M,D
Chemistry M,D
Civil Engineering M,D
Communication—General M,D
Computer Science M,D
Electrical Engineering M,D
Engineering and Applied Sciences—General M,D
Environmental Engineering M,D
Finance and Banking M
Industrial/Management Engineering M,D
Information Science M,D
International Business M
Manufacturing Engineering M,D
Marketing M
Mechanical Engineering M,D
Organic Chemistry M,D
Science Education M,D
Systems Engineering M,D

INSTITUTO TECNOLÓGICO Y DE ESTUDIOS SUPERIORES DE MONTERREY, CAMPUS QUERÉTARO

Business Administration and Management—General M

INSTITUTO TECNOLÓGICO Y DE ESTUDIOS SUPERIORES DE MONTERREY, CAMPUS SONORA NORTE

Business Administration and Management—General M
Education—General M
Information Science M

INSTITUTO TECNOLÓGICO Y DE ESTUDIOS SUPERIORES DE MONTERREY, CAMPUS TOLUCA

Business Administration and Management—General M

INTER AMERICAN UNIVERSITY OF PUERTO RICO, AGUADILLA CAMPUS

Accounting M
Business Administration and Management—General M
Counseling Psychology M
Criminal Justice and Criminology M
Educational Leadership and Administration M
Elementary Education M
Finance and Banking M
Human Resources Management M
Management Information Systems M
Marketing M

INTER AMERICAN UNIVERSITY OF PUERTO RICO, ARECIBO CAMPUS

Accounting M
Acute Care/Critical Care Nursing M
Business Administration and Management—General M
Counselor Education M
Curriculum and Instruction M
Education—General M
Educational Leadership and Administration M
Elementary Education M
English as a Second Language M
Finance and Banking M
Foreign Languages Education M
Human Resources Management M
Mathematics Education M
Medical/Surgical Nursing M
Nurse Anesthesia M
Nursing—General M
Science Education M
Social Sciences Education M

INTER AMERICAN UNIVERSITY OF PUERTO RICO, BARRANQUITAS CAMPUS

Accounting M
Business Administration and Management—General M
Curriculum and Instruction M
Education—General M
Educational Leadership and Administration M
Elementary Education M
English as a Second Language M
Finance and Banking M
Foreign Languages Education M
Library Science M
Mathematics Education M
Science Education M
Social Sciences Education M
Special Education M

INTER AMERICAN UNIVERSITY OF PUERTO RICO, BAYAMÓN CAMPUS

Biotechnology M
Ecology M
Electronic Commerce M
Human Resources Management M

INTER AMERICAN UNIVERSITY OF PUERTO RICO, GUAYAMA CAMPUS

Business Administration and Management—General M
Computer and Information Systems Security M
Computer Science M
Early Childhood Education M
Elementary Education M
Marketing M

INTER AMERICAN UNIVERSITY OF PUERTO RICO, METROPOLITAN CAMPUS

Accounting M
American Studies M,D
Athletic Training and Sports Medicine M
Business Administration and Management—General M
Business Education M
Clinical Laboratory Sciences/Medical Technology M
Computer Science M
Counseling Psychology M,D
Counselor Education M,D
Criminal Justice and Criminology M
Curriculum and Instruction M,D
Education—General M,D
Educational Leadership and Administration M,D
Educational Media/Instructional Technology M
Elementary Education M
English as a Second Language M
English M
Environmental Management and Policy M
Exercise and Sports Science M
Finance and Banking M
Foreign Languages Education M
Health Education M
Higher Education M
History M,D
Human Resources Development M
Human Resources Management M
Industrial and Labor Relations M,D
Industrial and Manufacturing Management M
Industrial and Organizational Psychology M,D
International Business M,D
Management Information Systems M
Marketing M
Mathematics Education M
Microbiology M
Molecular Biology M
Music Education M
Pastoral Ministry and Counseling D
Physical Education M
Psychology—General M,D
Religious Education D
School Psychology M,D
Science Education M
Social Sciences Education M
Social Work M
Spanish M
Special Education M
Theology D
Vocational and Technical Education M
Women's Studies M

INTER AMERICAN UNIVERSITY OF PUERTO RICO, PONCE CAMPUS

Accounting M
Criminal Justice and Criminology M
Elementary Education M
English as a Second Language M
Finance and Banking M
Human Resources Management M
Marketing M
Mathematics Education M
Science Education M
Social Sciences Education M
Spanish M

INTER AMERICAN UNIVERSITY OF PUERTO RICO, SAN GERMÁN CAMPUS

Accounting M,D
Applied Mathematics M
Art/Fine Arts M
Business Administration and Management—General M,D
Business Education M
Counseling Psychology M,D
Counselor Education M,D
Curriculum and Instruction D
Educational Leadership and Administration M,D
Elementary Education M
English as a Second Language M
Entrepreneurship D
Environmental Biology M
Environmental Sciences M
Finance and Banking M,D
Human Resources Development M,D
Human Resources Management M,D
Industrial and Manufacturing Management M,D
International Business D
Kinesiology and Movement Studies M
Library Science M
Management Information Systems M,D
Marketing M,D
Music Education M
Photography M
Physical Education M
Psychology—General M,D
School Psychology M,D
Science Education M
Special Education M
Water Resources M

*M—master's degree; P—first professional degree; D—doctorate; O—other advanced degree; *—Close-Up and/or Display in one of the other books in this series*

INTER AMERICAN UNIVERSITY OF PUERTO RICO SCHOOL OF LAW

Law P

INTER AMERICAN UNIVERSITY OF PUERTO RICO SCHOOL OF OPTOMETRY

Optometry P

INTERDENOMINATIONAL THEOLOGICAL CENTER

Theology P,M,D

INTERIOR DESIGNERS INSTITUTE

Interior Design M

INTERNATIONAL BAPTIST COLLEGE

Education—General M
Pastoral Ministry and Counseling M,D
Theology M

INTERNATIONAL COLLEGE OF THE CAYMAN ISLANDS

Business Administration and Management—General M
Business Education M
Human Resources Management M

INTERNATIONAL TECHNOLOGICAL UNIVERSITY

Business Administration and Management—General M
Computer Art and Design M
Computer Engineering M
Computer Science M
Electrical Engineering M,D
Engineering Management M
Industrial and Manufacturing Management M
Software Engineering M,D

THE INTERNATIONAL UNIVERSITY OF MONACO

Business Administration and Management—General M
Entrepreneurship M
Finance and Banking M
Financial Engineering M
International Business M
Marketing M

IONA COLLEGE

Accounting M,O
Advertising and Public Relations M
Business Administration and Management—General M,O*
Computer Science M
Counseling Psychology M
Criminal Justice and Criminology M
Education—General M
Educational Leadership and Administration M
English Education M
English M
Experimental Psychology M
Finance and Banking M,O
Foreign Languages Education M
Health Services Management and Hospital Administration M,O
History M
Human Resources Management M,O
Industrial and Organizational Psychology M
International Business M,O
Italian M
Journalism M
Management of Technology M,O
Marketing M,O
Marriage and Family Therapy M,O
Mass Communication M
Mathematics Education M
Pastoral Ministry and Counseling M,O
Psychology—General M
Reading Education M
School Psychology M
Science Education M
Social Sciences Education M
Spanish M
Telecommunications M

IOWA STATE UNIVERSITY OF SCIENCE AND TECHNOLOGY

Accounting M
Aerospace/Aeronautical Engineering M,D
Agricultural Economics and Agribusiness M,D
Agricultural Education M,D
Agricultural Engineering M,D
Agricultural Sciences—General M,D
Agronomy and Soil Sciences M,D
Animal Sciences M,D
Anthropology M
Applied Arts and Design—General M
Applied Mathematics M,D
Applied Physics M,D
Architecture M
Astronomy M,D
Astrophysics M,D
Biochemistry M,D*
Bioengineering M,D
Bioinformatics M,D
Biological and Biomedical Sciences—General M,D
Biophysics M,D
Biostatistics M,D
Biosystems Engineering M,D
Business Administration and Management—General M,D
Cell Biology M,D
Chemical Engineering M,D
Chemistry M,D
Child and Family Studies M,D
Civil Engineering M,D
Clothing and Textiles M,D
Cognitive Sciences D
Computational Biology M,D
Computer Engineering M,D
Computer Science M,D
Condensed Matter Physics M,D
Construction Engineering M,D
Consumer Economics M,D
Corporate and Organizational Communication M,D
Counseling Psychology D
Counselor Education M,D
Curriculum and Instruction M,D
Developmental Biology M,D
Ecology M,D
Economics M,D
Educational Leadership and Administration M,D
Educational Measurement and Evaluation M,D
Educational Media/Instructional Technology M,D
Electrical Engineering M,D
Elementary Education M,D
Engineering and Applied Sciences—General M,D
English M,D
Entomology M,D
Environmental Engineering M,D
Environmental Sciences M,D
Evolutionary Biology M,D
Family and Consumer Sciences-General M
Fish, Game, and Wildlife Management M,D
Food Science and Technology M,D
Forestry M,D
Foundations and Philosophy of Education M,D
Genetics M,D
Geology M,D
Geosciences M,D
Geotechnical Engineering M,D
Graphic Design M
Higher Education M,D
History of Science and Technology M,D
History M,D
Home Economics Education M,D
Horticulture M,D
Hospitality Management M,D
Human Development M,D
Human Resources Development M,D
Human-Computer Interaction M,D
Immunology M,D
Industrial/Management Engineering M,D
Information Science M
Interdisciplinary Studies M
Interior Design M
Journalism M
Kinesiology and Movement Studies M,D
Landscape Architecture M
Management Information Systems M
Mass Communication M
Materials Engineering M,D
Materials Sciences M,D
Mathematics Education M,D
Mathematics M,D
Mechanical Engineering M,D
Mechanics M,D
Meteorology M,D
Microbiology M,D
Molecular Biology M,D
Natural Resources M,D
Neuroscience M,D
Nutrition M,D
Operations Research M,D
Pathology M,D
Physics M,D
Plant Biology M,D
Plant Pathology M,D
Political Science M
Psychology—General D
Public Administration M
Rhetoric M,D
Rural Planning and Studies M,D
Rural Sociology M,D
Social Psychology D
Sociology M,D
Special Education M,D
Statistics M,D
Structural Biology M,D
Structural Engineering M,D
Sustainable Development M,D
Systems Engineering M
Toxicology M,D
Transportation and Highway Engineering M,D
Transportation Management M
Urban and Regional Planning M
Veterinary Medicine P,M
Veterinary Sciences M,D
Vocational and Technical Education M,D
Writing M,D

ITHACA COLLEGE

Accounting M
Allied Health—General M,D
Business Administration and Management—General M
Communication Disorders M
Communication—General M
Elementary Education M
English Education M
Exercise and Sports Science M
Foreign Languages Education M
Health Education M
Mathematics Education M
Music Education M
Music M
Occupational Therapy M
Physical Education M
Physical Therapy M,D
Science Education M
Secondary Education M
Social Sciences Education M
Sports Management M

ITT TECHNICAL INSTITUTE (IN)

Business Administration and Management—General M

JACKSON STATE UNIVERSITY

Accounting M
Biological and Biomedical Sciences—General M,D
Business Administration and Management—General M,D
Chemistry M,D
Clinical Psychology D
Communication Disorders M
Computer Science M
Counselor Education M
Criminal Justice and Criminology M
Early Childhood Education M,D,O
Education—General M,D,O
Educational Leadership and Administration M,D,O
Educational Media/Instructional Technology M,D,O
Elementary Education M,D,O
English Education M
English M
Environmental Sciences M,D
Health Education M
History M
Mass Communication M
Materials Sciences M
Mathematics Education M
Mathematics M
Music Education M
Physical Education M
Political Science M
Psychology—General D
Public Administration M,D
Public Affairs M,D
Public Policy M,D
Rehabilitation Counseling M
Science Education M
Secondary Education M,D,O
Social Work M,D
Sociology M
Special Education M,O
Urban and Regional Planning M,D
Vocational and Technical Education M

JACKSONVILLE STATE UNIVERSITY

Biological and Biomedical Sciences—General M

Business Administration and Management—General M
Computer Science M
Counselor Education M
Criminal Justice and Criminology M
Early Childhood Education M
Education—General M,O
Educational Leadership and Administration M,O
Educational Media/ Instructional Technology M
Elementary Education M
Emergency Management M,D
English M
History M
Liberal Studies M
Mathematics M
Music M
Nursing—General M
Physical Education M,O
Political Science M
Psychology—General M
Reading Education M
Secondary Education M
Software Engineering M
Special Education M

JACKSONVILLE UNIVERSITY

Business Administration and Management—General M
Computer Education M
Early Childhood Education M,O
Education—General M,O
Educational Media/ Instructional Technology M
Elementary Education M
Mathematics Education M
Music Education M
Nursing—General M
Oral and Dental Sciences O
Reading Education M

JAMES MADISON UNIVERSITY

Accounting M
Applied Science and Technology M
Art Education M
Art History M
Art/Fine Arts M
Biological and Biomedical Sciences—General M
Business Administration and Management—General M
Clinical Psychology M,D,O
Communication Disorders M,D
Computer Science M
Counseling Psychology M,O
Early Childhood Education M
Educational Leadership and Administration M
Elementary Education M
English M
Health Education M
History M
Kinesiology and Movement Studies M
Mathematics M
Middle School Education M
Music Education M,D
Music D
Nursing—General M
Occupational Therapy M
Photography M
Physician Assistant Studies M
Political Science M
Psychology—General M,D,O
Public Administration M
Reading Education M
School Psychology M,D,O
Secondary Education M
Special Education M
Statistics M
Technical Writing M

Textile Design M
Vocational and Technical Education M

JEFFERSON COLLEGE OF HEALTH SCIENCES

Nursing and Healthcare Administration M
Nursing Education M
Nursing—General M
Occupational Therapy M
Physician Assistant Studies M

THE JEWISH THEOLOGICAL SEMINARY

Jewish Studies M,D
Music M
Religion M,D
Religious Education M,D
Theology M,D,O
Women's Studies M,D

JEWISH UNIVERSITY OF AMERICA

Jewish Studies P,D
Pastoral Ministry and Counseling M,D
Religious Education M,D

JOHN BROWN UNIVERSITY

Business Administration and Management—General M
Counselor Education M
Educational Leadership and Administration M
Ethics M
Higher Education M
International Business M
International Development M
Marriage and Family Therapy M
Pastoral Ministry and Counseling M
Urban and Regional Planning M

JOHN CARROLL UNIVERSITY

Accounting M
Biological and Biomedical Sciences—General M
Business Administration and Management—General M
Corporate and Organizational Communication M
Counseling Psychology M,O
Counselor Education M,O
Early Childhood Education M
Education—General M
Educational Leadership and Administration M
Educational Psychology M
English M
History M
Humanities M
Mathematics M
Middle School Education M
Nonprofit Management M
Religion M
Science Education M
Secondary Education M

JOHN F. KENNEDY UNIVERSITY

Art/Fine Arts M
Business Administration and Management—General M,O
Comparative and Interdisciplinary Arts M
Counseling Psychology M
Education—General M
Health Education M
Health Psychology M

Human Resources Development M,O
Industrial and Organizational Psychology M,O
Interdisciplinary Studies M
Law P
Museum Studies M,O
Organizational Management M,O
Psychology—General M,D,O
Sport Psychology M
Transpersonal and Humanistic Psychology M

JOHN JAY COLLEGE OF CRIMINAL JUSTICE OF THE CITY UNIVERSITY OF NEW YORK

Criminal Justice and Criminology M,D
Forensic Psychology M,D
Forensic Sciences M,D
Legal and Justice Studies M,D
Organizational Behavior M,D
Public Administration M
Public Policy M,D

JOHN MARSHALL LAW SCHOOL

International Business P,M
Law P,M
Legal and Justice Studies P,M
Management Information Systems P,M
Real Estate P,M
Taxation P,M

THE JOHNS HOPKINS UNIVERSITY

Acute Care/Critical Care Nursing M,O
Addictions/Substance Abuse Counseling M,D
Adult Education M,O
Adult Nursing M,O
Allopathic Medicine P
Anatomy D
Anthropology D
Applied Economics M
Applied Mathematics M,D,O
Applied Physics M,O
Art History M,D
Asian Studies M,D,O
Astronomy D
Biochemistry M,D
Bioengineering M,D
Bioethics M,D
Bioinformatics M,D,O
Biological and Biomedical Sciences—General M,D
Biomedical Engineering M,D,O
Biophysics D
Biostatistics M,D
Biotechnology M
Business Administration and Management—General M,O
Cell Biology D
Chemical Engineering M,D
Chemistry D
Civil Engineering M,D
Classics D
Clinical Psychology M,D
Clinical Research M,D
Cognitive Sciences D
Communication—General M
Community Health Nursing M
Community Health M,D
Comparative Literature D
Computer and Information Systems Security M,O
Computer Engineering M,D,O
Computer Science M,D,O
Counselor Education M,O
Criminal Justice and Criminology M

Curriculum and Instruction M,O
Demography and Population Studies M,D
Developmental Biology D
Early Childhood Education M,D,O
Economics D
Education of the Gifted M,D,O
Education—General M,D,O
Educational Leadership and Administration M,D,O
Educational Media/ Instructional Technology M,D,O
Educational Psychology M,O
Electrical Engineering M,D,O
Elementary Education M,O
Emergency Management M,O
Engineering and Applied Sciences—General M,D,O
Engineering Management M
English as a Second Language M,D,O
English Education M,O
English D
Environmental and Occupational Health M,D
Environmental Engineering M,D,O
Environmental Management and Policy M,O
Environmental Sciences M
Epidemiology M,D
Evolutionary Biology D
Family Nurse Practitioner Studies M,O
Finance and Banking M,O
Foreign Languages Education M,O
French D
Genetic Counseling M,D
Genetics M,D
Geography M,D
Geosciences M,D
German D
Health Communication M,D
Health Education M,D
Health Informatics M
Health Services Management and Hospital Administration M,D,O
Health Services Research M,D
History of Science and Technology M,D
History D
Homeland Security M,O
Human Genetics D
Human Resources Development M,O
Immunology M,D
Infectious Diseases M,D
Information Science M
International Affairs M,D,O
International Development M,D,O
International Economics M,D,O
International Health M,D
Investment Management M,O
Italian D
Liberal Studies M,O
Management Information Systems M,O
Management of Technology M,O
Marketing M
Materials Engineering M,D
Materials Sciences M,D
Mathematical and Computational Finance M,D
Mathematics Education M,O
Mathematics D
Mechanical Engineering M,D
Mechanics M
Medical Illustration M
Microbiology M,D
Military and Defense Studies M
Molecular Biology M,D
Molecular Biophysics M,D
Molecular Medicine D
Museum Studies M
Music M,D,O
Nanotechnology M

*M—master's degree; P—first professional degree; D—doctorate; O—other advanced degree; *—Close-Up and/or Display in one of the other books in this series*

Near and Middle Eastern Studies D
Neuroscience D
Nursing and Healthcare Administration M,O
Nursing—General M,D,O
Nutrition M,D
Operations Research M,D
Pathobiology D
Pathology D
Pediatric Nursing M,O
Pharmaceutical Sciences M
Pharmacology D
Philosophy M,D
Physics D
Physiology M,D
Political Science M,D,O
Psychology—General D
Public Health—General M,D
Public Policy M
Reading Education M,D,O
Real Estate M
Romance Languages D
School Psychology M,O
Science Education M,O
Secondary Education M,O
Social Sciences Education M,O
Social Sciences M,D
Sociology M,D
Spanish D
Special Education M,D,O
Statistics M,D
Systems Engineering M,O
Technical Writing M
Telecommunications M,O
Toxicology M,D
Urban Education M,O
Women's Health Nursing M,O
Writing M

JOHNSON & WALES UNIVERSITY

Accounting M
Business Education M
Education—General M
Educational Leadership and Administration D
Elementary Education M,D
Higher Education D
Hospitality Management M
International Business M
Secondary Education M,D
Special Education M

JOHNSON STATE COLLEGE

Applied Behavior Analysis M
Art/Fine Arts M
Counselor Education M
Curriculum and Instruction M
Education of the Gifted M
Education—General M,O
Reading Education M
Science Education M
Secondary Education M,O
Special Education M

JOHNSON UNIVERSITY

Education—General M
Educational Media/Instructional Technology M
Marriage and Family Therapy M
Theology M

JONES INTERNATIONAL UNIVERSITY

Accounting M
Adult Education M
Business Administration and Management—General M
Computer and Information Systems Security M
Conflict Resolution and Mediation/Peace Studies M
Corporate and Organizational Communication M
Curriculum and Instruction M
Distance Education Development M
Education—General M
Educational Leadership and Administration M
Educational Media/Instructional Technology M
Elementary Education M
Entrepreneurship M
Finance and Banking M
Health Services Management and Hospital Administration M
Higher Education M
Management of Technology M
Organizational Management M
Project Management M
Secondary Education M

THE JUDGE ADVOCATE GENERAL'S SCHOOL, U.S. ARMY

Law M
Military and Defense Studies M

JUDSON UNIVERSITY

Architecture M
Education—General M
Organizational Management M
Reading Education M

THE JUILLIARD SCHOOL

Music M,D,O

KANSAS CITY UNIVERSITY OF MEDICINE AND BIOSCIENCES

Bioethics M
Biological and Biomedical Sciences—General M
Osteopathic Medicine P

KANSAS STATE UNIVERSITY

Accounting M
Adult Education M,D
Agricultural Economics and Agribusiness M,D
Agricultural Engineering M,D
Agricultural Sciences—General M,D
Agronomy and Soil Sciences M,D
Analytical Chemistry M,D
Animal Sciences M,D
Applied Arts and Design—General M
Architectural Engineering M
Architecture M
Art/Fine Arts M
Biochemistry M,D
Bioengineering M,D
Biological and Biomedical Sciences—General M,D
Business Administration and Management—General M
Chemical Engineering M,D
Chemistry M,D
Child and Family Studies M,D
Civil Engineering M,D
Clothing and Textiles M,D
Communication Disorders M
Communication—General M
Computer Science M,D
Consumer Economics D
Counselor Education M,D
Curriculum and Instruction M,D
Early Childhood Education M
Economics M,D
Education—General M,D
Educational Leadership and Administration M,D
Electrical Engineering M,D
Engineering and Applied Sciences—General M,D*
Engineering Management M,D
English M
Entomology M,D
Family and Consumer Sciences-General M,D
Food Science and Technology M,D
French M
Genetics M,D
Geography M,D
Geology M
German M
Higher Education M,D
History M,D
Horticulture M,D
Hospitality Management M,D
Human Development M,D
Human Services M
Industrial and Manufacturing Management M
Industrial/Management Engineering M,D
Information Science M,D
Inorganic Chemistry M,D
International Affairs M
Kinesiology and Movement Studies M
Landscape Architecture M
Manufacturing Engineering M,D
Marketing M
Marriage and Family Therapy M,D
Mass Communication M
Mathematics M,D
Mechanical Engineering M,D
Microbiology M,D
Music Education M
Music M
National Security M,D
Nuclear Engineering M,D
Nutrition M,D
Operations Research M,D
Organic Chemistry M,D
Pathobiology M,D
Physical Chemistry M,D
Physiology D
Plant Pathology M,D
Political Science M
Psychology—General M,D
Public Administration M
Range Science M,D
Rhetoric M
Sociology M,D
Software Engineering M,D
Spanish M
Special Education M,D
Speech and Interpersonal Communication M
Statistics M,D
Student Affairs M,D
Theater M
Urban and Regional Planning M
Veterinary Sciences M
Vocational and Technical Education M,D

KANSAS WESLEYAN UNIVERSITY

Business Administration and Management—General M
Sports Management M

KAPLAN UNIVERSITY, DAVENPORT CAMPUS

Business Administration and Management—General M
Computer and Information Systems Security M
Criminal Justice and Criminology M
Education—General M
Educational Leadership and Administration M
Educational Media/Instructional Technology M
Entrepreneurship M
Finance and Banking M
Health Services Management and Hospital Administration M,O
Higher Education M
Human Resources Management M
International Business M
Law M
Legal and Justice Studies M,O
Logistics M
Management Information Systems M
Marketing M
Mathematics Education M
Nursing and Healthcare Administration M
Nursing Education M
Nursing—General M
Organizational Management M
Political Science M,O
Project Management M
Reading Education M
Science Education M
Secondary Education M
Special Education M
Student Affairs M
Supply Chain Management M

KEAN UNIVERSITY

Accounting M
Addictions/Substance Abuse Counseling M
Adult Education M
Art Education M
Art/Fine Arts M
Biotechnology M
Business Administration and Management—General M
Clinical Psychology M,D
Communication Disorders M
Communication—General M
Community Health Nursing M
Counseling Psychology M
Counselor Education M
Criminal Justice and Criminology M
Curriculum and Instruction M
Early Childhood Education M
Education—General M
Educational Leadership and Administration M,D
English as a Second Language M
Environmental Management and Policy M
Exercise and Sports Science M
Foreign Languages Education M
Health Services Management and Hospital Administration M
Holocaust and Genocide Studies M
Industrial and Organizational Psychology M
International Business M
Liberal Studies M
Marriage and Family Therapy O
Mathematics Education M
Multilingual and Multicultural Education M
Nonprofit Management M

Nursing and Healthcare Administration M
Nursing—General M
Occupational Therapy M
Political Science M
Psychology—General M
Public Administration M
Reading Education M
School Nursing M
School Psychology D,O
Science Education M
Social Work M
Sociology M
Spanish M
Special Education M
Urban Education D
Writing M

KECK GRADUATE INSTITUTE OF APPLIED LIFE SCIENCES

Biological and Biomedical Sciences—General M,D,O
Computational Biology M,D,O

KEENE STATE COLLEGE

Counselor Education M,O
Curriculum and Instruction M,O
Education—General M,O
Educational Leadership and Administration M,O
School Psychology M,O
Special Education M,O

KEHILATH YAKOV RABBINICAL SEMINARY

Theology

KEISER UNIVERSITY

Accounting M
Business Administration and Management—General M,D
Criminal Justice and Criminology M
Education—General M
Educational Leadership and Administration M,D
Educational Media/Instructional Technology D
Health Services Management and Hospital Administration M
International Business M,D
Marketing M,D
Nursing—General M
Organizational Management D
Physician Assistant Studies M

KENNESAW STATE UNIVERSITY

Accounting M
American Studies M
Applied Statistics M
Art Education M
Business Administration and Management—General M,D
Computer Science M
Conflict Resolution and Mediation/Peace Studies M,D
Early Childhood Education M
Education—General M,D,O
Educational Leadership and Administration M,D,O
Educational Media/Instructional Technology M
Elementary Education M
English as a Second Language M
English Education M
Exercise and Sports Science M
Health Services Management and Hospital Administration M
Information Science M
International Affairs M
Mathematics Education M
Middle School Education M
Nursing—General M,D
Public Administration M
Science Education M
Secondary Education M
Social Work M
Special Education M
Writing M

KENRICK-GLENNON SEMINARY

Theology P,M

KENT STATE UNIVERSITY

Accounting M,D
Adult Nursing M,D
Analytical Chemistry M,D
Anthropology M
Applied Mathematics M,D
Architecture M,O
Art Education M
Art History M
Art/Fine Arts M
Athletic Training and Sports Medicine M
Biochemistry M,D
Biological and Biomedical Sciences—General M,D
Biological Anthropology D
Business Administration and Management—General M
Cell Biology M,D
Chemical Physics M,D
Chemistry M,D*
Child and Family Studies M
Classics M,D
Clinical Psychology M,D
Communication Disorders M,D
Communication—General M,D
Comparative Literature M,D
Computer Education M
Computer Science M,D
Counseling Psychology M
Counselor Education M,D,O
Criminal Justice and Criminology M
Curriculum and Instruction M,D,O
Early Childhood Education M
Ecology M,D
Economics M
Education of the Gifted M
Education—General M,D,O
Educational Leadership and Administration M,D,O
Educational Measurement and Evaluation M,D
Educational Media/Instructional Technology M
Educational Psychology M,D
Engineering and Applied Sciences—General M
English as a Second Language M,D
English Education M,D
English M,D
Exercise and Sports Science M,D
Experimental Psychology M,D
Family Nurse Practitioner Studies M,D
Finance and Banking D
Financial Engineering M
Foreign Languages Education M,D
Foundations and Philosophy of Education M,D
French M,D
Geography M,D
Geology M,D
German M,D
Gerontological Nursing M,D
Gerontology M
Graphic Design M
Health Education M,D
Health Promotion M,D
Higher Education M,D,O
Historic Preservation M,O
History M,D
Hospitality Management M
Human Development M,D
Human Services M,D,O
Illustration M
Information Science M
Inorganic Chemistry M,D
Japanese M,D
Journalism M
Liberal Studies M
Library Science M
Management Information Systems D
Marketing D
Mass Communication M
Mathematics M,D
Middle School Education M
Molecular Biology M,D
Music Education M,D
Music M,D
Neuroscience M,D
Nursing and Healthcare Administration M,D
Nursing—General M,D
Nutrition M
Organic Chemistry M,D
Pediatric Nursing M,D
Pharmacology M,D
Philosophy M
Physical Chemistry M,D
Physics M,D
Physiology M,D
Political Science M,D
Psychiatric Nursing M,D
Psychology—General M,D
Public Administration M
Public Policy M,D
Reading Education M
Recreation and Park Management M
Rehabilitation Counseling M,O
Rhetoric M,D
Russian M,D
School Psychology M,D,O
Secondary Education M
Sociology M,D
Spanish M,D
Special Education M,D,O
Sports Management M
Student Affairs M
Textile Design M
Theater M
Translation and Interpretation M,D
Travel and Tourism M
Urban Design M,O
Vocational and Technical Education M
Women's Health Nursing M,D
Writing M,D

KENT STATE UNIVERSITY AT STARK

Business Administration and Management—General M

KENTUCKY CHRISTIAN UNIVERSITY

Religion M
Theology M

KENTUCKY STATE UNIVERSITY

Accounting M
Aquaculture M
Business Administration and Management—General M
Computer and Information Systems Security M
Computer Science M
Environmental Sciences M
Finance and Banking M
Human Resources Development M
Information Science M
International Affairs M
Management Information Systems M
Marketing M
Nonprofit Management M
Public Administration M
Special Education M

KETTERING UNIVERSITY

Business Administration and Management—General M
Electrical Engineering M
Engineering Management M
Manufacturing Engineering M
Mechanical Engineering M

KEUKA COLLEGE

Business Administration and Management—General M
Criminal Justice and Criminology M
Early Childhood Education M
Nursing—General M
Occupational Therapy M

KING COLLEGE

Business Administration and Management—General M

KING'S COLLEGE

Business Administration and Management—General M
Health Services Management and Hospital Administration M
Physician Assistant Studies M
Reading Education M

KNOWLEDGE SYSTEMS INSTITUTE

Computer Science M
Information Science M

KNOX COLLEGE

Theology P,M,D

KNOX THEOLOGICAL SEMINARY

Missions and Missiology M
Pastoral Ministry and Counseling D
Religion M
Theology P,M,O

KOL YAAKOV TORAH CENTER

Theology O

KONA UNIVERSITY

Transpersonal and Humanistic Psychology M

KUTZTOWN UNIVERSITY OF PENNSYLVANIA

Art Education M,O
Business Administration and Management—General M
Computer Science M
Counseling Psychology M
Counselor Education M
Curriculum and Instruction M,O
Early Childhood Education M,O
Education—General M,O
Educational Leadership and Administration M
Educational Media/Instructional Technology M,O

*M—master's degree; P—first professional degree; D—doctorate; O—other advanced degree; *—Close-Up and/or Display in one of the other books in this series*

Elementary Education M,O
English Education M,O
English M
Library Science M,O
Marriage and Family Therapy M
Mathematics Education M,O
Media Studies M
Public Administration M
Reading Education M
School Nursing M,O
Science Education M,O
Secondary Education M,O
Social Sciences Education M,O
Social Work M
Special Education M,O

LAGRANGE COLLEGE

Curriculum and Instruction M
Education—General M
Middle School Education M
Organizational Management M
Secondary Education M

LAGUNA COLLEGE OF ART & DESIGN

Art/Fine Arts M

LAKE ERIE COLLEGE

Business Administration and Management—General M
Curriculum and Instruction M
Education—General M
Educational Leadership and Administration M
Health Services Management and Hospital Administration M
Reading Education M

LAKE ERIE COLLEGE OF OSTEOPATHIC MEDICINE

Biological and Biomedical Sciences—General P,M,O
Health Education P,M,O
Osteopathic Medicine P,M,O
Pharmacy P,M,O

LAKE FOREST COLLEGE

Education—General M
Liberal Studies M

LAKE FOREST GRADUATE SCHOOL OF MANAGEMENT

Business Administration and Management—General M
Health Services Management and Hospital Administration M
International Business M
Marketing M
Organizational Behavior M

LAKEHEAD UNIVERSITY

Biological and Biomedical Sciences—General M
Chemistry M
Clinical Psychology M,D
Computer Engineering M
Computer Science M
Economics M
Education—General M,D
Electrical Engineering M
Engineering and Applied Sciences—General M
English M
Environmental Engineering M
Exercise and Sports Science M
Experimental Psychology M,D
Forestry M,D
Geology M
Gerontology M,D
Health Services Research M
History M
Kinesiology and Movement Studies M
Mathematics M
Physics M
Psychology—General M,D
Social Work M
Sociology M
Women's Studies M,D

LAKELAND COLLEGE

Accounting M
Business Administration and Management—General M
Counselor Education M
Education—General M
Finance and Banking M
Health Services Management and Hospital Administration M
Project Management M
Theology M

LAMAR UNIVERSITY

Accounting M
Applied Arts and Design—General M
Art History M
Art/Fine Arts M
Biological and Biomedical Sciences—General M
Business Administration and Management—General M
Chemical Engineering M,D
Chemistry M
Civil Engineering M,D
Clinical Psychology M
Communication Disorders M,D
Computer Science M
Counselor Education M,D,O
Criminal Justice and Criminology M
Education—General M,D,O
Educational Leadership and Administration M,D,O
Educational Media/Instructional Technology M,D,O
Electrical Engineering M,D
Engineering and Applied Sciences—General M,D
Engineering Management M,D
English M
Entrepreneurship M
Environmental Engineering M,D
Environmental Management and Policy M,D
Family and Consumer Sciences-General M,O
Finance and Banking M
Health Services Management and Hospital Administration M
History M
Industrial and Organizational Psychology M
Industrial/Management Engineering M,D
Information Science M
Kinesiology and Movement Studies M
Management Strategy and Policy M
Mathematics M
Mechanical Engineering M,D
Music Education M
Music M
Nursing and Healthcare Administration M
Nursing Education M
Nursing—General M
Photography M
Political Science M
Psychology—General M
Public Administration M
Social Psychology M
Special Education M,D
Theater M

LANCASTER BIBLE COLLEGE

Counseling Psychology M,D
Counselor Education M,D
Elementary Education M,D
Marriage and Family Therapy M,D
Pastoral Ministry and Counseling M,D
Secondary Education M,D
Special Education M,D
Theology M,D

LANCASTER THEOLOGICAL SEMINARY

Art History P,M,D,O
Ethics P,M,D,O
Religion P,M,D,O
Religious Education P,M,D,O
Theology P,M,D,O

LANDER UNIVERSITY

Curriculum and Instruction M
Education—General M
Elementary Education M

LANGSTON UNIVERSITY

Education—General M
Elementary Education M
English as a Second Language M
Multilingual and Multicultural Education M
Physical Therapy D
Rehabilitation Counseling M
Urban Education M

LA ROCHE COLLEGE

Human Resources Management M,O
Nurse Anesthesia M
Nursing and Healthcare Administration M
Nursing Education M
Nursing—General M

LA SALLE UNIVERSITY

Business Administration and Management—General M,O
Clinical Psychology M,D
Communication Disorders M
Computer Science M
Corporate and Organizational Communication M
Counseling Psychology M
East European and Russian Studies M
Education—General M
Educational Media/Instructional Technology M
Hispanic Studies M
History M
Latin American Studies M
Management of Technology M
Marriage and Family Therapy D
Nursing—General M,O
Pastoral Ministry and Counseling M
Psychology—General D
Rehabilitation Counseling D
Religion M
Theology M

LASELL COLLEGE

Advertising and Public Relations M,O
Business Administration and Management—General M,O
Communication—General M,O
Corporate and Organizational Communication M,O
Education—General M
Elementary Education M
Hospitality Management M,O
Human Resources Management M,O
Marketing M,O
Nonprofit Management M,O
Project Management M,O
Special Education M
Sports Management M,O

LA SIERRA UNIVERSITY

Accounting M,O
Advertising and Public Relations M
Business Administration and Management—General M,O
Communication—General M
Counselor Education M,O
Curriculum and Instruction M,D,O
Education—General M,D,O
Educational Leadership and Administration M,D,O
Educational Psychology M,O
English M
Finance and Banking M,O
Human Resources Management M,O
Marketing M,O
Pastoral Ministry and Counseling P,M
Religion P,M
Religious Education P,M
School Psychology M,O
Writing M

LAURA AND ALVIN SIEGAL COLLEGE OF JUDAIC STUDIES

Holocaust and Genocide Studies M
Humanities M
Jewish Studies M
Religious Education M

LAUREL UNIVERSITY

Business Administration and Management—General M

LAURENTIAN UNIVERSITY

Analytical Chemistry M
Applied Physics M
Applied Psychology M
Applied Social Research M
Biochemistry M
Biological and Biomedical Sciences—General M,D
Business Administration and Management—General M
Chemistry M
Ecology M,D
Engineering and Applied Sciences—General M,D
Environmental Sciences M
Experimental Psychology M
Geology M,D
History M
Human Development M
Humanities M
Mineral/Mining Engineering M,D
Natural Resources M,D
Nursing—General M
Organic Chemistry M
Physical Chemistry M

Psychology—General M
Public Health—General D
Science Education O
Social Work M
Sociology M
Technical Writing O
Theoretical Chemistry M

LAWRENCE TECHNOLOGICAL UNIVERSITY

Architectural Engineering M,D
Architecture M
Automotive Engineering M,D
Business Administration and Management—General M,D
Civil Engineering M,D
Computer Engineering M,D
Computer Science M
Corporate and Organizational Communication M
Educational Media/Instructional Technology M
Electrical Engineering M,D
Engineering and Applied Sciences—General M,D
Engineering Management M,D
Industrial and Manufacturing Management M,D
Industrial/Management Engineering M,D
Interior Design M
International Business M,D
Management Information Systems M,D
Management of Technology M,D
Manufacturing Engineering M,D
Mechanical Engineering M,D
Project Management M,D
Science Education M
Technical Communication M
Urban Design M

LEBANESE AMERICAN UNIVERSITY

Business Administration and Management—General M
Computer Science M
International Affairs M
Pharmacy P

LEBANON VALLEY COLLEGE

Business Administration and Management—General M
Music Education M
Physical Therapy D
Science Education M

LEE UNIVERSITY

Child Development M
Counseling Psychology M
Counselor Education M
Education—General M,O
Educational Leadership and Administration M,O
Elementary Education M,O
Marriage and Family Therapy M
Music Education M
Music M
Pastoral Ministry and Counseling M
Religion M
Secondary Education M,O
Special Education M,O
Student Affairs M
Theology M

LEHIGH UNIVERSITY

Accounting M
American Studies M,D
Applied Mathematics M,D
Biochemistry M,D
Bioengineering M,D
Biological and Biomedical Sciences—General M,D
Business Administration and Management—General M,D,O
Chemical Engineering M,D
Chemistry M,D
Civil Engineering M,D
Computational Sciences M,D
Computer Engineering M,D
Computer Science M,D
Counseling Psychology M,D,O
Counselor Education M,D,O
Curriculum and Instruction M,D,O
Economics M,D
Education—General M,D,O
Educational Leadership and Administration M,D,O
Educational Media/Instructional Technology M,D,O
Electrical Engineering M,D
Elementary Education M,D,O
Energy and Power Engineering M
Engineering and Applied Sciences—General M,D
Engineering Management M,D
English as a Second Language M,O
English M,D
Environmental Engineering M,D
Environmental Law M,O
Environmental Management and Policy M,O
Environmental Sciences M,D
Finance and Banking M
Geology M,D
Geosciences M,D
History M,D
Human Development M,D
Human Services M,D,O
Industrial/Management Engineering M,D
Information Science M
Interdisciplinary Studies M,D
International and Comparative Education M,O
International Development M,O
Manufacturing Engineering M
Materials Engineering M,D
Materials Sciences M,D
Mathematics M,D
Mechanical Engineering M,D
Mechanics M,D
Molecular Biology M,D
Neuroscience M,D
Photonics M,D
Physics M,D
Political Science M
Polymer Science and Engineering M,D
Project Management M,D,O
Psychology—General M,D
Quantitative Analysis M
School Psychology D,O
Sociology M
Special Education M,D,O
Statistics M,D
Structural Engineering M,D
Student Affairs M,D,O
Supply Chain Management M,D,O
Systems Engineering M,D

LEHMAN COLLEGE OF THE CITY UNIVERSITY OF NEW YORK

Accounting M
Adult Nursing M
Art/Fine Arts M
Biological and Biomedical Sciences—General M
Business Education M
Communication Disorders M
Computer Science M
Counselor Education M
Early Childhood Education M
Education—General M
Elementary Education M
English as a Second Language M
English Education M
English M
Gerontological Nursing M
Health Education M
Health Promotion M
History M
Maternal and Child/Neonatal Nursing M
Mathematics Education M
Mathematics M
Multilingual and Multicultural Education M
Music Education M
Nursing—General M
Nutrition M
Pediatric Nursing M
Plant Sciences D
Reading Education M
Recreation and Park Management M
Science Education M
Social Sciences Education M
Spanish M
Special Education M

LE MOYNE COLLEGE

Business Administration and Management—General M
Early Childhood Education M,O
Education—General M,O
Educational Leadership and Administration M,O
Elementary Education M,O
English as a Second Language M,O
English Education M,O
Middle School Education M,O
Nursing and Healthcare Administration M,O
Nursing Education M,O
Nursing—General M,O
Physician Assistant Studies M
Reading Education M,O
Secondary Education M,O
Social Sciences Education M,O
Special Education M,O
Urban Studies M,O

LENOIR-RHYNE UNIVERSITY

Accounting M
Athletic Training and Sports Medicine M
Business Administration and Management—General M
Counselor Education M
Early Childhood Education M
Education—General M
Entrepreneurship M
Occupational Therapy M
School Psychology M
Social Psychology M

LESLEY UNIVERSITY

Art Education M,D,O
Art Therapy M,D,O
Art/Fine Arts M
Clinical Psychology M,D,O
Computer Education M,D,O
Counseling Psychology M
Curriculum and Instruction M,D,O
Early Childhood Education M,D,O
Ecology M,D,O
Education—General M,D,O
Elementary Education M,D,O
Environmental Education M,D,O
Health Psychology M
Interdisciplinary Studies M
International Affairs M,O
Middle School Education M,D,O
Psychology—General M,D,O
Reading Education M,D,O
School Psychology M
Science Education M,D,O
Social Psychology M,D,O
Special Education M,D,O
Sustainable Development M
Therapies—Dance, Drama, and Music M,D,O
Urban and Regional Planning M
Women's Studies M
Writing M

LETOURNEAU UNIVERSITY

Business Administration and Management—General M
Counselor Education M
Curriculum and Instruction M
Education—General M
Educational Leadership and Administration M
Engineering and Applied Sciences—General M
Management Strategy and Policy M
Psychology—General M

LEWIS & CLARK COLLEGE

Addictions/Substance Abuse Counseling M
Communication Disorders M
Counseling Psychology M,O
Cultural Studies M,O
Curriculum and Instruction M
Early Childhood Education M
Educational Leadership and Administration D,O
Elementary Education M
Environmental Law P,M
Law P,M
Marriage and Family Therapy M
Middle School Education M
Psychology—General M,O
School Psychology M,O
Secondary Education M
Social Psychology M
Special Education M

LEWIS UNIVERSITY

Accounting M
Adult Nursing M
Aviation Management M
Aviation M
Business Administration and Management—General M
Computer and Information Systems Security M
Counseling Psychology M
Counselor Education M
Criminal Justice and Criminology M
Curriculum and Instruction M
Education—General M,D,O
Educational Leadership and Administration M,D,O
Educational Media/Instructional Technology M
Electronic Commerce M
Elementary Education M
English as a Second Language M
Environmental and Occupational Health M
Finance and Banking M
Health Services Management and Hospital Administration M
Human Resources Management M
International Business M
Management Information Systems M
Management of Technology M

*M—master's degree; P—first professional degree; D—doctorate; O—other advanced degree; *—Close-Up and/or Display in one of the other books in this series*

Marketing M
Mathematics Education M
Nursing and Healthcare Administration M
Nursing Education M
Nursing—General M
Organizational Management M
Project Management M
Public Administration M
Reading Education M
Science Education M
Secondary Education M
Social Sciences Education M
Special Education M
Student Affairs M

LEXINGTON THEOLOGICAL SEMINARY

Theology P,M,D

LIBERTY UNIVERSITY

Business Administration and Management—General M
Communication—General M
Counseling Psychology M,D
Counselor Education M,D,O
Curriculum and Instruction M,D,O
Distance Education Development M,D,O
Early Childhood Education M,D,O
Education of the Gifted M,D,O
Education—General M,D,O
Educational Leadership and Administration M,D,O
Educational Media/ Instructional Technology M,D,O
Elementary Education M,D,O
Human Services M,D
Law P
Nursing—General M,D
Pastoral Ministry and Counseling M,D
Reading Education M,D,O
Religion P,M,D
Secondary Education M,D,O
Special Education M,D,O
Sports Management M,D,O
Theology P,M,D

LIFE CHIROPRACTIC COLLEGE WEST

Chiropractic P

LIFE UNIVERSITY

Chiropractic P
Exercise and Sports Science M

LIM COLLEGE

Business Administration and Management—General M
Entrepreneurship M
Textile Design M

LINCOLN CHRISTIAN SEMINARY

Pastoral Ministry and Counseling P,M,D
Religious Education P,M,D
Theology P,M,D

LINCOLN MEMORIAL UNIVERSITY

Business Administration and Management—General M
Counselor Education M,D,O
Curriculum and Instruction M,D,O
Education—General M,D,O
Educational Leadership and Administration M,D,O
English Education M,D,O
Family Nurse Practitioner Studies M
Higher Education M,D,O
Human Resources Development M,D,O
Law P
Nurse Anesthesia M
Nursing—General M
Osteopathic Medicine P
Psychiatric Nursing M

LINCOLN UNIVERSITY (CA)

Business Administration and Management—General M,D
Finance and Banking M,D
Human Resources Management M,D
International Business M,D
Investment Management M,D
Management Information Systems M,D

LINCOLN UNIVERSITY (MO)

Accounting M,O
Business Administration and Management—General M,O
Counselor Education M,O
Criminal Justice and Criminology M,O
Educational Leadership and Administration M,O
Elementary Education M,O
Entrepreneurship M,O
History M,O
Political Science M,O
Public Administration M,O
Public Policy M,O
Secondary Education M,O
Social Sciences M,O
Sociology M,O
Special Education M,O

LINCOLN UNIVERSITY (PA)

Business Administration and Management—General M
Early Childhood Education M
Elementary Education M
Finance and Banking M
Human Resources Management M
Human Services M
Reading Education M

LINDENWOOD UNIVERSITY

Accounting M
American Studies M
Art/Fine Arts M
Business Administration and Management—General M,O
Communication—General M,O
Counseling Psychology M,D,O
Criminal Justice and Criminology M,O
Education—General M,D,O
Educational Leadership and Administration M,D,O
Educational Media/ Instructional Technology M,D,O
Entrepreneurship M
Finance and Banking M
Gerontology M,O
Health Services Management and Hospital Administration M,O
Human Resources Management M,O
Human Services M
International Affairs M
International Business M
Management Information Systems M,O
Marketing M
Nonprofit Management M
Public Administration M
School Psychology M,D,O
Sports Management M
Theater M
Writing M,O

LINDSEY WILSON COLLEGE

Counseling Psychology M
Human Development M

LIPSCOMB UNIVERSITY

Accounting M
Business Administration and Management—General M
Conflict Resolution and Mediation/Peace Studies M,O
Counseling Psychology M,O
Curriculum and Instruction M,D
Education—General M,D
Educational Leadership and Administration M,D
Educational Media/ Instructional Technology M,D
English as a Second Language M,D
Exercise and Sports Science M
Finance and Banking M
Health Services Management and Hospital Administration M
Mathematics Education M,D
Nonprofit Management M
Nutrition M
Pharmacy P
Psychology—General M,O
Religion P,M
Special Education M,D
Sports Management M
Sustainability Management M
Sustainable Development M
Theology P,M

LOCK HAVEN UNIVERSITY OF PENNSYLVANIA

Education—General M
Elementary Education M
Liberal Studies M
Physician Assistant Studies M

LOGAN UNIVERSITY–COLLEGE OF CHIROPRACTIC

Chiropractic P,M
Exercise and Sports Science M
Nutrition M
Rehabilitation Sciences M

LOGOS EVANGELICAL SEMINARY

Theology P,M,D

LOMA LINDA UNIVERSITY

Adult Nursing M
Allied Health—General M,D
Allopathic Medicine P,M,D
Anatomy M,D
Biochemistry M,D
Bioethics M,O
Biological and Biomedical Sciences—General M,D
Biostatistics M,D,O
Child and Family Studies M,D,O
Communication Disorders M
Counselor Education M,D,O
Dentistry P,M,O
Environmental and Occupational Health M
Epidemiology M,D,O
Geosciences M,D
Gerontological Nursing M
Health Education M,D
Health Promotion M,D
Health Services Management and Hospital Administration M
International Health M
Microbiology M,D
Nursing and Healthcare Administration M
Nursing—General M
Nutrition M,D
Occupational Therapy M,D
Oral and Dental Sciences M,O
Pastoral Ministry and Counseling M,O
Pathology M,D
Pediatric Nursing M
Pharmacology M,D
Pharmacy P
Physical Therapy M,D
Physician Assistant Studies M
Physiology M,D
Psychology—General D
Public Health—General M,D,O
Religion M
Social Work M,D

LONG ISLAND UNIVERSITY AT RIVERHEAD

Applied Behavior Analysis M,O
Early Childhood Education M
Education—General M,O
Elementary Education M
Homeland Security M,O
Reading Education M
Special Education M

LONG ISLAND UNIVERSITY, BRENTWOOD CAMPUS

Counseling Psychology M
Counselor Education M
Criminal Justice and Criminology M
Early Childhood Education M
Education—General M
Reading Education M
Special Education M

LONG ISLAND UNIVERSITY, BROOKLYN CAMPUS

Accounting M
Adult Nursing M,O
Athletic Training and Sports Medicine M
Biological and Biomedical Sciences—General M
Business Administration and Management—General M
Chemistry M
Clinical Psychology D
Communication Disorders M
Community Health M
Comparative Literature M
Computer Art and Design M
Computer Science M
Counselor Education M,O
Economics M
Education—General M,O
Educational Leadership and Administration M
Educational Media/ Instructional Technology M
Elementary Education M
English as a Second Language M
English Education M
English M
Exercise and Sports Science M
Health Education M
Health Services Management and Hospital Administration M
History M,O
Human Resources Management M
International Affairs M,O

Mathematics Education	M
Multilingual and Multicultural Education	M
Nursing and Healthcare Administration	M
Nursing—General	M,O
Pharmaceutical Administration	M
Pharmaceutical Sciences	M,D
Pharmacology	M,D
Physical Education	M
Physical Therapy	D
Political Science	M
Psychology—General	M,D
Public Administration	M
Reading Education	M
School Psychology	M
Social Sciences	M,O
Special Education	M
Taxation	M
Toxicology	M,D
Urban Studies	M
Writing	M

LONG ISLAND UNIVERSITY, C.W. POST CAMPUS

Accounting	M,O
Addictions/Substance Abuse Counseling	M
Allied Health—General	M,O
Applied Mathematics	M
Archives/Archival Administration	M,D,O
Art Education	M
Art Therapy	M
Art/Fine Arts	M
Biological and Biomedical Sciences—General	M
Business Administration and Management—General	M,O
Cardiovascular Sciences	M
Clinical Laboratory Sciences/Medical Technology	M
Clinical Psychology	D
Communication Disorders	M
Computer Art and Design	M
Computer Education	M
Computer Science	M
Counselor Education	M
Criminal Justice and Criminology	M
Early Childhood Education	M
Education—General	M,D,O
Educational Leadership and Administration	M,D,O
Educational Media/Instructional Technology	M
Elementary Education	M
Engineering Management	M
English as a Second Language	M
English Education	M
English	M
Environmental Management and Policy	M
Family Nurse Practitioner Studies	M,O
Finance and Banking	M,O
Foreign Languages Education	M
Forensic Sciences	M
Genetic Counseling	M
Geosciences	M
Gerontology	M,O
Health Services Management and Hospital Administration	M,O
History	M
Immunology	M
Information Science	M
Information Studies	M,D,O
Interdisciplinary Studies	M
International Affairs	M
International Business	M,O
Internet and Interactive Multimedia	M
Library Science	M,D,O
Management Information Systems	M,O
Marketing	M,O
Mathematics Education	M
Mathematics	M
Medicinal and Pharmaceutical Chemistry	M
Microbiology	M
Middle School Education	M
Multilingual and Multicultural Education	M
Music Education	M
Music	M
Nonprofit Management	M,O
Nursing—General	M,O
Nutrition	M,O
Perfusion	M
Political Science	M
Psychology—General	M,D
Public Administration	M,O
Reading Education	M
Science Education	M
Secondary Education	M
Social Sciences	M
Social Work	M
Spanish	M
Special Education	M
Taxation	M,O
Theater	M

LONG ISLAND UNIVERSITY, ROCKLAND GRADUATE CAMPUS

Business Administration and Management—General	M,O
Counseling Psychology	M
Counselor Education	M
Early Childhood Education	M
Educational Leadership and Administration	M,O
Elementary Education	M
Entrepreneurship	M,O
Finance and Banking	M,O
Gerontology	M,O
Health Services Management and Hospital Administration	M,O
Pharmaceutical Sciences	M
Public Administration	M,O
Reading Education	M
Secondary Education	M
Special Education	M

LONG ISLAND UNIVERSITY, WESTCHESTER GRADUATE CAMPUS

Business Administration and Management—General	M
Counseling Psychology	M
Counselor Education	M
Early Childhood Education	M,O
Education—General	M,O
Educational Psychology	M
Elementary Education	M,O
English as a Second Language	M,O
Information Studies	M
Library Science	M
Multilingual and Multicultural Education	M,O
Reading Education	M,O
School Psychology	M
Secondary Education	M,O
Special Education	M,O

LONGWOOD UNIVERSITY

Business Administration and Management—General	M
Communication Disorders	M
Counselor Education	M
Criminal Justice and Criminology	M
Education—General	M
Educational Leadership and Administration	M
Educational Media/Instructional Technology	M
Elementary Education	M
English Education	M
English	M
Reading Education	M
Secondary Education	M
Special Education	M
Writing	M

LONGY SCHOOL OF MUSIC

Music	M,O

LORAS COLLEGE

Applied Psychology	M
Educational Leadership and Administration	M
Pastoral Ministry and Counseling	M
Special Education	M
Theology	M

LOUISIANA STATE UNIVERSITY AND AGRICULTURAL AND MECHANICAL COLLEGE

Accounting	M,D
Agricultural Economics and Agribusiness	M,D
Agricultural Education	M,D
Agricultural Engineering	M,D
Agricultural Sciences—General	M,D
Agronomy and Soil Sciences	M,D
Animal Sciences	M,D
Anthropology	M,D
Applied Arts and Design—General	M
Applied Science and Technology	M
Applied Statistics	M
Architecture	M
Art History	M
Art/Fine Arts	M
Astronomy	M,D
Astrophysics	M,D
Biochemistry	M,D
Bioengineering	M,D
Biological and Biomedical Sciences—General	M,D
Biopsychology	M,D
Business Administration and Management—General	M,D
Business Education	M,D
Chemical Engineering	M,D
Chemistry	M,D
Civil Engineering	M,D
Clinical Psychology	M,D
Cognitive Sciences	M,D
Communication Disorders	M,D
Communication—General	M,D
Comparative Literature	M,D
Computer Engineering	M,D
Computer Science	M,D
Counselor Education	M,D,O
Developmental Psychology	M,D
Economics	M,D
Education—General	M,D,O
Educational Leadership and Administration	M,D,O
Educational Measurement and Evaluation	M,D,O
Educational Media/Instructional Technology	M,D,O
Electrical Engineering	M,D
Elementary Education	M,D,O
Engineering and Applied Sciences—General	M,D
English	M,D
Entomology	M,D
Environmental Engineering	M,D
Environmental Management and Policy	M
Environmental Sciences	M,D
Family and Consumer Sciences-General	M,D
Finance and Banking	M,D
Fish, Game, and Wildlife Management	M,D
Food Science and Technology	M,D
Forestry	M,D
French	M,D
Geography	M,D
Geology	M,D
Geophysics	M,D
Geotechnical Engineering	M,D
Graphic Design	M
Higher Education	M,D,O
Hispanic Studies	M
History	M,D
Home Economics Education	M,D
Horticulture	M,D
Human Resources Development	M,D
Industrial and Organizational Psychology	M,D
Industrial/Management Engineering	M,D
Information Studies	M
International and Comparative Education	M,D
Kinesiology and Movement Studies	M,D
Landscape Architecture	M
Law	M,O
Liberal Studies	M
Library Science	M
Linguistics	M,D
Management Information Systems	M,D
Marine Affairs	M,D
Marketing	D
Mass Communication	M,D
Mathematics	M,D
Mechanical Engineering	M,D
Mechanics	M,D
Media Studies	M,D
Medical Physics	M,D
Music Education	M,D
Music	M,D
Natural Resources	M,D
Oceanography	M,D
Petroleum Engineering	M,D
Philosophy	M
Photography	M
Physics	M,D
Plant Pathology	M,D
Political Science	M,D
Psychology—General	M,D
Public Administration	M,D
School Psychology	M,D
Secondary Education	M,D,O
Social Work	M,D
Sociology	M,D
Statistics	M
Structural Engineering	M,D
Systems Science	M,D
Theater	M,D
Toxicology	M
Transportation and Highway Engineering	M,D
Veterinary Medicine	P
Veterinary Sciences	M,D
Vocational and Technical Education	M,D
Water Resources Engineering	M,D
Writing	M,D

LOUISIANA STATE UNIVERSITY HEALTH SCIENCES CENTER

Adult Nursing	M,D
Allopathic Medicine	P,M
Anatomy	M,D
Biological and Biomedical Sciences—General	M,D
Biostatistics	M,D

*M—master's degree; P—first professional degree; D—doctorate; O—other advanced degree; *—Close-Up and/or Display in one of the other books in this series*

Cell Biology M,D
Communication Disorders M,D
Community Health Nursing M,D
Community Health M,D
Dentistry P
Developmental Biology M,D
Environmental and Occupational Health M,D
Epidemiology M,D
Health Services Management and Hospital Administration M,D
Human Genetics M,D
Immunology M,D
Microbiology M,D
Neurobiology M,D
Neuroscience M,D
Nurse Anesthesia M,D
Nursing—General M,D
Occupational Therapy M
Parasitology M,D
Pathology M,D
Pharmacology M,D
Physical Therapy D
Physiology M,D
Public Health—General M,D
Rehabilitation Counseling M

LOUISIANA STATE UNIVERSITY HEALTH SCIENCES CENTER AT SHREVEPORT

Allopathic Medicine P
Anatomy M,D
Biochemistry M,D
Biological and Biomedical Sciences—General M,D
Cell Biology M,D
Immunology M,D
Microbiology M,D
Molecular Biology M,D
Pharmacology D
Physiology M,D

LOUISIANA STATE UNIVERSITY IN SHREVEPORT

Business Administration and Management—General M
Computer Science M
Counseling Psychology M
Counselor Education M
Curriculum and Instruction M
Education—General M
Educational Leadership and Administration M
Health Promotion M
Health Services Management and Hospital Administration M
Human Services M
Kinesiology and Movement Studies M
Liberal Studies M
Public Health—General M
School Psychology O
Systems Science M

LOUISIANA TECH UNIVERSITY

Accounting M,D
Applied Arts and Design—General M
Art/Fine Arts M
Biological and Biomedical Sciences—General M
Biomedical Engineering M,D
Business Administration and Management—General M,D
Business Education M,D
Chemical Engineering M,D
Chemistry M
Civil Engineering M,D
Communication Disorders M
Computer Science M
Counseling Psychology M,D
Counselor Education M,D
Curriculum and Instruction M,D
Economics M,D
Education—General M,D
Educational Leadership and Administration M,D
Electrical Engineering M,D
Engineering and Applied Sciences—General M,D
English Education M,D
English M
Exercise and Sports Science M
Family and Consumer Sciences-General M
Finance and Banking M,D
Foreign Languages Education M,D
Graphic Design M
Health Education M,D
History M
Industrial and Organizational Psychology M,D
Industrial/Management Engineering M
Interior Design M
Marketing M,D
Mathematics Education M,D
Mathematics M
Mechanical Engineering M,D
Modeling and Simulation M,D
Nutrition M
Photography M
Physical Education M,D
Physics M,D
Psychology—General M,D
Science Education M,D
Secondary Education M,D
Social Sciences Education M,D
Special Education M,D
Speech and Interpersonal Communication M
Statistics M

LOUISVILLE PRESBYTERIAN THEOLOGICAL SEMINARY

Religion P,M,D
Theology P,M,D

LOURDES COLLEGE

Education—General M
Educational Media/Instructional Technology M
Organizational Management M

LOYOLA MARYMOUNT UNIVERSITY

Bioethics M
Business Administration and Management—General M
Civil Engineering M
Computer Science M
Counselor Education M
Early Childhood Education M
Education—General M,D
Educational Leadership and Administration M,D
Electrical Engineering M
Elementary Education M
Engineering Management M
English as a Second Language M
English M
Environmental Sciences M
Film, Television, and Video Production M
Law P,M
Marriage and Family Therapy M
Mathematics Education M
Mechanical Engineering M
Multilingual and Multicultural Education M
Pastoral Ministry and Counseling M
Philosophy M
Reading Education M
Religious Education M
School Psychology M
Secondary Education M
Special Education M
Systems Engineering M
Taxation P,M
Theology M
Urban Education M
Writing M

LOYOLA UNIVERSITY CHICAGO

Accounting M
Acute Care/Critical Care Nursing M,O
Adult Nursing M,O
Allopathic Medicine P
Anatomy M,D
Applied Psychology M,D
Applied Statistics M
Biochemistry M,D
Biological and Biomedical Sciences—General M
Business Administration and Management—General M
Cardiovascular Sciences M,O
Cell Biology M,D
Chemistry M,D
Clinical Psychology M,D
Computer Science M
Corporate and Organizational Communication M
Counseling Psychology D
Counselor Education M,O
Criminal Justice and Criminology M
Curriculum and Instruction M,D
Developmental Psychology M,D
Education—General M,D,O
Educational Leadership and Administration M,D,O
Educational Measurement and Evaluation M,D
Educational Media/Instructional Technology M,O
Educational Policy M,D
Educational Psychology M
Elementary Education M,O
English as a Second Language M,O
English M,D
Environmental and Occupational Health M,O
Family Nurse Practitioner Studies M,O
Finance and Banking M
Health Law P,M,D
Health Services Management and Hospital Administration M
Higher Education M,D
History M,D
Human Resources Management M
Immunology M,D
Industrial and Labor Relations M
Infectious Diseases M,O
Information Science M
Law P,M,D
Legal and Justice Studies M,O
Management Information Systems M
Marketing M
Mathematics Education M,O
Mathematics M
Microbiology M,D
Molecular Biology M,D
Molecular Physiology M,D
Neurobiology M,D
Neuroscience M,D
Nursing and Healthcare Administration M
Nursing Informatics M,O
Nursing—General M,D
Nutrition M,O
Oncology Nursing M,O
Pastoral Ministry and Counseling M,O
Pharmacology M,D
Philosophy M,D
Physiology M,D
Political Science M,D
Psychology—General M,D
Public Health—General M
Public History M,D
Reading Education M,O
Religious Education M,O
School Psychology D,O
Science Education M,O
Secondary Education M,O
Social Psychology M,D
Social Work M,D,O
Sociology M,D
Software Engineering M
Spanish M
Special Education M,O
Statistics M
Theology P,M,D,O
Urban and Regional Planning M,O
Urban Studies M,D
Women's Health Nursing M

LOYOLA UNIVERSITY MARYLAND

Accounting M
Business Administration and Management—General M
Clinical Psychology M,D,O
Communication Disorders M,O
Computer Science M
Counseling Psychology M,O
Counselor Education M,O
Curriculum and Instruction M,O
Early Childhood Education M,O
Education—General M,O
Educational Leadership and Administration M,O
Educational Media/Instructional Technology M
Finance and Banking M
International Business M
Liberal Studies M
Management Information Systems M
Marketing M
Pastoral Ministry and Counseling M,D,O
Psychology—General M,D,O
Reading Education M,O
Software Engineering M
Special Education M,O

LOYOLA UNIVERSITY NEW ORLEANS

Adult Nursing M,D
Business Administration and Management—General M
Counselor Education M
Criminal Justice and Criminology M
Family Nurse Practitioner Studies M,D
Health Services Management and Hospital Administration M,D
Law P,M
Music M
Nursing—General M,D
Theology M,O
Therapies—Dance, Drama, and Music M

LUBBOCK CHRISTIAN UNIVERSITY

Theology M

LUTHERAN SCHOOL OF THEOLOGY AT CHICAGO

Pastoral Ministry and Counseling P,M,D
Theology P,M,D

LUTHERAN THEOLOGICAL SEMINARY

Ethics P,M,D
Pastoral Ministry and Counseling P,M,D
Religion P,M,D
Theology P,M,D

LUTHERAN THEOLOGICAL SEMINARY AT GETTYSBURG

Pastoral Ministry and Counseling P,M,D
Religion P,M,D
Theology P,M,D

THE LUTHERAN THEOLOGICAL SEMINARY AT PHILADELPHIA

Pastoral Ministry and Counseling P,M,D,O
Religion P,M,D,O
Theology P,M,D,O

LUTHERAN THEOLOGICAL SOUTHERN SEMINARY

Theology P,M,D

LUTHER RICE UNIVERSITY

Missions and Missiology P,M,D
Pastoral Ministry and Counseling P,M,D
Religious Education P,M,D
Theology P,M,D

LUTHER SEMINARY

Theology P,M,D

LYNCHBURG COLLEGE

Business Administration and Management—General M
Clinical Psychology M
Counseling Psychology M
Counselor Education M
Curriculum and Instruction M
Education—General M
Educational Leadership and Administration M,D
English M
History M
Music M
Nursing—General M
Physical Therapy D
Reading Education M
School Psychology M
Science Education M
Social Psychology M
Special Education M

LYNDON STATE COLLEGE

Counselor Education M
Curriculum and Instruction M
Education—General M
Reading Education M
Science Education M
Special Education M

LYNN UNIVERSITY

Applied Psychology M,O
Aviation Management M
Business Administration and Management—General M
Criminal Justice and Criminology M,O
Education of the Gifted M,D
Education—General M,D
Educational Leadership and Administration M,D
Emergency Management M,O
Hospitality Management M
International Business M
Investment Management M
Marketing M
Mass Communication M
Media Studies M
Music M,O
Special Education M,D
Sports Management M

MACHZIKEI HADATH RABBINICAL COLLEGE

Theology O

MADONNA UNIVERSITY

Adult Nursing M
Business Administration and Management—General M
Clinical Psychology M
Criminal Justice and Criminology M
Education—General M
Educational Leadership and Administration M
English as a Second Language M
Health Services Management and Hospital Administration M
Hospice Nursing M
International Business M
Liberal Studies M
Nursing and Healthcare Administration M
Nursing—General M
Pastoral Ministry and Counseling M
Psychology—General M
Quality Management M
Reading Education M
Special Education M
Theology M

MAHARISHI UNIVERSITY OF MANAGEMENT

Accounting M,D
Asian Studies M,D
Business Administration and Management—General M,D
Computer Science M
Education—General M
Elementary Education M
Secondary Education M
Sustainability Management M,D

MAINE COLLEGE OF ART

Art/Fine Arts M

MAINE MARITIME ACADEMY

International Business M,O
Logistics M,O
Supply Chain Management M,O
Transportation Management M,O

MALONE UNIVERSITY

Business Administration and Management—General M
Counselor Education M
Curriculum and Instruction M
Education—General M
Family Nurse Practitioner Studies M
Nursing—General M
Organizational Management M
Reading Education M
Special Education M
Theology M

MANCHESTER COLLEGE

Athletic Training and Sports Medicine M
Education—General M

MANHATTAN COLLEGE

Chemical Engineering M
Civil Engineering M
Computer Engineering M
Counselor Education M,O
Early Childhood Education M,O
Education—General M,O
Educational Leadership and Administration M,O
Electrical Engineering M
Engineering and Applied Sciences—General M
Environmental Engineering M
Mechanical Engineering M
Multilingual and Multicultural Education M,O
Special Education M,O
Student Affairs M,O

MANHATTAN SCHOOL OF MUSIC

Music M,D,O

MANHATTANVILLE COLLEGE

Art Education M
Early Childhood Education M
Education—General M,D*
Educational Leadership and Administration M,D
Elementary Education M
English as a Second Language M
English Education M
Exercise and Sports Science M
Finance and Banking M
Foreign Languages Education M
Human Resources Development M
International Business M
Liberal Studies M
Management Strategy and Policy M
Marketing M
Mathematics Education M
Middle School Education M
Music Education M
Organizational Management M
Reading Education M
Science Education M
Secondary Education M
Social Sciences Education M
Special Education M
Sports Management M
Writing M

MANSFIELD UNIVERSITY OF PENNSYLVANIA

Art Education M
Education—General M
Elementary Education M
Information Studies M
Library Science M
Music M
Nursing—General M
Organizational Management M
Psychology—General M
Secondary Education M

MAPLE SPRINGS BAPTIST BIBLE COLLEGE AND SEMINARY

Pastoral Ministry and Counseling P,M,D,O
Religious Education P,M,D,O
Theology P,M,D,O

MARANATHA BAPTIST BIBLE COLLEGE

Cultural Studies M
Pastoral Ministry and Counseling M
Religion M
Theology P,M

MARIAN UNIVERSITY (IN)

Education—General M

MARIAN UNIVERSITY (WI)

Adult Nursing M
Business Administration and Management—General M
Education—General M,D
Educational Leadership and Administration M,D
Nursing Education M
Nursing—General M
Organizational Management M
Quality Management M

MARIETTA COLLEGE

Corporate and Organizational Communication M
Education—General M
Physician Assistant Studies M
Psychology—General M

MARIST COLLEGE

Business Administration and Management—General M,O
Computer Science M,O
Corporate and Organizational Communication M
Counseling Psychology M,O
Education—General M,O
Industrial and Manufacturing Management M,O
Management Information Systems M,O
Management of Technology M,O
Psychology—General M,O
Public Administration M
School Psychology M,O
Software Engineering M,O

MARLBORO COLLEGE

Business Administration and Management—General M
Computer Education M
Education—General M
Educational Media/Instructional Technology M
Health Services Management and Hospital Administration M
Information Science M,O
Internet and Interactive Multimedia M
Legal and Justice Studies M
Project Management M,O
Sustainability Management M

*M—master's degree; P—first professional degree; D—doctorate; O—other advanced degree; *—Close-Up and/or Display in one of the other books in this series*

MARQUETTE UNIVERSITY

Accounting M
Acute Care/Critical Care Nursing M,D,O
Adult Nursing M,D,O
Advertising and Public Relations M,O
Analytical Chemistry M,D
Bioinformatics M,D
Biological and Biomedical Sciences—General M,D
Biomedical Engineering M,D
Business Administration and Management—General M
Cell Biology M,D
Chemical Physics M,D
Chemistry M,D
Civil Engineering M,D,O
Clinical Psychology M,D,O
Communication Disorders M,O
Communication—General M,O
Computational Sciences M,D
Computer Engineering M,D,O
Computer Science M,D
Conflict Resolution and Mediation/Peace Studies M,O
Construction Engineering M,D,O
Construction Management M,D,O
Counseling Psychology M,D,O
Counselor Education M,D,O
Criminal Justice and Criminology M,O
Dentistry P
Developmental Biology M,D
Ecology M,D
Economics M
Education—General M,D,O
Educational Leadership and Administration M,D,O
Educational Policy M,D,O
Educational Psychology M,D,O
Electrical Engineering M,D,O
Elementary Education M,D,O
Engineering and Applied Sciences—General M,D,O
Engineering Management M,D,O
English M,D
Entrepreneurship O
Environmental Engineering M,D,O
Ethics M,D
Finance and Banking M
Foreign Languages Education M
Foundations and Philosophy of Education M,D,O
Genetics M,D
Geotechnical Engineering M,D,O
Gerontological Nursing M,D,O
Hazardous Materials Management M,D,O
Health Communication M,O
Health Services Management and Hospital Administration M,O
History M,D
Human Resources Development M
Human Resources Management M
Industrial and Manufacturing Management M
Inorganic Chemistry M,D
Interdisciplinary Studies M,D
International Affairs M,D
International Business M
Jewish Studies M,D
Journalism M,O
Law P
Management Information Systems M
Management of Technology M,D
Marketing Research M
Marketing M
Mass Communication M,O
Maternal and Child/Neonatal Nursing M,D,O
Mathematics Education M,D
Mathematics M,D
Mechanical Engineering M,D,O
Media Studies M,O
Microbiology M,D
Molecular Biology M,D
Neuroscience M,D
Nonprofit Management M,O
Nurse Midwifery M,D,O
Nursing and Healthcare Administration M,D,O
Nursing—General M,D,O
Oral and Dental Sciences M
Organic Chemistry M,D
Pediatric Nursing M,D,O
Philosophy M,D
Physical Chemistry M,D
Physical Therapy D
Physician Assistant Studies M
Physiology M,D
Political Science M
Psychology—General D
Public Administration M,O
Reading Education M,D,O
Real Estate M
Religion M,D
Secondary Education M,D,O
Spanish M
Speech and Interpersonal Communication M,O
Sports Management M,O
Structural Engineering M,D,O
Student Affairs M,D,O
Supply Chain Management M
Theology M,D
Transportation and Highway Engineering M,D,O
Water Resources Engineering M,D,O
Water Resources M,D,O

MARSHALL UNIVERSITY

Adult Education M
Allopathic Medicine P
Art/Fine Arts M
Biological and Biomedical Sciences—General M,D
Business Administration and Management—General M,O
Chemistry M
Classics M
Clinical Psychology M,D
Communication Disorders M
Communication—General M
Counselor Education M,O
Criminal Justice and Criminology M
Early Childhood Education M
Education—General M,D,O
Educational Leadership and Administration M,D,O
Elementary Education M
Engineering and Applied Sciences—General M
Engineering Management M
English M
Environmental Engineering M
Environmental Sciences M
Exercise and Sports Science M
Family and Consumer Sciences-General M
Geography M
Health Education M
Health Services Management and Hospital Administration M,D
History M
Human Resources Management M
Humanities M
Industrial and Organizational Psychology M,D
Information Science M
Journalism M
Management of Technology M
Mass Communication M
Mathematics M
Music M
Nursing—General M
Nutrition M
Physics M
Political Science M
Psychology—General M,D
Reading Education M,O
School Psychology O
Secondary Education M
Sociology M
Spanish M
Special Education M
Sports Management M
Vocational and Technical Education M

MARS HILL GRADUATE SCHOOL

Counseling Psychology M
Religion M
Theology M

MARTIN LUTHER COLLEGE

Curriculum and Instruction M
Education—General M
Educational Leadership and Administration M
Special Education M

MARTIN UNIVERSITY

Pastoral Ministry and Counseling M
Psychology—General M
Social Psychology M

MARY BALDWIN COLLEGE

Education—General M
Elementary Education M
English M
Middle School Education M
Theater M

MARYGROVE COLLEGE

Education—General M
Educational Leadership and Administration M
Elementary Education M
English M
Human Resources Management M
Legal and Justice Studies M
Reading Education M
Secondary Education M
Translation and Interpretation O
Urban Education M

MARYLAND INSTITUTE COLLEGE OF ART

Applied Arts and Design—General M
Art Education M
Art/Fine Arts M,O
Business Administration and Management—General M
Graphic Design M
Illustration M
Museum Studies M
Photography M

MARYLHURST UNIVERSITY

Art Therapy M,O
Business Administration and Management—General M
Counseling Psychology M,O
Education—General M
Energy and Power Engineering M
Environmental Management and Policy M
Finance and Banking M
Health Services Management and Hospital Administration M
Interdisciplinary Studies M
Marketing M
Natural Resources M
Nonprofit Management M
Organizational Behavior M
Public Administration M
Public Policy M
Real Estate M
Sustainable Development M
Theology P,M

MARYMOUNT UNIVERSITY

Allied Health—General M,D,O
Business Administration and Management—General M,O
Computer and Information Systems Security M,O
Counseling Psychology M,O
Counselor Education M
Education—General M
Educational Leadership and Administration M,O
Elementary Education M
English as a Second Language M
English M
Family Nurse Practitioner Studies M,D,O
Forensic Psychology M
Health Promotion M
Health Services Management and Hospital Administration M,O
Human Resources Management M,O
Humanities M
Interior Design M
Legal and Justice Studies M,O
Management Information Systems M,O
Medical Informatics M,O
Nursing Education M,D,O
Nursing—General M,D,O
Organizational Management M,O
Pastoral Ministry and Counseling M,O
Physical Therapy D
Project Management M,O
Secondary Education M
Special Education M

MARYVILLE UNIVERSITY OF SAINT LOUIS

Accounting M,O
Actuarial Science M
Addictions/Substance Abuse Counseling M,O
Adult Nursing M,D
Allied Health—General M,D,O
Art Education M,D
Business Administration and Management—General M,O
Business Education M,O
Early Childhood Education M,D
Education of the Gifted M,D
Education—General M,D
Educational Leadership and Administration M,D
Elementary Education M,D
Entertainment Management M,O
Family Nurse Practitioner Studies M,D
Gerontological Nursing M,D
Higher Education M,D

Marketing M,O
Marriage and Family Therapy M,O
Middle School Education M,D
Nursing Education M,D
Nursing—General M,D
Occupational Therapy M
Organizational Management M
Physical Therapy D
Project Management M,O
Reading Education M,D
Rehabilitation Counseling M,O
Secondary Education M,D
Sports Management M,O
Therapies—Dance, Drama, and Music M

MARYWOOD UNIVERSITY

Architecture M
Art Education M
Art Therapy M,O
Art/Fine Arts M
Biotechnology M
Business Administration and Management—General M
Clinical Psychology M,D
Communication Disorders M
Communication—General M
Corporate and Organizational Communication M,O
Counseling Psychology M
Counselor Education M,O
Criminal Justice and Criminology M
Early Childhood Education M
Education—General M
Educational Leadership and Administration M,D
Educational Media/ Instructional Technology M,O
Electronic Commerce M,O
Elementary Education M
Exercise and Sports Science M
Film, Television, and Video Production M
Finance and Banking M
Gerontology M
Graphic Design M
Health Communication M,O
Health Education D
Health Services Management and Hospital Administration M
Higher Education M,D
Human Development D
Illustration M
Information Science M,O
Interdisciplinary Studies M
Interior Design M
Investment Management M
Kinesiology and Movement Studies M
Library Science M,O
Management Information Systems M
Media Studies M
Music Education M
Nonprofit Management M
Nursing and Healthcare Administration M
Nutrition M,O
Photography M
Physician Assistant Studies M
Psychology—General M
Public Administration M
Reading Education M
School Psychology O
Secondary Education M
Social Work M,D
Special Education M
Textile Design M
Therapies—Dance, Drama, and Music M,O

MASSACHUSETTS COLLEGE OF ART AND DESIGN

Applied Arts and Design—General M
Architecture M
Art Education M
Art/Fine Arts M
Education—General M
Film, Television, and Video Production M
Photography M
Textile Design M
Theater M

MASSACHUSETTS COLLEGE OF LIBERAL ARTS

Curriculum and Instruction M
Education—General M
Educational Leadership and Administration M
Reading Education M
Special Education M

MASSACHUSETTS COLLEGE OF PHARMACY AND HEALTH SCIENCES

Chemistry M,D
Community Health M
Health Services Management and Hospital Administration M
Nursing—General M
Oral and Dental Sciences M
Organic Chemistry M
Pharmaceutical Sciences M,D
Pharmacology M,D
Pharmacy P
Physician Assistant Studies M

MASSACHUSETTS INSTITUTE OF TECHNOLOGY

Aerospace/Aeronautical Engineering M,D,O
Archaeology M,D,O
Architectural History M,D
Architecture M,D
Art History M,D
Atmospheric Sciences M,D
Biochemistry D
Bioengineering M,D
Biological and Biomedical Sciences—General P,M,D
Biomedical Engineering M,D
Business Administration and Management—General M,D
Cell Biology D
Chemical Engineering M,D
Chemistry D
Civil Engineering M,D,O
Cognitive Sciences D
Communication Disorders D
Computational Biology D
Computational Sciences M
Computer Engineering M,D,O
Computer Science M,D,O
Construction Engineering M,D,O
Developmental Biology D
Economics M,D
Electrical Engineering M,D,O
Electronic Materials M,D,O
Engineering and Applied Sciences—General M,D,O
Engineering Management M,D
Environmental Biology M,D,O
Environmental Engineering M,D,O
Environmental Sciences M,D,O
Genetics D
Geochemistry M,D
Geology M,D
Geophysics M,D
Geosciences M,D
Geotechnical Engineering M,D,O
History of Science and Technology D
Hydrology M,D,O
Immunology D
Information Science M,D,O
Inorganic Chemistry D
Linguistics D
Logistics M,D
Manufacturing Engineering M,D,O
Marine Geology M,D
Materials Engineering M,D,O
Materials Sciences M,D,O
Mathematics D
Mechanical Engineering M,D,O
Media Studies M,D
Medical Informatics M
Medical Physics D
Metallurgical Engineering and Metallurgy M,D,O
Microbiology D
Molecular Biology D
Molecular Toxicology D
Neurobiology D
Neuroscience D
Nuclear Engineering M,D,O
Ocean Engineering M,D,O
Oceanography M,D,O
Operations Research M,D
Organic Chemistry M,D,O
Philosophy D
Physical Chemistry D
Physics M,D
Planetary and Space Sciences M,D
Political Science M,D
Polymer Science and Engineering M,D,O
Real Estate M
Social Sciences D
Structural Biology D
Structural Engineering M,D,O
Systems Biology D
Systems Engineering M,D
Technical Writing M
Technology and Public Policy M,D
Toxicology M,D
Transportation and Highway Engineering M,D,O
Urban and Regional Planning M,D
Urban Studies M,D
Writing M

MASSACHUSETTS MARITIME ACADEMY

Emergency Management M
Facilities Management M

MASSACHUSETTS SCHOOL OF LAW AT ANDOVER

Law P

MASSACHUSETTS SCHOOL OF PROFESSIONAL PSYCHOLOGY

Applied Psychology M,D,O
Clinical Psychology M,D,O
Community Health M,D,O
Counseling Psychology M,D,O
Forensic Psychology M,D,O
Industrial and Organizational Psychology M,D,O
International Health M,D,O
Psychology—General M,D,O
School Psychology M,D,O
Student Affairs M,D,O

THE MASTER'S COLLEGE AND SEMINARY

Pastoral Ministry and Counseling P,M,D
Theology P,M,D

MAYO GRADUATE SCHOOL

Biochemistry D
Biological and Biomedical Sciences—General D
Biomedical Engineering D
Cancer Biology/Oncology D
Cell Biology D
Genetics D
Immunology D
Molecular Biology D
Molecular Pharmacology D
Neuroscience D
Structural Biology D
Virology D

MAYO MEDICAL SCHOOL

Allopathic Medicine P

MAYO SCHOOL OF HEALTH SCIENCES

Nurse Anesthesia M
Physical Therapy D

McCORMICK THEOLOGICAL SEMINARY

Pastoral Ministry and Counseling P,M,D,O
Theology P,M,D,O

McDANIEL COLLEGE

Counselor Education M
Curriculum and Instruction M
Educational Leadership and Administration M
Educational Media/ Instructional Technology M
Elementary Education M
Human Resources Development M
Human Services M
Liberal Studies M
Library Science M
Physical Education M
Reading Education M
Secondary Education M
Special Education M

McGILL UNIVERSITY

Accounting M,D,O
Aerospace/Aeronautical Engineering M,D
Agricultural Economics and Agribusiness M
Agricultural Engineering M,D
Agricultural Sciences—General M,D,O
Agronomy and Soil Sciences M,D
Allopathic Medicine M,D
Anatomy M,D
Animal Sciences M,D
Anthropology M,D
Applied Mathematics M,D
Architecture M,D,O
Art History M,D
Asian Studies M,D
Atmospheric Sciences M,D
Biochemistry M,D
Bioengineering M,D
Bioethics M,D,O
Bioinformatics M,D
Biological and Biomedical Sciences—General M,D
Biomedical Engineering M,D
Biostatistics M,D,O
Biotechnology M,D,O
Business Administration and Management—General M,D,O
Cell Biology M,D
Chemical Engineering M,D
Chemistry M,D
Civil Engineering M,D
Clinical Psychology M,D
Communication Disorders M,D
Communication—General M,D
Community Health M,D,O
Computational Sciences M,D
Computer Engineering M,D
Computer Science M,D

*M—master's degree; P—first professional degree; D—doctorate; O—other advanced degree; *—Close-Up and/or Display in one of the other books in this series*

Counseling Psychology M,D,O
Curriculum and Instruction M,D,O
Dentistry P,M,D,O
Developmental Psychology M,D,O
Economics M,D
Education—General M,D,O
Educational Leadership and Administration M,D,O
Educational Psychology M,D,O
Electrical Engineering M,D
Engineering and Applied Sciences—General M,D,O
English M,D
Entomology M,D
Entrepreneurship M,D,O
Environmental and Occupational Health M,D,O
Environmental Engineering M,D
Environmental Management and Policy M,D
Epidemiology M,D,O
Experimental Psychology M,D
Family Nurse Practitioner Studies M,D,O
Finance and Banking M,D,O
Fish, Game, and Wildlife Management M,D
Food Science and Technology M,D
Foreign Languages Education M,D,O
Forensic Sciences M,D,O
Forestry M,D
Foundations and Philosophy of Education M,D,O
French M,D
Genetic Counseling M,D
Geography M,D
Geosciences M,D
Geotechnical Engineering M,D
German M,D
Health Services Management and Hospital Administration M,D,O
Hispanic Studies M,D
History of Medicine M,D
History M,D
Human Genetics M,D
Hydraulics M,D
Immunology M,D
Industrial and Manufacturing Management M,D,O
Information Studies M,D,O
International Business M,D,O
International Development M,D,O
Italian M,D
Jewish Studies M
Kinesiology and Movement Studies M,D,O
Law P,M,D,O
Library Science M,D,O
Linguistics M,D
Management Information Systems M,D,O
Management Strategy and Policy M,D,O
Marketing M,D,O
Materials Engineering M,D,O
Mathematics M,D
Mechanical Engineering M,D
Mechanics M,D
Medical Physics M,D
Meteorology M,D
Microbiology M,D
Mineral/Mining Engineering M,D,O
Music Education M,D
Music M,D
Natural Resources M,D
Near and Middle Eastern Studies M,D,O
Neuroscience M,D
Nursing—General M,D,O
Nutrition M,D,O
Oceanography M,D
Oral and Dental Sciences M,D,O
Parasitology M,D,O
Pathology M,D
Pharmacology M,D
Philosophy M,D
Physical Education M,D,O
Physics M,D
Physiology M,D
Planetary and Space Sciences M,D
Plant Sciences M,D,O
Political Science M,D
Psychology—General M,D
Rehabilitation Sciences M,D,O
Religion M,D
Russian M,D
School Psychology M,D,O
Social Work M,D,O
Sociology M,D,O
Statistics M,D,O
Structural Engineering M,D
Theology M,D
Transportation Management M,D
Urban and Regional Planning M,D
Water Resources Engineering M,D

McKENDREE UNIVERSITY

Business Administration and Management—General M
Counseling Psychology M
Education—General M
Educational Leadership and Administration M
Higher Education M
Human Resources Management M
International Business M
Music Education M
Nursing and Healthcare Administration M
Nursing Education M
Nursing—General M
Special Education M

McMASTER UNIVERSITY

Analytical Chemistry M,D
Anthropology M,D
Applied Statistics M
Astrophysics D
Biochemistry M,D
Biological and Biomedical Sciences—General M,D
Business Administration and Management—General M,D
Cancer Biology/Oncology M,D
Cardiovascular Sciences M,D
Cell Biology M,D
Chemical Engineering M,D
Chemical Physics M,D
Chemistry M,D
Civil Engineering M,D
Classics M,D
Computer Science M,D
Cultural Studies M,D
Economics M,D
Electrical Engineering M,D
Engineering and Applied Sciences—General M,D
Engineering Physics M,D
English M,D
French M
Genetics M,D
Geochemistry M,D
Geography M,D
Geology M,D
Geosciences M,D
Health Physics/Radiological Health M,D
Health Services Research M,D
History M,D
Human Resources Management M,D
Immunology M,D
Industrial and Labor Relations M
Inorganic Chemistry M,D
International Affairs M,D
Kinesiology and Movement Studies M,D
Management Information Systems D
Materials Engineering M,D
Materials Sciences M,D
Mathematics M,D
Mechanical Engineering M,D
Medical Physics M,D
Molecular Biology M,D
Neuroscience M,D
Nuclear Engineering M,D
Nursing—General M,D
Nutrition M,D
Occupational Therapy M
Organic Chemistry M,D
Pastoral Ministry and Counseling P,M,D,O
Pharmacology M,D
Philosophy M,D
Physical Chemistry M,D
Physical Therapy M
Physics D
Physiology M,D
Political Science M,D
Psychology—General M,D
Public Administration M,D
Public Affairs M,D
Public Policy M,D
Rehabilitation Sciences M,D
Religion M,D
Social Work M
Sociology M,D
Software Engineering M,D
Statistics M
Theology P,M,D,O
Virology M,D

McNEESE STATE UNIVERSITY

Accounting M
Addictions/Substance Abuse Counseling M
Agricultural Sciences—General M
Applied Behavior Analysis M
Business Administration and Management—General M
Chemical Engineering M
Chemistry M
Civil Engineering M
Computer Science M
Counseling Psychology M
Counselor Education M,O
Curriculum and Instruction M
Early Childhood Education M
Educational Leadership and Administration M,O
Educational Measurement and Evaluation M,O
Educational Media/Instructional Technology M,O
Electrical Engineering M
Elementary Education M,O
Engineering and Applied Sciences—General M
Engineering Management M
English M
Environmental Sciences M
Exercise and Sports Science M
Experimental Psychology M
Family Nurse Practitioner Studies M
Health Promotion M
Library Science M,O
Mathematics M
Mechanical Engineering M
Middle School Education M,O
Music Education M,O
Nursing and Healthcare Administration M
Nursing Education M
Nursing—General M
Nutrition M
Psychology—General M
Reading Education M
School Psychology M,O
Science Education M
Secondary Education M,O
Special Education M,O
Statistics M
Writing M

MEADVILLE LOMBARD THEOLOGICAL SCHOOL

Pastoral Ministry and Counseling P,M,D
Theology P,M,D

MEDAILLE COLLEGE

Business Administration and Management—General M
Counseling Psychology M
Curriculum and Instruction M
Education—General M
Elementary Education M
Organizational Management M
Psychology—General M
Reading Education M
Secondary Education M
Special Education M

MEDICAL COLLEGE OF WISCONSIN

Allopathic Medicine P
Biochemistry D
Bioethics M,O
Bioinformatics M
Biological and Biomedical Sciences—General M,D,O
Biophysics D*
Biostatistics D
Clinical Laboratory Sciences/Medical Technology M,D
Clinical Research
Community Health M,D,O
Environmental and Occupational Health M
Epidemiology M
Medical Imaging D
Medical Informatics M
Microbiology M,D
Molecular Genetics M,D
Neuroscience D
Pharmacology D
Physiology D
Public Health—General M,D,O
Toxicology D

MEDICAL UNIVERSITY OF SOUTH CAROLINA

Adult Nursing M
Allied Health—General M,D
Allopathic Medicine P
Biochemistry M,D
Biological and Biomedical Sciences—General M,D
Biostatistics M,D
Cancer Biology/Oncology D
Cardiovascular Sciences D
Cell Biology D
Clinical Research M
Dentistry P
Developmental Biology D
Epidemiology M,D
Family Nurse Practitioner Studies M
Genetics D
Health Services Management and Hospital Administration M,D
Health Services Research M
Immunology M,D
International Health M
Marine Sciences D
Maternal and Child/Neonatal Nursing M
Medical Imaging D

Medicinal and Pharmaceutical Chemistry D
Microbiology M,D
Molecular Biology M,D
Molecular Pharmacology M,D
Neuroscience M,D
Nurse Anesthesia M
Nursing and Healthcare Administration M
Nursing Education M
Nursing—General D
Occupational Therapy M
Pathobiology D
Pathology M,D
Pharmacy P
Physical Therapy D
Physician Assistant Studies M
Rehabilitation Sciences D
Toxicology D

MEHARRY MEDICAL COLLEGE

Allopathic Medicine P
Biological and Biomedical Sciences—General D
Cancer Biology/Oncology D
Community Health M
Dentistry P
Environmental and Occupational Health M
Health Services Management and Hospital Administration M
Immunology D
Microbiology D
Neuroscience D
Pharmacology D

MEMORIAL UNIVERSITY OF NEWFOUNDLAND

Adult Education M,D,O
Anthropology M,D
Applied Psychology M,D
Aquaculture M
Archaeology M,D
Biochemistry M,D
Biological and Biomedical Sciences—General M,D,O
Biopsychology M,D
Business Administration and Management—General M
Cancer Biology/Oncology M,D
Cardiovascular Sciences M,D
Chemistry M,D
Civil Engineering M,D
Classics M
Clinical Research M
Community Health M,D,O
Computational Sciences M
Computer Engineering M,D
Computer Science M,D
Condensed Matter Physics M,D
Cultural Anthropology M,D
Curriculum and Instruction M,D,O
Economics M
Education—General M,D,O
Educational Leadership and Administration M,D,O
Educational Media/Instructional Technology M,D,O
Educational Psychology M,D,O
Electrical Engineering M,D
Engineering and Applied Sciences—General M,D
English M,D
Environmental Engineering M
Environmental Sciences M
Epidemiology M,D,O
Exercise and Sports Science M
Experimental Psychology M,D
Fish, Game, and Wildlife Management M,O
Folklore M,D
Food Science and Technology M,D
French M
Gender Studies M,D
Geography M,D
Geology M,D
Geophysics M,D
Geosciences M,D
German M
History M,D
Human Genetics M,D
Humanities M
Immunology M,D
Industrial and Labor Relations M
Kinesiology and Movement Studies M
Linguistics M,D
Marine Affairs M,D,O
Marine Biology M,D
Marine Sciences M,O
Mathematics M,D
Mechanical Engineering M,D
Music M,D
Neuroscience M,D
Nursing—General M,O
Ocean Engineering M,D
Oceanography M,D
Pharmaceutical Sciences M,D
Philosophy M
Physical Education M
Physics M,D
Political Science M
Psychology—General M,D
Religion M
Social Psychology M,D
Social Work M
Sociology M,D
Sport Psychology M
Statistics M,D
Women's Studies M

MEMPHIS COLLEGE OF ART

Applied Arts and Design—General M
Art Education M*
Art/Fine Arts M*

MEMPHIS THEOLOGICAL SEMINARY

Theology P,M,D

MERCER UNIVERSITY

Allopathic Medicine P,M
Biomedical Engineering M
Business Administration and Management—General M
Computer Engineering M
Curriculum and Instruction M,D,O
Early Childhood Education M,D,O
Education—General M,D,O
Educational Leadership and Administration M,D,O
Electrical Engineering M
Engineering and Applied Sciences—General M
Engineering Management M
Environmental Engineering M
Environmental Sciences M
Law P
Management of Technology M
Mechanical Engineering M
Middle School Education M,D,O
Music P,M
Nursing—General M,D,O
Pharmaceutical Sciences P,M,D
Pharmacy P,M,D
Reading Education M,D,O
Secondary Education M,D,O
Software Engineering M
Theology P,M,D

MERCY COLLEGE

Accounting M
Addictions/Substance Abuse Counseling M,O
Allied Health—General M,D,O
Applied Behavior Analysis O
Business Administration and Management—General M
Communication Disorders M
Computer and Information Systems Security M
Counseling Psychology M,O
Counselor Education M,O
Early Childhood Education M
Education—General M,O
Educational Leadership and Administration M,O
Electronic Commerce M,O
Elementary Education M
English as a Second Language M,O
English M
Health Services Management and Hospital Administration M
Human Resources Management M,O
Internet and Interactive Multimedia M,O
Marriage and Family Therapy M,O
Middle School Education M
Multilingual and Multicultural Education M,O
Nursing and Healthcare Administration M,O
Nursing Education M,O
Nursing—General M,O
Occupational Therapy M
Organizational Management M
Physical Therapy D
Physician Assistant Studies M
Psychology—General M
Reading Education M
School Psychology M
Secondary Education M
Special Education M,O
Urban Education M

MERCYHURST COLLEGE

Biological Anthropology M
Criminal Justice and Criminology M,O
Educational Leadership and Administration M,O
Forensic Sciences M
Multilingual and Multicultural Education M,O
Organizational Management M,O
Special Education M,O

MEREDITH COLLEGE

Business Administration and Management—General M
Education—General M
Nutrition M,O

MERRIMACK COLLEGE

Early Childhood Education M,O
Education—General M,O
Educational Leadership and Administration M,O
Elementary Education M,O
English as a Second Language M,O
Higher Education M,O
Middle School Education M,O
Reading Education M,O
Secondary Education M,O
Special Education M,O

MESA STATE COLLEGE

Business Administration and Management—General M
Education—General M
Educational Leadership and Administration M
English as a Second Language M

MESIVTA OF EASTERN PARKWAY–YESHIVA ZICHRON MEILECH

Theology

MESIVTA TIFERETH JERUSALEM OF AMERICA

Theology

MESIVTA TORAH VODAATH RABBINICAL SEMINARY

Theology

MESSIAH COLLEGE

Art Education M
Clinical Psychology M,O
Counseling Psychology M,O
Counselor Education M,O
Marriage and Family Therapy M,O
Music M
Pastoral Ministry and Counseling M

METHODIST THEOLOGICAL SCHOOL IN OHIO

Theology P,M,D

METHODIST UNIVERSITY

Business Administration and Management—General M
Criminal Justice and Criminology M
Physician Assistant Studies M

METROPOLITAN COLLEGE OF NEW YORK

Business Administration and Management—General M
Corporate and Organizational Communication M
Elementary Education M
Media Studies M
Public Administration M

METROPOLITAN STATE UNIVERSITY

Business Administration and Management—General M,D,O
Community Health Nursing M,D
Computer and Information Systems Security M,D,O
Computer Science M
Information Studies M,D,O
Liberal Studies M
Management Information Systems M,D,O
Nonprofit Management M,D,O
Nursing and Healthcare Administration M,D
Nursing Education M,D
Nursing—General M,D
Project Management M,D,O
Psychology—General M,O
Public Administration M,D,O
Secondary Education M,O
Technical Writing M

*M—master's degree; P—first professional degree; D—doctorate; O—other advanced degree; *—Close-Up and/or Display in one of the other books in this series*

Urban Education	M,O
Women's Health Nursing	M,D

MGH INSTITUTE OF HEALTH PROFESSIONS

Communication Disorders	M,O
Gerontological Nursing	M,D,O
Medical Imaging	O
Nursing Education	M,D,O
Nursing—General	M,D,O
Pediatric Nursing	M,D,O
Physical Therapy	M,D,O
Psychiatric Nursing	M,D,O
Reading Education	M,O
Women's Health Nursing	M,D,O

MIAMI INTERNATIONAL UNIVERSITY OF ART & DESIGN

Art/Fine Arts	M
Computer Art and Design	M
Film, Television, and Video Production	M
Graphic Design	M*
Interior Design	M

MIAMI UNIVERSITY

Accounting	M
Architecture	M
Art Education	M
Art/Fine Arts	M
Biochemistry	M,D
Botany	M,D
Business Administration and Management—General	M
Chemistry	M,D
Child and Family Studies	M
Communication Disorders	M
Computational Sciences	M
Curriculum and Instruction	M,D
Early Childhood Education	M
Economics	M
Education—General	M,D,O
Educational Leadership and Administration	M,D
Educational Media/Instructional Technology	M,O
Educational Psychology	M,O
Elementary Education	M
Engineering and Applied Sciences—General	M,O
English	M,D
Environmental Sciences	M
Exercise and Sports Science	M
French	M
Geography	M
Geology	M,D
Gerontology	M,D
Higher Education	M,D
History	M
Mathematics Education	M
Mathematics	M
Microbiology	M,D
Music Education	M
Music	M
Paper and Pulp Engineering	M
Philosophy	M
Physics	M
Plant Biology	M,D
Plant Sciences	M,D
Political Science	M
Psychology—General	D
Reading Education	M
Religion	M
School Psychology	M,O
Secondary Education	M
Software Engineering	M,O
Special Education	M,O
Statistics	M
Student Affairs	M,D
Systems Science	M
Theater	M
Zoology	M,D

MICHIGAN SCHOOL OF PROFESSIONAL PSYCHOLOGY

Clinical Psychology	M,D
Educational Psychology	M,D
Psychology—General	M,D
Transpersonal and Humanistic Psychology	M,D

MICHIGAN STATE UNIVERSITY

Accounting	M,D
Adult Education	M,D,O
Advertising and Public Relations	M,D
African Studies	M,D
African-American Studies	M,D
Agricultural Economics and Agribusiness	M,D
Agricultural Sciences—General	M,D
Agronomy and Soil Sciences	M,D
Allopathic Medicine	P
American Studies	M,D
Animal Sciences	M,D
Anthropology	M,D
Applied Mathematics	M,D
Applied Statistics	M,D
Art/Fine Arts	M
Astronomy	M,D
Astrophysics	M,D
Biochemistry	M,D
Biological and Biomedical Sciences—General	M,D
Biosystems Engineering	M,D
Business Administration and Management—General	M,D
Cell Biology	M,D
Chemical Engineering	M,D
Chemical Physics	M,D
Chemistry	M,D
Child and Family Studies	M,D
Child Development	M,D
Civil Engineering	M,D
Clinical Laboratory Sciences/Medical Technology	M
Communication Disorders	M,D
Communication—General	M,D
Computer Art and Design	M
Computer Science	M,D
Construction Management	M,D
Counselor Education	M,D,O
Criminal Justice and Criminology	M,D
Curriculum and Instruction	M,D,O
Ecology	D
Economics	M,D
Education—General	M,D,O
Educational Leadership and Administration	M,D,O
Educational Measurement and Evaluation	M,D,O
Educational Media/Instructional Technology	M,D,O
Educational Policy	D
Educational Psychology	M,D,O
Electrical Engineering	M,D
Engineering and Applied Sciences—General	M,D
English as a Second Language	M,D
English	M,D
Entomology	M,D
Environmental Design	M,D
Environmental Engineering	M,D
Environmental Sciences	M,D
Epidemiology	M,D
Evolutionary Biology	D
Finance and Banking	M,D
Fish, Game, and Wildlife Management	M,D
Food Science and Technology	M,D
Foreign Languages Education	D
Forensic Sciences	M,D
Forestry	M,D
French	M,D
Game Design and Development	M
Genetics	M,D
Geography	M,D
Geosciences	M,D
German	M,D
Health Communication	M
Higher Education	M,D,O
Hispanic and Latin American Languages	M,D
Hispanic Studies	M,D
History	M,D
Horticulture	M,D
Hospitality Management	M
Human Resources Management	M,D
Industrial and Labor Relations	M,D
Interior Design	M,D
Journalism	M
Kinesiology and Movement Studies	M,D
Latin American Studies	D
Linguistics	M,D
Management Information Systems	M,D
Manufacturing Engineering	M,D
Marketing	M,D
Marriage and Family Therapy	M,D
Materials Engineering	M,D
Materials Sciences	M,D
Mathematics Education	M,D
Mathematics	M,D
Mechanical Engineering	M,D
Mechanics	M,D
Media Studies	M,D
Microbiology	M,D
Molecular Biology	M,D
Molecular Genetics	M,D
Music Education	M,D
Music	M,D
Natural Resources	M,D
Neuroscience	M,D
Nursing—General	M,D
Nutrition	M,D
Osteopathic Medicine	P
Pathobiology	M,D
Pathology	M,D
Pharmacology	M,D
Philosophy	M,D
Physics	M,D
Physiology	M,D
Plant Biology	M,D
Plant Pathology	M,D
Plant Sciences	M,D
Political Science	M,D
Portuguese	M,D
Psychology—General	M,D
Public Health—General	M
Reading Education	M
Recreation and Park Management	M,D
Rehabilitation Counseling	M,D,O
Rhetoric	M,D
Romance Languages	M,D
School Psychology	M,D,O
Science Education	M,D
Social Sciences Education	M,D
Social Work	M,D
Sociology	M,D
Spanish	M,D
Special Education	M,D,O
Statistics	M,D
Structural Biology	D
Supply Chain Management	M,D
Systems Biology	D
Telecommunications	M
Theater	M
Therapies—Dance, Drama, and Music	M,D
Toxicology	M,D
Urban and Regional Planning	M,D
Veterinary Medicine	P
Veterinary Sciences	M,D
Writing	M,D
Zoology	M,D

MICHIGAN STATE UNIVERSITY COLLEGE OF LAW

Law	P,M
Legal and Justice Studies	P,M

MICHIGAN TECHNOLOGICAL UNIVERSITY

Archaeology	M,D
Atmospheric Sciences	D
Biological and Biomedical Sciences—General	M,D
Biomedical Engineering	D
Business Administration and Management—General	M
Chemical Engineering	M,D
Chemistry	M,D
Civil Engineering	M,D
Computational Sciences	D
Computer Engineering	D
Computer Science	M,D
Ecology	M
Electrical Engineering	M,D
Engineering and Applied Sciences—General	M,D
Engineering Physics	D
Environmental Engineering	M,D
Environmental Management and Policy	M,D
Forestry	M,D
Geological Engineering	M,D
Geology	M,D
Geophysics	M
Historic Preservation	D
Materials Engineering	M,D
Mathematics	M,D
Mechanical Engineering	M,D
Mechanics	M
Metallurgical Engineering and Metallurgy	M,D
Mineral Economics	M
Mineral/Mining Engineering	M,D
Physics	M,D
Plant Molecular Biology	M,D
Rhetoric	M,D
Science Education	M
Sustainability Management	O
Sustainable Development	O
Technical Communication	M,D

MICHIGAN THEOLOGICAL SEMINARY

Counseling Psychology	P,M,O
Religion	P,M,O
Religious Education	P,M,O
Theology	P,M,O

MID-AMERICA BAPTIST THEOLOGICAL SEMINARY

Theology	P,M,D

MID-AMERICA BAPTIST THEOLOGICAL SEMINARY NORTHEAST BRANCH

Theology	P

MID-AMERICA CHRISTIAN UNIVERSITY

Business Administration and Management—General	M
Counseling Psychology	M
Marriage and Family Therapy	M
Organizational Management	M
Pastoral Ministry and Counseling	M
Public Administration	M

MIDAMERICA NAZARENE UNIVERSITY

Business Administration and Management—General	M
Counseling Psychology	M,O
Education—General	M
Educational Media/Instructional Technology	M
English as a Second Language	M
Finance and Banking	M
International Business	M
Nonprofit Management	M
Organizational Management	M
Special Education	M

MID-AMERICA REFORMED SEMINARY

Theology	P,M

MIDDLEBURY COLLEGE

Chinese	M
English	M
French	M,D
German	M,D
Italian	M,D
Russian	M,D
Spanish	M,D

MIDDLE TENNESSEE SCHOOL OF ANESTHESIA

Nurse Anesthesia	M

MIDDLE TENNESSEE STATE UNIVERSITY

Accounting	M
Aerospace/Aeronautical Engineering	M
Aviation Management	M
Biological and Biomedical Sciences—General	M
Biostatistics	M
Business Administration and Management—General	M
Business Education	M
Chemistry	M,D
Child and Family Studies	M
Child Development	M
Clinical Psychology	M,O
Computer Science	M
Counseling Psychology	M,O
Counselor Education	M,O
Criminal Justice and Criminology	M
Curriculum and Instruction	M,O
Early Childhood Education	M,O
Economics	M,D
Education—General	M,D,O
Educational Leadership and Administration	M,O
Educational Media/Instructional Technology	M,O
Elementary Education	M,O
English as a Second Language	M,O
English	M,D
Exercise and Sports Science	M,D
Experimental Psychology	M,O
Family Nurse Practitioner Studies	M,O
Food Science and Technology	M
Foreign Languages Education	M
Geosciences	O
Gerontology	O
Health Education	M
Health Services Management and Hospital Administration	O
History	M
Industrial and Organizational Psychology	M,O
Management Information Systems	M
Management Strategy and Policy	M,O
Marketing	M
Mass Communication	M
Mathematics Education	M,D
Mathematics	M,D
Medical Informatics	M
Middle School Education	M,O
Music	M
Nursing—General	M,O
Nutrition	M
Physical Education	M
Psychology—General	M
Public History	M,D
Reading Education	M,D
Recreation and Park Management	M
School Psychology	M,O
Science Education	M
Secondary Education	M,O
Social Sciences	M,O
Social Work	M
Sociology	M
Special Education	M,O
Vocational and Technical Education	M

MIDWAY COLLEGE

Business Administration and Management—General	M
Organizational Management	M

MIDWEST COLLEGE OF ORIENTAL MEDICINE

Acupuncture and Oriental Medicine	M,O

MIDWESTERN BAPTIST THEOLOGICAL SEMINARY

Archaeology	P,M,D,O
Linguistics	P,M,D,O
Missions and Missiology	P,M,D,O
Music	P,M,D,O
Pastoral Ministry and Counseling	P,M,D,O
Religion	P,M,D,O
Religious Education	P,M,D,O
Theology	P,M,D,O

MIDWESTERN STATE UNIVERSITY

Biological and Biomedical Sciences—General	M
Business Administration and Management—General	M
Computer Science	M
Counselor Education	M
Criminal Justice and Criminology	M
Curriculum and Instruction	M
Education—General	M
Educational Leadership and Administration	M
Educational Media/Instructional Technology	M
English	M
Family Nurse Practitioner Studies	M
Health Physics/Radiological Health	M
Health Services Management and Hospital Administration	M
History	M
Human Resources Development	M
Kinesiology and Movement Studies	M
Nursing Education	M
Nursing—General	M
Political Science	M
Psychiatric Nursing	M
Psychology—General	M
Public Administration	M
Reading Education	M
Special Education	M

MIDWESTERN UNIVERSITY, DOWNERS GROVE CAMPUS

Allied Health—General	M,D
Biological and Biomedical Sciences—General	M
Clinical Psychology	M,D
Occupational Therapy	M
Osteopathic Medicine	P
Pharmacy	P
Physical Therapy	D
Physician Assistant Studies	M

MIDWESTERN UNIVERSITY, GLENDALE CAMPUS

Allied Health—General	P,M,D,O
Bioethics	M,O
Biological and Biomedical Sciences—General	M
Cardiovascular Sciences	M
Clinical Psychology	D
Dentistry	P
Health Education	M
Nurse Anesthesia	M
Occupational Therapy	M
Optometry	P
Osteopathic Medicine	P
Pharmacy	P
Physical Therapy	D
Physician Assistant Studies	M
Podiatric Medicine	P

MIDWEST UNIVERSITY

English as a Second Language	P,M,D
Theology	P,M,D

MIDWIVES COLLEGE OF UTAH

Nurse Midwifery	M

MILLERSVILLE UNIVERSITY OF PENNSYLVANIA

Art Education	M
Clinical Psychology	M
Early Childhood Education	M
Education of the Gifted	M
Education—General	M
Elementary Education	M
Emergency Management	M
English Education	M
English	M
Foundations and Philosophy of Education	M
French	M
German	M
History	M
Mathematics Education	M
Nursing—General	M
Psychology—General	M
Reading Education	M
School Psychology	M
Social Work	M
Spanish	M
Special Education	M
Sports Management	M
Vocational and Technical Education	M

MILLIGAN COLLEGE

Business Administration and Management—General	M
Education—General	M
Occupational Therapy	M

MILLIKIN UNIVERSITY

Business Administration and Management—General	M
Nurse Anesthesia	M
Nursing and Healthcare Administration	M
Nursing Education	M
Nursing—General	M

MILLSAPS COLLEGE

Accounting	M
Business Administration and Management—General	M

MILLS COLLEGE

Art Education	M,D
Art/Fine Arts	M
Biological and Biomedical Sciences—General	O
Business Administration and Management—General	M
Computer Science	M,O
Curriculum and Instruction	M,D
Dance	M
Early Childhood Education	M,D
Education—General	M,D
Educational Leadership and Administration	M,D
Elementary Education	M,D
English Education	M,D
English	M
Foreign Languages Education	M,D
Health Education	M,D
Illustration	M
Interdisciplinary Studies	M,O
Mathematics Education	M,D
Music	M
Photography	M
Public Policy	M
Science Education	M,D
Secondary Education	M,D
Social Sciences Education	M,D
Writing	M

MILWAUKEE SCHOOL OF ENGINEERING

Business Administration and Management—General	M
Cardiovascular Sciences	M
Civil Engineering	M
Clinical Laboratory Sciences/Medical Technology	M
Engineering and Applied Sciences—General	M
Engineering Management	M
Environmental Engineering	M
Industrial and Manufacturing Management	M
International Business	M
Marketing	M
Medical Informatics	M
Perfusion	M
Structural Engineering	M

MINNEAPOLIS COLLEGE OF ART AND DESIGN

Applied Arts and Design—General	M
Art/Fine Arts	M,O
Computer Art and Design	O
Film, Television, and Video Production	M
Graphic Design	M,O
Illustration	M
Photography	M
Sustainable Development	O

*M—master's degree; P—first professional degree; D—doctorate; O—other advanced degree; *—Close-Up and/or Display in one of the other books in this series*

MINNESOTA STATE UNIVERSITY MANKATO

Allied Health—General M,D,O
Anthropology M
Art Education M
Art/Fine Arts M
Astronomy M
Automotive Engineering M
Biological and Biomedical Sciences—General M
Business Administration and Management—General M
Clinical Psychology M,D
Communication Disorders M
Communication—General M,O
Community Health M,O
Corporate and Organizational Communication M,O
Counseling Psychology M,D,O
Counselor Education M,D,O
Curriculum and Instruction M,O
Database Systems M,O
Early Childhood Education M,O
Education—General M,D,O
Educational Leadership and Administration M
Educational Media/Instructional Technology M,O
Electrical Engineering M
Elementary Education M,O
English as a Second Language M,O
English Education M,O
English M,O
Environmental Sciences M
Ethnic Studies M,O
Family Nurse Practitioner Studies M,D
French M
Gender Studies M,O
Geographic Information Systems M,O
Geography M,O
Gerontology M,O
Health Education M,O
Higher Education M
History M
Human Services M
Industrial and Organizational Psychology M,D
Interdisciplinary Studies M
Management Information Systems M,O
Manufacturing Engineering M
Marriage and Family Therapy M,D,O
Mathematics Education M
Mathematics M
Multilingual and Multicultural Education M,O
Music M
Nursing—General M,D
Physical Education M
Physics M
Psychology—General M,D
Public Administration M
Rehabilitation Counseling M
School Psychology M,D
Science Education M
Secondary Education M,O
Social Sciences Education M
Social Work M
Sociology M
Spanish M
Special Education M,O
Statistics M
Student Affairs M,D,O
Technical Communication M,O
Theater M
Urban and Regional Planning M,O
Urban Studies M,O
Women's Studies M,O
Writing M,O

MINNESOTA STATE UNIVERSITY MOORHEAD

Communication Disorders M
Counselor Education M
Curriculum and Instruction M
Education—General M,O
Educational Leadership and Administration M,O
Human Services M,O
Liberal Studies M
Nursing Education M
Nursing—General M,O
Public Administration M
Reading Education M
School Psychology M,O
Special Education M
Writing M

MINOT STATE UNIVERSITY

Business Administration and Management—General M
Communication Disorders M
Criminal Justice and Criminology M
Early Childhood Education M
Education of Students with Severe/Multiple Disabilities M
Elementary Education M
Management Information Systems M
Mathematics Education M
Music Education M
School Psychology O
Science Education M
Special Education M

MIRRER YESHIVA

Theology

MISERICORDIA UNIVERSITY

Allied Health—General M,D
Business Administration and Management—General M
Communication Disorders M
Curriculum and Instruction M
Education—General M
Nursing—General M
Occupational Therapy M,D
Organizational Management M
Physical Therapy M,D

MISSISSIPPI COLLEGE

Accounting M,O
Advertising and Public Relations M
Art Education M,D,O
Art/Fine Arts M
Biochemistry M
Biological and Biomedical Sciences—General M
Business Administration and Management—General M,O
Business Education M,D,O
Chemistry M
Communication—General M
Computer Education M,D,O
Computer Science M
Corporate and Organizational Communication M
Counseling Psychology M,O
Counselor Education M,O
Criminal Justice and Criminology M,O
Curriculum and Instruction M,D,O
Education—General M,D,O
Educational Leadership and Administration M,D,O
Elementary Education M,D,O
English as a Second Language M
English Education M,D,O
English M
Finance and Banking M,O
Health Services Management and Hospital Administration M
Higher Education M,D,O
History M,O
Kinesiology and Movement Studies M
Law P,O
Legal and Justice Studies M,O
Liberal Studies M
Marriage and Family Therapy M,O
Mathematics Education M,D,O
Mathematics M
Music Education M
Music M
Political Science M,O
Science Education M,D,O
Secondary Education M,D,O
Social Sciences Education M,D,O
Social Sciences M,O
Special Education M,D,O

MISSISSIPPI STATE UNIVERSITY

Accounting M,D
Aerospace/Aeronautical Engineering M,D
Agricultural Economics and Agribusiness M
Agricultural Education M,D
Agricultural Sciences—General M,D
Agronomy and Soil Sciences M,D
American Studies M,D
Animal Sciences M,D
Anthropology M
Applied Economics M,D
Applied Physics M,D
Architecture M
Atmospheric Sciences M,D
Biochemistry M,D
Bioengineering M,D
Biological and Biomedical Sciences—General M,D
Biomedical Engineering M,D
Business Administration and Management—General M,D
Chemical Engineering M,D
Chemistry M,D
Civil Engineering M,D
Clinical Psychology M,D
Cognitive Sciences M,D
Community College Education M,D,O
Computer Art and Design M
Computer Engineering M,D
Computer Science M,D
Counselor Education M,D,O
Curriculum and Instruction M,D,O
Economics M,D
Education—General M,D,O
Educational Leadership and Administration M,D,O
Educational Media/Instructional Technology M,D,O
Educational Psychology M,D,O
Electrical Engineering M,D
Elementary Education M,D,O
Engineering and Applied Sciences—General M,D
English M
Entomology M,D
Exercise and Sports Science M
Experimental Psychology M,D
Finance and Banking M,D
Fish, Game, and Wildlife Management M,D
Food Science and Technology M,D
Foreign Languages Education M
Forestry M,D
French M
Genetics M,D
Geosciences M,D
German M
Health Promotion M,D
History M,D
Horticulture M,D
Human Resources Development M,D,O
Industrial/Management Engineering M,D
Interdisciplinary Studies M,D
Kinesiology and Movement Studies M
Landscape Architecture M
Management Information Systems M,D
Marketing M,D
Mathematics M,D
Mechanical Engineering M,D
Molecular Biology M,D
Nutrition M,D
Physical Education M
Physics M,D
Plant Pathology M,D
Plant Sciences M,D
Political Science M,D
Project Management M
Psychology—General M,D
Public Administration M,D
Public Policy M,D
School Psychology M,D,O
Secondary Education M,D,O
Sociology M,D
Spanish M
Special Education M,D,O
Sports Management M
Statistics M,D
Student Affairs M,D,O
Systems Engineering M,D
Taxation M,D
Veterinary Medicine P
Veterinary Sciences M,D
Vocational and Technical Education M,D,O
Western European Studies M,D

MISSISSIPPI UNIVERSITY FOR WOMEN

Communication Disorders M,O
Curriculum and Instruction M
Education of the Gifted M
Education—General M
Educational Leadership and Administration M
Health Education M
Nursing—General M,O
Reading Education M

MISSISSIPPI VALLEY STATE UNIVERSITY

Bioinformatics M
Criminal Justice and Criminology M
Education—General M
Elementary Education M
Environmental and Occupational Health M

MISSOURI BAPTIST UNIVERSITY

Business Administration and Management—General M,O
Counselor Education M,O
Education—General M,O
Educational Leadership and Administration M,O
Pastoral Ministry and Counseling M,O

MISSOURI SOUTHERN STATE UNIVERSITY

Business Administration and Management—General M
Criminal Justice and Criminology M
Dental Hygiene M

Early Childhood Education	M
Education—General	M
Educational Media/ Instructional Technology	M
Nursing—General	M

MISSOURI STATE UNIVERSITY

Accounting	M
Agricultural Education	M
Agricultural Sciences—General	M
Anthropology	M
Applied Science and Technology	M
Art Education	M
Art/Fine Arts	M
Biological and Biomedical Sciences—General	M
Business Administration and Management—General	M
Cell Biology	M
Chemistry	M
Child and Family Studies	M
Clinical Psychology	M
Communication Disorders	M,D
Communication—General	M
Computer Science	M
Construction Management	M
Counselor Education	M
Criminal Justice and Criminology	M
Curriculum and Instruction	M
Early Childhood Education	M
Educational Leadership and Administration	M,O
Educational Media/ Instructional Technology	M
Elementary Education	M,O
English	M
Environmental Management and Policy	M
Experimental Psychology	M
Family and Consumer Sciences-General	M
Family Nurse Practitioner Studies	M
Foreign Languages Education	M
Geography	M
Geology	M
Geosciences	M
Health Promotion	M
Health Services Management and Hospital Administration	M
History	M
Industrial and Organizational Psychology	M
Interior Design	M
International Affairs	M
Management Information Systems	M
Materials Sciences	M
Mathematics	M
Military and Defense Studies	M
Molecular Biology	M
Music Education	M
Music	M
Natural Resources	M
Nurse Anesthesia	M
Nursing Education	M
Nursing—General	M
Physical Education	M
Physical Therapy	D
Physician Assistant Studies	M
Plant Sciences	M
Political Science	M
Project Management	M
Psychology—General	M
Public Administration	M
Public Health—General	M
Reading Education	M
Religion	M
Science Education	M
Secondary Education	M,O
Social Psychology	M
Social Sciences Education	M
Social Work	M
Spanish	M
Special Education	M,D
Sports Management	M
Student Affairs	M
Textile Design	M
Theater	M
Urban and Regional Planning	M

MISSOURI UNIVERSITY OF SCIENCE AND TECHNOLOGY

Aerospace/Aeronautical Engineering	M,D
Applied Mathematics	M,D
Biological and Biomedical Sciences—General	M
Ceramic Sciences and Engineering	M,D
Chemical Engineering	M,D
Chemistry	M,D
Civil Engineering	M,D
Computer Engineering	M,D
Computer Science	M,D
Construction Engineering	M,D
Electrical Engineering	M,D
Engineering and Applied Sciences—General	M,D
Engineering Management	M,D
Environmental Biology	M
Environmental Engineering	M,D
Geochemistry	M,D
Geological Engineering	M,D
Geology	M,D
Geophysics	M,D
Geotechnical Engineering	M,D
Hydraulics	M,D
Hydrology	M,D
Information Science	M
Manufacturing Engineering	M,D
Mathematics Education	M,D
Mathematics	M,D
Mechanical Engineering	M,D
Mechanics	M,D
Metallurgical Engineering and Metallurgy	M,D
Mineral/Mining Engineering	M,D
Nuclear Engineering	M,D
Petroleum Engineering	M,D
Physics	M,D
Statistics	M,D
Systems Engineering	M,D
Water Resources	M,D

MISSOURI WESTERN STATE UNIVERSITY

Chemistry	M
Educational Measurement and Evaluation	M
Engineering and Applied Sciences—General	M
English as a Second Language	M
Ergonomics and Human Factors	M
Forensic Sciences	M
Management Information Systems	M
Media Studies	M
Nursing and Healthcare Administration	M
Nursing—General	M
Rhetoric	M
Special Education	M
Technical Communication	M
Writing	M

MOLLOY COLLEGE

Accounting	M
Adult Nursing	M,O
Business Administration and Management—General	M
Criminal Justice and Criminology	M
Education—General	M,O
Family Nurse Practitioner Studies	M,O
Finance and Banking	M
Nursing and Healthcare Administration	M,O
Nursing Education	M,O
Nursing Informatics	M,O
Nursing—General	M,O
Pediatric Nursing	M,O
Psychiatric Nursing	M,O
Social Work	M
Therapies—Dance, Drama, and Music	M

MONMOUTH UNIVERSITY

Accounting	M,O
Adult Nursing	M,D,O
Advertising and Public Relations	M,O
American Studies	M
Business Administration and Management—General	M,O
Communication—General	M,O
Computer Science	M,O
Corporate and Organizational Communication	M,O
Counseling Psychology	M,O
Criminal Justice and Criminology	M,O
Education—General	M,O
Educational Leadership and Administration	M,O
Elementary Education	M,O
English as a Second Language	M,O
English	M
Family Nurse Practitioner Studies	M,D,O
Finance and Banking	M,O
Forensic Nursing	M,D,O
Health Services Management and Hospital Administration	M,O
History	M
Homeland Security	M,O
Liberal Studies	M
Mathematical and Computational Finance	M
Nursing and Healthcare Administration	M,D,O
Nursing Education	M,D,O
Nursing—General	M,D,O
Psychiatric Nursing	M,D,O
Psychology—General	M,O
Public Policy	M
Reading Education	M,O
Real Estate	M,O
Rhetoric	M
School Nursing	M,D,O
Secondary Education	M,O
Social Work	M,O
Software Engineering	M,O
Special Education	M,O
Western European Studies	M
Writing	M

MONROE COLLEGE

Business Administration and Management—General	M

MONTANA STATE UNIVERSITY

Accounting	M
Adult Education	M,D,O
Agricultural Education	M
Agricultural Sciences—General	M,D
American Indian/Native American Studies	M
Animal Sciences	M,D
Architecture	M
Art History	M
Art/Fine Arts	M
Biochemistry	M,D
Biological and Biomedical Sciences—General	M,D
Chemical Engineering	M,D
Chemistry	M,D
Civil Engineering	M,D
Computer Engineering	M,D
Computer Science	M,D
Construction Engineering	M,D
Curriculum and Instruction	M,D,O
Ecology	M,D
Education—General	M,D,O
Educational Leadership and Administration	M,D,O
Electrical Engineering	M,D
Engineering and Applied Sciences—General	M,D
English	M
Environmental Engineering	M,D
Environmental Sciences	M,D
Family Nurse Practitioner Studies	M,O
Film, Television, and Video Production	M
Fish, Game, and Wildlife Management	M,D
Geosciences	M,D
Health Education	M
Higher Education	M,D,O
History	M,D
Home Economics Education	M
Human Development	M
Immunology	M,D
Industrial/Management Engineering	M,D
Infectious Diseases	M,D
Mathematics Education	M,D
Mathematics	M,D
Mechanical Engineering	M,D
Mechanics	M,D
Microbiology	M,D
Natural Resources	M
Neuroscience	M,D
Nursing and Healthcare Administration	M,O
Nursing Education	M,O
Physics	M,D
Plant Pathology	M,D
Plant Sciences	M,D
Psychiatric Nursing	M,O
Psychology—General	M
Public Administration	M
Range Science	M,D
School Psychology	M,D,O
Statistics	M,D
Vocational and Technical Education	M,D,O

MONTANA STATE UNIVERSITY BILLINGS

Advertising and Public Relations	M
Athletic Training and Sports Medicine	M
Communication—General	M
Counselor Education	M
Curriculum and Instruction	M
Early Childhood Education	M
Education—General	M,O
Educational Media/ Instructional Technology	M
Health Services Management and Hospital Administration	M
Human Services	M
Interdisciplinary Studies	M
Physical Education	M
Psychology—General	M
Public Administration	M
Reading Education	M
Rehabilitation Counseling	M
Secondary Education	M
Special Education	M
Sports Management	M

*M—master's degree; P—first professional degree; D—doctorate; O—other advanced degree; *—Close-Up and/or Display in one of the other books in this series*

MONTANA STATE UNIVERSITY–NORTHERN

Counselor Education	M
Education—General	M

MONTANA TECH OF THE UNIVERSITY OF MONTANA

Electrical Engineering	M
Engineering and Applied Sciences—General	M
Environmental Engineering	M
Geochemistry	M
Geological Engineering	M
Geology	M
Geosciences	M
Hydrogeology	M
Industrial Hygiene	M
Industrial/Management Engineering	M
Interdisciplinary Studies	M
Metallurgical Engineering and Metallurgy	M
Mineral/Mining Engineering	M
Petroleum Engineering	M
Project Management	M
Technical Communication	M

MONTCLAIR STATE UNIVERSITY

Accounting	M,O
Addictions/Substance Abuse Counseling	M,D,O
Adult Education	M,D,O
Advertising and Public Relations	M
Anthropology	O
Applied Mathematics	M,D,O
Art Education	M,O
Art/Fine Arts	M,O
Arts Administration	M
Biochemistry	M,O
Biological and Biomedical Sciences—General	M,O
Business Administration and Management—General	M,O
Chemistry	M,O
Clinical Psychology	M,O
Communication Disorders	M,D,O
Communication—General	M
Community Health	M,O
Computer Science	M,O
Conflict Resolution and Mediation/Peace Studies	M,O
Corporate and Organizational Communication	M
Counseling Psychology	M,D,O
Counselor Education	M,D,O
Curriculum and Instruction	M,D,O
Early Childhood Education	M,O
Ecology	M,O
Education of Students with Severe/Multiple Disabilities	M,O
Education—General	M,D,O
Educational Leadership and Administration	M,D,O
Educational Media/Instructional Technology	M,O
Educational Psychology	M,O
Elementary Education	M,O
English as a Second Language	M,O
English Education	M,O
English	M,O
Environmental Management and Policy	M,D
Environmental Sciences	M,D,O
Evolutionary Biology	M,O
Exercise and Sports Science	M,O
Finance and Banking	M,O
Food Science and Technology	M,O
Foundations and Philosophy of Education	O
French	M,O
Geographic Information Systems	M,D,O
Geosciences	M,D,O
Health Education	M,O
History	M,O
Home Economics Education	M,O
Industrial and Organizational Psychology	M,O
Information Science	M,O
Intellectual Property Law	M,O
International Business	M,O
Italian	M,O
Law	M,O
Legal and Justice Studies	O
Linguistics	M,O
Management Information Systems	M,O
Marketing	M,O
Marriage and Family Therapy	M,O
Mathematics Education	M,D,O
Middle School Education	M,D,O
Molecular Biology	M,O
Museum Studies	M,O
Music Education	M,O
Music	M,O
Nutrition	M,O
Philosophy	D,O
Physical Education	M,O
Physiology	M,O
Political Science	M,O
Psychology—General	M,O
Public Health—General	M,O
Reading Education	M,O
School Psychology	M,O
Science Education	M,D,O
Social Psychology	M,D,O
Social Sciences Education	M,O
Social Sciences	M,O
Sociology	M
Spanish	M,O
Special Education	M,O
Sports Management	M,O
Statistics	M,D,O
Theater	M
Therapies—Dance, Drama, and Music	M,O
Translation and Interpretation	M,O
Urban and Regional Planning	O
Writing	M,O

MONTEREY INSTITUTE OF INTERNATIONAL STUDIES

Business Administration and Management—General	M
English as a Second Language	M
Environmental Management and Policy	M
Foreign Languages Education	M
International Affairs	M
International Business	M
International Trade Policy	M
Public Administration	M
Translation and Interpretation	M

MONTREAT COLLEGE

Business Administration and Management—General	M
Education—General	M
Elementary Education	M
Environmental Education	M

MOODY BIBLE INSTITUTE

Pastoral Ministry and Counseling	P,M,O
Theology	P,M,O
Urban Studies	P,M,O

MOORE COLLEGE OF ART & DESIGN

Art Education	M
Art/Fine Arts	M
Interior Design	M

MORAVIAN COLLEGE

Accounting	M
Allied Health—General	M
Business Administration and Management—General	M
Curriculum and Instruction	M
Human Resources Development	M
Human Resources Management	M
Nursing and Healthcare Administration	M
Nursing Education	M
Nursing—General	M
Supply Chain Management	M

MORAVIAN THEOLOGICAL SEMINARY

Pastoral Ministry and Counseling	P,M
Theology	P,M

MOREHEAD STATE UNIVERSITY

Adult Education	M,O
Agricultural Sciences—General	M
Art Education	M
Art/Fine Arts	M
Biological and Biomedical Sciences—General	M
Business Administration and Management—General	M
Business Education	M,O
Clinical Psychology	M
Communication—General	M
Counseling Psychology	M
Counselor Education	M,O
Criminal Justice and Criminology	M
Curriculum and Instruction	M,O
Education of the Gifted	M,O
Education—General	M,O
Educational Leadership and Administration	M,O
Educational Media/Instructional Technology	M,O
Elementary Education	M,O
English Education	M,O
English	M
Environmental Management and Policy	M
Exercise and Sports Science	M
Experimental Psychology	M
Foreign Languages Education	M
Gerontology	M
Graphic Design	M
Health Education	M
Higher Education	M,O
Industrial/Management Engineering	M
International and Comparative Education	M,O
Management Information Systems	M
Mathematics Education	M
Middle School Education	M,O
Music Education	M
Music	M
Physical Education	M
Psychology—General	M
Public Administration	M
Public Policy	M
Reading Education	M,O
Science Education	M
Secondary Education	M,O
Social Sciences Education	M,O
Sociology	M
Special Education	M,O
Sports Management	M
Vocational and Technical Education	M

MOREHOUSE SCHOOL OF MEDICINE

Allopathic Medicine	P
Biological and Biomedical Sciences—General	M,D*
Clinical Research	M
Epidemiology	M
Health Education	M
Health Promotion	M
Health Services Management and Hospital Administration	M
International Health	M
Public Health—General	M

MORGAN STATE UNIVERSITY

African-American Studies	M,D
Architecture	M
Bioinformatics	M
Biological and Biomedical Sciences—General	M,D
Business Administration and Management—General	D
Chemistry	M
Civil Engineering	M,D
Community College Education	D
Economics	M
Education—General	M,D
Educational Leadership and Administration	M,D
Electrical Engineering	M,D
Elementary Education	M
Engineering and Applied Sciences—General	M,D
English	M,D
Environmental Biology	D
Higher Education	D
History	M,D
Industrial/Management Engineering	M,D
International Affairs	M
Landscape Architecture	M
Mathematics Education	M,D
Mathematics	M
Middle School Education	M
Music	M
Nursing—General	M,D
Psychology—General	M,D
Public Health—General	M,D
Science Education	M,D
Secondary Education	M
Social Work	M,D
Sociology	M
Telecommunications Management	M
Transportation and Highway Engineering	M
Transportation Management	M
Urban and Regional Planning	M
Urban Education	M,D

MORNINGSIDE COLLEGE

Education—General	M
Special Education	M

MORRISON UNIVERSITY

Business Administration and Management—General	M

MOUNTAIN STATE UNIVERSITY

Allied Health—General	M
Criminal Justice and Criminology	M
Family Nurse Practitioner Studies	M

Interdisciplinary Studies M
Management Strategy and Policy M
Nursing and Healthcare Administration M
Nursing Education M
Nursing—General M
Organizational Management D
Physician Assistant Studies M
Psychology—General M,O

MOUNT ALLISON UNIVERSITY

Biological and Biomedical Sciences—General M
Chemistry M

MOUNT ALOYSIUS COLLEGE

Business Administration and Management—General M
Criminal Justice and Criminology M
Education—General M
Psychology—General M
Social Psychology M

MOUNT ANGEL SEMINARY

Theology P,M

MOUNT CARMEL COLLEGE OF NURSING

Adult Nursing M
Family Nurse Practitioner Studies M
Nursing and Healthcare Administration M
Nursing Education M
Nursing—General M

MOUNT HOLYOKE COLLEGE

Psychology—General M

MOUNT IDA COLLEGE

Business Administration and Management—General M
Interior Design M

MOUNT MARTY COLLEGE

Business Administration and Management—General M
Nurse Anesthesia M
Nursing—General M
Pastoral Ministry and Counseling M

MOUNT MARY COLLEGE

Art Therapy M
Business Administration and Management—General M
Counselor Education M
Education—General M
English M
Health Education M
Nutrition M
Occupational Therapy M
Pastoral Ministry and Counseling M
Social Psychology M

MOUNT MERCY UNIVERSITY

Business Administration and Management—General M
Education—General M
Reading Education M
Special Education M

MOUNT SAINT MARY COLLEGE

Adult Nursing M,O
Business Administration and Management—General M
Early Childhood Education M,O
Education—General M,O
Elementary Education M,O
Family Nurse Practitioner Studies M,O
Finance and Banking M
Middle School Education M,O
Nursing and Healthcare Administration M,O
Nursing Education M,O
Nursing—General M,O
Reading Education M,O
Secondary Education M,O
Special Education M,O

MOUNT ST. MARY'S COLLEGE

Adult Nursing M
Business Administration and Management—General M
Community Health M
Counseling Psychology M
Education—General M
Educational Leadership and Administration M
Elementary Education M
Humanities M
Marriage and Family Therapy M
Nursing and Healthcare Administration M
Nursing Education M
Nursing—General M
Physical Therapy D
Psychology—General M
Religion M
Secondary Education M
Special Education M

MOUNT ST. MARY'S UNIVERSITY

Business Administration and Management—General M
Education—General M
Philosophy M
Theology P,M

MOUNT SAINT VINCENT UNIVERSITY

Adult Education M
Child and Family Studies M
Curriculum and Instruction M
Education—General M
Educational Psychology M
Elementary Education M
English as a Second Language M
Foundations and Philosophy of Education M
Gerontology M
Middle School Education M
Nutrition M
Reading Education M
School Psychology M
Special Education M
Women's Studies M

MOUNT SINAI SCHOOL OF MEDICINE

Allopathic Medicine P
Bioethics M
Biological and Biomedical Sciences—General M,D
Clinical Research M,D
Community Health M,D
Genetic Counseling M,D
Neuroscience M,D

MOUNT VERNON NAZARENE UNIVERSITY

Business Administration and Management—General M
Education—General M
Theology M

MULTNOMAH UNIVERSITY

Counselor Education M
Education—General M
English as a Second Language M

MURRAY STATE UNIVERSITY

Accounting M
Agricultural Education M
Agricultural Sciences—General M
Biological and Biomedical Sciences—General M,D
Business Administration and Management—General M
Chemistry M
Clinical Psychology M
Communication Disorders M
Corporate and Organizational Communication M
Counselor Education M,O
Early Childhood Education M
Economics M
Education—General M,D,O
Educational Leadership and Administration M,O
Elementary Education M,O
English as a Second Language M
English M
Environmental and Occupational Health M
Environmental Sciences M
Exercise and Sports Science M
Family Nurse Practitioner Studies M
Geosciences M
History M
Human Services M
Hydrology M
Industrial Hygiene M
Leisure Studies M
Management of Technology M
Mass Communication M
Mathematics M
Middle School Education M,O
Music Education M
Music M
Nurse Anesthesia M
Nursing—General M
Physical Education M,O
Psychology—General M
Public Affairs M
Reading Education M,O
Safety Engineering M
Secondary Education M,O
Special Education M
Statistics M
Telecommunications Management M
Vocational and Technical Education M
Writing M

MUSKINGUM UNIVERSITY

Education—General M

NAROPA UNIVERSITY

Art Therapy M
Asian Languages M
Clinical Psychology M
Counseling Psychology M
Counselor Education M
Education—General M
Environmental Management and Policy M
Psychoanalysis and Psychotherapy M
Recreation and Park Management M
Religion M
Social Psychology M
Theater M
Theology P
Therapies—Dance, Drama, and Music M
Transpersonal and Humanistic Psychology M
Writing M

NASHOTAH HOUSE

Theology P,M,O

NATIONAL AMERICAN UNIVERSITY

Business Administration and Management—General M

NATIONAL COLLEGE OF MIDWIFERY

Nurse Midwifery M,D

NATIONAL COLLEGE OF NATURAL MEDICINE

Acupuncture and Oriental Medicine M
Naturopathic Medicine M,D

NATIONAL DEFENSE INTELLIGENCE COLLEGE

Military and Defense Studies M

NATIONAL DEFENSE UNIVERSITY

Conflict Resolution and Mediation/Peace Studies M
Homeland Security M
Military and Defense Studies M
National Security M

THE NATIONAL GRADUATE SCHOOL OF QUALITY MANAGEMENT

Business Administration and Management—General M
Electronic Commerce M
Quality Management M

NATIONAL-LOUIS UNIVERSITY

Adult Education M,D,O
Business Administration and Management—General M
Counselor Education M,D,O
Curriculum and Instruction M,D,O
Developmental Education M,D,O
Early Childhood Education M,D,O
Education—General M,D,O
Educational Leadership and Administration M,D,O
Educational Media/Instructional Technology M,D,O
Educational Psychology M,D,O
Elementary Education M,D,O
English Education M,D,O
Human Development M,D,O
Human Resources Development M
Human Resources Management M
Human Services M,D,O
Mathematics Education M,D,O
Psychology—General M,D,O
Public Policy M,D,O

*M—master's degree; P—first professional degree; D—doctorate; O—other advanced degree; *—Close-Up and/or Display in one of the other books in this series*

Reading Education M,D,O
School Psychology M,D,O
Science Education M,D,O
Secondary Education M,D,O
Special Education M,D,O
Writing M,D,O

NATIONAL THEATRE CONSERVATORY

Theater M,O

NATIONAL UNIVERSITY

Accounting M
Art/Fine Arts M
Business Administration and Management—General M
Communication Disorders M
Communication—General M
Community Health M
Computer Art and Design M
Computer Science M
Conflict Resolution and Mediation/Peace Studies M
Corporate and Organizational Communication M
Counseling Psychology M
Counselor Education M
Criminal Justice and Criminology M
Database Systems M
Economics M
Education—General M
Educational Leadership and Administration M
Educational Media/Instructional Technology M
Electronic Commerce M
Engineering and Applied Sciences—General M
Engineering Management M
English M
Environmental Engineering M
Finance and Banking M
Forensic Sciences M
Game Design and Development M
Health Informatics M
Health Services Management and Hospital Administration M
History M
Homeland Security M
Human Resources Management M
Human Services M
Humanities M
Information Science M
International Business M
Internet and Interactive Multimedia M
Management Information Systems M
Management of Technology M
Marketing M
Media Studies M
Multilingual and Multicultural Education M
Organizational Management M
Psychology—General M
Public Administration M
Public Health—General M
Safety Engineering M
School Psychology M
Software Engineering M
Special Education M
Systems Engineering M
Telecommunications M
Writing M

NATIONAL UNIVERSITY OF HEALTH SCIENCES

Acupuncture and Oriental Medicine P,M,D
Chiropractic P,M,D
Health Services Management and Hospital Administration M
Medical Imaging M
Naturopathic Medicine P,M,D

NATIONAL UNIVERSITY OF SINGAPORE

Public Administration M,D
Public Affairs M,D
Public Policy M,D

NAVAL POSTGRADUATE SCHOOL

Aerospace/Aeronautical Engineering M
Applied Mathematics M,D
Applied Physics M,D
Applied Science and Technology M
Business Administration and Management—General M
Computer Engineering M,D,O
Computer Science M,D
Electrical Engineering M,D,O
Human Resources Development M
Information Science M,O
International Affairs M
Management Information Systems M,O
Mathematics M,D
Mechanical Engineering M,D,O
Meteorology M,D
Military and Defense Studies M,D
Modeling and Simulation M,D
National Security M
Oceanography M,D
Operations Research M,D
Physics M,D
Political Science M
Software Engineering M,D
Systems Engineering M,D,O

NAVAL WAR COLLEGE

National Security M

NAZARENE THEOLOGICAL SEMINARY

Missions and Missiology P,M,D
Religious Education P,M,D
Theology P,M,D

NAZARETH COLLEGE OF ROCHESTER

Art Education M
Art Therapy M
Business Administration and Management—General M
Business Education M
Communication Disorders M
Early Childhood Education M
Education—General M
Educational Media/Instructional Technology M
Elementary Education M
English as a Second Language M
Gerontological Nursing M
Human Resources Management M
Liberal Studies M
Middle School Education M
Music Education M
Nursing—General M
Physical Therapy M,D
Reading Education M
Social Work M
Therapies—Dance, Drama, and Music M

NEBRASKA METHODIST COLLEGE

Health Promotion M
Health Services Management and Hospital Administration M
Nursing and Healthcare Administration M
Nursing Education M
Nursing—General M

NEBRASKA WESLEYAN UNIVERSITY

Forensic Sciences M
History M
Nursing—General M

NER ISRAEL RABBINICAL COLLEGE

Theology M,D,O

NER ISRAEL YESHIVA COLLEGE OF TORONTO

Theology

NEUMANN UNIVERSITY

Education—General M
Educational Leadership and Administration D
Management Strategy and Policy M
Nursing—General M
Pastoral Ministry and Counseling M,O
Physical Therapy D
Sports Management M

NEW BRUNSWICK THEOLOGICAL SEMINARY

Pastoral Ministry and Counseling D
Theology P,M,D

NEW ENGLAND COLLEGE

Accounting M
Business Administration and Management—General M
Counseling Psychology M
Education—General M
Educational Leadership and Administration M
Health Services Management and Hospital Administration M
Higher Education M
Human Services M
International Affairs M
Management Strategy and Policy M
Marketing M
Nonprofit Management M
Project Management M
Public Policy M
Recreation and Park Management M
Special Education M
Sports Management M
Writing M

NEW ENGLAND COLLEGE OF BUSINESS AND FINANCE

Ethics M
Finance and Banking M

THE NEW ENGLAND COLLEGE OF OPTOMETRY

Optometry P,M
Vision Sciences P,M

NEW ENGLAND CONSERVATORY OF MUSIC

Music M,D,O

NEW ENGLAND LAWÛBOSTON

Law P,M

NEW ENGLAND SCHOOL OF ACUPUNCTURE

Acupuncture and Oriental Medicine M

NEW JERSEY CITY UNIVERSITY

Accounting M
Allied Health—General M
Art Education M
Art/Fine Arts M
Business Administration and Management—General M
Community Health M
Counseling Psychology M
Criminal Justice and Criminology M
Early Childhood Education M
Educational Leadership and Administration M
Educational Media/Instructional Technology M
Educational Psychology M,O
Elementary Education M
English as a Second Language M
Finance and Banking M
Health Education M
Health Services Management and Hospital Administration M
Mathematics Education M
Multilingual and Multicultural Education M
Music Education M
Music M
Reading Education M
School Psychology M,O
Secondary Education M
Special Education M
Urban Education M
Urban Studies M

NEW JERSEY INSTITUTE OF TECHNOLOGY

Applied Mathematics M
Applied Physics M,D
Applied Statistics M
Architecture M
Bioinformatics M,D
Biological and Biomedical Sciences—General M,D
Biomedical Engineering M,D
Biostatistics M
Business Administration and Management—General M
Chemical Engineering M,D
Chemistry M,D
Civil Engineering M,D
Computational Biology M
Computer Engineering M,D
Computer Science M,D
Electrical Engineering M,D
Emergency Management M,D
Energy and Power Engineering M
Engineering and Applied Sciences—General M,D,O
Engineering Management M
Environmental Engineering M,D

Environmental Management and Policy M
Environmental Sciences M,D
History M
Industrial/Management Engineering M,D
Information Science M,D
Internet Engineering M
Management Information Systems M,D
Management of Technology M
Manufacturing Engineering M
Materials Engineering M,D
Materials Sciences M,D
Mathematics D
Mechanical Engineering M,D,O
Pharmaceutical Engineering M
Safety Engineering M
Software Engineering M,D
Technical Communication M
Transportation and Highway Engineering M,D
Transportation Management M,D
Urban Studies D

NEW LIFE THEOLOGICAL SEMINARY

Religion M

NEWMAN THEOLOGICAL COLLEGE

Educational Leadership and Administration M,O
Religious Education M,O
Theology P,M

NEWMAN UNIVERSITY

Business Administration and Management—General M
Curriculum and Instruction M
Education—General M
Educational Leadership and Administration M
English as a Second Language M
Finance and Banking M
International Business M
Management Information Systems M
Nurse Anesthesia M
Organizational Management M
Reading Education M
Social Work M
Theology M

NEW MEXICO HIGHLANDS UNIVERSITY

American Studies M
Anthropology M
Business Administration and Management—General M
Chemistry M
Clinical Psychology M
Computer Science M
Counselor Education M
Curriculum and Instruction M
Education—General M
Educational Leadership and Administration M
English M
Exercise and Sports Science M
Fish, Game, and Wildlife Management M
Health Education M
Human Resources Management M
International Business M
Internet and Interactive Multimedia M
Management Information Systems M
Media Studies M
Nonprofit Management M
Psychology—General M
Public Affairs M
Rhetoric M
School Psychology M
Social Work M
Special Education M
Sports Management M
Writing M

NEW MEXICO INSTITUTE OF MINING AND TECHNOLOGY

Applied Mathematics M,D
Astrophysics M,D
Atmospheric Sciences M,D
Biochemistry M,D
Biological and Biomedical Sciences—General M
Chemistry M,D
Computer Science M,D
Electrical Engineering M
Engineering Management M
Environmental Engineering M
Environmental Sciences M,D
Geochemistry M,D
Geology M,D
Geophysics M,D
Geosciences M,D
Hazardous Materials Management M
Hydrology M,D
Materials Engineering M,D
Mathematical Physics M,D
Mathematics M,D
Mechanics M
Mineral/Mining Engineering M
Operations Research M,D
Petroleum Engineering M,D
Physics M,D
Science Education M
Water Resources Engineering M

NEW MEXICO STATE UNIVERSITY

Accounting M
Adult Nursing M,D
Agricultural Economics and Agribusiness M,D
Agricultural Education M
Agricultural Sciences—General M
Animal Sciences M,D
Anthropology M
Applied Arts and Design—General M
Applied Statistics M,D
Art History M
Art/Fine Arts M
Astronomy M,D
Bioinformatics M,D
Biological and Biomedical Sciences—General M,D
Biotechnology M,D
Business Administration and Management—General M,D
Chemical Engineering M,D
Chemistry M,D
Civil Engineering M,D
Communication Disorders M,D
Communication—General M
Community Health Nursing M,D
Community Health M
Computer Engineering M,D
Computer Science M,D
Corporate and Organizational Communication M,D
Counseling Psychology M,D,O
Counselor Education M,D,O
Criminal Justice and Criminology M
Curriculum and Instruction M,D
Economic Development M,D
Economics M,D
Education—General M,D,O
Educational Leadership and Administration M,D
Electrical Engineering M,D
Engineering and Applied Sciences—General M,D
English M,D
Entomology M
Environmental Engineering M,D
Environmental Sciences M,D
Family and Consumer Sciences-General M
Fish, Game, and Wildlife Management M
Geography M
Geology M
Health Education M
History M
Horticulture M,D
Industrial/Management Engineering M,D
Interdisciplinary Studies M,D
Marketing D
Mathematics M,D
Mechanical Engineering M,D
Medical/Surgical Nursing M,D
Molecular Biology M,D
Multilingual and Multicultural Education M,D
Music Education M
Music M
Nursing and Healthcare Administration M,D
Nursing—General M,D
Photography M
Physics M,D
Plant Pathology M
Plant Sciences M,D
Political Science M
Psychiatric Nursing M,D
Psychology—General M,D
Public Health—General M
Range Science M,D
Rhetoric M,D
School Psychology M,D,O
Social Work M
Spanish M
Special Education M,D
Writing M,D

NEW ORLEANS BAPTIST THEOLOGICAL SEMINARY

Music P,M,D
Pastoral Ministry and Counseling P,M,D
Religious Education P,M,D
Theology P,M,D

NEW SAINT ANDREWS COLLEGE

Religion M,O
Theology M,O

THE NEW SCHOOL: A UNIVERSITY

Anthropology M,D
Applied Arts and Design—General M
Applied Social Research M,D
Architecture M
Art/Fine Arts M
Clinical Psychology M,D
Cognitive Sciences M,D
Computer Art and Design M
Decorative Arts M
Developmental Psychology M,D
Economics M,D
English as a Second Language M
Environmental Management and Policy M
Finance and Banking M,D
History M,D
Interior Design M
International Affairs M
International Economics M,D
Liberal Studies M
Lighting Design M
Media Studies M,O
Music M
Nonprofit Management M
Organizational Management M
Philosophy M,D
Photography M
Political Science M,D
Psychology—General M,D
Public Policy D
Social Sciences M,D
Sociology M,D
Sustainability Management M
Textile Design M
Theater M
Urban Design M
Urban Studies M
Writing M

NEWSCHOOL OF ARCHITECTURE & DESIGN

Architecture M

NEW YORK ACADEMY OF ART

Art/Fine Arts M

NEW YORK CHIROPRACTIC COLLEGE

Acupuncture and Oriental Medicine M
Anatomy M
Chiropractic P
Health Physics/Radiological Health M
Nutrition M

NEW YORK COLLEGE OF HEALTH PROFESSIONS

Acupuncture and Oriental Medicine M

NEW YORK COLLEGE OF PODIATRIC MEDICINE

Podiatric Medicine P

NEW YORK COLLEGE OF TRADITIONAL CHINESE MEDICINE

Acupuncture and Oriental Medicine M

NEW YORK FILM ACADEMY

Film, Television, and Video Production M
Photography M

NEW YORK INSTITUTE OF TECHNOLOGY

Accounting M,O
Architecture M
Art/Fine Arts M
Business Administration and Management—General M,O
Communication—General M
Computer and Information Systems Security M
Computer Art and Design M
Computer Engineering M
Computer Science M
Counseling Psychology M
Counselor Education M
Distance Education Development M,O

*M—master's degree; P—first professional degree; D—doctorate; O—other advanced degree; *—Close-Up and/or Display in one of the other books in this series*

Education—General M,O
Educational Leadership and Administration O
Educational Media/Instructional Technology M,O
Electrical Engineering M
Elementary Education M
Energy and Power Engineering M,O
Energy Management and Policy M,O
Engineering and Applied Sciences—General M,O
Environmental Engineering M
Environmental Management and Policy M,O
Finance and Banking M,O
Graphic Design M
Human Resources Management M,O
Industrial and Labor Relations M,O
International Business M,O
Management Information Systems M,O
Marketing M,O
Nutrition M
Occupational Therapy M
Osteopathic Medicine P
Physical Therapy D
Physician Assistant Studies M
Urban Design M

NEW YORK LAW SCHOOL

Finance and Banking P,M
Law P,M*
Taxation P,M

NEW YORK MEDICAL COLLEGE

Allopathic Medicine P
Anatomy M,D
Biochemistry M,D
Biological and Biomedical Sciences—General M,D*
Cell Biology M,D
Communication Disorders M
Emergency Management O
Environmental and Occupational Health M,O
Epidemiology M
Health Education O
Health Promotion M
Health Services Management and Hospital Administration M,D,O
Immunology M,D
Industrial Hygiene O
International Health O
Microbiology M,D
Molecular Biology M,D
Neuroscience M,D
Pathology M,D
Pharmacology M,D
Physical Therapy D
Physiology M,D
Public Health—General M,D,O

NEW YORK SCHOOL OF INTERIOR DESIGN

Interior Design M
Lighting Design M
Sustainable Development M

NEW YORK STUDIO SCHOOL OF DRAWING, PAINTING AND SCULPTURE

Art/Fine Arts M,O

NEW YORK THEOLOGICAL SEMINARY

Theology P,M,D

NEW YORK UNIVERSITY

Accounting M,D
Acute Care/Critical Care Nursing M,D,O
Adult Nursing M,D,O
Advertising and Public Relations M
African Studies M,D,O
Agricultural Engineering M,D
Allopathic Medicine P
American Studies M,D
Anthropology M,D
Applied Arts and Design—General M
Applied Economics M,D,O
Applied Psychology M,D,O
Archaeology M,D
Archives/Archival Administration M,D,O
Art Education M
Art History M,D
Art Therapy M
Art/Fine Arts M,D,O
Arts Administration M
Asian Studies M,D
Bioethics M
Biological and Biomedical Sciences—General M,D
Business Administration and Management—General P,M,D,O
Business Education M,O
Cancer Biology/Oncology P,M,D
Cell Biology P,M,D
Chemistry M,D
Classics M,D,O
Clinical Research P,M,D
Cognitive Sciences M,D,O
Communication Disorders M,D
Communication—General M,D
Community Health D
Comparative Literature M,D
Computational Biology D
Computer Art and Design M
Computer Science M,D
Conflict Resolution and Mediation/Peace Studies M
Construction Management M,O
Corporate and Organizational Communication M
Counseling Psychology M,D,O
Counselor Education M,D,O
Cultural Studies M,D,O
Curriculum and Instruction M,D,O
Dance M,D
Database Systems M,O
Dentistry P
Developmental Biology M,D
Developmental Psychology M,D
Early Childhood Education M,D
Economics M,D,O
Education—General M,D,O
Educational Leadership and Administration M,D,O
Educational Media/Instructional Technology M,D,O
Educational Policy M,D
Educational Psychology M,D
Elementary Education M,D
English as a Second Language M,D,O
English Education M,D,O
English M,D,O
Environmental and Occupational Health M,D
Environmental Education M
Environmental Management and Policy M
Epidemiology M,D
Ergonomics and Human Factors M,D
Film, Television, and Video Production M
Film, Television, and Video Theory and Criticism M,D
Finance and Banking M,D,O
Food Science and Technology M,D
Foreign Languages Education M,D,O
Foundations and Philosophy of Education M,D
French M,D,O
Genetics M,D
German M,D
Gerontological Nursing M,D,O
Gerontology D
Graphic Design M
Health Promotion M,D,O
Health Services Management and Hospital Administration M,O
Higher Education M,D
Hispanic Studies M,D
Historic Preservation
History M,D,O
Hospitality Management M,D,O
Human Development M,D,O
Human Resources Development M,O
Human Resources Management M,D,O
Humanities M,O
Immunology P,M,D
Industrial and Organizational Psychology M,D,O
Interdisciplinary Studies M
International Affairs M,D,O
International and Comparative Education M,D,O
International Business M,D,O
Internet and Interactive Multimedia M
Italian M,D
Jewish Studies M,D,O
Journalism M,D,O
Kinesiology and Movement Studies M,D,O
Latin American Studies M,D,O
Law P,M,D,O
Legal and Justice Studies M,D
Linguistics M,D,O
Management Information Systems M,D,O
Management Strategy and Policy M,D,O
Marketing M,D,O
Mathematical and Computational Finance M,D
Mathematics Education M
Mathematics M,D
Media Studies M,D
Medical Imaging P,M,D
Microbiology P,M,D
Molecular Biology P,M,D
Molecular Genetics M,D
Molecular Pharmacology D
Molecular Toxicology M,D
Multilingual and Multicultural Education M,D,O
Museum Studies M,O
Music Education M,D,O
Music M,D,O
National Security M
Near and Middle Eastern Studies M,D,O
Neurobiology M,D
Neuroscience P,M,D
Nonprofit Management M,D,O
Nurse Midwifery M,D,O
Nursing and Healthcare Administration M
Nursing Education M,O
Nursing Informatics M,O
Nursing—General M,D,O
Nutrition M,D
Occupational Therapy M,D
Oral and Dental Sciences M,D,O
Organizational Behavior M,D
Organizational Management M,D
Parasitology P,M,D
Pathobiology P,M,D
Pediatric Nursing M,D,O
Pharmacology P,M,D
Philosophy M,D
Physical Therapy M,D,O
Physics M,D
Physiology P,M,D
Plant Biology M,D
Political Science M,D
Portuguese M,D
Psychiatric Nursing M,D,O
Psychoanalysis and Psychotherapy M,D,O
Psychology—General M,D,O
Public Administration M,D,O
Public Health—General D
Public History M,D,O
Publishing M
Quantitative Analysis M,D,O
Reading Education M
Real Estate M,O
Religion M,O
Romance Languages M,D
Russian M
Science Education M
Secondary Education M,D,O
Slavic Languages M
Social Psychology M,D,O
Social Sciences Education M,D,O
Social Sciences M,O
Social Work M,D
Sociology M,D
Spanish M,D
Special Education M,D
Speech and Interpersonal Communication M,D
Sports Management M,O
Statistics M,D
Structural Biology P,M,D
Student Affairs M,D
Sustainable Development M,O
Taxation P,M,D,O
Theater M,D,O
Therapies—Dance, Drama, and Music M
Toxicology M,D
Translation and Interpretation M,D
Travel and Tourism M,O
Urban and Regional Planning M,O
Western European Studies M
Writing M,D

NIAGARA UNIVERSITY

Business Administration and Management—General M
Counselor Education M,O
Criminal Justice and Criminology M
Early Childhood Education M,O
Education—General M,O
Educational Leadership and Administration M,O
Elementary Education M,O
Foundations and Philosophy of Education M
Interdisciplinary Studies M
Middle School Education M,O
Reading Education M
School Psychology M,O
Secondary Education M,O
Special Education M,O

NICHOLLS STATE UNIVERSITY

Business Administration and Management—General M
Computer Science M
Counseling Psychology M,O
Counselor Education M
Curriculum and Instruction M
Education—General M
Educational Leadership and Administration M
Environmental Biology M
Marine Biology M
Mathematics Education M

Mathematics M
School Psychology M,O

NICHOLS COLLEGE

Business Administration and Management—General M
Criminal Justice and Criminology M
Sports Management M

THE NIGERIAN BAPTIST THEOLOGICAL SEMINARY

Music P,M,D,O
Pastoral Ministry and Counseling P,M,D,O
Religious Education P,M,D,O
Theology P,M,D,O

NIPISSING UNIVERSITY

Education—General M,O

NORFOLK STATE UNIVERSITY

Art/Fine Arts M
Clinical Psychology M
Communication—General M
Computer Engineering M
Computer Science M
Criminal Justice and Criminology M
Early Childhood Education M
Education of Students with Severe/Multiple Disabilities M
Education—General M
Educational Leadership and Administration M
Electrical Engineering M
Materials Sciences M
Media Studies M
Music Education M
Music M
Optical Sciences M
Psychology—General M,D
Secondary Education M
Social Psychology M
Social Work M,D
Sociology M
Special Education M
Urban Education M
Urban Studies M

NORTH CAROLINA AGRICULTURAL AND TECHNICAL STATE UNIVERSITY

Adult Education M,D
African-American Studies M
Agricultural Economics and Agribusiness M
Agricultural Education M
Agricultural Sciences—General M
Agronomy and Soil Sciences M
Animal Sciences M
Applied Economics M
Art Education M
Bioengineering M
Biological and Biomedical Sciences—General M
Business Administration and Management—General M,D
Chemical Engineering M,D
Chemistry M
Civil Engineering M
Computer Engineering M,D
Computer Science M
Construction Management M
Counselor Education M,D
Education—General M
Educational Leadership and Administration M,D
Educational Media/Instructional Technology M
Electrical Engineering M,D
Elementary Education M
Energy and Power Engineering M,D
Engineering and Applied Sciences—General M,D
English Education M
English M
Environmental and Occupational Health M
Environmental Sciences M
Health Education M
Human Resources Development M,D
Industrial/Management Engineering M,D
Management of Technology M,D
Mathematics Education M
Mechanical Engineering M,D
Nutrition M
Optical Sciences M,D
Organizational Management M,D
Physical Education M
Plant Sciences M
Reading Education M
Rehabilitation Counseling M,D
Science Education M
Social Sciences Education M
Social Work M
Systems Engineering M,D
Vocational and Technical Education M,D

NORTH CAROLINA CENTRAL UNIVERSITY

Applied Mathematics M
Biological and Biomedical Sciences—General M
Business Administration and Management—General M
Chemistry M
Communication Disorders M
Counselor Education M
Criminal Justice and Criminology M
Curriculum and Instruction M
Education—General M
Educational Leadership and Administration M
Educational Media/Instructional Technology M
Elementary Education M
English M
Family and Consumer Sciences-General M
Geosciences M
History M
Information Studies M
Law P
Library Science M
Mathematics Education M
Mathematics M
Middle School Education M
Music M
Physical Education M
Physics M
Psychology—General M
Public Administration M
Recreation and Park Management M
Social Psychology M
Sociology M
Special Education M
Sports Management M

NORTH CAROLINA STATE UNIVERSITY

Accounting M
Adult Education M,D
Aerospace/Aeronautical Engineering M,D
Agricultural Economics and Agribusiness M
Agricultural Education M,O
Agricultural Engineering M,D,O
Agricultural Sciences—General M,D,O
Agronomy and Soil Sciences M,D
Animal Sciences M,D
Anthropology M
Applied Arts and Design—General M,D
Applied Mathematics M,D
Architecture M
Atmospheric Sciences M,D
Biochemistry D
Bioengineering M,D,O
Bioinformatics M,D
Biological and Biomedical Sciences—General M,D,O
Biomathematics M,D
Biomedical Engineering M,D
Biotechnology M
Botany M,D
Business Administration and Management—General M*
Business Education M
Cell Biology M,D
Chemical Engineering M,D
Chemistry M,D
Civil Engineering M,D
Clothing and Textiles D
Communication—General M
Community College Education M,D
Computer Art and Design D
Computer Engineering M,D
Computer Science M,D
Counselor Education M,D
Cultural Anthropology M
Curriculum and Instruction M,D
Developmental Education M,D,O
Developmental Psychology D
Economics M,D
Education—General M,D,O
Educational Leadership and Administration M,D
Educational Measurement and Evaluation D
Educational Media/Instructional Technology M,D
Electrical Engineering M,D
Elementary Education M
Engineering and Applied Sciences—General M,D*
English Education M
English M
Entomology M,D
Entrepreneurship M
Epidemiology M,D
Ergonomics and Human Factors D
Experimental Psychology D
Financial Engineering M
Fish, Game, and Wildlife Management M,D
Food Science and Technology M,D
Forestry M,D
French M
Genetics M,D
Genomic Sciences M,D
Geographic Information Systems M,D
Geosciences M,D
Graphic Design M
Higher Education M,D
History M
Horticulture M,D,O
Human Resources Development M
Immunology M,D
Industrial and Organizational Psychology D
Industrial Design M
Industrial/Management Engineering M,D
Infectious Diseases M,D
International Affairs M
Landscape Architecture M
Liberal Studies M
Management of Technology D
Manufacturing Engineering M
Marine Sciences M,D
Materials Engineering M,D
Materials Sciences M,D
Mathematical and Computational Finance M
Mathematics Education M,D
Mathematics M,D
Mechanical Engineering M,D*
Meteorology M,D
Microbiology M,D
Middle School Education M
Molecular Toxicology M,D
Natural Resources M,D
Nonprofit Management M,D,O
Nuclear Engineering M,D
Nutrition M,D
Oceanography M,D
Operations Research M,D
Paper and Pulp Engineering M,D
Pathology M,D
Pharmacology M,D
Physics M,D
Physiology M,D
Plant Biology M,D
Plant Pathology M,D
Polymer Science and Engineering D
Psychology—General D
Public Administration M,D
Public History M
Recreation and Park Management M,D
Rhetoric D
School Psychology D
Science Education M,D
Secondary Education M
Social Psychology M
Social Sciences Education M
Social Work M
Sociology M,D
Spanish M
Special Education M
Sports Management M,D
Statistics M,D
Supply Chain Management M
Technical Communication M
Textile Sciences and Engineering M,D
Toxicology M,D
Travel and Tourism M,D
Veterinary Medicine P,M
Veterinary Sciences M,D
Writing M
Zoology M,D

NORTH CENTRAL COLLEGE

Business Administration and Management—General M
Computer Science M
Curriculum and Instruction M
Education—General M
Educational Leadership and Administration M
Finance and Banking M
Human Resources Management M
Internet and Interactive Multimedia M
Liberal Studies M
Management Information Systems M
Management Strategy and Policy M
Marketing M
Nonprofit Management M
Organizational Management M
Sports Management M
Technical Communication M

*M—master's degree; P—first professional degree; D—doctorate; O—other advanced degree; *—Close-Up and/or Display in one of the other books in this series*

NORTHCENTRAL UNIVERSITY

Program	Degrees
Business Administration and Management—General	M,D,O
Education—General	M,D,O
Marriage and Family Therapy	M,D,O
Psychology—General	M,D,O

NORTH DAKOTA STATE UNIVERSITY

Program	Degrees
Adult Education	M,D,O
Agricultural Economics and Agribusiness	M
Agricultural Education	M
Agricultural Engineering	M,D
Agricultural Sciences—General	M,D
Agronomy and Soil Sciences	M,D
Animal Sciences	M,D
Applied Mathematics	M,D
Applied Statistics	M,D,O
Biochemistry	M,D
Bioinformatics	M,D
Biological and Biomedical Sciences—General	M,D
Biosystems Engineering	M,D
Botany	M,D
Business Administration and Management—General	M
Cell Biology	M,D
Chemistry	M,D
Child and Family Studies	M,D
Child Development	M,D
Civil Engineering	M,D
Clinical Psychology	M,D
Cognitive Sciences	M,D
Communication—General	M,D
Computer Engineering	M,D
Computer Science	M,D,O
Conservation Biology	M,D
Construction Management	M
Consumer Economics	M,D
Counselor Education	M,D
Criminal Justice and Criminology	M,D
Ecology	M,D
Education—General	M,D,O
Educational Leadership and Administration	M,O
Electrical Engineering	M,D
Emergency Management	M,D
Engineering and Applied Sciences—General	M,D
English	M
Entomology	M,D
Environmental Engineering	M,D
Environmental Sciences	M,D
Exercise and Sports Science	M
Family and Consumer Sciences-General	M
Food Science and Technology	M,D
Genomic Sciences	M,D
Gerontology	M,D
Health Psychology	M,D
History	M,D
Human Development	D
Industrial/Management Engineering	M,D
Logistics	M,D
Manufacturing Engineering	M,D
Marriage and Family Therapy	M,D
Mass Communication	M,D
Materials Sciences	D
Mathematics Education	M,D,O
Mathematics	M,D
Mechanical Engineering	M,D
Mechanics	M,D
Microbiology	M,D
Molecular Biology	M,D
Molecular Pathogenesis	M,D
Music Education	M,D,O
Music	M,D
Nanotechnology	D
Natural Resources	M,D
Nursing—General	M,D
Nutrition	M
Operations Research	M,D,O
Pathology	M,D
Pharmaceutical Sciences	M,D
Physical Education	M
Physics	M,D
Plant Pathology	M,D
Plant Sciences	M,D
Polymer Science and Engineering	M,D
Psychology—General	M,D
Range Science	M,D
Science Education	M,D,O
Social Psychology	M,D
Social Sciences Education	M,D,O
Social Sciences	M,D
Sociology	M,D
Software Engineering	M,D,O
Speech and Interpersonal Communication	M,D
Sports Management	M
Statistics	M,D,O
Transportation Management	M,D
Veterinary Sciences	M,D
Vocational and Technical Education	M,D,O
Zoology	M,D

NORTHEASTERN ILLINOIS UNIVERSITY

Program	Degrees
Accounting	M
Biological and Biomedical Sciences—General	M
Business Administration and Management—General	M
Chemistry	M
Computer Science	M
Counselor Education	M
Education of the Gifted	M
Education—General	M
Educational Leadership and Administration	M
English as a Second Language	M
English Education	M
English	M
Environmental Management and Policy	M
Finance and Banking	M
Geography	M
Gerontology	M
History	M
Human Resources Development	M
Linguistics	M
Marketing	M
Mathematics Education	M
Mathematics	M
Multilingual and Multicultural Education	M
Music	M
Political Science	M
Reading Education	M
Rehabilitation Counseling	M
Special Education	M
Speech and Interpersonal Communication	M
Urban Education	M
Writing	M

NORTHEASTERN OHIO UNIVERSITIES COLLEGES OF MEDICINE AND PHARMACY

Program	Degrees
Allopathic Medicine	P
Pharmacy	P

NORTHEASTERN SEMINARY AT ROBERTS WESLEYAN COLLEGE

Program	Degrees
Theology	P,M,D

NORTHEASTERN STATE UNIVERSITY

Program	Degrees
Accounting	M
Addictions/Substance Abuse Counseling	M
American Studies	M
Business Administration and Management—General	M
Communication Disorders	M
Communication—General	M
Counseling Psychology	M
Counselor Education	M
Criminal Justice and Criminology	M
Early Childhood Education	M
Education—General	M
Educational Leadership and Administration	M
Educational Media/Instructional Technology	M
English	M
Finance and Banking	M
Foundations and Philosophy of Education	M
Health Education	M
Higher Education	M
Industrial and Manufacturing Management	M
Mathematics Education	M
Nursing Education	M
Optometry	P
Psychology—General	M
Reading Education	M
Science Education	M

NORTHEASTERN UNIVERSITY

Program	Degrees
Accounting	M
Acute Care/Critical Care Nursing	M,O
Allied Health—General	P,M,D,O
Analytical Chemistry	M,D
Applied Behavior Analysis	M
Applied Economics	M,D
Applied Mathematics	M,D
Applied Psychology	M,D,O
Architecture	M
Art/Fine Arts	M
Biochemistry	M,D
Bioinformatics	M
Biological and Biomedical Sciences—General	M,D
Biotechnology	M
Business Administration and Management—General	M,O
Chemical Engineering	M,D
Chemistry	M,D
Civil Engineering	M,D
Communication Disorders	M,D
Communication—General	M
Computer Engineering	M,D
Computer Science	M,D
Counseling Psychology	M,D,O
Counselor Education	M,O
Criminal Justice and Criminology	M,D
Cultural Studies	M
Economics	M,D
Electrical Engineering	M,D
Energy and Power Engineering	M
Engineering and Applied Sciences—General	M,D,O
Engineering Management	M,D
English	M,D
Entrepreneurship	M
Environmental Engineering	M,D
Exercise and Sports Science	M
Experimental Psychology	M,D
Health Informatics	M,D
Health Services Management and Hospital Administration	M,D,O
History	M,D
Industrial/Management Engineering	M,D
Information Science	M,D,O
Inorganic Chemistry	M,D
Interdisciplinary Studies	D
International Affairs	M,D,O
Law	P
Legal and Justice Studies	M,D
Management Information Systems	M,D
Manufacturing Engineering	M,D
Marine Biology	M,D
Maternal and Child/Neonatal Nursing	M,O
Mathematics	M,D
Mechanical Engineering	M,D
Media Studies	M
Nurse Anesthesia	M,O
Nursing and Healthcare Administration	M
Nursing—General	M,O
Operations Research	M,D
Organic Chemistry	M,D
Pediatric Nursing	M,O
Pharmaceutical Sciences	P,M,D
Physical Chemistry	M,D
Physical Therapy	D
Physician Assistant Studies	M
Physics	M,D
Political Science	M,D,O
Psychiatric Nursing	M,O
Public Administration	M,D,O
Public Affairs	M,D,O
Public Health—General	M
Public History	M,D
Public Policy	M,D
School Psychology	M,D,O
Sociology	M,D
Speech and Interpersonal Communication	D
Student Affairs	M,O
Telecommunications Management	M
Urban and Regional Planning	M,D,O
Urban Studies	M,D,O

NORTHERN ARIZONA UNIVERSITY

Program	Degrees
Allied Health—General	M,D,O
Anthropology	M
Applied Physics	M
Applied Statistics	M,O
Archaeology	M
Atmospheric Sciences	M
Biological and Biomedical Sciences—General	M,D
Business Administration and Management—General	M
Chemistry	M
Civil Engineering	M
Clinical Psychology	M
Communication Disorders	M
Communication—General	M
Community College Education	M,D,O
Computer Science	M
Counseling Psychology	M,D,O
Counselor Education	M,D,O
Criminal Justice and Criminology	M
Cultural Anthropology	M
Curriculum and Instruction	M,D,O
Early Childhood Education	M
Education—General	M,D,O
Educational Leadership and Administration	M,D,O
Educational Media/Instructional Technology	M,D,O
Educational Psychology	M,D,O
Electrical Engineering	M
Elementary Education	M
Engineering and Applied Sciences—General	M,D,O
English as a Second Language	M,D,O
English Education	M,D,O

English M,D,O
Environmental Engineering M
Environmental Management and Policy M
Environmental Sciences M
Ethnic Studies O
Family Nurse Practitioner Studies M,O
Foreign Languages Education M
Forestry M,D
Foundations and Philosophy of Education M,D,O
Gender Studies O
Geographic Information Systems M,O
Geography M,O
Geology M
Health Services Management and Hospital Administration O
Higher Education M,D,O
History M,D
Human Development O
Liberal Studies M
Linguistics M,D,O
Mathematics Education M,O
Mathematics M,O
Mechanical Engineering M
Meteorology M
Multilingual and Multicultural Education M,D,O
Music M,O
Nursing Education M,O
Nursing—General M,O
Physical Therapy D,O
Physics M
Political Science M,D,O
Psychology—General M
Public Administration M,D,O
Public Health—General O
School Psychology M,D,O
Science Education M,O
Secondary Education M
Sociology M
Spanish M
Special Education M,D,O
Statistics M,O
Student Affairs M,D,O
Sustainable Development M
Technical Writing M,D,O
Vocational and Technical Education M,D,O
Women's Studies O
Writing M,D,O

NORTHERN BAPTIST THEOLOGICAL SEMINARY

Pastoral Ministry and Counseling P,M,D
Theology P,M,D

NORTHERN ILLINOIS UNIVERSITY

Accounting M
Adult Education M,D
Anthropology M
Art/Fine Arts M
Biological and Biomedical Sciences—General M,D
Business Administration and Management—General M
Chemistry M,D
Child and Family Studies M
Communication Disorders M,D
Communication—General M
Computer Science M
Counselor Education M,D
Curriculum and Instruction M,D
Dance M
Early Childhood Education M,D
Economics M,D
Education—General M,D,O
Educational Leadership and Administration M,D,O
Educational Media/Instructional Technology M,D
Educational Psychology M,D,O
Electrical Engineering M
Elementary Education M,D
Engineering and Applied Sciences—General M
English M,D
Foundations and Philosophy of Education M,D,O
French M
Geography M,D
Geology M,D
Higher Education M,D
History M,D
Industrial and Manufacturing Management M
Industrial/Management Engineering M
Law P
Management Information Systems M
Mathematics M,D
Mechanical Engineering M
Music M,O
Nursing—General M
Nutrition M
Philosophy M
Physical Education M
Physical Therapy M
Physics M,D
Political Science M,D
Psychology—General M,D
Public Administration M
Public Health—General M
Reading Education M,D
Romance Languages M
Secondary Education M,D
Sociology M
Spanish M
Special Education M,D
Sports Management M
Statistics M
Taxation M
Theater M

NORTHERN KENTUCKY UNIVERSITY

Accounting M,O
Advertising and Public Relations M,O
Business Administration and Management—General M,O
Clinical Psychology M,O
Communication—General M,O
Computer and Information Systems Security M,O
Computer Science M,O
Counseling Psychology M,O
Counselor Education M,O
Cultural Studies M,O
Education—General M,D,O
Educational Leadership and Administration M,D,O
English M,O
Geographic Information Systems M,O
Health Informatics M,O
Health Psychology M,O
Industrial and Organizational Psychology M,O
Information Science M,O
Law P
Liberal Studies M,O
Management of Technology M
Marriage and Family Therapy M,O
Media Studies M,O
Music M,O
Nonprofit Management M,O
Nursing—General M,O
Organizational Management M
Public Administration M,O
Public History M,O
Rhetoric M,O
Social Psychology M,O
Social Work M
Software Engineering M,O
Special Education M,O
Student Affairs M,O
Taxation M,O
Writing M,O

NORTHERN MICHIGAN UNIVERSITY

Biological and Biomedical Sciences—General M
Counselor Education M
Criminal Justice and Criminology M
Education—General M,O
Educational Leadership and Administration M,O
Elementary Education M
English M
Exercise and Sports Science M
Nursing—General M
Psychology—General M
Public Administration M
Reading Education M,O
Science Education M
Secondary Education M
Special Education M
Writing M

NORTHERN STATE UNIVERSITY

Counselor Education M
Education—General M
Educational Leadership and Administration M
Educational Media/Instructional Technology M
Elementary Education M
Health Education M
Physical Education M
Secondary Education M

NORTH GEORGIA COLLEGE & STATE UNIVERSITY

Art Education M,O
Early Childhood Education M,O
Education—General M,O
Educational Leadership and Administration M,O
English Education M,O
Family Nurse Practitioner Studies M
Mathematics Education M,O
Middle School Education M,O
Nursing Education M
Physical Education M,O
Physical Therapy D
Public Administration M
Science Education M,O
Secondary Education M,O
Social Psychology M
Social Sciences Education M,O
Special Education M,O

NORTH GREENVILLE UNIVERSITY

Human Resources Management M
Pastoral Ministry and Counseling M

NORTH PARK THEOLOGICAL SEMINARY

Pastoral Ministry and Counseling M,O
Theology P,M,D

NORTH PARK UNIVERSITY

Adult Nursing M
Business Administration and Management—General M
Education—General M
Music M
Nonprofit Management M
Nursing and Healthcare Administration M
Nursing—General M

NORTH SHORE–LIJ GRADUATE SCHOOL OF MOLECULAR MEDICINE

Molecular Medicine D

NORTHWEST BAPTIST SEMINARY

Theology P,M,D,O

NORTHWEST CHRISTIAN UNIVERSITY

Business Administration and Management—General M
Counselor Education M
Education—General M

NORTHWESTERN COLLEGE

Organizational Management M
Theology M

NORTHWESTERN HEALTH SCIENCES UNIVERSITY

Acupuncture and Oriental Medicine M
Chiropractic P
Rehabilitation Sciences O

NORTHWESTERN OKLAHOMA STATE UNIVERSITY

Counseling Psychology M
Counselor Education M
Curriculum and Instruction M
Education—General M
Educational Leadership and Administration M
Elementary Education M
Reading Education M
Secondary Education M

NORTHWESTERN POLYTECHNIC UNIVERSITY

Business Administration and Management—General M
Computer Engineering M
Computer Science M
Electrical Engineering M
Engineering and Applied Sciences—General M

NORTHWESTERN STATE UNIVERSITY OF LOUISIANA

Adult Education M
Archaeology M
Art/Fine Arts M
Business Education M
Clinical Psychology M
Counselor Education M,O
Curriculum and Instruction M
Early Childhood Education M
Education—General M,O
Educational Leadership and Administration M,O
Educational Media/Instructional Technology M,O
Elementary Education M,O
English Education M
English M
Health Education M
Historic Preservation M
Home Economics Education M
Mathematics Education M
Middle School Education M
Music M
Nursing—General M

*M—master's degree; P—first professional degree; D—doctorate; O—other advanced degree; *—Close-Up and/or Display in one of the other books in this series*

Program	Degrees
Psychology—General	M
Reading Education	M,O
Science Education	M
Secondary Education	M,O
Social Sciences Education	M
Special Education	M,O
Student Affairs	M,O

NORTHWESTERN UNIVERSITY

Program	Degrees
Accounting	D
Advertising and Public Relations	M
African Studies	O
African-American Studies	D
Allopathic Medicine	
American Studies	M
Anthropology	D
Applied Mathematics	M,D
Art History	D
Art/Fine Arts	M
Astronomy	M,D
Astrophysics	M,D
Biochemistry	D
Biological and Biomedical Sciences—General	D
Biomedical Engineering	M,D
Biophysics	D
Biopsychology	D
Biotechnology	D
Broadcast Journalism	M
Business Administration and Management—General	M
Cancer Biology/Oncology	D
Cell Biology	D
Chemical Engineering	M,D
Chemistry	D
Civil Engineering	M,D
Clinical Psychology	D
Clinical Research	M,O
Cognitive Sciences	D
Communication Disorders	M,D*
Communication—General	M,D
Comparative Literature	M,D,O
Computer and Information Systems Security	M
Computer Engineering	M,D,O
Computer Science	M,D,O
Corporate and Organizational Communication	M
Counseling Psychology	M
Database Systems	M
Developmental Biology	D
Economics	M,D
Education—General	M,D*
Educational Media/Instructional Technology	M,D
Electrical Engineering	M,D,O
Electronic Commerce	M
Electronic Materials	M,D,O
Elementary Education	M
Engineering and Applied Sciences—General	M,D,O
Engineering Design	M
Engineering Management	M
English	M,D
Environmental Engineering	M,D
Ethics	M
Evolutionary Biology	D
Film, Television, and Video Production	M,D
Finance and Banking	D
French	D,O
Gender Studies	
Genetic Counseling	M
Genetics	D
Geology	M,D
Geosciences	M,D
Geotechnical Engineering	M,D
German	D
Higher Education	M
History	M,D
Human Development	D
Immunology	D
Industrial/Management Engineering	M,D
Information Science	M
International Affairs	P,M,O
Internet and Interactive Multimedia	M
Italian	D,O
Journalism	M
Kinesiology and Movement Studies	D
Law	P,M,O
Liberal Studies	M
Linguistics	M,D
Management Information Systems	M
Management Strategy and Policy	M,D
Marketing	M,D
Marriage and Family Therapy	M
Materials Engineering	M,D,O
Materials Sciences	M,D,O
Mathematics	D
Mechanical Engineering	M,D
Mechanics	M,D
Media Studies	M,D
Medical Informatics	M
Microbiology	D
Molecular Biology	D
Music Education	M,D
Music	M,D,O
Neurobiology	M,D
Neuroscience	D
Organizational Behavior	M,D
Organizational Management	M,D
Pharmacology	D
Philosophy	D
Physical Therapy	D
Physics	M,D
Physiology	M
Political Science	M,D
Project Management	M
Psychology—General	D
Public Administration	M
Public Health—General	M
Public Policy	M,D
Publishing	M
Quality Management	M
Rehabilitation Sciences	D
Religion	M
Reproductive Biology	D
Secondary Education	M
Slavic Languages	D
Social Psychology	D
Social Sciences	M,O
Sociology	D
Software Engineering	M
Special Education	M,D
Speech and Interpersonal Communication	M,D
Sports Management	M
Statistics	M,D
Structural Biology	D
Structural Engineering	M,D
Taxation	P,M
Theater	M,D
Toxicology	D
Transportation and Highway Engineering	M,D
Writing	M

NORTHWEST MISSOURI STATE UNIVERSITY

Program	Degrees
Accounting	M
Agricultural Economics and Agribusiness	M
Agricultural Education	M
Agricultural Sciences—General	M
Biological and Biomedical Sciences—General	M
Business Administration and Management—General	M
Computer Science	M,O
Counselor Education	M
Early Childhood Education	M
Education—General	M,O
Educational Leadership and Administration	M,O
Educational Media/Instructional Technology	M
Elementary Education	M,O
English as a Second Language	M,O
English Education	M
English	M
Geographic Information Systems	M,O
Geography	M,O
Health Education	M
Higher Education	M,O
History	M
Management Information Systems	M
Mathematics Education	M
Middle School Education	M
Music Education	M
Physical Education	M
Psychology—General	M
Reading Education	M
Recreation and Park Management	M
Science Education	M
Secondary Education	M,O
Social Sciences Education	M
Special Education	M

NORTHWEST NAZARENE UNIVERSITY

Program	Degrees
Business Administration and Management—General	M
Counselor Education	M
Curriculum and Instruction	M
Education—General	M
Educational Leadership and Administration	M
Marriage and Family Therapy	M
Missions and Missiology	P,M
Nursing and Healthcare Administration	M
Pastoral Ministry and Counseling	P,M
Reading Education	M
Religion	P,M
School Psychology	M
Social Psychology	M
Social Work	M
Special Education	M

NORTHWEST UNIVERSITY

Program	Degrees
Business Administration and Management—General	M
Counseling Psychology	M,D
Cultural Studies	M
Education—General	M
Missions and Missiology	M
Organizational Management	M
Pastoral Ministry and Counseling	M
Psychology—General	M,D
Theology	M

NORTHWOOD UNIVERSITY

Program	Degrees
Business Administration and Management—General	M

NORWICH UNIVERSITY

Program	Degrees
American Studies	M
Business Administration and Management—General	M
Civil Engineering	M
Computer and Information Systems Security	M
Conflict Resolution and Mediation/Peace Studies	M
Construction Management	M
Criminal Justice and Criminology	M
Environmental Engineering	M
Ethnic Studies	M
Finance and Banking	M
Gender Studies	M
Geotechnical Engineering	M
International Affairs	M
International Business	M
Management Information Systems	M
Military and Defense Studies	M
Nursing and Healthcare Administration	M
Nursing Education	M
Organizational Management	M
Project Management	M
Public Administration	M
Science Education	M
Structural Engineering	M
Water Resources Engineering	M

NOTRE DAME COLLEGE (OH)

Program	Degrees
Accounting	M,O
Business Administration and Management—General	M,O
Education—General	M,O
Finance and Banking	M,O
Homeland Security	M,O
Management Information Systems	M,O
Pastoral Ministry and Counseling	M,O
Reading Education	M,O
Special Education	M,O

NOTRE DAME DE NAMUR UNIVERSITY

Program	Degrees
Art Therapy	M
Biological and Biomedical Sciences—General	O
Business Administration and Management—General	M
Clinical Psychology	M
Education—General	M,O
Educational Leadership and Administration	M,O
English as a Second Language	M,O
English	M,O
Finance and Banking	M
Human Resources Management	M
Marketing	M
Marriage and Family Therapy	M
Music	M,O
Psychology—General	M
Public Administration	M
Public Affairs	M
Reading Education	M,O
Special Education	M,O

NOTRE DAME SEMINARY

Program	Degrees
Theology	P,M

NOVA SCOTIA AGRICULTURAL COLLEGE

Program	Degrees
Agricultural Sciences—General	M
Agronomy and Soil Sciences	M
Animal Sciences	M
Aquaculture	M
Botany	M
Ecology	M
Environmental Biology	M
Environmental Management and Policy	M
Environmental Sciences	M
Food Science and Technology	M
Horticulture	M
Physiology	M
Plant Pathology	M

Plant Physiology M
Water Resources M

NOVA SOUTHEASTERN UNIVERSITY

Accounting M,D
Adult Education D
Allied Health—General M,D
Art Education M,O
Bioinformatics M,O
Biological and Biomedical Sciences—General M,D
Business Administration and Management—General M,D
Child and Family Studies M,D
Clinical Psychology D,O
Communication Disorders M,D
Computer and Information Systems Security M,D
Computer Education M,D,O
Computer Science M,D
Conflict Resolution and Mediation/Peace Studies M,D
Counseling Psychology M
Counselor Education M
Criminal Justice and Criminology M
Curriculum and Instruction M,O
Dentistry P,M
Distance Education Development M,D
Early Childhood Education M,O
Education of the Gifted M,O
Education—General M,D,O
Educational Leadership and Administration M,D,O
Educational Media/Instructional Technology M,D,O
Elementary Education M,O
English as a Second Language M,O
English Education M,O
Environmental Education M,O
Environmental Sciences M
Finance and Banking D
Health Education M,D
Health Informatics M,O
Health Law M
Higher Education D
Human Resources Management M,D
Human Services M,D
Humanities M,O
Information Science M,D
Interdisciplinary Studies M
International Business M,D
Law P,M,O
Legal and Justice Studies M,O
Management Information Systems M,D
Marine Affairs M
Marine Biology M,D
Marine Sciences M
Marketing D
Marriage and Family Therapy M,D,O
Mathematics Education M,O
Medical Informatics M,O
Multilingual and Multicultural Education M,O
National Security M,O
Nursing—General M,D
Occupational Therapy M,D
Oceanography M,D
Optometry P,M
Organizational Management D
Osteopathic Medicine P,M,O
Pharmacology M
Pharmacy P,D*
Physical Therapy D
Physician Assistant Studies M
Psychology—General M,D,O
Public Administration M
Public Health—General M
Reading Education M,O
Real Estate M
School Psychology O
Science Education M,O
Secondary Education M,O
Social Sciences Education M,O
Social Sciences M,O
Spanish M,O
Special Education M,D,O
Sports Management M,O
Student Affairs M
Taxation M
Urban Education M,O
Vision Sciences P,M
Vocational and Technical Education D

NSCAD UNIVERSITY

Applied Arts and Design—General M
Art/Fine Arts M

NYACK COLLEGE

Business Administration and Management—General M
Counseling Psychology M
Counselor Education M
Education—General M
Elementary Education M
Marriage and Family Therapy M
Organizational Management M
Pastoral Ministry and Counseling P,M,D
Special Education M
Theology P,M,D

OAKLAND CITY UNIVERSITY

Business Administration and Management—General M
Education—General M,D
Educational Leadership and Administration M,D
Theology P,D

OAKLAND UNIVERSITY

Accounting M,O
Adult Nursing M
Allied Health—General M,D,O
Applied Mathematics M,D
Applied Statistics M
Biological and Biomedical Sciences—General M,D
Business Administration and Management—General M,O
Chemistry M,D
Computer Engineering M
Computer Science M
Counseling Psychology M,D,O
Early Childhood Education M,D,O
Economics O
Education—General M,D,O
Educational Leadership and Administration M,D,O
Educational Media/Instructional Technology O
Electrical Engineering M
Engineering and Applied Sciences—General M,D
Engineering Management M
English as a Second Language M,O
English M
Entrepreneurship M,O
Environmental and Occupational Health M
Environmental Sciences M,D
Exercise and Sports Science M,O
Family Nurse Practitioner Studies M,O
Finance and Banking M,O
Foundations and Philosophy of Education M
Gerontological Nursing M,O
Health Promotion O
Higher Education M,D,O
History M
Human Resources Development M
Human Resources Management M,O
Industrial and Manufacturing Management M,O
International Business M,O
Liberal Studies M
Linguistics M,O
Management Information Systems M,O
Marketing M,O
Maternal and Child Health M,D,O
Mathematics Education M,D,O
Mathematics M
Mechanical Engineering M,D
Medical Physics M,D
Music Education M,D
Music M,D
Nurse Anesthesia M,O
Nursing Education M,O
Nursing—General M,D,O
Physical Therapy M,D,O
Physics M,D
Public Administration M
Reading Education M,D,O
Secondary Education M
Software Engineering M
Special Education M,O
Statistics O
Systems Engineering M,D
Systems Science M

OAKWOOD UNIVERSITY

Pastoral Ministry and Counseling M

OBERLIN COLLEGE

Early Childhood Education M
Education—General M
Middle School Education M
Music M,O

OBLATE SCHOOL OF THEOLOGY

Pastoral Ministry and Counseling P,M,D,O
Religion P,M,D,O
Theology P,M,D,O

OCCIDENTAL COLLEGE

Biological and Biomedical Sciences—General M
Education—General M
Elementary Education M
English Education M
Foreign Languages Education M
Liberal Studies M
Mathematics Education M
Science Education M
Secondary Education M
Social Sciences Education M

OGI SCHOOL OF SCIENCE & ENGINEERING AT OREGON HEALTH & SCIENCE UNIVERSITY

Biochemistry M,D
Biomedical Engineering M,D
Business Administration and Management—General M,O
Computer Engineering M,D
Computer Science M,D
Electrical Engineering M,D
Environmental and Occupational Health M,D
Environmental Engineering M,D
Environmental Sciences M,D
Health Services Management and Hospital Administration M,O
Management of Technology M,O
Molecular Biology M,D
Ocean Engineering M,D

OGLALA LAKOTA COLLEGE

Business Administration and Management—General M
Educational Leadership and Administration M

OGLETHORPE UNIVERSITY

Early Childhood Education M
Education—General M

OHIO COLLEGE OF PODIATRIC MEDICINE

Podiatric Medicine P

OHIO DOMINICAN UNIVERSITY

Business Administration and Management—General M
Education—General M
English as a Second Language M
Liberal Studies M
Theology M

OHIO NORTHERN UNIVERSITY

Law P,M
Pharmacy P

THE OHIO STATE UNIVERSITY

Accounting M,D
African Studies M
African-American Studies M
Agricultural Economics and Agribusiness M,D
Agricultural Education M,D
Agricultural Engineering M,D
Agricultural Sciences—General M,D
Agronomy and Soil Sciences M,D
Allied Health—General M,D
Allopathic Medicine P
Anatomy M,D
Animal Sciences M,D
Anthropology M,D
Architecture M,D
Art Education M,D
Art History M,D
Art/Fine Arts M
Arts Administration M
Asian Languages M,D
Astronomy M,D
Atmospheric Sciences M,D
Biochemistry M,D
Bioengineering M,D
Biological and Biomedical Sciences—General D
Biomedical Engineering M,D
Biophysics M,D
Biostatistics M,D
Business Administration and Management—General M,D
Cell Biology M,D
Chemical Engineering M,D
Chemical Physics M,D
Chemistry M,D
Child and Family Studies M,D
Chinese M,D
Civil Engineering M,D
Classics M,D
Clinical Psychology M,D
Clothing and Textiles M,D
Cognitive Sciences M,D
Communication Disorders M,D
Communication—General M,D
Computer Engineering M,D

*M—master's degree; P—first professional degree; D—doctorate; O—other advanced degree; *—Close-Up and/or Display in one of the other books in this series*

Computer Science M,D
Consumer Economics M,D
Dance M,D
Dentistry P,M,D
Developmental Biology M,D
Developmental Psychology M,D
East European and Russian Studies M,D
Ecology M,D
Economics M,D
Education—General M,D
Educational Leadership and Administration M,D
Educational Policy M,D
Electrical Engineering M,D
Engineering and Applied Sciences—General M,D
English M,D
Entomology M,D
Environmental Sciences M,D
Evolutionary Biology M,D
Food Science and Technology M,D
French M,D
Genetics M,D
Geodetic Sciences M,D
Geography M,D
Geology M,D
German M,D
Health Services Management and Hospital Administration M,D
History M,D
Horticulture M,D
Hospitality Management M,D
Human Development M,D
Human Resources Management M,D
Immunology D
Industrial and Labor Relations M,D
Industrial Design M
Industrial/Management Engineering M,D
Information Science M,D
Interdisciplinary Studies M,D
Interior Design M
Italian M,D
Japanese M,D
Landscape Architecture M,D
Law P,M
Linguistics M,D
Logistics M
Management Information Systems M,D
Marketing M,D
Materials Engineering M,D
Materials Sciences M,D
Mathematics M,D
Mechanical Engineering M,D
Metallurgical Engineering and Metallurgy M,D
Microbiology M,D
Molecular Biology M,D
Molecular Genetics M,D
Music M,D
Natural Resources M,D
Near and Middle Eastern Languages M,D
Neuroscience M,D
Nuclear Engineering M,D
Nursing—General M,D
Nutrition M,D
Occupational Therapy M
Operations Research M
Optical Sciences P,M,D
Optometry P,M,D
Oral and Dental Sciences P,M,D
Pathobiology M,D
Pathology M
Pharmaceutical Administration P,M,D
Pharmacology P,M,D
Pharmacy P,M,D
Philosophy M,D
Physical Education M,D
Physical Therapy D
Physics M,D
Physiology M,D
Plant Pathology M,D
Political Science M,D
Portuguese M,D
Psychology—General M,D
Public Administration M,D
Public Affairs M,D
Public Health—General M,D
Public Policy M,D
Rehabilitation Sciences M,D
Rural Sociology M,D
Russian M,D
Slavic Languages M,D
Social Psychology M,D
Social Work M,D
Sociology M,D
Spanish M,D
Statistics M,D
Surveying Science and Engineering M,D
Systems Engineering M,D
Theater M,D
Toxicology M,D
Urban and Regional Planning M,D
Veterinary Sciences M,D
Virology D
Women's Studies M,D

THE OHIO STATE UNIVERSITY AT LIMA

Early Childhood Education M
Education—General M
Middle School Education M
Social Work M

THE OHIO STATE UNIVERSITY AT MARION

Early Childhood Education M
Education—General M
Middle School Education M

THE OHIO STATE UNIVERSITY–MANSFIELD CAMPUS

Early Childhood Education M
Education—General M
Middle School Education M
Social Work M

THE OHIO STATE UNIVERSITY–NEWARK CAMPUS

Early Childhood Education M
Education—General M
Middle School Education M
Social Work M

OHIO UNIVERSITY

African Studies M
Applied Economics M
Art History M
Art/Fine Arts M
Asian Studies M
Astronomy M,D
Athletic Training and Sports Medicine M
Biochemistry M,D
Biological and Biomedical Sciences—General M,D
Biomedical Engineering M,D
Business Administration and Management—General M
Cell Biology M,D
Chemical Engineering M,D
Child and Family Studies M
Child Development M
Civil Engineering M,D
Clinical Psychology D
Clothing and Textiles M
Communication Disorders M,D
Communication—General M,D
Comparative and Interdisciplinary Arts D
Computer Education M,D
Computer Science M,D
Construction Engineering M,D
Corporate and Organizational Communication M,D
Counselor Education M,D
Curriculum and Instruction M,D
Ecology M,D
Economics M
Education—General M,D
Educational Leadership and Administration M,D
Educational Measurement and Evaluation M,D
Educational Media/Instructional Technology M,D
Electrical Engineering M,D
Engineering and Applied Sciences—General M,D
English as a Second Language M
English M,D
Environmental Biology M,D
Environmental Engineering M,D
Environmental Management and Policy M
Evolutionary Biology M,D
Exercise and Sports Science M,D
Experimental Psychology D
Family and Consumer Sciences-General M
Family Nurse Practitioner Studies M
Film, Television, and Video Production M
Film, Television, and Video Theory and Criticism M
Finance and Banking M
French M
Geochemistry M
Geography M
Geology M
Geophysics M
Geotechnical Engineering M,D
Graphic Design M
Health Communication M,D
Health Services Management and Hospital Administration M
Higher Education M,D
History M,D
Hydrogeology M
Industrial and Organizational Psychology D
Industrial/Management Engineering M,D
International Affairs M
International Development M
Journalism M,D
Latin American Studies M
Linguistics M
Mathematics Education M,D
Mathematics M,D
Mechanical Engineering M,D
Mechanics M,D
Media Studies M,D
Microbiology M,D
Middle School Education M,D
Molecular Biology M,D
Multilingual and Multicultural Education M,D
Music Education M,O
Music M,O
Neuroscience M,D
Nursing and Healthcare Administration M
Nursing Education M
Nursing—General M
Nutrition M
Osteopathic Medicine P
Philosophy M
Photography M
Physical Education M
Physical Therapy D
Physics M,D*
Physiology M,D
Plant Biology M,D
Political Science M
Psychology—General D
Public Administration M
Public Health—General M
Reading Education M,D
Recreation and Park Management M
Rehabilitation Counseling M,D
Rhetoric M,D
Science Education M
Secondary Education M,D
Social Sciences Education M,D
Social Sciences M
Social Work M
Sociology M
Spanish M
Special Education M,D
Speech and Interpersonal Communication M,D
Sports Management M
Structural Engineering M,D
Student Affairs M,D
Systems Engineering M
Telecommunications M
Theater M
Therapies—Dance, Drama, and Music M,O
Transportation and Highway Engineering M,D
Water Resources Engineering M,D

OHIO VALLEY UNIVERSITY

Education—General M

OHR HAMEIR THEOLOGICAL SEMINARY

Theology

OKLAHOMA CHRISTIAN UNIVERSITY

Pastoral Ministry and Counseling P,M
Theology P,M

OKLAHOMA CITY UNIVERSITY

Accounting M
Applied Behavior Analysis M
Art/Fine Arts M
Business Administration and Management—General M
Comparative Literature M
Computer Science M
Corporate and Organizational Communication M
Criminal Justice and Criminology M
Dance M
Early Childhood Education M
Education—General M
Elementary Education M
English as a Second Language M
Finance and Banking M
Health Services Management and Hospital Administration M
International Business M
Law P
Liberal Studies M
Management Information Systems M
Marketing M
Mass Communication M
Music M
Nonprofit Management M
Nursing—General M,D
Philosophy M
Religion M
Sociology M
Theater M
Writing M

OKLAHOMA STATE UNIVERSITY

Accounting M,D

Agricultural Economics and Agribusiness	M,D
Agricultural Education	M,D
Agricultural Engineering	M,D
Agricultural Sciences—General	M,D
Agronomy and Soil Sciences	M,D
Animal Sciences	M,D
Applied Arts and Design—General	M,D
Applied Behavior Analysis	M,D,O
Applied Mathematics	M,D
Applied Psychology	M,D,O
Applied Science and Technology	M,D,O
Biochemistry	M,D
Bioengineering	M,D
Botany	M,D
Business Administration and Management—General	M,D
Chemical Engineering	M,D
Chemistry	M,D
Child and Family Studies	M,D
Civil Engineering	M,D
Clinical Psychology	M,D
Clothing and Textiles	M,D
Communication Disorders	M
Computer Engineering	M,D
Computer Science	M,D
Consumer Economics	M,D
Curriculum and Instruction	M,D
Economics	M,D
Education—General	M,D,O
Educational Leadership and Administration	M,D
Educational Psychology	M,D,O
Electrical Engineering	M,D
Emergency Management	M,D
Engineering and Applied Sciences—General	M,D*
English	M,D
Entomology	M,D
Environmental Engineering	M,D
Environmental Sciences	M,D,O
Family and Consumer Sciences-General	M,D
Finance and Banking	M,D
Fire Protection Engineering	M,D
Food Science and Technology	M,D
Forestry	M,D
Geography	M,D
Geology	M,D
Health Education	M,D,O
Higher Education	M,D
History	M,D
Horticulture	M,D
Hospitality Management	M,D
Human Development	M,D
Industrial/Management Engineering	M,D
Information Science	M,D
International Affairs	M,D,O
Landscape Architecture	M,D
Management Information Systems	M,D
Marketing	M,D
Marriage and Family Therapy	M,D
Mass Communication	M
Mathematics Education	M,D
Mathematics	M,D
Mechanical Engineering	M,D
Microbiology	M,D
Molecular Biology	M,D
Molecular Genetics	M,D
Music Education	M
Music	M
Natural Resources	M,D
Nutrition	M,D
Philosophy	M
Photonics	M,D,O
Physics	M,D
Plant Pathology	M,D
Plant Sciences	M,D,O
Political Science	M,D
Psychology—General	M,D
Quantitative Analysis	M,D
Sociology	M,D
Statistics	M,D
Telecommunications Management	M,D
Theater	M
Veterinary Medicine	P
Veterinary Sciences	M,D
Writing	M,D
Zoology	M,D

OKLAHOMA STATE UNIVERSITY CENTER FOR HEALTH SCIENCES

Biological and Biomedical Sciences—General	M,D
Forensic Psychology	M,O
Forensic Sciences	M,O
Health Services Management and Hospital Administration	M
Molecular Biology	M,O
Osteopathic Medicine	P
Toxicology	M,O

OLD DOMINION UNIVERSITY

Accounting	M
Aerospace/Aeronautical Engineering	M,D
Allied Health—General	M,D
Analytical Chemistry	M,D
Applied Economics	M
Applied Psychology	D
Athletic Training and Sports Medicine	M
Biochemistry	M,D
Biological and Biomedical Sciences—General	M,D
Business Administration and Management—General	M,D
Business Education	M,D
Chemistry	M,D
Civil Engineering	M,D
Clinical Psychology	D
Communication Disorders	M
Community College Education	M,D
Computer Art and Design	M
Computer Engineering	M,D
Computer Science	M,D
Counselor Education	M,D,O
Criminal Justice and Criminology	D
Curriculum and Instruction	M,D
Dental Hygiene	M
Early Childhood Education	M,D
Ecology	D
Economics	M
Education—General	M,D,O
Educational Leadership and Administration	M,D,O
Educational Media/Instructional Technology	M,D
Electrical Engineering	M,D
Elementary Education	M
Engineering and Applied Sciences—General	M,D
Engineering Management	M,D
English	M,D
Environmental and Occupational Health	M
Environmental Engineering	M,D
Ergonomics and Human Factors	D
Exercise and Sports Science	M
Experimental Psychology	D
Family Nurse Practitioner Studies	M
Finance and Banking	M,D
Health Promotion	M
Health Services Research	D
Higher Education	M,D,O
History	M
Human-Computer Interaction	M,D
Humanities	M
Industrial and Organizational Psychology	D
Information Science	D
International Affairs	M,D
International Business	M
Kinesiology and Movement Studies	D
Library Science	M
Linguistics	M
Management Information Systems	M
Management of Technology	M
Marine Affairs	M
Marketing	D
Mathematics	M,D
Mechanical Engineering	M,D
Middle School Education	M
Modeling and Simulation	M,D
Music Education	M
Nurse Anesthesia	M
Nurse Midwifery	M
Nursing and Healthcare Administration	M
Nursing Education	M
Nursing—General	M,D
Oceanography	M,D
Organic Chemistry	M,D
Physical Chemistry	M,D
Physical Education	M
Physical Therapy	D
Physics	M,D
Psychology—General	M,D
Public Administration	M,D
Public Health—General	M
Reading Education	M,D
Recreation and Park Management	M
Science Education	M
Secondary Education	M
Sociology	M
Special Education	M,D
Speech and Interpersonal Communication	M
Sports Management	M
Systems Engineering	M,D
Travel and Tourism	M
Urban Studies	D
Vocational and Technical Education	M,D
Women's Health Nursing	M
Women's Studies	M,D
Writing	M

OLIVET COLLEGE

Education—General	M

OLIVET NAZARENE UNIVERSITY

Business Administration and Management—General	M
Curriculum and Instruction	M
Education—General	M
Educational Leadership and Administration	M
Elementary Education	M
Library Science	M
Organizational Management	M
Reading Education	M
Religion	M
Secondary Education	M
Theology	M

ORAL ROBERTS UNIVERSITY

Accounting	M
Business Administration and Management—General	M
Curriculum and Instruction	M,D
Education—General	M,D
Educational Leadership and Administration	M,D
Entrepreneurship	M
Finance and Banking	M
Higher Education	M,D
International Business	M
Marketing	M
Marriage and Family Therapy	P,M,D
Missions and Missiology	P,M,D
Near and Middle Eastern Languages	P,M,D
Nonprofit Management	M
Pastoral Ministry and Counseling	P,M,D
Religious Education	P,M,D
Theology	P,M,D

OREGON COLLEGE OF ORIENTAL MEDICINE

Acupuncture and Oriental Medicine	M,D

OREGON HEALTH & SCIENCE UNIVERSITY

Allopathic Medicine	P
Biochemistry	M,D
Biological and Biomedical Sciences—General	M,D,O
Biomedical Engineering	M,D
Biopsychology	D
Biostatistics	M
Cancer Biology/Oncology	D
Cell Biology	D
Clinical Research	M,O
Community Health Nursing	M,O
Computational Biology	M,D,O
Computer Engineering	M,D
Computer Science	M,D
Dentistry	P,O
Developmental Biology	D
Electrical Engineering	M,D
Environmental Engineering	M,D
Environmental Sciences	M,D
Epidemiology	M
Family Nurse Practitioner Studies	M,O
Genetics	D
Gerontological Nursing	O
Gerontology	M,O
Health Informatics	M,D,O
Health Services Management and Hospital Administration	M
Immunology	D
Management of Technology	M
Medical Informatics	M,D,O
Microbiology	D
Molecular Biology	M,D
Neuroscience	D*
Nurse Anesthesia	M
Nurse Midwifery	M,O
Nursing Education	M,O
Nursing—General	M,D,O
Nutrition	M,O
Oral and Dental Sciences	P,M,O
Pharmacology	D
Physician Assistant Studies	M
Physiology	D
Psychiatric Nursing	M,O

OREGON STATE UNIVERSITY

Adult Education	M
Agricultural Economics and Agribusiness	M,D
Agricultural Education	M
Agricultural Sciences—General	M,D
Agronomy and Soil Sciences	M,D
Analytical Chemistry	M,D
Animal Sciences	M,D
Anthropology	M
Applied Physics	M,D
Atmospheric Sciences	M,D
Biochemistry	M,D

*M—master's degree; P—first professional degree; D—doctorate; O—other advanced degree; *—Close-Up and/or Display in one of the other books in this series*

Bioengineering M,D
Biophysics M,D
Botany M,D
Business Administration and Management—General M,O
Cell Biology M,D
Chemical Engineering M,D
Chemistry M,D
Child and Family Studies M,D
Civil Engineering M,D
Clothing and Textiles M,D
Computer Engineering M,D
Computer Science M,D
Construction Engineering M,D
Counselor Education M,D
Economics M,D
Education—General M,D
Educational Leadership and Administration M
Electrical Engineering M,D
Elementary Education M
Engineering and Applied Sciences—General M,D
English M
Environmental and Occupational Health M
Environmental Engineering M,D
Environmental Sciences M,D
Exercise and Sports Science M,D
Family and Consumer Sciences-General M
Fish, Game, and Wildlife Management M,D
Food Science and Technology M,D
Forestry M,D
Genetics M,D
Geography M,D
Geology M,D
Geophysics M,D
Geosciences M,D
Geotechnical Engineering M,D
Gerontology M
Health Physics/Radiological Health M,D
Health Promotion M,D
Health Services Management and Hospital Administration M,D
History of Science and Technology M,D
History M,D
Horticulture M,D
Human Development M,D
Industrial/Management Engineering M,D
Inorganic Chemistry M,D
Interdisciplinary Studies M
Kinesiology and Movement Studies M
Manufacturing Engineering M,D
Marine Affairs M
Marine Sciences M
Materials Sciences M,D
Mathematics Education M,D
Mathematics M,D
Mechanical Engineering M,D
Microbiology M,D
Molecular Biology M,D
Molecular Toxicology M,D
Music Education M
Nanotechnology M,D
Nuclear Engineering M,D
Nutrition M,D
Ocean Engineering M,D
Oceanography M,D
Operations Research M,D
Organic Chemistry M,D
Paper and Pulp Engineering M,D
Pharmaceutical Sciences P,M,D
Pharmacy P,M,D
Physical Chemistry M,D
Physics M,D
Plant Pathology M,D
Plant Physiology M,D
Public Health—General M,D
Range Science M,D
Reading Education M
Science Education M,D
Statistics M,D
Structural Engineering M,D
Student Affairs M
Systems Engineering M,D
Toxicology M,D
Transportation and Highway Engineering M,D
Veterinary Medicine P
Veterinary Sciences D
Water Resources Engineering M,D
Zoology M,D

OREGON STATE UNIVERSITY–CASCADES

Education—General M
School Psychology M
Social Psychology M

OTIS COLLEGE OF ART AND DESIGN

Art/Fine Arts M
Graphic Design M
Photography M
Writing M

OTTAWA UNIVERSITY

Art Therapy M
Business Administration and Management—General M
Counseling Psychology M
Counselor Education M
Curriculum and Instruction M
Early Childhood Education M
Education—General M
Educational Leadership and Administration M
Educational Media/Instructional Technology M
Elementary Education M
Finance and Banking M
Human Resources Development M
Human Resources Management M
Marketing M
Marriage and Family Therapy M
Pastoral Ministry and Counseling M
School Psychology M
Special Education M

OTTERBEIN UNIVERSITY

Adult Nursing M,O
Business Administration and Management—General M
Education—General M
Family Nurse Practitioner Studies M,O
Nursing and Healthcare Administration M,O
Nursing—General M,O

OUR LADY OF HOLY CROSS COLLEGE

Counselor Education M
Curriculum and Instruction M
Education—General M
Educational Leadership and Administration M
Marriage and Family Therapy M

OUR LADY OF THE LAKE COLLEGE

Nurse Anesthesia M
Nursing and Healthcare Administration M
Nursing Education M
Nursing—General M
Physician Assistant Studies M

OUR LADY OF THE LAKE UNIVERSITY OF SAN ANTONIO

Accounting M
Business Administration and Management—General M
Communication Disorders M
Communication—General M
Computer and Information Systems Security M
Counseling Psychology M,D
Counselor Education M
Curriculum and Instruction M
Early Childhood Education M
Education—General M,D
Educational Leadership and Administration M
Educational Media/Instructional Technology M
Elementary Education M
English as a Second Language M
English Education M
English M
Finance and Banking M
Health Services Management and Hospital Administration M
Human Development M
Management Information Systems M
Marriage and Family Therapy M,D
Mathematics Education M
Middle School Education M
Multilingual and Multicultural Education M
Nonprofit Management M
Organizational Management M,D
Psychology—General M,D
Reading Education M
School Psychology M,D
Science Education M
Secondary Education M
Social Work M
Special Education M
Vocational and Technical Education M
Writing M

OXFORD GRADUATE SCHOOL

Child and Family Studies M,D
Organizational Management M,D
Religion M,D
Sociology M,D

PACE UNIVERSITY

Accounting M
Addictions/Substance Abuse Counseling M
Art Education M,O
Business Administration and Management—General M,D,O
Clinical Psychology M,D
Computer and Information Systems Security M,D,O
Computer Science M,D,O
Counseling Psychology M
Curriculum and Instruction M,O
Early Childhood Education M,O
Economics M
Education—General M,O
Educational Leadership and Administration M,O
Electronic Commerce M,D,O
Elementary Education M,O
Environmental Law P,M,D
Environmental Management and Policy M
Environmental Sciences M
Family Nurse Practitioner Studies M,D,O
Finance and Banking M
Forensic Sciences M
Health Services Management and Hospital Administration M
Homeland Security M
Information Science M,D,O
International Business M
Internet and Interactive Multimedia M,D,O
Investment Management M
Law P,M,D
Legal and Justice Studies P,M,D
Management Information Systems M
Management Strategy and Policy M
Marketing Research M
Marketing M
Nonprofit Management M
Nursing and Healthcare Administration M,D,O
Nursing Education M,D,O
Nursing—General M,D,O
Physician Assistant Studies M
Psychology—General M
Public Administration M
Publishing M,O
Reading Education M,O
School Psychology M,D
Software Engineering M,D,O
Special Education M,O
Sustainable Development P,M,D
Taxation M
Telecommunications M,D,O
Theater M

PACIFICA GRADUATE INSTITUTE

Clinical Psychology M,D
Counseling Psychology M,D
Psychology—General M,D

PACIFIC COLLEGE OF ORIENTAL MEDICINE

Acupuncture and Oriental Medicine M,D

PACIFIC COLLEGE OF ORIENTAL MEDICINE-CHICAGO

Acupuncture and Oriental Medicine M

PACIFIC COLLEGE OF ORIENTAL MEDICINE-NEW YORK

Acupuncture and Oriental Medicine M

PACIFIC LUTHERAN THEOLOGICAL SEMINARY

Theology P,M,D,O

PACIFIC LUTHERAN UNIVERSITY

Business Administration and Management—General M
Curriculum and Instruction M
Education—General M
Educational Leadership and Administration M
Family Nurse Practitioner Studies M
Management of Technology M
Marriage and Family Therapy M
Nursing and Healthcare Administration M
Nursing—General M
Writing M

PACIFIC NORTHWEST COLLEGE OF ART

Applied Arts and Design—General M
Art/Fine Arts M

PACIFIC OAKS COLLEGE

Human Development M
Marriage and Family Therapy M

PACIFIC SCHOOL OF RELIGION

Religion P,M,D,O
Theology P,M,D,O

PACIFIC STATES UNIVERSITY

Accounting M,D
Business Administration and Management—General M,D
Computer Science M
Finance and Banking M,D
International Business M,D
Management Information Systems M,D
Management of Technology M,D
Real Estate M,D

PACIFIC UNION COLLEGE

Education—General M

PACIFIC UNIVERSITY

Early Childhood Education M
Education—General M
Elementary Education M
Health Services Management and Hospital Administration M
Middle School Education M
Occupational Therapy M
Pharmacy P
Physical Therapy D
Physician Assistant Studies M
Psychology—General M,D
Secondary Education M
Special Education M
Writing M

PALM BEACH ATLANTIC UNIVERSITY

Addictions/Substance Abuse Counseling M
Business Administration and Management—General M
Counseling Psychology M
Counselor Education M
Education—General M
Marriage and Family Therapy M
Organizational Management M
Pharmacy P

PALMER COLLEGE OF CHIROPRACTIC

Anatomy M
Chiropractic P
Clinical Research M

PALO ALTO UNIVERSITY

Biopsychology D
Clinical Psychology D
Psychology—General M,D

PARKER COLLEGE OF CHIROPRACTIC

Chiropractic P

PARK UNIVERSITY

Business Administration and Management—General M
Education—General M
Educational Leadership and Administration M
Emergency Management M
Entrepreneurship M
Health Services Management and Hospital Administration M
International Business M
Law M
Management Information Systems M
Middle School Education M
Multilingual and Multicultural Education M
Nonprofit Management M
Public Administration M
Public Affairs M
Secondary Education M
Special Education M

PAYNE THEOLOGICAL SEMINARY

Theology P

PENN STATE DICKINSON SCHOOL OF LAW

Law P,M

PENN STATE ERIE, THE BEHREND COLLEGE

Business Administration and Management—General M
Engineering and Applied Sciences—General M

PENN STATE GREAT VALLEY

Business Administration and Management—General M
Education—General M
Engineering and Applied Sciences—General M

PENN STATE HARRISBURG

American Studies M,D
Business Administration and Management—General M
Education—General M,D
Engineering and Applied Sciences—General M
Environmental Sciences M
Humanities M,D
Psychology—General M,D
Public Affairs M,D

PENN STATE HERSHEY MEDICAL CENTER

Allopathic Medicine P,M,D
Anatomy M,D
Biochemistry M,D
Bioengineering M,D
Biological and Biomedical Sciences—General M,D
Cell Biology M,D
Genetics M,D
Health Services Research M
Immunology M,D
Microbiology M,D
Molecular Biology M,D
Molecular Medicine M,D
Molecular Toxicology M,D
Neuroscience M,D
Pharmacology M,D
Physiology M,D
Public Health—General M
Veterinary Sciences M
Virology M,D

PENN STATE UNIVERSITY PARK

Acoustics M,D
Aerospace/Aeronautical Engineering M,D
Agricultural Economics and Agribusiness M,D
Agricultural Education M,D
Agricultural Engineering M,D
Agricultural Sciences—General M,D
Agronomy and Soil Sciences M,D
Animal Sciences M,D
Anthropology M,D
Applied Mathematics M,D
Architectural Engineering M,D
Architecture M,D
Art History M,D
Art/Fine Arts M,D
Astronomy M,D
Astrophysics M,D
Biochemistry M,D
Bioengineering M,D
Biological and Biomedical Sciences—General M,D
Biopsychology D
Business Administration and Management—General M,D
Chemical Engineering M,D
Chemistry M,D
Child and Family Studies M,D
Civil Engineering M,D
Communication Disorders M,D
Communication—General M,D
Computer Engineering M,D
Computer Science M,D
Counseling Psychology M,D
Counselor Education M,D
Curriculum and Instruction M,D
Ecology M,D
Economics M,D
Education—General M,D
Educational Media/Instructional Technology M,D
Educational Policy M,D
Educational Psychology M,D
Electrical Engineering M,D
Engineering and Applied Sciences—General M,D
English M,D
Entomology M,D
Environmental Engineering M,D
Environmental Management and Policy M
Environmental Sciences M
Food Science and Technology M,D
Forestry M,D
French M,D
Genetics M,D
Geography M,D
Geosciences M,D
Geotechnical Engineering M,D
German M,D
Health Services Management and Hospital Administration M,D
History M,D
Homeland Security M,D
Horticulture M,D
Hospitality Management M,D
Human Development M,D
Human Resources Development M
Human Resources Management M
Industrial and Labor Relations M
Industrial and Manufacturing Management M
Industrial/Management Engineering M,D
Information Science M,D
Kinesiology and Movement Studies M,D
Landscape Architecture M
Leisure Studies M,D
Linguistics M,D
Manufacturing Engineering M,D
Materials Engineering M,D
Materials Sciences M,D
Mathematics M,D
Mechanical Engineering M,D
Mechanics M,D
Meteorology M,D
Microbiology M,D
Mineral/Mining Engineering M,D
Molecular Biology M,D
Music M,D
Nuclear Engineering M,D
Nursing—General M,D
Nutrition M,D
Pathobiology D
Philosophy M,D
Physics M,D
Physiology M,D
Plant Pathology M,D
Plant Physiology M,D
Political Science M,D
Psychology—General M,D
Quality Management M
Recreation and Park Management M,D
Rural Sociology M,D
School Psychology M,D
Sociology M,D
Spanish M,D
Special Education M,D
Statistics M,D
Theater M
Travel and Tourism M,D
Veterinary Sciences D
Vocational and Technical Education M,D
Writing M,D

PENNSYLVANIA ACADEMY OF THE FINE ARTS

Art/Fine Arts M,O

PENTECOSTAL THEOLOGICAL SEMINARY

Pastoral Ministry and Counseling P,M,D
Theology P,M,D

PEPPERDINE UNIVERSITY

American Studies M
Business Administration and Management—General M
Clinical Psychology M
Communication—General M
Conflict Resolution and Mediation/Peace Studies M
Economics M
Education—General M,D
Educational Leadership and Administration M,D
Educational Media/Instructional Technology M,D
Film, Television, and Video Production M
Finance and Banking M
History M
Humanities M
International Affairs M
International Business M
Law P
Marriage and Family Therapy M
Organizational Management M
Pastoral Ministry and Counseling M
Political Science M
Psychology—General D
Public Administration M
Public Policy M
Religion P,M
Theology P
Writing M

*M—master's degree; P—first professional degree; D—doctorate; O—other advanced degree; *—Close-Up and/or Display in one of the other books in this series*

PERELANDRA COLLEGE
Counseling Psychology M
Writing M

PERU STATE COLLEGE
Curriculum and Instruction M
Economics M
Education—General M
Entrepreneurship M
Organizational Management M

PFEIFFER UNIVERSITY
Business Administration and Management—General M
Elementary Education M
Health Services Management and Hospital Administration M
Organizational Management M
Religious Education M
Theology M

PHILADELPHIA BIBLICAL UNIVERSITY
Curriculum and Instruction M
Education—General M
Educational Leadership and Administration M
Organizational Management M
Pastoral Ministry and Counseling M
Theology P,M

PHILADELPHIA COLLEGE OF OSTEOPATHIC MEDICINE
Biological and Biomedical Sciences—General M,O
Clinical Psychology M,D,O
Counseling Psychology M,D,O
Forensic Sciences M
Health Psychology M,D,O
Industrial and Organizational Psychology M,D,O
Osteopathic Medicine P
Physician Assistant Studies M
Psychology—General M,D,O*
School Psychology M,D,O

PHILADELPHIA UNIVERSITY
Architecture M
Business Administration and Management—General M
Clothing and Textiles M
Computer Art and Design M
Construction Management M
Emergency Management M
Finance and Banking M
Health Services Management and Hospital Administration M
International Business M
Marketing M
Nurse Midwifery M,O
Occupational Therapy M
Physician Assistant Studies M
Sustainable Development M
Taxation M
Textile Design M
Textile Sciences and Engineering M,D

PHILLIPS GRADUATE INSTITUTE
Counselor Education M
Marriage and Family Therapy M
Organizational Behavior D
School Psychology M

PHILLIPS THEOLOGICAL SEMINARY
Business Administration and Management—General P,M,D
Ethics P,M,D
Higher Education P,M,D
Missions and Missiology P,M,D
Music P,M,D
Pastoral Ministry and Counseling D
Religious Education P,M,D
Social Work P,M,D
Theology P,M,D

PHOENIX SEMINARY
Counseling Psychology P,M,D,O
Pastoral Ministry and Counseling P,M,D,O
Theology P,M,D,O

PIEDMONT BAPTIST COLLEGE AND GRADUATE SCHOOL
Theology M,D

PIEDMONT COLLEGE
Business Administration and Management—General M
Early Childhood Education M,D,O
Education—General M,D,O
Educational Leadership and Administration M,D,O
Middle School Education M,D,O
Secondary Education M,D,O
Special Education M,D,O

PIKEVILLE COLLEGE
Osteopathic Medicine P

PITTSBURGH THEOLOGICAL SEMINARY
Theology P,M,D

PITTSBURG STATE UNIVERSITY
Accounting M
Applied Physics M
Art Education M
Art/Fine Arts M
Biological and Biomedical Sciences—General M
Business Administration and Management—General M
Chemistry M
Communication—General M
Community College Education O
Construction Engineering M
Counselor Education M
Early Childhood Education M
Education—General M,O
Educational Leadership and Administration M,O
Educational Media/Instructional Technology M
Elementary Education M
Engineering and Applied Sciences—General M
English M
Graphic Design M
Higher Education M,O
History M
Human Resources Development M
Mathematics M
Music Education M
Music M
Nursing—General M
Physical Education M
Physics M
Psychology—General M
Reading Education M
School Psychology O
Secondary Education M
Social Psychology M
Special Education M
Theater M
Vocational and Technical Education M,O

PLYMOUTH STATE UNIVERSITY
Adult Education D
Athletic Training and Sports Medicine M
Business Administration and Management—General M
Counselor Education M
Education—General O
Educational Leadership and Administration M
Elementary Education M
English Education M
Environmental Management and Policy M
Health Education M
Mathematics Education M
Meteorology M
Middle School Education M
Reading Education M
Science Education M
Secondary Education M
Special Education M,D,O

POINT LOMA NAZARENE UNIVERSITY
Biological and Biomedical Sciences—General M
Business Administration and Management—General M
Education—General M,O
Nursing—General M,O
Religion M

POINT PARK UNIVERSITY
Business Administration and Management—General M
Communication—General M
Criminal Justice and Criminology M
Curriculum and Instruction M
Education—General M
Educational Leadership and Administration M
Engineering Management M
Environmental Management and Policy M
Journalism M
Mass Communication M
Music M
Organizational Management M
Theater M

POLYTECHNIC INSTITUTE OF NYU
Applied Physics M,D
Bioinformatics M
Biomedical Engineering M,D
Biotechnology M
Business Administration and Management—General M,D,O
Chemical Engineering M,D
Chemistry M,D
Civil Engineering M,D
Communication—General O
Computer and Information Systems Security O
Computer Engineering M,O
Computer Science M,D
Construction Management M,D,O
Criminal Justice and Criminology M,D,O
Electrical Engineering M,D
Electronic Commerce M,D,O
Engineering Physics M
Entrepreneurship M,D,O
Environmental Engineering M
Environmental Sciences M
Film, Television, and Video Production O
Finance and Banking M,O
Financial Engineering M,O
History of Science and Technology M
Human Resources Management M,D,O
Humanities M,O
Industrial/Management Engineering M
Interdisciplinary Studies M
Internet and Interactive Multimedia M,O
Journalism M
Management Information Systems M,D,O
Management of Technology M,D,O
Manufacturing Engineering M
Mathematical and Computational Finance M,O
Mathematics M,D
Mechanical Engineering M,D
Organizational Behavior M,O
Polymer Science and Engineering M
Project Management M,D,O
Psychology—General M,O
Software Engineering O
Systems Engineering M
Technical Writing M
Telecommunications Management M
Telecommunications M
Transportation and Highway Engineering M,D
Transportation Management M
Urban and Regional Planning M
Urban Studies M

POLYTECHNIC INSTITUTE OF NYU, LONG ISLAND GRADUATE CENTER
Aerospace/Aeronautical Engineering M
Bioinformatics M
Chemical Engineering M
Chemistry M
Civil Engineering M
Computer Engineering M
Computer Science M
Construction Management M
Electrical Engineering M
Engineering Design M
Engineering Physics M
Environmental Engineering M
Financial Engineering M,O
Industrial/Management Engineering M
Interdisciplinary Studies M
Management of Technology M
Manufacturing Engineering M
Mechanical Engineering M
Systems Engineering M
Telecommunications M
Transportation and Highway Engineering M

POLYTECHNIC INSTITUTE OF NYU, WESTCHESTER GRADUATE CENTER
Bioinformatics M
Business Administration and Management—General M
Chemistry M
Computer Engineering M
Computer Science M
Criminal Justice and Criminology M

Electrical Engineering M
Finance and Banking M,O
Financial Engineering M,O
Industrial/Management Engineering M
Information Science M
Interdisciplinary Studies M
Management Information Systems M,O
Management of Technology M
Manufacturing Engineering M
Mathematical and Computational Finance M,O
Telecommunications M

POLYTECHNIC UNIVERSITY OF PUERTO RICO

Business Administration and Management—General M
Civil Engineering M
Computer Engineering M
Computer Science M
Electrical Engineering M
Engineering Management M
Environmental Management and Policy M
Industrial and Manufacturing Management M
International Business M
Landscape Architecture M
Management Information Systems M
Management of Technology M
Manufacturing Engineering M
Mechanical Engineering M

POLYTECHNIC UNIVERSITY OF PUERTO RICO, MIAMI CAMPUS

Accounting M
Business Administration and Management—General M
Construction Management M
Environmental Engineering M
Environmental Management and Policy M
Finance and Banking M
Human Resources Management M
Industrial and Manufacturing Management M
International Business M
Logistics M
Marketing M
Project Management M
Supply Chain Management M

POLYTECHNIC UNIVERSITY OF PUERTO RICO, ORLANDO CAMPUS

Accounting M
Business Administration and Management—General M
Construction Management M
Engineering Management M
Environmental Engineering M
Environmental Management and Policy M
Finance and Banking M
Human Resources Management M
Industrial and Manufacturing Management M
International Business M
Management of Technology M

PONCE SCHOOL OF MEDICINE

Allopathic Medicine P
Biological and Biomedical Sciences—General D
Clinical Psychology D
Epidemiology M,D
Public Health—General M,D

PONTIFICAL CATHOLIC UNIVERSITY OF PUERTO RICO

Accounting M,O
Art/Fine Arts M
Biological and Biomedical Sciences—General M
Business Administration and Management—General M,D,O
Business Education M,D
Chemistry M
Clinical Laboratory Sciences/Medical Technology O
Clinical Psychology D
Counselor Education M
Criminal Justice and Criminology M
Curriculum and Instruction M,D
Education—General M,D
Educational Leadership and Administration D
Educational Psychology M
English as a Second Language M
Environmental Sciences M
Finance and Banking M
Hispanic Studies M,O
History M
Human Resources Management M,O
Human Services M,D
Industrial and Organizational Psychology D
International Business M
Law P
Logistics O
Management Information Systems M,O
Marketing M
Medical/Surgical Nursing M
Nursing—General M
Psychiatric Nursing M
Psychology—General M,D
Public Administration M
Rehabilitation Counseling M
Religious Education M
Social Work M
Spanish M,O
Theology P
Transportation Management O

PONTIFICAL COLLEGE JOSEPHINUM

Theology P,M

PONTIFICIA UNIVERSIDAD CATOLICA MADRE Y MAESTRA

Allopathic Medicine P
Architecture M
Building Science M
Business Administration and Management—General M
Clinical Psychology M
Criminal Justice and Criminology M
Developmental Psychology M
Early Childhood Education M
Engineering and Applied Sciences—General M
Entrepreneurship M
Finance and Banking M
Forensic Psychology M
Hospitality Management M
Human Resources Management M
Insurance M
Interior Design M
International Affairs M
International Business M
Landscape Architecture M
Law M
Logistics M
Management Strategy and Policy M
Marketing M
Psychology—General M
Real Estate M
Structural Engineering M
Travel and Tourism M

PORTLAND STATE UNIVERSITY

Adult Education M,D
Anthropology M,D,O
Applied Economics M,D
Applied Social Research M,D
Art/Fine Arts M
Artificial Intelligence/Robotics M,D,O
Biological and Biomedical Sciences—General M,D
Business Administration and Management—General M,D,O
Chemistry M,D
Civil Engineering M,D,O
Communication Disorders M
Computer Engineering M,D
Computer Science M,D
Conflict Resolution and Mediation/Peace Studies M
Counselor Education M,D
Criminal Justice and Criminology M,D
Curriculum and Instruction M,D
Early Childhood Education M,D
Economics M,D,O
Education—General M,D
Educational Leadership and Administration M,D
Educational Media/Instructional Technology M,D
Educational Policy M,D
Electrical Engineering M,D
Elementary Education M,D
Engineering and Applied Sciences—General M,D,O
Engineering Management M,D,O
English as a Second Language M
English M
Environmental Engineering M,D
Environmental Management and Policy M,D
Environmental Sciences M,D
Finance and Banking M
Foreign Languages Education M
French M
Geography M,D
Geology M,D
German M
Gerontology O
Health Education M,O
Health Promotion M,O
Health Services Management and Hospital Administration M
Higher Education M,D
History M
Industrial and Manufacturing Management M,D
International Business M
Japanese M
Management of Technology M,D
Manufacturing Engineering M,D
Mathematics Education M,D
Mathematics M,D,O
Mechanical Engineering M,D,O
Modeling and Simulation M,D,O
Music Education M
Music M
Physics M,D
Political Science M,D
Psychology—General M,D,O
Public Administration M,D
Public Health—General M,O
Reading Education M,D
Science Education M,D
Secondary Education M,D
Social Sciences Education M
Social Work M,D
Sociology M,D,O
Software Engineering M,D
Spanish M
Special Education M,D
Speech and Interpersonal Communication M,O
Statistics M,D
Systems Engineering M,O
Systems Science M,D,O
Theater M
Urban and Regional Planning M
Urban Studies M,D

POST UNIVERSITY

Business Administration and Management—General M
Education—General M
Educational Media/Instructional Technology M
Entrepreneurship M
Finance and Banking M
Human Services M
Marketing M

PRAIRIE VIEW A&M UNIVERSITY

Accounting M
Agricultural Economics and Agribusiness M
Agricultural Sciences—General M
Agronomy and Soil Sciences M
Animal Sciences M
Architecture M
Biological and Biomedical Sciences—General M
Business Administration and Management—General M
Chemistry M
Clinical Psychology M,D
Computer Science M,D
Counselor Education M,D
Curriculum and Instruction M
Education—General M,D
Educational Leadership and Administration M,D
Electrical Engineering M,D
Engineering and Applied Sciences—General M,D
English M
Family and Consumer Sciences-General M
Family Nurse Practitioner Studies M
Forensic Psychology M,D
Health Education M
Legal and Justice Studies M,D
Management Information Systems M,D
Mathematics M
Nursing and Healthcare Administration M
Nursing Education M
Nursing—General M
Physical Education M
Sociology M
Special Education M
Toxicology M
Urban Design M

PRATT INSTITUTE

Applied Arts and Design—General M,O*

*M—master's degree; P—first professional degree; D—doctorate; O—other advanced degree; *—Close-Up and/or Display in one of the other books in this series*

Program	Degrees
Architecture	M
Archives/Archival Administration	M,O
Art Education	M,O
Art History	M
Art Therapy	M
Art/Fine Arts	M
Arts Administration	M
Facilities Management	M
Graphic Design	M
Historic Preservation	M
Industrial Design	M
Information Studies	M,O*
Interior Design	M
Internet and Interactive Multimedia	M
Library Science	M,O
Photography	M
Special Education	M
Sustainable Development	M
Therapies—Dance, Drama, and Music	M
Urban and Regional Planning	M
Urban Design	M

PRESCOTT COLLEGE

Program	Degrees
Art Therapy	M
Counseling Psychology	M
Counselor Education	M,D
Early Childhood Education	M,D
Education—General	M,D
Educational Leadership and Administration	M,D
Elementary Education	M,D
Environmental Education	M,D
Environmental Management and Policy	M
Health Psychology	M
Humanities	M
Leisure Studies	M
Psychoanalysis and Psychotherapy	M
Secondary Education	M,D
Special Education	M,D

PRINCETON THEOLOGICAL SEMINARY

Program	Degrees
Religion	P,M,D
Theology	P,M,D

PRINCETON UNIVERSITY

Program	Degrees
Aerospace/Aeronautical Engineering	M,D
Anthropology	D
Applied Mathematics	D
Archaeology	D
Architecture	M,D
Asian Studies	D
Astronomy	D
Astrophysics	D
Atmospheric Sciences	D
Chemical Engineering	M,D
Chemistry	M,D*
Civil Engineering	M,D
Classics	D
Comparative Literature	D
Computational Biology	D
Computational Sciences	D
Computer Science	M,D
Demography and Population Studies	D,O
Ecology	D
Economics	D,O
Electrical Engineering	M,D
Electronic Materials	D
Engineering and Applied Sciences—General	M,D
English	D
Evolutionary Biology	D
Finance and Banking	M
Financial Engineering	M,D
French	D
Geosciences	D
German	D
History of Science and Technology	D
History	D
International Affairs	M,D
Marine Biology	D
Materials Sciences	D
Mathematics	D
Mechanical Engineering	M,D
Molecular Biology	D
Music	D
Near and Middle Eastern Studies	M,D
Neuroscience	D
Ocean Engineering	D
Oceanography	D
Operations Research	M,D
Philosophy	D
Photonics	D
Physics	D
Plasma Physics	D
Political Science	D
Portuguese	D
Psychology—General	D
Public Affairs	M,D,O
Public Policy	M,D
Religion	D
Russian	D
Slavic Languages	D
Sociology	D,O
Spanish	D

PROVIDENCE COLLEGE

Program	Degrees
Accounting	M
American Studies	M
Business Administration and Management—General	M
Counselor Education	M
Education—General	M
Educational Leadership and Administration	M
Elementary Education	M
Entrepreneurship	M
Finance and Banking	M
History	M
International Business	M
Marketing	M
Mathematics Education	M
Nonprofit Management	M
Reading Education	M
Religion	M
Secondary Education	M
Special Education	M
Theology	M

PROVIDENCE COLLEGE AND THEOLOGICAL SEMINARY

Program	Degrees
Counseling Psychology	P,M,D,O
English as a Second Language	P,M,D,O
Missions and Missiology	P,M,D,O
Pastoral Ministry and Counseling	P,M,D,O
Religious Education	P,M,D,O
Student Affairs	P,M,D,O
Theology	P,M,D,O

PURCHASE COLLEGE, STATE UNIVERSITY OF NEW YORK

Program	Degrees
Art History	M
Art/Fine Arts	M
Dance	M
Music	M
Theater	M

PURDUE UNIVERSITY

Program	Degrees
Aerospace/Aeronautical Engineering	M,D
Agricultural Economics and Agribusiness	M,D
Agricultural Education	M,D,O
Agricultural Engineering	M,D
Agricultural Sciences—General	M,D
Agronomy and Soil Sciences	M,D
American Studies	M,D
Analytical Chemistry	M,D
Anatomy	M,D
Animal Sciences	M,D
Anthropology	M,D
Applied Arts and Design—General	M
Aquaculture	M,D
Art Education	M,D,O
Art/Fine Arts	M
Atmospheric Sciences	M,D
Biochemistry	M,D
Biological and Biomedical Sciences—General	M,D
Biomedical Engineering	M,D
Biophysics	M,D
Botany	M,D
Business Administration and Management—General	M,D
Cell Biology	M,D
Chemical Engineering	M,D
Chemistry	M,D
Child and Family Studies	M,D
Child Development	M,D
Civil Engineering	M,D
Clothing and Textiles	M,D
Communication Disorders	M,D
Communication—General	M,D
Comparative Literature	M,D
Computer and Information Systems Security	M
Computer Engineering	M,D
Computer Science	M,D
Consumer Economics	M,D
Counselor Education	M,D,O
Curriculum and Instruction	M,D,O
Developmental Biology	M,D
Ecology	M,D
Economics	D
Education of the Gifted	M,D,O
Education—General	M,D,O
Educational Leadership and Administration	M,D,O
Educational Media/Instructional Technology	M,D,O
Educational Psychology	M,D,O
Electrical Engineering	M,D
Elementary Education	M,D,O
Engineering and Applied Sciences—General	M,D,O
English Education	M,D,O
English	M,D
Entomology	M,D
Environmental Management and Policy	M,D
Epidemiology	M,D
Evolutionary Biology	M,D
Exercise and Sports Science	M,D
Family and Consumer Sciences-General	M,D
Finance and Banking	M
Fish, Game, and Wildlife Management	M,D
Food Science and Technology	M,D
Foreign Languages Education	M,D,O
Forestry	M,D
Foundations and Philosophy of Education	M,D,O
French	M,D
Genetics	M,D
Geosciences	M,D
German	M,D
Health Promotion	M,D
Higher Education	M,D,O
History	M,D
Home Economics Education	M,D,O
Horticulture	M,D
Hospitality Management	M,D
Human Development	M,D
Human Resources Management	M,D
Immunology	M,D
Industrial and Manufacturing Management	M
Industrial/Management Engineering	M,D
Inorganic Chemistry	M,D
International Business	M
Linguistics	M,D
Marriage and Family Therapy	M,D
Materials Engineering	M,D
Mathematics Education	M,D,O
Mathematics	M,D
Mechanical Engineering	M,D,O
Medicinal and Pharmaceutical Chemistry	M,D
Microbiology	M,D
Molecular Biology	M,D
Molecular Pharmacology	M,D
Natural Resources	M,D
Neurobiology	M,D
Nuclear Engineering	M,D
Nutrition	M,D
Organic Chemistry	M,D
Organizational Behavior	D
Pathobiology	M,D
Pathology	M,D
Pharmaceutical Administration	M,D,O
Pharmaceutical Sciences	M,D
Pharmacology	M,D
Pharmacy	P
Philosophy	M,D
Physical Chemistry	M,D
Physical Education	M,D
Physics	M,D
Physiology	M,D
Plant Pathology	M,D
Plant Physiology	M,D
Political Science	M,D
Psychology—General	D
Public Health—General	M,D
Reading Education	M,D,O
Science Education	M,D,O
Social Sciences Education	M,D,O
Sociology	M,D
Spanish	M,D
Special Education	M,D,O
Sport Psychology	M,D
Statistics	M,D,O
Theater	M
Toxicology	M,D
Travel and Tourism	M,D
Veterinary Medicine	P
Veterinary Sciences	M,D
Virology	M,D
Vocational and Technical Education	M,D,O
Writing	M,D

PURDUE UNIVERSITY CALUMET

Program	Degrees
Accounting	M
Acute Care/Critical Care Nursing	M
Adult Nursing	M
Biological and Biomedical Sciences—General	M
Biotechnology	M
Business Administration and Management—General	M
Child and Family Studies	M
Child Development	M
Communication—General	M
Computer Engineering	M
Computer Science	M
Counseling Psychology	M
Counselor Education	M
Education—General	M
Educational Leadership and Administration	M
Educational Media/Instructional Technology	M
Electrical Engineering	M
Engineering and Applied Sciences—General	M
English	M
Family Nurse Practitioner Studies	M
History	M
Human Services	M
Marriage and Family Therapy	M
Mathematics Education	M
Mathematics	M

Mechanical Engineering M
Nursing and Healthcare Administration M
Nursing—General M
School Psychology M
Science Education M
Special Education M

PURDUE UNIVERSITY NORTH CENTRAL

Education—General M
Elementary Education M

QUEENS COLLEGE OF THE CITY UNIVERSITY OF NEW YORK

Accounting M
Art Education M,O
Art History M
Art/Fine Arts M
Biochemistry M
Biological and Biomedical Sciences—General M
Chemistry M
Clinical Psychology M
Communication Disorders M
Computer Science M
Counselor Education M
Early Childhood Education M,O
Education—General M,O
Educational Leadership and Administration O
Elementary Education M,O
English as a Second Language M
English Education M,O
English M
Environmental Sciences M
Exercise and Sports Science M
Family and Consumer Sciences-General M
Foreign Languages Education M,O
French M
Geology M
Hispanic and Latin American Languages M
History M
Home Economics Education M
Information Studies M,O
Italian M
Liberal Studies M
Library Science M,O
Linguistics M
Mathematics Education M,O
Mathematics M
Multilingual and Multicultural Education M,O
Music Education M,O
Music M
Physics M,D
Psychology—General M
Reading Education M
Romance Languages M
School Psychology M,O
Science Education M,O
Secondary Education M,O
Social Sciences Education M,O
Social Sciences M
Sociology M
Spanish M
Special Education M
Urban Studies M
Writing M

QUEEN'S UNIVERSITY AT KINGSTON

Allopathic Medicine P
Anatomy M,D
Biochemistry M,D
Biological and Biomedical Sciences—General M,D
Business Administration and Management—General M
Canadian Studies M,D
Cancer Biology/Oncology M,D
Cardiovascular Sciences M,D
Cell Biology M,D
Chemical Engineering M,D
Chemistry M,D
Civil Engineering M,D
Classics M
Clinical Psychology M,D
Cognitive Sciences M,D
Communication—General M,D
Computer Engineering M,D
Computer Science M,D
Developmental Psychology M,D
Education—General M,D
Electrical Engineering M,D
Engineering and Applied Sciences—General M,D
English M,D
Entrepreneurship M
Epidemiology M,D
Exercise and Sports Science M,D
Family Nurse Practitioner Studies M,D,O
Finance and Banking M
French M,D
Gender Studies M,D
Geography M,D
Geology M,D
German M,D
Health Services Management and Hospital Administration M,D
Hispanic Studies M
Immunology M,D
Industrial and Labor Relations M
Information Studies M,D
International Affairs M,D
Law P,M
Legal and Justice Studies M,D
Marketing M
Mathematics M,D
Mechanical Engineering M,D
Microbiology M,D
Mineral/Mining Engineering M,D
Molecular Biology M,D
Molecular Medicine M,D
Neurobiology M,D
Neuroscience M,D
Nursing—General M,D,O
Occupational Therapy M,D
Pathology M,D
Pediatric Nursing M,D,O
Pharmaceutical Sciences M,D
Pharmacology M,D
Philosophy M,D
Physical Therapy M,D
Physics M,D
Physiology M,D
Political Science M,D
Project Management M
Psychology—General M,D
Public Health—General M,D
Public Policy M
Rehabilitation Sciences M,D
Religion M
Reproductive Biology M,D
Social Psychology M,D
Sociology M,D
Spanish M
Sport Psychology M,D
Statistics M,D
Theology P,M,O
Toxicology M,D
Urban and Regional Planning M
Women's Health Nursing M,D,O
Women's Studies M,D

QUEENS UNIVERSITY OF CHARLOTTE

Business Administration and Management—General M
Corporate and Organizational Communication M
Education—General M
Educational Leadership and Administration M
Elementary Education M
Nursing and Healthcare Administration M
Nursing—General M
Reading Education M
Writing M

QUINCY UNIVERSITY

Business Administration and Management—General M
Clinical Psychology M
Counseling Psychology M
Counselor Education M
Curriculum and Instruction M
Education—General M
Educational Leadership and Administration M
Human Resources Management M
Reading Education M
School Psychology M
Special Education M
Theology M

QUINNIPIAC UNIVERSITY

Adult Nursing D
Advertising and Public Relations M
Allied Health—General M,D
Biological and Biomedical Sciences—General M
Business Administration and Management—General M
Cardiovascular Sciences M
Cell Biology M
Clinical Laboratory Sciences/Medical Technology M
Communication—General M
Community Health D
Education—General M
Elementary Education M
English Education M
Family Nurse Practitioner Studies D
Finance and Banking M
Foreign Languages Education M
Health Law P,M
Health Physics/Radiological Health M
Health Services Management and Hospital Administration M
Interdisciplinary Studies D
Internet and Interactive Multimedia M
Investment Management M
Journalism M
Law P,M
Management Information Systems M
Marketing M
Mathematics Education M
Microbiology M
Middle School Education M
Molecular Biology M
Nursing—General D
Occupational Therapy M
Organizational Management M
Pathology M
Perfusion M
Physical Therapy M,D
Physician Assistant Studies M
Science Education M
Secondary Education M
Social Sciences Education M
Supply Chain Management M
Women's Health Nursing D

RABBI ISAAC ELCHANAN THEOLOGICAL SEMINARY

Theology O

RABBINICAL ACADEMY MESIVTA RABBI CHAIM BERLIN

Theology O

RABBINICAL COLLEGE BETH SHRAGA

Theology

RABBINICAL COLLEGE BOBOVER YESHIVA B'NEI ZION

Theology

RABBINICAL COLLEGE CH'SAN SOFER

Theology

RABBINICAL COLLEGE OF LONG ISLAND

Theology

RABBINICAL SEMINARY M'KOR CHAIM

Theology

RABBINICAL SEMINARY OF AMERICA

Theology

RADFORD UNIVERSITY

Art/Fine Arts M
Business Administration and Management—General M
Clinical Psychology M
Communication Disorders M
Corporate and Organizational Communication M
Counseling Psychology M,D
Counselor Education M
Criminal Justice and Criminology M
Early Childhood Education M
Education—General M
Educational Leadership and Administration M
English M
Experimental Psychology M
Industrial and Organizational Psychology M
Music Education M
Music M
Nursing—General M,D
Occupational Therapy M
Psychology—General M
Reading Education M
School Psychology M,O
Social Work M
Special Education M
Student Affairs M
Therapies—Dance, Drama, and Music M

RAMAPO COLLEGE OF NEW JERSEY

Educational Media/Instructional Technology M
Liberal Studies M
Nursing Education M
Nursing—General M
Sustainable Development M

*M—master's degree; P—first professional degree; D—doctorate; O—other advanced degree; *—Close-Up and/or Display in one of the other books in this series*

RANDOLPH COLLEGE

Curriculum and Instruction M
Education—General M
Special Education M

RECONSTRUCTIONIST RABBINICAL COLLEGE

Jewish Studies P,M,D,O
Theology P,M,D,O
Women's Studies P,M,D,O

REED COLLEGE

Liberal Studies M

REFORMED PRESBYTERIAN THEOLOGICAL SEMINARY

Theology P,M,D

REFORMED THEOLOGICAL SEMINARY–ATLANTA CAMPUS

Theology P,M,D,O

REFORMED THEOLOGICAL SEMINARY–CHARLOTTE CAMPUS

Pastoral Ministry and Counseling P,M,D
Religion P,M,D
Theology P,M,D

REFORMED THEOLOGICAL SEMINARY–JACKSON CAMPUS

Marriage and Family Therapy P,M,D,O
Missions and Missiology P,M,D,O
Pastoral Ministry and Counseling P,M,D,O
Religious Education P,M,D,O
Theology P,M,D,O

REFORMED THEOLOGICAL SEMINARY–ORLANDO CAMPUS

Pastoral Ministry and Counseling P,M,D
Theology P,M,D

REFORMED THEOLOGICAL SEMINARY–WASHINGTON D.C.

Religion P,M
Theology P,M

REGENT COLLEGE

Theology P,M,O

REGENT'S AMERICAN COLLEGE LONDON

Business Administration and Management—General M
Finance and Banking M
Human Resources Management M
International Affairs M
International Business M
Management Information Systems M
Marketing M

REGENT UNIVERSITY

American Studies M
Business Administration and Management—General M,D,O
Clinical Psychology M,D,O
Communication—General M,D
Computer Art and Design M,D
Counseling Psychology M,D,O
Counselor Education M,D,O
Education—General M,D,O
Educational Leadership and Administration M,D,O
Elementary Education M,D,O
English as a Second Language M,D,O
Entrepreneurship M,D,O
Film, Television, and Video Production M,D
Journalism M,D
Law P,M
Legal and Justice Studies P,M
Management Strategy and Policy M,D,O
Mathematics Education M,D,O
Missions and Missiology P,M,D
Organizational Management M,D,O
Pastoral Ministry and Counseling P,M,D
Political Science M
Psychoanalysis and Psychotherapy M,D
Public Administration M
Religious Education M,D,O
Social Psychology M,D,O
Special Education M,D,O
Student Affairs M,D,O
Theater M,D
Theology P,M,D

REGIS COLLEGE (CANADA)

Pastoral Ministry and Counseling P,M,D,O
Philosophy P,M,D,O
Theology P,M,D,O

REGIS COLLEGE (MA)

Biotechnology M
Corporate and Organizational Communication M
Education—General M
Elementary Education M
Family Nurse Practitioner Studies M,D,O
Health Services Management and Hospital Administration M,D,O
Nursing Education M,D,O
Nursing—General M,D,O
Quality Management M
Reading Education M
Special Education M

REGIS UNIVERSITY

Accounting M,O
Adult Education M,O
Allied Health—General P,M,D,O
Arts Administration M,O
Business Administration and Management—General M,O
Communication—General M,O
Computer and Information Systems Security M,O
Computer Science M,O
Conflict Resolution and Mediation/Peace Studies M,O
Counseling Psychology M,O
Criminal Justice and Criminology M
Curriculum and Instruction M,O
Database Systems M,O
Education—General M,O
Educational Leadership and Administration M,O
Educational Media/Instructional Technology M,O
Electronic Commerce M,O
Family Nurse Practitioner Studies P,M,D,O
Finance and Banking M,O
Foundations and Philosophy of Education M,O
Health Education P,M,D,O
Health Services Management and Hospital Administration P,M,D,O
Human Resources Management M,O
Industrial and Manufacturing Management M,O
Information Science M,O
Interdisciplinary Studies M,O
International Business M,O
Management Information Systems M,O
Management of Technology M,O
Management Strategy and Policy M,O
Marketing M,O
Marriage and Family Therapy M,O
Maternal and Child/Neonatal Nursing P,M,D,O
Nonprofit Management M,O
Nursing and Healthcare Administration P,M,D,O
Nursing—General P,M,D,O
Organizational Management M,O
Pharmacy P,M,D,O
Physical Therapy P,M,D,O
Project Management M,O
Psychology—General M,O
Reading Education M,O
Science Education M,O
Social Psychology M,O
Software Engineering M,O
Special Education M,O
Systems Engineering M,O

REINHARDT UNIVERSITY

Business Administration and Management—General M
Early Childhood Education M
Education—General M
Music Education M
Music M

RENSSELAER AT HARTFORD

Business Administration and Management—General M
Computer Engineering M
Computer Science M
Electrical Engineering M
Engineering and Applied Sciences—General M
Information Science M
Mechanical Engineering M
Systems Science M

RENSSELAER POLYTECHNIC INSTITUTE

Acoustics M,D
Aerospace/Aeronautical Engineering M,D
Analytical Chemistry M,D
Applied Arts and Design—General M,D
Applied Mathematics M
Art/Fine Arts M,D
Biochemistry M,D
Bioengineering M,D
Biological and Biomedical Sciences—General M,D
Biomedical Engineering M,D
Biophysics M,D
Building Science M,D
Business Administration and Management—General M,D
Ceramic Sciences and Engineering M,D
Chemical Engineering M,D
Chemistry M,D
Civil Engineering M,D
Cognitive Sciences M,D
Computer Art and Design M,D
Computer Engineering M,D
Computer Science M,D
Electrical Engineering M,D
Engineering and Applied Sciences—General M,D
Engineering Management M,D
Engineering Physics M,D
Entrepreneurship M,D
Environmental Engineering M,D
Environmental Management and Policy D
Financial Engineering M,D
Geology M,D
Geotechnical Engineering M,D
History of Science and Technology M,D
Human-Computer Interaction M
Industrial/Management Engineering M,D
Information Science M
Inorganic Chemistry M,D
Interdisciplinary Studies M,D
Lighting Design M,D
Materials Engineering M,D
Materials Sciences M,D
Mathematics M,D
Mechanical Engineering M,D
Metallurgical Engineering and Metallurgy M,D
Nuclear Engineering M,D
Organic Chemistry M,D
Physical Chemistry M,D
Physics M,D
Polymer Science and Engineering M,D
Rhetoric M,D
Speech and Interpersonal Communication M,D
Structural Engineering M,D
Sustainable Development M,D
Systems Engineering M,D
Technical Communication M
Technology and Public Policy M,D
Transportation and Highway Engineering M,D

RESEARCH COLLEGE OF NURSING

Family Nurse Practitioner Studies M
Nursing and Healthcare Administration M
Nursing Education M
Nursing—General M

RESURRECTION UNIVERSITY

Nursing—General M

RHODE ISLAND COLLEGE

Accounting M,O
Art Education M
Art/Fine Arts M
Arts Administration M
Biological and Biomedical Sciences—General M,O
Counseling Psychology M,O
Counselor Education M,O
Early Childhood Education M
Education—General D
Educational Leadership and Administration M,O
Educational Psychology M,O
Elementary Education M
English as a Second Language M
English Education M
English M,O
Finance and Banking M,O
Foreign Languages Education M
Health Education M,O
Health Psychology M,O
History M
Mathematics Education M
Mathematics M,O
Music Education M
Nursing—General M
Physical Education M,O
Psychology—General M,O
Public Administration M

Reading Education M
School Psychology M,O
Secondary Education M
Social Sciences Education M
Social Work M
Special Education M,O
Vocational and Technical Education M
Writing M,O

RHODE ISLAND SCHOOL OF DESIGN

Applied Arts and Design—General M
Architecture M
Art Education M
Art/Fine Arts M
Computer Art and Design M
Graphic Design M
Industrial Design M
Interior Design M
Landscape Architecture M
Photography M
Textile Design M

RHODES COLLEGE

Accounting M

RICE UNIVERSITY

African Studies D
American Studies D
Anthropology M,D
Applied Mathematics M,D
Applied Physics M,D
Archaeology M,D
Architecture M,D
Art History D
Astronomy M,D
Biochemistry M,D
Bioengineering M,D
Bioinformatics M,D
Biomedical Engineering M,D
Biostatistics M,D
Business Administration and Management—General M
Cell Biology M,D
Chemical Engineering M,D
Chemistry M,D
Civil Engineering M,D
Cognitive Sciences M,D
Computational Sciences M,D
Computer Engineering M,D
Computer Science M,D
Cultural Anthropology M,D
Ecology M,D
Economics M,D
Education—General M
Electrical Engineering M,D
Engineering and Applied Sciences—General M,D
English M,D
Environmental Engineering M,D
Environmental Management and Policy M
Environmental Sciences M,D
Evolutionary Biology M,D
Geophysics M
Geosciences M,D
Health Services Management and Hospital Administration M
History M,D
Industrial and Organizational Psychology M,D
Inorganic Chemistry M,D
Jewish Studies D
Liberal Studies M
Linguistics M,D
Materials Sciences M,D
Mathematical and Computational Finance M,D
Mathematics D
Mechanical Engineering M,D
Music M,D
Near and Middle Eastern Studies D
Organic Chemistry M,D
Philosophy M,D
Physical Chemistry M,D
Physics M,D
Political Science D
Psychology—General M,D
Religion D
Science Education M,D
Sociology D
Statistics M,D
Urban Design M,D

THE RICHARD STOCKTON COLLEGE OF NEW JERSEY

Business Administration and Management—General M
Computational Sciences M
Criminal Justice and Criminology M
Education—General M
Educational Leadership and Administration M
Educational Media/Instructional Technology M
Environmental Sciences M
Holocaust and Genocide Studies M
Nursing—General M
Occupational Therapy M
Physical Therapy D
Social Work M

RICHMOND, THE AMERICAN INTERNATIONAL UNIVERSITY IN LONDON

Art History M
International Affairs M

RICHMONT GRADUATE UNIVERSITY

Counseling Psychology M
Marriage and Family Therapy M
Psychology—General M

RIDER UNIVERSITY

Accounting M
Business Administration and Management—General M
Business Education O
Counselor Education M,O
Curriculum and Instruction M,O
Education—General M,O
Educational Leadership and Administration M,O
Elementary Education O
English as a Second Language O
English Education O
Foreign Languages Education O
French O
German O
Mathematics Education O
Music Education M
Music M
Organizational Management M
Reading Education M,O
School Psychology O
Science Education O
Social Sciences Education O
Spanish O
Special Education M,O

RIVIER COLLEGE

Business Administration and Management—General M
Clinical Psychology M
Computer Science M
Counseling Psychology M,D,O
Counselor Education M,D,O
Curriculum and Instruction M,D,O
Early Childhood Education M,D,O
Education—General M,D,O
Educational Leadership and Administration M,D,O
Elementary Education M,D,O
English M
Experimental Psychology M
Family Nurse Practitioner Studies M
Foreign Languages Education M
Management Information Systems M
Mathematics M
Nursing Education M
Nursing—General M
Psychiatric Nursing M
Psychology—General M
Reading Education M,D,O
Social Sciences Education M
Special Education M,D,O
Writing M

THE ROBERT E. WEBBER INSTITUTE FOR WORSHIP STUDIES

Religion M,D

ROBERT MORRIS UNIVERSITY

Business Administration and Management—General M
Business Education M,D,O
Computer and Information Systems Security M,D
Education—General M,D,O
Educational Leadership and Administration M,D,O
Engineering and Applied Sciences—General M
Engineering Management M
Human Resources Management M
Information Science M,D
Internet and Interactive Multimedia M,D
Management Information Systems M,D
Nonprofit Management M
Nursing—General M,D
Organizational Management M,D
Project Management M,D
Taxation M

ROBERT MORRIS UNIVERSITY ILLINOIS

Accounting M
Business Administration and Management—General M
Educational Leadership and Administration M
Finance and Banking M
Health Services Management and Hospital Administration M
Human Resources Management M
Management Information Systems M

ROBERTS WESLEYAN COLLEGE

Business Administration and Management—General M,O
Child and Family Studies M
Counselor Education M
Early Childhood Education M,O
Education—General M,O
Health Services Management and Hospital Administration M
Human Services M
Management Strategy and Policy M,O
Marketing M,O
Middle School Education M,O
Nonprofit Management M,O
Nursing and Healthcare Administration M
Nursing Education M
Nursing—General M
Pastoral Ministry and Counseling M
Reading Education M,O
School Psychology M
Secondary Education M,O
Social Work M
Special Education M,O
Urban Education M,O

ROCHESTER COLLEGE

Missions and Missiology M
Religious Education M

ROCHESTER INSTITUTE OF TECHNOLOGY

Accounting M
Applied Mathematics M
Applied Statistics M,O
Architecture M
Art Education M
Art/Fine Arts M
Astrophysics M,D
Bioinformatics M
Biological and Biomedical Sciences—General M
Business Administration and Management—General M
Chemistry M
Clinical Laboratory Sciences/Medical Technology M
Communication—General M
Computer and Information Systems Security M,O
Computer Art and Design M
Computer Engineering M
Computer Science M,D,O
Criminal Justice and Criminology M
Database Systems M,O
Electrical Engineering M
Engineering and Applied Sciences—General M,D,O
Engineering Design M
Engineering Management M
Environmental Management and Policy M
Environmental Sciences M
Film, Television, and Video Production M
Finance and Banking M
Game Design and Development M
Gerontology M,O
Graphic Design M
Health Services Management and Hospital Administration M,O
Hospitality Management M
Human Resources Development M
Human-Computer Interaction M
Industrial and Manufacturing Management M
Industrial Design M
Industrial/Management Engineering M
Information Science M,D
Interdisciplinary Studies M
International Business M
Internet and Interactive Multimedia M,O
Management Information Systems M
Manufacturing Engineering M
Materials Engineering M

*M—master's degree; P—first professional degree; D—doctorate; O—other advanced degree; *—Close-Up and/or Display in one of the other books in this series*

Materials Sciences M
Mechanical Engineering M
Media Studies M
Medical Illustration M
Medical Informatics M
Optical Sciences M,D
Photography M
Psychology—General M
Public Policy M
Secondary Education M
Software Engineering M
Special Education M
Statistics M,O
Sustainability Management M,D
Sustainable Development M,D
Systems Engineering M,D
Technical Communication O
Technology and Public Policy M
Telecommunications M
Travel and Tourism M

THE ROCKEFELLER UNIVERSITY

Biological and Biomedical Sciences—General M,D*

ROCKFORD COLLEGE

Business Administration and Management—General M
Education—General M,O
Elementary Education M
Reading Education M
Secondary Education M,O
Special Education M,O

ROCKHURST UNIVERSITY

Business Administration and Management—General M
Communication Disorders M
Education—General M
Occupational Therapy M
Physical Therapy D

ROCKY MOUNTAIN COLLEGE

Accounting M
Educational Leadership and Administration M
Physician Assistant Studies M

ROCKY MOUNTAIN UNIVERSITY OF HEALTH PROFESSIONS

Athletic Training and Sports Medicine D
Exercise and Sports Science D
Family Nurse Practitioner Studies D
Health Promotion D
Nursing—General M,D
Occupational Therapy D
Pediatric Nursing D
Physical Therapy D
Physiology D

ROGER WILLIAMS UNIVERSITY

Architecture M
Construction Management M
Criminal Justice and Criminology M
Education—General M
Elementary Education M
Forensic Psychology M
Law P
Public Administration M
Reading Education M

ROLLINS COLLEGE

Business Administration and Management—General M
Counselor Education M
Education—General M
Elementary Education M
English Education M
Entrepreneurship M
Finance and Banking M
Human Resources Development M
Human Resources Management M
International Business M
Liberal Studies M
Management of Technology M
Marketing M
Mathematics Education M
Music Education M
Secondary Education M
Sustainable Development M
Urban Design M

ROOSEVELT UNIVERSITY

Accounting M
Actuarial Science M
Anthropology M
Applied Economics M
Biotechnology M
Business Administration and Management—General M
Chemistry M
Clinical Psychology M
Communication—General M
Computer Science M
Corporate and Organizational Communication M
Counselor Education M
Early Childhood Education M
Economics M
Education—General M,D
Educational Leadership and Administration M
Elementary Education M
English M
Gender Studies M,O
History M
Hospitality Management M
Human Resources Development M
Human Resources Management M
Industrial and Organizational Psychology M,D
International Business M
Journalism M
Management Information Systems M
Mathematics M
Music Education M,O
Music M,O
Organizational Management M,D
Pharmacy P
Political Science M
Psychology—General M,D
Public Administration M
Reading Education M
Real Estate M,O
Secondary Education M
Sociology M
Spanish M
Special Education M
Telecommunications M
Theater M
Women's Studies M,O
Writing M

ROSALIND FRANKLIN UNIVERSITY OF MEDICINE AND SCIENCE

Allied Health—General M,D,O
Allopathic Medicine P
Anatomy M,D
Biochemistry M,D
Biological and Biomedical Sciences—General M,D
Biophysics M,D
Cell Biology M,D
Health Education M
Health Services Management and Hospital Administration M,O
Immunology M,D
Interdisciplinary Studies D
Medical Physics M
Microbiology M,D
Molecular Biology M,D
Molecular Pharmacology M,D
Neuroscience D
Nurse Anesthesia M
Nutrition M
Pathology M
Physical Therapy M,D
Physician Assistant Studies M
Physiology M,D
Podiatric Medicine P
Psychology—General M,D
Women's Health Nursing M,O

ROSE-HULMAN INSTITUTE OF TECHNOLOGY

Biomedical Engineering M
Chemical Engineering M
Civil Engineering M
Computer Engineering M
Electrical Engineering M
Engineering and Applied Sciences—General M
Engineering Management M
Environmental Engineering M
Mechanical Engineering M
Optical Sciences M
Software Engineering M

ROSEMAN UNIVERSITY OF HEALTH SCIENCES

Business Administration and Management—General M
Oral and Dental Sciences M
Pharmacy P

ROSEMONT COLLEGE

Business Administration and Management—General M
Counseling Psychology M
Counselor Education M
Curriculum and Instruction M
Elementary Education M
English M
Human Services M
Publishing M
Writing M

ROWAN UNIVERSITY

Accounting M
Advertising and Public Relations M
Applied Behavior Analysis M
Applied Psychology M
Business Administration and Management—General M
Chemical Engineering M
Civil Engineering M
Clinical Psychology M
Construction Management M
Counseling Psychology M
Counselor Education M
Criminal Justice and Criminology M
Curriculum and Instruction M
Education—General M,D,O
Educational Leadership and Administration M,D,O
Electrical Engineering M
Elementary Education M
Engineering and Applied Sciences—General M
Engineering Management M
English as a Second Language O
Entrepreneurship M
Finance and Banking M
Foreign Languages Education M
Health Promotion M
Higher Education M
Library Science M
Management Information Systems M
Marketing M
Mathematics M
Mechanical Engineering M
Multilingual and Multicultural Education O
Music M
Project Management M
Psychology—General M
Reading Education M
School Psychology M,O
Secondary Education M
Special Education M
Theater M
Writing M

ROYAL MILITARY COLLEGE OF CANADA

Business Administration and Management—General M
Chemical Engineering M,D
Chemistry M,D
Civil Engineering M,D
Computer Engineering M,D
Computer Science M
Electrical Engineering M,D
Engineering and Applied Sciences—General M,D
Environmental Engineering M,D
Environmental Sciences M,D
Materials Sciences M,D
Mathematics M
Mechanical Engineering M,D
Military and Defense Studies M,D
Nuclear Engineering M,D
Physics M
Software Engineering M,D

ROYAL ROADS UNIVERSITY

Advertising and Public Relations O
Business Administration and Management—General M,O
Conflict Resolution and Mediation/Peace Studies M,O
Emergency Management M,O
Environmental Education M,O
Environmental Management and Policy M,O
Health Services Management and Hospital Administration O
Hospitality Management M,O
Human Resources Management M,O
Project Management O
Travel and Tourism M,O

RUSH UNIVERSITY

Acute Care/Critical Care Nursing M,D,O
Adult Nursing M,D,O
Allopathic Medicine P
Anatomy M,D
Biochemistry D
Bioethics M,O
Cell Biology M,D
Clinical Laboratory Sciences/Medical Technology M
Communication Disorders M,D
Community Health Nursing M,D,O

Family Nurse Practitioner Studies	M,D,O
Gerontological Nursing	M,D,O
Health Services Management and Hospital Administration	M,D
Immunology	M,D
Maternal and Child/ Neonatal Nursing	M,D,O
Medical Physics	M,D
Medical/Surgical Nursing	M,D,O
Microbiology	M,D
Neuroscience	M,D
Nurse Anesthesia	M,D,O
Nursing—General	M,D,O
Nutrition	M
Occupational Therapy	M
Pediatric Nursing	M,D,O
Pharmaceutical Sciences	M,D
Pharmacology	M,D
Physician Assistant Studies	M
Physiology	D
Psychiatric Nursing	M,D,O
Virology	M,D

RUTGERS, THE STATE UNIVERSITY OF NEW JERSEY, CAMDEN

Biological and Biomedical Sciences—General	M
Business Administration and Management—General	M
Chemistry	M
Child Development	M,D
Computer Science	M
Criminal Justice and Criminology	M
Educational Leadership and Administration	M
Educational Policy	M
English	M
History	M
International Affairs	M
International Development	M
Law	P
Liberal Studies	M
Mathematics	M
Physical Therapy	D
Psychology—General	M
Public Administration	M
Public History	M
Public Policy	M
Writing	M

RUTGERS, THE STATE UNIVERSITY OF NEW JERSEY, NEWARK

Accounting	D
Adult Nursing	M
American Studies	M,D
Analytical Chemistry	M,D
Applied Physics	M,D
Biochemistry	M,D
Biological and Biomedical Sciences—General	M,D
Biopsychology	D
Business Administration and Management—General	M,D
Chemistry	M,D
Cognitive Sciences	D*
Community Health Nursing	M
Computational Biology	M
Criminal Justice and Criminology	M,D
Economics	M,D
English	M
Environmental Sciences	M,D
Family Nurse Practitioner Studies	M
Finance and Banking	D
Geology	M
Gerontological Nursing	M
Health Services Management and Hospital Administration	M,D
History	M
Human Resources Management	M,D
Inorganic Chemistry	M,D
International Affairs	M,D
International Business	D
Law	P
Management Information Systems	D
Management of Technology	D
Marketing	D
Maternal and Child/ Neonatal Nursing	M
Mathematics	D
Music	M
Neuroscience	D
Nursing—General	M
Organic Chemistry	M,D
Organizational Management	D
Physical Chemistry	M,D
Political Science	M
Psychiatric Nursing	M
Psychology—General	D
Public Administration	M,D
Public Policy	M,D
Social Psychology	D
Supply Chain Management	D
Urban Studies	M,D
Writing	M

RUTGERS, THE STATE UNIVERSITY OF NEW JERSEY, NEW BRUNSWICK

Aerospace/Aeronautical Engineering	M,D
African Studies	D
African-American Studies	D
Agricultural Economics and Agribusiness	M
Animal Sciences	M,D
Anthropology	M,D
Applied Arts and Design—General	M
Applied Mathematics	M,D
Applied Psychology	M,D
Applied Statistics	M,D
Art History	M,D,O
Art/Fine Arts	M
Asian Studies	D
Astronomy	M,D
Atmospheric Sciences	M,D
Biochemical Engineering	M,D
Biochemistry	M,D
Biological and Biomedical Sciences—General	D
Biomedical Engineering	M,D
Biopsychology	D
Biostatistics	M,D
Cancer Biology/Oncology	M,D
Cell Biology	M,D
Chemical Engineering	M,D
Chemistry	M,D
Civil Engineering	M,D
Classics	M,D
Clinical Psychology	M,D
Cognitive Sciences	D
Communication—General	D
Comparative Literature	M,D
Computational Biology	D
Computer Engineering	M,D
Computer Science	M,D
Condensed Matter Physics	M,D
Counseling Psychology	M
Counselor Education	M
Developmental Biology	M,D
Developmental Education	M
Early Childhood Education	M,D
Ecology	M,D
Economics	M,D
Education—General	M,D
Educational Leadership and Administration	M,D
Educational Measurement and Evaluation	M
Educational Policy	D
Educational Psychology	M,D
Electrical Engineering	M,D
Elementary Education	M,D
English as a Second Language	M,D
English Education	M
English	D
Entomology	M,D
Environmental Biology	M,D
Environmental Engineering	M,D
Environmental Sciences	M,D
Evolutionary Biology	M,D
Food Science and Technology	M,D
Foreign Languages Education	M,D
Foundations and Philosophy of Education	M,D
French	M,D
Gender Studies	M,D
Genetics	M,D
Geography	M,D
Geology	M,D
German	M,D
Hazardous Materials Management	M,D
Health Psychology	D
Historic Preservation	M,D,O
History of Medicine	D
History of Science and Technology	D
History	D
Horticulture	M,D
Human Resources Management	M,D
Immunology	M,D
Industrial and Labor Relations	M,D
Industrial/Management Engineering	M,D
Information Studies	M,D
Inorganic Chemistry	M,D
Interdisciplinary Studies	D
International Affairs	D
Italian	M,D
Legal and Justice Studies	D
Library Science	M,D
Linguistics	D
Marine Biology	M,D
Materials Engineering	M,D
Materials Sciences	M,D
Mathematics Education	M,D
Mathematics	M,D
Mechanical Engineering	M,D
Mechanics	M,D
Media Studies	D
Medical Microbiology	M,D
Medicinal and Pharmaceutical Chemistry	M,D
Medieval and Renaissance Studies	D
Microbiology	M,D
Molecular Biology	M,D
Molecular Biophysics	D
Molecular Genetics	M,D
Molecular Pharmacology	D
Molecular Physiology	M,D
Multilingual and Multicultural Education	M,D
Music Education	M,D,O
Music	M,D,O
Neuroscience	M,D
Nutrition	M,D
Oceanography	M,D
Operations Research	D
Organic Chemistry	M,D
Pharmaceutical Sciences	M,D
Pharmacy	P,M,D
Philosophy	D
Physical Chemistry	M,D
Physics	M,D
Physiology	M,D
Plant Biology	M,D
Plant Molecular Biology	M,D
Plant Pathology	M,D
Political Science	D
Psychology—General	D
Public Health—General	M,D
Public Policy	M,D
Quality Management	M,D
Reading Education	M,D
Reproductive Biology	M,D
School Psychology	M,D
Science Education	M,D
Social Psychology	D
Social Sciences Education	M,D
Social Work	M,D
Sociology	M,D
Spanish	M,D
Special Education	M,D
Statistics	M,D
Student Affairs	M
Systems Biology	D
Systems Engineering	M,D
Theater	M
Theoretical Physics	M,D
Toxicology	M,D
Translation and Interpretation	M,D
Urban and Regional Planning	M,D
Virology	M,D
Water Resources	M,D
Women's Studies	M,D
Writing	M

RYERSON UNIVERSITY

Arts Administration	M

SACRED HEART MAJOR SEMINARY

Pastoral Ministry and Counseling	P,M
Theology	P,M

SACRED HEART SCHOOL OF THEOLOGY

Theology	P,M

SACRED HEART UNIVERSITY

Accounting	M
Business Administration and Management—General	M
Chemistry	M
Computer and Information Systems Security	M,O
Computer Science	M,O
Criminal Justice and Criminology	M
Database Systems	M,O
Education—General	M,O
Educational Leadership and Administration	M,O
Educational Media/ Instructional Technology	M,O
Elementary Education	M,O
Exercise and Sports Science	M,D
Family Nurse Practitioner Studies	M,D
Finance and Banking	M
Gerontology	M
Health Services Management and Hospital Administration	M,D
Information Science	M,O
Internet and Interactive Multimedia	M,O
Management Information Systems	M,O
Marketing	M
Nursing and Healthcare Administration	M,D
Nursing—General	M,D
Nutrition	M,D
Occupational Therapy	M
Physical Therapy	M,D
Reading Education	M,O
Religion	M
Secondary Education	M,O

*M—master's degree; P—first professional degree; D—doctorate; O—other advanced degree; *—Close-Up and/or Display in one of the other books in this series*

SAGE GRADUATE SCHOOL

- Adult Nursing M,O
- Applied Behavior Analysis M,O
- Art Education M
- Business Administration and Management—General M
- Child and Family Studies M
- Community Health Nursing M,O
- Community Health M
- Counseling Psychology M
- Counselor Education M,O
- Education—General M,D,O
- Educational Leadership and Administration D
- Elementary Education M
- English Education M
- Family Nurse Practitioner Studies M,O
- Finance and Banking M
- Forensic Psychology M,O
- Gerontological Nursing M,D,O
- Gerontology M,O
- Health Education M
- Health Services Management and Hospital Administration M,D,O
- Human Resources Management M
- Management Strategy and Policy M
- Marketing M
- Mathematics Education M
- Nursing and Healthcare Administration M,D,O
- Nursing Education D
- Nursing—General M,D,O
- Nutrition M,O
- Occupational Therapy M
- Organizational Management M
- Physical Therapy D
- Psychiatric Nursing M,O
- Psychology—General M
- Public Administration M
- Reading Education M
- Social Psychology M
- Social Sciences Education M
- Special Education M

SAGINAW VALLEY STATE UNIVERSITY

- Business Administration and Management—General M
- Communication—General M
- Distance Education Development M
- Early Childhood Education M
- Education—General M,O
- Educational Leadership and Administration M,O
- Educational Media/Instructional Technology M
- Elementary Education M
- Family Nurse Practitioner Studies M
- Health Services Management and Hospital Administration M
- Media Studies M
- Middle School Education M
- Nursing and Healthcare Administration M
- Nursing—General M
- Occupational Therapy M
- Physical Education M
- Public Administration M
- Reading Education M
- Science Education M
- Secondary Education M
- Special Education M

ST. AMBROSE UNIVERSITY

- Accounting M
- Business Administration and Management—General M,D
- Communication Disorders M
- Criminal Justice and Criminology M
- Education—General M
- Educational Leadership and Administration M
- Health Services Management and Hospital Administration M,D
- Human Resources Management M,D
- Management of Technology M
- Nursing—General M
- Occupational Therapy M
- Organizational Management M
- Pastoral Ministry and Counseling M
- Physical Therapy D
- Social Work M
- Special Education M

ST. ANDREW'S COLLEGE

- Theology P,M

ST. ANDREW'S COLLEGE IN WINNIPEG

- Theology P

SAINT ANTHONY COLLEGE OF NURSING

- Nursing—General M

ST. AUGUSTINE'S SEMINARY OF TORONTO

- Pastoral Ministry and Counseling P,M,O
- Religious Education P,M,O
- Theology P,M,O

SAINT BERNARD'S SCHOOL OF THEOLOGY AND MINISTRY

- Pastoral Ministry and Counseling P,M,O
- Theology P,M,O

ST. BONAVENTURE UNIVERSITY

- Business Administration and Management—General M
- Corporate and Organizational Communication M
- Counseling Psychology M,O
- Counselor Education M,O
- Early Childhood Education M
- Education—General M,O
- Educational Leadership and Administration M,O
- English M
- Middle School Education M
- Reading Education M
- Religion M
- Secondary Education M
- Social Psychology M,O
- Special Education M

ST. CATHERINE UNIVERSITY

- Adult Nursing M,D
- Curriculum and Instruction M
- Education—General M
- Gerontological Nursing M,D
- Information Studies M
- Library Science M
- Maternal and Child/Neonatal Nursing M,D
- Nursing Education M,D
- Nursing—General M,D
- Occupational Therapy M
- Organizational Management M
- Pastoral Ministry and Counseling M,O
- Pediatric Nursing M,D
- Physical Therapy D
- Public Health—General M
- Social Work M
- Theology M,O

ST. CHARLES BORROMEO SEMINARY, OVERBROOK

- Religion M
- Theology P,M

ST. CLOUD STATE UNIVERSITY

- Applied Behavior Analysis M
- Applied Economics M
- Applied Statistics M
- Archaeology M
- Biological and Biomedical Sciences—General M
- Biomedical Engineering M
- Business Administration and Management—General M
- Child and Family Studies M
- Communication Disorders M
- Computer and Information Systems Security M
- Computer Science M
- Counselor Education M
- Criminal Justice and Criminology M
- Curriculum and Instruction M
- Economics M
- Education—General M,D,O
- Educational Leadership and Administration M,D
- Educational Media/Instructional Technology M
- Electrical Engineering M
- Engineering and Applied Sciences—General M
- Engineering Management M
- English as a Second Language M
- English M
- Environmental Management and Policy M
- Exercise and Sports Science M
- Geography M
- Gerontology M
- Higher Education M,D
- Historic Preservation M
- History M
- Industrial and Organizational Psychology M
- Marriage and Family Therapy M
- Mass Communication M
- Mathematics M
- Mechanical Engineering M
- Music Education M
- Music M
- Nonprofit Management M
- Physical Education M
- Psychology—General M,D
- Rehabilitation Counseling M
- Social Psychology M
- Social Work M
- Special Education M
- Sports Management M
- Student Affairs M
- Technology and Public Policy M

ST. EDWARD'S UNIVERSITY

- Accounting M,O
- Business Administration and Management—General M,O
- Computer Art and Design M
- Conflict Resolution and Mediation/Peace Studies M,O
- Counseling Psychology M
- Education—General M,O
- Educational Leadership and Administration M,O
- Educational Media/Instructional Technology M,O
- Ethics M
- Finance and Banking M,O
- Human Resources Management M,O
- Humanities M,O
- International Business M,O
- Liberal Studies M,O
- Management Information Systems M,O
- Marketing M,O
- Media Studies M
- Organizational Management M
- Project Management M
- Social Sciences M,O
- Special Education M,O
- Sports Management M,O
- Student Affairs M

ST. FRANCIS COLLEGE

- Accounting M

SAINT FRANCIS MEDICAL CENTER COLLEGE OF NURSING

- Maternal and Child/Neonatal Nursing M,D,O
- Medical/Surgical Nursing M,D,O
- Nursing Education M,D,O
- Nursing—General M,D,O

SAINT FRANCIS SEMINARY

- Pastoral Ministry and Counseling P,M
- Theology P,M

SAINT FRANCIS UNIVERSITY

- Biological and Biomedical Sciences—General M
- Business Administration and Management—General M
- Education—General M
- Educational Leadership and Administration M
- Health Education M
- Human Resources Management M
- Occupational Therapy M
- Physical Therapy D
- Physician Assistant Studies M
- Reading Education M

ST. FRANCIS XAVIER UNIVERSITY

- Adult Education M
- Biological and Biomedical Sciences—General M
- Chemistry M
- Computer Science M
- Cultural Studies M
- Curriculum and Instruction M
- Education—General M
- Educational Leadership and Administration M
- Geology M
- Geosciences M
- Physics M

ST. JOHN FISHER COLLEGE

- Business Administration and Management—General M
- Counseling Psychology M
- Education—General M,D,O
- Educational Leadership and Administration M,D
- Elementary Education M
- English Education M
- Family Nurse Practitioner Studies M,O

Foreign Languages Education M
Human Resources Development M
International Affairs M
Mathematics Education M
Middle School Education M
Nursing Education M,O
Nursing—General M,D,O
Pharmacy P
Reading Education M
Science Education M
Social Sciences Education M
Special Education M,O

ST. JOHN'S COLLEGE (MD)

Liberal Studies M

ST. JOHN'S COLLEGE (NM)

Asian Languages M
Asian Studies M
Liberal Studies M

ST. JOHN'S SEMINARY (CA)

Pastoral Ministry and Counseling P,M
Theology P,M

SAINT JOHN'S SEMINARY (MA)

Religion P,M
Theology P,M

SAINT JOHN'S UNIVERSITY (MN)

Music P,M
Pastoral Ministry and Counseling P,M
Theology P,M

ST. JOHN'S UNIVERSITY (NY)

Accounting M,O
Actuarial Science M
African Studies M,O
Applied Mathematics M
Asian Studies M,O
Biological and Biomedical Sciences—General M,D
Biotechnology M
Business Administration and Management—General M,O
Chemistry M
Clinical Psychology M,D
Communication Disorders M,D
Computer Science M
Counselor Education M,O
Criminal Justice and Criminology M
Early Childhood Education M
Education—General M,D,O
Educational Leadership and Administration M,D,O
Elementary Education M
English as a Second Language M
English M,D
Experimental Psychology M
Finance and Banking M,O
History M,D
Information Studies M,O
Insurance M
International Affairs M
International Business M,O
Investment Management M,O
Law P
Legal and Justice Studies M
Liberal Studies M
Library Science M,O
Management Information Systems M,O
Marketing M,O
Mathematics M
Middle School Education M,O
Multilingual and Multicultural Education M
Pastoral Ministry and Counseling P,M,O
Pharmaceutical Administration M
Pharmaceutical Sciences M,D
Pharmacy P
Philosophy M
Political Science M
Psychology—General M,D
Quantitative Analysis M,O
Reading Education M,D,O
Rehabilitation Counseling M,D,O
School Psychology M,D
Secondary Education M
Sociology M
Spanish M
Special Education M
Sports Management M
Statistics M
Taxation M,O
Theology P,M,O
Toxicology M

SAINT JOSEPH COLLEGE

Biochemistry M
Biological and Biomedical Sciences—General M
Business Administration and Management—General M
Chemistry M
Counseling Psychology M
Counselor Education M
Education—General M
Gerontology M,O
Human Development M,O
Marriage and Family Therapy M
Nursing—General M
Nutrition M
Social Psychology M
Special Education M

SAINT JOSEPH'S COLLEGE

Music M,O

ST. JOSEPH'S COLLEGE, LONG ISLAND CAMPUS

Accounting M
Business Administration and Management—General M,O
Early Childhood Education M
Health Services Management and Hospital Administration M,O
Human Resources Management M,O
Nursing—General M
Organizational Management M,O
Reading Education M
Special Education M

ST. JOSEPH'S COLLEGE, NEW YORK

Accounting M
Business Administration and Management—General M
Early Childhood Education M
Education—General M*
Health Services Management and Hospital Administration M
Human Services M*
Nursing—General M*
Reading Education M
Special Education M

SAINT JOSEPH'S COLLEGE OF MAINE

Business Administration and Management—General M
Education—General M
Health Services Management and Hospital Administration M
Nursing and Healthcare Administration M,O
Nursing Education M,O
Nursing—General M,O
Quality Management M

ST. JOSEPH'S SEMINARY

Theology P,M

SAINT JOSEPH'S UNIVERSITY

Accounting M
Adult Education M,O
Biological and Biomedical Sciences—General M
Business Administration and Management—General M,O
Computer Science M,O
Criminal Justice and Criminology M,O
Education—General M,D
Educational Leadership and Administration M,D
Educational Media/Instructional Technology M,D
Elementary Education M,D
Environmental and Occupational Health M,O
Finance and Banking M
Gerontology M,O
Health Education M,O
Health Informatics M,O
Health Services Management and Hospital Administration M,O
Homeland Security M,O
Human Resources Management M
Human Services M,O
Industrial and Organizational Psychology M,O
International Business M
Law M,O
Management Information Systems M
Management Strategy and Policy M
Marketing M,O
Mathematics M,O
Nurse Anesthesia M,O
Organizational Management M,D,O
Psychology—General M,O
Reading Education M,D
School Nursing M,O
Secondary Education M,D
Special Education M,D
Writing M

ST. LAWRENCE UNIVERSITY

Counselor Education M,O
Education—General M,O
Educational Leadership and Administration M,O
Human Development M,O

SAINT LEO UNIVERSITY

Accounting M
Business Administration and Management—General M
Computer and Information Systems Security M
Criminal Justice and Criminology M
Curriculum and Instruction M,O
Education of the Gifted M,O
Education—General M,O
Educational Leadership and Administration M,O
Educational Media/Instructional Technology M,O
Forensic Sciences M
Health Services Management and Hospital Administration M
Higher Education M,O
Human Resources Management M
Marketing M
Pastoral Ministry and Counseling M
Reading Education M,O
Social Work M
Sports Management M
Theology M

ST. LOUIS COLLEGE OF PHARMACY

Pharmacy P

SAINT LOUIS UNIVERSITY

Accounting M
Allied Health—General M,D,O
Allopathic Medicine P
American Studies M,D
Anatomy M,D
Athletic Training and Sports Medicine M,D
Biochemistry D
Bioethics D,O
Biological and Biomedical Sciences—General M,D
Biomedical Engineering M,D
Business Administration and Management—General M
Chemistry M,D
Clinical Psychology M,D
Communication Disorders M
Communication—General M
Community Health M
Counselor Education M,D,O
Curriculum and Instruction M,D
Dentistry M
Education—General M,D
Educational Leadership and Administration M,D,O
English M,D
Experimental Psychology M,D
Finance and Banking M
Foundations and Philosophy of Education M,D
French M
Geographic Information Systems M,D,O
Geophysics M,D
Geosciences M,D
Health Services Management and Hospital Administration M,D
Higher Education M,D,O
History M,D
Human Development M,D,O
Immunology D
Industrial and Organizational Psychology M,D
International Business M,D
Law P,M
Marriage and Family Therapy M,D,O
Mathematics M,D
Meteorology M,D
Microbiology D
Molecular Biology D
Nursing—General M,D,O
Nutrition M
Occupational Therapy M
Oral and Dental Sciences M
Organizational Management M,D,O
Pathology D
Pharmacology D
Philosophy M,D
Physical Therapy M,D
Physician Assistant Studies M
Physiology D
Political Science M
Psychology—General M,D

*M—master's degree; P—first professional degree; D—doctorate; O—other advanced degree; *—Close-Up and/or Display in one of the other books in this series*

Public Administration M,D,O
Public Health—General M,D
Public Policy M,D,O
Social Work M
Spanish M
Special Education M,D
Student Affairs M,D,O
Theology M,D
Urban Studies M,D,O

SAINT LOUIS UNIVERSITY–MADRID CAMPUS

English M
Spanish M

SAINT MARTIN'S UNIVERSITY

Business Administration and Management—General M
Civil Engineering M
Counseling Psychology M
Counselor Education M
Education—General M
Educational Leadership and Administration M
Engineering Management M
English as a Second Language M
Reading Education M
Social Psychology M
Special Education M
Vocational and Technical Education M

SAINT MARY-OF-THE-WOODS COLLEGE

Art Therapy M,O
Environmental Management and Policy M
Management Strategy and Policy M
Pastoral Ministry and Counseling M,O
Theology M,O
Therapies—Dance, Drama, and Music M

SAINT MARY'S COLLEGE OF CALIFORNIA

Business Administration and Management—General M
Counselor Education M
Curriculum and Instruction M
Early Childhood Education M
Education—General M
Educational Leadership and Administration M
Exercise and Sports Science M
Kinesiology and Movement Studies M
Marriage and Family Therapy M
Reading Education M
Special Education M
Sports Management M
Writing M

ST. MARY'S COLLEGE OF MARYLAND

Education—General M

SAINT MARY SEMINARY AND GRADUATE SCHOOL OF THEOLOGY

Theology P,M,D

ST. MARY'S SEMINARY AND UNIVERSITY

Theology P,M,D,O

SAINT MARY'S UNIVERSITY (CANADA)

Applied Psychology M,D
Applied Science and Technology M
Astronomy M,D
Business Administration and Management—General M,D
Canadian Studies M,O
Criminal Justice and Criminology M
Gender Studies M
History M
Industrial and Organizational Psychology M,D
International Development M,O
Philosophy M
Psychology—General M,D
Religion M
Theology M
Women's Studies M

ST. MARY'S UNIVERSITY (UNITED STATES)

Accounting M
Addictions/Substance Abuse Counseling M,D,O
Business Administration and Management—General M
Clinical Psychology M
Communication—General M
Computer Engineering M
Computer Science M
Counseling Psychology M
Counselor Education D
Education—General M,O
Educational Leadership and Administration M,O
Electrical Engineering M
Engineering and Applied Sciences—General M
Engineering Management M
English M
Finance and Banking M
Human Services M,D,O
Industrial and Organizational Psychology M
Industrial/Management Engineering M
Information Science M
International Affairs M
International Business M
Law P
Marriage and Family Therapy M,D
Operations Research M
Pastoral Ministry and Counseling M
Political Science M
Psychology—General M
Public Administration M
Reading Education M
Social Psychology M
Software Engineering M
Theology M

SAINT MARY'S UNIVERSITY OF MINNESOTA

Arts Administration M
Business Administration and Management—General M
Counseling Psychology M,D,O
Education of the Gifted M,O
Education—General M,O
Educational Leadership and Administration M,D,O
Elementary Education M,O
Environmental and Occupational Health M
Geographic Information Systems M,O
Health Services Management and Hospital Administration M
Human Development M
Human Resources Management M
International Business M
Marriage and Family Therapy M,O
Nurse Anesthesia M
Organizational Management M
Pastoral Ministry and Counseling M,O
Philanthropic Studies M
Project Management M,O
Reading Education M,O
Religious Education M
Secondary Education M,O
Special Education M,O
Telecommunications M

SAINT MEINRAD SCHOOL OF THEOLOGY

Theology P,M

SAINT MICHAEL'S COLLEGE

Art Education M,O
Business Administration and Management—General M,O
Clinical Psychology M
Curriculum and Instruction M,O
Education—General M,O
Educational Leadership and Administration M,O
Educational Media/Instructional Technology M,O
English as a Second Language M,O
Reading Education M,O
Special Education M,O
Theology M,O

ST. NORBERT COLLEGE

Education—General M
Liberal Studies M
Theology M

ST. PATRICK'S SEMINARY & UNIVERSITY

Theology P,M

SAINT PAUL SCHOOL OF THEOLOGY

Theology P,M,D

SAINT PAUL UNIVERSITY

Conflict Resolution and Mediation/Peace Studies M
Counseling Psychology M
Marriage and Family Therapy M
Missions and Missiology M
Pastoral Ministry and Counseling M,D,O
Theology M,D,O

SAINT PETER'S COLLEGE

Accounting M
Adult Nursing M,D,O
Applied Behavior Analysis M,D,O
Business Administration and Management—General M
Counselor Education M,O
Criminal Justice and Criminology M
Education—General M,D,O
Educational Leadership and Administration M,D
Elementary Education M,O
Finance and Banking M
Health Services Management and Hospital Administration M
Human Resources Management M
International Business M
Management Information Systems M
Marketing M
Mathematics Education M,D,O
Middle School Education M,O
Nursing and Healthcare Administration M,D,O
Nursing—General M,D,O
Reading Education M,O
Secondary Education M,O
Special Education M,O

ST. PETER'S SEMINARY

Theology P,M

SAINTS CYRIL AND METHODIUS SEMINARY

Pastoral Ministry and Counseling P,M
Religious Education P,M
Theology P,M

ST. STEPHEN'S COLLEGE

Pastoral Ministry and Counseling M,D
Theology M,D

ST. THOMAS AQUINAS COLLEGE

Business Administration and Management—General M
Education—General M,O
Educational Leadership and Administration M,O
Elementary Education M,O
Finance and Banking M
Marketing M
Middle School Education M,O
Reading Education M,O
Secondary Education M,O
Special Education M,O

ST. THOMAS UNIVERSITY

Accounting M,O
Arts Administration M
Business Administration and Management—General M,O
Communication—General M,D,O
Counseling Psychology M
Counselor Education M,O
Criminal Justice and Criminology M,O
Education of the Gifted M,D,O
Education—General M,D,O
Educational Leadership and Administration M,D,O
Educational Media/Instructional Technology M,D,O
Elementary Education M,D,O
English as a Second Language M,D,O
Film, Television, and Video Production M
Geosciences M,D,O
Health Services Management and Hospital Administration M,O
Hispanic Studies M,O
Human Resources Management M,O
International Business M,O
Law P,M
Marriage and Family Therapy M,O
Pastoral Ministry and Counseling M,D,O
Planetary and Space Sciences M,D,O

Public Administration	M,O
Reading Education	M,D,O
Special Education	M,D,O
Sports Management	M,O
Taxation	P,M
Theology	M,D,O

ST. TIKHON'S ORTHODOX THEOLOGICAL SEMINARY

Theology	P

SAINT VINCENT COLLEGE

Curriculum and Instruction	M
Education—General	M
Educational Leadership and Administration	M
Educational Media/ Instructional Technology	M
Environmental Education	M
Nurse Anesthesia	M
Nursing and Healthcare Administration	M
Special Education	M

SAINT VINCENT DE PAUL REGIONAL SEMINARY

Theology	P,M

SAINT VINCENT SEMINARY

Theology	P,M

ST. VLADIMIR'S ORTHODOX THEOLOGICAL SEMINARY

Music	P,M,D
Religious Education	P,M,D
Theology	P,M,D

SAINT XAVIER UNIVERSITY

Adult Nursing	M,O
Business Administration and Management—General	M,O
Communication Disorders	M
Community Health Nursing	M,O
Computer Science	M
Counseling Psychology	M,O
Counselor Education	M
Curriculum and Instruction	M,O
Early Childhood Education	M,O
Education—General	M,O
Educational Leadership and Administration	M,O
Electronic Commerce	M,O
Elementary Education	M,O
English	M,O
Family Nurse Practitioner Studies	M,O
Finance and Banking	M,O
Health Services Management and Hospital Administration	M,O
Information Science	M
Marketing	M,O
Mathematics	M
Nonprofit Management	M,O
Nursing and Healthcare Administration	M,O
Nursing—General	M,O
Psychiatric Nursing	M,O
Psychology—General	M,O
Public Health—General	M,O
Reading Education	M,O
Secondary Education	M,O
Special Education	M,O
Travel and Tourism	M,O
Writing	M,O

SALEM COLLEGE

Early Childhood Education	M
Education—General	M
Elementary Education	M
English as a Second Language	M
Middle School Education	M
Reading Education	M
Secondary Education	M
Special Education	M

SALEM INTERNATIONAL UNIVERSITY

Business Administration and Management—General	M
Computer and Information Systems Security	M
Curriculum and Instruction	M
Education—General	M
Educational Leadership and Administration	M
International Business	M

SALEM STATE UNIVERSITY

Art Education	M
Business Administration and Management—General	M
Counseling Psychology	M,O
Counselor Education	M
Criminal Justice and Criminology	M
Early Childhood Education	M
Educational Leadership and Administration	M
Educational Media/ Instructional Technology	M
Elementary Education	M
English as a Second Language	M
English Education	M
English	M
Geography	M
Higher Education	M
History	M
Mathematics Education	M
Mathematics	M
Middle School Education	M
Nursing—General	M
Occupational Therapy	M
Physical Education	M
Psychology—General	M,O
Reading Education	M
Science Education	M
Secondary Education	M
Social Work	M
Spanish	M
Special Education	M

SALISBURY UNIVERSITY

Accounting	M
Business Administration and Management—General	M
Conflict Resolution and Mediation/Peace Studies	M
Education—General	M
Educational Leadership and Administration	M
English as a Second Language	M
English	M
Geographic Information Systems	M
History	M
Mathematics Education	M
Nursing—General	M
Physiology	M
Reading Education	M
Social Work	M
Writing	M

SALUS UNIVERSITY

Communication Disorders	D
Optometry	P
Physician Assistant Studies	M
Rehabilitation Sciences	M,O
Special Education	M,O
Vision Sciences	M,O

SALVE REGINA UNIVERSITY

Art Therapy	M,O
Business Administration and Management—General	M,O
Counseling Psychology	M,O
Criminal Justice and Criminology	M
Health Services Management and Hospital Administration	M,O
Homeland Security	M,O
Human Resources Development	M,O
Human Resources Management	M,O
Humanities	M,D,O
International Affairs	M,O
Legal and Justice Studies	M
Rehabilitation Counseling	M,O

SAMFORD UNIVERSITY

Business Administration and Management—General	M
Early Childhood Education	M,D,O
Education of the Gifted	M,D,O
Education—General	M,D,O
Educational Leadership and Administration	M,D,O
Elementary Education	M,D,O
Environmental Management and Policy	M
Family Nurse Practitioner Studies	M,D
Law	P,M
Music Education	M
Music	M
Nurse Anesthesia	M,D
Nursing and Healthcare Administration	M,D
Nursing Education	M,D
Nursing—General	M,D
Pharmacy	P
Secondary Education	M,D,O
Theology	P,M,D

SAM HOUSTON STATE UNIVERSITY

Accounting	M
Agricultural Sciences—General	M
Biological and Biomedical Sciences—General	M
Business Administration and Management—General	M
Chemistry	M
Clinical Psychology	M,D
Computational Sciences	M
Computer Science	M
Counselor Education	M,D
Criminal Justice and Criminology	M,D
Curriculum and Instruction	M
Dance	M
Education—General	M,D
Educational Leadership and Administration	M,D
Educational Media/ Instructional Technology	M
English	M
Family and Consumer Sciences-General	M
Finance and Banking	M
Forensic Sciences	M,D
History	M
Humanities	M,D
Industrial/Management Engineering	M
Information Science	M
Kinesiology and Movement Studies	M
Library Science	M
Mathematics	M
Music Education	M
Music	M
Nutrition	M
Political Science	M
Psychology—General	M,D
Public Administration	M
Reading Education	M,D
Sociology	M
Special Education	M,D
Speech and Interpersonal Communication	M,D
Statistics	M

SAMRA UNIVERSITY OF ORIENTAL MEDICINE

Acupuncture and Oriental Medicine	M,D

SAMUEL MERRITT UNIVERSITY

Family Nurse Practitioner Studies	M,O
Nurse Anesthesia	M,O
Nursing and Healthcare Administration	M,O
Nursing—General	M,O
Occupational Therapy	M
Physical Therapy	D
Physician Assistant Studies	M

SAN DIEGO STATE UNIVERSITY

Accounting	M
Advertising and Public Relations	M
Aerospace/Aeronautical Engineering	M,D
Anthropology	M
Applied Arts and Design—General	M
Applied Mathematics	M
Art History	M
Art/Fine Arts	M
Asian Studies	M
Astronomy	M
Biological and Biomedical Sciences—General	M,D
Biometry	M
Biostatistics	M,D
Business Administration and Management—General	M
Cell Biology	M,D
Chemistry	M,D
Child and Family Studies	M
Child Development	M
Civil Engineering	M
Clinical Psychology	M,D
Communication Disorders	M,D
Communication—General	M
Computational Sciences	M,D
Computer Science	M
Counselor Education	M
Criminal Justice and Criminology	M
Curriculum and Instruction	M
Ecology	M,D
Economics	M
Education—General	M,D
Educational Leadership and Administration	M
Educational Media/ Instructional Technology	M,D
Electrical Engineering	M
Elementary Education	M
Emergency Management	M,D
Emergency Medical Services	M,D
Engineering and Applied Sciences—General	M,D
Engineering Design	M,D
English as a Second Language	M,O
English	M
Entrepreneurship	M
Environmental and Occupational Health	M,D
Environmental Design	M
Epidemiology	M,D
Exercise and Sports Science	M

*M—master's degree; P—first professional degree; D—doctorate; O—other advanced degree; *—Close-Up and/or Display in one of the other books in this series*

Film, Television, and Video Production M
Finance and Banking M
Geography M,D
Geology M
Gerontology M
Graphic Design M
Health Physics/Radiological Health M
Health Promotion M,D
Health Psychology M,D
Health Services Management and Hospital Administration M,D
Higher Education M
History M
Human Resources Management M
Industrial and Manufacturing Management M
Industrial and Organizational Psychology M,D
Interdisciplinary Studies M
Interior Design M
International Business M
International Health M,D
Internet and Interactive Multimedia M
Kinesiology and Movement Studies M
Latin American Studies M
Liberal Studies M
Linguistics M,O
Management Information Systems M
Marketing M
Mathematics Education M,D
Mathematics M,D
Mechanical Engineering M,D
Mechanics M,D
Media Studies M
Microbiology M
Molecular Biology M,D
Multilingual and Multicultural Education M,D
Music Education M
Music M
Nursing—General M
Nutrition M
Pharmaceutical Administration M
Philosophy M
Physical Education M
Physics M
Political Science M
Psychology—General M,D
Public Administration M
Public Health—General M,D
Reading Education M
Rehabilitation Counseling M
Rhetoric M
Romance Languages M
School Psychology M
Science Education M,D
Secondary Education M
Social Work M
Sociology M
Spanish M
Special Education M
Sports Management M
Statistics M
Telecommunications Management M
Theater M
Toxicology M,D
Urban and Regional Planning M
Western European Studies M
Women's Studies M
Writing M

SAN FRANCISCO ART INSTITUTE

Applied Arts and Design—General M,O
Art History M
Art/Fine Arts M,O
Film, Television, and Video Production M,O
Museum Studies M
Photography M,O
Urban Studies M

SAN FRANCISCO CONSERVATORY OF MUSIC

Music M

SAN FRANCISCO STATE UNIVERSITY

Accounting M
Adult Education M,O
Anthropology M
Archaeology M
Art/Fine Arts M
Asian-American Studies M
Biochemistry M
Biological and Biomedical Sciences—General M
Biotechnology M
Business Administration and Management—General M
Cell Biology M
Chemistry M
Chinese M
Classics M
Clinical Psychology M
Communication Disorders M
Comparative Literature M
Computer Science M
Conservation Biology M
Counseling Psychology M
Cultural Anthropology M
Cultural Studies M
Developmental Biology M
Developmental Psychology M
Early Childhood Education M,D,O
Ecology M
Economics M
Education—General M,D,O
Educational Leadership and Administration M,D,O
Educational Media/Instructional Technology O
Elementary Education M
Engineering and Applied Sciences—General M
English as a Second Language M
English Education M,O
English M
Environmental Management and Policy M
Ethnic Studies M
Exercise and Sports Science M
Family and Consumer Sciences-General M
Family Nurse Practitioner Studies M
Film, Television, and Video Production M
Film, Television, and Video Theory and Criticism M
French M
Geographic Information Systems M
Geography M
Geosciences M
German M
Gerontology M
Health Education M
History M
Humanities M
Industrial and Organizational Psychology M
Industrial Design M
International Affairs M
Italian M
Japanese M
Kinesiology and Movement Studies M
Legal and Justice Studies M
Leisure Studies M
Linguistics M
Marine Biology M
Marine Sciences M
Marriage and Family Therapy M
Mathematics Education M
Mathematics M
Media Studies M
Microbiology M
Molecular Biology M
Museum Studies M
Music Education M
Music M
Natural Resources M
Nonprofit Management M
Nursing and Healthcare Administration M
Nursing Education M
Nursing—General M
Philosophy M,O
Physical Therapy M,D
Physics M
Physiology M
Political Science M
Psychology—General M
Public Administration M
Public Health—General M
Public Policy M
Reading Education M,O
Recreation and Park Management M
Rehabilitation Counseling M
School Psychology M
Secondary Education M
Social Psychology M
Social Work M
Software Engineering M
Spanish M
Special Education M,D,O
Speech and Interpersonal Communication M
Theater M
Women's Studies M
Writing M

SAN FRANCISCO THEOLOGICAL SEMINARY

Theology P,M,D

SAN JOAQUIN COLLEGE OF LAW

Law P

SAN JOSE STATE UNIVERSITY

Accounting M
Aerospace/Aeronautical Engineering M
Anthropology M
Applied Arts and Design—General M
Applied Economics M
Applied Mathematics M
Art History M
Art/Fine Arts M
Biological and Biomedical Sciences—General M
Business Administration and Management—General M
Chemical Engineering M
Chemistry M
Child and Family Studies M
Civil Engineering M
Clinical Psychology M
Communication Disorders M
Communication—General M
Comparative Literature M
Computer Art and Design M
Computer Engineering M
Computer Science M
Counselor Education M
Criminal Justice and Criminology M
Curriculum and Instruction M,O
Ecology M
Economics M
Education—General M,O
Educational Leadership and Administration M
Electrical Engineering M
Elementary Education M,O
Engineering and Applied Sciences—General M
English as a Second Language M,O
English M
Environmental Management and Policy M
Experimental Psychology M
Film, Television, and Video Production M
French M
Geographic Information Systems M,O
Geography M,O
Geology M
Gerontological Nursing M,O
Gerontology M,O
Health Education M,O
Higher Education M
Hispanic Studies M
History M
Illustration M
Industrial and Manufacturing Management M
Industrial and Organizational Psychology M
Industrial/Management Engineering M
Information Studies M,D
Interdisciplinary Studies M
Kinesiology and Movement Studies M
Library Science M,D
Linguistics M,O
Management Information Systems M
Marine Sciences M
Mass Communication M
Materials Engineering M
Mathematics Education M
Mathematics M
Mechanical Engineering M
Meteorology M
Microbiology M
Molecular Biology M
Music M
Nursing and Healthcare Administration M,O
Nursing Education M,O
Nursing—General M,O
Nutrition M
Occupational Therapy M
Philosophy M
Photography M
Physics M
Physiology M
Psychology—General M
Public Administration M
Public Health—General M,O
Quality Management M
Reading Education M,O
Recreation and Park Management M
Science Education M
Secondary Education O
Social Work M,O
Sociology M
Software Engineering M
Spanish M
Special Education M
Speech and Interpersonal Communication M
Statistics M
Student Affairs M
Systems Engineering M
Taxation M
Theater M
Transportation Management M

Urban and Regional Planning M,O

SAN JUAN BAUTISTA SCHOOL OF MEDICINE

Allopathic Medicine P

SANTA CLARA UNIVERSITY

Accounting M
Agricultural Economics and Agribusiness M
Applied Mathematics M
Business Administration and Management—General M
Civil Engineering M
Computer Engineering M,D,O
Computer Science M,D,O
Counseling Psychology M
Counselor Education M
Education—General M,O
Educational Leadership and Administration M,O
Electrical Engineering M,D,O
Energy and Power Engineering M,D,O
Energy Management and Policy M,D,O
Engineering and Applied Sciences—General M,D,O
Engineering Design M,D,O
Engineering Management M
Entrepreneurship M
Finance and Banking M
Intellectual Property Law P,M,O
International Business M
Law P,M,O
Management Information Systems M
Management of Technology M
Marketing M
Materials Engineering M,D,O
Mathematical and Computational Finance M
Mechanical Engineering M,D,O
Organizational Management M
Pastoral Ministry and Counseling M
Software Engineering M,D,O
Supply Chain Management M
Theology P,M,D,O

SANTA FE UNIVERSITY OF ART AND DESIGN

Education—General M

SARAH LAWRENCE COLLEGE

Child Development M
Dance M
Education—General M
Genetic Counseling M
History M
Human Genetics M
Interdisciplinary Studies M
Public Health—General M
Theater M
Women's Studies M
Writing M

SAVANNAH COLLEGE OF ART AND DESIGN

Advertising and Public Relations M
Applied Arts and Design—General M,O
Architectural History M
Architecture M
Art History M
Art/Fine Arts M*
Arts Administration M
Clothing and Textiles M,O
Computer Art and Design M,O
Cultural Studies M,O
Education—General M
Film, Television, and Video Production M
Film, Television, and Video Theory and Criticism M
Game Design and Development M,O
Graphic Design M
Historic Preservation M,O
Illustration M
Industrial Design M
Interior Design M
Internet and Interactive Multimedia M,O
Media Studies M
Music M,O
Photography M
Textile Design M
Theater M
Urban Design M
Writing M

SAVANNAH STATE UNIVERSITY

Business Administration and Management—General M
Marine Sciences M
Public Administration M
Social Work M
Urban Studies M

SAYBROOK UNIVERSITY

Clinical Psychology M,D
Counseling Psychology M
Health Psychology M,D
Marriage and Family Therapy M,D
Nutrition M,D,O
Organizational Behavior M,D
Organizational Management M,D
Psychology—General M,D
Sustainable Development M,D
Transpersonal and Humanistic Psychology M,D

SCHILLER INTERNATIONAL UNIVERSITY (GERMANY)

Business Administration and Management—General M
International Business M
Management Information Systems M

SCHILLER INTERNATIONAL UNIVERSITY

Business Administration and Management—General M
International Affairs M
International Business M

SCHILLER INTERNATIONAL UNIVERSITY (SPAIN)

Business Administration and Management—General M
International Business M

SCHILLER INTERNATIONAL UNIVERSITY

Business Administration and Management—General M
International Business M

SCHILLER INTERNATIONAL UNIVERSITY (UNITED KINGDOM)

Corporate and Organizational Communication M
Hospitality Management M
International Affairs M
International Business M
Management Information Systems M
Travel and Tourism M

SCHILLER INTERNATIONAL UNIVERSITY (UNITED STATES)

Business Administration and Management—General M
Finance and Banking M
Hospitality Management M
International Business M
Management Information Systems M
Travel and Tourism M

SCHOOL OF ADVANCED AIR AND SPACE STUDIES

Military and Defense Studies M

THE SCHOOL OF PROFESSIONAL PSYCHOLOGY AT FOREST INSTITUTE

Applied Behavior Analysis M,D,O
Clinical Psychology M,D,O
Counseling Psychology M,D,O
Marriage and Family Therapy M,D,O
Psychology—General M,D,O

SCHOOL OF THE ART INSTITUTE OF CHICAGO

Applied Arts and Design—General M
Architecture M
Art Education M
Art History M
Art Therapy M
Art/Fine Arts M*
Arts Administration M
Arts Journalism M
Film, Television, and Video Production M
Graphic Design M
Historic Preservation M
Interior Design M
Journalism M
Materials Sciences M
Music M
Photography M
Textile Design M,O
Writing M,O

SCHOOL OF THE MUSEUM OF FINE ARTS, BOSTON

Art/Fine Arts M

SCHOOL OF VISUAL ARTS (NY)

Applied Arts and Design—General M
Art Education M
Art Therapy M
Art/Fine Arts M
Computer Art and Design M
Film, Television, and Video Production M
Illustration M
Internet and Interactive Multimedia M
Photography M

SCHREINER UNIVERSITY

Education—General M

THE SCRIPPS RESEARCH INSTITUTE

Biological and Biomedical Sciences—General D
Chemistry D

SEABURY-WESTERN THEOLOGICAL SEMINARY

Music P,M,D,O
Theology P,M,D,O

SEATTLE INSTITUTE OF ORIENTAL MEDICINE

Acupuncture and Oriental Medicine M

SEATTLE PACIFIC UNIVERSITY

Adult Nursing M,O
Business Administration and Management—General M
Clinical Psychology D
Counselor Education M,D,O
Curriculum and Instruction M
Educational Leadership and Administration M,D,O
English as a Second Language M
Family Nurse Practitioner Studies M,O
Gerontological Nursing M,O
Industrial and Organizational Psychology M,D
Management Information Systems M
Marriage and Family Therapy M,O
Nursing and Healthcare Administration M,O
Nursing Education M,O
Nursing Informatics M,O
Nursing—General M,O
Reading Education M
Secondary Education M,O
Theology P,M
Writing M

SEATTLE UNIVERSITY

Accounting M
Adult Education M,O
Business Administration and Management—General M,O
Community Health Nursing M
Counselor Education M,O
Criminal Justice and Criminology M
Curriculum and Instruction M,O
Education—General M,D,O
Educational Leadership and Administration M,D,O
Engineering and Applied Sciences—General M
English as a Second Language M,O
Finance and Banking M,O
Law P,O
Nonprofit Management M
Nursing and Healthcare Administration M
Nursing—General M
Organizational Management M,O
Pastoral Ministry and Counseling M
Psychiatric Nursing M
Psychology—General M
Public Administration M
Reading Education M,O
School Psychology M,O
Software Engineering M
Special Education M,O

*M—master's degree; P—first professional degree; D—doctorate; O—other advanced degree; *—Close-Up and/or Display in one of the other books in this series*

Sports Management M
Theology P,M,O
Transpersonal and Humanistic Psychology M

SEMINARY OF THE IMMACULATE CONCEPTION

Pastoral Ministry and Counseling P,M,D,O
Theology P,M,D,O

SEMINARY OF THE SOUTHWEST

Pastoral Ministry and Counseling P,M,O
Religion P,M,O
Theology P,M,O

SETON HALL UNIVERSITY

Accounting M,O
Adult Nursing M,D
Advertising and Public Relations M
Allied Health—General M,D
Analytical Chemistry M,D
Art/Fine Arts M
Asian Languages M
Asian Studies M
Athletic Training and Sports Medicine M
Biochemistry M,D
Biological and Biomedical Sciences—General M,D
Business Administration and Management—General M,O
Chemistry M,D
Chinese M
Communication Disorders M
Communication—General M
Corporate and Organizational Communication M
Counseling Psychology M,D
Education—General M,D,O
Educational Leadership and Administration D,O
Educational Measurement and Evaluation M,D,O
Educational Media/Instructional Technology M
English M
Experimental Psychology M
Finance and Banking M
Gerontological Nursing M,D
Health Law P,M
Health Services Management and Hospital Administration M,D,O
Higher Education D
History M
Holocaust and Genocide Studies M
Inorganic Chemistry M,D
International Affairs M
International Business M,O
Jewish Studies M
Law P,M
Management of Technology M
Marketing M
Marriage and Family Therapy M,D,O
Microbiology M,D
Molecular Biology M,D
Multilingual and Multicultural Education O
Museum Education M
Museum Studies M
Neuroscience M,D
Nonprofit Management M,O
Nursing and Healthcare Administration M,D
Nursing Education M,D
Nursing—General M,D
Occupational Therapy M
Organic Chemistry M,D
Pastoral Ministry and Counseling P,M,O
Pediatric Nursing M,D
Physical Chemistry M,D
Physical Therapy D
Physician Assistant Studies M
Psychology—General M,D,O
Public Administration M,O
Public Policy M,O
Religion P,M,O
School Nursing M,D
School Psychology O
Speech and Interpersonal Communication M
Sports Management M
Student Affairs M
Supply Chain Management M
Taxation M,O
Theology P,M,O
Writing M

SETON HILL UNIVERSITY

Art Therapy M
Business Administration and Management—General M,O
Education—General M
Elementary Education M,O
Entrepreneurship M,O
Holocaust and Genocide Studies O
Marriage and Family Therapy M
Oral and Dental Sciences O
Physician Assistant Studies M
Special Education M,O
Writing M,O

SEWANEE: THE UNIVERSITY OF THE SOUTH

English M
Theology P,M,D
Writing M

SHASTA BIBLE COLLEGE

Educational Leadership and Administration M
Pastoral Ministry and Counseling M
Religious Education M

SHAWNEE STATE UNIVERSITY

Curriculum and Instruction M
Education—General M
Occupational Therapy M

SHAW UNIVERSITY

Curriculum and Instruction M
Theology P,M

SHENANDOAH UNIVERSITY

Allied Health—General M,D,O
Arts Administration M,D,O
Athletic Training and Sports Medicine M,O
Business Administration and Management—General M,O
Education—General M,D,O
Educational Leadership and Administration M,D,O
Elementary Education M,D,O
English as a Second Language M,D,O
Family Nurse Practitioner Studies M,D,O
Middle School Education M,D,O
Music Education M,D,O
Music M,D,O
Nurse Midwifery M,D,O
Nursing Education M,D,O
Nursing—General M,D,O
Occupational Therapy M
Organizational Management M,D,O
Pharmacy P
Physical Therapy D
Physician Assistant Studies M
Psychiatric Nursing M,D,O
Public Administration M,D,O
Reading Education M,D,O
Secondary Education M,D,O
Special Education M,D,O
Therapies—Dance, Drama, and Music M,D,O

SHEPHERD UNIVERSITY

Curriculum and Instruction M

SHERMAN COLLEGE OF CHIROPRACTIC

Chiropractic P

SHIPPENSBURG UNIVERSITY OF PENNSYLVANIA

Addictions/Substance Abuse Counseling M,O
Applied Psychology M
Biological and Biomedical Sciences—General M
Business Administration and Management—General M,O
Clinical Psychology M,O
Communication—General M
Computer Science M
Counseling Psychology M,O
Counselor Education M,O
Criminal Justice and Criminology M
Curriculum and Instruction M
Early Childhood Education M
Education—General M,O
Educational Leadership and Administration M
Elementary Education M
English Education M
Environmental Management and Policy M
Foreign Languages Education M
Geography M
Gerontology M,O
Higher Education M
History M,O
Marriage and Family Therapy M,O
Mathematics Education M
Middle School Education M
Organizational Management M
Psychology—General M
Public Administration M
Public History M,O
Reading Education M
Science Education M
Social Work M,O
Sociology M
Special Education M
Student Affairs M,O

SHORTER UNIVERSITY

Accounting M
Business Administration and Management—General M
Curriculum and Instruction M

SH'OR YOSHUV RABBINICAL COLLEGE

Theology

SIENA HEIGHTS UNIVERSITY

Early Childhood Education M
Education—General M
Educational Leadership and Administration M
Elementary Education M
Mathematics Education M
Middle School Education M
Reading Education M
Secondary Education M

SIERRA NEVADA COLLEGE

Education—General M
Educational Leadership and Administration M
Elementary Education M
Secondary Education M

SILICON VALLEY UNIVERSITY

Business Administration and Management—General M
Computer Engineering M
Computer Science M

SILVER LAKE COLLEGE

Business Administration and Management—General M
Education—General M
Educational Leadership and Administration M
Music Education M
Organizational Behavior M
Special Education M

SIMMONS COLLEGE

Applied Behavior Analysis M,D,O
Archives/Archival Administration O
Business Administration and Management—General M,O
Corporate and Organizational Communication M
Counselor Education M,D,O
Cultural Studies M
Education—General M,D,O
Educational Leadership and Administration M,D,O
Educational Media/Instructional Technology M,D,O
Elementary Education M,O
English as a Second Language M,O
English M
Gender Studies M
Health Education M,D,O
Health Promotion M,O
Health Services Management and Hospital Administration M,O
History M
Information Studies M,D
Library Science M,D
Middle School Education M,O
Nursing—General M,D,O
Nutrition M,O
Physical Therapy D
Psychology—General M,D
Public History O
Secondary Education M,O
Social Work M,D,O
Spanish M
Special Education M,D,O
Urban Education M,O

SIMON FRASER UNIVERSITY

Actuarial Science M,D
Anthropology M,D
Applied Mathematics M,D
Archaeology M,D
Art Education M,D
Biochemistry M,D
Biological and Biomedical Sciences—General M,D
Biophysics M,D
Biotechnology M,D
Business Administration and Management—General M,D
Chemical Physics M,D

Chemistry	M,D
Communication—General	M,D
Community Health	M
Comparative and Interdisciplinary Arts	M
Computational Sciences	M,D
Computer Science	M,D
Counselor Education	M
Criminal Justice and Criminology	M,D
Curriculum and Instruction	M,D
Economics	M,D
Education—General	M,D
Educational Leadership and Administration	M,D
Educational Media/ Instructional Technology	M,D
Educational Psychology	M,D
Engineering and Applied Sciences—General	M,D
English as a Second Language	M
English	M,D
Entomology	M,D
Environmental Management and Policy	M,D
Finance and Banking	M,D
Foundations and Philosophy of Education	M,D
French	M
Geography	M,D
Geosciences	M,D
Gerontology	M,D
History	M,D
Information Science	M,D
International Business	M,D
Internet and Interactive Multimedia	M,D
Kinesiology and Movement Studies	M,D
Latin American Studies	M
Liberal Studies	M
Linguistics	M,D
Management of Technology	M,D
Mathematics Education	M,D
Mathematics	M,D
Molecular Biology	M,D
Philosophy	M,D
Physics	M,D
Political Science	M,D
Psychology—General	M,D
Public Health—General	M
Public Policy	M
Publishing	M
Sociology	M,D
Statistics	M,D
Toxicology	M,D
Urban Studies	M,O
Women's Studies	M,D

SIMPSON COLLEGE

Criminal Justice and Criminology	M
Education—General	M
Secondary Education	M

SIMPSON UNIVERSITY

Counseling Psychology	M
Education—General	M
Educational Leadership and Administration	M
Missions and Missiology	P,M
Pastoral Ministry and Counseling	P,M

SINTE GLESKA UNIVERSITY

Education—General	M
Elementary Education	M

SIOUX FALLS SEMINARY

Marriage and Family Therapy	M
Pastoral Ministry and Counseling	P,M
Religion	M
Theology	M,D,O

SIT GRADUATE INSTITUTE

Business Administration and Management—General	M
Conflict Resolution and Mediation/Peace Studies	M
English as a Second Language	M
International Affairs	M
International and Comparative Education	M
International Business	M
Sustainable Development	M

SKIDMORE COLLEGE

Liberal Studies	M

SLIPPERY ROCK UNIVERSITY OF PENNSYLVANIA

Counselor Education	M
Criminal Justice and Criminology	M
Education—General	M
Educational Leadership and Administration	M
Elementary Education	M
English Education	M
Environmental Education	M
Environmental Management and Policy	M
History	M
Mathematics Education	M
Physical Education	M
Physical Therapy	D
Reading Education	M
Science Education	M
Secondary Education	M
Special Education	M
Student Affairs	M
Sustainable Development	M

SMITH COLLEGE

Biological and Biomedical Sciences—General	M
Chemistry	M
Dance	M
Education—General	M
Elementary Education	M
English Education	M
Exercise and Sports Science	M
Foreign Languages Education	M
French	M
History	M
Mathematics Education	M
Mathematics	O
Middle School Education	M
Science Education	M
Secondary Education	M
Social Sciences Education	M
Social Work	M,D
Special Education	M
Theater	M
Women's Studies	O

SOJOURNER-DOUGLASS COLLEGE

Human Services	M
Public Administration	M
Reading Education	M
Urban Education	M

SOKA UNIVERSITY OF AMERICA

English as a Second Language	O
Foreign Languages Education	O
Japanese	O

SONOMA STATE UNIVERSITY

Anthropology	M
Biological and Biomedical Sciences—General	M
Business Administration and Management—General	M
Counseling Psychology	M
Counselor Education	M
Curriculum and Instruction	M
Early Childhood Education	M
Education—General	M,D
Educational Leadership and Administration	M,D
Elementary Education	M
English	M
Environmental Biology	M
Family Nurse Practitioner Studies	M
History	M
Interdisciplinary Studies	M
Kinesiology and Movement Studies	M
Marriage and Family Therapy	M
Political Science	M
Public Administration	M
Public History	M
Reading Education	M
Special Education	M,D
Writing	M

SOTHEBY'S INSTITUTE OF ART–LONDON

Art/Fine Arts	M
Arts Administration	M
Decorative Arts	M
Photography	M

SOTHEBY'S INSTITUTE OF ART–NEW YORK

Art/Fine Arts	M
Arts Administration	M
Decorative Arts	M

SOUTH BAYLO UNIVERSITY

Acupuncture and Oriental Medicine	M

SOUTH CAROLINA STATE UNIVERSITY

Agricultural Economics and Agribusiness	M
Allied Health—General	M
Business Education	M,D,O
Child and Family Studies	M
Civil Engineering	M
Communication Disorders	M
Counselor Education	M,D,O
Early Childhood Education	M,D,O
Education—General	M,D,O
Educational Leadership and Administration	M,D,O
Elementary Education	M,D,O
English Education	M,D,O
Entrepreneurship	M
Family and Consumer Sciences-General	M
Home Economics Education	M,D,O
Human Services	M
Mathematics Education	M,D,O
Mechanical Engineering	M
Nutrition	M
Rehabilitation Counseling	M
Science Education	M,D,O
Secondary Education	M,D,O
Social Sciences Education	M,D,O
Special Education	M,D,O
Transportation and Highway Engineering	M
Vocational and Technical Education	M,D,O

SOUTH COLLEGE

Physician Assistant Studies	M

SOUTH DAKOTA SCHOOL OF MINES AND TECHNOLOGY

Artificial Intelligence/ Robotics	M
Atmospheric Sciences	M,D
Bioengineering	D
Biomedical Engineering	M,D
Chemical Engineering	M,D
Civil Engineering	M
Construction Management	M
Electrical Engineering	M
Engineering and Applied Sciences—General	M,D
Engineering Management	M
Environmental Sciences	D
Geological Engineering	M,D
Geology	M,D
Management of Technology	M
Materials Engineering	M,D
Materials Sciences	M,D
Mechanical Engineering	M,D
Nanotechnology	D
Paleontology	M,D
Physics	M,D

SOUTH DAKOTA STATE UNIVERSITY

Agricultural Engineering	M,D
Agricultural Sciences—General	M,D
Agronomy and Soil Sciences	M,D
Animal Sciences	M,D
Biological and Biomedical Sciences—General	M,D
Biosystems Engineering	M,D
Chemistry	M,D
Civil Engineering	M
Clothing and Textiles	M
Communication—General	M
Computational Sciences	M,D
Counselor Education	M
Curriculum and Instruction	M
Economics	M
Education—General	M,D
Educational Leadership and Administration	M
Electrical Engineering	M,D
Engineering and Applied Sciences—General	M,D
English	M
Family and Consumer Sciences-General	M
Fish, Game, and Wildlife Management	M,D
Food Science and Technology	M,D
Geography	M
Geosciences	D
Health Education	M
Hospitality Management	M,D
Human Development	M
Industrial/Management Engineering	M
Interior Design	M
Journalism	M
Mathematics	M,D
Mechanical Engineering	M
Microbiology	M,D
Nursing—General	M,D
Nutrition	M,D
Pharmaceutical Sciences	M,D
Pharmacy	P
Physical Education	M
Physics	M
Plant Sciences	M,D
Recreation and Park Management	M
Rural Sociology	M,D
Statistics	M,D
Veterinary Sciences	M,D

SOUTHEASTERN BAPTIST THEOLOGICAL SEMINARY

Ethics	P,M,D
Missions and Missiology	P,M,D
Music	P,M,D

*M—master's degree; P—first professional degree; D—doctorate; O—other advanced degree; *—Close-Up and/or Display in one of the other books in this series*

Philosophy P,M,D
Psychology—General P,M,D
Religious Education P,M,D
Theology P,M,D
Women's Studies P,M,D

SOUTHEASTERN LOUISIANA UNIVERSITY

Accounting M
Addictions/Substance Abuse Counseling M
Adult Nursing M
Applied Science and Technology M
Biological and Biomedical Sciences—General M
Business Administration and Management—General M
Chemistry M
Communication Disorders M
Communication—General M
Computer Science M
Counselor Education M
Criminal Justice and Criminology M
Curriculum and Instruction M
Education—General M,D
Educational Leadership and Administration M,D
Educational Media/Instructional Technology M,D
Elementary Education M
English Education M
English M
Family Nurse Practitioner Studies M
Health Education M
History M
Kinesiology and Movement Studies M
Management Information Systems M
Marriage and Family Therapy M
Mathematics M
Music M
Nursing and Healthcare Administration M
Nursing Education M
Nursing—General M
Physics M
Psychiatric Nursing M
Psychology—General M
Public Policy M
Reading Education M
Social Psychology M
Sociology M
Special Education M
Supply Chain Management M
Writing M

SOUTHEASTERN OKLAHOMA STATE UNIVERSITY

Aviation Management M
Aviation M
Biotechnology M
Business Administration and Management—General M
Clinical Psychology M
Counseling Psychology M
Counselor Education M
Education—General M
Educational Leadership and Administration M
Management Information Systems M
Mathematics Education M
Reading Education M
Special Education M

SOUTHEASTERN UNIVERSITY (FL)

Business Administration and Management—General M
Counseling Psychology M
Counselor Education M
Education—General M
Educational Leadership and Administration M
Elementary Education M
Human Services M
Pastoral Ministry and Counseling M

SOUTHEAST MISSOURI STATE UNIVERSITY

Accounting M
Biological and Biomedical Sciences—General M
Business Administration and Management—General M
Chemistry M
Communication Disorders M
Counseling Psychology M,O
Counselor Education M,O
Criminal Justice and Criminology M
Educational Leadership and Administration M,O
Educational Media/Instructional Technology M
Elementary Education M,O
English as a Second Language M
English M
Entrepreneurship M
Environmental Management and Policy M
Environmental Sciences M
Exercise and Sports Science M
Finance and Banking M
Foundations and Philosophy of Education M
Health Services Management and Hospital Administration M
Higher Education M,O
Historic Preservation M,O
History M,O
Industrial and Manufacturing Management M
International Business M
Leisure Studies M
Management of Technology M
Mathematics M
Middle School Education M
Nursing—General M
Nutrition M
Public Administration M
Public History M,O
School Psychology M,O
Science Education M
Secondary Education M,O
Social Psychology M,O
Special Education M
Sports Management M

SOUTHERN ADVENTIST UNIVERSITY

Accounting M
Acute Care/Critical Care Nursing M
Adult Nursing M
Business Administration and Management—General M
Counseling Psychology M
Counselor Education M
Education—General M
Educational Leadership and Administration M
Family Nurse Practitioner Studies M
Finance and Banking M
Health Services Management and Hospital Administration M
Marketing M
Missions and Missiology M
Nonprofit Management M
Nursing and Healthcare Administration M
Nursing—General M
Psychology—General M
Reading Education M
Recreation and Park Management M
Religion M
Religious Education M
Social Work M
Theology M

SOUTHERN ARKANSAS UNIVERSITY–MAGNOLIA

Agricultural Sciences—General M
Business Administration and Management—General M
Computer Science M
Counselor Education M
Curriculum and Instruction M
Education—General M
Educational Leadership and Administration M
Elementary Education M
English as a Second Language M
Kinesiology and Movement Studies M
Library Science M
Middle School Education M
Psychiatric Nursing M
Public Administration M
Reading Education M
Secondary Education M

SOUTHERN BAPTIST THEOLOGICAL SEMINARY

Higher Education P,M,D
Missions and Missiology P,M,D
Music P,M,D
Pastoral Ministry and Counseling P,M,D
Philosophy P,M,D
Religion P,M,D
Religious Education P,M,D
Theology P,M,D

SOUTHERN CALIFORNIA COLLEGE OF OPTOMETRY

Optometry P

SOUTHERN CALIFORNIA INSTITUTE OF ARCHITECTURE

Architecture M

SOUTHERN CALIFORNIA SEMINARY

Counseling Psychology P,M,D
Marriage and Family Therapy P,M,D
Psychology—General P,M,D
Religion P,M,D
Theology P,M,D

SOUTHERN CALIFORNIA UNIVERSITY OF HEALTH SCIENCES

Acupuncture and Oriental Medicine M
Chiropractic P

SOUTHERN COLLEGE OF OPTOMETRY

Optometry P

SOUTHERN CONNECTICUT STATE UNIVERSITY

Art Education M
Biological and Biomedical Sciences—General M
Business Administration and Management—General M
Chemistry M
Communication Disorders M
Computer Science M
Counselor Education M,O
Education—General M,D,O
Educational Leadership and Administration M,D,O
Educational Measurement and Evaluation M
Elementary Education M,O
English as a Second Language M
English M
Environmental Education M,O
Exercise and Sports Science M
Foundations and Philosophy of Education M,D,O
Health Education M
History M
Information Studies M,O
Leisure Studies M
Library Science M,O
Mathematics M
Multilingual and Multicultural Education M
Nursing and Healthcare Administration M
Nursing Education M
Nursing—General M
Physical Education M
Political Science M
Psychology—General M
Public Health—General M
Reading Education M,O
Recreation and Park Management M
School Psychology M,O
Science Education M,O
Social Work M
Sociology M
Special Education M,O
Sport Psychology M
Urban Studies M
Women's Studies M

SOUTHERN EVANGELICAL SEMINARY

Jewish Studies P,M,D,O
Missions and Missiology P,M,D,O
Near and Middle Eastern Studies P,M,D,O
Pastoral Ministry and Counseling P,M,D,O
Philosophy P,M,D,O
Religion P,M,D,O
Religious Education P,M,D,O
Theology P,M,D,O

SOUTHERN ILLINOIS UNIVERSITY CARBONDALE

Accounting M,D
Agricultural Economics and Agribusiness M
Agricultural Sciences—General M
Agronomy and Soil Sciences M
Animal Sciences M
Anthropology M,D
Applied Arts and Design—General M
Applied Physics M,D

Architecture	M
Art/Fine Arts	M
Biochemistry	M,D
Biological and Biomedical Sciences—General	M,D
Biomedical Engineering	M
Business Administration and Management—General	M,D
Chemistry	M,D
Civil Engineering	M
Clinical Psychology	M,D
Communication Disorders	M
Communication—General	M,D
Community Health	M
Computer Engineering	M,D
Computer Science	M,D
Counseling Psychology	M,D
Counselor Education	M,D
Criminal Justice and Criminology	M
Cultural Studies	M
Curriculum and Instruction	M,D
Economics	M,D
Education—General	M,D
Educational Leadership and Administration	M,D
Educational Measurement and Evaluation	M,D
Educational Psychology	M,D
Electrical Engineering	M,D
Energy and Power Engineering	D
Engineering and Applied Sciences—General	M,D
English as a Second Language	M
English	M,D
Environmental Sciences	D
Experimental Psychology	M,D
Forestry	M
Geography	M,D
Geology	M,D
Health Education	M,D
Health Law	M
Health Services Management and Hospital Administration	M
Higher Education	M
History	M,D
Horticulture	M
Human Development	M,D
Journalism	D
Law	P,M
Legal and Justice Studies	M
Linguistics	M
Manufacturing Engineering	M
Mass Communication	M
Mathematics	M,D
Mechanical Engineering	M
Mechanics	M,D
Media Studies	M
Microbiology	M,D
Mineral/Mining Engineering	M
Molecular Biology	M,D
Music Education	M
Music	M
Nutrition	M
Pharmacology	M,D
Philosophy	M,D
Physical Education	M
Physician Assistant Studies	M
Physics	M,D
Physiology	M,D
Plant Biology	M,D
Plant Sciences	M
Political Science	M,D
Psychology—General	M,D
Public Administration	M
Recreation and Park Management	M
Rehabilitation Counseling	M,D
Rhetoric	M,D
Social Work	M
Sociology	M,D
Special Education	M
Speech and Interpersonal Communication	M,D
Statistics	M,D
Theater	M,D
Vocational and Technical Education	M,D
Writing	M
Zoology	M,D

SOUTHERN ILLINOIS UNIVERSITY EDWARDSVILLE

Accounting	M
Art Education	M
Art Therapy	M
Art/Fine Arts	M
Biological and Biomedical Sciences—General	M
Biotechnology	M
Business Administration and Management—General	M
Chemistry	M
Civil Engineering	M
Clinical Psychology	M
Communication Disorders	M
Computer Science	M
Corporate and Organizational Communication	M,O
Curriculum and Instruction	M
Dentistry	P
Economics	M
Education—General	M,D,O
Educational Leadership and Administration	M,D,O
Educational Media/Instructional Technology	M,O
Electrical Engineering	M
Engineering and Applied Sciences—General	M
English as a Second Language	M,O
English Education	M,O
English	M,O
Environmental Management and Policy	M
Environmental Sciences	M
Family Nurse Practitioner Studies	M,D,O
Finance and Banking	M
Foreign Languages Education	M
Foundations and Philosophy of Education	M
Geography	M
Health Communication	M
Health Education	M
History	M
Industrial and Organizational Psychology	M
Industrial/Management Engineering	M
Kinesiology and Movement Studies	M
Management Information Systems	M
Marketing Research	M
Mass Communication	M
Mathematics Education	M
Mathematics	M
Mechanical Engineering	M
Media Studies	O
Museum Studies	O
Music Education	M,O
Music	M
Nurse Anesthesia	M,O
Nursing and Healthcare Administration	M,O
Nursing Education	M,O
Nursing—General	M,D,O
Pharmacy	P
Project Management	M
Psychology—General	M,O
Public Administration	M
Reading Education	M,O
School Psychology	O
Science Education	M
Secondary Education	M
Social Sciences Education	M
Social Work	M
Sociology	M
Special Education	M,O
Speech and Interpersonal Communication	M
Taxation	M
Writing	M

SOUTHERN METHODIST UNIVERSITY

Accounting	M
Advertising and Public Relations	M
Anthropology	M,D
Applied Economics	M,D
Applied Mathematics	M,D
Applied Science and Technology	M,D
Art History	M
Art/Fine Arts	M
Arts Administration	
Biological and Biomedical Sciences—General	M,D
Business Administration and Management—General	M
Chemistry	M,D
Civil Engineering	M,D
Clinical Psychology	D
Communication—General	M
Computational Sciences	M,D
Computer Engineering	M,D
Computer Science	M,D
Conflict Resolution and Mediation/Peace Studies	M,O
Counselor Education	M,O
Dance	M
Economics	M,D
Education of the Gifted	M,D,O
Education—General	M,D,O
Electrical Engineering	M,D
Engineering and Applied Sciences—General	M,D
Engineering Management	M,D
English	M,D
Entrepreneurship	M
Environmental Engineering	M,D
Environmental Sciences	M,D
Film, Television, and Video Production	M
Finance and Banking	M
Geology	M,D
Geophysics	M,D
History	M,D
Information Science	M,D
Law	P,M,D
Liberal Studies	M
Management Information Systems	M
Management Strategy and Policy	M
Manufacturing Engineering	M,D
Marketing	M
Mathematics	M,D
Mechanical Engineering	M,D
Medieval and Renaissance Studies	M
Multilingual and Multicultural Education	M,D,O
Music Education	M,O
Music	M,O
Operations Research	M,D
Photography	M
Physics	M,D
Psychology—General	D
Real Estate	M
Religion	M,D
Software Engineering	M,D
Statistics	M,D
Systems Engineering	M,D
Systems Science	M,D
Taxation	P,M,D
Telecommunications	M,D
Theater	M
Theology	P,M,D

SOUTHERN NAZARENE UNIVERSITY

Business Administration and Management—General	M
Counseling Psychology	M
Curriculum and Instruction	M
Education—General	M
Educational Leadership and Administration	M
Marriage and Family Therapy	M
Nursing and Healthcare Administration	M
Nursing Education	M
Nursing—General	M
Psychology—General	M
Religion	M
Theology	M

SOUTHERN NEW HAMPSHIRE UNIVERSITY

Accounting	M,D,O
Addictions/Substance Abuse Counseling	M,O
Business Administration and Management—General	M,D,O
Business Education	M,O
Child Development	M,O
Clinical Psychology	M,O
Community Health	M,O
Computer Education	M,O
Curriculum and Instruction	M,O
Economic Development	M,D
Education—General	M,O
Educational Leadership and Administration	M,O
Elementary Education	M,O
English as a Second Language	M,O
Finance and Banking	M,D,O
Hospitality Management	M,D,O
Human Resources Development	M,O
Human Resources Management	M,D,O
International Business	M,D,O
Management Information Systems	M,D,O
Marketing	M,D,O
Nonprofit Management	M,D,O
Organizational Management	M,D,O
Project Management	M,D,O
Psychology—General	M,O
Public Policy	M,D
Secondary Education	M,O
Special Education	M,O
Sports Management	M,D,O
Taxation	M,D,O
Vocational and Technical Education	M,O
Writing	M,O

SOUTHERN OREGON UNIVERSITY

Business Administration and Management—General	M
Computer Science	M
Counseling Psychology	M
Early Childhood Education	M
Education—General	M
Educational Leadership and Administration	M
Elementary Education	M
Environmental Education	M
Foreign Languages Education	M
Interdisciplinary Studies	M
Psychology—General	M
Reading Education	M
Secondary Education	M
Special Education	M

*M—master's degree; P—first professional degree; D—doctorate; O—other advanced degree; *—Close-Up and/or Display in one of the other books in this series*

SOUTHERN POLYTECHNIC STATE UNIVERSITY

Accounting M,O
Business Administration and Management—General M,O
Communication—General M,O
Computer and Information Systems Security M,O
Computer Engineering M
Computer Science M,O
Construction Management M
Educational Media/Instructional Technology M,O
Electrical Engineering M
Engineering and Applied Sciences—General M,O
Graphic Design M,O
Industrial/Management Engineering M,O
Information Science M,O
Internet and Interactive Multimedia M,O
Quality Management M,O
Software Engineering M,O
Systems Engineering M,O
Technical Communication M,O

SOUTHERN UNIVERSITY AND AGRICULTURAL AND MECHANICAL COLLEGE

Agricultural Sciences—General M
Analytical Chemistry M
Biochemistry M
Biological and Biomedical Sciences—General M
Business Administration and Management—General M
Chemistry M
Computer Science M
Counselor Education M
Criminal Justice and Criminology M
Education—General M,D
Educational Leadership and Administration M
Educational Media/Instructional Technology M
Elementary Education M
Engineering and Applied Sciences—General M
Environmental Sciences M
Family Nurse Practitioner Studies M,D,O
Forestry M
Gerontological Nursing M,D,O
History M
Inorganic Chemistry M
Law P
Mass Communication M
Mathematics Education D
Mathematics M
Nursing and Healthcare Administration M,D,O
Nursing Education M,D,O
Nursing—General M,D,O
Organic Chemistry M
Physical Chemistry M
Physics M
Political Science M
Psychology—General M
Public Administration M
Public Policy D
Recreation and Park Management M
Rehabilitation Counseling M
Science Education D
Secondary Education M
Social Sciences M
Special Education M,D

SOUTHERN UNIVERSITY AT NEW ORLEANS

Social Work M

SOUTHERN UTAH UNIVERSITY

Accounting M
Arts Administration M
Business Administration and Management—General M
Communication—General M
Education—General M
Exercise and Sports Science M
Forensic Sciences M
Public Administration M

SOUTHERN WESLEYAN UNIVERSITY

Business Administration and Management—General M
Education—General M
Pastoral Ministry and Counseling M

SOUTH TEXAS COLLEGE OF LAW

Law P

SOUTH UNIVERSITY (AL)

Business Administration and Management—General M*
Counseling Psychology M
Health Services Management and Hospital Administration M*

SOUTH UNIVERSITY (FL)

Business Administration and Management—General M*
Counseling Psychology M*
Health Services Management and Hospital Administration M

SOUTH UNIVERSITY (FL)

Health Services Management and Hospital Administration M*
Physician Assistant Studies M

SOUTH UNIVERSITY (GA)

Anesthesiologist Assistant Studies M
Business Administration and Management—General M*
Counseling Psychology M*
Criminal Justice and Criminology M
Entrepreneurship M
Hospitality Management M
Pharmacy P*
Physician Assistant Studies M*
Sustainability Management M

SOUTH UNIVERSITY (MI)

Business Administration and Management—General M*
Counseling Psychology M*

SOUTH UNIVERSITY (SC)

Business Administration and Management—General M*
Counseling Psychology M*
Criminal Justice and Criminology M*
Health Services Management and Hospital Administration M*
Pharmacy P*

SOUTH UNIVERSITY (TX)

Business Administration and Management—General M

SOUTH UNIVERSITY (VA)

Business Administration and Management—General M*
Counseling Psychology M*

SOUTH UNIVERSITY (VA)

Business Administration and Management—General M*
Counseling Psychology M*

SOUTHWEST ACUPUNCTURE COLLEGE

Acupuncture and Oriental Medicine M

SOUTHWEST BAPTIST UNIVERSITY

Business Administration and Management—General M
Education—General M,O
Educational Leadership and Administration M,O
Health Services Management and Hospital Administration M
Physical Therapy D

SOUTHWEST COLLEGE OF NATUROPATHIC MEDICINE AND HEALTH SCIENCES

Naturopathic Medicine D

SOUTHWESTERN ADVENTIST UNIVERSITY

Accounting M
Business Administration and Management—General M
Curriculum and Instruction M
Education—General M
Educational Leadership and Administration M
Finance and Banking M
Reading Education M

SOUTHWESTERN ASSEMBLIES OF GOD UNIVERSITY

Counseling Psychology M
Curriculum and Instruction M
Education—General M
Educational Leadership and Administration M
History M
Missions and Missiology P,M
Pastoral Ministry and Counseling P,M
Religion P,M
Religious Education M
Secondary Education M
Theology P,M

SOUTHWESTERN BAPTIST THEOLOGICAL SEMINARY

Music M,D,O
Religious Education M,D,O
Theology P,M,D,O

SOUTHWESTERN CHRISTIAN UNIVERSITY

Missions and Missiology M
Pastoral Ministry and Counseling M

SOUTHWESTERN COLLEGE (KS)

Business Administration and Management—General M
Criminal Justice and Criminology M
Curriculum and Instruction M
Education—General M
Music Education M
Music M
Organizational Management M
Special Education M
Theology M

SOUTHWESTERN COLLEGE (NM)

Art Therapy M
Counseling Psychology M,O
Health Psychology O
Psychology—General O
Social Psychology O
Thanatology M,O

SOUTHWESTERN LAW SCHOOL

Law P,M

SOUTHWESTERN OKLAHOMA STATE UNIVERSITY

Allied Health—General M
Art Education M
Business Administration and Management—General M
Counselor Education M
Early Childhood Education M
Education—General M
Educational Leadership and Administration M
Educational Measurement and Evaluation M
Elementary Education M
English Education M
Kinesiology and Movement Studies M
Mathematics Education M
Microbiology M
Music Education M
Music M
Pharmacy P
Recreation and Park Management M
School Psychology M
Science Education M
Secondary Education M
Social Sciences Education M
Special Education M

SOUTHWEST MINNESOTA STATE UNIVERSITY

Business Administration and Management—General M
Early Childhood Education M
Education—General M
Educational Leadership and Administration M
English as a Second Language M
Marketing M
Mathematics Education M
Reading Education M
Special Education M

SOUTHWEST UNIVERSITY

Business Administration and Management—General M

Criminal Justice and Criminology M
Organizational Management M

SPALDING UNIVERSITY

Adult Nursing M
Applied Behavior Analysis M
Business Administration and Management—General M
Clinical Psychology M,D
Communication—General M
Corporate and Organizational Communication M
Counselor Education M
Education—General M,D
Educational Leadership and Administration M,D
Elementary Education M
Family Nurse Practitioner Studies M
Middle School Education M
Nursing and Healthcare Administration M
Nursing—General M
Occupational Therapy M
Pediatric Nursing M
Psychology—General M,D
Secondary Education M
Social Work M
Special Education M
Writing M

SPERTUS INSTITUTE OF JEWISH STUDIES

Jewish Studies M,D
Nonprofit Management M
Religious Education M

SPRING ARBOR UNIVERSITY

Business Administration and Management—General M
Child and Family Studies M
Communication—General M
Counseling Psychology M
Education—General M
Nursing—General M
Organizational Management M
Pastoral Ministry and Counseling M
Special Education M
Theology M

SPRINGFIELD COLLEGE

Addictions/Substance Abuse Counseling M
Art Therapy M,O
Athletic Training and Sports Medicine M,D
Counseling Psychology M,O
Counselor Education M,O
Early Childhood Education M
Education—General M
Educational Leadership and Administration M
Elementary Education M
Exercise and Sports Science M,D
Health Education M,D,O
Health Promotion M,D
Health Services Management and Hospital Administration M
Human Services M
Industrial and Organizational Psychology M,O
Marriage and Family Therapy M,O
Occupational Therapy M,O
Organizational Management M
Physical Education M,D,O
Physical Therapy D
Physician Assistant Studies M
Recreation and Park Management M
Rehabilitation Counseling M
Secondary Education M
Social Psychology M
Social Work M
Special Education M
Sport Psychology M,D,O
Sports Management M,D,O
Student Affairs M,O

SPRING HILL COLLEGE

Art/Fine Arts M
Business Administration and Management—General M
Early Childhood Education M
Education—General M
Elementary Education M
English M
Ethics M
Foundations and Philosophy of Education M
History M
Liberal Studies M
Nursing—General M
Pastoral Ministry and Counseling M
Secondary Education M
Social Sciences Education M
Theology M

STANFORD UNIVERSITY

Aerospace/Aeronautical Engineering M,D,O
Allopathic Medicine P
Anthropology M,D
Applied Physics M,D
Art Education M,D
Art/Fine Arts M,D
Asian Studies M
Biochemistry D
Bioengineering M,D
Biological and Biomedical Sciences—General M,D
Biomedical Engineering M
Biophysics D
Business Administration and Management—General M,D
Cancer Biology/Oncology D
Chemical Engineering M,D,O
Chemistry D
Child and Family Studies D
Chinese M,D
Civil Engineering M,D,O
Classics M,D
Communication—General M,D
Comparative Literature D
Computational Sciences M,D
Computer Education M,D
Computer Science M,D
Counseling Psychology D
Cultural Anthropology M,D
Curriculum and Instruction M,D
Developmental Biology D
Developmental Psychology D
East European and Russian Studies M
Economics D
Education—General M,D
Educational Leadership and Administration M,D
Educational Measurement and Evaluation M,D
Educational Psychology D
Electrical Engineering M,D,O
Engineering and Applied Sciences—General M,D,O
Engineering Design M
Engineering Management M,D
English Education M,D
English M,D
Environmental Engineering M,D,O
Environmental Management and Policy M
Environmental Sciences M,D,O
Epidemiology M,D
Foreign Languages Education M
Foundations and Philosophy of Education M,D
French M,D
Genetics D
Geophysics M,D
Geosciences M,D,O
German M,D
Health Services Research M
Higher Education M,D
History M,D
Humanities M
Immunology D
Industrial/Management Engineering M,D
Interdisciplinary Studies M,D
International Affairs M
International and Comparative Education M,D
Italian M,D
Japanese M,D
Journalism M,D
Law P,M,D
Linguistics M,D
Materials Engineering M,D,O
Materials Sciences M,D,O
Mathematical and Computational Finance M,D
Mathematics Education M,D
Mathematics M,D
Mechanical Engineering M,D,O
Medical Informatics M,D
Microbiology D
Molecular Pharmacology D
Music M,D
Neuroscience D
Petroleum Engineering M,D,O
Philosophy M,D
Physics D
Physiology D
Political Science M,D
Psychology—General D
Religion M,D
Russian M,D
Science Education M,D
Slavic Languages M,D
Social Sciences Education M,D
Sociology D
Spanish M,D
Statistics M,D
Structural Biology D
Theater D

STARR KING SCHOOL FOR THE MINISTRY

Theology P

STATE UNIVERSITY OF NEW YORK AT BINGHAMTON

Accounting M,D
Analytical Chemistry M,D
Anthropology M,D
Applied Physics M,D
Art History M,D
Biological and Biomedical Sciences—General M,D
Biomedical Engineering M,D
Biopsychology M,D
Business Administration and Management—General M,D
Chemistry M,D
Clinical Psychology M,D
Cognitive Sciences M,D
Comparative Literature M,D
Computer Science M,D
Cultural Studies M,D
Early Childhood Education M
Economics M,D
Education—General M,D
Educational Leadership and Administration M
Electrical Engineering M,D
Engineering and Applied Sciences—General M,D
English Education M
English M,D
Finance and Banking M,D
Foreign Languages Education M
Foundations and Philosophy of Education D
French M
Geography M
Geology M,D
Health Services Management and Hospital Administration M,D
History M,D
Industrial/Management Engineering M,D
Inorganic Chemistry M,D
Italian M
Legal and Justice Studies M,D
Materials Engineering M,D
Materials Sciences M,D
Mathematics Education M
Mathematics M,D
Mechanical Engineering M,D
Music M
Nursing—General M,D,O
Organic Chemistry M,D
Philosophy M,D
Physical Chemistry M,D
Physics M,D
Political Science M,D
Psychology—General M,D
Public Administration M
Public Policy M,D
Reading Education M
Science Education M
Secondary Education M
Social Sciences Education M
Social Work M
Sociology M,D
Spanish M,O
Special Education M
Statistics M,D*
Student Affairs M
Systems Science M,D
Theater M
Translation and Interpretation M,O

STATE UNIVERSITY OF NEW YORK AT FREDONIA

Biological and Biomedical Sciences—General M
Chemistry M
Communication Disorders M
Education—General M,O
Educational Leadership and Administration O
Elementary Education M
English as a Second Language M
English M
Interdisciplinary Studies M
Mathematics M
Music Education M
Music M
Reading Education M
Science Education M
Secondary Education M

STATE UNIVERSITY OF NEW YORK AT NEW PALTZ

Accounting M
Art Education M
Art/Fine Arts M
Biological and Biomedical Sciences—General M
Business Administration and Management—General M
Chemistry M
Communication Disorders M
Computer Science M

*M—master's degree; P—first professional degree; D—doctorate; O—other advanced degree; *—Close-Up and/or Display in one of the other books in this series*

Counseling Psychology M
Counselor Education M
Early Childhood Education M
Education—General M,O
Educational Leadership and Administration M,O
Electrical Engineering M
Elementary Education M
English as a Second Language M
English Education M
English M
French M
Geosciences M
Multilingual and Multicultural Education M
Music M
Psychology—General M
Reading Education M
Science Education M
Secondary Education M
Social Sciences Education M
Spanish M
Special Education M
Therapies—Dance, Drama, and Music M

STATE UNIVERSITY OF NEW YORK AT OSWEGO

Agricultural Education M
Art Education M
Art/Fine Arts M
Business Administration and Management—General M
Business Education M
Chemistry M
Child and Family Studies M
Consumer Economics M
Counseling Psychology M,O
Early Childhood Education M
Education—General M,O
Educational Leadership and Administration O
Elementary Education M
English M
History M
Human-Computer Interaction M
Middle School Education M
Reading Education M
School Psychology M,O
Secondary Education M
Special Education M
Vocational and Technical Education M

STATE UNIVERSITY OF NEW YORK AT PLATTSBURGH

Communication Disorders M
Counselor Education M,O
Curriculum and Instruction M
Educational Leadership and Administration O
Elementary Education M
English Education M
Foreign Languages Education M
Liberal Studies M
Mathematics Education M
Organizational Management M
Psychology—General M,O
Reading Education M
School Psychology M,O
Science Education M
Secondary Education M
Social Sciences Education M
Special Education M

STATE UNIVERSITY OF NEW YORK COLLEGE AT CORTLAND

American Studies O
Early Childhood Education M
Education—General M,O
Educational Leadership and Administration O
English as a Second Language M
English Education M
English M
Exercise and Sports Science M
Foreign Languages Education M
Health Education M
History M
Mathematics Education M
Mathematics M
Physical Education M
Reading Education M
Recreation and Park Management M
Science Education M
Secondary Education M
Social Sciences Education M
Special Education M
Sports Management M

STATE UNIVERSITY OF NEW YORK COLLEGE AT GENESEO

Accounting M
Business Administration and Management—General M
Early Childhood Education M
Education—General M
Elementary Education M
Multilingual and Multicultural Education M
Reading Education M
Secondary Education M

STATE UNIVERSITY OF NEW YORK COLLEGE AT OLD WESTBURY

Accounting M

STATE UNIVERSITY OF NEW YORK COLLEGE AT ONEONTA

Biological and Biomedical Sciences—General M
Counselor Education M,O
Education—General M,O
Educational Media/ Instructional Technology M,O
Educational Psychology M,O
Elementary Education M
Family and Consumer Sciences-General M
Geosciences M
Home Economics Education M
Middle School Education M
Museum Studies M
Nutrition M
Reading Education M
Secondary Education M
Special Education M,O

STATE UNIVERSITY OF NEW YORK COLLEGE AT POTSDAM

Communication—General M
Curriculum and Instruction M
Early Childhood Education M
Educational Media/ Instructional Technology M
Elementary Education M
English M
Mathematics Education M
Mathematics M
Middle School Education M
Music Education M
Music M
Organizational Management M
Reading Education M
Science Education M
Secondary Education M
Social Sciences Education M
Special Education M

STATE UNIVERSITY OF NEW YORK COLLEGE OF ENVIRONMENTAL SCIENCE AND FORESTRY

Biochemistry M,D
Chemistry M,D
Communication—General M,D
Conservation Biology M,D
Construction Management M,D
Ecology M,D
Entomology M,D
Environmental Biology M,D
Environmental Engineering M,D
Environmental Management and Policy M,D
Environmental Sciences M,D
Fish, Game, and Wildlife Management M,D
Forestry M,D
Geodetic Sciences M,D
Geographic Information Systems M,D
Landscape Architecture M
Natural Resources M,D
Organic Chemistry M,D
Paper and Pulp Engineering M,D
Plant Pathology M,D
Plant Sciences M,D
Urban and Regional Planning M,D
Urban Design M
Water Resources Engineering M,D
Water Resources M,D

STATE UNIVERSITY OF NEW YORK COLLEGE OF OPTOMETRY

Optometry P
Vision Sciences D

STATE UNIVERSITY OF NEW YORK DOWNSTATE MEDICAL CENTER

Allopathic Medicine P,M
Biological and Biomedical Sciences—General M,D
Biomedical Engineering M,D
Cell Biology D
Community Health M
Family Nurse Practitioner Studies M,O
Medical/Surgical Nursing M,O
Molecular Biology D
Neuroscience D
Nurse Anesthesia M
Nurse Midwifery M,O
Nursing—General M,O
Public Health—General M

STATE UNIVERSITY OF NEW YORK EMPIRE STATE COLLEGE

Business Administration and Management—General M
Education—General M
Industrial and Labor Relations M
Liberal Studies M
Public Policy M

STATE UNIVERSITY OF NEW YORK INSTITUTE OF TECHNOLOGY

Accounting M
Adult Nursing M,O
Business Administration and Management—General M
Computer Science M
Engineering and Applied Sciences—General M
Family Nurse Practitioner Studies M,O
Gerontological Nursing M,O
Health Services Management and Hospital Administration M
Information Science M
Management of Technology M
Nursing and Healthcare Administration M,O
Nursing Education M,O
Nursing—General M,O
Sociology M
Telecommunications M

STATE UNIVERSITY OF NEW YORK MARITIME COLLEGE

Transportation Management M

STATE UNIVERSITY OF NEW YORK UPSTATE MEDICAL UNIVERSITY

Allopathic Medicine P
Anatomy M,D
Biochemistry M,D
Biological and Biomedical Sciences—General M,D
Cancer Biology/Oncology
Cardiovascular Sciences
Cell Biology M,D
Clinical Laboratory Sciences/Medical Technology M
Family Nurse Practitioner Studies M,O
Immunology M,D
Infectious Diseases
Microbiology M,D
Molecular Biology M,D
Neuroscience D
Nursing—General M,O
Pharmacology D
Physical Therapy D
Physiology M,D

STEPHEN F. AUSTIN STATE UNIVERSITY

Accounting M
Agricultural Education M
Applied Arts and Design—General M
Art/Fine Arts M
Athletic Training and Sports Medicine M
Biological and Biomedical Sciences—General M
Biotechnology M
Business Administration and Management—General M
Chemistry M
Communication Disorders M
Communication—General M
Computer Science M
Counselor Education M
Early Childhood Education M
Education—General M,D
Educational Leadership and Administration M,D
Elementary Education M
English M
Environmental Sciences M
Family and Consumer Sciences-General M
Forestry M,D
Geology M
History M
Interdisciplinary Studies M
Kinesiology and Movement Studies M
Marketing M
Mass Communication M
Mathematics Education M
Mathematics M
Music M

Physics M
Psychology—General M
Public Administration M
School Psychology M
Secondary Education M,D
Social Work M
Special Education M
Statistics M

STEPHENS COLLEGE

Business Administration and Management—General M
Counseling Psychology M
Counselor Education M
Curriculum and Instruction M
Health Informatics M,O
Marriage and Family Therapy M

STETSON UNIVERSITY

Accounting M
Business Administration and Management—General M
Counselor Education M
Education—General M,O
Educational Leadership and Administration M,O
English M
Law P,M
Marriage and Family Therapy M
Reading Education M

STEVENS INSTITUTE OF TECHNOLOGY

Aerospace/Aeronautical Engineering M,O
Analytical Chemistry M,D,O
Applied Mathematics M
Applied Statistics O
Biochemistry M,D,O
Bioinformatics M,D,O
Biomedical Engineering M,O
Business Administration and Management—General M
Chemical Engineering M,D,O
Chemistry M,D,O
Civil Engineering M,D,O
Communication—General M,D,O
Computer and Information Systems Security M,D,O
Computer Art and Design M,D,O
Computer Engineering M,D,O
Computer Science M,D,O
Construction Engineering M,O
Construction Management M,O
Corporate and Organizational Communication O
Database Systems M,D,O
Electrical Engineering M,D,O
Electronic Commerce M,O
Engineering and Applied Sciences—General M,D,O
Engineering Design M
Engineering Management M,D
Engineering Physics M,D,O
Entrepreneurship M,O
Environmental Engineering M,D,O
Finance and Banking M
Financial Engineering M
Health Informatics M,D,O
Human Resources Management M
Hydrology M,D,O
Industrial and Manufacturing Management M
Information Science M,O
International Business M
Internet and Interactive Multimedia M,D,O
Logistics M,D,O
Management Information Systems M,D,O
Management of Technology M,D,O
Management Strategy and Policy M
Manufacturing Engineering M
Marine Affairs M
Materials Engineering M,D
Mathematics M,D
Mechanical Engineering M,D,O
Modeling and Simulation M,D,O
Ocean Engineering M,D
Organic Chemistry M,D,O
Pharmaceutical Sciences M,O
Photonics M,D,O
Physical Chemistry M,D,O
Physics M,D,O
Polymer Science and Engineering M,D,O
Project Management M,O
Quality Management M,O
Software Engineering M,D,O
Statistics M,O
Structural Engineering M,D,O
Systems Engineering M,D,O
Systems Science M,D
Telecommunications Management M,D,O
Telecommunications M,D,O
Water Resources Engineering M,D,O

STEVENSON UNIVERSITY

Forensic Sciences M
Management of Technology M
Nursing—General M

STONY BROOK UNIVERSITY, STATE UNIVERSITY OF NEW YORK

Addictions/Substance Abuse Counseling M
Adult Nursing M,O
African Studies M
Allopathic Medicine P
Anatomy D
Anthropology M,D
Applied Mathematics M,D
Art History M,D
Art/Fine Arts M
Astronomy D
Atmospheric Sciences M,D
Biochemistry D
Biological and Biomedical Sciences—General D
Biomedical Engineering M,D,O
Biophysics D
Biopsychology D
Business Administration and Management—General M,O
Cell Biology M,D
Chemistry M,D
Clinical Psychology D
Community Health M,D
Comparative Literature M,D
Computer Education M
Computer Engineering M,D,O
Computer Science M,D,O
Cultural Studies M,D
Dentistry P,O
Developmental Biology M,D
Ecology M,D
Economics M,D
Educational Leadership and Administration M,O
Educational Media/Instructional Technology M,O
Electrical Engineering M,D
Engineering and Applied Sciences—General M,D,O
English as a Second Language M
English Education M,D,O
English M,D,O
Environmental and Occupational Health M,O
Environmental Management and Policy M,O
Evolutionary Biology M,D
Experimental Psychology D
Family Nurse Practitioner Studies M,O
Finance and Banking M,O
Foreign Languages Education M,O
French M
Genetics D
Geosciences M,D
Hazardous Materials Management M,O
Health Psychology D
Health Services Management and Hospital Administration M,D,O
Hispanic and Latin American Languages M,D
History M,D
Human Resources Management M,O
Immunology M,D
Italian M
Liberal Studies M,O
Linguistics M,D
Management Information Systems M,D,O
Management of Technology M
Marine Affairs M
Marine Sciences M,D
Marketing M,O
Materials Engineering M,D
Materials Sciences M,D
Maternal and Child/Neonatal Nursing M,O
Mathematics Education M,O
Mathematics M,D
Mechanical Engineering M,D
Medical Physics M,D
Microbiology D
Molecular Biology M,D
Molecular Genetics D
Molecular Physiology D
Music M,D
Neuroscience D
Nurse Midwifery M,O
Nursing—General M,D,O
Occupational Therapy M,D,O
Oral and Dental Sciences P,M,D,O
Pathology M,D
Pediatric Nursing M,O
Pharmacology D
Philosophy M,D
Physical Education M,O
Physical Therapy M,D,O
Physician Assistant Studies M,D,O
Physics M,D
Physiology D
Political Science M,D
Psychiatric Nursing M,O
Psychology—General D
Public Health—General M
Public Policy M
Romance Languages M
Science Education M,D,O
Social Psychology D
Social Sciences Education M,O
Social Sciences M,O
Social Work M,D
Sociology M,D
Software Engineering M,D,O
Statistics M,D
Structural Biology D
Systems Engineering M
Technology and Public Policy D
Theater M
Women's Health Nursing M,O
Women's Studies O
Writing M,O

STRATFORD UNIVERSITY

Accounting M
Business Administration and Management—General M
Computer and Information Systems Security M
Entrepreneurship M
Management Information Systems M
Software Engineering M
Telecommunications M

STRAYER UNIVERSITY

Accounting M
Business Administration and Management—General M
Computer and Information Systems Security M
Education—General M
Educational Media/Instructional Technology M
Finance and Banking M
Health Services Management and Hospital Administration M
Hospitality Management M
Human Resources Management M
Information Science M
Management Information Systems M
Marketing M
Public Administration M
Software Engineering M
Supply Chain Management M
Systems Science M
Taxation M
Telecommunications Management M
Travel and Tourism M

SUFFOLK UNIVERSITY

Accounting M,O
Adult Education M,O
Advertising and Public Relations M
Applied Arts and Design—General M
Business Administration and Management—General M,O
Clinical Psychology D
Communication—General M
Computer Science M
Corporate and Organizational Communication M
Counseling Psychology M,O
Counselor Education M,O
Criminal Justice and Criminology M
Economics M,D
Education—General M,O
Educational Leadership and Administration M,O
Entrepreneurship M,O
Ethics M
Finance and Banking M,O
Foundations and Philosophy of Education M,O
Graphic Design M
Health Education M
Health Law P,M
Health Services Management and Hospital Administration M,O
Human Resources Development M,O
Intellectual Property Law P,M
Interior Design M
International Business M,D,O
Law P,M
Management Strategy and Policy M,O
Marketing M,O
Middle School Education M,O
Nonprofit Management M,O

*M—master's degree; P—first professional degree; D—doctorate; O—other advanced degree; *—Close-Up and/or Display in one of the other books in this series*

Organizational Behavior	M,O
Organizational Management	M,O
Political Science	M,O
Psychology—General	D
Public Administration	M,O
Public Policy	M
Secondary Education	M,O
Taxation	M,O
Women's Studies	M

SULLIVAN UNIVERSITY

Business Administration and Management—General	P,M,D
Conflict Resolution and Mediation/Peace Studies	P,M,D
Management Information Systems	P,M,D
Management of Technology	P,M,D

SUL ROSS STATE UNIVERSITY

Animal Sciences	M
Applied Arts and Design—General	M
Art Education	M
Art History	M
Art/Fine Arts	M
Biological and Biomedical Sciences—General	M
Business Administration and Management—General	M
Counselor Education	M
Criminal Justice and Criminology	M
Education—General	M
Educational Leadership and Administration	M
Educational Measurement and Evaluation	M
Elementary Education	M
English	M
Fish, Game, and Wildlife Management	M
Geology	M
History	M
Multilingual and Multicultural Education	M
Physical Education	M
Political Science	M
Psychology—General	M
Public Administration	M
Range Science	M
Reading Education	M
Secondary Education	M
Textile Design	M

SWEDISH INSTITUTE, COLLEGE OF HEALTH SCIENCES

Acupuncture and Oriental Medicine	M

SWEET BRIAR COLLEGE

Education—General	M

SYRACUSE UNIVERSITY

Accounting	M,D
Addictions/Substance Abuse Counseling	O
Advertising and Public Relations	M
Aerospace/Aeronautical Engineering	M,D
African Studies	M
African-American Studies	M
Anthropology	M,D
Applied Arts and Design—General	M
Applied Statistics	M
Architecture	M
Art Education	M,O
Art History	M
Art/Fine Arts	M*
Arts Journalism	M
Biochemistry	D
Bioengineering	M,D
Biological and Biomedical Sciences—General	M,D
Biophysics	D
Broadcast Journalism	M
Business Administration and Management—General	M,D
Chemical Engineering	M,D
Chemistry	M,D
Child and Family Studies	M,D
Civil Engineering	M,D
Clinical Psychology	M,D
Communication Disorders	M,D
Communication—General	M,D
Community Health	M
Computer and Information Systems Security	O
Computer Art and Design	M
Computer Engineering	M,D,O
Computer Science	M
Conflict Resolution and Mediation/Peace Studies	O
Counselor Education	M,D,O
Curriculum and Instruction	M,D,O
Disability Studies	O
Early Childhood Education	M
Economics	M,D,O
Education of Students with Severe/Multiple Disabilities	M
Education—General	M,D,O
Educational Leadership and Administration	M,D,O
Educational Measurement and Evaluation	M,D,O
Educational Media/ Instructional Technology	M,O
Electrical Engineering	M,D,O
Engineering and Applied Sciences—General	M,D,O
Engineering Management	M
English as a Second Language	M,O
English Education	M,D
English	M,D
Entrepreneurship	M,O
Environmental Engineering	M
Exercise and Sports Science	M
Experimental Psychology	D
Film, Television, and Video Production	M
Film, Television, and Video Theory and Criticism	M
Finance and Banking	M,D
Forensic Sciences	M
Foundations and Philosophy of Education	M,D
French	M
Gender Studies	O
Geography	M,D
Geology	M,D
Health Services Management and Hospital Administration	O
Higher Education	M,D
Historic Preservation	O
History	M,D
Human Resources Development	D
Human Services	O
Illustration	M
Industrial and Manufacturing Management	D
Information Science	D,O
Information Studies	M,D*
International Affairs	M
Journalism	M
Latin American Studies	O
Law	P
Library Science	M,O
Linguistics	M
Management Information Systems	M,D,O
Management Strategy and Policy	D
Marketing	M,D
Marriage and Family Therapy	M
Mass Communication	M,D
Maternal and Child Health	M
Mathematics Education	M,D
Mathematics	M,D
Mechanical Engineering	M,D
Media Studies	M
Museum Studies	M
Music Education	M
Music	M
Near and Middle Eastern Studies	O
Nutrition	M
Organizational Behavior	D
Organizational Management	O
Philosophy	M,D
Photography	M
Physics	M,D
Political Science	M,D,O
Public Administration	M,D,O
Public Policy	O
Quantitative Analysis	D
Reading Education	M,D
Religion	M,D
Rhetoric	M,D
School Psychology	M,D,O
Science Education	M,D
Social Psychology	D
Social Sciences Education	M
Social Sciences	M,D
Social Work	M
Sociology	M,D
Spanish	M
Special Education	M,D
Structural Biology	D
Student Affairs	M
Supply Chain Management	M,D
Sustainability Management	O
Telecommunications Management	M,O
Telecommunications	M
Western European Studies	O
Women's Studies	O
Writing	M,D

TABOR COLLEGE

Accounting	M
Business Administration and Management—General	M

TAFT LAW SCHOOL

Law	P,M
Legal and Justice Studies	P,M
Taxation	P,M

TAI SOPHIA INSTITUTE

Acupuncture and Oriental Medicine	M,O

TALMUDIC COLLEGE OF FLORIDA

Theology	M

TARLETON STATE UNIVERSITY

Accounting	M
Agricultural Education	M
Agricultural Sciences—General	M
Biological and Biomedical Sciences—General	M
Business Administration and Management—General	M
Counseling Psychology	M,O
Counselor Education	M,O
Criminal Justice and Criminology	M
Curriculum and Instruction	M
Economics	M
Education—General	M,D,O
Educational Leadership and Administration	M,D,O
English	M
Environmental Sciences	M
Finance and Banking	M
History	M
Human Resources Management	M
Liberal Studies	M
Management Information Systems	M
Mathematics	M
Music Education	M
Physical Education	M
Political Science	M
School Psychology	M,O
Secondary Education	M,O
Special Education	M,O

TAYLOR COLLEGE AND SEMINARY

Cultural Studies	P,M,O
English as a Second Language	P,M,O
Missions and Missiology	P,M,O
Theology	P,M,O

TAYLOR UNIVERSITY

Business Administration and Management—General	M
Environmental Sciences	M
Higher Education	M
International Business	M
Management Strategy and Policy	M
Religion	M

TEACHER EDUCATION UNIVERSITY

Counselor Education	M
Education—General	M
Educational Leadership and Administration	M
Educational Media/ Instructional Technology	M
Elementary Education	M

TEACHERS COLLEGE, COLUMBIA UNIVERSITY

Adult Education	M,D
Anthropology	M,D
Applied Behavior Analysis	M,D
Applied Psychology	M,D
Art Education	M,D
Arts Administration	M
Clinical Psychology	D
Communication Disorders	M,D
Communication—General	M,D
Computer Education	M
Counseling Psychology	M,D
Counselor Education	M
Curriculum and Instruction	M,D
Developmental Psychology	M,D
Early Childhood Education	M,D
Economics	M,D
Education of Students with Severe/Multiple Disabilities	M
Education of the Gifted	M,D
Education—General	M,D,O
Educational Leadership and Administration	M,D
Educational Measurement and Evaluation	M,D
Educational Media/ Instructional Technology	M,D
Educational Policy	M,D
Educational Psychology	M,D
Elementary Education	M,D,O
English as a Second Language	M,D
English Education	M,D

Foundations and Philosophy of Education M,D
Health Education M,D
Higher Education M,D
History M,D
Industrial and Organizational Psychology M
Interdisciplinary Studies M,D
International and Comparative Education M,D
Kinesiology and Movement Studies M,D
Linguistics M,D
Management of Technology M
Mathematics Education M,D
Multilingual and Multicultural Education M
Music Education M,D
Neuroscience M
Nursing and Healthcare Administration M,D
Nursing Education M,D
Nutrition M,D
Organizational Management M
Physical Education M,D
Physiology M,D
Political Science M,D
Public Health—General M,D
Reading Education M
Rehabilitation Counseling M
School Psychology M,D
Science Education M,D
Social Psychology M
Social Sciences Education M,D
Sociology M,D
Special Education M,D,O
Student Affairs M,D
Urban Education D

TÉLÉ-UNIVERSITÉ

Computer Science M,D
Distance Education Development M,D
Finance and Banking M,D

TELSHE YESHIVA–CHICAGO

Jewish Studies O

TEMPLE BAPTIST SEMINARY

Archaeology P,M,D
Religion P,M,D
Religious Education P,M,D
Theology P,M,D

TEMPLE UNIVERSITY

Accounting M,D
Actuarial Science M
African-American Studies M,D
Allied Health—General M,D
Allopathic Medicine P
Anatomy M,D
Anthropology D
Applied Behavior Analysis M,D
Applied Mathematics M,D
Architecture M
Art Education M
Art History M,D
Art/Fine Arts M
Arts Administration M,D
Biochemistry M,D
Biological and Biomedical Sciences—General M,D
Business Administration and Management—General M,D
Cell Biology M,D
Chemistry M,D
Civil Engineering M
Clinical Psychology M,D
Cognitive Sciences M,D
Communication Disorders M,D
Communication—General M,D
Computational Sciences M,D
Computer Engineering M
Computer Science M,D
Corporate and Organizational Communication M
Counseling Psychology M,D
Criminal Justice and Criminology M,D
Dance M,D
Dentistry P
Developmental Psychology M,D
Early Childhood Education M,D
Economics M,D
Education—General M,D
Educational Leadership and Administration M,D
Educational Psychology M,D
Electrical Engineering M
Elementary Education M,D
Engineering and Applied Sciences—General M,D
English as a Second Language M,D
English Education M,D
English M,D
Entrepreneurship D
Environmental and Occupational Health M,D
Epidemiology M,D
Film, Television, and Video Production M
Finance and Banking M,D
Financial Engineering M
Foreign Languages Education M,D
Genetics M,D
Geography M,D
Geology M
Graphic Design M
Health Education M,D
Health Informatics M
Health Services Management and Hospital Administration M
History M,D
Hospitality Management M,D
Human Resources Management M
Immunology M,D
Industrial and Organizational Psychology M
Information Science M,D
Insurance D
International Business M,D
Journalism M
Kinesiology and Movement Studies M,D
Landscape Architecture M
Law P,M,D
Legal and Justice Studies P,M,D
Leisure Studies M
Liberal Studies M
Linguistics M,D
Management Information Systems D
Management Strategy and Policy D
Marketing M,D
Mass Communication D
Mathematics Education M,D
Mathematics M,D
Mechanical Engineering M
Media Studies M,D
Medicinal and Pharmaceutical Chemistry M,D
Microbiology M,D
Molecular Biology M,D
Music Education M,D
Music M,D
Neuroscience M,D
Nursing—General M
Occupational Therapy M,D
Oral and Dental Sciences M,O
Pathology D
Pharmaceutical Administration M
Pharmaceutical Sciences M
Pharmacology D
Pharmacy P
Philosophy M,D
Photography M
Physical Education M,D
Physical Therapy D
Physics M,D*
Physiology D
Podiatric Medicine P
Political Science M,D
Psychology—General M,D
Public Health—General M,D
Reading Education M,D
Recreation and Park Management M
Religion M,D
School Psychology M,D
Science Education M,D
Social Psychology M,D
Social Work M
Sociology M,D
Spanish M,D
Special Education M,D
Sports Management M,D
Statistics M,D
Taxation P,M,D
Textile Design M
Theater M
Therapies—Dance, Drama, and Music M,D
Travel and Tourism M
Urban and Regional Planning M
Urban Design M,D
Urban Education M,D
Urban Studies M,D
Vocational and Technical Education M,D
Writing M

TENNESSEE STATE UNIVERSITY

Agricultural Sciences—General M
Allied Health—General M,D
Biological and Biomedical Sciences—General M,D
Business Administration and Management—General M
Chemistry M
Communication Disorders M
Counseling Psychology M,D
Counselor Education M,D
Criminal Justice and Criminology M
Curriculum and Instruction M,D
Education—General M,D,O
Educational Leadership and Administration M,D,O
Elementary Education M,D
Engineering and Applied Sciences—General M,D
English M
Exercise and Sports Science M
Family and Consumer Sciences-General M
Family Nurse Practitioner Studies M
Mathematics M
Music Education M
Nursing Informatics M
Nursing—General M
Physical Education M
Physical Therapy M,D
Psychology—General M,D
Public Administration M,D
School Psychology M,D
Special Education M,D

TENNESSEE TECHNOLOGICAL UNIVERSITY

Accounting M
Applied Behavior Analysis D
Biological and Biomedical Sciences—General M,D
Business Administration and Management—General M
Chemical Engineering M,D
Chemistry M,D
Civil Engineering M,D
Computer Science M
Curriculum and Instruction M,O
Early Childhood Education M,O
Education of the Gifted D
Education—General M,D,O
Educational Leadership and Administration M,O
Educational Measurement and Evaluation D
Educational Psychology M,O
Electrical Engineering M,D
Elementary Education M,O
Engineering and Applied Sciences—General M,D
English M
Environmental Sciences D
Family Nurse Practitioner Studies M
Finance and Banking M
Fish, Game, and Wildlife Management M
Health Education M
Human Resources Management M
Insurance M
International Business M
Kinesiology and Movement Studies M
Library Science M
Management Information Systems M
Management Strategy and Policy M
Mathematics M
Mechanical Engineering M,D
Nursing and Healthcare Administration M
Nursing Education M
Nursing Informatics M
Nursing—General M
Physical Education M
Reading Education M,D,O
Secondary Education M,O
Special Education M,O
Student Affairs M,O

TENNESSEE TEMPLE UNIVERSITY

Curriculum and Instruction M
Education—General M
Educational Leadership and Administration M

TEXAS A&M HEALTH SCIENCE CENTER

Biological and Biomedical Sciences—General M,D
Cell Biology D
Dental Hygiene M
Dentistry P
Environmental and Occupational Health M
Epidemiology M
Health Education M
Health Services Management and Hospital Administration M
Immunology D
Materials Sciences M
Microbiology D
Molecular Biology D
Molecular Medicine D
Molecular Pathogenesis D
Neuroscience D
Oral and Dental Sciences P,M,D,O
Public Health—General M
Systems Biology D
Translational Biology D
Virology D

TEXAS A&M INTERNATIONAL UNIVERSITY

Accounting M

*M—master's degree; P—first professional degree; D—doctorate; O—other advanced degree; *—Close-Up and/or Display in one of the other books in this series*

Biological and Biomedical Sciences—General	M
Business Administration and Management—General	M
Counseling Psychology	M
Counselor Education	M
Criminal Justice and Criminology	M
Curriculum and Instruction	M
Early Childhood Education	M
Education—General	M
Educational Leadership and Administration	M
English	M,D
Family Nurse Practitioner Studies	M
Finance and Banking	M
Foreign Languages Education	M,D
Hispanic Studies	M,D
History	M
International Business	M
Management Information Systems	M
Mathematics	M
Nursing—General	M
Political Science	M
Psychology—General	M
Public Administration	M
Reading Education	M
Social Sciences	M
Sociology	M
Spanish	M,D
Special Education	M

TEXAS A&M UNIVERSITY

Accounting	M,D
Adult Education	M,D
Aerospace/Aeronautical Engineering	M,D
Agricultural Economics and Agribusiness	M,D
Agricultural Education	M,D
Agricultural Engineering	M,D
Agricultural Sciences—General	M,D
Agronomy and Soil Sciences	M,D
Animal Sciences	M,D
Anthropology	M,D
Applied Physics	M,D
Architecture	M,D
Art/Fine Arts	M,D
Asian Studies	M,O
Biochemistry	M,D
Bioengineering	M,D
Biological and Biomedical Sciences—General	M,D
Biomedical Engineering	M,D
Biophysics	M,D
Biopsychology	D
Botany	M,D
Business Administration and Management—General	M,D
Cell Biology	M,D
Chemical Engineering	M,D
Chemistry	M,D
Civil Engineering	M,D
Clinical Psychology	D
Cognitive Sciences	D
Communication—General	M,D
Computer Engineering	M,D
Computer Science	M,D
Construction Engineering	M,D
Construction Management	M,D
Counseling Psychology	M,D
Cultural Studies	M,D
Curriculum and Instruction	M,D
Developmental Psychology	D
Economics	M,D
Education—General	M,D
Educational Leadership and Administration	M,D
Educational Measurement and Evaluation	M,D
Educational Media/Instructional Technology	M,D
Educational Psychology	M,D
Electrical Engineering	M,D
Engineering and Applied Sciences—General	M,D
English as a Second Language	M,D
English Education	M,D
English	M,D
Entomology	M,D
Environmental Engineering	M,D
Epidemiology	M
Finance and Banking	M,D
Fish, Game, and Wildlife Management	M,D
Food Science and Technology	M,D
Forestry	M,D
Genetics	M,D
Geography	M,D
Geology	M,D
Geophysics	M,D
Geotechnical Engineering	M,D
Health Education	M,D
Health Physics/Radiological Health	M,D
Higher Education	M,D
History	M,D
Homeland Security	M,O
Horticulture	M,D
Human Development	M,D
Human Resources Development	M,D
Human Resources Management	M,D
Industrial and Manufacturing Management	M,D
Industrial and Organizational Psychology	D
Industrial/Management Engineering	M,D
International Affairs	M,O
Journalism	M
Kinesiology and Movement Studies	M,D
Landscape Architecture	M,D
Management Information Systems	M,D
Manufacturing Engineering	M
Marketing	M,D
Materials Engineering	M,D
Mathematics Education	M,D
Mathematics	M,D
Mechanical Engineering	M,D
Meteorology	M,D
Microbiology	M,D
Multilingual and Multicultural Education	M,D
National Security	M,O
Natural Resources	M,D
Neuroscience	M,D
Nonprofit Management	M,O
Nuclear Engineering	M,D
Nutrition	M,D
Ocean Engineering	M,D
Oceanography	M,D
Parasitology	M,D
Pathobiology	M,D
Pathology	M,D
Petroleum Engineering	M,D
Philosophy	M,D
Physical Education	M,D
Physics	M,D
Physiology	M,D
Plant Biology	M,D
Plant Pathology	M,D
Plant Sciences	M,D
Political Science	D
Psychology—General	D
Public Administration	M,O
Public Affairs	M,O
Public Health—General	M
Range Science	M,D
Reading Education	M,D
Real Estate	M
Recreation and Park Management	M,D
School Psychology	M,D
Science Education	M,D
Social Psychology	D
Sociology	M,D
Spanish	M,D
Special Education	M,D
Sports Management	M,D
Statistics	M,D
Structural Engineering	M,D
Toxicology	M,D
Transportation and Highway Engineering	M,D
Urban and Regional Planning	M,D
Urban Education	M,D
Veterinary Medicine	P,M
Veterinary Sciences	M
Water Resources Engineering	M,D
Zoology	M,D

TEXAS A&M UNIVERSITY AT GALVESTON

Marine Biology	M,D
Marine Sciences	M

TEXAS A&M UNIVERSITY–COMMERCE

Agricultural Education	M
Agricultural Sciences—General	M
Art History	M
Art/Fine Arts	M
Biological and Biomedical Sciences—General	M
Business Administration and Management—General	M
Chemistry	M
Cognitive Sciences	M,D
Computer Science	M
Counseling Psychology	M,D
Counselor Education	M,D
Curriculum and Instruction	M,D
Early Childhood Education	M,D
Economics	M
Education—General	M,D
Educational Leadership and Administration	M,D
Educational Media/Instructional Technology	M,D
Elementary Education	M,D
English as a Second Language	M,D
English Education	M,D
English	M,D
Exercise and Sports Science	M,D
Geosciences	M
Health Education	M,D
Health Promotion	M,D
Higher Education	M,D
History	M
Industrial/Management Engineering	M
Kinesiology and Movement Studies	M,D
Management of Technology	M
Mathematics	M
Multilingual and Multicultural Education	M,D
Music Education	M
Music	M
Physical Education	M,D
Physics	M
Psychology—General	M,D
Reading Education	M,D
Secondary Education	M,D
Social Sciences Education	M
Social Sciences	M
Social Work	M
Sociology	M
Spanish	M,D
Special Education	M,D
Speech and Interpersonal Communication	M
Theater	M

TEXAS A&M UNIVERSITY–CORPUS CHRISTI

Accounting	M
Applied Mathematics	M
Aquaculture	M
Art/Fine Arts	M
Biological and Biomedical Sciences—General	M
Business Administration and Management—General	M
Computer Science	M
Counselor Education	M,D
Curriculum and Instruction	M,D
Early Childhood Education	M,D
Education—General	M,D
Educational Leadership and Administration	M,D
Educational Media/Instructional Technology	M,D
Elementary Education	M
English	M
Environmental Sciences	M
Family Nurse Practitioner Studies	M
Health Services Management and Hospital Administration	M
History	M
International Business	M
Kinesiology and Movement Studies	M,D
Marine Sciences	D
Mathematics Education	M
Mathematics	M
Nursing and Healthcare Administration	M
Nursing—General	M
Psychology—General	M
Public Administration	M
Reading Education	M,D
Secondary Education	M
Special Education	M

TEXAS A&M UNIVERSITY–KINGSVILLE

Adult Education	M
Agricultural Economics and Agribusiness	M
Agricultural Education	M
Agricultural Sciences—General	M,D
Agronomy and Soil Sciences	M,D
Animal Sciences	M
Art/Fine Arts	M
Biological and Biomedical Sciences—General	M
Business Administration and Management—General	M
Chemical Engineering	M
Chemistry	M
Civil Engineering	M
Communication Disorders	M
Computer Science	M
Counselor Education	M
Early Childhood Education	M
Education—General	M,D
Educational Leadership and Administration	M,D
Electrical Engineering	M
Elementary Education	M
Engineering and Applied Sciences—General	M,D
English as a Second Language	M
English	M
Environmental Engineering	M,D
Family and Consumer Sciences-General	M
Fish, Game, and Wildlife Management	M,D

Foreign Languages Education M
Geology M
Gerontology M
Health Education M
Higher Education D
History M
Industrial/Management Engineering M
Kinesiology and Movement Studies M
Mathematics M
Mechanical Engineering M
Multilingual and Multicultural Education M,D
Music Education M
Petroleum Engineering M
Plant Sciences M,D
Political Science M
Psychology—General M
Range Science M
Reading Education M
Secondary Education M
Sociology M
Spanish M
Special Education M

TEXAS A&M UNIVERSITY–SAN ANTONIO

Business Administration and Management—General M
Computer and Information Systems Security M
Counselor Education M
Early Childhood Education M
Educational Leadership and Administration M
Educational Measurement and Evaluation M
English M
Finance and Banking M
Health Services Management and Hospital Administration M
Human Resources Management M
International Business M
Kinesiology and Movement Studies M
Management Information Systems M
Multilingual and Multicultural Education M
Project Management M
Reading Education M
Special Education M
Supply Chain Management M

TEXAS A&M UNIVERSITY–TEXARKANA

Accounting M
Adult Education M
Business Administration and Management—General M
Counseling Psychology M
Curriculum and Instruction M
Education—General M
Educational Leadership and Administration M
Educational Media/Instructional Technology M
English M
Interdisciplinary Studies M
Psychology—General M
Special Education M

TEXAS CHIROPRACTIC COLLEGE

Chiropractic P

TEXAS CHRISTIAN UNIVERSITY

Accounting M
Adult Nursing M,D
Advertising and Public Relations M
Allied Health—General M,D
Art History M
Art/Fine Arts M
Astrophysics M,D
Biochemistry M,D
Biological and Biomedical Sciences—General M
Business Administration and Management—General M,D
Chemistry M,D
Cognitive Sciences M,D
Communication Disorders M
Counselor Education M,O
Curriculum and Instruction M
Education—General M,D,O
Educational Leadership and Administration M,D,O
Educational Psychology M,D,O
Elementary Education M
English M,D
Environmental Sciences M
Experimental Psychology M,D
Geology M
Gerontological Nursing M,D
History M,D
Inorganic Chemistry M,D
International Business M
Journalism M
Kinesiology and Movement Studies M
Liberal Studies M
Mathematics M,D
Middle School Education M
Music Education M,D,O
Music M,D,O
Neuroscience M,D
Nurse Anesthesia M,D
Nursing and Healthcare Administration M,D
Nursing Education M,D
Nursing—General M,D
Organic Chemistry M,D
Pediatric Nursing M,D
Physical Chemistry M,D
Physics M,D
Psychology—General M,D
Rhetoric M,D
Science Education M
Secondary Education M
Social Psychology M,D
Special Education M
Speech and Interpersonal Communication M

TEXAS COLLEGE OF TRADITIONAL CHINESE MEDICINE

Acupuncture and Oriental Medicine M

TEXAS SOUTHERN UNIVERSITY

Art/Fine Arts M
Biological and Biomedical Sciences—General M
Business Administration and Management—General M
Chemistry M
Communication—General M
Computer Science M
Counselor Education M,D
Criminal Justice and Criminology M,D
Curriculum and Instruction M,D
Education—General M,D
Educational Leadership and Administration M,D
English M
Environmental Management and Policy M,D
Family and Consumer Sciences-General M
Health Education M
Higher Education M,D
History M
Human Services M
Industrial/Management Engineering M
Law P
Management Information Systems M
Mathematics M
Multilingual and Multicultural Education M,D
Music M
Pharmacy P,M,D
Physical Education M
Psychology—General M
Public Administration M
Secondary Education M,D
Sociology M
Toxicology M,D
Transportation and Highway Engineering M
Transportation Management M
Urban and Regional Planning M,D

TEXAS STATE UNIVERSITY–SAN MARCOS

Accounting M
Adult Education M,D
Agricultural Education M
Allied Health—General M,D
Anthropology M
Applied Mathematics M
Athletic Training and Sports Medicine M
Biochemistry M
Biological and Biomedical Sciences—General M
Business Administration and Management—General M
Chemistry M
Child and Family Studies M
Communication Disorders M
Communication—General M
Computer Art and Design M
Computer Science M
Conservation Biology M
Counselor Education M
Criminal Justice and Criminology M,D
Developmental Education M,D
Early Childhood Education M
Education—General M,D,O
Educational Leadership and Administration M
Elementary Education M
English M
Environmental Management and Policy M
Fish, Game, and Wildlife Management M
Geographic Information Systems M,D
Geography M,D
Graphic Design M
Health Education M
Health Psychology M
Health Services Management and Hospital Administration M
Health Services Research M
History M
Industrial/Management Engineering M
Interdisciplinary Studies M
International Affairs M
Legal and Justice Studies M
Leisure Studies M
Management Information Systems M
Management of Technology M
Marine Biology M,D
Mass Communication M
Materials Sciences D
Mathematics Education M,D
Mathematics M,D
Multilingual and Multicultural Education M
Music Education M
Music M
Nutrition M
Physical Education M
Physical Therapy D
Physics M
Political Science M
Psychology—General M
Public Administration M
Reading Education M
Recreation and Park Management M
Rhetoric M
School Psychology O
Science Education M
Secondary Education M
Social Sciences Education D
Social Work M
Sociology M
Software Engineering M
Spanish M
Special Education M
Technical Communication M
Theater M
Vocational and Technical Education M
Writing M

TEXAS TECH UNIVERSITY

Accounting M,D
Agricultural Economics and Agribusiness M,D
Agricultural Education M,D
Agricultural Sciences—General M,D
Agronomy and Soil Sciences M,D
Animal Sciences M,D
Anthropology M
Applied Economics M,D
Applied Physics M,D
Architecture M
Art Education M
Art History M
Art/Fine Arts M,D
Atmospheric Sciences M,D
Biological and Biomedical Sciences—General M,D
Biotechnology M
Business Administration and Management—General M,D
Chemical Engineering M,D
Chemistry M,D
Child and Family Studies M,D
Civil Engineering M,D
Classics M
Clinical Psychology M,D
Communication—General M
Computer Science M,D
Consumer Economics M,D
Counseling Psychology M,D
Counselor Education M,D
Curriculum and Instruction M,D
Dance D
Economics M,D
Education—General M,D
Educational Leadership and Administration M,D
Educational Media/Instructional Technology M,D
Educational Psychology M,D
Electrical Engineering M,D
Elementary Education M,D
Engineering and Applied Sciences—General M,D
Engineering Management M,D
English Education M,D
English M,D
Entrepreneurship M
Environmental Design M,D
Environmental Engineering M,D
Environmental Management and Policy D
Environmental Sciences M,D
Exercise and Sports Science M
Experimental Psychology M,D

*M—master's degree; P—first professional degree; D—doctorate; O—other advanced degree; *—Close-Up and/or Display in one of the other books in this series*

Program	Degrees
Family and Consumer Sciences-General	M,D
Finance and Banking	M,D
Fish, Game, and Wildlife Management	M,D
Food Science and Technology	M,D
French	M
Geosciences	M,D
German	M
Gerontology	M,D
Health Services Management and Hospital Administration	M,D
Higher Education	M,D
Historic Preservation	M
History	M,D
Home Economics Education	M,D
Horticulture	M,D
Hospitality Management	M,D
Human Development	M,D
Humanities	M,D
Industrial and Manufacturing Management	M,D
Industrial/Management Engineering	M,D
Interdisciplinary Studies	M
Interior Design	M,D*
International Business	M
Landscape Architecture	M
Law	P
Linguistics	M
Management Information Systems	M,D
Manufacturing Engineering	M,D
Marketing	M,D
Marriage and Family Therapy	M,D
Mass Communication	M,D
Mathematics	M,D
Mechanical Engineering	M,D
Microbiology	M,D
Multilingual and Multicultural Education	M,D
Museum Studies	M
Music Education	M,D
Music	M,D
Natural Resources	M,D
Nutrition	M,D
Petroleum Engineering	M,D
Philosophy	M
Physics	M,D
Plant Sciences	M,D
Political Science	M,D
Psychology—General	M,D
Quantitative Analysis	M,D
Range Science	M,D
Reading Education	M,D
Real Estate	M
Rhetoric	M,D
Romance Languages	M,D
Secondary Education	M,D
Sociology	M
Software Engineering	M,D
Spanish	M,D
Special Education	M,D
Statistics	M,D
Systems Engineering	M,D
Taxation	M,D
Technical Writing	M,D
Theater	M,D
Toxicology	M,D
Zoology	M,D

TEXAS TECH UNIVERSITY HEALTH SCIENCES CENTER

Program	Degrees
Acute Care/Critical Care Nursing	M,D,O
Allied Health—General	M,D
Allopathic Medicine	P
Athletic Training and Sports Medicine	M
Biochemistry	M,D
Biological and Biomedical Sciences—General	M,D
Biotechnology	M
Cell Biology	M,D
Communication Disorders	M,D
Family Nurse Practitioner Studies	M,D,O
Gerontological Nursing	M,D,O
Health Services Management and Hospital Administration	M
Medical Microbiology	M,D
Molecular Biophysics	M,D
Molecular Genetics	M,D
Molecular Pathology	M
Molecular Physiology	M,D
Neuroscience	M,D
Nursing and Healthcare Administration	M,D,O
Nursing Education	M,D,O
Nursing—General	M,D,O
Occupational Therapy	M
Pediatric Nursing	M,D,O
Pharmaceutical Sciences	M,D
Pharmacology	M,D
Physical Therapy	D
Physician Assistant Studies	M
Rehabilitation Counseling	M
Rehabilitation Sciences	D

TEXAS WESLEYAN UNIVERSITY

Program	Degrees
Business Administration and Management—General	M
Counseling Psychology	M,D
Counselor Education	M,D
Education—General	M,D
Health Services Management and Hospital Administration	M
Law	P
Marriage and Family Therapy	M,D
Nurse Anesthesia	M,D

TEXAS WOMAN'S UNIVERSITY

Program	Degrees
Acute Care/Critical Care Nursing	M,D
Adult Nursing	M,D
Allied Health—General	M,D
Art/Fine Arts	M
Biological and Biomedical Sciences—General	M,D
Business Administration and Management—General	M
Chemistry	M
Child and Family Studies	M,D
Child Development	M,D
Communication Disorders	M
Counseling Psychology	M,D,O
Counselor Education	M,D
Curriculum and Instruction	M,D
Dance	M,D
Early Childhood Education	M,D
Education—General	M,D
Educational Leadership and Administration	M,D
English	M,D
Exercise and Sports Science	M,D
Family Nurse Practitioner Studies	M,D
Food Science and Technology	M,D
Health Education	M,D
Health Services Management and Hospital Administration	M,D
History	M
Kinesiology and Movement Studies	M,D
Library Science	M,D
Marriage and Family Therapy	M,D
Mathematics Education	M
Mathematics	M
Molecular Biology	M,D
Music	M
Nursing and Healthcare Administration	M,D
Nursing Education	M,D
Nursing—General	M,D
Nutrition	M,D
Occupational Therapy	M,D
Pediatric Nursing	M,D
Physical Education	M,D
Physical Therapy	D
Political Science	M
Psychology—General	M,D,O
Reading Education	M,D
Rhetoric	M,D
School Psychology	M,D,O
Sociology	M,D
Special Education	M,D
Sports Management	M,D
Theater	M
Women's Health Nursing	M,D
Women's Studies	M,D

THOMAS COLLEGE

Program	Degrees
Business Administration and Management—General	M
Business Education	M
Computer Education	M
Human Resources Management	M

THOMAS EDISON STATE COLLEGE

Program	Degrees
Applied Science and Technology	O
Business Administration and Management—General	M
Distance Education Development	O
Educational Leadership and Administration	M
Educational Media/Instructional Technology	O
Epidemiology	O
Homeland Security	O
Human Resources Management	M,O
Liberal Studies	M
Nursing Education	O
Nursing—General	M
Organizational Management	O
Public Administration	O

THOMAS JEFFERSON SCHOOL OF LAW

Program	Degrees
Finance and Banking	M
International Business	M
Investment Management	M
Law	P,M
Legal and Justice Studies	M
Taxation	M

THOMAS JEFFERSON UNIVERSITY

Program	Degrees
Allopathic Medicine	P
Biochemistry	D
Biological and Biomedical Sciences—General	M,D,O
Biomedical Engineering	D
Biophysics	D
Biotechnology	D
Cell Biology	M,D
Clinical Laboratory Sciences/Medical Technology	M
Clinical Research	O
Developmental Biology	M,D
Epidemiology	M,D,O
Genetics	D
Health Education	M,D,O
Health Services Management and Hospital Administration	M,D,O
Health Services Research	M,D,O
Immunology	D
Marriage and Family Therapy	M
Microbiology	M,D
Molecular Biology	D
Molecular Pharmacology	D
Molecular Physiology	D
Neuroscience	D
Nursing—General	M
Occupational Therapy	M
Pharmacology	M
Pharmacy	P
Physical Therapy	M,D
Public Health—General	M,O
Structural Biology	D

THOMAS M. COOLEY LAW SCHOOL

Program	Degrees
Insurance	P,M
Law	P,M
Taxation	P,M

THOMAS MORE COLLEGE

Program	Degrees
Business Administration and Management—General	M
Education—General	M

THOMAS UNIVERSITY

Program	Degrees
Business Administration and Management—General	M
Education—General	M
Human Services	M
Nursing—General	M
Rehabilitation Counseling	M
Social Psychology	M

THOMPSON RIVERS UNIVERSITY

Program	Degrees
Business Administration and Management—General	M
Education—General	M
Environmental Sciences	M
Social Work	M

THUNDERBIRD SCHOOL OF GLOBAL MANAGEMENT

Program	Degrees
Business Administration and Management—General	M
International Business	M

TIFFIN UNIVERSITY

Program	Degrees
Business Administration and Management—General	M
Criminal Justice and Criminology	M
Finance and Banking	M
Forensic Psychology	M
Health Services Management and Hospital Administration	M
Homeland Security	M
Human Resources Management	M
Humanities	M
International Business	M
Marketing	M
Sports Management	M

TORONTO SCHOOL OF THEOLOGY

Program	Degrees
Theology	P,M,D

TOURO COLLEGE

Program	Degrees
Acupuncture and Oriental Medicine	M,D
Communication Disorders	M,D
Jewish Studies	M
Law	P,M
Occupational Therapy	M
Physical Therapy	M,D
Public Health—General	M,D

TOURO UNIVERSITY

Education—General	P,M
Osteopathic Medicine	P,M
Pharmacy	P,M
Physician Assistant Studies	P,M
Public Health—General	P,M

TOWSON UNIVERSITY

Accounting	M
Advertising and Public Relations	O
Allied Health—General	M
Applied Mathematics	M
Applied Physics	M
Art Education	M,O
Art/Fine Arts	M
Biological and Biomedical Sciences—General	M
Child and Family Studies	M,O
Clinical Psychology	M
Communication Disorders	M,D
Communication—General	M,O
Computer and Information Systems Security	M,D,O
Computer Science	M
Corporate and Organizational Communication	M
Counseling Psychology	O
Database Systems	M,D,O
Early Childhood Education	M,O
Education—General	M
Educational Media/ Instructional Technology	M,D
Elementary Education	M
Environmental and Occupational Health	D
Environmental Management and Policy	M
Environmental Sciences	M,O
Forensic Sciences	M
Geography	M
Gerontology	M,O
Health Services Management and Hospital Administration	O
Homeland Security	M,O
Human Resources Development	M
Humanities	M
Information Science	M,D,O
Internet and Interactive Multimedia	M,D,O
Jewish Studies	M,D,O
Kinesiology and Movement Studies	M
Liberal Studies	M
Management Information Systems	M,D,O
Management Strategy and Policy	O
Mathematics Education	M
Music Education	M,O
Music	M
Nursing Education	M,O
Nursing—General	M,O
Occupational Therapy	M
Organizational Behavior	O
Physician Assistant Studies	M
Reading Education	M,O
Religious Education	M,D,O
School Psychology	O
Science Education	M
Secondary Education	M
Social Sciences	M
Software Engineering	M,D,O
Special Education	M,O
Theater	M
Women's Studies	M,O
Writing	M

TOYOTA TECHNOLOGICAL INSTITUTE OF CHICAGO

Computer Science	D

TRADITIONAL CHINESE MEDICAL COLLEGE OF HAWAII

Acupuncture and Oriental Medicine	M

TRENT UNIVERSITY

American Indian/Native American Studies	M,D
Anthropology	M
Biological and Biomedical Sciences—General	M,D
Canadian Studies	M,D
Chemistry	M
Computer Science	M
Cultural Studies	D
Environmental Management and Policy	M,D
Geography	M,D
Materials Sciences	M
Modeling and Simulation	M,D
Physics	M

TREVECCA NAZARENE UNIVERSITY

Business Administration and Management—General	M
Counseling Psychology	M
Counselor Education	M,D
Curriculum and Instruction	M
Education—General	M,D
Educational Leadership and Administration	M,D
Educational Media/ Instructional Technology	M
Elementary Education	M
English as a Second Language	M
Information Science	M
Library Science	M
Management of Technology	M
Marriage and Family Therapy	M
Organizational Management	M
Physician Assistant Studies	M
Psychology—General	M,D
Reading Education	M
Religion	M
Secondary Education	M
Theology	M
Vocational and Technical Education	M

TRINE UNIVERSITY

Civil Engineering	M
Criminal Justice and Criminology	M
Engineering and Applied Sciences—General	M
Mechanical Engineering	M

TRINITY BAPTIST COLLEGE

Educational Leadership and Administration	M
Pastoral Ministry and Counseling	M
Special Education	M

TRINITY COLLEGE

American Studies	M
Economics	M
English	M
Public Policy	M

TRINITY INTERNATIONAL UNIVERSITY

Archaeology	P,M,D,O
Bioethics	M
Business Administration and Management—General	P,M,D,O
Communication—General	M
Counseling Psychology	P,M,D,O
Education—General	M
Educational Leadership and Administration	M
Law	P
Missions and Missiology	P,M,D,O
Pastoral Ministry and Counseling	P,M,D,O
Religious Education	P,M,D,O
Theology	P,M,D,O

TRINITY INTERNATIONAL UNIVERSITY, SOUTH FLORIDA CAMPUS

Counseling Psychology	M
Religion	M,O

TRINITY LUTHERAN SEMINARY

Music	P,M
Pastoral Ministry and Counseling	P,M
Religious Education	P,M
Theology	P,M

TRINITY SCHOOL FOR MINISTRY

Missions and Missiology	P,M,D,O
Pastoral Ministry and Counseling	P,M,D,O
Religion	P,M,D,O
Theology	P,M,D,O

TRINITY UNIVERSITY

Accounting	M
Business Administration and Management—General	M
Education—General	M
Educational Leadership and Administration	M
Health Services Management and Hospital Administration	M
School Psychology	M

TRINITY (WASHINGTON) UNIVERSITY

Business Administration and Management—General	M
Communication—General	M
Counselor Education	M
Curriculum and Instruction	M
Early Childhood Education	M
Education—General	M
Educational Leadership and Administration	M
Elementary Education	M
English as a Second Language	M
English Education	M
Human Resources Management	M
National Security	M
Nonprofit Management	M
Organizational Management	M
Public Health—General	M
Reading Education	M
Secondary Education	M
Social Sciences Education	M
Special Education	M

TRINITY WESTERN UNIVERSITY

Business Administration and Management—General	M
Counseling Psychology	M
Educational Leadership and Administration	M,O
English as a Second Language	M
English	M
Health Services Management and Hospital Administration	M,O
History	M
Humanities	M
Interdisciplinary Studies	M
International Business	M
Linguistics	M
Nonprofit Management	M,O
Nursing—General	M
Organizational Management	M,O
Pastoral Ministry and Counseling	P,M,D
Philosophy	M
Theology	P,M,D

TRI-STATE COLLEGE OF ACUPUNCTURE

Acupuncture and Oriental Medicine	M,O

TROPICAL AGRICULTURE RESEARCH AND HIGHER EDUCATION CENTER

Agricultural Economics and Agribusiness	M,D
Agricultural Sciences—General	M,D
Conservation Biology	M,D
Environmental Management and Policy	M,D
Forestry	M,D
Travel and Tourism	M,D
Water Resources	M,D

TROY UNIVERSITY

Accounting	M
Addictions/Substance Abuse Counseling	M,O
Adult Education	M
Adult Nursing	M,D,O
Art Education	M
Business Administration and Management—General	M
Clinical Psychology	M,O
Computer Education	M
Computer Science	M
Counselor Education	M,O
Criminal Justice and Criminology	M,O
Early Childhood Education	M,O
Economic Development	M
Education of the Gifted	M
Education—General	M,O
Educational Leadership and Administration	M,O
Educational Media/ Instructional Technology	M
Elementary Education	M,O
English Education	M
Environmental Management and Policy	M
Exercise and Sports Science	M
Family Nurse Practitioner Studies	M,D,O
Finance and Banking	M
Foundations and Philosophy of Education	M
Health Services Management and Hospital Administration	M
Higher Education	M
History	M
Hospitality Management	M
Human Resources Management	M
International Affairs	M
International Business	M
Management Information Systems	M
Maternal and Child Health	M,D,O
Mathematics Education	M
Music Education	M
Music	M
National Security	M
Nonprofit Management	M
Nursing Informatics	M,D,O
Nursing—General	M,D,O

*M—master's degree; P—first professional degree; D—doctorate; O—other advanced degree; *—Close-Up and/or Display in one of the other books in this series*

Organizational Management	M
Physical Education	M
Political Science	M
Public Administration	M
Reading Education	M
Rehabilitation Counseling	M,O
School Psychology	M,O
Science Education	M
Secondary Education	M
Social Psychology	M,O
Social Sciences Education	M
Social Work	M,O
Sports Management	M
Taxation	M,O

TRUMAN STATE UNIVERSITY

Accounting	M
Biological and Biomedical Sciences—General	M
Communication Disorders	M
Education—General	M
English	M
Music	M

TUFTS UNIVERSITY

Allopathic Medicine	P
Analytical Chemistry	M,D
Animal Sciences	M
Archaeology	M
Art History	M
Art/Fine Arts	M
Biochemistry	D
Bioengineering	M,D,O
Biological and Biomedical Sciences—General	P,M,D
Biomedical Engineering	M,D
Biostatistics	M,D
Biotechnology	O
Cell Biology	D
Chemical Engineering	M,D
Chemistry	M,D
Child and Family Studies	M,D,O
Child Development	M,D,O
Civil Engineering	M,D
Classics	M
Clinical Research	M,D
Computer Science	M,D,O
Conflict Resolution and Mediation/Peace Studies	M,D
Dentistry	P
Developmental Biology	D
Early Childhood Education	M,D,O
Economics	M
Education—General	M,D,O
Electrical Engineering	M,D,O
Engineering and Applied Sciences—General	M,D
Engineering Management	M
English	M,D
Environmental and Occupational Health	M,D
Environmental Engineering	M,D
Environmental Management and Policy	M,D,O
Environmental Sciences	M,D
Epidemiology	M,D,O
Ergonomics and Human Factors	M,D
Family and Consumer Sciences-General	M,D,O
French	M
Genetics	D
Geotechnical Engineering	M,D
German	M
Hazardous Materials Management	M,D
Health Communication	M
History	M,D
Human-Computer Interaction	O
Immunology	D
Inorganic Chemistry	M,D
International Affairs	M,D
International Business	M,D
International Development	M,D
International Health	M,D
Law	M,D
Management Strategy and Policy	O
Manufacturing Engineering	O
Mathematics	M,D
Mechanical Engineering	M,D
Microbiology	D
Middle School Education	M,D
Molecular Biology	D
Molecular Physiology	D
Museum Studies	O
Music	M
Neuroscience	D
Nonprofit Management	O
Nutrition	M,D
Occupational Therapy	M,D,O
Oral and Dental Sciences	M,O
Organic Chemistry	M,D
Pharmacology	D
Philosophy	M
Physical Chemistry	M,D
Physics	M,D
Physiology	D
Psychology—General	M,D
Public Administration	O
Public Health—General	M
Public Policy	M
School Psychology	M,O
Secondary Education	M,D
Structural Engineering	M,D
Theater	M,D
Urban and Regional Planning	M
Urban Studies	M
Veterinary Medicine	P,M,D
Water Resources Engineering	M,D

TUI UNIVERSITY

Adult Education	M
Business Administration and Management—General	M,D
Clinical Research	M,D,O
Computer and Information Systems Security	M,D
Conflict Resolution and Mediation/Peace Studies	M,D
Criminal Justice and Criminology	M,D
Early Childhood Education	M
Education—General	M,D
Educational Leadership and Administration	M,D
Educational Media/ Instructional Technology	M,D
Emergency Management	M,D,O
Environmental and Occupational Health	M,D,O
Finance and Banking	M,D
Health Education	M,D,O
Health Informatics	M,D,O
Health Services Management and Hospital Administration	M,D,O
Higher Education	M,D
Human Resources Management	M,D
International Business	M,D
International Health	M,D,O
Legal and Justice Studies	M,D,O
Logistics	M,D
Management Information Systems	M,D,O
Marketing	M,D
Nursing and Healthcare Administration	M,D,O
Project Management	M,D
Public Administration	M,D
Public Health—General	M,D,O
Quality Management	M,D,O
Reading Education	M

TULANE UNIVERSITY

Allopathic Medicine	P
Anthropology	M,D
Applied Mathematics	M,D
Architecture	M
Art History	M
Art/Fine Arts	M
Biochemistry	M,D
Biological and Biomedical Sciences—General	M,D
Biomedical Engineering	M,D
Biostatistics	M,D
Business Administration and Management—General	M,D
Cell Biology	M,D
Chemical Engineering	D
Chemistry	M,D
Classics	M
Dance	M
Ecology	M,D
Economics	M,D
English	M,D
Environmental and Occupational Health	M,D
Epidemiology	M,D
Evolutionary Biology	M,D
French	M,D
Health Communication	M
Health Education	M
Health Services Management and Hospital Administration	M,D
History	M,D
Human Genetics	M,D
Immunology	M,D
Infectious Diseases	M,D,O
Interdisciplinary Studies	D
International Development	M,D
International Health	M,D
Latin American Studies	M,D*
Law	P,M,D
Liberal Studies	M
Maternal and Child Health	M,D
Mathematics	M,D
Microbiology	M,D
Molecular Biology	M,D
Music	M
Neuroscience	M,D
Nutrition	M
Parasitology	M,D,O
Pharmacology	M,D
Philosophy	M,D
Physics	D
Physiology	M,D
Political Science	M,D
Portuguese	M,D
Psychology—General	M,D
Public Health—General	M,D,O
Social Work	M
Sociology	M,D
Spanish	M,D
Statistics	M,D
Structural Biology	M,D
Theater	M

TUSCULUM COLLEGE

Adult Education	M
Education—General	M
Organizational Management	M

TUSKEGEE UNIVERSITY

Agricultural Economics and Agribusiness	M
Agronomy and Soil Sciences	M
Animal Sciences	M
Biological and Biomedical Sciences—General	M,D
Chemistry	M
Electrical Engineering	M
Engineering and Applied Sciences—General	M,D
Environmental Sciences	M
Food Science and Technology	M
Materials Engineering	D
Mechanical Engineering	M
Nutrition	M
Plant Sciences	M
Veterinary Medicine	P,M
Veterinary Sciences	P,M

TYNDALE UNIVERSITY COLLEGE & SEMINARY

Missions and Missiology	P,M,O
Pastoral Ministry and Counseling	P,M,O
Theology	P,M,O

UNIFICATION THEOLOGICAL SEMINARY

Pastoral Ministry and Counseling	P,M,D
Religion	P,M,D
Religious Education	P,M,D
Theology	P,M,D

UNIFORMED SERVICES UNIVERSITY OF THE HEALTH SCIENCES

Biological and Biomedical Sciences—General	M,D
Cell Biology	D
Clinical Psychology	D
Environmental and Occupational Health	M,D
Family Nurse Practitioner Studies	M
Immunology	D
Infectious Diseases	D*
International Health	M,D
Medical/Surgical Nursing	M
Molecular Biology	D*
Neuroscience	D*
Nurse Anesthesia	M
Nursing—General	M
Psychiatric Nursing	M
Psychology—General	D
Public Health—General	M,D
Zoology	M,D

UNION COLLEGE (KY)

Clinical Psychology	M
Counseling Psychology	M
Education—General	M
Educational Leadership and Administration	M
Elementary Education	M
Health Education	M
Middle School Education	M
Music Education	M
Physical Education	M
Psychology—General	M
Reading Education	M
School Psychology	M
Secondary Education	M
Special Education	M

UNION COLLEGE (NE)

Physician Assistant Studies	M

UNION GRADUATE COLLEGE

Bioethics	M,O
Business Administration and Management—General	M,O
Chinese	M,O
Classics	M,O
Computer Science	M
Education—General	M,O
Educational Leadership and Administration	M,O
Electrical Engineering	M
Engineering and Applied Sciences—General	M
Engineering Management	M
English Education	M,O
Finance and Banking	M,O
Foreign Languages Education	M,O
Health Law	M,O
Health Services Management and Hospital Administration	M,O
Human Resources Management	M,O
Mathematics Education	M,O

Mechanical Engineering M
Middle School Education M,O
Science Education M,O
Social Sciences Education M,O

UNION INSTITUTE & UNIVERSITY

Adult Education M,D,O
Clinical Psychology M,D,O
Counseling Psychology M,D,O
Counselor Education M,D,O
Cultural Studies M
Curriculum and Instruction M,D,O
Developmental Psychology M,D,O
Education—General M,D,O
Educational Leadership and Administration M,D,O
Educational Psychology M,D,O
Ethics D
Health Promotion M,D,O
Higher Education M,D,O
History M
Human Development M,D,O
Humanities D
Industrial and Organizational Psychology M,D,O
Interdisciplinary Studies M,D
Psychology—General M,D,O
Public Policy M,D
Reading Education M,D,O
Writing M

UNION PRESBYTERIAN SEMINARY

Religious Education P,M,D

UNION THEOLOGICAL SEMINARY IN THE CITY OF NEW YORK

Theology P,M,D

UNION UNIVERSITY

Business Administration and Management—General M
Cultural Studies M
Education—General M,D,O
Educational Leadership and Administration M,D,O
Family Nurse Practitioner Studies M,D,O
Higher Education M,D,O
Nurse Anesthesia M,D,O
Nursing and Healthcare Administration M,D,O
Nursing Education M,D,O
Nursing—General M,D,O
Pastoral Ministry and Counseling M,D
Religion M,D

UNITED STATES ARMY COMMAND AND GENERAL STAFF COLLEGE

Military and Defense Studies M

UNITED STATES INTERNATIONAL UNIVERSITY

Addictions/Substance Abuse Counseling M
Business Administration and Management—General M
Conflict Resolution and Mediation/Peace Studies M
Counseling Psychology M
Entrepreneurship M
Finance and Banking M
Health Psychology M
Human Resources Management M
International Affairs M
International Business M
Management Information Systems M
Management Strategy and Policy M
Marketing M
Organizational Management M

UNITED STATES SPORTS ACADEMY

Athletic Training and Sports Medicine M
Exercise and Sports Science M
Physical Education M
Sports Management M,D

UNITED STATES UNIVERSITY

Family Nurse Practitioner Studies M

UNITED TALMUDICAL SEMINARY

Theology

UNITED THEOLOGICAL SEMINARY

Theology P,M,D

UNITED THEOLOGICAL SEMINARY OF THE TWIN CITIES

Art/Fine Arts P,M,D,O
Asian Studies P,M,D,O
Conflict Resolution and Mediation/Peace Studies P,M,D,O
Ethnic Studies P,M,D,O
Humanities P,M,D,O
Pastoral Ministry and Counseling P,M,D,O
Religion P,M,D,O
Theology P,M,D,O
Women's Studies P,M,D,O

UNIVERSIDAD ADVENTISTA DE LAS ANTILLAS

Curriculum and Instruction P,M
Educational Leadership and Administration P,M
Health Education P,M
Medical/Surgical Nursing P,M
Pastoral Ministry and Counseling P,M

UNIVERSIDAD AUTONOMA DE GUADALAJARA

Advertising and Public Relations M,D
Allopathic Medicine P
Architecture M,D
Business Administration and Management—General M,D
Computer Art and Design M,D
Computer Science M,D
Corporate and Organizational Communication M,D
Education—General M,D
Energy and Power Engineering M,D
Entertainment Management M,D
Environmental and Occupational Health M,D
Environmental Management and Policy M,D
Film, Television, and Video Production M,D
International Business M,D
Internet and Interactive Multimedia M,D
Law M,D
Legal and Justice Studies M,D
Manufacturing Engineering M,D
Marketing Research M,D
Mathematics Education M,D
Philosophy M,D
Public Policy M,D
Spanish M,D
Systems Science M,D
Translation and Interpretation M,D

UNIVERSIDAD CENTRAL DEL CARIBE

Addictions/Substance Abuse Counseling M
Allopathic Medicine P,M,D
Anatomy M,D
Biochemistry M,D
Biological and Biomedical Sciences—General M,D
Cell Biology M,D
Immunology M,D
Microbiology M,D
Molecular Biology M,D
Pharmacology M,D
Physiology M,D

UNIVERSIDAD CENTRAL DEL ESTE

Allopathic Medicine P
Dentistry P
Environmental Engineering M
Finance and Banking M
Higher Education M
Human Resources Development M
Law P

UNIVERSIDAD DE CIENCIAS MEDICAS

Allopathic Medicine P,M,O
Anatomy P,M,O
Biological and Biomedical Sciences—General P,M,O
Community Health P,M,O
Environmental and Occupational Health P,M,O
Health Services Management and Hospital Administration P,M,O
Pharmacy P,M,O

UNIVERSIDAD DE IBEROAMERICA

Acute Care/Critical Care Nursing P,M,D
Allopathic Medicine P,M,D
Clinical Psychology P,M,D
Educational Psychology P,M,D
Forensic Psychology P,M,D
Health Services Management and Hospital Administration P,M,D
Neuroscience P,M,D

UNIVERSIDAD DE LAS AMERICAS, A.C.

Business Administration and Management—General M
Education—General M
Finance and Banking M
International Affairs M
Marketing Research M
Marriage and Family Therapy M
Organizational Behavior M
Psychology—General M
Quality Management M

UNIVERSIDAD DE LAS AMÉRICAS–PUEBLA

American Studies M
Anthropology M
Archaeology M
Biotechnology M
Business Administration and Management—General M
Chemical Engineering M
Clinical Laboratory Sciences/Medical Technology M
Computer Art and Design M
Computer Science M,D
Construction Management M
Economics M
Education—General M
Electrical Engineering M
Engineering and Applied Sciences—General M,D
English M
Finance and Banking M
Food Science and Technology M
Industrial and Manufacturing Management M
Industrial/Management Engineering M
Linguistics M
Manufacturing Engineering M
Psychology—General M

UNIVERSIDAD DEL ESTE

Accounting M
Adult Education M
Agricultural Economics and Agribusiness M
Business Administration and Management—General M
Computer and Information Systems Security M
Criminal Justice and Criminology M
Electronic Commerce M
Elementary Education M
English as a Second Language M
Foreign Languages Education M
Human Resources Management M
Management Information Systems M
Management Strategy and Policy M
Public Policy M
Social Work M
Special Education M

UNIVERSIDAD DEL TURABO

Accounting M
Adult Nursing M
Art/Fine Arts M
Arts Administration M
Athletic Training and Sports Medicine M
Business Administration and Management—General M,D
Chemistry M,D
Communication Disorders M
Conflict Resolution and Mediation/Peace Studies M
Counseling Psychology M,D,O
Counselor Education M
Criminal Justice and Criminology M
Curriculum and Instruction M,D
Early Childhood Education M
Education—General M,D,O
Educational Leadership and Administration M,D,O
English as a Second Language M
Environmental Biology M,D
Environmental Management and Policy M,D
Environmental Sciences M,D
Family Nurse Practitioner Studies M
Forensic Sciences M

*M—master's degree; P—first professional degree; D—doctorate; O—other advanced degree; *—Close-Up and/or Display in one of the other books in this series*

Health Promotion	M
Human Resources Management	M
Human Services	M
Information Studies	M
Library Science	M,O
Logistics	M
Management Information Systems	M,D
Marketing	M
Naturopathic Medicine	D
Nursing—General	M
Physical Education	M
Project Management	M
Quality Management	M
Special Education	M
Telecommunications	M

UNIVERSIDAD FLET

Education—General	M
Theology	M

UNIVERSIDAD IBEROAMERICANA

Allopathic Medicine	P
Business Administration and Management—General	P,M
Dentistry	P,M
Educational Leadership and Administration	P,M
Human Resources Development	P,M
Law	P,M
Marketing	P,M
Real Estate	P,M
Special Education	P,M

UNIVERSIDAD METROPOLITANA

Accounting	M
Adult Education	M
Business Administration and Management—General	M
Counseling Psychology	M
Curriculum and Instruction	M
Education—General	M
Educational Leadership and Administration	M
Elementary Education	M
Environmental Management and Policy	M
Finance and Banking	M
Human Resources Management	M
International Business	M
Leisure Studies	M
Management Information Systems	M
Marketing	M
Natural Resources	M
Nursing and Healthcare Administration	M,O
Nursing—General	M,O
Oncology Nursing	M,O
Physical Education	M
Recreation and Park Management	M
Secondary Education	M
Special Education	M

UNIVERSIDAD NACIONAL PEDRO HENRIQUEZ URENA

Agricultural Sciences—General	M
Allopathic Medicine	P
Animal Sciences	M
Architecture	M
Dentistry	P
Ecology	M
Environmental Engineering	M
Environmental Sciences	M
Historic Preservation	M
Horticulture	M
International Affairs	M
Natural Resources	M
Political Science	M
Project Management	M
Science Education	M

UNIVERSITÉ DE MONCTON

Astronomy	M
Biochemistry	M
Biological and Biomedical Sciences—General	M
Business Administration and Management—General	M
Chemistry	M
Civil Engineering	M
Computer Science	M,O
Counselor Education	M
Economics	M
Education—General	M
Educational Leadership and Administration	M
Educational Psychology	M
Electrical Engineering	M
Engineering and Applied Sciences—General	M
Food Science and Technology	M
French	M,D
History	M
Industrial/Management Engineering	M
Mathematics	M
Mechanical Engineering	M
Nutrition	M
Physics	M
Public Administration	M
Social Work	M

UNIVERSITÉ DE MONTRÉAL

Allopathic Medicine	P
Anthropology	M,D
Art History	M,D
Biochemistry	M,D,O
Bioethics	M,D,O
Bioinformatics	M,D
Biological and Biomedical Sciences—General	M,D
Biomedical Engineering	M,D,O
Cell Biology	M,D
Chemistry	M,D
Classics	M
Communication Disorders	M,O
Communication—General	M,D
Community Health	M,D,O
Comparative Literature	M,D
Computer Science	M,D
Criminal Justice and Criminology	M,D
Curriculum and Instruction	M,D,O
Demography and Population Studies	M,D
Dental Hygiene	O
Developmental Psychology	M,D
Economics	M,D,O
Education—General	M,D,O
Educational Leadership and Administration	M,D,O
Educational Psychology	M,D,O
Electronic Commerce	M,D
Emergency Management	O
English	M,D
Environmental and Occupational Health	M
Environmental Design	M,D,O
Environmental Management and Policy	O
Ergonomics and Human Factors	O
Film, Television, and Video Theory and Criticism	M,D
French	M,D
Genetic Counseling	O
Genetics	O
Geography	M,D,O
German	M
Health Services Management and Hospital Administration	M,O
Hispanic and Latin American Languages	M,D
History	M,D
Human Services	D
Immunology	M,D
Industrial and Labor Relations	M,D,O
Information Studies	M,D
International Affairs	M,O
Kinesiology and Movement Studies	M,D,O
Law	P,M,D,O
Library Science	M,D
Linguistics	M,D,O
Mathematical and Computational Finance	M,D,O
Mathematics	M,D,O
Microbiology	M,D
Molecular Biology	M,D
Museum Studies	M
Music	M,D,O
Neuroscience	M,D
Nursing—General	M,D,O
Nutrition	M,D,O
Occupational Therapy	O
Optometry	P
Oral and Dental Sciences	M,O
Pathology	M,D
Pharmaceutical Sciences	M,D,O
Pharmacology	M,D
Philosophy	M,D
Physical Education	M,D,O
Physics	M,D
Physiology	M,D
Political Science	M,D
Psychology—General	M,D
Public Health—General	M,D,O
Public Policy	O
Rehabilitation Sciences	O
Religion	M,D,O
Social Work	O
Sociology	M,D
Spanish	M
Statistics	M,D,O
Taxation	P,M,D,O
Theology	M,D,O
Toxicology	O
Translation and Interpretation	M,D,O
Urban and Regional Planning	M,D,O
Veterinary Medicine	D
Veterinary Sciences	M,D
Virology	D
Vision Sciences	M,O

UNIVERSITÉ DE SHERBROOKE

Accounting	M
Allopathic Medicine	P
Biochemistry	M,D
Biological and Biomedical Sciences—General	M,D,O
Biophysics	M,D
Biotechnology	P,M,D,O
Business Administration and Management—General	P,M,D,O
Canadian Studies	M,D
Cell Biology	M,D
Chemical Engineering	M,D
Chemistry	M,D,O
Civil Engineering	M,D
Clinical Laboratory Sciences/Medical Technology	M,D
Comparative Literature	M,D
Computer and Information Systems Security	M
Conflict Resolution and Mediation/Peace Studies	P,M,D,O
Corporate and Organizational Communication	M
Economic Development	D
Economics	M
Education—General	M,O
Educational Leadership and Administration	M
Electrical Engineering	M,D
Electronic Commerce	M
Elementary Education	M,O
Engineering and Applied Sciences—General	M,D,O
Engineering Management	M,O
Environmental Engineering	M
Environmental Sciences	M,O
Ethics	M,D,O
Finance and Banking	M
French	M,D
Geography	M,D
Gerontology	M
Health Law	P,M,D,O
Higher Education	M,O
History	M
Immunology	M,D
Information Science	M,D
International Business	M
Kinesiology and Movement Studies	M,O
Law	P,M,D,O
Linguistics	M,D
Management Information Systems	M,O
Marketing	M
Mathematics	M,D
Mechanical Engineering	M,D
Microbiology	M,D
Organizational Behavior	M
Pharmacology	M,D
Philosophy	M,D,O
Physical Education	M,O
Physics	M,D
Physiology	M,D
Psychology—General	M
Public Administration	M
Radiation Biology	M,D
Religion	M,D,O
Social Work	M
Special Education	M,O
Taxation	M,O
Theater	M,D
Theology	M,D,O

UNIVERSITÉ DU QUÉBEC À CHICOUTIMI

Art/Fine Arts	M
Business Administration and Management—General	M
Canadian Studies	M
Comparative Literature	M
Education—General	M,D
Engineering and Applied Sciences—General	M,D
Environmental Management and Policy	M
Ethics	O
French	O
Genetics	M
Geosciences	M
Linguistics	M
Mineralogy	D
Project Management	M
Theology	M,D

UNIVERSITÉ DU QUÉBEC À MONTRÉAL

Accounting	M,O
Actuarial Science	O
Art History	M,D
Art/Fine Arts	M
Atmospheric Sciences	M,D,O
Biological and Biomedical Sciences—General	M,D
Business Administration and Management—General	M,D,O
Chemistry	M,D
Communication—General	M,D
Comparative Literature	M,D
Dance	M
Economics	M,D
Education—General	M,D,O

Environmental and Occupational Health	O
Environmental Education	M,D,O
Environmental Sciences	M,D,O
Ergonomics and Human Factors	O
Finance and Banking	O
Geographic Information Systems	O
Geography	M
Geology	M,D,O
Geosciences	M,D,O
History	M,D
Kinesiology and Movement Studies	M
Law	O
Linguistics	M,D
Management Information Systems	M
Mathematics	M,D
Meteorology	M,D,O
Mineralogy	M,D,O
Museum Studies	M
Natural Resources	M,D,O
Philosophy	M,D
Political Science	M,D
Project Management	M,O
Psychology—General	D
Public Administration	M
Religion	M,D
Social Work	M
Sociology	M,D
Urban Studies	M,D

UNIVERSITÉ DU QUÉBEC À RIMOUSKI

Business Administration and Management—General	M,O
Comparative Literature	M,D
Education—General	M,D,O
Engineering and Applied Sciences—General	M
Ethics	M,O
Fish, Game, and Wildlife Management	M,D,O
Marine Affairs	M,O
Nursing—General	M,O
Oceanography	M,D
Project Management	M,O
Social Psychology	M
Urban and Regional Planning	M,D,O

UNIVERSITÉ DU QUÉBEC À TROIS-RIVIÈRES

Accounting	M
Biophysics	M,D
Business Administration and Management—General	M,D
Chemistry	M
Chiropractic	P
Communication—General	M,O
Comparative Literature	M
Computer Science	M
Education—General	M,D
Educational Leadership and Administration	O
Educational Psychology	M,D
Electrical Engineering	M,D
Environmental Sciences	M,D
Finance and Banking	O
Industrial and Labor Relations	O
Industrial/Management Engineering	M,O
Leisure Studies	M,O
Mathematics	M
Nursing—General	M,O
Philosophy	M,D
Physical Education	M
Physics	M,D
Psychology—General	D,O
Travel and Tourism	M,O

UNIVERSITÉ DU QUÉBEC, ÉCOLE DE TECHNOLOGIE SUPÉRIEURE

Engineering and Applied Sciences—General	M,D,O

UNIVERSITÉ DU QUÉBEC, ÉCOLE NATIONALE D'ADMINISTRATION PUBLIQUE

International Business	M,O
Public Administration	D,O
Urban Studies	M

UNIVERSITÉ DU QUÉBEC EN ABITIBI-TÉMISCAMINGUE

Biological and Biomedical Sciences—General	M,D
Business Administration and Management—General	M
Education—General	M,D,O
Engineering and Applied Sciences—General	M,O
Environmental Sciences	M,D
Forestry	M,D
Mineral/Mining Engineering	M,O
Natural Resources	M,D
Project Management	M,O
Social Work	M

UNIVERSITÉ DU QUÉBEC EN OUTAOUAIS

Accounting	M,O
Adult Education	O
Computer Science	M,D
Education—General	M,D,O
Educational Psychology	M
Finance and Banking	M,O
Foreign Languages Education	O
Industrial and Labor Relations	M,D,O
Nursing—General	M,O
Project Management	M,O
Social Work	M
Software Engineering	O
Urban and Regional Planning	M

UNIVERSITÉ DU QUÉBEC, INSTITUT NATIONAL DE LA RECHERCHE SCIENTIFIQUE

Biological and Biomedical Sciences—General	M,D
Demography and Population Studies	M,D
Energy Management and Policy	M,D
Environmental Management and Policy	M,D
Geosciences	M,D
Hydrology	M,D
Immunology	M,D
Materials Sciences	M,D
Medical Microbiology	M,D
Microbiology	M,D
Telecommunications	M,D
Urban Studies	M,D
Virology	M,D

UNIVERSITÉ LAVAL

Accounting	M,O
Advertising and Public Relations	O
Aerospace/Aeronautical Engineering	M
Agricultural Economics and Agribusiness	M
Agricultural Engineering	M
Agricultural Sciences—General	M,D,O
Agronomy and Soil Sciences	M,D
Allopathic Medicine	P,O
Anatomy	M,D,O
Anesthesiologist Assistant Studies	O
Animal Sciences	M,D
Anthropology	M,D
Archaeology	M,D
Architecture	M
Art History	M,D
Art/Fine Arts	M
Biochemistry	M,D,O
Biological and Biomedical Sciences—General	M,D,O
Business Administration and Management—General	M,D,O
Cancer Biology/Oncology	O
Cardiovascular Sciences	O
Cell Biology	M,D
Chemical Engineering	M,D
Chemistry	M,D
Civil Engineering	M,D,O
Clinical Psychology	D
Communication Disorders	M
Community Health	M,D,O
Comparative Literature	M,D
Computer Science	M,D
Consumer Economics	O
Counselor Education	M,D
Curriculum and Instruction	M,D
Dentistry	P
Economics	M,D
Education—General	M,D,O
Educational Leadership and Administration	M,D,O
Educational Measurement and Evaluation	M,D,O
Educational Media/Instructional Technology	M,D
Educational Psychology	M,D
Electrical Engineering	M,D
Electronic Commerce	M,O
Emergency Medical Services	O
Engineering and Applied Sciences—General	M,D,O
English	M,D
Entrepreneurship	M,O
Environmental and Occupational Health	O
Environmental Engineering	M,D
Environmental Management and Policy	M,D,O
Environmental Sciences	M,D
Epidemiology	M,D
Ethics	O
Ethnic Studies	M,D
Facilities Management	M,O
Film, Television, and Video Theory and Criticism	M,D
Finance and Banking	M,O
Food Science and Technology	M,D
Forestry	M,D
Geodetic Sciences	M,D
Geographic Information Systems	M,O
Geography	M,D
Geology	M,D
Geosciences	M,D
Gerontology	O
Graphic Design	M
Health Physics/Radiological Health	O
History	M,D
Immunology	M,D
Industrial and Labor Relations	M,D
Industrial/Management Engineering	O
Infectious Diseases	O
International Affairs	M,D
International Business	M,O
Journalism	O
Kinesiology and Movement Studies	M,D
Law	M,D,O
Legal and Justice Studies	O
Linguistics	M,D
Management Information Systems	M,O
Marketing	M,O
Mass Communication	M,D
Mathematics	M,D
Mechanical Engineering	M,D
Metallurgical Engineering and Metallurgy	M,D
Microbiology	M,D
Mineral/Mining Engineering	M,D
Modeling and Simulation	M,O
Molecular Biology	M,D
Museum Studies	O
Music Education	M,D
Music	M,D
Neurobiology	M,D
Nursing—General	M,D,O
Nutrition	M,D
Oceanography	D
Oral and Dental Sciences	M,O
Organizational Management	M,O
Pathology	O
Pharmaceutical Sciences	M,D,O
Philosophy	M,D
Physics	M,D
Physiology	M,D
Plant Biology	M,D
Political Science	M,D
Psychology—General	D
Religion	M,D
Rural Planning and Studies	O
Social Psychology	D
Social Work	M,D
Sociology	M,D
Software Engineering	O
Spanish	M,D
Statistics	M
Theater	M,D
Theology	M,D
Translation and Interpretation	M,O
Urban and Regional Planning	M,D
Women's Studies	O

UNIVERSITY AT ALBANY, STATE UNIVERSITY OF NEW YORK

Accounting	M
African Studies	M
African-American Studies	M
Anthropology	M,D
Art/Fine Arts	M
Atmospheric Sciences	M,D
Biochemistry	M,D
Biological and Biomedical Sciences—General	M,D
Biopsychology	M,D,O
Biostatistics	M,D
Business Administration and Management—General	M
Cell Biology	M,D
Chemistry	M,D
Clinical Psychology	M,D,O
Communication—General	M,D
Computer Science	M,D
Conservation Biology	M
Counseling Psychology	M,D,O
Counselor Education	M,D,O
Criminal Justice and Criminology	M,D
Curriculum and Instruction	M,D,O
Demography and Population Studies	M,D,O
Developmental Biology	M,D
Ecology	M,D
Economics	M,D,O
Education—General	M,D,O
Educational Leadership and Administration	M,D,O
Educational Measurement and Evaluation	M,D,O
Educational Media/Instructional Technology	M,D,O
Educational Psychology	M,D,O
English	M,D

*M—master's degree; P—first professional degree; D—doctorate; O—other advanced degree; *—Close-Up and/or Display in one of the other books in this series*

Program	Degrees
Environmental and Occupational Health	M,D
Environmental Management and Policy	M
Environmental Sciences	M
Epidemiology	M,D
Evolutionary Biology	M,D
Experimental Psychology	M,D,O
Finance and Banking	M
Forensic Sciences	M,D
French	M,D
Genetics	M,D
Geographic Information Systems	M,O
Geography	M,O
Geology	M,D
Geosciences	M,D
Health Services Management and Hospital Administration	M
History	M,D,O
Human Resources Management	M
Immunology	M,D
Industrial and Organizational Psychology	M,D,O
Information Science	M,D,O
Information Studies	M,O
Italian	M
Latin American Studies	M,O
Liberal Studies	M
Management of Technology	M
Marketing	M
Mathematics Education	M,D
Mathematics	M,D
Molecular Biology	M,D
Molecular Pathogenesis	M,D
Nanotechnology	M,D
Neurobiology	M,D
Neuroscience	M,D
Philosophy	M,D
Physics	M,D
Political Science	M,D
Psychology—General	M,D,O
Public Administration	M,D,O
Public Health—General	M,D
Public History	M,D,O
Public Policy	M,D,O
Reading Education	M,D,O
Rehabilitation Counseling	M
Russian	M,O
School Psychology	M,D,O
Science Education	M,D
Social Psychology	M,D,O
Social Work	M,D
Sociology	M,D,O
Spanish	M,D
Special Education	M
Statistics	M,D,O
Structural Biology	M,D
Taxation	M
Theater	M
Toxicology	M,D
Translation and Interpretation	M,O
Urban and Regional Planning	M
Urban Studies	M,D,O
Women's Studies	M,D

UNIVERSITY AT BUFFALO, THE STATE UNIVERSITY OF NEW YORK

Program	Degrees
Accounting	M,D,O
Adult Nursing	D,O
Aerospace/Aeronautical Engineering	M,D
Allied Health—General	M,D,O
Allopathic Medicine	P
American Studies	M,D
Anatomy	M,D
Anthropology	M,D
Architecture	M
Art History	M,O
Art/Fine Arts	M,O
Biochemistry	M,D
Bioengineering	M,D
Biological and Biomedical Sciences—General	M,D
Biophysics	M,D
Biostatistics	M,D
Biotechnology	M
Business Administration and Management—General	M,D,O
Cancer Biology/Oncology	M,D
Cell Biology	D
Chemical Engineering	M,D
Chemistry	M,D
Civil Engineering	M,D
Classics	M,D,O
Clinical Laboratory Sciences/Medical Technology	M
Clinical Psychology	M,D
Cognitive Sciences	M,D
Communication Disorders	M,D
Communication—General	M,D
Comparative Literature	M,D
Computer Science	M,D
Counseling Psychology	M,D,O
Counselor Education	M,D,O
Cultural Studies	M
Dentistry	P,M,D,O
Early Childhood Education	M,D,O
Ecology	M,D,O
Economics	M,D,O
Education of the Gifted	M,D,O
Education—General	M,D,O
Educational Leadership and Administration	M,D,O
Educational Media/Instructional Technology	M,D,O
Educational Psychology	M,D,O
Electrical Engineering	M,D
Electronic Commerce	M,D,O
Elementary Education	M,D,O
Engineering and Applied Sciences—General	M,D
English as a Second Language	M,D,O
English Education	M,D,O
English	M,D
Environmental Engineering	M,D
Environmental Sciences	M,D,O
Epidemiology	M,D*
Evolutionary Biology	M,D,O
Exercise and Sports Science	M,D
Family Nurse Practitioner Studies	D,O
Finance and Banking	M,D,O
Financial Engineering	M,D,O
Foreign Languages Education	M,D,O
French	M,D,O
Geographic Information Systems	M,D,O
Geography	M,D,O
Geology	M,D
Geosciences	M,D,O
German	M,D,O
Higher Education	M,D,O
History	M,D
Human Resources Management	M,D,O
Immunology	M,D
Industrial/Management Engineering	M,D
Information Studies	M,O
International Business	M,D,O
Latin American Studies	M
Law	P,M
Library Science	M,O
Linguistics	M,D
Logistics	M,D,O
Management Information Systems	M,D,O
Materials Sciences	M
Mathematics Education	M,D,O
Mathematics	M,D
Mechanical Engineering	M,D
Media Studies	M,D,O
Medicinal and Pharmaceutical Chemistry	M,D
Microbiology	M,D
Modeling and Simulation	M,D,O
Molecular Biology	D
Molecular Pharmacology	D
Multilingual and Multicultural Education	M,D,O
Museum Studies	M,O
Music Education	M,D,O
Music	M,D
Neuroscience	M,D
Nursing—General	D,O
Nutrition	M,D
Occupational Therapy	M
Oral and Dental Sciences	M,D
Pathology	M,D
Pharmaceutical Sciences	M,D
Pharmacology	M,D
Pharmacy	P
Philosophy	M,D
Physical Therapy	D
Physics	M,D
Physiology	M,D
Political Science	M,D
Psychology—General	M,D
Public Health—General	M,D
Reading Education	M,D,O
Rehabilitation Counseling	M,D,O
Rehabilitation Sciences	M,D,O
Romance Languages	M,D
Science Education	M,D,O
Social Psychology	M,D
Social Sciences Education	M,D,O
Social Work	M,D*
Sociology	M,D
Spanish	M,D,O
Special Education	M,D,O
Structural Biology	M,D
Structural Engineering	M,D
Student Affairs	M,D,O
Toxicology	M,D
Urban and Regional Planning	M
Urban Design	M

UNIVERSITY OF ADVANCING TECHNOLOGY

Program	Degrees
Computer and Information Systems Security	M
Computer Science	M
Game Design and Development	M
Internet and Interactive Multimedia	M
Management of Technology	M

THE UNIVERSITY OF AKRON

Program	Degrees
Accounting	M
Applied Mathematics	M,D
Arts Administration	M
Biological and Biomedical Sciences—General	M,D
Biomedical Engineering	M,D
Business Administration and Management—General	M
Chemical Engineering	M,D
Chemistry	M,D
Child and Family Studies	M
Child Development	M
Civil Engineering	M,D
Clothing and Textiles	M
Communication Disorders	M,D
Communication—General	M
Computer Engineering	M,D
Computer Science	M
Counseling Psychology	M,D
Counselor Education	M,D
Economics	M
Education—General	M,D
Educational Leadership and Administration	M,D
Electrical Engineering	M,D
Electronic Commerce	M
Elementary Education	M,D
Engineering and Applied Sciences—General	M,D
Engineering Management	M
English	M
Entrepreneurship	M
Exercise and Sports Science	M
Finance and Banking	M
Geographic Information Systems	M
Geography	M
Geology	M
Geophysics	M
Geosciences	M
Health Services Management and Hospital Administration	M
Higher Education	M
History	M,D
Human Resources Management	M
Industrial and Organizational Psychology	M,D
International Business	M
Law	P,M
Management Information Systems	M
Management of Technology	M
Marketing	M
Marriage and Family Therapy	M
Mathematics	M
Mechanical Engineering	M,D
Music Education	M
Music	M
Nursing—General	M,D
Nutrition	M
Physical Education	M
Physics	M
Political Science	M
Polymer Science and Engineering	M,D
Psychology—General	M,D
Public Administration	M
Public Health—General	M,D
School Psychology	M
Secondary Education	M,D
Social Psychology	M
Social Work	M
Sociology	M,D
Spanish	M
Special Education	M
Statistics	M
Supply Chain Management	M
Taxation	M
Theater	M
Urban and Regional Planning	M
Urban Studies	M,D
Vocational and Technical Education	M
Writing	M

THE UNIVERSITY OF ALABAMA

Program	Degrees
Accounting	M,D
Advertising and Public Relations	M
Aerospace/Aeronautical Engineering	M,D
American Studies	M
Anthropology	M,D
Applied Mathematics	M,D
Applied Statistics	M,D
Art History	M
Art/Fine Arts	M
Biological and Biomedical Sciences—General	M,D
Business Administration and Management—General	M,D
Chemical Engineering	M,D
Child and Family Studies	M
Civil Engineering	M,D
Clinical Psychology	D
Clothing and Textiles	M
Communication Disorders	M
Communication—General	M,D
Community Health	M
Computer Engineering	M,D

Computer Science M,D
Construction Engineering M,D
Consumer Economics M
Counselor Education M,D,O
Criminal Justice and Criminology M
Economics M,D
Education of the Gifted M,D,O
Educational Leadership and Administration M,D,O
Electrical Engineering M,D
Elementary Education M,D,O
Engineering and Applied Sciences—General M,D
English as a Second Language M,D
English M,D
Environmental Engineering M,D
Ergonomics and Human Factors M
Exercise and Sports Science M,D
Experimental Psychology D
Family and Consumer Sciences-General M,D
Film, Television, and Video Production M
Finance and Banking M,D
French M,D
Geography M
Geology M,D
German M,D
Health Education M,D
Health Promotion M,D
Higher Education M,D
History M,D
Hospitality Management M
Human Development M
Information Studies M,D
Interdisciplinary Studies D
Interior Design M
Journalism M
Kinesiology and Movement Studies M,D
Law P,M
Library Science M,D
Marketing M,D
Mass Communication D
Materials Engineering M,D
Materials Sciences D
Mathematics M,D
Mechanical Engineering M,D
Mechanics M,D
Media Studies M
Metallurgical Engineering and Metallurgy M,D
Music Education M,D,O
Music M,D
Nursing—General M,D
Nutrition M
Photography M
Physical Education M,D
Physics M,D
Political Science M,D
Psychology—General D
Public Administration M,D
Quality Management M
Rhetoric M,D
Romance Languages M,D
Secondary Education M,D,O
Social Work M,D
Spanish M,D
Special Education M,D,O
Speech and Interpersonal Communication M
Sports Management M,D
Taxation M,D
Theater M
Women's Studies M
Writing M,D

THE UNIVERSITY OF ALABAMA AT BIRMINGHAM

Accounting M
Allied Health—General M,D
Allopathic Medicine P
Anthropology M
Applied Mathematics D
Art Education M
Art History M
Biochemistry D
Biological and Biomedical Sciences—General M,D*
Biomedical Engineering M,D
Biostatistics M,D
Business Administration and Management—General M
Cell Biology D
Chemistry M,D
Civil Engineering M,D
Communication—General M
Computer and Information Systems Security M
Computer Engineering D
Computer Science M,D
Construction Engineering M
Counselor Education M
Criminal Justice and Criminology M
Dentistry P
Early Childhood Education M,D
Education—General M,D,O
Educational Leadership and Administration M,D,O
Electrical Engineering M
Elementary Education M
Engineering and Applied Sciences—General M,D
English M
Environmental and Occupational Health D
Epidemiology D
Forensic Sciences M
Genetic Counseling M
Genetics D
Health Education M,D
Health Informatics M
Health Promotion D
Health Services Management and Hospital Administration M,D
History M
Information Science M,D
Interdisciplinary Studies D
Materials Engineering M,D
Materials Sciences D
Mathematics M
Mechanical Engineering M
Microbiology D
Molecular Biology D
Molecular Genetics D
Molecular Physiology D
Neurobiology D
Nurse Anesthesia M
Nursing—General M,D
Nutrition M,D
Occupational Therapy M
Optometry P
Oral and Dental Sciences M
Pathology D
Pharmacology D
Physical Education M
Physical Therapy D
Physician Assistant Studies M
Physics M,D
Psychology—General M,D
Public Administration M
Public Health—General M,D
Rehabilitation Sciences D
Safety Engineering M
Secondary Education M
Sociology M,D
Special Education M
Toxicology D
Vision Sciences M,D

THE UNIVERSITY OF ALABAMA IN HUNTSVILLE

Accounting M
Acute Care/Critical Care Nursing M,D,O
Aerospace/Aeronautical Engineering M,D
Applied Mathematics M,D
Atmospheric Sciences M,D
Biological and Biomedical Sciences—General M
Biotechnology D
Business Administration and Management—General M
Chemical Engineering M
Chemistry M
Civil Engineering M,D
Computer Engineering M,D
Computer Science M,D,O
Criminal Justice and Criminology M,O
Electrical Engineering M,D
Engineering and Applied Sciences—General M,D
Engineering Management M,D
English as a Second Language M,O
English M,O
Environmental Engineering M,D
Environmental Sciences M,D
Experimental Psychology M
Family Nurse Practitioner Studies M,D,O
Finance and Banking M
Geotechnical Engineering M,D
Health Services Management and Hospital Administration M,D,O
History M
Human Resources Management M
Industrial and Organizational Psychology M
Industrial/Management Engineering M,D
Interdisciplinary Studies M,D,O
Logistics M
Management Information Systems M,O
Marketing M
Materials Sciences M,D
Mathematics M,D
Mechanical Engineering M,D
Modeling and Simulation M,D,O
Nursing Education M,D,O
Nursing—General M,D,O
Operations Research M
Optical Sciences M,D
Photonics M,D
Physics M,D
Project Management M
Psychology—General M
Public Affairs M
Software Engineering M,D,O
Structural Engineering M,D
Supply Chain Management M
Systems Engineering M,D
Taxation M
Technical Writing M,O
Transportation and Highway Engineering M,D
Vision Sciences M,D
Water Resources Engineering M,D

UNIVERSITY OF ALASKA ANCHORAGE

Adult Education M
Anthropology M
Biological and Biomedical Sciences—General M
Business Administration and Management—General M
Civil Engineering M,O
Clinical Psychology M,D
Counselor Education M
Early Childhood Education M,O
Education—General M,O
Educational Leadership and Administration M,O
Engineering and Applied Sciences—General M,O
Engineering Management M
English M
Environmental Engineering M
Environmental Sciences M
Family Nurse Practitioner Studies M,O
Geological Engineering M
Interdisciplinary Studies M
Logistics M,O
Nursing Education M,O
Nursing—General M,O
Ocean Engineering M,O
Project Management M
Psychiatric Nursing M,O
Psychology—General M,D
Public Administration M
Public Health—General M
Social Psychology M,D
Social Work M,O
Special Education M,O
Writing M

UNIVERSITY OF ALASKA FAIRBANKS

Anthropology M,D
Art/Fine Arts M
Astrophysics M,D
Atmospheric Sciences M,D
Biochemistry M,D
Biological and Biomedical Sciences—General M,D
Botany M,D
Business Administration and Management—General M
Chemistry M,D
Civil Engineering M,D
Clinical Psychology D
Communication—General M
Computational Sciences M,D
Computer Art and Design M
Computer Engineering M,D
Computer Science M
Corporate and Organizational Communication M
Counselor Education M
Criminal Justice and Criminology M
Cultural Studies M
Curriculum and Instruction M,D,O
Economics M
Education—General M,D,O
Electrical Engineering M,D
Elementary Education M,D,O
Engineering and Applied Sciences—General M,D
Engineering Management M,D
English Education M,D,O
English M
Environmental Engineering M,D
Environmental Management and Policy M,D
Environmental Sciences M,D
Finance and Banking M
Fish, Game, and Wildlife Management M,D
Geography M,D
Geological Engineering M,D
Geology M,D
Geophysics M,D
History M
Interdisciplinary Studies M,D
Limnology M,D
Linguistics M
Marine Biology M,D
Marine Sciences M,D
Mathematics M,D
Mechanical Engineering M,D
Mineral/Mining Engineering M
Multilingual and Multicultural Education M,D,O
Music Education M
Music M
Natural Resources M,D
Northern Studies M
Nutrition M,D

*M—master's degree; P—first professional degree; D—doctorate; O—other advanced degree; *—Close-Up and/or Display in one of the other books in this series*

Oceanography M,D
Petroleum Engineering M,D
Photography M
Physics M,D
Psychology—General D
Reading Education M,D,O
Rural Planning and Studies M
Secondary Education M,D,O
Social Psychology M,D
Software Engineering M
Special Education M,D,O
Statistics M,D
Sustainable Development M,D
Water Resources M,D
Writing M
Zoology M,D

UNIVERSITY OF ALASKA SOUTHEAST

Business Administration and Management—General M
Early Childhood Education M
Education—General M
Educational Media/Instructional Technology M
Elementary Education M
Public Administration M
Secondary Education M

UNIVERSITY OF ALBERTA

Accounting D
Adult Education M,D,O
Agricultural Economics and Agribusiness M,D
Agricultural Sciences—General M,D
Agronomy and Soil Sciences M,D
Anthropology M,D
Applied Arts and Design—General M
Applied Mathematics M,D,O
Archaeology M,D
Art History M
Art/Fine Arts M
Asian Studies M
Astrophysics M,D
Biochemistry M,D
Biological and Biomedical Sciences—General P,M,D
Biomedical Engineering M,D
Biostatistics M,D,O
Biotechnology M,D
Business Administration and Management—General M,D
Cancer Biology/Oncology M,D
Cell Biology M,D
Chemical Engineering M,D
Chemistry M,D
Chinese M
Civil Engineering M,D
Classics M,D
Clinical Laboratory Sciences/Medical Technology M,D
Clothing and Textiles M,D
Communication Disorders M,D
Communication—General M
Community Health M,D
Computer Engineering M,D
Computer Science M,D
Condensed Matter Physics M,D
Conservation Biology M,D
Construction Engineering M,D
Counseling Psychology M,D
Counselor Education M,D
Criminal Justice and Criminology M,D
Demography and Population Studies M,D
Dental Hygiene O
Dentistry P
East European and Russian Studies M,D
Ecology M,D
Economics M,D
Educational Leadership and Administration M,D,O
Educational Media/Instructional Technology M,D
Educational Policy M,D,O
Educational Psychology M,D
Electrical Engineering M,D
Elementary Education M,D
Energy and Power Engineering M,D
Engineering Management M,D
English as a Second Language M,D
English M,D
Environmental and Occupational Health M,D
Environmental Biology M,D
Environmental Engineering M,D
Environmental Management and Policy M,D
Environmental Sciences M,D
Epidemiology M,D
Evolutionary Biology M,D
Exercise and Sports Science M,D
Family and Consumer Sciences-General M,D
Finance and Banking M,D
Folklore M,D
Forestry M,D
French M,D
Genetics M,D
Geophysics M,D
Geosciences M,D
Geotechnical Engineering M,D
German M,D
Health Physics/Radiological Health M,D
Health Promotion M,O
Health Services Management and Hospital Administration M,D
Health Services Research M,D
Hispanic Studies M,D
History M,D
Immunology M,D
Industrial and Labor Relations D
Information Studies M
International Business M
International Health M,D
Italian M,D
Japanese M
Law P,M
Library Science M
Linguistics M,D
Marketing D
Materials Engineering M,D
Maternal and Child/Neonatal Nursing P
Mathematical and Computational Finance M,D,O
Mathematical Physics M,D,O
Mathematics M,D,O
Mechanical Engineering M,D
Medical Microbiology M,D
Medical Physics M,D
Microbiology M,D
Mineral/Mining Engineering M,D
Molecular Biology M,D
Multilingual and Multicultural Education M
Music M,D
Nanotechnology M,D
Natural Resources M,D
Neuroscience M,D
Nursing—General M,D
Occupational Therapy M,D
Oral and Dental Sciences M,D
Organizational Management D
Pathology M,D
Petroleum Engineering M,D
Pharmaceutical Sciences M,D
Pharmacology M,D
Pharmacy M,D
Philosophy M,D
Physical Education M,D
Physical Therapy M,D
Physics M,D
Physiology M,D
Plant Biology M,D
Political Science M,D
Psychology—General M,D
Public Health—General M,D
Recreation and Park Management M,D
Rehabilitation Sciences D
Rural Sociology M,D
School Psychology M,D
Secondary Education M,D
Slavic Languages M,D
Sociology M,D
Special Education M,D
Sports Management M
Statistics M,D,O
Structural Engineering M,D
Systems Engineering M,D
Telecommunications M,D
Theater M
Vision Sciences M,D
Water Resources Engineering M,D

THE UNIVERSITY OF ARIZONA

Accounting M
Aerospace/Aeronautical Engineering M,D
Agricultural Economics and Agribusiness M
Agricultural Education M
Agricultural Engineering M,D
Agricultural Sciences—General M,D
Agronomy and Soil Sciences M,D
Allopathic Medicine P
American Indian/Native American Studies M,D
Anatomy D
Animal Sciences M,D
Anthropology M,D
Applied Mathematics M,D
Applied Physics M
Architecture M
Art Education M
Art History M,D
Art/Fine Arts M
Asian Studies M,D
Astronomy M,D
Atmospheric Sciences M,D
Biochemistry D
Biological and Biomedical Sciences—General M
Biomedical Engineering M,D
Biostatistics D
Biosystems Engineering M,D
Business Administration and Management—General M,D
Cancer Biology/Oncology D
Cell Biology M,D
Chemical Engineering M,D
Chemistry D
Child and Family Studies M
Civil Engineering M,D
Classics M
Communication Disorders M,D
Communication—General M,D
Computer Engineering M,D
Computer Science M,D
Counselor Education M
Dance M
Ecology M,D
Economics M,D
Education—General M,D,O
Educational Leadership and Administration M,D,O
Educational Psychology M,D,O
Electrical Engineering M,D
Engineering and Applied Sciences—General M,D,O
English as a Second Language M,D
English Education D
English M,D
Entomology M,D
Environmental Engineering M,D
Environmental Sciences M,D
Epidemiology M,D
Evolutionary Biology M,D
Family and Consumer Sciences-General M,D
Family Nurse Practitioner Studies M,D,O
Finance and Banking M,D
Fish, Game, and Wildlife Management M,D
Forestry M,D
French M
Gender Studies M,D
Genetics M,D
Geography M,D
Geological Engineering M,D,O
Geosciences M,D
German M
Higher Education M,D
History M,D
Human Development M
Hydrology M,D
Immunology M,D
Industrial/Management Engineering M,D
Information Studies M,D
Interdisciplinary Studies M,D
Landscape Architecture M
Latin American Studies M
Law P,M
Library Science M,D
Linguistics M,D
Management Information Systems M
Management Strategy and Policy D
Marketing M,D
Materials Engineering M,D
Materials Sciences M,D
Mathematics M,D
Mechanical Engineering M,D
Mechanics M,D
Media Studies M
Medical Informatics M,D,O
Microbiology M,D
Mineral/Mining Engineering M,O
Molecular Biology M,D
Multilingual and Multicultural Education M,D,O
Music Education M,D
Music M,D
Near and Middle Eastern Studies M,D
Neuroscience D
Nursing—General M,D,O
Nutrition M,D
Optical Sciences M,D
Pathobiology M,D
Perfusion M,D
Pharmaceutical Sciences M,D
Pharmacology M,D
Pharmacy P
Philosophy M,D
Physics M,D
Physiology M,D
Planetary and Space Sciences M,D
Plant Pathology M,D
Plant Sciences M,D
Political Science M,D
Psychology—General M,D
Public Administration M,D
Public Health—General M,D
Public Policy M,D
Range Science M,D
Reading Education M,D,O
Rehabilitation Counseling M,D
Reliability Engineering M
Rhetoric D
Russian M
School Psychology D,O
Sociology D
Spanish M,D
Special Education M,D,O
Statistics M,D

Systems Engineering M,D
Theater M
Urban and Regional Planning M
Water Resources M,D
Women's Studies M,D
Writing M

UNIVERSITY OF ARKANSAS

Accounting M
Agricultural Economics and Agribusiness M
Agricultural Education M
Agricultural Engineering M,D
Agricultural Sciences—General M,D
Agronomy and Soil Sciences M,D
Animal Sciences M,D
Anthropology M,D
Applied Physics M,D
Art/Fine Arts M
Athletic Training and Sports Medicine M
Bioengineering M
Biological and Biomedical Sciences—General M,D
Biomedical Engineering M
Business Administration and Management—General M,D
Cell Biology M,D
Chemical Engineering M,D
Chemistry M,D
Civil Engineering M,D
Communication Disorders M
Communication—General M
Comparative Literature M,D
Computer Engineering M,D
Computer Science M,D
Counselor Education M,D,O
Curriculum and Instruction D
Early Childhood Education M
Economics M,D
Education—General M,D,O
Educational Leadership and Administration M,D,O
Educational Measurement and Evaluation M,D
Educational Media/Instructional Technology M
Educational Policy D
Electrical Engineering M,D
Electronic Materials M,D
Elementary Education M,O
Engineering and Applied Sciences—General M,D
English M,D
Entomology M,D
Environmental Engineering M
Family and Consumer Sciences-General M
Food Science and Technology M,D
French M
Geography M
Geology M
German M
Health Education M,D
Higher Education M,D,O
History M,D
Horticulture M
Industrial and Manufacturing Management M
Industrial/Management Engineering M,D
Interdisciplinary Studies M,D
Journalism M
Kinesiology and Movement Studies M,D
Law P,M
Management Information Systems M
Mathematics Education M
Mathematics M,D
Mechanical Engineering M,D
Middle School Education M,D,O
Molecular Biology M,D
Music M
Nursing—General M
Operations Research M,D
Philosophy M,D
Photonics M,D
Physical Education M
Physics M,D
Planetary and Space Sciences M,D
Plant Pathology M
Plant Sciences D
Political Science M
Psychology—General M,D
Public Administration M
Public Policy D
Recreation and Park Management M,D
Rehabilitation Counseling M,D
Secondary Education M,O
Social Work M
Sociology M
Spanish M
Special Education M
Statistics M
Telecommunications M,D
Theater M
Translation and Interpretation M
Transportation and Highway Engineering M
Vocational and Technical Education M,D
Writing M

UNIVERSITY OF ARKANSAS AT LITTLE ROCK

Accounting M,O
Adult Education M
Allied Health—General M
Applied Mathematics M,O
Applied Psychology M
Applied Science and Technology M,D
Applied Statistics M,O
Art Education M
Art History M
Art/Fine Arts M
Bioinformatics M,D
Biological and Biomedical Sciences—General M
Business Administration and Management—General M,O
Chemistry M
Computer Science M
Conflict Resolution and Mediation/Peace Studies O
Construction Management M,O
Counselor Education M
Criminal Justice and Criminology M,D
Early Childhood Education M
Education of the Gifted M
Education—General M,D,O
Educational Leadership and Administration M,D,O
Educational Media/Instructional Technology M
English as a Second Language M
Foreign Languages Education M
Geosciences O
Gerontology O
Higher Education D
Information Science M
Journalism M
Law P
Liberal Studies M
Management Information Systems M,O
Management of Technology M,O
Marriage and Family Therapy O
Mass Communication M
Mathematics M,O
Middle School Education M
Nonprofit Management O
Psychology—General M
Public Administration M
Public Affairs M,O
Public History M
Reading Education M,O
Rehabilitation Counseling M,O
Rhetoric M
Secondary Education M
Social Work M
Special Education M,O
Speech and Interpersonal Communication M
Systems Engineering O
Taxation M,O
Technical Writing M
Writing M

UNIVERSITY OF ARKANSAS AT MONTICELLO

Education—General M
Educational Leadership and Administration M
Forestry M
Natural Resources M

UNIVERSITY OF ARKANSAS AT PINE BLUFF

Addictions/Substance Abuse Counseling M
Aquaculture M
Education—General M
Elementary Education M
Fish, Game, and Wildlife Management M
Physical Education M
Science Education M
Secondary Education M
Social Sciences Education M

UNIVERSITY OF ARKANSAS FOR MEDICAL SCIENCES

Allopathic Medicine P
Anatomy M,D
Biochemistry M,D
Biological and Biomedical Sciences—General M,D,O
Biophysics M,D
Communication Disorders M,D
Environmental and Occupational Health M,O
Genetic Counseling M
Health Promotion D
Health Services Research D
Immunology M,D
Microbiology M,D
Molecular Biology M,D
Neurobiology M,D
Nursing—General D
Nutrition M
Pathology M
Pharmaceutical Administration M
Pharmaceutical Sciences M
Pharmacology M,D
Pharmacy P,M
Physiology M,D
Toxicology M,D

UNIVERSITY OF ATLANTA

Business Administration and Management—General P,M,D,O
Computer Science P,M,D,O
Educational Leadership and Administration P,M,D,O
Health Services Management and Hospital Administration P,M,D,O
Law P,M,D,O
Management Information Systems P,M,D,O
Project Management P,M,D,O
Social Sciences P,M,D,O

UNIVERSITY OF BALTIMORE

Accounting M,O
Applied Arts and Design—General M
Applied Psychology M
Business Administration and Management—General M,O
Computer Art and Design M,D
Conflict Resolution and Mediation/Peace Studies M
Counseling Psychology M
Criminal Justice and Criminology M
Ethics M
Finance and Banking M
Graphic Design M,D
Health Services Management and Hospital Administration M
Human Services M
Human-Computer Interaction M,D
Industrial and Organizational Psychology M
Information Science M,D
Law M
Legal and Justice Studies M
Management Information Systems M,O
Marketing M
Public Administration M,D
Publishing M
Taxation M
Writing M

UNIVERSITY OF BRIDGEPORT

Acupuncture and Oriental Medicine M
Business Administration and Management—General M
Chiropractic P
Computer Education M,O
Computer Engineering M,D
Computer Science M,D
Conflict Resolution and Mediation/Peace Studies M
Dental Hygiene M
Early Childhood Education M,O
Education—General M,D,O
Educational Leadership and Administration D,O
Electrical Engineering M
Elementary Education M,O
Engineering and Applied Sciences—General M,D
Human Resources Development M
Human Services M
International Affairs M
International and Comparative Education M,O
Management of Technology M
Mechanical Engineering M
Naturopathic Medicine D
Nutrition M
Reading Education M,O
Secondary Education M,O
Student Affairs M

THE UNIVERSITY OF BRITISH COLUMBIA

Accounting D
Adult Education M,D
Agricultural Economics and Agribusiness M
Agricultural Sciences—General M,D
Agronomy and Soil Sciences M,D
Allopathic Medicine P,M
Anatomy M,D
Animal Sciences M,D
Anthropology M,D
Applied Mathematics M,D

*M—master's degree; P—first professional degree; D—doctorate; O—other advanced degree; *—Close-Up and/or Display in one of the other books in this series*

Archaeology	M,D
Architecture	M
Archives/Archival Administration	M,D
Art Education	M,D
Art History	M,D,O
Art/Fine Arts	M,D,O
Asian Studies	M,D
Astronomy	M,D
Atmospheric Sciences	M,D
Biochemistry	M,D
Biopsychology	M,D
Botany	M,D
Business Administration and Management—General	M,D
Business Education	M,D
Cell Biology	M,D
Chemical Engineering	M,D
Chemistry	M,D
Civil Engineering	M,D
Classics	M,D
Clinical Psychology	M,D
Cognitive Sciences	M,D
Communication Disorders	M,D
Computer Engineering	M,D
Computer Science	M,D
Counseling Psychology	M,D,O
Curriculum and Instruction	M,D
Dentistry	P
Developmental Psychology	M,D
Early Childhood Education	M,D
East European and Russian Studies	M,D
Economics	M,D
Education—General	M,D,O
Educational Leadership and Administration	M,D
Educational Measurement and Evaluation	M,D,O
Educational Policy	M,D
Electrical Engineering	M,D
Engineering and Applied Sciences—General	M,D
English as a Second Language	M,D
English	M,D
Environmental and Occupational Health	M,D
Epidemiology	M,D
Film, Television, and Video Production	M,O
Film, Television, and Video Theory and Criticism	M,O
Finance and Banking	D
Food Science and Technology	M,D
Forestry	M,D
Foundations and Philosophy of Education	M,D
French	M,D
Genetic Counseling	M
Genetics	M,D
Geography	M,D
Geological Engineering	M,D
Geology	M,D
Geophysics	M,D
German	M,D
Health Psychology	M,D
Health Services Management and Hospital Administration	M,D
Higher Education	M,D
Hispanic Studies	M,D
History	M,D
Home Economics Education	M,D
Human Development	M,D,O
Immunology	M,D
Information Studies	M,D
Interdisciplinary Studies	M
International Affairs	M
International Business	D
Journalism	M
Kinesiology and Movement Studies	M,D
Landscape Architecture	M
Law	M,D
Library Science	M,D
Linguistics	M,D
Management Information Systems	D
Management Strategy and Policy	D
Marine Sciences	M,D
Marketing	D
Materials Engineering	M,D
Materials Sciences	M,D
Mathematics Education	M,D
Mathematics	M,D
Mechanical Engineering	M,D
Metallurgical Engineering and Metallurgy	M,D
Microbiology	M,D
Mineral/Mining Engineering	M,D
Molecular Biology	M,D
Museum Studies	M,D,O
Music Education	M,D
Music	M,D
Natural Resources	M,D
Neuroscience	M,D
Nurse Anesthesia	M,D
Nursing—General	M,D
Nutrition	M,D
Occupational Therapy	M
Oceanography	M,D
Operations Research	M
Oral and Dental Sciences	M,D,O
Organizational Behavior	D
Pathology	M,D
Pharmaceutical Sciences	P,M,D
Pharmacology	M,D
Pharmacy	P,M,D
Philosophy	M,D
Physical Education	M,D
Physics	M,D
Physiology	M,D
Plant Sciences	M,D
Political Science	M,D
Psychology—General	M,D
Public Health—General	M,D
Quantitative Analysis	M,D
Reading Education	M,D
Rehabilitation Sciences	M,D
Religion	M,D
Reproductive Biology	M,D
School Psychology	M,D,O
Science Education	M,D
Social Psychology	M,D
Social Sciences Education	M,D
Social Work	M,D
Sociology	M,D
Software Engineering	M
Special Education	M,D,O
Statistics	M,D
Theater	M,D
Transportation Management	D
Urban and Regional Planning	M,D
Vocational and Technical Education	M,D
Writing	M,O
Zoology	M,D

UNIVERSITY OF CALGARY

Allopathic Medicine	P
Analytical Chemistry	M,D
Anthropology	M,D
Applied Psychology	M,D
Archaeology	M,D
Architecture	M,D
Art/Fine Arts	M
Astronomy	M,D
Biochemistry	M,D
Biological and Biomedical Sciences—General	M,D
Biomedical Engineering	M,D
Biotechnology	M
Business Administration and Management—General	M,D
Cancer Biology/Oncology	M,D
Cardiovascular Sciences	M,D
Chemical Engineering	M,D
Chemistry	M,D
Civil Engineering	M,D
Classics	M,D
Clinical Psychology	M,D
Communication—General	M,D
Community Health	M,D,O
Computer Engineering	M,D
Computer Science	M,D
Counseling Psychology	M,D
Curriculum and Instruction	M,D,O
Economics	M,D
Education of the Gifted	M,D,O
Educational Leadership and Administration	M,D,O
Educational Measurement and Evaluation	M,D,O
Educational Media/Instructional Technology	M,D,O
Electrical Engineering	M,D
Engineering and Applied Sciences—General	M,D
English as a Second Language	M,D,O
English	M,D
Environmental Design	M,D
Environmental Law	M,O
Environmental Management and Policy	M,D,O
Epidemiology	M,D
Exercise and Sports Science	M,D
Foreign Languages Education	M,D,O
Foundations and Philosophy of Education	M,D,O
Geography	M,D
Geology	M,D
Geophysics	M,D
Geotechnical Engineering	M,D
German	M
Health Education	M,D
Higher Education	M,D,O
History	M,D
Human Development	M,D
Immunology	M,D
Infectious Diseases	M,D
Inorganic Chemistry	M,D
Kinesiology and Movement Studies	M,D
Law	P,M,O
Legal and Justice Studies	M,O
Linguistics	M,D
Management Strategy and Policy	M,D
Manufacturing Engineering	M,D
Mathematics	M,D
Mechanical Engineering	M,D
Microbiology	M,D
Military and Defense Studies	M,D
Molecular Biology	M,D
Music	M,D
Neuroscience	M,D
Nursing—General	M,D,O
Organic Chemistry	M,D
Petroleum Engineering	M,D
Philosophy	M,D
Physical Chemistry	M,D
Physics	M,D
Political Science	M,D
Psychology—General	M,D
Religion	M,D
School Psychology	M,D
Social Work	M,D,O
Sociology	M,D
Software Engineering	M,D
Special Education	M,D
Statistics	M,D
Theater	M
Theoretical Chemistry	M,D
Vocational and Technical Education	M,D,O

UNIVERSITY OF CALIFORNIA, BERKELEY

Accounting	D,O
Addictions/Substance Abuse Counseling	O
African-American Studies	D
Agricultural Economics and Agribusiness	D
Allopathic Medicine	
Anthropology	D
Applied Arts and Design—General	M,O
Applied Mathematics	D
Applied Science and Technology	D
Archaeology	M,D
Architectural History	M,D
Architecture	M,D
Art History	D
Art/Fine Arts	M,O
Asian Languages	M,D
Asian Studies	M,D
Astrophysics	D
Biochemistry	D
Bioengineering	D
Biological and Biomedical Sciences—General	D
Biophysics	D
Biostatistics	M,D
Building Science	M,D
Business Administration and Management—General	M,D,O
Cell Biology	D
Chemical Engineering	M,D
Chemistry	D
Chinese	D
Civil Engineering	M,D
Classics	M,D
Clinical Research	O
Comparative Literature	D
Computer Science	M,D
Construction Management	O
Counseling Psychology	O
Demography and Population Studies	M,D
Economics	D
Education—General	M,D,O
Electrical Engineering	M,D
Energy Management and Policy	M,D
Engineering and Applied Sciences—General	M,D,O
Engineering Management	M,D
English as a Second Language	O
English	D
Environmental and Occupational Health	M,D
Environmental Design	M,D
Environmental Engineering	M,D
Environmental Management and Policy	M,D,O
Environmental Sciences	M,D
Epidemiology	M,D
Ethnic Studies	D
Facilities Management	O
Finance and Banking	D,O
Financial Engineering	M
Folklore	M
Forestry	M,D
French	D
Geography	D
Geology	M,D
Geophysics	M,D
Geotechnical Engineering	M,D
German	D
Health Services Management and Hospital Administration	D
Hispanic and Latin American Languages	D
History of Science and Technology	D
History	M,D
Human Development	M,D
Human Resources Management	O
Immunology	D
Industrial and Labor Relations	D
Industrial and Manufacturing Management	D

Industrial/Management Engineering M,D
Infectious Diseases M,D
Information Studies M,D
Interior Design O
International Affairs M,D
International Business O
Italian D
Japanese D
Jewish Studies D
Journalism M
Landscape Architecture M,D,O
Latin American Studies M
Law P,M,D
Legal and Justice Studies D
Linguistics D
Management Information Systems O
Marketing D,O
Materials Engineering M,D
Materials Sciences M,D
Mathematics Education M,D
Mathematics M,D
Mechanical Engineering M,D
Mechanics M,D
Microbiology D
Molecular Biology D
Molecular Toxicology D
Music D
Natural Resources M,D
Near and Middle Eastern Studies M,D
Neuroscience D*
Nuclear Engineering M,D
Nutrition D
Operations Research M,D
Optometry P,O
Organizational Behavior D
Philosophy D
Physics D
Physiology M,D
Plant Biology D
Political Science D
Project Management O
Psychology—General D
Public Health—General M,D
Public Policy M,D
Range Science M
Real Estate D
Religion D
Rhetoric D
Romance Languages D
Russian D
Scandinavian Languages D
Science Education M,D
Slavic Languages D
Social Work M,D
Sociology D
Spanish D
Special Education M,D
Statistics M,D
Structural Engineering M,D
Sustainability Management O
Sustainable Development O
Theater D
Transportation and Highway Engineering M,D
Urban and Regional Planning M,D
Urban Design M,D
Vision Sciences M,D
Water Resources Engineering M,D
Writing O

UNIVERSITY OF CALIFORNIA, DAVIS

Aerospace/Aeronautical Engineering M,D,O
Agricultural Economics and Agribusiness M,D
Agricultural Sciences—General M
Agronomy and Soil Sciences M,D
Allopathic Medicine P
American Indian/Native American Studies M,D
Animal Behavior D
Animal Sciences M,D
Anthropology M,D
Applied Mathematics M,D
Applied Science and Technology M,D
Art History M
Art/Fine Arts M
Atmospheric Sciences M,D
Biochemistry M,D
Bioengineering M,D
Biomedical Engineering M,D
Biophysics M,D
Biostatistics M,D
Business Administration and Management—General M
Cell Biology M,D
Chemical Engineering M,D
Chemistry M,D
Child Development M
Civil Engineering M,D,O
Clinical Research M
Clothing and Textiles M
Communication—General M
Comparative Literature D
Computer Engineering M,D
Computer Science M,D
Cultural Studies M,D
Curriculum and Instruction M,D
Developmental Biology M,D
Ecology M,D
Economics M,D
Education—General M,D
Educational Psychology M,D
Electrical Engineering M,D
Engineering and Applied Sciences—General M,D,O
English M,D
Entomology M,D
Environmental Engineering M,D,O
Environmental Sciences M,D
Epidemiology M,D
Evolutionary Biology D
Exercise and Sports Science M
Food Science and Technology M,D
Forensic Sciences M
French D
Genetics M,D
Geography M,D
Geology M,D
German M,D
History M,D
Horticulture M
Human Development D
Hydrology M,D
Immunology M,D
Law P,M
Linguistics M,D
Materials Engineering M,D
Materials Sciences M,D
Maternal and Child Health M
Mathematics M,D
Mechanical Engineering M,D,O
Medical Informatics M
Microbiology M,D
Molecular Biology M,D
Music M,D
Neuroscience D
Nutrition M,D
Pathology M,D
Pharmacology M,D
Philosophy M,D
Physics M,D
Physiology M,D
Plant Biology M,D
Plant Pathology M,D
Political Science M,D
Psychology—General D
Sociology M,D
Spanish M,D
Statistics M,D
Textile Design M
Theater M,D
Toxicology M,D
Transportation and Highway Engineering M,D
Transportation Management M,D
Urban and Regional Planning M
Veterinary Medicine P
Veterinary Sciences M,O
Viticulture and Enology M,D
Writing M,D
Zoology M

UNIVERSITY OF CALIFORNIA, HASTINGS COLLEGE OF THE LAW

Law P,M

UNIVERSITY OF CALIFORNIA, IRVINE

Aerospace/Aeronautical Engineering M,D
Allopathic Medicine P
Anatomy M,D
Anthropology M,D
Art History M,D
Art/Fine Arts M,D
Asian Languages M,D
Biochemical Engineering M,D
Biochemistry M,D
Biological and Biomedical Sciences—General M,D
Biomedical Engineering M,D
Biophysics D
Biotechnology M
Business Administration and Management—General M,D
Cell Biology M,D
Chemical Engineering M,D
Chemistry M,D
Chinese M,D
Civil Engineering M,D
Classics M,D
Comparative Literature M,D
Computational Biology D
Computer Science M,D
Criminal Justice and Criminology M,D
Cultural Studies D
Dance M
Demography and Population Studies M
Developmental Biology M,D
Ecology M,D
Economics M,D
Education—General M,D
Educational Leadership and Administration M,D
Electrical Engineering M,D
Elementary Education M,D
Engineering and Applied Sciences—General M,D
English M,D
Environmental Design D
Environmental Engineering M,D
Epidemiology M,D
Evolutionary Biology M,D
Foreign Languages Education M,D
French M,D
Genetic Counseling M
Genetics D
Geosciences M,D
German M,D
Health Services Management and Hospital Administration M
History M,D
Information Science M,D
Japanese M,D
Law P
Materials Engineering M,D
Materials Sciences M,D
Mathematics M,D
Mechanical Engineering M,D
Medicinal and Pharmaceutical Chemistry D
Microbiology M,D
Molecular Biology M,D
Molecular Genetics M,D
Music M
Neurobiology M,D
Neuroscience D
Nursing—General M
Pathology D
Pharmacology M,D*
Philosophy M,D
Physics M,D
Physiology D
Political Science D
Psychology—General D
Public Health—General M,D
Secondary Education M,D
Social Sciences M,D
Sociology M,D
Spanish M,D
Statistics M,D
Systems Biology D
Theater M,D
Toxicology M,D
Transportation and Highway Engineering M,D
Urban and Regional Planning M,D
Urban Studies M,D
Writing M

UNIVERSITY OF CALIFORNIA, LOS ANGELES

Accounting M,D
Aerospace/Aeronautical Engineering M,D
African Studies M
African-American Studies M
Allopathic Medicine P
American Indian/Native American Studies M
Anatomy D
Anthropology M,D
Applied Arts and Design—General M
Applied Social Research M,D
Archaeology M,D
Architecture M,D
Archives/Archival Administration M,D,O
Art History M,D
Art/Fine Arts M
Asian Languages M,D
Asian Studies M,D
Asian-American Studies M
Astronomy M,D
Astrophysics M,D
Atmospheric Sciences M,D
Biochemistry M,D
Bioinformatics M,D
Biological and Biomedical Sciences—General M,D
Biomathematics M,D
Biomedical Engineering M,D
Biometry M,D*
Biostatistics M,D
Business Administration and Management—General M,D*
Cell Biology D
Chemical Engineering M,D
Chemistry M,D
Civil Engineering M,D
Classics M,D
Clinical Research M
Community Health M,D
Comparative Literature M,D
Computer Science M,D
Dance M,D
Dentistry P,O
Developmental Biology D
Ecology M,D
Economics M,D
Education—General M,D
Educational Leadership and Administration D
Electrical Engineering M,D
Engineering and Applied Sciences—General M,D
English as a Second Language M,D,O

*M—master's degree; P—first professional degree; D—doctorate; O—other advanced degree; *—Close-Up and/or Display in one of the other books in this series*

English M,D
Environmental and Occupational Health M,D
Environmental Engineering M,D
Environmental Sciences M,D
Epidemiology M,D
Evolutionary Biology M,D
Film, Television, and Video Production M,D
Finance and Banking M,D
Financial Engineering M,D
French M,D
Geochemistry M,D
Geography M,D
Geology M,D
Geophysics M,D
Geosciences M,D
German M,D
Health Services Management and Hospital Administration M,D
Hispanic and Latin American Languages D
Historic Preservation M
History M,D
Human Genetics M,D
Human Resources Development M,D
Immunology M,D
Industrial and Manufacturing Management M,D
Information Studies M,D,O
International Business M,D
Italian M,D
Latin American Studies M
Law P,M,D
Library Science M,D,O
Linguistics M,D
Management Information Systems M,D
Management Strategy and Policy M,D
Manufacturing Engineering M
Marketing M,D
Materials Engineering M,D
Materials Sciences M,D
Mathematics M,D
Mechanical Engineering M,D
Medical Physics M,D
Microbiology M,D
Molecular Biology M,D
Molecular Genetics M,D
Molecular Toxicology D
Music M,D
Near and Middle Eastern Languages M,D
Near and Middle Eastern Studies M,D
Neurobiology D
Neuroscience D
Nursing—General M,D
Oral and Dental Sciences M,D
Organizational Behavior M,D
Pathology M,D
Pharmacology D
Philosophy M,D
Physics M,D
Physiology M,D
Planetary and Space Sciences M,D
Political Science M,D
Portuguese M
Psychology—General M,D
Public Health—General M,D
Public Policy M
Scandinavian Languages M
Science Education M,D
Slavic Languages M,D
Social Work M,D
Sociology M,D
Spanish M
Special Education D
Statistics M,D
Theater M,D
Toxicology D
Urban and Regional Planning M,D
Urban Design M,D
Women's Studies M,D

UNIVERSITY OF CALIFORNIA, MERCED

Applied Mathematics M,D
Bioengineering M,D
Biological and Biomedical Sciences—General M,D
Chemistry M,D
Cognitive Sciences M,D
Computer Science M,D
Electrical Engineering M,D
Engineering and Applied Sciences—General M,D
Environmental Sciences M,D
Mechanical Engineering M,D
Mechanics M,D
Physics M,D
Social Sciences M,D
Systems Biology M,D

UNIVERSITY OF CALIFORNIA, RIVERSIDE

Agronomy and Soil Sciences M,D
Anthropology M,D
Applied Statistics M,D
Archives/Archival Administration M,D
Art History M
Art/Fine Arts M
Artificial Intelligence/Robotics M,D
Asian Studies M
Biochemistry M,D
Bioengineering M,D
Bioinformatics D
Biological and Biomedical Sciences—General M,D
Botany M,D
Business Administration and Management—General M
Cell Biology M,D
Chemical Engineering M,D
Chemistry M,D
Classics D
Comparative Literature M,D
Computer Engineering M,D
Computer Science M,D
Curriculum and Instruction M,D
Dance M,D
Developmental Biology M,D
Ecology M,D
Economics M,D
Education—General M,D
Educational Leadership and Administration M,D
Educational Psychology M,D
Electrical Engineering M,D
English M,D
Entomology M,D
Environmental Engineering M,D
Environmental Sciences M,D
Ethnic Studies D
Evolutionary Biology M,D
Genetics D
Genomic Sciences D
Geology M,D
Higher Education M,D
Hispanic Studies M,D
Historic Preservation M,D
History M,D
Materials Engineering M,D
Materials Sciences M,D
Mathematics M,D
Mechanical Engineering M,D
Microbiology M,D
Molecular Biology M,D
Molecular Genetics D
Multilingual and Multicultural Education M,D
Museum Studies M,D
Music M,D
Nanotechnology M,D
Neuroscience D
Philosophy M,D
Physics M,D
Plant Biology M,D
Plant Pathology M,D
Plant Sciences M,D
Political Science M,D
Psychology—General M,D
Reading Education M,D
School Psychology M,D
Sociology M,D
Spanish M,D
Special Education M,D
Statistics M,D
Toxicology M,D
Water Resources M,D
Writing M

UNIVERSITY OF CALIFORNIA, SAN DIEGO

Aerospace/Aeronautical Engineering M,D
Allopathic Medicine P
Anthropology D
Applied Mathematics M,D
Applied Physics M,D
Art/Fine Arts M,D
Artificial Intelligence/Robotics M,D
Biochemistry M,D
Bioengineering M,D
Bioinformatics D
Biological and Biomedical Sciences—General M,D
Biophysics M,D
Business Administration and Management—General M
Cancer Biology/Oncology D
Cardiovascular Sciences D
Cell Biology D
Chemical Engineering M,D
Chemistry M,D
Clinical Psychology D
Clinical Research M
Cognitive Sciences D
Communication Disorders D
Communication—General M,D
Comparative Literature M,D
Computer Engineering M,D
Computer Science M,D
Developmental Biology D
Ecology D
Economics M,D
Education—General M,D
Electrical Engineering M,D
Engineering Physics M,D
English M
Epidemiology D
Ethnic Studies M,D
Evolutionary Biology D
French M
Genetics D
Geosciences D
German M
Health Law M
Health Services Management and Hospital Administration M
History of Science and Technology M,D
History M,D
Immunology D
International Affairs M,D
Jewish Studies M,D
Latin American Studies M
Law M
Legal and Justice Studies M
Linguistics D
Marine Biology D
Marine Sciences M
Materials Sciences M,D
Mathematics Education D
Mathematics M,D
Mechanical Engineering M,D
Mechanics M,D
Microbiology D
Modeling and Simulation M,D
Molecular Biology D
Molecular Pathology D
Music M,D
Neurobiology D
Neuroscience D
Ocean Engineering M,D
Oceanography D
Pacific Area/Pacific Rim Studies M,D
Pharmacology D
Pharmacy P
Philosophy D
Photonics M,D
Physics M,D
Physiology D
Plant Biology D
Plant Molecular Biology D
Political Science M,D
Psychology—General D
Public Health—General D
Science Education D
Sociology D
Spanish M
Statistics M,D
Structural Biology D
Structural Engineering M,D
Systems Biology D
Telecommunications M,D
Theater M,D
Virology D

UNIVERSITY OF CALIFORNIA, SAN FRANCISCO

Allopathic Medicine P,D
Anatomy D
Anthropology D
Biochemistry D
Bioengineering D
Bioinformatics D
Biological and Biomedical Sciences—General D
Biophysics D
Cell Biology D
Chemistry D
Dentistry P
Developmental Biology D
Epidemiology D
Genetics D
Genomic Sciences D
History of Science and Technology M,D
Immunology D
Medical Informatics D
Medicinal and Pharmaceutical Chemistry D
Microbiology D
Molecular Biology D
Neuroscience D
Nursing—General M,D
Oral and Dental Sciences M,D
Pathology D
Pharmaceutical Sciences D
Pharmacology D
Pharmacy P
Physical Therapy M,D
Physiology D
Sociology D

UNIVERSITY OF CALIFORNIA, SANTA BARBARA

Agricultural Economics and Agribusiness M,D
Anthropology M,D
Applied Mathematics M,D
Applied Statistics M,D
Archaeology M,D
Art History D
Art/Fine Arts M,D
Asian Languages M,D
Asian Studies M,D
Biochemistry D
Bioengineering D
Biophysics D
Cell Biology M,D
Chemical Engineering D
Chemistry M,D
Child and Family Studies M,D
Classics M,D
Clinical Psychology M,D

Cognitive Sciences M,D
Communication—General D
Comparative Literature D
Computational Sciences M,D
Computer Engineering M,D
Computer Science M,D
Counseling Psychology M,D
Cultural Anthropology M,D
Cultural Studies M
Developmental Biology M,D
Developmental Psychology M,D
Ecology M,D
Economics M,D
Education—General M,D
Educational Leadership and Administration M,D
Educational Measurement and Evaluation M,D
Electrical Engineering M,D
Engineering and Applied Sciences—General M,D
English D
Environmental Management and Policy M,D
Environmental Sciences M,D
Evolutionary Biology M,D
Film, Television, and Video Production D
French D
Geography M,D
Geology M,D
Geophysics M,D
Geosciences M,D
Hispanic and Latin American Languages M,D
Hispanic Studies M,D
History D
International Affairs M,D
International and Comparative Education M,D
Latin American Studies M
Linguistics M,D
Marine Biology M,D
Marine Sciences M,D
Materials Engineering M,D
Materials Sciences M,D
Mathematical and Computational Finance M,D
Mathematics M,D
Mechanical Engineering M,D
Media Studies M,D
Medieval and Renaissance Studies M,D
Molecular Biology M,D
Music M,D
Philosophy D
Photonics M,D
Physics D
Political Science M,D
Portuguese M,D
Psychology—General D
Quantitative Analysis M,D
Religion M,D
School Psychology M,D
Social Sciences D
Sociology M,D
Spanish M,D
Special Education M,D
Speech and Interpersonal Communication D
Statistics M,D
Sustainable Development M
Theater M,D
Translation and Interpretation M,D
Transportation Management M,D
Women's Studies M,D

UNIVERSITY OF CALIFORNIA, SANTA CRUZ

Anthropology D
Applied Economics M
Applied Mathematics M,D
Art/Fine Arts M,D
Astronomy D
Astrophysics D
Biochemistry M,D
Bioinformatics M,D
Cell Biology M,D
Chemistry M,D
Communication—General O
Comparative Literature M,D
Computer Art and Design M,D
Computer Engineering M,D
Computer Science M,D
Cultural Anthropology D
Developmental Biology M,D
Ecology M,D
Economics D
Education—General M,D
Electrical Engineering M,D
Engineering and Applied Sciences—General M,D
English M,D
Environmental Biology M,D
Environmental Management and Policy D
Evolutionary Biology M,D
Film, Television, and Video Theory and Criticism D
Finance and Banking M
Geosciences M,D
History M,D
Humanities D
Interdisciplinary Studies M,D
International Affairs D
Linguistics M,D
Management Information Systems M,D
Management of Technology M,D
Marine Sciences M,D
Mathematics M,D
Molecular Biology M,D
Music M,D
Philosophy M,D
Physics M,D
Planetary and Space Sciences M,D
Political Science D
Psychology—General D
Social Sciences Education M
Social Sciences D
Sociology D
Statistics M,D
Telecommunications M,D
Theater O
Toxicology M,D
Writing M

UNIVERSITY OF CENTRAL ARKANSAS

Accounting M
Applied Mathematics M
Biological and Biomedical Sciences—General M
Business Administration and Management—General M
Communication Disorders M,D
Computer Art and Design M
Computer Science M
Counseling Psychology M
Counselor Education M
Economic Development M,O
Economics M
Education—General M,O
Educational Leadership and Administration M,O
Educational Media/Instructional Technology M
English M
Family and Consumer Sciences-General M
Family Nurse Practitioner Studies M
Film, Television, and Video Production M
Foreign Languages Education M
Geographic Information Systems M,O
Geography M,O
Health Education M
History M
Kinesiology and Movement Studies M
Library Science M
Mathematics Education M
Mathematics M
Medical Physics M
Music Education M
Music M
Nursing—General M
Occupational Therapy M
Physical Therapy D
Psychology—General M,D
Reading Education M
School Psychology M,D
Social Psychology M
Special Education M
Student Affairs M
Urban and Regional Planning M,O

UNIVERSITY OF CENTRAL FLORIDA

Accounting M
Actuarial Science M,O
Adult Nursing M,D,O
Aerospace/Aeronautical Engineering M
Allopathic Medicine P,M
Anthropology M
Applied Mathematics M,D,O
Applied Psychology M,D
Art Education M
Art/Fine Arts M
Biological and Biomedical Sciences—General M,D,O
Biotechnology M
Business Administration and Management—General M,D,O
Chemistry M,D,O
Child and Family Studies M,O
Civil Engineering M,D,O
Clinical Psychology M,D
Communication Disorders M,D,O
Communication—General M
Community College Education M,D,O
Computer Art and Design M
Computer Engineering M,D
Computer Science M,D
Conservation Biology M,D,O
Construction Engineering M,D,O
Counselor Education M,D,O
Criminal Justice and Criminology M,O
Distance Education Development M,O
Early Childhood Education M
Education of the Gifted M,O
Educational Leadership and Administration M,D
Educational Media/Instructional Technology M,D,O
Electrical Engineering M,D,O
Elementary Education M,D
Emergency Management M,O
Engineering and Applied Sciences—General M,D,O
Engineering Design M,D,O
English as a Second Language M,D,O
English Education M
English M,O
Entrepreneurship M,O
Environmental Engineering M,D
Ergonomics and Human Factors M,D,O
Exercise and Sports Science M,D,O
Experimental Psychology M,D
Family Nurse Practitioner Studies M,D,O
Film, Television, and Video Production M
Forensic Sciences M,D,O
Game Design and Development M
Gerontological Nursing M,D,O
Gerontology M,O
Health Informatics M,O
Health Promotion M,O
Health Services Management and Hospital Administration M,O
Health Services Research M,O
Higher Education M,D
History M
Homeland Security M,O
Hospitality Management M,O
Industrial and Organizational Psychology M,D
Industrial/Management Engineering M,D,O
Interdisciplinary Studies M
International and Comparative Education M,O
Latin American Studies M,D,O
Marriage and Family Therapy M,O
Materials Engineering M,D
Materials Sciences M,D
Mathematics Education M,D,O
Mathematics M,D,O
Mechanical Engineering M,D,O
Middle School Education M
Modeling and Simulation M,D,O
Music M
Nonprofit Management M,O
Nursing and Healthcare Administration M,D,O
Nursing Education M,D,O
Nursing—General M,D,O
Operations Research M,D,O
Optical Sciences M,D
Photonics M,D
Physical Education M,O
Physical Therapy D
Physics M,D
Political Science M
Psychology—General M,D
Public Administration M,O
Public Affairs D
Reading Education M,D,O
Real Estate M
School Psychology O
Science Education M,D,O
Social Sciences Education M,D
Social Work M,O
Sociology M,D,O
Spanish M
Special Education M,D,O
Sports Management M
Statistics M,O
Structural Engineering M,D,O
Student Affairs M,D
Systems Engineering M,D,O
Taxation M
Theater M
Transportation and Highway Engineering M,D,O
Travel and Tourism M,O
Urban and Regional Planning M,O
Urban Education M,O
Vocational and Technical Education M
Writing M,O

UNIVERSITY OF CENTRAL MISSOURI

Accounting M
Aerospace/Aeronautical Engineering M,D
Applied Mathematics M,D
Biological and Biomedical Sciences—General M,D
Business Administration and Management—General M
Communication Disorders M
Computer Science M,D
Counseling Psychology M,D,O
Counselor Education M,D,O
Criminal Justice and Criminology M
Curriculum and Instruction M,D,O

*M—master's degree; P—first professional degree; D—doctorate; O—other advanced degree; *—Close-Up and/or Display in one of the other books in this series*

Program	Degrees
Education—General	M,D,O
Educational Leadership and Administration	M,D,O
Educational Media/Instructional Technology	M,D,O
Elementary Education	M,D,O
English as a Second Language	M
English	M
Environmental and Occupational Health	M
Environmental Management and Policy	M,D
Exercise and Sports Science	M
Finance and Banking	M
Foundations and Philosophy of Education	M,D,O
Gerontology	M
History	M
Human Services	M,D,O
Industrial and Manufacturing Management	M,D
Industrial Hygiene	M
Information Science	M,D,O
Library Science	M,D,O
Management Information Systems	M
Management of Technology	M,D
Management Strategy and Policy	M
Marketing	M
Mass Communication	M
Mathematics	M,D
Music	M
Nursing—General	M
Physical Education	M
Psychology—General	M
Reading Education	M,D,O
Secondary Education	M,D,O
Sociology	M
Special Education	M,D,O
Speech and Interpersonal Communication	M
Student Affairs	M,D,O
Theater	M
Vocational and Technical Education	M,D,O

UNIVERSITY OF CENTRAL OKLAHOMA

Program	Degrees
Addictions/Substance Abuse Counseling	M
Adult Education	M
American Studies	M
Applied Arts and Design—General	M
Applied Mathematics	M
Biological and Biomedical Sciences—General	M
Business Administration and Management—General	M
Chemistry	M
Communication Disorders	M
Computer Education	M
Computer Science	M
Counseling Psychology	M
Counselor Education	M
Criminal Justice and Criminology	M
Early Childhood Education	M
Education—General	M
Educational Leadership and Administration	M
Educational Media/Instructional Technology	M
Elementary Education	M
Engineering and Applied Sciences—General	M
English as a Second Language	M
English	M
Family and Consumer Sciences-General	M
Gerontology	M
Health Education	M
Higher Education	M
History	M
Home Economics Education	M
Human Development	M
Interior Design	M
International Affairs	M
Mathematics Education	M
Mathematics	M
Museum Studies	M
Music Education	M
Music	M
Nutrition	M
Physics	M
Political Science	M
Psychology—General	M
Reading Education	M
Secondary Education	M
Special Education	M
Statistics	M
Urban Studies	M
Writing	M

UNIVERSITY OF CHARLESTON

Program	Degrees
Accounting	M
Business Administration and Management—General	M
Legal and Justice Studies	M
Pharmacy	P

UNIVERSITY OF CHICAGO

Program	Degrees
Accounting	M
Allopathic Medicine	P
Anatomy	D
Anthropology	M,D
Applied Mathematics	M,D
Archaeology	M,D
Art History	M,D
Art/Fine Arts	M
Asian Languages	M,D
Asian Studies	M,D
Astronomy	M,D
Astrophysics	M,D
Atmospheric Sciences	M,D
Biochemistry	D
Biological and Biomedical Sciences—General	D
Biophysics	D
Business Administration and Management—General	M,D
Cancer Biology/Oncology	D
Cell Biology	D
Chemistry	D
Classics	M,D
Comparative Literature	M,D
Computer Science	M
Developmental Biology	D
Ecology	D
Economics	M,D
English	M,D
Entrepreneurship	M
Environmental Management and Policy	M,D
Environmental Sciences	M,D
Evolutionary Biology	D
Film, Television, and Video Theory and Criticism	M,D
Finance and Banking	M
French	M,D
Genetics	D
Genomic Sciences	D
Geophysics	M,D
Geosciences	M,D
German	M,D
Health Promotion	M,D
History	D
Human Development	D
Human Genetics	D
Human Resources Management	M
Humanities	M
Immunology	D
Interdisciplinary Studies	D
International Affairs	M
International Business	M
Italian	M,D
Latin American Studies	M
Law	P,M,D
Linguistics	M,D
Management Strategy and Policy	M
Marketing	M
Mathematical and Computational Finance	M
Mathematics	M,D
Media Studies	M,D
Medical Physics	D
Microbiology	D
Molecular Biology	D
Molecular Medicine	D
Molecular Pathogenesis	D
Molecular Physiology	D
Music	M,D
Near and Middle Eastern Languages	M,D
Near and Middle Eastern Studies	M,D
Neurobiology	D
Neuroscience	D
Nutrition	D
Organizational Behavior	M
Paleontology	M,D
Pathology	D
Pharmacology	D
Philosophy	M,D
Physics	M,D
Physiology	D
Planetary and Space Sciences	M,D
Political Science	D
Psychology—General	D
Public Policy	M,D
Religion	P,M,D
Romance Languages	M,D
Science Education	D
Slavic Languages	M,D
Social Sciences	M,D
Social Work	M,D
Sociology	D
Spanish	M,D
Statistics	M,D
Systems Biology	D
Theology	P,M,D
Vision Sciences	D
Zoology	D

UNIVERSITY OF CINCINNATI

Program	Degrees
Accounting	M,D
Acute Care/Critical Care Nursing	M,D
Adult Education	M,D,O
Adult Nursing	M,D
Aerospace/Aeronautical Engineering	M,D
Allopathic Medicine	P,M
Analytical Chemistry	M,D
Anthropology	M
Applied Arts and Design—General	M
Applied Mathematics	M,D
Architecture	M
Art Education	M
Art History	M
Art/Fine Arts	M
Arts Administration	M,D
Biochemistry	M,D
Bioinformatics	D
Biological and Biomedical Sciences—General	M,D
Biomedical Engineering	D
Biophysics	D
Biostatistics	M,D
Business Administration and Management—General	M,D
Cancer Biology/Oncology	D
Cell Biology	D
Chemical Engineering	M,D
Chemistry	M,D
Civil Engineering	M,D
Classics	M,D
Clinical Psychology	D
Communication Disorders	M,D,O
Communication—General	M
Community Health Nursing	M,D
Computer Engineering	M,D
Computer Science	M,D
Counselor Education	M,D,O
Criminal Justice and Criminology	M,D
Curriculum and Instruction	M,D
Developmental Biology	D
Early Childhood Education	M
Economics	M
Education—General	M,D,O
Educational Leadership and Administration	M,D,O
Electrical Engineering	M,D
Elementary Education	M
Engineering and Applied Sciences—General	M,D
English as a Second Language	M,D,O
English	M,D
Environmental and Occupational Health	M,D
Environmental Engineering	M,D
Environmental Sciences	M,D
Epidemiology	M,D
Ergonomics and Human Factors	M,D
Experimental Psychology	D
Finance and Banking	D
Foundations and Philosophy of Education	M,D
French	M,D
Genetic Counseling	M
Genomic Sciences	M,D
Geography	M,D
Geology	M,D
German	M,D
Graphic Design	M
Health Education	M,D
Health Physics/Radiological Health	M
History	M,D
Immunology	M,D
Industrial and Labor Relations	M
Industrial and Manufacturing Management	D
Industrial Design	M
Industrial Hygiene	M,D
Industrial/Management Engineering	M,D
Inorganic Chemistry	M,D
Interdisciplinary Studies	D
Interior Design	M
Law	P
Management Information Systems	M,D
Marketing	M,D
Materials Engineering	M,D
Materials Sciences	M,D
Maternal and Child/Neonatal Nursing	M,D
Mathematics Education	M,D
Mathematics	M,D
Mechanical Engineering	M,D
Mechanics	M,D
Medical Imaging	D
Medical Physics	M
Microbiology	M,D
Molecular Biology	M,D
Molecular Genetics	M,D
Molecular Medicine	D
Molecular Toxicology	M,D
Music Education	M
Music	M,D,O
Neuroscience	D
Nuclear Engineering	M,D
Nurse Anesthesia	M,D
Nurse Midwifery	M,D
Nursing and Healthcare Administration	M,D
Nursing—General	M,D
Nutrition	M
Occupational Health Nursing	M,D
Organic Chemistry	M,D

Organizational Management	M
Pathobiology	D
Pathology	D
Pediatric Nursing	M,D
Pharmaceutical Sciences	M,D
Pharmacology	D
Pharmacy	P
Philosophy	M,D
Physical Chemistry	M,D
Physics	M,D
Physiology	D
Political Science	M,D
Psychiatric Nursing	M,D
Psychology—General	D
Quantitative Analysis	M,D
Reading Education	M,D
Rehabilitation Sciences	D
Romance Languages	M,D
School Psychology	D,O
Science Education	M,D,O
Secondary Education	M
Social Sciences Education	M,D,O
Social Work	M
Sociology	M,D
Spanish	M,D
Special Education	M,D
Statistics	M,D
Textile Design	M
Theater	M,D
Urban and Regional Planning	M
Women's Health Nursing	M,D
Women's Studies	M,O

UNIVERSITY OF COLORADO AT COLORADO SPRINGS

Adult Nursing	M,D
Aerospace/Aeronautical Engineering	M
Applied Mathematics	M,D
Applied Science and Technology	M,D
Athletic Training and Sports Medicine	M
Biological and Biomedical Sciences—General	M
Business Administration and Management—General	M
Chemistry	M
Communication—General	M
Community Health Nursing	M,D
Computer Science	M,D
Counselor Education	M,D
Criminal Justice and Criminology	M
Curriculum and Instruction	M,D
Education—General	M,D
Educational Leadership and Administration	M,D
Electrical Engineering	M,D
Engineering and Applied Sciences—General	M,D
Engineering Management	M
Environmental Sciences	M
Family Nurse Practitioner Studies	M,D
Forensic Nursing	M,D
Geography	M
Health Promotion	M
History	M
Human Services	M,D
Information Science	M
Manufacturing Engineering	M
Maternal and Child/Neonatal Nursing	M,D
Mathematics	M,D
Mechanical Engineering	M
Nursing and Healthcare Administration	M,D
Nursing—General	M,D
Nutrition	M
Physics	M
Psychology—General	M,D
Public Administration	M
Public Affairs	M
Sociology	M
Software Engineering	M
Special Education	M,D
Women's Health Nursing	M,D

UNIVERSITY OF COLORADO BOULDER

Accounting	M,D
Aerospace/Aeronautical Engineering	M,D
Animal Behavior	M,D
Anthropology	M,D
Applied Mathematics	M,D
Architectural Engineering	M,D
Art History	M
Art/Fine Arts	M
Asian Studies	M,D
Astrophysics	M,D
Atmospheric Sciences	M,D
Biochemistry	M,D
Business Administration and Management—General	M*
Cell Biology	M,D
Chemical Engineering	M,D
Chemical Physics	M,D
Chemistry	M,D
Chinese	M,D
Civil Engineering	M,D
Classics	M,D
Communication Disorders	M,D
Communication—General	M,D
Comparative Literature	M,D
Computer Engineering	M,D
Computer Science	M,D
Construction Engineering	M,D
Curriculum and Instruction	M,D
Dance	M,D
Developmental Biology	M,D
Ecology	M,D
Economics	M,D
Education—General	M,D
Educational Measurement and Evaluation	D
Educational Policy	M,D
Educational Psychology	M,D
Electrical Engineering	M,D
Engineering and Applied Sciences—General	M,D
Engineering Management	M
English	M,D
Entrepreneurship	M,D
Environmental Engineering	M,D
Environmental Management and Policy	M,D
Evolutionary Biology	M,D
Finance and Banking	M,D
French	M,D
Genetics	M,D
Geography	M,D
Geology	M,D
Geophysics	M,D
Geotechnical Engineering	M,D
German	M
Hispanic and Latin American Languages	M,D
History	M,D
Hydrology	M,D
International Affairs	M,D
Japanese	M,D
Journalism	M,D
Kinesiology and Movement Studies	M,D
Law	P
Linguistics	M,D
Management Information Systems	M,D
Marine Biology	M,D
Marketing	M,D
Mass Communication	M,D
Mathematical Physics	M,D
Mathematics	M,D
Mechanical Engineering	M,D
Media Studies	D
Medical Physics	M,D
Microbiology	M,D
Molecular Biology	M,D
Multilingual and Multicultural Education	M,D
Museum Studies	M
Music Education	M,D
Music	M,D
Neurobiology	M,D
Oceanography	M,D
Operations Research	M
Optical Sciences	M,D
Organizational Management	M,D
Philosophy	M,D
Photography	M
Physics	M,D
Physiology	M,D
Plasma Physics	M,D
Political Science	M,D
Psychology—General	M,D
Public Policy	M,D
Religion	M
Sociology	D
Spanish	M,D
Structural Engineering	M,D
Telecommunications Management	M
Telecommunications	M
Theater	M,D
Water Resources Engineering	M,D
Writing	M,D

UNIVERSITY OF COLORADO DENVER

Accounting	M
Adult Education	M
Adult Nursing	M,D
Allopathic Medicine	P
American Studies	M
Anthropology	M
Applied Mathematics	M,D
Applied Science and Technology	M
Archaeology	M
Architectural History	D
Biochemistry	D
Bioengineering	M,D
Bioinformatics	D
Biological and Biomedical Sciences—General	M,D
Biostatistics	M,D
Business Administration and Management—General	M
Cancer Biology/Oncology	D
Cell Biology	D
Chemistry	M
Civil Engineering	M,D
Clinical Laboratory Sciences/Medical Technology	M,D
Clinical Psychology	M,D
Clinical Research	M,D
Communication—General	M
Community Health	M,D
Computational Biology	D
Computer Science	M,D
Corporate and Organizational Communication	M
Counseling Psychology	M
Counselor Education	M
Criminal Justice and Criminology	M,D
Dentistry	P
Developmental Biology	D
Distance Education Development	M
Early Childhood Education	M
Ecology	M
Economic Development	M
Economics	M
Education—General	M,D,O
Educational Leadership and Administration	M,D,O
Educational Measurement and Evaluation	M,D,O
Educational Media/Instructional Technology	M
Educational Policy	D
Educational Psychology	M,O
Electrical Engineering	M
Electronic Commerce	M
Elementary Education	M
Emergency Management	M,D
Energy Management and Policy	M
Engineering and Applied Sciences—General	M,D
English Education	M
English	M
Entrepreneurship	M,D
Environmental and Occupational Health	M,D
Environmental Education	M
Environmental Engineering	M,D
Environmental Law	M,D
Environmental Management and Policy	M,D
Environmental Sciences	M
Epidemiology	M,D
Family Nurse Practitioner Studies	M,D
Finance and Banking	M
Forensic Sciences	M
Gender Studies	M
Genetic Counseling	M
Genetics	D
Geographic Information Systems	M,D
Geotechnical Engineering	M,D
Hazardous Materials Management	M
Health Education	M,D
Health Services Management and Hospital Administration	M,D
Health Services Research	M,D
Historic Preservation	M
History	M
Homeland Security	M,D
Human Development	M,O
Human Resources Management	M
Humanities	M
Hydraulics	M,D
Hydrology	M,D
Immunology	D
Information Science	M,D
International Affairs	M
International Business	M
International Health	M
Landscape Architecture	M
Linguistics	M
Management Information Systems	M,D
Management of Technology	M,D
Management Strategy and Policy	M
Marketing Research	M
Marketing	M
Mathematics Education	M,D
Mathematics	M
Mechanical Engineering	M,D
Medical Imaging	M,D
Medical Informatics	M,D
Microbiology	D
Military and Defense Studies	M,D
Molecular Biology	D
Multilingual and Multicultural Education	M
Music	M
Neuroscience	D
Nonprofit Management	M,D
Nurse Midwifery	M,D
Nursing and Healthcare Administration	M,D
Nursing—General	M,D
Pediatric Nursing	M,D
Pharmaceutical Sciences	P,D
Pharmacology	D
Physical Therapy	D
Physician Assistant Studies	M
Physiology	D
Political Science	M,D
Psychiatric Nursing	M,D
Public Administration	M,D
Public Affairs	M,D

*M—master's degree; P—first professional degree; D—doctorate; O—other advanced degree; *—Close-Up and/or Display in one of the other books in this series*

Public Health—General	M,D
Public History	M
Quantitative Analysis	M
Reading Education	M
Rhetoric	M
School Psychology	M,O
Science Education	M,D
Secondary Education	M
Social Sciences	M
Sociology	M
Spanish	M
Special Education	M
Structural Engineering	M,D
Sustainability Management	M
Sustainable Development	M,D
Technical Communication	M
Toxicology	D
Transportation and Highway Engineering	M,D
Urban and Regional Planning	M,D
Urban Design	M,D
Water Resources	M
Western European Studies	M
Women's Health Nursing	M,D
Women's Studies	M
Writing	M

UNIVERSITY OF CONNECTICUT

Accounting	M,D
Actuarial Science	M,D
Adult Education	M,D
African Studies	M
Agricultural Economics and Agribusiness	M,D
Agricultural Education	M,D,O
Agricultural Sciences—General	M,D
Agronomy and Soil Sciences	M,D
Allied Health—General	M
Animal Sciences	M,D
Anthropology	M,D
Applied Mathematics	M
Art History	M
Art/Fine Arts	M
Biochemistry	M,D
Biological and Biomedical Sciences—General	D
Biomedical Engineering	M,D
Biophysics	M,D
Biopsychology	M,D,O
Botany	M,D
Business Administration and Management—General	M,D*
Cell Biology	M,D
Chemical Engineering	M,D
Chemistry	M,D
Child and Family Studies	M,D,O
Civil Engineering	M,D
Clinical Psychology	M,D,O
Clinical Research	M
Cognitive Sciences	M,D,O
Communication Disorders	M,D
Communication—General	M
Comparative Literature	M,D
Computer Science	M,D
Corporate and Organizational Communication	D
Counseling Psychology	M,D,O
Counselor Education	M,D,O
Developmental Biology	M,D
Developmental Psychology	M,D,O
Ecology	M,D,O
Economics	M,D
Education of the Gifted	M,D,O
Education—General	M,D,O
Educational Leadership and Administration	D,O
Educational Measurement and Evaluation	M,D,O
Educational Media/ Instructional Technology	M,D,O
Educational Psychology	M,D,O
Electrical Engineering	M,D
Elementary Education	M,D,O
Engineering and Applied Sciences—General	M,D
English Education	M,D,O
English	M,D
Entomology	M,D
Environmental and Occupational Health	M
Environmental Engineering	M,D
Exercise and Sports Science	M,D
Experimental Psychology	M,D,O
Finance and Banking	M,D,O
Foreign Languages Education	M,D,O
Foundations and Philosophy of Education	D
French	M,D
Genetics	M,D
Genomic Sciences	M
Geographic Information Systems	M,D,O
Geography	M,D,O
Geology	M,D
German	M,D
Health Psychology	M,D,O
Health Services Management and Hospital Administration	M,D
Higher Education	M
History	M,D
Homeland Security	M
Human Development	M,D,O
Human Resources Development	M
Human Resources Management	M
Industrial and Organizational Psychology	M,D,O
International Affairs	M
Italian	M,D
Jewish Studies	M
Latin American Studies	M
Law	P
Leisure Studies	M,D
Linguistics	M,D
Marine Sciences	M,D
Marketing	M,D
Materials Engineering	M,D
Materials Sciences	M,D
Mathematical and Computational Finance	M
Mathematics Education	M,D,O
Mathematics	M,D
Mechanical Engineering	M,D
Medicinal and Pharmaceutical Chemistry	M,D
Medieval and Renaissance Studies	M,D
Metallurgical Engineering and Metallurgy	M,D
Microbiology	M,D
Molecular Biology	M
Multilingual and Multicultural Education	M,D,O
Music Education	M,D,O
Music	M,D,O
Natural Resources	M,D
Neurobiology	M,D
Neuroscience	M,D,O
Nonprofit Management	M,O
Nursing—General	M,D,O
Nutrition	M,D
Oceanography	M,D
Oral and Dental Sciences	M
Pathobiology	M,D
Pharmaceutical Sciences	M,D
Pharmacology	M,D
Pharmacy	P
Philosophy	M,D
Physical Therapy	D
Physics	M,D
Physiology	M,D
Plant Biology	M,D
Plant Molecular Biology	M,D
Plant Sciences	M,D
Political Science	M,D
Polymer Science and Engineering	M,D
Psychology—General	M,D,O
Public Administration	M,O
Public Health—General	M
Quantitative Analysis	M,O
Reading Education	M,D,O
School Psychology	M,D,O
Science Education	M,D
Secondary Education	M,D,O
Social Psychology	M,D,O
Social Sciences Education	M,D,O
Sociology	M,D
Software Engineering	M,D
Spanish	M,D
Special Education	M,D,O
Statistics	M,D
Structural Biology	M,D
Sustainable Development	M
Theater	M
Toxicology	M,D
Western European Studies	M
Zoology	M,D

UNIVERSITY OF CONNECTICUT HEALTH CENTER

Allopathic Medicine	P
Biochemistry	D
Biological and Biomedical Sciences—General	D*
Cell Biology	D*
Clinical Research	M
Dentistry	P,O
Developmental Biology	D
Genetics	D
Immunology	D*
Molecular Biology	D*
Neuroscience	D
Oral and Dental Sciences	M,D*
Public Health—General	M

UNIVERSITY OF DALLAS

Accounting	M
American Studies	M
Art/Fine Arts	M
Business Administration and Management—General	M
Comparative Literature	D
English	M
Entertainment Management	M
Finance and Banking	M
Health Services Management and Hospital Administration	M
Human Resources Management	M
Humanities	M
International Business	M
Logistics	M
Management Information Systems	M
Management of Technology	M
Management Strategy and Policy	M
Marketing	M
Organizational Management	M
Pastoral Ministry and Counseling	M
Philosophy	M,D
Political Science	M,D
Project Management	M
Psychology—General	M
Sports Management	M
Supply Chain Management	M
Theology	M

UNIVERSITY OF DAYTON

Accounting	M
Aerospace/Aeronautical Engineering	M,D
Agricultural Engineering	M
Applied Mathematics	M
Art Education	M
Bioengineering	M
Biological and Biomedical Sciences—General	M,D
Biosystems Engineering	M
Business Administration and Management—General	M
Chemical Engineering	M
Chemistry	M
Civil Engineering	M
Clinical Psychology	M
Communication—General	M
Computer and Information Systems Security	M
Computer Engineering	M,D
Computer Science	M
Counselor Education	M,O
Early Childhood Education	M
Education—General	M,D,O
Educational Leadership and Administration	M,D,O
Educational Media/ Instructional Technology	M
Electrical Engineering	M,D
Electronic Commerce	M
Engineering and Applied Sciences—General	M,D
Engineering Management	M
English	M
Entrepreneurship	M
Environmental Engineering	M
Environmental Management and Policy	M,D
Exercise and Sports Science	M,D
Finance and Banking	M
Human Development	M,O
Industrial and Manufacturing Management	M
International Business	M
Law	P,M
Management Information Systems	M
Management Strategy and Policy	M
Marketing	M
Materials Engineering	M,D
Mathematical and Computational Finance	M
Mathematics Education	M
Mechanical Engineering	M,D
Mechanics	M
Middle School Education	M
Music Education	M
Optical Sciences	M,D
Pastoral Ministry and Counseling	M,D
Physical Education	M,D
Physical Therapy	M,D
Psychology—General	M
Public Administration	M
Reading Education	M
School Psychology	M,O
Secondary Education	M
Social Psychology	M,O
Special Education	M
Structural Engineering	M
Student Affairs	M,O
Theology	M,D
Transportation and Highway Engineering	M
Water Resources Engineering	M

UNIVERSITY OF DELAWARE

Accounting	M
Adult Nursing	M,O
Agricultural Economics and Agribusiness	M
Agricultural Education	M
Agricultural Sciences—General	M,D
Agronomy and Soil Sciences	M,D
American Studies	M

Animal Sciences M,D
Applied Arts and Design—General M
Applied Mathematics M,D
Art History M,D
Art/Fine Arts M
Astronomy M,D
Biochemistry M,D
Biological and Biomedical Sciences—General M,D
Biotechnology M,D
Business Administration and Management—General M,D
Business Education M,D
Cancer Biology/Oncology M,D
Cell Biology M,D
Chemical Engineering M,D
Chemistry M,D
Child and Family Studies M,D
Chinese M
Civil Engineering M,D
Clinical Psychology D
Clothing and Textiles M
Cognitive Sciences D
Communication—General M
Computer Engineering M,D
Computer Science M,D
Criminal Justice and Criminology M,D
Curriculum and Instruction M,D,O
Developmental Biology M,D
Ecology M,D
Economics M,D
Education—General M,D,O
Educational Leadership and Administration M,D,O
Electrical Engineering M,D
Energy Management and Policy M,D
Engineering and Applied Sciences—General M,D
English as a Second Language M,D,O
English M,D
Entomology M,D
Entrepreneurship M,D
Environmental Engineering M,D
Environmental Management and Policy M,D
Evolutionary Biology M,D
Exercise and Sports Science M
Family Nurse Practitioner Studies M,O
Finance and Banking M
Fish, Game, and Wildlife Management M,D
Food Science and Technology M,D
Foreign Languages Education M
French M
Genetics M,D
Geography M,D
Geology M,D
Geotechnical Engineering M,D
German M
Gerontological Nursing M,O
Health Promotion M
Higher Education M,D,O
Historic Preservation M,D
History of Science and Technology M,D
History M,D
HIV/AIDS Nursing M,O
Horticulture M
Hospitality Management M
Human Development M,D
Information Science M,D
International Affairs M,D
Kinesiology and Movement Studies M,D
Liberal Studies M
Linguistics M,D
Management Information Systems M
Management of Technology M
Marine Affairs M,D
Marine Geology M,D
Marine Sciences M,D
Materials Engineering M,D
Materials Sciences M,D
Maternal and Child/Neonatal Nursing M,O
Mathematics M,D
Mechanical Engineering M,D
Microbiology M,D
Molecular Biology M,D
Multilingual and Multicultural Education M,D,O
Music Education M
Music M
Natural Resources M
Neuroscience D
Nonprofit Management M,D
Nursing and Healthcare Administration M,O
Nursing—General M,O
Nutrition M
Ocean Engineering M,D
Oceanography M,D
Oncology Nursing M,O
Operations Research M,D
Pediatric Nursing M,O
Physical Therapy D
Physics M,D
Physiology M,D
Plant Sciences M,D
Political Science M,D
Psychiatric Nursing M,O
Psychology—General D
Public Administration M*
Public Policy M,D
School Psychology M,D,O
Social Psychology D
Sociology M,D
Spanish M
Statistics M
Structural Engineering M,D
Theater M
Translation and Interpretation M
Transportation and Highway Engineering M,D
Urban Studies M,D
Water Resources Engineering M,D
Women's Health Nursing M,O

UNIVERSITY OF DENVER

Accounting M
Adult Education M,D,O
Advertising and Public Relations M,O
Anthropology M
Applied Physics M,D
Archaeology M
Art History M
Art/Fine Arts M,O
Arts Administration M,O
Astronomy M,D
Bioengineering M,D
Biological and Biomedical Sciences—General M,D
Business Administration and Management—General M
Chemistry M,D
Child and Family Studies M,D,O
Clinical Psychology M,D
Computer and Information Systems Security M,O
Computer Art and Design M
Computer Engineering M,D
Computer Science M,D
Conflict Resolution and Mediation/Peace Studies M,O
Construction Management M
Corporate and Organizational Communication M,O
Counseling Psychology M,D,O
Criminal Justice and Criminology M,O
Cultural Anthropology M
Cultural Studies M,O
Curriculum and Instruction M,D,O
Database Systems M,O
Developmental Psychology D
Economics M
Education—General M,D,O
Educational Leadership and Administration M,D,O
Educational Measurement and Evaluation M,D,O
Educational Psychology M,D,O
Electrical Engineering M,D
Electronic Commerce M
Emergency Management M,O
Energy Management and Policy M,O
Engineering and Applied Sciences—General M,D
English M,D
Environmental and Occupational Health M,O
Environmental Management and Policy M,O
Finance and Banking M
Forensic Psychology M,D
Geographic Information Systems M,D,O
Geography M,D
Health Law M,O
Health Services Management and Hospital Administration M,O
Higher Education M,D,O
History M,O
Homeland Security M,D,O
Human Resources Development M,O
Human Resources Management M,O
Interdisciplinary Studies M,D
International Affairs M,D,O
International Business M,D,O
International Development M,D,O
International Economics M,D,O
International Health M,D,O
Internet and Interactive Multimedia M,O
Internet Engineering M,O
Law P,M
Legal and Justice Studies M,O
Library Science M,D,O
Management Information Systems M,O
Management of Technology M,O
Management Strategy and Policy M
Marketing M
Mass Communication M
Materials Engineering M,D
Materials Sciences M,D
Mathematics M,D
Mechanical Engineering M,D
Media Studies M
Museum Studies M
Music Education M,O
Music M,O
National Security M,D,O
Natural Resources M,O
Neuroscience D
Organizational Management M,O
Physics M,D
Project Management M,O
Psychology—General M,D
Public Policy M
Real Estate M
Religion M,D
Rhetoric M,D
School Psychology M,D,O
Social Psychology D
Social Work M,D,O
Software Engineering M,O
Speech and Interpersonal Communication M,D
Sport Psychology M,D
Statistics M
Systems Engineering M,D
Taxation M
Telecommunications M,O
Theology D
Translation and Interpretation M,O
Writing M,D,O

UNIVERSITY OF DETROIT MERCY

Addictions/Substance Abuse Counseling M,O
Allied Health—General M,O
Architectural Engineering M
Biochemistry M
Business Administration and Management—General M,O
Chemistry M
Civil Engineering M,D
Clinical Psychology M,D
Computer Education M
Computer Engineering M,D
Computer Science M
Counselor Education M
Criminal Justice and Criminology M
Curriculum and Instruction M
Dentistry P
Education—General M
Educational Leadership and Administration M
Electrical Engineering M,D
Engineering and Applied Sciences—General M,D
Engineering Management M
Environmental Engineering M,D
Family Nurse Practitioner Studies M,O
Health Services Management and Hospital Administration M
Industrial and Organizational Psychology M
Information Science M
Law P
Liberal Studies M
Management Information Systems M
Mathematics Education M
Mechanical Engineering M,D
Military and Defense Studies M
Nurse Anesthesia M
Oral and Dental Sciences M,O
Physician Assistant Studies M
Psychology—General M,D,O
Religion M
School Psychology O
Software Engineering M
Special Education M

UNIVERSITY OF DUBUQUE

Business Administration and Management—General M
Communication—General M
Theology P,M,D

UNIVERSITY OF EVANSVILLE

Business Administration and Management—General M
Computer Science M
Education—General M
Electrical Engineering M
Engineering and Applied Sciences—General M
Health Services Management and Hospital Administration M
Nursing—General M
Physical Therapy D
Public Administration M

*M—master's degree; P—first professional degree; D—doctorate; O—other advanced degree; *—Close-Up and/or Display in one of the other books in this series*

THE UNIVERSITY OF FINDLAY

Program	Degrees
Athletic Training and Sports Medicine	M
Business Administration and Management—General	M
Early Childhood Education	M
Education—General	M
Educational Leadership and Administration	M
Educational Media/Instructional Technology	M
Elementary Education	M
English as a Second Language	M
Environmental Management and Policy	M
Health Services Management and Hospital Administration	M
Hospitality Management	M
Multilingual and Multicultural Education	M
Occupational Therapy	M
Organizational Management	M
Pharmacy	P
Physical Therapy	D
Physician Assistant Studies	M
Public Administration	M
Special Education	M

UNIVERSITY OF FLORIDA

Program	Degrees
Accounting	M,D
Advertising and Public Relations	M
Aerospace/Aeronautical Engineering	M,D,O
African Studies	M,D,O
Agricultural Economics and Agribusiness	M,D
Agricultural Education	M,D
Agricultural Engineering	M,D,O
Agricultural Sciences—General	M,D
Agronomy and Soil Sciences	M,D
Allied Health—General	M,D
Allopathic Medicine	P
American Studies	M,D
Animal Sciences	M,D
Anthropology	M,D
Aquaculture	M,D
Architecture	M,D
Art Education	M,D
Art History	M,D
Art/Fine Arts	M,D
Arts Administration	M
Asian Studies	M,D
Astronomy	M,D
Athletic Training and Sports Medicine	M,D
Biochemistry	M,D
Bioengineering	M,D,O
Biological and Biomedical Sciences—General	D
Biomedical Engineering	M,D,O
Biostatistics	M
Botany	M,D
Building Science	M,D
Business Administration and Management—General	M,D,O
Cell Biology	M,D
Chemical Engineering	M,D
Chemistry	M,D
Civil Engineering	M,D,O
Classics	M,D
Clinical Psychology	D
Clinical Research	M
Cognitive Sciences	M,D
Communication Disorders	M,D
Communication—General	M,D
Computer Art and Design	M,D
Computer Engineering	M,D,O
Computer Science	M,D
Construction Engineering	M,D
Counseling Psychology	M,D
Counselor Education	M,D,O
Criminal Justice and Criminology	M,D
Curriculum and Instruction	M,D,O
Dentistry	P,O
Developmental Psychology	M,D
Early Childhood Education	M,D,O
Ecology	M,D
Economics	M,D
Education—General	M,D,O
Educational Leadership and Administration	M,D,O
Educational Measurement and Evaluation	M,D,O
Educational Psychology	M,D,O
Electrical Engineering	M,D,O
Electronic Commerce	M
Elementary Education	M,D,O
Engineering and Applied Sciences—General	M,D,O*
English as a Second Language	M,D,O
English Education	M,D,O
English	M,D
Entomology	M,D
Entrepreneurship	M,D,O
Environmental and Occupational Health	M
Environmental Engineering	M,D,O
Environmental Law	P,M,D
Epidemiology	M
Exercise and Sports Science	M,D
Family and Consumer Sciences-General	M
Finance and Banking	M,D,O
Fish, Game, and Wildlife Management	M,D
Food Science and Technology	M,D
Forensic Sciences	M,O
Forestry	M,D
Foundations and Philosophy of Education	M,D,O
French	M,D
Gender Studies	M,O
Genetics	D
Genomic Sciences	D
Geography	M,D
Geology	M,D
Geosciences	M,D
German	M,D
Graphic Design	M,D
Health Communication	M,D,O
Health Education	M,D,O
Health Psychology	D
Health Services Management and Hospital Administration	M,D
Health Services Research	M,D
Higher Education	M,D,O
Historic Preservation	D
History	M,D
Horticulture	M,D
Human Resources Management	M
Immunology	D
Industrial/Management Engineering	M,D,O
Information Science	M,D
Interior Design	M,D
International Affairs	M
International Business	P,M,D
International Development	M,D,O
Internet and Interactive Multimedia	M,D
Journalism	M
Kinesiology and Movement Studies	M,D
Landscape Architecture	M
Latin American Studies	M,D,O
Law	P,M,D
Limnology	M,D
Linguistics	M,D,O
Management Information Systems	M,D
Management Strategy and Policy	M
Marine Sciences	M,D
Marketing	M,D
Marriage and Family Therapy	M,D,O
Mass Communication	M,D
Materials Engineering	M,D,O
Materials Sciences	M,D,O
Mathematics Education	M,D,O
Mathematics	M,D
Mechanical Engineering	M,D,O
Media Studies	M
Medical Imaging	M,D
Medicinal and Pharmaceutical Chemistry	M,D
Microbiology	M,D
Molecular Biology	M,D
Molecular Genetics	M,D
Multilingual and Multicultural Education	M,D,O
Museum Studies	M,D
Music Education	M,D
Music	M,D
Natural Resources	M,D
Neuroscience	M,D
Nuclear Engineering	M,D,O
Nursing—General	M,D
Nutrition	M,D
Occupational Therapy	M
Ocean Engineering	M,D,O
Oral and Dental Sciences	M,D,O
Pathology	D
Pharmaceutical Administration	M,D
Pharmaceutical Sciences	M,D
Pharmacology	M,D
Pharmacy	P
Philosophy	M,D
Photography	M,D
Physical Education	M,D
Physical Therapy	D
Physician Assistant Studies	M
Physics	M,D
Physiology	M,D
Plant Biology	M,D
Plant Molecular Biology	M,D
Plant Pathology	M,D
Plant Sciences	D
Political Science	M,D,O
Psychology—General	M,D
Public Affairs	M,D,O
Public Health—General	M
Quantitative Analysis	M
Reading Education	M,D,O
Real Estate	M,D,O
Recreation and Park Management	M,D
Rehabilitation Sciences	D
Religion	M,D
School Psychology	M,D,O
Science Education	M,D,O
Social Psychology	M,D
Social Sciences Education	M,D,O
Social Sciences	M
Sociology	M,D
Spanish	M,D
Special Education	M,D,O
Sports Management	M,D
Statistics	M,D
Student Affairs	M,D,O
Supply Chain Management	M,D
Systems Engineering	M,D,O
Taxation	P,M,D
Theater	M
Toxicology	M,D,O
Urban and Regional Planning	M
Veterinary Medicine	P
Veterinary Sciences	M,D,O
Water Resources	M,D
Western European Studies	M,D
Women's Studies	M,O
Writing	M,D
Zoology	M,D

UNIVERSITY OF GEORGIA

Program	Degrees
Accounting	M
Adult Education	M,D,O
Agricultural Economics and Agribusiness	M,D
Agricultural Education	M
Agricultural Engineering	M,D
Agricultural Sciences—General	M,D
Agronomy and Soil Sciences	M,D
Analytical Chemistry	M,D
Anatomy	M
Animal Sciences	M,D
Anthropology	M,D
Applied Economics	M,D
Applied Mathematics	M,D
Archaeology	M,D
Art Education	M,D,O
Art History	M
Art/Fine Arts	M
Artificial Intelligence/Robotics	M
Biochemical Engineering	M
Biochemistry	M,D
Bioengineering	M,D
Bioinformatics	M,D,O
Biological and Biomedical Sciences—General	D
Biostatistics	M
Business Administration and Management—General	M,D
Cell Biology	M,D
Chemistry	M,D
Child and Family Studies	M,D,O
Classics	M
Clothing and Textiles	M,D
Communication Disorders	M,D,O
Communication—General	M,D
Comparative Literature	M,D
Computer Science	M,D
Consumer Economics	M,D
Counselor Education	M,D,O
Early Childhood Education	M,D,O
Ecology	M,D
Economics	M,D
Education—General	M,D,O
Educational Leadership and Administration	M,D,O
Educational Media/Instructional Technology	M,D,O
Educational Policy	M,D,O
Educational Psychology	M,D,O
Elementary Education	M,D,O
English Education	M,D,O
English	M,D
Entomology	M,D
Environmental and Occupational Health	M
Environmental Design	M
Environmental Engineering	M
Epidemiology	M
Family and Consumer Sciences-General	M,D
Food Science and Technology	M,D
Foreign Languages Education	M,D,O
Forestry	M,D
Foundations and Philosophy of Education	M,D,O
French	M
Genetics	M,D
Genomic Sciences	M,D
Geography	M,D
Geology	M,D
German	M
Gerontology	O
Health Education	M,D
Health Promotion	M,D
Health Services Management and Hospital Administration	M
Higher Education	D
Historic Preservation	M
History	M,D
Horticulture	M,D

Program	Degrees
Human Resources Management	M,D,O
Infectious Diseases	M,D
Inorganic Chemistry	M,D
Interior Design	M,D
Internet and Interactive Multimedia	M
Internet Engineering	M
Journalism	M,D
Kinesiology and Movement Studies	M,D
Landscape Architecture	M
Law	P,M
Leisure Studies	M,D,O
Linguistics	M,D
Management Information Systems	D
Marine Sciences	M,D
Marketing Research	M
Mass Communication	M,D
Mathematics Education	M,D,O
Mathematics	M,D
Microbiology	M,D
Middle School Education	M,D,O
Molecular Biology	M,D
Music Education	M,D,O
Music	M,D
Natural Resources	M,D
Neuroscience	D
Nonprofit Management	M,O
Nutrition	M,D
Organic Chemistry	M,D
Pathology	M,D
Pharmaceutical Sciences	M,D,O
Pharmacology	M,D
Pharmacy	P
Philosophy	M,D
Physical Chemistry	M,D
Physical Education	M,D
Physics	M,D
Physiology	M,D
Plant Biology	M,D
Plant Pathology	M,D
Plant Sciences	M,D
Political Science	M,D
Psychology—General	M,D
Public Administration	M,D
Public Policy	M,D
Reading Education	M,D,O
Religion	M
Romance Languages	M,D
Science Education	M,D,O
Social Sciences Education	M,D,O
Social Work	M,D,O
Sociology	M,D
Spanish	M
Special Education	M,D,O
Speech and Interpersonal Communication	M,D
Statistics	M,D
Student Affairs	M,D,O
Sustainable Development	M,D
Theater	M,D
Toxicology	M,D
Veterinary Medicine	P,M
Veterinary Sciences	M,D
Vocational and Technical Education	M,D,O
Women's Studies	O
Writing	M,D

UNIVERSITY OF GREAT FALLS

Program	Degrees
Counseling Psychology	M
Criminal Justice and Criminology	M
Education—General	M
Human Services	M
Secondary Education	M

UNIVERSITY OF GUAM

Program	Degrees
Art/Fine Arts	M
Biological and Biomedical Sciences—General	M
Business Administration and Management—General	M
Counselor Education	M
Education—General	M
Educational Leadership and Administration	M
English as a Second Language	M
English	M
Environmental Sciences	M
Graphic Design	M
Marine Biology	M
Pacific Area/Pacific Rim Studies	M
Public Administration	M
Reading Education	M
Secondary Education	M
Social Work	M
Special Education	M

UNIVERSITY OF GUELPH

Program	Degrees
Acute Care/Critical Care Nursing	M,D,O
Agricultural Economics and Agribusiness	M,D
Agricultural Sciences—General	M,D,O
Agronomy and Soil Sciences	M,D
Anatomy	M,D
Anesthesiologist Assistant Studies	M,D,O
Animal Sciences	M,D
Anthropology	M,D
Applied Mathematics	M,D
Applied Psychology	M,D
Applied Statistics	M,D
Aquaculture	M
Art/Fine Arts	M
Atmospheric Sciences	M,D
Biochemistry	M,D
Bioengineering	M,D
Biological and Biomedical Sciences—General	M,D
Biophysics	M,D
Biotechnology	M,D
Botany	M,D
Business Administration and Management—General	M,D
Cardiovascular Sciences	M,D,O
Cell Biology	M,D
Chemistry	M,D
Child and Family Studies	M,D
Clinical Psychology	M,D
Cognitive Sciences	M,D
Comparative Literature	D
Computer Science	M,D
Consumer Economics	M
Criminal Justice and Criminology	M,D
Demography and Population Studies	M,D
Ecology	M,D
Economics	M,D
Emergency Medical Services	M,D,O
Engineering and Applied Sciences—General	M,D
English	M
Entomology	M,D
Environmental Biology	M,D
Environmental Engineering	M,D
Environmental Management and Policy	M,D
Environmental Sciences	M,D
Epidemiology	M,D
Evolutionary Biology	M,D
Food Science and Technology	M,D
French	M
Geography	M,D
History	M,D
Horticulture	M,D
Hospitality Management	M
Human Development	M,D
Immunology	M,D,O
Industrial and Organizational Psychology	M,D
Infectious Diseases	M,D,O
International Development	M,D
Landscape Architecture	M
Marriage and Family Therapy	M,D
Mathematics	M,D
Medical Imaging	M,D,O
Medieval and Renaissance Studies	D
Microbiology	M,D
Molecular Biology	M,D
Molecular Genetics	M,D
Natural Resources	M,D
Neuroscience	M,D,O
Nutrition	M,D
Organizational Management	M
Pathology	M,D,O
Pharmacology	M,D
Philosophy	M,D
Physics	M,D
Physiology	M,D
Plant Pathology	M,D
Political Science	M
Psychology—General	M,D
Public Administration	M
Public Policy	M
Rural Planning and Studies	M,D
Social Psychology	M,D
Sociology	M,D
Statistics	M,D
Theater	M
Toxicology	M,D
Veterinary Medicine	M,D,O
Veterinary Sciences	M,D,O
Vision Sciences	M,D,O
Water Resources Engineering	M,D
Western European Studies	M
Zoology	M,D

UNIVERSITY OF HARTFORD

Program	Degrees
Accounting	M,O
Architecture	M
Art/Fine Arts	M
Biological and Biomedical Sciences—General	M
Business Administration and Management—General	M
Clinical Psychology	M,D
Communication—General	M
Community Health Nursing	M
Counselor Education	M,O
Early Childhood Education	M
Education—General	M,D,O
Educational Leadership and Administration	D,O
Educational Media/Instructional Technology	M
Elementary Education	M
Engineering and Applied Sciences—General	M
Experimental Psychology	M
Music Education	M,D,O
Music	M,D,O
Neuroscience	M
Nursing Education	M
Nursing—General	M
Organizational Behavior	M
Physical Therapy	M,D
Psychology—General	M,D
School Psychology	M
Taxation	M,O

UNIVERSITY OF HAWAII AT HILO

Program	Degrees
Asian Studies	M
Conservation Biology	M
Counseling Psychology	M
Cultural Studies	M,D
Education—General	M
Environmental Sciences	M
Foreign Languages Education	M,D
Marine Biology	M

UNIVERSITY OF HAWAII AT MANOA

Program	Degrees
Accounting	M,D
Adult Nursing	M,D,O
Agricultural Sciences—General	M,D
Allopathic Medicine	P
American Studies	M,D,O
Animal Sciences	M
Anthropology	M,D
Architecture	D
Art History	M
Art/Fine Arts	M
Asian Languages	M,D
Asian Studies	O
Astronomy	M,D
Bioengineering	M
Biological and Biomedical Sciences—General	M,D
Botany	M,D
Business Administration and Management—General	M
Chemistry	M,D
Chinese	M,D,O
Civil Engineering	M,D
Clinical Psychology	M,D,O
Communication Disorders	M
Communication—General	M,O
Community Health Nursing	M,D,O
Computer Science	M,D,O
Conflict Resolution and Mediation/Peace Studies	O
Conservation Biology	M,D
Cultural Studies	O
Curriculum and Instruction	M,D
Dance	M,D
Demography and Population Studies	O
Developmental Biology	M,D
Disability Studies	O
Early Childhood Education	M
Ecology	M,D
Economics	M,D
Education—General	M,D,O
Educational Leadership and Administration	M,D
Educational Media/Instructional Technology	M,D
Educational Policy	D
Educational Psychology	M,D
Electrical Engineering	M,D
Emergency Management	O
Engineering and Applied Sciences—General	M,D
English as a Second Language	M,D,O
English	M,D
Entomology	M,D
Entrepreneurship	M,O
Environmental Engineering	M,D
Environmental Management and Policy	M,D,O
Epidemiology	D
Evolutionary Biology	M,D
Family Nurse Practitioner Studies	M,D,O
Finance and Banking	M,D
Financial Engineering	M
Food Science and Technology	M
Foreign Languages Education	M,D,O
Foundations and Philosophy of Education	M,D
French	M
Genetics	M,D
Geochemistry	M,D
Geography	M,D,O
Geological Engineering	M,D
Geology	M,D
Geophysics	M,D
Historic Preservation	O
History	M,D
Horticulture	M,D
Human Resources Management	M

*M—master's degree; P—first professional degree; D—doctorate; O—other advanced degree; *—Close-Up and/or Display in one of the other books in this series*

Hydrogeology	M,D
Information Science	M,D
Information Studies	M,O
International Affairs	O
International Business	M,D
Japanese	M,D,O
Kinesiology and Movement Studies	M,D
Law	P,M,O
Library Science	M,O
Linguistics	M,D
Management Information Systems	M,D,O
Marine Biology	M,D
Marine Geology	M,D
Marine Sciences	O
Marketing	M,D
Mathematics	M,D
Mechanical Engineering	M,D
Medical Microbiology	M,D
Meteorology	M,D
Microbiology	M,D
Molecular Biology	M,D
Museum Studies	O
Music	M,D
Natural Resources	M,D
Nursing and Healthcare Administration	M,D,O
Nursing—General	M,D,O*
Nutrition	M,D
Ocean Engineering	M,D
Oceanography	M,D
Organizational Behavior	M
Organizational Management	M,D
Pacific Area/Pacific Rim Studies	M,O
Philosophy	M,D
Physics	M,D
Physiology	M,D
Planetary and Space Sciences	M,D
Plant Pathology	M,D
Plant Sciences	M,D
Political Science	M,D
Psychology—General	M,D,O
Public Administration	M,O
Public Health—General	M,D,O
Public Policy	O
Real Estate	M
Religion	M
Reproductive Biology	M,D
Social Psychology	M,D,O
Social Work	M,D
Sociology	M,D
Spanish	M
Special Education	M,D
Speech and Interpersonal Communication	M
Taxation	M
Telecommunications	O
Theater	M,D
Travel and Tourism	M
Urban and Regional Planning	M,D,O
Women's Studies	O
Zoology	M,D

UNIVERSITY OF HOUSTON

Accounting	M,D
Advertising and Public Relations	M
Anthropology	M
Applied Economics	M,D
Applied Mathematics	M,D
Architecture	M
Art History	M
Art/Fine Arts	M
Atmospheric Sciences	M,D
Biochemistry	M,D
Biological and Biomedical Sciences—General	M,D
Biomedical Engineering	D
Business Administration and Management—General	M,D
Chemical Engineering	M,D
Chemistry	M,D
Civil Engineering	M,D
Clinical Psychology	M,D
Communication Disorders	M
Communication—General	M
Comparative Literature	M
Computer and Information Systems Security	M
Computer Science	M,D
Construction Management	M
Counseling Psychology	M,D
Cultural Studies	M
Curriculum and Instruction	M,D
Developmental Psychology	M,D
Economics	M,D
Education—General	M,D
Educational Leadership and Administration	M,D
Educational Psychology	M,D
Electrical Engineering	M,D
Engineering and Applied Sciences—General	M,D
Environmental Law	P,M
Exercise and Sports Science	M,D
Family and Consumer Sciences-General	M
Finance and Banking	M
Foundations and Philosophy of Education	M,D
Geology	M,D
Geophysics	M,D
Health Communication	M
Health Education	M,D
Health Law	P,M
Higher Education	M,D
Hispanic Studies	M,D
History	M,D
Hospitality Management	M
Human Resources Development	M
Industrial and Organizational Psychology	M,D
Industrial/Management Engineering	M,D
Information Science	M,D
Intellectual Property Law	P,M
Kinesiology and Movement Studies	M,D
Law	P,M
Linguistics	M,D
Logistics	M
Marketing	D
Mass Communication	M
Mathematics	M,D
Mechanical Engineering	M,D
Music Education	M,D
Music	M,D
Nutrition	M,D
Optometry	P
Petroleum Engineering	M,D
Pharmaceutical Administration	P,M,D
Pharmaceutical Sciences	P,M,D
Pharmacology	P,M,D
Pharmacy	P,M,D
Philosophy	M
Physical Education	M,D
Physics	M,D
Planetary and Space Sciences	M,D
Political Science	M,D
Project Management	M
Psychology—General	M,D
Public Administration	M,D
Social Psychology	M,D
Social Work	M,D
Sociology	M
Spanish	M,D
Special Education	M,D
Speech and Interpersonal Communication	M
Supply Chain Management	M
Taxation	P,M
Telecommunications	M
Theater	M
Vision Sciences	M,D
Writing	M,D

UNIVERSITY OF HOUSTON–CLEAR LAKE

Accounting	M
Biological and Biomedical Sciences—General	M
Biotechnology	M
Business Administration and Management—General	M
Chemistry	M
Clinical Psychology	M
Computer Engineering	M
Computer Science	M
Counselor Education	M
Criminal Justice and Criminology	M
Cultural Studies	M
Curriculum and Instruction	M
Early Childhood Education	M
Education—General	M,D
Educational Leadership and Administration	M,D
Educational Media/Instructional Technology	M
English	M
Environmental Management and Policy	M
Environmental Sciences	M
Exercise and Sports Science	M
Finance and Banking	M
Foundations and Philosophy of Education	M
Health Services Management and Hospital Administration	M
History	M
Human Resources Management	M
Humanities	M
Information Science	M
Library Science	M
Management Information Systems	M
Marriage and Family Therapy	M
Mathematics	M
Multilingual and Multicultural Education	M
Physics	M
Psychology—General	M
Reading Education	M
School Psychology	M
Sociology	M
Software Engineering	M
Statistics	M
Systems Engineering	M

UNIVERSITY OF HOUSTON–DOWNTOWN

Criminal Justice and Criminology	M
Curriculum and Instruction	M
Elementary Education	M
English	M
Multilingual and Multicultural Education	M
Secondary Education	M
Technical Communication	M
Urban Education	M
Writing	M

UNIVERSITY OF HOUSTON–VICTORIA

Accounting	M
Business Administration and Management—General	M
Computer Science	M
Counseling Psychology	M
Counselor Education	M
Curriculum and Instruction	M
Economic Development	M
Education—General	M
Educational Leadership and Administration	M
Entrepreneurship	M
Finance and Banking	M
Interdisciplinary Studies	M
International Business	M
Marketing	M
Nursing—General	M
Psychology—General	M
Publishing	M
School Psychology	M
Special Education	M

UNIVERSITY OF IDAHO

Accounting	M
Agricultural Economics and Agribusiness	M
Agricultural Education	M
Agricultural Engineering	M,D
Agronomy and Soil Sciences	M,D
American Indian/Native American Studies	P
Animal Sciences	M,D
Anthropology	M
Applied Economics	M
Architecture	M
Art Education	M
Art/Fine Arts	M
Biochemistry	M,D
Bioengineering	M,D
Bioinformatics	M,D
Biological and Biomedical Sciences—General	M,D
Business Administration and Management—General	M
Chemical Engineering	M,D
Chemistry	M,D
Civil Engineering	M,D
Computational Biology	M,D
Computer Engineering	M
Computer Science	M,D
Consumer Economics	M
Counselor Education	M
Curriculum and Instruction	M,O
Economics	M
Education—General	M,D,O
Educational Leadership and Administration	M,O
Electrical Engineering	M,D
Engineering and Applied Sciences—General	M,D
Engineering Management	M
English as a Second Language	M
English	M
Entomology	M,D
Environmental Engineering	M
Environmental Law	P
Environmental Sciences	M,D
Fish, Game, and Wildlife Management	M,D
Food Science and Technology	M,D
Geography	M,D
Geological Engineering	M
Geology	M,D
Graphic Design	M
History	M,D
Hydrology	M
Interdisciplinary Studies	M
Landscape Architecture	M
Law	P
Materials Sciences	M,D
Mathematics	M,D
Metallurgical Engineering and Metallurgy	M,D
Microbiology	M,D
Mineral/Mining Engineering	M,D
Molecular Biology	M,D
Music	M
Natural Resources	M,D
Neuroscience	M,D
Nuclear Engineering	M,D
Physical Education	M
Physics	M,D
Plant Sciences	M,D
Political Science	M,D
Psychology—General	M
Public Administration	M

Program	Degrees
Public Affairs	M,D
Recreation and Park Management	M
School Psychology	O
Social Sciences	M,D
Special Education	M
Statistics	M
Theater	M
Urban and Regional Planning	M
Urban Design	M
Veterinary Sciences	M,D
Water Resources	M,D
Writing	M

UNIVERSITY OF ILLINOIS AT CHICAGO

Program	Degrees
Accounting	M
Acute Care/Critical Care Nursing	M
Adult Nursing	M
Allied Health—General	M,D
Allopathic Medicine	P
Anatomy	D
Anthropology	M,D
Applied Mathematics	M,D
Architecture	M
Art History	M,D
Art/Fine Arts	M
Biochemistry	D
Bioengineering	M,D
Biological and Biomedical Sciences—General	M,D
Biophysics	M,D
Biostatistics	M,D
Biotechnology	D
Business Administration and Management—General	M,D
Cell Biology	D
Chemical Engineering	M,D
Chemistry	M,D
Civil Engineering	M,D
Communication—General	M,D
Community Health Nursing	M
Community Health	M,D
Computer Engineering	M,D
Computer Science	M,D
Criminal Justice and Criminology	M,D
Curriculum and Instruction	M,D
Dentistry	P
Disability Studies	M,D
Economics	M,D
Education—General	M,D
Educational Leadership and Administration	M,D
Educational Policy	M,D
Educational Psychology	D
Electrical Engineering	M,D
Elementary Education	M,D
Engineering and Applied Sciences—General	M,D
English as a Second Language	M
English Education	M,D
English	M,D
Environmental and Occupational Health	M,D
Epidemiology	M,D
Family Nurse Practitioner Studies	M
Forensic Sciences	M
French	M
Genetics	D
Geography	M
Geology	M,D
Geosciences	M,D
German	M,D
Gerontological Nursing	M
Graphic Design	M
Health Education	M
Health Informatics	M
Health Services Management and Hospital Administration	M,D
Health Services Research	M,D
Hispanic and Latin American Languages	M,D
Hispanic Studies	M,D
History	M,D
Human Development	M,D
Immunology	D
Industrial Design	M
Industrial/Management Engineering	M,D
Kinesiology and Movement Studies	M,D
Linguistics	M
Management Information Systems	M,D
Materials Engineering	M,D
Maternal and Child/Neonatal Nursing	M
Mathematical and Computational Finance	M,D
Mathematics Education	M
Mathematics	M,D
Mechanical Engineering	M,D
Medical Illustration	M
Microbiology	D
Molecular Biology	D
Molecular Genetics	D
Multilingual and Multicultural Education	M,D
Neurobiology	D
Neuroscience	D
Nurse Midwifery	M
Nursing and Healthcare Administration	M
Nursing—General	M,D
Nutrition	M,D
Occupational Health Nursing	M
Occupational Therapy	M,D
Operations Research	D
Oral and Dental Sciences	M,D
Pediatric Nursing	M
Pharmaceutical Administration	M,D
Pharmaceutical Sciences	M,D
Pharmacology	D
Pharmacy	P,D
Philosophy	M,D
Photography	M
Physical Therapy	M,D
Physics	M,D
Physiology	M,D
Political Science	M,D
Psychiatric Nursing	M
Psychology—General	D
Public Administration	M,D
Public Health—General	M,D
Quantitative Analysis	M,D
Reading Education	M,D
Real Estate	M
School Nursing	M
Secondary Education	M,D
Social Work	M,D
Sociology	M,D
Spanish	M,D
Special Education	M,D
Statistics	M,D
Urban and Regional Planning	M,D
Urban Education	M,D
Women's Health Nursing	M
Writing	M,D

UNIVERSITY OF ILLINOIS AT SPRINGFIELD

Program	Degrees
Accounting	M
Addictions/Substance Abuse Counseling	M
Biological and Biomedical Sciences—General	M
Business Administration and Management—General	M
Child and Family Studies	M
Communication—General	M
Computer Science	M
Education—General	M
Educational Leadership and Administration	M
English	M
Environmental Management and Policy	M
Environmental Sciences	M
Gerontology	M
History	M
Human Development	M
Human Services	M
Interdisciplinary Studies	M
Journalism	M
Legal and Justice Studies	M
Management Information Systems	M
Political Science	M
Public Administration	M,D
Public Health—General	M
Public History	M
Social Sciences	M

UNIVERSITY OF ILLINOIS AT URBANA–CHAMPAIGN

Program	Degrees
Accounting	M,D
Actuarial Science	M,D
Advertising and Public Relations	M
Aerospace/Aeronautical Engineering	M,D
African Studies	M
Agricultural Economics and Agribusiness	M,D
Agricultural Education	M,D
Agricultural Engineering	M,D
Agricultural Sciences—General	M
Agronomy and Soil Sciences	M,D
Allopathic Medicine	
Animal Sciences	M,D
Anthropology	M,D
Applied Arts and Design—General	M,D
Applied Economics	M,D
Applied Mathematics	M,D
Applied Statistics	M,D
Architecture	M,D
Art Education	M,D
Art History	M,D
Art/Fine Arts	M
Asian Languages	M,D
Asian Studies	M,D
Astronomy	M,D
Atmospheric Sciences	M,D
Aviation	M
Biochemistry	M,D
Bioengineering	M,D
Bioinformatics	M,D,O
Biological and Biomedical Sciences—General	M,D
Biophysics	M,D
Business Administration and Management—General	M,D
Cell Biology	D
Chemical Engineering	M,D
Chemical Physics	M,D
Chemistry	M,D
Civil Engineering	M,D
Classics	M,D
Communication Disorders	M,D
Communication—General	M,D
Community Health	M,D
Comparative Literature	M,D
Computational Biology	M,D
Computer Engineering	M,D
Computer Science	M,D
Conservation Biology	M,D
Consumer Economics	M,D
Counselor Education	M,D,O
Curriculum and Instruction	M,D,O
Dance	M
Developmental Biology	D
East European and Russian Studies	M
Ecology	M,D
Economics	M,D
Education of Students with Severe/Multiple Disabilities	M,D,O
Education—General	M,D,O
Educational Leadership and Administration	M,D,O
Educational Policy	M,D,O
Educational Psychology	M,D,O
Electrical Engineering	M,D
Energy Management and Policy	M
Engineering and Applied Sciences—General	M,D
English as a Second Language	M,D
English	M,D
Entomology	M,D
Environmental Engineering	M,D
Environmental Sciences	M,D
Ergonomics and Human Factors	M
Evolutionary Biology	M,D
Finance and Banking	M,D
Financial Engineering	M
Food Science and Technology	M,D
Foreign Languages Education	M,D
French	M,D
Geography	M,D
Geology	M,D
Geosciences	M,D
German	M,D
Graphic Design	M
Health Informatics	M,D,O
History	M,D
Human Development	M,D
Human Resources Development	M,D,O
Human Resources Management	M,D,O
Human-Computer Interaction	M,D,O
Industrial and Labor Relations	M,D
Industrial Design	M
Industrial/Management Engineering	M,D
Information Science	M,D,O
Information Studies	M,D,O
Italian	M,D
Journalism	M
Kinesiology and Movement Studies	M,D
Landscape Architecture	M,D
Latin American Studies	M
Law	P,M,D
Leisure Studies	M,D
Library Science	M,D,O
Linguistics	M,D
Management of Technology	M,D
Management Strategy and Policy	M,D,O
Materials Engineering	M,D
Materials Sciences	M,D
Mathematics Education	M,D
Mathematics	M,D
Mechanical Engineering	M,D
Mechanics	M,D
Media Studies	M,D
Medical Informatics	M,D,O
Microbiology	M,D
Molecular Physiology	M,D
Music Education	M,D,O
Music	M,D,O
Natural Resources	M,D
Neuroscience	D
Nuclear Engineering	M,D
Nutrition	M,D
Pathobiology	M,D
Philosophy	M,D
Photography	M
Physics	M,D
Physiology	M,D
Plant Biology	M,D
Political Science	M,D
Portuguese	M,D
Psychology—General	M,D
Public Health—General	M,D
Rehabilitation Sciences	M,D
Science Education	M,D
Slavic Languages	M,D

*M—master's degree; P—first professional degree; D—doctorate; O—other advanced degree; *—Close-Up and/or Display in one of the other books in this series*

Program	Degrees
Social Work	M,D
Sociology	M,D
Spanish	M,D
Special Education	M,D,O
Statistics	M,D
Systems Engineering	M,D
Taxation	M,D
Theater	M,D
Urban and Regional Planning	M,D
Veterinary Medicine	P
Veterinary Sciences	M,D
Vocational and Technical Education	M,D,O
Western European Studies	M
Writing	M,D
Zoology	M,D

UNIVERSITY OF INDIANAPOLIS

Program	Degrees
Anthropology	M
Art Education	M
Art/Fine Arts	M
Biological and Biomedical Sciences—General	M
Business Administration and Management—General	M,O
Clinical Psychology	M,D
Counseling Psychology	M,D
Curriculum and Instruction	M
Education—General	M
Educational Leadership and Administration	M
Elementary Education	M
English Education	M
English	M
Foreign Languages Education	M
Gerontology	M,O
History	M
International Affairs	M
Mathematics Education	M
Nurse Midwifery	M
Nursing and Healthcare Administration	M
Nursing Education	M
Nursing—General	M
Occupational Therapy	M,D
Physical Education	M
Physical Therapy	M,D
Psychology—General	M,D
Science Education	M
Secondary Education	M
Social Sciences Education	M
Sociology	M

THE UNIVERSITY OF IOWA

Program	Degrees
Accounting	M,D
Actuarial Science	M,D
African-American Studies	M
Allopathic Medicine	P
American Studies	M,D
Anatomy	D
Anthropology	M,D
Applied Mathematics	D
Art Education	M,D
Art History	M,D
Art/Fine Arts	M
Asian Studies	M
Astronomy	M
Bacteriology	M,D
Biochemical Engineering	M,D
Biochemistry	M,D
Biological and Biomedical Sciences—General	M,D
Biomedical Engineering	M,D
Biophysics	M,D
Biostatistics	M,D
Business Administration and Management—General	M,D
Cell Biology	M,D
Chemical Engineering	M,D
Chemistry	M,D
Civil Engineering	M,D
Classics	M,D
Clinical Research	M,D
Communication Disorders	M,D
Communication—General	M,D
Community Health	M,D
Comparative Literature	M,D
Computational Biology	M,D,O
Computational Sciences	D
Computer Engineering	M,D
Computer Science	M,D
Counseling Psychology	M,D,O
Counselor Education	M,D
Curriculum and Instruction	M,D
Dance	M
Dentistry	P,M,D,O
Developmental Education	M,D
Early Childhood Education	M,D
Economics	D
Education—General	M,D,O
Educational Leadership and Administration	M,D,O
Educational Measurement and Evaluation	M,D,O
Educational Policy	M,D,O
Educational Psychology	M,D,O
Electrical Engineering	M,D
Elementary Education	M,D
Engineering and Applied Sciences—General	M,D
English Education	M,D
English	M,D
Environmental and Occupational Health	M,D,O
Environmental Engineering	M,D
Epidemiology	M,D
Ergonomics and Human Factors	M,D
Evolutionary Biology	M,D
Exercise and Sports Science	M,D
Film, Television, and Video Production	M
Film, Television, and Video Theory and Criticism	M,D
Finance and Banking	M,D
Foreign Languages Education	M,D
Foundations and Philosophy of Education	M,D,O
French	M,D
Genetics	M,D
Geography	M,D
Geosciences	M,D
German	M,D
Health Informatics	M,D,O
Health Services Management and Hospital Administration	M,D
Higher Education	M,D,O
History	M,D
Immunology	M,D
Industrial/Management Engineering	M,D
Information Science	M,D,O
Information Studies	M
Investment Management	M
Journalism	M
Law	P,M
Leisure Studies	M
Library Science	M
Linguistics	M,D
Management Strategy and Policy	M
Manufacturing Engineering	M,D
Marketing	M,D
Mass Communication	M,D
Mathematics Education	M,D
Mathematics	M,D
Mechanical Engineering	M,D
Media Studies	M,D
Microbiology	M,D
Molecular Biology	D
Music	M,D
Neurobiology	M,D
Neuroscience	D
Nursing—General	M,D
Operations Research	M,D
Oral and Dental Sciences	M,D,O
Pathology	M
Pharmacology	M,D
Pharmacy	M,D
Philosophy	M,D
Physical Education	M,D
Physical Therapy	D
Physician Assistant Studies	M
Physics	M,D
Physiology	M,D
Political Science	M,D
Psychology—General	M,D,O
Public Health—General	M,D,O
Radiation Biology	M,D
Recreation and Park Management	M
Rehabilitation Counseling	M,D
Rehabilitation Sciences	D
Religion	M,D
Rhetoric	M,D
School Psychology	M,D,O
Science Education	M,D
Secondary Education	M,D
Social Psychology	M,D
Social Sciences Education	M,D
Social Work	M,D
Sociology	M,D
Spanish	M,D
Special Education	M,D
Sport Psychology	M,D
Sports Management	M
Statistics	M,D,O
Student Affairs	M,D
Theater	M
Toxicology	M,D
Translation and Interpretation	M
Translational Biology	M,D
Urban and Regional Planning	M
Virology	M,D
Women's Studies	D
Writing	M,D

THE UNIVERSITY OF KANSAS

Program	Degrees
Accounting	M
Aerospace/Aeronautical Engineering	M,D
African Studies	M,O
African-American Studies	M,O
Allied Health—General	M,D,O
Allopathic Medicine	P
American Indian/Native American Studies	M
American Studies	M,D
Anatomy	M,D
Anthropology	M,D
Applied Arts and Design—General	M
Applied Behavior Analysis	M,D
Architectural Engineering	M
Architecture	M,D,O
Art Education	M
Art History	M,D
Art/Fine Arts	M
Asian Languages	M
Asian Studies	M
Astronomy	M,D
Atmospheric Sciences	M,D
Biochemistry	M,D
Bioengineering	M,D
Biological and Biomedical Sciences—General	M,D
Biophysics	M,D
Biostatistics	M,D
Biotechnology	M
Botany	M,D
Business Administration and Management—General	M,D
Cell Biology	M,D
Chemical Engineering	M,D
Chemistry	M,D
Civil Engineering	M,D
Classics	M
Clinical Psychology	M,D
Clinical Research	M
Cognitive Sciences	M,D
Communication Disorders	M,D
Communication—General	M,D
Community Health Nursing	M,D,O
Computational Sciences	M,D
Computer Art and Design	M
Computer Engineering	M
Computer Science	M,D
Construction Management	M
Counseling Psychology	M,D
Curriculum and Instruction	M,D
Developmental Biology	M,D
Developmental Psychology	M,D
East European and Russian Studies	M
Ecology	M,D
Economics	M,D
Education—General	M,D,O
Educational Leadership and Administration	M,D
Educational Measurement and Evaluation	M,D
Educational Policy	D
Educational Psychology	M,D
Electrical Engineering	M,D
Engineering and Applied Sciences—General	M,D
Engineering Management	M
English	M,D
Entomology	M,D
Environmental Engineering	M,D
Environmental Sciences	M,D
Epidemiology	M
Evolutionary Biology	M,D
Facilities Management	M,D,O
Family Nurse Practitioner Studies	M,D,O
Film, Television, and Video Theory and Criticism	M,D
Foundations and Philosophy of Education	D
French	M,D
Geography	M,D
Geology	M,D
German	M,D
Gerontology	M,D,O
Health Education	M,D,O
Health Informatics	M
Health Services Management and Hospital Administration	M,D
Higher Education	M,D
History	M,D
Interdisciplinary Studies	M,D
International Affairs	M
Journalism	M
Latin American Studies	M,O
Law	P
Linguistics	M,D
Management Information Systems	M
Mathematics	M,D
Mechanical Engineering	M,D
Media Studies	M,D
Medical Informatics	M,D,O
Medicinal and Pharmaceutical Chemistry	M,D
Microbiology	M,D
Molecular Biology	M,D
Museum Studies	M
Music Education	M,D
Music	M,D
Near and Middle Eastern Studies	M
Neuroscience	M,D
Nurse Anesthesia	M
Nurse Midwifery	M,D,O
Nursing and Healthcare Administration	M,D,O
Nursing—General	M,D,O
Nutrition	M,D,O
Occupational Therapy	M,D
Organizational Management	M,D,O
Pathology	M,D
Petroleum Engineering	M,D
Pharmaceutical Sciences	M
Pharmacology	M,D

Philosophy	M,D
Physical Education	M,D
Physical Therapy	D
Physics	M,D
Physiology	M,D
Political Science	M,D
Psychiatric Nursing	M,D,O
Psychology—General	M,D
Public Administration	M,D
Public Health—General	M
Rehabilitation Counseling	M,D
Rehabilitation Sciences	M,D
Religion	M
School Psychology	D,O
Slavic Languages	M,D
Social Psychology	M,D
Social Work	M,D
Sociology	M,D
Spanish	M,D
Special Education	M,D
Theater	M,D
Therapies—Dance, Drama, and Music	M
Toxicology	M,D
Urban and Regional Planning	M
Writing	M,D

UNIVERSITY OF KENTUCKY

Accounting	M
Agricultural Economics and Agribusiness	M,D
Agricultural Engineering	M,D
Agricultural Sciences—General	M,D
Agronomy and Soil Sciences	M,D
Allied Health—General	M,D
Allopathic Medicine	P
Anatomy	D
Animal Sciences	M,D
Anthropology	M,D
Applied Arts and Design—General	M
Applied Mathematics	M,D
Architecture	M
Art Education	M
Art History	M
Art/Fine Arts	M
Astronomy	M,D
Biochemistry	D
Biological and Biomedical Sciences—General	M,D
Biomedical Engineering	M,D
Business Administration and Management—General	M,D
Chemical Engineering	M,D
Chemistry	M,D
Child and Family Studies	M,D
Civil Engineering	M,D
Classics	M
Clinical Laboratory Sciences/Medical Technology	M,D
Clinical Psychology	M,D
Clothing and Textiles	M
Communication Disorders	M
Communication—General	M,D
Computer Science	M,D
Counseling Psychology	M,D,O
Curriculum and Instruction	M,D
Dentistry	P
Early Childhood Education	M,D
Economics	M,D
Education—General	M,D,O
Educational Leadership and Administration	M,D,O
Educational Measurement and Evaluation	M,D
Educational Media/Instructional Technology	M,D
Educational Policy	M,D
Educational Psychology	M,D,O
Electrical Engineering	M,D
Engineering and Applied Sciences—General	M,D
English	M,D
Entomology	M,D
Exercise and Sports Science	M,D
Experimental Psychology	M,D
Foreign Languages Education	M
Forestry	M
French	M
Geography	M,D
Geology	M,D
German	M
Gerontology	D
Health Physics/Radiological Health	M
Health Promotion	M,D
Health Services Management and Hospital Administration	M
Higher Education	M,D
Hispanic Studies	M,D
Historic Preservation	M
History	M,D
Hospitality Management	M
Interior Design	M
International Affairs	M
International Business	M
Kinesiology and Movement Studies	M,D
Law	P
Library Science	M*
Manufacturing Engineering	M
Materials Sciences	M,D
Mathematics	M,D
Mechanical Engineering	M,D
Medical Physics	M
Microbiology	D
Middle School Education	M,D
Mineral/Mining Engineering	M,D
Music Education	M,D
Music	M,D
Neurobiology	D
Nursing—General	M,D
Nutrition	M,D
Oral and Dental Sciences	M
Pharmaceutical Sciences	M,D
Pharmacology	D
Pharmacy	P
Philosophy	M,D
Physical Therapy	M
Physician Assistant Studies	M
Physics	M,D
Physiology	M,D
Plant Pathology	M,D
Plant Physiology	D
Plant Sciences	M
Political Science	M,D
Psychology—General	M,D
Public Administration	M,D
Public Health—General	M
Rehabilitation Counseling	M,D
Rehabilitation Sciences	D
School Psychology	M,D,O
Social Work	M,D
Sociology	M,D
Special Education	M,D
Statistics	M,D
Theater	M
Toxicology	M,D
Veterinary Sciences	M,D
Vocational and Technical Education	M

UNIVERSITY OF LA VERNE

Accounting	M
Business Administration and Management—General	M,O
Child and Family Studies	M
Child Development	M
Clinical Psychology	D
Counseling Psychology	M
Counselor Education	M,O
Education—General	M,O
Educational Leadership and Administration	M,D,O
Finance and Banking	M
Gerontology	M,O
Health Informatics	M
Health Services Management and Hospital Administration	M,O
Health Services Research	M
International Business	M
Law	P
Management Information Systems	M
Marketing	M
Marriage and Family Therapy	M
Multilingual and Multicultural Education	O
Nonprofit Management	M,O
Organizational Management	M,O
Psychology—General	M,D
Public Administration	M,D
Reading Education	M,O
Social Psychology	D
Special Education	M
Student Affairs	M

UNIVERSITY OF LETHBRIDGE

Accounting	M,D
Addictions/Substance Abuse Counseling	M,D
Agricultural Sciences—General	M,D
American Indian/Native American Studies	M,D
Anthropology	M,D
Archaeology	M,D
Art/Fine Arts	M,D
Biochemistry	M,D
Biological and Biomedical Sciences—General	M,D
Business Administration and Management—General	M,D
Canadian Studies	M,D
Chemistry	M,D
Computational Sciences	M,D
Computer Science	M,D
Counseling Psychology	M,D
Economics	M,D
Education—General	M,D
Educational Leadership and Administration	M,D
English	M,D
Environmental Sciences	M,D
Exercise and Sports Science	M,D
Finance and Banking	M,D
French	M,D
Geographic Information Systems	M,D
Geography	M,D
German	M,D
History	M,D
Human Resources Management	M,D
International Business	M,D
Kinesiology and Movement Studies	M,D
Management Information Systems	M,D
Management Strategy and Policy	M,D
Mathematics	M,D
Media Studies	M,D
Molecular Biology	M,D
Music	M,D
Neuroscience	M,D
Nursing—General	M,D
Philosophy	M,D
Physics	M,D
Political Science	M,D
Psychology—General	M,D
Religion	M,D
Social Sciences	M,D
Sociology	M,D
Spanish	M,D
Theater	M,D
Urban Studies	M,D
Women's Studies	M,D

UNIVERSITY OF LOUISIANA AT LAFAYETTE

American Studies	D
Architectural Engineering	M
Biological and Biomedical Sciences—General	M,D
Business Administration and Management—General	M
Chemical Engineering	M
Civil Engineering	M
Cognitive Sciences	D
Communication Disorders	M,D
Communication—General	M
Computer Engineering	M,D
Computer Science	M,D*
Counselor Education	M
Curriculum and Instruction	M
Education of the Gifted	M
Education—General	M,D
Educational Leadership and Administration	M,D
Engineering Management	M
English	M,D
Environmental Biology	M,D
Evolutionary Biology	M,D
Folklore	M,D
French	M,D
Geology	M
History	M
Mass Communication	M
Mathematics	M,D
Mechanical Engineering	M
Music Education	M
Music	M
Nursing—General	M
Petroleum Engineering	M
Physics	M
Psychology—General	M
Rehabilitation Counseling	M
Rhetoric	M,D
Telecommunications	M
Writing	M,D

UNIVERSITY OF LOUISIANA AT MONROE

Addictions/Substance Abuse Counseling	M
Biological and Biomedical Sciences—General	M
Business Administration and Management—General	M
Communication Disorders	M
Communication—General	M
Counselor Education	M
Criminal Justice and Criminology	M
Curriculum and Instruction	M,D
Education of the Gifted	M,D
Education—General	M,D,O
Educational Leadership and Administration	M,D
Educational Measurement and Evaluation	M,D
Elementary Education	M,D
English	M
Exercise and Sports Science	M
Experimental Psychology	M
Gerontology	M,O
History	M
Marriage and Family Therapy	M,D
Middle School Education	M
Music	M
Pharmaceutical Sciences	M
Pharmacy	D
Psychology—General	M,O
Reading Education	M,D
School Psychology	M,O
Secondary Education	M

UNIVERSITY OF LOUISVILLE

Accounting	M
Addictions/Substance Abuse Counseling	M,D,O
Adult Nursing	M,D

*M—master's degree; P—first professional degree; D—doctorate; O—other advanced degree; *—Close-Up and/or Display in one of the other books in this series*

African Studies M
African-American Studies M
Allopathic Medicine P
Analytical Chemistry M,D
Anatomy M,D
Anthropology M
Applied Mathematics M,D
Art Education M,D
Art History M,D
Art/Fine Arts M,D
Biochemistry M,D
Biological and Biomedical Sciences—General M,D
Biophysics M,D
Biostatistics M,D
Business Administration and Management—General M
Chemical Engineering M,D
Chemical Physics M,D
Chemistry M,D
Civil Engineering M,D
Clinical Psychology D
Clinical Research M,D,O
Communication Disorders M,D
Communication—General M
Community Health M
Computer and Information Systems Security M,D,O
Computer Engineering M,D,O
Computer Science M,D,O
Counselor Education M,D
Criminal Justice and Criminology M
Curriculum and Instruction M,D
Dentistry P,M
Early Childhood Education M,D
Education—General M,D,O
Educational Leadership and Administration M,D,O
Educational Psychology M,D
Electrical Engineering M,D
Elementary Education M,D
Engineering and Applied Sciences—General M,D,O
Engineering Management M,D,O
English M,D
Entrepreneurship M,D
Environmental and Occupational Health M,D
Environmental Biology M,D
Environmental Engineering M,D
Epidemiology M,D
Exercise and Sports Science M
Experimental Psychology D
Family Nurse Practitioner Studies M,D
French M
Geography M
Gerontology M,D,O
Health Education M,D
Health Promotion D
Health Services Management and Hospital Administration D
Higher Education M,D,O
History M,O
Human Resources Development M,D,O
Human Resources Management M,D
Humanities M,D
Immunology M,D
Industrial/Management Engineering M,D,O
Inorganic Chemistry M,D
Interdisciplinary Studies M,D
International Business M
Law P
Logistics M,D,O
Marriage and Family Therapy M,D,O
Maternal and Child/Neonatal Nursing M,D
Mathematics M,D
Mechanical Engineering M,D
Microbiology M,D
Middle School Education M,D
Molecular Biology M,D
Museum Studies M,D
Music Education M,D
Music M
Neurobiology M,D
Nonprofit Management M,D
Nursing—General M,D
Oral and Dental Sciences P,M
Organic Chemistry M,D
Pharmacology M,D
Philosophy M
Physical Chemistry M,D
Physical Education M
Physics M,D
Physiology M,D
Political Science M
Psychiatric Nursing M,D
Psychology—General D
Public Administration M,D
Public Affairs M,D
Public Health—General M,D
Public History M,O
Public Policy M,D
Reading Education M,D
Rhetoric M,D
Secondary Education M,D
Social Work M,D,O
Sociology M
Spanish M
Special Education M,D
Sports Management M
Student Affairs M,D
Supply Chain Management M,D,O
Theater M
Toxicology M,D
Urban and Regional Planning M,D
Urban Studies M,D
Women's Studies M,O
Writing M,D

UNIVERSITY OF MAINE

Accounting M
Agricultural Economics and Agribusiness M
Agricultural Sciences—General M,D,O
Agronomy and Soil Sciences M,D
American Studies M,D
Animal Sciences M
Asian Studies M,D
Astronomy M
Biochemistry M,D
Bioengineering M
Biological and Biomedical Sciences—General D
Biomedical Engineering D
Botany M
Business Administration and Management—General M
Canadian Studies M,D
Cell Biology D
Chemical Engineering M,D
Chemistry M,D
Civil Engineering M,D
Clinical Psychology M,D
Communication Disorders M
Communication—General M,D
Computer Engineering M,D
Computer Science M,D
Conflict Resolution and Mediation/Peace Studies M
Counselor Education M,D,O
Curriculum and Instruction M
Developmental Psychology M,D
Ecology M,D
Education—General M,D,O
Educational Leadership and Administration M,D,O
Educational Media/Instructional Technology M
Electrical Engineering M,D
Elementary Education M,O
Engineering and Applied Sciences—General M,D
Engineering Physics M
English Education M
English M
Entomology M
Environmental Management and Policy M,D
Environmental Sciences M,D
Exercise and Sports Science M
Experimental Psychology M,D
Family Nurse Practitioner Studies M,O
Finance and Banking M
Fish, Game, and Wildlife Management M,D
Food Science and Technology M,D
Foreign Languages Education M
Forestry M,D
French M
Gender Studies M
Genomic Sciences D
Geology M,D
Geosciences M,D
Higher Education M,D,O
History of Science and Technology M,D
History M,D
Horticulture M
Human Development M
Interdisciplinary Studies M,D
Kinesiology and Movement Studies M
Liberal Studies M
Management Information Systems M
Marine Affairs M
Marine Biology M,D
Marine Sciences M,D
Mass Communication M,D
Mathematics Education M
Mathematics M
Mechanical Engineering M,D
Media Studies M
Microbiology M,D
Molecular Biology M,D
Music M
Natural Resources M,D
Neuroscience D
Nursing—General M,O
Nutrition M,D
Ocean Engineering D
Oceanography M,D
Physical Education M
Physics M,D
Plant Biology M,D
Plant Pathology M
Plant Sciences M,D
Psychology—General M,D
Public Administration M,D
Reading Education M,D,O
Science Education M,O
Secondary Education M,O
Social Sciences Education M,O
Social Work M
Special Education M,O
Sustainability Management M
Toxicology D
Water Resources Engineering M,D
Water Resources M,D
Western European Studies M,D
Writing M
Zoology M,D

UNIVERSITY OF MAINE AT FARMINGTON

Early Childhood Education M
Education—General M
Educational Leadership and Administration M

UNIVERSITY OF MANAGEMENT AND TECHNOLOGY

Business Administration and Management—General M,D,O
Computer Science M,O
Criminal Justice and Criminology M
Information Science M,O
Management Information Systems M,O
Project Management M,D,O
Public Administration M,O
Software Engineering M,O

THE UNIVERSITY OF MANCHESTER

Accounting M,D
Actuarial Science M,D
Aerospace/Aeronautical Engineering M,D
Analytical Chemistry M,D
Anthropology M,D
Applied Mathematics M,D
Archaeology M,D
Architecture M,D
Art History D
Art/Fine Arts M,D
Arts Administration D
Asian Studies M,D
Astronomy M,D
Astrophysics M,D
Atmospheric Sciences M,D
Biochemical Engineering M,D
Biochemistry M,D
Bioinformatics M,D
Biological and Biomedical Sciences—General M,D
Biophysics M,D
Biotechnology M,D
Business Administration and Management—General M,D
Cancer Biology/Oncology M,D
Cell Biology M,D
Chemical Engineering M,D
Chemistry M,D
Chinese M,D
Civil Engineering M,D
Classics D
Clinical Psychology M,D
Clothing and Textiles M,D
Communication Disorders M,D
Computer Science M,D
Condensed Matter Physics M,D
Conflict Resolution and Mediation/Peace Studies D
Counseling Psychology M,D
Criminal Justice and Criminology M,D
Cultural Studies M,D
Dentistry M,D
Developmental Biology M,D
Developmental Psychology M,D
Ecology M,D
Economics D
Education—General M,D
Educational Psychology M,D
Electrical Engineering M,D
Engineering Management M,D
English as a Second Language M,D
English D
Environmental Biology M,D
Environmental Design M,D
Environmental Engineering M,D
Environmental Management and Policy M,D
Environmental Sciences M,D
Evolutionary Biology M,D
French M,D
Genetics M,D
Geochemistry M,D
Geography M,D
Geosciences M,D

German	M,D
Hazardous Materials Management	M,D
Health Law	M,D
Hispanic Studies	M,D
History of Medicine	M,D
History of Science and Technology	M,D
History	D
Immunology	M,D
Industrial and Manufacturing Management	M,D
Inorganic Chemistry	M,D
International Affairs	D
International Development	M,D
Italian	M,D
Japanese	M,D
Landscape Architecture	M,D
Latin American Studies	M,D
Law	M,D
Linguistics	M,D
Materials Sciences	M,D
Mathematical and Computational Finance	M,D
Mathematics	M,D
Mechanical Engineering	M,D
Metallurgical Engineering and Metallurgy	M,D
Microbiology	M,D
Modeling and Simulation	M,D
Molecular Biology	M,D
Molecular Genetics	M,D
Museum Studies	D
Music	D
Natural Resources	M,D
Near and Middle Eastern Languages	M,D
Near and Middle Eastern Studies	M,D
Neurobiology	M,D
Neuroscience	M,D
Nuclear Engineering	M,D
Nurse Midwifery	M,D
Nursing—General	M,D
Optometry	M,D
Oral and Dental Sciences	M,D
Organic Chemistry	M,D
Paleontology	M,D
Paper and Pulp Engineering	M,D
Pharmaceutical Sciences	M,D
Pharmacology	M,D
Pharmacy	M,D
Philosophy	M,D
Physical Chemistry	M,D
Physics	M,D
Physiology	M,D
Plant Sciences	M,D
Political Science	M,D
Polymer Science and Engineering	M,D
Psychology—General	M,D
Public Health—General	M,D
Religion	D
Russian	M,D
Slavic Languages	M,D
Social Sciences	M,D
Social Work	M,D
Sociology	M,D
Spanish	M,D
Statistics	M,D
Structural Biology	M,D
Structural Engineering	M,D
Textile Design	M,D
Theater	D
Theology	D
Theoretical Chemistry	M,D
Theoretical Physics	M,D
Toxicology	M,D
Translation and Interpretation	M,D
Vision Sciences	M,D
Writing	D

UNIVERSITY OF MANITOBA

Adult Education	M
Agricultural Economics and Agribusiness	M,D
Agricultural Sciences—General	M,D
Agronomy and Soil Sciences	M,D
American Indian/Native American Studies	M
Anatomy	M,D
Animal Sciences	M,D
Anthropology	M,D
Architecture	M
Archives/Archival Administration	M,D
Biochemistry	M,D
Biological and Biomedical Sciences—General	M,D,O
Biosystems Engineering	M,D
Botany	M,D
Business Administration and Management—General	M,D
Canadian Studies	M
Cancer Biology/Oncology	M
Chemistry	M,D
Child and Family Studies	M
Civil Engineering	M,D
Classics	M
Clinical Psychology	M,D
Clothing and Textiles	M
Community Health	M,D,O
Computational Sciences	M
Computer Engineering	M,D
Computer Science	M,D
Counselor Education	M
Curriculum and Instruction	M
Dentistry	P
Disability Studies	M
Ecology	M,D
Economics	M,D
Education—General	M,D
Educational Leadership and Administration	M
Educational Psychology	M
Electrical Engineering	M,D
Engineering and Applied Sciences—General	M,D
English as a Second Language	M
English Education	M
English	M,D
Entomology	M,D
Environmental Sciences	M,D
Family and Consumer Sciences-General	M
Food Science and Technology	M,D
Foundations and Philosophy of Education	M
French	M,D
Geography	M,D
Geology	M,D
Geophysics	M,D
German	M
Higher Education	M
History	M,D
Horticulture	M,D
Human Genetics	M,D
Immunology	M,D
Industrial/Management Engineering	M,D
Interdisciplinary Studies	M,D
Interior Design	M
Kinesiology and Movement Studies	M
Landscape Architecture	M
Law	M
Linguistics	M,D
Manufacturing Engineering	M,D
Mathematics	M,D
Mechanical Engineering	M,D
Medical Microbiology	M,D
Microbiology	M,D
Music	M
Natural Resources	M,D
Northern Studies	M
Nursing—General	M
Nutrition	M,D
Occupational Therapy	M,D
Oral and Dental Sciences	M,D
Pathology	M
Pharmaceutical Sciences	M,D
Pharmacology	M,D
Philosophy	M
Physical Education	M
Physical Therapy	M,D
Physics	M,D
Physiology	M,D
Plant Physiology	M,D
Plant Sciences	M,D
Political Science	M
Psychology—General	M,D
Public Administration	M
Recreation and Park Management	M
Rehabilitation Sciences	M,D
Religion	M,D
School Psychology	M,D
Slavic Languages	M
Social Work	M,D
Sociology	M,D
Special Education	M
Statistics	M,D
Urban and Regional Planning	M
Zoology	M,D

UNIVERSITY OF MARY

Accounting	M
Addictions/Substance Abuse Counseling	M
Business Administration and Management—General	M
Cardiovascular Sciences	M
Curriculum and Instruction	M
Early Childhood Education	M
Education—General	M
Educational Leadership and Administration	M
Family Nurse Practitioner Studies	M
Health Services Management and Hospital Administration	M
Higher Education	M
Human Resources Management	M
Management Strategy and Policy	M
Nursing and Healthcare Administration	M
Nursing Education	M
Nursing—General	M
Occupational Therapy	M
Physical Therapy	D
Project Management	M
Reading Education	M
School Psychology	M
Social Psychology	M
Special Education	M
Student Affairs	M

UNIVERSITY OF MARY HARDIN-BAYLOR

Accounting	M
Business Administration and Management—General	M
Clinical Psychology	M
Counseling Psychology	M
Counselor Education	M
Curriculum and Instruction	M,D
Education—General	M,D
Educational Leadership and Administration	M,D
Educational Psychology	M,D
Exercise and Sports Science	M,D
Management Information Systems	M
Marriage and Family Therapy	M
Nursing—General	M
Psychology—General	M
Reading Education	M,D
School Psychology	M

UNIVERSITY OF MARYLAND, BALTIMORE

Allopathic Medicine	P
Biochemistry	M,D
Biological and Biomedical Sciences—General	M,D
Biostatistics	M,D
Cancer Biology/Oncology	M,D
Cell Biology	M,D
Clinical Laboratory Sciences/Medical Technology	M
Clinical Research	M,D
Community Health Nursing	M
Dental Hygiene	M
Dentistry	P,O
Environmental Sciences	M,D
Epidemiology	M,D
Genetic Counseling	M
Genomic Sciences	M,D
Gerontological Nursing	M
Gerontology	M,D
Health Services Research	M,D
Human Genetics	M,D
Immunology	D
Law	P,M
Marine Sciences	M,D
Maternal and Child/Neonatal Nursing	M
Medical/Surgical Nursing	M
Microbiology	D
Molecular Biology	M,D
Molecular Medicine	M,D
Neurobiology	D
Neuroscience	D
Nurse Midwifery	M
Nursing and Healthcare Administration	M
Nursing Education	M
Nursing—General	M,D
Oral and Dental Sciences	P,M,D,O
Pathology	M
Pediatric Nursing	M
Pharmaceutical Administration	M,D
Pharmaceutical Sciences	D
Pharmacology	M,D
Pharmacy	P,M,D
Physical Therapy	D
Psychiatric Nursing	M
Rehabilitation Sciences	D
Social Work	M,D
Toxicology	M,D

UNIVERSITY OF MARYLAND, BALTIMORE COUNTY

Applied Behavior Analysis	M,D
Applied Mathematics	M,D
Applied Physics	M,D
Applied Psychology	D
Art Education	M
Art/Fine Arts	M
Astrophysics	M,D
Atmospheric Sciences	M,D
Biochemical Engineering	M,D,O
Biochemistry	M,D
Biological and Biomedical Sciences—General	M,D
Biostatistics	M,D
Biotechnology	O
Cell Biology	D
Chemical Engineering	M,D
Chemistry	M,D
Civil Engineering	M,D
Cognitive Sciences	D
Communication—General	M
Computer Engineering	M,D
Computer Science	M,D
Curriculum and Instruction	M,D,O
Dance	M
Developmental Psychology	D
Distance Education Development	M,O
Early Childhood Education	M
Economics	M,D
Education—General	M,D,O

*M—master's degree; P—first professional degree; D—doctorate; O—other advanced degree; *—Close-Up and/or Display in one of the other books in this series*

Educational Media/ Instructional Technology	M,O
Educational Policy	M,D
Electrical Engineering	M,D
Elementary Education	M
Engineering and Applied Sciences—General	M,D,O
Engineering Management	M,O
English as a Second Language	M,O
English Education	M
Environmental Management and Policy	M,D
Environmental Sciences	M,D
Epidemiology	M,O
Foreign Languages Education	M
Geographic Information Systems	M,O
Geography	M,D
Gerontology	M,D
Health Education	M,O
Health Services Management and Hospital Administration	M,D,O
History	M
Human Services	M,D
Industrial and Organizational Psychology	M
Information Science	M,D
Linguistics	M
Marine Sciences	M,D
Mathematics Education	M
Mechanical Engineering	M,D,O
Molecular Biology	M,D
Multilingual and Multicultural Education	M,D
Music Education	M
Music	O
Neuroscience	D
Nonprofit Management	M,O
Optical Sciences	M,D
Physics	M,D
Planetary and Space Sciences	M
Psychology—General	M,D
Public History	M,D
Public Policy	M,D
Reading Education	M,D,O
Science Education	M
Secondary Education	M
Social Sciences Education	M
Social Sciences	D
Sociology	M,O
Statistics	M,D
Systems Engineering	M,O
Theater	M
Urban Studies	M,D
Women's Studies	O

UNIVERSITY OF MARYLAND, COLLEGE PARK

Advertising and Public Relations	M,D
Aerospace/Aeronautical Engineering	M,D
Agricultural Economics and Agribusiness	M,D
Agricultural Sciences—General	P,M,D
American Studies	M,D
Analytical Chemistry	M,D
Animal Sciences	M,D
Anthropology	M
Applied Mathematics	M,D
Architecture	M
Art History	M,D
Art Therapy	M,D,O
Art/Fine Arts	M
Astronomy	M,D
Biochemistry	M,D
Bioengineering	M,D
Biological and Biomedical Sciences—General	M,D
Biophysics	D
Biostatistics	M,D
Broadcast Journalism	M,D
Business Administration and Management—General	M,D
Cell Biology	M,D
Chemical Engineering	M,D
Chemical Physics	M,D
Chemistry	M,D
Child and Family Studies	M,D
Civil Engineering	M,D
Classics	M
Clinical Psychology	M,D
Cognitive Sciences	D
Communication Disorders	M,D
Communication—General	M,D
Comparative Literature	M,D
Computer Engineering	M,D
Computer Science	M,D
Conservation Biology	M
Counseling Psychology	M,D,O
Counselor Education	M,D,O
Criminal Justice and Criminology	M,D
Curriculum and Instruction	M,D,O
Dance	M,D
Developmental Psychology	M,D
Early Childhood Education	M,D
Ecology	M,D
Economics	M,D
Education—General	M,D,O
Educational Leadership and Administration	M,D,O
Educational Measurement and Evaluation	M,D
Educational Media/ Instructional Technology	M,D,O
Educational Policy	M,D
Educational Psychology	M,D
Electrical Engineering	M,D
Engineering and Applied Sciences—General	M
English as a Second Language	M,D,O
English	M,D
Entomology	M,D
Environmental and Occupational Health	M,D
Environmental Engineering	M,D
Environmental Sciences	M,D
Epidemiology	M,D
Evolutionary Biology	M,D
Experimental Psychology	M,D
Family and Consumer Sciences-General	M,D
Fire Protection Engineering	M
Food Science and Technology	M,D
Foreign Languages Education	D
Foundations and Philosophy of Education	M,D,O
French	M,D
Geography	M,D
Geology	M,D
German	M,D
Health Education	M,D
Health Services Management and Hospital Administration	M,D
Higher Education	M,D
Historic Preservation	M,O
History	M,D
Horticulture	M,D
Human Development	M,D
Industrial and Organizational Psychology	M,D
Information Studies	M,D
Inorganic Chemistry	M,D
International and Comparative Education	M,D
Jewish Studies	M
Journalism	M,D
Kinesiology and Movement Studies	M,D
Landscape Architecture	M
Law	
Library Science	
Linguistics	M,D
Manufacturing Engineering	M,D
Marine Sciences	M,D
Marriage and Family Therapy	M,D
Materials Engineering	M,D
Materials Sciences	M,D
Maternal and Child Health	M,D
Mathematics	M,D
Mechanical Engineering	M,D
Mechanics	M,D
Media Studies	M,D
Meteorology	M,D
Molecular Biology	D
Molecular Genetics	M,D
Music Education	M,D
Music	M,D
Natural Resources	M,D
Near and Middle Eastern Languages	M,O
Neuroscience	M,D
Nuclear Engineering	M,D
Nutrition	M,D
Oceanography	M,D
Organic Chemistry	M,D
Philosophy	M,D
Physical Chemistry	M,D
Physics	M,D
Plant Biology	M,D
Political Science	D
Portuguese	M,D
Psychology—General	M,D
Public Administration	M
Public Health—General	M,D
Public Policy	M,D
Reading Education	M,D,O
Real Estate	M
Rehabilitation Counseling	M,D,O
Reliability Engineering	M,D
School Psychology	M,D,O
Secondary Education	M,D,O
Social Psychology	M,D
Social Work	
Sociology	M,D
Spanish	M,D
Special Education	M,D,O
Speech and Interpersonal Communication	M,D
Statistics	M,D
Student Affairs	M,D,O
Survey Methodology	M,D
Sustainable Development	M
Systems Engineering	M
Telecommunications	M
Theater	M
Urban and Regional Planning	M,D
Veterinary Medicine	P
Veterinary Sciences	M,D
Women's Studies	M,D
Writing	M,D

UNIVERSITY OF MARYLAND EASTERN SHORE

Agricultural Sciences—General	M,D
Computer Science	M
Counselor Education	M
Criminal Justice and Criminology	M
Education—General	M
Educational Leadership and Administration	D
Environmental Sciences	M,D
Food Science and Technology	M,D
Marine Sciences	M,D
Organizational Management	D
Physical Therapy	D
Rehabilitation Counseling	M
Rehabilitation Sciences	M
Special Education	M
Toxicology	M,D
Vocational and Technical Education	M

UNIVERSITY OF MARYLAND UNIVERSITY COLLEGE

Accounting	M,O
Biotechnology	M,O
Business Administration and Management—General	M,D,O
Computer and Information Systems Security	M,O
Distance Education Development	M,O
Education—General	M
Environmental Management and Policy	M,O
Finance and Banking	M,O
Health Informatics	M,O
Health Services Management and Hospital Administration	M,O
Information Science	M,O
International Business	M,O
Management Information Systems	M,O
Management of Technology	M,O

UNIVERSITY OF MARY WASHINGTON

Business Administration and Management—General	M
Education—General	M
Management Information Systems	M

UNIVERSITY OF MASSACHUSETTS AMHERST

Accounting	M
African-American Studies	M,D
Agricultural Economics and Agribusiness	M,D
Agronomy and Soil Sciences	M,D
Animal Behavior	M,D
Animal Sciences	M,D
Anthropology	M,D
Applied Arts and Design—General	M
Applied Mathematics	M
Architectural Engineering	M,D
Architecture	M
Art Education	M
Art History	M
Art/Fine Arts	M
Astronomy	M,D
Biochemistry	M,D
Biological and Biomedical Sciences—General	M,D
Biostatistics	M,D
Biotechnology	M,D
Business Administration and Management—General	M,D
Cell Biology	M,D
Chemical Engineering	M,D
Chemistry	M,D
Child and Family Studies	M,D,O
Chinese	M
Civil Engineering	M,D
Classics	M
Clinical Psychology	M,D
Cognitive Sciences	M,D
Communication Disorders	M,D
Communication—General	M,D
Community Health	M,D
Comparative Literature	M,D
Computer Engineering	M,D
Computer Science	M,D
Conflict Resolution and Mediation/Peace Studies	M,D
Counselor Education	M,D,O
Developmental Biology	D
Developmental Psychology	M,D
Early Childhood Education	M,D,O
Ecology	M,D
Economics	M,D
Education—General	M,D,O

Educational Leadership and Administration M,D,O
Educational Measurement and Evaluation M,D,O
Educational Media/Instructional Technology M,D,O
Educational Policy M,D,O
Electrical Engineering M,D
Elementary Education M,D,O
Engineering and Applied Sciences—General M,D
Engineering Management
English as a Second Language M,D,O
English M,D
Entertainment Management
Entomology M,D
Environmental and Occupational Health M,D
Environmental Biology M,D
Environmental Engineering M
Environmental Management and Policy M,D
Epidemiology M,D
Evolutionary Biology M,D
Fish, Game, and Wildlife Management M,D
Food Science and Technology M,D
Foreign Languages Education M
Forestry M,D
French M
Genetics M,D
Geography M
Geosciences M,D
German M,D
Health Education M,D
Health Services Management and Hospital Administration M,D
Higher Education M,D,O
Hispanic and Latin American Languages M,D
Historic Preservation M
History of Science and Technology M,D
History M,D
Hospitality Management M
Industrial and Labor Relations M
Industrial/Management Engineering M,D
Interior Design M
International and Comparative Education M,D,O
Italian M
Japanese M
Kinesiology and Movement Studies M,D
Landscape Architecture M
Linguistics M,D
Marine Sciences M,D
Mathematics M,D
Mechanical Engineering M,D
Microbiology M,D*
Molecular Biophysics D
Multilingual and Multicultural Education M,D,O
Music M,D
Neuroscience M,D
Nursing—General M,D
Nutrition M,D
Operations Research M,D
Philosophy M,D
Physics M,D
Physiology M,D
Plant Biology M,D
Plant Molecular Biology M,D
Plant Physiology M,D
Plant Sciences M,D
Political Science M,D
Polymer Science and Engineering M,D
Portuguese M,D
Psychology—General M,D
Public Administration M
Public Health—General M,D
Public History M,D
Public Policy M
Reading Education M,D,O
Scandinavian Languages M,D
School Psychology M,D,O
Science Education M,D,O
Secondary Education M,D,O
Social Psychology M,D
Sociology M,D
Spanish M,D
Special Education M,D,O
Sports Management M,D
Statistics M,D
Theater M
Travel and Tourism M
Urban and Regional Planning M,D
Water Resources M,D
Writing M,D

UNIVERSITY OF MASSACHUSETTS BOSTON

American Studies M
Applied Physics M
Archaeology M
Archives/Archival Administration M
Biological and Biomedical Sciences—General M
Biotechnology M
Business Administration and Management—General M
Cell Biology D
Chemistry M
Clinical Psychology D
Computer Science M,D
Conflict Resolution and Mediation/Peace Studies M,O
Counseling Psychology M,O
Counselor Education M,O
Curriculum and Instruction M
Education—General M,D,O
Educational Leadership and Administration M,D,O
Elementary Education M,D,O
English as a Second Language M
English M
Environmental Biology D
Environmental Sciences D
Foreign Languages Education M
Forensic Psychology M,O
Gerontology M,D,O
Health Services Management and Hospital Administration M,D,O
Higher Education M,D,O
History M
Human Services M
Linguistics M
Marine Sciences D
Marriage and Family Therapy M,O
Molecular Biology D
Multilingual and Multicultural Education M
Nursing—General M,D
Political Science M,D,O
Public Affairs M
Public Policy D
Rehabilitation Counseling M,O
School Psychology M,O
Secondary Education M,D,O
Sociology M
Special Education M
Urban Education M,D,O
Women's Studies M,D,O

UNIVERSITY OF MASSACHUSETTS DARTMOUTH

Accounting M,O
Acoustics M,D,O
Adult Nursing M,D,O
Applied Arts and Design—General M
Art Education M
Art/Fine Arts M,O
Biological and Biomedical Sciences—General M
Biomedical Engineering D
Biotechnology D
Business Administration and Management—General M,O
Chemistry M,D
Civil Engineering M
Clinical Psychology M,O
Community Health Nursing M,D,O
Computer Art and Design M
Computer Engineering M,D,O
Computer Science M,O
Education—General M,O
Electrical Engineering M,D,O
Electronic Commerce M,O
Elementary Education M,O
Engineering and Applied Sciences—General M,D,O
Environmental Engineering M
Environmental Management and Policy M,O
Finance and Banking M,O
Graphic Design M
Illustration M
Latin American Studies M,D
Law P
Marine Biology M
Marketing M,O
Mathematics Education D
Mechanical Engineering M
Middle School Education M,O
Nursing—General M,D,O
Organizational Management M,O
Photography M
Physics M
Portuguese M,D
Psychology—General M,O
Public Policy M,O
Secondary Education M,O
Software Engineering M,O
Supply Chain Management M,O
Telecommunications M,D,O
Textile Design M,O
Textile Sciences and Engineering M
Writing M,O

UNIVERSITY OF MASSACHUSETTS LOWELL

Allied Health—General M,D,O
Analytical Chemistry M,D
Applied Mathematics M,D
Applied Physics M,D
Atmospheric Sciences M,D
Biochemistry M,D
Biological and Biomedical Sciences—General M,D
Biotechnology M,D
Business Administration and Management—General M,O
Chemical Engineering M,D
Chemistry M,D
Civil Engineering M,D,O
Clinical Laboratory Sciences/Medical Technology M,O
Computational Sciences M,D
Computer Engineering M
Computer Science M,D
Criminal Justice and Criminology M
Curriculum and Instruction M,D,O
Economic Development M,O
Economics M,O
Education—General M,D,O
Educational Leadership and Administration M,D,O
Electrical Engineering M,D
Energy and Power Engineering M,D
Engineering and Applied Sciences—General M,D,O
Entrepreneurship M,O
Environmental Engineering M,D,O
Environmental Management and Policy M,D,O
Environmental Sciences M,D,O
Epidemiology M,D,O
Ergonomics and Human Factors M,D,O
Family Nurse Practitioner Studies M
Gerontological Nursing M,O
Health Informatics M,O
Health Physics/Radiological Health M
Health Promotion D
Health Services Management and Hospital Administration M,O
Industrial Hygiene M,D,O
Industrial/Management Engineering M,D,O
Inorganic Chemistry M,D
Materials Engineering M,D,O
Mathematics Education M,D,O
Mathematics M,D
Mechanical Engineering M,D
Mechanics M,D
Medical/Surgical Nursing M,D,O
Music Education M
Music M
Nuclear Engineering M,D
Nursing and Healthcare Administration D
Nursing Education M,D,O
Nursing—General M,D,O
Nutrition M,O
Optical Sciences M,D
Organic Chemistry M,D
Pathology M,O
Physical Therapy D
Physics M,D
Polymer Science and Engineering M,D,O
Psychiatric Nursing M,O
Psychology—General M
Public Health—General M,O
Reading Education M,D,O
Science Education M,D,O
Social Psychology M
Sociology M,O
Sustainable Development M,D,O

UNIVERSITY OF MASSACHUSETTS WORCESTER

Acute Care/Critical Care Nursing M,D,O
Adult Nursing M,D,O
Allopathic Medicine P
Biochemistry M,D
Bioinformatics M,D
Biological and Biomedical Sciences—General M,D
Cancer Biology/Oncology M,D
Cell Biology M,D
Clinical Research M,D
Computational Biology M,D
Epidemiology M,D
Family Nurse Practitioner Studies M,D,O
Gerontological Nursing M,D,O
Health Services Research M,D
Immunology M,D
Interdisciplinary Studies M,D
Microbiology M,D
Molecular Genetics M,D
Molecular Pharmacology M,D
Neuroscience M,D
Nursing and Healthcare Administration M,D,O
Nursing Education M,D,O
Nursing—General M,D,O
Virology M,D

*M—master's degree; P—first professional degree; D—doctorate; O—other advanced degree; *—Close-Up and/or Display in one of the other books in this series*

UNIVERSITY OF MEDICINE AND DENTISTRY OF NEW JERSEY

Program	Degrees
Adult Nursing	M,D,O
Allied Health—General	M,D,O
Allopathic Medicine	P
Biochemistry	M,D
Bioinformatics	M,D
Biological and Biomedical Sciences—General	M,D,O
Biomedical Engineering	M,D,O
Biostatistics	M,D,O
Cancer Biology/Oncology	D,O
Cardiovascular Sciences	M,D
Cell Biology	M,D
Clinical Laboratory Sciences/Medical Technology	M,D
Counseling Psychology	M,D,O
Dentistry	P,M,O
Developmental Biology	D,O
Emergency Management	M,D,O
Environmental and Occupational Health	M,D,O
Environmental Sciences	D
Epidemiology	M,D,O
Family Nurse Practitioner Studies	M,D,O
Health Education	M,D,O
Health Physics/Radiological Health	M
Health Services Management and Hospital Administration	M,D,O
Immunology	M,D,O
Infectious Diseases	D,O
Interdisciplinary Studies	M,D
Kinesiology and Movement Studies	M,D
Medical Imaging	M
Medical Informatics	M,D,O
Microbiology	M,D
Molecular Biology	M,D
Molecular Genetics	M,D
Molecular Medicine	D
Molecular Pathology	M,D,O
Molecular Pharmacology	M,D
Neuroscience	M,D
Nurse Anesthesia	M,D,O
Nurse Midwifery	M,O
Nursing Informatics	M
Nursing—General	M,O
Nutrition	M,D,O
Occupational Health Nursing	M,D,O
Oral and Dental Sciences	P,M,O
Osteopathic Medicine	P
Pathology	D
Pharmacology	D
Physical Therapy	M,D
Physician Assistant Studies	M
Physiology	M,D
Public Health—General	M,D,O
Public Policy	M,O
Quantitative Analysis	M,O
Rehabilitation Counseling	M,D
Toxicology	M,D
Transcultural Nursing	D
Women's Health Nursing	M,D,O

UNIVERSITY OF MEMPHIS

Program	Degrees
Accounting	M,D
Adult Education	M,D
African-American Studies	M,D,O
Analytical Chemistry	M,D
Anthropology	M
Applied Mathematics	M,D
Applied Statistics	M,D
Archaeology	M,D,O
Architecture	M
Art History	M,O
Art/Fine Arts	M,O
Biological and Biomedical Sciences—General	M,D
Biomedical Engineering	M,D
Biostatistics	M
Business Administration and Management—General	M,D
Chemistry	M,D
Civil Engineering	M,D
Clinical Psychology	M,D,O
Communication Disorders	M,D
Communication—General	M,D
Comparative Literature	M,D,O
Computer Engineering	M,D
Computer Science	M,D
Counseling Psychology	M,D
Counselor Education	M,D
Criminal Justice and Criminology	M
Curriculum and Instruction	M,D
Early Childhood Education	M,D
Economics	M,D
Education—General	M,D,O
Educational Leadership and Administration	M,D
Educational Measurement and Evaluation	M,D
Educational Media/Instructional Technology	M,D
Educational Psychology	M,D
Electrical Engineering	M,D
Elementary Education	M,D
Energy and Power Engineering	M,D
Engineering and Applied Sciences—General	M,D
English as a Second Language	M,D,O
English	M,D,O
Environmental and Occupational Health	M
Environmental Engineering	M,D
Epidemiology	M
Exercise and Sports Science	M
Experimental Psychology	M,D,O
Family and Consumer Sciences-General	M
Family Nurse Practitioner Studies	M,O
Film, Television, and Video Production	M,D
Finance and Banking	M,D
French	M
Geographic Information Systems	M,D,O
Geography	M,D,O
Geology	M,D,O
Geophysics	M,D,O
Graphic Design	M,O
Health Promotion	M
Health Services Management and Hospital Administration	M
Higher Education	M,D
History	M,D
Industrial/Management Engineering	M,D
Inorganic Chemistry	M,D
Interdisciplinary Studies	M,D,O
Interior Design	M,O
International Business	M,D
Journalism	M
Law	P
Leisure Studies	M
Liberal Studies	M
Linguistics	M,D,O
Management Information Systems	M,D
Manufacturing Engineering	M
Marketing	M,D
Mathematics	M,D
Mechanical Engineering	M,D
Middle School Education	M,D
Music Education	M,D
Music	M,D
Near and Middle Eastern Studies	M,D
Nonprofit Management	M
Nursing and Healthcare Administration	M,O
Nursing Education	M,O
Nursing Informatics	M,O
Nursing—General	M,O
Nutrition	M
Organic Chemistry	M,D
Philosophy	M,D
Photography	M,O
Physical Chemistry	M,D
Physical Education	M
Physics	M
Political Science	M
Psychology—General	M,D,O
Public Administration	M
Public Health—General	M
Public Policy	M
Reading Education	M,D
Real Estate	M,D
Rehabilitation Counseling	M,D
School Psychology	M,D,O
Secondary Education	M,D
Social Sciences	M
Sociology	M
Spanish	M
Special Education	M,D
Statistics	M,D
Structural Engineering	M,D
Supply Chain Management	M,D
Taxation	M
Theater	M
Transportation and Highway Engineering	M,D
Urban and Regional Planning	M
Water Resources Engineering	M,D
Writing	M,D,O

UNIVERSITY OF MIAMI

Program	Degrees
Accounting	M
Acute Care/Critical Care Nursing	M,D
Adult Nursing	M,D
Advertising and Public Relations	M,D
Aerospace/Aeronautical Engineering	M,D
Allopathic Medicine	P
Architectural Engineering	M,D
Architecture	M
Art History	M
Art/Fine Arts	M
Athletic Training and Sports Medicine	M
Biochemistry	D
Biological and Biomedical Sciences—General	M,D
Biomedical Engineering	M,D
Biophysics	D
Broadcast Journalism	M,D
Business Administration and Management—General	M
Cancer Biology/Oncology	D
Cell Biology	D
Chemistry	M,D
Civil Engineering	M,D
Clinical Psychology	M,D
Communication—General	M,D
Computer Engineering	M,D
Computer Science	M,D
Counseling Psychology	D
Counselor Education	M,O
Developmental Biology	D
Developmental Psychology	M,D
Early Childhood Education	M,O
Economic Development	M,D
Economics	M,D
Education—General	M,D,O
Educational Measurement and Evaluation	M,D
Electrical Engineering	M,D
Engineering and Applied Sciences—General	M,D
English	M,D
Environmental and Occupational Health	M
Environmental Management and Policy	M,D
Epidemiology	D
Ergonomics and Human Factors	M
Evolutionary Biology	M,D
Exercise and Sports Science	M,D
Family Nurse Practitioner Studies	M,D
Film, Television, and Video Production	M,D
Film, Television, and Video Theory and Criticism	M,D
Finance and Banking	M
Fish, Game, and Wildlife Management	M,D
French	D
Genetics	M,D
Geography	M
Geophysics	M,D
Graphic Design	M
Higher Education	M,D,O
History	M,D
Immunology	D
Industrial/Management Engineering	M,D
Inorganic Chemistry	M,D
International Affairs	M,D
International Business	M
International Economics	M,D
Internet and Interactive Multimedia	M
Journalism	M,D
Latin American Studies	M
Law	P,M
Liberal Studies	M
Management Information Systems	M
Management of Technology	M,D
Marine Affairs	M
Marine Biology	M,D
Marine Geology	M,D
Marine Sciences	M,D
Marketing	M
Marriage and Family Therapy	M,O
Mathematics Education	D
Mathematics	M,D
Mechanical Engineering	M,D
Meteorology	M,D
Microbiology	D
Molecular Biology	D
Multilingual and Multicultural Education	D
Music Education	M,D,O
Music	M,D,O
Neuroscience	M,D
Nurse Anesthesia	M,D
Nurse Midwifery	M,D
Nursing—General	M,D
Oceanography	M,D
Organic Chemistry	M,D
Pharmacology	D
Philosophy	M,D
Photography	M
Physical Chemistry	M,D
Physical Therapy	D
Physics	M,D
Physiology	D
Political Science	M
Psychology—General	M,D
Public Health—General	M
Reading Education	D
Romance Languages	D
Science Education	D
Sociology	M,D
Spanish	M,D
Special Education	M,D,O
Sports Management	M
Taxation	M
Therapies—Dance, Drama, and Music	M,D,O
Urban Design	M
Writing	M,D

UNIVERSITY OF MICHIGAN

Program	Degrees
Acute Care/Critical Care Nursing	M
Adult Nursing	M,O

Aerospace/Aeronautical Engineering	M,D
Allopathic Medicine	P
American Studies	M,D
Analytical Chemistry	D
Anthropology	D
Applied Arts and Design—General	M
Applied Economics	M
Applied Physics	D
Applied Statistics	M,D
Archaeology	D
Architecture	M,D
Archives/Archival Administration	M,D
Art History	D
Art/Fine Arts	M
Asian Languages	M,D
Asian Studies	M,D,O
Astronomy	D
Astrophysics	D
Atmospheric Sciences	M,D
Biochemistry	D
Bioinformatics	M,D
Biological and Biomedical Sciences—General	M,D
Biomedical Engineering	M,D
Biophysics	D
Biopsychology	D
Biostatistics	M,D
Business Administration and Management—General	D
Cell Biology	M,D
Chemical Engineering	M,D,O
Chemistry	D
Civil Engineering	M,D,O
Classics	M,D,O
Clinical Psychology	D
Clinical Research	M
Communication—General	D
Community Health Nursing	M,O
Comparative Literature	D
Computer Education	M,D
Computer Engineering	M,D
Computer Science	M,D
Conservation Biology	M,D
Construction Engineering	M,D,O
Curriculum and Instruction	M,D
Dance	M
Dental Hygiene	M
Dentistry	P
Developmental Biology	M,D
Developmental Psychology	D
Early Childhood Education	M,D
East European and Russian Studies	M,O
Ecology	M,D
Economics	M,D
Education—General	M,D
Educational Leadership and Administration	M,D
Educational Measurement and Evaluation	M,D
Educational Media/Instructional Technology	M,D
Electrical Engineering	M,D
Engineering and Applied Sciences—General	M,D,O
English as a Second Language	M,D
English Education	M,D
English	M,D,O
Environmental and Occupational Health	M,D
Environmental Engineering	M,D,O
Environmental Management and Policy	M,D
Environmental Sciences	M,D
Epidemiology	M,D
Evolutionary Biology	M,D
Experimental Psychology	D
Family Nurse Practitioner Studies	M,O
Film, Television, and Video Theory and Criticism	D,O
Foreign Languages Education	M,D
Foundations and Philosophy of Education	M,D
French	D
Genetic Counseling	M,D
Geology	M,D
German	M,D
Gerontological Nursing	M
Health Education	M,D
Health Informatics	M,D
Health Physics/Radiological Health	M,D,O
Health Promotion	M,D
Health Services Management and Hospital Administration	M,D
Higher Education	M,D
History	D,O
Human Genetics	M,D
Human-Computer Interaction	M,D
Immunology	D
Industrial Hygiene	M,D
Industrial/Management Engineering	M,D
Information Science	M,D
Information Studies	M,D
Inorganic Chemistry	D
International Health	M,D
Italian	D
Jewish Studies	M,D,O
Kinesiology and Movement Studies	M,D
Landscape Architecture	M,D
Law	P,M,D
Library Science	M,D
Linguistics	D
Marine Sciences	M,D
Mass Communication	D
Materials Engineering	M,D
Materials Sciences	M,D
Mathematics Education	M,D
Mathematics	M,D
Mechanical Engineering	M,D
Media Studies	M
Medical/Surgical Nursing	M
Medicinal and Pharmaceutical Chemistry	D
Medieval and Renaissance Studies	O
Microbiology	D
Molecular Biology	M,D
Molecular Pathology	D
Multilingual and Multicultural Education	M,D
Music Education	M,D,O
Music	M,D,O
Natural Resources	M,D
Near and Middle Eastern Languages	M,D
Near and Middle Eastern Studies	M,D
Neuroscience	D
Nuclear Engineering	M,D,O
Nurse Midwifery	M,O
Nursing and Healthcare Administration	M
Nursing—General	M,D,O
Nutrition	M,D
Occupational Health Nursing	M,O
Ocean Engineering	M,D,O
Operations Research	M,D
Oral and Dental Sciences	M,D
Organic Chemistry	D
Pathology	D
Pediatric Nursing	M,O
Pharmaceutical Administration	D
Pharmaceutical Sciences	D
Pharmacology	M,D
Pharmacy	P
Philosophy	M,D
Physical Chemistry	D
Physics	M,D
Physiology	D
Planetary and Space Sciences	M,D
Political Science	M,D
Psychiatric Nursing	M
Psychology—General	D,O
Public Health—General	M,D
Public Policy	M,D
Reading Education	M,D
Real Estate	M,O
Religion	M,D
Romance Languages	D
Russian	M,D
Science Education	M,D
Slavic Languages	M,D
Social Psychology	D
Social Sciences Education	M,D
Social Sciences	D
Social Work	M,D
Sociology	D,O
Spanish	D
Sports Management	M,D
Statistics	M,D
Structural Engineering	M,D,O
Survey Methodology	M,D,O
Sustainable Development	M,D
Taxation	P,M,D
Theater	M,D
Toxicology	M,D
Urban and Regional Planning	M,D,O
Urban Design	M
Women's Studies	D,O
Writing	M

UNIVERSITY OF MICHIGAN–DEARBORN

Accounting	M
Applied Mathematics	M
Automotive Engineering	M,D
Business Administration and Management—General	M
Clinical Psychology	M
Computational Sciences	M
Computer Engineering	M
Computer Science	M
Curriculum and Instruction	D
Education—General	M,D
Educational Leadership and Administration	M,D
Educational Measurement and Evaluation	M,O
Educational Psychology	D
Electrical Engineering	M
Engineering and Applied Sciences—General	M,D
Engineering Management	M,D
Environmental Sciences	M
Finance and Banking	M
Health Psychology	M
Industrial/Management Engineering	M,D
Information Science	M,D
International Business	M
Liberal Studies	M
Management Information Systems	M
Manufacturing Engineering	M
Marketing	M
Mechanical Engineering	M
Nonprofit Management	M,O
Project Management	M,D
Public Administration	M,O
Public Policy	M
Science Education	M
Software Engineering	M
Special Education	M,D
Supply Chain Management	M
Systems Engineering	M,D
Systems Science	M,D
Urban Education	D

UNIVERSITY OF MICHIGAN–FLINT

American Studies	M
Biological and Biomedical Sciences—General	M
Business Administration and Management—General	M
Computer Science	M
Education—General	M
Educational Media/Instructional Technology	M
Elementary Education	M
English	M
Health Education	M
Information Science	M
Nurse Anesthesia	M
Nursing—General	D
Physical Therapy	D
Public Administration	M
Reading Education	M
Social Sciences	M
Special Education	M

UNIVERSITY OF MINNESOTA, DULUTH

Allopathic Medicine	P
Anthropology	M
Applied Mathematics	M
Art/Fine Arts	M
Biochemistry	M,D
Biological and Biomedical Sciences—General	M,D
Biophysics	M,D
Business Administration and Management—General	M
Chemistry	M
Communication Disorders	M
Computational Sciences	M
Computer Engineering	M
Computer Science	M
Criminal Justice and Criminology	M
Education—General	D
Electrical Engineering	M
Engineering Management	M
English	M
Geology	M,D
Graphic Design	M
Immunology	M,D
Liberal Studies	M
Medical Microbiology	M,D
Molecular Biology	M,D
Music Education	M
Music	M
Pharmacology	M,D
Pharmacy	M,D
Physics	M
Physiology	M,D
Safety Engineering	M
Social Work	M
Sociology	M
Toxicology	M,D

UNIVERSITY OF MINNESOTA, TWIN CITIES CAMPUS

Accounting	M,D
Adult Education	M,D,O
Adult Nursing	M
Aerospace/Aeronautical Engineering	M,D
Agricultural Education	M,D
Agricultural Sciences—General	M,D
Agronomy and Soil Sciences	M,D
Allopathic Medicine	P
American Studies	D
Animal Behavior	M,D
Animal Sciences	M,D
Anthropology	M,D
Applied Arts and Design—General	M,D,O
Applied Economics	M,D
Archaeology	M,D
Architecture	M
Art Education	M,D,O
Art History	M,D
Art/Fine Arts	M
Asian Languages	D
Asian Studies	D
Astronomy	M,D

*M—master's degree; P—first professional degree; D—doctorate; O—other advanced degree; *—Close-Up and/or Display in one of the other books in this series*

Astrophysics M,D
Biochemistry D
Biological and Biomedical Sciences—General M
Biomedical Engineering M,D
Biophysics M,D
Biopsychology D
Biostatistics M,D
Biosystems Engineering M,D
Biotechnology M
Business Administration and Management—General M,D
Business Education M,D
Cancer Biology/Oncology D
Cell Biology M,D
Chemical Engineering M,D
Chemistry M,D
Child and Family Studies M,D
Child Development M,D
Civil Engineering M,D
Classics M,D
Clinical Psychology D
Clinical Research M
Clothing and Textiles M,D,O
Cognitive Sciences D
Communication Disorders M,D
Communication—General M,D,O
Community Health Nursing M
Community Health M
Comparative Literature D
Computational Sciences M,D
Computer and Information Systems Security M
Computer Engineering M,D
Computer Science M,D
Conservation Biology M,D
Counseling Psychology D
Counselor Education M,D,O
Cultural Studies D
Curriculum and Instruction M,D,O
Dance M,D
Dentistry P
Developmental Biology M,D
Early Childhood Education M,D,O
Ecology M,D
Economic Development M
Economics D
Education of the Gifted M,D,O
Education—General M,D,O
Educational Leadership and Administration M,D
Educational Measurement and Evaluation M,D
Educational Media/Instructional Technology M,D,O
Educational Policy M,D,O
Educational Psychology M,D,O
Electrical Engineering M,D
Elementary Education M,D,O
Engineering and Applied Sciences—General M,D
English as a Second Language M
English Education M
English M,D
Entomology M,D
Environmental and Occupational Health M,D,O
Environmental Education M,D,O
Environmental Management and Policy M
Epidemiology M,D
Evolutionary Biology M,D
Exercise and Sports Science M,D,O
Family Nurse Practitioner Studies M
Finance and Banking M,D
Food Science and Technology M,D
Foreign Languages Education M
Foundations and Philosophy of Education M,D,O
French M,D
Genetic Counseling M,D
Genetics M,D
Geographic Information Systems M
Geological Engineering M,D
Geology M,D
Geophysics M,D
German M,D
Gerontological Nursing M
Health Informatics M,D
Health Services Management and Hospital Administration M,D
Health Services Research M,D
Higher Education M,D
Hispanic and Latin American Languages M,D
History of Medicine M,D
History of Science and Technology M,D
History M,D
Human Resources Development M,D,O
Human Resources Management M,D
Immunology D
Industrial and Labor Relations M,D
Industrial and Manufacturing Management D
Industrial and Organizational Psychology D
Industrial Hygiene M,D
Industrial/Management Engineering M,D
Infectious Diseases M,D
Information Science M,D
Interdisciplinary Studies D
Interior Design M,D,O
International and Comparative Education M,D
International Development M
International Health M,D
Kinesiology and Movement Studies M,D
Landscape Architecture M
Law P,M
Leisure Studies M,D
Linguistics M,D
Logistics D
Management Information Systems M,D
Management of Technology M
Management Strategy and Policy D
Marketing M,D
Marriage and Family Therapy M,D
Mass Communication M,D
Materials Engineering M,D
Materials Sciences M,D
Maternal and Child Health M
Mathematics Education M
Mathematics M,D
Mechanical Engineering M,D
Mechanics M,D
Medical Physics M,D
Medicinal and Pharmaceutical Chemistry M,D
Medieval and Renaissance Studies M,D
Microbiology D
Molecular Biology M,D
Multilingual and Multicultural Education M
Music M,D
Natural Resources M,D
Neurobiology M,D
Neuroscience M,D
Nurse Anesthesia M
Nurse Midwifery M
Nursing and Healthcare Administration M
Nursing—General M,D
Nutrition M,D
Occupational Health Nursing M,D
Oral and Dental Sciences M,D,O
Pediatric Nursing M
Pharmaceutical Administration M,D
Pharmaceutical Sciences M,D
Pharmacology M,D
Pharmacy P,M,D
Philosophy M,D
Physical Education M,D,O
Physical Therapy D
Physics M,D
Physiology D
Plant Biology M,D
Plant Pathology M,D
Plant Sciences M,D
Political Science D
Portuguese M,D
Psychiatric Nursing M
Psychology—General D
Public Affairs M
Public Health—General M,D,O
Public Policy M
Reading Education M,D,O
Recreation and Park Management M,D
Religion M,D
Scandinavian Languages M,D
School Psychology M,D,O
Science Education M
Social Psychology D
Social Sciences Education M
Social Work M,D
Sociology M,D
Spanish M,D
Special Education M,D,O
Sports Management M,D,O
Statistics M,D
Structural Biology D
Student Affairs M,D,O
Supply Chain Management M
Systems Engineering M
Taxation M
Technology and Public Policy M
Textile Design M,D,O
Theater M,D
Toxicology M,D
Urban and Regional Planning M
Veterinary Medicine P
Veterinary Sciences M,D
Virology D
Vocational and Technical Education M,D,O
Water Resources M,D
Women's Health Nursing M
Women's Studies D

UNIVERSITY OF MISSISSIPPI

Accounting M,D
American Studies M
Anthropology M
Applied Science and Technology M,D
Art Education M
Art History M
Art/Fine Arts M
Biological and Biomedical Sciences—General M,D
Business Administration and Management—General M,D
Chemistry M,D
Clinical Psychology M,D
Communication Disorders M
Counselor Education M,D,O
Curriculum and Instruction M,D,O
Economics M,D
Education—General M,D,O
Educational Leadership and Administration M,D,O
Engineering and Applied Sciences—General M,D
English M,D
Exercise and Sports Science M,D
Experimental Psychology M,D
Family and Consumer Sciences-General M
French M
German M
Higher Education M,D,O
History M,D
Journalism M
Law P
Legal and Justice Studies M
Leisure Studies M,D
Management Information Systems M,D
Mathematics M,D
Medicinal and Pharmaceutical Chemistry M,D
Music M,D
Pharmaceutical Administration M,D
Pharmaceutical Sciences M,D
Pharmacology M,D
Pharmacy P
Philosophy M
Physics M,D
Political Science M,D
Psychology—General M,D
Recreation and Park Management M,D
Social Work M
Sociology M
Spanish M
Student Affairs M,D,O
Taxation M,D

UNIVERSITY OF MISSISSIPPI MEDICAL CENTER

Allied Health—General M
Allopathic Medicine P
Anatomy M,D
Biochemistry M,D
Biological and Biomedical Sciences—General M,D
Biophysics M,D
Clinical Laboratory Sciences/Medical Technology M,D
Dentistry P,M,D
Maternal and Child Health M
Microbiology M,D
Nursing—General M,D
Occupational Therapy M
Oral and Dental Sciences M,D
Pathology M,D
Pharmacology M,D
Physical Therapy M
Physiology M,D
Toxicology M,D

UNIVERSITY OF MISSOURI

Accounting M,D
Adult Education M,D,O
Aerospace/Aeronautical Engineering M,D
Agricultural Economics and Agribusiness M,D
Agricultural Education M,D,O
Agricultural Engineering M,D
Agricultural Sciences—General M,D,O
Agronomy and Soil Sciences M,D
Allopathic Medicine P
Analytical Chemistry M,D
Anatomy M
Animal Sciences M,D
Anthropology M,D
Applied Mathematics M
Archaeology M,D
Architecture M
Art Education M,D,O
Art History M,D
Art/Fine Arts M
Astronomy M,D
Atmospheric Sciences M,D
Biochemistry M,D
Bioengineering M,D
Bioinformatics D
Biological and Biomedical Sciences—General M,D

Program	Degrees
Business Administration and Management—General	M,D
Business Education	M,D,O
Cell Biology	M,D
Chemical Engineering	M,D
Chemistry	M,D
Child and Family Studies	M,D
Civil Engineering	M,D
Classics	M,D
Clothing and Textiles	M
Communication Disorders	M
Communication—General	M,D
Comparative Literature	M,D
Computer Art and Design	M
Computer Science	M,D*
Conflict Resolution and Mediation/Peace Studies	M
Consumer Economics	M
Counseling Psychology	M,D,O
Curriculum and Instruction	M,D,O
Early Childhood Education	M,D,O
Ecology	M,D
Economics	M,D
Education of the Gifted	M,D
Education—General	M,D,O
Educational Leadership and Administration	M,D,O
Educational Media/Instructional Technology	M,D,O
Educational Psychology	M,D,O
Electrical Engineering	M,D
Elementary Education	M,D,O
Engineering and Applied Sciences—General	M,D
English Education	M,D,O
English	M,D
Entomology	M,D
Environmental Design	M
Environmental Engineering	M,D
Evolutionary Biology	M,D
Exercise and Sports Science	M,D
Family and Consumer Sciences-General	M,D
Fish, Game, and Wildlife Management	M,D
Food Science and Technology	M,D
Foreign Languages Education	M,D,O
Forestry	M,D
French	M,D
Genetics	M,D
Geography	M
Geology	M,D
Geotechnical Engineering	M,D
German	M
Health Education	M,D,O
Health Informatics	M
Health Physics/Radiological Health	M,D
Health Services Management and Hospital Administration	M
Higher Education	M,D,O
History	M,D
Horticulture	M,D
Hospitality Management	M,D
Human Development	M,D
Immunology	M,D
Industrial/Management Engineering	M,D
Information Studies	M,D,O
Inorganic Chemistry	M,D
Journalism	M,D
Law	P,M
Library Science	M,D,O
Manufacturing Engineering	M,D
Mathematics Education	M,D,O
Mathematics	M,D
Mechanical Engineering	M,D
Medical Physics	M,D
Microbiology	M,D
Music Education	M,D,O
Music	M
Natural Resources	M
Neurobiology	M,D
Neuroscience	M,D
Nuclear Engineering	M,D
Nursing—General	M,D
Nutrition	M,D
Occupational Therapy	M
Organic Chemistry	M,D
Pathobiology	M,D
Pathology	M
Pharmacology	M,D
Philosophy	M,D
Physical Chemistry	M,D
Physical Therapy	M
Physics	M,D
Physiology	M,D
Plant Biology	M,D
Plant Sciences	M,D
Political Science	M,D
Psychology—General	M,D
Public Affairs	M
Public Health—General	M
Reading Education	M,D,O
Recreation and Park Management	M
Religion	M
Romance Languages	M,D
Rural Sociology	M,D
School Psychology	M,D,O
Science Education	M,D,O
Social Sciences Education	M,D,O
Social Work	M
Sociology	M,D
Spanish	M,D
Special Education	M,D
Statistics	M,D
Structural Engineering	M,D
Theater	M,D
Transportation and Highway Engineering	M,D
Veterinary Medicine	P
Veterinary Sciences	M,D
Vocational and Technical Education	M,D,O
Water Resources Engineering	M,D

UNIVERSITY OF MISSOURI–KANSAS CITY

Program	Degrees
Accounting	M,D
Adult Nursing	M,D
Allopathic Medicine	P,M
Analytical Chemistry	M,D
Anesthesiologist Assistant Studies	P,M
Art History	M,D
Art/Fine Arts	M,D
Biochemistry	D
Bioinformatics	P,M,D
Biological and Biomedical Sciences—General	M,D
Biophysics	D
Business Administration and Management—General	M,D
Cell Biology	D*
Chemistry	M,D
Civil Engineering	M,D
Clinical Psychology	M,D
Computer Engineering	M,D
Computer Science	M,D
Counseling Psychology	M,D,O
Criminal Justice and Criminology	M
Curriculum and Instruction	M,D,O
Dental Hygiene	P,M,D,O
Dentistry	P,M,D,O
Economics	M,D
Education—General	M,D,O
Educational Leadership and Administration	M,D,O
Electrical Engineering	M,D
Engineering and Applied Sciences—General	M,D
English	M,D
Entrepreneurship	M,D
Family Nurse Practitioner Studies	M,D
Geology	M,D
Geosciences	M,D
Health Psychology	M,D
History	M,D
Inorganic Chemistry	M,D
Interdisciplinary Studies	D
Law	P,M
Maternal and Child/Neonatal Nursing	M,D
Mathematics	M,D
Mechanical Engineering	M,D
Media Studies	M,D
Molecular Biology	D*
Music Education	M,D
Music	M,D
Nursing and Healthcare Administration	M,D
Nursing Education	M,D
Nursing—General	M,D
Oral and Dental Sciences	P,M,D,O
Organic Chemistry	M,D
Pediatric Nursing	M,D
Pharmaceutical Sciences	P,D
Pharmacy	P,D
Physical Chemistry	M,D
Physics	M,D
Political Science	M,D
Polymer Science and Engineering	M,D
Psychology—General	M,D
Public Administration	M,D
Public Affairs	M,D
Reading Education	M,D,O
Romance Languages	M
Social Psychology	M,D
Social Work	M
Sociology	M,D
Software Engineering	M,D
Special Education	M,D,O
Statistics	M,D
Taxation	P,M
Telecommunications	M,D
Theater	M
Women's Health Nursing	M,D
Writing	M,D

UNIVERSITY OF MISSOURI–ST. LOUIS

Program	Degrees
Accounting	M,O
Adult Education	M,D,O
Adult Nursing	M,D,O
American Studies	M,D
Applied Mathematics	M,D
Applied Physics	M,D
Astrophysics	M,D
Biochemistry	M,D
Biological and Biomedical Sciences—General	M,D,O
Biotechnology	M,D,O
Business Administration and Management—General	M,O
Cell Biology	M,D,O
Chemistry	M,D
Clinical Psychology	M,D,O
Communication—General	M
Computer Science	M,D
Conservation Biology	M,D,O
Counselor Education	M,D
Criminal Justice and Criminology	M,D
Cultural Studies	O
Curriculum and Instruction	M,O
Early Childhood Education	M,O
Ecology	M,D,O
Economics	M
Education—General	M,D,O
Educational Leadership and Administration	M,D,O
Educational Measurement and Evaluation	M,O
Educational Psychology	D
Elementary Education	M,O
English as a Second Language	M,O
English	M,O
Evolutionary Biology	M,D,O
Family Nurse Practitioner Studies	M,D,O
Finance and Banking	M,O
Gender Studies	O
Gerontology	M,O
Health Services Management and Hospital Administration	M,O
Higher Education	M,D,O
Human Resources Development	M,O
Human Resources Management	M,O
Industrial and Manufacturing Management	M,O
Industrial and Organizational Psychology	M,D,O
Inorganic Chemistry	M,D
Interdisciplinary Studies	O
Linguistics	M,O
Logistics	M,D,O
Management Information Systems	M,D,O
Marketing	M,O
Maternal and Child/Neonatal Nursing	M,D,O
Mathematics	M,D
Middle School Education	M,O
Molecular Biology	M,D,O
Museum Studies	M,O
Music Education	M
Neuroscience	M,D,O
Nonprofit Management	M,O
Nursing and Healthcare Administration	M,D,O
Nursing Education	M,D,O
Nursing—General	M,D,O
Optometry	P
Organic Chemistry	M,D
Pediatric Nursing	M,D,O
Philosophy	M
Physical Chemistry	M,D
Physics	M,D
Political Science	M,D,O
Psychiatric Nursing	M,D,O
Psychology—General	M,D,O
Public Administration	M,D,O
Public Policy	M,D,O
Reading Education	M,O
School Psychology	O
Secondary Education	M,O
Social Psychology	M,D,O
Social Work	M,O
Special Education	M,O
Supply Chain Management	M,D,O
Vision Sciences	M,D
Women's Health Nursing	M,D,O
Writing	M,O

UNIVERSITY OF MOBILE

Program	Degrees
Business Administration and Management—General	M
Education—General	M
Marriage and Family Therapy	M
Nursing—General	M
Religion	M
Theology	M

THE UNIVERSITY OF MONTANA

Program	Degrees
Accounting	M
Analytical Chemistry	M,D
Animal Behavior	M,D,O
Anthropology	M,D
Art/Fine Arts	M
Biochemistry	M,D
Biological and Biomedical Sciences—General	M,D
Business Administration and Management—General	M
Chemistry	M,D
Clinical Psychology	M,D,O
Communication—General	M
Computer Science	M
Counseling Psychology	M,D,O
Counselor Education	M,D,O
Criminal Justice and Criminology	M

*M—master's degree; P—first professional degree; D—doctorate; O—other advanced degree; *—Close-Up and/or Display in one of the other books in this series*

Curriculum and Instruction M,D
Developmental Psychology M,D,O
Ecology M,D
Economics M
Education—General M,D,O
Educational Leadership and Administration M,D,O
English Education M
English M
Environmental Management and Policy M
Environmental Sciences M
Exercise and Sports Science M
Experimental Psychology M,D,O
Fish, Game, and Wildlife Management M,D
Forestry M,D
French M
Geographic Information Systems M
Geography M
Geology M,D
Geosciences M,D
German M
Health Education M
Health Promotion M
History M,D
Infectious Diseases D
Inorganic Chemistry M,D
Interdisciplinary Studies M,D
Jewish Studies M
Journalism M
Law P
Linguistics M,D
Mathematics Education M,D
Mathematics M,D
Microbiology M,D
Music Education M
Music M
Natural Resources M,D
Neuroscience M,D
Organic Chemistry M,D
Pharmaceutical Sciences M,D
Pharmacy P,M,D
Philosophy M
Physical Chemistry M,D
Physical Education M
Physical Therapy D
Political Science M
Psychology—General M,D,O
Public Administration M
Public Health—General M,O
Recreation and Park Management M,D
Rural Planning and Studies M
Rural Sociology M
School Psychology M,D,O
Social Work M
Sociology M
Spanish M
Theater M
Toxicology M,D
Writing M
Zoology M,D

UNIVERSITY OF MONTEVALLO

Business Administration and Management—General M
Communication Disorders M
Counselor Education M
Education—General M,O
Educational Leadership and Administration M,O
Elementary Education M
English M
Marriage and Family Therapy M
Secondary Education M
Social Psychology M

UNIVERSITY OF NEBRASKA AT KEARNEY

Art Education M
Biological and Biomedical Sciences—General M
Business Administration and Management—General M
Communication Disorders M
Counselor Education M,O
Curriculum and Instruction M
Education—General M,O
Educational Leadership and Administration M,O
Educational Media/Instructional Technology M
English M
Exercise and Sports Science M
Foreign Languages Education M
History M
Music Education M
Physical Education M
Reading Education M
School Psychology M,O
Science Education M
Special Education M
Writing M

UNIVERSITY OF NEBRASKA AT OMAHA

Accounting M
Biological and Biomedical Sciences—General M
Biopsychology M,D,O
Business Administration and Management—General M
Communication Disorders M
Communication—General M
Computer Science M
Counselor Education M
Criminal Justice and Criminology M,D
Developmental Psychology M,D,O
Economics M
Education—General M,D,O
Educational Leadership and Administration M,D,O
Educational Media/Instructional Technology M,O
Educational Psychology M,D,O
Elementary Education M
English as a Second Language M,O
English M,O
Foreign Languages Education M
Geography M,O
Gerontology M,O
Health Education M
History M
Industrial and Organizational Psychology M,D,O
Information Science M,D,O
Management Information Systems M,D,O
Mathematics M
Music M
Physical Education M
Political Science M
Psychology—General M,D,O
Public Administration M,D,O
Reading Education M
Recreation and Park Management M
School Psychology M,D,O
Secondary Education M
Social Work M
Special Education M
Technical Communication M,O
Theater M
Urban Education M,O
Writing M,O

UNIVERSITY OF NEBRASKA–LINCOLN

Accounting M,D
Actuarial Science M
Adult Education M,D,O
Advertising and Public Relations M,D
Agricultural Economics and Agribusiness M,D
Agricultural Education M
Agricultural Engineering M,D
Agricultural Sciences—General M,D
Agronomy and Soil Sciences M,D
Analytical Chemistry M,D
Animal Sciences M,D
Anthropology M
Archaeology M,D
Architectural Engineering M,D
Architecture M,D
Art History M
Art/Fine Arts M
Astronomy M,D
Biochemistry M,D
Bioengineering M,D
Bioinformatics M,D
Biological and Biomedical Sciences—General M,D
Biopsychology M,D
Business Administration and Management—General M,D
Chemical Engineering M,D
Chemistry M,D
Child and Family Studies M,D
Child Development M,D
Civil Engineering M,D
Classics M
Clinical Psychology M,D
Clothing and Textiles M,D
Cognitive Sciences M,D,O
Communication Disorders M,D
Communication—General M,D
Comparative Literature M,D
Computer Engineering M,D
Computer Science M,D
Consumer Economics M,D
Corporate and Organizational Communication M,D
Counseling Psychology M,D,O
Curriculum and Instruction M,D,O
Developmental Psychology M,D,O
Distance Education Development M
Early Childhood Education M,D
Economics M,D
Educational Leadership and Administration M,D,O
Educational Measurement and Evaluation M,D,O
Educational Psychology M,D,O
Electrical Engineering M,D
Engineering and Applied Sciences—General M,D
Engineering Management M,D
English M,D
Entomology M,D
Environmental Engineering M,D
Exercise and Sports Science M,D
Family and Consumer Sciences-General M,D
Finance and Banking M,D
Food Science and Technology M,D
French M,D
Geography M,D
Geosciences M,D
German M,D
Gerontology M,D
Health Education M
Health Promotion M,D
History M,D
Home Economics Education M,D
Horticulture M,D
Human Development M,D,O
Industrial/Management Engineering M,D
Information Science M,D
Inorganic Chemistry M,D
Interior Design M,D
Journalism M
Law P,M
Legal and Justice Studies M
Management Information Systems M
Manufacturing Engineering M,D
Marketing M,D
Marriage and Family Therapy M,D
Mass Communication M
Materials Engineering M,D
Materials Sciences M,D
Mathematics M,D
Mechanical Engineering M,D*
Mechanics M,D
Metallurgical Engineering and Metallurgy M,D
Music Education M,D
Music M,D
Natural Resources M,D
Nutrition M,D
Organic Chemistry M,D
Philosophy M,D
Physical Chemistry M,D
Physics M,D
Political Science M,D,O
Psychology—General M,D
Public Policy M,D,O
Rhetoric M,D
School Psychology M,D,O
Social Psychology M,D
Sociology M,D
Spanish M,D
Special Education M,D,O
Speech and Interpersonal Communication M,D
Statistics M,D
Survey Methodology M,D
Theater M
Toxicology M,D
Urban and Regional Planning M,D
Veterinary Sciences M,D
Vocational and Technical Education M,D,O
Writing M,D

UNIVERSITY OF NEBRASKA MEDICAL CENTER

Allied Health—General M,D,O
Allopathic Medicine P,O
Anatomy M,D
Biochemistry M,D
Biological and Biomedical Sciences—General M,D
Cancer Biology/Oncology D
Cell Biology M,D
Clinical Laboratory Sciences/Medical Technology M,O
Dentistry P,M,D,O
Genetics M,D
Microbiology M,D
Molecular Biology M,D
Neuroscience M,D
Nursing—General M,D
Nutrition O
Pathology M,D
Perfusion M
Pharmaceutical Sciences M,D
Pharmacology M,D
Pharmacy P
Physical Therapy D
Physician Assistant Studies M
Physiology M,D
Public Health—General M
Toxicology M,D

UNIVERSITY OF NEVADA, LAS VEGAS

Accounting M,O
Aerospace/Aeronautical Engineering M,D
Allied Health—General M,D

Anthropology	M,D
Architecture	M
Art/Fine Arts	M
Astronomy	M,D
Biochemistry	M,D
Biological and Biomedical Sciences—General	M,D
Biomedical Engineering	M,D
Business Administration and Management—General	M
Chemistry	M,D
Civil Engineering	M,D
Clinical Psychology	M,O
Communication—General	M
Community Health	M,D,O
Computer Engineering	M,D
Computer Science	M,D
Construction Management	M
Counselor Education	M,O
Criminal Justice and Criminology	M
Curriculum and Instruction	M,D,O
Early Childhood Education	M,D,O
Economics	M
Education—General	M,D,O
Educational Leadership and Administration	M,D
Educational Media/ Instructional Technology	M,D,O
Educational Psychology	M,D,O
Electrical Engineering	M,D
Emergency Management	M,D,O
Engineering and Applied Sciences—General	M,D
English	M,D
Entrepreneurship	O
Environmental Engineering	M,D
Environmental Sciences	M,D,O
Ethics	M
Ethnic Studies	M,D
Exercise and Sports Science	M
Family Nurse Practitioner Studies	M,D,O
Film, Television, and Video Production	M
Finance and Banking	O
Forensic Sciences	M,O
Geosciences	M,D
Health Physics/ Radiological Health	M
Health Promotion	M
Health Services Management and Hospital Administration	M
Hispanic Studies	M
History	M,D
Hospitality Management	M,D
Information Science	M,D
Journalism	M
Kinesiology and Movement Studies	M
Law	P
Leisure Studies	M
Management Information Systems	M,O
Marriage and Family Therapy	M
Materials Engineering	M,D
Mathematics	M,D
Mechanical Engineering	M,D
Media Studies	M
Music	M,D
Nonprofit Management	M,D,O
Nuclear Engineering	M,D
Nursing Education	M,D,O
Nursing—General	M,D,O
Pediatric Nursing	M,D,O
Physical Education	M,D
Physical Therapy	D
Physics	M,D
Political Science	M,D
Psychology—General	M,D
Public Administration	M,D,O
Public Affairs	M,D,O
Public Health—General	M,D
Public Policy	M
Rehabilitation Counseling	M,O
Social Work	M,O
Sociology	M,D
Special Education	M,D,O
Sports Management	M,D
Theater	M
Transportation and Highway Engineering	M,D
Water Resources	M
Women's Studies	O
Writing	M,D

UNIVERSITY OF NEVADA, RENO

Accounting	M
Agricultural Economics and Agribusiness	M,D
Agricultural Sciences—General	M,D
Animal Sciences	M
Anthropology	M,D
Applied Economics	M,D
Art/Fine Arts	M
Atmospheric Sciences	M,D
Biochemistry	M,D*
Biological and Biomedical Sciences—General	M
Biomedical Engineering	M,D
Biotechnology	M
Business Administration and Management—General	M
Cell Biology	M,D
Chemical Engineering	M,D
Chemical Physics	D
Chemistry	M,D
Child and Family Studies	M
Civil Engineering	M,D
Clinical Psychology	D
Cognitive Sciences	M,D
Communication Disorders	M,D
Computer Engineering	M,D
Computer Science	M,D
Conservation Biology	D
Counselor Education	M,D,O
Criminal Justice and Criminology	M
Curriculum and Instruction	D
Ecology	D
Economics	M
Education—General	M,D,O
Educational Leadership and Administration	M,D,O
Educational Psychology	M,D,O
Electrical Engineering	M,D
Elementary Education	M
Engineering and Applied Sciences—General	M,D
English as a Second Language	M
English	M,D
Environmental and Occupational Health	M,D
Environmental Management and Policy	M
Environmental Sciences	M,D
Evolutionary Biology	D
Finance and Banking	M
Foreign Languages Education	M
French	M
Geochemistry	M,D
Geography	M,D
Geological Engineering	M,D
Geology	M,D
Geophysics	M,D
German	M
History	M,D
Human Development	M
Hydrogeology	M,D
Hydrology	M,D
Journalism	M
Legal and Justice Studies	M,D
Management Information Systems	M
Materials Engineering	M,D
Mathematics Education	M
Mathematics	M
Mechanical Engineering	M,D
Metallurgical Engineering and Metallurgy	M,D
Mineral/Mining Engineering	M
Molecular Biology	M,D
Molecular Pharmacology	D
Music	M
Nursing—General	M,D
Nutrition	M
Philosophy	M
Physics	M,D
Physiology	D
Political Science	M,D
Psychology—General	M,D
Public Administration	M
Public Health—General	M,D
Reading Education	M,D
Secondary Education	M
Social Psychology	D
Social Work	M
Sociology	M
Spanish	M
Special Education	M,D
Speech and Interpersonal Communication	M
Western European Studies	D

UNIVERSITY OF NEW BRUNSWICK FREDERICTON

Anthropology	M
Applied Economics	M
Biological and Biomedical Sciences—General	M,D
Business Administration and Management—General	M
Chemical Engineering	M,D
Chemistry	M,D
Civil Engineering	M,D
Classics	M
Computer Engineering	M,D
Computer Science	M,D
Conflict Resolution and Mediation/Peace Studies	M
Construction Engineering	M,D
Economics	M
Education—General	M,D
Electrical Engineering	M,D
Engineering and Applied Sciences—General	M,D,O
Engineering Management	M
English	M,D
Entrepreneurship	M
Environmental Engineering	M,D
Environmental Management and Policy	M,D
Exercise and Sports Science	M
Forestry	M,D
Geodetic Sciences	M,D,O
Geology	M,D
Geotechnical Engineering	M,D
Health Services Research	M
History	M,D
Hydrology	M,D
Interdisciplinary Studies	M,D
Law	P
Marketing	M,D
Materials Sciences	M,D
Mathematics	M,D
Mechanical Engineering	M,D
Mechanics	M,D
Nursing Education	M
Nursing—General	M
Philosophy	M
Physical Education	M
Physics	M,D
Political Science	M
Public Administration	M
Public Policy	M
Recreation and Park Management	M
Sociology	M,D
Sports Management	M
Statistics	M,D
Structural Engineering	M,D
Surveying Science and Engineering	M,D,O
Sustainable Development	M
Transportation and Highway Engineering	M,D
Water Resources	M,D

UNIVERSITY OF NEW BRUNSWICK SAINT JOHN

Applied Psychology	M,D
Biological and Biomedical Sciences—General	M,D
Business Administration and Management—General	M
Clinical Psychology	M,D
Electronic Commerce	M
Experimental Psychology	M,D
International Business	M
Natural Resources	M
Psychology—General	M,D

UNIVERSITY OF NEW ENGLAND

Addictions/Substance Abuse Counseling	M,O
Biological and Biomedical Sciences—General	M
Curriculum and Instruction	M,O
Education—General	M,O
Educational Leadership and Administration	M,O
Educational Measurement and Evaluation	M,O
Ethics	M,O
Gerontology	M,O
Health Education	P,M
Marine Sciences	M
Nurse Anesthesia	M
Occupational Therapy	M
Osteopathic Medicine	P
Pharmacy	P
Physical Therapy	D
Physician Assistant Studies	M
Public Health—General	M,O
Reading Education	M,O
Social Work	M,O
Special Education	M,O

UNIVERSITY OF NEW HAMPSHIRE

Accounting	M
Animal Sciences	M,D
Applied Mathematics	M,D,O
Art/Fine Arts	M
Biochemistry	M,D
Biological and Biomedical Sciences—General	M,D
Business Administration and Management—General	M,O
Chemical Engineering	M,D
Chemistry	M,D
Child and Family Studies	M
Civil Engineering	M,D
Communication Disorders	M,O
Comparative Literature	M,D
Computer Science	M,D,O
Counselor Education	M,O
Early Childhood Education	M
Economics	M,D
Education—General	M,D,O
Educational Leadership and Administration	M,O
Electrical Engineering	M,D
Elementary Education	M
English Education	M,D
English	M,D
Environmental Education	M
Environmental Management and Policy	M
Family Nurse Practitioner Studies	M,O
Fish, Game, and Wildlife Management	M
Forestry	M
Genetics	M,D
Geochemistry	M
Geology	M
Geosciences	M

*M—master's degree; P—first professional degree; D—doctorate; O—other advanced degree; *—Close-Up and/or Display in one of the other books in this series*

Higher Education M
History M,D
Hydrology M
International Development M,D,O
Kinesiology and Movement Studies M
Legal and Justice Studies M
Liberal Studies M
Linguistics M,D
Logistics M,D
Management of Technology M,O
Marine Sciences M
Marriage and Family Therapy M
Materials Sciences M,D
Mathematics Education M,D,O
Mathematics M,D,O
Mechanical Engineering M,D
Microbiology M,D
Museum Studies M,D
Music Education M
Music M
Natural Resources M,D
Nursing—General M,O
Nutrition M,D
Occupational Therapy M,O
Ocean Engineering M,D,O
Oceanography M,D,O
Physics M,D
Plant Biology M,D
Political Science M
Psychology—General D
Public Administration M,O
Public Health—General M,O
Reading Education M
Recreation and Park Management M
Science Education M,D
Secondary Education M
Social Work M,O
Sociology M,D
Software Engineering M,D,O
Spanish M
Special Education M,O
Statistics M,D,O
Water Resources M
Writing M,D
Zoology M,D

UNIVERSITY OF NEW HAVEN

Accounting M,O
Business Administration and Management—General M,O
Cell Biology M,O
Computational Sciences M,O
Computer and Information Systems Security M,O
Computer Engineering M
Computer Science M,D,O
Conflict Resolution and Mediation/Peace Studies M,O
Criminal Justice and Criminology M,D,O
Database Systems M,O
Ecology M,O
Education—General M
Electrical Engineering M
Emergency Management M,O
Engineering and Applied Sciences—General M,O
Engineering Management M
Environmental and Occupational Health M,O
Environmental Engineering M,O
Environmental Management and Policy M,O
Environmental Sciences M,O
Facilities Management M,O
Finance and Banking M,O
Fire Protection Engineering M,O
Forensic Psychology M,D,O
Forensic Sciences M,D,O
Geographic Information Systems M,O
Geosciences M,O
Hazardous Materials Management M,O
Health Services Management and Hospital Administration M,O
Homeland Security M,O
Human Resources Management M,O
Industrial and Labor Relations M,O
Industrial and Manufacturing Management M
Industrial and Organizational Psychology M,O
Industrial/Management Engineering M,O
Information Science M,O
International Business M,O
Management Strategy and Policy M,O
Marketing M,O
Mechanical Engineering M
Molecular Biology M,O
National Security M,O
Nutrition M
Organizational Management M,O
Public Administration M,O
Social Psychology M,O
Software Engineering M,O
Sports Management M,O
Systems Engineering M,O
Taxation M
Telecommunications Management M,O
Urban and Regional Planning M,O
Water Resources Engineering M,O

UNIVERSITY OF NEW MEXICO

Accounting M
Allopathic Medicine P
American Studies M,D
Anthropology M,D
Architecture M
Art Education M
Art History M,D
Art/Fine Arts M
Biochemistry M,D,O
Biological and Biomedical Sciences—General M,D,O
Biomedical Engineering D
Biophysics M,D
Business Administration and Management—General M
Cell Biology M,D,O
Chemical Engineering M,D
Chemistry M,D
Child and Family Studies M,D
Civil Engineering M,D
Clinical Laboratory Sciences/Medical Technology M,O
Clinical Psychology M,D
Communication Disorders M
Communication—General M,D
Comparative Literature M,D
Computational Sciences O
Computer and Information Systems Security M
Computer Engineering M,D,O
Computer Science M,D
Construction Management M
Counselor Education M,D
Curriculum and Instruction O
Dance M
Dental Hygiene M
Early Childhood Education D
Economics M,D
Education—General M,O
Educational Leadership and Administration M,D,O
Educational Media/Instructional Technology M,D,O
Educational Psychology M,D
Electrical Engineering M,D,O*
Elementary Education M
Engineering and Applied Sciences—General M,D,O
English M,D
Environmental Management and Policy M
Exercise and Sports Science D
Finance and Banking M,D
Foundations and Philosophy of Education M,D
French M,D
Genetics M,D,O
Geography M
Geosciences M,D
German M,D
Health Education M
Higher Education O
Historic Preservation O
History M,D
Human Resources Management M,D
Industrial and Labor Relations M,D
International Business M
International Development M,D
International Economics M,D
Landscape Architecture M
Latin American Studies M,D
Law P
Linguistics M,D
Management Information Systems M
Management of Technology M
Management Strategy and Policy M
Manufacturing Engineering M
Marketing M
Mathematics M,D
Mechanical Engineering M,D
Microbiology M,D,O
Molecular Biology M,D,O
Multilingual and Multicultural Education D
Music Education M
Music M
Nanotechnology M,D
Natural Resources M,D
Neuroscience M,D,O
Nuclear Engineering M,D
Nursing—General M,D
Nutrition M
Occupational Therapy M
Optical Sciences M,D
Organizational Management M
Pathology M,D,O
Pharmaceutical Sciences M,D
Pharmacy P
Philosophy M,D
Physical Education M,D
Physical Therapy D
Physician Assistant Studies M
Physics M,D
Physiology M,D,O
Planetary and Space Sciences M,D
Political Science M,D
Portuguese M,D
Psychology—General M,D
Public Administration M
Public Health—General M
Science Education O
Secondary Education M
Sociology M,D
Spanish M,D
Special Education M,D,O
Statistics M,D
Taxation M
Theater M
Toxicology M,D,O
Urban and Regional Planning M
Urban Design O
Water Resources M
Women's Studies O
Writing M,D

UNIVERSITY OF NEW ORLEANS

Accounting M
Art/Fine Arts M
Arts Administration M
Biological and Biomedical Sciences—General M,D
Business Administration and Management—General M
Chemistry M,D
Computer Science M
Counselor Education M,D,O
Curriculum and Instruction M,D,O
Economics D
Education—General M,D,O
Educational Leadership and Administration M,D,O
Engineering and Applied Sciences—General M,D,O
Engineering Management M,O
English M
Environmental Sciences M
Film, Television, and Video Production M
Finance and Banking M,D
Geography M
Geosciences M
Health Services Management and Hospital Administration M
History M
Hospitality Management M
Mathematics M
Mechanical Engineering M
Music M
Physics M,D
Political Science M,D
Psychology—General M,D
Public Administration M
Romance Languages M
Sociology M
Special Education M,D,O
Taxation M
Theater M
Travel and Tourism M
Urban and Regional Planning M
Urban Studies M,D

UNIVERSITY OF NORTH ALABAMA

Business Administration and Management—General M
Counselor Education M
Criminal Justice and Criminology M
Education—General M,O
Educational Leadership and Administration O
Elementary Education M
English M
History M
Nursing—General M
Secondary Education M
Special Education M

THE UNIVERSITY OF NORTH CAROLINA AT ASHEVILLE

Liberal Studies M

THE UNIVERSITY OF NORTH CAROLINA AT CHAPEL HILL

Accounting M,D
Adult Nursing M,D,O
Allied Health—General M,D
Allopathic Medicine P
Anthropology M,D
Archaeology M,D
Art History M,D
Art/Fine Arts M
Astronomy M,D
Astrophysics M,D
Athletic Training and Sports Medicine M
Atmospheric Sciences M,D
Biochemistry M,D

Program	Degree
Bioinformatics	D
Biological and Biomedical Sciences—General	M,D
Biomedical Engineering	M,D
Biophysics	M,D
Biostatistics	M,D
Botany	M,D
Business Administration and Management—General	M,D
Cell Biology	M,D
Chemistry	M,D
Classics	M,D
Clinical Psychology	D
Cognitive Sciences	D
Communication Disorders	M,D
Communication—General	D
Community Health Nursing	M
Computational Biology	D
Computer Science	M,D*
Counselor Education	M
Curriculum and Instruction	M,D
Dental Hygiene	M,D
Dentistry	P
Developmental Biology	M,D
Developmental Psychology	D
Early Childhood Education	M,D
East European and Russian Studies	M
Ecology	M,D
Economics	M,D
Education—General	M,D
Educational Leadership and Administration	M,D
Educational Measurement and Evaluation	M,D
Educational Psychology	M,D
English as a Second Language	M
English Education	M
English	M,D
Environmental and Occupational Health	M,D
Environmental Engineering	M,D
Environmental Management and Policy	M,D
Environmental Sciences	M,D
Epidemiology	M,D
Evolutionary Biology	M,D
Exercise and Sports Science	M
Experimental Psychology	D
Family Nurse Practitioner Studies	M,D,O
Finance and Banking	D
Folklore	M
Foreign Languages Education	M
French	M,D
Genetics	M,D
Geography	M,D
Geology	M,D
German	M,D
Health Education	M,D
Health Promotion	M
Health Services Management and Hospital Administration	M,D
History	M,D
Immunology	M,D
Industrial Hygiene	M,D
Information Studies	M,D,O
Italian	M,D
Kinesiology and Movement Studies	M,D
Latin American Studies	M,D,O
Law	P
Library Science	M,D,O
Linguistics	M,D
Management Information Systems	D
Management Strategy and Policy	D
Marine Sciences	M,D
Marketing	D
Mass Communication	M,D
Materials Sciences	M,D
Maternal and Child Health	M,D
Mathematics Education	M
Mathematics	M,D
Microbiology	M,D
Molecular Biology	M,D
Molecular Physiology	D
Music Education	M
Music	M,D
Neurobiology	D
Nursing and Healthcare Administration	M,D,O
Nursing—General	M,D,O
Nutrition	M,D
Occupational Health Nursing	M
Occupational Therapy	M,D
Operations Research	M,D
Oral and Dental Sciences	M,D
Organizational Behavior	D
Pathology	D
Pediatric Nursing	M,D,O
Pharmaceutical Sciences	M,D
Pharmacology	D
Philosophy	M,D
Physical Education	M
Physical Therapy	M,D
Physics	M,D
Political Science	M,D,O
Portuguese	M,D
Psychiatric Nursing	M,D,O
Psychology—General	D
Public Administration	M
Public Health—General	M,D
Public Policy	D
Reading Education	M,D
Rehabilitation Counseling	M,D
Religion	M,D
Romance Languages	M,D
Russian	M,D
School Psychology	M,D
Science Education	M
Secondary Education	M
Slavic Languages	M,D
Social Psychology	D
Social Sciences Education	M
Social Work	M,D
Sociology	M,D
Spanish	M,D
Sports Management	M
Statistics	M,D
Theater	M
Toxicology	M,D
Urban and Regional Planning	M,D
Women's Health Nursing	M,D,O

THE UNIVERSITY OF NORTH CAROLINA AT CHARLOTTE

Program	Degree
Accounting	M
Adult Nursing	M,O
Advertising and Public Relations	M
Applied Mathematics	M,D
Applied Physics	M,D
Architecture	M
Art Education	M,D
Arts Administration	M,D,O
Bioinformatics	M,O
Biological and Biomedical Sciences—General	M,D
Business Administration and Management—General	M,D,O
Chemistry	M,D
Child Development	M,D
Civil Engineering	M,D
Clinical Psychology	M,D,O
Communication—General	M
Community Health	M,D,O
Computer and Information Systems Security	M,D,O
Computer Engineering	M,D
Computer Science	M,O
Corporate and Organizational Communication	M
Counselor Education	M,D,O
Criminal Justice and Criminology	M
Curriculum and Instruction	M,D
Dance	M,D
Database Systems	M,O
Economics	M
Education of the Gifted	M,D
Educational Leadership and Administration	M,D
Educational Media/ Instructional Technology	M,D
Electrical Engineering	M,D
Elementary Education	M
Emergency Management	M,D,O
Engineering and Applied Sciences—General	M,D
Engineering Management	M
English Education	M,O
English	M,O
Environmental Engineering	M,D
Ethics	M,O
Ethnic Studies	M
Exercise and Sports Science	M
Family Nurse Practitioner Studies	M,O
Finance and Banking	M,D,O
Game Design and Development	M,D,O
Gender Studies	M
Geographic Information Systems	M,D
Geography	M,D
Geosciences	M,D
Gerontology	M,O
Health Communication	M
Health Informatics	M,D,O
Health Psychology	M,D,O
Health Services Management and Hospital Administration	M,D,O
Health Services Research	M,D,O
History	M
Industrial and Organizational Psychology	M,D,O
Information Science	M,D,O
Interdisciplinary Studies	M,O
Kinesiology and Movement Studies	M
Latin American Studies	M,O
Liberal Studies	M,O
Marketing	M,D,O
Mathematical and Computational Finance	M
Mathematics Education	M,D
Mathematics	M,D
Mechanical Engineering	M,D
Media Studies	M
Middle School Education	M,D
Music Education	M,D
Nonprofit Management	M,D,O
Nurse Anesthesia	M,O
Nursing Education	M,O
Nursing—General	M,O
Optical Sciences	M,D
Philosophy	M,O
Political Science	M
Psychiatric Nursing	M,O
Psychology—General	M,D,O
Public Administration	M,D,O
Public Health—General	M,D,O
Public Policy	M,D,O
Reading Education	M
Real Estate	M,D,O
Religion	M
Rhetoric	M
Secondary Education	M,D
Social Psychology	M,D,O
Social Sciences Education	M
Social Sciences	M
Social Work	M
Sociology	M
Spanish	M
Special Education	M,D
Sports Management	M,D,O
Systems Engineering	M,D
Theater	M,D
Urban and Regional Planning	M,D,O
Urban Design	M
Women's Studies	M,O
Writing	M,O

THE UNIVERSITY OF NORTH CAROLINA AT GREENSBORO

Program	Degree
Accounting	M,O
Adult Education	M,D,O
Adult Nursing	M,D,O
Applied Economics	M
Architecture	M,O
Art/Fine Arts	M
Biochemistry	M
Biological and Biomedical Sciences—General	M
Business Administration and Management—General	M,O
Chemistry	M
Child and Family Studies	M,D
Classics	M
Clinical Psychology	M,D
Cognitive Sciences	M,D
Communication Disorders	M,D
Communication—General	M
Community Health	M,D
Computer Science	M
Conflict Resolution and Mediation/Peace Studies	M,O
Counseling Psychology	M,D,O
Counselor Education	M,D,O
Criminal Justice and Criminology	M
Curriculum and Instruction	M,D,O
Dance	M
Developmental Psychology	M,D
Early Childhood Education	M,D,O
Economic Development	M,D,O
Economics	D
Education—General	M,D,O
Educational Leadership and Administration	M,D,O
Educational Measurement and Evaluation	D
Educational Media/ Instructional Technology	M,D,O
Elementary Education	D
English as a Second Language	M,D,O
English Education	M,D
English	M,D
Exercise and Sports Science	M,D
Family and Consumer Sciences-General	M,D,O
Film, Television, and Video Production	M
Finance and Banking	M,O
Foreign Languages Education	M,D,O
French	M
Gender Studies	M,O
Genetic Counseling	M
Geographic Information Systems	M,D,O
Geography	M,D,O
Gerontological Nursing	M,D,O
Gerontology	M,O
Higher Education	D
Hispanic and Latin American Languages	M,O
Hispanic Studies	M,O
Historic Preservation	M,O
History	M,D,O
Human Development	M,D
Information Studies	M
Interior Design	M,O
Liberal Studies	M
Library Science	M
Management Information Systems	M,D,O
Marketing	M,D
Marriage and Family Therapy	M,D,O
Mathematics Education	M,D,O
Mathematics	M,D
Media Studies	M
Middle School Education	M,D,O

*M—master's degree; P—first professional degree; D—doctorate; O—other advanced degree; *—Close-Up and/or Display in one of the other books in this series*

Multilingual and Multicultural Education	M,D,O
Museum Studies	M,D,O
Music Education	M,D
Music	M,D
Nonprofit Management	M,O
Nurse Anesthesia	M,D,O
Nursing and Healthcare Administration	M,D,O
Nursing Education	M,D,O
Nursing—General	M,D,O
Nutrition	M,D
Political Science	M,O
Psychology—General	M,D
Public Affairs	M,O
Reading Education	M,D,O
Recreation and Park Management	M
Rhetoric	M,D
School Psychology	M,D,O
Science Education	M,D,O
Social Psychology	M,D
Social Sciences Education	M,D,O
Social Work	M
Sociology	M
Spanish	M,O
Special Education	M,D,O
Supply Chain Management	M,D,O
Taxation	M,O
Technical Writing	M,D,O
Textile Design	M,D
Theater	M
Women's Studies	M,D,O
Writing	M

THE UNIVERSITY OF NORTH CAROLINA AT PEMBROKE

Art Education	M
Business Administration and Management—General	M
Counselor Education	M
Education—General	M
Educational Leadership and Administration	M
Elementary Education	M
English Education	M
Mathematics Education	M
Middle School Education	M
Music Education	M
Physical Education	M
Public Administration	M
Reading Education	M
Science Education	M
Social Sciences Education	M

UNIVERSITY OF NORTH CAROLINA SCHOOL OF THE ARTS

Arts Administration	M
Film, Television, and Video Production	M
Music	M
Theater	M

THE UNIVERSITY OF NORTH CAROLINA WILMINGTON

Accounting	M
Biological and Biomedical Sciences—General	M,D
Business Administration and Management—General	M
Chemistry	M
Computer Science	M
Criminal Justice and Criminology	M
Curriculum and Instruction	M
Education—General	M,D
Educational Leadership and Administration	M,D
Educational Media/ Instructional Technology	M
Elementary Education	M
English	M
Environmental Education	M
Environmental Management and Policy	M
Family Nurse Practitioner Studies	M
Geology	M
Geosciences	M
Gerontology	M
Hispanic Studies	M,O
History	M
Liberal Studies	M
Marine Biology	M,D
Marine Sciences	M,D
Mathematics	M
Middle School Education	M
Nursing Education	M
Nursing—General	M
Psychology—General	M
Public Administration	M
Reading Education	M
Secondary Education	M
Social Work	M
Sociology	M
Spanish	M,O
Systems Science	M
Writing	M

UNIVERSITY OF NORTH DAKOTA

Accounting	M
Allopathic Medicine	P
Anatomy	M,D
Applied Economics	M
Art/Fine Arts	M
Atmospheric Sciences	M,D
Aviation	M
Biochemistry	M,D
Biological and Biomedical Sciences—General	M,D
Botany	M,D
Business Administration and Management—General	M
Cell Biology	M,D
Chemical Engineering	M
Chemistry	M,D
Civil Engineering	M
Clinical Laboratory Sciences/Medical Technology	M
Clinical Psychology	M,D
Communication Disorders	M,D
Communication—General	M,D
Community Health Nursing	M,D
Computer Science	M,D
Counseling Psychology	M
Criminal Justice and Criminology	D
Early Childhood Education	M
Ecology	M,D
Education—General	M,D,O
Educational Leadership and Administration	M,D,O
Educational Measurement and Evaluation	D
Educational Media/ Instructional Technology	M
Electrical Engineering	M
Elementary Education	M,D
Engineering and Applied Sciences—General	D
English	M,D
Entomology	M,D
Environmental Biology	M,D
Environmental Engineering	M
Experimental Psychology	M,D
Family Nurse Practitioner Studies	M,D
Fish, Game, and Wildlife Management	M,D
Forensic Psychology	M,D
Genetics	M,D
Geography	M
Geological Engineering	M
Geology	M,D
Geosciences	M,D
Gerontological Nursing	M,D
History	M,D
Immunology	M,D
Kinesiology and Movement Studies	M
Law	P
Linguistics	M
Management of Technology	M
Mathematics	M
Mechanical Engineering	M
Microbiology	M,D
Mineral/Mining Engineering	M
Molecular Biology	M,D
Music Education	M,D
Music	M,D
Nurse Anesthesia	M,D
Nursing Education	M,D
Nursing—General	M,D
Occupational Therapy	M
Pharmacology	M,D
Physical Therapy	M,D
Physician Assistant Studies	M
Physics	M,D
Physiology	M,D
Planetary and Space Sciences	M
Psychiatric Nursing	M,D
Psychology—General	M,D
Public Administration	M
Reading Education	M
Secondary Education	D
Social Work	M
Sociology	M
Special Education	M,D
Structural Engineering	M
Theater	M
Zoology	M,D

UNIVERSITY OF NORTHERN BRITISH COLUMBIA

Community Health	M,D,O
Computer Science	M,D,O
Disability Studies	M,D,O
Education—General	M,D,O
Environmental Management and Policy	M,D,O
Gender Studies	M,D,O
History	M,D,O
Interdisciplinary Studies	M,D,O
International Affairs	M,D,O
Mathematics	M,D,O
Natural Resources	M,D,O
Political Science	M,D,O
Psychology—General	M,D,O
Social Work	M,D,O

UNIVERSITY OF NORTHERN COLORADO

Accounting	M
Applied Statistics	M,D
Art/Fine Arts	M
Biological and Biomedical Sciences—General	M
Chemistry	M,D
Communication Disorders	M,D
Communication—General	M
Counselor Education	M,D
Criminal Justice and Criminology	M
Early Childhood Education	M,D
Education—General	M,D,O
Educational Leadership and Administration	M,D,O
Educational Measurement and Evaluation	M,D
Educational Media/ Instructional Technology	M,D
Educational Psychology	M,D
English	M
Exercise and Sports Science	M,D
Family Nurse Practitioner Studies	M,D
Foreign Languages Education	M
Geosciences	M
Gerontology	M
Health Education	M
Higher Education	D
History	M
Library Science	M
Mathematics Education	M,D
Mathematics	M,D
Music Education	M,D
Music	M,D
Nursing Education	M,D
Nursing—General	M,D
Physical Education	M,D
Psychology—General	M,D
Public Health—General	M
Reading Education	M
Rehabilitation Counseling	M,D
School Psychology	D,O
Science Education	M,D
Sociology	M
Spanish	M
Special Education	M,D
Sports Management	M,D
Student Affairs	D

UNIVERSITY OF NORTHERN IOWA

Accounting	M
Actuarial Science	M
Applied Mathematics	M
Applied Physics	M
Art Education	M
Art/Fine Arts	M
Athletic Training and Sports Medicine	M,D
Biochemistry	M
Biological and Biomedical Sciences—General	M
Biotechnology	M
Business Administration and Management—General	M
Chemistry	M
Communication Disorders	M
Communication—General	M
Community Health	M,D
Computer Science	M
Counseling Psychology	M
Counselor Education	M
Criminal Justice and Criminology	M
Curriculum and Instruction	D
Early Childhood Education	M
Education of the Gifted	M
Education—General	M,D,O
Educational Leadership and Administration	M,D
Educational Media/ Instructional Technology	M
Educational Psychology	M,O
Elementary Education	M
English as a Second Language	M
English Education	M
English	M
Environmental Sciences	M
French	M
Gender Studies	M
Geography	M
Geosciences	M
German	M
Health Education	M,D
Higher Education	M
History	M
Human Services	M,D
Kinesiology and Movement Studies	M
Leisure Studies	M,D
Mathematics Education	M
Mathematics	M
Middle School Education	M
Modeling and Simulation	M
Music Education	M
Music	M
Natural Resources	M
Nonprofit Management	M
Physical Education	M
Physics	M
Political Science	M
Psychology—General	M
Public History	M

- Public Policy M
- Reading Education M
- Rehabilitation Sciences M,D
- School Psychology M,O
- Science Education M
- Secondary Education M
- Social Sciences M
- Social Work M
- Sociology M
- Spanish M
- Special Education M,D
- Student Affairs M
- Vocational and Technical Education M,D
- Women's Studies M
- Writing M

UNIVERSITY OF NORTH FLORIDA

- Accounting M
- Adult Education M
- Adult Nursing M,D,O
- Allied Health—General M,D,O
- Applied Behavior Analysis M
- Biological and Biomedical Sciences—General M
- Business Administration and Management—General M
- Civil Engineering M
- Communication Disorders M
- Community Health M,O
- Computer Science M
- Construction Management M
- Counseling Psychology M
- Counselor Education M,D
- Criminal Justice and Criminology M
- Economics M
- Education—General M,D
- Educational Leadership and Administration M,D
- Educational Media/Instructional Technology M,D
- Electrical Engineering M
- Electronic Commerce M
- Elementary Education M
- English as a Second Language M
- English M
- Ethics M,O
- Finance and Banking M
- Gerontology M,O
- Health Services Management and Hospital Administration M,O
- History M
- Human Resources Management M
- International Business M
- Logistics M
- Management Information Systems M
- Mathematics M
- Mechanical Engineering M
- Nonprofit Management M,O
- Nurse Anesthesia M,D,O
- Nursing and Healthcare Administration M,D,O
- Nursing—General M,D,O
- Nutrition M
- Philosophy M,O
- Physical Therapy D
- Psychology—General M
- Public Administration M,O
- Public Health—General M,O
- Reading Education M
- Rehabilitation Counseling M,O
- Secondary Education M
- Software Engineering M
- Special Education M
- Sports Management M,D
- Statistics M
- Translation and Interpretation M
- Writing M

UNIVERSITY OF NORTH TEXAS

- Accounting M,D
- Anthropology M
- Applied Arts and Design—General M
- Applied Economics M
- Art Education M,D,O
- Art History M,D,O
- Art/Fine Arts M
- Biochemistry M,D
- Biological and Biomedical Sciences—General M,D
- Business Administration and Management—General M,D
- Chemistry M,D
- Child and Family Studies M,O
- Clinical Psychology M,D
- Clothing and Textiles M
- Communication Disorders M,D
- Communication—General M
- Community Health M,D
- Computer Education M,D
- Computer Engineering M,D
- Computer Science M,D
- Counseling Psychology M,D
- Counselor Education M,D,O
- Criminal Justice and Criminology M
- Curriculum and Instruction M,D
- Early Childhood Education M,D,O
- Economics M
- Education—General M,D,O
- Educational Leadership and Administration M,D
- Educational Measurement and Evaluation D
- Educational Media/Instructional Technology M,D
- Educational Psychology M
- Electrical Engineering M
- Engineering and Applied Sciences—General M
- English M,D
- Environmental Sciences M,D
- Experimental Psychology M,D
- Film, Television, and Video Production M
- Finance and Banking M,D
- French M
- Geography M
- Gerontology M,D,O
- Health Psychology M,D
- Higher Education M,D,O
- History M,D
- Hospitality Management M
- Human Development M,O
- Industrial and Labor Relations M
- Information Studies M,D
- Interdisciplinary Studies M
- International and Comparative Education M,D
- Journalism M,O
- Kinesiology and Movement Studies M
- Leisure Studies M,O
- Library Science M,D
- Management Information Systems M,D
- Marketing D
- Materials Sciences M,D
- Mathematics M,D
- Molecular Biology M,D
- Museum Studies M,D,O
- Music Education M,D
- Music M,D
- Philosophy M,D
- Physics M,D
- Political Science M,D
- Psychology—General M,D
- Public Administration M,D
- Quantitative Analysis M,D
- Reading Education M,D
- Real Estate M,D
- Recreation and Park Management M,O
- Rehabilitation Counseling M
- Rehabilitation Sciences M
- Religion M,D
- School Psychology M
- Secondary Education M,O
- Sociology M,D
- Spanish M
- Special Education M,D,O
- Taxation M,D
- Vocational and Technical Education M,D
- Writing M,D

UNIVERSITY OF NORTH TEXAS HEALTH SCIENCE CENTER AT FORT WORTH

- Anatomy M,D
- Biochemistry M,D
- Biological and Biomedical Sciences—General M,D
- Biostatistics M,D
- Biotechnology M,D
- Community Health M,D
- Environmental and Occupational Health M,D
- Epidemiology M,D
- Forensic Sciences M,D
- Genetics M,D
- Health Services Management and Hospital Administration M,D
- Immunology M,D
- Microbiology M,D
- Molecular Biology M,D
- Osteopathic Medicine P,M
- Pharmacology M,D
- Physician Assistant Studies M
- Physiology M,D
- Public Health—General M,D
- Science Education M,D

UNIVERSITY OF NOTRE DAME

- Accounting M
- Aerospace/Aeronautical Engineering M,D
- Applied Arts and Design—General M
- Applied Mathematics M,D
- Architecture M
- Art History M
- Art/Fine Arts M
- Biochemistry M,D
- Bioengineering M,D
- Biological and Biomedical Sciences—General M,D
- Business Administration and Management—General M
- Cell Biology M,D
- Chemical Engineering M,D
- Chemistry M,D
- Civil Engineering M,D
- Cognitive Sciences D
- Comparative Literature D
- Computer Engineering M,D
- Computer Science M,D
- Conflict Resolution and Mediation/Peace Studies M,D
- Counseling Psychology D
- Developmental Psychology D
- Ecology M,D
- Economics M,D
- Education—General M
- Electrical Engineering M,D*
- Engineering and Applied Sciences—General M,D
- English M,D
- Environmental Engineering M,D
- Evolutionary Biology M,D
- French M
- Genetics M,D
- Geosciences M,D
- Graphic Design M
- History of Science and Technology M,D
- History M,D
- Industrial Design M
- Inorganic Chemistry M,D
- Italian M
- Latin American Studies M
- Law P,M,D
- Mathematics M,D
- Mechanical Engineering M,D
- Medieval and Renaissance Studies M,D
- Molecular Biology M,D
- Nonprofit Management M
- Organic Chemistry M,D
- Parasitology M,D
- Philosophy D
- Photography M
- Physical Chemistry M,D
- Physics M,D
- Physiology M,D
- Political Science D
- Psychology—General D
- Religion M
- Romance Languages M
- Sociology D
- Spanish M
- Taxation M
- Theology P,M,D
- Writing M

UNIVERSITY OF OKLAHOMA

- Accounting M
- Addictions/Substance Abuse Counseling M,O
- Adult Education M,D
- Advertising and Public Relations M
- Aerospace/Aeronautical Engineering M,D
- American Indian/Native American Studies M
- Anthropology M,D
- Applied Arts and Design—General M
- Applied Economics M,D
- Architecture M
- Art History M,D
- Art/Fine Arts M
- Biochemistry M,D
- Bioengineering M,D
- Bioinformatics M,D
- Botany M,D
- Broadcast Journalism M
- Business Administration and Management—General M,D*
- Chemical Engineering M,D
- Chemistry M,D
- Child and Family Studies M,O
- Civil Engineering M,D
- Communication—General M,D
- Computer Engineering M,D
- Computer Science M,D
- Construction Management M
- Counseling Psychology D
- Curriculum and Instruction M,D,O
- Dance M
- Early Childhood Education M,D,O
- Ecology D
- Economics M,D
- Education—General M,D,O
- Educational Leadership and Administration M,D,O
- Educational Measurement and Evaluation M,D
- Educational Media/Instructional Technology M,D
- Educational Psychology M,D
- Electrical Engineering M,D
- Elementary Education M,D,O
- Engineering and Applied Sciences—General M,D
- Engineering Management M,D
- Engineering Physics M,D
- English Education M,D,O
- English M,D
- Environmental Engineering M,D
- Environmental Sciences M,D
- Evolutionary Biology D
- Exercise and Sports Science M,D

*M—master's degree; P—first professional degree; D—doctorate; O—other advanced degree; *—Close-Up and/or Display in one of the other books in this series*

Program	Degrees
Film, Television, and Video Production	M
French	M,D
Gender Studies	O
Geography	M,D
Geological Engineering	M,D
Geology	M,D
Geophysics	M,D
German	M
Health Promotion	M,D
Health Services Management and Hospital Administration	M
Higher Education	M,D,O
History of Science and Technology	M,D
History	M,D
Human Resources Development	M,O
Human Resources Management	M
Human Services	M,O
Industrial and Organizational Psychology	M,D
Industrial/Management Engineering	M,D
Information Studies	M,O
Interdisciplinary Studies	M,D
International Affairs	M,O
Journalism	M
Landscape Architecture	M
Law	P,M
Legal and Justice Studies	M,O
Liberal Studies	M
Library Science	M,O
Management Information Systems	M,D,O
Mass Communication	M
Mathematics Education	M,D,O
Mathematics	M,D*
Mechanical Engineering	M,D
Meteorology	M,D
Microbiology	M,D
Multilingual and Multicultural Education	M,D,O
Museum Studies	M
Music Education	M,D
Music	M,D
Natural Resources	M,D
Neurobiology	M,D
Organizational Behavior	M
Petroleum Engineering	M,D
Philosophy	M,D
Photography	M
Physics	M,D
Political Science	M,D
Project Management	M
Psychology—General	M,D
Public Administration	M
Reading Education	M,D,O
Science Education	M,D,O
Secondary Education	M,D,O
Social Psychology	M
Social Sciences Education	M,D,O
Social Work	M
Sociology	M,D
Spanish	M,D
Special Education	M,D
Telecommunications	M
Theater	M
Urban and Regional Planning	M
Women's Studies	O
Writing	M,D
Zoology	M,D

UNIVERSITY OF OKLAHOMA HEALTH SCIENCES CENTER

Program	Degrees
Allied Health—General	M,D,O
Allopathic Medicine	P
Biochemistry	M,D
Biological and Biomedical Sciences—General	M,D
Biopsychology	M,D
Biostatistics	M,D
Cell Biology	M,D
Communication Disorders	M,D,O
Dentistry	P,O
Environmental and Occupational Health	M,D
Epidemiology	M,D
Genetic Counseling	M
Health Education	D
Health Physics/Radiological Health	M,D
Health Promotion	M,D
Health Services Management and Hospital Administration	M,D
Immunology	M,D
Medical Physics	M,D
Microbiology	M,D
Molecular Biology	M,D
Neuroscience	M,D
Nursing—General	M
Nutrition	M
Occupational Therapy	M
Oral and Dental Sciences	M
Pathology	D
Pharmaceutical Sciences	M,D
Pharmacy	P
Physical Therapy	M
Physiology	M,D
Public Health—General	M,D
Radiation Biology	M,D
Reading Education	M,D,O
Rehabilitation Sciences	M
Special Education	M,D,O

UNIVERSITY OF OKLAHOMA—TULSA

Program	Degrees
Telecommunications	M

UNIVERSITY OF OREGON

Program	Degrees
Accounting	M,D
Anthropology	M,D
Architecture	M
Art History	M,D
Art/Fine Arts	M
Arts Administration	M
Asian Languages	M,D
Asian Studies	M
Biochemistry	M,D
Biological and Biomedical Sciences—General	M,D
Biopsychology	M,D
Business Administration and Management—General	M,D
Chemistry	M,D
Chinese	M,D
Classics	M
Clinical Psychology	D
Cognitive Sciences	M,D
Communication—General	M,D
Comparative Literature	M,D
Computer Science	M,D
Dance	M
Developmental Psychology	M,D
Ecology	M,D
Economics	M,D
Education—General	M,D
English	M,D
Environmental Management and Policy	M,D
Evolutionary Biology	M,D
Finance and Banking	D
Folklore	M
French	M
Genetics	M,D
Geography	M,D
Geology	M,D
German	M,D
Historic Preservation	M
History	M,D
Information Science	M,D
Interdisciplinary Studies	M
Interior Design	M
International Affairs	M
Italian	M
Japanese	M,D
Journalism	M,D
Landscape Architecture	M
Law	P,M
Linguistics	M,D
Management Information Systems	M
Marine Biology	M,D
Marketing	D
Mathematics	M,D
Media Studies	M
Molecular Biology	M,D
Music Education	M,D
Music	M,D
Neuroscience	M,D
Philosophy	M,D
Physics	M,D
Physiology	M,D
Political Science	M,D
Psychology—General	M,D
Public Policy	M
Quantitative Analysis	M
Romance Languages	M,D
Russian	M
Social Psychology	M,D
Sociology	M,D
Spanish	M
Theater	M,D
Urban and Regional Planning	M
Writing	M

UNIVERSITY OF OTTAWA

Program	Degrees
Aerospace/Aeronautical Engineering	M,D
Allopathic Medicine	P,M,D
Anthropology	M
Biochemistry	M,D
Biological and Biomedical Sciences—General	M,D
Biomedical Engineering	M
Business Administration and Management—General	M*
Canadian Studies	D
Cell Biology	M,D
Chemical Engineering	M,D
Chemistry	M,D
Civil Engineering	M,D
Classics	M,D
Communication Disorders	M
Communication—General	M
Community Health	M,D,O
Computer Engineering	M,D
Computer Science	M,D
Criminal Justice and Criminology	M,D
Economics	M,D
Education—General	M,D,O
Electrical Engineering	M,D
Electronic Commerce	M,D,O
Engineering and Applied Sciences—General	M,D,O
Engineering Management	M,O
English	M,D
Epidemiology	M
Finance and Banking	D,O
French	M,D
Geography	M,D
Geosciences	M,D
Health Services Management and Hospital Administration	M
Health Services Research	D,O
History	M,D
Immunology	M,D
Information Science	M,O
Interdisciplinary Studies	D,O
International Development	M
Kinesiology and Movement Studies	M
Law	M,D
Linguistics	M,D
Mathematics	M,D
Mechanical Engineering	M,D
Microbiology	M,D
Molecular Biology	M,D
Music Education	M,O
Music	M,O
Nursing—General	M,D,O
Philosophy	M,D
Physics	M,D
Political Science	M,D
Project Management	M,O
Psychology—General	D
Public Administration	D,O
Public Health—General	D
Rehabilitation Sciences	M
Religion	M,D
Social Work	M
Sociology	M
Spanish	M,D
Statistics	M,D
Systems Science	M,D,O
Theater	M
Translation and Interpretation	M,D
Women's Studies	M

UNIVERSITY OF PENNSYLVANIA

Program	Degrees
Accounting	M,D
Acute Care/Critical Care Nursing	M
Adult Nursing	M
African Studies	M,D
Allopathic Medicine	P,O
Anthropology	M,D
Applied Economics	D
Applied Mathematics	D
Applied Psychology	M,D
Archaeology	M,D
Architecture	M,D,O
Art History	M,D
Art/Fine Arts	M
Asian Studies	M,D
Astrophysics	M,D
Biochemistry	D
Bioengineering	M,D
Biological and Biomedical Sciences—General	M,D
Biostatistics	M,D
Biotechnology	M
Business Administration and Management—General	M,D
Cancer Biology/Oncology	D
Cell Biology	D
Chemical Engineering	M,D
Chemistry	M,D
Classics	M,D
Clinical Laboratory Sciences/Medical Technology	M
Communication—General	D
Comparative Literature	M,D
Computational Biology	D
Computational Sciences	D
Computer Art and Design	M
Computer Science	M,D
Counseling Psychology	M,D
Criminal Justice and Criminology	M,D
Demography and Population Studies	M,D
Dentistry	P
Developmental Biology	D
Economics	M,D
Education—General	M,D
Educational Leadership and Administration	M,D
Educational Measurement and Evaluation	M,D
Educational Media/Instructional Technology	M
Educational Policy	M,D
Electrical Engineering	M,D
Elementary Education	M
Engineering and Applied Sciences—General	M,D,O*
English as a Second Language	M,D
English	M,D
Environmental and Occupational Health	M
Environmental Management and Policy	M
Environmental Sciences	M,D
Epidemiology	M,D
Ethics	M,D
Family Nurse Practitioner Studies	M,O
Finance and Banking	M,D
French	M,D

Genetics D
Genomic Sciences D
Geosciences M,D
German M,D
Health Services Management and Hospital Administration M,D
Health Services Research M
Historic Preservation M,O
History of Science and Technology M,D
History M,D
Human Development M,D
Immunology D
Information Science M,D
Insurance M,D
International Affairs M
International and Comparative Education M,D
International Business M
International Health M
Italian M,D
Landscape Architecture M,O
Law P,M,D
Legal and Justice Studies M,D
Liberal Studies M
Linguistics M,D
Management Information Systems M,D
Management of Technology M
Marketing M,D
Materials Engineering M,D
Materials Sciences M,D
Maternal and Child/ Neonatal Nursing M,O
Mathematics M,D
Mechanical Engineering M,D
Mechanics M,D
Medical Physics M,D
Microbiology D
Molecular Biology D
Molecular Biophysics D
Multilingual and Multicultural Education M,D
Music M,D
Near and Middle Eastern Studies M,D
Neuroscience D
Nurse Anesthesia M
Nurse Midwifery M
Nursing and Healthcare Administration M,D
Nursing—General M,D,O
Occupational Health Nursing M
Oncology Nursing M
Organizational Behavior M
Organizational Management M
Pediatric Nursing M
Pharmacology D
Philosophy M,D
Physics M,D
Physiology D
Political Science M,D
Psychiatric Nursing M
Psychology—General D
Public Administration M
Public Health—General M
Public Policy M,D
Reading Education M,D
Real Estate M,D
Religion D
Romance Languages M,D
Secondary Education M
Social Work M,D*
Sociology M,D
Spanish M,D
Statistics M,D
Systems Engineering M,D
Telecommunications Management M
Telecommunications M
Urban and Regional Planning M,D,O
Urban Design D
Veterinary Medicine P
Virology D
Women's Health Nursing M
Writing M,D

UNIVERSITY OF PHILOSOPHICAL RESEARCH

Psychology—General M
Theology M

UNIVERSITY OF PHOENIX

Accounting M
Adult Education M
Business Administration and Management—General M,D,O
Clinical Psychology M
Counseling Psychology M
Criminal Justice and Criminology M
Curriculum and Instruction M,D,O
Early Childhood Education M
Education—General M,D,O
Educational Leadership and Administration M,D,O
Educational Media/ Instructional Technology D,O
Elementary Education M
Energy Management and Policy M
Gerontology M
Health Education M
Health Informatics M
Health Services Management and Hospital Administration M,D,O
Higher Education D,O
Human Resources Management M
Industrial and Organizational Psychology D,O
International Business M
Management Information Systems M
Management of Technology M
Marketing M
Nursing Education M
Nursing Informatics M
Nursing—General M,D,O
Organizational Management D,O
Project Management M
Psychology—General M
Public Administration M
Secondary Education M
Social Psychology M
Special Education M

UNIVERSITY OF PHOENIX–ATLANTA CAMPUS

Accounting M
Business Administration and Management—General M
Health Services Management and Hospital Administration M
Human Resources Management M
International Business M
Management Information Systems M
Management of Technology M
Marketing M
Nursing Education M
Nursing—General M
Public Administration M

UNIVERSITY OF PHOENIX–AUGUSTA CAMPUS

Accounting M
Business Administration and Management—General M
Criminal Justice and Criminology M
Health Services Management and Hospital Administration M
Human Resources Management M
International Business M
Management Information Systems M
Management of Technology M
Marketing M
Nursing Education M
Nursing—General M
Public Administration M

UNIVERSITY OF PHOENIX–AUSTIN CAMPUS

Accounting M
Business Administration and Management—General M
Criminal Justice and Criminology M
Curriculum and Instruction M
Education—General M
Electronic Commerce M
Health Services Management and Hospital Administration M
Human Resources Management M
International Business M
Management Information Systems M
Management of Technology M
Marketing M
Nursing—General M
Public Administration M

UNIVERSITY OF PHOENIX–BIRMINGHAM CAMPUS

Accounting M
Business Administration and Management—General M
Community Health M
Criminal Justice and Criminology M
Gerontology M
Health Informatics M
Health Services Management and Hospital Administration M
Human Resources Management M
International Business M
Management Information Systems M
Management of Technology M
Marketing M
Nursing Education M
Nursing—General M
Psychology—General M
Public Administration M

UNIVERSITY OF PHOENIX–BOSTON CAMPUS

Business Administration and Management—General M
International Business M
Management Information Systems M
Management of Technology M

UNIVERSITY OF PHOENIX–CENTRAL FLORIDA CAMPUS

Accounting M
Business Administration and Management—General M
Computer Education M
Curriculum and Instruction M
Early Childhood Education M
Education—General M
Educational Leadership and Administration M
Elementary Education M
Health Services Management and Hospital Administration M
Human Resources Management M
International Business M
Management Information Systems M
Management of Technology M
Marketing M
Mathematics Education M
Nursing Education M
Nursing—General M
Public Administration M
Secondary Education M

UNIVERSITY OF PHOENIX–CENTRAL MASSACHUSETTS CAMPUS

Business Administration and Management—General M
Education—General M
Management of Technology M

UNIVERSITY OF PHOENIX–CENTRAL VALLEY CAMPUS

Accounting M
Business Administration and Management—General M
Community Health M
Computer Education M
Curriculum and Instruction M
Education—General M
Elementary Education M
Gerontology M
Health Services Management and Hospital Administration M
Human Resources Management M
International Business M
Management Information Systems M
Management of Technology M
Marketing M
Marriage and Family Therapy M
Nursing—General M
Public Administration M
Secondary Education M

UNIVERSITY OF PHOENIX–CHARLOTTE CAMPUS

Accounting M
Business Administration and Management—General M
Gerontology M
Health Education M
Health Informatics M
Health Services Management and Hospital Administration M
International Business M
Management Information Systems M
Management of Technology M
Nursing Education M
Nursing Informatics M
Nursing—General M

UNIVERSITY OF PHOENIX–CHATTANOOGA CAMPUS

Accounting M

*M—master's degree; P—first professional degree; D—doctorate; O—other advanced degree; *—Close-Up and/or Display in one of the other books in this series*

Business Administration and Management—General M
Community Health M
Curriculum and Instruction M
Education—General M
Educational Leadership and Administration M
Elementary Education M
Gerontology M
Health Services Management and Hospital Administration M
Human Resources Management M
Industrial and Organizational Psychology M,D
International Business M
Management Information Systems M
Management of Technology M
Marketing M
Nursing—General M
Psychology—General M,D
Public Administration M
Secondary Education M

UNIVERSITY OF PHOENIX–CHEYENNE CAMPUS

Business Administration and Management—General M
Criminal Justice and Criminology M
Health Services Management and Hospital Administration M
Human Resources Management M
International Business M
Management Information Systems M
Management of Technology M
Marketing M
Nursing Education M
Nursing—General M
Public Administration M

UNIVERSITY OF PHOENIX–CHICAGO CAMPUS

Business Administration and Management—General M
Electronic Commerce M
Human Resources Management M
International Business M
Management Information Systems M
Management of Technology M

UNIVERSITY OF PHOENIX–CINCINNATI CAMPUS

Accounting M
Business Administration and Management—General M
Electronic Commerce M
Human Resources Management M
Information Science M
International Business M
Management Information Systems M
Management of Technology M
Marketing M
Psychology—General M
Public Administration M

UNIVERSITY OF PHOENIX–CLEVELAND CAMPUS

Accounting M
Business Administration and Management—General M
Human Resources Management M
International Business M
Management Information Systems M
Management of Technology M
Marketing M
Nursing—General M,D
Public Administration M

UNIVERSITY OF PHOENIX–COLUMBIA CAMPUS

Business Administration and Management—General M
Management of Technology M

UNIVERSITY OF PHOENIX–COLUMBUS GEORGIA CAMPUS

Accounting M
Business Administration and Management—General M
Electronic Commerce M
Human Resources Management M
International Business M
Management Information Systems M
Management of Technology M
Marketing M
Nursing—General M
Public Administration M

UNIVERSITY OF PHOENIX–COLUMBUS OHIO CAMPUS

Accounting M
Business Administration and Management—General M
Human Resources Management M
International Business M
Management Information Systems M
Management of Technology M
Marketing M
Nursing—General M,D
Public Administration M

UNIVERSITY OF PHOENIX–DALLAS CAMPUS

Accounting M
Business Administration and Management—General M
Criminal Justice and Criminology M
Curriculum and Instruction M
Education—General M
Electronic Commerce M
Human Resources Management M
International Business M
Management Information Systems M
Management of Technology M
Marketing M
Public Administration M

UNIVERSITY OF PHOENIX–DENVER CAMPUS

Accounting M
Business Administration and Management—General M
Curriculum and Instruction M
Education—General M
Educational Leadership and Administration M
Electronic Commerce M
Elementary Education M
Health Services Management and Hospital Administration M
Human Resources Management M
International Business M
Management Information Systems M
Management of Technology M
Marketing M
Nursing—General M
Public Administration M
School Psychology M
Secondary Education M

UNIVERSITY OF PHOENIX–DES MOINES CAMPUS

Accounting M
Business Administration and Management—General M
Criminal Justice and Criminology M
Gerontology M,D
Health Education M,D
Health Informatics M,D
Health Services Management and Hospital Administration M,D
Human Resources Management M
International Business M
Management Information Systems M
Management of Technology M
Marketing M
Nursing Education M,D
Nursing Informatics M,D
Nursing—General M,D
Public Administration M

UNIVERSITY OF PHOENIX–EASTERN WASHINGTON CAMPUS

Accounting M
Business Administration and Management—General M
Human Resources Management M
Management Information Systems M
Management of Technology M
Marketing M
Public Administration M

UNIVERSITY OF PHOENIX–FAIRFIELD COUNTY CAMPUS

Business Administration and Management—General M

UNIVERSITY OF PHOENIX–HARRISBURG CAMPUS

Accounting M
Business Administration and Management—General M
Criminal Justice and Criminology M
Health Services Management and Hospital Administration M
Human Resources Management M
International Business M
Management Information Systems M
Management of Technology M
Marketing M
Nursing Education M
Nursing—General M
Public Administration M

UNIVERSITY OF PHOENIX–HAWAII CAMPUS

Accounting M
Business Administration and Management—General M
Community Health M
Curriculum and Instruction M
Education—General M
Educational Leadership and Administration M
Elementary Education M
Family Nurse Practitioner Studies M
Gerontology M
Health Services Management and Hospital Administration M
Human Resources Management M
International Business M
Management Information Systems M
Management of Technology M
Marketing M
Nursing Education M
Nursing—General M
Public Administration M
Secondary Education M
Special Education M

UNIVERSITY OF PHOENIX–HOUSTON CAMPUS

Accounting M
Business Administration and Management—General M
Curriculum and Instruction M
Education—General M
Electronic Commerce M
Health Services Management and Hospital Administration M
Human Resources Management M
International Business M
Management Information Systems M
Management of Technology M
Marketing M
Nursing—General M
Public Administration M

UNIVERSITY OF PHOENIX–IDAHO CAMPUS

Accounting M
Business Administration and Management—General M
Curriculum and Instruction M
Education—General M
Educational Leadership and Administration M
Elementary Education M
Human Resources Management M
International Business M
Management Information Systems M
Management of Technology M
Marketing M
Nursing Education M
Nursing—General M
Public Administration M
Secondary Education M

UNIVERSITY OF PHOENIX–INDIANAPOLIS CAMPUS

Accounting	M
Business Administration and Management—General	M
Education—General	M
Elementary Education	M
Health Services Management and Hospital Administration	M
Human Resources Management	M
International Business	M
Management Information Systems	M
Management of Technology	M
Marketing	M
Nursing Education	M
Nursing—General	M
Public Administration	M
Secondary Education	M

UNIVERSITY OF PHOENIX–JERSEY CITY CAMPUS

Accounting	M
Business Administration and Management—General	M
Criminal Justice and Criminology	M
Human Resources Management	M
International Business	M
Management Information Systems	M
Management of Technology	M
Marketing	M
Psychology—General	M
Public Administration	M

UNIVERSITY OF PHOENIX–KANSAS CITY CAMPUS

Accounting	M
Business Administration and Management—General	M
Criminal Justice and Criminology	M
Education—General	M
Educational Leadership and Administration	M
Human Resources Management	M
International Business	M
Management of Technology	M
Marketing	M
Public Administration	M

UNIVERSITY OF PHOENIX–LAS VEGAS CAMPUS

Accounting	M
Allied Health—General	M
Business Administration and Management—General	M
Counseling Psychology	M
Counselor Education	M
Curriculum and Instruction	M
Education—General	M
Educational Leadership and Administration	M
Elementary Education	M
Human Resources Management	M
International Business	M
Management Information Systems	M
Management of Technology	M
Marketing	M
Marriage and Family Therapy	M
Public Administration	M
School Psychology	M

UNIVERSITY OF PHOENIX–LITTLE ROCK CAMPUS

Business Administration and Management—General	M

UNIVERSITY OF PHOENIX–LOUISIANA CAMPUS

Accounting	M
Business Administration and Management—General	M
Curriculum and Instruction	M
Early Childhood Education	M
Education—General	M
Human Resources Management	M
International Business	M
Management Information Systems	M
Management of Technology	M
Marketing	M
Nursing—General	M
Public Administration	M

UNIVERSITY OF PHOENIX–LOUISVILLE CAMPUS

Business Administration and Management—General	M
Electronic Commerce	M
Gerontology	M
Health Education	M
Health Informatics	M
Health Services Management and Hospital Administration	M
Management of Technology	M
Nursing Education	M
Nursing Informatics	M
Nursing—General	M

UNIVERSITY OF PHOENIX–MADISON CAMPUS

Accounting	M
Business Administration and Management—General	M
Curriculum and Instruction	D,O
Education—General	D,O
Educational Leadership and Administration	D,O
Electronic Commerce	M
Higher Education	D,O
Human Resources Management	M
International Business	M
Internet and Interactive Multimedia	M
Management Information Systems	M
Management of Technology	M
Marketing	M
Public Administration	M

UNIVERSITY OF PHOENIX–MARYLAND CAMPUS

Accounting	M
Business Administration and Management—General	M
Electronic Commerce	M
Health Services Management and Hospital Administration	M
Human Resources Management	M
International Business	M
Management Information Systems	M
Management of Technology	M
Marketing	M
Nursing Education	M
Nursing—General	M
Public Administration	M

UNIVERSITY OF PHOENIX–MEMPHIS CAMPUS

Accounting	M
Business Administration and Management—General	M
Criminal Justice and Criminology	M
Curriculum and Instruction	M
Education—General	M
Educational Leadership and Administration	M
Electronic Commerce	M
Elementary Education	M
Health Services Management and Hospital Administration	M,D
Human Resources Management	M
International Business	M
Management Information Systems	M
Management of Technology	M
Marketing	M
Nursing—General	M,D
Public Administration	M
Secondary Education	M

UNIVERSITY OF PHOENIX–METRO DETROIT CAMPUS

Education—General	M
Educational Leadership and Administration	M
Elementary Education	M
Management Information Systems	M
Nursing Education	M
Nursing—General	M
Secondary Education	M
Special Education	M

UNIVERSITY OF PHOENIX–MILWAUKEE CAMPUS

Accounting	M,D
Business Administration and Management—General	M,D
Criminal Justice and Criminology	M
Curriculum and Instruction	M,D,O
Education—General	M,D,O
Educational Leadership and Administration	M,D,O
English as a Second Language	M,D,O
Gerontology	M,D
Health Education	M,D
Health Informatics	M,D
Health Services Management and Hospital Administration	M,D
Higher Education	M,D,O
Human Resources Management	M,D
Industrial and Organizational Psychology	M,D
Management Information Systems	M,D
Nursing Education	M,D
Nursing Informatics	M,D
Nursing—General	M,D
Organizational Management	M,D
Psychology—General	M,D
Public Administration	M,D

UNIVERSITY OF PHOENIX–MINNEAPOLIS/ST. LOUIS PARK CAMPUS

Accounting	M
Business Administration and Management—General	M
Human Resources Management	M
Human Services	M
International Business	M
Management of Technology	M
Marketing	M
Public Administration	M
Social Psychology	M

UNIVERSITY OF PHOENIX–NASHVILLE CAMPUS

Business Administration and Management—General	M
Curriculum and Instruction	M
Education—General	M
Educational Leadership and Administration	M
Elementary Education	M
Health Services Management and Hospital Administration	M
Human Resources Management	M
Management Information Systems	M
Management of Technology	M
Nursing—General	M
Secondary Education	M

UNIVERSITY OF PHOENIX–NEW MEXICO CAMPUS

Accounting	M
Business Administration and Management—General	M
Counselor Education	M
Curriculum and Instruction	M
Education—General	M
Educational Leadership and Administration	M
Electronic Commerce	M
Elementary Education	M
Health Services Management and Hospital Administration	M
Human Resources Management	M
International Business	M
Management Information Systems	M
Management of Technology	M
Marketing	M
Nursing Education	M
Nursing—General	M
Secondary Education	M

UNIVERSITY OF PHOENIX–NORTHERN NEVADA CAMPUS

Accounting	M
Business Administration and Management—General	M
Criminal Justice and Criminology	M
Curriculum and Instruction	M
Education—General	M
Educational Leadership and Administration	M
Elementary Education	M
Health Services Management and Hospital Administration	M
Human Resources Management	M
International Business	M

*M—master's degree; P—first professional degree; D—doctorate; O—other advanced degree; *—Close-Up and/or Display in one of the other books in this series*

Management Information Systems M
Management of Technology M
Marketing M
Nursing Education M
Nursing—General M
Public Administration M
Secondary Education M

UNIVERSITY OF PHOENIX–NORTHERN VIRGINIA CAMPUS

Accounting M
Business Administration and Management—General M
Criminal Justice and Criminology M
Education—General M
Educational Leadership and Administration M
Health Services Management and Hospital Administration M
Management Information Systems M
Nursing—General M
Public Administration M

UNIVERSITY OF PHOENIX–NORTH FLORIDA CAMPUS

Accounting M
Business Administration and Management—General M
Computer Education M
Curriculum and Instruction M
Early Childhood Education M
Education—General M
Educational Leadership and Administration M
Elementary Education M
Health Services Management and Hospital Administration M
Human Resources Management M
International Business M
Management Information Systems M
Marketing M
Mathematics Education M
Nursing Education M
Nursing—General M
Public Administration M
Secondary Education M

UNIVERSITY OF PHOENIX–NORTHWEST ARKANSAS CAMPUS

Accounting M
Business Administration and Management—General M
Criminal Justice and Criminology M
Health Services Management and Hospital Administration M
Human Resources Management M
International Business M
Management Information Systems M
Management of Technology M
Marketing M
Nursing Education M
Nursing—General M
Public Administration M

UNIVERSITY OF PHOENIX–OKLAHOMA CITY CAMPUS

Accounting M
Business Administration and Management—General M
Electronic Commerce M
Human Resources Management M
International Business M
Management Information Systems M
Management of Technology M
Marketing M
Nursing—General M

UNIVERSITY OF PHOENIX–OMAHA CAMPUS

Accounting M
Adult Education M
Business Administration and Management—General M
Computer Education M
Criminal Justice and Criminology M
Curriculum and Instruction M
Education—General M
Educational Leadership and Administration M
Elementary Education M
English as a Second Language M
English Education M
Health Services Management and Hospital Administration M
Human Resources Management M
International Business M
Management Information Systems M
Management of Technology M
Marketing M
Mathematics Education M
Nursing—General M
Public Administration M
Secondary Education M
Special Education M

UNIVERSITY OF PHOENIX–OREGON CAMPUS

Accounting M
Business Administration and Management—General M
Curriculum and Instruction M
Early Childhood Education M
Education—General M
Elementary Education M
Health Services Management and Hospital Administration M
Human Resources Management M
International Business M
Management Information Systems M
Management of Technology M
Marketing M
Middle School Education M
Nursing—General M
Public Administration M
Secondary Education M

UNIVERSITY OF PHOENIX–PHILADELPHIA CAMPUS

Accounting M
Business Administration and Management—General M
Human Resources Management M
International Business M
Management Information Systems M
Management of Technology M
Marketing M
Psychology—General M
Public Administration M

UNIVERSITY OF PHOENIX–PHOENIX CAMPUS

Accounting M
Business Administration and Management—General M
Counseling Psychology M
Curriculum and Instruction M
Education—General M
Educational Leadership and Administration M
Elementary Education M
Family Nurse Practitioner Studies M
Health Services Management and Hospital Administration M
Nursing Education M
Nursing Informatics M
Nursing—General M
Psychology—General M
Secondary Education M
Social Psychology M
Special Education M
Vocational and Technical Education M

UNIVERSITY OF PHOENIX–PITTSBURGH CAMPUS

Accounting M
Business Administration and Management—General M
Electronic Commerce M
Health Services Management and Hospital Administration M
Human Resources Management M
International Business M
Management Information Systems M
Management of Technology M
Marketing M
Nursing Education M
Nursing—General M
Public Administration M

UNIVERSITY OF PHOENIX–PUERTO RICO CAMPUS

Accounting M
Business Administration and Management—General M
Counseling Psychology M
Early Childhood Education M
Education—General M
Educational Leadership and Administration M
Energy Management and Policy M
Entrepreneurship M
Human Resources Management M
Human Services M
International Business M
Management of Technology M
Marketing M
Marriage and Family Therapy M
Project Management M
School Psychology M

UNIVERSITY OF PHOENIX–RALEIGH CAMPUS

Accounting M
Business Administration and Management—General M
Electronic Commerce M
Gerontology M,D
Health Education M,D
Health Informatics M,D
Health Services Management and Hospital Administration M,D
Human Resources Management M
International Business M
Management Information Systems M
Management of Technology M
Marketing M
Nursing Education M,D
Nursing Informatics M,D
Nursing—General M,D

UNIVERSITY OF PHOENIX–RICHMOND CAMPUS

Accounting M
Business Administration and Management—General M
Curriculum and Instruction M
Education—General M
Educational Leadership and Administration M
Health Services Management and Hospital Administration M
Human Resources Management M
International Business M
Management Information Systems M
Management of Technology M
Marketing M
Nursing Education M
Nursing—General M
Public Administration M

UNIVERSITY OF PHOENIX–SACRAMENTO VALLEY CAMPUS

Accounting M
Adult Education M,O
Business Administration and Management—General M
Curriculum and Instruction M,O
Education—General M,O
Elementary Education M,O
Family Nurse Practitioner Studies M
Health Services Management and Hospital Administration M
Human Resources Management M
International Business M
Management Information Systems M
Management of Technology M
Marketing M
Nursing Education M
Nursing—General M
Public Administration M
Secondary Education M,O

UNIVERSITY OF PHOENIX–ST. LOUIS CAMPUS

Accounting M
Business Administration and Management—General M
Criminal Justice and Criminology M
Human Resources Management M
International Business M
Management Information Systems M

Marketing	M
Public Administration	M

UNIVERSITY OF PHOENIX–SAN ANTONIO CAMPUS

Accounting	M
Business Administration and Management—General	M
Criminal Justice and Criminology	M
Curriculum and Instruction	M
Electronic Commerce	M
Health Services Management and Hospital Administration	M
Human Resources Management	M
International Business	M
Management Information Systems	M
Management of Technology	M
Marketing	M
Nursing—General	M
Public Administration	M

UNIVERSITY OF PHOENIX–SAN DIEGO CAMPUS

Accounting	M
Business Administration and Management—General	M
Computer Education	M
Curriculum and Instruction	M
Education—General	M
Elementary Education	M
English as a Second Language	M
Human Resources Management	M
International Business	M
Management Information Systems	M
Management of Technology	M
Marketing	M
Nursing Education	M
Nursing—General	M
Public Administration	M
Secondary Education	M

UNIVERSITY OF PHOENIX–SAVANNAH CAMPUS

Accounting	M
Business Administration and Management—General	M
Criminal Justice and Criminology	M
Health Services Management and Hospital Administration	M
Human Resources Management	M
International Business	M
Management Information Systems	M
Management of Technology	M
Marketing	M
Nursing Education	M
Nursing—General	M
Public Administration	M

UNIVERSITY OF PHOENIX–SOUTHERN ARIZONA CAMPUS

Accounting	M
Adult Education	M,O
Business Administration and Management—General	M
Counselor Education	M,O
Curriculum and Instruction	M,O
Education—General	M,O
Educational Leadership and Administration	M,O
Educational Psychology	M,O
Elementary Education	M,O
Human Resources Management	M
International Business	M
Management Information Systems	M
Management of Technology	M
Marketing	M
Psychology—General	M
Secondary Education	M,O
Special Education	M,O

UNIVERSITY OF PHOENIX–SOUTHERN CALIFORNIA CAMPUS

Adult Education	M
Computer Education	M
Counseling Psychology	M
Criminal Justice and Criminology	M
Curriculum and Instruction	M
Early Childhood Education	M
Education—General	M
Educational Leadership and Administration	M
English as a Second Language	M
English Education	M
Family Nurse Practitioner Studies	M
Marriage and Family Therapy	M
Mathematics Education	M
Nursing Education	M
Nursing—General	M
Psychology—General	M
School Psychology	M
Social Psychology	M
Special Education	M

UNIVERSITY OF PHOENIX–SOUTHERN COLORADO CAMPUS

Accounting	M
Business Administration and Management—General	M
Curriculum and Instruction	M,O
Education—General	M,O
Educational Leadership and Administration	M,O
Elementary Education	M,O
Gerontology	M
Health Education	M
Health Services Management and Hospital Administration	M
Human Resources Management	M
International Business	M
Management Information Systems	M
Management of Technology	M
Marketing	M
Nursing—General	M
Public Administration	M
School Psychology	M,O
Secondary Education	M,O

UNIVERSITY OF PHOENIX–SOUTH FLORIDA CAMPUS

Accounting	M
Business Administration and Management—General	M
Computer Education	M
Curriculum and Instruction	M
Early Childhood Education	M
Education—General	M
Educational Leadership and Administration	M
Elementary Education	M
Health Services Management and Hospital Administration	M
Human Resources Management	M
International Business	M
Management Information Systems	M
Marketing	M
Mathematics Education	M
Nursing Education	M
Nursing—General	M
Public Administration	M
Secondary Education	M

UNIVERSITY OF PHOENIX–SPRINGFIELD CAMPUS

Accounting	M
Business Administration and Management—General	M
Computer Education	M
Criminal Justice and Criminology	M
Curriculum and Instruction	M
Education—General	M
Educational Leadership and Administration	M
English as a Second Language	M
English Education	M
Health Services Management and Hospital Administration	M
Human Resources Management	M
International Business	M
Management Information Systems	M
Management of Technology	M
Marketing	M
Mathematics Education	M
Nursing—General	M
Public Administration	M

UNIVERSITY OF PHOENIX–TULSA CAMPUS

Accounting	M
Business Administration and Management—General	M
Human Resources Management	M
International Business	M
Management Information Systems	M
Management of Technology	M
Marketing	M
Nursing—General	M

UNIVERSITY OF PHOENIX–UTAH CAMPUS

Accounting	M
Business Administration and Management—General	M
Curriculum and Instruction	M
Education—General	M
Educational Leadership and Administration	M
Elementary Education	M
Human Resources Management	M
International Business	M
Management Information Systems	M
Management of Technology	M
Marketing	M
Nursing Education	M
Nursing—General	M
School Psychology	M
Secondary Education	M
Special Education	M

UNIVERSITY OF PHOENIX–VANCOUVER CAMPUS

Accounting	M
Business Administration and Management—General	M
Computer Education	M
Curriculum and Instruction	M
Education—General	M
Educational Leadership and Administration	M
Health Services Management and Hospital Administration	M
Human Resources Management	M
International Business	M
Management Information Systems	M
Management of Technology	M
Marketing	M
Nursing—General	M

UNIVERSITY OF PHOENIX–WASHINGTON CAMPUS

Business Administration and Management—General	M
Criminal Justice and Criminology	M

UNIVERSITY OF PHOENIX–WASHINGTON D.C. CAMPUS

Accounting	M,D
Adult Education	M,D,O
Business Administration and Management—General	M,D
Computer Education	M,D,O
Criminal Justice and Criminology	M
Curriculum and Instruction	M,D,O
Early Childhood Education	M,D,O
Education—General	M,D,O
Educational Leadership and Administration	M,D,O
Educational Media/Instructional Technology	M,D,O
Elementary Education	M,D,O
English as a Second Language	M,D,O
English Education	M,D,O
Gerontology	M,D
Health Education	M,D
Health Informatics	M,D
Health Services Management and Hospital Administration	M,D
Higher Education	M,D,O
Human Resources Management	M,D
Industrial and Organizational Psychology	M,D
Management Information Systems	M,D
Mathematics Education	M,D,O
Nursing Education	M,D
Nursing Informatics	M,D
Nursing—General	M,D
Organizational Management	M,D
Psychology—General	M,D
Public Administration	M,D
Secondary Education	M,D,O
Special Education	M,D,O

UNIVERSITY OF PHOENIX–WEST FLORIDA CAMPUS

Accounting	M
Business Administration and Management—General	M
Computer Education	M
Curriculum and Instruction	M
Early Childhood Education	M

*M—master's degree; P—first professional degree; D—doctorate; O—other advanced degree; *—Close-Up and/or Display in one of the other books in this series*

Education—General M
Educational Leadership and Administration M
Educational Media/ Instructional Technology M
Elementary Education M
Health Services Management and Hospital Administration M
Human Resources Management M
International Business M
Management Information Systems M
Management of Technology M
Marketing M
Mathematics Education M
Nursing Education M
Nursing—General M
Public Administration M
Secondary Education M

UNIVERSITY OF PHOENIX–WEST MICHIGAN CAMPUS

Business Administration and Management—General M

UNIVERSITY OF PHOENIX–WICHITA CAMPUS

Business Administration and Management—General M

UNIVERSITY OF PITTSBURGH

Accounting M,D
Acute Care/Critical Care Nursing M,D
Adult Nursing M,D
African Studies O
Allopathic Medicine P
Anthropology M,D
Applied Mathematics M,D
Applied Psychology M,D
Applied Statistics M,D
Architectural History M,D
Art History M,D
Artificial Intelligence/ Robotics M,D*
Asian Studies M,O
Athletic Training and Sports Medicine M
Bioengineering M,D
Bioethics M
Bioinformatics M,D,O
Biological and Biomedical Sciences—General D
Biostatistics M,D
Business Administration and Management—General M,D,O
Cell Biology M,D
Chemical Engineering M,D
Chemistry M,D*
Civil Engineering M,D
Classics M,D
Clinical Laboratory Sciences/Medical Technology D
Clinical Research M,D,O
Cognitive Sciences D
Communication Disorders M,D
Communication—General M,D
Community Health M,D,O
Computational Biology D
Computer Engineering M,D
Computer Science M,D
Criminal Justice and Criminology M,D
Cultural Studies M,D,O
Dentistry P,M,O
Developmental Biology M,D
Developmental Psychology M,D
Early Childhood Education M
East European and Russian Studies O
Ecology D
Economics M,D
Education—General M,D
Educational Leadership and Administration M,D
Educational Measurement and Evaluation M,D
Educational Policy D
Electrical Engineering M,D
Elementary Education M
Engineering and Applied Sciences—General M,D
English as a Second Language O
English Education M,D
English M,D
Environmental and Occupational Health M,D,O
Environmental Engineering M,D
Environmental Law M,O
Environmental Management and Policy M,O
Epidemiology M,D
Evolutionary Biology D
Exercise and Sports Science M,D
Family Nurse Practitioner Studies M,D
Film, Television, and Video Theory and Criticism O
Finance and Banking M,D,O
Foreign Languages Education M,D
Foundations and Philosophy of Education M,D
French M,D
Genetic Counseling M,D,O
Geographic Information Systems M,D
Geology M,D
German M,D
Gerontology M,D,O
Health Education M,D,O
Health Informatics M
Health Law M,O
Health Promotion M,D,O
Health Services Management and Hospital Administration M,D,O
Higher Education M,D
Hispanic and Latin American Languages M,D
History of Science and Technology M,D
History M,D
Human Genetics M,D,O
Human Resources Management M,D,O
Immunology M,D
Industrial and Manufacturing Management M,O
Industrial/Management Engineering M,D
Infectious Diseases M,D,O
Information Science M,D,O
Information Studies M,D,O
Intellectual Property Law M,O
Interdisciplinary Studies D
International Affairs M,D,O
International and Comparative Education M,D
International Business M
International Development M,O
Italian M
Latin American Studies O
Law P,M,O
Legal and Justice Studies M,O
Library Science M,D,O
Linguistics M,D
Management Information Systems M,D,O
Management Strategy and Policy M,O
Marketing M,D,O
Materials Sciences M,D
Maternal and Child/ Neonatal Nursing M,D
Mathematics Education M,D
Mathematics M,D
Mechanical Engineering M,D
Medieval and Renaissance Studies O
Microbiology M,D,O
Military and Defense Studies M
Molecular Biology D
Molecular Biophysics D
Molecular Genetics M,D
Molecular Pathology M,D
Molecular Pharmacology M,D
Molecular Physiology M,D
Music M,D
National Security M
Neuroscience D
Nonprofit Management M
Nurse Anesthesia M,D
Nursing and Healthcare Administration M,D
Nursing—General M,D
Nutrition M
Occupational Therapy M
Oral and Dental Sciences M,O
Organizational Behavior M,D,O
Pathology M,D
Pediatric Nursing M,D
Petroleum Engineering M,D
Pharmaceutical Administration M
Pharmaceutical Sciences M,D
Pharmacy P
Philosophy M,D
Physical Therapy M,D
Physician Assistant Studies M
Physics M,D
Planetary and Space Sciences M,D
Political Science M,D
Psychiatric Nursing M,D
Psychology—General M,D
Public Administration M,D,O
Public Health—General M,D,O
Public Policy M,D,O
Quantitative Analysis D
Reading Education M,D
Rehabilitation Counseling M
Rehabilitation Sciences M,D
Religion M,D
Science Education M,D
Secondary Education M,D
Slavic Languages M,D
Social Sciences Education M,D
Social Work M,D,O
Sociology M,D
Spanish M,D
Special Education M,D
Statistics M,D
Structural Biology D
Systems Biology D
Telecommunications M,D,O
Theater M,D
Urban and Regional Planning M,O
Virology M,D
Western European Studies O
Women's Studies O
Writing M,D

UNIVERSITY OF PORTLAND

Business Administration and Management—General M
Communication—General M
Corporate and Organizational Communication M
Education—General M
Engineering and Applied Sciences—General M
Entrepreneurship M
Finance and Banking M
Health Services Management and Hospital Administration M
Management of Technology M
Marketing M
Nonprofit Management M
Nursing—General M,D
Pastoral Ministry and Counseling M
Sustainability Management M
Theater M

UNIVERSITY OF PRINCE EDWARD ISLAND

Anatomy M,D
Bacteriology M,D
Biological and Biomedical Sciences—General M
Chemistry M
Education—General M
Educational Leadership and Administration M
Epidemiology M,D
Geography M
Immunology M,D
Parasitology M,D
Pathology M,D
Pharmacology M,D
Physiology M,D
Toxicology M,D
Veterinary Medicine P
Veterinary Sciences M,D
Virology M,D

UNIVERSITY OF PUERTO RICO, MAYAGÜEZ CAMPUS

Agricultural Economics and Agribusiness M
Agricultural Education M
Agricultural Sciences—General M
Agronomy and Soil Sciences M
Animal Sciences M
Applied Mathematics M
Biological and Biomedical Sciences—General M
Business Administration and Management—General M
Chemical Engineering M,D
Chemistry M,D
Civil Engineering M,D
Computational Sciences M
Computer Engineering M,D
Computer Science M,D
Electrical Engineering M,D
Engineering and Applied Sciences—General M,D
English Education M
English M
Finance and Banking M
Food Science and Technology M
Geology M
Hispanic Studies M
Horticulture M
Human Resources Management M
Industrial and Manufacturing Management M
Industrial/Management Engineering M
Information Science M,D
Marine Sciences M,D
Mathematics M
Mechanical Engineering M
Physical Education M

Physics M
Statistics M

UNIVERSITY OF PUERTO RICO, MEDICAL SCIENCES CAMPUS

Acute Care/Critical Care Nursing M
Adult Nursing M
Allied Health—General M,D,O
Allopathic Medicine P
Anatomy M,D
Biochemistry M,D
Biological and Biomedical Sciences—General M,D
Biostatistics M
Clinical Laboratory Sciences/Medical Technology M,O
Clinical Research M,O
Communication Disorders M,D
Community Health Nursing M
Demography and Population Studies M
Dentistry P
Environmental and Occupational Health M,D
Epidemiology M
Family Nurse Practitioner Studies M
Gerontological Nursing M
Gerontology M,O
Health Education M
Health Informatics M
Health Promotion O
Health Services Management and Hospital Administration M
Health Services Research M
Industrial Hygiene M
Maternal and Child Health M
Maternal and Child/Neonatal Nursing M
Microbiology M,D
Nurse Midwifery M,O
Nursing—General M
Nutrition M,D,O
Occupational Therapy M
Oral and Dental Sciences O
Pediatric Nursing M
Pharmaceutical Sciences P,M
Pharmacology M,D
Pharmacy P,M
Physical Therapy M
Physiology M,D
Psychiatric Nursing M
Special Education O
Toxicology M,D

UNIVERSITY OF PUERTO RICO, RÍO PIEDRAS

Accounting M,D
Architecture M
Biological and Biomedical Sciences—General M,D
Business Administration and Management—General M,D
Cell Biology M,D
Chemistry M,D
Clinical Psychology M,D
Communication—General M
Comparative Literature M
Counselor Education M,D
Curriculum and Instruction M,D
Early Childhood Education M
Ecology M,D
Economic Development M
Economics M
Education—General M,D
Educational Leadership and Administration M,D
Educational Measurement and Evaluation M
English as a Second Language M
English M,D
Environmental Management and Policy M
Environmental Sciences M,D
Evolutionary Biology M,D
Exercise and Sports Science M
Family and Consumer Sciences-General M
Finance and Banking M,D
Foreign Languages Education M,D
Genetics M,D
Hispanic Studies M,D
History M,D
Human Resources Management M,D
Industrial and Manufacturing Management M,D
Industrial and Organizational Psychology M,D
Information Science M,O
Information Studies M,O
International Business M,D
Journalism M
Law P,M
Library Science M,O
Linguistics M,D
Marketing M,D
Mass Communication M
Mathematics Education M,D
Mathematics M,D
Molecular Biology M,D
Neuroscience M,D
Nutrition M
Philosophy M
Physics M,D
Psychology—General M,D
Public Administration M
Public Policy M
Quantitative Analysis M,D
Rehabilitation Counseling M
Science Education M,D
Social Psychology M,D
Social Sciences Education M,D
Social Work M,D
Sociology M
Special Education M
Translation and Interpretation M,O
Urban and Regional Planning M

UNIVERSITY OF PUGET SOUND

Counseling Psychology M
Counselor Education M
Education—General M
Elementary Education M
Occupational Therapy M
Pastoral Ministry and Counseling M
Physical Therapy D
Secondary Education M

UNIVERSITY OF REDLANDS

Business Administration and Management—General M
Communication Disorders M
Education—General M,D,O
Geographic Information Systems M
Management Information Systems M
Music M

UNIVERSITY OF REGINA

Adult Education M
Analytical Chemistry M,D
Anthropology M
Applied Psychology M,D
Art/Fine Arts M
Biochemistry M,D
Biological and Biomedical Sciences—General M,D
Biophysics M,D
Business Administration and Management—General M,O
Canadian Studies M,D
Cancer Biology/Oncology M,D
Chemistry M,D
Clinical Psychology M,D
Computer Engineering M,D
Computer Science M,D
Criminal Justice and Criminology M
Curriculum and Instruction M
Economics M,D,O
Education—General M,D,O
Educational Leadership and Administration M
Educational Psychology M
Engineering and Applied Sciences—General M,D
English M
Environmental Engineering M,D
Experimental Psychology M,D
French M
Geography M
Geology M,D
Gerontology M
Health Services Management and Hospital Administration M,D,O
Health Services Research M,D,O
History M
Human Resources Development M
Human Resources Management M,O
Industrial/Management Engineering M,D
Inorganic Chemistry M,D
International Business M,O
Kinesiology and Movement Studies M,D
Linguistics M
Mathematics M,D
Media Studies M
Music M
Organic Chemistry M,D
Organizational Management M,O
Petroleum Engineering M,D
Philosophy M
Physics M,D
Political Science M
Project Management M,O
Psychology—General M,D
Public Administration M,D,O
Public Policy M,D,O
Religion M
Social Sciences M
Social Work M
Sociology M
Software Engineering M,D
Statistics M,D
Systems Engineering M,D
Theoretical Chemistry M,D
Women's Studies M

UNIVERSITY OF RHODE ISLAND

Accounting M,D
Adult Education M,D
Animal Sciences M,D
Applied Mathematics M,D,O
Aquaculture M,D
Biochemistry M,D
Biological and Biomedical Sciences—General M,D
Biomedical Engineering M,D,O
Biotechnology M,D
Business Administration and Management—General M,D
Cell Biology M,D
Chemical Engineering M,D
Chemistry M,D
Child and Family Studies M
Civil Engineering M,D
Clinical Laboratory Sciences/Medical Technology M,D
Clinical Psychology M,D
Clothing and Textiles M
Communication Disorders M
Communication—General M
Computer Engineering M,D,O
Computer Science M,D,O
Counseling Psychology M
Economics M,D
Education—General M,D
Electrical Engineering M,D,O
Elementary Education M,D
Engineering and Applied Sciences—General M,D,O
English M,D
Entomology M,D
Environmental Engineering M,D
Environmental Management and Policy M,D
Environmental Sciences M,D
Exercise and Sports Science M
Family Nurse Practitioner Studies M,D
Finance and Banking M,D
Fish, Game, and Wildlife Management M,D
Food Science and Technology M,D
Forensic Sciences M,D,O
Geosciences M,D
Gerontological Nursing M,D
Gerontology M,D
Health Education M
History M
Human Resources Management M
Industrial and Labor Relations M
Industrial and Manufacturing Management M,D
Information Studies M
International Affairs M
Library Science M
Marine Affairs M,D
Marine Sciences M,D
Marketing M,D
Mathematics M,D
Medicinal and Pharmaceutical Chemistry M,D
Microbiology M,D
Molecular Biology M,D
Molecular Genetics M,D
Music Education M,D
Music M
Natural Resources M,D
Nursing and Healthcare Administration M,D
Nursing Education M,D
Nursing—General M,D
Nutrition M,D
Ocean Engineering M,D
Oceanography M,D,O
Pharmaceutical Sciences M,D
Pharmacology M,D
Pharmacy M,D
Physical Education M
Physical Therapy D
Physics M,D
Plant Sciences M,D
Political Science M
Psychiatric Nursing M,D
Psychology—General M,D
Public Administration M
Public Policy M
Reading Education M,D
Recreation and Park Management M
School Psychology M,D
Secondary Education M,D
Spanish M
Special Education M,D
Sport Psychology M
Statistics M,D,O
Student Affairs M
Supply Chain Management M,D
Toxicology M,D

*M—master's degree; P—first professional degree; D—doctorate; O—other advanced degree; *—Close-Up and/or Display in one of the other books in this series*

UNIVERSITY OF RICHMOND

Business Administration and Management—General M
Law P

UNIVERSITY OF RIO GRANDE

Art Education M
Education—General M
Mathematics Education M
Reading Education M
Special Education M

UNIVERSITY OF ROCHESTER

Accounting
Acute Care/Critical Care Nursing M,D,O
Adult Nursing M,D,O
Allopathic Medicine P
Anatomy M,D
Applied Mathematics
Art History M,D
Art/Fine Arts M,D
Astronomy
Biochemistry M,D
Biological and Biomedical Sciences—General M,D
Biomedical Engineering M,D
Biophysics M,D
Biostatistics M,D
Business Administration and Management—General M,D
Chemical Engineering
Chemistry M,D
Clinical Psychology
Clinical Research M
Cognitive Sciences M,D
Comparative Literature
Computational Biology M,D
Computer Engineering M,D
Computer Science M,D
Counselor Education
Cultural Studies
Curriculum and Instruction
Developmental Psychology
Economics M,D
Education—General
Educational Leadership and Administration
Educational Policy
Electrical Engineering
Emergency Management M,D,O
Energy and Power Engineering
Engineering and Applied Sciences—General M,D
English
Entrepreneurship M
Epidemiology M,D
Family Nurse Practitioner Studies M,D,O
French
Genetics M,D
Geology M,D
Geosciences M,D
German
Gerontological Nursing M,D,O
Health Education M,D,O
Health Promotion M,D,O
Health Services Management and Hospital Administration M,D,O
Health Services Research M,D,O
Higher Education
History M,D
Human Development
Immunology
Linguistics
Marriage and Family Therapy M
Materials Sciences M,D
Maternal and Child/Neonatal Nursing M,D,O
Mathematics
Mechanical Engineering M,D
Microbiology
Music Education M
Music
Neurobiology M,D
Neuroscience M,D
Nursing and Healthcare Administration M,D,O
Nursing—General M,D,O
Optical Sciences M,D,O
Oral and Dental Sciences M
Pathology M,D
Pediatric Nursing M,D,O
Pharmacology M,D
Philosophy M,D
Physics
Physiology M,D
Political Science M,D
Psychiatric Nursing M,D,O
Psychology—General
Public Health—General M
Romance Languages
Social Psychology M,D
Spanish
Statistics M,D
Toxicology M,D
Translation and Interpretation

UNIVERSITY OF ST. AUGUSTINE FOR HEALTH SCIENCES

Occupational Therapy M,D
Physical Therapy M,D,O

UNIVERSITY OF ST. FRANCIS (IL)

Adult Nursing M,D
Allied Health—General M,D
Art Education M
Business Administration and Management—General M
Business Education M
Curriculum and Instruction M
Education—General M
Educational Leadership and Administration M
Elementary Education M
English Education M
Family Nurse Practitioner Studies M,D
Health Services Management and Hospital Administration M
Mathematics Education M
Nursing—General M,D
Physician Assistant Studies M
Reading Education M
Science Education M
Secondary Education M
Social Sciences Education M
Social Work M
Special Education M

UNIVERSITY OF SAINT FRANCIS (IN)

Allied Health—General M
Art/Fine Arts M
Business Administration and Management—General M
Counseling Psychology M
Counselor Education M
Education—General M
Nursing—General M
Pastoral Ministry and Counseling M
Physician Assistant Studies M
Psychology—General M
Special Education M

UNIVERSITY OF SAINT MARY

Business Administration and Management—General M
Curriculum and Instruction M
Education—General M
Psychology—General M
Special Education M

UNIVERSITY OF SAINT MARY OF THE LAKE–MUNDELEIN SEMINARY

Theology P,M,D

UNIVERSITY OF ST. MICHAEL'S COLLEGE

Jewish Studies P,M,D,O
Pastoral Ministry and Counseling P,M,D,O
Religious Education P,M,D,O
Theology P,M,D,O

UNIVERSITY OF ST. THOMAS (MN)

Accounting M
Art History M
Business Administration and Management—General M
Computer and Information Systems Security M,O
Corporate and Organizational Communication M
Counseling Psychology M,D,O
Curriculum and Instruction M,O
Early Childhood Education M,O
Education of the Gifted M,O
Education—General M,D,O
Educational Leadership and Administration M,D,O
Educational Media/Instructional Technology M,D,O
Educational Policy M,D,O
Elementary Education M,O
Engineering and Applied Sciences—General M,O
Engineering Management M,O
English as a Second Language M,O
English M
Health Services Management and Hospital Administration M
Human Development M,D,O
Human Resources Development M,D,O
Human Resources Management M,D,O
Law P
Management Information Systems M,O
Management of Technology M,O
Manufacturing Engineering M,O
Marriage and Family Therapy M,D,O
Mathematics Education M,O
Mechanical Engineering M,O
Multilingual and Multicultural Education M,O
Music Education M
Music M
Organizational Management M,D,O
Pastoral Ministry and Counseling P,M
Psychology—General M,D,O
Reading Education M,O
Real Estate M
Religion M
Religious Education P,M
Secondary Education M,O
Social Work M
Software Engineering M,O
Special Education M,O
Student Affairs M,D,O
Systems Engineering M,O
Theology P,M

UNIVERSITY OF ST. THOMAS (TX)

Business Administration and Management—General M*
Education—General M
Liberal Studies M
Philosophy M,D
Religion M
Theology P,M

UNIVERSITY OF SAN DIEGO

Accounting M
Adult Nursing M,D
Business Administration and Management—General M,O
Communication Disorders M
Conflict Resolution and Mediation/Peace Studies M
Counseling Psychology M
Counselor Education M
Curriculum and Instruction M
Education—General M,D,O
Educational Leadership and Administration M,D,O
English as a Second Language M
Family Nurse Practitioner Studies M,D
Gerontological Nursing M,D
Health Informatics M,D
Higher Education M,D,O
History M
International Affairs M
International Business M
Law P,M,O
Legal and Justice Studies P,M,O
Marine Affairs M
Marine Sciences M
Marriage and Family Therapy M
Nonprofit Management M,D,O
Nursing and Healthcare Administration M,D
Nursing—General M,D
Pediatric Nursing M,D
Psychiatric Nursing M,D
Reading Education M
Real Estate M,O
Special Education M
Supply Chain Management M,O
Taxation P,M,O
Theater M

UNIVERSITY OF SAN FRANCISCO

Asian Studies M
Biological and Biomedical Sciences—General M
Business Administration and Management—General M
Chemistry M
Computer Science M
Counseling Psychology M,D
Counselor Education M,D
Curriculum and Instruction M,D
Economics M
Education—General M,D
Educational Leadership and Administration M,D
Educational Media/Instructional Technology M,D
Electronic Commerce M
English as a Second Language M,D
Entrepreneurship M
Family Nurse Practitioner Studies D
Finance and Banking M
Health Services Management and Hospital Administration M
Intellectual Property Law M
International Affairs M

International and Comparative Education	M,D
International Business	M
International Development	M
Internet and Interactive Multimedia	M
Internet Engineering	M
Investment Management	M
Law	P,M
Management Information Systems	M
Marketing	M
Marriage and Family Therapy	M,D
Multilingual and Multicultural Education	M,D
Natural Resources	M
Nonprofit Management	M
Nursing and Healthcare Administration	D
Nursing—General	M,D
Organizational Management	M
Pacific Area/Pacific Rim Studies	M
Project Management	M
Public Administration	M
Public Affairs	M
Reading Education	M,D
Religious Education	M,D
Sports Management	M
Telecommunications Management	M
Writing	M

UNIVERSITY OF SASKATCHEWAN

Accounting	M
Agricultural Economics and Agribusiness	M,D,O
Agricultural Engineering	M,D
Agricultural Sciences—General	M,D,O
Agronomy and Soil Sciences	M,D,O
Allopathic Medicine	P
Anatomy	M,D
Animal Sciences	M,D
Anthropology	M
Archaeology	M,D
Art/Fine Arts	M
Biochemistry	M,D
Biological and Biomedical Sciences—General	M,D
Biomedical Engineering	M,D
Biotechnology	M
Business Administration and Management—General	M
Canadian Studies	M,D
Cell Biology	M,D
Chemical Engineering	M,D
Chemistry	M,D
Civil Engineering	M,D
Community Health	M,D
Computer Science	M,D
Curriculum and Instruction	M,D,O
Dentistry	P
East European and Russian Studies	M
Economics	M,O
Education—General	M,D,O
Educational Leadership and Administration	M,D,O
Educational Psychology	M,D,O
Electrical Engineering	M,D
Engineering and Applied Sciences—General	M,D,O
Engineering Physics	M,D
English	M,D
Environmental Engineering	M,D,O
Environmental Sciences	M
Epidemiology	M,D
Finance and Banking	M
Food Science and Technology	M,D
Foundations and Philosophy of Education	M,D,O
French	M
Gender Studies	M,D
Geography	M,D
Geology	M,D,O
German	M
Health Services Management and Hospital Administration	M
History	M,D
Immunology	M,D
Industrial and Labor Relations	M
International Business	M,D
Kinesiology and Movement Studies	M,D,O
Law	P,M
Marketing	M
Mathematics	M,D
Mechanical Engineering	M,D
Microbiology	M,D
Music	M
Nursing—General	M
Organizational Behavior	M
Pathology	M,D
Pharmaceutical Sciences	M,D
Pharmacology	M,D
Philosophy	M
Physics	M,D
Physiology	M,D
Plant Sciences	M,D
Political Science	M
Psychology—General	M,D
Public Affairs	M,D
Public Policy	M,D
Religion	M
Reproductive Biology	M,D
Sociology	M,D
Special Education	M,D,O
Statistics	M,D
Sustainability Management	M
Theater	M
Toxicology	M,D,O
Veterinary Medicine	P,M,D
Veterinary Sciences	M,D
Women's Studies	M,D

THE UNIVERSITY OF SCRANTON

Accounting	M
Adult Nursing	M,O
Biochemistry	M
Business Administration and Management—General	M
Chemistry	M
Counseling Psychology	M,O
Counselor Education	M
Curriculum and Instruction	M
Early Childhood Education	M
Education—General	M
Educational Leadership and Administration	M
Elementary Education	M
English as a Second Language	M
Family Nurse Practitioner Studies	M,O
Finance and Banking	M
Health Services Management and Hospital Administration	M
History	M
Human Resources Development	M
Human Resources Management	M
International Business	M
Management Information Systems	M
Marketing	M
Nurse Anesthesia	M,O
Nursing—General	M,O
Occupational Therapy	M
Organizational Management	M
Physical Therapy	M,D
Reading Education	M
Rehabilitation Counseling	M
Secondary Education	M
Social Psychology	M
Software Engineering	M
Special Education	M
Theology	M

UNIVERSITY OF SIOUX FALLS

Business Administration and Management—General	M
Education—General	M,O
Educational Leadership and Administration	M,O
Educational Media/Instructional Technology	M,O
Reading Education	M,O

UNIVERSITY OF SOUTH AFRICA

Accounting	M,D
Acute Care/Critical Care Nursing	M,D
Adult Education	M,D
Agricultural Sciences—General	M,D
Anthropology	M,D
Archaeology	M,D
Art History	M,D
Business Administration and Management—General	M,D
Chemical Engineering	M
Classics	M,D
Clinical Psychology	M,D
Communication—General	M,D
Counseling Psychology	M,D
Counselor Education	M,D
Criminal Justice and Criminology	M,D
Curriculum and Instruction	M,D
Economics	M,D
Education—General	M,D
Educational Leadership and Administration	M,D
Educational Media/Instructional Technology	M,D
Educational Psychology	M,D
Engineering and Applied Sciences—General	M
English as a Second Language	M,D
English	M,D
Environmental Education	M,D
Environmental Management and Policy	M,D
Environmental Sciences*	M,D
Ethics	M,D
Family and Consumer Sciences-General	M,D
Foundations and Philosophy of Education	M,D
French	M,D
Geography	M,D
German	M,D
Health Education	M,D
Health Services Management and Hospital Administration	M,D
History	M,D
Horticulture	M,D
Human Development	M,D
Human Resources Development	M,D
Industrial and Organizational Psychology	M,D
Information Science	M,D
International and Comparative Education	M,D
Italian	M,D
Law	M,D
Linguistics	M,D
Logistics	M,D
Management Information Systems	M
Marketing	M,D
Maternal and Child/Neonatal Nursing	M,D
Mathematics Education	M,D
Medical/Surgical Nursing	M,D
Missions and Missiology	M,D
Music	M,D
Natural Resources	M,D
Near and Middle Eastern Languages	M,D
Near and Middle Eastern Studies	M,D
Nurse Midwifery	M,D
Pastoral Ministry and Counseling	M,D
Philosophy	M,D
Political Science	M,D
Portuguese	M,D
Psychology—General	M,D
Public Administration	M,D
Public Health—General	M,D
Quantitative Analysis	M,D
Real Estate	M,D
Religion	M,D
Romance Languages	M,D
Russian	M,D
Science Education	M,D
Social Work	M,D
Sociology	M,D
Spanish	M,D
Statistics	M,D
Technology and Public Policy	M,D
Telecommunications Management	M,D
Theology	M,D
Travel and Tourism	M,D
Vocational and Technical Education	M,D

UNIVERSITY OF SOUTH ALABAMA

Accounting	M
Adult Nursing	M,D
Allied Health—General	M,D
Allopathic Medicine	P
Biological and Biomedical Sciences—General	M,D
Business Administration and Management—General	M
Chemical Engineering	M
Civil Engineering	M
Clinical Psychology	M,D
Communication Disorders	M,D
Communication—General	M
Community Health Nursing	M,D
Computer Science	M
Counseling Psychology	M,D
Counselor Education	M,D
Early Childhood Education	M,O
Education—General	M,D,O
Educational Leadership and Administration	M,O
Educational Media/Instructional Technology	M,D
Electrical Engineering	M
Elementary Education	M,O
Engineering and Applied Sciences—General	M
English	M
Environmental and Occupational Health	M
Exercise and Sports Science	M
Gerontology	O
Health Education	M
History	M
Information Science	M
Leisure Studies	M
Management Information Systems	M
Marine Sciences	M,D
Maternal and Child/Neonatal Nursing	M,D
Mathematics	M
Mechanical Engineering	M
Nursing—General	M,D
Occupational Therapy	M
Physical Education	M
Physical Therapy	D

*M—master's degree; P—first professional degree; D—doctorate; O—other advanced degree; *—Close-Up and/or Display in one of the other books in this series*

Physician Assistant Studies M
Psychology—General M,D
Public Administration M
Reading Education M,O
Recreation and Park Management M
Rehabilitation Counseling M,D
School Psychology M,D
Science Education M,O
Secondary Education M,O
Sociology M
Special Education M,O
Toxicology M

UNIVERSITY OF SOUTH CAROLINA

Accounting M
Acute Care/Critical Care Nursing M,O
Adult Nursing M
Allopathic Medicine P
Anthropology M,D
Applied Statistics M,D,O
Archives/Archival Administration M,O
Art Education M,D
Art History M
Art/Fine Arts M
Astronomy M,D
Biochemistry M,D
Biological and Biomedical Sciences—General M,D,O
Biostatistics M,D
Business Administration and Management—General M,D
Business Education M,D
Cell Biology M,D
Chemical Engineering M,D
Chemistry M,D
Civil Engineering M,D
Clinical Psychology M,D
Communication Disorders M,D
Community Health Nursing M
Comparative Literature M,D
Computer Engineering M,D
Computer Science M,D
Consumer Economics M
Counselor Education D,O
Criminal Justice and Criminology M,D
Curriculum and Instruction D
Developmental Biology M,D
Early Childhood Education M,D
Ecology M,D
Economics M,D
Education—General M,D,O
Educational Leadership and Administration M,D,O
Educational Measurement and Evaluation M,D
Educational Media/Instructional Technology M
Educational Psychology M,D
Electrical Engineering M,D
Elementary Education M,D
Engineering and Applied Sciences—General M,D
English as a Second Language M,D,O
English Education M,D
English M,D
Entertainment Management M
Environmental and Occupational Health M,D
Environmental Management and Policy M
Epidemiology M,D
Evolutionary Biology M,D
Exercise and Sports Science M,D
Experimental Psychology M,D
Family Nurse Practitioner Studies M
Foreign Languages Education M,D
Foundations and Philosophy of Education D
French M,D
Genetic Counseling M
Geography M,D
Geology M,D
Geosciences M,D
German M,D
Gerontology O
Hazardous Materials Management M,D
Health Education M,D,O
Health Promotion M,D,O
Health Services Management and Hospital Administration M,D
Higher Education M
Historic Preservation M,O
History M,D,O
Hospitality Management M
Human Resources Management M
Industrial Hygiene M,D
Information Studies M,D,O
International Affairs M,D
International Business M
Journalism M,D
Law P
Library Science M,D,O
Linguistics M,D,O
Marine Sciences M,D
Mathematics Education M,D
Mathematics M,D
Mechanical Engineering M,D
Media Studies M
Medical/Surgical Nursing M
Molecular Biology M,D
Museum Studies M,O
Music Education M,D,O
Music M,D,O
Nuclear Engineering M,D
Nurse Anesthesia M
Nursing and Healthcare Administration M
Nursing—General M,O
Pediatric Nursing M
Pharmaceutical Sciences M,D
Pharmacy P
Philosophy M,D
Physical Education M,D
Physics M,D
Political Science M,D
Psychiatric Nursing M,O
Psychology—General M,D
Public Administration M
Public Health—General M
Public History M,O
Reading Education M,D
Rehabilitation Counseling M,O
Rehabilitation Sciences M,O
Religion M
School Psychology D
Science Education M,D
Secondary Education M,D
Social Psychology M,D
Social Sciences Education M,D
Social Work M,D
Sociology M,D
Software Engineering M,D
Spanish M,D
Special Education M,D
Speech and Interpersonal Communication M,D
Sports Management M
Statistics M,D,O
Student Affairs M
Theater M,D
Travel and Tourism M
Women's Health Nursing M
Women's Studies O
Writing M,D

UNIVERSITY OF SOUTH CAROLINA AIKEN

Applied Psychology M
Clinical Psychology M
Educational Media/Instructional Technology M

UNIVERSITY OF SOUTH CAROLINA UPSTATE

Early Childhood Education M
Education—General M
Elementary Education M
Special Education M

THE UNIVERSITY OF SOUTH DAKOTA

Accounting M
Allied Health—General M,D
Allopathic Medicine P
Art/Fine Arts M
Biological and Biomedical Sciences—General M,D
Business Administration and Management—General M
Cardiovascular Sciences M,D
Cell Biology M,D
Chemistry M,D
Clinical Psychology M,D
Communication Disorders M,D
Communication—General M
Computational Sciences M,D
Computer Science M,D
Counselor Education M,D,O
Curriculum and Instruction M,D,O
Education—General M,D,O
Educational Leadership and Administration M,D,O
Educational Media/Instructional Technology M,O
Educational Psychology M,D,O
Elementary Education M
English M,D
Health Education M
History M
Immunology M,D
Interdisciplinary Studies M
Law P
Mathematics M
Microbiology M,D
Molecular Biology M,D
Music M
Neuroscience M,D
Occupational Therapy M
Pharmacology M,D
Physical Education M
Physical Therapy D
Physician Assistant Studies M
Physics M,D
Physiology M,D
Political Science M,D
Psychology—General M,D
Public Administration M,D
Secondary Education M
Special Education M
Statistics M,D
Theater M

UNIVERSITY OF SOUTHERN CALIFORNIA

Accounting M
Advertising and Public Relations M
Aerospace/Aeronautical Engineering M,D,O
Allopathic Medicine P
American Studies D
Applied Mathematics M,D
Architecture M,D
Art History M,D,O
Art/Fine Arts M,D,O
Artificial Intelligence/Robotics M,D
Arts Administration M
Asian Languages M,D
Asian Studies M,D
Biochemistry M,D
Bioinformatics D
Biological and Biomedical Sciences—General M,D
Biomedical Engineering M,D
Biophysics M,D
Biostatistics M,D
Broadcast Journalism M
Business Administration and Management—General M,D
Cell Biology M,D
Chemical Engineering M,D,O
Chemistry D
Child and Family Studies M,D
Civil Engineering M,D,O
Classics M,D
Clinical Psychology M,D
Clinical Research M,D,O
Cognitive Sciences M,D
Communication—General M,D*
Comparative Literature D
Computational Biology D
Computer and Information Systems Security M,D
Computer Art and Design M
Computer Engineering M,D,O
Computer Science M,D
Construction Management M,D,O
Corporate and Organizational Communication M,D
Counselor Education M
Cultural Studies D
Dentistry P
Developmental Psychology M,D
Economic Development M,D
Economics M,D
Education—General M,D
Educational Leadership and Administration D
Educational Policy D
Educational Psychology D
Electrical Engineering M,D,O
Engineering and Applied Sciences—General M,D,O
Engineering Management M,D,O
English as a Second Language M
English M,D
Environmental Biology M,D
Environmental Engineering M,D,O
Epidemiology M,D
Evolutionary Biology D
Film, Television, and Video Production M
Film, Television, and Video Theory and Criticism M,D
Food Science and Technology M,D,O
Game Design and Development M,D
Genetics M,D
Geographic Information Systems M,O
Geography M,O
Geosciences M,D
Gerontology M,D,O
Hazardous Materials Management M,D,O
Health Communication M,D
Health Promotion M
Health Services Management and Hospital Administration M,O
Health Services Research D
Higher Education D
History D
Homeland Security M,O
Immunology M,D
Industrial/Management Engineering M,D,O
International Affairs M,D
International Health M
Internet and Interactive Multimedia M,D,O
Journalism M
Kinesiology and Movement Studies M,D
Latin American Studies D
Law P,M
Linguistics M,D
Manufacturing Engineering M,D,O
Marine Biology M,D
Marine Sciences M,D

Marriage and Family Therapy M
Mass Communication M,D
Materials Engineering M,D,O
Materials Sciences M,D,O
Mathematical and Computational Finance M,D
Mathematics M,D
Mechanical Engineering M,D,O
Mechanics M,D,O
Media Studies M,D
Medical Imaging M,D
Microbiology M,D
Modeling and Simulation M,D
Molecular Biology M,D
Molecular Pharmacology M,D
Multilingual and Multicultural Education D
Music Education M,D,O
Music M,D,O
Neurobiology M,D
Neuroscience M,D
Nonprofit Management M,O
Occupational Therapy M,D
Oceanography M,D
Operations Research M,D,O
Oral and Dental Sciences M,D,O
Organizational Management M
Pathobiology M,D*
Pathology M,D
Petroleum Engineering M,D,O
Pharmaceutical Sciences M,D,O*
Pharmacy P
Philosophy M,D
Photography M
Physical Chemistry D
Physical Therapy M,D
Physician Assistant Studies M
Physics M,D
Physiology M,D
Political Science M,D
Psychology—General M,D
Public Administration M,O
Public Health—General M*
Public Policy M,D,O
Quantitative Analysis M,D
Real Estate M,O
Safety Engineering M,D,O
Slavic Languages M,D
Social Psychology M,D
Social Work M,D
Sociology D
Software Engineering M,D
Spanish D
Speech and Interpersonal Communication M,D
Statistics M,D
Student Affairs M
Supply Chain Management M,D,O
Sustainable Development M,D,O
Systems Biology D
Systems Engineering M,D,O
Taxation M
Telecommunications M,D,O
Theater M
Toxicology M,D
Transportation and Highway Engineering M,D,O
Urban and Regional Planning M,D,O
Urban Education D
Water Resources M,D,O
Writing M,D

UNIVERSITY OF SOUTHERN INDIANA

Business Administration and Management—General M
Communication—General M
Education—General M
Elementary Education M
Engineering and Applied Sciences—General M
Health Services Management and Hospital Administration M
Industrial and Manufacturing Management M
Liberal Studies M
Nursing—General M,D
Occupational Therapy M
Public Administration M
Secondary Education M
Social Work M

UNIVERSITY OF SOUTHERN MAINE

Adult Education M,O
Adult Nursing M,O
American Studies M
Applied Behavior Analysis M,O
Biological and Biomedical Sciences—General M
Business Administration and Management—General M
Computer Science M
Counseling Psychology M,O
Counselor Education M,O
Education of the Gifted M,O
Education—General M,D,O
Educational Leadership and Administration M,O
Educational Psychology M,O
English as a Second Language M,O
Family Nurse Practitioner Studies M,O
Finance and Banking M
Health Services Management and Hospital Administration M,O
Higher Education M,O
Immunology M
Law P
Manufacturing Engineering M
Medical/Surgical Nursing M,O
Middle School Education M,O
Molecular Biology M
Music M
Nonprofit Management M,O
Nursing and Healthcare Administration M,O
Nursing Education M,O
Nursing—General M,O
Occupational Therapy M
Psychiatric Nursing M,O
Public Policy M,D,O
Reading Education M,O
Rehabilitation Counseling M,O
School Psychology M,D
Social Work M
Special Education M,O
Sports Management M,O
Statistics M
Taxation M
Urban and Regional Planning M,O
Writing M

UNIVERSITY OF SOUTHERN MISSISSIPPI

Accounting M
Adult Education M,D,O
Advertising and Public Relations M,D
Analytical Chemistry M,D
Anthropology M
Biochemistry M,D
Biological and Biomedical Sciences—General M,D
Biostatistics M
Business Administration and Management—General M
Chemistry M,D
Child and Family Studies M
Clinical Laboratory Sciences/Medical Technology M
Clinical Psychology M,D
Communication Disorders M,D
Community College Education M,D,O
Computational Sciences M,D
Computer Science M,D
Construction Engineering M
Counseling Psychology M,D
Counselor Education M,D,O
Criminal Justice and Criminology M,D
Curriculum and Instruction M,D,O
Early Childhood Education M,D,O
Economic Development M,D
Economics M,D
Education of the Gifted M,D,O
Education—General M,D,O
Educational Leadership and Administration M,D,O
Educational Measurement and Evaluation M,D,O
Elementary Education M,D,O
English M,D
Environmental and Occupational Health M
Environmental Biology M,D
Epidemiology M
Exercise and Sports Science M,D
Experimental Psychology M,D
Family Nurse Practitioner Studies M,D
Foreign Languages Education M
Forensic Sciences M,D
Geography M,D
Geology M,D
Health Education M
Health Services Management and Hospital Administration M
Higher Education M,D,O
History M,D
Hydrology M,D
Inorganic Chemistry M,D
International Affairs M,D
International Development M,D
Leisure Studies M,D
Library Science M
Management Information Systems M
Marine Biology M,D
Marine Sciences M,D
Marriage and Family Therapy M
Mass Communication M,D
Maternal and Child/Neonatal Nursing M,D
Mathematics Education M,D
Mathematics M,D
Microbiology M,D
Molecular Biology M,D
Music Education M,D
Music M,D
Nursing and Healthcare Administration M,D
Nursing—General M,D
Nutrition M,D
Organic Chemistry M,D
Physical Chemistry M,D
Physical Education M,D
Physics M,D
Political Science M,D
Polymer Science and Engineering M,D
Psychiatric Nursing M,D
Psychology—General M,D
Public Health—General M
Reading Education M,D,O
Recreation and Park Management M,D
School Psychology M,D
Science Education M,D
Secondary Education M,D,O
Social Sciences Education M,D,O
Social Work M
Special Education M,D,O
Speech and Interpersonal Communication M,D
Sports Management M,D
Student Affairs M,D,O
Theater M
Vocational and Technical Education M
Writing M,D

UNIVERSITY OF SOUTH FLORIDA

Accounting M,D
Adult Education M,D,O
African Studies M
Allopathic Medicine P,M,D
American Studies M
Analytical Chemistry M,D
Anthropology M,D
Applied Behavior Analysis M
Applied Physics M,D
Architecture M
Art History M
Art/Fine Arts M
Biochemistry M,D
Biological and Biomedical Sciences—General M,D
Biomedical Engineering M,D
Biostatistics M,D
Business Administration and Management—General M,D
Cancer Biology/Oncology D
Cell Biology M,D
Chemical Engineering M,D
Chemistry M,D
Civil Engineering M,D
Classics M
Clinical Psychology D
Cognitive Sciences D
Communication Disorders M,D
Communication—General M,D
Community College Education M,D,O
Community Health M,D
Computer Engineering M,D
Computer Science M,D
Conservation Biology M,D
Counselor Education M,D,O
Criminal Justice and Criminology M,D
Curriculum and Instruction M,D,O
Early Childhood Education M,D,O
Economics M,D
Education of the Gifted M,D
Education—General M,D,O*
Educational Leadership and Administration M,D,O
Educational Measurement and Evaluation M,D,O
Educational Media/Instructional Technology M,D,O
Electrical Engineering M,D
Elementary Education M,D,O
Engineering and Applied Sciences—General M,D
Engineering Management M,D
English as a Second Language M,D,O
English Education M,D,O
English M,D
Entrepreneurship M,O
Environmental and Occupational Health M,D
Environmental Engineering M,D
Environmental Management and Policy M
Environmental Sciences M,D
Epidemiology M,D
Exercise and Sports Science M
Film, Television, and Video Theory and Criticism M
Finance and Banking M,D
Foreign Languages Education M,D,O
French M
Geography M,D
Geology M,D
Gerontology M,D

*M—master's degree; P—first professional degree; D—doctorate; O—other advanced degree; *—Close-Up and/or Display in one of the other books in this series*

Health Services Management and Hospital Administration	M,D
Higher Education	M,D,O
History	M,D
Humanities	M
Industrial and Organizational Psychology	D
Industrial/Management Engineering	M,D
Information Studies	M
Inorganic Chemistry	M,D
Interdisciplinary Studies	M,D
International Affairs	M,D
International Health	M,D
Latin American Studies	M,D
Library Science	M
Linguistics	M
Management Information Systems	M,D
Marine Biology	M,D
Marine Sciences	M,D
Marketing	M,D
Mass Communication	M
Mathematics Education	M,D,O
Mathematics	M,D
Mechanical Engineering	M,D
Molecular Biology	M,D
Music Education	M,D
Music	M,D
Neuroscience	D
Nursing—General	M,D
Oceanography	M,D
Organic Chemistry	M,D
Philosophy	M,D
Physical Chemistry	M,D
Physical Education	M
Physical Therapy	M,D
Physics	M,D
Political Science	M,D
Polymer Science and Engineering	M,D
Psychology—General	D
Public Administration	M,D
Public Health—General	M,D
Reading Education	M,D,O
Real Estate	M,D
Rehabilitation Counseling	M
Religion	M
School Psychology	M,D,O
Science Education	M,D,O
Secondary Education	M,D,O
Social Sciences Education	M,D,O
Social Work	M,D
Sociology	M,D
Spanish	M
Special Education	M,D
Statistics	M,D
Student Affairs	M,D,O
Vocational and Technical Education	M,D,O
Women's Studies	M

THE UNIVERSITY OF TAMPA

Accounting	M
Adult Nursing	M
Business Administration and Management—General	M
Curriculum and Instruction	M
Education—General	M
Educational Leadership and Administration	M
Entrepreneurship	M
Family Nurse Practitioner Studies	M
Finance and Banking	M
International Business	M
Management Information Systems	M
Marketing	M
Nonprofit Management	M
Nursing—General	M

THE UNIVERSITY OF TENNESSEE

Accounting	M,D
Adult Education	M,D
Advertising and Public Relations	M,D
Aerospace/Aeronautical Engineering	M,D
Agricultural Education	M
Agricultural Engineering	M
Agricultural Sciences—General	M,D
Analytical Chemistry	M,D
Anatomy	M,D
Animal Behavior	M,D
Animal Sciences	M,D
Anthropology	M,D
Applied Mathematics	M,D
Applied Psychology	M,D
Archaeology	M,D
Architecture	M
Art Education	M,D,O
Art/Fine Arts	M
Athletic Training and Sports Medicine	M,D
Aviation	M
Biochemistry	M,D
Bioethics	M,D
Biological and Biomedical Sciences—General	M,D
Biomedical Engineering	M,D
Biosystems Engineering	M,D
Business Administration and Management—General	M,D
Chemical Engineering	M,D
Chemical Physics	M,D
Chemistry	M,D
Child and Family Studies	M,D
Civil Engineering	M,D
Clinical Psychology	M,D
Clothing and Textiles	M,D
Communication Disorders	M,D,O
Communication—General	M,D
Community Health	M,D
Computer Engineering	M,D
Computer Science	M,D
Consumer Economics	M,D
Counseling Psychology	M,D
Counselor Education	M,D,O
Criminal Justice and Criminology	M,D
Cultural Anthropology	M,D
Curriculum and Instruction	M,D,O
Early Childhood Education	M,D,O
Ecology	M,D
Economics	M,D
Education—General	M,D,O
Educational Leadership and Administration	M,D,O
Educational Measurement and Evaluation	M,D,O
Educational Media/Instructional Technology	M,D,O
Educational Psychology	M,D,O
Electrical Engineering	M,D
Elementary Education	M,D,O
Engineering and Applied Sciences—General	M,D
Engineering Management	M,D
English as a Second Language	M,D,O
English Education	M,D,O
English	M,D
Entomology	M,D
Environmental Engineering	M
Environmental Management and Policy	M,D
Evolutionary Biology	M,D
Exercise and Sports Science	M,D,O
Experimental Psychology	M,D
Family and Consumer Sciences-General	D
Finance and Banking	M,D
Fish, Game, and Wildlife Management	M
Food Science and Technology	M,D
Foreign Languages Education	M,D,O
Forestry	M
Foundations and Philosophy of Education	M,D,O
French	M,D
Genetics	M,D
Genomic Sciences	M,D
Geography	M,D
Geology	M,D
German	M,D
Gerontology	M
Graphic Design	M
Health Education	M
Health Promotion	M
Health Services Management and Hospital Administration	M
History	M,D
Hospitality Management	M
Human Resources Development	M
Industrial and Manufacturing Management	M,D
Industrial and Organizational Psychology	D
Industrial/Management Engineering	M,D
Information Science	M,D
Inorganic Chemistry	M,D
Italian	D
Journalism	M,D
Kinesiology and Movement Studies	M,D
Landscape Architecture	M
Law	P
Leisure Studies	M,D
Linguistics	D
Logistics	M,D
Marketing	M,D
Materials Engineering	M,D
Materials Sciences	M,D
Mathematics Education	M,D,O
Mathematics	M,D
Mechanical Engineering	M,D
Media Studies	M,D
Microbiology	M,D
Multilingual and Multicultural Education	M,D,O
Music Education	M
Music	M
Nuclear Engineering	M,D
Nursing—General	M,D
Nutrition	M
Organic Chemistry	M,D
Philosophy	M,D
Photography	M
Physical Chemistry	M,D
Physics	M,D
Physiology	M,D
Plant Pathology	M,D
Plant Physiology	M,D
Plant Sciences	M
Political Science	M,D
Polymer Science and Engineering	M,D
Portuguese	D
Psychology—General	M,D
Public Administration	M
Public Health—General	M
Reading Education	M,D,O
Recreation and Park Management	M,D
Rehabilitation Counseling	M,D
Reliability Engineering	M,D
Religion	M,D
Russian	D
School Psychology	M,D,O
Science Education	M,D,O
Secondary Education	M,D,O
Social Sciences Education	M,D,O
Social Work	M,D
Sociology	M,D
Spanish	M,D
Special Education	M,D,O
Speech and Interpersonal Communication	M,D
Sports Management	M,D
Statistics	M,D
Student Affairs	M
Theater	M
Theoretical Chemistry	M,D
Transportation Management	M,D
Travel and Tourism	M
Veterinary Medicine	P

THE UNIVERSITY OF TENNESSEE AT CHATTANOOGA

Accounting	M
Athletic Training and Sports Medicine	M
Business Administration and Management—General	M
Chemical Engineering	M
Civil Engineering	M
Computational Sciences	M,D
Computer Science	M,O
Counselor Education	M
Criminal Justice and Criminology	M
Education—General	M,D,O
Educational Leadership and Administration	M,D,O
Educational Media/Instructional Technology	O
Electrical Engineering	M
Elementary Education	M,O
Energy and Power Engineering	M,O
Engineering and Applied Sciences—General	M,D,O
Engineering Management	M,O
English	M,O
Environmental Sciences	M
Experimental Psychology	M
Family Nurse Practitioner Studies	M,D,O
Industrial and Organizational Psychology	M
Industrial/Management Engineering	M
Mechanical Engineering	M
Medical Informatics	M,D,O
Music Education	M
Music	M
Nonprofit Management	M,O
Nurse Anesthesia	M,D,O
Nursing and Healthcare Administration	M,D,O
Nursing Education	M,D,O
Nursing—General	M,D,O
Physical Education	M
Physical Therapy	D
Project Management	M,O
Psychology—General	M
Public Administration	M,O
Quality Management	M,O
Rhetoric	M,O
School Psychology	O
Secondary Education	M,O
Social Psychology	M
Special Education	M,O
Writing	M,O

THE UNIVERSITY OF TENNESSEE AT MARTIN

Agricultural Sciences—General	M
Business Administration and Management—General	M
Child and Family Studies	M
Child Development	M
Counselor Education	M
Education—General	M
Educational Leadership and Administration	M
Family and Consumer Sciences-General	M
Food Science and Technology	M
Nutrition	M
Social Psychology	M

THE UNIVERSITY OF TENNESSEE HEALTH SCIENCE CENTER

Allied Health—General M,D
Allopathic Medicine P,M,D
Dentistry P,M,O
Nursing—General M,D
Oral and Dental Sciences P,M,O
Pharmacy P,M,D
Physical Therapy M,D

THE UNIVERSITY OF TENNESSEE–OAK RIDGE NATIONAL LABORATORY GRADUATE SCHOOL OF GENOME SCIENCE AND TECHNOLOGY

Biological and Biomedical Sciences—General M,D
Genomic Sciences M,D

THE UNIVERSITY OF TENNESSEE SPACE INSTITUTE

Aerospace/Aeronautical Engineering M,D
Applied Mathematics M
Aviation M
Computer Science M,D
Electrical Engineering M,D
Engineering and Applied Sciences—General M,D
Engineering Management M,D
Materials Engineering M
Materials Sciences M
Mechanical Engineering M,D
Mechanics M,D
Physics M,D

THE UNIVERSITY OF TEXAS AT ARLINGTON

Accounting M,D
Aerospace/Aeronautical Engineering M,D
Anthropology M
Applied Mathematics M,D
Architecture M
Art/Fine Arts M
Bioengineering M,D
Biological and Biomedical Sciences—General M,D
Business Administration and Management—General M,D
Chemistry M,D
Civil Engineering M,D
Communication—General M
Computer Engineering M,D
Computer Science M,D
Criminal Justice and Criminology M
Curriculum and Instruction M
Economics M
Education—General M
Electrical Engineering M,D
Engineering and Applied Sciences—General M,D
Engineering Management M
English as a Second Language M
English M,D
Environmental Sciences M,D
Experimental Psychology M,D
Family Nurse Practitioner Studies M,D
Film, Television, and Video Production M
Finance and Banking M,D
French M
Geology M,D
Health Psychology M,D
Health Services Management and Hospital Administration M
History M,D
Human Resources Management M
Industrial and Manufacturing Management M,D
Industrial and Organizational Psychology M,D
Industrial/Management Engineering M,D
Interdisciplinary Studies M
Landscape Architecture M
Linguistics M,D
Logistics M
Management Information Systems M,D
Marketing Research M,D
Marketing M,D
Materials Engineering M,D
Materials Sciences M,D
Mathematics Education M,D
Mathematics M,D
Mechanical Engineering M,D
Music Education M
Music M
Nursing and Healthcare Administration M,D
Nursing Education M,D
Nursing—General M,D
Physics M,D
Political Science M
Psychology—General M,D
Public Administration M
Public Affairs D
Quantitative Analysis M,D
Real Estate M,D
Social Work M,D
Sociology M
Software Engineering M,D
Spanish M
Systems Engineering M
Taxation M,D
Urban and Regional Planning M

THE UNIVERSITY OF TEXAS AT AUSTIN

Accounting M,D
Actuarial Science M,D
Advertising and Public Relations M,D
Aerospace/Aeronautical Engineering M,D
African Studies M,D
American Studies M,D
Analytical Chemistry M,D
Animal Behavior M,D
Anthropology M,D
Applied Arts and Design—General M
Applied Mathematics M,D
Applied Physics M,D
Archaeology M,D
Architectural Engineering M
Architectural History M,D
Architecture M,D
Art Education M
Art History M,D
Art/Fine Arts M
Asian Languages M,D
Asian Studies M,D
Astronomy M,D
Biochemistry M,D
Biological and Biomedical Sciences—General M,D
Biomedical Engineering M,D
Biopsychology D
Business Administration and Management—General M,D
Cell Biology D
Chemical Engineering M,D
Chemistry M,D
Child and Family Studies M,D
Child Development M,D
Civil Engineering M,D
Classics M,D
Cognitive Sciences M,D
Communication Disorders M,D
Communication—General M,D
Comparative Literature M,D
Computational Sciences M,D
Computer Engineering M,D
Computer Science M,D
Counseling Psychology M,D
Counselor Education M,D
Curriculum and Instruction M,D
Dance M,D
East European and Russian Studies M
Ecology M,D
Economics M,D
Education—General M,D
Educational Leadership and Administration M,D
Educational Psychology M,D
Electrical Engineering M,D
Engineering and Applied Sciences—General M,D
English M,D
Entrepreneurship M
Environmental Engineering M,D
Evolutionary Biology M,D
Family and Consumer Sciences-General M,D
Film, Television, and Video Production M,D
Finance and Banking D
Folklore M,D
Foreign Languages Education M,D
French M,D
Geography M,D
Geology M,D
Geosciences M,D
Geotechnical Engineering M,D
German M,D
Health Education M,D
Hispanic and Latin American Languages M,D
Hispanic Studies M
Historic Preservation M,D
History M,D
Human Development M,D
Industrial and Manufacturing Management D
Industrial/Management Engineering M,D
Information Studies M,D
Inorganic Chemistry M,D
Italian M,D
Journalism M,D
Kinesiology and Movement Studies M,D
Landscape Architecture M,D
Latin American Studies M,D
Law P,M,O
Linguistics M,D
Management Information Systems D
Marine Sciences M,D
Marketing D
Materials Engineering M,D
Materials Sciences M,D
Mathematics Education M,D
Mathematics M,D
Mechanical Engineering M,D
Mechanics M,D
Media Studies M,D
Microbiology D
Mineral Economics M
Mineral/Mining Engineering M
Molecular Biology D
Music M,D
Natural Resources M
Near and Middle Eastern Languages M,D
Near and Middle Eastern Studies M,D
Neurobiology D
Neuroscience D
Nursing—General M,D
Nutrition M,D
Operations Research M,D
Organic Chemistry M,D
Petroleum Engineering M,D
Pharmaceutical Sciences M,D
Pharmacy P
Philosophy D
Physical Chemistry M,D
Physics M,D
Plant Biology M,D
Political Science D
Portuguese M,D
Psychology—General D
Public Affairs M,D
Public History M,D
Public Policy M,D
Romance Languages M,D
School Psychology M,D
Science Education M,D
Slavic Languages M,D
Social Work M,D
Sociology M,D
Spanish M,D
Special Education M,D
Sport Psychology M,D
Statistics M
Supply Chain Management D
Technology and Public Policy M
Textile Sciences and Engineering M
Theater M,D
Urban and Regional Planning M,D
Urban Design M,D
Water Resources Engineering M,D
Writing M,D

THE UNIVERSITY OF TEXAS AT BROWNSVILLE

Biological and Biomedical Sciences—General M
Business Administration and Management—General M
Community Health Nursing M
Counselor Education M
Curriculum and Instruction M
Early Childhood Education M
Education—General M
Educational Leadership and Administration M
Educational Media/Instructional Technology M
English as a Second Language M
English M
History M
Interdisciplinary Studies M
Mathematics M
Multilingual and Multicultural Education M
Physics M
Political Science M
Psychology—General M
Public Administration M
Public Policy M
Reading Education M
Spanish M
Special Education M

THE UNIVERSITY OF TEXAS AT DALLAS

Accounting M,D
Applied Mathematics M,D
Biological and Biomedical Sciences—General M,D
Biomedical Engineering M,D
Biotechnology M,D
Business Administration and Management—General M,D*
Cell Biology M,D
Chemistry M,D
Child and Family Studies M,D
Cognitive Sciences M,D
Communication Disorders M,D
Communication—General M,D
Comparative Literature M,D
Computer and Information Systems Security M

*M—master's degree; P—first professional degree; D—doctorate; O—other advanced degree; *—Close-Up and/or Display in one of the other books in this series*

Computer Engineering	M,D
Computer Science	M,D
Criminal Justice and Criminology	M,D
Economics	M,D*
Electrical Engineering	M,D
Electronic Commerce	M
Engineering and Applied Sciences—General	M,D
English	M,D
Entrepreneurship	M
Finance and Banking	M,D
Financial Engineering	M
Geochemistry	M,D
Geographic Information Systems	M,D
Geophysics	M,D
Geosciences	M,D
Health Services Management and Hospital Administration	M
History	M,D
Humanities	M,D
Hydrogeology	M,D
Interdisciplinary Studies	M
International Business	M,D
Internet and Interactive Multimedia	M,D
Investment Management	M
Latin American Studies	M,D
Law	M,D
Management Information Systems	M,D
Management Strategy and Policy	M,D
Marketing	M,D
Materials Engineering	M,D
Materials Sciences	M,D
Mathematics Education	M
Mathematics	M,D
Mechanical Engineering	M
Molecular Biology	M,D
Neuroscience	M,D
Organizational Management	M
Paleontology	M,D
Philosophy	M,D
Physics	M,D
Political Science	M,D
Project Management	M
Psychology—General	M,D
Public Affairs	M,D
Public Policy	M,D
Real Estate	M
Science Education	M
Sociology	M
Software Engineering	M,D
Statistics	M,D
Supply Chain Management	M
Systems Engineering	M
Taxation	M
Telecommunications	M,D

THE UNIVERSITY OF TEXAS AT EL PASO

Accounting	M
Allied Health—General	D
Art Education	M
Art/Fine Arts	M
Bioinformatics	M,D
Biological and Biomedical Sciences—General	M,D
Business Administration and Management—General	M,D,O*
Chemistry	M,D
Civil Engineering	M,D,O
Clinical Psychology	M,D
Communication Disorders	M
Communication—General	M
Computational Sciences	M,D
Computer Engineering	M,D
Computer Science	M,D
Construction Management	M,D,O
Counselor Education	M
Curriculum and Instruction	M,D
Economics	M
Education—General	M,D
Educational Leadership and Administration	M,D
Educational Measurement and Evaluation	M
Educational Psychology	M
Electrical Engineering	M,D
Engineering and Applied Sciences—General	M,D,O
English as a Second Language	M,O
English Education	M,D,O
English	M,D,O
Environmental Engineering	M,D,O
Environmental Sciences	M,D
Experimental Psychology	M,D
Family Nurse Practitioner Studies	M,D,O
Gender Studies	O
Geology	M,D
Geophysics	M
Health Education	M
Health Promotion	M
Health Services Management and Hospital Administration	M,D,O
History	M,D
Homeland Security	M,O
Industrial/Management Engineering	M,O
Information Science	M,D
Interdisciplinary Studies	M
International Business	M,D,O*
Kinesiology and Movement Studies	M
Latin American Studies	M,O
Liberal Studies	M
Linguistics	M,O
Manufacturing Engineering	M,O
Materials Engineering	M,D
Materials Sciences	M,D
Mathematics Education	M
Mathematics	M
Mechanical Engineering	M
Metallurgical Engineering and Metallurgy	M,D
Military and Defense Studies	M,O
Multilingual and Multicultural Education	M,D,O
Music Education	M
Music	M
National Security	M,O
Nursing and Healthcare Administration	M,D,O
Nursing—General	M,D,O
Occupational Therapy	M
Philosophy	M
Physical Therapy	M
Physics	M
Political Science	M
Psychology—General	M,D
Public Administration	M,O
Public Health—General	M
Public Policy	M,O
Reading Education	M,D
Rehabilitation Counseling	M
Rhetoric	M,D,O
Science Education	M
Social Work	M
Sociology	M,O
Spanish	M,O
Special Education	M
Statistics	M
Systems Engineering	M,O
Women's Studies	O
Writing	M,D,O

THE UNIVERSITY OF TEXAS AT SAN ANTONIO

Accounting	M,D
Adult Education	M,D
Anthropology	M,D
Applied Mathematics	M
Applied Statistics	M,D
Architecture	M
Art History	M
Art/Fine Arts	M
Biological and Biomedical Sciences—General	M,D
Biomedical Engineering	M,D*
Biotechnology	M,D
Business Administration and Management—General	M,D
Chemistry	M,D*
Civil Engineering	M,D*
Communication—General	M
Computer and Information Systems Security	M,D
Computer Engineering	M,D
Computer Science	M,D
Construction Management	M
Counselor Education	M,D*
Criminal Justice and Criminology	M
Cultural Studies	M,D
Curriculum and Instruction	M,D*
Demography and Population Studies	D
Early Childhood Education	M,D
Economics	M
Educational Leadership and Administration	M,D*
Educational Media/Instructional Technology	M,D
Electrical Engineering	M,D*
Engineering and Applied Sciences—General	M,D
English as a Second Language	M,D*
English	M,D
Environmental Engineering	M,D
Environmental Sciences	M,D*
Finance and Banking	M,D
Geology	M
Health Education	M*
History	M
Information Science	M
Interdisciplinary Studies	M,D
International Business	M,D
Kinesiology and Movement Studies	M
Management Information Systems	M,D
Management of Technology	M,D
Manufacturing Engineering	M*
Marketing	M,D
Mathematics Education	M
Mathematics	M
Mechanical Engineering	M*
Multilingual and Multicultural Education	M,D*
Music	M,O
Neurobiology	M,D
Organizational Management	M,D
Physics	M,D
Political Science	M
Psychology—General	M
Public Administration	M
Reading Education	M,D
Real Estate	M
School Psychology	M*
Social Work	M
Sociology	M
Software Engineering	M,D
Spanish	M
Special Education	M,D
Statistics	M,D
Taxation	M,D

THE UNIVERSITY OF TEXAS AT TYLER

Art History	M
Art/Fine Arts	M
Biological and Biomedical Sciences—General	M
Business Administration and Management—General	M
Civil Engineering	M
Clinical Psychology	M
Communication—General	M
Computer Science	M
Counseling Psychology	M
Criminal Justice and Criminology	M
Early Childhood Education	M
Educational Leadership and Administration	M
Electrical Engineering	M
English	M
Environmental and Occupational Health	M
Environmental Engineering	M
Family Nurse Practitioner Studies	M,D
Health Education	M
Health Services Management and Hospital Administration	M
History	M
Human Resources Development	M,D
Industrial and Manufacturing Management	M,D
Interdisciplinary Studies	M
Kinesiology and Movement Studies	M
Marriage and Family Therapy	M
Mathematics	M
Mechanical Engineering	M
Nursing and Healthcare Administration	M,D
Nursing Education	M,D
Nursing—General	M,D
Political Science	M
Psychology—General	M
Public Administration	M
Reading Education	M
School Psychology	M
Social Sciences	M
Sociology	M
Special Education	M
Structural Engineering	M
Transportation and Highway Engineering	M
Vocational and Technical Education	M,D
Water Resources Engineering	M

THE UNIVERSITY OF TEXAS HEALTH SCIENCE CENTER AT HOUSTON

Allopathic Medicine	P
Biochemistry	M,D
Biological and Biomedical Sciences—General	M,D
Biomathematics	M,D
Biostatistics	M,D
Cancer Biology/Oncology	M,D*
Cell Biology	M,D
Dentistry	P,M
Developmental Biology	M,D
Genetic Counseling	M
Genetics	M,D
Health Informatics	M,D,O
Human Genetics	M,D
Immunology	M,D
Medical Physics	M,D
Microbiology	M,D
Molecular Biology	M,D
Molecular Genetics	M,D
Molecular Pathology	M,D
Neuroscience	M,D
Nursing—General	M,D
Public Health—General	M,D,O
Virology	M,D

THE UNIVERSITY OF TEXAS HEALTH SCIENCE CENTER AT SAN ANTONIO

Allopathic Medicine	P,M
Biochemistry	M,D
Biological and Biomedical Sciences—General	M,D
Cell Biology	M,D

Clinical Laboratory Sciences/Medical Technology	M
Clinical Research	M
Communication Disorders	M
Dental Hygiene	M
Dentistry	P,M,O
Immunology	D
Medical Physics	M,D
Microbiology	D
Molecular Medicine	M,D
Neuroscience	D
Nursing—General	M,D
Occupational Therapy	M
Oral and Dental Sciences	M,O
Pharmacology	D
Physical Therapy	M
Physician Assistant Studies	M
Physiology	M,D
Structural Biology	M,D

THE UNIVERSITY OF TEXAS MEDICAL BRANCH

Allied Health—General	M,D
Allopathic Medicine	P
Bacteriology	D
Biochemistry	D
Bioinformatics	D
Biological and Biomedical Sciences—General	M,D
Biophysics	D
Cell Biology	D
Clinical Laboratory Sciences/Medical Technology	M,D
Community Health	M,D
Computational Biology	D
Genetics	D
Humanities	M,D
Immunology	M,D
Infectious Diseases	D
Microbiology	M,D
Molecular Biophysics	M,D
Neuroscience	D
Nursing—General	M,D
Occupational Therapy	M
Pathology	D
Pharmacology	M,D
Physical Therapy	M,D
Physician Assistant Studies	M
Physiology	M,D
Public Health—General	M
Structural Biology	D
Toxicology	M,D
Virology	D

THE UNIVERSITY OF TEXAS OF THE PERMIAN BASIN

Accounting	M
Applied Psychology	M
Biological and Biomedical Sciences—General	M
Business Administration and Management—General	M
Clinical Psychology	M
Computer Science	M
Counselor Education	M
Criminal Justice and Criminology	M
Early Childhood Education	M
Education—General	M
Educational Leadership and Administration	M
English as a Second Language	M
English	M
Experimental Psychology	M
Foundations and Philosophy of Education	M
Geology	M
History	M
Kinesiology and Movement Studies	M
Political Science	M
Psychology—General	M
Reading Education	M
Spanish	M
Special Education	M

THE UNIVERSITY OF TEXAS–PAN AMERICAN

Accounting	M
Adult Nursing	M
Art/Fine Arts	M
Biological and Biomedical Sciences—General	M
Business Administration and Management—General	M,D
Chemistry	M
Clinical Psychology	M
Communication Disorders	M
Communication—General	M
Computer Science	M
Counselor Education	M
Criminal Justice and Criminology	M
Early Childhood Education	M
Economics	D
Education of the Gifted	M
Education—General	M,D
Educational Leadership and Administration	M,D
Educational Measurement and Evaluation	M
Educational Psychology	M
Electrical Engineering	M
Elementary Education	M
English as a Second Language	M
English	M
Experimental Psychology	M
Family Nurse Practitioner Studies	M
Finance and Banking	D
History	M
Interdisciplinary Studies	M
International Business	D
Kinesiology and Movement Studies	M
Management Information Systems	D
Manufacturing Engineering	M
Marketing	D
Mathematics Education	M
Mathematics	M
Mechanical Engineering	M
Multilingual and Multicultural Education	M
Music Education	M
Music	M
Nursing—General	M
Occupational Therapy	M
Pediatric Nursing	M
Psychology—General	M
Public Administration	M
Reading Education	M
Rehabilitation Counseling	M,D
School Psychology	M
Secondary Education	M
Social Work	M
Sociology	M
Spanish	M
Special Education	M
Theater	M

THE UNIVERSITY OF TEXAS SOUTHWESTERN MEDICAL CENTER AT DALLAS

Allopathic Medicine	P
Biochemistry	D
Biological and Biomedical Sciences—General	M,D
Biomedical Engineering	M,D
Cancer Biology/Oncology	D
Cell Biology	D
Clinical Psychology	D
Developmental Biology	D
Genetics	D
Immunology	D
Medical Illustration	M
Microbiology	D
Molecular Biophysics	D
Neuroscience	D
Nutrition	M
Physical Therapy	D
Physician Assistant Studies	M
Rehabilitation Counseling	M

THE UNIVERSITY OF THE ARTS

Art Education	M
Art/Fine Arts	M*
Industrial Design	M
Museum Education	M
Museum Studies	M
Music Education	M
Music	M

UNIVERSITY OF THE CUMBERLANDS

Business Administration and Management—General	M
Business Education	M,D,O
Clinical Psychology	D
Counseling Psychology	M
Counselor Education	M,D,O
Education—General	M,D,O
Educational Leadership and Administration	M,D,O
Elementary Education	M,D,O
Marketing	M,D,O
Middle School Education	M,D,O
Physician Assistant Studies	M
Reading Education	M,D,O
Religion	M
Secondary Education	M,D,O
Special Education	M,D,O
Student Affairs	M,D,O
Theater	M,D,O

UNIVERSITY OF THE DISTRICT OF COLUMBIA

Applied Statistics	M
Business Administration and Management—General	M
Cancer Biology/Oncology	M
Clinical Psychology	M
Communication Disorders	M
Computer Science	M
Counseling Psychology	M
Counselor Education	M
Early Childhood Education	M
Education—General	M
Electrical Engineering	M
Engineering and Applied Sciences—General	M
English	M
Law	P,M
Legal and Justice Studies	P,M
Mathematics Education	M
Nutrition	M
Public Administration	M
Special Education	M

UNIVERSITY OF THE FRASER VALLEY

Criminal Justice and Criminology	M

UNIVERSITY OF THE INCARNATE WORD

Accounting	M
Adult Education	M,D,O
Biological and Biomedical Sciences—General	M
Business Administration and Management—General	M,O
Communication—General	M,O
Early Childhood Education	M,D
Education—General	M,D
Educational Leadership and Administration	M,D
Educational Media/Instructional Technology	M,D,O
Elementary Education	M
Entrepreneurship	M,D
Health Promotion	M
Health Services Management and Hospital Administration	M,O
Higher Education	M,D
Interdisciplinary Studies	M
International Business	M,O
Kinesiology and Movement Studies	M,D
Mathematics	M
Multilingual and Multicultural Education	M,D
Nursing—General	M
Nutrition	M,O
Optometry	P
Organizational Management	M,D,O
Pharmacy	P
Physical Education	M,O
Project Management	M,O
Reading Education	M,D
Religion	M
Science Education	M
Secondary Education	M
Special Education	M,D
Sports Management	M,O
Statistics	M

UNIVERSITY OF THE PACIFIC

Biological and Biomedical Sciences—General	M
Business Administration and Management—General	M*
Communication Disorders	M
Communication—General	M
Criminal Justice and Criminology	P,M,D
Curriculum and Instruction	M,D
Education—General	M,D,O
Educational Leadership and Administration	M,D
Educational Psychology	M,D,O
Exercise and Sports Science	M
International Affairs	P,M,D
Law	P,M,D
Legal and Justice Studies	P,M,D
Music Education	M
Music	M
Pharmaceutical Sciences	M,D
Pharmacy	P
Physical Therapy	M,D
Psychology—General	M
Public Policy	P,M,D
School Psychology	M,D,O
Special Education	M,D
Taxation	P,M,D
Therapies—Dance, Drama, and Music	M
Water Resources	P,M,D

UNIVERSITY OF THE ROCKIES

Psychology—General	M,D

UNIVERSITY OF THE SACRED HEART

Accounting	M,O
Advertising and Public Relations	M
Broadcast Journalism	M,O
Business Administration and Management—General	M,O
Communication—General	M,O
Conflict Resolution and Mediation/Peace Studies	M
Cultural Studies	M
Early Childhood Education	M,O
Education—General	M,O
Educational Media/Instructional Technology	M
English Education	M,O
Environmental and Occupational Health	M

*M—master's degree; P—first professional degree; D—doctorate; O—other advanced degree; *—Close-Up and/or Display in one of the other books in this series*

Film, Television, and Video Production	M,O
Foreign Languages Education	M,O
Human Resources Management	M
Information Science	O
Internet and Interactive Multimedia	M,O
Legal and Justice Studies	M
Management Information Systems	M
Marketing	M
Mathematics Education	M,O
Nonprofit Management	M
Occupational Health Nursing	M
Taxation	M
Writing	M,O

UNIVERSITY OF THE SCIENCES IN PHILADELPHIA

Biochemistry	M,D
Bioinformatics	M
Biotechnology	M,D
Cell Biology	M,D
Chemistry	M,D
Health Psychology	M
Health Services Management and Hospital Administration	M,D
Medicinal and Pharmaceutical Chemistry	M,D
Molecular Biology	D
Pharmaceutical Administration	M
Pharmaceutical Sciences	M,D
Pharmacology	M,D
Public Health—General	M,D
Technical Writing	M,O
Toxicology	M,D

UNIVERSITY OF THE SOUTHWEST

Business Administration and Management—General	M
Counseling Psychology	M
Counselor Education	M
Curriculum and Instruction	M
Early Childhood Education	M
Education—General	M
Educational Leadership and Administration	M
Educational Measurement and Evaluation	M
Reading Education	M
Special Education	M
Sports Management	M

UNIVERSITY OF THE VIRGIN ISLANDS

Business Administration and Management—General	M
Education—General	M
Environmental Sciences	M
Marine Sciences	M
Mathematics Education	M
Public Administration	M

UNIVERSITY OF THE WEST

Business Administration and Management—General	M
Finance and Banking	M
International Business	M
Management Information Systems	M
Nonprofit Management	M
Psychology—General	M
Religion	M,D

THE UNIVERSITY OF TOLEDO

Accounting	M
Adult Nursing	M,O
Analytical Chemistry	M,D
Applied Mathematics	M,D
Art Education	M,D,O
Biochemistry	M,D
Bioengineering	M,D
Bioinformatics	M,O
Biological and Biomedical Sciences—General	M,D
Biomedical Engineering	D
Biostatistics	M,O
Business Administration and Management—General	M,D,O
Business Education	M,D,O
Cancer Biology/Oncology	M,D
Cardiovascular Sciences	M,D
Cell Biology	M,D
Chemical Engineering	M,D
Chemistry	M,D
Civil Engineering	M,D
Clinical Psychology	M,D
Communication Disorders	M,D
Communication—General	O
Community Health Nursing	M,O
Computer Science	M,D
Counselor Education	M,D,O
Criminal Justice and Criminology	M,O
Curriculum and Instruction	M,D,O
Early Childhood Education	M,D,O
Ecology	M,D
Economics	M,D,O
Education of the Gifted	M,D,O
Education—General	M,D,O
Educational Leadership and Administration	M,D,O
Educational Measurement and Evaluation	M,D,O
Educational Media/ Instructional Technology	M,D,O
Educational Psychology	M,D,O
Electrical Engineering	M,D
Elementary Education	M,D,O
Engineering and Applied Sciences—General	M
English as a Second Language	M,D,O
English Education	M,D,O
English	M,O
Entrepreneurship	M
Environmental and Occupational Health	M,O
Environmental Sciences	M
Epidemiology	M,O
Exercise and Sports Science	M,D
Experimental Psychology	M,D
Family Nurse Practitioner Studies	M,O
Finance and Banking	M
Foreign Languages Education	M,D,O
Foundations and Philosophy of Education	M,D,O
French	M
Genomic Sciences	M,O
Geographic Information Systems	M,D,O
Geography	M,D,O
Geology	M
Geosciences	M
German	M
Gerontology	M,O
Health Education	M,D,O
Health Promotion	M,D,O
Health Services Management and Hospital Administration	M,O
Higher Education	M,D,O
History	M,D
Homeland Security	M,O
Immunology	M,D
Industrial and Manufacturing Management	M,D,O
Industrial/Management Engineering	M,D
Inorganic Chemistry	M,D
Law	P
Liberal Studies	M
Management Information Systems	M,D,O
Mathematics Education	M,D,O
Mathematics	M,D
Mechanical Engineering	M,D
Medical Physics	M
Medicinal and Pharmaceutical Chemistry	M,D
Middle School Education	M,D,O
Music Education	M,D,O
Music	M
Neuroscience	M,D
Nonprofit Management	M,O
Nursing and Healthcare Administration	M,O
Nursing Education	M,O
Nursing—General	M,D,O
Nutrition	M,O
Occupational Therapy	M,D
Oral and Dental Sciences	M
Organic Chemistry	M,D
Pathology	O
Pediatric Nursing	M,O
Pharmaceutical Administration	M
Pharmaceutical Sciences	M
Pharmacology	M
Philosophy	M
Physical Chemistry	M,D
Physical Education	M
Physical Therapy	M,D
Physician Assistant Studies	M
Physics	M,D
Political Science	M,O
Psychiatric Nursing	M,O
Psychology—General	M,D
Public Administration	M,O
School Psychology	M,D,O
Science Education	M,D,O
Secondary Education	M,D,O
Social Psychology	M,D,O
Social Sciences Education	M,D,O
Social Work	M,O
Sociology	M
Spanish	M
Special Education	M,D,O
Statistics	M,D
Supply Chain Management	M,D,O
Urban and Regional Planning	M,D,O
Vocational and Technical Education	M,D,O
Writing	M,O

UNIVERSITY OF TORONTO

Accounting	M,D
Aerospace/Aeronautical Engineering	M,D
Allopathic Medicine	P,M,D
Anthropology	M,D
Architecture	M
Art History	M,D
Art/Fine Arts	M,D
Asian Studies	M,D
Astronomy	M,D
Astrophysics	M,D
Biochemistry	M,D
Bioethics	M,D
Biological and Biomedical Sciences—General	M,D
Biomedical Engineering	M,D
Biophysics	M,D
Biotechnology	M
Business Administration and Management—General	M,D
Cell Biology	M,D
Chemical Engineering	M,D
Chemistry	M,D
Civil Engineering	M,D
Classics	M,D
Communication Disorders	M,D
Comparative Literature	M,D
Computer Engineering	M,D
Computer Science	M,D
Criminal Justice and Criminology	M,D
Dentistry	P
East European and Russian Studies	M
Ecology	M,D
Economics	M,D
Education—General	M,D
Electrical Engineering	M,D
Engineering and Applied Sciences—General	M,D
English	M,D
Environmental Sciences	M,D
Evolutionary Biology	M,D
Film, Television, and Video Theory and Criticism	M
Finance and Banking	M
Forestry	M,D
French	M,D
Gender Studies	M
Genetic Counseling	M,D
Genetics	M,D
Geography	M,D
Geology	M,D
German	M,D
Health Informatics	M
Health Services Management and Hospital Administration	M,D
History of Science and Technology	M,D
History	M,D
Human Resources Management	M,D
Immunology	M,D
Industrial and Labor Relations	M,D
Industrial/Management Engineering	M,D
Information Studies	M,D,O
International Affairs	M
Italian	M,D
Law	P,M,D
Library Science	M,D,O
Linguistics	M,D
Management of Technology	M
Manufacturing Engineering	M
Materials Engineering	M,D
Materials Sciences	M,D
Mathematical and Computational Finance	M
Mathematics	M,D
Mechanical Engineering	M,D
Medieval and Renaissance Studies	M,D
Museum Studies	M,D
Music Education	M,D
Music	M,D
Near and Middle Eastern Studies	M,D
Nursing—General	M,D
Nutrition	M,D
Occupational Therapy	M
Oral and Dental Sciences	M,D
Pathobiology	M,D
Pharmaceutical Sciences	M,D
Pharmacology	M,D
Philosophy	M,D
Physical Education	M,D
Physical Therapy	M
Physics	M,D
Physiology	M,D
Political Science	M,D
Portuguese	M,D
Psychology—General	M,D
Public Health—General	M,D
Rehabilitation Sciences	M,D
Religion	M,D
Slavic Languages	M,D
Social Work	M,D
Sociology	M,D
Spanish	M,D
Statistics	M,D
Systems Biology	M,D
Theater	M,D
Toxicology	M,D

Urban and Regional Planning M,D
Urban Design M,D
Women's Studies M

UNIVERSITY OF TRINITY COLLEGE

Music P,M,D,O
Pastoral Ministry and Counseling P,M,D,O
Theology P,M,D,O

UNIVERSITY OF TULSA

Accounting M
American Indian/Native American Studies M
Anthropology M
Applied Mathematics
Art/Fine Arts M
Biochemistry M
Biological and Biomedical Sciences—General M,D
Business Administration and Management—General M
Chemical Engineering M,D
Chemistry M,D
Clinical Psychology M,D
Communication Disorders M
Computer Science M,D
Education—General M
Electrical Engineering M
Elementary Education M
Energy Management and Policy M
Engineering and Applied Sciences—General M,D
Engineering Physics M
English Education M
English M,D
Environmental Law P,M,O
Finance and Banking M
Financial Engineering M
Geosciences M,D
Health Law P,M,O
History M
Industrial and Organizational Psychology M,D
International Business M
Investment Management M
Law P,M,O
Management Information Systems M
Mathematics Education M
Mathematics M
Mechanical Engineering M,D
Museum Studies M
Petroleum Engineering M,D
Physics M
Psychology—General M,D
Public Policy P,M,O
Science Education M
Secondary Education M
Taxation M
Theater M

UNIVERSITY OF UTAH

Accounting M,D
Allopathic Medicine P
American Studies M,D
Anatomy D
Anthropology M,D
Architecture M
Art Education M
Art History M
Art/Fine Arts M
Asian Studies M
Atmospheric Sciences M,D
Biochemistry M,D
Bioengineering M,D*
Bioinformatics M,D,O
Biological and Biomedical Sciences—General M,D,O
Biostatistics M,D
Biotechnology M
Business Administration and Management—General M,D
Cancer Biology/Oncology M,D
Chemical Engineering M,D
Chemical Physics M,D
Chemistry M,D
Child and Family Studies M
Civil Engineering M,D*
Clinical Laboratory Sciences/Medical Technology M
Clinical Psychology D
Communication Disorders M,D
Communication—General M,D
Comparative Literature M,D
Computational Sciences M
Computer Science M,D
Consumer Economics M
Counseling Psychology M,D
Counselor Education M,D
Dance M
Early Childhood Education M,D
Economics M,D
Education—General M,D
Educational Leadership and Administration M,D
Educational Media/Instructional Technology M,D
Educational Psychology M,D
Electrical Engineering M,D
Elementary Education M,D
Engineering and Applied Sciences—General M,D
English M,D
Environmental Engineering M,D
Environmental Sciences M
Exercise and Sports Science M,D
Film, Television, and Video Production M
Finance and Banking M,D
Foreign Languages Education M,D
Foundations and Philosophy of Education M,D
French M,D
Geography M,D
Geological Engineering M,D
Geology M,D
Geophysics M,D
German M,D
Gerontological Nursing M,O
Gerontology M,O
Graphic Design M
Health Education M,D
Health Promotion M,D
Health Services Management and Hospital Administration M
History M,D
Human Development M
Human Genetics M,D
Humanities M
International Affairs M
Law P,M
Leisure Studies M,D
Linguistics M,D
Management Information Systems M
Materials Engineering M,D
Materials Sciences M,D
Mathematics M,D
Mechanical Engineering M,D
Medical Physics M,D
Medicinal and Pharmaceutical Chemistry M,D
Metallurgical Engineering and Metallurgy M,D
Mineral/Mining Engineering M,D
Molecular Biology D
Music M,D
Near and Middle Eastern Languages M,D
Near and Middle Eastern Studies M,D
Neurobiology D
Neuroscience D
Nuclear Engineering M,D
Nursing—General M,D
Nutrition M
Occupational Therapy M,D
Pathology M,D
Pharmaceutical Sciences M
Pharmacology D
Pharmacy P
Philosophy M,D
Photography M
Physical Therapy D,O
Physician Assistant Studies M
Physics M,D
Physiology D
Political Science M,D
Psychology—General D
Public Administration M
Public Health—General M,D
Reading Education M,D
Real Estate M
Recreation and Park Management M,D
Rehabilitation Sciences D,O
Rhetoric M,D
School Psychology M,D
Science Education M,D
Secondary Education M,D
Social Work M,D
Sociology M,D
Spanish M,D
Special Education M,D
Statistics M,D
Toxicology D
Urban and Regional Planning M,D
Writing M,D

UNIVERSITY OF VERMONT

Accounting M
Agricultural Economics and Agribusiness M
Agricultural Sciences—General M,D
Agronomy and Soil Sciences M,D
Allied Health—General M,D
Allopathic Medicine P
Animal Sciences M,D
Applied Economics M
Biochemistry M,D
Biological and Biomedical Sciences—General M,D
Biomedical Engineering M
Biophysics M,D
Biostatistics M
Business Administration and Management—General M
Cell Biology M,D
Chemistry M,D
Civil Engineering M,D
Classics M
Clinical Laboratory Sciences/Medical Technology M,D
Clinical Psychology D
Communication—General M
Computer Science M,D
Counseling Psychology M
Counselor Education M
Curriculum and Instruction M
Education—General M,D
Educational Leadership and Administration M,D
Electrical Engineering M,D
Engineering and Applied Sciences—General M,D
English M
Environmental Engineering M,D
Food Science and Technology D
Foreign Languages Education M
Forestry M,D
French M
Geology M
German M
Historic Preservation M
History M
Horticulture M,D
Interdisciplinary Studies M
Materials Sciences M,D
Mathematics Education M,D
Mathematics M,D
Mechanical Engineering M,D
Microbiology M,D
Molecular Biology M,D
Molecular Genetics M,D
Molecular Physiology M,D
Natural Resources M,D
Neuroscience D
Nursing—General M
Nutrition M,D
Pathology M
Pharmacology M,D
Physical Therapy D
Physics M
Plant Biology M,D
Plant Sciences M,D
Psychology—General D
Public Administration M
Reading Education M
Science Education M,D
Social Work M
Special Education M
Statistics M

UNIVERSITY OF VICTORIA

Anthropology M
Art Education M,D
Art History M,D
Art/Fine Arts M
Asian Studies M
Astronomy M,D
Astrophysics M,D
Biochemistry M,D
Biological and Biomedical Sciences—General M,D
Business Administration and Management—General M
Chemistry M,D
Child and Family Studies M,D
Classics M,D
Clinical Psychology M,D
Computer Art and Design M
Computer Engineering M,D
Computer Science M,D
Condensed Matter Physics M,D
Conflict Resolution and Mediation/Peace Studies M,D
Counseling Psychology M,D
Counselor Education M,D
Curriculum and Instruction M,D
Developmental Psychology M,D
Early Childhood Education M,D
Economics M,D
Education—General M,D
Educational Leadership and Administration M,D
Educational Measurement and Evaluation M,D
Educational Psychology M,D
Electrical Engineering M,D
Engineering and Applied Sciences—General M,D
English Education M,D
English M,D
Environmental Education M,D
Experimental Psychology M,D
Family Nurse Practitioner Studies M,D
Film, Television, and Video Production M
Foreign Languages Education M
Foundations and Philosophy of Education M,D
French M
Geography M,D
Geophysics M,D
Geosciences M,D
German M

*M—master's degree; P—first professional degree; D—doctorate; O—other advanced degree; *—Close-Up and/or Display in one of the other books in this series*

Health Informatics M
Hispanic Studies M
History M,D
Human Development M,D
Italian M
Kinesiology and Movement Studies M
Law P,M,D
Leisure Studies M
Linguistics M,D
Mathematics Education M,D
Mathematics M,D
Mechanical Engineering M,D
Medical Physics M,D
Microbiology M,D
Music Education M,D
Music M,D
Nursing and Healthcare Administration M,D
Nursing Education M,D
Nursing—General M,D
Oceanography M,D
Pacific Area/Pacific Rim Studies M
Philosophy M
Photography M
Physical Education M
Physics M,D
Political Science M,D
Psychology—General M,D
Public Administration M,D
Reading Education M,D
Science Education M,D
Social Psychology M,D
Social Sciences Education M,D
Social Work M
Sociology M,D
Special Education M,D
Statistics M,D
Theater M
Theoretical Physics M,D
Vocational and Technical Education M,D
Writing M

UNIVERSITY OF VIRGINIA

Accounting M
Acute Care/Critical Care Nursing M,D
Aerospace/Aeronautical Engineering M,D
Allopathic Medicine P,M,D
Anthropology M,D
Architectural History M,D
Art History M,D
Asian Studies M
Astronomy M,D
Biochemistry D
Bioethics M
Biological and Biomedical Sciences—General M,D
Biomedical Engineering M,D
Biophysics M,D
Business Administration and Management—General M,D
Cell Biology D
Chemical Engineering M,D
Chemistry M,D
Civil Engineering M,D
Classics M,D
Clinical Psychology D
Clinical Research M
Communication Disorders M
Community Health M,D
Computer Engineering M,D
Computer Science M,D
Counselor Education M,D,O
Curriculum and Instruction M,D,O
Early Childhood Education M,D
Economics M,D
Education of the Gifted M,D,O
Education—General M,D,O
Educational Leadership and Administration M,D,O
Educational Measurement and Evaluation M,D,O
Educational Media/Instructional Technology M,D,O
Educational Psychology M,D,O
Electrical Engineering M,D
Elementary Education M,D,O
Engineering and Applied Sciences—General M,D
Engineering Physics M,D
English Education M,D,O
English M,D,O
Environmental Sciences M,D
Finance and Banking M
Foreign Languages Education M,D,O
French M,D
German M,D
Health Education M,D
Health Informatics M
Health Services Management and Hospital Administration M
Health Services Research M
Higher Education M,D,O
History M,D
Interdisciplinary Studies M,D
International Affairs M,D
Italian M
Kinesiology and Movement Studies M,D
Landscape Architecture M
Law P,M,D,O
Linguistics M
Management Information Systems M
Marketing M
Materials Sciences M,D
Mathematics Education M,D,O
Mathematics M,D
Mechanical Engineering M,D
Microbiology D
Molecular Genetics D
Molecular Physiology M,D
Music M,D
Near and Middle Eastern Studies M
Neuroscience D
Nursing and Healthcare Administration M,D
Nursing—General M,D
Pathology D
Pharmacology D
Philosophy M,D
Physical Education M,D
Physics M,D
Physiology D
Political Science M,D
Psychiatric Nursing M,D
Psychology—General M,D
Public Health—General M,D
Public Policy M
Reading Education M,D,O
Religion M,D
Romance Languages M,D
School Psychology M,D
Science Education M,D,O
Slavic Languages M,D
Social Sciences Education M,D,O
Sociology M,D
Spanish M,D
Special Education M,D,O
Statistics M,D
Student Affairs M,D,O
Systems Engineering M,D
Theater M
Urban and Regional Planning M,O
Writing M

UNIVERSITY OF WASHINGTON

Accounting M,D
Aerospace/Aeronautical Engineering M,D
Allopathic Medicine P
Animal Behavior D
Anthropology M,D
Applied Arts and Design—General M
Applied Mathematics M,D
Applied Physics M,D
Architecture M,D,O
Art History M,D
Art/Fine Arts M
Asian Languages M,D
Asian Studies M,D
Astronomy M,D
Atmospheric Sciences M,D
Bacteriology D
Biochemistry D
Bioengineering M,D
Bioethics M
Bioinformatics M,D
Biological and Biomedical Sciences—General M,D
Biomedical Engineering M,D
Biophysics D
Biostatistics M,D
Biotechnology D
Business Administration and Management—General M,D
Business Education M,D
Cell Biology D
Ceramic Sciences and Engineering M,D
Chemical Engineering M,D
Chemistry M,D
Chinese M,D
Civil Engineering M,D
Classics M,D
Clinical Laboratory Sciences/Medical Technology M
Clinical Psychology D
Clinical Research M,D
Cognitive Sciences D
Communication Disorders M,D
Communication—General M,D
Community Health M,D
Comparative Literature M,D
Computational Sciences M,D
Computer Science M,D
Construction Engineering M,D
Construction Management M
Curriculum and Instruction M,D
Dance M
Demography and Population Studies M,D
Dentistry P
Developmental Psychology D
East European and Russian Studies M
Ecology M,D
Economics M,D
Education—General M,D,O
Educational Leadership and Administration M,D
Educational Measurement and Evaluation M,D
Educational Media/Instructional Technology M,D
Educational Policy M,D
Educational Psychology M,D
Electrical Engineering M,D
Energy Management and Policy M,D
Engineering and Applied Sciences—General M,D
English as a Second Language M,D
English Education M,D
English M,D
Environmental and Occupational Health M,D
Environmental Engineering M,D
Environmental Management and Policy M,D
Epidemiology M,D
Finance and Banking M,D
Fish, Game, and Wildlife Management M,D
Forestry M,D
Foundations and Philosophy of Education M,D
French M,D
Genetics M,D
Genomic Sciences D
Geography M,D
Geology M,D
Geophysics M,D
Geotechnical Engineering M,D
German M,D
Health Informatics M,D
Health Services Management and Hospital Administration M
Health Services Research M,D
Higher Education M,D
Hispanic and Latin American Languages M
Hispanic Studies M,D
Historic Preservation O
History M,D
Horticulture M,D
Human Development M,D
Hydrology M,D
Immunology D
Industrial Design M
Industrial/Management Engineering M,D
Information Science M,D
Intellectual Property Law P,M,D
International Affairs M
International Business M,D,O
International Health M,D
Italian M,D
Japanese M,D
Landscape Architecture M
Law P,M,D
Legal and Justice Studies P,M,D
Library Science M,D
Lighting Design M,D,O
Linguistics M,D
Logistics O
Management of Technology M,D
Marine Affairs M,O
Marine Geology M,D
Materials Engineering M,D
Materials Sciences M,D
Maternal and Child Health M,D
Mathematics Education M,D
Mathematics M,D
Mechanical Engineering M,D
Medical Informatics M,D
Medicinal and Pharmaceutical Chemistry D
Microbiology D
Molecular Biology D
Molecular Medicine D
Multilingual and Multicultural Education M,D
Museum Studies M
Music Education M,D
Music M,D
Nanotechnology M,D
Natural Resources M,D
Near and Middle Eastern Studies M,D
Neurobiology D
Nursing—General M,D,O
Nutrition M,D
Occupational Therapy M,D
Oceanography M,D
Oral and Dental Sciences P,M,O
Parasitology D
Pathobiology D
Pathology D
Pharmaceutical Sciences M,D
Pharmacology D
Pharmacy P,M,D
Philosophy M,D
Photography M
Physical Education M,D
Physical Therapy M,D
Physics M,D
Physiology D
Political Science M,D
Portuguese M
Psychology—General D
Public Administration M,D
Public Affairs M,D
Public Policy M,D
Reading Education M,D
Rehabilitation Sciences M,D
Religion M,D
Romance Languages M,D
Russian M,D
Scandinavian Languages M,D

School Psychology	M,D
Science Education	M,D
Slavic Languages	M,D
Social Psychology	D
Social Sciences Education	M,D
Social Sciences	M,D
Social Work	M,D
Sociology	M,D
Spanish	M
Special Education	M,D
Statistics	M,D
Structural Biology	D
Structural Engineering	M,D
Sustainable Development	P,M,D
Taxation	P,M,D
Technical Communication	M,D
Theater	M,D
Toxicology	M,D
Transportation and Highway Engineering	M,D
Transportation Management	O
Urban and Regional Planning	M,D
Urban Design	M,D,O
Veterinary Sciences	M
Water Resources Engineering	M,D
Women's Studies	D
Writing	M

UNIVERSITY OF WASHINGTON, BOTHELL

Business Administration and Management—General	M
Computer Engineering	M
Cultural Studies	M
Education—General	M
Educational Leadership and Administration	M
Middle School Education	M
Nursing—General	M
Public Policy	M
Secondary Education	M
Software Engineering	M

UNIVERSITY OF WASHINGTON, TACOMA

Accounting	M
Business Administration and Management—General	M
Community Health Nursing	M
Computer Engineering	M
Education—General	M
Educational Leadership and Administration	M
Elementary Education	M
Finance and Banking	M
Interdisciplinary Studies	M
Mathematics Education	M
Nursing and Healthcare Administration	M
Nursing Education	M
Nursing—General	M
Science Education	M
Social Work	M
Software Engineering	M
Special Education	M

UNIVERSITY OF WATERLOO

Accounting	M,D
Actuarial Science	M,D
Anthropology	M
Applied Mathematics	M,D
Architecture	M
Art/Fine Arts	M
Biochemistry	M,D
Biological and Biomedical Sciences—General	M,D
Biostatistics	M,D
Business Administration and Management—General	M
Chemical Engineering	M,D
Chemistry	M,D
Civil Engineering	M,D
Computer Engineering	M,D
Computer Science	M,D
Economic Development	M
Economics	M,D
Electrical Engineering	M,D
Engineering and Applied Sciences—General	M,D
Engineering Management	M,D
English	M,D
Entrepreneurship	M
Environmental Engineering	M,D
Environmental Management and Policy	M
Finance and Banking	M,D
French	M,D
Geography	M,D
Geosciences	M,D
German	M,D
Health Education	M,D
History	M,D
Information Science	M,D
International Affairs	M,D
Kinesiology and Movement Studies	M,D
Leisure Studies	M,D
Management of Technology	M,D
Mathematics	M,D
Mechanical Engineering	M,D
Near and Middle Eastern Studies	M
Operations Research	M,D
Optometry	M,D
Philosophy	M,D
Physics	M,D
Political Science	M,D
Psychology—General	M,D
Public Affairs	M
Public Health—General	M
Recreation and Park Management	M,D
Religion	D
Russian	M,D
Sociology	M,D
Software Engineering	M,D
Statistics	M,D
Systems Engineering	M,D
Taxation	M,D
Technical Writing	M,D
Travel and Tourism	M
Urban and Regional Planning	M,D
Vision Sciences	M,D

THE UNIVERSITY OF WEST ALABAMA

Adult Education	M
Athletic Training and Sports Medicine	M
Counselor Education	M
Early Childhood Education	M
Education—General	M
Educational Leadership and Administration	M
Educational Media/Instructional Technology	M
Elementary Education	M
English Education	M
Foundations and Philosophy of Education	M
Mathematics Education	M
Physical Education	M
Science Education	M
Secondary Education	M
Social Sciences Education	M
Special Education	M

THE UNIVERSITY OF WESTERN ONTARIO

Allopathic Medicine	P,M
Anatomy	M,D
Anthropology	M,D
Applied Mathematics	M,D
Astronomy	M,D
Biochemical Engineering	M,D
Biochemistry	M,D
Biophysics	M,D
Biostatistics	M,D
Business Administration and Management—General	M,D
Cell Biology	M,D
Chemical Engineering	M,D
Chemistry	M,D
Civil Engineering	M,D
Classics	M
Communication Disorders	M
Comparative Literature	M,D
Computer Engineering	M,D
Computer Science	M,D
Counseling Psychology	M
Curriculum and Instruction	M
Dentistry	P
Economics	M,D
Education—General	M
Educational Policy	M
Educational Psychology	M
Electrical Engineering	M,D
Engineering and Applied Sciences—General	M,D
English	M,D
Entrepreneurship	M,D
Environmental Engineering	M,D
Environmental Sciences	M,D
Epidemiology	M,D
Finance and Banking	M,D
French	M,D
Geography	M,D
Geology	M,D
Geophysics	M,D
Geosciences	M,D
Health Services Management and Hospital Administration	M,D
History	M,D
Immunology	M,D
Information Studies	M,D
Interdisciplinary Studies	M,D
International Business	M,D
Journalism	M
Kinesiology and Movement Studies	M,D
Law	P,M,O
Library Science	M,D
Management Strategy and Policy	M,D
Marketing	M,D
Materials Engineering	M,D
Mathematics	M,D
Mechanical Engineering	M,D
Media Studies	M,D
Microbiology	M,D
Molecular Biology	M,D
Music	M,D
Neuroscience	M,D
Nursing—General	M,D
Occupational Therapy	M
Oral and Dental Sciences	M
Pathology	M,D
Philosophy	M,D
Physical Therapy	M,O
Physics	M,D
Physiology	M,D
Plant Biology	M,D
Plant Sciences	M,D
Political Science	M,D
Psychology—General	M,D
Sociology	M,D
Spanish	M,D
Special Education	M
Statistics	M,D
Sustainable Development	M,D
Zoology	M,D

UNIVERSITY OF WESTERN STATES

Chiropractic	P

UNIVERSITY OF WEST FLORIDA

Accounting	M
Anthropology	M
Applied Statistics	M
Archaeology	M
Biochemistry	M
Biological and Biomedical Sciences—General	M
Biotechnology	M
Business Administration and Management—General	M
Communication—General	M
Community Health	M
Computer Science	M
Counseling Psychology	M
Counselor Education	M,D,O
Criminal Justice and Criminology	M
Curriculum and Instruction	M,D,O
Database Systems	M
Early Childhood Education	M,D
Educational Leadership and Administration	M,D,O
Educational Media/Instructional Technology	M,D
Elementary Education	M,D
English	M
Environmental and Occupational Health	M
Environmental Biology	M
Environmental Sciences	M
Exercise and Sports Science	M
Gerontology	M
Health Education	M
History	M
Industrial and Organizational Psychology	M
Leisure Studies	M
Management Strategy and Policy	M
Marine Affairs	M
Mathematics	M
Middle School Education	M,D,O
Military and Defense Studies	M
Nursing and Healthcare Administration	M
Pharmaceutical Administration	M
Physical Education	M
Political Science	M
Psychology—General	M
Public Administration	M
Public Health—General	M
Public History	M
Reading Education	M
Science Education	M
Secondary Education	M,D,O
Social Work	M
Sociology	M
Software Engineering	M
Special Education	M,D
Student Affairs	M,D,O
Vocational and Technical Education	M
Writing	M

UNIVERSITY OF WEST GEORGIA

Accounting	M
Applied Mathematics	M
Art Education	M,O
Biological and Biomedical Sciences—General	M
Business Administration and Management—General	M
Business Education	M,O
Communication Disorders	M,D,O
Computer Science	M,O
Counselor Education	M,D,O
Criminal Justice and Criminology	M
Early Childhood Education	M,O
Education—General	M,D,O
Educational Leadership and Administration	M,D,O
Educational Media/Instructional Technology	M,O
English Education	M,O
English	M

*M—master's degree; P—first professional degree; D—doctorate; O—other advanced degree; *—Close-Up and/or Display in one of the other books in this series*

Foreign Languages Education M,O
French M,O
Health Services Management and Hospital Administration M,O
History M,O
Mathematics Education M,O
Mathematics M
Middle School Education M,O
Museum Studies M,O
Music Education M
Music M
Nursing Education M,O
Nursing—General M,O
Physical Education M,O
Political Science M,O
Psychology—General M,D
Public Administration M,O
Public History M,O
Reading Education M,D,O
Rural Planning and Studies M,O
Science Education M,O
Secondary Education M,O
Social Sciences Education M,O
Sociology M
Software Engineering M,O
Spanish M,O
Special Education M,D,O
Sports Management M,O

UNIVERSITY OF WINDSOR

Applied Psychology M,D
Art/Fine Arts M
Biochemistry M,D
Biological and Biomedical Sciences—General M,D
Biopsychology M,D
Business Administration and Management—General M
Chemistry M,D
Civil Engineering M,D
Clinical Psychology M,D
Communication—General M
Computer Science M,D
Criminal Justice and Criminology M,D
Economics M
Education—General M,D
Electrical Engineering M,D
Engineering and Applied Sciences—General M,D
English M
Environmental Engineering M,D
Environmental Sciences M,D
Geosciences M,D
History M
Industrial/Management Engineering M,D
Kinesiology and Movement Studies M
Legal and Justice Studies M
Manufacturing Engineering M,D
Materials Engineering M,D
Mathematics M,D
Mechanical Engineering M,D
Nursing—General M
Philosophy M
Physics M,D
Political Science M
Psychology—General M,D
Social Psychology M,D
Social Work M
Sociology M,D
Statistics M,D
Writing M

THE UNIVERSITY OF WINNIPEG

History M
Marriage and Family Therapy P,M,O
Public Administration M
Religion M
Theology P,M,O

UNIVERSITY OF WISCONSIN–EAU CLAIRE

Adult Nursing M,D
Business Administration and Management—General M
Communication Disorders M
Education—General M
Elementary Education M
English M
Family Nurse Practitioner Studies M,D
Gerontological Nursing M,D
History M
Library Science M
Nursing and Healthcare Administration M,D
Nursing Education M,D
Nursing—General M,D
Psychology—General M,O
Reading Education M
School Psychology M,O
Secondary Education M
Special Education M
Writing M

UNIVERSITY OF WISCONSIN–GREEN BAY

Business Administration and Management—General M
Education—General M
Environmental Management and Policy M
Environmental Sciences M
Social Work M

UNIVERSITY OF WISCONSIN–LA CROSSE

Athletic Training and Sports Medicine M
Biological and Biomedical Sciences—General M
Business Administration and Management—General M
Cancer Biology/Oncology M
Cell Biology M
Community Health M
Education—General M
Elementary Education M
Exercise and Sports Science M
Health Education M
Marine Sciences M
Medical Microbiology M
Microbiology M
Molecular Biology M
Nurse Anesthesia M
Occupational Therapy M
Physical Education M
Physical Therapy M,D
Physician Assistant Studies M
Physiology M
Psychology—General M,O
Public Health—General M
Recreation and Park Management M
Rehabilitation Sciences M
School Psychology M,O
Secondary Education M
Software Engineering M
Special Education M
Student Affairs M

UNIVERSITY OF WISCONSIN–MADISON

Accounting M,D
Actuarial Science M
Adult Nursing D
African Studies M,D
African-American Studies M
Agricultural Economics and Agribusiness M,D
Agricultural Engineering M,D
Agricultural Sciences—General M,D
Agronomy and Soil Sciences M,D
Allopathic Medicine P
American Studies M,D
Animal Sciences M,D
Anthropology D
Applied Arts and Design—General M,D
Applied Economics M,D
Archaeology D
Art Education M,D
Art History M,D
Art/Fine Arts M
Arts Administration M
Asian Languages M,D
Asian Studies M,D
Astronomy D
Atmospheric Sciences M,D
Bacteriology M
Biochemistry M,D
Bioengineering M,D
Biological and Biomedical Sciences—General M,D
Biomedical Engineering M,D
Biometry M
Biophysics D
Biopsychology D
Botany M,D
Business Administration and Management—General M
Cancer Biology/Oncology D
Cell Biology D
Chemical Engineering M,D
Chemistry M,D
Child and Family Studies M,D
Chinese M,D
Civil Engineering M,D
Classics M,D
Clinical Psychology D
Clinical Research M,D
Cognitive Sciences D
Communication Disorders M,D
Communication—General M,D
Community Health M,D
Comparative Literature M,D
Computer and Information Systems Security M
Computer Science M,D
Conservation Biology M
Consumer Economics M,D
Counseling Psychology D
Counselor Education M
Cultural Anthropology D
Curriculum and Instruction M,D
Developmental Psychology D
Ecology M
Economics D
Education—General M,D,O
Educational Leadership and Administration M,D,O
Educational Policy M,D,O
Educational Psychology M,D
Electrical Engineering M,D
Energy and Power Engineering M,D
Engineering and Applied Sciences—General M,D
Engineering Management M
Engineering Physics M,D
English M,D
Entomology M,D
Entrepreneurship M
Environmental Biology M,D
Environmental Engineering M,D
Environmental Sciences M,D
Epidemiology M,D
Family and Consumer Sciences-General M,D
Film, Television, and Video Theory and Criticism M,D
Finance and Banking M,D
Fish, Game, and Wildlife Management M,D
Folklore M,D
Food Science and Technology M,D
Foreign Languages Education M,D
Forestry M,D
French M,D,O
Genetic Counseling M
Genetics M,D
Geographic Information Systems M,D,O
Geography M,D,O
Geological Engineering M,D
Geology M,D
Geophysics M,D
German M,D
Gerontological Nursing D
Health Services Research M,D
History of Science and Technology M,D
History M,D
Horticulture M,D
Human Development M,D
Human Resources Management M,D
Industrial/Management Engineering M,D
Information Studies M,D
Insurance M,D
Investment Management D
Italian M,D
Japanese M,D
Jewish Studies M,D
Journalism M,D
Kinesiology and Movement Studies M,D
Landscape Architecture M
Latin American Studies M,D
Law P,M,D
Legal and Justice Studies M,D
Library Science M,D
Limnology M,D
Linguistics M,D
Management Information Systems D
Management of Technology M
Management Strategy and Policy M
Manufacturing Engineering M
Marine Sciences M,D
Marketing Research M
Marketing D
Mass Communication M,D
Materials Engineering M,D
Materials Sciences M,D
Mathematics Education M,D
Mathematics D
Mechanical Engineering M,D
Mechanics M,D
Media Studies M,D
Medical Microbiology D
Medical Physics M,D
Microbiology D
Molecular Biology D
Music Education M,D
Music M,D
Natural Resources M,D
Near and Middle Eastern Languages M,D
Near and Middle Eastern Studies M,D
Neurobiology D
Neuroscience D
Nuclear Engineering M,D
Nursing—General D
Nutrition M,D
Occupational Therapy M,D
Oceanography M,D
Pathology D*
Pediatric Nursing D
Pharmaceutical Administration M,D
Pharmaceutical Sciences M,D
Pharmacology D
Pharmacy P
Philosophy M,D
Physics M,D
Physiology M,D
Plant Pathology M,D
Plant Sciences M,D

Political Science D
Polymer Science and Engineering M,D
Portuguese M,D
Psychiatric Nursing D
Psychology—General D
Public Affairs M
Real Estate M,D
Rehabilitation Counseling M,D
Rehabilitation Sciences M
Rhetoric M,D
Rural Sociology M,D
Scandinavian Languages M,D
Science Education M,D
Slavic Languages M,D
Social Psychology D
Social Sciences D
Social Work M,D
Sociology M,D
Spanish M,D
Special Education M,D
Speech and Interpersonal Communication M,D
Statistics M,D
Supply Chain Management M
Sustainable Development M
Systems Engineering M,D
Taxation M
Theater M,D
Toxicology M,D
Urban and Regional Planning M,D
Veterinary Medicine P
Veterinary Sciences M,D
Water Resources M
Women's Studies M,D
Writing M,D
Zoology M,D

UNIVERSITY OF WISCONSIN–MILWAUKEE

Adult Education D
African Studies D
Allied Health—General M,D,O
Anthropology M,D,O
Architecture M,D,O
Archives/Archival Administration M,D,O
Art Education M
Art History M,O
Art/Fine Arts M
Biochemistry M,D
Biological and Biomedical Sciences—General M,D
Business Administration and Management—General M,D,O
Chemistry M,D
Civil Engineering M,D,O
Classics M,O
Clinical Psychology M,D
Communication Disorders M,O
Communication—General M,D,O
Comparative Literature M,D,O
Computer Engineering M,D,O
Computer Science M,D
Conflict Resolution and Mediation/Peace Studies M,D,O
Counseling Psychology M,D
Counselor Education M,D
Criminal Justice and Criminology M
Curriculum and Instruction M,D
Dance M
Developmental Psychology M,D
Early Childhood Education M
Economics M,D
Education—General M,D,O
Educational Leadership and Administration M,D,O
Educational Measurement and Evaluation M,D
Educational Media/Instructional Technology D
Educational Psychology M,D
Electrical Engineering M,D,O
Elementary Education M
Engineering and Applied Sciences—General M,D,O
Engineering Management M,D,O
English M,D,O
Ergonomics and Human Factors M,D,O
Family Nurse Practitioner Studies M,D,O
Film, Television, and Video Production M
Foundations and Philosophy of Education M,D
French M,O
Geochemistry M,D
Geographic Information Systems M,O
Geography M,D
Geology M,D
German M,O
Gerontology M,D,O
Health Education M,D,O
Health Informatics M,O
Higher Education M,O
Historic Preservation M,D,O
History M,D
Human Resources Development M,O
Industrial and Labor Relations M,O
Industrial/Management Engineering M,D,O
Information Studies M,D,O
Interdisciplinary Studies D
International Business M,O
Investment Management M,D,O
Italian M,O
Jewish Studies M,O
Kinesiology and Movement Studies M
Liberal Studies M
Library Science M,D,O
Linguistics M,D,O
Manufacturing Engineering M,D,O
Marriage and Family Therapy M,D,O
Materials Engineering M,D,O
Mathematics M,D
Mechanical Engineering M,D,O
Mechanics M,D,O
Media Studies M,O
Medical Informatics D
Middle School Education M
Multilingual and Multicultural Education D
Museum Studies M,D,O
Music Education M,O
Music M,O
Nonprofit Management M,D,O
Nursing—General M,D,O
Occupational Therapy M,O
Philosophy M
Physical Therapy D
Physics M,D
Political Science M,D
Psychology—General M,D
Public Administration M
Public Health—General M,D,O
Reading Education M
Real Estate M,O
Recreation and Park Management M,O
Rhetoric M,D,O
School Psychology D,O
Secondary Education M
Slavic Languages M,O
Social Psychology M,D
Social Work M,D,O
Sociology M
Spanish M,O
Special Education M,D,O
Taxation M,D,O
Technical Communication M,D,O
Theater M
Translation and Interpretation M,O
Urban and Regional Planning M,O
Urban Education M,D
Urban Studies M,D
Water Resources M,D
Women's Studies M
Writing M,D,O

UNIVERSITY OF WISCONSIN–OSHKOSH

Adult Nursing M
Biological and Biomedical Sciences—General M
Botany M
Business Administration and Management—General M
Counselor Education M
Curriculum and Instruction M
Early Childhood Education M
Education—General M
Educational Leadership and Administration M
English M
Experimental Psychology M
Family Nurse Practitioner Studies M
Health Services Management and Hospital Administration M
Industrial and Organizational Psychology M
International Business M
Mathematics Education M
Microbiology M
Nursing—General M
Psychology—General M
Public Administration M
Reading Education M
Social Work M
Special Education M
Zoology M

UNIVERSITY OF WISCONSIN–PARKSIDE

Business Administration and Management—General M
Computer Science M
Information Science M
Molecular Biology M

UNIVERSITY OF WISCONSIN–PLATTEVILLE

Adult Education M
Computer Science M
Counselor Education M
Criminal Justice and Criminology M
Education—General M
Elementary Education M
Engineering and Applied Sciences—General M
English Education M
Middle School Education M
Project Management M
Secondary Education M

UNIVERSITY OF WISCONSIN–RIVER FALLS

Agricultural Education M
Agricultural Sciences—General M
Art/Fine Arts M
Business Administration and Management—General M
Communication Disorders M
Counselor Education M,O
Education—General M
Elementary Education M
English as a Second Language M
Mathematics Education M
Reading Education M
School Psychology M,O
Science Education M
Social Sciences Education M

UNIVERSITY OF WISCONSIN–STEVENS POINT

Advertising and Public Relations M
Business Administration and Management—General M
Communication Disorders M,D
Communication—General M
Corporate and Organizational Communication M
Counselor Education M
Education—General M
Educational Leadership and Administration M
Elementary Education M
English M
Family and Consumer Sciences-General M
Health Promotion M
History M
Human Development M
Mass Communication M
Music Education M
Natural Resources M
Nutrition M
Reading Education M
Science Education M
Special Education M
Speech and Interpersonal Communication M

UNIVERSITY OF WISCONSIN–STOUT

Applied Psychology M
Child and Family Studies M
Counseling Psychology M
Education—General M,O
Food Science and Technology M
Human Development M
Human Resources Development M
Industrial Hygiene M
Industrial/Management Engineering M
Information Science M
Management of Technology M
Manufacturing Engineering M
Marriage and Family Therapy M
Nutrition M
Rehabilitation Counseling M
School Psychology M,O
Telecommunications Management M
Vocational and Technical Education M,O

UNIVERSITY OF WISCONSIN–SUPERIOR

Art Education M
Art History M
Art Therapy M
Art/Fine Arts M
Communication—General M
Counselor Education M
Curriculum and Instruction M
Education—General M
Educational Leadership and Administration M,O
Mass Communication M
Reading Education M
School Psychology M
Social Psychology M
Special Education M
Speech and Interpersonal Communication M
Theater M

UNIVERSITY OF WISCONSIN–WHITEWATER

Accounting M

*M—master's degree; P—first professional degree; D—doctorate; O—other advanced degree; *—Close-Up and/or Display in one of the other books in this series*

Program	Degrees
Business Administration and Management—General	M*
Business Education	M
Communication Disorders	M
Communication—General	M
Corporate and Organizational Communication	M
Counselor Education	M
Curriculum and Instruction	M
Education—General	M
Educational Leadership and Administration	M
Environmental and Occupational Health	M
Finance and Banking	M
Higher Education	M
Human Resources Management	M
International Business	M
Management of Technology	M
Marketing	M
Mass Communication	M
Psychology—General	M,O
Reading Education	M
School Psychology	M,O
Secondary Education	M
Social Psychology	M
Special Education	M
Supply Chain Management	M

UNIVERSITY OF WYOMING

Program	Degrees
Accounting	M
Adult Education	M,D,O
Agricultural Economics and Agribusiness	M
Agricultural Sciences—General	M,D
Agronomy and Soil Sciences	M,D
American Studies	M
Animal Sciences	M,D
Anthropology	M,D
Applied Economics	M
Atmospheric Sciences	M,D
Biotechnology	D
Botany	M,D
Business Administration and Management—General	M
Cell Biology	D
Chemical Engineering	M,D
Chemistry	M,D
Child Development	M
Civil Engineering	M,D
Communication Disorders	M
Communication—General	M
Community Health	M,D
Computational Biology	D
Computer Science	M,D
Consumer Economics	M
Counselor Education	M,D
Curriculum and Instruction	M,D
Distance Education Development	M,D,O
Ecology	M,D
Economics	M,D
Educational Leadership and Administration	M,D,O
Educational Media/ Instructional Technology	M,D,O
Electrical Engineering	M,D
Engineering and Applied Sciences—General	M,D
English	M
Entomology	M,D
Environmental Engineering	M
Exercise and Sports Science	M
Finance and Banking	M
Food Science and Technology	M
French	M
Genetics	D
Geography	M
Geology	M,D
Geophysics	M,D
German	M
Health Education	M
Health Promotion	M
History	M
International Affairs	M
Kinesiology and Movement Studies	M
Law	P
Mathematics Education	M,D
Mathematics	M,D
Mechanical Engineering	M,D
Microbiology	D
Molecular Biology	M,D
Music Education	M
Music	M
Natural Resources	M,D
Nursing—General	M
Nutrition	M
Pathobiology	M
Petroleum Engineering	M,D
Pharmacy	P
Philosophy	M
Physical Education	M
Physiology	M,D
Political Science	M
Psychology—General	M,D
Public Administration	M
Range Science	M,D
Reproductive Biology	M,D
Rural Planning and Studies	M
Science Education	M
Social Work	M
Sociology	M
Spanish	M
Special Education	M,D,O
Statistics	M,D
Student Affairs	M,D
Water Resources	M,D
Writing	M
Zoology	M,D

UPPER IOWA UNIVERSITY

Program	Degrees
Accounting	M
Business Administration and Management—General	M
Criminal Justice and Criminology	M
Education—General	M
Educational Leadership and Administration	M
Finance and Banking	M
Higher Education	M
Homeland Security	M
Human Resources Management	M
Human Services	M
International Business	M
Organizational Management	M
Public Administration	M
Quality Management	M

URBANA UNIVERSITY

Program	Degrees
Business Administration and Management—General	M
Criminal Justice and Criminology	M
Education—General	M
Nursing—General	M

URSULINE COLLEGE

Program	Degrees
Art Education	M
Art Therapy	M
Business Administration and Management—General	M
Early Childhood Education	M
Education—General	M
Educational Leadership and Administration	M
Historic Preservation	M
Liberal Studies	M
Mathematics Education	M
Medical/Surgical Nursing	M,D
Middle School Education	M
Nursing and Healthcare Administration	M,D
Nursing Education	M,D
Nursing—General	M,D
Reading Education	M
Science Education	M
Social Sciences Education	M
Special Education	M
Theology	M

UTAH STATE UNIVERSITY

Program	Degrees
Accounting	M
Aerospace/Aeronautical Engineering	M,D
Agricultural Education	M
Agricultural Engineering	M,D
Agricultural Sciences—General	M,D
Agronomy and Soil Sciences	M,D
American Studies	M
Animal Sciences	M,D
Applied Economics	M
Applied Mathematics	M,D
Art/Fine Arts	M
Biochemistry	M,D
Biological and Biomedical Sciences—General	M,D
Business Administration and Management—General	M
Business Education	M,D
Chemistry	M,D
Child and Family Studies	M,D
Civil Engineering	M,D,O
Clinical Psychology	M,D
Communication Disorders	M,D,O
Communication—General	M
Computer Science	M,D
Consumer Economics	M
Counseling Psychology	M,D
Counselor Education	M,D
Curriculum and Instruction	D
Disability Studies	M,D,O
Ecology	M,D
Economics	M,D
Education—General	M,D,O
Educational Measurement and Evaluation	M,D
Educational Media/ Instructional Technology	M,D,O
Electrical Engineering	M,D
Elementary Education	M
Engineering and Applied Sciences—General	M,D,O
English	M
Environmental Engineering	M,D,O
Environmental Management and Policy	M,D
Family and Consumer Sciences-General	M,D
Fish, Game, and Wildlife Management	M,D
Folklore	M
Food Science and Technology	M,D
Forestry	M,D
Geography	M,D
Geology	M
Health Education	M
History	M
Home Economics Education	M
Human Development	M,D
Human Resources Management	M
Interior Design	M
Landscape Architecture	M
Management Information Systems	M,D
Marriage and Family Therapy	M,D
Mathematics	M,D
Mechanical Engineering	M,D
Meteorology	M,D
Microbiology	M,D
Molecular Biology	M,D
Multilingual and Multicultural Education	M
Natural Resources	M
Nutrition	M,D
Physical Education	M
Physics	M,D
Plant Sciences	M,D
Political Science	M
Psychology—General	M,D
Range Science	M,D
Recreation and Park Management	M,D
Rehabilitation Counseling	M
School Psychology	M,D
Secondary Education	M
Sociology	M,D
Special Education	M,D,O
Statistics	M,D
Theater	M
Toxicology	M,D
Urban and Regional Planning	M,D
Veterinary Sciences	M,D
Vocational and Technical Education	M
Water Resources Engineering	M,D
Water Resources	M,D
Writing	M

UTAH VALLEY UNIVERSITY

Program	Degrees
Education—General	M
Nursing—General	M

UTICA COLLEGE

Program	Degrees
Accounting	M
Computer and Information Systems Security	M
Criminal Justice and Criminology	M
Education—General	M,O
Forensic Sciences	M
Health Services Management and Hospital Administration	M
Liberal Studies	M
Occupational Therapy	M
Physical Therapy	D

VALDOSTA STATE UNIVERSITY

Program	Degrees
Business Administration and Management—General	M
Clinical Psychology	M,O
Counseling Psychology	M,O
Counselor Education	M,O
Criminal Justice and Criminology	M
Educational Leadership and Administration	M,D,O
English	M
History	M
Industrial and Organizational Psychology	M,O
Information Studies	M
Library Science	M
Marriage and Family Therapy	M
Middle School Education	M,O
Psychology—General	M,O
School Psychology	M,O
Secondary Education	M,O
Social Work	M
Sociology	M
Special Education	M,O

VALLEY CITY STATE UNIVERSITY

Program	Degrees
Education—General	M
Educational Media/ Instructional Technology	M
English as a Second Language	M
Library Science	M

- Vocational and Technical Education M

VALLEY FORGE CHRISTIAN COLLEGE

- Music M
- Religion M
- Theology M

VALPARAISO UNIVERSITY

- Arts Administration M
- Asian Studies M
- Business Administration and Management—General M,O
- Clinical Psychology M,O
- Communication—General M,O
- Counseling Psychology M,O
- Counselor Education
- Education—General M
- Educational Leadership and Administration M
- Engineering Management M,O
- English as a Second Language M,O
- English M,O
- Entertainment Management M
- Ethics M,O
- Finance and Banking M
- Gerontology M,O
- History M,O
- International Business M
- International Economics M
- Law P,M
- Legal and Justice Studies O
- Liberal Studies M,O
- Management Information Systems M
- Media Studies M,O
- Nursing Education M,O
- Nursing—General M,O
- Psychology—General M,O
- School Psychology
- Sports Management M
- Theology M,O

VANCOUVER ISLAND UNIVERSITY

- Business Administration and Management—General M

VANCOUVER SCHOOL OF THEOLOGY

- Theology P,M,O

VANDERBILT UNIVERSITY

- Accounting M
- Acute Care/Critical Care Nursing M,D
- Adult Nursing M,D
- Allopathic Medicine P,M,D
- Analytical Chemistry M,D
- Anthropology M,D
- Astronomy M,D
- Biochemistry M,D
- Bioinformatics M,D
- Biological and Biomedical Sciences—General M,D
- Biomedical Engineering M,D
- Biophysics M,D
- Business Administration and Management—General M
- Cancer Biology/Oncology M,D
- Cell Biology M,D
- Chemical Engineering M,D
- Chemistry M,D
- Child and Family Studies M
- Civil Engineering M,D
- Classics M
- Clinical Research M
- Communication Disorders M,D
- Computer Science M,D
- Counselor Education M
- Economic Development M,D
- Economics P,M,D
- Education—General M,D*
- Educational Leadership and Administration M,D
- Educational Measurement and Evaluation M,D
- Educational Policy M,D
- Electrical Engineering M,D
- Elementary Education M
- Engineering and Applied Sciences—General M,D
- English Education M
- English M,D
- Environmental Engineering M,D
- Environmental Management and Policy M,D
- Environmental Sciences M
- Family Nurse Practitioner Studies M,D
- Finance and Banking M
- Foreign Languages Education M,D
- French M,D
- German M,D
- Gerontological Nursing M,D
- Higher Education M,D
- History M,D
- Human Development M
- Human Genetics D
- Immunology M,D
- Inorganic Chemistry M,D
- International and Comparative Education M,D
- Latin American Studies M
- Law P,M,D
- Liberal Studies M
- Materials Sciences M,D
- Maternal and Child/Neonatal Nursing M,D
- Mathematics M,D
- Mechanical Engineering M,D
- Medical Physics M
- Medical/Surgical Nursing M,D
- Microbiology M,D
- Molecular Biology M,D
- Molecular Physiology M,D
- Multilingual and Multicultural Education M,D
- Nurse Midwifery M,D
- Nursing and Healthcare Administration M,D
- Nursing Informatics M,D
- Nursing—General M,D
- Nutrition M,D
- Organic Chemistry M,D
- Organizational Management M,D
- Pathology D
- Pediatric Nursing M,D
- Pharmacology D
- Philosophy M,D
- Physical Chemistry M,D
- Physics M,D
- Political Science M,D
- Portuguese M,D
- Psychiatric Nursing M,D
- Psychology—General M,D
- Public Health—General M
- Public Policy M,D
- Reading Education M
- Religion M,D
- Science Education M,D
- Secondary Education M
- Sociology M,D
- Spanish M,D
- Special Education M,D
- Theology P,M
- Theoretical Chemistry M,D
- Urban and Regional Planning M
- Urban Education M
- Women's Health Nursing M,D
- Writing M

VANDERCOOK COLLEGE OF MUSIC

- Music Education M

VANGUARD UNIVERSITY OF SOUTHERN CALIFORNIA

- Business Administration and Management—General M
- Clinical Psychology M
- Education—General M
- Religion M
- Theology M

VAUGHN COLLEGE OF AERONAUTICS AND TECHNOLOGY

- Aviation Management M

VERMONT COLLEGE OF FINE ARTS

- Art/Fine Arts M
- Graphic Design M
- Music M
- Writing M

VERMONT LAW SCHOOL

- Environmental Law M,O
- Environmental Management and Policy M,O
- Law P,O
- Legal and Justice Studies M,O

VICTORIA UNIVERSITY

- Theology P,M,D,O

VILLANOVA UNIVERSITY

- Accounting M
- Adult Nursing M,D,O
- American Studies M,O
- Applied Statistics M
- Artificial Intelligence/Robotics M,O
- Biochemical Engineering M,O
- Biological and Biomedical Sciences—General M
- Business Administration and Management—General M
- Chemical Engineering M,O
- Chemistry M
- Civil Engineering M
- Communication—General M
- Computer Engineering M,O
- Computer Science M,O
- Counselor Education M
- Education—General M
- Educational Leadership and Administration M
- Electrical Engineering M,O
- Elementary Education M
- Engineering and Applied Sciences—General M,D,O
- English M
- Environmental Engineering M,O
- Family Nurse Practitioner Studies M,D,O
- Finance and Banking M
- Health Services Management and Hospital Administration M,D,O
- Higher Education M
- Hispanic Studies M
- History M
- Human Resources Development M
- Humanities M
- International Business M
- Law P
- Liberal Studies M,O
- Management Information Systems M
- Management Strategy and Policy M
- Manufacturing Engineering M,O
- Marketing M
- Mathematics M
- Mechanical Engineering M,O
- Missions and Missiology M
- Nurse Anesthesia M,D,O
- Nursing and Healthcare Administration M,D,O
- Nursing Education M,D,O
- Nursing—General M,D,O
- Pediatric Nursing M,D,O
- Philosophy D
- Political Science M
- Psychology—General M
- Public Administration M
- Real Estate M
- Secondary Education M
- Software Engineering M
- Taxation M
- Theater M
- Theology M
- Water Resources Engineering M,O

VIRGINIA COLLEGE AT BIRMINGHAM

- Business Administration and Management—General M
- Criminal Justice and Criminology M

VIRGINIA COMMONWEALTH UNIVERSITY

- Accounting M,D
- Adult Education M
- Adult Nursing M,D,O
- Advertising and Public Relations M
- Allied Health—General D
- Allopathic Medicine P
- Analytical Chemistry M,D
- Anatomy D,O
- Applied Arts and Design—General M
- Applied Mathematics M
- Applied Physics M
- Applied Social Research M,O
- Architectural History M,D
- Art Education M
- Art History M,D
- Art/Fine Arts M,D
- Athletic Training and Sports Medicine M
- Biochemistry M,D,O
- Bioengineering M,D
- Bioinformatics M,D
- Biological and Biomedical Sciences—General M,D,O
- Biomedical Engineering M,D
- Biopsychology D
- Biostatistics M,D
- Business Administration and Management—General M,O
- Chemical Engineering M,D
- Chemical Physics M,D
- Chemistry M,D
- Clinical Laboratory Sciences/Medical Technology M,D
- Clinical Psychology D
- Communication—General D
- Computer Science M,D
- Counseling Psychology M,D,O
- Counselor Education M
- Criminal Justice and Criminology M,O
- Dentistry P,M
- Developmental Psychology D
- Early Childhood Education M,O
- Economics M
- Education—General M,D,O
- Educational Leadership and Administration D
- Educational Measurement and Evaluation D
- Educational Media/Instructional Technology M
- Educational Policy D
- Educational Psychology D
- Electrical Engineering M,D

*M—master's degree; P—first professional degree; D—doctorate; O—other advanced degree; *—Close-Up and/or Display in one of the other books in this series*

Elementary Education M,O
Emergency Management M,O
Engineering and Applied Sciences—General M,D
English M
Environmental Management and Policy M
Exercise and Sports Science M
Family Nurse Practitioner Studies M,O
Finance and Banking M
Forensic Sciences M
Genetics M,D
Geographic Information Systems O
Gerontology M,D,O
Health Education M,O
Health Physics/Radiological Health D
Health Psychology D
Health Services Management and Hospital Administration M,D
Health Services Research D
Historic Preservation O
History M,D
Homeland Security M,O
Human Genetics M,D,O
Human Resources Development M
Humanities M,D,O
Immunology M,D
Inorganic Chemistry M,D
Insurance M
Interdisciplinary Studies M
Interior Design M
Internet and Interactive Multimedia M
Journalism M
Management Information Systems M,D
Marketing M
Mass Communication M
Mathematics M
Mechanical Engineering M,D
Media Studies M,D
Medical Physics M,D
Medicinal and Pharmaceutical Chemistry M,D
Microbiology M,D,O
Molecular Biology M,D
Museum Studies M,D
Music Education M
Music M
Nanotechnology M,D
Neurobiology D
Neuroscience M,D,O
Nonprofit Management O
Nurse Anesthesia M,D
Nursing and Healthcare Administration M,D,O
Nursing Education M,D,O
Nursing—General M,D,O
Occupational Therapy M,D
Operations Research M
Organic Chemistry M,D
Pathology D
Pediatric Nursing M,D,O
Pharmaceutical Administration M,D
Pharmaceutical Sciences M,D
Pharmacology M,D,O
Pharmacy P
Photography M,D
Physical Chemistry M,D
Physical Education M,D,O
Physical Therapy M,D
Physics M
Physiology M,D,O
Political Science M,D,O
Psychiatric Nursing M,D,O
Psychology—General D
Public Administration M,O
Public Affairs M,D,O
Public Health—General M,D
Public Policy D
Quantitative Analysis M
Reading Education M,O
Real Estate M,O
Recreation and Park Management M
Rehabilitation Counseling M,O
Rehabilitation Sciences D
Rhetoric M
Secondary Education M,O
Social Psychology D
Social Work M,D
Sociology M,O
Special Education M,D,O
Statistics M
Student Affairs M
Systems Biology D
Taxation M
Theater M
Toxicology M,D,O
Urban and Regional Planning M
Urban Education D
Women's Health Nursing M,D,O
Writing M

VIRGINIA INTERNATIONAL UNIVERSITY

Accounting M,O
Business Administration and Management—General M,O
Computer Science M
English as a Second Language M,O
Finance and Banking M,O
Health Services Management and Hospital Administration M,O
Human Resources Management M,O
International Business M,O
Logistics M,O
Management Information Systems M
Marketing M,O

VIRGINIA POLYTECHNIC INSTITUTE AND STATE UNIVERSITY

Accounting M,D
Aerospace/Aeronautical Engineering M,D,O
Agricultural Economics and Agribusiness M,D
Agricultural Education M,D
Agricultural Engineering M,D
Agronomy and Soil Sciences M,D
Animal Sciences M,D
Applied Arts and Design—General M,D
Applied Economics M,D
Architecture M,D
Art/Fine Arts D,O
Biochemistry M,D
Bioengineering M,D
Bioinformatics D
Biological and Biomedical Sciences—General M,D
Biomedical Engineering M,D
Biotechnology M
Business Administration and Management—General M,D
Chemical Engineering M,D
Chemistry M,D
Civil Engineering M,D,O
Clothing and Textiles M,D
Cognitive Sciences M,D,O
Communication—General M
Computational Biology D
Computer and Information Systems Security M,D,O
Computer Engineering M,D,O
Computer Science M,O
Construction Engineering M
Consumer Economics M,D
Counselor Education M,D,O
Curriculum and Instruction M,D,O
Distance Education Development M,O
Economic Development M,D,O
Economics D
Educational Leadership and Administration M,D,O
Educational Measurement and Evaluation M,D,O
Educational Media/Instructional Technology M,O
Educational Policy M,D,O
Electrical Engineering M,D,O
Engineering and Applied Sciences—General M,D,O
Engineering Management M,O
English M,D
Entomology M,D
Environmental Design D
Environmental Engineering M,D,O
Environmental Management and Policy M,D,O
Environmental Sciences M,D,O
Finance and Banking M,D
Fish, Game, and Wildlife Management M,D
Food Science and Technology M,D,O
Foreign Languages Education M
Forestry M,D,O
Gender Studies M,D,O
Genetics D
Geographic Information Systems D,O
Geography M,D
Geosciences M,D
Gerontological Nursing M,D,O
Hazardous Materials Management M,D,O
Higher Education M,D,O
History of Science and Technology M,D,O
History M
Homeland Security M,D,O
Horticulture M,D
Hospitality Management M,D
Human-Computer Interaction M,D,O
Humanities D,O
Hydrology M,D,O
Industrial/Management Engineering M,D,O
Interdisciplinary Studies M,D,O
Interior Design M,D
International Affairs M,D,O
Internet and Interactive Multimedia M
Landscape Architecture M,D,O
Liberal Studies M,O
Management Information Systems M,D,O
Marketing M,D
Marriage and Family Therapy M,D,O
Materials Engineering M,D
Materials Sciences M,D
Mathematics Education D,O
Mathematics M,D
Mechanical Engineering M,D
Mechanics M,D,O
Microbiology D
Mineral/Mining Engineering M,D
Molecular Biology D
National Security M,O
Natural Resources M,O
Nonprofit Management M,D,O
Nutrition M,D
Ocean Engineering M,O
Philosophy M
Physics M,D
Plant Pathology M,D
Plant Physiology M,D
Political Science M,D,O
Psychology—General M,D
Public Administration M,D,O
Public Affairs M,D,O
Public Health—General M
Public Policy M,O
Quantitative Analysis M,O
Religion O
Social Sciences Education D,O
Sociology M,D,O
Software Engineering M,O
Statistics M,D
Systems Engineering M,D,O
Theater M
Transportation and Highway Engineering M,D,O
Travel and Tourism M,D
Urban and Regional Planning M,D,O
Veterinary Medicine P
Veterinary Sciences M,D
Vocational and Technical Education M,D,O
Water Resources Engineering M,D,O
Water Resources M,D,O
Women's Studies M,D,O

VIRGINIA STATE UNIVERSITY

Agricultural Sciences—General M
Biological and Biomedical Sciences—General M
Clinical Psychology M,D
Community Health M,D
Computer Science M
Economics M
Education—General M,O
Educational Leadership and Administration M
English M
Health Education M,D
Health Psychology M,D
History M
Interdisciplinary Studies M
Mathematics Education M
Mathematics M
Physics M
Plant Sciences M
Psychology—General M,D
Vocational and Technical Education M,O

VIRGINIA THEOLOGICAL SEMINARY

Theology P,M,D

VIRGINIA UNION UNIVERSITY

Theology P,D

VIRGINIA UNIVERSITY OF LYNCHBURG

Religion P

VITERBO UNIVERSITY

Business Administration and Management—General M
Education—General M
Nursing—General M

WAGNER COLLEGE

Accounting M
Biological and Biomedical Sciences—General M
Business Administration and Management—General M
Early Childhood Education M
Education—General M
Educational Leadership and Administration M
Elementary Education M
Family Nurse Practitioner Studies O
Finance and Banking M
Health Services Management and Hospital Administration M
International Business M
Marketing M
Microbiology M

Middle School Education	M
Nursing—General	M
Physician Assistant Studies	M
Reading Education	M
Secondary Education	M

WAKE FOREST UNIVERSITY

Accounting	M
Allopathic Medicine	P
Analytical Chemistry	M,D
Anatomy	D
Biochemistry	D
Biological and Biomedical Sciences—General	M,D
Biomedical Engineering	M,D
Business Administration and Management—General	M
Cancer Biology/Oncology	D
Chemistry	M,D
Communication—General	M
Computer Science	M
Counselor Education	M
Education—General	M
English	M
Entrepreneurship	M
Exercise and Sports Science	M
Finance and Banking	M
Genomic Sciences	D
Health Services Management and Hospital Administration	M
Health Services Research	M
Human Genetics	D
Immunology	D
Industrial and Manufacturing Management	M
Inorganic Chemistry	M,D
Law	P,M,D
Liberal Studies	M
Marketing	M
Mathematics	M
Microbiology	D
Molecular Biology	D
Molecular Genetics	D
Molecular Medicine	M,D
Neurobiology	D
Neuroscience	D
Organic Chemistry	M,D
Pathobiology	M,D
Pharmacology	D
Physical Chemistry	M,D
Physics	M,D
Physiology	D
Psychology—General	M
Religion	M
Secondary Education	M
Speech and Interpersonal Communication	M
Taxation	M

WALDEN UNIVERSITY

Accounting	M,D
Adult Education	M,D,O
Business Administration and Management—General	M,D
Child and Family Studies	M,D
Clinical Psychology	M,D,O
Clinical Research	M,D,O
Community College Education	M,D,O
Community Health	M,D,O
Computer and Information Systems Security	M,D
Conflict Resolution and Mediation/Peace Studies	M,D,O
Counseling Psychology	M,D,O
Counselor Education	M,D
Criminal Justice and Criminology	M,D,O
Curriculum and Instruction	M,D,O
Developmental Education	M,D,O
Developmental Psychology	M,D,O
Distance Education Development	M,D,O
Early Childhood Education	M,D,O
Education—General	M,D,O
Educational Leadership and Administration	M,D,O
Educational Measurement and Evaluation	M,D,O
Educational Media/Instructional Technology	M,D,O
Educational Policy	M,D,O
Elementary Education	M,D,O
Emergency Management	M,D,O
Engineering Management	M,D
English as a Second Language	M,D,O
Entrepreneurship	M,D
Epidemiology	M,D,O
Finance and Banking	M,D
Forensic Psychology	M,D,O
Health Informatics	M,D,O
Health Promotion	M,D,O
Health Psychology	M,D,O
Health Services Management and Hospital Administration	M,D,O
Higher Education	M,D,O
Homeland Security	M,D,O
Human Resources Development	M,D,O
Human Resources Management	M,D
Human Services	M,D
Industrial and Organizational Psychology	M,D,O
International Affairs	M,D,O
International and Comparative Education	M,D,O
International Business	M,D
International Development	M,D,O
Law	M,D,O
Management Information Systems	M,D
Management of Technology	M,D
Management Strategy and Policy	M,D
Marketing	M,D
Marriage and Family Therapy	M,D
Mathematics Education	M,D,O
Middle School Education	M,D,O
Multilingual and Multicultural Education	M,D,O
Nonprofit Management	M,D,O
Nursing and Healthcare Administration	M,O
Nursing Education	M,O
Nursing Informatics	M,O
Nursing—General	M,O
Organizational Management	M,D,O
Project Management	M,D
Psychology—General	M,D,O
Public Administration	M,D,O
Public Health—General	M,D,O
Public Policy	M,D,O
Quantitative Analysis	M,D
Reading Education	M,D,O
Science Education	M,D,O
Secondary Education	M,D,O
Social Psychology	M,D,O
Social Work	M,D
Software Engineering	M,D
Special Education	M,D,O
Supply Chain Management	M,D
Sustainability Management	M,D
Sustainable Development	M,D,O

WALLA WALLA UNIVERSITY

Biological and Biomedical Sciences—General	M
Counseling Psychology	M
Curriculum and Instruction	M
Education—General	M
Educational Leadership and Administration	M
Reading Education	M
Social Work	M
Special Education	M

WALSH COLLEGE OF ACCOUNTANCY AND BUSINESS ADMINISTRATION

Accounting	M
Business Administration and Management—General	M
Finance and Banking	M
Management Information Systems	M
Taxation	M

WALSH UNIVERSITY

Business Administration and Management—General	M
Corporate and Organizational Communication	M
Counseling Psychology	M
Counselor Education	M
Education—General	M
Health Services Management and Hospital Administration	M
Marketing	M
Physical Therapy	D
Theology	M

WARNER PACIFIC COLLEGE

Business Administration and Management—General	M
Education—General	M
Ethics	M
Organizational Management	M
Pastoral Ministry and Counseling	M
Religion	M
Theology	M

WARNER UNIVERSITY

Business Administration and Management—General	M
Education—General	M

WARREN WILSON COLLEGE

Writing	M

WARTBURG THEOLOGICAL SEMINARY

Theology	P,M

WASHBURN UNIVERSITY

Adult Nursing	M
Business Administration and Management—General	M
Clinical Psychology	M
Criminal Justice and Criminology	M
Curriculum and Instruction	M
Education—General	M
Educational Leadership and Administration	M
Family Nurse Practitioner Studies	M
Law	P
Liberal Studies	M
Nursing and Healthcare Administration	M
Nursing—General	M
Psychology—General	M
Reading Education	M
Social Work	M
Special Education	M

WASHINGTON ADVENTIST UNIVERSITY

Business Administration and Management—General	M
Counseling Psychology	M
Nursing and Healthcare Administration	M
Nursing—General	M
Public Administration	M
Religion	M

WASHINGTON AND LEE UNIVERSITY

Law	P,M

WASHINGTON COLLEGE

English	M
History	M
Psychology—General	M

WASHINGTON STATE UNIVERSITY

Accounting	M,D
Agricultural Economics and Agribusiness	M,D,O
Agricultural Engineering	M,D
Agricultural Sciences—General	M
Agronomy and Soil Sciences	M,D
American Studies	M,D
Animal Sciences	M,D
Anthropology	M,D
Applied Economics	M,D,O
Applied Mathematics	M,D
Applied Statistics	M
Archaeology	M,D
Architecture	M
Art/Fine Arts	M
Asian Studies	M,D
Biochemistry	M,D
Bioengineering	M,D
Biological and Biomedical Sciences—General	M
Biophysics	M,D
Botany	M,D
Business Administration and Management—General	M,D
Cell Biology	M,D
Chemical Engineering	M,D
Chemistry	M,D
Civil Engineering	M,D
Clinical Psychology	M,D
Clothing and Textiles	M,D
Communication—General	M,D
Computer Art and Design	M
Computer Engineering	M,D
Computer Science	M,D
Corporate and Organizational Communication	M,D
Counseling Psychology	M,D,O
Criminal Justice and Criminology	M,D
Cultural Anthropology	M,D
Cultural Studies	M,D
Curriculum and Instruction	M,D
Demography and Population Studies	M,D
Economics	M,D,O
Education—General	M,D,O
Educational Leadership and Administration	M,D
Educational Psychology	M,D,O
Electrical Engineering	M,D
Elementary Education	M,D
Engineering and Applied Sciences—General	M,D
English Education	M,D
English	M,D
Entomology	M,D
Environmental Engineering	M
Environmental Sciences	M,D
Ethnic Studies	M,D

*M—master's degree; P—first professional degree; D—doctorate; O—other advanced degree; *—Close-Up and/or Display in one of the other books in this series*

Exercise and Sports Science	M,D
Experimental Psychology	M,D
Finance and Banking	M,D
Food Science and Technology	M,D
Foreign Languages Education	M
Genetics	M,D
Geology	M,D
Geosciences	M,D
Health Communication	M,D
Health Services Management and Hospital Administration	M
Higher Education	M,D,O
History	M,D
Horticulture	M,D
Human Development	M
Industrial and Manufacturing Management	M,D
Interdisciplinary Studies	D
Interior Design	M,D
International Affairs	M,D
International Business	M,D,O
Landscape Architecture	M,D
Management Information Systems	M,D
Marketing	M,D
Materials Engineering	M
Materials Sciences	M,D
Mathematics Education	M,D
Mathematics	M,D
Mechanical Engineering	M,D
Media Studies	M,D
Microbiology	M,D
Molecular Biology	M,D
Multilingual and Multicultural Education	M,D
Music Education	M
Music	M
Natural Resources	M,D
Neuroscience	M,D
Nutrition	M,D
Pharmacy	P,D
Philosophy	M
Photography	M
Physics	M,D
Plant Molecular Biology	M,D
Plant Pathology	M,D
Political Science	M,D
Psychology—General	M,D
Public History	M,D
Public Policy	M,D
Reading Education	M,D
School Psychology	M,D,O
Secondary Education	M,D
Social Psychology	M,D
Sociology	M,D
Spanish	M
Sports Management	M,D,O
Statistics	M
Student Affairs	M,D,O
Taxation	M
Veterinary Medicine	P
Veterinary Sciences	M,D
Western European Studies	M,D
Women's Studies	M,D
Zoology	M,D

WASHINGTON STATE UNIVERSITY SPOKANE

Architecture	M,D
Communication Disorders	M
Criminal Justice and Criminology	M,D
Education—General	M,O
Educational Leadership and Administration	M,O
Engineering Management	M
Exercise and Sports Science	M
Health Services Management and Hospital Administration	M
Interior Design	M,D
Landscape Architecture	M,D
Nursing—General	M
Pharmacy	P

WASHINGTON STATE UNIVERSITY TRI-CITIES

Biological and Biomedical Sciences—General	M
Business Administration and Management—General	M
Chemistry	M,D
Computer Engineering	M,D
Computer Science	M,D
Counselor Education	M,D
Education—General	M,D
Educational Leadership and Administration	M,D
Electrical Engineering	M,D
Engineering and Applied Sciences—General	M,D
Environmental Sciences	M,D
Mechanical Engineering	M,D
Nursing—General	M
Reading Education	M,D
Secondary Education	M,D

WASHINGTON STATE UNIVERSITY VANCOUVER

Business Administration and Management—General	M
Computer Science	M
Education—General	M,D
Engineering and Applied Sciences—General	M
Environmental Sciences	M
History	M
Mechanical Engineering	M
Nursing—General	M
Public Affairs	M

WASHINGTON THEOLOGICAL UNION

Theology	P,M,D

WASHINGTON UNIVERSITY IN ST. LOUIS

Accounting	M
Aerospace/Aeronautical Engineering	M,D
Allied Health—General	M,D,O
Allopathic Medicine	P
Anthropology	D
Archaeology	M,D
Architecture	M
Art History	M,D
Art/Fine Arts	M*
Asian Languages	M,D
Asian Studies	M
Biochemistry	D
Biological and Biomedical Sciences—General	D
Biomedical Engineering	M,D
Business Administration and Management—General	M,D
Cell Biology	D
Chemical Engineering	M,D
Chemistry	D
Chinese	M,D
Classics	M
Clinical Psychology	D
Clinical Research	M
Communication Disorders	M,D
Comparative Literature	M,D
Computational Biology	D
Computer Engineering	M,D
Computer Science	M,D*
Developmental Biology	D
Ecology	D
Economics	D
Education—General	M,D
Educational Measurement and Evaluation	D
Electrical Engineering	M,D
Elementary Education	M
Engineering and Applied Sciences—General	M,D
English	M,D
Environmental Biology	D
Environmental Engineering	M,D
Evolutionary Biology	D
Experimental Psychology	D
Finance and Banking	M
French	M,D
Genetics	M,D,O
Genomic Sciences	M
Geosciences	M,D
German	M,D
History	M,D
Immunology	D
Japanese	M,D
Kinesiology and Movement Studies	D
Law	P,M,D
Mathematics	M,D
Mechanical Engineering	M,D
Microbiology	D
Molecular Biology	D
Molecular Biophysics	D
Molecular Genetics	D
Molecular Pathogenesis	D
Music	M,D
Neuroscience	D
Occupational Therapy	M,D
Philosophy	M,D
Physical Therapy	D,O
Physics	D
Planetary and Space Sciences	M,D
Plant Biology	D
Political Science	M,D
Psychology—General	D
Public Health—General	M,D
Public Policy	M
Romance Languages	M,D
Secondary Education	M
Social Psychology	D
Social Work	M,D
Spanish	M,D
Special Education	M,D
Speech and Interpersonal Communication	M,D
Statistics	M,D
Structural Engineering	M,D
Supply Chain Management	M
Systems Science	M,D
Translational Biology	M
Urban Design	M
Writing	M

WAYLAND BAPTIST UNIVERSITY

Business Administration and Management—General	M
Counseling Psychology	M
Criminal Justice and Criminology	M
Education—General	M
Educational Leadership and Administration	M
Educational Media/Instructional Technology	M
Health Services Management and Hospital Administration	M
Higher Education	M
Homeland Security	M
Human Resources Management	M
Interdisciplinary Studies	M
International Business	M
Management Information Systems	M
Organizational Management	M
Pastoral Ministry and Counseling	M
Public Administration	M
Religion	M
Special Education	M

WAYNESBURG UNIVERSITY

Addictions/Substance Abuse Counseling	M,D
Business Administration and Management—General	M,D
Clinical Psychology	M,D
Counseling Psychology	M,D
Education—General	M,D
Educational Media/Instructional Technology	M,D
Finance and Banking	M,D
Health Services Management and Hospital Administration	M,D
Human Resources Management	M,D
Medical/Surgical Nursing	M,D
Nursing and Healthcare Administration	M,D
Nursing Education	M,D
Nursing Informatics	M,D
Nursing—General	M,D
Organizational Management	M,D
Special Education	M,D

WAYNE STATE COLLEGE

Business Administration and Management—General	M
Business Education	M
Communication—General	M
Counselor Education	M
Curriculum and Instruction	M
Early Childhood Education	M
Education—General	M,O
Educational Leadership and Administration	M,O
Elementary Education	M
English as a Second Language	M
English Education	M
Exercise and Sports Science	M
Home Economics Education	M
Mathematics Education	M
Music Education	M
Organizational Management	M
Physical Education	M
Science Education	M
Social Sciences Education	M
Special Education	M
Sports Management	M
Vocational and Technical Education	M

WAYNE STATE UNIVERSITY

Accounting	M,D
Acute Care/Critical Care Nursing	M
Adult Education	M,D,O
Adult Nursing	M
Advertising and Public Relations	M,D
Allopathic Medicine	P
Anatomy	M,D
Anthropology	M,D
Applied Arts and Design—General	M
Applied Mathematics	M,D
Archives/Archival Administration	M,O
Art Education	M,D,O
Art History	M
Art/Fine Arts	M
Automotive Engineering	M,O
Biochemistry	M,D
Biological and Biomedical Sciences—General	M,D
Biomedical Engineering	M,D
Biopsychology	M,D
Business Administration and Management—General	M,D*
Business Education	M,D,O

Program	Degrees
Cancer Biology/Oncology	M,D*
Chemical Engineering	M,D
Chemistry	M,D
Civil Engineering	M,D
Classics	M
Clinical Psychology	M,D,O
Communication Disorders	M,D
Communication—General	M,D
Community Health Nursing	M
Community Health	M,O
Comparative Literature	M
Computer Engineering	M,D
Computer Science	M,D,O
Conflict Resolution and Mediation/Peace Studies	M,O
Corporate and Organizational Communication	M,D
Counselor Education	M,D,O
Criminal Justice and Criminology	M
Curriculum and Instruction	M,D,O
Early Childhood Education	M,D,O
Economics	M,D
Education—General	M,D,O
Educational Leadership and Administration	M,D,O
Educational Measurement and Evaluation	M,D,O
Educational Media/ Instructional Technology	M,D,O
Educational Policy	M,D,O
Educational Psychology	M,D,O
Electrical Engineering	M,D
Elementary Education	M,D,O
Engineering and Applied Sciences—General	M,D,O
Engineering Management	M
English Education	M,D,O
English	M,D
Environmental and Occupational Health	M,O
Food Science and Technology	M,D
Foreign Languages Education	M,D,O
Foundations and Philosophy of Education	M,D,O
French	M,D
Genetic Counseling	M
Genetics	M,D
Geography	M
Geology	M
German	M,D
Health Education	M,D,O
Health Physics/ Radiological Health	M,D
Higher Education	M,D,O
History	M,D
Immunology	M,D
Industrial and Organizational Psychology	M,D
Industrial/Management Engineering	M,D
Information Studies	M,O
Italian	M
Kinesiology and Movement Studies	M
Law	P,M,D
Library Science	M,O
Linguistics	M
Manufacturing Engineering	M
Materials Engineering	M,D,O
Materials Sciences	M,D,O
Maternal and Child/ Neonatal Nursing	M,O
Mathematics Education	M,D,O
Mathematics	M,D
Mechanical Engineering	M,D
Media Studies	M,D
Medical Physics	M,D
Medicinal and Pharmaceutical Chemistry	P,M,D
Metallurgical Engineering and Metallurgy	M,D,O
Microbiology	M,D
Molecular Biology	M,D
Multilingual and Multicultural Education	M,D,O
Music Education	M,O
Music	M,O
Near and Middle Eastern Languages	M
Near and Middle Eastern Studies	M
Neuroscience	M,D
Nurse Anesthesia	M,O
Nursing Education	M,O
Nursing—General	D
Nutrition	M,D
Occupational Therapy	M
Pathology	M,D
Pediatric Nursing	M,O
Pharmaceutical Administration	P,M,D,O
Pharmaceutical Sciences	P,M,D,O
Pharmacology	P,M,D
Pharmacy	P,M,D,O
Philosophy	M,D
Physical Education	M
Physical Therapy	D
Physician Assistant Studies	M
Physics	M,D
Physiology	M,D
Political Science	M,D
Polymer Science and Engineering	M,D,O
Psychiatric Nursing	M,O
Psychology—General	M,D
Public Administration	M
Public Health—General	M,O
Reading Education	M,D,O
Recreation and Park Management	M
Rehabilitation Counseling	M,D,O
Russian	M,D
School Psychology	M,D,O
Science Education	M,D,O
Secondary Education	M,D,O
Social Sciences Education	M,D,O
Social Work	M,D,O
Sociology	M,D
Spanish	M,D
Special Education	M,D,O
Speech and Interpersonal Communication	M,D
Sports Management	M
Statistics	M,D
Sustainable Development	O
Taxation	M,D
Theater	M,D
Toxicology	M,D
Urban and Regional Planning	M
Vocational and Technical Education	M,D,O
Writing	M,D

WEBBER INTERNATIONAL UNIVERSITY

Program	Degrees
Accounting	M
Business Administration and Management—General	M
Criminal Justice and Criminology	M
Sports Management	M

WEBER STATE UNIVERSITY

Program	Degrees
Accounting	M
Athletic Training and Sports Medicine	M
Business Administration and Management—General	M
Curriculum and Instruction	M
Education—General	M
English	M
Health Services Management and Hospital Administration	M
Legal and Justice Studies	M
Taxation	M

WEBSTER UNIVERSITY

Program	Degrees
Advertising and Public Relations	M
Aerospace/Aeronautical Engineering	M,D,O
Art/Fine Arts	M
Arts Administration	M
Business Administration and Management—General	M,D,O
Communication—General	M
Computer Science	M,O
Corporate and Organizational Communication	M
Counseling Psychology	M
Criminal Justice and Criminology	M,D,O
Early Childhood Education	M
Education—General	M,O
Educational Leadership and Administration	M,O
Educational Media/ Instructional Technology	M,O
Engineering Management	M
English as a Second Language	M
Environmental Management and Policy	M,D,O
Finance and Banking	M
Gerontology	M
Health Services Management and Hospital Administration	M,D,O
Human Resources Development	M,D,O
Human Resources Management	M,D,O
Intellectual Property Law	M,O
International Affairs	M
International Business	M
Legal and Justice Studies	M
Management Information Systems	M,D,O
Marketing	M,D,O
Mathematics Education	M,O
Media Studies	M
Music Education	M
Music	M
Nonprofit Management	M,D,O
Nurse Anesthesia	M
Nursing—General	M,O
Organizational Management	M
Public Administration	M,D,O
Quality Management	M,D,O
Social Sciences Education	M,O
Special Education	M,O
Telecommunications Management	M,D,O

WENTWORTH INSTITUTE OF TECHNOLOGY

Program	Degrees
Architecture	M*
Construction Management	M*

WESLEYAN COLLEGE

Program	Degrees
Business Administration and Management—General	M
Early Childhood Education	M
Education—General	M

WESLEYAN UNIVERSITY

Program	Degrees
Animal Behavior	D
Astronomy	M
Biochemistry	M,D
Bioinformatics	D
Biological and Biomedical Sciences—General	D
Cell Biology	D
Chemical Physics	M,D
Chemistry	M,D
Computer Science	M,D
Developmental Biology	D
Ecology	D
Environmental Sciences	M
Evolutionary Biology	D
Genetics	D
Genomic Sciences	D
Geosciences	M
Inorganic Chemistry	M,D
Liberal Studies	M,O
Mathematics	M,D*
Molecular Biology	D
Music	M,D
Neurobiology	D
Organic Chemistry	M,D
Physics	M,D
Theoretical Chemistry	M,D

WESLEY BIBLICAL SEMINARY

Program	Degrees
Marriage and Family Therapy	P,M
Missions and Missiology	P,M
Pastoral Ministry and Counseling	P,M
Religion	P,M
Religious Education	P,M
Theology	P,M

WESLEY COLLEGE

Program	Degrees
Business Administration and Management—General	M
Education—General	M
Environmental Management and Policy	M
Nursing—General	M

WESLEY THEOLOGICAL SEMINARY

Program	Degrees
Theology	P,M,D

WEST CHESTER UNIVERSITY OF PENNSYLVANIA

Program	Degrees
Anthropology	M,O
Applied Statistics	M,O
Astronomy	M,O
Athletic Training and Sports Medicine	M,O
Biological and Biomedical Sciences—General	M,O
Business Administration and Management—General	M,O
Chemistry	O
Clinical Psychology	M,O
Communication Disorders	M,O
Communication—General	M
Community Health Nursing	M,O
Community Health	M,O
Computer and Information Systems Security	M,O
Computer Science	M,O
Counselor Education	M,O
Criminal Justice and Criminology	M
Early Childhood Education	M,O
Education—General	M,O
Educational Media/ Instructional Technology	M,O
Elementary Education	M,O
Emergency Management	M,O
English as a Second Language	M,O
English	M,O
Entrepreneurship	M,O
Environmental and Occupational Health	M,O
Ethics	M,O
Exercise and Sports Science	M,O
Foreign Languages Education	M,O
French	M,O
Geographic Information Systems	M,O
Geography	M,O
Geology	M,O
Geosciences	M,O
Gerontology	M,O
Health Education	M,O

*M—master's degree; P—first professional degree; D—doctorate; O—other advanced degree; *—Close-Up and/or Display in one of the other books in this series*

Health Psychology M,O
Health Services Management and Hospital Administration M,O
History M,O
Holocaust and Genocide Studies M,O
Human Resources Management M,O
Industrial and Organizational Psychology M,O
Kinesiology and Movement Studies M,O
Management Information Systems M,O
Marketing M
Mathematics M,O
Music Education M,O
Music M,O
Nonprofit Management M,O
Nursing and Healthcare Administration M,O
Nursing Education M,O
Nursing—General M,O
Nutrition M,O
Philosophy M,O
Physical Education M,O
Planetary and Space Sciences M,O
Political Science M,O
Psychology—General M,O
Public Administration M,O
Public Affairs M,O
Public Health—General M,O
Reading Education M,O
School Nursing M,O
Science Education M,O
Secondary Education M,O
Social Work M
Sociology M,O
Spanish M,O
Special Education M,O
Sports Management M,O
Sustainable Development M,O
Urban and Regional Planning M,O

WESTERN CAROLINA UNIVERSITY

Accounting M
Applied Arts and Design—General M
Art/Fine Arts M
Biological and Biomedical Sciences—General M
Business Administration and Management—General M
Chemistry M
Communication Disorders M
Community College Education M
Computer Science M
Construction Management M
Counselor Education M
Education—General M,D,O
Educational Leadership and Administration M,D,O
English as a Second Language M
English M
Entrepreneurship M
Health Services Management and Hospital Administration M
Higher Education M
History M
Human Resources Development M
Industrial/Management Engineering M
Mathematics M
Music Education M
Music M
Nursing Education M,O
Nursing—General M,O
Physical Education M
Physical Therapy M
Project Management M
Psychology—General M
Public Affairs M
School Psychology M
Social Psychology M
Social Work M

WESTERN CONNECTICUT STATE UNIVERSITY

Accounting M
Adult Nursing M
Art/Fine Arts M
Biological and Biomedical Sciences—General M
Business Administration and Management—General M
Counselor Education M
Criminal Justice and Criminology M
Curriculum and Instruction M
Education—General M,D
Educational Leadership and Administration D
Educational Media/Instructional Technology M
English as a Second Language M
English Education M
English M
Environmental Sciences M
Geosciences M
Health Services Management and Hospital Administration M
History M
Illustration M
Mathematics Education M
Mathematics M
Music Education M
Nursing—General M
Planetary and Space Sciences M
Reading Education M
Science Education M
Secondary Education M
Social Psychology M
Special Education M
Writing M

WESTERN GOVERNORS UNIVERSITY

Business Administration and Management—General M
Computer and Information Systems Security M
Education—General M,O
Educational Leadership and Administration M,O
Educational Measurement and Evaluation M,O
Educational Media/Instructional Technology M,O
English Education M,O
Higher Education M,O
Management Information Systems M
Management Strategy and Policy M
Mathematics Education M,O
Science Education M,O

WESTERN ILLINOIS UNIVERSITY

Accounting M
Applied Arts and Design—General M
Applied Mathematics M,O
Biological and Biomedical Sciences—General M,O
Business Administration and Management—General M
Chemistry M
Clinical Psychology M,O
Communication Disorders M
Communication—General M
Computer Science M
Counselor Education M
Criminal Justice and Criminology M,O
Distance Education Development M,O
Economic Development M,O
Economics M,O
Education—General M,D,O
Educational Leadership and Administration M,D,O
Educational Media/Instructional Technology M,O
Elementary Education M
English as a Second Language M,O
English M,O
Foundations and Philosophy of Education M,O
Geographic Information Systems M,O
Geography M,O
Graphic Design M,O
Health Education M,O
Health Services Management and Hospital Administration M,O
History M
Internet and Interactive Multimedia M,O
Kinesiology and Movement Studies M
Liberal Studies M
Manufacturing Engineering M
Marine Biology M,O
Mathematics M,O
Museum Studies M,O
Music M
Physics M
Political Science M
Psychology—General M,O
Reading Education M
Recreation and Park Management M
School Psychology M,O
Social Psychology M,O
Sociology M
Special Education M
Sports Management M
Student Affairs M
Sustainable Development M,O
Technology and Public Policy M
Theater M
Travel and Tourism M
Writing M,O
Zoology M,O

WESTERN INTERNATIONAL UNIVERSITY

Business Administration and Management—General M
Finance and Banking M
International Business M
Management Information Systems M
Management Strategy and Policy M
Marketing M
Organizational Behavior M
Organizational Management M
Public Administration M
Systems Engineering M

WESTERN KENTUCKY UNIVERSITY

Adult Education M,D,O
Agricultural Sciences—General M
Anthropology M
Applied Economics M
Art Education M
Biological and Biomedical Sciences—General M
Business Administration and Management—General M
Chemistry M
Clinical Psychology M,O
Communication Disorders M
Communication—General M,O
Comparative Literature M
Computational Sciences M
Computer Science M
Corporate and Organizational Communication M,O
Counseling Psychology M
Counselor Education M
Criminal Justice and Criminology M
Early Childhood Education M,O
Educational Leadership and Administration M,D,O
Educational Media/Instructional Technology M,O
Elementary Education M,O
English as a Second Language M
English Education M
English M
Experimental Psychology M,O
Foreign Languages Education M
French M
Geology M
Geosciences M
German M
Health Services Management and Hospital Administration M
Higher Education M
History M
Homeland Security M
Industrial and Organizational Psychology M,O
Interdisciplinary Studies M,O
Management of Technology M
Marriage and Family Therapy M
Mathematics M
Middle School Education M,O
Music Education M
Nursing—General M
Physical Education M
Physics M
Political Science M
Psychology—General M,O
Public Administration M
Public Health—General M
Reading Education M,O
Recreation and Park Management M
School Psychology M,O
Secondary Education M,O
Social Work M
Sociology M
Spanish M
Special Education M,O
Sports Management M
Student Affairs M
Writing M

WESTERN MICHIGAN UNIVERSITY

Accounting M
Anthropology M
Applied Arts and Design—General M
Applied Economics M,D
Applied Mathematics M
Art Education M
Art/Fine Arts M
Athletic Training and Sports Medicine M
Biological and Biomedical Sciences—General M,D
Business Administration and Management—General M
Chemical Engineering M,D

Chemistry M,D
Civil Engineering M
Clinical Psychology M,D
Communication Disorders M,D
Communication—General M
Computational Sciences M
Computer Engineering M,D
Computer Science M,D
Construction Engineering M
Construction Management M
Corporate and Organizational Communication M
Counseling Psychology M,D
Counselor Education M,D
Economics M,D
Education—General M,D,O
Educational Leadership and Administration M,D,O
Educational Measurement and Evaluation M,D,O
Educational Media/ Instructional Technology M,D,O
Electrical Engineering M,D
Engineering and Applied Sciences—General M,D
Engineering Management M
English Education M,D
English M,D
Exercise and Sports Science M
Family and Consumer Sciences-General M
Finance and Banking M
Geographic Information Systems M,O
Geography M,O
Geosciences M,D
Health Education D
Health Services Management and Hospital Administration M,D,O
History M,D
Human Resources Development M,D
Industrial and Organizational Psychology M,D
Industrial/Management Engineering M,D
International Affairs M
Manufacturing Engineering M
Mathematics Education M,D
Mathematics M,D
Mechanical Engineering M,D
Medieval and Renaissance Studies M
Music Education M
Music M
Nonprofit Management M,D,O
Nursing—General M
Occupational Therapy M
Paper and Pulp Engineering M,D
Philosophy M
Physical Education M
Physician Assistant Studies M
Physics M,D
Physiology M
Political Science M,D
Psychology—General M,D
Public Administration M,D,O
Public Affairs M,D,O
Reading Education M,D
Rehabilitation Counseling M
Rehabilitation Sciences M
Religion M
Science Education M,D
Social Work M
Sociology M,D
Spanish M,D
Special Education M,D
Sports Management M
Statistics M,D
Structural Engineering M
Therapies—Dance, Drama, and Music M
Transportation and Highway Engineering M
Vocational and Technical Education M
Writing M,D

WESTERN NEW ENGLAND UNIVERSITY

Accounting M
Applied Behavior Analysis D,O
Business Administration and Management—General M
Electrical Engineering M
Elementary Education M
Engineering and Applied Sciences—General M,D
Engineering Management M,D
English Education M
Industrial/Management Engineering M
Law P,M
Manufacturing Engineering M
Mathematics Education M
Mechanical Engineering M
Sports Management M

WESTERN NEW MEXICO UNIVERSITY

Business Administration and Management—General M
Counselor Education M
Education—General M
Educational Leadership and Administration M
Elementary Education M
English as a Second Language M
Interdisciplinary Studies M
Multilingual and Multicultural Education M
Occupational Therapy M
Reading Education M
School Psychology M
Secondary Education M
Social Work M
Special Education M

WESTERN OREGON UNIVERSITY

Criminal Justice and Criminology M
Early Childhood Education M
Education—General M
Educational Media/ Instructional Technology M
Health Education M
Mathematics Education M
Multilingual and Multicultural Education M
Music M
Rehabilitation Counseling M
Science Education M
Secondary Education M
Social Sciences Education M
Special Education M

WESTERN SEMINARY

Human Resources Development M
Pastoral Ministry and Counseling P,M,D,O
Religion M,O
Theology P,M,O
Women's Studies M

WESTERN SEMINARY–SACRAMENTO CAMPUS

Marriage and Family Therapy M
Pastoral Ministry and Counseling M,O
Theology P,M,O
Women's Studies O

WESTERN SEMINARY–SAN JOSE CAMPUS

Marriage and Family Therapy P,M,O
Pastoral Ministry and Counseling P,M,O
Theology P,M,O

WESTERN STATE COLLEGE OF COLORADO

Education—General M*
Educational Leadership and Administration M
Film, Television, and Video Production M
Reading Education M
Writing M*

WESTERN STATE UNIVERSITY COLLEGE OF LAW

Law P

WESTERN THEOLOGICAL SEMINARY

Theology P,M,D

WESTERN UNIVERSITY OF HEALTH SCIENCES

Allied Health—General M,D
Biological and Biomedical Sciences—General M
Dentistry P
Family Nurse Practitioner Studies M,D
Health Education M
Nursing—General M,D
Optometry P
Osteopathic Medicine P
Pharmaceutical Sciences M
Pharmacy P
Physical Therapy D
Physician Assistant Studies M
Veterinary Medicine P

WESTERN WASHINGTON UNIVERSITY

Adult Education M
Anthropology M
Biological and Biomedical Sciences—General M
Business Administration and Management—General M
Chemistry M
Communication Disorders M
Computer Science M
Counseling Psychology M
Counselor Education M
Education of the Gifted M
Education—General M
Educational Leadership and Administration M
Elementary Education M
English M
Environmental Education M
Environmental Sciences M
Exercise and Sports Science M
Experimental Psychology M
Geography M
Geology M
Higher Education M
History M
Marine Sciences M
Mathematics M
Music M
Physical Education M
Political Science M
Psychology—General M
Rehabilitation Counseling M
Science Education M
Secondary Education M

WESTFIELD STATE UNIVERSITY

Applied Behavior Analysis M
Counseling Psychology M
Counselor Education M
Criminal Justice and Criminology M
Early Childhood Education M
Education—General M,O
Educational Leadership and Administration M,O
Educational Media/ Instructional Technology M
Elementary Education M
English M
History M
Physical Education M
Psychology—General M
Reading Education M
Secondary Education M
Special Education M
Vocational and Technical Education M,O

WEST LIBERTY UNIVERSITY

Education—General M

WESTMINSTER COLLEGE (PA)

Counselor Education M,O
Education—General M,O
Educational Leadership and Administration M,O
Reading Education M,O

WESTMINSTER COLLEGE (UT)

Accounting M,O
Business Administration and Management—General M,O
Communication—General M
Counseling Psychology M
Education—General M
Family Nurse Practitioner Studies M
Management of Technology M,O
Nurse Anesthesia M
Nursing Education M
Nursing—General M
Public Health—General M
Writing M

WESTMINSTER SEMINARY CALIFORNIA

Religion P,M
Theology P,M

WESTMINSTER THEOLOGICAL SEMINARY

Missions and Missiology P,M,D,O
Pastoral Ministry and Counseling P,M,D,O
Religion P,M,D,O
Theology P,M,D,O

WEST TEXAS A&M UNIVERSITY

Accounting M
Agricultural Economics and Agribusiness M
Agricultural Sciences—General M,D
Animal Sciences M
Art/Fine Arts M
Biological and Biomedical Sciences—General M
Business Administration and Management—General M
Chemistry M
Communication Disorders M
Communication—General M
Counselor Education M
Criminal Justice and Criminology M
Curriculum and Instruction M
Economics M

*M—master's degree; P—first professional degree; D—doctorate; O—other advanced degree; *—Close-Up and/or Display in one of the other books in this series*

Education—General M
Educational Leadership and Administration M
Educational Measurement and Evaluation M
Educational Media/ Instructional Technology M
Engineering and Applied Sciences—General M
English M
Environmental Sciences M
Exercise and Sports Science M
Finance and Banking M
History M
Interdisciplinary Studies M
Mathematics M
Music M
Nursing—General M
Plant Sciences M
Political Science M
Psychology—General M
Reading Education M
Special Education M

WEST VIRGINIA SCHOOL OF OSTEOPATHIC MEDICINE

Osteopathic Medicine P

WEST VIRGINIA STATE UNIVERSITY

Biotechnology M
Media Studies M

WEST VIRGINIA UNIVERSITY

Accounting M
Aerospace/Aeronautical Engineering M,D
African Studies M,D
African-American Studies M,D
Agricultural Economics and Agribusiness M
Agricultural Education M,D
Agricultural Sciences—General M,D
Agronomy and Soil Sciences D
Allopathic Medicine P
American Studies M,D
Analytical Chemistry M,D
Animal Sciences M,D
Applied Mathematics M,D
Applied Physics M,D
Applied Social Research M
Art Education M
Art History M
Art/Fine Arts M
Asian Studies M,D
Athletic Training and Sports Medicine M,D
Biochemistry M,D
Biological and Biomedical Sciences—General M,D
Business Administration and Management—General M
Cancer Biology/Oncology M,D
Cell Biology M,D
Chemical Engineering M,D
Chemical Physics M,D
Chemistry M,D
Child and Family Studies M
Civil Engineering M,D
Clinical Psychology M,D
Communication Disorders M,D
Communication—General M,D
Community Health M
Computer Engineering D
Computer Science M,D
Condensed Matter Physics M,D
Corporate and Organizational Communication M,D,O
Counseling Psychology D
Counselor Education M
Curriculum and Instruction M,D
Dentistry P
Developmental Biology M,D
Developmental Psychology M,D
Early Childhood Education M,D
Economic Development M,D
Economics M,D
Education of Students with Severe/Multiple Disabilities M,D
Education of the Gifted M,D
Education—General M,D
Educational Leadership and Administration M,D
Educational Media/ Instructional Technology M,D
Educational Psychology M
Electrical Engineering M,D
Elementary Education M
Engineering and Applied Sciences—General M,D
English as a Second Language M
English M,D
Entomology M,D
Environmental and Occupational Health D
Environmental Biology M,D
Environmental Education M,D
Environmental Engineering M,D
Environmental Management and Policy M,D
Evolutionary Biology M,D
Exercise and Sports Science M,D
Fish, Game, and Wildlife Management M
Food Science and Technology M,D
Forensic Sciences M,D
Forestry M,D
French M
Genetics M,D
Genomic Sciences M,D
Geographic Information Systems M,D
Geography M,D
Geology M,D
Geophysics M,D
Graphic Design M
Health Education M,D
Health Promotion M,D
Higher Education M,D
History of Science and Technology M,D
History M,D
Horticulture M,D
Human Development M,D
Human Genetics M,D
Human Services M
Hydrogeology M,D
Immunology M,D
Industrial and Labor Relations M
Industrial Hygiene M
Industrial/Management Engineering M,D
Inorganic Chemistry M,D
International Affairs M,D
International Economics M,D
Journalism M,O
Latin American Studies M,D
Law P
Legal and Justice Studies M
Liberal Studies M
Linguistics M
Marketing M
Mathematics Education M,D
Mathematics M,D
Mechanical Engineering M,D
Medicinal and Pharmaceutical Chemistry M,D
Microbiology M,D
Mineral/Mining Engineering M,D
Molecular Biology M,D
Music Education M,D
Music M,D
Natural Resources M,D
Neurobiology M,D
Neuroscience D
Nursing—General M,D,O
Nutrition M
Occupational Therapy M
Oral and Dental Sciences M
Organic Chemistry M,D
Paleontology M,D
Petroleum Engineering M,D
Pharmaceutical Administration M,D
Pharmaceutical Sciences M,D
Pharmacology M,D
Pharmacy P,M,D
Physical Chemistry M,D
Physical Education M,D
Physical Therapy D
Physics M,D
Physiology M,D
Plant Pathology M,D
Plant Sciences D
Plasma Physics M,D
Political Science M,D
Psychology—General M,D
Public Administration M
Public Health—General M
Public Policy M,D
Reading Education M
Recreation and Park Management M
Rehabilitation Counseling M
Reproductive Biology M,D
Safety Engineering M
Secondary Education M,D
Social Work M
Sociology M
Software Engineering M
Spanish M
Special Education M,D
Sport Psychology M,D
Sports Management M,D
Statistics M,D
Sustainable Development D
Teratology M,D
Theater M
Theoretical Chemistry M,D
Theoretical Physics M,D
Toxicology M,D
Urban and Regional Planning M,D
Writing M

WEST VIRGINIA UNIVERSITY INSTITUTE OF TECHNOLOGY

Engineering and Applied Sciences—General M
Systems Engineering M

WEST VIRGINIA WESLEYAN COLLEGE

Athletic Training and Sports Medicine M
Business Administration and Management—General M
Education—General M
Nursing—General M

WHEATON COLLEGE

American Studies M
Archaeology M
Clinical Psychology M,D
Cultural Studies M,O
Education—General M
Elementary Education M
English as a Second Language M,O
Missions and Missiology M,O
Pastoral Ministry and Counseling M,D
Psychology—General M,D
Religion M
Religious Education M
Secondary Education M
Theology M,D

WHEELING JESUIT UNIVERSITY

Accounting M
Business Administration and Management—General M
Nursing—General M
Organizational Management M
Physical Therapy D

WHEELOCK COLLEGE

Child and Family Studies M
Early Childhood Education M
Education—General M
Educational Leadership and Administration M
Elementary Education M
Human Development M
Reading Education M
Social Work M
Special Education M

WHITTIER COLLEGE

Child Development M
Education—General M
Educational Leadership and Administration M
Elementary Education M
Law P,M
Legal and Justice Studies P,M
Secondary Education M

WHITWORTH UNIVERSITY

Counselor Education M
Education of the Gifted M
Education—General M
Educational Leadership and Administration M
Elementary Education M
International Business M
Secondary Education M
Special Education M
Theology M

WICHITA STATE UNIVERSITY

Accounting M
Aerospace/Aeronautical Engineering M,D
Allied Health—General M,D
Anthropology M
Applied Mathematics M,D
Art/Fine Arts M
Biological and Biomedical Sciences—General M
Business Administration and Management—General M
Chemistry M,D
Clinical Psychology D
Communication Disorders M,D
Communication—General M
Computer Engineering M,D
Computer Science M,D
Counselor Education M,O
Criminal Justice and Criminology M
Curriculum and Instruction M
Early Childhood Education M
Economics M
Education of the Gifted M
Education—General M,D,O
Educational Leadership and Administration M,D,O
Educational Psychology M,O
Electrical Engineering M,D
Engineering and Applied Sciences—General M,D
English M
Environmental Sciences M
Exercise and Sports Science M
Family Nurse Practitioner Studies M,D
Geology M
Gerontology M
History M
Human Services M

Industrial/Management Engineering M,D
Liberal Studies M
Manufacturing Engineering M,D
Mathematics M,D
Mechanical Engineering M,D
Music Education M
Music M
Nurse Midwifery M,D
Nursing and Healthcare Administration M,D
Nursing—General M,D
Physical Therapy D
Physician Assistant Studies M
Psychology—General D
Public Administration M
School Psychology M,O
Social Psychology D
Social Work M
Sociology M
Spanish M
Special Education M
Sports Management M
Writing M

WIDENER UNIVERSITY

Accounting M
Adult Education M,D
Business Administration and Management—General M
Chemical Engineering M
Civil Engineering M
Clinical Psychology D
Computer Engineering M
Counselor Education M,D
Criminal Justice and Criminology M
Early Childhood Education M,D
Education—General M,D
Educational Leadership and Administration M,D
Educational Media/Instructional Technology M,D
Educational Psychology M,D
Elementary Education M,D
Engineering and Applied Sciences—General M
Engineering Management M
English Education M,D
Foundations and Philosophy of Education M,D
Health Education M,D
Health Law P,M,D
Health Services Management and Hospital Administration M
Human Resources Management M
Law P,M,D
Liberal Studies M
Mathematics Education M,D
Mechanical Engineering M
Middle School Education M,D
Nursing—General M,D,O
Physical Therapy M,D
Psychology—General
Public Administration M
Reading Education M,D
Science Education M,D
Social Sciences Education M,D
Social Work M,D
Software Engineering M
Special Education M,D
Taxation M
Telecommunications M

WILBERFORCE UNIVERSITY

Rehabilitation Counseling M

WILFRID LAURIER UNIVERSITY

Accounting M,D
American Studies M,D
Archaeology M
Biological and Biomedical Sciences—General M
Business Administration and Management—General M,D
Canadian Studies* M,D
Chemistry M
Classics M
Cognitive Sciences M,D
Communication—General M
Conflict Resolution and Mediation/Peace Studies D
Criminal Justice and Criminology M
Cultural Studies M,D
Developmental Psychology M,D
Economics M,D
English M,D
Environmental Management and Policy M,D
Environmental Sciences M,D
Film, Television, and Video Theory and Criticism M,D
Finance and Banking M,D
Gender Studies M,D
Geography M,D
Health Promotion M
History M,D
Human Resources Management M,D
International Affairs M,D
International Economics M
Kinesiology and Movement Studies M
Legal and Justice Studies D
Management of Technology M,D
Marketing M,D
Mathematics M
Media Studies M,D
Near and Middle Eastern Studies M
Neuroscience M,D
Organizational Behavior M,D
Organizational Management M,D
Pastoral Ministry and Counseling P,M,D,O
Philosophy M
Physical Education M
Political Science M,D
Psychology—General M,D
Public Policy M
Religion M,D
Social Psychology M,D
Social Sciences M
Social Work M,D
Sociology M
Supply Chain Management M,D
Theology P,M,D,O
Therapies—Dance, Drama, and Music M

WILKES UNIVERSITY

Accounting M
Business Administration and Management—General M
Computer Education M,D
Curriculum and Instruction M,D
Distance Education Development M,D
Early Childhood Education M,D
Education—General M,D
Educational Leadership and Administration M,D
Educational Measurement and Evaluation M,D
Educational Media/Instructional Technology M,D
Electrical Engineering M
Engineering and Applied Sciences—General M
Engineering Management M
English as a Second Language M,D
English Education M,D
Entrepreneurship M
Finance and Banking M
Health Services Management and Hospital Administration M
Higher Education M,D
Human Resources Management M
Industrial and Manufacturing Management M
International Business M
Marketing M
Mathematics Education M,D
Mathematics M
Mechanical Engineering M
Nursing—General M,D
Organizational Management M
Pharmacy P
Reading Education M,D
Science Education M,D
Secondary Education M,D
Social Sciences Education M,D
Special Education M,D
Writing M

WILLAMETTE UNIVERSITY

Business Administration and Management—General M
Education—General M
Environmental Management and Policy M
Law P,M
Reading Education M
Special Education M

WILLIAM CAREY UNIVERSITY

Art Education M,O
Business Administration and Management—General M
Counseling Psychology M
Education of the Gifted M,O
Education—General M,O
Elementary Education M,O
English Education M,O
Nursing—General M
Psychology—General M
Secondary Education M,O
Social Sciences Education M,O
Special Education M,O

WILLIAM HOWARD TAFT UNIVERSITY

Education—General M
Taxation M

WILLIAM MITCHELL COLLEGE OF LAW

Law P,M

WILLIAM PATERSON UNIVERSITY OF NEW JERSEY

Art/Fine Arts M
Biological and Biomedical Sciences—General M
Biotechnology M
Business Administration and Management—General M
Clinical Psychology M
Communication Disorders M
Communication—General M
Counseling Psychology M
Counselor Education M
Education—General M
Educational Leadership and Administration M
English M
History M
Music M
Nursing—General M
Public Policy M
Reading Education M
Sociology M
Special Education M

WILLIAMS COLLEGE

Art History M

WILLIAM WOODS UNIVERSITY

Agricultural Economics and Agribusiness M,O
Curriculum and Instruction M,O
Educational Leadership and Administration M,O
Elementary Education M,O
Health Services Management and Hospital Administration M,O
Human Resources Development M,O
Physical Education M,O
Secondary Education M,O
Special Education M,O

WILMINGTON COLLEGE

Education—General M
Reading Education M
Special Education M

WILMINGTON UNIVERSITY

Adult Nursing M
Business Administration and Management—General M
Computer and Information Systems Security M
Counselor Education M
Criminal Justice and Criminology M
Education of the Gifted M
Education—General M
Educational Leadership and Administration M,D
Educational Media/Instructional Technology M
Elementary Education M
Family Nurse Practitioner Studies M
Finance and Banking M
Gerontology M
Health Services Management and Hospital Administration M
Homeland Security M
Human Resources Management M
Human Services M
Internet and Interactive Multimedia M
Internet Engineering M
Logistics M
Management Information Systems M
Nursing—General M
Organizational Management M
Public Administration M
Reading Education M
Secondary Education M
Social Psychology M
Special Education M
Transportation Management M
Vocational and Technical Education M
Women's Health Nursing M

WILSON COLLEGE

Education—General M
Elementary Education M
Secondary Education M

WINEBRENNER THEOLOGICAL SEMINARY

Theology P,M,D

*M—master's degree; P—first professional degree; D—doctorate; O—other advanced degree; *—Close-Up and/or Display in one of the other books in this series*

WINGATE UNIVERSITY

Business Administration and Management—General M
Education—General M
Educational Leadership and Administration M
Elementary Education M
Pharmacy P
Physical Education M
Sports Management M

WINONA STATE UNIVERSITY

Adult Nursing M,D,O
Counselor Education M
Education—General M
Educational Leadership and Administration M,O
English M
Family Nurse Practitioner Studies M,D,O
Nursing and Healthcare Administration M,D,O
Nursing Education M,D,O
Nursing—General M,D,O
Recreation and Park Management M,O
Special Education M
Sports Management M,O

WINSTON-SALEM STATE UNIVERSITY

Business Administration and Management—General M
Computer Science M
Elementary Education M
Management Information Systems M
Nursing—General M
Occupational Therapy M
Physical Therapy M
Rehabilitation Counseling M

WINTHROP UNIVERSITY

Art Education M
Art/Fine Arts M
Arts Administration M
Biological and Biomedical Sciences—General M
Business Administration and Management—General M
Counselor Education M
Education—General M
Educational Leadership and Administration M
English M
History M
Liberal Studies M
Middle School Education M
Music Education M
Music M
Nutrition M
Physical Education M
Project Management M,O
Psychology—General M,O
Reading Education M
Secondary Education M
Social Work M
Software Engineering M,O
Spanish M
Special Education M

WISCONSIN SCHOOL OF PROFESSIONAL PSYCHOLOGY

Clinical Psychology M,D
Psychology—General M,D

WITTENBERG UNIVERSITY

Education—General M

WON INSTITUTE OF GRADUATE STUDIES

Acupuncture and Oriental Medicine M
Religion M

WOODBURY UNIVERSITY

Architecture M
Business Administration and Management—General M
Organizational Management M
Urban Design M

WOODS HOLE OCEANOGRAPHIC INSTITUTION

Marine Biology D
Marine Geology D
Ocean Engineering D
Oceanography D

WORCESTER POLYTECHNIC INSTITUTE

Applied Mathematics M,D,O
Applied Statistics M,D,O
Artificial Intelligence/Robotics M,D,O
Biochemistry M,D
Biological and Biomedical Sciences—General M,D
Biomedical Engineering M,D,O
Biotechnology M,D
Business Administration and Management—General M,O
Chemical Engineering M,D
Chemistry M,D
Civil Engineering M,D,O
Computer Engineering M,D,O
Computer Science M,D,O
Construction Management M,D,O
Electrical Engineering M,D,O
Energy and Power Engineering M,D
Engineering and Applied Sciences—General M,D,O
Engineering Design M,O
Environmental Engineering M,D,O
Fire Protection Engineering M,D,O
Interdisciplinary Studies M,D,O
Management Information Systems M,O
Manufacturing Engineering M,D
Marketing M,O
Materials Engineering M,D
Materials Sciences M,D
Mathematics M,D,O
Mechanical Engineering M,D,O
Modeling and Simulation M,D
Organizational Management M,O
Physics M,D
Social Sciences M,D,O
Systems Science M,D,O

WORCESTER STATE UNIVERSITY

Accounting M
Biotechnology M
Business Administration and Management—General M
Communication Disorders M
Community Health Nursing M
Early Childhood Education M
Education—General M,O
Educational Leadership and Administration M,O
Elementary Education M
English Education M
Foreign Languages Education M
Health Education M
Health Services Management and Hospital Administration M
History M
Middle School Education M
Nonprofit Management M
Nursing Education M
Occupational Therapy M
Organizational Management M
Reading Education M,O
School Psychology M,O
Secondary Education M
Social Sciences Education M
Spanish M
Special Education M

WORLD MEDICINE INSTITUTE OF ACUPUNCTURE AND HERBAL MEDICINE

Acupuncture and Oriental Medicine M

WRIGHT INSTITUTE

Clinical Psychology D
Counseling Psychology M
Psychology—General D

WRIGHT STATE UNIVERSITY

Accounting M
Acute Care/Critical Care Nursing M
Adult Education O
Adult Nursing M
Allopathic Medicine P
Anatomy M
Applied Behavior Analysis M
Applied Economics M
Applied Mathematics M
Applied Statistics M
Biochemistry M
Biological and Biomedical Sciences—General M,D
Biomedical Engineering M
Biophysics M
Business Administration and Management—General M
Business Education M
Chemistry M
Clinical Psychology D
Community Health Nursing M
Computer Education M
Computer Engineering M,D
Computer Science M,D
Counselor Education M
Criminal Justice and Criminology M
Curriculum and Instruction M,O
Early Childhood Education M
Economics M
Education of the Gifted M
Education—General M,O
Educational Leadership and Administration M,O
Electrical Engineering M
Elementary Education M
Engineering and Applied Sciences—General M,D
English as a Second Language M
English M
Environmental Sciences M,D
Ergonomics and Human Factors M,D
Family Nurse Practitioner Studies M
Finance and Banking M
Geology M
Geophysics M
Health Education M
Health Promotion M
Health Services Management and Hospital Administration M
Higher Education M,O
History M
Humanities M
Immunology M
Industrial and Organizational Psychology M,D
Interdisciplinary Studies M
International and Comparative Education M
International Business M
Library Science M
Logistics M
Management Information Systems M
Marketing M
Materials Engineering M
Materials Sciences M
Mathematics Education M
Mathematics M
Mechanical Engineering M
Medical Physics M
Microbiology M
Middle School Education M
Molecular Biology M
Music Education M
Music M
Nursing and Healthcare Administration M
Nursing—General M
Pediatric Nursing M
Pharmacology M
Physical Education M
Physics M
Physiology M
Project Management M
Psychology—General M,D
Public Administration M
Public Health—General M
Recreation and Park Management M
Rehabilitation Counseling M
Rhetoric M
School Nursing M
Science Education M
Secondary Education M
Special Education M
Supply Chain Management M
Toxicology M
Urban Studies M
Vocational and Technical Education M
Writing M

WYCLIFFE COLLEGE

Religion P,M,D,O
Theology P,M,D,O

XAVIER UNIVERSITY

Business Administration and Management—General M
Clinical Psychology M,D
Counselor Education M
Criminal Justice and Criminology M
Early Childhood Education M
Education—General M
Educational Leadership and Administration M
Elementary Education M
English M
Experimental Psychology M,D
Finance and Banking M
Health Law M
Health Services Management and Hospital Administration M
Human Resources Development M

Industrial and Organizational Psychology	M,D
International Business	M
Management Information Systems	M
Management Strategy and Policy	M
Marketing	M
Multilingual and Multicultural Education	M
Nursing and Healthcare Administration	M
Nursing Education	M
Nursing Informatics	M
Nursing—General	M
Occupational Therapy	M
Pastoral Ministry and Counseling	M
Psychology—General	M,D
Reading Education	M
Religious Education	M
Secondary Education	M
Special Education	M
Sports Management	M
Theology	M

XAVIER UNIVERSITY OF LOUISIANA

Counselor Education	M
Curriculum and Instruction	M
Education—General	M
Educational Leadership and Administration	M
Pastoral Ministry and Counseling	M
Pharmacy	P
Theology	M

YALE UNIVERSITY

Accounting	D
African Studies	M
African-American Studies	D
Allopathic Medicine	P
American Studies	D
Anthropology	M,D
Applied Arts and Design—General	M
Applied Mathematics	M,D
Applied Physics	M,D
Archaeology	M,D
Architecture	M,D
Art History	D
Art/Fine Arts	M
Asian Languages	D
Asian Studies	M
Astronomy	M,D
Astrophysics	M,D
Atmospheric Sciences	D
Biochemistry	D
Bioinformatics	D
Biological and Biomedical Sciences—General	D
Biomedical Engineering	M,D
Biophysics	D
Biostatistics	M,D,O
Business Administration and Management—General	M,D
Cancer Biology/Oncology	D
Cell Biology	D
Chemical Engineering	M,D
Chemistry	D
Classics	M,D
Clinical Psychology	D
Cognitive Sciences	D
Comparative Literature	D
Computational Biology	D
Computer Science	M,D
Developmental Biology	D
Developmental Psychology	D
East European and Russian Studies	M,D
Ecology	D
Economic Development	M
Economics	M,D
Electrical Engineering	M,D
Engineering and Applied Sciences—General	M,D
Engineering Physics	M,D
English	M,D
Environmental and Occupational Health	M,D,O
Environmental Design	M,D
Environmental Engineering	M,D
Environmental Management and Policy	M,D
Environmental Sciences	M,D
Epidemiology	M,D,O
Evolutionary Biology	D
Film, Television, and Video Theory and Criticism	D
Finance and Banking	D
Forestry	M,D
French	M,D
Genetics	D
Genomic Sciences	D
Geochemistry	D
Geology	D
Geophysics	D
Geosciences	D
German	D
Graphic Design	M
Health Services Management and Hospital Administration	M,D,O
History of Medicine	M,D
History of Science and Technology	M,D
History	M,D
Immunology	D
Infectious Diseases	D
Inorganic Chemistry	D
International Affairs	M
International Economics	M
International Health	M,D,O
Italian	D
Latin American Studies	D
Law	P,M,D
Linguistics	D
Marketing	D
Mathematics	M,D
Mechanical Engineering	M,D
Medieval and Renaissance Studies	M,D
Meteorology	D
Microbiology	D
Molecular Biology	D
Molecular Biophysics	D
Molecular Medicine	D
Molecular Pathology	D
Molecular Physiology	D
Music	M,D,O
Near and Middle Eastern Languages	M,D
Near and Middle Eastern Studies	M,D
Neurobiology	D
Neuroscience	D
Nursing—General	M,D,O
Oceanography	D
Organic Chemistry	D
Organizational Management	D
Paleontology	D
Pathobiology	D
Pathology	M,D
Pharmacology	D
Philosophy	D
Photography	M
Physical Chemistry	D
Physician Assistant Studies	M,O
Physics	D
Physiology	D
Planetary and Space Sciences	M,D
Plant Biology	D
Political Science	D
Portuguese	D
Psychology—General	D
Public Health—General	M,D,O
Religion	D
Russian	D
Slavic Languages	D
Social Psychology	D
Social Sciences	M,D,O
Sociology	D
Spanish	D
Statistics	M,D
Theater	M,D,O
Theology	P,M
Theoretical Chemistry	D
Virology	D

YESHIVA BETH MOSHE

Theology	O

YESHIVA DERECH CHAIM

Religion	D

YESHIVA KARLIN STOLIN RABBINICAL INSTITUTE

Theology	O

YESHIVA OF NITRA RABBINICAL COLLEGE

Theology	

YESHIVA SHAAR HATORAH TALMUDIC RESEARCH INSTITUTE

Theology	

YESHIVATH ZICHRON MOSHE

Theology	O

YESHIVA TORAS CHAIM TALMUDICAL SEMINARY

Theology	

YESHIVA UNIVERSITY

Accounting	M
Clinical Psychology	D
Conflict Resolution and Mediation/Peace Studies	P,M
Counseling Psychology	M
Educational Leadership and Administration	M,D,O
Health Psychology	D
Intellectual Property Law	P,M
Jewish Studies	M,D
Law	P,M
Psychology—General	M,D
Religious Education	M,D,O
School Psychology	D
Social Work	M,D*

YORK COLLEGE OF PENNSYLVANIA

Accounting	M
Business Administration and Management—General	M
Education—General	M
Educational Leadership and Administration	M
Finance and Banking	M
Marketing	M
Nursing—General	M
Reading Education	M

YORKTOWN UNIVERSITY

American Studies	M
Business Administration and Management—General	M
Economics	M
Entrepreneurship	M
Political Science	M
Sports Management	M

YORK UNIVERSITY

Anthropology	M,D
Applied Arts and Design—General	M
Applied Mathematics	M,D
Art History	M,D
Art/Fine Arts	M,D
Astronomy	M,D
Biological and Biomedical Sciences—General	M,D
Business Administration and Management—General	M,D*
Chemistry	M,D
Communication—General	M,D
Computer Science	M,D
Dance	M
Disability Studies	M,D
Economics	M,D
Education—General	M,D
Emergency Management	M
English	M,D
Environmental Management and Policy	M,D
Film, Television, and Video Production	M,D
Finance and Banking	M,D
French	M
Geography	M,D
Geosciences	M,D
History	M,D
Human Resources Management	M,D
Humanities	M,D
Interdisciplinary Studies	M
International Affairs	M
International Business	M,D
Kinesiology and Movement Studies	M,D
Law	P,M,D
Linguistics	M,D
Mathematics	M,D
Music	M,D
Nursing—General	M
Philosophy	M,D
Physics	M,D
Planetary and Space Sciences	M,D
Political Science	M,D
Psychology—General	M,D
Public Administration	M,D
Public Affairs	M
Public Policy	M
Social Sciences	M
Social Work	M,D
Sociology	M,D
Statistics	M,D
Theater	M,D
Translation and Interpretation	M
Women's Studies	M,D

YO SAN UNIVERSITY OF TRADITIONAL CHINESE MEDICINE

Acupuncture and Oriental Medicine	M

YOUNGSTOWN STATE UNIVERSITY

Accounting	M
Analytical Chemistry	M
Anatomy	M
Applied Behavior Analysis	M
Applied Mathematics	M
Biochemistry	M
Biological and Biomedical Sciences—General	M
Business Administration and Management—General	M,O
Chemistry	M
Civil Engineering	M
Computer Engineering	M
Computer Science	M
Counseling Psychology	M
Counselor Education	M
Criminal Justice and Criminology	M
Curriculum and Instruction	M
Early Childhood Education	M
Economics	M
Education of the Gifted	M

*M—master's degree; P—first professional degree; D—doctorate; O—other advanced degree; *—Close-Up and/or Display in one of the other books in this series*

Education—General	M,D
Educational Leadership and Administration	M,D
Educational Media/ Instructional Technology	M
Electrical Engineering	M
Engineering and Applied Sciences—General	M
English	M
Environmental Biology	M
Environmental Engineering	M
Environmental Management and Policy	M,O
Finance and Banking	M
Foundations and Philosophy of Education	M,D
Health Services Management and Hospital Administration	M
History	M
Human Services	M
Industrial/Management Engineering	M
Information Science	M
Inorganic Chemistry	M
Marketing	M
Mathematics Education	M
Mathematics	M
Mechanical Engineering	M
Microbiology	M
Middle School Education	M
Molecular Biology	M
Music Education	M
Music	M
Nursing—General	M
Organic Chemistry	M
Physical Chemistry	M
Physical Therapy	D
Physiology	M
Psychology—General	M
Reading Education	M
School Psychology	M
Science Education	M
Secondary Education	M
Special Education	M
Statistics	M

PROFILES OF INSTITUTIONS OFFERING GRADUATE AND PROFESSIONAL WORK

ABILENE CHRISTIAN UNIVERSITY, Abilene, TX 79699-9100

General Information Independent-religious, coed, comprehensive institution. CGS member. *Enrollment:* 4,728 graduate, professional, and undergraduate students; 286 full-time matriculated graduate/professional students (161 women), 603 part-time matriculated graduate/professional students (360 women). *Enrollment by degree level:* 809 master's, 22 doctoral, 58 other advanced degrees. *Graduate faculty:* 13 full-time (2 women), 78 part-time/adjunct (27 women). *Tuition:* Full-time $12,906; part-time $717 per hour. *Required fees:* $1250; $61.50 per unit. *Graduate housing:* On-campus housing not available. *Student services:* Campus employment opportunities, campus safety program, career counseling, exercise/wellness program, grant writing training, international student services, low-cost health insurance, multicultural affairs office, services for students with disabilities, teacher training, writing training. *Library facilities:* Brown Library. *Online resources:* library catalog, web page, access to other libraries' catalogs. *Collection:* 542,615 titles, 1,123 serial subscriptions, 65,617 audiovisual materials. *Research affiliation:* Fermilab (peanut toxins), Los Alamos National Laboratory (particle physics).

Computer facilities: Computer purchase and lease plans are available. 530 computers available on campus for general student use. A campuswide network can be accessed from student residence rooms and from off campus. Online class registration is available. *Web address:* http://www.acu.edu/.

General Application Contact: William Pittman, Graduate Admissions Counselor, 325-674-2656, Fax: 325-674-6717, E-mail: gradinfo@acu.edu.

GRADUATE UNITS

Graduate School Students: 286 full-time (161 women), 603 part-time (360 women); includes 103 Black or African American, non-Hispanic/Latino; 2 American Indian or Alaska Native, non-Hispanic/Latino; 11 Asian, non-Hispanic/Latino; 60 Hispanic/Latino; 15 Two or more races, non-Hispanic/Latino, 48 international. Average age 32. 793 applicants, 51% accepted, 346 enrolled. *Faculty:* 13 full-time (2 women), 78 part-time/adjunct (27 women). Expenses: Contact institution. *Financial support:* In 2010–11, 182 students received support, including 36 research assistantships with partial tuition reimbursements available (averaging $5,800 per year), 12 teaching assistantships with partial tuition reimbursements available (averaging $5,800 per year); career-related internships or fieldwork, Federal Work-Study, institutionally sponsored loans, scholarships/grants, and tuition waivers (partial) also available. Support available to part-time students. Financial award application deadline: 4/1; financial award applicants required to submit FAFSA. In 2010, 268 master's, 2 doctorates, 42 other advanced degrees awarded. *Degree program information:* Part-time and evening/weekend programs available. Postbaccalaureate distance learning degree programs offered (no on-campus study). Offers liberal arts (MLA). *Application deadline:* For fall admission, 4/1 priority date for domestic students; for spring admission, 11/1 priority date for domestic students. Applications are processed on a rolling basis. *Application fee:* $40. Electronic applications accepted. *Application Contact:* David Pittman, Graduate Admissions Counselor, 325-674-2656, Fax: 325-674-3717, E-mail: gradinfo@acu.edu. *Dean,* Dr. Carley Dodd, 325-674-2223, Fax: 325-674-6717, E-mail: gradinfo@acu.edu.

College of Arts and Sciences Students: 85 full-time (52 women), 222 part-time (156 women); includes 53 Black or African American, non-Hispanic/Latino; 3 Asian, non-Hispanic/Latino; 18 Hispanic/Latino; 5 Two or more races, non-Hispanic/Latino, 20 international. 343 applicants, 43% accepted, 123 enrolled. *Faculty:* 2 full-time (0 women), 36 part-time/adjunct (13 women). Expenses: Contact institution. *Financial support:* In 2010–11, 59 students received support, including 21 research assistantships (averaging $5,800 per year), 12 teaching assistantships (averaging $5,800 per year); career-related internships or fieldwork, Federal Work-Study, and tuition waivers (partial) also available. Support available to part-time students. Financial award application deadline: 4/1; financial award applicants required to submit FAFSA. In 2010, 78 master's, 42 other advanced degrees awarded. *Degree program information:* Part-time programs available. Postbaccalaureate distance learning degree programs offered (no on-campus study). Offers arts and sciences (MA, MS, Certificate, Specialist); clinical psychology (MS); communication (MA); composition/rhetoric (MA); conflict resolution (Certificate); conflict resolution and reconciliation (MA); conflict resolution for educators (Certificate); counseling psychology (MS); literature (MA); organizational and human resource development (MS); psychology (MS); school psychology (Specialist); writing (MA). *Application deadline:* For fall admission, 4/1 priority date for domestic students; for spring admission, 11/1 for domestic students. Applications are processed on a rolling basis. *Application fee:* $40. Electronic applications accepted. *Application Contact:* David Pittman, Graduate Admissions Counselor, 325-674-2656, Fax: 325-674-6717, E-mail: gradinfo@acu.edu. *Interim Dean,* Dr. Charles Mattis, 325-674-2209, Fax: 325-674-6800, E-mail: mattisc@acu.edu.

College of Biblical Studies Students: 95 full-time (32 women), 101 part-time (8 women); includes 9 Black or African American, non-Hispanic/Latino; 1 American Indian or Alaska Native, non-Hispanic/Latino; 3 Asian, non-Hispanic/Latino; 9 Hispanic/Latino; 1 Two or more races, non-Hispanic/Latino, 7 international. 121 applicants, 71% accepted, 66 enrolled. *Faculty:* 11 full-time (2 women), 10 part-time/adjunct (2 women). Expenses: Contact institution. *Financial support:* In 2010–11, 59 students received support; teaching assistantships, career-related internships or fieldwork and Federal Work-Study available. Support available to part-time students. Financial award application deadline: 4/1; financial award applicants required to submit FAFSA. In 2010, 56 master's, 2 doctorates awarded. *Degree program information:* Part-time and evening/weekend programs available. Offers Biblical studies (M Div, MA, MACM, MAMI, MMFT, D Min); Christian ministry (MACM); divinity (M Div); history and theology (MA); marriage and family therapy (MMFT); ministry (D Min); missions (MA, MAMI); New Testament (MA); Old Testament (MA). *Application deadline:* For fall admission, 4/1 priority date for domestic students; for spring admission, 11/1 for domestic students. Applications are processed on a rolling basis. *Application fee:* $40. *Application Contact:* David Pittman, Graduate Admissions Counselor, 325-674-2656, Fax: 325-674-6717, E-mail: gradinfo@acu.edu. *Dean,* Dr. Jack Reese, 325-674-3700, Fax: 325-674-6180, E-mail: reese@bible.acu.edu.

College of Business Administration Students: 32 full-time (14 women), 5 part-time (3 women); includes 2 Two or more races, non-Hispanic/Latino, 12 international. 23 applicants, 65% accepted, 14 enrolled. *Faculty:* 7 part-time/adjunct (0 women). Expenses: Contact institution. *Financial support:* In 2010–11, 24 students received support; teaching assistantships, Federal Work-Study available. Support available to part-time students. Financial award application deadline: 4/1; financial award applicants required to submit FAFSA. In 2010, 41 master's awarded. *Degree program information:* Part-time programs available. Offers business administration (M Acc). *Application deadline:* For fall admission, 4/1 priority date for domestic students; for spring admission, 11/1 for domestic students. Applications are processed on a rolling basis. *Application fee:* $40. Electronic applications accepted. *Application Contact:* David Pittman, Graduate Admissions Counselor, 325-674-2656, Fax: 325-674-6717, E-mail: gradinfo@acu.edu. *Department Chair,* Bill Fowler, 325-674-2080, Fax: 325-674-2564, E-mail: bill.fowler@coba.acu.edu.

College of Education and Human Services Students: 72 full-time (63 women), 267 part-time (189 women); includes 41 Black or African American, non-Hispanic/Latino; 4 Asian, non-Hispanic/Latino; 32 Hispanic/Latino; 6 Two or more races, non-Hispanic/Latino, 9 international. 302 applicants, 51% accepted, 140 enrolled. *Faculty:* 4 full-time (1 woman), 18 part-time/adjunct (8 women). Expenses: Contact institution. *Financial support:* In 2010–11, 38 students received support. Application deadline: 4/1. In 2010, 84 master's awarded. Offers communication sciences and disorders (MS); curriculum and instruction (M Ed); education and human services (M Ed, MS, MSSW, Post-Master's Certificate); higher education (M Ed); leadership of learning (M Ed); social work (MSSW); superintendency (Post-Master's Certificate). *Application deadline:* For fall admission, 4/1 priority date for domestic students; for spring admission, 11/1 for domestic students. Applications are processed on a rolling basis. *Application fee:* $40. Electronic applications accepted. *Application Contact:* David Pittman, Graduate Admissions Counselor, 325-674-2656, Fax: 325-674-6717, E-mail: gradinfo@acu.edu. *Dean,* Dr. Malesa Breeding, 325-674-2700.

School of Nursing Students: 1 full-time (0 women), 5 part-time (3 women); includes 1 American Indian or Alaska Native, non-Hispanic/Latino; 1 Asian, non-Hispanic/Latino; 1 Hispanic/Latino; 1 Two or more races, non-Hispanic/Latino. 2 applicants, 100% accepted, 2 enrolled. *Faculty:* 3 part-time/adjunct (all women). Expenses: Contact institution. *Financial support:* In 2010–11, 1 student received support. Application deadline: 4/1. In 2010, 7 master's awarded. *Degree program information:* Part-time programs available. Offers education and administration (MSN); family nurse practitioner (MSN). *Application deadline:* For fall admission, 4/1 priority date for domestic students; for spring admission, 11/1 for domestic students. Applications are processed on a rolling basis. *Application fee:* $40. Electronic applications accepted. *Application Contact:* David Pittman, Graduate Admissions Counselor, 325-674-2656, Fax: 325-674-6717, E-mail: gradinfo@acu.edu. *Graduate Director,* Dr. Amy Toone, 325-671-2361, Fax: 325-671-2386, E-mail: atoone@phssn.edu.

ACADEMY FOR FIVE ELEMENT ACUPUNCTURE, Hallandale, FL 33009

General Information Independent, coed, graduate-only institution.

GRADUATE UNITS

Graduate Program Offers acupuncture (M Ac).

ACADEMY OF ART UNIVERSITY, San Francisco, CA 94105-3410

General Information Proprietary, coed, comprehensive institution. *Enrollment:* 3,183 full-time matriculated graduate/professional students (1,837 women), 2,333 part-time matriculated graduate/professional students (1,468 women). *Enrollment by degree level:* 5,516 master's. *Graduate faculty:* 201 full-time (82 women), 334 part-time/adjunct (124 women). *Tuition:* Full-time $20,160; part-time $840 per semester hour. *Required fees:* $45 per semester. *Graduate housing:* Room and/or apartments guaranteed to single students; on-campus housing not available to married students. Typical cost: $9800 per year ($13,400 including board). Housing application deadline: 9/7. *Student services:* Campus employment opportunities, campus safety program, career counseling, international student services, low-cost health insurance, services for students with disabilities, teacher training, writing training. *Library facilities:* Academy of Art University Library. *Online resources:* library catalog, web page, access to other libraries' catalogs. *Collection:* 36,000 titles, 476 serial subscriptions, 3,500 audiovisual materials.

Computer facilities: 800 computers available on campus for general student use. A campuswide network can be accessed from off campus. Online class registration is available. *Web address:* http://www.academyart.edu/.

General Application Contact: Cindy Cai, Director of Graduate Domestic Admissions, 800-544-ARTS, Fax: 415-263-4130, E-mail: info@academyart.edu.

GRADUATE UNITS

Graduate Program Students: 3,183 full-time (1,837 women), 2,333 part-time (1,468 women); includes 322 Black or African American, non-Hispanic/Latino; 26 American Indian or Alaska Native, non-Hispanic/Latino; 336 Asian, non-Hispanic/Latino; 266 Hispanic/Latino; 4 Native Hawaiian or other Pacific Islander, non-Hispanic/Latino, 1,915 international. Average age 31. 1,863 applicants. *Faculty:* 201 full-time (82 women), 1,093 part-time/adjunct (468 women). Expenses: Contact institution. *Financial support:* Career-related internships or fieldwork and Federal Work-Study available. Support available to part-time students. Financial award application deadline: 8/10; financial award applicants required to submit FAFSA. In 2010, 520 master's awarded. *Degree program information:* Part-time and evening/weekend programs available. Postbaccalaureate distance learning degree programs offered (no on-campus study). *Application deadline:* For fall admission, 9/7 for domestic and international students; for spring admission, 2/2 for domestic and international students. Applications are processed on a rolling basis. *Application fee:* $100 ($500 for international students). Electronic applications accepted. *Application Contact:* 800-544-ARTS, Fax: 415-263-4130, E-mail: info@academyart.edu.

School of Advertising Students: 201 full-time (123 women), 95 part-time (64 women); includes 24 Black or African American, non-Hispanic/Latino; 20 Asian, non-Hispanic/Latino; 14 Hispanic/Latino, 115 international. Average age 28. 87 applicants. *Faculty:* 9 full-time (2 women), 51 part-time/adjunct (17 women). Expenses: Contact institution. *Financial support:* Career-related internships or fieldwork and Federal Work-Study available. Support available to part-time students. Financial award application deadline: 8/10; financial award applicants required to submit FAFSA. In 2010, 38 degrees awarded. *Degree program information:* Part-time programs available. Postbaccalaureate distance learning degree programs offered (no on-campus study). Offers advertising (MFA). *Application deadline:* For fall admission, 9/7 for domestic and international students; for spring admission, 2/2 for domestic and international students. Applications are processed on a rolling basis. *Application fee:* $100 ($500 for international students). Electronic applications accepted. *Application Contact:* 800-544-ARTS, Fax: 415-263-4130, E-mail: info@academyart.edu.

School of Animation and Visual Effects Students: 613 full-time (224 women), 340 part-time (118 women); includes 41 Black or African American, non-Hispanic/Latino; 3 American Indian or Alaska Native, non-Hispanic/Latino; 70 Asian, non-Hispanic/Latino; 47 Hispanic/Latino; 1 Native Hawaiian or other Pacific Islander, non-Hispanic/Latino, 448 international. Average age 29. 244 applicants. *Faculty:* 20 full-time (4 women), 90 part-time/adjunct (17 women). Expenses: Contact institution. *Financial support:* Career-related internships or fieldwork and Federal Work-Study available. Support available to part-time students. Financial award application deadline: 8/10; financial award applicants required to submit FAFSA. In 2010, 109 master's awarded. *Degree program information:* Part-time programs available. Postbaccalaureate distance learning degree programs offered (no on-campus study). Offers 2D animation (MFA); 3D animation (MFA); 3D modeling (MFA); visual effects (MFA). *Application deadline:* For fall admission, 9/7 for domestic and international students; for spring admission, 2/2 for domestic and international students. Applications are processed on a rolling basis. *Application fee:* $100 ($500 for international students). Electronic applications accepted.

School of Architecture Students: 153 full-time (70 women), 36 part-time (11 women); includes 7 Black or African American, non-Hispanic/Latino; 19 Asian, non-Hispanic/Latino; 10 Hispanic/Latino, 90 international. Average age 29. 147 applicants. *Faculty:* 2 full-time (1 woman), 27 part-time/adjunct (8 women). Expenses: Contact institution. *Financial support:* Career-related internships or fieldwork and Federal Work-Study available. Support available to part-time students. Financial award application deadline: 8/10; financial award applicants required to submit FAFSA. In 2010, 7 master's awarded. *Degree program information:* Part-time programs available. Postbaccalaureate distance learning degree programs offered (no on-campus study). Offers architecture (M Arch). *Application deadline:* For fall admission, 9/7 for domestic and international students; for spring admission, 2/2 for domestic and international students. Applications are processed on a rolling basis. *Application fee:* $100 ($500 for international students). Electronic applications accepted. *Application Contact:* Prospective Students Services, 800-544-ARTS, Fax: 415-263-4131, E-mail: info@academyart.edu.

School of Art Education Students: 7 full-time (6 women), 4 part-time (2 women); includes 1 Black or African American, non-Hispanic/Latino; 1 Hispanic/Latino, 4 international. Average age 29. 21 applicants. *Faculty:* 1 (woman) full-time, 1 (woman) part-time/adjunct. Expenses: Contact institution. *Financial support:* Career-related internships or fieldwork and Federal Work-Study available. Support available to part-time students. Financial award application deadline: 8/10; financial award applicants required to submit FAFSA. *Degree program information:* Part-time programs available. Postbaccalaureate distance learning degree programs offered (no on-campus study). Offers art education (MA). *Application deadline:* For fall admission, 9/7 for domestic and international students; for spring admission, 2/2 for domestic and international students. Applications are processed on a rolling basis. *Application fee:* $100 ($500 for international students). Electronic applications accepted.

School of Fashion Students: 487 full-time (445 women), 260 part-time (237 women); includes 73 Black or African American, non-Hispanic/Latino; 6 American Indian or Alaska Native, non-Hispanic/Latino; 45 Asian, non-Hispanic/Latino; 35 Hispanic/Latino, 310 international. Average age 29. 218 applicants. *Faculty:* 23 full-time (13 women), 110 part-time/adjunct (87 women). Expenses: Contact institution. *Financial support:* Career-related internships or fieldwork and Federal Work-Study available. Support available to part-time students. Financial award application deadline: 8/10; financial award applicants required to submit FAFSA. In 2010, 107 master's awarded. *Degree program information:* Part-time programs available. Postbaccalaureate distance learning degree programs offered (no on-campus study). Offers fashion design (MFA); fashion merchandising (MFA); fashion textiles (MFA); knitwear (MFA). *Application deadline:* For fall admission, 9/7 for domestic and international students; for spring admission, 2/2 for domestic and international students. Applications are processed on a rolling basis. *Application fee:* $100 ($500 for international students). Electronic applications accepted. *Application Contact:* Prospective Student Services, 800-544-ARTS, Fax: 415-263-4130, E-mail: info@academyart.edu.

School of Fine Art Students: 151 full-time (93 women), 266 part-time (193 women); includes 15 Black or African American, non-Hispanic/Latino; 1 American Indian or Alaska Native, non-Hispanic/Latino; 29 Asian, non-Hispanic/Latino; 22 Hispanic/Latino, 58 international. Average age 40. 115 applicants. *Faculty:* 19 full-time (7 women), 65 part-time/adjunct (28 women). Expenses: Contact institution. *Financial support:* Career-related internships or fieldwork and Federal Work-Study available. Support available to part-time students. Financial award application deadline: 8/10; financial award applicants required to submit FAFSA. In 2010, 38 master's awarded. *Degree program information:* Part-time programs available. Postbaccalaureate distance learning degree programs offered (no on-campus study). Offers figurative painting (MFA); non-figurative painting (MFA); printmaking (MFA); sculpture (MFA). *Application deadline:* For fall admission, 9/7 for domestic and international students; for spring admission, 2/2 for domestic and international students. Applications are processed on a rolling basis. *Application fee:* $100 ($500 for international students). Electronic applications accepted. *Application Contact:* Prospective Student Services, 800-544-ARTS, Fax: 415-263-4130, E-mail: info@academyart.edu.

School of Game Design Students: 58 full-time (13 women), 22 part-time (9 women); includes 5 Black or African American, non-Hispanic/Latino; 1 American Indian or Alaska Native, non-Hispanic/Latino; 7 Asian, non-Hispanic/Latino; 3 Hispanic/Latino; 1 Native Hawaiian or other Pacific Islander, non-Hispanic/Latino, 25 international. Average age 27. 80 applicants. *Faculty:* 3 full-time (0 women), 8 part-time/adjunct (1 woman). Expenses: Contact institution. *Financial support:* Career-related internships or fieldwork and Federal Work-Study available. Support available to part-time students. Financial award application deadline: 8/10; financial award applicants required to submit FAFSA. *Degree program information:* Part-time programs available. Postbaccalaureate distance learning degree programs offered (no on-campus study). Offers game design (MFA). *Application deadline:* For fall admission, 9/7 for domestic and international students; for spring admission, 2/2 for domestic and international students. Applications are processed on a rolling basis. *Application fee:* $100 ($500 for international students). Electronic applications accepted.

School of Graphic Design Students: 184 full-time (128 women), 217 part-time (158 women); includes 18 Black or African American, non-Hispanic/Latino; 1 American Indian or Alaska Native, non-Hispanic/Latino; 26 Asian, non-Hispanic/Latino; 18 Hispanic/Latino, 138 international. Average age 30. 170 applicants. *Faculty:* 9 full-time (3 women), 64 part-time/adjunct (28 women). Expenses: Contact institution. *Financial support:* Career-related internships or fieldwork and Federal Work-Study available. Support available to part-time students. Financial award application deadline: 8/10; financial award applicants required to submit FAFSA. In 2010, 15 master's awarded. *Degree program information:* Part-time programs available. Postbaccalaureate distance learning degree programs offered (no on-campus study). Offers graphic design (MFA). *Application deadline:* For fall admission, 9/7 for domestic and international students; for spring admission, 2/2 for domestic and international students. Applications are processed on a rolling basis. *Application fee:* $100 ($500 for international students). Electronic applications accepted. *Application Contact:* Prospective Student Services, 800-544-ARTS, Fax: 415-263-4130, E-mail: info@academyart.edu.

School of Illustration Students: 158 full-time (103 women), 185 part-time (95 women); includes 12 Black or African American, non-Hispanic/Latino; 5 American Indian or Alaska Native, non-Hispanic/Latino; 17 Asian, non-Hispanic/Latino; 11 Hispanic/Latino; 1 Native Hawaiian or other Pacific Islander, non-Hispanic/Latino, 87 international. Average age 32. 114 applicants. *Faculty:* 12 full-time (2 women), 45 part-time/adjunct (5 women). Expenses: Contact institution. *Financial support:* Career-related internships or fieldwork and Federal Work-Study available. Support available to part-time students. Financial award application deadline: 8/10; financial award applicants required to submit FAFSA. In 2010, 31 master's awarded. *Degree program information:* Part-time programs available. Postbaccalaureate distance learning degree programs offered (no on-campus study). Offers illustration (MFA). *Application deadline:* For fall admission, 9/7 for domestic and international students; for spring admission, 2/2 for domestic and international students. Applications are processed on a rolling basis. *Application fee:* $100 ($500 for international students). Electronic applications accepted. *Application Contact:* Prospective Student Services, 800-544-ARTS, Fax: 415-263-4130, E-mail: info@academyart.edu.

School of Industrial Design Students: 149 full-time (59 women), 53 part-time (19 women); includes 2 Black or African American, non-Hispanic/Latino; 12 Asian, non-Hispanic/Latino; 10 Hispanic/Latino, 120 international. Average age 28. 85 applicants. *Faculty:* 5 full-time (0 women), 41 part-time/adjunct (9 women). Expenses: Contact institution. *Financial support:* Career-related internships or fieldwork and Federal Work-Study available. Support available to part-time students. Financial award application deadline: 8/10; financial award applicants required to submit FAFSA. In 2010, 18 master's awarded. *Degree program information:* Part-time programs available. Postbaccalaureate distance learning degree programs offered (no on-campus study). Offers industrial design (MFA). *Application deadline:* For fall admission, 9/7 for domestic and international students; for spring admission, 2/2 for domestic and international students. Applications are processed on a rolling basis. *Application fee:* $100 ($500 for international students). Electronic applications accepted. *Application Contact:* 800-544-ARTS, Fax: 415-263-4130, E-mail: info@academyart.edu.

School of Interior Architecture and Design Students: 181 full-time (146 women), 185 part-time (160 women); includes 13 Black or African American, non-Hispanic/Latino; 21 Asian, non-Hispanic/Latino; 17 Hispanic/Latino, 107 international. Average age 32. 127 applicants. *Faculty:* 5 full-time (3 women), 55 part-time/adjunct (28 women). Expenses: Contact institution. *Financial support:* Career-related internships or fieldwork and Federal Work-Study available. Support available to part-time students. Financial award application deadline: 8/10; financial award applicants required to submit FAFSA. In 2010, 10 master's awarded. *Degree program information:* Part-time programs available. Postbaccalaureate distance learning degree programs offered (no on-campus study). Offers interior architecture and design (MFA). *Application deadline:* For fall admission, 9/7 for domestic and international students; for spring admission, 2/2 for domestic and international students. Applications are processed on a rolling basis. *Application fee:* $100 ($500 for international students). Electronic applications accepted. *Application Contact:* 800-544-ARTS, Fax: 415-263-4130, E-mail: info@academyart.edu.

School of Motion Pictures and Television Students: 253 full-time (105 women), 154 part-time (67 women); includes 43 Black or African American, non-Hispanic/Latino; 4 American Indian or Alaska Native, non-Hispanic/Latino; 14 Asian, non-Hispanic/Latino; 26 Hispanic/Latino; 1 Native Hawaiian or other Pacific Islander, non-Hispanic/Latino, 111 international. Average age 31. 153 applicants. *Faculty:* 10 full-time (3 women), 98 part-time/adjunct (33 women). Expenses: Contact institution. *Financial support:* Career-related internships or fieldwork and Federal Work-Study available. Support available to part-time students. Financial award application deadline: 8/10; financial award applicants required to submit FAFSA. In 2010, 58 master's awarded. *Degree program information:* Part-time programs available. Postbaccalaureate distance learning degree programs offered (no on-campus study). Offers motion pictures and television (MFA). *Application deadline:* For fall admission, 9/7 for domestic and international students; for spring admission, 2/2 for domestic and international students. Applications are processed on a rolling basis. *Application fee:* $100 ($500 for international students). Electronic applications accepted. *Application Contact:* 800-544-ARTS, Fax: 415-263-4130, E-mail: info@academyart.edu.

School of Multimedia Communications Students: 112 full-time (78 women), 38 part-time (25 women); includes 16 Black or African American, non-Hispanic/Latino; 1 American Indian or Alaska Native, non-Hispanic/Latino; 5 Asian, non-Hispanic/Latino; 7 Hispanic/Latino, 74 international. Average age 28. 77 applicants. *Faculty:* 3 full-time (1 woman), 24 part-time/adjunct (8 women). Expenses: Contact institution. *Financial support:* Career-related internships or fieldwork and Federal Work-Study available. Support available to part-time students. Financial award applicants required to submit FAFSA. In 2010, 4 master's awarded. *Degree program information:* Part-time programs available. Postbaccalaureate distance learning degree programs offered. Offers multimedia communications (MA). *Application deadline:* For fall admission, 9/7 for domestic and international students; for spring admission, 2/2 for domestic and international students. Applications are processed on a rolling basis. *Application fee:* $100 ($500 for international students). Electronic applications accepted.

School of Music Production and Sound Design for Visual Media Students: 26 full-time (10 women), 8 part-time (2 women); includes 1 Black or African American, non-Hispanic/Latino; 2 Asian, non-Hispanic/Latino; 2 Hispanic/Latino, 15 international. Average age 30. 19 applicants. *Faculty:* 1 full-time (0 women), 11 part-time/adjunct (2 women). Expenses: Contact institution. *Financial support:* Career-related internships or fieldwork and Federal Work-Study available. Support available to part-time students. Financial award application deadline: 8/10; financial award applicants required to submit FAFSA. *Degree program information:* Part-time programs available. Postbaccalaureate distance learning degree programs offered (no on-campus study). Offers music production and sound design for visual media (MFA). *Application deadline:* For fall admission, 9/7 for domestic and international students; for spring admission, 2/2 for domestic and international students. Applications are processed on a rolling basis. *Application fee:* $100 ($500 for international students). Electronic applications accepted.

School of Photography Students: 199 full-time (127 women), 275 part-time (167 women); includes 24 Black or African American, non-Hispanic/Latino; 3 American Indian or Alaska Native, non-Hispanic/Latino; 14 Asian, non-Hispanic/Latino; 23 Hispanic/Latino, 64 international. Average age 34. 143 applicants. *Faculty:* 16 full-time (6 women), 85 part-time/adjunct (28 women). Expenses: Contact institution. *Financial support:* Career-related internships or fieldwork and Federal Work-Study available. Support available to part-time students. Financial award application deadline: 8/10; financial award applicants required to submit FAFSA. In 2010, 48 master's awarded. *Degree program information:* Part-time programs available. Postbaccalaureate distance learning degree programs offered (no on-campus study). Offers photography (MFA). *Application deadline:* For fall admission, 9/7 for domestic and international students; for spring admission, 2/2 for domestic and international students. Applications are processed on a rolling basis. *Application fee:* $100 ($500 for international students). Electronic applications accepted. *Application Contact:* 800-544-ARTS, Fax: 415-263-4130, E-mail: info@academyart.edu.

School of Web Design and New Media Students: 224 full-time (117 women), 222 part-time (134 women); includes 27 Black or African American, non-Hispanic/Latino; 1 American Indian or Alaska Native, non-Hispanic/Latino; 35 Asian, non-Hispanic/Latino; 20 Hispanic/Latino, 149 international. Average age 31. 108 applicants. *Faculty:* 5 full-time (2 women), 58 part-time/adjunct (17 women). Expenses: Contact institution. *Financial support:* Career-related internships or fieldwork and Federal Work-Study available. Support available to part-time students. Financial award application deadline: 8/10; financial award applicants required to submit FAFSA. In 2010, 37 master's awarded. *Degree program information:* Part-time and evening/weekend programs available. Postbaccalaureate distance learning degree programs offered (no on-campus study). Offers Web design and new media (MFA). *Application deadline:* For fall admission, 9/7 for domestic and international students; for spring admission, 2/2 for domestic students, 9/2 for international students. Applications are processed on a rolling basis. *Application fee:* $100 ($500 for international students). Electronic applications accepted. *Application Contact:* 800-544-ARTS, Fax: 415-263-4130, E-mail: info@academyart.edu.

ACADEMY OF CHINESE CULTURE AND HEALTH SCIENCES, Oakland, CA 94612

General Information Private, coed, graduate-only institution. *Graduate housing:* On-campus housing not available.

GRADUATE UNITS

Program in Traditional Chinese Medicine *Degree program information:* Part-time and evening/weekend programs available. Offers traditional Chinese medicine (MS).

ACADEMY OF ORIENTAL MEDICINE AT AUSTIN, Austin, TX 78757

General Information Proprietary, coed, graduate-only institution. *Enrollment by degree level:* 213 master's. *Graduate faculty:* 10 full-time (3 women), 15 part-time/adjunct (8 women). *Tuition:* Full-time $11,883; part-time $195 per credit. One-time fee: $75. Part-time tuition and fees vary according to course load and program. *Student services:* Campus employment opportunities, campus safety program, career counseling, exercise/wellness program, international student services, services for students with disabilities. *Library facilities:* AOMA Library. *Online resources:* web page. *Collection:* 6 titles, 1 serial subscription, 615 audiovisual materials.

Computer facilities: 8 computers available on campus for general student use. A campuswide network can be accessed from off campus. Wireless Internet Access available. *Web address:* http://www.aoma.edu/.

General Application Contact: Hannah Thornton, Director of Admissions and Student Services, 512-492-3017, Fax: 512-454-7001, E-mail: admissions@aoma.edu.

GRADUATE UNITS

Master of Acupuncture and Oriental Medicine Program Students: 174 full-time (124 women), 39 part-time (32 women); includes 8 Black or African American, non-Hispanic/Latino; 21 Asian, non-Hispanic/Latino; 22 Hispanic/Latino. Average age 35. 43 applicants, 88% accepted, 32 enrolled. *Faculty:* 10 full-time (3 women), 15 part-time/adjunct (8 women). Expenses: Contact institution. *Financial support:* Scholarships/grants available. Financial award applicants required to submit FAFSA. In 2010, 41 master's awarded. Offers acupuncture and oriental medicine (MAcOM). *Application deadline:* For fall admission, 7/19 priority date for domestic students; for winter admission, 11/1 priority date for domestic students; for spring admission, 5/15 priority date for domestic students. Applications are processed on a rolling basis. *Application fee:* $75. Electronic applications accepted. *Application Contact:* Hannah Thornton, Director of Admissions and Student Services, 512-492-3017, Fax: 512-454-7001, E-mail: admissions@aoma.edu. *President,* Dr. William R. Morris, 512-454-1188, Fax: 512-454-7001, E-mail: info@aoma.edu.

ACADIA UNIVERSITY, Wolfville, NS B4P 2R6, Canada

General Information Province-supported, coed, comprehensive institution. *Enrollment:* 3,439 graduate, professional, and undergraduate students; 160 full-time matriculated graduate/professional students (81 women), 167 part-time matriculated graduate/professional students (106 women). *Enrollment by degree level:* 272 master's, 55 doctoral. *Graduate faculty:* 145 full-time (51 women), 86 part-time/adjunct (27 women). *Graduate housing:* Room and/or apartments available on a first-come, first-served basis to single students; on-campus housing not available to married students. Typical cost: $5520 Canadian dollars per year ($9200 Canadian dollars including board). Housing application deadline: 5/31. *Student services:* Campus employment opportunities, campus safety program, career counseling, exercise/wellness program, free psychological counseling, international student services, low-cost health insurance, services for students with disabilities, writing training. *Library facilities:* Vaughan Memorial Library. *Online resources:* library catalog, web page, access to other libraries' catalogs. *Collection:* 1.4 million titles, 34,962 serial subscriptions, 13,313 audiovisual materials. *Research affiliation:* Atlantic Research Laboratory.

Computer facilities: Computer purchase and lease plans are available. A campuswide network can be accessed from student residence rooms and from off campus. Online class registration is available. *Web address:* http://www.acadiau.ca/.

General Application Contact: Theresa Starratt, Graduate Studies Officer, 902-585-1914, Fax: 902-585-1096, E-mail: gradadmissions@acadiau.ca.

GRADUATE UNITS

Divinity College Students: 34 full-time (9 women), 29 part-time (11 women). Average age 43. *Faculty:* 12 full-time (2 women), 12 part-time/adjunct (1 woman). Expenses: Contact institution. *Financial support:* In 2010–11, 8 teaching assistantships (averaging $1,000 per year) were awarded; career-related internships or fieldwork, institutionally sponsored loans, and

Acadia University (continued)

scholarships/grants also available. Support available to part-time students. Financial award application deadline: 8/12. In 2010, 53 master's, 7 doctorates awarded. *Degree program information:* Part-time programs available. Offers divinity (M Div); theology (MA, D Min). *Application deadline:* For fall admission, 6/30 priority date for domestic students, 4/1 priority date for international students; for spring admission, 4/30 priority date for domestic students. Applications are processed on a rolling basis. *Application fee:* $50. *Application Contact:* Shawna Peverill, Registrar, 902-585-2215, Fax: 902-585-2233, E-mail: shawna.peverill@acadiau.ca. *President*, Dr. Harry Gardner, 902-585-2212, Fax: 902-585-2233, E-mail: harry.gardner@acadiau.ca.

Faculty of Arts Students: 17 full-time (10 women), 13 part-time (10 women). Average age 25. 50 applicants, 62% accepted, 17 enrolled. *Faculty:* 42 full-time (16 women), 3 part-time/adjunct (1 woman). Expenses: Contact institution. *Financial support:* Research assistantships, teaching assistantships, scholarships/grants and unspecified assistantships available. Financial award application deadline: 2/1. In 2010, 8 master's awarded. Offers arts (MA); English (MA); political science (MA); sociology (MA). *Application deadline:* For fall admission, 2/1 for domestic and international students. Applications are processed on a rolling basis. *Application fee:* $50. *Application Contact:* Dr. Robert J. Perrins, Dean, 902-585-1485, Fax: 902-585-1070, E-mail: robert.perrins@acadiau.ca. *Dean*, Dr. Robert J. Perrins, 902-585-1485, Fax: 902-585-1070, E-mail: robert.perrins@acadiau.ca.

Faculty of Professional Studies Students: 16 full-time (11 women), 85 part-time (71 women). 228 applicants, 59% accepted. *Faculty:* 22 full-time (13 women), 1 part-time/adjunct (0 women). Expenses: Contact institution. *Financial support:* Research assistantships, teaching assistantships available. Financial award application deadline: 2/1. In 2010, 135 master's awarded. *Application deadline:* Applications are processed on a rolling basis. *Application fee:* $50. *Application Contact:* Rosie Hare, Administrative Assistant, 902-585-1597, Fax: 902-585-1086, E-mail: rosie.hare@acadiau.ca. *Dean*, Dr. Heather Hemming, 902-585-1597, Fax: 902-585-1086, E-mail: heather.hemming@acadiau.ca.

School of Education Students: 13 full-time (9 women), 84 part-time (70 women). 228 applicants, 59% accepted. *Faculty:* 24 full-time (13 women), 1 part-time/adjunct (0 women). Expenses: Contact institution. *Financial support:* Research assistantships, teaching assistantships, unspecified assistantships available. Financial award application deadline: 2/1. In 2010, 135 master's awarded. Offers counseling (M Ed); cultural and media studies (M Ed); curriculum studies (M Ed); inclusive education (M Ed); leadership (M Ed); learning and technology (M Ed); science, math and technology (M Ed). *Application deadline:* Applications are processed on a rolling basis. *Application fee:* $50. *Application Contact:* Sheila Langille, Secretary, 902-585-1229, Fax: 902-585-1071, E-mail: sheila.langille@acadiau.ca. *Director*, Ann Vibert, 902-585-1229, E-mail: ann.vibert@acadiau.ca.

School of Recreation Management and Kinesiology Students: 3 full-time (2 women), 1 (woman) part-time. 5 applicants, 40% accepted, 2 enrolled. Expenses: Contact institution. *Financial support:* In 2010–11, teaching assistantships (averaging $9,000 per year); unspecified assistantships also available. Financial award application deadline: 2/1. Offers recreation management and kinesiology (MR). *Application deadline:* For fall admission, 2/1 priority date for domestic and international students. Applications are processed on a rolling basis. *Application fee:* $50. *Application Contact:* Dr. Rene Murphy, Director, 902-585-1559, Fax: 902-585-1702, E-mail: rene.murphy@acadiau.ca. *Director*, Dr. Rene Murphy, 902-585-1559, Fax: 902-585-1702, E-mail: rene.murphy@acadiau.ca.

Faculty of Pure and Applied Science Students: 58 full-time (32 women), 29 part-time (14 women). 125 applicants, 42% accepted, 38 enrolled. *Faculty:* 95 full-time (28 women), 16 part-time/adjunct (7 women). Expenses: Contact institution. *Financial support:* Fellowships, research assistantships, teaching assistantships, career-related internships or fieldwork, scholarships/grants, and unspecified assistantships available. Financial award application deadline: 2/1. In 2010, 22 master's awarded. Offers applied geomatics (M Sc); applied mathematics and statistics (M Sc); biology (M Sc); chemistry (M Sc); clinical psychology (M Sc); earth and environmental science (M Sc); pure and applied science (M Sc). *Application deadline:* For fall admission, 2/1 priority date for domestic and international students. Applications are processed on a rolling basis. *Application fee:* $50. *Application Contact:* Dr. Peter Williams, Dean, 902-585-1473, Fax: 902-585-1637, E-mail: peter.williams@acadiau.ca. *Dean*, Dr. Peter Williams, 902-585-1473, Fax: 902-585-1637, E-mail: peter.williams@acadiau.ca.

Jodrey School of Computer Science Students: 9 full-time (1 woman), 6 part-time (0 women). Average age 28. 40 applicants, 48% accepted, 11 enrolled. *Faculty:* 6 full-time (0 women), 5 part-time/adjunct (0 women). Expenses: Contact institution. *Financial support:* Research assistantships, teaching assistantships, career-related internships or fieldwork, scholarships/grants, and unspecified assistantships available. Financial award application deadline: 2/1. In 2010, 5 master's awarded. Offers computer science (M Sc). *Application deadline:* For fall admission, 2/1 priority date for domestic and international students. Applications are processed on a rolling basis. *Application fee:* $50. *Application Contact:* Dr. Andre Trudel, Graduate Coordinator, 902-585-1136, E-mail: andre.trudel@acadiau.ca. *Director*, Dr. Daniel L. Silver, 902-585-1331, Fax: 902-585-1067, E-mail: cs@acadiau.ca.

ACUPUNCTURE & INTEGRATIVE MEDICINE COLLEGE, BERKELEY, Berkeley, CA 94704

General Information Independent, coed, graduate-only institution. *Graduate housing:* On-campus housing not available.

GRADUATE UNITS

Program in Oriental Medicine *Degree program information:* Part-time and evening/weekend programs available. Offers Oriental medicine (MS).

ACUPUNCTURE AND MASSAGE COLLEGE, Miami, FL 33176

General Information Proprietary, coed, graduate-only institution.

GRADUATE UNITS

Program in Oriental Medicine Offers Oriental medicine (MOM).

ADAMS STATE COLLEGE, Alamosa, CO 81102

General Information State-supported, coed, comprehensive institution. CGS member. *Graduate housing:* Rooms and/or apartments available to single and married students. Housing application deadline: 5/15. *Research affiliation:* Sandia National Laboratories (science education).

GRADUATE UNITS

The Graduate School *Degree program information:* Part-time programs available. Postbaccalaureate distance learning degree programs offered. Offers art (MA); counseling (MA); education (MA); history (MA); human performance and physical education (MA); special education (MA).

ADELPHI UNIVERSITY, Garden City, NY 11530-0701

General Information Independent, coed, university. *Enrollment:* 7,917 graduate, professional, and undergraduate students; 1,040 full-time matriculated graduate/professional students (829 women), 1,879 part-time matriculated graduate/professional students (1,461 women). *Enrollment by degree level:* 2,687 master's, 232 doctoral. *Graduate faculty:* 311 full-time (163 women), 656 part-time/adjunct (426 women). *Graduate housing:* Room and/or apartments available on a first-come, first-served basis to single students; on-campus housing not available to married students. *Student services:* Campus employment opportunities, campus safety program, career counseling, child daycare facilities, exercise/wellness program, free psychological counseling, international student services, low-cost health insurance, multicultural affairs office, services for students with disabilities, teacher training, writing training. *Library facilities:* Swirbul Library plus 1 other. *Online resources:* library catalog, web page, access to other libraries' catalogs. *Collection:* 599,524 titles, 62,812 serial subscriptions, 25,438 audiovisual materials. *Research affiliation:* Teagle Foundation, World Anti-doping Agency, The National Science Foundation, The Research Corporation, The Horace Hagedorn Foundation, Albert Einstein College of Medicine.

Computer facilities: Computer purchase and lease plans are available. 880 computers available on campus for general student use. A campuswide network can be accessed from student residence rooms and from off campus. Online class registration, payment, drop/add classes, check application status are available. *Web address:* http://www.adelphi.edu/.

General Application Contact: Christine Murphy, Director of Admissions, 516-877-3050, Fax: 516-877-3039, E-mail: graduateadmissions@adelphi.edu.

GRADUATE UNITS

College of Arts and Sciences Students: 24 full-time (13 women), 74 part-time (44 women); includes 8 Black or African American, non-Hispanic/Latino; 2 Asian, non-Hispanic/Latino; 6 Hispanic/Latino, 17 international. Average age 29. 180 applicants, 52% accepted, 41 enrolled. *Faculty:* 118 full-time (49 women), 179 part-time/adjunct (92 women). Expenses: Contact institution. *Financial support:* In 2010–11, 35 research assistantships with full and partial tuition reimbursements (averaging $11,539 per year) were awarded; fellowships, teaching assistantships, career-related internships or fieldwork, Federal Work-Study, institutionally sponsored loans, tuition waivers (full and partial), and unspecified assistantships also available. Support available to part-time students. Financial award application deadline: 2/15; financial award applicants required to submit FAFSA. In 2010, 28 master's awarded. *Degree program information:* Part-time programs available. Offers arts and sciences (MA, MFA, MS); biology (MS); creative writing (MFA); environmental studies (MS); studio art (MA). *Application deadline:* For fall admission, 5/1 priority date for international students; for spring admission, 11/1 priority date for international students. Applications are processed on a rolling basis. *Application fee:* $50. Electronic applications accepted. *Application Contact:* Christine Murphy, Director of Admissions, 516-877-3050, Fax: 516-877-3039, E-mail: graduateadmissions@adelphi.edu. *Dean*, Dr. Sam L. Grogg, 516-877-4124, Fax: 516-877-4191, E-mail: sjr@adelphi.edu.

Derner Institute of Advanced Psychological Studies Students: 186 full-time (154 women), 111 part-time (94 women); includes 63 minority (24 Black or African American, non-Hispanic/Latino; 2 American Indian or Alaska Native, non-Hispanic/Latino; 15 Asian, non-Hispanic/Latino; 17 Hispanic/Latino; 1 Native Hawaiian or other Pacific Islander, non-Hispanic/Latino; 4 Two or more races, non-Hispanic/Latino), 16 international. Average age 28. 566 applicants, 36% accepted, 100 enrolled. *Faculty:* 24 full-time (11 women), 67 part-time/adjunct (38 women). Expenses: Contact institution. *Financial support:* In 2010–11, 107 research assistantships with full and partial tuition reimbursements (averaging $8,303 per year) were awarded; teaching assistantships, career-related internships or fieldwork, Federal Work-Study, institutionally sponsored loans, and unspecified assistantships also available. Financial award application deadline: 2/15; financial award applicants required to submit FAFSA. In 2010, 115 master's, 29 doctorates awarded. *Degree program information:* Part-time programs available. Offers clinical psychology (PhD); general psychology (MA); mental health counseling (MA); school psychology (MA). *Application deadline:* For fall admission, 4/1 priority date for domestic students, 5/1 priority date for international students; for spring admission, 11/1 priority date for international students. *Application fee:* $50. Electronic applications accepted. *Application Contact:* Christine Murphy, Director of Admissions, 516-877-3050, Fax: 516-877-3039, E-mail: graduateadmissions@adelphi.edu. *Dean*, Dr. Jacques P. Barber, 516-877-4803, E-mail: jcmuran@adelphi.edu.

School of Business Students: 145 full-time (67 women), 202 part-time (84 women); includes 34 Black or African American, non-Hispanic/Latino; 28 Asian, non-Hispanic/Latino; 21 Hispanic/Latino; 5 Two or more races, non-Hispanic/Latino, 111 international. Average age 30. 669 applicants, 29% accepted, 122 enrolled. *Faculty:* 39 full-time (8 women), 21 part-time/adjunct (4 women). Expenses: Contact institution. *Financial support:* In 2010–11, 36 research assistantships with partial tuition reimbursements (averaging $6,682 per year) were awarded; teaching assistantships, career-related internships or fieldwork, Federal Work-Study, institutionally sponsored loans, scholarships/grants, and unspecified assistantships also available. Financial award application deadline: 3/1; financial award applicants required to submit FAFSA. In 2010, 86 master's, 5 other advanced degrees awarded. *Degree program information:* Part-time and evening/weekend programs available. Offers accounting (MBA); business (MBA, Certificate); finance (MBA); human resources management (Certificate); management information systems (MBA); management/human resource management (MBA); marketing/e-commerce (MBA). *Application deadline:* For fall admission, 4/1 for international students; for spring admission, 11/1 for international students. Applications are processed on a rolling basis. *Application fee:* $50. Electronic applications accepted. *Application Contact:* Christine Murphy, Director of Admissions, 516-877-3050, Fax: 516-877-3039, E-mail: graduateadmissions@adelphi.edu. *Associate Dean*, Dr. Rakesh Gupta, 516-877-4629.

School of Education Students: 467 full-time (402 women), 688 part-time (532 women); includes 224 minority (88 Black or African American, non-Hispanic/Latino; 1 American Indian or Alaska Native, non-Hispanic/Latino; 22 Asian, non-Hispanic/Latino; 105 Hispanic/Latino; 1 Native Hawaiian or other Pacific Islander, non-Hispanic/Latino; 7 Two or more races, non-Hispanic/Latino), 19 international. Average age 28. 1,292 applicants, 52% accepted, 431 enrolled. *Faculty:* 66 full-time (42 women), 173 part-time/adjunct (119 women). Expenses: Contact institution. *Financial support:* In 2010–11, 126 teaching assistantships (averaging $7,700 per year) were awarded; career-related internships or fieldwork, Federal Work-Study, institutionally sponsored loans, tuition waivers (full), and unspecified assistantships also available. Support available to part-time students. Financial award application deadline: 2/15; financial award applicants required to submit FAFSA. In 2010, 496 master's, 7 doctorates, 73 other advanced degrees awarded. *Degree program information:* Part-time and evening/weekend programs available. Offers adolescent education (MA); aging (Certificate); art education (MA); audiology (MS, DA); birth-grade 12 (MS); birth-grade 6 (MS); community health education (MA, Certificate); early childhood education (Certificate); education (MA, MS, DA, Certificate); educational leadership and technology (MA, Certificate); elementary teachers pre K-6 (MA); grades 1-6 (MA); grades 5-12 (MS); in-service (MA); physical/educational human performance science (MA); pre-certification (MA); school health education (MA); special education (MS, Certificate); speech-language pathology (MS, DA); teaching English to speakers of other languages (MA, Certificate). *Application deadline:* For fall admission, 4/1 for international students; for spring admission, 11/1 for international students. Applications are processed on a rolling basis. *Application fee:* $50. Electronic applications accepted. *Application Contact:* Christine Murphy, Director of Admissions, 516-877-3050, Fax: 516-877-3039, E-mail: graduateadmissions@adelphi.edu. *Dean*, Dr. Jane Ashdown, 516-877-4065, E-mail: jashdown@adelphi.edu.

School of Nursing Students: 119 part-time (109 women); includes 72 minority (48 Black or African American, non-Hispanic/Latino; 11 Asian, non-Hispanic/Latino; 7 Hispanic/Latino; 1 Native Hawaiian or other Pacific Islander, non-Hispanic/Latino; 5 Two or more races, non-Hispanic/Latino). Average age 41. 114 applicants, 46% accepted, 38 enrolled. *Faculty:* 34 full-time (32 women), 94 part-time/adjunct (89 women). Expenses: Contact institution. *Financial support:* In 2010–11, 13 research assistantships (averaging $3,062 per year) were awarded; career-related internships or fieldwork, unspecified assistantships, and graduate achievement awards also available. Support available to part-time students. Financial award application deadline: 2/15; financial award applicants required to submit FAFSA. In 2010, 63 master's, 1 other advanced degree awarded. *Degree program information:* Part-time and evening/weekend programs available. Offers nursing (MS, PhD, Certificate). *Application deadline:* For fall admission, 3/15 for domestic students, 4/1 for international students; for spring admission, 11/1 for international students. *Application fee:* $50. Electronic applications accepted. *Application Contact:* Christine Murphy, Director of Admissions, 516-877-3050, Fax: 516-877-3039, E-mail: graduateadmissions@adelphi.edu. *Dean*, Dr. Patrick Coonan, 516-877-4511, E-mail: coonan@adelphi.edu.

School of Social Work Students: 218 full-time (193 women), 672 part-time (589 women); includes 400 minority (264 Black or African American, non-Hispanic/Latino; 1 American Indian or Alaska Native, non-Hispanic/Latino; 13 Asian, non-Hispanic/Latino; 106 Hispanic/Latino; 4 Native Hawaiian or other Pacific Islander, non-Hispanic/Latino; 12 Two or more races, non-Hispanic/Latino), 2 international. Average age 35. 698 applicants, 72% accepted, 323 enrolled. *Faculty:* 29 full-time (21 women), 100 part-time/adjunct (75 women). Expenses: Contact institution. *Financial support:* In 2010–11, 34 research assistantships (averaging $3,056 per year) were awarded; career-related internships or fieldwork, Federal Work-Study, institutionally sponsored loans, scholarships/grants, traineeships, tuition waivers (full and partial), and unspecified assistantships also available. Financial award application deadline: 2/15; financial award applicants required to submit FAFSA. In 2010, 300 master's, 2 doctorates awarded. *Degree program information:* Part-time and evening/weekend programs available. Offers social welfare (DSW); social work (MSW, PhD). *Application deadline:* For fall admission, 4/1 for international students; for spring admission, 12/1 for domestic students, 11/1 for international students. *Application fee:* $50. Electronic applications accepted. *Application Contact:* Christine Murphy, Director of Admissions, 516-877-3050, Fax: 516-877-3039, E-mail: graduateadmissions@adelphi.edu. *Dean*, Dr. Andrew Safyer, 516-877-4300, E-mail: asafyer@adelphi.edu.

University College Students: 8 part-time (4 women). Average age 35. 10 applicants, 50% accepted, 2 enrolled. *Faculty:* 1 full-time (0 women), 22 part-time/adjunct (9 women). Expenses: Contact institution. In 2010, 5 Certificates awarded. Offers emergency management (Certificate). *Application Contact:* Christine Murphy, Director of Admissions, 516-877-3050, Fax: 516-877-3039, E-mail: graduateadmissions@adelphi.edu. *Executive Director*, Shawn O'Riely, 516-877-3412, E-mail: ucinfo@adelphi.edu.

ADLER GRADUATE SCHOOL, Richfield, MN 55423

General Information Independent, coed, graduate-only institution. *Enrollment by degree level:* 442 master's. *Graduate faculty:* 11 full-time (4 women), 48 part-time/adjunct (28 women). *Tuition:* Part-time $455 per credit. *Graduate housing:* On-campus housing not available. *Student services:* Career counseling, multicultural affairs office, services for students with disabilities, writing training. *Library facilities:* Adler Graduate School Library. *Online resources:* web page. *Collection:* 11,200 titles, 6,500 serial subscriptions, 275 audiovisual materials.

Computer facilities: 12 computers available on campus for general student use. A campuswide network can be accessed. Online class registration is available. *Web address:* http://www.alfredadler.edu/.

General Application Contact: Evelyn B. Haas, Director of Student Services and Admissions, 612-861-7554 Ext. 103, Fax: 612-861-7559, E-mail: ev@alfredadler.edu.

GRADUATE UNITS

Program in Adlerian Counseling and Psychotherapy Students: 442 part-time (361 women). Average age 37. *Faculty:* 11 full-time (4 women), 48 part-time/adjunct (28 women). Expenses: Contact institution. *Financial support:* Career-related internships or fieldwork and tuition waivers available. Support available to part-time students. Financial award applicants required to submit FAFSA. *Degree program information:* Part-time and evening/weekend programs available. Offers art therapy (MA); clinical mental health counseling (MA); marriage and family therapy (MA); non-clinical Adlerian studies (MA); online Adlerian studies (MA); organizational wellness and transformation (MA); parent coaching (Certificate); personal and professional life coaching (Certificate); school counseling (MA). *Application deadline:* Applications are processed on a rolling basis. *Application fee:* $50. *Application Contact:* Evelyn B. Haas, Director of Student Services and Admissions, 612-861-7554 Ext. 103, Fax: 612-861-7559, E-mail: ev@alfredadler.edu. *President*, Dr. Dan Haugen, 612-861-7554 Ext. 107, Fax: 612-861-7559, E-mail: haugen@alfredadler.edu.

ADLER SCHOOL OF PROFESSIONAL PSYCHOLOGY, Chicago, IL 60602

General Information Independent, coed, graduate-only institution. *Enrollment by degree level:* 330 master's, 382 doctoral. *Graduate faculty:* 40 full-time (18 women), 61 part-time/adjunct (31 women). *Graduate housing:* On-campus housing not available. *Student services:* Campus employment opportunities, campus safety program, career counseling, exercise/wellness program, international student services, low-cost health insurance, services for students with disabilities, writing training. *Library facilities:* Sol and Elaine Mosak Library plus 1 other. *Online resources:* library catalog, web page, access to other libraries' catalogs. *Collection:* 12,869 titles, 24,652 serial subscriptions, 550 audiovisual materials. *Research affiliation:* Adler Institute on Social Exclusion, Adler Institute on Public Safety and Social Justice.

Computer facilities: 40 computers available on campus for general student use. A campuswide network can be accessed from off campus. Online class registration is available. *Web address:* http://www.adler.edu/.

General Application Contact: Michelle Brice, Director of Admissions, 312-662-4113, Fax: 312-662-4199, E-mail: admissions@adler.edu.

GRADUATE UNITS

Programs in Psychology Students: 688 full-time (532 women), 142 part-time (110 women). Average age 27. *Faculty:* 40 full-time (18 women), 61 part-time/adjunct (31 women). Expenses: Contact institution. *Financial support:* Career-related internships or fieldwork, Federal Work-Study, scholarships/grants, and tuition waivers (full and partial) available. Support available to part-time students. Financial award application deadline: 5/15; financial award applicants required to submit FAFSA. *Degree program information:* Part-time and evening/weekend programs available. Postbaccalaureate distance learning degree programs offered (minimal on-campus study). Offers advanced Adlerian psychotherapy (Certificate); art therapy (MA); clinical neuropsychology (Certificate); clinical psychology (Psy D); community psychology (MA); counseling and organizational psychology (MA); counseling psychology (MA); forensic psychology (MA); gerontological counseling (MA); marriage and family counseling (MA); marriage and family therapy (Certificate); organizational psychology (MA); police psychology (MA); rehabilitation counseling (MA); sport and health psychology (MA); substance abuse counseling (Certificate). *Application deadline:* For fall admission, 2/15 priority date for domestic students, 12/1 priority date for international students. Applications are processed on a rolling basis. *Application fee:* $50. Electronic applications accepted. *Application Contact:* Michelle Brice, Director of Admissions, 312-662-4113, Fax: 312-662-4199, E-mail: admissions@adler.edu.

AIR FORCE INSTITUTE OF TECHNOLOGY, Dayton, OH 45433-7765

General Information Federally supported, coed, primarily men, graduate-only institution. CGS member. *Graduate housing:* On-campus housing not available. *Research affiliation:* U. S. Air Force Office of Scientific Research, U. S. Air Force Research Laboratory, Dayton Area Graduate Studies Institute (aerospace), Department of Energy, National Security Agency.

GRADUATE UNITS

Graduate School of Engineering and Management *Degree program information:* Part-time programs available. Offers aeronautical engineering (MS, PhD); applied mathematics (MS, PhD); applied physics (MS, PhD); astronautical engineering (MS, PhD); computer engineering (MS, PhD); computer systems/science (MS); cost analysis (MS); electrical engineering (MS, PhD); electro-optics (MS, PhD); engineering and management (MS, PhD); environmental and engineering management (MS); environmental engineering science (MS); information resource/systems management (MS); logistics management (MS); materials science (MS, PhD); nuclear engineering (MS, PhD); operations research (MS, PhD); space operations (MS); space physics (MS); systems engineering (MS, PhD).

ALABAMA AGRICULTURAL AND MECHANICAL UNIVERSITY, Huntsville, AL 35811

General Information State-supported, coed, university. CGS member. *Graduate housing:* Rooms and/or apartments available on a first-come, first-served basis to single students and available to married students. Housing application deadline: 5/1. *Research affiliation:* National Aeronautics and Space Administration (NASA) (utilization of space resources), Boeing Defense and Space Group (plant science), Lawrence Livermore National Laboratory (chemistry, physics), Alabama Supercomputer Network, Nichols Research Corporation (computer science), Hughes Aircraft Corporation (physics).

GRADUATE UNITS

School of Graduate Studies Electronic applications accepted.

School of Agricultural and Environmental Sciences *Degree program information:* Part-time and evening/weekend programs available. Offers agribusiness (MS); agricultural and environmental sciences (MS, MURP, PhD); animal sciences (MS); environmental science (MS); family and consumer sciences (MS); food science (MS, PhD); plant and soil science (PhD); urban and regional planning (MURP). Electronic applications accepted.

School of Arts and Sciences *Degree program information:* Part-time and evening/weekend programs available. Offers arts and sciences (MS, MSW, PhD); biology (MS); physics (MS, PhD); social work (MSW). Electronic applications accepted.

School of Business *Degree program information:* Part-time and evening/weekend programs available. Offers business (MBA); management and marketing (MBA). Electronic applications accepted.

School of Education *Degree program information:* Part-time and evening/weekend programs available. Offers communicative disorders (M Ed, MS); early childhood education (MS Ed, Ed S); education (M Ed, Ed S); elementary education (MS Ed, Ed S); higher administration (MS); music (MS); music education (M Ed); physical education (M Ed, MS); psychology and counseling (MS, Ed S); special education (M Ed, MS). Electronic applications accepted.

School of Engineering and Technology *Degree program information:* Part-time and evening/weekend programs available. Offers computer science (MS); engineering and technology (M Ed, MS); industrial technology (M Ed, MS). Electronic applications accepted.

ALABAMA STATE UNIVERSITY, Montgomery, AL 36101-0271

General Information State-supported, coed, comprehensive institution. *Enrollment:* 5,705 graduate, professional, and undergraduate students; 313 full-time matriculated graduate/professional students (214 women), 473 part-time matriculated graduate/professional students (344 women). *Enrollment by degree level:* 538 master's, 172 doctoral, 76 other advanced degrees. Tuition, state resident: part-time $312 per hour. Tuition, nonresident: part-time $624 per hour. *Required fees:* $213 per semester. Tuition and fees vary according to course load. *Graduate housing:* Rooms and/or apartments available on a first-come, first-served basis to single and married students. Housing application deadline: 7/15. *Student services:* Campus employment opportunities, career counseling, child daycare facilities, free psychological counseling, international student services, low-cost health insurance, services for students with disabilities. *Library facilities:* Levi Watkins Learning Center plus 1 other. *Online resources:* library catalog, web page.

Computer facilities: A campuswide network can be accessed from student residence rooms and from off campus. Online class registration is available. *Web address:* http://www.alasu.edu/.

General Application Contact: Dr. Doris Screws, Dean of Graduate Studies, 334-229-4274, Fax: 334-229-4928, E-mail: dscrews@alasu.edu.

GRADUATE UNITS

College of Health Sciences Offers health sciences (DPT); physical therapy (DPT).

Department of Accounting and Finance Offers accountancy (M Acc).

Department of Biological Sciences *Degree program information:* Part-time programs available. Offers biological sciences (MS).

Department of Curriculum and Instruction *Degree program information:* Part-time programs available. Offers biology education (M Ed, Ed S); early childhood education (M Ed, Ed S); elementary education (M Ed, Ed S); English/language arts (M Ed); history education (M Ed, Ed S); mathematics education (M Ed); secondary education (M Ed, Ed S); social studies (Ed S); special education (M Ed).

Department of Earth and Environmental Sciences Offers earth and environmental sciences (MS, PhD). Electronic applications accepted.

Department of Health, Physical Education, and Recreation *Degree program information:* Part-time programs available. Offers health education (M Ed); physical education (M Ed).

Department of Instructional Support *Degree program information:* Part-time programs available. Offers educational administration (M Ed, Ed D, Ed S); educational leadership, policy and law (Ed D); general counseling (MS, Ed S); guidance and counseling (M Ed, MS, Ed S); library education media (M Ed, Ed S); school counseling (M Ed, Ed S).

Department of Mathematics and Computer Science *Degree program information:* Part-time programs available. Offers mathematics (M Ed, MS, Ed S).

Department of Music *Degree program information:* Part-time programs available. Offers instrumental music (M Ed); vocal/choral music (M Ed).

ALASKA PACIFIC UNIVERSITY, Anchorage, AK 99508-4672

General Information Independent, coed, comprehensive institution. *Graduate housing:* Room and/or apartments available on a first-come, first-served basis to single students; on-campus housing not available to married students. Housing application deadline: 8/15.

GRADUATE UNITS

Graduate Programs *Degree program information:* Part-time and evening/weekend programs available. Offers business administration (MBA); counseling psychology (MSCP); environmental science (MSES, MSOEE); health services administration (MBA); information and communication technology (MBAICT); investment (CGS); outdoor and environmental education (MSOEE); self-designed study (MA); teaching (MAT); teaching (K-8) (MAT). Electronic applications accepted.

ALBANY COLLEGE OF PHARMACY AND HEALTH SCIENCES, Albany, NY 12208

General Information Independent, coed, comprehensive institution. *Enrollment:* 1,597 graduate, professional, and undergraduate students; 467 full-time matriculated graduate/professional students (251 women), 2 part-time matriculated graduate/professional students (both women). *Enrollment by degree level:* 447 first professional, 22 master's. *Graduate faculty:* 59 full-time (25 women), 9 part-time/adjunct (3 women). *Tuition:* Full-time $28,830; part-time $815 per credit hour. *Required fees:* $670. *Graduate housing:* Room and/or apartments available on a first-come, first-served basis to single students; on-campus housing not available to married students. Typical cost: $7500 per year ($10,700 including board). Housing application deadline: 6/1. *Student services:* Campus employment opportunities, campus safety program, career counseling, exercise/wellness program, free psychological counseling, international student services, low-cost health insurance, writing training. *Library facilities:* George and Leona Lewis Library. *Online resources:* library catalog. *Collection:* 13,418 titles, 3,731 serial subscriptions, 950 audiovisual materials.

Computer facilities: Computer purchase and lease plans are available. 30 computers available on campus for general student use. A campuswide network can be accessed from student residence rooms and from off campus. Online class registration is available. *Web address:* http://www.acphs.edu/.

General Application Contact: Donna Myers, Pharmacy and Graduate Admissions Coordinator, 518-694-7149, Fax: 518-694-7063, E-mail: graduate@acphs.edu.

GRADUATE UNITS

Program in Pharmacy Students: 467 full-time (251 women), 2 part-time (both women); includes 19 Black or African American, non-Hispanic/Latino; 60 Asian, non-Hispanic/Latino; 3 Hispanic/Latino; 6 Two or more races, non-Hispanic/Latino, 52 international. Average age 26. 1,648 applicants, 8% accepted, 76 enrolled. *Faculty:* 59 full-time (25 women), 9 part-time/adjunct (3 women). Expenses: Contact institution. *Financial support:* Federal Work-Study and scholarships/grants available. Support available to part-time students. Financial award application deadline: 3/1; financial award applicants required to submit FAFSA. In 2010, 216 first professional degrees awarded. Offers biotechnology (MS); cytotechnology (MS); health outcomes research (MS); pharmaceutical sciences (MS); pharmacy (Pharm D); pharmacy administration (MS). *Application deadline:* For fall admission, 3/1 for domestic and international students. Applications are processed on a rolling basis. *Application fee:* $75. Electronic applications accepted. *Application Contact:* Donna Myers, Pharmacy and Graduate Admissions Counselor, 518-694-7149, Fax: 518-694-7063. *Provost*, Dr. Mehdi Boroujerdi, 518-694-7212, Fax: 518-694-7063.

ALBANY LAW SCHOOL, Albany, NY 12208-3494

General Information Independent, coed, graduate-only institution. *Enrollment by degree level:* 720 first professional, 8 master's, 6 other advanced degrees. *Graduate faculty:* 54 full-time (29 women), 48 part-time/adjunct (11 women). *Tuition:* Full-time $38,900; part-time $1345 per credit hour. One-time fee: $150 part-time. *Graduate housing:* On-campus housing not available. *Student services:* Campus employment opportunities, campus safety program, career counseling, free psychological counseling, low-cost health insurance, services for students with disabilities, writing training. *Library facilities:* Schaffer Law Library. *Online resources:* library catalog, web page. *Collection:* 88,936 titles, 2,755 serial subscriptions, 446 audiovisual materials.

Computer facilities: 95 computers available on campus for general student use. A campuswide network can be accessed from off campus. Online class registration is available. *Web address:* http://www.albanylaw.edu/.

General Application Contact: Gail S. Benson, Director of Admissions, 518-445-2326, Fax: 518-445-2369, E-mail: gbens@albanylaw.edu.

GRADUATE UNITS

Professional Program Students: 702 full-time (307 women), 32 part-time (19 women); includes 93 minority (21 Black or African American, non-Hispanic/Latino; 5 American Indian or Alaska Native, non-Hispanic/Latino; 37 Asian, non-Hispanic/Latino; 30 Hispanic/Latino), 17 international. *Faculty:* 54 full-time (29 women), 48 part-time/adjunct (11 women). Expenses: Contact institution. *Financial support:* Research assistantships, career-related internships or fieldwork, Federal Work-Study, institutionally sponsored loans, scholarships/grants, health care benefits, and tuition waivers (full and partial) available. Support available to part-time students. Financial award applicants required to submit FAFSA. In 2010, 219 first professional degrees, 9 master's awarded. *Degree program information:* Part-time programs available. Offers law (JD, LL M). JD/MBA offered jointly with The College of Saint Rose, The Sage Colleges, Union Graduate College, and University at Albany, State University of New York; JD/MPA, JD/MRP, and JD/MSW offered jointly with University at Albany, State University of New York. *Application deadline:* For fall admission, 3/1 priority date for domestic students. Applications are processed on a rolling basis. *Application fee:* $60. *Application Contact:* Gail S. Benson, Director of Admissions, 518-445-2326, Fax: 518-445-2369, E-mail: gbens@albanylaw.edu. *President and Dean,* Thomas F. Guernsey, 518-445-2321, Fax: 518-472-5865.

ALBANY MEDICAL COLLEGE, Albany, NY 12208-3479

General Information Independent, coed, graduate-only institution. *Enrollment by degree level:* 573 first professional, 144 master's, 62 doctoral. *Graduate faculty:* 168 full-time (50 women), 80 part-time/adjunct (30 women). *Graduate housing:* On-campus housing not available. *Student services:* Campus employment opportunities, campus safety program, child daycare facilities, exercise/wellness program, free psychological counseling, international student services, low-cost health insurance. *Library facilities:* Schaffer Library of the Health Sciences. *Online resources:* library catalog, web page, access to other libraries' catalogs. *Collection:* 150,417 titles, 20,355 serial subscriptions, 481 audiovisual materials. *Research affiliation:* X-Ray Optical Systems (diagnostic equipment), Integrated Tissue Dynamics INTIGYN (integrated tissue dynamics), Regenerative Research Foundation (biomedical research), Wadsworth Center for Laboratories and Research (biomedical research), ORDWAY Research Institute (biomedical research), General Electric Company (GE) (imaging).

Computer facilities: 95 computers available on campus for general student use. A campuswide network can be accessed from student residence rooms and from off campus. Online class registration is available. *Web address:* http://www.amc.edu/.

General Application Contact: Jean M. Cornwell, Admissions Coordinator, 518-262-5253, Fax: 518-262-5183, E-mail: graduate-studies@mail.amc.edu.

GRADUATE UNITS

Alden March Bioethics Institute Students: 4 full-time (2 women), 29 part-time (17 women); includes 5 minority (1 Black or African American, non-Hispanic/Latino; 2 Asian, non-Hispanic/Latino; 2 Two or more races, non-Hispanic/Latino), 1 international. Average age 40. 26 applicants, 100% accepted, 20 enrolled. *Faculty:* 5 full-time (2 women), 11 part-time/adjunct (4 women). Expenses: Contact institution. *Financial support:* Scholarships/grants, tuition waivers (full and partial), and employee discount available. In 2010, 19 master's, 9 other advanced degrees awarded. *Degree program information:* Part-time programs available. Postbaccalaureate distance learning degree programs offered (no on-campus study). Offers bioethics (MS); clinical ethics (Certificate). *Application deadline:* Applications are processed on a rolling basis. *Application fee:* $100. Electronic applications accepted. *Application Contact:* Hayley A. Dittus, Coordinator of Graduate Studies, 518-262-2639, Fax: 518-262-6856, E-mail: dittush@mail.amc.edu. *Director,* Dr. Bruce D. White, 518-262-6082, Fax: 518-262-6856, E-mail: whiteb@mail.amc.edu.

Center for Cardiovascular Sciences Students: 18 full-time (10 women); includes 1 Black or African American, non-Hispanic/Latino; 7 Asian, non-Hispanic/Latino; 1 Hispanic/Latino. Average age 25. 8 applicants, 75% accepted, 4 enrolled. *Faculty:* 18 full-time (3 women). Expenses: Contact institution. *Financial support:* In 2010–11, 9 students received support, including 9 research assistantships (averaging $24,000 per year); Federal Work-Study, scholarships/grants, and tuition waivers (full) also available. Financial award applicants required to submit FAFSA. In 2010, 1 doctorate awarded. *Degree program information:* Part-time programs available. Offers cardiovascular sciences (MS, PhD). *Application deadline:* For fall admission, 3/15 priority date for domestic and international students. Applications are processed on a rolling basis. *Application fee:* $60. *Application Contact:* Wendy M. Vienneau, Administrative Coordinator, 518-262-8102, Fax: 518-262-8101, E-mail: hobbw@mail.amc.edu. *Graduate Director,* Dr. Peter A. Vincent, 518-262-6296, Fax: 518-262-8101, E-mail: vincenp@mail.amc.edu.

Center for Cell Biology and Cancer Research Students: 22 full-time (19 women); includes 7 minority (1 Black or African American, non-Hispanic/Latino; 5 Asian, non-Hispanic/Latino; 1 Hispanic/Latino). Average age 26. 25 applicants, 44% accepted, 9 enrolled. *Faculty:* 14 full-time (4 women). Expenses: Contact institution. *Financial support:* In 2010–11, 10 research assistantships (averaging $24,000 per year) were awarded; Federal Work-Study, scholarships/grants, and tuition waivers (full) also available. Financial award applicants required to submit FAFSA. In 2010, 1 master's, 5 doctorates awarded. *Degree program information:* Part-time programs available. Offers cell biology and cancer research (MS, PhD). *Application deadline:* For fall admission, 3/15 priority date for domestic and international students. Applications are processed on a rolling basis. *Application Contact:* Dr. C. Michael DiPersio, Graduate Director, 518-262-5916, Fax: 518-262-5669, E-mail: dipersm@mail.amc.edu. *Graduate Director,* Dr. C. Michael DiPersio, 518-262-5916, Fax: 518-262-5669, E-mail: dipersm@mail.amc.edu.

Center for Immunology and Microbial Disease Students: 18 full-time (10 women); includes 1 Asian, non-Hispanic/Latino. Average age 25. 20 applicants, 45% accepted, 6 enrolled. *Faculty:* 19 full-time (4 women), 11 part-time/adjunct (6 women). Expenses: Contact institution. *Financial support:* In 2010–11, 10 research assistantships (averaging $24,000 per year) were awarded; Federal Work-Study, scholarships/grants, and tuition waivers (full) also available. Financial award applicants required to submit FAFSA. In 2010, 1 doctorate awarded. *Degree program information:* Part-time programs available. Offers immunology and microbial disease (MS, PhD). *Application deadline:* For fall admission, 3/15 priority date for domestic and international students. Applications are processed on a rolling basis. *Application fee:* $0 ($60 for international students). *Application Contact:* Dr. Thomas D. Friedrich, Graduate Director, 518-262-6750, Fax: 518-262-6161, E-mail: dgs_cimd@mail.amc.edu. *Graduate Director,* Dr. Thomas D. Friedrich, 518-262-6750, Fax: 518-262-6161, E-mail: dgs_cimd@mail.amc.edu.

Center for Neuropharmacology and Neuroscience Students: 16 full-time (5 women); includes 1 minority (Black or African American, non-Hispanic/Latino), 3 international. Average age 24. 31 applicants, 19% accepted, 6 enrolled. *Faculty:* 19 full-time (6 women), 8 part-time/adjunct (2 women). Expenses: Contact institution. *Financial support:* In 2010–11, 3 fellowships with partial tuition reimbursements (averaging $20,772 per year), 18 research assistantships with full tuition reimbursements (averaging $24,000 per year) were awarded; Federal Work-Study, scholarships/grants, and tuition waivers (full) also available. Financial award applicants required to submit FAFSA. In 2010, 1 master's, 3 doctorates awarded. Offers neuropharmacology and neuroscience (MS, PhD). *Application deadline:* For fall admission, 3/15 priority date for domestic and international students. Applications are processed on a rolling basis. *Application fee:* $0 ($60 for international students). *Application Contact:* Dr. Mark Fleck, Graduate Director, 518-262-5303, Fax: 518-262-5799, E-mail: cnninfo@mail.amc.edu. *Director,* Dr. Stanley D. Glick, 518-262-5303, Fax: 518-262-5799, E-mail: cnninfo@mail.amc.edu.

Center for Nurse Anesthesiology Students: 40 full-time (32 women); includes 2 Black or African American, non-Hispanic/Latino; 2 Asian, non-Hispanic/Latino; 1 Hispanic/Latino. Average age 31. 75 applicants, 31% accepted, 23 enrolled. *Faculty:* 3 full-time (all women), 1 (woman) part-time/adjunct. Expenses: Contact institution. *Financial support:* Scholarships/grants and traineeships available. Financial award applicants required to submit FAFSA. In 2010, 18 master's awarded. Offers nurse anesthesiology (MS). *Application deadline:* For fall admission, 3/1 for domestic students. Applications are processed on a rolling basis. *Application fee:* $100. Electronic applications accepted. *Application Contact:* Helene M. Gregory, Coordinator, 518-262-4303, Fax: 518-262-5170, E-mail: amcnap@mail.amc.edu. *Director,* Eileen Falcobe, 518-262-4303, Fax: 518-262-5170, E-mail: amcnap@mail.amc.edu.

Center for Physician Assistant Studies Students: 59 full-time (48 women); includes 7 minority (3 Black or African American, non-Hispanic/Latino; 2 Asian, non-Hispanic/Latino; 2 Hispanic/Latino). Average age 25. 743 applicants, 11% accepted, 35 enrolled. *Faculty:* 8 full-time (5 women), 17 part-time/adjunct (8 women). Expenses: Contact institution. *Financial support:* In 2010–11, 54 students received support. Scholarships/grants available. Financial award application deadline: 10/1; financial award applicants required to submit FAFSA. In 2010, 31 master's awarded. Offers physician assistant studies (MS). *Application deadline:* For winter admission, 11/1 for domestic and international students. Applications are processed on a rolling basis. *Application fee:* $60. Electronic applications accepted. *Application Contact:* Rosalyn Green, Admissions Coordinator, 518-262-5251, Fax: 518-262-0484, E-mail: greenr@mail.amc.edu. *Director,* Dr. David F. Irvine, 518-262-5251, Fax: 518-262-0484, E-mail: irvined@mail.amc.edu.

Professional Program Students: 573 full-time (265 women); includes 16 Black or African American, non-Hispanic/Latino; 1 American Indian or Alaska Native, non-Hispanic/Latino; 200 Asian, non-Hispanic/Latino; 16 Hispanic/Latino; 11 Two or more races, non-Hispanic/Latino, 10 international. Average age 26. 9,180 applicants, 3% accepted, 138 enrolled. *Faculty:* 82 full-time (23 women), 32 part-time/adjunct (9 women). Expenses: Contact institution. *Financial support:* Federal Work-Study, institutionally sponsored loans, and tuition waivers (partial) available. Financial award application deadline: 3/15; financial award applicants required to submit FAFSA. In 2010, 137 MDs awarded. Offers medicine (MD). *Application deadline:* For fall admission, 11/1 for domestic students. Applications are processed on a rolling basis. *Application fee:* $105. Electronic applications accepted. *Application Contact:* Joanne H. Nanos, Director of Admissions and Student Records, 518-262-5521, Fax: 518-262-5887. *Dean,* Dr. Vincent Verdile, 518-262-6008.

ALBANY STATE UNIVERSITY, Albany, GA 31705-2717

General Information State-supported, coed, comprehensive institution. *Enrollment:* 4,653 graduate, professional, and undergraduate students; 165 full-time matriculated graduate/professional students (135 women), 307 part-time matriculated graduate/professional students (227 women). *Enrollment by degree level:* 464 master's, 8 other advanced degrees. *Graduate faculty:* 41 full-time (18 women), 20 part-time/adjunct (13 women). Tuition, state resident: full-time $3060; part-time $170 per credit hour. Tuition, nonresident: full-time $12,204; part-time $678 per credit hour. *Required fees:* $1160. Part-time tuition and fees vary according to course load. *Graduate housing:* Room and/or apartments available on a first-come, first-served basis to single students; on-campus housing not available to married students. Typical cost: $8038 (including board). Room and board charges vary according to board plan. Housing application deadline: 6/30. *Student services:* Campus employment opportunities, campus safety program, career counseling, child daycare facilities, exercise/wellness program, free psychological counseling, grant writing training, international student services, low-cost health insurance, services for students with disabilities, teacher training, writing training. *Library facilities:* James Pendergrast Memorial Library. *Online resources:* library catalog, web page, access to other libraries' catalogs. *Collection:* 199,196 titles, 800,776 serial subscriptions, 2,780 audiovisual materials.

Computer facilities: Computer purchase and lease plans are available. A campuswide network can be accessed from student residence rooms and from off campus. Online class registration, academic advising tools, online payment, and campus one stop portal are available. *Web address:* http://www.asurams.edu/.

General Application Contact: Dr. Rani George, Dean, Graduate School, 229-430-4862, Fax: 229-430-6398.

GRADUATE UNITS

College of Arts and Humanities Students: 32 full-time (26 women), 51 part-time (34 women); includes 73 Black or African American, non-Hispanic/Latino, 1 international. Average age 34. 35 applicants, 83% accepted, 26 enrolled. *Faculty:* 7 full-time (3 women), 3 part-time/adjunct (1 woman). Expenses: Contact institution. *Financial support:* Application deadline: 4/15. In 2010, 20 master's awarded. *Degree program information:* Part-time programs available. Offers arts and humanities (MPA, MSW); community and economic development administration (MPA); criminal justice administration (MPA); fiscal management (MPA); general management (MPA); health administration and policy (MPA); human resources management (MPA); public policy (MPA); social work (MSW); water resource management and policy (MPA). *Application deadline:* For fall admission, 7/15 for domestic students, 5/15 for international students; for spring admission, 11/15 for domestic students, 9/15 for international students. Applications are processed on a rolling basis. *Application fee:* $20. Electronic applications accepted. *Application Contact:* Dr. Rani George, Dean, Graduate School, 229-430-5118, Fax: 229-430-6398, E-mail: rani.george@asurams.edu. *Dean,* Dr. Leroy Bynum, 229-430-4832, Fax: 229-430-4296, E-mail: leroy.bynum@asurams.edu.

College of Business Students: 8 full-time (6 women), 25 part-time (17 women); includes 27 minority (all Black or African American, non-Hispanic/Latino), 2 international. Average age 31. 12 applicants, 92% accepted, 11 enrolled. *Faculty:* 5 full-time (1 woman), 1 part-time/adjunct (0 women). Expenses: Contact institution. *Financial support:* Application deadline: 4/15. In 2010, 8 master's awarded. *Degree program information:* Part-time and evening/weekend programs available. Offers accounting (MBA); business administration (MBA). *Application deadline:* For fall admission, 7/15 for domestic students, 5/15 for international students; for spring admission, 11/15 for domestic students, 9/15 for international students. Applications are processed on a rolling basis. *Application fee:* $20. Electronic applications accepted. *Application Contact:* Dr. Rani George, Dean, Graduate School, 229-430-5118, Fax: 229-430-6398, E-mail: rani.george@asurams.edu. *Interim Dean,* Dr. Kathaleena Monds, 229-430-2749, Fax: 229-430-5119, E-mail: kathaleena.monds@asurams.edu.

College of Education Students: 84 full-time (69 women), 136 part-time (100 women); includes 183 Black or African American, non-Hispanic/Latino; 1 American Indian or Alaska Native, non-Hispanic/Latino, 1 international. Average age 34. 53 applicants, 92% accepted, 39 enrolled. *Faculty:* 12 full-time (7 women), 6 part-time/adjunct (5 women). Expenses: Contact institution. *Financial support:* Scholarships/grants available. Financial award application deadline: 4/15; financial award applicants required to submit FAFSA. In 2010, 90 master's, 7 other advanced degrees awarded. *Degree program information:* Part-time and evening/weekend programs available. Postbaccalaureate distance learning degree programs offered (minimal on-campus study). Offers early childhood education (M Ed); education (M Ed, Certificate, Ed S); educational leadership (M Ed, Ed S); health and physical education (M Ed); intellectual disabilities (M Ed); inter-related (M Ed); middle grades education (M Ed); school counseling (M Ed). *Application deadline:* For fall admission, 7/15 for domestic students, 5/15 for international students; for spring admission, 11/15 for domestic students, 9/15 for international students. Applications are processed on a rolling basis. *Application fee:* $34. Electronic applications accepted. *Application Contact:* Dr. Rani George, Dean, Graduate School, 229-430-5118, Fax: 229-430-6398, E-mail: rani.george@asurams.edu. *Dean,* Dr. Kimberly King-Jupiter, 229-430-1718, Fax: 229-430-4993, E-mail: kimberly.king-jupiter@asurams.edu.

College of Sciences and Health Professions Students: 41 full-time (34 women), 95 part-time (76 women); includes 95 Black or African American, non-Hispanic/Latino; 3 Asian, non-Hispanic/Latino; 1 Hispanic/Latino, 1 international. Average age 35. 50 applicants, 94% accepted, 34 enrolled. *Faculty:* 7 full-time (3 women), 3 part-time/adjunct (1 woman). Expenses: Contact institution. *Financial support:* Scholarships/grants and traineeships available. Financial award application deadline: 4/15; financial award applicants required to submit CSS PROFILE or FAFSA. In 2010, 23 master's awarded. *Degree program information:* Part-time and evening/weekend programs available. Postbaccalaureate distance learning degree programs offered. Offers criminal justice (MS); mathematics education (M Ed); RN to MSN family nurse practitioner (MSN); RN to MSN nurse educator (MSN); science education (M Ed); sciences and health professions (M Ed, MS, MSN). *Application deadline:* For fall admission, 7/15 for domestic students, 5/15 for international students; for spring admission, 11/15 for domestic students, 9/15 for international students. Applications are processed on a rolling basis. *Application fee:* $20. Electronic applications accepted. *Application Contact:* Rani George, Dean, Graduate School, 229-430-5118, Fax: 229-430-6398, E-mail: rani.george@asurams.edu. *Dean,* Dr. Joyce Johnson, 229-430-4724, Fax: 229-430-3937, E-mail: joyce.johnson@asurams.edu.

ALBERT EINSTEIN COLLEGE OF MEDICINE, Bronx, NY 10461

General Information Independent, coed, graduate-only institution. *Web address:* http://www.aecom.yu.edu.

General Application Contact: Noreen Kerrigan, Assistant Dean for Admissions, 718-430-2106, Fax: 718-430-8825, E-mail: admissions@aecom.yu.edu.

GRADUATE UNITS

Graduate Division of Biomedical Sciences Students: 377 full-time; includes 13 Black or African American, non-Hispanic/Latino; 24 Asian, non-Hispanic/Latino; 8 Hispanic/Latino, 101 international. Average age 25. 213 applicants, 20% accepted. *Faculty:* 172 full-time, 17 part-time/adjunct. Expenses: Contact institution. *Financial support:* In 2010–11, 229 fellowships were awarded. In 2010, 37 doctorates awarded. Offers anatomy (PhD); biochemistry (PhD); biomedical sciences (PhD); cell and developmental biology (PhD); microbiology and immunology (PhD); neuroscience (PhD); pathology (PhD); physiology and biophysics (PhD). *Application deadline:* For fall admission, 1/15 priority date for domestic students. *Application fee:* $0. *Application Contact:* Salvatore Calabro, Assistant Director of Admissions, 718-430-2345, Fax: 718-430-8655, E-mail: phd@einstein.yu.edu. *Assistant Dean for Graduate Studies,* Dr. Victoria H. Freedman, 718-430-2345, Fax: 718-430-8655.

Division of Biological Sciences Offers cell biology (PhD); computational genetics (PhD); developmental and molecular biology (PhD); genetics (PhD); molecular genetics (PhD); molecular pharmacology (PhD); translational genetics (PhD).

Medical Scientist Training Program

Professional Program in Medicine Offers medicine (MD).

ALBERTUS MAGNUS COLLEGE, New Haven, CT 06511-1189

General Information Independent-religious, coed, comprehensive institution. *Enrollment:* 1,961 graduate, professional, and undergraduate students; 281 full-time matriculated graduate/professional students (170 women), 109 part-time matriculated graduate/professional students (93 women). *Enrollment by degree level:* 390 master's. *Graduate faculty:* 31 full-time (14 women), 47 part-time/adjunct (23 women). *Tuition:* Full-time $12,582; part-time $2097 per course. *Required fees:* $90; $25 per course. *Graduate housing:* Room and/or apartments available to single students; on-campus housing not available to married students. Housing application deadline: 8/31. *Student services:* Campus employment opportunities, career counseling, free psychological counseling, international student services, teacher training. *Online resources:* library catalog. *Collection:* 111,603 titles, 51,000 serial subscriptions.

Computer facilities: 196 computers available on campus for general student use. A campuswide network can be accessed from student residence rooms and from off campus. Online class registration is available. *Web address:* http://www.albertus.edu/.

General Application Contact: Dr. John Donohue, Provost and Vice President for Academic Affairs, 203-777-8539, Fax: 203-777-3701, E-mail: jdonohue@albertus.edu.

GRADUATE UNITS

Master of Arts in Liberal Studies Program Students: 25 part-time (21 women); includes 2 Black or African American, non-Hispanic/Latino; 2 Hispanic/Latino. Average age 39. 8 applicants, 88% accepted, 6 enrolled. *Faculty:* 5 full-time (3 women), 4 part-time/adjunct (2 women). Expenses: Contact institution. *Financial support:* Available to part-time students. Application deadline: 8/15. In 2010, 3 master's awarded. *Degree program information:* Part-time and evening/weekend programs available. Offers liberal studies (MALS). *Application deadline:* For fall admission, 8/31 priority date for domestic students; for spring admission, 1/10 for domestic students. Applications are processed on a rolling basis. *Application fee:* $25. *Director,* Dr. Paul Robichaud, 203-773-8556, Fax: 203-773-3117, E-mail: probichaud@albertus.edu.

Master of Fine Arts in Writing Program Students: 4 full-time (all women), 5 part-time (all women); includes 2 Black or African American, non-Hispanic/Latino; 1 Hispanic/Latino. Average age 35. 12 applicants, 83% accepted, 9 enrolled. *Faculty:* 5 full-time (3 women), 2 part-time/adjunct (1 woman). Expenses: Contact institution. Offers writing (MFA). *Application deadline:* For fall admission, 8/15 for domestic students; for spring admission, 1/15 for domestic students. *Application fee:* $35. *Application Contact:* Sarah Wallman, Director of Master of Fine Arts Program, 203-777-4473, Fax: 203-777-3701, E-mail: swallman@albertus.edu. *Provost and Vice President for Academic Affairs,* Dr. John Donohue, 203-777-8539, Fax: 203-777-3701, E-mail: jdonohue@albertus.edu.

Master of Science in Education Program Students: 14 full-time (10 women), 2 part-time (0 women); includes 3 Black or African American, non-Hispanic/Latino; 3 Hispanic/Latino. 8 applicants, 88% accepted, 6 enrolled. *Faculty:* 4 full-time (1 woman), 2 part-time/adjunct (1 woman). Expenses: Contact institution. Offers education (MS Ed). *Application deadline:* For fall admission, 8/15 for domestic students; for spring admission, 1/15 for domestic students. *Application fee:* $35. Electronic applications accepted. *Application Contact:* Dr. John Donohue, Provost and Vice President for Academic Affairs, 203-777-8539, Fax: 203-777-3701, E-mail: jdonohue@albertus.edu. Dr. Irene Rios, 203-777-7100, Fax: 203-777-2112.

Master of Science in Human Services Program Students: 14 full-time (13 women); includes 3 Black or African American, non-Hispanic/Latino; 1 Hispanic/Latino. 16 applicants, 94% accepted, 14 enrolled. *Faculty:* 3 full-time (2 women), 2 part-time/adjunct (1 woman). Expenses: Contact institution. Offers human services (MS). *Application deadline:* For fall admission, 8/15 for domestic students; for spring admission, 1/15 for domestic students. *Application fee:* $35. *Application Contact:* Dr. Ragaa Mazen, Director of Master in Human Services Program, 203-777-8574, Fax: 203-777-3701, E-mail: rmazen@albertus.edu. *Provost and Vice President for Academic Affairs,* Dr. John Donohue, 203-777-8539, Fax: 203-777-3701, E-mail: jdonohue@albertus.edu.

Program in Art Therapy Students: 17 full-time (14 women), 41 part-time (40 women); includes 8 Black or African American, non-Hispanic/Latino; 10 Hispanic/Latino. Average age 35. 22 applicants, 82% accepted, 16 enrolled. *Faculty:* 7 full-time (6 women), 5 part-time/adjunct (3 women). Expenses: Contact institution. *Financial support:* Available to part-time students. Application deadline: 8/15. In 2010, 5 master's awarded. *Degree program information:* Part-time and evening/weekend programs available. Offers art therapy (MAAT). *Application deadline:* For fall admission, 8/30 for domestic students; for spring admission, 12/30 for domestic students. *Application fee:* $35. *Application Contact:* Donna Kaiser, Director, 203-773-8903, Fax: 203-773-3117. *Director,* Donna Kaiser, 203-773-8903, Fax: 203-773-3117.

Program in Leadership Students: 16 full-time (11 women), 11 part-time (6 women); includes 6 Black or African American, non-Hispanic/Latino; 1 Asian, non-Hispanic/Latino; 4 Hispanic/Latino. 4 applicants, 75% accepted, 2 enrolled. *Faculty:* 4 full-time (2 women). Expenses: Contact institution. Offers leadership (MA). *Application fee:* $35. *Application Contact:* Joseph Chadwick, Director of Program Development, 203-777-0800 Ext. 114, Fax: 203-777-2112. *Director,* Dr. Howard Fero, 203-977-7100, Fax: 203-777-2112, E-mail: hfero@albertus.edu.

Program in Management Students: 245 full-time (131 women), 22 part-time (14 women); includes 77 Black or African American, non-Hispanic/Latino; 2 American Indian or Alaska Native, non-Hispanic/Latino; 3 Asian, non-Hispanic/Latino; 20 Hispanic/Latino. Average age 35. 93 applicants, 83% accepted, 70 enrolled. *Faculty:* 9 full-time (4 women), 37 part-time/adjunct (16 women). Expenses: Contact institution. *Financial support:* Available to part-time students. In 2010, 233 master's awarded. *Degree program information:* Evening/weekend programs available. Offers business administration (MBA); management (MSM). Program also offered in East Hartford, CT. *Application deadline:* Applications are processed on a rolling basis. *Application fee:* $75. *Application Contact:* Dr. Irene Rios, Dean of New Dimensions, 203-777-7100 Ext. 108, Fax: 203-777-2112, E-mail: iriosi@albertus.edu. *Provost and Vice President, Academic Affairs,* Dr. John Donohue, 203-773-8068, Fax: 203-773-8525, E-mail: jdonohue@albertus.edu.

ALBRIGHT COLLEGE, Reading, PA 19612-5234

General Information Independent-religious, coed, comprehensive institution. *Graduate housing:* On-campus housing not available.

GRADUATE UNITS

Graduate Division *Degree program information:* Part-time and evening/weekend programs available. Offers early childhood education (MS); elementary education (MS); English as a second language (MA); general education (MA); special education (MS). Electronic applications accepted.

ALCORN STATE UNIVERSITY, Alcorn State, MS 39096-7500

General Information State-supported, coed, comprehensive institution. CGS member. *Graduate housing:* Room and/or apartments available on a first-come, first-served basis to single students; on-campus housing not available to married students.

GRADUATE UNITS

School of Graduate Studies *Degree program information:* Part-time programs available. Offers workforce education leadership (MS). Electronic applications accepted.

School of Agriculture and Applied Science Offers agricultural economics (MS Ag); agronomy (MS Ag); animal science (MS Ag).

School of Arts and Sciences Offers arts and sciences (MS); biology (MS); computer and information sciences (MS).

School of Business Offers business (MBA).

School of Nursing Offers rural nursing (MSN).

School of Psychology and Education Offers agricultural education (MS Ed); elementary education (MS Ed, Ed S); guidance and counseling (MS Ed); industrial education (MS Ed); secondary education (MS Ed); special education (MS Ed).

ALDERSON-BROADDUS COLLEGE, Philippi, WV 26416

General Information Independent-religious, coed, comprehensive institution. *Graduate housing:* Rooms and/or apartments available on a first-come, first-served basis to single and married students. Housing application deadline: 8/21.

GRADUATE UNITS

Program in Physician Assistant Studies Offers physician assistant studies (MPAS). Electronic applications accepted.

ALFRED UNIVERSITY, Alfred, NY 14802-1205

General Information Independent, coed, university. CGS member. *Research affiliation:* Polymer-Assisted Ceramics Manufacturing Center, New York State Center for Advanced Ceramic Technology, Laboratory for Electronic Ceramics, National Science Foundation Industry–University Center for Glass Research, Whitewares Research Center Industry University Center (whitewares processing, traditional ceramics), National Science Foundation Industry–University Center for Biosurfaces (bioceramics).

GRADUATE UNITS

Graduate School *Degree program information:* Part-time programs available. Offers school counseling (MS Ed, CAS); school psychology (MA, Psy D, CAS). Electronic applications accepted.

College of Business *Degree program information:* Part-time programs available. Offers business administration (MBA). Electronic applications accepted.

Division of Education *Degree program information:* Part-time programs available. Offers literacy teacher (MS Ed); numeracy (MS). Electronic applications accepted.

New York State College of Ceramics Offers biomedical materials engineering science (MS); ceramic art (MFA); ceramic engineering (MS); ceramics (MFA, MS, PhD); electrical engineering (MS); electronic integrated arts (MFA); glass art (MFA); glass science (MS, PhD); materials science and engineering (MS, PhD); mechanical engineering (MS); sculpture (MFA). Electronic applications accepted.

ALLEN COLLEGE, Waterloo, IA 50703

General Information Independent, coed, primarily women, comprehensive institution. *Enrollment:* 477 graduate, professional, and undergraduate students; 30 full-time matriculated graduate/professional students (29 women), 121 part-time matriculated graduate/professional students (118 women). *Enrollment by degree level:* 146 master's, 5 other advanced degrees. *Graduate faculty:* 2 full-time (both women), 8 part-time/adjunct (all women). *Tuition:* Full-time $13,709; part-time $677 per credit hour. *Required fees:* $827; $68 per credit hour. One-time fee: $425. Tuition and fees vary according to course load and program. *Graduate housing:* Room and/or apartments available on a first-come, first-served basis to single students; on-campus housing not available to married students. *Student services:* Career counseling, free psychological counseling, low-cost health insurance, multicultural affairs office. *Library facilities:* Barrett Library. *Online resources:* library catalog, web page, access to other libraries' catalogs. *Collection:* 3,300 titles, 214 serial subscriptions, 400 audiovisual materials.

Computer facilities: 29 computers available on campus for general student use. A campuswide network can be accessed from student residence rooms and from off campus. *Web address:* http://www.allencollege.edu/.

General Application Contact: Dina Dowden, Education Secretary, 319-226-2000, Fax: 319-226-2051, E-mail: allcucollegeadmissions@ihs.org.

GRADUATE UNITS

Program in Nursing Students: 29 full-time (28 women), 117 part-time (114 women); includes 1 Black or African American, non-Hispanic/Latino; 1 Asian, non-Hispanic/Latino; 4 Hispanic/Latino. Average age 36. 165 applicants, 38% accepted, 56 enrolled. *Faculty:* 2 full-time (both women), 8 part-time/adjunct (all women). Expenses: Contact institution. *Financial support:* In 2010–11, 41 students received support. Institutionally sponsored loans, scholarships/grants, and traineeships available. Support available to part-time students. Financial award application deadline: 8/15; financial award applicants required to submit FAFSA. In 2010, 23 master's, 6 other advanced degrees awarded. *Degree program information:* Part-time programs available. Offers acute care nurse practitioner (MSN, Post-Master's Certificate); adult nurse practitioner (MSN, Post-Master's Certificate); adult psychiatric-mental health nurse practitioner (MSN, Post-Master's Certificate); family nurse practitioner (MSN, Post-Master's Certificate); gerontological nurse practitioner (MSN, Post-Master's Certificate); health education (MSN); leadership in health care delivery (MSN, Post-Master's Certificate); nursing (DNP). *Application deadline:* For fall admission, 2/1 priority date for domestic students; for spring admission, 9/1 priority date for domestic students. Applications are processed on a rolling basis. *Application fee:* $50. Electronic applications accepted. *Application Contact:* Michelle Koehn, Admissions Counselor, 319-226-2002, Fax: 319-226-2051, E-mail: koehnml@ihs.org. *Dean, School of Nursing,* Kendra Williams-Perez, 319-226-2044, Fax: 319-226-2070, E-mail: williakb@ihs.org.

ALLIANT INTERNATIONAL UNIVERSITY–FRESNO, Fresno, CA 93727

General Information Independent, coed, graduate-only institution. *Graduate housing:* On-campus housing not available.

Alliant International University–Fresno (continued)

GRADUATE UNITS

California School of Professional Psychology Offers clinical psychology (PhD, Psy D); professional psychology (PhD, Psy D).

Center for Forensic Studies Offers forensic psychology (PhD, Psy D). Electronic applications accepted.

Graduate School of Education *Degree program information:* Part-time and evening/weekend programs available. Postbaccalaureate distance learning degree programs offered (no on-campus study). Offers education (MA, Ed D, Certificate, Credential); educational leadership and management (Ed D); teaching (MA); teaching English to speakers of other languages (MA, Ed D, Certificate). Electronic applications accepted.

Marshall Goldsmith School of Management *Degree program information:* Part-time and evening/weekend programs available. Offers management (MA, Psy D).

Organizational Psychology Division *Degree program information:* Part-time and evening/weekend programs available. Offers organizational behavior (MA); organizational development (Psy D). Electronic applications accepted.

ALLIANT INTERNATIONAL UNIVERSITY–IRVINE, Irvine, CA 92612

General Information Independent, coed, graduate-only institution.

GRADUATE UNITS

California School of Professional Psychology *Degree program information:* Part-time programs available. Offers marital and family therapy (MA, Psy D); professional psychology (MA, Psy D). Electronic applications accepted.

Center for Forensic Studies Offers forensic studies (Psy D).

Graduate School of Education *Degree program information:* Part-time and evening/weekend programs available. Postbaccalaureate distance learning degree programs offered. Offers auditory oral education (Certificate); CLAD (Certificate); education (MA, Ed D, Psy D, Certificate, Credential); educational administration (MA, Credential); educational leadership and management (K-12) (Ed D); educational psychology (Psy D); higher education (Ed D); preliminary administrative services (Credential); preliminary multiple subject (Credential); preliminary multiple subject with BCLAD (Credential); preliminary single subject (Credential); professional clear multiple subject (Credential); professional clear single subject (Credential); pupil personnel services (Credential); school psychology (MA); teaching (MA, Credential); teaching English to speakers of other languages (MA, Ed D); technology and learning (MA). Electronic applications accepted.

ALLIANT INTERNATIONAL UNIVERSITY–LOS ANGELES, Alhambra, CA 91803-1360

General Information Independent, coed, graduate-only institution. *Graduate housing:* Room and/or apartments available to single students; on-campus housing not available to married students.

GRADUATE UNITS

California School of Professional Psychology Offers biofeedback (MA); chemical dependency (MA); clinical psychology (PhD, Psy D); gerontology (MA); Latin American family therapy (MA); professional psychology (MA, PhD, Psy D). Electronic applications accepted.

Center for Forensic Studies Offers forensic psychology (Psy D).

Graduate School of Education *Degree program information:* Part-time and evening/weekend programs available. Postbaccalaureate distance learning degree programs offered (no on-campus study). Offers education (MA, Ed D, Psy D, Credential); educational administration (MA); educational leadership and management (K-12) (Ed D); educational psychology (Psy D); higher education (Ed D); preliminary administrative services (Credential); pupil personnel services (Credential); school psychology (MA); teaching (MA). Electronic applications accepted.

Marshall Goldsmith School of Management Offers management (MA, DBA, PhD).

Business Division Offers business (DBA).

Organizational Psychology Division *Degree program information:* Part-time programs available. Offers industrial/organizational psychology (MA, PhD). Electronic applications accepted.

ALLIANT INTERNATIONAL UNIVERSITY–MÉXICO CITY, CP06700 Mexico City, Mexico

General Information Independent, coed, comprehensive institution. *Graduate housing:* On-campus housing not available.

GRADUATE UNITS

California School of Professional Psychology Offers professional psychology (MA).

Graduate School of Education *Degree program information:* Part-time and evening/weekend programs available. Postbaccalaureate distance learning degree programs offered (no on-campus study). Offers teaching (MA).

International Studies Division Offers international relations (MA).

Marshall Goldsmith School of Management *Degree program information:* Part-time and evening/weekend programs available. Offers international business administration (MIBA); international relations (MA). Electronic applications accepted.

Programs in Arts and Science *Degree program information:* Part-time programs available. Offers counseling psychology (MA); international relations (MA). Electronic applications accepted.

ALLIANT INTERNATIONAL UNIVERSITY–SACRAMENTO, Sacramento, CA 95825

General Information Independent, coed, graduate-only institution.

GRADUATE UNITS

California School of Professional Psychology Offers clinical psychology (Psy D); marital and family therapy (MA); professional psychology (MA, Psy D). Electronic applications accepted.

Graduate School of Education Offers education (MA); teaching (MA).

Marshall Goldsmith School of Management Offers management (Psy D); organizational development (Psy D).

ALLIANT INTERNATIONAL UNIVERSITY–SAN DIEGO, San Diego, CA 92131-1799

General Information Independent, coed, graduate-only institution. *Graduate housing:* Rooms and/or apartments available on a first-come, first-served basis to single and married students.

GRADUATE UNITS

California School of Professional Psychology *Degree program information:* Part-time programs available. Offers clinical psychology (PhD, Psy D); marital and family therapy (MA, Psy D); professional psychology (MA, PhD, Psy D).

Graduate School of Education *Degree program information:* Part-time and evening/weekend programs available. Postbaccalaureate distance learning degree programs offered (no on-campus study). Offers education (MA, Ed D, Psy D, Certificate, Credential); educational administration (MA); educational leadership and management (K-12) (Ed D); educational psychology (Psy D); higher education (Ed D, Certificate); preliminary administrative services (Credential); preliminary single subject (Credential); professional clear multiple subject (Credential); professional clear single subject (Credential); pupil personnel services (Credential); school psychology (MA); student personnel services (Certificate); teacher education (MA); teaching English to speakers of other languages (MA, Ed D, Certificate). Electronic applications accepted.

Marshall Goldsmith School of Management *Degree program information:* Part-time and evening/weekend programs available. Offers management (MA, MBA, MIBA, MS, DBA, PhD).

Business and Management Division *Degree program information:* Part-time and evening/weekend programs available. Offers business administration (MBA); information and technology management (DBA); international business (MIBA, DBA); strategic business (DBA); sustainable management (MBA). Electronic applications accepted.

International Studies Division *Degree program information:* Part-time programs available. Offers international relations (MA).

Organizational Psychology Division *Degree program information:* Part-time and evening/weekend programs available. Offers clinical/industrial organizational psychology (PhD); consulting psychology (PhD); industrial/organizational psychology (MA, MS, PhD); organizational behavior (MA). Electronic applications accepted.

ALLIANT INTERNATIONAL UNIVERSITY–SAN FRANCISCO, San Francisco, CA 94133-1221

General Information Independent, coed, graduate-only institution. *Graduate housing:* On-campus housing not available.

GRADUATE UNITS

California School of Professional Psychology Offers clinical psychology (PhD, Psy D, Certificate); professional psychology (Post-Doctoral MS, PhD, Psy D, Certificate); psychopharmacology (Post-Doctoral MS). Electronic applications accepted.

Graduate School of Education *Degree program information:* Part-time and evening/weekend programs available. Postbaccalaureate distance learning degree programs offered (no on-campus study). Offers auditory oral education (Certificate); CLAD (Certificate); community college administration (Ed D); education (MA, Ed D, Psy D, Certificate, Credential); educational administration (MA); educational leadership and management (K-12) (Ed D); educational psychology (Psy D); higher education (Ed D); preliminary administrative services (Credential); preliminary multiple subject (Credential); preliminary multiple subject with BCLAD (Credential); preliminary single subject (Credential); professional clear multiple subject (Credential); professional clear single subject (Credential); pupil personnel services (Credential); school psychology (MA); teaching (MA); university administration (Ed D). Electronic applications accepted.

Marshall Goldsmith School of Management *Degree program information:* Part-time and evening/weekend programs available. Offers management (MA, MBA, PhD). Electronic applications accepted.

Organizational Psychology Division *Degree program information:* Part-time and evening/weekend programs available. Offers organization development (MA); organizational psychology (MA, PhD). Electronic applications accepted.

Presidio School of Management Offers sustainable management (MBA).

ALVERNIA UNIVERSITY, Reading, PA 19607-1799

General Information Independent-religious, coed, comprehensive institution. *Graduate housing:* On-campus housing not available.

GRADUATE UNITS

Graduate Studies *Degree program information:* Part-time and evening/weekend programs available. Offers business (MBA); community counseling (MA); leadership (PhD); liberal studies (MALS); occupational therapy (MSOT); urban education (M Ed). Electronic applications accepted.

ALVERNO COLLEGE, Milwaukee, WI 53234-3922

General Information Independent-religious, Undergraduate: women only; graduate: coed, comprehensive institution. *Enrollment:* 2,759 graduate, professional, and undergraduate students; 150 full-time matriculated graduate/professional students (141 women), 135 part-time matriculated graduate/professional students (120 women). *Enrollment by degree level:* 285 master's. *Graduate faculty:* 21 full-time (18 women), 21 part-time/adjunct (19 women). *Tuition:* Part-time $595 per credit. *Graduate housing:* On-campus housing not available. *Student services:* Campus employment opportunities, campus safety program, career counseling, child daycare facilities, exercise/wellness program, multicultural affairs office, services for students with disabilities. *Library facilities:* Alverno College Library. *Online resources:* library catalog, web page, access to other libraries' catalogs. *Collection:* 106,546 titles, 32,892 serial subscriptions, 5,075 audiovisual materials.

Computer facilities: 604 computers available on campus for general student use. A campuswide network can be accessed from student residence rooms and from off campus. Online class registration is available. *Web address:* http://www.alverno.edu/.

General Application Contact: Dianna K. Gaebler, Executive Director of Admissions, 414-382-6133, Fax: 414-382-6354, E-mail: dianna.gaebler@alverno.edu.

GRADUATE UNITS

School of Business Students: 83 full-time (74 women), 5 part-time (all women); includes 24 minority (10 Black or African American, non-Hispanic/Latino; 2 American Indian or Alaska Native, non-Hispanic/Latino; 2 Asian, non-Hispanic/Latino; 8 Hispanic/Latino; 2 Two or more races, non-Hispanic/Latino), 1 international. Average age 36. 68 applicants, 43% accepted, 26 enrolled. *Faculty:* 4 full-time (1 woman), 2 part-time/adjunct (both women). Expenses: Contact institution. *Financial support:* Federal Work-Study available. Support available to part-time students. Financial award application deadline: 4/15; financial award applicants required to submit FAFSA. In 2010, 39 master's awarded. *Degree program information:* Evening/weekend programs available. Offers business (MBA). *Application deadline:* For fall admission, 7/15 priority date for domestic and international students; for spring admission, 12/15 priority date for domestic and international students. Applications are processed on a rolling basis. *Application fee:* $50. Electronic applications accepted. *Application Contact:* Carolyn Wise, Graduate Recruiter, 414-382-6045, Fax: 414-382-6354, E-mail: carolyn.wise@alverno.edu. *MBA Program Director*, Patricia Jensen, 414-382-6321, E-mail: patricia.jensen@alverno.edu.

School of Education Students: 44 full-time (all women), 103 part-time (88 women); includes 34 minority (27 Black or African American, non-Hispanic/Latino; 1 American Indian or Alaska Native, non-Hispanic/Latino; 2 Asian, non-Hispanic/Latino; 4 Hispanic/Latino), 2 international. Average age 38. 208 applicants, 54% accepted, 78 enrolled. *Faculty:* 10 full-time (all women), 17 part-time/adjunct (15 women). Expenses: Contact institution. *Financial support:* In 2010–11, 7 students received support. Federal Work-Study available. Support available to part-time students. Financial award application deadline: 4/15; financial award applicants required to submit FAFSA. In 2010, 59 master's awarded. *Degree program information:* Part-time and evening/weekend programs available. Offers adaptive education (MA); administrative leadership (MA); adult education and organizational development (MA); adult educational and instructional design (MA); adult educational and instructional technology (MA); global connections in the humanities (MA); instructional leadership (MA); instructional technology for K-12 settings (MA); professional development (MA); reading education (MA); reading education with adaptive education (MA); science education (MA); teaching in alternative schools (MA). *Application deadline:* For fall admission, 7/15 priority date for domestic and international students; for spring admission, 12/15 priority date for domestic and international students. Applications are processed on a rolling basis. *Application fee:* $50. Electronic applications accepted. *Application Contact:* Angela Peterson-Adams, Graduate Recruiter, 414-382-6104, Fax: 414-382-6354, E-mail: angela.peterson-adams@alverno.edu. *Associate Dean, Graduate Program*, Dr. Desiree Pointer-Mace, 414-382-6345, Fax: 414-382-6332, E-mail: desiree.pointer-mace@alverno.edu.

School of Nursing Students: 23 full-time (all women), 27 part-time (all women); includes 9 minority (6 Black or African American, non-Hispanic/Latino; 1 Asian, non-Hispanic/Latino; 2 Hispanic/Latino), 1 international. Average age 39. 37 applicants, 41% accepted, 9 enrolled.

Faculty: 7 full-time (all women), 2 part-time/adjunct (both women). Expenses: Contact institution. *Financial support:* In 2010–11, 7 students received support. Federal Work-Study available. Support available to part-time students. Financial award application deadline: 4/15. In 2010, 11 master's awarded. *Degree program information:* Part-time and evening/weekend programs available. Offers nursing (MSN). *Application deadline:* For fall admission, 7/15 priority date for domestic and international students; for spring admission, 12/15 priority date for domestic and international students. Applications are processed on a rolling basis. *Application fee:* $50. Electronic applications accepted. *Application Contact:* Carolyn Wise, Graduate Recruiter, 414-382-6045, Fax: 414-382-6354, E-mail: carolyn.wise@alverno.edu. *Program Director,* Julie Millenbruch, 414-382-6278, Fax: 414-382-6354, E-mail: julie.millenbruch@alverno.edu.

AMBERTON UNIVERSITY, Garland, TX 75041-5595

General Information Independent-religious, coed, upper-level institution. *Graduate housing:* On-campus housing not available.

GRADUATE UNITS

Graduate School *Degree program information:* Part-time and evening/weekend programs available. Offers counseling (MA); general business (MBA); human relations and business (MA, MS); management (MBA); professional development (MA).

AMBROSE UNIVERSITY COLLEGE, Calgary, AB T2P 3T5, Canada

General Information Independent-religious, coed, comprehensive institution. *Enrollment by degree level:* 35 first professional, 56 master's, 60 other advanced degrees. *Graduate faculty:* 7 full-time (0 women), 24 part-time/adjunct (2 women). *Graduate tuition:* Tuition and fees charges are reported in Canadian dollars. *Tuition:* Full-time $9270 Canadian dollars; part-time $309 Canadian dollars per credit hour. *Required fees:* $510 Canadian dollars. *Graduate housing:* Room and/or apartments available on a first-come, first-served basis to single students; on-campus housing not available to married students. Typical cost: $2858 Canadian dollars per year ($5508 Canadian dollars including board). Room and board charges vary according to board plan. Housing application deadline: 8/20. *Student services:* Campus employment opportunities, career counseling, international student services, services for students with disabilities, writing training. *Library facilities:* Archibald Foundation Library. *Online resources:* library catalog, access to other libraries' catalogs. *Collection:* 65,000 titles, 546 serial subscriptions.

Computer facilities: A campuswide network can be accessed. *Web address:* http://www.ambrose.edu/.

General Application Contact: Helen Thiessen, Director of Enrollment Management, 403-410-2000 Ext. 2902, Fax: 403-571-2556, E-mail: enrolment@ambrose.edu.

GRADUATE UNITS

Ambrose Seminary Students: 55 full-time (16 women), 98 part-time (52 women); includes 49 minority (5 Black or African American, non-Hispanic/Latino; 2 American Indian or Alaska Native, non-Hispanic/Latino; 41 Asian, non-Hispanic/Latino; 1 Hispanic/Latino). Average age 41. *Faculty:* 7 full-time (0 women), 24 part-time/adjunct (2 women). Expenses: Contact institution. *Financial support:* Career-related internships or fieldwork and scholarships/grants available. Support available to part-time students. Financial award application deadline: 3/30. *Degree program information:* Part-time programs available. Offers biblical/theological studies (MA); Chinese ministries (Certificate); Christian studies (M Div, MA, Diploma); foundations for ministry (Certificate); intercultural ministries (M Div, MA, Certificate, Diploma); leadership and ministry (MA, Certificate, Diploma). *Application deadline:* For fall admission, 7/31 priority date for domestic students, 3/1 priority date for international students; for winter admission, 11/30 priority date for domestic students, 6/1 priority date for international students. Applications are processed on a rolling basis. *Application fee:* $50. Electronic applications accepted. *Application Contact:* Dr. Paul Spilsbury, Vice-President of Academic Affairs, 403-410-2000 Ext. 6905, Fax: 403-571-2556, E-mail: pspilsbury@ambrose.edu. *Vice-President of Academic Affairs,* Dr. Paul Spilsbury, 403-410-2000 Ext. 6905, Fax: 403-571-2556, E-mail: pspilsbury@ambrose.edu.

AMERICAN BAPTIST SEMINARY OF THE WEST, Berkeley, CA 94704-3029

General Information Independent-religious, coed, graduate-only institution. *Enrollment by degree level:* 53 first professional, 4 master's, 18 other advanced degrees. *Graduate faculty:* 6 full-time (4 women), 7 part-time/adjunct (2 women). *Tuition:* Full-time $14,040; part-time $540 per credit. *Required fees:* $240 per semester. One-time fee: $340. *Graduate housing:* Rooms and/or apartments available on a first-come, first-served basis to single and married students. Housing application deadline: 5/1. *Student services:* Campus employment opportunities, international student services, low-cost health insurance, services for students with disabilities, writing training. *Library facilities:* Graduate Theological Union (Flora Lamson Hewlett) Library.

Computer facilities: 3 computers available on campus for general student use. A campuswide network can be accessed. Online class registration is available. *Web address:* http://www.absw.edu/.

General Application Contact: Rev. Marie Onwubuariri, Director of Recruitment, 510-841-1905, Fax: 510-841-2446, E-mail: admissions@absw.edu.

GRADUATE UNITS

Graduate and Professional Programs Students: 42 full-time (13 women), 33 part-time (15 women); includes 38 Black or African American, non-Hispanic/Latino; 11 Asian, non-Hispanic/Latino; 1 Hispanic/Latino; 1 Native Hawaiian or other Pacific Islander, non-Hispanic/Latino, 16 international. *Faculty:* 6 full-time (4 women), 7 part-time/adjunct (2 women). Expenses: Contact institution. *Financial support:* Career-related internships or fieldwork, Federal Work-Study, institutionally sponsored loans, scholarships/grants, tuition waivers (partial), and tuition discount available. Support available to part-time students. Financial award application deadline: 4/15; financial award applicants required to submit FAFSA. In 2010, 22 first professional degrees awarded. *Degree program information:* Part-time and evening/weekend programs available. Offers community leadership (MA); theology (M Div, MA). MA program in theology offered jointly with Graduate Theological Union. *Application deadline:* For fall admission, 4/15 priority date for domestic students, 4/15 for international students. Applications are processed on a rolling basis. *Application fee:* $25. Electronic applications accepted. *Application Contact:* Rev. Michelle M. Holmes, Vice President, 510-841-1905 Ext. 225, Fax: 510-841-2446, E-mail: mmholmes@absw.edu. *President,* Dr. Paul M. Martin, 510-841-1905 Ext. 224, Fax: 510-841-2446, E-mail: pmartin@absw.edu.

THE AMERICAN COLLEGE, Bryn Mawr, PA 19010-2105

General Information Independent, coed, graduate-only institution. *Enrollment by degree level:* 629 master's. *Graduate faculty:* 20 full-time, 7 part-time/adjunct. *Graduate housing:* On-campus housing not available. *Student services:* Career counseling, international student services. *Library facilities:* Lucas Memorial Library. *Online resources:* library catalog. *Collection:* 12,500 titles, 620 serial subscriptions.

Computer facilities: 3 computers available on campus for general student use. Online class registration is available. *Web address:* http://www.theamericancollege.edu/.

General Application Contact: Leah Selekman, Coordinator, Graduate School, 610-526-1385, Fax: 610-526-1359, E-mail: leah.selekman@theamericancollege.edu.

GRADUATE UNITS

Graduate Programs Students: 629 part-time (141 women). *Faculty:* 20 full-time, 7 part-time/adjunct. Expenses: Contact institution. *Financial support:* Scholarships/grants available. Support available to part-time students. *Degree program information:* Part-time and evening/weekend programs available. Postbaccalaureate distance learning degree programs offered (minimal on-campus study). Offers financial services (MSFS); leadership (MSM). *Application deadline:* Applications are processed on a rolling basis. *Application fee:* $335. Electronic applications accepted. *Application Contact:* Joanne F. Patterson, Associate Director of Graduate School Administration, 610-526-1366, Fax: 610-526-1359, E-mail: joanne.patterson@theamericancollege.edu. *Vice President for Academics and Dean,* Dr. Walter J. Woerheide, 610-526-1398, Fax: 610-526-1359, E-mail: walt.woerheide@theamericancollege.edu.

AMERICAN COLLEGE OF ACUPUNCTURE AND ORIENTAL MEDICINE, Houston, TX 77063

General Information Proprietary, coed, graduate-only institution. *Research affiliation:* Baylor College of Medicine (acupuncture for osteoarthritis of the knee), Memorial Herman Healthcare System, Tianjing Hospital, China (traditional Chinese medicine), Montrose Clinic (HIV/AIDS research and treatment), Rice University Wellness Center (student and staff care).

GRADUATE UNITS

Graduate Studies *Degree program information:* Part-time programs available.

AMERICAN COLLEGE OF EDUCATION, Chicago, IL 60606

General Information Private, coed, graduate-only institution.

GRADUATE UNITS

Graduate Programs Offers curriculum and instruction (M Ed); educational leadership (M Ed); educational technology (M Ed).

AMERICAN COLLEGE OF HEALTHCARE SCIENCES, Portland, OR 97239-3719

General Information Independent, coed. *Graduate housing:* On-campus housing not available.

GRADUATE UNITS

Graduate Programs Postbaccalaureate distance learning degree programs offered. Offers complementary alternative medicine (MS).

AMERICAN COLLEGE OF THESSALONIKI, GR-555-10 Pylea, Thessaloniki, Greece

General Information Independent, coed, comprehensive institution.

GRADUATE UNITS

Department of Business Administration *Degree program information:* Part-time and evening/weekend programs available. Offers banking and finance (MBA); entrepreneurship (MBA, Certificate); finance (Certificate); management (MBA, Certificate); marketing (MBA, Certificate). Electronic applications accepted.

AMERICAN COLLEGE OF TRADITIONAL CHINESE MEDICINE, San Francisco, CA 94107

General Information Independent, coed, graduate-only institution. *Enrollment by degree level:* 264 master's, 19 doctoral, 2 other advanced degrees. *Graduate faculty:* 20 full-time (10 women), 58 part-time/adjunct (25 women). *Graduate housing:* On-campus housing not available. *Student services:* Campus employment opportunities, campus safety program, career counseling, free psychological counseling, international student services, low-cost health insurance, services for students with disabilities. *Library facilities:* ACTCM Shuji Goto Library. *Online resources:* library catalog, web page. *Collection:* 5,900 titles, 65 serial subscriptions, 475 audiovisual materials.

Computer facilities: 20 computers available on campus for general student use. A campuswide network can be accessed from off campus. *Web address:* http://www.actcm.edu/.

General Application Contact: Yuwen Chiu, Director of Admissions, 415-282-7600 Ext. 14, Fax: 415-282-0856, E-mail: admissions@actcm.edu.

GRADUATE UNITS

Graduate Program Students: 202 full-time (147 women), 83 part-time (63 women); includes 85 minority (3 Black or African American, non-Hispanic/Latino; 65 Asian, non-Hispanic/Latino; 17 Hispanic/Latino), 7 international. 60 applicants, 95% accepted, 40 enrolled. *Faculty:* 20 full-time (10 women), 58 part-time/adjunct (25 women). Expenses: Contact institution. *Financial support:* Teaching assistantships, Federal Work-Study, institutionally sponsored loans, and scholarships/grants available. Support available to part-time students. Financial award applicants required to submit FAFSA. In 2010, 58 master's, 13 doctorates awarded. *Degree program information:* Part-time programs available. Offers acupuncture and Oriental medicine (DAOM); dermatology (Certificate); shiatsu massage (Certificate); traditional Chinese medicine (MSTCM); tui na massage (Certificate). *Application deadline:* For fall admission, 9/1 for domestic and international students; for winter admission, 12/1 for domestic and international students; for spring admission, 3/1 for domestic and international students. Applications are processed on a rolling basis. *Application fee:* $100 ($150 for international students). *Application Contact:* Gina Rossi, Admissions Counselor, 415-282-7600 Ext. 14, Fax: 415-282-0856, E-mail: admissions@actcm.edu. *President,* Lixin Huang, 415-282-7600 Ext. 12, Fax: 415-282-0856, E-mail: lixinhuang@actcm.edu.

AMERICAN CONSERVATORY THEATER, San Francisco, CA 94108-5800

General Information Independent, coed, graduate-only institution. *Graduate housing:* On-campus housing not available.

GRADUATE UNITS

Program in Acting Offers acting (MFA, Certificate). Certificate open only to applicants with undergraduate degree from a non-accredited institution. Curriculum is the same as MFA Program in Acting.

AMERICAN FILM INSTITUTE CONSERVATORY, Los Angeles, CA 90027-1657

General Information Independent, coed, graduate-only institution. *Enrollment by degree level:* 356 master's. *Graduate faculty:* 13 full-time (1 woman), 65 part-time/adjunct (22 women). *Tuition:* Full-time $37,112. *Required fees:* $2484. *Student services:* Free psychological counseling, international student services. *Library facilities:* Louis B. Mayer Library. *Online resources:* library catalog. *Collection:* 6,500 titles, 20 serial subscriptions, 6,500 audiovisual materials.

Computer facilities: 31 computers available on campus for general student use. A campuswide network can be accessed. *Web address:* http://www.afi.com/.

General Application Contact: Karin Tucker, Admissions Manager, 323-856-7609, Fax: 323-856-7683, E-mail: ktucker@afi.com.

GRADUATE UNITS

Graduate Program Students: 356 full-time (117 women); includes 81 minority (23 Black or African American, non-Hispanic/Latino; 1 American Indian or Alaska Native, non-Hispanic/Latino; 23 Asian, non-Hispanic/Latino; 21 Hispanic/Latino; 13 Two or more races, non-Hispanic/Latino), 89 international. Average age 26. 629 applicants, 32% accepted, 136 enrolled. *Faculty:* 13 full-time (1 woman), 65 part-time/adjunct (22 women). Expenses: Contact institution. *Financial support:* In 2010–11, 198 students received support, including 16 teaching assistantships with partial tuition reimbursements available (averaging $3,000 per year); career-related internships or fieldwork, scholarships/grants, and unspecified assistantships also available. Financial award application deadline: 4/15; financial award applicants required to submit FAFSA. In 2010, 120 master's awarded. Offers cinematography (MFA); directing (MFA); editing (MFA); producing (MFA); production design (MFA); screenwriting (MFA). *Application deadline:* For fall admission, 12/1 for domestic and international students. Applications are processed on a rolling basis. *Application fee:* $75. *Application Contact:* Karin Tucker, Admissions Manager, 323-856-7609, Fax: 323-856-7683, E-mail: ktucker@afi.com.

AMERICAN GRADUATE SCHOOL IN PARIS, F-75006 Paris, France

General Information Independent, coed, graduate-only institution.

American Graduate School in Paris (continued)

GRADUATE UNITS

Program in International Relations and Diplomacy Offers international relations and diplomacy (MA, PhD).

AMERICAN GRADUATE UNIVERSITY, Covina, CA 91724

General Information Proprietary, coed, graduate-only institution. *Enrollment by degree level:* 909 master's. *Graduate faculty:* 17 part-time/adjunct (3 women). *Tuition:* Part-time $275 per credit. *Library facilities:* American Graduate University Library. *Online resources:* library catalog. *Collection:* 11,000 titles, 33 serial subscriptions.

Computer facilities: Online class registration is available. *Web address:* http://www.agu.edu/.

General Application Contact: Debbie McDonald, Registrar, 626-966-4576 Ext. 1001, Fax: 626-915-1709, E-mail: debbiemcdonald@agu.edu.

GRADUATE UNITS

Program in Acquisition Management Students: 366 part-time. *Faculty:* 2 full-time (1 woman), 15 part-time/adjunct (2 women). Expenses: Contact institution. In 2010, 49 master's, 10 Certificates awarded. *Degree program information:* Part-time programs available. Postbaccalaureate distance learning degree programs offered (no on-campus study). Offers acquisition management (MAM, Certificate). *Application deadline:* Applications are processed on a rolling basis. *Application fee:* $50. Electronic applications accepted. *Application Contact:* Marie Sirney, Admissions Director, 626-966-4576 Ext. 1003, Fax: 626-915-1709, E-mail: mariesirney@agu.edu. *President*, Paul McDonald, 626-966-4576 Ext. 1006, E-mail: paulmcdonald@agu.edu.

Program in Business Administration Students: 235 part-time. *Faculty:* 2 full-time (1 woman), 15 part-time/adjunct (2 women). Expenses: Contact institution. In 2010, 27 master's awarded. *Degree program information:* Part-time programs available. Postbaccalaureate distance learning degree programs offered (no on-campus study). Offers business administration (MBA). *Application deadline:* Applications are processed on a rolling basis. *Application fee:* $50. Electronic applications accepted. *Application Contact:* Marie J. Sirney, Executive Vice President, 626-966-4576, Fax: 626-915-1709, E-mail: mariesirney@agu.edu. *President*, Paul McDonald, 626-966-4576 Ext. 1006, E-mail: paulmcdonald@agu.edu.

Program in Contract Management Students: 250 part-time. *Faculty:* 2 full-time (1 woman), 15 part-time/adjunct (2 women). Expenses: Contact institution. In 2010, 27 master's awarded. *Degree program information:* Part-time programs available. Postbaccalaureate distance learning degree programs offered (no on-campus study). Offers contract management (MCM, Certificate). *Application deadline:* Applications are processed on a rolling basis. *Application fee:* $50. Electronic applications accepted. *Application Contact:* Marie Sirney, 626-966-4576 Ext. 1003, Fax: 626-915-1709, E-mail: mariesirney@agu.edu. *President*, Paul McDonald, 626-966-4576 Ext. 1006, E-mail: paulmcdonald@agu.edu.

Program in Project Management Students: 250 part-time. *Faculty:* 2 full-time (1 woman), 15 part-time/adjunct (2 women). Expenses: Contact institution. In 2010, 14 master's awarded. *Degree program information:* Part-time programs available. Postbaccalaureate distance learning degree programs offered (no on-campus study). Offers project management (MPM, Certificate). *Application deadline:* Applications are processed on a rolling basis. *Application fee:* $50. Electronic applications accepted. *Application Contact:* Marie Sirney, Director of Admissions, 626-966-4576 Ext. 1003, Fax: 626-915-1709, E-mail: mariesirney@agu.edu. *President*, Paul McDonald, 626-966-4576 Ext. 1006, E-mail: paulmcdonald@agu.edu.

AMERICAN INTERCONTINENTAL UNIVERSITY ATLANTA, Atlanta, GA 30328

General Information Proprietary, coed, comprehensive institution. CGS member. *Graduate housing:* On-campus housing not available.

GRADUATE UNITS

Program in Global Technology Management *Degree program information:* Part-time and evening/weekend programs available. Postbaccalaureate distance learning degree programs offered. Offers global technology management (MBA). Electronic applications accepted.

Program in Information Technology *Degree program information:* Part-time and evening/weekend programs available. Offers information technology (MIT). Electronic applications accepted.

AMERICAN INTERCONTINENTAL UNIVERSITY HOUSTON, Houston, TX 77042

General Information Proprietary, coed, comprehensive institution.

GRADUATE UNITS

School of Business Offers management (MBA).

AMERICAN INTERCONTINENTAL UNIVERSITY LONDON, London W1U 4RY, United Kingdom

General Information Proprietary, coed, comprehensive institution. *Graduate housing:* Room and/or apartments available on a first-come, first-served basis to single students. Housing application deadline: 9/18.

GRADUATE UNITS

Program in Business Administration Offers international business (MBA). Electronic applications accepted.

Program in Information Technology Offers information technology (MIT). Electronic applications accepted.

AMERICAN INTERCONTINENTAL UNIVERSITY ONLINE, Hoffman Estates, IL 60192

General Information Proprietary, coed, comprehensive institution.

GRADUATE UNITS

Program in Business Administration *Degree program information:* Evening/weekend programs available. Postbaccalaureate distance learning degree programs offered (no on-campus study). Offers accounting and finance (MBA); finance (MBA); healthcare management (MBA); human resource management (MBA); international business (MBA); management (MBA); marketing (MBA); operations management (MBA); organizational psychology and development (MBA); project management (MBA). Electronic applications accepted.

Program in Education *Degree program information:* Evening/weekend programs available. Postbaccalaureate distance learning degree programs offered (no on-campus study). Offers curriculum and instruction (M Ed); educational assessment and evaluation (M Ed); instructional technology (M Ed); leadership of educational organizations (M Ed). Electronic applications accepted.

Program in Information Technology *Degree program information:* Evening/weekend programs available. Postbaccalaureate distance learning degree programs offered (no on-campus study). Offers Internet security (MIT); IT project management (MIT). Electronic applications accepted.

AMERICAN INTERCONTINENTAL UNIVERSITY SOUTH FLORIDA, Weston, FL 33326

General Information Proprietary, coed, comprehensive institution.

GRADUATE UNITS

Program in Information Technology *Degree program information:* Part-time and evening/weekend programs available. Offers Internet security (MIT); wireless computer forensics (MIT). Electronic applications accepted.

Program in Instructional Technology *Degree program information:* Part-time and evening/weekend programs available. Offers instructional technology (M Ed). Electronic applications accepted.

Program in International Business *Degree program information:* Part-time and evening/weekend programs available. Postbaccalaureate distance learning degree programs offered. Offers accounting and finance (MBA); human resource management (MBA); management (MBA); marketing (MBA). Electronic applications accepted.

AMERICAN INTERNATIONAL COLLEGE, Springfield, MA 01109-3189

General Information Independent, coed, comprehensive institution. *Graduate housing:* Room and/or apartments available on a first-come, first-served basis to single students; on-campus housing not available to married students. Housing application deadline: 6/1.

GRADUATE UNITS

School of Arts, Education and Sciences *Degree program information:* Part-time and evening/weekend programs available. Offers arts, education and sciences (M Ed, MA, MS, Ed D, CAGS); clinical psychology (MA); early childhood education (M Ed, CAGS); educational leadership and supervision (Ed D); educational psychology (MA, Ed D); elementary education (M Ed, CAGS); forensic psychology (MS); middle/secondary education (M Ed, CAGS); moderate disabilities (M Ed, CAGS); reading (M Ed, CAGS); school adjustment counseling (MA, CAGS); school administration (M Ed, CAGS); school guidance counseling (MA, CAGS); teaching (MA, MS); teaching and learning (Ed D).

Center for Human Resource Development *Degree program information:* Evening/weekend programs available. Offers human resource development (MA). Electronic applications accepted.

School of Business Administration *Degree program information:* Part-time and evening/weekend programs available. Postbaccalaureate distance learning degree programs offered (minimal on-campus study). Offers accounting (MBA); accounting and taxation (MSAT); business administration (MBA, MPA, MS, MSAT); corporate/public communication (MBA); finance (MBA); general business (MBA); hospitality, hotel and service management (MBA); international business (MBA); international business practice (MBA); management (MBA); management information systems (MBA); marketing (MBA); nonprofit management (MS); organization development (MS); public administration (MPA).

School of Health Sciences *Degree program information:* Part-time and evening/weekend programs available. Postbaccalaureate distance learning degree programs offered (minimal on-campus study). Offers health sciences (MSN, MSOT, DPT); nursing administration (MSN); nursing education (MSN); occupational therapy (MSOT); physical therapy (DPT).

AMERICAN JEWISH UNIVERSITY, Bel Air, CA 90077-1599

General Information Independent-religious, coed, comprehensive institution. *Graduate housing:* Rooms and/or apartments available on a first-come, first-served basis to single and married students. Housing application deadline: 6/1.

GRADUATE UNITS

Graduate School of Education Offers education (MA Ed); education for working professionals (MA Ed).

Graduate School of Nonprofit Management *Degree program information:* Part-time and evening/weekend programs available. Offers general nonprofit administration (MBA); Jewish communal studies (MAJCS); Jewish nonprofit administration (MBA); nonprofit management (MAJCS, MBA).

Ziegler School of Rabbinic Studies Offers rabbinic studies (MARS).

AMERICAN PUBLIC UNIVERSITY SYSTEM, Charles Town, WV 25414

General Information Proprietary, coed, comprehensive institution. *Enrollment:* 39,296 graduate, professional, and undergraduate students; 956 full-time matriculated graduate/professional students (422 women), 8,476 part-time matriculated graduate/professional students (2,821 women). *Enrollment by degree level:* 9,432 master's. *Graduate faculty:* 253 full-time (134 women), 1,208 part-time/adjunct (570 women). *Graduate housing:* On-campus housing not available. *Student services:* Career counseling, international student services, teacher training. *Library facilities:* APUS Online Library. *Online resources:* library catalog, web page. *Collection:* 118,000 titles, 32,000 serial subscriptions.

Computer facilities: Online class registration is available. *Web address:* http://www.apus.edu/.

General Application Contact: Terry Grant, Director of Enrollment Management, 877-468-6268, Fax: 304-724-3780, E-mail: info@apus.edu.

GRADUATE UNITS

AMU/APU Graduate Programs Students: 956 full-time (422 women), 8,476 part-time (2,821 women); includes 2,511 minority (1,218 Black or African American, non-Hispanic/Latino; 68 American Indian or Alaska Native, non-Hispanic/Latino; 219 Asian, non-Hispanic/Latino; 705 Hispanic/Latino; 46 Native Hawaiian or other Pacific Islander, non-Hispanic/Latino; 255 Two or more races, non-Hispanic/Latino), 107 international. Average age 35. 9,550 applicants, 100% accepted. *Faculty:* 253 full-time (134 women), 1,208 part-time/adjunct (570 women). Expenses: Contact institution. *Financial support:* Applicants required to submit FAFSA. In 2010, 1,688 master's awarded. *Degree program information:* Part-time and evening/weekend programs available. Postbaccalaureate distance learning degree programs offered (no on-campus study). Offers accounting (MBA); administration and supervision (M Ed); air warfare (MA Military Studies); asymmetrical warfare (MA Military Studies); criminal justice (MA); emergency and disaster management (MA); entrepreneurship (MBA); environmental policy and management (MS); finance (MBA); general (MBA); global business management (MBA); guidance and counseling (M Ed); history (MA); homeland security (MA); homeland security resource allocation (MBA); humanities (MA); information technology (MS); information technology management (MBA); intelligence studies (MA); international relations and conflict resolution (MA); joint warfare (MA Military Studies); land warfare (MA Military Studies); legal studies (MA); management (MA); marketing (MBA); military history (MA); national security studies (MA); naval warfare (MA Military Studies); nonprofit management (MBA); political science (MA); psychology (MA); public administration (MA); public health (MA); security management (MA); space studies (MS); sports management (MS); strategic leadership (MA Military Studies); teaching (M Ed); transportation and logistics management (MA). Programs offered via distance learning only. *Application deadline:* Applications are processed on a rolling basis. *Application fee:* $0. Electronic applications accepted. *Application Contact:* Terry Grant, Director of Enrollment Management, 877-468-6268, Fax: 304-724-3780, E-mail: info@apus.edu. *Provost*, Dr. Frank McCluskey, 877-468-6268, Fax: 304-724-3780.

AMERICAN SENTINEL UNIVERSITY, Aurora, CO 80014

General Information Private, coed, comprehensive institution.

GRADUATE UNITS

Graduate Programs *Degree program information:* Part-time and evening/weekend programs available. Postbaccalaureate distance learning degree programs offered (no on-campus study). Electronic applications accepted.

AMERICAN UNIVERSITY, Washington, DC 20016-8001

General Information Independent-religious, coed, university. CGS member. *Enrollment:* 12,795 graduate, professional, and undergraduate students; 3,085 full-time matriculated graduate/professional students (1,851 women), 2,440 part-time matriculated graduate/professional students (1,507 women). *Enrollment by degree level:* 1,503 first professional, 3,384 master's, 439 doctoral, 199 other advanced degrees. *Graduate faculty:* 688 full-time (319 women), 547 part-time/adjunct (260 women). *Graduate housing:* On-campus housing not available. *Student services:* Campus employment opportunities, campus safety program, career counseling, child daycare facilities, exercise/wellness program, free psychological counseling, grant writing training, international student services, low-cost health insurance, multicultural affairs office, services for students with disabilities, teacher training. *Library facilities:* Bender Library plus 2 others. *Online resources:* library catalog, web page, access to other libraries' catalogs.

Computer facilities: A campuswide network can be accessed from student residence rooms and from off campus. Online class registration is available. *Web address:* http://www.american.edu/.

General Application Contact: 202-885-1000.

GRADUATE UNITS

College of Arts and Sciences Students: 451 full-time (308 women), 836 part-time (588 women); includes 212 minority (113 Black or African American, non-Hispanic/Latino; 7 American Indian or Alaska Native, non-Hispanic/Latino; 32 Asian, non-Hispanic/Latino; 56 Hispanic/Latino; 3 Native Hawaiian or other Pacific Islander, non-Hispanic/Latino; 1 Two or more races, non-Hispanic/Latino), 85 international. Average age 28. 1,735 applicants, 54% accepted, 382 enrolled. *Faculty:* 304 full-time (153 women), 253 part-time/adjunct (147 women). Expenses: Contact institution. *Financial support:* Fellowships, research assistantships with full and partial tuition reimbursements, teaching assistantships with full and partial tuition reimbursements, career-related internships or fieldwork, Federal Work-Study, institutionally sponsored loans, scholarships/grants, traineeships, tuition waivers (full and partial), and unspecified assistantships available. Support available to part-time students. Financial award applicants required to submit FAFSA. In 2010, 383 master's, 31 doctorates awarded. *Degree program information:* Part-time and evening/weekend programs available. Offers anthropology (PhD); applied microeconomics (Certificate); applied science (MS); applied statistics (Certificate); art history (MA); arts and sciences (M Ed, MA, MAT, MFA, MS, PhD, Certificate, Graduate Certificate); arts management (MA, Certificate); behavior, cognition, and neuroscience (PhD); biology (MA, MS); chemistry (MS); clinical psychology (PhD); computer science (MS, Certificate); creative writing (MFA); economics (MA, PhD); environmental assessment (Graduate Certificate); environmental science (MS); ethics, peace, and global affairs (MA); French (Certificate); history (MA, PhD); interdisciplinary studies (MA); international economic relations (Certificate); literature (MA); mathematics (MA); painting, sculpture and printmaking (MFA); philosophy (MA); pre-medical (Certificate); psychology (MA); public anthropology (MA, Certificate); Russian (Certificate); social research (Certificate); sociology (MA); Spanish: Latin American studies (MA, Certificate); statistics (MS); teaching English to speakers of other languages (MA, Certificate); toxicology (MS, Certificate). *Application deadline:* For fall admission, 2/1 for domestic students; for spring admission, 10/1 for domestic students. *Application fee:* $80. Electronic applications accepted. *Application Contact:* Kathleen Clowery, Director, Graduate Admissions, 202-885-3621, Fax: 202-885-1505. *Dean,* Dr. Peter Starr, 202-885-2446, Fax: 202-885-2429.

School of Education, Teaching, and Health Students: 80 full-time (68 women), 363 part-time (267 women); includes 85 minority (52 Black or African American, non-Hispanic/Latino; 7 American Indian or Alaska Native, non-Hispanic/Latino; 5 Asian, non-Hispanic/Latino; 18 Hispanic/Latino; 2 Native Hawaiian or other Pacific Islander, non-Hispanic/Latino; 1 Two or more races, non-Hispanic/Latino), 2 international. Average age 26. 263 applicants, 88% accepted, 154 enrolled. *Faculty:* 16 full-time (10 women), 39 part-time/adjunct (28 women). Expenses: Contact institution. *Financial support:* Fellowships, research assistantships with full and partial tuition reimbursements, teaching assistantships with full and partial tuition reimbursements, career-related internships or fieldwork, Federal Work-Study, and institutionally sponsored loans available. Support available to part-time students. Financial award application deadline: 2/1; financial award applicants required to submit FAFSA. In 2010, 185 master's awarded. *Degree program information:* Part-time and evening/weekend programs available. Offers curriculum and instruction (M Ed, Certificate); early childhood education (MAT, Certificate); elementary education (MAT); English for speakers of other languages (MAT, Certificate); health promotion management (MS); international training and development (MAT); international training and education (MA); nutrition education (Certificate); secondary teaching (MAT, Certificate); special education (MA); special education: learning disabilities (MA). *Application deadline:* For fall admission, 2/1 priority date for domestic students; for spring admission, 10/1 priority date for domestic students. Applications are processed on a rolling basis. *Application fee:* $80. *Application Contact:* Kathleen Clowery, Director, Graduate Admissions, 202-885-3621, Fax: 202-885-1505. *Dean,* Dr. Sarah Irvine-Belson, 202-885-3714, Fax: 202-885-1187, E-mail: educate@american.edu.

Kogod School of Business *Degree program information:* Part-time and evening/weekend programs available. Postbaccalaureate distance learning degree programs offered. Offers accounting (MBA, MS); business (MBA, MS, Certificate); consulting (MBA); corporate finance: commercial banking (MBA); corporate finance: corporate financial management (MBA); corporate finance: investment banking (MBA); entrepreneurship (MBA); finance (MS, Certificate); global emerging markets (MBA); international business (Certificate); international trade and global supply chain management (MBA); leadership (MBA); marketing management (MBA); marketing research (MBA); real estate (MBA, MS, Certificate); taxation (MS, Certificate).

School of Communication Students: 177 full-time (120 women), 199 part-time (119 women); includes 61 Black or African American, non-Hispanic/Latino; 1 American Indian or Alaska Native, non-Hispanic/Latino; 14 Asian, non-Hispanic/Latino; 14 Hispanic/Latino; 1 Two or more races, non-Hispanic/Latino, 22 international. Average age 27. 685 applicants, 64% accepted, 200 enrolled. *Faculty:* 44 full-time (23 women). Expenses: Contact institution. *Financial support:* In 2010–11, 64 students received support, including 6 fellowships with partial tuition reimbursements available (averaging $23,000 per year), 15 research assistantships with partial tuition reimbursements available (averaging $18,000 per year), 15 teaching assistantships with partial tuition reimbursements available (averaging $18,000 per year); career-related internships or fieldwork, Federal Work-Study, institutionally sponsored loans, scholarships/grants, and tuition waivers (partial) also available. Support available to part-time students. Financial award application deadline: 2/1; financial award applicants required to submit FAFSA. In 2010, 185 master's awarded. *Degree program information:* Part-time and evening/weekend programs available. Offers broadcast journalism (MA); communication (MA, MFA, PhD); film and electronic media (MFA); film and video (MA); interactive journalism (MA); international media (MA); media industries and institutions (PhD); media, public issues, and engagement (PhD); media, technology, and culture (PhD); news media studies (MA); political communication (MA); print journalism (MA); producing for film and video (MA); public communication (MA). *Application deadline:* For fall admission, 2/1 priority date for domestic students, 4/1 priority date for international students; for spring admission, 11/15 for domestic and international students. Applications are processed on a rolling basis. *Application fee:* $50. Electronic applications accepted. *Application Contact:* Sharmeen Ahsan-Bracciale, Director of Graduate Services, 202-885-2040, Fax: 202-885-2019, E-mail: sharmeen@american.edu. *Dean,* Larry Kirkman, 202-885-2058, Fax: 202-885-2099, E-mail: larry@american.edu.

School of International Service Students: 591 full-time (383 women), 367 part-time (229 women); includes 164 minority (51 Black or African American, non-Hispanic/Latino; 4 American Indian or Alaska Native, non-Hispanic/Latino; 42 Asian, non-Hispanic/Latino; 63 Hispanic/Latino; 4 Two or more races, non-Hispanic/Latino), 94 international. Average age 27. 2,115 applicants, 59% accepted, 360 enrolled. *Faculty:* 91 full-time (35 women), 48 part-time/adjunct (16 women). Expenses: Contact institution. *Financial support:* Career-related internships or fieldwork, Federal Work-Study, and institutionally sponsored loans available. Financial award application deadline: 1/15. In 2010, 370 master's, 7 doctorates awarded. *Degree program information:* Part-time and evening/weekend programs available. Offers comparative and regional studies (Certificate); cross-cultural communication (Certificate); development management (MS); ethics, peace, and global affairs (MA); European studies (Certificate); global environmental policy (MA, Certificate); international affairs (MA); international communication (MA, Certificate); international development (MA, Certificate); international development management (Certificate); international economic policy (Certificate); international economic relations (Certificate); international media (MA); international peace and conflict resolution (MA, Certificate); international relations (PhD); international service (MIS); peace building (Certificate); the Americas (Certificate); United States foreign policy (Certificate). *Application deadline:* For fall admission, 1/15 priority date for domestic students; for spring admission, 10/1 priority date for domestic students. Applications are processed on a rolling basis. *Application fee:* $50. *Application Contact:* Yasmin Quianzon, Director of Graduate Admissions and Financial Aid, 202-885-2496, Fax: 202-885-1109. *Dean,* Dr. Louis W. Goodman, 202-885-1600, Fax: 202-885-2494.

School of Public Affairs Students: 312 full-time (182 women), 309 part-time (193 women); includes 135 minority (83 Black or African American, non-Hispanic/Latino; 4 American Indian or Alaska Native, non-Hispanic/Latino; 23 Asian, non-Hispanic/Latino; 25 Hispanic/Latino), 23 international. Average age 29. 1,103 applicants, 68% accepted, 223 enrolled. *Faculty:* 73 full-time (37 women), 63 part-time/adjunct (17 women). Expenses: Contact institution. *Financial support:* Fellowships, research assistantships, teaching assistantships, career-related internships or fieldwork, Federal Work-Study, institutionally sponsored loans, and tuition waivers (full and partial) available. Financial award application deadline: 2/1. In 2010, 205 master's, 8 doctorates awarded. *Degree program information:* Part-time and evening/weekend programs available. Offers advanced organization development (Certificate); fundamentals of organization development (Certificate); justice, law and society (MS, PhD); key executive leadership (MPA); leadership for organizational change (Certificate); non-profit management (Certificate); organization development (MSOD); organizational change (Certificate); political science (MA, PhD); public administration (MPA, PhD); public affairs (MA, MPA, MPP, MS, MSOD, PhD, Certificate); public financial management (Certificate); public management (Certificate); public policy (MPP); public policy analysis (Certificate); women, policy and political leadership (Certificate). *Application deadline:* For fall admission, 2/1 for domestic students; for spring admission, 11/1 for domestic students. *Application fee:* $55. *Application Contact:* Brenda Manley, Admissions and Financial Aid Manager, 202-885-6202, Fax: 202-885-2355, E-mail: bmanley@american.edu. *Dean,* Dr. William Leo Grande, 202-885-6234.

Washington College of Law *Degree program information:* Part-time and evening/weekend programs available. Offers human rights and the law (Certificate); international legal studies (LL M, Certificate); judicial sciences (SJD); law (JD, LL M, SJD, Certificate); law and government (LL M).

THE AMERICAN UNIVERSITY IN CAIRO, 11511 Cairo, Egypt

General Information Independent, coed, comprehensive institution. *Graduate housing:* Room and/or apartments available to single students; on-campus housing not available to married students.

GRADUATE UNITS

Graduate School of Education Students: 5 full-time (3 women), 22 part-time (18 women). 53 applicants, 72% accepted, 25 enrolled. *Faculty:* 7 full-time (6 women). Expenses: Contact institution. *Financial support:* Fellowships with partial tuition reimbursements, scholarships/grants available. Financial award application deadline: 5/12. *Degree program information:* Part-time programs available. Offers international and comparative education (MA). *Application deadline:* For fall admission, 2/1 priority date for domestic and international students; for spring admission, 11/1 priority date for domestic and international students. Applications are processed on a rolling basis. *Application fee:* $50. Electronic applications accepted. *Application Contact:* Wesley Clark, Coordinator of Student Affairs, 212-646-810-9433 Ext. 4547, E-mail: wclark@aucnyo.edu. Dr. Samiha Peterson, 20-2-2615-1490, E-mail: peterss@aucegypt.edu.

School of Business, Economics and Communication Students: 117 full-time (60 women), 110 part-time (39 women). 327 applicants, 40% accepted, 55 enrolled. *Faculty:* 19 full-time (4 women), 4 part-time/adjunct (0 women). Expenses: Contact institution. *Financial support:* Fellowships with partial tuition reimbursements, research assistantships, teaching assistantships, career-related internships or fieldwork, scholarships/grants, and unspecified assistantships available. Financial award application deadline: 5/12; financial award applicants required to submit CSS PROFILE. In 2010, 88 master's awarded. *Degree program information:* Part-time programs available. Offers business, economics and communication (MA, MBA, Diploma); economics (MA); management (MBA, MPA, Diploma). *Application deadline:* For fall admission, 2/1 priority date for domestic and international students; for spring admission, 11/1 priority date for domestic and international students. Applications are processed on a rolling basis. *Application fee:* $50. Electronic applications accepted. *Application Contact:* Wesley Clark, Director of North American Admissions and Financial Aid, 212-646-810-9433 Ext. 4547, E-mail: wclark@aucnyo.edu. *Dean,* Dr. Sherif Kamel, 20-2-2615-3290, E-mail: skamel@aucegypt.edu.

School of Global Affairs and Public Policy Students: 156 full-time (106 women), 245 part-time (179 women). 457 applicants, 53% accepted, 127 enrolled. *Faculty:* 23 full-time (9 women), 11 part-time/adjunct (4 women). Expenses: Contact institution. *Financial support:* Fellowships, career-related internships or fieldwork, scholarships/grants, and unspecified assistantships available. Financial award application deadline: 5/12. In 2010, 86 master's awarded. *Degree program information:* Part-time programs available. Offers forced migration and refugee studies (Diploma); gender and development (MA, Diploma); gender and justice (MA, Diploma); gender and women's studies in the Middle East and North Africa (MA, Diploma); global affairs and public policy (LL M, MA, MPA, MPP, Diploma); international and comparative law (LL M); international human rights law (MA); journalism and mass communication (MA); Middle East studies (MA, Diploma); migration and refugee studies (MA); public policy and administration (MA, MPA, MPP, Diploma); television and digital journalism (MA). *Application deadline:* For fall admission, 2/1 for domestic and international students; for spring admission, 11/1 for domestic and international students. *Application fee:* $50. *Application Contact:* Wesley Clark, Director of North American Admissions and Financial Aid, 212-646-810-9433 Ext. 4547, E-mail: wclark@aucnyo.edu. *Dean,* Dr. Nabil Fahmy, 20-2-2615-4443, E-mail: nfahmy@aucegypt.edu.

School of Humanities and Social Sciences Students: 200 full-time (141 women), 94 part-time (59 women). 366 applicants, 36% accepted, 86 enrolled. *Faculty:* 37 full-time (19 women), 28 part-time/adjunct (17 women). Expenses: Contact institution. *Financial support:* Fellowships with partial tuition reimbursements, teaching assistantships, career-related internships or fieldwork and tuition waivers (partial) available. Support available to part-time students. Financial award application deadline: 5/12. *Degree program information:* Part-time programs available. Offers Arab language and literature (MA); English and comparative literature (MA); humanities and social sciences (MA, Diploma); Islamic art and architecture (MA); Islamic studies (Diploma); Middle East studies (MA, Diploma); Middle Eastern history (MA); political science (MA); sociology and anthropology (MA). *Application deadline:* For fall admission, 2/1 priority date for domestic and international students; for spring admission, 11/1 priority date for domestic and international students. Applications are processed on a rolling basis. *Application fee:* $50. Electronic applications accepted. *Application Contact:* Wesley Clark, Director of North American Admissions and Financial Aid, 212-646-810-9433 Ext. 4547, E-mail: wclark@aucnyo.edu. *Dean,* Dr. Bruce Ferguson, 20-2-2615-1594, E-mail: bferguson@aucegypt.edu.

Arabic Language Institute Offers teaching Arabic as a foreign language (MA).

English Language Institute *Degree program information:* Part-time programs available. Offers teaching English as a foreign language (MA, Diploma). Electronic applications accepted.

School of Sciences and Engineering Students: 91 full-time (42 women), 184 part-time (90 women). 375 applicants, 46% accepted, 102 enrolled. *Faculty:* 27 full-time (5 women), 9 part-time/adjunct (0 women). Expenses: Contact institution. *Financial support:* Fellowships with partial tuition reimbursements, teaching assistantships, scholarships/grants and unspecified assistantships available. Financial award application deadline: 5/12. In 2010, 56 master's awarded. *Degree program information:* Part-time programs available. Offers computer science and engineering (M Comp); construction engineering (M Eng, MS); electronics engineering (M Eng, MS); food chemistry (M Chem); management of technology (M Eng); mechanical engineering (MS); product development and systems management (M Eng); sciences and engineering (M Comp, M Eng, MS, PhD, Diploma). *Application deadline:* For fall admission, 2/1 priority date for domestic and international students; for spring admission, 11/1 priority date for domestic and international students. Applications are processed on a rolling basis. *Application fee:* $50. Electronic applications accepted. *Application Contact:* Wesley Clark,

The American University in Cairo (continued)

Director of North American Admissions and Financial Aid, 212-646-810-9433 Ext. 4547, E-mail: wclark@aucnyo.edu. *Dean*, Dr. Ezzat Fahmy, 20-2-2615-2926, E-mail: ezzat@aucegypt.edu.

THE AMERICAN UNIVERSITY IN DUBAI, Dubai, United Arab Emirates

General Information Proprietary, coed, comprehensive institution. *Graduate housing:* Room and/or apartments available on a first-come, first-served basis to single students; on-campus housing not available to married students. Housing application deadline: 7/31.

GRADUATE UNITS

Master in Business Administration Program *Degree program information:* Part-time and evening/weekend programs available. Offers general (MBA); healthcare management (MBA); international finance (MBA); international marketing (MBA); management of construction enterprises (MBA). Electronic applications accepted.

AMERICAN UNIVERSITY OF ARMENIA, Yerevan 3750198, Armenia

General Information Independent, coed, graduate-only institution.

GRADUATE UNITS

Graduate Programs

THE AMERICAN UNIVERSITY OF ATHENS, GR-115 25 Athens, Greece

General Information Independent, coed, comprehensive institution. *Graduate housing:* Room and/or apartments guaranteed to single students; on-campus housing not available to married students. *Research affiliation:* Dimokritos (engineering and physics), Pasteur Institute (biomedical sciences).

GRADUATE UNITS

School of Graduate Studies Offers biomedical sciences (MS); business (MBA); business communication (MA); computer sciences (MS); engineering and applied sciences (MS); politics and policy making (MA); systems engineering (MS); telecommunications (MS).

AMERICAN UNIVERSITY OF BEIRUT, Beirut 1107 2020, Lebanon

General Information Independent, coed, university. *Enrollment:* 7,985 graduate, professional, and undergraduate students; 659 full-time matriculated graduate/professional students (317 women), 902 part-time matriculated graduate/professional students (577 women). *Enrollment by degree level:* 334 first professional, 1,146 master's, 52 doctoral, 29 other advanced degrees. *Graduate faculty:* 424 full-time (111 women), 83 part-time/adjunct (12 women). *Tuition:* Full-time $12,294; part-time $683 per credit. *Required fees:* $499; $499 per credit. Tuition and fees vary according to course load and program. *Graduate housing:* Room and/or apartments available on a first-come, first-served basis to single students; on-campus housing not available to married students. Typical cost: $1933 per year. Room charges vary according to campus/location and housing facility selected. Housing application deadline: 7/29. *Student services:* Campus employment opportunities, campus safety program, career counseling, exercise/wellness program, free psychological counseling, grant writing training, international student services, low-cost health insurance, services for students with disabilities, teacher training, writing training. *Library facilities:* Jafet Memorial Library plus 2 others. *Online resources:* library catalog, web page. *Collection:* 363,108 titles, 58,808 serial subscriptions, 3,243 audiovisual materials. *Research affiliation:* University of Paris 7, Denis Diderot (medicine), University of Poitiers (medicine), Cornell University (agriculture), The University of Palermo, University of California, Davis (engineering), Lebanese American University (student exchange).

Computer facilities: 1,851 computers available on campus for general student use. A campuswide network can be accessed from student residence rooms and from off campus. Online class registration is available. *Web address:* http://www.aub.edu.lb/.

General Application Contact: Dr. Salim Kanaan, Director, Admissions Office, 961-135-0000 Ext. 2594, Fax: 961-175-0775, E-mail: sk00@aub.edu.lb.

GRADUATE UNITS

Graduate Programs Students: 659 full-time (317 women), 902 part-time (577 women). Average age 25. 1,436 applicants, 63% accepted, 509 enrolled. *Faculty:* 424 full-time (111 women), 83 part-time/adjunct (12 women). Expenses: Contact institution. *Financial support:* In 2010–11, 338 students received support, including 909 research assistantships (averaging $4,549 per year); career-related internships or fieldwork, institutionally sponsored loans, scholarships/grants, health care benefits, and unspecified assistantships also available. Financial award application deadline: 2/2; financial award applicants required to submit FAFSA. In 2010, 81 first professional degrees, 344 master's, 1 doctorate awarded. *Degree program information:* Part-time and evening/weekend programs available. *Application deadline:* For fall admission, 2/20 priority date for domestic and international students; for spring admission, 11/15 for domestic and international students. Applications are processed on a rolling basis. *Application fee:* $50. Electronic applications accepted. *Application Contact:* Dr. Salim Kanaan, Director, Admissions Office, 961-135-0000 Ext. 2594, Fax: 961-175-0775, E-mail: sk00@aub.edu.lb.

Faculty of Agricultural and Food Sciences Students: 6 full-time (3 women), 86 part-time (77 women). Average age 24. 94 applicants, 60% accepted, 15 enrolled. *Faculty:* 22 full-time (6 women). Expenses: Contact institution. *Financial support:* In 2010–11, 18 research assistantships with partial tuition reimbursements (averaging $13,132 per year), 42 teaching assistantships with full and partial tuition reimbursements (averaging $1,000 per year) were awarded; scholarships/grants, health care benefits, and unspecified assistantships also available. Financial award application deadline: 2/2. In 2010, 28 master's awarded. *Degree program information:* Part-time programs available. Offers agricultural economics (MS); animal sciences (MS); ecosystem management (MSES); food technology (MS); irrigation (MS); mechanization (MS); nutrition (MS); plant protection (MS); plant science (MS); poultry science (MS); soils (MS). *Application deadline:* For fall admission, 4/30 for domestic and international students; for spring admission, 11/1 for domestic and international students. Applications are processed on a rolling basis. *Application fee:* $50. Electronic applications accepted. *Application Contact:* Dr. Salim Kanaan, Director, Admissions Office, 961-135-0000 Ext. 2594, Fax: 961-175-0775, E-mail: sk00@aub.edu.lb. *Dean*, Prof. Nahla Hwalla, 961-134-3002 Ext. 4400, Fax: 961-174-4460, E-mail: nahla@aub.edu.lb.

Faculty of Arts and Sciences Students: 158 full-time (104 women), 263 part-time (171 women). Average age 25. 356 applicants, 59% accepted, 127 enrolled. *Faculty:* 229 full-time (98 women), 136 part-time/adjunct (79 women). Expenses: Contact institution. *Financial support:* In 2010–11, 33 students received support. Career-related internships or fieldwork, institutionally sponsored loans, scholarships/grants, health care benefits, and unspecified assistantships available. Financial award application deadline: 2/4; financial award applicants required to submit FAFSA. In 2010, 57 master's awarded. *Degree program information:* Part-time programs available. Offers anthropology (MA); Arabic language and literature (MA); archaeology (MA); biology (MS); chemistry (MS); computational science (MS); computer science (MS); economics (MA); education (MA); English language (MA); English literature (MA); environmental policy planning (MSES); financial economics (MAFE); geology (MS); history (MA); mathematics (MA, MS); Middle Eastern studies (MA); philosophy (MA); physics (MS); political studies (MA); psychology (MA); public administration (MA); sociology (MA); statistics (MA, MS). *Application deadline:* For fall admission, 4/30 for domestic and international students; for spring admission, 11/1 for domestic and international students. *Application fee:* $50. *Application Contact:* Dr. Salim Kanaan, Director, Admissions Office, 961-135-0000 Ext. 2594, Fax: 961-175-0775, E-mail: sk00@aub.edu.lb. *Dean*, Dr. Patrick McGreevy, 961-137-4374 Ext. 3800, Fax: 961-174-4461, E-mail: pm07@aub.edu.lb.

Faculty of Engineering and Architecture Students: 261 full-time (92 women), 58 part-time (20 women). Average age 25. 272 applicants, 79% accepted, 108 enrolled. *Faculty:* 57 full-time (12 women), 3 part-time/adjunct (0 women). Expenses: Contact institution. *Financial support:* In 2010–11, 10 fellowships with full tuition reimbursements (averaging $24,800 per year), 33 research assistantships with full tuition reimbursements (averaging $24,800 per year), 70 teaching assistantships with full tuition reimbursements (averaging $9,800 per year) were awarded; career-related internships or fieldwork, institutionally sponsored loans, scholarships/grants, health care benefits, and unspecified assistantships also available. In 2010, 70 master's, 1 doctorate awarded. *Degree program information:* Part-time programs available. Offers applied energy (MME); civil engineering (ME, PhD); electrical and computer engineering (ME, PhD); engineering management (MEM); environmental and water resources (ME); environmental and water resources engineering (PhD); environmental technology (MSES); mechanical engineering (ME, PhD); urban design (MUD); urban planning and policy (MUP). *Application deadline:* For fall admission, 2/5 priority date for domestic and international students; for spring admission, 11/1 priority date for domestic students, 11/1 for international students. Applications are processed on a rolling basis. *Application fee:* $50. Electronic applications accepted. *Application Contact:* Dr. Salim Kanaan, Director, Admissions Office, 961-135-0000 Ext. 2594, Fax: 961-175-0775, E-mail: sk00@aub.edu.lb. *Acting Dean*, Fadl H. Moukalled, 961-135-0000 Ext. 3400, Fax: 961-174-4462, E-mail: memouk@aub.edu.lb.

Faculty of Health Sciences Students: 64 full-time (55 women), 111 part-time (85 women). Average age 26. 209 applicants, 67% accepted, 75 enrolled. *Faculty:* 33 full-time (23 women), 8 part-time/adjunct (3 women). Expenses: Contact institution. *Financial support:* In 2010–11, 65 students received support. Scholarships/grants, health care benefits, and unspecified assistantships available. Financial award application deadline: 2/20. In 2010, 54 master's awarded. *Degree program information:* Part-time programs available. Offers environmental sciences (MSES); epidemiology (MS); epidemiology and biostatistics (MPH); health management and policy (MPH); health promotion and community health (MPH); population health (MS). *Application deadline:* For fall admission, 2/20 for domestic and international students; for spring admission, 11/1 for domestic and international students. *Application fee:* $50. Electronic applications accepted. *Application Contact:* Mitra Tauk, Assistant for Graduate Student Affairs, 961-135-0000 Ext. 4687, Fax: 961-174-4470, E-mail: mt12@aub.edu.lb. *Dean*, Iman Adel Nuwayhid, 961-134-0119, Fax: 961-174-4470, E-mail: nuwayhid@aub.edu.lb.

Faculty of Medicine Students: 346 full-time (135 women), 69 part-time (57 women). Average age 23. *Faculty:* 222 full-time (56 women), 58 part-time/adjunct (4 women). Expenses: Contact institution. *Financial support:* In 2010–11, 4 students received support. Career-related internships or fieldwork, institutionally sponsored loans, scholarships/grants, health care benefits, and unspecified assistantships available. Financial award application deadline: 2/2. In 2010, 81 first professional degrees, 19 master's awarded. *Degree program information:* Part-time programs available. Offers biochemistry (MS); human morphology (MS); medicine (MD); microbiology and immunology (MS); neuroscience (MS); pharmacology and therapeutics (MS); physiology (MS). *Application deadline:* For fall admission, 4/30 for domestic and international students; for spring admission, 11/1 for domestic and international students. *Application fee:* $50. *Application Contact:* Dr. Salim Kanaan, Director, Admissions Office, 961-135-0000 Ext. 2594, Fax: 961-175-0775, E-mail: sk00@aub.edu.lb. *Dean*, Dr. Mohamed Sayegh, 961-135-0000 Ext. 4700, Fax: 961-174-4464, E-mail: msayegh@aub.edu.lb.

Olayan School of Business Students: 86 full-time (30 women), 40 part-time (22 women). Average age 34. 186 applicants, 53% accepted, 70 enrolled. *Faculty:* 27 full-time (5 women), 8 part-time/adjunct (2 women). Expenses: Contact institution. *Financial support:* In 2010–11, 23 students received support. Unspecified assistantships available. Financial award application deadline: 2/2. In 2010, 26 master's awarded. *Degree program information:* Part-time and evening/weekend programs available. Offers business (EMBA, MBA); business administration (MBA); executive business administration (EMBA). *Application Contact:* Dr. Salim Kanaan, Director, Admissions Office, 961-135-0000 Ext. 2594, Fax: 961-175-0775, E-mail: sk00@aub.edu.lb. *Dean*, George Najjar, 961-134-0460 Ext. 3930, Fax: 961-175-0214, E-mail: gnajjar@aub.edu.lb.

School of Nursing Students: 3 full-time (all women), 54 part-time (41 women). Average age 28. 57 applicants, 72% accepted, 23 enrolled. *Faculty:* 4 full-time (3 women), 5 part-time/adjunct (all women). Expenses: Contact institution. *Financial support:* In 2010–11, 15 research assistantships with partial tuition reimbursements, 2 teaching assistantships with partial tuition reimbursements were awarded; career-related internships or fieldwork, institutionally sponsored loans, scholarships/grants, health care benefits, and unspecified assistantships also available. Support available to part-time students. Financial award application deadline: 2/2. In 2010, 18 master's awarded. *Degree program information:* Part-time programs available. Offers adult care nursing (MSN); community health nursing (MSN); nursing administration (MSN); psychiatry mental health nursing (MSN). *Application deadline:* For fall admission, 4/30 for domestic and international students; for spring admission, 11/1 for domestic and international students. Applications are processed on a rolling basis. *Application fee:* $50. *Application Contact:* Dr. Salim Kanaan, Director, Admissions Office, 961-135-0000 Ext. 2594, Fax: 961-175-0775, E-mail: sk00@aub.edu.lb. *Director*, Dr. Huda Huijer Abu-Saad, 961-137-4374 Ext. 5952, Fax: 961-174-4476, E-mail: hh35@aub.edu.lb.

THE AMERICAN UNIVERSITY OF PARIS, 75007 Paris, France

General Information Independent, coed, comprehensive institution. *Enrollment:* 927 graduate, professional, and undergraduate students; 151 full-time matriculated graduate/professional students (110 women), 56 part-time matriculated graduate/professional students (43 women). *Enrollment by degree level:* 207 master's. *Graduate faculty:* 14 full-time (3 women). *Graduate housing:* Room and/or apartments available on a first-come, first-served basis to single students; on-campus housing not available to married students. *Student services:* Career counseling, free psychological counseling, low-cost health insurance, writing training. *Library facilities:* AUP Library. *Online resources:* library catalog, web page, access to other libraries' catalogs. *Collection:* 76,000 titles, 1,000 serial subscriptions, 2,000 audiovisual materials.

Computer facilities: 100 computers available on campus for general student use. A campuswide network can be accessed from off campus. Online class registration is available. *Web address:* http://www.aup.edu/.

General Application Contact: International Admissions, 33-1 40 62 07 20, Fax: 33-1 47 05 34 32, E-mail: admissions@aup.edu.

GRADUATE UNITS

Graduate Programs Students: 151 full-time (110 women), 56 part-time (43 women). 271 applicants, 83% accepted, 104 enrolled. *Faculty:* 14 full-time (3 women). Expenses: Contact institution. *Financial support:* Scholarships/grants available. Financial award applicants required to submit FAFSA. In 2010, 67 master's awarded. Offers cross-cultural and sustainable business management (MA); cultural translation (MA); global communications (MA); global communications and civil society (MA); international affairs, conflict resolution and civil society development (MA); Middle East and Islamic studies (MA); Middle East and Islamic studies and international affairs (MA); public policy and international affairs (MA); public policy and international law (MA). *Application deadline:* For fall admission, 4/15 priority date for international students; for spring admission, 11/15 priority date for international students. Applications are processed on a rolling basis. *Application fee:* $75. Electronic applications accepted. *Application Contact:* International Admissions Counselor, 33-1 40 62 07 20, Fax: 33-1 47 05 34 32, E-mail: admissions@aup.edu. *President*, Dr. Celeste Schenck, 33 1 40 62 06 59, E-mail: president@aup.fr.

AMERICAN UNIVERSITY OF PUERTO RICO, Bayamón, PR 00960-2037

General Information Independent, coed, comprehensive institution. *Enrollment:* 103 full-time matriculated graduate/professional students (79 women), 46 part-time matriculated graduate/professional students (37 women). *Enrollment by degree level:* 149 master's. *Graduate faculty:* 1 full-time (0 women), 31 part-time/adjunct (7 women). *Library facilities:* Loida

Figueroa Meacado. *Collection:* 100,000 titles, 231 serial subscriptions, 2,091 audiovisual materials. *Web address:* http://www.aupr.edu/.

General Application Contact: Dr. Josephine Resto-Olivo, Chancellor, 787-620-2040 Ext. 2011, Fax: 787-620-2958, E-mail: jresto@aupr.edu.

GRADUATE UNITS

Program in Criminal Justice Students: 3 full-time (0 women), 4 part-time (0 women); includes all Hispanic/Latino. *Faculty:* 9 part-time/adjunct (1 woman). Expenses: Contact institution. *Financial support:* Applicants required to submit FAFSA. *Degree program information:* Evening/weekend programs available. Offers criminal justice (MA). *Application deadline:* For fall admission, 8/1 for domestic students; for winter admission, 10/15 for domestic students; for spring admission, 3/22 for domestic students. Applications are processed on a rolling basis. *Application fee:* $0. *Application Contact:* Information Contact, 787-620-2040, E-mail: oficnaadmisiones@aupr.edu.

Program in Education Students: 104 full-time (83 women), 45 part-time (40 women); includes all Hispanic/Latino. *Faculty:* 1 full-time (0 women), 22 part-time/adjunct (6 women). Expenses: Contact institution. Offers art history (M Ed); elementary education (4-6) (M Ed); elementary education (K-3) (M Ed); general science education (M Ed); physical education (M Ed); special education (transition) (M Ed); youth transition to adult life (Graduate Certificate). *Application deadline:* For fall admission, 8/1 for domestic students; for winter admission, 10/18 for domestic students; for spring admission, 3/15 for domestic students. Applications are processed on a rolling basis. *Application fee:* $50. *Application Contact:* Information Contact, 787-620-2040, E-mail: oficnaadmisiones@aupr.edu.

AMERICAN UNIVERSITY OF SHARJAH, Sharjah, United Arab Emirates

General Information Independent, coed, comprehensive institution. *Graduate housing:* Room and/or apartments available on a first-come, first-served basis to single students; on-campus housing not available to married students. Housing application deadline: 7/1. *Research affiliation:* Cambridge University (water resources and environmental engineering), Mohammed Bin Rashid Foundation (education), TESOL Arabian (TESOL education).

GRADUATE UNITS

Graduate Programs *Degree program information:* Part-time and evening/weekend programs available. Offers business (EMBA, GEMPA, MBA); chemical engineering (MS Ch E); civil engineering (MSCE); computer engineering (MS); electrical engineering (MSEE); mechanical engineering (MSME); mechatronics engineering (MS); public administration (MPA); teaching English to speakers of other languages (MA); translation and interpreting (MA); urban planning (MUP). Electronic applications accepted.

AMRIDGE UNIVERSITY, Montgomery, AL 36117

General Information Independent-religious, coed, university. *Enrollment:* 749 graduate, professional, and undergraduate students; 119 full-time matriculated graduate/professional students (54 women), 260 part-time matriculated graduate/professional students (149 women). *Enrollment by degree level:* 78 first professional, 231 master's, 70 doctoral. *Graduate faculty:* 39 full-time (6 women), 39 part-time/adjunct (5 women). *Graduate housing:* On-campus housing not available. *Student services:* Campus employment opportunities, campus safety program, career counseling, services for students with disabilities. *Library facilities:* Southern Christian University Library plus 1 other. *Online resources:* library catalog, web page, access to other libraries' catalogs. *Collection:* 80,000 titles, 1,200 serial subscriptions, 800 audiovisual materials.

Computer facilities: 5 computers available on campus for general student use. A campuswide network can be accessed from off campus. Online class registration, access to over 20 million monographs and journals online are available. *Web address:* http://www.amridgeuniversity.edu/.

General Application Contact: Ora Davis, Admissions Officer, 334-387-3877 Ext. 7524, Fax: 334-387-3878, E-mail: admissions@amridgeuniversity.edu.

GRADUATE UNITS

Graduate and Professional Programs Students: 119 full-time (54 women), 260 part-time (149 women); includes 160 minority (153 Black or African American, non-Hispanic/Latino; 1 Asian, non-Hispanic/Latino; 6 Hispanic/Latino). Average age 35. *Faculty:* 39 full-time (6 women), 39 part-time/adjunct (5 women). Expenses: Contact institution. *Financial support:* Federal Work-Study and scholarships/grants available. Support available to part-time students. Financial award applicants required to submit FAFSA. *Degree program information:* Part-time and evening/weekend programs available. Postbaccalaureate distance learning degree programs offered (no on-campus study). Offers behavioral leadership and management (MA); Biblical exposition (MA); biblical studies (MA, PhD); family therapy (D Min); historical and theological studies (MA); leadership and management (MS); marriage and family therapy (M Div, MA, PhD); ministerial leadership (M Div, MS); pastoral counseling (M Div, MS); practical ministry (MA); professional counseling (M Div, MA, PhD); theology (D Min). *Application deadline:* For fall admission, 9/1 priority date for domestic students; for spring admission, 1/1 priority date for domestic students. Applications are processed on a rolling basis. *Application fee:* $75. Electronic applications accepted. *Application Contact:* Ora Davis, Admissions Officer, 334-387-3877 Ext. 7524, Fax: 334-387-3878, E-mail: admissions@amridgeuniversity.edu. *Director of Enrollment Management*, 800-351-4040 Ext. 7513, Fax: 334-387-3878.

ANAHEIM UNIVERSITY, Anaheim, CA 92806-5150

General Information Proprietary, coed, graduate-only institution.

GRADUATE UNITS

Program in Teaching English to Speakers of Other Languages Postbaccalaureate distance learning degree programs offered (no on-campus study). Offers teaching English to speakers of other languages (MA, Certificate).

Programs in Business Administration Postbaccalaureate distance learning degree programs offered. Offers online global (MBA); online green (MBA); professional (MBA); sustainable management (Certificate, Diploma).

ANDERSON UNIVERSITY, Anderson, IN 46012-3495

General Information Independent-religious, coed, comprehensive institution. *Graduate housing:* Room and/or apartments available to single students; on-campus housing not available to married students. Housing application deadline: 6/1.

GRADUATE UNITS

Falls School of Business Offers accountancy (MA); business administration (MBA, DBA).

School of Education Offers education (M Ed).

School of Theology *Degree program information:* Part-time programs available. Offers missions (MA); theology (M Div, MTS, D Min).

ANDERSON UNIVERSITY, Anderson, SC 29621-4035

General Information Independent-religious, coed, comprehensive institution. *Enrollment:* 2,537 graduate, professional, and undergraduate students; 164 full-time matriculated graduate/professional students (84 women), 36 part-time matriculated graduate/professional students (14 women). *Enrollment by degree level:* 200 master's. *Tuition:* Part-time $320 per semester hour. *Library facilities:* Thrift Library. *Online resources:* library catalog, web page, access to other libraries' catalogs. *Collection:* 133,687 titles, 174 serial subscriptions, 6,688 audiovisual materials.

Computer facilities: 192 computers available on campus for general student use. A campuswide network can be accessed from student residence rooms and from off campus. Online class registration is available. *Web address:* http://www.andersonuniversity.edu/.

General Application Contact: Mallory Knight, Graduate Admission Counselor, 864-231-2182 Ext. 2182, Fax: 864-231-2115, E-mail: malloryknight@andersonuniversity.edu.

GRADUATE UNITS

College of Business Students: 7 full-time (0 women), 1 part-time (0 women). Expenses: Contact institution. Offers business (MBA). *Application Contact:* Dr. Douglas Goodwin, MBA Director/Associate Dean, 864-MBA-6000. *MBA Director/Associate Dean*, Dr. Douglas Goodwin, 864-MBA-6000.

College of Education *Faculty:* 4 full-time (1 woman), 8 part-time/adjunct (3 women). Expenses: Contact institution. Offers education (M Ed). *Application Contact:* Dr. Ray Locy, Dean, 864-231-2042. *Dean*, Dr. Ray Locy, 864-231-2042.

Command College Expenses: Contact institution. Postbaccalaureate distance learning degree programs offered. Offers executive leadership (MA).

School of Christian Ministry Expenses: Contact institution. Postbaccalaureate distance learning degree programs offered. Offers Christian ministry (M Min). *Application Contact:* Dr. Michael Duduit, Dean, 800-542-3594, E-mail: ministry@andersonuniversity.edu. *Dean*, Dr. Michael Duduit, 800-542-3594, E-mail: ministry@andersonuniversity.edu.

ANDOVER NEWTON THEOLOGICAL SCHOOL, Newton Centre, MA 02459-2243

General Information Independent-religious, coed, graduate-only institution. *Enrollment by degree level:* 212 first professional, 41 master's, 39 doctoral. *Graduate faculty:* 15 full-time (7 women), 49 part-time/adjunct (21 women). *Graduate housing:* Rooms and/or apartments available on a first-come, first-served basis to single and married students. Housing application deadline: 7/1. *Student services:* Campus employment opportunities, career counseling, international student services, low-cost health insurance. *Library facilities:* Franklin Trask Library. *Online resources:* library catalog, web page. *Collection:* 232,555 titles, 556 serial subscriptions, 67 audiovisual materials.

Computer facilities: 16 computers available on campus for general student use. A campuswide network can be accessed. *Web address:* http://www.ants.edu/.

General Application Contact: Alison McCarthy, Director of Admissions, 617-831-2430, Fax: 617-831-1630, E-mail: admissions@ants.edu.

GRADUATE UNITS

Graduate and Professional Programs Students: 58 full-time (28 women), 234 part-time (160 women). *Faculty:* 15 full-time (7 women), 49 part-time/adjunct (21 women). Expenses: Contact institution. *Financial support:* Teaching assistantships with partial tuition reimbursements, career-related internships or fieldwork, Federal Work-Study, scholarships/grants, and tuition waivers (full) available. Support available to part-time students. Financial award application deadline: 4/15; financial award applicants required to submit FAFSA. *Degree program information:* Part-time programs available. Offers divinity (M Div); religious education (MA); theological research (MA); theological studies (MA); theology (D Min). *Application deadline:* For fall admission, 7/1 priority date for domestic students, 4/1 for international students; for winter admission, 11/1 for domestic students; for spring admission, 12/1 priority date for domestic students. Applications are processed on a rolling basis. *Application fee:* $20 ($50 for international students). Electronic applications accepted. *Application Contact:* Margaret L. Carroll, Director of Enrollment, 800-964-2687 Ext. 2428, Fax: 617-558-9785, E-mail: admissions@ants.edu. *President*, Nick Carter, 617-964-1100 Ext. 2410, Fax: 617-965-9756, E-mail: ncarter@ants.edu.

ANDREW JACKSON UNIVERSITY, Birmingham, AL 35244

General Information Private, coed, comprehensive institution. *Graduate housing:* On-campus housing not available.

GRADUATE UNITS

Brian Tracy College of Business and Entrepreneurship *Degree program information:* Part-time and evening/weekend programs available. Postbaccalaureate distance learning degree programs offered (no on-campus study). Offers entrepreneurship (MBA); finance (MBA); health services management (MBA); hospitality and tourism management (MBA); human resource management (MBA); international business (MBA); management (MBA); marketing (MBA). Electronic applications accepted.

Jeffrey D. Rubenstein College of Criminal Justice *Degree program information:* Part-time and evening/weekend programs available. Postbaccalaureate distance learning degree programs offered (no on-campus study). Offers criminal justice (MPA, MS); public administration (MPA). Electronic applications accepted.

ANDREWS UNIVERSITY, Berrien Springs, MI 49104

General Information Independent-religious, coed, university. CGS member. *Graduate housing:* Rooms and/or apartments available on a first-come, first-served basis to single and married students. *Research affiliation:* RAND Corporation (drug abuse), Argonne National Laboratory (physics), Deutches Electronen Synchroton (physics).

GRADUATE UNITS

School of Graduate Studies *Degree program information:* Part-time and evening/weekend programs available. Postbaccalaureate distance learning degree programs offered (minimal on-campus study).

College of Arts and Sciences *Degree program information:* Part-time and evening/weekend programs available. Offers arts and sciences (M Mus, MA, MAT, MS, MSA, MSMT, MSW, Dr Sc PT, TDPT); biology (MAT, MS); clinical and laboratory sciences (MSMT); communication (MA); community services management (MSA); English (MA, MAT); history (MA, MAT); international development (MSA); international language studies (MAT); mathematics and physical science (MS); music (M Mus, MA); nursing (MS); nutrition (MS); physical therapy (DPT, Dr Sc PT, TDPT); social work (MSW).

College of Technology Offers software engineering (MS); technology (MS).

Division of Architecture Offers architecture (M Arch).

School of Business *Degree program information:* Part-time programs available. Offers business (MBA, MSA).

School of Education *Degree program information:* Part-time programs available. Offers community counseling (MA); counseling psychology (PhD); curriculum and instruction (MA, Ed D, PhD, Ed S); education (MA, MAT, MS, Ed D, PhD, Ed S); educational administration and leadership (MA, Ed D, PhD, Ed S); educational and developmental psychology (MA, Ed D, PhD); educational psychology (Ed D, PhD); elementary education (MAT); leadership (MA, Ed D, PhD); reading (MA); school counseling (MA); school psychology (Ed S); secondary education (MAT); special education (MS); special education/learning disabilities (MS); teacher education (MAT).

Seventh-day Adventist Theological Seminary Offers ministry (M Div, D Min); pastoral ministry (MA); religious education (MA, Ed D, PhD, Ed S); theology (M Th, Th D); youth ministry (MA).

ANGELO STATE UNIVERSITY, San Angelo, TX 76909

General Information State-supported, coed, comprehensive institution. CGS member. *Enrollment:* 6,856 graduate, professional, and undergraduate students; 219 full-time matriculated graduate/professional students (140 women), 309 part-time matriculated graduate/professional students (196 women). *Enrollment by degree level:* 508 master's, 20 doctoral. *Graduate faculty:* 126 full-time (52 women). Tuition, state resident: full-time $4560; part-time $152 per credit hour. Tuition, nonresident: full-time $13,860; part-time $462 per credit hour. *Required fees:* $2132. Tuition and fees vary according to course load. *Graduate housing:* Room and/or apartments available on a first-come, first-served basis to single students; on-campus housing not available to married students. Typical cost: $4066 per year ($6666 including board). Room and board charges vary according to board plan and housing facility selected. Housing application deadline: 7/15. *Student services:* Campus employment opportunities, campus safety program, career counseling, free psychological counseling, international student services, low-cost health insurance, multicultural affairs office. *Library facilities:* Porter Henderson Library plus 1 other. *Online resources:* library catalog, web page. *Collection:* 714,411 titles, 40,955 serial subscriptions, 20,288 audiovisual materials. *Research affiliation:*

Angelo State University (continued)

Zinpro Corporation (animal nutrition), Purina (animal nutrition), Texas Space Consortium (space research and technology), TASCO (animal nutrition), Mannatech, Inc. (nutrition).

Computer facilities: Computer purchase and lease plans are available. 610 computers available on campus for general student use. A campuswide network can be accessed from student residence rooms and from off campus. Online class registration, online courses, tuition payments, purchase books, purchase parking permits, university calendar, library card catalog and library resources. Discounted hardware and software programs for personally owned computers are available. *Web address:* http://www.angelo.edu/.

General Application Contact: Theresa Fortin, Graduate Admissions Assistant, 325-942-2169, Fax: 325-942-2194, E-mail: theresa.fortin@angelo.edu.

GRADUATE UNITS

College of Graduate Studies Students: 268 full-time (182 women), 441 part-time (307 women); includes 30 Black or African American, non-Hispanic/Latino; 3 American Indian or Alaska Native, non-Hispanic/Latino; 101 Hispanic/Latino; 8 Native Hawaiian or other Pacific Islander, non-Hispanic/Latino. Average age 32. 219 applicants, 94% accepted, 166 enrolled. *Faculty:* 126 full-time (52 women). Expenses: Contact institution. *Financial support:* In 2010–11, 274 students received support, including 9 research assistantships (averaging $9,887 per year), 16 teaching assistantships (averaging $10,251 per year); career-related internships or fieldwork, Federal Work-Study, scholarships/grants, and unspecified assistantships also available. Support available to part-time students. Financial award application deadline: 3/1. In 2010, 143 master's awarded. *Degree program information:* Part-time and evening/weekend programs available. Postbaccalaureate distance learning degree programs offered (no on-campus study). Offers interdisciplinary studies (MA, MS). *Application deadline:* For fall admission, 7/15 priority date for domestic students, 6/10 for international students; for spring admission, 12/1 priority date for domestic students, 11/1 for international students. Applications are processed on a rolling basis. *Application fee:* $40 ($50 for international students). Electronic applications accepted. *Application Contact:* Aly Hunter, Graduate Admissions Assistant, 325-942-2169, Fax: 325-942-2194, E-mail: aly.hunter@angelo.edu. *Dean,* Dr. Brian J. May, 325-942-2169, Fax: 325-942-2194, E-mail: brian.may@angelo.edu.

College of Business Students: 28 full-time (12 women), 32 part-time (15 women); includes 6 Hispanic/Latino, 5 international. Average age 27. 44 applicants, 50% accepted, 21 enrolled. *Faculty:* 10 full-time (1 woman). Expenses: Contact institution. *Financial support:* In 2010–11, 36 students received support. Career-related internships or fieldwork, Federal Work-Study, and scholarships/grants available. Support available to part-time students. Financial award application deadline: 3/1; financial award applicants required to submit FAFSA. In 2010, 25 master's awarded. *Degree program information:* Part-time and evening/weekend programs available. Offers accounting (MBA); business (MBA, MPAC); business administration (MBA); professional accountancy (MPAC). *Application deadline:* For fall admission, 7/15 priority date for domestic students, 6/10 for international students; for spring admission, 12/1 priority date for domestic students, 11/1 for international students. Applications are processed on a rolling basis. *Application fee:* $40 ($50 for international students). Electronic applications accepted. *Application Contact:* Aly Hunter, Graduate Admissions Assistant, 325-942-2169, Fax: 325-942-2194, E-mail: aly.hunter@angelo.edu. *Dean,* Dr. Corbett Gaulden, 325-942-2337, Fax: 325-942-2718, E-mail: corbett.gaulden@angelo.edu.

College of Education Students: 65 full-time (54 women), 270 part-time (192 women); includes 12 Black or African American, non-Hispanic/Latino; 1 American Indian or Alaska Native, non-Hispanic/Latino; 2 Asian, non-Hispanic/Latino; 63 Hispanic/Latino, 3 international. Average age 36. 54 applicants, 80% accepted, 41 enrolled. *Faculty:* 10 full-time (7 women). Expenses: Contact institution. *Financial support:* In 2010–11, 73 students received support. Career-related internships or fieldwork, Federal Work-Study, scholarships/grants, and unspecified assistantships available. Support available to part-time students. Financial award application deadline: 3/1; financial award applicants required to submit FAFSA. In 2010, 59 master's awarded. *Degree program information:* Part-time and evening/weekend programs available. Offers coaching, sport, recreation and fitness administration (M Ed); curriculum and instruction (MA); education (M Ed, MA, MS, Certificate); educational diagnostics (M Ed); guidance and counseling (M Ed); principal (Certificate); professional education (M Ed); reading specialist (M Ed); school administration (M Ed, Certificate); special education (M Ed); student development and leadership in higher education (M Ed); superintendent (Certificate). *Application deadline:* For fall admission, 7/15 priority date for domestic students, 6/10 for international students; for spring admission, 12/1 priority date for domestic students, 11/1 for international students. Applications are processed on a rolling basis. *Application fee:* $40 ($50 for international students). Electronic applications accepted. *Application Contact:* Aly Hunter, Graduate Admissions Assistant, 325-942-2169, Fax: 325-942-2194, E-mail: aly.hunter@angelo.edu. *Dean,* Dr. John J. Miazga, 325-942-2212, E-mail: john.miazga@angelo.edu.

College of Liberal and Fine Arts Students: 78 full-time (53 women), 44 part-time (23 women); includes 9 Black or African American, non-Hispanic/Latino; 1 American Indian or Alaska Native, non-Hispanic/Latino; 1 Asian, non-Hispanic/Latino; 19 Hispanic/Latino, 1 international. Average age 30. 79 applicants, 67% accepted, 51 enrolled. *Faculty:* 21 full-time (4 women). Expenses: Contact institution. *Financial support:* In 2010–11, 68 students received support, including 10 teaching assistantships (averaging $10,251 per year); career-related internships or fieldwork, Federal Work-Study, scholarships/grants, and unspecified assistantships also available. Support available to part-time students. Financial award application deadline: 3/1; financial award applicants required to submit FAFSA. In 2010, 31 master's awarded. *Degree program information:* Part-time and evening/weekend programs available. Offers communication systems management (MA); English (MA); history (MA); liberal and fine arts (MA, MPA, MS); psychology (MS); public administration (MPA). *Application deadline:* For fall admission, 7/15 priority date for domestic students, 6/10 for international students; for spring admission, 12/1 priority date for domestic students, 11/1 for international students. Applications are processed on a rolling basis. *Application fee:* $40 ($50 for international students). Electronic applications accepted. *Application Contact:* Aly Hunter, Graduate Admissions Assistant, 325-942-2169, Fax: 325-942-2194, E-mail: aly.hunter@angelo.edu. *Dean,* Dr. Kevin Lambert, 325-942-2115, Fax: 325-942-2340, E-mail: kevin.lambert@angelo.edu.

College of Nursing and Allied Health Students: 64 full-time (46 women), 54 part-time (50 women); includes 6 Black or African American, non-Hispanic/Latino; 4 Asian, non-Hispanic/Latino; 10 Hispanic/Latino, 1 international. Average age 33. 66 applicants, 71% accepted, 45 enrolled. Expenses: Contact institution. In 2010, 25 master's awarded. Offers advanced practice registered nurse (MSN); nurse educator (MSN); nursing—RN to MSN (MSN); nursing and allied health (MSN, DPT); physical therapy (DPT). *Application deadline:* For fall admission, 7/15 priority date for domestic students, 6/10 for international students; for spring admission, 12/1 priority date for domestic students, 11/1 for international students. *Application fee:* $40 ($50 for international students). *Application Contact:* Theresa Fortin, Graduate Admissions Assistant, 325-942-2169, Fax: 325-942-2194, E-mail: theresa.fortin@angelo.edu. *Dean,* Dr. Leslie M. Mayrand, 325-942-2060 Ext. 247, Fax: 325-942-2236, E-mail: leslie.mayrand@angelo.edu.

College of Sciences Students: 26 full-time (11 women), 18 part-time (6 women); includes 1 Hispanic/Latino. Average age 25. 22 applicants, 59% accepted, 12 enrolled. *Faculty:* 26 full-time (13 women), 1 part-time/adjunct (0 women). Expenses: Contact institution. *Financial support:* In 2010–11, 9 research assistantships (averaging $9,887 per year), 2 teaching assistantships (averaging $10,251 per year) were awarded; career-related internships or fieldwork, Federal Work-Study, scholarships/grants, and unspecified assistantships also available. Support available to part-time students. Financial award application deadline: 8/1; financial award applicants required to submit FAFSA. In 2010, 15 master's awarded. *Degree program information:* Part-time and evening/weekend programs available. Offers animal science (MS); biology (MS); sciences (MS). *Application deadline:* For fall admission, 7/15 priority date for domestic students, 6/10 for international students; for spring admission, 12/1 priority date for domestic students, 11/1 for international students. Applications are processed on a rolling basis. *Application fee:* $40 ($50 for international students). Electronic applications accepted. *Application Contact:* Aly Hunter, Graduate Admissions Assistant, 325-942-2169, Fax: 325-942-2194, E-mail: aly.hunter@angelo.edu. *Dean,* Dr. Grady Price Blount, 325-942-2024 Ext. 242, Fax: 325-942-2557, E-mail: grady.blount@angelo.edu.

ANNA MARIA COLLEGE, Paxton, MA 01612

General Information Independent-religious, coed, comprehensive institution. *Graduate housing:* On-campus housing not available.

GRADUATE UNITS

Graduate Division *Degree program information:* Part-time and evening/weekend programs available. Offers art and visual art (MA); business administration (MBA, AC); counseling psychology (MA); criminal justice (MS); early childhood education (M Ed); education (CAGS); elementary education (M Ed); emergency management (MS, Graduate Certificate); English language arts (M Ed); fire science (MA); justice administration (MS); occupational and environmental health and safety (MS); pastoral ministry (MA); public administration (MPA); security management (MA); teacher of visual art (M Ed); visual arts (M Ed). Electronic applications accepted.

ANTIOCH UNIVERSITY LOS ANGELES, Culver City, CA 90230

General Information Independent, coed, upper-level institution. *Graduate housing:* On-campus housing not available.

GRADUATE UNITS

Graduate Programs *Degree program information:* Part-time and evening/weekend programs available. Postbaccalaureate distance learning degree programs offered. Offers clinical psychology (MA); creative writing (MFA); education (MA); human resource development (MA); leadership (MA); organizational development (MA); pedagogy of creative writing (Certificate); psychology (MA).

ANTIOCH UNIVERSITY MIDWEST, Yellow Springs, OH 45387-1609

General Information Independent, coed, upper-level institution. *Enrollment:* 645 graduate, professional, and undergraduate students; 324 full-time matriculated graduate/professional students (217 women), 162 part-time matriculated graduate/professional students (117 women). *Enrollment by degree level:* 486 master's. *Graduate faculty:* 16 full-time (9 women), 23 part-time/adjunct (16 women). *Tuition:* Full-time $30,720; part-time $480 per credit hour. *Required fees:* $600; $150 per quarter. *Graduate housing:* On-campus housing not available. *Student services:* International student services, low-cost health insurance, teacher training, writing training. *Library facilities:* Olive Kettering Library plus 1 other. *Online resources:* library catalog, web page, access to other libraries' catalogs. *Collection:* 521,562 titles, 95,527 serial subscriptions, 6,400 audiovisual materials.

Computer facilities: 32 computers available on campus for general student use. A campuswide network can be accessed. Online class registration, online bill pay, and online view of financial aid award letter are available. *Web address:* http://midwest.antioch.edu/.

General Application Contact: Seth Gordon, Assistant Director of Admissions, 937-769-1800 Ext. 1825, Fax: 937-769-1804, E-mail: sgordon@antioch.edu.

GRADUATE UNITS

Graduate Programs Students: 324 full-time (217 women), 162 part-time (117 women); includes 141 Black or African American, non-Hispanic/Latino; 3 American Indian or Alaska Native, non-Hispanic/Latino; 3 Asian, non-Hispanic/Latino; 8 Hispanic/Latino. Average age 37. 241 applicants, 69% accepted, 150 enrolled. *Faculty:* 16 full-time (9 women), 23 part-time/adjunct (16 women). Expenses: Contact institution. *Financial support:* Federal Work-Study and scholarships/grants available. Financial award applicants required to submit FAFSA. In 2010, 155 master's awarded. *Degree program information:* Part-time and evening/weekend programs available. Postbaccalaureate distance learning degree programs offered (minimal on-campus study). Offers conflict analysis and management (MA); liberal and professional studies (MA); management (MA). *Application deadline:* For fall admission, 8/1 for domestic students; for winter admission, 12/1 for domestic students; for spring admission, 3/10 for domestic students. Applications are processed on a rolling basis. *Application fee:* $50. Electronic applications accepted. *Application Contact:* Seth Gordon, Assistant Director of Admissions, 937-769-1800 Ext. 1825, Fax: 937-769-1804, E-mail: sgordon@antioch.edu. *Dean of Students,* Darlene Robertson, 937-769-1800 Ext. 1820, Fax: 937-769-1804, E-mail: drobertson@antioch.edu.

School of Education Students: 252 full-time (169 women), 102 part-time (76 women); includes 113 Black or African American, non-Hispanic/Latino; 2 American Indian or Alaska Native, non-Hispanic/Latino; 1 Asian, non-Hispanic/Latino; 4 Hispanic/Latino. Average age 31. 194 applicants, 65% accepted, 116 enrolled. *Faculty:* 11 full-time (8 women), 14 part-time/adjunct (10 women). Expenses: Contact institution. *Financial support:* Federal Work-Study available. Financial award applicants required to submit FAFSA. In 2010, 123 master's awarded. *Degree program information:* Part-time and evening/weekend programs available. Offers education (M Ed). *Application deadline:* For fall admission, 9/7 for domestic students; for winter admission, 12/10 for domestic students; for spring admission, 3/10 for domestic students. Applications are processed on a rolling basis. *Application fee:* $50. Electronic applications accepted. *Application Contact:* Oscar Robinson, Director of Admissions, 937-769-1823, Fax: 937-769-1804, E-mail: orobinson@antioch.edu. *Director,* Dr. Zak Shariff, 937-769-1880, Fax: 937-769-1805, E-mail: zsharif@antioch.edu.

ANTIOCH UNIVERSITY NEW ENGLAND, Keene, NH 03431-3552

General Information Independent, coed, graduate-only institution. *Graduate housing:* On-campus housing not available. *Research affiliation:* Harris Center for Conservation Education (environmental studies), Cheshire Medical Center Cardiac Rehabilitation Program (clinical psychology), Northeast Foundation for Children (education), Pine Hill Waldorf School (education).

GRADUATE UNITS

Graduate School *Degree program information:* Evening/weekend programs available. Offers administration and supervision (M Ed); autism spectrum disorders (Certificate); clinical mental health counseling (MA); clinical psychology (Psy D); conservation biology (MS); dance/movement therapy and counseling (M Ed, MA); early childhood education (M Ed); elementary education (M Ed); environmental advocacy and organizing (MS); environmental education (MS); environmental studies (MS, PhD); experienced educators (M Ed); individualized study (MS); integrated learning (M Ed); marriage and family therapy (MA, PhD); organizational and environmental sustainability (MBA); organizational development (Certificate); organizational leadership and management (MS); resource management and conservation (MS); science teacher certification (MS); Waldorf teacher training (M Ed). Electronic applications accepted.

ANTIOCH UNIVERSITY SANTA BARBARA, Santa Barbara, CA 93101-1581

General Information Independent, coed, upper-level institution. *Graduate housing:* On-campus housing not available.

GRADUATE UNITS

Program in Clinical Psychology Offers clinical psychology (Psy D). Electronic applications accepted.

Program in Education/Teacher Credentialing *Degree program information:* Part-time programs available. Offers education/teacher credentialing (MA). Electronic applications accepted.

Program in Organizational Management *Degree program information:* Part-time and evening/weekend programs available. Postbaccalaureate distance learning degree programs offered (minimal on-campus study). Offers organizational management (MA). Electronic applications accepted.

Program in Psychology *Degree program information:* Part-time and evening/weekend programs available. Offers psychology (MA). Electronic applications accepted.

ANTIOCH UNIVERSITY SEATTLE, Seattle, WA 98121-1814

General Information Independent, coed, university. *Graduate housing:* On-campus housing not available.

GRADUATE UNITS

Graduate Programs *Degree program information:* Part-time and evening/weekend programs available. Offers education (MA); psychology (MA, Psy D). Electronic applications accepted.

Center for Creative Change *Degree program information:* Evening/weekend programs available. Offers environment and community (MA); management (MS); organizational psychology (MA); strategic communications (MA); whole system design (MA). Electronic applications accepted.

APEX SCHOOL OF THEOLOGY, Durham, NC 27703

General Information Independent-religious, coed, comprehensive institution. *Enrollment:* 294 graduate, professional, and undergraduate students; 111 full-time matriculated graduate/professional students (76 women), 27 part-time matriculated graduate/professional students (10 women). *Graduate faculty:* 4 full-time (1 woman), 11 part-time/adjunct (6 women). *Tuition:* Part-time $675 per course. *Graduate housing:* On-campus housing not available. *Student services:* Campus safety program, career counseling. *Web address:* http://www.apexsot.edu/.

General Application Contact: Dr. Henry Wells, Registrar, 919-572-1625, Fax: 919-572-1762, E-mail: registrar@apexsot.edu.

GRADUATE UNITS

Graduate Programs Students: 111 full-time (76 women), 27 part-time (10 women). Average age 45. *Faculty:* 4 full-time (1 woman), 11 part-time/adjunct (6 women). Expenses: Contact institution. *Application fee:* $50. *Application Contact:* Dr. Henry O. Wells, Registrar, 919-572-1625, Fax: 919-572-1762, E-mail: registrar@apexsot.edu. *Academic Dean,* Dr. LaFayette Maxwell, 919-572-1625, Fax: 919-572-1762, E-mail: lmaxwell@apexsot.edu.

APPALACHIAN BIBLE COLLEGE, Bradley, WV 25818

General Information Independent-religious, coed, comprehensive institution.

GRADUATE UNITS

Graduate School Postbaccalaureate distance learning degree programs offered (no on-campus study).

APPALACHIAN SCHOOL OF LAW, Grundy, VA 24614

General Information Independent, coed, graduate-only institution. *Enrollment by degree level:* 313 first professional. *Graduate faculty:* 19 full-time (5 women), 2 part-time/adjunct (1 woman). *Tuition:* Full-time $26,500. *Required fees:* $325. Full-time tuition and fees vary according to student level. *Graduate housing:* On-campus housing not available. *Student services:* Campus employment opportunities, career counseling, services for students with disabilities, writing training. *Library facilities:* ASL Library. *Online resources:* library catalog, web page. *Collection:* 136,175 titles, 4,051 serial subscriptions, 728 audiovisual materials.

Computer facilities: 29 computers available on campus for general student use. A campuswide network can be accessed. Online class registration, printing access are available. *Web address:* http://www.asl.edu/.

General Application Contact: Nancy M. Pruitt, Director of Student Services and Registrar, 276-935-4349 Ext. 1229, Fax: 276-935-8496, E-mail: npruitt@asl.edu.

GRADUATE UNITS

Professional Program in Law Students: 313 full-time (108 women); includes 37 minority (7 Black or African American, non-Hispanic/Latino; 2 American Indian or Alaska Native, non-Hispanic/Latino; 7 Asian, non-Hispanic/Latino; 9 Hispanic/Latino; 12 Two or more races, non-Hispanic/Latino), 1 international. Average age 26. 1,368 applicants, 60% accepted, 127 enrolled. *Faculty:* 19 full-time (5 women), 2 part-time/adjunct (1 woman). Expenses: Contact institution. *Financial support:* In 2010–11, 84 students received support; research assistantships, career-related internships or fieldwork, Federal Work-Study, institutionally sponsored loans, scholarships/grants, and tuition waivers (full and partial) available. Financial award application deadline: 7/1; financial award applicants required to submit FAFSA. In 2010, 107 JDs awarded. Offers law (JD). *Application deadline:* For fall admission, 6/1 for domestic students. Applications are processed on a rolling basis. *Application fee:* $60. Electronic applications accepted. *Application Contact:* Nancy M. Pruitt, Director of Student Services and Registrar, 276-935-4349 Ext. 1229, Fax: 276-935-8496, E-mail: npruitt@asl.edu. *Dean,* Clinton W. Shinn, 276-935-4349, Fax: 276-935-8261, E-mail: wshinn@asl.edu.

APPALACHIAN STATE UNIVERSITY, Boone, NC 28608

General Information State-supported, coed, comprehensive institution. CGS member. *Enrollment:* 17,222 graduate, professional, and undergraduate students; 830 full-time matriculated graduate/professional students (495 women), 1,028 part-time matriculated graduate/professional students (788 women). *Enrollment by degree level:* 1,778 master's, 80 doctoral. *Graduate faculty:* 474 full-time (189 women), 58 part-time/adjunct (33 women). Tuition, state resident: full-time $3428; part-time $428 per unit. Tuition, nonresident: full-time $14,518; part-time $1814 per unit. *Required fees:* $2320; $344 per unit. Tuition and fees vary according to campus/location. *Graduate housing:* On-campus housing not available. *Student services:* Campus employment opportunities, campus safety program, career counseling, child daycare facilities, exercise/wellness program, free psychological counseling, grant writing training, international student services, low-cost health insurance, multicultural affairs office, services for students with disabilities, teacher training, writing training. *Library facilities:* Carol Grotnes Belk Library plus 1 other. *Online resources:* library catalog, web page, access to other libraries' catalogs. *Collection:* 969,276 titles, 34,610 serial subscriptions, 26,235 audiovisual materials.

Computer facilities: 1,800 computers available on campus for general student use. A campuswide network can be accessed from student residence rooms and from off campus. Online class registration is available. *Web address:* http://www.appstate.edu/.

General Application Contact: Sandy Krause, Director of Admissions and Recruiting, 828-262-2130, Fax: 828-262-2709, E-mail: krausesl@appstate.edu.

GRADUATE UNITS

Cratis D. Williams Graduate School Students: 830 full-time (495 women), 1,028 part-time (788 women); includes 109 minority (60 Black or African American, non-Hispanic/Latino; 4 American Indian or Alaska Native, non-Hispanic/Latino; 17 Asian, non-Hispanic/Latino; 20 Hispanic/Latino; 8 Two or more races, non-Hispanic/Latino). 1,707 applicants, 66% accepted, 722 enrolled. *Faculty:* 474 full-time (189 women), 58 part-time/adjunct (33 women). Expenses: Contact institution. *Financial support:* In 2010–11, 30 fellowships (averaging $5,000 per year) were awarded; career-related internships or fieldwork, Federal Work-Study, institutionally sponsored loans, scholarships/grants, and unspecified assistantships also available. Financial award application deadline: 4/1; financial award applicants required to submit FAFSA. In 2010, 859 master's, 15 doctorates awarded. *Degree program information:* Part-time and evening/weekend programs available. Postbaccalaureate distance learning degree programs offered (no on-campus study). Offers accounting (MS); appropriate technology (MS); business administration (MBA); cell and molecular (MS); clinical health psychology (MA); clinical mental health counseling (MA); college student development (MA); computer science (MS); criminal justice (MS); curriculum specialist (MA); educational administration (Ed S); educational leadership (Ed D); educational media (MA); elementary education (MA); engineering physics (MS); English (MA); English education (MA); exercise science (MS); general (MS); general experimental psychology (MA); geography (MA); higher education (MA, Ed S); history (MA); industrial and organizational psychology (MA); library science (MLS); marriage and family therapy (MA); mathematics (MA); mathematics education (MA); middle grades education (MA); nutrition (MS); political science (MA); public administration (MPA); public history (MA); reading education (MA); romance languages (MA); school administration (MSA); school counseling (MA); social work (MSW); special education (MA); speech-language pathology (MS); technology (MS). *Application deadline:* For fall admission, 3/1 priority date for domestic students, 2/1 for international students; for spring admission, 11/1 for domestic students, 7/1 for international students. Applications are processed on a rolling basis. *Application fee:* $55. Electronic applications accepted. *Application Contact:* Sandy Krause, Director of Admissions and Recruiting, 828-262-2130, Fax: 828-262-2709, E-mail: krausesl@appstate.edu. *Dean of Research and Graduate Studies,* Dr. Edelma D. Huntley, 828-262-2130, E-mail: huntleyed@appstate.edu.

Center for Appalachian Studies Students: 25 full-time (15 women), 5 part-time (4 women); includes 1 Hispanic/Latino. 20 applicants, 85% accepted, 12 enrolled. *Faculty:* 14 full-time (5 women). Expenses: Contact institution. *Financial support:* In 2010–11, 8 research assistantships (averaging $8,000 per year) were awarded; fellowships, teaching assistantships, career-related internships or fieldwork, Federal Work-Study, scholarships/grants, and unspecified assistantships also available. Financial award application deadline: 4/1; financial award applicants required to submit FAFSA. In 2010, 11 master's awarded. *Degree program information:* Part-time programs available. Offers culture (MA); music (MA); sustainable development (MA). *Application deadline:* For fall admission, 7/1 for domestic students, 2/1 for international students; for spring admission, 11/1 for domestic students, 7/1 for international students. Applications are processed on a rolling basis. *Application fee:* $55. Electronic applications accepted. *Application Contact:* Dr. Katherine Ledford, Graduate Program Director, 828-262-4089, E-mail: ledfordke@appstate.edu. *Director,* Dr. Pat Beaver, 828-262-2550, E-mail: beaverpd@appstate.edu.

School of Music Students: 30 full-time (20 women), 4 part-time (3 women); includes 1 minority (Hispanic/Latino). 34 applicants, 82% accepted, 21 enrolled. *Faculty:* 28 full-time (8 women), 2 part-time/adjunct (1 woman). Expenses: Contact institution. *Financial support:* In 2010–11, 16 research assistantships (averaging $8,000 per year) were awarded; fellowships, teaching assistantships, career-related internships or fieldwork, Federal Work-Study, scholarships/grants, tuition waivers (partial), and unspecified assistantships also available. Financial award application deadline: 4/1; financial award applicants required to submit FAFSA. In 2010, 22 master's awarded. *Degree program information:* Part-time programs available. Offers music education (MM); music performance (MM); music therapy (MMT). *Application deadline:* For fall admission, 7/1 for domestic students, 2/1 for international students; for spring admission, 11/1 for domestic students, 7/1 for international students. Applications are processed on a rolling basis. *Application fee:* $55. Electronic applications accepted. *Application Contact:* Dr. Jennifer Snodgrass, Graduate Program Director, 828-262-6463, E-mail: snodgrassjs@appstate.edu. *Dean,* Dr. William Pelto, 828-262-6446, E-mail: peltowl@appstate.edu.

AQUINAS COLLEGE, Grand Rapids, MI 49506-1799

General Information Independent-religious, coed, comprehensive institution. *Enrollment:* 2,186 graduate, professional, and undergraduate students; 24 full-time matriculated graduate/professional students (16 women), 209 part-time matriculated graduate/professional students (159 women). *Enrollment by degree level:* 233 master's. *Graduate faculty:* 33 full-time (20 women), 39 part-time/adjunct (22 women). *Tuition:* Part-time $527 per credit. *Graduate housing:* On-campus housing not available. *Student services:* Campus employment opportunities, campus safety program, career counseling, child daycare facilities, exercise/wellness program, free psychological counseling, multicultural affairs office, services for students with disabilities, teacher training. *Library facilities:* Grace Hauenstein Library plus 1 other. *Online resources:* library catalog, web page, access to other libraries' catalogs. *Collection:* 101,540 titles, 402 serial subscriptions.

Computer facilities: Computer purchase and lease plans are available. 175 computers available on campus for general student use. A campuswide network can be accessed from student residence rooms and from off campus. Online class registration is available. *Web address:* http://www.aquinas.edu/.

General Application Contact: Mary Pastore, Assistant to the Associate Provost, 616-632-2435, Fax: 616-732-4465, E-mail: kwiatmar@aquinas.edu.

GRADUATE UNITS

School of Education Students: 13 full-time (10 women), 150 part-time (123 women); includes 18 minority (2 Black or African American, non-Hispanic/Latino; 3 Asian, non-Hispanic/Latino; 13 Hispanic/Latino). Average age 36. 96 applicants, 76% accepted, 53 enrolled. *Faculty:* 16 full-time (12 women), 16 part-time/adjunct (13 women). Expenses: Contact institution. *Financial support:* In 2010–11, 141 students received support. Scholarships/grants available. Support available to part-time students. Financial award application deadline: 3/15; financial award applicants required to submit FAFSA. In 2010, 68 master's awarded. *Degree program information:* Part-time and evening/weekend programs available. Offers education (MAT, ME, MS). *Application deadline:* Applications are processed on a rolling basis. *Application fee:* $0. *Application Contact:* Michele Polega, Coordinator of Graduate Education Programs, 616-632-2440, E-mail: pciegmic@aquinas.edu. *Dean,* Nanette Clatterbuck, 616-632-2973, Fax: 616-732-4465, E-mail: clattnan@aquinas.edu.

School of Management Students: 11 full-time (6 women), 59 part-time (36 women); includes 7 minority (3 Black or African American, non-Hispanic/Latino; 1 Asian, non-Hispanic/Latino; 3 Hispanic/Latino). Average age 35. 79 applicants, 90% accepted, 37 enrolled. *Faculty:* 11 full-time (3 women), 7 part-time/adjunct (0 women). Expenses: Contact institution. *Financial support:* In 2010–11, 26 students received support. Scholarships/grants available. Support available to part-time students. Financial award application deadline: 3/15; financial award applicants required to submit FAFSA. In 2010, 20 master's awarded. *Degree program information:* Part-time and evening/weekend programs available. Offers management (M Mgt). *Application deadline:* Applications are processed on a rolling basis. *Application Contact:* Lynn Atkins-Rykert, Executive Assistant, 616-632-2924, Fax: 616-732-4489, E-mail: atkinlyn@aquinas.edu. *Director,* Brian DiVita, 616-632-2922, Fax: 616-732-4489, E-mail: vangecyn@aquinas.edu.

AQUINAS INSTITUTE OF THEOLOGY, St. Louis, MO 63108

General Information Independent-religious, coed, graduate-only institution. *Graduate housing:* On-campus housing not available.

GRADUATE UNITS

Graduate and Professional Programs *Degree program information:* Part-time and evening/weekend programs available. Postbaccalaureate distance learning degree programs offered (minimal on-campus study). Offers biblical studies (Certificate); health care mission (MAHCM); ministry (M Div); pastoral care (Certificate); pastoral ministry (MAPM); pastoral studies (MAPS); preaching (D Min); spiritual direction (Certificate); theology (M Div, MA); Thomistic studies (Certificate).

ARCADIA UNIVERSITY, Glenside, PA 19038-3295

General Information Independent-religious, coed, comprehensive institution. *Enrollment:* 4,078 graduate, professional, and undergraduate students; 685 full-time matriculated graduate/professional students (541 women), 963 part-time matriculated graduate/professional students (711 women). *Enrollment by degree level:* 1,167 master's, 270 doctoral, 211 other advanced degrees. *Graduate faculty:* 71 full-time, 135 part-time/adjunct. *Required fees:* $645 per credit hour. *Graduate housing:* On-campus housing not available. *Student services:* Campus safety program, career counseling, international student services, low-cost health insurance, multicultural affairs office, writing training. *Library facilities:* Bette E. Landman Library. *Collection:* 157,438 titles, 982 serial subscriptions, 2,745 audiovisual materials.

Computer facilities: 120 computers available on campus for general student use. A campuswide network can be accessed from student residence rooms and from off campus. Online class registration is available. *Web address:* http://www.arcadia.edu/.

General Application Contact: Information Contact, 215-572-2910, Fax: 215-572-4049, E-mail: admiss@arcadia.edu.

GRADUATE UNITS

Graduate Studies Students: 685 full-time (541 women), 963 part-time (711 women); includes 217 minority (144 Black or African American, non-Hispanic/Latino; 1 American Indian or Alaska Native, non-Hispanic/Latino; 38 Asian, non-Hispanic/Latino; 11 Hispanic/Latino; 23 Two or more races, non-Hispanic/Latino), 40 international. Average age 30. *Faculty:* 71 full-time, 135 part-time/adjunct. Expenses: Contact institution. *Financial support:* Research assistantships, teaching assistantships, career-related internships or fieldwork, scholarships/grants, tuition waivers (partial), and unspecified assistantships available. Support available to

Arcadia University (continued)

part-time students. In 2010, 473 master's, 62 doctorates, 1 other advanced degree awarded. *Degree program information:* Part-time and evening/weekend programs available. Postbaccalaureate distance learning degree programs offered (minimal on-campus study). Offers allied health (MPH, MSHE, MSPH); art education (M Ed, MA Ed); biology education (MA Ed); business administration (MBA); chemistry education (MA Ed); child development (CAS); community counseling (MACP); computer education (M Ed, CAS); computer education 7-12 (MA Ed); early childhood education (M Ed, CAS); educational leadership (M Ed, CAS); educational psychology (CAS); elementary education (M Ed, CAS); English (MAE); English education (MA Ed); environmental education (MA Ed, CAS); fine arts, theater, and music (MAH); forensic science (MSFS); genetic counseling (MSGC); history education (MA Ed); history, philosophy, and religion (MAH); international peace and conflict resolution (MAIPCR); language arts (M Ed, CAS); literature and language (MAH); mathematics education (M Ed, MA Ed, CAS); medical science and community health (MM Sc, MPH, MSHE, MSPH); music education (MA Ed); physical therapy (DPT); psychology (MA Ed); pupil personnel services (CAS); reading (M Ed, CAS); school counseling (MACP); school library science (M Ed); science education (M Ed, CAS); secondary education (M Ed, CAS); special education (M Ed, Ed D, CAS); theater arts (MA Ed); written communication (MA Ed). *Application fee:* $50. Electronic applications accepted. *Application Contact:* 215-572-2910, Fax: 215-572-4049, E-mail: admiss@arcadia.edu. *Dean,* John Hoffman, 215-572-2925, Fax: 215-572-2081, E-mail: hoffman@arcadia.edu.

ARGOSY UNIVERSITY, ATLANTA, Atlanta, GA 30328

General Information Proprietary, coed, university.

GRADUATE UNITS

College of Business Offers accounting (DBA); corporate compliance (MBA); customized professional concentration (MBA, DBA); finance (MBA); healthcare administration (MBA); information systems (DBA); information systems management (MBA); international business (MBA, DBA); management (MBA, MSM, DBA); marketing (MBA, DBA).

College of Education Offers educational leadership (MAEd, Ed D, Ed S); teaching and learning (MAEd, Ed D, Ed S).

College of Health Sciences Offers public health (MPH).

College of Psychology and Behavioral Sciences Offers clinical psychology (MA, Psy D, Postdoctoral Respecialization Certificate); community counseling (MA); counselor education and supervision (Ed D); forensic psychology (MA); industrial organizational psychology (MA); marriage and family therapy (Certificate); sport-exercise psychology (MA).

ARGOSY UNIVERSITY, CHICAGO, Chicago, IL 60601

General Information Proprietary, coed, university.

GRADUATE UNITS

College of Business Postbaccalaureate distance learning degree programs offered (minimal on-campus study). Offers accounting (DBA); customized professional concentration (MBA, DBA); finance (MBA); fraud examination (MBA); global business sustainability (DBA); healthcare administration (MBA); information systems (DBA); information systems management (MBA); international business (MBA, DBA); management (MBA, MSM, DBA); marketing (MBA, DBA); organizational leadership (Ed D); public administration (MBA); sustainable management (MBA).

College of Education Postbaccalaureate distance learning degree programs offered (minimal on-campus study). Offers adult education and training (MA Ed); community college executive leadership (Ed D); educational leadership (MA Ed, Ed D, Ed S); instructional leadership (Ed D, Ed S).

College of Health Sciences Offers public health (MPH).

College of Psychology and Behavioral Sciences Postbaccalaureate distance learning degree programs offered (minimal on-campus study). Offers child and adolescent psychology (Psy D); client-centered and experiential psychotherapies (Psy D); clinical psychology (MA, Psy D); community counseling (MA); counseling psychology (Ed D); counselor education and supervision (Ed D); diversity and multicultural psychology (Psy D); family psychology (Psy D); forensic psychology (Psy D); health psychology (Psy D); industrial organizational psychology (MA); neuropsychology (Psy D); organizational consulting (Psy D); psychoanalytic psychology (Psy D); psychology and spirituality (Psy D).

ARGOSY UNIVERSITY, DALLAS, Farmers Branch, TX 75244

General Information Proprietary, coed, university.

GRADUATE UNITS

College of Business Offers accounting (DBA, AGC); corporate compliance (MBA, Graduate Certificate); customized professional concentration (MBA); finance (MBA, Graduate Certificate); fraud examination (MBA, Graduate Certificate); global business sustainability (DBA, AGC); healthcare administration (Graduate Certificate); healthcare management (MBA); information systems (MBA, DBA, AGC); information systems management (Graduate Certificate); international business (MBA, DBA, AGC, Graduate Certificate); management (MBA, DBA, AGC, Graduate Certificate); marketing (MBA, DBA, AGC, Graduate Certificate); public administration (MBA, Graduate Certificate); sustainable management (MBA, Graduate Certificate).

College of Education Offers educational administration (MA Ed); educational leadership (Ed D); higher and postsecondary education (MA Ed); instructional leadership (MA Ed); school psychology (MA).

College of Health Sciences Offers public health (MPH).

College of Psychology and Behavioral Sciences Offers clinical psychology (MA, Psy D); community counseling (MA); counselor education and supervision (Ed D); forensic psychology (MA); industrial organizational psychology (MA); psychology and behavioral sciences (MA, Ed D, Psy D).

ARGOSY UNIVERSITY, DENVER, Denver, CO 80231

General Information Proprietary, coed, university.

GRADUATE UNITS

College of Business Offers accounting (DBA); corporate compliance (MBA); customized professional concentration (MBA, DBA); finance (MBA); fraud examination (MBA); global business sustainability (DBA); healthcare administration (MBA); information systems (DBA); information systems management (MBA); international business (MBA, DBA); management (MBA, MSM, DBA); marketing (MBA, DBA); organizational leadership (Ed D); public administration (MBA); sustainable management (MBA).

College of Education Offers community college executive leadership (Ed D); educational leadership (MA Ed, Ed D); instructional leadership (MA Ed, Ed D).

College of Health Sciences Offers public health (MPH).

College of Psychology and Behavioral Sciences Offers clinical mental health counseling (MA); clinical psychology (MA, Psy D); counseling psychology (Ed D); counselor education and supervision (Ed D); forensic psychology (MA); industrial organizational psychology (MA); marriage and family therapy (MA, DMFT).

ARGOSY UNIVERSITY, HAWAI'I, Honolulu, HI 96813

General Information Proprietary, coed, university.

GRADUATE UNITS

College of Business Offers accounting (DBA); corporate compliance (MBA); customized professional concentration (MBA, DBA); finance (MBA, Certificate); fraud examination (MBA); global business sustainability (DBA); healthcare administration (MBA, Certificate); information systems (DBA); information systems management (MBA, Certificate); international business (MBA, DBA, Certificate); management (MBA, MSM, DBA); marketing (MBA, DBA, Certificate); organizational leadership (Ed D); public administration (MBA); sustainable management (MBA).

College of Education Offers adult education and training (MAEd); educational leadership (Ed D); instructional leadership (Ed D); school psychology (MA).

College of Psychology and Behavioral Sciences Offers clinical psychology (MA, Psy D, Postdoctoral Respecialization Certificate); counseling psychology (Ed D); forensic psychology (MA); marriage and family therapy (MA); psychology and behavioral sciences (MA, MS, Ed D, Psy D, Certificate, Postdoctoral Respecialization Certificate); psychopharmacology (MS, Certificate); substance abuse counseling (Certificate).

ARGOSY UNIVERSITY, INLAND EMPIRE, San Bernardino, CA 92408

General Information Proprietary, coed, university.

GRADUATE UNITS

College of Business Offers accounting (DBA); corporate compliance (MBA); customized professional concentration (MBA, DBA); finance (MBA); fraud examination (MBA); global business sustainability (DBA); healthcare administration (MBA); information systems (DBA); information systems management (MBA); international business (MBA, DBA); management (MBA, MSM, DBA); marketing (MBA, DBA); organizational leadership (Ed D); public administration (MBA); sustainable management (MBA).

College of Education Offers community college executive leadership (Ed D); educational leadership (MA Ed, Ed D); instructional leadership (MA Ed, Ed D).

College of Health Sciences Offers public health (MPH).

College of Psychology and Behavioral Sciences Offers clinical psychology/marriage and family therapy (MA); counseling psychology (Ed D); counseling psychology/marriage and family therapy (MA); forensic psychology (MA); industrial organizational psychology (MA); sport-exercise psychology (MA).

ARGOSY UNIVERSITY, LOS ANGELES, Santa Monica, CA 90045

General Information Proprietary, coed, university.

GRADUATE UNITS

College of Business Offers accounting (DBA); corporate compliance (MBA); customized professional concentration (MBA, DBA); finance (MBA); fraud examination (MBA); global business sustainability (DBA); healthcare administration (MBA); information systems (DBA); information systems management (MBA); international business (MBA, DBA); management (MBA, MSM, DBA); marketing (MBA, DBA); organizational leadership (Ed D); public administration (MBA); sustainable management (MBA).

College of Education Offers community college executive leadership (Ed D); educational leadership (MA Ed, Ed D); instructional leadership (MA Ed, Ed D).

College of Health Sciences Offers public health (MPH).

College of Psychology and Behavioral Sciences Offers clinical psychology/marriage and family therapy (MA); counseling psychology (Ed D); counseling psychology/marriage and family therapy (MA); forensic psychology (MA).

ARGOSY UNIVERSITY, NASHVILLE, Nashville, TN 37214

General Information Proprietary, coed, university.

GRADUATE UNITS

College of Business Offers accounting (DBA); customized professional concentration (MBA, DBA); finance (MBA); healthcare administration (MBA); information systems (MBA, DBA); international business (MBA, DBA); management (MBA, MSM, DBA); marketing (MBA, DBA).

College of Education Offers education (MA Ed, Ed D, Ed S); education technology (Ed D); educational leadership (MA Ed, Ed S); higher education administration (Ed D); instructional leadership (MA Ed, Ed S); K-12 education (Ed D).

College of Health Sciences Offers public health (MPH).

College of Psychology and Behavioral Sciences Offers counselor education and supervision (Ed D); mental health counseling (MA).

ARGOSY UNIVERSITY, ORANGE COUNTY, Orange, CA 92868

General Information Proprietary, coed, university.

GRADUATE UNITS

College of Business Offers accounting (DBA, Adv C); corporate compliance (MBA); customized professional concentration (MBA, DBA); finance (MBA, Certificate); fraud examination (MBA); global business sustainability (DBA); healthcare administration (MBA, Certificate); information systems (DBA, Adv C, Certificate); information systems management (MBA); international business (MBA, DBA, Adv C, Certificate); management (MBA, MSM, DBA, Adv C); marketing (MBA, DBA, Adv C, Certificate); organizational leadership (Ed D); public administration (MBA, Certificate); sustainable management (MBA).

College of Education Offers community college executive leadership (Ed D); educational leadership (MA Ed, Ed D); instructional leadership (MA Ed, Ed D).

College of Health Sciences Offers public health (MPH).

College of Psychology and Behavioral Sciences *Degree program information:* Part-time and evening/weekend programs available. Offers child and adolescent psychology (Psy D); counseling psychology (Ed D); forensic psychology (MA); marriage and family therapy (MA); psychology and behavioral sciences (MA, Ed D, Psy D); sport-exercise psychology (MA). Electronic applications accepted.

ARGOSY UNIVERSITY, PHOENIX, Phoenix, AZ 85021

General Information Proprietary, coed, university.

GRADUATE UNITS

College of Business Offers accounting (DBA); corporate compliance (MBA); customized professional concentration (MBA, DBA); finance (MBA); fraud examination (MBA); global business sustainability (DBA); healthcare administration (MBA); information systems (DBA); information systems management (MBA); international business (MBA, DBA); management (MBA, DBA); marketing (MBA, DBA); public administration (MBA); sustainable management (MBA).

College of Education Offers adult education and training (MA Ed); advanced educational administration (Ed D, Ed S); community college executive leadership (Ed D); educational administration (MA Ed); educational leadership (MA Ed, Ed D, Ed S); higher and postsecondary education (MA Ed); initial educational administration (Ed D, Ed S); school psychology (MA, Psy D); teaching and learning (MA Ed, Ed D, Ed S).

College of Health Sciences Offers public health (MPH).

College of Psychology and Behavioral Sciences Offers clinical psychology (MA); forensic psychology (MA); industrial organizational psychology (MA); mental health counseling (MA); neuropsychology (Psy D); psychology and behavioral sciences (MA, Psy D); sport–exercise psychology (MA); sports-exercise psychology (Psy D).

ARGOSY UNIVERSITY, SALT LAKE CITY, Draper, UT 84020

General Information Proprietary, coed, university.

GRADUATE UNITS

College of Business Offers accounting (DBA); corporate compliance (MBA); customized professional concentration (MBA, DBA); finance (MBA); fraud examination (MBA); global business sustainability (DBA); healthcare administration (MBA); information systems (DBA); information systems management (MBA); international business (MBA, DBA); management (MBA, DBA); marketing (MBA, DBA); public administration (MBA); sustainable management (MBA).

College of Education Offers educational leadership (MA Ed, Ed D).

College of Health Sciences Offers public health (MPH).

College of Psychology and Behavioral Sciences Offers counseling psychology (Ed D); counselor education and supervision (Ed D); forensic psychology (MA); marriage and family therapy (MA, DMFT); mental health counseling (MA).

ARGOSY UNIVERSITY, SAN DIEGO, San Diego, CA 92108

General Information Proprietary, coed, university.

GRADUATE UNITS

College of Business Offers accounting (DBA); corporate compliance (MBA); customized professional concentration (MBA, DBA); finance (MBA); fraud examination (MBA); global business sustainability (DBA); information systems (DBA); information systems management (MBA); international business (MBA, DBA); management (MBA, MSM, DBA); marketing (MBA, DBA); organizational leadership (Ed D); public administration (MBA).

College of Education Offers community college executive leadership (Ed D); educational leadership (MA Ed, Ed D); instructional leadership (MA Ed, Ed D).

College of Health Sciences Offers public health (MPH).

College of Psychology and Behavioral Sciences Offers clinical psychology/marriage and family therapy (MA); counseling psychology (Ed D); counseling psychology/marriage and family therapy (MA); forensic psychology (MA).

ARGOSY UNIVERSITY, SAN FRANCISCO BAY AREA, Alameda, CA 94501

General Information Proprietary, coed, university.

GRADUATE UNITS

College of Business Offers accounting (DBA); corporate compliance (MBA); customized professional concentration (MBA, DBA); finance (MBA); fraud examination (MBA); global business sustainability (DBA); healthcare administration (MBA); information systems (DBA); information systems management (MBA); international business (MBA, DBA); management (MBA, MSM, DBA); marketing (MBA, DBA); organizational leadership (Ed D); public administration (MBA); sustainable management (MBA).

College of Education Offers community college executive leadership (Ed D); educational leadership (MA Ed, Ed D); instructional leadership (MA Ed, Ed D).

College of Health Sciences Offers public health (MPH).

College of Psychology and Behavioral Sciences Offers clinical psychology (MA, Psy D); counseling psychology (MA, Ed D); forensic psychology (MA); sport-exercise psychology (MA).

ARGOSY UNIVERSITY, SARASOTA, Sarasota, FL 34235

General Information Proprietary, coed, university.

GRADUATE UNITS

College of Business Offers accounting (DBA, Adv C); corporate compliance (MBA, DBA, Certificate); customized professional concentration (MBA, DBA); finance (MBA, Certificate); fraud examination (MBA, Certificate); global business sustainability (DBA, Adv C); healthcare administration (MBA, Certificate); information systems (DBA, Adv C, Certificate); information systems management (MBA); international business (MBA, DBA, Adv C, Certificate); management (MBA, MSM, DBA, Adv C, Certificate); marketing (MBA, DBA, Adv C, Certificate); organizational leadership (Ed D); public administration (MBA, Certificate); sustainable management (MBA, Certificate).

College of Education Offers community college executive leadership (Ed D); educational leadership (MA Ed, Ed D, Ed S); school counseling (MA, Ed S); school psychology (MA); teaching and learning (MA Ed, Ed D, Ed S).

College of Psychology and Behavioral Sciences Offers community counseling (MA); counseling psychology (Ed D); counselor education and supervision (Ed D); forensic psychology (MA); marriage and family therapy (MA); mental health counseling (MA); pastoral community counseling (Ed D).

ARGOSY UNIVERSITY, SCHAUMBURG, Schaumburg, IL 60173-5403

General Information Proprietary, coed, university.

GRADUATE UNITS

College of Business Offers accounting (DBA, Adv C); customized professional concentration (MBA, DBA); finance (MBA, Certificate); fraud examination (MBA); global business sustainability (DBA); healthcare administration (MBA, Certificate); information systems (DBA, Adv C, Certificate); information systems management (MBA); international business (MBA, DBA, Adv C, Certificate); management (MBA, MSM, DBA, Adv C, Certificate); marketing (MBA, DBA, Adv C, Certificate); organizational leadership (Ed D); public administration (MBA); sustainable management (MBA).

College of Education Offers community college executive leadership (Ed D); educational leadership (MA Ed, Ed D, Ed S); instructional leadership (Ed D, Ed S).

College of Psychology and Behavioral Sciences Offers clinical health psychology (Post-Graduate Certificate); clinical psychology (MA, Psy D); community counseling (MA); counseling psychology (Ed D); counselor education and supervision (Ed D); forensic psychology (Post-Graduate Certificate); industrial organizational psychology (MA).

ARGOSY UNIVERSITY, SEATTLE, Seattle, WA 98121

General Information Proprietary, coed, university.

GRADUATE UNITS

College of Business Offers accounting (DBA); corporate compliance (MBA); customized professional concentration (MBA, DBA); finance (MBA); fraud examination (MBA); global business sustainability (DBA); healthcare administration (MBA); information systems (DBA); information systems management (MBA); international business (MBA, DBA); management (MBA, MSM, DBA); marketing (MBA, DBA); organizational leadership (Ed D); public administration (MBA); sustainable management (MBA).

College of Education Offers adult education and training (MA Ed); community college executive leadership (Ed D); educational leadership (MA Ed, Ed D); higher and postsecondary education (MA Ed); instructional leadership (MA Ed, Ed D).

College of Health Sciences Offers public health (MPH).

College of Psychology and Behavioral Sciences Offers clinical psychology (MA, Psy D, Postdoctoral Respecialization Certificate); counseling psychology (MA, Ed D); psychology and behavioral sciences (MA, Ed D, Psy D, Postdoctoral Respecialization Certificate).

ARGOSY UNIVERSITY, TAMPA, Tampa, FL 33607

General Information Proprietary, coed, university.

GRADUATE UNITS

College of Business Offers accounting (DBA); corporate compliance (MBA); customized professional concentration (MBA, DBA); finance (MBA); fraud examination (MBA); global business sustainability (DBA); healthcare administration (MBA); information systems (DBA); information systems management (MBA); international business (MBA, DBA); management (MBA, MSM, DBA); marketing (MBA, DBA); organizational leadership (Ed D); public administration (MBA); sustainable management (MBA).

College of Education Offers community college executive leadership (Ed D); educational leadership (MA Ed, Ed D, Ed S); school counseling (MA); teaching and learning (MA Ed, Ed D, Ed S).

College of Psychology and Behavioral Sciences Offers clinical psychology (MA, Psy D); counselor education and supervision (Ed D); industrial organizational psychology (MA); marriage and family therapy (MA); mental health counseling (MA).

ARGOSY UNIVERSITY, TWIN CITIES, Eagan, MN 55121

General Information Proprietary, coed, university.

GRADUATE UNITS

College of Business Offers accounting (DBA); customized professional concentration (MBA, DBA); finance (MBA); fraud examination (MBA); global business sustainability (DBA); healthcare administration (MBA); information systems (DBA); information systems management (MBA); international business (MBA, DBA); management (MBA, MSM, DBA); marketing (MBA, DBA); organizational leadership (Ed D); public administration (MBA); sustainable management (MBA).

College of Education Offers advanced educational administration (Ed D, Ed S); educational leadership (MA Ed, Ed D, Ed S); higher and postsecondary education (MA Ed); initial educational administration (Ed D, Ed S); instructional leadership (MA Ed, Ed D, Ed S).

College of Health Sciences Offers health services management (MS); public health (MPH).

College of Psychology and Behavioral Sciences Offers clinical psychology (MA, Psy D); forensic counseling (Post-Graduate Certificate); forensic psychology (MA); industrial organizational psychology (MA); marriage and family therapy (MA, DMFT).

ARGOSY UNIVERSITY, WASHINGTON DC, Arlington, VA 22209

General Information Proprietary, coed, university.

GRADUATE UNITS

College of Business Offers accounting (DBA); customized professional concentration (MBA, DBA); finance (MBA); fraud examination (MBA); global business sustainability (DBA); healthcare administration (MBA); information systems (DBA); information systems management (MBA); international business (MBA, DBA, Certificate); management (MBA, MSM, DBA); marketing (MBA, DBA, Certificate); organizational leadership (Ed D); public administration (MBA); sustainable management (MBA).

College of Education Offers community college executive leadership (Ed D); educational leadership (MA Ed, Ed D, Ed S); instructional leadership (MA Ed, Ed D, Ed S).

College of Health Sciences Offers public health (MPH).

College of Psychology and Behavioral Sciences Offers clinical psychology (MA, Psy D); community counseling (MA); counseling psychology (Ed D); counselor education and supervision (Ed D); forensic psychology (MA).

ARIZONA SCHOOL OF ACUPUNCTURE AND ORIENTAL MEDICINE, Tucson, AZ 85712

General Information Proprietary, coed, graduate-only institution.

GRADUATE UNITS

Graduate Programs Offers acupuncture (M Ac, M Ac OM).

ARIZONA STATE UNIVERSITY, Tempe, AZ 85287

General Information State-supported, coed, university. CGS member. *Enrollment:* 70,440 graduate, professional, and undergraduate students; 9,334 full-time matriculated graduate/professional students (4,668 women), 3,757 part-time matriculated graduate/professional students (2,052 women). *Enrollment by degree level:* 614 first professional, 8,424 master's, 3,989 doctoral, 64 other advanced degrees. *Graduate faculty:* 2,527 full-time (1,059 women), 231 part-time/adjunct (115 women). Tuition, state resident: full-time $8510; part-time $608 per credit. Tuition, nonresident: full-time $16,542; part-time $919 per credit. *Required fees:* $339; $110 per credit. Part-time tuition and fees vary according to course load. *Graduate housing:* Room and/or apartments available to single students; on-campus housing not available to married students. Typical cost: $7380 per year ($10,576 including board). *Student services:* Campus employment opportunities, campus safety program, career counseling, child daycare facilities, exercise/wellness program, free psychological counseling, grant writing training, international student services, low-cost health insurance, multicultural affairs office, services for students with disabilities, teacher training, writing training. *Library facilities:* Hayden Library plus 8 others. *Online resources:* library catalog, web page, access to other libraries' catalogs. *Collection:* 4.5 million titles, 92,272 serial subscriptions, 1.7 million audiovisual materials. *Research affiliation:* Arizona Public Service (electrical, computer and energy engineering), Banner Health (health, biomedical, life sciences), Honeywell (mechanical and aerospace engineering), Mayo Clinic (healthcare, biomedical Informatics), Raytheon (computer science and engineering), Translational Genomics Research Institute (TGEN) (biomedicine).

Computer facilities: Computer purchase and lease plans are available. 4,250 computers available on campus for general student use. A campuswide network can be accessed from student residence rooms and from off campus. Online class registration is available. *Web address:* http://www.asu.edu/.

General Application Contact: Graduate Admissions, 480-965-6113.

GRADUATE UNITS

College of Liberal Arts and Sciences Students: 1,787 full-time (954 women), 572 part-time (366 women); includes 377 minority (50 Black or African American, non-Hispanic/Latino; 24 American Indian or Alaska Native, non-Hispanic/Latino; 86 Asian, non-Hispanic/Latino; 198 Hispanic/Latino; 2 Native Hawaiian or other Pacific Islander, non-Hispanic/Latino; 17 Two or more races, non-Hispanic/Latino), 424 international. Average age 30. 4,057 applicants, 32% accepted, 655 enrolled. *Faculty:* 1,062 full-time (462 women), 73 part-time/adjunct (38 women). Expenses: Contact institution. *Financial support:* In 2010–11, 488 research assistantships with full and partial tuition reimbursements (averaging $15,586 per year), 894 teaching assistantships with full and partial tuition reimbursements (averaging $14,843 per year) were awarded; fellowships with full tuition reimbursements, career-related internships or fieldwork, Federal Work-Study, institutionally sponsored loans, scholarships/grants, and tuition waivers (full and partial) also available. Financial award application deadline: 3/1; financial award applicants required to submit FAFSA. In 2010, 384 master's, 184 doctorates, 32 other advanced degrees awarded. *Degree program information:* Part-time programs available. Postbaccalaureate distance learning degree programs offered (minimal on-campus study). Offers American media and popular culture (MAS); applied linguistics (PhD); applied mathematics (PhD); audiology (Au D); behavioral neuroscience (PhD); biochemistry (MS, PhD); chemistry (MS, PhD); clinical psychology (PhD); cognition, action and perception (PhD); communication disorders (MS); computational biosciences (PhD); creative writing (MFA); developmental psychology (PhD); English (MA, PhD); liberal arts and sciences (MA, MAS, MFA, MLS, MNS, MS, MTESOL, MUEP, PSM, PSM, Au D, PhD, Graduate Certificate); liberal studies (MLS); liberal studies (film and media studies) (MLS); linguistics (Graduate Certificate); mathematics (MA, MNS, PhD); mathematics education (PhD); nanoscience (PSM, PSM); physics (MNS, PhD); political science (MA, PhD); quantitative psychology (PhD); science and technology policy (PSM); social psychology (PhD); speech and hearing science (PhD); statistics (PhD); teaching English to speakers of other languages (MTESOL). *Application deadline:* For fall admission, 7/1 for domestic and international students; for spring admission, 12/1 for domestic and international students. Applications are processed on a rolling basis. *Application fee:* $70 ($90 for international students). Electronic applications accepted. *Application Contact:* Graduate Admissions, 480-965-6113. *Vice President and Dean,* Quentin Wheeler, 480-965-3391, E-mail: quentin.wheeler@asu.edu.

Hugh Downs School of Human Communication Students: 43 full-time (29 women), 15 part-time (10 women); includes 8 minority (1 Black or African American, non-Hispanic/Latino; 1 Asian, non-Hispanic/Latino; 6 Hispanic/Latino), 5 international. Average age 31. 120 applicants, 31% accepted, 12 enrolled. *Faculty:* 31 full-time (14 women), 11 part-time/adjunct (8 women). Expenses: Contact institution. *Financial support:* In 2010–11, 6 research assistantships with full and partial tuition reimbursements (averaging $11,771 per year), 33 teaching assistantships with full and partial tuition reimbursements (averaging $13,911 per year) were awarded; fellowships with full tuition reimbursements, career-related internships or fieldwork, Federal Work-Study, institutionally sponsored loans, scholarships/grants, and tuition waivers (full and partial) also available. Financial award application deadline: 3/1; financial award applicants required to submit FAFSA. In 2010, 12 doctorates awarded. *Degree program information:* Evening/weekend programs available. Offers communication (PhD). *Application deadline:* For fall admission, 1/5 for domestic and international students.

Arizona State University (continued)

Applications are processed on a rolling basis. *Application fee:* $70 ($90 for international students). Electronic applications accepted. *Application Contact:* Graduate Admissions, 480-965-6113. *Director*, Dr. Angela Trethewey, 480-965-5095, E-mail: atreth@asu.edu.

School of Earth and Space Exploration Students: 89 full-time (32 women), 16 part-time (8 women); includes 12 minority (2 American Indian or Alaska Native, non-Hispanic/Latino; 4 Asian, non-Hispanic/Latino; 6 Hispanic/Latino), 18 international. Average age 30. 181 applicants, 28% accepted, 28 enrolled. *Faculty:* 43 full-time (4 women), 2 part-time/adjunct (1 woman). Expenses: Contact institution. *Financial support:* In 2010–11, 52 research assistantships with full and partial tuition reimbursements (averaging $15,804 per year), 42 teaching assistantships with full and partial tuition reimbursements (averaging $15,169 per year) were awarded; fellowships with full tuition reimbursements, career-related internships or fieldwork, Federal Work-Study, institutionally sponsored loans, scholarships/grants, and tuition waivers (full and partial) also available. Financial award application deadline: 3/1; financial award applicants required to submit FAFSA. In 2010, 6 master's, 7 doctorates awarded. Offers astrophysics (MS, PhD); exploration systems design (PhD); geological sciences (MS, PhD). PhD in exploration systems design is offered in collaboration with the Fulton Schools of Engineering. *Application deadline:* For fall admission, 1/15 for domestic and international students; for spring admission, 10/1 for domestic and international students. Applications are processed on a rolling basis. *Application fee:* $70 ($90 for international students). Electronic applications accepted. *Application Contact:* Graduate Admissions, 480-965-6113. *Director*, Dr. Kip Hodges, 480-965-5331, Fax: 480-965-8102, E-mail: kvhodges@asu.edu.

School of Geographical Sciences Students: 125 full-time (40 women), 47 part-time (25 women); includes 24 minority (4 Black or African American, non-Hispanic/Latino; 1 American Indian or Alaska Native, non-Hispanic/Latino; 1 Asian, non-Hispanic/Latino; 16 Hispanic/Latino; 2 Two or more races, non-Hispanic/Latino), 34 international. Average age 30. 261 applicants, 56% accepted, 79 enrolled. *Faculty:* 34 full-time (9 women), 2 part-time/adjunct (both women). Expenses: Contact institution. *Financial support:* In 2010–11, 25 research assistantships with full and partial tuition reimbursements (averaging $15,546 per year), 50 teaching assistantships with full and partial tuition reimbursements (averaging $10,686 per year) were awarded; fellowships with full tuition reimbursements, career-related internships or fieldwork, Federal Work-Study, institutionally sponsored loans, scholarships/grants, and tuition waivers (full and partial) also available. Financial award application deadline: 3/1; financial award applicants required to submit FAFSA. In 2010, 76 master's, 3 doctorates, 13 other advanced degrees awarded. Offers atmospheric science (Graduate Certificate); geographic education (MAS); geographic information systems (MAS); geographical information science (Graduate Certificate); geography (MA, PhD); transportation systems (Graduate Certificate); urban and environmental planning (MUEP). *Application deadline:* For fall admission, 1/15 for domestic and international students. Applications are processed on a rolling basis. *Application fee:* $70 ($90 for international students). Electronic applications accepted. *Application Contact:* Graduate Admissions, 480-965-6113. *Chair and Director*, Dr. Luc Anselin, 480-965-7533, E-mail: luc.anselin@asu.edu.

School of Historical, Philosophical and Religious Studies Students: 125 full-time (58 women), 68 part-time (37 women); includes 21 minority (5 Black or African American, non-Hispanic/Latino; 3 American Indian or Alaska Native, non-Hispanic/Latino; 1 Asian, non-Hispanic/Latino; 11 Hispanic/Latino; 1 Two or more races, non-Hispanic/Latino), 16 international. Average age 34. 221 applicants, 51% accepted, 41 enrolled. *Faculty:* 70 full-time (29 women), 2 part-time/adjunct (0 women). Expenses: Contact institution. *Financial support:* In 2010–11, 26 research assistantships with full and partial tuition reimbursements (averaging $12,900 per year), 69 teaching assistantships with full and partial tuition reimbursements (averaging $11,771 per year) were awarded; fellowships with full tuition reimbursements, career-related internships or fieldwork, institutionally sponsored loans, scholarships/grants, and tuition waivers (partial) also available. Financial award application deadline: 3/1; financial award applicants required to submit FAFSA. In 2010, 24 master's, 10 doctorates, 3 other advanced degrees awarded. *Degree program information:* Part-time programs available. Offers East/Southeast Asian history (MA, PhD); European history (MA, PhD); Latin American studies (MA, PhD); North American history (MA, PhD); philosophy (MA, PhD); public history (MA); religious studies (MA, PhD); scholarly publishing (Graduate Certificate). *Application deadline:* For fall admission, 1/1 for domestic and international students. Applications are processed on a rolling basis. *Application fee:* $70 ($90 for international students). Electronic applications accepted. *Application Contact:* Graduate Admissions, 480-965-6113. *Director*, Mark Von Hagen, 480-965-4186, E-mail: mark.vonhagen@asu.edu.

School of Human Evolution and Social Change Students: 127 full-time (77 women), 52 part-time (37 women); includes 43 minority (8 Black or African American, non-Hispanic/Latino; 4 American Indian or Alaska Native, non-Hispanic/Latino; 4 Asian, non-Hispanic/Latino; 26 Hispanic/Latino; 1 Two or more races, non-Hispanic/Latino), 19 international. Average age 32. 250 applicants, 24% accepted, 25 enrolled. *Faculty:* 52 full-time (19 women), 4 part-time/adjunct (2 women). Expenses: Contact institution. *Financial support:* In 2010–11, 30 research assistantships with full and partial tuition reimbursements (averaging $14,993 per year), 63 teaching assistantships with full and partial tuition reimbursements (averaging $15,266 per year) were awarded; fellowships with full tuition reimbursements, career-related internships or fieldwork, Federal Work-Study, institutionally sponsored loans, scholarships/grants, and tuition waivers (full and partial) also available. Financial award application deadline: 3/1; financial award applicants required to submit FAFSA. In 2010, 8 master's, 18 doctorates, 7 other advanced degrees awarded. Offers anthropology (PhD); anthropology (archaeology) (PhD); anthropology (bioarchaeology) (PhD); anthropology (museum studies) (MA); anthropology (physical) (PhD); applied mathematics for the life and social sciences (PhD); environmental social science (PhD); environmental social science (urbanism) (PhD); global health (MA); global health (health and culture) (PhD); global health (urbanism) (PhD); immigration studies (Graduate Certificate). *Application deadline:* For fall admission, 12/15 for domestic students, 12/1 for international students. Applications are processed on a rolling basis. *Application fee:* $70 ($90 for international students). Electronic applications accepted. *Application Contact:* Graduate Admissions, 480-965-6113. *Director*, Dr. Sander van der Leeuw, 480-965-6214, E-mail: vanderle@asu.edu.

School of International Letters and Cultures Students: 86 full-time (55 women), 24 part-time (16 women); includes 43 minority (2 Black or African American, non-Hispanic/Latino; 7 Asian, non-Hispanic/Latino; 33 Hispanic/Latino; 1 Two or more races, non-Hispanic/Latino), 20 international. Average age 33. 90 applicants, 63% accepted, 34 enrolled. *Faculty:* 70 full-time (40 women), 1 part-time/adjunct (0 women). Expenses: Contact institution. *Financial support:* In 2010–11, 6 research assistantships with full and partial tuition reimbursements (averaging $15,333 per year), 76 teaching assistantships with full and partial tuition reimbursements (averaging $14,042 per year) were awarded; fellowships with full tuition reimbursements, career-related internships or fieldwork, Federal Work-Study, institutionally sponsored loans, scholarships/grants, and tuition waivers (full and partial) also available. Financial award application deadline: 3/1; financial award applicants required to submit FAFSA. In 2010, 16 master's, 3 doctorates awarded. Offers Asian languages and civilizations: Chinese (MA); Asian languages and civilizations: Japanese (MA); Chinese (MA, PhD); French (MA); French (linguistics) (MA); French (literature) (MA); German (MA); German (comparative literature) (MA); German (language and culture) (MA); German (literature) (MA); Japanese (MA); Spanish (MA, PhD); Spanish (cultural studies) (PhD); Spanish (linguistics) (MA); Spanish (literature and culture) (MA); Spanish (literature) (PhD). *Application deadline:* For fall admission, 12/15 for domestic and international students. Applications are processed on a rolling basis. *Application fee:* $70 ($90 for international students). Electronic applications accepted. *Application Contact:* Graduate Admissions, 480-965-6113. *Director*, Joe Cutter, 480-965-3762, E-mail: joe.cutter@asu.edu.

School of Justice and Social Inquiry Students: 52 full-time (37 women), 28 part-time (23 women); includes 23 minority (4 Black or African American, non-Hispanic/Latino; 1 American Indian or Alaska Native, non-Hispanic/Latino; 5 Asian, non-Hispanic/Latino; 12 Hispanic/Latino; 1 Two or more races, non-Hispanic/Latino), 12 international. Average age 32. 83 applicants, 41% accepted, 22 enrolled. *Faculty:* 55 full-time (37 women). Expenses: Contact institution. *Financial support:* In 2010–11, 4 research assistantships with full and partial tuition reimbursements (averaging $12,586 per year), 27 teaching assistantships with full and partial tuition reimbursements (averaging $14,093 per year) were awarded; fellowships with full tuition reimbursements, career-related internships or fieldwork, Federal Work-Study, institutionally sponsored loans, scholarships/grants, and tuition waivers (full) also available. Financial award application deadline: 3/1; financial award applicants required to submit FAFSA. In 2010, 8 master's, 12 doctorates, 3 other advanced degrees awarded. *Degree program information:* Part-time programs available. Offers African American diaspora studies (Graduate Certificate); gender studies (PhD, Graduate Certificate); justice studies (MS, PhD); socio-economic justice (Graduate Certificate). *Application deadline:* For fall admission, 12/14 for domestic and international students. Applications are processed on a rolling basis. *Application fee:* $70 ($90 for international students). Electronic applications accepted. *Application Contact:* Graduate Admissions, 480-965-6113. *Director*, Dr. Mary Margaret Fonow, 480-965-2358, E-mail: marymargaret.fonow@asu.edu.

School of Life Sciences Students: 188 full-time (95 women), 45 part-time (29 women); includes 31 minority (3 Black or African American, non-Hispanic/Latino; 2 American Indian or Alaska Native, non-Hispanic/Latino; 12 Asian, non-Hispanic/Latino; 12 Hispanic/Latino; 2 Two or more races, non-Hispanic/Latino), 39 international. Average age 30. 203 applicants, 41% accepted, 60 enrolled. *Faculty:* 102 full-time (26 women), 4 part-time/adjunct (1 woman). Expenses: Contact institution. *Financial support:* In 2010–11, 80 research assistantships with full and partial tuition reimbursements (averaging $17,888 per year), 101 teaching assistantships with full and partial tuition reimbursements (averaging $17,327 per year) were awarded; fellowships with full tuition reimbursements, career-related internships or fieldwork, Federal Work-Study, institutionally sponsored loans, scholarships/grants, and tuition waivers (full and partial) also available. Financial award application deadline: 3/1; financial award applicants required to submit FAFSA. In 2010, 17 master's, 21 doctorates awarded. Offers animal behavior (PhD); applied ethics (biomedical and health ethics) (MA); biological design (PhD); biology (MS, PhD); biology (biology and society) (MS, PhD); environmental life sciences (PhD); evolutionary biology (PhD); human and social dimensions of science and technology (PhD); microbiology (PhD); molecular and cellular biology (PhD); neuroscience (PhD); philosophy (history and philosophy of science) (MA); sustainability (PhD). *Application deadline:* For fall admission, 12/15 for domestic and international students. *Application fee:* $70 ($90 for international students). Electronic applications accepted. *Application Contact:* Graduate Admissions, 480-965-6113. *Director*, Dr. Robert E. Page, 480-965-0803, E-mail: robert.page@asu.edu.

School of Social and Family Dynamics Students: 91 full-time (82 women), 32 part-time (27 women); includes 28 minority (3 Black or African American, non-Hispanic/Latino; 2 American Indian or Alaska Native, non-Hispanic/Latino; 4 Asian, non-Hispanic/Latino; 17 Hispanic/Latino; 1 Native Hawaiian or other Pacific Islander, non-Hispanic/Latino; 1 Two or more races, non-Hispanic/Latino), 10 international. Average age 27. 186 applicants, 38% accepted, 44 enrolled. *Faculty:* 60 full-time (39 women), 2 part-time/adjunct (both women). Expenses: Contact institution. *Financial support:* In 2010–11, 22 research assistantships with full and partial tuition reimbursements (averaging $14,111 per year), 27 teaching assistantships with full and partial tuition reimbursements (averaging $12,750 per year) were awarded; fellowships with full tuition reimbursements, career-related internships or fieldwork, Federal Work-Study, institutionally sponsored loans, scholarships/grants, and tuition waivers (full and partial) also available. Financial award application deadline: 3/1; financial award applicants required to submit FAFSA. In 2010, 32 master's, 7 doctorates awarded. Offers family and human development (MS, PhD); infant-family practice (MAS); marriage and family therapy (MAS); sociology (MA, PhD). *Application deadline:* For fall admission, 1/15 for domestic and international students. *Application fee:* $70 ($90 for international students). Electronic applications accepted. *Application Contact:* Graduate Admissions, 480-965-6113. *Director*, Dr. Richard Fabes, 480-965-4892, E-mail: rf@asu.edu.

College of Nursing and Health Innovation Students: 269 full-time (227 women), 163 part-time (148 women); includes 94 minority (22 Black or African American, non-Hispanic/Latino; 11 American Indian or Alaska Native, non-Hispanic/Latino; 20 Asian, non-Hispanic/Latino; 34 Hispanic/Latino; 7 Two or more races, non-Hispanic/Latino), 22 international. Average age 36. 410 applicants, 62% accepted, 173 enrolled. *Faculty:* 111 full-time (95 women), 37 part-time/adjunct (34 women). Expenses: Contact institution. *Financial support:* In 2010–11, 32 research assistantships with full and partial tuition reimbursements (averaging $10,566 per year), 39 teaching assistantships with full and partial tuition reimbursements (averaging $11,266 per year) were awarded; fellowships with full tuition reimbursements, career-related internships or fieldwork, Federal Work-Study, institutionally sponsored loans, scholarships/grants, and tuition waivers (full and partial) also available. Financial award application deadline: 3/1; financial award applicants required to submit FAFSA. In 2010, 114 master's, 30 doctorates, 24 other advanced degrees awarded. Postbaccalaureate distance learning degree programs offered (minimal on-campus study). Offers advanced nursing practice (DNP); child/family mental health nurse practitioner (Graduate Certificate); clinical research management (MS); community and public health practice (Graduate Certificate); community health (MS); exercise and wellness (MS); family nurse practitioner (Graduate Certificate); healthcare innovation (MHI); international health for healthcare (Graduate Certificate); kinesiology (MS, PhD); nursing (MS, Graduate Certificate); nursing and healthcare innovation (PhD); nutrition (MS); physical activity nutrition and wellness (PhD); public health (MPH); regulatory science and health safety (MS). *Application deadline:* For fall admission, 7/1 for domestic and international students; for spring admission, 12/1 for domestic and international students. Applications are processed on a rolling basis. *Application fee:* $70 ($90 for international students). Electronic applications accepted. *Application Contact:* Graduate Admissions, 480-965-6113. *Dean*, Dr. Bernadette Melnyk, 602-496-2200, E-mail: bernadette.melnyk@asu.edu.

College of Public Programs Students: 887 full-time (686 women), 391 part-time (260 women); includes 368 minority (81 Black or African American, non-Hispanic/Latino; 31 American Indian or Alaska Native, non-Hispanic/Latino; 36 Asian, non-Hispanic/Latino; 202 Hispanic/Latino; 3 Native Hawaiian or other Pacific Islander, non-Hispanic/Latino; 15 Two or more races, non-Hispanic/Latino), 52 international. Average age 32. 1,178 applicants, 74% accepted, 560 enrolled. *Faculty:* 104 full-time (52 women), 8 part-time/adjunct (4 women). Expenses: Contact institution. *Financial support:* In 2010–11, 62 research assistantships with full and partial tuition reimbursements (averaging $13,584 per year), 7 teaching assistantships with full and partial tuition reimbursements (averaging $9,814 per year) were awarded; fellowships with full tuition reimbursements, career-related internships or fieldwork, Federal Work-Study, institutionally sponsored loans, scholarships/grants, and tuition waivers (full and partial) also available. Financial award application deadline: 3/1; financial award applicants required to submit FAFSA. In 2010, 407 master's, 8 doctorates, 12 other advanced degrees awarded. *Degree program information:* Part-time and evening/weekend programs available. Postbaccalaureate distance learning degree programs offered (minimal on-campus study). *Application deadline:* For fall admission, 7/1 for domestic and international students; for spring admission, 12/1 for domestic and international students. Applications are processed on a rolling basis. *Application fee:* $70 ($90 for international students). Electronic applications accepted. *Application Contact:* Graduate Admissions, 480-965-6113. *Dean*, Debra Friedman, 602-496-0402, Fax: 602-496-0955, E-mail: debra.friedman@asu.edu.

School of Community Resources and Development Students: 53 full-time (35 women), 72 part-time (55 women); includes 28 minority (6 Black or African American, non-Hispanic/Latino; 5 American Indian or Alaska Native, non-Hispanic/Latino; 1 Asian, non-Hispanic/Latino; 16 Hispanic/Latino), 12 international. Average age 33. 90 applicants, 73% accepted, 45 enrolled. *Faculty:* 19 full-time (8 women), 2 part-time/adjunct (both women). Expenses: Contact institution. *Financial support:* In 2010–11, 6 research assistantships with full and partial tuition reimbursements (averaging $8,949 per year), 5 teaching assistantships with full and partial tuition reimbursements (averaging $9,774 per year) were awarded; fellowships with full tuition reimbursements, career-related internships or fieldwork, Federal Work-Study, institutionally sponsored loans, scholarships/grants, and tuition waivers (full and partial) also available. Financial award application deadline: 3/1; financial award applicants required to submit FAFSA. In 2010, 37 master's, 3 other advanced degrees awarded. *Degree program information:* Part-time and evening/weekend programs available. Offers community resources and development (PhD); nonprofit leadership and management (Graduate Certificate); nonprofit studies (MNpS); recreation and tourism studies (MS). *Application deadline:* For fall admission, 3/1 for domestic and international students; for spring admission, 10/1 for domestic and international students. *Application fee:* $70 ($90 for international students). Electronic applications accepted. *Application Contact:* Graduate Admissions, 480-965-6113. *Director,* Dr. Kathleen Andereck, 602-496-1056, E-mail: kandereck@asu.edu.

School of Criminology and Criminal Justice Students: 89 full-time (47 women), 87 part-time (44 women); includes 61 minority (15 Black or African American, non-Hispanic/Latino; 4 American Indian or Alaska Native, non-Hispanic/Latino; 5 Asian, non-Hispanic/Latino; 31 Hispanic/Latino; 2 Native Hawaiian or other Pacific Islander, non-Hispanic/Latino; 4 Two or more races, non-Hispanic/Latino), 2 international. Average age 30. 159 applicants, 68% accepted, 70 enrolled. *Faculty:* 21 full-time (8 women), 1 part-time/adjunct (0 women). Expenses: Contact institution. *Financial support:* In 2010–11, 27 research assistantships with full and partial tuition reimbursements (averaging $14,444 per year) were awarded; fellowships with full tuition reimbursements, teaching assistantships with full and partial tuition reimbursements, career-related internships or fieldwork, Federal Work-Study, institutionally sponsored loans, scholarships/grants, and tuition waivers (full and partial) also available. Financial award application deadline: 3/1; financial award applicants required to submit FAFSA. In 2010, 24 master's awarded. *Degree program information:* Part-time and evening/weekend programs available. Postbaccalaureate distance learning degree programs offered (minimal on-campus study). Offers criminal justice (MA); criminology and criminal justice (MS, PhD). *Application deadline:* For fall admission, 2/1 for domestic and international students. Applications are processed on a rolling basis. *Application fee:* $50 ($90 for international students). Electronic applications accepted. *Application Contact:* Graduate Admissions, 480-965-6113. *Director,* Dr. Scott Decker, 602-496-2333, E-mail: scott.decker@asu.edu.

School of Public Affairs Students: 149 full-time (96 women), 106 part-time (62 women); includes 62 minority (14 Black or African American, non-Hispanic/Latino; 5 American Indian or Alaska Native, non-Hispanic/Latino; 9 Asian, non-Hispanic/Latino; 32 Hispanic/Latino; 2 Two or more races, non-Hispanic/Latino), 34 international. Average age 32. 227 applicants, 71% accepted, 87 enrolled. *Faculty:* 19 full-time (7 women), 1 part-time/adjunct (0 women). Expenses: Contact institution. *Financial support:* In 2010–11, 16 research assistantships with full and partial tuition reimbursements (averaging $14,106 per year), 2 teaching assistantships with full and partial tuition reimbursements (averaging $9,913 per year) were awarded; fellowships with full tuition reimbursements, career-related internships or fieldwork, Federal Work-Study, institutionally sponsored loans, scholarships/grants, and tuition waivers (full and partial) also available. Financial award application deadline: 3/1; financial award applicants required to submit FAFSA. In 2010, 68 master's, 4 doctorates awarded. *Degree program information:* Part-time and evening/weekend programs available. Offers public administration (nonprofit administration) (MPA); public administration (urban management) (MPA); public affairs (PhD); public policy (MPP). *Application deadline:* For fall admission, 1/15 for domestic and international students. *Application fee:* $70 ($90 for international students). Electronic applications accepted. *Application Contact:* Graduate Admissions, 480-965-6113. *Director,* Dr. Jonathan Koppell, 602-496-1101, E-mail: koppell@asu.edu.

School of Social Work Students: 596 full-time (508 women), 126 part-time (99 women); includes 217 minority (46 Black or African American, non-Hispanic/Latino; 17 American Indian or Alaska Native, non-Hispanic/Latino; 21 Asian, non-Hispanic/Latino; 123 Hispanic/Latino; 1 Native Hawaiian or other Pacific Islander, non-Hispanic/Latino; 9 Two or more races, non-Hispanic/Latino), 4 international. Average age 32. 702 applicants, 77% accepted, 358 enrolled. *Faculty:* 40 full-time (29 women), 1 (woman) part-time/adjunct. Expenses: Contact institution. *Financial support:* In 2010–11, 13 research assistantships with full and partial tuition reimbursements (averaging $13,295 per year) were awarded; fellowships with full tuition reimbursements, teaching assistantships with full and partial tuition reimbursements, career-related internships or fieldwork, Federal Work-Study, institutionally sponsored loans, scholarships/grants, and tuition waivers (full and partial) also available. Financial award application deadline: 3/1; financial award applicants required to submit FAFSA. In 2010, 278 master's, 4 doctorates, 9 other advanced degrees awarded. *Degree program information:* Part-time programs available. Offers assessment of integrative health modalities (Graduate Certificate); gerontology and geriatric care (Graduate Certificate); Latino cultural competency (Graduate Certificate); social work (PhD); social work (advanced direct practice) (MSW); social work (planning, administration and community practice) (MSW); trauma and bereavement (Graduate Certificate). *Application deadline:* For fall admission, 2/1 for domestic and international students. *Application fee:* $70 ($90 for international students). Electronic applications accepted. *Application Contact:* Graduate Admissions, 480-965-6113. *Director,* Dr. Steven G. Anderson, 602-496-0800, Fax: 602-496-0960, E-mail: steven.anderson.2@asu.edu.

College of Technology and Innovation Students: 149 full-time (41 women), 288 part-time (126 women); includes 96 minority (21 Black or African American, non-Hispanic/Latino; 8 American Indian or Alaska Native, non-Hispanic/Latino; 29 Asian, non-Hispanic/Latino; 34 Hispanic/Latino; 4 Two or more races, non-Hispanic/Latino), 84 international. Average age 33. 433 applicants, 85% accepted, 109 enrolled. *Faculty:* 101 full-time (25 women), 9 part-time/adjunct (2 women). Expenses: Contact institution. *Financial support:* In 2010–11, 17 research assistantships with full and partial tuition reimbursements (averaging $13,230 per year), 2 teaching assistantships with full and partial tuition reimbursements (averaging $12,263 per year) were awarded; career-related internships or fieldwork, Federal Work-Study, scholarships/grants, health care benefits, tuition waivers (full and partial), and unspecified assistantships also available. Support available to part-time students. Financial award application deadline: 3/1; financial award applicants required to submit FAFSA. In 2010, 71 master's awarded. *Degree program information:* Part-time and evening/weekend programs available. Offers applied biological sciences (MS); applied psychology (MS); computing studies (MCST); simulation, modeling, and applied cognitive science (PhD); technology (alternative energy technologies) (MS); technology (aviation management and human factors) (MS); technology (electronic systems engineering technology) (MS); technology (environmental technology management) (MS); technology (global technology and development) (MS); technology (graphic information technology) (MS); technology (integrated electronic systems) (MS); technology (management of technology) (MS); technology (manufacturing engineering technology) (MS); technology and innovation (MCST, MS, PhD). *Application deadline:* For fall admission, 7/1 for domestic and international students; for spring admission, 12/1 for domestic and international students. Applications are processed on a rolling basis. *Application fee:* $70 ($90 for international students). Electronic applications accepted. *Application Contact:* Graduate Admissions, 480-965-6113. *Vice Provost and Dean,* Dr. Mitzi Montoya, 480-727-1955, Fax: 480-727-1089, E-mail: mitzi.montoya@asu.edu.

Graduate College Students: 108 full-time (45 women), 30 part-time (17 women); includes 22 minority (1 American Indian or Alaska Native, non-Hispanic/Latino; 14 Asian, non-Hispanic/Latino; 4 Hispanic/Latino; 1 Native Hawaiian or other Pacific Islander, non-Hispanic/Latino; 2 Two or more races, non-Hispanic/Latino), 55 international. Average age 29. 248 applicants, 47% accepted, 69 enrolled. Expenses: Contact institution. *Financial support:* In 2010–11, 62 research assistantships with full and partial tuition reimbursements (averaging $18,052 per year), 10 teaching assistantships with full and partial tuition reimbursements (averaging $17,179 per year) were awarded; fellowships with full tuition reimbursements, career-related internships or fieldwork, Federal Work-Study, institutionally sponsored loans, scholarships/grants, tuition waivers (full and partial), and unspecified assistantships also available. Financial award application deadline: 3/1; financial award applicants required to submit FAFSA. In 2010, 20 master's, 17 other advanced degrees awarded. *Degree program information:* Part-time and evening/weekend programs available. Postbaccalaureate distance learning degree programs offered (minimal on-campus study). Offers biological design (PhD); biomedical informatics (MS, PhD); human and social dimensions of science and technology (PhD); neuroscience (PhD); statistics (MS, Graduate Certificate). *Application deadline:* For fall admission, 7/1 for domestic and international students; for spring admission, 12/1 for domestic and international students. Applications are processed on a rolling basis. *Application fee:* $70 ($90 for international students). Electronic applications accepted. *Application Contact:* Graduate Admissions, 480-965-6113, Fax: 480-965-5158. *Executive Vice Provost for Academic Affairs/Dean,* Dr. Maria T. Allison, 480-965-7279, Fax: 480-965-0375.

Herberger Institute for Design and the Arts Students: 662 full-time (351 women), 214 part-time (118 women); includes 129 minority (13 Black or African American, non-Hispanic/Latino; 4 American Indian or Alaska Native, non-Hispanic/Latino; 35 Asian, non-Hispanic/Latino; 67 Hispanic/Latino; 1 Native Hawaiian or other Pacific Islander, non-Hispanic/Latino; 9 Two or more races, non-Hispanic/Latino), 137 international. Average age 29. 1,122 applicants, 49% accepted, 283 enrolled. *Faculty:* 202 full-time (81 women), 8 part-time/adjunct (4 women). Expenses: Contact institution. *Financial support:* In 2010–11, 24 research assistantships with full and partial tuition reimbursements (averaging $10,477 per year), 253 teaching assistantships with full and partial tuition reimbursements (averaging $6,052 per year) were awarded; fellowships with full tuition reimbursements, career-related internships or fieldwork, Federal Work-Study, institutionally sponsored loans, scholarships/grants, and tuition waivers (full and partial) also available. Financial award application deadline: 3/1; financial award applicants required to submit FAFSA. In 2010, 176 master's, 51 doctorates awarded. Offers dance (MFA); dance (interdisciplinary digital media and performance) (MFA); design and the arts (M Arch, MA, MFA, MLA, MM, MS, MSD, MUD, DMA, PhD). *Application deadline:* For fall admission, 7/1 for domestic and international students; for spring admission, 12/1 for domestic and international students. Applications are processed on a rolling basis. *Application fee:* $70 ($90 for international students). Electronic applications accepted. *Application Contact:* Graduate Admissions, 480-965-6113. *Dean and Director,* Dr. Kwang-Wu Kim, 480-965-8561, Fax: 480-965-9073, E-mail: kwang-wu.kim@asu.edu.

School of Architecture and Landscape Architecture Students: 252 full-time (111 women), 45 part-time (21 women); includes 61 minority (3 Black or African American, non-Hispanic/Latino; 2 American Indian or Alaska Native, non-Hispanic/Latino; 13 Asian, non-Hispanic/Latino; 41 Hispanic/Latino; 1 Native Hawaiian or other Pacific Islander, non-Hispanic/Latino; 1 Two or more races, non-Hispanic/Latino), 58 international. Average age 29. 420 applicants, 61% accepted, 117 enrolled. *Faculty:* 41 full-time (9 women), 6 part-time/adjunct (3 women). Expenses: Contact institution. *Financial support:* In 2010–11, 9 research assistantships with full and partial tuition reimbursements (averaging $11,913 per year), 76 teaching assistantships with full and partial tuition reimbursements (averaging $6,294 per year) were awarded; fellowships with full and partial tuition reimbursements, scholarships/grants and tuition waivers (full and partial) also available. Financial award application deadline: 3/1; financial award applicants required to submit FAFSA. In 2010, 60 master's, 8 doctorates awarded. Offers architecture (M Arch); building design/built environment (MS); design (arts, media, and engineering) (MSD); design (healthcare and healing environments) (MSD); design (industrial design) (MSD); design (interior design) (MSD); design (new product innovation) (MSD); design (visual communication design) (MSD); design, environment and the arts (PhD); design, environment and the arts (design) (PhD); design, environment and the arts (healthcare and healing environments) (PhD); design, environment and the arts (history, theory, and criticism) (PhD); landscape architecture (MLA); urban design (MUD). *Application deadline:* For fall admission, 1/15 priority date for domestic and international students. *Application fee:* $70 ($90 for international students). Electronic applications accepted. *Application Contact:* Graduate Admissions, 480-965-6113. *Director,* Darren Petrucci, 480-965-3536, E-mail: darren.petrucci@asu.edu.

School of Art Students: 98 full-time (56 women), 21 part-time (18 women); includes 13 minority (2 American Indian or Alaska Native, non-Hispanic/Latino; 3 Asian, non-Hispanic/Latino; 8 Hispanic/Latino), 7 international. Average age 31. 206 applicants, 32% accepted, 37 enrolled. *Faculty:* 46 full-time (28 women). Expenses: Contact institution. *Financial support:* In 2010–11, 4 research assistantships with full and partial tuition reimbursements (averaging $7,475 per year), 55 teaching assistantships with full and partial tuition reimbursements (averaging $6,553 per year) were awarded; fellowships with full and partial tuition reimbursements, scholarships/grants and tuition waivers (full and partial) also available. Financial award application deadline: 3/1; financial award applicants required to submit FAFSA. In 2010, 26 master's, 1 doctorate awarded. Offers art (art education) (MA); art (art history) (MA); art (ceramics) (MFA); art (digital technology) (MFA); art (drawing) (MFA); art (fibers) (MFA); art (intermedia) (MFA); art (metals) (MFA); art (painting) (MFA); art (printmaking) (MFA); art (sculpture) (MFA); art (wood) (MFA); design, environment and the arts (history, theory and criticism) (PhD). *Application deadline:* For fall admission, 1/15 priority date for domestic and international students. Applications are processed on a rolling basis. *Application fee:* $70 ($90 for international students). Electronic applications accepted. *Application Contact:* Graduate Admissions, 480-965-6113. *Director,* Adriene Jenik, 480-965-8521, Fax: 480-965-8338, E-mail: ajenik@mainex1.asu.edu.

School of Arts, Media and Engineering Students: 13 full-time (8 women), 2 part-time (1 woman); includes 3 minority (1 Asian, non-Hispanic/Latino; 1 Hispanic/Latino; 1 Two or more races, non-Hispanic/Latino), 4 international. Average age 30. 18 applicants, 33% accepted, 3 enrolled. *Faculty:* 9 full-time (2 women), 1 part-time/adjunct (0 women). Expenses: Contact institution. *Financial support:* In 2010–11, 3 research assistantships with full and partial tuition reimbursements (averaging $15,000 per year) were awarded; fellowships with full and partial tuition reimbursements, career-related internships or fieldwork, scholarships/grants, traineeships, and tuition waivers (full and partial) also available. Financial award application deadline: 3/1; financial award applicants required to submit FAFSA. Offers media arts and sciences (PhD). *Application deadline:* For fall admission, 2/1 for domestic and international students. *Application fee:* $70 ($90 for international students). Electronic applications accepted. *Application Contact:* Graduate Admissions, 480-965-6113. *Director,* Dr. Thanassis Rikakis, 480-965-0972, Fax: 480-965—961, E-mail: thanassis.rikakis@asu.edu.

School of Music Students: 236 full-time (133 women), 133 part-time (71 women); includes 39 minority (6 Black or African American, non-Hispanic/Latino; 17 Asian, non-Hispanic/Latino; 13 Hispanic/Latino; 3 Two or more races, non-Hispanic/Latino), 63 international. Average age 29. 406 applicants, 47% accepted, 105 enrolled. *Faculty:* 66 full-time (21 women), 1 (woman) part-time/adjunct. Expenses: Contact institution. *Financial support:* In 2010–11, 1 research assistantship with full and partial tuition reimbursement (averaging $4,000 per year), 74 teaching assistantships with full and partial tuition reimbursements (averaging $4,191 per year) were awarded; fellowships with full and partial tuition reimbursements, Federal Work-Study, institutionally sponsored loans, scholarships/grants, and tuition waivers (full and partial) also available. Financial award application deadline: 3/1; financial award applicants required to submit FAFSA. In 2010, 81 master's, 40 doctorates awarded. Offers composition (MM); music (conducting) (DMA); music (ethnomusicology) (MA); music (interdisciplinary digital media/performance) (DMA); music (music history and literature) (MA); music (performance) (DMA); music education (MM, PhD); music therapy (MM); performance (MM). *Application deadline:* For fall admission, 12/1 for domestic and international students; for spring admission, 10/1 for domestic and international students. Applications are processed on a rolling basis. *Application fee:* $70 ($90 for international students). Electronic applications accepted. *Application Contact:* Graduate Admissions, 480-965-6113. *Director,* Dr. Kimberly Marshall, 480-727-6222, Fax: 480-965-2659, E-mail: kimberly.marshall@asu.edu.

School of Theatre and Film Students: 47 full-time (28 women), 12 part-time (6 women); includes 10 minority (3 Black or African American, non-Hispanic/Latino; 1 Asian, non-Hispanic/Latino; 4 Hispanic/Latino; 2 Two or more races, non-Hispanic/Latino), 4 international. Average age 30. 52 applicants, 48% accepted, 16 enrolled. *Faculty:* 28 full-time (12 women). Expenses: Contact institution. *Financial support:* In 2010–11, 4 research assistantships with full and partial tuition reimbursements (averaging $9,021 per year), 38 teaching assistantships with full and partial tuition reimbursements (averaging $8,322 per year) were awarded; fellowships with full and partial tuition reimbursements, Federal Work-Study, institutionally sponsored loans, scholarships/grants, and tuition waivers (full and partial) also available. Financial award application deadline: 3/1; financial award applicants required to submit FAFSA. In 2010, 4 master's, 2 doctorates awarded. Offers theatre (MA, MFA); theatre (directing) (MFA); theatre (dramatic writing) (MFA); theatre (interdisciplinary digital media and performance) (MFA); theatre (performance design) (MFA); theatre (performance) (MFA); theatre (theatre and performance of the Americas) (PhD); theatre (theatre for youth) (PhD). *Application deadline:* For fall admission, 1/15 for domestic and international students. *Application fee:* $70 ($90 for international students). Electronic applications accepted. *Application Contact:* Graduate Admissions, 480-965-6113. *Interim Director,* Guillermo Reyes, 480-965-0519, E-mail: guillermo.reyes@asu.edu.

Arizona State University (continued)

Ira A. Fulton School of Engineering Students: 1,373 full-time (291 women), 824 part-time (141 women); includes 289 minority (41 Black or African American, non-Hispanic/Latino; 8 American Indian or Alaska Native, non-Hispanic/Latino; 125 Asian, non-Hispanic/Latino; 104 Hispanic/Latino; 1 Native Hawaiian or other Pacific Islander, non-Hispanic/Latino; 10 Two or more races, non-Hispanic/Latino), 1,141 international. Average age 28. 3,762 applicants, 59% accepted, 739 enrolled. *Faculty:* 234 full-time (42 women), 34 part-time/adjunct (7 women). Expenses: Contact institution. *Financial support:* In 2010–11, 545 research assistantships with full and partial tuition reimbursements (averaging $14,785 per year), 122 teaching assistantships with full and partial tuition reimbursements (averaging $12,879 per year) were awarded; fellowships with full tuition reimbursements, career-related internships or fieldwork, Federal Work-Study, institutionally sponsored loans, scholarships/grants, and tuition waivers (full and partial) also available. Financial award application deadline: 3/1; financial award applicants required to submit FAFSA. In 2010, 521 master's, 115 doctorates awarded. *Degree program information:* Part-time and evening/weekend programs available. Postbaccalaureate distance learning degree programs offered (minimal on-campus study). Offers aerospace engineering (MS, MSE, PhD); chemical engineering (MS, MSE, PhD); construction (MS); electrical engineering (MS, MSE, PhD); embedded systems (M Eng); engineering (M Eng, MA, MCS, MS, MSE, PhD, Graduate Certificate); enterprise systems innovation and management (MSE); materials science and engineering (MS, PhD); mechanical engineering (MS, MSE, PhD); modeling and simulation (M Eng); nuclear power generation (Graduate Certificate); quality and reliability engineering (M Eng); software engineering (MSE); systems engineering (M Eng). *Application deadline:* For fall admission, 1/31 for domestic and international students; for spring admission, 7/1 for domestic and international students. Applications are processed on a rolling basis. *Application fee:* $70 ($90 for international students). Electronic applications accepted. *Application Contact:* Graduate Admissions, 480-965-6113. *Dean*, Paul C. Johnson, 480-965-9235, E-mail: paul.c.johnson@asu.edu.

Del E. Webb School of Construction Students: 149 full-time (51 women), 85 part-time (17 women); includes 32 minority (6 Black or African American, non-Hispanic/Latino; 2 American Indian or Alaska Native, non-Hispanic/Latino; 13 Asian, non-Hispanic/Latino; 10 Hispanic/Latino; 1 Native Hawaiian or other Pacific Islander, non-Hispanic/Latino), 69 international. Average age 29. 379 applicants, 53% accepted, 77 enrolled. *Faculty:* 40 full-time (4 women), 6 part-time/adjunct (1 woman). Expenses: Contact institution. *Financial support:* In 2010–11, 67 research assistantships with full and partial tuition reimbursements (averaging $16,393 per year), 17 teaching assistantships with full and partial tuition reimbursements (averaging $13,812 per year) were awarded; fellowships with full and partial tuition reimbursements, career-related internships or fieldwork, institutionally sponsored loans, scholarships/grants, traineeships, and tuition waivers (full and partial) also available. Financial award application deadline: 3/1; financial award applicants required to submit FAFSA. In 2010, 44 master's, 10 doctorates awarded. *Degree program information:* Part-time and evening/weekend programs available. Postbaccalaureate distance learning degree programs offered (minimal on-campus study). Offers civil, environmental and sustainable engineering (MS, MSE, PhD); construction (MS, MSE, PhD); construction engineering (MSE). *Application deadline:* For fall admission, 1/1 for domestic and international students; for spring admission, 7/1 for domestic and international students. *Application fee:* $70 ($90 for international students). Electronic applications accepted. *Application Contact:* Graduate Admissions, 480-965-6113. *Director*, Dr. G. Edward Gibson, 480-965-7972, E-mail: edd.gibson@asu.edu.

School of Biological and Health Systems Engineering Students: 71 full-time (25 women), 15 part-time (4 women); includes 18 minority (2 Black or African American, non-Hispanic/Latino; 10 Asian, non-Hispanic/Latino; 5 Hispanic/Latino; 1 Two or more races, non-Hispanic/Latino), 19 international. Average age 27. 188 applicants, 41% accepted, 40 enrolled. *Faculty:* 21 full-time (2 women), 1 part-time/adjunct (0 women). Expenses: Contact institution. *Financial support:* In 2010–11, 30 research assistantships with partial tuition reimbursements (averaging $18,265 per year), 3 teaching assistantships with partial tuition reimbursements (averaging $14,500 per year) were awarded; fellowships with full and partial tuition reimbursements, institutionally sponsored loans, scholarships/grants, and tuition waivers (full and partial) also available. Financial award application deadline: 3/1; financial award applicants required to submit FAFSA. In 2010, 16 master's, 19 doctorates awarded. *Degree program information:* Part-time and evening/weekend programs available. Offers biomedical engineering (MS, PhD). *Application deadline:* For fall admission, 12/31 priority date for domestic and international students; for spring admission, 8/31 priority date for domestic and international students. Applications are processed on a rolling basis. *Application fee:* $70 ($90 for international students). Electronic applications accepted. *Application Contact:* Graduate Admissions, 480-965-6113. *Director*, Dr. William Ditto, 480-965-3676, E-mail: william.ditto@asu.edu.

School of Computing, Informatics, and Decision Systems Engineering Students: 365 full-time (76 women), 168 part-time (36 women); includes 60 minority (10 Black or African American, non-Hispanic/Latino; 1 American Indian or Alaska Native, non-Hispanic/Latino; 29 Asian, non-Hispanic/Latino; 18 Hispanic/Latino; 2 Two or more races, non-Hispanic/Latino), 352 international. Average age 28. 1,016 applicants, 53% accepted, 152 enrolled. *Faculty:* 58 full-time (14 women), 5 part-time/adjunct (2 women). Expenses: Contact institution. *Financial support:* In 2010–11, 156 research assistantships with full and partial tuition reimbursements (averaging $13,688 per year), 41 teaching assistantships with full and partial tuition reimbursements (averaging $10,940 per year) were awarded; fellowships with full and partial tuition reimbursements, institutionally sponsored loans, scholarships/grants, and tuition waivers (full and partial) also available. Financial award application deadline: 3/1; financial award applicants required to submit FAFSA. In 2010, 138 master's, 22 doctorates awarded. *Degree program information:* Part-time and evening/weekend programs available. Postbaccalaureate distance learning degree programs offered (minimal on-campus study). Offers computer science (MCS, MS, PhD); industrial engineering (MS, PhD). *Application deadline:* For fall admission, 12/1 for domestic and international students; for spring admission, 8/1 for domestic and international students. *Application fee:* $70 ($90 for international students). Electronic applications accepted. *Application Contact:* Graduate Admissions, 480-965-6113. *Director*, Dr. Ronald Askin, 480-965-2567, E-mail: ron.askin@asu.edu.

Mary Lou Fulton Teachers College Students: 1,475 full-time (1,052 women), 944 part-time (700 women); includes 637 minority (142 Black or African American, non-Hispanic/Latino; 66 American Indian or Alaska Native, non-Hispanic/Latino; 91 Asian, non-Hispanic/Latino; 302 Hispanic/Latino; 6 Native Hawaiian or other Pacific Islander, non-Hispanic/Latino; 30 Two or more races, non-Hispanic/Latino), 78 international. Average age 32. 1,594 applicants, 73% accepted, 867 enrolled. *Faculty:* 147 full-time (96 women), 6 part-time/adjunct (5 women). Expenses: Contact institution. *Financial support:* In 2010–11, 75 research assistantships with full and partial tuition reimbursements (averaging $11,146 per year), 112 teaching assistantships with full and partial tuition reimbursements (averaging $11,375 per year) were awarded; fellowships with full tuition reimbursements, career-related internships or fieldwork, Federal Work-Study, institutionally sponsored loans, scholarships/grants, and tuition waivers (full and partial) also available. Financial award application deadline: 3/1; financial award applicants required to submit FAFSA. In 2010, 1,053 master's, 83 doctorates, 16 other advanced degrees awarded. *Degree program information:* Part-time and evening/weekend programs available. Postbaccalaureate distance learning degree programs offered (minimal on-campus study). Offers autism spectrum disorder (Graduate Certificate); curriculum and instruction (M Ed, MA, PhD); education (M Ed, MA, MC, MPE, Ed D, PhD, Graduate Certificate); educational administration and supervision (M Ed); educational leadership and policy studies (PhD); educational technology (M Ed, PhD); elementary education (M Ed); higher and postsecondary education (M Ed); instructional design and performance improvement (Graduate Certificate); leadership and innovation (Ed D); online teaching for grades K-12 (Graduate Certificate); physical education (MPE); secondary education (M Ed); social and philosophical foundations of education (MA); special education (M Ed, MA). *Application deadline:* For fall admission, 7/1 for domestic and international students; for spring admission, 11/15 for domestic and international students. Applications are processed on a rolling basis. *Application fee:* $70 ($90 for international students). Electronic applications accepted. *Application Contact:* Graduate Admissions, 480-965-6113. *Dean*, Dr. Mari Koerner, 602-543-6358, Fax: 602-543-6900, E-mail: mari.koerner@asu.edu.

New College of Interdisciplinary Arts and Sciences Students: 97 full-time (65 women), 82 part-time (54 women); includes 39 minority (17 Black or African American, non-Hispanic/Latino; 5 American Indian or Alaska Native, non-Hispanic/Latino; 4 Asian, non-Hispanic/Latino; 11 Hispanic/Latino; 2 Two or more races, non-Hispanic/Latino), 8 international. Average age 31. 159 applicants, 72% accepted, 74 enrolled. *Faculty:* 109 full-time (53 women), 4 part-time/adjunct (3 women). Expenses: Contact institution. *Financial support:* In 2010–11, 10 research assistantships with full and partial tuition reimbursements (averaging $6,102 per year) were awarded; teaching assistantships with full and partial tuition reimbursements, career-related internships or fieldwork, Federal Work-Study, institutionally sponsored loans, scholarships/grants, and tuition waivers (full and partial) also available. Support available to part-time students. Financial award application deadline: 3/1; financial award applicants required to submit FAFSA. In 2010, 35 master's awarded. *Degree program information:* Part-time and evening/weekend programs available. Offers applied ethics and the professions (MA); communication studies (MA); interdisciplinary studies (MA); psychology (MS); social justice and human rights (MA). *Application deadline:* For fall admission, 7/1 for domestic and international students; for spring admission, 12/1 for domestic and international students. Applications are processed on a rolling basis. *Application fee:* $70 ($90 for international students). Electronic applications accepted. *Application Contact:* Sheryl Gordon, Coordinator, Student Support Services, 602-543-6241, Fax: 602-543-6032, E-mail: sheryl.gordon@asu.edu. *Vice President and Dean*, Dr. Elizabeth Langland, 602-543-6033, Fax: 602-543-6032, E-mail: elizabeth.langland@asu.edu.

Sandra Day O'Connor College of Law Students: 643 full-time (286 women), 14 part-time (6 women); includes 161 minority (19 Black or African American, non-Hispanic/Latino; 36 American Indian or Alaska Native, non-Hispanic/Latino; 25 Asian, non-Hispanic/Latino; 70 Hispanic/Latino; 11 Two or more races, non-Hispanic/Latino), 8 international. Average age 28. 2,457 applicants, 24% accepted, 191 enrolled. *Faculty:* 63 full-time (20 women), 29 part-time/adjunct (4 women). Expenses: Contact institution. *Financial support:* In 2010–11, 280 students received support; research assistantships, teaching assistantships, career-related internships or fieldwork, Federal Work-Study, institutionally sponsored loans, scholarships/grants, tuition waivers (full and partial), and unspecified assistantships available. Financial award application deadline: 3/15; financial award applicants required to submit FAFSA. In 2010, 167 first professional degrees awarded. Offers biotechnology and genomics (LL M); global legal studies (LL M); law (JD); law (customized) (LL M); legal studies (MLS); tribal policy, law and government (LL M). JD/MD offered jointly with Mayo Medical School. *Application deadline:* For fall admission, 11/15 priority date for domestic and international students; for spring admission, 2/1 for domestic and international students. Applications are processed on a rolling basis. *Application fee:* $60. Electronic applications accepted. *Application Contact:* Chitra Damania, Director of Operations, 480-965-1474, Fax: 480-727-7930, E-mail: law.admissions@asu.edu. *Dean/Professor*, Paul Schiff Berman, 480-965-6188, Fax: 480-965-6521, E-mail: paul.berman@asu.edu.

School of Letters and Sciences Students: 160 full-time (120 women), 62 part-time (44 women); includes 68 minority (18 Black or African American, non-Hispanic/Latino; 5 American Indian or Alaska Native, non-Hispanic/Latino; 10 Asian, non-Hispanic/Latino; 30 Hispanic/Latino; 5 Two or more races, non-Hispanic/Latino), 9 international. Average age 35. 343 applicants, 38% accepted, 84 enrolled. *Faculty:* 90 full-time (49 women), 16 part-time/adjunct (11 women). Expenses: Contact institution. *Financial support:* In 2010–11, 11 research assistantships with full and partial tuition reimbursements (averaging $8,236 per year), 26 teaching assistantships with full and partial tuition reimbursements (averaging $9,600 per year) were awarded; fellowships with full tuition reimbursements, career-related internships or fieldwork, Federal Work-Study, institutionally sponsored loans, scholarships/grants, and tuition waivers (full and partial) also available. Financial award application deadline: 3/1; financial award applicants required to submit FAFSA. In 2010, 29 master's, 4 doctorates awarded. *Degree program information:* Part-time and evening/weekend programs available. Postbaccalaureate distance learning degree programs offered (minimal on-campus study). Offers applied ethics and the professions (biomedical and health ethics) (MA); applied ethics and the professions (ethics and emerging technologies) (MA); applied ethics and the professions (public administration, policy and ethics) (MA); applied ethics and the professions (science, technology and ethics) (MA); behavioral health (DBH); counseling (MC); counseling psychology (PhD); letters and sciences (MA, MC, DBH, PhD). *Application deadline:* For fall admission, 7/1 for domestic and international students; for spring admission, 12/1 for domestic and international students. Applications are processed on a rolling basis. *Application fee:* $70 ($90 for international students). Electronic applications accepted. *Application Contact:* Graduate Admissions, 480-965-6113. *Director*, Frederick C. Corey, 602-496-0624, E-mail: frederick.corey@asu.edu.

School of Sustainability Students: 60 full-time (30 women), 26 part-time (12 women); includes 17 minority (2 Black or African American, non-Hispanic/Latino; 4 Asian, non-Hispanic/Latino; 9 Hispanic/Latino; 2 Two or more races, non-Hispanic/Latino), 18 international. Average age 32. 216 applicants, 25% accepted, 30 enrolled. *Faculty:* 9 full-time (3 women). Expenses: Contact institution. *Financial support:* In 2010–11, 25 research assistantships with full and partial tuition reimbursements (averaging $16,992 per year), 39 teaching assistantships with full and partial tuition reimbursements (averaging $16,179 per year) were awarded; fellowships with full tuition reimbursements, career-related internships or fieldwork, Federal Work-Study, institutionally sponsored loans, scholarships/grants, and tuition waivers (full and partial) also available. Financial award application deadline: 3/1; financial award applicants required to submit FAFSA. In 2010, 11 master's, 1 doctorate, 3 other advanced degrees awarded. *Degree program information:* Part-time and evening/weekend programs available. Offers sustainability (MA, MS, PhD); sustainable technology and management (Graduate Certificate). *Application deadline:* For fall admission, 7/1 for domestic and international students; for spring admission, 12/1 for domestic and international students. Applications are processed on a rolling basis. *Application fee:* $70 ($90 for international students). Electronic applications accepted. *Application Contact:* Graduate Admissions, 480-965-6113. *Dean*, Sander Van Der Leeuw, 480-965-2975, Fax: 480-965-8087, E-mail: vanderle@asu.edu.

Walter Cronkite School of Journalism and Mass Communication Students: 47 full-time (33 women), 1 (woman) part-time; includes 6 minority (2 Black or African American, non-Hispanic/Latino; 1 Native Hawaiian or other Pacific Islander, non-Hispanic/Latino; 3 Two or more races, non-Hispanic/Latino), 3 international. Average age 28. 170 applicants, 48% accepted, 28 enrolled. *Faculty:* 30 full-time (11 women), 1 part-time/adjunct (0 women). Expenses: Contact institution. *Financial support:* In 2010–11, 17 teaching assistantships with full and partial tuition reimbursements (averaging $10,968 per year) were awarded; fellowships with full tuition reimbursements, research assistantships with full and partial tuition reimbursements, career-related internships or fieldwork, Federal Work-Study, institutionally sponsored loans, scholarships/grants, and tuition waivers (full and partial) also available. Financial award application deadline: 3/1; financial award applicants required to submit FAFSA. In 2010, 28 degrees awarded. Offers journalism and mass communication (PhD); mass communication (MMC). *Application deadline:* For fall admission, 7/1 for domestic and international students; for spring admission, 12/1 for domestic and international students. Applications are processed on a rolling basis. *Application fee:* $70 ($90 for international students). Electronic applications accepted. *Application Contact:* Graduate Admissions, 480-965-6113. *Dean*, Christopher Callahan, 602-496-5012, Fax: 602-496-7041, E-mail: christopher.callahan@asu.edu.

W. P. Carey School of Business Students: 1,648 full-time (505 women), 115 part-time (43 women); includes 327 minority (43 Black or African American, non-Hispanic/Latino; 13 American Indian or Alaska Native, non-Hispanic/Latino; 141 Asian, non-Hispanic/Latino; 113 Hispanic/Latino; 4 Native Hawaiian or other Pacific Islander, non-Hispanic/Latino; 13 Two or more races, non-Hispanic/Latino), 249 international. Average age 31. 2,658 applicants, 47% accepted, 833 enrolled. *Faculty:* 214 full-time (53 women), 21 part-time/adjunct (3 women). Expenses: Contact institution. *Financial support:* In 2010–11, 31 research assistantships with full and partial tuition reimbursements (averaging $12,557 per year), 217 teaching assistantships with full and partial tuition reimbursements (averaging $10,872 per year) were awarded; fellowships with full tuition reimbursements, career-related internships or fieldwork, Federal Work-Study, institutionally sponsored loans, scholarships/grants, and tuition waivers (full and partial) also available. Financial award application deadline: 3/1; financial award applicants required to submit FAFSA. In 2010, 1,040 master's, 14 doctorates, 72 other advanced degrees awarded. *Degree program information:* Part-time and evening/weekend programs available. Postbaccalaureate distance learning degree programs offered (minimal on-campus study). Offers accountancy (PhD); agribusiness (PhD); business (M Acc, M Tax, MBA, MRED, MS, PhD, Graduate Certificate); business administration (MBA); business administration (computer information systems) (PhD); business administration (marketing) (PhD); economics (PhD); finance (PhD); financial management and markets (MBA); information management (MBA, MS); information systems (PhD); management (PhD); marketing (PhD); real estate development (MRED); strategic marketing and services leadership (MBA); supply chain financial management (MBA); supply chain management (MBA, PhD). *Application deadline:* For fall admission, 7/1 for domestic and international students; for spring admission, 12/1 for domestic and international students. Applications are processed on a rolling basis. *Application fee:* $70 ($90 for international students). Electronic applications accepted. *Application Contact:* Graduate Admissions, 480-965-6113. *Dean,* Dr. Robert E. Mittelstaedt, 480-965-2468, Fax: 480-965-5539, E-mail: mittelsr@asu.edu.

Morrison School of Agribusiness and Resource Management Students: 8 full-time (3 women), 3 part-time (2 women); includes 3 minority (1 American Indian or Alaska Native, non-Hispanic/Latino; 2 Hispanic/Latino), 2 international. Average age 29. 6 applicants, 83% accepted, 3 enrolled. *Faculty:* 12 full-time (1 woman), 1 part-time/adjunct (0 women). Expenses: Contact institution. *Financial support:* In 2010–11, 2 research assistantships with partial tuition reimbursements (averaging $4,988 per year) were awarded; fellowships with full and partial tuition reimbursements, teaching assistantships with partial tuition reimbursements, career-related internships or fieldwork, institutionally sponsored loans, scholarships/grants, and tuition waivers (full and partial) also available. Financial award application deadline: 3/1; financial award applicants required to submit CSS PROFILE or FAFSA. In 2010, 18 master's awarded. *Degree program information:* Part-time and evening/weekend programs available. Offers agribusiness (MS). *Application deadline:* For fall admission, 2/1 priority date for domestic and international students; for spring admission, 10/15 priority date for domestic and international students. Applications are processed on a rolling basis. *Application fee:* $70 ($90 for international students). Electronic applications accepted. *Application Contact:* Graduate Admissions, 480-965-6113. *Chair,* Dr. Timothy Richards, 480-727-1488, Fax: 480-727-1186, E-mail: trichards@asu.edu.

School of Accountancy Students: 145 full-time (68 women), 15 part-time (9 women); includes 32 minority (17 Asian, non-Hispanic/Latino; 15 Hispanic/Latino), 28 international. Average age 25. 431 applicants, 55% accepted, 145 enrolled. *Faculty:* 28 full-time (11 women), 3 part-time/adjunct (0 women). Expenses: Contact institution. *Financial support:* In 2010–11, 16 teaching assistantships with partial tuition reimbursements (averaging $6,491 per year) were awarded; fellowships with full and partial tuition reimbursements, research assistantships with partial tuition reimbursements, career-related internships or fieldwork, institutionally sponsored loans, scholarships/grants, and tuition waivers (full and partial) also available. Financial award application deadline: 3/1; financial award applicants required to submit FAFSA. In 2010, 109 master's awarded. *Degree program information:* Part-time and evening/weekend programs available. Offers accountancy (M Acc, M Tax); business administration (accountancy) (PhD). *Application deadline:* For fall admission, 3/1 for domestic and international students. *Application fee:* $70 ($90 for international students). Electronic applications accepted. *Application Contact:* Graduate Admissions, 480-965-6113. *Director,* Dr. Mike Mikhail, 480-727-7198, Fax: 480-965-8392, E-mail: michael.mikhail@asu.edu.

ARKANSAS STATE UNIVERSITY, Jonesboro, State University, AR 72467

General Information State-supported, coed, comprehensive institution. CGS member. *Enrollment:* 13,415 graduate, professional, and undergraduate students; 697 full-time matriculated graduate/professional students (405 women), 2,667 part-time matriculated graduate/professional students (1,942 women). *Enrollment by degree level:* 2,904 master's, 208 doctoral, 252 other advanced degrees. *Graduate faculty:* 225 full-time (87 women), 60 part-time/adjunct (33 women). *International tuition:* $8376 full-time. Tuition, state resident: full-time $3888; part-time $216 per credit hour. Tuition, nonresident: full-time $9918; part-time $551 per credit hour. *Required fees:* $932; $49 per credit hour. $25 per term. One-time fee: $30. Tuition and fees vary according to course load and program. *Graduate housing:* Rooms and/or apartments available on a first-come, first-served basis to single and married students. Typical cost: $5068 per year for single students; $5068 per year for married students. Housing application deadline: 8/22. *Student services:* Campus employment opportunities, campus safety program, career counseling, child daycare facilities, exercise/wellness program, free psychological counseling, international student services, multicultural affairs office, services for students with disabilities. *Library facilities:* Dean B. Ellis Library. *Online resources:* library catalog, web page. *Collection:* 638,942 titles, 10,931 serial subscriptions, 25,004 audiovisual materials. *Research affiliation:* Radiance Technologies, Alaka'i Consulting and Engineering.

Computer facilities: Computer purchase and lease plans are available. 510 computers available on campus for general student use. A campuswide network can be accessed from student residence rooms and from off campus. Online class registration is available. *Web address:* http://www.astate.edu/.

General Application Contact: Dr. Andrew Sustich, Dean of the Graduate School, 870-972-3029, Fax: 870-972-3857, E-mail: sustich@astate.edu.

GRADUATE UNITS

Graduate School Students: 697 full-time (405 women), 2,667 part-time (1,942 women); includes 548 minority (428 Black or African American, non-Hispanic/Latino; 17 American Indian or Alaska Native, non-Hispanic/Latino; 12 Asian, non-Hispanic/Latino; 41 Hispanic/Latino; 3 Native Hawaiian or other Pacific Islander, non-Hispanic/Latino; 47 Two or more races, non-Hispanic/Latino), 236 international. Average age 34. 2,881 applicants, 64% accepted, 1139 enrolled. *Faculty:* 223 full-time (85 women), 60 part-time/adjunct (33 women). Expenses: Contact institution. *Financial support:* In 2010–11, 304 students received support; fellowships, research assistantships, teaching assistantships, career-related internships or fieldwork, scholarships/grants, and unspecified assistantships available. Financial award application deadline: 7/1; financial award applicants required to submit FAFSA. In 2010, 669 master's, 16 doctorates, 42 other advanced degrees awarded. *Degree program information:* Part-time programs available. Postbaccalaureate distance learning degree programs offered (no on-campus study). *Application deadline:* Applications are processed on a rolling basis. *Application fee:* $50. Electronic applications accepted. *Application Contact:* Dr. Andrew Sustich, Dean of the Graduate School, 870-972-3029, Fax: 870-972-3857, E-mail: sustich@astate.edu. *Dean of the Graduate School,* Dr. Andrew Sustich, 870-972-3029, Fax: 870-972-3857, E-mail: sustich@astate.edu.

College of Agriculture and Technology Students: 12 full-time (4 women), 26 part-time (13 women); includes 14 minority (2 Black or African American, non-Hispanic/Latino; 12 Hispanic/Latino). Average age 32. 14 applicants, 93% accepted, 7 enrolled. *Faculty:* 8 full-time (0 women), 3 part-time/adjunct (1 woman). Expenses: Contact institution. *Financial support:* In 2010–11, 4 students received support; teaching assistantships, career-related internships or fieldwork, scholarships/grants, and unspecified assistantships available. Financial award application deadline: 7/1; financial award applicants required to submit FAFSA. In 2010, 7 master's awarded. *Degree program information:* Part-time programs available. Offers agricultural education (SCCT); agriculture (MSA); vocational-technical administration (SCCT). *Application deadline:* For fall admission, 7/1 for domestic and international students; for spring admission, 11/15 for domestic students, 11/14 for international students. Applications are processed on a rolling basis. *Application fee:* $30 ($40 for international students). Electronic applications accepted. *Application Contact:* Dr. Andrew Sustich, Dean of the Graduate School, 870-972-3029, Fax: 870-972-3857, E-mail: sustich@astate.edu. *Dean,* Dr. Gregory Phillips, 870-972-2085, Fax: 870-972-3885, E-mail: gphillips@astate.edu.

College of Business Students: 92 full-time (48 women), 139 part-time (67 women); includes 31 minority (20 Black or African American, non-Hispanic/Latino; 1 American Indian or Alaska Native, non-Hispanic/Latino; 5 Asian, non-Hispanic/Latino; 2 Hispanic/Latino; 1 Native Hawaiian or other Pacific Islander, non-Hispanic/Latino; 2 Two or more races, non-Hispanic/Latino), 72 international. Average age 29. 213 applicants, 83% accepted, 105 enrolled. *Faculty:* 31 full-time (7 women), 2 part-time/adjunct (1 woman). Expenses: Contact institution. *Financial support:* In 2010–11, 29 students received support; teaching assistantships, career-related internships or fieldwork, scholarships/grants, and unspecified assistantships available. Financial award application deadline: 7/1; financial award applicants required to submit FAFSA. In 2010, 69 master's awarded. *Degree program information:* Part-time and evening/weekend programs available. Offers accountancy (M Acc); business (M Acc, MBA, MS, MSE, SCCT); business administration (MBA); business education (SCCT); business technology education (MSE); information systems and e-commerce (MS). *Application deadline:* For fall admission, 7/1 for domestic and international students; for spring admission, 11/15 for domestic students, 11/14 for international students. Applications are processed on a rolling basis. *Application fee:* $30 ($40 for international students). Electronic applications accepted. *Application Contact:* Dr. Andrew Sustich, Dean of the Graduate School, 870-972-3029, Fax: 870-972-3857, E-mail: sustich@astate.edu. *Dean,* Dr. Len Frey, 870-972-3035, Fax: 870-972-3744, E-mail: lfrey@astate.edu.

College of Communications Students: 33 full-time (20 women), 31 part-time (19 women); includes 27 minority (all Black or African American, non-Hispanic/Latino), 24 international. Average age 27. 63 applicants, 73% accepted, 29 enrolled. *Faculty:* 13 full-time (5 women), 1 part-time/adjunct (0 women). Expenses: Contact institution. *Financial support:* In 2010–11, 23 students received support. Career-related internships or fieldwork, scholarships/grants, and unspecified assistantships available. Financial award application deadline: 7/1; financial award applicants required to submit FAFSA. In 2010, 14 master's awarded. *Degree program information:* Part-time programs available. Offers communication studies and theatre arts (MA); communication studies and theatre arts education (SCCT); communications (MA, MSMC, SCCT); journalism (MSMC); radio-television (MSMC). *Application deadline:* For fall admission, 7/1 for domestic and international students; for spring admission, 11/15 for domestic students, 11/14 for international students. Applications are processed on a rolling basis. *Application fee:* $30 ($40 for international students). Electronic applications accepted. *Application Contact:* Dr. Andrew Sustich, Dean of the Graduate School, 870-972-3029, Fax: 870-972-3857, E-mail: sustich@astate.edu. *Interim Dean,* Dr. Osabuohien Amienyi, 870-972-2468, Fax: 870-972-3856, E-mail: osami@astate.edu.

College of Education Students: 103 full-time (76 women), 2,016 part-time (1,538 women); includes 352 minority (277 Black or African American, non-Hispanic/Latino; 11 American Indian or Alaska Native, non-Hispanic/Latino; 2 Asian, non-Hispanic/Latino; 33 Hispanic/Latino; 29 Two or more races, non-Hispanic/Latino), 11 international. Average age 36. 1,843 applicants, 63% accepted, 666 enrolled. *Faculty:* 37 full-time (17 women), 29 part-time/adjunct (16 women). Expenses: Contact institution. *Financial support:* In 2010–11, 66 students received support; fellowships, teaching assistantships, career-related internships or fieldwork, scholarships/grants, and unspecified assistantships available. Financial award application deadline: 7/1; financial award applicants required to submit FAFSA. In 2010, 378 master's, 13 doctorates, 39 other advanced degrees awarded. *Degree program information:* Part-time programs available. Postbaccalaureate distance learning degree programs offered (no on-campus study). Offers college student personnel services (MS); community college administration education (SCCT); curriculum and instruction (MSE); early childhood education (MAT, MSE); early childhood services (MS); education (MAT, MRC, MS, MSE, Ed D, PhD, Certificate, Ed S, SCCT); education theory and practice (MSE); educational leadership (MSE, Ed D, PhD, Ed S); exercise science (MS); mental health counseling (Certificate); middle level education (MAT, MSE); physical education (MSE, SCCT); psychology and counseling (Ed S); reading (MSE, SCCT); rehabilitation counseling (MRC); school counseling (MSE); special education (MSE); sports administration (MS); student affairs (Certificate). *Application deadline:* Applications are processed on a rolling basis. *Application fee:* $50. Electronic applications accepted. *Application Contact:* Dr. Andrew Sustich, Dean of the Graduate School, 870-972-3029, Fax: 870-972-3857, E-mail: sustich@astate.edu. *Dean,* Dr. Don Maness, 870-972-3057, Fax: 870-972-3828, E-mail: dmaness@astate.edu.

College of Engineering Students: 8 full-time (0 women), 7 part-time (1 woman); includes 2 minority (1 Black or African American, non-Hispanic/Latino; 1 Asian, non-Hispanic/Latino), 12 international. Average age 26. 16 applicants, 88% accepted, 10 enrolled. *Faculty:* 3 part-time/adjunct (0 women). Expenses: Contact institution. *Financial support:* In 2010–11, 3 students received support. Career-related internships or fieldwork, scholarships/grants, and unspecified assistantships available. Financial award application deadline: 7/1; financial award applicants required to submit FAFSA. In 2010, 11 master's awarded. *Degree program information:* Part-time programs available. Offers engineering (MEM). *Application deadline:* For fall admission, 6/1 for domestic and international students; for spring admission, 10/15 for domestic and international students. Applications are processed on a rolling basis. *Application fee:* $30 ($40 for international students). Electronic applications accepted. *Application Contact:* Dr. Andrew Sustich, Dean of the Graduate School, 870-972-3029, Fax: 870-972-3857, E-mail: sustich@astate.edu. *Dean,* Dr. David Beasley, 870-972-2088, Fax: 870-972-3539, E-mail: dbbeasley@astate.edu.

College of Fine Arts Students: 8 full-time (4 women), 11 part-time (6 women), 1 international. Average age 29. 22 applicants, 64% accepted, 11 enrolled. *Faculty:* 26 full-time (8 women), 2 part-time/adjunct (both women). Expenses: Contact institution. *Financial support:* In 2010–11, 13 students received support; teaching assistantships, career-related internships or fieldwork, scholarships/grants, and unspecified assistantships available. Financial award application deadline: 7/1; financial award applicants required to submit FAFSA. In 2010, 10 master's, 3 other advanced degrees awarded. *Degree program information:* Part-time programs available. Offers art (MA); communication studies and theatre arts (MA); communication studies and theatre arts education (SCCT); fine arts (MA, MM, MME, SCCT); music education (MME, SCCT); performance (MM). *Application deadline:* Applications are processed on a rolling basis. *Application fee:* $30 ($40 for international students). Electronic applications accepted. *Application Contact:* Dr. Andrew Sustich, Dean of the Graduate School, 870-972-3029, Fax: 870-972-3857, E-mail: sustich@astate.edu. *Dean,* Dr. Daniel Reeves, 870-972-3053, Fax: 870-972-3932, E-mail: dreeves@astate.edu.

College of Humanities and Social Sciences Students: 79 full-time (53 women), 120 part-time (65 women); includes 40 minority (36 Black or African American, non-Hispanic/Latino; 2 American Indian or Alaska Native, non-Hispanic/Latino; 1 Hispanic/Latino; 1 Two or more races, non-Hispanic/Latino), 15 international. Average age 33. 127 applicants, 73% accepted, 68 enrolled. *Faculty:* 46 full-time (20 women), 5 part-time/adjunct (4 women). Expenses: Contact institution. *Financial support:* In 2010–11, 64 students received support; fellowships, teaching assistantships, career-related internships or fieldwork, scholarships/grants, and unspecified assistantships available. Financial award application deadline: 7/1; financial award applicants required to submit FAFSA. In 2010, 50 master's, 2 doctorates awarded. *Degree program information:* Part-time programs available. Offers criminal justice (MA, Certificate); English (MA); English education (MSE, SCCT); heritage studies (MA, PhD); history (MA); history education (MSE, SCCT); humanities and social sciences (MA, MPA, MSE, PhD, Certificate, SCCT); political science (MA); political science education (SCCT); public administration (MPA); social science education (MSE); sociology (MA); sociology education (SCCT). *Application deadline:* Applications are processed on a rolling basis. *Application fee:* $50. Electronic applications accepted. *Application Contact:* Dr. Andrew Sustich, Dean of the Graduate School, 870-972-3029, Fax: 870-972-3857, E-mail: sustich@astate.edu. *Interim Dean,* Dr. Carol O'Connor, 870-972-3973, Fax: 870-972-3976, E-mail: coconnor@astate.edu.

College of Nursing and Health Professions Students: 251 full-time (155 women), 179 part-time (158 women); includes 64 minority (48 Black or African American, non-Hispanic/Latino; 2 Asian, non-Hispanic/Latino; 2 Hispanic/Latino; 1 Native Hawaiian or other Pacific Islander, non-Hispanic/Latino; 11 Two or more races, non-Hispanic/Latino), 4 international. Average age 31. 355 applicants, 42% accepted, 135 enrolled. *Faculty:* 19 full-time (13 women), 8 part-time/adjunct (6 women). Expenses: Contact institution. *Financial support:* In 2010–11, 25 students received support; fellowships, career-related internships or fieldwork, scholarships/grants, and unspecified assistantships available. Financial award application deadline: 7/1; financial award applicants required to submit FAFSA. In 2010, 114 master's awarded. *Degree program information:* Part-time programs available. Offers aging studies (Certificate); communication disorders (MCD); health care management (Certificate); health communications (Certificate); health sciences (MS); health sciences education (Certificate); nurse anesthesia (MSN); nursing (MSN); nursing and health professions (MCD, MPT, MS, MSN, MSW, DPT, Certificate); physical therapy (MPT, DPT); social work (MSW). *Applica-*

Arkansas State University (continued)

tion deadline: Applications are processed on a rolling basis. *Application fee:* $50. Electronic applications accepted. *Application Contact:* Dr. Andrew Sustich, Dean of the Graduate School, 870-972-3029, Fax: 870-972-3857, E-mail: sustich@astate.edu. *Dean*, Dr. Susan Hanrahan, 870-972-3112, Fax: 870-972-2040, E-mail: hanrahan@astate.edu.

College of Sciences and Mathematics Students: 107 full-time (42 women), 64 part-time (26 women); includes 14 minority (6 Black or African American, non-Hispanic/Latino; 2 American Indian or Alaska Native, non-Hispanic/Latino; 1 Asian, non-Hispanic/Latino; 2 Hispanic/Latino; 1 Native Hawaiian or other Pacific Islander, non-Hispanic/Latino; 2 Two or more races, non-Hispanic/Latino), 86 international. Average age 28. 137 applicants, 77% accepted, 62 enrolled. *Faculty:* 38 full-time (12 women), 7 part-time/adjunct (3 women). Expenses: Contact institution. *Financial support:* In 2010–11, 76 students received support; fellowships, teaching assistantships, career-related internships or fieldwork, scholarships/grants, and unspecified assistantships available. Financial award application deadline: 7/1; financial award applicants required to submit FAFSA. In 2010, 16 master's, 1 doctorate awarded. *Degree program information:* Part-time programs available. Offers biological sciences (MA); biology (MS); biology education (MSE, SCCT); biotechnology (Certificate); chemistry (MS); chemistry education (MSE, SCCT); computer science (MS); environmental sciences (MS, PhD); mathematics (MS); mathematics education (MSE); molecular biosciences (PhD); sciences and mathematics (MA, MS, MSE, PhD, Certificate, SCCT). *Application deadline:* Applications are processed on a rolling basis. *Application fee:* $50. Electronic applications accepted. *Application Contact:* Dr. Andrew Sustich, Dean of the Graduate School, 870-972-3029, Fax: 870-972-3857, E-mail: sustich@astate.edu. *Dean*, Dr. Andy Novobilski, 870-972-3079, Fax: 870-972-3827, E-mail: anovobilski@astate.edu.

ARKANSAS TECH UNIVERSITY, Russellville, AR 72801

General Information State-supported, coed, comprehensive institution. *Enrollment:* 9,815 graduate, professional, and undergraduate students; 190 full-time matriculated graduate/professional students (85 women), 477 part-time matriculated graduate/professional students (338 women). *Enrollment by degree level:* 644 master's, 23 other advanced degrees. *Graduate faculty:* 66 full-time (27 women), 6 part-time/adjunct (4 women). Tuition, state resident: full-time $4680; part-time $195 per credit hour. Tuition, nonresident: full-time $9360; part-time $390 per credit hour. *Required fees:* $714; $14 per credit hour. One-time fee: $326 part-time. Tuition and fees vary according to course load. *Graduate housing:* Room and/or apartments available on a first-come, first-served basis to single students; on-campus housing not available to married students. Typical cost: $3248 per year ($5394 including board). Room and board charges vary according to board plan, campus/location and housing facility selected. Housing application deadline: 8/1. *Student services:* Campus employment opportunities, campus safety program, career counseling, exercise/wellness program, free psychological counseling, international student services, low-cost health insurance, multicultural affairs office, services for students with disabilities, teacher training. *Library facilities:* Ross Pendergraft Library and Technology Center. *Online resources:* library catalog, web page. *Collection:* 285,397 titles, 791 serial subscriptions, 12,637 audiovisual materials.

Computer facilities: Computer purchase and lease plans are available. 700 computers available on campus for general student use. A campuswide network can be accessed from student residence rooms and from off campus. Online class registration is available. *Web address:* http://www.atu.edu/.

General Application Contact: Dr. Mary B. Gunter, Dean of Graduate College, 479-968-0398, Fax: 479-964-0542, E-mail: graduate.school@atu.edu.

GRADUATE UNITS

Graduate College Students: 190 full-time (85 women), 477 part-time (338 women); includes 67 minority (35 Black or African American, non-Hispanic/Latino; 7 American Indian or Alaska Native, non-Hispanic/Latino; 5 Asian, non-Hispanic/Latino; 16 Hispanic/Latino; 4 Two or more races, non-Hispanic/Latino), 80 international. Average age 33. *Faculty:* 66 full-time (27 women), 6 part-time/adjunct (4 women). Expenses: Contact institution. *Financial support:* In 2010–11, teaching assistantships with full tuition reimbursements (averaging $4,000 per year); research assistantships, career-related internships or fieldwork, Federal Work-Study, scholarships/grants, health care benefits, and unspecified assistantships also available. Support available to part-time students. Financial award application deadline: 4/15; financial award applicants required to submit FAFSA. In 2010, 209 master's, 1 other advanced degree awarded. *Degree program information:* Part-time and evening/weekend programs available. Postbaccalaureate distance learning degree programs offered (no on-campus study). *Application deadline:* For fall admission, 3/1 priority date for domestic students, 5/1 priority date for international students; for spring admission, 10/1 priority date for domestic and international students. Applications are processed on a rolling basis. *Application fee:* $0 ($50 for international students). Electronic applications accepted. *Application Contact:* Dr. Mary B. Gunter, Dean of Graduate College, 479-968-0398, Fax: 479-964-0542, E-mail: graduate.school@atu.edu. *Dean of Graduate College*, Dr. Mary B. Gunter, 479-968-0398, Fax: 479-964-0542, E-mail: graduate.school@atu.edu.

College of Applied Sciences Students: 86 full-time (24 women), 53 part-time (21 women); includes 14 minority (5 Black or African American, non-Hispanic/Latino; 2 American Indian or Alaska Native, non-Hispanic/Latino; 1 Asian, non-Hispanic/Latino; 4 Hispanic/Latino; 2 Two or more races, non-Hispanic/Latino), 60 international. Average age 31. Expenses: Contact institution. *Financial support:* In 2010–11, teaching assistantships with full tuition reimbursements (averaging $4,000 per year); research assistantships, career-related internships or fieldwork, Federal Work-Study, scholarships/grants, health care benefits, and unspecified assistantships also available. Support available to part-time students. Financial award application deadline: 4/15; financial award applicants required to submit FAFSA. In 2010, 44 master's awarded. *Degree program information:* Part-time programs available. Offers emergency management (MS); engineering (M Engr); information technology (MS). *Application deadline:* For fall admission, 3/1 priority date for domestic students, 5/1 priority date for international students; for spring admission, 10/1 priority date for domestic and international students. Applications are processed on a rolling basis. *Application fee:* $0 ($30 for international students). Electronic applications accepted. *Application Contact:* Dr. Mary B. Gunter, Dean of Graduate College, 479-968-0398, Fax: 479-964-0542, E-mail: graduate.school@atu.edu. *Dean*, Dr. William Hoefler, 479-968-0353 Ext. 501, E-mail: whoeflerjr@atu.edu.

College of Arts and Humanities Students: 39 full-time (23 women), 87 part-time (69 women); includes 13 minority (3 Black or African American, non-Hispanic/Latino; 1 American Indian or Alaska Native, non-Hispanic/Latino; 1 Asian, non-Hispanic/Latino; 8 Hispanic/Latino), 14 international. Average age 32. Expenses: Contact institution. *Financial support:* In 2010–11, teaching assistantships with full tuition reimbursements (averaging $4,000 per year); research assistantships, career-related internships or fieldwork, Federal Work-Study, scholarships/grants, health care benefits, and unspecified assistantships also available. Support available to part-time students. Financial award application deadline: 4/15; financial award applicants required to submit FAFSA. In 2010, 54 degrees awarded. *Degree program information:* Part-time programs available. Offers communication (MLA); English (M Ed, MA); fine arts (MLA); history (MA); multi-media journalism (MA); psychology (MS); social science (MLA); Spanish (MA, MLA); teaching English as a second language (MA, MLA). *Application deadline:* For fall admission, 3/1 priority date for domestic students, 5/1 priority date for international students; for spring admission, 10/1 priority date for domestic and international students. Applications are processed on a rolling basis. *Application fee:* $0 ($50 for international students). Electronic applications accepted. *Application Contact:* Dr. Mary B. Gunter, Dean of Graduate College, 479-968-0398, Fax: 479-964-0542, E-mail: graduate.school@atu.edu. *Dean*, Dr. Micheal Tarver, 479-968-0274, Fax: 479-964-0812, E-mail: mtarver@atu.edu.

College of Education Students: 56 full-time (34 women), 184 part-time (140 women); includes 33 minority (23 Black or African American, non-Hispanic/Latino; 2 American Indian or Alaska Native, non-Hispanic/Latino; 3 Asian, non-Hispanic/Latino; 3 Hispanic/Latino; 2 Two or more races, non-Hispanic/Latino), 4 international. Average age 31. Expenses: Contact institution. *Financial support:* In 2010–11, teaching assistantships with full tuition reimbursements (averaging $4,000 per year); research assistantships, career-related internships or fieldwork, Federal Work-Study, scholarships/grants, health care benefits, and unspecified assistantships also available. Support available to part-time students. Financial award application deadline: 4/15; financial award applicants required to submit FAFSA. In 2010, 70 master's, 1 other advanced degree awarded. *Degree program information:* Part-time and evening/weekend programs available. Postbaccalaureate distance learning degree programs offered (no on-campus study). Offers college student personnel (MS); educational leadership (M Ed, Ed S); English education (M Ed); instructional improvement (M Ed); secondary education (M Ed); teaching (MAT); teaching, learning and leadership (M Ed). *Application deadline:* For fall admission, 3/1 priority date for domestic students, 5/1 priority date for international students; for spring admission, 10/1 priority date for domestic and international students. Applications are processed on a rolling basis. *Application fee:* $0 ($50 for international students). Electronic applications accepted. *Application Contact:* Dr. Mary B. Gunter, Dean of Graduate College, 479-968-0398, Fax: 479-964-0542, E-mail: graduate.school@atu.edu. *Dean*, Dr. Eldon G. Clary, 479-968-0350, Fax: 479-968-0350, E-mail: eclary@atu.edu.

College of Natural and Health Sciences Students: 9 full-time (4 women), 25 part-time (21 women); includes 1 minority (Black or African American, non-Hispanic/Latino), 2 international. Average age 36. Expenses: Contact institution. *Financial support:* In 2010–11, teaching assistantships with full tuition reimbursements (averaging $4,000 per year); research assistantships, career-related internships or fieldwork, Federal Work-Study, scholarships/grants, health care benefits, and unspecified assistantships also available. Support available to part-time students. Financial award application deadline: 4/15; financial award applicants required to submit FAFSA. In 2010, 9 master's awarded. Offers fisheries and wildlife biology (MS); health informatics (MS); nursing (MSN). *Application deadline:* For fall admission, 3/1 priority date for domestic students, 5/1 priority date for international students; for spring admission, 10/1 priority date for domestic and international students. Applications are processed on a rolling basis. *Application fee:* $0 ($30 for international students). Electronic applications accepted. *Application Contact:* Dr. Mary B. Gunter, Dean of Graduate College, 479-968-0398, Fax: 479-964-0542, E-mail: graduate.school@atu.edu. *Dean*, Dr. Richard Cohoon, 479-964-0816, E-mail: richard.cohoon@atu.edu.

ARMSTRONG ATLANTIC STATE UNIVERSITY, Savannah, GA 31419-1997

General Information State-supported, coed, comprehensive institution. *Graduate housing:* Room and/or apartments available on a first-come, first-served basis to single students; on-campus housing not available to married students.

GRADUATE UNITS

School of Graduate Studies *Degree program information:* Part-time and evening/weekend programs available. Postbaccalaureate distance learning degree programs offered (minimal on-campus study). Offers adult education (M Ed); computer science (MS); criminal justice (MS); curriculum and instruction (M Ed); early childhood education (M Ed); education (M Ed); elementary education (M Ed); health services administration (MHSA); history (MA); liberal and professional studies (MALPS); middle grades education (M Ed); nursing (MSN); physical therapy (DPT); public health (MPH); secondary education (M Ed); special education (M Ed); sports health sciences (MSSM). Electronic applications accepted.

ART ACADEMY OF CINCINNATI, Cincinnati, OH 45202

General Information Independent, coed, comprehensive institution. *Graduate housing:* Rooms and/or apartments available on a first-come, first-served basis to single and married students. Housing application deadline: 5/1.

GRADUATE UNITS

Program in Art Education *Degree program information:* Part-time programs available. Offers art education (MAAE). Offered during summer only. Electronic applications accepted.

ART CENTER COLLEGE OF DESIGN, Pasadena, CA 91103

General Information Independent, coed, comprehensive institution. *Enrollment:* 1,737 graduate, professional, and undergraduate students; 130 full-time matriculated graduate/professional students (47 women), 52 part-time matriculated graduate/professional students (17 women). *Enrollment by degree level:* 182 master's. *Graduate faculty:* 15 full-time (4 women), 32 part-time/adjunct (12 women). *Tuition:* Part-time $17,220 per term. *Graduate housing:* On-campus housing not available. *Student services:* Campus employment opportunities, career counseling, free psychological counseling, international student services, low-cost health insurance. *Library facilities:* James LeMont Fogg Library plus 2 others. *Online resources:* library catalog, web page, access to other libraries' catalogs. *Collection:* 80,848 titles, 359 serial subscriptions, 13,000 audiovisual materials.

Computer facilities: Computer purchase and lease plans are available. 250 computers available on campus for general student use. A campuswide network can be accessed from off campus. Online class registration is available. *Web address:* http://www.artcenter.edu/.

General Application Contact: Kit Baron, Vice President of Admission and Enrollment Management, 626-396-2373, Fax: 626-795-0578.

GRADUATE UNITS

Graduate Division Students: 130 full-time (47 women), 51 part-time (16 women); includes 49 minority (10 Black or African American, non-Hispanic/Latino; 23 Asian, non-Hispanic/Latino; 9 Hispanic/Latino; 4 Native Hawaiian or other Pacific Islander, non-Hispanic/Latino; 3 Two or more races, non-Hispanic/Latino), 55 international. Average age 30. *Faculty:* 15 full-time (4 women), 32 part-time/adjunct (12 women). Expenses: Contact institution. *Financial support:* In 2010–11, 149 students received support; teaching assistantships, career-related internships or fieldwork, Federal Work-Study, and scholarships/grants available. Financial award application deadline: 3/1. Offers broadcast cinema (MFA); environmental design (MS); fine arts (MFA); media design (MFA); product design (MS). *Application deadline:* For fall admission, 2/1 priority date for domestic and international students; for spring admission, 10/1 priority date for domestic and international students. Applications are processed on a rolling basis. *Application Contact:* Kit Baron, Vice President of Admission and Enrollment Management, 626-396-2373. *Vice President of Admission and Enrollment Management*, Kit Baron, 626-396-2373.

THE ART INSTITUTE OF ATLANTA, Atlanta, GA 30328

General Information Proprietary, coed, comprehensive institution.

GRADUATE UNITS

Program in Business Administration Offers business administration (MBA). Program offered jointly with South University.

THE ART INSTITUTE OF BOSTON AT LESLEY UNIVERSITY, Boston, MA 02215-2598

General Information Independent, coed, comprehensive institution.

GRADUATE UNITS

Program in Visual Arts Offers visual arts (MFA).

THE ART INSTITUTE OF CALIFORNIA–SAN FRANCISCO, San Francisco, CA 94102

General Information Proprietary, coed, comprehensive institution. *Web address:* http://www.artinstitutes.edu/sanfrancisco/.

GRADUATE UNITS

Master of Fine Arts Program Expenses: Contact institution. Offers computer animation (MFA).

ASBURY THEOLOGICAL SEMINARY, Wilmore, KY 40390-1199

General Information Independent-religious, coed, primarily men, graduate-only institution. *Enrollment by degree level:* 835 first professional, 448 master's, 272 doctoral, 19 other advanced degrees. *Graduate faculty:* 64 full-time (12 women), 77 part-time/adjunct (14 women). *Tuition:* Full-time $12,120; part-time $505 per credit hour. One-time fee: $100. *Graduate housing:* Rooms and/or apartments available on a first-come, first-served basis to single and married students. Typical cost: $945 per year ($3488 including board) for single students; $3600 per year for married students. Room and board charges vary according to board plan and housing facility selected. Housing application deadline: 8/15. *Student services:* Campus employment opportunities, campus safety program, exercise/wellness program, free psychological counseling, international student services, low-cost health insurance, multicultural affairs office, services for students with disabilities, writing training. *Library facilities:* B. L. Fisher Library plus 1 other. *Online resources:* library catalog, web page. *Collection:* 345,500 titles, 1,125 serial subscriptions, 43,773 audiovisual materials.

Computer facilities: 38 computers available on campus for general student use. A campuswide network can be accessed from student residence rooms and from off campus. Online class registration, course management system are available. *Web address:* http://www.asburyseminary.edu/.

General Application Contact: Kevin Bish, Vice President of Enrollment Management, 859-858-2211, Fax: 859-858-2287, E-mail: admissions.office@asburyseminary.edu.

GRADUATE UNITS

Graduate and Professional Programs Students: 719 full-time (251 women), 855 part-time (276 women); includes 178 minority (87 Black or African American, non-Hispanic/Latino; 4 American Indian or Alaska Native, non-Hispanic/Latino; 35 Asian, non-Hispanic/Latino; 40 Hispanic/Latino; 3 Native Hawaiian or other Pacific Islander, non-Hispanic/Latino; 9 Two or more races, non-Hispanic/Latino), 109 international. Average age 38. 772 applicants, 71% accepted, 406 enrolled. *Faculty:* 63 full-time (12 women), 74 part-time/adjunct (14 women). Expenses: Contact institution. *Financial support:* In 2010–11, 1,317 students received support. Career-related internships or fieldwork, Federal Work-Study, institutionally sponsored loans, and scholarships/grants available. Support available to part-time students. Financial award applicants required to submit FAFSA. In 2010, 101 master's, 37 doctorates, 3 other advanced degrees awarded. *Degree program information:* Part-time programs available. Postbaccalaureate distance learning degree programs offered (minimal on-campus study). Offers theology (MA, MACE, MACL, MAMFC, MAMHC, MAPC, MAYM, Th M, PhD, Certificate). *Application deadline:* Applications are processed on a rolling basis. *Application fee:* $50. Electronic applications accepted. *Application Contact:* Kevin Bush, Vice President of Enrollment Management, 859-858-2211, Fax: 859-858-2287, E-mail: admissions.office@asburyseminary.edu. *Provost,* Dr. Leslie A. Andrews, 859-858-2206, Fax: 859-858-2025, E-mail: leslie.andrews@asburyseminary.edu.

ASBURY UNIVERSITY, Wilmore, KY 40390-1198

General Information Independent-religious, coed, comprehensive institution. *Graduate housing:* On-campus housing not available.

GRADUATE UNITS

School of Graduate and Professional Studies *Degree program information:* Part-time programs available. Offers biology: alternative certificate (MA Ed); chemistry: alternative certificate (MA Ed); child and family services (MSW); English (MA Ed); English as a second language (MA Ed); ESL (MA Ed); French (MA Ed); Latin: alternative certificate (MA Ed); mathematics: alternative certificate (MA Ed); reading/writing endorsement (MA Ed); social studies (MA Ed); social work (MSW); Spanish (MA Ed); special education (MA Ed); special education: alternative certificate (MA Ed); teacher as leader endorsement (MA Ed). Electronic applications accepted.

ASHLAND THEOLOGICAL SEMINARY, Ashland, OH 44805

General Information Independent-religious, coed, graduate-only institution. *Enrollment by degree level:* 493 master's, 88 doctoral. *Graduate faculty:* 23 full-time (6 women), 38 part-time/adjunct (15 women). *Graduate housing:* Rooms and/or apartments available on a first-come, first-served basis to single and married students. Housing application deadline: 8/30. *Student services:* Campus employment opportunities, free psychological counseling, international student services, low-cost health insurance, services for students with disabilities, writing training. *Library facilities:* Darling Memorial Library. *Online resources:* library catalog, web page, access to other libraries' catalogs. *Collection:* 84,121 titles, 316 serial subscriptions, 1,256 audiovisual materials. *Research affiliation:* Tel Gezer Excavation and Study Program (archaeological studies).

Computer facilities: 20 computers available on campus for general student use. A campuswide network can be accessed. Online class registration is available. *Web address:* http://www.ashland.edu/seminary/.

General Application Contact: Glenn Black, Director of Enrollment Management, 419-289-5115, Fax: 419-289-5969, E-mail: gblack@ashland.edu.

GRADUATE UNITS

Graduate Programs Students: 464 full-time (258 women), 117 part-time (70 women); includes 240 minority (221 Black or African American, non-Hispanic/Latino; 4 American Indian or Alaska Native, non-Hispanic/Latino; 8 Asian, non-Hispanic/Latino; 7 Hispanic/Latino), 11 international. Average age 43. 89 applicants, 100% accepted, 88 enrolled. *Faculty:* 23 full-time (6 women), 38 part-time/adjunct (15 women). Expenses: Contact institution. *Financial support:* In 2010–11, 156 students received support, including 17 teaching assistantships; research assistantships, career-related internships or fieldwork, institutionally sponsored loans, scholarships/grants, and unspecified assistantships also available. Support available to part-time students. Financial award application deadline: 5/15; financial award applicants required to submit FAFSA. In 2010, 34 first professional degrees, 100 master's, 27 doctorates, 2 other advanced degrees awarded. *Degree program information:* Part-time programs available. Offers biblical and theological studies (MA, MAR); Christian ministry (MAPT); Christian studies (Diploma); clinical counseling (MAC, MACC); historical studies (MA); ministry (D Min); pastoral ministry (M Div); theological studies (MA). *Application deadline:* For fall admission, 8/30 for domestic students. Applications are processed on a rolling basis. *Application fee:* $30. Electronic applications accepted. *Application Contact:* Glenn Black, Director of Enrollment Management, 419-289-5151, Fax: 419-289-5969, E-mail: gblack@ashland.edu. *President,* Dr. John C. Shultz, 419-289-5160, Fax: 419-289-5969, E-mail: jshultz@ashland.edu.

ASHLAND UNIVERSITY, Ashland, OH 44805-3702

General Information Independent-religious, coed, comprehensive institution. CGS member. *Enrollment:* 6,491 graduate, professional, and undergraduate students; 795 full-time matriculated graduate/professional students (469 women), 1,144 part-time matriculated graduate/professional students (740 women). *Enrollment by degree level:* 1,889 master's, 50 doctoral. *Graduate faculty:* 68 full-time (35 women), 183 part-time/adjunct (73 women). *Tuition:* Part-time $451 per semester hour. Tuition and fees vary according to course load and program. *Graduate housing:* On-campus housing not available. *Student services:* Campus employment opportunities, campus safety program, career counseling, exercise/wellness program, free psychological counseling, international student services, low-cost health insurance, multicultural affairs office, services for students with disabilities, teacher training, writing training. *Library facilities:* Ashland Library plus 2 others. *Online resources:* library catalog, web page. *Collection:* 205,200 titles, 1,625 serial subscriptions, 3,550 audiovisual materials. *Research affiliation:* Teacher Quality Project (TQP) (education).

Computer facilities: Computer purchase and lease plans are available. 760 computers available on campus for general student use. A campuswide network can be accessed from student residence rooms and from off campus. Online class registration is available. *Web address:* http://www.exploreashland.com/.

General Application Contact: Dr. W. Gregory Gerrick, Dean, Graduate School, 419-289-5750, Fax: 419-289-5949, E-mail: ggerrick@ashland.edu.

GRADUATE UNITS

College of Arts and Sciences Students: 115 full-time (67 women), 65 part-time (31 women); includes 17 minority (2 Black or African American, non-Hispanic/Latino; 4 American Indian or Alaska Native, non-Hispanic/Latino; 4 Asian, non-Hispanic/Latino; 7 Hispanic/Latino). Average age 37. 124 applicants, 78% accepted, 62 enrolled. *Faculty:* 6 full-time (0 women), 46 part-time/adjunct (8 women). Expenses: Contact institution. *Financial support:* Application deadline: 4/15. In 2010, 16 master's awarded. *Degree program information:* Part-time programs available. Offers American history and government (MAHG); arts and sciences (MAHG, MFA); creative writing (MFA). *Application deadline:* Applications are processed on a rolling basis. *Application fee:* $30. Electronic applications accepted. *Application Contact:* Dr. W. Gregory Gerrick, Dean, Graduate School, 419-289-5750, Fax: 419-289-5949, E-mail: ggerrick@ashland.edu. *Dean,* Dr. Dawn Weber, 419-289-5107.

Dauch College of Business and Economics Students: 305 full-time (131 women), 290 part-time (125 women); includes 83 minority (59 Black or African American, non-Hispanic/Latino; 5 American Indian or Alaska Native, non-Hispanic/Latino; 6 Asian, non-Hispanic/Latino; 9 Hispanic/Latino; 3 Native Hawaiian or other Pacific Islander, non-Hispanic/Latino; 1 Two or more races, non-Hispanic/Latino), 80 international. Average age 33. 205 applicants, 98% accepted, 146 enrolled. *Faculty:* 16 full-time (5 women), 21 part-time/adjunct (6 women). Expenses: Contact institution. *Financial support:* In 2010–11, 21 students received support. Tuition waivers (partial) and unspecified assistantships available. Financial award application deadline: 4/15; financial award applicants required to submit FAFSA. In 2010, 191 master's awarded. *Degree program information:* Part-time and evening/weekend programs available. Offers business and economics (MBA). *Application deadline:* For fall admission, 8/1 priority date for domestic students; for spring admission, 12/1 priority date for domestic students. Applications are processed on a rolling basis. *Application fee:* $30. Electronic applications accepted. *Application Contact:* Stephen W. Krispinsky, Executive Director of MBA Program, 419-289-5236, Fax: 419-289-5910, E-mail: skrispin@ashland.edu. *Chair,* Dr. Beverly Heimann, 419-289-5216, E-mail: bheimann@ashland.edu.

Dwight Schar College of Education Students: 375 full-time (271 women), 789 part-time (584 women); includes 87 minority (71 Black or African American, non-Hispanic/Latino; 3 American Indian or Alaska Native, non-Hispanic/Latino; 3 Asian, non-Hispanic/Latino; 10 Hispanic/Latino), 18 international. Average age 33. 321 applicants, 96% accepted, 282 enrolled. *Faculty:* 47 full-time (29 women), 116 part-time/adjunct (59 women). Expenses: Contact institution. *Financial support:* In 2010–11, 238 students received support; teaching assistantships with partial tuition reimbursements available, scholarships/grants available. Financial award application deadline: 4/15. In 2010, 596 master's, 4 doctorates awarded. *Degree program information:* Part-time and evening/weekend programs available. Offers adapted physical education (M Ed); applied exercise science (M Ed); curriculum and instruction (M Ed); curriculum specialist (M Ed); education (M Ed, Ed D); educational leadership studies (Ed D); intervention specialist, mild/moderate (M Ed); intervention specialist, moderate/intensive (M Ed); literacy (M Ed); principalship (M Ed); pupil services (M Ed); sport education (M Ed); sport management (M Ed); talented and gifted (M Ed); technology facilitator (M Ed). *Application deadline:* For fall admission, 8/27 for domestic students; for spring admission, 1/14 for domestic students. Applications are processed on a rolling basis. *Application fee:* $30. *Application Contact:* Dr. Linda Billman, Director and Chair, Graduate Studies in Education/Associate Dean, 419-289-5369, Fax: 419-289-5331, E-mail: lbillman@ashland.edu. *Dean,* Dr. James P. Van Keuren, 419-289-5377, E-mail: jvankeu1@ashland.edu.

ASHWORTH COLLEGE, Norcross, GA 30092

General Information Proprietary, coed, comprehensive institution. *Enrollment:* 57,650 graduate, professional, and undergraduate students; 299 matriculated graduate/professional students. *Enrollment by degree level:* 299 master's. *Graduate faculty:* 5 part-time/adjunct (1 woman). *Tuition:* Full-time $9230; part-time $250 per credit hour.

Computer facilities: Online class registration is available. *Web address:* http://www.ashworthcollege.edu/.

General Application Contact: Dr. Leslie A. Gargiulo, Vice President of Education, 770-729-8400, E-mail: lgargiulo@ashworthcollege.edu.

GRADUATE UNITS

Graduate Programs Students: 299. *Faculty:* 5 part-time/adjunct (1 woman). Expenses: Contact institution. Offers business administration (MBA); criminal justice (MS); health care administration (MBA, MS); human resource management (MBA, MS); international business (MBA); management (MS); marketing (MBA, MS). *Application Contact:* Dr. Leslie A. Gargiulo, Vice President of Education, 770-729-8400, E-mail: lgargiulo@ashworthcollege.edu. *Vice President of Education,* Dr. Leslie A. Gargiulo, 770-729-8400, E-mail: lgargiulo@ashworthcollege.edu.

ASPEN UNIVERSITY, Denver, CO 80246

General Information Independent, coed, comprehensive institution. *Graduate housing:* On-campus housing not available.

GRADUATE UNITS

Program in Business Administration *Degree program information:* Part-time and evening/weekend programs available. Postbaccalaureate distance learning degree programs offered (no on-campus study). Offers business administration (MBA); finance (MBA); information management (MBA); project management (MBA, Certificate). Electronic applications accepted.

Program in Information Technology *Degree program information:* Part-time and evening/weekend programs available. Postbaccalaureate distance learning degree programs offered (no on-campus study). Offers information technology (MS, Certificate). Electronic applications accepted.

Programs in Information Management *Degree program information:* Part-time and evening/weekend programs available. Postbaccalaureate distance learning degree programs offered (no on-campus study). Offers information management (MS); information systems (Certificate). Electronic applications accepted.

ASSEMBLIES OF GOD THEOLOGICAL SEMINARY, Springfield, MO 65802

General Information Independent-religious, coed, graduate-only institution. *Enrollment by degree level:* 87 first professional, 166 master's, 134 doctoral. *Graduate faculty:* 12 full-time (3 women), 20 part-time/adjunct (6 women). *Tuition:* Full-time $12,192; part-time $508 per credit hour. *Graduate housing:* On-campus housing not available. *Student services:* Career counseling, free psychological counseling, international student services, services for students with disabilities, writing training. *Library facilities:* Cordas C. Burnett Library. *Online resources:* library catalog, web page, access to other libraries' catalogs. *Collection:* 99,173 titles, 321 serial subscriptions, 5,453 audiovisual materials.

Computer facilities: 18 computers available on campus for general student use. A campuswide network can be accessed. Online class registration is available. *Web address:* http://www.agts.edu/.

General Application Contact: Natalia Guerreiro, 417-268-1000, Fax: 417-268-1001.

GRADUATE UNITS

Graduate and Professional Programs Students: 176 full-time (59 women), 211 part-time (48 women); includes 55 minority (16 Black or African American, non-Hispanic/Latino; 7 American Indian or Alaska Native, non-Hispanic/Latino; 16 Asian, non-Hispanic/Latino; 14 Hispanic/Latino; 2 Native Hawaiian or other Pacific Islander, non-Hispanic/Latino), 9 international. Average age 40. 96 applicants, 79% accepted, 53 enrolled. *Faculty:* 12 full-time (3 women), 20 part-time/adjunct (6 women). Expenses: Contact institution. *Financial support:* Career-related internships or fieldwork, Federal Work-Study, and scholarships/grants available. Support available to part-time students. Financial award application deadline: 7/15; financial award applicants required to submit FAFSA. In 2010, 26 first professional degrees, 65 master's, 9 doctorates awarded. *Degree program information:* Part-time and evening/weekend programs available. Postbaccalaureate distance learning degree programs offered (minimal on-campus study). Offers Christian ministries (MA); counseling (MA); divinity (M Div); intercultural ministry (MA); intercultural studies (PhD); ministry (D Min); missiology (D Miss); theological studies (MA). *Application deadline:* For fall admission, 7/1 priority date for domestic students, 6/1 priority date for international students; for spring admission, 12/1 priority date for domestic students, 11/1 priority date for international students. Applications are processed on a rolling basis. *Application fee:* $75. Electronic applications accepted. *Application Contact:* Stephen Lim, Academic Dean, 417-268-1000, Fax: 417-268-1001, E-mail: slim@agts.edu. *Academic Dean,* Stephen Lim, 417-268-1000, Fax: 417-268-1001, E-mail: slim@agts.edu.

ASSOCIATED MENNONITE BIBLICAL SEMINARY, Elkhart, IN 46517-1999

General Information Independent-religious, coed, graduate-only institution. *Graduate housing:* Rooms and/or apartments available on a first-come, first-served basis to single and married students. Housing application deadline: 5/1.

GRADUATE UNITS

Graduate and Professional Programs *Degree program information:* Part-time programs available. Offers Christian formation (MA); divinity (M Div); mission and evangelism (MA); peace studies (MA); theological studies (MA, Certificate). Electronic applications accepted.

ASSUMPTION COLLEGE, Worcester, MA 01609-1296

General Information Independent-religious, coed, comprehensive institution. CGS member. *Enrollment:* 2,562 graduate, professional, and undergraduate students; 195 full-time matriculated graduate/professional students (158 women), 279 part-time matriculated graduate/professional students (199 women). *Enrollment by degree level:* 474 master's. *Graduate faculty:* 14 full-time (4 women), 51 part-time/adjunct (21 women). *Tuition:* Part-time $503 per credit. *Required fees:* $20 per semester. One-time fee: $100. Part-time tuition and fees vary according to campus/location. *Graduate housing:* On-campus housing not available. *Student services:* Campus employment opportunities, campus safety program, career counseling, exercise/wellness program, international student services, low-cost health insurance, multicultural affairs office, services for students with disabilities. *Library facilities:* Emmanuel d'Alzon Library. *Online resources:* library catalog, web page, access to other libraries' catalogs.
Computer facilities: Computer purchase and lease plans are available. A campuswide network can be accessed from student residence rooms and from off campus. Online class registration is available. *Web address:* http://www.assumption.edu/.
General Application Contact: Daniel Provost, Assistant Director of Graduate Student Services, 508-767-7426, Fax: 508-767-7030, E-mail: dprovost@assumption.edu.

GRADUATE UNITS

Graduate School Students: 195 full-time (158 women), 279 part-time (199 women); includes 65 minority (31 Black or African American, non-Hispanic/Latino; 1 American Indian or Alaska Native, non-Hispanic/Latino; 7 Asian, non-Hispanic/Latino; 22 Hispanic/Latino; 4 Two or more races, non-Hispanic/Latino), 5 international. Average age 25. 351 applicants, 88% accepted. *Faculty:* 14 full-time (4 women), 51 part-time/adjunct (21 women). Expenses: Contact institution. *Financial support:* In 2010–11, 44 students received support, including 41 fellowships with partial tuition reimbursements available (averaging $6,283 per year), 3 teaching assistantships with partial tuition reimbursements available (averaging $8,403 per year); scholarships/grants, traineeships, and unspecified assistantships also available. Financial award application deadline: 7/1; financial award applicants required to submit FAFSA. In 2010, 139 master's, 17 other advanced degrees awarded. *Degree program information:* Part-time and evening/weekend programs available. Postbaccalaureate distance learning degree programs offered (minimal on-campus study). Offers accounting (MBA); business administration (CAGS); child and family interventions (MA); cognitive-behavioral therapies (MA); counseling psychology (CAGS); finance/economics (MBA); general business (MBA); general psychology (MA); human resources (MBA); international business (MBA); management (MBA); marketing (MBA); nonprofit leadership (MBA); positive behavior support (CAGS); rehabilitation counseling (MA, CAGS); school counseling (MA, CAGS); special education (MA). *Application deadline:* For fall admission, 6/1 priority date for domestic students, 5/1 priority date for international students; for spring admission, 11/1 priority date for domestic students, 9/1 priority date for international students. Applications are processed on a rolling basis. *Application fee:* $30. Electronic applications accepted. *Application Contact:* Daniel Provost, Assistant Director of Graduate Student Services, 508-767-7426, Fax: 508-767-7030, E-mail: dprovost@assumption.edu. *Acting Dean of Graduate Studies*, Dr. Jeffrey G. Hunter, 508-767-7246, Fax: 508-767-7252, E-mail: jhunter@assumption.edu.

ATHABASCA UNIVERSITY, Athabasca, AB T9S 3A3, Canada

General Information Province-supported, coed, comprehensive institution. *Graduate housing:* On-campus housing not available. *Research affiliation:* SAP (software), IBM (software).

GRADUATE UNITS

Centre for Distance Education *Degree program information:* Part-time programs available. Postbaccalaureate distance learning degree programs offered (no on-campus study). Offers distance education (MDE); distance education technology (Advanced Diploma). Electronic applications accepted.

Centre for Innovative Management *Degree program information:* Part-time and evening/weekend programs available. Postbaccalaureate distance learning degree programs offered (no on-campus study). Offers business administration (MBA); information technology management (MBA); management (GDM); project management (MBA, GDM). Electronic applications accepted.

Centre for Integrated Studies *Degree program information:* Part-time and evening/weekend programs available. Postbaccalaureate distance learning degree programs offered (no on-campus study). Offers adult education (MA); community studies (MA); cultural studies (MA); educational studies (MA); global change (MA); work, organization, and leadership (MA). Electronic applications accepted.

Centre for Nursing and Health Studies *Degree program information:* Part-time programs available. Postbaccalaureate distance learning degree programs offered. Offers advanced nursing practice (MN, Advanced Diploma); generalist (MN); health studies-leadership (MHS). Electronic applications accepted.

Graduate Centre for Applied Psychology Offers art therapy (MC); career counseling (MC); counseling (Advanced Certificate); counseling psychology (MC); school counseling (MC).

School of Computing and Information Systems *Degree program information:* Part-time programs available. Postbaccalaureate distance learning degree programs offered (no on-campus study). Offers information systems (M Sc). Electronic applications accepted.

THE ATHENAEUM OF OHIO, Cincinnati, OH 45230-5900

General Information Independent-religious, coed, graduate-only institution. *Graduate housing:* Room and/or apartments guaranteed to single students; on-campus housing not available to married students.

GRADUATE UNITS

Graduate Programs *Degree program information:* Part-time and evening/weekend programs available. Offers biblical studies (MABS); divinity (M Div); lay ministry (Certificate); pastoral counseling (MAPC); pastoral ministry (MA); theology (MA Th).

ATLANTA'S JOHN MARSHALL LAW SCHOOL, Atlanta, GA 30309

General Information Private, coed, graduate-only institution. *Enrollment by degree level:* 630 first professional, 9 other advanced degrees. *Graduate faculty:* 40 full-time (21 women), 17 part-time/adjunct (6 women). *Tuition:* Full-time $32,250; part-time $19,350 per year. *Required fees:* $715; $715 per year. *Student services:* Campus employment opportunities, career counseling, free psychological counseling, low-cost health insurance, services for students with disabilities, writing training. *Library facilities:* Atlanta's John Marshall Law School Library. *Online resources:* library catalog, web page. *Collection:* 168,663 titles, 2,723 serial subscriptions, 548 audiovisual materials.
Computer facilities: 24 computers available on campus for general student use. A campuswide network can be accessed from off campus. Online class registration is available. *Web address:* http://www.johnmarshall.edu/.
General Application Contact: Crystal Ridgley, Assistant Director of Admissions, 404-872-3593 Ext. 265, Fax: 404-873-8302, E-mail: cridgley@johnmarshalal.edu.

GRADUATE UNITS

Graduate Program Students: 455 full-time (207 women), 184 part-time (101 women); includes 118 minority (84 Black or African American, non-Hispanic/Latino; 6 American Indian or Alaska Native, non-Hispanic/Latino; 2 Asian, non-Hispanic/Latino; 15 Hispanic/Latino; 11 Native Hawaiian or other Pacific Islander, non-Hispanic/Latino). Average age 24. 1,969 applicants, 42% accepted, 265 enrolled. *Faculty:* 40 full-time (21 women), 17 part-time/adjunct (6 women). Expenses: Contact institution. *Financial support:* In 2010–11, 514 students received support. Applicants required to submit FAFSA. In 2010, 166 first professional degrees awarded. *Degree program information:* Part-time and evening/weekend programs available. Postbaccalaureate distance learning degree programs offered (minimal on-campus study). Offers employment law (LL M); law (JD). *Application deadline:* Applications are processed on a rolling basis. *Application fee:* $50. Electronic applications accepted. *Application Contact:* Crystal Ridgley, Assistant Director of Admissions, 404-872-3593 Ext. 265, Fax: 404-873-3802, E-mail: cridgley@johnmarshall.edu. *Associate Dean for Academic Affairs*, Kevin Cieply, 404-872-3593 Ext. 264, Fax: 404-873-3802, E-mail: kcieply@johnmarshall.edu.

ATLANTIC COLLEGE, Guaynabo, PR 00970

General Information Independent, coed, comprehensive institution.

GRADUATE UNITS

Program in Graphic Arts *Degree program information:* Part-time programs available. Offers digital graphic design (MGD).

ATLANTIC INSTITUTE OF ORIENTAL MEDICINE, Fort Lauderdale, FL 33301

General Information Independent, coed, graduate-only institution. *Enrollment by degree level:* 134 master's. *Graduate faculty:* 8 full-time (1 woman), 18 part-time/adjunct (7 women). *Tuition:* Full-time $13,000. *Required fees:* $725. Full-time tuition and fees vary according to course level and campus/location. *Student services:* Campus employment opportunities, campus safety program, career counseling, exercise/wellness program, international student services. *Collection:* 2,751 titles.
Computer facilities: 3 computers available on campus for general student use. *Web address:* http://www.atom.edu/.
General Application Contact: Karen Gemignani, Admissions Counselor, 954-763-9840 Ext. 213, Fax: 954-763-9844, E-mail: admissions@atom.edu.

GRADUATE UNITS

Graduate Program Students: 134 full-time (100 women); includes 23 minority (3 Black or African American, non-Hispanic/Latino; 7 Asian, non-Hispanic/Latino; 13 Hispanic/Latino), 7 international. *Faculty:* 8 full-time (1 woman), 18 part-time/adjunct (7 women). Expenses: Contact institution. *Degree program information:* Evening/weekend programs available. Offers Oriental medicine (MS). *Application deadline:* For fall admission, 7/1 for domestic students, 5/1 for international students; for spring admission, 11/30 for domestic students, 2/28 for international students. Applications are processed on a rolling basis. *Application fee:* $20 ($100 for international students). *Application Contact:* Milagros Ferreira, Registrar, 954-763-9840 Ext. 207, Fax: 954-763-9844, E-mail: registrar@atom.edu. *President*, Dr. Johanna C. Yen, 954-763-9840 Ext. 202, Fax: 954-763-9844, E-mail: president@atom.edu.

ATLANTIC SCHOOL OF THEOLOGY, Halifax, NS B3H 3B5, Canada

General Information Independent, coed, graduate-only institution. *Graduate housing:* Rooms and/or apartments available on a first-come, first-served basis to single and married students. Housing application deadline: 6/1.

GRADUATE UNITS

Graduate and Professional Programs *Degree program information:* Part-time programs available. Postbaccalaureate distance learning degree programs offered (minimal on-campus study). Offers ministry (M Div); theological studies (Graduate Certificate).

ATLANTIC UNION COLLEGE, South Lancaster, MA 01561-1000

General Information Independent-religious, coed, comprehensive institution. *Graduate housing:* Room and/or apartments available to single students; on-campus housing not available to married students.

GRADUATE UNITS

Graduate Education Program *Degree program information:* Part-time programs available. Postbaccalaureate distance learning degree programs offered (minimal on-campus study). Offers education (M Ed). Offered during summer only.

ATLANTIC UNIVERSITY, Virginia Beach, VA 23451-2061

General Information Independent, coed, primarily women, graduate-only institution. *Enrollment by degree level:* 174 master's. *Graduate faculty:* 23 part-time/adjunct (10 women). *Required fees:* $795 per course. One-time fee: $50 part-time. *Graduate housing:* On-campus housing not available.
Computer facilities: We're an online university available. *Web address:* http://www.atlanticuniv.edu/.
General Application Contact: Candis Collins, Director of Admissions, 757-631-8101, Fax: 757-631-8096, E-mail: candis.collins@atlanticuniv.edu.

GRADUATE UNITS

Program in Transpersonal Studies Students: 174 part-time (122 women); includes 8 minority (3 Black or African American, non-Hispanic/Latino; 3 Asian, non-Hispanic/Latino; 2 Hispanic/Latino), 5 international. Average age 46. 109 applicants, 33% accepted, 36 enrolled. *Faculty:* 23 part-time/adjunct (10 women). Expenses: Contact institution. In 2010, 15 master's awarded. *Degree program information:* Part-time and evening/weekend programs available. Postbaccalaureate distance learning degree programs offered (no on-campus study). Offers transpersonal studies (MA). *Application deadline:* Applications are processed on a rolling basis. *Application fee:* $50. Electronic applications accepted. *Application Contact:* Candis Collins, Director of Admissions, 757-631-8101, Fax: 757-631-8096, E-mail: candis.collins@atlanticuniv.edu. *Chief Executive Officer*, Kevin J. Todeschi, 757-631-8101, Fax: 757-631-8096.

A.T. STILL UNIVERSITY OF HEALTH SCIENCES, Kirksville, MO 63501

General Information Independent, coed, graduate-only institution. *Enrollment by degree level:* 1,371 first professional, 911 master's, 1,186 doctoral, 96 other advanced degrees. *Graduate faculty:* 146 full-time (60 women), 466 part-time/adjunct (221 women). *Graduate housing:* Rooms and/or apartments available on a first-come, first-served basis to single and married students. Typical cost: $4740 (including board) for single students; $4740 (including board) for married students. Housing application deadline: 4/1. *Student services:* Campus employment opportunities, career counseling, exercise/wellness program, free psychological counseling, services for students with disabilities. *Library facilities:* A. T. Still Memorial Library. *Online resources:* library catalog, web page, access to other libraries' catalogs. *Collection:* 70,608 titles, 7,092 serial subscriptions, 2,713 audiovisual materials. *Research affiliation:* Truman State University (osteopathic clinical research), University of Arizona College of Medicine-Phoenix (osteopathic/biomedical clinical research), British School of Osteopathy (osteopathic manual medicine), European School of Osteopathy (osteopathic manual medicine), Nordic Academy of Osteopathy (osteopathic clinical research), Ridgway Integrative Medicine (osteopathic clinical research).
Computer facilities: 45 computers available on campus for general student use. A campuswide network can be accessed from student residence rooms and from off campus. *Web address:* http://www.atsu.edu/.
General Application Contact: Donna Sparks, Associate Director for Admissions, 660-626-2237, Fax: 660-626-2969, E-mail: admissions@atsu.edu.

GRADUATE UNITS

Arizona School of Dentistry and Oral Health Students: 271 full-time (133 women); includes 7 Black or African American, non-Hispanic/Latino; 10 American Indian or Alaska Native, non-Hispanic/Latino; 46 Asian, non-Hispanic/Latino; 19 Hispanic/Latino. Average age 27. 3,178 applicants, 4% accepted, 70 enrolled. *Faculty:* 27 full-time (12 women), 116 part-time/adjunct (38 women). Expenses: Contact institution. *Financial support:* In 2010–11, 12 students received support. Federal Work-Study and scholarships/grants available. Financial award application deadline: 5/1; financial award applicants required to submit FAFSA. In 2010, 60 DMDs, 4 other advanced degrees awarded. Offers dental medicine (DMD); orthodontics (Certificate). *Application deadline:* For fall admission, 12/1 for domestic and international students. Applications are processed on a rolling basis. *Application fee:* $60. Electronic applications accepted. *Application Contact:* Donna Sparks, Associate Director for Admissions, 660-626-2237, Fax: 660-626-2969, E-mail: admissions@atsu.edu. *Dean,* Dr. Jack Dillenberg, 480-219-6000, Fax: 480-219-6110, E-mail: jdillenberg@atsu.edu.

Arizona School of Health Sciences Students: 523 full-time (367 women), 1,048 part-time (703 women); includes 73 Black or African American, non-Hispanic/Latino; 21 American Indian or Alaska Native, non-Hispanic/Latino; 184 Asian, non-Hispanic/Latino; 38 Hispanic/Latino; 10 Native Hawaiian or other Pacific Islander, non-Hispanic/Latino, 4 international. Average age 35. 3,049 applicants, 10% accepted, 184 enrolled. *Faculty:* 42 full-time (26 women), 237 part-time/adjunct (141 women). Expenses: Contact institution. *Financial support:* In 2010–11, 13 students received support. Federal Work-Study and scholarships/grants available. Financial award application deadline: 5/1; financial award applicants required to submit FAFSA. In 2010, 255 master's, 514 doctorates awarded. Postbaccalaureate distance learning degree programs offered (no on-campus study). Offers advanced occupational therapy (MS); advanced physician assistant (MS); athletic training (MS); audiology (Au D); health sciences (DHSc); human movement (MS); occupational therapy (MS); physical therapy (DPT); physician assistant (MS); transitional audiology (Au D); transitional physical therapy (DPT). *Application deadline:* For fall admission, 8/1 priority date for domestic and international students. Applications are processed on a rolling basis. *Application fee:* $60. *Application Contact:* Donna Sparks, Associate Director for Admissions, 660-626-2237, Fax: 660-626-2969, E-mail: admissions@atsu.edu. *Interim Dean,* Dr. Barbara Maxwell, 480-219-6000, Fax: 480-219-6110, E-mail: bmaxwell@atsu.edu.

Kirksville College of Osteopathic Medicine Students: 716 full-time (286 women), 9 part-time (3 women); includes 115 minority (13 Black or African American, non-Hispanic/Latino; 5 American Indian or Alaska Native, non-Hispanic/Latino; 75 Asian, non-Hispanic/Latino; 19 Hispanic/Latino; 2 Native Hawaiian or other Pacific Islander, non-Hispanic/Latino; 1 Two or more races, non-Hispanic/Latino), 11 international. Average age 26. 3,483 applicants, 11% accepted, 172 enrolled. *Faculty:* 34 full-time (6 women), 17 part-time/adjunct (3 women). Expenses: Contact institution. *Financial support:* In 2010–11, 192 students received support, including 20 fellowships with full tuition reimbursements available (averaging $16,000 per year); Federal Work-Study and scholarships/grants also available. Financial award application deadline: 5/1; financial award applicants required to submit FAFSA. In 2010, 165 first professional degrees, 9 master's awarded. Offers biomedical sciences (MS); osteopathic medicine (DO). *Application deadline:* For fall admission, 2/1 for domestic and international students. Applications are processed on a rolling basis. *Application fee:* $60. Electronic applications accepted. *Application Contact:* Donna Sparks, Associate Director for Admissions, 660-626-2237, Fax: 660-626-2969, E-mail: admissions@atsu.edu. *Acting Dean,* Dr. Jeff Suzewits, 660-626-2354, Fax: 660-626-2080, E-mail: jsuzewits@atsu.edu.

School of Health Management Students: 87 full-time (59 women), 503 part-time (340 women); includes 147 minority (74 Black or African American, non-Hispanic/Latino; 7 American Indian or Alaska Native, non-Hispanic/Latino; 38 Asian, non-Hispanic/Latino; 26 Hispanic/Latino; 1 Native Hawaiian or other Pacific Islander, non-Hispanic/Latino; 1 Two or more races, non-Hispanic/Latino). Average age 34. 121 applicants, 100% accepted, 105 enrolled. *Faculty:* 12 full-time (6 women), 65 part-time/adjunct (29 women). Expenses: Contact institution. *Financial support:* In 2010–11, 10 students received support. Scholarships/grants available. Financial award application deadline: 5/1; financial award applicants required to submit FAFSA. In 2010, 141 master's, 40 doctorates awarded. *Degree program information:* Part-time and evening/weekend programs available. Postbaccalaureate distance learning degree programs offered (minimal on-campus study). Offers dental emphasis (MPH); geriatric healthcare (MGH); health administration (MHA); health education (MH Ed, DH Ed); public health (MPH). *Application deadline:* For fall admission, 7/9 for domestic and international students; for winter admission, 10/23 for domestic students, 10/1 for international students; for spring admission, 1/15 for domestic students, 1/14 for international students. Applications are processed on a rolling basis. *Application fee:* $60. Electronic applications accepted. *Application Contact:* Sarah Spencer, Director of Recruitment, 660-626-2820 Ext. 2669, Fax: 660-626-2826, E-mail: sbartlett@atsu.edu. *Interim Dean,* Dr. Kimberly O'Reilly, 660-626-2820, Fax: 660-626-2826, E-mail: koreilley@atsu.edu.

School of Osteopathic Medicine in Arizona Students: 407 full-time (196 women); includes 10 Black or African American, non-Hispanic/Latino; 12 American Indian or Alaska Native, non-Hispanic/Latino; 100 Asian, non-Hispanic/Latino; 37 Hispanic/Latino; 2 Native Hawaiian or other Pacific Islander, non-Hispanic/Latino. Average age 28. 3,630 applicants, 9% accepted, 108 enrolled. *Faculty:* 30 full-time (9 women), 34 part-time/adjunct (10 women). Expenses: Contact institution. *Financial support:* In 2010–11, 284 students received support. Federal Work-Study and scholarships/grants available. Financial award application deadline: 5/1; financial award applicants required to submit FAFSA. Offers osteopathic medicine (DO). *Application deadline:* For fall admission, 3/1 for domestic students. Applications are processed on a rolling basis. *Application fee:* $60. Electronic applications accepted. *Application Contact:* Donna Sparks, Associate Director for Admissions, 660-626-2237, Fax: 660-626-2969, E-mail: admissions@atsu.edu. *Interim Dean,* Dr. Thomas McWilliams, 480-219-6000, Fax: 480-219-6110, E-mail: tmcwilliams@atsu.edu.

AUBURN UNIVERSITY, Auburn University, AL 36849

General Information State-supported, coed, university. CGS member. *Enrollment:* 25,078 graduate, professional, and undergraduate students; 2,609 full-time matriculated graduate/professional students (1,430 women), 2,067 part-time matriculated graduate/professional students (950 women). *Enrollment by degree level:* 987 first professional, 2,262 master's, 1,365 doctoral, 62 other advanced degrees. *Graduate faculty:* 1,143 full-time (374 women), 131 part-time/adjunct (61 women). *International tuition:* $22,116 full-time. Tuition, state resident: full-time $7002. Tuition, nonresident: full-time $21,898. *Required fees:* $892. Tuition and fees vary according to course load and program. *Graduate housing:* Rooms and/or apartments available on a first-come, first-served basis to single and married students. Typical cost: $9630 (including board) for married students. *Student services:* Campus employment opportunities, campus safety program, career counseling, exercise/wellness program, free psychological counseling, international student services, low-cost health insurance, multicultural affairs office, services for students with disabilities, teacher training, writing training. *Library facilities:* R. B. Draughon Library plus 2 others. *Online resources:* library catalog, web page, access to other libraries' catalogs. *Collection:* 3.5 million titles, 256,354 serial subscriptions, 121,403 audiovisual materials. *Research affiliation:* National Center of Excellence for Airliner Cabin Environmental Research (aerospace, polymer and fibers engineering), National Textile Center Consortium (polymer and fibers engineering), National Asphalt Pavement Association (asphalt technology, civil engineering), Consortium for Vehicle Electronics (mechanical and automotive, electrical engineering), Tay-Sachs Gene Therapy Consortium (veterinary medicine, clinical sciences), Higher Education Consortium for Special Education (special and rehabilitative education).

Computer facilities: Computer purchase and lease plans are available. 1,722 computers available on campus for general student use. A campuswide network can be accessed from student residence rooms and from off campus. Online class registration, pay Bursar online, course materials available online are available. *Web address:* http://www.auburn.edu/.

General Application Contact: Dr. George Flowers, Dean of the Graduate School, 334-844-2125, E-mail: flowegt@auburn.edu.

GRADUATE UNITS

College of Veterinary Medicine Students: 389 full-time (270 women), 71 part-time (49 women); includes 9 Black or African American, non-Hispanic/Latino; 2 American Indian or Alaska Native, non-Hispanic/Latino; 5 Asian, non-Hispanic/Latino; 9 Hispanic/Latino, 22 international. Average age 26. *Faculty:* 100 full-time (40 women), 5 part-time/adjunct (1 woman). Expenses: Contact institution. *Financial support:* Fellowships, research assistantships, teaching assistantships, Federal Work-Study available. Support available to part-time students. Financial award application deadline: 3/15; financial award applicants required to submit FAFSA. In 2010, 96 first professional degrees, 12 master's, 7 doctorates awarded. *Degree program information:* Part-time programs available. Offers biomedical sciences (MS, PhD); veterinary medicine (DVM, MS, PhD). *Application deadline:* For fall admission, 7/7 for domestic students. Applications are processed on a rolling basis. *Application fee:* $50 ($60 for international students). *Application Contact:* Dr. George Flowers, Interim Dean of the Graduate School, 334-844-4700. *Dean,* Dr. Timothy R. Boosinger, 334-844-4546.

Graduate School Students: 2,609 full-time (1,430 women), 2,067 part-time (950 women); includes 382 Black or African American, non-Hispanic/Latino; 22 American Indian or Alaska Native, non-Hispanic/Latino; 121 Asian, non-Hispanic/Latino; 83 Hispanic/Latino, 834 international. Average age 29. 4,237 applicants, 55% accepted, 1398 enrolled. *Faculty:* 1,143 full-time (374 women), 131 part-time/adjunct (61 women). Expenses: Contact institution. *Financial support:* Fellowships, research assistantships, teaching assistantships, career-related internships or fieldwork and Federal Work-Study available. Support available to part-time students. Financial award applicants required to submit FAFSA. In 2010, 865 master's, 213 doctorates, 8 other advanced degrees awarded. *Degree program information:* Part-time and evening/weekend programs available. Offers cell and molecular biology (PhD); integrated textile and apparel sciences (PhD); rural sociology (MS); sociology (MA, MS); sociology and rural sociology (MA, MS). *Application deadline:* For fall admission, 7/7 for domestic students; for spring admission, 11/24 for domestic students. *Application fee:* $50 ($60 for international students). *Application Contact:* Dr. George Flowers, Dean of the Graduate School, 334-844-4700, E-mail: gradadm@auburn.edu. *Dean,* Dr. George Flowers, 334-844-4700, E-mail: gradadm@auburn.edu.

College of Agriculture Students: 133 full-time (54 women), 123 part-time (48 women); includes 8 Black or African American, non-Hispanic/Latino; 2 American Indian or Alaska Native, non-Hispanic/Latino; 6 Asian, non-Hispanic/Latino; 3 Hispanic/Latino, 106 international. Average age 29. 204 applicants, 45% accepted, 55 enrolled. *Faculty:* 150 full-time (30 women), 1 part-time/adjunct (0 women). Expenses: Contact institution. *Financial support:* Fellowships, research assistantships, teaching assistantships, Federal Work-Study available. Support available to part-time students. Financial award application deadline: 3/15; financial award applicants required to submit FAFSA. In 2010, 48 master's, 17 doctorates awarded. *Degree program information:* Part-time programs available. Offers agricultural economics (M Ag, MS); agriculture (M Ag, M Aq, MS, PhD); agronomy and soils (M Ag, MS, PhD); animal sciences (M Ag, MS, PhD); applied economics (PhD); entomology (M Ag, MS, PhD); fisheries and allied aquacultures (M Aq, MS, PhD); horticulture (M Ag, MS, PhD); plant pathology (M Ag, MS, PhD); poultry science (M Ag, MS, PhD). *Application deadline:* For fall admission, 7/7 for domestic students; for spring admission, 11/24 for domestic students. Applications are processed on a rolling basis. *Application fee:* $50 ($60 for international students). Electronic applications accepted. *Application Contact:* Dr. George Flowers, Dean of the Graduate School, 334-844-2125. *Dean,* William Batchelor, 334-844-2345.

College of Architecture, Design, and Construction Students: 111 full-time (41 women), 43 part-time (12 women); includes 8 Black or African American, non-Hispanic/Latino; 1 Asian, non-Hispanic/Latino; 3 Hispanic/Latino, 22 international. Average age 26. 250 applicants, 58% accepted, 97 enrolled. *Faculty:* 61 full-time (12 women), 6 part-time/adjunct (2 women). Expenses: Contact institution. *Financial support:* Fellowships, Federal Work-Study available. Support available to part-time students. Financial award application deadline: 3/15; financial award applicants required to submit FAFSA. In 2010, 37 master's awarded. *Degree program information:* Part-time programs available. Offers architecture, design, and construction (MBS, MCP, MDB, MID, MLA); building science (MBS); community planning (MCP); construction management (MBS); design-build (MDB); industrial design (MID); landscape architecture (MLA). *Application deadline:* For fall admission, 7/7 for domestic students; for spring admission, 11/24 for domestic students. Applications are processed on a rolling basis. *Application fee:* $50 ($60 for international students). Electronic applications accepted. *Application Contact:* Dr. George Flowers, Dean of the Graduate School, 334-844-2125. *Dean,* Dr. Vini Nathan, 334-844-4285.

College of Business Students: 168 full-time (75 women), 424 part-time (123 women); includes 36 Black or African American, non-Hispanic/Latino; 4 American Indian or Alaska Native, non-Hispanic/Latino; 23 Asian, non-Hispanic/Latino; 18 Hispanic/Latino, 39 international. Average age 32. 742 applicants, 48% accepted, 225 enrolled. *Faculty:* 75 full-time (17 women), 15 part-time/adjunct (6 women). Expenses: Contact institution. *Financial support:* Fellowships, research assistantships, teaching assistantships, career-related internships or fieldwork and Federal Work-Study available. Support available to part-time students. Financial award application deadline: 3/15; financial award applicants required to submit FAFSA. In 2010, 224 master's, 6 doctorates awarded. *Degree program information:* Part-time programs available. Offers accountancy (M Acc); business (M Acc, MBA, MRED, MS, PhD); business administration (MBA); finance (MS); human resource management (PhD); management (MS, PhD); management information systems (MS, PhD). *Application deadline:* For fall admission, 7/7 for domestic students; for spring admission, 11/24 for domestic students. Applications are processed on a rolling basis. *Application fee:* $50 ($60 for international students). Electronic applications accepted. *Application Contact:* Dr. George Flowers, Dean of the Graduate School, 334-844-2125. *Dean,* Dr. Bill Hardgrave.

College of Education Students: 363 full-time (258 women), 476 part-time (328 women); includes 177 Black or African American, non-Hispanic/Latino; 2 American Indian or Alaska Native, non-Hispanic/Latino; 9 Asian, non-Hispanic/Latino; 15 Hispanic/Latino, 26 international. Average age 33. 699 applicants, 61% accepted, 303 enrolled. *Faculty:* 85 full-time (52 women), 23 part-time/adjunct (15 women). Expenses: Contact institution. *Financial support:* Fellowships, research assistantships, teaching assistantships, career-related internships or fieldwork and Federal Work-Study available. Support available to part-time students. Financial award application deadline: 3/15; financial award applicants required to submit FAFSA. In 2010, 207 master's, 50 doctorates, 8 other advanced degrees awarded. *Degree program information:* Part-time programs available. Offers adult education (M Ed, MS, Ed D); business education (M Ed, MS, PhD); collaborative teacher special education (M Ed, MS); curriculum and instruction (M Ed, MS, Ed D, Ed S); curriculum supervision (M Ed, MS, Ed D, Ed S); early childhood education (M Ed, MS, PhD, Ed S); early childhood special education (M Ed, MS); education (M Ed, MS, Ed D, PhD, Ed S); educational psychology (PhD); elementary education (M Ed, MS, PhD, Ed S); exercise science (M Ed, MS, PhD); foreign languages (M Ed, MS); health promotion (M Ed, MS); higher education administration (M Ed, MS, Ed D, Ed S); kinesiology (PhD); media instructional design (MS); media specialist (M Ed); music education (M Ed, MS, PhD, Ed S); physical education/teacher education (M Ed, MS, Ed D, Ed S); postsecondary education (PhD); reading education (PhD, Ed S); rehabilitation counseling (M Ed, MS, PhD); school administration (M Ed, MS, Ed D, Ed S); secondary education (M Ed, MS, PhD, Ed S). *Application fee:* $50 ($60 for international students). Electronic applications accepted. *Application Contact:* Dr. George Flowers, Dean of the Graduate School, 334-844-2125. *Dean,* Dr. Frances Kochan, 334-844-4446.

College of Human Sciences Students: 49 full-time (39 women), 46 part-time (34 women); includes 19 Black or African American, non-Hispanic/Latino; 6 Asian, non-Hispanic/Latino; 3 Hispanic/Latino, 15 international. Average age 29. 151 applicants, 47% accepted, 30 enrolled. *Faculty:* 50 full-time (33 women), 2 part-time/adjunct (both women). Expenses: Contact institution. *Financial support:* Fellowships, research assistantships, teaching assistantships, career-related internships or fieldwork and Federal Work-Study available. Support available to part-time students. Financial award application deadline: 3/15; financial award applicants required to submit FAFSA. In 2010, 33 master's, 7 doctorates awarded. *Degree program information:* Part-time programs available. Offers apparel and textiles (MS); human development and family studies (MS, PhD); human sciences (MS, PhD); nutrition and food science (MS, PhD). *Application deadline:* For fall admission, 7/7 for domestic students; for spring admission, 11/24 for domestic students. Applications are processed on a rolling basis. *Application fee:* $50 ($60 for international students). Electronic

Auburn University (continued)

applications accepted. *Application Contact:* Dr. George Flowers, Dean of the Graduate School, 334-844-2125. *Dean*, Dr. June Henton, 334-844-3790, E-mail: jhenton@humsci.auburn.edu.

College of Liberal Arts Students: 233 full-time (159 women), 214 part-time (126 women); includes 29 Black or African American, non-Hispanic/Latino; 9 Asian, non-Hispanic/Latino; 14 Hispanic/Latino, 15 international. Average age 28. 688 applicants, 31% accepted, 154 enrolled. *Faculty:* 229 full-time (109 women), 53 part-time/adjunct (29 women). Expenses: Contact institution. *Financial support:* Fellowships, research assistantships, teaching assistantships, career-related internships or fieldwork and Federal Work-Study available. Support available to part-time students. Financial award application deadline: 3/15; financial award applicants required to submit FAFSA. In 2010, 118 master's, 30 doctorates awarded. *Degree program information:* Part-time programs available. Offers applied behavior analysis in developmental disabilities (MS); audiology (MCD, MS, Au D); clinical psychology (PhD); communication (MA); economics (MS); English (MA, MTPC, PhD); experimental psychology (PhD); history (MA, PhD); industrial/organizational psychology (PhD); liberal arts (MA, MCD, MHS, MPA, MS, MTPC, Au D, PhD); mass communications (MA); public administration (MPA, PhD); Spanish (MA, MHS); speech pathology (MCD, MS). *Application deadline:* For fall admission, 7/7 for domestic students; for spring admission, 11/24 for domestic students. Applications are processed on a rolling basis. *Application fee:* $50 ($60 for international students). Electronic applications accepted. *Application Contact:* Dr. George Flowers, Dean of the Graduate School, 334-844-2125. *Dean*, Dr. Anne-Katrin Gramberg, 334-844-2185.

College of Sciences and Mathematics Students: 165 full-time (51 women), 158 part-time (70 women); includes 10 Black or African American, non-Hispanic/Latino; 1 American Indian or Alaska Native, non-Hispanic/Latino; 6 Asian, non-Hispanic/Latino; 6 Hispanic/Latino, 128 international. Average age 28. 457 applicants, 37% accepted, 57 enrolled. *Faculty:* 151 full-time (25 women), 6 part-time/adjunct (2 women). Expenses: Contact institution. *Financial support:* Fellowships, research assistantships, teaching assistantships, career-related internships or fieldwork and Federal Work-Study available. Support available to part-time students. Financial award applicants required to submit FAFSA. In 2010, 49 master's, 38 doctorates awarded. *Degree program information:* Part-time programs available. Offers analytical chemistry (MS, PhD); applied mathematics (MAM, MS); biochemistry (MS, PhD); botany (MS, PhD); geography (MS); geology (MS); inorganic chemistry (MS, PhD); mathematics (MS, PhD); microbiology (MS, PhD); organic chemistry (MS, PhD); physical chemistry (MS, PhD); physics (MS, PhD); probability and statistics (M Prob S); sciences and mathematics (M Prob S, MAM, MS, PhD); statistics (MS); zoology (MS, PhD). *Application deadline:* For fall admission, 7/7 for domestic students; for spring admission, 11/24 for domestic students. Applications are processed on a rolling basis. *Application fee:* $50 ($60 for international students). *Application Contact:* Dr. George Flowers, Dean of the Graduate School, 334-844-2125. *Interim Dean*, Charles Savrda, 334-844-5737.

Ginn College of Engineering Students: 407 full-time (96 women), 347 part-time (70 women); includes 40 Black or African American, non-Hispanic/Latino; 2 American Indian or Alaska Native, non-Hispanic/Latino; 15 Asian, non-Hispanic/Latino; 8 Hispanic/Latino, 385 international. Average age 28. 1,512 applicants, 44% accepted, 162 enrolled. *Faculty:* 146 full-time (12 women), 17 part-time/adjunct (2 women). Expenses: Contact institution. *Financial support:* Fellowships, research assistantships, teaching assistantships, Federal Work-Study available. Support available to part-time students. Financial award application deadline: 3/15; financial award applicants required to submit FAFSA. In 2010, 125 master's, 48 doctorates awarded. *Degree program information:* Part-time programs available. Offers aerospace engineering (MAE, MS, PhD); chemical engineering (M Ch E, MS, PhD); computer science and software engineering (MS, MSWE, PhD); construction engineering and management (MCE, MS, PhD); electrical and computer engineering (MEE, MS, PhD); engineering (M Ch E, M Mtl E, MAE, MCE, MEE, MISE, MME, MS, MSWE, PhD); environmental engineering (MCE, MS, PhD); geotechnical/materials engineering (MCE, MS, PhD); hydraulics/hydrology (MCE, MS, PhD); industrial and systems engineering (MISE, MS, PhD); materials engineering (M Mtl E, MS, PhD); mechanical engineering (MME, MS, PhD); structural engineering (MCE, MS, PhD); transportation engineering (MCE, MS, PhD). *Application deadline:* For fall admission, 7/7 for domestic students; for spring admission, 11/24 for domestic students. Applications are processed on a rolling basis. *Application fee:* $50 ($60 for international students). Electronic applications accepted. *Application Contact:* Dr. George Flowers, Dean of the Graduate School, 334-844-2125. *Dean*, Dr. Larry Benefield, 334-844-2308.

School of Forestry and Wildlife Sciences Students: 29 full-time (12 women), 53 part-time (17 women); includes 1 Black or African American, non-Hispanic/Latino; 1 Asian, non-Hispanic/Latino; 1 Hispanic/Latino, 28 international. Average age 28. 55 applicants, 44% accepted, 17 enrolled. *Faculty:* 28 full-time (5 women), 2 part-time/adjunct (0 women). Expenses: Contact institution. *Financial support:* Fellowships, research assistantships, teaching assistantships, Federal Work-Study available. Support available to part-time students. Financial award application deadline: 3/15; financial award applicants required to submit FAFSA. In 2010, 5 master's, 3 doctorates awarded. *Degree program information:* Part-time programs available. Offers forest economics (PhD); forestry (MS, PhD); natural resource conservation (MNR); wildlife sciences (MS, PhD). *Application deadline:* For fall admission, 7/7 for domestic students; for spring admission, 11/24 for domestic students. Applications are processed on a rolling basis. *Application fee:* $50 ($60 for international students). Electronic applications accepted. *Application Contact:* Dr. George Flowers, Dean of the Graduate School, 334-844-2125. *Dean*, Dr. James P. Shepard, 334-844-4000, Fax: 334-844-1084, E-mail: brinker@forestry.auburn.edu.

School of Nursing Expenses: Contact institution. Offers nursing (MSN). *Application Contact:* Dr. George Flowers, Dean of the Graduate School, 334-844-4700, E-mail: gradadm@auburn.edu. *Dean*, Dr. Gregg Newschwander, 334-844-3658, E-mail: gen0002@auburn.edu.

Harrison School of Pharmacy Students: 535 full-time (361 women), 53 part-time (34 women); includes 40 Black or African American, non-Hispanic/Latino; 8 American Indian or Alaska Native, non-Hispanic/Latino; 33 Asian, non-Hispanic/Latino; 3 Hispanic/Latino, 22 international. Average age 25. *Faculty:* 48 full-time (27 women), 1 (woman) part-time/adjunct. Expenses: Contact institution. *Financial support:* Fellowships, research assistantships, teaching assistantships, Federal Work-Study available. Support available to part-time students. Financial award applicants required to submit FAFSA. In 2010, 119 first professional degrees, 2 master's, 4 doctorates awarded. *Degree program information:* Part-time programs available. Offers pharmacal sciences (MS, PhD); pharmaceutical sciences (PhD); pharmacy (Pharm D, MS, PhD); pharmacy care systems (MS, PhD). *Application deadline:* For fall admission, 7/7 for domestic students; for spring admission, 11/24 for domestic students. Applications are processed on a rolling basis. *Application fee:* $50 ($60 for international students). Electronic applications accepted. *Application Contact:* Dr. George Flowers, Dean of the Graduate School, 334-844-2125. *Dean*, Dr. R. Lee Evans, 334-844-8348.

AUBURN UNIVERSITY MONTGOMERY, Montgomery, AL 36124-4023

General Information State-supported, coed, comprehensive institution. *Graduate housing:* Rooms and/or apartments available to single students and available on a first-come, first-served basis to married students.

GRADUATE UNITS

School of Business *Degree program information:* Part-time and evening/weekend programs available. Offers business (MBA). Electronic applications accepted.

School of Education *Degree program information:* Part-time and evening/weekend programs available. Offers counseling (M Ed, Ed S); early childhood education (M Ed, Ed S); education (M Ed, Ed S); education administration (M Ed, Ed S); elementary education (M Ed, Ed S); physical education (M Ed); reading education (M Ed, Ed S); secondary education (M Ed, Ed S); special education (M Ed, Ed S). Electronic applications accepted.

School of Liberal Arts *Degree program information:* Part-time and evening/weekend programs available. Offers liberal arts (MLA). Electronic applications accepted.

School of Sciences *Degree program information:* Part-time and evening/weekend programs available. Offers justice and public safety (MSJPS); psychology (MSPG); public administration and political science (MPA, MPS, PhD); sciences (MPA, MPS, MSJPS, MSPG, PhD). Electronic applications accepted.

AUGSBURG COLLEGE, Minneapolis, MN 55454-1351

General Information Independent-religious, coed, comprehensive institution. *Enrollment:* 4,073 graduate, professional, and undergraduate students; 616 full-time matriculated graduate/professional students (405 women), 304 part-time matriculated graduate/professional students (239 women). *Enrollment by degree level:* 899 master's, 21 doctoral. *Graduate faculty:* 30 full-time (19 women), 18 part-time/adjunct (8 women). *Tuition:* Part-time $2274 per course. *Graduate housing:* On-campus housing not available. *Student services:* Career counseling, exercise/wellness program, free psychological counseling, international student services, multicultural affairs office, services for students with disabilities. *Library facilities:* James G. Lindell Library. *Online resources:* library catalog, web page, access to other libraries' catalogs. *Collection:* 146,433 titles, 754 serial subscriptions.

Computer facilities: 260 computers available on campus for general student use. A campuswide network can be accessed from student residence rooms and from off campus. Online class registration is available. *Web address:* http://www.augsburg.edu/.

General Application Contact: Nathan Gorr, Director, Weekend College and Graduate Admissions, 612-330-1101 Ext. 1390, E-mail: gorr@augsburg.edu.

GRADUATE UNITS

Program in Business Administration *Degree program information:* Evening/weekend programs available. Offers business administration (MBA). Electronic applications accepted.

Program in Education *Degree program information:* Part-time and evening/weekend programs available. Offers education (MAE). Electronic applications accepted.

Program in Leadership *Degree program information:* Part-time and evening/weekend programs available. Offers leadership (MA).

Program in Physicians Assistant Studies Offers physicians assistant studies (MS).

Program in Social Work *Degree program information:* Part-time and evening/weekend programs available. Offers social work (MSW).

Program in Transcultural Community Health Nursing Offers transcultural community health nursing (MA).

AUGUSTANA COLLEGE, Sioux Falls, SD 57197

General Information Independent-religious, coed, comprehensive institution. *Enrollment:* 1,820 graduate, professional, and undergraduate students; 1 full-time matriculated graduate/professional student, 25 part-time matriculated graduate/professional students (9 women). *Enrollment by degree level:* 24 master's. *Graduate faculty:* 9 full-time (5 women), 1 (woman) part-time/adjunct. *Graduate housing:* Rooms and/or apartments available on a first-come, first-served basis to single and married students. Typical cost: $3048 per year for single students. Room charges vary according to board plan. Housing application deadline: 6/1. *Student services:* Campus safety program, career counseling, child daycare facilities, exercise/wellness program, international student services, low-cost health insurance, services for students with disabilities, writing training. *Library facilities:* Mikkelsen Library. *Online resources:* library catalog, web page, access to other libraries' catalogs. *Collection:* 254,791 titles, 3,576 serial subscriptions, 6,004 audiovisual materials.

Computer facilities: Computer purchase and lease plans are available. 270 computers available on campus for general student use. A campuswide network can be accessed from student residence rooms and from off campus. Online class registration is available. *Web address:* http://www.augie.edu/.

General Application Contact: Nancy Wright, Assistant, Graduate Education, 605-274-5417, Fax: 605-274-4450, E-mail: nancy.wright@augie.edu.

GRADUATE UNITS

Department of Education Expenses: Contact institution. *Financial support:* Career-related internships or fieldwork, Federal Work-Study, institutionally sponsored loans, scholarships/grants, tuition waivers (partial), and unspecified assistantships available. Financial award application deadline: 3/1; financial award applicants required to submit FAFSA. *Degree program information:* Part-time and evening/weekend programs available. Offers education (MA). *Application deadline:* For fall admission, 6/1 priority date for domestic and international students. Applications are processed on a rolling basis. *Application Contact:* Nancy Wright, Graduate Coordinator, 274-274-4043, Fax: 274-274-4450, E-mail: graduate@augie.edu. *Professor*, Dr. Sheryl Feinstein, 605-274-5211.

Program in Sports Administration and Leadership Students: 15 part-time. *Faculty:* 9 full-time (5 women), 1 (woman) part-time/adjunct. Expenses: Contact institution. Offers sports administration and leadership (MA). *Application Contact:* Nancy Wright, Assistant, Graduate Education, 605-274-5417, Fax: 605-274-4450, E-mail: nancy.wright@augie.edu. Dr. Sherry Barkley.

AUGUSTA STATE UNIVERSITY, Augusta, GA 30904-2200

General Information State-supported, coed, comprehensive institution. *Enrollment:* 413 full-time matriculated graduate/professional students (305 women), 433 part-time matriculated graduate/professional students (312 women). *Enrollment by degree level:* 780 master's, 66 other advanced degrees. *Graduate faculty:* 50 full-time (24 women), 34 part-time/adjunct (25 women). Tuition, state resident: part-time $165 per hour. Tuition, nonresident: part-time $615 per hour. *Graduate housing:* Room and/or apartments available on a first-come, first-served basis to single students; on-campus housing not available to married students. *Student services:* Campus employment opportunities, career counseling, child daycare facilities, low-cost health insurance, services for students with disabilities, teacher training. *Library facilities:* Reese Library. *Online resources:* library catalog, web page, access to other libraries' catalogs. *Research affiliation:* Veterans Administration Hospital (psychology).

Computer facilities: A campuswide network can be accessed from off campus. Online class registration is available. *Web address:* http://www.aug.edu/.

General Application Contact: Katherine Sweeney, Director of Admissions/Registrar, 706-737-1405, Fax: 706-667-4355, E-mail: ksweeney@aug.edu.

GRADUATE UNITS

Graduate Studies *Degree program information:* Part-time and evening/weekend programs available.

College of Arts and Sciences *Degree program information:* Part-time and evening/weekend programs available. Offers arts and sciences (MPA, MS); political science (MPA); psychology (MS).

College of Education *Degree program information:* Part-time and evening/weekend programs available. Offers counseling/guidance (M Ed); curriculum/instruction (M Ed); education (M Ed, MAT, Ed S); educational leadership (M Ed, Ed S); health and physical education (M Ed); special education (M Ed, Ed S); teacher leadership (M Ed); teaching/learning (MAT, Ed S).

Hull College of Business *Degree program information:* Part-time and evening/weekend programs available. Offers business (MBA).

AURORA UNIVERSITY, Aurora, IL 60506-4892

General Information Independent, coed, comprehensive institution. *Enrollment:* 388 full-time matriculated graduate/professional students (298 women), 1,417 part-time matriculated graduate/professional students (1,015 women). *Enrollment by degree level:* 1,668 master's, 131 doctoral. *Graduate faculty:* 39 full-time (19 women), 168 part-time/adjunct (89 women). *Graduate housing:* On-campus housing not available. *Student services:* Campus employment opportunities, campus safety program, career counseling, exercise/wellness program, free psychological counseling, international student services, low-cost health insurance, multicultural affairs office, services for students with disabilities, teacher training, writing training.

Library facilities: Charles B. Phillips Library. *Online resources:* library catalog, web page, access to other libraries' catalogs. *Collection:* 95,869 titles, 30,124 serial subscriptions, 7,100 audiovisual materials.

Computer facilities: 90 computers available on campus for general student use. A campuswide network can be accessed from student residence rooms and from off campus. Moodle Learning Management System available. *Web address:* http://www.aurora.edu/.

General Application Contact: Dr. Donna DeSpain, Dean of Adult and Graduate Studies, 800-742-5281, Fax: 630-844-5535, E-mail: auadmission@aurora.edu.

GRADUATE UNITS

College of Arts and Sciences Students: 3 full-time (0 women), 118 part-time (77 women); includes 1 Black or African American, non-Hispanic/Latino; 2 Asian, non-Hispanic/Latino; 9 Hispanic/Latino. Average age 35. 18 applicants, 94% accepted, 12 enrolled. *Faculty:* 6 full-time (3 women), 4 part-time/adjunct (2 women). Expenses: Contact institution. *Financial support:* Teaching assistantships, Federal Work-Study, scholarships/grants, and unspecified assistantships available. Support available to part-time students. Financial award application deadline: 4/15; financial award applicants required to submit FAFSA. In 2010, 10 master's awarded. *Degree program information:* Part-time and evening/weekend programs available. Offers elementary math and science (MATL); life science (MATL); mathematics (MATL, MS). *Application deadline:* For fall admission, 7/15 priority date for domestic students, 3/1 for international students; for spring admission, 12/15 for domestic students, 7/1 for international students. Applications are processed on a rolling basis. *Application fee:* $25. Electronic applications accepted. *Application Contact:* Marcia Koenen, Director of Adult and Graduate Studies, 800-742-5281, Fax: 630-844-6854, E-mail: auadmission@aurora.edu. *Dean,* Dr. Saib Othman, 630-844-4229, E-mail: sothman@aurora.edu.

College of Education Students: 89 full-time (65 women), 905 part-time (650 women); includes 41 Black or African American, non-Hispanic/Latino; 6 American Indian or Alaska Native, non-Hispanic/Latino; 16 Asian, non-Hispanic/Latino; 93 Hispanic/Latino. Average age 35. 393 applicants, 95% accepted, 305 enrolled. *Faculty:* 22 full-time (11 women), 114 part-time/adjunct (63 women). Expenses: Contact institution. *Financial support:* In 2010–11, 215 students received support. Federal Work-Study and scholarships/grants available. Support available to part-time students. Financial award application deadline: 4/15; financial award applicants required to submit FAFSA. In 2010, 441 master's, 25 doctorates awarded. *Degree program information:* Part-time and evening/weekend programs available. Offers curriculum and instruction (MA, Ed D); early childhood and special education (MA); education (MAT); education and administration (Ed D); educational leadership (MEL); educational technology (MATL); reading instruction (MA); special education (MA). *Application deadline:* For fall admission, 8/15 priority date for domestic students, 3/1 for international students; for spring admission, 12/15 for domestic students, 7/1 for international students. Applications are processed on a rolling basis. *Application fee:* $25. Electronic applications accepted. *Application Contact:* Marcia Koenen, Director of Adult and Graduate Studies, 800-742-5281, Fax: 630-844-6854, E-mail: auadmission@aurora.edu. *Dean,* Dr. Donald C. Wold, 630-844-1542, Fax: 630-844-5530, E-mail: dwold@aurora.edu.

College of Professional Studies Students: 275 full-time (220 women), 261 part-time (184 women); includes 75 Black or African American, non-Hispanic/Latino; 2 American Indian or Alaska Native, non-Hispanic/Latino; 4 Asian, non-Hispanic/Latino; 43 Hispanic/Latino. Average age 32. 274 applicants, 96% accepted, 197 enrolled. *Faculty:* 22 full-time (7 women), 30 part-time/adjunct (15 women). Expenses: Contact institution. *Financial support:* In 2010–11, 250 students received support; fellowships, research assistantships, teaching assistantships available. Financial award application deadline: 4/15; financial award applicants required to submit FAFSA. In 2010, 208 master's awarded. *Degree program information:* Part-time and evening/weekend programs available. Offers business (MBA); criminal justice (MS); nursing (MSN); social work (MSW, DSW). *Application deadline:* For fall admission, 8/15 priority date for domestic students, 3/1 for international students; for spring admission, 12/15 for domestic students, 7/1 for international students. Applications are processed on a rolling basis. *Application fee:* $25. Electronic applications accepted. *Application Contact:* Marcia Koenen, Director of Adult and Graduate Studies, 800-742-5281, Fax: 630-844-6854, E-mail: auadmission@aurora.edu. *Dean,* Dr. Fred McKenzie, 630-844-5420, E-mail: mckenzie@aurora.edu.

Dunham School of Business Students: 50 full-time (23 women), 109 part-time (52 women); includes 27 Black or African American, non-Hispanic/Latino; 2 Asian, non-Hispanic/Latino; 12 Hispanic/Latino. Average age 33. 59 applicants, 92% accepted, 37 enrolled. *Faculty:* 11 full-time (2 women), 15 part-time/adjunct (5 women). Expenses: Contact institution. *Financial support:* In 2010–11, 35 students received support. Federal Work-Study and scholarships/grants available. Support available to part-time students. Financial award application deadline: 4/15; financial award applicants required to submit FAFSA. In 2010, 72 master's awarded. *Degree program information:* Part-time and evening/weekend programs available. Offers business (MBA). *Application deadline:* For fall admission, 8/15 priority date for domestic students, 3/1 for international students; for spring admission, 12/15 for domestic students, 7/1 for international students. Applications are processed on a rolling basis. *Application fee:* $25. Electronic applications accepted. *Application Contact:* Marcia Koenen, Director of Adult and Graduate Studies, 800-742-5281, Fax: 630-844-6854, E-mail: auadmission@aurora.edu. *Director,* Charles Edwards, 630-844-3847, Fax: 630-844-7830, E-mail: cedwards@aurora.edu.

School of Social Work Students: 225 full-time (197 women), 152 part-time (132 women); includes 48 Black or African American, non-Hispanic/Latino; 2 American Indian or Alaska Native, non-Hispanic/Latino; 2 Asian, non-Hispanic/Latino; 31 Hispanic/Latino. Average age 32. 215 applicants, 97% accepted, 160 enrolled. *Faculty:* 11 full-time (5 women), 15 part-time/adjunct (10 women). Expenses: Contact institution. *Financial support:* In 2010–11, 201 students received support. Federal Work-Study and scholarships/grants available. Support available to part-time students. Financial award application deadline: 4/15; financial award applicants required to submit FAFSA. In 2010, 136 master's awarded. *Degree program information:* Part-time and evening/weekend programs available. Offers social work (MSW, DSW). *Application deadline:* For fall admission, 8/15 priority date for domestic students, 3/1 for international students; for spring admission, 12/15 for domestic students, 7/1 for international students. Applications are processed on a rolling basis. *Application fee:* $25. Electronic applications accepted. *Application Contact:* Marcia Koenen, Director of Adult and Graduate Studies, 800-742-5281, Fax: 630-844-6854, E-mail: auadmission@aurora.edu. *Director,* Dr. Stephanie Brzuzy, 630-844-7842, E-mail: sbrzuzy@aurora.edu.

George Williams College of Aurora University Students: 11 full-time (5 women), 4 part-time (all women); includes 1 Black or African American, non-Hispanic/Latino. Average age 28. 16 applicants. *Faculty:* 2 full-time (0 women), 2 part-time/adjunct (1 woman). Expenses: Contact institution. *Financial support:* In 2010–11, 8 students received support. Federal Work-Study, scholarships/grants, and unspecified assistantships available. Support available to part-time students. Financial award application deadline: 4/15. In 2010, 20 master's awarded. *Degree program information:* Part-time and evening/weekend programs available. Offers recreation administration (MS). *Application deadline:* For fall admission, 8/15 priority date for domestic students, 3/1 for international students; for spring admission, 12/15 priority date for domestic students, 7/1 for international students. Applications are processed on a rolling basis. *Application fee:* $25. Electronic applications accepted. *Application Contact:* Kelly Brand, Director of Enrollment, 262-245-8571, E-mail: kbrand@aurora.edu. *Assistant Provost,* Dr. Donette Considine, 262-245-8542, E-mail: dconsidi@aurora.edu.

AUSTIN COLLEGE, Sherman, TX 75090-4400

General Information Independent-religious, coed, comprehensive institution. *Enrollment:* 1,314 graduate, professional, and undergraduate students; 19 full-time matriculated graduate/professional students (16 women), 2 part-time matriculated graduate/professional students (1 woman). *Enrollment by degree level:* 21 master's. *Graduate faculty:* 5 full-time (4 women), 1 (woman) part-time/adjunct. *Tuition:* Full-time $34,545. *Required fees:* $160. *Graduate housing:* Room and/or apartments available on a first-come, first-served basis to single students; on-campus housing not available to married students. Housing application deadline: 5/1. *Student services:* Campus employment opportunities, campus safety program, career counseling, free psychological counseling, teacher training. *Library facilities:* Abell Library. *Online resources:* library catalog, web page, access to other libraries' catalogs. *Collection:* 230,222 titles, 10,352 serial subscriptions, 6,368 audiovisual materials.

Computer facilities: 160 computers available on campus for general student use. A campuswide network can be accessed from student residence rooms and from off campus. Online class registration is available. *Web address:* http://www.austincollege.edu/.

General Application Contact: Dr. Barbara Sylvester, Director of Teaching Program, 903-813-2327, E-mail: bsylvester@austincollege.edu.

GRADUATE UNITS

Program in Education Students: 19 full-time (16 women), 2 part-time (1 woman); includes 1 minority (Hispanic/Latino). Average age 23. *Faculty:* 5 full-time (4 women), 1 (woman) part-time/adjunct. Expenses: Contact institution. *Financial support:* Career-related internships or fieldwork, Federal Work-Study, scholarships/grants, and unspecified assistantships available. Support available to part-time students. Financial award application deadline: 4/1; financial award applicants required to submit FAFSA. In 2010, 24 master's awarded. *Degree program information:* Part-time programs available. Offers art education (MA); elementary education (MA); middle school education (MA); music education (MA); physical education and coaching (MA); secondary education (MA); theatre education (MA). *Application deadline:* For fall admission, 5/1 priority date for domestic students; for spring admission, 1/15 priority date for domestic students. Applications are processed on a rolling basis. *Application fee:* $35. Electronic applications accepted. *Application Contact:* Dr. Barbara Sylvester, Director of Teaching Program, 903-813-2327, E-mail: bsylvester@austincollege.edu. *Director of Teaching Program,* Dr. Barbara Sylvester, 903-813-2327, E-mail: bsylvester@austincollege.edu.

AUSTIN GRADUATE SCHOOL OF THEOLOGY, Austin, TX 78752

General Information Independent-religious, coed, upper-level institution. *Graduate housing:* On-campus housing not available.

GRADUATE UNITS

Program in Theological Studies *Degree program information:* Part-time programs available. Offers theological studies (MATS).

AUSTIN PEAY STATE UNIVERSITY, Clarksville, TN 37044

General Information State-supported, coed, comprehensive institution. CGS member. *Enrollment:* 10,723 graduate, professional, and undergraduate students; 300 full-time matriculated graduate/professional students (231 women), 570 part-time matriculated graduate/professional students (411 women). *Enrollment by degree level:* 841 master's, 29 other advanced degrees. *Graduate faculty:* 111 full-time (60 women), 15 part-time/adjunct (11 women). Tuition, state resident: full-time $6480; part-time $324 per credit hour. Tuition, nonresident: full-time $17,960; part-time $898 per credit hour. *Required fees:* $1244; $61.20 per credit hour. *Graduate housing:* Rooms and/or apartments available on a first-come, first-served basis to single and married students. Typical cost: $5900 per year ($8390 including board) for single students; $6600 per year ($9090 including board) for married students. *Student services:* Campus employment opportunities, campus safety program, career counseling, child daycare facilities, exercise/wellness program, free psychological counseling, international student services, low-cost health insurance, multicultural affairs office, services for students with disabilities, teacher training, writing training. *Library facilities:* Felix G. Woodward Library. *Online resources:* library catalog, web page, access to other libraries' catalogs. *Collection:* 417,033 titles, 34,166 serial subscriptions, 6,019 audiovisual materials.

Computer facilities: Computer purchase and lease plans are available. 790 computers available on campus for general student use. A campuswide network can be accessed from student residence rooms and from off campus. Online class registration is available. *Web address:* http://www.apsu.edu/.

General Application Contact: Dr. Dixie Dennis, Dean, College of Graduate Studies, 931-221-7662, Fax: 931-221-7641, E-mail: dennisdi@apsu.edu.

GRADUATE UNITS

College of Graduate Studies Students: 294 full-time (227 women), 533 part-time (381 women); includes 169 minority (95 Black or African American, non-Hispanic/Latino; 5 American Indian or Alaska Native, non-Hispanic/Latino; 8 Asian, non-Hispanic/Latino; 26 Hispanic/Latino; 4 Native Hawaiian or other Pacific Islander, non-Hispanic/Latino; 31 Two or more races, non-Hispanic/Latino), 4 international. Average age 33. 471 applicants, 95% accepted, 288 enrolled. *Faculty:* 111 full-time (60 women), 15 part-time/adjunct (11 women). Expenses: Contact institution. *Financial support:* In 2010–11, 109 students received support, including 109 research assistantships with full tuition reimbursements available (averaging $5,174 per year); career-related internships or fieldwork, Federal Work-Study, institutionally sponsored loans, scholarships/grants, and unspecified assistantships also available. Support available to part-time students. Financial award application deadline: 3/1; financial award applicants required to submit FAFSA. In 2010, 273 master's, 4 other advanced degrees awarded. *Degree program information:* Part-time and evening/weekend programs available. Postbaccalaureate distance learning degree programs offered. *Application deadline:* For fall admission, 7/27 priority date for domestic students; for spring admission, 12/17 priority date for domestic students. Applications are processed on a rolling basis. *Application fee:* $25. Electronic applications accepted. *Application Contact:* Dr. Dixie Dennis, Dean, College of Graduate Studies, 931-221-7662, Fax: 931-221-7641, E-mail: dennisdi@apsu.edu. *Dean, College of Graduate Studies,* Dr. Dixie Dennis, 931-221-7662, Fax: 931-221-7641, E-mail: dennisdi@apsu.edu.

College of Arts and Letters Students: 57 full-time (28 women), 118 part-time (63 women); includes 30 minority (18 Black or African American, non-Hispanic/Latino; 2 Asian, non-Hispanic/Latino; 1 Hispanic/Latino; 3 Native Hawaiian or other Pacific Islander, non-Hispanic/Latino; 6 Two or more races, non-Hispanic/Latino), 2 international. Average age 33. 111 applicants, 96% accepted, 66 enrolled. *Faculty:* 43 full-time (19 women), 8 part-time/adjunct (5 women). Expenses: Contact institution. *Financial support:* In 2010–11, research assistantships with full tuition reimbursements (averaging $5,174 per year); career-related internships or fieldwork, Federal Work-Study, institutionally sponsored loans, scholarships/grants, and unspecified assistantships also available. Support available to part-time students. Financial award application deadline: 3/1; financial award applicants required to submit FAFSA. In 2010, 49 master's awarded. *Degree program information:* Part-time programs available. Postbaccalaureate distance learning degree programs offered. Offers arts and letters (M Mu, MA); communication arts (MA); English (MA); military history (MA); music education (M Mu); music performance (M Mu). *Application deadline:* For fall admission, 7/27 priority date for domestic students; for spring admission, 12/17 priority date for domestic students. Applications are processed on a rolling basis. *Application fee:* $25. Electronic applications accepted. *Application Contact:* Dr. Dixie Dennis, Dean, College of Graduate Studies, 931-221-7662, Fax: 931-221-7641, E-mail: dennisdi@apsu.edu. *Interim Dean,* Dixie Webb, 931-221-6445, Fax: 931-221-1024, E-mail: webbd@apsu.edu.

College of Behavioral and Health Sciences Students: 128 full-time (111 women), 118 part-time (101 women); includes 49 minority (29 Black or African American, non-Hispanic/Latino; 1 American Indian or Alaska Native, non-Hispanic/Latino; 5 Asian, non-Hispanic/Latino; 4 Hispanic/Latino; 10 Two or more races, non-Hispanic/Latino), 1 international. Average age 34. 147 applicants, 93% accepted, 96 enrolled. *Faculty:* 28 full-time (18 women), 1 (woman) part-time/adjunct. Expenses: Contact institution. *Financial support:* In 2010–11, research assistantships with full tuition reimbursements (averaging $5,174 per year); career-related internships or fieldwork, Federal Work-Study, institutionally sponsored loans, scholarships/grants, and unspecified assistantships also available. Support available to part-time students. Financial award application deadline: 3/1; financial award applicants required to submit FAFSA. In 2010, 79 master's awarded. *Degree program information:* Part-time and evening/weekend programs available. Postbaccalaureate distance learning degree programs offered. Offers advanced practice (MSN); behavioral and health sciences (MA, MS, MSN, MSW, Ed S); counseling (MS); counseling and guidance (Ed S); health leadership (MS); nursing administration (MSN); nursing education (MSN); nursing informatics (MSN); psychology (MA); social work (MSW). *Application deadline:* For fall admission, 7/27 priority date for domestic students; for spring admission, 12/17 priority date for domestic students. Applications are processed on a rolling basis. *Application fee:* $25. Electronic applications accepted. *Application Contact:* Dr. Dixie Dennis, Dean, College of

Austin Peay State University (continued)

Graduate Studies, 931-221-7662, Fax: 931-221-7641, E-mail: dennisdi@apsu.edu. *Dean*, Dr. David Denton, 931-221-7423, E-mail: dentond@apsu.edu.

College of Business Students: 7 full-time (4 women), 79 part-time (49 women); includes 30 minority (21 Black or African American, non-Hispanic/Latino; 1 American Indian or Alaska Native, non-Hispanic/Latino; 1 Asian, non-Hispanic/Latino; 5 Hispanic/Latino; 2 Two or more races, non-Hispanic/Latino). Average age 34. 37 applicants, 95% accepted, 23 enrolled. *Faculty:* 5 full-time (0 women). Expenses: Contact institution. *Financial support:* In 2010–11, research assistantships with full tuition reimbursements (averaging $5,174 per year); career-related internships or fieldwork, Federal Work-Study, institutionally sponsored loans, scholarships/grants, and unspecified assistantships also available. Support available to part-time students. Financial award application deadline: 3/1; financial award applicants required to submit FAFSA. In 2010, 46 master's awarded. *Degree program information:* Part-time and evening/weekend programs available. Postbaccalaureate distance learning degree programs offered (no on-campus study). Offers management (MS). *Application deadline:* For fall admission, 7/27 priority date for domestic students; for spring admission, 12/17 priority date for domestic students. Applications are processed on a rolling basis. *Application fee:* $25. Electronic applications accepted. *Application Contact:* Dr. Dixie Dennis, Dean, College of Graduate Studies, 931-221-7662, Fax: 931-221-7641, E-mail: dennisdi@apsu.edu. *Dean*, Dr. William Rupp, 931-221-7674, Fax: 931-221-7355, E-mail: ruppw@apsu.edu.

College of Education Students: 96 full-time (78 women), 201 part-time (160 women); includes 58 minority (25 Black or African American, non-Hispanic/Latino; 3 American Indian or Alaska Native, non-Hispanic/Latino; 2 Asian, non-Hispanic/Latino; 14 Hispanic/Latino; 1 Native Hawaiian or other Pacific Islander, non-Hispanic/Latino; 13 Two or more races, non-Hispanic/Latino). Average age 34. 148 applicants, 97% accepted, 81 enrolled. *Faculty:* 20 full-time (15 women), 6 part-time/adjunct (5 women). Expenses: Contact institution. *Financial support:* In 2010–11, research assistantships with full tuition reimbursements (averaging $5,174 per year); career-related internships or fieldwork, Federal Work-Study, institutionally sponsored loans, scholarships/grants, and unspecified assistantships also available. Support available to part-time students. Financial award application deadline: 3/1; financial award applicants required to submit FAFSA. In 2010, 88 master's, 4 other advanced degrees awarded. *Degree program information:* Part-time and evening/weekend programs available. Postbaccalaureate distance learning degree programs offered. Offers administration and supervision (Ed S); curriculum and instruction (MA Ed); education (MA Ed, MAT, Ed S); education leadership (MA Ed); elementary education (Ed S); elementary education K-6 (MAT); reading (MA Ed); secondary education (Ed S); secondary education 7-12 (MAT); special education (MA Ed); special education K-12 (MAT). *Application deadline:* For fall admission, 7/27 priority date for domestic students; for spring admission, 12/17 priority date for domestic students. Applications are processed on a rolling basis. *Application fee:* $25. Electronic applications accepted. *Application Contact:* Dr. Dixie Dennis, Dean, College of Graduate Studies, 931-221-7662, Fax: 931-221-7641, E-mail: dennisdi@apsu.edu. *Director*, Dr. Carlette Hardin, 931-221-7696, Fax: 931-221-1292, E-mail: forbusl@apsu.edu.

College of Science and Mathematics Students: 6 full-time (all women), 17 part-time (8 women); includes 4 minority (2 Black or African American, non-Hispanic/Latino; 2 Hispanic/Latino), 1 international. Average age 29. 15 applicants, 100% accepted, 11 enrolled. *Faculty:* 13 full-time (6 women). Expenses: Contact institution. *Financial support:* In 2010–11, research assistantships with full tuition reimbursements (averaging $5,174 per year); career-related internships or fieldwork, Federal Work-Study, institutionally sponsored loans, scholarships/grants, and unspecified assistantships also available. Support available to part-time students. Financial award application deadline: 3/1; financial award applicants required to submit FAFSA. In 2010, 6 master's awarded. *Degree program information:* Part-time programs available. Offers clinical laboratory science (MS); radiologic science (MS); science and mathematics (MS). *Application deadline:* For fall admission, 7/27 priority date for domestic students; for spring admission, 12/17 priority date for domestic students. Applications are processed on a rolling basis. *Application fee:* $25. Electronic applications accepted. *Application Contact:* Dr. Dixie Dennis, Dean, College of Graduate Studies, 931-221-7662, Fax: 931-221-7641, E-mail: dennisdi@apsu.edu. *Dean*, Dr. Jaime Taylor, 931-221-7971, E-mail: taylorj@apsu.edu.

AUSTIN PRESBYTERIAN THEOLOGICAL SEMINARY, Austin, TX 78705-5797

General Information Independent-religious, coed, graduate-only institution. *Enrollment by degree level:* 132 master's, 62 doctoral, 2 other advanced degrees. *Graduate faculty:* 18 full-time (5 women), 6 part-time/adjunct (2 women). *Tuition:* Part-time $190 per credit. *Required fees:* $30 per semester. One-time fee: $150 part-time. Tuition and fees vary according to degree level and program. *Graduate housing:* Rooms and/or apartments available on a first-come, first-served basis to single and married students. Typical cost: $1670 (including board) for single students; $6305 (including board) for married students. Housing application deadline: 5/31. *Student services:* Campus employment opportunities, campus safety program, career counseling, free psychological counseling, international student services, services for students with disabilities, writing training. *Library facilities:* David and Jane Stitt Library. *Online resources:* library catalog, web page, access to other libraries' catalogs. *Collection:* 160,340 titles, 439 serial subscriptions, 5,921 audiovisual materials.

Computer facilities: 20 computers available on campus for general student use. A campuswide network can be accessed from off campus. Biblical Theological Research available. *Web address:* http://www.austinseminary.edu/.

General Application Contact: Dr. Jack Barden, Director of Admissions, 512-404-4827, Fax: 512-472-7089, E-mail: admissions@austinseminary.edu.

GRADUATE UNITS

Graduate and Professional Programs Students: 96 full-time (56 women), 100 part-time (49 women); includes 27 minority (15 Black or African American, non-Hispanic/Latino; 1 American Indian or Alaska Native, non-Hispanic/Latino; 5 Asian, non-Hispanic/Latino; 6 Hispanic/Latino), 6 international. 89 applicants, 61% accepted, 41 enrolled. *Faculty:* 18 full-time (5 women), 6 part-time/adjunct (2 women). Expenses: Contact institution. *Financial support:* In 2010–11, 130 students received support; fellowships, career-related internships or fieldwork, institutionally sponsored loans, scholarships/grants, and tutorships available. Support available to part-time students. Financial award application deadline: 6/1; financial award applicants required to submit FAFSA. In 2010, 52 first professional degrees, 10 master's, 5 doctorates awarded. *Degree program information:* Part-time programs available. Offers divinity (M Div); ministry (D Min); theological studies (MA). *Application deadline:* For fall admission, 5/1 for domestic students, 1/1 for international students; for spring admission, 9/1 for domestic students. Applications are processed on a rolling basis. *Application fee:* $65. *Application Contact:* Dr. Jack Barden, Director of Admissions, 512-404-4827, Fax: 512-472-7089, E-mail: admissions@austinseminary.edu. *Academic Dean*, Rev. Dr. Allan Hugh Cole, 512-404-4821, Fax: 512-479-0738, E-mail: dean@austinseminary.edu.

AVE MARIA SCHOOL OF LAW, Naples, FL 34119

General Information Independent-religious, coed, graduate-only institution. *Enrollment by degree level:* 468 first professional. *Graduate faculty:* 27 full-time (7 women), 14 part-time/adjunct (3 women). *Graduate housing:* Rooms and/or apartments available on a first-come, first-served basis to single and married students. Housing application deadline: 5/1. *Student services:* Campus employment opportunities, campus safety program, career counseling, international student services, services for students with disabilities, writing training. *Library facilities:* Ave Maria School of Law Library. *Online resources:* library catalog, web page. *Collection:* 60,583 titles, 25,650 serial subscriptions, 1,104 audiovisual materials.

Computer facilities: 28 computers available on campus for general student use. A campuswide network can be accessed from off campus. Online class registration is available. *Web address:* http://www.avemarialaw.edu/.

General Application Contact: Monique McCarthy, Assistant Dean for Admissions, 239-687-5420, Fax: 239-352-2890, E-mail: info@avemarialaw.edu.

GRADUATE UNITS

School of Law Students: 468 full-time (210 women); includes 64 minority (13 Black or African American, non-Hispanic/Latino; 2 American Indian or Alaska Native, non-Hispanic/Latino; 17 Asian, non-Hispanic/Latino; 32 Hispanic/Latino), 9 international. Average age 26. 1,775 applicants, 50% accepted, 210 enrolled. *Faculty:* 27 full-time (7 women), 14 part-time/adjunct (3 women). Expenses: Contact institution. *Financial support:* In 2010–11, 193 students received support. Career-related internships or fieldwork, Federal Work-Study, and scholarships/grants available. Financial award application deadline: 6/1; financial award applicants required to submit FAFSA. In 2010, 87 JDs awarded. Offers law (JD). *Application deadline:* For fall admission, 4/1 priority date for domestic and international students. Applications are processed on a rolling basis. *Application fee:* $50. Electronic applications accepted. *Application Contact:* Monique McCarthy, Assistant Dean for Admissions, 239-687-5420, Fax: 239-352-2890, E-mail: info@avemarialaw.edu. *President/Dean*, Eugene R. Milhizer, 239-687-5300.

AVE MARIA UNIVERSITY, Ave Maria, FL 34142

General Information Independent-religious, coed, comprehensive institution. *Graduate housing:* Room and/or apartments available on a first-come, first-served basis to single students; on-campus housing not available to married students. Housing application deadline: 7/15.

GRADUATE UNITS

Graduate Programs

Institute for Pastoral Theology *Degree program information:* Part-time and evening/weekend programs available. Offers pastoral theology (MTS).

AVERETT UNIVERSITY, Danville, VA 24541-3692

General Information Independent-religious, coed, comprehensive institution. *Enrollment:* 893 graduate, professional, and undergraduate students; 314 full-time matriculated graduate/professional students (240 women), 491 part-time matriculated graduate/professional students (309 women). *Enrollment by degree level:* 805 master's. *Graduate faculty:* 14 full-time (4 women), 58 part-time/adjunct (25 women). *Graduate housing:* On-campus housing not available. *Student services:* Campus employment opportunities, campus safety program, career counseling, exercise/wellness program, free psychological counseling, international student services, services for students with disabilities, teacher training, writing training. *Library facilities:* Blount Library.

Computer facilities: 150 computers available on campus for general student use. A campuswide network can be accessed from student residence rooms. Online class registration is available. *Web address:* http://www.averett.edu/.

General Application Contact: Dr. Lynn H. Wolf, Chair/Associate Professor/Director of Education, 434-791-5844, Fax: 434-791-5850, E-mail: lynn.wolf@averett.edu.

GRADUATE UNITS

Master in Education Program Students: 189 full-time (161 women), 108 part-time (90 women); includes 100 Black or African American, non-Hispanic/Latino; 1 American Indian or Alaska Native, non-Hispanic/Latino; 3 Asian, non-Hispanic/Latino; 5 Hispanic/Latino. Average age 37. 119 applicants, 99% accepted, 98 enrolled. *Faculty:* 4 full-time (3 women), 36 part-time/adjunct (22 women). Expenses: Contact institution. *Financial support:* Career-related internships or fieldwork, Federal Work-Study, and scholarships/grants available. Financial award application deadline: 4/1; financial award applicants required to submit FAFSA. In 2010, 92 master's awarded. *Degree program information:* Part-time and evening/weekend programs available. Offers art education (M Ed); biology (M Ed); biology education (M Ed); chemistry (M Ed); chemistry education (M Ed); curriculum and instruction (M Ed); elementary education (M Ed); English (M Ed); English education (M Ed); health and physical education (M Ed); history and social studies education (M Ed); math (M Ed); mathematics education (M Ed); physical science (M Ed); reading specialization (M Ed); special education (learning disabilities specialization PK-12) (M Ed). Program also offered at Richmond, VA regional campus location. *Application deadline:* Applications are processed on a rolling basis. *Application Contact:* Dr. Lynn H. Wolf, Associate Professor/Director, 434-793-3995, Fax: 434-791-4392, E-mail: lynn.wolf@averett.edu. *Associate Professor/Director*, Dr. Lynn H. Wolf, 434-793-3995, Fax: 434-791-4392, E-mail: lynn.wolf@averett.edu.

Program in Business Administration Students: 125 full-time (79 women), 383 part-time (219 women); includes 209 Black or African American, non-Hispanic/Latino; 2 American Indian or Alaska Native, non-Hispanic/Latino; 8 Asian, non-Hispanic/Latino; 11 Hispanic/Latino. Average age 37. 164 applicants, 99% accepted, 135 enrolled. *Faculty:* 10 full-time (1 woman), 22 part-time/adjunct (3 women). Expenses: Contact institution. *Financial support:* Institutionally sponsored loans available. Support available to part-time students. In 2010, 159 master's awarded. *Degree program information:* Part-time programs available. Offers business administration (MBA). *Application deadline:* Applications are processed on a rolling basis. *Application fee:* $50. *Application Contact:* Dr. Eugene Steadman, 434-791-5600, E-mail: eugene.steadman@averett.edu. Dr. Eugene Steadman, 434-791-5600, E-mail: eugene.steadman@averett.edu.

AVILA UNIVERSITY, Kansas City, MO 64145-1698

General Information Independent-religious, coed, comprehensive institution. *Enrollment:* 1,876 graduate, professional, and undergraduate students; 475 full-time matriculated graduate/professional students (341 women), 173 part-time matriculated graduate/professional students (114 women). *Enrollment by degree level:* 648 master's. *Graduate faculty:* 23 full-time (13 women), 59 part-time/adjunct (25 women). *Tuition:* Full-time $5580; part-time $465 per credit hour. *Required fees:* $348; $29 per credit hour. *Graduate housing:* Room and/or apartments available on a first-come, first-served basis to single students; on-campus housing not available to married students. Typical cost: $3150 per year ($6350 including board). Room and board charges vary according to board plan and housing facility selected. *Student services:* Campus employment opportunities, campus safety program, career counseling, child daycare facilities, exercise/wellness program, free psychological counseling, international student services, low-cost health insurance, multicultural affairs office, services for students with disabilities, teacher training, writing training. *Library facilities:* Hooley Bundshu Library. *Online resources:* library catalog, web page, access to other libraries' catalogs. *Collection:* 80,845 titles, 22,464 serial subscriptions.

Computer facilities: 180 computers available on campus for general student use. A campuswide network can be accessed from student residence rooms and from off campus. Online class registration is available. *Web address:* http://www.avila.edu/.

General Application Contact: Office of Admissions, 816-501-2400.

GRADUATE UNITS

Department of Psychology Students: 122 full-time (96 women), 21 part-time (16 women); includes 35 minority (26 Black or African American, non-Hispanic/Latino; 2 Asian, non-Hispanic/Latino; 6 Hispanic/Latino; 1 Two or more races, non-Hispanic/Latino), 6 international. Average age 32. 76 applicants, 53% accepted, 28 enrolled. *Faculty:* 6 full-time (5 women), 20 part-time/adjunct (9 women). Expenses: Contact institution. *Financial support:* In 2010–11, 132 students received support, including 1 research assistantship with partial tuition reimbursement available, 1 teaching assistantship (averaging $2,400 per year); career-related internships or fieldwork, scholarships/grants, and unspecified assistantships also available. Support available to part-time students. Financial award applicants required to submit FAFSA. In 2010, 3,631 master's awarded. *Degree program information:* Part-time and evening/weekend programs available. Offers counseling psychology (MS); general psychology (MS). *Application deadline:* Applications are processed on a rolling basis. *Application fee:* $0. Electronic applications accepted. *Application Contact:* Jennifer A. Manczuk, Graduate Program Liaison, 816-501-3698, Fax: 816-501-2455, E-mail: gradpsych@avila.edu. *Director of Graduate Psychology*, Robin M. Schluter, 816-501-2969, Fax: 816-501-2455, E-mail: robin.schluter@avila.edu.

Program in Organizational Development Students: 72 full-time (61 women), 36 part-time (24 women); includes 35 minority (28 Black or African American, non-Hispanic/Latino; 2 American Indian or Alaska Native, non-Hispanic/Latino; 2 Asian, non-Hispanic/Latino; 2 Hispanic/Latino; 1 Native Hawaiian or other Pacific Islander, non-Hispanic/Latino), 4 international. Average age 36. 47 applicants, 64% accepted, 27 enrolled. *Faculty:* 2 full-time

(1 woman), 10 part-time/adjunct (7 women). Expenses: Contact institution. *Financial support:* In 2010–11, 69 students received support. Unspecified assistantships available. Support available to part-time students. Financial award applicants required to submit FAFSA. In 2010, 18 master's awarded. *Degree program information:* Part-time and evening/weekend programs available. Postbaccalaureate distance learning degree programs offered (no on-campus study). Offers fundraising (Graduate Certificate); management (MA); organizational development (MS); project management (Graduate Certificate). *Application deadline:* Applications are processed on a rolling basis. *Application fee:* $0. Electronic applications accepted. *Application Contact:* Linda Dubar, School of Professional Studies, 816-501-3737, Fax: 816-941-4650, E-mail: advantage@avila.edu. *Dean*, Dr. Steve Iliff, 816-501-3737, Fax: 816-941-4650, E-mail: advantage@avila.edu.

School of Business Students: 123 full-time (68 women), 87 part-time (52 women); includes 44 minority (30 Black or African American, non-Hispanic/Latino; 1 American Indian or Alaska Native, non-Hispanic/Latino; 6 Asian, non-Hispanic/Latino; 6 Hispanic/Latino; 1 Native Hawaiian or other Pacific Islander, non-Hispanic/Latino), 46 international. Average age 33. 62 applicants, 79% accepted, 49 enrolled. *Faculty:* 9 full-time (3 women), 24 part-time/adjunct (6 women). Expenses: Contact institution. *Financial support:* In 2010–11, 102 students received support. Career-related internships or fieldwork and Competitive Merit Scholarship available. Support available to part-time students. Financial award applicants required to submit FAFSA. In 2010, 80 master's awarded. *Degree program information:* Part-time and evening/weekend programs available. Offers accounting (MBA); finance (MBA); general management (MBA); health care administration (MBA); international business (MBA); management information systems (MBA); marketing (MBA). *Application deadline:* For fall admission, 7/30 priority date for domestic students, 7/30 for international students; for winter admission, 11/30 priority date for domestic students, 11/30 for international students; for spring admission, 2/28 priority date for domestic students, 2/28 for international students. Applications are processed on a rolling basis. *Application fee:* $0. Electronic applications accepted. *Application Contact:* JoAnna Giffin, MBA Admissions Director, 816-501-3601, Fax: 816-501-2463, E-mail: joanna.giffin@avila.edu. *Dean*, Dr. Richard Woodall, 816-501-3720, Fax: 816-501-2463, E-mail: richard.woodall@avila.edu.

School of Education Students: 158 full-time (116 women), 29 part-time (22 women); includes 23 minority (14 Black or African American, non-Hispanic/Latino; 3 American Indian or Alaska Native, non-Hispanic/Latino; 1 Asian, non-Hispanic/Latino; 2 Hispanic/Latino; 3 Two or more races, non-Hispanic/Latino). Average age 33. 57 applicants, 65% accepted, 23 enrolled. *Faculty:* 6 full-time (4 women), 5 part-time/adjunct (3 women). Expenses: Contact institution. *Financial support:* In 2010–11, 64 students received support, including 1 research assistantship; career-related internships or fieldwork also available. Support available to part-time students. Financial award applicants required to submit FAFSA. In 2010, 51 master's awarded. *Degree program information:* Part-time and evening/weekend programs available. Offers education (MA); English for speakers of other languages (Advanced Certificate). *Application deadline:* Applications are processed on a rolling basis. *Application fee:* $0. Electronic applications accepted. *Application Contact:* Margaret Longstreet, 816-501-2464, E-mail: margaret.longstreet@avila.edu. *Director of Graduate Education*, Deana Angotti, 816-501-2446, Fax: 816-501-2915, E-mail: deana.augotti@avila.edu.

AZUSA PACIFIC UNIVERSITY, Azusa, CA 91702-7000

General Information Independent-religious, coed, university. CGS member. *Enrollment:* 9,258 graduate, professional, and undergraduate students; 1,755 full-time matriculated graduate/professional students (1,204 women), 1,992 part-time matriculated graduate/professional students (1,319 women). *Enrollment by degree level:* 220 first professional, 2,865 master's, 385 doctoral, 236 other advanced degrees. *Graduate faculty:* 144 full-time (86 women), 26 part-time/adjunct (10 women). *Graduate housing:* On-campus housing not available. *Student services:* Campus employment opportunities, campus safety program, career counseling, exercise/wellness program, free psychological counseling, international student services, low-cost health insurance, multicultural affairs office, services for students with disabilities, teacher training. *Library facilities:* Marshburn Memorial Library. *Online resources:* library catalog, web page.

Computer facilities: Computer purchase and lease plans are available. A campuswide network can be accessed from off campus. Online class registration is available. *Web address:* http://www.apu.edu/.

General Application Contact: Linda Witte, Graduate Admissions Office, 626-969-3434.

GRADUATE UNITS

Center for Adult and Professional Studies Students: 1 full-time (0 women), 89 part-time (50 women); includes 29 minority (10 Black or African American, non-Hispanic/Latino; 4 Asian, non-Hispanic/Latino; 15 Hispanic/Latino), 1 international. Average age 38. Expenses: Contact institution. In 2010, 42 master's awarded. Postbaccalaureate distance learning degree programs offered. Offers leadership and organizational studies (MA). *Application fee:* $45 ($65 for international students). *Application Contact:* Linda Witte, Graduate Admissions Office, 626-969-3434. *Dean*, Dr. Fred G. Garlett, 626-815-5301, E-mail: fgarlett@apu.edu.

College of Liberal Arts and Sciences Students: 73 full-time (55 women), 67 part-time (43 women); includes 31 minority (3 Black or African American, non-Hispanic/Latino; 8 Asian, non-Hispanic/Latino; 18 Hispanic/Latino; 2 Native Hawaiian or other Pacific Islander, non-Hispanic/Latino), 12 international. Average age 34. *Faculty:* 3 full-time (2 women). Expenses: Contact institution. *Financial support:* Teaching assistantships, career-related internships or fieldwork available. Support available to part-time students. In 2010, 38 master's awarded. *Degree program information:* Part-time and evening/weekend programs available. Postbaccalaureate distance learning degree programs offered. Offers fine arts in visual art (MFA); liberal arts and sciences (MA, MFA); teaching English to speakers of other languages (MA); transformational urban leadership (MA). *Application deadline:* Applications are processed on a rolling basis. *Application fee:* $45 ($65 for international students). *Application Contact:* Director of Graduate Admissions, 626-812-3037, Fax: 626-969-7180. *Dean*, Dr. David Weeks, 626-969-3434 Ext. 3500, E-mail: dweeks@apu.edu.

Haggard Graduate School of Theology Students: 197 full-time (51 women), 158 part-time (52 women); includes 164 minority (48 Black or African American, non-Hispanic/Latino; 65 Asian, non-Hispanic/Latino; 51 Hispanic/Latino), 75 international. Average age 39. *Faculty:* 12 full-time (3 women), 2 part-time/adjunct (0 women). Expenses: Contact institution. *Financial support:* Teaching assistantships, career-related internships or fieldwork available. Support available to part-time students. Financial award application deadline: 6/1; financial award applicants required to submit FAFSA. In 2010, 33 first professional degrees, 39 master's awarded. *Degree program information:* Part-time and evening/weekend programs available. Offers biblical studies (MA); Christian education in youth ministry (MA); church leadership and development (MAPS); divinity (M Div); ministry (D Min); religion: Biblical studies (MAR); religion: theology and ethics (MA); theology (M Div, MA, MAPS, MAR, D Min); urban studies (MAPS); worship leadership (MAPS); youth and family ministry (MAPS). *Application deadline:* For fall admission, 6/1 for international students; for spring admission, 10/7 for international students. *Application fee:* $45 ($65 for international students). *Application Contact:* Dr. Scott Daniels, Dean, 626-387-5750, E-mail: ezone@apu.edu. *Dean*, Dr. Scott Daniels, 626-387-5750, E-mail: ezone@apu.edu.

School of Behavioral and Applied Sciences Students: 473 full-time (339 women), 376 part-time (248 women); includes 238 minority (48 Black or African American, non-Hispanic/Latino; 3 American Indian or Alaska Native, non-Hispanic/Latino; 65 Asian, non-Hispanic/Latino; 120 Hispanic/Latino; 2 Native Hawaiian or other Pacific Islander, non-Hispanic/Latino), 79 international. Average age 32. *Faculty:* 37 full-time (25 women), 5 part-time/adjunct (1 woman). Expenses: Contact institution. In 2010, 215 master's, 58 doctorates awarded. Offers behavioral and applied sciences (M Ed, MA, MSW, DPT, Ed D, PhD, Psy D); clinical psychology (MA, Psy D); college student affairs (M Ed); educational leadership (Ed D); entry-level (DPT); global leadership (MA); higher education leadership (Ed D); organizational leadership (MA); social work (MSW); transitional (DPT). *Application Contact:* Linda Witte, Graduate Admissions Office, 626-969-3434. *Interim Dean*, Dr. Rosemary Liegler, 626-815-6000 Ext. 5518.

School of Business and Management Students: 75 full-time (41 women), 96 part-time (46 women); includes 65 minority (15 Black or African American, non-Hispanic/Latino; 15 Asian, non-Hispanic/Latino; 34 Hispanic/Latino; 1 Native Hawaiian or other Pacific Islander, non-Hispanic/Latino), 17 international. Average age 30. *Faculty:* 19 full-time (5 women), 2 part-time/adjunct (1 woman). Expenses: Contact institution. *Financial support:* Scholarships/grants available. In 2010, 82 master's awarded. *Degree program information:* Part-time and evening/weekend programs available. Offers business administration (MBA); diversity for strategic advantage (MA); entrepreneurship (MBA); finance (MBA); human and organizational development (MA); human resources and organizational development (MBA); human resources management (MA); international business (MBA); marketing (MBA); non-profit management (MA); organizational development and change (MA); performance improvement (MA); public administration (MA); strategic management (MBA). *Application deadline:* For fall admission, 8/15 priority date for domestic students. Applications are processed on a rolling basis. *Application fee:* $45 ($65 for international students). *Application Contact:* Dr. Ilene Bezjian, Dean, 626-815-3090, Fax: 626-815-3802, E-mail: ibezjian@apu.edu. *Dean*, Dr. Ilene Bezjian, 626-815-3090, Fax: 626-815-3802, E-mail: ibezjian@apu.edu.

School of Education Students: 725 full-time (550 women), 935 part-time (661 women); includes 100 Black or African American, non-Hispanic/Latino; 5 American Indian or Alaska Native, non-Hispanic/Latino; 81 Asian, non-Hispanic/Latino; 361 Hispanic/Latino; 6 Native Hawaiian or other Pacific Islander, non-Hispanic/Latino, 4 international. Average age 34. *Faculty:* 59 full-time (32 women), 14 part-time/adjunct (6 women). Expenses: Contact institution. *Financial support:* Career-related internships or fieldwork available. Support available to part-time students. Financial award applicants required to submit FAFSA. In 2010, 736 master's, 12 doctorates awarded. *Degree program information:* Part-time and evening/weekend programs available. Offers curriculum and instruction in multicultural contexts (MA Ed); digital teaching and learning (MA Ed); education (M Ed, MA, MA Ed, Ed D, Credential); educational counseling (MA); educational psychology (MA); educational technology (M Ed); educational technology and learning (MA); physical education (M Ed); school administration (MA); school librarianship (MA); special education (MA Ed); special education and educational technology (M Ed); teacher librarian services (Credential); teaching (MA Ed). *Application fee:* $45 ($65 for international students). *Application Contact:* Linda Witte, Graduate Admissions Office, 626-969-3434. *Dean*, Dr. Helen E. Williams, 626-815-5376, E-mail: pgray@apu.edu.

School of Music Students: 25 full-time (7 women), 24 part-time (11 women); includes 3 Black or African American, non-Hispanic/Latino; 1 Asian, non-Hispanic/Latino; 5 Hispanic/Latino, 9 international. Average age 29. Expenses: Contact institution. *Financial support:* In 2010–11, 7 students received support. Career-related internships or fieldwork available. Support available to part-time students. Financial award applicants required to submit FAFSA. In 2010, 22 master's awarded. *Degree program information:* Part-time and evening/weekend programs available. Offers education (M Mus); performance (M Mus). *Application fee:* $45 ($65 for international students). *Application Contact:* Graduate Admissions, 626-815-5470, Fax: 626-815-3867, E-mail: dfunderburk@apu.edu. *Acting Dean*, Dr. Donald Neufeld, 626-812-3848, E-mail: dfunderburk@apu.edu.

School of Nursing Students: 186 full-time (161 women), 206 part-time (181 women); includes 160 minority (36 Black or African American, non-Hispanic/Latino; 4 American Indian or Alaska Native, non-Hispanic/Latino; 78 Asian, non-Hispanic/Latino; 37 Hispanic/Latino; 5 Native Hawaiian or other Pacific Islander, non-Hispanic/Latino), 13 international. Average age 35. *Faculty:* 25 full-time (22 women), 2 part-time/adjunct (1 woman). Expenses: Contact institution. *Financial support:* Teaching assistantships, scholarships/grants, traineeships, and unspecified assistantships available. Support available to part-time students. Financial award application deadline: 10/15. In 2010, 31 master's, 6 doctorates awarded. *Degree program information:* Part-time and evening/weekend programs available. Offers nursing (MSN); nursing education (PhD). *Application deadline:* Applications are processed on a rolling basis. *Application fee:* $45 ($65 for international students). *Application Contact:* Barb Barthelmess, Graduate Program Secretary, 626-815-5391, Fax: 626-815-5414. *Dean/Professor*, Dr. Aja Lesh, 626-815-5386, E-mail: alesh@apu.edu.

BABEL UNIVERSITY SCHOOL OF TRANSLATION, Honolulu, HI 96815-1302

General Information Proprietary, coed, primarily women, graduate-only institution. *Graduate housing:* On-campus housing not available.

GRADUATE UNITS

Program in Translation *Degree program information:* Part-time and evening/weekend programs available. Postbaccalaureate distance learning degree programs offered (no on-campus study). Offers translation (MS).

BABSON COLLEGE, Wellesley, Babson Park, MA 02457-0310

General Information Independent, coed, comprehensive institution. *Enrollment:* 486 full-time matriculated graduate/professional students (145 women), 838 part-time matriculated graduate/professional students (236 women). *Enrollment by degree level:* 1,319 master's, 5 other advanced degrees. *Graduate faculty:* 142 full-time (39 women), 41 part-time/adjunct (9 women). *Tuition:* Full-time $46,000; part-time $1220 per credit. *Required fees:* $1946. Full-time tuition and fees vary according to course load, program and student level. *Graduate housing:* Rooms and/or apartments available on a first-come, first-served basis to single and married students. Typical cost: $12,000 per year ($16,568 including board) for single students; $13,000 per year ($17,568 including board) for married students. Room and board charges vary according to housing facility selected. Housing application deadline: 5/1. *Student services:* Campus employment opportunities, campus safety program, career counseling, exercise/wellness program, free psychological counseling, international student services, low-cost health insurance, multicultural affairs office, services for students with disabilities, writing training. *Library facilities:* Horn Library plus 1 other. *Online resources:* library catalog, web page, access to other libraries' catalogs. *Collection:* 131,436 titles, 626 serial subscriptions.

Computer facilities: Computer purchase and lease plans are available. 290 computers available on campus for general student use. A campuswide network can be accessed from student residence rooms and from off campus. Online class registration, network drives and folders; students are also issued an IBM Thinkpad are available. *Web address:* http://www.babson.edu/.

General Application Contact: Kathy Longee, Office Manager, 781-239-4317, Fax: 781-239-4194, E-mail: mbaadmission@babson.edu.

GRADUATE UNITS

F. W. Olin Graduate School of Business Students: 486 full-time (145 women), 838 part-time (236 women); includes 199 minority (22 Black or African American, non-Hispanic/Latino; 1 American Indian or Alaska Native, non-Hispanic/Latino; 127 Asian, non-Hispanic/Latino; 29 Hispanic/Latino; 1 Native Hawaiian or other Pacific Islander, non-Hispanic/Latino; 19 Two or more races, non-Hispanic/Latino), 263 international. Average age 33. 877 applicants, 56% accepted, 283 enrolled. *Faculty:* 142 full-time (39 women), 41 part-time/adjunct (9 women). Expenses: Contact institution. *Financial support:* In 2010–11, 286 students received support, including 48 fellowships (averaging $28,489 per year); career-related internships or fieldwork, Federal Work-Study, institutionally sponsored loans, scholarships/grants, health care benefits, and unspecified assistantships also available. Financial award application deadline: 4/15. In 2010, 723 master's, 2 other advanced degrees awarded. *Degree program information:* Part-time and evening/weekend programs available. Postbaccalaureate distance learning degree programs offered (minimal on-campus study). Offers accounting (MSA); advanced management (Certificate); business administration (MBA); global entrepreneurship (MS); technological entrepreneurship (MS). *Application deadline:* For fall admission, 11/1 priority date for domestic and international students; for winter admission, 1/15 priority date for domestic and international students; for spring admission, 4/15 priority date for domestic students. Applications are processed on a rolling basis. *Application fee:* $100. Electronic applications accepted. *Application Contact:* Kathy Longee, Admission Services Team, 781-239-4317, Fax: 781-239-4194, E-mail: mbaadmission@babson.edu. *Dean*, Dr. Raghu Tadepalli, 781-239-5237, E-mail: rtadepalli@babson.edu.

BAKER COLLEGE CENTER FOR GRADUATE STUDIES—ONLINE, Flint, MI 48507-9843

General Information Independent, coed, graduate-only institution. CGS member. *Graduate housing:* On-campus housing not available.

Baker College Center for Graduate Studies—Online (continued)

GRADUATE UNITS

Graduate Programs *Degree program information:* Part-time and evening/weekend programs available. Postbaccalaureate distance learning degree programs offered. Offers accounting (MBA); business administration (DBA); finance (MBA); general business (MBA); health care management (MBA); human resources management (MBA); information management (MBA); leadership studies (MBA); management information systems (MSIS); marketing (MBA). Electronic applications accepted.

BAKER UNIVERSITY, Baldwin City, KS 66006-0065

General Information Independent-religious, coed, comprehensive institution. *Enrollment:* 386 full-time matriculated graduate/professional students (234 women), 1,133 part-time matriculated graduate/professional students (729 women). *Enrollment by degree level:* 1,395 master's, 124 doctoral. *Graduate housing:* On-campus housing not available. *Student services:* Campus safety program, international student services, services for students with disabilities. *Library facilities:* Collins Library. *Online resources:* library catalog, web page, access to other libraries' catalogs. *Collection:* 106,549 titles, 160 serial subscriptions, 6,366 audiovisual materials.

Computer facilities: 222 computers available on campus for general student use. A campuswide network can be accessed from student residence rooms. Online class registration is available. *Web address:* http://www.bakeru.edu/.

General Application Contact: Kelly Belk, Director of Marketing, 913-491-4432, Fax: 913-491-0470, E-mail: kbelk@bakeru.edu.

GRADUATE UNITS

School of Education Students: 90 full-time (75 women), 699 part-time (501 women); includes 42 Black or African American, non-Hispanic/Latino; 5 American Indian or Alaska Native, non-Hispanic/Latino; 4 Asian, non-Hispanic/Latino; 18 Hispanic/Latino; 5 Two or more races, non-Hispanic/Latino. Average age 35. Expenses: Contact institution. *Financial support:* Applicants required to submit FAFSA. In 2010, 427 master's, 15 doctorates awarded. *Degree program information:* Part-time and evening/weekend programs available. Offers education (MA Ed, MASL, MSSE, MSSL, MST, Ed D). Master-level programs also offered in Wichita, KS. *Application deadline:* Applications are processed on a rolling basis. *Application fee:* $20. *Application Contact:* Judy Favor, Director of Graduate Program, 913-491-4432, Fax: 913-491-0470, E-mail: jfavor@bakeru.edu. *Vice President and Dean,* Dr. Peggy Harris, 785-594-8492, Fax: 785-594-8363, E-mail: peggy.harris@bakeru.edu.

School of Professional and Graduate Studies Students: 296 full-time (159 women), 434 part-time (228 women); includes 156 minority (82 Black or African American, non-Hispanic/Latino; 11 American Indian or Alaska Native, non-Hispanic/Latino; 19 Asian, non-Hispanic/Latino; 38 Hispanic/Latino; 1 Native Hawaiian or other Pacific Islander, non-Hispanic/Latino; 5 Two or more races, non-Hispanic/Latino). Average age 34. Expenses: Contact institution. *Financial support:* Applicants required to submit FAFSA. In 2010, 405 master's awarded. *Degree program information:* Part-time and evening/weekend programs available. Postbaccalaureate distance learning degree programs offered (minimal on-campus study). Offers business (MBA, MSM); conflict management and dispute resolution (MA); liberal arts (MLA). *Application deadline:* Applications are processed on a rolling basis. *Application fee:* $45. *Application Contact:* Kelly Belk, Director of Marketing, 913-491-4432, Fax: 913-491-0470, E-mail: kbelk@bakeru.edu. *Vice President and Dean,* Dr. Peggy Harris, 785-594-8492, Fax: 785-594-8363, E-mail: peggy.harris@bakeru.edu.

BAKKE GRADUATE UNIVERSITY, Seattle, WA 98104

General Information Independent-religious, coed, primarily men, graduate-only institution. *Enrollment by degree level:* 146 master's, 197 doctoral, 36 other advanced degrees. *Graduate faculty:* 7 full-time (2 women), 30 part-time/adjunct (4 women). *Tuition:* Full-time $5000; part-time $500 per credit. *Required fees:* $175; $50 per course. *Graduate housing:* On-campus housing not available. *Student services:* Career counseling, writing training. *Library facilities:* Bakke Graduate University Library. *Online resources:* web page. *Collection:* 5,000 titles, 69 serial subscriptions, 125 audiovisual materials.

Computer facilities: 4 computers available on campus for general student use. A campuswide network can be accessed. Online class registration is available. *Web address:* http://www.bgu.edu/.

General Application Contact: Ruby Tice, Admissions Coordinator, 206-246-9100 Ext. 122, Fax: 206-246-8828, E-mail: rubyt@bgu.edu.

GRADUATE UNITS

Programs in Pastoral Ministry and Business Students: 78 full-time (15 women), 301 part-time (105 women); includes 199 minority (99 Black or African American, non-Hispanic/Latino; 1 American Indian or Alaska Native, non-Hispanic/Latino; 90 Asian, non-Hispanic/Latino; 9 Hispanic/Latino). Average age 38. 41 applicants, 98% accepted, 25 enrolled. *Faculty:* 7 full-time (2 women), 30 part-time/adjunct (4 women). Expenses: Contact institution. *Financial support:* In 2010–11, 140 students received support. Scholarships/grants and tuition waivers (partial) available. Financial award applicants required to submit FAFSA. In 2010, 11 master's, 37 doctorates awarded. *Degree program information:* Part-time programs available. Postbaccalaureate distance learning degree programs offered (minimal on-campus study). Offers business (MBA); global urban leadership (MA); social and civic entrepreneurship (MA); transformational leadership for the global city (D Min). *Application deadline:* For fall admission, 7/1 priority date for domestic students; for winter admission, 12/1 for domestic students; for spring admission, 3/15 for domestic students. Applications are processed on a rolling basis. *Application fee:* $75. Electronic applications accepted. *Application Contact:* Addie Tolle, Registrar, 206-246-9100 Ext. 110, Fax: 206-264-8828. *Academic Dean,* Dr. Gwen Dewey, 206-264-9100 Ext. 119, Fax: 206-264-8828, E-mail: gwend@bgu.edu.

BALDWIN-WALLACE COLLEGE, Berea, OH 44017-2088

General Information Independent-religious, coed, comprehensive institution. *Enrollment:* 4,352 graduate, professional, and undergraduate students; 344 full-time matriculated graduate/professional students (205 women), 310 part-time matriculated graduate/professional students (195 women). *Enrollment by degree level:* 654 master's. *Graduate faculty:* 30 full-time (8 women), 28 part-time/adjunct (9 women). *Tuition:* Full-time $16,750; part-time $712 per credit hour. Tuition and fees vary according to program. *Graduate housing:* Room and/or apartments available to single students; on-campus housing not available to married students. *Student services:* Campus employment opportunities, campus safety program, career counseling, exercise/wellness program, free psychological counseling, international student services, low-cost health insurance, multicultural affairs office, services for students with disabilities, teacher training, writing training. *Library facilities:* Ritter Library plus 2 others. *Online resources:* library catalog, web page, access to other libraries' catalogs. *Collection:* 200,000 titles, 22,000 serial subscriptions. *Research affiliation:* Cleveland State University (Science, Technology, Engineering, and Math (STEM)), Ohio Board of Regents (science and science teaching), Parma City Schools/Ohio Board of Regents (Science, Technology, Engineering, and Math (STEM)).

Computer facilities: 565 computers available on campus for general student use. A campuswide network can be accessed from student residence rooms. Online class registration is available. *Web address:* http://www.bw.edu/.

General Application Contact: Winifred W. Gerhardt, Director of Admission for the Evening and Weekend College, 440-826-2222, Fax: 440-826-3830, E-mail: admission@bw.edu.

GRADUATE UNITS

Graduate Programs Students: 344 full-time (205 women), 310 part-time (195 women); includes 105 minority (64 Black or African American, non-Hispanic/Latino; 2 American Indian or Alaska Native, non-Hispanic/Latino; 14 Asian, non-Hispanic/Latino; 16 Hispanic/Latino; 9 Two or more races, non-Hispanic/Latino), 13 international. Average age 34. 319 applicants, 71% accepted, 146 enrolled. *Faculty:* 30 full-time (8 women), 28 part-time/adjunct (9 women). Expenses: Contact institution. *Financial support:* Career-related internships or fieldwork available. Support available to part-time students. Financial award application deadline: 5/1; financial award applicants required to submit FAFSA. In 2010, 257 master's awarded. *Degree program information:* Part-time and evening/weekend programs available. *Application deadline:* Applications are processed on a rolling basis. *Application fee:* $25. Electronic applications accepted. *Application Contact:* Winifred W. Gerhardt, Director of Admission for the Evening and Weekend College, 440-826-2222, Fax: 440-826-3830, E-mail: admission@bw.edu. *Vice President for Academic Affairs and Dean of the College,* Mary Lou Higgerson, 440-826-2251, Fax: 440-826-2329, E-mail: mlhiggers@bw.edu.

Division of Business Students: 233 full-time (119 women), 218 part-time (119 women); includes 82 minority (47 Black or African American, non-Hispanic/Latino; 2 American Indian or Alaska Native, non-Hispanic/Latino; 14 Asian, non-Hispanic/Latino; 14 Hispanic/Latino; 5 Two or more races, non-Hispanic/Latino), 13 international. Average age 35. 162 applicants, 77% accepted, 88 enrolled. *Faculty:* 21 full-time (4 women), 22 part-time/adjunct (5 women). Expenses: Contact institution. *Financial support:* Career-related internships or fieldwork available. Support available to part-time students. Financial award application deadline: 5/1; financial award applicants required to submit FAFSA. In 2010, 183 master's awarded. *Degree program information:* Part-time and evening/weekend programs available. Postbaccalaureate distance learning degree programs offered (minimal on-campus study). Offers accounting (MBA); business administration-systems management (MBA); entrepreneurship (MBA); executive management (MBA); health care management (MBA); human resources (MBA); international management (MBA); sustainability (MBA). *Application deadline:* For fall admission, 7/25 priority date for domestic students, 4/30 priority date for international students; for spring admission, 12/15 priority date for domestic students, 9/30 priority date for international students. Applications are processed on a rolling basis. *Application fee:* $25. Electronic applications accepted. *Application Contact:* Laura Spencer, Graduate Application Specialist, 440-826-2191, Fax: 440-826-3868, E-mail: lspencer@bw.edu. *Chairperson,* Peter Kelly, 440-826-2394, Fax: 440-826-3868, E-mail: pkelly@bw.edu.

Division of Education Students: 111 full-time (86 women), 92 part-time (76 women); includes 23 minority (17 Black or African American, non-Hispanic/Latino; 2 Hispanic/Latino; 4 Two or more races, non-Hispanic/Latino). Average age 31. 155 applicants, 66% accepted, 58 enrolled. *Faculty:* 9 full-time (4 women), 6 part-time/adjunct (4 women). Expenses: Contact institution. *Financial support:* Career-related internships or fieldwork available. Support available to part-time students. Financial award application deadline: 5/1; financial award applicants required to submit FAFSA. In 2010, 74 master's awarded. *Degree program information:* Part-time and evening/weekend programs available. Postbaccalaureate distance learning degree programs offered (no on-campus study). Offers educational technology (MA Ed); leadership in higher education (MA Ed); literacy (MA Ed); mild/moderate educational needs (MA Ed); school leadership (MA Ed); teaching and learning (MA Ed). *Application deadline:* For fall admission, 8/15 priority date for domestic students; for spring admission, 12/15 priority date for domestic students. Applications are processed on a rolling basis. *Application fee:* $25. Electronic applications accepted. *Application Contact:* Winifred W. Gerhardt, Director of Admission for the Evening and Weekend College, 440-826-2222, Fax: 440-826-3830, E-mail: admission@bw.edu. *Chair,* Karen Kaye, 440-826-2168, Fax: 440-826-3779, E-mail: kkaye@bw.edu.

BALL STATE UNIVERSITY, Muncie, IN 47306-1099

General Information State-supported, coed, university. CGS member. *Enrollment:* 22,083 graduate, professional, and undergraduate students; 1,269 full-time matriculated graduate/professional students (705 women), 2,605 part-time matriculated graduate/professional students (1,776 women). *Enrollment by degree level:* 3,342 master's, 417 doctoral, 115 other advanced degrees. *Graduate faculty:* 712. Tuition, state resident: full-time $6160; part-time $299 per credit hour. Tuition, nonresident: full-time $16,020; part-time $783 per credit hour. *Required fees:* $2278; $95 per credit hour. *Graduate housing:* Rooms and/or apartments available on a first-come, first-served basis to single and married students. Typical cost: $8964 (including board) for single students; $7020 per year for married students. Housing application deadline: 3/1. *Student services:* Campus employment opportunities, campus safety program, career counseling, child daycare facilities, exercise/wellness program, free psychological counseling, international student services, low-cost health insurance, multicultural affairs office, services for students with disabilities, teacher training. *Library facilities:* Bracken Library plus 2 others. *Online resources:* library catalog, web page. *Collection:* 1.1 million titles, 2,217 serial subscriptions, 65,080 audiovisual materials.

Computer facilities: Computer purchase and lease plans are available. 865 computers available on campus for general student use. A campuswide network can be accessed from student residence rooms and from off campus. Online class registration, room reservations, testing and test results, manage and pay tuition, order/buy textbooks, request room repairs, order transcripts, manage meal plan, manage and prepay long distance service, undergraduate degree progress report are available. *Web address:* http://www.bsu.edu/.

General Application Contact: Dr. Robert J. Morris, Associate Provost for Research and Dean of the Graduate School, 765-285-1300, Fax: 765-285-1994, E-mail: rmorris@bsu.edu.

GRADUATE UNITS

Graduate School Students: 1,269 full-time (705 women), 2,605 part-time (1,776 women); includes 235 minority (117 Black or African American, non-Hispanic/Latino; 11 American Indian or Alaska Native, non-Hispanic/Latino; 20 Asian, non-Hispanic/Latino; 57 Hispanic/Latino; 3 Native Hawaiian or other Pacific Islander, non-Hispanic/Latino; 27 Two or more races, non-Hispanic/Latino), 323 international. 2,540 applicants, 55% accepted, 848 enrolled. *Faculty:* 705. Expenses: Contact institution. *Financial support:* In 2010–11, 921 students received support, including 48 research assistantships with full and partial tuition reimbursements available (averaging $9,444 per year), 629 teaching assistantships with full and partial tuition reimbursements available (averaging $9,685 per year); fellowships, career-related internships or fieldwork, Federal Work-Study, tuition waivers (partial), and unspecified assistantships also available. Support available to part-time students. Financial award application deadline: 3/1. In 2010, 1,211 master's, 50 doctorates, 104 other advanced degrees awarded. *Degree program information:* Part-time and evening/weekend programs available. Postbaccalaureate distance learning degree programs offered (no on-campus study). *Application deadline:* For fall admission, 3/1 priority date for domestic students, 1/1 priority date for international students; for spring admission, 12/1 priority date for domestic students, 7/1 priority date for international students. Applications are processed on a rolling basis. *Application fee:* $35 ($40 for international students). Electronic applications accepted. *Application Contact:* Dr. Carolyn A. Kapinus, Associate Dean, 765-285-1297, Fax: 765-285-1328, E-mail: ckapinus@bsu.edu. *Associate Provost for Research and Dean of the Graduate School,* Dr. Robert J. Morris, 765-285-1300, Fax: 765-285-1994, E-mail: rmorris@bsu.edu.

College of Applied Science and Technology Students: 82 full-time (45 women), 666 part-time (521 women); includes 48 minority (26 Black or African American, non-Hispanic/Latino; 1 American Indian or Alaska Native, non-Hispanic/Latino; 2 Asian, non-Hispanic/Latino; 14 Hispanic/Latino; 5 Two or more races, non-Hispanic/Latino), 18 international. Average age 29. 487 applicants, 40% accepted, 113 enrolled. *Faculty:* 80. Expenses: Contact institution. *Financial support:* In 2010–11, 7 research assistantships with full tuition reimbursements (averaging $10,114 per year), 85 teaching assistantships with full tuition reimbursements (averaging $10,343 per year) were awarded; career-related internships or fieldwork and tuition waivers (full) also available. Financial award application deadline: 3/1. In 2010, 243 master's, 3 doctorates, 6 other advanced degrees awarded. *Degree program information:* Part-time and evening/weekend programs available. Postbaccalaureate distance learning degree programs offered (no on-campus study). Offers applied gerontology (MA); applied science and technology (MA, MAE, MS, DNP, PhD, Graduate Certificate); family and consumer sciences (MA, MS); human bioenergetics (PhD); industry and technology (MA, MAE); nursing (MS, DNP); physical education (MA, MAE, MS, PhD); wellness management (MA, MS). *Application deadline:* For fall admission, 1/1 for international students; for spring admission, 7/1 for international students. Applications are processed on a rolling basis. *Application fee:* $50. Electronic applications accepted. *Application Contact:* Dr. Robert Morris, Associate Provost for Research and Dean of the Graduate School, 765-285-5723, Fax: 765-285-1328, E-mail: rmorris@bsu.edu. *Dean,* Dr. Mitchell Whaley, 765-285-5816, E-mail: mwhaley@bsu.edu.

College of Architecture and Planning Students: 166 full-time (72 women), 45 part-time (20 women); includes 8 minority (2 Black or African American, non-Hispanic/Latino; 1 American Indian or Alaska Native, non-Hispanic/Latino; 1 Asian, non-Hispanic/Latino; 2 Hispanic/

Latino; 2 Two or more races, non-Hispanic/Latino), 44 international. Average age 27. 279 applicants, 63% accepted, 72 enrolled. *Faculty:* 47. Expenses: Contact institution. *Financial support:* In 2010–11, 73 research assistantships with full tuition reimbursements (averaging $6,629 per year) were awarded; career-related internships or fieldwork also available. Support available to part-time students. Financial award application deadline: 3/1. In 2010, 73 master's awarded. *Degree program information:* Part-time programs available. Offers architecture (M Arch); architecture and planning (M Arch, MLA, MS, MUD, MURP); historic preservation (M Arch, MS); landscape architecture (MLA); urban design (MUD); urban planning (MURP). *Application deadline:* For fall admission, 1/1 priority date for international students. Applications are processed on a rolling basis. *Application fee:* $50. Electronic applications accepted. *Application Contact:* Dr. Robert Morris, Associate Provost for Research and Dean of the Graduate School, 765-285-1300, E-mail: rmorris@bsu.edu. *Dean*, Dr. Guillermo Vasquez de Velasco, 765-285-5861, Fax: 765-285-3726.

College of Communication, Information, and Media Students: 141 full-time (58 women), 74 part-time (35 women); includes 9 Black or African American, non-Hispanic/Latino; 1 American Indian or Alaska Native, non-Hispanic/Latino; 1 Asian, non-Hispanic/Latino; 3 Hispanic/Latino; 2 Two or more races, non-Hispanic/Latino, 32 international. Average age 25. 223 applicants, 61% accepted, 91 enrolled. *Faculty:* 31. Expenses: Contact institution. *Financial support:* In 2010–11, 8 research assistantships with full tuition reimbursements (averaging $6,668 per year), 66 teaching assistantships with full tuition reimbursements (averaging $7,976 per year) were awarded; career-related internships or fieldwork also available. Financial award application deadline: 3/1. In 2010, 92 master's awarded. *Degree program information:* Part-time programs available. Postbaccalaureate distance learning degree programs offered (no on-campus study). Offers communication, information, and media (MA, MS); digital storytelling (MA); information and communication sciences (MS); journalism (MA); public relations (MA); speech, public address, forensics, and rhetoric (MA). *Application deadline:* For fall admission, 1/1 priority date for international students; for spring admission, 7/1 priority date for international students. Applications are processed on a rolling basis. *Application fee:* $50. Electronic applications accepted. *Application Contact:* Dr. Robert Morris, Associate Provost for Research and Dean of the Graduate School, 765-285-4723, Fax: 765-285-1328, E-mail: rmorris@bsu.edu. *Dean*, Roger Lavery, 765-285-6000, Fax: 765-285-6002.

College of Fine Arts Students: 64 full-time (36 women), 63 part-time (32 women); includes 8 minority (2 Black or African American, non-Hispanic/Latino; 1 American Indian or Alaska Native, non-Hispanic/Latino; 1 Asian, non-Hispanic/Latino; 2 Hispanic/Latino; 2 Two or more races, non-Hispanic/Latino), 30 international. Average age 26. 99 applicants, 72% accepted, 47 enrolled. *Faculty:* 69. Expenses: Contact institution. *Financial support:* In 2010–11, 2 research assistantships (averaging $6,700 per year), 58 teaching assistantships with full tuition reimbursements (averaging $9,019 per year) were awarded; fellowships with full tuition reimbursements also available. Support available to part-time students. Financial award application deadline: 3/1. In 2010, 28 master's, 8 doctorates, 5 other advanced degrees awarded. *Degree program information:* Part-time programs available. Offers art (MA); art education (MA, MAE); fine arts (MA, MAE, MFA, MM, DA, Graduate Certificate); music education (MA, MM, DA). *Application deadline:* For fall admission, 1/1 priority date for international students; for spring admission, 6/1 priority date for international students. Applications are processed on a rolling basis. *Application fee:* $50. Electronic applications accepted. *Application Contact:* Dr. Robert Morris, Associate Provost for Research and Dean of the Graduate School, 765-285-1300, E-mail: rmorris@bsu.edu. *Dean*, Dr. Robert Kvam, 765-285-5495, Fax: 765-285-3790, E-mail: rkvam@bsu.edu.

College of Sciences and Humanities Students: 395 full-time (223 women), 297 part-time (159 women); includes 57 minority (11 Black or African American, non-Hispanic/Latino; 8 American Indian or Alaska Native, non-Hispanic/Latino; 8 Asian, non-Hispanic/Latino; 10 Hispanic/Latino; 10 Native Hawaiian or other Pacific Islander, non-Hispanic/Latino; 10 Two or more races, non-Hispanic/Latino), 113 international. Average age 26. 821 applicants, 45% accepted, 218 enrolled. *Faculty:* 301. Expenses: Contact institution. *Financial support:* In 2010–11, 11 research assistantships with full tuition reimbursements (averaging $10,467 per year), 225 teaching assistantships with full tuition reimbursements (averaging $11,415 per year) were awarded; career-related internships or fieldwork and Federal Work-Study also available. Support available to part-time students. Financial award application deadline: 3/1. In 2010, 210 master's, 9 doctorates, 19 other advanced degrees awarded. *Degree program information:* Part-time programs available. Postbaccalaureate distance learning degree programs offered (minimal on-campus study). Offers actuarial science (MA); anthropology (MA); applied linguistics (PhD); biology (MA, MAE, MS); biology education (Ed D); chemistry (MA, MS); clinical psychology (MA); cognitive and social processes (MA); computer science (MA, MS); criminal justice (MPA); English (MA, PhD); geography (MS); geology (MA, MS); history (MA); linguistics (MA, PhD); linguistics and teaching English to speakers of other languages (MA); mathematics (MA, MS); mathematics education (MA); natural resources (MA, MS); physics (MA, MAE, MS); physiology (MA, MS); political science (MA); public administration (MPA); sciences and humanities (MA, MAE, MPA, MS, Au D, Ed D, PhD, Graduate Certificate); sociology (MA); speech pathology and audiology (MA, Au D); statistics (MA); teaching English to speakers of other languages (MA). *Application deadline:* For fall admission, 1/1 priority date for international students; for spring admission, 7/1 priority date for international students. Applications are processed on a rolling basis. *Application fee:* $50. Electronic applications accepted. *Application Contact:* Dr. Robert Morris, Associate Provost for Research and Dean of the Graduate School, 765-285-1300, E-mail: rmorris@bsu.edu. *Dean*, Dr. Michael Maggioto, 765-285-1042, Fax: 765-285-8980.

Miller College of Business Students: 97 full-time (31 women), 183 part-time (71 women); includes 4 Black or African American, non-Hispanic/Latino; 1 Asian, non-Hispanic/Latino; 2 Two or more races, non-Hispanic/Latino, 24 international. Average age 26. 206 applicants, 55% accepted, 93 enrolled. *Faculty:* 60. Expenses: Contact institution. *Financial support:* In 2010–11, 39 teaching assistantships with full tuition reimbursements (averaging $9,065 per year) were awarded; fellowships with full tuition reimbursements, research assistantships, unspecified assistantships also available. Support available to part-time students. Financial award application deadline: 3/1. In 2010, 92 master's awarded. *Degree program information:* Part-time and evening/weekend programs available. Offers accounting (MS); business (MAE, MBA, MS); business administration (MBA); business education (MAE). *Application fee:* $50. *Application Contact:* Jennifer Bott, Graduate Coordinator, 765-285-1931, Fax: 765-285-8818, E-mail: jbott@bsu.edu. *Interim Dean*, Dr. Rajib Sanyal, 765-285-8192, Fax: 765-285-5117.

Teachers College Students: 324 full-time (240 women), 1,231 part-time (909 women); includes 98 minority (60 Black or African American, non-Hispanic/Latino; 3 American Indian or Alaska Native, non-Hispanic/Latino; 6 Asian, non-Hispanic/Latino; 24 Hispanic/Latino; 1 Native Hawaiian or other Pacific Islander, non-Hispanic/Latino; 4 Two or more races, non-Hispanic/Latino), 62 international. Average age 28. 553 applicants, 76% accepted, 406 enrolled. *Faculty:* 98. Expenses: Contact institution. *Financial support:* In 2010–11, 6 research assistantships with full tuition reimbursements (averaging $10,409 per year), 121 teaching assistantships with full tuition reimbursements (averaging $9,925 per year) were awarded; career-related internships or fieldwork and Federal Work-Study also available. Support available to part-time students. Financial award application deadline: 3/1. In 2010, 454 master's, 26 doctorates, 14 other advanced degrees awarded. *Degree program information:* Part-time and evening/weekend programs available. Postbaccalaureate distance learning degree programs offered (no on-campus study). Offers adult and community education (MA); adult education (MA, Ed D); adult, community, and higher education (Ed D); applied behavior analysis (MA); counseling psychology (MA, PhD); curriculum (MAE, Ed S); education (MA, MAE, Ed D, PhD, Ed S, Graduate Certificate); educational administration (MAE, Ed D); educational psychology (MA, PhD, Ed S); educational studies (MAE, PhD); elementary education (MAE, Ed D, PhD); executive development (MA); school psychology (MA, PhD, Ed S); school superintendency (Ed S); secondary education (MA); social psychology (MA); special education (MA, MAE, Ed D, Ed S); student affairs administration in higher education (MA). *Application deadline:* For fall admission, 1/1 priority date for international students. *Application fee:* $50. *Application Contact:* Dr. Robert Morris, Associate Provost for Research and Dean of the Graduate School, 765-285-1300, E-mail: rmorris@bsu.edu. *Dean*, Dr. John E. Jacobson, 765-285-5251, Fax: 765-285-5455, E-mail: jejacobson@bsu.edu.

BALTIMORE INTERNATIONAL COLLEGE, Baltimore, MD 21202-3230

General Information Independent, coed, comprehensive institution.

GRADUATE UNITS

Program in International Hospitality Management *Degree program information:* Part-time and evening/weekend programs available. Postbaccalaureate distance learning degree programs offered. Offers international hospitality management (MS).

BANGOR THEOLOGICAL SEMINARY, Bangor, ME 04401-4699

General Information Independent-religious, coed, graduate-only institution. *Graduate housing:* On-campus housing not available.

GRADUATE UNITS

Professional Program *Degree program information:* Part-time programs available. Offers theology (M Div, MA, MTS, D Min). M Div not offered at Portland, ME campus.

BANK STREET COLLEGE OF EDUCATION, New York, NY 10025

General Information Independent, coed, graduate-only institution. *Enrollment by degree level:* 904 master's. *Graduate faculty:* 72 full-time (61 women), 56 part-time/adjunct (47 women). *Student services:* Campus employment opportunities, campus safety program, career counseling, child daycare facilities, international student services, services for students with disabilities, teacher training, writing training. *Library facilities:* Bank Street College Library. *Online resources:* library catalog, web page, access to other libraries' catalogs. *Collection:* 119,537 titles, 28,658 serial subscriptions, 3,140 audiovisual materials. *Research affiliation:* American Association of Colleges for Teacher Education (education), Columbia Mailman School of Public Health (education), Educational Development Corporation (education), Mathematica Policy Research, Inc. (education), Center for Teaching Quality (education).

Computer facilities: 60 computers available on campus for general student use. A campuswide network can be accessed from off campus. Online class registration, wireless campus—ports not necessary (#10b) are available. *Web address:* http://www.bankstreet.edu/.

General Application Contact: Ann Morgan, Director of Graduate Admissions, 212-875-4403, Fax: 212-873-4678, E-mail: gradcourses@bankstreet.edu.

GRADUATE UNITS

Graduate School Students: 353 full-time (310 women), 551 part-time (487 women); includes 208 minority (78 Black or African American, non-Hispanic/Latino; 4 American Indian or Alaska Native, non-Hispanic/Latino; 32 Asian, non-Hispanic/Latino; 68 Hispanic/Latino; 1 Native Hawaiian or other Pacific Islander, non-Hispanic/Latino; 25 Two or more races, non-Hispanic/Latino), 9 international. Average age 30. 602 applicants, 80% accepted, 348 enrolled. *Faculty:* 72 full-time (61 women), 56 part-time/adjunct (47 women). Expenses: Contact institution. *Financial support:* In 2010–11, 674 students received support. Career-related internships or fieldwork, Federal Work-Study, scholarships/grants, and unspecified assistantships available. Support available to part-time students. Financial award application deadline: 4/15; financial award applicants required to submit FAFSA. In 2010, 366 master's awarded. Offers advanced literacy specialization (Ed M); bilingual childhood special education (Ed M); bilingual early childhood general education (MS Ed); bilingual early childhood special and general education (MS Ed); bilingual early childhood special education (Ed M, MS Ed); bilingual elementary/childhood general education (MS Ed); bilingual elementary/childhood special and general education (MS Ed); bilingual elementary/childhood special education (MS Ed); child life (MS); early childhood and elementary/childhood education (MS Ed); early childhood education (MS Ed); early childhood leadership (MS Ed); early childhood special and general education (MS Ed); early childhood special education (Ed M, MS Ed); education (Ed M, MS, MS Ed); educational leadership (MS Ed); elementary/childhood education (MS Ed); elementary/childhood special and general education (MS Ed); elementary/childhood special education (MS Ed); elementary/childhood special education certification (Ed M); infant and family development (MS Ed); infant and family early childhood special and general education (MS Ed); infant and family/early childhood special education (Ed M); leadership for educational change (Ed M, MS Ed); leadership in mathematics education (MS Ed); leadership in museum education (MS Ed); leadership in the arts: creative writing (MS Ed); leadership in the arts: visual arts (MS Ed); museum education (MS Ed); museum education: elementary education certification (MS Ed); museum education: middle school certification (MS Ed); reading and literacy (MS Ed); teaching literacy (MS Ed); teaching literacy and childhood general education (MS Ed). *Application deadline:* For fall admission, 2/15 priority date for domestic and international students; for spring admission, 11/1 priority date for domestic and international students. Applications are processed on a rolling basis. *Application fee:* $65. Electronic applications accepted. *Application Contact:* Ann Morgan, Director of Graduate Admissions, 212-875-4403, Fax: 212-875-4678, E-mail: amorgan@bankstreet.edu. *Dean*, Dr. Virginia Casper, 212-875-4703, Fax: 212-875-4753, E-mail: vcasper@bankstreet.edu.

BAPTIST BIBLE COLLEGE, Springfield, MO 65803-3498

General Information Independent-religious, coed, comprehensive institution. *Graduate housing:* Rooms and/or apartments available on a first-come, first-served basis to single students and available to married students.

GRADUATE UNITS

Graduate School of Theology *Degree program information:* Part-time programs available. Offers biblical counseling (MA); biblical studies (MA); church ministry (MA); intercultural studies (MA); theology (M Div). Electronic applications accepted.

BAPTIST BIBLE COLLEGE OF PENNSYLVANIA, Clarks Summit, PA 18411-1297

General Information Independent-religious, coed, comprehensive institution. *Enrollment:* 858 graduate, professional, and undergraduate students; 116 full-time matriculated graduate/professional students (21 women), 147 part-time matriculated graduate/professional students (41 women). *Enrollment by degree level:* 220 master's, 31 doctoral, 12 other advanced degrees. *Graduate faculty:* 12 full-time (0 women), 1 part-time/adjunct (0 women). *Tuition:* Full-time $7488; part-time $416 per credit. *Required fees:* $522; $29 per credit. Full-time tuition and fees vary according to degree level and campus/location. *Graduate housing:* Room and/or apartments available on a first-come, first-served basis to single students; on-campus housing not available to married students. Typical cost: $2300 per year ($6150 including board). Room and board charges vary according to board plan. *Student services:* Campus employment opportunities, campus safety program, career counseling, free psychological counseling, international student services. *Library facilities:* Murphy Memorial Library. *Online resources:* library catalog, web page. *Collection:* 97,376 titles, 26,314 serial subscriptions, 6,038 audiovisual materials.

Computer facilities: 25 computers available on campus for general student use. A campuswide network can be accessed from student residence rooms. Online class registration is available. *Web address:* http://www.bbc.edu/.

General Application Contact: Howard Hicks, Director of Admissions, 570-585-9345, Fax: 570-586-1753, E-mail: gradadmissions@bbc.edu.

GRADUATE UNITS

Baptist Bible Seminary Students: 71 full-time (0 women), 79 part-time (0 women); includes 16 minority (10 Black or African American, non-Hispanic/Latino; 4 Asian, non-Hispanic/Latino; 2 Hispanic/Latino), 7 international. Average age 38. *Faculty:* 10 full-time (0 women). Expenses: Contact institution. *Financial support:* Career-related internships or fieldwork and scholarships/grants available. Support available to part-time students. In 2010, 23 master's, 4 doctorates awarded. *Degree program information:* Part-time and evening/weekend programs available. Postbaccalaureate distance learning degree programs offered (minimal on-campus study).

Baptist Bible College of Pennsylvania (continued)

Offers biblical studies (PhD); church planting (M Div); global missions (M Div); military chaplaincy (M Div); ministry (M Min, D Min); pastor of church education (M Div); pastor of outreach (M Div); pastoral counseling (M Div); pastoral leadership (M Div); theology (M Div, Th M); youth pastor (M Div). *Application deadline:* Applications are processed on a rolling basis. *Application fee:* $30. Electronic applications accepted. *Application Contact:* Paul Golden, Director of Seminary Admissions, 570-586-9396, Fax: 570-585-4057, E-mail: pgolden@bbc.edu. *Seminary Academic Dean*, Dr. Michael Stallard, 570-585-9348, Fax: 570-585-4057, E-mail: mstallard@bbc.edu.

Graduate School Students: 45 full-time (21 women), 68 part-time (41 women); includes 10 minority (9 Black or African American, non-Hispanic/Latino; 1 Hispanic/Latino), 1 international. Average age 31. *Faculty:* 2 full-time (0 women), 1 part-time/adjunct (0 women). Expenses: Contact institution. *Financial support:* In 2010–11, 75 students received support. Institutionally sponsored loans and scholarships/grants available. Financial award application deadline: 8/20; financial award applicants required to submit FAFSA. In 2010, 14 master's awarded. *Degree program information:* Part-time and evening/weekend programs available. Postbaccalaureate distance learning degree programs offered (no on-campus study). Offers Bible (MA); counseling (MS); education (MS). *Application deadline:* Applications are processed on a rolling basis. *Application fee:* $30. *Application Contact:* Drew Whipple, Assistant Director of Enrollment, 570-585-9370, Fax: 570-585-9299, E-mail: gradadmissions@bbc.edu. *Provost*, Dr. James Lytle, 570-586-2400 Ext. 9222, Fax: 570-586-1753.

BAPTIST MISSIONARY ASSOCIATION THEOLOGICAL SEMINARY, Jacksonville, TX 75766-5407

General Information Independent-religious, coed, primarily men, comprehensive institution. *Graduate housing:* Rooms and/or apartments available on a first-come, first-served basis to single and married students. Housing application deadline: 6/1.

GRADUATE UNITS

Graduate and Professional Programs *Degree program information:* Part-time programs available. Offers theology (M Div, MAR). Electronic applications accepted.

BAPTIST THEOLOGICAL SEMINARY AT RICHMOND, Richmond, VA 23227

General Information Independent-religious, coed, graduate-only institution. *Enrollment by degree level:* 87 first professional, 6 master's, 8 doctoral. *Graduate faculty:* 8 full-time (2 women), 19 part-time/adjunct (7 women). *Tuition:* Full-time $9000; part-time $900 per credit. *Required fees:* $135 per year. *Graduate housing:* Rooms and/or apartments available on a first-come, first-served basis to single and married students. Typical cost: $5715 per year for single students; $7110 per year for married students. Housing application deadline: 6/1. *Student services:* Campus employment opportunities, campus safety program, exercise/wellness program, free psychological counseling, international student services, services for students with disabilities, writing training. *Library facilities:* Morton Library. *Online resources:* library catalog, web page, access to other libraries' catalogs. *Collection:* 309,610 titles, 1,358 serial subscriptions, 34,252 audiovisual materials.

Computer facilities: 4 computers available on campus for general student use. A campuswide network can be accessed from student residence rooms and from off campus. *Web address:* http://www.btsr.edu/.

General Application Contact: Tiffany Kellogg Pittman, Director of Admissions, 804-204-1208, Fax: 804-355-8182, E-mail: admissions@btsr.edu.

GRADUATE UNITS

Graduate and Professional Programs Students: 71 full-time (36 women), 30 part-time (13 women); includes 10 minority (9 Black or African American, non-Hispanic/Latino; 1 Hispanic/Latino), 3 international. Average age 46. 40 applicants, 88% accepted, 30 enrolled. *Faculty:* 8 full-time (2 women), 19 part-time/adjunct (7 women). Expenses: Contact institution. *Financial support:* In 2010–11, 12 teaching assistantships (averaging $1,650 per year) were awarded; scholarships/grants and tuition waivers (partial) also available. Financial award application deadline: 2/1. In 2010, 24 first professional degrees, 4 doctorates awarded. *Degree program information:* Part-time programs available. Postbaccalaureate distance learning degree programs offered (minimal on-campus study). Offers biblical interpretation (M Div); Christian education (M Div); theological studies (MATS); theology (D Min); youth and student ministries (M Div). *Application deadline:* For fall admission, 8/1 priority date for domestic students, 5/1 priority date for international students; for winter admission, 12/1 priority date for domestic students, 9/1 priority date for international students; for spring admission, 1/1 priority date for domestic students, 10/1 priority date for international students. Applications are processed on a rolling basis. *Application fee:* $35. *Application Contact:* Tiffany Kellogg Pittman, Director of Admissions, 804-204-1208, Fax: 804-355-8182, E-mail: admissions@btsr.edu. *President*, Dr. Ronald W. Crawford, 804-204-1201, Fax: 804-355-8182, E-mail: rcrawford@btsr.edu.

BARD COLLEGE, Annandale-on-Hudson, NY 12504

General Information Independent, coed, comprehensive institution. *Graduate housing:* Room and/or apartments available on a first-come, first-served basis to single students; on-campus housing not available to married students.

GRADUATE UNITS

Bard Center for Environmental Policy Students: 58 full-time (41 women). Average age 26. 75 applicants, 77% accepted, 28 enrolled. *Faculty:* 10 full-time (5 women), 6 part-time/adjunct (3 women). Expenses: Contact institution. *Financial support:* In 2010–11, 58 students received support, including 58 fellowships (averaging $7,000 per year), 6 research assistantships (averaging $6,000 per year), 1 teaching assistantship (averaging $6,000 per year); career-related internships or fieldwork, scholarships/grants, tuition waivers (full), and unspecified assistantships also available. Support available to part-time students. Financial award application deadline: 2/15; financial award applicants required to submit FAFSA. In 2010, 13 master's awarded. *Degree program information:* Part-time programs available. Offers climate science and policy (MS, Professional Certificate); environmental policy (MS, Professional Certificate); sustainability (MBA). *Application deadline:* For winter admission, 1/15 priority date for domestic and international students; for spring admission, 5/15 for domestic and international students. Applications are processed on a rolling basis. *Application fee:* $65. Electronic applications accepted. *Application Contact:* Molly Williams, Admissions Coordinator, 845-758-7071, Fax: 845-758-7636, E-mail: mwilliam@bard.edu. *Director*, Dr. Eban Goodstein, 845-758-7067, Fax: 845-758-7636, E-mail: ebangood@bard.edu.

Center for Curatorial Studies Offers curatorial studies (MA). Electronic applications accepted.

Conservatory of Music Offers music (MFA, MM); vocal arts (MM).

The Conductors Institute Offers conducting (MFA).

International Center of Photography Offers advanced photographic studies (MFA).

Master of Arts in Teaching Program Offers teaching (MAT). Electronic applications accepted.

Milton Avery Graduate School of the Arts Offers arts (MFA). Electronic applications accepted.

BARD GRADUATE CENTER: DECORATIVE ARTS, DESIGN HISTORY, MATERIAL CULTURE, New York, NY 10024-3602

General Information Independent, coed, primarily women, graduate-only institution. *Graduate housing:* Rooms and/or apartments available on a first-come, first-served basis to single and married students. Housing application deadline: 4/15. *Research affiliation:* Brooklyn Museum of Art, Metropolitan Museum of Art, New York Historical Society, American Museum of Natural History.

GRADUATE UNITS

Graduate Studies *Degree program information:* Part-time programs available. Offers decorative arts, design history, and material culture (M Phil, MA, PhD).

BARRY UNIVERSITY, Miami Shores, FL 33161-6695

General Information Independent-religious, coed, university. *Graduate housing:* On-campus housing not available. *Research affiliation:* Baxter Corporation (immunology, diagnostics), Coulter Corporation (immunology, cytology), Cordis Corporation (cardiac product development), Diamedix (immunological diagnostics), Noven Pharmaceutical, Sano Pharmaceuticals.

GRADUATE UNITS

Andreas School of Business *Degree program information:* Part-time and evening/weekend programs available. Offers accounting (MSA); business (MBA, MSA, MSM, Certificate); business administration (MBA); finance (Certificate); health services administration (Certificate); international business (Certificate); management (MSM); management information systems (Certificate); marketing (Certificate). Electronic applications accepted.

College of Health Sciences *Degree program information:* Part-time and evening/weekend programs available. Offers anesthesiology (MS); biology (MS); biomedical sciences (MS); health care leadership (Certificate); health care planning and informatics (Certificate); health sciences (MS, Certificate); health services administration (MS); histotechnology (Certificate); long term care management (Certificate); medical group practice management (Certificate); occupational therapy (MS); quality improvement and outcomes management (Certificate). Electronic applications accepted.

School of Adult and Continuing Education *Degree program information:* Part-time and evening/weekend programs available. Offers administrative studies (MA); adult and continuing education (MA, MPA, MS); information technology (MS); public administration (MPA). Electronic applications accepted.

School of Arts and Sciences *Degree program information:* Part-time and evening/weekend programs available. Offers arts and sciences (MA, MFA, MS, D Min, Certificate, SSP); broadcasting (Certificate); clinical psychology (MS); communication (MA); liberal studies (MA); ministry (D Min); organizational communication (MS); pastoral ministry for Hispanics (MA); pastoral theology (MA); photography (MA, MFA); practical theology (MA); school psychology (MS, SSP). Electronic applications accepted.

School of Education *Degree program information:* Part-time and evening/weekend programs available. Postbaccalaureate distance learning degree programs offered. Offers accomplished teacher (Ed S); advanced teaching and learning with technology (Certificate); counseling (MS, PhD, Ed S); culture, language and literacy (TESOL) (PhD); curriculum evaluation and research (PhD); distance education (Certificate); early childhood (Ed S); early childhood education (PhD); education (MS, Ed D, PhD, Certificate, Ed S); education for teachers of students with hearing impairments (MS); educational computing and technology (MS, Ed S); educational leadership (MS, Ed D, Certificate, Ed S); educational technology (PhD); elementary (Ed S); elementary education (MS, PhD); elementary education/ESOL (MS); ESOL (Ed S); exceptional student education (MS, Ed S); gifted (Ed S); higher education administration (MS); higher education technology integration (Certificate); human resource development (PhD); human resource development and administration (MS); human resources: not for profit and religious organizations (Certificate); K-12 technology integration (Certificate); leadership (PhD); marital, couple and family counseling/therapy (MS, Ed S); mental health counseling (MS, Ed S); Montessori (Ed S); Montessori education (MS, Ed S); PKP/elementary (Ed S); pre-k/primary (MS); pre-k/primary/ESOL (MS); reading (Ed S); reading, language and cognition (PhD); rehabilitation counseling (MS, Ed S); school counseling (MS, Ed S); technology and TESOL (MS, Ed S); TESOL (MS); TESOL international (MS). Electronic applications accepted.

School of Graduate Medical Sciences Offers anatomy (MS); medical sciences (DPM, MCMS, MPH, MS); physician assistant (MCMS); podiatric medicine and surgery (DPM); public health (MPH). Electronic applications accepted.

School of Human Performance and Leisure Sciences *Degree program information:* Part-time and evening/weekend programs available. Offers athletic training (MS); biomechanics (MS); exercise science (MS); general movement science (MS); human performance and leisure sciences (MS); sport and exercise psychology (MS); sport management (MS). Electronic applications accepted.

School of Law Offers law (JD).

School of Nursing *Degree program information:* Part-time and evening/weekend programs available. Offers acute care nurse practitioner (MSN); family nurse practitioner (MSN); nurse practitioner (Certificate); nursing (MSN, PhD, Certificate); nursing administration (MSN, PhD, Certificate); nursing education (MSN, Certificate). Electronic applications accepted.

School of Social Work *Degree program information:* Part-time and evening/weekend programs available. Offers social work (MSW, PhD). Electronic applications accepted.

See Display on next page and Close-Up on page 925.

BASTYR UNIVERSITY, Kenmore, WA 98028-4966

General Information Independent, coed, upper-level institution. *Enrollment:* 996 graduate, professional, and undergraduate students; 638 full-time matriculated graduate/professional students (528 women), 105 part-time matriculated graduate/professional students (93 women). *Enrollment by degree level:* 465 first professional, 255 master's, 12 doctoral, 11 other advanced degrees. *Graduate faculty:* 53 full-time (29 women), 100 part-time/adjunct (73 women). *Tuition:* Full-time $19,995; part-time $528 per credit hour. *Graduate housing:* Room and/or apartments available on a first-come, first-served basis to single students; on-campus housing not available to married students. *Student services:* Campus employment opportunities, career counseling, child daycare facilities, free psychological counseling, international student services, low-cost health insurance, writing training. *Library facilities:* Bastyr University Library. *Online resources:* library catalog, web page. *Collection:* 19,859 titles, 177 serial subscriptions, 5,876 audiovisual materials. *Research affiliation:* Cleavage Creek Winery (oncology), Benaroya Research Institute at Virginia Mason (health), University of Washington (health), Fred Hutchinson Cancer Research Center (oncology).

Computer facilities: 71 computers available on campus for general student use. A campuswide network can be accessed from student residence rooms and from off campus. *Web address:* http://www.bastyr.edu/.

General Application Contact: Information Contact, 425-602-3330, Fax: 425-602-2090, E-mail: admissions@bastyr.edu.

GRADUATE UNITS

School of Acupuncture and Oriental Medicine Students: 83 full-time (61 women), 36 part-time (28 women). Average age 31. Expenses: Contact institution. *Financial support:* Career-related internships or fieldwork, Federal Work-Study, and scholarships/grants available. Support available to part-time students. Financial award application deadline: 3/15; financial award applicants required to submit FAFSA. In 2010, 50 master's, 5 doctorates, 2 other advanced degrees awarded. Offers acupuncture (MS); acupuncture and Oriental medicine (MS, DAOM); Chinese herbal medicine (Certificate). *Application deadline:* For fall admission, 3/15 priority date for domestic and international students. Applications are processed on a rolling basis. *Application fee:* $75. *Application Contact:* Admissions Office, 425-602-3330, Fax: 425-602-3090, E-mail: admissions@bastyr.edu. *Dean*, Terry Courtney, 425-823-1300, Fax: 425-823-6222.

School of Naturopathic Medicine Students: 444 full-time (357 women), 21 part-time (19 women); includes 89 minority (11 Black or African American, non-Hispanic/Latino; 3 American Indian or Alaska Native, non-Hispanic/Latino; 38 Asian, non-Hispanic/Latino; 13 Hispanic/Latino; 1 Native Hawaiian or other Pacific Islander, non-Hispanic/Latino; 23 Two or more races, non-Hispanic/Latino), 33 international. Average age 30. 274 applicants, 67% accepted, 117 enrolled. Expenses: Contact institution. *Financial support:* Career-related internships or fieldwork, Federal Work-Study, and scholarships/grants available. Support available to part-time students. Financial award application deadline: 4/15; financial award applicants required to submit FAFSA. Offers naturopathic medicine (ND). *Application deadline:* For fall admission, 2/1 priority date for domestic and international students. Applications are processed on a rolling basis. *Application fee:* $75. *Application Contact:* Admissions Office, 425-602-3330, Fax: 425-602-3090, E-mail: admissions@bastyr.edu. *Dean*, Dr. Jane Guiltinan, 425-823-1300, Fax: 425-823-6222.

School of Nutrition and Exercise Science Students: 91 full-time (88 women), 26 part-time (25 women). Average age 31. Expenses: Contact institution. *Financial support:* Career-related internships or fieldwork, Federal Work-Study, and scholarships/grants available. Support available to part-time students. Financial award application deadline: 4/15; financial award applicants required to submit FAFSA. In 2010, 36 master's awarded. *Degree program information:* Part-time programs available. Offers nutrition (MS); nutrition and clinical health psychology (MS). *Application deadline:* For fall admission, 3/15 priority date for domestic and international students. Applications are processed on a rolling basis. *Application fee:* $75. *Application Contact:* Admissions Office, 425-602-3330, Fax: 425-602-3090, E-mail: admissions@bastyr.edu. *Chair,* Debra Boutin, 425-823-1300, Fax: 425-823-6222.

BAYAMÓN CENTRAL UNIVERSITY, Bayamón, PR 00960-1725

General Information Independent-religious, coed, comprehensive institution. *Graduate housing:* On-campus housing not available.

GRADUATE UNITS

Graduate Programs *Degree program information:* Part-time and evening/weekend programs available. Offers accounting (MBA); administration and supervision (MA Ed); commercial education (MA Ed); elementary education (K–3) (MA Ed); family counseling (Graduate Certificate); finance (MBA); general business (MBA); guidance and counseling (MA Ed); management (MBA); marketing (MBA); organizational psychology (MA); pre-elementary teacher (MA Ed); rehabilitation counseling (MA Ed); special education (MA Ed).

BAYLOR COLLEGE OF MEDICINE, Houston, TX 77030-3498

General Information Independent, coed, graduate-only institution. CGS member. *Enrollment by degree level:* 725 first professional, 156 master's, 608 doctoral. *Graduate faculty:* 1,744 full-time, 460 part-time/adjunct. *Tuition:* Full-time $11,000. *Required fees:* $4900. *Graduate housing:* On-campus housing not available. *Student services:* Campus employment opportunities, campus safety program, career counseling, exercise/wellness program, free psychological counseling, grant writing training, international student services, low-cost health insurance, multicultural affairs office, services for students with disabilities. *Library facilities:* Houston Academy of Medicine–Texas Medical Center Library. *Online resources:* library catalog, web page, access to other libraries' catalogs. *Collection:* 270,649 titles, 4,447 serial subscriptions, 786 audiovisual materials. *Research affiliation:* Veterans Affairs Medical Center (biomedical research), Texas Children's Hospital (pediatric biomedical research), The Methodist Hospital (biomedical research), National Space Biomedical Research Institute, Harris County Hospital District (biomedical research), Children's Nutrition Research Center (pediatric nutrition).

Computer facilities: 60 computers available on campus for general student use. A campuswide network can be accessed from off campus. Online class registration is available. *Web address:* http://www.bcm.edu/.

General Application Contact: Dr. Lloyd H. Michael, Interim Senior Associate Dean of the Medical School, 713-798-4842, Fax: 713-798-5563, E-mail: lmichael@bcm.edu.

GRADUATE UNITS

Graduate School of Biomedical Sciences Students: 608 full-time (314 women); includes 25 Black or African American, non-Hispanic/Latino; 3 American Indian or Alaska Native, non-Hispanic/Latino; 63 Asian, non-Hispanic/Latino; 52 Hispanic/Latino, 221 international. Average age 28. 1,112 applicants, 20% accepted, 117 enrolled. *Faculty:* 417 full-time (105 women). Expenses: Contact institution. *Financial support:* In 2010–11, 177 fellowships with full tuition reimbursements (averaging $26,000 per year), 431 research assistantships with full tuition reimbursements (averaging $26,000 per year) were awarded; teaching assistantships, career-related internships or fieldwork, Federal Work-Study, institutionally sponsored loans, health care benefits, and students receive a scholarship unless there are grant funds available to pay tuition also available. Financial award applicants required to submit FAFSA. In 2010, 11 master's, 74 doctorates awarded. Offers biochemistry (PhD); biochemistry and molecular biology (PhD); biomedical sciences (MS, PhD); cardiovascular sciences (PhD); cell and molecular biology (PhD); clinical scientist training (MS, PhD); developmental biology (PhD); genetics (PhD); human genetics (PhD); immunology (PhD); microbiology (PhD); molecular and cellular biology (PhD); molecular and human genetics (PhD); molecular physiology and biophysics (PhD); molecular virology and microbiology (PhD); neuroscience (PhD); pharmacology (PhD); structural and computational biology and molecular biophysics (PhD); translational biology and molecular medicine (PhD); virology (PhD). *Application deadline:* For fall admission, 1/1 priority date for domestic students. Applications are processed on a rolling basis. *Application fee:* $0. Electronic applications accepted. *Application Contact:* Melissa Houghton, Administrator for GSBS Admissions, 713-798-4031, Fax: 713-798-6325, E-mail: melissah@bcm.edu. *Dean of Graduate Sciences,* Dr. William R. Brinkley, 713-798-5263, Fax: 713-798-6325, E-mail: brinkley@bcm.tmc.edu.

Medical School Students: 725 full-time (362 women); includes 39 Black or African American, non-Hispanic/Latino; 11 American Indian or Alaska Native, non-Hispanic/Latino; 263 Asian, non-Hispanic/Latino; 112 Hispanic/Latino, 1 international. Average age 24. 4,588 applicants, 7% accepted, 186 enrolled. Expenses: Contact institution. *Financial support:* In 2010–11, 568 students received support. Career-related internships or fieldwork, Federal Work-Study, institutionally sponsored loans, scholarships/grants, traineeships, and tuition waivers (full and partial) available. Financial award application deadline: 5/11; financial award applicants required to submit FAFSA. In 2010, 157 MDs awarded. Offers medicine (MD). *Application deadline:* For fall admission, 11/1 for domestic students. Applications are processed on a rolling basis. *Application fee:* $90. Electronic applications accepted. *Application Contact:* Dr. Florence F. Eddins-Folensbee, Senior Associate Dean of the Medical School, 713-798-4842, Fax: 713-798-5563, E-mail: florence@bcm.edu. *Senior Vice President/Dean of Medical Education,* Dr. Stephen B. Greenberg, 713-798-8878, Fax: 713-798-3096, E-mail: stepheng@bcm.edu.

Program in Cell and Molecular Biology of Aging Expenses: Contact institution. Offers cell and molecular biology of aging (PhD). *Application Contact:* Dr. Lloyd H. Michael, Senior Associate Dean of the Medical School, 713-798-4842, Fax: 713-798-5563, E-mail: lmichael@bcm.edu.

School of Allied Health Sciences Students: 169 full-time (132 women); includes 41 minority (7 Black or African American, non-Hispanic/Latino; 17 Asian, non-Hispanic/Latino; 12 Hispanic/Latino; 4 Native Hawaiian or other Pacific Islander, non-Hispanic/Latino; 1 Two or more races, non-Hispanic/Latino). Average age 29. 955 applicants, 7% accepted, 55 enrolled. *Faculty:* 18 full-time (11 women), 5 part-time/adjunct (3 women). Expenses: Contact institution. *Financial support:* In 2010–11, 130 students received support. Career-related internships or fieldwork, Federal Work-Study, institutionally sponsored loans, scholarships/grants, and traineeships available. Financial award applicants required to submit FAFSA. In 2010, 48 master's awarded. Offers allied health sciences (MS, DNP); nurse anesthesia (MS, DNP); physician assistant (MS). *Application deadline:* For fall admission, 10/1 for domestic students; for spring admission, 7/1 for domestic students. Electronic applications accepted. *Application Contact:* Dr. J. David Holcomb, Dean, 713-798-4613, Fax: 713-798-7694, E-mail: jholcomb@bcm.edu. *Dean,* Dr. J. David Holcomb, 713-798-4613, Fax: 713-798-7694, E-mail: jholcomb@bcm.edu.

BAYLOR UNIVERSITY, Waco, TX 76798

General Information Independent-religious, coed, university. CGS member. *Enrollment:* 2,157 full-time matriculated graduate/professional students (1,026 women), 354 part-time matriculated graduate/professional students (190 women). *Enrollment by degree level:* 777 first professional, 1,018 master's, 692 doctoral, 24 other advanced degrees. *Graduate faculty:* 350. *Graduate housing:* Rooms and/or apartments available to single and married students. *Student services:* Campus employment opportunities, campus safety program, career counseling, exercise/wellness program, free psychological counseling, international student services, low-cost health insurance, multicultural affairs office, services for students with disabilities. *Library facilities:* Moody Memorial Library plus 8 others. *Online resources:* library catalog, web page, access to other libraries' catalogs. *Collection:* 2.3 million titles, 8,429 serial subscriptions. *Research affiliation:* Sandia National Laboratories (physics), National Center for Supercomputing Applications (physics), Zyvex Corporation (physics), OXiGENE, Inc. (pharmaceuticals), Brookhaven National Laboratory (physics), Fermi National Accelerator Laboratory (physics).

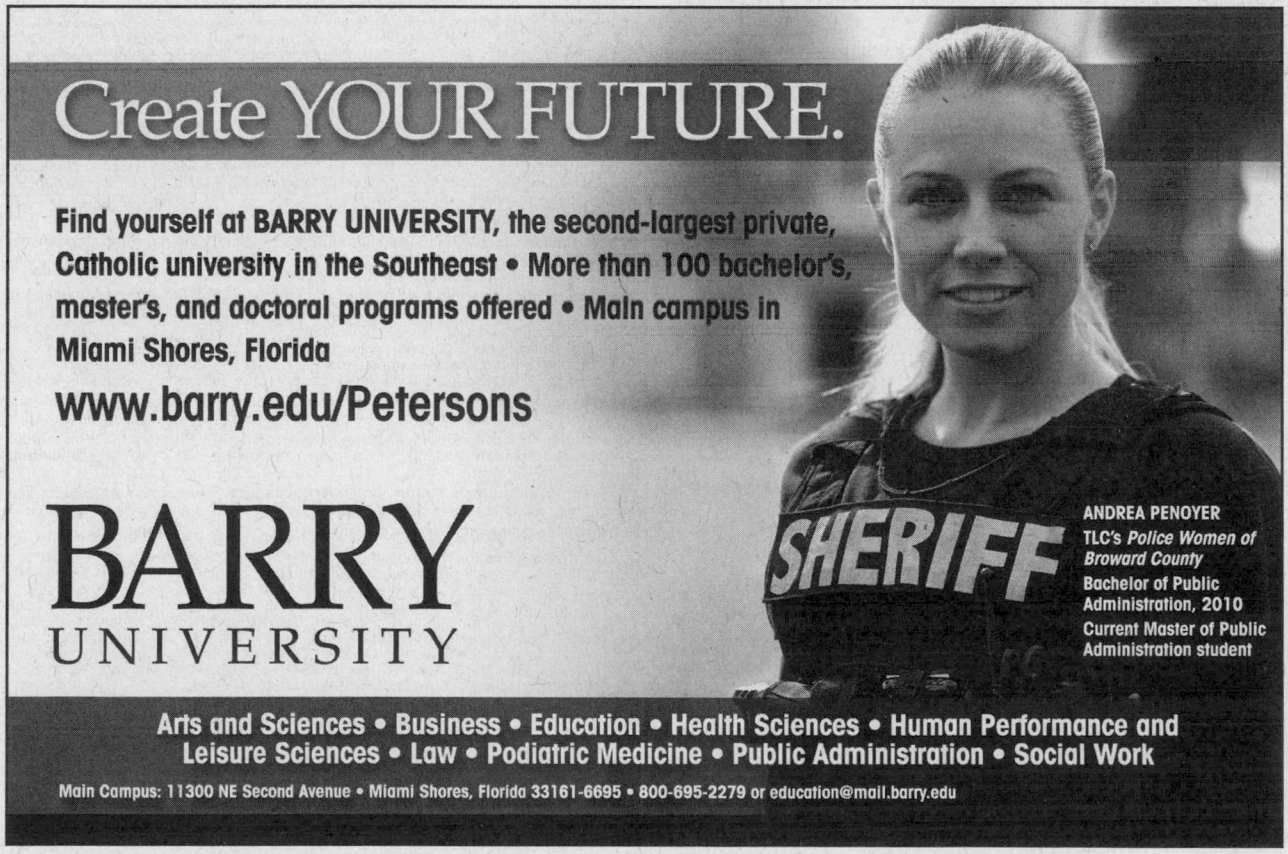

Baylor University (continued)

Computer facilities: Computer purchase and lease plans are available. 1,656 computers available on campus for general student use. A campuswide network can be accessed from student residence rooms and from off campus. Online class registration is available. *Web address:* http://www.baylor.edu/.

General Application Contact: Suzanne Keener, Administrative Assistant, 254-710-3588, Fax: 254-710-3870.

GRADUATE UNITS

George W. Truett Theological Seminary Students: 289 full-time (107 women), 80 part-time (28 women); includes 76 minority (41 Black or African American, non-Hispanic/Latino; 1 American Indian or Alaska Native, non-Hispanic/Latino; 3 Asian, non-Hispanic/Latino; 20 Hispanic/Latino; 1 Native Hawaiian or other Pacific Islander, non-Hispanic/Latino; 10 Two or more races, non-Hispanic/Latino), 23 international. Average age 29. 144 applicants, 94% accepted, 102 enrolled. *Faculty:* 17 full-time (3 women), 7 part-time/adjunct (1 woman). Expenses: Contact institution. *Financial support:* In 2010–11, 207 students received support, including 1 research assistantship, 12 teaching assistantships; career-related internships or fieldwork, institutionally sponsored loans, scholarships/grants, tuition waivers (partial), and unspecified assistantships also available. Support available to part-time students. Financial award application deadline: 8/1; financial award applicants required to submit FAFSA. In 2010, 68 first professional degrees, 112 master's, 6 doctorates awarded. Offers theology (M Div, MTS, D Min). *Application deadline:* For fall admission, 5/1 for domestic and international students; for spring admission, 11/1 for domestic and international students. Applications are processed on a rolling basis. *Application fee:* $35. Electronic applications accepted. *Application Contact:* Dr. Edward Grear Howard, Director of Student Services, 254-710-6087, Fax: 254-710-7233, E-mail: grear_howard@baylor.edu. *Dean,* Dr. David E. Garland, 254-710-3755, Fax: 254-710-3753, E-mail: david_e_garland@baylor.edu.

Graduate School Students: 1,342 full-time (630 women), 263 part-time (156 women); includes 236 minority (43 Black or African American, non-Hispanic/Latino; 7 American Indian or Alaska Native, non-Hispanic/Latino; 55 Asian, non-Hispanic/Latino; 86 Hispanic/Latino; 4 Native Hawaiian or other Pacific Islander, non-Hispanic/Latino; 41 Two or more races, non-Hispanic/Latino), 173 international. 1,435 applicants, 46% accepted, 465 enrolled. *Faculty:* 350. Expenses: Contact institution. *Financial support:* Fellowships, research assistantships with full and partial tuition reimbursements, teaching assistantships with full and partial tuition reimbursements, career-related internships or fieldwork, Federal Work-Study, institutionally sponsored loans, scholarships/grants, tuition waivers (full and partial), and unspecified assistantships available. Support available to part-time students. In 2010, 549 master's, 124 doctorates, 7 other advanced degrees awarded. *Degree program information:* Part-time and evening/weekend programs available. Postbaccalaureate distance learning degree programs offered (minimal on-campus study). Offers clinical orthopedics (D Sc); emergency medicine (D Sc PA); health care administration (MHA); health sciences (MHA, MPT, MS, D Sc, D Sc PA, DPT); nutrition (MS); physical therapy (MPT, DPT). *Application deadline:* Applications are processed on a rolling basis. *Application fee:* $25. *Application Contact:* Lori McNamara, Graduate Admissions Coordinator, 254-710-3584, Fax: 254-710-3870, E-mail: lori_mcnamara@baylor.edu. *Dean,* Dr. Larry Lyon, 254-710-3588, Fax: 254-710-3870, E-mail: larry_lyon@baylor.edu.

College of Arts and Sciences Students: 623 full-time (313 women), 83 part-time (41 women); includes 83 minority (7 Black or African American, non-Hispanic/Latino; 4 American Indian or Alaska Native, non-Hispanic/Latino; 21 Asian, non-Hispanic/Latino; 30 Hispanic/Latino; 21 Two or more races, non-Hispanic/Latino), 107 international. Expenses: Contact institution. *Financial support:* Fellowships, research assistantships with partial tuition reimbursements, teaching assistantships, career-related internships or fieldwork, Federal Work-Study, institutionally sponsored loans, scholarships/grants, tuition waivers (full and partial), and laboratory assistantships, practicum stipends available. Support available to part-time students. In 2010, 124 master's, 55 doctorates awarded. *Degree program information:* Part-time and evening/weekend programs available. Offers air science and environment (IMES); American studies (MA); applied sociology (PhD); arts and sciences (IMES, MA, MES, MFA, MIJ, MPPA, MS, MSCP, MSCSD, MSW, PhD, Psy D); biology (MA, MS, PhD); chemistry (MS, PhD); church-state studies (MA, PhD); clinical psychology (MSCP, Psy D); communication sciences and disorders (MA, MSCSD); communication studies (MA); directing (MFA); earth science (MA); ecological, earth and environmental sciences (PhD); English (MA, PhD); environmental biology (MS); environmental studies (MES, MS); geology (MS, PhD); history (MA); international journalism (MIJ); international studies (MA); journalism (MA); limnology (MS); mathematics (MS, PhD); museum studies (MA); philosophy (MA, PhD); physics (MA, MS, PhD); political science (MA, PhD); psychology (MA, PhD); public policy and administration (MPPA); religion (MA, PhD); sociology (MA); Spanish (MA); statistics (MA, PhD). *Application deadline:* Applications are processed on a rolling basis. *Application fee:* $25. Electronic applications accepted. *Application Contact:* Suzanne Keener, Administrative Assistant, 254-710-3588, Fax: 254-710-3870.

Hankamer School of Business Students: 273 full-time (82 women), 15 part-time (7 women); includes 50 minority (10 Black or African American, non-Hispanic/Latino; 1 American Indian or Alaska Native, non-Hispanic/Latino; 11 Asian, non-Hispanic/Latino; 22 Hispanic/Latino; 6 Two or more races, non-Hispanic/Latino), 29 international. Expenses: Contact institution. *Financial support:* Research assistantships, teaching assistantships, career-related internships or fieldwork, Federal Work-Study, and institutionally sponsored loans available. In 2010, 206 master's awarded. *Degree program information:* Part-time programs available. Offers accounting and business law (M Acc, MT); business (M Acc, MA, MBA, MS, MS Eco, MSIS, MT); business administration (MBA); economics (MS Eco); information systems (MSIS); information systems management (MBA); international economics (MA, MS). *Application deadline:* For fall admission, 8/1 for domestic students; for spring admission, 12/1 for domestic students. Applications are processed on a rolling basis. *Application fee:* $25. *Application Contact:* Laurie Wilson, Director, Graduate Business Programs, 254-710-4163, Fax: 254-710-1066, E-mail: laurie_wilson@baylor.edu. *Associate Dean,* Dr. Gary Carini, 254-710-3718, Fax: 254-710-1092, E-mail: gary_carini@baylor.edu.

Institute of Biomedical Studies Students: 29 full-time (17 women); includes 3 minority (1 Asian, non-Hispanic/Latino; 1 Hispanic/Latino; 1 Two or more races, non-Hispanic/Latino), 9 international. Expenses: Contact institution. *Financial support:* Research assistantships, teaching assistantships available. In 2010, 3 master's, 3 doctorates awarded. Offers biomedical studies (MS, PhD). *Application deadline:* Applications are processed on a rolling basis. *Application fee:* $25. *Application Contact:* Rhonda Bellert, Administrative Assistant, 254-710-2514, Fax: 254-710-3870, E-mail: rhonda_bellert@baylor.edu. *Graduate Program Director,* Dr. Chris Kearney, 254-710-2131, Fax: 254-710-3878, E-mail: chris_kearney@baylor.edu.

Louise Herrington School of Nursing Students: 37 full-time (34 women), 36 part-time (35 women); includes 18 minority (3 Black or African American, non-Hispanic/Latino; 1 American Indian or Alaska Native, non-Hispanic/Latino; 5 Asian, non-Hispanic/Latino; 6 Hispanic/Latino; 3 Two or more races, non-Hispanic/Latino), 1 international. Expenses: Contact institution. In 2010, 21 master's awarded. Offers family nurse practitioner (MSN); neonatal nurse practitioner (MSN); nursing administration and management (MSN). *Application deadline:* For fall admission, 8/1 for domestic students; for spring admission, 12/1 for domestic students. Applications are processed on a rolling basis. *Application fee:* $25. *Application Contact:* Beverly Kurfees, Administrative Assistant, 214-820-4111, Fax: 254-710-3870, E-mail: beverly_kurfees@baylor.edu. *Graduate Program Director,* Dr. Mary Brucker, 214-820-4111, Fax: 214-818-8692, E-mail: mary_brucker@baylor.edu.

School of Education Students: 149 full-time (102 women), 83 part-time (46 women); includes 37 minority (12 Black or African American, non-Hispanic/Latino; 8 Asian, non-Hispanic/Latino; 13 Hispanic/Latino; 4 Two or more races, non-Hispanic/Latino), 10 international. Expenses: Contact institution. *Financial support:* Research assistantships, teaching assistantships, career-related internships or fieldwork, Federal Work-Study, institutionally sponsored loans, scholarships/grants, and tuition waivers (partial) available. In 2010, 104 master's, 20 doctorates, 7 other advanced degrees awarded. *Degree program information:* Part-time programs available. Postbaccalaureate distance learning degree programs offered (minimal on-campus study). Offers curriculum and instruction (MA, MS Ed, Ed D, Ed S); education (MA, MS Ed, Ed D, PhD, Ed S); educational administration (MS Ed, Ed S); educational psychology (MA, MS Ed, PhD, Ed S); exercise, nutrition and preventive health (PhD); health, human performance and recreation (MS Ed). *Application deadline:* Applications are processed on a rolling basis. *Application fee:* $25. Electronic applications accepted. *Application Contact:* Julie Baker, Administrative Assistant, 254-710-3050, Fax: 254-710-3870, E-mail: julie_baker@baylor.edu. *Dean,* Dr. Jon Engelhardt, 254-710-3111, Fax: 254-710-3987.

School of Engineering and Computer Science Students: 46 full-time (6 women), 8 part-time (2 women); includes 14 minority (3 Black or African American, non-Hispanic/Latino; 3 Asian, non-Hispanic/Latino; 5 Hispanic/Latino; 3 Two or more races, non-Hispanic/Latino), 16 international. Expenses: Contact institution. *Financial support:* Teaching assistantships available. Financial award application deadline: 3/15. In 2010, 10 master's awarded. *Degree program information:* Part-time programs available. Offers biomedical engineering (MSBE); computer science (MS); electrical and computer engineering (MSECE, PhD); engineering (ME); engineering and computer science (ME, MS, MSBE, MSECE, MSME, PhD); mechanical engineering (MSME). *Application deadline:* For fall admission, 8/1 for domestic students; for spring admission, 12/1 for domestic students. Applications are processed on a rolling basis. *Application fee:* $25. *Application Contact:* Suzanne Keener, Administrative Assistant, 254-710-3588, Fax: 254-710-3870. *Graduate Program Director,* Dr. Greg Speegle, 254-710-3876, Fax: 254-710-3839, E-mail: greg_speegle@baylor.edu.

School of Music Students: 13 full-time (6 women), 38 part-time (25 women); includes 6 minority (1 Asian, non-Hispanic/Latino; 2 Hispanic/Latino; 3 Two or more races, non-Hispanic/Latino), 10 international. Expenses: Contact institution. *Financial support:* In 2010–11, 43 teaching assistantships with full tuition reimbursements (averaging $5,990 per year) were awarded; Federal Work-Study and institutionally sponsored loans also available. In 2010, 29 master's awarded. Offers church music (MM); collaborative piano (MM); composition (MM); conducting (MM); music history and literature (MM); music theory (MM); performance (MM); piano pedagogy and performance (MM). *Application deadline:* For fall admission, 8/1 for domestic students; for spring admission, 12/1 for domestic students. Applications are processed on a rolling basis. *Application fee:* $25. *Application Contact:* Melinda Coates, Administrative Assistant, 254-710-2360, Fax: 254-710-3870, E-mail: melinda_coats@baylor.edu. *Graduate Program Director,* Dr. David Music, 254-710-2360, Fax: 254-710-1191, E-mail: david_music@baylor.edu.

School of Law Students: 457 full-time (228 women), 9 part-time (4 women); includes 97 minority (9 Black or African American, non-Hispanic/Latino; 2 American Indian or Alaska Native, non-Hispanic/Latino; 33 Asian, non-Hispanic/Latino; 37 Hispanic/Latino; 2 Native Hawaiian or other Pacific Islander, non-Hispanic/Latino; 14 Two or more races, non-Hispanic/Latino). Average age 24. 2,360 applicants, 32% accepted, 86 enrolled. *Faculty:* 27 full-time (6 women), 13 part-time/adjunct (2 women). Expenses: Contact institution. *Financial support:* In 2010–11, 397 students received support. Career-related internships or fieldwork, Federal Work-Study, institutionally sponsored loans, and scholarships/grants available. Financial award application deadline: 2/1; financial award applicants required to submit FAFSA. In 2010, 165 first professional degrees awarded. Offers law (JD). *Application deadline:* For fall admission, 5/1 for domestic students; for spring admission, 11/1 for domestic students. Applications are processed on a rolling basis. *Application fee:* $40. Electronic applications accepted. *Application Contact:* Becky Beck, Assistant Dean of Admission, 254-710-1911, Fax: 254-710-2316, E-mail: becky_beck@baylor.edu. *Dean,* Dr. Bradley J. B. Toben, 254-710-1911, Fax: 254-710-2316.

School of Social Work Students: 69 full-time (61 women), 2 part-time (both women); includes 23 minority (9 Black or African American, non-Hispanic/Latino; 1 American Indian or Alaska Native, non-Hispanic/Latino; 2 Asian, non-Hispanic/Latino; 8 Hispanic/Latino; 3 Two or more races, non-Hispanic/Latino), 4 international. Average age 27. 190 applicants, 72% accepted. *Faculty:* 11 full-time (5 women), 13 part-time/adjunct (7 women). Expenses: Contact institution. *Financial support:* In 2010–11, 12 research assistantships with tuition reimbursements (averaging $6,800 per year) were awarded; career-related internships or fieldwork, Federal Work-Study, institutionally sponsored loans, scholarships/grants, traineeships, tuition waivers (full and partial), and unspecified assistantships also available. Support available to part-time students. Financial award application deadline: 6/1; financial award applicants required to submit FAFSA. In 2010, 58 master's awarded. *Degree program information:* Part-time programs available. Offers social work (MSW). *Application deadline:* For spring admission, 3/15 for domestic and international students. Applications are processed on a rolling basis. *Application fee:* $45. Electronic applications accepted. *Application Contact:* Tracey Kelley, Director of Recruitment/Career Services, 254-710-4479, Fax: 254-710-6455, E-mail: tracey_kelley@baylor.edu. *Associate Dean for Graduate Studies,* Dr. Dennis Myers, 254-710-6404, E-mail: dennis_myers@baylor.edu.

BAY PATH COLLEGE, Longmeadow, MA 01106-2292

General Information Independent, Undergraduate: women only; graduate: coed, comprehensive institution. *Graduate housing:* Room and/or apartments available on a first-come, first-served basis to single students; on-campus housing not available to married students. Housing application deadline: 7/2.

GRADUATE UNITS

Program in Communications and Information Management *Degree program information:* Part-time and evening/weekend programs available. Offers information management (MS); information systems (MS). Electronic applications accepted.

Program in Entrepreneurial Thinking and Innovative Practices *Degree program information:* Part-time and evening/weekend programs available. Offers entrepreneurial thinking and innovative practices (MBA). Electronic applications accepted.

Program in Higher Education Administration Postbaccalaureate distance learning degree programs offered (no on-campus study). Offers enrollment management (MS); general administration (MS); institutional advancement (MS). Electronic applications accepted.

Program in Nonprofit Management and Philanthropy Postbaccalaureate distance learning degree programs offered. Offers nonprofit management and philanthropy (MS).

Program in Occupational Therapy *Degree program information:* Part-time and evening/weekend programs available. Offers occupational therapy (MOT, MS). Electronic applications accepted.

Program in Strategic Fundraising and Philanthropy Postbaccalaureate distance learning degree programs offered. Offers strategic fundraising and philanthropy (MS).

BELHAVEN UNIVERSITY, Jackson, MS 39202-1789

General Information Independent-religious, coed, comprehensive institution. *Enrollment:* 3,099 graduate, professional, and undergraduate students; 492 full-time matriculated graduate/professional students (365 women), 140 part-time matriculated graduate/professional students (110 women). *Enrollment by degree level:* 463 master's. *Graduate faculty:* 17 full-time (7 women), 37 part-time/adjunct (15 women). *Tuition:* Full-time $6456; part-time $538 per credit hour. Tuition and fees vary according to campus/location. *Graduate housing:* On-campus housing not available. *Student services:* Career counseling, free psychological counseling. *Library facilities:* Hood Library. *Online resources:* library catalog, web page. *Collection:* 140,025 titles, 433 serial subscriptions, 2,456 audiovisual materials.

Computer facilities: 36 computers available on campus for general student use. A campuswide network can be accessed from student residence rooms and from off campus. Online class registration is available. *Web address:* http://www.belhaven.edu/.

General Application Contact: Dr. Audrey Kelleher, Vice President for Adult and Graduate Marketing and Development, 407-804-1424, Fax: 407-620-5210, E-mail: akelleher@belhaven.edu.

GRADUATE UNITS

School of Business Students: 316 full-time (231 women), 39 part-time (25 women); includes 15 Black or African American, non-Hispanic/Latino; 1 Hispanic/Latino. Average age 36. 329 applicants, 54% accepted, 124 enrolled. *Faculty:* 13 full-time (3 women), 24 part-time/adjunct (6 women). Expenses: Contact institution. *Financial support:* Applicants required to submit FAFSA. In 2010, 103 master's awarded. *Degree program information:* Evening/weekend programs available. Offers business administration (MBA); leadership (MSL); public administration (MPA). MBA program also offered in Houston, TX, Memphis, TN and Orlando, FL. *Application deadline:* Applications are processed on a rolling basis. *Application fee:* $25. Electronic applications accepted. *Application Contact:* Dr. Audrey Kelleher, Vice President of Adult and Graduate Marketing and Development, 407-804-1424, Fax: 407-620-5210, E-mail: akelleher@belhaven.edu. *Dean,* Dr. Ralph Mason, 601-968-8949, Fax: 601-968-8951, E-mail: cmason@belhaven.edu.

School of Education Students: 138 full-time (103 women), 47 part-time (39 women); includes 7 Black or African American, non-Hispanic/Latino; 1 Hispanic/Latino. Average age 34. 392 applicants, 70% accepted, 140 enrolled. *Faculty:* 4 full-time (all women), 13 part-time/adjunct (9 women). Expenses: Contact institution. *Financial support:* Federal Work-Study, scholarships/grants, tuition waivers (full), and unspecified assistantships available. Support available to part-time students. Financial award applicants required to submit FAFSA. In 2010, 94 master's awarded. *Degree program information:* Part-time and evening/weekend programs available. Offers elementary education (M Ed, MAT); secondary education (M Ed, MAT). *Application deadline:* Applications are processed on a rolling basis. *Application fee:* $25. Electronic applications accepted. *Application Contact:* Jenny Mixon, Director of Graduate and Online Admission, 601-968-8947, Fax: 601-968-5953, E-mail: gradadmission@belhaven.edu. *Dean,* Dr. Sandra L. Rasberry, 601-968-8703, Fax: 601-974-6461, E-mail: srasberry@belhaven.edu.

BELLARMINE UNIVERSITY, Louisville, KY 40205-0671

General Information Independent-religious, coed, comprehensive institution. *Enrollment:* 3,342 graduate, professional, and undergraduate students; 313 full-time matriculated graduate/professional students (190 women), 417 part-time matriculated graduate/professional students (290 women). *Enrollment by degree level:* 590 master's, 140 doctoral. *Graduate faculty:* 48 full-time (25 women), 36 part-time/adjunct (22 women). *Graduate housing:* Room and/or apartments available on a first-come, first-served basis to single students; on-campus housing not available to married students. Housing application deadline: 5/1. *Student services:* Campus employment opportunities, campus safety program, career counseling, exercise/wellness program, free psychological counseling, grant writing training, international student services, multicultural affairs office, services for students with disabilities, teacher training, writing training. *Library facilities:* W.L. Lyons Brown Library. *Online resources:* library catalog, web page. *Collection:* 135,303 titles, 420 serial subscriptions, 5,547 audiovisual materials.

Computer facilities: 434 computers available on campus for general student use. A campuswide network can be accessed from student residence rooms and from off campus. Online class registration is available. *Web address:* http://www.bellarmine.edu/.

General Application Contact: Dr. Sara Pettingill, Dean of Graduate Admission, 502-272-8401, Fax: 502-272-8002, E-mail: spettingill@bellarmine.edu.

GRADUATE UNITS

Annsley Frazier Thornton School of Education Students: 83 full-time (63 women), 159 part-time (128 women); includes 23 Black or African American, non-Hispanic/Latino; 7 Asian, non-Hispanic/Latino; 1 Hispanic/Latino, 2 international. Average age 32. *Faculty:* 12 full-time (6 women), 19 part-time/adjunct (15 women). Expenses: Contact institution. *Financial support:* Scholarships/grants available. Financial award applicants required to submit FAFSA. In 2010, 113 master's awarded. *Degree program information:* Part-time and evening/weekend programs available. Offers early elementary education (MA Ed, MAT); education and social change (PhD); learning and behavior disorders (MA Ed, MAT); middle school education (MA Ed, MAT); principalship (Ed S); reading and writing endorsement (MA Ed); secondary school education (MAT); teacher leadership, grades P-12 (MA Ed). *Application deadline:* Applications are processed on a rolling basis. *Application fee:* $25. *Application Contact:* Theresa Klapheke, Administrative Director of Graduate Programs, 502-272-8271, Fax: 502-272-8002, E-mail: tklapheke@bellarmine.edu. *Dean,* Dr. Robert Cooter, 502-272-8191, Fax: 502-272-8189, E-mail: rcooter@bellarmine.edu.

Bellarmine College of Arts and Sciences Students: 13 part-time (11 women); includes 1 Black or African American, non-Hispanic/Latino. Average age 43. *Faculty:* 3 full-time (1 woman), 3 part-time/adjunct (1 woman). Expenses: Contact institution. In 2010, 1 master's awarded. Offers spirituality (MA). *Application deadline:* For spring admission, 3/15 for domestic students. *Application fee:* $25. *Application Contact:* Sara Pettingill, Dean of Graduate Admission, 502-272-8401, E-mail: spettingill@bellarmine.edu. *Program Director,* Dr. Gregory Hillis, 502-272-3800, E-mail: ghillis@bellarmine.edu.

Donna and Allan Lansing School of Nursing and Health Sciences Students: 136 full-time (96 women), 86 part-time (77 women); includes 4 Black or African American, non-Hispanic/Latino; 1 American Indian or Alaska Native, non-Hispanic/Latino; 2 Asian, non-Hispanic/Latino; 3 Hispanic/Latino. Average age 31. *Faculty:* 17 full-time (12 women), 7 part-time/adjunct (6 women). Expenses: Contact institution. *Financial support:* Career-related internships or fieldwork and scholarships/grants available. In 2010, 24 master's, 47 doctorates awarded. *Degree program information:* Part-time and evening/weekend programs available. Offers family nurse practitioner (MSN); nursing administration (MSN); nursing education (MSN); nursing practice (DNP); physical therapy (DPT). *Application fee:* $25. Electronic applications accepted. *Application Contact:* Julie Armstrong-Binnix, Health Science Recruiter, 800-274-4723 Ext. 8364, E-mail: julieab@bellarmine.edu. *Dean,* Dr. Susan H. Davis, 800-274-4723 Ext. 8217, E-mail: sdavis@bellarmine.edu.

School of Communication Students: 40 part-time (30 women); includes 1 Black or African American, non-Hispanic/Latino; 2 Hispanic/Latino. Average age 33. *Faculty:* 4 full-time (all women). Expenses: Contact institution. In 2010, 14 master's awarded. *Degree program information:* Part-time and evening/weekend programs available. Offers communication (MA). *Application deadline:* Applications are processed on a rolling basis. *Application fee:* $30. *Application Contact:* Dr. Sara Pettingill, Dean of Graduate Admission, 502-272-8401, Fax: 502-272-8002, E-mail: spettingill@bellarmine.edu. *Executive Director,* Edward Manasssah, 502-272-8324, E-mail: emahassah@bellarmine.edu.

School of Continuing and Professional Studies Students: 13 full-time (0 women), 9 part-time (3 women); includes 2 Black or African American, non-Hispanic/Latino. Average age 30. *Faculty:* 1 full-time (0 women), 2 part-time/adjunct (0 women). Expenses: Contact institution. In 2010, 6 master's awarded. *Degree program information:* Part-time and evening/weekend programs available. Offers technology and entrepreneurship (MAIT). *Application fee:* $25. *Application Contact:* Dr. Sara Pettingill, Dean of Graduate Admission, 502-272-8401, E-mail: spettingill@bellarmine.edu. *Dean,* Dr. Michael D. Mattei, 502-272-8441, E-mail: mmattei@bellarmine.edu.

W. Fielding Rubel School of Business Students: 81 full-time (31 women), 108 part-time (40 women); includes 11 Black or African American, non-Hispanic/Latino; 3 Asian, non-Hispanic/Latino; 1 Hispanic/Latino, 1 international. Average age 30. *Faculty:* 10 full-time (2 women), 7 part-time/adjunct (0 women). Expenses: Contact institution. *Financial support:* Career-related internships or fieldwork, scholarships/grants, and unspecified assistantships available. Support available to part-time students. Financial award application deadline: 7/1. In 2010, 84 master's awarded. *Degree program information:* Part-time and evening/weekend programs available. Offers business (EMBA, MBA). *Application deadline:* Applications are processed on a rolling basis. *Application fee:* $25. Electronic applications accepted. *Application Contact:* Dr. Sara Pettingill, Dean of Graduate Admission, 800-274-4723 Ext. 8258, Fax: 502-272-8002, E-mail: spettingill@bellarmine.edu. *Dean,* Dr. Daniel L. Bauer, 800-274-4723 Ext. 8026, Fax: 502-272-8013, E-mail: dbauer@bellarmine.edu.

BELLEVUE UNIVERSITY, Bellevue, NE 68005-3098

General Information Independent, coed, comprehensive institution. *Graduate housing:* Room and/or apartments available on a first-come, first-served basis to single students; on-campus housing not available to married students.

GRADUATE UNITS

Graduate School *Degree program information:* Part-time and evening/weekend programs available. Postbaccalaureate distance learning degree programs offered (no on-campus study). Offers acquisition and contract management (MS); business administration (MBA); clinical counseling (MS); computer information systems (MS); healthcare administration (MA, MHA, MS); human capital management (MS, PhD); human services (MA, MS); instructional design and development (MS); leadership (MA); management (MA); management information systems (MS); organizational performance (MS); public administration (MPA); public health (MPH); security management (MS).

BELLIN COLLEGE, Green Bay, WI 54305

General Information Independent, coed, primarily women, comprehensive institution.

GRADUATE UNITS

Program in Nursing Offers administrator (MSN); educator (MSN).

BELMONT UNIVERSITY, Nashville, TN 37212-3757

General Information Independent-religious, coed, comprehensive institution. *Enrollment:* 5,896 graduate, professional, and undergraduate students; 579 full-time matriculated graduate/professional students (425 women), 706 part-time matriculated graduate/professional students (437 women). *Enrollment by degree level:* 214 first professional, 878 master's, 164 doctoral, 5 other advanced degrees. *Graduate faculty:* 128 full-time (68 women), 73 part-time/adjunct (42 women). *Tuition:* Part-time $1800 per course. *Required fees:* $295 per semester. Tuition and fees vary according to degree level and program. *Graduate housing:* On-campus housing not available. *Student services:* Campus employment opportunities, campus safety program, career counseling, exercise/wellness program, free psychological counseling, international student services, low-cost health insurance, multicultural affairs office. *Library facilities:* Lila D. Bunch Library. *Online resources:* library catalog, web page, access to other libraries' catalogs. *Collection:* 228,427 titles, 1,084 serial subscriptions, 32,810 audiovisual materials.

Computer facilities: Computer purchase and lease plans are available. 500 computers available on campus for general student use. A campuswide network can be accessed from student residence rooms and from off campus. Online class registration, individual student information via BANNER Web are available. *Web address:* http://www.belmont.edu/.

General Application Contact: David Mee, Dean of Enrollment Services, 615-460-6785, Fax: 615-460-5434, E-mail: david.mee@belmont.edu.

GRADUATE UNITS

College of Arts and Sciences Students: 119 full-time (81 women), 409 part-time (274 women); includes 98 minority (81 Black or African American, non-Hispanic/Latino; 1 American Indian or Alaska Native, non-Hispanic/Latino; 7 Asian, non-Hispanic/Latino; 9 Hispanic/Latino), 6 international. Average age 30. 145 applicants, 60% accepted, 67 enrolled. *Faculty:* 26 full-time (20 women), 26 part-time/adjunct (15 women). Expenses: Contact institution. *Financial support:* In 2010–11, 50 students received support; fellowships with partial tuition reimbursements available, teaching assistantships with partial tuition reimbursements available, Federal Work-Study, institutionally sponsored loans, scholarships/grants, tuition waivers (partial), and unspecified assistantships available. Financial award application deadline: 4/15; financial award applicants required to submit FAFSA. In 2010, 134 master's awarded. *Degree program information:* Part-time and evening/weekend programs available. Offers arts and sciences (M Ed, MA, MAT, MSA); education (M Ed); elementary education (MAT); English (MAT); history (MAT); literature (MA); mathematics (MAT); middle grade education (MAT); science (MAT); secondary education (MAT); special education (MAT); sport administration (MSA); sports administration (MSA); writing (MA). *Application deadline:* For fall admission, 8/1 for domestic students; for spring admission, 12/1 for domestic students. Applications are processed on a rolling basis. *Application fee:* $50. Electronic applications accepted. *Application Contact:* Dr. Bryce Sullivan, Dean, 615-460-6437, Fax: 615-385-5084, E-mail: bryce.sullivan@belmont.edu. *Dean,* Dr. Bryce Sullivan, 615-460-6437, Fax: 615-385-5084, E-mail: bryce.sullivan@belmont.edu.

College of Health Sciences Students: 462 full-time (356 women), 42 part-time (41 women); includes 82 minority (34 Black or African American, non-Hispanic/Latino; 2 American Indian or Alaska Native, non-Hispanic/Latino; 31 Asian, non-Hispanic/Latino; 14 Hispanic/Latino; 1 Two or more races, non-Hispanic/Latino), 6 international. Average age 26. 928 applicants, 44% accepted, 261 enrolled. *Faculty:* 41 full-time (28 women), 27 part-time/adjunct (20 women). Expenses: Contact institution. *Financial support:* In 2010–11, 204 students received support, including teaching assistantships with full tuition reimbursements available (averaging $7,020 per year); career-related internships or fieldwork, scholarships/grants, and traineeships also available. Financial award application deadline: 3/1; financial award applicants required to submit FAFSA. In 2010, 43 master's, 54 doctorates awarded. *Degree program information:* Part-time programs available. Postbaccalaureate distance learning degree programs offered (minimal on-campus study). Offers health sciences (Pharm D, MSN, MSOT, DPT, OTD). *Application deadline:* Applications are processed on a rolling basis. *Application fee:* $50. Electronic applications accepted. *Application Contact:* David Mee, Dean of Enrollment Services, 615-460-6785, Fax: 615-460-5434, E-mail: david.mee@belmont.edu. *Dean,* 615-460-6916, Fax: 615-460-6750.

School of Nursing Students: 13 full-time (12 women), 42 part-time (41 women); includes 5 Black or African American, non-Hispanic/Latino; 1 Asian, non-Hispanic/Latino; 3 Hispanic/Latino, 1 international. Average age 30. 20 applicants, 85% accepted, 15 enrolled. *Faculty:* 1 (woman) full-time, 3 part-time/adjunct (all women). Expenses: Contact institution. *Financial support:* In 2010–11, 21 students received support. Scholarships/grants and traineeships available. Financial award application deadline: 3/1; financial award applicants required to submit FAFSA. In 2010, 7 master's awarded. *Degree program information:* Part-time programs available. Offers family nurse practitioner (MSN). *Application deadline:* For fall admission, 8/1 for domestic students, 3/1 priority date for international students; for spring admission, 10/15 priority date for domestic students, 10/1 priority date for international students. Applications are processed on a rolling basis. *Application fee:* $50. Electronic applications accepted. *Application Contact:* Heather Germain, Program Assistant, 615-460-6142, Fax: 615-460-6125, E-mail: hether.germain@belmont.edu. *Director, Graduate Program,* Dr. Leslie J. Higgins, 615-460-6027, Fax: 615-460-6125, E-mail: leslie.higgins@belmont.edu.

School of Occupational Therapy Students: 131 full-time (120 women); includes 9 Black or African American, non-Hispanic/Latino; 1 American Indian or Alaska Native, non-Hispanic/Latino; 3 Asian, non-Hispanic/Latino; 4 Hispanic/Latino, 1 international. Average age 27. 183 applicants, 42% accepted, 62 enrolled. *Faculty:* 9 full-time (8 women), 11 part-time/adjunct (8 women). Expenses: Contact institution. *Financial support:* Fellowships, research assistantships, teaching assistantships available. Financial award applicants required to submit FAFSA. In 2010, 28 master's, 22 doctorates awarded. *Degree program information:* Evening/weekend programs available. Offers occupational therapy (MSOT, OTD). *Application deadline:* For fall admission, 3/1 priority date for domestic students. *Application fee:* $50. Electronic applications accepted. *Application Contact:* Kelly Rockey, Admissions Assistant, 615-460-6798, Fax: 615-460-6475, E-mail: otd@belmont.edu. *Associate Dean,* Dr. Scott D. McPhee, 615-460-6700, Fax: 615-460-6475, E-mail: scott.mcphee@belmont.edu.

School of Pharmacy Students: 214 full-time (138 women); includes 49 minority (20 Black or African American, non-Hispanic/Latino; 21 Asian, non-Hispanic/Latino; 7 Hispanic/Latino; 1 Two or more races, non-Hispanic/Latino), 4 international. Average age 25. 354 applicants, 32% accepted, 75 enrolled. *Faculty:* 22 full-time (14 women). Expenses: Contact institution. *Financial support:* In 2010–11, 8 students received support. Applicants required to submit FAFSA. Offers pharmacy (Pharm D). *Application deadline:* For fall admission, 8/31 priority date for domestic students; for spring admission, 3/1 for domestic students. Applications are processed on a rolling basis. *Application fee:* $50. Electronic applications accepted. *Application Contact:* Dr. Elinor Gray, Dean of Enrollment Services, 615-460-6747, Fax: 615-460-6741, E-mail: elinor.gray@belmont.edu. *Dean,* Dr. Phil Johnston, 615-460-6746, Fax: 615-460-6741, E-mail: phil.johnston@belmont.edu.

School of Physical Therapy Students: 97 full-time (79 women); includes 1 American Indian or Alaska Native, non-Hispanic/Latino. Average age 24. 309 applicants, 27% accepted, 34 enrolled. *Faculty:* 9 full-time (5 women), 12 part-time/adjunct (8 women). Expenses: Contact institution. *Financial support:* In 2010–11, 38 students received support. Scholarships/grants available. Financial award applicants required to submit FAFSA. In 2010, 31 doctorates awarded. Offers physical therapy (DPT). *Application deadline:* For fall admission, 8/31 priority date for domestic and international students; for spring admission, 5/15 for domestic

Belmont University (continued)

students, 5/16 for international students. Applications are processed on a rolling basis. *Application fee:* $50. Electronic applications accepted. *Application Contact:* Lucy Baltimore, Program Assistant, 615-460-6722, Fax: 615-460-6729, E-mail: pt@belmont.edu. *Associate Dean*, Dr. John S. Halle, 615-460-6727, Fax: 615-460-6729, E-mail: john.halle@belmont.edu.

College of Visual and Performing Arts Students: 10 full-time (4 women), 43 part-time (24 women); includes 4 minority (all Black or African American, non-Hispanic/Latino), 1 international. Average age 28. 19 applicants, 89% accepted, 13 enrolled. *Faculty:* 26 full-time (8 women), 15 part-time/adjunct (6 women). Expenses: Contact institution. *Financial support:* In 2010–11, 15 fellowships (averaging $2,000 per year), 5 teaching assistantships (averaging $2,000 per year) were awarded; career-related internships or fieldwork, scholarships/grants, and unspecified assistantships also available. Financial award application deadline: 3/1; financial award applicants required to submit FAFSA. In 2010, 15 master's awarded. *Degree program information:* Part-time programs available. Offers visual and performing arts (MM). *Application deadline:* For fall admission, 5/1 priority date for domestic students, 5/11 for international students; for spring admission, 11/1 priority date for domestic students, 11/1 for international students. Applications are processed on a rolling basis. *Application fee:* $50. Electronic applications accepted. *Application Contact:* Russ Cornwall, Graduate Secretary, 615-460-8117, Fax: 615-386-0239, E-mail: cornwallr@mail.belmont.edu. *Dean*, Dr. Cynthia R. Curtis, 615-460-8118.

School of Music Students: 10 full-time (4 women), 43 part-time (24 women); includes 4 minority (all Black or African American, non-Hispanic/Latino), 1 international. Average age 28. 19 applicants, 89% accepted, 13 enrolled. *Faculty:* 26 full-time (8 women), 12 part-time/adjunct (3 women). Expenses: Contact institution. *Financial support:* In 2010–11, 15 fellowships (averaging $2,000 per year), 5 teaching assistantships (averaging $2,000 per year) were awarded; career-related internships or fieldwork, scholarships/grants, and unspecified assistantships also available. Financial award application deadline: 3/1; financial award applicants required to submit FAFSA. In 2010, 16 master's awarded. *Degree program information:* Part-time programs available. Offers church music (MM); composition (MM); music education (MM); pedagogy (MM); performance (MM). *Application deadline:* For fall admission, 5/1 priority date for domestic students, 5/1 for international students; for spring admission, 11/1 priority date for domestic students, 11/1 for international students. Applications are processed on a rolling basis. *Application fee:* $50. Electronic applications accepted. *Application Contact:* Russ Cornwall, Graduate Secretary, 615-460-8117, Fax: 615-386-0239, E-mail: cornwallr@mail.belmont.edu. *Director*, Dr. Robert Gregg, 615-460-8111, Fax: 615-386-0239, E-mail: greggr@mail.belmont.edu.

Jack C. Massey Graduate School of Business Students: 45 full-time (23 women), 212 part-time (98 women); includes 43 minority (20 Black or African American, non-Hispanic/Latino; 1 American Indian or Alaska Native, non-Hispanic/Latino; 13 Asian, non-Hispanic/Latino; 9 Hispanic/Latino), 2 international. Average age 29. 181 applicants, 54% accepted, 72 enrolled. *Faculty:* 34 full-time (11 women), 6 part-time/adjunct (2 women). Expenses: Contact institution. *Financial support:* In 2010–11, 22 students received support. Scholarships/grants, tuition waivers (partial), and unspecified assistantships available. Financial award application deadline: 7/1; financial award applicants required to submit FAFSA. In 2010, 112 master's awarded. *Degree program information:* Part-time and evening/weekend programs available. Offers business (M Acc, MBA). *Application deadline:* For fall admission, 7/1 for domestic and international students; for spring admission, 11/1 for domestic and international students. Applications are processed on a rolling basis. *Application fee:* $50. Electronic applications accepted. *Application Contact:* Tonya Hollin, Admissions Assistant, 615-460-6480, Fax: 615-460-6353, E-mail: masseyadmissions@.belmont.edu. *Dean*, Dr. Patrick Raines, 615-460-6480, Fax: 615-460-6455, E-mail: patraines@belmont.edu.

BEMIDJI STATE UNIVERSITY, Bemidji, MN 56601-2699

General Information State-supported, coed, comprehensive institution. *Enrollment:* 5,365 graduate, professional, and undergraduate students; 82 full-time matriculated graduate/professional students (51 women), 350 part-time matriculated graduate/professional students (210 women). *Enrollment by degree level:* 432 master's. *Graduate faculty:* 142 full-time (61 women), 37 part-time/adjunct (22 women). Tuition, state resident: full-time $6605; part-time $330 per credit. Tuition, nonresident: full-time $6605; part-time $330 per credit. *Required fees:* $107.97 per credit. *Graduate housing:* Room and/or apartments available on a first-come, first-served basis to single students; on-campus housing not available to married students. Typical cost: $6480 per year ($6480 including board). Room and board charges vary according to board plan and housing facility selected. Housing application deadline: 8/1. *Student services:* Campus employment opportunities, campus safety program, career counseling, child daycare facilities, exercise/wellness program, free psychological counseling, grant writing training, international student services, low-cost health insurance, multicultural affairs office, services for students with disabilities, teacher training, writing training. *Library facilities:* A. C. Clark Library. *Online resources:* library catalog, web page, access to other libraries' catalogs. *Collection:* 407,573 titles, 35,000 serial subscriptions, 5,538 audiovisual materials.

Computer facilities: Computer purchase and lease plans are available. 1,200 computers available on campus for general student use. A campuswide network can be accessed from student residence rooms and from off campus. Online class registration is available. *Web address:* http://www.bemidjistate.edu/.

General Application Contact: Joan Miller, Senior Office and Administrative Specialist, 218-755-2027, Fax: 218-755-2258, E-mail: jmiller@bemidjistate.edu.

GRADUATE UNITS

School of Graduate Studies Students: 82 full-time (51 women), 350 part-time (210 women); includes 21 minority (6 Black or African American, non-Hispanic/Latino; 3 American Indian or Alaska Native, non-Hispanic/Latino; 6 Asian, non-Hispanic/Latino; 6 Hispanic/Latino), 8 international. Average age 35. 491 applicants, 93% accepted, 307 enrolled. *Faculty:* 142 full-time (61 women), 37 part-time/adjunct (22 women). Expenses: Contact institution. *Financial support:* In 2010–11, 110 students received support, including 40 research assistantships with partial tuition reimbursements available (averaging $7,196 per year), 40 teaching assistantships with partial tuition reimbursements available (averaging $7,196 per year); career-related internships or fieldwork, Federal Work-Study, scholarships/grants, health care benefits, and unspecified assistantships also available. Support available to part-time students. Financial award application deadline: 4/15; financial award applicants required to submit FAFSA. In 2010, 97 master's awarded. *Degree program information:* Part-time programs available. Postbaccalaureate distance learning degree programs offered (no on-campus study). Offers biology (MS); counseling psychology (MS); education (M Ed, MS); English (MA, MS); environmental studies (MS); mathematics (MS); mathematics (elementary and middle level education) (MS); special education (M Sp Ed, MS). *Application deadline:* Applications are processed on a rolling basis. *Application fee:* $20. Electronic applications accepted. *Application Contact:* Joan Miller, Senior Office and Administrative Specialist, 218-755-2027, Fax: 218-755-2258, E-mail: jmiller@bemidjistate.edu. *Dean*, Dr. Patricia Rogers, 218-755-2027, Fax: 218-755-2258, E-mail: progers@bemidjistate.edu.

BENEDICTINE COLLEGE, Atchison, KS 66002-1499

General Information Independent-religious, coed, comprehensive institution. *Enrollment:* 1,959 graduate, professional, and undergraduate students; 29 full-time matriculated graduate/professional students (13 women), 44 part-time matriculated graduate/professional students (21 women). *Enrollment by degree level:* 73 master's. *Graduate faculty:* 9 full-time (3 women), 20 part-time/adjunct (5 women). *Graduate housing:* On-campus housing not available. *Student services:* Campus employment opportunities, career counseling, exercise/wellness program, free psychological counseling, international student services, services for students with disabilities, teacher training. *Library facilities:* Benedictine College Library plus 1 other. *Online resources:* library catalog, web page, access to other libraries' catalogs. *Collection:* 207,316 titles, 32,834 serial subscriptions, 1,032 audiovisual materials.

Computer facilities: Computer purchase and lease plans are available. 100 computers available on campus for general student use. A campuswide network can be accessed from student residence rooms and from off campus. Online class registration is available. *Web address:* http://www.benedictine.edu/.

General Application Contact: Donna Bonnel, Administrative Assistant of Graduate Programs, 913-367-5340 Ext. 2524, Fax: 913-367-5462, E-mail: emba@benedictine.edu.

GRADUATE UNITS

Executive Master of Business Administration Program Students: 20 full-time (6 women); includes 8 minority (all Black or African American, non-Hispanic/Latino). Average age 37. 22 applicants, 91% accepted, 20 enrolled. *Faculty:* 5 full-time (0 women), 7 part-time/adjunct (2 women). Expenses: Contact institution. *Financial support:* In 2010–11, 6 students received support. Scholarships/grants and tuition waivers (full and partial) available. Financial award application deadline: 4/15; financial award applicants required to submit FAFSA. In 2010, 12 master's awarded. *Degree program information:* Evening/weekend programs available. Offers business administration (EMBA). *Application deadline:* For fall admission, 7/15 priority date for domestic students, 7/1 for international students; for spring admission, 4/15 priority date for domestic students, 4/1 for international students. Applications are processed on a rolling basis. *Application fee:* $100. Electronic applications accepted. *Application Contact:* Donna Bonnel, Administrator of Graduate Programs, 913-367-5340 Ext. 7589, Fax: 913-360-7301, E-mail: dbonnel@benedictine.edu. *Executive Director, Graduate Business Programs*, Dave Geenens, 913-367-5340 Ext. 7633, Fax: 913-360-7301, E-mail: emba@benedictine.edu.

Master of Arts Program in School Leadership Students: 28 part-time (16 women). Average age 32. 12 applicants, 83% accepted, 10 enrolled. *Faculty:* 2 full-time (both women), 9 part-time/adjunct (3 women). Expenses: Contact institution. *Financial support:* Scholarships/grants available. Support available to part-time students. Financial award applicants required to submit FAFSA. In 2010, 7 master's awarded. *Degree program information:* Part-time and evening/weekend programs available. Offers school leadership (MA). *Application deadline:* For fall admission, 8/15 priority date for domestic students; for spring admission, 5/15 priority date for domestic students. Applications are processed on a rolling basis. *Application fee:* $35. *Application Contact:* Donna Bonnel, Administrative Assistant, 913-360-7589 Ext. 7589, Fax: 913-360-7301, E-mail: emba@benedictine.edu. *Director*, Dr. Cheryl Reding, 913-360-7384, E-mail: creding@benedictine.edu.

Master of Education Program in Teacher Leadership Expenses: Contact institution. Offers teacher leadership (M Ed). *Application Contact:* Donna Bonnel, Administrative Assistant, 913-367-5340 Ext. 2524, Fax: 913-367-5462, E-mail: emba@benedictine.edu.

Traditional Business Administration Program Students: 9 full-time (7 women), 16 part-time (5 women); includes 3 minority (2 Asian, non-Hispanic/Latino; 1 Hispanic/Latino). Average age 22. 28 applicants, 89% accepted, 25 enrolled. *Faculty:* 2 full-time (1 woman), 4 part-time/adjunct (0 women). Expenses: Contact institution. *Financial support:* In 2010–11, 7 students received support. Scholarships/grants and unspecified assistantships available. Support available to part-time students. Financial award application deadline: 3/15; financial award applicants required to submit FAFSA. In 2010, 18 master's awarded. *Degree program information:* Part-time and evening/weekend programs available. Offers business administration (MBA). *Application deadline:* For fall admission, 8/1 priority date for domestic students, 7/1 priority date for international students; for winter admission, 1/7 priority date for domestic students, 12/1 priority date for international students; for spring admission, 5/1 priority date for domestic students, 4/1 priority date for international students. Applications are processed on a rolling basis. *Application fee:* $50. Electronic applications accepted. *Application Contact:* Donna Bonnel, Administrative Specialist, 913-360-7589, Fax: 913-360-7301, E-mail: dbonnel@benedictine.edu. *Executive Director, Graduate Business Programs*, Dave Geenens, 913-367-5340 Ext. 7633, Fax: 913-360-7301, E-mail: emba@benedictine.edu.

BENEDICTINE UNIVERSITY, Lisle, IL 60532-0900

General Information Independent-religious, coed, comprehensive institution. *Enrollment:* 6,892 graduate, professional, and undergraduate students; 1,039 full-time matriculated graduate/professional students (653 women), 2,127 part-time matriculated graduate/professional students (1,540 women). *Enrollment by degree level:* 3,082 master's, 84 doctoral. *Graduate faculty:* 27 full-time (14 women), 283 part-time/adjunct (157 women). *Graduate housing:* Rooms and/or apartments available on a first-come, first-served basis to single and married students. *Student services:* Campus employment opportunities, campus safety program, career counseling, free psychological counseling, international student services, services for students with disabilities. *Library facilities:* Benedictine Library. *Online resources:* library catalog, web page, access to other libraries' catalogs. *Collection:* 135,810 titles, 38,136 serial subscriptions, 3,292 audiovisual materials.

Computer facilities: 200 computers available on campus for general student use. A campuswide network can be accessed from student residence rooms and from off campus. Online class registration is available. *Web address:* http://www.ben.edu/.

General Application Contact: Kari Gibbons, Director, Admissions, 630-829-6200, Fax: 630-829-6584, E-mail: kgibbons@ben.edu.

GRADUATE UNITS

Graduate Programs Students: 1,039 full-time (653 women), 2,127 part-time (1,540 women); includes 1,003 minority (427 Black or African American, non-Hispanic/Latino; 9 American Indian or Alaska Native, non-Hispanic/Latino; 465 Asian, non-Hispanic/Latino; 99 Hispanic/Latino; 3 Native Hawaiian or other Pacific Islander, non-Hispanic/Latino), 63 international. Average age 33. 1,624 applicants, 85% accepted, 833 enrolled. *Faculty:* 27 full-time (14 women), 283 part-time/adjunct (157 women). Expenses: Contact institution. *Financial support:* Career-related internships or fieldwork and health care benefits available. Support available to part-time students. In 2010, 1,020 master's, 9 doctorates awarded. *Degree program information:* Part-time and evening/weekend programs available. Postbaccalaureate distance learning degree programs offered (no on-campus study). Offers accountancy (MS); accounting (MBA); administration of health care institutions (MPH); clinical exercise physiology (MS); clinical psychology (MS); curriculum and instruction and collaborative teaching (M Ed); dietetics (MPH); disaster management (MPH); elementary education (MA Ed); entrepreneurship and managing innovation (MBA); financial management (MBA); health administration (MBA); health education (MPH); health information systems (MPH); higher education and organizational change (Ed D); human resource management (MBA); information systems security (MBA); international business (MBA); leadership and administration (M Ed); management and organizational behavior (MS); management consulting (MBA); management information systems (MBA); marketing management (MBA); nursing (MSN); nutrition and wellness (MS); operations management and logistics (MBA); organizational development (PhD); organizational leadership (MBA); reading and literacy (M Ed); science content and process (MSSCP); secondary education (MA Ed); special education (MA Ed). *Application deadline:* For fall admission, 9/1 for domestic students; for winter admission, 12/1 for domestic students; for spring admission, 2/15 for domestic students. Applications are processed on a rolling basis. *Application fee:* $40. Electronic applications accepted. *Application Contact:* Kari Gibbons, Director, Admissions, 630-829-6200, Fax: 630-829-6584, E-mail: kgibbons@ben.edu. *Provost and Vice President for Academic Affairs*, Dr. Donald B. Taylor, 630-829-6240, Fax: 630-829-6369.

BENEDICTINE UNIVERSITY AT SPRINGFIELD, Springfield, IL 62702

General Information Independent-religious, coed.

GRADUATE UNITS

Program in Business Administration *Degree program information:* Part-time and evening/weekend programs available. Offers health administration (MBA); organizational leadership (MBA).

Program in Elementary Education Offers elementary education (MA Ed).

Program in Management and Organizational Behavior *Degree program information:* Evening/weekend programs available. Offers management and organizational behavior (MS).

Program in Organization Development *Degree program information:* Evening/weekend programs available. Offers organization development (PhD).

Program in Reading/Literacy Offers reading/literacy (M Ed).

BENNINGTON COLLEGE, Bennington, VT 05201

General Information Independent, coed, comprehensive institution. *Enrollment:* 811 graduate, professional, and undergraduate students; 121 full-time matriculated graduate/professional students (82 women), 22 part-time matriculated graduate/professional students (19 women). *Enrollment by degree level:* 135 master's, 8 other advanced degrees. *Graduate faculty:* 45 full-time (20 women), 20 part-time/adjunct (12 women). *Tuition:* Full-time $20,950; part-time $2935 per course. One-time fee: $75. Tuition and fees vary according to program. *Graduate housing:* Room and/or apartments available on a first-come, first-served basis to single students; on-campus housing not available to married students. Typical cost: $5800 per year ($11,160 including board). *Student services:* Campus employment opportunities, campus safety program, career counseling, exercise/wellness program, free psychological counseling, international student services, low-cost health insurance, teacher training, writing training. *Library facilities:* Crossett Library plus 1 other. *Online resources:* library catalog, web page, access to other libraries' catalogs. *Collection:* 127,322 titles, 15,943 serial subscriptions, 7,451 audiovisual materials.

Computer facilities: 100 computers available on campus for general student use. A campuswide network can be accessed from student residence rooms and from off campus. *Web address:* http://www.bennington.edu/.

General Application Contact: Ken Himmelman, Dean of Admissions and Financial Aid, 802-440-4312, Fax: 802-440-4320, E-mail: admissions@bennington.edu.

GRADUATE UNITS

Graduate Programs Students: 121 full-time (82 women), 22 part-time (19 women); includes 18 minority (3 Black or African American, non-Hispanic/Latino; 1 American Indian or Alaska Native, non-Hispanic/Latino; 6 Asian, non-Hispanic/Latino; 8 Hispanic/Latino). Average age 39. 245 applicants, 44% accepted, 50 enrolled. *Faculty:* 45 full-time (20 women), 20 part-time/adjunct (12 women). Expenses: Contact institution. *Financial support:* In 2010–11, 20 students received support, including 1 fellowship (averaging $7,000 per year), 5 teaching assistantships (averaging $13,618 per year); scholarships/grants and unspecified assistantships also available. Financial award application deadline: 4/1; financial award applicants required to submit FAFSA. In 2010, 71 master's, 10 other advanced degrees awarded. *Degree program information:* Part-time programs available. Postbaccalaureate distance learning degree programs offered (minimal on-campus study). Offers allied and health sciences (Certificate); art education (MAT); creative writing (MFA); dance (MFA); early childhood (MAT); education (MATSL); elementary education (MAT); English education (MAT); foreign language education (MAT, MATSL); French (MATSL); K-12 education (MAT); mathematics education (MAT); music (MFA); music education (MAT); science education (MAT); secondary education (MAT); social studies education (MAT); Spanish (MATSL); theater arts (MAT). *Application deadline:* Applications are processed on a rolling basis. *Application fee:* $60. *Application Contact:* Ken Himmelman, Dean of Admissions and Financial Aid, 802-440-4312, Fax: 802-440-4320, E-mail: admissions@bennington.edu. *Associate Dean of the College*, Duncan Dobbelmann, 802-440-4400, Fax: 802-440-4876, E-mail: duncand@bennington.edu.

BENTLEY UNIVERSITY, Waltham, MA 02452-4705

General Information Independent, coed, comprehensive institution. *Enrollment:* 5,695 graduate, professional, and undergraduate students; 497 full-time matriculated graduate/professional students (273 women), 933 part-time matriculated graduate/professional students (408 women). *Enrollment by degree level:* 1,375 master's, 34 doctoral, 21 other advanced degrees. *Graduate faculty:* 74 full-time (22 women), 21 part-time/adjunct (5 women). *Tuition:* Full-time $28,224; part-time $1176 per credit. *Required fees:* $404. Part-time tuition and fees vary according to course load. *Graduate housing:* Room and/or apartments available on a first-come, first-served basis to single students; on-campus housing not available to married students. Typical cost: $9670 per year ($14,660 including board). Room and board charges vary according to board plan and housing facility selected. *Student services:* Campus employment opportunities, campus safety program, career counseling, exercise/wellness program, free psychological counseling, international student services, low-cost health insurance, multicultural affairs office, services for students with disabilities. *Library facilities:* Bentley Library plus 1 other. *Online resources:* library catalog, web page, access to other libraries' catalogs. *Collection:* 173,000 titles, 53,300 serial subscriptions, 7,100 audiovisual materials.

Computer facilities: Computer purchase and lease plans are available. 4,523 computers available on campus for general student use. A campuswide network can be accessed from student residence rooms and from off campus. Online class registration, Grade checking, online admission, Blackboard, resume review, student employment, interlibrary loan, free software are available. *Web address:* http://www.bentley.edu/.

General Application Contact: Sharon Hill, Assistant Dean/Director of Graduate Admissions, 781-891-2108, Fax: 781-891-2464, E-mail: bentleygraduateadmissions@bentley.edu.

GRADUATE UNITS

McCallum Graduate School of Business Students: 497 full-time (273 women), 933 part-time (408 women); includes 170 minority (17 Black or African American, non-Hispanic/Latino; 16 American Indian or Alaska Native, non-Hispanic/Latino; 97 Asian, non-Hispanic/Latino; 37 Hispanic/Latino; 3 Two or more races, non-Hispanic/Latino), 344 international. Average age 29. 1,822 applicants, 63% accepted, 553 enrolled. *Faculty:* 74 full-time (22 women), 21 part-time/adjunct (5 women). Expenses: Contact institution. *Financial support:* In 2010–11, 234 students received support, including 39 research assistantships (averaging $17,545 per year); scholarships/grants and unspecified assistantships also available. Financial award application deadline: 6/1; financial award applicants required to submit CSS PROFILE or FAFSA. In 2010, 558 master's, 21 other advanced degrees awarded. *Degree program information:* Part-time and evening/weekend programs available. Postbaccalaureate distance learning degree programs offered. Offers accountancy (PhD); accounting (GBC); accounting information systems (GBC); business (GSS); business administration (MBA); business ethics (GBC); data analysis (GBC); finance (MSF); financial planning (GBC); fraud and forensic accounting (GBC); human factors in information design (MSHFID); information technology (MSIT); marketing analytics (MSMA); taxation (MST). *Application deadline:* For fall admission, 12/1 priority date for domestic and international students; for spring admission, 10/1 priority date for domestic and international students. *Application fee:* $50. Electronic applications accepted. *Application Contact:* Sharon Hill, Director of Graduate Admissions, 781-891-2108, Fax: 781-891-2464, E-mail: bentleygraduateadmissions@bentley.edu. *Dean*, Dr. Roy A. Wiggins, 781-891-3166.

BERNARD M. BARUCH COLLEGE OF THE CITY UNIVERSITY OF NEW YORK, New York, NY 10010-5585

General Information State and locally supported, coed, comprehensive institution. *Graduate housing:* On-campus housing not available.

GRADUATE UNITS

School of Public Affairs Students: 246 full-time (177 women), 727 part-time (486 women); includes 213 Black or African American, non-Hispanic/Latino; 2 American Indian or Alaska Native, non-Hispanic/Latino; 79 Asian, non-Hispanic/Latino; 155 Hispanic/Latino; 30 Two or more races, non-Hispanic/Latino. Average age 33. 630 applicants, 69% accepted, 324 enrolled. *Faculty:* 71 full-time (27 women), 51 part-time/adjunct (23 women). Expenses: Contact institution. *Financial support:* In 2010–11, 32 students received support, including 15 fellowships (averaging $2,250 per year), 23 research assistantships (averaging $12,000 per year); teaching assistantships, career-related internships or fieldwork, Federal Work-Study, scholarships/grants, tuition waivers (partial), and unspecified assistantships also available. Support available to part-time students. Financial award application deadline: 5/15; financial award applicants required to submit FAFSA. In 2010, 270 master's awarded. *Degree program information:* Part-time and evening/weekend programs available. Offers educational leadership (MS Ed); health care policy (MPA); higher education administration (MS Ed); nonprofit administration (MPA); policy analysis and evaluation (MPA); public affairs (MPA, MS Ed, Advanced Certificate); public management (MPA); school building leadership (Advanced Certificate); school district leadership (Advanced Certificate). *Application deadline:* For fall admission, 4/1 priority date for domestic and international students; for spring admission, 11/15 priority date for domestic and international students. Applications are processed on a rolling basis. *Application fee:* $125. Electronic applications accepted. *Application Contact:* Michael J. Lovaglio, Director of Student Affairs and Graduate Admissions, 646-660-6750, Fax: 646-660-6751, E-mail: michael.lovaglio@baruch.cuny.edu. *Dean*, David Birdsell, 646-660-6700, Fax: 646-660-6721, E-mail: david.birdsell@baruch.cuny.edu.

Weissman School of Arts and Sciences Offers arts and sciences (MA, MS); corporate communication (MA); financial engineering (MS); industrial organizational psychology (MS).

Zicklin School of Business *Degree program information:* Part-time and evening/weekend programs available. Offers accounting (MBA, MS, PhD); business (MBA, MS, PhD, Certificate); business administration (MBA); computer information systems (MBA, MS, PhD); decision sciences (MBA, MS); economics (MBA); entrepreneurship (MBA); finance (MBA, MS, PhD); general business (MBA); general management and policy (MBA); health care administration (MBA); human resources management (MBA); industrial and labor relations (MS); industrial and organizational psychology (MBA, MS, PhD, Certificate); international executive education (MBA); management planning systems (PhD); management science (MBA); marketing (MBA, MS, PhD); organization and policy studies (PhD); organizational behavior (MBA); statistics (MBA, MS); taxation (MBA, MS). JD/MBA offered jointly with Brooklyn Law School and New York Law School. Electronic applications accepted.

BERRY COLLEGE, Mount Berry, GA 30149-0159

General Information Independent-religious, coed, comprehensive institution. *Enrollment:* 2,087 graduate, professional, and undergraduate students; 42 full-time matriculated graduate/professional students (29 women), 117 part-time matriculated graduate/professional students (85 women). *Enrollment by degree level:* 121 master's, 38 other advanced degrees. *Graduate faculty:* 22 part-time/adjunct (11 women). *Tuition:* Full-time $7992; part-time $444 per credit hour. *Required fees:* $150. Tuition and fees vary according to program. *Graduate housing:* On-campus housing not available. *Student services:* Campus employment opportunities, campus safety program, career counseling, child daycare facilities, exercise/wellness program, free psychological counseling, grant writing training, international student services, low-cost health insurance, multicultural affairs office. *Library facilities:* Memorial Library plus 1 other. *Online resources:* library catalog, web page. *Collection:* 280,360 titles, 2,188 serial subscriptions, 8,591 audiovisual materials. *Research affiliation:* Georgia Forestry Commission (biology), American Library Association (academic services), American Chestnut Foundation (biology), Research Corporation, University of Hawaii (biology), University of Georgia (animal science), University of Chicago (government and international studies).

Computer facilities: 140 computers available on campus for general student use. A campuswide network can be accessed from student residence rooms and from off campus. Online class registration is available. *Web address:* http://www.berry.edu/.

General Application Contact: Brett Kennedy, Director of Admissions, 706-236-2215, Fax: 706-290-2178, E-mail: admissions@berry.edu.

GRADUATE UNITS

Graduate Programs Students: 42 full-time (29 women), 117 part-time (85 women); includes 12 minority (6 Black or African American, non-Hispanic/Latino; 1 American Indian or Alaska Native, non-Hispanic/Latino; 3 Hispanic/Latino; 2 Two or more races, non-Hispanic/Latino), 1 international. Average age 32. *Faculty:* 22 part-time/adjunct (11 women). Expenses: Contact institution. *Financial support:* In 2010–11, 50 students received support, including 26 research assistantships with full tuition reimbursements available (averaging $4,137 per year); scholarships/grants, tuition waivers (partial), and unspecified assistantships also available. Support available to part-time students. Financial award application deadline: 4/1; financial award applicants required to submit FAFSA. In 2010, 41 master's, 5 other advanced degrees awarded. *Degree program information:* Part-time and evening/weekend programs available. Offers curriculum and instruction (Ed S); early childhood education (M Ed, MAT); educational leadership (Ed S); leadership in curriculum and instruction (Ed S); middle-grades education and reading (M Ed); secondary education (M Ed). *Application deadline:* For fall admission, 7/22 for domestic students, 5/1 for international students; for spring admission, 12/9 for domestic students, 2/1 for international students. Applications are processed on a rolling basis. *Application fee:* $25 ($30 for international students). *Application Contact:* Brett Kennedy, Director of Admissions, 706-236-2215, Fax: 706-290-2178, E-mail: admissions@berry.edu. *Provost*, Dr. Katherine Whatley, 706-236-2216, Fax: 706-290-2179, E-mail: kwhatley@berry.edu.

Campbell School of Business Students: 4 full-time (2 women), 27 part-time (13 women); includes 3 minority (2 Black or African American, non-Hispanic/Latino; 1 American Indian or Alaska Native, non-Hispanic/Latino), 1 international. Average age 27. *Faculty:* 6 part-time/adjunct (2 women). Expenses: Contact institution. *Financial support:* In 2010–11, 17 students received support, including 14 research assistantships with full tuition reimbursements available (averaging $4,376 per year); scholarships/grants, tuition waivers (partial), and unspecified assistantships also available. Support available to part-time students. Financial award application deadline: 4/1; financial award applicants required to submit FAFSA. In 2010, 15 master's awarded. *Degree program information:* Part-time and evening/weekend programs available. Offers business (MBA). *Application deadline:* For fall admission, 7/22 for domestic students; for spring admission, 12/9 for domestic students. Applications are processed on a rolling basis. *Application fee:* $25 ($30 for international students). *Application Contact:* Brett Kennedy, Director of Admissions, 706-236-2215, Fax: 706-290-2178, E-mail: admissions@berry.edu. *Dean*, Dr. John Grout, 706-236-2233, Fax: 706-802-6728, E-mail: jgrout@berry.edu.

BETHANY THEOLOGICAL SEMINARY, Richmond, IN 47374-4019

General Information Independent-religious, coed, graduate-only institution. *Graduate housing:* On-campus housing not available.

GRADUATE UNITS

Graduate and Professional Programs *Degree program information:* Part-time programs available. Postbaccalaureate distance learning degree programs offered (minimal on-campus study). Offers biblical studies (MA Th); ministry studies (M Div); peace studies (M Div, MA Th); theological studies (MA Th, CATS); youth ministry (M Div).

BETHANY UNIVERSITY, Scotts Valley, CA 95066-2820

General Information Independent-religious, coed, comprehensive institution. *Graduate housing:* Rooms and/or apartments available to single students and available on a first-come, first-served basis to married students. Housing application deadline: 7/31.

GRADUATE UNITS

Program in Clinical Psychology *Degree program information:* Part-time and evening/weekend programs available. Offers clinical psychology (MS).

Program in Teacher Education *Degree program information:* Part-time and evening/weekend programs available. Offers education (MA); educational leadership (MA).

BETHEL COLLEGE, Mishawaka, IN 46545-5591

General Information Independent-religious, coed, comprehensive institution. *Enrollment:* 2,152 graduate, professional, and undergraduate students; 45 full-time matriculated graduate/professional students (29 women), 182 part-time matriculated graduate/professional students (95 women). *Enrollment by degree level:* 227 master's. *Graduate faculty:* 1 full-time (0 women), 33 part-time/adjunct (18 women). Tuition and fees vary according to program. *Graduate housing:* On-campus housing not available. *Student services:* Campus employment opportunities, campus safety program, career counseling, international student services, services for students with disabilities, writing training. *Library facilities:* Otis and Elizabeth Bowen Library. *Online resources:* library catalog, web page, access to other libraries' catalogs. *Collection:* 145,302 titles, 1,437 serial subscriptions, 3,159 audiovisual materials.

Computer facilities: 160 computers available on campus for general student use. A campuswide network can be accessed from student residence rooms. Online class registration is available. *Web address:* http://www.bethelcollege.edu/.

Bethel College (continued)

General Application Contact: Dr. Bradley D. Smith, Dean, 574-257-3363, Fax: 574-257-7616.

GRADUATE UNITS

Division of Graduate Studies Students: 45 full-time (29 women), 182 part-time (95 women); includes 26 minority (19 Black or African American, non-Hispanic/Latino; 5 Hispanic/Latino; 2 Two or more races, non-Hispanic/Latino), 3 international. Average age 37. 153 applicants, 90% accepted, 109 enrolled. *Faculty:* 1 full-time (0 women), 33 part-time/adjunct (18 women). Expenses: Contact institution. *Financial support:* Career-related internships or fieldwork available. Financial award applicants required to submit FAFSA. In 2010, 70 master's awarded. *Degree program information:* Part-time and evening/weekend programs available. Offers business administration (MBA); Christian ministries (M Min); education (M Ed, MAT); nursing (MSN); theological studies (MATS). *Application deadline:* For fall admission, 5/1 for international students; for spring admission, 10/1 for international students. Applications are processed on a rolling basis. *Application fee:* $25. Electronic applications accepted. *Application Contact:* Dr. Bradley D. Smith, Dean, 574-257-3363, Fax: 574-257-3357, E-mail: smithb@bethelcollege.edu. *Dean,* Dr. Bradley D. Smith, 574-257-3363, Fax: 574-257-3357, E-mail: smithb@bethelcollege.edu.

BETHEL SEMINARY, St. Paul, MN 55112-6998

General Information Independent-religious, coed, graduate-only institution. *Enrollment by degree level:* 370 first professional, 483 master's, 102 doctoral, 48 other advanced degrees. *Graduate faculty:* 26 full-time (3 women), 74 part-time/adjunct (29 women). *Graduate housing:* Rooms and/or apartments available on a first-come, first-served basis to single and married students. *Student services:* Campus employment opportunities, campus safety program, career counseling, child daycare facilities, free psychological counseling, international student services, multicultural affairs office, writing training. *Library facilities:* Carl H. Lundquist Library plus 1 other. *Online resources:* library catalog, web page, access to other libraries' catalogs. *Collection:* 170,750 titles, 517 serial subscriptions, 8,875 audiovisual materials.

Computer facilities: 19 computers available on campus for general student use. A campuswide network can be accessed from student residence rooms and from off campus. Online class registration is available. *Web address:* http://www.bethel.edu/.

General Application Contact: Joseph V. Dworak, Director of Admissions, 651-638-6288, Fax: 651-638-6002, E-mail: j-dworak@bethel.edu.

GRADUATE UNITS

Graduate and Professional Programs Students: 729 full-time (275 women), 274 part-time (118 women); includes 75 minority (34 Black or African American, non-Hispanic/Latino; 1 American Indian or Alaska Native, non-Hispanic/Latino; 12 Asian, non-Hispanic/Latino; 16 Hispanic/Latino; 1 Native Hawaiian or other Pacific Islander, non-Hispanic/Latino; 11 Two or more races, non-Hispanic/Latino), 16 international. Average age 38. 525 applicants, 76% accepted, 265 enrolled. *Faculty:* 26 full-time (3 women), 74 part-time/adjunct (29 women). Expenses: Contact institution. *Financial support:* In 2010–11, 655 students received support, including 18 teaching assistantships; career-related internships or fieldwork, Federal Work-Study, scholarships/grants, and tuition waivers (full) also available. Financial award application deadline: 7/15; financial award applicants required to submit FAFSA. In 2010, 149 master's, 13 doctorates awarded. *Degree program information:* Part-time and evening/weekend programs available. Postbaccalaureate distance learning degree programs offered (minimal on-campus study). Offers Anglican studies (Certificate); applied ministry (MA, Certificate); biblical studies (Certificate); children's and family ministry (MACFM); Christian education (MACE); Christian thought (MACT); community ministry leadership (MA, Certificate); global and contextual studies (MA); Greek and Hebrew language (M Div); Greek language (M Div); Hebrew language (M Div); lay ministry (Certificate); marriage and family therapy (MAMFT, Certificate); men's ministry leadership (Certificate); ministry (D Min); ministry leadership (Certificate); spiritual formation (Certificate); theological studies (MATS, Certificate); transformational leadership (MATL, Certificate); young life youth ministry (Certificate). *Application deadline:* For fall admission, 8/1 priority date for domestic students, 3/1 for international students; for winter admission, 12/1 priority date for domestic students; for spring admission, 3/1 priority date for domestic students. Applications are processed on a rolling basis. *Application fee:* $20. Electronic applications accepted. *Application Contact:* Joseph V. Dworak, Director of Admissions, 651-638-6288, Fax: 651-638-6002, E-mail: j-dworak@bethel.edu. *Vice President and Dean,* Dr. David Ridder, 651-638-6553.

BETHEL UNIVERSITY, St. Paul, MN 55112-6999

General Information Independent-religious, coed, comprehensive institution. *Enrollment:* 5,391 graduate, professional, and undergraduate students; 601 full-time matriculated graduate/professional students (402 women), 401 part-time matriculated graduate/professional students (259 women). *Enrollment by degree level:* 912 master's, 90 doctoral. *Graduate faculty:* 7 full-time (3 women), 52 part-time/adjunct (23 women). *Tuition:* Full-time $5400; part-time $450 per credit. Tuition and fees vary according to course level, course load, degree level and program. *Graduate housing:* On-campus housing not available. *Student services:* Campus employment opportunities, campus safety program, career counseling, international student services, low-cost health insurance, multicultural affairs office, services for students with disabilities, writing training. *Library facilities:* Bethel University Library plus 1 other. *Online resources:* library catalog, web page, access to other libraries' catalogs. *Collection:* 193,728 titles, 26,264 serial subscriptions, 12,016 audiovisual materials.

Computer facilities: Computer purchase and lease plans are available. 460 computers available on campus for general student use. A campuswide network can be accessed from student residence rooms and from off campus. Online class registration is available. *Web address:* http://www.bethel.edu/.

General Application Contact: Paul Ives, Director of Admissions, 651-635-8000, Fax: 651-635-8004, E-mail: gs@bethel.edu.

GRADUATE UNITS

Graduate School Students: 601 full-time (402 women), 401 part-time (259 women); includes 64 minority (26 Black or African American, non-Hispanic/Latino; 1 American Indian or Alaska Native, non-Hispanic/Latino; 10 Asian, non-Hispanic/Latino; 17 Hispanic/Latino; 1 Native Hawaiian or other Pacific Islander, non-Hispanic/Latino; 9 Two or more races, non-Hispanic/Latino), 17 international. Average age 36. 397 applicants, 84% accepted, 252 enrolled. *Faculty:* 7 full-time (3 women), 52 part-time/adjunct (23 women). Expenses: Contact institution. *Financial support:* Applicants required to submit FAFSA. In 2010, 268 master's, 5 doctorates awarded. *Degree program information:* Part-time and evening/weekend programs available. Postbaccalaureate distance learning degree programs offered (minimal on-campus study). Offers business administration (MBA); child and adolescent and community counseling (MA); communication (MA); education K-12 (MA); educational administration (Ed D); gerontology (MA); healthcare leadership (MA); literacy (Certificate); literacy education (MA); nursing education (MA, Certificate); organizational leadership (MA); post-secondary teaching (Certificate); special education (MA); teaching (MA). *Application deadline:* Applications are processed on a rolling basis. Electronic applications accepted. *Application Contact:* Paul Ives, Director of Admissions, 651-635-8000, Fax: 651-635-8004, E-mail: gs@bethel.edu. *Acting Vice President and Dean,* Dr. Lori Jass, 651-635-8000, Fax: 651-635-8039, E-mail: l-jass@bethel.edu.

BETHEL UNIVERSITY, McKenzie, TN 38201

General Information Independent-religious, coed, comprehensive institution. *Enrollment:* 3,141 graduate, professional, and undergraduate students; 93 full-time matriculated graduate/professional students (68 women), 27 part-time matriculated graduate/professional students (18 women). *Enrollment by degree level:* 120 master's. *Graduate faculty:* 7 full-time (4 women), 2 part-time/adjunct (both women). *Graduate housing:* Room and/or apartments available on a first-come, first-served basis to single students; on-campus housing not available to married students. Housing application deadline: 7/31. *Student services:* Career counseling, free psychological counseling, international student services. *Library facilities:* Burroughs Learning Center plus 1 other. *Online resources:* library catalog, web page. *Collection:* 45,000 titles, 111,700 serial subscriptions, 538 audiovisual materials.

Computer facilities: Computer purchase and lease plans are available. 12 computers available on campus for general student use. A campuswide network can be accessed from student residence rooms. Online class registration is available. *Web address:* http://www.bethel-college.edu/.

General Application Contact: Dr. Ben G. McClure, Chair, Division of Education and Health Sciences, 731-352-4025, Fax: 731-352-4097, E-mail: graduate@bethel-college.edu.

GRADUATE UNITS

Graduate Programs Students: 93 full-time (68 women), 27 part-time (18 women); includes 42 minority (27 Black or African American, non-Hispanic/Latino; 15 Asian, non-Hispanic/Latino). Average age 32. 120 applicants, 100% accepted, 120 enrolled. *Faculty:* 7 full-time (4 women), 2 part-time/adjunct (both women). Expenses: Contact institution. *Financial support:* In 2010–11, 61 students received support. Career-related internships or fieldwork available. Support available to part-time students. Financial award application deadline: 6/1; financial award applicants required to submit FAFSA. *Degree program information:* Part-time and evening/weekend programs available. Offers administration and supervision (MA Ed); business administration (MBA); conflict resolution (MA); physician assistant studies (MS). *Application deadline:* For fall admission, 8/23 priority date for domestic and international students; for spring admission, 1/11 priority date for domestic and international students. Applications are processed on a rolling basis. *Application fee:* $30. *Application Contact:* Dr. Ben G. McClure, Chair, Division of Education and Health Sciences, 731-352-4025, Fax: 731-352-4097. *Dean of Graduate Studies,* J. Bentley Rawdon, 731-352-4028, Fax: 731-352-4097.

BETHESDA CHRISTIAN UNIVERSITY, Anaheim, CA 92801

General Information Independent-religious, coed, comprehensive institution.

GRADUATE UNITS

Graduate and Professional Programs Offers biblical studies (MA); music (MA); theology (M Div).

BETH HAMEDRASH SHAAREI YOSHER INSTITUTE, Brooklyn, NY 11204

General Information Independent-religious, men only, comprehensive institution.

GRADUATE UNITS

Graduate Programs

BETH HATALMUD RABBINICAL COLLEGE, Brooklyn, NY 11214

General Information Independent-religious, men only, comprehensive institution.

GRADUATE UNITS

Graduate Programs

BETH MEDRASH GOVOHA, Lakewood, NJ 08701-2797

General Information Independent-religious, men only, comprehensive institution.

GRADUATE UNITS

Graduate Programs

BETHUNE-COOKMAN UNIVERSITY, Daytona Beach, FL 32114-3099

General Information Independent-religious, coed, comprehensive institution.

GRADUATE UNITS

School of Graduate and Professional Studies Postbaccalaureate distance learning degree programs offered (minimal on-campus study). Offers transformative leadership (MS). Electronic applications accepted.

BEULAH HEIGHTS UNIVERSITY, Atlanta, GA 30316

General Information Independent-religious, coed, comprehensive institution.

GRADUATE UNITS

Graduate School Offers biblical studies (MA); leadership studies (MA). Electronic applications accepted.

BEXLEY HALL EPISCOPAL SEMINARY, Columbus, OH 43209-2325

General Information Independent-religious, coed, graduate-only institution.

GRADUATE UNITS

Graduate Programs Offers ministry (M Div, MA).

BIBLICAL THEOLOGICAL SEMINARY, Hatfield, PA 19440-2499

General Information Independent-religious, coed, graduate-only institution. *Enrollment by degree level:* 140 first professional, 60 master's, 17 doctoral, 51 other advanced degrees. *Graduate faculty:* 11 full-time (0 women), 27 part-time/adjunct (9 women). *Tuition:* Full-time $10,728; part-time $447 per credit. *Required fees:* $25 per term. One-time fee: $30. *Graduate housing:* Rooms and/or apartments available on a first-come, first-served basis to single and married students. Typical cost: $8260 per year ($8260 including board) for single students; $8260 per year ($8260 including board) for married students. Housing application deadline: 8/30. *Student services:* Campus employment opportunities, career counseling, international student services. *Online resources:* library catalog. *Collection:* 52,000 titles, 210 serial subscriptions. *Research affiliation:* Christian Counseling and Education Foundation (psychology).

Computer facilities: 20 computers available on campus for general student use. A campuswide network can be accessed from off campus. *Web address:* http://www.biblical.edu/.

General Application Contact: Rev. Darryl John Lang, Director of Recruitment and Student Life, 215-368-5000 Ext. 147, Fax: 215-368-7002, E-mail: dlang@biblical.edu.

GRADUATE UNITS

Graduate and Professional Programs 205 applicants, 52% accepted, 84 enrolled. *Faculty:* 11 full-time (0 women), 27 part-time/adjunct (9 women). Expenses: Contact institution. *Financial support:* In 2010–11, 174 students received support. Career-related internships or fieldwork, institutionally sponsored loans, and scholarships/grants available. Support available to part-time students. Financial award application deadline: 8/30; financial award applicants required to submit FAFSA. In 2010, 23 first professional degrees, 24 master's, 10 doctorates awarded. *Degree program information:* Part-time and evening/weekend programs available. Offers advanced missional leadership (D Min); advanced pastoral studies (Certificate); biblical counseling (Certificate); biblical studies (MA, Certificate); counseling (MA); ministry (M Div, MA); missional theology (MA). *Application deadline:* Applications are processed on a rolling basis. *Application fee:* $30. *Application Contact:* Rev. Darryl John Lang, Director of Recruitment and Student Life, 215-368-5000 Ext. 147, Fax: 215-368-7002, E-mail: dlang@biblical.edu. *Vice President for Student Advancement,* Pamela Jean Smith, 215-368-5000 Ext. 122, Fax: 215-368-7002, E-mail: psmith@biblical.edu.

BIOLA UNIVERSITY, La Mirada, CA 90639-0001

General Information Independent-religious, coed, university. *Enrollment:* 6,101 graduate, professional, and undergraduate students; 724 full-time matriculated graduate/professional students (263 women), 1,160 part-time matriculated graduate/professional students (457 women). *Graduate faculty:* 97 full-time (21 women), 107 part-time/adjunct (33 women). *Graduate housing:* Rooms and/or apartments available on a first-come, first-served basis to single and married students. *Student services:* Campus employment opportunities, campus safety program, career counseling, international student services, low-cost health insurance, multicultural affairs office, services for students with disabilities, teacher training, writing training. *Library facilities:* Biola University Library. *Online resources:* library catalog, web page, access to other libraries' catalogs. *Collection:* 330,173 titles, 264,053 serial subscriptions, 7,461 audiovisual materials.

Computer facilities: A campuswide network can be accessed from student residence rooms and from off campus. Online class registration is available. *Web address:* http://www.biola.edu/.

General Application Contact: Roy M. Allinson, Director of Graduate Admissions, 562-903-4752, Fax: 562-903-4709, E-mail: admissions@biola.edu.

GRADUATE UNITS

Crowell School of Business Students: 25 part-time (7 women); includes 2 Black or African American, non-Hispanic/Latino; 10 Asian, non-Hispanic/Latino. 22 applicants, 73% accepted, 13 enrolled. *Faculty:* 7 full-time (1 woman), 5 part-time/adjunct (0 women). Expenses: Contact institution. *Financial support:* Institutionally sponsored loans and scholarships/grants available. Support available to part-time students. In 2010, 8 master's awarded. *Degree program information:* Part-time and evening/weekend programs available. Offers business (MBA). *Application deadline:* For fall admission, 4/30 priority date for domestic students. *Application fee:* $45. Electronic applications accepted. *Application Contact:* Christina Bullock, Program Coordinator, 562-777-4015, E-mail: mba@biola.edu. *Dean,* Larry D. Strand, 562-777-4015, Fax: 562-906-4545, E-mail: mba@biola.edu.

Rosemead School of Psychology Students: 86 full-time (57 women), 10 part-time (7 women); includes 5 Black or African American, non-Hispanic/Latino; 21 Asian, non-Hispanic/Latino; 4 Hispanic/Latino, 6 international. 135 applicants, 33% accepted, 24 enrolled. *Faculty:* 17 full-time (5 women), 6 part-time/adjunct (3 women). Expenses: Contact institution. *Financial support:* Research assistantships, teaching assistantships, career-related internships or fieldwork, institutionally sponsored loans, scholarships/grants, and unspecified assistantships available. Support available to part-time students. Financial award application deadline: 3/2; financial award applicants required to submit FAFSA. In 2010, 17 doctorates awarded. Offers psychology (PhD, Psy D). *Application deadline:* For fall admission, 1/15 for domestic and international students. *Application fee:* $45. Electronic applications accepted. *Application Contact:* Roy M. Allinson, Director of Graduate Admissions, 562-903-4752, Fax: 562-903-4709, E-mail: admissions@biola.edu. *Administrative Dean,* Dr. Clark Campbell, 562-903-4867, Fax: 562-903-4864.

School of Arts and Sciences Students: 26 full-time (5 women), 173 part-time (38 women); includes 35 minority (7 Black or African American, non-Hispanic/Latino; 14 Asian, non-Hispanic/Latino; 9 Hispanic/Latino; 5 Two or more races, non-Hispanic/Latino), 6 international. 118 applicants, 85% accepted, 83 enrolled. *Faculty:* 8 full-time (5 women), 10 part-time/adjunct (7 women). Expenses: Contact institution. *Financial support:* Career-related internships or fieldwork, institutionally sponsored loans, and scholarships/grants available. Support available to part-time students. Financial award application deadline: 3/2; financial award applicants required to submit FAFSA. In 2010, 49 master's awarded. *Degree program information:* Part-time and evening/weekend programs available. Offers science and religion (MS). *Application deadline:* For fall admission, 7/1 for domestic students; for spring admission, 12/1 for domestic students. Applications are processed on a rolling basis. *Application fee:* $45. Electronic applications accepted. *Application Contact:* Roy M. Allinson, Director of Graduate Admissions, 562-903-4752, Fax: 562-903-4709, E-mail: admissions@biola.edu.

School of Intercultural Studies Students: 66 full-time (39 women), 126 part-time (72 women); includes 48 minority (6 Black or African American, non-Hispanic/Latino; 40 Asian, non-Hispanic/Latino; 2 Two or more races, non-Hispanic/Latino), 30 international. 136 applicants, 70% accepted, 59 enrolled. *Faculty:* 16 full-time (5 women), 6 part-time/adjunct (1 woman). Expenses: Contact institution. *Financial support:* Teaching assistantships, career-related internships or fieldwork, institutionally sponsored loans, and scholarships/grants available. Support available to part-time students. Financial award application deadline: 3/2; financial award applicants required to submit FAFSA. In 2010, 27 master's, 10 doctorates awarded. *Degree program information:* Part-time and evening/weekend programs available. Offers anthropology (MA); applied linguistics (MA); Biblical languages and linguistics (MA); intercultural education (PhD); intercultural studies (MAICS); linguistics (Certificate); missiology (D Miss); missions (MA); teaching English to speakers of other languages (MA, Certificate). *Application deadline:* For fall admission, 7/1 for domestic students; for spring admission, 1/1 for domestic students. Applications are processed on a rolling basis. *Application fee:* $45. Electronic applications accepted. *Application Contact:* Roy M. Allinson, Director of Graduate Admissions, 562-903-4752, Fax: 562-903-4709, E-mail: admissions@biola.edu. *Dean,* Dr. Douglas Pennoyer, 562-903-4844, Fax: 562-903-4748, E-mail: douglas.pennoyer@biola.edu.

School of Professional Studies Students: 5 full-time (2 women), 44 part-time (22 women); includes 6 Black or African American, non-Hispanic/Latino; 6 Asian, non-Hispanic/Latino; 6 Hispanic/Latino. 184 applicants, 65% accepted. *Faculty:* 4 full-time (0 women), 40 part-time/adjunct (12 women). Expenses: Contact institution. *Financial support:* Institutionally sponsored loans and scholarships/grants available. Support available to part-time students. Financial award application deadline: 3/2; financial award applicants required to submit FAFSA. In 2010, 72 master's awarded. *Degree program information:* Part-time and evening/weekend programs available. Offers Christian apologetics (MA); organizational leadership (MA). *Application deadline:* For fall admission, 7/1 for domestic students; for spring admission, 12/1 for domestic students. Applications are processed on a rolling basis. *Application fee:* $45. Electronic applications accepted. *Application Contact:* Roy M. Allinson, Director of Graduate Admissions, 562-903-4752, Fax: 562-903-4709, E-mail: admissions@biola.edu. *Dean,* Dr. Ed Norman, 562-903-4715, E-mail: ed.norman@biola.edu.

Talbot School of Theology Students: 611 full-time (123 women), 573 part-time (144 women); includes 382 minority (48 Black or African American, non-Hispanic/Latino; 1 American Indian or Alaska Native, non-Hispanic/Latino; 300 Asian, non-Hispanic/Latino; 5 Native Hawaiian or other Pacific Islander, non-Hispanic/Latino; 28 Two or more races, non-Hispanic/Latino), 153 international. Average age 31. 515 applicants, 76% accepted, 277 enrolled. *Faculty:* 45 full-time (5 women), 40 part-time/adjunct (10 women). Expenses: Contact institution. *Financial support:* Research assistantships, teaching assistantships, career-related internships or fieldwork, institutionally sponsored loans, and scholarships/grants available. Support available to part-time students. Financial award application deadline: 3/2; financial award applicants required to submit FAFSA. In 2010, 47 first professional degrees, 152 master's, 9 doctorates awarded. *Degree program information:* Part-time and evening/weekend programs available. Offers Biblical studies (MA); Christian education (MACE); Christian ministry and leadership (MA); divinity (M Div); education (PhD); ministry (MA Min); New Testament (MA); Old Testament (MA); philosophy of religion and ethics (MA); spiritual formation (MA); spiritual formation and soul care (MA); theological studies (MA); theology (MA, Th M, D Min). *Application deadline:* For fall admission, 7/1 for domestic students; for spring admission, 1/1 for domestic students. Applications are processed on a rolling basis. *Application fee:* $45. *Application Contact:* Roy M. Allinson, Director of Graduate Admissions, 562-903-4752, Fax: 562-903-4709, E-mail: admissions@biola.edu. *Dean,* Dr. Dennis Dirks, 562-903-4816, Fax: 562-903-4748, E-mail: dennis_dirks@peter.biola.edu.

BISHOP'S UNIVERSITY, Sherbrooke, QC J1M 0C8, Canada

General Information Province-supported, coed, comprehensive institution. *Graduate housing:* Room and/or apartments available on a first-come, first-served basis to single students; on-campus housing not available to married students. Housing application deadline: 7/1.

GRADUATE UNITS

School of Education *Degree program information:* Part-time programs available. Postbaccalaureate distance learning degree programs offered (minimal on-campus study). Offers advanced studies in education (Diploma); education (M Ed, MA); teaching English as a second language (Certificate).

BLACK HILLS STATE UNIVERSITY, Spearfish, SD 57799

General Information State-supported, coed, comprehensive institution. *Graduate housing:* Room and/or apartments available on a first-come, first-served basis to single students; on-campus housing not available to married students. Housing application deadline: 3/1.

GRADUATE UNITS

Graduate Studies Offers business administration (MBA); curriculum and instruction (MS); integrative genomics (MS); strategic leadership (MS).

BLESSED JOHN XXIII NATIONAL SEMINARY, Weston, MA 02493-2618

General Information Independent-religious, men only, graduate-only institution. *Graduate housing:* Room and/or apartments available to single students; on-campus housing not available to married students. Housing application deadline: 8/1.

GRADUATE UNITS

School of Theology Offers theology (M Div).

BLESSING-RIEMAN COLLEGE OF NURSING, Quincy, IL 62305-7005

General Information Independent, coed, primarily women, comprehensive institution. *Enrollment:* 7 part-time matriculated graduate/professional students (all women). *Enrollment by degree level:* 7 master's. *Graduate faculty:* 7 full-time (all women). *Tuition:* Part-time $450 per credit hour. *Graduate housing:* Rooms and/or apartments available on a first-come, first-served basis to single and married students. Typical cost: $9540 per year for single students; $9540 per year for married students. *Student services:* Child daycare facilities, free psychological counseling, services for students with disabilities, teacher training, writing training. *Library facilities:* Blessing Health Professions Library plus 1 other. *Online resources:* library catalog, web page, access to other libraries' catalogs. *Collection:* 3,767 titles, 125 serial subscriptions.

Computer facilities: 28 computers available on campus for general student use. A campuswide network can be accessed. *Web address:* http://www.brcn.edu/.

General Application Contact: Heather Mutter, Admissions Counselor, 217-228-5520 Ext. 6964, Fax: 217-223-4661, E-mail: hmutter@brcn.edu.

GRADUATE UNITS

Program in Nursing Students: 7 part-time (all women). *Faculty:* 7 full-time (all women). Expenses: Contact institution. *Degree program information:* Part-time programs available. Offers nursing (MSN). *Application deadline:* For fall admission, 4/1 for domestic students. *Application Contact:* Heather Mutter, Admissions Counselor, 217-228-5520 Ext. 6964, Fax: 217-223-4661, E-mail: hmutter@brcn.edu. *Administrative Coordinator, Program Evaluation and Instructional Design/Director,* Dr. Karen Mayville, 217-228-5520 Ext. 6968, Fax: 217-223-4661, E-mail: kmayville@brcn.edu.

BLOOMSBURG UNIVERSITY OF PENNSYLVANIA, Bloomsburg, PA 17815-1301

General Information State-supported, coed, comprehensive institution. CGS member. *Graduate housing:* Room and/or apartments available to single students; on-campus housing not available to married students. *Research affiliation:* Marine Science Consortium (biology), American Chemical Society Petroleum Research Fund (chemistry), Consortium of Big Ten Universities Research and Training Reactors (physics), Melanoma Research Fund (biology), Merck & Company, Inc. (biology).

GRADUATE UNITS

School of Graduate Studies *Degree program information:* Part-time and evening/weekend programs available. Electronic applications accepted.

College of Business Offers business (M Ed, MBA); business administration (MBA); business education (M Ed). Electronic applications accepted.

College of Liberal Arts *Degree program information:* Part-time programs available. Offers clinical athletic training (MS); exercise science (MS); liberal arts (MS). Electronic applications accepted.

College of Professional Studies Offers adult and family nurse practitioner (MSN); adult health and illness (MSN); audiology (Au D); community health (MSN); curriculum and instruction (M Ed); early childhood education (MS); education (M Ed, MS); education of the deaf/hard of hearing (MS); elementary education (M Ed); exceptionality programs (MS); guidance counseling and student affairs (M Ed); health sciences (MS, MSN, Au D); nursing (MSN); nursing administration (MSN); reading (M Ed); special education (MS); speech pathology (MS). Electronic applications accepted.

College of Science and Technology Offers biology (MS); biology education (M Ed); instructional technology (MS); radiologist assistant (MS); science and technology (M Ed, MS).

BLUE MOUNTAIN COLLEGE, Blue Mountain, MS 38610-9509

General Information Independent-religious, coed, comprehensive institution.

GRADUATE UNITS

Program in Elementary Education Offers elementary education (M Ed). Electronic applications accepted.

BLUFFTON UNIVERSITY, Bluffton, OH 45817

General Information Independent-religious, coed, comprehensive institution.

GRADUATE UNITS

Program in Education *Degree program information:* Part-time programs available. Offers education (MA Ed). Electronic applications accepted.

Programs in Business *Degree program information:* Evening/weekend programs available. Offers business administration (MBA); organizational management (MA). Electronic applications accepted.

BOB JONES UNIVERSITY, Greenville, SC 29614

General Information Independent-religious, coed, university.

GRADUATE UNITS

Graduate Programs

BOISE STATE UNIVERSITY, Boise, ID 83725-0399

General Information State-supported, coed, university. CGS member. *Graduate housing:* Rooms and/or apartments available on a first-come, first-served basis to single and married students. Housing application deadline: 6/1. *Research affiliation:* American Chemical Society (petroleum research), Federal Aviation Administration (airliner cabin environment research), Lee Pesky Learning Center (elementary mathematics education), Prewitt & Associates, Inc. (C-130 drop zones), Bechtel BWXT Idaho, LLC (energy policy analysis), Argonne National Laboratory (energy policy analysis).

GRADUATE UNITS

Graduate College *Degree program information:* Part-time programs available. Postbaccalaureate distance learning degree programs offered (no on-campus study). Electronic applications accepted.

College of Arts and Sciences *Degree program information:* Part-time programs available. Offers art education (MA); arts and sciences (MA, MFA, MM, MS, PhD); biology (MA, MS); creative writing (MFA); earth science (MS); English (MA, MFA); geology (MS, PhD); geophysics (MS, PhD); interdisciplinary studies (MA, MS); music (MM); music education (MM); pedagogy (MM); performance (MM); raptor biology (MS); technical communication (MA); visual arts (MFA). Electronic applications accepted.

College of Business and Economics *Degree program information:* Part-time programs available. Offers accountancy (MSA); business administration (MBA); business and economics (MBA, MSA); information technology management (MBA); taxation (MSA). Electronic applications accepted.

Boise State University (continued)

College of Education *Degree program information:* Part-time programs available. Offers counseling (MA); counselor education (MA); curriculum and instruction (Ed D); curriculum instruction (MA); early childhood education (M Ed, MA); education (M Ed, MA, MET, MPE, MS, MS Ed, Ed D); educational leadership (M Ed); educational technology (MET, MS, MS Ed); exercise and sports studies (MS); physical education (MS); reading (MA); special education (M Ed, MA). Electronic applications accepted.

College of Engineering *Degree program information:* Part-time programs available. Post-baccalaureate distance learning degree programs offered (no on-campus study). Offers civil engineering (M Engr, MS); computer engineering (M Engr, MS); computer science (MS); electrical and computer engineering (PhD); electrical engineering (M Engr, MS); engineering (M Engr, MS, PhD); instructional and performance technology (MS); materials science and engineering (M Engr, MS); mechanical engineering (M Engr, MS). Electronic applications accepted.

College of Health Science *Degree program information:* Part-time programs available. Offers health science (MHS). Electronic applications accepted.

College of Social Sciences and Public Affairs *Degree program information:* Part-time programs available. Offers communication (MA); criminal justice administration (MA); environmental and natural resources policy and administration (MPA); general public administration (MPA); history (MA); social sciences and public affairs (MA, MPA, MSW); social work (MSW); state and local government policy and administration (MPA). Electronic applications accepted.

BORICUA COLLEGE, New York, NY 10032-1560

General Information Independent, coed, comprehensive institution.

GRADUATE UNITS

Program in Human Services (Brooklyn Campus) *Degree program information:* Evening/weekend programs available. Offers human services (MS).

Program in Human Services (Manhattan Campus) *Degree program information:* Evening/weekend programs available. Offers human services (MS).

Program in Latin American and Caribbean Studies (Brooklyn Campus) *Degree program information:* Evening/weekend programs available. Offers Latin American and Caribbean studies (MA).

Program in Latin American and Caribbean Studies (Manhattan Campus) *Degree program information:* Evening/weekend programs available. Offers Latin American and Caribbean studies (MA).

BOSTON ARCHITECTURAL COLLEGE, Boston, MA 02115-2795

General Information Independent, coed, comprehensive institution.

GRADUATE UNITS

Graduate Programs Offers architecture (M Arch); interior design (MID). Electronic applications accepted.

BOSTON COLLEGE, Chestnut Hill, MA 02467-3800

General Information Independent-religious, coed, university. CGS member. *Graduate housing:* Rooms and/or apartments available on a first-come, first-served basis to single and married students.

GRADUATE UNITS

Carroll School of Management Students: 374 full-time (147 women), 503 part-time (163 women); includes 9 Black or African American, non-Hispanic/Latino; 1 American Indian or Alaska Native, non-Hispanic/Latino; 69 Asian, non-Hispanic/Latino; 21 Hispanic/Latino, 153 international. Average age 28. 2,018 applicants, 31% accepted, 330 enrolled. *Faculty:* 96 full-time (33 women), 109 part-time/adjunct (21 women). Expenses: Contact institution. *Financial support:* In 2010–11, 262 fellowships with full tuition reimbursements, 221 research assistantships with full and partial tuition reimbursements were awarded; teaching assistantships, career-related internships or fieldwork, Federal Work-Study, institutionally sponsored loans, scholarships/grants, tuition waivers (full and partial), and unspecified assistantships also available. Support available to part-time students. Financial award application deadline: 3/1; financial award applicants required to submit FAFSA. In 2010, 411 master's, 15 doctorates awarded. *Degree program information:* Part-time and evening/weekend programs available. Offers accounting (MSA); business administration (MBA); finance (MSF, PhD); management (MBA, MSA, MSF, PhD); organization studies (PhD). *Application fee:* $100. Electronic applications accepted. *Application Contact:* Shelley A. Burt, Director of Graduate Enrollment, 617-552-3920, Fax: 617-552-8078, E-mail: bcmba@bc.edu. *Associate Dean for Graduate Programs,* Dr. Jeffrey L. Ringuest, 617-552-9100, Fax: 617-552-0514, E-mail: jeffrey.ringuest@bc.edu.

Graduate School of Arts and Sciences *Degree program information:* Part-time programs available. Offers arts and sciences (M Div, MA, MS, MST, MTS, Th M, PhD, STD, STL); biochemistry (PhD); biology (PhD); classics (MA); economics (PhD); English (MA, PhD); European national studies (MA); French (MA, PhD); geology and geophysics (MS); Greek (MA); history (MA, PhD); inorganic chemistry (PhD); Italian (MA); Latin (MA); linguistics (MA); mathematics (PhD); medieval language (PhD); medieval studies (MA); organic chemistry (PhD); philosophy (MA, PhD); physical chemistry (PhD); physics (MS, PhD); political science (MA, PhD); psychology (MA, PhD); Russian and Slavic languages and literature (MA); science education (MST); Slavic studies (MA); sociology (MA, PhD); Spanish (MA, PhD); theology (PhD). Electronic applications accepted.

Graduate School of Social Work *Degree program information:* Part-time programs available. Offers social work (MSW, PhD).

Law School Offers law (JD). Electronic applications accepted.

Lynch Graduate School of Education Students: 693 full-time (516 women), 233 part-time (159 women); includes 46 Black or African American, non-Hispanic/Latino; 2 American Indian or Alaska Native, non-Hispanic/Latino; 49 Asian, non-Hispanic/Latino; 47 Hispanic/Latino, 89 international. 2,160 applicants, 48% accepted, 449 enrolled. *Faculty:* 55 full-time (32 women), 36 part-time/adjunct (23 women). Expenses: Contact institution. In 2010, 351 master's, 32 doctorates, 11 other advanced degrees awarded. Offers applied developmental and educational psychology (MA, PhD); counseling psychology (MA, PhD); curriculum and instruction (M Ed, PhD, CAES); early childhood education (M Ed); education (M Ed, MA, MAT, MST, Ed D, PhD, CAES); educational leadership (M Ed, Ed D, CAES); educational research, measurement, and evaluation (M Ed, PhD); elementary education (M Ed, MAT); higher education (MA, PhD); reading and literacy (M Ed, MAT, CAES); religious education (M Ed, CAES); secondary education (M Ed, MAT, MST); special needs: moderate disabilities (M Ed, CAES); special needs: severe disabilities (M Ed, CAES). *Application fee:* $65. Electronic applications accepted. *Application Contact:* Adam Poluzzi, Director, Graduate Admission and Financial Aid, 617-552-4214, Fax: 617-552-0398, E-mail: poluzzi@bc.edu. *Interim Dean,* Dr. Maureen Kenny, 617-552-4030, Fax: 617-552-0812.

School of Theology and Ministry *Degree program information:* Part-time programs available. Offers church leadership (MA); divinity (M Div); pastoral ministry (MA); religious education (MA, PhD); sacred theology (STD, STL); social justice/social ministry (MA); spiritual direction (MA); theological studies (MTS); theology (Th M, PhD); youth ministry (MA). Electronic applications accepted.

William F. Connell School of Nursing Students: 263 full-time (240 women), 83 part-time (79 women); includes 19 Black or African American, non-Hispanic/Latino; 3 American Indian or Alaska Native, non-Hispanic/Latino; 21 Asian, non-Hispanic/Latino; 4 Hispanic/Latino, 9 international. Average age 32. 388 applicants, 44% accepted, 106 enrolled. *Faculty:* 48 full-time (46 women), 31 part-time/adjunct (29 women). Expenses: Contact institution. *Financial support:* In 2010–11, 146 students received support, including 11 fellowships with partial tuition reimbursements available (averaging $15,000 per year), 5 teaching assistantships (averaging $13,346 per year); research assistantships, Federal Work-Study, institutionally sponsored loans, scholarships/grants, traineeships, health care benefits, and tuition waivers (partial) also available. Support available to part-time students. Financial award application deadline: 3/1; financial award applicants required to submit FAFSA. In 2010, 108 master's, 10 doctorates awarded. *Degree program information:* Part-time programs available. Offers adult health nursing (MS); community health nursing (MS); family health (MS); forensic nursing (MS); gerontology (MS); maternal/child health nursing (MS); nurse anesthesia (MS); nursing (PhD); palliative care (MS); psychiatric-mental health nursing (MS). *Application deadline:* For fall admission, 11/1 for domestic and international students; for winter admission, 12/31 for domestic and international students; for spring admission, 9/15 for domestic and international students. Applications are processed on a rolling basis. *Application fee:* $40. Electronic applications accepted. *Application Contact:* MaryBeth Crowley, Graduate Programs Assistant, 617-552-4928, Fax: 617-552-2121, E-mail: csongrad@bc.edu. *Dean,* Dr. Susan Gennaro, 617-552-4251, Fax: 617-552-0931, E-mail: susan.gennaro@bc.edu.

THE BOSTON CONSERVATORY, Boston, MA 02215

General Information Independent, coed, comprehensive institution. *Graduate housing:* Room and/or apartments available on a first-come, first-served basis to single students; on-campus housing not available to married students. Housing application deadline: 12/1.

GRADUATE UNITS

Graduate Division *Degree program information:* Part-time programs available. Offers choral conducting (MM); composition (MM); music (MM, ADP, Certificate); music education (MM); music performance (MM, ADP, Certificate); opera (MM, ADP, Certificate); theater (MM). Electronic applications accepted.

BOSTON GRADUATE SCHOOL OF PSYCHOANALYSIS, Brookline, MA 02446-4602

General Information Independent, coed, graduate-only institution. *Enrollment by degree level:* 69 master's, 87 doctoral, 8 other advanced degrees. *Graduate faculty:* 15 full-time (11 women), 35 part-time/adjunct (14 women). *Tuition:* Full-time $13,500; part-time $500 per credit. *Required fees:* $50; $860 per semester. *Graduate housing:* On-campus housing not available. *Student services:* Campus employment opportunities, career counseling, international student services, teacher training, writing training. *Library facilities:* Boston Graduate School of Psychoanalysis Library. *Online resources:* library catalog, web page. *Collection:* 11,000 titles, 20 serial subscriptions, 750 audiovisual materials. *Research affiliation:* Boston Institute for Psychotherapy (psychotherapy).

Computer facilities: 5 computers available on campus for general student use. A campuswide network can be accessed. *Web address:* http://www.bgsp.edu/.

General Application Contact: Dr. Mara Wagner, Director of Admissions, 617-277-3915, Fax: 617-277-0312, E-mail: admissions@bgsp.edu.

GRADUATE UNITS

Master's, Certificate, and Doctoral Programs Students: 17 full-time (14 women), 80 part-time (59 women); includes 2 Black or African American, non-Hispanic/Latino; 5 Asian, non-Hispanic/Latino; 6 Hispanic/Latino, 14 international. 10 applicants, 70% accepted, 5 enrolled. *Faculty:* 11 full-time (7 women), 16 part-time/adjunct (8 women). Expenses: Contact institution. *Financial support:* In 2010–11, 17 students received support. Career-related internships or fieldwork and unspecified assistantships available. Financial award applicants required to submit FAFSA. In 2010, 8 master's, 3 doctorates awarded. *Degree program information:* Part-time programs available. Offers psychoanalysis (MA, Psya D, Certificate). *Application deadline:* For fall admission, 4/15 priority date for domestic and international students; for spring admission, 11/15 priority date for domestic and international students. Applications are processed on a rolling basis. *Application fee:* $100. *Application Contact:* Stephanie Woolbert, Admissions Coordinator, 617-277-3915, Fax: 617-277-0312, E-mail: bgsp@bgsp.edu. *President,* Dr. Jane Snyder, 617-277-3915, E-mail: snyderj@bgsp.edu.

Master's Program—New York Students: 8 full-time (4 women), 24 part-time (16 women). 16 applicants, 100% accepted, 13 enrolled. *Faculty:* 12 full-time (10 women), 11 part-time/adjunct (7 women). Expenses: Contact institution. *Financial support:* Career-related internships or fieldwork available. Financial award applicants required to submit FAFSA. In 2010, 4 master's awarded. *Degree program information:* Part-time programs available. Offers psychoanalysis (MA). *Application deadline:* Applications are processed on a rolling basis. *Application fee:* $100. *Application Contact:* Stephen Guttman, Registrar, 212-260-7050, Fax: 212-228-6410, E-mail: bgsp-ny.registrar@bgsp.edu. *Dean,* Dr. Mimi Crowell, 212-260-7050, Fax: 212-228-6410, E-mail: bgsp-ny.registrar@bgsp.edu.

Program in Psychoanalytic Counseling Students: 18 full-time (12 women), 1 (woman) part-time; includes 2 Black or African American, non-Hispanic/Latino; 2 Asian, non-Hispanic/Latino; 1 Hispanic/Latino, 4 international. 36 applicants, 86% accepted. *Faculty:* 11 full-time (7 women), 16 part-time/adjunct (8 women). Expenses: Contact institution. *Financial support:* Career-related internships or fieldwork and unspecified assistantships available. Financial award applicants required to submit FAFSA. In 2010, 9 master's awarded. Offers psychoanalytic counseling (MA). *Application deadline:* For fall admission, 4/15 priority date for domestic and international students; for spring admission, 11/15 priority date for domestic and international students. Applications are processed on a rolling basis. *Application fee:* $100. *Application Contact:* Stephanie Woolbert, Admissions Coordinator, 617-277-3915, Fax: 617-277-0312, E-mail: admissions@bgsp.edu. *President,* Dr. Jane Snyder, 617-277-3915.

Programs in Psychoanalysis and Culture Students: 2 full-time (1 woman), 12 part-time (7 women); includes 1 Black or African American, non-Hispanic/Latino, 2 international. 11 applicants, 82% accepted, 6 enrolled. *Faculty:* 2 full-time (1 woman), 20 part-time/adjunct (6 women). Expenses: Contact institution. *Financial support:* In 2010–11, 3 students received support. Unspecified assistantships available. Financial award applicants required to submit FAFSA. In 2010, 1 master's, 1 doctorate awarded. *Degree program information:* Part-time programs available. Offers psychoanalysis and culture (MA, Psya D). *Application deadline:* For fall admission, 4/15 priority date for domestic and international students; for spring admission, 11/15 priority date for domestic and international students. Applications are processed on a rolling basis. *Application fee:* $100. *Application Contact:* Stephanie Woolbert, Admissions Coordinator, 617-277-3915, Fax: 617-277-0312, E-mail: admissions@bgsp.edu. *Director,* Dr. Siamak Movahedi, 617-277-3915, E-mail: bgsp@bgsp.edu.

BOSTON UNIVERSITY, Boston, MA 02215

General Information Independent, coed, university. CGS member. *Enrollment:* 32,727 graduate, professional, and undergraduate students; 9,293 full-time matriculated graduate/professional students (5,063 women), 4,663 part-time matriculated graduate/professional students (2,461 women). *Enrollment by degree level:* 2,251 first professional, 9,262 master's, 2,265 doctoral, 146 other advanced degrees. *Tuition:* Full-time $39,314; part-time $1228 per credit. *Required fees:* $40 per semester. *Graduate housing:* On-campus housing not available. *Student services:* Campus employment opportunities, campus safety program, career counseling, child daycare facilities, exercise/wellness program, free psychological counseling, international student services, low-cost health insurance, services for students with disabilities, writing training. *Library facilities:* Mugar Memorial Library plus 18 others. *Online resources:* library catalog, web page, access to other libraries' catalogs. *Collection:* 3 million titles, 65,037 serial subscriptions, 69,901 audiovisual materials. *Research affiliation:* NASA–Ames Research Center, Society for the Preservation of New England Antiquities, Massachusetts Historical Society, Woods Hole Oceanographic Institution–Marine Biological Laboratory.

Computer facilities: Computer purchase and lease plans are available. 250 computers available on campus for general student use. A campuswide network can be accessed from student residence rooms and from off campus. Online class registration, research and educational networks are available. *Web address:* http://www.bu.edu/.

GRADUATE UNITS

College of Communication Students: 252 full-time (178 women), 30 part-time (15 women); includes 29 minority (9 Black or African American, non-Hispanic/Latino; 8 Asian, non-Hispanic/Latino; 11 Hispanic/Latino; 1 Two or more races, non-Hispanic/Latino), 56 international. Average age 25. 875 applicants, 48% accepted. *Faculty:* 57 full-time, 81 part-time/adjunct. Expenses: Contact institution. *Financial support:* In 2010–11, 18 teaching assistantships with partial tuition reimbursements were awarded; career-related internships or fieldwork, Federal

Work-Study, institutionally sponsored loans, scholarships/grants, and unspecified assistantships also available. Support available to part-time students. Financial award application deadline: 2/1; financial award applicants required to submit FAFSA. In 2010, 148 master's awarded. *Degree program information:* Part-time programs available. Offers advertising (MS); broadcast journalism (MS); business and economics journalism (MS); communication (MFA, MS); communication research (MS); communication studies (MS); film production (MFA); film studies (MFA); media ventures (MS); photojournalism (MS); print journalism (MS); public relations (MS); science journalism (MS); screenwriting (MFA); television production (MS). *Application deadline:* For fall admission, 2/1 for domestic and international students. *Application fee:* $70. Electronic applications accepted. *Application Contact:* Jennifer Healey, Administrator of Graduate Services, 617-353-3481, Fax: 617-358-0399, E-mail: comgrad@bu.edu. *Dean,* Thomas Fiedler, 617-353-3450, Fax: 617-358-0399, E-mail: com@bu.edu.

College of Engineering Students: 551 full-time (112 women), 60 part-time (13 women); includes 75 minority (6 Black or African American, non-Hispanic/Latino; 1 American Indian or Alaska Native, non-Hispanic/Latino; 49 Asian, non-Hispanic/Latino; 17 Hispanic/Latino; 2 Two or more races, non-Hispanic/Latino), 271 international. Average age 26. 1,931 applicants, 25% accepted, 245 enrolled. *Faculty:* 112 full-time (12 women), 9 part-time/adjunct (1 woman). Expenses: Contact institution. *Financial support:* In 2010–11, 458 students received support, including 70 fellowships with full tuition reimbursements available (averaging $28,200 per year), 241 research assistantships with full tuition reimbursements available (averaging $18,800 per year), 62 teaching assistantships with full tuition reimbursements available (averaging $18,800 per year); career-related internships or fieldwork, Federal Work-Study, institutionally sponsored loans, scholarships/grants, traineeships, health care benefits, and tuition waivers (full and partial) also available. Financial award application deadline: 1/15; financial award applicants required to submit FAFSA. In 2010, 124 master's, 41 doctorates awarded. *Degree program information:* Part-time programs available. Postbaccalaureate distance learning degree programs offered (no on-campus study). Offers biomedical engineering (M Eng, MS, PhD); computer engineering (M Eng, MS, PhD); electrical engineering (M Eng, MS, PhD); engineering (M Eng, MS, PhD); general engineering (MS); global manufacturing (MS); manufacturing engineering (M Eng, MS); materials science and engineering (M Eng, MS, PhD); mechanical engineering (M Eng, MS, PhD); photonics (M Eng, MS); systems engineering (M Eng, MS, PhD). *Application deadline:* For fall admission, 4/1 for domestic and international students; for spring admission, 10/1 for domestic and international students. Applications are processed on a rolling basis. *Application fee:* $70. Electronic applications accepted. *Application Contact:* Stephen Doherty, Director of Graduate Programs, 617-353-9760, Fax: 617-353-0259, E-mail: enggrad@bu.edu. *Dean,* Dr. Kenneth R. Lutchen, 617-353-2800, Fax: 617-358-3468, E-mail: klutch@bu.edu.

College of Fine Arts Students: 1,114 full-time (701 women), 100 part-time (51 women); includes 125 minority (11 Black or African American, non-Hispanic/Latino; 7 American Indian or Alaska Native, non-Hispanic/Latino; 34 Asian, non-Hispanic/Latino; 53 Hispanic/Latino; 2 Native Hawaiian or other Pacific Islander, non-Hispanic/Latino; 18 Two or more races, non-Hispanic/Latino), 192 international. Average age 29. 1,335 applicants, 38% accepted. *Faculty:* 70 full-time, 38 part-time/adjunct. Expenses: Contact institution. *Financial support:* Fellowships, teaching assistantships, Federal Work-Study and scholarships/grants available. Support available to part-time students. Financial award application deadline: 1/1. In 2010, 261 master's, 43 doctorates, 13 other advanced degrees awarded. *Degree program information:* Part-time programs available. Offers art education (MA); collaborative piano (MM, DMA); composition (MM, DMA); conducting (MM, Artist Diploma, Performance Diploma); costume design (MFA); costume production (MFA); directing (MFA); fine arts (MA, MFA, MM, DMA, Artist Diploma, Certificate, Performance Diploma); graphic design (MFA); historical performance (MM, DMA, Artist Diploma, Performance Diploma); lighting design (MFA); music education (MM, DMA); music theory (MM); musicology (MM); opera performance (Certificate); painting (MFA); performance (MM, DMA, Artist Diploma, Performance Diploma); scene design (MFA); sculpture (MFA); studio teaching (MA); technical production (MFA, Certificate); theatre crafts (Certificate); theatre education (MFA). *Application deadline:* For fall admission, 1/15 priority date for domestic and international students. *Application fee:* $70. Electronic applications accepted. *Application Contact:* Mark Krone, Manager, Graduate Admissions, 617-353-3350, E-mail: arts@bu.edu. *Dean,* Benjamin E. Juarez, 617-353-3350.

College of Health and Rehabilitation Sciences: Sargent College Students: 392 full-time (348 women), 79 part-time (61 women); includes 74 minority (4 Black or African American, non-Hispanic/Latino; 1 American Indian or Alaska Native, non-Hispanic/Latino; 43 Asian, non-Hispanic/Latino; 14 Hispanic/Latino; 4 Native Hawaiian or other Pacific Islander, non-Hispanic/Latino; 8 Two or more races, non-Hispanic/Latino), 26 international. Average age 27. 763 applicants, 42% accepted, 110 enrolled. *Faculty:* 54 full-time (42 women), 44 part-time/adjunct (28 women). Expenses: Contact institution. *Financial support:* In 2010–11, 300 students received support, including 119 fellowships with full and partial tuition reimbursements available (averaging $15,000 per year), 9 research assistantships with partial tuition reimbursements available (averaging $18,000 per year), 15 teaching assistantships with partial tuition reimbursements available (averaging $6,000 per year); career-related internships or fieldwork, Federal Work-Study, institutionally sponsored loans, scholarships/grants, and health care benefits also available. Support available to part-time students. Financial award application deadline: 4/15; financial award applicants required to submit FAFSA. In 2010, 88 master's, 62 doctorates awarded. Postbaccalaureate distance learning degree programs offered (minimal on-campus study). Offers applied anatomy and physiology (MS, PhD); audiology (PhD); health and rehabilitation sciences (MS, MSOT, D Sc, DPT, OTD, PhD, CAGS); nutrition (MS); occupational therapy (MSOT, OTD); physical therapy (DPT); rehabilitation sciences (D Sc); speech-language pathology (MS, PhD, CAGS). *Application deadline:* For fall admission, 2/1 priority date for domestic students. Applications are processed on a rolling basis. *Application fee:* $70. Electronic applications accepted. *Application Contact:* Sharon Sankey, Director, Student Services, 617-353-2713, Fax: 617-353-7500, E-mail: ssankey@bu.edu. *Dean,* Dr. Gloria S. Waters, 617-353-2704, Fax: 617-353-7500, E-mail: gwaters@bu.edu.

Graduate School of Arts and Sciences Students: 1,784 full-time (884 women), 216 part-time (116 women); includes 234 minority (42 Black or African American, non-Hispanic/Latino; 3 American Indian or Alaska Native, non-Hispanic/Latino; 99 Asian, non-Hispanic/Latino; 57 Hispanic/Latino; 1 Native Hawaiian or other Pacific Islander, non-Hispanic/Latino; 32 Two or more races, non-Hispanic/Latino), 583 international. Average age 29. 6,819 applicants, 24% accepted, 567 enrolled. Expenses: Contact institution. *Financial support:* In 2010–11, 1,200 students received support, including 102 fellowships with full tuition reimbursements available, 544 research assistantships with full tuition reimbursements available, 430 teaching assistantships with full tuition reimbursements available; career-related internships or fieldwork, Federal Work-Study, scholarships/grants, traineeships, health care benefits, and unspecified assistantships also available. Support available to part-time students. Financial award application deadline: 1/15; financial award applicants required to submit FAFSA. In 2010, 387 master's, 187 doctorates awarded. Offers African American studies (MA); African studies (Certificate); American and New England studies (PhD); anthropology (PhD); applied anthropology (MA); applied linguistics (MA, PhD); archaeological heritage management (MA); archaeology (MA, PhD); art history (MA, PhD); arts and sciences (MA, MAEP, MAPE, MFA, MS, PhD, Certificate); astronomy (MA, PhD); bioinformatics (MS, PhD); biology (MA, PhD); biostatistics (MA, PhD); cellular biophysics (PhD); chemistry (MA, PhD); classical studies (MA, PhD); cognitive and neural systems (MA, PhD); composition (MA); computer science (MA, PhD); creative writing (MFA); earth sciences (MA, PhD); economic policy (MAEP); economics (MA, PhD); energy and environmental analysis (MA); English (MA, PhD); environmental remote sensing and GIs (MA); French language and literature (MA, PhD); geoarchaeology (MA); geography (MA); geography and environment (PhD); Hispanic language and literatures (MA, PhD); history (MA, PhD); international relations (MA); international relations and environmental policy (MA); international relations and environmental policy management (MA); international relations and international communication (MA); mathematics (MA, PhD); molecular biology, cell biology, and biochemistry (MA, PhD); museum studies (Certificate); music education (MA); music history/theory (PhD); musicology (MA, PhD); philosophy (MA, PhD); physics (MA, PhD); political economy (MAPE); political science (MA, PhD); preservation studies (MA); psychology (MA, PhD); religious and theological studies (MA, PhD); sociology (MA, PhD); sociology and social work (PhD). *Application deadline:* For fall admission, 1/15 priority date for domestic and international students; for spring admission, 10/15 priority date for domestic and international students. *Application fee:* $70. Electronic applications accepted. *Application Contact:* Rebekah Alexander, Assistant Director of Admissions and Financial Aid, 617-353-2696, Fax: 617-358-5492, E-mail: grs@bu.edu. *Associate Dean,* W. Jeffrey Hughes, 617-353-2690, Fax: 617-358-5492.

Editorial Institute Students: 14 full-time (9 women), 2 part-time (0 women), 1 international. Average age 39. 13 applicants, 38% accepted, 5 enrolled. Expenses: Contact institution. *Financial support:* In 2010–11, 14 students received support, including 3 teaching assistantships with full tuition reimbursements available (averaging $18,800 per year); Federal Work-Study, scholarships/grants, and unspecified assistantships also available. Support available to part-time students. Financial award application deadline: 1/15; financial award applicants required to submit FAFSA. Offers editorial studies (MA, PhD). *Application deadline:* For fall admission, 3/30 for domestic and international students. *Application fee:* $70. Electronic applications accepted. *Application Contact:* Katy Evans, Administrative Assistant, 617-358-1937, Fax: 617-353-6917, E-mail: editinst@bu.edu. *Co-Director,* Archie Burnett, 617-353-6631, E-mail: burnetta@bu.edu.

Henry M. Goldman School of Dental Medicine Students: 794 full-time (382 women); includes 168 minority (8 Black or African American, non-Hispanic/Latino; 1 American Indian or Alaska Native, non-Hispanic/Latino; 111 Asian, non-Hispanic/Latino; 43 Hispanic/Latino; 4 Native Hawaiian or other Pacific Islander, non-Hispanic/Latino; 1 Two or more races, non-Hispanic/Latino), 320 international. Average age 27. Expenses: Contact institution. *Financial support:* In 2010–11, 480 students received support. Career-related internships or fieldwork and institutionally sponsored loans available. Financial award application deadline: 4/15; financial award applicants required to submit CSS PROFILE or FAFSA. In 2010, 188 first professional degrees, 25 master's, 4 doctorates, 67 other advanced degrees awarded. Offers advanced general dentistry (CAGS); dental medicine (DMD, MS, MSD, D Sc, D Sc D, PhD, CAGS); dental public health (MS, MSD, D Sc D, CAGS); dentistry (DMD); endodontics (MSD, D Sc D, CAGS); implantology (CAGS); operative dentistry (MSD, D Sc D, CAGS); oral and maxillofacial surgery (MSD, D Sc D, CAGS); oral biology (MSD, D Sc, D Sc D, PhD); orthodontics (MSD, D Sc D, CAGS); pediatric dentistry (MSD, D Sc D, CAGS); periodontology (MSD, D Sc D, CAGS); prosthodontics (MSD, D Sc D, CAGS). *Application deadline:* Applications are processed on a rolling basis. *Application fee:* $70 ($100 for international students). Electronic applications accepted. *Application Contact:* Admissions Representative, 617-638-4787, Fax: 617-638-4798, E-mail: sdmadmis@bu.edu. *Dean,* Dr. Jeffrey W. Hutter, 617-638-4780.

Metropolitan College Students: 208 full-time (100 women), 2,263 part-time (1,039 women); includes 447 minority (147 Black or African American, non-Hispanic/Latino; 7 American Indian or Alaska Native, non-Hispanic/Latino; 152 Asian, non-Hispanic/Latino; 107 Hispanic/Latino; 5 Native Hawaiian or other Pacific Islander, non-Hispanic/Latino; 29 Two or more races, non-Hispanic/Latino), 322 international. Average age 33. 1,275 applicants, 71% accepted, 609 enrolled. *Faculty:* 35 full-time (6 women), 103 part-time/adjunct (21 women). Expenses: Contact institution. *Financial support:* In 2010–11, 948 students received support; research assistantships, teaching assistantships, career-related internships or fieldwork, scholarships/grants, tuition waivers (full and partial), and unspecified assistantships available. Support available to part-time students. Financial award applicants required to submit FAFSA. In 2010, 928 master's awarded. *Degree program information:* Part-time and evening/weekend programs available. Offers actuarial science (MS); advertising (MS); arts administration (MS, Graduate Certificate); banking and financial management (MSM); business (MLA); business continuity in emergency management (MSM); city planning (MCP); communications (MLA); computer information systems (MS); computer science (MS); criminal justice (MCJ); economics development and tourism management (MSAS); electronic commerce, systems, and technology (MSAS); financial economics (MSAS); food policy (MLA); fundraising management (Graduate Certificate); health communication (MS); history and culture (MLA); innovation and technology (MSAS); insurance management (MSM); international market management (MSM); multinational commerce (MSAS); project management (MSM); security (MS); telecommunications (MS); urban affairs (MUA). *Application deadline:* Applications are processed on a rolling basis. *Application fee:* $70. Electronic applications accepted. *Application Contact:* Dr. Jay Halfond, Dean, 617-353-6776, Fax: 617-353-6066, E-mail: jhalfond@bu.edu. *Dean,* Dr. Jay Halfond, 617-353-6776, Fax: 617-353-6066, E-mail: jhalfond@bu.edu.

School of Education Students: 245 full-time (191 women), 376 part-time (274 women); includes 83 minority (14 Black or African American, non-Hispanic/Latino; 2 American Indian or Alaska Native, non-Hispanic/Latino; 28 Asian, non-Hispanic/Latino; 31 Hispanic/Latino; 2 Native Hawaiian or other Pacific Islander, non-Hispanic/Latino; 6 Two or more races, non-Hispanic/Latino), 79 international. Average age 30. 1,270 applicants, 66% accepted, 292 enrolled. *Faculty:* 57 full-time, 39 part-time/adjunct. Expenses: Contact institution. *Financial support:* In 2010–11, 276 students received support, including 31 fellowships with full tuition reimbursements available, 16 research assistantships, 26 teaching assistantships with partial tuition reimbursements available; career-related internships or fieldwork, Federal Work-Study, and scholarships/grants also available. Support available to part-time students. Financial award applicants required to submit FAFSA. In 2010, 273 master's, 15 doctorates, 7 other advanced degrees awarded. *Degree program information:* Part-time programs available. Offers counseling (Ed M, CAGS); counseling psychology (Ed D); curriculum and teaching (Ed M, Ed D, CAGS); developmental studies (Ed D); developmental studies in literacy and language education (Ed M, CAGS); early childhood education (Ed M, CAGS); education of the deaf (Ed M, CAGS); educational leadership and development (Ed D); educational media and technology (Ed M, CAGS); elementary education (Ed M); English and language arts (Ed M, CAGS); English education (MAT); health education (Ed M, CAGS); Latin and classical studies (MAT); mathematics education (Ed M, MAT, CAGS); mathematics for teaching (MMT); modern foreign language education (MAT); physical education and coaching (Ed M, CAGS); policy, planning, and administration (Ed M, CAGS); reading education (Ed M, CAGS); science education (Ed M, MAT, CAGS); social studies education (Ed M, MAT, CAGS); special education (Ed M, Ed D, CAGS); teaching English as a second language (Ed M, CAGS). *Application deadline:* For fall admission, 1/15 priority date for domestic and international students; for spring admission, 9/15 priority date for domestic and international students. Applications are processed on a rolling basis. *Application fee:* $70. Electronic applications accepted. *Application Contact:* Dana Fernandez, Director of Enrollment, 617-353-4237, Fax: 617-353-8937, E-mail: sedgrad@bu.edu. *Dean,* Dr. Hardin Coleman, 617-353-3213.

School of Law Students: 973 full-time (490 women), 66 part-time (32 women); includes 235 minority (44 Black or African American, non-Hispanic/Latino; 5 American Indian or Alaska Native, non-Hispanic/Latino; 84 Asian, non-Hispanic/Latino; 79 Hispanic/Latino; 2 Native Hawaiian or other Pacific Islander, non-Hispanic/Latino; 21 Two or more races, non-Hispanic/Latino), 131 international. Average age 26. 7,660 applicants, 23% accepted, 271 enrolled. *Faculty:* 65 full-time (26 women), 88 part-time/adjunct (32 women). Expenses: Contact institution. *Financial support:* In 2010–11, 533 students received support. Career-related internships or fieldwork, Federal Work-Study, institutionally sponsored loans, and scholarships/grants available. Financial award application deadline: 3/1; financial award applicants required to submit FAFSA. In 2010, 206 first professional degrees, 207 master's awarded. Offers American law (LL M); banking (LL M); intellectual property law (LL M); law (JD); taxation (LL M). *Application deadline:* For fall admission, 3/1 for domestic and international students. Applications are processed on a rolling basis. *Application fee:* $75. Electronic applications accepted. *Application Contact:* Alissa Leonard, Director of Admissions and Financial Aid, 617-353-3100, Fax: 617-353-0578, E-mail: bulawadm@bu.edu. *Dean,* Maureen A. O'Rourke, 617-353-3112, Fax: 617-353-7400, E-mail: lawdean@bu.edu.

School of Management Students: 525 full-time (206 women), 743 part-time (272 women); includes 14 Black or African American, non-Hispanic/Latino; 134 Asian, non-Hispanic/Latino; 19 Hispanic/Latino, 247 international. Average age 30. 1,387 applicants, 28% accepted, 160 enrolled. *Faculty:* 185 full-time (49 women), 60 part-time/adjunct (15 women). Expenses: Contact institution. *Financial support:* Career-related internships or fieldwork, Federal Work-Study, institutionally sponsored loans, scholarships/grants, and tuition waivers (partial) available. Financial award applicants required to submit FAFSA. In 2010, 532 master's, 5 doctorates awarded. *Degree program information:* Part-time and evening/weekend programs available. Offers business administration (MBA); executive business administration (EMBA); investment management (MS); management (PhD); mathematical finance (MS, PhD). *Application deadline:* For fall admission, 1/5 for domestic and international students; for spring admission, 11/1 for

Boston University (continued)

domestic students. *Application fee:* $125. Electronic applications accepted. *Application Contact:* Patti Cudney, Assistant Dean, Graduate Admissions, 617-353-2670, Fax: 617-353-7368, E-mail: mba@bu.edu. *Professor/Dean,* Kenneth W. Freeman, 617-353-9720, Fax: 617-353-5581, E-mail: kfreeman@bu.edu.

School of Medicine Students: 1,474 full-time (803 women), 155 part-time (106 women); includes 536 minority (104 Black or African American, non-Hispanic/Latino; 4 American Indian or Alaska Native, non-Hispanic/Latino; 298 Asian, non-Hispanic/Latino; 97 Hispanic/Latino; 7 Native Hawaiian or other Pacific Islander, non-Hispanic/Latino; 26 Two or more races, non-Hispanic/Latino), 122 international. Average age 25. Expenses: Contact institution. *Financial support:* Fellowships, research assistantships, teaching assistantships, career-related internships or fieldwork, Federal Work-Study, and institutionally sponsored loans available. Support available to part-time students. In 2010, 153 first professional degrees, 263 master's, 41 doctorates awarded. *Degree program information:* Part-time and evening/weekend programs available. Offers medicine (MD, MA, MS, PhD). *Application Contact:* Dr. Robert Witzburg, Associate Dean for Admissions, 617-638-4630. *Dean,* Dr. Karen H. Antman, 617-638-5300.

Division of Graduate Medical Sciences Students: 775 full-time (432 women), 106 part-time (75 women); includes 221 minority (33 Black or African American, non-Hispanic/Latino; 2 American Indian or Alaska Native, non-Hispanic/Latino; 126 Asian, non-Hispanic/Latino; 41 Hispanic/Latino; 4 Native Hawaiian or other Pacific Islander, non-Hispanic/Latino; 15 Two or more races, non-Hispanic/Latino), 99 international. Average age 25. 2,060 applicants, 37% accepted, 373 enrolled. *Faculty:* 1,019 full-time (460 women), 517 part-time/adjunct (212 women). Expenses: Contact institution. *Financial support:* In 2010–11, 261 students received support, including 19 fellowships with tuition reimbursements available (averaging $30,500 per year), 157 research assistantships with full and partial tuition reimbursements available (averaging $30,500 per year), 1 teaching assistantship with tuition reimbursement available (averaging $30,500 per year); Federal Work-Study, scholarships/grants, and traineeships also available. Financial award applicants required to submit FAFSA. In 2010, 261 master's, 47 doctorates awarded. *Degree program information:* Part-time programs available. Offers anatomy and neurobiology (MA, PhD); behavioral neuroscience (PhD); biochemistry (MA, PhD); bioimaging (MA); biomedical forensic sciences (MS); cell and molecular biology (PhD); clinical investigation (MA); forensic anthropology (MS); genetic counseling (MS); genetics and genomics (PhD); healthcare emergency management (MS); immunology (PhD); medical anthropology and cross cultural practice (MA); medical nutrition sciences (MA, PhD); medical sciences (MA, MS, PhD); mental health counseling and behavioral medicine (MA); microbiology (MA); molecular medicine (PhD); neuroscience (MA, PhD); oral biology (PhD); pathology and laboratory medicine (PhD); pharmacology and experimental therapeutics (MA, PhD); physiology and biophysics (MA, PhD). *Application deadline:* For fall admission, 1/31 priority date for domestic and international students; for spring admission, 10/15 priority date for domestic and international students. Applications are processed on a rolling basis. *Application fee:* $75. Electronic applications accepted. *Application Contact:* Michelle Hall, Associate Director of Admissions, 617-638-5121, Fax: 617-638-5740, E-mail: natashah@bu.edu. *Associate Provost,* Dr. Linda E. Hyman, 617-638-5255, Fax: 617-638-5740, E-mail: askgms@bu.edu.

School of Public Health Students: 437 full-time (351 women), 349 part-time (292 women); includes 172 minority (38 Black or African American, non-Hispanic/Latino; 1 American Indian or Alaska Native, non-Hispanic/Latino; 85 Asian, non-Hispanic/Latino; 29 Hispanic/Latino; 3 Native Hawaiian or other Pacific Islander, non-Hispanic/Latino; 16 Two or more races, non-Hispanic/Latino), 70 international. Average age 28. 2,439 applicants, 48% accepted, 337 enrolled. *Faculty:* 153 full-time, 271 part-time/adjunct. Expenses: Contact institution. *Financial support:* Fellowships, career-related internships or fieldwork, Federal Work-Study, institutionally sponsored loans, scholarships/grants, traineeships, and tuition waivers (partial) available. Support available to part-time students. Financial award application deadline: 3/1; financial award applicants required to submit FAFSA. In 2010, 318 master's, 14 doctorates awarded. *Degree program information:* Part-time and evening/weekend programs available. Offers biostatistics (MA, MPH, PhD); environmental health (MPH, MS, PhD); epidemiology (MPH, MS, PhD); health law, bioethics and human rights (MPH); health policy and management (MPH); health services research (MS, PhD); international health (MPH, Dr PH); maternal and child health (MPH, Dr PH); public health (MA, MPH, MS, Dr PH, PhD); social and behavioral sciences (Dr PH). *Application deadline:* For fall admission, 2/1 priority date for domestic and international students; for spring admission, 10/15 priority date for domestic and international students. Applications are processed on a rolling basis. *Application fee:* $115. Electronic applications accepted. *Application Contact:* LePhan Quan, Associate Director of Admissions, 617-638-4640, Fax: 617-638-5299, E-mail: asksph@bu.edu. *Dean,* Dr. Robert F. Meenan, 617-638-4640, Fax: 617-638-5299, E-mail: asksph@bu.edu.

School of Social Work Students: 222 full-time (194 women), 210 part-time (187 women); includes 73 minority (19 Black or African American, non-Hispanic/Latino; 3 American Indian or Alaska Native, non-Hispanic/Latino; 12 Asian, non-Hispanic/Latino; 30 Hispanic/Latino; 9 Two or more races, non-Hispanic/Latino), 4 international. Average age 29. 920 applicants, 68% accepted, 209 enrolled. *Faculty:* 28 full-time (20 women), 27 part-time/adjunct (20 women). Expenses: Contact institution. *Financial support:* In 2010–11, 4 fellowships (averaging $10,000 per year), 2 research assistantships with full tuition reimbursements (averaging $24,000 per year), 3 teaching assistantships (averaging $3,000 per year) were awarded; career-related internships or fieldwork, Federal Work-Study, institutionally sponsored loans, and scholarships/grants also available. Support available to part-time students. Financial award application deadline: 3/1; financial award applicants required to submit FAFSA. In 2010, 131 master's awarded. *Degree program information:* Part-time and evening/weekend programs available. Postbaccalaureate distance learning degree programs offered (minimal on-campus study). Offers clinical practice with individuals, families, and groups (MSW); macro social work practice (MSW); social work (MSW); social work and sociology (PhD). *Application deadline:* For fall admission, 3/1 for domestic and international students. Applications are processed on a rolling basis. *Application fee:* $70. Electronic applications accepted. *Application Contact:* Ken Schulman, Associate Dean for Enrollment Services and External Relations, 617-353-3750, Fax: 617-353-5612, E-mail: busswad@bu.edu. *Dean,* Gail Steketee, 617-353-3760, Fax: 617-353-5612.

School of Theology Students: 252 full-time (110 women), 19 part-time (7 women); includes 38 minority (13 Black or African American, non-Hispanic/Latino; 2 American Indian or Alaska Native, non-Hispanic/Latino; 10 Asian, non-Hispanic/Latino; 10 Hispanic/Latino; 3 Two or more races, non-Hispanic/Latino), 77 international. Average age 34. *Faculty:* 24 full-time (10 women), 18 part-time/adjunct (5 women). Expenses: Contact institution. *Financial support:* Fellowships, research assistantships, teaching assistantships, Federal Work-Study, institutionally sponsored loans, and scholarships/grants available. Support available to part-time students. Financial award application deadline: 7/15; financial award applicants required to submit FAFSA. In 2010, 25 first professional degrees, 38 master's, 8 doctorates awarded. *Degree program information:* Part-time programs available. Offers theology (M Div, MSM, MTS, STM, D Min, Th D). *Application deadline:* For fall admission, 1/15 priority date for domestic students; for spring admission, 10/1 priority date for domestic students. Applications are processed on a rolling basis. *Application fee:* $70. Electronic applications accepted. *Application Contact:* Anastasia Kidd, Director of Admissions, 617-353-3036, Fax: 617-358-0140, E-mail: sthadmis@bu.edu. *Interim Dean,* Mary Elizabeth Moore, 617-353-3050, Fax: 617-353-3061.

BOWIE STATE UNIVERSITY, Bowie, MD 20715-9465

General Information State-supported, coed, comprehensive institution. CGS member. *Enrollment:* 5,578 graduate, professional, and undergraduate students; 409 full-time matriculated graduate/professional students (281 women), 768 part-time matriculated graduate/professional students (559 women). *Enrollment by degree level:* 1,134 master's, 43 doctoral. *Graduate faculty:* 61 full-time (32 women), 57 part-time/adjunct (20 women). Tuition, state resident: full-time $4080; part-time $340 per credit. Tuition, nonresident: full-time $7752; part-time $646 per credit. *Required fees:* $2128; $340 per credit. *Graduate housing:* Room and/or apartments available on a first-come, first-served basis to single students; on-campus housing not available to married students. Typical cost: $5702 per year ($8570 including board). Housing application deadline: 8/1. *Student services:* Campus employment opportunities, campus safety program, career counseling, free psychological counseling, international student services, low-cost health insurance, writing training. *Library facilities:* Thurgood Marshall Library. *Online resources:* library catalog, web page, access to other libraries' catalogs. *Collection:* 285,815 titles, 770 serial subscriptions, 7,570 audiovisual materials.

Computer facilities: 3,144 computers available on campus for general student use. A campuswide network can be accessed from student residence rooms and from off campus. Online class registration is available. *Web address:* http://www.bowiestate.edu/.

General Application Contact: Dr. Cosmas Nwkeafor, Interim Dean, 301-860-3406, Fax: 301-860-3414, E-mail: graduatestudiesandresearch@bowiestate.edu.

GRADUATE UNITS

Graduate Programs *Degree program information:* Part-time and evening/weekend programs available. Offers administration of nursing services (MS); applied and computational mathematics (MS); business administration (MBA); computer science (MS, App Sc D); counseling psychology (MA); educational leadership (Ed D); elementary and secondary school administration (M Ed); elementary education (M Ed); English (MA); family nurse practitioner (MS); guidance and counseling (M Ed); human resource development (MA); information systems analyst (Certificate); management information systems (MS); mental health counseling (MA); nursing education (MS); organizational communication (MA, Certificate); public administration (MPA); reading education (M Ed); school administration and supervision (M Ed); secondary education (M Ed); special education (M Ed); teaching (MAT). Electronic applications accepted.

BOWLING GREEN STATE UNIVERSITY, Bowling Green, OH 43403

General Information State-supported, coed, university. CGS member. *Graduate housing:* On-campus housing not available. *Research affiliation:* Spectra Group, Inc. (photoscience).

GRADUATE UNITS

Graduate College *Degree program information:* Part-time and evening/weekend programs available. Electronic applications accepted.

College of Arts and Sciences *Degree program information:* Part-time programs available. Offers 2-D studio art (MA, MFA); 3-D studio art (MA, MFA); American culture studies (MA, PhD); applied philosophy (PhD); applied statistics (MS); art education (MA); art history (MA); arts and sciences (MA, MAT, MFA, MPA, MS, PhD); biological sciences (MAT, MS, PhD); chemistry (MAT, MS); clinical psychology (MA, PhD); communication studies (MA, PhD); computer art (MA); computer science (MS); creative writing (MFA); demography and population studies (MA); design (MFA); developmental psychology (MA, PhD); digital arts (MFA); English (MA, PhD); experimental psychology (MA, PhD); fiction (MFA); French (MA, MAT); French education (MAT); geology (MS); geophysics (MS); German (MA, MAT); graphics (MFA); history (MA, MAT, PhD); industrial/organizational psychology (MA, PhD); institutional theory and history (PhD); literature (MA); mathematics (MA, MAT, PhD); philosophy (MA); photochemical sciences (PhD); physics (MAT, MS); poetry (MFA); popular culture (MA); public administration (MPA); public history (MA); quantitative psychology (MA, PhD); rhetoric and writing (PhD); scientific and technical communication (MA); social psychology (MA); sociology (PhD); Spanish (MA, MAT); Spanish education (MAT); statistics (PhD); theatre and film (MA, PhD). Electronic applications accepted.

College of Business Administration *Degree program information:* Part-time and evening/weekend programs available. Offers accountancy (M Acc); applied statistics (MS); business (MBA); business administration (M Acc, MA, MBA, MOD, MS); economics (MA); organization development (MOD). Electronic applications accepted.

College of Education and Human Development *Degree program information:* Part-time and evening/weekend programs available. Offers assistive technology (M Ed); business education (M Ed); classroom technology (M Ed); college student personnel (MA); counseling (M Ed, MA); cross-cultural and international education (MA); curriculum (M Ed); curriculum and teaching (M Ed); developmental kinesiology (M Ed); early childhood intervention (M Ed); education and human development (M Ed, MA, MFCS, MRC, Ed D, PhD, Ed S, Sp Ed); education and intervention services (M Ed, MA, MRC, Ed S, Sp Ed); educational administration and supervision (M Ed, Ed S); food and nutrition (MFCS); gifted education (M Ed); hearing impaired intervention (M Ed); higher education administration (PhD); human development and family studies (MFCS); leadership and policy studies (M Ed, MA, Ed D, PhD, Ed S); leadership studies (Ed D); master teaching (M Ed); mental health counseling (MA); mild/moderate intervention (M Ed); moderate/intensive intervention (M Ed); reading (M Ed, Ed S); recreation and leisure (M Ed); rehabilitation counseling (MRC); school counseling (M Ed); school psychology (M Ed, Sp Ed); special education (M Ed); sport administration (M Ed). Electronic applications accepted.

College of Health and Human Services *Degree program information:* Part-time and evening/weekend programs available. Offers communication disorders (PhD); criminal justice (MSCJ); health and human services (MPH, MS, MSCJ, PhD); public health (MPH); speech-language pathology (MS). Electronic applications accepted.

College of Musical Arts *Degree program information:* Part-time programs available. Offers composition (MM); contemporary music (DMA); ethnomusicology (MM); music education (MM); music history (MM); music theory (MM); performance (MM). Electronic applications accepted.

College of Technology *Degree program information:* Part-time programs available. Offers career and technology education (M Ed); construction management (MIT); manufacturing technology (MIT); technology (M Ed, MIT). Electronic applications accepted.

Interdisciplinary Studies *Degree program information:* Part-time programs available. Offers interdisciplinary studies (M Ed, MA, MS, PhD). Electronic applications accepted.

See Display on next page and Close-Up on page 927.

BRADLEY UNIVERSITY, Peoria, IL 61625-0002

General Information Independent, coed, comprehensive institution. CGS member. *Graduate housing:* Room and/or apartments available to single students; on-campus housing not available to married students. *Research affiliation:* Northern Research Laboratory, Peoria School of Medicine, Caterpillar, Inc., Ford Motor Credit/Visteon, Illinois Manufacturing Extension Center.

GRADUATE UNITS

Graduate School *Degree program information:* Part-time and evening/weekend programs available.

College of Education and Health Sciences *Degree program information:* Part-time and evening/weekend programs available. Offers curriculum and instruction (MA, Certificate); education and health sciences (MA, MSN, DPT, Certificate); human development counseling (MA); leadership in educational administration (MA); leadership in human service administration (MA); nurse administered anesthesia (MSN); nursing administration (MSN); physical therapy (DPT).

College of Engineering and Technology *Degree program information:* Part-time and evening/weekend programs available. Offers civil engineering and construction (MSCE); electrical engineering (MSEE); engineering and technology (MSCE, MSEE, MSIE, MSME, MSMFE); industrial engineering (MSIE); manufacturing engineering (MSIE); mechanical engineering (MSME).

College of Liberal Arts and Sciences *Degree program information:* Part-time and evening/weekend programs available. Offers biology (MS); chemistry (MS); computer information systems (MS); computer science (MS); English (MA); liberal arts and sciences (MA, MLS, MS); liberal studies (MLS).

Foster College of Business Administration *Degree program information:* Part-time and evening/weekend programs available. Offers accounting (MSA); business administration (MBA, MSA).

Slane College of Communications and Fine Arts *Degree program information:* Part-time and evening/weekend programs available. Offers ceramics (MA, MFA); communications and fine arts (MA, MFA); drawing/illustration (MA, MFA); interdisciplinary art (MA, MFA); painting (MA, MFA); photography (MA, MFA); printmaking (MA, MFA); sculpture (MA, MFA); visual communication and design (MA, MFA).

BRANDEIS UNIVERSITY, Waltham, MA 02454-9110

General Information Independent, coed, university. *Graduate housing:* Room and/or apartments available on a first-come, first-served basis to single students; on-campus housing not available to married students. Housing application deadline: 6/1.

GRADUATE UNITS

Graduate School of Arts and Sciences Students: 872 full-time (437 women), 28 part-time (19 women); includes 20 Black or African American, non-Hispanic/Latino; 2 American Indian or Alaska Native, non-Hispanic/Latino; 23 Asian, non-Hispanic/Latino; 27 Hispanic/Latino; 1 Two or more races, non-Hispanic/Latino, 200 international. Average age 30. 2,350 applicants, 34% accepted, 355 enrolled. *Faculty:* 309 full-time (121 women), 106 part-time/adjunct (57 women). Expenses: Contact institution. *Financial support:* Fellowships with full and partial tuition reimbursements, research assistantships with full and partial tuition reimbursements, teaching assistantships with full and partial tuition reimbursements, career-related internships or fieldwork, institutionally sponsored loans, scholarships/grants, health care benefits, tuition waivers (full and partial), and unspecified assistantships available. Support available to part-time students. Financial award applicants required to submit FAFSA. In 2010, 176 master's, 53 doctorates, 14 other advanced degrees awarded. *Degree program information:* Part-time programs available. Offers acting (MFA); ancient Greek and Roman studies (MA, Graduate Certificate); anthropology (MA, PhD); anthropology and women's and gender studies (MA); arts and sciences (MA, MAT, MFA, MS, PhD, Certificate, Graduate Certificate, Postbaccalaureate Certificate); biochemistry and biophysics (PhD); biotechnology (MS); brain, body and behavior (PhD); cognitive neuroscience (PhD); composition and theory (MA, MFA, PhD); computational linguistics (MA); computer science (MA, PhD, Certificate); computer science and IT entrepreneurship (MA); elementary education (public) (MAT); English (MA, PhD); English and women's and gender studies (MA); general psychology (MA); genetic counseling (MS); genetics (PhD); global studies (MA); history (MA, PhD); inorganic chemistry (MS, PhD); Jewish day school (MAT); mathematics (MA, PhD, Postbaccalaureate Certificate); microbiology (PhD); molecular and cell biology (MS, PhD); molecular biology (PhD); music and women's and gender studies (MA); musicology (MA, MFA, PhD); Near Eastern and Judaic studies (MA, PhD); Near Eastern and Judaic studies and sociology (PhD); Near Eastern and Judaic studies and women's and gender studies (MA); neurobiology (PhD); neuroscience (MS, PhD); organic chemistry (MS, PhD); philosophy (MA); physical chemistry (MS, PhD); physics (MS, PhD); politics (MA, PhD); premedical studies (Postbaccalaureate Certificate); public policy and women's and gender studies (MA); secondary education (English, history, biology, chemistry, physics, Bible) (MAT); social policy and sociology (PhD); social/developmental psychology (PhD); sociology (MA, PhD); sociology and women's and gender studies (MA); studio art (Certificate); sustainable international development and women's/gender studies (MA); teaching of Hebrew (MAT); women's and gender studies (MA). *Application deadline:* For fall admission, 1/15 priority date for domestic and international students; for spring admission, 11/1 for domestic and international students. Applications are processed on a rolling basis. *Application fee:* $75. Electronic applications accepted. *Application Contact:* David F. Cotter, Associate Dean, 781-736-3410, Fax: 781-736-3412, E-mail: gradschool@brandeis.edu. *Dean*, Dr. Malcolm Watson, 781-736-3410, Fax: 781-736-3412, E-mail: gradschool@brandeis.edu.

The Heller School for Social Policy and Management Students: 575 full-time (345 women); includes 57 minority (19 Black or African American, non-Hispanic/Latino; 25 Asian, non-Hispanic/Latino; 13 Hispanic/Latino), 259 international. Average age 30. 1,349 applicants, 87% accepted, 238 enrolled. *Faculty:* 36 full-time, 107 part-time/adjunct. Expenses: Contact institution. *Financial support:* In 2010–11, 15 fellowships with full and partial tuition reimbursements (averaging $20,000 per year) were awarded; research assistantships, teaching assistantships, institutionally sponsored loans, scholarships/grants, traineeships, health care benefits, tuition waivers (full and partial), and unspecified assistantships also available. Financial award application deadline: 2/15; financial award applicants required to submit FAFSA. In 2010, 138 master's, 8 doctorates awarded. *Degree program information:* Part-time programs available. Offers aging (MPP); assets and inequalities (PhD); behavioral health (MPP); child, youth, and family management (MBA); children, youth and families (MPP, PhD); coexistence and conflict (MA); general social policy (MPP); global health and development (PhD); health (MPP); health and behavioral health (PhD); health care management (MBA); international development (MA); international health policy and management (MS); poverty alleviation and development (MPP); social impact management (MBA); social policy and management (MA, MBA, MPP, MS, PhD); sustainable development (MA, MBA). *Application deadline:* For fall admission, 3/15 for domestic and international students. Applications are processed on a rolling basis. *Application fee:* $55. Electronic applications accepted. *Application Contact:* Margaret Haley, Assistant Director for Admissions and Financial Aid, 781-736-3792, Fax: 781-736-3881, E-mail: haley@brandeis.edu. *Dean*, Dr. Lisa M. Lynch, 781-736-3883, E-mail: lmlynch@brandeis.edu.

International Business School *Degree program information:* Part-time and evening/weekend programs available. Offers finance (MSF); international business (MBAi); international economics and finance (MA, PhD); international finance/international economics (MBAi). Electronic applications accepted.

Rabb School of Continuing Studies, Division of Graduate Professional Studies Students: 2 full-time (0 women), 215 part-time (47 women); includes 10 Black or African American, non-Hispanic/Latino; 29 Asian, non-Hispanic/Latino; 10 Hispanic/Latino, 1 international. Average age 35. 44 applicants, 100% accepted, 38 enrolled. *Faculty:* 2 full-time (both women), 33 part-time/adjunct (5 women). Expenses: Contact institution. In 2010, 130 master's, 8 other advanced degrees awarded. *Degree program information:* Part-time and evening/weekend programs available. Postbaccalaureate distance learning degree programs offered (no on-campus study). Offers bioinformatics (MS, Graduate Certificate); health and medical informatics (MS, Graduate Certificate); information assurance (MS, Graduate Certificate); information technology management (MS, Graduate Certificate); management of projects and programs (MS, Graduate Certificate); software engineering (MSE, Graduate Certificate); virtual team management and communication (MS, Graduate Certificate). *Application deadline:* For fall admission, 6/15 priority date for domestic students; for winter admission, 10/15 priority date for domestic students; for spring admission, 2/15 priority date for domestic students. Applications are processed on a rolling basis. *Application fee:* $50. Electronic applications accepted. *Application Contact:* Frances Stearns, Associate Director of Admissions and Student Services, 781-736-8785, Fax: 781-736-3420, E-mail: fstearns@brandeis.edu. *Executive Director*, Sybil P. Smith, 781-736-3443, Fax: 781-736-3420, E-mail: sysmith@brandeis.edu.

BRANDON UNIVERSITY, Brandon, MB R7A 6A9, Canada

General Information Province-supported, coed, comprehensive institution. *Graduate housing:* Room and/or apartments available on a first-come, first-served basis to single students; on-campus housing not available to married students.

GRADUATE UNITS

Department of Rural Development Offers rural development (MRD, Diploma). Electronic applications accepted.

Faculty of Education Offers curriculum and instruction (M Ed, Diploma); educational administration (M Ed, Diploma); guidance and counseling (M Ed, Diploma); special education (M Ed, Diploma).

School of Music Students: 11 full-time (4 women), 1 part-time (0 women), 2 international. Average age 25. 2 applicants, 100% accepted. *Faculty:* 7 full-time (5 women). Expenses: Contact institution. *Financial support:* In 2010–11, 4 students received support, including 1 research assistantship, 5 teaching assistantships (averaging $3,250 per year). Financial award application deadline: 5/1. In 2010, 2 master's awarded. *Degree program information:* Part-time programs available. Offers composition (M Mus); music education (M Mus); performance and literature (M Mus). *Application deadline:* For spring admission, 5/1 priority date for domestic students. Applications are processed on a rolling basis. *Application fee:* $60 ($125 for international students). Electronic applications accepted. *Application Contact:* Dr.

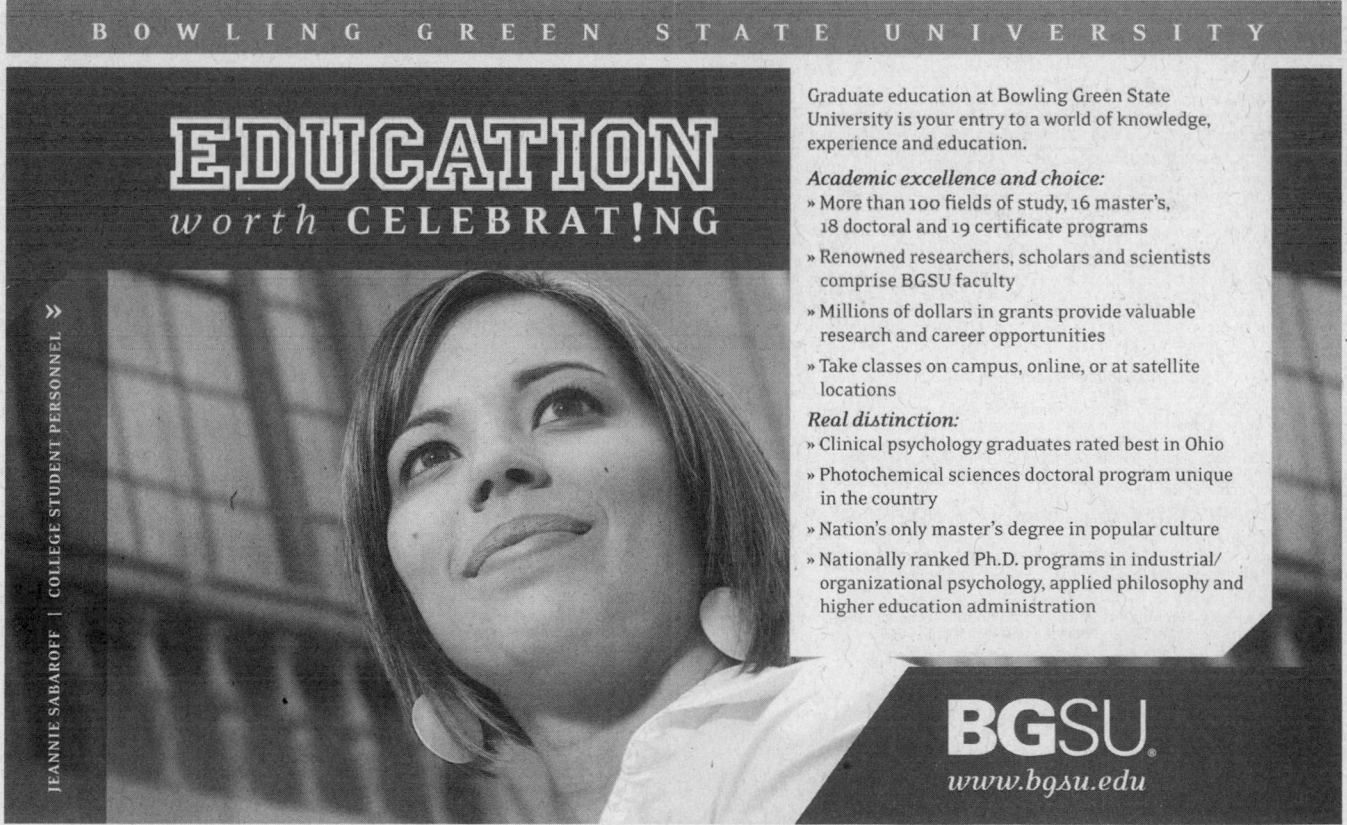

Brandon University (continued)

Patrick Carrabre, Joint Chair of Graduate Music Department (Performance and Literature), 204-727-9666, Fax: 204-728-6839. *Dean*, Dr. Michael Kim, 204-727-9633, Fax: 204-728-6839, E-mail: kimm@brandonu.ca.

BRENAU UNIVERSITY, Gainesville, GA 30501

General Information Independent, women only, comprehensive institution. *Enrollment:* 374 full-time matriculated graduate/professional students (321 women), 582 part-time matriculated graduate/professional students (460 women). *Enrollment by degree level:* 936 master's, 20 other advanced degrees. *Graduate faculty:* 42 full-time (29 women), 47 part-time/adjunct (31 women). *Tuition:* Part-time $494 per credit hour. *Required fees:* $130 per semester. Tuition and fees vary according to campus/location and program. *Graduate housing:* Room and/or apartments available on a first-come, first-served basis to single students; on-campus housing not available to married students. *Student services:* Career counseling, free psychological counseling, international student services, writing training. *Library facilities:* Trustee Library. *Online resources:* library catalog, web page. *Collection:* 87,297 titles, 19,597 serial subscriptions, 3,203 audiovisual materials.

Computer facilities: 130 computers available on campus for general student use. A campuswide network can be accessed from student residence rooms. Online class registration, students can create own Web sites, videos and other things made possible by Google apps are available. *Web address:* http://www.brenau.edu/.

General Application Contact: Christina White, Dean of Graduate Admissions, 770-718-5320, E-mail: cwhite@brenau.edu.

GRADUATE UNITS

Sydney O. Smith Graduate School Students: 374 full-time (321 women), 582 part-time (460 women); includes 228 Black or African American, non-Hispanic/Latino; 4 American Indian or Alaska Native, non-Hispanic/Latino; 19 Asian, non-Hispanic/Latino; 31 Hispanic/Latino; 15 Two or more races, non-Hispanic/Latino, 43 international. Average age 35. *Faculty:* 42 full-time (29 women), 47 part-time/adjunct (31 women). Expenses: Contact institution. *Financial support:* Scholarships/grants and traineeships available. Support available to part-time students. Financial award applicants required to submit FAFSA. In 2010, 320 master's, 20 other advanced degrees awarded. *Degree program information:* Part-time and evening/weekend programs available. Postbaccalaureate distance learning degree programs offered (no on-campus study). *Application deadline:* Applications are processed on a rolling basis. Electronic applications accepted. *Application Contact:* Christina White, Dean of Graduate Admissions, 770-718-5320, E-mail: cwhite@brenau.edu. *Dean*, Dr. Gale Starich, 770-718-5305.

College of Health and Science Students: 136 full-time (129 women), 106 part-time (96 women); includes 82 minority (61 Black or African American, non-Hispanic/Latino; 1 American Indian or Alaska Native, non-Hispanic/Latino; 4 Asian, non-Hispanic/Latino; 12 Hispanic/Latino; 4 Two or more races, non-Hispanic/Latino), 1 international. Average age 33. *Faculty:* 14 full-time (12 women), 9 part-time/adjunct (all women). Expenses: Contact institution. *Financial support:* In 2010–11, 32 students received support. Scholarships/grants and traineeships available. Support available to part-time students. Financial award application deadline: 7/15; financial award applicants required to submit FAFSA. In 2010, 35 master's awarded. *Degree program information:* Part-time and evening/weekend programs available. Offers family nurse practitioner (MSN); nurse educator (MSN); nursing management (MSN); occupational therapy (MS); psychology (MS). *Application deadline:* Applications are processed on a rolling basis. *Application fee:* $35. Electronic applications accepted. *Application Contact:* Christina White, Admissions Coordinator, 770-718-5320, Fax: 770-770-5338, E-mail: cwhite@brenau.edu. *Dean*, Dr. Gale Starich, 777-718-5305, Fax: 770-297-5929, E-mail: gstarich@brenau.edu.

School of Business and Mass Communication Students: 124 full-time (89 women), 348 part-time (250 women); includes 130 Black or African American, non-Hispanic/Latino; 2 American Indian or Alaska Native, non-Hispanic/Latino; 7 Asian, non-Hispanic/Latino; 13 Hispanic/Latino; 9 Two or more races, non-Hispanic/Latino, 42 international. Average age 35. *Faculty:* 12 full-time (7 women), 24 part-time/adjunct (10 women). Expenses: Contact institution. *Financial support:* In 2010–11, 1 student received support. Application deadline: 7/15. In 2010, 125 master's awarded. *Degree program information:* Part-time and evening/weekend programs available. Postbaccalaureate distance learning degree programs offered (no on-campus study). Offers accounting (MBA); business administration (MBA); healthcare management (MBA); organizational leadership (MS); project management (MBA). *Application deadline:* Applications are processed on a rolling basis. Electronic applications accepted. *Application Contact:* Christina White, Graduate Admissions Specialist, 770-718-5320, Fax: 770-718-5338, E-mail: cwhite@brenau.edu. *Dean*, Dr. William S. Lightfoot, 770-538-5330, Fax: 770-537-4701, E-mail: wlightfoot@brenau.edu.

School of Education Students: 107 full-time (96 women), 122 part-time (108 women); includes 35 Black or African American, non-Hispanic/Latino; 1 American Indian or Alaska Native, non-Hispanic/Latino; 8 Asian, non-Hispanic/Latino; 5 Hispanic/Latino; 2 Two or more races, non-Hispanic/Latino. Average age 36. 163 applicants, 34% accepted, 47 enrolled. *Faculty:* 13 full-time (7 women), 14 part-time/adjunct (12 women). Expenses: Contact institution. *Financial support:* In 2010–11, 2 students received support. Scholarships/grants available. Support available to part-time students. Financial award application deadline: 7/15; financial award applicants required to submit FAFSA. In 2010, 20 other advanced degrees awarded. *Degree program information:* Part-time and evening/weekend programs available. Postbaccalaureate distance learning degree programs offered (no on-campus study). Offers early childhood (Ed S); early childhood education (M Ed, MAT); middle grades (Ed S); middle grades education (M Ed, MAT); secondary education (MAT); special education (M Ed, MAT). *Application deadline:* Applications are processed on a rolling basis. *Application fee:* $35. Electronic applications accepted. *Application Contact:* Christina White, Dean of Admissions, 770-718-5320, Fax: 770-718-5337, E-mail: cwhite@brenau.edu. *Interim Dean*, Dr. David Barnett, 770-531-3172, Fax: 770-718-5329, E-mail: lbailey@brenau.edu.

School of Fine Arts and Humanities Students: 7 full-time (all women), 6 part-time (all women); includes 2 Black or African American, non-Hispanic/Latino; 1 Hispanic/Latino. Average age 42. *Faculty:* 3 full-time (all women). Expenses: Contact institution. In 2010, 6 master's awarded. *Degree program information:* Part-time programs available. Offers interior design (MID). *Application deadline:* Applications are processed on a rolling basis. *Application fee:* $35. Electronic applications accepted. *Application Contact:* Christina White, Dean of Admissions, 770-718-5320, Fax: 770-718-5338. *Dean*, Dr. Andrea Birch, 710-718-5325, E-mail: abirch@brenau.edu.

BRESCIA UNIVERSITY, Owensboro, KY 42301-3023

General Information Independent-religious, coed, comprehensive institution. *Graduate housing:* Room and/or apartments available on a first-come, first-served basis to single students; on-campus housing not available to married students.

GRADUATE UNITS

Program in Business Administration *Degree program information:* Part-time and evening/weekend programs available. Offers business administration (MBA).

Program in Curriculum and Instruction *Degree program information:* Part-time and evening/weekend programs available. Offers curriculum and instruction (MSCI). Electronic applications accepted.

Program in Management *Degree program information:* Part-time and evening/weekend programs available. Offers management (MSM).

BRIAR CLIFF UNIVERSITY, Sioux City, IA 51104-0100

General Information Independent-religious, coed, comprehensive institution. *Enrollment:* 1,156 graduate, professional, and undergraduate students; 9 full-time matriculated graduate/professional students (7 women), 81 part-time matriculated graduate/professional students (70 women). *Enrollment by degree level:* 90 master's. *Graduate faculty:* 5 full-time (3 women), 4 part-time/adjunct (2 women). *Tuition:* Full-time $5904; part-time $492 per credit hour. *Required fees:* $276; $23 per credit hour. Tuition and fees vary according to program. *Graduate housing:* Room and/or apartments available on a first-come, first-served basis to single students; on-campus housing not available to married students. Typical cost: $4014 per year ($7557 including board). Housing application deadline: 6/1. *Student services:* Campus employment opportunities, campus safety program, career counseling, free psychological counseling, international student services, services for students with disabilities. *Library facilities:* Bishop Mueller Library. *Online resources:* library catalog, web page. *Collection:* 82,007 titles, 151 serial subscriptions, 1,244 audiovisual materials.

Computer facilities: 112 computers available on campus for general student use. A campuswide network can be accessed from student residence rooms and from off campus. *Web address:* http://www.briarcliff.edu/.

General Application Contact: Cheryl Olson, Continuing Studies Admissions Representative, 712-279-1777, Fax: 712-279-1632, E-mail: cheryl.olson@briarcliff.edu.

GRADUATE UNITS

Program in Human Resource Management Students: 1 full-time (0 women), 2 part-time (1 woman). Average age 36. 32 applicants, 66% accepted. *Faculty:* 1 full-time (0 women), 2 part-time/adjunct (1 woman). Expenses: Contact institution. *Financial support:* Application deadline: 8/1. In 2010, 9 master's awarded. *Degree program information:* Part-time and evening/weekend programs available. Offers human resource management (MA). *Application deadline:* For fall admission, 4/1 for domestic students. *Application fee:* $25. Electronic applications accepted. *Application Contact:* Cheryl Olson, Continuing Studies Admissions Representative, 712-279-1777, Fax: 712-279-1632, E-mail: cheryl.olson@briarcliff.edu. *Director*, Barb Redmond, 712-279-5561, Fax: 712-279-1698, E-mail: barb.redmond@briarcliff.edu.

Program in Nursing Students: 5 full-time (all women), 51 part-time (48 women). Average age 38. 16 applicants, 81% accepted, 10 enrolled. *Faculty:* 4 full-time (3 women), 2 part-time/adjunct (both women). Expenses: Contact institution. *Financial support:* Application deadline: 8/1. In 2010, 3 master's awarded. *Degree program information:* Part-time and evening/weekend programs available. Offers nursing (MSN). *Application deadline:* For fall admission, 8/1 for domestic students. *Application fee:* $25. *Application Contact:* Cheryl Olson, Continuing Studies Admissions Representative, 712-279-1777, Fax: 712-279-1632, E-mail: cheryl.olson@briarcliff.edu. *Director*, Dr. Richard Peterson, 712-279-1662, Fax: 712-279-1698, E-mail: richard.petersen@briarcliff.edu.

BRIDGEWATER STATE UNIVERSITY, Bridgewater, MA 02325-0001

General Information State-supported, coed, comprehensive institution. *Graduate housing:* On-campus housing not available.

GRADUATE UNITS

School of Graduate Studies *Degree program information:* Part-time and evening/weekend programs available.

School of Arts and Sciences *Degree program information:* Part-time and evening/weekend programs available. Offers art (MAT); arts and sciences (MA, MAT, MPA, MS, MSW); biological sciences (MAT); computer science (MS); criminal justice (MS); English (MA, MAT); history (MAT); mathematics (MAT); physical sciences (MAT); physics (MAT); psychology (MA); public administration (MPA); social work (MSW).

School of Business *Degree program information:* Part-time and evening/weekend programs available. Offers accounting and finance (MSM); business (MSM); management (MSM).

School of Education and Allied Studies *Degree program information:* Part-time and evening/weekend programs available. Offers counseling (M Ed, CAGS); early childhood education (M Ed); education and allied studies (M Ed, MAT, MS, CAGS); educational leadership (M Ed, CAGS); elementary education (M Ed); health promotion (M Ed); instructional technology (M Ed); physical education (MS); reading (M Ed, CAGS); secondary education (MAT); special education (M Ed).

BRIERCREST SEMINARY, Caronport, SK S0H 0S0, Canada

General Information Independent-religious, coed, graduate-only institution. *Graduate housing:* Rooms and/or apartments guaranteed to single students and available on a first-come, first-served basis to married students.

GRADUATE UNITS

Graduate Programs *Degree program information:* Part-time programs available. Offers Biblical studies (M Div); leadership (MA); leadership and management (M Div); marriage and family counseling (MA); missions (MA); New Testament (MATS); Old Testament (MATS); organizational leadership (MA); pastoral counseling (M Div, MA); pastoral ministry (M Div); theological studies (M Div); theology (MATS); worship (M Div, MA); youth and family ministry (M Div, MA).

BRIGHAM YOUNG UNIVERSITY, Provo, UT 84602-1001

General Information Independent-religious, coed, university. CGS member. *Enrollment:* 33,841 graduate, professional, and undergraduate students; 2,140 full-time matriculated graduate/professional students (755 women), 1,132 part-time matriculated graduate/professional students (430 women). *Enrollment by degree level:* 443 first professional, 2,263 master's, 509 doctoral, 57 other advanced degrees. *Graduate faculty:* 1,080 full-time (187 women), 5 part-time/adjunct (1 woman). *Tuition:* Full-time $5580; part-time $310 per credit hour. Tuition and fees vary according to program and student's religious affiliation. *Graduate housing:* Rooms and/or apartments available on a first-come, first-served basis to single and married students. Typical cost: $4400 per year ($8400 including board) for single students; $5200 per year ($9200 including board) for married students. Room and board charges vary according to board plan and housing facility selected. Housing application deadline: 2/1. *Student services:* Campus employment opportunities, campus safety program, career counseling, exercise/wellness program, free psychological counseling, international student services, low-cost health insurance, multicultural affairs office, services for students with disabilities, teacher training, writing training. *Library facilities:* Harold B. Lee Library plus 2 others. *Online resources:* library catalog, web page, access to other libraries' catalogs.

Computer facilities: Computer purchase and lease plans are available. A campuswide network can be accessed from student residence rooms and from off campus. Online class registration is available. *Web address:* http://www.byu.edu/.

General Application Contact: Graduate Studies, 801-422-4091, Fax: 801-422-0270, E-mail: gradstudies@byu.edu.

GRADUATE UNITS

Graduate Studies Students: 2,140 full-time (755 women), 1,132 part-time (430 women); includes 278 minority (13 Black or African American, non-Hispanic/Latino; 9 American Indian or Alaska Native, non-Hispanic/Latino; 57 Asian, non-Hispanic/Latino; 114 Hispanic/Latino; 26 Native Hawaiian or other Pacific Islander, non-Hispanic/Latino; 59 Two or more races, non-Hispanic/Latino), 366 international. Average age 30. 2,571 applicants, 57% accepted, 1134 enrolled. *Faculty:* 1,080 full-time (187 women), 5 part-time/adjunct (1 woman). Expenses: Contact institution. *Financial support:* Fellowships, research assistantships, teaching assistantships, career-related internships or fieldwork, institutionally sponsored loans, and tuition waivers (full and partial) available. Support available to part-time students. Financial award applicants required to submit FAFSA. In 2010, 156 first professional degrees, 1,044 master's, 89 doctorates, 39 other advanced degrees awarded. *Degree program information:* Part-time and evening/weekend programs available. *Application deadline:* For fall admission, 12/1 priority date for domestic and international students; for winter admission, 8/15 priority date for domestic students, 6/15 priority date for international students; for spring admission, 2/1 priority date for domestic and international students. Applications are processed on a rolling basis. *Application fee:* $50. Electronic applications accepted. *Application Contact:* Kevin Green, Adviser, 801-422-7308, Fax: 801-422-0270, E-mail: gradstudies@byu.edu. *Dean*, Wynn Stirling, 801-422-4465, Fax: 801-422-0270, E-mail: gradstudies@byu.edu.

College of Family, Home, and Social Sciences Students: 290 full-time (169 women), 10 part-time (7 women); includes 30 minority (3 American Indian or Alaska Native, non-Hispanic/Latino; 9 Asian, non-Hispanic/Latino; 15 Hispanic/Latino; 2 Native Hawaiian or other Pacific Islander, non-Hispanic/Latino; 1 Two or more races, non-Hispanic/Latino), 14 international.

Average age 28. 401 applicants, 36% accepted, 114 enrolled. *Faculty:* 107 full-time (22 women), 17 part-time/adjunct (10 women). Expenses: Contact institution. *Financial support:* In 2010–11, 23 fellowships (averaging $1,777 per year), 122 research assistantships (averaging $9,020 per year), 52 teaching assistantships (averaging $10,681 per year) were awarded. Financial award applicants required to submit FAFSA. In 2010, 81 master's, 22 doctorates awarded. Offers anthropology (MA); clinical psychology (PhD); family, home, and social sciences (MA, MPP, MS, MSW, PhD); general psychology (MS); geography (MS); marriage and family therapy (MS, PhD); marriage, family and human development (MS, PhD); psychology (PhD); public policy (MPP); social work (MSW); sociology (MS). Electronic applications accepted. *Application Contact:* Adviser, 801-422-4541, Fax: 801-378-5238, E-mail: gradstudies@byu.edu. *Dean,* Dr. David B. Magleby, 801-422-2083, Fax: 801-422-2084, E-mail: david_magleby@byu.edu.

College of Fine Arts and Communications Students: 118 full-time (85 women), 47 part-time (23 women); includes 1 Black or African American, non-Hispanic/Latino; 7 Asian, non-Hispanic/Latino; 2 Hispanic/Latino; 2 Native Hawaiian or other Pacific Islander, non-Hispanic/Latino, 1 international. Average age 29. 133 applicants, 47% accepted, 56 enrolled. *Faculty:* 108 full-time (24 women), 1 (woman) part-time/adjunct. Expenses: Contact institution. *Financial support:* In 2010–11, 135 students received support, including 19 research assistantships with full and partial tuition reimbursements available (averaging $4,188 per year), 65 teaching assistantships with full and partial tuition reimbursements available (averaging $4,867 per year); career-related internships or fieldwork, institutionally sponsored loans, scholarships/grants, health care benefits, tuition waivers (partial), unspecified assistantships, and administrative aides, supplementary awards also available. Support available to part-time students. Financial award applicants required to submit FAFSA. In 2010, 36 master's awarded. Offers art education (MA); art history (MA); composition (MM); conducting (MM); fine arts and communications (MA, MFA, MM); mass communications (MA); music education (MA, MM); musicology (MA); performance (MM); studio art (MFA); theatre and media arts (MA). *Application fee:* $50. Electronic applications accepted. *Application Contact:* Adviser, 801-422-4541, Fax: 801-378-5238, E-mail: gradstudies@byu.edu. *Dean,* Dr. Stephen M. Jones, 801-422-8271, Fax: 801-422-0253, E-mail: amber_louw@byu.edu.

College of Humanities Students: 187 full-time (120 women), 43 part-time (25 women); includes 6 Asian, non-Hispanic/Latino; 10 Hispanic/Latino; 1 Native Hawaiian or other Pacific Islander, non-Hispanic/Latino, 6 international. Average age 25. 236 applicants, 50% accepted, 96 enrolled. *Faculty:* 176 full-time (42 women), 5 part-time/adjunct (all women). Expenses: Contact institution. *Financial support:* In 2010–11, 170 students received support, including 68 fellowships with partial tuition reimbursements available (averaging $1,494 per year), 108 research assistantships with partial tuition reimbursements available (averaging $2,133 per year), 205 teaching assistantships with partial tuition reimbursements available (averaging $4,894 per year); career-related internships or fieldwork, institutionally sponsored loans, tuition waivers (full and partial), and student instructorships also available. Support available to part-time students. In 2010, 74 master's, 61 other advanced degrees awarded. *Degree program information:* Part-time programs available. Offers comparative studies (MA); creative writing (MFA); French studies (MA); general linguistics (MA); Hispanic literature (MA); humanities (MA, MFA, Certificate); literature (MA); Portuguese linguistics (MA); Portuguese literature (MA); rhetoric/composition (MA); second language teaching (MA); Spanish linguistics (MA); Spanish teaching (MA); teaching English as a second language (MA, Certificate). *Application fee:* $50. Electronic applications accepted. *Application Contact:* Adviser, 801-422-4541, Fax: 801-378-5238, E-mail: gradstudies@byu.edu. *Dean,* Dr. John R. Rosenberg, 801-422-2779, Fax: 801-422-0308, E-mail: john_rosenberg@byu.edu.

College of Life Sciences Students: 213 full-time (100 women), 31 part-time (13 women); includes 29 minority (2 Black or African American, non-Hispanic/Latino; 14 Asian, non-Hispanic/Latino; 12 Hispanic/Latino; 1 Native Hawaiian or other Pacific Islander, non-Hispanic/Latino). Average age 27. 169 applicants, 51% accepted, 73 enrolled. *Faculty:* 127 full-time (16 women), 3 part-time/adjunct (1 woman). Expenses: Contact institution. *Financial support:* In 2010–11, 183 students received support, including 21 fellowships with full and partial tuition reimbursements available (averaging $4,630 per year), 52 research assistantships with full and partial tuition reimbursements available (averaging $12,840 per year), 9 teaching assistantships with full and partial tuition reimbursements available (averaging $15,996 per year); scholarships/grants and tuition waivers (partial) also available. Financial award application deadline: 2/1. In 2010, 62 master's, 9 doctorates awarded. Offers athletic training (MS); biological science education (MS); biology (MS, PhD); environmental science (MS); exercise physiology (MS, PhD); exercise science (MS); food science (MS); genetics and biotechnology (MS); health promotion (MS, PhD); health science (MPH); life sciences (MPH, MS, PhD); microbiology (MS, PhD); molecular biology (MS, PhD); neuroscience (MS, PhD); nutrition (MS); physical medicine and rehabilitation (PhD); physiology and developmental biology (MS, PhD); wildlife and wildlands conservation (MS, PhD). *Application deadline:* For fall admission, 2/1 for domestic and international students. Electronic applications accepted. *Application Contact:* Sue Pratley, Application Contact, 801-422-3963, Fax: 801-422-0050, E-mail: sue_pratley@byu.edu. *Dean,* Dr. Rodney J. Brown, 801-422-3963, Fax: 801-422-0050.

College of Nursing Students: 28 full-time (19 women), 3 part-time (2 women); includes 3 Asian, non-Hispanic/Latino. Average age 36. 41 applicants, 34% accepted, 14 enrolled. *Faculty:* 14 full-time (13 women), 4 part-time/adjunct (3 women). Expenses: Contact institution. *Financial support:* In 2010–11, 31 students received support, including 2 research assistantships with full and partial tuition reimbursements available (averaging $10,000 per year), 3 teaching assistantships with full and partial tuition reimbursements available (averaging $10,000 per year); institutionally sponsored loans, scholarships/grants, tuition waivers (full), and unspecified assistantships also available. Support available to part-time students. Financial award application deadline: 2/1; financial award applicants required to submit FAFSA. In 2010, 14 master's awarded. Offers family nurse practitioner (MS). *Application deadline:* For spring admission, 12/1 for domestic students. Applications are processed on a rolling basis. *Application fee:* $50. Electronic applications accepted. *Application Contact:* Stephanie Wilson, Graduate Secretary, 801-422-4142, Fax: 801-422-0538, E-mail: stephanie-wilson@byu.edu. *Dean,* Dr. Beth Vaughan Cole, 801-422-8296, Fax: 801-422-0536, E-mail: beth-cole@byu.edu.

College of Physical and Mathematical Sciences Students: 315 full-time (80 women), 32 part-time (9 women); includes 2 Black or African American, non-Hispanic/Latino; 1 American Indian or Alaska Native, non-Hispanic/Latino; 21 Asian, non-Hispanic/Latino; 4 Hispanic/Latino; 3 Native Hawaiian or other Pacific Islander, non-Hispanic/Latino, 61 international. Average age 27. 229 applicants, 63% accepted, 108 enrolled. *Faculty:* 160 full-time (12 women), 5 part-time/adjunct (0 women). Expenses: Contact institution. *Financial support:* In 2010–11, 309 students received support, including 10 fellowships with full tuition reimbursements available (averaging $21,250 per year), 183 research assistantships with full and partial tuition reimbursements available (averaging $16,824 per year), 137 teaching assistantships with full and partial tuition reimbursements available (averaging $15,928 per year); career-related internships or fieldwork, institutionally sponsored loans, scholarships/grants, health care benefits, tuition waivers (full and partial), and unspecified assistantships also available. Support available to part-time students. In 2010, 57 master's, 24 doctorates awarded. *Degree program information:* Part-time programs available. Offers applied statistics (MS); biochemistry (MS, PhD); chemistry (MS, PhD); computer science (MS, PhD); geological sciences (MS); mathematics (MS, PhD); mathematics education (MA); physical and mathematical sciences (MA, MS, PhD); physics (MS, PhD); physics and astronomy (PhD). *Application deadline:* Applications are processed on a rolling basis. *Application fee:* $50. Electronic applications accepted. *Application Contact:* Lynn Patten, Executive Secretary, 801-422-4022, Fax: 801-422-0550, E-mail: lynn_patten@byu.edu. *Dean,* Dr. Scott D. Sommerfeldt, 801-422-2205, Fax: 801-422-0550, E-mail: scott_sommerfeldt@byu.edu.

College of Religious Education Students: 16 full-time (0 women), 11 part-time (1 woman). Average age 32. *Faculty:* 56 full-time (4 women). Expenses: Contact institution. *Financial support:* Scholarships/grants available. In 2010, 4 master's awarded. Offers religious education (MA). *Application deadline:* For fall admission, 12/1 for domestic and international students. *Application fee:* $50. Electronic applications accepted. *Application Contact:* Dr. Ray L. Huntington, Professor of Ancient Scripture, 801-422-3125, Fax: 801-422-0616, E-mail: ray_huntington@byu.edu. *Dean,* Dr. Terry B. Ball, 801-422-2736, Fax: 801-422-0616, E-mail: terry_ball@byu.edu.

David O. McKay School of Education Students: 161 full-time (102 women), 127 part-time (70 women); includes 17 minority (1 Black or African American, non-Hispanic/Latino; 3 American Indian or Alaska Native, non-Hispanic/Latino; 5 Asian, non-Hispanic/Latino; 6 Hispanic/Latino; 2 Native Hawaiian or other Pacific Islander, non-Hispanic/Latino), 14 international. Average age 31. 234 applicants, 44% accepted, 88 enrolled. *Faculty:* 61 full-time (26 women), 12 part-time/adjunct (2 women). Expenses: Contact institution. *Financial support:* In 2010–11, 150 students received support, including 75 research assistantships with full and partial tuition reimbursements available (averaging $10,107 per year), 35 teaching assistantships with full and partial tuition reimbursements available (averaging $5,414 per year); fellowships, career-related internships or fieldwork, institutionally sponsored loans, scholarships/grants, tuition waivers (partial), and unspecified assistantships also available. Support available to part-time students. Financial award applicants required to submit FAFSA. In 2010, 83 master's, 32 doctorates, 10 other advanced degrees awarded. *Degree program information:* Part-time programs available. Offers communication disorders (MS); counseling psychology (PhD); education (M Ed, MA, MS, Ed D, PhD, Ed S); educational leadership and foundations (M Ed, Ed D, PhD); instructional psychology and technology (MS, PhD); integrative science-technology-engineering-mathematics (STEM) (MA); literacy education (MA); school psychology (Ed S); special education (MS); teacher education (MA). *Application deadline:* For fall admission, 2/1 for domestic and international students; for winter admission, 2/1 for domestic and international students; for spring admission, 2/15 for domestic and international students. *Application fee:* $50. Electronic applications accepted. *Application Contact:* Jeanna Nochols, Director, Education Student Services, 801-422-3695, Fax: 801-422-0195. *Dean,* Dr. K. Richard Young, 801-422-3695, Fax: 801-422-0200, E-mail: richard_young@byu.edu.

Ira A. Fulton College of Engineering and Technology Students: 387 full-time (36 women), 41 part-time (5 women); includes 67 minority (4 Black or African American, non-Hispanic/Latino; 8 American Indian or Alaska Native, non-Hispanic/Latino; 34 Asian, non-Hispanic/Latino; 19 Hispanic/Latino; 2 Native Hawaiian or other Pacific Islander, non-Hispanic/Latino), 36 international. Average age 27. 227 applicants, 77% accepted, 133 enrolled. *Faculty:* 104 full-time (1 woman), 14 part-time/adjunct (0 women). Expenses: Contact institution. *Financial support:* In 2010–11, 197 students received support, including 22 fellowships with full and partial tuition reimbursements available (averaging $15,050 per year), 200 research assistantships with full and partial tuition reimbursements available (averaging $11,883 per year), 98 teaching assistantships with full and partial tuition reimbursements available (averaging $10,029 per year); career-related internships or fieldwork, institutionally sponsored loans, scholarships/grants, and unspecified assistantships also available. Support available to part-time students. Financial award application deadline: 6/30; financial award applicants required to submit FAFSA. In 2010, 102 master's, 15 doctorates awarded. Offers chemical engineering (MS, PhD); civil engineering (MS, PhD); construction management (MS); electrical and computer engineering (MS, PhD); engineering and technology (MS, PhD); information technology (MS); manufacturing systems (MS); mechanical engineering (MS, PhD); technology and engineering education (MS). *Application deadline:* For fall admission, 1/15 for domestic and international students; for winter admission, 6/15 for domestic and international students; for spring admission, 1/15 for domestic and international students. *Application fee:* $50. Electronic applications accepted. *Application Contact:* Claire A. DeWitt, Adviser, 801-422-4541, Fax: 801-422-0270, E-mail: gradstudies@byu.edu. *Dean,* Dr. Alan R. Parkinson, 801-422-4327, Fax: 801-422-0218, E-mail: college@et.byu.edu.

J. Reuben Clark Law School Students: 449 full-time (154 women); includes 6 Black or African American, non-Hispanic/Latino; 3 American Indian or Alaska Native, non-Hispanic/Latino; 20 Asian, non-Hispanic/Latino; 25 Hispanic/Latino; 16 Native Hawaiian or other Pacific Islander, non-Hispanic/Latino, 4 international. Average age 25. 772 applicants, 28% accepted, 150 enrolled. *Faculty:* 37 full-time (10 women), 43 part-time/adjunct (11 women). Expenses: Contact institution. *Financial support:* In 2010–11, 159 students received support, including 159 fellowships (averaging $5,746 per year); research assistantships, teaching assistantships, career-related internships or fieldwork, institutionally sponsored loans, scholarships/grants, and health care benefits also available. Financial award application deadline: 6/1; financial award applicants required to submit FAFSA. In 2010, 145 first professional degrees, 8 master's awarded. Offers law (JD, LL M). *Application deadline:* For fall admission, 3/1 priority date for domestic students. Applications are processed on a rolling basis. *Application fee:* $50. Electronic applications accepted. *Application Contact:* GaeLynn Kuchar, Admissions Director, 801-422-4277, Fax: 801-422-0389, E-mail: kucharg@lawgate.byu.edu. *Dean,* James R. Rasband, 801-422-6383, Fax: 801-422-0389, E-mail: rasbandj@law.byu.edu.

Marriott School of Management Students: 696 full-time (154 women), 268 part-time (57 women); includes 8 Black or African American, non-Hispanic/Latino; 5 American Indian or Alaska Native, non-Hispanic/Latino; 48 Asian, non-Hispanic/Latino; 28 Hispanic/Latino, 65 international. Average age 30. 1,200 applicants, 55% accepted, 535 enrolled. *Faculty:* 126 full-time (10 women), 72 part-time/adjunct (24 women). Expenses: Contact institution. *Financial support:* In 2010–11, 439 students received support. Career-related internships or fieldwork, institutionally sponsored loans, scholarships/grants, and tuition waivers (full and partial) available. Financial award application deadline: 4/15; financial award applicants required to submit FAFSA. In 2010, 528 master's awarded. Offers accountancy (M Acc); business administration (MBA); finance (MPA); human resources (MPA); information systems (MISM); local government (MPA); management (EMPA, M Acc, MBA, MISM, MPA, MS); nonprofit management (MPA); public administration (EMPA, MPA); youth and family recreation (MS). *Application fee:* $50. Electronic applications accepted. *Application Contact:* Adviser, 801-422-4541, Fax: 801-378-5238, E-mail: gradstudies@byu.edu. *Dean,* Dr. Gary C. Cornia, 801-422-4121, Fax: 801-422-4501.

BROADVIEW UNIVERSITY, West Jordan, UT 84088

General Information Proprietary, coed, comprehensive institution.

GRADUATE UNITS

Graduate Programs

BROCK UNIVERSITY, St. Catharines, ON L2S 3A1, Canada

General Information Province-supported, coed, university. *Graduate housing:* Room and/or apartments available on a first-come, first-served basis to single students; on-campus housing not available to married students. *Research affiliation:* Registered Nurses Association of Ontario (nursing best practices), Canadian Honey Council (agriculture, therapeutic product development), Fly Fishing Canada/Trout Unlimited Canada (fisheries management), Henry Ford Health Centre (cancer epidemiology).

GRADUATE UNITS

Faculty of Graduate Studies *Degree program information:* Part-time and evening/weekend programs available. Electronic applications accepted.

Faculty of Applied Health Sciences Offers applied health sciences (M Sc, MA, PhD). Electronic applications accepted.

Faculty of Business *Degree program information:* Part-time programs available. Offers accountancy (M Acc); business (M Acc, M Sc, MBA); business administration (MBA); management (M Sc). Electronic applications accepted.

Faculty of Education *Degree program information:* Part-time and evening/weekend programs available. Offers education (M Ed, PhD). Electronic applications accepted.

Faculty of Humanities *Degree program information:* Part-time programs available. Offers applied linguistics (MA); classics (MA); English (MA); history (MA); humanities (MA); philosophy (MA); studies in comparative literatures and arts (MA). Electronic applications accepted.

Faculty of Mathematics and Science *Degree program information:* Part-time programs available. Offers biological sciences (M Sc, PhD); biotechnology (M Sc, PhD); chemistry

Brock University (continued)
(M Sc, PhD); computer science (M Sc); earth sciences (M Sc); mathematics and science (M Sc, PhD); mathematics and statistics (M Sc); physics (M Sc). Electronic applications accepted.

Faculty of Social Sciences *Degree program information:* Part-time programs available. Offers applied disability studies (MA, MADS, Diploma); behavioral neuroscience (MA, PhD); business economics (MBE); Canadian politics (MA); child and youth studies (MA); comparative politics (MA); critical sociology (MA); geography (MA); international relations (MA); life span development (MA, PhD); political theory or philosophy (MA); popular culture (MA); public policy (MA); social justice and equity studies (MA); social personality (MA, PhD); social sciences (MA, MADS, MBE, PhD, Diploma). Electronic applications accepted.

BROOKLYN COLLEGE OF THE CITY UNIVERSITY OF NEW YORK, Brooklyn, NY 11210-2889

General Information State and locally supported, coed, comprehensive institution. *Enrollment:* 587 full-time matriculated graduate/professional students (440 women), 2,918 part-time matriculated graduate/professional students (1,968 women). *Enrollment by degree level:* 3,353 master's, 152 other advanced degrees. Tuition, state resident: full-time $7360; part-time $310 per credit hour. Tuition, nonresident: full-time $13,800; part-time $575 per credit hour. *Required fees:* $190 per semester. *Graduate housing:* Room and/or apartments available on a first-come, first-served basis to single students; on-campus housing not available to married students. *Student services:* Campus employment opportunities, career counseling, child daycare facilities, exercise/wellness program, free psychological counseling, international student services, low-cost health insurance, multicultural affairs office, services for students with disabilities, writing training. *Library facilities:* Brooklyn College Library plus 1 other. *Online resources:* library catalog, web page, access to other libraries' catalogs. *Collection:* 1.3 million titles, 13,500 serial subscriptions, 21,731 audiovisual materials. *Research affiliation:* Donald Danforth Plant Science Center/DOEnergy FlowThru (biofuels), Crohn's and Colitis Foundation of America (Crohn's, ulcerative colitis, and other inflammatory bowel diseases), NARSAD (diffusion tensor imaging and structural MRI in youth at-risk for depression), Ajinomoto, Inc. (psychology), New York Hall of Science Motorola Foundation (education), National Geographic Society (anthropology and archaeology).

Computer facilities: 1,000 computers available on campus for general student use. A campuswide network can be accessed from off campus. Online class registration is available. *Web address:* http://www.brooklyn.cuny.edu/.

General Application Contact: Office of Admissions, 718-951-4536, Fax: 718-951-4506, E-mail: grads@brooklyn.cuny.edu.

GRADUATE UNITS

Division of Graduate Studies Students: 587 full-time (440 women), 2,918 part-time (1,968 women); includes 1,409 minority (842 Black or African American, non-Hispanic/Latino; 3 American Indian or Alaska Native, non-Hispanic/Latino; 244 Asian, non-Hispanic/Latino; 320 Hispanic/Latino), 311 international. Average age 31. 3,660 applicants, 52% accepted, 1155 enrolled. Expenses: Contact institution. *Financial support:* Career-related internships or fieldwork, Federal Work-Study, institutionally sponsored loans, and scholarships/grants available. Support available to part-time students. Financial award application deadline: 5/1; financial award applicants required to submit FAFSA. In 2010, 1,127 master's, 51 other advanced degrees awarded. *Degree program information:* Part-time and evening/weekend programs available. Offers accounting (MS); acting (MFA); art history (MA, PhD); audiology (Au D); biology (MA, PhD); business economics (MS); chemistry (MA, PhD); community health (MA, MPH, MS); community health education (MA); community-public health (MPH); computer science (MA, PhD); computer science and health science (MS); creative writing (MFA); criticism and history (MA); design and technical production (MFA); digital art (MFA); directing (MFA); drawing and painting (MFA); earth and environmental Sciences (MA, PhD); economics (MA); English (MA, PhD); exercise science and rehabilitation (MS); experimental psychology (MA); fiction (MFA); French (MA); grief counseling (CAS); health care management (MPH); health care policy and administration (MPH); history (MA, PhD); human relations (MA); industrial and organizational psychology (MA); information systems (MS); international affairs (MA); Judaic studies (MA); liberal studies (MA); mathematics (MA, PhD); media studies (MS); mental health counseling (MA); modern languages and literature (PhD); nutrition (MS); organizational behavior (MA); parallel and distributed computing (Advanced Certificate); performance and interactive media arts (MFA, CAS); performing arts management (MFA); photography (MFA); physical education (MS); physics (MA, PhD); playwriting (MFA); poetry (MFA); political science (MA, PhD); political science, urban policy and administration (MA); printmaking (MFA); psychology (PhD); public health (MPH); sculpture (MFA); sociology (MA, PhD); Spanish (MA); speech (MA); speech and hearing sciences (PhD); speech pathology (MS); television production (MFA); thanatology (MA); theater (PhD). *Application deadline:* For fall admission, 3/1 priority date for domestic students, 2/1 priority date for international students; for spring admission, 11/1 priority date for domestic students, 10/1 priority date for international students. Applications are processed on a rolling basis. *Application fee:* $125. Electronic applications accepted. *Application Contact:* Hernan Sierra, Graduate Admissions Coordinator, 718-951-4536, Fax: 718-951-4506, E-mail: grads@brooklyn.cuny.edu.

Conservatory of Music Students: 2 full-time (1 woman), 78 part-time (50 women); includes 19 minority (3 Black or African American, non-Hispanic/Latino; 4 Asian, non-Hispanic/Latino; 12 Hispanic/Latino), 14 international. Average age 29. 68 applicants, 74% accepted, 28 enrolled. Expenses: Contact institution. *Financial support:* Career-related internships or fieldwork, Federal Work-Study, institutionally sponsored loans, and scholarships/grants available. Support available to part-time students. Financial award application deadline: 5/1; financial award applicants required to submit FAFSA. In 2010, 22 master's awarded. *Degree program information:* Part-time programs available. Offers composition (MM); music (DMA, PhD); music education (MA); musicology (MA); performance (MM); performance practice (MA). *Application deadline:* For fall admission, 3/1 priority date for domestic students, 2/1 priority date for international students; for spring admission, 11/1 priority date for domestic students, 10/1 priority date for international students. Applications are processed on a rolling basis. *Application fee:* $125. Electronic applications accepted. *Application Contact:* Hernan Sierra, Graduate Admissions Coordinator, 718-951-4536, Fax: 718-951-4506, E-mail: grads@brooklyn.cuny.edu. *Chairperson,* Dr. Bruce MacIntyre, 718-951-5286, E-mail: brucem@brooklyn.cuny.edu.

School of Education Students: 254 full-time (198 women), 1,385 part-time (1,051 women); includes 684 minority (409 Black or African American, non-Hispanic/Latino; 3 American Indian or Alaska Native, non-Hispanic/Latino; 97 Asian, non-Hispanic/Latino; 175 Hispanic/Latino), 38 international. Average age 31. 1,102 applicants, 71% accepted, 552 enrolled. Expenses: Contact institution. *Financial support:* Fellowships, career-related internships or fieldwork, Federal Work-Study, institutionally sponsored loans, scholarships/grants, and tuition waivers (full and partial) available. Support available to part-time students. Financial award application deadline: 5/1; financial award applicants required to submit FAFSA. In 2010, 631 master's, 46 other advanced degrees awarded. *Degree program information:* Part-time and evening/weekend programs available. Offers adolescence science education (MAT); art teacher (MA); bilingual education (MS Ed); biology (MA); biology teacher (MA); birth-grade 2 (MS Ed); chemistry (MA); chemistry teacher (MA); earth science (MA); earth science teacher (MAT); education (MA, MAT, MS Ed, CAS); educational leadership (MS Ed); English teacher (MA); French teacher (MA); general science (MA); health and nutrition sciences: health teacher (MS Ed); liberal arts (MS Ed); mathematics (MS Ed); mathematics teacher (MA); middle childhood education (math) (MS Ed); music education (CAS); music teacher (MA); physical education teacher (MS Ed); physics (MA); physics teacher (MA); school counseling (MS Ed, CAS); school psychologist (MS Ed, CAS); school psychologist-bilingual (CAS); science/environmental education (MS Ed); social studies teacher (MA); Spanish teacher (MA); teacher of students with disabilities (MS Ed). *Application deadline:* For fall admission, 3/1 priority date for domestic students, 2/1 priority date for international students; for spring admission, 11/1 priority date for domestic students, 10/1 priority date for international students. Applications are processed on a rolling basis. *Application fee:* $125. Electronic applications accepted. *Application Contact:* Hernan Sierra, Graduate Admissions Coordinator, 718-951-4536, Fax: 718-951-4506, E-mail: grads@brooklyn.cuny.edu. *Dean,* Dr. Deborah Shanley, 718-951-5214, Fax: 718-951-4816, E-mail: dshanley@brooklyn.cuny.edu.

BROOKLYN LAW SCHOOL, Brooklyn, NY 11201-3798

General Information Independent, coed, graduate-only institution. *Graduate housing:* Rooms and/or apartments available to single students and guaranteed to married students. Housing application deadline: 5/1.

GRADUATE UNITS

Professional Program *Degree program information:* Part-time and evening/weekend programs available. Offers law (JD). JD/MBA offered jointly with Bernard M. Baruch College of the City University of New York; JD/MS with Pratt Institute; JD/MUP with Hunter College of the City University of New York; and JD/MA with Brooklyn College of the City University of New York. Electronic applications accepted.

BROOKS INSTITUTE, Santa Barbara, CA 93101

General Information Proprietary, coed, comprehensive institution. *Graduate housing:* On-campus housing not available.

GRADUATE UNITS

Graduate Program in Professional Photography *Degree program information:* Evening/weekend programs available. Offers professional photography (MFA). Electronic applications accepted.

BROWN UNIVERSITY, Providence, RI 02912

General Information Independent, coed, university. CGS member. *Graduate housing:* Room and/or apartments available to single students; on-campus housing not available to married students. *Research affiliation:* Woods Hole Oceanographic Institution–Marine Biological Laboratory, Rhode Island Reactor, International Center for Numismatic Studies, Meeting Street School.

GRADUATE UNITS

Graduate School *Degree program information:* Part-time programs available. Offers acting and directing (MFA); American civilization (MA, PhD); ancient Judaism (PhD); anthropology (AM, PhD); behavioral neuroscience (PhD); biochemistry (PhD); biology (MAT); chemistry (AM, Sc M, PhD); classics (MA, PhD); cognitive processes (PhD); cognitive science (Sc M, PhD); comparative literature (PhD); computer science (Sc M, PhD); early Christianity (PhD); economics (PhD); Egyptology (AM, PhD); electronic music and multimedia (PhD); elementary education (MAT); English (MAT); ethnomusicology (PhD); French studies (PhD); geological sciences (MA, Sc M, PhD); German (PhD); Hispanic studies (MA, PhD); history (MA, PhD); history of art and architecture (MA, PhD); history/social studies (MAT); Italian studies (PhD); linguistics (AM, PhD); literatures and cultures in English (MA, PhD); mathematics (M Sc, MA, PhD); museum studies (AM); neuroscience (PhD); nonfiction writing (MFA); philosophy (MA, PhD); physics (Sc M, PhD); playwriting (MFA); political science (PhD); public humanities (MA); religion and critical thought (PhD); religion in the ancient Mediterranean (PhD); religion, culture, and comparison (PhD); Russian language and literature (AM); sensation and perception (PhD); Slavic languages (AM); Slavic studies (PhD); social/developmental (PhD); sociology (AM, MA, PhD); teaching (MAT); theatre and performance studies (PhD); urban education policy (AM).

A. Alfred Taubman Center for Public Policy and American Institutions Offers public policy and American institutions (MPA, MPP).

Center for Environmental Studies *Degree program information:* Part-time programs available. Offers environmental studies (AM). Electronic applications accepted.

Center for Portuguese and Brazilian Studies Offers Brazilian studies (AM); Portuguese and Brazilian studies (AM, PhD); Portuguese Bilingual Education and Cross-Cultural Studies (AM).

Division of Applied Mathematics Offers applied mathematics (Sc M, PhD).

Division of Biology and Medicine *Degree program information:* Part-time programs available. Offers artificial organs, biomaterials, and cell technology (MA, Sc M, PhD); biochemistry (M Med Sc, Sc M, PhD); biology (MA, PhD); biology and medicine (M Med Sc, MA, MPH, MS, Sc M, PhD); biomedical engineering (MS, PhD); biostatistics (MS, PhD); cancer biology (PhD); cell biology (M Med Sc, Sc M, PhD); developmental biology (M Med Sc, Sc M, PhD); ecology and evolutionary biology (PhD); epidemiology (MS, PhD); health services research (MS, PhD); immunology (M Med Sc, Sc M, PhD); immunology and infection (PhD); medical science (PhD); molecular microbiology (M Med Sc, Sc M, PhD); molecular pharmacology and physiology (MA, Sc M, PhD); neuroscience (PhD); pathobiology (Sc M); public health (MPH); statistical science (MS, PhD); toxicology and environmental pathology (PhD). Electronic applications accepted.

Division of Engineering Offers biomedical engineering (Sc M, PhD); electrical sciences and computer engineering (Sc M, PhD); fluid, thermal and chemical processes (Sc M, PhD); materials science and engineering (Sc M, PhD); mechanics of solids (Sc M, PhD).

Joukowsky Institute for Archaeology and the Ancient World Offers archaeology and the ancient world (PhD).

National Institutes of Health Sponsored Programs Offers neuroscience (PhD).

Program in Medicine Offers medicine (MD).

BRYAN COLLEGE, Dayton, TN 37321-7000

General Information Independent-religious, coed, comprehensive institution.

GRADUATE UNITS

MBA Program Offers business administration (MBA).

BRYANLGH COLLEGE OF HEALTH SCIENCES, Lincoln, NE 68506-1398

General Information Independent, coed, comprehensive institution.

GRADUATE UNITS

School of Nurse Anesthesia Offers nurse anesthesia (MS).

BRYANT UNIVERSITY, Smithfield, RI 02917

General Information Independent, coed, comprehensive institution. *Enrollment:* 3,606 graduate, professional, and undergraduate students; 103 full-time matriculated graduate/professional students (44 women), 177 part-time matriculated graduate/professional students (69 women). *Enrollment by degree level:* 280 master's. *Graduate faculty:* 40 full-time (10 women), 12 part-time/adjunct (1 woman). *Tuition:* Full-time $32,580; part-time $2580 per course. One-time fee: $800. Tuition and fees vary according to program. *Graduate housing:* On-campus housing not available. *Student services:* Campus employment opportunities, campus safety program, career counseling, exercise/wellness program, free psychological counseling, international student services, low-cost health insurance, multicultural affairs office, services for students with disabilities, writing training. *Library facilities:* Douglas and Judith Krupp Library plus 1 other. *Online resources:* library catalog, web page, access to other libraries' catalogs. *Collection:* 282,176 titles, 68,915 serial subscriptions, 2,137 audiovisual materials.

Computer facilities: Computer purchase and lease plans are available. 478 computers available on campus for general student use. A campuswide network can be accessed from student residence rooms and from off campus. Online class registration, e-mail, online library, wireless network, student Web hosts are available. *Web address:* http://www.bryant.edu/.

General Application Contact: Kristopher T. Sullivan, Assistant Dean of the Graduate School, 401-232-6230, Fax: 401-232-6494, E-mail: gradprog@bryant.edu.

GRADUATE UNITS

Graduate School of Business Students: 103 full-time (44 women), 177 part-time (69 women); includes 7 Black or African American, non-Hispanic/Latino; 1 American Indian or Alaska Native, non-Hispanic/Latino; 5 Asian, non-Hispanic/Latino; 8 Hispanic/Latino, 7 international. Average age 29. 206 applicants, 75% accepted, 90 enrolled. *Faculty:* 40 full-time (10 women), 12 part-time/adjunct (1 woman). Expenses: Contact institution. *Financial support:* In 2010–11, 40 students received support, including 20 research assistantships (averaging $14,475 per year); scholarships/grants and unspecified assistantships also available. Support available to part-time students. Financial award application deadline: 2/15; financial award applicants required to submit FAFSA. In 2010, 168 master's awarded. *Degree program information:* Part-time and evening/weekend programs available. Offers business administration (MBA); general business (MBA); professional accountancy (MPAC); taxation (MST). *Application deadline:* For fall admission, 7/15 for domestic and international students; for spring admission, 11/15 for domestic and international students. Applications are processed on a rolling basis. *Application fee:* $80. Electronic applications accepted. *Application Contact:* Ellen Hudon, Associate Director, 401-232-6230, Fax: 401-232-6494, E-mail: ehudon@bryant.edu. *Assistant Dean*, Kristopher T. Sullivan, 401-232-6230, Fax: 401-232-6494, E-mail: sullivan@bryant.edu.

BRYN ATHYN COLLEGE OF THE NEW CHURCH, Bryn Athyn, PA 19009-0717

General Information Independent-religious, coed, comprehensive institution. *Graduate housing:* Room and/or apartments available on a first-come, first-served basis to single students; on-campus housing not available to married students. Housing application deadline: 1/31.

GRADUATE UNITS

Academy of the New Church Theological School *Degree program information:* Part-time programs available. Postbaccalaureate distance learning degree programs offered (minimal on-campus study). Offers divinity (M Div); religious studies (MA).

BRYN MAWR COLLEGE, Bryn Mawr, PA 19010-2899

General Information Independent, Undergraduate: women only; graduate: coed, university. CGS member. *Enrollment:* 1,755 graduate, professional, and undergraduate students; 235 full-time matriculated graduate/professional students (194 women), 136 part-time matriculated graduate/professional students (121 women). *Enrollment by degree level:* 37 master's, 334 doctoral. *Graduate faculty:* 82. *Graduate housing:* Room and/or apartments available on a first-come, first-served basis to single students. *Student services:* Campus employment opportunities, career counseling, exercise/wellness program, international student services, low-cost health insurance, multicultural affairs office, services for students with disabilities. *Online resources:* library catalog.

Computer facilities: 200 computers available on campus for general student use. A campuswide network can be accessed from student residence rooms and from off campus. Online class registration is available. *Web address:* http://www.brynmawr.edu/.

General Application Contact: Office of Admissions, 610-526-5152.

GRADUATE UNITS

Graduate School of Arts and Sciences Students: 125 full-time (98 women), 63 part-time (55 women); includes 14 Black or African American, non-Hispanic/Latino; 7 Asian, non-Hispanic/Latino; 4 Hispanic/Latino; 1 Two or more races, non-Hispanic/Latino, 8 international. Average age 31. 190 applicants, 24% accepted, 29 enrolled. *Faculty:* 52. Expenses: Contact institution. *Financial support:* In 2010–11, 53 fellowships (averaging $10,995 per year) were awarded; career-related internships or fieldwork, Federal Work-Study, institutionally sponsored loans, unspecified assistantships, and tuition awards also available. Support available to part-time students. Financial award application deadline: 1/3. In 2010, 22 master's, 11 doctorates awarded. *Degree program information:* Part-time programs available. Offers arts and sciences (MA, PhD); chemistry (MA, PhD); classical and Near Eastern archaeology (MA, PhD); French (MA, PhD); Greek, Latin, and Classical studies (MA, PhD); history of art (MA, PhD); mathematics (MA, PhD); physics (MA, PhD). *Application deadline:* For fall admission, 1/3 for domestic and international students. Applications are processed on a rolling basis. *Application fee:* $50. *Application Contact:* Teri A. Lobo, Secretary, 610-526-5072, Fax: 610-526-5076, E-mail: lrmiller@brynmawr.edu. *Dean*, Dr. Elizabeth McCormack, 610-526-5073, Fax: 610-526-5076, E-mail: graddean@brynmawr.edu.

Graduate School of Social Work and Social Research Students: 110 full-time (96 women), 73 part-time (66 women); includes 44 minority (27 Black or African American, non-Hispanic/Latino; 7 Asian, non-Hispanic/Latino; 5 Hispanic/Latino; 5 Two or more races, non-Hispanic/Latino). Average age 34. 248 applicants, 64% accepted, 108 enrolled. *Faculty:* 14 full-time (7 women), 16 part-time/adjunct (2 women). Expenses: Contact institution. *Financial support:* In 2010–11, 183 students received support, including 29 fellowships with full and partial tuition reimbursements available (averaging $2,517 per year), 1 research assistantship with full and partial tuition reimbursement available (averaging $9,333 per year), 7 teaching assistantships with full and partial tuition reimbursements available (averaging $8,680 per year); career-related internships or fieldwork, Federal Work-Study, institutionally sponsored loans, scholarships/grants, tuition waivers (full and partial), and dissertation award (PhD) also available. Support available to part-time students. Financial award application deadline: 3/1; financial award applicants required to submit FAFSA. In 2010, 89 master's, 7 doctorates awarded. *Degree program information:* Part-time and evening/weekend programs available. Offers social work and social research (MLSP, MSS, PhD). *Application deadline:* For fall admission, 3/31 priority date for domestic and international students. Applications are processed on a rolling basis. *Application fee:* $50. Electronic applications accepted. *Application Contact:* Diane D. Craw, Assistant to the Dean and Administrative Director, Social Work, 610-520-2612, Fax: 610-520-2613, E-mail: dcraw@brynmawr.edu. *Dean*, Dr. Darlyne Bailey, 610-520-2610, Fax: 610-520-2613, E-mail: dbailey01@brynmawr.edu.

BUCKNELL UNIVERSITY, Lewisburg, PA 17837

General Information Independent, coed, comprehensive institution. CGS member. *Enrollment:* 3,615 graduate, professional, and undergraduate students; 57 full-time matriculated graduate/professional students (30 women), 21 part-time matriculated graduate/professional students (14 women). *Enrollment by degree level:* 78 master's. *Graduate faculty:* 140 full-time (50 women), 5 part-time/adjunct (2 women). *Tuition:* Full-time $36,992; part-time $4624 per course. *Graduate housing:* On-campus housing not available. *Student services:* Campus employment opportunities, campus safety program, career counseling, free psychological counseling, international student services, low-cost health insurance, multicultural affairs office, services for students with disabilities, teacher training, writing training. *Library facilities:* Ellen Clarke Bertrand Library plus 2 others. *Online resources:* library catalog, web page, access to other libraries' catalogs. *Collection:* 917,328 titles, 36,242 serial subscriptions, 22,457 audiovisual materials.

Computer facilities: 970 computers available on campus for general student use. A campuswide network can be accessed from student residence rooms and from off campus. Online class registration is available. *Web address:* http://www.bucknell.edu/.

General Application Contact: Dr. James P. Rice, Dean of Graduate Studies, 570-577-1304, Fax: 570-577-3760, E-mail: gradstds@bucknell.edu.

GRADUATE UNITS

Graduate Studies Students: 57 full-time (30 women), 21 part-time (14 women); includes 1 Asian, non-Hispanic/Latino, 4 international. 113 applicants, 35% accepted, 31 enrolled. *Faculty:* 140 full-time (50 women), 5 part-time/adjunct (2 women). Expenses: Contact institution. *Financial support:* In 2010–11, 69 students received support, including 52 teaching assistantships with tuition reimbursements available; fellowships, research assistantships, scholarships/grants, tuition waivers (partial), and unspecified assistantships also available. Financial award application deadline: 2/1. In 2010, 46 master's awarded. *Degree program information:* Part-time programs available. *Application deadline:* For fall admission, 2/1 priority date for domestic students, 1/1 priority date for international students; for spring admission, 12/1 priority date for domestic students. *Application fee:* $25. *Application Contact:* Gretchen H. Fegley, Coordinator, 570-577-3655, Fax: 570-577-3760, E-mail: gfegley@bucknell.edu. *Associate Provost/Dean*, Dr. James P. Rice, 570-577-3655, Fax: 570-577-3760, E-mail: gradstds@bucknell.edu.

College of Arts and Sciences *Degree program information:* Part-time programs available. Offers animal behavior (MA, MS); arts and sciences (MA, MS, MS Ed); biology (MA, MS); chemistry (MA, MS); classroom teaching (MS Ed); college student personnel (MS Ed); educational research (MS Ed); elementary and secondary counseling (MA, MS Ed); elementary and secondary principalship (MA, MS Ed); English (MA); mathematics (MA, MS); psychology (MA, MS); reading (MA, MS Ed); school psychology (MS Ed); supervision of curriculum and instruction (MA, MS Ed).

College of Engineering *Degree program information:* Part-time programs available. Offers chemical engineering (MS, MS Ch E); civil and environmental engineering (MS, MSCE, MSEV); electrical engineering (MS, MSEE); engineering (MS, MS Ch E, MSCE, MSEE, MSEV, MSME); mechanical engineering (MS, MSME).

BUENA VISTA UNIVERSITY, Storm Lake, IA 50588

General Information Independent-religious, coed, comprehensive institution. *Graduate housing:* Room and/or apartments available on a first-come, first-served basis to single students; on-campus housing not available to married students. Housing application deadline: 5/1.

GRADUATE UNITS

School of Education *Degree program information:* Part-time and evening/weekend programs available. Postbaccalaureate distance learning degree programs offered (minimal on-campus study). Offers curriculum and instruction (M Ed); school guidance and counseling (MS Ed). Program offered in summer only. Electronic applications accepted.

BUFFALO STATE COLLEGE, STATE UNIVERSITY OF NEW YORK, Buffalo, NY 14222-1095

General Information State-supported, coed, comprehensive institution. CGS member. *Graduate housing:* Room and/or apartments available on a first-come, first-served basis to single students; on-campus housing not available to married students. Housing application deadline: 8/15. *Research affiliation:* Friends of Buffalo River, Research Institute on Addictions at the University of Buffalo, Roswell Park Memorial Institute, Hauptman-Woodward Medical Research Institute, Ecology and Environment Corporation, Phillip Morris Foundation.

GRADUATE UNITS

The Graduate School *Degree program information:* Part-time and evening/weekend programs available. Postbaccalaureate distance learning degree programs offered (no on-campus study). Offers multidisciplinary studies (MA, MS).

Faculty of Applied Science and Education *Degree program information:* Part-time and evening/weekend programs available. Postbaccalaureate distance learning degree programs offered (no on-campus study). Offers adult education (MS, Certificate); applied science and education (MPS, MS, MS Ed, CAS, Certificate); business and marketing education (MS Ed); career and technical education (MS Ed); childhood education (grades 1-6) (MS Ed); creative studies (MS); criminal justice (MS); early childhood and childhood curriculum and instruction (MS Ed); early childhood education (birth-grade 2) (MS Ed); educational computing (MS Ed); educational leadership (CAS); elementary education (MS Ed); human resources development (Certificate); industrial technology (MS); literacy specialist (MPS, MS Ed); literacy specialist (birth-grade 6) (MS Ed); literacy specialist (grades 5-12) (MPS); special education (MS Ed); special education: adolescents (MS Ed); special education: childhood (MS Ed); special education: early childhood (MS Ed); speech-language pathology (MS Ed); student personnel administration (MS); teaching bilingual exceptional individuals (MS Ed); technology education (MS Ed).

Faculty of Arts and Humanities *Degree program information:* Part-time and evening/weekend programs available. Offers art conservation (CAS); art education (MS Ed); arts and humanities (MA, MS Ed, CAS); conservation of historic works and art works (MA); English (MA); secondary education (MS Ed).

Faculty of Natural and Social Sciences *Degree program information:* Part-time and evening/weekend programs available. Offers applied economics (MA); biology (MA); chemistry (MA); history (MA); mathematics education (MS Ed); natural and social sciences (MA, MS Ed); secondary education (MS Ed); secondary education physics (MS Ed).

BUTLER UNIVERSITY, Indianapolis, IN 46208-3485

General Information Independent, coed, comprehensive institution. *Enrollment:* 4,640 graduate, professional, and undergraduate students; 359 full-time matriculated graduate/professional students (223 women), 384 part-time matriculated graduate/professional students (209 women). *Enrollment by degree level:* 239 first professional, 504 master's. *Graduate faculty:* 73 full-time (31 women), 27 part-time/adjunct (14 women). *Tuition:* Full-time $29,740; part-time $1250 per credit. *Required fees:* $818; $430 per credit. Tuition and fees vary according to program. *Graduate housing:* Room and/or apartments available on a first-come, first-served basis to single students; on-campus housing not available to married students. Housing application deadline: 8/1. *Student services:* Campus employment opportunities, campus safety program, career counseling, free psychological counseling, international student services, low-cost health insurance, multicultural affairs office. *Library facilities:* Irwin Library System plus 1 other. *Online resources:* library catalog, web page, access to other libraries' catalogs.

Computer facilities: 450 computers available on campus for general student use. A campuswide network can be accessed from student residence rooms and from off campus. Online class registration is available. *Web address:* http://www.butler.edu/.

General Application Contact: Pamela Bender, Student Services Specialist, 317-940-8100, Fax: 317-940-8250, E-mail: pbender@butler.edu.

GRADUATE UNITS

College of Business Administration Students: 37 full-time (11 women), 163 part-time (53 women); includes 11 minority (7 Black or African American, non-Hispanic/Latino; 4 Asian, non-Hispanic/Latino), 13 international. Average age 32. 195 applicants, 53% accepted, 45 enrolled. *Faculty:* 17 full-time (4 women), 4 part-time/adjunct (0 women). Expenses: Contact institution. *Financial support:* Career-related internships or fieldwork and institutionally sponsored loans available. Support available to part-time students. Financial award application deadline: 7/15; financial award applicants required to submit FAFSA. In 2010, 94 master's awarded. *Degree program information:* Part-time and evening/weekend programs available. Offers business administration (MBA, MP Acc). *Application deadline:* For fall admission, 8/15 priority date for domestic students. Applications are processed on a rolling basis. *Application fee:* $35. Electronic applications accepted. *Application Contact:* Stephanie Judge, Director of Marketing, 317-940-9886, Fax: 317-940-9455, E-mail: sjudge@butler.edu. *Dean*, Dr. Chuck Williams, 317-940-8491, Fax: 317-940-9455, E-mail: crwillia@butler.edu.

College of Education Students: 11 full-time (8 women), 136 part-time (108 women); includes 22 minority (18 Black or African American, non-Hispanic/Latino; 1 Asian, non-Hispanic/Latino; 2 Hispanic/Latino; 1 Two or more races, non-Hispanic/Latino), 7 international. Average age 31. 66 applicants, 62% accepted, 24 enrolled. *Faculty:* 11 full-time (8 women), 9 part-time/adjunct (7 women). Expenses: Contact institution. *Financial support:* Institutionally sponsored loans available. Support available to part-time students. Financial award application deadline: 7/15; financial award applicants required to submit FAFSA. In 2010, 52 master's awarded. *Degree program information:* Part-time and evening/weekend programs available. Offers administration (MS); elementary education (MS); reading (MS); school counseling (MS); secondary education (MS); special education (MS). *Application deadline:* For fall admission, 8/15 priority date for domestic students. Applications are processed on a rolling basis. *Application fee:* $35. Electronic applications accepted. *Application Contact:* Karen Farrell, Department Secretary, 317-940-9220, E-mail: kfarrell@butler.edu. *Dean*, Dr. Ena Shelley, 317-940-9752, Fax: 317-940-6481.

College of Liberal Arts and Sciences Students: 4 full-time (1 woman), 48 part-time (29 women); includes 3 minority (1 Black or African American, non-Hispanic/Latino; 1 Asian, non-Hispanic/Latino; 1 Two or more races, non-Hispanic/Latino), 3 international. Average age 37. 55 applicants, 56% accepted, 17 enrolled. *Faculty:* 6 full-time (3 women). Expenses: Contact institution. *Financial support:* Career-related internships or fieldwork, institutionally sponsored loans, and tuition waivers (full and partial) available. Support available to part-time students. Financial award applicants required to submit FAFSA. In 2010, 3 master's awarded.

Butler University (continued)

Degree program information: Part-time and evening/weekend programs available. Offers English (MA); history (MA); liberal arts and sciences (MA). *Application deadline:* For fall admission, 8/15 priority date for domestic students. Applications are processed on a rolling basis. *Application fee:* $35. Electronic applications accepted. *Application Contact:* Pamela Bender, Student Services Specialist, 317-940-8100, Fax: 317-940-8250, E-mail: pbender@butler.edu. *Dean*, Dr. Jay Howard, 317-940-9874, E-mail: jrhoward@butler.edu.

College of Pharmacy Students: 284 full-time (192 women), 14 part-time (7 women); includes 22 minority (6 Black or African American, non-Hispanic/Latino; 9 Asian, non-Hispanic/Latino; 7 Hispanic/Latino), 15 international. Average age 24. 63 applicants, 6% accepted, 3 enrolled. *Faculty:* 20 full-time (12 women), 1 (woman) part-time/adjunct. Expenses: Contact institution. *Financial support:* Applicants required to submit FAFSA. In 2010, 107 first professional degrees, 50 master's awarded. *Degree program information:* Part-time and evening/weekend programs available. Offers pharmaceutical science (Pharm D, MS); physician assistance studies (MS). *Application deadline:* For fall admission, 8/1 priority date for domestic students; for spring admission, 12/15 for domestic students. Applications are processed on a rolling basis. *Application fee:* $35. Electronic applications accepted. *Application Contact:* Dr. Bruce Clayton, Professor, 317-940-9830, E-mail: bclayton@butler.edu. *Dean*, Dr. Mary Andritz, 317-940-9451, Fax: 317-940-6172, E-mail: mandritz@butler.edu.

Jordan College of Fine Arts Students: 23 full-time (11 women), 23 part-time (12 women), 5 international. Average age 27. 45 applicants, 69% accepted, 17 enrolled. *Faculty:* 19 full-time (4 women), 13 part-time/adjunct (6 women). Expenses: Contact institution. *Financial support:* In 2010–11, 15 teaching assistantships with full tuition reimbursements (averaging $2,500 per year) were awarded; fellowships, career-related internships or fieldwork, institutionally sponsored loans, and scholarships/grants also available. Support available to part-time students. Financial award application deadline: 7/15; financial award applicants required to submit FAFSA. In 2010, 16 master's awarded. *Degree program information:* Part-time and evening/weekend programs available. Offers composition (MM); conducting (MM); fine arts (MM); music (MM); music education (MM); music history (MM); organ (MM); performance (MM). *Application deadline:* For fall admission, 8/15 priority date for domestic students. Applications are processed on a rolling basis. *Application fee:* $35. Electronic applications accepted. *Application Contact:* Kathy Lang, Admission Representative, 317-940-9646, Fax: 317-940-9658, E-mail: klang@butler.edu. *Interim Dean*, Michelle Jarvis, 317-940-9961, Fax: 317-940-9658, E-mail: mjarvis@butler.edu.

CABRINI COLLEGE, Radnor, PA 19087-3698

General Information Independent-religious, coed, comprehensive institution. CGS member. *Enrollment:* 3,440 graduate, professional, and undergraduate students; 175 full-time matriculated graduate/professional students (119 women), 1,850 part-time matriculated graduate/professional students (1,423 women). *Enrollment by degree level:* 2,025 master's. *Graduate faculty:* 4 full-time (3 women), 141 part-time/adjunct (87 women). *Tuition:* Part-time $575 per credit. *Graduate housing:* On-campus housing not available. *Student services:* Campus safety program, career counseling, exercise/wellness program, free psychological counseling, international student services, low-cost health insurance, multicultural affairs office, services for students with disabilities, teacher training. *Library facilities:* Holy Spirit Library. *Online resources:* library catalog, web page. *Collection:* 93,388 titles, 61,397 serial subscriptions, 2,833 audiovisual materials.

Computer facilities: 469 computers available on campus for general student use. A campuswide network can be accessed from student residence rooms. Online class registration, account balances and other services are available. *Web address:* http://www.cabrini.edu/.

General Application Contact: Bruce D. Bryde, Director of Enrollment and Recruiting, 610-902-8291, Fax: 610-902-8522, E-mail: bruce.d.bryde@cabrini.edu.

GRADUATE UNITS

Graduate and Professional Studies Students: 175 full-time (119 women), 1,850 part-time (1,423 women); includes 273 minority (186 Black or African American, non-Hispanic/Latino; 3 American Indian or Alaska Native, non-Hispanic/Latino; 24 Asian, non-Hispanic/Latino; 48 Hispanic/Latino; 5 Native Hawaiian or other Pacific Islander, non-Hispanic/Latino; 7 Two or more races, non-Hispanic/Latino), 3 international. Average age 34. 724 applicants, 74% accepted, 496 enrolled. *Faculty:* 4 full-time (3 women), 141 part-time/adjunct (87 women). Expenses: Contact institution. *Financial support:* Career-related internships or fieldwork and unspecified assistantships available. Support available to part-time students. Financial award applicants required to submit FAFSA. In 2010, 728 master's awarded. *Degree program information:* Part-time and evening/weekend programs available. Offers education (M Ed); organization leadership (MS). *Application deadline:* For fall admission, 7/29 priority date for domestic students, 7/29 for international students; for spring admission, 12/9 for domestic and international students. Applications are processed on a rolling basis. *Application fee:* $50. Electronic applications accepted. *Application Contact:* Bruce D. Bryde, Director of Enrollment and Recruiting, 610-902-8291, Fax: 610-902-8522, E-mail: bruce.d.bryde@cabrini.edu. *Interim Dean*, Dr. Dennis R. Dougherty, 610-902-8501, Fax: 610-902-8522, E-mail: dennis.dougherty@cabrini.edu.

CALDWELL COLLEGE, Caldwell, NJ 07006-6195

General Information Independent-religious, coed, comprehensive institution. CGS member. *Graduate housing:* On-campus housing not available.

GRADUATE UNITS

Graduate Studies *Degree program information:* Part-time and evening/weekend programs available. Postbaccalaureate distance learning degree programs offered (minimal on-campus study). Offers accounting (MBA); applied behavior analysis (MA, PhD); art therapy (MA); business administration (MBA); counseling psychology (MA); curriculum and instruction (MA); educational administration (MA); pastoral ministry (MA); school counseling (MA); special education (MA). Electronic applications accepted.

CALIFORNIA BAPTIST UNIVERSITY, Riverside, CA 92504-3206

General Information Independent-religious, coed, comprehensive institution. *Enrollment:* 4,715 graduate, professional, and undergraduate students; 414 full-time matriculated graduate/professional students (305 women), 503 part-time matriculated graduate/professional students (399 women). *Enrollment by degree level:* 917 master's. *Graduate faculty:* 65 full-time (31 women), 37 part-time/adjunct (20 women). *Tuition:* Full-time $8532; part-time $474 per unit. *Required fees:* $355 per semester. One-time fee: $45 full-time. Tuition and fees vary according to course load and program. *Graduate housing:* Rooms and/or apartments available on a first-come, first-served basis to single and married students. Typical cost: $3300 per year for single students; $3900 per year for married students. *Student services:* Campus employment opportunities, campus safety program, career counseling, exercise/wellness program, free psychological counseling, international student services, low-cost health insurance, services for students with disabilities, teacher training, writing training. *Library facilities:* Annie Gabriel Library. *Online resources:* library catalog, web page, access to other libraries' catalogs. *Collection:* 207,053 titles, 22,925 serial subscriptions, 6,292 audiovisual materials.

Computer facilities: Computer purchase and lease plans are available. 279 computers available on campus for general student use. A campuswide network can be accessed from student residence rooms and from off campus. Online class registration is available. *Web address:* http://www.calbaptist.edu/.

General Application Contact: Gail Ronveaux, Dean of Graduate Enrollment, 951-343-5045, Fax: 951-343-5095, E-mail: graduateadmissions@calbaptist.edu.

GRADUATE UNITS

Program in Athletic Training Students: 30 full-time (19 women); includes 4 Black or African American, non-Hispanic/Latino; 1 American Indian or Alaska Native, non-Hispanic/Latino; 1 Asian, non-Hispanic/Latino; 3 Hispanic/Latino; 1 Native Hawaiian or other Pacific Islander, non-Hispanic/Latino, 1 international. 37 applicants, 73% accepted, 15 enrolled. *Faculty:* 3 full-time (2 women). Expenses: Contact institution. *Financial support:* Federal Work-Study, scholarships/grants, and unspecified assistantships available. Financial award applicants required to submit FAFSA. In 2010, 12 master's awarded. Offers athletic training (MS). *Application deadline:* For fall admission, 8/1 priority date for domestic students, 7/1 for international students; for spring admission, 12/1 priority date for domestic students, 10/15 for international students. Applications are processed on a rolling basis. *Application fee:* $45. Electronic applications accepted. *Application Contact:* Gail Ronveaux, Dean of Graduate Enrollment, 951-343-5045, Fax: 951-343-5095, E-mail: graduateadmissions@calbaptist.edu. *Director*, Dr. Nicole MacDonald, 951-343-4379.

Program in Business Administration Students: 37 full-time (19 women), 17 part-time (9 women); includes 7 Black or African American, non-Hispanic/Latino; 3 Asian, non-Hispanic/Latino; 10 Hispanic/Latino, 7 international. 24 applicants, 92% accepted, 16 enrolled. *Faculty:* 8 full-time (2 women), 1 (woman) part-time/adjunct. Expenses: Contact institution. *Financial support:* Federal Work-Study and scholarships/grants available. Support available to part-time students. Financial award applicants required to submit FAFSA. In 2010, 43 master's awarded. *Degree program information:* Part-time and evening/weekend programs available. Offers accounting (PhD); management (MBA). *Application deadline:* For fall admission, 8/1 priority date for domestic students, 7/1 for international students; for spring admission, 12/1 priority date for domestic students, 10/15 for international students. Applications are processed on a rolling basis. *Application fee:* $45. Electronic applications accepted. *Application Contact:* Gail Ronveaux, Dean of Graduate Enrollment, 951-343-5045, Fax: 951-343-5095, E-mail: graduateadmissions@calbaptist.edu. *Dean, School of Business*, Dr. Andrew Herrity, 951-343-4427, Fax: 951-343-4361, E-mail: aherrity@calbaptist.edu.

Program in Counseling Ministry Students: 8 full-time (all women), 3 part-time (2 women); includes 4 Black or African American, non-Hispanic/Latino; 2 Hispanic/Latino. 3 applicants, 100% accepted, 3 enrolled. *Faculty:* 4 full-time (0 women). Expenses: Contact institution. *Financial support:* Federal Work-Study and scholarships/grants available. Support available to part-time students. Financial award applicants required to submit FAFSA. In 2010, 1 master's awarded. *Degree program information:* Part-time programs available. Offers counseling ministry (MA). *Application deadline:* For fall admission, 8/1 priority date for domestic students, 7/1 for international students; for spring admission, 12/1 priority date for domestic students, 10/15 for international students. Applications are processed on a rolling basis. *Application fee:* $45. Electronic applications accepted. *Application Contact:* Gail Ronveaux, Dean of Graduate Enrollment, 951-343-5045, Fax: 951-343-5095, E-mail: graduateadmissions@calbaptist.edu. *Director*, Dr. Nathan Lewis, 951-343-4348, Fax: 951-343-4569, E-mail: nlewis@calbaptist.edu.

Program in Counseling Psychology Students: 151 full-time (126 women), 50 part-time (42 women); includes 107 minority (34 Black or African American, non-Hispanic/Latino; 2 American Indian or Alaska Native, non-Hispanic/Latino; 7 Asian, non-Hispanic/Latino; 61 Hispanic/Latino; 3 Two or more races, non-Hispanic/Latino), 1 international. 97 applicants, 91% accepted, 76 enrolled. *Faculty:* 13 full-time (8 women), 15 part-time/adjunct (8 women). Expenses: Contact institution. *Financial support:* Career-related internships or fieldwork, Federal Work-Study, scholarships/grants, traineeships, and unspecified assistantships available. Support available to part-time students. Financial award applicants required to submit FAFSA. In 2010, 51 master's awarded. *Degree program information:* Part-time programs available. Offers professional counseling (MS); professional ministry (MS). *Application deadline:* For fall admission, 9/1 for domestic students, 7/1 for international students; for spring admission, 1/3 for domestic students, 10/15 for international students. Applications are processed on a rolling basis. *Application fee:* $45. Electronic applications accepted. *Application Contact:* Gail Ronveaux, Dean of Graduate Enrollment, 951-343-5045, Fax: 951-343-5095, E-mail: graduateadmissions@calbaptist.edu. *Director*, Dr. Mischa Routon, 951-343-4206, Fax: 951-343-4569, E-mail: mrouton@calbaptist.edu.

Program in Education Students: 69 full-time (55 women), 346 part-time (279 women); includes 148 minority (32 Black or African American, non-Hispanic/Latino; 4 American Indian or Alaska Native, non-Hispanic/Latino; 11 Asian, non-Hispanic/Latino; 97 Hispanic/Latino; 3 Native Hawaiian or other Pacific Islander, non-Hispanic/Latino; 1 Two or more races, non-Hispanic/Latino). 134 applicants, 100% accepted, 118 enrolled. *Faculty:* 15 full-time (10 women), 8 part-time/adjunct (6 women). Expenses: Contact institution. *Financial support:* Career-related internships or fieldwork, Federal Work-Study, and scholarships/grants available. Support available to part-time students. Financial award applicants required to submit FAFSA. In 2010, 53 master's awarded. *Degree program information:* Part-time programs available. Offers educational leadership for faith-based instruction (MS); educational leadership for public institutions (MS); educational technology (MS); instructional computer applications (MS); international education (MS); reading (MS); school counseling (MS); school psychology (MS); special education (MS); special education in mild/moderate disabilities (MS); special education in moderate/severe disabilities (MS); teaching (MS); teaching and learning (MS Ed). *Application deadline:* For fall admission, 8/1 priority date for domestic students, 7/1 for international students; for spring admission, 12/1 priority date for domestic students, 10/15 priority date for international students. Applications are processed on a rolling basis. *Application fee:* $45. Electronic applications accepted. *Application Contact:* Gail Ronveaux, Dean of Graduate Enrollment, 951-343-5045, Fax: 951-343-5095, E-mail: graduateadmissions@calbaptist.edu. *Dean, School of Education*, Dr. Mary Crist, 951-343-4313, Fax: 951-343-4516, E-mail: mcrist@calbaptist.edu.

Program in English Students: 7 full-time (5 women), 20 part-time (17 women); includes 1 Hispanic/Latino, 5 international. 11 applicants, 82% accepted, 6 enrolled. *Faculty:* 4 full-time (3 women). Expenses: Contact institution. *Financial support:* Federal Work-Study and scholarships/grants available. Support available to part-time students. Financial award applicants required to submit FAFSA. In 2010, 8 master's awarded. *Degree program information:* Part-time programs available. Offers English pedagogy (MA); literature (MA); teaching English as a second language (TESOL) (MA). *Application deadline:* For fall admission, 8/1 priority date for domestic students, 7/1 for international students; for spring admission, 12/1 priority date for domestic students, 10/15 for international students. Applications are processed on a rolling basis. *Application fee:* $45. Electronic applications accepted. *Application Contact:* Gail Ronveaux, Dean of Graduate Enrollment, 951-343-5045, Fax: 951-343-5095, E-mail: graduateadmissions@calbaptist.edu. *Director*, Dr. Jennifer Newton, 951-343-4276, Fax: 951-343-4661, E-mail: jnewton@calbaptist.edu.

Program in Forensic Psychology Students: 13 full-time (11 women), 7 part-time (5 women); includes 1 Black or African American, non-Hispanic/Latino; 3 Asian, non-Hispanic/Latino; 7 Hispanic/Latino. 10 applicants, 100% accepted, 9 enrolled. *Faculty:* 3 full-time (2 women), 2 part-time/adjunct (1 woman). Expenses: Contact institution. *Financial support:* Federal Work-Study and scholarships/grants available. Support available to part-time students. Financial award applicants required to submit FAFSA. In 2010, 9 master's awarded. *Degree program information:* Part-time programs available. Offers forensic psychology (MA). *Application deadline:* For fall admission, 8/1 priority date for domestic students, 7/1 for international students; for spring admission, 12/1 priority date for domestic students, 10/15 for international students. Applications are processed on a rolling basis. *Application fee:* $45. Electronic applications accepted. *Application Contact:* Gail Ronveaux, Dean of Graduate Enrollment, 951-343-5045, Fax: 951-343-5095, E-mail: graduateadmissions@calbaptist.edu. *Director*, Dr. Anne-Marie Larsen, 951-343-4761, E-mail: alarsen@calbaptist.edu.

Program in Kinesiology Students: 23 full-time (10 women), 8 part-time (5 women); includes 4 Black or African American, non-Hispanic/Latino; 3 Asian, non-Hispanic/Latino; 3 Hispanic/Latino; 1 Two or more races, non-Hispanic/Latino, 11 international. 19 applicants, 100% accepted, 13 enrolled. *Faculty:* 3 full-time (0 women), 9 part-time/adjunct (2 women). Expenses: Contact institution. *Financial support:* Federal Work-Study, scholarships/grants, and unspecified assistantships available. Support available to part-time students. Financial award applicants required to submit FAFSA. In 2010, 19 master's awarded. *Degree program information:* Part-time programs available. Offers exercise science (MS); physical education pedagogy (MS); sport management (MS). *Application deadline:* For fall admission, 8/1 priority date for domestic students, 7/1 for international students; for spring admission, 12/1 priority date for domestic students, 10/15 for international students. Applications are processed on a rolling basis. *Application fee:* $45. Electronic applications accepted. *Application Contact:* Gail Ronveaux, Dean of Graduate Enrollment, 951-343-5045, Fax: 951-343-5095, E-mail: graduateadmissions@calbaptist.edu. *Chair, Department of Kinesiology*, Dr. Sean Sullivan, 951-343-4528, E-mail: ssullivan@calbaptist.edu.

Program in Music Students: 14 full-time (9 women), 4 part-time (3 women); includes 5 minority (2 Black or African American, non-Hispanic/Latino; 1 Asian, non-Hispanic/Latino; 2 Hispanic/Latino), 7 international. 9 applicants, 89% accepted, 7 enrolled. *Faculty:* 5 full-time (2 women), 1 (woman) part-time/adjunct. Expenses: Contact institution. *Financial support:* Federal Work-Study and scholarships/grants available. Support available to part-time students. Financial award applicants required to submit FAFSA. In 2010, 6 master's awarded. *Degree program information:* Part-time programs available. Offers conducting (MM); music education (MM); performance (MM). *Application deadline:* For fall admission, 8/1 priority date for domestic students, 7/1 for international students; for spring admission, 12/1 priority date for domestic students, 10/15 for international students. Applications are processed on a rolling basis. *Application fee:* $45. Electronic applications accepted. *Application Contact:* Gail Ronveaux, Dean of Graduate Enrollment, 951-343-5045, Fax: 951-343-5095, E-mail: graduateadmissions@calbaptist.edu. *Dean, School of Music,* Dr. Gary Bonner, 951-343-4251, Fax: 951-343-4570, E-mail: gbonner@calbaptist.edu.

Program in Nursing Students: 14 full-time (12 women), 3 part-time (all women). 96 applicants, 65% accepted. *Faculty:* 6 full-time (1 woman), 1 (woman) part-time/adjunct. Expenses: Contact institution. *Financial support:* Federal Work-Study and scholarships/grants available. Support available to part-time students. Financial award applicants required to submit FAFSA. *Degree program information:* Part-time programs available. Offers nursing (MSN). *Application deadline:* For fall admission, 8/1 for domestic students; for spring admission, 12/1 for domestic students. *Application fee:* $45. Electronic applications accepted. *Application Contact:* Gail Ronveaux, Dean of Graduate Enrollment, 951-343-5045, Fax: 951-343-5095, E-mail: graduateadmissions@calbaptist.edu. *Dean, School of Nursing,* Dr. Constance Milton, 951-343-4700, E-mail: cmilton@calbaptist.edu.

Program in Public Administration Students: 34 full-time (22 women), 18 part-time (11 women); includes 11 Black or African American, non-Hispanic/Latino; 2 Asian, non-Hispanic/Latino; 12 Hispanic/Latino; 1 Two or more races, non-Hispanic/Latino, 2 international. 21 applicants, 95% accepted, 18 enrolled. *Faculty:* 1 (woman) full-time. Expenses: Contact institution. *Financial support:* Federal Work-Study and scholarships/grants available. Support available to part-time students. Financial award applicants required to submit FAFSA. In 2010, 34 master's awarded. *Degree program information:* Part-time programs available. Offers public administration (MPA). *Application deadline:* For fall admission, 8/1 priority date for domestic students, 7/1 for international students; for spring admission, 12/1 priority date for domestic students, 10/15 for international students. Applications are processed on a rolling basis. *Application fee:* $45. Electronic applications accepted. *Application Contact:* Gail Ronveaux, Dean of Graduate Enrollment, 951-343-5045, Fax: 951-343-5095, E-mail: graduateadmissions@calbaptist.edu. *Director,* Dr. Elaine Ahumada, 951-343-4306, Fax: 951-343-4661, E-mail: eahumada@calbaptist.edu.

CALIFORNIA COAST UNIVERSITY, Santa Ana, CA 92701

General Information Proprietary, coed, comprehensive institution.

GRADUATE UNITS

School of Administration and Management Postbaccalaureate distance learning degree programs offered (no on-campus study). Offers business marketing (MBA); health care management (MBA); human resource management (MBA); management (MBA, MS). Electronic applications accepted.

School of Behavioral Science Postbaccalaureate distance learning degree programs offered (no on-campus study). Offers psychology (MS).

School of Criminal Justice Offers criminal justice (MS).

School of Education Postbaccalaureate distance learning degree programs offered (no on-campus study). Offers administration (M Ed); curriculum and instruction (M Ed); educational administration (Ed D); educational psychology (Ed D); organizational leadership (Ed D).

CALIFORNIA COLLEGE OF THE ARTS, San Francisco, CA 94107

General Information Independent, coed, comprehensive institution. *Enrollment:* 1,881 graduate, professional, and undergraduate students; 445 full-time matriculated graduate/professional students (271 women), 26 part-time matriculated graduate/professional students (16 women). *Enrollment by degree level:* 471 master's. *Graduate faculty:* 31 full-time (2 women), 149 part-time/adjunct (64 women). *Tuition:* Full-time $38,550; part-time $1285 per unit. One-time fee: $185 full-time. *Graduate housing:* Room and/or apartments available on a first-come, first-served basis to single students; on-campus housing not available to married students. Housing application deadline: 4/1. *Student services:* Campus employment opportunities, career counseling, free psychological counseling, international student services, low-cost health insurance, services for students with disabilities. *Library facilities:* CCA Library plus 1 other. *Online resources:* library catalog, web page. *Collection:* 73,000 titles, 3,250 serial subscriptions, 3,800 audiovisual materials.

Computer facilities: Computer purchase and lease plans are available. 346 computers available on campus for general student use. A campuswide network can be accessed from student residence rooms and from off campus. Online class registration is available. *Web address:* http://www.cca.edu/.

General Application Contact: Heidi Geis, Assistant Director of Graduate Admissions, 415-703-9533 Ext. 9533, Fax: 415-703-9539, E-mail: graduateprograms@cca.edu.

GRADUATE UNITS

Graduate Programs Students: 445 full-time (271 women), 26 part-time (16 women); includes 18 Black or African American, non-Hispanic/Latino; 4 American Indian or Alaska Native, non-Hispanic/Latino; 61 Asian, non-Hispanic/Latino; 66 Hispanic/Latino, 41 international. Average age 30. 1,234 applicants, 53% accepted, 240 enrolled. *Faculty:* 52 full-time (23 women), 149 part-time/adjunct (64 women). Expenses: Contact institution. *Financial support:* In 2010–11, 48 fellowships (averaging $18,958 per year), teaching assistantships (averaging $2,000 per year) were awarded. In 2010, 173 master's awarded. Offers architecture (M Arch); ceramics (MFA); curatorial practice (MA); design (MFA); design strategy (MBA); film/video/performance (MFA); glass (MFA); jewelry/metal arts (MFA); painting/drawing (MFA); photography (MFA); printmaking (MFA); sculpture (MFA); textiles (MFA); visual and critical studies (MA); wood/furniture (MFA); writing (MFA). *Application deadline:* For fall admission, 1/5 for domestic and international students. *Application fee:* $70. *Application Contact:* Heidi Geis, Assistant Director of Graduate Admissions, 415-703-9523 Ext. 9533, Fax: 415-703-9539, E-mail: hgeis@cca.edu. *Unit Head,* 800-477-1ART.

CALIFORNIA INSTITUTE OF INTEGRAL STUDIES, San Francisco, CA 94103

General Information Independent, coed, upper-level institution. CGS member. *Enrollment:* 1,106 full-time matriculated graduate/professional students (791 women), 210 part-time matriculated graduate/professional students (154 women). *Enrollment by degree level:* 748 master's, 567 doctoral, 1 other advanced degree. *Graduate faculty:* 55 full-time (26 women), 105 part-time/adjunct (61 women). *Tuition:* Full-time $15,660; part-time $870 per semester hour. *Required fees:* $95 per semester. *Graduate housing:* On-campus housing not available. *Student services:* Campus employment opportunities, campus safety program, career counseling, grant writing training, international student services, low-cost health insurance, multicultural affairs office, services for students with disabilities, writing training. *Library facilities:* The Laurance S. Rockefeller. *Research affiliation:* Bay Area Reference Service.

Computer facilities: A campuswide network can be accessed from off campus. *Web address:* http://www.ciis.edu/.

General Application Contact: Cori Watkins, Admissions Inquiries Coordinator, 415-575-6151, Fax: 415-575-1268, E-mail: cwatkins@ciis.edu.

GRADUATE UNITS

School of Consciousness and Transformation Students: 455 full-time (315 women), 133 part-time (90 women); includes 47 Black or African American, non-Hispanic/Latino; 3 American Indian or Alaska Native, non-Hispanic/Latino; 21 Asian, non-Hispanic/Latino; 41 Hispanic/Latino, 40 international. Average age 37. 265 applicants, 91% accepted, 163 enrolled. Expenses: Contact institution. *Financial support:* In 2010–11, 255 students received support; research assistantships, teaching assistantships, career-related internships or fieldwork, Federal Work-Study, scholarships/grants, and tuition waivers (partial) available. Support available to part-time students. Financial award application deadline: 4/15; financial award applicants required to submit FAFSA. In 2010, 64 master's, 22 doctorates awarded. *Degree program information:* Part-time and evening/weekend programs available. Postbaccalaureate distance learning degree programs offered (minimal on-campus study). Offers creative inquiry/interdisciplinary arts (MFA); cultural anthropology and social transformation (MA); East-West psychology (MA, PhD); integrative health studies (MA); philosophy and religion (MA, PhD); social and cultural anthropology (PhD); transformative leadership (MA); transformative studies (PhD); writing and consciousness (MFA). *Application deadline:* For fall admission, 2/1 priority date for domestic and international students; for spring admission, 10/15 priority date for domestic and international students. Applications are processed on a rolling basis. *Application fee:* $65. Electronic applications accepted. *Application Contact:* Allyson Werner, Associate Director of Admissions, 415-575-6155, Fax: 415-575-1268.

School of Professional Psychology Students: 651 full-time (476 women), 74 part-time (62 women); includes 146 minority (32 Black or African American, non-Hispanic/Latino; 1 American Indian or Alaska Native, non-Hispanic/Latino; 53 Asian, non-Hispanic/Latino; 43 Hispanic/Latino; 17 Two or more races, non-Hispanic/Latino), 52 international. Average age 37. 556 applicants, 72% accepted, 247 enrolled. Expenses: Contact institution. *Financial support:* Research assistantships with tuition reimbursements, teaching assistantships with tuition reimbursements, career-related internships or fieldwork, Federal Work-Study, scholarships/grants, and tuition waivers (partial) available. Support available to part-time students. Financial award application deadline: 4/15; financial award applicants required to submit FAFSA. In 2010, 148 master's, 27 doctorates awarded. *Degree program information:* Part-time and evening/weekend programs available. Offers clinical psychology (Psy D); community mental health (MA); drama therapy (MA); expressive arts therapy (MA); integral counseling psychology (MA); integral counseling psychology-weekend (MA); somatic psychology (MA). *Application deadline:* For fall admission, 2/1 priority date for domestic and international students; for spring admission, 10/15 priority date for domestic and international students. Applications are processed on a rolling basis. *Application fee:* $65. Electronic applications accepted. *Application Contact:* David Townes, Senior Admissions Counselor, 415-575-6152, Fax: 415-575-1268, E-mail: dtownes@ciis.edu.

CALIFORNIA INSTITUTE OF TECHNOLOGY, Pasadena, CA 91125-0001

General Information Independent, coed, university. CGS member. *Graduate housing:* Rooms and/or apartments available on a first-come, first-served basis to single students and available to married students. Housing application deadline: 5/1. *Research affiliation:* Scripps Institute of Oceanography, Stanford Linear Accelerator Center (high-energy physics), European Center for Nuclear Research (high-energy physics), National Science Foundation Center for Research in Parallel Computing, Cosmic Gravitational Waves Observatory (laser interferometer gravitational waves).

GRADUATE UNITS

Division of Biology Students: 78 full-time (41 women); includes 3 Black or African American, non-Hispanic/Latino; 5 Hispanic/Latino. 176 applicants, 18% accepted, 11 enrolled. *Faculty:* 40 full-time (9 women). Expenses: Contact institution. *Financial support:* In 2010–11, fellowships with full tuition reimbursements (averaging $23,766 per year), teaching assistantships with full tuition reimbursements (averaging $4,782 per year) were awarded; research assistantships with full tuition reimbursements, institutionally sponsored loans, scholarships/grants, and unspecified assistantships also available. Financial award application deadline: 1/1. In 2010, 18 doctorates awarded. Offers biochemistry and molecular biophysics (PhD); cell biology and biophysics (PhD); developmental biology (PhD); genetics (PhD); immunology (PhD); molecular biology (PhD); neurobiology (PhD). *Application deadline:* For fall admission, 1/1 for domestic and international students. *Application fee:* $80. Electronic applications accepted. *Application Contact:* Elizabeth M. Ayala, Graduate Program Coordinator, 626-395-4497, Fax: 626-683-3343, E-mail: biograd@caltech.edu. *Chairman,* Prof. Stephen L. Mayo, 626-395-4951, Fax: 626-683-3343.

Division of Chemistry and Chemical Engineering Students: 323 full-time (122 women). Average age 26. 643 applicants, 22% accepted, 47 enrolled. *Faculty:* 41 full-time (8 women). Expenses: Contact institution. *Financial support:* In 2010–11, 319 students received support; fellowships, research assistantships, teaching assistantships, Federal Work-Study, institutionally sponsored loans, scholarships/grants, traineeships, health care benefits, and unspecified assistantships available. Financial award application deadline: 1/1. In 2010, 11 master's, 61 doctorates awarded. *Degree program information:* Part-time and evening/weekend programs available. Postbaccalaureate distance learning degree programs offered (minimal on-campus study). Offers biochemistry and molecular biophysics (MS, PhD); chemical engineering (MS, PhD); chemistry (MS, PhD). *Application deadline:* For fall admission, 1/1 for domestic and international students. *Application fee:* $80. Electronic applications accepted. *Application Contact:* Natalie Gilmore, Graduate Office, 626-395-3812, Fax: 626-577-9246, E-mail: ngilmore@its.caltech.edu. *Chair,* Prof. Jacqueline K. Barton, 626-395-3646, Fax: 626-395-6948, E-mail: jkbarton@caltech.edu.

Division of Engineering and Applied Science Students: 556 full-time (128 women). 2,592 applicants, 8% accepted, 67 enrolled. *Faculty:* 85 full-time (11 women). Expenses: Contact institution. *Financial support:* In 2010–11, 122 fellowships, 355 research assistantships, 110 teaching assistantships were awarded; Federal Work-Study and institutionally sponsored loans also available. Support available to part-time students. In 2010, 71 master's, 84 doctorates awarded. Offers aeronautics (MS, PhD, Engr); applied and computational mathematics (MS, PhD); applied mechanics (MS, PhD); applied physics (MS, PhD); bioengineering (MS, PhD); civil engineering (MS, PhD, Engr); computation and neural systems (MS, PhD); computer science (MS, PhD); control and dynamical systems (MS, PhD); electrical engineering (MS, PhD, Engr); environmental science and engineering (MS, PhD); materials science (MS, PhD); mechanical engineering (MS, PhD, Engr). *Application deadline:* For fall admission, 1/1 for domestic students. *Application fee:* $50. Electronic applications accepted. *Application Contact:* Natalie Gilmore, Assistant Dean of Graduate Studies, 626-395-3812, Fax: 626-577-9246, E-mail: ngilmore@caltech.edu. *Chair,* Dr. Ares J. Rosakis, 626-395-4100, E-mail: arosakis@caltech.edu.

Division of Geological and Planetary Sciences Students: 76 full-time (39 women); includes 1 Black or African American, non-Hispanic/Latino; 4 Asian, non-Hispanic/Latino; 1 Hispanic/Latino, 28 international. Average age 26. 102 applicants, 28% accepted, 9 enrolled. *Faculty:* 38 full-time (6 women). Expenses: Contact institution. *Financial support:* In 2010–11, 75 students received support, including 14 fellowships with full tuition reimbursements available (averaging $27,000 per year), 62 research assistantships with full tuition reimbursements available (averaging $27,000 per year); teaching assistantships with full tuition reimbursements available, institutionally sponsored loans, scholarships/grants, health care benefits, and unspecified assistantships also available. Financial award applicants required to submit FAFSA. In 2010, 12 master's, 14 doctorates awarded. Offers geobiology (MS, PhD); geochemistry (MS, PhD); geology (MS, PhD); geophysics (MS, PhD); planetary science (MS, PhD). *Application deadline:* For fall admission, 1/1 for domestic and international students. *Application fee:* $80. Electronic applications accepted. *Application Contact:* Dr. Robert W. Clayton, Academic Officer, 626-395-6909, Fax: 626-795-6028, E-mail: dianb@gps.caltech.edu. *Chairman,* Dr. Kenneth A. Farley, 626-395-6111, Fax: 626-795-6028, E-mail: dianb@gps.caltech.edu.

Division of Physics, Mathematics and Astronomy Offers astronomy (PhD); mathematics (PhD); physics (PhD).

Division of the Humanities and Social Sciences Students: 34 full-time (8 women); includes 2 minority (both Asian, non-Hispanic/Latino), 18 international. Average age 26. 300 applicants, 10% accepted, 12 enrolled. *Faculty:* 27 full-time (3 women). Expenses: Contact institution. *Financial support:* In 2010–11, 35 students received support, including 20 fellowships with tuition reimbursements available (averaging $28,000 per year), 6 research assistantships with tuition reimbursements available (averaging $28,000 per year), 8 teaching assistantships with tuition reimbursements available (averaging $28,000 per year); Federal Work-Study,

California Institute of Technology (continued)

institutionally sponsored loans, and scholarships/grants also available. In 2010, 6 master's, 7 doctorates awarded. Offers humanities and social sciences (MS, PhD); social science (MS, PhD). *Application deadline:* For fall admission, 12/15 for domestic and international students. *Application fee:* $80. Electronic applications accepted. *Application Contact:* Laurel Auchampaugh, Option Secretary, 626-395-4206, Fax: 626-405-9841, E-mail: gradsec@hss.caltech.edu. Dr. Jonathan Katz.

CALIFORNIA INSTITUTE OF THE ARTS, Valencia, CA 91355-2340

General Information Independent, coed, comprehensive institution. *Graduate housing:* Room and/or apartments available on a first-come, first-served basis to single students; on-campus housing not available to married students. Housing application deadline: 7/1.

GRADUATE UNITS

School of Art Offers art (MFA, Adv C); graphic design (MFA, Adv C); photography (MFA, Adv C). Electronic applications accepted.

School of Critical Studies Offers writing (MFA, Adv C).

School of Dance Offers dance (MFA, Adv C).

School of Film/Video Offers experimental animation (MFA); film directing (MFA, Adv C); film/video (Adv C). Electronic applications accepted.

School of Music *Degree program information:* Part-time programs available. Offers African music (MFA, Adv C); composition (MFA, Adv C); composition/new media (MFA, Adv C); Indonesian music (MFA, Adv C); jazz (MFA, Adv C); North Indian music (MFA, Adv C); performance (MFA, Adv C); performer/composer (MFA, Adv C); voice (MFA, Adv C); world music performance (MFA). Electronic applications accepted.

School of Theatre Offers acting (MFA, Adv C); design and technology (Adv C); directing (MFA); performing arts design and technology (MFA); theater management (MFA, Adv C); writing for performance (MFA). Electronic applications accepted.

CALIFORNIA INTERCONTINENTAL UNIVERSITY, Diamond Bar, CA 91765

General Information Proprietary, coed, comprehensive institution.

GRADUATE UNITS

Hollywood College of the Entertainment Industry Offers Hollywood and entertainment management (MBA).

School of Business Offers banking and finance (MBA); entrepreneurship and business management (DBA); global business leadership (DBA); international management and marketing (MBA); organizational management and human resource management (MBA).

School of Healthcare Offers healthcare management and leadership (MBA, DBA).

School of Information Technology Offers information systems and enterprise resource management (DBA); information systems and knowledge management (MBA); project and quality management (MBA).

CALIFORNIA INTERNATIONAL BUSINESS UNIVERSITY, San Diego, CA 92101

General Information Independent, coed, graduate-only institution.

GRADUATE UNITS

Graduate Programs Offers business (MBA, MSIM, DBA).

CALIFORNIA LUTHERAN UNIVERSITY, Thousand Oaks, CA 91360-2787

General Information Independent-religious, coed, comprehensive institution. CGS member. *Enrollment:* 925 full-time matriculated graduate/professional students (613 women), 461 part-time matriculated graduate/professional students (254 women). *Enrollment by degree level:* 1,256 master's, 90 doctoral, 40 other advanced degrees. *Graduate faculty:* 155 full-time (70 women), 202 part-time/adjunct (93 women). *Graduate housing:* Rooms and/or apartments available on a first-come, first-served basis to single and married students. *Student services:* Campus employment opportunities, career counseling, free psychological counseling, international student services, low-cost health insurance, multicultural affairs office, services for students with disabilities, writing training. *Library facilities:* Pearson Library. *Online resources:* library catalog, web page. *Collection:* 132,744 titles, 1,497 serial subscriptions.

Computer facilities: 300 computers available on campus for general student use. A campuswide network can be accessed from student residence rooms and from off campus. Online class registration is available. *Web address:* http://www.callutheran.edu/.

General Application Contact: Information Contact, 805-493-3127, Fax: 805-493-3542, E-mail: clugrad@clunet.edu.

GRADUATE UNITS

Graduate Studies Students: 925 full-time (613 women), 461 part-time (254 women); includes 400 minority (46 Black or African American, non-Hispanic/Latino; 2 American Indian or Alaska Native, non-Hispanic/Latino; 69 Asian, non-Hispanic/Latino; 237 Hispanic/Latino; 9 Native Hawaiian or other Pacific Islander, non-Hispanic/Latino; 37 Two or more races, non-Hispanic/Latino), 213 international. Average age 32. 841 applicants, 76% accepted, 395 enrolled. *Faculty:* 34 full-time (18 women), 80 part-time/adjunct (42 women). Expenses: Contact institution. *Financial support:* In 2010–11, 159 students received support. Scholarships/grants and unspecified assistantships available. Support available to part-time students. Financial award applicants required to submit FAFSA. In 2010, 435 master's, 32 doctorates awarded. *Degree program information:* Part-time and evening/weekend programs available. Offers clinical psychology (MS, Psy D); marital and family therapy (MS); public policy and administration (MPPA). *Application deadline:* Applications are processed on a rolling basis. *Application fee:* $50. Electronic applications accepted. *Application Contact:* 805-493-3127, Fax: 805-493-3542, E-mail: clugrad@clunet.edu. *Provost/Vice President for Academic Affairs,* Dr. Leanne Neilson, 805-493-3145, E-mail: neilson@clunet.edu.

Graduate School of Education Students: 367 full-time (286 women), 146 part-time (119 women); includes 171 minority (15 Black or African American, non-Hispanic/Latino; 1 American Indian or Alaska Native, non-Hispanic/Latino; 16 Asian, non-Hispanic/Latino; 119 Hispanic/Latino; 4 Native Hawaiian or other Pacific Islander, non-Hispanic/Latino; 16 Two or more races, non-Hispanic/Latino), 14 international. Average age 33. 199 applicants, 86% accepted, 134 enrolled. *Faculty:* 22 full-time (15 women), 36 part-time/adjunct (24 women). Expenses: Contact institution. *Financial support:* In 2010–11, 323 students received support. In 2010, 110 master's, 32 doctorates awarded. *Degree program information:* Part-time and evening/weekend programs available. Offers counseling and guidance (MS); educational leadership (MA, Ed D); special education (MS); teacher leadership (M Ed); teaching (M Ed). *Application deadline:* For fall admission, 7/1 priority date for domestic students; for spring admission, 11/1 priority date for domestic students. Applications are processed on a rolling basis. *Application fee:* $50. *Application Contact:* 805-493-3127, Fax: 805-493-3542, E-mail: clugrad@clunet.edu. *Dean,* Dr. George J. Perterson, 805-493-3421.

School of Management Students: 350 full-time (162 women), 262 part-time (99 women); includes 21 Black or African American, non-Hispanic/Latino; 44 Asian, non-Hispanic/Latino; 56 Hispanic/Latino; 4 Native Hawaiian or other Pacific Islander, non-Hispanic/Latino; 12 Two or more races, non-Hispanic/Latino, 185 international. Average age 32. 379 applicants, 74% accepted, 138 enrolled. *Faculty:* 12 full-time (3 women), 27 part-time/adjunct (6 women). Expenses: Contact institution. In 2010, 231 master's awarded. *Degree program information:* Part-time and evening/weekend programs available. Postbaccalaureate distance learning degree programs offered (no on-campus study). Offers business (IMBA); computer science (MS); econometrics (MBA); economics (MS); entrepreneurship (MBA, Certificate); finance (MBA, Certificate); financial planning (MBA, Certificate); information systems and technology (MS); information technology management (MBA, Certificate); international business (MBA, Certificate); management and organization behavior (MBA); management and organizational behavior (Certificate); marketing (MBA, Certificate); microeconomics (MBA); nonprofit and social enterprise (MBA). *Application deadline:* Applications are processed on a rolling basis. *Application fee:* $50. *Application Contact:* 805-493-3127, Fax: 805-493-3542, E-mail: clugrad@clunet.edu. *Dean,* Dr. Charles Maxey, 805-493-3360.

CALIFORNIA MIRAMAR UNIVERSITY, San Diego, CA 92126

General Information Proprietary, coed, comprehensive institution.

GRADUATE UNITS

Program in Business Administration Offers business administration (MBA).

Program in Strategic Leadership Offers strategic leadership (MS).

Program in Taxation and Trade for Executives Offers taxation and trade for executives (MT).

Program in Telecommunications Management Offers telecommunications management (MST).

CALIFORNIA NATIONAL UNIVERSITY FOR ADVANCED STUDIES, Northridge, CA 91325

General Information Proprietary, coed, comprehensive institution.

GRADUATE UNITS

College of Business Administration *Degree program information:* Part-time programs available. Postbaccalaureate distance learning degree programs offered (no on-campus study). Offers business administration (MBA, MHRM). Electronic applications accepted.

College of Engineering *Degree program information:* Part-time programs available. Postbaccalaureate distance learning degree programs offered (no on-campus study). Offers engineering (MS Eng). Electronic applications accepted.

College of Quality and Engineering Management *Degree program information:* Part-time programs available. Offers quality and engineering management (MEM).

CALIFORNIA POLYTECHNIC STATE UNIVERSITY, SAN LUIS OBISPO, San Luis Obispo, CA 93407

General Information State-supported, coed, comprehensive institution. CGS member. *Enrollment:* 18,360 graduate, professional, and undergraduate students; 621 full-time matriculated graduate/professional students (267 women), 287 part-time matriculated graduate/professional students (109 women). *Enrollment by degree level:* 908 master's. *Graduate faculty:* 50 full-time (13 women), 9 part-time/adjunct (8 women). Tuition, state resident: full-time $5386; part-time $3124 per year. Tuition, nonresident: full-time $11,160; part-time $248 per unit. *Required fees:* $2250; $614 per term. One-time fee: $2250 full-time; $1842 part-time. *Graduate housing:* Room and/or apartments available on a first-come, first-served basis to single students; on-campus housing not available to married students. Typical cost: $6495 per year. Room charges vary according to housing facility selected. *Student services:* Campus employment opportunities, campus safety program, career counseling, child daycare facilities, exercise/wellness program, free psychological counseling, grant writing training, international student services, low-cost health insurance, multicultural affairs office, services for students with disabilities, teacher training, writing training. *Library facilities:* Robert E. Kennedy Library. *Online resources:* library catalog, web page, access to other libraries' catalogs. *Collection:* 833,538 titles, 50,487 serial subscriptions, 8,486 audiovisual materials.

Computer facilities: A campuswide network can be accessed from student residence rooms and from off campus. Online class registration is available. *Web address:* http://www.calpoly.edu/.

General Application Contact: Dr. James Maraviglia, Associate Vice Provost for Marketing and Enrollment Development, 805-756-2311, Fax: 805-756-5400, E-mail: admissions@calpoly.edu.

GRADUATE UNITS

College of Agriculture, Food and Environmental Sciences Students: 60 full-time (41 women), 40 part-time (24 women); includes 11 minority (1 American Indian or Alaska Native, non-Hispanic/Latino; 7 Hispanic/Latino; 3 Two or more races, non-Hispanic/Latino), 6 international. Average age 28. 96 applicants, 55% accepted, 44 enrolled. *Faculty:* 8 full-time (1 woman). Expenses: Contact institution. *Financial support:* Fellowships, research assistantships, teaching assistantships, career-related internships or fieldwork, Federal Work-Study, institutionally sponsored loans, and scholarships/grants available. Support available to part-time students. Financial award application deadline: 3/2; financial award applicants required to submit FAFSA. In 2010, 39 master's awarded. *Degree program information:* Part-time programs available. Offers agribusiness (MS); agricultural education and communication (MAE); agriculture (MS); agriculture, food and environmental sciences (MAE, MS); forestry sciences (MS). *Application deadline:* For fall admission, 4/1 for domestic students, 11/30 for international students; for winter admission, 10/1 for domestic students, 6/30 for international students; for spring admission, 10/1 for domestic students. Applications are processed on a rolling basis. *Application fee:* $55. Electronic applications accepted. *Application Contact:* Dr. Mark Shelton, Associate Dean/Graduate Coordinator, 805-756-2161, Fax: 805-756-6577, E-mail: mshelton@calpoly.edu. *Dean,* Dr. David J. Wehner, 805-756-2161, Fax: 805-756-6577, E-mail: dwehner@calpoly.edu.

College of Architecture and Environmental Design Students: 72 full-time (38 women), 6 part-time (3 women); includes 21 minority (11 Asian, non-Hispanic/Latino; 6 Hispanic/Latino; 4 Two or more races, non-Hispanic/Latino), 2 international. Average age 28. 183 applicants, 37% accepted, 47 enrolled. *Faculty:* 6 full-time (1 woman), 1 part-time/adjunct (0 women). Expenses: Contact institution. *Financial support:* Research assistantships, teaching assistantships, career-related internships or fieldwork, Federal Work-Study, and institutionally sponsored loans available. Support available to part-time students. Financial award application deadline: 3/2; financial award applicants required to submit FAFSA. In 2010, 35 master's awarded. *Degree program information:* Part-time programs available. Offers architecture (MS); architecture and environmental design (MAE, MCRP, MS); city and regional planning (MCRP). *Application deadline:* For fall admission, 7/1 for domestic students, 11/30 for international students; for winter admission, 11/1 for domestic students, 6/30 for international students. Applications are processed on a rolling basis. *Application fee:* $55. Electronic applications accepted. *Application Contact:* Dr. James Maraviglia, Assistant Vice President for Admissions, Recruitment and Financial Aid, 805-756-2311, Fax: 805-756-5400, E-mail: admissions@calpoly.edu. *Dean,* R. Thomas Jones, 805-756-1414, Fax: 805-756-2765, E-mail: rtjones@calpoly.edu.

College of Engineering Students: 249 full-time (34 women), 110 part-time (16 women); includes 105 minority (6 Black or African American, non-Hispanic/Latino; 2 American Indian or Alaska Native, non-Hispanic/Latino; 67 Asian, non-Hispanic/Latino; 27 Hispanic/Latino; 3 Two or more races, non-Hispanic/Latino), 13 international. Average age 25. 394 applicants, 56% accepted, 143 enrolled. *Faculty:* 15 full-time (3 women), 1 (woman) part-time/adjunct. Expenses: Contact institution. *Financial support:* Fellowships, research assistantships, teaching assistantships, career-related internships or fieldwork, Federal Work-Study, institutionally sponsored loans, and unspecified assistantships available. Support available to part-time students. Financial award application deadline: 3/2; financial award applicants required to submit FAFSA. In 2010, 200 master's awarded. *Degree program information:* Part-time programs available. Offers aerospace engineering (MS); biomedical and general engineering (MS); civil and environmental engineering (MS); computer science (MS); electrical engineering (MS); engineering (MS); industrial engineering (MS); mechanical engineering (MS). *Application deadline:* For fall admission, 7/1 for domestic students, 11/30 for international students; for winter admission, 11/1 for domestic students, 6/30 for international students; for spring admission, 2/1 for domestic students. Applications are processed on a rolling basis. *Application fee:* $55. Electronic applications accepted. *Application Contact:* Dr. Erling Smith, Dean, 805-756-2132, Fax: 805-756-6503, E-mail: esmith21@calpoly.edu. *Dean,* Dr. Erling Smith, 805-756-2132, Fax: 805-756-6503, E-mail: esmith21@calpoly.edu.

College of Liberal Arts Students: 85 full-time (59 women), 68 part-time (36 women); includes 37 minority (2 Black or African American, non-Hispanic/Latino; 3 Asian, non-Hispanic/Latino; 21 Hispanic/Latino; 11 Two or more races, non-Hispanic/Latino). Average age 29. 181 applicants, 52% accepted, 58 enrolled. *Faculty:* 7 full-time (2 women). Expenses: Contact institution. *Financial support:* Teaching assistantships, career-related internships or fieldwork, Federal Work-Study, institutionally sponsored loans, scholarships/grants, and tutorships, writing laboratory assistantships available. Support available to part-time students. Financial award application deadline: 3/2; financial award applicants required to submit FAFSA. In 2010, 33 master's awarded. *Degree program information:* Part-time programs available. Offers English (MA); history (MA); liberal arts (MA, MPP, MS); political science (MPP); psychology (MS). *Application deadline:* For fall admission, 5/1 for domestic students, 11/30 for international students; for winter admission, 11/1 for domestic students, 6/30 for international students; for spring admission, 2/1 for domestic students. *Application fee:* $55. *Application Contact:* Dr. Linda Halisky, Dean, 805-756-2706, Fax: 805-756-5748, E-mail: lhalisky@calpoly.edu. *Dean,* Dr. Linda Halisky, 805-756-2706, Fax: 805-756-5748, E-mail: lhalisky@calpoly.edu.

College of Science and Mathematics Students: 117 full-time (81 women), 49 part-time (24 women); includes 37 minority (2 Black or African American, non-Hispanic/Latino; 7 Asian, non-Hispanic/Latino; 18 Hispanic/Latino; 10 Two or more races, non-Hispanic/Latino), 2 international. Average age 27. 238 applicants, 52% accepted, 92 enrolled. *Faculty:* 9 full-time (4 women), 7 part-time/adjunct (all women). Expenses: Contact institution. *Financial support:* Research assistantships, teaching assistantships, career-related internships or fieldwork and Federal Work-Study available. Support available to part-time students. Financial award application deadline: 3/2; financial award applicants required to submit FAFSA. In 2010, 83 master's awarded. *Degree program information:* Part-time programs available. Offers biological sciences (MS); kinesiology (MS); mathematics (MS); polymers and coating science (MS); science and mathematics (MA, MS). *Application deadline:* For fall admission, 7/1 for domestic students, 11/30 for international students; for winter admission, 11/1 for domestic students, 6/30 for international students; for spring admission, 2/1 for domestic students. *Application fee:* $55. Electronic applications accepted. *Application Contact:* Dr. James Maraviglia, Assistant Vice President for Admissions, Recruitment and Financial Aid, 805-756-2311, Fax: 805-756-5400, E-mail: admissions@calpoly.edu. *Dean,* Dr. Philip S. Bailey, 805-756-2226, Fax: 805-756-1670, E-mail: pbailey@calpoly.edu.

School of Education Students: 74 full-time (59 women), 4 part-time (2 women); includes 21 minority (4 Asian, non-Hispanic/Latino; 11 Hispanic/Latino; 6 Two or more races, non-Hispanic/Latino), 1 international. Average age 30. 143 applicants, 52% accepted, 61 enrolled. *Faculty:* 5 full-time (2 women), 5 part-time/adjunct (all women). Expenses: Contact institution. *Financial support:* Research assistantships, career-related internships or fieldwork, Federal Work-Study, and institutionally sponsored loans available. Support available to part-time students. Financial award application deadline: 3/2; financial award applicants required to submit FAFSA. In 2010, 56 master's awarded. *Degree program information:* Part-time and evening/weekend programs available. Offers education (MA). *Application deadline:* For fall admission, 2/1 priority date for domestic students, 11/30 for international students. *Application fee:* $55. *Application Contact:* Dr. James Maraviglia, Assistant Vice President for Admissions, Recruitment, and Financial Aid, 805-756-2311, Fax: 805-756-5400, E-mail: admissions@calpoly.edu. *Director,* Dr. Patricia Mulligan, 805-756-1505, Fax: 805-756-7430, E-mail: pmulliga@calpoly.edu.

Orfalea College of Business Students: 38 full-time (14 women), 14 part-time (6 women); includes 8 minority (4 Asian, non-Hispanic/Latino; 3 Hispanic/Latino; 1 Native Hawaiian or other Pacific Islander, non-Hispanic/Latino). Average age 26. 112 applicants, 46% accepted, 38 enrolled. *Faculty:* 5 full-time (2 women). Expenses: Contact institution. *Financial support:* Career-related internships or fieldwork, Federal Work-Study, institutionally sponsored loans, scholarships/grants, and unspecified assistantships available. Support available to part-time students. Financial award application deadline: 3/2; financial award applicants required to submit FAFSA. In 2010, 69 master's awarded. Offers business (MBA); business and technology (MS); taxation (MSA). *Application deadline:* For fall admission, 7/1 for domestic students, 11/30 for international students. Applications are processed on a rolling basis. *Application fee:* $55. Electronic applications accepted. *Application Contact:* Dr. Brian Tietje, Associate Dean, 805-756-1757, Fax: 805-756-0110, E-mail: btietje@calpoly.edu. *Dean,* Dr. David P. Christy, 805-756-2705, Fax: 805-756-5452, E-mail: dchristy@calpoly.edu.

CALIFORNIA SCHOOL OF PODIATRIC MEDICINE AT SAMUEL MERRITT UNIVERSITY, Oakland, CA 94609

General Information Independent, coed, graduate-only institution. *Enrollment by degree level:* 161 first professional. *Graduate faculty:* 16 full-time (3 women), 8 part-time/adjunct (1 woman). *Tuition:* Full-time $30,968. *Required fees:* $2240. *Student services:* Campus employment opportunities, career counseling, exercise/wellness program, free psychological counseling, low-cost health insurance, services for students with disabilities, writing training. *Library facilities:* John A. Graziano Memorial Library. *Online resources:* web page. *Collection:* 41,496 titles, 9,373 serial subscriptions, 5,035 audiovisual materials. *Research affiliation:* University of Southern California–Los Angeles County Medical Center, University of California, San Francisco Health Sciences Center, University of Texas Health Science Center–San Antonio.

Computer facilities: 102 computers available on campus for general student use. A campuswide network can be accessed. Online class registration is available. *Web address:* http://www.samuelmerritt.edu/podiatric_medicine.

General Application Contact: Dr. David Tran, Assistant Director of Admission, 510-869-6789, Fax: 510-869-6525, E-mail: dtran@samuelmerritt.edu.

GRADUATE UNITS

Graduate and Professional Programs Students: 158 full-time (70 women), 3 part-time (0 women); includes 85 minority (7 Black or African American, non-Hispanic/Latino; 1 American Indian or Alaska Native, non-Hispanic/Latino; 64 Asian, non-Hispanic/Latino; 9 Hispanic/Latino; 4 Two or more races, non-Hispanic/Latino). Average age 27. 341 applicants, 32% accepted, 41 enrolled. *Faculty:* 16 full-time (3 women), 8 part-time/adjunct (1 woman). Expenses: Contact institution. *Financial support:* In 2010–11, 92 students received support; fellowships, Federal Work-Study and institutionally sponsored loans available. Financial award application deadline: 3/2; financial award applicants required to submit FAFSA. In 2010, 35 DPMs awarded. Offers podiatric medicine (DPM). *Application deadline:* For fall admission, 4/1 priority date for domestic students. Applications are processed on a rolling basis. *Application fee:* $50. *Application Contact:* Dr. David Tran, Assistant Director of Admission, 510-869-6789, Fax: 510-869-6525, E-mail: dtran@samuelmerritt.edu. *Associate Dean for Administrative Affairs,* Irma Walker-Adame, 510-869-8742, E-mail: iadame@samuelmerritt.edu.

CALIFORNIA STATE POLYTECHNIC UNIVERSITY, POMONA, Pomona, CA 91768-2557

General Information State-supported, coed, comprehensive institution. CGS member. *Enrollment:* 20,747 graduate, professional, and undergraduate students; 452 full-time matriculated graduate/professional students (244 women), 1,079 part-time matriculated graduate/professional students (507 women). *Enrollment by degree level:* 1,531 master's. *Graduate faculty:* 504 full-time (207 women), 451 part-time/adjunct (164 women). Tuition, state resident: full-time $5386; part-time $2850 per year. Tuition, nonresident: full-time $12,082; part-time $248 per credit. *Required fees:* $577; $248 per credit. $577 per year. Tuition and fees vary according to course load and program. *Graduate housing:* Room and/or apartments available on a first-come, first-served basis to single students; on-campus housing not available to married students. Typical cost: $6327 per year ($10,011 including board). Room and board charges vary according to board plan and housing facility selected. Housing application deadline: 5/1. *Student services:* Campus employment opportunities, campus safety program, career counseling, child daycare facilities, free psychological counseling, international student services, low-cost health insurance, multicultural affairs office, services for students with disabilities. *Library facilities:* University Library. *Online resources:* library catalog, web page, access to other libraries' catalogs. *Collection:* 832,132 titles, 4,663 serial subscriptions, 10,886 audiovisual materials.

Computer facilities: Computer purchase and lease plans are available. 1,875 computers available on campus for general student use. A campuswide network can be accessed from student residence rooms and from off campus. Online class registration is available. *Web address:* http://www.csupomona.edu/.

General Application Contact: Scott J. Duncan, Director, Admissions, 909-869-3258, Fax: 909-869-4529, E-mail: sjduncan@csupomona.edu.

GRADUATE UNITS

Academic Affairs Students: 452 full-time (244 women), 1,079 part-time (507 women); includes 709 minority (51 Black or African American, non-Hispanic/Latino; 6 American Indian or Alaska Native, non-Hispanic/Latino; 305 Asian, non-Hispanic/Latino; 303 Hispanic/Latino; 4 Native Hawaiian or other Pacific Islander, non-Hispanic/Latino; 40 Two or more races, non-Hispanic/Latino), 161 international. Average age 31. 1,930 applicants, 43% accepted, 536 enrolled. *Faculty:* 504 full-time (207 women), 451 part-time/adjunct (164 women). Expenses: Contact institution. *Financial support:* In 2010–11, 4 fellowships, 5 research assistantships, 3 teaching assistantships were awarded; career-related internships or fieldwork, Federal Work-Study, institutionally sponsored loans, and unspecified assistantships also available. Support available to part-time students. Financial award application deadline: 3/2; financial award applicants required to submit FAFSA. In 2010, 403 master's awarded. *Degree program information:* Part-time programs available. *Application deadline:* Applications are processed on a rolling basis. *Application fee:* $55. Electronic applications accepted. *Application Contact:* Scott J. Duncan, Director, Admissions, 909-869-3258, Fax: 909-869-4529, E-mail: sjduncan@csupomona.edu. *Provost/Vice President for Academic Affairs,* Dr. Marten L. denBoer, 909-869-3443, E-mail: mdenboer@csupomona.edu.

College of Agriculture Students: 15 full-time (14 women), 45 part-time (36 women); includes 24 minority (3 Black or African American, non-Hispanic/Latino; 3 American Indian or Alaska Native, non-Hispanic/Latino; 8 Asian, non-Hispanic/Latino; 7 Hispanic/Latino; 3 Two or more races, non-Hispanic/Latino), 6 international. Average age 29. 68 applicants, 37% accepted, 22 enrolled. *Faculty:* 28 full-time (9 women), 21 part-time/adjunct (14 women). Expenses: Contact institution. *Financial support:* Career-related internships or fieldwork, Federal Work-Study, and institutionally sponsored loans available. Support available to part-time students. Financial award application deadline: 3/2; financial award applicants required to submit FAFSA. In 2010, 16 master's awarded. *Degree program information:* Part-time programs available. Offers agriculture (MS). *Application deadline:* For fall admission, 5/1 priority date for domestic students; for winter admission, 10/15 priority date for domestic students; for spring admission, 1/2 priority date for domestic students. Applications are processed on a rolling basis. *Application fee:* $55. Electronic applications accepted. *Application Contact:* Dan Hostetler, Chair/Professor, 909-869-2189, Fax: 909-869-5036, E-mail: dghostetler@csupomona.edu. *Dean,* Dr. Lester C. Young, 909-869-2203, E-mail: lcyoung@csupomona.edu.

College of Business Administration Students: 31 full-time (17 women), 145 part-time (59 women); includes 71 minority (2 Black or African American, non-Hispanic/Latino; 45 Asian, non-Hispanic/Latino; 22 Hispanic/Latino; 2 Two or more races, non-Hispanic/Latino), 48 international. Average age 31. 250 applicants, 35% accepted, 48 enrolled. *Faculty:* 68 full-time (24 women), 51 part-time/adjunct (13 women). Expenses: Contact institution. *Financial support:* In 2010–11, 5 research assistantships, 3 teaching assistantships were awarded; career-related internships or fieldwork, Federal Work-Study, and institutionally sponsored loans also available. Support available to part-time students. Financial award application deadline: 3/2; financial award applicants required to submit FAFSA. In 2010, 45 master's awarded. *Degree program information:* Part-time programs available. Postbaccalaureate distance learning degree programs offered (minimal on-campus study). Offers accountancy (MS); business administration (MBA, MS); information systems auditing (MS); professional business administration (PMBA). *Application deadline:* For fall admission, 5/1 priority date for domestic students; for winter admission, 10/15 priority date for domestic students; for spring admission, 1/2 priority date for domestic students. Applications are processed on a rolling basis. *Application fee:* $55. Electronic applications accepted. *Application Contact:* Dr. Steven Curl, Associate Dean, 909-869-4244, E-mail: scurl@csupomona.edu. *Dean,* Dr. Richard S. Lapidus, 909-869-2400, E-mail: rslapidus@csupomona.edu.

College of Education and Integrative Studies Students: 67 full-time (52 women), 173 part-time (120 women); includes 134 minority (16 Black or African American, non-Hispanic/Latino; 1 American Indian or Alaska Native, non-Hispanic/Latino; 30 Asian, non-Hispanic/Latino; 83 Hispanic/Latino; 4 Two or more races, non-Hispanic/Latino), 7 international. Average age 36. 96 applicants, 68% accepted, 47 enrolled. *Faculty:* 37 full-time (24 women), 37 part-time/adjunct (24 women). Expenses: Contact institution. *Financial support:* Career-related internships or fieldwork, Federal Work-Study, and institutionally sponsored loans available. Support available to part-time students. Financial award application deadline: 3/2; financial award applicants required to submit FAFSA. In 2010, 116 master's awarded. *Degree program information:* Part-time programs available. Offers education and integrative studies (MA). *Application deadline:* For fall admission, 5/1 priority date for domestic students; for winter admission, 10/15 priority date for domestic students; for spring admission, 1/20 priority date for domestic students. Applications are processed on a rolling basis. *Application fee:* $55. Electronic applications accepted. *Application Contact:* Dr. Dorothy MacNevin, Co-Chair, Graduate Education Department, 909-869-2311, Fax: 909-869-4822, E-mail: dmacnevin@csupomona.edu. *Dean,* Dr. Peggy Kelly, 909-869-2307, E-mail: pkelly@csupomona.edu.

College of Engineering Students: 48 full-time (7 women), 227 part-time (37 women); includes 139 minority (3 Black or African American, non-Hispanic/Latino; 2 American Indian or Alaska Native, non-Hispanic/Latino; 78 Asian, non-Hispanic/Latino; 49 Hispanic/Latino; 7 Two or more races, non-Hispanic/Latino), 31 international. Average age 28. 397 applicants, 51% accepted, 122 enrolled. *Faculty:* 83 full-time (15 women), 75 part-time/adjunct (9 women). Expenses: Contact institution. *Financial support:* In 2010–11, 1 fellowship, 6 research assistantships, 5 teaching assistantships were awarded; career-related internships or fieldwork, Federal Work-Study, institutionally sponsored loans, and unspecified assistantships also available. Support available to part-time students. Financial award application deadline: 3/2; financial award applicants required to submit FAFSA. In 2010, 47 master's awarded. *Degree program information:* Part-time programs available. Offers aerospace engineering (MSE); civil engineering (MS); electrical engineering (MSEE); engineering (MS, MSE, MSEE); engineering management (MS); mechanical engineering (MS). *Application deadline:* For fall admission, 5/1 priority date for domestic students; for winter admission, 10/15 priority date for domestic students; for spring admission, 1/2 priority date for domestic students. Applications are processed on a rolling basis. *Application fee:* $55. Electronic applications accepted. *Application Contact:* Scott J. Duncan, Director, Admissions, 909-869-3258, E-mail: sjduncan@csupomona.edu. *Interim Dean,* Dr. Donald P. Coduto, 909-869-2472, Fax: 909-869-4370, E-mail: dpcoduto@csupomona.edu.

College of Environmental Design Students: 152 full-time (81 women), 75 part-time (35 women); includes 80 minority (3 Black or African American, non-Hispanic/Latino; 37 Asian, non-Hispanic/Latino; 27 Hispanic/Latino; 13 Two or more races, non-Hispanic/Latino), 14 international. Average age 30. 418 applicants, 31% accepted, 81 enrolled. *Faculty:* 46 full-time (22 women), 45 part-time/adjunct (16 women). Expenses: Contact institution. *Financial support:* Career-related internships or fieldwork, Federal Work-Study, and institutionally sponsored loans available. Support available to part-time students. Financial award application deadline: 3/2; financial award applicants required to submit FAFSA. In 2010, 66 master's awarded. *Degree program information:* Part-time programs available. Offers architecture (M Arch); environmental design (M Arch, M Land Arch, MS, MURP); landscape architecture (M Land Arch); regenerative studies (MS); urban and regional planning (MURP). *Application deadline:* For fall admission, 5/1 priority date for domestic students; for winter admission, 10/15 priority date for domestic students; for spring admission, 1/20 priority date for domestic students. Applications are processed on a rolling basis. *Application fee:* $55. Electronic applications accepted. *Application Contact:* Scott J. Duncan, Director, Admissions, 909-869-3258, Fax: 909-869-4529, E-mail: sjduncan@csupomona.edu. *Dean,* Michael Woo, 909-869-2667, E-mail: mwoo@csupomona.edu.

College of Letters, Arts, and Social Sciences Students: 75 full-time (46 women), 239 part-time (140 women); includes 164 minority (19 Black or African American, non-Hispanic/

California State Polytechnic University, Pomona (continued)

Latino; 2 American Indian or Alaska Native, non-Hispanic/Latino; 50 Asian, non-Hispanic/Latino; 85 Hispanic/Latino; 2 Native Hawaiian or other Pacific Islander, non-Hispanic/Latino; 6 Two or more races, non-Hispanic/Latino), 17 international. Average age 31. 409 applicants, 44% accepted, 108 enrolled. *Faculty:* 116 full-time (65 women), 138 part-time/adjunct (62 women). Expenses: Contact institution. *Financial support:* In 2010–11, 2 fellowships were awarded; Federal Work-Study and institutionally sponsored loans also available. Support available to part-time students. Financial award application deadline: 3/2; financial award applicants required to submit FAFSA. In 2010, 68 master's awarded. *Degree program information:* Part-time programs available. Offers economics (MS); English (MA); history (MA); kinesiology (MS); letters, arts, and social sciences (MA, MPA, MS); psychology (MS); public administration (MPA). *Application deadline:* Applications are processed on a rolling basis. *Application fee:* $55. Electronic applications accepted. *Application Contact:* Scott J. Duncan, Director, Admissions, 909-869-3258, Fax: 909-869-4529, E-mail: sjduncan@csupomona.edu. *Dean,* Dr. Carol P. Richardson, 909-869-3943, E-mail: cprichardson@csupomona.edu.

College of Science Students: 64 full-time (27 women), 175 part-time (80 women); includes 100 minority (5 Black or African American, non-Hispanic/Latino; 1 American Indian or Alaska Native, non-Hispanic/Latino; 57 Asian, non-Hispanic/Latino; 30 Hispanic/Latino; 2 Native Hawaiian or other Pacific Islander, non-Hispanic/Latino; 5 Two or more races, non-Hispanic/Latino), 38 international. Average age 28. 293 applicants, 50% accepted, 82 enrolled. *Faculty:* 106 full-time (39 women), 79 part-time/adjunct (24 women). Expenses: Contact institution. *Financial support:* Career-related internships or fieldwork, Federal Work-Study, and institutionally sponsored loans available. Support available to part-time students. Financial award application deadline: 3/2; financial award applicants required to submit FAFSA. In 2010, 45 master's awarded. *Degree program information:* Part-time programs available. Offers applied biotechnology (MBT); applied mathematics (MS); biological sciences (MS); chemistry (MS); computer science (MS); pure mathematics (MS); science (MBT, MS). *Application deadline:* For fall admission, 5/1 priority date for domestic students; for winter admission, 10/15 priority date for domestic students; for spring admission, 1/20 priority date for domestic students. Applications are processed on a rolling basis. *Application fee:* $55. Electronic applications accepted. *Application Contact:* Scott J. Duncan, Director, Admissions, 909-869-3258, Fax: 909-869-4529, E-mail: sjduncan@csupomona.edu. *Interim Dean,* Dr. Mandayam Srinivas, 909-869-3437, E-mail: masrinivas@csupomona.edu.

CALIFORNIA STATE UNIVERSITY, BAKERSFIELD, Bakersfield, CA 93311

General Information State-supported, coed, comprehensive institution. *Graduate housing:* Room and/or apartments available on a first-come, first-served basis to single students; on-campus housing not available to married students. Housing application deadline: 8/1.

GRADUATE UNITS

Division of Graduate Studies *Degree program information:* Part-time and evening/weekend programs available. Postbaccalaureate distance learning degree programs offered (no on-campus study). Offers administration (MS); interdisciplinary studies (MA).

School of Business and Public Administration Offers business administration (MBA); business and public administration (MBA, MPA, MSA); health care management (MSA); public administration (MPA).

School of Education Offers bilingual/multicultural education (MA Ed); curriculum and instruction (MA Ed); early childhood education (MA); education (MA, MA Ed, MS, Certificate); educational administration (MA); educational technology (MA Ed); reading/literacy (MA Ed, Certificate); school counseling (MS); special education (MA); student affairs (MS).

School of Humanities and Social Sciences *Degree program information:* Part-time and evening/weekend programs available. Offers anthropology (MA); counseling psychology (MS); English (MA); history (MA); humanities and social sciences (MA, MS, MSW); psychology (MA); social work (MSW); sociology (MA); Spanish (MA).

School of Natural Sciences and Mathematics Offers biology (MS); geology (MS); hydrogeology (MS); natural sciences and mathematics (MA, MS); nursing (MS); petroleum geology (MS); teaching mathematics (MA).

CALIFORNIA STATE UNIVERSITY CHANNEL ISLANDS, Camarillo, CA 93012

General Information State-supported, coed, comprehensive institution. *Graduate housing:* Room and/or apartments available on a first-come, first-served basis to single students; on-campus housing not available to married students. Housing application deadline: 6/1.

GRADUATE UNITS

Extended Education *Degree program information:* Part-time and evening/weekend programs available. Offers biotechnology and bioinformatics (MS); business administration (MBA); computer science (MS); educational leadership (MAEd); mathematics (MS).

CALIFORNIA STATE UNIVERSITY, CHICO, Chico, CA 95929-0722

General Information State-supported, coed, comprehensive institution. CGS member. *Enrollment:* 15,989 graduate, professional, and undergraduate students; 826 full-time matriculated graduate/professional students (566 women), 491 part-time matriculated graduate/professional students (294 women). *Enrollment by degree level:* 1,317 master's. *Graduate faculty:* 533 full-time (203 women), 432 part-time/adjunct (212 women). *Graduate housing:* Room and/or apartments available on a first-come, first-served basis to single students; on-campus housing not available to married students. Housing application deadline: 3/22. *Student services:* Campus employment opportunities, campus safety program, career counseling, child daycare facilities, free psychological counseling, grant writing training, international student services, low-cost health insurance, services for students with disabilities, teacher training. *Library facilities:* Meriam Library. *Online resources:* library catalog, web page, access to other libraries' catalogs. *Collection:* 942,304 titles, 22,000 serial subscriptions, 25,765 audiovisual materials. *Research affiliation:* Hewlett-Packard (computer science).

Computer facilities: Computer purchase and lease plans are available. 1,212 computers available on campus for general student use. A campuswide network can be accessed from student residence rooms and from off campus. Online class registration, student account information, calendar, transcripts are available. *Web address:* http://www.csuchico.edu/.

General Application Contact: Office of Graduate Studies, 530-898-6880, Fax: 530-898-3342, E-mail: graduatestudies@csuchico.edu.

GRADUATE UNITS

Graduate School Students: 833 full-time (574 women), 398 part-time (248 women); includes 232 minority (17 Black or African American, non-Hispanic/Latino; 13 American Indian or Alaska Native, non-Hispanic/Latino; 43 Asian, non-Hispanic/Latino; 130 Hispanic/Latino; 2 Native Hawaiian or other Pacific Islander, non-Hispanic/Latino; 27 Two or more races, non-Hispanic/Latino), 107 international. Average age 31. 1,087 applicants, 52% accepted, 338 enrolled. Expenses: Contact institution. *Financial support:* Fellowships, research assistantships, teaching assistantships, career-related internships or fieldwork, Federal Work-Study, scholarships/grants, unspecified assistantships, and stipends available. Support available to part-time students. In 2010, 355 master's awarded. *Degree program information:* Part-time programs available. Postbaccalaureate distance learning degree programs offered (no on-campus study). Offers interdisciplinary studies (MA, MS); science teaching (MS); simulation science (MS); teaching international languages (MA). *Application deadline:* For fall admission, 3/1 priority date for domestic students, 3/1 for international students; for spring admission, 9/15 priority date for domestic students, 9/15 for international students. Applications are processed on a rolling basis. *Application fee:* $55. Electronic applications accepted. *Application Contact:* School of Graduate, International, and Interdisciplinary Studies, 530-898-6880, Fax: 530-898-6889, E-mail: grin@csuchico.edu. *School of Graduate, International, and Interdisciplinary Studies,* Dr. Susan E. Place, 530-898-6880, Fax: 530-898-6889, E-mail: splace@csuchico.edu.

College of Behavioral and Social Sciences Students: 255 full-time (190 women), 96 part-time (58 women); includes 98 minority (10 Black or African American, non-Hispanic/Latino; 7 American Indian or Alaska Native, non-Hispanic/Latino; 15 Asian, non-Hispanic/Latino; 54 Hispanic/Latino; 2 Native Hawaiian or other Pacific Islander, non-Hispanic/Latino; 10 Two or more races, non-Hispanic/Latino), 11 international. Average age 31. 406 applicants, 47% accepted, 129 enrolled. Expenses: Contact institution. *Financial support:* Fellowships, teaching assistantships, career-related internships or fieldwork, Federal Work-Study, scholarships/grants, and unspecified assistantships available. Support available to part-time students. In 2010, 104 master's awarded. *Degree program information:* Part-time programs available. Offers applied psychology (MA); behavioral and social sciences (MA, MPA, MS, MSW); geography (MA); health administration (MPA); local government management (MPA); marriage and family therapy (MS); museum studies (MA); political science (MA, MPA); psychological science (MA); psychology (MA); public administration (MPA); rural and town planning (MA); social science (MA); social science education (MA); social work (MSW). *Application deadline:* For fall admission, 3/1 for domestic and international students; for spring admission, 9/15 for domestic and international students. Applications are processed on a rolling basis. *Application fee:* $55. Electronic applications accepted. *Application Contact:* School of Graduate, International, and Interdisciplinary Studies, 530-898-6880, Fax: 530-898-6889, E-mail: grin@csuchico.edu. *Dean,* Gayle Hutchinson, 530-898-6171.

College of Business Students: 53 full-time (28 women), 33 part-time (15 women); includes 7 Asian, non-Hispanic/Latino; 2 Hispanic/Latino; 1 Two or more races, non-Hispanic/Latino, 38 international. Average age 26. 97 applicants, 73% accepted, 44 enrolled. Expenses: Contact institution. In 2010, 33 master's awarded. *Degree program information:* Part-time programs available. Offers business (MBA); business administration (MBA). *Application deadline:* For fall admission, 3/1 for domestic and international students; for spring admission, 9/15 for domestic and international students. Applications are processed on a rolling basis. *Application fee:* $55. Electronic applications accepted. *Application Contact:* Dr. Ray Boykin, Head, 530-898-5895. *Dean,* Dr. Willie Hopkins, 530-898-6271.

College of Communication and Education Students: 152 full-time (112 women), 100 part-time (76 women); includes 4 Black or African American, non-Hispanic/Latino; 2 American Indian or Alaska Native, non-Hispanic/Latino; 8 Asian, non-Hispanic/Latino; 25 Hispanic/Latino; 3 Two or more races, non-Hispanic/Latino, 18 international. Average age 31. 275 applicants, 43% accepted, 79 enrolled. Expenses: Contact institution. *Financial support:* Fellowships, teaching assistantships, career-related internships or fieldwork, Federal Work-Study, and stipends available. Support available to part-time students. In 2010, 107 master's awarded. *Degree program information:* Part-time programs available. Offers communication and education (MA); communication science and disorders (MA); communication studies (MA); curriculum and instruction (MA); education (MA); kinesiology (MA); recreation administration (MA); special education (MA); teaching English learners (MA). *Application deadline:* For fall admission, 3/1 for domestic and international students; for spring admission, 9/15 for domestic and international students. Applications are processed on a rolling basis. *Application fee:* $55. Electronic applications accepted. *Application Contact:* School of Graduate, International, and Interdisciplinary Studies, 530-898-6880, Fax: 530-898-6889, E-mail: grin@csuchico.edu. *Dean,* Dr. Phyllis Fernlund, 530-898-4015.

College of Engineering, Computer Science, and Technology Students: 23 full-time (2 women), 18 part-time (1 woman); includes 1 Asian, non-Hispanic/Latino, 29 international. Average age 26. 123 applicants, 63% accepted, 13 enrolled. Expenses: Contact institution. *Financial support:* Fellowships, research assistantships, teaching assistantships, career-related internships or fieldwork and Federal Work-Study available. Support available to part-time students. In 2010, 51 master's awarded. *Degree program information:* Part-time programs available. Postbaccalaureate distance learning degree programs offered. Offers computer engineering (MS); computer science (MS); electronics engineering (MS); engineering, computer science, and technology (MS). *Application deadline:* For fall admission, 3/1 priority date for domestic students, 3/1 for international students; for spring admission, 9/15 priority date for domestic students, 9/15 for international students. Applications are processed on a rolling basis. *Application fee:* $55. Electronic applications accepted. *Application Contact:* School of Graduate, International, and Interdisciplinary Studies, 530-898-6880, Fax: 530-898-6889, E-mail: grin@csuchico.edu. *Dean,* Dr. Kenneth Derucher, 530-898-5963.

College of Humanities and Fine Arts Students: 46 full-time (31 women), 34 part-time (14 women); includes 1 American Indian or Alaska Native, non-Hispanic/Latino; 8 Hispanic/Latino; 1 Two or more races, non-Hispanic/Latino, 2 international. Average age 33. 50 applicants, 60% accepted, 21 enrolled. Expenses: Contact institution. *Financial support:* Teaching assistantships, career-related internships or fieldwork and Federal Work-Study available. Support available to part-time students. In 2010, 16 master's awarded. Offers art history (MA); English (MA); fine arts (MFA); history (MA); humanities and fine arts (MA, MFA); music (MA). *Application deadline:* For fall admission, 3/1 priority date for domestic students, 3/1 for international students; for spring admission, 9/15 priority date for domestic students, 9/15 for international students. Applications are processed on a rolling basis. *Application fee:* $55. Electronic applications accepted. *Application Contact:* School of Graduate, International, and Interdisciplinary Studies, 530-898-6880, Fax: 530-898-6889, E-mail: grin@csuchico.edu. *Dean,* Dr. Joel Zimbelman, 530-898-5351.

College of Natural Sciences Students: 47 full-time (33 women), 48 part-time (36 women); includes 2 Black or African American, non-Hispanic/Latino; 1 American Indian or Alaska Native, non-Hispanic/Latino; 5 Asian, non-Hispanic/Latino; 8 Hispanic/Latino; 5 Two or more races, non-Hispanic/Latino, 5 international. Average age 32. 130 applicants, 56% accepted, 49 enrolled. Expenses: Contact institution. *Financial support:* Fellowships, research assistantships, teaching assistantships, career-related internships or fieldwork and Federal Work-Study available. Support available to part-time students. In 2010, 17 master's awarded. *Degree program information:* Part-time programs available. Offers biological sciences (MS); botany (MS); environmental science (MS); geosciences (MS); hydrology/hydrogeology (MS); math education (MS); natural sciences (MS); nursing (MS); nutrition education (MS); nutritional sciences (MS). *Application deadline:* For fall admission, 3/1 priority date for domestic students, 3/1 for international students; for spring admission, 9/15 priority date for domestic students, 9/15 for international students. Applications are processed on a rolling basis. *Application fee:* $55. Electronic applications accepted. *Application Contact:* School of Graduate, International, and Interdisciplinary Studies, 530-898-6880, Fax: 530-898-6889, E-mail: grin@csuchico.edu. *Dean,* Dr. James Houpis, 530-898-6121.

CALIFORNIA STATE UNIVERSITY, DOMINGUEZ HILLS, Carson, CA 90747-0001

General Information State-supported, coed, comprehensive institution. CGS member. *Enrollment:* 13,854 graduate, professional, and undergraduate students; 1,283 full-time matriculated graduate/professional students (950 women), 1,624 part-time matriculated graduate/professional students (1,253 women). *Enrollment by degree level:* 2,242 master's, 665 other advanced degrees. *Graduate faculty:* 105 full-time (68 women), 99 part-time/adjunct (70 women). *Graduate housing:* Rooms and/or apartments available on a first-come, first-served basis to single and married students. Housing application deadline: 4/15. *Student services:* Campus employment opportunities, campus safety program, career counseling, child daycare facilities, free psychological counseling, international student services, low-cost health insurance, multicultural affairs office, services for students with disabilities. *Library facilities:* Leo F. Cain Educational Resource Center. *Online resources:* library catalog, web page, access to other libraries' catalogs. *Collection:* 442,893 titles, 27,960 serial subscriptions, 4,289 audiovisual materials. *Research affiliation:* Los Angeles Biomedical Research Institute at Harbor UCLA Medical Center (biomedical science), Hewlett Packard (catalyst initiative grant).

Computer facilities: 256 computers available on campus for general student use. A campuswide network can be accessed from student residence rooms. Online class registration is available. *Web address:* http://www.csudh.edu/.

General Application Contact: Brandy McLelland, Director of Student Records and Student Information Services, 310-243-3645, E-mail: bmclelland@csudh.edu.

GRADUATE UNITS

College of Arts and Humanities Students: 47 full-time (28 women), 282 part-time (188 women); includes 84 Black or African American, non-Hispanic/Latino; 2 American Indian or Alaska Native, non-Hispanic/Latino; 13 Asian, non-Hispanic/Latino; 50 Hispanic/Latino; 4 Two or more races, non-Hispanic/Latino, 8 international. Average age 39. 207 applicants, 76% accepted, 79 enrolled. *Faculty:* 30 full-time (15 women), 12 part-time/adjunct (4 women). Expenses: Contact institution. *Financial support:* Institutionally sponsored loans available. Support available to part-time students. In 2010, 41 master's awarded. *Degree program information:* Part-time and evening/weekend programs available. Offers arts and humanities (MA, MS, Certificate); English (MA); negotiation, conflict resolution and peacebuilding (MA); rhetoric and composition (Certificate); teaching English as a second language (Certificate). *Application deadline:* For fall admission, 6/1 for domestic students. *Application fee:* $55. *Application Contact:* Brandy McLelland, Interim Director, Student Information Services, 310-243-3645, E-mail: bmclelland@csudh.edu. *Dean,* Dr. George Arasimowicz, 310-243-3389, E-mail: garasimowicz@csudh.edu.

College of Business Administration and Public Policy Students: 79 full-time (37 women), 140 part-time (70 women); includes 35 Black or African American, non-Hispanic/Latino; 28 Asian, non-Hispanic/Latino; 32 Hispanic/Latino; 1 Native Hawaiian or other Pacific Islander, non-Hispanic/Latino; 2 Two or more races, non-Hispanic/Latino, 9 international. Average age 35. 622 applicants, 34% accepted, 55 enrolled. *Faculty:* 18 full-time (10 women), 18 part-time/adjunct (8 women). Expenses: Contact institution. In 2010, 130 master's awarded. *Degree program information:* Part-time and evening/weekend programs available. Postbaccalaureate distance learning degree programs offered (no on-campus study). Offers business administration (MBA); business administration and public policy (MBA, MPA); public administration (MPA). *Application deadline:* For fall admission, 4/1 for domestic and international students; for spring admission, 11/1 for domestic students, 10/1 for international students. *Application fee:* $55. *Application Contact:* Eileen Hall, Graduate Advisor, 310-243-3465, E-mail: ehall@csudh.edu. *Acting Dean,* Dr. Kaye Bragg, 310-243-3548, E-mail: kbragg@csudh.edu.

College of Extended and International Education Students: 10 full-time (5 women), 582 part-time (314 women); includes 32 Black or African American, non-Hispanic/Latino; 3 American Indian or Alaska Native, non-Hispanic/Latino; 51 Asian, non-Hispanic/Latino; 47 Hispanic/Latino; 3 Native Hawaiian or other Pacific Islander, non-Hispanic/Latino, 27 international. Average age 42. 191 applicants, 77% accepted, 110 enrolled. *Faculty:* 8 full-time (4 women), 52 part-time/adjunct (17 women). Expenses: Contact institution. In 2010, 121 master's awarded. *Degree program information:* Part-time and evening/weekend programs available. Postbaccalaureate distance learning degree programs offered. Offers extended and international education (MA, MS); humanities (MA); quality assurance (MS). *Application fee:* $55. Electronic applications accepted. *Application Contact:* Dr. Timothy Mozia, Director of Operations, 310-243-3741, E-mail: tmozia@csudh.edu. *Dean,* Dr. Margaret Gordon, 310-243-3737, Fax: 310-516-4423, E-mail: mgordon@csudh.edu.

College of Natural and Behavioral Sciences Students: 79 full-time (51 women), 152 part-time (97 women); includes 163 minority (57 Black or African American, non-Hispanic/Latino; 21 Asian, non-Hispanic/Latino; 79 Hispanic/Latino; 2 Native Hawaiian or other Pacific Islander, non-Hispanic/Latino; 4 Two or more races, non-Hispanic/Latino), 12 international. Average age 34. 182 applicants, 66% accepted, 72 enrolled. *Faculty:* 29 full-time (11 women), 24 part-time/adjunct (7 women). Expenses: Contact institution. In 2010, 30 master's awarded. Offers biology (MS); clinical psychology (MA); computer science (MSCS); environmental science (MS); natural and behavioral sciences (MA, MS, MSCS, Certificate); social research (Certificate); sociology (MA); teaching of mathematics (MA). *Application Contact:* Brandy McLelland, Interim Director, Student Information Services, 310-243-3645, E-mail: bmclelland@csudh.edu. *Acting Dean,* Dr. Laura Robles, 310-243-2547, E-mail: lrobles@csudh.edu.

College of Professional Studies Students: 1,085 full-time (826 women), 1,193 part-time (963 women); includes 1,433 minority (426 Black or African American, non-Hispanic/Latino; 10 American Indian or Alaska Native, non-Hispanic/Latino; 292 Asian, non-Hispanic/Latino; 658 Hispanic/Latino; 7 Native Hawaiian or other Pacific Islander, non-Hispanic/Latino; 40 Two or more races, non-Hispanic/Latino), 14 international. Average age 36. 1,403 applicants, 66% accepted, 586 enrolled. *Faculty:* 84 full-time (61 women), 56 part-time/adjunct (35 women). Expenses: Contact institution. In 2010, 533 master's awarded. *Application fee:* $55. Electronic applications accepted. *Application Contact:* Brandy McLelland, Interim Director, Student Information Services, 310-243-3645, E-mail: bmclelland@csudh.edu. *Dean,* Dr. Larry Ortiz, 301-243-2046, Fax: 310-217-6800, E-mail: lortiz@csudh.edu.

School of Education Students: 692 full-time (491 women), 633 part-time (469 women); includes 893 minority (251 Black or African American, non-Hispanic/Latino; 8 American Indian or Alaska Native, non-Hispanic/Latino; 117 Asian, non-Hispanic/Latino; 482 Hispanic/Latino; 6 Native Hawaiian or other Pacific Islander, non-Hispanic/Latino; 29 Two or more races, non-Hispanic/Latino), 9 international. Average age 37. 668 applicants, 72% accepted, 200 enrolled. *Faculty:* 53 full-time (35 women), 33 part-time/adjunct (17 women). Expenses: Contact institution. In 2010, 284 master's awarded. *Degree program information:* Part-time and evening/weekend programs available. Offers counseling (MA); curriculum and instruction (MA); early childhood (MA); education (MA, Certificate); educational administration (MA); individualized education (MA); mild/moderate (MA); moderate/severe (MA); multicultural education (MA); special education (MA); technology-based education (MA, Certificate). *Application deadline:* For fall admission, 6/1 priority date for domestic students; for spring admission, 10/1 priority date for domestic students. Applications are processed on a rolling basis. *Application fee:* $55. *Acting Director,* Cynthia Grutzik, 310-243-3510, Fax: 310-243-3518, E-mail: cgrutzik@csudh.edu.

School of Health and Human Services Students: 393 full-time (335 women), 560 part-time (494 women); includes 540 minority (175 Black or African American, non-Hispanic/Latino; 2 American Indian or Alaska Native, non-Hispanic/Latino; 175 Asian, non-Hispanic/Latino; 176 Hispanic/Latino; 1 Native Hawaiian or other Pacific Islander, non-Hispanic/Latino; 11 Two or more races, non-Hispanic/Latino), 5 international. Average age 37. 713 applicants, 60% accepted, 245 enrolled. *Faculty:* 34 full-time (26 women), 47 part-time/adjunct (42 women). Expenses: Contact institution. In 2010, 249 master's awarded. Offers health and human services (MA, MS, MSN, MSW); marital and family therapy (MS); nursing (MSN); occupational therapy (MS); physical education administration (MA); social work (MSW). *Application deadline:* For fall admission, 6/1 for domestic students. *Application fee:* $55. *Application Contact:* Brandy McLelland, Interim Director, Student Information Services, 310-243-3645, E-mail: bmclelland@csudh.edu. *Acting Director,* Dr. Anupama Joshi, 310-243-1003, Fax: 310-217-6800, E-mail: ajoshi@csudh.edu.

CALIFORNIA STATE UNIVERSITY, EAST BAY, Hayward, CA 94542-3000

General Information State-supported, coed, comprehensive institution. CGS member. *Enrollment:* 825 full-time matriculated graduate/professional students (580 women), 1,125 part-time matriculated graduate/professional students (660 women). *Enrollment by degree level:* 1,912 master's, 38 doctoral. *Graduate faculty:* 366 full-time (176 women), 454 part-time/adjunct (272 women). *Graduate housing:* Room and/or apartments available on a first-come, first-served basis to single students; on-campus housing not available to married students. Typical cost: $7963 per year. Housing application deadline: 12/1. *Student services:* Campus employment opportunities, campus safety program, career counseling, child daycare facilities, free psychological counseling, international student services, low-cost health insurance, services for students with disabilities. *Library facilities:* Hayward Campus Library. *Online resources:* library catalog, web page. *Research affiliation:* Stanford University (complex learning), Lawrence Livermore National Laboratory (technology transfer), NASA–Ames Research Center, Academy of Economy, Moscow (business management training), Sandia National Laboratories (technology marketing assessment), Pacific Telesis (urban education).

Computer facilities: Computer purchase and lease plans are available. 700 computers available on campus for general student use. A campuswide network can be accessed from student residence rooms and from off campus. Online class registration is available. *Web address:* http://www.csueastbay.edu/.

General Application Contact: Dr. Donna Wiley, Interim Associate Director, 510-885-2928, Fax: 510-885-4777, E-mail: donna.wiley@csueastbay.edu.

GRADUATE UNITS

Office of Academic Programs and Graduate Studies Students: 825 full-time (580 women), 1,125 part-time (660 women); includes 870 minority (185 Black or African American, non-Hispanic/Latino; 9 American Indian or Alaska Native, non-Hispanic/Latino; 397 Asian, non-Hispanic/Latino; 208 Hispanic/Latino; 11 Native Hawaiian or other Pacific Islander, non-Hispanic/Latino; 60 Two or more races, non-Hispanic/Latino), 405 international. Average age 32. 3,052 applicants, 46% accepted, 664 enrolled. *Faculty:* 366 full-time (176 women), 454 part-time/adjunct (272 women). Expenses: Contact institution. *Financial support:* Fellowships, teaching assistantships, career-related internships or fieldwork, Federal Work-Study, institutionally sponsored loans, and scholarships/grants available. Support available to part-time students. Financial award application deadline: 3/2; financial award applicants required to submit FAFSA. In 2010, 1,146 master's awarded. *Degree program information:* Part-time and evening/weekend programs available. Postbaccalaureate distance learning degree programs offered (no on-campus study). Offers interdisciplinary studies (MA, MS). *Application deadline:* For fall admission, 6/30 for domestic and international students. Applications are processed on a rolling basis. *Application fee:* $55. Electronic applications accepted. *Application Contact:* Dr. Donna Wiley, Interim Associate Director, 510-885-2928, Fax: 510-885-4777, E-mail: donna.wiley@csueastbay.edu. *Associate Vice President,* Dr. Susan Opp, 510-885-3716, Fax: 510-885-4777, E-mail: susan.opp@csueastbay.edu.

College of Business and Economics Students: 143 full-time (66 women), 197 part-time (101 women); includes 123 minority (13 Black or African American, non-Hispanic/Latino; 83 Asian, non-Hispanic/Latino; 16 Hispanic/Latino; 4 Native Hawaiian or other Pacific Islander, non-Hispanic/Latino; 7 Two or more races, non-Hispanic/Latino), 116 international. Average age 32. 389 applicants, 53% accepted, 92 enrolled. *Faculty:* 37 full-time (7 women), 8 part-time/adjunct (3 women). Expenses: Contact institution. *Financial support:* Fellowships, career-related internships or fieldwork, Federal Work-Study, institutionally sponsored loans, and scholarships/grants available. Support available to part-time students. Financial award application deadline: 3/2; financial award applicants required to submit FAFSA. In 2010, 248 master's awarded. *Degree program information:* Part-time and evening/weekend programs available. Postbaccalaureate distance learning degree programs offered (no on-campus study). Offers accounting/finance (MBA); business and economics (MA, MBA, MS); economics (MA); entrepreneurship (MBA); finance (MBA); human resources and organizational behavior (MBA); information technology management (MBA); marketing management (MBA); operations and supply chain management (MBA); strategy and international business (MBA); taxation (MS). *Application deadline:* For fall admission, 6/30 for domestic and international students. Applications are processed on a rolling basis. *Application fee:* $55. Electronic applications accepted. *Application Contact:* Dr. Donna Wiley, Interim Associate Director, 510-885-2928, Fax: 510-885-4777, E-mail: donna.wiley@csueastbay.edu. *Dean,* Dr. Terri Swartz, 510-885-3291, Fax: 510-885-4884, E-mail: terri.swartz@csueastbay.edu.

College of Education and Allied Studies Students: 363 full-time (297 women), 190 part-time (130 women); includes 210 minority (58 Black or African American, non-Hispanic/Latino; 4 American Indian or Alaska Native, non-Hispanic/Latino; 58 Asian, non-Hispanic/Latino; 68 Hispanic/Latino; 2 Native Hawaiian or other Pacific Islander, non-Hispanic/Latino; 20 Two or more races, non-Hispanic/Latino), 3 international. Average age 35. 762 applicants, 36% accepted, 125 enrolled. *Faculty:* 56 full-time (31 women), 11 part-time/adjunct (7 women). Expenses: Contact institution. *Financial support:* Career-related internships or fieldwork, Federal Work-Study, and institutionally sponsored loans available. Support available to part-time students. Financial award application deadline: 3/2; financial award applicants required to submit FAFSA. In 2010, 294 master's awarded. *Degree program information:* Part-time and evening/weekend programs available. Postbaccalaureate distance learning degree programs offered. Offers counseling (MS); education (MS); education and allied studies (MS, Ed D); educational leadership (MS, Ed D); exercise physiology (MS); humanities/cultural studies (MS); professional perspectives (MS); recreation and tourism (MS); skill acquisition/sport psychology (MS); special education (MS); specializing in urban teaching leadership (MS). *Application deadline:* For fall admission, 6/30 for domestic and international students. *Application fee:* $55. Electronic applications accepted. *Application Contact:* Dr. Donna Wiley, Interim Associate Director, 510-885-2928, Fax: 510-885-4777, E-mail: donna.wiley@csueastbay.edu. *Dean,* Dr. Carolyn Nelson, 510-885-3942, Fax: 510-885-2283, E-mail: carolyn.nelson@csueastbay.edu.

College of Letters, Arts, and Social Sciences Students: 275 full-time (190 women), 399 part-time (280 women); includes 344 minority (93 Black or African American, non-Hispanic/Latino; 3 American Indian or Alaska Native, non-Hispanic/Latino; 122 Asian, non-Hispanic/Latino; 94 Hispanic/Latino; 4 Native Hawaiian or other Pacific Islander, non-Hispanic/Latino; 28 Two or more races, non-Hispanic/Latino), 48 international. Average age 34. 1,128 applicants, 44% accepted, 260 enrolled. *Faculty:* 74 full-time (36 women), 21 part-time/adjunct (8 women). Expenses: Contact institution. *Financial support:* Fellowships, research assistantships, teaching assistantships, career-related internships or fieldwork, Federal Work-Study, institutionally sponsored loans, and scholarships/grants available. Support available to part-time students. Financial award application deadline: 3/2; financial award applicants required to submit FAFSA. In 2010, 412 master's awarded. *Degree program information:* Part-time and evening/weekend programs available. Offers anthropology (MA); communication (MA); English (MA); geography (MA); health care administration (MS); history (MA); letters, arts, and social sciences (MA, MPA, MS, MSW); multimedia (MA); music (MA); public administration (MPA); social work (MSW); speech pathology and audiology (MS). *Application deadline:* For fall admission, 6/30 for domestic and international students; for winter admission, 10/31 for domestic students; for spring admission, 11/30 for domestic and international students. Applications are processed on a rolling basis. *Application fee:* $55. Electronic applications accepted. *Application Contact:* Dr. Donna Wiley, Interim Associate Director, 510-885-2928, Fax: 510-885-4777, E-mail: donna.wiley@csueastbay.edu. *Dean,* Dr. Kathleen Rountree, 510-885-3161, Fax: 510-885-3164, E-mail: kathleen.rountree@csueastbay.edu.

College of Science Students: 173 full-time (83 women), 469 part-time (213 women); includes 193 minority (21 Black or African American, non-Hispanic/Latino; 2 American Indian or Alaska Native, non-Hispanic/Latino; 134 Asian, non-Hispanic/Latino; 30 Hispanic/Latino; 1 Native Hawaiian or other Pacific Islander, non-Hispanic/Latino; 5 Two or more races, non-Hispanic/Latino), 247 international. Average age 31. 768 applicants, 56% accepted, 187 enrolled. *Faculty:* 52 full-time (24 women). Expenses: Contact institution. *Financial support:* Career-related internships or fieldwork, Federal Work-Study, and institutionally sponsored loans available. Support available to part-time students. Financial award application deadline: 3/2; financial award applicants required to submit FAFSA. In 2010, 191 master's awarded. *Degree program information:* Part-time and evening/weekend programs available. Offers applied math (MS); biochemistry (MS); biological sciences (MA, MS); biostatistics (MS); chemistry (MS); computer networks (MS); computer science (MS); construction management (MS); engineering management (MS); geology (MS); marine science (MS); mathematics (MS); mathematics teaching (MS); science (MA, MS); statistics (MS). *Application deadline:* For fall admission, 6/30 for domestic and international students. *Application fee:* $55. Electronic applications accepted. *Application Contact:* Dr. Donna Wiley, Interim Associate Director, 510-885-2928, Fax: 510-885-4777, E-mail: donna.wiley@csueastbay.edu. *Dean,* Dr. Michael Leung, 510-885-3441, Fax: 510-885-2035, E-mail: michael.leung@csueastbay.edu.

CALIFORNIA STATE UNIVERSITY, FRESNO, Fresno, CA 93740-8027

General Information State-supported, coed, comprehensive institution. CGS member. *Graduate housing:* Room and/or apartments available on a first-come, first-served basis to single students; on-campus housing not available to married students. Housing application deadline: 4/1. *Research affiliation:* Coleman Foundation (administration), Starburst Foundation (engineering), Garabedian Foundation (agribusiness), California Endowment (arts and humanities).

GRADUATE UNITS

Division of Graduate Studies *Degree program information:* Part-time and evening/weekend programs available. Electronic applications accepted.

California State University, Fresno (continued)

College of Agricultural Sciences and Technology *Degree program information:* Part-time and evening/weekend programs available. Offers agricultural sciences and technology (MS); animal science (MS); family and consumer sciences (MS); food science and nutritional sciences (MS); industrial technology (MS); plant science (MS); viticulture and enology (MS). Electronic applications accepted.

College of Arts and Humanities *Degree program information:* Part-time and evening/weekend programs available. Offers art (MA); arts and humanities (MA, MFA); communication (MA); composition theory (MA); creative writing (MFA); linguistics (MA); literature (MA); mass communication and journalism (MA); music (MA); music education (MA); performance (MA); Spanish (MA). Electronic applications accepted.

College of Engineering and Computer Science *Degree program information:* Part-time and evening/weekend programs available. Offers civil engineering (MS); electrical engineering (MS); engineering and computer science (MS); mechanical engineering (MS). Electronic applications accepted.

College of Health and Human Services *Degree program information:* Part-time and evening/weekend programs available. Offers communicative disorders (MA); exercise science (MA); health and human services (MA, MPH, MPT, MS, MSW, DPT); health policy and management (MPH); health promotion (MPH); nursing (MS); physical therapy (MPT, DPT); social work education (MSW); sport psychology (MA). Electronic applications accepted.

College of Science and Mathematics *Degree program information:* Part-time and evening/weekend programs available. Offers biology (MA); biotechnology (MBT); chemistry (MS); computer science (MS); geology (MS); marine sciences (MS); mathematics (MA); physics (MS); psychology (MA, MS); science and mathematics (MA, MBT, MS); teaching (MA). Electronic applications accepted.

College of Social Sciences *Degree program information:* Part-time and evening/weekend programs available. Offers criminology (MS); history-teaching option (MA); history-traditional track (MA); international relations (MA); public administration (MPA); social sciences (MA, MPA, MS). Electronic applications accepted.

Craig School of Business *Degree program information:* Part-time programs available. Offers accountancy (MS); business (MBA, MS); business administration (MBA). Electronic applications accepted.

School of Education and Human Development *Degree program information:* Part-time and evening/weekend programs available. Offers counseling and student services (MS); education (MA); education and human development (MA, MS, Ed D); educational leadership (Ed D); marriage and family therapy (MS); rehabilitation counseling (MS); special education (MA). Electronic applications accepted.

CALIFORNIA STATE UNIVERSITY, FULLERTON, Fullerton, CA 92834-9480

General Information State-supported, coed, comprehensive institution. CGS member. *Enrollment:* 35,590 graduate, professional, and undergraduate students; 1,706 full-time matriculated graduate/professional students (1,024 women), 2,809 part-time matriculated graduate/professional students (1,611 women). *Enrollment by degree level:* 4,404 master's, 111 doctoral. *Graduate housing:* On-campus housing not available. *Student services:* Campus employment opportunities, campus safety program, career counseling, child daycare facilities, exercise/wellness program, free psychological counseling, international student services, low-cost health insurance, multicultural affairs office, services for students with disabilities, teacher training, writing training. *Library facilities:* Pollack Library. *Online resources:* library catalog, web page, access to other libraries' catalogs. *Collection:* 1.3 million titles, 23,295 serial subscriptions, 29,489 audiovisual materials.

Computer facilities: 2,000 computers available on campus for general student use. A campuswide network can be accessed from student residence rooms and from off campus. Online class registration is available. *Web address:* http://www.fullerton.edu/.

General Application Contact: Admissions/Applications, 657-278-2371, E-mail: admissions@fullerton.edu.

GRADUATE UNITS

Graduate Studies Students: 1,706 full-time (1,024 women), 2,809 part-time (1,611 women); includes 136 Black or African American, non-Hispanic/Latino; 10 American Indian or Alaska Native, non-Hispanic/Latino; 880 Asian, non-Hispanic/Latino; 691 Hispanic/Latino; 96 Two or more races, non-Hispanic/Latino, 576 international. Average age 31. 6,376 applicants, 42% accepted, 1671 enrolled. Expenses: Contact institution. *Financial support:* Research assistantships, teaching assistantships, career-related internships or fieldwork, Federal Work-Study, institutionally sponsored loans, and scholarships/grants available. Support available to part-time students. Financial award application deadline: 3/1; financial award applicants required to submit FAFSA. In 2010, 1,394 master's, 7 doctorates awarded. *Degree program information:* Part-time and evening/weekend programs available. Postbaccalaureate distance learning degree programs offered (no on-campus study). *Application deadline:* For fall admission, 3/1 for domestic and international students; for spring admission, 10/1 for domestic and international students. Applications are processed on a rolling basis. *Application fee:* $55. Electronic applications accepted. *Application Contact:* Admissions/Applications, 657-278-2371, Fax: 657-278-2356, E-mail: admissions@fullerton.edu. *Associate Vice President, Graduate Programs and Research,* Dr. Dorota Huizinga, 657-278-2618.

College of Business and Economics Students: 364 full-time (179 women), 405 part-time (151 women); includes 10 Black or African American, non-Hispanic/Latino; 1 American Indian or Alaska Native, non-Hispanic/Latino; 228 Asian, non-Hispanic/Latino; 61 Hispanic/Latino; 15 Two or more races, non-Hispanic/Latino, 196 international. Average age 29. 1,076 applicants, 42% accepted, 223 enrolled. Expenses: Contact institution. *Financial support:* Career-related internships or fieldwork, Federal Work-Study, institutionally sponsored loans, and scholarships/grants available. Support available to part-time students. Financial award application deadline: 3/1; financial award applicants required to submit FAFSA. In 2010, 207 master's awarded. *Degree program information:* Part-time programs available. Offers accounting (MBA, MS); business and economics (MA, MBA, MS); business economics (MBA); e-commerce (MBA); economics (MA); entrepreneurship (MBA); finance (MBA); information systems (MS); information systems (decision sciences) (MS); information systems (e-commerce) (MS); information technology (MS); international business (MBA); management (MBA); management science (MBA); marketing (MBA); taxation (MS). *Application deadline:* Applications are processed on a rolling basis. *Application fee:* $55. Electronic applications accepted. *Application Contact:* Admissions/Applications, 657-278-2371. *Dean,* Dr. Anil Puri, 657-773-2592.

College of Communications Students: 93 full-time (74 women), 80 part-time (59 women); includes 11 Black or African American, non-Hispanic/Latino; 28 Asian, non-Hispanic/Latino; 33 Hispanic/Latino; 4 Two or more races, non-Hispanic/Latino, 11 international. Average age 30. 510 applicants, 19% accepted, 68 enrolled. Expenses: Contact institution. *Financial support:* Teaching assistantships, career-related internships or fieldwork, Federal Work-Study, institutionally sponsored loans, and scholarships/grants available. Support available to part-time students. Financial award application deadline: 3/1; financial award applicants required to submit FAFSA. In 2010, 70 master's awarded. *Degree program information:* Part-time programs available. Offers advertising (MA); communications (MA, MFA); communicative disorders (MA); entertainment and tourism (MA); journalism (MA); public relations (MA); speech communication (MA). *Application fee:* $55. *Application Contact:* Admissions/Applications, 657-278-2371. *Dean,* Dr. William G. Briggs, 657-278-3355.

College of Education Students: 119 full-time (98 women), 715 part-time (569 women); includes 39 Black or African American, non-Hispanic/Latino; 2 American Indian or Alaska Native, non-Hispanic/Latino; 113 Asian, non-Hispanic/Latino; 192 Hispanic/Latino; 16 Two or more races, non-Hispanic/Latino, 8 international. Average age 34. 559 applicants, 64% accepted, 292 enrolled. Expenses: Contact institution. *Financial support:* Research assistantships, teaching assistantships available. Financial award application deadline: 3/1; financial award applicants required to submit FAFSA. In 2010, 301 master's, 7 doctorates awarded. Offers bilingual/bicultural education (MS); education (MS, Ed D); educational leadership (MS, Ed D); elementary curriculum and instruction (MS); instructional design and technology (MS); middle school mathematics (MS); reading (MS); secondary education (MS); special education (MS); teacher induction (MS). *Application fee:* $55. *Application Contact:* Admissions/Applications, 657-278-2371. *Dean,* Dr. Claire Cavallaro, 657-278-4021.

College of Engineering and Computer Science Students: 210 full-time (38 women), 522 part-time (124 women); includes 17 Black or African American, non-Hispanic/Latino; 186 Asian, non-Hispanic/Latino; 47 Hispanic/Latino; 9 Two or more races, non-Hispanic/Latino, 268 international. Average age 29. 1,052 applicants, 67% accepted, 315 enrolled. Expenses: Contact institution. *Financial support:* Career-related internships or fieldwork, Federal Work-Study, institutionally sponsored loans, and scholarships/grants available. Support available to part-time students. Financial award application deadline: 3/1; financial award applicants required to submit FAFSA. In 2010, 207 master's awarded. *Degree program information:* Part-time programs available. Offers civil engineering and engineering mechanics (MS); computer science (MS); electrical engineering (MS); engineering and computer science (MS); mechanical engineering (MS); software engineering (MS); systems engineering (MS). *Application fee:* $55. *Application Contact:* Admissions/Applications, 657-278-2371. *Dean,* Dr. Raman Unnikrishnan, 657-278-3362.

College of Health and Human Development Students: 462 full-time (359 women), 377 part-time (314 women); includes 34 Black or African American, non-Hispanic/Latino; 1 American Indian or Alaska Native, non-Hispanic/Latino; 163 Asian, non-Hispanic/Latino; 162 Hispanic/Latino; 18 Two or more races, non-Hispanic/Latino, 21 international. Average age 32. 1,648 applicants, 26% accepted, 329 enrolled. Expenses: Contact institution. *Financial support:* Career-related internships or fieldwork, Federal Work-Study, institutionally sponsored loans, and scholarships/grants available. Support available to part-time students. Financial award application deadline: 3/1; financial award applicants required to submit FAFSA. In 2010, 245 master's awarded. *Degree program information:* Part-time programs available. Offers counseling (MS); health and human development (MPH, MS, MSW); kinesiology (MS); nursing (MS); public health (MPH); social work (MSW). *Application fee:* $55. *Application Contact:* Admissions/Applications, 657-278-2371. *Acting Dean,* Dr. Shari McMahan, 657-278-3311.

College of Humanities and Social Sciences Students: 310 full-time (198 women), 477 part-time (264 women); includes 19 Black or African American, non-Hispanic/Latino; 6 American Indian or Alaska Native, non-Hispanic/Latino; 88 Asian, non-Hispanic/Latino; 154 Hispanic/Latino; 27 Two or more races, non-Hispanic/Latino, 39 international. Average age 30. 1,032 applicants, 44% accepted, 313 enrolled. Expenses: Contact institution. *Financial support:* Career-related internships or fieldwork, Federal Work-Study, institutionally sponsored loans, and scholarships/grants available. Support available to part-time students. Financial award application deadline: 3/1; financial award applicants required to submit FAFSA. In 2010, 286 master's awarded. *Degree program information:* Part-time programs available. Offers American studies (MA); analysis of specific language structures (MA); anthropological linguistics (MA); anthropology (MA); applied linguistics (MA); clinical/community psychology (MS); communication and semantics (MA); comparative literature (MA); disorders of communication (MA); English (MA); environmental sciences (MS); experimental phonetics (MA); French (MA); geography (MA); German (MA); gerontology (MS); history (MA); humanities and social sciences (MA, MPA, MS); political science (MA); psychology (MA); public administration (MPA); sociology (MA); Spanish (MA); teaching English to speakers of other languages (MS). *Application fee:* $55. *Application Contact:* Admissions/Applications, 657-278-2371. *Dean,* Dr. Angela Della-Volpe, 657-278-3528.

College of Natural Science and Mathematics Students: 62 full-time (28 women), 157 part-time (87 women); includes 2 Black or African American, non-Hispanic/Latino; 51 Asian, non-Hispanic/Latino; 24 Hispanic/Latino; 6 Two or more races, non-Hispanic/Latino, 20 international. Average age 29. 308 applicants, 47% accepted, 86 enrolled. Expenses: Contact institution. *Financial support:* Research assistantships, teaching assistantships, career-related internships or fieldwork, Federal Work-Study, institutionally sponsored loans, and scholarships/grants available. Support available to part-time students. Financial award application deadline: 3/1; financial award applicants required to submit FAFSA. In 2010, 63 master's awarded. *Degree program information:* Part-time programs available. Offers applied mathematics (MA); biological science (MS); chemistry (MS); geochemistry (MS); geological sciences (MS); mathematics (MA); mathematics for secondary school teachers (MA); natural science and mathematics (MA, MAT, MS); physics (MA); teaching science (MAT). *Application fee:* $55. *Application Contact:* Admissions/Applications, 657-278-2371. *Dean,* Dr. Robert Koch, 657-278-2638.

College of the Arts Students: 86 full-time (50 women), 76 part-time (43 women); includes 4 Black or African American, non-Hispanic/Latino; 23 Asian, non-Hispanic/Latino; 18 Hispanic/Latino; 1 Two or more races, non-Hispanic/Latino, 13 international. Average age 32. 191 applicants, 28% accepted, 45 enrolled. Expenses: Contact institution. *Financial support:* Teaching assistantships, career-related internships or fieldwork, Federal Work-Study, institutionally sponsored loans, and scholarships/grants available. Support available to part-time students. Financial award application deadline: 3/1; financial award applicants required to submit FAFSA. In 2010, 37 master's awarded. *Degree program information:* Part-time programs available. Offers acting (MFA); acting and directing (MA); art (MA, MFA); art history (MA); arts (MA, MFA, MM); dance (MA); design (MA); directing (MFA); dramatic literature/criticism (MA); music education (MA); music history and literature (MA); oral interpretation (MA); performance (MM); piano pedagogy (MA); playwriting (MA); technical theater (MA); technical theater and design (MFA); television (MA); theatre for children (MA); theatre history (MA); theory-composition (MM). *Application fee:* $55. *Application Contact:* Admissions/Applications, 657-278-2371. *Dean,* Jerry Samuelson, 657-278-3256.

CALIFORNIA STATE UNIVERSITY, LONG BEACH, Long Beach, CA 90840

General Information State-supported, coed, comprehensive institution. CGS member. *Enrollment:* 33,416 graduate, professional, and undergraduate students; 2,038 full-time matriculated graduate/professional students (1,251 women), 2,561 part-time matriculated graduate/professional students (1,518 women). *Enrollment by degree level:* 4,506 master's, 93 doctoral. *Graduate faculty:* 495 full-time (219 women), 153 part-time/adjunct (84 women). *Graduate housing:* Room and/or apartments available on a first-come, first-served basis to single students; on-campus housing not available to married students. Typical cost: $11,294 (including board). Housing application deadline: 4/1. *Student services:* Campus employment opportunities, campus safety program, career counseling, child daycare facilities, exercise/wellness program, free psychological counseling, grant writing training, international student services, low-cost health insurance, multicultural affairs office, services for students with disabilities, teacher training, writing training. *Library facilities:* University Library. *Online resources:* library catalog, web page, access to other libraries' catalogs. *Collection:* 2.4 million titles, 12,264 serial subscriptions, 1.5 million audiovisual materials. *Research affiliation:* The Boeing Company (aerospace engineering and manufacturing).

Computer facilities: 2,000 computers available on campus for general student use. A campuswide network can be accessed from off campus. *Web address:* http://www.csulb.edu/.

General Application Contact: Linda Fontes, Communication Specialist, 562-985-4129, Fax: 562-985-1680, E-mail: lfontes@csulb.edu.

GRADUATE UNITS

Graduate Studies Students: 2,038 full-time (1,251 women), 2,561 part-time (1,518 women); includes 258 Black or African American, non-Hispanic/Latino; 51 American Indian or Alaska Native, non-Hispanic/Latino; 834 Asian, non-Hispanic/Latino; 973 Hispanic/Latino, 449 international. Average age 31. 7,762 applicants, 39% accepted, 1623 enrolled. *Faculty:* 495 full-time (219 women), 153 part-time/adjunct (84 women). Expenses: Contact institution. *Financial support:* Fellowships, research assistantships, teaching assistantships, career-related internships or fieldwork, Federal Work-Study, institutionally sponsored loans, scholarships/grants, traineeships, tuition waivers (partial), and unspecified assistantships available. Financial award application deadline: 3/2; financial award applicants required to submit FAFSA. In 2010, 1,816 master's, 13 doctorates awarded. *Degree program information:* Part-time and evening/weekend programs available. Postbaccalaureate distance learning degree programs offered (no on-campus study). Offers interdisciplinary studies (MA, MS). *Application deadline:* For fall admission, 7/1 for domestic and international students; for spring admission, 12/1 for domestic and international students. Applications are processed on a rolling basis. *Application fee:* $55. Electronic applications accepted. *Application Contact:* Rachel Brophy, Student Programs Coordinator, 562-985-4546, Fax: 562-985-7786, E-mail: rpbrophy@csulb.edu. *Director*, Dr. Cecile Lindsay, 562-985-8225, Fax: 562-985-1680, E-mail: clindsay@csulb.edu.

College of Business Administration Students: 69 full-time (28 women), 175 part-time (79 women); includes 6 Black or African American, non-Hispanic/Latino; 51 Asian, non-Hispanic/Latino; 27 Hispanic/Latino, 33 international. Average age 30. 557 applicants, 36% accepted, 65 enrolled. *Faculty:* 20 full-time (5 women), 6 part-time/adjunct (1 woman). Expenses: Contact institution. *Financial support:* Career-related internships or fieldwork and scholarships/grants available. Financial award application deadline: 3/2; financial award applicants required to submit FAFSA. In 2010, 147 master's awarded. *Degree program information:* Part-time and evening/weekend programs available. Offers business administration (MBA). *Application deadline:* For fall admission, 3/30 for domestic students. Applications are processed on a rolling basis. *Application fee:* $55. Electronic applications accepted. *Application Contact:* Dr. H. Michael Chung, Director, Graduate Programs and Executive Education, 562-985-5565, Fax: 562-985-5742, E-mail: hmchung@csulb.edu. *Dean*, Dr. Michael E. Solt, 562-985-5306, Fax: 562-985-5742, E-mail: msolt@csulb.edu.

College of Education Students: 256 full-time (196 women), 541 part-time (426 women); includes 78 Black or African American, non-Hispanic/Latino; 19 American Indian or Alaska Native, non-Hispanic/Latino; 101 Asian, non-Hispanic/Latino; 253 Hispanic/Latino, 21 international. Average age 32. 1,048 applicants, 38% accepted, 333 enrolled. *Faculty:* 48 full-time (30 women), 28 part-time/adjunct (20 women). Expenses: Contact institution. *Financial support:* Federal Work-Study, institutionally sponsored loans, and scholarships/grants available. Financial award application deadline: 3/2. In 2010, 269 master's, 13 doctorates awarded. *Degree program information:* Part-time and evening/weekend programs available. Offers counseling (MS); education (MA, Ed D); educational administration (MA, Ed D); educational psychology (MA); elementary education (MA); marriage and family therapy (MS); school counseling (MS); secondary education (MA); special education (MS); student development in higher education (MS). *Application deadline:* For fall admission, 3/1 for domestic students. Applications are processed on a rolling basis. *Application fee:* $55. Electronic applications accepted. *Application Contact:* Nancy L. McGlothin, Coordinator for Graduate Studies and Research, 562-985-8476, Fax: 562-985-4951, E-mail: nmcgloth@csulb.edu. *Dean*, Dr. Marquita Grenot-Scheyer, 562-985-1609, Fax: 562-985-4951, E-mail: cedinfo@csulb.edu.

College of Engineering Students: 331 full-time (66 women), 408 part-time (68 women); includes 27 Black or African American, non-Hispanic/Latino; 3 American Indian or Alaska Native, non-Hispanic/Latino; 193 Asian, non-Hispanic/Latino; 77 Hispanic/Latino, 238 international. Average age 29. 1,169 applicants, 61% accepted, 300 enrolled. *Faculty:* 51 full-time (10 women), 12 part-time/adjunct (0 women). Expenses: Contact institution. *Financial support:* Research assistantships, teaching assistantships, career-related internships or fieldwork, Federal Work-Study, institutionally sponsored loans, scholarships/grants, and unspecified assistantships available. Financial award application deadline: 3/2. In 2010, 200 master's awarded. *Degree program information:* Part-time and evening/weekend programs available. Offers aerospace engineering (MSAE); chemical engineering (MS); civil engineering (MSCE); computer engineering (MSCS); computer science (MSCS); electrical engineering (MSEE); engineering (MS, MSAE, MSCE, MSCS, MSE, MSEE, MSME, PhD); engineering and industrial applied mathematics (PhD); interdisciplinary engineering (MSE); management engineering (MSE); mechanical engineering (MSME). *Application deadline:* For fall admission, 4/20 for domestic students. *Application fee:* $55. Electronic applications accepted. *Application Contact:* Dr. Sandra Cynar, Special Assistant to the Dean for Outreach, 562-985-1512, Fax: 562-985-7561, E-mail: cynar@csulb.edu. *Dean*, Dr. Forouzan Golshani, 562-985-5123, Fax: 562-985-7561, E-mail: coe-dean@csulb.edu.

College of Health and Human Services Students: 806 full-time (638 women), 670 part-time (515 women); includes 126 Black or African American, non-Hispanic/Latino; 11 American Indian or Alaska Native, non-Hispanic/Latino; 297 Asian, non-Hispanic/Latino; 392 Hispanic/Latino, 57 international. Average age 31. 3,128 applicants, 29% accepted, 428 enrolled. *Faculty:* 96 full-time (60 women), 54 part-time/adjunct (38 women). Expenses: Contact institution. *Financial support:* Fellowships, research assistantships, teaching assistantships, career-related internships or fieldwork, Federal Work-Study, institutionally sponsored loans, and scholarships/grants available. Financial award application deadline: 3/2; financial award applicants required to submit FAFSA. In 2010, 844 master's awarded. *Degree program information:* Part-time and evening/weekend programs available. Postbaccalaureate distance learning degree programs offered (no on-campus study). Offers adapted physical education (MA); coaching and student athlete development (MA); communicative disorders (MA); criminal justice (MS); emergency services administration (MS); exercise physiology and nutrition (MS); exercise science (MS); family and consumer sciences (MA); food science (MS); gerontology (MS); health and human services (MA, MPA, MPH, MPT, MS, MSN, MSW); health care administration (MS); health science (MPH, MS); hospitality foodservice and hotel management (MS); individualized studies (MA); kinesiology (MA); nursing (MSN); nutritional science (MS); pedagogical studies (MA); physical therapy (MPT); public policy and administration (MPA); recreation administration (MS); social work (MSW); sport and exercise psychology (MS); sport management (MA); sports medicine and injury studies (MS). *Application deadline:* For fall admission, 7/1 for domestic students; for spring admission, 12/1 for domestic students. Applications are processed on a rolling basis. *Application fee:* $55. Electronic applications accepted. *Application Contact:* Kenneth I. Millar, Dean, 562-985-4194, Fax: 562-985-7581. *Dean*, Kenneth I. Millar, 562-985-4194, Fax: 562-985-7581.

College of Liberal Arts Students: 289 full-time (174 women), 380 part-time (230 women); includes 15 Black or African American, non-Hispanic/Latino; 11 American Indian or Alaska Native, non-Hispanic/Latino; 70 Asian, non-Hispanic/Latino; 126 Hispanic/Latino, 42 international. Average age 30. 1,014 applicants, 40% accepted, 264 enrolled. *Faculty:* 134 full-time (62 women), 10 part-time/adjunct (4 women). Expenses: Contact institution. *Financial support:* Research assistantships, teaching assistantships, career-related internships or fieldwork, Federal Work-Study, institutionally sponsored loans, and scholarships/grants available. Financial award application deadline: 3/2. In 2010, 194 master's awarded. *Degree program information:* Part-time and evening/weekend programs available. Offers Africa and the Middle East (MA); ancient/medieval Europe (MA); anthropology (MA); applied anthropology (MA); Asia (MA); Asian studies (MA); communication studies (MA); creative writing (MFA); economics (MA); English (MA); French and Francophone studies (MA); general linguistics (MA); geography (MA); German (MA); global logistics (MA); human factors (MS); industrial/organizational psychology (MS); language and culture (MA); Latin America (MA); liberal arts (MA, MFA, MS); modern Europe (MA); philosophy (MA); political science (MA); psychology (MA); religious studies (MA); Spanish (MA); special concentration (MA); teaching English as a second language (MA); United States (MA); world (MA). *Application deadline:* For fall admission, 7/1 for domestic and international students; for spring admission, 12/1 for international students. Applications are processed on a rolling basis. *Application fee:* $55. Electronic applications accepted. *Application Contact:* Dr. Mark Wiley, Associate Dean, 562-985-5381, Fax: 562-985-2463, E-mail: mwiley@csulb.edu. *Dean*, Dr. Gerry Riposa, 562-985-5381, Fax: 562-985-2463, E-mail: cla@csulb.edu.

College of Natural Sciences and Mathematics Students: 111 full-time (47 women), 279 part-time (121 women); includes 10 Black or African American, non-Hispanic/Latino; 2 American Indian or Alaska Native, non-Hispanic/Latino; 87 Asian, non-Hispanic/Latino; 53 Hispanic/Latino, 35 international. Average age 30. 435 applicants, 59% accepted, 155 enrolled. *Faculty:* 77 full-time (23 women), 7 part-time/adjunct (5 women). Expenses: Contact institution. *Financial support:* Research assistantships, teaching assistantships, Federal Work-Study, institutionally sponsored loans, scholarships/grants, traineeships, and unspecified assistantships available. Financial award application deadline: 3/2. In 2010, 78 master's awarded. *Degree program information:* Part-time programs available. Offers biochemistry (MS); biology (MS); chemistry (MS); geology (MS); geophysics (MS); mathematics (MS); microbiology (MS); natural sciences and mathematics (MS); physics (MS); science education (MS). *Application deadline:* For fall admission, 7/1 for domestic students. Applications are processed on a rolling basis. *Application fee:* $55. Electronic applications accepted. *Application Contact:* Dr. Henry Fung, Associate Dean for Curriculum and Instruction, 562-985-7898, Fax: 562-985-2315, E-mail: hcfung@csulb.edu. *Dean*, Dr. Laura Kingsford, 562-985-1521, Fax: 562-985-2315, E-mail: lking@csulb.edu.

College of the Arts Students: 174 full-time (101 women), 57 part-time (36 women); includes 1 Black or African American, non-Hispanic/Latino; 1 American Indian or Alaska Native, non-Hispanic/Latino; 22 Asian, non-Hispanic/Latino; 28 Hispanic/Latino, 23 international. Average age 31. 409 applicants, 27% accepted, 77 enrolled. *Faculty:* 71 full-time (30 women), 37 part-time/adjunct (16 women). Expenses: Contact institution. *Financial support:* Research assistantships, teaching assistantships, Federal Work-Study, institutionally sponsored loans, scholarships/grants, and traineeships available. Financial award application deadline: 3/2. In 2010, 81 master's awarded. *Degree program information:* Part-time programs available. Offers acting (MFA); art education (MA); art history (MA); arts (MA, MFA, MM); composition (MM); conducting-choral (MM); conducting-instrumental (MM); dance (MA, MFA); design (MFA); instrument/vocal performance (MM); jazz studies (MM); music (MA); opera performance (MM); studio art (MA, MFA); theatre management (MFA). *Application deadline:* For fall admission, 1/31 for domestic students. Applications are processed on a rolling basis. *Application fee:* $55. Electronic applications accepted. *Application Contact:* Jay Kvapil, Interim Dean, 562-985-4364, Fax: 562-985-7883, E-mail: cota@csulb.edu. *Interim Dean*, Jay Kvapil, 562-985-4364, Fax: 562-985-7883, E-mail: cota@csulb.edu.

CALIFORNIA STATE UNIVERSITY, LOS ANGELES, Los Angeles, CA 90032-8530

General Information State-supported, coed, comprehensive institution. CGS member. *Enrollment:* 20,142 graduate, professional, and undergraduate students; 1,858 full-time matriculated graduate/professional students (1,246 women), 2,184 part-time matriculated graduate/professional students (1,345 women). *Enrollment by degree level:* 4,018 master's, 24 doctoral. *Graduate faculty:* 189 full-time (97 women), 154 part-time/adjunct (75 women). *Graduate housing:* Room and/or apartments available on a first-come, first-served basis to single students; on-campus housing not available to married students. Typical cost: $9105 (including board). *Student services:* Campus employment opportunities, career counseling, child daycare facilities, free psychological counseling, international student services, multicultural affairs office, services for students with disabilities, writing training. *Library facilities:* John F. Kennedy Memorial Library plus 1 other. *Online resources:* library catalog, web page. *Collection:* 1.3 million titles, 26,104 serial subscriptions, 11,812 audiovisual materials.

Computer facilities: 1,500 computers available on campus for general student use. A campuswide network can be accessed from student residence rooms and from off campus. Online class registration is available. *Web address:* http://www.calstatela.edu/.

General Application Contact: Dr. Alan Muchlinski, Interim Dean of Graduate Studies, 323-343-3820, Fax: 323-343-5653, E-mail: amuchli@exchange.calstatela.edu.

GRADUATE UNITS

Graduate Studies Students: 1,858 full-time (1,246 women), 2,184 part-time (1,345 women); includes 2,192 minority (218 Black or African American, non-Hispanic/Latino; 7 American Indian or Alaska Native, non-Hispanic/Latino; 638 Asian, non-Hispanic/Latino; 1,274 Hispanic/Latino; 3 Native Hawaiian or other Pacific Islander, non-Hispanic/Latino; 52 Two or more races, non-Hispanic/Latino), 502 international. Average age 32. 2,017 applicants, 99% accepted, 1216 enrolled. *Faculty:* 189 full-time (97 women), 154 part-time/adjunct (75 women). Expenses: Contact institution. *Financial support:* Fellowships, teaching assistantships, career-related internships or fieldwork and Federal Work-Study available. Support available to part-time students. Financial award application deadline: 3/1. In 2010, 1,351 master's awarded. *Degree program information:* Part-time and evening/weekend programs available. *Application deadline:* For fall admission, 5/1 for domestic and international students. Applications are processed on a rolling basis. *Application fee:* $55. Electronic applications accepted. *Application Contact:* Dr. Alan Muchlinski, Dean of Graduate Studies, 323-343-3820, Fax: 323-343-5653, E-mail: amuchli@exchange.calstatela.edu. *Dean of Graduate Studies*, Dr. Alan Muchlinski, 323-343-3820, Fax: 323-343-5653, E-mail: amuchli@exchange.calstatela.edu.

Charter College of Education Students: 729 full-time (533 women), 734 part-time (571 women); includes 889 minority (80 Black or African American, non-Hispanic/Latino; 1 American Indian or Alaska Native, non-Hispanic/Latino; 181 Asian, non-Hispanic/Latino; 610 Hispanic/Latino; 1 Native Hawaiian or other Pacific Islander, non-Hispanic/Latino; 16 Two or more races, non-Hispanic/Latino), 59 international. Average age 33. 507 applicants, 99% accepted, 357 enrolled. *Faculty:* 41 full-time (26 women), 21 part-time/adjunct (13 women). Expenses: Contact institution. *Financial support:* Career-related internships or fieldwork and Federal Work-Study available. Support available to part-time students. Financial award application deadline: 3/1. In 2010, 450 master's awarded. *Degree program information:* Part-time and evening/weekend programs available. Offers applied and advanced studies in education (MA); counseling (MS); education (MA, MS, PhD); elementary teaching (MA); reading (MA); secondary teaching (MA); special education (MA, PhD). *Application deadline:* For fall admission, 5/1 for domestic and international students. Applications are processed on a rolling basis. *Application fee:* $55. Electronic applications accepted. *Application Contact:* Dr. Alan Muchlinski, Dean of Graduate Studies, 323-343-3820, Fax: 323-343-5653, E-mail: amuchli@exchange.calstatela.edu. *Dean*, Dr. Mary Falvey, 323-343-4300, Fax: 323-343-4318, E-mail: mfalvey@calstatela.edu.

College of Arts and Letters Students: 192 full-time (110 women), 234 part-time (127 women); includes 176 minority (30 Black or African American, non-Hispanic/Latino; 1 American Indian or Alaska Native, non-Hispanic/Latino; 30 Asian, non-Hispanic/Latino; 105 Hispanic/Latino; 10 Two or more races, non-Hispanic/Latino), 53 international. Average age 34. 252 applicants, 99% accepted, 133 enrolled. *Faculty:* 45 full-time (24 women), 26 part-time/adjunct (10 women). Expenses: Contact institution. *Financial support:* Career-related internships or fieldwork and Federal Work-Study available. Support available to part-time students. Financial award application deadline: 3/1. In 2010, 155 master's awarded. *Degree program information:* Part-time and evening/weekend programs available. Offers art (MA); arts and letters (MA, MFA, MM); English (MA); fine arts (MFA); French (MA); music composition (MM); music education (MA); musicology (MA); performance (MM); philosophy (MA); Spanish (MA); speech communication (MA); television, film and theatre (MFA); theater arts (MA). *Application deadline:* For fall admission, 5/1 for domestic and international students. Applications are processed on a rolling basis. *Application fee:* $55. Electronic applications accepted. *Application Contact:* Dr. Alan Muchlinski, Dean of Graduate Studies, 323-343-3820, Fax: 323-343-5653, E-mail: amuchli@exchange.calstatela.edu. *Dean*, Peter McAllister, 323-343-4001, Fax: 323-343-6440.

College of Business and Economics Students: 76 full-time (36 women), 186 part-time (99 women); includes 100 minority (3 Black or African American, non-Hispanic/Latino; 70 Asian, non-Hispanic/Latino; 24 Hispanic/Latino; 3 Two or more races, non-Hispanic/Latino), 106 international. Average age 31. 167 applicants, 100% accepted, 95 enrolled. *Faculty:* 23 full-time (8 women), 9 part-time/adjunct (0 women). Expenses: Contact institution. *Financial support:* Fellowships, career-related internships or fieldwork and Federal Work-Study available. Support available to part-time students. Financial award application deadline: 3/1. In 2010, 129 master's awarded. *Degree program information:* Part-time and evening/weekend programs available. Offers accountancy (MS); accounting (MBA); analytical quantitative economics (MA); business and economics (MA, MBA, MS); business economics (MA, MBA, MS); business information systems (MBA); economics (MA); finance and banking (MBA, MS); health care management (MS); international business (MBA, MS); management (MBA, MS); management information systems (MS); marketing management (MBA, MS); office management (MBA). *Application deadline:* For fall admission, 5/1 for international students. Applications are processed on a rolling basis. *Application fee:* $55. Electronic applications accepted. *Application Contact:* Dr. Alan Muchlinski, Dean of Graduate Studies, 323-343-3820, Fax: 323-343-5653, E-mail: amuchli@exchange.calstatela.edu. *Acting Dean*, Dr. Dong-Woo Lee, 323-343-2800, Fax: 323-343-2813, E-mail: dwlee@calstatela.edu.

College of Engineering, Computer Science, and Technology Students: 172 full-time (51 women), 268 part-time (49 women); includes 160 minority (18 Black or African American, non-Hispanic/Latino; 82 Asian, non-Hispanic/Latino; 59 Hispanic/Latino; 1 Two or more races, non-Hispanic/Latino), 206 international. Average age 29. 308 applicants, 99% accepted, 123 enrolled. *Faculty:* 16 full-time (5 women), 13 part-time/adjunct (2 women).

California State University, Los Angeles (continued)

Expenses: Contact institution. *Financial support:* Federal Work-Study available. Support available to part-time students. Financial award application deadline: 3/1. In 2010, 161 master's awarded. *Degree program information:* Part-time and evening/weekend programs available. Offers civil engineering (MS); computer science (MS); electrical engineering (MS); engineering, computer science, and technology (MA, MS); industrial and technical studies (MA); mechanical engineering (MS). *Application deadline:* For fall admission, 5/1 for domestic and international students. Applications are processed on a rolling basis. *Application fee:* $55. Electronic applications accepted. *Application Contact:* Dr. Alan Muchlinski, Dean of Graduate Studies, 323-343-3820, Fax: 323-343-5653, E-mail: amuchli@exchange.calstatela.edu. *Dean,* Dr. Keith Moo-Young, 323-343-4500, Fax: 323-343-4555, E-mail: kmooyou@exchange.calstatela.edu.

College of Health and Human Services Students: 436 full-time (363 women), 299 part-time (250 women); includes 455 minority (47 Black or African American, non-Hispanic/Latino; 3 American Indian or Alaska Native, non-Hispanic/Latino; 182 Asian, non-Hispanic/Latino; 212 Hispanic/Latino; 1 Native Hawaiian or other Pacific Islander, non-Hispanic/Latino; 10 Two or more races, non-Hispanic/Latino), 30 international. Average age 32. 398 applicants, 99% accepted, 271 enrolled. *Faculty:* 27 full-time (18 women), 41 part-time/adjunct (31 women). Expenses: Contact institution. *Financial support:* Career-related internships or fieldwork and Federal Work-Study available. Support available to part-time students. Financial award application deadline: 3/1. In 2010, 234 master's awarded. *Degree program information:* Part-time and evening/weekend programs available. Offers child development (MA); criminal justice (MS); criminalistics (MS); health and human services (MA, MS, MSW); health science (MA); nursing (MS); nutritional science (MS); physical education and kinesiology (MA, MS); social work (MSW); speech and hearing (MA); speech-language pathology (MA). *Application deadline:* For fall admission, 5/1 for domestic and international students. Applications are processed on a rolling basis. *Application fee:* $55. Electronic applications accepted. *Application Contact:* Dr. Alan Muchlinski, Dean of Graduate Studies, 323-343-3820, Fax: 323-343-5653, E-mail: amuchli@exchange.calstatela.edu. *Dean,* Dr. Beatrice Yorker, 323-343-4600, Fax: 323-343-5598, E-mail: byorker@calstatela.edu.

College of Natural and Social Sciences Students: 252 full-time (146 women), 446 part-time (241 women); includes 395 minority (38 Black or African American, non-Hispanic/Latino; 2 American Indian or Alaska Native, non-Hispanic/Latino; 87 Asian, non-Hispanic/Latino; 255 Hispanic/Latino; 1 Native Hawaiian or other Pacific Islander, non-Hispanic/Latino; 12 Two or more races, non-Hispanic/Latino), 48 international. Average age 31. 385 applicants, 98% accepted, 237 enrolled. *Faculty:* 36 full-time (16 women), 43 part-time/adjunct (19 women). Expenses: Contact institution. *Financial support:* Teaching assistantships, career-related internships or fieldwork and Federal Work-Study available. Support available to part-time students. Financial award application deadline: 3/1. In 2010, 221 master's awarded. *Degree program information:* Part-time and evening/weekend programs available. Offers analytical chemistry (MS); anthropology (MA); biochemistry (MS); biology (MS); chemistry (MS); geography (MA); geological sciences (MS); history (MA); inorganic chemistry (MS); Latin American studies (MA); mathematics (MS); Mexican-American studies (MA); natural and social sciences (MA, MS); organic chemistry (MS); physical chemistry (MS); physics (MS); political science (MA); psychology (MA, MS); public administration (MS); sociology (MA). *Application deadline:* For fall admission, 5/1 for domestic and international students. Applications are processed on a rolling basis. *Application fee:* $55. *Application Contact:* Dr. Alan Muchlinski, Dean of Graduate Studies, 323-343-3820, Fax: 323-343-5653, E-mail: amuchli@exchange.calstatela.edu. *Dean,* Dr. James Henderson, 323-343-2000, Fax: 323-343-2011, E-mail: jhender3@calstatela.edu.

CALIFORNIA STATE UNIVERSITY, MONTEREY BAY, Seaside, CA 93955-8001

General Information State-supported, coed, comprehensive institution. *Graduate housing:* Rooms and/or apartments available on a first-come, first-served basis to single and married students.

GRADUATE UNITS

College of Professional Studies *Degree program information:* Part-time and evening/weekend programs available. Postbaccalaureate distance learning degree programs offered. Offers professional studies (EMBA, MA, MPP); public policy (MPP); social work (MSW). Electronic applications accepted.

Institute for Advanced Studies in Education *Degree program information:* Part-time and evening/weekend programs available. Offers education (MA). Electronic applications accepted.

School of Business *Degree program information:* Part-time and evening/weekend programs available. Postbaccalaureate distance learning degree programs offered (no on-campus study). Offers business (EMBA). Electronic applications accepted.

College of Science, Media Arts and Technology *Degree program information:* Part-time programs available. Offers coastal and watershed science and policy (MS, PSM); marine science (MS); science, media arts and technology (MA, MS, MSMIT, PSM). Electronic applications accepted.

School of Information Technology and Communication Design Offers interdisciplinary studies (MA); management and information technology (MA). Electronic applications accepted.

CALIFORNIA STATE UNIVERSITY, NORTHRIDGE, Northridge, CA 91330

General Information State-supported, coed, comprehensive institution. CGS member. *Graduate housing:* Room and/or apartments available to single students; on-campus housing not available to married students. *Research affiliation:* California Institute of Technology (science), Haagen Company (archaeology), Northridge Hospital (biology), Warner Center Institute (child care), Jet Propulsion Laboratory (engineering), Hughes Aircraft Corporation (engineering).

GRADUATE UNITS

Graduate Studies *Degree program information:* Part-time and evening/weekend programs available. Offers interdisciplinary studies (MA, MS).

College of Arts, Media, and Communication *Degree program information:* Part-time and evening/weekend programs available. Offers art education (MA); art history (MA); arts, media, and communication (MA, MFA, MM); communication studies (MA); composition (MM); conducting (MM); mass communication (MA); music education (MA); performance (MM); screenwriting (MA); studio art (MA, MFA); theatre (MA); visual communications (MA, MFA).

College of Business and Economics *Degree program information:* Part-time programs available. Offers business and economics (MBA).

College of Education *Degree program information:* Part-time and evening/weekend programs available. Offers counseling (MS); curriculum and instruction (MA); early childhood special education (MA); education (MA, MA Ed, MS, Ed D); education of the deaf and hard of hearing (MA); educational administration (MA); educational leadership (Ed D); educational psychology (MA Ed); educational technology (MA); educational therapy (MA); English education (MA); language and literacy (MA); mathematics education (MA); mild/moderate disabilities (MA); moderate/severe disabilities (MA); multilingual/multicultural education (MA); secondary science education (MA); teaching and learning (MA).

College of Engineering and Computer Science *Degree program information:* Part-time and evening/weekend programs available. Offers computer science (MS); electrical engineering (MS); engineering (MS); engineering and computer science (MS); engineering automation (MS); engineering management (MS); manufacturing systems engineering (MS); materials engineering (MS); mechanical engineering (MS); software engineering (MS).

College of Health and Human Development *Degree program information:* Part-time and evening/weekend programs available. Offers audiology (MS); environmental and occupational health (MS); family and consumer sciences (MS); health administration (MS); health and human development (MPH, MPT, MS); hospitality and tourism (MS); industrial hygiene (MS); kinesiology (MS); physical therapy (MPT); public health (MPH); recreational sport management/campus recreation (MS); speech language pathology (MS).

College of Humanities *Degree program information:* Part-time and evening/weekend programs available. Offers Chicana and Chicano studies (MA); creative writing (MA); humanities (MA); linguistics (MA); literature (MA); rhetoric and composition theory (MA); Spanish (MA).

College of Science and Mathematics *Degree program information:* Part-time and evening/weekend programs available. Offers applied mathematics (MS); biochemistry (MS); biology (MS); chemistry (MS); geology (MS); mathematics (MS); mathematics for educational careers (MS); physics (MS); science and mathematics (MS).

College of Social and Behavioral Sciences *Degree program information:* Part-time and evening/weekend programs available. Offers clinical psychology (MA); general anthropology (MA); general-experimental psychology (MA); geography (MA); history (MA); human factors and applied experimental psychology (MA); political science (MA); public archaeology (MA); social and behavioral sciences (MA, MSW); social work (MSW); sociology (MA).

The Tseng College of Extended Learning Offers knowledge management (MKM); public administration (MPA); taxation (MS).

CALIFORNIA STATE UNIVERSITY, SACRAMENTO, Sacramento, CA 95819

General Information State-supported, coed, comprehensive institution. CGS member. *Graduate housing:* Room and/or apartments available on a first-come, first-served basis to single students; on-campus housing not available to married students.

GRADUATE UNITS

Graduate Studies *Degree program information:* Part-time and evening/weekend programs available. Electronic applications accepted.

College of Arts and Letters *Degree program information:* Part-time and evening/weekend programs available. Offers arts and letters (MA, MM); communication studies (MA); creative writing (MA); foreign languages (MA); music (MM); public history (MA); studio art (MA); teaching English to speakers of other languages (MA); theatre and dance (MA). Electronic applications accepted.

College of Business Administration *Degree program information:* Part-time and evening/weekend programs available. Offers accountancy (MS); business administration (MBA); human resources (MBA); management information science (MS); urban land development (MBA). Electronic applications accepted.

College of Education *Degree program information:* Part-time programs available. Offers bilingual/multicultural education (MA); career counseling (MS); curriculum and instruction (MA); early childhood education (MA); education (MA, MS); educational leadership (MA); generic counseling (MS); guidance (MA); reading education (MA); school counseling (MS); school psychology (MS); special education (MA); vocational rehabilitation (MS). Electronic applications accepted.

College of Engineering and Computer Science *Degree program information:* Part-time and evening/weekend programs available. Offers civil engineering (MS); computer systems (MS); electrical engineering (MS); engineering and computer science (MS); mechanical engineering (MS); software engineering (MS). Electronic applications accepted.

College of Health and Human Services *Degree program information:* Part-time programs available. Offers audiology (MS); criminal justice (MS); family and children's services (MSW); health and human services (MS, MSW); health care (MSW); mental health (MSW); nursing (MS); physical education (MS); recreation administration (MS); social justice and corrections (MSW); speech pathology (MS). Electronic applications accepted.

College of Natural Sciences and Mathematics *Degree program information:* Part-time programs available. Offers biological sciences (MA, MS); chemistry (MS); immunohematology (MS); marine science (MS); mathematics and statistics (MA); natural sciences and mathematics (MA, MS). Electronic applications accepted.

College of Social Sciences and Interdisciplinary Studies *Degree program information:* Part-time programs available. Offers anthropology (MA); counseling psychology (MA); French (MA); German (MA); government (MA); international affairs (MA); public policy and administration (MPPA); social sciences and interdisciplinary studies (MA, MPPA); sociology (MA); Spanish (MA); theater arts (MA). Electronic applications accepted.

CALIFORNIA STATE UNIVERSITY, SAN BERNARDINO, San Bernardino, CA 92407-2397

General Information State-supported, coed, comprehensive institution. CGS member. *Graduate housing:* Room and/or apartments available on a first-come, first-served basis to single students; on-campus housing not available to married students. Housing application deadline: 8/1.

GRADUATE UNITS

Graduate Studies *Degree program information:* Part-time and evening/weekend programs available. Offers interdisciplinary studies (MA). Electronic applications accepted.

College of Arts and Letters *Degree program information:* Part-time and evening/weekend programs available. Offers art (MA); art/graphics (MA); arts and letters (MA, MFA); communication studies (MA); creative writing (MFA); English composition (MA); integrated marketing communication (MA); Spanish (MA); theatre arts (MA); theatre education (MA); theatre for youth (MA).

College of Business and Public Administration *Degree program information:* Part-time and evening/weekend programs available. Offers business administration (MBA); business and public administration (MBA, MPA); for executives (MBA); public administration (MPA).

College of Education *Degree program information:* Part-time and evening/weekend programs available. Offers bilingual/cross-cultural education (MA); correctional and alternative education (MA); counseling and guidance (MS); curriculum and instruction (MA); educational administration (MA); educational leadership and curriculum (Ed D); educational psychology and counseling (MA, MS); elementary education (MA); English as a second language (MA); environmental education (MA); general education (MA); history and English for secondary teachers (MA); instructional technology (MA); reading (MA); rehabilitation counseling (MA); secondary education (MA); special education (MA); special education and rehabilitation counseling (MA); teaching of science (MA); vocational and career education (MA).

College of Extended Learning *Degree program information:* Part-time and evening/weekend programs available. Offers executive business administration (MBA); TESOL (MA Ed).

College of Natural Sciences *Degree program information:* Part-time programs available. Offers biology (MS); computer science (MS); health science (MS); health services administration (MS); kinesiology (MA Ed); mathematics (MA); natural sciences (MA, MA Ed, MAT, MPH, MS); nursing (MS); public health (MPH); teaching mathematics (MAT).

College of Social and Behavioral Sciences *Degree program information:* Part-time and evening/weekend programs available. Offers child development (MA); clinical psychology (MS); clinical/counseling psychology (MS); criminal justice (MA); environmental sciences (MS); general/experimental psychology (MA); industrial/organizational psychology (MS); national security studies (MA); organizational psychology (MS); psychology (MA); psychology-life span (MA); social and behavioral sciences (MA, MS, MSW); social sciences (MA); social work (MSW).

CALIFORNIA STATE UNIVERSITY, SAN MARCOS, San Marcos, CA 92096-0001

General Information State-supported, coed, comprehensive institution. CGS member. *Graduate housing:* Room and/or apartments available on a first-come, first-served basis to single students; on-campus housing not available to married students. Housing application deadline: 10/1.

GRADUATE UNITS

College of Arts and Sciences *Degree program information:* Part-time and evening/weekend programs available. Offers arts and sciences (MA, MS); biological sciences (MS); computer science (MS); literature and writing studies (MA); mathematics (MS); psychology (MA); sociological practice (MA); Spanish (MA). Electronic applications accepted.

College of Business Administration *Degree program information:* Evening/weekend programs available. Offers business management (MBA); government management (MBA).

College of Education *Degree program information:* Part-time and evening/weekend programs available. Offers education (MA).

CALIFORNIA STATE UNIVERSITY, STANISLAUS, Turlock, CA 95382

General Information State-supported, coed, comprehensive institution. CGS member. *Enrollment:* 8,305 graduate, professional, and undergraduate students; 427 full-time matriculated graduate/professional students (291 women), 496 part-time matriculated graduate/professional students (358 women). *Enrollment by degree level:* 870 master's, 53 doctoral. Tuition and fees vary according to program. *Graduate housing:* Room and/or apartments available on a first-come, first-served basis to single students; on-campus housing not available to married students. Typical cost: $7450 per year ($8250 including board). Room and board charges vary according to board plan and housing facility selected. Housing application deadline: 7/15. *Student services:* Campus employment opportunities, campus safety program, career counseling, child daycare facilities, exercise/wellness program, free psychological counseling, international student services, low-cost health insurance, services for students with disabilities, teacher training. *Library facilities:* Vasche Library. *Online resources:* library catalog, web page, access to other libraries' catalogs. *Collection:* 496,592 titles, 31,646 serial subscriptions, 5,527 audiovisual materials. *Research affiliation:* Kaiser Permanente (healthcare), California Campus Compact–Carnegie Fellowship Program (teaching development for faculty), Valley Mountain Regional Center (development disability), Friends of Turlock Library (public library), EDAW, Inc. (environmental sustainable development), Mathematical Association of America (mathematics).

Computer facilities: 200 computers available on campus for general student use. A campuswide network can be accessed from student residence rooms and from off campus. Online class registration is available. *Web address:* http://www.csustan.edu/.

General Application Contact: Graduate School, 209-667-3129, Fax: 209-664-7025, E-mail: graduate_school@csustan.edu.

GRADUATE UNITS

College of Business Administration Expenses: Contact institution. *Financial support:* Fellowships, Federal Work-Study available. Financial award application deadline: 3/1; financial award applicants required to submit FAFSA. *Degree program information:* Part-time and evening/weekend programs available. Offers accounting and finance (MS); business administration (EMBA, MBA, MS). *Application deadline:* For fall admission, 6/30 for domestic students; for winter admission, 11/30 for domestic students; for spring admission, 11/30 for domestic students. *Application fee:* $55. *Application Contact:* Dr. Randall Brown, Director, 209-667-3280, Fax: 209-667-3080. *Dean,* Dr. Nael Aly, 209-667-3288, Fax: 209-667-3080.

College of Education Expenses: Contact institution. *Financial support:* Fellowships, career-related internships or fieldwork and Federal Work-Study available. Financial award application deadline: 3/1; financial award applicants required to submit FAFSA. *Degree program information:* Part-time and evening/weekend programs available. Offers community college leadership (Ed D); curriculum and instruction (MA); education (MA, Ed D, Graduate Certificate); P-12 leadership (Ed D); school administration (MA); school counseling (MA). *Application deadline:* For fall admission, 6/30 for domestic students; for winter admission, 11/30 for domestic students; for spring admission, 11/30 for domestic students. *Application fee:* $55. *Dean,* Dr. Carl Brown, 209-667-3652.

College of Human and Health Sciences Expenses: Contact institution. Offers behavior analysis (MS); counseling psychology (MS); gerontological nursing (MS); human and health sciences (MA, MS, MSW, Graduate Certificate); nursing education (MS); psychology (MA); social work (MSW). *Dean,* Dr. Gary Novak, 209-667-3155, Fax: 209-667-7113, E-mail: chhs@csustan.edu.

College of Humanities and Social Sciences Expenses: Contact institution. Offers criminal justice (MA); history (MA); humanities and social sciences (MA, MPA, MS, Certificate); interdisciplinary studies (MA, MS); international relations (MA); literature (Certificate); public administration (MPA); rhetoric and teaching writing (MA); secondary school teachers (MA); teaching English to speakers of other languages (MA). *Dean,* Dr. Carolyn Stefanco, 209-667-3531.

College of Natural Sciences Expenses: Contact institution. Offers ecological conservation (MS); ecological economics (MS); genetic counseling (MS); natural sciences (MS). *Dean,* Dr. Roger McNeil, 209-667-3153.

CALIFORNIA UNIVERSITY OF PENNSYLVANIA, California, PA 15419-1394

General Information State-supported, coed, comprehensive institution. CGS member. *Graduate housing:* Room and/or apartments available on a first-come, first-served basis to single students; on-campus housing not available to married students. *Research affiliation:* The Center for Rural Pennsylvania (agriculture), The Technology Collaborative (robotics), International Technical Education Association (curricular development), NCAA (tobacco use), Gettysburg Travel Council (travel and tourism), National Aeronautics and Space Administration (NASA) (space grant consortium).

GRADUATE UNITS

School of Graduate Studies and Research *Degree program information:* Part-time and evening/weekend programs available. Postbaccalaureate distance learning degree programs offered (no on-campus study). Offers legal studies (MS). Electronic applications accepted.

College of Education and Human Services *Degree program information:* Part-time and evening/weekend programs available. Postbaccalaureate distance learning degree programs offered (minimal on-campus study). Offers athletic training (MS); communication disorders (MS); community and agency counseling (MS); education and human services (M Ed, MAT, MS, MSW); intercollegiate athletic administration (MS); mentally and/or physically handicapped education (M Ed); performance enhancement and injury prevention (MS); reading specialist (M Ed); rehabilitation science (MS); school administration (M Ed); school counseling (M Ed); school psychology (MS); secondary education (MAT); social work (MSW); sport management (MS); sport psychology (MS); sports counseling (MS); technology education (M Ed); wellness and fitness (MS). Electronic applications accepted.

College of Liberal Arts *Degree program information:* Part-time and evening/weekend programs available. Offers liberal arts (MA); social science—criminal justice (MA). Electronic applications accepted.

School of Science and Technology *Degree program information:* Part-time and evening/weekend programs available. Postbaccalaureate distance learning degree programs offered. Offers business administration (MSBA); multimedia technology (MS); science and technology (MS, MSBA). Electronic applications accepted.

CALIFORNIA WESTERN SCHOOL OF LAW, San Diego, CA 92101-3090

General Information Independent, coed, graduate-only institution. *Graduate housing:* On-campus housing not available.

GRADUATE UNITS

Graduate and Professional Programs *Degree program information:* Part-time programs available. Offers law (JD, LL M). JD/MSW and JD/MBA offered jointly with San Diego State University; JD/PhD with University of California, San Diego. Electronic applications accepted.

CALUMET COLLEGE OF SAINT JOSEPH, Whiting, IN 46394-2195

General Information Independent-religious, coed, comprehensive institution.

GRADUATE UNITS

Program in Leadership in Teaching Offers leadership in teaching (MS Ed).

Program in Public Safety Administration Offers public safety administration (MS).

Program in Quality Assurance Offers quality assurance (MS).

CALVARY BAPTIST THEOLOGICAL SEMINARY, Landsdale, PA 19446

General Information Independent-religious, coed, graduate-only institution.

GRADUATE UNITS

Graduate Programs Offers theology (M Div, MACM, MATS, Th M, D Min).

CALVARY BIBLE COLLEGE AND THEOLOGICAL SEMINARY, Kansas City, MO 64147-1341

General Information Independent-religious, coed, comprehensive institution. *Enrollment:* 332 graduate, professional, and undergraduate students; 14 full-time matriculated graduate/professional students (5 women), 36 part-time matriculated graduate/professional students (10 women). *Enrollment by degree level:* 50 master's. *Graduate faculty:* 5 full-time, 2 part-time/adjunct. *Tuition:* Full-time $5580; part-time $310 per hour. *Required fees:* $258 per semester. *Graduate housing:* Rooms and/or apartments available on a first-come, first-served basis to single and married students. *Student services:* Campus employment opportunities, services for students with disabilities, writing training. *Library facilities:* Hilda Kroeker Library. *Online resources:* library catalog, web page, access to other libraries' catalogs.

Computer facilities: 23 computers available on campus for general student use. Online class registration is available. *Web address:* http://www.calvary.edu/.

General Application Contact: Bob Crank, Director of Admissions, 800-326-3960 Ext. 1321, Fax: 816-331-4474, E-mail: admissions@calvary.edu.

GRADUATE UNITS

Calvary Theological Seminary Students: 14 full-time (5 women), 36 part-time (10 women); includes 4 Black or African American, non-Hispanic/Latino; 1 Asian, non-Hispanic/Latino; 1 Native Hawaiian or other Pacific Islander, non-Hispanic/Latino. Average age 40. *Faculty:* 5 full-time, 2 part-time/adjunct. Expenses: Contact institution. *Financial support:* Scholarships/grants available. Financial award application deadline: 11/5. In 2010, 14 master's awarded. *Degree program information:* Part-time and evening/weekend programs available. Offers Bible and theology (MS); Biblical counseling (MA); Biblical studies (MA); Christian ministry (MA); Christian studies (MS); Christian theology (MA); New Testament (MA); Old Testament (MA); pastoral studies (M Div). *Application deadline:* For fall admission, 7/15 priority date for domestic and international students; for spring admission, 12/1 priority date for domestic and international students. *Application fee:* $25. *Application Contact:* Bob Crank, Director of Admissions, 800-326-3960 Ext. 1321, Fax: 816-331-4474, E-mail: admissions@calvary.edu. *Academic Dean,* Dr. Thomas Baurain, 816-322-0110 Ext. 1502, Fax: 816-331-4474, E-mail: thomas.baurain@calvary.edu.

CALVIN COLLEGE, Grand Rapids, MI 49546-4388

General Information Independent-religious, coed, comprehensive institution. *Enrollment:* 3,991 graduate, professional, and undergraduate students; 11 full-time matriculated graduate/professional students (6 women), 106 part-time matriculated graduate/professional students (74 women). *Enrollment by degree level:* 117 master's. *Graduate faculty:* 3 full-time (2 women), 4 part-time/adjunct (1 woman). *Tuition:* Full-time $10,080. *Graduate housing:* Room and/or apartments available on a first-come, first-served basis to single students; on-campus housing not available to married students. Housing application deadline: 5/1. *Student services:* Campus employment opportunities, campus safety program, career counseling, exercise/wellness program, free psychological counseling, international student services, low-cost health insurance, multicultural affairs office, services for students with disabilities, writing training. *Library facilities:* Hekman Library. *Online resources:* library catalog, web page. *Collection:* 1.3 million titles, 28,017 serial subscriptions, 12,946 audiovisual materials.

Computer facilities: Computer purchase and lease plans are available. 1,004 computers available on campus for general student use. A campuswide network can be accessed from student residence rooms and from off campus. Online class registration is available. *Web address:* http://www.calvin.edu/.

General Application Contact: Cindi Hoekstra, Graduate Program Coordinator, 616-516-6158, Fax: 616-526-6505, E-mail: choekstr@calvin.edu.

GRADUATE UNITS

Graduate Programs in Education Students: 11 full-time (6 women), 106 part-time (74 women); includes 1 Black or African American, non-Hispanic/Latino; 9 Asian, non-Hispanic/Latino; 2 Hispanic/Latino; 1 Two or more races, non-Hispanic/Latino. Average age 29. *Faculty:* 3 full-time (2 women), 4 part-time/adjunct (1 woman). Expenses: Contact institution. *Financial support:* Federal Work-Study, scholarships/grants, and tuition waivers (full and partial) available. Support available to part-time students. Financial award application deadline: 4/3. In 2010, 17 master's awarded. *Degree program information:* Part-time programs available. Offers curriculum and instruction (M Ed); educational leadership (M Ed); learning disabilities (M Ed); literacy (M Ed). *Application deadline:* For fall admission, 1/1 priority date for domestic students, 3/1 priority date for international students; for spring admission, 1/1 priority date for domestic students, 3/1 priority date for international students. Applications are processed on a rolling basis. *Application fee:* $0. Electronic applications accepted. *Application Contact:* Cindi Hoekstra, Program Coordinator, 616-526-6158, Fax: 616-526-6505, E-mail: choekstr@calvin.edu. *Graduate Program Director,* Dr. Debra Buursma, 616-526-6231, Fax: 616-526-6505, E-mail: dbuursma@calvin.edu.

CALVIN THEOLOGICAL SEMINARY, Grand Rapids, MI 49546-4387

General Information Independent-religious, coed, graduate-only institution. *Graduate housing:* Rooms and/or apartments available on a first-come, first-served basis to single and married students. Housing application deadline: 4/1.

GRADUATE UNITS

Graduate and Professional Programs *Degree program information:* Part-time programs available. Offers Bible and theology (MA); divinity (M Div); educational ministry (MA); historical theology (PhD); missions and evangelism (MA); pastoral care (MA); philosophical and moral theology (PhD); systematic theology (PhD); theological studies (MTS); theology (Th M); worship (MA); youth and family ministries (MA). Electronic applications accepted.

CAMBRIDGE COLLEGE, Cambridge, MA 02138-5304

General Information Independent, coed, comprehensive institution. *Enrollment:* 4,458 graduate, professional, and undergraduate students; 1,504 full-time matriculated graduate/professional students (1,136 women), 1,456 part-time matriculated graduate/professional students (1,098 women). *Enrollment by degree level:* 2,652 master's, 39 doctoral, 269 other advanced degrees. *Graduate faculty:* 18 full-time (7 women), 382 part-time/adjunct (240 women). *Tuition:* Full-time $10,944; part-time $456 per credit. *Required fees:* $50. *Graduate housing:* On-campus housing not available. *Student services:* Career counseling, free psychological counseling, international student services, services for students with disabilities, writing training. *Library facilities:* Cambridge College Online Library. *Online resources:* web page. *Collection:* 55,331 titles, 19,069 serial subscriptions.

Computer facilities: Computer purchase and lease plans are available. A campuswide network can be accessed from off campus. Online class registration is available. *Web address:* http://www.cambridgecollege.edu/.

General Application Contact: Elaine M. Lapomardo, Dean of Enrollment Management, 617-873-0274, Fax: 617-349-3561, E-mail: elaine.lapomardo@cambridgecollege.edu.

GRADUATE UNITS

School of Education Students: 846 full-time (664 women), 930 part-time (714 women); includes 972 minority (802 Black or African American, non-Hispanic/Latino; 3 American Indian

Cambridge College (continued)

or Alaska Native, non-Hispanic/Latino; 18 Asian, non-Hispanic/Latino; 148 Hispanic/Latino; 1 Two or more races, non-Hispanic/Latino), 23 international. Average age 38. *Faculty:* 8 full-time (2 women), 245 part-time/adjunct (166 women). Expenses: Contact institution. *Financial support:* Career-related internships or fieldwork, Federal Work-Study, and scholarships/grants available. Financial award applicants required to submit FAFSA. In 2010, 724 master's, 162 other advanced degrees awarded. *Degree program information:* Part-time and evening/weekend programs available. Postbaccalaureate distance learning degree programs offered (minimal on-campus study). Offers autism specialist (M Ed); autism/behavior analyst (M Ed); behavior analyst (Post-Master's Certificate); behavioral management (M Ed); early childhood teacher (M Ed); education specialist in curriculum and instruction (CAGS); educational leadership (Ed D); elementary teacher (M Ed); English as a second language (M Ed, Certificate); general science (M Ed); health education (Post-Master's Certificate); health/family and consumer sciences (M Ed); history (M Ed); individualized (M Ed); information technology literacy (M Ed); instructional technology (M Ed); interdisciplinary studies (M Ed); library teacher (M Ed); literacy education (M Ed); mathematics (M Ed); mathematics specialist (Certificate); middle school mathematics and science (M Ed); school administration (M Ed, CAGS); school guidance counselor (M Ed); school nurse education (M Ed); school social worker/school adjustment counselor (M Ed); special education administrator (CAGS); special education/moderate disabilities (M Ed); teaching skills and methodologies (M Ed). *Application deadline:* Applications are processed on a rolling basis. *Application fee:* $30. Electronic applications accepted. *Application Contact:* Elaine M. Lapomardo, Dean of Enrollment Management, 617-873-0274, Fax: 617-349-3561, E-mail: elaine.lapomardo@cambridgecollege.edu. *Interim Associate Dean,* Dr. N. Alan Sheppard, 617-873-0619, E-mail: alan.sheppard@cambridgecollege.edu.

School of Management Students: 222 full-time (121 women), 175 part-time (110 women); includes 127 minority (89 Black or African American, non-Hispanic/Latino; 2 American Indian or Alaska Native, non-Hispanic/Latino; 9 Asian, non-Hispanic/Latino; 25 Hispanic/Latino; 2 Two or more races, non-Hispanic/Latino), 125 international. Average age 37. *Faculty:* 6 full-time (3 women), 54 part-time/adjunct (26 women). Expenses: Contact institution. *Financial support:* Career-related internships or fieldwork, Federal Work-Study, and scholarships/grants available. Financial award applicants required to submit FAFSA. In 2010, 221 master's awarded. *Degree program information:* Part-time and evening/weekend programs available. Offers business negotiation and conflict resolution (M Mgt); general business (M Mgt); health care informatics (M Mgt); health care management (M Mgt); leadership in human and organizational dynamics (M Mgt); non-profit and public organization management (M Mgt); small business development (M Mgt); technology management (M Mgt). *Application deadline:* Applications are processed on a rolling basis. *Application fee:* $30. Electronic applications accepted. *Application Contact:* Elaine M. Lapomardo, Dean of Enrollment Management, 617-873-0274, Fax: 617-349-3561, E-mail: elaine.lapomardo@cambridgecollege.edu. *Acting Dean,* Dr. Mary Ann Joseph, 617-873-0227, E-mail: maryann.joseph@cambridgecollege.edu.

School of Psychology and Counseling Students: 436 full-time (351 women), 351 part-time (274 women); includes 321 Black or African American, non-Hispanic/Latino; 3 American Indian or Alaska Native, non-Hispanic/Latino; 4 Asian, non-Hispanic/Latino; 87 Hispanic/Latino; 4 Two or more races, non-Hispanic/Latino, 6 international. Average age 37. *Faculty:* 4 full-time (2 women), 83 part-time/adjunct (48 women). Expenses: Contact institution. *Financial support:* Career-related internships or fieldwork, Federal Work-Study, and scholarships/grants available. Financial award applicants required to submit FAFSA. In 2010, 284 master's, 16 other advanced degrees awarded. *Degree program information:* Part-time and evening/weekend programs available. Offers addiction counseling (M Ed); alcohol and drug counseling (Certificate); counseling psychology (M Ed, CAGS); counseling psychology: forensic counseling (M Ed); marriage and family therapy (M Ed); mental health and addiction counseling (M Ed); mental health counseling (M Ed); mental health counseling for school guidance counselors (Post Master's Certificate); psychological studies (M Ed); school adjustment and mental health counseling (M Ed); school adjustment, mental health and addiction counseling (M Ed); school guidance counselor (M Ed); trauma studies (Certificate). *Application deadline:* Applications are processed on a rolling basis. *Application fee:* $30. Electronic applications accepted. *Application Contact:* Elaine M. Lapomardo, Dean of Enrollment Management, 617-873-0274, Fax: 617-349-3561, E-mail: elaine.lapomardo@cambridgecollege.edu. *Dean,* Dr. Niti Seth, 617-873-0208, Fax: 617-349-3561, E-mail: nseth@cambridgecollege.edu.

CAMERON UNIVERSITY, Lawton, OK 73505-6377

General Information State-supported, coed, comprehensive institution. *Graduate housing:* Room and/or apartments available on a first-come, first-served basis to single students; on-campus housing not available to married students. *Research affiliation:* Telos-Ok (simulations), Army Research Institute (human factors), Advanced Systems Technology, Inc. (informational systems), Dynamics Research Corporation (multimedia systems), Eagle Systems, Inc. (multimedia systems), Halliburton (energy systems).

GRADUATE UNITS

Office of Graduate Studies *Degree program information:* Part-time and evening/weekend programs available. Postbaccalaureate distance learning degree programs offered (no on-campus study). Offers behavioral sciences (MS); business administration (MBA); education (M Ed); educational leadership (MS); entrepreneurial studies (MS); teaching (MAT). Electronic applications accepted.

CAMPBELLSVILLE UNIVERSITY, Campbellsville, KY 42718-2799

General Information Independent-religious, coed, comprehensive institution. *Enrollment:* 3,431 graduate, professional, and undergraduate students; 336 full-time matriculated graduate/professional students (205 women), 117 part-time matriculated graduate/professional students (72 women). *Enrollment by degree level:* 453 master's. *Graduate faculty:* 60 full-time (26 women), 47 part-time/adjunct (23 women). *Tuition:* Full-time $7110; part-time $395 per contact hour. *Required fees:* $250; $75 per course. *Graduate housing:* Rooms and/or apartments available on a first-come, first-served basis to single and married students. Typical cost: $6740 (including board) for single students. Housing application deadline: 6/30. *Student services:* Campus employment opportunities, campus safety program, career counseling, exercise/wellness program, international student services, teacher training, writing training. *Library facilities:* Montgomery Library plus 2 others. *Online resources:* library catalog, web page. *Collection:* 172,000 titles, 12,777 serial subscriptions.

Computer facilities: 175 computers available on campus for general student use. A campuswide network can be accessed from student residence rooms and from off campus. *Web address:* http://www.campbellsville.edu/.

General Application Contact: Monica Bamwine, Assistant Director of Admissions, 270-789-5221, Fax: 270-789-5071, E-mail: mkbamwine@campbellsville.edu.

GRADUATE UNITS

Carver School of Social Work *Degree program information:* Evening/weekend programs available. Electronic applications accepted.

College of Arts and Sciences *Degree program information:* Part-time programs available. Offers social science (MA). Electronic applications accepted.

School of Business and Economics *Degree program information:* Part-time and evening/weekend programs available. Offers business administration (MBA). Electronic applications accepted.

School of Education *Degree program information:* Part-time and evening/weekend programs available. Postbaccalaureate distance learning degree programs offered (minimal on-campus study). Offers curriculum and instruction (MAE); special education (MASE). Electronic applications accepted.

School of Music *Degree program information:* Part-time programs available. Offers church music (MM); music (MA); music education (MM). Electronic applications accepted.

School of Theology *Degree program information:* Part-time programs available. Offers theology (M Th). Electronic applications accepted.

CAMPBELL UNIVERSITY, Buies Creek, NC 27506

General Information Independent-religious, coed, university. *Graduate housing:* Rooms and/or apartments available on a first-come, first-served basis to single and married students. Housing application deadline: 6/2.

GRADUATE UNITS

Graduate and Professional Programs *Degree program information:* Part-time and evening/weekend programs available.

Divinity School Offers Christian education (MA); divinity (M Div); ministry (D Min).

Lundy-Fetterman School of Business *Degree program information:* Part-time and evening/weekend programs available. Offers business (MBA, MTIM).

Norman Adrian Wiggins School of Law Offers law (JD). Dual degree offered in partnership with North Carolina State University. Electronic applications accepted.

School of Education *Degree program information:* Part-time and evening/weekend programs available. Offers administration (MSA); community counseling (MA); elementary education (M Ed); English education (M Ed); interdisciplinary studies (M Ed); mathematics education (M Ed); middle grades education (M Ed); physical education (M Ed); school counseling (M Ed); secondary education (M Ed); social science education (M Ed).

School of Pharmacy *Degree program information:* Part-time and evening/weekend programs available. Offers clinical research (MS); pharmaceutical science (MS); pharmacy (Pharm D). Electronic applications accepted.

CANADIAN COLLEGE OF NATUROPATHIC MEDICINE, Toronto, ON M2K 1E2, Canada

General Information Independent, coed, primarily women, graduate-only institution. *Graduate housing:* Room and/or apartments available on a first-come, first-served basis to single students; on-campus housing not available to married students. *Research affiliation:* Ottawa Regional Cancer Centre, McMaster University, University of Oxford, Hospital for Sick Children, Mayo Clinic, Johns Hopkins University.

GRADUATE UNITS

Doctor of Naturopathic Medicine Program Offers naturopathic medicine (ND).

CANADIAN MEMORIAL CHIROPRACTIC COLLEGE, Toronto, ON M2H 3J1, Canada

General Information Independent, coed, graduate-only institution. *Graduate housing:* On-campus housing not available. *Research affiliation:* University of Waterloo, University of Calgary, University of Toronto.

GRADUATE UNITS

Certificate Programs Offers chiropractic clinical sciences (Certificate); chiropractic radiology (Certificate); chiropractic sports sciences (Certificate); clinical acupuncture (Certificate).

Professional Program Offers chiropractic (DC).

CANADIAN SOUTHERN BAPTIST SEMINARY, Cochrane, AB T4C 2G1, Canada

General Information Independent-religious, coed, graduate-only institution. *Enrollment by degree level:* 35 master's. *Graduate faculty:* 8 full-time (0 women), 2 part-time/adjunct (0 women). *Tuition:* Full-time $5800; part-time $240 per credit hour. *Required fees:* $20 per credit hour. *Graduate housing:* Rooms and/or apartments available on a first-come, first-served basis to single and married students. Typical cost: $4000 per year for single students; $9000 per year for married students. Room charges vary according to housing facility selected. Housing application deadline: 6/30. *Student services:* Campus employment opportunities, free psychological counseling. *Library facilities:* Keith C. Willis Library. *Online resources:* library catalog, access to other libraries' catalogs. *Collection:* 37,203 titles, 12,594 serial subscriptions, 2,581 audiovisual materials.

Computer facilities: 12 computers available on campus for general student use. A campuswide network can be accessed from off campus. Online class registration is available. *Web address:* http://www.csbs.edu/.

General Application Contact: Alain Laundriault, Recruitment Director, 403-932-6622 Ext. 251, Fax: 403-932-7049, E-mail: alain.laundriault@csbs.ca.

GRADUATE UNITS

Graduate Programs Students: 7 full-time (2 women), 28 part-time (6 women); includes 2 Black or African American, non-Hispanic/Latino; 12 Asian, non-Hispanic/Latino; 3 Hispanic/Latino, 1 international. 11 applicants, 91% accepted, 8 enrolled. *Faculty:* 8 full-time (0 women), 2 part-time/adjunct (0 women). Expenses: Contact institution. In 2010, 9 master's awarded. *Degree program information:* Part-time programs available. Offers Christian education (MACE); ministry (M Div). *Application deadline:* For fall admission, 7/1 priority date for domestic and international students; for winter admission, 11/15 priority date for domestic and international students. Applications are processed on a rolling basis. *Application fee:* $50. *Application Contact:* Kathleen McNaughton, Registrar, 403-932-6622 Ext. 221, E-mail: kathleen.mcnaughton@csbs.ca. *Academic Dean,* Steve Booth, 403-932-6622.

CANISIUS COLLEGE, Buffalo, NY 14208-1098

General Information Independent-religious, coed, comprehensive institution. *Enrollment:* 5,111 graduate, professional, and undergraduate students; 886 full-time matriculated graduate/professional students (534 women), 829 part-time matriculated graduate/professional students (458 women). *Enrollment by degree level:* 1,715 master's. *Graduate faculty:* 103 full-time (39 women), 143 part-time/adjunct (76 women). *Tuition:* Part-time $694 per credit hour. *Required fees:* $11 per credit hour. $90 per semester. *Graduate housing:* Room and/or apartments available on a first-come, first-served basis to single students; on-campus housing not available to married students. Typical cost: $6670 per year ($10,556 including board). Housing application deadline: 5/1. *Student services:* Campus employment opportunities, campus safety program, career counseling, exercise/wellness program, free psychological counseling, international student services, multicultural affairs office, services for students with disabilities, teacher training. *Library facilities:* Andrew L. Bouwhuis Library plus 1 other. *Online resources:* library catalog, web page, access to other libraries' catalogs. *Collection:* 425,000 titles, 24,000 serial subscriptions, 12,250 audiovisual materials.

Computer facilities: Computer purchase and lease plans are available. 700 computers available on campus for general student use. A campuswide network can be accessed from student residence rooms and from off campus. Online class registration, online accounts are available. *Web address:* http://www.canisius.edu/.

General Application Contact: Donna Shaffner, Admissions Office, 716-888-2502, Fax: 716-888-3290, E-mail: graded@canisius.edu.

GRADUATE UNITS

Graduate Division Students: 886 full-time (534 women), 829 part-time (458 women); includes 167 minority (109 Black or African American, non-Hispanic/Latino; 6 American Indian or Alaska Native, non-Hispanic/Latino; 22 Asian, non-Hispanic/Latino; 27 Hispanic/Latino; 3 Two or more races, non-Hispanic/Latino), 188 international. Average age 28. 1,043 applicants, 75% accepted, 496 enrolled. *Faculty:* 103 full-time (39 women), 143 part-time/adjunct (76 women). Expenses: Contact institution. *Financial support:* Career-related internships or fieldwork, Federal Work-Study, scholarships/grants, tuition waivers (partial), and unspecified assistantships available. Support available to part-time students. Financial award application deadline: 7/1; financial award applicants required to submit FAFSA. In 2010, 632 master's awarded. *Degree program information:* Part-time and evening/weekend programs available. Postbaccalaureate distance learning degree programs offered (minimal on-campus study). *Application deadline:* Applications are processed on a rolling basis. *Application fee:* $25. Electronic applications accepted. *Application Contact:* Donna Shaffner, Dean of Admissions, 716-888-2200, Fax: 716-888-3230, E-mail: admissions@canisius.edu. *Vice President for Academic Affairs,* Dr. Scott A. Chadwick, 716-888-2120, Fax: 716-888-2120, E-mail: chadwics@canisius.edu.

College of Arts and Sciences Students: 10 full-time (6 women), 32 part-time (20 women); includes 4 minority (2 Black or African American, non-Hispanic/Latino; 2 Hispanic/Latino), 1 international. Average age 28. 23 applicants, 61% accepted, 8 enrolled. *Faculty:* 11 full-time (4 women), 3 part-time/adjunct (0 women). Expenses: Contact institution. *Financial support:* Career-related internships or fieldwork, Federal Work-Study, scholarships/grants, tuition waivers (partial), and unspecified assistantships available. Support available to part-time students. Financial award application deadline: 7/1; financial award applicants required to submit FAFSA. In 2010, 12 master's awarded. *Degree program information:* Part-time and evening/weekend programs available. Offers arts and sciences (MS); communication and leadership (MS). *Application deadline:* For fall admission, 7/15 priority date for domestic students; for spring admission, 4/15 priority date for domestic students. Applications are processed on a rolling basis. *Application fee:* $25. Electronic applications accepted. *Application Contact:* Stephanie Q. Cattarin, Assistant Director, Graduate Programs, 716-888-2212, E-mail: cattaris@canisius.edu. *Dean,* Dr. David Ewing, 716-888-2150, E-mail: ewingd@canisius.edu.

Richard J. Wehle School of Business Students: 143 full-time (51 women), 191 part-time (79 women); includes 33 minority (17 Black or African American, non-Hispanic/Latino; 1 American Indian or Alaska Native, non-Hispanic/Latino; 11 Asian, non-Hispanic/Latino; 4 Hispanic/Latino), 15 international. Average age 28. 207 applicants, 71% accepted, 117 enrolled. *Faculty:* 43 full-time (8 women), 7 part-time/adjunct (3 women). Expenses: Contact institution. *Financial support:* Career-related internships or fieldwork, Federal Work-Study, scholarships/grants, and unspecified assistantships available. Support available to part-time students. Financial award application deadline: 7/1; financial award applicants required to submit FAFSA. In 2010, 115 master's awarded. *Degree program information:* Part-time and evening/weekend programs available. Offers accelerated business administration (1 year) (MBA); accounting (MBA); business (MBA, MS); business administration (MBA); forensic accounting (MS); international business (MS); professional accounting (MBA). *Application deadline:* For fall admission, 7/1 priority date for domestic students; for spring admission, 11/1 priority date for domestic students. Applications are processed on a rolling basis. *Application fee:* $25. Electronic applications accepted. *Application Contact:* Jim Bagwell, Director, Graduate Admissions, 716-888-2545, Fax: 716-888-3290, E-mail: bagwellj@canisius.edu. *Dean,* Dr. Antone Alber, 716-888-2160, Fax: 716-888-2145, E-mail: gradubus@canisius.edu.

School of Education and Human Services Students: 733 full-time (477 women), 606 part-time (359 women); includes 130 minority (90 Black or African American, non-Hispanic/Latino; 5 American Indian or Alaska Native, non-Hispanic/Latino; 11 Asian, non-Hispanic/Latino; 21 Hispanic/Latino; 3 Two or more races, non-Hispanic/Latino), 172 international. Average age 28. 813 applicants, 77% accepted, 371 enrolled. *Faculty:* 49 full-time (27 women), 133 part-time/adjunct (73 women). Expenses: Contact institution. *Financial support:* Career-related internships or fieldwork, Federal Work-Study, scholarships/grants, tuition waivers (partial), and unspecified assistantships available. Support available to part-time students. Financial award application deadline: 7/1; financial award applicants required to submit FAFSA. In 2010, 513 master's awarded. *Degree program information:* Part-time and evening/weekend programs available. Postbaccalaureate distance learning degree programs offered (minimal on-campus study). Offers adolescent education (MS Ed); adolescent special education (MS); advanced special education (MS); business and marketing education (MS Ed); childhood education (MS Ed); childhood special education (MS); childhood special education, grades 1-6 (MS); college student personnel (MS); community mental health counseling (MS); deaf education (MS); deaf/adolescent education, grades 7-12 (MS); deaf/childhood education, grades 1-6 (MS); differentiated instruction (MS Ed); education administration (MS); education and human services (MS, MS Ed, Certificate); general education (MS Ed); gifted education extension (Certificate); health and human performance (MS); literacy (MS Ed); literacy (online) (MS Ed); physical education (MS Ed); physical education, birth-12 (MS Ed); school agency counseling (MS); school building leadership (Certificate); school building leadership (online) (MS); sport administration (MS); sport administration (online) (MS); teacher leader (Certificate). *Application deadline:* Applications are processed on a rolling basis. *Application fee:* $25. Electronic applications accepted. *Application Contact:* Jim Bagwell, Director of Graduate Recruitment and Admissions, 716-888-2544, E-mail: bagwellj@canisius.edu. *Dean,* Dr. Michael J. Pardales, 716-888-3294, E-mail: pardalem@canisius.edu.

CAPE BRETON UNIVERSITY, Sydney, NS B1P 6L2, Canada

General Information Province-supported, coed, comprehensive institution. *Enrollment:* 211 full-time matriculated graduate/professional students (119 women). *Enrollment by degree level:* 211 master's. *Graduate faculty:* 6 full-time (3 women). *Graduate tuition:* Tuition and fees charges are reported in Canadian dollars. *International tuition:* $28,848 Canadian dollars full-time. *Tuition, area resident:* Full-time $19,520 Canadian dollars; part-time $1220 Canadian dollars per course. One-time fee: $480 Canadian dollars full-time. *Graduate housing:* Room and/or apartments available on a first-come, first-served basis to single students; on-campus housing not available to married students. Typical cost: $5400 Canadian dollars per year ($9100 Canadian dollars including board). Room and board charges vary according to board plan. Housing application deadline: 3/31. *Student services:* Campus employment opportunities, career counseling, child daycare facilities, exercise/wellness program, international student services, services for students with disabilities, writing training. *Library facilities:* Cape Breton University Library plus 1 other. *Online resources:* web page. *Collection:* 100,000 titles. *Research affiliation:* Hyperspectral Data International (marine remote sensing), Sable Offshore Energy, Inc. (petroleum resources), Fortress Louisbourg National Historic Park (museum/heritage projects), Dynagen Industrial Mine Technology (mining industry equipment), Atlantic Geomatics (computer networking and software development), Advanced Glazing, Limited (transparent insulation).

Computer facilities: A campuswide network can be accessed. Online class registration is available. *Web address:* http://www.cbu.ca/.

General Application Contact: Cheryl Livingstone, Admissions Officer, 902-563-1166, E-mail: cheryl_livingstone@cbu.ca.

GRADUATE UNITS

Shannon School of Business Students: 211 full-time (119 women). 251 applicants, 92% accepted. *Faculty:* 6 full-time (3 women). Expenses: Contact institution. In 2010, 1 master's awarded. *Degree program information:* Part-time programs available. Offers business (MBA). *Application deadline:* For fall admission, 5/31 for domestic and international students; for spring admission, 3/31 for domestic and international students. Applications are processed on a rolling basis. *Application fee:* $80. Electronic applications accepted. *Application Contact:* Anne Michele Chiasson, MBA Program Coordinator, 902-563-1664, E-mail: anne_chiasson@cbu.ca. *MBA Program Coordinator,* Anne Michele Chiasson, 902-563-1664, E-mail: anne_chiasson@cbu.ca.

CAPELLA UNIVERSITY, Minneapolis, MN 55402

General Information Proprietary, coed, upper-level institution. CGS member. *Enrollment:* 1,395 full-time matriculated graduate/professional students (1,052 women), 29,704 part-time matriculated graduate/professional students (22,606 women). *Enrollment by degree level:* 18,717 master's, 11,840 doctoral, 542 other advanced degrees. *Tuition:* Full-time $11,880; part-time $440 per credit hour. *Library facilities:* Capella University Library.

Computer facilities: Online class registration is available. *Web address:* http://www.capella.edu/.

General Application Contact: Enrollment Services Office, 888-CAPELLA, Fax: 612-977-5060, E-mail: info@capella.edu.

GRADUATE UNITS

Harold Abel School of Psychology *Degree program information:* Part-time and evening/weekend programs available. Postbaccalaureate distance learning degree programs offered (minimal on-campus study). Offers child and adolescent development (MS); clinical psychology (MS, Psy D); counseling psychology (MS); educational psychology (MS, PhD); evaluation, research, and measurement (MS); general psychology (MS, PhD); industrial/organizational psychology (MS, PhD); leadership coaching psychology (MS); organizational leader development (MS); school psychology (MS); sport psychology (MS). Electronic applications accepted.

School of Business and Technology *Degree program information:* Part-time and evening/weekend programs available. Postbaccalaureate distance learning degree programs offered (minimal on-campus study). Offers accounting (MBA); business (Certificate); finance (MBA); general business (MBA); health care management (MBA); information technology (MS, Certificate); information technology management (MBA); marketing (MBA); organization and management (MBA, MS, PhD); project management (MBA). Electronic applications accepted.

School of Public Service Leadership Offers criminal justice (MS, PhD); emergency management (MS, PhD); general human services (MS, PhD); general public administration (MPA, DPA); gerontology (MS); health care administration (MS, PhD); health management and policy (MSPH); management of nonprofit agencies (MS, PhD); nurse educator (MS); public safety leadership (MS, PhD); social and community services (MS, PhD); social behavioral sciences (MSPH).

CAPITAL BIBLE SEMINARY, Lanham, MD 20706-3599

General Information Independent-religious, coed, graduate-only institution. *Graduate housing:* Rooms and/or apartments available on a first-come, first-served basis to single and married students. Housing application deadline: 7/15.

GRADUATE UNITS

Graduate and Professional Programs *Degree program information:* Part-time and evening/weekend programs available. Offers biblical studies (MA, Certificate); Christian counseling (MA); Christian counseling and discipleship (Certificate); ministry leadership (MA); theology (M Div, Th M).

CAPITAL UNIVERSITY, Columbus, OH 43209-2394

General Information Independent-religious, coed, comprehensive institution. *Graduate housing:* On-campus housing not available.

GRADUATE UNITS

Conservatory of Music *Degree program information:* Part-time programs available. Offers music education (MM). Program offered only in summer. Electronic applications accepted.

Law School *Degree program information:* Part-time and evening/weekend programs available. Offers business (LL M); business and taxation (LL M); law (JD, LL M, MT); taxation (LL M, MT). Electronic applications accepted.

School of Management *Degree program information:* Part-time and evening/weekend programs available. Offers management (MBA). Electronic applications accepted.

School of Nursing *Degree program information:* Part-time and evening/weekend programs available. Offers administration (MSN); legal studies (MSN); theological studies (MSN).

CAPITOL COLLEGE, Laurel, MD 20708-9759

General Information Independent, coed, comprehensive institution. *Graduate housing:* On-campus housing not available.

GRADUATE UNITS

Graduate Programs *Degree program information:* Part-time and evening/weekend programs available. Postbaccalaureate distance learning degree programs offered (no on-campus study). Offers business administration (MBA); computer science (MS); electrical engineering (MS); information and telecommunications systems management (MS); information architecture (MS); network security (MS). Electronic applications accepted.

CARDINAL STRITCH UNIVERSITY, Milwaukee, WI 53217-3985

General Information Independent-religious, coed, comprehensive institution. *Enrollment:* 1,557 full-time matriculated graduate/professional students (1,003 women), 1,301 part-time matriculated graduate/professional students (1,006 women). *Graduate faculty:* 7 full-time. *Graduate housing:* Room and/or apartments available on a first-come, first-served basis to single students; on-campus housing not available to married students. *Student services:* Career counseling, international student services, multicultural affairs office, services for students with disabilities, teacher training, writing training. *Library facilities:* Cardinal Stritch University Library. *Online resources:* library catalog, web page, access to other libraries' catalogs. *Collection:* 124,897 titles, 667 serial subscriptions.

Computer facilities: 290 computers available on campus for general student use. A campuswide network can be accessed from student residence rooms and from off campus. *Web address:* http://www.stritch.edu/.

General Application Contact: Information Contact, 800-347-8822 Ext. 4042, E-mail: gradadm@stritch.edu.

GRADUATE UNITS

College of Arts and Sciences *Degree program information:* Part-time and evening/weekend programs available. Offers arts and sciences (MA, MM, MS); clinical psychology (MA); history (MA); lay ministries (MA); ministry (MA); piano (MM); religious studies (MA); sport management (MS); visual studies (MA).

College of Business and Management *Degree program information:* Part-time and evening/weekend programs available. Offers business and management (MBA, MSM). Programs also offered in Madison, WI and Minneapolis-St. Paul, MN.

College of Education *Degree program information:* Part-time and evening/weekend programs available. Offers education (MA, MAT, ME, MS, Ed D, PhD); educational leadership (MS); instructional technology (ME, MS); leadership for the advancement of learning and service (Ed D, PhD); literacy/English as a second language (MA); reading/language arts (MA); reading/learning disability (MA); special education (MA); teaching (MAT); urban education (MA).

College of Nursing *Degree program information:* Part-time and evening/weekend programs available. Offers nursing (MSN). Electronic applications accepted.

CAREY THEOLOGICAL COLLEGE, Vancouver, BC V6T 1J6, Canada

General Information Independent-religious, coed, graduate-only institution. *Graduate housing:* Rooms and/or apartments available on a first-come, first-served basis to single and married students. Housing application deadline: 5/31.

GRADUATE UNITS

Graduate Programs *Degree program information:* Part-time programs available. Offers theology (M Div, MASF, D Min). Electronic applications accepted.

CARIBBEAN UNIVERSITY, Bayamón, PR 00960-0493

General Information Independent, coed, comprehensive institution.

GRADUATE UNITS

Graduate School

CARLETON UNIVERSITY, Ottawa, ON K1S 5B6, Canada

General Information Province-supported, coed, university. *Graduate housing:* Room and/or apartments guaranteed to single students; on-campus housing not available to married students. Housing application deadline: 5/31.

GRADUATE UNITS

Faculty of Graduate Studies *Degree program information:* Part-time and evening/weekend programs available. Electronic applications accepted.

Faculty of Arts and Social Sciences *Degree program information:* Part-time and evening/weekend programs available. Offers anthropology (MA); applied language studies (MA); art history: art and its institutions (MA); arts and social sciences (M Sc, MA, PhD); Canadian studies (MA, PhD); cognitive science (PhD); cultural mediations (PhD); English (MA, PhD); film studies (MA); French (MA); geography (M Sc, MA, PhD); history (MA, PhD); music and culture (MA); neuroscience (M Sc); philosophy (MA); psychology (MA, PhD); sociology (MA, PhD).

Carleton University (continued)

Faculty of Business Offers business (MBA, PhD); business administration (MBA); management (PhD).

Faculty of Engineering and Design Offers aerospace engineering (M Eng, MA Sc, PhD); biomedical engineering (MA Sc); civil and environmental engineering (M Eng, MA Sc, PhD); design studies (M Arch); electrical engineering (M Eng, M Sc, MA Sc, PhD); engineering and design (M Arch, M Des, M Eng, M Sc, MA Sc, PhD); industrial design (M Des); information and systems science (M Sc); materials engineering (M Eng, MA Sc); mechanical engineering (M Eng, MA Sc, PhD); technology innovation management (M Eng, MA Sc).

Faculty of Public Affairs and Management *Degree program information:* Part-time programs available. Offers communication (MA, PhD); conflict resolution (Certificate); economics (MA, PhD); European and European Union studies (MA); European integration studies (Diploma); international affairs (MA, PhD); journalism (MJ); legal studies (MA); political economy (MA, PhD); political science (MA, PhD); public administration (MA, DPA); public affairs and management (MA, MJ, MSW, DPA, PhD, Certificate, Diploma); public policy (PhD); Russian, Eurasian and transition studies (MA); social work (MSW).

Faculty of Science *Degree program information:* Part-time and evening/weekend programs available. Offers biology (M Sc, PhD); chemistry (M Sc, PhD); computer science (MCS, PhD); earth sciences (M Sc, PhD); information and system science (M Sc); information and systems science (M Sc); mathematics (M Sc, PhD); physics (M Sc, PhD); science (M Sc, MCS, PhD).

CARLOS ALBIZU UNIVERSITY, San Juan, PR 00901

General Information Independent, coed, primarily women, university. *Graduate housing:* On-campus housing not available.

GRADUATE UNITS

Graduate Programs *Degree program information:* Part-time and evening/weekend programs available. Offers clinical psychology (MS, PhD, Psy D); general psychology (PhD); industrial/organizational psychology (MS, PhD); speech and language pathology (MS).

CARLOS ALBIZU UNIVERSITY, MIAMI CAMPUS, Miami, FL 33172-2209

General Information Independent, coed, primarily women, comprehensive institution. *Enrollment:* 1,169 graduate, professional, and undergraduate students; 496 full-time matriculated graduate/professional students (400 women), 242 part-time matriculated graduate/professional students (192 women). *Enrollment by degree level:* 395 master's, 343 doctoral. *Graduate faculty:* 21 full-time (12 women), 37 part-time/adjunct (18 women). *Tuition:* Full-time $9360; part-time $520 per credit. *Required fees:* $298 per term. Tuition and fees vary according to course load, degree level and program. *Graduate housing:* On-campus housing not available. *Student services:* Campus employment opportunities, campus safety program, career counseling, exercise/wellness program, international student services, services for students with disabilities, teacher training, writing training. *Library facilities:* Albizu Library. *Online resources:* library catalog, web page. *Collection:* 26,418 titles, 366 serial subscriptions, 1,863 audiovisual materials.

Computer facilities: 116 computers available on campus for general student use. A campuswide network can be accessed. *Web address:* http://www.mia.albizu.edu/.

General Application Contact: Vanessa Almendarez, Secretary, 305-593-1223 Ext. 137, Fax: 305-593-1854, E-mail: valmendarez@albizu.edu.

GRADUATE UNITS

Graduate Programs Students: 496 full-time (400 women), 242 part-time (192 women); includes 590 minority (58 Black or African American, non-Hispanic/Latino; 2 American Indian or Alaska Native, non-Hispanic/Latino; 5 Asian, non-Hispanic/Latino; 523 Hispanic/Latino; 2 Two or more races, non-Hispanic/Latino), 15 international. Average age 36. 141 applicants, 84% accepted, 118 enrolled. *Faculty:* 21 full-time (12 women), 37 part-time/adjunct (18 women). Expenses: Contact institution. *Financial support:* In 2010–11, 106 students received support. Federal Work-Study, scholarships/grants, and tuition discounts available. Financial award application deadline: 6/1; financial award applicants required to submit FAFSA. In 2010, 159 master's, 20 doctorates awarded. *Degree program information:* Part-time and evening/weekend programs available. Offers clinical psychology (Psy D); entrepreneurship (MBA); exceptional student education (MS); industrial/organizational psychology (MS); marriage and family therapy (MS); mental health counseling (MS); nonprofit management (MBA); organizational management (MBA); psychology (MS); school counseling (MS); teaching English as a second language (MS). *Application deadline:* For fall admission, 8/1 priority date for domestic students; for spring admission, 11/30 priority date for domestic students. Applications are processed on a rolling basis. *Application fee:* $50. Electronic applications accepted. *Application Contact:* Vanessa Almendarez, Secretary, 305-593-1223 Ext. 137, Fax: 305-593-1854, E-mail: valmendarez@albizu.edu. *Chancellor*, Dr. Carmen S. Roca, 305-593-1223 Ext. 120, Fax: 305-629-8052, E-mail: croca@albizu.edu.

CARLOW UNIVERSITY, Pittsburgh, PA 15213-3165

General Information Independent-religious, coed, primarily women, comprehensive institution. CGS member. *Enrollment:* 2,803 graduate, professional, and undergraduate students; 631 full-time matriculated graduate/professional students (563 women), 201 part-time matriculated graduate/professional students (179 women). *Enrollment by degree level:* 730 master's, 73 doctoral, 29 other advanced degrees. *Graduate faculty:* 19 full-time (16 women), 67 part-time/adjunct (46 women). *Tuition:* Full-time $9900; part-time $660 per credit. Tuition and fees vary according to course load, degree level and program. *Graduate housing:* Room and/or apartments available on a first-come, first-served basis to single students; on-campus housing not available to married students. Typical cost: $4500 per year ($8900 including board). Room and board charges vary according to board plan. *Student services:* Campus employment opportunities, campus safety program, career counseling, child daycare facilities, exercise/wellness program, free psychological counseling, grant writing training, international student services, low-cost health insurance, services for students with disabilities, teacher training, writing training. *Library facilities:* Grace Library. *Online resources:* library catalog, web page, access to other libraries' catalogs. *Collection:* 135,011 titles, 15,496 serial subscriptions.

Computer facilities: 162 computers available on campus for general student use. A campuswide network can be accessed from student residence rooms. Online class registration is available. *Web address:* http://www.carlow.edu/.

General Application Contact: Jo Danhires, Administrative Assistant, Admissions, 412-578-8764, Fax: 412-578-6321, E-mail: gradstudies@carlow.edu.

GRADUATE UNITS

Humanities Division Students: 34 part-time (31 women); includes 3 Black or African American, non-Hispanic/Latino. Average age 41. 1 applicant, 100% accepted, 1 enrolled. Expenses: Contact institution. *Financial support:* Career-related internships or fieldwork, Federal Work-Study, and scholarships/grants available. Support available to part-time students. Financial award application deadline: 4/1; financial award applicants required to submit FAFSA. In 2010, 11 master's awarded. *Degree program information:* Part-time and evening/weekend programs available. Postbaccalaureate distance learning degree programs offered (minimal on-campus study). Offers creative writing (MFA). *Application deadline:* For fall admission, 6/15 priority date for domestic and international students; for spring admission, 11/15 priority date for domestic and international students. Applications are processed on a rolling basis. *Application fee:* $20. *Application Contact:* Jo Danhires, Administrative Assistant of Admissions, 412-578-6059, Fax: 412-578-6321, E-mail: gradstudies@carlow.edu. *Director of MFA Program*, Dr. Ellie Wymard, 412-578-6597, Fax: 412-578-8706, E-mail: wymardex@carlow.edu.

School for Social Change Students: 206 full-time (184 women), 21 part-time (18 women); includes 41 Black or African American, non-Hispanic/Latino; 1 American Indian or Alaska Native, non-Hispanic/Latino; 2 Asian, non-Hispanic/Latino; 3 Hispanic/Latino. Average age 31. 298 applicants, 36% accepted, 71 enrolled. Expenses: Contact institution. *Financial support:* Federal Work-Study available. Financial award application deadline: 4/1; financial award applicants required to submit FAFSA. In 2010, 50 master's awarded. *Degree program information:* Part-time and evening/weekend programs available. Offers counseling psychology (Psy D); professional counseling (MS); professional counseling: school counseling (MS). *Application deadline:* For fall admission, 6/15 priority date for domestic and international students; for spring admission, 11/15 priority date for domestic and international students. Applications are processed on a rolling basis. *Application fee:* $20. Electronic applications accepted. *Application Contact:* Jo Danhires, Administrative Assistant of Admissions, 412-578-6059, Fax: 412-578-6321, E-mail: gradstudies@carlow.edu. *Chair, Department of Psychology and Counseling*, Dr. Robert A. Reed, 412-575-6349, E-mail: reedra@carlow.edu.

School of Education Students: 158 full-time (134 women), 83 part-time (73 women); includes 28 Black or African American, non-Hispanic/Latino; 1 Asian, non-Hispanic/Latino; 1 Hispanic/Latino. Average age 34. 146 applicants, 62% accepted, 65 enrolled. Expenses: Contact institution. *Financial support:* Application deadline: 4/1. In 2010, 63 master's awarded. *Degree program information:* Part-time and evening/weekend programs available. Offers art education (M Ed); early childhood education (M Ed); early childhood supervision (M Ed); education (M Ed); educational leadership (M Ed); instructional technology specialist (M Ed); middle level education (M Ed); secondary education (M Ed); special education (M Ed). *Application deadline:* For fall admission, 6/15 priority date for domestic and international students; for spring admission, 11/15 priority date for domestic and international students. Applications are processed on a rolling basis. *Application fee:* $20. Electronic applications accepted. *Application Contact:* Jo Danhires, Administrative Assistant of Admissions, 412-578-6059, Fax: 412-578-6321, E-mail: gradstudies@carlow.edu. *Associate Dean and Director*, Dr. Roberta Schomburg, 412-578-6312, Fax: 412-578-8816, E-mail: schomburgrl@carlow.edu.

School of Management Students: 83 full-time (71 women), 18 part-time (14 women); includes 18 Black or African American, non-Hispanic/Latino; 1 American Indian or Alaska Native, non-Hispanic/Latino; 1 Asian, non-Hispanic/Latino; 1 Hispanic/Latino, 2 international. Average age 37. 91 applicants, 48% accepted, 38 enrolled. Expenses: Contact institution. *Financial support:* Federal Work-Study and scholarships/grants available. Support available to part-time students. Financial award application deadline: 4/1; financial award applicants required to submit FAFSA. In 2010, 33 master's awarded. *Degree program information:* Part-time and evening/weekend programs available. Postbaccalaureate distance learning degree programs offered (no on-campus study). Offers business administration (MBA). *Application deadline:* For fall admission, 6/15 priority date for domestic and international students; for spring admission, 11/15 priority date for domestic and international students. Applications are processed on a rolling basis. *Application fee:* $20. Electronic applications accepted. *Application Contact:* Jo Danhires, Administrative Assistant, Admissions, 412-578-6088, Fax: 412-578-6321, E-mail: gradstudies@carlow.edu. *Director, MBA Program*, Dr. Enrique Mu, 412-578-8729, Fax: 412-587-6367, E-mail: muex@carlow.edu.

School of Nursing Students: 184 full-time (174 women), 45 part-time (43 women); includes 6 Black or African American, non-Hispanic/Latino; 2 Asian, non-Hispanic/Latino; 1 Native Hawaiian or other Pacific Islander, non-Hispanic/Latino, 2 international. Average age 38. 191 applicants, 50% accepted, 70 enrolled. Expenses: Contact institution. *Financial support:* Application deadline: 4/1. In 2010, 47 master's, 10 doctorates awarded. *Degree program information:* Part-time and evening/weekend programs available. Postbaccalaureate distance learning degree programs offered (minimal on-campus study). Offers family nurse practitioner (MSN); nursing (DNP); nursing leadership and education (MSN). *Application deadline:* For fall admission, 6/15 priority date for domestic and international students; for spring admission, 11/15 priority date for domestic and international students. Applications are processed on a rolling basis. *Application fee:* $20. Electronic applications accepted. *Application Contact:* Jo Danhires, Administrative Assistant, Admissions, 412-578-6059, Fax: 412-578-6321, E-mail: gradstudies@carlow.edu. *Associate Dean and Director*, Dr. Clare M. Hopkins, 412-578-6108, Fax: 412-578-6114, E-mail: hopkinscm@carlow.edu.

CARNEGIE MELLON UNIVERSITY, Pittsburgh, PA 15213-3891

General Information Independent, coed, university. CGS member. *Graduate housing:* On-campus housing not available. *Research affiliation:* National Census Data Research Center (public policy), Robotics Engineering Consortium (computer science and engineering), Software Engineering Institute (computer science and engineering), Carnegie Bosch Institute for Applied Studies in International Management (business and management), Pittsburgh Supercomputer Center.

GRADUATE UNITS

Carnegie Institute of Technology *Degree program information:* Part-time and evening/weekend programs available. Offers advanced infrastructure systems (MS, PhD); bioengineering (MS, PhD); chemical engineering (M Ch E, MS, PhD); civil and environmental engineering (MS, PhD); civil and environmental engineering/engineering and public policy (PhD); civil engineering (MS, PhD); colloids, polymers and surfaces (MS); computational mechanics (MS, PhD); computational science and engineering (MS, PhD); electrical and computer engineering (MS, PhD); engineering and public policy (PhD); environmental engineering (MS, PhD); environmental management and science (MS, PhD); materials science and engineering (MS, PhD); mechanical engineering (MS, PhD); product development (MPD); technology (M Ch E, MPD, MS, PhD).

Information Networking Institute Offers information networking (MS); information security technology and management (MS); information technology—information security (MS); information technology—mobility (MS); information technology—software management (MS).

Center for the Neural Basis of Cognition Offers neural basis of cognition (PhD).

College of Fine Arts *Degree program information:* Part-time programs available. Offers fine arts (M Des, M Sc, MAM, MET, MFA, MM, MPD, MS, MSA, PhD). Electronic applications accepted.

School of Architecture Offers architectural engineering construction management (M Sc); architecture (MSA); architecture, engineering, and construction management (PhD); building performance and diagnostics (M Sc, PhD); computational design (M Sc, PhD); sustainable design (M Sc); urban design (M Sc).

School of Art Offers art (MFA).

School of Design Offers communication planning and information design (M Des); design (PhD); design theory (PhD); interaction design (M Des, PhD); new product development (PhD); product development (MPD); typography and information design (PhD).

School of Drama Offers design (MFA); directing (MFA); dramatic writing (MFA); production technology and management (MFA).

School of Music *Degree program information:* Part-time programs available. Offers composition (MM); conducting (MM); instrumental performance (MM); music and technology (MS); music education (MM); vocal performance (MM).

College of Humanities and Social Sciences *Degree program information:* Part-time programs available. Offers African and African-American diaspora (PhD); behavioral decision research (PhD); behavioral decision research and psychology (PhD); cognitive neuroscience (PhD); cognitive psychology (PhD); communication planning and design (M Des); culture and power (PhD); developmental psychology (PhD); editing and publishing (MAPW); gender and the family (PhD); history (MA, MS); history and policy (MA); humanities and social sciences (M Des, MA, MAPW, MS, PhD); labor and politics (PhD); literary and cultural studies (MA, PhD); logic, computation and methodology (MS, PhD); machine learning and statistics (PhD); mathematical finance (PhD); philosophy (MA); policy and non-profit communication (MAPW); professional writing (MAPW); public and media relations / corporate communications (MAPW); rhetoric (MA, PhD); science or healthcare communication (MAPW); science, technology, medicine and environment (PhD); second language acquisition (PhD); social and decision science (PhD); social/personality/health psychology (PhD); statistics (MS, PhD); statistics and public policy (PhD); strategy, entrepeneurship, and technological change (PhD); technical writing (MAPW); writing for new media (MAPW); writing for print media (MAPW). Electronic applications accepted.

Center for Innovation in Learning Offers instructional science (PhD).

Heinz College Australia Offers information technology (MSIT); public policy and management (MS).

H. John Heinz III College *Degree program information:* Part-time and evening/weekend programs available. Offers public policy and information systems (MAM, MEIM, MIS, MISM, MMM, MPM, MS, MSED, MSHCPM, MSISPM, MSIT, PhD). Electronic applications accepted.

School of Information Systems and Management Offers information security policy and management (MSISPM); information systems and management (MISM, MSISPM, MSIT); information systems management (MISM); information technology (MSIT).

School of Public Policy and Management Offers arts management (MAM); biotechnology and management (MS); entertainment industry management (MEIM); health care policy and management (MSHCPM); medical management (MMM); public management (MPM); public policy and management (MMM, MPM, MS, MSHCPM, PhD).

Joint CMU-Pitt PhD Program in Computational Biology Offers computational biology (PhD).

Mellon College of Science *Degree program information:* Part-time programs available. Offers algorithms, combinatorics, and optimization (PhD); applied mathematics (PhD); applied physics (PhD); biochemistry (PhD); biophysics (PhD); biotechnology and management (MS); cell biology (PhD); chemistry (PhD); colloids, polymers and surfaces (MS); computational biology (MS); computational finance (MS); developmental biology (PhD); genetics (PhD); mathematical finance (PhD); mathematical sciences (MS, DA, PhD); molecular biology (PhD); molecular biophysics and structural biology (PhD); neuroscience (PhD); physics (MS, PhD); pure and applied logic (PhD); science (MS, DA, PhD). Electronic applications accepted.

School of Computer Science Offers algorithms, combinatorics, and optimization (PhD); computer science (MS, PhD); entertainment technology (MET); human-computer interaction (MHCI, PhD); machine learning (PhD); pure and applied logic (PhD); software engineering (MSE, PhD).

Language Technologies Institute Offers language technologies (MLT, PhD).

Robotics Institute Offers robotic systems development (MS); robotics (MS, PhD); robotics technology (MS).

Tepper School of Business *Degree program information:* Part-time programs available. Offers accounting (PhD); algorithms, combinatorics, and optimization (PhD); business management and software engineering (MBMSE); civil engineering and industrial management (MS); computational finance (MSCF); economics (MS, PhD); electronic commerce (MS); environmental engineering and management (MEEM); finance (PhD); financial economics (PhD); industrial administration (MBA); information systems (PhD); management of manufacturing and automation (PhD); marketing (PhD); mathematical finance (PhD); operations research (PhD); organizational behavior and theory (PhD); political economy (PhD); production and operations management (PhD); public policy and management (MS, MSED); software engineering and business management (MS). JD/MSIA offered jointly with University of Pittsburgh.

CAROLINA EVANGELICAL DIVINITY SCHOOL, High Point, NC 27265

General Information Independent-religious, coed, graduate-only institution.

GRADUATE UNITS

Divinity Program Offers divinity (M Div).

Ministry Program Offers ministry (D Min).

Program in Theological Studies Offers theological studies (MA).

CARROLL UNIVERSITY, Waukesha, WI 53186-5593

General Information Independent-religious, coed, comprehensive institution. *Enrollment:* 3,385 graduate, professional, and undergraduate students; 94 full-time matriculated graduate/professional students (73 women), 205 part-time matriculated graduate/professional students (136 women). *Enrollment by degree level:* 221 master's, 78 doctoral. *Graduate faculty:* 18 full-time (12 women), 19 part-time/adjunct (18 women). *Tuition:* Full-time $24,749; part-time $440 per credit hour. *Required fees:* $550. *Graduate housing:* On-campus housing not available. *Student services:* Campus employment opportunities, campus safety program, career counseling, exercise/wellness program, free psychological counseling, international student services, multicultural affairs office, services for students with disabilities. *Library facilities:* Todd Wehr Memorial Library. *Online resources:* library catalog, web page, access to other libraries' catalogs. *Collection:* 150,000 titles, 65,200 serial subscriptions, 2,539 audiovisual materials.

Computer facilities: Computer purchase and lease plans are available. 400 computers available on campus for general student use. A campuswide network can be accessed from student residence rooms and from off campus. Online class registration is available. *Web address:* http://www.carrollu.edu/.

General Application Contact: Tami Bartunek, Graduate Admission Counselor, 262-524-7643, E-mail: tbartune@carrollu.edu.

GRADUATE UNITS

Graduate Program in Education Students: 11 full-time (10 women), 163 part-time (125 women); includes 3 Black or African American, non-Hispanic/Latino; 3 American Indian or Alaska Native, non-Hispanic/Latino; 2 Asian, non-Hispanic/Latino; 3 Hispanic/Latino, 1 international. Average age 34. 96 applicants, 38% accepted, 18 enrolled. *Faculty:* 7 full-time (5 women), 14 part-time/adjunct (all women). Expenses: Contact institution. *Financial support:* Available to part-time students. Application deadline: 3/15. In 2010, 43 master's awarded. *Degree program information:* Part-time and evening/weekend programs available. Offers education (M Ed); learning and teaching (M Ed). *Application deadline:* For fall admission, 8/15 priority date for domestic students. Applications are processed on a rolling basis. *Application fee:* $0. Electronic applications accepted. *Application Contact:* Tami Bartunek, Graduate Admission Counselor, 262-524-7643, E-mail: tbartune@carrollu.edu. *Chair,* Dr. Wilma Robinson, 262-524-7287, Fax: 262-524-7139, E-mail: wrobinso@carrollu.edu.

Program in Business Administration Students: 15 part-time (6 women). Average age 28. 54 applicants, 43% accepted. *Faculty:* 2 full-time (both women). Expenses: Contact institution. *Degree program information:* Part-time programs available. Offers business administration (MBA). *Application deadline:* Applications are processed on a rolling basis. Electronic applications accepted. *Application Contact:* Tami Bartunek, Graduate Admission Counselor, 262-524-7643, E-mail: tbartune@carrollu.edu. *Professor,* Dr. Richard J. Penlesky, 262-951-3023, E-mail: rpenlesk@carrollu.edu.

Program in Physical Therapy Students: 78 full-time (59 women); includes 4 minority (2 Asian, non-Hispanic/Latino; 2 Hispanic/Latino). Average age 24. 150 applicants, 69% accepted, 57 enrolled. *Faculty:* 6 full-time (3 women), 5 part-time/adjunct (4 women). Expenses: Contact institution. *Financial support:* Available to part-time students. Application deadline: 3/15. In 2010, 33 doctorates awarded. Offers physical therapy (MPT, DPT). *Application deadline:* For fall admission, 7/14 for domestic students. Applications are processed on a rolling basis. *Application fee:* $25. *Application Contact:* Tami Bartunek, Graduate Admission Counselor, 262-524-7643, E-mail: tbartune@carrollu.edu. *Dean, Natural and Health Sciences,* Dr. Jane F. Hopp, 262-524-7294, E-mail: jhopp@carrollu.edu.

Program in Physician Assistant Studies 167 applicants, 16% accepted, 22 enrolled. Expenses: Contact institution. *Financial support:* Applicants required to submit FAFSA. Offers physician assistant studies (MS). *Application fee:* $0. *Application Contact:* Tami Bartunek, Graduate Admission Counselor, 262-524-7643, E-mail: tbartune@carrollu.edu. *Director,* Dr. Russell W. Harland, 262-524-7399, E-mail: rharland@carrollu.edu.

Program in Software Engineering Students: 5 full-time (4 women), 27 part-time (5 women); includes 3 minority (1 Black or African American, non-Hispanic/Latino; 1 Asian, non-Hispanic/Latino; 1 Hispanic/Latino), 7 international. Average age 34. 29 applicants, 76% accepted, 8 enrolled. *Faculty:* 4 full-time (1 woman). Expenses: Contact institution. *Financial support:* In 2010–11, 2 students received support. Institutionally sponsored loans available. Support available to part-time students. In 2010, 8 master's awarded. *Degree program information:* Part-time and evening/weekend programs available. Offers software engineering (MSE). *Application deadline:* For fall admission, 9/15 priority date for domestic students. Applications are processed on a rolling basis. *Application fee:* $0. Electronic applications accepted. *Application Contact:* Tami Bartunek, Graduate Admission Counselor, 262-524-7643, E-mail: tbartune@carrollu.edu. *Associate Professor of Computer Science and Program Director,* Dr. Chenglie Hu, 262-524-7170, E-mail: chu@carrollu.edu.

CARSON-NEWMAN COLLEGE, Jefferson City, TN 37760

General Information Independent-religious, coed, comprehensive institution. *Enrollment:* 2,065 graduate, professional, and undergraduate students; 147 full-time matriculated graduate/professional students (102 women), 155 part-time matriculated graduate/professional students (88 women). *Enrollment by degree level:* 302 master's. *Graduate faculty:* 5 full-time (2 women), 10 part-time/adjunct (3 women). *Tuition:* Full-time $6750; part-time $375 per credit hour. *Required fees:* $200. *Graduate housing:* Rooms and/or apartments available to single and married students. Housing application deadline: 7/15. *Student services:* Campus employment opportunities, career counseling, free psychological counseling, international student services, low-cost health insurance. *Library facilities:* Stephens-Burnett Library plus 1 other. *Online resources:* library catalog, web page. *Collection:* 218,371 titles, 3,966 serial subscriptions.

Computer facilities: 200 computers available on campus for general student use. A campuswide network can be accessed from student residence rooms and from off campus. *Web address:* http://www.cn.edu/.

General Application Contact: Graduate Admissions and Services Adviser, 865-473-3468, Fax: 865-472-3475.

GRADUATE UNITS

Department of Nursing Students: 22 full-time (20 women), 31 part-time (22 women); includes 1 Asian, non-Hispanic/Latino; 1 Hispanic/Latino; 1 Two or more races, non-Hispanic/Latino. Average age 32. *Faculty:* 2 full-time (both women), 10 part-time/adjunct (9 women). Expenses: Contact institution. In 2010, 19 master's awarded. Offers family nurse practitioner (MSN); nurse educator (MSN). *Application deadline:* For fall admission, 7/15 priority date for domestic students. Applications are processed on a rolling basis. *Application fee:* $50. *Application Contact:* Graduate Admissions and Services Adviser, 865-473-3468, Fax: 865-472-3475. *Dean,* Dr. Gregory A. Casalenuovo, 865-471-3426.

Graduate Program in Education Students: 118 full-time (79 women), 87 part-time (49 women); includes 9 Black or African American, non-Hispanic/Latino; 1 Asian, non-Hispanic/Latino, 22 international. Average age 32. 78 applicants, 97% accepted. *Faculty:* 5 full-time (2 women), 10 part-time/adjunct (3 women). Expenses: Contact institution. *Financial support:* In 2010–11, 41 students received support. Federal Work-Study and unspecified assistantships available. Financial award application deadline: 4/1; financial award applicants required to submit FAFSA. In 2010, 62 master's awarded. *Degree program information:* Part-time and evening/weekend programs available. Offers curriculum and instruction (M Ed); educational leadership (M Ed); elementary education (MAT); school counseling (MS); secondary education (MAT); teaching English as a second language (MATESL). *Application deadline:* For fall admission, 7/15 priority date for domestic students. Applications are processed on a rolling basis. *Application fee:* $25 ($50 for international students). *Application Contact:* Graduate Admissions and Services Adviser, 865-471-3460, Fax: 865-471-3875. *Chair,* Dr. Sharon Teets, 865-471-3461.

Program in Applied Theology Students: 12 part-time (4 women). *Faculty:* 2 full-time (0 women). Expenses: Contact institution. Offers applied theology (MA). *Application deadline:* For fall admission, 7/15 priority date for domestic students. Applications are processed on a rolling basis. *Application Contact:* Graduate Admissions and Services Adviser, 865-473-3468, Fax: 865-472-3475.

Program in Business Administration Students: 7 full-time (3 women), 22 part-time (11 women); includes 1 Black or African American, non-Hispanic/Latino; 1 Hispanic/Latino, 2 international. *Faculty:* 6 full-time (3 women). Expenses: Contact institution. Offers business administration (MBA). *Application deadline:* For fall admission, 7/15 priority date for domestic students. *Application fee:* $50. *Application Contact:* Graduate Admissions and Services Adviser, 865-473-3468, Fax: 865-472-3475. Dr. Clyde Herring.

CARTHAGE COLLEGE, Kenosha, WI 53140

General Information Independent-religious, coed, comprehensive institution. *Graduate housing:* On-campus housing not available.

GRADUATE UNITS

Division of Teacher Education *Degree program information:* Part-time and evening/weekend programs available. Offers classroom guidance and counseling (M Ed); creative arts (M Ed); gifted and talented children (M Ed); language arts (M Ed); modern language (M Ed); natural sciences (M Ed); reading (M Ed, Certificate); social sciences (M Ed); teacher leadership (M Ed).

CASE WESTERN RESERVE UNIVERSITY, Cleveland, OH 44106

General Information Independent, coed, university. CGS member. *Enrollment:* 9,837 graduate, professional, and undergraduate students; 4,379 full-time matriculated graduate/professional students (2,171 women), 1,012 part-time matriculated graduate/professional students (649 women). *Enrollment by degree level:* 1,740 first professional, 1,997 master's, 1,601 doctoral, 53 other advanced degrees. *Graduate faculty:* 2,822 full-time (996 women). *Graduate housing:* On-campus housing not available. *Student services:* Campus employment opportunities, campus safety program, career counseling, exercise/wellness program, free psychological counseling, grant writing training, international student services, low-cost health insurance, multicultural affairs office, services for students with disabilities, teacher training, writing training. *Library facilities:* University Library plus 6 others. *Online resources:* library catalog, web page, access to other libraries' catalogs. *Collection:* 2.8 million titles, 75,083 serial subscriptions, 57,386 audiovisual materials. *Research affiliation:* Cleveland Clinic Foundation (biomedical science), Bayer Materials Science (wind materials research), Cleveland Hearing and Speech Center (speech-language pathology and audiology), Holden Arboretum (plant sciences and ecology), Swagelok Company (surface analysis and materials technology), University Hospitals of Cleveland (biomedical science).

Computer facilities: Computer purchase and lease plans are available. 265 computers available on campus for general student use. A campuswide network can be accessed from student residence rooms and from off campus. Online class registration, software library, online reference databases, electronic books and journals are available. *Web address:* http://www.case.edu/.

General Application Contact: Susan M. Benedict, Admissions Coordinator, 216-368-4400, Fax: 216-368-4250, E-mail: susan.benedict@case.edu.

GRADUATE UNITS

Frances Payne Bolton School of Nursing Students: 250 full-time (210 women), 257 part-time (235 women); includes 71 minority (27 Black or African American, non-Hispanic/Latino; 38 Asian, non-Hispanic/Latino; 6 Hispanic/Latino). 394 applicants, 62% accepted, 164 enrolled. *Faculty:* 58 full-time (53 women), 10 part-time/adjunct (9 women). Expenses: Contact institution. *Financial support:* In 2010–11, 32 research assistantships (averaging $4,448 per year), 17 teaching assistantships (averaging $12,038 per year) were awarded; fellowships, Federal Work-Study, institutionally sponsored loans, scholarships/grants, and tuition waivers (partial) also available. Support available to part-time students. Financial award application deadline: 5/15; financial award applicants required to submit FAFSA. In 2010, 72 master's, 87 doctorates awarded. *Degree program information:* Part-time programs available. Post-baccalaureate distance learning degree programs offered (minimal on-campus study). Offers acute care cardiovascular nursing (MSN); acute care nurse practitioner (MSN, DNP); acute care/flight nurse (MSN); adult gerontology nurse practitioner (MSN, DNP); advanced public health nursing (MSN, DNP); educational leadership (DNP); family nurse practitioner (MSN, DNP); family systems psychiatric mental health nursing (DNP); midwifery/family nursing (DNP); neonatal nurse practitioner (MSN, DNP); nurse anesthesia (MSN); nurse midwifery (MSN); nurse practitioner (MSN); nursing (MN, MSN, DNP, PhD); nursing informatics (MSN); pediatric nurse practitioner (MSN, DNP); practice leadership (DNP); pre-licensure generalist nursing (MN); women's health nurse practitioner (MSN, DNP). *Application deadline:* Applications are processed on a rolling basis. *Application fee:* $75. *Application Contact:* Donna

Case Western Reserve University (continued)

Hassik, Admissions Coordinator, Graduate Programs, 216-368-5253, Fax: 216-368-0124, E-mail: donna.hassik@case.edu. *Dean*, Dr. May L. Wykle, 216-368-2545, Fax: 216-368-5050, E-mail: may.wykle@case.edu.

Mandel School of Applied Social Sciences *Degree program information:* Evening/weekend programs available. Offers social administration (MSSA); social welfare (PhD). Electronic applications accepted.

School of Dental Medicine Offers advanced general dentistry (Certificate); dental medicine (DMD, MSD, Certificate); dentistry (DMD, MSD, Certificate); endodontics (MSD, Certificate); oral surgery (Certificate); orthodontics (MSD, Certificate); pedodontics (MSD, Certificate); periodontics (MSD, Certificate). Electronic applications accepted.

School of Graduate Studies Students: 1,719 full-time (791 women), 320 part-time (162 women); includes 78 Black or African American, non-Hispanic/Latino; 4 American Indian or Alaska Native, non-Hispanic/Latino; 133 Asian, non-Hispanic/Latino; 39 Hispanic/Latino; 12 Two or more races, non-Hispanic/Latino, 654 international. Average age 30. 4,585 applicants, 24% accepted, 506 enrolled. *Faculty:* 2,822 full-time (996 women). Expenses: Contact institution. *Financial support:* Fellowships with tuition reimbursements, research assistantships with tuition reimbursements, teaching assistantships with tuition reimbursements, career-related internships or fieldwork, Federal Work-Study, institutionally sponsored loans, scholarships/grants, traineeships, health care benefits, tuition waivers (full and partial), and unspecified assistantships available. Support available to part-time students. Financial award applicants required to submit FAFSA. In 2010, 429 master's, 211 doctorates awarded. *Degree program information:* Part-time and evening/weekend programs available. Offers acting (MFA); anthropology (MA, PhD); applied mathematics (MS, PhD); art education (MA); art history (MA, PhD); art history and museum studies (MA, PhD); astronomy (MS, PhD); biology (MS, PhD); chemistry (MS, PhD); clinical psychology (PhD); cognitive linguistics (MA); contemporary dance (MFA); dance (MA); early music (MA, D Mus A); English (MA, PhD); experimental psychology (PhD); French (MA); geological sciences (MS, PhD); history (MA, PhD); mathematics (MS, PhD); music education (MA, PhD); music history (MA); musicology (PhD); physics (MS, PhD); political science (MA, PhD); sociology (MA, PhD); speech-language pathology (MA, PhD); statistics (MS, PhD); theater (MFA); world literature (MA). *Application deadline:* For fall admission, 3/1 for domestic students; for spring admission, 11/1 for domestic students. *Application fee:* $50. Electronic applications accepted. *Application Contact:* Susan M. Benedict, Admissions Coordinator, 216-368-4400, Fax: 216-368-4250, E-mail: susan.benedict@case.edu. *Dean*, Dr. Charles E. Rozek, 216-368-4400, Fax: 216-368-4250, E-mail: charles.rozek@case.edu.

Case School of Engineering Students: 561 full-time (122 women), 84 part-time (21 women); includes 14 Black or African American, non-Hispanic/Latino; 3 American Indian or Alaska Native, non-Hispanic/Latino; 50 Asian, non-Hispanic/Latino; 9 Hispanic/Latino, 310 international. 1,480 applicants, 22% accepted, 105 enrolled. *Faculty:* 106 full-time (12 women). Expenses: Contact institution. *Financial support:* Fellowships with full and partial tuition reimbursements, research assistantships with full and partial tuition reimbursements, teaching assistantships, career-related internships or fieldwork, Federal Work-Study, and institutionally sponsored loans available. Support available to part-time students. Financial award applicants required to submit FAFSA. In 2010, 134 master's, 56 doctorates awarded. *Degree program information:* Part-time and evening/weekend programs available. Postbaccalaureate distance learning degree programs offered (minimal on-campus study). Offers biomedical engineering (MS, PhD); chemical engineering (MS, PhD); civil engineering (MS, PhD); computer engineering (MS, PhD); computing and information sciences (MS, PhD); electrical engineering (MS, PhD); engineering (ME, MEM, MS, PhD); integration of management and engineering (MEM); macromolecular science and engineering (MS, PhD); materials science and engineering (MS, PhD); mechanical and aerospace engineering (MS, PhD); systems and control engineering (MS, PhD). *Application deadline:* Applications are processed on a rolling basis. *Application fee:* $50. Electronic applications accepted. *Application Contact:* Dr. Patrick Crago, Associate Dean and Professor of Biomedical Engineering, 216-368-4436, Fax: 216-368-6939, E-mail: cseinfo@case.edu. *Dean/Professor*, Norman C. Tien, 216-368-4436, Fax: 216-368-6939, E-mail: norman.tien@case.edu.

Cleveland Clinic Lerner Research Institute–Molecular Medicine PhD Program Students: 16 full-time (7 women), 17 part-time (11 women); includes 6 Black or African American, non-Hispanic/Latino; 4 Asian, non-Hispanic/Latino; 1 Hispanic/Latino, 7 international. Average age 26. 79 applicants, 22% accepted, 7 enrolled. *Faculty:* 137 full-time (41 women). Expenses: Contact institution. *Financial support:* Fellowships with full tuition reimbursements, health care benefits and stipends available. In 2010, 1 doctorate awarded. Offers molecular medicine (PhD). *Application deadline:* For fall admission, 11/1 priority date for domestic students, 11/1 for international students. *Application fee:* $50. Electronic applications accepted. *Application Contact:* John Pounardjian, Recruiting and Development Coordinator, 216-445-9417, E-mail: molmedphd@ccf.org. *Program Director*, Dr. Martha Cathcart, 216-444-5222, E-mail: molmedphd@ccf.org.

School of Law Students: 677 full-time (295 women), 4 part-time (all women); includes 24 Black or African American, non-Hispanic/Latino; 2 American Indian or Alaska Native, non-Hispanic/Latino; 49 Asian, non-Hispanic/Latino; 12 Hispanic/Latino; 5 Two or more races, non-Hispanic/Latino, 37 international. Average age 24. 2,193 applicants, 38% accepted, 236 enrolled. *Faculty:* 50 full-time (16 women), 36 part-time/adjunct (13 women). Expenses: Contact institution. *Financial support:* In 2010–11, 599 students received support. Career-related internships or fieldwork, Federal Work-Study, institutionally sponsored loans, and scholarships/grants available. Financial award application deadline: 5/1; financial award applicants required to submit FAFSA. In 2010, 223 first professional degrees, 46 master's awarded. *Degree program information:* Part-time programs available. Offers intellectual property (LL M); international business law (LL M); law (JD); U. S. legal studies (LL M). *Application deadline:* For fall admission, 4/1 priority date for domestic and international students. Applications are processed on a rolling basis. *Application fee:* $40. Electronic applications accepted. *Application Contact:* Elaine Greaves, Assistant Dean for Admissions, 216-368-3600, Fax: 216-368-1042, E-mail: lawadmissions@case.edu. *Dean*, Lawrence E. Mitchell, 216-368-3283.

School of Medicine *Degree program information:* Part-time programs available. Offers clinical research (MS); medicine (MD, MA, MPH, MS, PhD).

Graduate Programs in Medicine *Degree program information:* Part-time programs available. Offers anesthesiology (MS); applied anatomy (MS); biochemical research (MS); biochemistry (MS, PhD); bioethics (MA); biological anthropology (MS); biomedical sciences (PhD); biostatistics (MS, PhD); cancer biology (PhD); cell and molecular physiology (MS); cell biology (MS, PhD); cell physiology (PhD); cellular biology (MS, PhD); dietetics (MS); epidemiology (MS, PhD); genetic and molecular epidemiology (MS, PhD); genetic counseling (MS); health services research (MS, PhD); human, molecular, and developmental genetics and genomics (PhD); immunology (MS, PhD); medicine (MA, MPH, MS, PhD); microbiology (PhD); molecular biology (PhD); molecular medicine (PhD); molecular virology (PhD); molecular/cellular biophysics (PhD); neurobiology (PhD); neuroscience (PhD); nutrition (MS, PhD); pathology (MS, PhD); pharmacology (PhD); physiology and biophysics (PhD); public health (MPH); public health nutrition (MS); RNA biology (PhD); systems physiology (PhD). Electronic applications accepted.

Weatherhead School of Management *Degree program information:* Part-time and evening/weekend programs available. Offers accountancy (M Acc, PhD); banking and finance (MBA); business administration (EMBA, MBA); economics (MBA); information systems (MBA); labor and human resource policy (MBA); management (EMBA, M Acc, MBA, MNO, MPOD, MS, MSM, EDM, PhD, CNM); management for liberal arts graduates (MSM); management policy (MBA); marketing (MBA); operations research (MSM, PhD); organizational behavior and analysis (MBA, MPOD, MS); positive organization development and change (MS); supply chain (MSM). Electronic applications accepted.

Mandel Center for Nonprofit Organizations Offers nonprofit management (MNO, CNM).

CASTLETON STATE COLLEGE, Castleton, VT 05735

General Information State-supported, coed, comprehensive institution. *Graduate housing:* Room and/or apartments available on a first-come, first-served basis to single students; on-campus housing not available to married students. Housing application deadline: 5/19.

GRADUATE UNITS

Division of Graduate Studies *Degree program information:* Part-time and evening/weekend programs available. Offers curriculum and instruction (MA Ed); educational leadership (MA Ed, CAGS); forensic psychology (MA); language arts and reading (MA Ed, CAGS); special education (MA Ed, CAGS).

CATAWBA COLLEGE, Salisbury, NC 28144-2488

General Information Independent-religious, coed, comprehensive institution. *Enrollment:* 35 part-time matriculated graduate/professional students (34 women). *Enrollment by degree level:* 35 master's. *Graduate faculty:* 4 full-time (3 women). *Tuition:* Part-time $160 per credit hour. *Graduate housing:* On-campus housing not available. *Student services:* Campus safety program, career counseling, exercise/wellness program, teacher training. *Library facilities:* Corriher-Linn-Black Memorial Library plus 1 other. *Online resources:* library catalog, access to other libraries' catalogs. *Collection:* 204,645 titles, 1,435 serial subscriptions, 2,909 audiovisual materials.

Computer facilities: 97 computers available on campus for general student use. A campuswide network can be accessed from student residence rooms and from off campus. *Web address:* http://www.catawba.edu/.

General Application Contact: Dr. Lou W. Kasias, Director, Graduate Program, 704-637-4462, Fax: 704-637-4732, E-mail: lakasias@catawba.edu.

GRADUATE UNITS

Program in Education Students: 35 part-time (34 women). Average age 36. 3 applicants, 100% accepted, 3 enrolled. *Faculty:* 4 full-time (3 women). Expenses: Contact institution. *Financial support:* Scholarships/grants available. Financial award applicants required to submit FAFSA. In 2010, 10 master's awarded. *Degree program information:* Part-time and evening/weekend programs available. Offers elementary education (M Ed). *Application deadline:* For fall admission, 7/1 for domestic students; for spring admission, 12/1 for domestic students. Applications are processed on a rolling basis. *Application fee:* $25. *Application Contact:* Dr. Lou W. Kasias, Director, Graduate Program, 704-637-4462, Fax: 704-637-4732, E-mail: lakasias@catawba.edu. *Chair, Department of Teacher Education*, Dr. Rhonda Truitt, 704-637-4468, Fax: 704-637-4732, E-mail: rltruitt@catawba.edu.

THE CATHOLIC DISTANCE UNIVERSITY, Hamilton, VA 20158

General Information Independent-religious, coed, graduate-only institution. *Graduate housing:* On-campus housing not available.

GRADUATE UNITS

Graduate Programs *Degree program information:* Part-time and evening/weekend programs available. Postbaccalaureate distance learning degree programs offered (no on-campus study). Offers religious studies (MRS); theology (MA).

CATHOLIC THEOLOGICAL UNION AT CHICAGO, Chicago, IL 60615-5698

General Information Independent-religious, coed, graduate-only institution. *Graduate housing:* Rooms and/or apartments available on a first-come, first-served basis to single and married students. Housing application deadline: 7/1.

GRADUATE UNITS

Graduate and Professional Programs *Degree program information:* Part-time and evening/weekend programs available. Offers biblical spirituality (Certificate); cross-cultural ministries (D Min); cross-cultural missions (Certificate); divinity (M Div); liturgical studies (Certificate); liturgy (D Min); pastoral studies (MAPS, Certificate); spiritual formation (Certificate); spirituality (D Min); theology (MA). M Div/PhD offered jointly with University of Chicago; M Div/MSW with Loyola University Chicago and University of Chicago.

THE CATHOLIC UNIVERSITY OF AMERICA, Washington, DC 20064

General Information Independent-religious, coed, university. CGS member. *Enrollment:* 6,967 graduate, professional, and undergraduate students; 1,481 full-time matriculated graduate/professional students (784 women), 1,820 part-time matriculated graduate/professional students (942 women). *Enrollment by degree level:* 905 first professional, 1,441 master's, 922 doctoral, 33 other advanced degrees. *Graduate faculty:* 385 full-time (155 women), 361 part-time/adjunct (142 women). *Tuition:* Full-time $33,580; part-time $1315 per credit hour. *Required fees:* $80; $40 per semester hour. One-time fee: $425. *Graduate housing:* Room and/or apartments available on a first-come, first-served basis to single students; on-campus housing not available to married students. Typical cost: $10,000 per year ($15,198 including board). Room and board charges vary according to board plan and housing facility selected. Housing application deadline: 5/15. *Student services:* Campus employment opportunities, campus safety program, career counseling, exercise/wellness program, free psychological counseling, international student services, low-cost health insurance, multicultural affairs office, services for students with disabilities, teacher training, writing training. *Library facilities:* Mullen Library plus 7 others. *Online resources:* library catalog, web page, access to other libraries' catalogs. *Collection:* 1.6 million titles, 10,047 serial subscriptions, 41,944 audiovisual materials. *Research affiliation:* EnergySolutions (waste vitrification), Christopher and Dana Reeve Foundation (medical device development), American Cancer Society (graduate social work education), Henry Jackson Foundation (medical research), Lily Foundation (religion and young Americans), Catholic dioceses (secondary school development).

Computer facilities: Computer purchase and lease plans are available. 500 computers available on campus for general student use. A campuswide network can be accessed from student residence rooms and from off campus. Online class registration, Internet 2, video streaming, online voting, pedagogical software are available. *Web address:* http://www.cua.edu/.

General Application Contact: Andrew Woodall, Director of Graduate Admissions, 202-319-5057, Fax: 202-319-6533, E-mail: cua-admissions@cua.edu.

GRADUATE UNITS

The Benjamin T. Rome School of Music Students: 43 full-time (27 women), 89 part-time (49 women); includes 4 Black or African American, non-Hispanic/Latino; 10 Asian, non-Hispanic/Latino; 6 Hispanic/Latino, 26 international. Average age 34. 108 applicants, 61% accepted, 30 enrolled. *Faculty:* 18 full-time (5 women), 20 part-time/adjunct (8 women). Expenses: Contact institution. *Financial support:* Fellowships, research assistantships, teaching assistantships, Federal Work-Study, scholarships/grants, tuition waivers (full and partial), and unspecified assistantships available. Financial award application deadline: 2/1; financial award applicants required to submit FAFSA. In 2010, 16 master's, 14 doctorates awarded. *Degree program information:* Part-time programs available. Offers music (MA, MM, MMSM, DMA, PhD, Certificate). *Application deadline:* For fall admission, 8/1 priority date for domestic students, 7/15 for international students; for spring admission, 12/1 priority date for domestic students, 10/15 for international students. Applications are processed on a rolling basis. *Application fee:* $55. Electronic applications accepted. *Application Contact:* Andrew Woodall, Director of Graduate Admissions, 202-319-5057, Fax: 202-319-6533, E-mail: cua-admissions@cua.edu. *Dean*, Murry Sidlin, 202-319-5417, Fax: 202-319-6280, E-mail: cua-music@cua.edu.

Columbus School of Law Students: 562 full-time (320 women), 296 part-time (131 women); includes 159 minority (39 Black or African American, non-Hispanic/Latino; 1 American Indian or Alaska Native, non-Hispanic/Latino; 82 Asian, non-Hispanic/Latino; 28 Hispanic/Latino; 3 Native Hawaiian or other Pacific Islander, non-Hispanic/Latino; 6 Two or more races, non-Hispanic/Latino), 4 international. Average age 25. 3,372 applicants, 34% accepted, 274 enrolled. *Faculty:* 66 full-time (29 women), 108 part-time/adjunct (39 women). Expenses:

Contact institution. *Financial support:* In 2010–11, 140 students received support; research assistantships, career-related internships or fieldwork, Federal Work-Study, institutionally sponsored loans, and scholarships/grants available. Support available to part-time students. Financial award application deadline: 6/1; financial award applicants required to submit FAFSA. *Degree program information:* Part-time and evening/weekend programs available. Offers law (JD). *Application deadline:* For fall admission, 3/12 priority date for domestic students, 3/12 for international students. Applications are processed on a rolling basis. *Application fee:* $65. Electronic applications accepted. *Application Contact:* Shani J. P. Butts, Director of Admissions, 202-319-5151, Fax: 202-319-6285, E-mail: butts@law.edu. *Dean*, Veryl Miles, 202-319-5139, Fax: 202-319-5473.

Metropolitan School of Professional Studies Students: 21 full-time (15 women), 153 part-time (88 women); includes 51 Black or African American, non-Hispanic/Latino; 1 American Indian or Alaska Native, non-Hispanic/Latino; 4 Asian, non-Hispanic/Latino; 16 Hispanic/Latino, 15 international. Average age 36. 176 applicants, 47% accepted, 65 enrolled. *Faculty:* 44 part-time/adjunct (20 women). Expenses: Contact institution. In 2010, 34 master's awarded. *Degree program information:* Part-time and evening/weekend programs available. Offers human resource management (MA); management (MSM). *Application deadline:* For fall admission, 8/1 priority date for domestic students, 7/15 for international students; for spring admission, 12/1 priority date for domestic students, 10/15 for international students. *Application fee:* $55. *Application Contact:* Andrew Woodall, Director of Graduate Admissions, 202-319-5057, Fax: 202-319-6533, E-mail: cua-admissions@cua.edu. *Dean*, Dr. Sara Thompson, 202-319-5256, Fax: 202-319-6032, E-mail: thompsons@cua.edu.

National Catholic School of Social Service Students: 168 full-time (145 women), 159 part-time (134 women); includes 36 Black or African American, non-Hispanic/Latino; 10 Asian, non-Hispanic/Latino; 18 Hispanic/Latino; 1 Native Hawaiian or other Pacific Islander, non-Hispanic/Latino, 34 international. Average age 33. 316 applicants, 74% accepted, 130 enrolled. *Faculty:* 18 full-time (15 women), 25 part-time/adjunct (19 women). Expenses: Contact institution. *Financial support:* Fellowships, research assistantships, teaching assistantships, Federal Work-Study, scholarships/grants, tuition waivers (full and partial), and unspecified assistantships available. Financial award application deadline: 2/1; financial award applicants required to submit FAFSA. In 2010, 71 master's, 8 doctorates awarded. *Degree program information:* Part-time programs available. Offers social service (MSW, PhD). *Application deadline:* For fall admission, 7/15 priority date for domestic students, 7/15 for international students; for spring admission, 12/1 priority date for domestic students, 10/15 for international students. Applications are processed on a rolling basis. *Application fee:* $55. Electronic applications accepted. *Application Contact:* Andrew Woodall, Director of Graduate Admissions, 202-319-5057, Fax: 202-319-6533, E-mail: cua-admissions@cua.edu. *Dean*, Dr. James R. Zabora, 202-319-5454, Fax: 202-319-5093, E-mail: zabora@cua.edu.

School of Architecture and Planning Students: 116 full-time (55 women), 31 part-time (13 women); includes 11 Black or African American, non-Hispanic/Latino; 6 Asian, non-Hispanic/Latino; 11 Hispanic/Latino, 11 international. Average age 27. 167 applicants, 70% accepted, 56 enrolled. *Faculty:* 25 full-time (6 women), 38 part-time/adjunct (9 women). Expenses: Contact institution. *Financial support:* Fellowships, research assistantships, teaching assistantships, Federal Work-Study, scholarships/grants, tuition waivers (full and partial), and unspecified assistantships available. Financial award application deadline: 2/1; financial award applicants required to submit FAFSA. In 2010, 55 master's awarded. *Degree program information:* Part-time programs available. Offers architecture studies (MS Arch St); sustainable design (MSSD). *Application deadline:* For fall admission, 1/15 priority date for domestic students, 1/15 for international students; for spring admission, 10/15 priority date for domestic students, 10/15 for international students. Applications are processed on a rolling basis. *Application fee:* $55. Electronic applications accepted. *Application Contact:* Andrew Woodall, Director of Graduate Admissions, 202-319-5057, Fax: 202-319-6533, E-mail: cua-admissions@cua.edu. *Dean*, Randall Ott, 202-319-5784, Fax: 202-319-2023, E-mail: ott@cua.edu.

School of Arts and Sciences Students: 191 full-time (105 women), 336 part-time (184 women); includes 22 Black or African American, non-Hispanic/Latino; 2 American Indian or Alaska Native, non-Hispanic/Latino; 20 Asian, non-Hispanic/Latino; 24 Hispanic/Latino, 43 international. Average age 31. 695 applicants, 45% accepted, 151 enrolled. *Faculty:* 157 full-time (68 women), 86 part-time/adjunct (31 women). Expenses: Contact institution. *Financial support:* Fellowships, research assistantships, teaching assistantships, Federal Work-Study, scholarships/grants, tuition waivers (full and partial), and unspecified assistantships available. Financial award application deadline: 2/1; financial award applicants required to submit FAFSA. In 2010, 92 master's, 35 doctorates, 2 other advanced degrees awarded. *Degree program information:* Part-time programs available. Offers acting, directing, and playwriting (MFA); American government (MA, PhD); Ancient Near East (Biblical Hebrew/Aramaic) (MA, PhD); anthropology (MA); applied experimental psychology (PhD); Arabic (PhD); arts and sciences (MA, MFA, MS, MSBA, PhD, Certificate); Catholic educational leadership and policy studies (PhD); Catholic school leadership (MA); cell and microbial biology (MS, PhD); Christian Near East (Biblical Hebrew/Aramaic) (MA); clinical laboratory science (MS, PhD); clinical psychology (PhD); Congressional and presidential studies (MA); Coptic (MA, PhD); early Christian studies (MA, PhD); education (Certificate); educational psychology (PhD); English language and literature (MA, PhD); general psychology (MA); Greek (Certificate); Greek and Latin (MA, PhD, Certificate); history (MA, PhD); human factors (MA); international affairs (MA); international political economics (MA); Latin (MA, Certificate); medieval and Byzantine studies (MA, PhD, Certificate); physics (MS, PhD); political theory (MA, PhD); religion and society in the late medieval and early modern world (MA); rhetoric (Certificate); secondary education (MA); sociology (MA, PhD); Spanish (MA, PhD); special education (MA); Syriac (MA); theatre education (MA); theatre history and criticism (MA); world politics (MA, PhD). *Application deadline:* For fall admission, 8/1 priority date for domestic students, 7/15 for international students; for spring admission, 12/1 priority date for domestic students, 10/15 for international students. Applications are processed on a rolling basis. *Application fee:* $55. Electronic applications accepted. *Application Contact:* Andrew Woodall, Director of Graduate Admissions, 202-319-5057, Fax: 202-319-6533, E-mail: cua-admissions@cua.edu. *Dean*, Dr. Lawrence R. Poos, 202-319-5115, Fax: 202-319-6076, E-mail: poos@cua.edu.

School of Canon Law Students: 37 full-time (8 women), 49 part-time (3 women); includes 2 Black or African American, non-Hispanic/Latino; 4 Asian, non-Hispanic/Latino; 6 Hispanic/Latino, 13 international. Average age 40. 40 applicants, 65% accepted, 22 enrolled. *Faculty:* 6 full-time (1 woman), 1 part-time/adjunct (0 women). Expenses: Contact institution. *Financial support:* Fellowships, research assistantships, teaching assistantships, Federal Work-Study, scholarships/grants, tuition waivers (full and partial), and unspecified assistantships available. Financial award application deadline: 2/1; financial award applicants required to submit FAFSA. In 2010, 5 doctorates awarded. *Degree program information:* Part-time programs available. Offers canon law (JCD, JCL). *Application deadline:* For fall admission, 8/1 priority date for domestic students, 7/15 for international students; for spring admission, 12/1 priority date for domestic students, 10/15 for international students. Applications are processed on a rolling basis. *Application fee:* $55. Electronic applications accepted. *Application Contact:* Andrew Woodall, Director of Graduate Admissions, 202-319-5057, Fax: 202-319-6533, E-mail: cua-admissions@cua.edu. *Dean*, Rev. Robert Kaslyn, SJ, 202-319-5492, Fax: 202-319-4187, E-mail: cua-canonlaw@cua.edu.

School of Engineering Students: 49 full-time (13 women), 116 part-time (27 women); includes 13 Black or African American, non-Hispanic/Latino; 7 Asian, non-Hispanic/Latino; 8 Hispanic/Latino, 47 international. Average age 32. 200 applicants, 53% accepted, 46 enrolled. *Faculty:* 28 full-time (4 women), 27 part-time/adjunct (1 woman). Expenses: Contact institution. *Financial support:* Fellowships, research assistantships, teaching assistantships, Federal Work-Study, scholarships/grants, tuition waivers (full and partial), and unspecified assistantships available. Financial award application deadline: 2/1; financial award applicants required to submit FAFSA. In 2010, 67 master's, 3 doctorates awarded. *Degree program information:* Part-time programs available. Offers biomedical engineering (MBE, PhD); electrical engineering and computer science (MEE, MSCS, D Engr, PhD); engineering (MBE, MCE, MEE, MME, MS, MSCS, MSE, D Engr, PhD, Certificate); engineering management (MSE, Certificate); environmental engineering (PhD); materials science and engineering (MS); mechanical engineering (MME, MSE, PhD). *Application deadline:* For fall admission, 8/1 priority date for domestic students, 7/15 for international students; for spring admission, 12/1 priority date for domestic students, 10/15 for international students. Applications are processed on a rolling basis. *Application fee:* $55. Electronic applications accepted. *Application Contact:* Andrew Woodall, Director of Graduate Admissions, 202-319-5057, Fax: 202-319-6533, E-mail: cua-admissions@cua.edu. *Dean*, Dr. Charles C. Nguyen, 202-319-5160, Fax: 202-319-4499, E-mail: nguyen@cua.edu.

School of Library and Information Science Students: 35 full-time (28 women), 193 part-time (152 women); includes 22 Black or African American, non-Hispanic/Latino; 8 Asian, non-Hispanic/Latino; 7 Hispanic/Latino; 1 Native Hawaiian or other Pacific Islander, non-Hispanic/Latino, 3 international. Average age 34. 213 applicants, 75% accepted, 93 enrolled. *Faculty:* 6 full-time (4 women), 17 part-time/adjunct (9 women). Expenses: Contact institution. *Financial support:* Fellowships, research assistantships, teaching assistantships, Federal Work-Study, scholarships/grants, tuition waivers (full and partial), and unspecified assistantships available. Financial award application deadline: 2/1; financial award applicants required to submit FAFSA. In 2010, 82 master's awarded. *Degree program information:* Part-time programs available. Offers library and information science (MSLS). *Application deadline:* For fall admission, 8/1 priority date for domestic students, 7/15 for international students; for spring admission, 11/1 priority date for domestic students, 10/15 for international students. Applications are processed on a rolling basis. *Application fee:* $55. Electronic applications accepted. *Application Contact:* Andrew Woodall, Director of Graduate Admissions, 202-319-5057, Fax: 202-319-6533, E-mail: cua-admissions@cua.edu. *Acting Dean*, Dr. Ingrid Hsieh-Yee, 202-319-5085, Fax: 202-319-5574, E-mail: hsiehyee@cua.edu.

School of Nursing Students: 30 full-time (28 women), 72 part-time (69 women); includes 27 Black or African American, non-Hispanic/Latino; 6 Asian, non-Hispanic/Latino; 3 Hispanic/Latino, 5 international. Average age 42. 80 applicants, 66% accepted, 32 enrolled. *Faculty:* 19 full-time (17 women), 28 part-time/adjunct (26 women). Expenses: Contact institution. *Financial support:* Fellowships, research assistantships, teaching assistantships, Federal Work-Study, scholarships/grants, tuition waivers (full and partial), and unspecified assistantships available. Financial award application deadline: 2/1; financial award applicants required to submit FAFSA. In 2010, 16 master's, 7 doctorates awarded. *Degree program information:* Part-time programs available. Offers nursing (MSN, DNP, PhD, Certificate). *Application deadline:* For fall admission, 8/1 priority date for domestic students, 7/15 for international students; for spring admission, 12/1 priority date for domestic students, 10/15 for international students. Applications are processed on a rolling basis. *Application fee:* $55. Electronic applications accepted. *Application Contact:* Andrew Woodall, Director of Graduate Admissions, 202-319-5057, Fax: 202-319-6533, E-mail: cua-admissions@cua.edu. *Dean*, Dr. Patricia McMullen, 202-319-5403, Fax: 202-319-6485, E-mail: mcmullep@cua.edu.

School of Philosophy Students: 62 full-time (8 women), 76 part-time (16 women); includes 1 Black or African American, non-Hispanic/Latino; 3 Asian, non-Hispanic/Latino; 6 Hispanic/Latino, 9 international. Average age 31. 134 applicants, 58% accepted, 41 enrolled. *Faculty:* 20 full-time (5 women), 2 part-time/adjunct (1 woman). Expenses: Contact institution. *Financial support:* Fellowships, research assistantships, teaching assistantships, Federal Work-Study, scholarships/grants, tuition waivers (full and partial), and unspecified assistantships available. Financial award application deadline: 2/1; financial award applicants required to submit FAFSA. In 2010, 18 master's, 8 doctorates awarded. *Degree program information:* Part-time programs available. Offers philosophy (MA, PhD, Ph L). *Application deadline:* For fall admission, 8/1 priority date for domestic students, 7/15 for international students; for spring admission, 12/1 priority date for domestic students, 10/15 for international students. Applications are processed on a rolling basis. *Application fee:* $55. Electronic applications accepted. *Application Contact:* Andrew Woodall, Director of Graduate Admissions, 202-319-5057, Fax: 202-319-6533, E-mail: cua-admissions@cua.edu. *Interim Dean*, Dr. John McCarthy, OP, 202-319-6649, Fax: 202-319-4731, E-mail: mccartjc@cua.edu.

School of Theology and Religious Studies Students: 161 full-time (28 women), 235 part-time (61 women); includes 7 Black or African American, non-Hispanic/Latino; 1 American Indian or Alaska Native, non-Hispanic/Latino; 10 Asian, non-Hispanic/Latino; 11 Hispanic/Latino; 1 Native Hawaiian or other Pacific Islander, non-Hispanic/Latino, 69 international. Average age 36. 259 applicants, 64% accepted, 73 enrolled. *Faculty:* 40 full-time (6 women), 10 part-time/adjunct (2 women). Expenses: Contact institution. *Financial support:* Fellowships, research assistantships, teaching assistantships, Federal Work-Study, scholarships/grants, tuition waivers (full and partial), and unspecified assistantships available. Financial award application deadline: 2/1; financial award applicants required to submit FAFSA. In 2010, 7 first professional degrees, 29 master's, 29 doctorates awarded. *Degree program information:* Part-time programs available. Offers theology and religious studies (M Div, STB, MA, MRE, D Min, PhD, STD, Certificate, STL). *Application deadline:* For fall admission, 8/1 priority date for domestic students, 7/15 for international students; for spring admission, 12/1 priority date for domestic students, 10/15 for international students. Applications are processed on a rolling basis. *Application fee:* $55. Electronic applications accepted. *Application Contact:* Andrew Woodall, Director of Graduate Admissions, 202-319-5057, Fax: 202-319-6533, E-mail: cua-admissions@cua.edu. *Dean*, Msgr. Kevin W. Irwin, 202-319-5684, Fax: 202-319-5704, E-mail: irwin@cua.edu.

CEDAR CREST COLLEGE, Allentown, PA 18104-6196

General Information Independent-religious, coed, primarily women, comprehensive institution.

GRADUATE UNITS

Department of Education *Degree program information:* Part-time and evening/weekend programs available. Offers education (M Ed).

Program in Forensic Science Offers forensic science (MS). Electronic applications accepted.

CEDARS-SINAI MEDICAL CENTER, Los Angeles, CA 90048

General Information Independent, coed, graduate-only institution. *Graduate housing:* On-campus housing not available.

GRADUATE UNITS

Graduate Program in Biomedical Sciences and Translational Medicine Offers biomedical sciences and translational medicine (PhD).

CEDARVILLE UNIVERSITY, Cedarville, OH 45314-0601

General Information Independent-religious, coed, comprehensive institution. *Graduate housing:* Room and/or apartments available on a first-come, first-served basis to single students; on-campus housing not available to married students. Housing application deadline: 5/1.

GRADUATE UNITS

Graduate Programs *Degree program information:* Part-time and evening/weekend programs available. Offers education (M Ed). Electronic applications accepted.

CENTENARY COLLEGE, Hackettstown, NJ 07840-2100

General Information Independent-religious, coed, comprehensive institution. *Graduate housing:* Room and/or apartments available on a first-come, first-served basis to single students; on-campus housing not available to married students. Housing application deadline: 6/1.

GRADUATE UNITS

Program in Business Administration *Degree program information:* Part-time and evening/weekend programs available. Postbaccalaureate distance learning degree programs offered (minimal on-campus study). Offers business administration (MBA).

Program in Counseling Psychology *Degree program information:* Part-time and evening/weekend programs available. Postbaccalaureate distance learning degree programs offered (minimal on-campus study). Offers counseling (MA); counseling psychology (MA).

Program in Education *Degree program information:* Part-time and evening/weekend programs available. Postbaccalaureate distance learning degree programs offered (minimal on-campus study). Offers educational leadership (MA); instructional leadership (MA); special education (MA).

Centenary College (continued)

Program in Professional Accounting *Degree program information:* Part-time and evening/weekend programs available. Postbaccalaureate distance learning degree programs offered (minimal on-campus study). Offers professional accounting (MS).

CENTENARY COLLEGE OF LOUISIANA, Shreveport, LA 71104

General Information Independent-religious, coed, comprehensive institution. *Graduate housing:* Rooms and/or apartments available on a first-come, first-served basis to single students and available to married students.

GRADUATE UNITS

Graduate Programs *Degree program information:* Part-time and evening/weekend programs available. Offers administration (M Ed); elementary education (MAT); secondary education (MAT); supervision of instruction (M Ed).

Frost School of Business *Degree program information:* Part-time and evening/weekend programs available. Offers business (MBA).

CENTRAL BAPTIST THEOLOGICAL SEMINARY, Shawnee, KS 66226

General Information Independent-religious, coed, graduate-only institution. *Graduate housing:* On-campus housing not available.

GRADUATE UNITS

Graduate and Professional Programs *Degree program information:* Part-time programs available. Offers missional church studies (MA); theological studies (MA); theology (M Div, Diploma). Electronic applications accepted.

CENTRAL BAPTIST THEOLOGICAL SEMINARY OF VIRGINIA BEACH, Virginia Beach, VA 23464

General Information Independent-religious, coed, graduate-only institution.

GRADUATE UNITS

Graduate Programs Offers biblical studies (M Div, MBS, Th M). Electronic applications accepted.

CENTRAL CONNECTICUT STATE UNIVERSITY, New Britain, CT 06050-4010

General Information State-supported, coed, comprehensive institution. CGS member. *Enrollment:* 12,477 graduate, professional, and undergraduate students; 613 full-time matriculated graduate/professional students (393 women), 1,542 part-time matriculated graduate/professional students (1,029 women). *Enrollment by degree level:* 1,662 master's, 45 doctoral, 448 other advanced degrees. *Graduate faculty:* 346 full-time (137 women), 453 part-time/adjunct (196 women). *Tuition, area resident:* Full-time $5012; part-time $470 per credit. Tuition, state resident: full-time $7518; part-time $482 per credit. Tuition, nonresident: full-time $13,962; part-time $482 per credit. *Required fees:* $3772. One-time fee: $62 part-time. *Graduate housing:* Room and/or apartments available on a first-come, first-served basis to single students; on-campus housing not available to married students. Typical cost: $5368 per year ($9372 including board). Housing application deadline: 4/1. *Student services:* Campus employment opportunities, campus safety program, career counseling, child daycare facilities, exercise/wellness program, free psychological counseling, international student services, low-cost health insurance, multicultural affairs office, services for students with disabilities, teacher training, writing training. *Library facilities:* Elihu Burritt Library plus 1 other. *Online resources:* library catalog, web page, access to other libraries' catalogs. *Collection:* 732,480 titles, 40,128 serial subscriptions, 14,227 audiovisual materials.

Computer facilities: 750 computers available on campus for general student use. A campuswide network can be accessed from student residence rooms and from off campus. Online class registration is available. *Web address:* http://www.ccsu.edu/.

General Application Contact: Patricia Gardner, Associate Director of Graduate Studies, 860-832-2350, Fax: 860-832-2352, E-mail: graduateadmissions@ccsu.edu.

GRADUATE UNITS

School of Graduate Studies Students: 613 full-time (393 women), 1,542 part-time (1,029 women); includes 338 minority (122 Black or African American, non-Hispanic/Latino; 7 American Indian or Alaska Native, non-Hispanic/Latino; 53 Asian, non-Hispanic/Latino; 133 Hispanic/Latino; 23 Two or more races, non-Hispanic/Latino), 43 international. Average age 33. 1,376 applicants, 64% accepted, 557 enrolled. *Faculty:* 346 full-time (137 women), 453 part-time/adjunct (196 women). Expenses: Contact institution. *Financial support:* In 2010–11, 179 students received support, including 66 research assistantships (averaging $4,800 per year); career-related internships or fieldwork, Federal Work-Study, scholarships/grants, and unspecified assistantships also available. Support available to part-time students. Financial award application deadline: 2/15; financial award applicants required to submit FAFSA. In 2010, 596 master's, 10 doctorates, 103 other advanced degrees awarded. *Degree program information:* Part-time and evening/weekend programs available. *Application deadline:* For fall admission, 7/1 for domestic students, 5/1 for international students; for spring admission, 12/1 for domestic students, 11/1 for international students. Applications are processed on a rolling basis. *Application fee:* $50. Electronic applications accepted. *Application Contact:* Patricia Gardner, Associate Director of Graduate Studies, 860-832-2350, Fax: 860-832-2352, E-mail: graduateadmissions@ccsu.edu. *Associate Director of Graduate Studies,* Patricia Gardner, 860-832-2350, Fax: 860-832-2352, E-mail: graduateadmissions@ccsu.edu.

School of Arts and Sciences Students: 331 full-time (194 women), 464 part-time (268 women); includes 134 minority (36 Black or African American, non-Hispanic/Latino; 2 American Indian or Alaska Native, non-Hispanic/Latino; 29 Asian, non-Hispanic/Latino; 54 Hispanic/Latino; 13 Two or more races, non-Hispanic/Latino), 25 international. Average age 32. 498 applicants, 63% accepted, 184 enrolled. *Faculty:* 224 full-time (94 women), 303 part-time/adjunct (128 women). Expenses: Contact institution. *Financial support:* In 2010–11, 78 students received support, including 38 research assistantships; career-related internships or fieldwork, Federal Work-Study, scholarships/grants, and unspecified assistantships also available. Support available to part-time students. Financial award application deadline: 2/15; financial award applicants required to submit FAFSA. In 2010, 181 master's, 29 other advanced degrees awarded. *Degree program information:* Part-time and evening/weekend programs available. Offers art education (MS, Certificate); arts and sciences (MA, MS, Certificate, Sixth Year Certificate); biological sciences (MA, MS); biology (Certificate); community psychology (MA); computer information technology (MS); criminal justice (MS); data mining (MS, Certificate); English (MA, MS, Certificate); French (MA, Certificate); general psychology (MA); geography (MS); German (Certificate); graphic information design (MA); health psychology (MA); history (MA, Certificate); international studies (MS); Italian (Certificate); mathematics (MA, MS, Certificate, Sixth Year Certificate); modern language (MA, Certificate); music education (MS, Certificate); natural sciences (MS); organizational communication (MS); public history (MA); public relations/promotions (Certificate); science education (Certificate); social studies (Certificate); Spanish (MS, Certificate); Spanish language and Hispanic culture (MA); teaching English to speakers of other languages (MS, Certificate). *Application deadline:* For fall admission, 7/1 for domestic students, 5/1 for international students; for spring admission, 12/1 for domestic students, 11/1 for international students. Applications are processed on a rolling basis. *Application fee:* $50. Electronic applications accepted. *Application Contact:* Dr. Susan Pease, Dean, 860-832-2600, E-mail: pease@ccsu.edu. *Dean,* Dr. Susan Pease, 860-832-2600, E-mail: pease@ccsu.edu.

School of Education and Professional Studies Students: 243 full-time (185 women), 949 part-time (731 women); includes 166 minority (74 Black or African American, non-Hispanic/Latino; 5 American Indian or Alaska Native, non-Hispanic/Latino; 7 Asian, non-Hispanic/Latino; 71 Hispanic/Latino; 9 Two or more races, non-Hispanic/Latino), 10 international. Average age 33. 764 applicants, 62% accepted, 315 enrolled. *Faculty:* 66 full-time (32 women), 100 part-time/adjunct (59 women). Expenses: Contact institution. *Financial support:* In 2010–11, 89 students received support, including 20 research assistantships; career-related internships or fieldwork, Federal Work-Study, scholarships/grants, and unspecified assistantships also available. Support available to part-time students. Financial award application deadline: 2/15; financial award applicants required to submit FAFSA. In 2010, 360 master's, 10 doctorates, 71 other advanced degrees awarded. *Degree program information:* Part-time and evening/weekend programs available. Offers early childhood education (MS); education and professional studies (MAT, MS, Ed D, Certificate, Sixth Year Certificate); educational foundations policy/secondary education (MS); educational leadership (MS, Ed D, Sixth Year Certificate); educational technology and media (MS); elementary education (MS, Certificate); marriage and family therapy (MS); physical education (MS, Certificate); professional counseling (MS, Certificate); reading and language arts (MS, Sixth Year Certificate); school counseling (MS); special education (Certificate); special education for special educators (MS); special education for teachers certified in areas other than education (MS); student development in higher education (MS); teacher education (MAT). *Application deadline:* For fall admission, 7/1 for domestic students, 5/1 for international students; for spring admission, 12/1 for domestic students, 11/1 for international students. Applications are processed on a rolling basis. *Application fee:* $50. Electronic applications accepted. *Application Contact:* Dr. Mitchell Sakofs, Dean, 860-832-2100, E-mail: sakofsm@ccsu.edu. *Dean,* Dr. Mitchell Sakofs, 860-832-2100, E-mail: sakofsm@ccsu.edu.

School of Technology Students: 39 full-time (14 women), 129 part-time (30 women); includes 38 minority (12 Black or African American, non-Hispanic/Latino; 17 Asian, non-Hispanic/Latino; 8 Hispanic/Latino; 1 Two or more races, non-Hispanic/Latino), 8 international. Average age 33. 114 applicants, 80% accepted, 58 enrolled. *Faculty:* 45 full-time (9 women), 41 part-time/adjunct (7 women). Expenses: Contact institution. *Financial support:* In 2010–11, 12 students received support, including 8 research assistantships; career-related internships or fieldwork, Federal Work-Study, scholarships/grants, and unspecified assistantships also available. Support available to part-time students. Financial award application deadline: 2/15; financial award applicants required to submit FAFSA. In 2010, 52 master's, 1 other advanced degree awarded. *Degree program information:* Part-time and evening/weekend programs available. Offers biomolecular sciences (MS); construction management (MS, Certificate); engineering (MS); lean manufacturing and Six Sigma (Certificate); supply chain and logistics (Certificate); technology (MA, MS, Certificate); technology engineering education (MS, Certificate); technology management (MS). *Application deadline:* For fall admission, 7/1 for domestic students, 5/1 for international students; for spring admission, 12/1 for domestic students, 11/1 for international students. Applications are processed on a rolling basis. *Application fee:* $50. Electronic applications accepted. *Application Contact:* Dr. Zdzislaw Kremens, Dean, 860-832-1800, E-mail: kremensz@ccsu.edu. *Dean,* Dr. Zdzislaw Kremens, 860-832-1800, E-mail: kremensz@ccsu.edu.

CENTRAL EUROPEAN UNIVERSITY, H-1051 Budapest, Hungary

General Information Independent, coed, graduate-only institution. *Enrollment by degree level:* 824 master's, 441 doctoral. *Graduate faculty:* 133 full-time (39 women), 19 part-time/adjunct (9 women). *Graduate tuition:* Tuition and fees charges are reported in euros. *Tuition:* Full-time 11,000 euros. *Required fees:* 250 euros. One-time fee: 200 euros full-time. Tuition and fees vary according to degree level, program, reciprocity agreements and student level. *Graduate housing:* Room and/or apartments guaranteed to single students; on-campus housing not available to married students. *Student services:* Campus employment opportunities, campus safety program, career counseling, exercise/wellness program, free psychological counseling, grant writing training, international student services, low-cost health insurance, multicultural affairs office, services for students with disabilities, teacher training, writing training. *Library facilities:* Central European University Library plus 1 other. *Online resources:* library catalog, web page, access to other libraries' catalogs. *Collection:* 190,000 titles, 1,650 serial subscriptions, 600 audiovisual materials. *Research affiliation:* Open Society Archives, Institute of Human Sciences Vienna (social sciences), Open Society Institute.

Computer facilities: 700 computers available on campus for general student use. A campuswide network can be accessed from student residence rooms and from off campus. Online class registration, laptop area, PC in dormitory rooms are available. *Web address:* http://www.ceu.hu/.

General Application Contact: Zsuzsanna Jaszberenyi, Admissions Officer, 361-327-3009, Fax: 361-327-3211, E-mail: admissions@ceu.hu.

GRADUATE UNITS

CEU Business School Students: 71 full-time (30 women), 142 part-time (47 women). Average age 34. 144 applicants, 36% accepted, 32 enrolled. *Faculty:* 16 full-time (4 women), 2 part-time/adjunct (1 woman). Expenses: Contact institution. *Financial support:* In 2010–11, 4 students received support. Tuition waivers (partial) available. In 2010, 64 master's awarded. *Degree program information:* Part-time and evening/weekend programs available. Offers executive business administration (EMBA); finance (MBA); general management (MBA); information technology management (MBA); marketing (MBA); real estate management (MBA). *Application deadline:* For fall admission, 5/15 priority date for domestic students, 5/22 for international students; for winter admission, 11/15 priority date for domestic students, 11/10 for international students. Applications are processed on a rolling basis. *Application fee:* $0. Electronic applications accepted. *Application Contact:* Agnes Schram, MBA Program Manager, 361-887-5511, Fax: 361-887-5133, E-mail: mba@ceubusiness.com. *Dean and Managing Director,* Dr. Mel Horwitch, 361-887-5050, E-mail: mhorwitch@ceubusiness.com.

Graduate Studies Students: 1,044 full-time (572 women), 8 part-time (4 women). Average age 28. 5,384 applicants, 19% accepted, 599 enrolled. *Faculty:* 117 full-time (35 women), 126 part-time/adjunct (9 women). Expenses: Contact institution. *Financial support:* In 2010–11, 582 students received support, including 599 fellowships with full and partial tuition reimbursements available (averaging $6,100 per year); career-related internships or fieldwork, institutionally sponsored loans, scholarships/grants, health care benefits, and tuition waivers (full and partial) also available. Financial award application deadline: 1/5. In 2010, 420 master's, 44 doctorates awarded. Offers comparative Constitutional law (LL M); economic and legal studies (LL M, MA); environmental sciences and policy (MS, PhD); history (MA, PhD); human rights (LL M, MA); international business law (LL M); legal studies (SJD). *Application deadline:* For fall admission, 1/15 priority date for domestic and international students. *Application fee:* $0. Electronic applications accepted. *Application Contact:* Zsuzsanna Jaszberenyi, Admissions Officer, 361-324-3009, Fax: 367-327-3211, E-mail: admissions@ceu.hu. *Provost/Academic Pro Rector,* Dr. Katalin Farkas, 361-327-3000 Ext. 2227, Fax: 361-327-3211, E-mail: farkask@ceu.hu.

School of Social Sciences and Humanities Students: 732 full-time (404 women). Average age 28. 3,639 applicants, 22% accepted, 416 enrolled. *Faculty:* 90 full-time (29 women), 13 part-time/adjunct (7 women). Expenses: Contact institution. *Financial support:* In 2010–11, 402 students received support, including 416 fellowships with full and partial tuition reimbursements available (averaging $6,200 per year); career-related internships or fieldwork, institutionally sponsored loans, and scholarships/grants also available. Financial award application deadline: 1/5. In 2010, 278 master's, 16 doctorates awarded. Offers economics (MA, PhD); gender studies (MA, PhD); international relations and European studies (MA, PhD); mathematics and its applications (MS, PhD); medieval studies (MA, PhD); nationalism studies (MA, PhD); philosophy (MA, PhD); political science (MA, PhD); public policy (MA, PhD); sociology and social anthropology (MA, PhD). *Application deadline:* For fall admission, 1/15 priority date for domestic and international students. *Application fee:* $0. Electronic applications accepted. *Application Contact:* Zsuzsanna Jaszberenyi, Admissions Officer, 361-327-3009, Fax: 361-327-3211, E-mail: admissions@ceu.hu. *Provost/Academic Pro Rector,* Dr. Katalin Farkas, 361-327-3000 Ext. 2227, E-mail: farkask@ceu.hu.

CENTRAL METHODIST UNIVERSITY, Fayette, MO 65248-1198

General Information Independent-religious, coed, comprehensive institution. *Enrollment:* 35 full-time matriculated graduate/professional students (28 women), 128 part-time matriculated graduate/professional students (105 women). *Enrollment by degree level:* 163 master's. *Graduate faculty:* 31 part-time/adjunct (12 women). *Tuition:* Part-time $260 per credit hour. *Required fees:* $5 per credit hour. Tuition and fees vary according to program. *Graduate housing:* Rooms and/or apartments available on a first-come, first-served basis to single and married students. Typical cost: $3125 per year ($6250 including board) for single students. Room and board charges vary according to board plan, campus/location and housing facility selected. *Student services:* Campus employment opportunities, campus safety program, career counseling, free psychological counseling, low-cost health insurance, services for students with disabilities, teacher training, writing training. *Library facilities:* Smiley Library plus 1 other. *Online resources:* library catalog, web page, access to other libraries' catalogs. *Collection:* 97,793 titles, 316 serial subscriptions, 379 audiovisual materials.

Computer facilities: 72 computers available on campus for general student use. A campuswide network can be accessed from student residence rooms and from off campus. *Web address:* http://www.centralmethodist.edu/.

General Application Contact: Aimee Sage, Lead Admissions Counselor, 660-248-6651, Fax: 660-248-6392, E-mail: asage@centralmethodist.edu.

GRADUATE UNITS

College of Graduate and Extended Studies Students: 35 full-time (28 women), 128 part-time (105 women); includes 8 Black or African American, non-Hispanic/Latino; 2 Asian, non-Hispanic/Latino; 1 Hispanic/Latino. Average age 36. *Faculty:* 31 part-time/adjunct (12 women). Expenses: Contact institution. *Financial support:* Tuition waivers available. Support available to part-time students. Financial award application deadline: 6/5; financial award applicants required to submit FAFSA. In 2010, 22 master's awarded. *Degree program information:* Part-time and evening/weekend programs available. Postbaccalaureate distance learning degree programs offered (no on-campus study). Offers clinical counseling (MS); clinical nurse leader (MSN); education (M Ed). *Application deadline:* Applications are processed on a rolling basis. *Application fee:* $25. Electronic applications accepted. *Application Contact:* Aimee Sage, Lead Admissions Counselor, 660-248-6651, Fax: 660-248-6392, E-mail: asage@centralmethodist.edu. *Vice President and Dean,* Dr. Rita Gulstad, 660-248-6292, Fax: 660-248-6392, E-mail: rgulstad@centralmethodist.edu.

CENTRAL MICHIGAN UNIVERSITY, Mount Pleasant, MI 48859

General Information State-supported, coed, university. CGS member. *Enrollment:* 28,292 graduate, professional, and undergraduate students; 1,007 full-time matriculated graduate/professional students (583 women), 915 part-time matriculated graduate/professional students (530 women). *Enrollment by degree level:* 1,387 master's, 405 doctoral. *Graduate faculty:* 368 full-time (142 women), 51 part-time/adjunct (19 women). Tuition, state resident: full-time $8208; part-time $456 per credit hour. Tuition, nonresident: full-time $13,788; part-time $766 per credit hour. One-time fee: $25. *Graduate housing:* Rooms and/or apartments available on a first-come, first-served basis to single and married students. Typical cost: $4248 per year ($5539 including board) for single students; $5301 per year ($6592 including board) for married students. Room and board charges vary according to board plan, campus/location and housing facility selected. *Student services:* Campus employment opportunities, campus safety program, career counseling, exercise/wellness program, free psychological counseling, grant writing training, international student services, low-cost health insurance, multicultural affairs office, services for students with disabilities, teacher training, writing training. *Library facilities:* Charles V. Park Library plus 1 other. *Online resources:* library catalog, web page. *Collection:* 1.2 million titles, 13,821 serial subscriptions, 34,190 audiovisual materials. *Research affiliation:* SAP (information technology), IBM (information technology), Dendritic Nanotechnologies, Inc. (chemistry, physics), Dow Corning Corporation (silicon-based technology), Dow Chemical Company (chemicals and plastics), SAS (business analysis).

Computer facilities: Computer purchase and lease plans are available. 3,000 computers available on campus for general student use. A campuswide network can be accessed from student residence rooms and from off campus. Online class registration, Blackboard are available. *Web address:* http://www.cmich.edu.

General Application Contact: Judith L. Prince, Director of Graduate Student Services, 989-774-4723, Fax: 989-774-1587, E-mail: judith.l.prince@cmich.edu.

GRADUATE UNITS

Central Michigan University Off-Campus Programs Students: 845 full-time (498 women), 3,675 part-time (2,406 women); includes 2,026 minority (1,670 Black or African American, non-Hispanic/Latino; 29 American Indian or Alaska Native, non-Hispanic/Latino; 88 Asian, non-Hispanic/Latino; 158 Hispanic/Latino; 6 Native Hawaiian or other Pacific Islander, non-Hispanic/Latino; 75 Two or more races, non-Hispanic/Latino), 156 international. Average age 38. 1,979 applicants, 87% accepted, 1240 enrolled. *Faculty:* 1,130 part-time/adjunct. Expenses: Contact institution. *Financial support:* Scholarships/grants and tuition waivers (partial) available. Support available to part-time students. Financial award applicants required to submit FAFSA. In 2010, 1,406 master's, 27 doctorates, 117 other advanced degrees awarded. *Degree program information:* Part-time and evening/weekend programs available. Postbaccalaureate distance learning degree programs offered (no on-campus study). Offers acquisitions administration (MSA, Certificate); adult education (MA); community college (MA); education (MA); educational administration (Ed S); educational administration and community leadership (Ed D); educational leadership (MA); educational technology (MA); general administration (MSA, Certificate); guidance and development (MA); health administration (DHA); health services administration (MSA, Certificate); human resources administration (MSA, Certificate); information resource management (MSA, Certificate); instructional (MA); international administration (MSA, Certificate); international health (Certificate); leadership (MSA, Certificate); logistics management (MBA, Certificate); nutrition and dietetics (MS); professional counseling (MA); public administration (MSA, Certificate); public management (MPA); reading and literacy K-12 (MA); SAP (MBA, Certificate); school counseling (MA); school principalship (MA); sport administration (MA); state and local government (MPA); value-driven organization (MBA); vehicle design and manufacturing administration (Certificate). *Application deadline:* Applications are processed on a rolling basis. *Application fee:* $50. Electronic applications accepted. *Application Contact:* Off-Campus Programs Call Center, 877-268-4636, Fax: 989-774-2461, E-mail: cmuoffcampus@cmich.edu. *Vice President and Executive Director,* Dr. Merodie Hancock, 989-774-3865, Fax: 989-774-3542.

College of Graduate Studies Students: 915 full-time (530 women), 1,007 part-time (583 women); includes 45 Black or African American, non-Hispanic/Latino; 21 American Indian or Alaska Native, non-Hispanic/Latino; 35 Asian, non-Hispanic/Latino; 27 Hispanic/Latino, 332 international. Average age 29. *Faculty:* 368 full-time (142 women), 51 part-time/adjunct (19 women). Expenses: Contact institution. *Financial support:* Fellowships with full and partial tuition reimbursements, research assistantships with full and partial tuition reimbursements, teaching assistantships with full and partial tuition reimbursements, career-related internships or fieldwork, Federal Work-Study, unspecified assistantships, and out-of-state merit awards, non-resident graduate awards available. *Degree program information:* Part-time and evening/weekend programs available. Postbaccalaureate distance learning degree programs offered (no on-campus study). Offers acquisitions administration (MSA, Graduate Certificate); general administration (MSA, Graduate Certificate); health services administration (MSA, Graduate Certificate); human resource administration (Graduate Certificate); human resources administration (MSA); information resource management (MSA, Graduate Certificate); international administration (MSA, Graduate Certificate); leadership (MSA, Graduate Certificate); organizational communication (MSA, Graduate Certificate); public administration (MSA, Graduate Certificate); recreation and park administration (MSA); sport administration (MSA). *Application deadline:* For fall admission, 6/1 for international students; for spring admission, 10/1 for international students. Applications are processed on a rolling basis. *Application fee:* $35 ($45 for international students). Electronic applications accepted. *Application Contact:* Judith L. Prince, Director of Graduate Student Services, 989-774-1059, Fax: 989-774-1857, E-mail: judith.l.prince@cmich.edu. *Interim Dean, College of Graduate Studies,* Dr. Roger Coles, 989-774-6099, Fax: 989-774-3439, E-mail: grad@cmich.edu.

College of Business Administration Students: 144 full-time (56 women), 99 part-time (40 women); includes 3 Black or African American, non-Hispanic/Latino; 4 American Indian or Alaska Native, non-Hispanic/Latino; 6 Asian, non-Hispanic/Latino, 102 international. Average age 27. *Faculty:* 43 full-time (9 women), 4 part-time/adjunct (0 women). Expenses: Contact institution. *Financial support:* Fellowships with tuition reimbursements, research assistantships with tuition reimbursements, teaching assistantships with tuition reimbursements, career-related internships or fieldwork, Federal Work-Study, unspecified assistantships, and out-of-state merit awards, non-resident graduate awards available. *Degree program information:* Part-time and evening/weekend programs available. Offers accounting (MBA); business computing (Graduate Certificate); business economics (MBA); business information systems (MS, Graduate Certificate); economics (MA); finance (MBA); finance and law (MBA); human resource management (MBA); information systems (MS); international business (MBA); management (MBA); management information systems (MBA); management information systems/SAP (MBA); marketing (MBA); marketing and hospitality services administration (MBA). *Application deadline:* For fall admission, 6/1 for international students; for spring admission, 10/1 for international students. Applications are processed on a rolling basis. *Application fee:* $35 ($45 for international students). Electronic applications accepted. *Application Contact:* Dr. Daniel Vetter, Senior Associate Dean, 989-774-7966, Fax: 989-774-1329, E-mail: vette1de@cmich.edu. *Dean,* Dr. Charles T. Crespy, 989-774-3337, Fax: 989-774-1320, E-mail: cresp1ct@cmich.edu.

College of Communication and Fine Arts Students: 47 full-time (20 women), 72 part-time (40 women); includes 3 Black or African American, non-Hispanic/Latino; 1 American Indian or Alaska Native, non-Hispanic/Latino; 1 Asian, non-Hispanic/Latino; 4 Hispanic/Latino, 10 international. Average age 28. *Faculty:* 61 full-time (22 women), 7 part-time/adjunct (3 women). Expenses: Contact institution. *Financial support:* Fellowships with tuition reimbursements, research assistantships with tuition reimbursements, teaching assistantships with tuition reimbursements, career-related internships or fieldwork, Federal Work-Study, unspecified assistantships, and out-of-state merit awards, non-resident graduate awards available. *Degree program information:* Part-time programs available. Offers communication and fine arts (MA, MM); conducting (MM); electronic media management (MA); electronic media production (MA); electronic media studies (MA); film theory and criticism (MA); interpersonal and public communication (MA); music composition (MM); music education (MM); music performance (MM); piano pedagogy (MM). *Application deadline:* For fall admission, 6/1 for international students; for spring admission, 10/1 for international students. *Application fee:* $35 ($45 for international students). Electronic applications accepted. *Application Contact:* Dr. Shelly S. Hinck, Associate Dean, 989-774-3951, Fax: 989-774-1890, E-mail: hinck1ss@cmich.edu. *Dean,* Dr. Salma Ghanem, 989-774-1885, Fax: 989-774-1890, E-mail: ghane1si@cmich.edu.

College of Education and Human Services Students: 85 full-time (59 women), 209 part-time (164 women); includes 11 Black or African American, non-Hispanic/Latino; 2 American Indian or Alaska Native, non-Hispanic/Latino; 6 Hispanic/Latino, 6 international. Average age 32. *Faculty:* 61 full-time (41 women), 13 part-time/adjunct (11 women). Expenses: Contact institution. *Financial support:* Fellowships with tuition reimbursements, research assistantships with tuition reimbursements, teaching assistantships with tuition reimbursements, career-related internships or fieldwork, Federal Work-Study, unspecified assistantships, and out-of-state merit awards, non-resident graduate awards available. *Degree program information:* Part-time and evening/weekend programs available. Offers apparel product development and merchandising technology (MS); autism (Graduate Certificate); counseling (MA); education and human services (MA, MS, Ed D, Ed S, Graduate Certificate); educational leadership (MA, Ed D); educational technology (MA, Graduate Certificate); elementary education (MA); general educational administration (Ed S); gerontology (Graduate Certificate); human development and family studies (MA); middle level education (MA); nutrition and dietetics (MS); reading and literacy K-12 (MA); recreation and park administration (MA); school principalship (MA); secondary education (MA); special education (MA); teacher leadership (MA); therapeutic recreation (MA). *Application deadline:* For fall admission, 6/1 for international students; for spring admission, 10/1 for international students. Applications are processed on a rolling basis. *Application fee:* $35 ($45 for international students). Electronic applications accepted. *Application Contact:* Dr. Raymond W. Francis, Interim Associate Dean, 989-774-3888, Fax: 989-774-1999, E-mail: franc1rw@cmich.edu. *Interim Dean,* Dr. Kathy Koch, 989-774-6995, Fax: 989-774-1999, E-mail: koch1ke@cmich.edu.

College of Humanities and Social and Behavioral Sciences Students: 152 full-time (76 women), 215 part-time (124 women); includes 7 Black or African American, non-Hispanic/Latino; 6 American Indian or Alaska Native, non-Hispanic/Latino; 4 Asian, non-Hispanic/Latino; 6 Hispanic/Latino, 38 international. Average age 29. *Faculty:* 85 full-time (34 women), 3 part-time/adjunct (0 women). Expenses: Contact institution. *Financial support:* Fellowships with tuition reimbursements, research assistantships with tuition reimbursements, teaching assistantships with tuition reimbursements, career-related internships or fieldwork, Federal Work-Study, unspecified assistantships, and out-of-state merit awards, non-resident tuition awards available. *Degree program information:* Part-time and evening/weekend programs available. Offers applied experimental psychology (PhD); clinical psychology (PhD); English composition and communication (MA); English language and literature (MA); European history (Graduate Certificate); experimental psychology (MS, PhD); history (MA, PhD); humanities (MA); humanities and social and behavioral sciences (MA, MPA, MS, PhD, Graduate Certificate, S Psy S); industrial and organizational psychology (MA, PhD); modern history (Graduate Certificate); neuroscience (MS, PhD); occupational health psychology (PhD); political science (MA); professional development in public administration (Graduate Certificate); public administration (MPA, Graduate Certificate); public management (MPA); school psychology (PhD, S Psy S); Spanish (MA); state and local government (MPA); teaching English to speakers of other languages (MA); United States history (Graduate Certificate). *Application deadline:* For fall admission, 6/1 for international students; for spring admission, 10/1 for international students. Applications are processed on a rolling basis. *Application fee:* $35 ($45 for international students). Electronic applications accepted. *Application Contact:* Dr. Rick S. Kurtz, Associate Dean, 989-774-3436, Fax: 989-774-7106, E-mail: kurtz1rs@cmich.edu. *Dean,* Dr. Pamela Gates, 989-774-3341, Fax: 989-774-7106, E-mail: gates1ps@cmich.edu.

College of Science and Technology Students: 77 full-time (25 women), 128 part-time (43 women); includes 3 Black or African American, non-Hispanic/Latino; 1 American Indian or Alaska Native, non-Hispanic/Latino; 4 Asian, non-Hispanic/Latino; 3 Hispanic/Latino, 76 international. Average age 29. *Faculty:* 73 full-time (18 women), 4 part-time/adjunct (1 woman). Expenses: Contact institution. *Financial support:* Fellowships with tuition reimbursements, research assistantships with tuition reimbursements, teaching assistantships with tuition reimbursements, career-related internships or fieldwork, Federal Work-Study, unspecified assistantships, and out-of-state merit awards, non-resident graduate awards available. *Degree program information:* Part-time and evening/weekend programs available. Offers biology (MS); chemistry (MS); computer science (MS); conservation biology (MS); industrial management and technology (MA); mathematics (MA, PhD); physics (MS); science and technology (MA, MAT, MS, PhD, Graduate Certificate); science of advanced materials (PhD); teaching chemistry (MA). *Application deadline:* For fall admission, 6/1 for international students; for spring admission, 10/1 for international students. Applications are processed on a rolling basis. *Application fee:* $35 ($45 for international students). Electronic applications accepted. *Application Contact:* Dr. Jane M. Matty, Associate Dean, 989-774-1870, Fax: 989-774-1874, E-mail: matty1jm@cmich.edu. *Dean,* Dr. Ian R. Davison, 989-774-1870, Fax: 989-774-1874, E-mail: davis1ir@cmich.edu.

The Herbert H. and Grace A. Dow College of Health Professions Students: 359 full-time (271 women), 48 part-time (22 women); includes 5 Black or African American, non-Hispanic/Latino; 4 American Indian or Alaska Native, non-Hispanic/Latino; 7 Asian, non-Hispanic/Latino; 6 Hispanic/Latino, 7 international. Average age 26. *Faculty:* 44 full-time (18 women), 15 part-time/adjunct (4 women). Expenses: Contact institution. *Financial support:* Fellowships with tuition reimbursements, research assistantships with tuition reimbursements, teaching assistantships with tuition reimbursements, career-related internships or fieldwork, Federal Work-Study, unspecified assistantships, and out-of-state merit awards, non-resident graduate awards available. *Degree program information:* Part-time programs available. Offers audiology (Au D); exercise science (MA); health administration (DHA); health professions (MA, MS, Au D, DHA, DPT, Graduate Certificate); physical education (MA); physical therapy (DPT); physician assistant (MS); speech-language pathology (MA); sport administration (MA). *Application deadline:* For fall admission, 6/1 for international students; for spring admission, 10/1 for international students. *Application fee:* $35 ($45 for international students). Electronic applications accepted. *Application Contact:* Clint Fitzpatrick, Director of Admissions and Enrollment Management, 989-774-1730, Fax: 989-774-2223, E-mail: fitzp1tc@cmich.edu. *Dean,* Dr. Chris Ingersoll, 989-774-1850, Fax: 989-774-1853, E-mail: inger1c@cmich.edu.

CENTRAL STATE UNIVERSITY, Wilberforce, OH 45384

General Information State-supported, coed, comprehensive institution. *Graduate housing:* Room and/or apartments available on a first-come, first-served basis to single students; on-campus housing not available to married students. Housing application deadline: 6/15.

GRADUATE UNITS

Program in Education *Degree program information:* Part-time and evening/weekend programs available. Offers education (M Ed).

CENTRAL WASHINGTON UNIVERSITY, Ellensburg, WA 98926

General Information State-supported, coed, comprehensive institution. CGS member. *Graduate housing:* Rooms and/or apartments available on a first-come, first-served basis to single and married students. *Research affiliation:* JPL, East-West Center (Pacific area studies), Associated Western Universities (science and engineering).

GRADUATE UNITS

Graduate Studies and Research *Degree program information:* Part-time and evening/weekend programs available. Offers individual studies (M Ed, MA, MS). Electronic applications accepted.

College of Arts and Humanities *Degree program information:* Part-time programs available. Offers art (MA, MFA); arts and humanities (MA, MFA, MM); English (MA); history (MA); music (MM); teaching English as a second language (MA); theatre production (MA); theatre studies (MA). Electronic applications accepted.

College of Business *Degree program information:* Part-time programs available. Offers accounting (MPA); business (MPA). Electronic applications accepted.

College of Education and Professional Studies *Degree program information:* Part-time programs available. Offers education and professional studies (M Ed, MS); engineering technology (MS); exercise science (MS); family and consumer sciences education (MS); family studies (MS); master teacher (M Ed); nutrition (MS); reading education (M Ed); special education (M Ed). Electronic applications accepted.

College of the Sciences *Degree program information:* Part-time and evening/weekend programs available. Offers biological sciences (MS); chemistry (MS); experimental psychology (MS); geological sciences (MS); mathematics (MAT); mental health counseling (MS); resource management (MS); school counseling (M Ed); school psychology (M Ed); sciences (M Ed, MAT, MS). Electronic applications accepted.

CENTRAL YESHIVA TOMCHEI TMIMIM-LUBAVITCH, Brooklyn, NY 11230

General Information Independent-religious, men only, comprehensive institution.

GRADUATE UNITS

Graduate Programs Offers Jewish/Judaic studies (MA); Talmudic studies (MA).

CENTRO DE ESTUDIOS AVANZADOS DE PUERTO RICO Y EL CARIBE, Old San Juan, PR 00902-3970

General Information Independent, coed, graduate-only institution. *Graduate housing:* On-campus housing not available. *Research affiliation:* Museo de las Americas, Museo Hombre Dominicano, Archivo General, Museo Universidad del Turabo.

GRADUATE UNITS

Graduate Program in Puerto Rican and Caribbean Studies *Degree program information:* Part-time and evening/weekend programs available. Offers Puerto Rican and Caribbean history (MA, PhD); Puerto Rican and Caribbean literature (MA, PhD); Puerto Rican studies (MA).

CHADRON STATE COLLEGE, Chadron, NE 69337

General Information State-supported, coed, comprehensive institution. *Graduate housing:* Rooms and/or apartments available on a first-come, first-served basis to single and married students. Housing application deadline: 6/1.

GRADUATE UNITS

School of Professional and Graduate Studies *Degree program information:* Part-time and evening/weekend programs available. Postbaccalaureate distance learning degree programs offered (minimal on-campus study). Offers business (MA Ed); business and economics (MBA); community counseling (MA Ed); educational administration (MS Ed, Sp Ed); elementary education (MS Ed); history (MA Ed); language and literature (MA Ed); secondary administration (MS Ed); secondary education (MS Ed). Electronic applications accepted.

CHAMINADE UNIVERSITY OF HONOLULU, Honolulu, HI 96816-1578

General Information Independent-religious, coed, comprehensive institution. *Graduate housing:* On-campus housing not available.

GRADUATE UNITS

Graduate Services *Degree program information:* Part-time and evening/weekend programs available. Offers business administration (MBA); counseling psychology (MSCP); criminal justice administration (MSCJA); forensic science (MSFS); homeland security (Certificate); pastoral leadership (MAPL); pastoral theology (MPT); social science via peace education (M Ed). Electronic applications accepted.

CHAMPLAIN COLLEGE, Burlington, VT 05402-0670

General Information Independent, coed, comprehensive institution. CGS member. *Enrollment:* 2,374 graduate, professional, and undergraduate students; 304 full-time matriculated graduate/professional students (144 women), 2 part-time matriculated graduate/professional students (both women). *Enrollment by degree level:* 306 master's. *Graduate faculty:* 6 full-time (0 women), 7 part-time/adjunct (0 women). *Tuition:* Part-time $740 per credit hour. Part-time tuition and fees vary according to program. *Student services:* Campus employment opportunities, campus safety program, career counseling, exercise/wellness program, multicultural affairs office, services for students with disabilities, writing training. *Library facilities:* Miller Information Commons. *Online resources:* library catalog, web page. *Collection:* 120,000 titles, 50,268 serial subscriptions, 1,262 audiovisual materials.

Computer facilities: 260 computers available on campus for general student use. A campuswide network can be accessed from student residence rooms and from off campus. Online class registration, wireless laptops available are available. *Web address:* http://www.champlain.edu/.

General Application Contact: R. J. Sweeney, Associate Director, Graduate Admission, 802-865-5483, E-mail: sweeney@champlain.edu.

GRADUATE UNITS

Graduate Studies Students: 304 full-time (144 women), 2 part-time (both women). Average age 30. 271 applicants, 90% accepted, 216 enrolled. *Faculty:* 14 full-time (0 women), 24 part-time/adjunct (9 women). Expenses: Contact institution. *Financial support:* Applicants required to submit FAFSA. In 2010, 8 master's awarded. *Degree program information:* Part-time programs available. Postbaccalaureate distance learning degree programs offered (no on-campus study). Offers business (MBA); digital forensic management (MS); education (M Ed); emergent media (MFA); health care management (MS); law (MS); managing innovation and information technology (MS); mediation and applied conflict studies (MS). *Application deadline:* For fall admission, 8/1 priority date for domestic and international students; for spring admission, 1/1 priority date for domestic and international students. Applications are processed on a rolling basis. *Application fee:* $50. Electronic applications accepted. *Application Contact:* Jon Walsh, Assistant Vice President, Graduate Admission, 800-570-5858, E-mail: walsh@champlain.edu. *Associate Provost*, Dr. Donald Haggerty, 802-865-6403, Fax: 802-865-6447.

CHANCELLOR UNIVERSITY, Cleveland, OH 44114-4624

General Information Independent, coed, comprehensive institution. *Graduate housing:* On-campus housing not available.

GRADUATE UNITS

College of Business *Degree program information:* Part-time and evening/weekend programs available. Postbaccalaureate distance learning degree programs offered (no on-campus study). Offers business (MBA, MMG).

CHAPMAN UNIVERSITY, Orange, CA 92866

General Information Independent-religious, coed, comprehensive institution. *Enrollment:* 6,881 graduate, professional, and undergraduate students; 1,422 full-time matriculated graduate/professional students (760 women), 540 part-time matriculated graduate/professional students (333 women). *Enrollment by degree level:* 577 first professional, 1,114 master's, 209 doctoral, 62 other advanced degrees. *Graduate faculty:* 233 full-time (86 women), 190 part-time/adjunct (68 women). *Graduate housing:* Rooms and/or apartments available on a first-come, first-served basis to single and married students. Housing application deadline: 6/1. *Student services:* Campus employment opportunities, campus safety program, career counseling, exercise/wellness program, free psychological counseling, grant writing training, international student services, low-cost health insurance, services for students with disabilities, teacher training, writing training. *Library facilities:* Leatherby Libraries plus 1 other. *Online resources:* library catalog, web page, access to other libraries' catalogs. *Collection:* 249,503 titles, 51,534 serial subscriptions, 14,743 audiovisual materials. *Research affiliation:* National Science Foundation (science, engineering), National Endowment for the Arts (NEA) (art), U. S. Department of Education (DOE) (education), U. S. Geological Survey (USGS) (earth sciences), U. S. Department of Agriculture (USDA) (agriculture, food, nutrition).

Computer facilities: Computer purchase and lease plans are available. A campuswide network can be accessed from student residence rooms and from off campus. Online class registration is available. *Web address:* http://www.chapman.edu/.

General Application Contact: Saundra Hoover, Director of Graduate Admissions, 714-997-6786, Fax: 714-997-6713, E-mail: shoover@chapman.edu.

GRADUATE UNITS

Graduate Studies Students: 1,355 full-time (719 women), 551 part-time (344 women); includes 37 Black or African American, non-Hispanic/Latino; 10 American Indian or Alaska Native, non-Hispanic/Latino; 224 Asian, non-Hispanic/Latino; 198 Hispanic/Latino, 96 international. Average age 28. 4,775 applicants, 39% accepted, 710 enrolled. *Faculty:* 215 full-time (77 women), 180 part-time/adjunct (57 women). Expenses: Contact institution. *Financial support:* Fellowships, Federal Work-Study and scholarships/grants available. Financial award application deadline: 6/30; financial award applicants required to submit FAFSA. In 2010, 158 first professional degrees, 417 master's, 37 doctorates awarded. *Degree program information:* Part-time and evening/weekend programs available. *Application fee:* $55. Electronic applications accepted. *Application Contact:* Saundra Hoover, Director of Graduate Admissions, 714-997-6786, Fax: 714-997-6713, E-mail: shoover@chapman.edu. *Associate Provost*, Dr. Raymond Sfeir, 714-997-6733, Fax: 714-628-7358, E-mail: sfeir@chapman.edu.

College of Educational Studies Students: 237 full-time (208 women), 208 part-time (167 women); includes 166 minority (11 Black or African American, non-Hispanic/Latino; 3 American Indian or Alaska Native, non-Hispanic/Latino; 54 Asian, non-Hispanic/Latino; 92 Hispanic/Latino; 3 Native Hawaiian or other Pacific Islander, non-Hispanic/Latino; 3 Two or more races, non-Hispanic/Latino), 1 international. Average age 29. 477 applicants, 45% accepted, 155 enrolled. *Faculty:* 23 full-time (15 women), 31 part-time/adjunct (22 women). Expenses: Contact institution. *Financial support:* Fellowships, scholarships/grants available. Financial award application deadline: 6/30; financial award applicants required to submit FAFSA. In 2010, 132 master's, 4 doctorates awarded. *Degree program information:* Part-time and evening/weekend programs available. Offers administrative services (Tier I) (Credential); communication sciences and disorders (MS); cultural and curricular studies (PhD); disability studies (PhD); education (MA); education: disability studies (PhD); education: school psychology (PhD); educational studies (MA, MS, PhD, Credential, Ed S); elementary education (MA); mild/moderate level I (Credential); mild/moderate level II (Credential); moderate/severe level I (Credential); moderate/severe level II (Credential); multiple subjects with bilingual emphasis (Credential); reading education (MA, Credential); school counseling (MA, Credential); school psychology (MA, Credential, Ed S); secondary education (MA); single subject (Credential); special education (MA); teaching: secondary education (MA). *Application deadline:* Applications are processed on a rolling basis. *Application fee:* $60. Electronic applications accepted. *Application Contact:* Admissions Coordinator, 714-997-6714. *Dean*, Dr. Don Cardinal, 714-997-6781, E-mail: cardinal@chapman.edu.

Dodge College of Film and Media Arts Students: 270 full-time (87 women), 11 part-time (3 women); includes 64 minority (16 Black or African American, non-Hispanic/Latino; 2 American Indian or Alaska Native, non-Hispanic/Latino; 19 Asian, non-Hispanic/Latino; 23 Hispanic/Latino; 1 Native Hawaiian or other Pacific Islander, non-Hispanic/Latino; 3 Two or more races, non-Hispanic/Latino), 31 international. Average age 26. 501 applicants, 39% accepted, 118 enrolled. *Faculty:* 39 full-time (9 women), 69 part-time/adjunct (22 women). Expenses: Contact institution. *Financial support:* Fellowships, Federal Work-Study and scholarships/grants available. Financial award applicants required to submit FAFSA. In 2010, 90 master's awarded. *Degree program information:* Part-time and evening/weekend programs available. Offers film and media arts (MA, MFA); film and television producing (MFA); film production (MFA); film studies (MA); production design (MFA); screenwriting (MFA). *Application deadline:* For fall admission, 2/1 priority date for domestic students. *Application fee:* $60. Electronic applications accepted. *Application Contact:* Graduate Assistants, 714-628-2764. *Chair, Graduate Conservatory*, Alexandra Rose, 714-744-7941, E-mail: arose@chapman.edu.

The George L. Argyros School of Business and Economics Students: 153 full-time (53 women), 111 part-time (33 women); includes 63 minority (4 Black or African American, non-Hispanic/Latino; 26 Asian, non-Hispanic/Latino; 30 Hispanic/Latino; 1 Native Hawaiian or other Pacific Islander, non-Hispanic/Latino; 2 Two or more races, non-Hispanic/Latino), 23 international. Average age 29. 252 applicants, 62% accepted, 90 enrolled. *Faculty:* 52 full-time (11 women), 25 part-time/adjunct (4 women). Expenses: Contact institution. *Financial support:* Fellowships, Federal Work-Study and scholarships/grants available. Financial award applicants required to submit FAFSA. In 2010, 125 master's awarded. *Degree program information:* Part-time and evening/weekend programs available. Offers business administration (Exec MBA, MBA). *Application fee:* $60. Electronic applications accepted. *Application Contact:* Debra Gonda, Associate Dean, 714-997-6894, E-mail: gonda@chapman.edu. *Dean*, Dr. Arthur Kraft, 714-997-6684.

Schmid College of Science Students: 157 full-time (111 women), 117 part-time (87 women); includes 82 minority (4 Black or African American, non-Hispanic/Latino; 1 American Indian or Alaska Native, non-Hispanic/Latino; 53 Asian, non-Hispanic/Latino; 19 Hispanic/Latino; 5 Two or more races, non-Hispanic/Latino), 16 international. Average age 26. 989 applicants, 27% accepted, 97 enrolled. *Faculty:* 38 full-time (15 women), 16 part-time/adjunct (9 women). Expenses: Contact institution. *Financial support:* Fellowships, Federal Work-Study and scholarships/grants available. Financial award applicants required to submit FAFSA. In 2010, 39 master's, 40 doctorates awarded. *Degree program information:* Part-time programs available. Offers food science (MS); health communication (MS); marriage and family therapy (MA); physical therapy (DPT); science (MA, MS, DPT). *Application fee:* $60. *Application Contact:* Saundra Hoover, Director of Graduate Admissions, 714-997-6786, Fax: 714-997-6713, E-mail: shoover@chapman.edu. *Dean*, Dr. Menas Kafatos, 714-628-7223, E-mail: jhill@chapman.edu.

School of Law Students: 580 full-time (283 women), 64 part-time (22 women); includes 132 minority (5 Black or African American, non-Hispanic/Latino; 1 American Indian or Alaska Native, non-Hispanic/Latino; 77 Asian, non-Hispanic/Latino; 37 Hispanic/Latino; 1 Native Hawaiian or other Pacific Islander, non-Hispanic/Latino; 11 Two or more races, non-Hispanic/Latino), 8 international. Average age 27. 2,779 applicants, 28% accepted, 212 enrolled. *Faculty:* 57 full-time (25 women), 26 part-time/adjunct (4 women). Expenses: Contact institution. *Financial support:* Fellowships, Federal Work-Study and scholarships/grants available. Financial award applicants required to submit FAFSA. In 2010, 173 first professional degrees, 19 master's awarded. *Degree program information:* Part-time and evening/

weekend programs available. Offers advocacy and dispute resolution (JD); entertainment law (JD); environmental, land use, and real estate (JD); international law (JD); law (LL M); prosecutorial science (LL M); tax law (JD); taxation (LL M). *Application deadline:* For fall admission, 4/15 priority date for domestic students. Applications are processed on a rolling basis. *Application fee:* $65. Electronic applications accepted. *Application Contact:* Marissa Vargas, Assistant Director of Admission and Financial Aid, 877-CHAPLAW, E-mail: mvargas@chapman.edu. *Dean,* Dr. Tom Campbell, 714-628-2500.

Wilkinson College of Humanities and Social Sciences Students: 55 full-time (32 women), 29 part-time (21 women); includes 25 minority (6 Black or African American, non-Hispanic/Latino; 4 Asian, non-Hispanic/Latino; 13 Hispanic/Latino; 2 Two or more races, non-Hispanic/Latino), 3 international. Average age 31. 98 applicants, 62% accepted, 31 enrolled. *Faculty:* 22 full-time (11 women), 23 part-time/adjunct (7 women). Expenses: Contact institution. *Financial support:* Fellowships, Federal Work-Study and scholarships/grants available. Financial award applicants required to submit FAFSA. In 2010, 26 master's awarded. *Degree program information:* Part-time and evening/weekend programs available. Offers creative writing (MFA); English (MA); humanities and social sciences (MA, MFA); international studies (MA). *Application fee:* $60. *Application Contact:* Saundra Hoover, Director of Graduate Admissions, 714-997-6786, Fax: 714-997-6713, E-mail: shoover@chapman.edu. *Dean,* Dr. Patrick Quinn, 714-997-6947, E-mail: pjquinn@chapman.edu.

See Display on this page and Close-Up on page 929.

CHARLES DREW UNIVERSITY OF MEDICINE AND SCIENCE, Los Angeles, CA 90059

General Information Independent, coed, comprehensive institution. *Graduate housing:* On-campus housing not available.

GRADUATE UNITS

College of Science and Health

Professional Program in Medicine Offers medicine (MD).

CHARLESTON SOUTHERN UNIVERSITY, Charleston, SC 29423-8087

General Information Independent-religious, coed, comprehensive institution. *Graduate housing:* On-campus housing not available. *Research affiliation:* Santee Lynches Council of Governments (economic forecasting), Waccamaw Regional Planning and Development Council (economic forecasting), Metro Charleston Chamber of Commerce (economic forecasting).

GRADUATE UNITS

Department of Criminal Justice *Degree program information:* Part-time and evening/weekend programs available. Offers criminal justice (MSCJ).

Program in Business *Degree program information:* Part-time and evening/weekend programs available. Offers accounting (MBA); finance (MBA); health care administration (MBA); information systems (MBA); organizational development (MBA).

School of Education *Degree program information:* Part-time and evening/weekend programs available. Offers administration and supervision (M Ed); elementary education (M Ed); secondary education (M Ed).

CHARLOTTE SCHOOL OF LAW, Charlotte, NC 28204

General Information Independent, coed, graduate-only institution.

GRADUATE UNITS

Professional Program Offers law (JD).

CHATHAM UNIVERSITY, Pittsburgh, PA 15232-2826

General Information Independent, Undergraduate: women only; graduate: coed, university. CGS member. *Graduate housing:* Rooms and/or apartments available on a first-come, first-served basis to single and married students.

GRADUATE UNITS

Program in Accounting *Degree program information:* Part-time and evening/weekend programs available. Offers accounting (M Acc, MAC). Electronic applications accepted.

Program in Biology *Degree program information:* Part-time programs available. Offers environmental biology-non-thesis track (MS); environmental biology-thesis track (MS); human biology-non-thesis track (MS); human biology-thesis track (MS). Electronic applications accepted.

Program in Business Administration *Degree program information:* Part-time and evening/weekend programs available. Offers business administration (MBA); healthcare professionals (MBA). Electronic applications accepted.

Program in Counseling Psychology *Degree program information:* Part-time and evening/weekend programs available. Offers child, adolescent and family (MSCP); counseling psychology (Psy D); health and holistic (MSCP); infant mental health (MSCP); organization and supervision (MSCP); sport and exercise (MSCP). Electronic applications accepted.

Program in Education Offers early childhood education (MAT); elementary education (MAT); English—secondary (MAT); environmental education (K-12) (MAT); secondary art (MAT); secondary biology education (MAT); secondary chemistry education (MAT); secondary English education (MAT); secondary math education (MAT); secondary physics education (MAT); secondary social studies education (MAT); special education (MAT). Electronic applications accepted.

Program in Film and Digital Technology *Degree program information:* Part-time and evening/weekend programs available. Offers emerging media (MFA). Electronic applications accepted.

Program in Interior Architecture *Degree program information:* Part-time and evening/weekend programs available. Postbaccalaureate distance learning degree programs offered (no on-campus study). Offers interior architecture (MIA). Electronic applications accepted.

Program in Landscape Architecture *Degree program information:* Part-time and evening/weekend programs available. Offers landscape architecture (ML Arch); landscape studies (MA). Electronic applications accepted.

Program in Nursing Offers education/leadership (MSN); nursing (DNP). Electronic applications accepted.

Program in Occupational Therapy Offers occupational therapy (MOT, OTD). Electronic applications accepted.

Program in Physical Therapy Offers physical therapy (DPT, TDPT).

Program in Physician Assistant Studies Offers physician assistant studies (MPAS).

Program in Writing *Degree program information:* Part-time and evening/weekend programs available. Postbaccalaureate distance learning degree programs offered (minimal on-campus study). Offers children's writing (MFA); fiction (MFA); non-fiction (MFA); poetry (MFA); professional writing (MPW); screenwriting (MFA). Electronic applications accepted.

CHESTNUT HILL COLLEGE, Philadelphia, PA 19118-2693

General Information Independent-religious, coed, comprehensive institution. CGS member. *Enrollment:* 2,414 graduate, professional, and undergraduate students; 223 full-time matriculated graduate/professional students (185 women), 617 part-time matriculated graduate/professional students (479 women). *Enrollment by degree level:* 726 master's, 114 doctoral. *Graduate faculty:* 26 full-time (17 women), 93 part-time/adjunct (62 women). *Tuition:* Part-time $560 per credit hour. One-time fee: $55. Tuition and fees vary according to degree level and program. *Graduate housing:* On-campus housing not available. *Student services:* Campus employment opportunities, career counseling, free psychological counseling, international student services, low-cost health insurance, services for students with disabilities, teacher

Chestnut Hill College (continued)

training, writing training. *Library facilities:* Logue Library. *Online resources:* library catalog, web page, access to other libraries' catalogs. *Collection:* 132,434 titles, 1,296 serial subscriptions, 4,893 audiovisual materials.

Computer facilities: 60 computers available on campus for general student use. A campuswide network can be accessed from student residence rooms. Online class registration is available. *Web address:* http://www.chc.edu/.

General Application Contact: Jayne Mashett, Director of Graduate Admissions, 215-248-7020, Fax: 215-248-7161, E-mail: mashettj@chc.edu.

GRADUATE UNITS

School of Graduate Studies Students: 223 full-time (185 women), 617 part-time (479 women); includes 121 minority (83 Black or African American, non-Hispanic/Latino; 16 Asian, non-Hispanic/Latino; 20 Hispanic/Latino; 2 Two or more races, non-Hispanic/Latino), 11 international. Average age 31. 418 applicants, 70% accepted, 214 enrolled. *Faculty:* 26 full-time (17 women), 93 part-time/adjunct (62 women). Expenses: Contact institution. *Financial support:* Unspecified assistantships available. In 2010, 205 master's, 7 doctorates awarded. *Degree program information:* Part-time and evening/weekend programs available. Offers administration of human services (MS); clinical and counseling psychology (MA, MS, CAS); clinical psychology (Psy D); early childhood education (M Ed); educational leadership (M Ed); elementary education (M Ed); holistic spirituality (MA); holistic spirituality and healthcare (MA); holistic spirituality and spiritual direction (MA); holistic spirituality/health care (CAS); instructional technology (MS, CAS); secondary education (M Ed); spiritual direction (CAS); spirituality (CAS); supervision of spiritual directors (CAS). *Application deadline:* For fall admission, 7/1 priority date for domestic students; for winter admission, 11/1 priority date for domestic students; for spring admission, 4/1 priority date for domestic students. Applications are processed on a rolling basis. *Application fee:* $55. *Application Contact:* Amy Boorse, Administrative Assistant, School of Graduate Studies Office, 215-248-7170, Fax: 215-248-7161, E-mail: gradadmissions@chc.edu. *Dean,* Dr. Steven Guerriero, 215-248-7120, Fax: 215-248-7161, E-mail: guerrieros@chc.edu.

See Display below and Close-Up on page 931.

CHEYNEY UNIVERSITY OF PENNSYLVANIA, Cheyney, PA 19319

General Information State-supported, coed, comprehensive institution. *Enrollment:* 19 full-time matriculated graduate/professional students (all women), 59 part-time matriculated graduate/professional students (35 women). *Enrollment by degree level:* 71 master's, 7 other advanced degrees. *Graduate faculty:* 9 full-time (2 women), 3 part-time/adjunct (2 women). Tuition, state resident: full-time $3483; part-time $2322 per semester. Tuition, nonresident: full-time $5573; part-time $3714 per semester. *Required fees:* $270 per semester. Tuition and fees vary according to course load. *Graduate housing:* On-campus housing not available. *Student services:* Career counseling, international student services, low-cost health insurance. *Library facilities:* Leslie Pickney Hill. *Online resources:* library catalog.

Computer facilities: Computer purchase and lease plans are available. A campuswide network can be accessed from student residence rooms and from off campus. Online class registration, online tutorials, various software packages, online payment/online Praxis study guide are available. *Web address:* http://www.cheyney.edu/.

General Application Contact: Dr. Ivan Banks, Provost, 610-399-2271, Fax: 610-399-2070, E-mail: ibanks@cheyney.edu.

GRADUATE UNITS

School of Education and Professional Studies *Degree program information:* Part-time and evening/weekend programs available. Offers adult and continuing education (MS); early childhood education (Certificate); education and professional studies (M Ed, MAT, MPA, MS, Certificate); educational administration and supervision (M Ed, Certificate); educational administration of adult and continuing education (M Ed, MS); elementary and secondary principalship (Certificate); elementary education (M Ed, MAT); public administration (MPA); special education (M Ed, MS). Electronic applications accepted.

THE CHICAGO SCHOOL OF PROFESSIONAL PSYCHOLOGY, Chicago, IL 60610

General Information Independent, coed, primarily women, graduate-only institution. CGS member. *Graduate housing:* On-campus housing not available.

GRADUATE UNITS

Program in Applied Behavior Analysis Offers applied behavior analysis (Psy D); clinical psychology (applied behavior analysis specialization) (MA).

Program in Business Psychology Offers business psychology (Psy D).

Program in Clinical Forensic Psychology Offers clinical forensic psychology (Psy D).

Program in Clinical Psychology Offers applied behavior analysis (MA); clinical psychology (Psy D); counseling (MA). Electronic applications accepted.

Program in Forensic Psychology Offers forensic psychology (MA).

Program in Industrial and Organizational Psychology *Degree program information:* Part-time and evening/weekend programs available. Offers business psychology (Psy D); industrial and organizational psychology (MA).

Program in School Psychology *Degree program information:* Part-time programs available. Offers school psychology (Ed S).

THE CHICAGO SCHOOL OF PROFESSIONAL PSYCHOLOGY AT DOWNTOWN LOS ANGELES, Los Angeles, CA 90017

General Information Independent, coed, graduate-only institution.

GRADUATE UNITS

Program in Applied Behavior Analysis Offers applied behavior analysis (Psy D).

Program in Clinical Forensic Psychology Offers clinical forensic psychology (Psy D).

Program in Clinical Psychology Offers applied behavior analysis (MA); clinical psychology (Psy D); marital and family therapy (MA).

Program in Industrial and Organizational Psychology Offers industrial and organizational psychology (MA).

THE CHICAGO SCHOOL OF PROFESSIONAL PSYCHOLOGY AT GRAYSLAKE, Grayslake, IL 60030

General Information Independent, coed, graduate-only institution. *Graduate housing:* On-campus housing not available.

GRADUATE UNITS

Program in Clinical Counseling Psychology Offers counseling (MA).

Program in School Psychology Offers school psychology (Ed S).

THE CHICAGO SCHOOL OF PROFESSIONAL PSYCHOLOGY AT IRVINE, Irvine, CA 92612

General Information Independent, coed, graduate-only institution.

GRADUATE UNITS

Program in Clinical Forensic Psychology Offers clinical forensic psychology (Psy D).

Program in Marital and Family Therapy Offers clinical psychology (MA); management practice (Psy D); psychodynamic psychotherapy (Psy D).

Program in Psychology Offers generalist (Psy D); psychodynamic psychotherapy (Psy D).

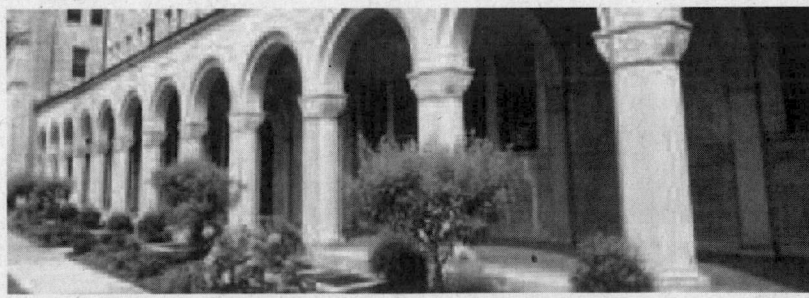

THE CHICAGO SCHOOL OF PROFESSIONAL PSYCHOLOGY AT WESTWOOD, Los Angeles, CA 90024

General Information Independent, coed, graduate-only institution.

GRADUATE UNITS

Program in Clinical Psychology Offers marital and family therapy (MA).

Program in Marital and Family Therapy Offers management practice (Psy D); psychodynamic psychotherapy (Psy D).

Program in Psychology Offers generalist (Psy D); psychodynamic psychotherapy (Psy D).

THE CHICAGO SCHOOL OF PROFESSIONAL PSYCHOLOGY: ONLINE, Chicago, IL 60654

General Information Independent, coed, graduate-only institution. *Graduate housing:* On-campus housing not available.

GRADUATE UNITS

PhD Program in Organizational Leadership Offers organizational leadership (PhD).

Program in Applied Forensic Psychology Services Offers applied forensic psychology services (MA, Certificate).

Program in Applied Industrial and Organizational Psychology Offers applied industrial and organizational psychology (MA, Certificate).

Program in International Psychology Offers international psychology (PhD).

Program in Psychology Offers child and adolescent psychology (MA); generalist (MA); gerontology (MA); international psychology (MA); organizational leadership (MA); sport and exercise psychology (MA).

CHICAGO STATE UNIVERSITY, Chicago, IL 60628

General Information State-supported, coed, comprehensive institution. *Graduate housing:* Room and/or apartments available on a first-come, first-served basis to single students; on-campus housing not available to married students.

GRADUATE UNITS

School of Graduate and Professional Studies *Degree program information:* Part-time and evening/weekend programs available. Electronic applications accepted.

College of Arts and Sciences *Degree program information:* Part-time and evening/weekend programs available. Offers arts and sciences (MA, MFA, MS, MSW); biological sciences (MS); computer science (MS); counseling (MA); creative writing (MFA); criminal justice (MS); English (MA); geography and economic development (MA); history, philosophy, and political science (MA); mathematics (MS); social work (MSW).

College of Education *Degree program information:* Part-time programs available. Offers bilingual education (M Ed); curriculum and instruction (MS Ed); early childhood education (MAT, MS Ed); education (M Ed, MA, MAT, MS Ed, Ed D); educational leadership (MA, Ed D); elementary education (MAT); general administration (MA); higher education administration (MA); instructional foundations (MS Ed); library information and media studies (MS Ed); middle school education (MAT); physical education (MS Ed); reading (MS Ed); secondary education (MAT); special education (M Ed); teaching of reading (MS Ed); technology and education (MS Ed).

CHICAGO THEOLOGICAL SEMINARY, Chicago, IL 60637-1507

General Information Independent-religious, coed, graduate-only institution. *Graduate housing:* On-campus housing not available.

GRADUATE UNITS

Graduate and Professional Programs *Degree program information:* Part-time programs available. Offers preaching (D Min); religion and health (D Min); religious studies (MA); spirituality and spiritual direction (D Min); theology (M Div); theology, ethics and the human sciences (PhD).

CHRISTENDOM COLLEGE, Front Royal, VA 22630-5103

General Information Independent-religious, coed, comprehensive institution. *Graduate housing:* On-campus housing not available.

GRADUATE UNITS

Notre Dame Graduate School *Degree program information:* Part-time and evening/weekend programs available. Offers theological studies (MA). Electronic applications accepted.

CHRISTIAN BROTHERS UNIVERSITY, Memphis, TN 38104-5581

General Information Independent-religious, coed, comprehensive institution. *Enrollment:* 1,828 graduate, professional, and undergraduate students; 66 full-time matriculated graduate/professional students (47 women), 411 part-time matriculated graduate/professional students (208 women). *Enrollment by degree level:* 477 master's. *Graduate faculty:* 8 full-time (3 women), 21 part-time/adjunct (14 women). *Tuition:* Full-time $11,520; part-time $640 per credit hour. *Required fees:* $140; $140 per course. $70 per semester. Tuition and fees vary according to program. *Graduate housing:* On-campus housing not available. *Student services:* Campus safety program, career counseling, free psychological counseling, low-cost health insurance. *Library facilities:* Plough Memorial Library and Media Center. *Online resources:* library catalog, web page, access to other libraries' catalogs. *Collection:* 101,898 titles, 371 serial subscriptions, 2,004 audiovisual materials.

Computer facilities: 310 computers available on campus for general student use. A campuswide network can be accessed from student residence rooms and from off campus. Online class registration, online class listings, course assignments are available. *Web address:* http://www.cbu.edu/.

General Application Contact: Dr. Mike R. Ryan, Dean, Graduate and Professional Studies Programs, 901-321-3296, E-mail: mryan@cbu.edu.

GRADUATE UNITS

School of Arts Students: 51 full-time (42 women), 154 part-time (119 women); includes 77 minority (67 Black or African American, non-Hispanic/Latino; 3 Asian, non-Hispanic/Latino; 4 Hispanic/Latino; 1 Native Hawaiian or other Pacific Islander, non-Hispanic/Latino; 2 Two or more races, non-Hispanic/Latino), 3 international. Average age 33. *Faculty:* 6 full-time (3 women), 13 part-time/adjunct (11 women). Expenses: Contact institution. *Financial support:* Institutionally sponsored loans available. Support available to part-time students. In 2010, 89 master's awarded. *Degree program information:* Part-time and evening/weekend programs available. Offers Catholic studies (MACS); educational leadership (MSEL); teacher-leadership (M Ed); teaching (MAT). *Application deadline:* Applications are processed on a rolling basis. *Application fee:* $35. *Application Contact:* Dr. Talana L. Vogel, Director, 901-321-4101, Fax: 901-321-3408, E-mail: tvogel@cbu.edu. *Dean,* Dr. Paul A. Haught, 901-321-3579, Fax: 901-321-4340, E-mail: phaught@cbu.edu.

School of Business Students: 11 full-time (4 women), 180 part-time (67 women); includes 57 minority (40 Black or African American, non-Hispanic/Latino; 8 Asian, non-Hispanic/Latino; 7 Hispanic/Latino; 2 Two or more races, non-Hispanic/Latino), 9 international. Average age 35. *Faculty:* 1 full-time (0 women), 5 part-time/adjunct (1 woman). Expenses: Contact institution. *Financial support:* Institutionally sponsored loans available. Support available to part-time students. In 2010, 46 master's awarded. *Degree program information:* Part-time and evening/weekend programs available. Offers business (MBA); financial planning (Certificate); project management (Certificate). *Application deadline:* Applications are processed on a rolling basis. *Application fee:* $50. *Application Contact:* Dr. Scott Lawyer, Director, Graduate Business Programs, 901-321-3104, Fax: 901-321-3566, E-mail: mlawyer@cbu.edu. *Director,* Dr. Scott Lawyer, 901-321-3104, Fax: 901-321-3566, E-mail: mlawyer@cbu.edu.

School of Engineering Students: 4 full-time (1 woman), 70 part-time (20 women); includes 18 minority (14 Black or African American, non-Hispanic/Latino; 2 Asian, non-Hispanic/Latino; 1 Hispanic/Latino; 1 Two or more races, non-Hispanic/Latino), 31 international. Average age 33. *Faculty:* 1 full-time (0 women), 2 part-time/adjunct (1 woman). Expenses: Contact institution. *Financial support:* Institutionally sponsored loans available. In 2010, 9 master's awarded. *Degree program information:* Part-time and evening/weekend programs available. Post-baccalaureate distance learning degree programs offered (no on-campus study). Offers engineering (MEM, MSEM). *Application fee:* $50. *Application Contact:* Dr. Neal Jackson, Director, 901-321-3283, Fax: 901-321-3494, E-mail: njackson@cbu.edu. *Dean,* Dr. Eric B. Welch, 901-321-3425, Fax: 901-321-3402, E-mail: ewelch@cbu.edu.

CHRISTIAN THEOLOGICAL SEMINARY, Indianapolis, IN 46208-3301

General Information Independent-religious, coed, graduate-only institution. *Graduate housing:* Rooms and/or apartments available on a first-come, first-served basis to single and married students.

GRADUATE UNITS

Graduate and Professional Programs *Degree program information:* Part-time programs available. Offers educational and arts ministries (MA); marriage and family therapy (MA); pastoral care and counseling (D Min); psychotherapy and faith (MA); theological studies (MTS); theology (M Div). Electronic applications accepted.

CHRISTIE'S EDUCATION, New York, NY 10036

General Information Proprietary, coed, primarily women, graduate-only institution. *Graduate housing:* On-campus housing not available.

GRADUATE UNITS

Program in Modern Art, Connoisseurship, and the History of the Art Market Offers modern art, connoisseurship, and the history of the art market (MA).

CHRISTOPHER NEWPORT UNIVERSITY, Newport News, VA 23606-2998

General Information State-supported, coed, comprehensive institution. *Enrollment:* 4,916 graduate, professional, and undergraduate students; 83 full-time matriculated graduate/professional students (66 women), 44 part-time matriculated graduate/professional students (19 women). *Enrollment by degree level:* 127 master's. *Graduate faculty:* 36 full-time (18 women), 13 part-time/adjunct (8 women). Tuition, state resident: part-time $418 per credit hour. Tuition, nonresident: part-time $769 per credit hour. *Graduate housing:* On-campus housing not available. *Student services:* Campus employment opportunities, campus safety program, career counseling, exercise/wellness program, free psychological counseling, grant writing training, international student services, multicultural affairs office, services for students with disabilities, teacher training, writing training. *Library facilities:* Paul and Rosemary Trible Library. *Online resources:* library catalog, web page, access to other libraries' catalogs. *Collection:* 201,174 titles, 36,104 serial subscriptions, 6,137 audiovisual materials. *Research affiliation:* Langley Research Center, Center for Distance Learning (flow visualization), Thomas Jefferson National Accelerator Facility (instrument and nuclear physics), Applied Research Center (biology, engineering, physics), National Science Foundation (science), National Science Foundation (science).

Computer facilities: 450 computers available on campus for general student use. A campuswide network can be accessed from student residence rooms and from off campus. Online class registration, online degree audit; 80% of campus is wireless are available. *Web address:* http://www.cnu.edu/.

General Application Contact: Lyn Sawyer, Associate Director, Graduate Admissions, 757-594-7544, Fax: 757-594-7649, E-mail: gradstdy@cnu.edu.

GRADUATE UNITS

Graduate Studies Students: 83 full-time (66 women), 44 part-time (19 women); includes 11 minority (4 Black or African American, non-Hispanic/Latino; 6 Hispanic/Latino; 1 Native Hawaiian or other Pacific Islander, non-Hispanic/Latino). Average age 26. 22 applicants, 91% accepted, 8 enrolled. *Faculty:* 36 full-time (18 women), 13 part-time/adjunct (8 women). Expenses: Contact institution. *Financial support:* In 2010–11, 15 students received support, including 6 research assistantships with full and partial tuition reimbursements available (averaging $6,000 per year); teaching assistantships, career-related internships or fieldwork, Federal Work-Study, institutionally sponsored loans, scholarships/grants, and unspecified assistantships also available. Support available to part-time students. Financial award application deadline: 3/1; financial award applicants required to submit FAFSA. In 2010, 104 master's awarded. *Degree program information:* Part-time and evening/weekend programs available. Offers applied physics and computer science (MS); art (PK-12) (MAT); biology (6-12) (MAT); chemistry (6-12) (MAT); computer science (6-12) (MAT); elementary (PK-6) (MAT); English (6-12) (MAT); English as second language (PK-12) (MAT); environmental science (MS); French (PK-12) (MAT); history and social science (6-12) (MAT); mathematics (6-12) (MAT); music (PK-12) (MAT); physics (6-12) (MAT); Spanish (PK-12) (MAT). *Application deadline:* For fall admission, 8/15 for domestic students, 4/1 for international students; for spring admission, 10/15 for domestic students, 10/1 for international students. Applications are processed on a rolling basis. *Application fee:* $50. Electronic applications accepted. *Application Contact:* Lyn Sawyer, Associate Director, Graduate Admissions and Records, 757-594-7544, Fax: 757-594-7649, E-mail: gradstdy@cnu.edu. *Director/Associate Provost,* Dr. Bobbye Bartels, 757-594-7050, E-mail: bbartels@cnu.edu.

CHRIST THE KING SEMINARY, East Aurora, NY 14052

General Information Independent-religious, coed, graduate-only institution. *Graduate faculty:* 9 full-time (0 women), 11 part-time/adjunct (3 women). *Tuition:* Full-time $7110. *Required fees:* $220. *Graduate housing:* On-campus housing not available. *Student services:* Writing training. *Library facilities:* Main library plus 1 other. *Collection:* 180,000 titles, 436 serial subscriptions, 1,684 audiovisual materials.

Computer facilities: 4 computers available on campus for general student use. A campuswide network can be accessed from student residence rooms. Online class registration is available. *Web address:* http://www.cks.edu/.

General Application Contact: Dr. Dennis Castillo, Assistant to the Academic Dean, 716-652-8900 Ext. 7090, Fax: 716-652-8903, E-mail: dcastillo@cks.edu.

GRADUATE UNITS

Graduate and Professional Programs Students: 22 full-time (4 women), 60 part-time (34 women); includes 12 minority (8 Black or African American, non-Hispanic/Latino; 4 Hispanic/Latino). Average age 38. 20 applicants, 90% accepted, 17 enrolled. *Faculty:* 9 full-time (0 women), 11 part-time/adjunct (3 women). Expenses: Contact institution. *Financial support:* Career-related internships or fieldwork and scholarships/grants available. Support available to part-time students. Financial award application deadline: 8/1; financial award applicants required to submit FAFSA. In 2010, 5 first professional degrees, 12 master's awarded. *Degree program information:* Part-time and evening/weekend programs available. Offers divinity (M Div); pastoral ministry (MA); theology (MA). *Application deadline:* For fall admission, 8/15 priority date for domestic students; for spring admission, 1/5 priority date for domestic students. Applications are processed on a rolling basis. *Application fee:* $40. *Application Contact:* Cindy Vogel, Assistant to the Academic Dean, 716-652-8900 Ext. 7088, Fax: 716-652-8903, E-mail: cvogel@cks.edu. *Academic Dean,* Dr. Dennis Castillo, 716-652-8900, E-mail: dcastillo@cks.edu.

CHURCH DIVINITY SCHOOL OF THE PACIFIC, Berkeley, CA 94709-1217

General Information Independent-religious, coed, graduate-only institution. *Graduate housing:* Rooms and/or apartments available on a first-come, first-served basis to single and married students. Housing application deadline: 5/1.

GRADUATE UNITS

Graduate and Professional Programs *Degree program information:* Part-time programs available. Offers theology (M Div, MA, MTS, D Min, Certificate). MA program offered jointly with Graduate Theological Union. Electronic applications accepted.

CINCINNATI CHRISTIAN UNIVERSITY, Cincinnati, OH 45204-3200

General Information Independent-religious, coed, comprehensive institution. *Graduate housing:* On-campus housing not available.

GRADUATE UNITS

Graduate School *Degree program information:* Part-time programs available. Offers biblical studies (MA); church history (MA); counseling (MAC); divinity (M Div); ministry (M Min); practical ministries (MA); theological studies (MA). Electronic applications accepted.

THE CITADEL, THE MILITARY COLLEGE OF SOUTH CAROLINA, Charleston, SC 29409

General Information State-supported, coed, primarily men, comprehensive institution. *Enrollment:* 3,402 graduate, professional, and undergraduate students; 197 full-time matriculated graduate/professional students (130 women), 630 part-time matriculated graduate/professional students (356 women). *Enrollment by degree level:* 725 master's, 102 other advanced degrees. *Graduate faculty:* 80 full-time (24 women), 10 part-time/adjunct (5 women). Tuition, state resident: part-time $460 per credit hour. Tuition, nonresident: part-time $756 per credit hour. *Required fees:* $40 per term. *Graduate housing:* On-campus housing not available. *Student services:* Campus employment opportunities, career counseling, exercise/wellness program, free psychological counseling, international student services, low-cost health insurance, multicultural affairs office, services for students with disabilities, teacher training, writing training. *Library facilities:* Daniel Library. *Online resources:* library catalog, web page, access to other libraries' catalogs. *Collection:* 333,742 titles, 254 serial subscriptions, 7,433 audiovisual materials.

Computer facilities: 350 computers available on campus for general student use. A campuswide network can be accessed from student residence rooms and from off campus. Online class registration is available. *Web address:* http://www.citadel.edu/.

General Application Contact: Dr. Steve A. Nida, Associate Provost, The Citadel Graduate College, 843-953-5089, Fax: 843-953-7630, E-mail: cgc@citadel.edu.

GRADUATE UNITS

Citadel Graduate College Students: 197 full-time (130 women), 630 part-time (356 women); includes 70 Black or African American, non-Hispanic/Latino; 2 American Indian or Alaska Native, non-Hispanic/Latino; 7 Asian, non-Hispanic/Latino; 13 Hispanic/Latino, 9 international. Average age 29. *Faculty:* 69 full-time (22 women), 21 part-time/adjunct (7 women). Expenses: Contact institution. *Financial support:* Fellowships, research assistantships, career-related internships or fieldwork, health care benefits, and unspecified assistantships available. Support available to part-time students. Financial award application deadline: 7/1; financial award applicants required to submit FAFSA. In 2010, 258 master's, 7 other advanced degrees awarded. *Degree program information:* Part-time and evening/weekend programs available. Offers biology (MA); computer and information science (MS); English (MA); health, exercise, and sport science (MS); history (MA); mathematics education (MAE); physical education (MAT); psychology (MA); school psychology (Ed S); social science (MA). *Application deadline:* For fall admission, 8/1 priority date for domestic students. Applications are processed on a rolling basis. *Application fee:* $30. Electronic applications accepted. *Application Contact:* Dr. Steve A. Nida, Associate Provost, The Citadel Graduate College, 843-953-5089, Fax: 843-953-7630, E-mail: cgc@citadel.edu. *Provost/Dean of the College,* Brig. Gen. Samuel M. Hines, 843-953-5007, Fax: 843-953-7240, E-mail: sam.hines@citadel.edu.

School of Business Administration Students: 62 full-time (23 women), 204 part-time (77 women); includes 15 Black or African American, non-Hispanic/Latino; 1 American Indian or Alaska Native, non-Hispanic/Latino; 2 Asian, non-Hispanic/Latino; 2 Hispanic/Latino, 4 international. Average age 28. *Faculty:* 16 full-time (3 women), 6 part-time/adjunct (1 woman). Expenses: Contact institution. *Financial support:* Fellowships, career-related internships or fieldwork, health care benefits, and unspecified assistantships available. Support available to part-time students. Financial award application deadline: 7/1; financial award applicants required to submit FAFSA. In 2010, 92 master's awarded. *Degree program information:* Part-time and evening/weekend programs available. Offers business administration (MBA). *Application deadline:* For fall admission, 7/20 for domestic students; for spring admission, 12/1 for domestic students. *Application fee:* $30. Electronic applications accepted. *Application Contact:* Lt. Col. Kathy Jones, Director, MBA Program, 843-953-5257, Fax: 843-953-6764, E-mail: kathy.jones@citadel.edu. *Dean,* Dr. Ronald F. Green, 843-953-5056, Fax: 843-953-6764, E-mail: ron.green@citadel.edu.

School of Education Students: 44 full-time (34 women), 212 part-time (160 women); includes 35 Black or African American, non-Hispanic/Latino; 2 Asian, non-Hispanic/Latino; 6 Hispanic/Latino. Average age 30. *Faculty:* 12 full-time (7 women), 8 part-time/adjunct (5 women). Expenses: Contact institution. *Financial support:* Fellowships, career-related internships or fieldwork, health care benefits, and unspecified assistantships available. Support available to part-time students. Financial award application deadline: 7/1; financial award applicants required to submit FAFSA. In 2010, 132 master's, 7 other advanced degrees awarded. *Degree program information:* Part-time and evening/weekend programs available. Offers biology (MAT); education (M Ed, MAT, Ed S); elementary/secondary school administration and supervision (M Ed); elementary/secondary school counseling (M Ed); English language arts (MAT); literacy education (M Ed); mathematics (MAT); school superintendency (Ed S); social studies (MAT); student affairs and college counseling (M Ed). *Application deadline:* Applications are processed on a rolling basis. *Application fee:* $30. Electronic applications accepted. *Application Contact:* Dr. Steve A. Nida, Associate Provost, The Citadel Graduate College, 843-953-5089, Fax: 843-953-7630, E-mail: cgc@citadel.edu. *Dean,* Dr. Tony W. Johnson, 843-953-5871, Fax: 843-953-7258, E-mail: tony.johnson@citadel.edu.

CITY COLLEGE OF THE CITY UNIVERSITY OF NEW YORK, New York, NY 10031-9198

General Information State and locally supported, coed, comprehensive institution. *Enrollment:* 15,553 graduate, professional, and undergraduate students; 373 full-time matriculated graduate/professional students (194 women), 2,975 part-time matriculated graduate/professional students (1,817 women). *Enrollment by degree level:* 3,348 master's. *Graduate faculty:* 519 full-time (199 women), 610 part-time/adjunct (291 women). *Graduate housing:* Room and/or apartments available on a first-come, first-served basis to single students; on-campus housing not available to married students. *Student services:* Campus employment opportunities, campus safety program, career counseling, child daycare facilities, exercise/wellness program, free psychological counseling, international student services, multicultural affairs office, services for students with disabilities. *Library facilities:* Morris Raphael Cohen Library plus 3 others. *Online resources:* library catalog, web page, access to other libraries' catalogs. *Collection:* 50,096 serial subscriptions, 273,031 audiovisual materials. *Research affiliation:* New York Center for Biological Structures, Lucent Laboratories (engineering), Hospital for Joint Diseases (biomedical engineering), Museum of Natural History.

Computer facilities: Computer purchase and lease plans are available. 2,500 computers available on campus for general student use. A campuswide network can be accessed from off campus. Online class registration is available. *Web address:* http://www.ccny.cuny.edu/.

General Application Contact: Pauline Pabon, Assistant Director of Graduate Admissions, 212-650-6977, Fax: 212-650-6417, E-mail: graduateadmissions@ccny.cuny.edu.

GRADUATE UNITS

Graduate School Students: 373 full-time (194 women), 2,975 part-time (1,817 women); includes 885 Black or African American, non-Hispanic/Latino; 1 American Indian or Alaska Native, non-Hispanic/Latino; 577 Asian, non-Hispanic/Latino; 1,007 Hispanic/Latino, 462 international. 1,723 applicants, 70% accepted. Expenses: Contact institution. *Financial support:* Fellowships, research assistantships, teaching assistantships, career-related internships or fieldwork, Federal Work-Study, institutionally sponsored loans, scholarships/grants, health care benefits, tuition waivers (full and partial), and unspecified assistantships available. Support available to part-time students. Financial award applicants required to submit FAFSA. In 2010, 953 master's awarded. *Degree program information:* Part-time and evening/weekend programs available. Offers sustainability in the urban environment (MS). *Application deadline:* Applications are processed on a rolling basis. *Application fee:* $125. *Application Contact:* 212-650-6977, Fax: 212-650-6417, E-mail: graduateadmissions@ccny.cuny.edu.

College of Liberal Arts and Science 559 applicants, 59% accepted. Expenses: Contact institution. *Financial support:* Fellowships, research assistantships, teaching assistantships, career-related internships or fieldwork, Federal Work-Study, institutionally sponsored loans, scholarships/grants, and tuition waivers (full and partial) available. Support available to part-time students. Financial award applicants required to submit FAFSA. In 2010, 280 master's awarded. *Degree program information:* Part-time and evening/weekend programs available. Offers advertising design (MFA); art history (MA); art history and museum studies (MA); biochemistry (MA, PhD); biology (MA, PhD); ceramic design (MFA); chemistry (MA, PhD); clinical psychology (PhD); creative writing (MA, MFA); earth and environmental science (PhD); earth systems science (MA); economics (MA); English and American literature (MA); experimental cognition (PhD); fine arts (MFA); general psychology (MA); history (MA); humanities and arts (MA, MFA); international relations (MA); language and literacy (MA); liberal arts and science (MA, MFA, MPA, PhD); mathematics (MA); media arts production (MFA); mental health counseling (MA); museum studies (MA); music (MA); painting (MFA); physics (MA, PhD); printmaking (MFA); psychology (MA, PhD); public service management (MPA); science (MA, PhD); sculpture (MFA); sociology (MA); Spanish (MA); wood and metal design (MFA). *Application deadline:* For fall admission, 5/1 for domestic and international students; for spring admission, 11/15 for domestic and international students. Applications are processed on a rolling basis. *Application fee:* $125. Electronic applications accepted. *Application Contact:* 212-650-6977, Fax: 212-650-6417, E-mail: gradadm@ccny.cuny.edu.

Grove School of Engineering *Degree program information:* Part-time programs available. Offers biomedical engineering (ME, PhD); chemical engineering (ME, MS, PhD); civil engineering (ME, MS, PhD); computer sciences (MS, PhD); electrical engineering (ME, MS, PhD); engineering (ME, MS, PhD); mechanical engineering (ME, MS, PhD).

School of Architecture and Environmental Studies *Degree program information:* Part-time programs available. Offers architecture (M Arch); landscape architecture (MLA); urban design (MUP).

School of Education *Degree program information:* Part-time and evening/weekend programs available. Offers adolescent mathematics education (MA, AC); bilingual education (MS); bilingual special education (MS Ed); childhood education (MS); education (MA, MS, AC); educational leadership (MS, AC); English education (MA); middle school mathematics education (MS); science education (MA); social studies education (AC); teacher of students with disabilities in childhood education (MS Ed); teacher of students with disabilities in middle childhood education (MS Ed); teaching students with disabilities (MA).

CITY OF HOPE NATIONAL MEDICAL CENTER/BECKMAN RESEARCH INSTITUTE, Duarte, CA 91010

General Information Independent, coed, graduate-only institution. *Enrollment by degree level:* 79 doctoral. *Graduate faculty:* 81 full-time (21 women). *Required fees:* $150. *Graduate housing:* Rooms and/or apartments available on a first-come, first-served basis to single and married students. Typical cost: $7200 per year for single students; $7200 per year for married students. Room charges vary according to housing facility selected. Housing application deadline: 7/31. *Student services:* Campus employment opportunities, campus safety program, career counseling, free psychological counseling, grant writing training, international student services, low-cost health insurance, services for students with disabilities, teacher training, writing training. *Library facilities:* Graff Medical and Scientific Library. *Online resources:* library catalog, web page. *Collection:* 59,066 titles, 26,437 serial subscriptions, 75 audiovisual materials.

Computer facilities: 100 computers available on campus for general student use. A campuswide network can be accessed from student residence rooms and from off campus. Online class registration, on-line application are available. *Web address:* http://www.cityofhope.org/gradschool/.

General Application Contact: Lee Ann Cornell, Graduate Education Program Director, 626-471-7396, Fax: 626-301-8105, E-mail: lcornell@coh.org.

GRADUATE UNITS

Irell and Manella Graduate School of Biological Sciences Students: 75 full-time (42 women); includes 1 Black or African American, non-Hispanic/Latino; 3 Asian, non-Hispanic/Latino; 3 Hispanic/Latino; 2 Native Hawaiian or other Pacific Islander, non-Hispanic/Latino; 1 Two or more races, non-Hispanic/Latino, 25 international. Average age 24. 181 applicants, 14% accepted, 15 enrolled. *Faculty:* 81 full-time (21 women). Expenses: Contact institution. *Financial support:* In 2010–11, 55 fellowships with full tuition reimbursements (averaging $30,000 per year) were awarded; teaching assistantships, health care benefits and tuition waivers (full) also available. Financial award application deadline: 4/15. In 2010, 11 doctorates awarded. Offers biological sciences (PhD). *Application deadline:* For fall admission, 1/1 priority date for domestic and international students. *Application fee:* $0. Electronic applications accepted. *Application Contact:* Lee Ann Cornell, Graduate Education Program Director, 626-471-7396, Fax: 626-301-8105, E-mail: lcornell@coh.org. *Dean,* Dr. John J. Rossi, 626-256-8775, Fax: 626-301-8105, E-mail: gradschool@coh.org.

CITY UNIVERSITY OF NEW YORK SCHOOL OF LAW AT QUEENS COLLEGE, Flushing, NY 11367-1358

General Information State and locally supported, coed, graduate-only institution. *Enrollment by degree level:* 430 first professional. *Graduate faculty:* 51 full-time (35 women), 9 part-time/adjunct (6 women). Tuition, state resident: full-time $10,495; part-time $425 per credit. Tuition, nonresident: full-time $17,445; part-time $750 per credit. *Required fees:* $1712. *Graduate housing:* On-campus housing not available. *Student services:* Campus employment opportunities, campus safety program, career counseling, child daycare facilities, exercise/wellness program, free psychological counseling, low-cost health insurance, services for students with disabilities, writing training. *Library facilities:* City University of New York School of Law Library. *Online resources:* library catalog, web page, access to other libraries' catalogs. *Collection:* 225,375 titles, 72,424 serial subscriptions, 257 audiovisual materials.

Computer facilities: 104 computers available on campus for general student use. A campuswide network can be accessed from off campus. Online class registration, free wireless internet access are available. *Web address:* http://www.law.cuny.edu/.

General Application Contact: Yvonne Cherena-Pacheco, Assistant Dean for Enrollment Management and Director of Admissions, 718-340-4210, Fax: 718-340-4435, E-mail: admissions@mail.law.cuny.edu.

GRADUATE UNITS

Professional Program Students: 430 full-time (275 women); includes 159 minority (39 Black or African American, non-Hispanic/Latino; 1 American Indian or Alaska Native, non-Hispanic/Latino; 46 Asian, non-Hispanic/Latino; 61 Hispanic/Latino; 1 Native Hawaiian or other Pacific Islander, non-Hispanic/Latino; 11 Two or more races, non-Hispanic/Latino), 7 international. Average age 27. 2,137 applicants, 25% accepted, 163 enrolled. *Faculty:* 51 full-time (35 women), 9 part-time/adjunct (6 women). Expenses: Contact institution. *Financial support:* In 2010–11, 125 students received support, including 125 fellowships (averaging $4,188 per year), 51 research assistantships (averaging $1,469 per year), 34 teaching assistantships (averaging $11,517 per year); career-related internships or fieldwork, Federal Work-Study, scholarships/grants, and tuition waivers (partial) also available. Financial award application deadline: 5/3; financial award applicants required to submit FAFSA. In 2010, 126 JDs awarded. Offers law (JD). *Application deadline:* For fall admission, 3/15 priority date for domestic students. Applications are processed on a rolling basis. *Application fee:* $50. Electronic applications accepted. *Application Contact:* Yvonne Cherena-Pacheco, Assistant Dean for Enrollment Management and Director of Admissions, 718-340-4210, Fax: 718-340-4435, E-mail: admissions@mail.law.cuny.edu. *Dean/Professor of Law,* Michelle J. Anderson, 718-340-4201, Fax: 718-340-4482.

CITY UNIVERSITY OF SEATTLE, Bellevue, WA 98005

General Information Independent, coed, comprehensive institution. *Graduate housing:* On-campus housing not available.

GRADUATE UNITS

Graduate Division *Degree program information:* Part-time and evening/weekend programs available. Postbaccalaureate distance learning degree programs offered (no on-campus study). Electronic applications accepted.

Albright School of Education *Degree program information:* Part-time and evening/weekend programs available. Postbaccalaureate distance learning degree programs offered (no on-campus study). Offers administrator certification (Certificate); curriculum and instruction (M Ed); elementary education (MIT); guidance and counseling (M Ed); leadership (M Ed); leadership and school counseling (M Ed); reading and literacy (M Ed); special education (MIT); superintendent certification (Certificate). Electronic applications accepted.

Division of Arts and Sciences *Degree program information:* Part-time and evening/weekend programs available. Offers counseling psychology (MA). Electronic applications accepted.

School of Management *Degree program information:* Part-time and evening/weekend programs available. Postbaccalaureate distance learning degree programs offered (no on-campus study). Offers accounting (Certificate); change leadership (MBA, Certificate); computer systems (MS); finance (Certificate); financial management (MBA); general management (MBA); general management-Europe (MBA); global marketing (MBA); human resources management (Certificate); individualized study (MBA); information security (MS); information systems (MBA); leadership (MA); marketing (MBA, Certificate); project management (MBA, MS, Certificate); sustainable business (Certificate); technology management (MBA, Certificate). Electronic applications accepted.

CLAFLIN UNIVERSITY, Orangeburg, SC 29115

General Information Independent-religious, coed, comprehensive institution. *Enrollment:* 1,902 graduate, professional, and undergraduate students; 71 full-time matriculated graduate/professional students (48 women), 18 part-time matriculated graduate/professional students (11 women). *Enrollment by degree level:* 89 master's. *Tuition:* Full-time $8532; part-time $474 per credit hour. *Required fees:* $312. *Graduate housing:* Room and/or apartments available to single students; on-campus housing not available to married students. Housing application deadline: 4/15. *Student services:* Campus employment opportunities, career counseling, services for students with disabilities. *Library facilities:* H. V. Manning Library plus 1 other. *Online resources:* library catalog, web page. *Collection:* 215,641 titles, 468 serial subscriptions, 1,201 audiovisual materials.

Computer facilities: 530 computers available on campus for general student use. A campuswide network can be accessed from student residence rooms and from off campus. Online class registration is available. *Web address:* http://www.claflin.edu/.

GRADUATE UNITS

Graduate Programs Students: 71 full-time (48 women), 18 part-time (11 women); includes 72 minority (all Black or African American, non-Hispanic/Latino), 15 international. Expenses: Contact institution. *Financial support:* Research assistantships, teaching assistantships available. Financial award application deadline: 4/15; financial award applicants required to submit FAFSA. *Degree program information:* Part-time programs available. Offers biotechnology (MS); business administration (MBA). *Application deadline:* For fall admission, 8/1 for domestic students; for spring admission, 12/1 for domestic students. *Application fee:* $40 ($55 for international students). *Application Contact:* Dr. Gloria Seabrook, Interim Executive Director of Professional and Continuing Studies, 803-535-5574, Fax: 803-535-5576, E-mail: gseabrook@claflin.edu. *Interim Executive Director of Professional and Continuing Studies,* Dr. Gloria Seabrook, 803-535-5574, Fax: 803-535-5576, E-mail: gseabrook@claflin.edu.

CLAREMONT GRADUATE UNIVERSITY, Claremont, CA 91711-6160

General Information Independent, coed, graduate-only institution. CGS member. *Enrollment by degree level:* 941 master's, 1,297 doctoral, 21 other advanced degrees. *Graduate faculty:* 110 full-time (40 women), 23 part-time/adjunct (6 women). *Tuition:* Full-time $35,748; part-time $1554 per unit. *Required fees:* $215 per semester. *Graduate housing:* Rooms and/or apartments available on a first-come, first-served basis to single and married students. *Student services:* Campus employment opportunities, campus safety program, career counseling, free psychological counseling, international student services, low-cost health insurance, multicultural affairs office, teacher training, writing training. *Library facilities:* Honnold Library plus 3 others. *Online resources:* library catalog, web page, access to other libraries' catalogs. *Collection:* 3.4 million titles, 6,000 serial subscriptions, 606 audiovisual materials. *Research affiliation:* Claremont School of Theology (religion), Rancho Santa Ana Botanic Garden (botany, native plants).

Computer facilities: A campuswide network can be accessed. Online class registration is available. *Web address:* http://www.cgu.edu/.

General Application Contact: Julia Evans, Director of Central Recruitment, 909-607-3689, Fax: 909-607-7285, E-mail: admiss@cgu.edu.

GRADUATE UNITS

Graduate Programs Students: 1,874 full-time (957 women), 385 part-time (218 women); includes 723 minority (137 Black or African American, non-Hispanic/Latino; 10 American Indian or Alaska Native, non-Hispanic/Latino; 235 Asian, non-Hispanic/Latino; 267 Hispanic/Latino; 12 Native Hawaiian or other Pacific Islander, non-Hispanic/Latino; 62 Two or more races, non-Hispanic/Latino), 362 international. Average age 34. *Faculty:* 110 full-time (40 women), 23 part-time/adjunct (6 women). Expenses: Contact institution. *Financial support:* Fellowships, research assistantships, teaching assistantships, career-related internships or fieldwork, Federal Work-Study, institutionally sponsored loans, scholarships/grants, tuition waivers (full and partial), and unspecified assistantships available. Support available to part-time students. Financial award application deadline: 2/15; financial award applicants required to submit FAFSA. In 2010, 459 master's, 134 doctorates, 88 other advanced degrees awarded. *Degree program information:* Part-time programs available. Offers arts management (MA); botany (MS, PhD); financial engineering (MSFE); public policy and evaluation (MA). *Application deadline:* For fall admission, 2/1 priority date for domestic and international students; for spring admission, 11/1 priority date for domestic and international students. Applications are processed on a rolling basis. *Application fee:* $60. Electronic applications accepted. *Application Contact:* Deborah A. Freund, President, 909-607-3305, Fax: 909-607-9103, E-mail: deborah.freund@cgu.edu. *President,* Deborah A. Freund, 909-607-3305, Fax: 909-607-9103, E-mail: deborah.freund@cgu.edu.

Peter F. Drucker and Masatoshi Ito Graduate School of Management Students: 165 full-time (77 women), 90 part-time (34 women); includes 102 minority (10 Black or African American, non-Hispanic/Latino; 1 American Indian or Alaska Native, non-Hispanic/Latino; 46 Asian, non-Hispanic/Latino; 38 Hispanic/Latino; 1 Native Hawaiian or other Pacific Islander, non-Hispanic/Latino; 6 Two or more races, non-Hispanic/Latino), 45 international. Average age 35. *Faculty:* 11 full-time (3 women), 3 part-time/adjunct (0 women). Expenses: Contact institution. *Financial support:* Fellowships, research assistantships, teaching assistantships, Federal Work-Study, institutionally sponsored loans, and scholarships/grants available. Support available to part-time students. Financial award application deadline: 2/15; financial award applicants required to submit FAFSA. In 2010, 99 master's, 1 doctorate, 71 other advanced degrees awarded. *Degree program information:* Part-time programs available. Offers advanced management (MS); executive management (EMBA); leadership (Certificate); management (EMBA, MA, MBA, MS, PhD, Certificate); strategy (Certificate). *Application deadline:* For fall admission, 2/15 priority date for domestic students. Applications are processed on a rolling basis. *Application fee:* $60. Electronic applications accepted. *Application Contact:* Albert Ramos, Program Coordinator, 909-621-8067, Fax: 909-621-8551, E-mail: albert.ramos@cgu.edu. *Dean/Professor,* Ira A. Jackson, 909-607-9209, Fax: 909-621-8543, E-mail: ira.jackson@cgu.edu.

School of Arts and Humanities Students: 361 full-time (194 women), 31 part-time (22 women); includes 116 minority (21 Black or African American, non-Hispanic/Latino; 2 American Indian or Alaska Native, non-Hispanic/Latino; 33 Asian, non-Hispanic/Latino; 42 Hispanic/Latino; 1 Native Hawaiian or other Pacific Islander, non-Hispanic/Latino; 17 Two or more races, non-Hispanic/Latino), 25 international. Average age 35. *Faculty:* 19 full-time (9 women), 6 part-time/adjunct (2 women). Expenses: Contact institution. *Financial support:* Fellowships, research assistantships, teaching assistantships, Federal Work-Study, institutionally sponsored loans, and scholarships/grants available. Support available to part-time students. Financial award application deadline: 2/15; financial award applicants required to submit FAFSA. In 2010, 78 master's, 26 doctorates, 3 other advanced degrees awarded. *Degree program information:* Part-time programs available. Offers Africana history (Certificate); Africana studies (Certificate); American studies (MA, PhD); American studies and U. S. history (MA, PhD); applied women's studies (MA); archival studies (MA); arts and humanities (M Phil, MA, MFA, DCM, DMA, PhD, Certificate); church music (MA, DCM); composition (MA, DMA); critical theory (MA, PhD); cultural studies (MA, PhD); digital media (MA, MFA); drawing (MA, MFA); early modern studies (MA, PhD); English (M Phil, MA, PhD); European studies (MA, PhD); historical performance practices (MA, DMA); installation (MA, MFA); literary theory (PhD); literature (MA, PhD); literature and creative writing (MA); literature and film (MA); media studies (MA, PhD); museum studies (MA); musicology (MA, PhD); new genre (MA, MFA); oral history (MA, PhD); painting (MA, MFA); performance (MA, MFA, DMA); philosophy (MA, PhD); photography (MA, MFA); sculpture (MA, MFA). *Application deadline:* For fall admission, 2/1 priority date for domestic students. Applications are processed on a rolling basis. *Application fee:* $60. Electronic applications accepted. *Application Contact:* Susan Hampson, Admissions and Academic Support, 909-607-1278, Fax: 909-607-1221, E-mail: susan.hampson@cgu.edu. *Administrative Director,* Lisa Flores Griffith, 909-607-3877, Fax: 909-607-3877, E-mail: elysabeth.flores@cgu.edu.

School of Behavioral and Organizational Sciences Students: 281 full-time (189 women), 22 part-time (15 women); includes 80 minority (16 Black or African American, non-Hispanic/Latino; 1 American Indian or Alaska Native, non-Hispanic/Latino; 30 Asian, non-Hispanic/Latino; 23 Hispanic/Latino; 3 Native Hawaiian or other Pacific Islander, non-Hispanic/Latino; 7 Two or more races, non-Hispanic/Latino), 50 international. Average age 30. *Faculty:* 15 full-time (6 women), 5 part-time/adjunct (2 women). Expenses: Contact institution. *Financial support:* Fellowships, research assistantships, teaching assistantships, Federal Work-Study, institutionally sponsored loans, scholarships/grants, and tuition waivers (full and partial) available. Support available to part-time students. Financial award application deadline: 2/15; financial award applicants required to submit FAFSA. In 2010, 58 master's, 21 doctorates, 4 other advanced degrees awarded. *Degree program information:* Part-time programs available. Offers advanced study in evaluation (Certificate); behavioral and organizational sciences (MA, MS, PhD, Certificate); cognitive psychology (MA, PhD); developmental psychology (MA, PhD); evaluation and applied research methods (MA, PhD); health behavior research and evaluation (MA, PhD); human resource development and evaluation (MA); human resources design (MS); industrial/organizational psychology (MA, PhD); organizational behavior (MA, PhD); organizational psychology (MA, PhD); social psychology (MA, PhD). *Application deadline:* For fall admission, 1/15 priority date for domestic students. Applications are processed on a rolling basis. *Application fee:* $60. Electronic applications accepted. *Application Contact:* Paul Thomas, Director, External Affairs, 909-607-9016, Fax: 909-621-8905, E-mail: paul.thomas@cgu.edu. *Dean,* Stewart Donaldson, 909-607-9001, E-mail: stewart.donaldson@cgu.edu.

School of Community and Global Health Students: 24 full-time (18 women), 5 part-time (3 women); includes 2 Black or African American, non-Hispanic/Latino; 1 American Indian or Alaska Native, non-Hispanic/Latino; 5 Asian, non-Hispanic/Latino; 7 Hispanic/Latino; 1 Two or more races, non-Hispanic/Latino, 1 international. Average age 31. *Faculty:* 9 full-time (3 women). Expenses: Contact institution. *Financial support:* Fellowships, research assistantships, teaching assistantships, Federal Work-Study, institutionally sponsored loans, and scholarships/grants available. Support available to part-time students. Financial award application deadline: 2/15; financial award applicants required to submit FAFSA. Offers health promotion science (PhD); public health (MPH). *Application deadline:* For fall admission, 2/1 priority date for domestic students; for spring admission, 11/1 priority date for domestic students. Applications are processed on a rolling basis. *Application fee:* $60. Electronic applications accepted. *Application Contact:* C. Anderson Johnson, Dean, 909-607-8235, E-mail: andy.johnson@cgu.edu. *Dean,* C. Anderson Johnson, 909-607-8235, E-mail: andy.johnson@cgu.edu.

School of Educational Studies Students: 296 full-time (200 women), 154 part-time (112 women); includes 228 minority (55 Black or African American, non-Hispanic/Latino; 4 American Indian or Alaska Native, non-Hispanic/Latino; 48 Asian, non-Hispanic/Latino; 99 Hispanic/Latino; 3 Native Hawaiian or other Pacific Islander, non-Hispanic/Latino; 19 Two or more races, non-Hispanic/Latino), 11 international. Average age 38. *Faculty:* 16 full-time (8 women), 2 part-time/adjunct (1 woman). Expenses: Contact institution. *Financial support:* Fellowships, research assistantships, Federal Work-Study, institutionally sponsored loans, and scholarships/grants available. Support available to part-time students. Financial award application deadline: 2/15; financial award applicants required to submit FAFSA. In 2010, 83 master's, 26 doctorates, 9 other advanced degrees awarded. *Degree program information:* Part-time programs available. Offers Africana education (Certificate); education and policy (MA, PhD); higher education/student affairs (MA, PhD); human development (MA, PhD); public school administration (MA, PhD); quantitative evaluation (MA, PhD); special education (MA, PhD); teacher education (MA); teaching and learning (MA, PhD); urban leadership (PhD). PhD program offered jointly with San Diego State University. *Application deadline:* For fall admission, 2/1 priority date for domestic students. Applications are processed on a rolling basis. *Application fee:* $60. Electronic applications accepted. *Application Contact:* Margaret Grogan, Dean, 909-621-8075, Fax: 909-621-8734, E-mail: margaret.grogan@cgu.edu. *Dean,* Margaret Grogan, 909-621-8075, Fax: 909-621-8734, E-mail: margaret.grogan@cgu.edu.

School of Information Systems and Technology Students: 87 full-time (24 women), 22 part-time (8 women); includes 31 minority (6 Black or African American, non-Hispanic/Latino; 1 American Indian or Alaska Native, non-Hispanic/Latino; 18 Asian, non-Hispanic/Latino; 3 Hispanic/Latino; 1 Native Hawaiian or other Pacific Islander, non-Hispanic/Latino; 2 Two or more races, non-Hispanic/Latino), 37 international. Average age 37. *Faculty:* 6 full-time (1 woman), 1 part-time/adjunct (0 women). Expenses: Contact institution. *Financial support:* Fellowships, research assistantships, teaching assistantships, Federal Work-Study, institutionally sponsored loans, and scholarships/grants available. Support available to part-time students. Financial award application deadline: 2/15; financial award applicants required to submit FAFSA. In 2010, 30 master's, 6 doctorates awarded. *Degree program information:* Part-time programs available. Offers electronic commerce (MS, PhD); health information management (MS); information systems (Certificate); knowledge management (MS, PhD); systems development (MS, PhD); telecommunications and networking (MS, PhD). *Application deadline:* For fall admission, 2/1 priority date for domestic students. Applications are processed on a rolling basis. *Application fee:* $60. Electronic applications accepted. *Application Contact:* Matt Hutter, Director of External Affairs, 909-621-3180, Fax: 909-621-8564, E-mail: matt.hutter@cgu.edu. *Dean,* Terry Ryan, 909-607-9591, Fax: 909-621-8564, E-mail: terry.ryan@cgu.edu.

School of Mathematical Sciences Students: 50 full-time (15 women), 11 part-time (1 woman); includes 2 Black or African American, non-Hispanic/Latino; 9 Asian, non-Hispanic/Latino; 7 Hispanic/Latino; 3 Two or more races, non-Hispanic/Latino, 13 international. Average age 36. *Faculty:* 6 full-time (0 women). Expenses: Contact institution. *Financial support:* Fellowships, research assistantships, Federal Work-Study, institutionally sponsored loans, scholarships/grants, and tuition waivers (full and partial) available. Support available to part-time students. Financial award application deadline: 2/15; financial award applicants required to submit FAFSA. In 2010, 17 master's, 11 doctorates awarded. *Degree program information:* Part-time programs available. Offers computational and systems biology (PhD); computational mathematics and numerical analysis (MA, MS); computational science (PhD); engineering and industrial applied mathematics (PhD); mathematics (PhD); operations research and statistics (MA, MS); physical applied mathematics (MA, MS); pure mathematics (MA, MS); scientific computing (MA, MS); systems and control theory (MA, MS). *Application deadline:* For fall admission, 2/1 priority date for domestic students. Applications are processed on a rolling basis. *Application fee:* $60. Electronic applications accepted.

Claremont Graduate University (continued)

Application Contact: Susan Townzen, Program Coordinator, 909-621-8080, Fax: 909-607-8261, E-mail: susan.n.townzen@cgu.edu. *Dean,* John Angus, 909-621-8080, Fax: 909-607-8261, E-mail: john.angus@cgu.edu.

School of Politics and Economics Students: 293 full-time (104 women), 32 part-time (11 women); includes 64 minority (8 Black or African American, non-Hispanic/Latino; 22 Asian, non-Hispanic/Latino; 26 Hispanic/Latino; 3 Native Hawaiian or other Pacific Islander, non-Hispanic/Latino; 5 Two or more races, non-Hispanic/Latino), 110 international. Average age 32. *Faculty:* 16 full-time (5 women), 4 part-time/adjunct (1 woman). Expenses: Contact institution. *Financial support:* Fellowships, research assistantships, teaching assistantships, Federal Work-Study, institutionally sponsored loans, and scholarships/grants available. Support available to part-time students. Financial award application deadline: 2/15; financial award applicants required to submit FAFSA. In 2010, 29 master's, 29 doctorates, 1 other advanced degree awarded. *Degree program information:* Part-time programs available. Offers American politics (MA, PhD); business and financial economics (MA, PhD); comparative politics (PhD); economic development (Certificate); economics (PhD); industrial organization (PhD); international and development economics (PhD); international economics policy and development (MA); international money and finance (PhD); international political economy (MA); international studies (MA); neuroeconomics (PhD); political economy and public policy (MA); political philosophy (PhD); political science (PhD); politics and economics (MA, PhD, Certificate); politics, economics and business (MA); public choice and public economics (PhD); public policy (MA, PhD); world politics (PhD). *Application deadline:* For fall admission, 2/1 priority date for domestic students. Applications are processed on a rolling basis. *Application fee:* $60. Electronic applications accepted. *Application Contact:* Lesa Hiben, Admissions Coordinator, 909-621-8699, Fax: 909-621-7545, E-mail: lesa.hiben@cga.edu. *Dean,* Jean Schroedel, 909-621-8696, Fax: 909-621-8545, E-mail: jean.schroedel@cgu.edu.

School of Religion Students: 218 full-time (87 women), 10 part-time (4 women); includes 13 Black or African American, non-Hispanic/Latino; 11 Asian, non-Hispanic/Latino; 12 Hispanic/Latino; 1 Two or more races, non-Hispanic/Latino, 29 international. Average age 37. *Faculty:* 6 full-time (2 women), 2 part-time/adjunct (0 women). Expenses: Contact institution. *Financial support:* Fellowships, research assistantships, teaching assistantships, Federal Work-Study, institutionally sponsored loans, and scholarships/grants available. Support available to part-time students. Financial award application deadline: 2/15; financial award applicants required to submit FAFSA. In 2010, 13 master's, 12 doctorates awarded. *Degree program information:* Part-time programs available. Offers Hebrew Bible (MA, PhD); history of Christianity and religions of North America (MA, PhD); New Testament (MA, PhD); philosophy of religion and theology (MA, PhD); theology, ethics and culture (MA, PhD); women's studies in religion (MA, PhD). *Application deadline:* For fall admission, 2/1 priority date for domestic students. Applications are processed on a rolling basis. *Application fee:* $60. Electronic applications accepted. *Application Contact:* Brent Smith, Recruiter, 909-607-2653, Fax: 909-607-9587, E-mail: brent.smith@cgu.edu. *Dean,* Anselm Min, 909-607-3214, Fax: 909-621-9587, E-mail: anselm.min@cgu.edu.

CLAREMONT MCKENNA COLLEGE, Claremont, CA 91711

General Information Independent, coed, comprehensive institution. *Enrollment:* 1,278 graduate, professional, and undergraduate students; 17 matriculated graduate/professional students (3 women). *Enrollment by degree level:* 17 master's. *Graduate faculty:* 9 full-time (2 women), 1 part-time/adjunct (0 women). *Tuition:* Full-time $46,725. *Library facilities:* Honnold Library plus 2 others. *Online resources:* library catalog, web page, access to other libraries' catalogs. *Collection:* 2.6 million titles, 47,450 serial subscriptions, 15,000 audiovisual materials.

Computer facilities: Computer purchase and lease plans are available. 220 computers available on campus for general student use. A campuswide network can be accessed from student residence rooms and from off campus. Online class registration is available. *Web address:* http://www.claremontmckenna.edu/.

General Application Contact: Darren Filson, Director of Graduate Programs, 909-607-6796, E-mail: darren.filson@claremontmckenna.edu.

GRADUATE UNITS

Robert Day School of Economics and Finance Students: 17 (3 women); includes 2 Asian, non-Hispanic/Latino, 5 international. Average age 23. 125 applicants, 16% accepted, 17 enrolled. *Faculty:* 9 full-time (2 women), 1 part-time/adjunct (0 women). Expenses: Contact institution. *Financial support:* In 2010–11, 17 students received support, including 17 fellowships with full and partial tuition reimbursements available. Financial award applicants required to submit FAFSA. In 2010, 20 master's awarded. Offers finance (MAF). *Application deadline:* For fall admission, 11/2 for domestic and international students; for winter admission, 1/15 for domestic students; for spring admission, 3/9 for domestic students, 2/10 for international students. *Application fee:* $70. Electronic applications accepted. *Application Contact:* Kevin Arnold, Director of Graduate Programs, 909-607-3347, E-mail: karnold@cmc.edu. *Dean,* Brock Blomberg, 909-607-9597, E-mail: bblomberg@cmc.edu.

CLAREMONT SCHOOL OF THEOLOGY, Claremont, CA 91711-3199

General Information Independent-religious, coed, graduate-only institution. *Graduate housing:* Rooms and/or apartments guaranteed to single and married students. Housing application deadline: 6/1. *Research affiliation:* Moore Multicultural Resource and Research Center, Institute for Antiquity and Christianity, Center for Process Studies, National United Methodist Native American Center, Center for Pacific and Asian-American Ministries, Ancient Biblical Manuscript Center.

GRADUATE UNITS

Graduate and Professional Programs *Degree program information:* Part-time programs available. Offers divinity (M Div); ministry (D Min); practical theology (PhD); religion (PhD); religion and theology (MA); religious education (MARE). Electronic applications accepted.

CLARION UNIVERSITY OF PENNSYLVANIA, Clarion, PA 16214

General Information State-supported, coed, comprehensive institution. CGS member. *Graduate housing:* Room and/or apartments available on a first-come, first-served basis to single students; on-campus housing not available to married students.

GRADUATE UNITS

Office of Research and Graduate Studies *Degree program information:* Part-time and evening/weekend programs available.

College of Arts and Sciences *Degree program information:* Part-time programs available. Offers arts and sciences (MA, MS); biology (MS); English (MA); mass media arts, journalism, and communication studies (MS). Electronic applications accepted.

College of Business Administration *Degree program information:* Part-time and evening/weekend programs available. Offers business administration (MBA). Electronic applications accepted.

College of Education and Human Services *Degree program information:* Part-time programs available. Offers curriculum and instruction (M Ed); early childhood (M Ed); education (M Ed); education and human services (M Ed, MS, MSLS, CAS); English (M Ed); history (M Ed); library science (MSLS, CAS); literacy (M Ed); reading (M Ed); rehabilitative sciences (MS); science (M Ed); science education (M Ed); special education (MS); speech language pathology (MS); technology (M Ed).

School of Nursing Offers nursing (MSN).

CLARK ATLANTA UNIVERSITY, Atlanta, GA 30314

General Information Independent-religious, coed, university. CGS member. *Enrollment:* 3,941 graduate, professional, and undergraduate students; 324 full-time matriculated graduate/professional students (226 women), 350 part-time matriculated graduate/professional students (225 women). *Enrollment by degree level:* 462 master's, 205 doctoral, 7 other advanced degrees. *Graduate faculty:* 86 full-time (33 women), 32 part-time/adjunct (16 women). *Tuition:* Full-time $12,942; part-time $719 per credit hour. *Required fees:* $710; $355 per semester. *Graduate housing:* Room and/or apartments available on a first-come, first-served basis to single students; on-campus housing not available to married students. Typical cost: $8124 (including board). Housing application deadline: 6/1. *Student services:* Campus employment opportunities, campus safety program, career counseling, free psychological counseling, international student services, low-cost health insurance. *Library facilities:* Robert W. Woodruff Library. *Online resources:* library catalog, web page, access to other libraries' catalogs. *Collection:* 352,587 titles, 31,197 serial subscriptions, 7,597 audiovisual materials.

Computer facilities: 700 computers available on campus for general student use. A campuswide network can be accessed from student residence rooms. Online class registration is available. *Web address:* http://www.cau.edu/.

General Application Contact: Michelle Clark-Davis, Graduate Program Admissions, 404-880-6605, E-mail: cauadmissions@cau.edu.

GRADUATE UNITS

School of Arts and Sciences Students: 89 full-time (56 women), 172 part-time (107 women); includes 219 Black or African American, non-Hispanic/Latino; 3 American Indian or Alaska Native, non-Hispanic/Latino; 2 Asian, non-Hispanic/Latino; 1 Hispanic/Latino, 18 international. Average age 33. 113 applicants, 91% accepted, 60 enrolled. *Faculty:* 43 full-time (10 women), 9 part-time/adjunct (4 women). Expenses: Contact institution. *Financial support:* Fellowships, research assistantships, teaching assistantships, career-related internships or fieldwork, Federal Work-Study, institutionally sponsored loans, scholarships/grants, and unspecified assistantships available. Support available to part-time students. Financial award application deadline: 4/30; financial award applicants required to submit FAFSA. In 2010, 30 master's, 6 doctorates awarded. *Degree program information:* Part-time programs available. Offers African-American studies (MA, DAH); Africana women's studies (MA, DAH); arts and sciences (MA, MPA, MS, DAH, PhD); biology (MS, PhD); chemistry (MS, PhD); computer and information science (MS); criminal justice (MA); English (MA, DAH); history (MA, DAH); mathematical sciences (MS); physics (MS); political science (MA, PhD); public administration (MPA); Romance languages (MA, DAH); sociology (MA). *Application deadline:* For fall admission, 4/1 for domestic and international students; for spring admission, 11/1 for domestic and international students. Applications are processed on a rolling basis. *Application fee:* $40 ($55 for international students). *Application Contact:* Michelle Clark-Davis, Graduate Program Admissions, 404-880-6605, E-mail: cauadmissions@cau.edu. *Dean,* Dr. Shirley Williams-Kirksey, 404-880-6774, E-mail: skirksey@cau.edu.

School of Business Administration Students: 73 full-time (38 women), 14 part-time (8 women); includes 70 Black or African American, non-Hispanic/Latino; 1 Asian, non-Hispanic/Latino; 1 Hispanic/Latino, 10 international. Average age 27. 81 applicants, 89% accepted, 43 enrolled. *Faculty:* 19 full-time (6 women). Expenses: Contact institution. *Financial support:* Career-related internships or fieldwork, scholarships/grants, and unspecified assistantships available. Support available to part-time students. Financial award application deadline: 4/30; financial award applicants required to submit FAFSA. In 2010, 54 master's awarded. *Degree program information:* Part-time programs available. Offers accounting (MA); business administration (MA, MBA); economics (MA). *Application deadline:* For fall admission, 4/1 for domestic and international students; for spring admission, 11/1 for domestic and international students. Applications are processed on a rolling basis. *Application fee:* $40 ($55 for international students). Electronic applications accepted. *Application Contact:* Michelle Clark-Davis, Graduate Program Admissions, 404-880-6605, E-mail: cauadmissions@cau.edu. *Dean,* Dr. Lydia Floyd, 404-880-8454, E-mail: lfloyd@cau.edu.

School of Education Students: 44 full-time (33 women), 104 part-time (60 women); includes 137 Black or African American, non-Hispanic/Latino; 1 American Indian or Alaska Native, non-Hispanic/Latino; 1 Asian, non-Hispanic/Latino; 1 Hispanic/Latino, 2 international. Average age 33. 68 applicants, 79% accepted, 36 enrolled. *Faculty:* 15 full-time (10 women), 9 part-time/adjunct (6 women). Expenses: Contact institution. *Financial support:* Career-related internships or fieldwork, Federal Work-Study, scholarships/grants, and unspecified assistantships available. Support available to part-time students. Financial award application deadline: 4/30; financial award applicants required to submit FAFSA. In 2010, 27 master's, 9 doctorates awarded. *Degree program information:* Part-time and evening/weekend programs available. Offers counseling and psychological studies (MA); education (MA, MAT, Ed D, Ed S); educational leadership (MA, Ed D, Ed S); special education general curriculum (MA); teaching math and science (MAT). *Application deadline:* For fall admission, 4/1 for domestic and international students; for spring admission, 11/1 for domestic and international students. Applications are processed on a rolling basis. *Application fee:* $40 ($55 for international students). Electronic applications accepted. *Application Contact:* Michelle Clark-Davis, Graduate Program Admissions, 404-880-6605, E-mail: cauadmissions@cau.edu. *Interim Dean,* Dr. Sean Warner, 404-880-8504, E-mail: swarner@cau.edu.

School of Social Work Students: 118 full-time (99 women), 60 part-time (50 women); includes 162 Black or African American, non-Hispanic/Latino, 2 international. Average age 32. 113 applicants, 93% accepted, 83 enrolled. *Faculty:* 9 full-time (7 women), 14 part-time/adjunct (6 women). Expenses: Contact institution. *Financial support:* Career-related internships or fieldwork, Federal Work-Study, scholarships/grants, and unspecified assistantships available. Support available to part-time students. Financial award application deadline: 4/30; financial award applicants required to submit FAFSA. In 2010, 61 master's, 12 doctorates awarded. *Degree program information:* Part-time programs available. Offers social work (MSW, PhD). *Application deadline:* For fall admission, 4/1 for domestic and international students; for spring admission, 11/1 for domestic and international students. Applications are processed on a rolling basis. *Application fee:* $40 ($55 for international students). Electronic applications accepted. *Application Contact:* Michelle Clark-Davis, Graduate Program Admissions, 404-880-6605, E-mail: cauadmissions@cau.edu. *Interim Dean,* Dr. Vimala Pillari, 404-880-8006, E-mail: rlyle@cau.edu.

CLARKE UNIVERSITY, Dubuque, IA 52001-3198

General Information Independent-religious, coed, comprehensive institution. *Graduate housing:* On-campus housing not available.

GRADUATE UNITS

Department of Nursing and Health *Degree program information:* Part-time programs available. Offers administration of nursing systems (MSN); advanced practice nursing (MSN); education (MSN); family nurse practitioner (MSN, PMC). Electronic applications accepted.

Physical Therapy Program Offers physical therapy (DPT). Freshman-entry master's degree program. Entry to the MSPT is determined after junior year of BS program.

Program in Business Administration *Degree program information:* Part-time and evening/weekend programs available. Offers business administration (MBA). Electronic applications accepted.

Program in Education *Degree program information:* Part-time and evening/weekend programs available. Postbaccalaureate distance learning degree programs offered (minimal on-campus study). Offers early childhood/special education (MAE); educational administration: elementary and secondary (MAE); educational media: elementary and secondary (MAE); multi-categorical resource k-12 (MAE); multidisciplinary studies (MAE); reading: elementary (MAE); technology in education (MAE). Electronic applications accepted.

CLARKSON COLLEGE, Omaha, NE 68131-2739

General Information Independent, coed, primarily women, comprehensive institution. *Graduate housing:* Room and/or apartments available on a first-come, first-served basis to single students; on-campus housing not available to married students. Housing application deadline: 6/30.

GRADUATE UNITS

Master of Science in Nursing Program *Degree program information:* Part-time and evening/weekend programs available. Postbaccalaureate distance learning degree programs offered (minimal on-campus study). Offers adult nurse practitioner (MSN, Post-Master's Certificate); family nurse practitioner (MSN, Post-Master's Certificate); nursing education (MSN, Post-Master's Certificate); nursing health care leadership (MSN, Post-Master's Certificate). Electronic applications accepted.

Program in Health Care Administration *Degree program information:* Part-time and evening/weekend programs available. Postbaccalaureate distance learning degree programs offered (no on-campus study). Offers health care administration (MHCA). Electronic applications accepted.

CLARKSON UNIVERSITY, Potsdam, NY 13699

General Information Independent, coed, university. *Enrollment:* 3,330 graduate, professional, and undergraduate students; 423 full-time matriculated graduate/professional students (138 women), 50 part-time matriculated graduate/professional students (20 women). *Enrollment by degree level:* 52 first professional, 281 master's, 140 doctoral. *Graduate faculty:* 183 full-time (48 women), 20 part-time/adjunct (11 women). *Tuition:* Part-time $1136 per credit hour. *Graduate housing:* On-campus housing not available. *Student services:* Campus employment opportunities, campus safety program, career counseling, free psychological counseling, international student services, low-cost health insurance, multicultural affairs office, services for students with disabilities. *Library facilities:* Harriet Call Burnap Memorial Library plus 1 other. *Online resources:* library catalog, web page. *Collection:* 356,695 titles, 18,739 serial subscriptions, 364 audiovisual materials.

Computer facilities: Computer purchase and lease plans are available. 350 computers available on campus for general student use. A campuswide network can be accessed from student residence rooms and from off campus. Online class registration is available. *Web address:* http://www.clarkson.edu/.

GRADUATE UNITS

Graduate School Students: 423 full-time (138 women), 50 part-time (20 women); includes 25 minority (2 Black or African American, non-Hispanic/Latino; 2 American Indian or Alaska Native, non-Hispanic/Latino; 7 Asian, non-Hispanic/Latino; 8 Hispanic/Latino; 6 Two or more races, non-Hispanic/Latino), 186 international. Average age 27. 928 applicants, 51% accepted, 163 enrolled. *Faculty:* 183 full-time (48 women), 20 part-time/adjunct (11 women). Expenses: Contact institution. *Financial support:* In 2010–11, 390 students received support, including 21 fellowships with full tuition reimbursements available (averaging $21,580 per year), 133 research assistantships with full tuition reimbursements available (averaging $21,580 per year), 100 teaching assistantships with full tuition reimbursements available (averaging $21,580 per year); scholarships/grants, tuition waivers (partial), and unspecified assistantships also available. In 2010, 112 master's, 26 doctorates awarded. *Degree program information:* Part-time and evening/weekend programs available. *Application deadline:* For fall admission, 1/30 priority date for domestic and international students; for spring admission, 9/1 priority date for domestic and international students. Applications are processed on a rolling basis. *Application fee:* $25 ($35 for international students). Electronic applications accepted.

Institute for a Sustainable Environment Students: 30 full-time (16 women), 1 (woman) part-time, 16 international. Average age 27. 7 applicants, 100% accepted, 7 enrolled. *Faculty:* 4 full-time (2 women). Expenses: Contact institution. *Financial support:* In 2010–11, 29 students received support, including fellowships with full tuition reimbursements available (averaging $21,580 per year), 17 research assistantships with full tuition reimbursements available (averaging $21,580 per year), 10 teaching assistantships with full tuition reimbursements available (averaging $21,580 per year); scholarships/grants, tuition waivers (partial), and unspecified assistantships also available. In 2010, 5 master's, 2 doctorates awarded. *Degree program information:* Part-time programs available. Offers environmental science and engineering (MS, PhD); sustainable environment (MS, PhD). *Application deadline:* For fall admission, 1/30 priority date for domestic and international students; for spring admission, 9/1 priority date for domestic and international students. Applications are processed on a rolling basis. *Application fee:* $25 ($35 for international students). Electronic applications accepted. *Application Contact:* Suzann Cheney, Administrative Secretary, 315-268-3856, Fax: 315-268-4291, E-mail: scheney@clarkson.edu. *Director*, Dr. Philip Hopke, 315-268-3856, Fax: 315-268-4291, E-mail: hopkepk@clarkson.edu.

School of Arts and Sciences Students: 161 full-time (70 women), 3 part-time (2 women); includes 11 minority (2 Black or African American, non-Hispanic/Latino; 3 Asian, non-Hispanic/Latino; 4 Hispanic/Latino; 2 Two or more races, non-Hispanic/Latino), 60 international. Average age 26. 311 applicants, 41% accepted, 53 enrolled. *Faculty:* 64 full-time (18 women), 12 part-time/adjunct (7 women). Expenses: Contact institution. *Financial support:* In 2010–11, 153 students received support, including 8 fellowships with full tuition reimbursements available (averaging $21,580 per year), 32 research assistantships with full tuition reimbursements available (averaging $21,580 per year), 43 teaching assistantships with full tuition reimbursements available (averaging $21,580 per year); scholarships/grants, tuition waivers (partial), and unspecified assistantships also available. In 2010, 20 master's, 8 doctorates awarded. *Degree program information:* Part-time programs available. Offers arts and sciences (MS, DPT, PhD); basic science (MS); chemistry (MS, PhD); computer science (MS); information technology (MS); mathematics (MS, PhD); physical therapy (DPT); physics (MS, PhD). *Application deadline:* For fall admission, 1/30 priority date for domestic and international students; for spring admission, 9/1 priority date for domestic and international students. Applications are processed on a rolling basis. *Application fee:* $25 ($35 for international students). Electronic applications accepted. *Application Contact:* Jennifer Reed, Graduate School Coordinator, School of Arts and Sciences, 315-268-3802, Fax: 315-268-3989, E-mail: sciencegrad@clarkson.edu. *Dean*, Dr. Peter Turner, 315-268-6544, Fax: 315-268-3989, E-mail: pturner@clarkson.edu.

School of Business Students: 62 full-time (18 women), 43 part-time (15 women); includes 5 minority (1 American Indian or Alaska Native, non-Hispanic/Latino; 1 Asian, non-Hispanic/Latino; 2 Hispanic/Latino; 1 Two or more races, non-Hispanic/Latino), 16 international. Average age 28. 167 applicants, 67% accepted, 66 enrolled. *Faculty:* 38 full-time (10 women), 1 part-time/adjunct (0 women). Expenses: Contact institution. *Financial support:* In 2010–11, 64 students received support. Scholarships/grants available. In 2010, 49 master's awarded. *Degree program information:* Part-time and evening/weekend programs available. Offers business (MBA, MS); business administration (MBA); engineering and global operations management (MS). *Application deadline:* For fall admission, 1/30 priority date for domestic and international students; for spring admission, 9/1 priority date for domestic and international students. Applications are processed on a rolling basis. *Application fee:* $25 ($35 for international students). Electronic applications accepted. *Application Contact:* Karen Fuhr, Assistant to the Graduate Director, 315-268-6613, Fax: 315-268-3810, E-mail: fuhrk@clarkson.edu. *Dean*, Dr. Timothy Sugrue, 315-268-2300, Fax: 315-268-3810, E-mail: sugrue@clarkson.edu.

Wallace H. Coulter School of Engineering Students: 170 full-time (34 women), 3 part-time (2 women); includes 9 minority (1 American Indian or Alaska Native, non-Hispanic/Latino; 3 Asian, non-Hispanic/Latino; 2 Hispanic/Latino; 3 Two or more races, non-Hispanic/Latino), 94 international. Average age 27. 387 applicants, 53% accepted, 37 enrolled. *Faculty:* 77 full-time (18 women), 7 part-time/adjunct (4 women). Expenses: Contact institution. *Financial support:* In 2010–11, 144 students received support, including 13 fellowships with full tuition reimbursements available (averaging $21,580 per year), 84 research assistantships with full tuition reimbursements available (averaging $21,580 per year), 47 teaching assistantships with full tuition reimbursements available (averaging $21,580 per year); scholarships/grants, tuition waivers (partial), and unspecified assistantships also available. In 2010, 38 master's, 16 doctorates awarded. *Degree program information:* Part-time programs available. Offers chemical engineering (ME, MS, PhD); civil engineering (ME, MS); electrical and computer engineering (PhD); electrical engineering (ME, MS); engineering (ME, MS, PhD); interdisciplinary engineering science (MS, PhD); mechanical engineering (ME, MS, PhD). *Application deadline:* For fall admission, 1/30 priority date for domestic and international students; for spring admission, 9/1 priority date for domestic and international students. Applications are processed on a rolling basis. *Application fee:* $25 ($35 for international students). Electronic applications accepted. *Application Contact:* Kelly Sharlow, Assistant to the Dean, 315-268-7929, Fax: 315-268-4494, E-mail: ksharlow@clarkson.edu. *Dean*, Dr. Goodarz Ahmadi, 315-268-6446, Fax: 315-268-4494, E-mail: gahmadi@clarkson.edu.

CLARK UNIVERSITY, Worcester, MA 01610-1477

General Information Independent, coed, university. CGS member. *Enrollment:* 3,451 graduate, professional, and undergraduate students; 859 full-time matriculated graduate/professional students (476 women), 235 part-time matriculated graduate/professional students (109 women). *Enrollment by degree level:* 904 master's, 189 doctoral, 1 other advanced degree. *Graduate faculty:* 194 full-time (89 women), 33 part-time/adjunct (12 women). *Tuition:* Full-time $37,000; part-time $1156 per credit hour. *Required fees:* $30; $1156 per credit hour. *Graduate housing:* Rooms and/or apartments available on a first-come, first-served basis to single and married students. Typical cost: $6700 per year ($9800 including board) for single students. *Student services:* Campus employment opportunities, campus safety program, career counseling, exercise/wellness program, free psychological counseling, grant writing training, international student services, low-cost health insurance, multicultural affairs office, services for students with disabilities, teacher training, writing training. *Library facilities:* Robert Hutchings Goddard Library plus 4 others. *Online resources:* library catalog, web page, access to other libraries' catalogs. *Collection:* 325,172 titles, 2,152 serial subscriptions, 1,531 audiovisual materials. *Research affiliation:* Massachusetts Biotechnology Research Institute, Worcester Area Computation Center, Worcester Foundation for Experimental Biology.

Computer facilities: 115 computers available on campus for general student use. A campuswide network can be accessed from student residence rooms and from off campus. Online class registration, online course support are available. *Web address:* http://www.clarku.edu/.

General Application Contact: Denise Robertson, Graduate School Coordinator, 508-793-7676, Fax: 508-793-8834, E-mail: gradadmissions@clarku.edu.

GRADUATE UNITS

Graduate School Students: 859 full-time (476 women), 235 part-time (109 women); includes 73 minority (29 Black or African American, non-Hispanic/Latino; 3 American Indian or Alaska Native, non-Hispanic/Latino; 15 Asian, non-Hispanic/Latino; 21 Hispanic/Latino; 5 Two or more races, non-Hispanic/Latino), 517 international. Average age 28. 2,462 applicants, 56% accepted, 508 enrolled. *Faculty:* 194 full-time (89 women), 33 part-time/adjunct (12 women). Expenses: Contact institution. *Financial support:* In 2010–11, 6 fellowships with full and partial tuition reimbursements (averaging $16,250 per year), 44 research assistantships with full and partial tuition reimbursements (averaging $16,250 per year), 76 teaching assistantships with full and partial tuition reimbursements (averaging $16,250 per year) were awarded; career-related internships or fieldwork, Federal Work-Study, institutionally sponsored loans, scholarships/grants, and tuition waivers (full and partial) also available. Support available to part-time students. In 2010, 435 master's, 32 doctorates, 1 other advanced degree awarded. *Degree program information:* Part-time and evening/weekend programs available. Offers American history (MA, PhD); biology (MA, PhD); chemistry (MA, PhD); clinical psychology (PhD); community development and planning (MA); developmental psychology (PhD); economics (PhD); education (MAT); English (MA); environmental science and policy (MA); geographic information science (MA); geographic information science for development and environment (MA); geography (PhD); history (MA, CAGS); Holocaust history (PhD); international development and social change (MA); physics (MA, PhD); social-personality psychology (PhD). *Application deadline:* Applications are processed on a rolling basis. *Application fee:* $50. Electronic applications accepted. *Application Contact:* Denise Robertson, Coordinator, 508-793-7676, Fax: 508-793-8834, E-mail: gradadmissions@clarku.edu. *Director*, Dr. Pricilla Elsass, 508-793-7274.

College of Professional and Continuing Education Students: 69 full-time (51 women), 61 part-time (30 women); includes 4 Black or African American, non-Hispanic/Latino; 1 American Indian or Alaska Native, non-Hispanic/Latino; 5 Asian, non-Hispanic/Latino; 2 Hispanic/Latino; 1 Two or more races, non-Hispanic/Latino, 31 international. Average age 30. 73 applicants, 100% accepted, 54 enrolled. *Faculty:* 13 part-time/adjunct (4 women). Expenses: Contact institution. *Financial support:* Career-related internships or fieldwork available. Support available to part-time students. In 2010, 76 master's, 1 other advanced degree awarded. *Degree program information:* Part-time and evening/weekend programs available. Offers information technology (MSIT); liberal studies (MALA); professional and continuing education (MALA, MPA, MSIT, MSPC, CAGS, Certificate); professional communication (MSPC); public administration (MPA, Certificate). *Application deadline:* Applications are processed on a rolling basis. *Application fee:* $50. Electronic applications accepted. *Application Contact:* Julia Parent, Director of Marketing, Communications, and Admissions, 508-793-7217, Fax: 508-793-7232, E-mail: jparent@clarku.edu. *Director*, Dr. Thomas Massey, 508-793-7217.

Graduate School of Management Students: 362 full-time (195 women), 133 part-time (57 women); includes 24 minority (10 Black or African American, non-Hispanic/Latino; 1 American Indian or Alaska Native, non-Hispanic/Latino; 6 Asian, non-Hispanic/Latino; 5 Hispanic/Latino; 2 Two or more races, non-Hispanic/Latino), 317 international. Average age 27. 1,302 applicants, 61% accepted, 215 enrolled. *Faculty:* 23 full-time (10 women), 8 part-time/adjunct (2 women). Expenses: Contact institution. *Financial support:* In 2010–11, 14 research assistantships with partial tuition reimbursements (averaging $4,800 per year), 14 teaching assistantships with partial tuition reimbursements (averaging $4,800 per year) were awarded; fellowships, career-related internships or fieldwork, Federal Work-Study, institutionally sponsored loans, and tuition waivers (partial) also available. Support available to part-time students. Financial award application deadline: 5/31. In 2010, 183 master's awarded. *Degree program information:* Part-time and evening/weekend programs available. Offers accounting (MBA); finance (MBA); global business (MBA); health care management (MBA); management (MBA, MSF); management of information technology (MBA); marketing (MBA). *Application deadline:* For fall admission, 6/1 priority date for domestic students; for spring admission, 12/1 priority date for domestic students. Applications are processed on a rolling basis. *Application fee:* $50. Electronic applications accepted. *Application Contact:* Lynn Davis, Enrollment and Marketing Director, 508-793-7406, Fax: 508-793-8822, E-mail: clarkmba@clarku.edu. *Dean*, Dr. Joseph Sarkis, 508-793-7406, Fax: 508-793-8822.

CLAYTON STATE UNIVERSITY, Morrow, GA 30260-0285

General Information State-supported, coed, comprehensive institution. *Graduate housing:* On-campus housing not available.

GRADUATE UNITS

School of Graduate Studies Offers business administration (MBA); English (MAT); health administration (MHA); liberal studies (MALS); mathematics (MAT); nursing (MSN). Electronic applications accepted.

CLEARWATER CHRISTIAN COLLEGE, Clearwater, FL 33759-4595

General Information Independent-religious, coed, comprehensive institution. *Enrollment:* 575 graduate, professional, and undergraduate students; 4 full-time matriculated graduate/professional students (3 women), 3 part-time matriculated graduate/professional students (all women). *Enrollment by degree level:* 7 master's. *Graduate faculty:* 9. *Tuition:* Part-time $390 per credit hour. *Library facilities:* Easter Library. *Online resources:* library catalog, access to other libraries' catalogs. *Collection:* 112,000 titles, 12,000 serial subscriptions, 7,600 audiovisual materials.

Computer facilities: 25 computers available on campus for general student use. A campuswide network can be accessed from student residence rooms and from off campus. *Web address:* http://www.clearwater.edu/.

General Application Contact: Debbie Edson, Secretary for Graduate Studies, 727-726-1153 Ext. 232, E-mail: graduatestudies@clearwater.edu.

GRADUATE UNITS

Program in Educational Leadership Students: 4 full-time (3 women), 3 part-time (all women). *Faculty:* 9. Expenses: Contact institution. *Financial support:* Applicants required to submit FAFSA. In 2010, 2 master's awarded. *Degree program information:* Part-time programs available. Postbaccalaureate distance learning degree programs offered (no on-campus study). Offers educational leadership (M Ed). *Application deadline:* For fall admission, 8/1 for domestic students; for spring admission, 1/3 for domestic students. Applications are processed on a rolling basis. *Application fee:* $50. Electronic applications accepted. *Application Contact:* Dr. Gary Smith, Chair of Graduate Studies, 727-726-1153 Ext. 257. *Chair of Graduate Studies*, Dr. Gary Smith, 727-726-1153 Ext. 257.

CLEARY UNIVERSITY, Ann Arbor, MI 48105-2659

General Information Independent, coed, comprehensive institution. *Enrollment:* 762 graduate, professional, and undergraduate students; 1 (woman) full-time matriculated graduate/professional student, 115 part-time matriculated graduate/professional students (67 women). *Enrollment by degree level:* 116 master's. *Graduate faculty:* 1 (woman) full-time, 20 part-time/adjunct (8 women). *Graduate housing:* On-campus housing not available. *Student services:* Campus employment opportunities, career counseling, writing training. *Library facilities:* Cleary Online Library. *Online resources:* web page.

Computer facilities: 60 computers available on campus for general student use. A campuswide network can be accessed from off campus. *Web address:* http://www.cleary.edu/.

General Application Contact: Carrie Bonofiglio, Director of Student Recruiting, 800-686-1883, Fax: 517-552-7805, E-mail: cbono@cleary.edu.

GRADUATE UNITS

Online Program in Business Administration Students: 1 (woman) full-time, 115 part-time (67 women); includes 30 minority (21 Black or African American, non-Hispanic/Latino; 1 American Indian or Alaska Native, non-Hispanic/Latino; 6 Asian, non-Hispanic/Latino; 2 Hispanic/Latino), 7 international. Average age 34. 62 applicants, 77% accepted, 36 enrolled. *Faculty:* 1 (woman) full-time, 20 part-time/adjunct (8 women). Expenses: Contact institution. *Financial support:* In 2010–11, 80 students received support, including 80 fellowships (averaging $12,501 per year); Federal Work-Study and scholarships/grants also available. Support available to part-time students. Financial award application deadline: 8/15; financial award applicants required to submit FAFSA. In 2010, 22 master's awarded. *Degree program information:* Part-time and evening/weekend programs available. Postbaccalaureate distance learning degree programs offered (no on-campus study). Offers financial planning (MBA); financial planning (Graduate Certificate); green business strategy (MBA, Graduate Certificate); management (MBA); nonprofit management (MBA, Graduate Certificate); organizational leadership (MBA); public accounting (MBA). *Application deadline:* For fall admission, 8/15 for domestic students, 7/15 for international students; for spring admission, 4/2 for domestic students, 1/2 for international students. Applications are processed on a rolling basis. *Application fee:* $50. Electronic applications accepted. *Application Contact:* Carrie Bonofiglio, Director of Student Recruiting, 800-686-1883, Fax: 517-552-7805, E-mail: cbono@cleary.edu. *Provost and Vice President for Academic Affairs,* Dr. Vincent Linder, 800-686-1883, Fax: 734-332-4646, E-mail: vlinder@cleary.edu.

CLEMSON UNIVERSITY, Clemson, SC 29634

General Information State-supported, coed, university. CGS member. *Enrollment:* 18,317 graduate, professional, and undergraduate students; 2,640 full-time matriculated graduate/professional students (1,075 women), 979 part-time matriculated graduate/professional students (493 women). *Enrollment by degree level:* 2,237 master's, 1,375 doctoral, 7 other advanced degrees. *Graduate faculty:* 795 full-time (233 women), 97 part-time/adjunct (30 women). Tuition, state resident: full-time $6492; part-time $400 per credit hour. Tuition, nonresident: full-time $13,634; part-time $800 per credit hour. *Required fees:* $262 per semester. Part-time tuition and fees vary according to course load and program. *Graduate housing:* Room and/or apartments available to single students; on-campus housing not available to married students. *Student services:* Campus employment opportunities, campus safety program, career counseling, exercise/wellness program, free psychological counseling, grant writing training, international student services, low-cost health insurance, multicultural affairs office, services for students with disabilities. *Library facilities:* Robert Muldrow Cooper Library plus 1 other. *Online resources:* library catalog, web page. *Collection:* 1.2 million titles, 5,587 serial subscriptions. *Research affiliation:* Fluor Corporation (supply chain logistics), Savannah National Research Lab (energy), BMW (automotive, electrical and mechanical engineering), Greenville Hospital System (biological sciences), South Carolina Universities Research and Education Foundation (energy), Oak Ridge National Laboratory (materials science, physics).

Computer facilities: Computer purchase and lease plans are available. 1,250 computers available on campus for general student use. A campuswide network can be accessed from student residence rooms and from off campus. Online class registration is available. *Web address:* http://www.clemson.edu/.

General Application Contact: Dr. Tristam Aldridge, Interim Associate Dean, 864-656-3195, E-mail: gradapp@clemson.edu.

GRADUATE UNITS

Graduate School Students: 2,640 full-time (1,075 women), 979 part-time (493 women); includes 177 Black or African American, non-Hispanic/Latino; 9 American Indian or Alaska Native, non-Hispanic/Latino; 63 Asian, non-Hispanic/Latino; 49 Hispanic/Latino; 40 Two or more races, non-Hispanic/Latino, 973 international. Average age 30. 6,296 applicants, 45% accepted, 1290 enrolled. *Faculty:* 795 full-time (233 women), 97 part-time/adjunct (30 women). Expenses: Contact institution. *Financial support:* In 2010–11, 1,970 students received support, including 233 fellowships with full and partial tuition reimbursements available (averaging $7,354 per year), 803 research assistantships with partial tuition reimbursements available (averaging $14,206 per year), 1,106 teaching assistantships with partial tuition reimbursements available (averaging $11,587 per year); career-related internships or fieldwork, institutionally sponsored loans, scholarships/grants, health care benefits, and unspecified assistantships also available. Support available to part-time students. Financial award application deadline: 1/1; financial award applicants required to submit FAFSA. In 2010, 992 master's, 176 doctorates, 10 other advanced degrees awarded. *Degree program information:* Part-time and evening/weekend programs available. Postbaccalaureate distance learning degree programs offered. Offers international family and community studies (PhD); policy studies (PhD, Certificate); public administration (MPA). *Application deadline:* Applications are processed on a rolling basis. *Application fee:* $70 ($80 for international students). Electronic applications accepted. *Application Contact:* Dr. Tristam Aldridge, Interim Associate Dean, 864-656-2561, Fax: 864-656-5344, E-mail: saldrid@clemson.edu. *Dean,* Dr. J. Bruce Rafert, 864-656-4172, Fax: 864-656-5344, E-mail: jbruce@mail.clemson.edu.

College of Agriculture, Forestry and Life Sciences Students: 291 full-time (158 women), 78 part-time (41 women); includes 21 minority (10 Black or African American, non-Hispanic/Latino; 4 Asian, non-Hispanic/Latino; 5 Hispanic/Latino; 2 Two or more races, non-Hispanic/Latino), 87 international. Average age 30. 431 applicants, 39% accepted, 118 enrolled. *Faculty:* 180 full-time (52 women), 20 part-time/adjunct (7 women). Expenses: Contact institution. *Financial support:* In 2010–11, 259 students received support, including 41 fellowships with full and partial tuition reimbursements available, 159 research assistantships with partial tuition reimbursements available, 162 teaching assistantships with partial tuition reimbursements available; career-related internships or fieldwork, Federal Work-Study, institutionally sponsored loans, scholarships/grants, and unspecified assistantships also available. Financial award applicants required to submit FAFSA. In 2010, 80 master's, 23 doctorates awarded. *Degree program information:* Part-time programs available. Offers agricultural education (M Ag Ed); agriculture, forestry and life sciences (M Ag Ed, MFR, MS, PhD); animal and veterinary sciences (MS, PhD); biochemistry and molecular biology (PhD); biological sciences (MS, PhD); entomology (MS, PhD); environmental toxicology (MS, PhD); food technology (PhD); food, nutrition, and culinary science (MS); forest resources (MFR, MS, PhD); genetics (PhD); microbiology (MS, PhD); packaging science (MS); plant and environmental sciences (MS, PhD); wildlife and fisheries biology (MS, PhD). *Application deadline:* For fall admission, 4/15 for domestic and international students; for spring admission, 10/1 for domestic students, 9/15 for international students. Applications are processed on a rolling basis. *Application fee:* $70 ($80 for international students). Electronic applications accepted. *Application Contact:* Dr. Joseph Culin, Associate Dean for Research and Graduate Studies, 864-656-2810, E-mail: jculin@clemson.edu. *Dean,* Dr. Thomas Scott, 864-656-7592, Fax: 864-656-1286.

College of Architecture, Arts, and Humanities Students: 370 full-time (160 women), 40 part-time (17 women); includes 13 Black or African American, non-Hispanic/Latino; 3 American Indian or Alaska Native, non-Hispanic/Latino; 6 Asian, non-Hispanic/Latino; 13 Hispanic/Latino; 6 Two or more races, non-Hispanic/Latino, 35 international. Average age 29. 720 applicants, 49% accepted, 161 enrolled. *Faculty:* 106 full-time (43 women), 18 part-time/adjunct (6 women). Expenses: Contact institution. *Financial support:* In 2010–11, 246 students received support, including 58 fellowships with full and partial tuition reimbursements available (averaging $17,475 per year), 3 research assistantships with partial tuition reimbursements available (averaging $40,830 per year), 175 teaching assistantships with partial tuition reimbursements available (averaging $92,329 per year); career-related internships or fieldwork, Federal Work-Study, institutionally sponsored loans, scholarships/grants, health care benefits, and unspecified assistantships also available. Financial award applicants required to submit FAFSA. In 2010, 152 master's, 8 doctorates awarded. *Degree program information:* Part-time programs available. Offers architecture (M Arch, MS); architecture, arts, and humanities (M Arch, MA, MCRP, MCSM, MFA, MLA, MRED, MS, PhD); city and regional planning (MCRP); construction science and management (MCSM); developmental planning (MCRP); English (MA); historic preservation (MS); history (MA); landscape architecture (MLA); planning, design and the built environment (PhD); professional communication (MA); real estate development (MRED); rhetorics, communication and information design (PhD); visual arts (MFA). *Application deadline:* For fall admission, 4/15 for international students; for spring admission, 9/15 for international students. Applications are processed on a rolling basis. *Application fee:* $70 ($80 for international students). Electronic applications accepted. *Application Contact:* Dr. James B. London, Associate Dean for Research and Graduate Studies, 864-656-3927, E-mail: london1@clemson.edu. *Interim Dean,* Dr. Clifton Egan, 864-656-3084, Fax: 964-656-0204.

College of Business and Behavioral Science Students: 328 full-time (141 women), 185 part-time (55 women); includes 13 Black or African American, non-Hispanic/Latino; 14 Asian, non-Hispanic/Latino; 6 Hispanic/Latino; 6 Two or more races, non-Hispanic/Latino, 106 international. Average age 29. 997 applicants, 43% accepted, 213 enrolled. *Faculty:* 134 full-time (39 women), 12 part-time/adjunct (3 women). Expenses: Contact institution. *Financial support:* In 2010–11, 200 students received support, including 27 fellowships with full and partial tuition reimbursements available (averaging $33,981 per year), 42 research assistantships with partial tuition reimbursements available (averaging $60,715 per year), 126 teaching assistantships with partial tuition reimbursements available (averaging $90,689 per year); career-related internships or fieldwork, institutionally sponsored loans, scholarships/grants, health care benefits, and unspecified assistantships also available. Support available to part-time students. Financial award applicants required to submit FAFSA. In 2010, 203 master's, 18 doctorates awarded. *Degree program information:* Part-time and evening/weekend programs available. Offers accountancy and finance (MP Acc); applied economics and statistics (MS, PhD); applied psychology (MS); applied sociology (MS); business administration (MBA); business and behavioral science (MA, MBA, MP Acc, MS, PhD); economics (MA, PhD); graphic communications (MS); human factors psychology (PhD); industrial/organizational psychology (PhD); management (MS, PhD); marketing (MS). *Application deadline:* Applications are processed on a rolling basis. *Application fee:* $70 ($80 for international students). Electronic applications accepted. *Application Contact:* Dr. Raju Balakrishnan, Senior Associate Dean, 864-656-3177, Fax: 864-656-5344, E-mail: scaron@clemson.edu. *Dean,* Dr. Claude C. Lilly, 864-656-3178, Fax: 864-656-5344.

College of Engineering and Science Students: 1,238 full-time (323 women), 214 part-time (62 women); includes 51 Black or African American, non-Hispanic/Latino; 5 American Indian or Alaska Native, non-Hispanic/Latino; 34 Asian, non-Hispanic/Latino; 11 Hispanic/Latino; 13 Two or more races, non-Hispanic/Latino, 699 international. Average age 28. 2,797 applicants, 51% accepted, 487 enrolled. *Faculty:* 282 full-time (40 women), 41 part-time/adjunct (11 women). Expenses: Contact institution. *Financial support:* In 2010–11, 1,014 students received support, including 83 fellowships with full and partial tuition reimbursements available, 498 research assistantships with partial tuition reimbursements available, 526 teaching assistantships with partial tuition reimbursements available; career-related internships or fieldwork, institutionally sponsored loans, scholarships/grants, health care benefits, and unspecified assistantships also available. Support available to part-time students. Financial award applicants required to submit FAFSA. In 2010, 281 master's, 86 doctorates awarded. *Degree program information:* Part-time programs available. Offers applied and pure mathematics (MS, PhD); automotive engineering (MS, PhD); bioengineering (MS, PhD); biosystems engineering (MS, PhD); chemical and biomolecular engineering (MS, PhD); chemistry (MS, PhD); civil engineering (MS, PhD); computational mathematics (MS, PhD); computer engineering (MS, PhD); computer science (MS, PhD); computing (MFA, MS, PhD); digital production arts (MFA); electrical engineering (M Engr, MS, PhD); engineering and science (M Eng, M Engr, MFA, MS, PhD); environmental engineering and science (M Engr, MS, PhD); environmental health physics (MS); hydrogeology (MS); industrial engineering (M Eng, MS, PhD); materials science and engineering (MS, PhD); mechanical engineering (MS, PhD); operations research (MS, PhD); physics (MS, PhD); statistics (MS, PhD). *Application fee:* $70 ($80 for international students). Electronic applications accepted. *Application Contact:* Dr. R. Larry Dooley, Associate Dean for Research and Graduate Studies, 864-656-3200, Fax: 864-656-4466, E-mail: dooley@eng.clemson.edu. *Dean,* Dr. Esin Gulari, 864-656-3202.

College of Health, Education, and Human Development Students: 354 full-time (259 women), 421 part-time (298 women); includes 83 Black or African American, non-Hispanic/Latino; 1 American Indian or Alaska Native, non-Hispanic/Latino; 4 Asian, non-Hispanic/Latino; 14 Hispanic/Latino, 28 international. Average age 33. 1,227 applicants, 34% accepted, 276 enrolled. *Faculty:* 93 full-time (59 women), 6 part-time/adjunct (3 women). Expenses: Contact institution. *Financial support:* In 2010–11, 204 students received support, including 16 fellowships with full and partial tuition reimbursements available (averaging $23,700 per year), 30 research assistantships with partial tuition reimbursements available (averaging $90,677 per year), 89 teaching assistantships with partial tuition reimbursements available (averaging $68,730 per year); career-related internships or fieldwork, Federal Work-Study, tuition waivers (full and partial), and unspecified assistantships also available. Support available to part-time students. Financial award applicants required to submit FAFSA. In 2010, 255 master's, 33 doctorates, 10 other advanced degrees awarded. *Degree program information:* Part-time and evening/weekend programs available. Postbaccalaureate distance learning degree programs offered. Offers administration and supervision (K-12) (M Ed, Ed S); clinical mental health counseling (M Ed); community mental health (M Ed); counselor education (M Ed); curriculum and instruction (PhD); early childhood education (M Ed); early childhood education (M Ed); educational leadership (PhD); elementary education (M Ed); health, education, and human development (M Ed, MAT, MHRD, MPRTM, MS, PhD, Ed S); healthcare genetics (PhD); higher education (PhD); human resource development (MHRD); K-12 (PhD); middle grades education (MAT); nursing (MS); parks, recreation, and tourism management (MPRTM, MS, PhD); reading literacy (M Ed); school counseling (K-12) (M Ed); secondary education: math and science (MAT); secondary English (M Ed); secondary math (M Ed); secondary science (M Ed); secondary social studies (M Ed); special education (M Ed); student affairs (higher education) (M Ed); teaching and learning (M Ed); youth development (MS). *Application deadline:* Applications are processed on a rolling basis. *Application fee:* $70 ($80 for international students). Electronic applications accepted. *Application Contact:* Dr. Kathy Headley, Associate Dean for Research and Graduate Programs, 864-656-2181, Fax: 864-656-5488, E-mail: ksn1177@clemson.edu. *Dean,* Dr. Larry Allen, 864-656-7640, Fax: 864-656-5488, E-mail: lalln@clemson.edu.

CLEVELAND CHIROPRACTIC COLLEGE–KANSAS CITY CAMPUS, Overland Park, KS 66210

General Information Independent, coed, comprehensive institution. *Graduate housing:* On-campus housing not available.

GRADUATE UNITS

Professional Program *Degree program information:* Part-time programs available. Offers chiropractic (DC). Electronic applications accepted.

Program in Health Promotion Offers health promotion (MSHP).

CLEVELAND CHIROPRACTIC COLLEGE–LOS ANGELES CAMPUS, Los Angeles, CA 90004-2196

General Information Independent, coed, comprehensive institution. *Enrollment:* 315 graduate, professional, and undergraduate students; 201 full-time matriculated graduate/professional students (70 women), 22 part-time matriculated graduate/professional students (8 women). *Enrollment by degree level:* 223 first professional. *Graduate faculty:* 23 full-time (9 women),

10 part-time/adjunct (2 women). *Tuition:* Full-time $17,472; part-time $8736 per year. *Required fees:* $825; $825. *Graduate housing:* On-campus housing not available. *Student services:* Campus employment opportunities, campus safety program, career counseling, international student services, services for students with disabilities. *Library facilities:* Carl Cleveland Jr. Memorial Library plus 1 other. *Online resources:* library catalog, web page, access to other libraries' catalogs. *Collection:* 24,830 titles, 45 serial subscriptions, 1,425 audiovisual materials. *Research affiliation:* Unihealth Foundation (chiropractic), Unihealth Foundation (chiropractic), Unihealth Foundation (chiropractic).

Computer facilities: 30 computers available on campus for general student use. A campuswide network can be accessed from off campus. Internet available. *Web address:* http://www.clevelandchiropractic.edu/.

General Application Contact: Sunshine Garcia, Director of Admission, 800-466-CCLA, Fax: 323-906-2094, E-mail: sunshine.garcia@cleveland.edu.

GRADUATE UNITS

Professional Program Students: 240 full-time (99 women), 33 part-time (11 women); includes 10 Black or African American, non-Hispanic/Latino; 1 American Indian or Alaska Native, non-Hispanic/Latino; 48 Asian, non-Hispanic/Latino; 26 Hispanic/Latino, 14 international. Average age 29. 41 applicants, 76% accepted, 31 enrolled. *Faculty:* 23 full-time (9 women), 10 part-time/adjunct (2 women). Expenses: Contact institution. *Financial support:* Fellowships, research assistantships with partial tuition reimbursements, Federal Work-Study and scholarships/grants available. Financial award application deadline: 7/1. Offers chiropractic medicine (DC). *Application deadline:* For fall admission, 8/10 priority date for domestic and international students; for spring admission, 12/1 priority date for domestic students, 12/7 priority date for international students. Applications are processed on a rolling basis. *Application fee:* $50. Electronic applications accepted. *Application Contact:* Brian Kane, Director of Admission, 800-466-CCLA, Fax: 323-906-2094, E-mail: brian.kane@cleveland.edu. *Vice President for Academic Affairs,* Dr. Ruth Sandefur, 816-501-0100, Fax: 323-660-5387.

Program in Health Promotion Expenses: Contact institution. Offers health promotion (MSHP). *Application Contact:* Brian Kane, Director of Admission, 800-466-CCLA, Fax: 323-906-2094, E-mail: dan.justin@cleveland.edu.

CLEVELAND INSTITUTE OF MUSIC, Cleveland, OH 44106-1776

General Information Independent, coed, comprehensive institution. *Graduate housing:* Room and/or apartments available on a first-come, first-served basis to single students; on-campus housing not available to married students. Housing application deadline: 5/30.

GRADUATE UNITS

Graduate Programs Offers performance (MM, DMA, AD, CPS). DMA and MM programs offered jointly with Case Western Reserve University. Electronic applications accepted.

CLEVELAND STATE UNIVERSITY, Cleveland, OH 44115

General Information State-supported, coed, university. CGS member. *Enrollment:* 17,323 graduate, professional, and undergraduate students; 2,100 full-time matriculated graduate/professional students (1,147 women), 3,127 part-time matriculated graduate/professional students (1,854 women). *Enrollment by degree level:* 221 first professional, 3,211 master's, 153 doctoral, 100 other advanced degrees. *Graduate faculty:* 384 full-time (155 women), 211 part-time/adjunct (89 women). Tuition, state resident: full-time $8447; part-time $469 per credit hour. Tuition, nonresident: full-time $16,020; part-time $890 per credit hour. *Required fees:* $50. *Graduate housing:* Room and/or apartments available on a first-come, first-served basis to single students; on-campus housing not available to married students. Typical cost: $6985 per year ($10,285 including board). Housing application deadline: 7/15. *Student services:* Campus employment opportunities, campus safety program, career counseling, child daycare facilities, exercise/wellness program, free psychological counseling, grant writing training, international student services, low-cost health insurance, multicultural affairs office, services for students with disabilities, teacher training, writing training. *Library facilities:* Michael Schwartz Library plus 1 other. *Online resources:* library catalog, web page, access to other libraries' catalogs. *Collection:* 521,811 titles, 11,135 serial subscriptions, 35,159 audiovisual materials. *Research affiliation:* Metro Health System, Cleveland Clinic Foundation.

Computer facilities: Computer purchase and lease plans are available. 800 computers available on campus for general student use. A campuswide network can be accessed from student residence rooms and from off campus. Online class registration, each general purpose computer lab has a scanner and printer, and students are allowed free black and white printing up to 2,000 pages per semester are available. *Web address:* http://www.csuohio.edu/.

General Application Contact: Deborah L. Brown, Interim Assistant Director, Graduate Admissions, 216-523-7572, Fax: 216-687-9214, E-mail: d.l.brown@csuohio.edu.

GRADUATE UNITS

Cleveland-Marshall College of Law Students: 453 full-time (176 women), 157 part-time (73 women); includes 58 Black or African American, non-Hispanic/Latino; 1 American Indian or Alaska Native, non-Hispanic/Latino; 10 Asian, non-Hispanic/Latino; 13 Hispanic/Latino, 7 international. Average age 26. 1,765 applicants, 36% accepted, 195 enrolled. *Faculty:* 45 full-time (22 women), 33 part-time/adjunct (7 women). Expenses: Contact institution. *Financial support:* In 2010–11, 206 students received support, including 23 fellowships (averaging $2,400 per year), 50 research assistantships (averaging $900 per year), 8 teaching assistantships with partial tuition reimbursements available (averaging $1,650 per year); career-related internships or fieldwork, Federal Work-Study, scholarships/grants, tuition waivers (full and partial), and unspecified assistantships also available. Support available to part-time students. Financial award application deadline: 5/1; financial award applicants required to submit FAFSA. In 2010, 183 first professional degrees, 3 master's awarded. *Degree program information:* Part-time and evening/weekend programs available. Offers business law (JD); civil litigation and dispute resolution (JD); criminal law (JD); employment labor law (JD); international and comparative law (JD); law (LL M). *Application deadline:* For fall admission, 5/1 for domestic and international students. Applications are processed on a rolling basis. *Application fee:* $0. Electronic applications accepted. *Application Contact:* Christopher Lucak, Assistant Dean for Admissions, 216-687-4692, Fax: 216-687-6881, E-mail: christopher.lucak@law.csuohio.edu. *Dean,* Phyllis L. Crocker, 216-687-2300, Fax: 216-687-6881, E-mail: phyllis.crocker@law.csuohio.edu.

College of Graduate Studies Students: 1,833 full-time (1,096 women), 1,852 part-time (1,157 women); includes 572 Black or African American, non-Hispanic/Latino; 9 American Indian or Alaska Native, non-Hispanic/Latino; 374 Asian, non-Hispanic/Latino; 76 Hispanic/Latino. Average age 33. 4,010 applicants, 60% accepted. *Faculty:* 383 full-time (145 women), 151 part-time/adjunct (55 women). Expenses: Contact institution. *Financial support:* In 2010–11, 306 research assistantships with full and partial tuition reimbursements (averaging $3,480 per year), 123 teaching assistantships with full and partial tuition reimbursements (averaging $3,480 per year) were awarded; career-related internships or fieldwork, scholarships/grants, tuition waivers (full and partial), and unspecified assistantships also available. In 2010, 1,336 master's, 77 doctorates awarded. *Degree program information:* Part-time and evening/weekend programs available. Postbaccalaureate distance learning degree programs offered (minimal on-campus study). *Application deadline:* For fall admission, 7/15 priority date for domestic students, 5/15 priority date for international students; for spring admission, 12/8 priority date for domestic students, 11/1 priority date for international students. Applications are processed on a rolling basis. *Application fee:* $30. Electronic applications accepted. *Application Contact:* Deborah L. Brown, Interim Assistant Director, Graduate Admissions, 216-523-7572, Fax: 216-687-9214, E-mail: d.l.brown@csuohio.edu. *Dean,* Dr. Vera Vogelsang-Coombs, 216-687-3595, Fax: 216-687-9214, E-mail: dean.graduatestudies@csuohio.edu.

College of Education and Human Services Students: 315 full-time (241 women), 1,255 part-time (988 women); includes 372 Black or African American, non-Hispanic/Latino; 1 American Indian or Alaska Native, non-Hispanic/Latino; 18 Asian, non-Hispanic/Latino; 32 Hispanic/Latino, 36 international. Average age 35. 809 applicants, 61% accepted, 368 enrolled. *Faculty:* 86 full-time (60 women), 106 part-time/adjunct (81 women). Expenses: Contact institution. *Financial support:* In 2010–11, 64 students received support, including 38 research assistantships with full tuition reimbursements available (averaging $6,960 per year), 2 teaching assistantships with full tuition reimbursements available (averaging $7,800 per year); career-related internships or fieldwork, Federal Work-Study, scholarships/grants, tuition waivers (partial), and unspecified assistantships also available. Support available to part-time students. Financial award application deadline: 8/1; financial award applicants required to submit FAFSA. In 2010, 409 master's, 18 doctorates, 20 other advanced degrees awarded. *Degree program information:* Part-time and evening/weekend programs available. Postbaccalaureate distance learning degree programs offered (minimal on-campus study). Offers accelerated degree in adult learning and development (M Ed); adult learning and development (M Ed); art education (M Ed); chemical dependency counseling (Certificate); clinical nursing leader (MSN); community agency counseling (M Ed); community health education (M Ed); counseling (PhD); counseling and pupil personnel administration (Ed S); counseling psychology (PhD); early childhood education (M Ed); early childhood mental health counseling (Certificate); education and human services (M Ed, MPH, MSN, PhD, Certificate, Ed S); educational administration and supervision (M Ed); executive track (MSN); exercise science (M Ed); foreign language education (M Ed); forensic nursing (MSN); human performance (M Ed); leadership and lifelong learning (PhD); learning and development (PhD); mathematics and science education (M Ed); middle childhood education (M Ed); nursing education (MSN); physical education pedagogy (M Ed); policy studies (PhD); population health nursing (MSN); public health (MPH); school administration (PhD, Ed S); school counseling (M Ed); school health education (M Ed); special education (M Ed); sport and exercise psychology (M Ed); sports management (M Ed); teaching English to speakers of other languages (M Ed). *Application deadline:* For fall admission, 7/15 priority date for domestic students, 5/15 for international students; for spring admission, 12/8 priority date for domestic students, 11/1 for international students. Applications are processed on a rolling basis. *Application fee:* $30. Electronic applications accepted. *Application Contact:* Deborah L. Brown, Interim Assistant Director of Graduate Admissions, 216-687-5599, Fax: 216-687-5400, E-mail: d.l.brown@csuohio.edu. *Dean,* Dr. James A. McLoughlin, 216-687-3737, Fax: 216-687-5415, E-mail: j.mcloughlin@csuohio.edu.

College of Liberal Arts and Social Sciences Students: 243 full-time (180 women), 239 part-time (161 women); includes 107 Black or African American, non-Hispanic/Latino; 4 Asian, non-Hispanic/Latino; 10 Hispanic/Latino, 18 international. Average age 34. 439 applicants, 49% accepted, 151 enrolled. *Faculty:* 156 full-time (64 women), 184 part-time/adjunct (79 women). Expenses: Contact institution. *Financial support:* In 2010–11, 99 research assistantships with full and partial tuition reimbursements (averaging $4,172 per year), 67 teaching assistantships with full and partial tuition reimbursements (averaging $4,657 per year) were awarded; fellowships, career-related internships or fieldwork, Federal Work-Study, institutionally sponsored loans, tuition waivers (full and partial), and unspecified assistantships also available. Support available to part-time students. In 2010, 178 master's awarded. *Degree program information:* Part-time and evening/weekend programs available. Offers applied communication theory and methodology (MA); art education (M Ed); art history (MA); bioethics (MA, Certificate); composition (MM); creative writing (MFA); culture, communication and health care (Certificate); economics (MA); English (MA); French (M Ed); history (MA); liberal arts and social sciences (M Ed, MA, MFA, MM, MSW, Certificate); museum studies (MA); music education (MM); performance (MM); philosophy (MA); social work (MSW); sociology (MA); Spanish (M Ed, MA). *Application deadline:* For fall admission, 7/15 priority date for domestic students; for spring admission, 12/2 priority date for domestic students. Applications are processed on a rolling basis. *Application fee:* $30. Electronic applications accepted. *Application Contact:* Deborah L. Brown, Interim Assistant Director, Graduate Admissions, 216-523-7572, Fax: 216-687-5400, E-mail: d.l.brown@csuohio.edu. *Dean,* Dr. Gregory M. Sadlek, 216-687-3660.

College of Sciences and Health Professions Students: 382 full-time (266 women), 226 part-time (152 women); includes 44 Black or African American, non-Hispanic/Latino; 1 American Indian or Alaska Native, non-Hispanic/Latino; 12 Asian, non-Hispanic/Latino; 13 Hispanic/Latino, 95 international. Average age 29. 758 applicants, 39% accepted, 173 enrolled. *Faculty:* 107 full-time (35 women), 76 part-time/adjunct (43 women). Expenses: Contact institution. *Financial support:* In 2010–11, 174 students received support, including 47 research assistantships with full tuition reimbursements available (averaging $17,000 per year), 127 teaching assistantships with full and partial tuition reimbursements available (averaging $10,700 per year); unspecified assistantships also available. In 2010, 149 master's, 43 doctorates, 4 other advanced degrees awarded. *Degree program information:* Part-time and evening/weekend programs available. Postbaccalaureate distance learning degree programs offered (no on-campus study). Offers adult development and aging (PhD); analytical chemistry (MS); applied optics (MS); biology (MS); clinical chemistry (MS); clinical psychology (MA); clinical/bioanalytical chemistry (PhD); condensed matter physics (MS); consumer/industrial research (MA); diversity management (MA); environmental chemistry (MS); environmental science (MS); experimental research psychology (MA); health sciences (MS); inorganic chemistry (MS); mathematics (MA, MS); medical physics (MS); museum studies for natural historians (MS); occupational therapy (MOT); online health sciences (MS); optics and materials (MS); optics and medical imaging (MS); pharmaceutical/organic chemistry (MS); physical chemistry (MS); physical therapy (DPT); physician's assistant (MS); regulatory biology (PhD); school psychology (Psy S); sciences and health professions (MA, MOT, MS, DPT, PhD, Psy S); speech pathology and audiology (MA). *Application deadline:* For fall admission, 7/15 priority date for domestic and international students; for spring admission, 12/8 priority date for domestic and international students. Applications are processed on a rolling basis. *Application fee:* $30. *Application Contact:* Dr. Deborah L. Brown, Interim Assistant Director, Graduate Admissions, 216-523-7572, Fax: 216-687-5400, E-mail: d.l.brown@csuohio.edu. *Dean,* Dr. Bette R. Bonder, 216-687-5580, E-mail: b.bonder@csuohio.edu.

Fenn College of Engineering Students: 129 full-time (31 women), 242 part-time (36 women); includes 9 Black or African American, non-Hispanic/Latino; 8 Asian, non-Hispanic/Latino; 2 Hispanic/Latino, 238 international. Average age 27. 686 applicants, 52% accepted, 80 enrolled. *Faculty:* 54 full-time (5 women), 12 part-time/adjunct (0 women). Expenses: Contact institution. *Financial support:* In 2010–11, 93 students received support, including 1 fellowship with full tuition reimbursement available, 120 research assistantships with full and partial tuition reimbursements available (averaging $8,694 per year), 20 teaching assistantships with full and partial tuition reimbursements available (averaging $8,082 per year); career-related internships or fieldwork, institutionally sponsored loans, scholarships/grants, tuition waivers (full and partial), and unspecified assistantships also available. Support available to part-time students. Financial award application deadline: 3/30. In 2010, 99 master's, 8 doctorates awarded. *Degree program information:* Part-time and evening/weekend programs available. Offers accelerated program civil engineering (MS); accelerated program environmental engineering (MS); applied biomedical engineering (D Eng); chemical engineering (MS, D Eng); civil engineering (MS, D Eng); electrical engineering (MS, D Eng); engineering (MS, D Eng); engineering mechanics (MS); environmental engineering (MS); industrial engineering (MS, D Eng); mechanical engineering (MS, D Eng); software engineering (MS). *Application deadline:* For fall admission, 7/15 for domestic students, 5/15 for international students; for spring admission, 12/5 for domestic students, 11/1 for international students. Applications are processed on a rolling basis. *Application fee:* $30. Electronic applications accepted. *Application Contact:* Dr. Paul P. Lin, Associate Dean, 216-687-2556, Fax: 216-687-9280, E-mail: p.lin@csuohio.edu. *Associate Dean,* Dr. Paul P. Lin, 216-687-2556, Fax: 216-687-9280, E-mail: p.lin@csuohio.edu.

Maxine Goodman Levin College of Urban Affairs Students: 88 full-time (43 women), 199 part-time (115 women); includes 54 Black or African American, non-Hispanic/Latino; 1 American Indian or Alaska Native, non-Hispanic/Latino; 2 Asian, non-Hispanic/Latino; 8 Hispanic/Latino, 39 international. Average age 32. 353 applicants, 52% accepted, 99 enrolled. *Faculty:* 22 full-time (9 women), 8 part-time/adjunct (4 women). Expenses: Contact institution. *Financial support:* In 2010–11, 60 students received support, including 40 research assistantships with full tuition reimbursements available (averaging $8,000 per year), 15 teaching assistantships with full and partial tuition reimbursements available (averaging $7,000 per year); career-related internships or fieldwork, Federal Work-Study, institutionally sponsored loans, scholarships/grants, and unspecified assistantships also available. Support available to part-time students. Financial award application deadline: 3/1; financial award applicants required to submit FAFSA. In 2010, 74 master's, 7 doctorates, 23 other advanced degrees awarded. *Degree program information:* Part-time and

Cleveland State University (continued)

evening/weekend programs available. Offers environmental studies (MAES); geographic information systems (Certificate); local and urban management (Certificate); non-profit management (Certificate); nonprofit administration and leadership (MNAL); nonprofit management (Certificate); public administration (MPA); urban affairs (MAES, MNAL, MPA, MS, MUPDD, PhD, Certificate); urban economic development (Certificate); urban planning, design, and development (MUPDD); urban real estate development (Certificate); urban real estate development and finance (Certificate); urban studies (MS); urban studies and public affairs (PhD). *Application deadline:* For fall admission, 7/15 priority date for domestic students, 5/15 for international students; for spring admission, 11/1 for international students. Applications are processed on a rolling basis. *Application fee:* $30. Electronic applications accepted. *Application Contact:* Graduate Program Coordinator, 216-523-7522, Fax: 216-687-5398, E-mail: urbanprograms@csuohio.edu. *Dean,* Dr. Edward W. Hill, 216-687-2135, E-mail: e.hill@csuohio.edu.

Nance College of Business Administration Students: 356 full-time (164 women), 600 part-time (258 women); includes 69 Black or African American, non-Hispanic/Latino; 1 American Indian or Alaska Native, non-Hispanic/Latino; 34 Asian, non-Hispanic/Latino; 10 Hispanic/Latino, 186 international. Average age 30. 708 applicants, 62% accepted, 245 enrolled. *Faculty:* 48 full-time (16 women), 33 part-time/adjunct (12 women). Expenses: Contact institution. *Financial support:* In 2010–11, 110 students received support, including 45 research assistantships with full tuition reimbursements available (averaging $6,960 per year), 1 teaching assistantship with full tuition reimbursement available (averaging $7,800 per year); career-related internships or fieldwork, scholarships/grants, tuition waivers (full), and unspecified assistantships also available. Financial award application deadline: 5/15; financial award applicants required to submit FAFSA. In 2010, 374 master's, 4 doctorates, 2 other advanced degrees awarded. *Degree program information:* Part-time and evening/weekend programs available. Offers business administration (AMBA, EMBA, M Acc, MBA, MCIS, MLRHR, DBA, Graduate Certificate); computer and information science (MCIS); executive business administration (EMBA); finance (DBA); financial accounting/audit (M Acc); global business (Graduate Certificate); health care administration (MBA); information systems (DBA); labor relations and human resources (MLRHR); marketing (MBA, DBA); marketing analytics (Graduate Certificate); off-campus programs (MBA); operations management (DBA); taxation (M Acc). *Application deadline:* For fall admission, 7/15 priority date for domestic students, 5/15 for international students; for spring admission, 12/15 priority date for domestic students, 11/1 for international students. Applications are processed on a rolling basis. *Application fee:* $30. Electronic applications accepted. *Application Contact:* Kenneth Dippong, Director, Student Services, 216-523-7545, Fax: 216-687-9354, E-mail: k.dippong@csuohio.edu. *Dean,* Dr. Robert F. Scherer, 216-687-3786, Fax: 216-687-9354, E-mail: r.scherer@csuohio.edu.

COASTAL CAROLINA UNIVERSITY, Conway, SC 29528-6054

General Information State-supported, coed, comprehensive institution. *Enrollment:* 8,706 graduate, professional, and undergraduate students; 127 full-time matriculated graduate/professional students (76 women), 204 part-time matriculated graduate/professional students (144 women). *Enrollment by degree level:* 331 master's. *Graduate faculty:* 45 full-time (17 women), 6 part-time/adjunct (4 women). Tuition, state resident: full-time $10,080; part-time $420 per credit hour. Tuition, nonresident: full-time $12,840; part-time $535 per credit hour. *Required fees:* $80; $40 per semester. Tuition and fees vary according to program. *Graduate housing:* On-campus housing not available. *Student services:* Campus employment opportunities, campus safety program, career counseling, exercise/wellness program, free psychological counseling, grant writing training, international student services, low-cost health insurance, multicultural affairs office, services for students with disabilities, teacher training, writing training. *Library facilities:* Kimbel Library. *Online resources:* library catalog, web page, access to other libraries' catalogs. *Collection:* 213,886 titles, 24,551 serial subscriptions, 7,833 audiovisual materials.

Computer facilities: Computer purchase and lease plans are available. 700 computers available on campus for general student use. A campuswide network can be accessed from student residence rooms. Online class registration is available. *Web address:* http://www.coastal.edu/.

General Application Contact: Dr. Deborah A. Vrooman, Interim Director of Graduate Studies, 843-349-2783, Fax: 843-349-6444, E-mail: vroomand@coastal.edu.

GRADUATE UNITS

College of Natural and Applied Sciences Students: 16 full-time (11 women), 18 part-time (11 women); includes 1 minority (Hispanic/Latino). Average age 25. 39 applicants, 49% accepted, 13 enrolled. *Faculty:* 16 full-time (2 women). Expenses: Contact institution. *Financial support:* Fellowships, research assistantships, unspecified assistantships available. Support available to part-time students. Financial award application deadline: 3/1; financial award applicants required to submit FAFSA. In 2010, 10 master's awarded. *Degree program information:* Part-time and evening/weekend programs available. Offers coastal marine and wetland studies (MS). *Application deadline:* For fall admission, 3/1 priority date for domestic and international students; for spring admission, 11/1 priority date for domestic and international students. Applications are processed on a rolling basis. *Application fee:* $45. Electronic applications accepted. *Application Contact:* Dr. Deborah A. Vrooman, Interim Director of Graduate Studies, 843-349-2783, Fax: 843-349-6444, E-mail: vroomand@coastal.edu. *Dean,* Dr. Michael H. Roberts, 843-349-2282, Fax: 843-349-2545, E-mail: mroberts@coastal.edu.

Thomas W. and Robin W. Edwards College of Humanities and Fine Arts Students: 1 full-time (0 women), 9 part-time (6 women). Average age 39. 18 applicants, 67% accepted, 10 enrolled. *Faculty:* 6 full-time (5 women), 2 part-time/adjunct (1 woman). Expenses: Contact institution. *Financial support:* Fellowships, research assistantships, unspecified assistantships available. Support available to part-time students. Financial award application deadline: 3/1; financial award applicants required to submit FAFSA. *Degree program information:* Part-time and evening/weekend programs available. Offers writing (MA). *Application deadline:* For fall admission, 5/1 priority date for domestic and international students; for spring admission, 11/15 priority date for domestic and international students. Applications are processed on a rolling basis. *Application fee:* $45. Electronic applications accepted. *Application Contact:* Dr. Deborah A. Vrooman, Interim Director of Graduate Studies, 843-349-2783, Fax: 843-349-6444, E-mail: vroomand@coastal.edu. *Associate Dean,* Jason E. Ockert, 843-349-2531, E-mail: jockert@coastal.edu.

Wall College of Business Administration Students: 43 full-time (18 women), 13 part-time (5 women); includes 2 minority (both Black or African American, non-Hispanic/Latino), 6 international. Average age 27. 37 applicants, 68% accepted, 21 enrolled. *Faculty:* 9 full-time (4 women). Expenses: Contact institution. *Financial support:* Application deadline: 3/1. In 2010, 25 master's awarded. *Degree program information:* Part-time and evening/weekend programs available. Offers accounting (MBA); business (MBA). *Application deadline:* For fall admission, 3/15 priority date for domestic and international students; for spring admission, 10/15 priority date for domestic and international students. Applications are processed on a rolling basis. *Application fee:* $45. Electronic applications accepted. *Application Contact:* Dr. Deborah A. Vrooman, Interim Director of Graduate Studies, 843-349-2783, Fax: 843-349-6444, E-mail: vroomand@coastal.edu. *MBA Director,* John O. Lox, 843-349-2469, Fax: 843-349-2455, E-mail: jlox@coastal.edu.

William L. Spadoni College of Education Students: 67 full-time (47 women), 164 part-time (122 women); includes 30 minority (24 Black or African American, non-Hispanic/Latino; 2 American Indian or Alaska Native, non-Hispanic/Latino; 1 Native Hawaiian or other Pacific Islander, non-Hispanic/Latino; 3 Two or more races, non-Hispanic/Latino), 3 international. Average age 33. 172 applicants, 87% accepted, 109 enrolled. *Faculty:* 14 full-time (6 women), 4 part-time/adjunct (3 women). Expenses: Contact institution. *Financial support:* Fellowships, research assistantships, unspecified assistantships available. Support available to part-time students. Financial award application deadline: 3/1; financial award applicants required to submit FAFSA. In 2010, 67 master's awarded. *Degree program information:* Part-time and evening/weekend programs available. Offers education (MAT); educational leadership (M Ed); learning and teaching (M Ed); secondary education (M Ed). *Application deadline:* For fall admission, 7/1 priority date for domestic and international students; for spring admission, 11/15 priority date for domestic and international students. Applications are processed on a rolling basis. *Application fee:* $45. Electronic applications accepted. *Application Contact:* Dr. Deborah A. Vrooman, Interim Director of Graduate Studies, 843-349-2783, Fax: 843-349-6444, E-mail: vroomand@coastal.edu. *Interim Dean,* Dr. Edward Jadallah, 843-349-2773, Fax: 843-349-2106, E-mail: ejadalla@coastal.edu.

COE COLLEGE, Cedar Rapids, IA 52402-5092

General Information Independent-religious, coed, comprehensive institution. *Graduate housing:* On-campus housing not available.

GRADUATE UNITS

Department of Education *Degree program information:* Part-time programs available. Offers education (MAT).

COLD SPRING HARBOR LABORATORY, WATSON SCHOOL OF BIOLOGICAL SCIENCES, Cold Spring Harbor, NY 11724

General Information Independent, coed, graduate-only institution. *Enrollment by degree level:* 47 doctoral. *Graduate faculty:* 47 full-time (7 women). *Graduate housing:* Rooms and/or apartments guaranteed to single and married students. Housing application deadline: 5/1. *Student services:* Campus safety program, career counseling, child daycare facilities, exercise/wellness program, free psychological counseling, grant writing training, international student services, low-cost health insurance, teacher training, writing training. *Library facilities:* Cold Spring Harbor Library. *Online resources:* library catalog, web page. *Collection:* 18,500 titles, 600 serial subscriptions, 300 audiovisual materials.

Computer facilities: 100 computers available on campus for general student use. A campuswide network can be accessed from student residence rooms and from off campus. *Web address:* http://www.cshl.edu/gradschool/.

General Application Contact: Dawn Pologruto, Director of Admissions, Recruitment and Student Affairs, 516-367-6911, Fax: 516-367-6919, E-mail: gradschool@cshl.edu.

GRADUATE UNITS

Graduate Program Students: 46 full-time (20 women); includes 6 minority (1 Black or African American, non-Hispanic/Latino; 1 Asian, non-Hispanic/Latino; 2 Hispanic/Latino; 1 Native Hawaiian or other Pacific Islander, non-Hispanic/Latino; 1 Two or more races, non-Hispanic/Latino), 25 international. Average age 23. 257 applicants. *Faculty:* 47 full-time (7 women). Expenses: Contact institution. *Financial support:* In 2010–11, 44 students received support, including 44 fellowships with full tuition reimbursements available (averaging $30,500 per year); health care benefits and tuition waivers (full) also available. Financial award application deadline: 12/1. In 2010, 10 doctorates awarded. Offers biological sciences (PhD). *Application deadline:* For fall admission, 12/1 for domestic and international students. *Application fee:* $60. Electronic applications accepted. *Application Contact:* Dawn Pologruto, Director of Admissions, Recruitment and Student Affairs, 516-367-6911, Fax: 516-367-6919, E-mail: gradschool@cshl.edu. *Dean,* Dr. Leemor Joshua-Tor, 516-367-6890, Fax: 516-367-6919, E-mail: gradschool@cshl.edu.

COLEMAN UNIVERSITY, San Diego, CA 92123

General Information Independent, coed, comprehensive institution. *Graduate housing:* On-campus housing not available.

GRADUATE UNITS

Program in Business and Technology Management *Degree program information:* Evening/weekend programs available. Postbaccalaureate distance learning degree programs offered (no on-campus study). Offers business and technology management (MS).

Program in Information Technology *Degree program information:* Evening/weekend programs available. Offers information technology (MSIT).

COLGATE ROCHESTER CROZER DIVINITY SCHOOL, Rochester, NY 14620-2530

General Information Independent-religious, coed, graduate-only institution. *Enrollment by degree level:* 74 first professional, 5 master's, 33 doctoral, 2 other advanced degrees. *Graduate faculty:* 8 full-time (4 women), 14 part-time/adjunct (6 women). *Tuition:* Full-time $12,640; part-time $1580 per course. *Required fees:* $215; $35 per course. Tuition and fees vary according to degree level and program. *Graduate housing:* Rooms and/or apartments available on a first-come, first-served basis to single and married students. Typical cost: $7000 per year for single students; $7000 per year for married students. Housing application deadline: 7/1. *Student services:* Campus employment opportunities, low-cost health insurance, services for students with disabilities. *Library facilities:* Ambrose Swasey Library plus 1 other. *Online resources:* library catalog, access to other libraries' catalogs. *Collection:* 18,327 titles, 63 serial subscriptions, 754 audiovisual materials.

Computer facilities: 8 computers available on campus for general student use. A campuswide network can be accessed from student residence rooms and from off campus. Online class registration is available. *Web address:* http://www.crcds.edu/.

General Application Contact: Melissa M. Morral, Vice President for Enrollment Services, 585-340-9500, Fax: 585-340-9644, E-mail: mmorral@crcds.edu.

GRADUATE UNITS

Graduate and Professional Programs Students: 79 full-time, 35 part-time; includes 28 Black or African American, non-Hispanic/Latino; 2 Asian, non-Hispanic/Latino; 2 Hispanic/Latino, 4 international. Average age 42. 35 applicants, 86% accepted, 26 enrolled. *Faculty:* 8 full-time (4 women), 14 part-time/adjunct (6 women). Expenses: Contact institution. *Financial support:* In 2010–11, 63 students received support. Scholarships/grants available. Financial award application deadline: 9/1; financial award applicants required to submit FAFSA. In 2010, 15 first professional degrees, 6 master's, 6 doctorates awarded. *Degree program information:* Part-time programs available. Postbaccalaureate distance learning degree programs offered (minimal on-campus study). Offers theology (M Div, MA, D Min, Certificate). *Application deadline:* For fall admission, 7/1 priority date for domestic students, 3/1 for international students; for spring admission, 12/1 priority date for domestic students, 9/1 for international students. Applications are processed on a rolling basis. *Application fee:* $35. *Application Contact:* Melissa M. Morral, Vice President for Enrollment Services, 585-340-9500, Fax: 585-340-9644, E-mail: mmorral@crcds.edu. *President,* Rev. Jack M. McKelvey, 585-271-1320 Ext. 680, Fax: 585-271-8013.

COLGATE UNIVERSITY, Hamilton, NY 13346-1386

General Information Independent, coed, comprehensive institution. *Enrollment:* 2,903 graduate, professional, and undergraduate students; 7 full-time matriculated graduate/professional students (4 women), 1 (woman) part-time matriculated graduate/professional student. *Enrollment by degree level:* 8 master's. *Graduate faculty:* 5 full-time (4 women), 3 part-time/adjunct (2 women). *Tuition:* Full-time $41,585; part-time $4621 per course. *Required fees:* $285. Tuition and fees vary according to course load. *Graduate housing:* On-campus housing not available. *Student services:* Campus safety program, career counseling, exercise/wellness program, free psychological counseling, low-cost health insurance, services for students with disabilities, teacher training, writing training. *Library facilities:* Case Library and Geyer Cnter for Information Technology plus 1 other. *Online resources:* library catalog, web page, access to other libraries' catalogs. *Collection:* 1.2 million titles, 29,632 serial subscriptions, 16,184 audiovisual materials.

Computer facilities: Computer purchase and lease plans are available. A campuswide network can be accessed from student residence rooms and from off campus. Online class registration, software applications are available. *Web address:* http://www.colgate.edu/.

General Application Contact: Ginger Babich, Administrative Assistant, Department of Educational Studies, 315-228-7256, Fax: 315-228-7857, E-mail: gbabich@colgate.edu.

GRADUATE UNITS

Master of Arts in Teaching Program Students: 7 full-time (4 women), 1 (woman) part-time; includes 2 minority (1 American Indian or Alaska Native, non-Hispanic/Latino; 1 Two or more races, non-Hispanic/Latino), 1 international. Average age 24. 10 applicants, 90% accepted, 4 enrolled. *Faculty:* 5 full-time (4 women), 3 part-time/adjunct (2 women). Expenses: Contact institution. *Financial support:* In 2010–11, 8 students received support. Scholarships/grants, unspecified assistantships, and grants available. Financial award application deadline: 2/15; financial award applicants required to submit FAFSA. In 2010, 2 master's awarded. Offers adolescence education NY state certification (MAT). *Application deadline:* For fall admission, 2/15 for domestic students. *Application fee:* $50. *Application Contact:* Ginger Babich, Administrative Assistant, 315-228-7256, Fax: 315-228-7857, E-mail: gbabich@colgate.edu. *Associate Dean of the Faculty*, Dr. Nancy Pruitt, 315-228-7220.

THE COLLEGE AT BROCKPORT, STATE UNIVERSITY OF NEW YORK, Brockport, NY 14420-2997

General Information State-supported, coed, comprehensive institution. CGS member. *Enrollment:* 389 full-time matriculated graduate/professional students (266 women), 789 part-time matriculated graduate/professional students (528 women). *Enrollment by degree level:* 1,021 master's, 157 other advanced degrees. *Graduate housing:* Room and/or apartments available on a first-come, first-served basis to single students; on-campus housing not available to married students. Housing application deadline: 6/1. *Student services:* Campus employment opportunities, campus safety program, career counseling, child daycare facilities, exercise/wellness program, free psychological counseling, grant writing training, international student services, low-cost health insurance, multicultural affairs office, services for students with disabilities, teacher training, writing training. *Library facilities:* Drake Memorial Library.

Computer facilities: 700 computers available on campus for general student use. A campuswide network can be accessed from student residence rooms and from off campus. Online class registration is available. *Web address:* http://www.brockport.edu/.

General Application Contact: Danielle A. Welch, Graduate Admissions Counselor, 585-395-5465, Fax: 585-395-2515.

GRADUATE UNITS

Office of the Vice Provost Students: 25 full-time (15 women), 24 part-time (16 women); includes 3 Black or African American, non-Hispanic/Latino; 2 American Indian or Alaska Native, non-Hispanic/Latino; 2 Asian, non-Hispanic/Latino; 1 Hispanic/Latino. 42 applicants, 69% accepted, 26 enrolled. Expenses: Contact institution. In 2010, 20 master's awarded. Offers accounting (MS); forensic accounting (MS); liberal studies (MA). *Application Contact:* Danielle A. Welch, Graduate Admissions Counselor, 585-395-5465, Fax: 585-395-2515. *Vice Provost*, Dr. P. Michael Fox, 585-395-2524, Fax: 585-395-2401, E-mail: mmallory@brockport.edu.

School of Education and Human Services Students: 185 full-time (138 women), 581 part-time (413 women); includes 102 minority (66 Black or African American, non-Hispanic/Latino; 13 Asian, non-Hispanic/Latino; 23 Hispanic/Latino). 360 applicants, 48% accepted, 146 enrolled. Expenses: Contact institution. In 2010, 244 master's awarded. Offers adolescence biology education (MS Ed); adolescence chemistry education (MS Ed); adolescence earth science education (MS Ed); adolescence education (MS Ed); adolescence English education (MS Ed); adolescence mathematics education (MS Ed); adolescence physics education (MS Ed); adolescence social studies education (MS Ed); alternate adolescence English inclusive education (MS Ed); alternate adolescence inclusive education (MS Ed); alternate adolescence mathematics inclusive education (MS Ed); alternate adolescence science inclusive education (MS Ed); alternate adolescence social studies inclusive education (MS Ed); arts administration (AGC); bilingual education (MS Ed, AGC); childhood curriculum specialist (MS Ed); childhood literacy (MS Ed); college counseling (MS Ed); education and human services (MPA, MS, MS Ed, MSW, AGC, CAS); educational administration (CAS); mental health counseling (MS); nonprofit management (AGC); public administration (MPA); school business administration (CAS); school counseling (MS Ed, CAS); social work (MSW). *Application Contact:* Danielle A. Welch, Graduate Admissions Counselor, 585-395-5465, Fax: 585-395-2515. *Dean*, Dr. Douglas Scheidt, 585-395-2510, Fax: 585-395-2172.

School of Health and Human Performance Students: 43 full-time (24 women), 70 part-time (34 women); includes 1 American Indian or Alaska Native, non-Hispanic/Latino; 1 Asian, non-Hispanic/Latino; 3 Hispanic/Latino. 76 applicants, 57% accepted, 37 enrolled. Expenses: Contact institution. In 2010, 52 master's awarded. Offers health and human performance (MS, MS Ed); health education (MS Ed); physical education (MS Ed); recreation and leisure (MS). *Application Contact:* Danielle A. Welch, Graduate Admissions Counselor, 585-395-5465, Fax: 585-395-2515. *Dean*, Dr. Frank X. Short, 585-395-2350, E-mail: fshort@brockport.edu.

School of Science and Mathematics Students: 40 full-time (24 women), 31 part-time (16 women); includes 1 Black or African American, non-Hispanic/Latino; 1 Asian, non-Hispanic/Latino; 2 Hispanic/Latino. 69 applicants, 54% accepted, 29 enrolled. Expenses: Contact institution. In 2010, 20 master's awarded. Offers biological sciences (MS); computational science (MS); environmental science and biology (MS); mathematics (MA); psychology (MA); science and mathematics (MA, MS). *Application Contact:* Danielle A. Welch, Graduate Admissions Counselor, 585-395-5465, Fax: 585-395-2515. *Dean*, Dr. Stuart Appelle, 585-395-2394, Fax: 585-395-2172, E-mail: kkifer@brockport.edu.

School of the Arts, Humanities and Social Sciences Students: 96 full-time (65 women), 83 part-time (49 women); includes 3 Black or African American, non-Hispanic/Latino; 2 American Indian or Alaska Native, non-Hispanic/Latino; 5 Asian, non-Hispanic/Latino; 6 Hispanic/Latino. 132 applicants, 63% accepted, 71 enrolled. Expenses: Contact institution. In 2010, 46 master's awarded. Offers arts, humanities and social sciences (MA, MFA); communication (MA); dance (MA, MFA); English (MA); history (MA); visual studies (MFA). *Application Contact:* Danielle A. Welch, Graduate Admissions Counselor, 585-395-5465, Fax: 585-395-2515. *Dean*, Dr. Darwin Prioleau, 585-395-5806, Fax: 585-395-5808, E-mail: dprioleau@brockport.edu.

COLLÈGE DOMINICAIN DE PHILOSOPHIE ET DE THÉOLOGIE, Ottawa, ON K1R 7G3, Canada

General Information Independent-religious, coed, university. *Graduate housing:* Room and/or apartments available on a first-come, first-served basis to single students; on-campus housing not available to married students.

GRADUATE UNITS

Graduate Programs *Degree program information:* Part-time and evening/weekend programs available.

Faculty of Philosophy Offers philosophy (MA Ph, PhD).

Faculty of Theology *Degree program information:* Part-time and evening/weekend programs available. Offers theology (M Th, MA Th, PhD, Th D, L Th).

COLLEGE FOR FINANCIAL PLANNING, Greenwood Village, CO 80111

General Information Proprietary, coed, primarily men, graduate-only institution. *Enrollment by degree level:* 850 master's. *Graduate faculty:* 4 full-time (0 women), 8 part-time/adjunct (2 women). *Tuition:* Full-time $4875. *Graduate housing:* On-campus housing not available. *Library facilities:* Apollo University Library. *Online resources:* web page. *Collection:* 20 million titles.

Computer facilities: A campuswide network can be accessed from off campus. Online class registration is available. *Web address:* http://www.cffp.edu/.

General Application Contact: Brett Sanborn, Director of Enrollment, 303-220-4951, Fax: 303-220-1810, E-mail: brett.sanborn@cffp.edu.

GRADUATE UNITS

Graduate Programs Expenses: Contact institution. *Financial support:* In 2010–11, 5 students received support. *Degree program information:* Part-time and evening/weekend programs available. Postbaccalaureate distance learning degree programs offered (no on-campus study). Offers finance (MSF); financial analysis (MSF); personal financial planning (MS). *Application deadline:* Applications are processed on a rolling basis. Electronic applications accepted. *Application Contact:* Brett Sanborn, Director of Enrollment, 303-220-4951, Fax: 303-220-1810, E-mail: brett.sanborn@cffp.edu.

COLLEGE OF CHARLESTON, Charleston, SC 29424-0001

General Information State-supported, coed, comprehensive institution. CGS member. *Enrollment:* 11,532 graduate, professional, and undergraduate students; 355 full-time matriculated graduate/professional students (254 women), 222 part-time matriculated graduate/professional students (148 women). *Enrollment by degree level:* 567 master's, 10 other advanced degrees. *Graduate faculty:* 211 full-time (100 women), 40 part-time/adjunct (25 women). *Student services:* Campus employment opportunities, campus safety program, career counseling, child daycare facilities, exercise/wellness program, free psychological counseling, grant writing training, international student services, low-cost health insurance, multicultural affairs office, services for students with disabilities, teacher training, writing training. *Library facilities:* Marlene and Nathan Addlestone Library plus 1 other. *Online resources:* library catalog, web page, access to other libraries' catalogs. *Collection:* 797,550 titles, 3,067 serial subscriptions, 10,936 audiovisual materials. *Research affiliation:* Oak Ridge Associated Universities (science), South Carolina Department of Natural Resources, Marine Resources Division (marine biology, environmental studies), National Institute of Standards and Technology (NIST) (marine biology, environmental studies), National Oceanic and Atmospheric Administration (NOAA) (marine biology, environmental studies), U. S. Department of Agriculture (USDA) (environmental studies), South Carolina Aquarium (marine biology, environmental studies).

Computer facilities: Computer purchase and lease plans are available. 578 computers available on campus for general student use. A campuswide network can be accessed from student residence rooms and from off campus. Online class registration is available. *Web address:* http://www.cofc.edu/.

General Application Contact: Susan Hallatt, Director of Admissions, 843-953-5614, Fax: 843-953-1434, E-mail: hallatts@cofc.edu.

GRADUATE UNITS

Graduate School Students: 355 full-time (254 women), 222 part-time (148 women); includes 57 minority (32 Black or African American, non-Hispanic/Latino; 2 American Indian or Alaska Native, non-Hispanic/Latino; 3 Asian, non-Hispanic/Latino; 11 Hispanic/Latino; 1 Native Hawaiian or other Pacific Islander, non-Hispanic/Latino; 8 Two or more races, non-Hispanic/Latino), 17 international. Average age 28. 528 applicants, 51% accepted, 241 enrolled. *Faculty:* 211 full-time (100 women), 40 part-time/adjunct (25 women). Expenses: Contact institution. *Financial support:* In 2010–11, 160 students received support, including 5 fellowships (averaging $22,000 per year), 30 research assistantships (averaging $18,000 per year), 32 teaching assistantships (averaging $13,300 per year); career-related internships or fieldwork, Federal Work-Study, institutionally sponsored loans, scholarships/grants, tuition waivers (partial), and unspecified assistantships also available. Support available to part-time students. Financial award application deadline: 5/1; financial award applicants required to submit FAFSA. In 2010, 239 master's, 16 other advanced degrees awarded. *Degree program information:* Part-time and evening/weekend programs available. *Application deadline:* For fall admission, 4/1 priority date for domestic students, 4/1 for international students; for spring admission, 10/1 priority date for domestic students, 8/1 for international students. *Application fee:* $45. Electronic applications accepted. *Application Contact:* Susan Hallatt, Director of Admissions, 843-953-5614, Fax: 843-953-1434, E-mail: hallatts@cofc.edu. *Dean*, Dr. Amy Thompson McCandless, 843-953-5730, Fax: 843-953-1434, E-mail: mccandlessa@cofc.edu.

School of Business Students: 49 full-time (23 women), 5 part-time (all women); includes 3 minority (2 Black or African American, non-Hispanic/Latino; 1 Hispanic/Latino), 1 international. Average age 24. 105 applicants, 54% accepted, 49 enrolled. *Faculty:* 12 full-time (5 women). Expenses: Contact institution. *Financial support:* In 2010–11, 2 research assistantships were awarded; scholarships/grants and unspecified assistantships also available. Support available to part-time students. Financial award applicants required to submit FAFSA. In 2010, 46 master's awarded. Offers accountancy (MS); business (MBA, MS); business administration (MBA). *Application deadline:* For fall admission, 7/1 for domestic students. Applications are processed on a rolling basis. *Application fee:* $45. Electronic applications accepted. *Application Contact:* Susan Hallatt, Director of Graduate Admissions, 843-953-5614, Fax: 843-953-1434, E-mail: hallatts@cofc.edu. *Dean*, Dr. Alan Shao, 843-953-6651, Fax: 843-953-5697, E-mail: shaoa@cofc.edu.

School of Education, Health, and Human Performance Students: 142 full-time (118 women), 71 part-time (62 women); includes 30 minority (21 Black or African American, non-Hispanic/Latino; 1 American Indian or Alaska Native, non-Hispanic/Latino; 4 Hispanic/Latino; 1 Native Hawaiian or other Pacific Islander, non-Hispanic/Latino; 3 Two or more races, non-Hispanic/Latino), 1 international. Average age 29. 118 applicants, 58% accepted, 69 enrolled. *Faculty:* 34 full-time (27 women), 13 part-time/adjunct (all women). Expenses: Contact institution. *Financial support:* In 2010–11, research assistantships (averaging $19,000 per year), teaching assistantships (averaging $13,300 per year) were awarded; career-related internships or fieldwork, Federal Work-Study, scholarships/grants, and unspecified assistantships also available. Support available to part-time students. Financial award application deadline: 4/1; financial award applicants required to submit FAFSA. In 2010, 55 master's awarded. *Degree program information:* Part-time and evening/weekend programs available. Offers early childhood education (MAT); education, health, and human performance (M Ed, MAT, Certificate); elementary education (MAT); English to speakers of other languages (Certificate); languages (M Ed); performing arts education (MAT); science and mathematics for teachers (M Ed); special education (MAT); teaching, learning and advocacy (M Ed). *Application deadline:* For fall admission, 4/1 for domestic students; for spring admission, 11/1 for domestic students. Applications are processed on a rolling basis. *Application fee:* $45. Electronic applications accepted. *Application Contact:* Susan Hallatt, Director of Graduate Admissions, 843-953-5614, Fax: 843-953-1434, E-mail: hallatts@cofc.edu. *Dean*, Dr. Frances Welch, 843-953-5613, Fax: 843-953-5407, E-mail: welchf@cofc.edu.

School of Humanities and Social Sciences Students: 88 full-time (60 women), 62 part-time (45 women); includes 16 minority (8 Black or African American, non-Hispanic/Latino; 1 American Indian or Alaska Native, non-Hispanic/Latino; 3 Hispanic/Latino; 4 Two or more races, non-Hispanic/Latino), 1 international. Average age 28. 124 applicants, 54% accepted, 62 enrolled. *Faculty:* 82 full-time (40 women), 6 part-time/adjunct (1 woman). Expenses: Contact institution. *Financial support:* In 2010–11, research assistantships (averaging $19,000 per year), teaching assistantships (averaging $13,000 per year) were awarded; fellowships, career-related internships or fieldwork, Federal Work-Study, scholarships/grants, and unspecified assistantships also available. Support available to part-time students. Financial award application deadline: 4/1; financial award applicants required to submit FAFSA. In 2010, 63 master's, 8 other advanced degrees awarded. *Degree program information:* Part-time and evening/weekend programs available. Offers communication (MA); English (MA); history (MA); humanities and social sciences (MA, MPA, Certificate); public administration (MPA); urban and regional planning (Certificate). *Application fee:* $45. Electronic applications accepted. *Application Contact:* Susan Hallatt, Director of Graduate Admissions, 843-953-5614, Fax: 843-953-1434, E-mail: hallatts@cofc.edu. *Dean*, Dr. Cynthia Lowenthal, 843-953-0760, Fax: 843-953-0758.

School of Sciences and Mathematics Students: 76 full-time (53 women), 81 part-time (35 women); includes 6 minority (1 Black or African American, non-Hispanic/Latino; 2 Asian, non-Hispanic/Latino; 2 Hispanic/Latino; 1 Two or more races, non-Hispanic/Latino), 4 international. Average age 27. 158 applicants, 42% accepted, 50 enrolled. *Faculty:* 80 full-time (26 women), 17 part-time/adjunct (7 women). Expenses: Contact institution. *Financial support:* In 2010–11, 5 fellowships (averaging $20,000 per year), 20 research assistantships (averaging $19,000 per year), 30 teaching assistantships (averaging $16,000 per year) were awarded; career-related internships or fieldwork, Federal Work-Study, institutionally sponsored loans, scholarships/grants, and unspecified assistantships also available. Support available to part-time students. Financial award application deadline: 4/1; financial award applicants required to submit FAFSA. In 2010, 62 master's awarded. *Degree program information:* Part-time and evening/weekend programs available. Offers computer and information sciences (MS); environmental studies (MS); marine biology (MS); mathematics (MS); sciences and mathematics (MS, Certificate). *Application deadline:* Applications are processed on a rolling basis. *Application fee:* $45. Electronic applications accepted. *Applica-*

College of Charleston (continued)

tion Contact: Susan Hallatt, Director of Graduate Admissions, 843-953-5614, Fax: 843-953-1434, E-mail: hallatts@cofc.edu. *Dean,* Dr. Mike Auerbach, 843-953-5991, E-mail: auerbachmj@cofc.edu.

School of the Arts Students: 25 full-time (19 women), 1 part-time (0 women); includes 2 minority (1 Asian, non-Hispanic/Latino; 1 Hispanic/Latino). Average age 25. 2 applicants, 50% accepted, 0 enrolled. *Faculty:* 10 full-time (5 women). Expenses: Contact institution. *Financial support:* Scholarships/grants and unspecified assistantships available. Financial award application deadline: 4/1; financial award applicants required to submit FAFSA. In 2010, 10 master's, 5 other advanced degrees awarded. Offers arts (MPA, MS, Certificate); arts management (MPA, Certificate); historic preservation (MS). *Application fee:* $45. *Application Contact:* Susan Hallatt, Director of Graduate Admissions, 843-953-5614, Fax: 843-953-1434, E-mail: hallatts@cofc.edu. *Dean,* Dr. Valerie B. Morris, 843-953-8222, Fax: 843-953-4988, E-mail: morrisv@cofc.edu.

COLLEGE OF EMMANUEL AND ST. CHAD, Saskatoon, SK S7N 0W6, Canada

General Information Independent-religious, coed, graduate-only institution. *Graduate housing:* Room and/or apartments available on a first-come, first-served basis to single students; on-campus housing not available to married students. Housing application deadline: 6/15.

GRADUATE UNITS

Bachelor of Theology Program *Degree program information:* Part-time programs available. Postbaccalaureate distance learning degree programs offered (minimal on-campus study). Offers theology (B Th).

Graduate Programs *Degree program information:* Part-time programs available. Offers theology (M Div, MTS, STM). STM program offered jointly with Lutheran Theological Seminary and St. Andrew's College.

THE COLLEGE OF IDAHO, Caldwell, ID 83605

General Information Independent, coed, comprehensive institution. *Graduate housing:* Rooms and/or apartments available on a first-come, first-served basis to single and married students.

GRADUATE UNITS

Program in Teacher Education Offers teacher education (MAT).

COLLEGE OF MOUNT ST. JOSEPH, Cincinnati, OH 45233-1670

General Information Independent-religious, coed, comprehensive institution. CGS member. *Enrollment:* 2,474 graduate, professional, and undergraduate students; 220 full-time matriculated graduate/professional students (164 women), 180 part-time matriculated graduate/professional students (133 women). *Enrollment by degree level:* 309 master's, 90 doctoral, 1 other advanced degree. *Graduate faculty:* 43 full-time (23 women), 39 part-time/adjunct (26 women). *Graduate housing:* Room and/or apartments available on a first-come, first-served basis to single students; on-campus housing not available to married students. Housing application deadline: 3/31. *Student services:* Campus employment opportunities, campus safety program, career counseling, child daycare facilities, exercise/wellness program, free psychological counseling, international student services, multicultural affairs office, services for students with disabilities, teacher training, writing training. *Library facilities:* Archbishop Alter Library. *Online resources:* library catalog, web page, access to other libraries' catalogs. *Collection:* 96,897 titles, 9,489 serial subscriptions, 4,172 audiovisual materials.

Computer facilities: Computer purchase and lease plans are available. 140 computers available on campus for general student use. A campuswide network can be accessed from student residence rooms and from off campus. Online class registration, computer-aided instruction are available. *Web address:* http://www.msj.edu/.

General Application Contact: Marilyn Hoskins, Assistant Director for Graduate Recruitment, 513-244-4723, Fax: 513-244-4629, E-mail: marilyn_hoskins@mail.msj.edu.

GRADUATE UNITS

Graduate Education Program Students: 87 full-time (64 women), 89 part-time (67 women); includes 19 Black or African American, non-Hispanic/Latino; 1 Asian, non-Hispanic/Latino; 1 Hispanic/Latino; 1 Two or more races, non-Hispanic/Latino. Average age 35. 106 applicants, 94% accepted, 80 enrolled. *Faculty:* 18 full-time (11 women), 7 part-time/adjunct (6 women). Expenses: Contact institution. *Financial support:* In 2010–11, 45 students received support. Scholarships/grants available. Financial award applicants required to submit FAFSA. In 2010, 83 master's awarded. *Degree program information:* Part-time and evening/weekend programs available. Offers adolescent young adult education (MA); art (MA); inclusive early childhood education (MA); instructional leadership (MA); middle childhood education (MA); multi-age education (MA); multicultural special education (MA); music (MA); reading (MA). *Application deadline:* Applications are processed on a rolling basis. *Application fee:* $50. Electronic applications accepted. *Application Contact:* Marilyn Hoskins, Assistant Director of Graduate Recruitment, 513-244-4723, Fax: 513-244-4629, E-mail: marilyn_hoskins@mail.msj.edu. *Chair,* Dr. Mary West, 513-244-3263, Fax: 513-244-4867, E-mail: mary_west@mail.msj.edu.

Graduate Program in Religious Studies Students: 24 part-time (17 women); includes 1 minority (Black or African American, non-Hispanic/Latino). Average age 47. 20 applicants, 90% accepted, 10 enrolled. *Faculty:* 4 full-time (3 women). Expenses: Contact institution. *Financial support:* In 2010–11, 20 students received support. Scholarships/grants available. Financial award applicants required to submit FAFSA. In 2010, 5 master's awarded. *Degree program information:* Part-time and evening/weekend programs available. Offers religious education (Certificate); spiritual and pastoral care (MA, Certificate); spiritual direction (Certificate). *Application deadline:* Applications are processed on a rolling basis. *Application fee:* $50. Electronic applications accepted. *Application Contact:* Marilyn Hoskins, Assistant Director of Graduate Recruitment, 513-244-4723, Fax: 513-244-4629, E-mail: marilyn_hoskins@mail.msj.edu. *Chair of Religious/Pastoral Studies,* Dr. John Trokan, 513-244-4272, Fax: 513-244-4222, E-mail: john_trokan@mail.msj.edu.

Master of Nursing Program Students: 43 full-time (37 women); includes 3 minority (2 Black or African American, non-Hispanic/Latino; 1 Hispanic/Latino). Average age 30. 129 applicants, 98% accepted. *Faculty:* 4 full-time (3 women), 11 part-time/adjunct (all women). Expenses: Contact institution. *Financial support:* In 2010–11, 10 students received support. Scholarships/grants available. Financial award applicants required to submit FAFSA. In 2010, 17 master's awarded. Offers nursing (MN). *Application deadline:* Applications are processed on a rolling basis. *Application fee:* $50. Electronic applications accepted. *Application Contact:* Marilyn Hoskins, Assistant Director of Graduate Recruitment, 513-244-4723, Fax: 513-244-4629, E-mail: marilyn_hoskins@mail.msj.edu. *Chair,* Dr. Mary Kishman, 513-244-4726, Fax: 513-451-2547, E-mail: mary_kishman@mail.msj.edu.

Master of Science in Organizational Leadership Program Students: 66 part-time (48 women); includes 10 minority (8 Black or African American, non-Hispanic/Latino; 1 American Indian or Alaska Native, non-Hispanic/Latino; 1 Asian, non-Hispanic/Latino). Average age 41. 7 applicants, 57% accepted, 2 enrolled. *Faculty:* 6 full-time (3 women), 1 part-time/adjunct (0 women). Expenses: Contact institution. *Financial support:* In 2010–11, 2 students received support. Application deadline: 6/1. In 2010, 7 master's awarded. *Degree program information:* Part-time and evening/weekend programs available. Offers organizational leadership (MS). *Application deadline:* Applications are processed on a rolling basis. *Application fee:* $50. Electronic applications accepted. *Application Contact:* Marilyn Hoskins, Assistant Director of Graduate Recruitment, 513-244-4723, Fax: 513-244-4629, E-mail: marilyn_hoskins@mail.msj.edu. *Chair,* Daryl Smith, 513-244-4920, Fax: 513-244-4270, E-mail: daryl_smith@mail.msj.edu.

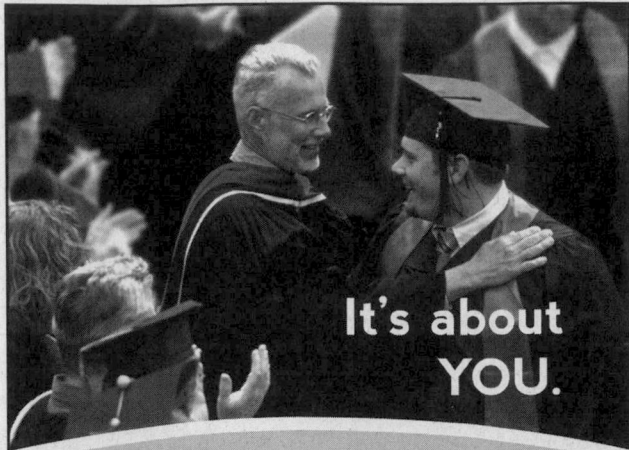

Physical Therapy Program Students: 90 full-time (63 women); includes 6 minority (1 Black or African American, non-Hispanic/Latino; 1 American Indian or Alaska Native, non-Hispanic/Latino; 2 Asian, non-Hispanic/Latino; 1 Hispanic/Latino; 1 Two or more races, non-Hispanic/Latino). Average age 24. 127 applicants, 43% accepted, 31 enrolled. *Faculty:* 8 full-time (4 women), 4 part-time/adjunct (2 women). Expenses: Contact institution. *Financial support:* In 2010–11, 3 students received support. Applicants required to submit FAFSA. In 2010, 18 doctorates awarded. Offers physical therapy (DPT). *Application fee:* $50. Electronic applications accepted. *Application Contact:* Marilyn Hoskins, Assistant Director of Graduate Recruitment, 513-244-4723, Fax: 513-244-4629, E-mail: marilyn_hoskins@mail.msj.edu. *Chair,* Dr. Karen Holtgrefe, 513-244-3299, Fax: 513-451-2547, E-mail: karen_holtgrefe@mail.msj.edu.

See Display on previous page and Close-Up on page 933.

COLLEGE OF MOUNT SAINT VINCENT, Riverdale, NY 10471-1093

General Information Independent, coed, comprehensive institution. *Graduate housing:* On-campus housing not available.

GRADUATE UNITS

School of Professional and Continuing Studies Offers adult nurse practitioner (MSN, PMC); family nurse practitioner (MSN, PMC); instructional technology and global perspectives (Certificate); middle level education (Certificate); multicultural studies (Certificate); nurse educator (PMC); nursing administration (MSN); nursing for the adult and aged (MSN); urban and multicultural education (MS Ed).

THE COLLEGE OF NEW JERSEY, Ewing, NJ 08628

General Information State-supported, coed, comprehensive institution. CGS member. *Enrollment:* 7,115 graduate, professional, and undergraduate students; 207 full-time matriculated graduate/professional students (170 women), 448 part-time matriculated graduate/professional students (366 women). *Enrollment by degree level:* 523 master's, 132 other advanced degrees. *Student services:* Campus employment opportunities, campus safety program, career counseling, exercise/wellness program, free psychological counseling, international student services, low-cost health insurance, services for students with disabilities, teacher training. *Library facilities:* New Library. *Online resources:* library catalog, web page. *Collection:* 675,900 titles, 69,419 serial subscriptions, 39,407 audiovisual materials.

Computer facilities: Computer purchase and lease plans are available. 631 computers available on campus for general student use. A campuswide network can be accessed from student residence rooms and from off campus. Online class registration is available. *Web address:* http://www.tcnj.edu/.

General Application Contact: Susan L. Hydro, Assistant Dean, Office of Graduate Studies, 609-771-2300, Fax: 609-637-5105, E-mail: graduate@tcnj.edu.

GRADUATE UNITS

Graduate Division Students: 207 full-time (170 women), 448 part-time (366 women); includes 106 minority (29 Black or African American, non-Hispanic/Latino; 2 American Indian or Alaska Native, non-Hispanic/Latino; 25 Asian, non-Hispanic/Latino; 42 Hispanic/Latino; 5 Native Hawaiian or other Pacific Islander, non-Hispanic/Latino; 3 Two or more races, non-Hispanic/Latino), 4 international. 891 applicants, 56% accepted, 349 enrolled. Expenses: Contact institution. *Financial support:* Tuition waivers (partial) and unspecified assistantships available. Financial award application deadline: 5/1; financial award applicants required to submit FAFSA. In 2010, 326 master's, 118 other advanced degrees awarded. *Degree program information:* Part-time and evening/weekend programs available. Offers overseas education (M Ed, Certificate). *Application deadline:* For fall admission, 2/1 priority date for domestic students; for spring admission, 10/1 priority date for domestic students. *Application fee:* $75. Electronic applications accepted. *Application Contact:* Susan L. Hydro, Assistant Dean, Office of Graduate Studies, 609-771-2300, Fax: 609-637-5105, E-mail: graduate@tcnj.edu.

School of Culture and Society Students: 6 full-time (all women), 32 part-time (24 women); includes 3 minority (1 Black or African American, non-Hispanic/Latino; 2 Hispanic/Latino). 38 applicants, 55% accepted, 11 enrolled. Expenses: Contact institution. *Financial support:* Tuition waivers (partial) and unspecified assistantships available. Financial award application deadline: 5/1; financial award applicants required to submit FAFSA. In 2010, 5 master's awarded. *Degree program information:* Part-time programs available. Offers culture and society (MA); English (MA). *Application deadline:* For fall admission, 2/1 priority date for domestic students; for spring admission, 10/1 priority date for domestic students. *Application fee:* $70. Electronic applications accepted. *Application Contact:* Susan L. Hydro, Assistant Dean, Office of Graduate Studies, 609-771-2300, Fax: 609-637-5105, E-mail: graduate@tcnj.edu. *Dean,* Dr. Benjamin Rifkin, 609-771-3434, Fax: 609-637-5173.

School of Education Students: 188 full-time (156 women), 322 part-time (274 women); includes 80 minority (22 Black or African American, non-Hispanic/Latino; 2 American Indian or Alaska Native, non-Hispanic/Latino; 16 Asian, non-Hispanic/Latino; 34 Hispanic/Latino; 4 Native Hawaiian or other Pacific Islander, non-Hispanic/Latino; 2 Two or more races, non-Hispanic/Latino), 2 international. 634 applicants, 55% accepted, 250 enrolled. Expenses: Contact institution. *Financial support:* Tuition waivers (partial) and unspecified assistantships available. Financial award application deadline: 5/1; financial award applicants required to submit FAFSA. In 2010, 274 master's, 57 other advanced degrees awarded. *Degree program information:* Part-time and evening/weekend programs available. Offers community counseling: human services (MA); community counseling: substance abuse and addiction (MA, Certificate); developmental reading (M Ed); education (M Ed, MA, MAT, Certificate, Ed S); educational leadership (M Ed, Certificate); elementary education (M Ed, MAT); elementary teaching (MAT); English as a second language (M Ed); marriage and family therapy (Ed S); reading certification (Certificate); school counseling (MA); school personnel licensure: preschool-grade 3 (M Ed, MAT); secondary education (MAT); special education (M Ed, MAT); special education with learning disabilities (Certificate); teaching English as a second language (M Ed, Certificate). *Application deadline:* For fall admission, 2/1 priority date for domestic students; for spring admission, 10/1 priority date for domestic students. *Application fee:* $70. Electronic applications accepted. *Application Contact:* Susan L. Hydro, Assistant Dean, Office of Graduate Studies, 609-771-2300, Fax: 609-637-5105, E-mail: graduate@tcnj.edu. *Dean,* Dr. William Behre, 609-771-2100.

School of Nursing, Health and Exercise Science Students: 12 full-time (7 women), 27 part-time (26 women); includes 6 Black or African American, non-Hispanic/Latino; 3 Asian, non-Hispanic/Latino; 1 Hispanic/Latino; 1 Native Hawaiian or other Pacific Islander, non-Hispanic/Latino; 1 Two or more races, non-Hispanic/Latino, 2 international. 24 applicants, 46% accepted, 4 enrolled. *Faculty:* 3. Expenses: Contact institution. *Financial support:* Tuition waivers (partial) and unspecified assistantships available. Financial award application deadline: 5/1; financial award applicants required to submit FAFSA. In 2010, 13 master's, 2 other advanced degrees awarded. *Degree program information:* Part-time programs available. Offers health (MAT); health education (M Ed, MAT); nursing (MSN, Certificate); nursing, health and exercise science (M Ed, MAT, MSN, Certificate); physical education (M Ed, MAT). *Application deadline:* For fall admission, 2/1 priority date for domestic students; for spring admission, 10/1 priority date for domestic students. *Application fee:* $70. Electronic applications accepted. *Application Contact:* Susan L. Hydro, Assistant Dean, Office of Graduate Studies, 609-771-2300, Fax: 609-637-5105, E-mail: graduate@tcnj.edu. *Dean,* Dr. Susan Bakewell-Sachs, 609-771-2541, Fax: 609-637-5159.

See Display below and Close-Up on page 935.

THE COLLEGE OF NEW ROCHELLE, New Rochelle, NY 10805-2308

General Information Independent, coed, primarily women, comprehensive institution. CGS member. *Graduate housing:* Room and/or apartments available on a first-come, first-served basis to single students; on-campus housing not available to married students. Housing application deadline: 8/1.

GRADUATE UNITS

Graduate School *Degree program information:* Part-time and evening/weekend programs available. Offers acute care nurse practitioner (MS, Certificate); clinical specialist in holistic nursing (MS, Certificate); family nurse practitioner (MS, Certificate); nursing and health care management (MS); nursing education (Certificate).

Division of Art and Communication Studies *Degree program information:* Part-time and evening/weekend programs available. Offers art education (MA); art therapy (MS); art therapy/counseling (MS); communication studies (MS, Certificate); studio art (MS).

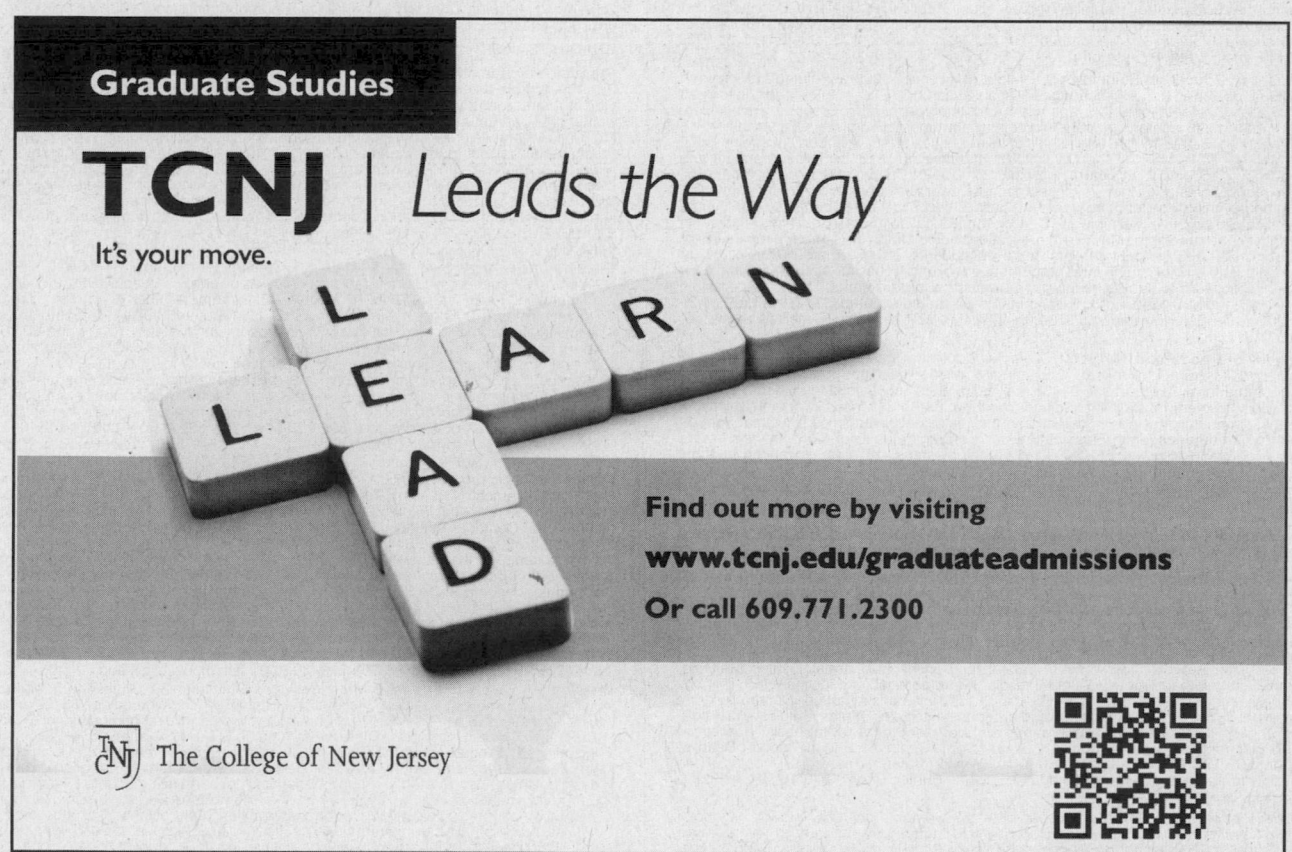

The College of New Rochelle (continued)

Division of Education *Degree program information:* Part-time and evening/weekend programs available. Offers bilingual education (Certificate); creative teaching and learning (MS Ed, Certificate); dual certification: school building leader/school district leader (MS); elementary education/early childhood education (MS Ed); literacy education (MS Ed); school administration and supervision (MS, Advanced Certificate, Advanced Diploma); school building leader (MS, Advanced Certificate); school district leader (MS, Advanced Diploma); special education (MS Ed); teaching English as a second language (MS Ed); teaching English as a second language and multilingual/multicultural education (MS Ed, Certificate).

Division of Human Services *Degree program information:* Part-time and evening/weekend programs available. Offers career development (MS); community-school psychology (MS); gerontology (MS, Certificate); guidance and counseling (MS); mental health counseling (Certificate).

COLLEGE OF NOTRE DAME OF MARYLAND, Baltimore, MD 21210-2476

General Information Independent-religious, coed, primarily women, comprehensive institution. *Graduate housing:* On-campus housing not available.

GRADUATE UNITS

Graduate Studies *Degree program information:* Part-time and evening/weekend programs available. Offers contemporary communication (MA); instructional leadership for changing populations (PhD); leadership in teaching (MA); liberal studies (MA); management (MA); nonprofit management (MA); teaching (MA); teaching English to speakers of other languages (MA). Electronic applications accepted.

COLLEGE OF SAINT ELIZABETH, Morristown, NJ 07960-6989

General Information Independent-religious, coed, primarily women, comprehensive institution. CGS member. *Enrollment:* 2,112 graduate, professional, and undergraduate students; 152 full-time matriculated graduate/professional students (130 women), 696 part-time matriculated graduate/professional students (583 women). *Enrollment by degree level:* 594 master's, 55 doctoral, 199 other advanced degrees. *Graduate faculty:* 29 full-time (16 women), 45 part-time/adjunct (29 women). *Tuition:* Part-time $857 per credit. *Required fees:* $70 per credit. *Graduate housing:* On-campus housing not available. *Student services:* Campus employment opportunities, campus safety program, career counseling, exercise/wellness program, free psychological counseling, international student services, low-cost health insurance, multicultural affairs office, services for students with disabilities, teacher training, writing training. *Library facilities:* Mahoney Library. *Online resources:* library catalog, web page, access to other libraries' catalogs. *Collection:* 119,438 titles, 977 serial subscriptions, 1,744 audiovisual materials. *Research affiliation:* Cornell University and University of Texas Houston (food biotechnology (attitude research)), National Figure Skating Association (sports nutrition), National Institute of Mental Health (mental health service).

Computer facilities: 127 computers available on campus for general student use. A campuswide network can be accessed from student residence rooms and from off campus. *Web address:* http://www.cse.edu/.

General Application Contact: Donna Tatarka, Dean of Admission, 973-290-4705, Fax: 973-290-4710, E-mail: dtatarka@cse.edu.

GRADUATE UNITS

Department of Business Administration and Economics Students: 10 full-time (all women), 62 part-time (51 women); includes 11 Black or African American, non-Hispanic/Latino; 5 Asian, non-Hispanic/Latino; 6 Hispanic/Latino; 1 Two or more races, non-Hispanic/Latino, 5 international. Average age 34. 38 applicants, 87% accepted, 21 enrolled. *Faculty:* 3 full-time (1 woman), 2 part-time/adjunct (both women). Expenses: Contact institution. *Financial support:* Career-related internships or fieldwork, tuition waivers (partial), and unspecified assistantships available. Support available to part-time students. Financial award application deadline: 3/15; financial award applicants required to submit FAFSA. In 2010, 39 master's awarded. *Degree program information:* Part-time and evening/weekend programs available. Offers management (MS). *Application deadline:* Applications are processed on a rolling basis. *Application fee:* $35. Electronic applications accepted. *Application Contact:* Donna Tatarka, Dean of Admission, 973-290-4705, Fax: 973-290-4710, E-mail: dtatarka@cse.edu. *Director of the Graduate Program in Management*, Dr. Kathleen Reddick, 973-290-4041, Fax: 973-290-4177, E-mail: kreddick@cse.edu.

Department of Education Students: 79 full-time (61 women), 298 part-time (259 women); includes 33 Black or African American, non-Hispanic/Latino; 3 Asian, non-Hispanic/Latino; 18 Hispanic/Latino, 1 international. Average age 37. 123 applicants, 72% accepted, 75 enrolled. *Faculty:* 11 full-time (3 women), 19 part-time/adjunct (9 women). Expenses: Contact institution. *Financial support:* Career-related internships or fieldwork, tuition waivers (partial), and unspecified assistantships available. Support available to part-time students. Financial award application deadline: 3/15; financial award applicants required to submit FAFSA. In 2010, 116 master's, 7 doctorates, 97 other advanced degrees awarded. *Degree program information:* Part-time and evening/weekend programs available. Offers accelerated certification for teachers (Certificate); assistive technology (Certificate); education: human services leadership (MA); educational leadership (MA, Ed D); educational technology (MA). *Application deadline:* For fall admission, 6/30 priority date for domestic students; for spring admission, 11/30 for domestic students. Applications are processed on a rolling basis. *Application fee:* $35. Electronic applications accepted. *Application Contact:* Donna Tatarka, Dean of Admission, 973-290-4705, Fax: 973-290-4710, E-mail: dtatarka@cse.edu. *Director of Graduate Education Programs*, Dr. Alan H. Markowitz, 973-290-4374, Fax: 973-290-4389, E-mail: amarkowitz@cse.edu.

Department of Foods and Nutrition Students: 8 full-time (all women), 17 part-time (16 women); includes 2 Black or African American, non-Hispanic/Latino; 2 Asian, non-Hispanic/Latino, 1 international. Average age 31. 38 applicants, 84% accepted, 24 enrolled. *Faculty:* 2 full-time (both women), 2 part-time/adjunct (both women). Expenses: Contact institution. *Financial support:* Tuition waivers (partial) and unspecified assistantships available. Support available to part-time students. Financial award application deadline: 3/15; financial award applicants required to submit FAFSA. In 2010, 10 master's, 18 other advanced degrees awarded. *Degree program information:* Part-time and evening/weekend programs available. Offers dietetic internship (Certificate); nutrition (MS). *Application deadline:* Applications are processed on a rolling basis. *Application fee:* $35. Electronic applications accepted. *Application Contact:* Donna Tatarka, Dean of Admission, 973-290-4705, Fax: 973-290-4710, E-mail: dtatarka@cse.edu. *Director of the Graduate Program in Nutrition*, Dr. Jean C. Burge, 973-290-4127, Fax: 973-290-4167, E-mail: nutrition@cse.edu.

Department of Health Professions and Related Sciences Students: 4 full-time (3 women), 179 part-time (137 women); includes 19 Black or African American, non-Hispanic/Latino; 1 American Indian or Alaska Native, non-Hispanic/Latino; 14 Asian, non-Hispanic/Latino; 12 Hispanic/Latino; 1 Native Hawaiian or other Pacific Islander, non-Hispanic/Latino, 2 international. Average age 45. 65 applicants, 71% accepted, 36 enrolled. *Faculty:* 3 full-time (all women), 4 part-time/adjunct (2 women). Expenses: Contact institution. *Financial support:* Career-related internships or fieldwork, tuition waivers (partial), and unspecified assistantships available. Support available to part-time students. Financial award application deadline: 3/15; financial award applicants required to submit FAFSA. In 2010, 7 master's awarded. *Degree program information:* Part-time and evening/weekend programs available. Offers health care management (MS). *Application deadline:* Applications are processed on a rolling basis. *Application fee:* $35. Electronic applications accepted. *Application Contact:* Donna Tatarka, Dean of Admission, 973-290-4705, Fax: 973-290-4710, E-mail: dtatarka@cse.edu. *Director of the Graduate Program in Health Care Management*, Linda Hunter, 973-290-4040, Fax: 973-290-4167, E-mail: lhunter@cse.edu.

Department of Nursing Students: 35 part-time (33 women); includes 3 Black or African American, non-Hispanic/Latino; 2 Asian, non-Hispanic/Latino; 3 Hispanic/Latino. Average age 49. 18 applicants, 78% accepted, 10 enrolled. *Faculty:* 2 full-time (both women), 2 part-time/adjunct (both women). Expenses: Contact institution. In 2010, 13 master's awarded. *Degree program information:* Part-time and evening/weekend programs available. Offers nursing (MSN). *Application fee:* $35. *Application Contact:* Donna Tatarka, Dean of Admission, 973-290-4705, Fax: 973-290-4710, E-mail: dtatarka@cse.edu. *Director of Graduate Program*, Dr. Sharon Hellwig, 973-290-1074, E-mail: shellwig@cse.edu.

Department of Psychology Students: 33 full-time (31 women), 67 part-time (57 women); includes 13 Black or African American, non-Hispanic/Latino; 4 Asian, non-Hispanic/Latino; 12 Hispanic/Latino, 2 international. Average age 30. 86 applicants, 41% accepted, 27 enrolled. *Faculty:* 4 full-time (3 women), 9 part-time/adjunct (all women). Expenses: Contact institution. *Financial support:* Career-related internships or fieldwork, tuition waivers (partial), and unspecified assistantships available. Support available to part-time students. Financial award application deadline: 3/15; financial award applicants required to submit FAFSA. In 2010, 22 master's awarded. *Degree program information:* Part-time and evening/weekend programs available. Offers counseling psychology (MA); forensic psychology (MA); student affairs in higher education (Certificate). *Application deadline:* For fall admission, 4/1 priority date for domestic students; for spring admission, 11/15 for domestic students. Applications are processed on a rolling basis. *Application fee:* $35. Electronic applications accepted. *Application Contact:* Donna Tatarka, Dean of Admission, 973-290-4705, Fax: 973-290-4710, E-mail: dtatarka@cse.edu. *Director of the Graduate Program in Counseling Psychology*, Dr. Valerie Scott, 973-290-4102, Fax: 973-290-4676, E-mail: vscott@cse.edu.

Department of Theology Students: 12 part-time (8 women); includes 1 Black or African American, non-Hispanic/Latino; 1 Asian, non-Hispanic/Latino. Average age 53. 7 applicants, 71% accepted, 4 enrolled. *Faculty:* 3 full-time (2 women), 4 part-time/adjunct (0 women). Expenses: Contact institution. *Financial support:* Tuition waivers (partial) and unspecified assistantships available. Support available to part-time students. Financial award applicants required to submit FAFSA. In 2010, 8 master's awarded. *Degree program information:* Part-time and evening/weekend programs available. Offers theology (MA). *Application deadline:* For fall admission, 3/1 priority date for domestic students; for spring admission, 9/1 for domestic students. Applications are processed on a rolling basis. *Application fee:* $35. Electronic applications accepted. *Application Contact:* Donna Tatarka, Dean of Admission, 973-290-4705, Fax: 973-290-4710, E-mail: dtatarka@cse.edu. *Director of the Graduate Program*, Sr. Kathleen Flanagan, 973-290-4336, Fax: 973-290-4312, E-mail: kflanagan@cse.edu.

Program in Justice Studies Students: 3 full-time (2 women), 13 part-time (9 women); includes 5 Black or African American, non-Hispanic/Latino; 2 Hispanic/Latino. Average age 33. 10 applicants, 80% accepted, 7 enrolled. *Faculty:* 1 full-time (0 women), 2 part-time/adjunct (both women). Expenses: Contact institution. *Financial support:* Unspecified assistantships available. Support available to part-time students. Financial award applicants required to submit FAFSA. In 2010, 1 master's awarded. *Degree program information:* Part-time and evening/weekend programs available. Offers justice administration and public service (MA). *Application deadline:* Applications are processed on a rolling basis. *Application fee:* $35. Electronic applications accepted. *Application Contact:* Donna Tatarka, Dean of Admission, 973-290-4705, Fax: 973-290-4710, E-mail: dtatarka@cse.edu. *Associate Professor*, Dr. James Ford, 973-290-4324, E-mail: jford@cse.edu.

COLLEGE OF ST. JOSEPH, Rutland, VT 05701-3899

General Information Independent-religious, coed, comprehensive institution. *Enrollment:* 418 graduate, professional, and undergraduate students; 50 full-time matriculated graduate/professional students (40 women), 95 part-time matriculated graduate/professional students (69 women). *Enrollment by degree level:* 145 master's. *Graduate faculty:* 10 full-time (4 women), 19 part-time/adjunct (8 women). *Tuition:* Full-time $14,200; part-time $400 per credit hour. *Required fees:* $45 per semester. *Graduate housing:* Room and/or apartments guaranteed to single students; on-campus housing not available to married students. Typical cost: $5000 per year. Housing application deadline: 7/1. *Student services:* Campus employment opportunities, campus safety program, career counseling, free psychological counseling, low-cost health insurance, services for students with disabilities, teacher training, writing training. *Library facilities:* Giorgetti Library. *Online resources:* library catalog, access to other libraries' catalogs. *Collection:* 58,422 titles, 80 serial subscriptions, 5,229 audiovisual materials.

Computer facilities: 33 computers available on campus for general student use. A campuswide network can be accessed. *Web address:* http://www.csj.edu/.

General Application Contact: Alan Young, Dean of Admissions, 802-773-5900 Ext. 3227, Fax: 802-776-5258, E-mail: alanyoung@csj.edu.

GRADUATE UNITS

Graduate Programs Students: 50 full-time (40 women), 95 part-time (69 women); includes 1 Black or African American, non-Hispanic/Latino; 2 Asian, non-Hispanic/Latino; 1 Hispanic/Latino. Average age 28. 59 applicants, 93% accepted, 51 enrolled. *Faculty:* 9 full-time (4 women), 14 part-time/adjunct (8 women). Expenses: Contact institution. *Financial support:* In 2010–11, 4 students received support. Career-related internships or fieldwork, Federal Work-Study, tuition waivers (partial), and unspecified assistantships available. Support available to part-time students. Financial award application deadline: 3/1. In 2010, 41 master's awarded. *Degree program information:* Part-time and evening/weekend programs available. *Application deadline:* Applications are processed on a rolling basis. *Application fee:* $35. Electronic applications accepted. *Application Contact:* Alan Young, Dean of Admissions, 802-773-5900 Ext. 3227, Fax: 802-776-5310, E-mail: alanyoung@csj.edu. *Academic Dean*, Dr. Nancy Kline, 802-773-5900 Ext. 3213, Fax: 802-776-5258, E-mail: nkline@csj.edu.

Division of Business Students: 3 full-time (1 woman), 22 part-time (11 women); includes 1 Asian, non-Hispanic/Latino; 1 Hispanic/Latino. Average age 35. 12 applicants, 92% accepted, 10 enrolled. *Faculty:* 3 full-time (0 women), 3 part-time/adjunct (0 women). Expenses: Contact institution. *Financial support:* In 2010–11, 1 student received support, including 1 teaching assistantship with full tuition reimbursement available (averaging $3,000 per year); Federal Work-Study and unspecified assistantships also available. Support available to part-time students. Financial award application deadline: 3/1. In 2010, 10 master's awarded. *Degree program information:* Part-time and evening/weekend programs available. Offers business administration (MBA). *Application deadline:* Applications are processed on a rolling basis. *Application fee:* $35. Electronic applications accepted. *Application Contact:* Alan Young, Dean of Admissions, 802-773-5900 Ext. 3227, Fax: 802-776-5310, E-mail: alanyoung@csj.edu. *Chair*, Robert Foley, 802-773-5900 Ext. 3248, Fax: 802-776-5258, E-mail: rfoley@csj.edu.

Division of Education Students: 17 full-time (14 women), 40 part-time (31 women); includes 1 Black or African American, non-Hispanic/Latino. Average age 33. 36 applicants, 92% accepted, 24 enrolled. *Faculty:* 3 full-time (all women), 5 part-time/adjunct (all women). Expenses: Contact institution. *Financial support:* Career-related internships or fieldwork, Federal Work-Study, and unspecified assistantships available. Support available to part-time students. Financial award application deadline: 3/1. In 2010, 19 master's awarded. *Degree program information:* Part-time and evening/weekend programs available. Offers elementary education (M Ed); English (M Ed); general education (M Ed); reading (M Ed); secondary education (M Ed); social studies (M Ed); special education (M Ed). *Application deadline:* Applications are processed on a rolling basis. *Application fee:* $35. Electronic applications accepted. *Application Contact:* Alan Young, Dean of Admissions, 802-773-5900 Ext. 3227, Fax: 802-776-5310, E-mail: alanyoung@csj.edu. *Chair*, Dr. Maria Bove, 802-773-5900 Ext. 3243, Fax: 802-776-5258, E-mail: mbove@csj.edu.

Division of Psychology and Human Services Students: 30 full-time (25 women), 32 part-time (26 women); includes 1 Asian, non-Hispanic/Latino. Average age 35. 22 applicants, 91% accepted, 17 enrolled. *Faculty:* 4 full-time (1 woman), 8 part-time/adjunct (4 women). Expenses: Contact institution. *Financial support:* In 2010–11, 3 students received support, including teaching assistantships with tuition reimbursements available (averaging $3,000 per year); career-related internships or fieldwork, Federal Work-Study, and unspecified assistantships also available. Support available to part-time students. Financial award application deadline: 3/1. In 2010, 12 master's awarded. *Degree program information:* Part-time and evening/weekend programs available. Offers alcohol and substance abuse counseling (MS); clinical mental health counseling (MS); clinical psychology (MS); community counseling (MS); school guidance counseling (MS). *Application deadline:* Applications are processed on a rolling basis. *Application fee:* $35. Electronic applications accepted. *Application Contact:* Alan Young, Dean of Admissions, 802-773-5900 Ext. 3227, Fax:

802-776-5310, E-mail: alanyoung@csj.edu. *Chair*, Dr. Craig Knapp, 802-773-5900 Ext. 3219, Fax: 802-776-5258, E-mail: cknapp@csj.edu.

COLLEGE OF SAINT MARY, Omaha, NE 68106

General Information Independent-religious, women only, comprehensive institution.

GRADUATE UNITS

Program in Education *Degree program information:* Part-time programs available. Offers assessment leadership (MSE); English as a second language (MSE).

Program in Health Professions Education *Degree program information:* Part-time programs available. Offers health professions education (Ed D).

Program in Nursing *Degree program information:* Part-time programs available. Offers nursing (MSN).

Program in Occupational Therapy Offers occupational therapy (MOT).

Program in Organizational Leadership *Degree program information:* Part-time and evening/weekend programs available. Offers organizational leadership (MOL). Electronic applications accepted.

Program in Teaching *Degree program information:* Evening/weekend programs available. Offers teaching (MAT).

THE COLLEGE OF SAINT ROSE, Albany, NY 12203-1419

General Information Independent, coed, comprehensive institution. CGS member. *Graduate housing:* On-campus housing not available.

GRADUATE UNITS

Graduate Studies *Degree program information:* Part-time and evening/weekend programs available. Electronic applications accepted.

School of Arts and Humanities *Degree program information:* Part-time and evening/weekend programs available. Offers art education (MS Ed, Certificate); arts and humanities (MA, MS Ed, Certificate); English (MA); history/political science (MA); music (MA); music education (MS Ed, Certificate); public communications (MA).

School of Business *Degree program information:* Part-time and evening/weekend programs available. Offers accounting (MS); business (MBA, MS, Certificate); business administration (MBA); not-for-profit management (Certificate). Electronic applications accepted.

School of Education *Degree program information:* Part-time and evening/weekend programs available. Offers applied technology education (MS Ed); bilingual pupil personnel services (Certificate); business and marketing (MS Ed); childhood education (MS Ed); college student personnel (MS Ed); college student services administration (MS Ed); communication disorders (MS Ed); community counseling (MS Ed); counseling (MS Ed); curriculum and instruction (MS Ed); early childhood education (MS Ed); education (MS, MS Ed, Certificate); educational administration and supervision (MS Ed, Certificate); educational leadership and administration (MS Ed); educational leadership and administrationûschool building leader (Certificate); educational leadership and administrationûschool district leader (Certificate); educational psychology (MS Ed); elementary education (K-6) (MS Ed); literacy: birth-grade 6 (MS Ed); literacy: grades 5-12 (MS Ed); reading (Certificate); school administrator and supervisor (Certificate); school counseling (MS Ed); school psychology (MS, Certificate); secondary education (MS Ed, Certificate); special education (MS Ed); teacher education (MS Ed, Certificate). Electronic applications accepted.

School of Mathematics and Sciences *Degree program information:* Part-time and evening/weekend programs available. Offers computer information systems (MS); mathematics and sciences (MS). Electronic applications accepted.

THE COLLEGE OF ST. SCHOLASTICA, Duluth, MN 55811-4199

General Information Independent-religious, coed, comprehensive institution. *Enrollment:* 3,898 graduate, professional, and undergraduate students; 401 full-time matriculated graduate/professional students (318 women), 306 part-time matriculated graduate/professional students (219 women). *Enrollment by degree level:* 111 first professional, 540 master's, 56 other advanced degrees. *Graduate faculty:* 50 full-time (33 women), 35 part-time/adjunct (25 women). *Graduate housing:* Room and/or apartments available on a first-come, first-served basis to single students; on-campus housing not available to married students. Housing application deadline: 2/5. *Student services:* Campus employment opportunities, campus safety program, career counseling, exercise/wellness program, free psychological counseling, international student services, low-cost health insurance, multicultural affairs office, services for students with disabilities, writing training. *Library facilities:* College of St. Scholastica Library. *Online resources:* library catalog, web page, access to other libraries' catalogs. *Collection:* 118,042 titles, 55,088 serial subscriptions, 5,843 audiovisual materials.

Computer facilities: 394 computers available on campus for general student use. A campuswide network can be accessed from student residence rooms and from off campus. Online class registration, student account information and transcripts online are available. *Web address:* http://www.css.edu/.

General Application Contact: Chad J. Oppelt, Graduate Recruitment Counselor, 218-723-6285, Fax: 218-733-2275, E-mail: gradstudies@css.edu.

GRADUATE UNITS

Graduate Studies Students: 677 full-time (504 women), 355 part-time (259 women); includes 68 minority (22 Black or African American, non-Hispanic/Latino; 15 American Indian or Alaska Native, non-Hispanic/Latino; 14 Asian, non-Hispanic/Latino; 7 Hispanic/Latino; 10 Two or more races, non-Hispanic/Latino), 7 international. Average age 35. 467 applicants, 76% accepted. *Faculty:* 50 full-time (33 women), 35 part-time/adjunct (25 women). Expenses: Contact institution. *Financial support:* In 2010–11, 362 students received support, including 16 teaching assistantships (averaging $1,583 per year); scholarships/grants and traineeships also available. Support available to part-time students. Financial award applicants required to submit FAFSA. In 2010, 189 master's, 64 doctorates awarded. *Degree program information:* Part-time and evening/weekend programs available. Postbaccalaureate distance learning degree programs offered (minimal on-campus study). Offers computer information systems (MA, Certificate); educational media and technology (M Ed); exercise physiology (MA); health information management (MA, Certificate); management (MA, Certificate); nursing (MA, PMC); occupational therapy (MA); physical therapy (DPT); teaching (M Ed, Certificate). *Application deadline:* For fall admission, 8/1 priority date for domestic students, 8/1 for international students; for spring admission, 11/15 priority date for domestic students, 11/15 for international students. Applications are processed on a rolling basis. *Application fee:* $50. Electronic applications accepted. *Application Contact:* Lindsey Lahti, Director of Graduate and Extended Studies Recruitment, 218-733-2240, Fax: 218-733-2275, E-mail: gradstudies@css.edu. *Vice President for Academic Affairs*, Dr. Beth Domholt, 218-723-6012, Fax: 218-723-6278, E-mail: bdomhold@css.edu.

COLLEGE OF STATEN ISLAND OF THE CITY UNIVERSITY OF NEW YORK, Staten Island, NY 10314-6600

General Information State and locally supported, coed, comprehensive institution. CGS member. *Enrollment:* 13,894 graduate, professional, and undergraduate students; 124 full-time matriculated graduate/professional students (28 women), 854 part-time matriculated graduate/professional students (235 women). *Enrollment by degree level:* 929 master's, 49 other advanced degrees. *Graduate faculty:* 74 full-time (38 women), 58 part-time/adjunct (31 women). Tuition, state resident: full-time $7730; part-time $325 per credit. Tuition, nonresident: full-time $14,520; part-time $605 per credit. *Required fees:* $378. *Graduate housing:* On-campus housing not available. *Student services:* Campus employment opportunities, campus safety program, career counseling, child daycare facilities, exercise/wellness program, free psychological counseling, international student services, low-cost health insurance, multicultural affairs office, services for students with disabilities, teacher training, writing training. *Library facilities:* College of Staten Island Library. *Online resources:* library catalog, web page, access to other libraries' catalogs. *Collection:* 350,000 titles, 42,800 serial subscriptions, 5,000 audiovisual materials. *Research affiliation:* PALL Corp (service agreement), Nulastin, Inc. (improvement of wound care preparations), Applied Nano Works, Inc. (catalysts and catalysts composite

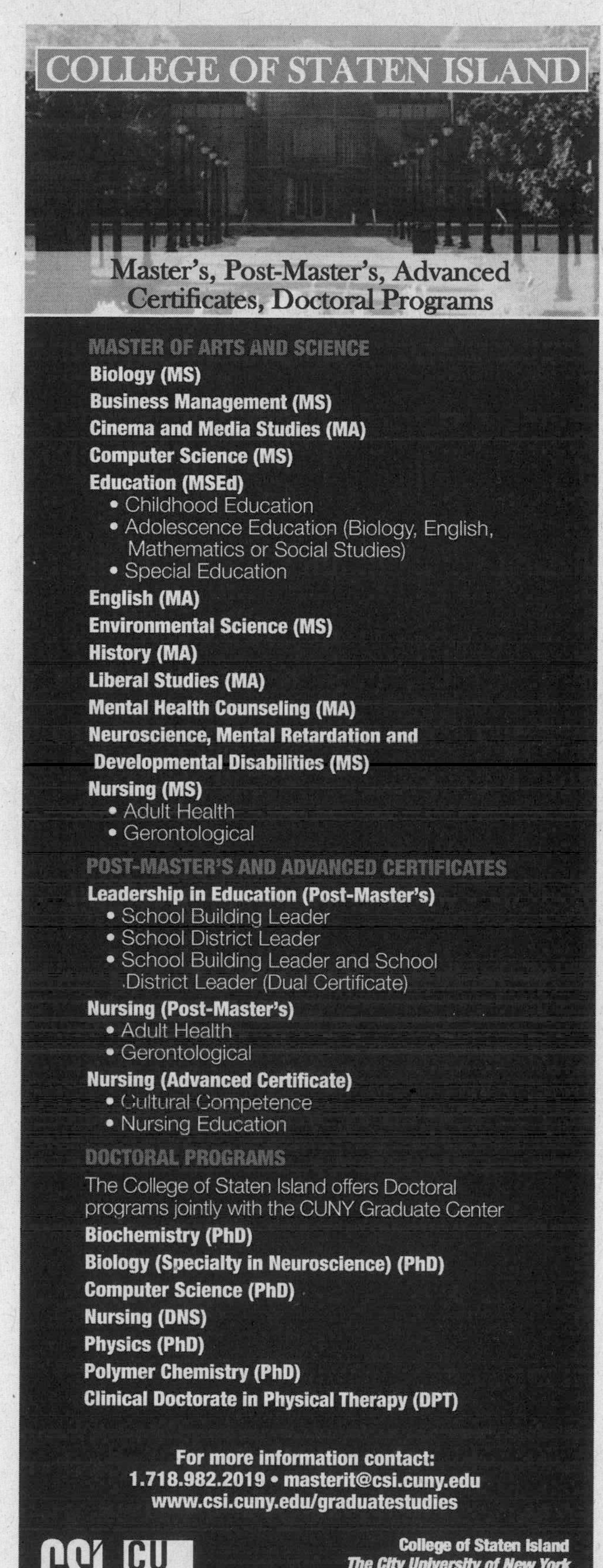

College of Staten Island of the City University of New York (continued)

beads), Kuraray America (polycetal research and acetal ring), Nulastin (polymer based wound care preparations involving tropelastin).

Computer facilities: 1,254 computers available on campus for general student use. A campuswide network can be accessed from off campus. Online class registration is available. *Web address:* http://www.csi.cuny.edu/.

General Application Contact: Sasha Spence, Assistant Director of Graduate Recruitment and Admissions, 718-982-2699, Fax: 718-982-2500, E-mail: sasha.spence@csi.cuny.edu.

GRADUATE UNITS

Graduate Programs Students: 124 full-time (96 women), 854 part-time (619 women); includes 154 minority (38 Black or African American, non-Hispanic/Latino; 51 Asian, non-Hispanic/Latino; 64 Hispanic/Latino; 1 Two or more races, non-Hispanic/Latino), 35 international. Average age 30. *Faculty:* 74 full-time (38 women), 58 part-time/adjunct (31 women). Expenses: Contact institution. In 2010, 238 master's, 15 other advanced degrees awarded. Offers adolescence education (MS Ed); adult health nursing (MS, 6th Year Certificate); biology (MS); business management (MS); childhood education (MS Ed); cinema and media studies (MA); computer science (MS); cultural competence (6th Year Certificate); English (MA); gerontological nursing (MS, 6th Year Certificate); history (MA); leadership in education (6th Year Certificate); liberal studies (MA); mental health counseling (MA); nursing education (6th Year Certificate); special education (MS Ed). *Application Contact:* Sasha Spence, Assistant Director of Graduate Recruitment and Admissions, 718-982-2699, Fax: 718-982-2500, E-mail: sasha.spence@csi.cuny.edu. *Provost/Senior Vice President for Academic Affairs*, Dr. William J. Fritz, 718-982-2440, Fax: 718-982-2442, E-mail: william.fritz@csi.cuny.edu.

Center for Developmental Neuroscience and Developmental Disabilities Students: 1 (woman) full-time, 32 part-time (18 women); includes 1 Black or African American, non-Hispanic/Latino; 4 Asian, non-Hispanic/Latino; 2 Hispanic/Latino, 2 international. Average age 27. 26 applicants, 58% accepted, 10 enrolled. *Faculty:* 7 full-time (1 woman), 3 part-time/adjunct (1 woman). Expenses: Contact institution. *Financial support:* In 2010–11, 1 student received support. Career-related internships or fieldwork and Federal Work-Study available. Financial award applicants required to submit FAFSA. In 2010, 2 master's awarded. *Degree program information:* Part-time and evening/weekend programs available. Offers neuroscience, mental retardation and developmental disabilities (MS). *Application deadline:* Applications are processed on a rolling basis. *Application fee:* $125. Electronic applications accepted. *Application Contact:* Sasha Spence, Assistant Director of Graduate Recruitment and Admissions, 718-982-2699, Fax: 718-982-2500, E-mail: sasha.spence@csi.cuny.edu. *Coordinator*, Dr. Probal Banerjee, 718-982-3950, Fax: 718-982-3953, E-mail: banerjee@mail.csi.cuny.edu.

Center for Environmental Science Students: 33 part-time (17 women); includes 9 minority (3 Black or African American, non-Hispanic/Latino; 5 Asian, non-Hispanic/Latino; 1 Hispanic/Latino), 4 international. Average age 30. 19 applicants, 84% accepted, 7 enrolled. *Faculty:* 5 full-time (3 women), 4 part-time/adjunct (2 women). Expenses: Contact institution. *Financial support:* In 2010–11, 6 research assistantships (averaging $2,000 per year) were awarded; career-related internships or fieldwork, Federal Work-Study, and scholarships/grants also available. Support available to part-time students. Financial award applicants required to submit FAFSA. In 2010, 6 master's awarded. *Degree program information:* Part-time and evening/weekend programs available. Offers environmental science (MS). *Application deadline:* Applications are processed on a rolling basis. *Application fee:* $125. Electronic applications accepted. *Application Contact:* Sasha Spence, Assistant Director of Graduate Recruitment and Admissions, 718-982-2699, Fax: 718-982-2500, E-mail: sasha.spence@csi.cuny.edu. *Director*, Dr. Alfred Levine, 718-982-2822, Fax: 718-982-3923, E-mail: envirscimasters@mail.csi.cuny.edu.

See Display on previous page and Close-Up on page 937.

COLLEGE OF THE ATLANTIC, Bar Harbor, ME 04609-1198

General Information Independent, coed, comprehensive institution. *Graduate housing:* Room and/or apartments available to single students; on-campus housing not available to married students. Housing application deadline: 6/1. *Research affiliation:* Acadia National Park, National Park Service (research management, environmental education), Mount Desert Island Biological Laboratory, Jackson Laboratory (genetics), Society for Human Ecology (ecological decision making in society).

GRADUATE UNITS

Program in Human Ecology Offers human ecology (M Phil).

COLLEGE OF THE HUMANITIES AND SCIENCES, HARRISON MIDDLETON UNIVERSITY, Tempe, AZ 85282

General Information Independent, coed, comprehensive institution. *Enrollment:* 152 graduate, professional, and undergraduate students; 52 full-time matriculated graduate/professional students (20 women). *Enrollment by degree level:* 16 master's, 36 doctoral. *Graduate faculty:* 17 full-time (7 women), 5 part-time/adjunct (2 women). *Tuition:* Part-time $300 per credit hour. One-time fee: $350 part-time. *Student services:* Career counseling, teacher training, writing training. *Web address:* http://www.hmu.edu/.

General Application Contact: Deborah Deacon, Dean of Graduate Studies, 877-248-6724, Fax: 800-762-1622, E-mail: ddeacon@hmu.edu.

GRADUATE UNITS

Graduate Program Students: 52 full-time (20 women). *Faculty:* 17 full-time (7 women), 14 part-time/adjunct (6 women). Expenses: Contact institution. In 2010, 4 master's awarded. *Degree program information:* Part-time and evening/weekend programs available. Post-baccalaureate distance learning degree programs offered (no on-campus study). Offers education (MA, Ed D); humanities (MA); imaginative literature (MA); interdisciplinary studies (DA); jurisprudence (MA); natural science (MA); philosophy and religion (MA); social science (MA). *Application deadline:* Applications are processed on a rolling basis. *Application fee:* $50. Electronic applications accepted. *Application Contact:* Deborah Deacon, Dean of Graduate Studies, 877-248-6724, Fax: 800-762-1622, E-mail: ddeacon@hmu.edu.

THE COLLEGE OF WILLIAM AND MARY, Williamsburg, VA 23187-8795

General Information State-supported, coed, university. CGS member. *Enrollment:* 8,000 graduate, professional, and undergraduate students; 1,664 full-time matriculated graduate/professional students (861 women), 355 part-time matriculated graduate/professional students (162 women). *Enrollment by degree level:* 630 first professional, 967 master's, 399 doctoral, 23 other advanced degrees. *Graduate faculty:* 658 full-time (257 women), 173 part-time/adjunct (77 women). Tuition, state resident: full-time $6400; part-time $345 per credit hour. Tuition, nonresident: full-time $19,720; part-time $920 per credit hour. *Required fees:* $4368. *Graduate housing:* Room and/or apartments available on a first-come, first-served basis to single students; on-campus housing not available to married students. Housing application deadline: 2/14. *Student services:* Campus employment opportunities, campus safety program, career counseling, child daycare facilities, exercise/wellness program, free psychological counseling, grant writing training, international student services, low-cost health insurance, multicultural affairs office, services for students with disabilities, teacher training, writing training. *Library facilities:* Swem Library plus 8 others. *Online resources:* library catalog, web page. *Collection:* 2.2 million titles, 102,516 serial subscriptions, 39,823 audiovisual materials. *Research affiliation:* Center for Excellence in Aging and Geriatric Health (public policy, kinesiology), Colonial Williamsburg (archaeology, history), Thomas Jefferson National Accelerator Facility (nuclear physics), Court Records Solutions (law and technology), AidData (online portal of global aid flows and development finance), James City County Business and Technology Incubator (economic development).

Computer facilities: Computer purchase and lease plans are available. 350 computers available on campus for general student use. A campuswide network can be accessed from student residence rooms. Online class registration is available. *Web address:* http://www.wm.edu/.

General Application Contact: Dr. Susan Bosworth, Associate Provost of Institutional Analysis and Effectiveness, 757-221-3584, Fax: 757-221-2080, E-mail: slbosw@wm.edu.

GRADUATE UNITS

Faculty of Arts and Sciences Students: 384 full-time (182 women), 22 part-time (12 women); includes 34 minority (13 Black or African American, non-Hispanic/Latino; 2 American Indian or Alaska Native, non-Hispanic/Latino; 6 Asian, non-Hispanic/Latino; 8 Hispanic/Latino; 5 Two or more races, non-Hispanic/Latino), 98 international. Average age 28. 839 applicants, 29% accepted, 119 enrolled. *Faculty:* 463 full-time (181 women), 103 part-time/adjunct (46 women). Expenses: Contact institution. *Financial support:* Fellowships, research assistantships, teaching assistantships, career-related internships or fieldwork, Federal Work-Study, institutionally sponsored loans, and unspecified assistantships available. Financial award applicants required to submit FAFSA. In 2010, 113 master's, 27 doctorates awarded. *Degree program information:* Part-time programs available. Offers American studies (MA, PhD); anthropology (MA, PhD); applied science (MS, PhD); arts and sciences (MA, MPP, MS, PhD); biology (MS); chemistry (MA, MS); computational operations research (MS); computer science (MS, PhD); history (MA, PhD); physics (MS, PhD); psychology (MA); public policy (MPP). *Application fee:* $45. *Application Contact:* Wanda Carter, Administrator of Graduate Student Services, 757-221-2467, Fax: 757-221-4874, E-mail: wdcart@wm.edu. *Dean of Graduate Studies and Research*, Dr. Laurie Sanderson, 757-221-2468, E-mail: slsand@wm.edu.

Mason School of Business Students: 324 full-time (124 women), 185 part-time (44 women); includes 52 minority (15 Black or African American, non-Hispanic/Latino; 19 Asian, non-Hispanic/Latino; 14 Hispanic/Latino; 2 Native Hawaiian or other Pacific Islander, non-Hispanic/Latino; 2 Two or more races, non-Hispanic/Latino), 91 international. Average age 29. 761 applicants, 51% accepted, 224 enrolled. *Faculty:* 52 full-time (13 women), 11 part-time/adjunct (1 woman). Expenses: Contact institution. *Financial support:* In 2010–11, 10 fellowships, 62 research assistantships with partial tuition reimbursements were awarded; career-related internships or fieldwork, scholarships/grants, and unspecified assistantships also available. Financial award application deadline: 3/7; financial award applicants required to submit FAFSA. In 2010, 255 master's awarded. *Degree program information:* Part-time and evening/weekend programs available. Offers accounting (M Acc); business administration (EMBA, MBA). *Application deadline:* For fall admission, 11/1 for domestic students, 11/6 for international students; for winter admission, 1/10 for domestic and international students; for spring admission, 3/5 for domestic students, 3/7 for international students. *Application fee:* $100. Electronic applications accepted. *Application Contact:* Amanda K. Barth, Director, Full-time MBA Admissions, 757-221-2944, Fax: 757-221-2958, E-mail: amanda.barth@mason.wm.edu. *Dean*, Dr. Lawrence Pulley, 757-221-2891, Fax: 757-221-2937, E-mail: larry.pulley@mason.wm.edu.

School of Education Students: 208 full-time (165 women), 159 part-time (116 women); includes 63 minority (43 Black or African American, non-Hispanic/Latino; 5 Asian, non-Hispanic/Latino; 9 Hispanic/Latino; 6 Two or more races, non-Hispanic/Latino), 8 international. Average age 33. 529 applicants, 51% accepted, 163 enrolled. *Faculty:* 40 full-time (22 women), 50 part-time/adjunct (39 women). Expenses: Contact institution. *Financial support:* In 2010–11, 168 students received support, including 1 fellowship with full tuition reimbursement available (averaging $20,000 per year), 112 research assistantships with full and partial tuition reimbursements available (averaging $13,000 per year); career-related internships or fieldwork, Federal Work-Study, institutionally sponsored loans, scholarships/grants, and unspecified assistantships also available. Financial award application deadline: 1/15; financial award applicants required to submit FAFSA. In 2010, 117 master's, 20 doctorates, 12 other advanced degrees awarded. *Degree program information:* Part-time and evening/weekend programs available. Offers community and addictions counseling (M Ed); community counseling (M Ed); counselor education (PhD); curriculum and educational technology (Ed D, PhD); curriculum leadership (Ed D, PhD); education (M Ed, MA Ed, Ed D, PhD, Ed S); educational leadership (M Ed); educational policy, planning, and leadership (Ed D, PhD); elementary education (MA Ed); family counseling (M Ed); gifted education (MA Ed); gifted education administration (M Ed); math specialist (MA Ed); reading education (MA Ed); school counseling (M Ed); school psychology (M Ed, Ed S); secondary education (MA Ed); special education (MA Ed). *Application deadline:* For fall admission, 1/15 for domestic and international students; for spring admission, 10/1 for domestic and international students. *Application fee:* $50. Electronic applications accepted. *Application Contact:* Dorothy Smith Osborne, Assistant Dean for Admission, 757-221-2317, Fax: 757-221-2293, E-mail: dsosbo@wm.edu. *Dean*, Dr. Virginia McLaughlin, 757-221-2317, E-mail: vamcla@wm.edu.

Virginia Institute of Marine Science Students: 100 full-time (66 women), 6 part-time (4 women); includes 11 minority (3 Black or African American, non-Hispanic/Latino; 1 American Indian or Alaska Native, non-Hispanic/Latino; 2 Asian, non-Hispanic/Latino; 2 Hispanic/Latino; 2 Native Hawaiian or other Pacific Islander, non-Hispanic/Latino; 1 Two or more races, non-Hispanic/Latino), 13 international. Average age 28. 118 applicants, 29% accepted, 27 enrolled. *Faculty:* 53 full-time (14 women), 8 part-time/adjunct (0 women). Expenses: Contact institution. *Financial support:* In 2010–11, 97 students received support, including 16 fellowships with full tuition reimbursements available (averaging $19,005 per year), 73 research assistantships with full tuition reimbursements available (averaging $19,005 per year), 8 teaching assistantships with partial tuition reimbursements available (averaging $6,500 per year); career-related internships or fieldwork, Federal Work-Study, scholarships/grants, health care benefits, and unspecified assistantships also available. Support available to part-time students. Financial award application deadline: 6/15; financial award applicants required to submit FAFSA. In 2010, 10 master's, 15 doctorates awarded. Offers marine science (MS, PhD). *Application deadline:* For fall admission, 1/15 for domestic and international students. *Application fee:* $50. Electronic applications accepted. *Application Contact:* Fonda J. Powell, Admissions Coordinator, 804-684-7105, Fax: 804-684-7881, E-mail: fonda@vims.edu. *Dean/Director*, Dr. John T. Wells, 804-684-7102, Fax: 804-684-7009, E-mail: wells@vims.edu.

William and Mary Law School Students: 649 full-time (323 women); includes 126 minority (81 Black or African American, non-Hispanic/Latino; 25 Asian, non-Hispanic/Latino; 12 Hispanic/Latino; 8 Two or more races, non-Hispanic/Latino), 19 international. Average age 25. 6,502 applicants, 20% accepted, 233 enrolled. *Faculty:* 39 full-time (17 women), 45 part-time/adjunct (12 women). Expenses: Contact institution. *Financial support:* In 2010–11, 371 students received support, including 194 fellowships with partial tuition reimbursements available (averaging $4,000 per year), 16 research assistantships (averaging $1,575 per year), 36 teaching assistantships (averaging $4,000 per year); career-related internships or fieldwork, scholarships/grants, and unspecified assistantships also available. Financial award application deadline: 2/15; financial award applicants required to submit FAFSA. In 2010, 214 first professional degrees, 25 master's awarded. Offers law (JD, LL M). *Application deadline:* For fall admission, 3/1 priority date for domestic and international students. *Application fee:* $50. Electronic applications accepted. *Application Contact:* Faye F. Shealy, Associate Dean for Admission, 757-221-3785, Fax: 757-221-3261, E-mail: ffshea@wm.edu. *Dean/Professor*, Davison M. Douglas, 757-221-3790, Fax: 757-221-3261, E-mail: dmdoug@wm.edu.

COLLÈGE UNIVERSITAIRE DE SAINT-BONIFACE, Saint-Boniface, MB R2H 0H7, Canada

General Information Independent-religious, coed, comprehensive institution.

GRADUATE UNITS

Department of Education Offers education (M Ed).

Program in Canadian Studies Offers Canadian studies (MA).

COLORADO CHRISTIAN UNIVERSITY, Lakewood, CO 80226

General Information Independent-religious, coed, comprehensive institution. *Enrollment:* 234 full-time matriculated graduate/professional students (160 women), 162 part-time matriculated graduate/professional students (122 women). *Enrollment by degree level:* 230 master's, 15 other advanced degrees. *Graduate faculty:* 27 full-time (15 women), 170 part-time/adjunct (102 women). *Graduate housing:* On-campus housing not available. *Student services:* Campus employment opportunities, campus safety program, free psychological counseling, teacher training, writing training. *Library facilities:* Clifton Fowler Library plus 1 other. *Online resources:* library catalog, web page.

Computer facilities: A campuswide network can be accessed from student residence rooms and from off campus. Online class registration is available. *Web address:* http://www.ccu.edu/.

General Application Contact: College of Adult and Graduate Studies, 303-963-3300, Fax: 303-963-3301, E-mail: agsadmission@ccu.edu.

GRADUATE UNITS

Program in Business Administration Students: 65 full-time (33 women), 35 part-time (19 women); includes 6 Black or African American, non-Hispanic/Latino; 2 Asian, non-Hispanic/Latino; 9 Hispanic/Latino. Average age 37. 25 applicants, 20% accepted. *Faculty:* 10 full-time (7 women), 35 part-time/adjunct (17 women). Expenses: Contact institution. *Financial support:* In 2010–11, 27 students received support. Scholarships/grants and tuition waivers (full and partial) available. Support available to part-time students. Financial award application deadline: 3/1; financial award applicants required to submit FAFSA. *Degree program information:* Part-time and evening/weekend programs available. Postbaccalaureate distance learning degree programs offered (minimal on-campus study). Offers corporate training (MBA); information security (MA); leadership (MBA); project management (MBA). *Application deadline:* For fall admission, 8/25 priority date for domestic and international students; for spring admission, 1/12 priority date for domestic and international students. Applications are processed on a rolling basis. *Application fee:* $40. Electronic applications accepted. *Application Contact:* Dr. Mellani Day, Dean of Business and Technology, 303-963-3300, Fax: 303-963-3301, E-mail: agsadmission@ccu.edu. *Dean of Business and Technology*, Dr. Mellani Day, 303-963-3300, Fax: 303-963-3301, E-mail: agsadmission@ccu.edu.

Program in Counseling Students: 35 full-time (28 women), 71 part-time (57 women); includes 5 Black or African American, non-Hispanic/Latino; 3 Asian, non-Hispanic/Latino; 11 Hispanic/Latino. 33 applicants, 21% accepted. *Faculty:* 12 full-time (5 women), 56 part-time/adjunct (39 women). Expenses: Contact institution. *Financial support:* In 2010–11, 27 students received support. Scholarships/grants and tuition waivers (full and partial) available. Support available to part-time students. Financial award application deadline: 3/1; financial award applicants required to submit FAFSA. *Degree program information:* Part-time and evening/weekend programs available. Offers counseling (MAC). *Application deadline:* For fall admission, 8/25 priority date for domestic and international students; for spring admission, 1/12 priority date for domestic and international students. Applications are processed on a rolling basis. *Application fee:* $40. Electronic applications accepted. *Application Contact:* College of Adult and Graduate Studies, 303-963-3300, Fax: 303-963-3301, E-mail: agsadmission@ccu.edu. *Dean of Social Sciences and Humanities*, Dr. Laverne Jordan, 303-963-3300, Fax: 303-963-3301, E-mail: agsadmission@ccu.edu.

Program in Curriculum and Instruction Students: 35 full-time (28 women), 71 part-time (57 women); includes 5 Black or African American, non-Hispanic/Latino; 2 Asian, non-Hispanic/Latino; 4 Hispanic/Latino. Average age 36. 13 applicants, 38% accepted. *Faculty:* 5 full-time (3 women), 79 part-time/adjunct (45 women). Expenses: Contact institution. *Financial support:* Scholarships/grants and tuition waivers (full and partial) available. Support available to part-time students. Financial award application deadline: 3/1; financial award applicants required to submit FAFSA. In 2010, 70 master's awarded. *Degree program information:* Part-time and evening/weekend programs available. Offers corporate education (MACI); early childhood educator (MACI); elementary educator (MACI); instructional technology (MACI); master educator (MACI); online course developer (MACI); online teaching and learning (MACI); special education generalist (MACI). *Application deadline:* For fall admission, 8/25 priority date for domestic and international students; for spring admission, 1/12 priority date for domestic and international students. Applications are processed on a rolling basis. *Application fee:* $40. Electronic applications accepted. *Application Contact:* Dr. Wendy Wendover, Dean, 303-963-3300, Fax: 303-963-3301, E-mail: agsadmission@ccu.edu. *Dean*, Dr. Wendy Wendover, 303-963-3300, Fax: 303-963-3301, E-mail: agsadmission@ccu.edu.

THE COLORADO COLLEGE, Colorado Springs, CO 80903-3294

General Information Independent, coed, comprehensive institution. *Graduate housing:* On-campus housing not available.

GRADUATE UNITS

Department of Education Offers art teaching (K-12) (MAT); arts and humanities (MAT); elementary education (MAT); elementary school teaching (MAT); English teaching (MAT); foreign language teaching (MAT); liberal arts (MAT); mathematics teaching (MAT); music teaching (MAT); science teaching (MAT); secondary education (MAT); social studies teaching (MAT); Southwest studies (MAT).

COLORADO SCHOOL OF MINES, Golden, CO 80401-1887

General Information State-supported, coed, university. CGS member. *Enrollment:* 5,093 graduate, professional, and undergraduate students; 1,052 full-time matriculated graduate/professional students (289 women), 169 part-time matriculated graduate/professional students (44 women). *Enrollment by degree level:* 734 master's, 487 doctoral. *Graduate faculty:* 323 full-time (74 women), 100 part-time/adjunct (26 women). Tuition, state resident: full-time $11,550; part-time $641 per credit. Tuition, nonresident: full-time $25,980; part-time $1444 per credit. *Required fees:* $1874; $937 per semester. *Graduate housing:* Rooms and/or apartments available on a first-come, first-served basis to single and married students. Typical cost: $7452 per year ($11,378 including board) for single students; $8748 per year for married students. *Student services:* Campus employment opportunities, campus safety program, career counseling, exercise/wellness program, free psychological counseling, international student services, low-cost health insurance, services for students with disabilities, teacher training, writing training. *Library facilities:* Arthur Lakes Library. *Online resources:* library catalog, web page, access to other libraries' catalogs. *Collection:* 412,560 titles, 26,399 serial subscriptions, 306 audiovisual materials.

Computer facilities: Computer purchase and lease plans are available. 400 computers available on campus for general student use. A campuswide network can be accessed from student residence rooms and from off campus. Online class registration is available. *Web address:* http://www.mines.edu/.

General Application Contact: Kay Leaman, Graduate Admissions Coordinator, 303-273-3249, Fax: 303-273-3244, E-mail: grad-app@mines.edu.

GRADUATE UNITS

Graduate School Students: 1,052 full-time (289 women), 169 part-time (44 women); includes 98 minority (10 Black or African American, non-Hispanic/Latino; 10 American Indian or Alaska Native, non-Hispanic/Latino; 31 Asian, non-Hispanic/Latino; 44 Hispanic/Latino; 1 Native Hawaiian or other Pacific Islander, non-Hispanic/Latino; 2 Two or more races, non-Hispanic/Latino), 331 international. Average age 29. 1,751 applicants, 50% accepted, 416 enrolled. *Faculty:* 323 full-time (74 women), 100 part-time/adjunct (26 women). Expenses: Contact institution. *Financial support:* In 2010–11, 699 students received support, including 82 fellowships with full tuition reimbursements available (averaging $20,000 per year), 420 research assistantships with full tuition reimbursements available (averaging $20,000 per year), 197 teaching assistantships with full tuition reimbursements available (averaging $20,000 per year); career-related internships or fieldwork, Federal Work-Study, institutionally sponsored loans, scholarships/grants, health care benefits, and unspecified assistantships also available. Financial award application deadline: 1/15; financial award applicants required to submit FAFSA. In 2010, 325 master's, 49 doctorates awarded. *Degree program information:* Part-time programs available. Offers applied chemistry (PhD); applied physics (MS, PhD); chemical engineering (MS, PhD); chemistry (MS, PhD); engineer of mines (ME); geochemistry (MS, PhD); geological engineering (ME, MS, PhD); geology (MS, PhD); geophysical engineering (ME, MS, PhD); geophysics (MS, PhD); materials science (MS, PhD); mathematical and computer sciences (MS, PhD); metallurgical and materials engineering (ME, MS, PhD); mineral exploration and mining geosciences (PMS); mining and earth systems engineering (MS); mining engineering (PhD); nuclear engineering (MS, PhD); petroleum engineering (ME, MS, PhD); petroleum reservoir systems (PMS). *Application deadline:* For fall admission, 1/15 priority date for domestic and international students; for spring admission, 10/15 priority date for domestic and international students. *Application fee:* $50 ($70 for international students). Electronic applications accepted. *Application Contact:* Kay Leaman, Graduate Admissions Coordinator, 303-273-3249, Fax: 303-273-3244, E-mail: grad-app@mines.edu. *Dean of Graduate Studies*, Dr. Tom M. Boyd, 303-273-3020, Fax: 303-273-3244, E-mail: tboyd@mines.edu.

Division of Economics and Business Students: 121 full-time (22 women), 23 part-time (5 women); includes 1 Black or African American, non-Hispanic/Latino; 2 American Indian or Alaska Native, non-Hispanic/Latino; 1 Asian, non-Hispanic/Latino; 6 Hispanic/Latino, 31 international. Average age 29. 179 applicants, 72% accepted, 63 enrolled. *Faculty:* 12 full-time (3 women), 8 part-time/adjunct (1 woman). Expenses: Contact institution. *Financial support:* In 2010–11, 45 students received support, including 6 fellowships with full tuition reimbursements available (averaging $20,000 per year), 11 research assistantships with full tuition reimbursements available (averaging $20,000 per year), 28 teaching assistantships with full tuition reimbursements available (averaging $20,000 per year); scholarships/grants, health care benefits, and unspecified assistantships also available. Financial award application deadline: 1/15; financial award applicants required to submit FAFSA. In 2010, 70 master's, 3 doctorates awarded. *Degree program information:* Part-time programs available. Offers engineering and technology management (MS); mineral economics (MS, PhD). *Application deadline:* For fall admission, 1/15 priority date for domestic and international students; for spring admission, 10/15 priority date for domestic and international students. *Application fee:* $50 ($70 for international students). Electronic applications accepted. *Application Contact:* Kathleen A. Feighny, Administrative Faculty, 303-273-3979, Fax: 303-273-3416, E-mail: kfeighny@mines.edu. *Division Head*, Dr. Rod Eggert, 303-273-3981, Fax: 303-273-3416, E-mail: reggert@mines.edu.

Division of Engineering Students: 171 full-time (34 women), 53 part-time (5 women); includes 1 Black or African American, non-Hispanic/Latino; 1 American Indian or Alaska Native, non-Hispanic/Latino; 9 Asian, non-Hispanic/Latino; 12 Hispanic/Latino, 41 international. Average age 30. 245 applicants, 74% accepted, 73 enrolled. *Faculty:* 39 full-time (7 women), 21 part-time/adjunct (4 women). Expenses: Contact institution. *Financial support:* In 2010–11, 102 students received support, including 29 fellowships with full tuition reimbursements available (averaging $20,000 per year), 53 research assistantships with full tuition reimbursements available (averaging $20,000 per year), 20 teaching assistantships with full tuition reimbursements available (averaging $20,000 per year); scholarships/grants, health care benefits, and unspecified assistantships also available. Financial award application deadline: 1/15; financial award applicants required to submit FAFSA. In 2010, 69 master's, 4 doctorates awarded. *Degree program information:* Part-time programs available. Offers engineering systems (ME, MS, PhD). *Application deadline:* For fall admission, 1/15 priority date for domestic and international students; for spring admission, 10/15 priority date for domestic and international students. *Application fee:* $50 ($70 for international students). Electronic applications accepted. *Application Contact:* Sara Perna, Administrative Assistant, 303-384-2394, Fax: 303-273-3602, E-mail: sperna@mines.edu. *Division Director*, Dr. Kevin Moore, 303-273-3899, Fax: 303-273-3602, E-mail: kmoore@mines.edu.

Division of Environmental Science and Engineering Students: 90 full-time (45 women), 22 part-time (12 women); includes 3 Black or African American, non-Hispanic/Latino; 3 Asian, non-Hispanic/Latino; 8 Hispanic/Latino; 1 Two or more races, non-Hispanic/Latino, 9 international. Average age 28. 154 applicants, 54% accepted, 36 enrolled. *Faculty:* 22 full-time (5 women), 8 part-time/adjunct (3 women). Expenses: Contact institution. *Financial support:* In 2010–11, 41 students received support, including 1 fellowship with full tuition reimbursement available (averaging $20,000 per year), 38 research assistantships with full tuition reimbursements available (averaging $20,000 per year), 2 teaching assistantships with full tuition reimbursements available (averaging $20,000 per year); scholarships/grants, health care benefits, and unspecified assistantships also available. Financial award application deadline: 1/15; financial award applicants required to submit FAFSA. In 2010, 37 master's, 4 doctorates awarded. *Degree program information:* Part-time programs available. Offers environmental science and engineering (MS, PhD). *Application deadline:* For fall admission, 1/15 priority date for domestic and international students; for spring admission, 10/15 priority date for domestic and international students. *Application fee:* $50 ($70 for international students). Electronic applications accepted. *Application Contact:* Tim VanHaverbeke, Research Faculty, 303-273-3467, Fax: 303-273-3413, E-mail: tvanhave@mines.edu. *Division Director*, Dr. John McCray, 303-384-3490, Fax: 303-273-3413, E-mail: jmccray@mines.edu.

Division of Liberal Arts and International Studies Students: 17 full-time (6 women), 2 part-time (1 woman); includes 2 Asian, non-Hispanic/Latino; 1 Hispanic/Latino, 4 international. Average age 28. 16 applicants, 88% accepted, 11 enrolled. *Faculty:* 20 full-time (9 women), 18 part-time/adjunct (8 women). Expenses: Contact institution. *Financial support:* In 2010–11, 11 students received support, including fellowships with full tuition reimbursements available (averaging $20,000 per year), research assistantships with full tuition reimbursements available (averaging $20,000 per year), 11 teaching assistantships with full tuition reimbursements available (averaging $20,000 per year); scholarships/grants, health care benefits, and unspecified assistantships also available. Financial award application deadline: 1/15. In 2010, 7 master's awarded. *Degree program information:* Part-time programs available. Offers international political economy (Graduate Certificate); liberal arts and international studies (MIPER); science and technology policy (Graduate Certificate). *Application deadline:* For fall admission, 1/15 priority date for domestic and international students; for spring admission, 10/15 priority date for domestic and international students. *Application fee:* $50 ($70 for international students). Electronic applications accepted. *Application Contact:* Connie Warren, Program Assistant, 303-273-3590, Fax: 303-273-3751, E-mail: cwarren@mines.edu. *Director*, Dr. Elizabeth Davis, 303-273-3567, Fax: 303-273-3751, E-mail: edavis@mines.edu.

COLORADO SCHOOL OF TRADITIONAL CHINESE MEDICINE, Denver, CO 80206-2127

General Information Independent, coed, graduate-only institution. *Enrollment by degree level:* 120 master's. *Graduate faculty:* 52 part-time/adjunct (20 women). *Tuition:* Full-time $16,000; part-time $15.50 per credit hour. *Required fees:* $1050; $15.50 per credit hour. $350 per trimester. One-time fee: $50. Part-time tuition and fees vary according to course load. *Graduate housing:* On-campus housing not available. *Student services:* Campus employment opportunities. *Library facilities:* CSTCM Library. *Collection:* 7,400 titles, 80 audiovisual materials.

Computer facilities: 4 computers available on campus for general student use. Wireless Internet available. *Web address:* http://www.cstcm.edu/.

General Application Contact: Chris Duxbury-Edwards, Recruiting Director, 303-329-6355 Ext. 21, Fax: 303-388-8165, E-mail: recruiting@cstcm.edu.

GRADUATE UNITS

Graduate Program Students: 113 full-time (86 women), 7 part-time (6 women). Average age 33. 62 applicants, 100% accepted, 62 enrolled. *Faculty:* 52 part-time/adjunct (20 women). Expenses: Contact institution. *Financial support:* Scholarships/grants available. Financial award applicants required to submit FAFSA. In 2010, 25 master's awarded. *Degree program information:* Part-time programs available. Offers acupuncture (MS); traditional Chinese medicine (MS). *Application deadline:* For fall admission, 8/26 for domestic and international students; for winter admission, 12/23 for domestic and international students; for spring admission, 3/15 for domestic students, 3/22 for international students. Applications are processed on a rolling basis. *Application fee:* $50. *Application Contact:* Vanessa Stockmar, Registrar, 303-329-6355 Ext. 12, Fax: 303-388-8165, E-mail: registrar@cstcm.edu. *Administrative Director*, Vladimir Dibrigida, 303-329-6355 Ext. 11, Fax: 303-388-8165, E-mail: director@cstcm.edu.

COLORADO STATE UNIVERSITY, Fort Collins, CO 80523-0015

General Information State-supported, coed, university. CGS member. *Enrollment:* 29,932 graduate, professional, and undergraduate students; 3,189 full-time matriculated graduate/professional students (1,830 women), 3,764 part-time matriculated graduate/professional students (1,612 women). *Enrollment by degree level:* 539 first professional, 4,747 master's, 1,667 doctoral. *Graduate faculty:* 934 full-time (308 women), 41 part-time/adjunct (7 women). Tuition, state resident: full-time $7434; part-time $413 per credit. Tuition, nonresident: full-time $19,022; part-time $1057 per credit. *Required fees:* $1729; $88 per credit. *Graduate housing:* Rooms and/or apartments available on a first-come, first-served basis to single and

Colorado State University (continued)

married students. Typical cost: $4322 per year ($8744 including board) for single students; $6363 per year for married students. Room and board charges vary according to board plan and housing facility selected. *Student services:* Campus employment opportunities, campus safety program, career counseling, child daycare facilities, exercise/wellness program, free psychological counseling, international student services, low-cost health insurance, multicultural affairs office, services for students with disabilities, teacher training, writing training. *Library facilities:* William E. Morgan Library plus 3 others. *Online resources:* library catalog, web page, access to other libraries' catalogs. *Collection:* 2.4 million titles, 53,774 serial subscriptions, 2,272 audiovisual materials. *Research affiliation:* Natural Resources Research Center/Agencies of U. S. Departments of Agriculture (USDA) and Interior (infectious disease), Department of Commerce/National Oceanic and Atmospheric Administration (NOAA) Joint Institutes (meteorological satellite imagery), National Center for Genetic Resources Preservation (genetic resources of crops), National Wildlife Research Center (interactions of wild animals and society), National Centers for Atmospheric Research (climate, meteorology), Solix (biofuels (algae produced)).

Computer facilities: Computer purchase and lease plans are available. 2,500 computers available on campus for general student use. A campuswide network can be accessed from student residence rooms and from off campus. Online class registration, personalized portal services including transcripts and financials (billing, financial aid) are available. *Web address:* http://www.colostate.edu/.

General Application Contact: Sandra Dailey, Graduate School Administrative Assistant III, 970-491-6817, Fax: 970-491-2194, E-mail: gschool@grad.colostate.edu.

GRADUATE UNITS

College of Veterinary Medicine and Biomedical Sciences Students: 773 full-time (577 women), 144 part-time (92 women); includes 132 minority (2 Black or African American, non-Hispanic/Latino; 6 American Indian or Alaska Native, non-Hispanic/Latino; 30 Asian, non-Hispanic/Latino; 69 Hispanic/Latino; 1 Native Hawaiian or other Pacific Islander, non-Hispanic/Latino; 24 Two or more races, non-Hispanic/Latino), 41 international. Average age 28. 2,074 applicants, 16% accepted, 277 enrolled. *Faculty:* 145 full-time (52 women), 8 part-time/adjunct (2 women). Expenses: Contact institution. *Financial support:* In 2010–11, 164 students received support, including 58 fellowships with full tuition reimbursements available (averaging $33,092 per year), 89 research assistantships with full tuition reimbursements available (averaging $22,034 per year), 17 teaching assistantships with partial tuition reimbursements available (averaging $11,855 per year); Federal Work-Study, institutionally sponsored loans, scholarships/grants, tuition waivers (partial), and unspecified assistantships also available. Financial award application deadline: 10/3; financial award applicants required to submit FAFSA. In 2010, 131 first professional degrees, 100 master's, 20 doctorates awarded. Offers biomedical sciences (MS, PhD); clinical sciences (MS, PhD); environmental health (MS, PhD); microbiology (MS, PhD); pathology (PhD); radiological health sciences (MS, PhD); veterinary medicine (DVM); veterinary medicine and biomedical sciences (DVM, MS, PhD). *Application deadline:* For fall admission, 10/3 for domestic and international students. *Application fee:* $60. Electronic applications accepted. *Application Contact:* Dr. Terry Nett, Associate Dean for Research and Graduate Education, 970-491-7053, Fax: 970-491-2250, E-mail: terry.nett@colostate.edu. *Dean,* Dr. Lance Perryman, 970-491-7051, Fax: 970-491-2250, E-mail: lance.perryman@colostate.edu.

Graduate School Students: 2,416 full-time (1,253 women), 3,620 part-time (1,520 women); includes 786 minority (108 Black or African American, non-Hispanic/Latino; 35 American Indian or Alaska Native, non-Hispanic/Latino; 201 Asian, non-Hispanic/Latino; 339 Hispanic/Latino; 10 Native Hawaiian or other Pacific Islander, non-Hispanic/Latino; 93 Two or more races, non-Hispanic/Latino), 653 international. Average age 33. 5,220 applicants, 47% accepted, 1546 enrolled. *Faculty:* 789 full-time (256 women), 33 part-time/adjunct (5 women). Expenses: Contact institution. *Financial support:* Fellowships, research assistantships, teaching assistantships, career-related internships or fieldwork, Federal Work-Study, institutionally sponsored loans, scholarships/grants, traineeships, tuition waivers (full and partial), and unspecified assistantships available. Support available to part-time students. In 2010, 1,320 master's, 183 doctorates awarded. *Degree program information:* Part-time programs available. Postbaccalaureate distance learning degree programs offered (no on-campus study). Offers cell and molecular biology (MS, PhD); ecology (MS, PhD); molecular, cellular and integrative neurosciences (PhD). *Application deadline:* For fall admission, 4/1 for domestic and international students; for spring admission, 9/1 for domestic and international students. *Application fee:* $50. Electronic applications accepted. *Application Contact:* Sandra Dailey, Graduate School Administrative Assistant III, 970-491-6817, Fax: 970-491-2194, E-mail: gschool@grad.colostate.edu. *Vice Provost for Graduate Studies,* Dr. Peter K. Dorhout, 970-491-6817, Fax: 970-491-2194, E-mail: peter.dorhout@colostate.edu.

College of Agricultural Sciences Students: 160 full-time (73 women), 153 part-time (73 women); includes 26 minority (3 Black or African American, non-Hispanic/Latino; 6 American Indian or Alaska Native, non-Hispanic/Latino; 12 Hispanic/Latino; 5 Two or more races, non-Hispanic/Latino), 53 international. Average age 31. 253 applicants, 67% accepted, 95 enrolled. *Faculty:* 100 full-time (18 women), 2 part-time/adjunct (0 women). Expenses: Contact institution. *Financial support:* In 2010–11, 148 students received support, including 15 fellowships (averaging $29,039 per year), 103 research assistantships (averaging $14,170 per year), 30 teaching assistantships (averaging $10,272 per year); scholarships/grants and unspecified assistantships also available. Financial award applicants required to submit FAFSA. In 2010, 41 master's, 21 doctorates awarded. *Degree program information:* Part-time and evening/weekend programs available. Postbaccalaureate distance learning degree programs offered (no on-campus study). Offers agricultural and resource economics (MS, PhD); agricultural sciences (M Agr, MLA, MS, PhD); animal sciences (MS, PhD); entomology (MS, PhD); horticulture (MS, PhD); landscape architecture (MLA); plant pathology and weed science (MS, PhD); soil and crop sciences (MS, PhD). *Application deadline:* For fall admission, 7/1 for domestic and international students; for spring admission, 1/1 for domestic and international students. Applications are processed on a rolling basis. *Application fee:* $50. Electronic applications accepted. *Application Contact:* Pam Schell, Administrative Assistant, 970-491-2410, Fax: 970-491-4895, E-mail: pam.schell@colostate.edu. *Dean,* Dr. Craig Beyrouty, 970-491-6274, Fax: 970-491-4895, E-mail: craig.beyrouty@colostate.edu.

College of Applied Human Sciences Students: 546 full-time (428 women), 713 part-time (457 women); includes 183 minority (37 Black or African American, non-Hispanic/Latino; 8 American Indian or Alaska Native, non-Hispanic/Latino; 20 Asian, non-Hispanic/Latino; 96 Hispanic/Latino; 4 Native Hawaiian or other Pacific Islander, non-Hispanic/Latino; 18 Two or more races, non-Hispanic/Latino), 49 international. Average age 35. 1,105 applicants, 35% accepted, 257 enrolled. *Faculty:* 104 full-time (54 women), 5 part-time/adjunct (1 woman). Expenses: Contact institution. *Financial support:* In 2010–11, 124 students received support, including 1 fellowship with full and partial tuition reimbursement available (averaging $37,368 per year), 49 research assistantships with full tuition reimbursements available (averaging $10,372 per year), 74 teaching assistantships with full and partial tuition reimbursements available (averaging $10,240 per year); career-related internships or fieldwork, Federal Work-Study, institutionally sponsored loans, scholarships/grants, traineeships, tuition waivers (full and partial), and unspecified assistantships also available. Support available to part-time students. Financial award application deadline: 2/15; financial award applicants required to submit FAFSA. In 2010, 396 master's, 38 doctorates awarded. *Degree program information:* Part-time programs available. Postbaccalaureate distance learning degree programs offered. Offers adult education and training (M Ed); applied human sciences (M Ed, MOT, MS, MSW, PhD); community college leadership (PhD); construction management (MS); counseling and career development (M Ed); design and merchandising (MS); education and human resource studies (M Ed, PhD); educational leadership (M Ed, PhD); exercise science and nutrition (MS); food science and human nutrition (MS, PhD); health and exercise science (MS); human bioenergetics (PhD); human development and family studies (MS, PhD); interdisciplinary studies (PhD); occupational therapy (MOT, MS); organizational performance and change (M Ed, PhD); social work (MSW); student affairs in higher education (MS). *Application deadline:* For fall admission, 2/15 priority date for domestic and international students. Applications are processed on a rolling basis. *Application fee:* $50. Electronic applications accepted. *Application Contact:* Thomas Mazzarisi, Assistant to Dean, 970-491-5236, Fax: 970-491-7859, E-mail: thomas.mazzarisi@colostate.edu. *Interim Dean,* Dr. Nancy Hartley, 977-491-5841, Fax: 970-491-7859, E-mail: nancy.hartley@colostate.edu.

College of Business Students: 417 full-time (162 women), 875 part-time (234 women); includes 230 minority (35 Black or African American, non-Hispanic/Latino; 6 American Indian or Alaska Native, non-Hispanic/Latino; 97 Asian, non-Hispanic/Latino; 70 Hispanic/Latino; 3 Native Hawaiian or other Pacific Islander, non-Hispanic/Latino; 19 Two or more races, non-Hispanic/Latino), 105 international. Average age 35. 630 applicants, 93% accepted, 474 enrolled. *Faculty:* 58 full-time (15 women). Expenses: Contact institution. *Financial support:* In 2010–11, 1 student received support, including 1 research assistantship with full and partial tuition reimbursement available (averaging $10,275 per year); fellowships, teaching assistantships with full and partial tuition reimbursements available, career-related internships or fieldwork, Federal Work-Study, scholarships/grants, and unspecified assistantships also available. Financial award application deadline: 6/1; financial award applicants required to submit FAFSA. In 2010, 403 master's awarded. *Degree program information:* Part-time and evening/weekend programs available. Postbaccalaureate distance learning degree programs offered. Offers accounting (M Acc); business (M Acc, MBA, MMP, MS, MSBA); business administration (MBA); computer information systems (MSBA); financial risk management (MSBA); global social and sustainable enterprise (MSBA); management practice (MMP). *Application deadline:* For fall admission, 7/15 for domestic students, 6/1 for international students; for spring admission, 11/15 for domestic students, 11/1 for international students. Applications are processed on a rolling basis. *Application fee:* $50. Electronic applications accepted. *Application Contact:* Rachel Stoll, Admissions Coordinator, 970-491-3704, Fax: 970-491-3481, E-mail: rachel.stoll@colostate.edu. *Associate Dean,* Dr. John Hoxmeier, 970-491-2142, Fax: 970-491-0596, E-mail: john.hoxmeier@colostate.edu.

College of Engineering Students: 310 full-time (81 women), 348 part-time (66 women); includes 52 minority (4 Black or African American, non-Hispanic/Latino; 1 American Indian or Alaska Native, non-Hispanic/Latino; 11 Asian, non-Hispanic/Latino; 22 Hispanic/Latino; 1 Native Hawaiian or other Pacific Islander, non-Hispanic/Latino; 13 Two or more races, non-Hispanic/Latino), 196 international. Average age 30. 764 applicants, 52% accepted, 192 enrolled. *Faculty:* 94 full-time (11 women), 7 part-time/adjunct (0 women). Expenses: Contact institution. *Financial support:* In 2010–11, 297 students received support, including 28 fellowships with full tuition reimbursements available (averaging $29,656 per year), 223 research assistantships with full tuition reimbursements available (averaging $17,494 per year), 46 teaching assistantships with full tuition reimbursements available (averaging $9,102 per year); career-related internships or fieldwork, Federal Work-Study, institutionally sponsored loans, scholarships/grants, traineeships, health care benefits, and unspecified assistantships also available. Financial award application deadline: 1/15; financial award applicants required to submit FAFSA. In 2010, 94 master's, 38 doctorates awarded. *Degree program information:* Part-time programs available. Offers atmospheric science (MS, PhD); chemical engineering (MS, PhD); civil engineering (ME, MS, PhD); electrical engineering (MEE, MS, PhD); engineering (ME, MEE, MS, PhD); mechanical engineering (ME, MS, PhD). *Application deadline:* For fall admission, 2/1 priority date for domestic and international students; for spring admission, 9/1 priority date for domestic and international students. Applications are processed on a rolling basis. *Application fee:* $50. Electronic applications accepted. *Application Contact:* Dr. Tom Siller, Associate Dean, 970-491-6220, Fax: 970-491-3429, E-mail: thomas.siller@colostate.edu. *Dean,* Dr. Sandra L. Woods, 970-491-3366, Fax: 970-491-5569, E-mail: sandra.woods@colostate.edu.

College of Liberal Arts Students: 412 full-time (238 women), 306 part-time (181 women); includes 64 minority (2 Black or African American, non-Hispanic/Latino; 2 American Indian or Alaska Native, non-Hispanic/Latino; 10 Asian, non-Hispanic/Latino; 41 Hispanic/Latino; 9 Two or more races, non-Hispanic/Latino), 61 international. Average age 30. 991 applicants, 40% accepted, 227 enrolled. *Faculty:* 218 full-time (93 women), 8 part-time/adjunct (4 women). Expenses: Contact institution. *Financial support:* In 2010–11, 259 students received support, including 13 research assistantships (averaging $12,258 per year), 246 teaching assistantships with full and partial tuition reimbursements available (averaging $11,484 per year); fellowships, career-related internships or fieldwork, Federal Work-Study, institutionally sponsored loans, scholarships/grants, traineeships, and unspecified assistantships also available. Support available to part-time students. Financial award application deadline: 3/1; financial award applicants required to submit FAFSA. In 2010, 210 master's, 9 doctorates awarded. *Degree program information:* Part-time programs available. Offers anthropology (MA); art (MFA); communication studies (MA); creative writing (MFA); economics (MA, PhD); English (MA); foreign languages and literatures (MA); history (MA); liberal arts (MA, MFA, MM, MS, PhD); music (MM); philosophy (MA); political science (MA, PhD); public communication and technology (MS, PhD); sociology (MA, PhD); technical communication (MS). *Application deadline:* For fall admission, 2/15 priority date for domestic and international students; for spring admission, 7/15 priority date for domestic and international students. Applications are processed on a rolling basis. *Application fee:* $50. Electronic applications accepted. *Application Contact:* Dr. Pattie Cowell, Associate Dean for Graduate Studies, 970-491-3486, Fax: 970-491-0528, E-mail: pattie.cowell@colostate.edu. *Dean,* Dr. Ann Gill, 970-491-5421, Fax: 970-491-0528, E-mail: ann.gill@colostate.edu.

College of Natural Sciences Students: 301 full-time (129 women), 458 part-time (136 women); includes 102 minority (7 Black or African American, non-Hispanic/Latino; 2 American Indian or Alaska Native, non-Hispanic/Latino; 34 Asian, non-Hispanic/Latino; 42 Hispanic/Latino; 17 Two or more races, non-Hispanic/Latino), 130 international. Average age 29. 1,005 applicants, 30% accepted, 170 enrolled. *Faculty:* 160 full-time (49 women), 9 part-time/adjunct (0 women). Expenses: Contact institution. *Financial support:* In 2010–11, 623 students received support, including 78 fellowships (averaging $27,916 per year), 238 research assistantships with full tuition reimbursements available (averaging $13,557 per year), 307 teaching assistantships with full tuition reimbursements available (averaging $13,002 per year); health care benefits also available. Financial award application deadline: 2/15; financial award applicants required to submit FAFSA. In 2010, 117 master's, 53 doctorates awarded. Postbaccalaureate distance learning degree programs offered (no on-campus study). Offers biochemistry (MS, PhD); botany (MS, PhD); chemistry (MS, PhD); computer science (MCS, MS, PhD); mathematics (MAT, MS, PhD); natural sciences (MA/OP, MAT, MCS, MS, PhD); physics (MS, PhD); psychology (MS, PhD); statistics (MS, PhD); zoology (MS, PhD). *Application deadline:* For fall admission, 2/15 priority date for domestic and international students; for spring admission, 9/15 priority date for domestic and international students. Applications are processed on a rolling basis. *Application fee:* $50. Electronic applications accepted. *Application Contact:* Dr. Don Mykles, Associate Dean for Graduate Education, 970-491-6864, Fax: 970-491-6639, E-mail: donald.mykles@colostate.edu. *Dean,* Dr. Jan Nerger, 970-491-6864, Fax: 970-491-6639, E-mail: jan.nerger@colostate.edu.

School of Biomedical Engineering Students: 22 full-time (10 women), 12 part-time (4 women); includes 6 minority (2 Asian, non-Hispanic/Latino; 3 Hispanic/Latino; 1 Two or more races, non-Hispanic/Latino). Average age 28. 64 applicants, 55% accepted, 13 enrolled. Expenses: Contact institution. *Financial support:* In 2010–11, 19 students received support, including 14 research assistantships with full tuition reimbursements available (averaging $12,764 per year), 5 teaching assistantships with full tuition reimbursements available (averaging $7,418 per year); fellowships, unspecified assistantships also available. Financial award application deadline: 2/15; financial award applicants required to submit FAFSA. *Degree program information:* Part-time and evening/weekend programs available. Offers biomedical engineering (ME, MS, PhD). *Application deadline:* For fall admission, 1/15 priority date for domestic and international students; for spring admission, 9/1 priority date for domestic students, 8/1 priority date for international students. Applications are processed on a rolling basis. *Application fee:* $50. Electronic applications accepted. *Application Contact:* Sara Neys, Academic Advisor, 970-491-7157, E-mail: sara.neys@colostate.edu. *Director,* Dr. Stuart Tobet, 970-491-1672, Fax: 970-491-3827, E-mail: stuart.tobet@colostate.edu.

Warner College of Natural Resources Students: 125 full-time (59 women), 151 part-time (57 women); includes 23 minority (1 Black or African American, non-Hispanic/Latino; 3 American Indian or Alaska Native, non-Hispanic/Latino; 3 Asian, non-Hispanic/Latino; 15 Hispanic/Latino; 1 Two or more races, non-Hispanic/Latino), 21 international. Average age

32. 222 applicants, 55% accepted, 81 enrolled. *Faculty:* 55 full-time (16 women), 2 part-time/adjunct (0 women). Expenses: Contact institution. *Financial support:* In 2010–11, 136 students received support, including 8 fellowships (averaging $29,711 per year), 86 research assistantships (averaging $13,863 per year), 42 teaching assistantships with tuition reimbursements available (averaging $7,664 per year); career-related internships or fieldwork, Federal Work-Study, institutionally sponsored loans, scholarships/grants, traineeships, and unspecified assistantships also available. Support available to part-time students. Financial award applicants required to submit FAFSA. In 2010, 48 master's, 10 doctorates awarded. *Degree program information:* Part-time programs available. Offers earth sciences (PhD); fish, wildlife and conservation biology (MFWCB); fishery and wildlife biology (MFWB, MS, PhD); forest sciences (MS, PhD); geosciences (MS); human dimensions of natural resources (MS, PhD); natural resources (MFWB, MFWCB, MNRS, MS, PhD); natural resources stewardship (MNRS); rangeland ecosystem science (MS, PhD); watershed science (MS). *Application deadline:* For fall admission, 2/15 priority date for domestic and international students; for spring admission, 7/15 priority date for domestic and international students. Applications are processed on a rolling basis. *Application fee:* $50. Electronic applications accepted. *Application Contact:* Ethan Billingsley, Coordinator, 970-491-4994, Fax: 970-491-0279, E-mail: ethan.billingsley@colostate.edu. *Dean,* Dr. Joyce Berry, 970-491-1649, Fax: 970-491-0279, E-mail: joyce.berry@colostate.edu.

COLORADO STATE UNIVERSITY–PUEBLO, Pueblo, CO 81001-4901

General Information State-supported, coed, comprehensive institution. *Graduate housing:* Room and/or apartments available on a first-come, first-served basis to single students; on-campus housing not available to married students. Housing application deadline: 8/1.

GRADUATE UNITS

College of Education, Engineering and Professional Studies *Degree program information:* Part-time and evening/weekend programs available. Offers art education (M Ed); education, engineering and professional studies (M Ed, MS); foreign language education (M Ed); health and physical education (M Ed); industrial and systems engineering (MS); instructional technology (M Ed); linguistically diverse education (M Ed); music education (M Ed); nursing (MS); special education (M Ed). Electronic applications accepted.

College of Science and Mathematics *Degree program information:* Part-time and evening/weekend programs available. Offers applied natural science (MS).

Malik and Seeme Hasan School of Business *Degree program information:* Part-time and evening/weekend programs available. Offers business (MBA).

COLORADO TECHNICAL UNIVERSITY COLORADO SPRINGS, Colorado Springs, CO 80907-3896

General Information Proprietary, coed, university. *Graduate housing:* On-campus housing not available.

GRADUATE UNITS

Graduate Studies *Degree program information:* Part-time and evening/weekend programs available. Offers accounting (MBA, MSA); business administration (MBA); computer engineering (MSCE); computer science (DCS); computer systems security (MSCS); criminal justice (MSM); database systems (MSCS); electrical engineering (MSEE); finance (MBA); human resources management (MBA); information systems security (MSM); logistics/supply chain management (MBA); management (DM); marketing (MBA); mediation and dispute resolution (MBA); operations management (MBA); project management (MBA); software engineering (MSCS); systems engineering (MS); technology management (MBA).

COLORADO TECHNICAL UNIVERSITY DENVER, Greenwood Village, CO 80111

General Information Proprietary, coed, comprehensive institution. *Graduate housing:* On-campus housing not available.

GRADUATE UNITS

Program in Computer Engineering Offers computer engineering (MS).

Program in Computer Science *Degree program information:* Part-time and evening/weekend programs available. Offers computer systems security (MSCS); database systems (MSCS); software engineering (MSCS).

Program in Electrical Engineering Offers electrical engineering (MS).

Program in Information Science Offers information systems security (MSM).

Program in Systems Engineering Offers systems engineering (MS).

Programs in Business Administration and Management *Degree program information:* Part-time and evening/weekend programs available. Offers accounting (MBA); business administration (MBA); business administration and management (EMBA); finance (MBA); human resource management (MBA); marketing (MBA); mediation and dispute resolution (MBA); operations management (MBA); project management (MBA); technology management (MBA).

COLORADO TECHNICAL UNIVERSITY SIOUX FALLS, Sioux Falls, SD 57108

General Information Proprietary, coed, comprehensive institution. *Graduate housing:* On-campus housing not available.

GRADUATE UNITS

Program in Computing Offers computer systems security (MSCS); software engineering (MSCS).

Program in Criminal Justice Offers criminal justice (MSM).

Programs in Business Administration and Management *Degree program information:* Evening/weekend programs available. Offers business administration (MBA); business management (MSM); health science management (MSM); human resources management (MSM); information technology (MSM); organizational leadership (MSM); project management (MBA); technology management (MBA).

COLUMBIA COLLEGE, Columbia, MO 65216-0002

General Information Independent-religious, coed, comprehensive institution. *Enrollment:* 1,327 graduate, professional, and undergraduate students; 124 full-time matriculated graduate/professional students (80 women), 757 part-time matriculated graduate/professional students (468 women). *Enrollment by degree level:* 881 master's. *Graduate faculty:* 12 full-time (7 women), 67 part-time/adjunct (30 women). *Tuition:* Part-time $299 per credit hour. Tuition and fees vary according to course load. *Graduate housing:* On-campus housing not available. *Student services:* Campus employment opportunities, campus safety program, career counseling, exercise/wellness program, free psychological counseling, international student services, low-cost health insurance, services for students with disabilities, teacher training, writing training. *Library facilities:* Stafford Library. *Online resources:* library catalog, web page, access to other libraries' catalogs. *Collection:* 73,986 titles, 218 serial subscriptions, 1,857 audiovisual materials.

Computer facilities: Computer purchase and lease plans are available. 83 computers available on campus for general student use. A campuswide network can be accessed from student residence rooms and from off campus. Online class registration is available. *Web address:* http://www.ccis.edu/.

General Application Contact: White Samantha, Director of Admissions, 573-875-7352, Fax: 573-875-7506, E-mail: sjwhite@ccis.edu.

GRADUATE UNITS

Master of Arts in Military Studies Program Expenses: Contact institution. Postbaccalaureate distance learning degree programs offered (no on-campus study). Offers military studies (MA). *Application Contact:* Samantha White, Director of Admissions, 573-875-7343, Fax: 573-875-7506, E-mail: sjwhite@ccis.edu.

Master of Arts in Teaching Program Students: 31 full-time (24 women), 160 part-time (128 women); includes 10 minority (6 Black or African American, non-Hispanic/Latino; 2 American Indian or Alaska Native, non-Hispanic/Latino; 1 Asian, non-Hispanic/Latino; 1 Hispanic/Latino), 2 international. Average age 32. 78 applicants, 58% accepted, 26 enrolled. *Faculty:* 5 full-time (4 women), 7 part-time/adjunct (4 women). Expenses: Contact institution. *Financial support:* In 2010–11, 19 students received support. Career-related internships or fieldwork, Federal Work-Study, and scholarships/grants available. Financial award application deadline: 3/15; financial award applicants required to submit FAFSA. In 2010, 45 master's awarded. *Degree program information:* Evening/weekend programs available. Postbaccalaureate distance learning degree programs offered (no on-campus study). Offers teaching (MAT). *Application deadline:* For fall admission, 8/9 priority date for domestic and international students; for spring admission, 12/27 priority date for domestic and international students. Applications are processed on a rolling basis. *Application fee:* $55. Electronic applications accepted. *Application Contact:* Samantha White, Director of Admissions, 573-875-7352, Fax: 573-875-7506, E-mail: sjwhite@ccis.edu. *Graduate Program Coordinator,* Dr. Kristina Miller, 573-875-7590, Fax: 573-876-4493, E-mail: kmiller@ccis.edu.

Master of Business Administration Program Students: 87 full-time (52 women), 480 part-time (278 women); includes 117 minority (75 Black or African American, non-Hispanic/Latino; 10 American Indian or Alaska Native, non-Hispanic/Latino; 7 Asian, non-Hispanic/Latino; 21 Hispanic/Latino; 4 Two or more races, non-Hispanic/Latino), 12 international. Average age 36. 157 applicants, 65% accepted, 55 enrolled. *Faculty:* 7 full-time (2 women), 48 part-time/adjunct (18 women). Expenses: Contact institution. *Financial support:* In 2010–11, 25 students received support. Federal Work-Study and scholarships/grants available. Financial award applicants required to submit FAFSA. In 2010, 219 master's awarded. *Degree program information:* Evening/weekend programs available. Postbaccalaureate distance learning degree programs offered (no on-campus study). Offers business administration (MBA). *Application deadline:* For fall admission, 8/9 priority date for domestic and international students; for spring admission, 12/27 priority date for domestic and international students. Applications are processed on a rolling basis. *Application fee:* $55. Electronic applications accepted. *Application Contact:* Samantha White, Director of Admissions, 573-875-7352, Fax: 573-875-7506, E-mail: sjwhite@ccis.edu. *Coordinator,* Dr. Diane Suhler, 573-875-7640, Fax: 573-876-4493, E-mail: drsuhler@ccis.edu.

Master of Science in Criminal Justice Program Students: 6 full-time (4 women), 117 part-time (62 women); includes 17 Black or African American, non-Hispanic/Latino; 1 American Indian or Alaska Native, non-Hispanic/Latino; 2 Asian, non-Hispanic/Latino; 6 Hispanic/Latino; 1 Two or more races, non-Hispanic/Latino. Average age 37. 48 applicants, 54% accepted, 21 enrolled. *Faculty:* 4 full-time (0 women), 15 part-time/adjunct (6 women). Expenses: Contact institution. *Financial support:* In 2010–11, 1 student received support. Federal Work-Study and scholarships/grants available. Financial award applicants required to submit FAFSA. In 2010, 46 master's awarded. *Degree program information:* Evening/weekend programs available. Postbaccalaureate distance learning degree programs offered (no on-campus study). Offers criminal justice (MSCJ). *Application deadline:* For fall admission, 8/9 priority date for domestic and international students; for spring admission, 12/27 priority date for domestic and international students. Applications are processed on a rolling basis. *Application fee:* $55. Electronic applications accepted. *Application Contact:* Samantha White, Director of Admissions, 573-875-7352, Fax: 573-875-7506, E-mail: sjwhite@ccis.edu. *Coordinator,* Dr. Mike Lyman, 573-875-7472, E-mail: mlyman@ccis.edu.

COLUMBIA COLLEGE, Columbia, SC 29203-5998

General Information Independent-religious, Undergraduate: women only; graduate: coed, comprehensive institution. *Enrollment:* 1,369 graduate, professional, and undergraduate students; 175 full-time matriculated graduate/professional students (156 women), 30 part-time matriculated graduate/professional students (22 women). *Enrollment by degree level:* 186 master's, 19 other advanced degrees. *Graduate faculty:* 3 full-time (1 woman), 18 part-time/adjunct (10 women). *Tuition:* Part-time $395 per credit hour. *Graduate housing:* On-campus housing not available. *Student services:* Campus safety program, career counseling. *Library facilities:* J. Drake Edens Library plus 1 other. *Online resources:* library catalog, web page, access to other libraries' catalogs. *Collection:* 144,571 titles, 185 serial subscriptions, 45,474 audiovisual materials.

Computer facilities: Computer purchase and lease plans are available. 150 computers available on campus for general student use. A campuswide network can be accessed from student residence rooms. Online class registration is available. *Web address:* http://www.columbiacollegesc.edu/.

General Application Contact: Carolyn Emeneker, Director of Graduate School and Evening College Admissions, 803-786-3766, Fax: 803-786-3674, E-mail: emeneker@colacoll.edu.

GRADUATE UNITS

Graduate Programs *Degree program information:* Part-time and evening/weekend programs available. Postbaccalaureate distance learning degree programs offered (minimal on-campus study). Offers divergent learning (M Ed); human behavior and conflict management (MA); interpersonal relations/conflict management (Certificate); organizational behavior/conflict management (Certificate). Electronic applications accepted.

COLUMBIA COLLEGE CHICAGO, Chicago, IL 60605-1996

General Information Independent, coed, comprehensive institution. *Enrollment:* 11,922 graduate, professional, and undergraduate students; 324 full-time matriculated graduate/professional students (205 women), 200 part-time matriculated graduate/professional students (139 women). *Enrollment by degree level:* 522 master's, 2 other advanced degrees. *Tuition:* Full-time $16,966; part-time $684 per credit. *Required fees:* $520; $113 per semester. One-time fee: $150 full-time. Tuition and fees vary according to course load and program. *Graduate housing:* Room and/or apartments available on a first-come, first-served basis to single students; on-campus housing not available to married students. Typical cost: $12,000 per year ($13,680 including board). Room and board charges vary according to board plan, campus/location and housing facility selected. Housing application deadline: 5/1. *Student services:* Campus employment opportunities, campus safety program, career counseling, exercise/wellness program, free psychological counseling, grant writing training, international student services, low-cost health insurance, multicultural affairs office, services for students with disabilities, teacher training, writing training. *Library facilities:* Columbia College Chicago Library plus 2 others. *Online resources:* library catalog, web page, access to other libraries' catalogs. *Collection:* 290,556 titles, 40,838 serial subscriptions, 33,067 audiovisual materials.

Computer facilities: Computer purchase and lease plans are available. 851 computers available on campus for general student use. A campuswide network can be accessed from student residence rooms and from off campus. Online class registration is available. *Web address:* http://www.colum.edu/.

General Application Contact: Cate Lagueux, Director of Graduate Admissions and Services, 312-369-7260, Fax: 312-369-8047, E-mail: gradstudy@colum.edu.

GRADUATE UNITS

Graduate School Students: 312 full-time (194 women), 148 part-time (105 women); includes 112 minority (60 Black or African American, non-Hispanic/Latino; 4 American Indian or Alaska Native, non-Hispanic/Latino; 12 Asian, non-Hispanic/Latino; 31 Hispanic/Latino; 5 Two or more races, non-Hispanic/Latino), 23 international. Average age 29. 938 applicants, 42% accepted, 169 enrolled. Expenses: Contact institution. *Financial support:* Fellowships with full and partial tuition reimbursements, research assistantships, teaching assistantships, career-related internships or fieldwork, Federal Work-Study, scholarships/grants, and tuition waivers (partial) available. Support available to part-time students. Financial award application deadline: 8/13; financial award applicants required to submit FAFSA. In 2010, 169 master's awarded. *Degree program information:* Part-time and evening/weekend programs available. Offers arts, entertainment and media management (MA); creative writing (MFA); dance/movement

Columbia College Chicago (continued)

therapy (MA, Certificate); elementary education (MAT); English (MAT); film and video (MFA); interdisciplinary arts (MA, MAT); interdisciplinary book and paper arts (MFA); multicultural education (MA); music composition for the screen (MFA); nonfiction writing (MFA); photography (MA, MFA); poetry (MFA); public affairs journalism (MA); teaching of writing (MA); urban teaching (MA). *Application deadline:* Applications are processed on a rolling basis. *Application fee:* $55. Electronic applications accepted. *Application Contact:* Steven Kapelke, Provost/Senior Vice President, 312-369-7493, Fax: 312-369-8022, E-mail: skapelke@colum.edu. *Provost/Senior Vice President*, Steven Kapelke, 312-369-7493, Fax: 312-369-8022, E-mail: skapelke@colum.edu.

COLUMBIA INTERNATIONAL UNIVERSITY, Columbia, SC 29230-3122

General Information Independent-religious, coed, university. *Graduate housing:* Room and/or apartments available on a first-come, first-served basis to single students; on-campus housing not available to married students. Housing application deadline: 8/27.

GRADUATE UNITS

Columbia Biblical Seminary and School of Missions *Degree program information:* Part-time and evening/weekend programs available. Offers academic ministries (M Div); bible exposition (M Div, MABE); biblical studies (Certificate); counseling ministries (Certificate); divinity (M Div); educational ministries (M Div, MAEM, Certificate); intercultural studies (M Div, MAIS, Certificate); leadership (D Min); leadership for evangelism/mobilization (MALM); member care (D Min); ministry (Certificate); missions (D Min); pastoral counseling and spiritual formation (M Div, MAPS); preaching (D Min); theology (MA). Electronic applications accepted.

Columbia Graduate School *Degree program information:* Part-time and evening/weekend programs available. Offers Bible teaching (MABT); Christian higher education leadership (Ed D); Christian school educational leadership (Ed D); counseling (MACN); curriculum and instruction (M Ed); early childhood and elementary education (MAT); educational administration (M Ed); teaching English as a foreign language (Certificate); teaching English as a foreign language and intercultural studies (MATF). Electronic applications accepted.

COLUMBIA SOUTHERN UNIVERSITY, Orange Beach, AL 36561

General Information Proprietary, coed, comprehensive institution. *Graduate housing:* On-campus housing not available.

GRADUATE UNITS

College of Safety and Emergency Services *Degree program information:* Part-time and evening/weekend programs available. Postbaccalaureate distance learning degree programs offered (no on-campus study). Offers criminal justice (MS); environmental management (MS); occupational safety and health (MS); occupational safety and health/environmental management (MS). Electronic applications accepted.

DBA Program *Degree program information:* Part-time and evening/weekend programs available. Postbaccalaureate distance learning degree programs offered (minimal on-campus study). Offers business administration (DBA). Electronic applications accepted.

MBA Program *Degree program information:* Part-time and evening/weekend programs available. Postbaccalaureate distance learning degree programs offered (no on-campus study). Offers electronic business and technology (MBA); finance (MBA); general (MBA); healthcare management (MBA); hospitality and tourism (MBA); human resources management (MBA); international management (MBA); marketing (MBA); project management (MBA); public administration (MBA); sport management (MBA). Electronic applications accepted.

COLUMBIA THEOLOGICAL SEMINARY, Decatur, GA 30031-0520

General Information Independent-religious, coed, graduate-only institution. *Graduate housing:* Rooms and/or apartments available on a first-come, first-served basis to single students and available to married students. Housing application deadline: 4/30.

GRADUATE UNITS

Graduate and Professional Programs Offers theology (M Div, MATS, Th M, D Min, Th D). Th D program offered jointly with Emory University; D Min with Interdenominational Theological Center.

COLUMBIA UNIVERSITY, New York, NY 10027

General Information Independent, coed, university. CGS member. *Graduate housing:* Rooms and/or apartments available on a first-come, first-served basis to single and married students. Housing application deadline: 7/10. *Research affiliation:* Long Island Biological Laboratory, Brookhaven National Laboratory, New York Botanical Gardens, American Museum of Natural History, Marine Biological Laboratory, Goddard Space Flight Center.

GRADUATE UNITS

College of Dental Medicine Offers advanced education in general dentistry (Certificate); biomedical informatics (MA, PhD); dental and oral surgery (DDS); dental medicine (DDS, MA, MS, PhD, Certificate); endodontics (Certificate); orthodontics (MS, Certificate); periodontics (MS, Certificate); prosthodontics (MS, Certificate); science education (MA).

College of Physicians and Surgeons *Degree program information:* Part-time programs available. Offers anatomy (M Phil, MA, PhD); anatomy and cell biology (PhD); biochemistry and molecular biophysics (M Phil, PhD); biomedical informatics (M Phil, MA, PhD); biomedical sciences (M Phil, MA, PhD); biophysics (PhD); cellular, molecular, structural and genetic studies (PhD); genetics (M Phil, MA, PhD); medicine (MD, M Phil, MA, MS, DN Sc, DPT, Ed D, PhD, Adv C); movement science (Ed D); neurobiology and behavior (PhD); occupational therapy (professional) (MS); occupational therapy administration or education (post-professional) (MS); pathobiology (M Phil, MA, PhD); pharmacology (M Phil, MA, PhD); pharmacology-toxicology (M Phil, MA, PhD); physical therapy (DPT); physiology and cellular biophysics (M Phil, MA, PhD).

Institute of Human Nutrition *Degree program information:* Part-time and evening/weekend programs available. Offers nutrition (MS, PhD).

Columbia University Mailman School of Public Health Students: 539 full-time (442 women), 542 part-time (390 women); includes 92 Black or African American, non-Hispanic/Latino; 5 American Indian or Alaska Native, non-Hispanic/Latino; 162 Asian, non-Hispanic/Latino; 63 Hispanic/Latino, 146 international. Average age 30. 1,889 applicants, 61% accepted, 430 enrolled. *Faculty:* 312 full-time (155 women), 284 part-time/adjunct (128 women). Expenses: Contact institution. *Financial support:* In 2010–11, 600 students received support; fellowships, research assistantships, teaching assistantships, career-related internships or fieldwork, Federal Work-Study, and traineeships available. Support available to part-time students. Financial award application deadline: 2/1; financial award applicants required to submit FAFSA. In 2010, 431 master's, 20 doctorates awarded. *Degree program information:* Part-time and evening/weekend programs available. Offers biostatistics (MPH, MS, Dr PH, PhD); environmental health sciences (MPH, Dr PH, PhD); epidemiology (MPH, MS, Dr PH, PhD); health policy and management (Exec MPH, MPH); population and family health (MPH); public health (Exec MPH, MPH, MS, Dr PH, PhD); sociomedical sciences (MPH, Dr PH, PhD). PhD offered in cooperation with the Graduate School of Arts and Sciences. *Application deadline:* For fall admission, 1/5 for domestic students, 1/1 for international students. *Application fee:* $60. Electronic applications accepted. *Application Contact:* Dr. Joseph Korevec, Director of Admissions and Financial Aid, 212-305-8698, Fax: 212-342-1861, E-mail: ph-admit@columbia.edu. *Dean/Professor*, Dr. Linda P. Fried, 212-305-9300, Fax: 212-305-9342, E-mail: lpfried@columbia.edu.

Fu Foundation School of Engineering and Applied Science Students: 1,387 full-time (349 women), 452 part-time (118 women); includes 159 minority (12 Black or African American, non-Hispanic/Latino; 2 American Indian or Alaska Native, non-Hispanic/Latino; 108 Asian, non-Hispanic/Latino; 25 Hispanic/Latino; 12 Two or more races, non-Hispanic/Latino), 1,228 international. Average age 28. 5,142 applicants, 27% accepted, 727 enrolled. *Faculty:* 203 full-time (22 women), 148 part-time/adjunct (11 women). Expenses: Contact institution. *Financial support:* In 2010–11, 643 students received support, including 72 fellowships with full and partial tuition reimbursements available (averaging $25,954 per year), 424 research assistantships with full tuition reimbursements available (averaging $29,525 per year), 147 teaching assistantships with full and partial tuition reimbursements available (averaging $26,844 per year); career-related internships or fieldwork, traineeships, health care benefits, and unspecified assistantships also available. Financial award application deadline: 12/1; financial award applicants required to submit FAFSA. In 2010, 817 master's, 129 doctorates, 6 other advanced degrees awarded. *Degree program information:* Part-time programs available. Postbaccalaureate distance learning degree programs offered (no on-campus study). Offers applied physics (Eng Sc D); applied physics and applied mathematics (MS, PhD, Engr); biomedical engineering (MS, Eng Sc D, PhD); chemical engineering (MS, Eng Sc D, PhD); civil engineering (MS, Eng Sc D, PhD, Engr); computer engineering (MS); computer science (MS, Eng Sc D, PhD, Engr); computer science and journalism (MS); construction engineering and management (MS); earth and environmental engineering (MS, Eng Sc D, PhD); electrical engineering (MS, Eng Sc D, PhD, Engr); engineering and applied science (MS, Eng Sc D, PhD, Engr); engineering mechanics (MS, Eng Sc D, PhD, Engr); financial engineering (MS); industrial engineering (Engr); industrial engineering and operations research (MS, Eng Sc D, PhD); materials science and engineering (MS, Eng Sc D, PhD); mechanical engineering (MS, Eng Sc D, PhD, Engr); medical physics (MS); metallurgical engineering (Engr); mining engineering (Engr); solid state science and engineering (MS, Eng Sc D, PhD). *Application deadline:* For fall admission, 12/1 priority date for domestic and international students; for spring admission, 10/1 priority date for domestic and international students. *Application fee:* $95. Electronic applications accepted. *Application Contact:* Jocelyn Morales, Assistant Director, 212-854-6901, Fax: 212-854-5900, E-mail: seasgradmit@columbia.edu. *Dean*, Dr. Feniosky Pena-Mora, 212-854-2993, Fax: 212-864-0104, E-mail: dean@seas.columbia.edu.

Graduate School of Architecture, Planning, and Preservation Offers advanced architectural design (MS); architecture (M Arch, PhD); architecture, planning, and preservation (M Arch, MS, PhD, Certificate); historic preservation (MS, Certificate); real estate development (MS); urban planning (MS, PhD). PhD offered through the Graduate School of Arts and Sciences.

Graduate School of Arts and Sciences *Degree program information:* Part-time and evening/weekend programs available. Offers African-American studies (MA); American studies (MA); arts and sciences (M Phil, MA, DMA, PhD, Certificate); climate and society (MA); conservation biology (MA); East Asian regional studies (MA); East Asian studies (MA); French cultural studies (MA); history and literature (MA); human rights studies (MA); Islamic culture studies (MA); Jewish studies (MA); medieval studies (MA); modern European studies (MA); quantitative methods in the social sciences (MA); Russian, Eurasian and East European regional studies (MA); South Asian studies (MA); sustainable development (PhD); theatre (M Phil, MA, PhD); Yiddish studies (MA).

Division of Humanities *Degree program information:* Part-time programs available. Offers archaeology (M Phil, MA, PhD); art history and archaeology (M Phil, MA, PhD); classics (M Phil, MA, PhD); comparative literature (M Phil, MA, PhD); East Asian languages and cultures (M Phil, MA, PhD); English literature (M Phil, MA, PhD); French and Romance philology (M Phil, PhD); Germanic languages (M Phil, MA, PhD); Hebrew language and literature (M Phil, MA, PhD); humanities (M Phil, MA, DMA, PhD); Italian (M Phil, MA, PhD); Jewish studies (M Phil, MA, PhD); literature-writing (M Phil, MA, PhD); Middle Eastern languages and cultures (M Phil, MA, PhD); modern art (MA); music (M Phil, MA, DMA, PhD); Oriental studies (M Phil, MA, PhD); philosophy (M Phil, MA, PhD); religion (M Phil, MA, PhD); Romance languages (MA); Russian literature (M Phil, MA, PhD); Slavic languages (M Phil, MA, PhD); South Asian languages and cultures (M Phil, MA, PhD); Spanish and Portuguese (M Phil, MA, PhD).

Division of Natural Sciences *Degree program information:* Part-time programs available. Offers astronomy (M Phil, MA, PhD); atmospheric and planetary science (M Phil, PhD); biological sciences (M Phil, MA, PhD); chemical physics (M Phil, PhD); conservation biology (MA, Certificate); ecology and evolutionary biology (PhD); environmental policy (Certificate); evolutionary primatology (PhD); experimental psychology (M Phil, MA, PhD); geochemistry (M Phil, MA, PhD); geodetic sciences (M Phil, MA, PhD); geophysics (M Phil, MA, PhD); inorganic chemistry (M Phil, MA, PhD); mathematics (M Phil, MA, PhD); natural sciences (M Phil, MA, PhD, Certificate); oceanography (M Phil, MA, PhD); organic chemistry (M Phil, MA, PhD); philosophical foundations of physics (MA); physics (M Phil, PhD); psychobiology (M Phil, MA, PhD); social psychology (M Phil, MA, PhD); statistics (M Phil, MA, PhD).

Division of Social Sciences *Degree program information:* Part-time programs available. Offers American history (M Phil, MA, PhD); anthropology (M Phil, MA, PhD); economics (M Phil, MA, PhD); history (M Phil, MA, PhD); political science (M Phil, MA, PhD); social sciences (M Phil, MA, PhD); sociology (M Phil, MA, PhD).

Graduate School of Business Offers accounting (MBA); business (EMBA, MBA, PhD); business administration (EMBA, MBA); decision, risk, and operations (MBA); entrepreneurship (MBA); finance and economics (MBA); global business administration (EMBA); healthcare and pharmaceutical management (MBA); human resource management (MBA); international business (MBA); leadership and ethics (MBA); management (MBA); marketing (MBA); media (MBA); private equity (MBA); real estate (MBA); social enterprise (MBA); value investing (MBA). Electronic applications accepted.

Graduate School of Journalism *Degree program information:* Part-time programs available. Offers journalism (MA, MS, PhD).

School of Continuing Education *Degree program information:* Part-time and evening/weekend programs available. Offers actuarial science (MS); bioethics (MS); communications practice (MS); construction administration (MS); fundraising management (MS); information and archive management (MS); landscape design (MS); narrative medicine (MS); negotiation and conflict resolution (MS); sports management (MS); strategic communications (MS); sustainability management (MS); technology management (Exec MS). Electronic applications accepted.

School of International and Public Affairs Offers development practice (MPA); environmental science and policy (MPA); international affairs (MIA); international and public affairs (MA, MIA, MPA, Certificate); public policy and administration (MPA). Electronic applications accepted.

The East Central Europe Center Offers East Central European studies (Certificate). Students must be enrolled in a separate graduate degree program at Columbia University. Electronic applications accepted.

The Harriman Institute *Degree program information:* Part-time programs available. Offers Russian, Eurasian, and Eastern European studies (Certificate). Students must be enrolled in a separate graduate degree program at Columbia University. Electronic applications accepted.

Institute for the Study of Europe Offers European studies (Certificate). Students must be enrolled in a separate graduate degree program at Columbia University. Electronic applications accepted.

Institute of African Studies Offers African studies (Certificate). Students must be enrolled in a separate graduate degree program at Columbia University. Electronic applications accepted.

Institute of Latin American Studies Offers Latin American and Caribbean studies (MA); Latin American studies (Certificate). Students must also be enrolled in a separate graduate degree program at Columbia University. Electronic applications accepted.

Middle East Institute Offers Middle East studies (Certificate). Students must also be enrolled in a separate graduate degree program at Columbia University. Electronic applications accepted.

Weatherhead East Asian Institute Offers Asian studies (Certificate). Students must be enrolled in a separate graduate degree program at Columbia University. Electronic applications accepted.

School of Law Offers law (JD, LL M, JSD). Electronic applications accepted.

School of Nursing *Degree program information:* Part-time programs available. Offers acute care nurse practitioner (MS, Adv C); adult nurse practitioner (MS, Adv C); family nurse practitioner (MS, Adv C); geriatric nurse practitioner (MS, Adv C); neonatal nurse practitioner (MS, Adv C); nurse anesthesia (MS, Adv C); nurse midwifery (MS); nursing (MS, DN Sc,

DNP, Adv C); nursing practice (DNP); nursing science (DN Sc); oncology nursing (MS, Adv C); pediatric nurse practitioner (MS, Adv C); psychiatric mental health nursing (MS, Adv C); women's health nurse practitioner (Adv C). Electronic applications accepted.

School of Social Work Students: 850. Average age 26. 1,104 applicants, 425 enrolled. *Faculty:* 50 full-time. Expenses: Contact institution. *Financial support:* Fellowships, research assistantships with partial tuition reimbursements, teaching assistantships with partial tuition reimbursements, career-related internships or fieldwork, Federal Work-Study, institutionally sponsored loans, scholarships/grants, health care benefits, and unspecified assistantships available. Support available to part-time students. Financial award application deadline: 2/1; financial award applicants required to submit FAFSA. In 2010, 437 master's, 17 doctorates awarded. Offers social work (MSSW, PhD). MS/MS Ed offered jointly with Bank Street College of Education; MS/M Div with Union Theological Seminary in the City of New York; MS/MA with The Jewish Theological Seminary. *Application deadline:* For fall admission, 1/3 priority date for domestic students; for winter admission, 10/15 priority date for domestic students. Applications are processed on a rolling basis. *Application fee:* $65. Electronic applications accepted. *Application Contact:* Debbie Lesperance, Director of Admissions, 212-851-2211, Fax: 212-851-2305, E-mail: dl635@columbia.edu. *Dean,* Dr. Jeanette Takamura, 212-851-2289.

School of the Arts Offers arts (MA, MFA); creative producing (MFA); directing (MFA); fiction (MFA); film studies (MA); new genres (MFA); nonfiction (MFA); painting (MFA); photography (MFA); poetry (MFA); printmaking (MFA); screenwriting (MFA); sculpture (MFA). Electronic applications accepted.

Theatre Arts Division Offers acting (MFA); directing (MFA); dramaturgy (MFA); playwriting (MFA); stage management (MFA); theater management (MFA). Electronic applications accepted.

South Asia Institute Offers South Asian studies (Certificate). Students must be enrolled in a separate graduate degree program at Columbia University. Electronic applications accepted.

COLUMBUS STATE UNIVERSITY, Columbus, GA 31907-5645

General Information State-supported, coed, comprehensive institution. *Enrollment:* 8,298 graduate, professional, and undergraduate students; 457 full-time matriculated graduate/professional students (286 women), 762 part-time matriculated graduate/professional students (431 women). *Enrollment by degree level:* 1,049 master's, 32 doctoral, 138 other advanced degrees. *Graduate faculty:* 81 full-time (34 women), 47 part-time/adjunct (22 women). Tuition, state resident: full-time $5573; part-time $232 per semester hour. Tuition, nonresident: full-time $13,968; part-time $582 per semester hour. *Required fees:* $1300; $650 per semester. Tuition and fees vary according to degree level and program. *Graduate housing:* Room and/or apartments available on a first-come, first-served basis to single students; on-campus housing not available to married students. Typical cost: $4100 per year ($7280 including board). Room and board charges vary according to board plan, campus/location and housing facility selected. Housing application deadline: 6/30. *Student services:* Campus employment opportunities, campus safety program, career counseling, exercise/wellness program, free psychological counseling, international student services, low-cost health insurance, multicultural affairs office, services for students with disabilities, teacher training. *Library facilities:* Simon Schwob Memorial Library plus 2 others. *Online resources:* library catalog, web page, access to other libraries' catalogs. *Collection:* 373,574 titles, 1,394 serial subscriptions, 12,122 audiovisual materials.

Computer facilities: 1,135 computers available on campus for general student use. A campuswide network can be accessed from student residence rooms and from off campus. Online class registration is available. *Web address:* http://www.columbusstate.edu/.

General Application Contact: Katie Thornton, Graduate Admissions Specialist, 706-568-2035, Fax: 706-568-2462, E-mail: thornton_katie@colstate.edu.

GRADUATE UNITS

Graduate Studies Students: 457 full-time (286 women), 762 part-time (431 women); includes 390 minority (319 Black or African American, non-Hispanic/Latino; 8 American Indian or Alaska Native, non-Hispanic/Latino; 18 Asian, non-Hispanic/Latino; 28 Hispanic/Latino; 2 Native Hawaiian or other Pacific Islander, non-Hispanic/Latino; 15 Two or more races, non-Hispanic/Latino), 24 international. Average age 35. 605 applicants, 66% accepted, 301 enrolled. *Faculty:* 81 full-time (34 women), 47 part-time/adjunct (22 women). Expenses: Contact institution. *Financial support:* In 2010–11, 584 students received support, including 103 research assistantships with partial tuition reimbursements available (averaging $3,000 per year); career-related internships or fieldwork, Federal Work-Study, institutionally sponsored loans, scholarships/grants, tuition waivers (partial), and unspecified assistantships also available. Support available to part-time students. Financial award application deadline: 5/1; financial award applicants required to submit FAFSA. In 2010, 382 master's, 54 other advanced degrees awarded. *Degree program information:* Part-time and evening/weekend programs available. Postbaccalaureate distance learning degree programs offered (minimal on-campus study). *Application deadline:* For fall admission, 6/30 for domestic and international students; for spring admission, 11/1 for domestic and international students. Applications are processed on a rolling basis. *Application fee:* $30. Electronic applications accepted. *Application Contact:* Katie Thornton, Graduate Admissions Specialist, 706-568-2035, Fax: 706-568-2462, E-mail: thornton_katie@colstate.edu. *Interim Provost and Vice President for Academic Affairs,* Dr. Paul Tom Hackett, 706-568-2061, Fax: 706-569-3168, E-mail: hackett_paul@colstate.edu.

College of Education and Health Professions Students: 275 full-time (223 women), 400 part-time (314 women); includes 239 minority (210 Black or African American, non-Hispanic/Latino; 3 American Indian or Alaska Native, non-Hispanic/Latino; 6 Asian, non-Hispanic/Latino; 15 Hispanic/Latino; 1 Native Hawaiian or other Pacific Islander, non-Hispanic/Latino; 4 Two or more races, non-Hispanic/Latino), 2 international. Average age 35. 346 applicants, 67% accepted, 168 enrolled. *Faculty:* 30 full-time (18 women), 30 part-time/adjunct (21 women). Expenses: Contact institution. *Financial support:* In 2010–11, 425 students received support, including 55 research assistantships with partial tuition reimbursements available (averaging $3,000 per year); career-related internships or fieldwork, Federal Work-Study, institutionally sponsored loans, scholarships/grants, tuition waivers (partial), and unspecified assistantships also available. Support available to part-time students. Financial award application deadline: 5/1; financial award applicants required to submit FAFSA. In 2010, 193 master's, 54 other advanced degrees awarded. *Degree program information:* Part-time and evening/weekend programs available. Postbaccalaureate distance learning degree programs offered (minimal on-campus study). Offers accomplished teaching (M Ed); community counseling (MS); curriculum and leadership (Ed D); early childhood education (M Ed, Ed S); education and health professions (M Ed, MAT, MPA, MS, Ed D, Ed S); educational leadership (M Ed, Ed S); health administration (MPA); middle grades education (M Ed, Ed S); physical education (M Ed); school counseling (M Ed); secondary education (M Ed, MAT, Ed S); special education (M Ed). *Application deadline:* For fall admission, 6/30 for domestic students, 5/1 for international students; for spring admission, 11/1 for domestic and international students. Applications are processed on a rolling basis. *Application fee:* $30. Electronic applications accepted. *Application Contact:* Katie Thornton, Graduate Admissions Specialist, 706-568-2035, Fax: 706-568-2462, E-mail: thornton_katie@colstate.edu. *Interim Dean,* Dr. Ellen Roberts, 706-568-5015, Fax: 706-569-3134, E-mail: roberts_ellen@colstate.edu.

College of Letters and Sciences Students: 123 full-time (44 women), 215 part-time (62 women); includes 106 minority (89 Black or African American, non-Hispanic/Latino; 2 American Indian or Alaska Native, non-Hispanic/Latino; 9 Hispanic/Latino; 1 Native Hawaiian or other Pacific Islander, non-Hispanic/Latino; 5 Two or more races, non-Hispanic/Latino), 3 international. Average age 39. 90 applicants, 79% accepted, 59 enrolled. *Faculty:* 13 full-time (2 women), 16 part-time/adjunct (1 woman). Expenses: Contact institution. *Financial support:* In 2010–11, 76 students received support, including 18 research assistantships with tuition reimbursements available (averaging $3,000 per year); career-related internships or fieldwork, Federal Work-Study, institutionally sponsored loans, scholarships/grants, tuition waivers (partial), and unspecified assistantships also available. Support available to part-time students. Financial award application deadline: 5/1; financial award applicants required to submit FAFSA. In 2010, 125 master's awarded. *Degree program information:* Part-time and evening/weekend programs available. Postbaccalaureate distance learning degree programs offered (no on-campus study). Offers environmental science (MS); justice administration (MPA); letters and sciences (MPA, MS). *Application deadline:* For fall admission, 6/30 for domestic students, 5/1 for international students; for spring admission, 11/1 for domestic students, 4/1 for international students. Applications are processed on a rolling basis. *Application fee:* $30. Electronic applications accepted. *Application Contact:* Katie Thornton, Graduate Admissions Specialist, 706-568-2035, Fax: 706-568-2462, E-mail: thornton_katie@colstate.edu. *Dean,* Dr. David Lanoue, 706-568-2056, E-mail: lanoue_david@colstate.edu.

College of the Arts Students: 23 full-time (10 women), 2 part-time (1 woman); includes 1 Black or African American, non-Hispanic/Latino; 1 Hispanic/Latino, 8 international. Average age 26. 36 applicants, 47% accepted, 16 enrolled. *Faculty:* 23 full-time (12 women), 1 part-time/adjunct (0 women). Expenses: Contact institution. *Financial support:* In 2010–11, 21 students received support, including 19 research assistantships with partial tuition reimbursements available (averaging $3,000 per year); career-related internships or fieldwork, Federal Work-Study, institutionally sponsored loans, scholarships/grants, tuition waivers (partial), and unspecified assistantships also available. Support available to part-time students. Financial award application deadline: 5/1; financial award applicants required to submit FAFSA. In 2010, 5 master's awarded. *Degree program information:* Part-time and evening/weekend programs available. Postbaccalaureate distance learning degree programs offered (minimal on-campus study). Offers art education (M Ed); artist diploma (Post-baccalaureate Certificate); arts (M Ed, MM, Postbaccalaureate Certificate); music education (MM). *Application deadline:* For fall admission, 6/30 for domestic students, 5/1 for international students; for spring admission, 11/1 for domestic and international students. Applications are processed on a rolling basis. *Application fee:* $30. Electronic applications accepted. *Application Contact:* Katie Thornton, Graduate Admissions Specialist, 706-568-2035, Fax: 706-568-2462, E-mail: thornton_katie@colstate.edu. *Interim Dean,* Gary Wortley, 706-507-8043, E-mail: wortley_gary@colstate.edu.

D. Abbott Turner College of Business and Computer Science Students: 36 full-time (9 women), 145 part-time (54 women); includes 43 minority (19 Black or African American, non-Hispanic/Latino; 3 American Indian or Alaska Native, non-Hispanic/Latino; 12 Asian, non-Hispanic/Latino; 3 Hispanic/Latino; 6 Two or more races, non-Hispanic/Latino), 11 international. Average age 33. 133 applicants, 61% accepted, 58 enrolled. *Faculty:* 15 full-time (2 women). Expenses: Contact institution. *Financial support:* In 2010–11, 62 students received support, including 11 research assistantships (averaging $3,000 per year). Financial award application deadline: 5/1. In 2010, 59 master's awarded. Offers applied computer science (MS); business administration (MBA); modeling and simulation (Certificate); organizational leadership (MS). *Application deadline:* For fall admission, 6/30 for domestic students, 5/1 for international students; for spring admission, 11/1 for domestic and international students. Applications are processed on a rolling basis. *Application fee:* $30. Electronic applications accepted. *Application Contact:* Katie Thornton, Graduate Admissions Specialist, 706-568-2035, Fax: 706-568-2462, E-mail: thornton_katie@colstate.edu. *Dean,* Dr. Linda U. Hadley, 706-568-2044, Fax: 706-568-2184, E-mail: hadley_linda@colstate.edu.

CONCORDIA COLLEGE, Moorhead, MN 56562

General Information Independent-religious, coed, comprehensive institution.

GRADUATE UNITS

Program in Education Offers world language instruction (M Ed).

CONCORDIA LUTHERAN SEMINARY, Edmonton, AB T5B 4E3, Canada

General Information Independent-religious, coed, primarily men, graduate-only institution. *Graduate housing:* On-campus housing not available.

GRADUATE UNITS

Graduate and Professional Programs *Degree program information:* Part-time programs available. Offers theology (M Div, Graduate Certificate).

CONCORDIA SEMINARY, St. Louis, MO 63105-3199

General Information Independent-religious, coed, primarily men, graduate-only institution. *Graduate housing:* Rooms and/or apartments guaranteed to single students and available to married students. Housing application deadline: 3/4. *Research affiliation:* Center for Reformation Research, Concordia Historical Institute.

GRADUATE UNITS

Graduate Programs Offers theology (M Div, MA, STM, D Min, PhD, Certificate).

CONCORDIA THEOLOGICAL SEMINARY, Fort Wayne, IN 46825-4996

General Information Independent-religious, coed, primarily men, graduate-only institution. *Graduate housing:* Room and/or apartments available to single students; on-campus housing not available to married students.

GRADUATE UNITS

Graduate and Professional Programs *Degree program information:* Part-time programs available. Offers theology (M Div, MA, STM, D Min, PhD).

CONCORDIA UNIVERSITY, Irvine, CA 92612-3299

General Information Independent-religious, coed, comprehensive institution. *Enrollment:* 2,927 graduate, professional, and undergraduate students; 876 full-time matriculated graduate/professional students (469 women), 493 part-time matriculated graduate/professional students (259 women). *Enrollment by degree level:* 1,312 master's, 57 other advanced degrees. *Graduate faculty:* 34 full-time (14 women), 98 part-time/adjunct (31 women). *Tuition:* Full-time $6375; part-time $425 per unit. One-time fee: $125. Tuition and fees vary according to campus/location and program. *Graduate housing:* Room and/or apartments available on a first-come, first-served basis to single students; on-campus housing not available to married students. Typical cost: $4800 per year ($8380 including board). Room and board charges vary according to board plan and housing facility selected. *Student services:* Campus employment opportunities, campus safety program, career counseling, exercise/wellness program, free psychological counseling, international student services, multicultural affairs office, services for students with disabilities, teacher training, writing training. *Library facilities:* Concordia University Library. *Online resources:* library catalog, web page. *Collection:* 79,725 titles, 30,196 serial subscriptions, 1,898 audiovisual materials.

Computer facilities: Computer purchase and lease plans are available. 103 computers available on campus for general student use. A campuswide network can be accessed from student residence rooms and from off campus. Online class registration is available. *Web address:* http://www.cui.edu/.

General Application Contact: Rick Hardy, Associate Vice President for Enrollment Management, 949-214-3147, E-mail: rick.hardy@cui.edu.

GRADUATE UNITS

School of Arts and Sciences Students: 314 full-time (72 women), 166 part-time (27 women); includes 68 minority (24 Black or African American, non-Hispanic/Latino; 5 Asian, non-Hispanic/Latino; 39 Hispanic/Latino), 1 international. Average age 34. 249 applicants, 90% accepted, 187 enrolled. *Faculty:* 7 full-time (1 woman), 24 part-time/adjunct (4 women). Expenses: Contact institution. *Financial support:* In 2010–11, 399 students received support. Tuition waivers (full and partial) and unspecified assistantships available. Financial award applicants required to submit FAFSA. In 2010, 188 master's awarded. *Degree program information:* Part-time and evening/weekend programs available. Postbaccalaureate distance learning degree programs offered (no on-campus study). Offers coaching and athletic administration (MA). *Application deadline:* For fall admission, 8/10 for domestic students, 6/1 for international students; for spring admission, 2/15 for domestic students, 10/1 for international students. *Application fee:* $50 ($125 for international students). Electronic applications accepted.

Concordia University (continued)

Application Contact: Chris Lewis, Associate Director of Graduate Admissions, 949-214-3025, Fax: 949-854-6894, E-mail: chris.lewis@cui.edu. *Dean*, Dr. Timothy Preuss, 949-214-3286, E-mail: tim.preuss@cui.edu.

School of Business and Professional Studies Students: 80 full-time (37 women), 48 part-time (22 women); includes 28 minority (6 Black or African American, non-Hispanic/Latino; 12 Asian, non-Hispanic/Latino; 10 Hispanic/Latino), 8 international. Average age 30. 52 applicants, 44% accepted, 15 enrolled. *Faculty:* 3 full-time (0 women), 19 part-time/adjunct (3 women). Expenses: Contact institution. *Financial support:* In 2010–11, 107 students received support. Tuition waivers (full and partial) and unspecified assistantships available. Financial award applicants required to submit FAFSA. In 2010, 66 master's awarded. *Degree program information:* Part-time and evening/weekend programs available. Offers business administration: business practice (MBA); international studies (MA). *Application deadline:* For fall admission, 8/1 for domestic students, 6/1 for international students; for spring admission, 1/1 for domestic students, 11/1 for international students. *Application fee:* $50 ($125 for international students). Electronic applications accepted. *Application Contact:* Sherry Powers, MBA Admissions Coordinator, 949-214-3032, Fax: 949-854-6894, E-mail: sherry.powers@cui.edu. *Dean*, Dr. Timothy Peters, 949-214-3363, E-mail: tim.peters@cui.edu.

School of Education Students: 452 full-time (357 women), 272 part-time (207 women); includes 220 minority (47 Black or African American, non-Hispanic/Latino; 43 Asian, non-Hispanic/Latino; 130 Hispanic/Latino). Average age 40. 349 applicants, 81% accepted, 262 enrolled. *Faculty:* 16 full-time (10 women), 53 part-time/adjunct (24 women). Expenses: Contact institution. *Financial support:* In 2010–11, 634 students received support. Scholarships/grants and unspecified assistantships available. Financial award applicants required to submit FAFSA. In 2010, 329 degrees awarded. *Degree program information:* Part-time and evening/weekend programs available. Postbaccalaureate distance learning degree programs offered (no on-campus study). Offers curriculum and instruction (MA); education and preliminary teaching credential (M Ed); educational administration and preliminary administrative services credential (MA). *Application deadline:* For fall admission, 7/15 priority date for domestic students, 6/1 for international students; for spring admission, 11/30 priority date for domestic students, 10/1 for international students. Applications are processed on a rolling basis. *Application fee:* $50 ($125 for international students). Electronic applications accepted. *Application Contact:* Aaron Stewart, Assistant Director of Graduate Admissions, 949-214-3024, Fax: 949-854-6894, E-mail: aaron.stewart@cui.edu. *Dean*, Dr. Janice Nelson, 949-214-3334, E-mail: janice.nelson@cui.edu.

School of Theology Students: 30 full-time (3 women), 7 part-time (3 women); includes 5 minority (1 Black or African American, non-Hispanic/Latino; 1 Asian, non-Hispanic/Latino; 3 Hispanic/Latino), 4 international. Average age 34. 11 applicants, 55% accepted, 5 enrolled. *Faculty:* 8 full-time (1 woman), 2 part-time/adjunct (0 women). Expenses: Contact institution. *Financial support:* Scholarships/grants and unspecified assistantships available. Financial award applicants required to submit FAFSA. In 2010, 2 master's awarded. *Degree program information:* Part-time and evening/weekend programs available. Offers Christian leadership (MA); research in theology (MA); theology and culture (MA). *Application deadline:* For fall admission, 7/1 priority date for domestic students, 6/1 for international students; for spring admission, 11/30 priority date for domestic students, 10/1 for international students. Applications are processed on a rolling basis. *Application fee:* $50 ($125 for international students). Electronic applications accepted. *Application Contact:* Carrie Donohoe, Christ College Program Coordinator, 949-214-3389, E-mail: carrie.donohoe@cui.edu. *Dean of Graduate Studies*, Rev. Dr. James Bachman, 949-214-3387, E-mail: james.bachman@cui.edu.

CONCORDIA UNIVERSITY, Montréal, QC H3G 1M8, Canada

General Information Province-supported, coed, university. CGS member. *Graduate housing:* On-campus housing not available. *Research affiliation:* Blue Metropolis Literary Series (English), Canadian Journalism Project (journalism), Canadian Rural Revitalization Foundation (sociology), Centre de Recherche en Plasturgie et Composites (CREPEC) (mechanical and industrial engineering), Centre de Recherche Informatique de Montréal (CRIM) (computer science), Center d'experise et de services en application Multimédia (multimedia).

GRADUATE UNITS

School of Graduate Studies *Degree program information:* Part-time and evening/weekend programs available. Offers individualized research (M Sc, MA, PhD).

Faculty of Arts and Science Offers écriture (Certificate); adult education (Diploma); anglais-français en langue et techniques de localisation (Certificate); applied linguistics (MA); arts and science (M Sc, MA, MTM, PhD, Certificate, Diploma); biology (M Sc, PhD); biotechnology and genomics (Diploma); chemistry (M Sc, PhD); child study (MA); communication (PhD); communication studies (Diploma); community economic development (Diploma); creative writing (MA); economics (MA, PhD, Diploma); educational studies (MA); educational technology (MA, PhD); English (MA); environmental impact assessment (Diploma); exercise science (M Sc); geography, urban and environmental studies (M Sc); history (MA, PhD); history and philosophy of religion (MA); human systems intervention (MA); humanities (PhD); instructional technology (Diploma); journalism (Diploma); Judaic studies (MA); littératures francophones et résonances médiatiques (MA); mathematics (M Sc, MA, PhD); media studies (MA); philosophy (MA); physics (M Sc, PhD); political science (PhD); psychology (clinical) (MA, PhD, Certificate); psychology (general) (MA, PhD); public policy and public administration (MA); religion (PhD); social and cultural anthropology (MA); sociology (MA); teaching English as a second language (Certificate); teaching of mathematics (MTM); theological studies (MA); traductologie (MA); translation (Diploma).

Faculty of Engineering and Computer Science Offers 3D graphics and game development (Certificate); aerospace engineering (M Eng); building engineering (M Eng, MA Sc, PhD, Certificate); civil engineering (M Eng, MA Sc, PhD); composites (M Eng); computer science (M App Comp Sc, M Comp Sc, PhD, Diploma); electrical and computer engineering (M Eng, MA Sc, PhD); engineering and computer science (M App Comp Sc, M Comp Sc, M Eng, MA Sc, PhD, Certificate, Diploma); environmental engineering (Certificate); industrial engineering (M Eng, MA Sc); information systems security (M Eng, MA Sc); mechanical engineering (M Eng, MA Sc, PhD, Certificate); quality systems engineering (M Eng, MA Sc); service engineering and network management (Certificate); software engineering (MA Sc); software systems for industrial engineering (Certificate).

Faculty of Fine Arts *Degree program information:* Part-time programs available. Offers advanced music performance studies (Diploma); art education (MA, PhD); art history (MA, PhD); creative arts therapies (MA); digital technologies in design art practice (Certificate); film studies (MA); fine arts (MA, MFA, PhD, Certificate, Diploma); studio arts (MFA).

John Molson School of Business *Degree program information:* Part-time and evening/weekend programs available. Offers administration (M Sc, Diploma); aviation management (Certificate, Diploma); business administration (MBA, UA Undergraduate Associate, PhD); chartered accountancy (Diploma); community organizational development (Certificate); event management and fundraising (Certificate); executive business administration (EMBA); investment management (Diploma); investment management option (MBA); management accounting (Certificate); management of healthcare organizations (Certificate); sport administration (Diploma). PhD program offered jointly with HEC Montreal, McGill University, and Université du Québec à Montréal.

CONCORDIA UNIVERSITY, Ann Arbor, MI 48105-2797

General Information Independent-religious, coed, comprehensive institution. *Graduate housing:* On-campus housing not available.

GRADUATE UNITS

Graduate Programs *Degree program information:* Part-time and evening/weekend programs available. Offers curriculum and instruction (MS); educational leadership (MS); organizational leadership and administration (MS).

CONCORDIA UNIVERSITY, Portland, OR 97211-6099

General Information Independent-religious, coed, comprehensive institution. *Graduate housing:* Room and/or apartments available on a first-come, first-served basis to single students; on-campus housing not available to married students. Housing application deadline: 8/1.

GRADUATE UNITS

College of Education *Degree program information:* Part-time programs available. Postbaccalaureate distance learning degree programs offered (no on-campus study). Offers curriculum and instruction (elementary) (M Ed); educational administration (M Ed); elementary education (MAT); secondary education (MAT). Electronic applications accepted.

School of Management *Degree program information:* Evening/weekend programs available. Offers management (MBA).

CONCORDIA UNIVERSITY CHICAGO, River Forest, IL 60305-1499

General Information Independent-religious, coed, comprehensive institution. CGS member. *Graduate housing:* Rooms and/or apartments available on a first-come, first-served basis to single and married students.

GRADUATE UNITS

College of Education Offers Christian education (MA); curriculum and instruction (MA); early childhood education (MAT); elementary education (MAT); reading education (MA); school leadership (MA, Ed D, CAS); secondary education (MAT).

College of Graduate and Innovative Programs Offers business administration (MBA); church music (MCM); community counseling (MA); educational technology (MA); gerontology (MA); human services (MA); liberal studies (MA); music (MA); psychology (MA); religion (MA); school counseling (MA, CAS).

CONCORDIA UNIVERSITY COLLEGE OF ALBERTA, Edmonton, AB T5B 4E4, Canada

General Information Independent-religious, coed, comprehensive institution.

GRADUATE UNITS

Program in Biblical and Christian Studies Offers Biblical and Christian studies (MA).

Program in Information Systems Security Management Offers information systems security management (MA).

CONCORDIA UNIVERSITY, NEBRASKA, Seward, NE 68434-1599

General Information Independent-religious, coed, comprehensive institution. *Graduate housing:* Rooms and/or apartments available on a first-come, first-served basis to single and married students.

GRADUATE UNITS

Graduate Programs in Education *Degree program information:* Part-time and evening/weekend programs available. Offers early childhood education (M Ed); education (M Ed, MPE, MS); elementary and secondary education (M Ed); elementary education (M Ed); family life ministry (MS); parish education (MPE); reading education (M Ed); secondary education (M Ed). Electronic applications accepted.

CONCORDIA UNIVERSITY, ST. PAUL, St. Paul, MN 55104-5494

General Information Independent-religious, coed, comprehensive institution. *Enrollment:* 2,808 graduate, professional, and undergraduate students; 1,063 full-time matriculated graduate/professional students (785 women), 3 part-time matriculated graduate/professional students (2 women). *Enrollment by degree level:* 1,038 master's, 28 other advanced degrees. *Graduate faculty:* 29 full-time (15 women), 106 part-time/adjunct (57 women). *Tuition:* Full-time $7500; part-time $460 per credit. *Required fees:* $460 per credit. Tuition and fees vary according to program. *Student services:* Campus employment opportunities, campus safety program, career counseling, child daycare facilities, exercise/wellness program, free psychological counseling, international student services, low-cost health insurance, multicultural affairs office, services for students with disabilities, teacher training, writing training. *Library facilities:* Library Technology Center. *Online resources:* library catalog, web page, access to other libraries' catalogs. *Collection:* 174,592 titles, 323 serial subscriptions, 1,859 audiovisual materials.

Computer facilities: A campuswide network can be accessed from student residence rooms and from off campus. Online class registration is available. *Web address:* http://www.csp.edu/.

General Application Contact: Kimberly Craig, Director of Graduate and Cohort Admission, 651-603-6223, Fax: 651-603-6320, E-mail: craig@csp.edu.

GRADUATE UNITS

College of Arts and Sciences Students: 15 full-time (8 women); includes 1 Two or more races, non-Hispanic/Latino. Average age 32. 23 applicants, 83% accepted. *Faculty:* 3 full-time (2 women), 3 part-time/adjunct (0 women). Expenses: Contact institution. *Financial support:* Applicants required to submit FAFSA. *Degree program information:* Evening/weekend programs available. Offers strategic communication management (MA). *Application deadline:* Applications are processed on a rolling basis. *Application fee:* $50. Electronic applications accepted. *Application Contact:* Kimberly Craig, Director of Graduate and Cohort Admission, 651-603-6223, Fax: 651-603-6320, E-mail: craig@csp.edu. *Dean*, Dr. Marilyn Reineck, 651-641-8850, E-mail: reineck@csp.edu.

College of Business and Organizational Leadership Students: 338 full-time (203 women), 2 part-time (1 woman); includes 24 Black or African American, non-Hispanic/Latino; 3 American Indian or Alaska Native, non-Hispanic/Latino; 11 Asian, non-Hispanic/Latino; 3 Hispanic/Latino; 3 Two or more races, non-Hispanic/Latino. Average age 34. 191 applicants, 65% accepted, 117 enrolled. *Faculty:* 14 full-time (6 women), 30 part-time/adjunct (8 women). Expenses: Contact institution. *Financial support:* Applicants required to submit FAFSA. In 2010, 125 master's awarded. *Degree program information:* Evening/weekend programs available. Postbaccalaureate distance learning degree programs offered (minimal on-campus study). Offers business and organizational leadership (MBA); criminal justice leadership (MA); health care management (MBA); human resources management (MA); leadership and management (MA). *Application deadline:* Applications are processed on a rolling basis. *Application fee:* $50. Electronic applications accepted. *Application Contact:* Kimberly Craig, Director of Graduate and Cohort Admission, 651-603-6223, Fax: 651-603-6320, E-mail: craig@csp.edu. *Dean*, Dr. Bruce Corrie, 651-641-8226, Fax: 651-641-8807, E-mail: corrie@csp.edu.

College of Education Students: 699 full-time (566 women), 1 (woman) part-time; includes 26 Black or African American, non-Hispanic/Latino; 2 American Indian or Alaska Native, non-Hispanic/Latino; 20 Asian, non-Hispanic/Latino; 7 Hispanic/Latino; 8 Two or more races, non-Hispanic/Latino. Average age 36. 311 applicants, 78% accepted, 230 enrolled. *Faculty:* 11 full-time (7 women), 69 part-time/adjunct (47 women). Expenses: Contact institution. *Financial support:* Applicants required to submit FAFSA. In 2010, 172 master's, 83 other advanced degrees awarded. *Degree program information:* Evening/weekend programs available. Postbaccalaureate distance learning degree programs offered (minimal on-campus study). Offers curriculum and instruction (MA Ed); differentiated instruction (MA Ed); early childhood education (MA Ed); educational leadership (MA Ed); family life education (MA); K-12 reading endorsement (Certificate); special education (Certificate); sports management (MA). *Application deadline:* Applications are processed on a rolling basis. *Application fee:* $50. Electronic applications accepted. *Application Contact:* Kimberly Craig, Director of Graduate and Cohort Admission, 651-603-6223, Fax: 651-603-6320, E-mail: craig@csp.edu. *Dean*, Dr. Donald Helmstetter, 651-641-8227, Fax: 651-641-8807, E-mail: helmstetter@csp.edu.

College of Vocation and Ministry Students: 11 full-time (3 women); includes 1 Asian, non-Hispanic/Latino. Average age 40. *Faculty:* 2 full-time (0 women), 5 part-time/adjunct (2 women). Expenses: Contact institution. *Financial support:* Applicants required to submit FAFSA. In 2010, 7 master's awarded. *Degree program information:* Evening/weekend programs available. Postbaccalaureate distance learning degree programs offered (minimal on-campus study). Offers Christian education (Certificate); Christian outreach (MA, Certificate). *Application deadline:* Applications are processed on a rolling basis. *Application fee:* $50. Electronic applications accepted. *Application Contact:* Kimberly Craig, Director of Graduate and Cohort Admission, 651-603-6223, Fax: 651-603-6320, E-mail: craig@csp.edu. *Dean*, Dr. David Lumpp, 651-641-8217, E-mail: lumpp@csp.edu.

CONCORDIA UNIVERSITY TEXAS, Austin, TX 78726

General Information Independent-religious, coed, comprehensive institution.

GRADUATE UNITS

College of Education *Degree program information:* Part-time and evening/weekend programs available. Offers education (M Ed).

CONCORDIA UNIVERSITY WISCONSIN, Mequon, WI 53097-2402

General Information Independent-religious, coed, comprehensive institution. *Graduate housing:* Room and/or apartments available to single students; on-campus housing not available to married students. Housing application deadline: 8/1.

GRADUATE UNITS

Graduate Programs *Degree program information:* Part-time and evening/weekend programs available. Postbaccalaureate distance learning degree programs offered (minimal on-campus study). Offers art education (MS Ed); curriculum and instruction (MS Ed); early childhood (MS Ed); educational administration (MS Ed); environmental education (MS Ed); family studies (MS Ed); professional counseling (MPC); reading (MS Ed); school counseling (MS Ed); special education (MS Ed). Electronic applications accepted.

School of Arts and Sciences Offers arts and sciences (MCM); church music (MCM).

School of Business and Legal Studies Offers business and legal studies (MBA, MSSPA); finance (MBA); health care administration (MBA); human resource management (MBA); international business (MBA); international business-bilingual English/Chinese (MBA); management (MBA); management information systems (MBA); managerial communications (MBA); marketing (MBA); public administration (MBA); risk management (MBA); student personnel administration (MSSPA).

School of Health and Human Services Offers family nurse practitioner (MSN); geriatric nurse practitioner (MSN); health and human services (MOT, MSN, MSPT, MSRS, DPT); nurse educator (MSN); occupational therapy (MOT); physical therapy (MSPT, DPT); rehabilitation science (MSRS).

CONCORD LAW SCHOOL, Los Angeles, CA 90024

General Information Proprietary, coed, graduate-only institution.

GRADUATE UNITS

Program in Law *Degree program information:* Part-time and evening/weekend programs available. Postbaccalaureate distance learning degree programs offered (no on-campus study). Offers law (EJD, JD). Electronic applications accepted.

CONCORD UNIVERSITY, Athens, WV 24712-1000

General Information State-supported, coed, comprehensive institution. *Enrollment:* 2,937 graduate, professional, and undergraduate students; 2 full-time matriculated graduate/professional students (both women), 247 part-time matriculated graduate/professional students (173 women). *Enrollment by degree level:* 249 master's. *Graduate faculty:* 16 full-time (7 women). Tuition, state resident: full-time $2674; part-time $297 per credit hour. Tuition, nonresident: full-time $4697; part-time $522 per credit hour. *Required fees:* $18 per term. One-time fee: $25. Tuition and fees vary according to course load. *Student services:* Campus employment opportunities, career counseling, child daycare facilities, free psychological counseling, international student services, multicultural affairs office, services for students with disabilities. *Library facilities:* J. Frank Marsh Library. *Online resources:* library catalog, web page, access to other libraries' catalogs. *Collection:* 163,292 titles, 140 serial subscriptions.

Computer facilities: 250 computers available on campus for general student use. A campuswide network can be accessed from student residence rooms and from off campus. Online class registration is available. *Web address:* http://www.concord.edu/.

General Application Contact: Wendy Bailey, 304-384-6223, E-mail: baileyw@concord.edu.

GRADUATE UNITS

Graduate Studies Students: 2 full-time (both women), 247 part-time (173 women); includes 6 Black or African American, non-Hispanic/Latino; 1 American Indian or Alaska Native, non-Hispanic/Latino; 2 Asian, non-Hispanic/Latino. Average age 36. 124 applicants, 71% accepted, 88 enrolled. *Faculty:* 16 full-time (7 women). Expenses: Contact institution. *Financial support:* Tuition waivers and unspecified assistantships available. In 2010, 27 master's awarded. *Degree program information:* Part-time and evening/weekend programs available. Postbaccalaureate distance learning degree programs offered (no on-campus study). Offers educational leadership and supervision (M Ed); geography (M Ed); health promotion (M Ed); reading specialist (M Ed). *Application deadline:* Applications are processed on a rolling basis. *Application fee:* $25. Electronic applications accepted. *Application Contact:* Wendy Bailey, 304-384-6223, E-mail: baileyw@concord.edu. *Interim Director*, Dr. Cheryl Barnes, 304-384-5148, E-mail: ctrull@concord.edu.

CONNECTICUT COLLEGE, New London, CT 06320-4196

General Information Independent, coed, comprehensive institution. *Enrollment:* 1,887 graduate, professional, and undergraduate students; 5 full-time matriculated graduate/professional students (all women), 2 part-time matriculated graduate/professional students (both women). *Enrollment by degree level:* 7 master's. *Tuition:* Part-time $44.13 per credit hour. *Graduate housing:* On-campus housing not available. *Student services:* Campus employment opportunities, career counseling, low-cost health insurance, services for students with disabilities. *Library facilities:* Charles Shain Library plus 1 other. *Online resources:* library catalog, web page, access to other libraries' catalogs. *Collection:* 496,817 titles, 2,279 serial subscriptions. *Research affiliation:* Hartford Hospital (neuropsychology and clinical psychology).

Computer facilities: Computer purchase and lease plans are available. A campuswide network can be accessed from student residence rooms and from off campus. Online class registration is available. *Web address:* http://www.connecticutcollege.edu/.

General Application Contact: Ann W. Whitlatch, Senior Associate Registrar, 860-439-2062, Fax: 860-439-5421, E-mail: awwhi@conncoll.edu.

GRADUATE UNITS

Department of Psychology *Degree program information:* Part-time programs available. Offers psychology (MA).

CONSERVATORIO DE MUSICA, San Juan, PR 00907

General Information Public, coed, comprehensive institution.

GRADUATE UNITS

Program in Musical Performance Offers guitar (Diploma); orchestral instruments (Diploma); piano (Diploma); vocal performance (Diploma).

Program in Music Education Offers music education (MM Ed).

CONVERSE COLLEGE, Spartanburg, SC 29302-0006

General Information Independent, Undergraduate: women only; graduate: coed, comprehensive institution. *Enrollment:* 185 full-time matriculated graduate/professional students (147 women), 363 part-time matriculated graduate/professional students (303 women). *Graduate faculty:* 35 full-time (16 women), 17 part-time/adjunct (8 women). *Tuition:* Part-time $365 per credit hour. *Graduate housing:* On-campus housing not available. *Student services:* Campus employment opportunities, campus safety program, career counseling, international student services, teacher training. *Library facilities:* Mickel Library. *Online resources:* library catalog, web page, access to other libraries' catalogs. *Collection:* 155,731 titles, 48,179 serial subscriptions, 21,668 audiovisual materials.

Computer facilities: 140 computers available on campus for general student use. A campuswide network can be accessed from student residence rooms and from off campus. Online class registration is available. *Web address:* http://www.converse.edu/.

General Application Contact: Dr. Kathy Good, Dean of the School of Education and Graduate Studies, 864-596-9082, Fax: 864-596-9221, E-mail: kathy.good@converse.edu.

GRADUATE UNITS

Carroll McDaniel Petrie School of Music *Degree program information:* Part-time and evening/weekend programs available. Offers instrumental performance (M Mus); music education (M Mus); piano pedagogy (M Mus); vocal performance (M Mus). Electronic applications accepted.

School of Education and Graduate Studies *Degree program information:* Part-time and evening/weekend programs available. Offers administration and supervision (Ed S); art education (M Ed); biology (MAT); chemistry (MAT); curriculum and instruction (Ed S); early childhood education (MAT); education (Ed S); elementary education (M Ed, MAT); English (M Ed, MAT, MLA); gifted education (M Ed); history (MLA); leadership (M Ed); learning disabilities (MAT); liberal arts (MLA); marriage and family therapy (Ed S); mathematics (M Ed, MAT); mental disabilities (MAT); natural sciences (M Ed); political science (MLA); secondary education (M Ed, MAT); social sciences (M Ed, MAT); special education (M Ed, MAT). Electronic applications accepted.

CONWAY SCHOOL OF LANDSCAPE DESIGN, Conway, MA 01341-0179

General Information Independent, coed, graduate-only institution. *Graduate housing:* On-campus housing not available.

GRADUATE UNITS

Graduate Program in Landscape Design Offers landscape design (MA).

COOPER UNION FOR THE ADVANCEMENT OF SCIENCE AND ART, New York, NY 10003-7120

General Information Independent, coed, comprehensive institution. *Enrollment:* 1,000 graduate, professional, and undergraduate students; 65 full-time matriculated graduate/professional students (18 women), 25 part-time matriculated graduate/professional students (1 woman). *Enrollment by degree level:* 90 master's. *Graduate faculty:* 27 full-time (1 woman), 15 part-time/adjunct (2 women). *Tuition:* Full-time $35,000; part-time $1100 per credit. *Required fees:* $825 per semester. *Graduate housing:* Room and/or apartments available to single students; on-campus housing not available to married students. *Student services:* Campus employment opportunities, campus safety program, career counseling, international student services, low-cost health insurance, writing training. *Library facilities:* Cooper Union Library. *Online resources:* library catalog, web page, access to other libraries' catalogs. *Collection:* 136,711 titles, 3,427 serial subscriptions, 1,837 audiovisual materials. *Research affiliation:* Consolidated Edison (Con Ed), ITT, Albert Einstein School of Medicine, Science House, Iridescent, Maxentric.

Computer facilities: Computer purchase and lease plans are available. 400 computers available on campus for general student use. A campuswide network can be accessed from student residence rooms and from off campus. *Web address:* http://www.cooper.edu/.

General Application Contact: Student Contact, 212-353-4120, E-mail: admissions@cooper.edu.

GRADUATE UNITS

Albert Nerken School of Engineering Students: 57 full-time (15 women), 25 part-time (1 woman); includes 2 Black or African American, non-Hispanic/Latino; 1 American Indian or Alaska Native, non-Hispanic/Latino; 22 Asian, non-Hispanic/Latino; 2 Hispanic/Latino, 16 international. Average age 24. 72 applicants, 39% accepted, 27 enrolled. *Faculty:* 27 full-time (1 woman), 15 part-time/adjunct (2 women). Expenses: Contact institution. *Financial support:* Fellowships with full tuition reimbursements, career-related internships or fieldwork, Federal Work-Study, tuition waivers (full), and all admitted students receive full-tuition scholarships available. Support available to part-time students. Financial award application deadline: 5/1; financial award applicants required to submit CSS PROFILE or FAFSA. In 2010, 25 master's awarded. *Degree program information:* Part-time programs available. Offers chemical engineering (ME); civil engineering (ME); electrical engineering (ME); mechanical engineering (ME). *Application deadline:* For fall admission, 2/15 for domestic and international students. *Application fee:* $65. *Application Contact:* Student Contact, 212-353-4120, E-mail: admissions@cooper.edu. *Acting Dean*, Dr. Simon Ben-Avi, 212-353-4285, E-mail: benavi@cooper.edu.

Irwin S. Chanin School of Architecture Students: 8 full-time (3 women), 4 international. Average age 25. 122 applicants, 10% accepted, 8 enrolled. *Faculty:* 14 full-time (3 women), 19 part-time/adjunct (6 women). Expenses: Contact institution. *Financial support:* In 2010–11, 7 students received support. Tuition waivers and all admitted students receive a full-tuition scholarship for the length of their study available. Financial award application deadline: 5/1; financial award applicants required to submit CSS PROFILE or FAFSA. In 2010, 7 master's awarded. Offers architecture (M Arch II). *Application deadline:* For fall admission, 2/1 for domestic students. *Application fee:* $65. *Application Contact:* Susan Cohen, Student Contact, 212-353-4120, E-mail: admissions@cooper.edu. *Dean*, Dr. Anthony Vidler.

COPPIN STATE UNIVERSITY, Baltimore, MD 21216-3698

General Information State-supported, coed, comprehensive institution. CGS member. *Graduate housing:* On-campus housing not available.

GRADUATE UNITS

Division of Graduate Studies *Degree program information:* Part-time and evening/weekend programs available. Postbaccalaureate distance learning degree programs offered.

Division of Arts and Sciences *Degree program information:* Part-time and evening/weekend programs available. Offers alcohol and substance abuse counseling (MS); arts and sciences (M Ed, MA, MS); criminal justice (MS); human services administration (MS); rehabilitation counseling (M Ed).

Division of Education *Degree program information:* Part-time and evening/weekend programs available. Postbaccalaureate distance learning degree programs offered. Offers adult and general education (MS); curriculum and instruction (M Ed, MAT, MS); reading education (MS); special education (M Ed); teacher education (MAT); teaching (MAT).

Helene Fuld School of Nursing *Degree program information:* Part-time and evening/weekend programs available. Offers family nurse practitioner (PMC); nursing (MSN).

CORBAN UNIVERSITY, Salem, OR 97301-9392

General Information Independent-religious, coed, comprehensive institution.

GRADUATE UNITS

Graduate School Offers counseling (MA); education (MS Ed); management (MBA); non-profit management (MBA).

CORCORAN COLLEGE OF ART AND DESIGN, Washington, DC 20006-4804

General Information Independent, coed, comprehensive institution. *Graduate housing:* Rooms and/or apartments available on a first-come, first-served basis to single and married students. Housing application deadline: 5/15.

GRADUATE UNITS

Graduate Programs *Degree program information:* Part-time programs available.

CORNELL UNIVERSITY, Ithaca, NY 14853-0001

General Information Independent, coed, university. CGS member. *Enrollment:* 20,939 graduate, professional, and undergraduate students; 7,004 full-time matriculated graduate/professional students (3,011 women). *Enrollment by degree level:* 974 first professional, 3,083 master's, 2,947 doctoral. *Graduate faculty:* 1,488 full-time (404 women), 86 part-time/

Cornell University (continued)

adjunct (17 women). *Tuition:* Full-time $29,500. *Required fees:* $76. Tuition and fees vary according to degree level and program. *Graduate housing:* Rooms and/or apartments available on a first-come, first-served basis to single and married students. Typical cost: $7500 per year ($12,600 including board) for single students; $11,040 per year ($16,140 including board) for married students. Room and board charges vary according to board plan and housing facility selected. Housing application deadline: 7/1. *Student services:* Campus employment opportunities, campus safety program, career counseling, exercise/wellness program, free psychological counseling, grant writing training, international student services, low-cost health insurance, multicultural affairs office, services for students with disabilities, teacher training, writing training. *Library facilities:* Main library plus 18 others. *Online resources:* library catalog, web page, access to other libraries' catalogs. *Collection:* 8.2 million titles, 98,000 serial subscriptions, 145,802 audiovisual materials. *Research affiliation:* Brookhaven National Laboratory (physics, biology, medicine, chemistry, energy, engineering, environmental science), Fermi National Accelerator Laboratory, Boyce Thompson Institute for Plant Research (plant research).

Computer facilities: Computer purchase and lease plans are available. 2,650 computers available on campus for general student use. A campuswide network can be accessed from student residence rooms and from off campus. Online class registration is available. *Web address:* http://www.cornell.edu/.

General Application Contact: Graduate School Application Requests, 607-255-5820, Fax: 607-255-1816, E-mail: gradadmissions@cornell.edu.

GRADUATE UNITS

College of Veterinary Medicine Students: 347 full-time (267 women); includes 56 minority (8 Black or African American, non-Hispanic/Latino; 2 American Indian or Alaska Native, non-Hispanic/Latino; 17 Asian, non-Hispanic/Latino; 26 Hispanic/Latino; 3 Two or more races, non-Hispanic/Latino), 1 international. Average age 26. 946 applicants, 12% accepted, 102 enrolled. *Faculty:* 176 full-time (69 women). Expenses: Contact institution. *Financial support:* In 2010–11, 317 students received support; fellowships, research assistantships, teaching assistantships, Federal Work-Study, institutionally sponsored loans, and scholarships/grants available. Financial award application deadline: 2/1; financial award applicants required to submit CSS PROFILE or FAFSA. Offers veterinary medicine (DVM). *Application deadline:* For fall admission, 10/1 for domestic and international students. *Application fee:* $60. Electronic applications accepted. *Application Contact:* Jennifer A. Mailey, Director of Admissions, 607-253-3700, Fax: 607-253-3709, E-mail: jam333@cornell.edu. *Dean,* Dr. Michael Kotlikoff, 607-253-3771, Fax: 607-253-3701.

Cornell Law School Offers law (JD, LL M, JSD). JD/MLLP offered jointly with Humboldt University, Berlin; JD/DESS offered jointly with Institut d'etudes Politiques de Paris ('Sciences Po") and Paris I. Electronic applications accepted.

Graduate School Students: 5,228 full-time (2,266 women); includes 127 Black or African American, non-Hispanic/Latino; 14 American Indian or Alaska Native, non-Hispanic/Latino; 415 Asian, non-Hispanic/Latino; 211 Hispanic/Latino, 2,079 international. Average age 27. 17,659 applicants, 24% accepted, 2300 enrolled. *Faculty:* 2,761 full-time (684 women). Expenses: Contact institution. *Financial support:* In 2010–11, 3,013 students received support, including 929 fellowships with full tuition reimbursements available, 1,204 research assistantships with full tuition reimbursements available, 1,176 teaching assistantships with full tuition reimbursements available; career-related internships or fieldwork, institutionally sponsored loans, scholarships/grants, traineeships, tuition waivers (full and partial), and unspecified assistantships also available. Financial award applicants required to submit FAFSA. In 2010, 1,385 master's, 500 doctorates awarded. Offers acarology (MS, PhD); advanced composites and structures (M Eng); advanced materials processing (M Eng, MS, PhD); aerospace engineering (M Eng, MS, PhD); African history (MA, PhD); African studies (MPS); African-American literature (PhD); African-American studies (MPS); agricultural education (MAT); agriculture and life sciences (M Eng, MAT, MFS, MLA, MPS, MS, PhD); agronomy (MS, PhD); algorithms (M Eng, PhD); American art (PhD); American history (MA, PhD); American literature after 1865 (PhD); American literature to 1865 (PhD); American politics (PhD); American studies (PhD); analytical chemistry (PhD); ancient art and archaeology (PhD); ancient history (MA, PhD); ancient Near Eastern studies (MA, PhD); ancient philosophy (PhD); animal breeding (MS, PhD); animal cytology (MS, PhD); animal genetics (MS, PhD); animal nutrition (MPS, MS, PhD); apiculture (MS, PhD); apparel design (MA, MPS); applied economics (PhD); applied economics and management (MPS, MS, PhD); applied entomology (MS, PhD); applied linguistics (MA, PhD); applied logic and automated reasoning (M Eng, PhD); applied mathematics (PhD); applied mathematics and computational methods (M Eng, MS, PhD); applied physics (PhD); applied probability and statistics (PhD); applied research in human-environment relations (MS); applied statistics (MPS); aquatic entomology (MS, PhD); aquatic science (MPS, MS, PhD); Arabic and Islamic studies (MA, PhD); archaeological anthropology (PhD); architectural design (M Arch); architectural science (MS); architecture, art and planning (M Arch, MA, MFA, MPSRE, MRP, MS, PhD); artificial intelligence (M Eng, PhD); arts and sciences (MA, MFA, MPA, MPS, MS, DMA, PhD); Asian art (PhD); Asian religions (PhD); astronomy (PhD); astrophysics (PhD); atmospheric science (MS, PhD); Baroque art (PhD); basic analytical economics (PhD); behavioral biology (PhD); behavioral physiology (MS, PhD); biblical studies (MA, PhD); bio-organic chemistry (PhD); biochemical engineering (M Eng, MS, PhD); biochemistry (PhD); biological anthropology (PhD); biological control (MS, PhD); biological engineering (M Eng, MPS, MS, PhD); biology (7-12) (MAT); biomechanical engineering (M Eng, MS, PhD); biomedical engineering (M Eng, MS, PhD); biometry (MS, PhD); biophysical chemistry (PhD); biophysics (PhD); biopsychology (PhD); building technology and environmental science (MS); cardiovascular and respiratory physiology (MS, PhD); cell biology (PhD); cellular and molecular medicine (MS, PhD); cellular and molecular toxicology (MS, PhD); cellular immunology (MS, PhD); chemical biology (PhD); chemical physics (PhD); chemical reaction engineering (M Eng, MS, PhD); chemistry (7-12) (MAT); Chinese linguistics (MA, PhD); Chinese philology (MA, PhD); city and regional planning (MRP, PhD); classical and statistical thermodynamics (M Eng, MS, PhD); classical archaeology (PhD); classical Chinese literature (MA, PhD); classical Japanese literature (MA, PhD); classical myth (PhD); classical rhetoric (PhD); cognition (PhD); collective bargaining, labor law and labor history (MILR, MPS, MS, PhD); colonial and postcolonial literature (PhD); combustion (M Eng, MS, PhD); communication (MPS, MS, PhD); communication research methods (MS, PhD); community and regional society (MS); community and regional sociology (MPS, PhD); community nutrition (MPS, MS, PhD); comparative and functional anatomy (MS, PhD); comparative biomedical sciences (MS, PhD); comparative literature (PhD); comparative politics (PhD); composition (DMA); computational behavioral biology (PhD); computational biology (PhD); computational cell biology (PhD); computational ecology (PhD); computational macromolecular biology (PhD); computational organismal biology (PhD); computer engineering (M Eng, PhD); computer graphics (M Eng, MS, PhD); computer science (M Eng, PhD); computer vision (M Eng, PhD); concurrency and distributed computing (M Eng, PhD); consumer policy (PhD); controlled environment agriculture (MPS, PhD); controlled environment horticulture (MS); creative visual arts (MFA); creative writing (MFA); cultural studies (PhD); curriculum and instruction (MPS, MS, PhD); cytology (MS, PhD); dairy science (MPS, MS, PhD); decision theory (MS, PhD); development policy (MPS); developmental and reproductive biology (MS, PhD); developmental biology (MS, PhD); developmental psychology (PhD); drama and the theatre (PhD); dramatic literature (PhD); dynamics and space mechanics (MS, PhD); early modern European history (MA, PhD); earth science (7-12) (MAT); East Asian linguistics (MA, PhD); East Asian studies (MA); ecological and environmental plant pathology (MPS, MS, PhD); ecology (MS, PhD); econometrics and economic statistics (PhD); economic and social statistics (MILR, MS, PhD); economic development and planning (PhD); economic geology (M Eng, MS, PhD); economic theory (PhD); economy and society (MA, PhD); ecotoxicology and environmental chemistry (MS, PhD); electrical engineering (M Eng, PhD); electrical systems (M Eng, PhD); electrophysics (M Eng, PhD); endocrinology (MS, PhD); energy (M Eng, MPS, MS, PhD); energy and power systems (M Eng, MS, PhD); engineering (M Eng, MPS, MS, PhD); engineering geology (M Eng, MS, PhD); engineering management (M Eng, MS, PhD); engineering physics (M Eng); engineering statistics (MS, PhD); English history (MA, PhD); English linguistics (MA, PhD); English poetry (PhD); English Renaissance to 1660 (PhD); environmental and comparative physiology (MS, PhD); environmental archaeology (MA); environmental engineering (M Eng, MPS, MS, PhD); environmental fluid mechanics and hydrology (M Eng, MS, PhD); environmental geophysics (M Eng, MS, PhD); environmental information science (MS, PhD); environmental management (MPS); environmental planning and design (MRP, PhD); environmental studies (MA, MS, PhD); environmental systems engineering (M Eng, MS, PhD); epidemiological plant pathology (MPS, MS, PhD); evaluation (PhD); evolutionary biology (PhD); experimental design (MS, PhD); experimental physics (MS, PhD); extension, and adult education (MPS, MS, PhD); facilities planning and management (MS); family and social welfare policy (PhD); fiber science (MS, PhD); field crop science (MS, PhD); fishery science (MPS, MS, PhD); fluid dynamics, rheology and biorheology (M Eng, MS, PhD); fluid mechanics (M Eng, MS, PhD); food chemistry (MPS, MS, PhD); food engineering (MPS, MS, PhD); food microbiology (MPS, MS, PhD); food processing engineering (M Eng, MPS, MS, PhD); food processing waste technology (MPS, MS, PhD); food science (MFS, MPS, MS, PhD); forest science (MPS, MS, PhD); French history (MA, PhD); French linguistics (PhD); French literature (PhD); gastrointestinal and metabolic physiology (MS, PhD); gender and life course (MA, PhD); general geology (M Eng, MS, PhD); general linguistics (MA, PhD); general space sciences (PhD); genetics (PhD); geobiology (M Eng, MS, PhD); geochemistry and isotope geology (M Eng, MS, PhD); geohydrology (M Eng, MS, PhD); geomorphology (M Eng, MS, PhD); geophysics (M Eng, MS, PhD); geotechnical engineering (M Eng, MS, PhD); geotectonics (M Eng, MS, PhD); German area studies (MA, PhD); German history (MA, PhD); German intellectual history (MA, PhD); Germanic linguistics (MA, PhD); Germanic literature (MA, PhD); Greek and Latin language and linguistics (PhD); Greek language and literature (PhD); greenhouse crops (MPS, MS, PhD); health administration (MHA); health management and policy (PhD); heat and mass transfer (M Eng, MS, PhD); heat transfer (M Eng, MS, PhD); Hebrew and Judaic studies (MA, PhD); Hispanic literature (PhD); histology (MS, PhD); historic preservation planning (MA); historical archaeology (MA); history and philosophy of science and technology (MA, PhD); history of architecture (MA, PhD); history of science (MA, PhD); history of urban development (MA, PhD); horticultural business management (MPS, MS, PhD); horticultural physiology (MPS, MS, PhD); hospitality management (MMH); hotel administration (MS, PhD); housing and design (MS); human computer interaction (PhD); human development and family studies (PhD); human ecology (MA, MHA, MPS, MS, PhD); human experimental psychology (PhD); human factors and ergonomics (MS); human nutrition (MPS, MS, PhD); human resource studies (MILR, MPS, MS, PhD); human-environment relations (MS); immunochemistry (MS, PhD); immunogenetics (MS, PhD); immunopathology (MS, PhD); Indo-European linguistics (MA, PhD); industrial and labor relations problems (MILR, MPS, MS, PhD); industrial organization and control (PhD); infection and immunity (MS, PhD); infectious diseases (MS, PhD); information organization and retrieval (M Eng, PhD); information systems (PhD); infrared astronomy (PhD); inorganic chemistry (PhD); insect behavior (MS, PhD); insect biochemistry (MS, PhD); insect ecology (MS, PhD); insect genetics (MS, PhD); insect morphology (MS, PhD); insect pathology (MS, PhD); insect physiology (MS, PhD); insect systematics (MS, PhD); insect toxicology and insecticide chemistry (MS, PhD); integrated pest management (MS, PhD); interior design (MA, MPS); international agriculture (M Eng, MPS, MS, PhD); international agriculture and development (MPS); international and comparative labor (MILR, MPS, MS, PhD); international communication (MS, PhD); international development planning (MRP, PhD); international economics (PhD); international food science (MPS, MS, PhD); international nutrition (MPS, MS, PhD); international planning (MPS); international population (MPS); international relations (PhD); international spatial problems (MA, MS, PhD); Italian linguistics (PhD); Italian literature (PhD); Japanese linguistics (MA, PhD); kinetics and catalysis (M Eng, MS, PhD); Korean literature (MA, PhD); labor economics (MILR, MPS, MS, PhD); landscape architecture (MLA); landscape horticulture (MPS, MS, PhD); Latin American archaeology (MA); Latin American history (MA, PhD); Latin language and literature (PhD); lesbian, bisexual, and gay literature studies (PhD); literary criticism and theory (PhD); local roads (M Eng, MPS, MS, PhD); location theory (MA, MS, PhD); machine systems (M Eng, MPS, MS, PhD); manufacturing systems engineering (PhD); marine geology (MS, PhD); materials and manufacturing engineering (M Eng, MS, PhD); materials chemistry (PhD); materials engineering (M Eng, PhD); materials science (M Eng, PhD); mathematical programming (PhD); mathematical statistics (MS, PhD); mathematics (PhD); mathematics (7-12) (MAT); mechanical systems and design (M Eng, MS, PhD); mechanics of materials (MS, PhD); medical and veterinary entomology (MS, PhD); medieval and Renaissance Latin literature (PhD); medieval archaeology (MA, PhD); medieval art (PhD); medieval Chinese history (MA, PhD); medieval history (MA, PhD); medieval literature (PhD); medieval music (PhD); medieval philology and linguistics (PhD); medieval philosophy (PhD); Mediterranean and Near Eastern archaeology (MA); membrane and epithelial physiology (MS, PhD); methodology (MA, PhD); methods of social research (MPS, MS, PhD); microbiology (PhD); mineralogy (M Eng, MS, PhD); modern art (PhD); modern Chinese history (MA, PhD); modern Chinese literature (MA, PhD); modern European history (MA, PhD); modern Japanese history (MA, PhD); modern Japanese literature (MA, PhD); molecular and cell biology (PhD); molecular and cellular physiology (MS, PhD); molecular biology (PhD); molecular plant pathology (MPS, MS, PhD); monetary and macroeconomics (PhD); multiphase flows (M Eng, MS, PhD); multiregional economic analysis (MA, MS, PhD); musicology (PhD); mycology (MPS, MS, PhD); neural and sensory physiology (MS, PhD); neurobiology (PhD); nineteenth century (PhD); nursery crops (MPS, MS, PhD); nutrition of horticultural crops (MPS, MS, PhD); nutritional and food toxicology (MS, PhD); nutritional biochemistry (MPS, MS, PhD); Old and Middle English (PhD); old Norse (MA, PhD); operating systems (M Eng, PhD); operations research and industrial engineering (M Eng); organic chemistry (PhD); organizational behavior (MILR, MPS, MS, PhD); organizations (MA, PhD); organometallic chemistry (PhD); paleobotany (MS, PhD); paleontology (M Eng, MS, PhD); parallel computing (M Eng, PhD); peace science (MA, MS, PhD); performance practice (DMA); personality and social psychology (PhD); petroleum geology (M Eng, MS, PhD); petrology (M Eng, MS, PhD); pharmacology (MS, PhD); philosophy (PhD); phonetics (MA, PhD); phonological theory (MA, PhD); physical chemistry (PhD); physics (MS, PhD); physics (7-12) (MAT); physiological genomics (MS, PhD); planetary geology (M Eng, MS, PhD); planetary studies (PhD); planning methods (MA, MS, PhD); planning theory and systems analysis (MRP, PhD); plant breeding (MPS, MS, PhD); plant cell biology (MS, PhD); plant disease epidemiology (MPS, MS, PhD); plant ecology (MS, PhD); plant genetics (MPS, MS, PhD); plant molecular biology (MS, PhD); plant morphology, anatomy and biomechanics (MS, PhD); plant pathology (MPS, MS, PhD); plant physiology (MS, PhD); plant propagation (MPS, MS, PhD); plant protection (MPS); policy analysis (MA, PhD); political methodology (PhD); political sociology/social movements (MA, PhD); political thought (PhD); polymer chemistry (PhD); polymer science (MS, PhD); polymers (M Eng, MS, PhD); population and development (MPS, MS, PhD); population medicine and epidemiology (MS, PhD); Precambrian geology (M Eng, MS, PhD); premodern Islamic history (MA, PhD); premodern Japanese history (MA, PhD); probability (MS, PhD); programming environments (M Eng, PhD); programming languages and methodology (M Eng, PhD); prose fiction (PhD); public affairs (MPA); public finance (PhD); public garden management (MPS, MS, PhD); public policy (MPA, PhD); Quaternary geology (M Eng, MS, PhD); racial and ethnic relations (MA, PhD); radio astronomy (PhD); radiophysics (PhD); real estate (MPSRE); regional economics and development planning (MRP, PhD); regional science (MRP, PhD); remote sensing (M Eng, MS, PhD); Renaissance art (PhD); Renaissance history (MA, PhD); reproductive physiology (MS, PhD); resource policy and management (MPS, MS, PhD); Restoration and eighteenth century (PhD); restoration ecology (MPS, MS, PhD); risk assessment, management and public policy (MS, PhD); robotics (M Eng, PhD); rock mechanics (M Eng, MS, PhD); Romance linguistics (MA, PhD); rural and environmental sociology (MPS, MS, PhD); Russian history (MA, PhD); sampling (MS, PhD); science and environmental communication (MS, PhD); science and technology policy (MPS); scientific computing (M Eng, PhD); second language acquisition (MA, PhD); sedimentology (M Eng, MS, PhD); seismology (M Eng, MS, PhD); semantics (MA, PhD); sensory evaluation (MPS, MS, PhD); Slavic linguistics (MA, PhD); social and health systems planning (MRP, PhD); social aspects of information (PhD); social networks (MA, PhD); social psychology (MA, PhD); social psychology of communication (MS, PhD); social stratification (MA, PhD); social studies of science and technology (MA, PhD); sociocultural anthropology (PhD); sociolinguistics (MA, PhD); soil and water engineering (M Eng, MPS, MS, PhD); soil science (MS, PhD); solid mechanics (MS, PhD); South Asian linguistics (MA, PhD); South Asian studies (MA); Southeast Asian art (PhD); Southeast Asian history (MA, PhD); Southeast Asian linguistics (MA, PhD); Southeast Asian studies (MA); Spanish linguistics (PhD); state, economy, and society (MPS, MS, PhD); statistical computing (MS, PhD); stochastic processes (MS, PhD); Stone Age archaeology (MA); stratigraphy (M Eng, MS,

PhD); structural and functional biology (MS, PhD); structural engineering (M Eng, MS, PhD); structural geology (M Eng, MS, PhD); structural mechanics (M Eng, MS); structures and environment (M Eng, MPS, MS, PhD); surface science (M Eng, MS, PhD); syntactic theory (MA, PhD); systematic botany (MS, PhD); systems engineering (M Eng); taxonomy of ornamental plants (MPS, MS, PhD); textile science (MS, PhD); theatre history (PhD); theatre theory and aesthetics (PhD); theoretical astrophysics (PhD); theoretical chemistry (PhD); theoretical physics (MS, PhD); theory and criticism (PhD); theory and criticism of architecture (M Arch); theory of computation (M Eng, PhD); theory of music (MA); transportation engineering (MS, PhD); transportation systems engineering (M Eng); turfgrass science (MPS, MS, PhD); twentieth century (PhD); urban and regional economics (MA, MS, PhD); urban and regional theory (MRP, PhD); urban design (M Arch); urban horticulture (MPS, MS, PhD); urban planning history (MRP, PhD); uses and effects of communication (MS, PhD); water resource systems (M Eng, MS, PhD); weed science (MPS, MS, PhD); wildlife science (MPS, MS, PhD); women's literature (PhD). *Application deadline:* For fall admission, 1/15 for domestic and international students; for spring admission, 11/1 for domestic and international students. *Application fee:* $70. Electronic applications accepted. *Application Contact:* Graduate School Application Requests, 607-255-5816, E-mail: gradadmissions@cornell.edu. *Dean,* Dr. Barbara Knuth, 607-255-5417.

Graduate Field in the Law School Students: 15 full-time (6 women); includes 1 Black or African American, non-Hispanic/Latino; 1 Hispanic/Latino, 8 international. Average age 30. 33 applicants, 27% accepted, 8 enrolled. *Faculty:* 48 full-time (14 women). Expenses: Contact institution. *Financial support:* In 2010–11, 1 fellowship with full tuition reimbursement was awarded; research assistantships with full tuition reimbursements, teaching assistantships with full tuition reimbursements, institutionally sponsored loans, scholarships/grants, health care benefits, tuition waivers (full and partial), and unspecified assistantships also available. Financial award applicants required to submit FAFSA. In 2010, 1 doctorate awarded. Offers law (JSD). *Application deadline:* For fall admission, 5/1 for domestic students. *Application fee:* $70. Electronic applications accepted. *Application Contact:* Graduate Field Assistant, 607-255-5141, E-mail: gradlaw@law.mail.cornell.edu. *Director of Graduate Studies,* 607-255-5141.

Graduate Field of Management Students: 41 full-time (12 women); includes 5 Asian, non-Hispanic/Latino, 23 international. Average age 29. 436 applicants, 4% accepted, 12 enrolled. *Faculty:* 55 full-time (9 women). Expenses: Contact institution. *Financial support:* In 2010–11, 38 students received support, including 4 fellowships with full tuition reimbursements available, 34 research assistantships with full tuition reimbursements available, 1 teaching assistantship with full tuition reimbursement available; institutionally sponsored loans, scholarships/grants, health care benefits, tuition waivers (full and partial), and unspecified assistantships also available. Financial award applicants required to submit FAFSA. In 2010, 5 doctorates awarded. Offers accounting (PhD); behavioral decision theory (PhD); finance (PhD); marketing (PhD); organizational behavior (PhD); production and operations management (PhD). *Application deadline:* For fall admission, 1/3 for domestic students. *Application fee:* $70. Electronic applications accepted. *Application Contact:* Graduate Field Assistant, 607-255-9431, E-mail: js_phd@cornell.edu. *Director of Graduate Studies,* 607-255-3669.

Johnson Graduate School of Management Students: 989 full-time (264 women); includes 163 minority (29 Black or African American, non-Hispanic/Latino; 104 Asian, non-Hispanic/Latino; 25 Hispanic/Latino; 5 Two or more races, non-Hispanic/Latino), 330 international. Average age 32. 2,283 applicants, 501 enrolled. *Faculty:* 47 full-time (9 women), 4 part-time/adjunct (0 women). Expenses: Contact institution. *Financial support:* Fellowships, research assistantships, career-related internships or fieldwork, Federal Work-Study, institutionally sponsored loans, and tuition waivers (full and partial) available. Financial award application deadline: 2/15; financial award applicants required to submit FAFSA. In 2010, 468 master's awarded. Offers management (MBA). *Application deadline:* For fall admission, 3/15 for domestic students, 1/1 for international students. *Application fee:* $200. Electronic applications accepted. *Application Contact:* 800-847-2082, Fax: 607-255-0065, E-mail: mba@johnson.cornell.edu. *Dean,* Dr. L. Joseph Thomas, 607-255-4854, E-mail: ljt3@cornell.edu.

CORNELL UNIVERSITY, JOAN AND SANFORD I. WEILL MEDICAL COLLEGE AND GRADUATE SCHOOL OF MEDICAL SCIENCES, New York, NY 10065

General Information Independent, coed, graduate-only institution. *Enrollment by degree level:* 396 first professional, 167 master's, 446 doctoral. *Graduate faculty:* 1,160 full-time (464 women), 3,784 part-time/adjunct (1,157 women). *Tuition:* Full-time $45,545. *Required fees:* $2805. *Graduate housing:* Rooms and/or apartments guaranteed to single students and available on a first-come, first-served basis to married students. Typical cost: $760 per year for married students. Room charges vary according to housing facility selected. Housing application deadline: 4/30. *Student services:* Campus employment opportunities, campus safety program, career counseling, free psychological counseling, grant writing training, international student services, low-cost health insurance, multicultural affairs office, services for students with disabilities. *Library facilities:* Samuel J. Wood Library. *Online resources:* library catalog, web page, access to other libraries' catalogs. *Collection:* 192,181 titles, 9,764 serial subscriptions, 1,000 audiovisual materials. *Research affiliation:* Strong Cancer Prevention Center (cancer prevention), Burke Medical Research Institute (neurology).

Computer facilities: 200 computers available on campus for general student use. A campuswide network can be accessed from student residence rooms and from off campus. Online class registration is available. *Web address:* http://www.med.cornell.edu/.

General Application Contact: Laurie Nicolaysen, Assistant Dean of Admissions, 212-746-1067, Fax: 212-746-8052, E-mail: cumc-admissions@med.cornell.edu.

GRADUATE UNITS

Weill Cornell Graduate School of Medical Sciences Students: 558 full-time (339 women); includes 16 Black or African American, non-Hispanic/Latino; 53 Asian, non-Hispanic/Latino; 26 Hispanic/Latino, 183 international. Average age 24. 682 applicants, 20% accepted, 55 enrolled. *Faculty:* 267 full-time (76 women). Expenses: Contact institution. *Financial support:* In 2010–11, 48 fellowships (averaging $23,221 per year) were awarded; scholarships/grants, health care benefits, and stipends (given to all students) also available. In 2010, 50 master's, 54 doctorates awarded. Offers biochemistry, cell and molecular biology (MS, PhD); chemical biology (PhD); clinical epidemiology and health services research (MS); computational biology and medicine (PhD); health sciences (MS); immunology (MS, PhD); medical sciences (MS, PhD); neuroscience (MS, PhD); pharmacology (MS, PhD); physiology, biophysics and systems biology (MS, PhD). *Application deadline:* For fall admission, 12/1 for domestic students. *Application fee:* $60. Electronic applications accepted. *Application Contact:* Dr. Randi Silver, Associate Dean, 212-746-6565, Fax: 212-746-8906, E-mail: gsms@med.cornell.edu. *Dean,* Dr. David P. Hajjar, 212-746-6900, E-mail: dphajjar@med.cornell.edu.

Weill Cornell/Rockefeller/Sloan-Kettering Tri-Institutional MD-PhD Program Students: 107 full-time (42 women); includes 17 Black or African American, non-Hispanic/Latino; 9 Asian, non-Hispanic/Latino; 14 Hispanic/Latino, 2 international. 477 applicants, 8% accepted, 13 enrolled. *Faculty:* 278 full-time (83 women). Expenses: Contact institution. *Financial support:* In 2010–11, 107 students received support, including 107 fellowships with full tuition reimbursements available (averaging $31,600 per year); health care benefits, tuition waivers (full), and stipends, research supplements, dental insurance also available. Offered jointly with The Rockefeller University and Sloan-Kettering Institute. *Application deadline:* For fall admission, 10/15 for domestic and international students. Applications are processed on a rolling basis. *Application fee:* $0. Electronic applications accepted. *Application Contact:* Ruth Gotian, Administrative Director, 212-746-6023, Fax: 212-746-8678, E-mail: mdphd@med.cornell.edu. *Director,* Dr. Olaf S. Andersen, 212-746-6023, Fax: 212-746-8678, E-mail: mdphd@med.cornell.edu.

CORNERSTONE UNIVERSITY, Grand Rapids, MI 49525-5897

General Information Independent-religious, coed, comprehensive institution. *Graduate housing:* Rooms and/or apartments available on a first-come, first-served basis to single and married students.

GRADUATE UNITS

Graduate Programs *Degree program information:* Part-time programs available. Postbaccalaureate distance learning degree programs offered. Offers business administration (MBA); education (MA Ed); management (MSM); teaching English to speakers of other languages (MA, Graduate Certificate). Programs also offered at Holland, Kalamazoo, and Troy, MI campuses. Electronic applications accepted.

COVENANT COLLEGE, Lookout Mountain, GA 30750

General Information Independent-religious, coed, comprehensive institution. *Enrollment:* 1,049 graduate, professional, and undergraduate students; 43 full-time matriculated graduate/professional students (15 women), 20 part-time matriculated graduate/professional students (16 women). *Enrollment by degree level:* 63 master's. *Graduate faculty:* 6 full-time (2 women), 5 part-time/adjunct (0 women). *Tuition:* Full-time $4455; part-time $495 per credit hour. *Required fees:* $169. *Graduate housing:* Room and/or apartments available on a first-come, first-served basis to single students; on-campus housing not available to married students. Housing application deadline: 5/1. *Student services:* Career counseling. *Library facilities:* Kresge Memorial Library. *Online resources:* library catalog, web page, access to other libraries' catalogs.

Computer facilities: A campuswide network can be accessed from student residence rooms and from off campus. Online class registration, online student information system are available. *Web address:* http://www.covenant.edu/.

General Application Contact: Rebecca Dodson, Associate Director, Program in Education, 706-419-1406, Fax: 706-820-0672, E-mail: rdodson@covenant.edu.

GRADUATE UNITS

Program in Education Students: 43 full-time (15 women), 20 part-time (16 women); includes 5 minority (2 Black or African American, non-Hispanic/Latino; 2 Asian, non-Hispanic/Latino; 1 Hispanic/Latino), 1 international. Average age 37. 26 applicants, 100% accepted, 22 enrolled. *Faculty:* 6 full-time (2 women), 5 part-time/adjunct (0 women). Expenses: Contact institution. *Financial support:* In 2010–11, 30 students received support. Institutionally sponsored loans, scholarships/grants, and tuition waivers (partial) available. Support available to part-time students. Financial award application deadline: 3/1; financial award applicants required to submit FAFSA. In 2010, 14 master's awarded. *Degree program information:* Part-time programs available. Offers education (M Ed). *Application deadline:* For fall admission, 3/31 priority date for domestic students. Applications are processed on a rolling basis. *Application fee:* $50. *Application Contact:* Rebecca Dodson, Associate Director, 706-419-1406, Fax: 706-820-0672, E-mail: rdodson@covenant.edu. *Director,* Dr. Jim Drexler, 706-419-1408.

COVENANT THEOLOGICAL SEMINARY, St. Louis, MO 63141-8697

General Information Independent-religious, coed, graduate-only institution. *Graduate housing:* Rooms and/or apartments available on a first-come, first-served basis to single and married students.

GRADUATE UNITS

Graduate and Professional Programs *Degree program information:* Part-time and evening/weekend programs available. Postbaccalaureate distance learning degree programs offered (minimal on-campus study). Offers theology (M Div, MA, MAC, MAEM, Th M, D Min, Certificate). Electronic applications accepted.

COX COLLEGE, Springfield, MO 65802

General Information Independent, coed, primarily women, comprehensive institution.

GRADUATE UNITS

Programs in Nursing Offers clinical nurse leader (MSN); family nurse practitioner (MSN); nurse educator (MSN). Electronic applications accepted.

CRANBROOK ACADEMY OF ART, Bloomfield Hills, MI 48303-0801

General Information Independent, coed, graduate-only institution. *Graduate housing:* Room and/or apartments available on a first-come, first-served basis to single students; on-campus housing not available to married students. Housing application deadline: 2/1.

GRADUATE UNITS

Graduate School Offers architecture (M Arch); ceramics (MFA); design (MFA); fiber arts (MFA); metalsmithing (MFA); painting (MFA); photography (MFA); printmaking (MFA); sculpture (MFA).

CREIGHTON UNIVERSITY, Omaha, NE 68178-0001

General Information Independent-religious, coed, university. CGS member. *Enrollment:* 7,662 graduate, professional, and undergraduate students; 2,711 full-time matriculated graduate/professional students (1,501 women), 745 part-time matriculated graduate/professional students (383 women). *Enrollment by degree level:* 2,429 first professional, 917 master's, 110 doctoral. *Graduate faculty:* 320 full-time (99 women). *Tuition:* Full-time $12,168; part-time $676 per credit hour. *Required fees:* $131 per semester. Tuition and fees vary according to program. *Graduate housing:* Rooms and/or apartments available on a first-come, first-served basis to single and married students. Typical cost: $0 per year for single students; $0 per year for married students. Room charges vary according to housing facility selected. Housing application deadline: 5/1. *Student services:* Campus employment opportunities, campus safety program, career counseling, child daycare facilities, exercise/wellness program, free psychological counseling, international student services, low-cost health insurance, multicultural affairs office, services for students with disabilities, teacher training, writing training. *Library facilities:* Reinert Alumni Memorial Library plus 2 others. *Online resources:* library catalog, web page, access to other libraries' catalogs. *Collection:* 619,314 titles, 45,032 serial subscriptions, 11,031 audiovisual materials. *Research affiliation:* U. S. Department of Education (student support services), Creighton University Medical Center, National Institutes of Health (asthma), U. S. Department of Commerce (atmospheric science), National Science Foundation (business and education).

Computer facilities: Computer purchase and lease plans are available. 550 computers available on campus for general student use. A campuswide network can be accessed from student residence rooms and from off campus. Online class registration, financial aid information are available. *Web address:* http://www.creighton.edu/.

General Application Contact: Taunya Plater, Senior Program Coordinator, 402-280-2870, Fax: 402-280-2899, E-mail: taunyaplater@creighton.edu.

GRADUATE UNITS

Graduate School Students: 319 full-time (180 women), 633 part-time (294 women); includes 108 minority (35 Black or African American, non-Hispanic/Latino; 1 American Indian or Alaska Native, non-Hispanic/Latino; 27 Asian, non-Hispanic/Latino; 33 Hispanic/Latino; 4 Native Hawaiian or other Pacific Islander, non-Hispanic/Latino; 8 Two or more races, non-Hispanic/Latino), 63 international. Average age 32. 763 applicants, 65% accepted, 392 enrolled. *Faculty:* 320 full-time (99 women). Expenses: Contact institution. *Financial support:* In 2010–11, research assistantships with tuition reimbursements (averaging $15,700 per year), teaching assistantships with tuition reimbursements (averaging $15,700 per year) were awarded; career-related internships or fieldwork, institutionally sponsored loans, and tuition waivers (partial) also available. Support available to part-time students. Financial award applicants required to submit FAFSA. In 2010, 200 master's, 6 doctorates awarded. *Degree program information:* Part-time and evening/weekend programs available. Postbaccalaureate distance learning degree programs offered (minimal on-campus study). *Application deadline:* For fall admission, 3/1 priority date for domestic and international students; for winter admission, 10/1 for domestic students, 7/1 for international students; for spring admission, 4/1 for domestic students, 10/1 for international students. Applications are processed on a rolling basis. *Application fee:* $50. Electronic applications accepted. *Application Contact:* Taunya Plater,

Creighton University (continued)

Senior Program Coordinator, 402-280-2870, Fax: 402-280-2899, E-mail: taunyaplater@creighton.edu. *Dean,* Dr. Gail M. Jensen, 402-280-2870, Fax: 402-280-2899, E-mail: gjenson@creighton.edu.

College of Arts and Sciences Students: 67 full-time (35 women), 197 part-time (125 women); includes 21 minority (7 Black or African American, non-Hispanic/Latino; 3 American Indian or Alaska Native, non-Hispanic/Latino; 2 Asian, non-Hispanic/Latino; 9 Hispanic/Latino), 16 international. Average age 33. 80 applicants, 70% accepted, 46 enrolled. *Faculty:* 147 full-time (43 women). Expenses: Contact institution. *Financial support:* In 2010–11, teaching assistantships with full tuition reimbursements (averaging $10,698 per year); tuition waivers (partial) also available. Financial award applicants required to submit FAFSA. In 2010, 62 master's awarded. *Degree program information:* Part-time and evening/weekend programs available. Postbaccalaureate distance learning degree programs offered (minimal on-campus study). Offers arts and sciences (M Ed, MA, MLS, MS); atmospheric sciences (MS); Christian spirituality (MA); college student affairs (MS); community counseling (MS); counselor education (MS); creative writing (MA); educational leadership (MS); elementary school administration (MS); elementary school guidance (MS); elementary teaching (M Ed); international relations (MA); liberal studies (MLS); ministry (MA); physics (MS); secondary school administration (MS); secondary school guidance (MS); secondary teaching (M Ed); special populations in education (MS); teacher leadership (MS); teaching (M Ed); theology (MA). *Application deadline:* For fall admission, 3/1 for domestic and international students; for winter admission, 10/1 for domestic students, 7/1 for international students; for spring admission, 4/1 for domestic students, 10/1 for international students. Applications are processed on a rolling basis. *Application fee:* $50. Electronic applications accepted. *Application Contact:* Taunya Plater, Senior Program Coordinator, 402-280-2870, Fax: 402-280-2899, E-mail: taunyaplater@creighton.edu. *Dean,* Dr. Robert J. Lueger, 402-280-2431, E-mail: robertlueger@creighton.edu.

Eugene C. Eppley College of Business Administration Students: 42 full-time (13 women), 268 part-time (51 women); includes 32 minority (17 Black or African American, non-Hispanic/Latino; 12 Asian, non-Hispanic/Latino; 3 Hispanic/Latino), 20 international. Average age 30. 133 applicants, 80% accepted, 100 enrolled. *Faculty:* 37 full-time (7 women). Expenses: Contact institution. *Financial support:* In 2010–11, 10 fellowships with partial tuition reimbursements (averaging $8,112 per year) were awarded; career-related internships or fieldwork, tuition waivers (partial), and unspecified assistantships also available. Financial award application deadline: 3/1. In 2010, 77 master's awarded. *Degree program information:* Part-time and evening/weekend programs available. Postbaccalaureate distance learning degree programs offered (minimal on-campus study). Offers business administration (MBA); information technology management (MS); securities and portfolio management (MSAPM). *Application deadline:* For fall admission, 7/1 priority date for domestic students, 3/1 for international students; for winter admission, 10/1 priority date for domestic students, 7/1 for international students; for spring admission, 4/1 priority date for domestic students, 10/1 for international students. Applications are processed on a rolling basis. *Application fee:* $50. Electronic applications accepted. *Application Contact:* Gail Hafer, Assistant Dean, 402-280-2829, Fax: 402-280-2172, E-mail: ghafer@creighton.edu. *Associate Dean for Graduate Programs,* Dr. Deborah Wells, 402-280-2841, E-mail: deborahwells@creighton.edu.

School of Dentistry Offers dentistry (DDS).

School of Law Students: 459 full-time (186 women), 12 part-time (6 women); includes 44 minority (13 Black or African American, non-Hispanic/Latino; 1 American Indian or Alaska Native, non-Hispanic/Latino; 15 Asian, non-Hispanic/Latino; 14 Hispanic/Latino; 1 Two or more races, non-Hispanic/Latino), 6 international. Average age 25. 1,387 applicants, 48% accepted, 145 enrolled. *Faculty:* 33 full-time (9 women), 35 part-time/adjunct (13 women). Expenses: Contact institution. *Financial support:* In 2010–11, 228 students received support. Career-related internships or fieldwork, institutionally sponsored loans, and scholarships/grants available. Support available to part-time students. Financial award application deadline: 7/1; financial award applicants required to submit FAFSA. In 2010, 140 first professional degrees awarded. *Degree program information:* Part-time programs available. Offers law (JD, MS, Certificate); negotiation and dispute resolution (MS, Certificate). *Application deadline:* For fall admission, 5/1 priority date for domestic and international students. Applications are processed on a rolling basis. *Application fee:* $50. Electronic applications accepted. *Application Contact:* Andrea D. Bashara, Assistant Dean, 402-280-2586, Fax: 402-280-3161, E-mail: bashara@creighton.edu. *Dean/Professor,* Marianne B. Culhane, 402-280-2874, Fax: 402-280-3161.

School of Medicine Offers biomedical sciences (MS, PhD); clinical anatomy (MS); medical microbiology and immunology (MS, PhD); medicine (MD, MS, PhD); pharmaceutical sciences (MS); pharmacology (MS, PhD). Electronic applications accepted.

School of Nursing Students: 49 full-time (48 women), 131 part-time (127 women); includes 2 Black or African American, non-Hispanic/Latino; 3 Asian, non-Hispanic/Latino; 5 Hispanic/Latino. Average age 33. 41 applicants, 85% accepted, 27 enrolled. *Faculty:* 1 (woman) full-time, 14 part-time/adjunct (13 women). Expenses: Contact institution. *Financial support:* Career-related internships or fieldwork, Federal Work-Study, institutionally sponsored loans, and traineeships available. Financial award applicants required to submit FAFSA. In 2010, 12 master's, 2 doctorates awarded. *Degree program information:* Part-time programs available. Postbaccalaureate distance learning degree programs offered (minimal on-campus study). Offers nursing (MS, DNP). *Application deadline:* For fall admission, 3/15 priority date for domestic and international students; for spring admission, 10/15 priority date for domestic and international students. Applications are processed on a rolling basis. *Application fee:* $50. Electronic applications accepted. *Application Contact:* Dr. Mary Kunes-Connell, Associate Dean for Academic and Clinical Affairs, 402-280-2024, Fax: 402-280-2045, E-mail: mkc@creighton.edu. *Dean,* Dr. Eleanor V. Howell, 402-280-2004, Fax: 402-280-2045, E-mail: howell@creighton.edu.

School of Pharmacy and Health Professions Postbaccalaureate distance learning degree programs offered (minimal on-campus study). Offers occupational therapy (OTD); pharmaceutical sciences (MS); pharmacy (Pharm D); pharmacy and health professions (Pharm D, MS, DPT, OTD); physical therapy (DPT). Electronic applications accepted.

THE CRISWELL COLLEGE, Dallas, TX 75246-1537

General Information Independent-religious, coed, comprehensive institution. *Graduate housing:* On-campus housing not available.

GRADUATE UNITS

Graduate School of the Bible *Degree program information:* Part-time programs available. Offers biblical studies (M Div); Christian leadership (MA); counseling (MA); Jewish studies (MA); ministry (MA); theological and biblical studies (MA). Electronic applications accepted.

CROWN COLLEGE, St. Bonifacius, MN 55375-9001

General Information Independent-religious, coed, comprehensive institution. *Enrollment:* 1,176 graduate, professional, and undergraduate students; 138 full-time matriculated graduate/professional students (53 women), 27 part-time matriculated graduate/professional students (11 women). *Enrollment by degree level:* 165 master's. *Graduate faculty:* 10 full-time (2 women), 19 part-time/adjunct (6 women). *Graduate housing:* Room and/or apartments available on a first-come, first-served basis to married students; on-campus housing not available to single students. Housing application deadline: 7/1. *Student services:* Campus employment opportunities, career counseling, free psychological counseling, teacher training. *Library facilities:* Peter Watne Memorial Library. *Online resources:* library catalog, web page, access to other libraries' catalogs. *Collection:* 148,561 titles, 29,308 serial subscriptions, 1,706 audiovisual materials.

Computer facilities: 95 computers available on campus for general student use. A campuswide network can be accessed from student residence rooms and from off campus. Online class registration is available. *Web address:* http://www.crown.edu/.

General Application Contact: Nate Erickson, Enrollment Coordinator, 952-446-4370, Fax: 952-446-4349, E-mail: grad@crown.edu.

GRADUATE UNITS

Adult and Graduate Studies Students: 138 full-time (53 women), 27 part-time (11 women); includes 16 minority (4 Black or African American, non-Hispanic/Latino; 1 American Indian or Alaska Native, non-Hispanic/Latino; 8 Asian, non-Hispanic/Latino; 3 Hispanic/Latino). Average age 37. 53 applicants, 91% accepted, 44 enrolled. *Faculty:* 10 full-time (2 women), 19 part-time/adjunct (6 women). Expenses: Contact institution. *Financial support:* In 2010–11, 71 students received support, including 3 teaching assistantships with full tuition reimbursements available (averaging $7,200 per year); scholarships/grants also available. Financial award application deadline: 8/1; financial award applicants required to submit FAFSA. In 2010, 40 master's awarded. *Degree program information:* Part-time and evening/weekend programs available. Postbaccalaureate distance learning degree programs offered (no on-campus study). Offers Christian studies (MA); instructional leadership (MA); international leadership (MA); ministry leadership (MA); organizational leadership (MA). *Application deadline:* For fall admission, 8/1 priority date for domestic students; for winter admission, 1/1 priority date for domestic students; for spring admission, 6/1 priority date for domestic students. Applications are processed on a rolling basis. *Application fee:* $20. Electronic applications accepted. *Application Contact:* Nate Erickson, Enrollment Coordinator, 952-446-4370, Fax: 952-446-4349, E-mail: grad@crown.edu. *Director,* Matt Newby, 952-446-4224, Fax: 952-416-4349, E-mail: grad@crown.edu.

CUMBERLAND UNIVERSITY, Lebanon, TN 37087

General Information Independent, coed, comprehensive institution. *Graduate housing:* Room and/or apartments available on a first-come, first-served basis to single students; on-campus housing not available to married students.

GRADUATE UNITS

Program in Business Administration *Degree program information:* Part-time and evening/weekend programs available. Offers business administration (MBA).

Program in Education *Degree program information:* Part-time and evening/weekend programs available. Postbaccalaureate distance learning degree programs offered (no on-campus study). Offers education (MAE).

Program in Public Service Administration *Degree program information:* Part-time and evening/weekend programs available. Offers public service administration (MS).

CUNY GRADUATE SCHOOL OF JOURNALISM, New York, NY 10018

General Information City-supported, coed, graduate-only institution. *Enrollment by degree level:* 163 master's. *Graduate faculty:* 10 full-time (3 women), 54 part-time/adjunct (26 women). Tuition, state resident: full-time $7730. *Required fees:* $1795. *Student services:* Campus employment opportunities, career counseling, free psychological counseling, international student services, low-cost health insurance, services for students with disabilities, writing training. *Library facilities:* Research Center. *Online resources:* library catalog, web page, access to other libraries' catalogs. *Collection:* 2,177 titles, 63 serial subscriptions, 47 audiovisual materials.

Computer facilities: 80 computers available on campus for general student use. A campuswide network can be accessed from off campus. Blogs, software available. *Web address:* http://www.journalism.cuny.edu.

General Application Contact: Colleen Marshall, Admissions/Outreach Counselor, 646-758-7852, Fax: 646-758-7709, E-mail: colleen.marshall@journalism.cuny.edu.

GRADUATE UNITS

Graduate Program Students: 163 full-time (101 women); includes 56 minority (18 Black or African American, non-Hispanic/Latino; 18 Asian, non-Hispanic/Latino; 20 Hispanic/Latino). Average age 27. 329 applicants, 50% accepted, 84 enrolled. *Faculty:* 10 full-time (3 women), 54 part-time/adjunct (26 women). Expenses: Contact institution. *Financial support:* Career-related internships or fieldwork, Federal Work-Study, and scholarships/grants available. Financial award application deadline: 3/1; financial award applicants required to submit FAFSA. In 2010, 58 master's awarded. Offers journalism (MA). *Application deadline:* For fall admission, 12/15 for domestic students. *Application fee:* $65. Electronic applications accepted. *Application Contact:* Colleen Marshall, Admissions/Outreach Counselor, 646-758-7852, Fax: 646-758-7709, E-mail: colleen.marshall@journalism.cuny.edu. *Dean,* Stephen B. Shepard, 646-758-7700.

CURRY COLLEGE, Milton, MA 02186-9984

General Information Independent, coed, comprehensive institution. *Enrollment:* 2,983 graduate, professional, and undergraduate students; 351 part-time matriculated graduate/professional students (178 women). *Enrollment by degree level:* 351 master's. *Graduate faculty:* 16 full-time (6 women), 19 part-time/adjunct (11 women). *Graduate housing:* On-campus housing not available. *Student services:* Campus safety program, career counseling, free psychological counseling, grant writing training, international student services, low-cost health insurance, services for students with disabilities, teacher training, writing training. *Library facilities:* Levin Library plus 1 other. *Online resources:* library catalog, web page, access to other libraries' catalogs. *Collection:* 139,600 titles, 33,700 serial subscriptions, 3,400 audiovisual materials. *Research affiliation:* Public School Systems, Literacy Centers/GED Programs.

Computer facilities: 185 computers available on campus for general student use. A campuswide network can be accessed from student residence rooms and from off campus. Online class registration, library online catalog and research databases are available. *Web address:* http://www.curry.edu/.

General Application Contact: John Bresnahan, Director of Graduate Enrollment and Student Services, 617-333-2243, Fax: 617-979-3535, E-mail: jbresnah0104@curry.edu.

GRADUATE UNITS

Graduate Studies Students: 347 part-time (174 women). Average age 36. *Faculty:* 16 full-time (6 women), 19 part-time/adjunct (11 women). Expenses: Contact institution. *Financial support:* Applicants required to submit FAFSA. In 2010, 133 master's awarded. *Degree program information:* Part-time and evening/weekend programs available. Offers business administration (MBA); criminal justice (MA); elementary education (M Ed); finance (Certificate); foundations (non-license) (M Ed); nursing (MSN); reading (M Ed, Certificate); special education (M Ed). *Application deadline:* Applications are processed on a rolling basis. *Application Contact:* John Bresnahan, Director of Graduate Enrollment and Student Services, 617-333-2243, Fax: 617-979-3535, E-mail: jbresnah0104@curry.edu. *Dean of Continuing Education and Graduate Studies,* 617-333-2134, Fax: 617-333-2045.

CURTIS INSTITUTE OF MUSIC, Philadelphia, PA 19103-6107

General Information Independent, coed, comprehensive institution. *Graduate housing:* On-campus housing not available.

GRADUATE UNITS

Graduate Studies Offers opera (MM).

DAEMEN COLLEGE, Amherst, NY 14226-3592

General Information Independent, coed, comprehensive institution. *Enrollment:* 606 full-time matriculated graduate/professional students (516 women), 257 part-time matriculated graduate/professional students (213 women). *Enrollment by degree level:* 744 master's, 108 doctoral, 11 other advanced degrees. *Graduate faculty:* 30 full-time (19 women), 67 part-time/adjunct (50 women). *Tuition:* Part-time $830 per credit hour. Tuition and fees vary according to course load and reciprocity agreements. *Graduate housing:* Room and/or apartments available on a first-come, first-served basis to single students; on-campus housing not available to married students. Typical cost: $10,840 (including board). Housing application deadline: 7/15. *Student services:* Campus employment opportunities, campus safety program, career counseling, exercise/wellness program, international student services, low-cost health insurance, services for students with disabilities, teacher training. *Library facilities:* Research and Information Commons plus 1 other. *Online resources:* library catalog, web page, access to other libraries' catalogs. *Collection:* 136,883 titles, 31,925 serial subscriptions, 2,315 audiovisual materials.

Computer facilities: 146 computers available on campus for general student use. A campuswide network can be accessed from student residence rooms and from off campus. Online class registration is available. *Web address:* http://www.daemen.edu/.

General Application Contact: Scott Rowe, Associate Director of Graduate Programs, 716-839-8225, Fax: 716-839-8229, E-mail: srowe@daemen.edu.

GRADUATE UNITS

Department of Accounting/Information Systems Students: 19 full-time (16 women), 5 part-time (1 woman); includes 1 minority (Black or African American, non-Hispanic/Latino), 18 international. Average age 28. *Faculty:* 1 full-time (0 women), 1 part-time/adjunct (0 women). Expenses: Contact institution. *Financial support:* Institutionally sponsored loans, scholarships/grants, and scholarships available. Financial award application deadline: 2/15; financial award applicants required to submit FAFSA. In 2010, 12 master's awarded. *Degree program information:* Part-time and evening/weekend programs available. Offers global business (MS). *Application deadline:* For fall admission, 3/1 priority date for domestic and international students; for spring admission, 10/1 priority date for domestic and international students. Applications are processed on a rolling basis. *Application fee:* $25. Electronic applications accepted. *Application Contact:* Scott Rowe, Associate Director of Graduate Admissions, 716-839-8225, Fax: 716-839-8229, E-mail: srowe@daemen.edu. *Chair,* S. Sgt. Sharlene S. Buszka, 716-839-8428, Fax: 716-839-8261, E-mail: sbuszka@daemen.edu.

Department of Nursing Students: 10 full-time (all women), 113 part-time (107 women); includes 20 minority (14 Black or African American, non-Hispanic/Latino; 3 Asian, non-Hispanic/Latino; 3 Hispanic/Latino), 3 international. Average age 42. *Faculty:* 4 full-time (all women), 6 part-time/adjunct (all women). Expenses: Contact institution. *Financial support:* Institutionally sponsored loans, scholarships/grants, and scholarships available. Financial award application deadline: 2/15; financial award applicants required to submit FAFSA. In 2010, 19 master's awarded. *Degree program information:* Part-time programs available. Offers adult nurse practitioner (MS, Post Master's Certificate); nurse executive leadership (Post Master's Certificate); nursing education (MS, Post Master's Certificate); nursing executive leadership (MS); nursing practice (DNP); palliative care nursing (Post Master's Certificate). *Application deadline:* For fall admission, 3/1 priority date for domestic and international students; for spring admission, 10/1 priority date for domestic and international students. Applications are processed on a rolling basis. *Application fee:* $25. Electronic applications accepted. *Application Contact:* Scott Rowe, Associate Director of Graduate Programs, 716-839-8225, Fax: 716-839-8229, E-mail: srowe@daemen.edu. *Chair,* Dr. Mary Lou Rusin, 716-839-8387, Fax: 716-839-8403, E-mail: mrusin@daemen.edu.

Department of Physical Therapy Students: 99 full-time (70 women), 9 part-time (3 women); includes 4 minority (1 Asian, non-Hispanic/Latino; 3 Hispanic/Latino), 2 international. Average age 26. *Faculty:* 10 full-time (6 women), 9 part-time/adjunct (5 women). Expenses: Contact institution. *Financial support:* Teaching assistantships, institutionally sponsored loans available. Financial award application deadline: 2/15; financial award applicants required to submit FAFSA. In 2010, 40 doctorates, 7 other advanced degrees awarded. *Degree program information:* Part-time programs available. Offers orthopedic manual physical therapy (Advanced Certificate); physical therapy-direct entry (DPT); transitional (DPT). *Application deadline:* For fall admission, 3/1 priority date for domestic and international students; for spring admission, 10/1 priority date for domestic and international students. Applications are processed on a rolling basis. *Application fee:* $25. Electronic applications accepted. *Application Contact:* Scott Rowe, Associate Director of Graduate Programs, 716-839-8225, Fax: 716-839-8229, E-mail: srowe@daemen.edu. *Chair,* Dr. Sharon L. Held, 716-839-8344, Fax: 716-839-8537, E-mail: sheld@daemen.edu.

Education Department Students: 388 full-time (350 women), 116 part-time (91 women); includes 10 minority (7 Black or African American, non-Hispanic/Latino; 3 Two or more races, non-Hispanic/Latino), 59 international. Average age 25. *Faculty:* 12 full-time (9 women), 47 part-time/adjunct (38 women). Expenses: Contact institution. *Financial support:* Institutionally sponsored loans available. Financial award application deadline: 2/15; financial award applicants required to submit FAFSA. In 2010, 305 master's awarded. *Degree program information:* Part-time programs available. Offers adolescence education (MS); childhood education (MS); childhood special education (MS); childhood special-alternative certification (MS); early childhood special-alternative certification (MS). *Application deadline:* For fall admission, 3/1 priority date for domestic and international students; for spring admission, 10/1 priority date for domestic and international students. Applications are processed on a rolling basis. *Application fee:* $25. Electronic applications accepted. *Application Contact:* Scott Rowe, Associate Director of Graduate Admissions, 716-839-8225, Fax: 716-839-8229, E-mail: srowe@daemen.edu. *Chair and Associate Dean,* Dr. Julius G. Adams, 716-839-8530, Fax: 716-566-7821, E-mail: jadams@daemen.edu.

Physician Assistant Department Students: 74 full-time (60 women), 1 (woman) part-time; includes 4 minority (1 Asian, non-Hispanic/Latino; 2 Hispanic/Latino; 1 Two or more races, non-Hispanic/Latino). Average age 24. *Faculty:* 2 full-time (0 women). Expenses: Contact institution. *Financial support:* Institutionally sponsored loans available. Financial award application deadline: 2/15; financial award applicants required to submit FAFSA. In 2010, 39 master's awarded. Offers physician assistant (MS). *Application deadline:* For fall admission, 3/1 priority date for domestic and international students; for spring admission, 10/1 priority date for domestic and international students. Applications are processed on a rolling basis. *Application fee:* $25. Electronic applications accepted. *Application Contact:* Marcy Moore, Director of Graduate Admissions, 716-839-8383, Fax: 716-839-8252, E-mail: mmoore@daemen.edu. *Director,* Gregg L. Shutts, 716-839-8316, Fax: 716-839-8252, E-mail: shutts@daemen.edu.

Program in Executive Leadership and Change Students: 8 full-time (5 women), 12 part-time (9 women); includes 3 minority (all Black or African American, non-Hispanic/Latino). Average age 38. *Faculty:* 1 full-time (0 women), 4 part-time/adjunct (1 woman). Expenses: Contact institution. *Financial support:* In 2010–11, 1 student received support. Institutionally sponsored loans available. Financial award application deadline: 2/15; financial award applicants required to submit FAFSA. In 2010, 5 master's awarded. *Degree program information:* Part-time and evening/weekend programs available. Offers business (MS); health professions (MS); not-for-profit organizations (MS). *Application deadline:* For fall admission, 3/1 priority date for domestic and international students; for spring admission, 10/1 priority date for domestic and international students. Applications are processed on a rolling basis. *Application fee:* $25. Electronic applications accepted. *Application Contact:* Scott Rowe, Associate Director of Graduate Admissions, 716-839-8225, Fax: 716-839-8229, E-mail: srowe@daemen.edu. *Executive Director,* Dr. John S. Frederick, 716-839-8342, Fax: 716-839-8261, E-mail: jfrederi@daemen.edu.

DAKOTA STATE UNIVERSITY, Madison, SD 57042-1799

General Information State-supported, coed, comprehensive institution. CGS member. *Enrollment:* 3,058 graduate, professional, and undergraduate students; 37 full-time matriculated graduate/professional students (7 women), 192 part-time matriculated graduate/professional students (55 women). *Enrollment by degree level:* 176 master's, 53 doctoral. *Graduate faculty:* 50 full-time (19 women), 4 part-time/adjunct (1 woman). *Graduate housing:* Room and/or apartments available on a first-come, first-served basis to single students; on-campus housing not available to married students. *Student services:* Campus employment opportunities, campus safety program, career counseling, exercise/wellness program, free psychological counseling, grant writing training, international student services, low-cost health insurance, multicultural affairs office, services for students with disabilities, writing training. *Library facilities:* Karl E. Mundt Library plus 1 other. *Online resources:* library catalog, web page, access to other libraries' catalogs. *Collection:* 127,243 titles, 299 serial subscriptions, 2,235 audiovisual materials. *Research affiliation:* SBS–Secure Banking Solutions, LLC (information security).

Computer facilities: Computer purchase and lease plans are available. 165 computers available on campus for general student use. A campuswide network can be accessed from student residence rooms and from off campus. Online class registration, wireless computing initiative requires full-time students to have a tablet computer are available. *Web address:* http://www.dsu.edu/.

General Application Contact: Pam Iverson, Secretary, Office of Graduate Studies and Research, 605-256-5799, Fax: 605-256-5093, E-mail: pamela.iverson@dsu.edu.

GRADUATE UNITS

College of Business and Information Systems Students: 37 full-time (7 women), 164 part-time (41 women); includes 24 minority (7 Black or African American, non-Hispanic/Latino; 2 American Indian or Alaska Native, non-Hispanic/Latino; 5 Asian, non-Hispanic/Latino; 6 Hispanic/Latino; 1 Native Hawaiian or other Pacific Islander, non-Hispanic/Latino; 3 Two or more races, non-Hispanic/Latino), 49 international. Average age 36. 143 applicants, 60% accepted, 59 enrolled. *Faculty:* 28 full-time (7 women), 2 part-time/adjunct (1 woman). Expenses: Contact institution. *Financial support:* In 2010–11, 54 students received support, including 11 fellowships with partial tuition reimbursements available (averaging $31,837 per year), 15 research assistantships with partial tuition reimbursements available (averaging $11,116 per year), 2 teaching assistantships with partial tuition reimbursements available (averaging $31,837 per year); Federal Work-Study, scholarships/grants, unspecified assistantships, and administrative assistantships also available. Support available to part-time students. Financial award applicants required to submit FAFSA. In 2010, 49 master's, 3 doctorates awarded. *Degree program information:* Part-time and evening/weekend programs available. Postbaccalaureate distance learning degree programs offered (minimal on-campus study). Offers business and information systems (MBA, MSHI, MSIA, MSIS, D Sc IS). *Application deadline:* For fall admission, 6/15 for domestic and international students; for spring admission, 11/15 for domestic and international students. Applications are processed on a rolling basis. *Application fee:* $35 ($85 for international students). *Application Contact:* Pam Iverson, Secretary, Office of Graduate Studies and Research, 605-256-5799, Fax: 605-256-5093, E-mail: pamela.iverson@dsu.edu. *Dean,* Dr. Tom Halverson, 605-256-5165, Fax: 605-256-5060, E-mail: tom.halverson@dsu.edu.

College of Education Students: 28 part-time (14 women); includes 2 minority (1 Hispanic/Latino; 1 Two or more races, non-Hispanic/Latino). Average age 32. 5 applicants, 80% accepted, 3 enrolled. *Faculty:* 6 full-time (3 women), 2 part-time/adjunct (0 women). Expenses: Contact institution. *Financial support:* In 2010–11, 9 students received support, including 1 research assistantship with partial tuition reimbursement available (averaging $11,116 per year); teaching assistantships, Federal Work-Study, scholarships/grants, tuition waivers (partial), unspecified assistantships, and administrative assistantships also available. Support available to part-time students. Financial award applicants required to submit FAFSA. In 2010, 9 master's awarded. *Degree program information:* Part-time and evening/weekend programs available. Postbaccalaureate distance learning degree programs offered (minimal on-campus study). Offers instructional technology (MSET). *Application deadline:* For fall admission, 6/15 for domestic and international students; for spring admission, 11/15 for domestic and international students. Applications are processed on a rolling basis. *Application fee:* $35 ($85 for international students). *Application Contact:* Pam Iverson, Secretary, Office of Graduate Studies and Research, 605-256-5799, Fax: 605-256-5093, E-mail: pamela.iverson@dsu.edu. *Dean,* Dr. Judy Dittman, 605-256-5177, Fax: 605-256-7300, E-mail: judy.dittman@dsu.edu.

DAKOTA WESLEYAN UNIVERSITY, Mitchell, SD 57301-4398

General Information Independent-religious, coed, comprehensive institution. *Enrollment:* 770 graduate, professional, and undergraduate students; 23 part-time matriculated graduate/professional students (9 women). *Enrollment by degree level:* 23 master's. *Graduate faculty:* 12 part-time/adjunct (7 women). *Tuition:* Full-time $5760; part-time $320 per credit hour. *Student services:* Campus employment opportunities, career counseling, child daycare facilities, exercise/wellness program, free psychological counseling, international student services, low-cost health insurance, multicultural affairs office, services for students with disabilities, teacher training, writing training. *Library facilities:* George and Eleanor McGovern Library plus 1 other. *Online resources:* library catalog. *Collection:* 70,241 titles, 839 serial subscriptions, 4,402 audiovisual materials.

Computer facilities: 100 computers available on campus for general student use. A campuswide network can be accessed from student residence rooms and from off campus. Online class registration, portal, course management system are available. *Web address:* http://www.dwu.edu/.

General Application Contact: Coordinator of Graduate Admissions, 605-995-2650, Fax: 605-995-2699, E-mail: admissions@dwu.edu.

GRADUATE UNITS

Program in Education Students: 23 part-time (9 women); includes 4 minority (all Black or African American, non-Hispanic/Latino). *Faculty:* 12 part-time/adjunct (7 women). Expenses: Contact institution. *Degree program information:* Part-time and evening/weekend programs available. Offers curriculum and instruction (MA Ed); educational policy and administration (MA Ed); preK-12 principal certification (MA Ed); secondary certification (MA Ed). *Application deadline:* For fall admission, 8/1 priority date for domestic and international students; for winter admission, 12/1 priority date for domestic students; for spring admission, 4/1 priority date for domestic students, 12/1 priority date for international students. Applications are processed on a rolling basis. *Application fee:* $50. Electronic applications accepted. *Application Contact:* Coordinator of Graduate Admissions, 605-995-2650, Fax: 605-995-2699, E-mail: admissions@dwu.edu. *Director of Graduate Studies,* Dr. Ruth Haidle, 605-995-2630, Fax: 605-995-2609, E-mail: ruhaidle@dwu.edu.

DALHOUSIE UNIVERSITY, Halifax, NS B3H 4R2, Canada

General Information Province-supported, coed, university. CGS member. *Graduate housing:* Rooms and/or apartments available on a first-come, first-served basis to single and married students. Housing application deadline: 8/1.

GRADUATE UNITS

Faculty of Architecture and Planning Offers architecture and planning (M Arch, M Eng, M Plan, MEDS, MPS). Electronic applications accepted.

School of Planning Offers planning (M Eng, M Plan, MPS). Electronic applications accepted.

Faculty of Arts and Social Science *Degree program information:* Part-time programs available. Offers arts and social science (MA, PhD); classics (MA, PhD); English (MA, PhD); French (MA, PhD); German (MA); history (MA, PhD); international development studies (MA); musicology (MA); philosophy (MA, PhD); political science (MA, PhD); social anthropology (MA, PhD); sociology (MA, PhD). Electronic applications accepted.

Faculty of Computer Science Offers computational biology and bioinformatics (M Sc); computer science (PhD); computer science (project-based) (MA Sc); computer science (thesis-based) (MC Sc); electronic commerce (MEC); health informatics (MHI). Electronic applications accepted.

Faculty of Dentistry Offers dentistryoral and maxillofacial surgery.

Faculty of Engineering Offers biological engineering (M Eng, MA Sc, PhD); biomedical engineering (MA Sc, PhD); chemical engineering (M Eng, MA Sc, PhD); civil and resource engineering (M Eng, MA Sc, PhD); electrical and computer engineering (M Eng, MA Sc, PhD); engineering (M Eng, M Sc, MA Sc, PhD); engineering mathematics (M Sc, PhD); environmental engineering (M Eng, MA Sc, PhD); food science and technology (M Sc, PhD); industrial engineering (M Eng, MA Sc, PhD); internetworking (M Eng); materials engineering (M Eng, MA Sc, PhD); mechanical engineering (M Eng, MA Sc, PhD); mineral resource engineering (M Eng, MA Sc, PhD).

Faculty of Graduate Studies *Degree program information:* Part-time programs available. Postbaccalaureate distance learning degree programs offered. Offers anatomy and neurobiology (M Sc, PhD); interdisciplinary studies (PhD); medicine (M Sc, PhD); neuroscience (M Sc, PhD); pathology (M Sc, PhD); pharmacology (M Sc, PhD). Electronic applications accepted.

Dalhousie Law School *Degree program information:* Part-time programs available. Offers law (LL M, JSD). Electronic applications accepted.

Dalhousie University (continued)

Nova Scotia Agricultural College *Degree program information:* Part-time programs available. Offers agriculture (M Sc). Electronic applications accepted.

Faculty of Health Professions *Degree program information:* Part-time programs available. Postbaccalaureate distance learning degree programs offered. Offers health professions (M Sc, MA, MAHSR, MHA, MN, MPH, MSW, PhD).

School of Health Administration *Degree program information:* Part-time programs available. Postbaccalaureate distance learning degree programs offered (minimal on-campus study). Offers health administration (MAHSR, MHA, MPH, PhD). Electronic applications accepted.

School of Health and Human Performance *Degree program information:* Part-time programs available. Offers health and human performance (M Sc, MA); health promotion (MA); kinesiology (M Sc); leisure studies (MA). Electronic applications accepted.

School of Human Communication Disorders Offers audiology (M Sc); speech-language pathology (M Sc). Electronic applications accepted.

School of Nursing *Degree program information:* Part-time programs available. Postbaccalaureate distance learning degree programs offered (minimal on-campus study). Offers nursing (MN, PhD). Electronic applications accepted.

School of Occupational Therapy *Degree program information:* Part-time and evening/weekend programs available. Postbaccalaureate distance learning degree programs offered (no on-campus study). Offers occupational therapy (entry to profession) (M Sc); occupational therapy (post-professional) (M Sc). Electronic applications accepted.

School of Physiotherapy Offers physiotherapy (entry to profession) (M Sc); physiotherapy (rehabilitation research) (M Sc). Electronic applications accepted.

School of Social Work *Degree program information:* Part-time programs available. Postbaccalaureate distance learning degree programs offered (minimal on-campus study). Offers social work (MSW). Electronic applications accepted.

Faculty of Management *Degree program information:* Part-time programs available. Offers management (MBA, MEC, MES, MIM, MLIS, MMM, MPA, MREM, GDPA); marine affairs (MMM). Electronic applications accepted.

Centre for Advanced Management Education *Degree program information:* Part-time programs available. Postbaccalaureate distance learning degree programs offered. Offers financial services (MBA); information management (MIM); management (MPA); natural resources (MBA). Electronic applications accepted.

School for Resource and Environmental Studies *Degree program information:* Part-time programs available. Offers resource and environmental studies (MES, MREM). Electronic applications accepted.

School of Business Administration *Degree program information:* Part-time programs available. Offers business administration (MBA); financial services (MBA). Electronic applications accepted.

School of Information Management *Degree program information:* Part-time programs available. Offers information management (MIM, MLIS). Electronic applications accepted.

School of Public Administration *Degree program information:* Part-time programs available. Offers management (MPA); public administration (MPA, GDPA). Electronic applications accepted.

Faculty of Medicine Offers biochemistry and molecular biology (M Sc, PhD); community health and epidemiology (M Sc); medicine (MD, M Sc, PhD); microbiology and immunology (M Sc, PhD); physiology and biophysics (M Sc, PhD). Electronic applications accepted.

Faculty of Science Offers biology (M Sc, PhD); chemistry (M Sc, PhD); clinical psychology (PhD); earth sciences (M Sc, PhD); economics (MA, MDE, PhD); mathematics (M Sc, PhD); oceanography (M Sc, PhD); physics and atmospheric science (M Sc, PhD); psychology (M Sc, PhD); psychology/neuroscience (M Sc, PhD); science (M Sc, MA, MDE, PhD); statistics (M Sc, PhD). Electronic applications accepted.

DALLAS BAPTIST UNIVERSITY, Dallas, TX 75211-9299

General Information Independent-religious, coed, comprehensive institution. *Enrollment:* 5,470 graduate, professional, and undergraduate students; 644 full-time matriculated graduate/professional students (392 women), 1,303 part-time matriculated graduate/professional students (843 women). *Enrollment by degree level:* 1,777 master's, 170 doctoral. *Graduate faculty:* 81 full-time (35 women), 170 part-time/adjunct (67 women). *Tuition:* Full-time $11,394; part-time $633 per credit hour. *Graduate housing:* Rooms and/or apartments available on a first-come, first-served basis to single and married students. Typical cost: $2326 per year ($5868 including board) for single students. Room and board charges vary according to board plan and housing facility selected. Housing application deadline: 6/19. *Student services:* Campus employment opportunities, campus safety program, career counseling, free psychological counseling, international student services, low-cost health insurance, services for students with disabilities, writing training. *Library facilities:* Vance Memorial Library. *Online resources:* library catalog, web page, access to other libraries' catalogs. *Collection:* 292,846 titles, 362 serial subscriptions, 7,644 audiovisual materials.

Computer facilities: 208 computers available on campus for general student use. A campuswide network can be accessed from student residence rooms and from off campus. Online class registration is available. *Web address:* http://www.dbu.edu/.

General Application Contact: Kit P. Montgomery, Director of Graduate Programs, 214-333-5242, Fax: 214-333-5579, E-mail: graduate@dbu.edu.

GRADUATE UNITS

College of Adult Education *Degree program information:* Part-time and evening/weekend programs available. Offers accounting (MA); adult education (MA, MLA); arts (MLA); Christian ministry (MLA); church leadership (MA); counseling (MA); criminal justice (MA); English (MLA); English as a second language (MA, MLA); finance (MA); fine arts (MLA); higher education (MA); history (MLA); leadership studies (MA); management (MA); management information systems (MA); marketing (MA); missions (MA, MLA); political science (MLA). Electronic applications accepted.

College of Business *Degree program information:* Part-time and evening/weekend programs available. Postbaccalaureate distance learning degree programs offered (no on-campus study). Offers accounting (MBA); business (MA, MBA); business communication (MA, MBA); conflict resolution management (MA, MBA); e-business (MBA); entrepreneurship (MBA); finance (MBA); general management (MA); health care management (MA, MBA); human resource management (MA); international business (MBA); leading the non-profit organization (MBA); management (MBA); management information systems (MBA); marketing (MBA); performance management (MA); project management (MBA); technology and engineering management (MBA). Electronic applications accepted.

College of Humanities and Social Sciences *Degree program information:* Part-time and evening/weekend programs available. Offers counseling (MA); humanities and social sciences (MA). Electronic applications accepted.

Dorothy M. Bush College of Education *Degree program information:* Part-time and evening/weekend programs available. Offers curriculum and instruction (M Ed); education (M Ed, MAT); educational leadership (M Ed); elementary (MAT); English as a second language (M Ed, MAT); hi-level (MAT); kinesiology (M Ed); master reading teacher (M Ed); reading specialist (M Ed); school counseling (M Ed); secondary (MAT). Electronic applications accepted.

Gary Cook School of Leadership *Degree program information:* Part-time and evening/weekend programs available. Offers adult ministry (MA); business communication (MA); business ministry (MA); childhood ministry (MA); Christian education and business administration (MA, MBA); Christian education/missions (MA); Christian education: childhood ministry (MA); Christian education: student ministry (MA); collegiate ministry (MA); communication ministry (MA); counseling ministry (MA); education in higher education (M Ed); education ministry (MA); ESL (MA); general ministry (MA); general studies (MA); global studies (MA); international business (MA); leadership (M Ed, MA, MBA); missions (MA); missions ministry (MA); student ministry (MA); worship leadership (MA); worship ministry (MA); worship/missions (MA). Electronic applications accepted.

DALLAS THEOLOGICAL SEMINARY, Dallas, TX 75204-6499

General Information Independent, coed, graduate-only institution. *Graduate housing:* Rooms and/or apartments available on a first-come, first-served basis to single and married students.

GRADUATE UNITS

Graduate Programs *Degree program information:* Part-time and evening/weekend programs available. Offers academic ministries (Th M); Bible translation (Th M); biblical and theological studies (CGS); biblical counseling (MA, Th M); biblical exegesis and linguistics (MA); biblical exposition (PhD); biblical studies (MA); Christian education (MA, D Min); cross-cultural ministries (MA, Th M); educational leadership (Th M); evangelism and discipleship (Th M); interdisciplinary studies (Th M); media and communication (MA); media arts in ministry (Th M); ministry (D Min); New Testament studies (Th M, PhD); Old Testament studies (PhD); parachurch ministries (Th M); pastoral ministries (Th M); sacred theology (STM); theological studies (PhD); women's ministry (Th M). Electronic applications accepted.

DANIEL WEBSTER COLLEGE, Nashua, NH 03063-1300

General Information Independent, coed, comprehensive institution.

GRADUATE UNITS

MBA Program *Degree program information:* Part-time and evening/weekend programs available. Offers applied management (MBA). Electronic applications accepted.

MBA Program for Aviation Professionals *Degree program information:* Part-time and evening/weekend programs available. Offers business administration for aviation professionals (MBA). Electronic applications accepted.

DANIEL WEBSTER COLLEGE–PORTSMOUTH CAMPUS, Portsmouth, NH 03801

General Information Independent, coed, comprehensive institution. *Graduate housing:* On-campus housing not available.

GRADUATE UNITS

MBA Program *Degree program information:* Part-time and evening/weekend programs available. Offers applied management (MBA). Electronic applications accepted.

DARKEI NOAM RABBINICAL COLLEGE, Brooklyn, NY 11210

General Information Independent-religious, men only, comprehensive institution.

GRADUATE UNITS

Graduate Programs

DARTMOUTH COLLEGE, Hanover, NH 03755

General Information Independent, coed, university. CGS member. *Graduate housing:* Rooms and/or apartments available to single and married students. Housing application deadline: 5/15.

GRADUATE UNITS

Arts and Sciences Graduate Programs Offers arts and sciences (AM, MALS, MS, PhD); biomedical physiology (PhD); cancer biology and molecular therapeutics (PhD); cardiovascular diseases (PhD); chemistry (PhD); cognitive neuroscience (PhD); comparative literature (AM); computer science (MS, PhD); earth sciences (MS, PhD); ecology and evolutionary biology (PhD); electro-acoustic music (AM); liberal studies (MALS); mathematics (PhD); molecular pharmacology, toxicology and experimental therapeutics (PhD); neuroscience (PhD); pharmacology and toxicology (PhD); physics and astronomy (MS, PhD); physiology (PhD); psychology (PhD). Electronic applications accepted.

The Dartmouth Institute *Degree program information:* Part-time programs available. Offers evaluative clinical sciences (MS, PhD); public health (MPH).

Dartmouth Medical School Offers medicine (MD).

Graduate Program in Molecular and Cellular Biology Offers biochemistry (PhD); biological sciences (PhD); genetics (PhD); immunologymicrobiology and immunology (PhD); molecular and cellular biology (PhD); molecular pathogenesis (PhD). Electronic applications accepted.

Program in Experimental and Molecular Medicine Offers biomedical physiology (PhD); cancer biology and molecular therapeutics (PhD); cardiovascular diseases (PhD); molecular pharmacology, toxicology and experimental therapeutics (PhD); neuroscience (PhD). Electronic applications accepted.

Thayer School of Engineering Students: 200 full-time (57 women); includes 3 Black or African American, non-Hispanic/Latino; 1 American Indian or Alaska Native, non-Hispanic/Latino; 10 Asian, non-Hispanic/Latino; 3 Hispanic/Latino; 1 Two or more races, non-Hispanic/Latino, 102 international. Average age 24. 583 applicants, 27% accepted, 70 enrolled. *Faculty:* 51 full-time (7 women), 36 part-time/adjunct (4 women). Expenses: Contact institution. *Financial support:* In 2010–11, 187 students received support, including 5 fellowships with full tuition reimbursements available (averaging $22,920 per year), 96 research assistantships with full tuition reimbursements available (averaging $22,920 per year); 40 teaching assistantships with partial tuition reimbursements available (averaging $7,200 per year); career-related internships or fieldwork, institutionally sponsored loans, scholarships/grants, and tuition waivers (full and partial) also available. Financial award application deadline: 2/15; financial award applicants required to submit CSS PROFILE. In 2010, 44 master's, 7 doctorates awarded. Offers biomedical engineering (MS, PhD); biotechnology and biochemical engineering (MS, PhD); computer engineering (MS, PhD); electrical engineering (MS, PhD); engineering (MEM, MS, PhD); engineering management (MEM); engineering physics (MS, PhD); environmental engineering (MS, PhD); manufacturing systems (MS, PhD); materials sciences and engineering (MS, PhD); mechanical engineering (MS, PhD). *Application deadline:* For fall admission, 1/1 priority date for domestic and international students. Applications are processed on a rolling basis. *Application fee:* $45. Electronic applications accepted. *Application Contact:* Candace S. Potter, Graduate Admissions Administrator, 603-646-3844, Fax: 603-646-1620, E-mail: candace.potter@dartmouth.edu. *Dean*, Dr. Joseph J. Helbie, 603-646-2238, Fax: 603-646-2580, E-mail: joseph.j.helbie@dartmouth.edu.

Tuck School of Business at Dartmouth Students: 537 full-time (181 women); includes 29 Black or African American, non-Hispanic/Latino; 50 Asian, non-Hispanic/Latino; 20 Hispanic/Latino, 170 international. Average age 28. 2,528 applicants, 20% accepted, 280 enrolled. *Faculty:* 46 full-time (11 women). Expenses: Contact institution. *Financial support:* In 2010–11, 387 students received support. Institutionally sponsored loans and scholarships/grants available. Financial award application deadline: 4/15; financial award applicants required to submit FAFSA. In 2010, 253 master's awarded. Offers business (MBA). *Application deadline:* For fall admission, 10/15 for domestic and international students; for winter admission, 1/31 for domestic and international students; for spring admission, 4/1 for domestic and international students. *Application fee:* $225. Electronic applications accepted. *Application Contact:* Dawna Clarke, Director of Admissions, 603-646-3162, Fax: 603-646-1441, E-mail: tuck.admissions@dartmouth.edu. *Dean*, Paul Danos, 603-646-2460, Fax: 603-646-1308, E-mail: tuck.public.relations@dartmouth.edu.

DAVENPORT UNIVERSITY, Dearborn, MI 48126-3799

General Information Independent, coed, comprehensive institution. *Graduate housing:* On-campus housing not available.

GRADUATE UNITS

Sneden Graduate School *Degree program information:* Part-time and evening/weekend programs available. Postbaccalaureate distance learning degree programs offered (no on-campus study). Offers accounting (MBA); business administration (EMBA); finance (MBA); health care management (MBA); human resources management (MBA); information assurance (MS); marketing (MBA); public health (MPH); strategic management (MBA).

DAVENPORT UNIVERSITY, Grand Rapids, MI 49512

General Information Independent, coed, comprehensive institution. *Graduate housing:* Room and/or apartments available on a first-come, first-served basis to single students;

on-campus housing not available to married students. *Research affiliation:* Human Synergistic Center for Applied Research, Inc. (leadership, organizational culture, strategy).

GRADUATE UNITS

Sneden Graduate School *Degree program information:* Evening/weekend programs available. Offers accounting (MBA); business administration (EMBA); finance (MBA); health care management (MBA); human resources (MBA); information assurance (MS); public health (MPH); strategic management (MBA). Electronic applications accepted.

DAVENPORT UNIVERSITY, Warren, MI 48092-5209

General Information Independent, coed, comprehensive institution.

GRADUATE UNITS

Sneden Graduate School Offers accounting (MBA); business administration (EMBA); finance (MBA); health care management (MBA); human resources management (MBA); information assurance (MS); public health (MPH); strategic management (MBA).

DEFIANCE COLLEGE, Defiance, OH 43512-1610

General Information Independent-religious, coed, comprehensive institution. *Graduate housing:* On-campus housing not available.

GRADUATE UNITS

Program in Business Administration *Degree program information:* Part-time and evening/weekend programs available. Offers criminal justice (MBA); health care (MBA); leadership (MBA).

Program in Education *Degree program information:* Part-time programs available. Offers adolescent and young adult (MA); mild and moderate intervention specialist (MA); sport science (MA).

DELAWARE STATE UNIVERSITY, Dover, DE 19901-2277

General Information State-supported, coed, university. CGS member. *Graduate housing:* Room and/or apartments available on a first-come, first-served basis to single students; on-campus housing not available to married students.

GRADUATE UNITS

Graduate Programs *Degree program information:* Part-time and evening/weekend programs available. Offers applied chemistry (MS, PhD); applied mathematics (MS); applied mathematics and theoretical physics (PhD); applied optics (MS); biological sciences (MA, MS); biology education (MS); chemistry (MS, PhD); French (MA); historic preservation (MA); mathematics (MS); mathematics education (MS); molecular and cellular neuroscience (MS); natural resources (MS); neuroscience (PhD); optics (PhD); physics (MS); physics teaching (MS); plant science (MS); Spanish (MA).

College of Business *Degree program information:* Part-time and evening/weekend programs available. Offers business administration (MBA). Electronic applications accepted.

College of Education, Health and Public Policy *Degree program information:* Part-time and evening/weekend programs available. Offers adult literacy and basic education (MA); art education (MA); curriculum and instruction (MA); education, health and public policy (MA, MS, MSW, Ed D); educational leadership (MA, Ed D); nursing (MS); science education (MA); social work (MSW); special education (MA); sport administration (MS); teaching (MA). Electronic applications accepted.

DELAWARE VALLEY COLLEGE, Doylestown, PA 18901-2697

General Information Independent, coed, comprehensive institution. *Graduate housing:* On-campus housing not available.

GRADUATE UNITS

MBA Program *Degree program information:* Part-time and evening/weekend programs available. Postbaccalaureate distance learning degree programs offered (no on-campus study). Offers accounting (MBA); food and agribusiness (MBA); general business (MBA); online global executive leadership (MBA).

Program in Educational Leadership *Degree program information:* Part-time and evening/weekend programs available. Offers instruction, curriculum and technology (MS); school administration and leadership (MS).

DELL'ARTE INTERNATIONAL SCHOOL OF PHYSICAL THEATRE, Blue Lake, CA 95525

General Information Independent, coed, graduate-only institution. *Graduate housing:* Rooms and/or apartments available on a first-come, first-served basis to single and married students.

GRADUATE UNITS

MFA Program Offers ensemble based physical theatre (MFA). Electronic applications accepted.

DELTA STATE UNIVERSITY, Cleveland, MS 38733-0001

General Information State-supported, coed, comprehensive institution. *Enrollment:* 4,327 graduate, professional, and undergraduate students; 571 full-time matriculated graduate/professional students (374 women), 808 part-time matriculated graduate/professional students (610 women). *Enrollment by degree level:* 1,215 master's, 60 doctoral, 104 other advanced degrees. *Graduate faculty:* 73 full-time (38 women), 24 part-time/adjunct (17 women). Tuition, state resident: full-time $4347; part-time $202 per credit hour. Tuition, nonresident: full-time $12,052; part-time $523 per credit hour. *Required fees:* $504. *Graduate housing:* Rooms and/or apartments available on a first-come, first-served basis to single and married students. Typical cost: $5850 (including board) for single students; $5850 (including board) for married students. Room and board charges vary according to housing facility selected. Housing application deadline: 6/1. *Student services:* Campus employment opportunities, campus safety program, career counseling, child daycare facilities, exercise/wellness program, free psychological counseling, grant writing training, international student services, low-cost health insurance, services for students with disabilities, teacher training, writing training. *Library facilities:* Roberts-LaForge Library. *Online resources:* library catalog, web page. *Collection:* 434,579 titles, 25,133 serial subscriptions, 20,611 audiovisual materials.

Computer facilities: Computer purchase and lease plans are available. 534 computers available on campus for general student use. A campuswide network can be accessed from student residence rooms. Online class registration is available. *Web address:* http://www.deltastate.edu/.

General Application Contact: Dr. Albert Nylander, Dean of Graduate Studies, 662-846-4875, Fax: 662-846-4313, E-mail: grad-info@deltastate.edu.

GRADUATE UNITS

Graduate Programs *Degree program information:* Part-time and evening/weekend programs available. Postbaccalaureate distance learning degree programs offered (minimal on-campus study). Electronic applications accepted.

College of Arts and Sciences *Degree program information:* Part-time programs available. Offers arts and sciences (M Ed, MSCD, MSCJ, MSJC, MSNS); community development (MS); history (M Ed); natural sciences (MSNS); secondary education (M Ed); social justice and criminology (MSJC); social science secondary education (M Ed).

College of Business *Degree program information:* Part-time and evening/weekend programs available. Postbaccalaureate distance learning degree programs offered (minimal on-campus study). Offers accountancy (MPA); business (MBA, MCA, MPA); business administration (MBA); commercial aviation (MCA).

College of Education *Degree program information:* Part-time and evening/weekend programs available. Offers counseling (M Ed); counselor education (Ed D); education (M Ed, MAT, MS, Ed D, Ed S); educational administration and supervision (M Ed, Ed S); educational leadership (Ed D); elementary education (M Ed, MAT, Ed D, Ed S); health, physical education, and recreation (M Ed); higher education (Ed D); professional studies (Ed D); special education (M Ed); sport and human performance (MS); teaching (alternate route) (MAT).

School of Nursing *Degree program information:* Part-time programs available. Offers family nurse practitioner (MSN); nurse administrator (MSN); nurse educator (MSN). Electronic applications accepted.

DENVER SEMINARY, Littleton, CO 80120

General Information Independent-religious, coed, graduate-only institution. *Graduate housing:* Rooms and/or apartments available on a first-come, first-served basis to single and married students. Housing application deadline: 6/1.

GRADUATE UNITS

Graduate and Professional Programs *Degree program information:* Part-time and evening/weekend programs available. Postbaccalaureate distance learning degree programs offered. Offers apologetics (Certificate); biblical studies (MA); Christian formation and soul care (MA, Certificate); Christian studies (MA, Certificate); church and parachurch leadership (D Min); counseling licensure (MA); counseling ministry (MA); intercultural ministry (Certificate); leadership (MA, Certificate); marriage and family counseling (D Min); pastoral ministry (D Min); philosophy of religion (MA); spiritual guidance (Certificate); theology (M Div, Certificate); worship (Certificate); youth and family ministry (MA). Electronic applications accepted.

DEPAUL UNIVERSITY, Chicago, IL 60604-2287

General Information Independent-religious, coed, university. CGS member. *Graduate housing:* On-campus housing not available. *Research affiliation:* Civic Federation (public services), Metro Chicago Information Center (public services), International Institute of Higher Studies in the Criminal Sciences (law).

GRADUATE UNITS

Charles H. Kellstadt Graduate School of Business *Degree program information:* Part-time and evening/weekend programs available. Offers applied economics (MBA); behavioral finance (MBA); brand management (MBA); business (M Acc, MA, MBA, MS, MSA, MSEPA, MSF, MSHR, MSMA, MSRE, MST); business strategy (MBA); computational finance (MS); customer relationship management (MBA); economics and policy analysis (MA); entrepreneurship (MBA); finance (MBA, MSF); financial analysis (MBA); financial management and control (MBA); health sector management (MBA); human resource management (MBA, MSHR); integrated marketing communication (MBA); international business (MBA); international marketing and finance (MBA); leadership/change management (MBA); management planning and strategy (MBA); managerial finance (MBA); marketing analysis (MSMA); marketing and management (MBA); marketing strategy and analysis (MBA); marketing strategy and planning (MBA); new product management (MBA); operations management (MBA); real estate (MS); real estate finance and investment (MBA); sales leadership (MBA); strategy, execution and valuation (MBA). Electronic applications accepted.

School of Accountancy and Management Information Systems Students: 207 full-time (112 women), 208 part-time (92 women); includes 7 Black or African American, non-Hispanic/Latino; 34 Asian, non-Hispanic/Latino; 19 Hispanic/Latino; 2 Two or more races, non-Hispanic/Latino, 76 international. *Faculty:* 30 full-time (9 women), 54 part-time/adjunct (7 women). Expenses: Contact institution. *Financial support:* In 2010–11, 7 research assistantships with full tuition reimbursements (averaging $4,100 per year) were awarded; institutionally sponsored loans also available. Financial award application deadline: 4/2. In 2010, 141 master's awarded. *Degree program information:* Part-time and evening/weekend programs available. Offers accountancy (M Acc, MSA); business information technology (MS); e-business (MBA, MS); financial management and control (MBA); management accounting (MBA); management information systems (MBA); taxation (MST). *Application deadline:* For fall admission, 7/1 for domestic students; for winter admission, 10/1 for domestic students; for spring admission, 2/1 for domestic students. Applications are processed on a rolling basis. *Application fee:* $60. *Application Contact:* Christopher E. Kinsella, Director of Cohort MBA Programs, 312-362-8810, Fax: 312-362-6677, E-mail: kgsb@depaul.edu. *Director*, Kevin Stevens, 312-362-6989, E-mail: kstevens@depaul.edu.

College of Communication Students: 170 full-time (129 women), 70 part-time (52 women); includes 29 Black or African American, non-Hispanic/Latino; 9 Asian, non-Hispanic/Latino; 20 Hispanic/Latino; 7 Two or more races, non-Hispanic/Latino, 17 international. Average age 29. 354 applicants, 44% accepted, 79 enrolled. *Faculty:* 31 full-time (17 women), 15 part-time/adjunct (7 women). Expenses: Contact institution. *Financial support:* In 2010–11, 8 students received support, including 4 research assistantships with partial tuition reimbursements available, 2 teaching assistantships with full tuition reimbursements available (averaging $12,000 per year); fellowships with full tuition reimbursements available, career-related internships or fieldwork, scholarships/grants, and tuition waivers (partial) also available. Support available to part-time students. Financial award applicants required to submit FAFSA. In 2010, 64 master's awarded. *Degree program information:* Part-time and evening/weekend programs available. Offers journalism (MA); media, culture and society (MA); organizational and multicultural communication (MA); public relations and advertising (MA). *Application fee:* $40. Electronic applications accepted. *Application Contact:* Ann Spittle, Director of Graduate Admission, 773-325-7315, Fax: 773-325-2395, E-mail: gradcom@depaul.edu. *Dean*, Dr. Jacqueline Taylor, 773-325-7216, Fax: 773-325-7584, E-mail: jtaylor@depaul.edu.

College of Computing and Digital Media Students: 952 full-time (230 women), 927 part-time (226 women); includes 557 minority (205 Black or African American, non-Hispanic/Latino; 2 American Indian or Alaska Native, non-Hispanic/Latino; 167 Asian, non-Hispanic/Latino; 136 Hispanic/Latino; 7 Native Hawaiian or other Pacific Islander, non-Hispanic/Latino; 40 Two or more races, non-Hispanic/Latino), 292 international. Average age 31. 896 applicants, 70% accepted, 324 enrolled. *Faculty:* 51 full-time (11 women), 50 part-time/adjunct (9 women). Expenses: Contact institution. *Financial support:* In 2010–11, 102 students received support, including 4 fellowships with full tuition reimbursements available (averaging $24,435 per year), 6 research assistantships (averaging $21,100 per year), 92 teaching assistantships with full and partial tuition reimbursements available (averaging $6,904 per year); Federal Work-Study, scholarships/grants, tuition waivers (full and partial), and unspecified assistantships also available. Support available to part-time students. Financial award application deadline: 4/30; financial award applicants required to submit FAFSA. In 2010, 417 master's, 6 doctorates awarded. *Degree program information:* Part-time and evening/weekend programs available. Postbaccalaureate distance learning degree programs offered (no on-campus study). Offers animation (MA, MFA); applied technology (MS); business information technology (MS); cinema (MFA); cinema production (MS); computational finance (MS); computer and information sciences (PhD); computer game development (MS); computer graphics and motion technology (MS); computer information and network security (MS); computer science (MS); e-commerce technology (MS); human-computer interaction (MS); information systems (MS); information technology (MA); information technology project management (MS); network engineering and management (MS); predictive analytics (MS); screenwriting (MFA); software engineering (MS). *Application deadline:* For fall admission, 8/15 priority date for domestic students, 6/1 priority date for international students; for winter admission, 12/15 priority date for domestic students, 9/15 priority date for international students; for spring admission, 3/1 priority date for domestic students, 12/15 priority date for international students. Applications are processed on a rolling basis. *Application fee:* $25. Electronic applications accepted. *Application Contact:* Dr. Liz Friedman, Assistant Dean of Student Services, 312-362-8714, Fax: 312-362-5179, E-mail: efriedm2@cdm.depaul.edu. *Dean*, Dr. David Miller, 312-362-8381, Fax: 312-362-5185.

College of Law Students: 853 full-time (404 women), 220 part-time (109 women); includes 234 minority (65 Black or African American, non-Hispanic/Latino; 6 American Indian or Alaska Native, non-Hispanic/Latino; 73 Asian, non-Hispanic/Latino; 90 Hispanic/Latino), 13 international. Average age 24. 5,770 applicants, 40% accepted, 312 enrolled. *Faculty:* 54 full-time (24 women), 65 part-time/adjunct (25 women). Expenses: Contact institution. *Financial support:* In 2010–11, 583 students received support, including 51 fellowships with partial tuition reimbursements available (averaging $5,000 per year), 106 research assistantships (averaging $1,400 per year); career-related internships or fieldwork, scholarships/grants, and tuition waivers (partial) also available. Support available to part-time students. Financial award application deadline: 3/1; financial award applicants required to submit FAFSA. In 2010, 323 first professional degrees awarded. *Degree program information:* Part-time and evening/weekend programs available. Offers health law (LL M); intellectual property law (LL M);

DePaul University (continued)

international law (LL M); law (JD); tax law (LL M). *Application deadline:* For fall admission, 3/1 for domestic and international students. Applications are processed on a rolling basis. *Application fee:* $60. Electronic applications accepted. *Application Contact:* Michael S. Burns, Director of Law Admission and Associate Dean, 312-362-6831, Fax: 312-362-5280, E-mail: lawinfo@depaul.edu. *Interim Dean,* Hon. Warren Wolfson, 312-362-8989, E-mail: wwolfson@depaul.edu.

College of Liberal Arts and Sciences *Degree program information:* Part-time and evening/weekend programs available. Postbaccalaureate distance learning degree programs offered (minimal on-campus study). Offers adult nursing (MS); applied mathematics (MS); applied physics (MS); applied statistics (MS, Certificate); biochemistry (MS); biological sciences (MA, MS); chemistry (MS); clinical psychology (MA, PhD); English (MA); experimental psychology (MA, PhD); family nursing (MS); general psychology (MS); generalist nursing (MS); history (MA); industrial/organizational psychology (MA, PhD); interdisciplinary studies (MA, MS); liberal arts and sciences (MA, MS, PhD, Certificate); mathematics education (MA); nurse anesthesia (MS); philosophy (MA, PhD); polymer chemistry and coatings technology (MS); sociology (MA); writing and publishing (MA). Electronic applications accepted.

School for New Learning Students: 15 full-time (6 women), 132 part-time (97 women); includes 58 Black or African American, non-Hispanic/Latino; 3 Asian, non-Hispanic/Latino; 8 Hispanic/Latino; 3 Two or more races, non-Hispanic/Latino, 1 international. Average age 42. 53 applicants, 60% accepted, 29 enrolled. *Faculty:* 11 full-time (6 women), 12 part-time/adjunct (8 women). Expenses: Contact institution. *Financial support:* In 2010–11, 7 students received support. Scholarships/grants and tuition waivers (partial) available. Financial award applicants required to submit FAFSA. In 2010, 20 master's awarded. *Degree program information:* Part-time and evening/weekend programs available. Offers applied professional studies (MA); applied technology (MS); educating adults (MA). *Application deadline:* For fall admission, 9/1 priority date for domestic students; for spring admission, 3/1 priority date for domestic students. Applications are processed on a rolling basis. *Application fee:* $25. Electronic applications accepted. *Application Contact:* Sarah Hellstrom, Assistant Director, 312-362-5744, Fax: 312-362-8809, E-mail: shellstr@depaul.edu. *Program Director,* Dr. Russ Rogers, 312-362-8512, Fax: 312-362-8809, E-mail: rrogers@depaul.edu.

School of Education Students: 944 full-time (753 women), 534 part-time (415 women); includes 355 minority (166 Black or African American, non-Hispanic/Latino; 1 American Indian or Alaska Native, non-Hispanic/Latino; 41 Asian, non-Hispanic/Latino; 124 Hispanic/Latino; 3 Native Hawaiian or other Pacific Islander, non-Hispanic/Latino; 20 Two or more races, non-Hispanic/Latino), 21 international. Average age 30. 635 applicants, 74% accepted, 318 enrolled. *Faculty:* 61 full-time (40 women), 66 part-time/adjunct (41 women). Expenses: Contact institution. *Financial support:* In 2010–11, 14 research assistantships with tuition reimbursements (averaging $5,800 per year) were awarded; career-related internships or fieldwork also available. In 2010, 604 master's, 5 doctorates awarded. *Degree program information:* Part-time and evening/weekend programs available. Offers bilingual and bicultural education (M Ed, MA); curriculum studies (M Ed, MA, Ed D); educational leadership (M Ed, MA, Ed D); human development and learning (MA); human services and counseling (M Ed, MA); reading and learning disabilities (M Ed, MA); social culture studies in education and development (M Ed, MA); teaching and learning (early childhood, elementary and secondary) (M Ed); teaching and learning (early childhood, elementary, and secondary) (MA). *Application deadline:* Applications are processed on a rolling basis. *Application fee:* $40. Electronic applications accepted. *Application Contact:* Brandon Washington, Data Project Manager, 773-325-1152, Fax: 773-325-2270, E-mail: bwashin3@depaul.edu. *Dean,* Dr. Marie Donovan, 773-325-7581, Fax: 773-325-7713, E-mail: mdonovan@depaul.edu.

School of Music Students: 50 full-time (29 women), 73 part-time (38 women); includes 5 Black or African American, non-Hispanic/Latino; 5 Asian, non-Hispanic/Latino; 5 Hispanic/Latino; 1 Two or more races, non-Hispanic/Latino, 28 international. Average age 24. 312 applicants, 31% accepted, 50 enrolled. *Faculty:* 11 full-time (2 women), 50 part-time/adjunct (14 women). Expenses: Contact institution. *Financial support:* In 2010–11, 4 fellowships with partial tuition reimbursements were awarded; teaching assistantships, career-related internships or fieldwork, Federal Work-Study, scholarships/grants, and tuition waivers also available. Support available to part-time students. Financial award application deadline: 1/15. In 2010, 40 master's, 5 Certificates awarded. *Degree program information:* Part-time and evening/weekend programs available. Offers applied music (performance) (MM, Certificate); jazz studies (MM); music composition (MM); music education (MM). *Application deadline:* For fall admission, 1/15 priority date for domestic and international students. Applications are processed on a rolling basis. *Application fee:* $40. Electronic applications accepted. *Application Contact:* Ross Beacraft, Director of Admissions, 773-325-7444, Fax: 773-325-7429, E-mail: rbeacraf@depaul.edu. *Dean,* Dr. Donald E. Casey, 773-325-7256, E-mail: dcasey@depaul.edu.

School of Public Service Students: 372 full-time (256 women), 324 part-time (237 women); includes 156 Black or African American, non-Hispanic/Latino; 33 Asian, non-Hispanic/Latino; 65 Hispanic/Latino; 18 Two or more races, non-Hispanic/Latino, 18 international. Average age 26. 162 applicants, 100% accepted, 94 enrolled. *Faculty:* 14 full-time (3 women), 43 part-time/adjunct (24 women). Expenses: Contact institution. *Financial support:* In 2010–11, 60 students received support, including 3 research assistantships with full tuition reimbursements available (averaging $7,000 per year); career-related internships or fieldwork, Federal Work-Study, institutionally sponsored loans, scholarships/grants, tuition waivers (partial), and unspecified assistantships also available. Support available to part-time students. Financial award application deadline: 7/1; financial award applicants required to submit FAFSA. In 2010, 108 master's awarded. *Degree program information:* Part-time and evening/weekend programs available. Postbaccalaureate distance learning degree programs offered (minimal on-campus study). Offers financial administration management (Certificate); health administration (Certificate); health law and policy (MS); international public services (MS); leadership and policy studies (MS); metropolitan planning (Certificate); public administration (MPA); public service management (MS); public services (Certificate). *Application deadline:* Applications are processed on a rolling basis. *Application fee:* $40. Electronic applications accepted. *Application Contact:* Megan B. Balderston, Director of Admissions and Marketing, 312-362-5565, Fax: 312-362-5506, E-mail: pubserv@depaul.edu. *Director,* Dr. J. Patrick Murphy, 312-362-5608, Fax: 312-362-5506, E-mail: jpmurphy@depaul.edu.

The Theatre School Students: 39 full-time (19 women); includes 8 Black or African American, non-Hispanic/Latino; 1 Asian, non-Hispanic/Latino; 1 Hispanic/Latino. Average age 28. 261 applicants, 8% accepted, 14 enrolled. *Faculty:* 21 full-time (12 women), 21 part-time/adjunct (10 women). Expenses: Contact institution. *Financial support:* In 2010–11, 39 students received support, including 39 fellowships (averaging $17,800 per year); career-related internships or fieldwork, Federal Work-Study, institutionally sponsored loans, and scholarships/grants also available. Financial award application deadline: 2/15; financial award applicants required to submit FAFSA. In 2010, 14 master's awarded. Offers acting (MFA); arts leadership (MFA); directing (MFA). *Application deadline:* For fall admission, 1/1 priority date for domestic and international students. *Application fee:* $25. Electronic applications accepted. *Application Contact:* Jason Beck, Director of Admissions, 773-325-7999, Fax: 773-325-7920, E-mail: jbeck1@depaul.edu. *Dean,* John Culbert, 773-325-7954, Fax: 773-325-7920, E-mail: jculbert@depaul.edu.

DeSALES UNIVERSITY, Center Valley, PA 18034-9568

General Information Independent-religious, coed, comprehensive institution. *Enrollment:* 3,199 graduate, professional, and undergraduate students; 66 full-time matriculated graduate/professional students (46 women), 767 part-time matriculated graduate/professional students (484 women). *Enrollment by degree level:* 833 master's. *Tuition:* Full-time $18,200; part-time $690 per credit. *Required fees:* $1200. *Student services:* Campus safety program, career counseling, free psychological counseling, international student services, low-cost health insurance, multicultural affairs office, services for students with disabilities, teacher training. *Library facilities:* Trexler Library plus 1 other. *Online resources:* library catalog, web page. *Collection:* 173,241 titles, 16,495 serial subscriptions, 13,333 audiovisual materials.

Computer facilities: Computer purchase and lease plans are available. 200 computers available on campus for general student use. A campuswide network can be accessed from student residence rooms and from off campus. Online class registration is available. *Web address:* http://www.desales.edu/.

General Application Contact: Caryn Stopper, Director of Graduate Admissions, 610-282-1100 Ext. 1768, Fax: 610-282-0525, E-mail: caryn.stopper@desales.edu.

GRADUATE UNITS

Graduate Division Expenses: Contact institution. *Financial support:* Career-related internships or fieldwork available. Support available to part-time students. Offers accounting (MBA); adult advanced practice nurse specialist (MSN); certified nurse midwives (MSN); certified nurse practitioners (MSN); computer information systems (MBA); criminal justice (MACJ); digital forensics (online) (MACJ); ESL endorsement (M Ed); family nurse practitioner (MSN); finance (MBA); health care systems management (MBA); health care systems management (online) (MBA); human resource management (MBA); information systems (MSIS); instructional technology for K-12 (M Ed); instructional technology for K-12 (online) (M Ed); interdisciplinary (M Ed); investigative forensics (online) (MACJ); management (MBA); management (online) (MBA); marketing (MBA); marketing (online) (MBA); nurse educator (MSN); nurse practitioner (Post-Master's Certificate); physician assistant studies (MSPAS); physician's track (MBA); project management (MBA); project management (online) (MBA); self-design (MBA); self-design (online) (MBA); TESOL/ESL (M Ed). *Application Contact:* Caryn Stopper, Director of Graduate Admissions, 610-282-1100 Ext. 1768, Fax: 610-282-0525, E-mail: caryn.stopper@desales.edu. *Director of Graduate Admissions,* Caryn Stopper, 610-282-1100 Ext. 1768, Fax: 610-282-0525, E-mail: caryn.stopper@desales.edu.

DES MOINES UNIVERSITY, Des Moines, IA 50312-4104

General Information Independent, coed, graduate-only institution. *Enrollment:* 1,425 full-time matriculated graduate/professional students (784 women), 357 part-time matriculated graduate/professional students (197 women). *Enrollment by degree level:* 1,409 first professional, 373 master's. *Graduate faculty:* 68 full-time (28 women), 22 part-time/adjunct (6 women). *Graduate housing:* On-campus housing not available. *Student services:* Campus employment opportunities, campus safety program, career counseling, exercise/wellness program, free psychological counseling, international student services, low-cost health insurance, multicultural affairs office. *Library facilities:* Des Moines University Library. *Online resources:* library catalog, web page, access to other libraries' catalogs. *Collection:* 58,039 titles, 581 serial subscriptions, 5,074 audiovisual materials.

Computer facilities: A campuswide network can be accessed from off campus. Online class registration, online classes are available. *Web address:* http://www.dmu.edu/.

General Application Contact: Margie Gehringer, Director of Enrollment Management, 515-271-7498, Fax: 515-271-7190, E-mail: margie.gehringer@dmu.edu.

GRADUATE UNITS

College of Health Sciences Students: 308 full-time (169 women), 318 part-time (175 women); includes 25 Black or African American, non-Hispanic/Latino; 1 American Indian or Alaska Native, non-Hispanic/Latino; 68 Asian, non-Hispanic/Latino; 5 Hispanic/Latino. Average age 24. 1,117 applicants, 40% accepted, 358 enrolled. *Faculty:* 14 full-time (7 women), 5 part-time/adjunct (3 women). Expenses: Contact institution. *Financial support:* Career-related internships or fieldwork, institutionally sponsored loans, scholarships/grants, and university employment available. Support available to part-time students. Financial award application deadline: 4/15; financial award applicants required to submit FAFSA. In 2010, 48 master's, 48 doctorates awarded. *Degree program information:* Part-time and evening/weekend programs available. Offers health sciences (MHA, MPH, MS, DPT); healthcare administration (MHA); physical therapy (DPT); physician assistant (MS); public health (MPH). *Application deadline:* Applications are processed on a rolling basis. Electronic applications accepted. *Application Contact:* Josh Kvinlaug, Admissions Coordinator, 515-271-7875, Fax: 515-271-7145, E-mail: paadmit@dmu.edu. *Dean,* Dr. Jodi Cahalan, 515-271-1415, E-mail: jodi.cahalan@dmu.edu.

College of Osteopathic Medicine Students: 872 full-time (413 women); includes 5 Black or African American, non-Hispanic/Latino; 1 American Indian or Alaska Native, non-Hispanic/Latino; 80 Asian, non-Hispanic/Latino; 18 Hispanic/Latino, 16 international. Average age 25. 3,350 applicants, 14% accepted, 221 enrolled. *Faculty:* 40 full-time (16 women), 22 part-time/adjunct (4 women). Expenses: Contact institution. *Financial support:* In 2010–11, 102 students received support, including 9 fellowships with tuition reimbursements available (averaging $6,000 per year); institutionally sponsored loans, scholarships/grants, and university employment also available. Support available to part-time students. Financial award application deadline: 7/15; financial award applicants required to submit FAFSA. In 2010, 204 first professional degrees awarded. Offers anatomy (MS); biomedical sciences (MS); osteopathic medicine (DO, MS). *Application deadline:* For fall admission, 2/1 for domestic students, 2/1 priority date for international students. Applications are processed on a rolling basis. *Application fee:* $50. Electronic applications accepted. *Application Contact:* Jamie Rehmann, Director of Admissions, 515-271-1451, Fax: 515-271-7163, E-mail: doadmit@dmu.edu. *Dean,* Dr. Kendall Reed, 515-271-1515, Fax: 515-271-1532, E-mail: kendall.reed@dmu.edu.

College of Podiatric Medicine and Surgery Students: 226 full-time (77 women); includes 3 Black or African American, non-Hispanic/Latino; 1 American Indian or Alaska Native, non-Hispanic/Latino; 9 Asian, non-Hispanic/Latino; 4 Hispanic/Latino, 3 international. Average age 24. 392 applicants, 27% accepted, 58 enrolled. *Faculty:* 5 full-time (1 woman), 1 part-time/adjunct (0 women). Expenses: Contact institution. *Financial support:* In 2010–11, 82 students received support. Institutionally sponsored loans, scholarships/grants, and university employment available. Support available to part-time students. Financial award application deadline: 7/15; financial award applicants required to submit FAFSA. In 2010, 45 DPMs awarded. Offers podiatric medicine and surgery (DPM). *Application deadline:* For fall admission, 6/1 for domestic and international students. Applications are processed on a rolling basis. *Application fee:* $0. Electronic applications accepted. *Application Contact:* Gina Smith, Admissions Coordinator, 515-271-7497, E-mail: cpmsadmit@dmu.edu. *Dean,* Dr. Robert Yoho, 515-271-1464, Fax: 515-271-1521, E-mail: robert.yoho@dmu.edu.

DEVRY COLLEGE OF NEW YORK, Long Island City, NY 11101

General Information Proprietary, coed, comprehensive institution. *Enrollment:* 1,784 graduate, professional, and undergraduate students; 68 full-time matriculated graduate/professional students (33 women), 229 part-time matriculated graduate/professional students (111 women). *Enrollment by degree level:* 297 master's. *Library facilities:* Learning Resource Center. *Online resources:* library catalog, web page.

Computer facilities: Computer purchase and lease plans are available. A campuswide network can be accessed from off campus. Online class registration is available. *Web address:* http://www.devry.edu/.

GRADUATE UNITS

Keller Graduate School of Management Students: 68 full-time (33 women), 229 part-time (111 women). Expenses: Contact institution. In 2010, 19 master's awarded. Offers management (MAFM, MBA, MISM).

DEVRY UNIVERSITY, Houston, TX 77041

General Information Proprietary, coed, comprehensive institution. *Enrollment:* 2,348 graduate, professional, and undergraduate students; 91 full-time matriculated graduate/professional students (47 women), 295 part-time matriculated graduate/professional students (165 women). *Enrollment by degree level:* 386 master's. *Web address:* http://www.devry.edu/.

GRADUATE UNITS

Keller Graduate School of Management Students: 91 full-time (47 women), 295 part-time (165 women). Expenses: Contact institution. In 2010, 74 master's awarded. Offers management (MAFM, MBA, MHRM, MISM, MNCM, MPA, MPM). *Application Contact:* Student Application Contact, 713-973-3100.

DEVRY UNIVERSITY, Columbus, OH 43209-2705

General Information Proprietary, coed, comprehensive institution. *Enrollment:* 3,807 graduate, professional, and undergraduate students; 55 full-time matriculated graduate/professional students (29 women), 341 part-time matriculated graduate/professional students (199 women). *Enrollment by degree level:* 396 master's. *Library facilities:* Learning Resource Center. *Online resources:* library catalog, web page.

Computer facilities: A campuswide network can be accessed from off campus. Online class registration is available. *Web address:* http://www.devry.edu/.

GRADUATE UNITS

Keller Graduate School of Management Students: 55 full-time (29 women), 341 part-time (199 women). Expenses: Contact institution. In 2010, 90 master's awarded. Offers management (MAFM, MBA, MHRM, MISM, MNCM, MPA, MPM). *Application Contact:* Student Application Contact, 614-253-7291.

DEVRY UNIVERSITY, Phoenix, AZ 85021-2995

General Information Proprietary, coed, comprehensive institution. *Enrollment:* 1,915 graduate, professional, and undergraduate students; 41 full-time matriculated graduate/professional students (15 women), 237 part-time matriculated graduate/professional students (120 women). *Enrollment by degree level:* 278 master's. *Library facilities:* Learning Resource Center. *Online resources:* library catalog, web page.

Computer facilities: Computer purchase and lease plans are available. A campuswide network can be accessed from off campus. Online class registration is available. *Web address:* http://www.devry.edu/.

General Application Contact: Student Application Contact, 602-870-9222.

GRADUATE UNITS

Keller Graduate School of Management Students: 41 full-time (15 women), 237 part-time (120 women). Expenses: Contact institution. In 2010, 83 master's awarded. Offers management (MAFM, MBA, MHRM, MISM, MNCM, MPA, MPM). *Application Contact:* Student Application Contact, 602-870-9222.

DEVRY UNIVERSITY, Tampa, FL 33607-5901

General Information Proprietary, coed, comprehensive institution.

GRADUATE UNITS

Keller Graduate School of Management Offers management (MAFM, MBA, MHRM, MISM, MNCM, MPA, MPM, Graduate Certificate).

DEVRY UNIVERSITY, Orlando, FL 32839

General Information Proprietary, coed, comprehensive institution. *Enrollment:* 2,367 graduate, professional, and undergraduate students; 56 full-time matriculated graduate/professional students (24 women), 235 part-time matriculated graduate/professional students (130 women). *Enrollment by degree level:* 291 master's. *Library facilities:* Learning Resource Center. *Online resources:* library catalog, web page.

Computer facilities: Computer purchase and lease plans are available. A campuswide network can be accessed from off campus. Online class registration is available. *Web address:* http://www.devry.edu/.

GRADUATE UNITS

Keller Graduate School of Management Students: 56 full-time (24 women), 235 part-time (130 women). Expenses: Contact institution. In 2010, 66 master's awarded. Offers management (MAFM, MBA, MHRM, MISM, MNCM, MPA, MPM). *Application Contact:* Student Application Contact, 407-345-2800.

DEVRY UNIVERSITY, Bellevue, WA 98004-5110

General Information Proprietary, coed, comprehensive institution.

GRADUATE UNITS

Keller Graduate School of Management Offers management (MAFM, MBA, MHRM, MISM, MNCM, MPA, MPM, Graduate Certificate).

DEVRY UNIVERSITY, Columbus, OH 43240

General Information Proprietary, coed, comprehensive institution.

GRADUATE UNITS

Keller Graduate School of Management Offers management (MAFM, MBA, MHRM, MISM, MNCM, MPA, MPM).

DEVRY UNIVERSITY, Mesa, AZ 85210-2011

General Information Proprietary, coed, comprehensive institution.

GRADUATE UNITS

Keller Graduate School of Management Offers management (MAFM, MBA, MHRM, MISM, MNCM, MPA, MPM, Graduate Certificate).

DEVRY UNIVERSITY, Alhambra, CA 91803

General Information Proprietary, coed, comprehensive institution.

GRADUATE UNITS

Keller Graduate School of Management Offers management (MAFM, MBA, MHRM, MISM, MNCM, MPA, MPM).

DEVRY UNIVERSITY, Anaheim, CA 92806-6136

General Information Proprietary, coed, comprehensive institution.

GRADUATE UNITS

Keller Graduate School of Management Offers management (MAFM, MBA, MHRM, MISM, MNCM, MPA, MPM).

DEVRY UNIVERSITY, Daly City, CA 94014-3899

General Information Proprietary, coed, comprehensive institution.

GRADUATE UNITS

Keller Graduate School of Management Offers management (MAFM, MBA, MHRM, MISM, MNCM, MPA, MPM).

DEVRY UNIVERSITY, Elk Grove, CA 95758

General Information Proprietary, coed, comprehensive institution.

GRADUATE UNITS

Keller Graduate School of Management Offers management (MAFM, MBA, MHRM, MISM, MNCM, MPA, MPM, Graduate Certificate).

DEVRY UNIVERSITY, Fremont, CA 94555

General Information Proprietary, coed, comprehensive institution.

GRADUATE UNITS

Keller Graduate School of Management Offers management (MAFM, MBA, MHRM, MISM, MNCM, MPA, MPM).

DEVRY UNIVERSITY, Irvine, CA 92602-1303

General Information Proprietary, coed, comprehensive institution.

GRADUATE UNITS

Keller Graduate School of Management Offers management (MAFM, MBA, MHRM, MISM, MNCM, MPA, MPM, Graduate Certificate).

DEVRY UNIVERSITY, Long Beach, CA 90806

General Information Proprietary, coed, comprehensive institution.

GRADUATE UNITS

Keller Graduate School of Management Offers management (MAFM, MBA, MHRM, MISM, MNCM, MPA, MPM).

DEVRY UNIVERSITY, Oakland, CA 94612

General Information Proprietary, coed, comprehensive institution.

GRADUATE UNITS

Keller Graduate School of Management Offers management (MAFM, MBA, MHRM, MISM, MNCM, MPA, MPM).

DEVRY UNIVERSITY, Palmdale, CA 93551

General Information Proprietary, coed, comprehensive institution.

GRADUATE UNITS

Keller Graduate School of Management Offers management (MAFM, MBA, MHRM, MPM, Graduate Certificate).

DEVRY UNIVERSITY, Pomona, CA 91768-2642

General Information Proprietary, coed, comprehensive institution. *Enrollment:* 3,339 graduate, professional, and undergraduate students; 73 full-time matriculated graduate/professional students (31 women), 322 part-time matriculated graduate/professional students (148 women). *Enrollment by degree level:* 395 master's.

Computer facilities: Computer purchase and lease plans are available. A campuswide network can be accessed from off campus. Online class registration is available. *Web address:* http://www.devry.edu/.

GRADUATE UNITS

Keller Graduate School of Management Students: 73 full-time (31 women), 322 part-time (148 women). Expenses: Contact institution. In 2010, 92 master's awarded. Offers management (MAFM, MBA, MHRM, MISM, MNCM, MPA, MPM). *Application Contact:* Student Application Contact, 909-622-8866.

DEVRY UNIVERSITY, San Diego, CA 92108-1633

General Information Proprietary, coed, comprehensive institution.

GRADUATE UNITS

Keller Graduate School of Management Offers management (MAFM, MBA, MHRM, MISM, MNCM, MPA, MPM, Graduate Certificate).

DEVRY UNIVERSITY, Kansas City, MO 64105-2112

General Information Proprietary, coed, comprehensive institution.

GRADUATE UNITS

Keller Graduate School of Management Offers management (MAFM, MBA, MHRM, MISM, MNCM, MPA, MPM, Graduate Certificate).

DEVRY UNIVERSITY, Colorado Springs, CO 80920

General Information Proprietary, coed, comprehensive institution.

GRADUATE UNITS

Keller Graduate School of Management Offers management (MAFM, MBA, MHRM, MISM, MNCM, MPA, MPM, Graduate Certificate).

DEVRY UNIVERSITY, Atlanta, GA 30305-1543

General Information Proprietary, coed, graduate-only institution.

GRADUATE UNITS

Keller Graduate School of Management Offers management (MAFM, MBA, MHRM, MISM, MNCM, MPA, MPM, Graduate Certificate).

DEVRY UNIVERSITY, Jacksonville, FL 32256-6040

General Information Proprietary, coed, comprehensive institution.

GRADUATE UNITS

Keller Graduate School of Management Offers management (MAFM, MBA, MHRM, MISM, MNCM, MPA, MPM).

DEVRY UNIVERSITY, Miami, FL 33174-2535

General Information Proprietary, coed, comprehensive institution.

GRADUATE UNITS

Keller Graduate School of Management Offers management (MAFM, MBA, MHRM, MISM, MNCM, MPA, MPM, Graduate Certificate).

DEVRY UNIVERSITY, Miramar, FL 33027-4150

General Information Proprietary, coed, comprehensive institution. *Enrollment:* 1,577 graduate, professional, and undergraduate students; 57 full-time matriculated graduate/professional students (33 women), 200 part-time matriculated graduate/professional students (117 women). *Enrollment by degree level:* 257 master's.

Computer facilities: Computer purchase and lease plans are available. *Web address:* http://www.devry.edu/.

GRADUATE UNITS

Keller Graduate School of Management Students: 57 full-time (33 women), 200 part-time (117 women). Expenses: Contact institution. In 2010, 64 master's awarded. Offers management (MAFM, MBA, MHRM, MISM, MNCM, MPA, MPM). *Application Contact:* Student Application Contact, 954-499-9700.

DEVRY UNIVERSITY, Alpharetta, GA 30009

General Information Proprietary, coed, comprehensive institution.

GRADUATE UNITS

Keller Graduate School of Management Offers management (MAFM, MBA, MHRM, MISM, MNCM, MPA, MPM).

DEVRY UNIVERSITY, Decatur, GA 30030-2556

General Information Proprietary, coed, comprehensive institution. *Enrollment:* 3,912 graduate, professional, and undergraduate students; 82 full-time matriculated graduate/professional students (47 women), 369 part-time matriculated graduate/professional students (241 women). *Enrollment by degree level:* 451 master's. *Library facilities:* Learning Resource Center. *Online resources:* library catalog, web page.

Computer facilities: Computer purchase and lease plans are available. A campuswide network can be accessed from off campus. Online class registration is available. *Web address:* http://www.devry.edu/.

GRADUATE UNITS

Keller Graduate School of Management Students: 82 full-time (47 women), 369 part-time (241 women). Expenses: Contact institution. In 2010, 132 master's awarded. Offers management (MAFM, MBA, MHRM, MISM, MNCM, MPA, MPM). *Application Contact:* Student Application Contact, 404-270-2700.

DEVRY UNIVERSITY, Duluth, GA 30096-7671

General Information Proprietary, coed, comprehensive institution.

GRADUATE UNITS

Keller Graduate School of Management Offers management (MAFM, MBA, MHRM, MISM, MNCM, MPA, MPM, Graduate Certificate).

DEVRY UNIVERSITY, Downers Grove, IL 60515

General Information Proprietary, coed, comprehensive institution. *Graduate housing:* On-campus housing not available.

DeVry University (continued)

GRADUATE UNITS

Keller Graduate School of Management Offers accounting and financial management (MAFM); business administration (MBA); human resources management (MHRM); information systems management (MISM); network and communications management (MNCM); project management (MPM); public administration (MPA).

DEVRY UNIVERSITY, Elgin, IL 60123

General Information Proprietary, coed, comprehensive institution.

GRADUATE UNITS

Keller Graduate School of Management Offers management (MAFM, MBA, MHRM, MISM, MNCM, MPA, MPM, Graduate Certificate).

DEVRY UNIVERSITY, Gurnee, IL 60031-9126

General Information Proprietary, coed, comprehensive institution.

GRADUATE UNITS

Keller Graduate School of Management Offers management (MAFM, MBA, MHRM, MISM, MNCM, MPA, MPM, Graduate Certificate).

DEVRY UNIVERSITY, Lincolnshire, IL 60069-4460

General Information Proprietary, coed, graduate-only institution.

GRADUATE UNITS

Keller Graduate School of Management Offers management (MAFM, MBA, MHRM, MISM, MNCM, MPA, MPM, Graduate Certificate).

DEVRY UNIVERSITY, Naperville, IL 60563-2361

General Information Proprietary, coed, comprehensive institution.

GRADUATE UNITS

Keller Graduate School of Management Offers management (MAFM, MBA, MHRM, MISM, MNCM, MPA, MPM, Graduate Certificate).

DEVRY UNIVERSITY, Schaumburg, IL 60173-5009

General Information Proprietary, coed, graduate-only institution.

GRADUATE UNITS

Keller Graduate School of Management Offers management (MAFM, MBA, MHRM, MISM, MNCM, MPA, MPM, Graduate Certificate).

DEVRY UNIVERSITY, Tinley Park, IL 60477

General Information Proprietary, coed, comprehensive institution.

GRADUATE UNITS

Keller Graduate School of Management Offers management (MAFM, MBA, MHRM, MISM, MNCM, MPA, MPM).

DEVRY UNIVERSITY, Indianapolis, IN 46240-2158

General Information Proprietary, coed, comprehensive institution.

GRADUATE UNITS

Keller Graduate School of Management Offers management (MAFM, MBA, MHRM, MISM, MNCM, MPA, MPM).

DEVRY UNIVERSITY, Merrillville, IN 46410-5673

General Information Proprietary, coed, comprehensive institution.

GRADUATE UNITS

Keller Graduate School of Management Offers management (MAFM, MBA, MHRM, MISM, MNCM, MPA, MPM, Graduate Certificate).

DEVRY UNIVERSITY, Bethesda, MD 20814-3304

General Information Proprietary, coed, comprehensive institution.

GRADUATE UNITS

Keller Graduate School of Management Offers management (MAFM, MBA, MHRM, MISM, MNCM, MPA, MPM).

DEVRY UNIVERSITY, St. Louis, MO 63146-4020

General Information Proprietary, coed, comprehensive institution.

GRADUATE UNITS

Keller Graduate School of Management Offers management (MAFM, MBA, MHRM, MISM, MNCM, MPA, MPM, Graduate Certificate).

DEVRY UNIVERSITY, Henderson, NV 89074-7120

General Information Proprietary, coed, comprehensive institution.

GRADUATE UNITS

Keller Graduate School of Management Offers management (MAFM, MBA, MHRM, MISM, MNCM, MPA, MPM).

DEVRY UNIVERSITY, North Brunswick, NJ 08902-3362

General Information Proprietary, coed, comprehensive institution. *Enrollment:* 1,905 graduate, professional, and undergraduate students; 40 full-time matriculated graduate/professional students (21 women), 92 part-time matriculated graduate/professional students (46 women). *Enrollment by degree level:* 132 master's. *Library facilities:* Learning Resource Center. *Online resources:* library catalog, web page.

Computer facilities: Computer purchase and lease plans are available. A campuswide network can be accessed from off campus. Online class registration is available. *Web address:* http://www.devry.edu/.

GRADUATE UNITS

Keller Graduate School of Management Students: 40 full-time (21 women), 92 part-time (46 women). Expenses: Contact institution. Offers management (MBA).

DEVRY UNIVERSITY, Paramus, NJ 07652

General Information Proprietary, coed, comprehensive institution.

GRADUATE UNITS

Keller Graduate School of Management Offers management (MBA).

DEVRY UNIVERSITY, Charlotte, NC 28273-4068

General Information Proprietary, coed, comprehensive institution.

GRADUATE UNITS

Keller Graduate School of Management Offers management (MAFM, MBA, MHRM, MISM, MNCM, MPA, MPM).

DEVRY UNIVERSITY, Phoenix, AZ 85054

General Information Proprietary, coed, graduate-only institution.

GRADUATE UNITS

Keller Graduate School of Management Offers management (MAFM, MBA, MHRM, MISM, MNCM, MPA, MPM, Graduate Certificate).

DEVRY UNIVERSITY, Seven Hills, OH 44131

General Information Proprietary, coed, comprehensive institution.

GRADUATE UNITS

Keller Graduate School of Management Offers management (MAFM, MBA, MHRM, MISM, MNCM, MPA, MPM, Graduate Certificate).

DEVRY UNIVERSITY, Portland, OR 97225-6651

General Information Proprietary, coed, comprehensive institution.

GRADUATE UNITS

Keller Graduate School of Management Offers management (MAFM, MBA, MHRM, MISM, MNCM, MPA, MPM).

DEVRY UNIVERSITY, Fort Washington, PA 19034

General Information Proprietary, coed, comprehensive institution. *Enrollment:* 1,300 graduate, professional, and undergraduate students; 32 full-time matriculated graduate/professional students (18 women), 191 part-time matriculated graduate/professional students (99 women). *Enrollment by degree level:* 223 master's. *Library facilities:* Learning Resource Center. *Online resources:* library catalog, web page.

Computer facilities: Computer purchase and lease plans are available. A campuswide network can be accessed from off campus. Online class registration is available. *Web address:* http://www.devry.edu/.

GRADUATE UNITS

Keller Graduate School of Management Students: 32 full-time (18 women), 191 part-time (99 women). Expenses: Contact institution. In 2010, 40 master's awarded. Offers management (MAFM, MBA, MHRM, MISM, MNCM, MPA, MPM). *Application Contact:* Student Application Contact, 215-591-5700.

DEVRY UNIVERSITY, King of Prussia, PA 19406-2926

General Information Proprietary, coed, comprehensive institution.

GRADUATE UNITS

Keller Graduate School of Management Offers management (MAFM, MBA, MHRM, MISM, MNCM, MPA, MPM, Graduate Certificate).

DEVRY UNIVERSITY, Pittsburgh, PA 15222-2606

General Information Proprietary, coed, comprehensive institution.

GRADUATE UNITS

Keller Graduate School of Management Offers management (MAFM, MBA, MHRM, MISM, MNCM, MPA, MPM, Graduate Certificate).

DEVRY UNIVERSITY, Memphis, TN 38119

General Information Proprietary, coed, comprehensive institution.

GRADUATE UNITS

Keller Graduate School of Management Offers management (MAFM, MBA, MHRM, MISM, MNCM, MPA, MPM).

DEVRY UNIVERSITY, Nashville, TN 37211-4147

General Information Proprietary, coed, comprehensive institution.

GRADUATE UNITS

Keller Graduate School of Management Offers management (MAFM, MBA, MHRM, MISM, MNCM, MPA, MPM).

DEVRY UNIVERSITY, Irving, TX 75063-2439

General Information Proprietary, coed, comprehensive institution. *Enrollment:* 2,292 graduate, professional, and undergraduate students; 87 full-time matriculated graduate/professional students (35 women), 306 part-time matriculated graduate/professional students (137 women). *Enrollment by degree level:* 393 master's. *Library facilities:* Learning Resource Center. *Online resources:* library catalog, web page.

Computer facilities: Computer purchase and lease plans are available. A campuswide network can be accessed from off campus. Online class registration is available. *Web address:* http://www.devry.edu/.

GRADUATE UNITS

Keller Graduate School of Management Students: 87 full-time (35 women), 306 part-time (137 women). Expenses: Contact institution. In 2010, 60 master's awarded. Offers management (MAFM, MBA, MHRM, MISM, MPM). *Application Contact:* Student Application Contact, 972-929-6777.

DEVRY UNIVERSITY, Richardson, TX 75080

General Information Proprietary, coed, comprehensive institution.

GRADUATE UNITS

Keller Graduate School of Management Offers management (MBA, Graduate Certificate).

DEVRY UNIVERSITY, Sandy, UT 84070

General Information Proprietary, coed, comprehensive institution.

GRADUATE UNITS

Keller Graduate School of Management Offers management (MAFM, MBA, MHRM, MISM, MNCM, MPA, MPM).

DEVRY UNIVERSITY, Arlington, VA 22202

General Information Proprietary, coed, comprehensive institution. *Enrollment:* 1,026 graduate, professional, and undergraduate students; 61 full-time matriculated graduate/professional students (30 women), 216 part-time matriculated graduate/professional students (89 women). *Enrollment by degree level:* 277 master's. *Library facilities:* Learning Resource Center. *Online resources:* library catalog, web page.

Computer facilities: Computer purchase and lease plans are available. A campuswide network can be accessed from off campus. Online class registration is available. *Web address:* http://www.devry.edu/.

GRADUATE UNITS

Keller Graduate School of Management Students: 61 full-time (30 women), 216 part-time (89 women). Expenses: Contact institution. In 2010, 36 master's awarded. Offers management (MAFM, MBA, MHRM, MISM, MNCM, MPA, MPM). *Application Contact:* Student Application Contact, 703-414-4000.

DEVRY UNIVERSITY, Chesapeake, VA 23320-3671

General Information Proprietary, coed, comprehensive institution.

GRADUATE UNITS

Keller Graduate School of Management Offers management (MAFM, MBA, MHRM, MISM, MNCM, MPA, MPM).

DEVRY UNIVERSITY, Manassas, VA 20109-3173

General Information Proprietary, coed, comprehensive institution.

GRADUATE UNITS

Keller Graduate School of Management Offers management (MAFM, MBA, MHRM, MISM, MNCM, MPA, MPM, Graduate Certificate).

DEVRY UNIVERSITY, Federal Way, WA 98001

General Information Proprietary, coed, comprehensive institution. *Enrollment:* 1,008 graduate, professional, and undergraduate students; 24 full-time matriculated graduate/professional students (13 women), 148 part-time matriculated graduate/professional students (55 women). *Enrollment by degree level:* 172 master's. *Library facilities:* Learning Resource Center.

Computer facilities: Computer purchase and lease plans are available. A campuswide network can be accessed from off campus. Online class registration is available. *Web address:* http://www.devry.edu/.

GRADUATE UNITS

Keller Graduate School of Management Students: 24 full-time (13 women), 148 part-time (55 women). Expenses: Contact institution. In 2010, 44 master's awarded. Offers management (MAFM, MBA, MHRM, MISM, MNCM, MPA, MPM). *Application Contact:* Student Application Contact, 253-943-2800.

DEVRY UNIVERSITY, Milwaukee, WI 53202

General Information Proprietary, coed, comprehensive institution.

GRADUATE UNITS

Keller Graduate School of Management Offers management (MAFM, MBA, MHRM, MISM, MNCM, MPA, MPM).

DEVRY UNIVERSITY, Waukesha, WI 53188-1157

General Information Proprietary, coed, comprehensive institution.

GRADUATE UNITS

Keller Graduate School of Management Offers management (MAFM, MBA, MHRM, MISM, MNCM, MPA, MPM, Graduate Certificate).

DEVRY UNIVERSITY ONLINE, Addison, IL 60101-6106

General Information Proprietary, coed, comprehensive institution. *Enrollment:* 30,564 graduate, professional, and undergraduate students; 903 full-time matriculated graduate/professional students (522 women), 5,326 part-time matriculated graduate/professional students (3,245 women). *Enrollment by degree level:* 6,229 master's. *Web address:* http://www.devry.edu/.

GRADUATE UNITS

Keller Graduate School of Management Students: 903 full-time (522 women), 5,326 part-time (3,245 women). Expenses: Contact institution. In 2010, 1,422 master's awarded. Offers management (MAFM, MBA, MEE, MET, MHRM, MISM, MNCM, MPA, MPM).

DIGIPEN INSTITUTE OF TECHNOLOGY, Redmond, WA 98052

General Information Proprietary, coed, comprehensive institution. *Enrollment:* 933 graduate, professional, and undergraduate students; 26 full-time matriculated graduate/professional students (5 women), 27 part-time matriculated graduate/professional students (2 women). *Enrollment by degree level:* 53 master's. *Graduate faculty:* 11 full-time (1 woman), 2 part-time/adjunct (0 women). *Tuition:* Full-time $12,004; part-time $8056 per semester. *Required fees:* $658 per credit. $80 per semester. One-time fee: $150. Tuition and fees vary according to course load. *Graduate housing:* On-campus housing not available. *Student services:* Campus employment opportunities, career counseling, free psychological counseling, international student services, services for students with disabilities. *Library facilities:* DigiPen Library plus 1 other. *Online resources:* library catalog, web page. *Collection:* 13,233 titles, 29 serial subscriptions, 866 audiovisual materials.

Computer facilities: Computer purchase and lease plans are available. 650 computers available on campus for general student use. A campuswide network can be accessed. Online class registration is available. *Web address:* http://www.digipen.edu/.

General Application Contact: Office of Admissions, 866-478-5236, Fax: 425-558-0378, E-mail: admissions@digipen.edu.

GRADUATE UNITS

Master of Science in Computer Science Program Students: 26 full-time (5 women), 27 part-time (2 women); includes 15 minority (1 Black or African American, non-Hispanic/Latino; 5 Asian, non-Hispanic/Latino; 5 Hispanic/Latino; 1 Native Hawaiian or other Pacific Islander, non-Hispanic/Latino; 3 Two or more races, non-Hispanic/Latino), 9 international. Average age 25. 77 applicants, 53% accepted, 30 enrolled. *Faculty:* 11 full-time (1 woman), 2 part-time/adjunct (0 women). Expenses: Contact institution. *Financial support:* In 2010–11, 2 students received support, including 1 fellowship with full and partial tuition reimbursement available (averaging $15,184 per year); career-related internships or fieldwork and scholarships/grants also available. Financial award application deadline: 5/1; financial award applicants required to submit FAFSA. In 2010, 9 degrees awarded. *Degree program information:* Part-time programs available. Offers computer science (MS). *Application deadline:* For fall admission, 2/1 priority date for domestic students; for spring admission, 7/1 for domestic students. Applications are processed on a rolling basis. *Application fee:* $35. Electronic applications accepted. *Application Contact:* Angela Kugler, Admissions Office, 425-558-0299, Fax: 425-558-0378, E-mail: admissions@digipen.edu. *Associate Professor*, Dr. Dmitri Volper, 425-629-5018, E-mail: dvolper@digipen.edu.

DIGITAL MEDIA ARTS COLLEGE, Boca Raton, FL 33431

General Information Proprietary, coed, comprehensive institution.

GRADUATE UNITS

Graduate Programs Offers graphic design (MFA); special FX animation (MFA).

DOANE COLLEGE, Crete, NE 68333-2430

General Information Independent-religious, coed, comprehensive institution. *Enrollment:* 1,049 graduate, professional, and undergraduate students; 402 full-time matriculated graduate/professional students (300 women), 609 part-time matriculated graduate/professional students (494 women). *Enrollment by degree level:* 852 master's. *Graduate faculty:* 5 full-time (2 women), 31 part-time/adjunct (9 women). *Tuition:* Part-time $299 per credit hour. Part-time tuition and fees vary according to program. *Graduate housing:* On-campus housing not available. *Student services:* Career counseling, teacher training. *Library facilities:* Perkins Library plus 1 other. *Online resources:* library catalog, web page, access to other libraries' catalogs. *Collection:* 335,481 titles, 54,528 serial subscriptions, 8,190 audiovisual materials.

Computer facilities: Computer purchase and lease plans are available. 250 computers available on campus for general student use. A campuswide network can be accessed from student residence rooms and from off campus. Online class registration is available. *Web address:* http://www.doane.edu/.

General Application Contact: Wilma Daddario, Assistant Dean, 402-466-4774, Fax: 404-466-4228, E-mail: wilma.daddario@doane.edu.

GRADUATE UNITS

Program in Counseling Students: 131 full-time (111 women), 30 part-time (27 women); includes 16 minority (4 Black or African American, non-Hispanic/Latino; 1 American Indian or Alaska Native, non-Hispanic/Latino; 1 Asian, non-Hispanic/Latino; 9 Hispanic/Latino; 1 Two or more races, non-Hispanic/Latino). Average age 34. *Faculty:* 2 full-time (0 women), 11 part-time/adjunct (6 women). Expenses: Contact institution. *Financial support:* Unspecified assistantships available. Financial award application deadline: 6/1; financial award applicants required to submit FAFSA. In 2010, 25 master's awarded. *Degree program information:* Evening/weekend programs available. Offers counseling (MAC). *Application deadline:* Applications are processed on a rolling basis. *Application fee:* $25. *Application Contact:* Wilma Daddario, Assistant Dean, 402-466-4774, Fax: 404-466-4228, E-mail: wilma.daddario@doane.edu. *Dean*, Thomas Gilligan, 402-466-4774, Fax: 402-466-4228, E-mail: tom.gilligan@doane.edu.

Program in Education Students: 162 full-time (126 women), 568 part-time (461 women); includes 23 minority (6 Black or African American, non-Hispanic/Latino; 4 American Indian or Alaska Native, non-Hispanic/Latino; 2 Asian, non-Hispanic/Latino; 9 Hispanic/Latino; 2 Native Hawaiian or other Pacific Islander, non-Hispanic/Latino), 2 international. Average age 33. *Faculty:* 12 full-time, 14 part-time/adjunct. Expenses: Contact institution. *Financial support:* Applicants required to submit FAFSA. In 2010, 274 master's awarded. *Degree program information:* Part-time and evening/weekend programs available. Offers curriculum and instruction (M Ed); educational leadership (M Ed). *Application deadline:* Applications are processed on a rolling basis. *Application fee:* $25. Electronic applications accepted. *Application Contact:* Wilma Daddario, Assistant Dean, 402-464-1223, Fax: 402-466-4228, E-mail: wdaddario@doane.edu. *Dean*, Lyn C. Forester, 402-826-8604, Fax: 402-826-8278.

Program in Management Students: 109 full-time (63 women), 11 part-time (6 women); includes 12 minority (5 Black or African American, non-Hispanic/Latino; 1 Asian, non-Hispanic/Latino; 5 Hispanic/Latino; 1 Two or more races, non-Hispanic/Latino). Average age 36. *Faculty:* 2 full-time (1 woman), 21 part-time/adjunct (9 women). Expenses: Contact institution. *Financial support:* Application deadline: 6/1. In 2010, 20 master's awarded. *Degree program information:* Part-time and evening/weekend programs available. Offers management (MA). *Application deadline:* Applications are processed on a rolling basis. *Application fee:* $25. *Application Contact:* Janice Hedfield, Dean, 880-333-6263, E-mail: janice.hedfield@doane.edu. *Dean*, Janice Hedfield, 880-333-6263, E-mail: janice.hedfield@doane.edu.

DOMINICAN COLLEGE, Orangeburg, NY 10962-1210

General Information Independent, coed, comprehensive institution. *Enrollment:* 2,070 graduate, professional, and undergraduate students; 143 full-time matriculated graduate/professional students (117 women), 243 part-time matriculated graduate/professional students (145 women). *Enrollment by degree level:* 235 master's, 151 doctoral. *Graduate faculty:* 15 full-time (11 women), 31 part-time/adjunct (22 women). *Tuition:* Part-time $700 per credit. *Graduate housing:* Room and/or apartments available on a first-come, first-served basis to single students; on-campus housing not available to married students. *Student services:* Campus employment opportunities, campus safety program, career counseling, free psychological counseling, services for students with disabilities, teacher training, writing training. *Library facilities:* Sullivan Library plus 1 other. *Online resources:* library catalog, web page, access to other libraries' catalogs. *Collection:* 125,000 titles, 450 serial subscriptions, 24,000 audiovisual materials.

Computer facilities: 150 computers available on campus for general student use. A campuswide network can be accessed from student residence rooms and from off campus. Web portal, Black Board available. *Web address:* http://www.dc.edu/.

General Application Contact: Joyce Elbe, Director of Admissions, 845-848-7896 Ext. 15, Fax: 845-365-3150, E-mail: admissions@dc.edu.

GRADUATE UNITS

Division of Allied Health Students: 108 full-time (84 women), 128 part-time (57 women); includes 8 Black or African American, non-Hispanic/Latino; 1 American Indian or Alaska Native, non-Hispanic/Latino; 87 Asian, non-Hispanic/Latino; 9 Hispanic/Latino. Average age 37. *Faculty:* 10 full-time (7 women), 22 part-time/adjunct (12 women). Expenses: Contact institution. In 2010, 66 master's, 58 doctorates awarded. *Degree program information:* Part-time and evening/weekend programs available. Postbaccalaureate distance learning degree programs offered (minimal on-campus study). Offers allied health (MS, DPT); occupational therapy (MS); physical therapy (MS, DPT). *Application deadline:* Applications are processed on a rolling basis. *Application Contact:* Joyce Elbe, Director of Admissions, 845-848-7896 Ext. 15, Fax: 845-365-3150, E-mail: admissions@dc.edu. *Division Director*, Dr. Sandra Countee, 845-848-6039, Fax: 845-398-4893, E-mail: sandra.countee@dc.edu.

Division of Nursing Students: 9 full-time (8 women), 22 part-time (21 women); includes 3 Black or African American, non-Hispanic/Latino; 8 Asian, non-Hispanic/Latino; 1 Hispanic/Latino. Expenses: Contact institution. *Financial support:* Applicants required to submit FAFSA. In 2010, 15 master's awarded. *Degree program information:* Part-time and evening/weekend programs available. Offers family nurse practitioner (MSN); nursing (MSN). *Application deadline:* Applications are processed on a rolling basis. *Application fee:* $50. *Application Contact:* Joyce Elbe, Director of Admissions, 845-848-7896 Ext. 15, Fax: 845-365-3150, E-mail: admissions@dc.edu. *Director*, Dr. Nancy DiDona, 845-848-6051, Fax: 845-398-4891, E-mail: nancydidona@dc.edu.

Division of Teacher Education Students: 20 full-time (all women), 72 part-time (54 women); includes 2 Black or African American, non-Hispanic/Latino; 1 Asian, non-Hispanic/Latino; 1 Hispanic/Latino. *Faculty:* 4 full-time (2 women), 4 part-time/adjunct (2 women). Expenses: Contact institution. *Financial support:* Application deadline: 2/15. In 2010, 22 master's awarded. *Degree program information:* Part-time and evening/weekend programs available. Postbaccalaureate distance learning degree programs offered (minimal on-campus study). Offers childhood education (MS Ed); teacher education (MS Ed); teacher of students with disabilities (MS Ed); teacher of visually impaired (MS Ed). *Application deadline:* Applications are processed on a rolling basis. *Application Contact:* Joyce Elbe, Director of Admissions, 845-848-7896 Ext. 15, Fax: 845-365-3150, E-mail: admissions@dc.edu. *Director*, Dr. Roger Tesi, 845-848-4082, Fax: 845-359-7802, E-mail: roger.tesi@dc.edu.

MBA Program Students: 2 full-time (both women), 19 part-time (9 women); includes 3 Asian, non-Hispanic/Latino; 3 Hispanic/Latino. Expenses: Contact institution. In 2010, 5 master's awarded. *Degree program information:* Evening/weekend programs available. Offers business administration (MBA). Electronic applications accepted. *Application Contact:* Joyce Elbe, Director of Admissions, 845-848-7896 Ext. 15, Fax: 845-365-3150, E-mail: admissions@dc.edu. *MBA Director*, Ken Mias, 845-848-4102, E-mail: ken.mias@dc.edu.

DOMINICAN HOUSE OF STUDIES, PONTIFICAL FACULTY OF THE IMMACULATE CONCEPTION, Washington, DC 20017-1585

General Information Independent-religious, coed, primarily men, graduate-only institution. *Enrollment by degree level:* 47 first professional, 8 master's, 16 other advanced degrees. *Graduate faculty:* 17 full-time (1 woman), 7 part-time/adjunct (3 women). *Tuition:* Full-time $15,120; part-time $630 per credit. *Required fees:* $50 per semester. One-time fee: $50. *Graduate housing:* On-campus housing not available. *Student services:* Career counseling, writing training. *Library facilities:* Dominican Theological Library. *Online resources:* library catalog, web page, access to other libraries' catalogs. *Collection:* 75,000 titles, 233 serial subscriptions, 350 audiovisual materials. *Research affiliation:* Washington Theological Consortium (theology, ecumenism), The Thomist (theological journal).

Computer facilities: 8 computers available on campus for general student use. A campuswide network can be accessed. Online course descriptions and academic calendar available. *Web address:* http://www.dhs.edu/.

General Application Contact: Tobias John Nathe, Registrar, 202-495-3836, Fax: 202-495-3873, E-mail: registrar@dhs.edu.

GRADUATE UNITS

Graduate and Professional Programs in Theology Students: 56 full-time (4 women), 15 part-time (5 women); includes 2 Asian, non-Hispanic/Latino; 3 Hispanic/Latino, 13 international. Average age 33. 33 applicants, 94% accepted, 22 enrolled. *Faculty:* 17 full-time (1 woman), 6 part-time/adjunct (2 women). Expenses: Contact institution. *Financial support:* In 2010–11, 8 students received support. Career-related internships or fieldwork and Federal Work-Study available. Support available to part-time students. Financial award application deadline: 6/30; financial award applicants required to submit FAFSA. In 2010, 10 first professional degrees, 6 master's, 10 other advanced degrees awarded. *Degree program information:* Part-time programs available. Offers moral theology (STL); sacred scripture (STL); systematic theology (STL); theology (M Div, STB, MA); Thomistic studies (MA, STL). *Application deadline:* For fall admission, 7/1 priority date for domestic and international students; for spring admission, 12/1 priority date for domestic and international students. Applications are processed on a rolling basis. *Application fee:* $50. *Application Contact:* Tobias John Nathe, Registrar, 202-495-3836, Fax: 202-495-3873, E-mail: registrar@dhs.edu. *Vice-President/Academic Dean*, Rev. Gabriel O'Donnell, 202-495-3832, Fax: 202-495-3873, E-mail: dean@dhs.edu.

DOMINICAN SCHOOL OF PHILOSOPHY AND THEOLOGY, Berkeley, CA 94708

General Information Independent-religious, coed, graduate-only institution. *Enrollment:* 72 full-time matriculated graduate/professional students (10 women), 24 part-time matriculated

Dominican School of Philosophy and Theology (continued)

graduate/professional students (12 women). *Enrollment by degree level:* 19 first professional, 58 master's, 19 other advanced degrees. *Graduate faculty:* 12 full-time (2 women), 10 part-time/adjunct (2 women). *Tuition:* Full-time $14,160; part-time $590 per unit. *Graduate housing:* Rooms and/or apartments available on a first-come, first-served basis to single and married students. *Student services:* Campus employment opportunities, career counseling, international student services, low-cost health insurance. *Library facilities:* Flora Lamson Hewlett Library. *Online resources:* web page. *Collection:* 450,000 titles, 1,500 serial subscriptions.

Computer facilities: 6 computers available on campus for general student use. Online class registration is available. *Web address:* http://www.dspt.edu/.

General Application Contact: John D. Knutsen, Director of Admissions, 510-883-2073, Fax: 510-849-1372, E-mail: admissions@dspt.edu.

GRADUATE UNITS

Graduate Programs Students: 72 full-time (10 women), 24 part-time (12 women); includes 36 minority (1 American Indian or Alaska Native, non-Hispanic/Latino; 16 Asian, non-Hispanic/Latino; 9 Hispanic/Latino; 10 Two or more races, non-Hispanic/Latino). Average age 35. 57 applicants, 95% accepted, 38 enrolled. *Faculty:* 12 full-time (2 women), 13 part-time/adjunct (2 women). Expenses: Contact institution. *Financial support:* In 2010–11, 42 students received support. Institutionally sponsored loans, scholarships/grants, and tuition waivers (partial) available. Financial award application deadline: 3/15; financial award applicants required to submit FAFSA. In 2010, 1 first professional degree, 20 master's awarded. *Degree program information:* Part-time programs available. Offers philosophy (MA); theology (M Div, MTS, Certificate). *Application deadline:* For fall admission, 3/15 priority date for domestic and international students; for spring admission, 10/15 priority date for domestic and international students. Applications are processed on a rolling basis. *Application fee:* $40. Electronic applications accepted. *Application Contact:* John D. Knutsen, Director of Admissions, 510-883-2073, Fax: 510-849-1372, E-mail: admissions@dspt.edu. *Academic Dean*, Fr. Christopher Renz, OP, 510-883-2084, Fax: 510-849-1372, E-mail: crenz@dspt.edu.

DOMINICAN UNIVERSITY, River Forest, IL 60305-1099

General Information Independent-religious, coed, comprehensive institution. *Graduate housing:* Room and/or apartments available on a first-come, first-served basis to single students; on-campus housing not available to married students. Housing application deadline: 7/1.

GRADUATE UNITS

Edward A. and Lois L. Brennan School of Business *Degree program information:* Part-time and evening/weekend programs available. Offers accounting (MSA); business administration (MBA). JD/MBA offered jointly with John Marshall Law School. Electronic applications accepted.

Graduate School of Library and Information Science *Degree program information:* Part-time and evening/weekend programs available. Postbaccalaureate distance learning degree programs offered (minimal on-campus study). Offers library and information science (MLIS, PhD); special studies (CSS). MLIS/M Div offered jointly with McCormick Theological Seminary; MLIS/MA with Loyola University Chicago; and MLIS/MM with Northwestern University.

Graduate School of Social Work *Degree program information:* Part-time programs available. Offers social work (MSW). Electronic applications accepted.

School of Education *Degree program information:* Part-time and evening/weekend programs available. Postbaccalaureate distance learning degree programs offered. Offers curriculum and instruction (MA Ed); early childhood education (MS); education (MAT); educational administration (MA); elementary (online) (MS); English as a second language (online) (MS); reading (online) (MS); special education (MS).

School of Leadership and Continuing Studies *Degree program information:* Part-time and evening/weekend programs available. Offers family ministry (MA); organizational leadership (MSOL).

DOMINICAN UNIVERSITY OF CALIFORNIA, San Rafael, CA 94901-2298

General Information Independent-religious, coed, comprehensive institution. *Enrollment:* 2,267 graduate, professional, and undergraduate students; 399 full-time matriculated graduate/professional students (287 women), 270 part-time matriculated graduate/professional students (186 women). *Enrollment by degree level:* 455 master's, 214 other advanced degrees. *Graduate housing:* On-campus housing not available. *Student services:* Career counseling, free psychological counseling, international student services. *Library facilities:* Archbishop Alemany Library. *Online resources:* library catalog, web page, access to other libraries' catalogs. *Collection:* 119,755 titles, 61,145 serial subscriptions, 1,531 audiovisual materials.

Computer facilities: 200 computers available on campus for general student use. A campuswide network can be accessed from student residence rooms. Online class registration, Microsoft Office Applications (Word, Excel, PowerPoint) are available. *Web address:* http://www.dominican.edu/.

General Application Contact: Larry Schwartz, Director, 415-458-3748, Fax: 415-485-3214, E-mail: larry.schwartz@dominican.edu.

GRADUATE UNITS

Graduate Programs Students: 399 full-time (287 women), 270 part-time (186 women); includes 155 minority (23 Black or African American, non-Hispanic/Latino; 3 American Indian or Alaska Native, non-Hispanic/Latino; 36 Asian, non-Hispanic/Latino; 70 Hispanic/Latino; 2 Native Hawaiian or other Pacific Islander, non-Hispanic/Latino; 21 Two or more races, non-Hispanic/Latino), 30 international. Average age 35. 448 applicants, 67% accepted, 223 enrolled. Expenses: Contact institution. *Financial support:* In 2010–11, 267 students received support. Application deadline: 3/2. In 2010, 283 master's, 88 other advanced degrees awarded. *Degree program information:* Part-time and evening/weekend programs available. *Application deadline:* For fall admission, 3/2 priority date for domestic students. Applications are processed on a rolling basis. *Application fee:* $40. Electronic applications accepted. *Application Contact:* Larry Schwartz, Director, 415-458-3748, Fax: 415-485-3214, E-mail: larry.schwartz@dominican.edu. *Executive Vice President and Chief Academic Officer*, Dr. Lu??s Calingo, 415-458-3759, Fax: 415-257-0165, E-mail: luis.calingo@dominican.edu.

School of Arts, Humanities and Social Sciences Students: 10 full-time (6 women), 35 part-time (26 women); includes 7 minority (2 Black or African American, non-Hispanic/Latino; 1 Asian, non-Hispanic/Latino; 3 Hispanic/Latino; 1 Two or more races, non-Hispanic/Latino), 2 international. Average age 42. 38 applicants, 71% accepted, 20 enrolled. Expenses: Contact institution. *Financial support:* In 2010–11, 16 students received support. Federal Work-Study and scholarships/grants available. Support available to part-time students. Financial award application deadline: 3/2; financial award applicants required to submit FAFSA. In 2010, 9 master's awarded. *Degree program information:* Part-time and evening/weekend programs available. Offers arts, humanities and social sciences (MA); humanities (MA). *Application deadline:* For fall admission, 6/15 priority date for domestic and international students; for spring admission, 11/15 priority date for domestic and international students. Applications are processed on a rolling basis. *Application fee:* $40. Electronic applications accepted. *Application Contact:* Larry Schwartz, Director, 415-458-3748, Fax: 415-485-3214, E-mail: larry.schwartz@dominican.edu. *Interim Dean*, Dr. Philip Novak, 415-485-3279, Fax: 415-257-0120, E-mail: philip.novak@dominican.edu.

School of Business and Leadership Students: 85 full-time (42 women), 97 part-time (49 women); includes 45 minority (6 Black or African American, non-Hispanic/Latino; 11 Asian, non-Hispanic/Latino; 21 Hispanic/Latino; 7 Two or more races, non-Hispanic/Latino), 22 international. Average age 33. 89 applicants, 62% accepted, 36 enrolled. *Faculty:* 7 full-time (3 women), 19 part-time/adjunct (8 women). Expenses: Contact institution. *Financial support:* In 2010–11, 56 students received support. Tuition discounts available. Financial award application deadline: 3/2; financial award applicants required to submit FAFSA. In 2010, 69 master's awarded. *Degree program information:* Part-time and evening/weekend programs available. Offers business and leadership (MAM, MBA); global management (MBA); management (MAM); strategic leadership (MBA); sustainable enterprise (MBA). Programs also offered in Ukiah, CA. *Application deadline:* For fall admission, 6/15 priority date for domestic and international students; for spring admission, 11/15 priority date for domestic and international students. Applications are processed on a rolling basis. *Application fee:* $40. Electronic applications accepted. *Application Contact:* Robbie Hayes, Assistant Director, 415-458-3771, Fax: 415-485-3214, E-mail: robbie.hayes@dominican.edu. *Dean*, Dr. Dan Moshavi, 415-458-3760, Fax: 415-458-3790, E-mail: dan.moshavi@dominican.edu.

School of Education and Counseling Psychology Students: 200 full-time (157 women), 130 part-time (105 women); includes 55 minority (9 Black or African American, non-Hispanic/Latino; 3 American Indian or Alaska Native, non-Hispanic/Latino; 4 Asian, non-Hispanic/Latino; 29 Hispanic/Latino; 10 Two or more races, non-Hispanic/Latino), 5 international. Average age 36. 204 applicants, 75% accepted, 119 enrolled. *Faculty:* 14 full-time (12 women), 60 part-time/adjunct (46 women). Expenses: Contact institution. *Financial support:* In 2010–11, 121 students received support, including 38 fellowships (averaging $2,704 per year); scholarships/grants also available. Support available to part-time students. Financial award application deadline: 3/2; financial award applicants required to submit FAFSA. In 2010, 32 master's, 88 other advanced degrees awarded. *Degree program information:* Part-time programs available. Offers counseling psychology (MFT, MS); education (MS); education and counseling psychology (MFT, MS, Credential); multiple subject teaching (Credential); single subject teaching (Credential); special education (Credential). *Application deadline:* Applications are processed on a rolling basis. *Application fee:* $40. Electronic applications accepted. *Application Contact:* Moriah Dunning, Associate Director, 415-485-3246, Fax: 415-485-3214, E-mail: moriah.dunning@dominican.edu. *Dean*, Dr. Ed Kujawa, 415-485-3245, Fax: 415-458-3790, E-mail: kujawa@dominican.edu.

School of Health and Natural Sciences Students: 104 full-time (82 women), 8 part-time (6 women); includes 48 minority (6 Black or African American, non-Hispanic/Latino; 20 Asian, non-Hispanic/Latino; 17 Hispanic/Latino; 2 Native Hawaiian or other Pacific Islander, non-Hispanic/Latino; 3 Two or more races, non-Hispanic/Latino), 1 international. Average age 32. 125 applicants, 54% accepted, 48 enrolled. Expenses: Contact institution. *Financial support:* In 2010–11, 78 students received support. Scholarships/grants available. Financial award application deadline: 3/2; financial award applicants required to submit FAFSA. In 2010, 27 master's awarded. Offers biology (MS); clinical nurse leader (MS); health and natural sciences (MS); occupational therapy (MS). *Application fee:* $40. *Application Contact:* Larry Schwartz, Director, 415-458-3748, Fax: 415-485-3214, E-mail: larry.schwartz@dominican.edu. *Dean*, Dr. Martha Nelson, 415-457-4440.

DONGGUK UNIVERSITY LOS ANGELES, Los Angeles, CA 90020

General Information Independent, coed, graduate-only institution. *Graduate housing:* On-campus housing not available.

GRADUATE UNITS

Program in Oriental Medicine *Degree program information:* Part-time and evening/weekend programs available. Offers Oriental medicine (MS).

DORDT COLLEGE, Sioux Center, IA 51250-1697

General Information Independent-religious, coed, comprehensive institution. *Graduate housing:* Rooms and/or apartments available to single and married students.

GRADUATE UNITS

Program in Education *Degree program information:* Part-time programs available. Postbaccalaureate distance learning degree programs offered (minimal on-campus study). Offers education (M Ed). Electronic applications accepted.

DOWLING COLLEGE, Oakdale, NY 11769-1999

General Information Independent, coed, comprehensive institution. *Enrollment:* 5,198 graduate, professional, and undergraduate students; 808 full-time matriculated graduate/professional students (494 women), 1,225 part-time matriculated graduate/professional students (779 women). *Graduate faculty:* 46 full-time (20 women), 141 part-time/adjunct (65 women). *Tuition:* Part-time $884 per credit hour. Part-time tuition and fees vary according to degree level and campus/location. *Graduate housing:* Room and/or apartments available on a first-come, first-served basis to single students; on-campus housing not available to married students. Housing application deadline: 9/1. *Student services:* Campus employment opportunities, campus safety program, career counseling, international student services, low-cost health insurance, services for students with disabilities. *Library facilities:* Dowling College Library plus 2 others. *Online resources:* library catalog, web page, access to other libraries' catalogs. *Collection:* 149,031 titles, 3,131 serial subscriptions, 2,955 audiovisual materials.

Computer facilities: 253 computers available on campus for general student use. A campuswide network can be accessed from student residence rooms and from off campus. Online class registration is available. *Web address:* http://www.dowling.edu/.

General Application Contact: Ronnie MacDonald, Vice President for Enrollment and Student Services, 631-244-3357, Fax: 631-244-1059.

GRADUATE UNITS

Graduate Programs in Education Students: 510 full-time (361 women), 756 part-time (567 women); includes 104 minority (37 Black or African American, non-Hispanic/Latino; 2 American Indian or Alaska Native, non-Hispanic/Latino; 1 Asian, non-Hispanic/Latino; 59 Hispanic/Latino; 5 Native Hawaiian or other Pacific Islander, non-Hispanic/Latino). Average age 32. 326 applicants, 94% accepted, 201 enrolled. *Faculty:* 30 full-time (15 women), 85 part-time/adjunct (58 women). Expenses: Contact institution. *Financial support:* Career-related internships or fieldwork and Federal Work-Study available. Support available to part-time students. Financial award application deadline: 6/30; financial award applicants required to submit FAFSA. In 2010, 451 master's, 30 doctorates, 37 other advanced degrees awarded. *Degree program information:* Part-time and evening/weekend programs available. Postbaccalaureate distance learning degree programs offered. Offers adolescence education with middle childhood extension (MS); advanced certificate in gifted education (AC); childhood and early childhood education (MS); childhood and gifted education (MS); computers in education (AC); early childhood education (MS); educational administration (Ed D); educational technology specialist (AC); literacy education (MS); literary education (AC); school building leader (AC); school district business leader (MBA, AC); school district leader (AC); special education (MS). *Application deadline:* For fall admission, 9/1 priority date for domestic students; for winter admission, 1/1 priority date for domestic students; for spring admission, 2/1 priority date for domestic students. Applications are processed on a rolling basis. *Application fee:* $50. Electronic applications accepted. *Application Contact:* Ronnie S. Macdonald, Assistant Vice President for Enrollment Services/Dean of Admissions, 631-244-3357, Fax: 631-244-1059, E-mail: macdonar@dowling.edu. *Dean of the School of Education*, Dr. Clyde Payne, 631-244-3404, Fax: 631-589-6644, E-mail: paynec@dowling.edu.

Programs in Arts and Sciences Students: 3 full-time (2 women), 9 part-time (6 women); includes 1 minority (Asian, non-Hispanic/Latino). Average age 33. 14 applicants, 79% accepted, 6 enrolled. *Faculty:* 6 full-time (1 woman). Expenses: Contact institution. *Financial support:* Federal Work-Study available. Support available to part-time students. Financial award application deadline: 6/30; financial award applicants required to submit FAFSA. In 2010, 1 master's awarded. *Degree program information:* Part-time and evening/weekend programs available. Offers integrated math and science (MS); liberal studies (MA). *Application deadline:* For fall admission, 9/1 priority date for domestic students; for winter admission, 1/1 priority date for domestic students; for spring admission, 2/1 priority date for domestic students. Applications are processed on a rolling basis. *Application fee:* $50. Electronic applications accepted. *Application Contact:* Ronnie S. Macdonald, Assistant Vice President for Enrollment Services/Dean of Admissions, 631-244-3357, Fax: 631-244-1059, E-mail: macdonar@dowling.edu. *Dean*, Dr. Paul Abramson, 631-244-3162, Fax: 631-244-1035, E-mail: abramsop@dowling.edu.

School of Business Students: 295 full-time (131 women), 460 part-time (206 women); includes 219 minority (97 Black or African American, non-Hispanic/Latino; 14 Asian, non-

Hispanic/Latino; 35 Hispanic/Latino; 73 Native Hawaiian or other Pacific Islander, non-Hispanic/Latino), 3 international. Average age 33. 327 applicants, 85% accepted, 160 enrolled. *Faculty:* 10 full-time (4 women), 56 part-time/adjunct (7 women). Expenses: Contact institution. *Financial support:* Career-related internships or fieldwork and Federal Work-Study available. Support available to part-time students. Financial award application deadline: 6/30; financial award applicants required to submit FAFSA. In 2010, 33 master's, 1 other advanced degree awarded. *Degree program information:* Part-time and evening/weekend programs available. Offers aviation management (MBA, Certificate); banking and finance (MBA, Certificate); corporate finance (MBA); financial planning (Certificate); health care management (MBA, Certificate); human resource management (Certificate); information systems management (MBA); management and leadership (MBA); marketing (Certificate); project management (Certificate); public management (MBA, Certificate); sport, event and entertainment management (Certificate). *Application deadline:* For fall admission, 9/1 priority date for domestic students; for winter admission, 1/1 priority date for domestic students; for spring admission, 2/1 priority date for domestic students. Applications are processed on a rolling basis. *Application fee:* $50. Electronic applications accepted. *Application Contact:* Ronnie S. Macdonald, Assistant Vice President for Enrollment Services/Dean of Admissions, 631-244-3357, Fax: 631-244-1059, E-mail: macdonar@dowling.edu. *Assistant Dean,* Antonia Loschiavo, 631-244-3266, Fax: 631-244-1018, E-mail: loschiat@dowling.edu.

DRAKE UNIVERSITY, Des Moines, IA 50311-4516

General Information Independent, coed, university. *Enrollment:* 5,616 graduate, professional, and undergraduate students; 1,062 full-time matriculated graduate/professional students (582 women), 953 part-time matriculated graduate/professional students (621 women). *Enrollment by degree level:* 907 first professional, 977 master's, 72 doctoral, 43 other advanced degrees. *Graduate faculty:* 110 full-time (50 women), 74 part-time/adjunct (44 women). *Tuition:* Part-time $538 per credit hour. *Graduate housing:* Room and/or apartments available on a first-come, first-served basis to single students; on-campus housing not available to married students. Housing application deadline: 8/1. *Student services:* Campus employment opportunities, campus safety program, career counseling, exercise/wellness program, free psychological counseling, international student services, low-cost health insurance, services for students with disabilities, teacher training, writing training. *Library facilities:* Cowles Library plus 2 others. *Online resources:* library catalog, web page, access to other libraries' catalogs. *Collection:* 949,476 titles, 1,406 serial subscriptions, 2,732 audiovisual materials. *Research affiliation:* NASA through Iowa State University (arts and sciences), Albertson's, Inc. (pharmacy), U. S. Department of Agriculture (USDA) (agriculture), U. S. Department of Education (DOE) (education), National Science Foundation (biology, physics), Iowa Department of Education (education).

Computer facilities: 1,000 computers available on campus for general student use. A campuswide network can be accessed from student residence rooms and from off campus. Online class registration is available. *Web address:* http://www.drake.edu/.

General Application Contact: Ann J. Martin, Graduate Coordinator, 515-271-2034, Fax: 515-271-2831, E-mail: ann.martin@drake.edu.

GRADUATE UNITS

College of Business and Public Administration *Degree program information:* Part-time and evening/weekend programs available. Offers business and public administration (M Acc, MBA, MFM, MPA). Electronic applications accepted.

College of Pharmacy and Health Sciences Offers pharmacy and health sciences (Pharm D). Electronic applications accepted.

Law School Offers law (JD). JD/MA and JD/MS offered jointly with Iowa State University of Science and Technology; JD/MSW with The University of Iowa. Electronic applications accepted.

School of Education *Degree program information:* Part-time and evening/weekend programs available. Offers education (MAT, MS, MSE, MST, Ed D, Ed S). Electronic applications accepted.

School of Journalism and Mass Communication Offers journalism and mass communication (MCL).

DREW UNIVERSITY, Madison, NJ 07940-1493

General Information Independent-religious, coed, university. CGS member. *Graduate housing:* Rooms and/or apartments available on a first-come, first-served basis to single and married students. Housing application deadline: 7/1. *Research affiliation:* Center for Research Libraries (humanities), Dana Rise Institute (science), St. Barnabas Medical Center (medical humanities), Overlook Hospital (medical humanities), Methodist Archives (religion).

GRADUATE UNITS

Caspersen School of Graduate Studies *Degree program information:* Part-time and evening/weekend programs available. Offers biology (MAT); chemistry (MAT); English (MAT); French (MAT); holocaust and genocide studies (Certificate); intellectual history (MA, PhD); interdisciplinary studies (M Litt, D Litt); Italian (MAT); math (MAT); medical humanities (MMH, DMH, CMH); physics (MAT); poetry (MFA); poetry in translation (MFA); social studies (MAT); Spanish (MAT); theatre arts (MAT).

Theological School Students: 200 full-time (114 women), 165 part-time (81 women); includes 111 minority (85 Black or African American, non-Hispanic/Latino; 1 American Indian or Alaska Native, non-Hispanic/Latino; 15 Asian, non-Hispanic/Latino; 10 Hispanic/Latino), 73 international. Average age 35. 237 applicants, 57% accepted, 76 enrolled. *Faculty:* 25 full-time (11 women), 24 part-time/adjunct (12 women). Expenses: Contact institution. *Financial support:* Fellowships, career-related internships or fieldwork, Federal Work-Study, institutionally sponsored loans, and scholarships/grants available. Support available to part-time students. Financial award application deadline: 4/15; financial award applicants required to submit FAFSA. In 2010, 68 master's, 22 doctorates awarded. *Degree program information:* Part-time programs available. Postbaccalaureate distance learning degree programs offered (minimal on-campus study). Offers theology (M Div, MA, MA Min, STM, D Min, Certificate). *Application deadline:* For fall admission, 3/1 priority date for domestic and international students; for spring admission, 12/1 priority date for domestic students, 10/1 priority date for international students. Applications are processed on a rolling basis. *Application fee:* $35. Electronic applications accepted. *Application Contact:* Rev. Dr. Kevin D. Miller, Director of Theological Admissions, 973-408-3111, Fax: 973-408-3242, E-mail: kmiller@drew.edu. *Dean,* Dr. Kah-Jin Jeffrey Kuan, 973-408-3258, Fax: 973-408-3534, E-mail: jkuan@drew.edu.

See Display below and Close-Up on page 939.

DREXEL UNIVERSITY, Philadelphia, PA 19104-2875

General Information Independent, coed, university. CGS member. *Graduate housing:* On-campus housing not available.

GRADUATE UNITS

Antoinette Westphal College of Media Arts and Design *Degree program information:* Part-time and evening/weekend programs available. Offers arts administration (MS); digital media (MS); fashion design (MS); interior architecture and design (MS); television management (MS). Electronic applications accepted.

College of Arts and Sciences *Degree program information:* Part-time and evening/weekend programs available. Offers arts and sciences (MA, MS, PhD); biological sciences (MS, PhD); chemistry (MS, PhD); clinical psychology (PhD); communication (MS); environmental policy (MS); environmental science (MS, PhD); forensic psychology (PhD); health psychology (PhD); human nutrition (MS); law-psychology (PhD); mathematics (MS, PhD); neuropsychology (PhD); physics (MS, PhD); psychology (MS); public communication (MS); publication management (MS); science communication (MS); science, technology and society (MS); technical communication (MS). Electronic applications accepted.

College of Engineering *Degree program information:* Part-time and evening/weekend programs available. Offers architectural / building systems engineering (PhD); architectural/building systems engineering (MS); biochemical engineering (MS); chemical engineering (MS, PhD); civil engineering (MS, PhD); computer engineering (MS); computer science (MS, PhD); electrical and computer engineering (PhD); electrical engineering (MSEE); engineering (MS, MSEE, MSSE, PhD, Certificate); engineering management (MS, Certificate); environ-

Drexel University (continued)

mental engineering (MS, PhD); geotechnical, geoenvironmental and geosynthetics (MS, PhD); geotechnical, geoenvironmental and geosynthetics engineering (MS, PhD); hydraulics, hydrology and water resources engineering (MS, PhD); materials engineering (MS, PhD); mechanical engineering (MS, PhD); software engineering (MSSE); structures (MS); telecommunications engineering (MSEE). Electronic applications accepted.

College of Medicine *Degree program information:* Part-time programs available. Offers medicine (MD, MLAS, MMS, MS, PhD, Certificate). Electronic applications accepted.

Biomedical Graduate Programs *Degree program information:* Part-time programs available. Offers biochemistry (MS, PhD); biomedical sciences (MLAS, MMS, MS, PhD, Certificate); laboratory animal science (MLAS); medical science (MMS, Certificate); microbiology and immunology (MS, PhD); molecular and cell biology and genetics (MS, PhD); molecular medicine (MS); molecular pathobiology (MS, PhD); neuroscience (MS, PhD); pharmacology and physiology (MS, PhD). Electronic applications accepted.

College of Nursing and Health Professions *Degree program information:* Part-time and evening/weekend programs available. Offers art therapy (MA, PMC); couples and family therapy (PhD); dance/movement therapy (MA, PMC); emergency and public safety services (MS); family therapy (MFT); hand and upper quarter rehabilitation (MHS, Certificate, PPDPT); movement science (PhD); music therapy (MA, PMC); nurse anesthesia (MSN); nursing (MSN); nursing and health professions (MA, MFT, MHS, MS, MSN, DPT, PhD, Certificate, PMC, PPDPT); orthopedics (MHS, PhD, PPDPT); pediatrics (MHS, PhD, PPDPT); physical therapy (DPT); physician assistant studies (MHS). Electronic applications accepted.

The iSchool at Drexel, College of Information Science and Technology Students: 278 full-time (187 women), 662 part-time (451 women); includes 123 minority (46 Black or African American, non-Hispanic/Latino; 7 American Indian or Alaska Native, non-Hispanic/Latino; 36 Asian, non-Hispanic/Latino; 34 Hispanic/Latino), 44 international. Average age 34. 674 applicants, 68% accepted, 343 enrolled. *Faculty:* 33 full-time (21 women), 26 part-time/adjunct (12 women). Expenses: Contact institution. *Financial support:* In 2010–11, 250 students received support, including 264 fellowships with partial tuition reimbursements available (averaging $22,500 per year), 22 research assistantships with full tuition reimbursements available (averaging $22,500 per year), 8 teaching assistantships with full tuition reimbursements available (averaging $25,000 per year); institutionally sponsored loans, scholarships/grants, health care benefits, tuition waivers (partial), and unspecified assistantships also available. Support available to part-time students. Financial award applicants required to submit FAFSA. In 2010, 288 master's, 7 doctorates, 19 other advanced degrees awarded. *Degree program information:* Part-time and evening/weekend programs available. Postbaccalaureate distance learning degree programs offered (no on-campus study). Offers archival studies (MS); competitive intelligence and knowledge management (MS); digital libraries (MS); healthcare informatics (Certificate); information science and technology (PMC); information studies (PhD); information studies and technology (Advanced Certificate); information systems (MSIS); library and information science (MS); library and information services (MS); school library media (MS); software engineering (MSSE); youth services (MS). *Application deadline:* For fall admission, 9/1 for domestic and international students; for spring admission, 3/4 for domestic students, 2/15 for international students. Applications are processed on a rolling basis. Electronic applications accepted. *Application Contact:* Matthew Lechtenberg, Graduate Admissions Manager, 215-895-1951, Fax: 215-895-2303, E-mail: ml333@drexel.edu. *Dean/Professor of Information Science,* Dr. David E. Fenske, 215-895-2475, Fax: 215-895-6378, E-mail: fenske@drexel.edu.

LeBow College of Business *Degree program information:* Part-time and evening/weekend programs available. Offers accounting (MS); business (MBA, MS, PhD, APC); business administration (MBA, PhD, APC); finance (MS). Electronic applications accepted.

School of Biomedical Engineering, Science and Health Systems Offers biomedical engineering (MS, PhD); biomedical science (MS, PhD); biostatistics (MS); clinical/rehabilitation engineering (MS). Electronic applications accepted.

School of Education Students: 113 full-time, 1,345 part-time; includes 204 Black or African American, non-Hispanic/Latino; 14 American Indian or Alaska Native, non-Hispanic/Latino; 58 Asian, non-Hispanic/Latino; 102 Hispanic/Latino. *Faculty:* 33 full-time. Expenses: Contact institution. *Financial support:* Research assistantships, teaching assistantships, unspecified assistantships available. Financial award applicants required to submit FAFSA. In 2010, 232 master's awarded. *Degree program information:* Part-time and evening/weekend programs available. Postbaccalaureate distance learning degree programs offered. Offers education leadership development and learning technologies (PhD); educational administration: collaborative leadership (MS); educational leadership and management (Ed D); educational leadership development and learning technologies (PhD); global and international education (MS); higher education (MS); human resource development (MS); human resources development (MS); learning technologies (MS); mathematics learning and teaching (MS); mathematics, learning and teaching (MS); science of instruction (MS); special education (MS); teaching, learning and curriculum (MS). *Application deadline:* For fall admission, 9/1 for domestic students; for winter admission, 12/2 for domestic students; for spring admission, 3/2 for domestic students. Applications are processed on a rolling basis. Electronic applications accepted. *Application Contact:* Callie Cash, Director of Graduate Admissions, 215-895-6400, Fax: 215-895-5939, E-mail: enroll@drexel.edu. *Dean,* Dr. William F. Lynch, 215-895-6770, Fax: 215-895-5879, E-mail: education@drexel.edu.

School of Journalism Offers journalism (MA).

School of Public Health Offers biostatistics (MS); epidemiology (PhD); epidemiology and biostatistics (Certificate); public health (MPH, MS, PhD, Certificate). Electronic applications accepted.

School of Technology and Professional Studies Postbaccalaureate distance learning degree programs offered. Offers construction management (MS); engineering technology (MS); food science (MS); hospitality management (MS); professional studies: creativity studies (MS); professional studies: e-learning leadership (MS); professional studies: homeland security management (MS); project management (MS); property management (MS); sport management (MS).

DRURY UNIVERSITY, Springfield, MO 65802

General Information Independent, coed, comprehensive institution. *Graduate housing:* Rooms and/or apartments available on a first-come, first-served basis to single and married students. *Research affiliation:* Yale University (child development).

GRADUATE UNITS

Breech School of Business Administration *Degree program information:* Part-time and evening/weekend programs available. Offers business administration (MBA). Electronic applications accepted.

Graduate Programs in Education *Degree program information:* Part-time and evening/weekend programs available. Offers elementary education (M Ed); gifted education (M Ed); human services (M Ed); instructional mathematics K-8 (M Ed); instructional technology (M Ed); middle school teaching (M Ed); secondary education (M Ed); special education (M Ed); special reading (M Ed). Electronic applications accepted.

Hammons School of Architecture Offers architecture (M Arch).

Program in Communication *Degree program information:* Part-time and evening/weekend programs available. Offers communication (MA). Electronic applications accepted.

Program in Criminology/Criminal Justice *Degree program information:* Part-time and evening/weekend programs available. Offers criminal justice (MS); criminology (MA). Electronic applications accepted.

Program in Studio Art and Theory Offers studio art and theory (MA). Electronic applications accepted.

DUKE UNIVERSITY, Durham, NC 27708-0586

General Information Independent-religious, coed, university. CGS member. *Enrollment:* 7,744 full-time matriculated graduate/professional students. *Graduate faculty:* 3,138 full-time. *Graduate housing:* Rooms and/or apartments available on a first-come, first-served basis to single students and available to married students. *Student services:* Campus employment opportunities, campus safety program, career counseling, free psychological counseling, international student services, low-cost health insurance, multicultural affairs office, services for students with disabilities, teacher training, writing training. *Library facilities:* Perkins Library plus 14 others. *Online resources:* library catalog, web page, access to other libraries' catalogs. *Collection:* 6 million titles, 62,639 serial subscriptions, 137,868 audiovisual materials. *Research affiliation:* Highlands Biological Station, U. S. Forest Sciences Laboratory, Organization for Tropical Studies.

Computer facilities: Computer purchase and lease plans are available. 500 computers available on campus for general student use. A campuswide network can be accessed from student residence rooms and from off campus. Online class registration is available. *Web address:* http://www.duke.edu/.

General Application Contact: Cynthia Robertson, Associate Dean for Academic Services, 919-684-3913, Fax: 919-684-2277, E-mail: grad-admissions@duke.edu.

GRADUATE UNITS

Divinity School *Degree program information:* Part-time programs available. Offers theology (M Div, MTS, Th M, Th D). Electronic applications accepted.

The Fuqua School of Business *Degree program information:* Evening/weekend programs available. Postbaccalaureate distance learning degree programs offered. Offers business (EMBA, GEMBA, MBA, MMS, WEMBA, PhD, Certificate); cross continent executive business administration (EMBA); executive business administration (EMBA); global executive business administration (GEMBA); health sector management (Certificate); weekend executive business administration (WEMBA). Electronic applications accepted.

Graduate School Students: 2,901 (1,342 women); includes 112 Black or African American, non-Hispanic/Latino; 11 American Indian or Alaska Native, non-Hispanic/Latino; 142 Asian, non-Hispanic/Latino; 97 Hispanic/Latino, 1,015 international. 8,983 applicants, 19% accepted, 730 enrolled. *Faculty:* 1,627 full-time. Expenses: Contact institution. *Financial support:* In 2010–11, 2,455 students received support; fellowships with full tuition reimbursements available, research assistantships with full tuition reimbursements available, teaching assistantships with full tuition reimbursements available, career-related internships or fieldwork, Federal Work-Study, institutionally sponsored loans, scholarships/grants, traineeships, and unspecified assistantships available. Support available to part-time students. Financial award application deadline: 4/15; financial award applicants required to submit FAFSA. In 2010, 345 master's, 333 doctorates awarded. *Degree program information:* Part-time and evening/weekend programs available. Offers art, art history and visual studies (PhD); biological psychology (PhD); biology (PhD); business administration (PhD); cell biology (PhD); cellular and molecular biology (Certificate); chemistry (PhD); classical studies (PhD); clinical psychology (PhD); cognitive neuroscience (PhD, Certificate); cognitive psychology (PhD); computational biology and bioinformatics (PhD, Certificate); computer science (MS, PhD); crystallography of macromolecules (PhD); developmental biology (Certificate); developmental psychology (PhD); East Asian studies (AM, Certificate); ecology (PhD, Certificate); economics (AM, PhD); English (PhD); environmental policy (PhD); enzyme mechanisms (PhD); experimental psychology (PhD); French (PhD); genetics and genomics (PhD); German studies (PhD); gross anatomy and physical anthropology (PhD); health psychology (PhD); history (AM, PhD); human social development (PhD); humanities (AM); immunology (PhD); integrated toxicology and environmental health (PhD, Certificate); Latin American studies (PhD); liberal studies (AM); lipid biochemistry (PhD); literature (PhD); marine science and conservation (MS); mathematics (PhD); medical physics (MS, PhD); membrane structure and function (PhD); molecular cancer biology (PhD); molecular genetics (PhD); molecular genetics and microbiology (PhD); music composition (AM, PhD); musicology (AM, PhD); natural resource economics/policy (PhD); natural resource science/ecology (PhD); natural resource systems science (PhD); neuroanatomy (PhD); neurobiology (PhD); neurochemistry (PhD); nucleic acid structure and function (PhD); pathology (PhD); performance practice (AM, PhD); pharmacology (PhD); philosophy (AM, PhD); physical anthropology (PhD); physics (PhD); political science (AM, PhD); protein structure and function (PhD); public policy (PhD); religion (MA, PhD); Slavic and Eurasian studies (AM, Certificate); social/cultural anthropology (PhD); sociology (AM, PhD); Spanish (PhD); statistical science (PhD); structural biology and biophysics (Certificate); teaching (MAT). *Application deadline:* For fall admission, 12/8 priority date for domestic and international students; for winter admission, 12/8 for domestic and international students; for spring admission, 10/15 for domestic and international students. *Application fee:* $75. Electronic applications accepted. *Application Contact:* Elizabeth Hutton, Director of Admissions, 919-684-3913, Fax: 919-684-2277, E-mail: grad-admissions@duke.edu. *Dean,* Jo Rae Wright, 919-681-3257.

Center for Documentary Studies *Faculty:* 26 full-time. Expenses: Contact institution. Offers experimental and documentary arts (MFA). *Application deadline:* For fall admission, 1/30 priority date for domestic students. Applications are processed on a rolling basis. *Application Contact:* Elizabeth Hutton, Director of Admissions, 919-684-3913, Fax: 919-684-2277, E-mail: grad-admissions@duke.edu. *Program Director,* Stanley Abe, 919-660-3661, Fax: 919-681-7600, E-mail: stanley.abe@duke.edu.

Division of Earth and Ocean Sciences Students: 23 full-time (12 women); includes 1 Asian, non-Hispanic/Latino, 5 international. 35 applicants, 17% accepted, 4 enrolled. *Faculty:* 11 full-time. Expenses: Contact institution. *Financial support:* Fellowships, research assistantships, teaching assistantships, Federal Work-Study available. Financial award application deadline: 12/8. In 2010, 1 doctorate awarded. *Degree program information:* Part-time programs available. Offers earth and ocean sciences (MS, PhD). *Application deadline:* For fall admission, 12/8 priority date for domestic and international students; for spring admission, 10/15 for domestic and international students. *Application fee:* $75. Electronic applications accepted. *Application Contact:* Elizabeth Hutton, Director of Admissions, 919-684-3913, Fax: 919-684-2277, E-mail: grad-admissions@duke.edu. *Director of Graduate Studies,* Alan Boudreau, 919-681-4426, Fax: 919-684-5833, E-mail: cabrera@duke.edu.

Duke Global Health Institute Students: 35 full-time (25 women); includes 1 Black or African American, non-Hispanic/Latino; 5 Asian, non-Hispanic/Latino, 10 international. 71 applicants, 65% accepted, 20 enrolled. *Faculty:* 49 full-time. Expenses: Contact institution. Offers global health (MS). *Application deadline:* For fall admission, 1/30 priority date for domestic and international students. *Application fee:* $75. *Application Contact:* Elizabeth Hutton, Director of Admissions, 919-684-3913, Fax: 919-684-2277, E-mail: grad-admissions@duke.edu. *Director of Graduate Studies,* Dr. Christopher Woods, 919-681-7916, Fax: 919-681-7748, E-mail: s.martin@duke.edu.

Duke Sanford Institute of Public Policy 157 applicants, 8% accepted, 2 enrolled. *Faculty:* 42 full-time, 19 part-time/adjunct. Expenses: Contact institution. *Financial support:* Career-related internships or fieldwork and Federal Work-Study available. Financial award application deadline: 12/31. Offers international development policy (AM, Certificate); public policy (AM, MPP, PhD, Certificate). *Application deadline:* For fall admission, 12/8 priority date for domestic students, 12/8 for international students. *Application fee:* $75. Electronic applications accepted. *Application Contact:* Jacob Vigdor, Director, 919-613-9214. *Director,* Jacob Vigdor, 919-613-9214.

Pratt School of Engineering Expenses: Contact institution. *Financial support:* Fellowships, research assistantships, teaching assistantships, Federal Work-Study available. Financial award application deadline: 12/31. *Degree program information:* Part-time programs available. Offers biomedical engineering (MS, PhD); civil and environmental engineering (MS, PhD); civil engineering (M Eng); electrical and computer engineering (M Eng); engineering (M Eng, MEM, MS, PhD); engineering management (MEM); environmental engineering (M Eng, MS, PhD); materials science (MS, PhD); materials science and engineering (M Eng); mechanical engineering (M Eng, MS, PhD); photonics and optical sciences (M Eng). *Application Contact:* Cynthia Robertson, Associate Dean for Enrollment Services, 919-684-3913, Fax: 919-684-2277, E-mail: grad-admissions@duke.edu. *Dean,* Robert Clark, 919-660-5286, Fax: 919-660-5469, E-mail: rws6@duke.edu.

Nicholas School of the Environment *Degree program information:* Part-time programs available. Offers coastal environmental management (MEM); DEL-environmental leadership (MEM); energy and environment (MEM); environmental economics and policy (MEM); environmental health and security (MEM); forest resource management (MF); global environmental change (MEM); resource ecology (MEM); water and air resources (MEM). Electronic applications accepted.

School of Law Offers law (JD, LL M, MLS, SJD). LL M and SJD offered only to international students. Electronic applications accepted.

School of Medicine Students: 779 full-time (479 women), 89 part-time (48 women); includes 92 Black or African American, non-Hispanic/Latino; 5 American Indian or Alaska Native, non-Hispanic/Latino; 144 Asian, non-Hispanic/Latino; 44 Hispanic/Latino, 36 international. 5,156 applicants, 11% accepted, 324 enrolled. *Faculty:* 1,461 full-time (483 women), 89 part-time/adjunct (35 women). Expenses: Contact institution. *Financial support:* In 2010–11, 248 students received support. Institutionally sponsored loans and scholarships/grants available. Financial award application deadline: 5/1; financial award applicants required to submit CSS PROFILE or FAFSA. In 2010, 103 master's, 154 doctorates awarded. *Degree program information:* Part-time programs available. Offers biostatistics (MS); clinical leadership (MHS); clinical research (MHS); medicine (MD, MHS, MS, DPT); pathologists' assistant (MHS); physician assistant (MHS). *Application Contact:* Dr. Brenda E. Armstrong, Director of Admissions, 919-684-2985, Fax: 919-684-8893, E-mail: mcdadm@mc.duke.edu. *Vice Dean, Medical Education,* Dr. Edward G. Buckley, 919-668-3381, Fax: 919-660-7040, E-mail: buckl002@mc.duke.edu.

Physical Therapy Division Students: 186 full-time (150 women); includes 5 Black or African American, non-Hispanic/Latino; 11 Asian, non-Hispanic/Latino; 6 Hispanic/Latino. 502 applicants, 22% accepted, 62 enrolled. *Faculty:* 16 full-time (10 women), 12 part-time/adjunct (5 women). Expenses: Contact institution. *Financial support:* In 2010–11, 161 students received support; fellowships, research assistantships, teaching assistantships, Federal Work-Study available. Financial award application deadline: 5/1; financial award applicants required to submit FAFSA. In 2010, 49 doctorates awarded. Offers physical therapy (DPT). *Application deadline:* For fall admission, 12/1 priority date for domestic and international students. Applications are processed on a rolling basis. *Application fee:* $0. Electronic applications accepted. *Application Contact:* Anita Aiken, Admissions Coordinator, 919-668-5206, Fax: 919-688-3024, E-mail: anita.aiken@duke.edu. *Interim Chief,* Victoria Kaprielian, 919-681-4380, Fax: 919-684-1846, E-mail: kapri001@mc.duke.edu.

School of Nursing Students: 114 full-time (91 women), 320 part-time (288 women); includes 62 minority (27 Black or African American, non-Hispanic/Latino; 3 American Indian or Alaska Native, non-Hispanic/Latino; 16 Asian, non-Hispanic/Latino; 10 Hispanic/Latino; 1 Native Hawaiian or other Pacific Islander, non-Hispanic/Latino; 5 Two or more races, non-Hispanic/Latino), 9 international. Average age 35. 337 applicants, 59% accepted, 146 enrolled. *Faculty:* 56 full-time (47 women), 2 part-time/adjunct (1 woman). Expenses: Contact institution. *Financial support:* Career-related internships or fieldwork, institutionally sponsored loans, scholarships/grants, traineeships, and tuition waivers (partial) available. Support available to part-time students. Financial award application deadline: 4/1; financial award applicants required to submit FAFSA. In 2010, 92 master's, 22 doctorates, 29 other advanced degrees awarded. *Degree program information:* Part-time programs available. Postbaccalaureate distance learning degree programs offered (minimal on-campus study). Offers adult acute care (Certificate); adult cardiovascular (Certificate); adult oncology (Certificate); adult primary care (Certificate); clinical nurse specialist (MSN); clinical research management (MSN, Certificate); family (Certificate); gerontology (Certificate); health and nursing ministries (MSN, Certificate); health systems leadership and outcomes (Certificate); neonatal (Certificate); neonatal/pediatric in rural health (MSN, Certificate); nurse anesthetist (MSN, Certificate); nurse practitioner (MSN); nursing (MSN, DNP, PhD, Certificate); nursing and healthcare leadership (MSN); nursing education (MSN); nursing informatics (MSN, Certificate); pediatric (Certificate); pediatric acute care (Certificate). *Application deadline:* For fall admission, 7/2 priority date for domestic students, 7/1 priority date for international students; for spring admission, 11/15 priority date for domestic and international students. Applications are processed on a rolling basis. *Application fee:* $50. Electronic applications accepted. *Application Contact:* Bebe T. Mills, Director of Admissions, 919-684-9151, Fax: 919-668-4693, E-mail: mills031@mc.duke.edu. *Dean/Vice Chancellor for Nursing Affairs,* Dr. Catherine L. Gilliss, 919-684-9444, Fax: 919-684-9414, E-mail: gilli025@mc.duke.edu.

DUQUESNE UNIVERSITY, Pittsburgh, PA 15282-0001

General Information Independent-religious, coed, university. CGS member. *Enrollment:* 10,161 graduate, professional, and undergraduate students; 3,668 full-time matriculated graduate/professional students (2,174 women), 748 part-time matriculated graduate/professional students (425 women). *Enrollment by degree level:* 1,490 first professional, 1,999 master's, 776 doctoral, 151 other advanced degrees. *Graduate faculty:* 382 full-time (159 women), 376 part-time/adjunct (140 women). *Tuition:* Part-time $884 per credit. *Required fees:* $84 per credit. Tuition and fees vary according to course load. *Graduate housing:* Rooms and/or apartments available on a first-come, first-served basis to single and married students. Typical cost: $5168 per year ($9476 including board) for single students; $12,400 per year for married students. Room and board charges vary according to housing facility selected. Housing application deadline: 8/22. *Student services:* Campus employment opportunities, campus safety program, career counseling, child daycare facilities, exercise/wellness program, free psychological counseling, international student services, low-cost health insurance, multicultural affairs office, services for students with disabilities, teacher training, writing training. *Library facilities:* Gumberg Library. *Online resources:* library catalog, web page, access to other libraries' catalogs. *Collection:* 721,569 titles, 77,747 serial subscriptions, 77,148 audiovisual materials.

Computer facilities: Computer purchase and lease plans are available. 850 computers available on campus for general student use. A campuswide network can be accessed from student residence rooms and from off campus. Online class registration is available. *Web address:* http://www.duq.edu/.

General Application Contact: Dr. Ralph L. Pearson, Provost and Vice President for Academic Affairs, 412-396-6054, E-mail: pearsonrl@duq.edu.

GRADUATE UNITS

Bayer School of Natural and Environmental Sciences Students: 128 full-time (61 women), 25 part-time (15 women); includes 4 Black or African American, non-Hispanic/Latino; 3 Asian, non-Hispanic/Latino; 1 Hispanic/Latino, 30 international. Average age 26. 137 applicants, 60% accepted, 57 enrolled. *Faculty:* 35 full-time (10 women), 15 part-time/adjunct (4 women). Expenses: Contact institution. *Financial support:* In 2010–11, 95 students received support, including 3 fellowships with full tuition reimbursements available (averaging $20,266 per year), 25 research assistantships with full tuition reimbursements available (averaging $21,400 per year), 57 teaching assistantships with full tuition reimbursements available (averaging $21,400 per year); career-related internships or fieldwork, scholarships/grants, tuition waivers (partial), and unspecified assistantships also available. Financial award application deadline: 5/31. In 2010, 39 master's, 6 doctorates awarded. *Degree program information:* Part-time programs available. Offers biological sciences (MS, PhD); biotechnology (MS); chemistry (MS, PhD); environmental management (MEM, Certificate); environmental science (Certificate); environmental science and management (MS); forensic science and law (MS); natural and environmental sciences (MEM, MS, PhD, Certificate). *Application deadline:* For fall admission, 2/15 priority date for domestic students, 2/15 for international students; for spring admission, 10/1 priority date for domestic students, 10/1 for international students. Applications are processed on a rolling basis. *Application fee:* $40 for international students. Electronic applications accepted. *Application Contact:* Heather Costello, Graduate Academic Advisor, 412-396-6339, Fax: 412-396-4881, E-mail: costelloh@duq.edu. *Dean,* Dr. David W. Seybert, 412-396-4877, Fax: 412-396-4881, E-mail: seybert@duq.edu.

Graduate School of Liberal Arts Students: 614 full-time (323 women), 90 part-time (54 women); includes 16 Black or African American, non-Hispanic/Latino; 3 Hispanic/Latino, 59 international. Average age 30. 604 applicants, 48% accepted, 166 enrolled. *Faculty:* 111 full-time (35 women), 66 part-time/adjunct (33 women). Expenses: Contact institution. *Financial support:* In 2010–11, 39 research assistantships with full tuition reimbursements (averaging $10,000 per year), 79 teaching assistantships with full tuition reimbursements (averaging $14,000 per year) were awarded; fellowships with full tuition reimbursements, career-related internships or fieldwork, Federal Work-Study, institutionally sponsored loans, scholarships/grants, and tuition waivers (full and partial) also available. Support available to part-time students. Financial award application deadline: 5/1. In 2010, 121 master's, 41 doctorates awarded. *Degree program information:* Part-time and evening/weekend programs available. Offers archival, museum, and editing studies (MA); clinical psychology (PhD); communication (MA); computational mathematics (MA, MS); English (MA, PhD); health care ethics (MA, DHCE, PhD, Certificate); history (MA); liberal arts (MA, MS, DHCE, PhD, Certificate); multimedia technology (MS, Certificate); pastoral ministry (MA); philosophy (MA, PhD); religious education (MA); rhetoric (PhD); systematic theology (PhD); theology (MA). *Application deadline:* For fall admission, 8/1 for domestic students, 5/1 for international students; for spring admission, 11/1 for domestic students, 9/1 for international students. Applications are processed on a rolling basis. Electronic applications accepted. *Application Contact:* Linda L. Rendulic, Assistant to the Dean, 412-396-6400, Fax: 412-396-5265, E-mail: rendulic@duq.edu. *Dean,* Dr. Christopher Duncan, 412-396-6400.

Graduate Center for Social and Public Policy Students: 52 full-time (26 women), 9 part-time (4 women); includes 1 Black or African American, non-Hispanic/Latino, 5 international. Average age 27. 38 applicants, 95% accepted, 17 enrolled. *Faculty:* 15 full-time (3 women), 1 (woman) part-time/adjunct. Expenses: Contact institution. *Financial support:* In 2010–11, 20 students received support, including 12 research assistantships with full and partial tuition reimbursements available (averaging $9,000 per year), 4 teaching assistantships with full and partial tuition reimbursements available (averaging $9,000 per year); career-related internships or fieldwork, institutionally sponsored loans, scholarships/grants, tuition waivers (full and partial), and unspecified assistantships also available. Support available to part-time students. Financial award application deadline: 5/1. In 2010, 11 master's awarded. *Degree program information:* Part-time and evening/weekend programs available. Offers conflict resolution and peace studies (Certificate); social and public policy (MA, Certificate). *Application deadline:* For fall admission, 4/30 priority date for domestic and international students; for spring admission, 11/1 priority date for domestic and international students. Applications are processed on a rolling basis. Electronic applications accepted. *Application Contact:* Dr. Joseph Yenerall, Assistant to the Dean, 412-396-6485. *Director,* Dr. Joseph Yenerall, 412-396-6485, Fax: 412-396-5265, E-mail: socialpolicy@duq.edu.

John F. Donahue Graduate School of Business Students: 97 full-time (45 women), 234 part-time (91 women); includes 5 Black or African American, non-Hispanic/Latino; 1 Asian, non-Hispanic/Latino; 2 Hispanic/Latino; 4 Native Hawaiian or other Pacific Islander, non-Hispanic/Latino, 29 international. Average age 31. 289 applicants, 43% accepted, 82 enrolled. *Faculty:* 24 full-time (5 women), 14 part-time/adjunct (0 women). Expenses: Contact institution. *Financial support:* In 2010–11, 40 students received support, including 12 fellowships with partial tuition reimbursements available, 28 research assistantships with partial tuition reimbursements available; career-related internships or fieldwork, scholarships/grants, and unspecified assistantships also available. Financial award application deadline: 7/1; financial award applicants required to submit FAFSA. In 2010, 120 master's awarded. *Degree program information:* Part-time and evening/weekend programs available. Offers accountancy (MS); business administration (MBA); information systems management (MSISM); sustainability (MBA). *Application deadline:* For fall admission, 5/1 priority date for domestic students, 5/1 for international students; for spring admission, 10/1 for domestic and international students. Applications are processed on a rolling basis. *Application fee:* $0. Electronic applications accepted. *Application Contact:* Patricia Moore, Assistant Director, 412-396-6276, Fax: 412-396-1726, E-mail: moorep@duq.edu. *Dean,* Alan R. Miciak, 412-396-5848, Fax: 412-396-5304, E-mail: miciaka@duq.edu.

John G. Rangos, Sr. School of Health Sciences Students: 327 full-time (263 women), 5 part-time (4 women); includes 8 minority (4 Black or African American, non-Hispanic/Latino; 2 Asian, non-Hispanic/Latino; 2 Hispanic/Latino), 4 international. Average age 23. 392 applicants, 19% accepted, 27 enrolled. *Faculty:* 34 full-time (23 women), 20 part-time/adjunct (11 women). Expenses: Contact institution. *Financial support:* Federal Work-Study available. In 2010, 113 master's, 30 doctorates awarded. Offers health management systems (MHMS); occupational therapy (MS); physical therapy (DPT); physician assistant studies (MPAS); rehabilitation science (MS, PhD); speech-language pathology (MS). *Application deadline:* Applications are processed on a rolling basis. Electronic applications accepted. *Application Contact:* Christopher R. Hilf, Recruiter/Academic Advisor, 412-396-5653, Fax: 412-396-5554, E-mail: hilfc@duq.edu. *Dean,* Dr. Gregory H. Frazer, 412-396-5303, Fax: 412-396-5554, E-mail: frazer@duq.edu.

Mary Pappert School of Music Students: 78 full-time (40 women), 22 part-time (12 women); includes 3 Black or African American, non-Hispanic/Latino; 14 Asian, non-Hispanic/Latino; 3 Hispanic/Latino. Average age 23. 105 applicants, 66% accepted, 50 enrolled. *Faculty:* 26 full-time (10 women), 72 part-time/adjunct (16 women). Expenses: Contact institution. *Financial support:* In 2010–11, 57 students received support. Career-related internships or fieldwork, institutionally sponsored loans, scholarships/grants, tuition waivers (full and partial), unspecified assistantships, and assistantships ($11,938) available. Financial award application deadline: 4/1. In 2010, 40 master's awarded. *Degree program information:* Part-time programs available. Offers music composition (MM); music education (MM); music performance (MM, AD); music technology (MM); music theory (MM); sacred music (MM). *Application deadline:* For fall admission, 7/1 priority date for domestic and international students; for spring admission, 12/1 priority date for domestic and international students. Applications are processed on a rolling basis. *Application fee:* $50. Electronic applications accepted. *Application Contact:* Peggy Eiseman, Administrative Assistant of Admissions, 412-396-5064, Fax: 412-396-5719, E-mail: eiseman@duq.edu. *Dean,* Dr. Edward W. Kocher, 412-396-6082, Fax: 412-396-1524, E-mail: kocher@duq.edu.

Mylan School of Pharmacy Students: 1,188 full-time (725 women), 17 part-time (13 women); includes 63 minority (17 Black or African American, non-Hispanic/Latino; 1 American Indian or Alaska Native, non-Hispanic/Latino; 33 Asian, non-Hispanic/Latino; 10 Hispanic/Latino; 2 Two or more races, non-Hispanic/Latino), 59 international. *Faculty:* 48 full-time (20 women), 2 part-time/adjunct (0 women). Expenses: Contact institution. In 2010, 178 first professional degrees, 2 master's, 7 doctorates awarded. Offers pharmacy (Pharm D, MS, PhD). *Application fee:* $50. *Application Contact:* Dr. J. Douglas Bricker, Dean, 412-396-6380. *Dean,* Dr. J. Douglas Bricker, 412-396-6380.

Graduate School of Pharmaceutical Sciences Students: 58 full-time (29 women), 1 part-time (0 women); includes 1 Black or African American, non-Hispanic/Latino, 43 international. 149 applicants, 15% accepted, 14 enrolled. *Faculty:* 22 full-time (7 women). Expenses: Contact institution. *Financial support:* In 2010–11, 10 research assistantships with full tuition reimbursements, 48 teaching assistantships with full tuition reimbursements were awarded; unspecified assistantships also available. In 2010, 2 master's, 7 doctorates awarded. Offers medicinal chemistry (MS, PhD); pharmaceutical administration (MS); pharmaceutics (MS, PhD); pharmacology (MS, PhD); pharmacy administration (MS). *Application deadline:* For fall admission, 2/1 priority date for domestic and international students; for spring admission, 10/1 priority date for domestic and international students. Applications are processed on a rolling basis. *Application fee:* $50. Electronic applications accepted. *Application Contact:* Information Contact, 412-396-1172, E-mail: gsps-adm@duq.edu. *Associate Dean for Research and Graduate Programs,* Dr. James K. Drennen, 412-396-5520.

School of Education Students: 609 full-time (444 women), 88 part-time (71 women); includes 35 Black or African American, non-Hispanic/Latino; 7 Asian, non-Hispanic/Latino; 8 Hispanic/Latino, 17 international. Average age 34. 559 applicants, 51% accepted, 149 enrolled. *Faculty:* 55 full-time (32 women), 35 part-time/adjunct (22 women). Expenses: Contact institution. *Financial support:* Research assistantships, teaching assistantships with tuition reimbursements, career-related internships or fieldwork, Federal Work-Study, institutionally sponsored loans, and tuition waivers available. Support available to part-time students. In 2010, 214 master's, 11 doctorates, 9 other advanced degrees awarded. *Degree program information:* Part-time and evening/weekend programs available. Offers child psychology (MS Ed); community counseling (MS Ed); community mental health (MS Ed); counselor education (MS Ed, Ed D); counselor education and supervision (Ed D); early childhood education (MS Ed); education (MS Ed, Ed D, PhD, CAGS, Post-Master's Certificate); educational leadership (Ed D); educational studies (MS Ed); elementary education (MS Ed); elementary education/early childhood (MS Ed); English as a second language (MS Ed); instructional technology

Duquesne University (continued)

(MS Ed, Ed D); marriage and family therapy (MS Ed); reading and language arts (MS Ed); school administration (MS Ed, Post-Master's Certificate); school administration and supervision (MS Ed, Post-Master's Certificate); school counseling (MS Ed); school psychology (MS Ed, PhD, CAGS); school supervision (MS Ed); secondary education (MS Ed); special education (MS Ed). *Application deadline:* For fall admission, 3/1 for domestic students; for spring admission, 9/1 for domestic students. Applications are processed on a rolling basis. *Application fee:* $0. Electronic applications accepted. *Application Contact:* Michael Dolinger, Director of Student and Academic Services, 412-396-6647, Fax: 412-396-5585, E-mail: dolingerm@duq.edu. *Dean*, Dr. Olga Welch, 412-396-6102, Fax: 412-396-5585.

School of Law Students: 687 full-time (329 women); includes 41 minority (15 Black or African American, non-Hispanic/Latino; 1 American Indian or Alaska Native, non-Hispanic/Latino; 10 Asian, non-Hispanic/Latino; 12 Hispanic/Latino; 3 Two or more races, non-Hispanic/Latino), 3 international. Average age 26. *Faculty:* 26 full-time (4 women), 51 part-time/adjunct (11 women). Expenses: Contact institution. *Financial support:* In 2010–11, 267 students received support; research assistantships, teaching assistantships, career-related internships or fieldwork, Federal Work-Study, scholarships/grants, and tuition waivers (partial) available. Support available to part-time students. Financial award application deadline: 5/31. In 2010, 204 first professional degrees, 1 master's awarded. *Degree program information:* Part-time and evening/weekend programs available. Offers law (JD, LL M). JD/M Div offered jointly with Pittsburgh Theological Seminary. *Application deadline:* For fall admission, 4/1 for domestic students. Applications are processed on a rolling basis. *Application fee:* $60. *Application Contact:* Joseph P. Campion, Director, Admissions, 412-396-6296, Fax: 412-396-6659, E-mail: campion@duq.edu. *Interim Dean*, Ken Gormley, 412-396-6300, Fax: 412-396-6659, E-mail: gormley@duq.edu.

School of Leadership and Professional Advancement Students: 275 full-time, 171 part-time; includes 20 Black or African American, non-Hispanic/Latino; 1 American Indian or Alaska Native, non-Hispanic/Latino; 6 Asian, non-Hispanic/Latino; 3 Hispanic/Latino. Average age 31. 161 applicants, 73% accepted, 103 enrolled. *Faculty:* 1 full-time (0 women), 70 part-time/adjunct (35 women). Expenses: Contact institution. *Financial support:* Applicants required to submit FAFSA. In 2010, 108 master's awarded. *Degree program information:* Part-time and evening/weekend programs available. Postbaccalaureate distance learning degree programs offered (no on-campus study). Offers leadership (MS). *Application deadline:* Applications are processed on a rolling basis. *Application fee:* $0. Electronic applications accepted. *Application Contact:* Marianne Leister, Director of Student Services, 412-396-4933, Fax: 412-396-5072, E-mail: leister@duq.edu. *Dean*, Dr. Dorothy Bassett, 412-396-2141, Fax: 412-396-4711, E-mail: bassettd@duq.edu.

School of Nursing Students: 127 full-time (122 women), 84 part-time (79 women); includes 23 minority (11 Black or African American, non-Hispanic/Latino; 1 American Indian or Alaska Native, non-Hispanic/Latino; 5 Asian, non-Hispanic/Latino; 6 Hispanic/Latino), 2 international. Average age 40. 120 applicants, 77% accepted, 71 enrolled. *Faculty:* 22 full-time (20 women), 5 part-time/adjunct (4 women). Expenses: Contact institution. *Financial support:* In 2010–11, 102 students received support, including 17 research assistantships with partial tuition reimbursements available (averaging $940 per year), 8 teaching assistantships with partial tuition reimbursements available (averaging $740 per year); institutionally sponsored loans, scholarships/grants, traineeships, tuition waivers (partial), and unspecified assistantships also available. Support available to part-time students. Financial award application deadline: 7/1; financial award applicants required to submit FAFSA. In 2010, 30 master's, 19 doctorates, 3 other advanced degrees awarded. *Degree program information:* Part-time and evening/weekend programs available. Postbaccalaureate distance learning degree programs offered (minimal on-campus study). Offers family nurse practitioner (MSN, Post-Master's Certificate); forensic nursing (MSN, Post-Master's Certificate); nursing (MSN, DNP, PhD, Post-Master's Certificate); nursing education (MSN); nursing practice (DNP); transcultural/international nursing (Post-Master's Certificate). *Application Contact:* Susan Hardner, Nurse Recruiter, 412-396-4945, Fax: 412-396-6346, E-mail: nursing@duq.edu. *Dean/Professor*, Dr. Eileen Zungolo, 412-396-6554, Fax: 412-396-5974, E-mail: zungolo@duq.edu.

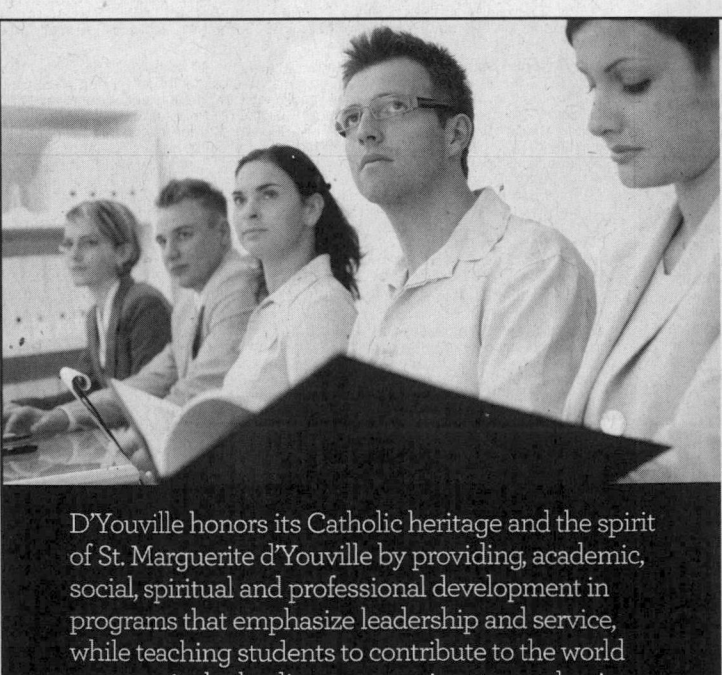

D'YOUVILLE COLLEGE, Buffalo, NY 14201-1084

General Information Independent, coed, comprehensive institution. *Enrollment:* 1,151 full-time matriculated graduate/professional students (816 women), 379 part-time matriculated graduate/professional students (305 women). *Enrollment by degree level:* 148 first professional, 1,290 master's, 75 doctoral, 17 other advanced degrees. *Tuition:* Part-time $790 per credit hour. Part-time tuition and fees vary according to degree level. *Graduate housing:* Room and/or apartments available on a first-come, first-served basis to single students; on-campus housing not available to married students. Housing application deadline: 8/1. *Student services:* Campus employment opportunities, campus safety program, career counseling, exercise/wellness program, free psychological counseling, grant writing training, international student services, low-cost health insurance, multicultural affairs office, services for students with disabilities, writing training. *Library facilities:* Montante Family Library. *Online resources:* library catalog, web page, access to other libraries' catalogs. *Collection:* 116,237 titles, 725 serial subscriptions, 3,668 audiovisual materials.

Computer facilities: 72 computers available on campus for general student use. A campuswide network can be accessed from student residence rooms and from off campus. Online class registration is available. *Web address:* http://www.dyc.edu/.

General Application Contact: Linda Fisher, Graduate Admissions Director, 716-829-8400, Fax: 716-829-7900, E-mail: graduateadmissions@dyc.edu.

GRADUATE UNITS

Department of Business Students: 63 full-time (46 women), 31 part-time (15 women); includes 24 minority (14 Black or African American, non-Hispanic/Latino; 2 American Indian or Alaska Native, non-Hispanic/Latino; 1 Asian, non-Hispanic/Latino; 6 Hispanic/Latino; 1 Two or more races, non-Hispanic/Latino), 19 international. Average age 30. 86 applicants, 62% accepted, 22 enrolled. *Faculty:* 4 full-time (1 woman), 7 part-time/adjunct (2 women). Expenses: Contact institution. *Financial support:* In 2010–11, 1 research assistantship with partial tuition reimbursement (averaging $3,000 per year) was awarded; career-related internships or fieldwork, Federal Work-Study, and scholarships/grants also available. Support available to part-time students. Financial award application deadline: 3/1; financial award applicants required to submit FAFSA. In 2010, 19 master's awarded. *Degree program information:* Part-time and evening/weekend programs available. Offers business administration (MBA); international business (MS). *Application deadline:* For fall admission, 5/1 priority date for international students; for spring admission, 9/1 priority date for international students. Applications are processed on a rolling basis. *Application fee:* $25. Electronic applications accepted. *Application Contact:* Linda Fisher, Graduate Admissions Director, 716-829-8400, Fax: 716-829-7900, E-mail: graduateadmissions@dyc.edu. *Chair*, Dr. Susan Kowalewski, 716-829-7839, Fax: 716-829-7760.

Department of Dietetics Students: 64 full-time (60 women), 9 part-time (all women); includes 4 minority (1 Black or African American, non-Hispanic/Latino; 1 American Indian or Alaska Native, non-Hispanic/Latino; 1 Asian, non-Hispanic/Latino; 1 Two or more races, non-Hispanic/Latino), 4 international. Average age 24. 106 applicants, 61% accepted, 18 enrolled. *Faculty:* 2 full-time (1 woman), 3 part-time/adjunct (all women). Expenses: Contact institution. In 2010, 10 master's awarded. Offers dietetics (MS). Five-year program begins at freshman entry. *Application deadline:* For fall admission, 5/1 priority date for international students; for spring admission, 9/1 priority date for international students. Applications are processed on a rolling basis. *Application fee:* $25. Electronic applications accepted. *Application Contact:* Dr. Steven Smith, Director of Admissions, 716-829-7600, Fax: 716-829-7900, E-mail: admiss@dyc.edu. *Chair*, Dr. Charlotte Baumgart, 716-829-7752, Fax: 716-829-8137.

Department of Education Students: 302 full-time (208 women), 52 part-time (37 women); includes 13 minority (7 Black or African American, non-Hispanic/Latino; 1 American Indian or Alaska Native, non-Hispanic/Latino; 2 Asian, non-Hispanic/Latino; 3 Hispanic/Latino), 235 international. Average age 30. 354 applicants, 45% accepted, 96 enrolled. *Faculty:* 29 full-time (18 women), 29 part-time/adjunct (17 women). Expenses: Contact institution. *Financial support:* In 2010–11, 1 research assistantship with partial tuition reimbursement (averaging $3,000 per year) was awarded; career-related internships or fieldwork, Federal Work-Study, institutionally sponsored loans, scholarships/grants, tuition waivers (full and partial), and unspecified assistantships also available. Support available to part-time students. Financial award application deadline: 3/1; financial award applicants required to submit FAFSA. In 2010, 296 master's, 4 other advanced degrees awarded. *Degree program information:* Part-time and evening/weekend programs available. Offers elementary education (MS Ed, Teaching Certificate); secondary education (MS Ed, Teaching Certificate); special education (MS Ed). *Application deadline:* For fall admission, 5/1 priority date for international students; for spring admission, 9/1 priority date for international students. Applications are processed on a rolling basis. *Application fee:* $25. Electronic applications accepted. *Application Contact:* Linda Fisher, Graduate Admissions Director, 716-829-8400, Fax: 716-829-7900, E-mail: graduateadmissions@dyc.edu. *Chair*, Dr. David Gorlewski, 716-829-8140, Fax: 716-829-7660.

Department of Health Services Administration Students: 21 full-time (17 women), 52 part-time (45 women); includes 21 minority (20 Black or African American, non-Hispanic/Latino; 1 Hispanic/Latino), 14 international. Average age 36. 48 applicants, 63% accepted, 22 enrolled. *Faculty:* 4 full-time (2 women), 4 part-time/adjunct (0 women). Expenses: Contact institution. *Financial support:* In 2010–11, 1 research assistantship with partial tuition reimbursement (averaging $3,000 per year) was awarded; career-related internships or fieldwork, Federal Work-Study, and scholarships/grants also available. Support available to part-time students. Financial award application deadline: 3/1; financial award applicants required to submit FAFSA. In 2010, 9 master's awarded. *Degree program information:* Part-time and evening/weekend programs available. Offers clinical research associate (Certificate); health services administration (MS, Certificate); long term care administration (Certificate). *Application deadline:* For fall admission, 5/1 priority date for international students; for spring admission, 9/1 priority date for international students. Applications are processed on a rolling basis. *Application fee:* $25. Electronic applications accepted. *Application Contact:* Linda Fisher, Graduate Admissions Director, 716-829-8400, Fax: 716-829-7900, E-mail: graduateadmissions@dyc.edu. *Chair*, Dr. Walter Iwanenko, 716-829-7612, Fax: 716-829-8184.

Department of Holistic Health Studies Students: 81 full-time (36 women), 5 part-time (3 women); includes 8 minority (5 Black or African American, non-Hispanic/Latino; 3 Asian, non-Hispanic/Latino), 17 international. Average age 27. 62 applicants, 58% accepted, 13 enrolled. *Faculty:* 10 full-time (2 women), 23 part-time/adjunct (6 women). Expenses: Contact institution. In 2010, 18 DCs awarded. Offers chiropractic (DC). *Application deadline:* Applications are processed on a rolling basis. *Application fee:* $25. Electronic applications accepted. *Application Contact:* Linda Fisher, Graduate Admissions Director, 716-829-8400, Fax: 716-829-7900, E-mail: graduateadmissions@dyc.edu. *Executive Director, Chiropractic Department*, Dr. Kathleen Linaker, 716-829-7725 Ext. 7793, Fax: 716-829-7893.

Department of Physical Therapy Students: 130 full-time (68 women), 14 part-time (7 women); includes 10 minority (8 Black or African American, non-Hispanic/Latino; 1 Asian, non-Hispanic/Latino; 1 Two or more races, non-Hispanic/Latino), 52 international. Average age 25. 184 applicants, 53% accepted, 53 enrolled. *Faculty:* 7 full-time (4 women), 4 part-time/adjunct (3 women). Expenses: Contact institution. *Financial support:* In 2010–11, 3 research assistantships with partial tuition reimbursements were awarded; Federal Work-Study and scholarships/grants also available. Financial award application deadline: 3/1; financial award applicants required to submit FAFSA. In 2010, 42 doctorates awarded. *Degree program information:* Part-time programs available. Postbaccalaureate distance learning degree programs offered (minimal on-campus study). Offers advanced orthopedic physical therapy (Certificate); manual physical therapy (Certificate); physical therapy (MPT, MS, DPT). *Application deadline:* For fall admission, 5/1 priority date for international students; for spring admission, 9/1 priority date for international students. Applications are processed on a rolling basis. *Application fee:* $25. Electronic applications accepted. *Application Contact:* Linda Fisher, Graduate Admissions Director, 716-829-8400, Fax: 716-829-7900, E-mail: graduateadmissions@dyc.edu. *Chair*, Dr. Lynn Rivers, 716-829-7708 Ext. 7708, Fax: 716-829-8137, E-mail: riversl@dyc.edu.

Doctoral Programs Students: 16 full-time (10 women), 50 part-time (39 women); includes 3 minority (2 Black or African American, non-Hispanic/Latino; 1 Asian, non-Hispanic/Latino), 16 international. Average age 46. 26 applicants, 62% accepted, 12 enrolled. *Faculty:* 6 full-time (2 women), 23 part-time/adjunct (13 women). Expenses: Contact institution. *Financial support:* In 2010–11, research assistantships with tuition reimbursements (averaging $3,000 per year); scholarships/grants also available. In 2010, 9 doctorates awarded. *Degree program information:* Part-time and evening/weekend programs available. Offers educational leadership (Ed D); health education (Ed D); health policy (Ed D). *Application Contact:* Linda Fisher, Graduate Admissions Director, 716-829-8400, Fax: 716-829-7900, E-mail: graduateadmissions@dyc.edu. *Director of Doctoral Programs*, Dr. Mark Garrison, 716-829-8125, E-mail: garrisonm@dyc.edu.

Occupational Therapy Department Students: 152 full-time (138 women), 16 part-time (15 women); includes 18 minority (8 Black or African American, non-Hispanic/Latino; 1 American Indian or Alaska Native, non-Hispanic/Latino; 2 Asian, non-Hispanic/Latino; 4 Hispanic/Latino; 3 Two or more races, non-Hispanic/Latino), 28 international. Average age 24. 215 applicants, 67% accepted, 64 enrolled. *Faculty:* 8 full-time (all women), 2 part-time/adjunct (both women). Expenses: Contact institution. *Financial support:* In 2010–11, 1 research assistantship with partial tuition reimbursement (averaging $3,000 per year) was awarded; scholarships/grants, tuition waivers (partial), and unspecified assistantships also available. In 2010, 30 master's awarded. Offers occupational therapy (MS). *Application deadline:* For fall admission, 5/1 priority date for international students; for spring admission, 9/1 priority date for international students. Applications are processed on a rolling basis. *Application fee:* $25. Electronic applications accepted. *Application Contact:* Linda Fisher, Graduate Admissions Director, 716-829-8400, Fax: 716-829-7900, E-mail: graduateadmissions@dyc.edu. *Chair*, Dr. Amy Nwora, 716-829-7707, Fax: 716-829-8137.

Physician Assistant Department Students: 163 full-time (117 women), 5 part-time (all women); includes 16 minority (3 Black or African American, non-Hispanic/Latino; 3 American Indian or Alaska Native, non-Hispanic/Latino; 6 Asian, non-Hispanic/Latino; 4 Hispanic/Latino), 8 international. Average age 27. 248 applicants, 23% accepted, 32 enrolled. *Faculty:* 5 full-time (4 women), 1 part-time/adjunct (0 women). Expenses: Contact institution. In 2010, 29 master's awarded. Offers physician assistant (MS). *Application deadline:* For fall admission, 5/1 priority date for international students; for spring admission, 9/1 priority date for international students. Applications are processed on a rolling basis. *Application fee:* $25. Electronic applications accepted. *Application Contact:* Linda Fisher, Graduate Admissions Director, 716-829-8400, Fax: 716-829-7900, E-mail: graduateadmissions@dyc.edu. *Chair*, Dr. Maureen F. Finney, 716-829-7730, E-mail: finneym@dyc.edu.

School of Nursing Students: 97 full-time (90 women), 145 part-time (130 women); includes 34 minority (30 Black or African American, non-Hispanic/Latino; 3 Hispanic/Latino; 1 Two or more races, non-Hispanic/Latino), 105 international. Average age 35. 288 applicants, 46% accepted, 58 enrolled. *Faculty:* 7 full-time (all women), 7 part-time/adjunct (6 women). Expenses: Contact institution. *Financial support:* Federal Work-Study, scholarships/grants, traineeships, and unspecified assistantships available. Support available to part-time students. Financial award application deadline: 3/1; financial award applicants required to submit FAFSA. In 2010, 50 master's, 4 other advanced degrees awarded. *Degree program information:* Part-time programs available. Offers community health nursing/education (MSN); community health nursing/management (MSN); family nurse practitioner (MS, Post-Master's Certificate); nursing and health-related professions (Certificate); nursing with clinical focus choice (MSN). *Application deadline:* For fall admission, 5/1 priority date for international students; for spring admission, 9/1 priority date for international students. Applications are processed on a rolling basis. *Application fee:* $25. Electronic applications accepted. *Application Contact:* Linda Fisher, Graduate Admissions Director, 716-829-8400, Fax: 716-829-7900, E-mail: graduateadmissions@dyc.edu. *Chair*, Dr. Abigail Mitchell, 716-829-8218, Fax: 716-829-8159.

School of Pharmacy Students: 62 full-time (26 women); includes 10 minority (2 Black or African American, non-Hispanic/Latino; 5 Asian, non-Hispanic/Latino; 2 Hispanic/Latino; 1 Two or more races, non-Hispanic/Latino), 2 international. Average age 24. 6 applicants, 67% accepted, 3 enrolled. Expenses: Contact institution. Offers pharmacy (Pharm D). *Application Contact:* Linda Fisher, Graduate Admissions Director, 716-829-8400, Fax: 716-829-7900, E-mail: graduateadmissions@dyc.edu. *Assistant Dean of Faculty and Student Affairs*, Dr. Canio Marasco, 716-829-7846, Fax: 716-829-7760, E-mail: pharmacyadmissions@dyc.edu.

See Display on previous page and Close-Up on page 941.

EARLHAM COLLEGE, Richmond, IN 47374-4095

General Information Independent-religious, coed, comprehensive institution. *Graduate housing:* On-campus housing not available.

GRADUATE UNITS

Graduate Programs Offers education (M Ed, MAT).

EARLHAM SCHOOL OF RELIGION, Richmond, IN 47374-5360

General Information Independent-religious, coed, graduate-only institution. *Enrollment by degree level:* 119 first professional, 30 master's. *Graduate faculty:* 9 full-time (4 women), 8 part-time/adjunct (5 women). *Graduate housing:* On-campus housing not available. *Student services:* Campus employment opportunities, campus safety program, career counseling, exercise/wellness program, international student services, low-cost health insurance. *Library facilities:* Lilly Library plus 2 others. *Online resources:* library catalog, web page, access to other libraries' catalogs. *Collection:* 406,699 titles, 24,708 serial subscriptions, 56,384 audiovisual materials.

Computer facilities: 125 computers available on campus for general student use. A campuswide network can be accessed from student residence rooms and from off campus. Online class registration is available. *Web address:* http://www.esr.earlham.edu/.

General Application Contact: Valerie Neverman, Director of Recruitment and Admissions, 765-983-1523, Fax: 765-983-1688, E-mail: neverva@earlham.edu.

GRADUATE UNITS

Graduate Programs Students: 111 full-time (71 women), 38 part-time (21 women); includes 2 Black or African American, non-Hispanic/Latino; 1 American Indian or Alaska Native, non-Hispanic/Latino; 1 Asian, non-Hispanic/Latino; 3 Hispanic/Latino, 6 international. Average age 45. 37 applicants, 97% accepted, 34 enrolled. *Faculty:* 9 full-time (4 women), 8 part-time/adjunct (5 women). Expenses: Contact institution. *Financial support:* Scholarships/grants and tuition waivers (full and partial) available. Financial award application deadline: 4/15; financial award applicants required to submit FAFSA. In 2010, 15 first professional degrees, 2 master's awarded. *Degree program information:* Part-time programs available. Postbaccalaureate distance learning degree programs offered (minimal on-campus study). Offers religion (MA); theology (M Div, M Min). *Application deadline:* For fall admission, 7/15 priority date for domestic students; for winter admission, 12/15 priority date for domestic students. Applications are processed on a rolling basis. *Application fee:* $35. Electronic applications accepted. *Application Contact:* Valerie K. Hurwitz, Director of Recruitment and Admissions, 800-432-1377, Fax: 765-983-1688, E-mail: hurwiva@earlham.edu. *Dean*, Jay W. Marshall, 800-432-1377, Fax: 765-983-1688, E-mail: marshja@earlham.edu.

EAST CAROLINA UNIVERSITY, Greenville, NC 27858-4353

General Information State-supported, coed, university. CGS member. *Enrollment:* 2,562 full-time matriculated graduate/professional students (1,637 women), 2,950 part-time matriculated graduate/professional students (2,035 women). *Enrollment by degree level:* 399 first professional, 4,658 master's, 410 doctoral, 45 other advanced degrees. *Graduate faculty:* 1,053 full-time (451 women), 53 part-time/adjunct (26 women). Tuition, state resident: full-time $3130; part-time $391.25 per credit hour. Tuition, nonresident: full-time $13,817; part-time $1727.13 per credit hour. *Required fees:* $1916; $239.50 per credit hour. Tuition and fees vary according to campus/location and program. *Graduate housing:* Room and/or apartments available on a first-come, first-served basis to single students; on-campus housing not available to married students. Typical cost: $4819 per year ($8104 including board). Housing application deadline: 5/1. *Student services:* Campus employment opportunities, campus safety program, career counseling, exercise/wellness program, free psychological counseling, grant writing training, international student services, low-cost health insurance, multicultural affairs office, services for students with disabilities, teacher training, writing training. *Library facilities:* Joyner Library. *Online resources:* library catalog, web page.

Computer facilities: Computer purchase and lease plans are available. A campuswide network can be accessed from student residence rooms and from off campus. Online class registration is available. *Web address:* http://www.ecu.edu/.

General Application Contact: Robin Armstrong, Director of Admissions, 252-328-6012, Fax: 252-328-6071, E-mail: gradschool@ecu.edu.

GRADUATE UNITS

Brody School of Medicine Offers anatomy and cell biology (PhD); biochemistry and molecular biology (PhD); medicine (MD, MPH, PhD); microbiology and immunology (PhD); Pathology (PhD); pharmacology (PhD); physiology (PhD); public health (MPH).

Graduate School *Degree program information:* Part-time and evening/weekend programs available. Postbaccalaureate distance learning degree programs offered (no on-campus study). Offers coastal resources management (PhD).

College of Business *Degree program information:* Part-time and evening/weekend programs available. Offers accounting (MS); business (MBA, MS, MSA); management (MBA).

College of Education *Degree program information:* Part-time and evening/weekend programs available. Postbaccalaureate distance learning degree programs offered (no on-campus study). Offers adult education (MA Ed); behavior/emotional disabilities (MA Ed); counselor education (MS, Ed S); education (MA, MA Ed, MLS, MS, MSA, Ed D, CAS, Ed S); educational administration and supervision (Ed S); educational leadership (Ed D); elementary education (MA Ed); English education (MA Ed); higher education administration (Ed D); information technologies (MS); instruction technology specialist (MA Ed); learning disabilities (MA Ed); library science (MLS, CAS); low incidence disabilities (MA Ed); mathematics (MA Ed); mental retardation (MA Ed); middle grade education (MA Ed); reading education (MA Ed); school administration (MSA); science education (MA, MA Ed); social studies education (MA Ed); supervision (MA Ed); vocation education (MA Ed).

College of Fine Arts and Communication Offers art and design (MA, MA Ed, MFA); fine arts and communication (MA, MA Ed, MFA, MM); health communication (MA); music education (MM); music therapy (MM); performance (MM); theory and composition (MM).

College of Health and Human Performance *Degree program information:* Part-time and evening/weekend programs available. Offers bioenergetics (PhD); environmental health (MS); exercise and sport science (MA, MA Ed); health and human performance (MA, MA Ed, MS, PhD); health education (MA, MA Ed); recreation and leisure services administration (MS); therapeutic recreation administration (MS).

College of Human Ecology *Degree program information:* Part-time programs available. Offers child development and family relations (MS); criminal justice (MS); human ecology (MS, MSW); marriage and family therapy (MS); nutrition (MS); social work (MSW).

College of Nursing *Degree program information:* Part-time programs available. Offers nursing (MSN, PhD).

College of Technology and Computer Science *Degree program information:* Part-time programs available. Offers computer network professional (Certificate); computer science (MS); industrial technology (MS); information assurance (Certificate); occupational safety (MS); technology and computer science (MS, PhD, Certificate); technology management (PhD); Website developer (Certificate).

School of Allied Health Sciences *Degree program information:* Part-time and evening/weekend programs available. Postbaccalaureate distance learning degree programs offered (no on-campus study). Offers allied health sciences (MPT, MS, MSOT, DPT, PhD); communication sciences and disorders (PhD); occupational therapy (MSOT); physical therapy (MPT, DPT); physician assistant studies (MS); rehabilitation counseling (MS); speech, language and auditory pathology (MS); substance abuse and clinical counseling (MS); vocational evaluation (MS).

Thomas Harriot College of Arts and Sciences *Degree program information:* Part-time and evening/weekend programs available. Offers American history (MA); anthropology (MA); applied and biomedical physics (MS); applied mathematics (MA); applied resource econom-

East Carolina University (continued)

ics (MS); arts and sciences (MA, MA Ed, MPA, MS, PhD); biology (MS); chemistry (MS); clinical psychology (MA); English (MA); European history (MA); general psychology (MA); geography (MA); geology (MS); health psychology (PhD); international studies (MA); maritime history (MA); mathematics (MA); medical physics (MS); molecular biology/biotechnology (MS); physics (PhD); public administration (MPA); sociology (MA).

EAST CENTRAL UNIVERSITY, Ada, OK 74820-6899

General Information State-supported, coed, comprehensive institution. CGS member. *Graduate housing:* Rooms and/or apartments available on a first-come, first-served basis to single and married students.

GRADUATE UNITS

School of Graduate Studies *Degree program information:* Part-time and evening/weekend programs available. Offers administration (MSHR); counseling (MSHR); criminal justice (MSHR); education (M Ed); psychology (MSPS); rehabilitation counseling (MSHR). Electronic applications accepted.

EASTERN CONNECTICUT STATE UNIVERSITY, Willimantic, CT 06226-2295

General Information State-supported, coed, comprehensive institution. *Enrollment:* 63 full-time matriculated graduate/professional students (43 women), 176 part-time matriculated graduate/professional students (122 women). *Enrollment by degree level:* 239 master's. *Graduate faculty:* 11 full-time (6 women), 16 part-time/adjunct (10 women). Tuition, state resident: full-time $5012; part-time $3440 per year. Tuition, nonresident: full-time $13,962; part-time $3488 per year. *Required fees:* $4147; $80 per semester. *Graduate housing:* On-campus housing not available. *Student services:* Campus employment opportunities, campus safety program, career counseling, child daycare facilities, exercise/wellness program, free psychological counseling, grant writing training, international student services, low-cost health insurance, multicultural affairs office, services for students with disabilities, teacher training, writing training. *Library facilities:* J. Eugene Smith Library. *Online resources:* library catalog, web page, access to other libraries' catalogs. *Collection:* 239,218 titles, 1,729 serial subscriptions. *Research affiliation:* Department of Education (early childhood education, mathematics and science education).

Computer facilities: Computer purchase and lease plans are available. 637 computers available on campus for general student use. A campuswide network can be accessed from student residence rooms and from off campus. Online class registration is available. *Web address:* http://www.easternct.edu/.

General Application Contact: Graduate Division, School of Education and Professional Studies, 860-465-5292, E-mail: graduateadmissions@easternct.edu.

GRADUATE UNITS

School of Education and Professional Studies/Graduate Division Students: 64 full-time (43 women), 175 part-time (122 women); includes 18 minority (7 Black or African American, non-Hispanic/Latino; 2 Asian, non-Hispanic/Latino; 9 Hispanic/Latino), 2 international. Average age 33. 89 applicants, 62% accepted, 51 enrolled. *Faculty:* 11 full-time (6 women), 16 part-time/adjunct (10 women). Expenses: Contact institution. *Financial support:* Teaching assistantships, career-related internships or fieldwork, scholarships/grants, and unspecified assistantships available. Support available to part-time students. Financial award application deadline: 3/15. In 2010, 99 master's awarded. *Degree program information:* Part-time and evening/weekend programs available. Offers early childhood education (MS); education and professional studies (MS); educational technology (MS); elementary education (MS); organizational management (MS); reading and language arts (MS); science education (MS); secondary education (MS). *Application deadline:* For fall admission, 7/6 priority date for domestic and international students; for spring admission, 11/3 priority date for domestic and international students. Applications are processed on a rolling basis. *Application fee:* $50. *Application Contact:* Graduate Division, School of Education and Professional Studies, 860-465-5292, E-mail: graduateadmissions@easternct.edu. *Dean,* Dr. Patricia A. Kleine, 860-465-5293, Fax: 860-465-4538, E-mail: kleinep@easternct.edu.

EASTERN ILLINOIS UNIVERSITY, Charleston, IL 61920-3099

General Information State-supported, coed, comprehensive institution. CGS member. *Graduate housing:* Rooms and/or apartments available to single and married students.

GRADUATE UNITS

Graduate School *Degree program information:* Part-time and evening/weekend programs available. Electronic applications accepted.

College of Arts and Humanities *Degree program information:* Part-time programs available. Offers art (MA); art education (MA); arts and humanities (MA); communication studies (MA); English (MA); historical administration (MA); history (MA); music (MA).

College of Education and Professional Studies *Degree program information:* Part-time and evening/weekend programs available. Offers clinical counseling (MS); college student affairs (MS); education and professional studies (MS, MS Ed, Ed S); educational leadership (MS Ed, Ed S); elementary education (MS Ed); kinesiology and sports studies (MS); school counseling (MS); special education (MS Ed).

College of Sciences *Degree program information:* Part-time programs available. Offers biological sciences (MS); chemistry (MS); clinical psychology (MA); communication disorders and sciences (MS); economics (MA); mathematics (MA); mathematics and computer science (MA); mathematics education (MA); natural sciences (MS); political science (MA); psychology (MA, SSP); school psychology (SSP).

Lumpkin College of Business and Applied Sciences *Degree program information:* Part-time and evening/weekend programs available. Offers accountancy (MBA, Certificate); business and applied sciences (MA, MBA, MS, Certificate); computer technology (Certificate); dietetics (MS); family and consumer sciences (MS); general management (MBA); gerontology (MA); quality systems (Certificate); technology (MS); technology security (Certificate); work performance improvement (Certificate).

EASTERN KENTUCKY UNIVERSITY, Richmond, KY 40475-3102

General Information State-supported, coed, comprehensive institution. CGS member. *Graduate housing:* Rooms and/or apartments guaranteed to single students and available to married students.

GRADUATE UNITS

The Graduate School *Degree program information:* Part-time and evening/weekend programs available. Postbaccalaureate distance learning degree programs offered. Electronic applications accepted.

College of Arts and Sciences *Degree program information:* Part-time and evening/weekend programs available. Offers arts and sciences (MA, MFA, MM, MPA, MS, PhD, Psy S); biological sciences (MS); chemistry (MS); choral conducting (MM); clinical psychology (MS); community development (MPA); community health administration (MPA); creative writing (MFA); ecology (MS); English (MA); general public administration (MPA); geology (MS, PhD); history (MA); industrial/organizational psychology (MS); mathematical sciences (MS); performance (MM); political science (MA); school psychology (Psy S); theory/composition (MM).

College of Business and Technology *Degree program information:* Part-time programs available. Offers business administration (MBA); business and technology (MBA, MS); industrial education (MS); industrial technology (MS); occupational training and development (MS); technical administration (MS); technology education (MS).

College of Education *Degree program information:* Part-time programs available. Postbaccalaureate distance learning degree programs offered (minimal on-campus study). Offers communication disorders (MA Ed); education (MA, MA Ed, MAT); elementary education (MA Ed); human services (MA); instructional leadership (MA Ed); library science (MA Ed); mental health counseling (MA); music education (MA Ed); school counseling (MA Ed); secondary and higher education (MA Ed); secondary education (MA Ed); teaching (MAT).

College of Health Sciences *Degree program information:* Part-time programs available. Offers community health (MPH); community nutrition (MS); environmental health science (MPH); exercise and sport science (MS); exercise and wellness (MS); health sciences (MPH, MS, MSN); occupational therapy (MS); recreation and park administration (MS); rural community health care (MSN); rural health family nurse practitioner (MSN); sports administration (MS).

College of Justice and Safety *Degree program information:* Part-time programs available. Offers correctional and juvenile justice studies (MS); criminal justice (MS); criminal justice education (MS); justice and safety (MS); loss prevention and safety (MS); police studies (MS).

EASTERN MENNONITE UNIVERSITY, Harrisonburg, VA 22802-2462

General Information Independent-religious, coed, comprehensive institution. *Graduate housing:* Rooms and/or apartments available on a first-come, first-served basis to single and married students. Housing application deadline: 4/15.

GRADUATE UNITS

Eastern Mennonite Seminary *Degree program information:* Part-time programs available. Offers church leadership (MA); divinity (M Div); ministry studies (Certificate); online theological studies (Certificate); religion (MA); theological studies (Certificate).

Program in Business Administration *Degree program information:* Part-time and evening/weekend programs available. Offers business administration (MBA).

Program in Conflict Transformation *Degree program information:* Part-time programs available. Offers conflict transformation (MA, Graduate Certificate). Electronic applications accepted.

Program in Counseling *Degree program information:* Part-time programs available. Offers counseling (MA).

Program in Education *Degree program information:* Part-time programs available. Offers education (MA).

EASTERN MICHIGAN UNIVERSITY, Ypsilanti, MI 48197

General Information State-supported, coed, comprehensive institution. CGS member. *Enrollment:* 23,504 graduate, professional, and undergraduate students; 1,057 full-time matriculated graduate/professional students (630 women), 3,649 part-time matriculated graduate/professional students (2,333 women). *Enrollment by degree level:* 3,881 master's, 236 doctoral, 589 other advanced degrees. *Graduate faculty:* 669 full-time (314 women). *Graduate housing:* Rooms and/or apartments available on a first-come, first-served basis to single and married students. *Student services:* Campus employment opportunities, campus safety program, career counseling, child daycare facilities, exercise/wellness program, free psychological counseling, grant writing training, international student services, low-cost health insurance, multicultural affairs office, services for students with disabilities, teacher training, writing training. *Library facilities:* Bruce T. Halle Library. *Online resources:* library catalog, web page, access to other libraries' catalogs. *Collection:* 1.1 million titles, 7,547 serial subscriptions, 17,025 audiovisual materials. *Research affiliation:* TRACO (coatings research), 3M (coatings research), Toyota (coatings research), Beckers-Fusion (coatings research), Dima-Shield (coatings research), Signal Medical Corporation (textiles research).

Computer facilities: 1,500 computers available on campus for general student use. A campuswide network can be accessed from student residence rooms. Online class registration is available. *Web address:* http://www.emich.edu/.

General Application Contact: Graduate Admissions, 734-487-2400, Fax: 734-487-6559, E-mail: graduate.admissions@emich.edu.

GRADUATE UNITS

Graduate School Students: 1,057 full-time (630 women), 3,649 part-time (2,333 women); includes 940 minority (680 Black or African American, non-Hispanic/Latino; 29 American Indian or Alaska Native, non-Hispanic/Latino; 114 Asian, non-Hispanic/Latino; 92 Hispanic/Latino; 5 Native Hawaiian or other Pacific Islander, non-Hispanic/Latino; 20 Two or more races, non-Hispanic/Latino), 443 international. Average age 33. 3,893 applicants, 53% accepted, 1287 enrolled. *Faculty:* 669 full-time (314 women). Expenses: Contact institution. *Financial support:* In 2010–11, 1,346 students received support; fellowships, research assistantships with full tuition reimbursements available, teaching assistantships with full tuition reimbursements available, career-related internships or fieldwork, Federal Work-Study, institutionally sponsored loans, scholarships/grants, tuition waivers (partial), and unspecified assistantships available. Support available to part-time students. Financial award applicants required to submit FAFSA. In 2010, 1,212 master's, 21 doctorates, 239 other advanced degrees awarded. *Degree program information:* Part-time and evening/weekend programs available. Postbaccalaureate distance learning degree programs offered (minimal on-campus study). *Application deadline:* For fall admission, 2/15 priority date for domestic students, 5/1 priority date for international students; for winter admission, 10/15 priority date for domestic students, 10/1 priority date for international students; for spring admission, 3/15 priority date for domestic students, 3/1 priority date for international students. Applications are processed on a rolling basis. *Application fee:* $35. Electronic applications accepted. *Application Contact:* Dr. Deborah deLaski-Smith, Interim Dean, 734-487-0042, Fax: 734-487-0050, E-mail: deb.delaski-smith@emich.edu. *Interim Dean,* Dr. Deborah deLaski-Smith, 734-487-0042, Fax: 734-487-0050, E-mail: deb.delaski-smith@emich.edu.

Academic Affairs Division Students: 36 full-time (28 women), 49 part-time (35 women); includes 24 minority (20 Black or African American, non-Hispanic/Latino; 2 American Indian or Alaska Native, non-Hispanic/Latino; 1 Asian, non-Hispanic/Latino; 1 Hispanic/Latino), 1 international. Average age 32. 444 applicants, 77% accepted. Expenses: Contact institution. In 2010, 34 master's awarded. Offers individualized studies (MA, MS); integrated marketing communications (MS). *Application Contact:* Dr. Deborah de Laski-Smith, Interim Dean, 734-487-0042, Fax: 734-487-0050, E-mail: deb.delaski-smith@emich.edu. *Interim Dean,* Dr. Deborah de Laski-Smith, 734-487-0042, Fax: 734-487-0050, E-mail: deb.delaski-smith@emich.edu.

College of Arts and Sciences Students: 333 full-time (195 women), 876 part-time (510 women); includes 195 minority (127 Black or African American, non-Hispanic/Latino; 6 American Indian or Alaska Native, non-Hispanic/Latino; 24 Asian, non-Hispanic/Latino; 30 Hispanic/Latino; 8 Two or more races, non-Hispanic/Latino), 141 international. Average age 32. 1,124 applicants, 49% accepted, 347 enrolled. *Faculty:* 363 full-time (149 women). Expenses: Contact institution. *Financial support:* Fellowships, research assistantships with full tuition reimbursements, teaching assistantships with full tuition reimbursements, career-related internships or fieldwork, Federal Work-Study, institutionally sponsored loans, and tuition waivers (partial) available. Support available to part-time students. Financial award applicants required to submit FAFSA. In 2010, 300 master's, 9 doctorates, 35 other advanced degrees awarded. *Degree program information:* Part-time and evening/weekend programs available. Offers African-American studies (Graduate Certificate); applied economics (MA); applied statistics (MA); art (MA); art education (MA); artificial intelligence (Graduate Certificate); arts administration (MA); arts and sciences (MA, MFA, MLS, MM, MPA, MS, PhD, Graduate Certificate); cell and molecular biology (MS); chemistry (MS); children's literature (MA); clinical behavioral psychology (MS); clinical psychology (MS, PhD); communication (MA); community college biology teaching (MS); computer science (MA, MS); creative writing (MA); criminology and criminal justice (MA); drama/theatre for the young (MA, MFA); earth science education (MS); ecology and organismal biology (MS); economics (MA); English linguistics (MA); English studies for teachers (MA); experimental psychology (MS); foreign languages (MA, Graduate Certificate); French (MA); general biology (MS); general science (MS); geographic information systems (MS, Graduate Certificate); geography (MA, MS); geography and geology (MA, MS, Graduate Certificate); German (MA); German for business (Graduate Certificate); gerontology-dementia (Graduate Certificate); GIS educator (Graduate Certificate); GIS professional (Graduate Certificate); GIS-planning (MS); health economics (MA); heritage interpretation and tourism (MS); Hispanic language and cultures (Graduate Certificate); historic preservation (MS, Graduate Certificate); history (MA, Graduate Certificate); international economics and development

(MA); interpretation/performance studies (MA); Japanese business practices (Graduate Certificate); language and international trade (MA); language technology (Graduate Certificate); literature (MA, Graduate Certificate); local government management (Graduate Certificate); management of public healthcare services (Graduate Certificate); mathematics (MA); mathematics education (MA); music composition (MM); music education (MM); music pedagogy (MM); music performance (MM); physics (MS); physics education (MS); public administration (MPA, Graduate Certificate); public budget management (Graduate Certificate); public land planning (Graduate Certificate); public management (Graduate Certificate); public personnel management (Graduate Certificate); public policy analysis (Graduate Certificate); schools, society and violence (MA); social science (MA, Graduate Certificate); social science and American culture (MLS); social sciences (MA, MLS, Graduate Certificate); sociology (MA); sociology—family specialty (MA); Spanish (MA); state and local history (Graduate Certificate); studio art (MA, MFA); teaching English to speakers of other languages (MA, Graduate Certificate); teaching of writing (MA, Graduate Certificate); technical communications (MA, Graduate Certificate); theatre arts (MA); theatre arts-arts administration (MA); trade and development (MA); urban and regional planning (MS); water resources (MS, Graduate Certificate); women's and gender studies (MA, Graduate Certificate); written communication (MA, Graduate Certificate); written communications (MA). *Application deadline:* Applications are processed on a rolling basis. *Application fee:* $35. *Application Contact:* Dr. Thomas Venner, Dean, 734-487-4344, Fax: 734-485-9592, E-mail: tom.venner@emich.edu. *Dean*, Dr. Thomas Venner, 734-487-4344, Fax: 734-485-9592, E-mail: tom.venner@emich.edu.

College of Business Students: 218 full-time (103 women), 578 part-time (311 women); includes 186 minority (130 Black or African American, non-Hispanic/Latino; 5 American Indian or Alaska Native, non-Hispanic/Latino; 40 Asian, non-Hispanic/Latino; 11 Hispanic/Latino), 138 international. Average age 31. 481 applicants, 61% accepted, 193 enrolled. *Faculty:* 73 full-time (27 women). Expenses: Contact institution. *Financial support:* Fellowships, research assistantships with full tuition reimbursements, teaching assistantships with full tuition reimbursements, career-related internships or fieldwork, Federal Work-Study, institutionally sponsored loans, traineeships, tuition waivers (partial), and unspecified assistantships available. Support available to part-time students. Financial award applicants required to submit FAFSA. In 2010, 248 master's, 53 other advanced degrees awarded. *Degree program information:* Part-time and evening/weekend programs available. Postbaccalaureate distance learning degree programs offered (minimal on-campus study). Offers accounting (MS); accounting information systems (MS); business (MBA, MS, MSHROD, MSIS, Graduate Certificate); business administration (MBA, Graduate Certificate); computer information systems (Graduate Certificate); e-business (MBA, Graduate Certificate); enterprise business intelligence (MBA); entrepreneurship (MBA, Graduate Certificate); finance (MBA, Graduate Certificate); human resources (MBA); human resources management (Graduate Certificate); human resources management and organizational development (MSHROD); information systems (MBA, MSIS); internal auditing (MBA); international business (MBA, Graduate Certificate); marketing management (Graduate Certificate); nonprofit management (MBA); organizational development (Graduate Certificate); supply chain management (MBA, Graduate Certificate). *Application deadline:* Applications are processed on a rolling basis. *Application fee:* $35. *Application Contact:* K. Michelle Henry, Interim Director, Graduate Programs, 734-487-4444, Fax: 734-483-1316, E-mail: mhenry1@emich.edu. *Dean*, Dr. David Mielke, 734-487-4140, Fax: 734-487-7099, E-mail: dmielke@emich.edu.

College of Education Students: 202 full-time (151 women), 1,140 part-time (886 women); includes 253 minority (187 Black or African American, non-Hispanic/Latino; 12 American Indian or Alaska Native, non-Hispanic/Latino; 19 Asian, non-Hispanic/Latino; 25 Hispanic/Latino; 3 Native Hawaiian or other Pacific Islander, non-Hispanic/Latino; 7 Two or more races, non-Hispanic/Latino), 17 international. Average age 34. 789 applicants, 47% accepted, 278 enrolled. *Faculty:* 90 full-time (65 women). Expenses: Contact institution. *Financial support:* Fellowships, research assistantships with full tuition reimbursements, teaching assistantships with full tuition reimbursements, career-related internships or fieldwork, Federal Work-Study, institutionally sponsored loans, scholarships/grants, tuition waivers (partial), and unspecified assistantships available. Support available to part-time students. Financial award applicants required to submit FAFSA. In 2010, 265 master's, 10 doctorates, 104 other advanced degrees awarded. *Degree program information:* Part-time and evening/weekend programs available. Postbaccalaureate distance learning degree programs offered (minimal on-campus study). Offers autism spectrum disorders (MA); cognitive impairment (MA); college counseling (MA); college student personnel (MA); community college leadership (Graduate Certificate); community counseling (MA); counseling (MA, Graduate Certificate, Post Master's Certificate); culture and diversity (MA); curriculum and instruction (MA); early childhood education (MA); education (MA, Ed D, PhD, Graduate Certificate, Post Master's Certificate, SPA); educational assessment (Graduate Certificate); educational leadership (MA, Ed D, SPA); educational media and technology (MA, Graduate Certificate); educational psychology (MA); educational psychology and assessment (MA, Graduate Certificate); educational studies (PhD); elementary education (MA); emotional impairment (MA); hearing impairment (MA); helping interventions in a multicultural society (Graduate Certificate); higher education general administration (MA); higher education student affairs (MA); K-12 administration (MA); K-12 basic administration (Post Master's Certificate); K-12 education (MA); leadership (MA, Ed D, Graduate Certificate, Post Master's Certificate, SPA); learning disabilities (MA); mentally impaired (MA); middle school education (MA); physical/other health impairment (MA); reading (MA); school counseling (MA); school counselor (MA); school counselor licensure (Post Master's Certificate); secondary school education (MA); social foundations (MA); special education (MA, SPA); special education-administration and supervision (SPA); special education-curriculum development (SPA); speech and language pathology (MA); visual impairment (MA). *Application deadline:* Applications are processed on a rolling basis. *Application fee:* $35. *Application Contact:* Dr. Jann Joseph, Dean, 734-487-1414, Fax: 734-484-6471. *Dean*, Dr. Jann Joseph, 734-487-1414, Fax: 734-484-6471.

College of Health and Human Services Students: 170 full-time (122 women), 577 part-time (446 women); includes 197 minority (159 Black or African American, non-Hispanic/Latino; 3 American Indian or Alaska Native, non-Hispanic/Latino; 15 Asian, non-Hispanic/Latino; 13 Hispanic/Latino; 2 Native Hawaiian or other Pacific Islander, non-Hispanic/Latino; 5 Two or more races, non-Hispanic/Latino), 49 international. Average age 33. 720 applicants, 47% accepted, 242 enrolled. *Faculty:* 89 full-time (58 women). Expenses: Contact institution. *Financial support:* Fellowships, research assistantships with full tuition reimbursements, teaching assistantships with full tuition reimbursements, career-related internships or fieldwork, Federal Work-Study, institutionally sponsored loans, scholarships/grants, tuition waivers (partial), and unspecified assistantships available. Support available to part-time students. Financial award applicants required to submit FAFSA. In 2010, 213 master's, 39 other advanced degrees awarded. *Degree program information:* Part-time and evening/weekend programs available. Postbaccalaureate distance learning degree programs offered (minimal on-campus study). Offers adapted physical education (MS); clinical research administration (MS, Graduate Certificate); community building (Graduate Certificate); exercise physiology (MS); family and children's services (MSW); health administration (MHA, MS, Graduate Certificate); health and human services (MHA, MOT, MS, MSN, MSW, Graduate Certificate); health education (MS); health promotion and human performance (MS, Graduate Certificate); health sciences (MHA, MOT, MS, Graduate Certificate); human nutrition (MS); human nutrition-coordinated track in dietetics (MS); mental health and chemical dependency (MSW); non-profit management (Graduate Certificate); nursing (MSN); occupational therapy (MOT, MS); orthotics (Graduate Certificate); orthotics/prosthetics (MS); physical education pedagogy (MS); prosthetics (Graduate Certificate); quality improvement in health care systems (Graduate Certificate); services to the aging (MSW); sports management (MS); sports medicine-biomechanics (MS); sports medicine-corporate adult fitness (MS); sports medicine-exercise physiology (MS); teaching in health care systems (MSN, Graduate Certificate). *Application deadline:* Applications are processed on a rolling basis. *Application fee:* $35. *Application Contact:* Dr. Murali Nair, Dean, 734-487-0077, Fax: 734-487-8536, E-mail: mnair@emich.edu. *Dean*, Dr. Murali Nair, 734-487-0077, Fax: 734-487-8536, E-mail: mnair@emich.edu.

College of Technology Students: 98 full-time (31 women), 429 part-time (145 women); includes 85 minority (57 Black or African American, non-Hispanic/Latino; 1 American Indian or Alaska Native, non-Hispanic/Latino; 15 Asian, non-Hispanic/Latino; 12 Hispanic/Latino), 97 international. Average age 35. 335 applicants, 53% accepted, 99 enrolled. *Faculty:* 54 full-time (15 women). Expenses: Contact institution. *Financial support:* Fellowships, research assistantships with full tuition reimbursements, teaching assistantships with full tuition reimbursements, career-related internships or fieldwork, Federal Work-Study, institutionally sponsored loans, scholarships/grants, tuition waivers (partial), and unspecified assistantships available. Support available to part-time students. Financial award applicants required to submit FAFSA. In 2010, 152 master's, 2 doctorates, 8 other advanced degrees awarded. *Degree program information:* Part-time and evening/weekend programs available. Postbaccalaureate distance learning degree programs offered (minimal on-campus study). Offers apparel, textile merchandising (MS); CAD/CAM (MS); career, technical and workforce education (MS); computer aided technology (MS); construction management (MS); engineering management (MS); engineering technology (MS, Graduate Certificate); hotel and restaurant management (MS, Graduate Certificate); information assurance (MLS, Graduate Certificate); interdisciplinary technology (MLS); interior design (MS); polymer technology (MS); quality (MS, Graduate Certificate); quality management (MS); technology (MLS, MS, PhD, Graduate Certificate); technology studies (MLS, MS). *Application deadline:* Applications are processed on a rolling basis. *Application fee:* $35. *Application Contact:* Dr. Morell Boone, Dean, 734-487-0354, Fax: 734-487-0843, E-mail: mboone@emich.edu. *Dean*, Dr. Morell Boone, 734-487-0354, Fax: 734-487-0843, E-mail: mboone@emich.edu.

EASTERN NAZARENE COLLEGE, Quincy, MA 02170

General Information Independent-religious, coed, comprehensive institution. *Graduate housing:* Rooms and/or apartments available to single students and available on a first-come, first-served basis to married students.

GRADUATE UNITS

Adult and Graduate Studies *Degree program information:* Part-time and evening/weekend programs available. Offers management (MSM); marriage and family therapy (MS).

Division of Teacher Education *Degree program information:* Part-time and evening/weekend programs available. Offers administration (M Ed); early childhood education (M Ed, Certificate); elementary education (M Ed, Certificate); English as a second language (Certificate); instructional enrichment and development (Certificate); middle school education (M Ed, Certificate); moderate special needs education (Certificate); principal (Certificate); program development and supervision (Certificate); secondary education (M Ed, Certificate); special education administrator (Certificate); special needs (M Ed); supervisor (Certificate); teacher of reading (M Ed, Certificate). M Ed and Certificate also available through weekend program for administration, special needs, and reading only.

EASTERN NEW MEXICO UNIVERSITY, Portales, NM 88130

General Information State-supported, coed, comprehensive institution. CGS member. *Enrollment:* 5,080 graduate, professional, and undergraduate students; 255 full-time matriculated graduate/professional students (180 women), 486 part-time matriculated graduate/professional students (327 women). *Enrollment by degree level:* 741 master's. *Graduate faculty:* 104 full-time (46 women), 17 part-time/adjunct (13 women). Tuition, state resident: full-time $3210; part-time $130 per credit hour. Tuition, nonresident: full-time $8652; part-time $360.50 per credit hour. *Required fees:* $1212; $50.50 per credit hour. Tuition and fees vary according to course load. *Graduate housing:* Rooms and/or apartments available on a first-come, first-served basis to single and married students. Typical cost: $4400 per year ($7350 including board) for single students; $3700 per year ($6600 including board) for married students. Room and board charges vary according to housing facility selected. Housing application deadline: 8/1. *Student services:* Campus employment opportunities, campus safety program, career counseling, child daycare facilities, exercise/wellness program, free psychological counseling, international student services, low-cost health insurance, multicultural affairs office, services for students with disabilities, writing training. *Library facilities:* Golden Library plus 2 others. *Online resources:* library catalog, web page, access to other libraries' catalogs. *Collection:* 815,320 titles, 63,091 serial subscriptions, 22,763 audiovisual materials. *Research affiliation:* National Institute of Health (GSS).

Computer facilities: 446 computers available on campus for general student use. A campuswide network can be accessed from student residence rooms and from off campus. Online class registration, Wifi in most student buildings are available. *Web address:* http://www.enmu.edu/.

General Application Contact: Dr. Linda Weems, Dean, Graduate School, 575-562-2147, Fax: 575-562-2500, E-mail: linda.weems@enmu.edu.

GRADUATE UNITS

Graduate School Students: 255 full-time (180 women), 486 part-time (327 women); includes 216 minority (23 Black or African American, non-Hispanic/Latino; 13 American Indian or Alaska Native, non-Hispanic/Latino; 3 Asian, non-Hispanic/Latino; 158 Hispanic/Latino; 3 Native Hawaiian or other Pacific Islander, non-Hispanic/Latino; 16 Two or more races, non-Hispanic/Latino), 23 International. Average age 34. 427 applicants, 51% accepted; 175 enrolled. *Faculty:* 104 full-time (46 women), 17 part-time/adjunct (13 women). Expenses: Contact institution. *Financial support:* In 2010–11, 3 fellowships (averaging $5,313 per year), 72 research assistantships with partial tuition reimbursements (averaging $4,250 per year), 44 teaching assistantships with partial tuition reimbursements (averaging $4,250 per year) were awarded; career-related internships or fieldwork, tuition waivers (partial), and unspecified assistantships also available. Support available to part-time students. Financial award application deadline: 7/1; financial award applicants required to submit FAFSA. In 2010, 128 master's awarded. *Degree program information:* Part-time and evening/weekend programs available. Postbaccalaureate distance learning degree programs offered (no on-campus study). *Application deadline:* For fall admission, 7/20 priority date for domestic students, 6/20 priority date for international students; for spring admission, 12/15 priority date for domestic students, 11/15 priority date for international students. Applications are processed on a rolling basis. *Application fee:* $10. Electronic applications accepted. *Application Contact:* Gail Crozier, Receptionist/Records Clerk, 575-562-2147, Fax: 575-562-2500, E-mail: gail.crozier@enmu.edu. *Dean*, Dr. Linda Weems, 575-562-2147, Fax: 575-562-2500, E-mail: linda.weems@enmu.edu.

College of Business Students: 25 full-time (12 women), 78 part-time (49 women); includes 31 minority (5 Black or African American, non-Hispanic/Latino; 1 American Indian or Alaska Native, non-Hispanic/Latino; 1 Asian, non-Hispanic/Latino; 20 Hispanic/Latino; 1 Native Hawaiian or other Pacific Islander, non-Hispanic/Latino; 3 Two or more races, non-Hispanic/Latino), 10 international. Average age 35. 49 applicants, 96% accepted, 34 enrolled. *Faculty:* 12 full-time (2 women). Expenses: Contact institution. *Financial support:* In 2010–11, 10 research assistantships with partial tuition reimbursements (averaging $4,250 per year) were awarded; tuition waivers (partial) and unspecified assistantships also available. Support available to part-time students. Financial award applicants required to submit FAFSA. In 2010, 14 master's awarded. *Degree program information:* Part-time and evening/weekend programs available. Postbaccalaureate distance learning degree programs offered (no on-campus study). Offers business (MBA). *Application deadline:* For fall admission, 7/20 priority date for domestic students, 6/20 priority date for international students; for spring admission, 12/15 priority date for domestic students, 11/15 priority date for international students. Applications are processed on a rolling basis. *Application fee:* $10. Electronic applications accepted. *Application Contact:* Dr. Veena Parboteeah, MBA Graduate Coordinator, 575-562-2442, Fax: 575-562-4331, E-mail: veena.parboteeah@enmu.edu. *MBA Graduate Coordinator*, Dr. Veena Parboteeah, 575-562-2442, Fax: 575-562-4331, E-mail: veena.parboteeah@enmu.edu.

College of Education and Technology Students: 130 full-time (102 women), 325 part-time (216 women); includes 129 minority (13 Black or African American, non-Hispanic/Latino; 8 American Indian or Alaska Native, non-Hispanic/Latino; 1 Asian, non-Hispanic/Latino; 99 Hispanic/Latino; 1 Native Hawaiian or other Pacific Islander, non-Hispanic/Latino; 7 Two or more races, non-Hispanic/Latino). Average age 36. 128 applicants, 98% accepted, 93 enrolled. *Faculty:* 32 full-time (21 women), 7 part-time/adjunct (6 women). Expenses: Contact institution. *Financial support:* In 2010–11, 1 fellowship with partial tuition reimbursement (averaging $5,313 per year), 17 research assistantships with partial tuition reimbursements (averaging $8,500 per year), 12 teaching assistantships with partial tuition reimburse-

Eastern New Mexico University (continued)

ments (averaging $8,500 per year) were awarded; career-related internships or fieldwork, tuition waivers (partial), and unspecified assistantships also available. Support available to part-time students. Financial award applicants required to submit FAFSA. In 2010, 66 master's awarded. *Degree program information:* Part-time programs available. Post-baccalaureate distance learning degree programs offered (minimal on-campus study). Offers bilingual education (M Ed); counseling (MA); early childhood special education (M Sp Ed); education (M Ed); education and technology (M Ed, M Sp Ed, MA, MS); educational technology (M Ed); elementary education (M Ed); English as a second language (M Ed); general (M Sp Ed); pedagogy and learning (M Ed); physical education (MS); professional technical education (M Ed); reading/literacy (M Ed); school counseling (M Ed); special education (M Sp Ed). *Application deadline:* For fall admission, 7/20 priority date for domestic students, 6/20 priority date for international students; for spring admission, 12/15 priority date for domestic students, 11/15 priority date for international students. Applications are processed on a rolling basis. *Application fee:* $10. Electronic applications accepted. *Application Contact:* Cheryl Reeves, Senior Secretary, 575-562-2443, Fax: 575-562-2559, E-mail: cheryl.reeves@enmu.edu. *Dean,* Dr. Jerry Harmon, 575-562-2443, Fax: 575-562-2559, E-mail: jerry.harmon@enmu.edu.

College of Fine Arts Students: 17 full-time (8 women), 11 part-time (6 women); includes 12 minority (1 Black or African American, non-Hispanic/Latino; 1 Asian, non-Hispanic/Latino; 10 Hispanic/Latino), 3 international. Average age 30. 26 applicants, 23% accepted, 6 enrolled. *Faculty:* 3 full-time (2 women), 1 part-time/adjunct (0 women). Expenses: Contact institution. *Financial support:* In 2010–11, 1 fellowship (averaging $5,312 per year), 1 research assistantship with partial tuition reimbursement (averaging $8,500 per year), 9 teaching assistantships with partial tuition reimbursements (averaging $8,500 per year) were awarded; unspecified assistantships also available. Support available to part-time students. Financial award applicants required to submit FAFSA. In 2010, 20 master's awarded. *Degree program information:* Part-time programs available. Postbaccalaureate distance learning degree programs offered (minimal on-campus study). Offers communicative arts and sciences (MA). *Application deadline:* For fall admission, 7/20 priority date for domestic students, 6/20 priority date for international students; for spring admission, 12/15 priority date for domestic students, 11/15 priority date for international students. Applications are processed on a rolling basis. *Application fee:* $10. Electronic applications accepted. *Application Contact:* Simon Chavez, Department Secretary, Communicative Arts and Sciences, 575-562-2130, Fax: 575-562-2847, E-mail: simon.chavez@enmu.edu. *Communicative Arts and Sciences Department Chair/Interim Graduate Coordinator,* Dr. Patty Dobson, 575-562-2130, Fax: 575-562-2847, E-mail: patricia.dobson@enmu.edu.

College of Liberal Arts and Sciences Students: 78 full-time (54 women), 61 part-time (49 women); includes 43 minority (4 Black or African American, non-Hispanic/Latino; 4 American Indian or Alaska Native, non-Hispanic/Latino; 29 Hispanic/Latino; 1 Native Hawaiian or other Pacific Islander, non-Hispanic/Latino; 5 Two or more races, non-Hispanic/Latino), 10 international. Average age 29. 107 applicants, 25% accepted, 25 enrolled. *Faculty:* 47 full-time (16 women), 6 part-time/adjunct (4 women). Expenses: Contact institution. *Financial support:* In 2010–11, 3 fellowships (averaging $5,312 per year), 36 research assistantships with partial tuition reimbursements (averaging $4,250 per year), 32 teaching assistantships with partial tuition reimbursements (averaging $4,250 per year) were awarded; career-related internships or fieldwork and tuition waivers (partial) also available. Support available to part-time students. Financial award applicants required to submit FAFSA. In 2010, 28 master's awarded. *Degree program information:* Part-time and evening/weekend programs available. Postbaccalaureate distance learning degree programs offered (minimal on-campus study). Offers anthropology (MA); applied ecology (MS); cell, molecular biology and bio-technology (MS); chemistry (MS); education (non-thesis) (MS); English (MA); liberal arts and sciences (MA, MS); mathematical sciences (MA); microbiology (MS); plant biology (MS); speech pathology and audiology (MS); zoology (MS). *Application deadline:* For fall admission, 7/20 priority date for domestic students, 6/20 priority date for international students; for spring admission, 12/15 priority date for domestic students, 11/15 priority date for international students. Applications are processed on a rolling basis. *Application fee:* $10. Electronic applications accepted. *Application Contact:* Maggie Gardls, Dean's Secretary, 575-562-2421, Fax: 575-562-2555, E-mail: mary.gardels@enmu.edu. *Dean,* Dr. Mary Ayala, 575-562-2421, Fax: 575-562-2555, E-mail: mary.ayala@enmu.edu.

EASTERN OREGON UNIVERSITY, La Grande, OR 97850-2899

General Information State-supported, coed, comprehensive institution. *Graduate housing:* Rooms and/or apartments available to single and married students.

GRADUATE UNITS

Master of Science Program *Degree program information:* Part-time programs available. Postbaccalaureate distance learning degree programs offered (no on-campus study). Offers education (MS).

Program in Business Administration *Degree program information:* Part-time programs available. Postbaccalaureate distance learning degree programs offered (minimal on-campus study). Offers business administration (MBA).

Program in Elementary Education *Degree program information:* Part-time programs available. Postbaccalaureate distance learning degree programs offered (minimal on-campus study). Offers elementary education (MAT).

Program in Secondary Education *Degree program information:* Part-time programs available. Postbaccalaureate distance learning degree programs offered (minimal on-campus study). Offers secondary education (MAT).

EASTERN UNIVERSITY, St. Davids, PA 19087-3696

General Information Independent-religious, coed, comprehensive institution. *Graduate housing:* On-campus housing not available.

GRADUATE UNITS

Department of Counseling Psychology Offers community/clinical counseling (MA); school counseling (MA, Certificate); school psychology (MS, Certificate).

Graduate Education Programs *Degree program information:* Part-time programs available. Offers multicultural education (M Ed); school health services (M Ed); school nurse (Certificate).

Office of Interdisciplinary Programs Offers organizational leadership (PhD).

Palmer Theological Seminary *Degree program information:* Part-time and evening/weekend programs available. Offers marriage and family (D Min); renewal of the church for mission (D Min); theology (M Div, MTS, D Min).

School for Social Change Offers urban studies (MA).

School of Leadership and Development *Degree program information:* Part-time and evening/weekend programs available. Offers economic development (MBA); international development (MA); nonprofit management (MS); organizational leadership (MA).

School of Management Studies Offers health administration (MBA); management (MBA).

EASTERN VIRGINIA MEDICAL SCHOOL, Norfolk, VA 23501-1980

General Information Independent, coed, graduate-only institution. *Enrollment by degree level:* 470 first professional, 348 master's, 62 doctoral, 24 other advanced degrees. *Graduate faculty:* 320 full-time (121 women), 1,255 part-time/adjunct (312 women). *Graduate housing:* On-campus housing not available. *Student services:* Campus employment opportunities, campus safety program, career counseling, low-cost health insurance. *Library facilities:* Edward E. Brickell Medical Library. *Online resources:* web page. *Collection:* 100,000 titles, 2,200 serial subscriptions.

Computer facilities: 70 computers available on campus for general student use. A campuswide network can be accessed from student residence rooms and from off campus. *Web address:* http://www.evms.edu/.

General Application Contact: Rose Mwayungu, Admissions and Enrollment Manager, 757-446-7153, Fax: 757-446-6179, E-mail: mwayunra@evms.edu.

GRADUATE UNITS

Doctoral Program in Biomedical Sciences Students: 26. 22 applicants, 27% accepted, 4 enrolled. Expenses: Contact institution. *Financial support:* Research assistantships with full tuition reimbursements available. In 2010, 6 doctorates awarded. Offers biomedical sciences (PhD). Program offered jointly with Old Dominion University. *Application deadline:* For fall admission, 2/1 for domestic students. Applications are processed on a rolling basis. *Application fee:* $60. Electronic applications accepted. *Application Contact:* Leah Solomon, Administrative Support Coordinator, 757-446-5944, Fax: 757-446-6179, E-mail: solomolj@evms.edu. *Director,* Dr. Earl Godfrey, 757-446-5609, Fax: 757-624-2255, E-mail: godfreew@evms.edu.

Graduate Art Therapy and Counseling Program 42 applicants, 74% accepted, 20 enrolled. *Faculty:* 3 full-time, 1 part-time/adjunct. Expenses: Contact institution. *Financial support:* Institutionally sponsored loans available. In 2010, 13 master's awarded. Offers art therapy and counseling (MS). *Application deadline:* For fall admission, 1/1 priority date for domestic and international students. *Application fee:* $60. Electronic applications accepted. *Application Contact:* Rose Mwayungu, Admissions and Enrollment Manager for Health Professions, 757-446-7153, Fax: 757-446-8915, E-mail: mwayunra@evms.edu. *Director,* Abby Calisch, 757-446-5895, Fax: 757-446-6179, E-mail: artthrpy@evms.edu.

Master of Physician Assistant Program Students: 149 full-time (106 women); includes 11 Black or African American, non-Hispanic/Latino; 1 Asian, non-Hispanic/Latino; 3 Hispanic/Latino. 1,004 applicants, 6% accepted, 53 enrolled. *Faculty:* 9 full-time (4 women). Expenses: Contact institution. *Financial support:* Applicants required to submit FAFSA. In 2010, 47 master's awarded. Offers physician assistant (MPA). *Application deadline:* For spring admission, 3/1 for domestic students. Applications are processed on a rolling basis. *Application fee:* $60. Electronic applications accepted. *Application Contact:* Rose Mwayungu, Admissions and Enrollment Manager, 757-446-7153, Fax: 757-446-8915, E-mail: mwayunra@evms.edu. *Director,* Dr. Thomas Parish, 757-446-7126, Fax: 757-446-7403, E-mail: parishtg@evms.edu.

Master of Public Health Program Students: 64 full-time (46 women); includes 21 Black or African American, non-Hispanic/Latino; 8 Asian, non-Hispanic/Latino; 3 Hispanic/Latino. 116 applicants, 69% accepted, 57 enrolled. *Faculty:* 6 full-time (3 women), 31 part-time/adjunct (17 women). Expenses: Contact institution. *Financial support:* Applicants required to submit FAFSA. In 2010, 29 master's awarded. *Degree program information:* Evening/weekend programs available. Offers public health (MPH). Program offered jointly with Old Dominion University. *Application deadline:* For fall admission, 4/30 for domestic and international students. Applications are processed on a rolling basis. *Application fee:* $60. Electronic applications accepted. *Application Contact:* Michelle Knight, Administrative Support Coordinator, 757-446-6120, Fax: 757-446-6121, E-mail: swartzpm@evms.edu. *Director,* Dr. David O. Matson, 757-466-6120, Fax: 757-446-6121, E-mail: matsondo@evms.edu.

Master's Program in Biomedical Sciences (Medical Master's) Students: 23 full-time (14 women); includes 6 Asian, non-Hispanic/Latino. 287 applicants, 12% accepted, 23 enrolled. *Faculty:* 25. Expenses: Contact institution. *Financial support:* Institutionally sponsored loans available. In 2010, 22 master's awarded. Offers biomedical sciences (MS). *Application deadline:* For fall admission, 4/1 for domestic students. Applications are processed on a rolling basis. *Application fee:* $60. Electronic applications accepted. *Application Contact:* Leah Solomon, Administrative Support Coordinator, 757-446-5944, Fax: 757-446-6179, E-mail: solomolj@evms.edu. *Director,* Dr. Donald Meyer, 757-446-5615, Fax: 757-446-6179, E-mail: meyerdc@evms.edu.

Master's Program in Biomedical Sciences Research Students: 9 full-time (7 women); includes 1 Black or African American, non-Hispanic/Latino; 2 Asian, non-Hispanic/Latino. 22 applicants, 50% accepted, 7 enrolled. *Faculty:* 57. Expenses: Contact institution. In 2010, 2 master's awarded. Offers biomedical sciences research (MS). *Application deadline:* For fall admission, 3/1 for domestic students. Applications are processed on a rolling basis. *Application fee:* $60. Electronic applications accepted. *Application Contact:* Leah Solomon, Administrative Support Coordinator, 757-446-5944, Fax: 757-446-6179, E-mail: solomolj@evms.edu. *Director,* Dr. Earl Godfrey, 757-446-5609, Fax: 757-624-2255, E-mail: godfreew@evms.edu.

Master's Program in Clinical Embryology and Andrology Students: 66 full-time (44 women); includes 6 Black or African American, non-Hispanic/Latino; 10 Asian, non-Hispanic/Latino; 10 Hispanic/Latino. 35 applicants, 69% accepted, 23 enrolled. *Faculty:* 12 full-time, 8 part-time/adjunct. Expenses: Contact institution. In 2010, 14 master's awarded. Post-baccalaureate distance learning degree programs offered (minimal on-campus study). Offers clinical embryology and andrology (MS). *Application deadline:* For fall admission, 1/14 for domestic and international students. Applications are processed on a rolling basis. *Application fee:* $60. Electronic applications accepted. *Application Contact:* Nancy Garcia, Administrator, 757-446-8935, Fax: 757-446-5905, E-mail: garcianw@evms.edu. *Director,* Dr. Jacob Mayer, 757-446-5049, Fax: 757-446-5905.

Ophthalmic Technology Program Students: 10 full-time (8 women); includes 4 Black or African American, non-Hispanic/Latino. 17 applicants, 35% accepted, 6 enrolled. *Faculty:* 1 (woman) full-time, 1 (woman) part-time/adjunct. Expenses: Contact institution. Offers ophthalmic technology (Certificate). *Application deadline:* For fall admission, 4/1 for domestic students. Applications are processed on a rolling basis. *Application fee:* $60. Electronic applications accepted. *Application Contact:* Rose Mwayungu, Admissions and Enrollment Manager, 757-446-7153, Fax: 757-446-6179, E-mail: mwayunra@evms.edu. *Director,* Lori J. Wood, 757-388-3747, E-mail: optech@evms.edu.

Professional Program in Medicine Students: 470 full-time (219 women); includes 31 Black or African American, non-Hispanic/Latino; 109 Asian, non-Hispanic/Latino; 6 Hispanic/Latino. 4,958 applicants, 118 enrolled. Expenses: Contact institution. In 2010, 99 first professional degrees awarded. Offers medicine (MD). *Application deadline:* For fall admission, 11/15 priority date for domestic students. Applications are processed on a rolling basis. *Application fee:* $95. Electronic applications accepted. *Application Contact:* Susan Castora, Director of Admissions, 757-446-5812, Fax: 757-446-5896, E-mail: castorsl@evms.edu. *Associate Dean for Medical Admissions,* Dr. Michael J. Solhaug, 757-446-5805, Fax: 757-446-5896, E-mail: solhaumj@evms.edu.

Surgical Assistant Program Students: 23 full-time (20 women); includes 1 Black or African American, non-Hispanic/Latino; 2 Asian, non-Hispanic/Latino; 2 Hispanic/Latino. 19 applicants, 79% accepted, 12 enrolled. *Faculty:* 8. Expenses: Contact institution. Offers surgical assistant (Graduate Certificate). *Application deadline:* For fall admission, 2/1 for domestic students. Applications are processed on a rolling basis. *Application fee:* $60. Electronic applications accepted. *Application Contact:* Nancy Stromann, Health Professions Office Coordinator, 757-446-6100, Fax: 757-446-6179, E-mail: stromand@evms.edu. *Program Director,* R. Clinton Crews, 757-446-8961, Fax: 757-446-6179, E-mail: crewsrc@evms.edu.

The Virginia Consortium Program in Clinical Psychology Students: 44 full-time (33 women); includes 4 Black or African American, non-Hispanic/Latino; 5 Asian, non-Hispanic/Latino; 4 Hispanic/Latino. 169 applicants, 4% accepted, 6 enrolled. *Faculty:* 33. Expenses: Contact institution. In 2010, 14 doctorates awarded. Offers clinical psychology (Psy D). Program offered jointly with The College of William and Mary, Norfolk State University, and Old Dominion University. *Application deadline:* For fall admission, 1/15 for domestic students. *Application fee:* $40. *Application Contact:* Eileen O'Neill, Administrative Coordinator, 757-368-1820, Fax: 757-446-8401, E-mail: exoneill@odu.edu. *Director,* Dr. Michael L. Stutts, 757-446-8400, Fax: 757-446-8401, E-mail: stuttsml@evms.edu.

EASTERN WASHINGTON UNIVERSITY, Cheney, WA 99004-2431

General Information State-supported, coed, comprehensive institution. CGS member. *Graduate housing:* Rooms and/or apartments available on a first-come, first-served basis to single and married students. Housing application deadline: 5/1.

GRADUATE UNITS

Graduate Studies *Degree program information:* Part-time and evening/weekend programs available. Offers interdisciplinary studies (MA, MS).

College of Arts and Letters *Degree program information:* Part-time programs available. Offers arts and letters (M Ed, MA, MFA); composition (MA); creative writing (MFA); French education (M Ed); instrumental/vocal performance (MA); literature (MA); music education

(MA); music history and literature (MA); rhetoric, composition, and technical communication (MA); teaching English as a second language (MA).

College of Business and Public Administration *Degree program information:* Part-time and evening/weekend programs available. Offers business administration (MBA); business and public administration (MBA, MPA, MURP); public administration (MPA); urban and regional planning (MURP).

College of Education and Human Development *Degree program information:* Part-time programs available. Offers adult education (M Ed); applied psychology (MS); curriculum development (M Ed); early childhood education (M Ed); education and human development (M Ed, MS); educational leadership (M Ed); elementary teaching (M Ed); exercise science (MS); foundations of education (M Ed); instructional media and technology (M Ed); literacy (M Ed); mental health counseling (MS); school counseling (MS); school psychology (MS); special education (M Ed); sport and exercise psychology (MS); sports administration/pedagogy (MS).

College of Science, Health and Engineering *Degree program information:* Part-time programs available. Offers biology (MS); communication disorders (MS); computer and technology-supported education (M Ed); computer science (MS); dental hygiene (MS); mathematics (MS); occupational therapy (MOT); physical therapy (DPT); science, health and engineering (M Ed, MA, MOT, MS, DPT); teaching mathematics (MA).

College of Social and Behavioral Sciences *Degree program information:* Part-time and evening/weekend programs available. Offers clinical psychology (MS); communication studies (MSC); experimental psychology (MS); history (MA); psychology (MS); school psychology (MS); social and behavioral sciences (MA, MS, MSC).

School of Social Work and Human Services *Degree program information:* Part-time programs available. Offers social work and human services (MSW).

EAST STROUDSBURG UNIVERSITY OF PENNSYLVANIA, East Stroudsburg, PA 18301-2999

General Information State-supported, coed, comprehensive institution. CGS member. *Graduate housing:* Room and/or apartments available on a first-come, first-served basis to single students; on-campus housing not available to married students. Housing application deadline: 5/1.

GRADUATE UNITS

Graduate School *Degree program information:* Part-time and evening/weekend programs available.

College of Arts and Sciences *Degree program information:* Part-time and evening/weekend programs available. Offers arts and sciences (M Ed, MA, MS); biology (M Ed, MS); computer science (MS); history (M Ed, MA); political science (M Ed, MA).

College of Business and Management *Degree program information:* Part-time and evening/weekend programs available. Offers business and management (MS); management and leadership (MS); sports management (MS).

College of Education *Degree program information:* Part-time and evening/weekend programs available. Offers education (M Ed); elementary education (M Ed); instructional technology (M Ed); professional and secondary education (M Ed); reading (M Ed); special education (M Ed).

College of Health Sciences *Degree program information:* Part-time and evening/weekend programs available. Offers cardiac rehabilitation and exercise science (MS); community health education (MPH); health and physical education (M Ed); health education (MS); health sciences (M Ed, MPH, MS); speech pathology and audiology (MS).

EAST TENNESSEE STATE UNIVERSITY, Johnson City, TN 37614

General Information State-supported, coed, university. CGS member. *Enrollment:* 14,952 graduate, professional, and undergraduate students; 1,769 full-time matriculated graduate/professional students (1,038 women), 961 part-time matriculated graduate/professional students (692 women). *Enrollment by degree level:* 570 first professional, 1,686 master's, 446 doctoral, 28 other advanced degrees. *Graduate faculty:* 482 full-time (177 women), 42 part-time/adjunct (11 women). *Graduate housing:* Rooms and/or apartments available on a first-come, first-served basis to single and married students. Housing application deadline: 7/1. *Student services:* Campus employment opportunities, campus safety program, career counseling, child daycare facilities, exercise/wellness program, free psychological counseling, grant writing training, international student services, low-cost health insurance, multicultural affairs office, services for students with disabilities, teacher training. *Library facilities:* Sherrod Library plus 2 others. *Online resources:* library catalog, web page. *Collection:* 1.1 million titles, 3,714 serial subscriptions. *Research affiliation:* Oak Ridge National Laboratory (biomedical physical science), Eastman Chemical Corporation (biomedical science), Tennessee Mouse Genome Consortium (biomedical science), Tennessee Biotechnology Association (biotechnology), Siemens (scientific and biomedical manufacturing), Marshall Space Flight Center (general).

Computer facilities: Computer purchase and lease plans are available. 1,400 computers available on campus for general student use. A campuswide network can be accessed from student residence rooms. Online class registration is available. *Web address:* http://www.etsu.edu/.

General Application Contact: Dr. Jeffrey Beck, Assistant Dean, 423-439-4221, Fax: 423-439-5624, E-mail: powersbj@etsu.edu.

GRADUATE UNITS

College of Pharmacy Students: 311 full-time (171 women), 1 part-time (0 women); includes 30 minority (7 Black or African American, non-Hispanic/Latino; 11 Asian, non-Hispanic/Latino; 4 Hispanic/Latino; 2 Native Hawaiian or other Pacific Islander, non-Hispanic/Latino; 6 Two or more races, non-Hispanic/Latino). Average age 26. Expenses: Contact institution. In 2010, 64 Pharm Ds awarded. Offers pharmacy (Pharm D). *Application Contact:* Admissions and Records Clerk, 423-439-4221, Fax: 423-439-5624, E-mail: gradsch@etsu.edu. *Dean,* Dr. Larry D. Calhoun, 423-439-2068, Fax: 423-439-6310, E-mail: calhoun@etsu.edu.

James H. Quillen College of Medicine Students: 285 full-time (139 women), 4 part-time (2 women); includes 45 minority (9 Black or African American, non-Hispanic/Latino; 1 American Indian or Alaska Native, non-Hispanic/Latino; 24 Asian, non-Hispanic/Latino; 5 Hispanic/Latino; 6 Two or more races, non-Hispanic/Latino), 5 international. Average age 27. 1,206 applicants, 9% accepted, 67 enrolled. *Faculty:* 164 full-time (48 women), 36 part-time/adjunct (9 women). Expenses: Contact institution. *Financial support:* In 2010–11, 7 research assistantships with full tuition reimbursements (averaging $15,000 per year) were awarded; teaching assistantships with full tuition reimbursements, career-related internships or fieldwork, Federal Work-Study, institutionally sponsored loans, scholarships/grants, and tuition waivers (full) also available. Financial award applicants required to submit FAFSA. In 2010, 62 first professional degrees, 2 doctorates awarded. *Degree program information:* Part-time programs available. Offers anatomy (PhD); biochemistry (PhD); medicine (MD, PhD); microbiology (PhD); pharmacology (PhD); physiology (PhD). *Application deadline:* Applications are processed on a rolling basis. *Application fee:* $25 ($35 for international students). *Application Contact:* Edwin D. Taylor, Assistant Dean for Admissions and Records, 423-439-4753, Fax: 423-439-8206. *Vice President for Health Affairs/Dean,* Dr. Philip Bagnell, 423-439-6316, Fax: 423-439-8090, E-mail: bagnell@etsu.edu.

School of Graduate Studies Students: 1,173 full-time (728 women), 956 part-time (690 women); includes 182 minority (87 Black or African American, non-Hispanic/Latino; 8 American Indian or Alaska Native, non-Hispanic/Latino; 21 Asian, non-Hispanic/Latino; 39 Hispanic/Latino; 27 Two or more races, non-Hispanic/Latino), 121 international. Average age 33. 1,999 applicants, 41% accepted, 497 enrolled. *Faculty:* 318 full-time (129 women), 6 part-time/adjunct (2 women). Expenses: Contact institution. *Financial support:* In 2010–11, 162 research assistantships with full tuition reimbursements (averaging $6,000 per year), 81 teaching assistantships with full tuition reimbursements (averaging $6,000 per year) were awarded. Financial award application deadline: 7/1; financial award applicants required to submit FAFSA. In 2010, 623 master's, 64 doctorates, 39 other advanced degrees awarded. *Application deadline:* For fall admission, 6/1 for domestic students, 4/30 for international students; for spring admission, 11/1 for domestic students, 9/30 for international students. *Application fee:* $25 ($35 for international students). *Application Contact:* Admissions and Records Clerk, 423-439-4221, Fax: 423-439-5624, E-mail: gradsch@etsu.edu. *Dean,* Dr. Cecilia McIntosh, 423-439-6146, Fax: 423-439-5624, E-mail: gradsch@etsu.edu.

College of Arts and Sciences Students: 324 full-time (185 women), 99 part-time (66 women); includes 39 minority (18 Black or African American, non-Hispanic/Latino; 4 American Indian or Alaska Native, non-Hispanic/Latino; 2 Asian, non-Hispanic/Latino; 8 Hispanic/Latino; 7 Two or more races, non-Hispanic/Latino), 54 international. Average age 30. 489 applicants, 40% accepted, 123 enrolled. *Faculty:* 136 full-time (43 women). Expenses: Contact institution. *Financial support:* In 2010–11, 30 research assistantships with full tuition reimbursements (averaging $6,000 per year), 57 teaching assistantships with full tuition reimbursements (averaging $6,000 per year) were awarded; tuition waivers (full) also available. Financial award application deadline: 7/1; financial award applicants required to submit FAFSA. In 2010, 141 master's, 7 other advanced degrees awarded. Offers applied sociology (MA); arts and sciences (MA, MCM, MFA, MPA, MS, MSW, PhD, Certificate); biology (MS); chemistry (MS); city management (MCM); clinical psychology (PhD); communication (MA); criminal justice and criminology (MA, Certificate); experiential psychology (PhD); general psychology (MA); general sociology (MA); history (MA); languages and literature (MA, Certificate); mathematics (MS); microbiology (MS); not-for-profit (MPA); paleontology (MS); planning and development (MPA); political science (MPA); public financial management (MPA); social work (MSW); studio art (MFA). *Application fee:* $25 ($35 for international students). *Application Contact:* Admissions and Records Clerk, 423-439-4221, Fax: 423-439-5624, E-mail: gradsch@etsu.edu. *Dean,* Dr. Gordon K. Anderson, 423-439-5671, Fax: 423-439-4645, E-mail: andersgk@etsu.edu.

College of Business and Technology Students: 187 full-time (67 women), 91 part-time (32 women); includes 30 minority (9 Black or African American, non-Hispanic/Latino; 1 American Indian or Alaska Native, non-Hispanic/Latino; 5 Asian, non-Hispanic/Latino; 10 Hispanic/Latino; 5 Two or more races, non-Hispanic/Latino), 31 international. Average age 30. 280 applicants, 57% accepted, 103 enrolled. *Faculty:* 68 full-time (16 women). Expenses: Contact institution. *Financial support:* In 2010–11, 27 research assistantships with full tuition reimbursements (averaging $6,000 per year) were awarded. Financial award application deadline: 7/1; financial award applicants required to submit FAFSA. In 2010, 121 master's, 8 other advanced degrees awarded. Offers accountancy (M Acc); applied computer science (MS); business administration (MBA, Certificate); business and technology (M Acc, MBA, MS, Certificate); digital media (MS); engineering technology (MS); entrepreneurial leadership (MS, Certificate); health care management (Certificate); information technology (MS). *Application fee:* $25 ($35 for international students). Electronic applications accepted. *Application Contact:* Dr. Linda Garceau, Dean, 423-439-5276, Fax: 423-439-5274, E-mail: garceaul@etsu.edu. *Dean,* Dr. Linda Garceau, 423-439-5276, Fax: 423-439-5274, E-mail: garceaul@etsu.edu.

College of Clinical and Rehabilitative Health Sciences Students: 181 full-time (144 women), 34 part-time (25 women); includes 17 minority (8 Black or African American, non-Hispanic/Latino; 3 Asian, non-Hispanic/Latino; 5 Hispanic/Latino; 1 Two or more races, non-Hispanic/Latino), 3 international. Average age 28. 281 applicants, 37% accepted, 37 enrolled. Expenses: Contact institution. In 2010, 51 master's, 37 doctorates awarded. Offers allied health science (MSAH); audiology (Au D); clinical and rehabilitative health sciences (MS, MSAH, Au D, DPT); clinical nutrition (MS); physical therapy (DPT); speech pathology (MS). *Application Contact:* Admissions and Records Clerk, 423-439-4221, Fax: 423-439-5624, E-mail: gradsch@etsu.edu. *Dean,* Dr. Nancy J. Scherer, 423-439-7454, Fax: 423-439-4240, E-mail: scherern@etsu.edu.

College of Education Students: 334 full-time (222 women), 392 part-time (295 women); includes 52 minority (30 Black or African American, non-Hispanic/Latino; 1 American Indian or Alaska Native, non-Hispanic/Latino; 7 Asian, non-Hispanic/Latino; 5 Hispanic/Latino; 9 Two or more races, non-Hispanic/Latino), 12 international. Average age 35. 480 applicants, 43% accepted, 130 enrolled. *Faculty:* 50 full-time (27 women), 6 part-time/adjunct (2 women). Expenses: Contact institution. *Financial support:* In 2010–11, 32 research assistantships with full tuition reimbursements (averaging $6,000 per year), 7 teaching assistantships with full tuition reimbursements (averaging $5,500 per year) were awarded; career-related internships or fieldwork, Federal Work-Study, institutionally sponsored loans, scholarships/grants, and unspecified assistantships also available. Financial award application deadline: 7/1; financial award applicants required to submit FAFSA. In 2010, 184 master's, 24 doctorates, 6 other advanced degrees awarded. Offers 7-12 (MAT); administrative endorsement (M Ed, Ed D, Ed S); advanced practitioner (M Ed); classroom leadership (Ed D); classroom technology (M Ed); community agency counseling (M Ed, MA); comprehensive concentration (M Ed); counseling (M Ed, MA); counselor leadership (Ed S); early childhood (PhD); early childhood education (M Ed, MA); early childhood general (M Ed); early childhood special education (M Ed); early childhood teaching (M Ed); education (M Ed, MA, MAT, Ed D, PhD, Ed S); educational communication (M Ed); educational media/educational technology (M Ed); elementary and secondary (school counseling) (M Ed, MA); elementary education (M Ed, MAT); exercise physiology and performance (MA); K-12 (MAT); K-12 physical education (MA); marriage and family therapy (M Ed, MA); modified concentration (M Ed); motorsport operations (MA); post secondary and private sector leadership (Ed D); reading and storytelling (M Ed, MA); reading education (M Ed, MA); school leadership (Ed D); school library media (M Ed); school system leadership (Ed S); secondary education (M Ed, MAT); sport performance (PhD); sport physiology (PhD); sports management (MA); teacher leadership (Ed S). *Application fee:* $25 ($35 for international students). Electronic applications accepted. *Application Contact:* Admissions and Records Clerk, 423-439-4221, Fax: 423-439-5624, E-mail: gradsch@etsu.edu. *Dean,* Dr. Hal Knight, 423-439-4159, Fax: 423-439-7560, E-mail: knighth@etsu.edu.

College of Nursing Students: 65 full-time (62 women), 166 part-time (148 women); includes 13 minority (4 Black or African American, non-Hispanic/Latino; 1 American Indian or Alaska Native, non-Hispanic/Latino; 6 Hispanic/Latino; 2 Two or more races, non-Hispanic/Latino), 2 international. Average age 39. 259 applicants, 21% accepted, 44 enrolled. *Faculty:* 32 full-time (30 women). Expenses: Contact institution. *Financial support:* In 2010–11, 6 research assistantships with full tuition reimbursements (averaging $5,500 per year), 4 teaching assistantships with full tuition reimbursements (averaging $5,500 per year) were awarded; career-related internships or fieldwork, institutionally sponsored loans, scholarships/grants, and unspecified assistantships also available. Financial award application deadline: 7/1; financial award applicants required to submit FAFSA. In 2010, 73 master's, 3 doctorates, 10 other advanced degrees awarded. *Degree program information:* Part-time and evening/weekend programs available. Postbaccalaureate distance learning degree programs offered (no on-campus study). Offers acute care nurse practitioner (DNP); administration (MSN); adult/gerontological nurse practitioner (DNP); advanced nursing practice (Post Master's Certificate); advanced practice (MSN); executive leadership (DNP); family nurse practitioner (DNP); health care management (Certificate); informatics (MSN); nursing (MSN, PhD); nursing education (MSN); psychiatric/mental health nurse practitioner (DNP). *Application deadline:* For fall admission, 2/1 for domestic and international students; for spring admission, 7/1 for domestic and international students. *Application fee:* $25 ($35 for international students). Electronic applications accepted. *Application Contact:* Dr. Wendy Nehring, Dean, 423-439-7051, Fax: 423-439-4522, E-mail: nehringw@etsu.edu. *Dean,* Dr. Wendy Nehring, 423-439-7051, Fax: 423-439-4522, E-mail: nehringw@etsu.edu.

College of Public Health Students: 56 full-time (33 women), 36 part-time (24 women); includes 16 minority (11 Black or African American, non-Hispanic/Latino; 4 Asian, non-Hispanic/Latino; 1 Hispanic/Latino), 19 international. Average age 32. 163 applicants, 38% accepted, 35 enrolled. *Faculty:* 30 full-time (12 women). Expenses: Contact institution. *Financial support:* In 2010–11, 20 research assistantships with full tuition reimbursements (averaging $5,500 per year) were awarded; teaching assistantships with full tuition reimbursements. Financial award application deadline: 7/1; financial award applicants required to submit FAFSA. In 2010, 39 master's, 6 other advanced degrees awarded. *Degree program information:* Part-time and evening/weekend programs available. Offers administrative (MSEH); biostatistics (MPH); community health (MPH, DPH); environmental health (PhD); environmental health sciences (MPH); epidemiology (MPH, Certificate); gerontology (Certificate); health care management (Certificate); health services administration (MPH); public health (MPH, MSEH, DPH, PhD, Certificate); rural health (Certificate).

East Tennessee State University (continued)

Application fee: $25 ($35 for international students). *Application Contact:* Admissions and Records Clerk, 423-439-4221, Fax: 423-439-5624, E-mail: gradsch@etsu.edu. *Dean,* Dr. Randy Wykoff, 423-439-4243, Fax: 423-439-5238, E-mail: wykoff@etsu.edu.

Division of Cross-Disciplinary Studies Students: 14 full-time (9 women), 61 part-time (51 women); includes 11 minority (5 Black or African American, non-Hispanic/Latino; 1 American Indian or Alaska Native, non-Hispanic/Latino; 3 Hispanic/Latino; 2 Two or more races, non-Hispanic/Latino). Average age 42. 47 applicants, 66% accepted, 25 enrolled. *Faculty:* 2 full-time (1 woman). Expenses: Contact institution. *Financial support:* In 2010–11, 2 research assistantships with full tuition reimbursements (averaging $5,500 per year) were awarded; teaching assistantships with full tuition reimbursements, institutionally sponsored loans, scholarships/grants, and unspecified assistantships also available. Financial award application deadline: 7/1; financial award applicants required to submit FAFSA. In 2010, 14 master's, 2 other advanced degrees awarded. *Degree program information:* Part-time programs available. Postbaccalaureate distance learning degree programs offered (no on-campus study). Offers archival studies (MALS); strategic leadership (MPS); training and development (MPS). *Application deadline:* For fall admission, 6/1 for domestic students, 4/30 for international students; for spring admission, 11/1 for domestic students, 9/30 for international students. *Application fee:* $25 ($35 for international students). Electronic applications accepted. *Application Contact:* Admissions and Records Clerk, 423-439-4221, Fax: 423-439-5624, E-mail: gradsch@etsu.edu. *Associate Dean,* Dr. Rick E. Osborn, 423-439-4223, Fax: 423-439-7091, E-mail: osbornr@etsu.edu.

EAST WEST COLLEGE OF NATURAL MEDICINE, Sarasota, FL 34234

General Information Proprietary, coed, graduate-only institution.

GRADUATE UNITS

Graduate Programs Offers Oriental medicine (MSOM).

ECOLE HÔTELIÈRE DE LAUSANNE, CH-1000 Lausanne 25, Switzerland

General Information Independent, coed, comprehensive institution.

GRADUATE UNITS

Program in Hospitality Administration Offers hospitality administration (MHA).

ÉCOLE POLYTECHNIQUE DE MONTRÉAL, Montréal, QC H3C 3A7, Canada

General Information Province-supported, coed, university. *Graduate housing:* Room and/or apartments available on a first-come, first-served basis to single students; on-campus housing not available to married students. Housing application deadline: 2/1. *Research affiliation:* Hydro-Québec (energy), Bell Canada (telecommunications), Bombardier, Inc. (aircraft and aviation), IBM (computer), Pratt and Whitney (aircraft and aviation), Ubisoft (video games).

GRADUATE UNITS

Graduate Programs *Degree program information:* Part-time and evening/weekend programs available. Offers aerothermics (M Eng, M Sc A, PhD); applied mechanics (M Eng, M Sc A, PhD); automation (M Eng, M Sc A, PhD); chemical engineering (M Eng, M Sc A, PhD, DESS); civil, geological and mining engineering (DESS); computer science (M Eng, M Sc A, PhD); electrical engineering (DESS); electrotechnology (M Eng, M Sc A, PhD); environmental engineering (M Eng, M Sc A, PhD); ergonomy (M Eng, M Sc A, DESS); geotechnical engineering (M Eng, M Sc A, PhD); hydraulics engineering (M Eng, M Sc A, PhD); mathematical method in CA engineering (M Eng, M Sc A, PhD); microelectronics (M Eng, M Sc A, PhD); microwave technology (M Eng, M Sc A, PhD); operational research (M Eng, M Sc A, PhD); optical engineering (M Eng, M Sc A, PhD); production (M Eng, M Sc A); solid-state physics and engineering (M Eng, M Sc A, PhD); structural engineering (M Eng, M Sc A, PhD); technology management (M Eng, M Sc A); tool design (M Eng, M Sc A, PhD); transportation engineering (M Eng, M Sc A, PhD). Electronic applications accepted.

Institute of Biomedical Engineering *Degree program information:* Part-time programs available. Offers biomedical engineering (M Sc A, PhD, DESS). M Sc A and PhD programs offered jointly with Université de Montréal.

Institute of Nuclear Engineering Offers nuclear engineering (M Eng, PhD, DESS); nuclear engineering, socio-economics of energy (M Sc A).

ECUMENICAL THEOLOGICAL SEMINARY, Detroit, MI 48201

General Information Independent-religious, coed, graduate-only institution. *Graduate housing:* On-campus housing not available.

GRADUATE UNITS

Professional Program Offers theology (M Div).

Program in Ministry Offers ministry (D Min).

EDEN THEOLOGICAL SEMINARY, St. Louis, MO 63119-3192

General Information Independent-religious, coed, graduate-only institution. *Graduate housing:* Rooms and/or apartments available on a first-come, first-served basis to single and married students. Housing application deadline: 7/30.

GRADUATE UNITS

Graduate and Professional Programs Offers theology (M Div, MAPS, MTS, D Min). Electronic applications accepted.

EDGEWOOD COLLEGE, Madison, WI 53711-1997

General Information Independent-religious, coed, primarily women, comprehensive institution. *Enrollment:* 2,626 graduate, professional, and undergraduate students; 220 full-time matriculated graduate/professional students (127 women), 314 part-time matriculated graduate/professional students (207 women). *Enrollment by degree level:* 408 master's, 126 doctoral. *Tuition:* Part-time $719 per credit hour. *Graduate housing:* On-campus housing not available. *Student services:* Campus employment opportunities, career counseling, free psychological counseling, international student services, low-cost health insurance, multicultural affairs office, services for students with disabilities, writing training. *Library facilities:* Oscar Rennebohm Library. *Online resources:* library catalog, web page. *Collection:* 93,480 titles, 1,085 serial subscriptions, 3,279 audiovisual materials.

Computer facilities: Computer purchase and lease plans are available. 100 computers available on campus for general student use. A campuswide network can be accessed from student residence rooms and from off campus. Online class registration is available. *Web address:* http://www.edgewood.edu/.

General Application Contact: Joann Eastman, Admissions Counselor, 608-663-3250, Fax: 608-663-2214, E-mail: jeastman@edgewood.edu.

GRADUATE UNITS

Program in Business Students: 38 full-time (20 women), 98 part-time (42 women); includes 9 minority (1 Black or African American, non-Hispanic/Latino; 5 Asian, non-Hispanic/Latino; 1 Hispanic/Latino; 2 Two or more races, non-Hispanic/Latino), 6 international. Average age 33. Expenses: Contact institution. *Financial support:* Career-related internships or fieldwork available. In 2010, 45 master's awarded. *Degree program information:* Part-time and evening/weekend programs available. Offers accountancy (MS); business (MBA). *Application deadline:* For fall admission, 8/26 for domestic students, 8/1 for international students; for spring admission, 1/10 for domestic students, 10/1 for international students. Applications are processed on a rolling basis. *Application fee:* $25. Electronic applications accepted. *Application Contact:* Joann Eastman, Admissions Counselor, 608-663-3250, Fax: 608-663-2214, E-mail: gps@edgewood.edu. *Dean,* Martin Preizler, 608-663-2898, Fax: 608-663-3291, E-mail: martinpreizler@edgewood.edu.

Program in Education Students: 151 full-time (81 women), 156 part-time (110 women); includes 46 minority (16 Black or African American, non-Hispanic/Latino; 1 American Indian or Alaska Native, non-Hispanic/Latino; 6 Asian, non-Hispanic/Latino; 16 Hispanic/Latino; 1 Native Hawaiian or other Pacific Islander, non-Hispanic/Latino; 6 Two or more races, non-Hispanic/Latino), 7 international. Average age 36. Expenses: Contact institution. In 2010, 34 master's, 23 doctorates awarded. *Degree program information:* Part-time and evening/weekend programs available. Offers director of instruction (Certificate); director of special education and pupil services (Certificate); education (MA Ed); educational administration (MA); educational leadership (Ed D); program coordinator (Certificate); school business administration (Certificate); school principalship K-12 (Certificate). *Application deadline:* For fall admission, 8/24 for domestic students, 8/1 for international students; for spring admission, 1/10 for domestic students, 10/1 for international students. Applications are processed on a rolling basis. *Application fee:* $25. Electronic applications accepted. *Application Contact:* Joann Eastman, Admissions Counselor, 608-663-3250, Fax: 608-663-2214, E-mail: gps@edgewood.edu. *Dean,* Dr. Jane Belmore, 608-663-8336, Fax: 608-663-3291, E-mail: jbelmore@edgewood.edu.

Program in Marriage and Family Therapy Students: 30 full-time (25 women), 17 part-time (16 women); includes 5 minority (2 Asian, non-Hispanic/Latino; 1 Hispanic/Latino; 1 Native Hawaiian or other Pacific Islander, non-Hispanic/Latino; 1 Two or more races, non-Hispanic/Latino), 1 international. Average age 31. Expenses: Contact institution. In 2010, 13 master's awarded. *Degree program information:* Part-time and evening/weekend programs available. Offers marriage and family therapy (MS). *Application deadline:* For fall admission, 3/1 for domestic students. *Application fee:* $25. Electronic applications accepted. *Application Contact:* Joann Eastman, Admissions Counselor, 608-663-3250, Fax: 608-663-2214, E-mail: gps@edgewood.edu. *Chair,* Dr. Peter Fabian, 608-663-2233, Fax: 608-663-3291, E-mail: fabian@edgewood.edu.

Program in Nursing Students: 1 (woman) full-time, 43 part-time (39 women); includes 2 minority (1 Black or African American, non-Hispanic/Latino; 1 Asian, non-Hispanic/Latino). Average age 39. Expenses: Contact institution. In 2010, 6 master's awarded. Offers nursing (MS). *Application deadline:* For fall admission, 8/24 priority date for domestic students, 8/1 for international students; for spring admission, 1/10 priority date for domestic students, 10/1 for international students. Applications are processed on a rolling basis. *Application fee:* $25. Electronic applications accepted. *Application Contact:* Joann Eastman, Admissions Counselor, 608-663-3250, Fax: 608-663-2214, E-mail: gps@edgewood.edu. *Chair and Dean,* Dr. Margaret Noreuil, 608-663-2820, Fax: 608-663-3291, E-mail: mnoreuil@edgewood.edu.

Program in Religious Studies Expenses: Contact institution. *Financial support:* Career-related internships or fieldwork, institutionally sponsored loans, scholarships/grants, and tuition waivers (partial) available. In 2010, 1 master's awarded. *Degree program information:* Part-time and evening/weekend programs available. Offers religious studies (MA). *Application deadline:* For fall admission, 8/24 for domestic students, 8/1 for international students; for spring admission, 1/10 for domestic students, 10/1 for international students. Applications are processed on a rolling basis. *Application fee:* $25. Electronic applications accepted. *Application Contact:* Joann Eastman, Admissions Counselor, 608-663-3250, Fax: 608-663-2214, E-mail: gps@edgewood.edu. *Chair,* Dr. John Leonard, 608-663-2823, Fax: 608-663-3291, E-mail: jleonard@edgewood.edu.

EDINBORO UNIVERSITY OF PENNSYLVANIA, Edinboro, PA 16444

General Information State-supported, coed, comprehensive institution. *Enrollment:* 8,642 graduate, professional, and undergraduate students; 554 full-time matriculated graduate/professional students (395 women), 1,257 part-time matriculated graduate/professional students (995 women). *Enrollment by degree level:* 1,633 master's, 178 other advanced degrees. *Graduate faculty:* 110 full-time (63 women), 24 part-time/adjunct (15 women). Tuition, state resident: full-time $6966; part-time $387 per credit. Tuition, nonresident: full-time $11,146; part-time $619 per credit. *Required fees:* $2402; $96.25 per credit. *Graduate housing:* Room and/or apartments available on a first-come, first-served basis to single students; on-campus housing not available to married students. Housing application deadline: 4/3. *Student services:* Campus employment opportunities, campus safety program, career counseling, exercise/wellness program, free psychological counseling, international student services, low-cost health insurance, multicultural affairs office, services for students with disabilities, teacher training. *Library facilities:* Baron-Forness Library. *Online resources:* library catalog, web page, access to other libraries' catalogs. *Collection:* 500,152 titles, 1,194 serial subscriptions, 10,231 audiovisual materials. *Research affiliation:* Pennsylvania Department of Education (technical education), Mid-Continent Research for Education and Learning (education and learning), ASM International (materials research), U. S. Department of Justice (criminal justice, forensics), Center for Rural Pennsylvania (food availability), Center for Rural Pennsylvania (microfinancing).

Computer facilities: Computer purchase and lease plans are available. 998 computers available on campus for general student use. A campuswide network can be accessed from student residence rooms. Online class registration, software are available. *Web address:* http://www.edinboro.edu/.

General Application Contact: Dr. Alan Biel, Dean of Graduate Studies and Research, 814-732-2856, Fax: 814-732-2611, E-mail: abiel@edinboro.edu.

GRADUATE UNITS

College of Arts and Sciences Students: 191 full-time (131 women), 167 part-time (131 women); includes 24 minority (15 Black or African American, non-Hispanic/Latino; 2 American Indian or Alaska Native, non-Hispanic/Latino; 3 Asian, non-Hispanic/Latino; 3 Hispanic/Latino; 1 Native Hawaiian or other Pacific Islander, non-Hispanic/Latino). Average age 33. *Faculty:* 66 full-time (29 women), 8 part-time/adjunct (6 women). Expenses: Contact institution. *Financial support:* In 2010–11, 66 research assistantships with full and partial tuition reimbursements (averaging $4,050 per year) were awarded; career-related internships or fieldwork, Federal Work-Study, institutionally sponsored loans, scholarships/grants, and unspecified assistantships also available. Support available to part-time students. Financial award application deadline: 2/15; financial award applicants required to submit FAFSA. In 2010, 112 master's, 14 other advanced degrees awarded. *Degree program information:* Part-time and evening/weekend programs available. Offers art (MA); arts and sciences (MA, MFA, MS, MSN, MSW, Certificate); biology (MS); communications studies (Certificate); conflict management (MA); fine arts (MFA); nurse educator (Certificate); nursing (MSN); palliative and end-of-life care (Certificate); social sciences (MA); social work (MSW); speech language pathology (MA). *Application deadline:* Applications are processed on a rolling basis. *Application fee:* $30. Electronic applications accepted. *Application Contact:* Dr. R. Scott Baldwin, Dean, 814-732-2752, Fax: 814-732-2268, E-mail: sbaldwin@edinboro.edu. *Dean,* Dr. Terry L. Smith, 814-732-2477, Fax: 814-732-2629, E-mail: tlsmith@edinboro.edu.

School of Education Students: 363 full-time (264 women), 1,090 part-time (864 women); includes 32 Black or African American, non-Hispanic/Latino; 3 American Indian or Alaska Native, non-Hispanic/Latino; 2 Asian, non-Hispanic/Latino; 9 Hispanic/Latino. Average age 32. *Faculty:* 44 full-time (34 women), 16 part-time/adjunct (9 women). Expenses: Contact institution. *Financial support:* In 2010–11, 78 research assistantships with full and partial tuition reimbursements (averaging $4,050 per year) were awarded; career-related internships or fieldwork, Federal Work-Study, institutionally sponsored loans, scholarships/grants, and unspecified assistantships also available. Support available to part-time students. Financial award application deadline: 2/15; financial award applicants required to submit FAFSA. In 2010, 435 master's, 74 other advanced degrees awarded. *Degree program information:* Part-time and evening/weekend programs available. Offers behavior management (Certificate); character education (Certificate); counseling (MA); education (M Ed, MA, MS, Certificate); educational leadership (M Ed); educational psychology (M Ed); educational specialist school psychology (MS); elementary education (M Ed); elementary principal (Certificate); elementary school guidance counselor (Certificate); K-12 school administration (Certificate); letter of eligibility (Certificate); middle/secondary instruction (M Ed); online special education (M Ed); reading (M Ed); reading specialist (Certificate); school psychology (Certificate); school supervision (Certificate); special education (M Ed). *Application deadline:* Applications are processed on a rolling basis. *Application fee:* $30. Electronic applications accepted. *Application Contact:*

Dr. James Bolton, Interim Dean, 814-732-2752, Fax: 814-732-2268, E-mail: jbolton@edinboro.edu. *Interim Dean*, Dr. James Bolton, 814-732-2752, Fax: 814-732-2268, E-mail: jbolton@edinboro.edu.

EDWARD VIA VIRGINIA COLLEGE OF OSTEOPATHIC MEDICINE, Blacksburg, VA 24060

General Information Independent, coed, graduate-only institution. *Enrollment by degree level:* 723 first professional. *Graduate faculty:* 47 full-time (18 women), 921 part-time/adjunct (214 women). *Tuition:* Full-time $35,277. *Required fees:* $828. *Student services:* Career counseling, exercise/wellness program, free psychological counseling, low-cost health insurance, services for students with disabilities. *Library facilities:* VCOM Library. *Online resources:* library catalog, web page. *Collection:* 1,893 titles, 771 serial subscriptions, 248 audiovisual materials. *Research affiliation:* Virginia Tech (biomedical research).

Computer facilities: 16 computers available on campus for general student use. A campuswide network can be accessed from off campus. Online class registration, Wireless Campus are available. *Web address:* http://www.vcom.vt.edu/.

General Application Contact: Julianne Smartt, Admissions Coordinator, 540-231-6138, Fax: 540-231-5252, E-mail: admissions@vcom.vt.edu.

GRADUATE UNITS

Graduate Program Students: 723 full-time (360 women). Average age 25. *Faculty:* 47 full-time (18 women), 921 part-time/adjunct (214 women). Expenses: Contact institution. *Financial support:* In 2010–11, 610 students received support. Scholarships/grants available. *Application deadline:* For fall admission, 2/1 for domestic and international students. Applications are processed on a rolling basis. *Application fee:* $85. *Application Contact:* Tyler Corvin, Director of Admissions, 540-231-6138, Fax: 540-231-5252, E-mail: admissions@vcom.vt.edu.

ELIZABETH CITY STATE UNIVERSITY, Elizabeth City, NC 27909-7806

General Information State-supported, coed, comprehensive institution. CGS member. *Graduate housing:* Room and/or apartments available on a first-come, first-served basis to single students; on-campus housing not available to married students. Housing application deadline: 5/31.

GRADUATE UNITS

School of Education and Psychology *Degree program information:* Part-time and evening/weekend programs available. Offers education and psychology (M Ed, MSA); elementary education (M Ed); school administration (MSA). Electronic applications accepted.

School of Mathematics, Science and Technology *Degree program information:* Part-time and evening/weekend programs available. Offers biology (MS); mathematics (MS); mathematics, science and technology (MS). Electronic applications accepted.

ELIZABETHTOWN COLLEGE, Elizabethtown, PA 17022-2298

General Information Independent-religious, coed, comprehensive institution.

GRADUATE UNITS

Department of Occupational Therapy Offers occupational therapy (MS).

ELLIS UNIVERSITY, Chicago, IL 60606-7204

General Information Proprietary, coed, comprehensive institution.

GRADUATE UNITS

MBA Program Offers e-commerce (MBA); finance (MBA); general business (MBA); global management (MBA); health care administration (MBA); leadership (MBA); management of information systems (MBA); marketing (MBA); professional accounting (MBA); project management (MBA); public accounting (MBA); risk management (MBA).

Program in Education Offers early childhood education (MA Ed); education (MA Ed); teacher as a leader (MA Ed).

Program in Instructional Technology Offers instructional technology (MS).

Program in Management Offers management (MS).

ELMHURST COLLEGE, Elmhurst, IL 60126-3296

General Information Independent-religious, coed, comprehensive institution. *Enrollment:* 3,430 graduate, professional, and undergraduate students; 22 full-time matriculated graduate/professional students (16 women), 263 part-time matriculated graduate/professional students (160 women). *Enrollment by degree level:* 285 master's. *Graduate faculty:* 17 full-time (10 women), 18 part-time/adjunct (5 women). *Tuition:* Part-time $785 per credit hour. *Required fees:* $60 per year. Tuition and fees vary according to program. *Graduate housing:* On-campus housing not available. *Student services:* Campus employment opportunities, campus safety program, career counseling, child daycare facilities, exercise/wellness program, free psychological counseling, international student services, low-cost health insurance, multicultural affairs office, services for students with disabilities, teacher training, writing training. *Library facilities:* Buehler Library. *Online resources:* library catalog, web page, access to other libraries' catalogs. *Collection:* 230,055 titles, 1,859 serial subscriptions, 8,327 audiovisual materials.

Computer facilities: 800 computers available on campus for general student use. A campuswide network can be accessed from student residence rooms and from off campus. Online class registration is available. *Web address:* http://www.elmhurst.edu/.

General Application Contact: Elizabeth D. Kuebler, Director of Adult and Graduate Admission, 630-617-3300, Fax: 630-617-5501, E-mail: sal@elmhurst.edu.

GRADUATE UNITS

Graduate Programs Students: 22 full-time (16 women), 263 part-time (160 women); includes 17 Black or African American, non-Hispanic/Latino; 19 Asian, non-Hispanic/Latino; 14 Hispanic/Latino; 2 Two or more races, non-Hispanic/Latino, 1 international. Average age 29. 289 applicants, 66% accepted, 134 enrolled. *Faculty:* 17 full-time (10 women), 18 part-time/adjunct (5 women). Expenses: Contact institution. *Financial support:* In 2010–11, 56 students received support. Federal Work-Study and scholarships/grants available. Support available to part-time students. Financial award application deadline: 6/1; financial award applicants required to submit FAFSA. In 2010, 134 master's awarded. *Degree program information:* Part-time and evening/weekend programs available. Postbaccalaureate distance learning degree programs offered (minimal on-campus study). Offers business administration (MBA); computer network systems (MS); early childhood special education (M Ed); English studies (MA); industrial/organizational psychology (MA); nursing (MSN); professional accountancy (MPA); supply chain management (MS); teacher leadership (M Ed). *Application deadline:* For fall admission, 5/1 priority date for domestic and international students. Applications are processed on a rolling basis. *Application fee:* $0. Electronic applications accepted. *Application Contact:* Elizabeth D. Kuebler, Director of Adult and Graduate Admission, 630-617-3300, Fax: 630-617-5501, E-mail: sal@elmhurst.edu. *Director of Adult and Graduate Admission*, Elizabeth D. Kuebler, 630-617-3300, Fax: 630-617-5501, E-mail: sal@elmhurst.edu.

ELMS COLLEGE, Chicopee, MA 01013-2839

General Information Independent-religious, coed, primarily women, comprehensive institution. *Graduate housing:* On-campus housing not available.

GRADUATE UNITS

Division of Communication Sciences and Disorders *Degree program information:* Part-time programs available. Offers autism spectrum disorders (MS, CAGS); autism spectrum disorders with practicum (MS, CAGS); communication sciences and disorders (CAGS).

Division of Education *Degree program information:* Part-time and evening/weekend programs available. Offers early childhood education (MAT); education (M Ed, CAGS); elementary education (MAT); English as a second language (MAT); reading (MAT); secondary education (MAT); special education (MAT).

Division of Nursing *Degree program information:* Part-time and evening/weekend programs available. Offers nursing and health services management (MSN); nursing education (MSN).

Religious Studies Department *Degree program information:* Part-time and evening/weekend programs available. Offers religious studies (MAAT).

ELON UNIVERSITY, Elon, NC 27244-2010

General Information Independent-religious, coed, comprehensive institution. *Enrollment:* 5,709 graduate, professional, and undergraduate students; 538 full-time matriculated graduate/professional students (285 women), 139 part-time matriculated graduate/professional students (81 women). *Enrollment by degree level:* 456 first professional, 221 master's. *Graduate faculty:* 93 full-time (44 women), 42 part-time/adjunct (12 women). *Graduate housing:* On-campus housing not available. *Student services:* Campus employment opportunities, campus safety program, career counseling, exercise/wellness program, free psychological counseling, international student services, low-cost health insurance, multicultural affairs office, services for students with disabilities, teacher training, writing training. *Library facilities:* Carol Grotnes Belk. *Online resources:* library catalog, web page, access to other libraries' catalogs. *Collection:* 348,426 titles, 36,922 serial subscriptions, 21,925 audiovisual materials.

Computer facilities: Computer purchase and lease plans are available. 1,200 computers available on campus for general student use. A campuswide network can be accessed from student residence rooms and from off campus. Online class registration is available. *Web address:* http://www.elon.edu/.

General Application Contact: Art Fadde, Director of Graduate Admissions, 800-334-8448 Ext. 3, Fax: 336-278-7699, E-mail: afadde@elon.edu.

GRADUATE UNITS

Program in Business Administration Students: 137 part-time (52 women); includes 11 Black or African American, non-Hispanic/Latino; 1 American Indian or Alaska Native, non-Hispanic/Latino; 7 Asian, non-Hispanic/Latino; 2 Hispanic/Latino, 10 international. Average age 31. 107 applicants, 63% accepted, 52 enrolled. *Faculty:* 20 full-time (7 women), 1 (woman) part-time/adjunct. Expenses: Contact institution. *Financial support:* In 2010–11, 1 student received support. Federal Work-Study and scholarships/grants available. Support available to part-time students. Financial award application deadline: 3/15; financial award applicants required to submit FAFSA. In 2010, 53 master's awarded. *Degree program information:* Part-time and evening/weekend programs available. Offers business administration (MBA). *Application deadline:* For fall admission, 8/1 priority date for domestic students; for spring admission, 2/1 priority date for domestic students. Applications are processed on a rolling basis. *Application fee:* $50. Electronic applications accepted. *Application Contact:* Art Fadde, Director of Graduate Admissions, 800-334-8448 Ext. 3, Fax: 336-278-7699, E-mail: afadde@elon.edu. *Director*, Dr. William Burpitt, 336-278-5949, Fax: 336-278-5952, E-mail: wburpitt@elon.edu.

Program in Education Students: 68 part-time (57 women); includes 9 Black or African American, non-Hispanic/Latino; 1 Hispanic/Latino. Average age 32. 43 applicants, 79% accepted, 29 enrolled. *Faculty:* 15 full-time (11 women). Expenses: Contact institution. *Financial support:* In 2010–11, 6 students received support. Federal Work-Study and scholarships/grants available. Support available to part-time students. Financial award application deadline: 6/1; financial award applicants required to submit FAFSA. In 2010, 35 master's awarded. *Degree program information:* Part-time programs available. Offers elementary education (M Ed); gifted education (M Ed); special education (M Ed). *Application deadline:* For winter admission, 6/1 priority date for domestic students. Applications are processed on a rolling basis. *Application fee:* $50. Electronic applications accepted. *Application Contact:* Art Fadde, Director of Graduate Admissions, 800-334-8448 Ext. 3, Fax: 336-278-7699, E-mail: afadde@elon.edu. *Director*, Dr. Judith B. Howard, 336-278-5885, Fax: 336-278-5919, E-mail: howardj@elon.edu.

Program in Interactive Media Students: 37 full-time (25 women); includes 2 Black or African American, non-Hispanic/Latino; 1 Hispanic/Latino; 1 Two or more races, non-Hispanic/Latino, 1 international. Average age 25. 76 applicants, 86% accepted, 37 enrolled. *Faculty:* 16 full-time (5 women). Expenses: Contact institution. *Financial support:* In 2010–11, 19 students received support. Federal Work-Study and scholarships/grants available. Financial award application deadline: 3/15; financial award applicants required to submit FAFSA. In 2010, 36 master's awarded. Offers interactive media (MA). *Application deadline:* For fall admission, 5/1 priority date for domestic students. Applications are processed on a rolling basis. *Application fee:* $50. Electronic applications accepted. *Application Contact:* Art Fadde, Director of Graduate Admissions, 800-334-8448 Ext. 3, Fax: 336-278-7699, E-mail: afadde@elon.edu. *Director*, Dr. David Alan Copeland, 336-278-5662, Fax: 336-278-5734, E-mail: dcopeland@elon.edu.

Program in Law Students: 342 full-time (157 women); includes 24 Black or African American, non-Hispanic/Latino; 2 American Indian or Alaska Native, non-Hispanic/Latino; 7 Asian, non-Hispanic/Latino; 2 Hispanic/Latino, 2 international. Average age 26. 873 applicants, 41% accepted, 132 enrolled. *Faculty:* 29 full-time (12 women), 34 part-time/adjunct (7 women). Expenses: Contact institution. *Financial support:* In 2010–11, 279 students received support. Federal Work-Study and scholarships/grants available. Financial award applicants required to submit FAFSA. In 2010, 98 JDs awarded. Offers law (JD). *Application deadline:* For spring admission, 4/1 priority date for domestic students. Applications are processed on a rolling basis. *Application fee:* $50. Electronic applications accepted. *Application Contact:* Alan Woodlief, Associate Dean of School of Law/Director of Law School Admissions, 336-279-9203, E-mail: awoodlief@elon.edu. *Dean*, George Johnson, 336-279-9201, E-mail: gjohnson8@elon.edu.

Program in Physical Therapy Students: 114 full-time (84 women); includes 2 Black or African American, non-Hispanic/Latino; 1 American Indian or Alaska Native, non-Hispanic/Latino; 1 Asian, non-Hispanic/Latino; 2 Hispanic/Latino. Average age 25. 300 applicants, 24% accepted, 38 enrolled. *Faculty:* 13 full-time (9 women), 7 part-time/adjunct (4 women). Expenses: Contact institution. *Financial support:* In 2010–11, 9 students received support. Federal Work-Study and scholarships/grants available. Financial award application deadline: 10/1; financial award applicants required to submit FAFSA. Offers physical therapy (DPT). *Application deadline:* For winter admission, 12/1 priority date for domestic students. Applications are processed on a rolling basis. *Application fee:* $50. Electronic applications accepted. *Application Contact:* Art Fadde, Director of Graduate Admissions, 800-334-8448 Ext. 3, Fax: 336-278-7699, E-mail: afadde@elon.edu. *Chair*, Dr. Elizabeth A. Rogers, 336-278-6400, Fax: 336-278-6414, E-mail: rogers@elon.edu.

EMBRY-RIDDLE AERONAUTICAL UNIVERSITY–DAYTONA, Daytona Beach, FL 32114-3900

General Information Independent, coed, comprehensive institution. *Enrollment:* 5,089 graduate, professional, and undergraduate students; 456 full-time matriculated graduate/professional students (109 women), 133 part-time matriculated graduate/professional students (36 women). *Enrollment by degree level:* 584 master's, 5 doctoral. *Graduate faculty:* 65 full-time (8 women), 18 part-time/adjunct (4 women). *Tuition:* Full-time $14,040; part-time $1170 per credit hour. *Graduate housing:* Room and/or apartments available on a first-come, first-served basis to single students; on-campus housing not available to married students. Housing application deadline: 6/30. *Student services:* Campus employment opportunities, campus safety program, career counseling, free psychological counseling, international student services, low-cost health insurance, services for students with disabilities. *Library facilities:* Jack R. Hunt Memorial Library. *Online resources:* library catalog, web page. *Collection:* 142,244 titles, 971 serial subscriptions, 5,615 audiovisual materials. *Research affiliation:* Federal Aviation Administration (commercial space transportation), The Boeing Company (passenger behavior and modeling for enplane/deplane efficiency), Lockheed Martin Corporation (transportation and security), Gulfstream Aerospace (design and delivery of courses), U. S. Department of Energy (green technology engineering), FAA, Lockheed Martin, Barco, Boeing, CSC, ENSCO, Harris Corporation (satellite-based air traffic control system).

Computer facilities: 1,049 computers available on campus for general student use. A campuswide network can be accessed from student residence rooms and from off campus. Online class registration is available. *Web address:* http://www.embryriddle.edu/.

Embry-Riddle Aeronautical University–Daytona (continued)

General Application Contact: Keith Deaton, Associate Director, International and Graduate Admissions, 800-388-3728, Fax: 386-226-7070, E-mail: graduate.admissions@erau.edu.

GRADUATE UNITS

Daytona Beach Campus Graduate Program Students: 456 full-time (109 women), 133 part-time (36 women); includes 97 minority (29 Black or African American, non-Hispanic/Latino; 3 American Indian or Alaska Native, non-Hispanic/Latino; 26 Asian, non-Hispanic/Latino; 32 Hispanic/Latino; 7 Two or more races, non-Hispanic/Latino), 169 international. Average age 26. 452 applicants, 61% accepted, 175 enrolled. *Faculty:* 65 full-time (8 women), 18 part-time/adjunct (4 women). Expenses: Contact institution. *Financial support:* In 2010–11, 197 students received support, including 57 research assistantships with full and partial tuition reimbursements available (averaging $6,939 per year), 67 teaching assistantships with full and partial tuition reimbursements available (averaging $8,382 per year); career-related internships or fieldwork, Federal Work-Study, and unspecified assistantships also available. Support available to part-time students. Financial award applicants required to submit FAFSA. In 2010, 110 master's awarded. *Degree program information:* Part-time and evening/weekend programs available. Postbaccalaureate distance learning degree programs offered. Offers aerospace engineering (MSAE); applied aviation sciences (MSA); business administration (MBA); business administration aviation management (MBA-AM); electrical/computer engineering (MSECE); engineering physics (PhD); human factors engineering (MSHFS); mechanical engineering (MSME); multidisciplinary engineering (MSE); software engineering (MSE); systems engineering (MSHFS). *Application deadline:* For fall admission, 8/1 priority date for domestic students; for spring admission, 12/1 priority date for domestic students. Applications are processed on a rolling basis. *Application fee:* $50. Electronic applications accepted. *Application Contact:* Keith Deaton, Associate Director, International and Graduate Admissions, 800-388-3728, Fax: 386-226-7070, E-mail: graduate.admissions@erau.edu. *Executive Vice President and Chief Academic Officer,* Dr. Richard H. Heist, 386-226-6216.

EMBRY-RIDDLE AERONAUTICAL UNIVERSITY–PRESCOTT, Prescott, AZ 86301-3720

General Information Independent, coed, comprehensive institution. *Enrollment:* 1,705 graduate, professional, and undergraduate students; 45 full-time matriculated graduate/professional students (11 women), 4 part-time matriculated graduate/professional students (2 women). *Enrollment by degree level:* 49 master's. *Graduate faculty:* 5 full-time (1 woman). *Tuition:* Full-time $14,040; part-time $1170 per credit hour. *Graduate housing:* Room and/or apartments available on a first-come, first-served basis to single students; on-campus housing not available to married students. Housing application deadline: 6/30. *Student services:* Campus employment opportunities, campus safety program, career counseling, free psychological counseling, international student services, low-cost health insurance, services for students with disabilities. *Library facilities:* Christine & Steven F. Udvar-Hazy Library & Learning Center. *Online resources:* library catalog, web page. *Collection:* 44,638 titles, 420 serial subscriptions, 2,584 audiovisual materials. *Research affiliation:* FAA (commercial space transportation topics: airspace standards, infrastructure, risk and capacity studies), U. S. Department of Energy & General Motors (engineering design of EcoCar Challenge), The Boeing Company (human factors analysis of passenger restraints and interferences while boarding aircraft).

Computer facilities: 470 computers available on campus for general student use. A campuswide network can be accessed from student residence rooms and from off campus. Online class registration is available. *Web address:* http://www.embryriddle.edu/.

General Application Contact: Debra Cates-Foster, Graduate Admissions Coordinator, 928-777-6697, Fax: 928-777-6958.

GRADUATE UNITS

Program in Safety Science Students: 45 full-time (11 women), 4 part-time (2 women); includes 6 minority (1 Black or African American, non-Hispanic/Latino; 3 Hispanic/Latino; 2 Two or more races, non-Hispanic/Latino), 9 international. Average age 28. 38 applicants, 63% accepted, 15 enrolled. *Faculty:* 5 full-time (1 woman). Expenses: Contact institution. *Financial support:* In 2010–11, 36 students received support, including 8 research assistantships with full and partial tuition reimbursements available (averaging $1,215 per year); career-related internships or fieldwork, Federal Work-Study, and unspecified assistantships also available. Support available to part-time students. Financial award application deadline: 4/15; financial award applicants required to submit FAFSA. In 2010, 17 master's awarded. Offers safety science (MSSS). *Application deadline:* For fall admission, 8/1 priority date for domestic students; for spring admission, 12/1 priority date for domestic students. Applications are processed on a rolling basis. *Application fee:* $50. Electronic applications accepted. *Application Contact:* Debra Cates-Foster, Graduate Admissions Coordinator, 928-777-6687, E-mail: debra.cates@erau.edu. *Dean, College of Aviation,* Dr. Gary Northam, 928-777-3964, Fax: 928-777-6958.

EMBRY-RIDDLE AERONAUTICAL UNIVERSITY–WORLDWIDE, Daytona Beach, FL 32114-3900

General Information Independent, coed, comprehensive institution. *Enrollment:* 16,423 graduate, professional, and undergraduate students; 2,594 full-time matriculated graduate/professional students (459 women), 2,618 part-time matriculated graduate/professional students (393 women). *Enrollment by degree level:* 5,189 master's, 23 doctoral. *Graduate faculty:* 41 full-time (2 women), 268 part-time/adjunct (24 women). *Student services:* Career counseling. *Library facilities:* Jack R. Hunt Memorial Library. *Online resources:* library catalog, web page. *Collection:* 142,244 titles, 971 serial subscriptions, 5,615 audiovisual materials. *Web address:* http://www.embryriddle.edu/.

General Application Contact: Linda Dammer, Director of Admissions, 386-226-6396 Ext. 1, Fax: 386-226-6984, E-mail: worldwide@erau.edu.

GRADUATE UNITS

Worldwide Headquarters Students: 2,594 full-time (459 women), 2,618 part-time (393 women); includes 1,042 minority (407 Black or African American, non-Hispanic/Latino; 28 American Indian or Alaska Native, non-Hispanic/Latino; 163 Asian, non-Hispanic/Latino; 370 Hispanic/Latino; 9 Native Hawaiian or other Pacific Islander, non-Hispanic/Latino; 65 Two or more races, non-Hispanic/Latino), 31 international. Average age 33. 1,553 applicants, 87% accepted, 872 enrolled. *Faculty:* 41 full-time (2 women), 268 part-time/adjunct (24 women). Expenses: Contact institution. *Financial support:* In 2010–11, 1,243 students received support. Available to part-time students. Applicants required to submit FAFSA. In 2010, 1,039 master's awarded. *Degree program information:* Part-time and evening/weekend programs available. Postbaccalaureate distance learning degree programs offered (no on-campus study). Offers aeronautics (MAS); aviation (PhD); business administration for aviation (MBAA); logistics and supply chain management (MSLSCM); management (MSM, MSM/MBAA); project management (MSPM); space education (MSSE); technical management (MSTM). *Application deadline:* Applications are processed on a rolling basis. *Application fee:* $50. Electronic applications accepted. *Application Contact:* Linda Dammer, Director of Admissions, 386-226-6396 Ext. 1, Fax: 386-226-6984, E-mail: worldwide@erau.edu. *Executive Vice President/Chief Academic Officer,* Dr. John R. Watret, 386-226-6970, E-mail: john.watret@erau.edu.

EMERSON COLLEGE, Boston, MA 02116-4624

General Information Independent, coed, comprehensive institution. CGS member. *Graduate housing:* On-campus housing not available.

GRADUATE UNITS

Graduate Studies *Degree program information:* Part-time and evening/weekend programs available. Electronic applications accepted.

School of Communication Offers communication (MA, MS); communication disorders (MS); communication management (MA); global marketing communication and advertising (MA); health communication (MA); integrated marketing communication (MA); journalism (MA). Electronic applications accepted.

School of the Arts *Degree program information:* Part-time programs available. Offers arts (MA, MFA); creative writing (MFA); media art (MFA); publishing and writing (MA); theatre education (MA); visual and media arts (MFA). Electronic applications accepted.

EMILY CARR UNIVERSITY OF ART + DESIGN, Vancouver, BC V6H 3R9, Canada

General Information Province-supported, coed, comprehensive institution. *Graduate housing:* On-campus housing not available. *Research affiliation:* Children's Hospital, Vancouver BC (health care research), Aldrich Pears and Associates (experience design), Kodak Communications Group (interaction design), Donat Group (e-learning), Paperny Films (television and film production), Fuel Cell Research Centre, National Research Council (clean technology).

GRADUATE UNITS

Program in Applied Arts Offers design (MAA); media arts (MAA); visual arts (MAA). Electronic applications accepted.

Program in Digital Media Offers digital media (MDM). Electronic applications accepted.

EMMANUEL CHRISTIAN SEMINARY, Johnson City, TN 37601-9438

General Information Independent-religious, coed, primarily men, graduate-only institution. *Enrollment by degree level:* 106 first professional, 29 master's, 10 doctoral, 2 other advanced degrees. *Graduate faculty:* 9 full-time (2 women), 9 part-time/adjunct (1 woman). *Tuition:* Full-time $11,700; part-time $390 per credit hour. *Required fees:* $162.50 per semester. One-time fee: $240. Tuition and fees vary according to reciprocity agreements. *Graduate housing:* Rooms and/or apartments available on a first-come, first-served basis to single and married students. Typical cost: $2700 per year for single students; $5400 per year for married students. Housing application deadline: 8/1. *Student services:* Campus employment opportunities, career counseling, international student services, low-cost health insurance, services for students with disabilities. *Library facilities:* ECS Library. *Online resources:* library catalog, web page, access to other libraries' catalogs. *Collection:* 149,890 titles, 735 serial subscriptions, 10,856 audiovisual materials. *Research affiliation:* American Schools of Oriental Research (Ancient Near East), Disciples of Christ Historical Society (church history (Stone-Campbell tradition)).

Computer facilities: 10 computers available on campus for general student use. A campuswide network can be accessed from student residence rooms and from off campus. *Web address:* http://www.esr.edu/.

General Application Contact: Erin Layton, Director of Admissions, 423-461-1535, Fax: 423-926-6198, E-mail: elayton@ecs.edu.

GRADUATE UNITS

Graduate and Professional Programs Students: 90 full-time (27 women), 57 part-time (10 women); includes 2 Black or African American, non-Hispanic/Latino; 3 Hispanic/Latino, 17 international. Average age 27. 30 applicants, 97% accepted, 22 enrolled. *Faculty:* 9 full-time (2 women), 9 part-time/adjunct (1 woman). Expenses: Contact institution. *Financial support:* In 2010–11, 136 students received support; teaching assistantships with partial tuition reimbursements available, career-related internships or fieldwork, scholarships/grants, and tuition waivers (partial) available. Support available to part-time students. Financial award application deadline: 3/1; financial award applicants required to submit FAFSA. In 2010, 17 first professional degrees, 1 master's, 1 doctorate awarded. *Degree program information:* Part-time programs available. Offers Christian care and counseling (M Div); Christian doctrine (MAR); Christian education (M Div); Christian ministry (M Div); church history (MAR); divinity (M Div); ministry (D Min); New Testament (MAR); Old Testament (MAR); urban ministry (M Div); world missions (M Div). *Application deadline:* For fall admission, 8/1 for domestic and international students; for spring admission, 1/20 for domestic and international students. Applications are processed on a rolling basis. *Application fee:* $25. *Application Contact:* Erin Layton, Director of Admissions, 423-461-1535, Fax: 423-926-6198, E-mail: elayton@ecs.edu. *Dean and Professor of Christian Care and Counseling,* Dr. Jack Holland, 423-461-1524, Fax: 423-926-6198, E-mail: jholland@ecs.edu.

EMMANUEL COLLEGE, Boston, MA 02115

General Information Independent-religious, coed, comprehensive institution. *Graduate housing:* On-campus housing not available.

GRADUATE UNITS

Graduate Programs *Degree program information:* Part-time and evening/weekend programs available. Postbaccalaureate distance learning degree programs offered. Offers biopharmaceutical leadership (MSM); educational leadership (CAGS); elementary education (MAT); human resource management (MS, Certificate); management (MSM); management and leadership (Certificate); research administration (MSM, Certificate); school administration (M Ed); secondary education (MAT). Electronic applications accepted.

EMORY & HENRY COLLEGE, Emory, VA 24327-0947

General Information Independent-religious, coed, comprehensive institution. *Graduate housing:* Room and/or apartments guaranteed to single students; on-campus housing not available to married students.

GRADUATE UNITS

Graduate Programs *Degree program information:* Part-time and evening/weekend programs available.

EMORY UNIVERSITY, Atlanta, GA 30322-1100

General Information Independent-religious, coed, university. CGS member. *Enrollment:* 13,381 graduate, professional, and undergraduate students; 5,273 full-time matriculated graduate/professional students (3,030 women), 620 part-time matriculated graduate/professional students (309 women). *Enrollment by degree level:* 1,683 first professional, 2,360 master's, 1,839 doctoral, 11 other advanced degrees. *Graduate faculty:* 2,952 full-time (1,124 women), 557 part-time/adjunct (252 women). *Tuition:* Full-time $33,800. *Required fees:* $1300. *Graduate housing:* Rooms and/or apartments available on a first-come, first-served basis to single and married students. *Student services:* Campus employment opportunities, campus safety program, career counseling, child daycare facilities, exercise/wellness program, free psychological counseling, grant writing training, international student services, low-cost health insurance, multicultural affairs office, services for students with disabilities, teacher training, writing training. *Library facilities:* Robert W. Woodruff Library plus 8 others. *Online resources:* library catalog, web page, access to other libraries' catalogs. *Collection:* 3.6 million titles, 85,044 serial subscriptions, 105,006 audiovisual materials. *Research affiliation:* BILL AND MELINDA GATES FOUNDATION, GARDEN CITY GROUP, GEORGIA CANCER COALITION, FOUNDATION FOR NATIONAL INSTITUTE OF HEALTH, DANA FARBER CANCER INSTITUTE, JUVENILE DIABETES RESEARCH FOUNDATION.

Computer facilities: Computer purchase and lease plans are available. 1,000 computers available on campus for general student use. A campuswide network can be accessed from student residence rooms and from off campus. Online class registration, Computer Repair System, Online Library, iTunes University are available. *Web address:* http://www.emory.edu/.

General Application Contact: Kharen Fulton, Director of Admissions, 404-727-0184, Fax: 404-727-4990, E-mail: gradkef@emory.edu.

GRADUATE UNITS

Candler School of Theology Students: 411 full-time (206 women), 44 part-time (29 women); includes 113 Black or African American, non-Hispanic/Latino; 1 American Indian or Alaska Native, non-Hispanic/Latino; 8 Asian, non-Hispanic/Latino; 8 Hispanic/Latino; 1 Two or more races, non-Hispanic/Latino, 40 international. Average age 32. 603 applicants, 74% accepted, 191 enrolled. *Faculty:* 45 full-time (11 women), 26 part-time/adjunct (12 women). Expenses: Contact institution. *Financial support:* In 2010–11, 422 students received support, including 343 fellowships (averaging $12,216 per year); career-related internships or fieldwork, institutionally sponsored loans, scholarships/grants, and student employment also available. Support available to part-time students. Financial award application deadline: 1/15; financial award applicants required to submit FAFSA. In 2010, 141 first professional degrees, 48 master's, 1 doctorate awarded. *Degree program information:* Part-time programs available. Offers formation and witness (M Div); history, scripture and tradition (MTS); leadership in church and community (M Div); modern religious thought and experience (MTS); pastoral counseling (Th D); religion and race (M Div); religion, health and science (M Div); scripture and interpretation (M Div); society and personality (M Div); theology (Th M); theology and ethics (M Div); theology and the arts (M Div); traditions of the church (M Div); women and religion (M Div). *Application deadline:* For fall admission, 7/1 for domestic and international students; for spring admission, 11/1 for domestic and international students. Applications are processed on a rolling basis. *Application fee:* $50. Electronic applications accepted. *Application Contact:* Mary Lou Greenwood Boice, Associate Dean of Admissions and Financial Aid, 404-727-6326, Fax: 404-727-2915, E-mail: candleradmissions@emory.edu. *Registrar*, Shelly E. Hart, 404-727-6480, Fax: 404-727-4373, E-mail: candlerregistrar@emory.edu.

Goizueta Business School Students: 481 full-time (149 women), 308 part-time (78 women); includes 198 minority (63 Black or African American, non-Hispanic/Latino; 1 American Indian or Alaska Native, non-Hispanic/Latino; 102 Asian, non-Hispanic/Latino; 31 Hispanic/Latino; 1 Two or more races, non-Hispanic/Latino), 180 international. 1,577 applicants, 35% accepted, 267 enrolled. *Faculty:* 82 full-time (18 women), 26 part-time/adjunct (12 women). Expenses: Contact institution. *Financial support:* In 2010–11, 469 students received support; fellowships with full tuition reimbursements available, research assistantships, teaching assistantships, career-related internships or fieldwork, Federal Work-Study, institutionally sponsored loans, and scholarships/grants available. Support available to part-time students. Financial award application deadline: 4/1; financial award applicants required to submit FAFSA. In 2010, 419 master's, 8 doctorates awarded. *Degree program information:* Part-time and evening/weekend programs available. Postbaccalaureate distance learning degree programs offered (minimal on-campus study). Offers accounting (PhD); business (MBA, PhD); business administration (MBA); finance (PhD); information systems (PhD); marketing (PhD); organization and management (PhD). *Application deadline:* For fall admission, 3/15 priority date for domestic students, 2/1 priority date for international students; for winter admission, 10/1 priority date for domestic students; for spring admission, 3/1 priority date for domestic students. Applications are processed on a rolling basis. Electronic applications accepted. *Application Contact:* Julie Barefoot, Associate Dean, 404-727-6311, Fax: 404-727-4612, E-mail: admissions@bus.emory.edu. *Dean*, Lawrence Benveniste, 404-727-6377, Fax: 404-727-0868, E-mail: larry_benveniste@bus.emory.edu.

Laney Graduate School Offers anthropology (PhD); art history (PhD); biophysics (PhD); biostatistics (MPH, MSPH, PhD); chemistry (PhD); choral conducting (MM, MSM); clinical psychology (PhD); clinical research (MS); cognition and development (PhD); comparative literature (PhD, Certificate); computer science (MS, PhD); condensed matter physics (PhD); development practice (MDP); economics (PhD); English (Certificate); film studies (Certificate); French (PhD, Certificate); French and educational studies (PhD); history (PhD); Jewish studies (MA); mathematics (MS, PhD); Middle Eastern studies (PhD); neuroscience and animal behavior (PhD); non-linear physics (PhD); nursing (PhD); organ performance (MM, MSM); philosophy (PhD); political science (PhD); psychoanalytic studies (PhD); public health informatics (MSPH); radiological physics (PhD); religion (PhD); sociology (MA, PhD); soft condensed matter physics (PhD); solid-state physics (PhD); Spanish (PhD, Certificate); statistical physics (PhD); women studies (Certificate); women's studies (Certificate). Electronic applications accepted.

Division of Biological and Biomedical Sciences Students: 447 full-time (288 women); includes 28 Black or African American, non-Hispanic/Latino; 1 American Indian or Alaska Native, non-Hispanic/Latino; 21 Asian, non-Hispanic/Latino; 20 Hispanic/Latino, 63 international. Average age 27. 1,066 applicants, 15% accepted, 77 enrolled. *Faculty:* 325 full-time (81 women). Expenses: Contact institution. *Financial support:* In 2010–11, 142 students received support, including 142 fellowships with full tuition reimbursements available (averaging $25,000 per year); institutionally sponsored loans, scholarships/grants, health care benefits, and tuition waivers (full) also available. In 2010, 60 doctorates awarded. Offers biochemistry, cell and developmental biology (PhD); biological and biomedical sciences (PhD); cancer biology (PhD); genetics and molecular biology (PhD); immunology and molecular pathogenesis (PhD); microbiology and molecular genetics (PhD); molecular and systems pharmacology (PhD); neuroscience (PhD); nutrition and health sciences (PhD); population biology, ecology and evolution (PhD). *Application deadline:* For fall admission, 12/1 for domestic and international students. *Application fee:* $75. Electronic applications accepted. *Application Contact:* Kathy Smith, Director of Recruitment and Admissions, 404-727-2547, Fax: 404-727-3322, E-mail: kathy.smith@emory.edu. *Director*, Dr. Keith Wilkinson, 404-727-2545, Fax: 404-727-3322, E-mail: genekdw@emory.edu.

Division of Educational Studies Offers educational studies (MA, PhD, DAST); middle grades teaching (M Ed, MAT); secondary teaching (M Ed, MAT). Electronic applications accepted.

Division of Religion Offers religion (PhD). Electronic applications accepted.

Graduate Institute of Liberal Arts Offers liberal arts (PhD). Electronic applications accepted.

Nell Hodgson Woodruff School of Nursing *Degree program information:* Part-time programs available. Offers adult and elder health advanced practice nursing (MSN); emergency nurse practitioner (MSN); family nurse practitioner (MSN); family nurse-midwife (MSN); nurse midwifery (MSN); pediatric nurse practitioner acute and primary care (MSN); public health nursing leadership (MSN); women's health nurse practitioner (MSN); women's health title x (MSN); women's health/adult health nurse practitioner (MSN). Electronic applications accepted.

Rollins School of Public Health *Degree program information:* Part-time and evening/weekend programs available. Postbaccalaureate distance learning degree programs offered (minimal on-campus study). Offers applied epidemiology (MPH); behavioral sciences and health education (MPH); biostatistics and bioinformatics (MPH, MSPH); environmental and occupational health (MPH, MSPH); epidemiology (MPH, MSPH, PhD); global demography (MSPH); global environmental health (MPH); health policy (MPH); health policy research (MSPH); health services management (MPH); healthcare outcomes (MPH); prevention science (MPH); public health (MPH, MSPH, PhD, MM Sc/MPH); public health informatics (MSPH); public nutrition (MSPH). Electronic applications accepted.

School of Law Students: 824 full-time (382 women); includes 56 Black or African American, non-Hispanic/Latino; 6 American Indian or Alaska Native, non-Hispanic/Latino; 88 Asian, non-Hispanic/Latino; 77 Hispanic/Latino; 16 Two or more races, non-Hispanic/Latino, 35 international. Average age 24. 4,583 applicants, 27% accepted, 293 enrolled. *Faculty:* 65 full-time (29 women), 36 part-time/adjunct (8 women). Expenses: Contact institution. *Financial support:* In 2010–11, 529 students received support, including 13 fellowships with full tuition reimbursements available (averaging $3,000 per year), 57 research assistantships (averaging $9,880 per year); career-related internships or fieldwork, Federal Work-Study, institutionally sponsored loans, scholarships/grants, and tuition waivers (full and partial) also available. Financial award application deadline: 3/1; financial award applicants required to submit FAFSA. In 2010, 255 first professional degrees, 9 other advanced degrees awarded. Offers law (JD, LL M, Certificate). *Application deadline:* For fall admission, 3/1 for domestic and international students. Applications are processed on a rolling basis. *Application fee:* $70. Electronic applications accepted. *Application Contact:* Ethan Rosenzweig, Assistant Dean for Admission, 404-727-6802, Fax: 404-727-2477, E-mail: lawinfo@law.emory.edu. *Dean*, David F. Partlett, 404-712-8815, Fax: 404-727-0866, E-mail: david.partlett@emory.edu.

School of Medicine Students: 922 full-time (561 women); includes 245 minority (92 Black or African American, non-Hispanic/Latino; 2 American Indian or Alaska Native, non-Hispanic/Latino; 110 Asian, non-Hispanic/Latino; 36 Hispanic/Latino; 5 Two or more races, non-Hispanic/Latino), 19 international. Average age 26. 5,758 applicants, 9% accepted, 292 enrolled. *Faculty:* 2,104 full-time (754 women), 1,200 part-time/adjunct (458 women). Expenses: Contact institution. *Financial support:* In 2010–11, 662 students received support. Institutionally sponsored loans and scholarships/grants available. Financial award application deadline: 3/1; financial award applicants required to submit CSS PROFILE or FAFSA. In 2010, 128 first professional degrees, 89 master's, 41 doctorates awarded. Offers anesthesiology (MM Sc); medicine (MD, MM Sc, DPT, PhD); physical therapy (DPT); physician assistant (MM Sc). *Application deadline:* Applications are processed on a rolling basis. Electronic applications accepted. *Application Contact:* Dr. John William Eley, Executive Associate Dean, Medical Education and Student Affairs, 404-727-5655, Fax: 404-727-0045, E-mail: jeley@emory.edu. *Executive Associate Dean, Medical Education and Student Affairs*, Dr. John William Eley, 404-727-5655, Fax: 404-727-0045, E-mail: jeley@emory.edu.

See Close-Up on page 943.

EMPEROR'S COLLEGE OF TRADITIONAL ORIENTAL MEDICINE, Santa Monica, CA 90403

General Information Private, coed, graduate-only institution. *Graduate housing:* On-campus housing not available. *Research affiliation:* UCLA Ashe Center (student health), Lotus Herbs (herbs), LA Free Clinic (herbs).

GRADUATE UNITS

Graduate Programs *Degree program information:* Part-time and evening/weekend programs available. Offers oriental medicine (MTOM, DAOM).

EMPORIA STATE UNIVERSITY, Emporia, KS 66801-5087

General Information State-supported, coed, comprehensive institution. CGS member. *Enrollment:* 6,262 graduate, professional, and undergraduate students; 345 full-time matriculated graduate/professional students (214 women), 1,483 part-time matriculated graduate/professional students (1,062 women). *Enrollment by degree level:* 1,801 master's, 17 doctoral, 10 other advanced degrees. *Graduate faculty:* 214 full-time (96 women), 14 part-time/adjunct (11 women). Tuition, state resident: full-time $4382; part-time $183 per credit hour. Tuition, nonresident: full-time $13,572; part-time $566 per credit hour. *Required fees:* $1022; $62 per credit hour. Tuition and fees vary according to course level, course load and campus/location. *Graduate housing:* Rooms and/or apartments available on a first-come, first-served basis to single and married students. Typical cost: $3180 per year ($6230 including board) for single students; $3060 per year ($6110 including board) for married students. Housing application deadline: 8/25. *Student services:* Campus employment opportunities, campus safety program, career counseling, child daycare facilities, exercise/wellness program, free psychological counseling, grant writing training, international student services, low-cost health insurance, multicultural affairs office, services for students with disabilities, teacher training, writing training. *Library facilities:* William Allen White Library. *Online resources:* library catalog, web page, access to other libraries' catalogs. *Collection:* 2.5 million titles, 41,417 serial subscriptions, 9,165 audiovisual materials.

Computer facilities: 410 computers available on campus for general student use. A campuswide network can be accessed from student residence rooms and from off campus. Online class registration, various software packages are available. *Web address:* http://www.emporia.edu/.

General Application Contact: Mary Sewell, Admissions Coordinator, 800-950-GRAD, Fax: 620-341-5909, E-mail: msewell@emporia.edu.

GRADUATE UNITS

Graduate School Students: 345 full-time (214 women), 1,483 part-time (1,062 women); includes 139 minority (40 Black or African American, non-Hispanic/Latino; 6 American Indian or Alaska Native, non-Hispanic/Latino; 22 Asian, non-Hispanic/Latino; 45 Hispanic/Latino; 14 Native Hawaiian or other Pacific Islander, non-Hispanic/Latino; 12 Two or more races, non-Hispanic/Latino), 143 international. Average age 34. 486 applicants, 83% accepted, 312 enrolled. *Faculty:* 253 full-time (114 women), 25 part-time/adjunct (19 women). Expenses: Contact institution. *Financial support:* In 2010–11, 27 research assistantships with full tuition reimbursements (averaging $6,596 per year), 85 teaching assistantships with full tuition reimbursements (averaging $6,698 per year) were awarded; career-related internships or fieldwork, Federal Work-Study, institutionally sponsored loans, scholarships/grants, health care benefits, and unspecified assistantships also available. Financial award application deadline: 3/15; financial award applicants required to submit FAFSA. In 2010, 609 master's, 1 doctorate, 19 other advanced degrees awarded. *Degree program information:* Part-time and evening/weekend programs available. Postbaccalaureate distance learning degree programs offered (no on-campus study). *Application deadline:* Applications are processed on a rolling basis. *Application fee:* $30 ($75 for international students). Electronic applications accepted. *Application Contact:* Mary Sewell, Admissions Coordinator, 800-950-GRAD, Fax: 620-341-5909, E-mail: msewell@emporia.edu. *Dean*, Dr. Kathy Ermler, 620-341-5403, Fax: 620-341-5909, E-mail: kermler@emporia.edu.

College of Liberal Arts and Sciences Students: 52 full-time (26 women), 117 part-time (62 women); includes 14 minority (3 Black or African American, non-Hispanic/Latino; 2 American Indian or Alaska Native, non-Hispanic/Latino; 2 Asian, non-Hispanic/Latino; 3 Hispanic/Latino; 2 Native Hawaiian or other Pacific Islander, non-Hispanic/Latino; 2 Two or more races, non-Hispanic/Latino), 27 international. 48 applicants, 94% accepted, 35 enrolled. *Faculty:* 98 full-time (35 women), 10 part-time/adjunct (8 women). Expenses: Contact institution. *Financial support:* In 2010–11, 12 research assistantships with full tuition reimbursements (averaging $5,981 per year), 45 teaching assistantships with full tuition reimbursements (averaging $6,890 per year) were awarded; career-related internships or fieldwork, Federal Work-Study, institutionally sponsored loans, health care benefits, and unspecified assistantships also available. Financial award application deadline: 3/15; financial award applicants required to submit FAFSA. In 2010, 47 master's awarded. *Degree program information:* Part-time programs available. Offers American history (MA, MAT); anthropology (MAT); botany (MS); earth science (MS); economics (MAT); English (MA); environmental biology (MS); general biology (MS); geography (MAT); geospatial analysis (Postbaccalaureate Certificate); history (MA); liberal arts and sciences (MA, MAT, MM, MS, Postbaccalaureate Certificate); mathematics (MS); microbial and cellular biology (MS); music education (MM); performance (MM); physical science (MS); political science (MAT); social sciences (MAT); social studies education (MAT); sociology (MAT); teaching English to speakers of other languages (MA); world history (MA, MAT); zoology (MS). *Application deadline:* For fall admission, 8/15 priority date for domestic students. Applications are processed on a rolling basis. *Application fee:* $30 ($75 for international students). Electronic applications accepted. *Application Contact:* Mary Sewell, Admissions Coordinator, 800-950-GRAD, Fax: 620-341-5909, E-mail: msewell@emporia.edu. *Dean*, Dr. Steven Brown, 620-341-5278, Fax: 620-341-5681, E-mail: sbrown10@emporia.edu.

School of Business Students: 97 full-time (56 women), 67 part-time (38 women); includes 10 minority (4 Black or African American, non-Hispanic/Latino; 3 Asian, non-Hispanic/Latino; 3 Hispanic/Latino), 80 international. 58 applicants, 67% accepted, 31 enrolled. *Faculty:* 30 full-time (8 women). Expenses: Contact institution. *Financial support:* In 2010–11, 5 research assistantships with full tuition reimbursements (averaging $6,353 per year), 11 teaching assistantships with full tuition reimbursements (averaging $7,059 per year) were awarded; career-related internships or fieldwork, Federal Work-Study, institutionally sponsored loans, health care benefits, and unspecified assistantships also available. Financial award application deadline: 3/15; financial award applicants required to submit FAFSA. In 2010, 49 master's awarded. *Degree program information:* Part-time programs available. Postbaccalaureate distance learning degree programs offered (minimal on-campus study). Offers business (MBA, MS); business administration (MBA); business education (MS). *Application deadline:* For fall admission, 8/15 priority date for domestic students. Applications are processed on a rolling basis. *Application fee:* $30 ($75 for international students). Electronic applications accepted. *Application Contact:* Dr. Donald Miller, Director, MBA Program, 620-341-5456, Fax: 620-341-6523, E-mail: dmiller1@emporia.edu. *Dean*, Dr. Joseph Wen, 620-341-5274, Fax: 620-341-5892, E-mail: hwen@emporia.edu.

School of Library and Information Management Students: 23 full-time (17 women), 338 part-time (280 women); includes 32 minority (4 Black or African American, non-Hispanic/Latino; 1 American Indian or Alaska Native, non-Hispanic/Latino; 12 Asian, non-Hispanic/Latino; 9 Hispanic/Latino; 5 Native Hawaiian or other Pacific Islander, non-Hispanic/Latino; 1 Two or more races, non-Hispanic/Latino), 4 international. 98 applicants, 95% accepted, 77 enrolled. *Faculty:* 5 full-time (3 women). Expenses: Contact institution. *Financial support:* In 2010–11, 4 research assistantships (averaging $7,059 per year), 8 teaching assistantships with full tuition reimbursements (averaging $7,059 per year) were awarded; Federal Work-Study, institutionally sponsored loans, and unspecified assistantships also available. Financial award application deadline: 3/15; financial award applicants required to submit FAFSA. In 2010, 127 master's, 1 doctorate, 5 other advanced degrees awarded. *Degree*

Emporia State University (continued)

program information: Part-time and evening/weekend programs available. Postbaccalaureate distance learning degree programs offered (minimal on-campus study). Offers archives studies (Certificate); legal information management (Certificate); library and information management (MLS, PhD, Certificate). *Application deadline:* For fall admission, 8/15 priority date for domestic students. Applications are processed on a rolling basis. *Application fee:* $30 ($75 for international students). Electronic applications accepted. *Application Contact:* Candace Boardman, Director, Kansas MLS Program, 620-341-6159, E-mail: cboardma@emporia.edu. *Interim Dean*, Dr. Gwen Alexander, 620-341-5203, Fax: 620-341-5233, E-mail: galexan1@emporia.edu.

Teachers College Students: 173 full-time (115 women), 961 part-time (682 women); includes 83 minority (29 Black or African American, non-Hispanic/Latino; 3 American Indian or Alaska Native, non-Hispanic/Latino; 5 Asian, non-Hispanic/Latino; 30 Hispanic/Latino; 7 Native Hawaiian or other Pacific Islander, non-Hispanic/Latino; 9 Two or more races, non-Hispanic/Latino), 32 international. 282 applicants, 79% accepted, 169 enrolled. *Faculty:* 81 full-time (50 women), 4 part-time/adjunct (3 women). Expenses: Contact institution. *Financial support:* In 2010–11, 2 research assistantships (averaging $7,059 per year), 25 teaching assistantships with full tuition reimbursements (averaging $6,471 per year) were awarded; career-related internships or fieldwork, Federal Work-Study, institutionally sponsored loans, health care benefits, and unspecified assistantships also available. Financial award application deadline: 3/15; financial award applicants required to submit FAFSA. In 2010, 386 master's, 11 other advanced degrees awarded. *Degree program information:* Part-time programs available. Postbaccalaureate distance learning degree programs offered (no on-campus study). Offers art therapy (MS); behavior disorders (MS); clinical psychology (MS); curriculum and instruction (MS); curriculum leadership (MS); early childhood curriculum (MS); early childhood education (MS); early childhood special education (MS); education (M Ed, MS, Ed S); educational administration (MS); effective practitioner (MS); elementary administration (MS); elementary subject matter (MS); elementary/secondary administration (MS); English as a second language (MS); general psychology (MS); gifted, talented, and creative (MS); industrial/organizational psychology (MS); instructional design and technology (MS); instructional leadership (MS); interrelated special education (MS); learning disabilities (MS); master teacher (MS); mental health counseling (MS); mental retardation (MS); national board certification (MS); physical education (MS); psychology (MS); reading (MS); rehabilitation counseling (MS); school counseling (MS); school psychology (MS, Ed S); secondary administration (MS); secondary subject matter (MS); special education (MS); teaching (M Ed). *Application deadline:* Applications are processed on a rolling basis. *Application fee:* $30 ($75 for international students). Electronic applications accepted. *Application Contact:* Mary Sewell, Admissions Coordinator, 800-950-GRAD, Fax: 620-341-5909, E-mail: msewell@emporia.edu. *Dean*, Dr. J. Phillip Bennett, 620-341-5367, Fax: 620-341-5785, E-mail: pbennett@emporia.edu.

See Close-Up on page 945.

ENDICOTT COLLEGE, Beverly, MA 01915-2096

General Information Independent, coed, comprehensive institution. *Enrollment:* 4,105 graduate, professional, and undergraduate students; 313 full-time matriculated graduate/professional students (192 women), 299 part-time matriculated graduate/professional students (221 women). *Enrollment by degree level:* 589 master's, 23 other advanced degrees. *Graduate faculty:* 17 full-time (6 women), 87 part-time/adjunct (46 women). *Graduate housing:* Room and/or apartments available on a first-come, first-served basis to single students; on-campus housing not available to married students. *Student services:* Campus employment opportunities, campus safety program, career counseling, free psychological counseling, international student services, low-cost health insurance, multicultural affairs office, services for students with disabilities, teacher training, writing training. *Library facilities:* Diane M. Halle Library. *Online resources:* library catalog, web page, access to other libraries' catalogs. *Collection:* 122,350 titles, 69,870 serial subscriptions, 1,637 audiovisual materials. *Research affiliation:* North Shore Consortium (special needs), Peabody Essex Museum (history).

Computer facilities: Computer purchase and lease plans are available. 158 computers available on campus for general student use. A campuswide network can be accessed from student residence rooms and from off campus. Online class registration is available. *Web address:* http://www.endicott.edu/.

General Application Contact: Dr. Mary Huegel, Vice President and Dean of the School of Graduate and Professional Studies, 978-232-2084, Fax: 978-232-3000, E-mail: mhuegel@endicott.edu.

GRADUATE UNITS

Apicius International School of Hospitality Expenses: Contact institution. *Financial support:* Applicants required to submit FAFSA. Offers organizational management (M Ed). Program held entirely in Florence, Italy. *Application deadline:* For fall admission, 6/30 for domestic and international students. *Application fee:* $50. *Application Contact:* Dr. Mary Huegel, Dean of Graduate and Professional Studies, 978-232-2084, Fax: 978-232-3000, E-mail: mhuegel@endicott.edu.

Van Loan School of Graduate and Professional Studies Students: 313 full-time (192 women), 299 part-time (221 women). Average age 35. *Faculty:* 17 full-time (6 women), 87 part-time/adjunct (46 women). Expenses: Contact institution. *Financial support:* Career-related internships or fieldwork, Federal Work-Study, institutionally sponsored loans, and tuition waivers (partial) available. In 2010, 129 master's awarded. *Degree program information:* Part-time and evening/weekend programs available. Postbaccalaureate distance learning degree programs offered (minimal on-campus study). Offers arts and learning (M Ed); athletic administration (M Ed); business administration (MBA); information technology (MSIT); initial and professional licensure (M Ed); integrative learning (M Ed); interior design (MA, MFA); Montessori integrative learning (M Ed); nursing (MSN); organizational management (M Ed); special needs (M Ed). *Application deadline:* Applications are processed on a rolling basis. *Application fee:* $50. *Application Contact:* Dr. Mary Huegel, Dean, 978-232-2084, Fax: 978-232-3000, E-mail: mhuegel@endicott.edu. *Dean*, Dr. Mary Huegel, 978-232-2084, Fax: 978-232-3000, E-mail: mhuegel@endicott.edu.

EPISCOPAL DIVINITY SCHOOL, Cambridge, MA 02138-3494

General Information Independent-religious, coed, graduate-only institution. *Graduate housing:* Rooms and/or apartments available on a first-come, first-served basis to single and married students. Housing application deadline: 7/31. *Research affiliation:* Boston Theological Institute.

GRADUATE UNITS

Graduate and Professional Programs *Degree program information:* Part-time programs available.

ERIKSON INSTITUTE, Chicago, IL 60654

General Information Independent, coed, primarily women, graduate-only institution. *Enrollment by degree level:* 192 master's, 41 other advanced degrees. *Graduate faculty:* 16 full-time (12 women), 18 part-time/adjunct (all women). *Tuition:* Part-time $810 per credit. *Required fees:* $420 per year. *Student services:* Campus employment opportunities, career counseling, international student services, low-cost health insurance, multicultural affairs office, services for students with disabilities, teacher training, writing training. *Library facilities:* Edward Neisser Library. *Online resources:* library catalog, web page, access to other libraries' catalogs. *Collection:* 14,380 titles, 80 serial subscriptions, 670 audiovisual materials.

Computer facilities: 30 computers available on campus for general student use. A campuswide network can be accessed from off campus. Online class registration, EriksonOnline learning platform are available. *Web address:* http://www.erikson.edu/.

General Application Contact: Valerie Williams, Associate Director, Admission and Multicultural Student Affairs, 312-893-7142, Fax: 312-755-0928, E-mail: vwilliams@erikson.edu.

GRADUATE UNITS

Academic Programs *Degree program information:* Part-time and evening/weekend programs available. Offers administration (Certificate); bilingual/ESL (Certificate); child development (MS); early childhood education (MS); infant mental health (Certificate); infant studies (Certificate). MS/MSW offered jointly with Loyola University Chicago.

ERSKINE THEOLOGICAL SEMINARY, Due West, SC 29639-0668

General Information Independent-religious, coed, graduate-only institution. *Graduate housing:* Room and/or apartments available on a first-come, first-served basis to single students; on-campus housing not available to married students. Housing application deadline: 6/1.

GRADUATE UNITS

Graduate and Professional Programs *Degree program information:* Part-time and evening/weekend programs available. Offers theology (M Div, MACE, MACM, MAPM, MATS, MCM, D Min). M Div program offered jointly with Columbia International University, Interdenominational Theological Center, Lutheran Theological Southern Seminary, and Reformed Theological Seminary–Charlotte Campus; D Min with Columbia Theological Seminary, Interdenominational Theological Center, and Emory University's Candler School of Theology. Electronic applications accepted.

EVANGELICAL SEMINARY OF PUERTO RICO, San Juan, PR 00925-2207

General Information Independent-religious, coed, graduate-only institution. *Enrollment by degree level:* 168 first professional, 43 master's, 29 doctoral. *Graduate faculty:* 8 full-time (1 woman), 11 part-time/adjunct (0 women). *Graduate housing:* Rooms and/or apartments available on a first-come, first-served basis to single and married students. Housing application deadline: 12/15. *Student services:* Campus safety program, career counseling, international student services. *Library facilities:* Juan de Valdés Library. *Online resources:* library catalog, web page, access to other libraries' catalogs. *Collection:* 70,334 titles, 599 serial subscriptions, 2,140 audiovisual materials.

Computer facilities: 7 computers available on campus for general student use. A campuswide network can be accessed from off campus. *Web address:* http://www.se-pr.edu/.

General Application Contact: Marie L. Rivera, Registrar, 787-763-6700 Ext. 224, Fax: 787-766-0938, E-mail: registro@seminarioevangelicopr.org.

GRADUATE UNITS

Graduate and Professional Programs Students: 59 full-time (27 women), 181 part-time (82 women); includes all Hispanic/Latino. Average age 45. *Faculty:* 8 full-time (1 woman), 11 part-time/adjunct (0 women). Expenses: Contact institution. *Financial support:* Scholarships/grants available. Support available to part-time students. Financial award application deadline: 8/30; financial award applicants required to submit FAFSA. In 2010, 15 first professional degrees, 6 master's awarded. *Degree program information:* Part-time programs available. Offers theology (M Div, MAR, D Min). *Application deadline:* For fall admission, 5/31 priority date for domestic students; for spring admission, 10/30 priority date for domestic students. *Application fee:* $50. *Application Contact:* Marie L. Rivera, Registrar, 787-763-6700 Ext. 224, Fax: 787-766-0938, E-mail: registro@seminarioevangelicopr.org. *President*, Dr. Sergio Ojeda, 787-763-6700 Ext. 243, Fax: 787-751-0847.

EVANGELICAL THEOLOGICAL SEMINARY, Myerstown, PA 17067-1212

General Information Independent-religious, coed, graduate-only institution. *Graduate housing:* Rooms and/or apartments available on a first-come, first-served basis to single and married students. Housing application deadline: 6/1.

GRADUATE UNITS

Graduate and Professional Programs *Degree program information:* Part-time programs available. Postbaccalaureate distance learning degree programs offered (minimal on-campus study). Offers Biblical studies (MAR); congregational ministry (M Div); global and contextual studies (M Div, MAR); historical and theological studies (MAR); interdisciplinary studies (MAR); marriage and family counseling (M Div); marriage and family therapy (MA); New Testament (MAR); Old Testament (MAR); spiritual formation (MAR); teaching ministry (M Div); youth ministry (M Div).

EVANGEL UNIVERSITY, Springfield, MO 65802

General Information Independent-religious, coed, comprehensive institution. *Enrollment:* 2,072 graduate, professional, and undergraduate students; 114 full-time matriculated graduate/professional students (74 women), 220 part-time matriculated graduate/professional students (183 women). *Enrollment by degree level:* 334 master's. *Graduate faculty:* 16 full-time (8 women), 31 part-time/adjunct (15 women). *Graduate housing:* Rooms and/or apartments available on a first-come, first-served basis to single and married students. Housing application deadline: 5/1. *Student services:* Campus employment opportunities, campus safety program, career counseling, exercise/wellness program, free psychological counseling, international student services, multicultural affairs office, services for students with disabilities, teacher training, writing training. *Library facilities:* Claude Kendrick Library.

Computer facilities: A campuswide network can be accessed from student residence rooms. Online class registration, online payment are available. *Web address:* http://www.evangel.edu/.

General Application Contact: Charity H. Fahlstrom, Admissions Representative, Graduate and Professional Studies, 417-865-2811 Ext. 7227, Fax: 417-575-5484.

GRADUATE UNITS

Department of Education Students: 5 full-time (3 women), 126 part-time (111 women). Average age 33. 14 applicants, 86% accepted, 11 enrolled. *Faculty:* 6 full-time (3 women), 10 part-time/adjunct (8 women). Expenses: Contact institution. *Financial support:* In 2010–11, 3 students received support. Career-related internships or fieldwork, institutionally sponsored loans, and scholarships/grants available. Support available to part-time students. Financial award application deadline: 3/1; financial award applicants required to submit FAFSA. In 2010, 23 master's awarded. *Degree program information:* Part-time and evening/weekend programs available. Offers educational leadership (M Ed); reading education (M Ed); secondary teaching (M Ed); teaching (MA). *Application deadline:* For fall admission, 7/15 priority date for domestic students; for spring admission, 11/15 priority date for domestic students. Applications are processed on a rolling basis. *Application fee:* $25. *Application Contact:* Charity H. Fahlstrom, Admissions Representative, Graduate and Professional Studies, 417-865-2811 Ext. 7227, Fax: 417-865-9599. *Program Coordinator*, Dr. Matt Stringer, 417-865-2815 Ext. 8563, E-mail: stringerm@evangel.edu.

Department of Psychology Students: 23 full-time (15 women), 18 part-time (14 women). Average age 27. 17 applicants, 100% accepted, 15 enrolled. *Faculty:* 3 full-time (2 women), 9 part-time/adjunct (4 women). Expenses: Contact institution. *Financial support:* In 2010–11, 6 students received support. Career-related internships or fieldwork, scholarships/grants, and unspecified assistantships available. Support available to part-time students. Financial award application deadline: 3/1; financial award applicants required to submit FAFSA. In 2010, 8 master's awarded. *Degree program information:* Part-time programs available. Offers clinical psychology (MS); counseling psychology (MS). *Application deadline:* For fall admission, 2/1 priority date for domestic students; for spring admission, 10/15 priority date for domestic students. Applications are processed on a rolling basis. *Application fee:* $25. Electronic applications accepted. *Application Contact:* Charity H. Fahlstrom, Admissions Representative, Graduate and Professional Studies, 417-865-2815 Ext. 7227, Fax: 417-575-5484, E-mail: fahlstromc@evangel.edu. *Chair*, Dr. Grant Jones, 417-865-2815 Ext. 8619, E-mail: jonesg@evangel.edu.

Organizational Leadership Program Students: 61 full-time (37 women), 8 part-time (3 women); includes 1 Black or African American, non-Hispanic/Latino; 1 Asian, non-Hispanic/Latino. Average age 37. 20 applicants, 60% accepted, 8 enrolled. *Faculty:* 5 full-time (1 woman), 7 part-time/adjunct (0 women). Expenses: Contact institution. *Financial support:* In 2010–11, 9 students received support. Career-related internships or fieldwork and scholarships/grants available. Support available to part-time students. Financial award application deadline: 3/1; financial award applicants required to submit FAFSA. In 2010, 8 master's awarded. *Degree program information:* Part-time and evening/weekend programs available. Postbaccalaureate distance learning degree programs offered (minimal on-campus study). Offers organizational leadership (MOL). *Application deadline:* For fall admission, 7/15 priority date for domestic and international students; for spring admission, 11/15 priority date for domestic and international students. Applications are processed on a rolling basis. *Application fee:* $25. Electronic applications accepted. *Application Contact:* Charity H. Fahlstrom, Admissions Representative, Graduate and Professional Studies, 417-865-2815 Ext. 7227, Fax: 417-575-5484, E-mail: fahlstromc@evangel.edu. *Director of Graduate Studies*, Dr. Jeff Fulks, 417-865-2815 Ext. 8260, Fax: 417-575-5484, E-mail: fulksj@evangel.edu.

School Counseling Program Students: 25 full-time (19 women), 68 part-time (55 women). Average age 32. 17 applicants, 94% accepted, 14 enrolled. *Faculty:* 2 full-time (both women), 5 part-time/adjunct (3 women). Expenses: Contact institution. *Financial support:* In 2010–11, 2 students received support. Career-related internships or fieldwork, scholarships/grants, and unspecified assistantships available. Support available to part-time students. Financial award application deadline: 3/1; financial award applicants required to submit FAFSA. In 2010, 9 master's awarded. *Degree program information:* Part-time programs available. Offers school counseling (MS). *Application deadline:* For fall admission, 7/15 priority date for domestic and international students; for spring admission, 11/15 priority date for domestic and international students. Applications are processed on a rolling basis. *Application fee:* $25. Electronic applications accepted. *Application Contact:* Charity H. Fahlstrom, Admissions Representative, Graduate and Professional Studies, 417-865-2815 Ext. 7227, Fax: 417-575-5484, E-mail: fahlstromc@evangel.edu. *Chair*, Debbie Bicket, 417-865-2815 Ext. 8567, Fax: 417-575-5484, E-mail: bicketd@evangel.edu.

EVEREST UNIVERSITY, Tampa, FL 33614-5899

General Information Proprietary, coed, comprehensive institution. *Graduate housing:* On-campus housing not available.

GRADUATE UNITS

Department of Business Administration *Degree program information:* Part-time and evening/weekend programs available. Offers accounting (MBA); human resources (MBA); international business (MBA).

EVEREST UNIVERSITY, Tampa, FL 33619

General Information Proprietary, coed, comprehensive institution. *Enrollment:* 12,695 graduate, professional, and undergraduate students; 6 full-time matriculated graduate/professional students (5 women), 31 part-time matriculated graduate/professional students (21 women). *Enrollment by degree level:* 37 master's. *Graduate faculty:* 2 part-time/adjunct (1 woman). *Tuition:* Full-time $12,120; part-time $55 per credit hour. *Required fees:* $60 per quarter. *Graduate housing:* On-campus housing not available. *Student services:* Campus employment opportunities, career counseling. *Library facilities:* Everest University Library. *Online resources:* library catalog, web page. *Collection:* 73,608 titles, 103 serial subscriptions, 338 audiovisual materials.

Computer facilities: 200 computers available on campus for general student use. A campuswide network can be accessed. *Web address:* http://www.everest.edu/.

General Application Contact: Shandretta Pointer, Director, 813-621-0091 Ext. 106, E-mail: spointer@cci.edu.

GRADUATE UNITS

Program in Business Administration Students: 2 full-time (both women), 17 part-time (12 women); includes 12 minority (8 Black or African American, non-Hispanic/Latino; 3 Hispanic/Latino; 1 Two or more races, non-Hispanic/Latino). Average age 38. *Faculty:* 1 (woman) part-time/adjunct. Expenses: Contact institution. *Financial support:* Institutionally sponsored loans and scholarships/grants available. In 2010, 10 master's awarded. *Degree program information:* Part-time and evening/weekend programs available. Postbaccalaureate distance learning degree programs offered (minimal on-campus study). Offers business administration (MBA). *Application deadline:* Applications are processed on a rolling basis. *Application fee:* $25. *Application Contact:* Shandretta Pointer, Admissions Office, 813-621-0041 Ext. 106, Fax: 813-628-0919, E-mail: spointer@cci.edu. *Chair*, James Jehs, 813-621-0041 Ext. 140, Fax: 813-623-5769, E-mail: jjehs@cci.edu.

Program in Criminal Justice Students: 4 full-time (3 women), 14 part-time (9 women); includes 12 minority (10 Black or African American, non-Hispanic/Latino; 2 Hispanic/Latino). Average age 41. *Faculty:* 1 part-time/adjunct (0 women). Expenses: Contact institution. *Financial support:* Institutionally sponsored loans and scholarships/grants available. In 2010, 1 master's awarded. *Degree program information:* Part-time and evening/weekend programs available. Postbaccalaureate distance learning degree programs offered (minimal on-campus study). Offers criminal justice (MS). *Application deadline:* Applications are processed on a rolling basis. *Application fee:* $25. *Application Contact:* Shandretta Pointer, Admissions Office, 813-621-0041 Ext. 106, Fax: 813-628-0919, E-mail: spointer@cci.edu. *Chair*, Seth Kanowitz, 813-621-0041 Ext. 219, Fax: 813-623-5769, E-mail: skanowitz@cci.edu.

EVEREST UNIVERSITY, Orlando, FL 32810-5674

General Information Proprietary, coed, comprehensive institution. *Graduate housing:* On-campus housing not available.

GRADUATE UNITS

Division of Business Administration *Degree program information:* Part-time and evening/weekend programs available. Offers business administration (MBA).

EVEREST UNIVERSITY, Orlando, FL 32819

General Information Proprietary, coed, comprehensive institution. *Graduate housing:* On-campus housing not available.

GRADUATE UNITS

Program in Business Administration Offers accounting (MBA); general management (MBA); human resources (MBA); international management (MBA).

EVEREST UNIVERSITY, Jacksonville, FL 32256

General Information Proprietary, coed, comprehensive institution.

GRADUATE UNITS

Graduate Programs

EVEREST UNIVERSITY, Lakeland, FL 33801

General Information Proprietary, coed, comprehensive institution.

GRADUATE UNITS

Program in Criminal Justice Offers criminal justice (MS).

EVEREST UNIVERSITY, Melbourne, FL 32935-6657

General Information Proprietary, coed, comprehensive institution.

GRADUATE UNITS

Program in Business Administration Offers business administration (MBA).

EVEREST UNIVERSITY, Pompano Beach, FL 33062

General Information Proprietary, coed, comprehensive institution. *Graduate housing:* On-campus housing not available.

GRADUATE UNITS

Program in Criminal Justice Offers criminal justice (MS).

School of Business *Degree program information:* Part-time and evening/weekend programs available. Offers business (MBA).

EVERGLADES UNIVERSITY, Boca Raton, FL 33431

General Information Independent, coed, comprehensive institution.

GRADUATE UNITS

Graduate Programs Offers aviation science (MSA); business administration (MBA); information technology (MIT). Electronic applications accepted.

THE EVERGREEN STATE COLLEGE, Olympia, WA 98505

General Information State-supported, coed, comprehensive institution. *Enrollment:* 4,833 graduate, professional, and undergraduate students; 196 full-time matriculated graduate/professional students (123 women), 123 part-time matriculated graduate/professional students (73 women). *Enrollment by degree level:* 319 master's. *Graduate faculty:* 20 full-time (10 women), 9 part-time/adjunct (2 women). Tuition, state resident: part-time $252.10 per credit. Tuition, nonresident: part-time $668.10 per credit. *Graduate housing:* Rooms and/or apartments available on a first-come, first-served basis to single and married students. Housing application deadline: 6/1. *Student services:* Campus employment opportunities, campus safety program, career counseling, child daycare facilities, exercise/wellness program, free psychological counseling, grant writing training, international student services, multicultural affairs office, services for students with disabilities, teacher training, writing training. *Library facilities:* Daniel J. Evans Library. *Online resources:* library catalog, web page, access to other libraries' catalogs. *Collection:* 289,504 titles, 27,372 serial subscriptions, 9,823 audiovisual materials. *Research affiliation:* Washington State Institute for Public Policy (public policy).

Computer facilities: 408 computers available on campus for general student use. A campuswide network can be accessed from student residence rooms and from off campus. Online class registration, online payment and student accounts history, online housing application are available. *Web address:* http://www.evergreen.edu/.

General Application Contact: Admissions, 360-867-6170, E-mail: admissions@evergreen.edu.

GRADUATE UNITS

Graduate Programs Students: 196 full-time (123 women), 123 part-time (73 women); includes 16 Black or African American, non-Hispanic/Latino; 31 American Indian or Alaska Native, non-Hispanic/Latino; 11 Asian, non-Hispanic/Latino; 16 Hispanic/Latino; 6 Native Hawaiian or other Pacific Islander, non-Hispanic/Latino. Average age 37. 243 applicants, 84% accepted, 139 enrolled. *Faculty:* 20 full-time (10 women), 9 part-time/adjunct (2 women). Expenses: Contact institution. *Financial support:* In 2010–11, 151 students received support, including 56 fellowships (averaging $8,181 per year); research assistantships, career-related internships or fieldwork, Federal Work-Study, scholarships/grants, tuition waivers (partial), and unspecified assistantships also available. Support available to part-time students. Financial award application deadline: 3/15; financial award applicants required to submit FAFSA. In 2010, 104 master's awarded. *Degree program information:* Part-time and evening/weekend programs available. Offers environmental studies (MES); public administration (MPA); teaching (MIT). *Application deadline:* For fall admission, 3/3 priority date for domestic and international students. Applications are processed on a rolling basis. *Application fee:* $50. Electronic applications accepted. *Application Contact:* Dr. Ken Tabbutt, Interim Vice President and Provost, 360-867-6400, Fax: 360-867-6745, E-mail: tabbuttk@evergreen.edu. *Interim Vice President and Provost*, Dr. Ken Tabbutt, 360-867-6400, Fax: 360-867-6745, E-mail: tabbuttk@evergreen.edu.

EXCELSIOR COLLEGE, Albany, NY 12203-5159

General Information Independent, coed, comprehensive institution.

GRADUATE UNITS

School of Business and Technology *Degree program information:* Part-time and evening/weekend programs available. Postbaccalaureate distance learning degree programs offered (no on-campus study). Offers business and technology (MBA).

School of Health Sciences *Degree program information:* Part-time and evening/weekend programs available. Postbaccalaureate distance learning degree programs offered (no on-campus study). Offers healthcare informatics (Certificate); hospice and palliative care (Certificate); nursing management (Certificate). Electronic applications accepted.

School of Liberal Arts *Degree program information:* Part-time and evening/weekend programs available. Postbaccalaureate distance learning degree programs offered (no on-campus study). Offers liberal studies (MA). Electronic applications accepted.

School of Nursing *Degree program information:* Part-time and evening/weekend programs available. Postbaccalaureate distance learning degree programs offered (no on-campus study). Offers clinical systems management (MS); nursing (MS). Electronic applications accepted.

FACULTAD DE DERECHO EUGENIO MARÍA DE HOSTOS, Mayagüez, PR 00681

General Information Independent, coed, graduate-only institution.

GRADUATE UNITS

School of Law Offers law (JD).

FAIRFIELD UNIVERSITY, Fairfield, CT 06824-5195

General Information Independent-religious, coed, comprehensive institution. *Enrollment:* 5,181 graduate, professional, and undergraduate students; 387 full-time matriculated graduate/professional students (257 women), 921 part-time matriculated graduate/professional students (635 women). *Enrollment by degree level:* 1,287 master's, 21 other advanced degrees. *Graduate faculty:* 141 full-time (75 women), 65 part-time/adjunct (24 women). *Tuition:* Part-time $600 per hour. Part-time tuition and fees vary according to degree level and program. *Graduate housing:* On-campus housing not available. *Student services:* Campus employment opportunities, campus safety program, career counseling, child daycare facilities, exercise/wellness program, free psychological counseling, international student services, low-cost health insurance, multicultural affairs office, services for students with disabilities, teacher training. *Library facilities:* DiMenna-Nyselius Library. *Online resources:* library catalog, web page. *Collection:* 397,874 titles, 46,817 serial subscriptions, 13,399 audiovisual materials.

Computer facilities: Computer purchase and lease plans are available. 220 computers available on campus for general student use. A campuswide network can be accessed from student residence rooms and from off campus. Online class registration is available. *Web address:* http://www.fairfield.edu/.

General Application Contact: Marianne Gumpper, Director of Graduate and Continuing Studies Admissions, 203-254-4184, Fax: 203-254-4100, E-mail: gradadmis@mail.fairfield.edu.

GRADUATE UNITS

Charles F. Dolan School of Business Students: 89 full-time (32 women), 127 part-time (54 women); includes 4 Black or African American, non-Hispanic/Latino; 2 Asian, non-Hispanic/Latino; 4 Hispanic/Latino; 1 Two or more races, non-Hispanic/Latino, 17 international. Average age 29. 108 applicants, 62% accepted, 46 enrolled. *Faculty:* 42 full-time (15 women), 8 part-time/adjunct (1 woman). Expenses: Contact institution. *Financial support:* In 2010–11, 48 students received support. Scholarships/grants, unspecified assistantships, and merit based one-time entrance scholarship available. Financial award applicants required to submit FAFSA. In 2010, 79 master's awarded. *Degree program information:* Part-time and evening/weekend programs available. Offers accounting (MBA, MS, CAS); accounting information systems (MBA); entrepreneurship (MBA); finance (MBA, MS, CAS); general management (MBA, CAS); human resource management (MBA, CAS); information systems and operations (MBA); information systems and operations management (CAS); international business (MBA, CAS); marketing (MBA, CAS); taxation (MBA, CAS). *Application deadline:* For fall admission, 5/15 for international students; for spring admission, 10/15 for international students. Applications are processed on a rolling basis. *Application fee:* $60. Electronic applications accepted. *Application Contact:* Marianne Gumpper, Director of Graduate and Continuing Studies Admissions, 203-254-4184, Fax: 203-254-4073, E-mail: gradadmis@fairfield.edu. *Dean*, Dr. Norman A. Solomon, 203-254-4000 Ext. 4070, Fax: 203-254-4105, E-mail: nsolomon@fairfield.edu.

Fairfield University (continued)

College of Arts and Sciences Students: 96 full-time (65 women), 97 part-time (63 women); includes 7 Black or African American, non-Hispanic/Latino; 5 Hispanic/Latino; 2 Two or more races, non-Hispanic/Latino, 7 international. Average age 41. 114 applicants, 62% accepted, 38 enrolled. *Faculty:* 46 full-time (20 women), 15 part-time/adjunct (7 women). Expenses: Contact institution. *Financial support:* In 2010–11, 19 students received support. Unspecified assistantships available. Financial award applicants required to submit FAFSA. In 2010, 36 master's awarded. *Degree program information:* Part-time and evening/weekend programs available. Postbaccalaureate distance learning degree programs offered (minimal on-campus study). Offers American studies (MA); communication (MA); creative writing (MFA); mathematics (MS). *Application deadline:* For fall admission, 5/15 for international students; for spring admission, 10/15 for international students. Applications are processed on a rolling basis. *Application fee:* $60. Electronic applications accepted. *Application Contact:* Marianne Gumpper, Director of Graduate and Continuing Studies Admissions, 203-254-4184, Fax: 203-254-4073, E-mail: gradadmis@fairfield.edu. *Dean*, Dr. Robbin Crabtree, 203-254-4000 Ext. 3263, Fax: 203-254-4119, E-mail: rcrabtree@fairfield.edu.

Graduate School of Education and Allied Professions Students: 168 full-time (145 women), 447 part-time (364 women); includes 17 Black or African American, non-Hispanic/Latino; 10 Asian, non-Hispanic/Latino; 43 Hispanic/Latino; 3 Two or more races, non-Hispanic/Latino, 4 international. Average age 33. 302 applicants, 50% accepted, 93 enrolled. *Faculty:* 22 full-time (17 women), 31 part-time/adjunct (16 women). Expenses: Contact institution. *Financial support:* In 2010–11, 189 students received support. Career-related internships or fieldwork and unspecified assistantships available. Financial award applicants required to submit FAFSA. In 2010, 147 master's, 19 other advanced degrees awarded. *Degree program information:* Part-time and evening/weekend programs available. Offers applied psychology (MA); bilingual education (CAS); clinical mental health counseling (MA, CAS); education and allied professions (MA, CAS); educational technology (MA); elementary education (MA); family studies (MA); marriage and family therapy (MA); media/educational technology (MA); school counseling (MA, CAS); school library media specialist (MA); school psychology (MA, CAS); secondary education (MA); special education (MA, CAS); teaching and foundations (MA, CAS); TESOL, foreign language and bilingual/multicultural education (MA, CAS). *Application deadline:* For fall admission, 2/15 for international students; for spring admission, 10/1 for international students. *Application fee:* $60. Electronic applications accepted. *Application Contact:* Marianne Gumpper, Director of Graduate and Continuing Studies Admissions, 203-254-4184, Fax: 203-254-4073, E-mail: gradadmis@fairfield.edu. *Dean*, Dr. Susan D. Franzosa, 203-254-4000 Ext. 4250, Fax: 203-254-4241, E-mail: sfranzosa@fairfield.edu.

School of Engineering Students: 31 full-time (12 women), 98 part-time (20 women); includes 28 minority (5 Black or African American, non-Hispanic/Latino; 17 Asian, non-Hispanic/Latino; 4 Hispanic/Latino; 1 Native Hawaiian or other Pacific Islander, non-Hispanic/Latino; 1 Two or more races, non-Hispanic/Latino), 26 international. Average age 35. 120 applicants, 55% accepted, 15 enrolled. *Faculty:* 8 full-time (1 woman), 11 part-time/adjunct (0 women). Expenses: Contact institution. *Financial support:* In 2010–11, 25 students received support. Unspecified assistantships available. Financial award applicants required to submit FAFSA. In 2010, 52 master's awarded. *Degree program information:* Part-time and evening/weekend programs available. Offers electrical and computer engineering (MS); management of technology (MS); mechanical engineering (MS); software engineering (MS). *Application deadline:* For fall admission, 5/15 for international students; for spring admission, 10/15 for international students. Applications are processed on a rolling basis. *Application fee:* $60. Electronic applications accepted. *Application Contact:* Marianne Gumpper, Director of Graduate and Continuing Studies Admissions, 203-254-4184, Fax: 203-254-4073, E-mail: gradadmis@fairfield.edu. *Dean*, Dr. Jack Beal, 203-254-4000 Ext. 4147, Fax: 203-254-4013, E-mail: jwbeal@fairfield.edu.

School of Nursing Students: 3 full-time (all women), 152 part-time (134 women); includes 7 Black or African American, non-Hispanic/Latino; 1 American Indian or Alaska Native, non-Hispanic/Latino; 7 Asian, non-Hispanic/Latino; 5 Hispanic/Latino; 1 Native Hawaiian or other Pacific Islander, non-Hispanic/Latino, 2 international. Average age 39. 87 applicants, 45% accepted, 31 enrolled. *Faculty:* 23 full-time (22 women). Expenses: Contact institution. *Financial support:* In 2010–11, 43 students received support. Traineeships, unspecified assistantships, and traineeships available. Financial award applicants required to submit FAFSA. In 2010, 10 master's awarded. *Degree program information:* Part-time programs available. Offers clinical nurse leader (MSN); family nurse practitioner (MSN, DNP); healthcare management (MSN); nurse anesthesia (DNP); psychiatric nurse practitioner (MSN, DNP). *Application deadline:* For fall admission, 5/15 for international students; for spring admission, 10/15 for international students. Applications are processed on a rolling basis. *Application fee:* $60. Electronic applications accepted. *Application Contact:* Marianne Gumpper, Director of Graduate and Continuing Studies Admissions, 203-254-4184, Fax: 203-254-4073, E-mail: gradadmis@fairfield.edu. *Dean*, Dr. Jeanne M. Novotny, 203-254-4000 Ext. 2701, Fax: 203-254-4126, E-mail: jnovotny@fairfield.edu.

FAIRLEIGH DICKINSON UNIVERSITY, COLLEGE AT FLORHAM, Madison, NJ 07940-1099

General Information Independent, coed, comprehensive institution. *Enrollment:* 3,288 graduate, professional, and undergraduate students; 352 full-time matriculated graduate/professional students (234 women), 481 part-time matriculated graduate/professional students (217 women). *Enrollment by degree level:* 824 master's, 9 other advanced degrees. *Graduate housing:* Room and/or apartments available on a first-come, first-served basis to single students; on-campus housing not available to married students. *Student services:* Campus employment opportunities, career counseling, exercise/wellness program, free psychological counseling, international student services, teacher training, writing training. *Library facilities:* College of Florham Library. *Online resources:* library catalog, access to other libraries' catalogs. *Collection:* 151,370 titles, 1,149 serial subscriptions, 845 audiovisual materials.

Computer facilities: Computer purchase and lease plans are available. 120 computers available on campus for general student use. A campuswide network can be accessed from student residence rooms and from off campus. Online class registration is available. *Web address:* http://www.fdu.edu/.

General Application Contact: Susan Brooman, University Director, Graduate Admissions, 973-443-8905, Fax: 973-443-8088, E-mail: grad@fdu.edu.

GRADUATE UNITS

Anthony J. Petrocelli College of Continuing Studies Students: 4 full-time (all women), 35 part-time (16 women), 1 international. Average age 34. 15 applicants, 87% accepted, 10 enrolled. Expenses: Contact institution. In 2010, 7 master's awarded. Offers continuing studies (MAS, MPA, MS, MSA); sports administration (MSA). *Application deadline:* Applications are processed on a rolling basis. *Application fee:* $40. *Application Contact:* Susan Brooman, University Director, Graduate Admissions, 973-443-8905, Fax: 973-443-8088, E-mail: grad@fdu.edu. *Dean*, Kenneth Vehrkens, 973-443-8500.

International School of Hospitality and Tourism Management Students: 4 full-time (all women), 33 part-time (16 women), 1 international. Average age 34. 13 applicants, 92% accepted, 10 enrolled. Expenses: Contact institution. In 2010, 7 master's awarded. Offers hospitality management studies (MS). *Application deadline:* Applications are processed on a rolling basis. *Application fee:* $40. *Application Contact:* Susan Brooman, University Director, Graduate Admissions, 973-443-8905, Fax: 973-443-8088, E-mail: grad@fdu.edu.

Public Administration Institute 1 applicant, 0% accepted, 0 enrolled. Expenses: Contact institution. In 2010, 1 master's awarded. Offers public administration (MPA). *Application fee:* $40. *Application Contact:* Susan Brooman, University Director, Graduate Admissions, 973-443-8905, Fax: 973-443-8088, E-mail: grad@fdu.edu. *Head*, Dr. William Roberts, 973-443-8500.

School of Administrative Science Students: 1 part-time (0 women). Average age 33. Expenses: Contact institution. Offers administrative science (MAS). *Application fee:* $40. *Application Contact:* Susan Brooman, University Director, Graduate Admissions, 973-443-8905, Fax: 973-443-8088, E-mail: grad@fdu.edu.

Maxwell Becton College of Arts and Sciences Students: 210 full-time (135 women), 105 part-time (66 women), 78 international. Average age 29. 272 applicants, 67% accepted, 75 enrolled. Expenses: Contact institution. In 2010, 110 master's awarded. Offers arts and sciences (MA, MFA, MS, Certificate); biology (MS); chemistry (MS); clinical mental health counseling (MA); computer science (MS); corporate and organizational communication (MA); counseling (MA); creative writing (MFA); creative writing and literature for educators (MA); industrial/organizational psychology (MA); organizational behavior (MA, Certificate); organizational leadership (Certificate). *Application deadline:* Applications are processed on a rolling basis. *Application fee:* $40. *Application Contact:* Susan Brooman, University Director, Graduate Admissions, 973-443-8905, Fax: 973-443-8088, E-mail: grad@fdu.edu. *Dean*, Dr. Geoffrey Weinman, 973-443-8500.

Silberman College of Business Students: 81 full-time (49 women), 305 part-time (112 women), 34 international. Average age 32. 163 applicants, 72% accepted, 62 enrolled. Expenses: Contact institution. In 2010, 157 master's awarded. *Degree program information:* Part-time and evening/weekend programs available. Offers accounting (MS); business (EMBA, MBA, MS, Certificate); business administration (MBA); entrepreneurial studies (MBA, Certificate); evolving technology (Certificate); finance (MBA, Certificate); health care and life sciences (EMBA); international business (MBA, Certificate); international taxation (Certificate); management (EMBA, MBA, Certificate); managing sustainability (Certificate); marketing (MBA, Certificate); pharmaceutical studies (MBA, Certificate); taxation (MS, Certificate). *Application deadline:* Applications are processed on a rolling basis. *Application fee:* $40. *Application Contact:* Susan Brooman, University Director of Graduate Admissions. *Dean*, Dr. William Moore, 973-443-8500.

Center for Human Resource Management Studies Students: 8 full-time (6 women), 8 part-time (5 women), 3 international. Average age 30. 4 applicants, 50% accepted, 0 enrolled. Expenses: Contact institution. In 2010, 6 master's awarded. Offers human resource management (MBA); human resource management studies (MBA). *Application fee:* $40.

University College: Arts, Sciences, and Professional Studies Students: 57 full-time (46 women), 36 part-time (23 women). Average age 27. 63 applicants, 89% accepted, 45 enrolled. Expenses: Contact institution. In 2010, 70 master's awarded. Offers arts, sciences, and professional studies (MA, MAT, Certificate). *Application deadline:* Applications are processed on a rolling basis. *Application fee:* $40. *Application Contact:* Susan Brooman, University Director, Graduate Admissions, 973-443-8905, Fax: 973-443-8088, E-mail: grad@fdu.edu. *Dean*, Patti Mills, 973-443-8500.

Peter Sammartino School of Education Students: 57 full-time (46 women), 36 part-time (23 women). Average age 27. 63 applicants, 89% accepted, 45 enrolled. Expenses: Contact institution. In 2010, 70 master's awarded. Offers education for certified teachers (MA, Certificate); educational leadership (MA); instructional technology (Certificate); literacy/reading (Certificate); teaching (MAT). *Application deadline:* Applications are processed on a rolling basis. *Application fee:* $40. *Application Contact:* Susan Brooman, University Director, Graduate Admissions, 973-443-8905, Fax: 973-443-8088, E-mail: grad@fdu.edu.

FAIRLEIGH DICKINSON UNIVERSITY, METROPOLITAN CAMPUS, Teaneck, NJ 07666-1914

General Information Independent, coed, comprehensive institution. *Enrollment:* 9,105 graduate, professional, and undergraduate students; 1,136 full-time matriculated graduate/professional students (609 women), 1,500 part-time matriculated graduate/professional students (963 women). *Enrollment by degree level:* 2,191 master's, 194 doctoral, 251 other advanced degrees. *Graduate housing:* Room and/or apartments available on a first-come, first-served basis to single students; on-campus housing not available to married students. *Student services:* Campus employment opportunities, career counseling, exercise/wellness program, free psychological counseling, international student services, teacher training, writing training. *Library facilities:* Weiner Library plus 3 others. *Online resources:* library catalog, web page, access to other libraries' catalogs.

Computer facilities: Computer purchase and lease plans are available. 200 computers available on campus for general student use. A campuswide network can be accessed from student residence rooms and from off campus. Online class registration is available. *Web address:* http://www.fdu.edu/.

General Application Contact: Susan Brooman, University Director of Graduate Admissions, 201-692-2554, Fax: 201-692-2560, E-mail: globaleducation@fdu.edu.

GRADUATE UNITS

Anthony J. Petrocelli College of Continuing Studies Students: 249 full-time (115 women), 642 part-time (293 women), 140 international. Average age 36. 425 applicants, 88% accepted, 225 enrolled. Expenses: Contact institution. In 2010, 406 master's awarded. Offers continuing studies (MAS, MPA, MS, MSA, MSHS, Certificate); sports administration (MSA). *Application deadline:* Applications are processed on a rolling basis. *Application fee:* $40. *Application Contact:* Susan Brooman, University Director of Graduate Admissions, 201-692-2554, Fax: 201-692-2560, E-mail: globaleducation@fdu.edu. *Dean*, Kenneth T. Vehrkens, 201-692-2000.

International School of Hospitality and Tourism Management Students: 11 full-time (10 women), 14 part-time (8 women), 14 international. Average age 32. 17 applicants, 71% accepted, 6 enrolled. Expenses: Contact institution. In 2010, 8 master's awarded. Offers hospitality management (MS). *Application deadline:* Applications are processed on a rolling basis. *Application fee:* $40. *Application Contact:* Susan Brooman, University Director of Graduate Admissions, 201-692-2554, Fax: 201-692-2560, E-mail: globaleducation@fdu.edu. *Director*, Dr. Richard Wisch, 201-692-2000.

Public Administration Institute Students: 116 full-time (49 women), 123 part-time (64 women), 97 international. Average age 32. 165 applicants, 76% accepted, 56 enrolled. Expenses: Contact institution. In 2010, 104 master's awarded. Offers public administration (MPA, Certificate); public non-profit management (Certificate). *Application deadline:* Applications are processed on a rolling basis. *Application fee:* $40. *Application Contact:* Susan Brooman, University Director of Graduate Admissions, 201-692-2554, Fax: 201-692-2560, E-mail: globaleducation@fdu.edu. *Director*, Dr. William Roberts, 201-692-2000.

School of Administrative Science Students: 87 full-time (46 women), 463 part-time (206 women), 24 international. Average age 38. 210 applicants, 97% accepted, 140 enrolled. Expenses: Contact institution. In 2010, 294 master's awarded. Offers administrative science (MAS, MSHS, Certificate); homeland security (MSHS). *Application deadline:* Applications are processed on a rolling basis. *Application fee:* $40. *Application Contact:* Susan Brooman, University Director of Graduate Admissions, 201-692-2554, Fax: 201-692-2560, E-mail: globaleducation@fdu.edu. *Director/Executive Associate Dean*, Ronald Calissi, 201-692-2000.

Silberman College of Business Students: 338 full-time (136 women), 112 part-time (53 women), 221 international. Average age 28. 451 applicants, 60% accepted, 106 enrolled. Expenses: Contact institution. In 2010, 199 master's awarded. Offers accounting (MBA, MS, Certificate); business (EMBA, MBA, MS, Certificate); business administration (MBA); chemical studies (Certificate); entrepreneurial studies (MBA, Certificate); executive management (EMBA); finance (MBA, Certificate); healthcare and life sciences (EMBA); international business (MBA); management (MBA, Certificate); management information systems (Certificate); marketing (MBA, Certificate); pharmaceutical studies (MBA, Certificate); taxation (MS). *Application deadline:* Applications are processed on a rolling basis. *Application fee:* $40. *Application Contact:* Susan Brooman, University Director of Graduate Admissions, 201-692-2554, Fax: 201-692-2560, E-mail: globaleducation@fdu.edu. *Dean*, Dr. William Moore, 201-692-2000.

Center for Human Resources Management Studies Students: 5 full-time (all women), 6 part-time (5 women), 4 international. Average age 28. 5 applicants, 20% accepted, 0 enrolled. Expenses: Contact institution. In 2010, 4 master's awarded. Offers human resource management (MBA, Certificate); human resources management studies (MBA, Certificate). *Application deadline:* Applications are processed on a rolling basis. *Application fee:* $40. *Application Contact:* Susan Brooman, University Director of Graduate Admissions, 201-692-2554, Fax: 201-692-2560, E-mail: globaleducation@fdu.edu.

University College: Arts, Sciences, and Professional Studies Students: 549 full-time (358 women), 746 part-time (617 women), 197 international. Average age 34. 1,181 applicants,

66% accepted, 375 enrolled. Expenses: Contact institution. In 2010, 402 master's, 24 doctorates awarded. Offers arts, sciences, and professional studies (MA, MAT, MS, MSEE, MSN, DNP, PhD, Psy D, Certificate); English and literature (MA); systems science (MS). *Application deadline:* Applications are processed on a rolling basis. *Application fee:* $40. *Application Contact:* Susan Brooman, University Director of Graduate Admissions, 201-692-2554, Fax: 201-692-2560, E-mail: globaleducation@fdu.edu. *Dean*, Patti Mills, 201-692-2000.

Henry P. Becton School of Nursing and Allied Health Students: 63 full-time (59 women), 157 part-time (135 women), 4 international. Average age 42. 126 applicants, 79% accepted, 74 enrolled. Expenses: Contact institution. In 2010, 23 master's, 9 doctorates awarded. Offers medical technology (MS); nursing (MSN, Certificate); nursing practice (DNP). *Application deadline:* Applications are processed on a rolling basis. *Application fee:* $40. *Application Contact:* Susan Brooman, University Director of Graduate Admissions, 201-692-2554, Fax: 201-692-2560, E-mail: globaleducation@fdu.edu.

Peter Sammartino School of Education Students: 83 full-time (69 women), 443 part-time (394 women), 10 international. Average age 36. 218 applicants, 90% accepted, 144 enrolled. Expenses: Contact institution. In 2010, 141 master's awarded. *Degree program information:* Part-time programs available. Offers dyslexia specialist (Certificate); education for certified teachers (MA); educational leadership (MA); instructional technology (Certificate); learning disabilities (MA); literacy/reading (Certificate); multilingual education (MA); teacher of the handicapped (Certificate); teaching (MAT). *Application deadline:* Applications are processed on a rolling basis. *Application fee:* $40. *Application Contact:* Susan Brooman, University Director of Graduate Admissions, 201-692-2554, Fax: 201-692-2560, E-mail: globaleducation@fdu.edu. *Director*, Dr. Vicki Cohen, 201-692-2525, Fax: 201-692-2603, E-mail: vicki_cohen@fdu.edu.

School of Art and Media Studies Students: 14 full-time (9 women), 10 part-time (8 women), 5 international. Average age 29. 16 applicants, 81% accepted, 7 enrolled. Expenses: Contact institution. In 2010, 16 master's awarded. Offers art and media studies (MA); media and communications (MA). *Application deadline:* Applications are processed on a rolling basis. *Application fee:* $40. *Application Contact:* Susan Brooman, University Director of Graduate Admissions, 201-692-2554, Fax: 201-692-2560, E-mail: globaleducation@fdu.edu.

School of Computer Sciences and Engineering Students: 114 full-time (34 women), 51 part-time (26 women), 109 international. Average age 27. 441 applicants, 57% accepted, 55 enrolled. Expenses: Contact institution. In 2010, 101 master's awarded. Offers computer engineering (MS); computer science (MS); e-commerce (MS); electrical engineering (MSEE); management information systems (MS); mathematical foundation (MS). *Application deadline:* Applications are processed on a rolling basis. *Application fee:* $40. *Application Contact:* Susan Brooman, University Director of Graduate Admissions, 201-692-2554, Fax: 201-692-2560, E-mail: globaleducation@fdu.edu. *Director*, Dr. Alfredo Tan, 201-692-2000.

School of Criminal Justice and Legal Studies Expenses: Contact institution. Offers criminal justice (MA). *Application Contact:* Susan Brooman, University Director of Graduate Admissions, 201-692-2554, Fax: 201-692-2560, E-mail: globaleducation@fdu.edu. *Director*, Dr. Robert F. Vodde, 201-692-2465, E-mail: rvodde@fdu.edu.

School of History, Political and International Studies Students: 5 full-time (3 women), 10 part-time (5 women), 3 international. Average age 29. 17 applicants, 47% accepted, 5 enrolled. Expenses: Contact institution. In 2010, 1 master's awarded. Offers history (MA); international studies (MA); political science (MA). *Application deadline:* Applications are processed on a rolling basis. *Application fee:* $40. *Application Contact:* Susan Brooman, University Director of Graduate Admissions, 201-692-2554, Fax: 201-692-2560, E-mail: globaleducation@fdu.edu.

School of Natural Sciences Students: 64 full-time (42 women), 29 part-time (20 women), 57 international. Average age 26. 174 applicants, 42% accepted, 24 enrolled. Expenses: Contact institution. In 2010, 69 master's awarded. Offers biology (MS); chemistry (MS); cosmetic science (MS); science (MA). *Application deadline:* Applications are processed on a rolling basis. *Application fee:* $40. *Application Contact:* Susan Brooman, University Director of Graduate Admissions, 201-692-2554, Fax: 201-692-2560, E-mail: globaleducation@fdu.edu.

School of Psychology Students: 205 full-time (141 women), 47 part-time (30 women), 8 international. Average age 32. 183 applicants, 73% accepted, 66 enrolled. Expenses: Contact institution. In 2010, 47 master's, 15 doctorates awarded. Offers clinical psychology (MA, PhD); clinical psychopharmacology (MA); forensic psychology (MA); general-theoretical psychology (MA, Certificate); school psychology (MA, Psy D). *Application deadline:* Applications are processed on a rolling basis. *Application fee:* $40. *Application Contact:* Susan Brooman, University Director of Graduate Admissions, 201-692-2554, Fax: 201-692-2560, E-mail: globaleducation@fdu.edu.

FAIRMONT STATE UNIVERSITY, Fairmont, WV 26554

General Information State-supported, coed, comprehensive institution. CGS member.

GRADUATE UNITS

Graduate Studies Offers business administration (MBA); criminal justice (MS); education (MAT); human and community service administration (MS); leadership studies (M Ed); nursing administration (MS); nursing education (MS); online learning (M Ed); professional studies (M Ed); reading (M Ed); special education (M Ed).

FAITH BAPTIST BIBLE COLLEGE AND THEOLOGICAL SEMINARY, Ankeny, IA 50023

General Information Independent-religious, coed, comprehensive institution. *Enrollment:* 364 graduate, professional, and undergraduate students; 14 full-time matriculated graduate/professional students (1 woman), 25 part-time matriculated graduate/professional students. *Enrollment by degree level:* 16 first professional, 13 master's. *Graduate faculty:* 4 full-time (0 women), 4 part-time/adjunct (0 women). *Graduate housing:* Rooms and/or apartments available on a first-come, first-served basis to single and married students. Housing application deadline: 8/1. *Student services:* Campus employment opportunities, career counseling, free psychological counseling, international student services, low-cost health insurance. *Library facilities:* Patten Hall. *Online resources:* library catalog, web page. *Collection:* 73,625 titles, 378 serial subscriptions, 7,283 audiovisual materials.

Computer facilities: 45 computers available on campus for general student use. A campuswide network can be accessed from student residence rooms and from off campus. Online class registration is available. *Web address:* http://www.faith.edu/.

General Application Contact: Patrick Odle, Vice President of Enrollment, 888-FAITH4U, Fax: 515-964-1638, E-mail: odlep@faith.edu.

GRADUATE UNITS

Graduate Program Students: 14 full-time (1 woman), 25 part-time (0 women); includes 3 Asian, non-Hispanic/Latino, 1 international. Average age 29. *Faculty:* 4 full-time (0 women), 4 part-time/adjunct (0 women). Expenses: Contact institution. *Financial support:* Career-related internships or fieldwork and scholarships/grants available. Support available to part-time students. Financial award application deadline: 3/1; financial award applicants required to submit FAFSA. In 2010, 5 first professional degrees, 14 master's awarded. *Degree program information:* Part-time programs available. Offers biblical studies (MA); pastoral studies (M Div); pastoral training (MA); religion (MA); theological studies (MA). *Application deadline:* For fall admission, 8/1 priority date for domestic students, 8/1 for international students; for spring admission, 12/15 for domestic and international students. Applications are processed on a rolling basis. *Application fee:* $25. *Application Contact:* Carrie Johnson, Admissions Administrative Assistant, 888-FAITH4U, Fax: 515-964-1638, E-mail: admissions@faith.edu. *Dean of Seminary*, Dr. Ernest Schmidt, 515-964-0601, E-mail: schmidte@faith.edu.

FAITH EVANGELICAL LUTHERAN SEMINARY, Tacoma, WA 98407

General Information Independent-religious, coed, graduate-only institution.

GRADUATE UNITS

Graduate and Professional Programs *Degree program information:* Part-time and evening/weekend programs available. Postbaccalaureate distance learning degree programs offered (minimal on-campus study). Offers theology (B Th, M Div, MCM, MTS, D Min).

FAITH THEOLOGICAL SEMINARY, Baltimore, MD 21212

General Information Independent-religious, coed, comprehensive institution.

GRADUATE UNITS

Graduate Programs Offers theology (M Div, D Min, Th D).

FASHION INSTITUTE OF TECHNOLOGY, New York, NY 10001-5992

General Information State and locally supported, coed, primarily women, comprehensive institution. *Graduate housing:* Room and/or apartments available on a first-come, first-served basis to single students; on-campus housing not available to married students. *Research affiliation:* IDEO (design and management innovation), Grove Dictionary of Art, Oxford University Press (costume history), Exhibition Designers and Producers Association (exhibition design), Society for Environmental Graphic Design (exhibition design), Lolita S. A. (global fashion management).

GRADUATE UNITS

School of Graduate Studies *Degree program information:* Part-time and evening/weekend programs available. Offers art market: principles and practices (MA); cosmetics and fragrance marketing and management (MPS); exhibition design (MA); fashion and textile studies: history, theory, museum practice (MA); global fashion management (MPS); illustration (MA); sustainable interior environments (MA). Electronic applications accepted.

FAULKNER UNIVERSITY, Montgomery, AL 36109-3398

General Information Independent-religious, coed, comprehensive institution. *Graduate housing:* On-campus housing not available.

GRADUATE UNITS

Alabama Christian College of Arts and Sciences Offers arts and sciences (M Ed, MCJ, MLA, MS); counseling (MS); criminal justice (MCJ); education (M Ed); liberal arts (MLA).

College of Biblical Studies Offers ministry (MABS); missions (MABS); New Testament (MABS); Old Testament (MABS); youth and family ministry (MABS).

Great Books Honors College Offers Western civilization (M Litt).

Harris College of Business and Executive Education Offers management (MSM).

Thomas Goode Jones School of Law Offers law (JD). Electronic applications accepted.

FAYETTEVILLE STATE UNIVERSITY, Fayetteville, NC 28301-4298

General Information State-supported, coed, comprehensive institution. CGS member. *Enrollment:* 5,781 graduate, professional, and undergraduate students; 257 full-time matriculated graduate/professional students (196 women), 421 part-time matriculated graduate/professional students (307 women). *Enrollment by degree level:* 364 master's, 48 doctoral. *Graduate faculty:* 135 full-time (60 women), 14 part-time/adjunct (4 women). *Graduate housing:* On-campus housing not available. *Student services:* Career counseling, child daycare facilities, free psychological counseling, low-cost health insurance. *Library facilities:* Charles W. Chestnut Library. *Online resources:* library catalog, web page, access to other libraries' catalogs. *Collection:* 317,412 titles, 4,725 serial subscriptions, 19,751 audiovisual materials. *Research affiliation:* Research Triangle Park.

Computer facilities: Computer purchase and lease plans are available. 538 computers available on campus for general student use. A campuswide network can be accessed from student residence rooms and from off campus. Online class registration is available. *Web address:* http://www.uncfsu.edu/.

General Application Contact: Karina Hoffman, Graduate Admissions Officer, 910-672-1374, Fax: 910-672-1470, E-mail: khoffman1@uncfsu.edu.

GRADUATE UNITS

Graduate School Students: 257 full-time (196 women), 421 part-time (307 women); includes 251 Black or African American, non-Hispanic/Latino; 8 American Indian or Alaska Native, non-Hispanic/Latino; 5 Asian, non-Hispanic/Latino; 10 Hispanic/Latino; 2 Native Hawaiian or other Pacific Islander, non-Hispanic/Latino, 3 international. Average age 35. 140 applicants, 95% accepted, 133 enrolled. *Faculty:* 135 full-time (60 women), 14 part-time/adjunct (4 women). Expenses: Contact institution. *Financial support:* In 2010–11, 327 students received support, including 19 research assistantships (averaging $4,000 per year); institutionally sponsored loans and unspecified assistantships also available. Support available to part-time students. Financial award application deadline: 3/1; financial award applicants required to submit FAFSA. In 2010, 152 master's, 11 doctorates awarded. *Degree program information:* Part-time and evening/weekend programs available. Offers biology (MA Ed, MS); business administration (MBA); criminal justice (MA); educational leadership (Ed D); elementary education (MA Ed); English (MA); history (MA, MA Ed); mathematics (MA Ed, MS); middle grades (MA Ed); political science (MA, MA Ed); psychology (MA); reading (MA Ed); school administration (MSA); social work (MSW); sociology (MA Ed); special education (MA Ed). *Application deadline:* For fall admission, 4/1 for domestic students, 3/1 for international students; for spring admission, 10/15 for domestic students. Applications are processed on a rolling basis. *Application fee:* $35. *Application Contact:* Katrina Hoffman, Graduate Admissions Officer, 910-672-1374, Fax: 910-672-1470, E-mail: khoffman1@uncfsu.edu. *Dean of Graduate Studies*, Dr. LaDelle Olion, 910-672-1681, E-mail: lolion@uncfsu.edu.

FELICIAN COLLEGE, Lodi, NJ 07644-2117

General Information Independent-religious, coed, comprehensive institution. *Graduate housing:* Room and/or apartments available on a first-come, first-served basis to single students; on-campus housing not available to married students.

GRADUATE UNITS

Doctor of Nursing Practice Program Postbaccalaureate distance learning degree programs offered (no on-campus study). Offers nursing (DNP).

Program in Business *Degree program information:* Part-time and evening/weekend programs available. Offers innovation and entrepreneurship (MBA).

Program in Counseling Psychology Offers counseling psychology (MA).

Program in Education *Degree program information:* Part-time and evening/weekend programs available. Offers education (MA); educational leadership (principal/supervision) (MA); educational supervision (PMC); principal (PMC); school nursing and health education (MA, Certificate).

Program in Health Care Administration Offers health care administration (MSHA).

Program in Nursing *Degree program information:* Part-time and evening/weekend programs available. Postbaccalaureate distance learning degree programs offered (no on-campus study). Offers adult nurse practitioner (MSN, PMC); family nurse practitioner (MSN, PMC); nursing (MSN); nursing education (MSN).

Program in Religious Education *Degree program information:* Part-time and evening/weekend programs available. Postbaccalaureate distance learning degree programs offered (no on-campus study). Offers religious education (MA, Certificate).

FERRIS STATE UNIVERSITY, Big Rapids, MI 49307

General Information State-supported, coed, comprehensive institution. CGS member. *Enrollment:* 14,381 graduate, professional, and undergraduate students; 754 full-time matriculated graduate/professional students (391 women), 457 part-time matriculated graduate/professional students (288 women). *Enrollment by degree level:* 672 first professional, 511 master's, 28 doctoral. *Graduate faculty:* 107 full-time (56 women), 126 part-time/adjunct (53

Ferris State University (continued)

women). *Graduate housing:* Rooms and/or apartments available on a first-come, first-served basis to single and married students. *Student services:* Campus employment opportunities, campus safety program, career counseling, child daycare facilities, exercise/wellness program, free psychological counseling, international student services, low-cost health insurance, multicultural affairs office, services for students with disabilities, teacher training. *Library facilities:* Ferris Library for Information, Technology and Education (FLITE). *Online resources:* library catalog, web page, access to other libraries' catalogs. *Collection:* 436,092 titles, 61,289 serial subscriptions, 4,882 audiovisual materials. *Research affiliation:* AERE American Education Research Association (education), Vistakon-Johnson & Johnson (optometry), Allergan-Hydron (optometry), Bausch & Lomb (optometry), Ciba Vision (optometry).

Computer facilities: 1,950 computers available on campus for general student use. A campuswide network can be accessed from student residence rooms and from off campus. Online class registration is available. *Web address:* http://www.ferris.edu/.

General Application Contact: Dr. Kristen Salomonson, Dean, Enrollment Services/Director, Admissions and Records, 231-591-2100, Fax: 231-591-3944, E-mail: admissions@ferris.edu.

GRADUATE UNITS

College of Allied Health Sciences Students: 1 (woman) full-time, 69 part-time (63 women); includes 1 Two or more races, non-Hispanic/Latino. Average age 44. *Faculty:* 6 full-time (all women). Expenses: Contact institution. *Financial support:* In 2010–11, 3 students received support. Career-related internships or fieldwork and scholarships/grants available. Financial award application deadline: 4/15; financial award applicants required to submit FAFSA. In 2010, 18 master's awarded. *Degree program information:* Part-time and evening/weekend programs available. Postbaccalaureate distance learning degree programs offered (no on-campus study). Offers allied health sciences (MSN). *Application deadline:* For fall admission, 7/15 priority date for domestic students; for spring admission, 10/5 for domestic students. *Application fee:* $30. *Application Contact:* Debby Buck, Off Campus Student Support, 231-591-2094, Fax: 231-591-3788, E-mail: buckd@ferris.edu. *Interim MSN Program Coordinator*, Dr. Marrietta Bell-Scriber, 231-591-2288, Fax: 231-591-3788, E-mail: bellscm@ferris.edu.

School of Nursing Students: 1 (woman) full-time, 69 part-time (63 women); includes 1 Two or more races, non-Hispanic/Latino. Average age 44. *Faculty:* 6 full-time (all women). Expenses: Contact institution. *Financial support:* In 2010–11, 4 students received support; fellowships, research assistantships, teaching assistantships, scholarships/grants available. Financial award application deadline: 4/15. In 2010, 18 master's awarded. *Degree program information:* Part-time and evening/weekend programs available. Postbaccalaureate distance learning degree programs offered (minimal on-campus study). Offers nursing (MSN); nursing administration (MSN); nursing education (MSN); nursing informatics (MSN). *Application deadline:* For fall admission, 7/15 priority date for domestic students; for spring admission, 11/15 for domestic students. Applications are processed on a rolling basis. *Application fee:* $30. Electronic applications accepted. *Application Contact:* Debby Buck, Off Campus Program Secretary, 231-591-2270, Fax: 231-591-3788, E-mail: buckd@ferris.edu. *Program Coordinator*, Dr. Marietta Bell-Scriber, 231-591-2288, Fax: 231-591-2325, E-mail: bellscm@ferris.edu.

College of Business Students: 34 full-time (9 women), 112 part-time (55 women); includes 3 Black or African American, non-Hispanic/Latino; 4 American Indian or Alaska Native, non-Hispanic/Latino; 3 Asian, non-Hispanic/Latino; 3 Hispanic/Latino; 4 Two or more races, non-Hispanic/Latino, 16 international. Average age 32. 68 applicants, 35% accepted, 15 enrolled. *Faculty:* 10 full-time (3 women), 2 part-time/adjunct (both women). Expenses: Contact institution. *Financial support:* Career-related internships or fieldwork, Federal Work-Study, scholarships/grants, and unspecified assistantships available. Support available to part-time students. Financial award application deadline: 3/15; financial award applicants required to submit FAFSA. In 2010, 62 master's awarded. *Degree program information:* Part-time and evening/weekend programs available. Offers application development (MSISM); business intelligence and informatics (MBA); database administration (MSISM); design and innovation management process (MBA); e-business (MSISM); networking (MSISM); quality management (MBA); security (MSISM). *Application deadline:* For fall admission, 7/1 priority date for domestic students, 6/15 for international students; for winter admission, 11/1 priority date for domestic students, 10/15 for international students; for spring admission, 3/1 priority date for domestic students, 2/15 for international students. Applications are processed on a rolling basis. *Application fee:* $30. Electronic applications accepted. *Application Contact:* Shannon Yost, Department Secretary, 231-591-2168, Fax: 231-591-3548, E-mail: yosts@ferris.edu. *Department Chair*, Dr. David Steenstra, 231-591-2168, Fax: 231-591-3548, E-mail: yosts@ferris.edu.

College of Education and Human Services Students: 33 full-time (19 women), 218 part-time (135 women); includes 33 Black or African American, non-Hispanic/Latino; 2 American Indian or Alaska Native, non-Hispanic/Latino; 1 Asian, non-Hispanic/Latino; 7 Hispanic/Latino; 2 Two or more races, non-Hispanic/Latino, 3 international. Average age 35. 64 applicants, 56% accepted, 28 enrolled. *Faculty:* 20 full-time (12 women), 11 part-time/adjunct (5 women). Expenses: Contact institution. *Financial support:* In 2010–11, 2 research assistantships (averaging $4,850 per year) were awarded; career-related internships or fieldwork, Federal Work-Study, scholarships/grants, and unspecified assistantships also available. Support available to part-time students. Financial award applicants required to submit FAFSA. In 2010, 72 master's awarded. *Degree program information:* Part-time and evening/weekend programs available. Postbaccalaureate distance learning degree programs offered (minimal on-campus study). Offers education and human services (M Ed, MSCJ, MSCTE). *Application deadline:* For fall admission, 7/1 priority date for domestic and international students; for spring admission, 11/1 priority date for domestic and international students. Applications are processed on a rolling basis. *Application fee:* $30. *Application Contact:* Michelle Johnston, Dean, 231-591-3646, Fax: 231-592-3792, E-mail: michelle_johnston@ferris.edu. *Dean*, Michelle Johnston, 231-591-3646, Fax: 231-592-3792, E-mail: michelle_johnston@ferris.edu.

School of Criminal Justice Students: 22 full-time (13 women), 49 part-time (24 women); includes 15 Black or African American, non-Hispanic/Latino; 2 American Indian or Alaska Native, non-Hispanic/Latino; 5 Hispanic/Latino; 2 Two or more races, non-Hispanic/Latino, 1 international. Average age 31. 18 applicants, 61% accepted, 11 enrolled. *Faculty:* 10 full-time (5 women). Expenses: Contact institution. *Financial support:* In 2010–11, 2 research assistantships (averaging $4,850 per year) were awarded; Federal Work-Study and unspecified assistantships also available. Support available to part-time students. Financial award applicants required to submit FAFSA. In 2010, 23 master's awarded. *Degree program information:* Part-time and evening/weekend programs available. Offers criminal justice administration (MSCJ). *Application deadline:* For fall admission, 8/15 for domestic students; for winter admission, 12/15 for domestic students; for spring admission, 3/15 for domestic students. Applications are processed on a rolling basis. *Application fee:* $30. Electronic applications accepted. *Application Contact:* Dr. Nancy L. Hogan, Assistant Professor, 231-591-2664, Fax: 231-591-3792, E-mail: hogann@ferris.edu. *Graduate Program Coordinator*, Dr. Nancy L. Hogan, 231-591-2664, Fax: 231-591-3792, E-mail: hogann@ferris.edu.

School of Education Students: 11 full-time (6 women), 169 part-time (111 women); includes 18 Black or African American, non-Hispanic/Latino; 1 Asian, non-Hispanic/Latino; 2 Hispanic/Latino, 2 international. Average age 37. 46 applicants, 54% accepted, 17 enrolled. *Faculty:* 10 full-time (7 women), 11 part-time/adjunct (5 women). Expenses: Contact institution. *Financial support:* Career-related internships or fieldwork and scholarships/grants available. Support available to part-time students. Financial award applicants required to submit FAFSA. In 2010, 49 master's awarded. *Degree program information:* Part-time and evening/weekend programs available. Postbaccalaureate distance learning degree programs offered (minimal on-campus study). Offers administration (MSCTE); curriculum and instruction (M Ed); education technology (MSCTE); instructor (MSCTE); post-secondary administration (MSCTE); training and development (MSCTE). *Application deadline:* For fall admission, 7/1 priority date for domestic and international students; for spring admission, 11/1 priority date for domestic and international students. Applications are processed on a rolling basis. *Application fee:* $30. Electronic applications accepted. *Application Contact:* Kimisue Worrall, Secretary, 231-591-5361, Fax: 231-591-2043. *Graduate Program Coordinator*, Dr. Liza Ing, 231-591-5362, Fax: 231-591-2043.

College of Pharmacy Students: 514 full-time (263 women), 15 part-time (6 women); includes 9 Black or African American, non-Hispanic/Latino; 1 American Indian or Alaska Native, non-Hispanic/Latino; 38 Asian, non-Hispanic/Latino; 4 Hispanic/Latino; 7 Two or more races, non-Hispanic/Latino, 25 international. Average age 24. 401 applicants, 15% accepted, 58 enrolled. *Faculty:* 37 full-time (21 women), 3 part-time/adjunct (2 women). Expenses: Contact institution. *Financial support:* Institutionally sponsored loans and scholarships/grants available. Financial award applicants required to submit FAFSA. In 2010, 125 Pharm Ds awarded. Offers pharmacy (Pharm D). *Application deadline:* For fall admission, 12/15 for domestic students. *Application fee:* $0. *Application Contact:* Tara M. Lee, Administrative Specialist, Admissions, 231-591-3780, Fax: 231-591-3829, E-mail: leet@ferris.edu. *Interim Dean*, Dr. Stephen Durst, 231-591-2254, Fax: 231-591-3829, E-mail: dursts@ferris.edu.

College of Professional and Technological Studies Students: 28 part-time (19 women); includes 4 Black or African American, non-Hispanic/Latino; 1 Two or more races, non-Hispanic/Latino. Average age 45. *Faculty:* 9 part-time/adjunct (5 women). Expenses: Contact institution. *Financial support:* In 2010–11, 10 students received support. Applicants required to submit FAFSA. *Degree program information:* Evening/weekend programs available. Postbaccalaureate distance learning degree programs offered (minimal on-campus study). Offers community college leadership (Ed D). *Application deadline:* For spring admission, 4/15 for domestic and international students. Applications are processed on a rolling basis. *Application fee:* $30. Electronic applications accepted. *Application Contact:* Andrea Wirgau, Coordinator, 231-591-2710, Fax: 231-591-3539, E-mail: andreawirgau@ferris.edu. *Director*, Dr. Roberta Teahen, 231-591-3805, E-mail: robertateahen@ferris.edu.

Kendall College of Art and Design Students: 29 full-time (19 women), 15 part-time (10 women); includes 1 American Indian or Alaska Native, non-Hispanic/Latino; 1 Asian, non-Hispanic/Latino; 1 Two or more races, non-Hispanic/Latino. Average age 31. 37 applicants, 70% accepted, 13 enrolled. *Faculty:* 15 full-time (10 women). Expenses: Contact institution. *Financial support:* In 2010–11, 30 students received support, including 7 fellowships (averaging $13,370 per year); scholarships/grants, unspecified assistantships, and half-tuition scholarships ($6317 average), graduate assistantships ($5309 average) also available. Support available to part-time students. Financial award application deadline: 2/15; financial award applicants required to submit FAFSA. In 2010, 15 master's awarded. *Degree program information:* Part-time programs available. Offers art and design (MFA). *Application deadline:* For fall admission, 2/15 priority date for domestic and international students; for spring admission, 11/1 priority date for domestic and international students. Applications are processed on a rolling basis. *Application fee:* $30. *Application Contact:* Sandra Britton, Director of Enrollment Management, 616-451-2787, Fax: 616-831-9689, E-mail: kcadadmissions@ferris.edu. *President and Vice Chancellor*, Dr. Oliver H. Evans, 616-451-2787.

Michigan College of Optometry Students: 143 full-time (80 women); includes 9 minority (5 Asian, non-Hispanic/Latino; 1 Hispanic/Latino; 3 Two or more races, non-Hispanic/Latino), 8 international. Average age 24. 476 applicants, 8% accepted, 33 enrolled. *Faculty:* 19 full-time (4 women), 101 part-time/adjunct (39 women). Expenses: Contact institution. *Financial support:* Fellowships, research assistantships, teaching assistantships, career-related internships or fieldwork, Federal Work-Study, and scholarships/grants available. Financial award application deadline: 3/15; financial award applicants required to submit FAFSA. In 2010, 38 ODs awarded. Offers optometry (OD). *Application deadline:* For fall admission, 4/1 for domestic and international students. Applications are processed on a rolling basis. *Application fee:* $30. Electronic applications accepted. *Application Contact:* Colleen Olson, Assistant to the Associate Dean, 231-591-3703, Fax: 231-591-2394, E-mail: olsonc@ferris.edu. *Dean*, Dr. Michael Cron, 231-591-3706, Fax: 231-591-2394, E-mail: cronm@ferris.edu.

FIELDING GRADUATE UNIVERSITY, Santa Barbara, CA 93105-3538

General Information Independent, coed, graduate-only institution. CGS member. *Enrollment by degree level:* 168 master's, 1,164 doctoral, 174 other advanced degrees. *Graduate faculty:* 69 full-time (35 women), 34 part-time/adjunct (16 women). *Tuition:* Full-time $22,365; part-time $720 per credit. *Student services:* International student services, low-cost health insurance, services for students with disabilities, writing training. *Library facilities:* The Fielding Graduate University Library Services. *Online resources:* web page. *Collection:* 70,936 titles, 38,125 serial subscriptions.

Computer facilities: Online class registration is available. *Web address:* http://www.fielding.edu/.

General Application Contact: Admission Office, 800-340-1099, Fax: 805-687-9793, E-mail: admission@fielding.edu.

GRADUATE UNITS

Graduate Programs Students: 1,288 full-time (936 women), 218 part-time (161 women); includes 420 minority (193 Black or African American, non-Hispanic/Latino; 20 American Indian or Alaska Native, non-Hispanic/Latino; 52 Asian, non-Hispanic/Latino; 117 Hispanic/Latino; 1 Native Hawaiian or other Pacific Islander, non-Hispanic/Latino; 37 Two or more races, non-Hispanic/Latino), 89 international. Average age 46. 562 applicants, 59% accepted, 218 enrolled. *Faculty:* 69 full-time (35 women), 34 part-time/adjunct (16 women). Expenses: Contact institution. *Financial support:* In 2010–11, 154 students received support. Scholarships/grants, health care benefits, and tuition waivers (partial) available. Support available to part-time students. In 2010, 104 master's, 110 doctorates, 90 other advanced degrees awarded. Postbaccalaureate distance learning degree programs offered (minimal on-campus study). *Application deadline:* For fall admission, 2/15 for domestic and international students; for spring admission, 8/15 for domestic and international students. *Application fee:* $75. Electronic applications accepted. *Application Contact:* Kathy Bellway, Admission Assistant, 800-340-1099, Fax: 805-687-9793, E-mail: admission@fielding.edu. *President*, Dr. Richard S. Meyers, 805-898-2903, Fax: 805-687-4590, E-mail: rmeyers@fielding.edu.

School of Educational Leadership and Change Students: 299 full-time (215 women), 1 (woman) part-time; includes 149 minority (83 Black or African American, non-Hispanic/Latino; 7 American Indian or Alaska Native, non-Hispanic/Latino; 8 Asian, non-Hispanic/Latino; 40 Hispanic/Latino; 1 Native Hawaiian or other Pacific Islander, non-Hispanic/Latino; 10 Two or more races, non-Hispanic/Latino), 4 international. Average age 47. 50 applicants, 96% accepted, 33 enrolled. *Faculty:* 17 full-time (9 women), 15 part-time/adjunct (11 women). Expenses: Contact institution. *Financial support:* In 2010–11, 48 students received support. Scholarships/grants, health care benefits, and tuition waivers (partial) available. Support available to part-time students. In 2010, 46 master's, 39 doctorates, 19 other advanced degrees awarded. Postbaccalaureate distance learning degree programs offered (minimal on-campus study). Offers collaborative educational leadership (MA); educational leadership and change (Ed D); teaching in the virtual classroom (Graduate Certificate). *Application deadline:* For fall admission, 6/10 for domestic and international students; for spring admission, 11/19 for domestic and international students. *Application fee:* $75. Electronic applications accepted. *Application Contact:* Admission Counselor, 800-340-1099, Fax: 805-687-9793, E-mail: elcadmissions@fielding.edu. *Dean*, Dr. Judy Witt, 805-898-2940, E-mail: jwitt@fielding.edu.

School of Human and Organization Development Students: 455 full-time (325 women), 148 part-time (112 women); includes 124 minority (69 Black or African American, non-Hispanic/Latino; 6 American Indian or Alaska Native, non-Hispanic/Latino; 19 Asian, non-Hispanic/Latino; 20 Hispanic/Latino; 10 Two or more races, non-Hispanic/Latino), 65 international. Average age 48. 179 applicants, 94% accepted, 109 enrolled. *Faculty:* 25 full-time (11 women), 11 part-time/adjunct (3 women). Expenses: Contact institution. *Financial support:* In 2010–11, 27 students received support. Scholarships/grants and health care benefits available. Support available to part-time students. In 2010, 49 master's, 32 doctorates, 55 other advanced degrees awarded. Postbaccalaureate distance learning degree programs offered (minimal on-campus study). Offers evidence-based coaching (Certificate); human and organizational systems (PhD); human development (PhD); integral studies (Certificate); organization management and development (MA, Certificate). *Application deadline:* For fall admission, 3/1 for domestic and international students; for spring admission, 9/1 for domestic and international students. *Application fee:* $75. Electronic applications accepted. *Application Contact:* Carmen Kuchera, Admission Counselor, 800-340-

1099, Fax: 805-687-9793, E-mail: hodadmissions@fielding.edu. *Dean*, Dr. Charles McClintock, 805-898-2930, Fax: 805-687-4590, E-mail: cmcclintock@fielding.edu.

School of Psychology Students: 534 full-time (396 women), 69 part-time (48 women); includes 147 minority (41 Black or African American, non-Hispanic/Latino; 7 American Indian or Alaska Native, non-Hispanic/Latino; 25 Asian, non-Hispanic/Latino; 57 Hispanic/Latino; 17 Two or more races, non-Hispanic/Latino), 20 international. Average age 42. 333 applicants, 35% accepted, 76 enrolled. *Faculty:* 27 full-time (15 women), 8 part-time/adjunct (2 women). Expenses: Contact institution. *Financial support:* In 2010–11, 79 students received support. Scholarships/grants and health care benefits available. Support available to part-time students. In 2010, 9 master's, 39 doctorates, 16 other advanced degrees awarded. Postbaccalaureate distance learning degree programs offered (minimal on-campus study). Offers clinical psychology (PhD); clinical psychology respecialization (Post-Doctoral Certificate); media psychology (PhD); media psychology and social change (MA); neuropsychology (Post-Doctoral Certificate). *Application deadline:* For fall admission, 2/25 for domestic and international students; for spring admission, 8/25 for domestic and international students. *Application fee:* $75. Electronic applications accepted. *Application Contact:* Admission Counselor, 800-340-1099, Fax: 805-687-9793, E-mail: psyadmissions@fielding.edu. *Interim Dean*, Dr. Gerardo Rodriguez-.Menendez, 805-898-2909, E-mail: grodriguez@fielding.edu.

FISK UNIVERSITY, Nashville, TN 37208-3051

General Information Independent-religious, coed, comprehensive institution. *Graduate housing:* Rooms and/or apartments available on a first-come, first-served basis to single and married students. Housing application deadline: 4/6. *Research affiliation:* Oak Ridge Associated Universities (physics).

GRADUATE UNITS

Division of Graduate Studies *Degree program information:* Part-time programs available. Offers biology (MA); chemistry (MA); clinical psychology (MA); physics (MA); psychology (MA). Electronic applications accepted.

FITCHBURG STATE UNIVERSITY, Fitchburg, MA 01420-2697

General Information State-supported, coed, comprehensive institution. *Enrollment:* 6,771 graduate, professional, and undergraduate students; 186 full-time matriculated graduate/professional students (115 women), 876 part-time matriculated graduate/professional students (653 women). *Enrollment by degree level:* 968 master's, 94 other advanced degrees. *Tuition, area resident:* Part-time $150 per credit. Tuition, state resident: part-time $150 per credit. Tuition, nonresident: part-time $150 per credit. *Required fees:* $127 per credit. *Graduate housing:* On-campus housing not available. *Student services:* Campus employment opportunities, campus safety program, career counseling, exercise/wellness program, free psychological counseling, international student services, low-cost health insurance, multicultural affairs office, services for students with disabilities, teacher training, writing training. *Library facilities:* Amelia V. Galucci-Cirio Library. *Online resources:* library catalog, web page, access to other libraries' catalogs. *Collection:* 252,331 titles, 2,098 serial subscriptions, 2,445 audiovisual materials.

Computer facilities: Computer purchase and lease plans are available. 500 computers available on campus for general student use. A campuswide network can be accessed from student residence rooms and from off campus. Online class registration is available. *Web address:* http://www.fitchburgstate.edu/.

General Application Contact: Kay Reynolds, Director of Admissions, 978-665-3144, Fax: 978-665-4540, E-mail: admissions@fitchburgstate.edu.

GRADUATE UNITS

Division of Graduate and Continuing Education Students: 186 full-time (115 women), 876 part-time (653 women); includes 17 Black or African American, non-Hispanic/Latino; 1 American Indian or Alaska Native, non-Hispanic/Latino; 21 Hispanic/Latino, 66 international. Average age 35. 339 applicants, 96% accepted, 244 enrolled. Expenses: Contact institution. *Financial support:* In 2010–11, research assistantships with partial tuition reimbursements (averaging $5,500 per year); Federal Work-Study, scholarships/grants, and unspecified assistantships also available. Support available to part-time students. Financial award application deadline: 3/1; financial award applicants required to submit FAFSA. In 2010, 461 master's, 55 other advanced degrees awarded. *Degree program information:* Part-time and evening/weekend programs available. Postbaccalaureate distance learning degree programs offered (minimal on-campus study). Offers accounting (MBA); applied communications (MS, Certificate); arts education (M Ed); biology and teaching biology (secondary level) (MA, MAT, Certificate); computer science (MS); curriculum and teaching (M Ed); early childhood education (M Ed); educational technology (Certificate); elementary education (M Ed); elementary school guidance counseling (MS); English and teaching English (secondary level) (MA, MAT, Certificate); fine arts director (Certificate); forensic nursing (MS, Certificate); guided studies (M Ed); health communication (MS); higher education administration (CAGS); history and teaching history (secondary level) (MA, MAT, Certificate); human resource management (MBA); interdisciplinary studies (CAGS); library media (MS); management (MBA); mental health counseling (MS); middle school education (M Ed); non-licensure (M Ed, CAGS); occupational education (M Ed); reading specialist (M Ed); school principal (M Ed, CAGS); science education (M Ed); secondary education (M Ed); secondary school guidance counseling (MS); supervisor/director (M Ed, CAGS); teaching students with moderate disabilities (M Ed); teaching students with severe disabilities (M Ed); technical and professional writing (MS); technology education (M Ed); technology leader (M Ed, CAGS). *Application deadline:* Applications are processed on a rolling basis. *Application fee:* $25 ($50 for international students). *Application Contact:* Kay Reynolds, Director of Admissions, 978-665-3144, Fax: 978-665-4540, E-mail: admissions@fitchburgstate.edu. *Dean*, Catherine Canney, 978-665-3182, Fax: 978-665-3658, E-mail: gce@fitchburgstate.edu.

FIVE BRANCHES UNIVERSITY: GRADUATE SCHOOL OF TRADITIONAL CHINESE MEDICINE, Santa Cruz, CA 95062

General Information Independent, coed, graduate-only institution. *Graduate housing:* On-campus housing not available.

GRADUATE UNITS

Program in Traditional Chinese Medicine Offers traditional Chinese medicine (MTCM). Electronic applications accepted.

FIVE TOWNS COLLEGE, Dix Hills, NY 11746-6055

General Information Independent, coed, comprehensive institution. *Enrollment:* 1,447 graduate, professional, and undergraduate students; 18 full-time matriculated graduate/professional students (5 women), 38 part-time matriculated graduate/professional students (9 women). *Enrollment by degree level:* 38 master's, 18 doctoral. *Graduate faculty:* 6 full-time (2 women), 15 part-time/adjunct (4 women). *Tuition:* Full-time $13,200; part-time $550 per credit. *Required fees:* $300 per semester. One-time fee: $85. Tuition and fees vary according to course level, course load, degree level, program and student level. *Graduate housing:* On-campus housing not available. *Student services:* Campus employment opportunities, campus safety program, career counseling, international student services, low-cost health insurance, teacher training, writing training. *Library facilities:* Five Towns College Library. *Online resources:* library catalog, access to other libraries' catalogs. *Collection:* 40,000 titles, 565 serial subscriptions, 650 audiovisual materials.

Computer facilities: 110 computers available on campus for general student use. A campuswide network can be accessed from student residence rooms. Online class registration is available. *Web address:* http://www.ftc.edu/.

General Application Contact: Jerry Cohen, Dean of Enrollment, 631-656-2121, Fax: 631-656-2172, E-mail: admissions@ftc.edu.

GRADUATE UNITS

Department of Music Students: 18 full-time (5 women), 23 part-time (4 women); includes 4 minority (3 Black or African American, non-Hispanic/Latino; 1 Hispanic/Latino), 10 international. Average age 28. 20 applicants, 70% accepted, 6 enrolled. *Faculty:* 6 full-time (2 women), 15 part-time/adjunct (4 women). Expenses: Contact institution. *Financial support:* Fellowships with tuition reimbursements, tuition waivers (partial) available. Financial award applicants required to submit FAFSA. In 2010, 3 master's awarded. *Degree program information:* Part-time programs available. Offers jazz/commercial music (MM); music (DMA); music education (MM). *Application deadline:* For fall admission, 9/1 for domestic and international students; for spring admission, 1/25 for domestic and international students. Applications are processed on a rolling basis. *Application fee:* $50. *Application Contact:* Jerry Cohen, Dean of Enrollment, 631-656-2121, Fax: 631-656-2172, E-mail: jcohen@ftc.edu. *Dean of Graduate Studies*, Dr. Jill Miller-Thorn, 631-656-2142, Fax: 631-656-2172, E-mail: jmillerthorn@ftc.edu.

FLORIDA AGRICULTURAL AND MECHANICAL UNIVERSITY, Tallahassee, FL 32307-3200

General Information State-supported, coed, university. CGS member. *Graduate housing:* Rooms and/or apartments available on a first-come, first-served basis to single and married students. Housing application deadline: 6/1. *Research affiliation:* The Boeing Company (aerospace science), Minority Health Professions Foundation (health science), Pfizer, Inc.

GRADUATE UNITS

College of Law *Degree program information:* Part-time and evening/weekend programs available. Offers law (JD).

Division of Graduate Studies, Research, and Continuing Education *Degree program information:* Part-time and evening/weekend programs available.

College of Arts and Sciences *Degree program information:* Part-time programs available. Offers African American history (MASS); arts and sciences (MASS, MS, MSW, PhD); biology (MS); chemistry (MS); community psychology (MS); criminal justice (MASS); economics (MASS); history (MASS); history and political sciences (MASS, MSW); physics (MS, PhD); political science (MASS); public administration (MASS); public management (MASS); school psychology (MS); social work (MASS); sociology (MASS); software engineering (MS).

College of Education *Degree program information:* Part-time and evening/weekend programs available. Offers administration and supervision (M Ed, MS Ed, PhD); adult education (M Ed, MS Ed); biology (M Ed); business education (MBE); chemistry (MS Ed); early childhood and elementary education (M Ed, MS Ed); education (M Ed, MBE, MS Ed, PhD); educational leadership (PhD); English (MS Ed); guidance and counseling (M Ed, MS Ed); health, physical education, and recreation (M Ed, MS Ed); history (MS Ed); industrial education (M Ed, MS Ed); math (MS Ed); physics (MS Ed).

College of Engineering Science, Technology, and Agriculture Offers agribusiness (MS); animal science (MS); engineering science, technology, and agriculture (MS); engineering technology (MS); entomology (MS); food science (MS); international programs (MS); plant science (MS).

College of Pharmacy and Pharmaceutical Sciences Offers environmental toxicology (PhD); medicinal chemistry (MS, PhD); pharmaceutics (MS, PhD); pharmacology/toxicology (MS, PhD); pharmacy administration (MS); pharmacy and pharmaceutical sciences (Pharm D, MPH, MS, Ex Doc, PhD); public health (MPH).

FAMU-FSU College of Engineering Offers biomedical engineering (MS, PhD); chemical engineering (MS, PhD); civil engineering (MS, PhD); electrical engineering (MS, PhD); engineering (MS, PhD); environmental engineering (MS, PhD); industrial engineering (MS, PhD); mechanical engineering (MS, PhD). College administered jointly by Florida State University.

School of Allied Health Sciences Offers health administration (MS); occupational therapy (MOT); physical therapy (MPT).

School of Architecture *Degree program information:* Part-time programs available. Offers architectural studies (MS Arch); architecture (professional) (M Arch); landscape architecture (MLA).

School of Business and Industry Offers accounting (MBA); finance (MBA); management information systems (MBA); marketing (MBA).

School of Journalism and Graphic Communication Offers journalism (MS).

School of Nursing Offers nursing (MS).

Environmental Sciences Institute Students: 26 full-time (23 women), 3 part-time (0 women); includes 20 Black or African American, non-Hispanic/Latino; 3 Asian, non-Hispanic/Latino; 2 Hispanic/Latino, 3 international. Average age 25. 21 applicants, 14% accepted, 3 enrolled. *Faculty:* 10 full-time (2 women). Expenses: Contact institution. *Financial support:* In 2010–11, 28 students received support, including 10 fellowships with full and partial tuition reimbursements available, 18 research assistantships with tuition reimbursements available; career-related internships or fieldwork, institutionally sponsored loans, scholarships/grants, and unspecified assistantships also available. Financial award application deadline: 6/10; financial award applicants required to submit FAFSA. In 2010, 3 master's, 2 doctorates awarded. Offers environmental sciences (MS, PhD). *Application deadline:* For fall admission, 6/1 priority date for domestic students, 4/1 priority date for international students; for spring admission, 11/1 priority date for domestic and international students. *Application fee:* $9 for international students. *Application Contact:* Ora S. Mukes, Coordinator, Academic Support Services, 850-561-2641, Fax: 850-412-5504, E-mail: ora.mukes@famu.edu. *Director*, Dr. Michael Abazinge, 850-599-3550, Fax: 850-599-8183, E-mail: michael.abazinge@famu.edu.

FLORIDA ATLANTIC UNIVERSITY, Boca Raton, FL 33431-0991

General Information State-supported, coed, university. CGS member. *Enrollment:* 28,325 graduate, professional, and undergraduate students; 1,719 full-time matriculated graduate/professional students (984 women), 2,527 part-time matriculated graduate/professional students (1,622 women). *Enrollment by degree level:* 3,467 master's, 779 doctoral. *Graduate faculty:* 1,058 full-time (483 women), 505 part-time/adjunct (260 women). Tuition, state resident: part-time $319.96 per credit. Tuition, nonresident: part-time $926.42 per credit. *Graduate housing:* Room and/or apartments available on a first-come, first-served basis to single students; on-campus housing not available to married students. Housing application deadline: 5/1. *Student services:* Campus employment opportunities, campus safety program, career counseling, exercise/wellness program, free psychological counseling, international student services, low-cost health insurance, multicultural affairs office, services for students with disabilities, teacher training. *Library facilities:* S. E. Wimberly Library plus 2 others. *Online resources:* library catalog, web page, access to other libraries' catalogs. *Collection:* 1.3 million titles, 12,811 serial subscriptions. *Research affiliation:* Smithsonian Marine Station (marine resources characterization), Harbor Branch Oceanographic Institution (harnessing ocean power), Motorola Corporation (engineering), Children's Services Council (urban redevelopment), Shell Oil Company (engineering), Florida Power & Light (solar energy).

Computer facilities: 1,000 computers available on campus for general student use. A campuswide network can be accessed from student residence rooms and from off campus. Online class registration is available. *Web address:* http://www.fau.edu/.

General Application Contact: Joanna Arlington, Manager, Graduate Admissions, 561-297-2428, Fax: 561-297-2117, E-mail: arlingto@fau.edu.

GRADUATE UNITS

Charles E. Schmidt College of Science Students: 323 full-time (157 women), 95 part-time (53 women); includes 71 minority (17 Black or African American, non-Hispanic/Latino; 22 Asian, non-Hispanic/Latino; 31 Hispanic/Latino; 1 Two or more races, non-Hispanic/Latino), 94 international. Average age 31. 392 applicants, 42% accepted, 108 enrolled. *Faculty:* 155 full-time (36 women), 25 part-time/adjunct (6 women). Expenses: Contact institution. *Financial support:* Fellowships with partial tuition reimbursements, research assistantships with partial tuition reimbursements, teaching assistantships with partial tuition reimbursements, career-related internships or fieldwork, Federal Work-Study, institutionally sponsored loans, scholarships/grants, tuition waivers (partial), and unspecified assistantships available. In 2010, 69 master's, 31 doctorates awarded. *Degree program information:* Part-time programs available. Offers applied mathematics and statistics (MS); biological sciences (MS, MST); chemistry (MS, MST, PhD); environmental sciences (MS); geography (MA); geology (MS); geosciences (PhD); mathematical sciences (MS, MST, PhD); physics (MS, PhD); psychology (MA, PhD); science (MA, MS, MST, PhD). *Application deadline:* For fall admission, 6/1 for

Florida Atlantic University (continued)

domestic students, 2/15 for international students; for spring admission, 11/1 for domestic students, 8/15 for international students. Applications are processed on a rolling basis. *Application fee:* $30. Electronic applications accepted. *Application Contact:* Dr. Leslie Terry, Associate Dean of External Affairs and Community Relations, 561-297-0347, Fax: 561-297-3388. *Dean*, Dr. Gary W. Perry, 561-297-3288, Fax: 561-297-3792.

Center for Complex Systems and Brain Sciences Students: 39 full-time (25 women), 10 part-time (7 women); includes 8 minority (2 Black or African American, non-Hispanic/Latino; 3 Asian, non-Hispanic/Latino; 3 Hispanic/Latino), 4 international. Average age 34. 16 applicants, 25% accepted, 4 enrolled. *Faculty:* 6 full-time (3 women), 1 part-time/adjunct (0 women). Expenses: Contact institution. *Financial support:* Fellowships with full tuition reimbursements, research assistantships with partial tuition reimbursements, teaching assistantships with partial tuition reimbursements, Federal Work-Study, traineeships, and unspecified assistantships available. In 2010, 5 doctorates awarded. Offers complex systems and brain sciences (PhD). *Application deadline:* For fall admission, 1/15 priority date for domestic and international students. *Application fee:* $30. *Application Contact:* Rhona Frankel, Associate Director, 561-297-2230, E-mail: frankel@fau.edu. *Director*, Dr. Janet Blanks, 561-297-2229, Fax: 561-297-3634, E-mail: blanks@ccs.fau.edu.

Christine E. Lynn College of Nursing Students: 17 full-time (15 women), 351 part-time (326 women); includes 156 minority (86 Black or African American, non-Hispanic/Latino; 2 American Indian or Alaska Native, non-Hispanic/Latino; 17 Asian, non-Hispanic/Latino; 48 Hispanic/Latino; 3 Two or more races, non-Hispanic/Latino), 1 international. Average age 40. 205 applicants, 34% accepted, 65 enrolled. *Faculty:* 44 full-time (41 women), 16 part-time/adjunct (13 women). Expenses: Contact institution. *Financial support:* Research assistantships with partial tuition reimbursements, teaching assistantships with partial tuition reimbursements, career-related internships or fieldwork, Federal Work-Study, institutionally sponsored loans, scholarships/grants, and traineeships available. Support available to part-time students. In 2010, 139 master's, 6 doctorates awarded. *Degree program information:* Part-time programs available. Offers nursing (MS, DNP, PhD, Post Master's Certificate). *Application deadline:* For fall admission, 6/1 for domestic students, 2/15 for international students; for spring admission, 10/1 for domestic students, 7/15 for international students. Applications are processed on a rolling basis. *Application fee:* $30. *Application Contact:* Carol Kruse, Graduate Coordinator, 561-297-3261, Fax: 561-297-0088, E-mail: ckruse@fau.edu. *Dean*, Dr. Marlaine Smith, 561-297-3206, Fax: 561-297-3687, E-mail: msmit230@fau.edu.

College of Biomedical Science Students: 36 full-time (25 women), 7 part-time (3 women); includes 17 minority (4 Black or African American, non-Hispanic/Latino; 3 Asian, non-Hispanic/Latino; 9 Hispanic/Latino; 1 Two or more races, non-Hispanic/Latino), 5 international. Average age 26. 61 applicants, 28% accepted, 13 enrolled. *Faculty:* 35 full-time (14 women), 13 part-time/adjunct (2 women). Expenses: Contact institution. *Financial support:* Research assistantships available. In 2010, 22 master's awarded. Offers biomedical science (MS); integrative biology (PhD). *Application deadline:* For fall admission, 5/1 for domestic students, 3/15 for international students; for spring admission, 10/1 for domestic and international students. *Application fee:* $30. *Application Contact:* Julie Sivigny, Academic Program Specialist for Graduate Studies, 561-297-2216, E-mail: jsivigny@fau.edu. *Dean*, Dr. Michael L. Friedland, 561-297-4341.

College of Business Students: 440 full-time (216 women), 825 part-time (414 women); includes 420 minority (138 Black or African American, non-Hispanic/Latino; 79 Asian, non-Hispanic/Latino; 182 Hispanic/Latino; 1 Native Hawaiian or other Pacific Islander, non-Hispanic/Latino; 20 Two or more races, non-Hispanic/Latino), 59 international. Average age 31. 860 applicants, 43% accepted, 289 enrolled. *Faculty:* 134 full-time (45 women), 87 part-time/adjunct (23 women). Expenses: Contact institution. *Financial support:* Fellowships with partial tuition reimbursements, research assistantships with partial tuition reimbursements, teaching assistantships with full tuition reimbursements, career-related internships or fieldwork, Federal Work-Study, institutionally sponsored loans, tuition waivers (full and partial), and unspecified assistantships available. Support available to part-time students. Financial award application deadline: 3/1. In 2010, 369 master's, 6 doctorates awarded. *Degree program information:* Part-time and evening/weekend programs available. Postbaccalaureate distance learning degree programs offered (minimal on-campus study). Offers business (Exec MBA, M Ac, M Tax, MBA, MHA, MS, PhD, Certificate); economics (MS); finance (MS, PhD); global entrepreneurship (MBA); international business (MBA, MS); management (PhD); management information systems (MS). *Application deadline:* For fall admission, 7/15 priority date for domestic students, 2/15 priority date for international students; for winter admission, 11/1 priority date for domestic students, 8/15 priority date for international students; for spring admission, 4/1 priority date for domestic students, 1/15 priority date for international students. Applications are processed on a rolling basis. *Application fee:* $30. *Application Contact:* Fredrick G. Taylor, Graduate Adviser, 561-297-3196, Fax: 561-297-1315, E-mail: ftaylor@fau.edu. *Dean*, Dr. Dennis Coates, 561-297-3635, Fax: 561-297-3686, E-mail: coates@fau.edu.

School of Accounting Students: 81 full-time (43 women), 320 part-time (195 women); includes 112 minority (42 Black or African American, non-Hispanic/Latino; 26 Asian, non-Hispanic/Latino; 41 Hispanic/Latino; 3 Two or more races, non-Hispanic/Latino), 6 international. Average age 31. 347 applicants, 46% accepted, 134 enrolled. *Faculty:* 27 full-time (13 women), 21 part-time/adjunct (6 women). Expenses: Contact institution. *Financial support:* Fellowships, research assistantships with partial tuition reimbursements, teaching assistantships, career-related internships or fieldwork, Federal Work-Study, institutionally sponsored loans, scholarships/grants, and tuition waivers (partial) available. Support available to part-time students. Financial award application deadline: 3/1. In 2010, 153 master's awarded. *Degree program information:* Part-time and evening/weekend programs available. Postbaccalaureate distance learning degree programs offered (minimal on-campus study). Offers accounting (M Ac, M Tax, PhD); taxation (M Tax). *Application deadline:* For fall admission, 7/1 priority date for domestic students, 2/15 priority date for international students; for spring admission, 11/1 priority date for domestic students, 7/15 priority date for international students. Applications are processed on a rolling basis. *Application fee:* $30. *Application Contact:* Dr. Kim Dunn, Graduate Adviser, 561-297-3643, Fax: 561-297-1315, E-mail: kdunn@fau.edu. *Director*, Dr. Somnath Bhattacharya, 561-297-3638, Fax: 561-297-7023, E-mail: sbhatt@fau.edu.

College of Design and Social Inquiry Students: 160 full-time (120 women), 282 part-time (140 women); includes 139 minority (67 Black or African American, non-Hispanic/Latino; 1 American Indian or Alaska Native, non-Hispanic/Latino; 7 Asian, non-Hispanic/Latino; 59 Hispanic/Latino; 5 Two or more races, non-Hispanic/Latino), 9 international. Average age 32. 442 applicants, 43% accepted, 132 enrolled. *Faculty:* 77 full-time (32 women), 55 part-time/adjunct (21 women). Expenses: Contact institution. *Financial support:* Fellowships with partial tuition reimbursements, research assistantships with partial tuition reimbursements, teaching assistantships with partial tuition reimbursements, career-related internships or fieldwork, Federal Work-Study, and institutionally sponsored loans available. Support available to part-time students. Financial award application deadline: 4/1. In 2010, 111 master's, 4 doctorates awarded. *Degree program information:* Part-time and evening/weekend programs available. Offers design and social inquiry (MNM, MPA, MS, MSW, MURP, PhD, Certificate). *Application deadline:* For fall admission, 7/1 for domestic students, 2/15 for international students; for spring admission, 11/1 for domestic students, 7/15 for international students. Applications are processed on a rolling basis. *Application fee:* $30. *Application Contact:* Dr. Sofia Do Espirito Santo, 954-762-5158, E-mail: ssanto@fau.edu. *Dean*, Dr. Rosalyn Carter, 954-762-5660, Fax: 954-762-5673, E-mail: rcarter@fau.edu.

School of Criminology and Criminal Justice Students: 8 full-time (6 women), 22 part-time (13 women); includes 12 minority (6 Black or African American, non-Hispanic/Latino; 1 Asian, non-Hispanic/Latino; 5 Hispanic/Latino). Average age 28. 29 applicants, 59% accepted, 13 enrolled. *Faculty:* 13 full-time (6 women), 12 part-time/adjunct (3 women). Expenses: Contact institution. *Financial support:* Research assistantships with partial tuition reimbursements, institutionally sponsored loans, scholarships/grants, and unspecified assistantships available. Financial award application deadline: 4/1. In 2010, 6 master's awarded. *Degree program information:* Part-time and evening/weekend programs available. Postbaccalaureate distance learning degree programs offered. Offers criminology and criminal justice (MS). *Application deadline:* For fall admission, 7/1 priority date for domestic students, 2/15 for international students; for spring admission, 11/1 priority date for domestic students, 7/15 for international students. Applications are processed on a rolling basis. *Application fee:* $30. Electronic applications accepted. *Application Contact:* Dr. Maria Schiff, Graduate Program Coordinator, 954-762-5638, Fax: 954-762-5673, E-mail: mschiff@fau.edu. *Chair*, Dr. Gordon Bazemore, 561-297-3240.

School of Public Administration Students: 41 full-time (22 women), 82 part-time (47 women); includes 40 minority (24 Black or African American, non-Hispanic/Latino; 2 Asian, non-Hispanic/Latino; 12 Hispanic/Latino; 2 Two or more races, non-Hispanic/Latino), 6 international. Average age 34. 87 applicants, 43% accepted, 25 enrolled. *Faculty:* 13 full-time (4 women), 2 part-time/adjunct (0 women). Expenses: Contact institution. *Financial support:* Fellowships with full tuition reimbursements, research assistantships with partial tuition reimbursements, teaching assistantships with partial tuition reimbursements, career-related internships or fieldwork, Federal Work-Study, institutionally sponsored loans, and tuition waivers (partial) available. Support available to part-time students. Financial award application deadline: 4/1. In 2010, 30 master's, 4 doctorates awarded. *Degree program information:* Part-time and evening/weekend programs available. Offers nonprofit management (MNM); public administration (MNM, MPA, PhD). *Application deadline:* For fall admission, 7/1 priority date for domestic students, 2/15 for international students; for spring admission, 11/1 for domestic students, 7/15 for international students. Applications are processed on a rolling basis. *Application fee:* $30. *Application Contact:* Dr. Khi Thai, Director, 954-762-5650, Fax: 954-762-5693, E-mail: thai@fau.edu. *Director*, Dr. Khi Thai, 954-762-5650, Fax: 954-762-5693, E-mail: thai@fau.edu.

School of Social Work Students: 87 full-time (74 women), 94 part-time (81 women); includes 70 minority (33 Black or African American, non-Hispanic/Latino; 1 American Indian or Alaska Native, non-Hispanic/Latino; 3 Asian, non-Hispanic/Latino; 30 Hispanic/Latino; 3 Two or more races, non-Hispanic/Latino), 1 international. Average age 33. 271 applicants, 44% accepted, 82 enrolled. *Faculty:* 21 full-time (12 women), 19 part-time/adjunct (14 women). Expenses: Contact institution. *Financial support:* Fellowships with tuition reimbursements, research assistantships with tuition reimbursements, career-related internships or fieldwork, Federal Work-Study, institutionally sponsored loans, and tuition waivers (partial) available. Financial award application deadline: 4/1. In 2010, 62 master's awarded. *Degree program information:* Part-time and evening/weekend programs available. Offers social work (MSW). *Application deadline:* For fall admission, 5/1 priority date for domestic students, 2/15 for international students. Applications are processed on a rolling basis. *Application fee:* $30. *Application Contact:* Dr. Elwood Hamlin, Coordinator, 501-297-3234, E-mail: ehamlin@fau.edu. *Director*, Dr. Michele Hawkins, 561-297-3234, Fax: 561-297-2866, E-mail: mhawkins@fau.edu.

School of Urban and Regional Planning Students: 24 full-time (18 women), 12 part-time (1 woman); includes 17 minority (4 Black or African American, non-Hispanic/Latino; 1 American Indian or Alaska Native, non-Hispanic/Latino; 12 Hispanic/Latino), 2 international. Average age 30. 55 applicants, 35% accepted, 12 enrolled. *Faculty:* 8 full-time (5 women), 2 part-time/adjunct (1 woman). Expenses: Contact institution. *Financial support:* Fellowships with full tuition reimbursements, research assistantships, career-related internships or fieldwork, Federal Work-Study, institutionally sponsored loans, and tuition waivers (partial) available. Financial award application deadline: 4/1. In 2010, 13 master's awarded. *Degree program information:* Part-time and evening/weekend programs available. Offers economic development and tourism (Certificate); environmental planning (Certificate); sustainable community planning (Certificate); urban and regional planning (MURP); visual planning technology (Certificate). *Application deadline:* For fall admission, 7/1 priority date for domestic students, 2/15 for international students; for spring admission, 11/1 priority date for domestic students, 7/15 for international students. Applications are processed on a rolling basis. *Application fee:* $30. *Application Contact:* Dr. Jaap Vos, Chair, 954-762-5653, Fax: 954-762-5673, E-mail: jvos@fau.edu. *Chair*, Dr. Jaap Vos, 954-762-5653, Fax: 954-762-5673, E-mail: jvos@fau.edu.

College of Education Students: 331 full-time (261 women), 679 part-time (523 women); includes 279 minority (132 Black or African American, non-Hispanic/Latino; 27 Asian, non-Hispanic/Latino; 113 Hispanic/Latino; 7 Two or more races, non-Hispanic/Latino), 15 international. Average age 33. 716 applicants, 47% accepted, 246 enrolled. *Faculty:* 165 full-time (114 women), 187 part-time/adjunct (138 women). Expenses: Contact institution. *Financial support:* Fellowships with partial tuition reimbursements, research assistantships with partial tuition reimbursements, teaching assistantships with partial tuition reimbursements, career-related internships or fieldwork, Federal Work-Study, and unspecified assistantships available. In 2010, 338 master's, 23 doctorates awarded. *Degree program information:* Part-time and evening/weekend programs available. Offers adult and community education (M Ed, PhD, Ed S); counselor education (M Ed, PhD, Ed S); curriculum and instruction (M Ed, Ed D, Ed S); early childhood education (M Ed); education (M Ed, MS, Ed D, PhD, Ed S); educational leadership (M Ed, PhD, Ed S); elementary education (M Ed); environmental education (M Ed); exceptional student education (M Ed, Ed D); exercise science and health promotion (MS); higher education (M Ed, PhD); K-12 school leadership (M Ed, PhD, Ed S); marriage and family therapy (Ed S); mental health counseling (M Ed, Ed S); multicultural education (M Ed); reading education (M Ed); rehabilitation counseling (M Ed); school counseling (M Ed, Ed S); social foundations of education (M Ed); speech-language pathology (MS); teaching English to speakers of other languages (TESOL) (M Ed). *Application deadline:* Applications are processed on a rolling basis. *Application fee:* $30. Electronic applications accepted. *Application Contact:* Dr. Eliah Watlington, Associate Dean, 561-296-8520, Fax: 261-297-2991, E-mail: ewatling@fau.edu. *Dean*, Dr. Valerie J. Bristor, 561-297-3564, E-mail: bristor@fau.edu.

College of Engineering and Computer Science Students: 158 full-time (33 women), 157 part-time (37 women); includes 96 minority (23 Black or African American, non-Hispanic/Latino; 1 American Indian or Alaska Native, non-Hispanic/Latino; 24 Asian, non-Hispanic/Latino; 46 Hispanic/Latino; 2 Two or more races, non-Hispanic/Latino), 88 international. Average age 30. 226 applicants, 50% accepted, 74 enrolled. *Faculty:* 81 full-time (10 women), 10 part-time/adjunct (1 woman). Expenses: Contact institution. *Financial support:* In 2010–11, research assistantships with partial tuition reimbursements (averaging $15,000 per year), teaching assistantships with partial tuition reimbursements (averaging $15,000 per year) were awarded; fellowships, career-related internships or fieldwork, Federal Work-Study, and unspecified assistantships also available. Support available to part-time students. Financial award applicants required to submit FAFSA. In 2010, 88 master's, 14 doctorates awarded. *Degree program information:* Part-time and evening/weekend programs available. Postbaccalaureate distance learning degree programs offered (minimal on-campus study). Offers civil engineering (MS); computer engineering (MS, PhD); computer science (MS, PhD); electrical engineering (MS, PhD); engineering and computer science (MS, PhD); mechanical engineering (MS, PhD); ocean engineering (MS, PhD). *Application deadline:* For fall admission, 7/1 for domestic students, 2/15 for international students; for spring admission, 11/1 for domestic students, 7/15 for international students. Applications are processed on a rolling basis. *Application fee:* $30. *Application Contact:* Dr. Karl K. Stevens, Dean, 561-297-3400, Fax: 561-297-2659, E-mail: stevens@fau.edu. *Dean*, Dr. Karl K. Stevens, 561-297-3400, Fax: 561-297-2659, E-mail: stevens@fau.edu.

Dorothy F. Schmidt College of Arts and Letters Students: 254 full-time (157 women), 203 part-time (124 women); includes 112 minority (26 Black or African American, non-Hispanic/Latino; 4 American Indian or Alaska Native, non-Hispanic/Latino; 7 Asian, non-Hispanic/Latino; 70 Hispanic/Latino; 5 Two or more races, non-Hispanic/Latino), 30 international. Average age 33. 357 applicants, 43% accepted, 123 enrolled. *Faculty:* 242 full-time (122 women), 80 part-time/adjunct (35 women). Expenses: Contact institution. *Financial support:* Fellowships with partial tuition reimbursements, research assistantships, teaching assistantships, career-related internships or fieldwork, Federal Work-Study, institutionally sponsored loans, and tuition waivers (partial) available. Support available to part-time students. In 2010, 83 master's, 8 doctorates awarded. *Degree program information:* Part-time programs available. Offers acting (MFA); anthropology (MA); art education (MAT); arts and letters (MA, MAT, MFA, PhD, Certificate); British and American literature (MA); ceramics (MFA); commercial music (MA); comparative literature (MA); comparative studies (PhD); computer art (MFA); creative nonfiction (MFA); creative writing (MFA); design and technology (MFA); environmental studies (Certificate); fiction (MFA); French (MA); graphic design (MFA); history (MA); liberal studies (MA); linguistics (MA); multicultural literatures and literacies (MA); music history/

literature (MA); painting (MFA); performance (MA); poetry (MFA); political science (MA, MAT); science fiction and fantasy (MA); sociology (MA); Spanish (MA); teaching English (MAT). *Application deadline:* For fall admission, 6/1 priority date for domestic students. Applications are processed on a rolling basis. *Application fee:* $30. Electronic applications accepted. *Application Contact:* Dr. Emily Stockard, Associate Dean, 561-297-2817, Fax: 561-297-2744, E-mail: stockard@fau.edu. *Dean,* Dr. Manjunath Pendakur, 561-297-3803.

School of Communication and Multimedia Studies Students: 19 full-time (15 women), 15 part-time (11 women); includes 8 minority (3 Black or African American, non-Hispanic/Latino; 1 American Indian or Alaska Native, non-Hispanic/Latino; 1 Asian, non-Hispanic/Latino; 1 Hispanic/Latino; 2 Two or more races, non-Hispanic/Latino), 6 international. Average age 28. 42 applicants, 26% accepted, 8 enrolled. *Faculty:* 28 full-time (10 women), 14 part-time/adjunct (3 women). Expenses: Contact institution. *Financial support:* Teaching assistantships with partial tuition reimbursements, Federal Work-Study and institutionally sponsored loans available. Support available to part-time students. Financial award application deadline: 3/1. In 2010, 3 master's awarded. *Degree program information:* Part-time programs available. Offers communication studies (MA); film and video (Certificate); film studies (MA); multimedia journalism studies (MA). *Application deadline:* For fall admission, 7/1 priority date for domestic students, 4/1 for international students; for spring admission, 11/1 for domestic students, 10/1 for international students. Applications are processed on a rolling basis. *Application fee:* $30. Electronic applications accepted. *Application Contact:* Dr. Eric M. Freedman, Graduate Coordinator, 561-297-2534, Fax: 561-297-2615, E-mail: efreedma@fau.edu. *Director,* Dr. Susan S. Reilly, 561-297-1095, Fax: 561-297-2615, E-mail: sreilly@fau.edu.

Women's Studies Center Students: 6 full-time (5 women), 3 part-time (all women); includes 1 minority (Hispanic/Latino), 2 international. Average age 32. 9 applicants, 67% accepted, 4 enrolled. *Faculty:* 2 full-time (both women), 3 part-time/adjunct (all women). Expenses: Contact institution. *Financial support:* Fellowships with full and partial tuition reimbursements, teaching assistantships with full and partial tuition reimbursements, career-related internships or fieldwork, Federal Work-Study, institutionally sponsored loans, scholarships/grants, and unspecified assistantships available. Support available to part-time students. In 2010, 2 master's awarded. Offers women's studies (MA, Certificate). *Application deadline:* For fall admission, 7/1 for domestic students, 2/15 for international students; for spring admission, 11/1 for domestic students, 7/15 for international students. Applications are processed on a rolling basis. *Application fee:* $30. *Application Contact:* Dr. Jane Caputi, Professor, 561-297-2056, Fax: 561-297-2127, E-mail: jcaputi@fau.edu. *Director,* Dr. Josephine Beoku-Betts, 561-297-3865, Fax: 561-297-2127.

FLORIDA COASTAL SCHOOL OF LAW, Jacksonville, FL 32256

General Information Proprietary, coed, graduate-only institution.

GRADUATE UNITS

Professional Program *Degree program information:* Part-time programs available. Offers law (JD). Electronic applications accepted.

FLORIDA COLLEGE OF INTEGRATIVE MEDICINE, Orlando, FL 32809

General Information Proprietary, coed, graduate-only institution. *Graduate housing:* On-campus housing not available.

GRADUATE UNITS

Graduate Program *Degree program information:* Evening/weekend programs available. Offers Oriental medicine (MSOM). Electronic applications accepted.

FLORIDA GULF COAST UNIVERSITY, Fort Myers, FL 33965-6565

General Information State-supported, coed, comprehensive institution. CGS member. *Enrollment:* 12,034 graduate, professional, and undergraduate students; 788 full-time matriculated graduate/professional students (523 women), 365 part-time matriculated graduate/professional students (257 women). *Enrollment by degree level:* 1,086 master's, 67 doctoral. *Graduate faculty:* 376 full-time (176 women), 213 part-time/adjunct (103 women). Tuition, state resident: part-time $322.08 per credit hour. Tuition, nonresident: part-time $1117.08 per credit hour. *Graduate housing:* Room and/or apartments available on a first-come, first-served basis to single students; on-campus housing not available to married students. Typical cost: $4728 per year ($8150 including board). Room and board charges vary according to board plan. Housing application deadline: 4/1. *Student services:* Campus employment opportunities, campus safety program, career counseling, child daycare facilities, exercise/wellness program, free psychological counseling, international student services, low-cost health insurance, multicultural affairs office, services for students with disabilities, teacher training. *Library facilities:* Library Services plus 1 other. *Online resources:* library catalog, web page, access to other libraries' catalogs. *Collection:* 387,860 titles, 12,374 serial subscriptions, 10,406 audiovisual materials.

Computer facilities: Computer purchase and lease plans are available. 871 computers available on campus for general student use. A campuswide network can be accessed from student residence rooms and from off campus. Online class registration, online admissions and advising are available. *Web address:* http://www.fgcu.edu/.

General Application Contact: Jennifer Paulke, Assistant Director, Graduate Studies, 239-590-7881, Fax: 239-590-7843, E-mail: graduate@fgcu.edu.

GRADUATE UNITS

College of Arts and Sciences Students: 69 full-time (37 women), 37 part-time (16 women); includes 4 Black or African American, non-Hispanic/Latino; 6 Hispanic/Latino, 1 international. Average age 33. 86 applicants, 67% accepted, 48 enrolled. *Faculty:* 187 full-time (78 women), 177 part-time/adjunct (70 women). Expenses: Contact institution. In 2010, 18 master's awarded. *Degree program information:* Part-time programs available. Offers arts and sciences (MA, MS); English (MA); environmental science (MS); history (MA). *Application deadline:* For fall admission, 2/15 priority date for domestic students; for spring admission, 10/1 for domestic students. Applications are processed on a rolling basis. *Application fee:* $30. Electronic applications accepted. *Application Contact:* Patricia Rice, Executive Secretary, 239-590-7196, Fax: 239-590-7200, E-mail: price@fgcu.edu. *Dean,* Dr. Donna Price Henry, 239-590-7155, Fax: 239-590-7200, E-mail: dhenry@fgcu.edu.

College of Education Students: 234 full-time (180 women), 98 part-time (84 women); includes 18 Black or African American, non-Hispanic/Latino; 4 American Indian or Alaska Native, non-Hispanic/Latino; 4 Asian, non-Hispanic/Latino; 29 Hispanic/Latino, 2 international. Average age 34. 202 applicants, 81% accepted, 128 enrolled. *Faculty:* 33 full-time (24 women), 43 part-time/adjunct (30 women). Expenses: Contact institution. In 2010, 122 master's awarded. *Degree program information:* Part-time and evening/weekend programs available. Postbaccalaureate distance learning degree programs offered (minimal on-campus study). Offers behavior disorders (MA); counseling (MA); early childhood education (M Ed); education (M Ed, MA); educational leadership (M Ed, MA); educational technology (M Ed, MA); elementary curriculum (M Ed); elementary education (MA); English education (M Ed); mental retardation (MA); reading education (M Ed); specific learning disabilities (MA); varying exceptionalities (MA). *Application deadline:* For fall admission, 7/1 priority date for domestic students; for spring admission, 10/15 for domestic students. Applications are processed on a rolling basis. *Application fee:* $30. Electronic applications accepted. *Application Contact:* Edward Beckett, Adviser/Counselor, 239-590-7759, Fax: 239-590-7801, E-mail: ebeckett@fgcu.edu. *Dean,* Dr. Marci Greene, 239-590-7781, Fax: 239-590-7801, E-mail: mgreene@fgcu.edu.

College of Health Professions Students: 155 full-time (114 women), 76 part-time (58 women); includes 14 Black or African American, non-Hispanic/Latino; 3 American Indian or Alaska Native, non-Hispanic/Latino; 9 Asian, non-Hispanic/Latino; 15 Hispanic/Latino, 1 international. Average age 31. 289 applicants, 31% accepted, 79 enrolled. *Faculty:* 45 full-time (35 women), 28 part-time/adjunct (18 women). Expenses: Contact institution. *Financial support:* Career-related internships or fieldwork, Federal Work-Study, and institutionally sponsored loans available. In 2010, 75 master's awarded. *Degree program information:* Part-time and evening/weekend programs available. Postbaccalaureate distance learning degree programs offered (minimal on-campus study). Offers health professions (MS, MSN, DPT); health sciences (MS); occupational therapy (MS); physical therapy (MS, DPT). *Application deadline:* Applications are processed on a rolling basis. *Application fee:* $30. Electronic applications accepted. *Application Contact:* Lynn O'Hare, Administrative Assistant, 239-590-7451, Fax: 239-590-7474, E-mail: lohare@fgcu.edu. *Dean,* Dr. Denise Heinemann, 239-590-7511, Fax: 239-590-7474.

School of Nursing Students: 3 full-time (all women). Average age 36. 3 applicants, 0% accepted, 0 enrolled. *Faculty:* 45 full-time (35 women), 28 part-time/adjunct (18 women). Expenses: Contact institution. In 2010, 21 master's awarded. *Degree program information:* Part-time programs available. Offers nursing (MSN). *Application deadline:* For fall admission, 4/15 priority date for domestic students; for spring admission, 6/1 for domestic students. Applications are processed on a rolling basis. *Application fee:* $30. Electronic applications accepted. *Application Contact:* Lynn O'Hare, Administrative Assistant, 239-590-7451, Fax: 239-590-7474, E-mail: lohare@fgcu.edu. *Director,* Dr. Marianne Rodgers, 239-590-7454, Fax: 239-590-7474, E-mail: mrodgers@fgcu.edu.

College of Professional Studies Students: 144 full-time (105 women), 73 part-time (59 women); includes 22 Black or African American, non-Hispanic/Latino; 3 American Indian or Alaska Native, non-Hispanic/Latino; 1 Asian, non-Hispanic/Latino; 19 Hispanic/Latino, 3 international. Average age 32. 153 applicants, 69% accepted, 87 enrolled. *Faculty:* 35 full-time (15 women), 34 part-time/adjunct (12 women). Expenses: Contact institution. *Financial support:* Research assistantships, career-related internships or fieldwork and tuition waivers (full and partial) available. Support available to part-time students. In 2010, 49 master's awarded. *Degree program information:* Part-time and evening/weekend programs available. Offers criminal forensic studies (MS); criminal justice (MPA); criminal justice studies (MS); environmental policy (MPA); general public administration (MPA); management (MPA); professional studies (MPA, MS, MSW); social work (MSW). *Application deadline:* Applications are processed on a rolling basis. *Application fee:* $30. Electronic applications accepted. *Application Contact:* Dr. Kenneth Millar, Dean, 239-590-7724, Fax: 239-590-7846, E-mail: kmillar@fgcu.edu. *Dean,* Dr. Kenneth Millar, 239-590-7724, Fax: 239-590-7846, E-mail: kmillar@fgcu.edu.

Lutgert College of Business Students: 185 full-time (86 women), 81 part-time (40 women); includes 6 Black or African American, non-Hispanic/Latino; 2 American Indian or Alaska Native, non-Hispanic/Latino; 11 Asian, non-Hispanic/Latino; 27 Hispanic/Latino, 8 international. Average age 29. 172 applicants, 66% accepted, 74 enrolled. *Faculty:* 67 full-time (21 women), 5 part-time/adjunct (1 woman). Expenses: Contact institution. In 2010, 96 master's awarded. *Degree program information:* Part-time and evening/weekend programs available. Offers accounting and taxation (MS); business (MBA, MS); business administration (MBA); computer and information systems (MS). *Application deadline:* For fall admission, 7/1 priority date for domestic students; for spring admission, 11/1 for domestic students. Applications are processed on a rolling basis. *Application fee:* $30. Electronic applications accepted. *Application Contact:* Carol Burnette, Associate Dean, 239-590-7350, Fax: 239-590-7330, E-mail: burnette@fgcu.edu. *Dean,* Dr. Richard Pegnetter, 239-590-7310, Fax: 239-590-7330, E-mail: epegnett@fgcu.edu.

FLORIDA HOSPITAL COLLEGE OF HEALTH SCIENCES, Orlando, FL 32803

General Information Independent, coed, comprehensive institution.

GRADUATE UNITS

Program in Nurse Anesthesia Offers nurse anesthesia (MS).

FLORIDA INSTITUTE OF TECHNOLOGY, Melbourne, FL 32901-6975

General Information Independent, coed, university. *Enrollment:* 8,985 graduate, professional, and undergraduate students; 885 full-time matriculated graduate/professional students (386 women), 2,481 part-time matriculated graduate/professional students (1,050 women). *Enrollment by degree level:* 3,024 master's, 342 doctoral. *Graduate faculty:* 159 full-time (26 women), 176 part-time/adjunct (37 women). *Tuition:* Part-time $1040 per credit hour. Tuition and fees vary according to campus/location. *Graduate housing:* Room and/or apartments available on a first-come, first-served basis to single students; on-campus housing not available to married students. *Student services:* Campus employment opportunities, career counseling, exercise/wellness program, free psychological counseling, international student services, low-cost health insurance, services for students with disabilities, writing training. *Library facilities:* Evans Library. *Online resources:* library catalog, web page, access to other libraries' catalogs. *Collection:* 358,230 titles, 56,414 serial subscriptions, 6,304 audiovisual materials. *Research affiliation:* IBM (software technology, information assurance), Harris Institute for Assured Information (information security), Boeing Corporation (digital signal processing aeronautics), General Electric-Harris (software testing), Microsoft Corporation (simulation software development), Lockheed Martin Corporation (biological sciences).

Computer facilities: 415 computers available on campus for general student use. A campuswide network can be accessed from student residence rooms and from off campus. Online class registration is available. *Web address:* http://www.fit.edu/.

General Application Contact: Cheryl A. Brown, Associate Director of Graduate Admissions, 321-674-7581, Fax: 321-723-9468, E-mail: cbrown@fit.edu.

GRADUATE UNITS

Graduate Programs Students: 885 full-time (386 women), 2,481 part-time (1,050 women); includes 904 minority (557 Black or African American, non-Hispanic/Latino; 21 American Indian or Alaska Native, non-Hispanic/Latino; 97 Asian, non-Hispanic/Latino; 185 Hispanic/Latino; 11 Native Hawaiian or other Pacific Islander, non-Hispanic/Latino; 33 Two or more races, non-Hispanic/Latino), 476 international. Average age 33. 3,119 applicants, 47% accepted, 782 enrolled. *Faculty:* 159 full-time (26 women), 176 part-time/adjunct (37 women). Expenses: Contact institution. *Financial support:* In 2010–11, 16 fellowships with full and partial tuition reimbursements (averaging $11,014 per year), 88 research assistantships with full and partial tuition reimbursements (averaging $8,324 per year), 136 teaching assistantships with full and partial tuition reimbursements (averaging $9,155 per year) were awarded; career-related internships or fieldwork, institutionally sponsored loans, tuition waivers (partial), unspecified assistantships, and tuition remissions also available. Support available to part-time students. Financial award application deadline: 3/1; financial award applicants required to submit FAFSA. In 2010, 954 master's, 38 doctorates awarded. *Degree program information:* Part-time and evening/weekend programs available. Postbaccalaureate distance learning degree programs offered (no on-campus study). *Application deadline:* For fall admission, 4/1 priority date for international students; for spring admission, 9/30 for international students. Applications are processed on a rolling basis. *Application fee:* $50. Electronic applications accepted. *Application Contact:* Cheryl A. Brown, Associate Director of Graduate Admissions, 321-674-7581, Fax: 321-723-9468, E-mail: cbrown@fit.edu. *Director,* Dr. Rosemary Layne, 321-674-8137, Fax: 321-674-7052, E-mail: rlayne@fit.edu.

College of Aeronautics Students: 23 full-time (3 women), 11 part-time (3 women); includes 3 minority (2 Asian, non-Hispanic/Latino; 1 Hispanic/Latino), 15 international. Average age 26. 36 applicants, 53% accepted, 9 enrolled. *Faculty:* 9 full-time (0 women). Expenses: Contact institution. *Financial support:* Career-related internships or fieldwork, institutionally sponsored loans, tuition waivers (partial), and tuition remissions available. Support available to part-time students. Financial award application deadline: 3/1; financial award applicants required to submit FAFSA. In 2010, 15 master's awarded. *Degree program information:* Part-time and evening/weekend programs available. Offers airport development and management (MSA); applied aviation safety option (MSA); aviation human factors (MS); human factors in aeronautics (MS). *Application deadline:* For fall admission, 4/1 for international students; for spring admission, 9/30 for international students. Applications are processed on a rolling basis. *Application fee:* $50. Electronic applications accepted. *Application Contact:* Cheryl A. Brown, Associate Director of Graduate Admissions, 321-674-7581, Fax: 321-723-9468, E-mail: cbrown@fit.edu. *Dean,* Dr. Winston E. Scott, 321-674-8971, Fax: 321-674-7368, E-mail: wscott@fit.edu.

Florida Institute of Technology (continued)

College of Engineering Students: 319 full-time (70 women), 183 part-time (37 women); includes 37 minority (13 Black or African American, non-Hispanic/Latino; 10 Asian, non-Hispanic/Latino; 11 Hispanic/Latino; 3 Two or more races, non-Hispanic/Latino), 261 international. Average age 29. 1,131 applicants, 53% accepted, 134 enrolled. *Faculty:* 60 full-time (2 women), 6 part-time/adjunct (0 women). Expenses: Contact institution. *Financial support:* In 2010–11, 5 fellowships with full and partial tuition reimbursements (averaging $7,240 per year), 23 research assistantships with full and partial tuition reimbursements (averaging $4,970 per year), 51 teaching assistantships with full and partial tuition reimbursements (averaging $6,698 per year) were awarded; career-related internships or fieldwork, institutionally sponsored loans, unspecified assistantships, and tuition remissions also available. Support available to part-time students. Financial award application deadline: 3/1; financial award applicants required to submit FAFSA. In 2010, 185 master's, 12 doctorates awarded. *Degree program information:* Part-time and evening/weekend programs available. Offers aerospace engineering (MS, PhD); chemical engineering (MS, PhD); civil engineering (MS, PhD); computer engineering (MS, PhD); computer science (MS, PhD); earth remote sensing (MS); electrical engineering (MS, PhD); engineering (MS, PhD); engineering management (MS); environmental resource management (MS); environmental science (MS, PhD); mechanical engineering (MS, PhD); meteorology (MS); ocean engineering (MS, PhD); oceanography (MS, PhD); software engineering (MS); systems engineering (MS, PhD). *Application deadline:* For fall admission, 4/1 for international students; for spring admission, 9/30 for international students. Applications are processed on a rolling basis. *Application fee:* $50. Electronic applications accepted. *Application Contact:* Cheryl A. Brown, Associate Director of Graduate Admissions, 321-674-7581, Fax: 321-723-9468, E-mail: cbrown@fit.edu. *Interim Dean,* Dr. Fredric M. Ham, 321-674-8138, Fax: 321-674-7270, E-mail: fmh@fit.edu.

College of Psychology and Liberal Arts Students: 231 full-time (174 women), 17 part-time (15 women); includes 30 minority (7 Black or African American, non-Hispanic/Latino; 1 American Indian or Alaska Native, non-Hispanic/Latino; 5 Asian, non-Hispanic/Latino; 17 Hispanic/Latino), 23 international. Average age 27. 383 applicants, 42% accepted, 81 enrolled. *Faculty:* 24 full-time (13 women), 7 part-time/adjunct (3 women). Expenses: Contact institution. *Financial support:* In 2010–11, 4 fellowships with full and partial tuition reimbursements (averaging $3,775 per year), 32 research assistantships with full and partial tuition reimbursements (averaging $5,602 per year), 8 teaching assistantships with full and partial tuition reimbursements (averaging $4,570 per year) were awarded; career-related internships or fieldwork, institutionally sponsored loans, tuition waivers (partial), unspecified assistantships, and tuition remissions also available. Support available to part-time students. Financial award application deadline: 3/1; financial award applicants required to submit FAFSA. In 2010, 59 master's, 13 doctorates awarded. *Degree program information:* Part-time programs available. Offers applied behavior analysis (MS); applied behavior analysis and organizational behavior management (MS); behavior analysis (PhD); clinical psychology (Psy D); industrial/organizational psychology (MS, PhD); organizational behavior management (MS); psychology and liberal arts (MS, PhD, Psy D); technical and professional communication (MS). *Application deadline:* For fall admission, 4/1 for international students; for spring admission, 9/30 for international students. Applications are processed on a rolling basis. *Application fee:* $50. Electronic applications accepted. *Application Contact:* Cheryl A. Brown, Associate Director of Graduate Admissions, 321-674-7581, Fax: 321-723-9468, E-mail: cbrown@fit.edu. *Dean,* Dr. Mary Beth Kenkel, 321-674-8142, Fax: 321-674-7105, E-mail: mkenkel@fit.edu.

College of Science Students: 185 full-time (88 women), 55 part-time (22 women); includes 21 minority (6 Black or African American, non-Hispanic/Latino; 4 Asian, non-Hispanic/Latino; 10 Hispanic/Latino; 1 Two or more races, non-Hispanic/Latino), 97 international. Average age 29. 467 applicants, 46% accepted, 71 enrolled. *Faculty:* 45 full-time (5 women), 4 part-time/adjunct (2 women). Expenses: Contact institution. *Financial support:* In 2010–11, 5 fellowships with full and partial tuition reimbursements (averaging $20,737 per year), 33 research assistantships with full and partial tuition reimbursements (averaging $13,302 per year), 77 teaching assistantships with full and partial tuition reimbursements (averaging $11,258 per year) were awarded; career-related internships or fieldwork, institutionally sponsored loans, tuition waivers (partial), unspecified assistantships, and tuition remissions also available. Support available to part-time students. Financial award application deadline: 3/1; financial award applicants required to submit FAFSA. In 2010, 37 master's, 13 doctorates awarded. *Degree program information:* Part-time and evening/weekend programs available. Offers applied mathematics (MS, PhD); biochemistry (MS); biological sciences (PhD); biotechnology (MS); cell and molecular biology (MS); chemistry (MS, PhD); computer education (MS); ecology (MS); ecology and marine biology (MS); elementary science education (M Ed); environmental education (MS); interdisciplinary science (MS); marine biology (MS); mathematics education (MS, Ed D, PhD, Ed S); operations research (MS, PhD); physics (MS, PhD); science (M Ed, MAT, MS, Ed D, PhD, Ed S); science education (M Ed, MS, Ed D, PhD, Ed S); space sciences (MS, PhD); teaching (MAT). *Application deadline:* For fall admission, 3/1 for domestic students, 4/1 for international students; for spring admission, 9/1 for domestic students, 9/30 for international students. Applications are processed on a rolling basis. *Application fee:* $50. Electronic applications accepted. *Application Contact:* Cheryl A. Brown, Associate Director of Graduate Admissions, 321-674-7581, Fax: 321-723-9468, E-mail: cbrown@fit.edu. *Dean,* Dr. Hamid K. Rassoul, 321-674-7260, Fax: 321-674-8864, E-mail: rassoul@fit.edu.

Extended Studies Division Students: 69 full-time (23 women), 907 part-time (369 women); includes 385 minority (242 Black or African American, non-Hispanic/Latino; 15 American Indian or Alaska Native, non-Hispanic/Latino; 44 Asian, non-Hispanic/Latino; 52 Hispanic/Latino; 3 Native Hawaiian or other Pacific Islander, non-Hispanic/Latino; 29 Two or more races, non-Hispanic/Latino), 17 international. 517 applicants, 49% accepted, 245 enrolled. *Faculty:* 11 full-time (3 women), 118 part-time/adjunct (24 women). Expenses: Contact institution. *Financial support:* Application deadline: 3/1. In 2010, 430 degrees awarded. *Degree program information:* Part-time and evening/weekend programs available. Postbaccalaureate distance learning degree programs offered (no on-campus study). Offers acquisition and contract management (MS); aerospace engineering (MS); business administration (MBA); computer information systems (MS); computer science (MS); electrical engineering (MS); engineering management (MS); human resources management (MS); logistics management (MS); management (MS); material acquisition management (MS); mechanical engineering (MS); operations research (MS); project management (MS); public administration (MPA); quality management (MS); software engineering (MS); space systems (MS); space systems management (MS); systems management (MS). *Application deadline:* For fall admission, 4/1 for international students; for spring admission, 9/30 for international students. Applications are processed on a rolling basis. *Application fee:* $50. Electronic applications accepted. *Application Contact:* Carolyn Farrior, Director of Graduate Admissions, Online Learning and Off-Campus Programs, 321-674-7118, Fax: 321-674-8216, E-mail: cfarrior@fit.edu. *Senior Associate Dean,* Dr. Theodore Richardson, 321-674-8123, Fax: 321-674-7597, E-mail: trichardson@fit.edu.

Nathan M. Bisk College of Business Students: 127 full-time (51 women), 2,215 part-time (973 women); includes 813 minority (531 Black or African American, non-Hispanic/Latino; 20 American Indian or Alaska Native, non-Hispanic/Latino; 76 Asian, non-Hispanic/Latino; 146 Hispanic/Latino; 11 Native Hawaiian or other Pacific Islander, non-Hispanic/Latino; 29 Two or more races, non-Hispanic/Latino), 80 international. Average age 36. 1,102 applicants, 487 enrolled. *Faculty:* 21 full-time (6 women), 159 part-time/adjunct (32 women). Expenses: Contact institution. *Financial support:* In 2010–11, 1 fellowship (averaging $500 per year) was awarded; career-related internships or fieldwork, institutionally sponsored loans, and unspecified assistantships also available. Support available to part-time students. Financial award application deadline: 3/1; financial award applicants required to submit FAFSA. In 2010, 658 master's awarded. *Degree program information:* Part-time programs available. Postbaccalaureate distance learning degree programs offered (no on-campus study). Offers accounting (MBA); accounting and finance (MBA); business (MBA, MPA, MS); finance (MBA); healthcare management (MBA); information technology (MS); information technology management (MBA); Internet marketing (MBA); management (MBA); marketing (MBA); project management (MBA). Program held jointly with College of Engineering, College of Science. *Application deadline:* For fall admission, 4/1 for international students; for spring admission, 9/30 for international students. Applications are processed on a rolling basis. *Application fee:* $50. Electronic applications accepted. *Application Contact:* Cheryl A. Brown, Associate Director of Graduate Admissions, 321-674-7581, Fax: 321-723-9468, E-mail: cbrown@fit.edu. *Dean,* Dr. Robert E. Niebuhr, 321-674-7327, Fax: 321-674-8896, E-mail: rniebuhr@fit.edu.

FLORIDA INTERNATIONAL UNIVERSITY, Miami, FL 33199

General Information State-supported, coed, university. CGS member. *Enrollment:* 42,287 graduate, professional, and undergraduate students; 5,106 full-time matriculated graduate/professional students (2,966 women), 3,059 part-time matriculated graduate/professional students (1,949 women). *Enrollment by degree level:* 85 first professional, 6,792 master's, 1,288 doctoral. *Graduate faculty:* 891 full-time (330 women). *Graduate housing:* Rooms and/or apartments available on a first-come, first-served basis to single and married students. *Student services:* Campus employment opportunities, campus safety program, career counseling, child daycare facilities, exercise/wellness program, free psychological counseling, international student services, low-cost health insurance, multicultural affairs office, services for students with disabilities, writing training. *Library facilities:* Steven and Dorothea Green Library plus 4 others. *Online resources:* library catalog, web page, access to other libraries' catalogs. *Research affiliation:* National Institute of Justice (chemistry), National Science Foundation (biological sciences), Howard Hughes Medical Institute (physics), National Institute of Child Health and Human Development (social work), The Boeing Company (mechanical engineering), American Heart Association (biomedical engineering).

Computer facilities: A campuswide network can be accessed from student residence rooms and from off campus. Online class registration, online financial and cashier's information; class schedule, financial, campus maps information available on cell phones are available. *Web address:* http://www.fiu.edu/.

General Application Contact: Nanett Rojas, Assistant Director of Graduate Admissions, 305-348-7442, Fax: 305-348-7441, E-mail: gradadm@fiu.edu.

GRADUATE UNITS

Alvah H. Chapman, Jr. Graduate School of Business Students: 1,080 full-time (533 women), 576 part-time (301 women); includes 175 Black or African American, non-Hispanic/Latino; 3 American Indian or Alaska Native, non-Hispanic/Latino; 56 Asian, non-Hispanic/Latino; 779 Hispanic/Latino; 1 Native Hawaiian or other Pacific Islander, non-Hispanic/Latino, 329 international. Average age 30. 3,279 applicants, 45% accepted, 1293 enrolled. *Faculty:* 92 full-time (29 women), 46 part-time/adjunct (10 women). Expenses: Contact institution. *Financial support:* Institutionally sponsored loans and scholarships/grants available. Financial award application deadline: 3/1; financial award applicants required to submit FAFSA. In 2010, 860 master's, 8 doctorates awarded. *Degree program information:* Part-time and evening/weekend programs available. Offers business (EMBA, IMBA, M Acc, MBA, MIB, MS, MSF, MSHRM, MSMIS, MSRE, MST, PMBA, PhD); business administration (EMBA, IMBA, MBA, PMBA, PhD); decision sciences and information systems (MSMIS); finance (MSF); human resources management (MSHRM); international business (MIB); international real estate (MS); management and international business (PhD); real estate (MS). *Application deadline:* For fall admission, 6/1 for domestic students, 4/1 for international students; for spring admission, 10/1 for domestic students, 9/1 for international students. Applications are processed on a rolling basis. *Application fee:* $30. Electronic applications accepted. *Application Contact:* Nanett Rojas, Coordinator of Graduate Admissions, 305-348-7442, Fax: 305-348-7441, E-mail: gradadm@fiu.edu. *Director of Admissions and Recruiting, Chapman Graduate School of Business,* Anna M. Pietraszek, 305-348-7299, Fax: 305-348-2368, E-mail: pietrasa@fiu.edu.

School of Accounting Students: 129 full-time (78 women), 35 part-time (24 women); includes 15 Black or African American, non-Hispanic/Latino; 7 Asian, non-Hispanic/Latino; 119 Hispanic/Latino, 5 international. Average age 30. 393 applicants, 49% accepted. *Faculty:* 20 full-time (5 women), 16 part-time/adjunct (4 women). Expenses: Contact institution. *Financial support:* Institutionally sponsored loans and scholarships/grants available. Financial award application deadline: 3/1; financial award applicants required to submit FAFSA. In 2010, 164 master's awarded. *Degree program information:* Part-time and evening/weekend programs available. Offers accounting (M Acc); taxation (MST). *Application deadline:* For fall admission, 6/1 for domestic students, 4/1 for international students; for spring admission, 10/1 for domestic students, 9/1 for international students. Applications are processed on a rolling basis. *Application fee:* $30. Electronic applications accepted. *Application Contact:* Teresita Brunken, 305-348-4224, Fax: 305-348-2914, E-mail: brunkent@fiu.edu. *Director, School of Accounting,* Dr. Sharon Lassar, 305-348-3501, Fax: 305-348-2914, E-mail: sharon.lassar@fiu.edu.

College of Architecture and the Arts Students: 404 full-time (227 women), 61 part-time (35 women); includes 23 Black or African American, non-Hispanic/Latino; 2 American Indian or Alaska Native, non-Hispanic/Latino; 11 Asian, non-Hispanic/Latino; 292 Hispanic/Latino, 21 international. Average age 26. 315 applicants, 29% accepted, 81 enrolled. *Faculty:* 64 full-time (21 women), 80 part-time/adjunct (38 women). Expenses: Contact institution. *Financial support:* Institutionally sponsored loans and scholarships/grants available. Financial award application deadline: 3/1; financial award applicants required to submit FAFSA. In 2010, 70 master's awarded. *Degree program information:* Part-time and evening/weekend programs available. Offers architecture and the arts (M Arch, MA, MFA, MID, MLA, MM, MS). *Application deadline:* For fall admission, 6/1 for domestic students, 4/1 for international students; for spring admission, 10/1 for domestic students, 9/1 for international students. Applications are processed on a rolling basis. *Application fee:* $30. Electronic applications accepted. *Application Contact:* Nanett Rojas, Assistant Director of Graduate Admissions, 305-348-7442, Fax: 305-348-7441, E-mail: gradadm@fiu.edu. *Dean,* Dr. Brian Schriner, 305-348-3181, Fax: 305-348-6716, E-mail: brian.schriner@fiu.edu.

School of Architecture Students: 364 full-time (207 women), 46 part-time (29 women); includes 21 Black or African American, non-Hispanic/Latino; 10 Asian, non-Hispanic/Latino; 268 Hispanic/Latino, 16 international. Average age 26. 239 applicants, 30% accepted, 62 enrolled. *Faculty:* 16 full-time (5 women), 23 part-time/adjunct (13 women). Expenses: Contact institution. *Financial support:* Institutionally sponsored loans and scholarships/grants available. Financial award application deadline: 3/1; financial award applicants required to submit FAFSA. In 2010, 51 master's awarded. *Degree program information:* Part-time and evening/weekend programs available. Offers architecture (M Arch, MA); interior design (MA, MID); landscape architecture (MA, MLA). *Application deadline:* For fall admission, 2/1 for domestic and international students. *Application fee:* $30. Electronic applications accepted. *Application Contact:* Nanett Rojas, Assistant Director of Graduate Admissions, 305-348-7441, Fax: 305-348-7442, E-mail: gradadm@fiu.edu. *Interim Dean,* Dr. Brian Schriner, 305-348-6442, Fax: 305-348-2650, E-mail: schriner@fiu.edu.

School of Art and Art History Students: 10 full-time (6 women), 1 (woman) part-time; includes 1 Black or African American, non-Hispanic/Latino; 4 Hispanic/Latino, 1 international. Average age 27. 34 applicants, 12% accepted, 4 enrolled. *Faculty:* 14 full-time (6 women), 4 part-time/adjunct (0 women). Expenses: Contact institution. *Financial support:* Institutionally sponsored loans and scholarships/grants available. Financial award application deadline: 3/1; financial award applicants required to submit FAFSA. In 2010, 4 master's awarded. *Degree program information:* Part-time and evening/weekend programs available. Offers visual arts (MFA). *Application deadline:* For fall admission, 2/1 for domestic and international students. *Application fee:* $30. Electronic applications accepted. *Application Contact:* Evelyn Martinez, Graduate Secretary, 305-348-6268, Fax: 305-348-0513, E-mail: emart022@fiu.edu. *Chair,* Dr. Juan Martinez, 305-348-3539, Fax: 305-348-0513, E-mail: juan.martinez@fiu.edu.

School of Music Students: 29 full-time (13 women), 11 part-time (3 women); includes 1 Black or African American, non-Hispanic/Latino; 1 Asian, non-Hispanic/Latino; 20 Hispanic/Latino. Average age 27. 42 applicants, 43% accepted, 18 enrolled. *Faculty:* 19 full-time (4 women), 11 part-time/adjunct (3 women). Expenses: Contact institution. *Financial support:* Institutionally sponsored loans and scholarships/grants available. Financial award application deadline: 3/1; financial award applicants required to submit FAFSA. In 2010, 15 master's awarded. *Degree program information:* Part-time and evening/weekend programs available. Offers music (MM); music education (MS). *Application deadline:* For fall admission, 6/1 for domestic students, 4/1 for international students; for spring admission, 10/1 for domestic students, 9/1 for international students. Applications are processed on a rolling basis. *Application fee:* $30. Electronic applications accepted. *Application Contact:* Joel Galand, Graduate Program Director, 305-348-2896, Fax: 305-348-4073, E-mail: joel.galand@fiu.edu. *Chair,* Orlando Garcia, 305-348-3357, Fax: 305-348-4073, E-mail: orlando.garcia@fiu.edu.

College of Arts and Sciences Students: 870 full-time (503 women), 625 part-time (383 women); includes 198 Black or African American, non-Hispanic/Latino; 7 American Indian or Alaska Native, non-Hispanic/Latino; 44 Asian, non-Hispanic/Latino; 574 Hispanic/Latino; 1 Native Hawaiian or other Pacific Islander, non-Hispanic/Latino, 225 international. Average age 29. 1,956 applicants, 32% accepted, 602 enrolled. *Faculty:* 388 full-time (135 women), 241 part-time/adjunct (126 women). Expenses: Contact institution. *Financial support:* Career-related internships or fieldwork, Federal Work-Study, institutionally sponsored loans, and scholarships/grants available. Financial award application deadline: 3/1; financial award applicants required to submit FAFSA. In 2010, 275 master's, 53 doctorates awarded. *Degree program information:* Part-time and evening/weekend programs available. Offers African-new world studies (MA); arts and sciences (MA, MFA, MPA, MS, PhD); Asian studies (MA); Atlantic civilization (PhD); biological sciences (MS, PhD); chemistry (MS, PhD); comparative sociology (MA, PhD); creative writing (MFA); criminal justice (MS); economics (MA, PhD); English (MA); environmental studies (MS); forensic science (MS); geosciences (MS, PhD); history (MA); international relations (MA, PhD); international studies (MA); Latin American and Caribbean studies (MA); liberal studies (MA); linguistics (MA); literature (MA); mathematical sciences (MS); physics (MS, PhD); political science (MA, PhD); psychology (MS, PhD); public administration (MPA); public management (PhD); religious studies (MA); Spanish (MA, PhD); statistics (MS). *Application deadline:* For fall admission, 6/1 for domestic students, 4/1 for international students; for spring admission, 10/1 for domestic students, 9/1 for international students. Applications are processed on a rolling basis. *Application fee:* $30. Electronic applications accepted. *Application Contact:* Nanett Rojas, Assistant Director of Graduate Admissions, 305-348-7442, Fax: 305-348-7441, E-mail: gradadm@fiu.edu. *Dean,* Dr. Kenneth Furton, 305-348-2864, Fax: 305-348-4172, E-mail: casdean@fiu.edu.

College of Education Students: 296 full-time (230 women), 640 part-time (516 women); includes 179 Black or African American, non-Hispanic/Latino; 4 American Indian or Alaska Native, non-Hispanic/Latino; 15 Asian, non-Hispanic/Latino; 446 Hispanic/Latino, 64 international. Average age 31. 895 applicants, 41% accepted, 312 enrolled. *Faculty:* 47 full-time (28 women), 81 part-time/adjunct (58 women). Expenses: Contact institution. *Financial support:* Career-related internships or fieldwork, Federal Work-Study, institutionally sponsored loans, and tuition waivers (full and partial) available. Support available to part-time students. In 2010, 298 master's, 14 doctorates, 25 other advanced degrees awarded. *Degree program information:* Part-time and evening/weekend programs available. Offers adult education (MS); adult education in human resource development (Ed D); art education (MAT, MS, Ed D); clinical mental health counseling (MS); conflict resolution and consensus building (Certificate); counselor education (MS); curriculum and instruction (Ed S); curriculum development (MS); curriculum studies (PhD); early childhood education (MS, Ed D); education (MAT, MS, Ed D, PhD, Certificate, Ed S); educational administration and supervision (Ed D); educational leadership (MS, Certificate, Ed S); elementary education (MS, Ed D); English education (MAT, MS, Ed D); foreign language education—teaching English to speakers of other languages (TESOL) (Certificate); foreign language education- teaching English to speakers of other languages (TESOL) (MS); French education—initial teacher preparation (MAT); higher education (Ed D); higher education administration (MS); human resource development (MS); instruction in urban settings (MS); international and intercultural development education (Ed D); international and intercultural developmental education (MS); international/intercultural education (MS); language, literacy and culture (PhD); learning technologies (MS, Ed D, PhD); mathematics education (MAT, MS, Ed D, PhD); modern language education/bilingual education (MS, Ed D); multicultural-bilingual (MS); multicultural-TESOL (MS); physical education (MS); reading education (MS, Ed D); recreation and sport management (MS); recreation therapy (MS); rehabilitation counseling (MS); school counseling (MS); school psychology (Ed S); science education (MAT, MS, Ed D, PhD); social studies education (MAT, MS, Ed D); Spanish education—initial teacher preparation (MAT); special education (MS); urban education (MS). *Application deadline:* For fall admission, 6/1 priority date for domestic students, 4/1 for international students; for winter admission, 10/1 priority date for domestic students, 9/1 for international students; for spring admission, 3/1 priority date for domestic students, 2/1 for international students. Applications are processed on a rolling basis. *Application fee:* $30. Electronic applications accepted. *Application Contact:* Nanette Rojas, Graduate Admissions, 305-348-7442, Fax: 305-348-7441, E-mail: nanette.rojas@fiu.edu. *Unit Head,* Dr. Delia Garcia, 305-348-3202, Fax: 305-348-3205, E-mail: delia.garcia@fiu.edu.

College of Engineering and Computing Students: 467 full-time (125 women), 360 part-time (87 women); includes 63 Black or African American, non-Hispanic/Latino; 1 American Indian or Alaska Native, non-Hispanic/Latino; 26 Asian, non-Hispanic/Latino; 242 Hispanic/Latino, 376 international. Average age 28. 1,840 applicants, 27% accepted, 394 enrolled. *Faculty:* 95 full-time (9 women), 31 part-time/adjunct (0 women). Expenses: Contact institution. *Financial support:* Career-related internships or fieldwork, Federal Work-Study, institutionally sponsored loans, scholarships/grants, and unspecified assistantships available. Financial award application deadline: 3/1; financial award applicants required to submit FAFSA. In 2010, 293 master's, 35 doctorates awarded. *Degree program information:* Part-time and evening/weekend programs available. Postbaccalaureate distance learning degree programs offered. Offers biomedical engineering (MS, PhD); civil engineering (MS, PhD); computer engineering (MS); construction management (MS); electrical engineering (MS, PhD); engineering and computing (MS, PhD); environmental engineering (MS); materials science and engineering (MS, PhD); mechanical engineering (MS, PhD); telecommunications and networking (MS). *Application deadline:* For fall admission, 6/1 for domestic students, 4/1 for international students; for spring admission, 10/1 for domestic students, 9/1 for international students. Applications are processed on a rolling basis. *Application fee:* $30. Electronic applications accepted. *Application Contact:* Maria Parrilla, Assistant Director of Graduate Admissions, 305-348-1890, Fax: 305-348-6142, E-mail: grad_eng@fiu.edu. *Dean,* Dr. Amir Mirmiran, 305-348-2522, Fax: 305-348-1401, E-mail: amir.mirmiran@fiu.edu.

School of Computing and Information Sciences Students: 96 full-time (24 women), 67 part-time (12 women); includes 7 Black or African American, non-Hispanic/Latino; 4 Asian, non-Hispanic/Latino; 47 Hispanic/Latino, 84 international. Average age 31. 433 applicants, 21% accepted, 77 enrolled. *Faculty:* 29 full-time (2 women), 5 part-time/adjunct (0 women). Expenses: Contact institution. *Financial support:* Research assistantships, teaching assistantships, institutionally sponsored loans, scholarships/grants, and unspecified assistantships available. Financial award application deadline: 3/1; financial award applicants required to submit FAFSA. In 2010, 25 master's, 5 doctorates awarded. *Degree program information:* Part-time and evening/weekend programs available. Offers computer science (MS, PhD); computing and information sciences (MS, PhD); telecommunications and networking (MS). *Application deadline:* For fall admission, 6/1 for domestic students, 4/1 for international students; for spring admission, 10/1 for domestic students, 9/1 for international students. Applications are processed on a rolling basis. *Application fee:* $30. Electronic applications accepted. *Application Contact:* Maria Parrilla, Graduate Admissions Assistant, 305-348-1890, Fax: 305-348-6142, E-mail: grad_eng@fiu.edu. *Interim Director,* Dr. Jainendra Navlakha, 305-348-2023, Fax: 305-348-3549, E-mail: navlakha@cis.fiu.edu.

College of Law Students: 565 full-time (291 women), 22 part-time (8 women); includes 56 Black or African American, non-Hispanic/Latino; 5 American Indian or Alaska Native, non-Hispanic/Latino; 22 Asian, non-Hispanic/Latino; 249 Hispanic/Latino, 1 international. Average age 33. 2,565 applicants, 19% accepted, 163 enrolled. *Faculty:* 26 full-time (11 women), 18 part-time/adjunct (7 women). Expenses: Contact institution. *Financial support:* Application deadline: 3/1. In 2010, 144 JDs awarded. *Degree program information:* Part-time and evening/weekend programs available. Offers law (JD). *Application deadline:* For fall admission, 5/1 for domestic and international students. Applications are processed on a rolling basis. *Application fee:* $20. Electronic applications accepted. *Application Contact:* Alma Miro, Director of Admissions and Financial Aid, 305-348-8006, Fax: 305-348-2965, E-mail: lawadmit@fiu.edu. *Dean,* Dr. R. Alex Acosta, 305-348-1118, Fax: 305-348-1159, E-mail: acosta@fiu.edu.

College of Nursing and Health Sciences Students: 541 full-time (435 women), 273 part-time (226 women); includes 138 Black or African American, non-Hispanic/Latino; 54 Asian, non-Hispanic/Latino; 401 Hispanic/Latino; 2 Native Hawaiian or other Pacific Islander, non-Hispanic/Latino, 16 international. Average age 33. 1,629 applicants, 17% accepted, 251 enrolled. *Faculty:* 49 full-time (38 women), 65 part-time/adjunct (53 women). Expenses: Contact institution. *Financial support:* Career-related internships or fieldwork, Federal Work-Study, institutionally sponsored loans, and scholarships/grants available. Financial award application deadline: 3/1; financial award applicants required to submit FAFSA. In 2010, 210 master's, 32 doctorates awarded. *Degree program information:* Part-time and evening/weekend programs available. Offers athletic training (MS); entry level professional (MS); nursing (MSN, PhD); nursing and health sciences (MS, MSN, DPT, PhD); physical therapy (DPT); speech-language pathology (MS). *Application fee:* $30. Electronic applications accepted. *Application Contact:* Nanett Rojas, Assistant Director of Graduate Admissions, 305-348-7441, Fax: 305-348-7442, E-mail: gradadm@fiu.edu. *Interim Dean,* Dr. Sharon Pontious, 305-348-7703, Fax: 305-348-7764, E-mail: sharon.pontious@fiu.edu.

Herbert Wertheim College of Medicine Students: 85 full-time (30 women); includes 6 Black or African American, non-Hispanic/Latino; 1 American Indian or Alaska Native, non-Hispanic/Latino; 12 Asian, non-Hispanic/Latino; 32 Hispanic/Latino. Average age 26. 3,536 applicants, 1% accepted, 43 enrolled. *Faculty:* 34 full-time (13 women), 14 part-time/adjunct (3 women). Expenses: Contact institution. *Financial support:* Institutionally sponsored loans and scholarships/grants available. Financial award application deadline: 3/1; financial award applicants required to submit FAFSA. Offers medicine (MD). *Application deadline:* For fall admission, 12/15 for domestic students. *Application fee:* $160. Electronic applications accepted. *Application Contact:* Betty Monfort, Director of Admissions and Records, 305-348-0644, Fax: 305-348-0650, E-mail: med.admissions@fiu.edu. *Dean,* Dr. John Rock, 305-348-0644, Fax: 305-348-0650, E-mail: med.admissions@fiu.edu.

School of Hospitality and Tourism Management Students: 214 full-time (144 women), 86 part-time (56 women); includes 28 Black or African American, non-Hispanic/Latino; 1 American Indian or Alaska Native, non-Hispanic/Latino; 7 Asian, non-Hispanic/Latino; 47 Hispanic/Latino, 150 international. Average age 29. 528 applicants, 42% accepted, 197 enrolled. *Faculty:* 17 full-time (5 women), 23 part-time/adjunct (8 women). Expenses: Contact institution. *Financial support:* Institutionally sponsored loans and scholarships/grants available. Financial award application deadline: 3/1; financial award applicants required to submit FAFSA. In 2010, 81 master's awarded. *Degree program information:* Part-time and evening/weekend programs available. Postbaccalaureate distance learning degree programs offered (no on-campus study). Offers hospitality and tourism management (MS); hospitality management (MS). *Application deadline:* For fall admission, 6/1 for domestic students, 4/1 for international students; for spring admission, 10/1 for domestic students, 9/1 for international students. Applications are processed on a rolling basis. *Application fee:* $30. Electronic applications accepted. *Application Contact:* Nanett Rojas, Assistant Director of Graduate Admissions, 305-348-7442, Fax: 305-348-7441, E-mail: gradadm@fiu.edu. *Interim Dean,* Joan Remington, 305-919-4500, Fax: 305-919-4555, E-mail: joan.remington@fiu.edu.

School of Journalism and Mass Communication Students: 94 full-time (71 women), 88 part-time (69 women); includes 26 Black or African American, non-Hispanic/Latino; 1 American Indian or Alaska Native, non-Hispanic/Latino; 6 Asian, non-Hispanic/Latino; 100 Hispanic/Latino, 21 international. Average age 27. 197 applicants, 30% accepted, 56 enrolled. *Faculty:* 21 full-time (13 women), 9 part-time/adjunct (7 women). Expenses: Contact institution. *Financial support:* Institutionally sponsored loans and scholarships/grants available. Financial award application deadline: 3/1; financial award applicants required to submit FAFSA. In 2010, 57 master's awarded. *Degree program information:* Part-time and evening/weekend programs available. Offers mass communication (MS). *Application deadline:* For fall admission, 6/1 for domestic students, 4/1 for international students; for spring admission, 10/1 for domestic students, 9/1 for international students. Applications are processed on a rolling basis. *Application fee:* $30. Electronic applications accepted. *Application Contact:* Nanett Rojas, Assistant Director of Graduate Admissions, 305-348-7442, Fax: 305-348-7441, E-mail: gradadm@fiu.edu. *Dean,* Dr. Lillian Kopenhaver, 305-919-5674, Fax: 305-919-5203, E-mail: kopenha@fiu.edu.

Stempel College of Public Health and Social Work Students: 455 full-time (377 women), 328 part-time (268 women); includes 241 Black or African American, non-Hispanic/Latino; 1 American Indian or Alaska Native, non-Hispanic/Latino; 41 Asian, non-Hispanic/Latino; 292 Hispanic/Latino, 78 international. Average age 31. 1,159 applicants, 36% accepted, 370 enrolled. *Faculty:* 45 full-time (24 women), 44 part-time/adjunct (22 women). Expenses: Contact institution. *Financial support:* Institutionally sponsored loans, scholarships/grants, and unspecified assistantships available. Financial award application deadline: 3/1; financial award applicants required to submit FAFSA. In 2010, 217 master's, 4 doctorates awarded. *Degree program information:* Part-time and evening/weekend programs available. Postbaccalaureate distance learning degree programs offered (no on-campus study). Offers biostatistics (MPH); dietetics and nutrition (MS, PhD); environmental and occupational health (MPH, PhD); epidemiology (MPH, PhD); health policy and management (MPH); health promotion and disease prevention (PhD); health promotion and diseases prevention (MPH); public health and social work (MHSA, MPH, MS, MSW, PhD). *Application deadline:* For fall admission, 6/1 for domestic students, 4/1 for international students; for spring admission, 10/1 for domestic students, 9/1 for international students. Applications are processed on a rolling basis. *Application fee:* $30. Electronic applications accepted. *Application Contact:* Nanett Rojas, Assistant Director of Graduate Admissions, 305-348-7442, Fax: 305-348-7441, E-mail: gradadm@fiu.edu. *Interim Dean,* Dr. Michele Ciccazzo, 305-348-5344, Fax: 305-348-7782, E-mail: michele.ciccazzo@fiu.edu.

School of Social Work Students: 145 full-time (124 women), 73 part-time (65 women); includes 71 Black or African American, non-Hispanic/Latino; 7 Asian, non-Hispanic/Latino; 102 Hispanic/Latino, 1 international. Average age 33. 257 applicants, 48% accepted, 115 enrolled. *Faculty:* 16 full-time (8 women), 16 part-time/adjunct (3 women). Expenses: Contact institution. *Financial support:* Institutionally sponsored loans and scholarships/grants available. Financial award application deadline: 3/1; financial award applicants required to submit FAFSA. In 2010, 82 master's awarded. *Degree program information:* Part-time and evening/weekend programs available. Offers social welfare (PhD); social work (MSW). *Application deadline:* For fall admission, 6/1 for domestic students, 4/1 for international students; for spring admission, 10/1 for domestic students, 9/1 for international students. Applications are processed on a rolling basis. *Application fee:* $30. Electronic applications accepted. *Application Contact:* Zoraya Arguello, Admissions Advisor, 305-348-5880, Fax: 305-348-5312, E-mail: arguello@fiu.edu. *Director,* Maria Gutierrez, 305-348-5880, Fax: 305-348-5312, E-mail: gutierm@fiu.edu.

FLORIDA MEMORIAL UNIVERSITY, Miami-Dade, FL 33054

General Information Independent-religious, coed, comprehensive institution.

GRADUATE UNITS

School of Business *Degree program information:* Part-time programs available. Offers business (MBA).

School of Education Offers elementary education (MS); exceptional student education (MS); reading (MS).

FLORIDA SOUTHERN COLLEGE, Lakeland, FL 33801-5698

General Information Independent-religious, coed, comprehensive institution. *Enrollment:* 2,149 graduate, professional, and undergraduate students; 49 full-time matriculated graduate/professional students (19 women), 116 part-time matriculated graduate/professional students (82 women). *Enrollment by degree level:* 165 master's. *Graduate faculty:* 24 full-time (9 women), 11 part-time/adjunct (7 women). *Tuition:* Full-time $6660; part-time $370 per credit hour. *Required fees:* $50 per semester. Tuition and fees vary according to course load and program. *Graduate housing:* On-campus housing not available. *Student services:* Campus employment opportunities, campus safety program, career counseling, exercise/wellness program, free psychological counseling, international student services, multicultural affairs office, services for students with disabilities, teacher training. *Library facilities:* Roux Library. *Online resources:* library catalog, web page. *Collection:* 249,436 titles, 3,030 serial subscriptions, 13,853 audiovisual materials.

Florida Southern College (continued)

Computer facilities: Computer purchase and lease plans are available. 450 computers available on campus for general student use. A campuswide network can be accessed from student residence rooms and from off campus. Online class registration, campus portal are available. *Web address:* http://www.flsouthern.edu/.

General Application Contact: Craig Story, Evening Program Director, 863-680-4205, Fax: 863-680-3872, E-mail: cstory@flsouthern.edu.

GRADUATE UNITS

Program in Business Administration Students: 27 full-time (8 women), 16 part-time (8 women); includes 2 Black or African American, non-Hispanic/Latino; 1 Hispanic/Latino, 4 international. Average age 26. 41 applicants, 51% accepted, 19 enrolled. *Faculty:* 14 full-time (2 women), 1 part-time/adjunct (0 women). Expenses: Contact institution. *Financial support:* In 2010–11, 6 students received support. Scholarships/grants available. Support available to part-time students. Financial award applicants required to submit FAFSA. In 2010, 9 master's awarded. *Degree program information:* Part-time and evening/weekend programs available. Offers business administration (MBA). *Application deadline:* For fall admission, 6/1 for domestic and international students. Applications are processed on a rolling basis. *Application fee:* $30. *Application Contact:* Kathy Connelly, Evening Program Assistant Director, 863-680-4205, Fax: 863-680-3872, E-mail: cconnelly@flsouthern.edu. *Program Coordinator,* Dr. Larry Ross, 863-680-4285, Fax: 863-680-4355, E-mail: lross@flsouthern.edu.

Program in Nursing Students: 11 full-time (9 women), 70 part-time (64 women); includes 6 Black or African American, non-Hispanic/Latino; 1 Asian, non-Hispanic/Latino; 3 Hispanic/Latino. Average age 43. 53 applicants, 51% accepted, 27 enrolled. *Faculty:* 5 full-time (4 women), 4 part-time/adjunct (all women). Expenses: Contact institution. *Financial support:* In 2010–11, 5 students received support. Scholarships/grants and traineeships available. Support available to part-time students. Financial award applicants required to submit FAFSA. In 2010, 22 master's awarded. *Degree program information:* Part-time and evening/weekend programs available. Offers clinical nurse specialist (MSN); nurse educator (MSN); nurse practitioner (MSN). *Application deadline:* For fall admission, 6/1 for domestic and international students; for spring admission, 10/1 for domestic and international students. Applications are processed on a rolling basis. *Application fee:* $30. *Application Contact:* Kathy Connelly, Evening Program Assistant Director, 863-680-4205, Fax: 863-680-3872, E-mail: kconnelly@flsouthern.edu. *Dean,* Dr. John Welton, 863-680-4310, Fax: 863-680-3872, E-mail: jwelton@flsouthern.edu.

Programs in Teaching Students: 26 full-time (17 women), 15 part-time (10 women); includes 3 Black or African American, non-Hispanic/Latino, 1 international. Average age 30. 25 applicants, 48% accepted, 12 enrolled. *Faculty:* 5 full-time (3 women), 6 part-time/adjunct (3 women). Expenses: Contact institution. *Financial support:* In 2010–11, 3 students received support. Scholarships/grants available. Support available to part-time students. Financial award applicants required to submit FAFSA. In 2010, 30 master's awarded. *Degree program information:* Part-time and evening/weekend programs available. Offers teaching (M Ed, MAT). *Application deadline:* For fall admission, 8/1 for domestic and international students; for winter admission, 4/1 for domestic and international students; for spring admission, 12/1 for domestic and international students. Applications are processed on a rolling basis. *Application fee:* $30. *Application Contact:* Kathy Connelly, Evening Program Assistant Director, 863-680-4205, Fax: 863-680-3872, E-mail: kconnelly@flsouthern.edu. *Dean,* Dr. Tracey Tedder, 863-680-4177, Fax: 863-680-4102, E-mail: ttedder@flsouthern.edu.

FLORIDA STATE UNIVERSITY, Tallahassee, FL 32306

General Information State-supported, coed, university. CGS member. *Enrollment:* 40,416 graduate, professional, and undergraduate students; 5,989 full-time matriculated graduate/professional students (3,026 women), 2,493 part-time matriculated graduate/professional students (1,551 women). *Enrollment by degree level:* 1,247 first professional, 4,413 master's, 2,704 doctoral, 118 other advanced degrees. *Graduate faculty:* 1,161 full-time (423 women), 140 part-time/adjunct (67 women). Tuition, state resident: full-time $8238. *Graduate housing:* Rooms and/or apartments available on a first-come, first-served basis to single students and available to married students. *Student services:* Campus employment opportunities, campus safety program, career counseling, child daycare facilities, exercise/wellness program, free psychological counseling, grant writing training, international student services, low-cost health insurance, multicultural affairs office, services for students with disabilities, teacher training, writing training. *Library facilities:* Robert Manning Strozier Library plus 7 others. *Online resources:* library catalog, access to other libraries' catalogs. *Collection:* 3 million titles, 78,300 serial subscriptions, 256,310 audiovisual materials. *Research affiliation:* Fermi National Accelerator Laboratory (high energy physics), National Center for Atmospheric Research (atmospheric Research), Oak Ridge National Laboratory (materials science), CERN (high energy research), Jefferson Laboratory (nuclear physics), Bruker, Inc. (nuclear magnetic resonance).

Computer facilities: 3,821 computers available on campus for general student use. A campuswide network can be accessed from student residence rooms and from off campus. Online class registration, course home pages, course search, online fee payment are available. *Web address:* http://www.fsu.edu/.

General Application Contact: Melanie Booker, Associate Director for Graduate Admissions, 850-644-3420, Fax: 850-644-0197, E-mail: mbooker@admin.fsu.edu.

GRADUATE UNITS

College of Law Students: 786 full-time (313 women), 3 part-time (1 woman); includes 60 Black or African American, non-Hispanic/Latino; 2 American Indian or Alaska Native, non-Hispanic/Latino; 23 Asian, non-Hispanic/Latino; 71 Hispanic/Latino, 1 international. Average age 24. 3,649 applicants, 22% accepted, 205 enrolled. *Faculty:* 50 full-time (22 women), 30 part-time/adjunct (8 women). Expenses: Contact institution. *Financial support:* In 2010–11, 282 students received support, including 282 fellowships (averaging $2,000 per year), 58 research assistantships (averaging $3,300 per year), 14 teaching assistantships (averaging $1,034 per year); scholarships/grants and unspecified assistantships also available. Financial award application deadline: 3/1; financial award applicants required to submit FAFSA. In 2010, 245 first professional degrees awarded. Offers American law for foreign lawyers (LL M); environmental law and policy (LL M); law (JD). *Application deadline:* For fall admission, 5/1 priority date for domestic students. Applications are processed on a rolling basis. *Application fee:* $30. Electronic applications accepted. *Application Contact:* Jennifer L. Kessinger, Director of Admissions and Records, 850-644-3787, Fax: 850-644-7284, E-mail: jkessing@law.fsu.edu. *Dean,* Donald J. Weidner, 850-644-3400, Fax: 850-644-5487, E-mail: dweidner@law.fsu.edu.

College of Medicine Students: 478 full-time (246 women); includes 40 Black or African American, non-Hispanic/Latino; 3 American Indian or Alaska Native, non-Hispanic/Latino; 74 Asian, non-Hispanic/Latino; 43 Hispanic/Latino; 1 Native Hawaiian or other Pacific Islander, non-Hispanic/Latino. Average age 25. 3,584 applicants, 6% accepted, 120 enrolled. *Faculty:* 134 full-time (58 women), 53 part-time/adjunct (17 women). Expenses: Contact institution. *Financial support:* In 2010–11, 223 students received support. Scholarships/grants and tuition waivers available. Financial award application deadline: 7/1; financial award applicants required to submit FAFSA. In 2010, 94 first professional degrees awarded. Offers biomedical sciences (PhD); medicine (MD, PhD); neuroscience (PhD). *Application deadline:* Applications are processed on a rolling basis. *Application fee:* $30. Electronic applications accepted. *Application Contact:* Dana Urrutia, Admissions Coordinator, 850-644-1857, Fax: 850-645-2846, E-mail: medadmissions@med.fsu.edu. *Dean,* Dr. John Fogarty, 850-644-1855, Fax: 850-645-1420, E-mail: john.fogarty@med.fsu.edu.

The Graduate School Students: 5,989 full-time (3,026 women), 2,507 part-time (1,558 women); includes 720 Black or African American, non-Hispanic/Latino; 54 American Indian or Alaska Native, non-Hispanic/Latino; 294 Asian, non-Hispanic/Latino; 599 Hispanic/Latino, 1,011 international. Average age 31. 11,908 applicants, 37% accepted, 1958 enrolled. *Faculty:* 1,161 full-time (423 women), 140 part-time/adjunct (67 women). Expenses: Contact institution. *Financial support:* Fellowships, research assistantships, teaching assistantships, career-related internships or fieldwork, Federal Work-Study, institutionally sponsored loans, scholarships/grants, traineeships, health care benefits, tuition waivers (partial), and unspecified assistantships available. Support available to part-time students. Financial award applicants required to submit FAFSA. In 2010, 2,006 master's, 390 doctorates, 49 other advanced degrees awarded. *Degree program information:* Part-time and evening/weekend programs available. Offers computational materials science and mechanics (MS); functional materials (MS); nanoscale materials, composite materials, and interfaces (MS); polymers and bio-inspired materials (MS). *Application deadline:* For fall admission, 7/1 for domestic and international students. *Application fee:* $30. Electronic applications accepted. *Application Contact:* Melanie Booker, Associate Director for Graduate Admissions, 850-644-3420, Fax: 850-644-0197, E-mail: mbooker@admin.fsu.edu. *Dean,* Dr. Nancy Marcus, 850-644-3500, Fax: 850-644-2969, E-mail: nmarcus@fsu.edu.

College of Arts and Sciences Students: 1,561 full-time (622 women), 218 part-time (107 women); includes 85 Black or African American, non-Hispanic/Latino; 12 American Indian or Alaska Native, non-Hispanic/Latino; 50 Asian, non-Hispanic/Latino; 102 Hispanic/Latino, 386 international. Average age 31. *Faculty:* 430 full-time (103 women). Expenses: Contact institution. *Financial support:* Fellowships, research assistantships, teaching assistantships, career-related internships or fieldwork, institutionally sponsored loans, scholarships/grants, traineeships, and unspecified assistantships available. Support available to part-time students. Financial award applicants required to submit FAFSA. In 2010, 254 master's, 151 doctorates awarded. *Degree program information:* Part-time programs available. Offers analytical chemistry (MS, PhD); applied behavior analysis (MS); applied computational mathematics (MS, PhD); applied statistics (MS); aquatic environmental science (MS); arts and sciences (MA, MFA, MS, MST, PhD); biochemistry (MS, PhD); biochemistry, molecular and cell biology (PhD); biomedical mathematics (MS, PhD); biostatistics (MS, PhD); cell and molecular biology and genetics (MS, PhD); classical archaeology (MA); classical civilization (MA); classics (MA, PhD); clinical psychology (PhD); cognitive psychology (PhD); computational science (MS, PhD); computational structural biology (PhD); computer science (MS, PhD); creative writing (MFA); developmental psychology (PhD); ecology and evolutionary biology (MS, PhD); English (PhD); financial mathematics (MS, PhD); French (MA, PhD); geological sciences (MS, PhD); geophysical fluid dynamics (PhD); German (MA); Greek (MA); Greek and Latin (MA); historical administration (MA); history (MA, PhD); history and philosophy of science (MA); humanities (PhD); information security (MS); inorganic chemistry (MS, PhD); Italian (MA); Italian studies (MA); Latin (MA); literature (MA); materials chemistry (PhD); mathematical statistics (MS, PhD); meteorology (MS, PhD); molecular biophysics (PhD); neuroscience (PhD); oceanography (MS, PhD); organic chemistry (MS, PhD); philosophy (MA, PhD); physical chemistry (MS, PhD); physics (MS, PhD); plant biology (MS, PhD); pure mathematics (MS, PhD); religion (MA, PhD); rhetoric and composition (MA); science teaching (MST); Slavic languages and literatures (MA); Slavic languages/Russian (MA); social psychology (PhD); Spanish (MA, PhD); structural biology (MS, PhD). *Application fee:* $30. *Application Contact:* Ginger Martin, Senior Graduate Academic Coordinator, 850-644-1081, Fax: 850-644-9656, E-mail: vmartin@fsu.edu. *Dean,* Dr. Joseph Travis, 850-644-1081.

College of Business Students: 196 full-time (76 women), 310 part-time (109 women); includes 27 Black or African American, non-Hispanic/Latino; 1 American Indian or Alaska Native, non-Hispanic/Latino; 31 Asian, non-Hispanic/Latino; 30 Hispanic/Latino. Average age 30. 702 applicants, 33% accepted, 205 enrolled. *Faculty:* 107 full-time (31 women). Expenses: Contact institution. *Financial support:* In 2010–11, 86 students received support, including 12 fellowships with full tuition reimbursements available (averaging $7,161 per year), 30 research assistantships with full tuition reimbursements available (averaging $6,000 per year), 43 teaching assistantships with full tuition reimbursements available (averaging $15,000 per year); career-related internships or fieldwork, scholarships/grants, health care benefits, tuition waivers (full and partial), and unspecified assistantships also available. Support available to part-time students. Financial award application deadline: 1/1. In 2010, 268 master's, 17 doctorates awarded. *Degree program information:* Part-time programs available. Postbaccalaureate distance learning degree programs offered (no on-campus study). Offers accounting (M Acc); business administration (MBA, PhD); finance (MS); insurance (MSM); management information systems (MS). *Application deadline:* For fall admission, 6/1 for domestic students, 5/1 for international students; for spring admission, 10/1 for domestic students, 9/1 for international students. Applications are processed on a rolling basis. *Application fee:* $30. Electronic applications accepted. *Application Contact:* Lisa Beverly, Director, Graduate Programs Admissions, 850-644-6458, Fax: 850-644-0588, E-mail: lbeverly@cob.fsu.edu. *Dean,* Dr. Caryn Beck-Dudley, 850-644-3090, Fax: 850-644-0915.

College of Communication and Information Students: 241 full-time (181 women), 701 part-time (526 women); includes 256 minority (83 Black or African American, non-Hispanic/Latino; 3 American Indian or Alaska Native, non-Hispanic/Latino; 85 Asian, non-Hispanic/Latino; 80 Hispanic/Latino; 1 Native Hawaiian or other Pacific Islander, non-Hispanic/Latino; 4 Two or more races, non-Hispanic/Latino), 18 international. Average age 28. 823 applicants, 63% accepted, 314 enrolled. *Faculty:* 70 full-time (38 women), 29 part-time/adjunct (16 women). Expenses: Contact institution. *Financial support:* In 2010–11, 408 students received support, including 9 fellowships with full tuition reimbursements available, 94 research assistantships with full and partial tuition reimbursements available, 107 teaching assistantships with full and partial tuition reimbursements available; career-related internships or fieldwork, Federal Work-Study, institutionally sponsored loans, scholarships/grants, health care benefits, tuition waivers (partial), and unspecified assistantships also available. Support available to part-time students. Financial award applicants required to submit FAFSA. In 2010, 373 master's, 17 doctorates, 8 other advanced degrees awarded. *Degree program information:* Part-time and evening/weekend programs available. Postbaccalaureate distance learning degree programs offered (no on-campus study). Offers communication and information (Adv M, MA, MS, PhD, Specialist); communication science and disorders (Adv M, MS, PhD); corporate and public communication (MS); integrated marketing communication (MA, MS); library and information studies (MA, MS, PhD, Specialist); mass communication (PhD); media and communication studies (MA, MS); speech communication (PhD). *Application deadline:* For fall admission, 7/1 priority date for domestic students, 7/1 for international students; for winter admission, 3/1 priority date for domestic students, 3/1 for international students; for spring admission, 11/1 priority date for domestic students, 11/1 for international students. Applications are processed on a rolling basis. *Application fee:* $30. Electronic applications accepted. *Application Contact:* Dr. Lawrence C. Dennis, Dean, 850-644-9698, Fax: 850-644-0611, E-mail: larry.dennis@cci.fsu.edu. *Dean,* Dr. Lawrence C. Dennis, 850-644-9698, Fax: 850-644-0611, E-mail: larry.dennis@cci.fsu.edu.

College of Criminology and Criminal Justice Students: 93 full-time (56 women), 98 part-time (56 women); includes 40 minority (19 Black or African American, non-Hispanic/Latino; 2 American Indian or Alaska Native, non-Hispanic/Latino; 6 Asian, non-Hispanic/Latino; 13 Hispanic/Latino), 5 international. 192 applicants, 59% accepted, 58 enrolled. *Faculty:* 19 full-time (4 women). Expenses: Contact institution. *Financial support:* In 2010–11, 1 fellowship with full tuition reimbursement (averaging $19,000 per year), 20 research assistantships with full tuition reimbursements (averaging $14,500 per year), 1 teaching assistantship with full tuition reimbursement (averaging $14,500 per year) were awarded; Federal Work-Study, institutionally sponsored loans, scholarships/grants, tuition waivers (partial), and unspecified assistantships also available. Financial award application deadline: 1/15; financial award applicants required to submit FAFSA. In 2010, 40 master's, 9 doctorates awarded. *Degree program information:* Part-time programs available. Postbaccalaureate distance learning degree programs offered (no on-campus study). Offers criminology and criminal justice (MA, MSC, PhD). *Application deadline:* For fall admission, 7/1 for domestic and international students; for spring admission, 11/1 for domestic and international students. Applications are processed on a rolling basis. *Application fee:* $30. Electronic applications accepted. *Application Contact:* Margarita Frankeberger, Graduate Student Coordinator, 850-644-7373, Fax: 850-644-9614, E-mail: mfrankeberger@fsu.edu. *Dean,* Dr. Thomas G. Blomberg, 850-644-7365, Fax: 850-644-9614.

College of Education Students: 656 full-time (439 women), 499 part-time (335 women); includes 250 minority (138 Black or African American, non-Hispanic/Latino; 8 American Indian or Alaska Native, non-Hispanic/Latino; 30 Asian, non-Hispanic/Latino; 73 Hispanic/Latino; 1 Two or more races, non-Hispanic/Latino), 144 international. Average age 31. 1,055 applicants, 56% accepted, 331 enrolled. *Faculty:* 110 full-time (69 women), 68 part-time/adjunct (43 women). Expenses: Contact institution. *Financial support:* In 2010–11, 114 students received support, including 17 fellowships with full and partial tuition reimbursements available, 154 research assistantships with full and partial tuition reimbursements available, 292 teaching assistantships with full and partial tuition reimbursements available; career-related internships or fieldwork, scholarships/grants, traineeships, health care benefits, and unspecified assistantships also available. Financial award application deadline: 1/15; financial award applicants required to submit FAFSA. In 2010, 376 master's, 57 doctorates, 43 other advanced degrees awarded. *Degree program information:* Part-time and evening/weekend programs available. Postbaccalaureate distance learning degree programs offered. Offers counseling/school psychology (PhD); early childhood education (MS, Ed D, PhD, Ed S); education (MS, Ed D, PhD, Ed S); educational administration/leadership (MS, Ed D, PhD, Ed S); educational leadership/administration (MS, Ed D, PhD, Ed S); educational policy and planning analysis (PhD, Ed S); educational psychology (MS, PhD, Ed S); elementary education (MS, Ed D, PhD, Ed S); emotional disturbance/learning disabilities (MS); English education (MS, PhD, Ed S); higher education (MS, Ed D, PhD, Ed S); history and philosophy of education (MS, PhD, Ed S); instructional systems (MS, PhD, Ed S); international and intercultural education (PhD); learning and cognition (MS, PhD, Ed S); mathematics education (MS, PhD, Ed S); measurement and statistics (MS, PhD, Ed S); mental health counseling (PhD); mental retardation (MS); open and distance learning (MS); performance improvement and human resources (MS); program evaluation (MS, PhD, Ed S); psychological services (MS, PhD, Ed S); reading education/language arts (MS, Ed D, PhD, Ed S); rehabilitation counseling (MS, PhD, Ed S); school psychology (MS, Ed S); science education (MS, PhD, Ed S); social science education (MS, PhD, Ed S); social, historical and philosophical foundations of education (MS, PhD, Ed S); sociocultural and international developmental education (MS, PhD, Ed S); special education (MS, PhD, Ed S); sport management (MS, Ed D, PhD); sports psychology (MS, PhD); visual disabilities (MS). *Application deadline:* For fall admission, 7/1 for domestic and international students; for winter admission, 11/1 for domestic and international students; for spring admission, 3/1 for domestic and international students. Applications are processed on a rolling basis. *Application fee:* $30. Electronic applications accepted. *Application Contact:* Dr. Pamela S. Carroll, Academic Dean, 850-644-0372, Fax: 850-644-1258, E-mail: pcarroll@fsu.edu. *Dean,* Dr. Marcy P. Driscoll, 850-644-6885, Fax: 850-644-2725, E-mail: mdriscoll@fsu.edu.

College of Human Sciences Students: 135 full-time (87 women), 35 part-time (27 women); includes 20 Black or African American, non-Hispanic/Latino; 4 Asian, non-Hispanic/Latino; 10 Hispanic/Latino; 1 Two or more races, non-Hispanic/Latino, 31 international. 198 applicants, 47% accepted, 44 enrolled. *Faculty:* 41 full-time (27 women). Expenses: Contact institution. *Financial support:* In 2010–11, 105 students received support, including 2 fellowships with partial tuition reimbursements available (averaging $12,650 per year), 30 research assistantships with partial tuition reimbursements available (averaging $6,980 per year), 70 teaching assistantships with partial tuition reimbursements available (averaging $10,051 per year); career-related internships or fieldwork, Federal Work-Study, institutionally sponsored loans, scholarships/grants, and unspecified assistantships also available. Financial award application deadline: 1/15; financial award applicants required to submit FAFSA. In 2010, 45 master's, 18 doctorates awarded. *Degree program information:* Part-time programs available. Offers exercise science (MS, PhD); family and child sciences (MS); family relations (PhD); human sciences (MS, PhD); marriage and family therapy (PhD); nutrition and food sciences (MS, PhD). *Application deadline:* For fall admission, 7/1 for domestic and international students; for spring admission, 11/1 for domestic and international students. Applications are processed on a rolling basis. *Application fee:* $30. Electronic applications accepted. *Application Contact:* Tara L. Hartman, Academic Program Specialist, 850-644-7221, Fax: 850-644-0700, E-mail: thartman@fsu.edu. *Dean,* Dr. Billie J. Collier, 850-644-1281, Fax: 850-644-0700, E-mail: bcollier@fsu.edu.

College of Motion Picture Arts Students: 61 full-time (24 women); includes 6 Black or African American, non-Hispanic/Latino; 8 Hispanic/Latino, 6 international. Average age 27. 182 applicants, 23% accepted, 30 enrolled. *Faculty:* 13 full-time (2 women), 4 part-time/adjunct (1 woman). Expenses: Contact institution. *Financial support:* In 2010–11, 22 students received support, including 1 fellowship with partial tuition reimbursement available (averaging $6,300 per year), 22 teaching assistantships with partial tuition reimbursements available (averaging $4,100 per year); Federal Work-Study and unspecified assistantships also available. Financial award application deadline: 1/1; financial award applicants required to submit FAFSA. In 2010, 28 master's awarded. Offers production (MFA); screen and play writing (MFA). *Application deadline:* For fall admission, 12/1 for domestic and international students. *Application fee:* $30. *Application Contact:* Carrie Lewis, Coordinator of Student Services, 850-644-8524, Fax: 850-644-2626, E-mail: clewis@film.fsu.edu. *Dean,* Frank Patterson, 850-644-0453, Fax: 850-644-2626.

College of Music Students: 406 full-time (211 women); includes 28 Black or African American, non-Hispanic/Latino; 38 Asian, non-Hispanic/Latino; 32 Hispanic/Latino. Average age 26. 525 applicants, 38% accepted, 145 enrolled. *Faculty:* 88 full-time, 13 part-time/adjunct. Expenses: Contact institution. *Financial support:* In 2010–11, 225 students received support, including 3 fellowships with full tuition reimbursements available (averaging $15,000 per year), 9 research assistantships with full tuition reimbursements available (averaging $4,000 per year), 173 teaching assistantships with full tuition reimbursements available (averaging $4,000 per year); career-related internships or fieldwork, Federal Work-Study, and tuition waivers (partial) also available. Support available to part-time students. Financial award application deadline: 2/28; financial award applicants required to submit FAFSA. In 2010, 102 master's, 41 doctorates awarded. Offers accompanying (MM); arts administration (MA); choral conducting (MM); composition (MM, DM); ethnomusicology (MM); general music (MA); instrumental accompanying (MM); instrumental conducting (MM); jazz studies (MM); music education (MM Ed, PhD); music theory (MM, PhD); music therapy (MM); musicology (MM, PhD); opera (MM); performance (MM, DM); piano pedagogy (MM); piano technology (MA); vocal accompanying (MM). *Application deadline:* For fall admission, 7/1 for domestic students, 5/2 for international students; for spring admission, 11/3 for domestic students, 9/1 for international students. Applications are processed on a rolling basis. *Application fee:* $30. Electronic applications accepted. *Application Contact:* Dr. Seth Beckman, Senior Associate Dean for Academic Affairs/Director of Graduate Studies, 850-644-5848, Fax: 850-644-2033, E-mail: sbeckman@admin.fsu.edu. *Dean,* Dr. Don Gibson, 850-644-4361, Fax: 850-644-2033.

College of Nursing Students: 17 full-time (13 women), 65 part-time (63 women); includes 4 Black or African American, non-Hispanic/Latino; 2 Asian, non-Hispanic/Latino; 3 Hispanic/Latino; 1 Native Hawaiian or other Pacific Islander, non-Hispanic/Latino. Average age 38. 72 applicants, 53% accepted, 35 enrolled. *Faculty:* 13 full-time (12 women). Expenses: Contact institution. *Financial support:* In 2010–11, 75 students received support, including fellowships with partial tuition reimbursements available (averaging $6,300 per year), research assistantships with partial tuition reimbursements available (averaging $3,000 per year), 3 teaching assistantships with partial tuition reimbursements available (averaging $3,000 per year); career-related internships or fieldwork, Federal Work-Study, institutionally sponsored loans, scholarships/grants, traineeships, and tuition waivers (partial) also available. Financial award application deadline: 4/15; financial award applicants required to submit FAFSA. In 2010, 38 master's awarded. *Degree program information:* Part-time programs available. Postbaccalaureate distance learning degree programs offered (no on-campus study). Offers family nurse practitioner (DNP); health systems leadership (DNP); nurse educator (MSN, Certificate). *Application deadline:* For fall admission, 7/1 for domestic and international students. *Application fee:* $30. Electronic applications accepted. *Application Contact:* Brenda Pereira, Director of Student Services, 850-644-5638, Fax: 850-645-7249, E-mail: bpereira@fsu.edu. *Dean,* Dr. Lisa Ann Plowfield, 850-644-3297, Fax: 850-644-7660, E-mail: lplowfield@nursing.fsu.edu.

College of Social Sciences and Public Policy Expenses: Contact institution. *Financial support:* Fellowships with full and partial tuition reimbursements, research assistantships with full and partial tuition reimbursements, teaching assistantships with full and partial tuition reimbursements, career-related internships or fieldwork, Federal Work-Study, institutionally sponsored loans, scholarships/grants, health care benefits, tuition waivers (full and partial), and unspecified assistantships available. Support available to part-time students. Financial award application deadline: 1/15; financial award applicants required to submit FAFSA. *Degree program information:* Part-time and evening/weekend programs available. Offers Asian studies (MA); demography and population health (MS); economics (MS, PhD); geographic information science (MS); geography (MA, MS, PhD); international affairs (MA, MS); political science (MA, MS, PhD); public administration and policy (MPA, PhD, Certificate); public health (MPH); Russian and East European studies (MA); social sciences and public policy (MA, MPA, MPH, MS, MSP, PhD, Certificate); sociology (MA, MS, PhD); urban and regional planning (MSP, PhD). *Application deadline:* For fall admission, 7/1 priority date for domestic and international students; for spring admission, 11/1 priority date for domestic students, 9/1 priority date for international students. Applications are processed on a rolling basis. Electronic applications accepted. *Application Contact:* Melanie Booker, Associate Director for Graduate Admissions, 850-644-3420, Fax: 850-644-0197, E-mail: mbooker@admin.fsu.edu. *Dean,* Dr. David W. Rasmussen, 850-644-5488, Fax: 850-645-4923, E-mail: drasmuss@coss.fsu.edu.

College of Social Work Students: 271 full-time (235 women), 215 part-time (186 women); includes 153 minority (95 Black or African American, non-Hispanic/Latino; 9 American Indian or Alaska Native, non-Hispanic/Latino; 11 Asian, non-Hispanic/Latino; 30 Hispanic/Latino; 1 Native Hawaiian or other Pacific Islander, non-Hispanic/Latino; 7 Two or more races, non-Hispanic/Latino), 3 international. Average age 28. 311 applicants, 75% accepted, 178 enrolled. *Faculty:* 35 full-time (22 women). Expenses: Contact institution. *Financial support:* In 2010–11, 54 students received support, including 3 fellowships with full tuition reimbursements available (averaging $22,000 per year), 49 research assistantships with partial tuition reimbursements available (averaging $3,500 per year), 12 teaching assistantships with full tuition reimbursements available (averaging $15,000 per year); career-related internships or fieldwork, Federal Work-Study, institutionally sponsored loans, scholarships/grants, traineeships, health care benefits, tuition waivers (partial), and unspecified assistantships also available. Support available to part-time students. Financial award application deadline: 3/1; financial award applicants required to submit FAFSA. In 2010, 166 master's, 7 doctorates awarded. *Degree program information:* Part-time and evening/weekend programs available. Postbaccalaureate distance learning degree programs offered (no on-campus study). Offers clinical social work (MSW); social policy and administration (MSW); social work (PhD). *Application deadline:* For fall admission, 5/1 priority date for domestic students; for winter admission, 3/1 priority date for domestic students; for spring admission, 10/1 priority date for domestic students. Applications are processed on a rolling basis. *Application fee:* $30. Electronic applications accepted. *Application Contact:* Craig Stanley, Director of the MSW Program, 800-378-9550, Fax: 850-644-1201, E-mail: grad@csw.fsu.edu. *Dean,* Dr. Nicholas Mazza, 850-644-4752, Fax: 850-644-9750.

College of Visual Arts, Theatre and Dance Students: 290 full-time (220 women), 60 part-time (35 women); includes 20 Black or African American, non-Hispanic/Latino; 15 Asian, non-Hispanic/Latino; 13 Hispanic/Latino, 4 international. Average age 26. 315 applicants, 37% accepted, 97 enrolled. *Faculty:* 88 full-time (46 women), 13 part-time/adjunct (12 women). Expenses: Contact institution. *Financial support:* In 2010–11, 5 fellowships with partial tuition reimbursements (averaging $18,000 per year), 90 research assistantships with partial tuition reimbursements (averaging $4,957 per year), 78 teaching assistantships with partial tuition reimbursements (averaging $8,001 per year) were awarded; career-related internships or fieldwork, Federal Work-Study, institutionally sponsored loans, scholarships/grants, and unspecified assistantships also available. Support available to part-time students. Financial award applicants required to submit FAFSA. In 2010, 95 master's, 20 doctorates, 7 other advanced degrees awarded. *Degree program information:* Part-time programs available. Offers American dance studies (MA); art (MFA); art education (MA, MS, Ed D, PhD, Ed S); art history (MA, PhD); dance (MFA); interior design (MA, MFA, MS); museum studies (Certificate); studio and related studies (MA); visual arts, theatre and dance (MA, MFA, MS, Ed D, PhD, Certificate, Ed S). *Application deadline:* For fall admission, 7/1 priority date for domestic students; for spring admission, 11/1 priority date for domestic students. Applications are processed on a rolling basis. *Application fee:* $30. Electronic applications accepted. *Application Contact:* Melanie Booker, Associate Director for Graduate Admissions, 850-644-3420, Fax: 850-644-0197, E-mail: mbooker@admin.fsu.edu. *Dean,* Dr. Sally E. McRorie, 850-664-5244, Fax: 850-644-2604, E-mail: smcrorie@mailer.fsu.edu.

FAMU-FSU College of Engineering Students: 251 full-time (54 women), 28 part-time (9 women); includes 41 Black or African American, non-Hispanic/Latino; 1 American Indian or Alaska Native, non-Hispanic/Latino; 5 Asian, non-Hispanic/Latino; 15 Hispanic/Latino, 124 international. Average age 29. 455 applicants, 43% accepted, 63 enrolled. *Faculty:* 76 full-time (9 women), 11 part-time/adjunct (2 women). Expenses: Contact institution. *Financial support:* In 2010–11, 233 students received support, including 8 fellowships with full tuition reimbursements available (averaging $18,000 per year), 113 research assistantships with full tuition reimbursements available (averaging $15,000 per year), 73 teaching assistantships with full tuition reimbursements available (averaging $15,000 per year); career-related internships or fieldwork, Federal Work-Study, institutionally sponsored loans, scholarships/grants, tuition waivers (full), and unspecified assistantships also available. Financial award application deadline: 6/15. In 2010, 53 master's, 23 doctorates awarded. *Degree program information:* Part-time programs available. Offers biomedical engineering (MS, PhD); chemical engineering (MS, PhD); civil and environmental engineering (MS, PhD); electrical engineering (MS, PhD); engineering (MS, PhD); industrial engineering (MS, PhD); mechanical engineering (MS, PhD); sustainable energy (MS). *Application deadline:* For fall admission, 7/1 for domestic and international students; for spring admission, 11/1 for domestic and international students. Applications are processed on a rolling basis. *Application fee:* $30. *Application Contact:* Dr. John Collier, Interim Dean and Professor, 850-410-6161, Fax: 850-410-6546, E-mail: dean@eng.fsu.edu. *Interim Dean and Professor,* Dr. John Collier, 850-410-6161, Fax: 850-410-6546, E-mail: dean@eng.fsu.edu.

School of Theatre Students: 103 full-time (51 women), 9 part-time (6 women); includes 3 Black or African American, non-Hispanic/Latino; 1 Asian, non-Hispanic/Latino; 4 Hispanic/Latino. Average age 25. 139 applicants, 24% accepted, 27 enrolled. *Faculty:* 20 full-time (10 women). Expenses: Contact institution. *Financial support:* In 2010–11, 1 fellowship with full tuition reimbursement (averaging $18,000 per year), 30 research assistantships with full tuition reimbursements (averaging $8,300 per year), 57 teaching assistantships with full tuition reimbursements (averaging $8,900 per year) were awarded; career-related internships or fieldwork, Federal Work-Study, institutionally sponsored loans, scholarships/grants, health care benefits, and unspecified assistantships also available. Financial award application deadline: 1/1; financial award applicants required to submit FAFSA. In 2010, 28 master's, 1 doctorate awarded. Offers acting (MFA); directing (MFA); lighting, costume, and scenic design (MFA); technical production (MFA); theater management (MFA); theatre (MA, MS, PhD). *Application deadline:* For fall admission, 2/15 priority date for domestic and international students. Applications are processed on a rolling basis. *Application fee:* $30. Electronic applications accepted. *Application Contact:* Barbara Thomas, Program Assistant, 850-644-7234, Fax: 850-644-7246, E-mail: bgthomas@admin.fsu.edu. *Director,* Cameron Jackson, 850-644-7257, Fax: 850-644-7408, E-mail: ccjackson@admin.fsu.edu.

FONTBONNE UNIVERSITY, St. Louis, MO 63105-3098

General Information Independent-religious, coed, comprehensive institution. *Enrollment:* 2,532 graduate, professional, and undergraduate students; 291 full-time matriculated graduate/professional students (226 women), 522 part-time matriculated graduate/professional students (401 women). *Enrollment by degree level:* 813 master's. *Graduate faculty:* 19 full-time (11 women), 49 part-time/adjunct (37 women). *Tuition:* Full-time $11,328. Full-time tuition and fees vary according to program. *Graduate housing:* Room and/or apartments available on a first-come, first-served basis to single students; on-campus housing not available to married students. Typical cost: $9000 (including board). Housing application deadline: 3/8. *Student services:* Career counseling, exercise/wellness program, free psychological counseling, international student services, multicultural affairs office, services for students with disabilities. *Library facilities:* The Jack C. Taylor Library at Fontbonne University. *Online resources:* library catalog, web page, access to other libraries' catalogs. *Collection:* 88,063 titles, 19,532 serial subscriptions, 3,084 audiovisual materials.

Computer facilities: Computer purchase and lease plans are available. 285 computers available on campus for general student use. A campuswide network can be accessed from student residence rooms and from off campus. Online class registration is available. *Web address:* http://www.fontbonne.edu/.

Fontbonne University (continued)

General Application Contact: Vice President of Enrollment Management, 314-889-1400, Fax: 314-889-1451.

GRADUATE UNITS

Graduate Programs Students: 291 full-time (226 women), 522 part-time (401 women); includes 255 Black or African American, non-Hispanic/Latino; 2 American Indian or Alaska Native, non-Hispanic/Latino; 6 Asian, non-Hispanic/Latino; 3 Hispanic/Latino, 46 international. Average age 35. *Faculty:* 19 full-time (11 women), 49 part-time/adjunct (37 women). Expenses: Contact institution. *Financial support:* Fellowships with full tuition reimbursements, teaching assistantships with partial tuition reimbursements available. Support available to part-time students. Financial award application deadline: 4/1; financial award applicants required to submit FAFSA. In 2010, 374 master's awarded. *Degree program information:* Part-time and evening/weekend programs available. Offers art (MA); computer education (MS); early intervention in deaf education (MA); education (MA); family and consumer sciences (MA); fine arts (MFA); speech-language pathology (MS); theater education (MA). *Application deadline:* For fall admission, 8/1 for international students; for spring admission, 12/1 for international students. Applications are processed on a rolling basis. *Application fee:* $25 ($30 for international students). Electronic applications accepted. *Application Contact:* Dr. Greg Taylor, Executive Vice President, 314-889-1400, E-mail: gtaylor@fontbonne.edu. *Vice President for Academic and Student Affairs,* Dr. John Bruno, 314-889-1401, Fax: 314-889-1451, E-mail: jbruno@fontbonne.edu.

College of Global Business and Professional Studies Students: 129 full-time (90 women), 254 part-time (166 women); includes 164 Black or African American, non-Hispanic/Latino; 1 American Indian or Alaska Native, non-Hispanic/Latino; 4 Asian, non-Hispanic/Latino; 1 Hispanic/Latino, 35 international. Average age 36. *Faculty:* 1 (woman) full-time, 24 part-time/adjunct (10 women). Expenses: Contact institution. *Financial support:* Available to part-time students. Application deadline: 4/1. In 2010, 213 master's awarded. *Degree program information:* Part-time and evening/weekend programs available. Offers accounting (MS); business administration (MBA); management (MM); taxation (MST). *Application deadline:* For fall admission, 8/1 priority date for domestic students. Applications are processed on a rolling basis. *Application fee:* $25. *Application Contact:* Fontbonne University OPTIONS, 314-863-2220, E-mail: options@fontbonne.edu. *Dean,* Linda Maurer, 314-889-1423, E-mail: lmaurer@fontbonne.edu.

FORDHAM UNIVERSITY, New York, NY 10458

General Information Independent-religious, coed, university. CGS member. *Enrollment:* 3,896 full-time matriculated graduate/professional students (2,343 women), 2,630 part-time matriculated graduate/professional students (1,547 women). *Enrollment by degree level:* 1,446 first professional, 4,121 master's, 848 doctoral, 111 other advanced degrees. *Graduate housing:* Room and/or apartments available on a first-come, first-served basis to single students; on-campus housing not available to married students. Housing application deadline: 4/10. *Student services:* Campus employment opportunities, campus safety program, career counseling, free psychological counseling, international student services, low-cost health insurance, services for students with disabilities, teacher training, writing training. *Library facilities:* Walsh Library plus 3 others. *Online resources:* library catalog, web page, access to other libraries' catalogs. *Collection:* 2.4 million titles, 32,300 serial subscriptions, 32,621 audiovisual materials. *Research affiliation:* Equator Initiative /UNDP, Folger Shakespeare Library, New York Botanical Gardens, New York Ocean Science Library, Wildlife Conservation Society, Memorial Sloan-Kettering Cancer Center.

Computer facilities: Computer purchase and lease plans are available. 1,400 computers available on campus for general student use. A campuswide network can be accessed from student residence rooms and from off campus. Online class registration is available. *Web address:* http://www.fordham.edu/.

General Application Contact: Charlene Dundie, Director of Graduate Admissions, 718-817-4420, Fax: 718-817-3566, E-mail: dundie@fordham.edu.

GRADUATE UNITS

Graduate School of Arts and Sciences Students: 313 full-time (159 women), 644 part-time (313 women); includes 34 Black or African American, non-Hispanic/Latino; 5 American Indian or Alaska Native, non-Hispanic/Latino; 30 Asian, non-Hispanic/Latino; 51 Hispanic/Latino, 260 international. Average age 30. 1,512 applicants, 32% accepted, 165 enrolled. *Faculty:* 249 full-time (81 women). Expenses: Contact institution. *Financial support:* In 2010–11, 26 fellowships with full and partial tuition reimbursements (averaging $22,625 per year), 114 research assistantships with full and partial tuition reimbursements (averaging $18,900 per year), 139 teaching assistantships with full and partial tuition reimbursements (averaging $20,400 per year) were awarded; career-related internships or fieldwork, Federal Work-Study, institutionally sponsored loans, scholarships/grants, health care benefits, tuition waivers (full and partial), and unspecified assistantships also available. Support available to part-time students. Financial award application deadline: 1/4; financial award applicants required to submit FAFSA. In 2010, 212 master's, 44 doctorates, 20 other advanced degrees awarded. *Degree program information:* Part-time and evening/weekend programs available. Offers applied developmental psychology (PhD); arts and sciences (MA, MS, PhD, Certificate); biological sciences (MS, PhD); classical Greek and Latin literature (MA); classics (PhD); clinical psychology (PhD); computer science (MS); economics (MA, PhD); elections and campaign management (MA); English language and literature (MA, PhD); history (MA, PhD); humanities and sciences (MA); international humanitarian action (MA); international political economy and development (MA, Certificate); Latin American and Latino studies (MA, Certificate); philosophical resources (MA); philosophy (MA, PhD); psychometrics (PhD); public communications (MA); sociology (MA); theology (MA, PhD); urban studies (MA). *Application deadline:* For fall admission, 1/4 priority date for domestic and international students; for spring admission, 10/31 for domestic and international students. *Application fee:* $70. Electronic applications accepted. *Application Contact:* Charlene Dundie, Director of Graduate Admissions, 718-817-4420, Fax: 718-817-3566, E-mail: dundie@fordham.edu. *Dean,* Dr. Nancy A. Busch, 718-817-4400, Fax: 718-817-4474, E-mail: busch@fordham.edu.

Center for Ethics Education Students: 4 full-time (2 women), 10 part-time (7 women); includes 1 Hispanic/Latino, 1 international. 9 applicants, 100% accepted, 8 enrolled. Expenses: Contact institution. *Financial support:* In 2010–11, 1 student received support. Federal Work-Study, institutionally sponsored loans, scholarships/grants, tuition waivers (partial), and unspecified assistantships available. Financial award application deadline: 1/4. *Degree program information:* Part-time programs available. Offers ethics and society (MA); health care ethics (Certificate). *Application deadline:* For fall admission, 1/4 priority date for domestic students; for spring admission, 10/31 for domestic students. *Application fee:* $65. Electronic applications accepted. *Application Contact:* Charlene Dundie, Director of Graduate Admissions, 718-817-4420, Fax: 718-817-3566, E-mail: dundie@fordham.edu. *Director,* Dr. Celia Fisher, 718-817-3793, Fax: 212-759-2009, E-mail: fisher@fordham.edu.

Center for Medieval Studies Students: 12 full-time (4 women), 11 part-time (9 women); includes 1 Asian, non-Hispanic/Latino. Average age 28. 34 applicants, 59% accepted, 9 enrolled. Expenses: Contact institution. *Financial support:* In 2010–11, 4 students received support, including 4 research assistantships with tuition reimbursements available (averaging $17,915 per year); institutionally sponsored loans, tuition waivers (full and partial), and unspecified assistantships also available. Financial award application deadline: 1/4; financial award applicants required to submit FAFSA. In 2010, 5 master's awarded. *Degree program information:* Part-time and evening/weekend programs available. Offers medieval studies (MA, Certificate). *Application deadline:* For fall admission, 1/4 priority date for domestic students; for spring admission, 11/1 for domestic students. *Application fee:* $70. Electronic applications accepted. *Application Contact:* Charlene Dundie, Director of Graduate Admissions, 718-817-4420, Fax: 718-817-3566, E-mail: dundie@fordham.edu. *Director,* Dr. Maryanne Kowaleski, 718-817-4655, E-mail: kowaleski@fordham.edu.

Graduate School of Business *Degree program information:* Part-time and evening/weekend programs available. Offers accounting (MBA); business (EMBA, MBA, MS, MTA); communications and media management (MBA); executive business administration (EMBA); finance (MBA, MS); information systems (MBA, MS); management systems (MBA); marketing (MBA); media management (MS); taxation (MS); taxation and accounting (MTA). MBA/MIM offered jointly with Thunderbird School of Global Management. Electronic applications accepted.

Graduate School of Education *Degree program information:* Part-time and evening/weekend programs available. Offers education (MAT, MS, MSE, MST, Ed D, PhD, Adv C).

Division of Curriculum and Teaching Offers adult education (MS, MSE); bilingual teacher education (MSE); curriculum and teaching (MSE); early childhood education (MSE); elementary education (MST); language, literacy, and learning (PhD); reading education (MSE, Adv C); secondary education (MAT, MSE); special education (MSE, Adv C); teaching English as a second language (MSE).

Division of Educational Leadership, Administration and Policy Offers administration and supervision (MSE, Adv C); administration and supervision for church leaders (PhD); educational administration and supervision (Ed D, PhD); human resource program administration (MS).

Division of Psychological and Educational Services Offers counseling and personnel services (MSE, Adv C); counseling psychology (PhD); educational psychology (MSE, PhD); school psychology (PhD); urban and urban bilingual school psychology (Adv C).

Graduate School of Religion and Religious Education *Degree program information:* Part-time programs available. Offers pastoral counseling and spiritual care (MA); pastoral ministry/spirituality/pastoral counseling (D Min); religion and religious education (MA); religious education (MS, PhD, PD); spiritual direction (Certificate). Electronic applications accepted.

Graduate School of Social Service *Degree program information:* Part-time and evening/weekend programs available. Offers social work (PhD). Electronic applications accepted.

School of Law *Degree program information:* Part-time and evening/weekend programs available. Offers banking, corporate and finance law (LL M); intellectual property and information law (LL M); international business and trade law (LL M); law (JD). Electronic applications accepted.

See Close-Up on page 947.

FORT HAYS STATE UNIVERSITY, Hays, KS 67601-4099

General Information State-supported, coed, comprehensive institution. CGS member. *Graduate housing:* Rooms and/or apartments available to single and married students. Housing application deadline: 8/1.

GRADUATE UNITS

Graduate School *Degree program information:* Part-time programs available. Electronic applications accepted.

College of Arts and Sciences *Degree program information:* Part-time programs available. Offers arts and sciences (MA, MFA, MLS, MS, Ed S); communication (MS); English (MA); geography (MS); geology (MS); geosciences (MS); history (MA); liberal studies (MLS); psychology (MS); school psychology (Ed S); studio art (MFA). Electronic applications accepted.

College of Business and Leadership *Degree program information:* Part-time programs available. Offers business and leadership (MBA); management (MBA). Electronic applications accepted.

College of Education and Technology *Degree program information:* Part-time programs available. Offers counseling (MS); education (MSE); education and technology (MS, MSE, Ed S); educational administration (MS, Ed S); instructional technology (MS); special education (MS). Electronic applications accepted.

College of Health and Life Sciences *Degree program information:* Part-time programs available. Offers biology (MS); health and human performance (MS); health and life sciences (MS, MSN); nursing (MSN); speech-language pathology (MS). Electronic applications accepted.

FORT VALLEY STATE UNIVERSITY, Fort Valley, GA 31030

General Information State-supported, coed, comprehensive institution. *Graduate housing:* Room and/or apartments available on a first-come, first-served basis to single students; on-campus housing not available to married students. Housing application deadline: 7/21.

GRADUATE UNITS

College of Graduate Studies and Extended Education *Degree program information:* Part-time programs available. Offers animal science (MS); environmental health (MPH); guidance and counseling (Ed S); mental health counseling (MS); rehabilitation counseling (MS).

FRAMINGHAM STATE UNIVERSITY, Framingham, MA 01701-9101

General Information State-supported, coed, comprehensive institution. *Graduate housing:* On-campus housing not available.

GRADUATE UNITS

Division of Graduate and Continuing Education *Degree program information:* Part-time and evening/weekend programs available. Offers art (M Ed); business administration (MBA); counseling psychology (MA); curriculum and instructional technology (M Ed); dietetics (MS); early childhood education (M Ed); educational leadership (MA); elementary education (M Ed); English (M Ed); food science and nutrition science (MS); health care administration (MA); history (M Ed); human nutrition: education and media technologies (MS); human resource management (MA); literacy and language (M Ed); mathematics (M Ed); nursing education (MSN); nursing leadership (MSN); public administration (MA); Spanish (M Ed); special education (M Ed); teaching of English as a second language (M Ed).

FRANCISCAN SCHOOL OF THEOLOGY, Berkeley, CA 94709-1294

General Information Independent-religious, coed, graduate-only institution. *Graduate housing:* Rooms and/or apartments available on a first-come, first-served basis to single and married students. Housing application deadline: 5/15.

GRADUATE UNITS

Graduate and Professional Programs *Degree program information:* Part-time programs available. Offers theology (M Div, MA, MAMC, MTS).

FRANCISCAN UNIVERSITY OF STEUBENVILLE, Steubenville, OH 43952-1763

General Information Independent-religious, coed, comprehensive institution. *Graduate housing:* On-campus housing not available.

GRADUATE UNITS

Graduate Programs *Degree program information:* Part-time and evening/weekend programs available. Postbaccalaureate distance learning degree programs offered (minimal on-campus study). Offers administration (MS Ed); business (MBA); counseling (MA); nursing (MSN); philosophy (MA); teaching (MS Ed); theology and Christian ministry (MA).

FRANCIS MARION UNIVERSITY, Florence, SC 29502-0547

General Information State-supported, coed, comprehensive institution. *Enrollment:* 4,032 graduate, professional, and undergraduate students; 37 full-time matriculated graduate/professional students (29 women), 149 part-time matriculated graduate/professional students (111 women). *Enrollment by degree level:* 186 master's. *Graduate faculty:* 118 full-time (45 women), 5 part-time/adjunct (4 women). Tuition, state resident: full-time $8667; part-time $433.35 per credit hour. Tuition, nonresident: full-time $17,334; part-time $866.70 per credit hour. *Required fees:* $335; $12.25 per credit hour. $30 per semester. *Graduate housing:* Room and/or apartments available on a first-come, first-served basis to single students; on-campus housing not available to married students. Typical cost: $3730 per year ($6620 including board). Housing application deadline: 8/1. *Student services:* Campus employment opportunities, campus safety program, career counseling, child daycare facilities, free psychological counseling, international student services, low-cost health insurance, multicultural affairs office, services for students with disabilities, teacher training. *Library facilities:* James A. Rogers Library plus 1 other. *Online resources:* library catalog, web page, access to other libraries' catalogs. *Collection:* 409,684 titles, 1,158 serial subscriptions, 9,503 audiovisual materials.

Computer facilities: 590 computers available on campus for general student use. A campuswide network can be accessed from student residence rooms and from off campus. Online class registration, Blackboard are available. *Web address:* http://www.fmarion.edu/.

General Application Contact: Rannie Gamble, Administrative Manager, 843-661-1286, Fax: 843-661-4688, E-mail: rgamble@fmarion.edu.

GRADUATE UNITS

Graduate Programs Students: 37 full-time (29 women), 149 part-time (111 women); includes 37 Black or African American, non-Hispanic/Latino; 2 Asian, non-Hispanic/Latino; 1 Hispanic/Latino, 5 international. Average age 30. 253 applicants, 93% accepted, 81 enrolled. *Faculty:* 118 full-time (45 women), 5 part-time/adjunct (4 women). Expenses: Contact institution. *Financial support:* In 2010–11, 5 research assistantships (averaging $6,400 per year), 3 teaching assistantships (averaging $8,000 per year) were awarded; career-related internships or fieldwork and unspecified assistantships also available. Support available to part-time students. Financial award application deadline: 3/1; financial award applicants required to submit FAFSA. In 2010, 73 master's awarded. *Degree program information:* Part-time and evening/weekend programs available. Offers applied psychology (MS); school psychology (SSP). *Application deadline:* For fall admission, 3/15 priority date for domestic students; for spring admission, 10/15 priority date for domestic students. Applications are processed on a rolling basis. *Application fee:* $30. *Application Contact:* Provost's Office, 843-661-1284, Fax: 843-661-4688. *Provost's Office*, 843-661-1284, Fax: 843-661-4688.

School of Business Students: 9 full-time (6 women), 40 part-time (14 women); includes 11 Black or African American, non-Hispanic/Latino; 1 Hispanic/Latino, 3 international. Average age 30. 18 applicants, 100% accepted, 12 enrolled. *Faculty:* 17 full-time (4 women). Expenses: Contact institution. *Financial support:* Research assistantships, unspecified assistantships available. Support available to part-time students. Financial award application deadline: 3/1; financial award applicants required to submit FAFSA. In 2010, 15 master's awarded. *Degree program information:* Part-time and evening/weekend programs available. Offers business (MBA); health management (MBA). *Application deadline:* For fall admission, 3/15 priority date for domestic students; for spring admission, 10/15 priority date for domestic students. Applications are processed on a rolling basis. *Application fee:* $30. *Application Contact:* Dr. M. Barry O'Brien, Dean, 843-661-1419, Fax: 843-661-1432, E-mail: mbobrien@fmarion.edu. *Dean*, Dr. M. Barry O'Brien, 843-661-1419, Fax: 843-661-1432, E-mail: mbobrien@fmarion.edu.

School of Education Students: 11 full-time (7 women), 83 part-time (72 women); includes 20 Black or African American, non-Hispanic/Latino; 2 Asian, non-Hispanic/Latino, 2 international. Average age 32. 191 applicants, 100% accepted, 55 enrolled. *Faculty:* 21 full-time (16 women). Expenses: Contact institution. *Financial support:* In 2010–11, 3 research assistantships (averaging $6,000 per year) were awarded; unspecified assistantships also available. Support available to part-time students. Financial award application deadline: 3/1; financial award applicants required to submit FAFSA. In 2010, 49 master's awarded. *Degree program information:* Part-time programs available. Offers early childhood education (M Ed); elementary education (M Ed); learning disabilities (M Ed, MAT); remedial education (M Ed); secondary education (M Ed). *Application deadline:* For fall admission, 3/15 priority date for domestic students; for spring admission, 10/15 priority date for domestic students. Applications are processed on a rolling basis. *Application fee:* $30. *Application Contact:* Dr. James R. Faulkenberry, Dean, 843-661-1460, Fax: 843-661-4647. *Dean*, Dr. James R. Faulkenberry, 843-661-1460, Fax: 843-661-4647.

FRANKLIN PIERCE LAW CENTER, Concord, NH 03301-4197

General Information Independent, coed, graduate-only institution. *Graduate housing:* On-campus housing not available. *Research affiliation:* Patent, Trademark, and Copyright Research Foundation, Institute for Health Law and Ethics, Academy of Applied Science.

GRADUATE UNITS

Professional Program Offers intellectual property (Diploma); intellectual property, commerce and technology (LL M, MIP); law (JD). Diploma awarded as part of Intellectual Property Summer Institute. Electronic applications accepted.

FRANKLIN PIERCE UNIVERSITY, Rindge, NH 03461-0060

General Information Independent, coed, university. *Enrollment:* 2,396 graduate, professional, and undergraduate students; 100 full-time matriculated graduate/professional students (63 women), 487 part-time matriculated graduate/professional students (306 women). *Enrollment by degree level:* 342 master's, 245 doctoral. *Graduate faculty:* 28 full-time (18 women), 72 part-time/adjunct (44 women). *Tuition:* Part-time $573 per credit hour. Part-time tuition and fees vary according to degree level and program. *Graduate housing:* On-campus housing not available. *Student services:* Campus employment opportunities, career counseling, exercise/wellness program, low-cost health insurance, services for students with disabilities. *Library facilities:* Frank S. DiPietro Library plus 1 other. *Online resources:* library catalog, web page. *Collection:* 144,770 titles, 30,093 serial subscriptions, 10,312 audiovisual materials.

Computer facilities: Computer purchase and lease plans are available. 60 computers available on campus for general student use. A campuswide network can be accessed from student residence rooms. Online class registration is available. *Web address:* http://www.franklinpierce.edu/.

General Application Contact: Graduate Studies, 800-437-0048, Fax: 603-626-4815, E-mail: cgps@franklinpierce.edu.

GRADUATE UNITS

Graduate Studies Students: 100 full-time (63 women), 487 part-time (306 women); includes 42 minority (25 Black or African American, non-Hispanic/Latino; 10 Asian, non-Hispanic/Latino; 6 Hispanic/Latino; 1 Two or more races, non-Hispanic/Latino), 67 international. Average age 38. 227 applicants, 97% accepted, 185 enrolled. *Faculty:* 28 full-time (18 women), 72 part-time/adjunct (44 women). Expenses: Contact institution. *Financial support:* In 2010–11, 121 students received support, including 32 teaching assistantships with full and partial tuition reimbursements available (averaging $8,000 per year); career-related internships or fieldwork and unspecified assistantships also available. Support available to part-time students. Financial award applicants required to submit FAFSA. In 2010, 76 master's, 46 doctorates awarded. *Degree program information:* Part-time programs available. Postbaccalaureate distance learning degree programs offered (no on-campus study). Offers curriculum and instruction (M Ed); emerging network technologies (Graduate Certificate); energy and sustainability studies (MBA); health administration (MBA, Graduate Certificate); human resource management (MBA, Graduate Certificate); information technology (MBA); information technology management (MS); leadership (MBA, DA); nursing (MS); physical therapy (DPT); physician assistant studies (MPAS); special education (M Ed); sports management (MBA). *Application deadline:* Applications are processed on a rolling basis. *Application fee:* $0. Electronic applications accepted. *Interim Dean of Graduate and Professional Studies*, Dr. Patricia Brown, 603-899-4316, Fax: 603-229-4580, E-mail: brownp@franklinpierce.edu.

FRANKLIN UNIVERSITY, Columbus, OH 43215-5399

General Information Independent, coed, comprehensive institution. *Enrollment:* 8,018 graduate, professional, and undergraduate students; 726 full-time matriculated graduate/professional students (405 women), 217 part-time matriculated graduate/professional students (131 women). *Enrollment by degree level:* 943 master's. *Tuition:* Full-time $9720; part-time $540 per credit hour. One-time fee: $30. Tuition and fees vary according to program. *Graduate housing:* On-campus housing not available. *Student services:* Campus employment opportunities, international student services, services for students with disabilities, writing training. *Library facilities:* Franklin University Library. *Online resources:* library catalog, web page, access to other libraries' catalogs.

Computer facilities: A campuswide network can be accessed. Online class registration is available. *Web address:* http://www.franklin.edu/.

General Application Contact: Graduate Services Office, 614-797-4700, Fax: 614-221-7723, E-mail: gradschl@franklin.edu.

GRADUATE UNITS

Computer Science Program Students: 22 full-time (6 women), 22 part-time (8 women); includes 8 minority (3 Black or African American, non-Hispanic/Latino; 5 Asian, non-Hispanic/Latino), 13 international. Average age 35. Expenses: Contact institution. *Financial support:* Application deadline: 6/15. In 2010, 23 master's awarded. *Degree program information:* Part-time and evening/weekend programs available. Offers computer science (MS). *Application deadline:* For fall admission, 8/1 priority date for domestic students, 6/1 for international students; for winter admission, 12/1 priority date for domestic students, 10/1 for international students; for spring admission, 3/15 priority date for domestic students, 2/1 for international students. Applications are processed on a rolling basis. *Application fee:* $30. Electronic applications accepted. *Application Contact:* 614-797-4700, Fax: 614-221-7723, E-mail: gradschl@franklin.edu. *Program Chair*, Dr. Ron Hartung, 614-947-6139, Fax: 614-224-4025, E-mail: hartung@franklin.edu.

Graduate School of Business Students: 585 full-time (316 women), 158 part-time (95 women); includes 132 minority (106 Black or African American, non-Hispanic/Latino; 18 Asian, non-Hispanic/Latino; 8 Hispanic/Latino), 65 international. Average age 33. Expenses: Contact institution. *Financial support:* Application deadline: 6/15. In 2010, 368 master's awarded. *Degree program information:* Part-time and evening/weekend programs available. Postbaccalaureate distance learning degree programs offered (no on-campus study). Offers business (MBA). *Application deadline:* For fall admission, 9/1 priority date for domestic students, 6/1 for international students; for winter admission, 1/15 priority date for domestic students, 10/1 for international students; for spring admission, 4/15 priority date for domestic students, 2/1 for international students. Applications are processed on a rolling basis. *Application fee:* $30. Electronic applications accepted. *Application Contact:* Graduate Services Office, 614-797-4700, Fax: 614-221-7723, E-mail: gradschl@franklin.edu. *Program Chair*, Dr. Doug Ross, 614-947-6149, Fax: 614-224-4025.

Marketing and Communications Program Students: 109 full-time (77 women), 37 part-time (28 women); includes 21 minority (17 Black or African American, non-Hispanic/Latino; 3 Asian, non-Hispanic/Latino; 1 Hispanic/Latino), 2 international. Average age 34. Expenses: Contact institution. *Financial support:* Application deadline: 6/30. In 2010, 33 master's awarded. *Degree program information:* Part-time and evening/weekend programs available. Offers marketing and communications (MS). *Application deadline:* For fall admission, 8/1 priority date for domestic students, 6/1 for international students; for winter admission, 12/1 priority date for domestic students, 10/1 for international students; for spring admission, 4/15 priority date for domestic students, 2/1 for international students. Applications are processed on a rolling basis. *Application fee:* $30. Electronic applications accepted. *Application Contact:* Graduate Services Office, 614-797-4700, Fax: 614-224-7723, E-mail: gradschl@franklin.edu. *Program Chair*, Dr. Doug Ross, 614-947-6149.

FRANK LLOYD WRIGHT SCHOOL OF ARCHITECTURE, Scottsdale, AZ 85261-4430

General Information Independent, coed, graduate-only institution. *Graduate housing:* Rooms and/or apartments guaranteed to single students and available on a first-come, first-served basis to married students.

GRADUATE UNITS

Graduate Program Offers architecture (M Arch). Summer session held in Spring Green, WI.

FREDERICK S. PARDEE RAND GRADUATE SCHOOL, Santa Monica, CA 90407-2138

General Information Independent, coed, graduate-only institution. *Enrollment by degree level:* 102 doctoral. *Graduate faculty:* 1 full-time (0 women), 142 part-time/adjunct (38 women). *Tuition:* Full-time $25,000. Full-time tuition and fees vary according to student level. *Graduate housing:* On-campus housing not available. *Student services:* Campus employment opportunities, career counseling, free psychological counseling, grant writing training, international student services, low-cost health insurance, writing training. *Library facilities:* RAND Corporation Library. *Collection:* 240,000 titles, 9,300 serial subscriptions, 1,290 audiovisual materials. *Research affiliation:* RAND Corporation (not-for-profit research).

Computer facilities: 96 computers available on campus for general student use. A campuswide network can be accessed from student residence rooms and from off campus. Online class registration is available. *Web address:* http://www.prgs.edu/.

General Application Contact: Dr. Stefanie Stern, Assistant Dean, 310-393-0411 Ext. 8224, Fax: 310-451-6978, E-mail: stern@rand.org.

GRADUATE UNITS

Program in Policy Analysis Students: 102 full-time (44 women); includes 1 Black or African American, non-Hispanic/Latino; 7 Asian, non-Hispanic/Latino; 2 Hispanic/Latino, 43 international. Average age 28. 126 applicants, 24% accepted, 22 enrolled. *Faculty:* 1 full-time (0 women), 142 part-time/adjunct (38 women). Expenses: Contact institution. *Financial support:* Fellowships, research assistantships, teaching assistantships, career-related internships or fieldwork available. Offers policy analysis (PhD). *Application deadline:* For fall admission, 1/5 for domestic and international students. *Application fee:* $50. Electronic applications accepted. *Application Contact:* Dr. Stefanie Stern, Assistant Dean, 310-393-0411 Ext. 8224, Fax: 310-451-6978, E-mail: stern@rand.org. *Dean*, Dr. Susan L. Marquis, 310-393-0411 Ext. 7075, Fax: 310-451-6978.

FREED-HARDEMAN UNIVERSITY, Henderson, TN 38340-2399

General Information Independent-religious, coed, comprehensive institution. *Graduate housing:* Room and/or apartments available on a first-come, first-served basis to single students; on-campus housing not available to married students. Housing application deadline: 8/22.

GRADUATE UNITS

Program in Business Administration *Degree program information:* Part-time and evening/weekend programs available. Postbaccalaureate distance learning degree programs offered (no on-campus study). Offers accounting (MBA); corporate responsibility (MBA); leadership (MBA).

Program in Counseling *Degree program information:* Part-time and evening/weekend programs available. Offers counseling (MS).

Program in Education *Degree program information:* Part-time and evening/weekend programs available. Offers curriculum and instruction (M Ed); school counseling (M Ed); school leadership (Ed S).

School of Biblical Studies *Degree program information:* Part-time programs available. Offers biblical studies (M Div, M Min, MA); divinity (M Div); ministry (M Min); New Testament (MA).

FRESNO PACIFIC UNIVERSITY, Fresno, CA 93702-4709

General Information Independent-religious, coed, comprehensive institution. *Graduate housing:* On-campus housing not available.

GRADUATE UNITS

Fresno Pacific Biblical Seminary *Degree program information:* Part-time programs available. Postbaccalaureate distance learning degree programs offered (minimal on-campus study). Offers Christian ministry (MA); divinity (M Div); intercultural mission (MA); marriage, family, and child counseling (MAMFCC, Diploma); New Testament (MA); Old Testament (MA); theology (MA).

Graduate Programs *Degree program information:* Part-time and evening/weekend programs available. Offers individualized study (MA); kinesiology (MA); leadership and organizational studies (MA); peacemaking and conflict studies (MA). Electronic applications accepted.

Fresno Pacific University (continued)

School of Education *Degree program information:* Part-time and evening/weekend programs available. Offers administration (MA Ed); administrative services (MA Ed); bilingual/cross-cultural education (MA Ed); curriculum and teaching (MA Ed); educational technology (MA Ed); elementary and middle school mathematics (MA Ed); foundations, curriculum and teaching (MA Ed); integrated mathematics/science education (MA Ed); language development (MA Ed); language, literacy, and culture (MA Ed); literacy in multilingual contexts (MA Ed); mathematics education (MA Ed); mathematics/science/computer education (MA Ed); mild/moderate (MA Ed); moderate/severe (MA Ed); physical and health impairments (MA Ed); pupil personnel services (MA Ed); reading (MA Ed); reading/English as a second language (MA Ed); reading/language arts (MA Ed); school counseling (MA Ed); school library and information technology (MA Ed); school psychology (MA Ed); secondary school mathematics (MA Ed); special education (MA Ed); teaching English to speakers of other languages (MA). Electronic applications accepted.

FRIENDS UNIVERSITY, Wichita, KS 67213

General Information Independent-religious, coed, comprehensive institution. *Enrollment:* 2,800 graduate, professional, and undergraduate students; 166 full-time matriculated graduate/professional students (122 women), 507 part-time matriculated graduate/professional students (290 women). *Enrollment by degree level:* 673 master's. *Graduate faculty:* 14 full-time (5 women), 2 part-time/adjunct (1 woman). Tuition and fees vary according to course load, campus/location and program. *Graduate housing:* Rooms and/or apartments available on a first-come, first-served basis to single and married students. Typical cost: $2650 per year ($5790 including board) for single students; $2650 per year ($5790 including board) for married students. Room and board charges vary according to board plan and housing facility selected. Housing application deadline: 8/1. *Student services:* Campus employment opportunities, campus safety program, career counseling, free psychological counseling, international student services, services for students with disabilities, teacher training, writing training. *Library facilities:* Edmund Stanley Library plus 1 other. *Online resources:* library catalog, web page. *Collection:* 110,945 titles, 22,127 serial subscriptions, 7,371 audiovisual materials.

Computer facilities: 360 computers available on campus for general student use. A campuswide network can be accessed from student residence rooms and from off campus. *Web address:* http://www.friends.edu/.

General Application Contact: Jeanette Hanson, Executive Director of Adult Recruitment, 800-794-6945, Fax: 316-295-5050, E-mail: jeanette@friends.edu.

GRADUATE UNITS

Graduate School Students: 166 full-time (122 women), 507 part-time (290 women); includes 134 minority (64 Black or African American, non-Hispanic/Latino; 6 American Indian or Alaska Native, non-Hispanic/Latino; 24 Asian, non-Hispanic/Latino; 30 Hispanic/Latino; 1 Native Hawaiian or other Pacific Islander, non-Hispanic/Latino; 9 Two or more races, non-Hispanic/Latino). Average age 38. 445 applicants, 69% accepted, 236 enrolled. *Faculty:* 14 full-time (5 women), 2 part-time/adjunct (1 woman). Expenses: Contact institution. *Financial support:* Applicants required to submit FAFSA. In 2010, 345 master's awarded. *Degree program information:* Part-time and evening/weekend programs available. Postbaccalaureate distance learning degree programs offered (minimal on-campus study). Offers accounting (MBA); business administration (MBA); business law (MBL); Christian ministry (MACM); family therapy (MSFT); global leadership and management (MA); health care leadership (MHCL); management information systems (MMIS); operations management (MSOM); organization development (MSOD); teaching (MAT). *Application deadline:* Applications are processed on a rolling basis. *Application fee:* $45 ($65 for international students). Electronic applications accepted. *Application Contact:* Jeanette Hanson, Executive Director of Adult Recruitment, 800-794-6945, Fax: 316-295-5050, E-mail: jeanette@friends.edu. *Dean,* Dr. Evelyn Hume, 800-794-6945 Ext. 5859, Fax: 316-295-5040, E-mail: evelyn_hume@friends.edu.

FRONTIER SCHOOL OF MIDWIFERY AND FAMILY NURSING, Hyden, KY 41749

General Information Independent, coed, primarily women, graduate-only institution.

GRADUATE UNITS

Graduate Programs

FROSTBURG STATE UNIVERSITY, Frostburg, MD 21532-1099

General Information State-supported, coed, comprehensive institution. *Graduate housing:* Room and/or apartments available to single students; on-campus housing not available to married students. Housing application deadline: 6/1.

GRADUATE UNITS

Graduate School *Degree program information:* Part-time and evening/weekend programs available. Electronic applications accepted.

College of Business *Degree program information:* Part-time and evening/weekend programs available. Offers business (MBA); business administration (MBA). Electronic applications accepted.

College of Education *Degree program information:* Part-time and evening/weekend programs available. Offers curriculum and instruction (M Ed); education (M Ed, MAT, MS); educational administration and supervision (M Ed); educational technology (M Ed); elementary (M Ed); elementary education (M Ed); elementary teaching (MAT); interdisciplinary education (M Ed); parks and recreational management (MS); reading (M Ed); school counseling (M Ed); secondary (M Ed); secondary education (M Ed); secondary teaching (MAT); special education (M Ed). Electronic applications accepted.

College of Liberal Arts and Sciences *Degree program information:* Part-time and evening/weekend programs available. Offers applied computer science (MS); applied ecology and conservation biology (MS); counseling psychology (MS); fisheries and wildlife management (MS); liberal arts and sciences (MS). Electronic applications accepted.

FULLER THEOLOGICAL SEMINARY, Pasadena, CA 91182

General Information Independent-religious, coed, graduate-only institution. *Graduate housing:* Rooms and/or apartments available on a first-come, first-served basis to single students and available to married students.

GRADUATE UNITS

Graduate School of Psychology Offers clinical psychology (PhD, Psy D); family studies (MA); marital and family therapy (MS); marriage and family enrichment (Certificate); psychology (MA, MS, PhD, Psy D, Certificate).

Graduate School of Theology *Degree program information:* Part-time and evening/weekend programs available. Offers Christian leadership (MACL); evangelism (MA); family life education (MA); ministry (M Div, D Min); pastoral ministry (MA); recovery ministry (MA); theology (MAT, Th M, PhD); worship music ministry (MA); worship, theology, and the arts (MA); youth, family, and culture (MA). M Div offered jointly with Denver Conservative Baptist Seminary; D Min with Tyndale University College & Seminary.

School of Intercultural Studies *Degree program information:* Part-time and evening/weekend programs available. Offers cross-cultural studies (MA); global leadership (MA); global ministries (D Min); global ministry (Korean language) (D Min); intercultural studies (MA, Th M, PhD); intercultural studies (Korean language) (MA); missiology (D Miss); missiology (Korean language) (Th M).

FULL SAIL UNIVERSITY, Winter Park, FL 32792-7437

General Information Proprietary, coed, primarily men, comprehensive institution. *Graduate housing:* On-campus housing not available.

GRADUATE UNITS

Creative Writing Master of Fine Arts Program—Online Postbaccalaureate distance learning degree programs offered (no on-campus study). Offers creative writing (MFA).

Education Media Design and Technology Master of Science Program—Online Postbaccalaureate distance learning degree programs offered (no on-campus study). Offers education media design and technology (MS).

Entertainment Business Master of Science Program—Campus Offers entertainment business (MS).

Entertainment Business Master of Science Program—Online Postbaccalaureate distance learning degree programs offered. Offers entertainment business (MS).

Game Design Master of Science Program—Campus Offers game design (MS).

Internet Marketing Master of Science Program—Online Postbaccalaureate distance learning degree programs offered. Offers Internet marketing (MS).

Media Design Master of Fine Arts Program—Online Postbaccalaureate distance learning degree programs offered. Offers media design (MFA).

New Media Journalism Master of Arts Program—Online Offers new media journalism (MA).

FURMAN UNIVERSITY, Greenville, SC 29613

General Information Independent, coed, comprehensive institution. *Enrollment:* 2,996 graduate, professional, and undergraduate students; 2 full-time matriculated graduate/professional students, 232 part-time matriculated graduate/professional students (177 women). *Enrollment by degree level:* 234 master's. *Graduate faculty:* 23 full-time (11 women), 11 part-time/adjunct (7 women). *Graduate housing:* On-campus housing not available. *Student services:* Campus employment opportunities, campus safety program, career counseling, child daycare facilities, exercise/wellness program, free psychological counseling, international student services, multicultural affairs office, services for students with disabilities, teacher training. *Library facilities:* James Buchanan Duke Library plus 2 others. *Online resources:* library catalog, web page, access to other libraries' catalogs. *Collection:* 526,690 titles, 13,200 serial subscriptions.

Computer facilities: Computer purchase and lease plans are available. 425 computers available on campus for general student use. A campuswide network can be accessed from student residence rooms and from off campus. Online class registration is available. *Web address:* http://www.furman.edu/.

General Application Contact: Dr. Troy M. Terry, Director of Graduate Studies, 864-294-2213, Fax: 864-294-3579, E-mail: troy.terry@furman.edu.

GRADUATE UNITS

Graduate Division Students: 2 full-time (0 women), 232 part-time (177 women); includes 22 minority (16 Black or African American, non-Hispanic/Latino; 4 Asian, non-Hispanic/Latino; 2 Hispanic/Latino). Average age 29. 80 applicants, 100% accepted, 75 enrolled. *Faculty:* 23 full-time (11 women), 11 part-time/adjunct (7 women). Expenses: Contact institution. *Financial support:* In 2010–11, 35 students received support, including 5 fellowships (averaging $4,350 per year); career-related internships or fieldwork, scholarships/grants, and unspecified assistantships also available. Financial award application deadline: 5/15; financial award applicants required to submit FAFSA. In 2010, 35 master's awarded. *Degree program information:* Part-time programs available. Postbaccalaureate distance learning degree programs offered (minimal on-campus study). Offers chemistry (MS); curriculum and instruction (MA); early childhood education (MA); educational leadership (Ed S); English as a second language (MA); literacy (MA); school leadership (MA); special education (MA). *Application deadline:* For fall admission, 8/1 priority date for domestic and international students; for spring admission, 12/1 priority date for domestic students, 12/2 priority date for international students. Applications are processed on a rolling basis. *Application fee:* $50. *Application Contact:* Helen Reynolds, Department Assistant, 864-294-2213, Fax: 864-294-3579, E-mail: helen.reynolds@furman.edu. *Director of Graduate Studies,* Dr. Troy M. Terry, 864-294-2213, Fax: 864-294-3579, E-mail: troy.terry@furman.edu.

FUTURE GENERATIONS GRADUATE SCHOOL, Franklin, WV 26807

General Information Independent, coed, graduate-only institution.

GRADUATE UNITS

Program in Applied Community Change and Conservation Offers applied community change and conservation (MA).

GALLAUDET UNIVERSITY, Washington, DC 20002-3625

General Information Independent, coed, university. CGS member. *Enrollment:* 1,533 graduate, professional, and undergraduate students; 291 full-time matriculated graduate/professional students (224 women), 122 part-time matriculated graduate/professional students (97 women). *Enrollment by degree level:* 250 master's, 136 doctoral, 27 other advanced degrees. *Graduate faculty:* 116 full-time (86 women). *Tuition:* Full-time $11,930; part-time $663 per credit. *Required fees:* $188 per semester. *Graduate housing:* Rooms and/or apartments available on a first-come, first-served basis to single and married students. Typical cost: $5460 per year ($9860 including board) for single students; $5460 per year ($9860 including board) for married students. Room and board charges vary according to board plan. Housing application deadline: 4/1. *Student services:* Campus employment opportunities, campus safety program, career counseling, child daycare facilities, exercise/wellness program, free psychological counseling, grant writing training, international student services, low-cost health insurance, multicultural affairs office, services for students with disabilities, teacher training, writing training. *Library facilities:* Merrill Learning Center. *Online resources:* library catalog, web page, access to other libraries' catalogs. *Collection:* 260,000 titles, 2,000 serial subscriptions, 8,000 audiovisual materials. *Research affiliation:* University of Connecticut (bimodal bilingualism development), University of Maryland (audiology), University of Wisconsin Madison (telecommunications access), Arizona State University (early childhood education), National Science Foundation (linguistics, visual language and visual learning), U.S. Department of Education; National Institute on Disability (rehabilitation and hearing enhancement).

Computer facilities: A campuswide network can be accessed from student residence rooms and from off campus. Online class registration is available. *Web address:* http://www.gallaudet.edu/.

General Application Contact: Wednesday Luria, Coordinator of Prospective Graduate Student Services, 202-651-5400, Fax: 202-651-5295, E-mail: graduate.school@gallaudet.edu.

GRADUATE UNITS

The Graduate School Students: 291 full-time (224 women), 122 part-time (97 women); includes 142 minority (36 Black or African American, non-Hispanic/Latino; 3 American Indian or Alaska Native, non-Hispanic/Latino; 13 Asian, non-Hispanic/Latino; 29 Hispanic/Latino; 61 Two or more races, non-Hispanic/Latino), 28 international. Average age 30. 442 applicants, 52% accepted, 145 enrolled. *Faculty:* 116 full-time (86 women). Expenses: Contact institution. *Financial support:* In 2010–11, 219 students received support; fellowships, research assistantships, teaching assistantships, career-related internships or fieldwork, Federal Work-Study, scholarships/grants, tuition waivers (partial), and unspecified assistantships available. Support available to part-time students. Financial award applicants required to submit FAFSA. In 2010, 116 master's, 17 doctorates, 16 other advanced degrees awarded. *Degree program information:* Part-time programs available. Offers administration (MS); audiology (Au D, PhD); change leadership in education (Ed S); clinical psychology (PhD); deaf education (Ed D, PhD); deaf education: advanced studies (MA); deaf education: special programs in deaf education (MA); deaf history (Certificate); deaf studies (MA); education: teacher preparation (MA, MA Missions); hearing, speech and language sciences (MS); international development (MA); interpretation (MA, PhD); leadership (Certificate); leisure services administration (MS); linguistics (MA, PhD); management (Certificate); mental health counseling (MA); school counseling (MA); school counseling (summer session) (MA); school psychology (Psy S); sign language teaching (MA); social work (MSW); special education administration (PhD); speech-language pathology (PhD). *Application deadline:* For fall admission, 2/15 for domestic students. Applications are processed on a rolling basis. *Application fee:* $50. Electronic applications accepted. *Application Contact:* Wednesday Luria, Coordinator of Prospective Graduate

Student Services, 202-651-5400, Fax: 202-651-5295, E-mail: graduate.school@gallaudet.edu. *Dean*, Dr. Carol J. Erting, 202-651-5520, Fax: 202-651-5027, E-mail: carol.erting@gallaudet.edu.

GANNON UNIVERSITY, Erie, PA 16541-0001

General Information Independent-religious, coed, university. CGS member. *Enrollment:* 4,219 graduate, professional, and undergraduate students; 588 full-time matriculated graduate/professional students (300 women), 622 part-time matriculated graduate/professional students (430 women). *Enrollment by degree level:* 120 first professional, 887 master's, 53 doctoral, 150 other advanced degrees. *Graduate faculty:* 78 full-time (38 women), 61 part-time/adjunct (22 women). *Tuition:* Full-time $14,670; part-time $815 per credit. *Required fees:* $430; $18 per credit. Tuition and fees vary according to class time, course load, degree level, campus/location and program. *Graduate housing:* Rooms and/or apartments available on a first-come, first-served basis to single students and available to married students. Typical cost: $6880 per year ($11,550 including board) for single students; $6880 per year ($11,550 including board) for married students. Room and board charges vary according to board plan and housing facility selected. *Student services:* Campus employment opportunities, campus safety program, career counseling, exercise/wellness program, free psychological counseling, grant writing training, international student services, low-cost health insurance, multicultural affairs office, services for students with disabilities, teacher training, writing training. *Library facilities:* Nash Library. *Online resources:* library catalog, web page. *Collection:* 266,136 titles, 58,039 serial subscriptions, 4,079 audiovisual materials. *Research affiliation:* PSI Medical Catheter Care, LLC (development of a software prototype for catheters), Procurex, Inc. (software development), Ben Franklin (producing syngas from glycerin), CE Convergence (software research and development), PA-DCED (computer information science innovation grant), AirBorn (PPS software enhancer).

Computer facilities: 380 computers available on campus for general student use. A campuswide network can be accessed from student residence rooms and from off campus. Online class registration is available. *Web address:* http://www.gannon.edu/.

General Application Contact: Kara Morgan, Assistant Director of Graduate Admissions, 814-871-5831, Fax: 814-871-5827, E-mail: graduate@gannon.edu.

GRADUATE UNITS

School of Graduate Studies Students: 588 full-time (300 women), 622 part-time (430 women); includes 43 minority (29 Black or African American, non-Hispanic/Latino; 10 Asian, non-Hispanic/Latino; 4 Hispanic/Latino), 208 international. Average age 30. 1,637 applicants, 68% accepted, 233 enrolled. *Faculty:* 78 full-time (38 women), 61 part-time/adjunct (22 women). Expenses: Contact institution. *Financial support:* In 2010–11, 40 fellowships (averaging $4,105 per year), 5 teaching assistantships (averaging $6,426 per year) were awarded; career-related internships or fieldwork, Federal Work-Study, scholarships/grants, traineeships, tuition waivers (partial), unspecified assistantships, and administrative assistantships also available. Support available to part-time students. Financial award application deadline: 7/1; financial award applicants required to submit FAFSA. In 2010, 540 master's, 40 doctorates, 5 other advanced degrees awarded. *Degree program information:* Part-time and evening/weekend programs available. *Application deadline:* Applications are processed on a rolling basis. *Application fee:* $25. Electronic applications accepted. *Application Contact:* Kara Morgan, Assistant Director of Graduate Admissions, 814-871-5831, Fax: 814-871-5827, E-mail: graduate@gannon.edu.

College of Engineering and Business Students: 250 full-time (50 women), 131 part-time (62 women); includes 11 minority (7 Black or African American, non-Hispanic/Latino; 3 Asian, non-Hispanic/Latino; 1 Hispanic/Latino), 198 international. Average age 28. 1,078 applicants, 73% accepted, 98 enrolled. *Faculty:* 39 full-time (12 women), 9 part-time/adjunct (0 women). Expenses: Contact institution. *Financial support:* In 2010–11, 13 fellowships (averaging $2,848 per year) were awarded; career-related internships or fieldwork, Federal Work-Study, scholarships/grants, traineeships, and administrative assistantships also available. Financial award application deadline: 7/1; financial award applicants required to submit FAFSA. In 2010, 154 master's, 2 other advanced degrees awarded. *Degree program information:* Part-time and evening/weekend programs available. Postbaccalaureate distance learning degree programs offered (no on-campus study). Offers accounting (Certificate); business (MBA, MPA, Certificate); business administration (MBA); computer and information science (MCIS); electrical engineering (MSEE); embedded software engineering (MSES); engineering and business (M Ed, MBA, MCIS, MPA, MS, MSEE, MSEM, MSES, MSME, Certificate); engineering and computer science (M Ed, MCIS, MS, MSEE, MSEM, MSES, MSME, Certificate); engineering management (MSEM); environmental and occupational science and health (Certificate); environmental science and engineering (MS); finance (Certificate); human resources management (Certificate); investments (Certificate); marketing (Certificate); mechanical engineering (MSME); natural and environmental sciences (M Ed); organizational leadership (Certificate); public administration (MPA, Certificate); risk management (Certificate). *Application deadline:* Applications are processed on a rolling basis. *Application fee:* $25. Electronic applications accepted. *Application Contact:* Kara Morgan, Assistant Director of Graduate Admissions, 814-871-5831, Fax: 814-871-5827, E-mail: graduate@gannon.edu. *Dean*, Dr. Melanie Hatch, 814-871-7582, Fax: 814-871-7616, E-mail: hatch004@gannon.edu.

College of Humanities, Education, and Social Sciences Students: 98 full-time (66 women), 437 part-time (323 women); includes 15 Black or African American, non-Hispanic/Latino; 3 Asian, non-Hispanic/Latino; 1 Hispanic/Latino, 3 international. Average age 34. 244 applicants, 84% accepted, 77 enrolled. *Faculty:* 20 full-time (11 women), 41 part-time/adjunct (19 women). Expenses: Contact institution. *Financial support:* In 2010–11, 9 fellowships (averaging $5,653 per year), 5 teaching assistantships (averaging $6,426 per year) were awarded; career-related internships or fieldwork, Federal Work-Study, scholarships/grants, traineeships, and unspecified assistantships also available. Financial award application deadline: 7/1; financial award applicants required to submit FAFSA. In 2010, 289 master's, 1 doctorate awarded. *Degree program information:* Part-time and evening/weekend programs available. Postbaccalaureate distance learning degree programs offered. Offers advanced counselor studies (Certificate); community counseling (MS, Certificate); counseling psychology (PhD); curriculum and instruction (M Ed); early intervention (MS); education (M Ed, MS, PhD, Certificate); educational computing technology (M Ed); educational leadership (M Ed); English (MA); English as a second language (Certificate); gerontology (Certificate); humanities (MA, MS, PhD, Certificate); humanities, education, and social sciences (M Ed, MA, MS, PhD, Certificate); organizational learning and leadership (PhD); pastoral studies (MA, Certificate); principal certification (Certificate); reading (M Ed, Certificate); school counselor preparation (Certificate); superintendent letter of eligibility (Certificate). *Application deadline:* Applications are processed on a rolling basis. *Application fee:* $25. Electronic applications accepted. *Application Contact:* Kara Morgan, Assistant Director of Graduate Admissions, 814-871-5831, Fax: 814-871-5827, E-mail: graduate@gannon.edu. *Dean*, Dr. Timothy Downs, 814-871-7549, Fax: 814-871-7652, E-mail: downs001@gannon.edu.

Morosky College of Health Professions and Sciences Students: 240 full-time (184 women), 54 part-time (45 women); includes 7 Black or African American, non-Hispanic/Latino; 4 Asian, non-Hispanic/Latino; 2 Hispanic/Latino, 7 international. Average age 27. 315 applicants, 41% accepted, 58 enrolled. *Faculty:* 24 full-time (19 women), 11 part-time/adjunct (3 women). Expenses: Contact institution. *Financial support:* In 2010–11, 11 fellowships (averaging $2,649 per year) were awarded; career-related internships or fieldwork, Federal Work-Study, scholarships/grants, traineeships, and unspecified assistantships also available. Financial award application deadline: 7/1; financial award applicants required to submit FAFSA. In 2010, 97 master's, 3 other advanced degrees awarded. *Degree program information:* Part-time and evening/weekend programs available. Offers anesthesia (MSN); business administration (MSN); family nurse practitioner (Certificate); health professions (MPAS, MS, MSN, DPT, Certificate); health professions and sciences (MPAS, MS, MSN, DPT, Certificate); medical-surgical nursing (MSN); nurse anesthesia (Certificate); nursing rural practitioner (MSN); occupational therapy (MS); physical therapy (DPT); physician assistant (MPAS). *Application fee:* $25. Electronic applications accepted. *Application Contact:* Kara Morgan, Assistant Director of Graduate Admissions, 814-871-5831, Fax: 814-871-5827, E-mail: graduate@gannon.edu. *Dean*, Dr. Carolynn Masters, 814-871-7605, E-mail: masters004@gannon.edu.

GARDNER-WEBB UNIVERSITY, Boiling Springs, NC 28017

General Information Independent-religious, coed, comprehensive institution. *Enrollment:* 4,310 graduate, professional, and undergraduate students; 196 full-time matriculated graduate/professional students (93 women), 1,279 part-time matriculated graduate/professional students (864 women). *Enrollment by degree level:* 198 first professional, 1,083 master's, 194 doctoral. *Graduate faculty:* 43 full-time (14 women), 14 part-time/adjunct (5 women). *Tuition:* Part-time $325 per credit hour. *Graduate housing:* Room and/or apartments available on a first-come, first-served basis to single students; on-campus housing not available to married students. *Student services:* Campus employment opportunities, campus safety program, career counseling, exercise/wellness program, free psychological counseling, international student services, low-cost health insurance, services for students with disabilities, teacher training, writing training. *Library facilities:* Dover Memorial Library plus 1 other. *Online resources:* library catalog, web page. *Collection:* 244,133 titles, 108,251 serial subscriptions, 12,494 audiovisual materials.

Computer facilities: Computer purchase and lease plans are available. 100 computers available on campus for general student use. A campuswide network can be accessed from student residence rooms and from off campus. Online class registration is available. *Web address:* http://www.gardner-webb.edu/.

General Application Contact: Office of Graduate Admisisons, 877-498-4723, Fax: 704-406-3895, E-mail: gradinfo@gardner-webb.edu.

GRADUATE UNITS

Graduate School Students: 26 part-time (17 women); includes 6 Black or African American, non-Hispanic/Latino. Average age 28. *Faculty:* 4 full-time (3 women). Expenses: Contact institution. *Financial support:* Fellowships, Federal Work-Study, institutionally sponsored loans, and unspecified assistantships available. Support available to part-time students. In 2010, 7 master's awarded. *Degree program information:* Part-time and evening/weekend programs available. Offers English (MA); English education (MA); religion (MA); sport science and pedagogy (MA). *Application deadline:* Applications are processed on a rolling basis. *Application fee:* $40. Electronic applications accepted. *Application Contact:* Office of Graduate Admisisons, 877-498-4723, Fax: 704-406-3895, E-mail: gradinfo@gardner-webb.edu. *Dean*, Dr. Gayle B. Price, 704-406-4723, Fax: 704-406-4329, E-mail: gradschool@gardner-webb.edu.

School of Education Students: 10 full-time (5 women), 576 part-time (413 women); includes 167 Black or African American, non-Hispanic/Latino; 3 American Indian or Alaska Native, non-Hispanic/Latino; 6 Asian, non-Hispanic/Latino; 5 Hispanic/Latino. Average age 37. *Faculty:* 10 full-time (4 women), 20 part-time/adjunct (7 women). Expenses: Contact institution. *Financial support:* Unspecified assistantships available. In 2010, 116 master's, 10 doctorates awarded. *Degree program information:* Part-time and evening/weekend programs available. Offers curriculum and instruction (Ed D); educational leadership (Ed D); elementary education (MA); executive leadership studies (MA); middle grades education (MA); school administration (MA). *Application deadline:* For fall admission, 8/1 priority date for domestic students. Applications are processed on a rolling basis. *Application fee:* $40. Electronic applications accepted. *Application Contact:* Office of Graduate Admisisons, 877-498-4723, Fax: 704-406-3895, E-mail: gradinfo@gardner-webb.edu. *Dean*, Dr. Alan D. Eury, 704-406-4402, Fax: 704-406-3921, E-mail: dsimmons@gardner-webb.edu.

School of Nursing Students: 7 full-time (6 women), 137 part-time (127 women); includes 18 Black or African American, non-Hispanic/Latino; 1 American Indian or Alaska Native, non-Hispanic/Latino; 1 Asian, non-Hispanic/Latino; 1 Hispanic/Latino. Average age 42. *Faculty:* 4 full-time (all women), 3 part-time/adjunct (all women). Expenses: Contact institution. In 2010, 38 master's awarded. *Degree program information:* Part-time programs available. Postbaccalaureate distance learning degree programs offered (no on-campus study). Offers nursing (MSN, DNP, PMC). *Application Contact:* Office of Graduate Admisisons, 877-498-4723, Fax: 704-406-3895, E-mail: gradinfo@gardner-webb.edu. *Dean*, Dr. Suzie B. Little, 704-406-4358, Fax: 704-406-4329, E-mail: gradschool@gardner-webb.edu.

School of Psychology Students: 3 full-time (all women), 88 part-time (75 women); includes 17 Black or African American, non-Hispanic/Latino; 1 Asian, non-Hispanic/Latino; 2 Hispanic/Latino. Average age 36. *Faculty:* 6 full-time (3 women). Expenses: Contact institution. *Financial support:* Unspecified assistantships available. In 2010, 22 master's awarded. *Degree program information:* Part-time and evening/weekend programs available. Offers mental health counseling (MA); school counseling (MA). *Application deadline:* For fall admission, 7/1 priority date for domestic students. Applications are processed on a rolling basis. *Application fee:* $40. Electronic applications accepted. *Application Contact:* Office of Graduate Admisisons, 877-498-4723, Fax: 704-406-3895, E-mail: gradinfo@gardner-webb.edu. *Chair*, Dr. David Carscaddon, 704-406-4437, Fax: 704-406-4329, E-mail: dcarscaddon@gardner-webb.edu.

Graduate School of Business Students: 38 full-time (16 women), 370 part-time (205 women); includes 87 Black or African American, non-Hispanic/Latino; 1 American Indian or Alaska Native, non-Hispanic/Latino; 9 Asian, non-Hispanic/Latino; 5 Hispanic/Latino, 3 international. Average age 35. 147 applicants, 80% accepted, 116 enrolled. *Faculty:* 14 full-time (3 women), 3 part-time/adjunct (0 women). Expenses: Contact institution. *Financial support:* In 2010–11, 23 students received support. Unspecified assistantships available. Support available to part-time students. Financial award applicants required to submit FAFSA. In 2010, 145 master's awarded. *Degree program information:* Part-time and evening/weekend programs available. Postbaccalaureate distance learning degree programs offered (no on-campus study). Offers business (IMBA, M Acc, MBA). *Application deadline:* For fall admission, 8/25 for domestic students; for spring admission, 1/15 for domestic students. Applications are processed on a rolling basis. *Application fee:* $40. Electronic applications accepted. *Application Contact:* Jeremy J. Fern, Director of Admissions, 800-457-4622, Fax: 704-434-3895, E-mail: jfern@gardner-webb.edu. *Director*, Dr. Anthony Negbenebor, 704-406-4622, Fax: 704-406-3895, E-mail: anegbenebor@gardner-webb.edu.

School of Divinity Students: 138 full-time (63 women), 81 part-time (26 women); includes 74 Black or African American, non-Hispanic/Latino; 1 Asian, non-Hispanic/Latino; 3 Hispanic/Latino, 2 international. Average age 40. *Faculty:* 11 full-time (9 women), 5 part-time/adjunct (2 women). Expenses: Contact institution. *Financial support:* Fellowships, institutionally sponsored loans and unspecified assistantships available. Support available to part-time students. Financial award application deadline: 5/15. In 2010, 56 first professional degrees, 1 doctorate awarded. *Degree program information:* Part-time programs available. Offers biblical studies (M Div); Christian education and formation (M Div); ministry (D Min); missiology (M Div); pastoral care and counseling (M Div); pastoral studies (M Div). *Application deadline:* For fall admission, 8/1 priority date for domestic students; for spring admission, 12/15 priority date for domestic students. Applications are processed on a rolling basis. *Application fee:* $40. *Application Contact:* Jeremy Fern, Director of Admissions, 704-406-3205, Fax: 704-406-3935, E-mail: jfern@gardner-webb.edu. *Dean*, Dr. Robert W. Canoy, 704-406-4400, Fax: 704-406-3935, E-mail: rcanoy@gardner-webb.edu.

GARRETT-EVANGELICAL THEOLOGICAL SEMINARY, Evanston, IL 60201-3298

General Information Independent-religious, coed, graduate-only institution. *Graduate housing:* Rooms and/or apartments guaranteed to single students and available to married students. Housing application deadline: 4/1.

GRADUATE UNITS

Graduate and Professional Programs *Degree program information:* Part-time programs available. Offers Bible and culture (PhD); Christian education (MA); Christian education and congregational studies (PhD); contemporary theology and culture (PhD); divinity (M Div); ethics, church, and society (MA); liturgical studies (PhD); ministry (D Min); music ministry (MA); pastoral care and counseling (MA); pastoral theology, personality, and culture (PhD); spiritual formation and evangelism (MA); theological studies (MTS). M Div/MSW offered jointly with Loyola University Chicago. Electronic applications accepted.

GENERAL THEOLOGICAL SEMINARY, New York, NY 10011-4977

General Information Independent-religious, coed, graduate-only institution. *Graduate housing:* Rooms and/or apartments available to single and married students. Housing application deadline: 6/1.

GRADUATE UNITS

Graduate and Professional Programs *Degree program information:* Part-time and evening/weekend programs available. Offers Anglican studies (STM, Th D, Certificate); ascetical theology (Certificate); biblical studies (Certificate); congregational development (Certificate); divinity (M Div); historical and theological studies (Certificate); spiritual direction (MASD, STM, Certificate); theology (MA).

GENEVA COLLEGE, Beaver Falls, PA 15010-3599

General Information Independent-religious, coed, comprehensive institution. *Graduate housing:* On-campus housing not available.

GRADUATE UNITS

Program in Business Administration *Degree program information:* Part-time and evening/weekend programs available. Offers business administration (MBA). Electronic applications accepted.

Program in Cardiovascular Science Offers cardiovascular science (MS). Electronic applications accepted.

Program in Counseling *Degree program information:* Part-time and evening/weekend programs available. Offers marriage and family (MA); mental health (MA); school counseling (MA). Electronic applications accepted.

Program in Higher Education *Degree program information:* Part-time and evening/weekend programs available. Postbaccalaureate distance learning degree programs offered (minimal on-campus study). Offers campus ministry (MA); college teaching (MA); educational leadership (MA); student affairs administration (MA). Electronic applications accepted.

Program in Organizational Leadership *Degree program information:* Evening/weekend programs available. Offers organizational leadership (MS). Electronic applications accepted.

Program in Reading *Degree program information:* Part-time and evening/weekend programs available. Offers reading (M Ed). Electronic applications accepted.

Program in Special Education *Degree program information:* Part-time and evening/weekend programs available. Offers special education (M Ed). Electronic applications accepted.

See Display on this page and Close-Up on page 949.

GEORGE FOX UNIVERSITY, Newberg, OR 97132-2697

General Information Independent-religious, coed, university. *Enrollment:* 3,555 graduate, professional, and undergraduate students; 504 full-time matriculated graduate/professional students (304 women), 797 part-time matriculated graduate/professional students (398 women). *Enrollment by degree level:* 93 first professional, 908 master's, 295 doctoral, 5 other advanced degrees. *Graduate faculty:* 61 full-time (26 women), 79 part-time/adjunct (39 women). *Graduate housing:* On-campus housing not available. *Student services:* Campus employment opportunities, career counseling, international student services, low-cost health insurance, services for students with disabilities, writing training. *Library facilities:* Murdock Learning Resource Center. *Online resources:* library catalog, web page, access to other libraries' catalogs. *Collection:* 221,199 titles, 4,996 serial subscriptions, 8,365 audiovisual materials.

Computer facilities: 130 computers available on campus for general student use. A campuswide network can be accessed from student residence rooms and from off campus. Online class registration, online acceptance of financial aid are available. *Web address:* http://www.georgefox.edu/.

General Application Contact: Bonnie Nakashimada, Director for Graduate and ADP Admissions and Regional Sites, 503-554-6149, Fax: 503-554-3110, E-mail: bnakashimada@georgefox.edu.

GRADUATE UNITS

Department of Physical Therapy Expenses: Contact institution. Offers physical therapy (DPT). *Application deadline:* For fall admission, 12/1 for domestic students. *Application fee:* $40. *Application Contact:* Patrick Kelley, Admissions Counselor, 503-554-2223, Fax: 503-554-3110, E-mail: dpt@georgefox.edu. *Director/Assistant Professor,* Dr. Tyler Cuddeford, 503-554-2452, E-mail: tcuddeford@georgefox.edu.

George Fox Evangelical Seminary Students: 122 full-time (41 women), 236 part-time (76 women); includes 6 Black or African American, non-Hispanic/Latino; 2 American Indian or Alaska Native, non-Hispanic/Latino; 11 Asian, non-Hispanic/Latino; 4 Hispanic/Latino; 4 Two or more races, non-Hispanic/Latino, 14 international. Average age 40. 141 applicants, 94% accepted, 95 enrolled. *Faculty:* 7 full-time (2 women), 23 part-time/adjunct (6 women). Expenses: Contact institution. *Financial support:* Career-related internships or fieldwork and scholarships/grants available. Financial award application deadline: 5/1; financial award applicants required to submit FAFSA. In 2010, 19 first professional degrees, 33 master's, 17 doctorates, 3 other advanced degrees awarded. *Degree program information:* Part-time programs available. Postbaccalaureate distance learning degree programs offered (minimal on-campus study). Offers Biblical studies (M Div); Christian earthkeeping (M Div); Christian history and theology (M Div); clinical pastoral education and hospital chaplaincy (M Div); leadership and spiritual formation (D Min); military chaplaincy (M Div); ministry leadership (MA); pastoral studies (M Div); spiritual formation (MA, Certificate); spiritual formation and discipleship (M Div); theological studies (MA). *Application deadline:* For fall admission, 7/1 for domestic and international students; for winter admission, 11/1 for domestic and international students; for spring admission, 4/1 for domestic and international students. Applications are processed on a rolling basis. *Application fee:* $40. Electronic applications accepted. *Application Contact:* Sheila Bartlett, Admissions Counselor, 800-631-0921, Fax: 503-554-6122, E-mail: gfes@georgefox.edu. *Professor of Theology/Vice President and Dean,* Dr. Chuck Conniry, 503-554-6152, E-mail: cconniry@georgefox.edu.

Program in Clinical Psychology Students: 92 full-time (62 women), 12 part-time (7 women); includes 1 Black or African American, non-Hispanic/Latino; 1 American Indian or Alaska Native, non-Hispanic/Latino; 4 Asian, non-Hispanic/Latino; 5 Hispanic/Latino; 1 Native Hawaiian or other Pacific Islander, non-Hispanic/Latino, 2 international. Average age 29. 81 applicants, 56% accepted, 20 enrolled. *Faculty:* 9 full-time (4 women), 3 part-time/adjunct (1 woman). Expenses: Contact institution. *Financial support:* Scholarships/grants available. Financial award application deadline: 5/15; financial award applicants required to submit FAFSA. In 2010, 21 master's, 18 doctorates awarded. Offers clinical psychology (MA, Psy D). *Application deadline:* For fall admission, 1/15 priority date for domestic and international students. *Application fee:* $40. Electronic applications accepted. *Application Contact:* Adina McConaughey, Admission Counselor, 800-631-0921 Ext. 2263, Fax: 503-554-2263, E-mail: psyd@georgefox.edu. *Professor and Director, Graduate Department of Clinical Psychology,* Dr. Wayne Adams, 800-765-4369 Ext. 2372, E-mail: wadams@georgefox.edu.

School of Business Students: 21 full-time (7 women), 247 part-time (87 women); includes 4 Black or African American, non-Hispanic/Latino; 2 American Indian or Alaska Native, non-Hispanic/Latino; 13 Asian, non-Hispanic/Latino; 13 Hispanic/Latino; 2 Two or more races, non-Hispanic/Latino, 12 international. Average age 37. 101 applicants, 93% accepted, 72 enrolled. *Faculty:* 9 full-time (2 women), 8 part-time/adjunct (3 women). Expenses: Contact institution. *Financial support:* In 2010–11, 2 students received support. Applicants required to submit FAFSA. In 2010, 82 master's awarded. *Degree program information:* Part-time and evening/weekend programs available. Postbaccalaureate distance learning degree programs offered (minimal on-campus study). Offers finance (MBA); management (DBA); management/general (MBA); marketing (DBA); organizational strategy (MBA); strategic human resource management (MBA). MBA offered part-time and full-time, also offered in Portland, OR, and Boise, ID. *Application deadline:* For fall admission, 8/1 for domestic and international students; for spring admission, 12/1 for domestic and international students. Applications are processed on a rolling basis. *Application fee:* $40. Electronic applications accepted. *Application Contact:*

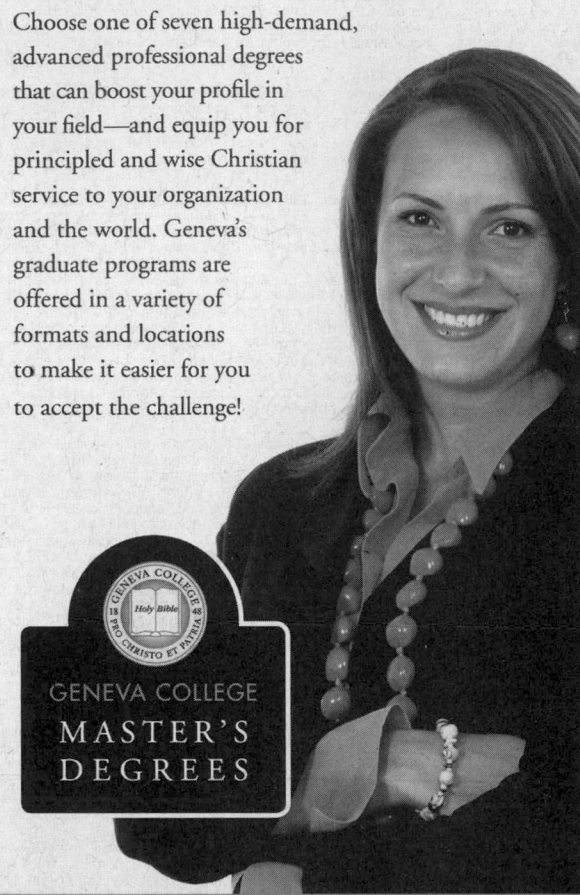

Robin Halverson, Admissions Counselor, 800-493-4937, Fax: 503-554-6111, E-mail: mba@georgefox.edu. *Professor/Dean*, Dr. Dirk Barram, 800-631-0921.

School of Education Expenses: Contact institution. Offers clinical mental health counseling (MA); continuing administrator license (Certificate); curriculum and instruction (M Ed); education (M Ed, MA, MAT, MS, Ed D, Certificate, Ed S); educational leadership (M Ed, Ed D); higher education (M Ed); initial administrator license (Certificate); instructional leadership (Ed S); library media (M Ed, Certificate); literacy (M Ed); marriage, couple and family counseling (MA, Certificate); mental health trauma (Certificate); reading (M Ed); school counseling (MA, Certificate); school psychology (Certificate, Ed S); secondary education (M Ed); teaching (MAT); teaching plus ESOL (MAT); teaching plus ESOL/bilingual (MAT); teaching plus reading (MAT). *Application Contact:* Bonnie Nakashimada, Director for Graduate and SPS Admissions and Regional Sites, 503-554-6149, Fax: 503-554-3110, E-mail: bnakashimada@georgefox.edu.

GEORGE MASON UNIVERSITY, Fairfax, VA 22030

General Information State-supported, coed, university. CGS member. *Enrollment:* 3,098 full-time matriculated graduate/professional students (1,716 women), 7,698 part-time matriculated graduate/professional students (4,405 women). *Enrollment by degree level:* 731 first professional, 7,449 master's, 2,120 doctoral, 496 other advanced degrees. *Graduate faculty:* 1,329 full-time (524 women), 1,015 part-time/adjunct (527 women). Tuition, state resident: full-time $8192; part-time $440 per credit hour. Tuition, nonresident: full-time $22,952; part-time $1055 per credit hour. *Required fees:* $2364; $99 per credit hour. *Graduate housing:* On-campus housing not available. *Student services:* Campus employment opportunities, campus safety program, career counseling, child daycare facilities, exercise/wellness program, free psychological counseling, grant writing training, international student services, low-cost health insurance, multicultural affairs office, services for students with disabilities, teacher training, writing training. *Library facilities:* Fenwick Library plus 4 others. *Online resources:* library catalog, web page, access to other libraries' catalogs. *Collection:* 1.9 million titles, 56,433 serial subscriptions, 43,289 audiovisual materials. *Research affiliation:* Gannon Technologies (high-tech communication technology), Northrop Grumman Corporation (high-tech communication technology), Science Applications International Corporation (science and technology), L3 Communications (high-tech communication technology), Lockheed Martin Corporation (science and technology), Inova Health System (health care and medical research).

Computer facilities: Computer purchase and lease plans are available. 1,437 computers available on campus for general student use. A campuswide network can be accessed from student residence rooms and from off campus. Online class registration is available. *Web address:* http://www.gmu.edu/.

General Application Contact: Dan Robb, Director of Graduate Admissions, 703-993-2424, Fax: 703-993-2392, E-mail: drobb@gmu.edu.

GRADUATE UNITS

College of Education and Human Development Students: 472 full-time (390 women), 2,189 part-time (1,783 women); includes 395 minority (165 Black or African American, non-Hispanic/Latino; 5 American Indian or Alaska Native, non-Hispanic/Latino; 87 Asian, non-Hispanic/Latino; 116 Hispanic/Latino; 2 Native Hawaiian or other Pacific Islander, non-Hispanic/Latino; 20 Two or more races, non-Hispanic/Latino), 59 international. Average age 33. 1,556 applicants, 71% accepted, 828 enrolled. *Faculty:* 117 full-time (77 women), 215 part-time/adjunct (168 women). Expenses: Contact institution. *Financial support:* In 2010–11, 94 students received support, including 3 fellowships with full tuition reimbursements available (averaging $18,000 per year), 80 research assistantships with full and partial tuition reimbursements available (averaging $8,846 per year), 21 teaching assistantships with full and partial tuition reimbursements available (averaging $7,427 per year); career-related internships or fieldwork, Federal Work-Study, scholarships/grants, unspecified assistantships, and health care benefits (full-time research or teaching assistantship recipients) also available. Support available to part-time students. Financial award application deadline: 3/1; financial award applicants required to submit FAFSA. In 2010, 960 master's, 26 doctorates awarded. *Degree program information:* Part-time and evening/weekend programs available. Post-baccalaureate distance learning degree programs offered (minimal on-campus study). Offers counseling and development (M Ed); curriculum and instruction (M Ed); education (PhD); education and human development (M Ed, MA, MS, PhD); education leadership (M Ed); educational psychology (MS); special education (M Ed); teaching (MA). *Application fee:* $100. Electronic applications accepted. *Dean*, Mark Ginsberg, 703-993-2004, Fax: 703-993-2001, E-mail: mginsber@gmu.edu.

School of Recreation, Health and Tourism Students: 9 full-time (4 women), 18 part-time (10 women); includes 2 minority (1 Black or African American, non-Hispanic/Latino; 1 Asian, non-Hispanic/Latino). Average age 32. 23 applicants, 70% accepted, 13 enrolled. *Faculty:* 27 full-time (11 women), 58 part-time/adjunct (33 women). Expenses: Contact institution. *Financial support:* In 2010–11, 3 students received support, including 3 research assistantships with full and partial tuition reimbursements available (averaging $5,963 per year); career-related internships or fieldwork, Federal Work-Study, scholarships/grants, unspecified assistantships, and health care benefits (full-time research or teaching assistantship recipients) also available. Financial award application deadline: 3/1; financial award applicants required to submit FAFSA. In 2010, 5 master's awarded. Offers exercise, fitness, and health promotion (MS); sport and recreation studies (MS). *Application deadline:* For fall admission, 11/1 priority date for domestic students, 11/1 for international students; for spring admission, 4/1 for domestic and international students. *Application fee:* $100. Electronic applications accepted. *Application Contact:* Dr. Pierre Rodgers, Associate Professor/Co-Coordinator of Graduate Programs, 703-993-8317, E-mail: prodgers@gmu.edu. *Director*, David Wiggins, 703-993-2057, E-mail: dwiggin1@gmu.edu.

College of Health and Human Services Students: 279 full-time (232 women), 602 part-time (528 women); includes 320 minority (153 Black or African American, non-Hispanic/Latino; 1 American Indian or Alaska Native, non-Hispanic/Latino; 102 Asian, non-Hispanic/Latino; 48 Hispanic/Latino; 1 Native Hawaiian or other Pacific Islander, non-Hispanic/Latino; 15 Two or more races, non-Hispanic/Latino), 45 international. Average age 35. 784 applicants, 58% accepted, 250 enrolled. *Faculty:* 82 full-time (58 women), 113 part-time/adjunct (100 women). Expenses: Contact institution. *Financial support:* In 2010–11, 34 students received support, including 30 research assistantships with full and partial tuition reimbursements available (averaging $13,805 per year), 5 teaching assistantships with full and partial tuition reimbursements available (averaging $15,496 per year); career-related internships or fieldwork, Federal Work-Study, scholarships/grants, unspecified assistantships, and health care benefits (full-time research or teaching assistantship recipients) also available. Financial award application deadline: 3/1; financial award applicants required to submit FAFSA. In 2010, 201 master's, 2 doctorates, 22 other advanced degrees awarded. Offers biostatistics (Certificate); epidemiology (Certificate); epidemiology and biostatistics (MS); gerontology (Certificate); global health (MS, Certificate); health and human services (MPH, MS, MSN, MSW, DNP, PhD, Certificate); health and medical policy (MS); health information systems (Certificate); health science (MS); health systems management (MS); nutrition (Certificate); public health (MPH, Certificate); quality improvement and outcomes management in health care systems (Certificate); rehabilitation science (Certificate); risk management and patient safety (Certificate); senior housing administration (MS, Certificate); social work (MSW). *Application fee:* $100. Electronic applications accepted. *Application Contact:* Sandy Kellerhals, Administrative Office Specialist, 703-993-2120, E-mail: skelleh@gmu.edu. *Dean*, Dr. Shirley S. Travis, 703-993-1918.

School of Nursing Students: 51 full-time (48 women), 303 part-time (289 women); includes 110 minority (50 Black or African American, non-Hispanic/Latino; 38 Asian, non-Hispanic/Latino; 17 Hispanic/Latino; 5 Two or more races, non-Hispanic/Latino), 12 international. Average age 41. 209 applicants, 64% accepted, 94 enrolled. *Faculty:* 36 full-time (all women), 53 part-time/adjunct (51 women). Expenses: Contact institution. *Financial support:* In 2010–11, 5 students received support, including 4 research assistantships with full and partial tuition reimbursements available (averaging $14,583 per year), 1 teaching assistantship with full and partial tuition reimbursement available (averaging $20,000 per year); career-related internships or fieldwork, Federal Work-Study, scholarships/grants, unspecified assistantships, and nurse faculty loan, health care benefits (full-time research or teaching assistantship recipients) also available. Financial award application deadline: 3/1; financial award applicants required to submit FAFSA. In 2010, 88 master's, 2 doctorates, 4 other advanced degrees awarded. Offers forensic nursing (Certificate); nursing (MSN, PhD); nursing administration (Certificate); nursing education (Certificate); nursing practice (DNP). *Application deadline:* For fall admission, 4/1 priority date for domestic students; for spring admission, 11/1 priority date for domestic students. Applications are processed on a rolling basis. *Application fee:* $75. Electronic applications accepted. *Application Contact:* Janice Lee-Beverly, Program Support, 703-993-1947, E-mail: jleebev1@gmu.edu. *Dean*, Dr. Shirley S. Travis, 703-993-1918.

College of Humanities and Social Sciences Students: 574 full-time (316 women), 1,373 part-time (802 women); includes 262 minority (85 Black or African American, non-Hispanic/Latino; 2 American Indian or Alaska Native, non-Hispanic/Latino; 73 Asian, non-Hispanic/Latino; 85 Hispanic/Latino; 1 Native Hawaiian or other Pacific Islander, non-Hispanic/Latino; 16 Two or more races, non-Hispanic/Latino), 101 international. Average age 32. 2,843 applicants, 46% accepted, 590 enrolled. *Faculty:* 408 full-time (185 women), 245 part-time/adjunct (120 women). Expenses: Contact institution. *Financial support:* In 2010–11, 364 students received support, including 25 fellowships with full tuition reimbursements available (averaging $18,000 per year), 165 research assistantships with full and partial tuition reimbursements available (averaging $12,296 per year), 203 teaching assistantships with full and partial tuition reimbursements available (averaging $9,947 per year); career-related internships or fieldwork, Federal Work-Study, scholarships/grants, unspecified assistantships, and health care benefits (full-time research or teaching assistantship recipients) also available. Support available to part-time students. Financial award application deadline: 3/1; financial award applicants required to submit FAFSA. In 2010, 511 master's, 52 doctorates, 33 other advanced degrees awarded. *Degree program information:* Part-time and evening/weekend programs available. Offers anthropology (MA); art history (MA); association management (Certificate); aviation psychology (Certificate); biodefense (MS, PhD); cognitive neuroscience (Certificate); college teaching (Certificate); communications (MA, PhD); community college education (DA Ed); creative writing (MFA); criminology, law and society (MA, PhD); cultural studies (PhD); economic systems design (Graduate Certificate); economics (MA, PhD); emergency management and homeland security (Certificate); English (MA); folklore studies (Certificate); foreign languages (MA); higher education administration (Certificate); history (MA, PhD); humanities and social sciences (MA, MAIS, MFA, MPA, MS, DA Ed, PhD, Certificate, Graduate Certificate); interdisciplinary studies (MAIS); linguistics (PhD); nonprofit management (Certificate); philosophy (MA); political science (MA, PhD); professional writing and rhetoric (Certificate); psychology (MA, PhD); public administration (MPA); public management (Certificate); school psychology (Certificate); sociology (MA, PhD); teaching English as a second language (Certificate); usability (Certificate). *Application deadline:* Applications are processed on a rolling basis. *Application fee:* $100. Electronic applications accepted. *Application Contact:* Laura Layland, Graduate Admissions Assistant, 703-993-2409, E-mail: llayland@gmu.edu. *Dean*, Jack Censer, 703-993-8715, Fax: 703-993-8714, E-mail: jcenser@gmu.edu.

College of Science Students: 223 full-time (97 women), 716 part-time (305 women); includes 180 minority (36 Black or African American, non-Hispanic/Latino; 2 American Indian or Alaska Native, non-Hispanic/Latino; 90 Asian, non-Hispanic/Latino; 47 Hispanic/Latino; 1 Native Hawaiian or other Pacific Islander, non-Hispanic/Latino; 4 Two or more races, non-Hispanic/Latino), 144 international. Average age 33. 894 applicants, 59% accepted, 315 enrolled. *Faculty:* 262 full-time (73 women), 62 part-time/adjunct (23 women). Expenses: Contact institution. *Financial support:* In 2010–11, 233 students received support, including 26 fellowships with tuition reimbursements available (averaging $18,000 per year), 104 research assistantships with tuition reimbursements available (averaging $15,616 per year), 107 teaching assistantships (averaging $12,215 per year); career-related internships or fieldwork, Federal Work-Study, scholarships/grants, and health care benefits (full time research or teaching assistantship recipients) also available. Support available to part-time students. Financial award application deadline: 2/1; financial award applicants required to submit FAFSA. In 2010, 95 master's, 32 doctorates, 27 other advanced degrees awarded. *Degree program information:* Part-time and evening/weekend programs available. Offers actuarial sciences (Certificate); advanced biomedical sciences (Certificate); applied and engineering physics (MS); bioinformatics and computational biology (MS, PhD, Certificate); biology (MS); biosciences (PhD); chemistry (MS); chemistry and biochemistry (MS, PhD); climate dynamics (PhD); computational and data sciences (MS, PhD, Certificate); computational sciences (MS); computational sciences and informatics (PhD); computational techniques and applications (Certificate); earth system science (MS); earth systems and geoinformation sciences (PhD); environmental management (Certificate); environmental science and policy (MS, PhD, Certificate); environmental science and public policy (PhD); forensic science (MS); forensics (Certificate); geographic and cartographic sciences (MS); geographic information sciences (Certificate); geography and geoinformation science (MS, PhD, Certificate); geoinformatics and geospatial intelligence (MS); geospatial intelligence (Certificate); mathematical sciences (MS, PhD, Certificate); mathematics (MS, PhD); molecular and microbiology (MS, PhD); neuroscience (PhD); physical sciences (PhD); physics (PhD); physics and astronomy (MS, PhD); remote sensing (Certificate). *Application deadline:* For fall admission, 3/1 priority date for domestic students, 2/1 for international students; for spring admission, 11/1 priority date for domestic students. Applications are processed on a rolling basis. *Application fee:* $100. Electronic applications accepted. *Application Contact:* Dr. Tim Born, Associate Dean for Graduate Programs, 703-993-4171, Fax: 703-993-9034, E-mail: tborn@gmu.edu. *Director*, Dr. Vikas E. Chandhoke, 703-993-3622, Fax: 703-993-1993, E-mail: cosinfo@gmu.edu.

College of Visual and Performing Arts Students: 98 full-time (72 women), 104 part-time (79 women); includes 7 Black or African American, non-Hispanic/Latino; 10 Asian, non-Hispanic/Latino; 12 Hispanic/Latino; 5 Two or more races, non-Hispanic/Latino, 11 international. Average age 29. 242 applicants, 50% accepted, 74 enrolled. *Faculty:* 63 full-time (28 women), 80 part-time/adjunct (49 women). Expenses: Contact institution. *Financial support:* In 2010–11, 1 student received support, including 1 teaching assistantship with partial tuition reimbursement available (averaging $11,913 per year); career-related internships or fieldwork, Federal Work-Study, scholarships/grants, unspecified assistantships, and health care benefits (full-time research or teaching assistantship recipients) also available. Financial award application deadline: 3/1; financial award applicants required to submit FAFSA. In 2010, 73 master's, 1 other advanced degree awarded. *Degree program information:* Part-time and evening/weekend programs available. Offers art and visual technology (MFA); art education (MAT); arts entrepreneurship (Certificate); arts management (MA); dance (MFA); fund raising and development in the arts (Certificate); public relations and marketing in the arts (Certificate); special events management in the arts (Certificate); visual and performing arts (MA, MAT, MFA, MM, DMA, PhD, Certificate). *Application fee:* $100. Electronic applications accepted. *Application Contact:* Patricia Diefenbach, Graduate Studies Assistant, 703-993-9773, E-mail: pdiefenb@gmu.edu. *Dean*, William Reeder, 703-993-8624, Fax: 703-993-8883.

School of Music Students: 19 full-time (6 women), 38 part-time (25 women); includes 1 Black or African American, non-Hispanic/Latino; 5 Asian, non-Hispanic/Latino; 3 Hispanic/Latino; 1 Two or more races, non-Hispanic/Latino. Average age 30. 65 applicants, 54% accepted, 21 enrolled. *Faculty:* 20 full-time (8 women), 20 part-time/adjunct (12 women). Expenses: Contact institution. *Financial support:* Career-related internships or fieldwork, Federal Work-Study, scholarships/grants, unspecified assistantships, and health care benefits (full-time research or teaching assistantship recipients) available. Financial award application deadline: 3/1; financial award applicants required to submit FAFSA. In 2010, 24 master's awarded. *Degree program information:* Part-time and evening/weekend programs available. Offers instrumental performance artist (Certificate); music (MM); music education (PhD); musical arts (DMA); piano performance artist (Certificate); vocal performance artist (Certificate). *Application deadline:* For fall admission, 4/1 priority date for domestic students; for spring admission, 11/1 priority date for domestic students. Applications are processed on a rolling basis. *Application fee:* $100. Electronic applications accepted. *Application Contact:* Victoria Salmon, Graduate Studies, 703-993-4541, E-mail: vsalmon@gmu.edu. *Director*, James Gardner, 703-993-1380, E-mail: jgviolin@gmu.edu.

School for Conflict Analysis and Resolution Students: 80 full-time (40 women), 196 part-time (113 women); includes 46 minority (27 Black or African American, non-Hispanic/Latino; 1 American Indian or Alaska Native, non-Hispanic/Latino; 6 Asian, non-Hispanic/Latino; 11 Hispanic/Latino; 1 Two or more races, non-Hispanic/Latino), 43 international. Average age 35. 398 applicants, 38% accepted, 76 enrolled. *Faculty:* 20 full-time (9 women), 14 part-time/adjunct (5 women). Expenses: Contact institution. *Financial support:* In 2010–11,

George Mason University (continued)

24 students received support, including 3 fellowships with full tuition reimbursements available (averaging $18,000 per year), 15 research assistantships with full and partial tuition reimbursements available (averaging $13,674 per year), 7 teaching assistantships with full and partial tuition reimbursements available (averaging $9,523 per year); career-related internships or fieldwork, Federal Work-Study, scholarships/grants, unspecified assistantships, and health care benefits (full-time research or teaching assistantship recipients) also available. Financial award application deadline: 3/1; financial award applicants required to submit FAFSA. In 2010, 44 master's, 8 doctorates, 26 other advanced degrees awarded. *Degree program information:* Part-time and evening/weekend programs available. Offers conflict analysis and resolution (MS, PhD); conflict analysis and resolution advanced skills (Certificate); conflict analysis and resolution for collaborative leadership in community planning (Certificate); conflict analysis and resolution for prevention, reconstruction, and stabilization contexts (Certificate); environmental conflict resolution and collaboration (Certificate); world religions, diplomacy, and conflict resolution (Certificate). *Application deadline:* For fall admission, 2/1 for domestic students. *Application fee:* $100. Electronic applications accepted. *Application Contact:* Erin Ogilvie, Graduate Admissions and Student Services Director, 703-993-9683, E-mail: eogilvie@gmu.edu. *Director,* Andrea Bartoli, 703-993-9716, Fax: 703-993-1302, E-mail: abartoli@gmu.edu.

School of Law Students: 505 full-time (211 women), 227 part-time (87 women); includes 9 Black or African American, non-Hispanic/Latino; 6 American Indian or Alaska Native, non-Hispanic/Latino; 75 Asian, non-Hispanic/Latino; 22 Hispanic/Latino; 3 Two or more races, non-Hispanic/Latino, 14 international. Average age 25. 5,227 applicants, 26% accepted, 303 enrolled. *Faculty:* 45 full-time (10 women), 177 part-time/adjunct (35 women). Expenses: Contact institution. *Financial support:* In 2010–11, 2 fellowships with full tuition reimbursements (averaging $36,278 per year) were awarded; career-related internships or fieldwork, scholarships/grants, health care benefits, and tuition waivers (partial) also available. Support available to part-time students. Financial award applicants required to submit FAFSA. In 2010, 231 first professional degrees, 2 master's awarded. *Degree program information:* Part-time and evening/weekend programs available. Offers intellectual property (LL M); law (JD); law and economics (LL M). *Application deadline:* For fall admission, 4/1 for domestic and international students. Applications are processed on a rolling basis. *Application fee:* $35. Electronic applications accepted. *Application Contact:* Alison H. Price, Associate Dean/Director of Admission, 703-993-8010, Fax: 703-993-8088, E-mail: lawadmit@gmu.edu. *Dean,* Daniel D. Polsby, 703-993-8006, Fax: 703-993-8088.

School of Management Students: 188 full-time (70 women), 353 part-time (111 women); includes 18 Black or African American, non-Hispanic/Latino; 1 American Indian or Alaska Native, non-Hispanic/Latino; 52 Asian, non-Hispanic/Latino; 17 Hispanic/Latino; 2 Two or more races, non-Hispanic/Latino, 40 international. Average age 31. 467 applicants, 58% accepted, 164 enrolled. *Faculty:* 80 full-time (26 women), 51 part-time/adjunct (15 women). Expenses: Contact institution. *Financial support:* In 2010–11, 38 students received support, including 21 research assistantships with full and partial tuition reimbursements available (averaging $7,176 per year), 20 teaching assistantships with full and partial tuition reimbursements available (averaging $7,255 per year); career-related internships or fieldwork, Federal Work-Study, scholarships/grants, unspecified assistantships, and health care benefits (full-time research or teaching assistantship recipients) also available. Support available to part-time students. Financial award application deadline: 3/1; financial award applicants required to submit FAFSA. In 2010, 203 master's awarded. *Degree program information:* Part-time and evening/weekend programs available. Offers accounting (MS); business administration (EMBA, MBA); real estate development (MS); taxation (MS); technology management (MS). *Application deadline:* Applications are processed on a rolling basis. *Application fee:* $100. Electronic applications accepted. *Application Contact:* Melanie Pflugshaupt, Administrative Coordinator to Dean's Office, 703-993-3638, E-mail: mpflugsh@gmu.edu. *Dean,* Jorge Haddock, 703-993-1875, E-mail: jhaddock@gmu.edu.

School of Public Policy Students: 344 full-time (199 women), 607 part-time (310 women); includes 55 Black or African American, non-Hispanic/Latino; 1 American Indian or Alaska Native, non-Hispanic/Latino; 33 Asian, non-Hispanic/Latino; 55 Hispanic/Latino; 5 Two or more races, non-Hispanic/Latino, 106 international. Average age 31. 842 applicants, 62% accepted, 280 enrolled. *Faculty:* 66 full-time (24 women), 15 part-time/adjunct (3 women). Expenses: Contact institution. *Financial support:* In 2010–11, 43 students received support, including 2 fellowships with full tuition reimbursements available (averaging $18,000 per year), 41 research assistantships with full and partial tuition reimbursements available (averaging $18,104 per year), 2 teaching assistantships (averaging $10,408 per year); career-related internships or fieldwork, Federal Work-Study, scholarships/grants, unspecified assistantships, and health care benefits (full-time research or teaching assistantship recipients) also available. Financial award application deadline: 3/1; financial award applicants required to submit FAFSA. In 2010, 291 master's, 15 doctorates, 12 other advanced degrees awarded. *Degree program information:* Part-time and evening/weekend programs available. Offers culture and values in social policy (Certificate); global medical policy (Certificate); global trade management (Certificate); health and medical policy (MS); international commerce and policy (MA); national security and public policy (Certificate); organization development and knowledge management (MS); peace operations (MS); public policy (EMPP, MPP, PhD); transportation and logistics policy (Certificate); transportation policy, operations and logistics (MA). *Application deadline:* Applications are processed on a rolling basis. *Application fee:* $100. Electronic applications accepted. *Application Contact:* Tennille Haegele, Director of Graduate Admissions, School of Public Policy, 703-993-3183, Fax: 703-993-4876, E-mail: thaegele@gmu.edu. *Dean,* Dr. Edward Rhodes, 703-993-2280, Fax: 703-993-8215, E-mail: edrhodes@gmu.edu.

Volgenau School of Engineering Students: 328 full-time (87 women), 1,293 part-time (279 women); includes 75 Black or African American, non-Hispanic/Latino; 5 American Indian or Alaska Native, non-Hispanic/Latino; 192 Asian, non-Hispanic/Latino; 57 Hispanic/Latino; 7 Two or more races, non-Hispanic/Latino, 471 international. Average age 31. 1,791 applicants, 63% accepted, 441 enrolled. *Faculty:* 147 full-time (29 women), 140 part-time/adjunct (23 women). Expenses: Contact institution. *Financial support:* In 2010–11, 257 students received support, including 9 fellowships with full tuition reimbursements available (averaging $18,000 per year), 105 research assistantships with full and partial tuition reimbursements available (averaging $15,300 per year), 144 teaching assistantships with full and partial tuition reimbursements available (averaging $11,126 per year); career-related internships or fieldwork, Federal Work-Study, scholarships/grants, unspecified assistantships, and health care benefits (full-time research or teaching assistantship recipients) also available. Financial award application deadline: 3/1; financial award applicants required to submit FAFSA. In 2010, 476 master's, 23 doctorates, 109 other advanced degrees awarded. *Degree program information:* Part-time and evening/weekend programs available. Offers advanced networking protocols for telecommunications (Certificate); applied information technology (MS); architecture-based systems integration (Certificate); biometrics (Certificate); biostatistics (Certificate); civil and infrastructure engineering (MS, PhD); civil infrastructure and security engineering (Certificate); command, control, communication, computing and intelligence (Certificate); communications and networking (Certificate); computational modeling (Certificate); computer engineering (MS); computer forensics (MS); computer games technology (Certificate); computer networking (Certificate); computer science (MS, PhD); data mining (Certificate); database management (Certificate); discovery, design and innovation (Certificate); electrical and computer engineering (PhD); electrical engineering (MS); electronic commerce (Certificate); engineering (MS, PhD, Certificate, Engr); federal statistics (Certificate); foundations of information systems (Certificate); information engineering (Certificate); information security and assurance (MS, Certificate); information systems (MS); information technology (PhD, Engr); intelligent agents (Certificate); leading technical enterprises (Certificate); military operations research (Certificate); network technology and applications (Certificate); networks, system integration and testing (Certificate); operations research (MS); signal processing (Certificate); software architecture (Certificate); software engineering (MS, Certificate); statistical science (MS, PhD); sustainability and the environment (Certificate); systems engineering (MS); systems engineering analysis and architecture (Certificate); systems engineering and operations research (PhD); systems engineering of software intensive systems (Certificate); telecom systems modeling (Certificate); telecommunications (MS); telecommunications forensics and security (Certificate); VLSI design/manufacturing (Certificate); water resources engineering (Certificate); Web-based software engineering (Certificate); wireless communication (Certificate). *Application fee:* $100. Electronic applications accepted. *Application Contact:* Nicole Sealey, Graduate Admission and Enrollment Services Director, 703-993-3932, E-mail: nsealey@gmu.edu. *Dean,* Lloyd Griffiths, 703-993-1500, Fax: 703-993-1734, E-mail: lgriff@gmu.edu.

GEORGETOWN COLLEGE, Georgetown, KY 40324-1696

General Information Independent-religious, coed, comprehensive institution. *Graduate housing:* On-campus housing not available.

GRADUATE UNITS

Department of Education *Degree program information:* Part-time programs available. Offers reading and writing (MA Ed); special education (MA Ed); teaching (MA Ed).

GEORGETOWN UNIVERSITY, Washington, DC 20057

General Information Independent-religious, coed, university. CGS member. *Graduate housing:* On-campus housing not available.

GRADUATE UNITS

Graduate School of Arts and Sciences Offers American government (MA, PhD); analytical chemistry (PhD); Arab studies (MA, Certificate); Arabic area studies (PhD); arts and sciences (IEMBA, MA, MALS, MAT, MBA, MPM, MPP, MPS, MS, DLS, PhD, Certificate); bilingual education (Certificate); biochemistry (PhD); bioethics (MA); biology (MS, PhD); British and American literature (MA); communication, culture, and technology (MA); comparative government (PhD); computational chemistry (PhD); computer science (MS); conflict resolution (MA); democracy and governance (MA); econometrics (PhD); economic development (PhD); economic theory (PhD); German (MA, MS, PhD); global history (MA); global, international and comparative history (MA); history (MA, PhD); industrial organization (PhD); inorganic chemistry (PhD); international law and government (MA); international macro and finance (PhD); international relations (PhD); international trade (PhD); Islamic studies (MA, PhD); labor economics (PhD); language and communication (MA); linguistics (MA, MS, PhD); macroeconomics (PhD); materials chemistry (PhD); mathematics and statistics (MS); organic chemistry (PhD); philosophy (PhD); physical chemistry (PhD); political theory (PhD); psychology (PhD); public economics and political economics (PhD); Russian and East European studies (MA); Spanish (MS, PhD); teaching English as a second language (MAT, Certificate); teaching English as a second language and bilingual education (MAT); theology (PhD); theoretical chemistry (PhD).

BMW Center for German and European Studies Offers German and European studies (MA).

Center for Latin American Studies Offers Latin American studies (MA).

Edmund A. Walsh School of Foreign Service Students: 207 full-time (93 women), 78 international. Average age 28. 1,173 applicants. *Faculty:* 32 full-time (7 women), 42 part-time/adjunct (7 women). Expenses: Contact institution. *Financial support:* Career-related internships or fieldwork and tuition waivers (full and partial) available. Financial award application deadline: 1/15. In 2010, 96 master's awarded. Offers foreign service (MS); security studies (MA). *Application deadline:* For fall admission, 1/15 for domestic students. *Application fee:* $75. Electronic applications accepted. *Application Contact:* Information Contact, 202-687-5763, E-mail: msfsinfo@georgetown.edu. *Director, MS in Foreign Service Program,* Dr. Anthony Arend, 202-687-5763.

The Georgetown Public Policy Institute Offers public policy (MPM, MPP).

McDonough School of Business Offers business administration (IEMBA, MBA).

Programs in Biomedical Sciences Offers biochemistry and molecular biology (MS, PhD); biohazardous threat agents and emerging infectious diseases (MS); biomedical sciences (MS, PhD); biostatistics (MS); cell biology (PhD); general microbiology and immunology (MS); global infectious diseases (PhD); health physics (MS); microbiology and immunology research (PhD); neuroscience (PhD); pathology (MS, PhD); pharmacology (MS, PhD); physiology and biophysics (MS, PhD); radiobiology (MS); science policy and advocacy (MS).

School of Continuing Studies Offers American studies (MALS); Catholic studies (MALS); classical civilizations (MALS); disability studies (MPS); ethics and the professions (MALS); human resources management (MPS); humanities (MALS); individualized study (MALS); international affairs (MALS); Islam and Muslim-Christian relations (MALS); journalism (MPS); liberal studies (DLS); literature and society (MALS); medieval and early modern European studies (MALS); public relations and corporate communications (MPS); real estate (MPS); religious studies (MALS); social and public policy (MALS); sports industry management (MPS); the theory and practice of American democracy (MALS); visual culture (MALS).

School of Nursing and Health Studies Offers acute care nurse practitioner (MS); clinical nurse specialist (MS); family nurse practitioner (MS); nurse anesthesia (MS); nurse-midwifery (MS); nursing education (MS).

Law Center *Degree program information:* Part-time and evening/weekend programs available. Offers general (LL M); global health law (LL M); international and comparative law (LL M); international business and economic law (LL M); international legal studies (LL M); law (JD, SJD); securities and financial regulation (LL M); taxation (LL M).

National Institutes of Health Sponsored Programs Offers biomedical sciences (MS, PhD).

School of Medicine Offers medicine (MD).

THE GEORGE WASHINGTON UNIVERSITY, Washington, DC 20052

General Information Independent, coed, university. CGS member. *Enrollment:* 6,913 full-time matriculated graduate/professional students (3,924 women), 7,399 part-time matriculated graduate/professional students (4,107 women). *Enrollment by degree level:* 2,428 first professional, 8,720 master's, 2,052 doctoral, 1,112 other advanced degrees. *Graduate faculty:* 1,906 full-time (858 women), 3,392 part-time/adjunct (1,234 women). *Graduate housing:* On-campus housing not available. *Student services:* Campus employment opportunities, campus safety program, career counseling, exercise/wellness program, free psychological counseling, international student services, low-cost health insurance, multicultural affairs office, services for students with disabilities, teacher training, writing training. *Library facilities:* Gelman Library. *Online resources:* library catalog, web page, access to other libraries' catalogs. *Research affiliation:* Goddard Space Flight Center (radar modeling analysis, space systems technologies), Library of Congress, Smithsonian Institution, National Institutes of Health (biostatistics), NASA–Langley Research Center (aeroacoustics, aeronautics, astronautics), Children's Hospital National Medical Center.

Computer facilities: A campuswide network can be accessed from student residence rooms and from off campus. *Web address:* http://www.gwu.edu/.

General Application Contact: Kristin Williams, Assistant Vice President for Graduate and Special Enrollment Management, 202-994-0467, Fax: 202-994-0371, E-mail: ksw@gwu.edu.

GRADUATE UNITS

College of Professional Studies Students: 171 full-time (75 women), 782 part-time (503 women); includes 207 minority (90 Black or African American, non-Hispanic/Latino; 7 American Indian or Alaska Native, non-Hispanic/Latino; 30 Asian, non-Hispanic/Latino; 71 Hispanic/Latino; 4 Native Hawaiian or other Pacific Islander, non-Hispanic/Latino; 5 Two or more races, non-Hispanic/Latino), 36 international. Average age 34. 847 applicants, 89% accepted, 430 enrolled. *Faculty:* 14 full-time (4 women), 19 part-time/adjunct (6 women). Expenses: Contact institution. In 2010, 328 master's, 60 other advanced degrees awarded. Offers healthcare corporate compliance (Graduate Certificate); law firm management (MPS, Graduate Certificate); molecular biotechnology (MPS); paralegal studies (MPS, Graduate Certificate); publishing (MPS). *Application Contact:* Kristin Williams, Assistant Vice President for Graduate and Special Enrollment Management, 202-994-0467, Fax: 202-994-0371, E-mail: ksw@gwu.edu. *Dean,* Kathleen M. Burke, 202-994-9711.

Graduate School of Political Management Students: 50 full-time (15 women), 205 part-time (94 women); includes 37 minority (11 Black or African American, non-Hispanic/Latino; 2 American Indian or Alaska Native, non-Hispanic/Latino; 7 Asian, non-Hispanic/Latino; 14

Hispanic/Latino; 2 Native Hawaiian or other Pacific Islander, non-Hispanic/Latino; 1 Two or more races, non-Hispanic/Latino), 19 international. Average age 29. 210 applicants, 90% accepted, 84 enrolled. *Faculty:* 5 full-time (0 women). Expenses: Contact institution. *Financial support:* In 2010–11, 18 students received support; fellowships with tuition reimbursements available, scholarships/grants and tuition waivers available. Financial award application deadline: 2/1. In 2010, 104 master's, 2 other advanced degrees awarded. Offers legislative affairs (MA); PAC management (Graduate Certificate); political management (MA). *Application deadline:* For fall admission, 6/15 priority date for domestic students, 4/1 priority date for international students; for spring admission, 11/15 priority date for domestic students, 10/1 priority date for international students. Applications are processed on a rolling basis. *Application fee:* $75. Electronic applications accepted. *Application Contact:* Information Contact, 202-994-6000, Fax: 202-994-6006. *Dean,* Dr. Christopher Arterton, 202-994-5843, Fax: 202-994-5806, E-mail: gspmmail@gwu.edu.

Columbian College of Arts and Sciences Students: 1,219 full-time (827 women), 1,093 part-time (715 women); includes 345 minority (105 Black or African American, non-Hispanic/Latino; 13 American Indian or Alaska Native, non-Hispanic/Latino; 121 Asian, non-Hispanic/Latino; 97 Hispanic/Latino; 5 Native Hawaiian or other Pacific Islander, non-Hispanic/Latino; 4 Two or more races, non-Hispanic/Latino), 334 international. Average age 29. 5,351 applicants, 44% accepted, 664 enrolled. *Faculty:* 472 full-time (211 women), 482 part-time/adjunct (246 women). Expenses: Contact institution. *Financial support:* Fellowships with tuition reimbursements, research assistantships, teaching assistantships with tuition reimbursements, career-related internships or fieldwork, Federal Work-Study, scholarships/grants, tuition waivers, and unspecified assistantships available. Support available to part-time students. Financial award application deadline: 2/1. In 2010, 528 master's, 124 doctorates, 60 other advanced degrees awarded. *Degree program information:* Part-time and evening/weekend programs available. Offers American studies (PhD); analytical chemistry (MS, PhD); anthropology (MA); applied mathematics (MA, MS, PhD); applied social psychology (PhD); art history (MA); art therapy (MA); arts and sciences (MA, MFA, MFS, MPA, MPP, MS, PhD, Psy D, Certificate, Graduate Certificate); biological sciences (MS, PhD); biostatistics (MS, PhD); ceramics (MFA); classical acting (MFA); clinical psychology (PhD); cognitive neuroscience (PhD); crime scene investigation (MFS); criminology (MA); dance (MFA); design (MFA); drawing/painting (MFA); economics (MA, PhD); English (MA, PhD); environmental and resource policy (MA); epidemiology (MS, PhD); folklife (MA); forensic chemistry (MFS); forensic molecular biology (MFS); forensic toxicology (MFS); geography (MA); high-technology crime investigation (MFS); Hinduism and Islam (MA); historic preservation (MA); history (MA, PhD); hominid paleobiology (MS, PhD); human resources management (MA); industrial/organizational psychology (PhD); inorganic chemistry (MS, PhD); interior design (MFA); international development (MA); material culture (MA); materials science (MS, PhD); museum studies (MA, Certificate); museum training (MA); new media (MFA); organic chemistry (MS, PhD); organizational management (MA); philosophy and social policy (MA); photography (MFA); physical chemistry (MS, PhD); physics (MA, PhD); political science (MA, PhD); professional psychology (Psy D); pure mathematics (MA, MS, PhD); sculpture (MFA); security management (MFS); sociology (MA); speech-language pathology (MA); statistics (MS, PhD); survey design and data analysis (Graduate Certificate); women's studies (MA, Certificate). *Application deadline:* For fall admission, 1/15 priority date for domestic and international students; for spring admission, 10/1 priority date for domestic and international students. Applications are processed on a rolling basis. *Application fee:* $75. Electronic applications accepted. *Application Contact:* 202-994-6210, Fax: 202-994-6213, E-mail: askccas@gwu.edu. *Dean,* Peg Barratt, 202-994-6130, E-mail: barratt@gwu.edu.

Institute for Biomedical Sciences Students: 16 full-time (8 women), 32 part-time (22 women); includes 2 Black or African American, non-Hispanic/Latino; 1 American Indian or Alaska Native, non-Hispanic/Latino; 3 Asian, non-Hispanic/Latino; 1 Hispanic/Latino, 6 international. Average age 30. 203 applicants, 7% accepted, 13 enrolled. Expenses: Contact institution. *Financial support:* In 2010–11, 24 students received support; fellowships with full tuition reimbursements available, Federal Work-Study, institutionally sponsored loans, and tuition waivers available. In 2010, 2 doctorates awarded. *Degree program information:* Part-time and evening/weekend programs available. Offers biochemistry and molecular genetics (PhD); microbiology and immunology (PhD); molecular and cellular oncology (PhD); molecular medicine (PhD); neurosciences (PhD); pharmacology and physiology (PhD). *Application deadline:* For fall admission, 12/15 priority date for domestic and international students. Applications are processed on a rolling basis. *Application fee:* $60. Electronic applications accepted. *Application Contact:* 202-994-2179, Fax: 202-994-0967, E-mail: gwibs@gwu.edu. *Director,* Dr. Linda L. Werling, 202-994-2918, Fax: 202-994-0967.

School of Media and Public Affairs Students: 22 full-time (14 women), 17 part-time (15 women); includes 1 Black or African American, non-Hispanic/Latino; 3 Asian, non-Hispanic/Latino; 1 Hispanic/Latino, 5 international. Average age 26. 119 applicants, 55% accepted, 21 enrolled. *Faculty:* 24 full-time (7 women), 16 part-time/adjunct (5 women). Expenses: Contact institution. *Financial support:* In 2010–11, fellowships with tuition reimbursements (averaging $10,000 per year), teaching assistantships with tuition reimbursements (averaging $5,000 per year) were awarded. Financial award application deadline: 1/15. In 2010, 11 master's awarded. Offers media and public affairs (MA). *Application deadline:* For fall admission, 4/1 priority date for domestic students, 1/15 priority date for international students; for spring admission, 10/1 priority date for domestic students, 9/1 priority date for international students. Applications are processed on a rolling basis. *Application fee:* $75. Electronic applications accepted. *Application Contact:* Information Contact, 202-994-6227, Fax: 202-994-5806, E-mail: smpa@gwu.edu. *Director,* Lee W. Huebner, 202-994-6227, E-mail: huebner@gwu.edu.

Trachtenberg School of Public Policy and Public Administration Students: 286 full-time (182 women), 163 part-time (123 women); includes 18 Black or African American, non-Hispanic/Latino; 1 American Indian or Alaska Native, non-Hispanic/Latino; 30 Asian, non-Hispanic/Latino; 12 Hispanic/Latino; 1 Native Hawaiian or other Pacific Islander, non-Hispanic/Latino. Average age 26. 1,102 applicants, 49% accepted, 146 enrolled. *Faculty:* 37 full-time (13 women), 19 part-time/adjunct (10 women). Expenses: Contact institution. *Financial support:* In 2010–11, 65 students received support; fellowships, research assistantships, teaching assistantships available. Financial award application deadline: 1/15. In 2010, 113 master's awarded. *Degree program information:* Part-time and evening/weekend programs available. Offers public administration (MPA). *Application deadline:* For fall admission, 1/15 priority date for domestic and international students; for spring admission, 10/1 priority date for domestic students, 9/1 priority date for international students. *Application fee:* $60. Electronic applications accepted. *Application Contact:* Bethany Pope, Program Coordinator, 202-994-6295, Fax: 202-994-6295, E-mail: tspppa@gwu.edu. *Director,* Dr. Kathyrn E. Newcomer, 202-994-3959, Fax: 202-994-3959, E-mail: newcomer@gwu.edu.

Elliott School of International Affairs Students: 540 full-time (286 women), 299 part-time (178 women); includes 16 Black or African American, non-Hispanic/Latino; 1 American Indian or Alaska Native, non-Hispanic/Latino; 50 Asian, non-Hispanic/Latino; 38 Hispanic/Latino; 6 Two or more races, non-Hispanic/Latino, 99 international. Average age 27. 2,152 applicants, 47% accepted, 314 enrolled. Expenses: Contact institution. *Financial support:* In 2010–11, 155 students received support; fellowships with tuition reimbursements available, research assistantships with tuition reimbursements available, teaching assistantships with tuition reimbursements available, career-related internships or fieldwork, Federal Work-Study, institutionally sponsored loans, and tuition waivers (full and partial) available. Financial award application deadline: 1/15; financial award applicants required to submit FAFSA. In 2010, 332 master's awarded. *Degree program information:* Part-time and evening/weekend programs available. Offers Asian studies (MA); European and Eurasian studies (MA); global communication (MA); international affairs (MA, MIPP, MIS); international development studies (MA); international policy and practice (MIPP); international science and technology policy (MA); international studies (MIS); international trade and investment policy (MA); Latin American and hemispheric studies (MA); Middle East studies (MA); security policy studies (MA). *Application deadline:* For fall admission, 2/1 for domestic and international students; for spring admission, 10/1 for domestic and international students. *Application fee:* $75. Electronic applications accepted. *Application Contact:* Jeff V. Miles, Director of Graduate Admissions, 202-994-7050, Fax: 202-994-9537, E-mail: esiagrad@gwu.edu. *Dean,* Michael Brown, 202-994-6241, Fax: 202-994-0335, E-mail: esiadean@gwu.edu.

Graduate School of Education and Human Development Students: 447 full-time (351 women), 1,240 part-time (908 women); includes 471 minority (321 Black or African American, non-Hispanic/Latino; 7 American Indian or Alaska Native, non-Hispanic/Latino; 59 Asian, non-Hispanic/Latino; 78 Hispanic/Latino; 1 Native Hawaiian or other Pacific Islander, non-Hispanic/Latino; 5 Two or more races, non-Hispanic/Latino), 69 international. Average age 36. 1,401 applicants, 86% accepted, 628 enrolled. *Faculty:* 78 full-time (49 women), 85 part-time/adjunct (57 women). Expenses: Contact institution. *Financial support:* In 2010–11, 279 students received support; fellowships with tuition reimbursements available, research assistantships with tuition reimbursements available, teaching assistantships with tuition reimbursements available, career-related internships or fieldwork, Federal Work-Study, and tuition waivers (full and partial) available. Support available to part-time students. Financial award application deadline: 1/15. In 2010, 518 master's, 77 doctorates, 210 other advanced degrees awarded. *Degree program information:* Part-time and evening/weekend programs available. Postbaccalaureate distance learning degree programs offered (no on-campus study). Offers community counseling (MA Ed); counseling (PhD, Ed S); counseling: school, community and rehabilitation (MA Ed); curriculum and instruction (MA Ed, Ed D, Ed S); early childhood special education (MA Ed); education and human development (M Ed, MA Ed, MAT, Ed D, PhD, Certificate, Ed S, Graduate Certificate); education policy (Ed D); education policy studies (MA Ed); educational administration (Ed D); educational administration and policy studies (Ed D); educational leadership and administration (MA Ed, Certificate, Ed S); educational technology leadership (MA Ed); elementary education (M Ed); higher education administration (MA Ed, Ed D, Ed S); human and organizational learning (MA Ed, Ed D, Graduate Certificate); human resource development (MA Ed); international education (MA Ed); leadership development (Graduate Certificate); museum education (MAT); rehabilitation counseling (MA Ed); school counseling (MA Ed); secondary education (M Ed); special education (Ed D, Ed S); special education for children with emotional and behavioral disabilities (MA Ed); transition special education (MA Ed, Certificate). *Application deadline:* For fall admission, 1/15 priority date for domestic students; for spring admission, 10/1 for domestic students. Applications are processed on a rolling basis. *Application fee:* $75. Electronic applications accepted. *Application Contact:* Sarah Lang, Director of Graduate Admissions, 202-994-1447, Fax: 202-994-7207, E-mail: slang@gwu.edu. *Dean,* Dr. Mary Hatwood Futrell, 202-994-6161, Fax: 202-994-7207, E-mail: mfutrell@gwu.edu.

Law School Students: 1,666 full-time (787 women), 445 part-time (164 women); includes 124 Black or African American, non-Hispanic/Latino; 8 American Indian or Alaska Native, non-Hispanic/Latino; 179 Asian, non-Hispanic/Latino; 123 Hispanic/Latino; 7 Native Hawaiian or other Pacific Islander, non-Hispanic/Latino, 140 international. Average age 28. 255 applicants, 100% accepted, 195 enrolled. *Faculty:* 89 full-time (35 women), 192 part-time/adjunct (62 women). Expenses: Contact institution. *Financial support:* Research assistantships, career-related internships or fieldwork, Federal Work-Study, institutionally sponsored loans, scholarships/grants, and tuition waivers (full and partial) available. Support available to part-time students. Financial award application deadline: 3/1; financial award applicants required to submit CSS PROFILE or FAFSA. In 2010, 496 first professional degrees, 198 master's, 1 doctorate awarded. *Degree program information:* Part-time and evening/weekend programs available. Offers law (JD, LL M, SJD). *Application deadline:* For fall admission, 3/1 for domestic students. Applications are processed on a rolling basis. *Application fee:* $75. *Application Contact:* Robert V. Stanek, Assistant Dean of Admissions and Financial Aid, 202-739-0648, Fax: 202-739-0624, E-mail: jd@admit.nlc.gwu.edu. *Dean,* Frederick M. Lawrence, 202-994-6288, Fax: 202-994-5157, E-mail: flawrence@law.gwu.edu.

School of Business Students: 961 full-time (448 women), 961 part-time (433 women); includes 458 minority (173 Black or African American, non-Hispanic/Latino; 11 American Indian or Alaska Native, non-Hispanic/Latino; 178 Asian, non-Hispanic/Latino; 87 Hispanic/Latino; 3 Native Hawaiian or other Pacific Islander, non-Hispanic/Latino; 6 Two or more races, non-Hispanic/Latino), 390 international. Average age 32. 2,544 applicants, 52% accepted, 662 enrolled. *Faculty:* 126 full-time (40 women), 57 part-time/adjunct (15 women). Expenses: Contact institution. *Financial support:* In 2010–11, 194 students received support; fellowships with tuition reimbursements available, teaching assistantships with tuition reimbursements available, career-related internships or fieldwork, Federal Work-Study, institutionally sponsored loans, and tuition waivers (partial) available. Financial award application deadline: 4/1. In 2010, 756 master's, 11 doctorates awarded. *Degree program information:* Part-time and evening/weekend programs available. Offers accountancy (M Accy, MBA, PhD); business (M Accy, MBA, MS, MSF, MSIST, MTA, PMBA, PhD, Professional Certificate); event and meeting management (MTA); event management (Professional Certificate); finance (MSF, PhD); finance and investments (MBA); hospitality management (MTA, Professional Certificate); information and decision systems (PhD); information systems (MSIST); information systems development (MSIST); information systems management (MBA); information systems project management (MSIST); international business (MBA, PhD); management (MBA, PhD); management information systems (MSIST); management of science, technology, and innovation (MBA, PhD); marketing (MBA, PhD); project management (MS); real estate and urban development (MBA); sport management (MTA); sports business management (Professional Certificate); strategic management and public policy (MBA, PhD); sustainable tourism destination management (MTA); tourism administration (MTA); tourism and hospitality management (MBA); tourism destination management (Professional Certificate). PMBA program also offered in Alexandria and Ashburn, VA. *Application deadline:* For fall admission, 4/1 priority date for domestic students; for spring admission, 10/1 for domestic students. Applications are processed on a rolling basis. *Application fee:* $75. Electronic applications accepted. *Application Contact:* Kristin Williams, Assistant Vice President for Graduate and Special Enrollment Management, 202-994-0467, Fax: 202-994-0371, E-mail: ksw@gwu.edu. *Dean,* Dr. Susan M. Phillips, 202-994-6380, Fax: 202-994-6382.

School of Engineering and Applied Science Students: 405 full-time (115 women), 1,516 part-time (355 women); includes 394 minority (162 Black or African American, non-Hispanic/Latino; 10 American Indian or Alaska Native, non-Hispanic/Latino; 148 Asian, non-Hispanic/Latino; 66 Hispanic/Latino; 6 Native Hawaiian or other Pacific Islander, non-Hispanic/Latino; 2 Two or more races, non-Hispanic/Latino), 417 international. Average age 33. 1,396 applicants, 81% accepted, 459 enrolled. *Faculty:* 82 full-time (10 women), 66 part-time/adjunct (9 women). Expenses: Contact institution. *Financial support:* In 2010–11, 216 students received support; fellowships with full and partial tuition reimbursements available, research assistantships with full and partial tuition reimbursements available, teaching assistantships with full and partial tuition reimbursements available, career-related internships or fieldwork, Federal Work-Study, institutionally sponsored loans, and tuition waivers (full and partial) available. Financial award application deadline: 3/1; financial award applicants required to submit FAFSA. In 2010, 520 master's, 47 doctorates, 169 other advanced degrees awarded. *Degree program information:* Part-time and evening/weekend programs available. Offers civil and environmental engineering (MS, D Sc, App Sc, Engr); computer science (MS, D Sc); electrical and computer engineering (MS, D Sc); engineering and applied science (MS, D Sc, App Sc, Engr, Graduate Certificate); engineering management and systems engineering (MS, D Sc, App Sc, Engr, Graduate Certificate); mechanical and aerospace engineering (MS, D Sc, App Sc, Engr, Graduate Certificate); telecommunication and computers (MS). *Application deadline:* For fall admission, 3/1 for domestic students; for spring admission, 10/1 for domestic students. Applications are processed on a rolling basis. *Application fee:* $75. *Application Contact:* Adina Lav, Marketing, Recruiting and Admissions, 202-994-5827, Fax: 202-994-0909, E-mail: engineering@gwu.edu. *Dean,* David S. Dolling, 202-994-6080, E-mail: dolling@gwu.edu.

School of Medicine and Health Sciences Students: 992 full-time (613 women), 343 part-time (248 women); includes 418 minority (147 Black or African American, non-Hispanic/Latino; 5 American Indian or Alaska Native, non-Hispanic/Latino; 217 Asian, non-Hispanic/Latino; 40 Hispanic/Latino; 6 Native Hawaiian or other Pacific Islander, non-Hispanic/Latino; 3 Two or more races, non-Hispanic/Latino), 56 international. Average age 29. 1,175 applicants, 51% accepted, 218 enrolled. *Faculty:* 860 full-time (418 women), 2,030 part-time/adjunct (625 women). Expenses: Contact institution. *Financial support:* Career-related internships or fieldwork, Federal Work-Study, and institutionally sponsored loans available. In 2010, 177 first professional degrees, 183 master's, 52 doctorates, 71 other advanced degrees awarded. Offers adult nurse practitioner (MSN, Post Master's Certificate); biochemistry and molecular biology (MS); biochemistry and molecular genetics (PhD); clinical practice management (MSHS); clinical research administration (MSHS); clinical research administration for nurses (MSN); emergency services management (MSHS); end-of-life care (MSHS, MSN); family

The George Washington University (continued)

nurse practitioner (MSN, Post Master's Certificate); immunohematology (MSHS); medicine (MD); medicine and health sciences (MD, MS, MSHS, MSN, DNP, DPT, PhD, Post Master's Certificate); molecular biochemistry and bioinformatics (MS); nursing (DNP); nursing leadership and management (MSN); physical therapy (DPT); physician assistant (MSHS). *Application deadline:* Applications are processed on a rolling basis. *Application fee:* $75. *Application Contact:* Admissions, 202-994-3748, Fax: 202-994-1753, E-mail: medadmit@gwu.edu. *Senior Associate Dean,* Dr. James L. Scott, 202-994-3725, E-mail: hspjej@gwumc.edu.

School of Nursing Students: 14 full-time (12 women), 267 part-time (237 women); includes 21 Black or African American, non-Hispanic/Latino; 8 American Indian or Alaska Native, non-Hispanic/Latino; 20 Asian, non-Hispanic/Latino; 6 Hispanic/Latino, 12 international. Average age 41. 328 applicants, 54% accepted, 106 enrolled. *Faculty:* 19 full-time (all women), 36 part-time/adjunct (33 women). Expenses: Contact institution. In 2010, 7 master's awarded. Offers nursing (MSN, DNP, Post-Master's Certificate). *Application Contact:* Kristin Williams, Assistant Vice President for Graduate and Special Enrollment Management, 202-994-0467, Fax: 202-994-0371, E-mail: ksw@gwu.edu. *Dean,* Jean E. Johnson, 202-994-3725, E-mail: sonjej@gwumc.edu.

School of Public Health and Health Services Students: 498 full-time (410 women), 453 part-time (366 women); includes 347 minority (135 Black or African American, non-Hispanic/Latino; 5 American Indian or Alaska Native, non-Hispanic/Latino; 142 Asian, non-Hispanic/Latino; 52 Hispanic/Latino; 2 Native Hawaiian or other Pacific Islander, non-Hispanic/Latino; 11 Two or more races, non-Hispanic/Latino), 59 international. Average age 29. 1,361 applicants, 79% accepted, 355 enrolled. *Faculty:* 95 full-time (56 women), 294 part-time/adjunct (146 women). Expenses: Contact institution. *Financial support:* In 2010–11, 71 students received support. Career-related internships or fieldwork, Federal Work-Study, institutionally sponsored loans, scholarships/grants, and tuition waivers (partial) available. Support available to part-time students. Financial award application deadline: 2/15. In 2010, 281 master's, 3 doctorates, 24 other advanced degrees awarded. *Degree program information:* Part-time and evening/weekend programs available. Offers biostatistics (MPH); environmental health science and policy (MPH); epidemiology (MPH); exercise science (MS); global health (MPH); health management and leadership (MHSA); health policy (MPH, MS); health services administration (Specialist); microbiology and emerging infectious diseases (MSPH); public health (MPH); public health and health services (MHSA, MPH, MS, MSPH, Dr PH, Specialist); public health management (MPH). *Application deadline:* For fall admission, 2/15 priority date for domestic students, 2/15 for international students. Applications are processed on a rolling basis. *Application Contact:* Jane Smith, Director of Admissions, 202-994-2160, Fax: 202-994-1860, E-mail: sphhsinfo@gwumc.edu. *Associate Dean,* Dr. Josef J. Reum, 202-994-5179, E-mail: josefr@gwu.edu.

GEORGIA CAMPUS–PHILADELPHIA COLLEGE OF OSTEOPATHIC MEDICINE, Suwanee, GA 30024

General Information Independent, coed, graduate-only institution.

GRADUATE UNITS

Program in Biomedical Sciences Offers biomedical sciences (MS, Certificate).

Program in Osteopathic Medicine Offers osteopathic medicine (DO).

GEORGIA COLLEGE & STATE UNIVERSITY, Milledgeville, GA 31061

General Information State-supported, coed, comprehensive institution. *Enrollment:* 6,737 graduate, professional, and undergraduate students; 387 full-time matriculated graduate/professional students (236 women), 635 part-time matriculated graduate/professional students (406 women). *Enrollment by degree level:* 887 master's, 135 other advanced degrees. *Graduate faculty:* 316 full-time (171 women). Tuition, state resident: full-time $4806; part-time $267 per hour. Tuition, nonresident: full-time $17,802; part-time $989 per hour. Tuition and fees vary according to course load. *Graduate housing:* Room and/or apartments available on a first-come, first-served basis to single students; on-campus housing not available to married students. Typical cost: $6934 per year. Room charges vary according to board plan, campus/location and housing facility selected. Housing application deadline: 3/1. *Student services:* Campus employment opportunities, campus safety program, career counseling, exercise/wellness program, free psychological counseling, international student services, multicultural affairs office, services for students with disabilities, teacher training. *Library facilities:* Ina Dillard Russell Library. *Online resources:* library catalog, web page, access to other libraries' catalogs. *Collection:* 206,641 titles, 55,049 serial subscriptions, 11,949 audiovisual materials.

Computer facilities: Computer purchase and lease plans are available. 180 computers available on campus for general student use. A campuswide network can be accessed from student residence rooms and from off campus. Online class registration is available. *Web address:* http://www.gcsu.edu/.

General Application Contact: Kate Marshall, Graduate Admissions Coordinator, 478-445-1184, Fax: 478-445-1336, E-mail: grad-admit@gcsu.edu.

GRADUATE UNITS

Graduate School Students: 387 full-time (236 women), 635 part-time (406 women); includes 226 minority (177 Black or African American, non-Hispanic/Latino; 2 American Indian or Alaska Native, non-Hispanic/Latino; 15 Asian, non-Hispanic/Latino; 19 Hispanic/Latino; 13 Two or more races, non-Hispanic/Latino), 27 international. Average age 31. 494 applicants, 85% accepted, 284 enrolled. *Faculty:* 316 full-time (171 women). Expenses: Contact institution. *Financial support:* In 2010–11, 157 research assistantships with full tuition reimbursements were awarded; career-related internships or fieldwork, scholarships/grants, and unspecified assistantships also available. Support available to part-time students. Financial award application deadline: 3/1. In 2010, 353 master's, 114 other advanced degrees awarded. *Degree program information:* Part-time and evening/weekend programs available. Postbaccalaureate distance learning degree programs offered (minimal on-campus study). *Application deadline:* For fall admission, 7/1 priority date for domestic students, 4/1 priority date for international students; for spring admission, 11/15 priority date for domestic students, 9/1 priority date for international students. Applications are processed on a rolling basis. *Application fee:* $40. Electronic applications accepted. *Application Contact:* Kate Marshall, Graduate Admissions Coordinator, 478-445-1184, Fax: 478-445-1336, E-mail: grad-admit@gcsu.edu. *Graduate Admissions Coordinator,* Kate Marshall, 478-445-1184, Fax: 478-445-1336, E-mail: grad-admit@gcsu.edu.

College of Arts and Sciences Students: 87 full-time (43 women), 234 part-time (142 women); includes 70 minority (52 Black or African American, non-Hispanic/Latino; 2 American Indian or Alaska Native, non-Hispanic/Latino; 1 Asian, non-Hispanic/Latino; 8 Hispanic/Latino; 7 Two or more races, non-Hispanic/Latino), 10 international. 164 applicants, 73% accepted, 91 enrolled. *Faculty:* 179 full-time (83 women). Expenses: Contact institution. *Financial support:* In 2010–11, 74 research assistantships with tuition reimbursements were awarded; career-related internships or fieldwork and unspecified assistantships also available. Support available to part-time students. Financial award application deadline: 3/1; financial award applicants required to submit FAFSA. In 2010, 95 master's awarded. *Degree program information:* Part-time and evening/weekend programs available. Offers arts and sciences (MA, MFA, MM Ed, MPA, MS, MSA); biology (MS); creative writing (MFA); criminal justice (MS); English (MA); history (advanced studies) (MA); history (predoctoral) (MA); logistics (MSA); logistics management (MSA); music (MM Ed); public administration (MPA); public history (MA). *Application deadline:* For fall admission, 7/1 priority date for domestic students, 4/1 priority date for international students; for spring admission, 11/15 priority date for domestic students, 9/1 priority date for international students. Applications are processed on a rolling basis. *Application fee:* $40. Electronic applications accepted. *Application Contact:* Kenneth Proctor, Dean, 478-445-4441, E-mail: ken.proctor@gcsu.edu. *Dean,* Kenneth Proctor, 478-445-4441, E-mail: ken.proctor@gcsu.edu.

College of Health Sciences Students: 51 full-time (33 women), 71 part-time (65 women); includes 19 Black or African American, non-Hispanic/Latino; 2 Asian, non-Hispanic/Latino; 2 Hispanic/Latino, 5 international. Average age 31. 53 applicants, 89% accepted, 33 enrolled. *Faculty:* 39 full-time (29 women). Expenses: Contact institution. *Financial support:* In 2010–11, 29 research assistantships with tuition reimbursements were awarded; career-related internships or fieldwork and unspecified assistantships also available. Support available to part-time students. Financial award applicants required to submit FAFSA. In 2010, 24 master's awarded. *Degree program information:* Part-time and evening/weekend programs available. Offers adult health (MSN); family nurse practitioner (MSN); health promotion (M Ed); health sciences (M Ed, MAT, MMT, MSN); human performance (M Ed); kinesiology (MAT); music therapy (MMT); nursing administration (MSN); outdoor education (M Ed). *Application deadline:* For fall admission, 7/1 priority date for domestic students, 4/1 priority date for international students; for spring admission, 11/15 for domestic students, 9/1 priority date for international students. Applications are processed on a rolling basis. *Application fee:* $40. Electronic applications accepted. *Application Contact:* Dr. Sandra Gangstead, Dean, 478-445-4092, E-mail: sandra.gangstead@gcsu.edu. *Dean,* Dr. Sandra Gangstead, 478-445-4092, E-mail: sandra.gangstead@gcsu.edu.

The John H. Lounsbury College of Education Students: 200 full-time (142 women), 183 part-time (152 women); includes 90 minority (81 Black or African American, non-Hispanic/Latino; 1 Asian, non-Hispanic/Latino; 6 Hispanic/Latino; 2 Two or more races, non-Hispanic/Latino), 1 international. Average age 32. 164 applicants, 97% accepted, 93 enrolled. *Faculty:* 51 full-time (38 women). Expenses: Contact institution. *Financial support:* In 2010–11, 22 research assistantships were awarded; career-related internships or fieldwork, Federal Work-Study, and unspecified assistantships also available. Support available to part-time students. Financial award application deadline: 3/1; financial award applicants required to submit FAFSA. In 2010, 177 master's, 93 other advanced degrees awarded. *Degree program information:* Part-time programs available. Offers curriculum and instruction (Ed S); early childhood education (M Ed, Ed S); education (M Ed, MAT, Ed S); educational technology (M Ed); educational leadership (M Ed, Ed S); educational technology (M Ed); middle grades education (M Ed, Ed S); secondary education (M Ed, MAT); special education (M Ed, MAT, Ed S); special education and educational leadership (M Ed, MAT, Ed S). *Application deadline:* For fall admission, 7/1 priority date for domestic students; for spring admission, 11/15 priority date for domestic students. Applications are processed on a rolling basis. *Application fee:* $40. Electronic applications accepted. *Application Contact:* Shanda Brand, Graduate Coordinator, 478-445-1383, Fax: 478-445-6582, E-mail: shanda.brand@gcsu.edu. *Dean,* Dr. Jane Hinson, 478-445-4546, E-mail: jane.hinson@gcsu.edu.

The J. Whitney Bunting School of Business Students: 53 full-time (22 women), 157 part-time (53 women); includes 35 minority (18 Black or African American, non-Hispanic/Latino; 9 Asian, non-Hispanic/Latino; 5 Hispanic/Latino; 3 Two or more races, non-Hispanic/Latino), 11 international. Average age 30. 111 applicants, 83% accepted, 61 enrolled. *Faculty:* 46 full-time (20 women). Expenses: Contact institution. *Financial support:* In 2010–11, 33 research assistantships with full tuition reimbursements were awarded; career-related internships or fieldwork and unspecified assistantships also available. Support available to part-time students. Financial award application deadline: 3/1; financial award applicants required to submit FAFSA. In 2010, 121 master's awarded. *Degree program information:* Part-time and evening/weekend programs available. Postbaccalaureate distance learning degree programs offered (no on-campus study). Offers accountancy (MACCT); accounting (MBA); business (MBA); health services administration (MBA); information systems (MIS); management information services (MBA). *Application deadline:* For fall admission, 7/1 priority date for domestic students, 4/1 priority date for international students; for spring admission, 11/15 priority date for domestic students, 8/1 priority date for international students. Applications are processed on a rolling basis. *Application fee:* $40. Electronic applications accepted. *Application Contact:* Lynn Hanson, Director of Graduate Programs, 478-445-5115, E-mail: lynn.hanson@gcsu.edu. *Dean,* Dr. Matthew Liao-Troth, 478-445-5497, E-mail: matthew.liao-troth@gcsu.edu.

GEORGIA HEALTH SCIENCES UNIVERSITY, Augusta, GA 30912

General Information State-supported, coed, upper-level institution. CGS member. *Enrollment:* 2,438 graduate, professional, and undergraduate students; 1,827 full-time matriculated graduate/professional students (1,042 women), 126 part-time matriculated graduate/professional students (102 women). *Enrollment by degree level:* 1,066 first professional, 579 master's, 300 doctoral, 8 other advanced degrees. *Graduate faculty:* 643 full-time (238 women), 114 part-time/adjunct (57 women). Tuition, state resident: full-time $7500; part-time $313 per semester hour. Tuition, nonresident: full-time $24,772; part-time $1033 per semester hour. *Required fees:* $1112. *Graduate housing:* Rooms and/or apartments available on a first-come, first-served basis to single and married students. *Student services:* Campus employment opportunities, campus safety program, career counseling, child daycare facilities, exercise/wellness program, free psychological counseling, international student services, low-cost health insurance, multicultural affairs office. *Library facilities:* Robert B. Greenblatt MD Library. *Online resources:* library catalog, web page, access to other libraries' catalogs. *Collection:* 166,744 titles, 4,674 serial subscriptions, 1,681 audiovisual materials. *Research affiliation:* Georgia Center of Innovation for Life Sciences (research commercialization and economic development), Georgia Research Alliance (science and technology development), Georgia Cancer Coalition (cancer research programs), Advanced Technology Development Center (biotechnology transfer), Medical College of Georgia Research Institute, Inc. (biomedical research).

Computer facilities: 250 computers available on campus for general student use. A campuswide network can be accessed. Online class registration is available. *Web address:* http://www.georgiahealth.edu.

General Application Contact: Heather Metress, Interim Director of Academic Admissions, 706-721-2725, Fax: 706-721-7279, E-mail: admissions@georgiahealth.edu.

GRADUATE UNITS

College of Dental Medicine Students: 262 full-time (115 women), 2 part-time (1 woman); includes 28 Black or African American, non-Hispanic/Latino; 1 American Indian or Alaska Native, non-Hispanic/Latino; 24 Asian, non-Hispanic/Latino; 10 Hispanic/Latino; 6 Two or more races, non-Hispanic/Latino. Average age 26. 309 applicants, 26% accepted, 70 enrolled. *Faculty:* 53 full-time (10 women), 14 part-time/adjunct (4 women). Expenses: Contact institution. *Financial support:* Federal Work-Study and scholarships/grants available. Financial award application deadline: 5/1; financial award applicants required to submit FAFSA. In 2010, 61 DMDs awarded. Offers dental medicine (DMD). *Application deadline:* For fall admission, 10/15 for domestic students. *Application fee:* $30. Electronic applications accepted. *Application Contact:* Dr. Carole M. Hanes, Associate Dean for Student and Alumni Affairs, 706-721-3587, Fax: 706-721-6276, E-mail: chanes@georgiahealth.edu. *Dean,* Dr. Connie Drisko, 706-721-2117, Fax: 706-721-6276, E-mail: cdrisko@georgiahealth.edu.

College of Graduate Studies Students: 471 full-time (355 women), 122 part-time (101 women); includes 60 Black or African American, non-Hispanic/Latino; 2 American Indian or Alaska Native, non-Hispanic/Latino; 33 Asian, non-Hispanic/Latino; 15 Hispanic/Latino; 12 Two or more races, non-Hispanic/Latino, 81 international. Average age 31. 451 applicants, 44% accepted, 125 enrolled. *Faculty:* 225 full-time (74 women), 7 part-time/adjunct (4 women). Expenses: Contact institution. *Financial support:* In 2010–11, 10 fellowships with partial tuition reimbursements (averaging $26,000 per year), 111 research assistantships with partial tuition reimbursements (averaging $23,000 per year) were awarded; teaching assistantships, career-related internships or fieldwork, Federal Work-Study, institutionally sponsored loans, scholarships/grants, traineeships, and unspecified assistantships also available. Support available to part-time students. Financial award application deadline: 5/31; financial award applicants required to submit FAFSA. In 2010, 104 master's, 33 doctorates awarded. *Degree program information:* Part-time programs available. Postbaccalaureate distance learning degree programs offered (no on-campus study). Offers biochemistry and molecular biology (MS, PhD); biostatistics (MS, PhD); cellular biology and anatomy (MS, PhD); clinical and translational science (MCTS, CCTS); clinical nurse leader (MSN); dental hygiene (MS); family nurse practitioner (MSN, Post-Master's Certificate); genomic medicine (MS, PhD); medical illustration (MS); molecular medicine (MS, PhD); neuroscience (MS, PhD); nursing (PhD); nursing anesthesia (MSN); nursing practice (DNP); oral biology and maxillofacial pathology (MS, PhD); pediatric nurse practitioner (MSN, Post-Master's Certificate); pharmacology (MS, PhD); physiology (MS, PhD); public health–informatics (MPH); vascular biology (MS, PhD). *Application fee:* $30. Electronic applications accepted. *Application Contact:* Heather Metress, Interim

Director of Admissions, 706-721-2725, Fax: 706-721-7279, E-mail: hmetress@georgiahealth.edu. *Dean,* Dr. Gretchen B. Caughman, 706-721-3278, Fax: 706-721-6829, E-mail: gcaughma@mail.mcg.edu.

Medical College of Georgia Students: 800 full-time (354 women), 2 part-time (0 women); includes 56 Black or African American, non-Hispanic/Latino; 188 Asian, non-Hispanic/Latino; 23 Hispanic/Latino; 17 Two or more races, non-Hispanic/Latino. Average age 25. 2,055 applicants, 15% accepted, 190 enrolled. *Faculty:* 438 full-time (133 women), 80 part-time/adjunct (37 women). Expenses: Contact institution. *Financial support:* Fellowships with tuition reimbursements, career-related internships or fieldwork, Federal Work-Study, institutionally sponsored loans, and scholarships/grants available. Support available to part-time students. Financial award application deadline: 5/1; financial award applicants required to submit FAFSA. In 2010, 178 first professional degrees awarded. Offers medicine (MD). *Application deadline:* For fall admission, 11/1 for domestic students. Applications are processed on a rolling basis. *Application fee:* $0. *Application Contact:* Dr. Geoffrey H. Young, Associate Dean for Admissions, 706-721-3186, Fax: 706-721-0959, E-mail: geyoung@georgiahealth.edu. *Dean,* Dr. Peter Buckley, 706-721-2231, Fax: 706-721-7035, E-mail: pbuckley@georgiahealth.edu.

GEORGIA INSTITUTE OF TECHNOLOGY, Atlanta, GA 30332-0001

General Information State-supported, coed, university. CGS member. *Graduate housing:* Rooms and/or apartments available on a first-come, first-served basis to single and married students. Housing application deadline: 5/1. *Research affiliation:* Oak Ridge National Laboratory (energy, health, environment), Yerkes Regional Primate Research Center (biomedicine, physiology and behavior), Skidaway Institute of Oceanography (marine geology), Southeastern Universities Research Association (high-energy physics), Emory University Medical School (biomedical engineering), Zoo Atlanta (environmental design, environmental psychology).

GRADUATE UNITS

Graduate Studies and Research *Degree program information:* Part-time and evening/weekend programs available. Postbaccalaureate distance learning degree programs offered. Offers algorithms, combinatorics, and optimization (PhD); statistics (MS Stat). Electronic applications accepted.

College of Architecture Offers architecture (M Arch, MCRP, MS, PhD); building construction (PhD); city and regional planning (PhD); economic development (MCRP); environmental planning and management (MCRP); geographic information systems (MCRP); integrated facility management (MS); integrated project delivery systems (MS); land and community development (MCRP); land use planning (MCRP); residential construction development (MS); transportation (MCRP); urban design (MCRP). Electronic applications accepted.

College of Computing *Degree program information:* Part-time programs available. Postbaccalaureate distance learning degree programs offered. Offers algorithms, combinatorics, and optimization (PhD); computational science and engineering (MS, PhD); computer science (MS, MSCS, PhD); human computer interaction (MSHCI); human-centered computing (PhD); information security (MS).

College of Engineering *Degree program information:* Part-time programs available. Postbaccalaureate distance learning degree programs offered. Offers aerospace engineering (MS, MSAE, PhD); algorithms, combinatorics, and optimization (PhD); bioengineering (MS Bio E, PhD); bioinformatics (PhD); biomedical engineering (MS Bio E, PhD); chemical engineering (MS Ch E, PhD); civil engineering (MS, MSCE, PhD); electrical and computer engineering (MS, MSEE, PhD); engineering (MS, MS Bio E, MS Ch E, MS Env E, MS Poly, MS Stat, MSAE, MSCE, MSEE, MSESM, MSHS, MSIE, MSME, MSNE, MSOR, PhD); engineering science and mechanics (MS, MSESM, PhD); environmental engineering (MS, MS Env E, PhD); health systems (MSHS); industrial and systems engineering (MS, MS Stat, MSIE, PhD); industrial engineering (MS, MSIE); materials science and engineering (MS, PhD); mechanical engineering (MS, MS Bio E, MSME, PhD); medical physics (MS); nuclear and radiological engineering (MSNE, PhD); nuclear and radiological engineering and medical physics (MS, MSNE, PhD); operations research (MSOR, PhD); paper science and engineering (MS, PhD); polymer, textile and fiber engineering (MS, PhD); polymers (MS Poly); statistics (MS Stat). Electronic applications accepted.

College of Management Offers accounting (MBA, PhD); e-commerce (Certificate); engineering entrepreneurship (MBA); entrepreneurship (Certificate); finance (MBA, PhD); information technology management (MBA, PhD); international business (MBA, Certificate); management (EMBA, MBA, MS, PhD, Certificate); management of technology (Certificate); marketing (MBA, PhD); operations management (MBA, PhD); organizational behavior (MBA, PhD); quantitative and computational finance (MS); strategic management (MBA, PhD). Electronic applications accepted.

College of Sciences *Degree program information:* Part-time programs available. Offers algorithms, combinatorics, and optimization (PhD); applied biology (MS, PhD); applied mathematics (MS); atmospheric chemistry, aerosols and clouds (MS, PhD); bioinformatics (MS, PhD); biology (MS); chemistry and biochemistry (MS, MS Chem, PhD); dynamics of weather and climate (MS, PhD); geochemistry (MS, PhD); geophysics (MS, PhD); human computer interaction (MSHCI); mathematics (PhD); oceanography (MS, PhD); paleoclimate (MS, PhD); physics (MS, PhD); planetary science (MS, PhD); prosthetics and orthotics (MS); psychology (MS, MS Psy, PhD); quantitative and computational finance (MS); remote sensing (MS, PhD); sciences (MS, MS Chem, MS Phys, MS Psy, MS Stat, MSA Phy, MSHCI, PhD); statistics (MS Stat). Electronic applications accepted.

Ivan Allen College of Policy and International Affairs *Degree program information:* Part-time and evening/weekend programs available. Offers digital media (MS, PhD); economics (MS); history and sociology of technology and science (MS, PhD); human computer interaction (MSHCI); international affairs (MS Int A, PhD); policy and international affairs (MS, MS Int A, MS Pub P, MSHCI, MSIDT, PhD); public policy (MS Pub P, PhD). Electronic applications accepted.

GEORGIAN COURT UNIVERSITY, Lakewood, NJ 08701-2697

General Information Independent-religious, coed, primarily women, comprehensive institution. *Enrollment:* 2,885 graduate, professional, and undergraduate students; 281 full-time matriculated graduate/professional students (237 women), 635 part-time matriculated graduate/professional students (526 women). *Enrollment by degree level:* 686 master's, 230 other advanced degrees. *Graduate faculty:* 53 full-time (31 women), 52 part-time/adjunct (39 women). *Tuition:* Full-time $12,510; part-time $695 per credit. *Required fees:* $416 per year. Tuition and fees vary according to campus/location and program. *Graduate housing:* On-campus housing not available. *Student services:* Campus employment opportunities, campus safety program, career counseling, exercise/wellness program, free psychological counseling, low-cost health insurance, services for students with disabilities, teacher training. *Library facilities:* The Sister Mary Joseph Cunningham Library. *Online resources:* library catalog, web page, access to other libraries' catalogs. *Collection:* 129,837 titles, 1,727 serial subscriptions, 5,248 audiovisual materials.

Computer facilities: 197 computers available on campus for general student use. A campuswide network can be accessed. Online class registration is available. *Web address:* http://www.georgian.edu/.

General Application Contact: Patrick Givens, Assistant Director of Admissions, 732-987-2736, Fax: 732-987-2084, E-mail: graduateadmissions@georgian.edu.

GRADUATE UNITS

School of Arts and Sciences Students: 61 full-time (59 women), 143 part-time (113 women); includes 20 minority (5 Black or African American, non-Hispanic/Latino; 3 Asian, non-Hispanic/Latino; 11 Hispanic/Latino; 1 Two or more races, non-Hispanic/Latino), 1 international. Average age 39. 139 applicants, 59% accepted, 50 enrolled. *Faculty:* 19 full-time (11 women), 7 part-time/adjunct (5 women). Expenses: Contact institution. *Financial support:* Scholarships/grants, health care benefits, and unspecified assistantships available. Financial award application deadline: 4/15; financial award applicants required to submit FAFSA. In 2010, 5 master's awarded. *Degree program information:* Part-time and evening/weekend programs available. Offers biology (MA); Catholic school leadership (Certificate); clinical mental health counseling (MA); holistic health studies (MA); mathematics (MA); pastoral ministry (Certificate); religious education (Certificate); school psychology (Certificate); theology (MA, Certificate). *Application deadline:* For fall admission, 8/1 priority date for domestic students, 4/1 for international students; for spring admission, 1/1 priority date for domestic students, 7/1 for international students. Applications are processed on a rolling basis. *Application fee:* $40. Electronic applications accepted. *Application Contact:* Patrick Givens, Assistant Director of Admissions, 732-987-2736, Fax: 732-987-2084, E-mail: graduateadmissions@georgian.edu. *Dean,* Dr. Linda James, 732-987-2617, Fax: 732-987-2007.

School of Business Students: 63 full-time (47 women), 65 part-time (42 women); includes 29 minority (14 Black or African American, non-Hispanic/Latino; 1 American Indian or Alaska Native, non-Hispanic/Latino; 2 Asian, non-Hispanic/Latino; 11 Hispanic/Latino; 1 Native Hawaiian or other Pacific Islander, non-Hispanic/Latino), 1 international. Average age 32. 85 applicants, 67% accepted, 41 enrolled. *Faculty:* 8 full-time (4 women), 7 part-time/adjunct (4 women). Expenses: Contact institution. *Financial support:* Scholarships/grants, health care benefits, and unspecified assistantships available. Financial award application deadline: 4/15; financial award applicants required to submit FAFSA. In 2010, 62 master's, 7 other advanced degrees awarded. *Degree program information:* Part-time and evening/weekend programs available. Offers accounting (Certificate); business administration (MBA). *Application deadline:* For fall admission, 8/1 priority date for domestic students, 4/1 for international students; for spring admission, 1/1 priority date for domestic students, 7/1 for international students. Applications are processed on a rolling basis. *Application fee:* $40. Electronic applications accepted. *Application Contact:* Patrick Givens, Assistant Director of Admissions, 732-987-2736, Fax: 732-987-2084, E-mail: graduateadmissions@georgian.edu. *Dean,* Dr. Joseph Monahan, 732-987-2724, Fax: 732-987-2024, E-mail: monahanj@georgian.edu.

School of Education Students: 156 full-time (130 women), 420 part-time (365 women); includes 52 minority (9 Black or African American, non-Hispanic/Latino; 2 American Indian or Alaska Native, non-Hispanic/Latino; 4 Asian, non-Hispanic/Latino; 36 Hispanic/Latino; 1 Two or more races, non-Hispanic/Latino). Average age 32. 481 applicants, 77% accepted, 191 enrolled. *Faculty:* 26 full-time (16 women), 38 part-time/adjunct (30 women). Expenses: Contact institution. *Financial support:* Scholarships/grants, health care benefits, and unspecified assistantships available. Financial award application deadline: 4/15; financial award applicants required to submit FAFSA. In 2010, 118 master's awarded. *Degree program information:* Part-time and evening/weekend programs available. Offers administration and leadership (MA); education (MA). *Application deadline:* For fall admission, 8/1 priority date for domestic students, 4/1 for international students; for spring admission, 1/1 priority date for domestic students, 7/1 for international students. Applications are processed on a rolling basis. *Application fee:* $40. Electronic applications accepted. *Application Contact:* Patrick Givens, Assistant Director of Admissions, 732-987-2736, Fax: 732-987-2084, E-mail: graduateadmissions@georgian.edu. *Dean,* Dr. Jacqueline Kress, 732-987-2525.

GEORGIA SOUTHERN UNIVERSITY, Statesboro, GA 30460

General Information State-supported, coed, university. CGS member. *Enrollment:* 19,691 graduate, professional, and undergraduate students; 941 full-time matriculated graduate/professional students (538 women), 1,605 part-time matriculated graduate/professional students (1,096 women). *Enrollment by degree level:* 1,763 master's, 510 doctoral, 273 other advanced degrees. *Graduate faculty:* 525 full-time (236 women), 23 part-time/adjunct (10 women). Tuition, state resident: full-time $6000; part-time $250 per semester hour. Tuition, nonresident: full-time $23,976; part-time $999 per semester hour. *Required fees:* $1644. *Graduate housing:* Room and/or apartments available to single students; on-campus housing not available to married students. Housing application deadline: 5/1. *Student services:* Campus employment opportunities, campus safety program, career counseling, exercise/wellness program, free psychological counseling, grant writing training, international student services, low-cost health insurance, multicultural affairs office, services for students with disabilities, teacher training, writing training. *Library facilities:* Henderson Library. *Online resources:* library catalog, web page, access to other libraries' catalogs. *Collection:* 613,593 titles, 39,997 serial subscriptions, 29,437 audiovisual materials. *Research affiliation:* Oak Ridge National Laboratory (physical sciences), Mount Desert Island Biological Laboratory (marine biology), Space Telescope Science Institute (astronomy, physics), St. Catherine's Island Foundation (marine science, life sciences), Skidaway Institute of Oceanography (marine sciences).

Computer facilities: 3,260 computers available on campus for general student use. A campuswide network can be accessed from student residence rooms and from off campus. Online class registration is available. *Web address:* http://www.georgiasouthern.edu/.

General Application Contact: Office of Graduate Admissions, 912-478-5384, Fax: 912-478-0740, E-mail: gradadmissions@georgiasouthern.edu.

GRADUATE UNITS

Jack N. Averitt College of Graduate Studies Students: 941 full-time (538 women), 1,605 part-time (1,096 women); includes 678 minority (559 Black or African American, non-Hispanic/Latino; 7 American Indian or Alaska Native, non-Hispanic/Latino; 30 Asian, non-Hispanic/Latino; 51 Hispanic/Latino; 2 Native Hawaiian or other Pacific Islander, non-Hispanic/Latino; 29 Two or more races, non-Hispanic/Latino), 97 international. Average age 32. 1,037 applicants, 80% accepted, 552 enrolled. *Faculty:* 497 full-time (224 women), 27 part-time/adjunct (16 women). Expenses: Contact institution. *Financial support:* In 2010–11, 1,737 students received support, including 192 research assistantships with partial tuition reimbursements available (averaging $7,200 per year), teaching assistantships with partial tuition reimbursements available (averaging $7,200 per year); career-related internships or fieldwork, Federal Work-Study, scholarships/grants, traineeships, tuition waivers (partial), unspecified assistantships, and doctoral stipends also available. Support available to part-time students. Financial award application deadline: 4/15; financial award applicants required to submit FAFSA. In 2010, 601 master's, 69 doctorates, 78 other advanced degrees awarded. *Degree program information:* Part-time and evening/weekend programs available. Postbaccalaureate distance learning degree programs offered. *Application deadline:* For fall admission, 3/1 priority date for domestic and international students; for spring admission, 10/1 priority date for domestic students, 10/1 for international students. Applications are processed on a rolling basis. *Application fee:* $50. Electronic applications accepted. *Application Contact:* Dr. Charles Ziglar, Coordinator for Graduate Student Recruitment, 912-478-5635, Fax: 912-478-0740, E-mail: gradadmissions@georgiasouthern.edu. *Associate Vice President for Research/Dean,* Dr. Charles E. Patterson, 912-478-0851, Fax: 912-478-0605, E-mail: cpatterson@georgiasouthern.edu.

Allen E. Paulson College of Science and Technology Students: 97 full-time (30 women), 30 part-time (8 women); includes 20 Black or African American, non-Hispanic/Latino; 1 American Indian or Alaska Native, non-Hispanic/Latino; 3 Asian, non-Hispanic/Latino; 4 Hispanic/Latino; 4 Two or more races, non-Hispanic/Latino, 22 international. Average age 27. 57 applicants, 86% accepted, 34 enrolled. *Faculty:* 91 full-time (25 women), 4 part-time/adjunct (0 women). Expenses: Contact institution. *Financial support:* In 2010–11, 106 students received support, including 38 research assistantships with partial tuition reimbursements available (averaging $7,200 per year), teaching assistantships with partial tuition reimbursements available (averaging $7,200 per year); career-related internships or fieldwork, Federal Work-Study, scholarships/grants, tuition waivers (partial), and unspecified assistantships also available. Support available to part-time students. Financial award application deadline: 4/15; financial award applicants required to submit FAFSA. In 2010, 33 master's awarded. *Degree program information:* Part-time programs available. Offers biology (MS); mathematics (MS); mechanical and electrical engineering technology (M Tech, MSAE, Certificate); science and technology (M Tech, MS, MSAE, Certificate). *Application deadline:* For fall admission, 3/1 priority date for domestic and international students; for spring admission, 10/1 priority date for domestic students, 10/1 for international students. Applications are processed on a rolling basis. *Application fee:* $50. Electronic applications accepted. *Application Contact:* Dr. Charles Ziglar, Coordinator for Graduate Student Recruitment, 912-478-5635, Fax: 912-478-0740, E-mail: gradadmissions@georgiasouthern.edu. *Dean,* Dr. Bret Danilowicz, 912-478-5111, Fax: 912-478-0836, E-mail: bdanilowicz@georgiasouthern.edu.

College of Business Administration Students: 191 full-time (65 women), 254 part-time (105 women); includes 86 minority (57 Black or African American, non-Hispanic/Latino; 1 American Indian or Alaska Native, non-Hispanic/Latino; 13 Asian, non-Hispanic/Latino; 8 Hispanic/Latino; 1 Native Hawaiian or other Pacific Islander, non-Hispanic/Latino; 6 Two or more races, non-Hispanic/Latino), 33 international. Average age 29. 292 applicants, 78%

Georgia Southern University (continued)

accepted, 155 enrolled. *Faculty:* 70 full-time (24 women), 1 part-time/adjunct (0 women). Expenses: Contact institution. *Financial support:* In 2010–11, 272 students received support, including 23 research assistantships with partial tuition reimbursements available (averaging $7,200 per year), teaching assistantships with partial tuition reimbursements available (averaging $7,200 per year); career-related internships or fieldwork, Federal Work-Study, scholarships/grants, tuition waivers (partial), and unspecified assistantships also available. Support available to part-time students. Financial award application deadline: 4/15; financial award applicants required to submit FAFSA. In 2010, 151 master's awarded. *Degree program information:* Part-time and evening/weekend programs available. Postbaccalaureate distance learning degree programs offered (no on-campus study). Offers accounting (M Acc); applied economics (MS); business administration (M Acc, MBA, MS, PhD); logistics/supply chain management (PhD). *Application deadline:* For fall admission, 3/1 priority date for domestic and international students; for spring admission, 10/1 priority date for domestic students, 10/1 for international students. Applications are processed on a rolling basis. *Application fee:* $50. Electronic applications accepted. *Application Contact:* Dr. Charles Ziglar, Coordinator for Graduate Student Recruitment, 912-478-5635, Fax: 912-478-0740, E-mail: gradadmissions@georgiasouthern.edu. *Dean,* Dr. Ron Shiffler, 912-478-2622, Fax: 912-478-0292, E-mail: shiffler@georgiasouthern.edu.

College of Education Students: 322 full-time (249 women), 1,051 part-time (823 women); includes 364 Black or African American, non-Hispanic/Latino; 2 American Indian or Alaska Native, non-Hispanic/Latino; 7 Asian, non-Hispanic/Latino; 22 Hispanic/Latino; 14 Two or more races, non-Hispanic/Latino, 10 international. Average age 35. 314 applicants, 95% accepted, 191 enrolled. *Faculty:* 73 full-time (51 women), 12 part-time/adjunct (10 women). Expenses: Contact institution. *Financial support:* In 2010–11, 851 students received support, including 26 research assistantships with partial tuition reimbursements available (averaging $7,200 per year), teaching assistantships with partial tuition reimbursements available (averaging $7,200 per year); career-related internships or fieldwork, Federal Work-Study, scholarships/grants, tuition waivers (partial), unspecified assistantships, and doctoral stipends also available. Support available to part-time students. Financial award application deadline: 4/15; financial award applicants required to submit FAFSA. In 2010, 242 master's, 68 doctorates, 78 other advanced degrees awarded. *Degree program information:* Part-time and evening/weekend programs available. Postbaccalaureate distance learning degree programs offered (no on-campus study). Offers accomplished teaching (M Ed); art education (M Ed, MAT); business education (M Ed, MAT); counselor education (M Ed, Ed S); curriculum studies (Ed D); early childhood education (MAT); education (M Ed, MAT, Ed D, Ed S); educational administration (Ed D); educational leadership (M Ed, Ed S); English education (M Ed, MAT); French education (M Ed); higher education (M Ed); instructional technology (M Ed); mathematics education (M Ed, MAT); middle grades education (M Ed, MAT); reading education (M Ed); school psychology (M Ed, Ed S); science education (M Ed, MAT); social science education (M Ed, MAT); Spanish education (MAT); special education (M Ed, MAT); teaching and learning (M Ed, Ed S). *Application deadline:* For fall admission, 3/1 priority date for domestic and international students; for spring admission, 10/1 priority date for domestic students, 10/1 for international students. Applications are processed on a rolling basis. *Application fee:* $50. Electronic applications accepted. *Application Contact:* Dr. Charles Ziglar, Coordinator of Graduate Student Recruitment, 912-478-5635, Fax: 912-478-0740, E-mail: gradadmissions@georgiasouthern.edu. *Dean,* Dr. Thomas Koballa, 912-478-5648, Fax: 912-478-5093, E-mail: tkoballa@georgiasouthern.edu.

College of Health and Human Sciences Students: 88 full-time (52 women), 149 part-time (98 women); includes 40 Black or African American, non-Hispanic/Latino; 1 American Indian or Alaska Native, non-Hispanic/Latino; 7 Hispanic/Latino; 1 Native Hawaiian or other Pacific Islander, non-Hispanic/Latino, 5 international. Average age 31. 135 applicants, 62% accepted, 67 enrolled. *Faculty:* 59 full-time (37 women), 1 (woman) part-time/adjunct. Expenses: Contact institution. *Financial support:* In 2010–11, 215 students received support, including 57 research assistantships with partial tuition reimbursements available (averaging $7,200 per year), teaching assistantships with partial tuition reimbursements available (averaging $7,200 per year); career-related internships or fieldwork, Federal Work-Study, scholarships/grants, traineeships, tuition waivers (partial), and unspecified assistantships also available. Support available to part-time students. Financial award application deadline: 4/15; financial award applicants required to submit FAFSA. In 2010, 93 master's awarded. *Degree program information:* Part-time and evening/weekend programs available. Postbaccalaureate distance learning degree programs offered (no on-campus study). Offers clinical nurse specialist (MSN, Certificate); health and human sciences (MS, MSN, DNP, Certificate); health and kinesiology (MS); nurse practitioner (MSN, Certificate); nursing science (DNP); rural community health nurse practitioner (MSN); rural community health nurse specialist (Certificate); rural family nurse practitioner (MSN, Certificate); sport management (MS); women's health nurse practitioner (MSN, Certificate). *Application deadline:* For fall admission, 3/1 priority date for domestic students, 3/1 for international students; for spring admission, 10/1 priority date for domestic students, 10/1 for international students. Applications are processed on a rolling basis. *Application fee:* $50. Electronic applications accepted. *Application Contact:* Dr. Charles Ziglar, Coordinator for Graduate Student Recruitment, 912-478-5635, Fax: 912-478-0740, E-mail: gradadmissions@georgiasouthern.edu. *Dean,* Dr. Jjean Bartels, 912-478-5322, Fax: 912-478-5349, E-mail: jbartels@georgiasouthern.edu.

College of Information Technology Students: 2 full-time (1 woman), 11 part-time (2 women); includes 3 Black or African American, non-Hispanic/Latino; 1 Asian, non-Hispanic/Latino. Average age 30. 16 applicants, 100% accepted, 10 enrolled. *Faculty:* 21 full-time (4 women), 1 part-time/adjunct (0 women). Expenses: Contact institution. *Financial support:* In 2010–11, 7 students received support. Postbaccalaureate distance learning degree programs offered. Offers computer science (MS). *Application Contact:* Dr. Lixin Li, Graduate Director, 912-478-7646, Fax: 912-478-7672, E-mail: mscs@georgiasouthern.edu. *Interim Dean,* Dr. Ron Shiffler, 912-478-7454, E-mail: shiffler@georgiasouthern.edu.

College of Liberal Arts and Social Sciences Students: 158 full-time (88 women), 79 part-time (36 women); includes 36 Black or African American, non-Hispanic/Latino; 2 American Indian or Alaska Native, non-Hispanic/Latino; 2 Asian, non-Hispanic/Latino; 10 Hispanic/Latino; 3 Two or more races, non-Hispanic/Latino, 6 international. Average age 28. 152 applicants, 69% accepted, 71 enrolled. *Faculty:* 155 full-time (71 women), 7 part-time/adjunct (5 women). Expenses: Contact institution. *Financial support:* In 2010–11, 198 students received support, including fellowships with full tuition reimbursements available (averaging $12,000 per year), 46 research assistantships with partial tuition reimbursements available (averaging $7,200 per year), teaching assistantships with partial tuition reimbursements available (averaging $7,200 per year); career-related internships or fieldwork, Federal Work-Study, scholarships/grants, tuition waivers (partial), and unspecified assistantships also available. Support available to part-time students. Financial award application deadline: 4/15; financial award applicants required to submit FAFSA. In 2010, 53 master's awarded. *Degree program information:* Part-time programs available. Offers English (MA); fine arts (MFA); history (MA); liberal arts and social sciences (MA, MFA, MM, MPA, MS, Psy D); music (MM); psychology (MS, Psy D); public administration (MPA); sociology and anthropology (MA); Spanish (MA). *Application deadline:* For fall admission, 3/1 priority date for domestic and international students; for spring admission, 10/1 priority date for domestic students, 10/1 for international students. Applications are processed on a rolling basis. *Application fee:* $50. Electronic applications accepted. *Application Contact:* Charles Ziglar, Coordinator for Graduate Student Recruitment, 912-478-5635, Fax: 912-478-0740, E-mail: gradadmissions@georgiasouthern.edu. *Dean,* Dr. Michael R. Smith, 912-478-2527, Fax: 912-478-5346, E-mail: msmith@georgiasouthern.edu.

Jiann-Ping Hsu College of Public Health Students: 83 full-time (53 women), 31 part-time (24 women); includes 43 Black or African American, non-Hispanic/Latino; 4 Asian, non-Hispanic/Latino; 2 Two or more races, non-Hispanic/Latino, 21 international. Average age 30. 71 applicants, 66% accepted, 24 enrolled. *Faculty:* 28 full-time (12 women), 1 part-time/adjunct (0 women). Expenses: Contact institution. *Financial support:* In 2010–11, 88 students received support, including research assistantships with partial tuition reimbursements available (averaging $7,200 per year), teaching assistantships with partial tuition reimbursements available (averaging $7,200 per year); career-related internships or fieldwork, Federal Work-Study, scholarships/grants, tuition waivers (partial), and unspecified assistantships also available. Support available to part-time students. Financial award application deadline: 4/15; financial award applicants required to submit FAFSA. In 2010, 29 master's, 1 doctorate awarded. *Degree program information:* Part-time programs available. Offers biostatistics (MPH, Dr PH); community health behavior and education (Dr PH); community health education (MPH); environmental health sciences (MPH); epidemiology (MPH); health services policy management (MPH); healthcare administration (MHA); public health (MHA, MPH, Dr PH); public health leadership (Dr PH). *Application deadline:* For fall admission, 3/1 priority date for domestic and international students; for spring admission, 10/1 priority date for domestic students, 10/1 for international students. Applications are processed on a rolling basis. *Application fee:* $50. Electronic applications accepted. *Application Contact:* Sarah Peterson, Coordinator for Graduate Student Recruitment, 912-478-2413, Fax: 912-478-5811, E-mail: speterson@georgiasouthern.edu. *Dean,* Dr. Charles Hardy, 912-478-5653, Fax: 912-478-5605, E-mail: chardy@georgiasouthern.edu.

GEORGIA SOUTHWESTERN STATE UNIVERSITY, Americus, GA 31709-4693

General Information State-supported, coed, comprehensive institution. *Graduate housing:* Room and/or apartments available on a first-come, first-served basis to single students; on-campus housing not available to married students. Housing application deadline: 8/1.

GRADUATE UNITS

Graduate Studies *Degree program information:* Part-time programs available. Electronic applications accepted.

School of Business Administration Offers business administration (MBA). Electronic applications accepted.

School of Computer and Information Sciences *Degree program information:* Part-time programs available. Offers computer information systems (MS); computer science (MS). Electronic applications accepted.

School of Education Offers early childhood education (M Ed, Ed S); health and physical education (M Ed); middle grades education (M Ed, Ed S); reading (M Ed); secondary education (M Ed); special education (M Ed). Electronic applications accepted.

GEORGIA STATE UNIVERSITY, Atlanta, GA 30302-3083

General Information State-supported, coed, university. CGS member. *Graduate housing:* Rooms and/or apartments available on a first-come, first-served basis to single and married students. *Research affiliation:* Lowell Observatory (astronomy), Brookhaven National Laboratory (physics), Argonne National Laboratory, Advanced Photon Source (crystallography), Cerro Tololo Interamerican Observatory (astronomy), Research Atlanta, Inc. (policy studies), Oak Ridge National Laboratory (environmental policy).

GRADUATE UNITS

Andrew Young School of Policy Studies *Degree program information:* Part-time and evening/weekend programs available. Offers disaster management (Certificate); economics (MA, PhD); non-profit management (Certificate); planning and economic development (Certificate); policy studies (MA, MPA, MPP, MS, PhD, Certificate); public administration (MPA); public policy (MPP, PhD). Electronic applications accepted.

College of Arts and Sciences *Degree program information:* Part-time and evening/weekend programs available. Offers anthropology (MA); applied and environmental microbiology (MS, PhD); applied linguistics (MA, PhD); arts and sciences (M Mu, MA, MA Ed, MFA, MHP, MS, PhD, Certificate, Graduate Certificate); astronomy (PhD); cellular and molecular biology and physiology (MS, PhD); chemistry (MS, PhD); computer science (MS, PhD); creative writing (MA, MFA, PhD); English (MA, PhD); fiction (MFA); fiction/poetry (MA, MFA); film/video/digital imaging (MA); French (MA, Certificate); geographic information systems (Certificate); geography (MA); geology (MA); German (MA, Certificate); heritage preservation (MHP, Certificate); history (MA, PhD); human communication and social influence (MA); hydrogeology (Certificate); Latin American studies (Certificate); literary studies (MA, PhD); mass communication (MA); mathematics (MA, MS); mathematics and statistics (PhD); molecular genetics and biochemistry (MS, PhD); moving image studies (PhD); neurobiology and behavior (MS, PhD); philosophy (MA); physics (MS, PhD); poetry (MFA); political science (MA, PhD); psychology (MA, PhD); public communication (PhD); religious studies (MA); rhetoric and composition (MA, PhD); sociology (MA, PhD); Spanish (MA, Certificate); translation and interpretation (Certificate). Electronic applications accepted.

Ernest G. Welch School of Art and Design Offers art and design (MA, MA Ed, MFA); art education (MA Ed); art history (MA); studio art (MFA). Electronic applications accepted.

Gerontology Institute *Degree program information:* Part-time programs available. Offers gerontology (MA). Electronic applications accepted.

School of Music *Degree program information:* Part-time and evening/weekend programs available. Offers music (M Mu). Electronic applications accepted.

Women's Studies Institute *Degree program information:* Part-time programs available. Offers women's studies (MA, Graduate Certificate).

College of Education *Degree program information:* Part-time and evening/weekend programs available. Postbaccalaureate distance learning degree programs offered (no on-campus study). Offers art education (Ed S); behavior and learning disabilities (M Ed); communication disorders (M Ed); counseling psychology (PhD); counselor education and practice (PhD); early childhood education (M Ed, MAT, PhD, Ed S); education (M Ed, MAT, MLM, MS, PhD, Ed S); education of students with exceptionalities (PhD); educational leadership (M Ed, PhD, Ed S); educational psychology (MS, PhD); educational research (MS, PhD); English education (M Ed, Ed S); exercise science (MS); health and physical education (M Ed); instructional technology (MS, PhD, Ed S); kinesiology (PhD); library media technology (MLM, PhD, Ed S); library science/media (MLM, MS, PhD, Ed S); mathematics education (M Ed, PhD, Ed S); middle childhood education (M Ed, Ed S); multiple and severe disabilities (M Ed, MAT); music education (PhD); professional counseling (MS, PhD, Ed S); reading instruction (M Ed, PhD, Ed S); reading, language and literacy (M Ed); reading, language, and literacy (PhD, Ed S); rehabilitation counseling (MS); research, measurements and statistics (PhD); school counseling (M Ed, Ed S); school psychology (M Ed, PhD, Ed S); science education (M Ed, PhD, Ed S); secondary education (M Ed, PhD, Ed S); social foundations of education (MS, PhD); social studies education (M Ed, PhD, Ed S); sports administration (MS); sports medicine (MS); teaching English as a second language (M Ed). Electronic applications accepted.

College of Health and Human Sciences *Degree program information:* Part-time and evening/weekend programs available. Offers criminal justice (MS); health and human sciences (MPH, MS, MSW, DPT, PhD, Certificate). Electronic applications accepted.

Byrdine F. Lewis School of Nursing *Degree program information:* Part-time and evening/weekend programs available. Postbaccalaureate distance learning degree programs offered (minimal on-campus study). Offers adult health (MS); adult health nursing (Certificate); child health (MS); family nurse practitioner (MS, Certificate); health promotion, protection and restoration (PhD); perinatal/women's health (MS); psychiatric mental health nursing (Certificate); psychiatric/mental health (MS); women's health nursing (Certificate). Electronic applications accepted.

Institute of Public Health *Degree program information:* Part-time and evening/weekend programs available. Offers public health (MPH, Certificate). Electronic applications accepted.

School of Health Professions Offers health professions (MS, DPT); nutrition (MS); physical therapy (DPT); respiratory therapy (MS).

School of Social Work *Degree program information:* Part-time programs available. Offers community partnerships (MSW). Electronic applications accepted.

College of Law *Degree program information:* Part-time and evening/weekend programs available. Offers law (JD). Electronic applications accepted.

J. Mack Robinson College of Business *Degree program information:* Part-time and evening/weekend programs available. Offers accounting/information systems (MBA); actuarial science (MAS, MBA); business (EMBA, MAS, MBA, MHA, MIB, MPA, MS, MSHA, MSIS, MSRE, MTX, PMBA, EDB, PhD, Certificate); business analysis (MBA, MS); computer information systems (MBA, MSIS, PhD); decision sciences (PhD); economics (MBA, MS); enterprise risk management (MBA); entrepreneurship (MBA); finance (MBA, MS, PhD); general business (MBA); general business administration (EMBA, PMBA); human resources management (MBA, MS); information systems consulting (MBA); information systems risk management (MBA); international business and information technology (MBA); international entrepreneurship (MBA); management (MBA, PhD); marketing (MBA, MS, PhD); operations management (MBA, MS); organization change (MS); personal financial planning (MBA, MS, Certificate); personnel employee relations (PhD); real estate (MBA, MSRE, PhD, Certificate); risk management and insurance (MBA, MS, PhD, Certificate); strategic management (PhD). Electronic applications accepted.

Institute of Health Administration Offers health administration (MBA, MHA, MSHA). Electronic applications accepted.

Institute of International Business *Degree program information:* Part-time and evening/weekend programs available. Offers international business (MBA, MIB). Electronic applications accepted.

School of Accountancy *Degree program information:* Part-time and evening/weekend programs available. Offers accountancy (MBA, MPA, MTX, PhD, Certificate); taxation (MTX). Electronic applications accepted.

GERSTNER SLOAN-KETTERING GRADUATE SCHOOL OF BIOMEDICAL SCIENCES, New York, NY 10021

General Information Independent, coed, graduate-only institution. *Enrollment by degree level:* 52 doctoral. *Graduate faculty:* 116 full-time (19 women). *Graduate housing:* Rooms and/or apartments available on a first-come, first-served basis to single and married students. *Student services:* Campus safety program, child daycare facilities, grant writing training, multicultural affairs office, services for students with disabilities. *Library facilities:* Memorial Sloan-Kettering Library. *Online resources:* library catalog. *Collection:* 1,100 titles.

Computer facilities: A campuswide network can be accessed from student residence rooms and from off campus. Online class registration is available. *Web address:* http://www.sloankettering.edu/gerstner.

General Application Contact: Graduate School Main Office, 646-888-6639, Fax: 646-422-2351, E-mail: gradstudies@sloankettering.edu.

GRADUATE UNITS

Program in Cancer Biology Students: 52 full-time (28 women); includes 6 minority (1 Black or African American, non-Hispanic/Latino; 4 Asian, non-Hispanic/Latino; 1 Hispanic/Latino), 4 international. *Faculty:* 116 full-time (19 women). Expenses: Contact institution. *Financial support:* Fellowship package including stipend ($32,637), full-tuition scholarship, first-year allowance, and comprehensive medical and dental insurance available. Offers cancer biology (PhD). Electronic applications accepted. *Application Contact:* Main Office, 646-888-6639, Fax: 646-422-2351, E-mail: gradstudies@sloankettering.edu. *Dean,* Dr. Kenneth Marians, 212-639-5890, E-mail: kmarians@sloankettering.edu.

GLION INSTITUTE OF HIGHER EDUCATION, CH-1823 Glion-sur-Montreux, Switzerland

General Information Proprietary, coed, comprehensive institution.

GRADUATE UNITS

Graduate Programs *Degree program information:* Evening/weekend programs available.

GLOBAL UNIVERSITY, Springfield, MO 65804

General Information Independent-religious, coed, comprehensive institution. *Graduate housing:* On-campus housing not available.

GRADUATE UNITS

Graduate School of Theology *Degree program information:* Part-time and evening/weekend programs available. Postbaccalaureate distance learning degree programs offered (no on-campus study). Offers biblical studies (MA); divinity (M Div); ministerial studies (MA). Electronic applications accepted.

GLOBE UNIVERSITY, Woodbury, MN 55125

General Information Proprietary, coed, comprehensive institution.

GRADUATE UNITS

Minnesota School of Business Offers business administration (MBA); health care management (MSM); information technology (MSM); managerial leadership (MSM).

GODDARD COLLEGE, Plainfield, VT 05667-9432

General Information Independent, coed, comprehensive institution. *Graduate housing:* On-campus housing not available.

GRADUATE UNITS

Graduate Division *Degree program information:* Part-time programs available. Postbaccalaureate distance learning degree programs offered (minimal on-campus study). Offers community education (MA); consciousness studies (MA); creative writing (MFA); environmental studies (MA); health arts and sciences (MA); interdisciplinary arts (MFA); organizational development (MA); psychology and counseling (MA); sexual orientation (MA); sustainable business and communities (MA); teacher licensure (MA); transformative language arts (MA). Electronic applications accepted.

GOLDEN GATE BAPTIST THEOLOGICAL SEMINARY, Mill Valley, CA 94941-3197

General Information Independent-religious, coed, graduate-only institution. *Graduate housing:* Rooms and/or apartments available on a first-come, first-served basis to single and married students. Housing application deadline: 6/15.

GRADUATE UNITS

Graduate and Professional Programs *Degree program information:* Part-time and evening/weekend programs available. Offers divinity (M Div); early childhood education (Certificate); education leadership (MAEL, Diploma); ministry (D Min); theological studies (MTS); theology (Th M); youth ministry (Certificate). Electronic applications accepted.

GOLDEN GATE UNIVERSITY, San Francisco, CA 94105-2968

General Information Independent, coed, university. *Enrollment:* 1,150 full-time matriculated graduate/professional students (637 women), 1,810 part-time matriculated graduate/professional students (986 women). *Enrollment by degree level:* 865 first professional, 2,057 master's, 38 doctoral. *Graduate faculty:* 36 full-time (9 women), 458 part-time/adjunct (139 women). *Graduate housing:* On-campus housing not available. *Student services:* Campus employment opportunities, career counseling, international student services, low-cost health insurance, services for students with disabilities. *Library facilities:* Golden Gate University Library plus 1 other. *Online resources:* library catalog, access to other libraries' catalogs. *Collection:* 79,204 titles, 3,335 serial subscriptions.

Computer facilities: Computer purchase and lease plans are available. 52 computers available on campus for general student use. A campuswide network can be accessed. Online class registration is available. *Web address:* http://www.ggu.edu/.

General Application Contact: Angela Melero, Enrollment Services, 415-442-7800, Fax: 415-442-7807, E-mail: info@ggu.edu.

GRADUATE UNITS

Ageno School of Business Students: 421 full-time (235 women), 744 part-time (425 women); includes 526 minority (114 Black or African American, non-Hispanic/Latino; 2 American Indian or Alaska Native, non-Hispanic/Latino; 296 Asian, non-Hispanic/Latino; 73 Hispanic/Latino; 29 Native Hawaiian or other Pacific Islander, non-Hispanic/Latino; 12 Two or more races, non-Hispanic/Latino), 100 international. Average age 32. 681 applicants, 78% accepted, 270 enrolled. *Faculty:* 16 full-time (4 women), 241 part-time/adjunct (72 women). Expenses: Contact institution. *Financial support:* Career-related internships or fieldwork, Federal Work-Study, institutionally sponsored loans, and scholarships/grants available. Support available to part-time students. Financial award applicants required to submit FAFSA. In 2010, 550 master's, 13 doctorates awarded. *Degree program information:* Part-time and evening/weekend programs available. Offers accounting (MBA); business administration (EMBA, MBA, PMBA, DBA); finance (MBA, MS, Certificate); financial planning (MS, Certificate); healthcare information systems (Certificate); human resource management (MBA, MS); human resources management (Certificate); information systems (MS); information technology (MBA); information technology management (Certificate); integrated marketing and communications (MS, Certificate); international business (MBA); management (MBA); marketing (MBA, MS, Certificate); operations supply chain management (Certificate); psychology (MA, Certificate); public administration (EMPA); public relations (MS, Certificate); technical market analysis (Certificate). *Application deadline:* For fall admission, 5/15 for domestic and international students; for winter admission, 1/15 for domestic and international students; for spring admission, 9/15 for domestic and international students. Applications are processed on a rolling basis. *Application fee:* $70 ($110 for international students). Electronic applications accepted. *Application Contact:* Angela Melero, Enrollment Services, 415-442-7800, Fax: 415-442-7807, E-mail: info@ggu.edu. *Dean,* Dr. Paul Fouts, 415-442-7026, Fax: 415-442-6579.

School of Accounting Students: 129 full-time (84 women), 168 part-time (98 women); includes 127 minority (6 Black or African American, non-Hispanic/Latino; 1 American Indian or Alaska Native, non-Hispanic/Latino; 100 Asian, non-Hispanic/Latino; 15 Hispanic/Latino; 3 Native Hawaiian or other Pacific Islander, non-Hispanic/Latino; 2 Two or more races, non-Hispanic/Latino), 40 international. Average age 31. 132 applicants, 80% accepted, 52 enrolled. *Faculty:* 5 full-time (2 women), 35 part-time/adjunct (12 women). Expenses: Contact institution. *Financial support:* Career-related internships or fieldwork, Federal Work-Study, institutionally sponsored loans, and scholarships/grants available. Support available to part-time students. Financial award applicants required to submit FAFSA. In 2010, 61 master's awarded. *Degree program information:* Part-time and evening/weekend programs available. Offers accounting (M Ac, Graduate Certificate); forensic (M Ac); forensic accounting (Graduate Certificate); taxation (M Ac). *Application deadline:* For fall admission, 5/15 for international students; for winter admission, 1/15 for international students; for spring admission, 9/15 for international students. Applications are processed on a rolling basis. *Application fee:* $70 ($110 for international students). Electronic applications accepted. *Application Contact:* Angela Melero, Enrollment Services, 415-442-7800, Fax: 415-442-7807, E-mail: info@ggu.edu. Mary Canning, 415-442-6559, Fax: 415-543-2607.

School of Law Students: 612 full-time (346 women), 253 part-time (127 women); includes 230 minority (30 Black or African American, non-Hispanic/Latino; 5 American Indian or Alaska Native, non-Hispanic/Latino; 147 Asian, non-Hispanic/Latino; 48 Hispanic/Latino), 83 international. *Faculty:* 41 full-time (19 women), 67 part-time/adjunct (27 women). Expenses: Contact institution. *Financial support:* Fellowships, research assistantships, teaching assistantships, career-related internships or fieldwork, Federal Work-Study, institutionally sponsored loans, scholarships/grants, tuition waivers (full and partial), and unspecified assistantships available. Support available to part-time students. Financial award application deadline: 3/1; financial award applicants required to submit FAFSA. In 2010, 249 first professional degrees, 60 master's, 9 doctorates awarded. *Degree program information:* Part-time and evening/weekend programs available. Offers environmental law (LL M); intellectual property law (LL M); international legal studies (LL M, SJD); law (JD); taxation (LL M); U. S. legal studies (LL M). *Application deadline:* For fall admission, 4/1 for domestic and international students. Applications are processed on a rolling basis. *Application fee:* $60. Electronic applications accepted. *Application Contact:* Greg Egertson, Associate Dean and Director of Admissions, 415-442-6636, Fax: 415-442-6609, E-mail: lawadmit@ggu.edu. *Dean,* Drucilla Ramey, 415-442-6600, Fax: 415-442-6609.

School of Taxation Students: 66 full-time (39 women), 641 part-time (359 women); includes 238 minority (20 Black or African American, non-Hispanic/Latino; 165 Asian, non-Hispanic/Latino; 35 Hispanic/Latino; 15 Native Hawaiian or other Pacific Islander, non-Hispanic/Latino; 3 Two or more races, non-Hispanic/Latino), 22 international. Average age 37. 337 applicants, 87% accepted, 148 enrolled. *Faculty:* 6 full-time (1 woman), 65 part-time/adjunct (15 women). Expenses: Contact institution. *Financial support:* Career-related internships or fieldwork, Federal Work-Study, institutionally sponsored loans, and scholarships/grants available. Support available to part-time students. Financial award applicants required to submit FAFSA. In 2010, 242 master's awarded. *Degree program information:* Part-time and evening/weekend programs available. Offers advanced studies in taxation (Certificate); estate planning (Certificate); international tax (Certificate); tax (Certificate); taxation (MS). *Application deadline:* For fall admission, 5/15 for international students; for winter admission, 1/15 for international students; for spring admission, 9/15 for international students. Applications are processed on a rolling basis. *Application fee:* $70 ($110 for international students). Electronic applications accepted. *Application Contact:* Angela Melero, Enrollment Services, 415-442-7800, Fax: 415-442-7807, E-mail: info@ggu.edu. *Dean,* Mary Canning, 415-442-7885, Fax: 415-442-7807.

GOLDEY-BEACOM COLLEGE, Wilmington, DE 19808-1999

General Information Independent, coed, comprehensive institution. *Enrollment:* 1,171 graduate, professional, and undergraduate students; 55 full-time matriculated graduate/professional students (28 women), 393 part-time matriculated graduate/professional students (164 women). *Enrollment by degree level:* 448 master's. *Graduate faculty:* 20 full-time (8 women), 28 part-time/adjunct (10 women). *Tuition:* Full-time $14,796; part-time $822 per credit. *Required fees:* $180; $10 per credit. *Graduate housing:* Room and/or apartments available on a first-come, first-served basis to single students; on-campus housing not available to married students. *Student services:* Campus employment opportunities, campus safety program, career counseling, free psychological counseling, international student services, low-cost health insurance, services for students with disabilities. *Library facilities:* J. Wilbur Hirons Library. *Online resources:* web page. *Collection:* 47,709 titles, 41,446 serial subscriptions, 1,665 audiovisual materials.

Computer facilities: 159 computers available on campus for general student use. A campuswide network can be accessed from student residence rooms and from off campus. Campus Web available. *Web address:* http://www.gbc.edu/.

General Application Contact: Larry W. Eby, Director of Admissions, 302-225-6289, Fax: 302-996-5408, E-mail: ebylw@gbc.edu.

GRADUATE UNITS

Graduate Program Students: 55 full-time (28 women), 393 part-time (164 women); includes 252 minority (51 Black or African American, non-Hispanic/Latino; 2 American Indian or Alaska Native, non-Hispanic/Latino; 183 Asian, non-Hispanic/Latino; 13 Hispanic/Latino; 1 Native Hawaiian or other Pacific Islander, non-Hispanic/Latino; 2 Two or more races, non-Hispanic/Latino). Average age 27. *Faculty:* 20 full-time (8 women), 28 part-time/adjunct (10 women). Expenses: Contact institution. *Financial support:* Scholarships/grants available. Support available to part-time students. Financial award application deadline: 4/1; financial award applicants required to submit FAFSA. In 2010, 231 master's awarded. *Degree program information:* Part-time and evening/weekend programs available. Offers business administration (MBA); finance (MS); financial management (MBA); human resource management (MBA); information technology (MBA); international business management (MBA); major finance (MBA); major taxation (MBA); management (MM); marketing management (MBA); taxation (MBA, MS). *Application deadline:* Applications are processed on a rolling basis. Electronic applications accepted. *Application Contact:* Ashley E. Mashington, Graduate Admissions Representative, 302-225-6259, Fax: 302-996-5408, E-mail: mashina@gbc.edu. *Director of Admissions,* Larry W. Eby, 302-225-6289, Fax: 302-996-5408, E-mail: ebylw@gbc.edu.

GOLDFARB SCHOOL OF NURSING AT BARNES-JEWISH COLLEGE, St. Louis, MO 63110

General Information Independent, coed, primarily women, comprehensive institution. *Enrollment:* 660 graduate, professional, and undergraduate students; 67 full-time matriculated graduate/professional students (59 women), 63 part-time matriculated graduate/professional students (59 women). *Enrollment by degree level:* 123 master's, 7 doctoral. *Graduate faculty:* 30 full-time (28 women), 16 part-time/adjunct (12 women). *Tuition:* Full-time $9000; part-time

Goldfarb School of Nursing at Barnes-Jewish College (continued)

$600 per credit hour. *Required fees:* $250; $15 per term. *Graduate housing:* On-campus housing not available. *Student services:* Campus employment opportunities, campus safety program, international student services, services for students with disabilities. *Online resources:* library catalog, web page, access to other libraries' catalogs. *Collection:* 1,070 titles, 47 serial subscriptions, 142 audiovisual materials.

Computer facilities: 110 computers available on campus for general student use. A campuswide network can be accessed from off campus. Software, research databases available. *Web address:* http://www.barnesjewishcollege.edu/.

General Application Contact: Margaret O'Connor, Manager for Enrollment, 314-454-7557, Fax: 314-454-9250, E-mail: maoconnor@bjc.org.

GRADUATE UNITS

Graduate Programs Students: 67 full-time (59 women), 63 part-time (59 women); includes 34 minority (27 Black or African American, non-Hispanic/Latino; 6 Asian, non-Hispanic/Latino; 1 Hispanic/Latino), 3 international. Average age 38. *Faculty:* 30 full-time (28 women), 16 part-time/adjunct (12 women). Expenses: Contact institution. *Financial support:* Fellowships, research assistantships, Federal Work-Study, institutionally sponsored loans, and scholarships/grants available. Support available to part-time students. Financial award applicants required to submit FAFSA. *Degree program information:* Part-time and evening/weekend programs available. Postbaccalaureate distance learning degree programs offered (minimal on-campus study). Offers adult acute care nurse practitioner (MSN); adult nurse practitioner (MSN); nurse anesthesia (MSN); nurse educator (MSN); nurse executive (MSN). *Application deadline:* For fall admission, 2/1 priority date for international students; for spring admission, 10/1 priority date for international students. Applications are processed on a rolling basis. *Application fee:* $50. *Application Contact:* Dr. Michael Ward, Associate Dean for Student Programs, 314-362-9155, Fax: 314-362-0984, E-mail: mward@bjc.org. *Dean,* Dr. Michael L. Evans, 314-362-6289, Fax: 314-362-0984, E-mail: mevans@bjc.org.

GONZAGA UNIVERSITY, Spokane, WA 99258

General Information Independent-religious, coed, comprehensive institution. *Graduate housing:* Rooms and/or apartments available on a first-come, first-served basis to single and married students.

GRADUATE UNITS

College of Arts and Sciences *Degree program information:* Part-time programs available. Offers arts and sciences (MA); pastoral ministry (MA); philosophy (MA); religious studies (MA); spirituality (MA).

Program in Teaching English as a Second Language Offers teaching English as a second language (MATESL). Electronic applications accepted.

School of Business Administration *Degree program information:* Part-time and evening/weekend programs available. Offers business administration (M Acc, MBA).

School of Education *Degree program information:* Part-time and evening/weekend programs available. Offers administration and curriculum (MAA); anesthesiology education (M Anesth Ed); counseling psychology (MAC, MAP); education (M Anesth Ed, M Ed, MA Ed Ad, MAA, MAC, MAP, MASPAA, MAT, MES, MIT); educational administration (MA Ed Ad); initial teaching (MIT); literacy (M Ed); special education (MES); sports and athletic administration (MASPAA); teaching at-risk students (MAT).

School of Law *Degree program information:* Part-time programs available. Offers law (JD).

School of Professional Studies Offers communication and leadership studies (MA); leadership studies (PhD); nursing (MSN); organizational leadership (MOL).

GOODING INSTITUTE OF NURSE ANESTHESIA, Panama City, FL 32401

General Information County-supported, coed, graduate-only institution. *Graduate housing:* On-campus housing not available.

GRADUATE UNITS

Program in Nurse Anesthesia Offers nurse anesthesia (MS).

GORDON COLLEGE, Wenham, MA 01984-1899

General Information Independent-religious, coed, comprehensive institution. *Graduate housing:* On-campus housing not available.

GRADUATE UNITS

Graduate Education *Degree program information:* Part-time and evening/weekend programs available. Offers education (M Ed, MAT); music education (MME).

GORDON-CONWELL THEOLOGICAL SEMINARY, South Hamilton, MA 01982-2395

General Information Independent-religious, coed, graduate-only institution. *Graduate housing:* Rooms and/or apartments available to single and married students. Housing application deadline: 4/1.

GRADUATE UNITS

Graduate and Professional Programs *Degree program information:* Part-time and evening/weekend programs available. Offers Biblical languages (MABL); church history (MACH); counseling (MACO); ministry (D Min); missions/evangelism (MAME); New Testament (MANT); Old Testament (MAOT); religion (MAR); theology (M Div, MATH, Th M, Th D).

GOSHEN COLLEGE, Goshen, IN 46526-4794

General Information Independent-religious, coed, comprehensive institution. *Enrollment:* 6 full-time matriculated graduate/professional students (5 women), 35 part-time matriculated graduate/professional students (29 women). *Enrollment by degree level:* 41 master's. *Graduate faculty:* 2 full-time (1 woman), 12 part-time/adjunct (8 women). *Tuition:* Full-time $23,500. *Required fees:* $530 per credit hour. *Library facilities:* The Harold and Wilma Good Library plus 1 other. *Online resources:* library catalog, web page, access to other libraries' catalogs. *Collection:* 137,000 titles, 350 serial subscriptions, 2,948 audiovisual materials.

Computer facilities: 160 computers available on campus for general student use. A campuswide network can be accessed from student residence rooms and from off campus. Online class registration is available. *Web address:* http://www.goshen.edu/.

General Application Contact: Nina Mishler, 574-535-7527, Fax: 574-535-7609, E-mail: ninajm@goshen.edu.

GRADUATE UNITS

Merry Lea Environmental Learning Center Offers environmental education (MA).

Program in Nursing *Degree program information:* Part-time and evening/weekend programs available. Offers clinical nurse leader (MSN); family nurse practitioner (MSN).

GOUCHER COLLEGE, Baltimore, MD 21204-2794

General Information Independent, coed, comprehensive institution. CGS member. *Enrollment:* 2,299 graduate, professional, and undergraduate students; 148 full-time matriculated graduate/professional students (99 women), 670 part-time matriculated graduate/professional students (551 women). *Enrollment by degree level:* 786 master's, 32 other advanced degrees. *Graduate faculty:* 10 full-time (3 women), 179 part-time/adjunct (118 women). *Graduate housing:* On-campus housing not available. *Student services:* Career counseling, low-cost health insurance. *Library facilities:* Goucher College Library. *Online resources:* library catalog, web page. *Collection:* 300,000 titles, 25,900 serial subscriptions, 6,190 audiovisual materials. *Research affiliation:* Sheppard-Pratt Hospital (education).

Computer facilities: Computer purchase and lease plans are available. 200 computers available on campus for general student use. A campuswide network can be accessed from student residence rooms and from off campus. Online class registration, transcripts, financial aid information, billing, ePortfolios, academic progress reports, study abroad plan are available. *Web address:* http://www.goucher.edu/.

General Application Contact: Megan Cornett, Director of Marketing and Communications, 410-337-6200, Fax: 410-337-6085, E-mail: mcornett@goucher.edu.

GRADUATE UNITS

Historic Preservation Program Students: 3 full-time (2 women), 31 part-time (24 women); includes 2 Black or African American, non-Hispanic/Latino, 1 international. Average age 42. *Faculty:* 18 part-time/adjunct (8 women). Expenses: Contact institution. *Financial support:* Career-related internships or fieldwork available. Support available to part-time students. Financial award application deadline: 3/15; financial award applicants required to submit FAFSA. In 2010, 7 master's awarded. *Degree program information:* Part-time and evening/weekend programs available. Postbaccalaureate distance learning degree programs offered (minimal on-campus study). Offers historic preservation (MA). *Application deadline:* For fall admission, 2/18 for domestic students. *Application fee:* $50. *Application Contact:* Megan Cornett, Director of Marketing and Communications, 410-337-6200, Fax: 410-337-6085, E-mail: mcornett@goucher.edu. *Director,* Richard Wagner, 410-337-6200, Fax: 410-337-6085, E-mail: rwagner@goucher.edu.

Program in Arts Administration Students: 20 full-time (17 women), 7 part-time (6 women); includes 2 Black or African American, non-Hispanic/Latino, 1 international. Average age 35. *Faculty:* 16 part-time/adjunct (10 women). Expenses: Contact institution. *Financial support:* Institutionally sponsored loans available. Financial award application deadline: 3/15. In 2010, 10 master's awarded. *Degree program information:* Part-time programs available. Postbaccalaureate distance learning degree programs offered (minimal on-campus study). Offers arts administration (MA). *Application deadline:* For fall admission, 3/15 for domestic students. *Application fee:* $50. *Application Contact:* Megan Cornett, Director of Marketing and Communications, 410-337-6200, Fax: 410-337-6085, E-mail: mcornett@goucher.edu. *Director,* Dr. Ramona Baker, 410-337-6200, Fax: 410-337-6085, E-mail: ramona.baker@goucher.edu.

Program in Creative Nonfiction Students: 41 full-time (28 women), 3 part-time (2 women); includes 2 Black or African American, non-Hispanic/Latino. Average age 40. *Faculty:* 9 part-time/adjunct (4 women). Expenses: Contact institution. *Financial support:* Career-related internships or fieldwork and institutionally sponsored loans available. Financial award application deadline: 3/15; financial award applicants required to submit FAFSA. In 2010, 16 master's awarded. *Degree program information:* Part-time and evening/weekend programs available. Postbaccalaureate distance learning degree programs offered (minimal on-campus study). Offers creative nonfiction (MFA). *Application deadline:* For fall admission, 2/26 for domestic students. Applications are processed on a rolling basis. *Application fee:* $50. *Application Contact:* Megan Cornett, Director of Marketing and Communications, 410-337-6200, Fax: 410-337-6085, E-mail: mcornett@goucher.edu. *Director,* Patsy Sims, 410-337-6200, Fax: 410-337-6085, E-mail: psims@goucher.edu.

Program in Cultural Sustainability Students: 22 full-time (20 women), 1 (woman) part-time; includes 2 Black or African American, non-Hispanic/Latino. *Faculty:* 13 part-time/adjunct (5 women). Expenses: Contact institution. *Financial support:* Application deadline: 3/15. *Degree program information:* Part-time programs available. Postbaccalaureate distance learning degree programs offered (minimal on-campus study). Offers cultural sustainability (MA). *Application deadline:* For fall admission, 4/20 for domestic students; for spring admission, 10/15 for domestic students. *Application fee:* $50. *Application Contact:* Megan Cornett, Director of Marketing and Communications, 410-337-6200, Fax: 410-337-6085, E-mail: mcornett@goucher.edu. *Program Director,* Rory Turner, 410-337-6296.

Program in Digital Arts *Faculty:* 5 part-time/adjunct (1 woman). Expenses: Contact institution. *Financial support:* Application deadline: 3/15. *Degree program information:* Part-time programs available. Postbaccalaureate distance learning degree programs offered (minimal on-campus study). Offers digital arts (MA). *Application deadline:* For fall admission, 4/20 for domestic students; for spring admission, 10/15 for domestic students. *Application Contact:* Megan Cornett, Director of Marketing and Communications, 410-337-6200, Fax: 410-337-6085, E-mail: mcornett@goucher.edu. *Academic Director,* Michael E. Scott-Nelson, 410-337-6200, Fax: 410-337-6085, E-mail: michael.scott-nelson@goucher.edu.

Program in Post-Baccalaureate Premedical Studies Students: 32 full-time (16 women); includes 1 Black or African American, non-Hispanic/Latino; 3 Asian, non-Hispanic/Latino; 1 Hispanic/Latino. Average age 24. *Faculty:* 10 full-time (3 women). Expenses: Contact institution. *Financial support:* In 2010–11, 5 fellowships (averaging $4,000 per year) were awarded; institutionally sponsored loans and scholarships/grants also available. Financial award application deadline: 3/1; financial award applicants required to submit FAFSA. In 2010, 32 Certificates awarded. Offers premedical studies (Certificate). *Application deadline:* Applications are processed on a rolling basis. *Application fee:* $50. *Application Contact:* Theresa Reifsnider, Associate Dean for Graduate and Professional Studies, 410-337-3437, Fax: 410-337-6461, E-mail: pbpm@goucher.edu. *Director,* Betsy Merideth, 800-414-3437, Fax: 410-337-6461, E-mail: bmerideth@goucher.edu.

Programs in Education Students: 40 full-time (26 women), 628 part-time (518 women); includes 53 Black or African American, non-Hispanic/Latino; 1 American Indian or Alaska Native, non-Hispanic/Latino; 1 Asian, non-Hispanic/Latino; 3 Hispanic/Latino. Average age 34. 40 applicants, 88% accepted, 25 enrolled. *Faculty:* 3 full-time (all women), 118 part-time/adjunct (28 women). Expenses: Contact institution. *Financial support:* In 2010–11, 3 research assistantships with tuition reimbursements (averaging $4,500 per year) were awarded; career-related internships or fieldwork and need-based awards also available. Support available to part-time students. Financial award application deadline: 8/15; financial award applicants required to submit FAFSA. In 2010, 78 master's awarded. *Degree program information:* Part-time and evening/weekend programs available. Offers education (M Ed, MAT). *Application deadline:* For fall admission, 9/1 priority date for domestic students; for spring admission, 1/15 for domestic students. Applications are processed on a rolling basis. *Application fee:* $25. *Application Contact:* Megan Cornett, Associate Director, Administrative Student Services, 410-337-6200, Fax: 410-337-6394, E-mail: mcornett@goucher.edu. *Director,* Dr. Phyllis Sunshine, 410-337-6047, Fax: 410-337-6394, E-mail: psunshin@goucher.edu.

GOVERNORS STATE UNIVERSITY, University Park, IL 60466-0975

General Information State-supported, coed, upper-level institution. CGS member. *Enrollment:* 5,674 graduate, professional, and undergraduate students; 748 full-time matriculated graduate/professional students (561 women), 1,919 part-time matriculated graduate/professional students (1,424 women). *Enrollment by degree level:* 2,492 master's, 175 doctoral. *Graduate faculty:* 212 full-time (116 women), 177 part-time/adjunct (97 women). Tuition, state resident: full-time $5400; part-time $225 per credit hour. Tuition, nonresident: full-time $16,200; part-time $675 per credit hour. *Required fees:* $1358; $46 per credit hour. $126 per term. Tuition and fees vary according to degree level and program. *Graduate housing:* On-campus housing not available. *Student services:* Campus employment opportunities, campus safety program, career counseling, child daycare facilities, exercise/wellness program, free psychological counseling, international student services, services for students with disabilities, teacher training. *Library facilities:* University Library. *Online resources:* library catalog, web page.

Computer facilities: A campuswide network can be accessed from off campus. Online class registration, student portal are available. *Web address:* http://www.govst.edu/.

General Application Contact: Dr. Sharon Evans, Interim Director of Admission, 708-534-4493, Fax: 708-534-1640, E-mail: sevans@govst.edu.

GRADUATE UNITS

College of Arts and Sciences *Degree program information:* Part-time and evening/weekend programs available. Offers analytical chemistry (MS); art (MA); arts and sciences (MA, MS); communication studies (MA); computer science (MS); English (MA); environmental biology (MS); instructional and training technology (MA); media communication (MA); political and justice studies (MA).

College of Business and Public Administration *Degree program information:* Part-time and evening/weekend programs available. Offers accounting (MS); business administration (MBA); business and public administration (MBA, MPA, MS); management information systems (MS); public administration (MPA).

College of Education *Degree program information:* Part-time and evening/weekend programs available. Offers counseling (MA); early childhood education (MA); education (MA); educational administration and supervision (MA); multi-categorical special education (MA); psychology (MA); reading (MA).

College of Health Professions *Degree program information:* Part-time and evening/weekend programs available. Offers addictions studies (MHS); communication disorders (MHS); health administration (MHA); health professions (MHA, MHS, MOT, MPT, MSN, MSW, DPT); nursing (MSN); occupational therapy (MOT); physical therapy (MPT, DPT); social work (MSW).

GRACE COLLEGE, Winona Lake, IN 46590-1294

General Information Independent-religious, coed, comprehensive institution. *Graduate housing:* On-campus housing not available.

GRADUATE UNITS

Graduate School in Counseling and Interpersonal Relations *Degree program information:* Part-time programs available. Offers counseling (MA); counseling and interpersonal relations (MA); interpersonal relations (MA). Electronic applications accepted.

GRACELAND UNIVERSITY, Lamoni, IA 50140

General Information Independent-religious, coed, comprehensive institution. *Enrollment:* 2,271 graduate, professional, and undergraduate students; 535 full-time matriculated graduate/professional students (431 women), 268 part-time matriculated graduate/professional students (227 women). *Enrollment by degree level:* 803 master's. *Graduate faculty:* 23 full-time (21 women), 36 part-time/adjunct (24 women). *Tuition:* Part-time $410 per semester hour. *Required fees:* $75 per course. One-time fee: $75 part-time. *Graduate housing:* On-campus housing not available. *Student services:* Campus safety program, career counseling, free psychological counseling, services for students with disabilities, teacher training, writing training. *Library facilities:* F. M. Smith Library. *Online resources:* library catalog, web page, access to other libraries' catalogs. *Collection:* 119,345 titles, 526 serial subscriptions, 3,778 audiovisual materials.

Computer facilities: 139 computers available on campus for general student use. A campuswide network can be accessed from student residence rooms and from off campus. Online class registration is available. *Web address:* http://www.graceland.edu/.

General Application Contact: Cathy Porter, Program Consultant, 816-833-0524 Ext. 4816, Fax: 816-833-2990, E-mail: cgporter@graceland.edu.

GRADUATE UNITS

Community of Christ Seminary Students: 4 full-time (all women), 13 part-time (8 women); includes 1 Black or African American, non-Hispanic/Latino, 1 international. Average age 41. 15 applicants, 80% accepted, 7 enrolled. *Faculty:* 2 full-time (1 woman), 9 part-time/adjunct (3 women). Expenses: Contact institution. *Financial support:* Scholarships/grants available. Financial award application deadline: 12/15; financial award applicants required to submit FAFSA. In 2010, 6 master's awarded. *Degree program information:* Part-time programs available. Postbaccalaureate distance learning degree programs offered (minimal on-campus study). Offers Christian ministry (MACM); religion (MAR). *Application deadline:* For fall admission, 8/15 priority date for domestic students; for winter admission, 10/15 priority date for domestic students; for spring admission, 4/15 priority date for domestic students. Applications are processed on a rolling basis. *Application fee:* $50. *Application Contact:* Judy K. Luffman, Executive Assistant, 816-833-0524 Ext. 4508, Fax: 816-833-2990, E-mail: luffman@graceland.edu. *Dean,* Dr. Don H. Compier, 800-833-0524 Ext. 4900, Fax: 816-833-2990, E-mail: dcompier@graceland.edu.

Gleazer School of Education Students: 368 full-time (278 women), 74 part-time (59 women); includes 5 Black or African American, non-Hispanic/Latino; 1 American Indian or Alaska Native, non-Hispanic/Latino; 2 Asian, non-Hispanic/Latino; 4 Hispanic/Latino, 7 international. Average age 37. 140 applicants, 97% accepted, 121 enrolled. *Faculty:* 8 full-time (7 women), 21 part-time/adjunct (15 women). Expenses: Contact institution. *Financial support:* Institutionally sponsored loans and scholarships/grants available. Financial award application deadline: 12/15; financial award applicants required to submit FAFSA. In 2010, 217 master's awarded. *Degree program information:* Part-time and evening/weekend programs available. Postbaccalaureate distance learning degree programs offered (no on-campus study). Offers collaborative learning and teaching (M Ed); differentiated instruction (M Ed); instructional leadership (M Ed); mild/moderate special education (M Ed); quality schools (M Ed); technology integration (M Ed). *Application deadline:* For fall admission, 7/15 for domestic students; for winter admission, 10/15 for domestic students; for spring admission, 1/15 priority date for domestic students. *Application fee:* $50. Electronic applications accepted. *Application Contact:* Cathy Porter, Program Consultant, 816-833-0524 Ext. 4516, E-mail: cgporter@graceland.edu. *Dean,* Dr. Tammy Everett, 641-784-5000 Ext. 5226, E-mail: teverett@graceland.edu.

School of Nursing Students: 167 full-time (153 women), 167 part-time (149 women); includes 8 Black or African American, non-Hispanic/Latino; 1 American Indian or Alaska Native, non-Hispanic/Latino; 4 Asian, non-Hispanic/Latino; 1 Hispanic/Latino. Average age 40. 263 applicants, 71% accepted, 138 enrolled. *Faculty:* 9 full-time (all women), 9 part-time/adjunct (7 women). Expenses: Contact institution. *Financial support:* Institutionally sponsored loans and traineeships available. Support available to part-time students. Financial award applicants required to submit FAFSA. In 2010, 88 master's, 2 other advanced degrees awarded. *Degree program information:* Part-time programs available. Postbaccalaureate distance learning degree programs offered (minimal on-campus study). Offers family nurse practitioner (MSN, PMC); nurse educator (MSN, PMC). *Application deadline:* For fall admission, 6/1 priority date for domestic students; for winter admission, 10/1 priority date for domestic students; for spring admission, 3/1 priority date for domestic students. *Application fee:* $50. Electronic applications accepted. *Application Contact:* Cara Hakes, Program Consultant, 816-833-0524 Ext. 4803, Fax: 816-833-2990, E-mail: chakes@graceland.edu. *Dean,* Dr. Claudia D. Horton, 816-833-0524 Ext. 4214, Fax: 816-833-2990, E-mail: horton@graceland.edu.

GRACE THEOLOGICAL SEMINARY, Winona Lake, IN 46590-9907

General Information Independent-religious, coed, primarily men, graduate-only institution. *Graduate housing:* On-campus housing not available.

GRADUATE UNITS

Graduate and Professional Programs *Degree program information:* Part-time programs available. Postbaccalaureate distance learning degree programs offered (no on-campus study). Offers biblical studies (Certificate); camp administration (MA); counseling (M Div); exegetical studies (MA); intercultural studies (M Div, MA); local church studies (MA); pastoral studies (M Div); theological studies (MA); theology (D Min, Diploma). Electronic applications accepted.

GRACE UNIVERSITY, Omaha, NE 68108

General Information Independent-religious, coed, comprehensive institution. *Graduate housing:* Rooms and/or apartments available on a first-come, first-served basis to single and married students.

GRADUATE UNITS

College of Graduate Studies *Degree program information:* Part-time and evening/weekend programs available. Offers Bible (MA); counseling (MA). Electronic applications accepted.

GRADUATE INSTITUTE OF APPLIED LINGUISTICS, Dallas, TX 75236

General Information Independent, coed, graduate-only institution.

GRADUATE UNITS

Graduate Programs *Degree program information:* Part-time programs available. Offers applied linguistics (MA, Certificate); language development (MA). Electronic applications accepted.

GRADUATE SCHOOL AND UNIVERSITY CENTER OF THE CITY UNIVERSITY OF NEW YORK, New York, NY 10016-4039

General Information State and locally supported, coed, graduate-only institution. CGS member. *Graduate housing:* Rooms and/or apartments available to single and married students. Housing application deadline: 5/1. *Research affiliation:* American Museum of Natural History (anthropology), Roche Institute of Molecular Biology (biological sciences), New York Botanical Gardens (biological sciences).

GRADUATE UNITS

Graduate Studies Offers accounting (PhD); anthropological linguistics (PhD); archaeology (PhD); architecture (PhD); audiology (Au D); basic applied neurocognition (PhD); behavioral science (PhD); biochemistry (PhD); biology (PhD); biomedical engineering (PhD); biopsychology (PhD); chemical engineering (PhD); chemistry (PhD); civil engineering (PhD); classics (MA, PhD); clinical psychology (PhD); comparative literature (MA, PhD); computer science (PhD); criminal justice (PhD); cultural anthropology (PhD); developmental psychology (PhD); earth and environmental sciences (PhD); economics (PhD); educational psychology (PhD); electrical engineering (PhD); English (PhD); environmental psychology (PhD); experimental psychology (PhD); finance (PhD); French (PhD); Germanic languages and literatures (MA, PhD); graphic arts (PhD); Hispanic and Luso-Brazilian literatures and languages (PhD); history (PhD); industrial psychology (PhD); learning processes (PhD); liberal studies (MA); linguistics (MA, PhD); management planning systems (PhD); mathematics (PhD); mechanical engineering (PhD); music (DMA, PhD); neuropsychology (PhD); nursing science (DNS); painting (PhD); philosophy (MA, PhD); photography (PhD); physical anthropology (PhD); physical therapy (DPT); physics (PhD); political science (MA, PhD); psychology (PhD); public health (DPH); sculpture (PhD); social personality (PhD); social welfare (DSW, PhD); sociology (PhD); speech and hearing sciences (PhD); theatre (PhD); urban education (PhD). Electronic applications accepted.

Interdisciplinary Studies Offers language in social context (PhD); medieval studies (PhD); public policy (MA, PhD); urban studies (MA, PhD); women's studies (MA, PhD).

GRADUATE THEOLOGICAL UNION, Berkeley, CA 94709-1212

General Information Independent-religious, coed, graduate-only institution. *Graduate housing:* Rooms and/or apartments available on a first-come, first-served basis to single and married students. Housing application deadline: 6/1.

GRADUATE UNITS

Graduate Programs Offers art and religion (MA, PhD, Th D); biblical languages (MA); biblical studies (MA); Biblical studies (PhD, Th D); Buddhist studies (MA); Christian spirituality (MA, PhD, Th D); cultural and historical studies of religions (MA, PhD, Th D); ethics and social theory (PhD, Th D); history (MA, PhD, Th D); homiletics (MA, PhD, Th D); interdisciplinary studies (PhD, Th D); Jewish studies (MA, PhD, Th D, Certificate); liturgical studies (MA, PhD, Th D); Near Eastern religions (PhD, Th D); Orthodox Christian studies (MA); religion and psychology (MA, PhD, Th D); religion and society/ethics and social theory (MA); systematic and philosophical theology (MA, PhD, Th D). PhD programs in Jewish studies and Near Eastern religions offered jointly with University of California, Berkeley. Electronic applications accepted.

GRAMBLING STATE UNIVERSITY, Grambling, LA 71245

General Information State-supported, coed, university. CGS member. *Graduate housing:* On-campus housing not available. *Research affiliation:* National Science Foundation (science and engineering), National Aeronautics and Space Administration (NASA) (aeronautics research), U. S. Environmental Protection Agency (human health and environment).

GRADUATE UNITS

School of Graduate Studies and Research *Degree program information:* Part-time and evening/weekend programs available. Electronic applications accepted.

College of Arts and Sciences *Degree program information:* Part-time programs available. Offers arts and sciences (MAT, MPA); health service administration (MPA); human resource management (MPA); public management (MPA); social sciences (MAT); state and local government (MPA). Electronic applications accepted.

College of Education *Degree program information:* Part-time and evening/weekend programs available. Offers curriculum and instruction (Ed D); developmental education (MS, Ed D); education (MS, Ed D); educational leadership (MS, Ed D); sports administration (MS). Electronic applications accepted.

College of Professional Studies *Degree program information:* Part-time programs available. Offers criminal justice (MS); family nurse practitioner (MSN, PMC); mass communication (MA); nurse educator (MSN); social work (MSW). Electronic applications accepted.

GRAND CANYON UNIVERSITY, Phoenix, AZ 85017-1097

General Information Independent-religious, coed, comprehensive institution. CGS member. *Enrollment by degree level:* 14,564 master's, 1,219 doctoral. *Graduate faculty:* 21 full-time (14 women), 696 part-time/adjunct (457 women). *Graduate housing:* Rooms and/or apartments available on a first-come, first-served basis to single and married students. *Student services:* Campus employment opportunities, campus safety program, career counseling, exercise/wellness program, free psychological counseling, international student services, low-cost health insurance, services for students with disabilities, teacher training, writing training. *Library facilities:* Grand Canyon University Library. *Online resources:* library catalog, web page. *Collection:* 156,511 titles, 53,122 serial subscriptions, 1,278 audiovisual materials.

Computer facilities: 65 computers available on campus for general student use. A campuswide network can be accessed from student residence rooms and from off campus. Online class registration is available. *Web address:* http://www.gcu.edu/.

General Application Contact: Becky Schildt, Online Enrollment Manager, 800-557-9551, Fax: 888-695-6316, E-mail: bschildt@online.gcu.edu.

GRADUATE UNITS

College of Business Students: 1 full-time (0 women), 2,121 part-time (1,165 women); includes 341 minority (249 Black or African American, non-Hispanic/Latino; 17 American Indian or Alaska Native, non-Hispanic/Latino; 15 Asian, non-Hispanic/Latino; 29 Hispanic/Latino; 4 Native Hawaiian or other Pacific Islander, non-Hispanic/Latino; 27 Two or more races, non-Hispanic/Latino), 20 international. Average age 38. *Faculty:* 8 full-time (3 women), 147 part-time/adjunct (49 women). Expenses: Contact institution. *Financial support:* Federal Work-Study available. Support available to part-time students. Financial award applicants required to submit FAFSA. In 2010, 569 master's awarded. *Degree program information:* Part-time and evening/weekend programs available. Postbaccalaureate distance learning degree programs offered (no on-campus study). Offers accounting (MBA); corporate business administration (MBA); disaster preparedness and crisis management (MBA); executive fire service leadership (MS); finance (MBA); general management (MBA); government and policy (MPA); health care management (MPA); health systems management (MBA); human resource management (MBA); innovation (MBA); leadership (MBA, MS); management of information system (MBA); marketing (MBA); project-based (MBA); six sigma (MBA); strategic human resource management (MBA). *Application deadline:* For fall admission, 8/21 for domestic students, 7/2 for international students; for spring admission, 12/24 for domestic students, 11/1 for international students. Applications are processed on a rolling basis. *Application fee:* $0. Electronic applications accepted. *Application Contact:* Matt Tidwell, Enrollment Manager, 602-639-6020, E-mail: mtidwell@gcu.edu. *Dean,* Kim Donaldson, 602-639-6597, E-mail: kdonaldson@gcu.edu.

College of Doctoral Studies Students: 968 part-time (711 women); includes 316 minority (283 Black or African American, non-Hispanic/Latino; 12 American Indian or Alaska Native, non-Hispanic/Latino; 3 Asian, non-Hispanic/Latino; 11 Hispanic/Latino; 1 Native Hawaiian or

Grand Canyon University (continued)

other Pacific Islander, non-Hispanic/Latino; 6 Two or more races, non-Hispanic/Latino). *Faculty:* 2 full-time (1 woman), 12 part-time/adjunct (5 women). Expenses: Contact institution. Offers business administration (DBA); general psychology (PhD); organizational leadership (Ed D, PhD). *Application fee:* $0. *Application Contact:* Hector Leal, Associate Vice President of Internet Enrollment, 800-639-7144, E-mail: hector.leal@.gcu.edu. *Dean*, Dr. Hank Radda, 602-639-7255, E-mail: hank.radda@gcu.edu.

College of Education Students: 8 full-time (6 women), 9,043 part-time (7,284 women); includes 1,387 minority (1,143 Black or African American, non-Hispanic/Latino; 32 American Indian or Alaska Native, non-Hispanic/Latino; 31 Asian, non-Hispanic/Latino; 112 Hispanic/Latino; 13 Native Hawaiian or other Pacific Islander, non-Hispanic/Latino; 56 Two or more races, non-Hispanic/Latino). Average age 38. *Faculty:* 4 full-time (all women), 415 part-time/adjunct (322 women). Expenses: Contact institution. *Financial support:* Federal Work-Study available. Support available to part-time students. Financial award applicants required to submit FAFSA. In 2010, 3,980 master's awarded. *Degree program information:* Part-time and evening/weekend programs available. Postbaccalaureate distance learning degree programs offered (no on-campus study). Offers curriculum and instruction (M Ed); education administration (M Ed); elementary education (M Ed); secondary education (M Ed); special education (M Ed); teaching (MA). *Application deadline:* For fall admission, 8/21 for domestic students, 7/2 for international students; for spring admission, 12/24 for domestic students, 11/1 for international students. Applications are processed on a rolling basis. *Application fee:* $100. Electronic applications accepted. *Application Contact:* Jaime Klatt, Vice President of Enrollment, 602-639-6476, E-mail: jaime.klatt@gcu.edu. *Dean*, Dr. Kimberly L. LaPrade, 602-639-6360, E-mail: kimberly.laprada@gcu.edu.

College of Nursing Students: 1,228 part-time (1,094 women); includes 142 minority (60 Black or African American, non-Hispanic/Latino; 11 American Indian or Alaska Native, non-Hispanic/Latino; 15 Asian, non-Hispanic/Latino; 27 Hispanic/Latino; 2 Native Hawaiian or other Pacific Islander, non-Hispanic/Latino; 27 Two or more races, non-Hispanic/Latino), 1 international. *Faculty:* 5 full-time (all women), 42 part-time/adjunct (38 women). Expenses: Contact institution. *Financial support:* Federal Work-Study available. Support available to part-time students. Financial award applicants required to submit FAFSA. In 2010, 235 master's, 3 other advanced degrees awarded. *Degree program information:* Part-time and evening/weekend programs available. Postbaccalaureate distance learning degree programs offered (no on-campus study). Offers acute care nurse practitioner (MS, PMC); clinical nurse specialist (PMC); family nurse practitioner (MS); leadership in health care systems (MS); nurse education (MS). *Application fee:* $0. *Application Contact:* Chanelle Ison, Assistant Vice President of Enrollment, 602-639-7996, E-mail: chanelle.ison@gcu.edu. *Dean*, Dr. Anne McNamara, 602-639-6165, Fax: 602-589-2810, E-mail: anne.mcnamara@gcu.edu.

College of Nursing and Health Sciences Students: 2 full-time (both women), 1,818 part-time (1,476 women); includes 414 minority (346 Black or African American, non-Hispanic/Latino; 14 American Indian or Alaska Native, non-Hispanic/Latino; 4 Asian, non-Hispanic/Latino; 29 Hispanic/Latino; 3 Native Hawaiian or other Pacific Islander, non-Hispanic/Latino; 18 Two or more races, non-Hispanic/Latino), 1 international. Average age 44. *Faculty:* 2 full-time (1 woman), 54 part-time/adjunct (36 women). Expenses: Contact institution. *Financial support:* Federal Work-Study available. Support available to part-time students. Financial award applicants required to submit FAFSA. In 2010, 103 master's awarded. *Degree program information:* Part-time and evening/weekend programs available. Postbaccalaureate distance learning degree programs offered (no on-campus study). Offers addiction counseling (MS); health care administration (MS); health care informatics (MS); marriage and family therapy (MS); professional counseling (MS); public health (MS). *Application deadline:* For fall admission, 8/21 for domestic students, 7/2 for international students; for spring admission, 12/24 for domestic students, 11/1 for international students. *Application fee:* $0. *Application Contact:* Andrea Wolochuk, Information Contact, 602-639-6429, E-mail: awolochuk@gcu.edu. *Dean*, Dr. Mark Wooden, 602-639-6815, E-mail: mark.wooden@gcu.edu.

GRAND RAPIDS THEOLOGICAL SEMINARY OF CORNERSTONE UNIVERSITY, Grand Rapids, MI 49525-5897

General Information Independent-religious, coed, graduate-only institution. *Graduate housing:* Rooms and/or apartments available on a first-come, first-served basis to single and married students. Housing application deadline: 6/1.

GRADUATE UNITS

Graduate Programs *Degree program information:* Part-time programs available. Postbaccalaureate distance learning degree programs offered (minimal on-campus study). Offers Biblical counseling (M Div); biblical counseling (MA); chaplaincy (M Div); Christian education (M Div, MA); intercultural studies (M Div, MA); New Testament (MA, Th M); Old Testament (MA, Th M); pastoral studies (M Div); systematic theology (MA); theology (Th M). Electronic applications accepted.

GRAND VALLEY STATE UNIVERSITY, Allendale, MI 49401-9403

General Information State-supported, coed, comprehensive institution. CGS member. *Graduate housing:* Rooms and/or apartments available on a first-come, first-served basis to single and married students. Housing application deadline: 2/1. *Research affiliation:* Elkins Innovations (life sciences), Progressive AE (water quality).

GRADUATE UNITS

College of Community and Public Service *Degree program information:* Part-time and evening/weekend programs available. Postbaccalaureate distance learning degree programs offered (no on-campus study). Offers community and public service (MHA, MPA, MS, MSW). Electronic applications accepted.

School of Criminal Justice *Degree program information:* Part-time and evening/weekend programs available. Offers criminal justice (MS).

School of Public and Nonprofit Administration *Degree program information:* Part-time and evening/weekend programs available. Offers health administration (MHA); public and nonprofit administration (MHA, MPA). Electronic applications accepted.

School of Social Work *Degree program information:* Part-time programs available. Offers social work (MSW). Electronic applications accepted.

College of Education *Degree program information:* Part-time and evening/weekend programs available. Postbaccalaureate distance learning degree programs offered (minimal on-campus study). Offers adult and higher education (M Ed); cognitive impairment (M Ed); college student affairs leadership (M Ed); early childhood developmental delay (M Ed); early childhood education (M Ed); education (M Ed, Ed S); educational differentiation (M Ed); educational leadership (M Ed); educational technology integration (M Ed); elementary education (M Ed); emotional impairment (M Ed); higher education (M Ed); instruction and curriculum (M Ed); leadership (Ed S); learning disabilities (M Ed); literacy studies (M Ed); middle level education (M Ed); reading and language arts (M Ed); school counseling (M Ed); school library media services (M Ed); secondary level education (M Ed); special education endorsements (M Ed); teaching English to speakers of other languages (M Ed). Electronic applications accepted.

College of Health Professions Offers health professions (MPAS, MS, DPT); occupational therapy (MS); physical therapy (DPT); physician assistant studies (MPAS). Electronic applications accepted.

College of Liberal Arts and Sciences *Degree program information:* Part-time and evening/weekend programs available. Offers biology (MS); biomedical sciences (MHS); biostatistics (MS); cell and molecular biology (MS); English (MA); liberal arts and sciences (MA, MHS, MS). Electronic applications accepted.

School of Communications *Degree program information:* Part-time and evening/weekend programs available. Offers communications (MS). Electronic applications accepted.

Kirkhof College of Nursing *Degree program information:* Part-time programs available. Offers advanced practice (MSN); case management (MSN); nursing administration (MSN); nursing education (MSN); nursing practice (DNP). Electronic applications accepted.

Padnos College of Engineering and Computing *Degree program information:* Part-time programs available. Offers engineering and computing (MS, MSE); medical and bioinformatics (MS). Electronic applications accepted.

School of Computing and Information Systems *Degree program information:* Part-time and evening/weekend programs available. Offers computer information systems (MS). Electronic applications accepted.

School of Engineering *Degree program information:* Part-time and evening/weekend programs available. Offers electrical and computer engineering (MSE); manufacturing operations (MSE); mechanical engineering (MSE); product design and manufacturing engineering (MSE). Electronic applications accepted.

Seidman College of Business *Degree program information:* Part-time and evening/weekend programs available. Offers accounting (MSA); business (MBA, MSA, MST); business administration (MBA); taxation (MST). Electronic applications accepted.

GRAND VIEW UNIVERSITY, Des Moines, IA 50316-1599

General Information Independent-religious, coed, comprehensive institution.

GRADUATE UNITS

Program in Innovative Leadership Offers business (MS); education (MS); nursing (MS). Electronic applications accepted.

GRANITE STATE COLLEGE, Concord, NH 03301

General Information State and locally supported, coed, comprehensive institution.

GRADUATE UNITS

Program in Project Management Offers project management (MS).

GRANTHAM UNIVERSITY, Kansas City, MO 64153

General Information Proprietary, coed, comprehensive institution. *Enrollment:* 116 full-time matriculated graduate/professional students (52 women), 954 part-time matriculated graduate/professional students (329 women). *Enrollment by degree level:* 1,070 master's. *Graduate faculty:* 14 full-time (8 women), 166 part-time/adjunct (80 women). *Tuition:* Full-time $7950; part-time $265 per credit hour. One-time fee: $30. *Student services:* Career counseling, international student services, services for students with disabilities, writing training. *Library facilities:* Grantham Online Library. *Collection:* 2,044 titles, 18,139 serial subscriptions, 803 audiovisual materials.

Computer facilities: Online class registration is available. *Web address:* http://www.grantham.edu/.

General Application Contact: Dan King, Vice President of Admissions, 800-955-2527, Fax: 816-595-5757, E-mail: admissions@grantham.edu.

GRADUATE UNITS

College of Arts and Sciences Students: 40 full-time (20 women), 389 part-time (152 women); includes 181 minority (139 Black or African American, non-Hispanic/Latino; 4 American Indian or Alaska Native, non-Hispanic/Latino; 13 Asian, non-Hispanic/Latino; 24 Hispanic/Latino; 1 Two or more races, non-Hispanic/Latino). Expenses: Contact institution. *Financial support:* Institutionally sponsored loans and scholarships/grants available. *Degree program information:* Part-time and evening/weekend programs available. Postbaccalaureate distance learning degree programs offered (no on-campus study). Offers case management (MSN); health systems management (MS); healthcare administration (MHA); nursing (MSN); nursing education (MSN); nursing informatics (MSN); nursing management and organizational leadership (MSN). *Application deadline:* Applications are processed on a rolling basis. Electronic applications accepted. *Application Contact:* Dan King, Vice President of Enrollment Management, 800-955-2527, Fax: 816-595-5757, E-mail: admissions@grantham.edu. *Dean*, Dr. Paul Illian, 800-955-2527, Fax: 816-595-5757, E-mail: admissions@grantham.edu.

Mark Skousen School of Business Students: 74 full-time (32 women), 565 part-time (177 women); includes 218 minority (142 Black or African American, non-Hispanic/Latino; 6 American Indian or Alaska Native, non-Hispanic/Latino; 31 Asian, non-Hispanic/Latino; 37 Hispanic/Latino; 1 Native Hawaiian or other Pacific Islander, non-Hispanic/Latino; 1 Two or more races, non-Hispanic/Latino). Expenses: Contact institution. *Financial support:* Institutionally sponsored loans and scholarships/grants available. In 2010, 126 master's awarded. *Degree program information:* Part-time and evening/weekend programs available. Postbaccalaureate distance learning degree programs offered (no on-campus study). Offers business administration (MBA); business intelligence (MS); information management (MBA); information management technology (MS); information technology (MS); performance improvement (MS); project management (MBA, MSIM). *Application deadline:* Applications are processed on a rolling basis. *Application fee:* $0. Electronic applications accepted. *Application Contact:* Dan King, Vice President of Admissions, 800-955-2527, Fax: 816-595-5757, E-mail: admissions@grantham.edu. *Dean*, Niccole Buckley, 800-955-2527, Fax: 816-595-5757, E-mail: admissions@grantham.edu.

GRATZ COLLEGE, Melrose Park, PA 19027

General Information Independent-religious, coed, comprehensive institution. *Graduate housing:* On-campus housing not available.

GRADUATE UNITS

Graduate Programs *Degree program information:* Part-time and evening/weekend programs available. Postbaccalaureate distance learning degree programs offered (minimal on-campus study). Offers classical studies (MA); education (MA); Holocaust studies (Certificate); Jewish communal service (MA, Certificate); Jewish education (MA, Ed D, Certificate); Jewish music (MA, Certificate); Jewish studies (MA, Certificate); modern studies (MA).

GREEN MOUNTAIN COLLEGE, Poultney, VT 05764-1199

General Information Independent, coed, comprehensive institution.

GRADUATE UNITS

Program in Business Administration Postbaccalaureate distance learning degree programs offered (no on-campus study). Offers business administration (MBA). Distance learning only. Electronic applications accepted.

Program in Environmental Studies *Degree program information:* Part-time and evening/weekend programs available. Postbaccalaureate distance learning degree programs offered (no on-campus study). Offers environmental studies (MS). Distance learning only. Electronic applications accepted.

GREENSBORO COLLEGE, Greensboro, NC 27401-1875

General Information Independent-religious, coed, comprehensive institution. *Graduate housing:* Rooms and/or apartments guaranteed to single and married students. Housing application deadline: 6/1.

GRADUATE UNITS

Program in Education *Degree program information:* Part-time and evening/weekend programs available. Offers elementary education (M Ed); special education (M Ed). Electronic applications accepted.

Program in Teaching English to Speakers of Other Languages *Degree program information:* Part-time and evening/weekend programs available. Offers teaching English to speakers of other languages (MA). Electronic applications accepted.

GREENVILLE COLLEGE, Greenville, IL 62246-0159

General Information Independent-religious, coed, comprehensive institution. *Graduate housing:* On-campus housing not available.

GRADUATE UNITS

Program in Education Offers education (MAT); elementary education (MAE); secondary education (MAE). Electronic applications accepted.

Program in Leadership and Ministry *Degree program information:* Part-time programs available. Offers leadership and ministry (MA). Electronic applications accepted.

GWYNEDD-MERCY COLLEGE, Gwynedd Valley, PA 19437-0901

General Information Independent-religious, coed, comprehensive institution. *Enrollment:* 126 full-time matriculated graduate/professional students (84 women), 282 part-time matriculated graduate/professional students (220 women). *Enrollment by degree level:* 408 master's. *Graduate faculty:* 9 full-time (7 women), 17 part-time/adjunct (11 women). *Tuition:* Part-time $620 per credit hour. *Graduate housing:* On-campus housing not available. *Student services:* Campus employment opportunities, campus safety program, career counseling, free psychological counseling, international student services, low-cost health insurance, services for students with disabilities, teacher training. *Library facilities:* Lourdes Library plus 1 other. *Online resources:* library catalog, web page, access to other libraries' catalogs. *Collection:* 105,070 titles, 667 serial subscriptions, 11,448 audiovisual materials.

Computer facilities: Computer purchase and lease plans are available. 218 computers available on campus for general student use. A campuswide network can be accessed from student residence rooms and from off campus. Online class registration is available. *Web address:* http://www.gmc.edu/.

General Application Contact: Information Contact, 800-342-5462, Fax: 215-641-5556.

GRADUATE UNITS

Center for Lifelong Learning Offers lifelong learning (MSM).

School of Education *Degree program information:* Part-time and evening/weekend programs available. Offers educational administration (MS); master teacher (MS); reading (MS); school counseling (MS); special education (MS).

School of Nursing Offers clinical nurse specialist (MSN); nurse practitioner (MSN). Electronic applications accepted.

HAMLINE UNIVERSITY, St. Paul, MN 55104-1284

General Information Independent-religious, coed, comprehensive institution. *Enrollment:* 5,003 graduate, professional, and undergraduate students; 1,420 full-time matriculated graduate/professional students (804 women), 1,124 part-time matriculated graduate/professional students (771 women). *Enrollment by degree level:* 655 first professional, 1,788 master's, 76 doctoral, 25 other advanced degrees. *Graduate faculty:* 86 full-time (46 women), 218 part-time/adjunct (128 women). *Tuition:* Full-time $7248; part-time $453 per credit hour. *Required fees:* $7 per credit hour. One-time fee: $210. Tuition and fees vary according to degree level, campus/location and program. *Graduate housing:* Rooms and/or apartments available on a first-come, first-served basis to single and married students. Typical cost: $4172 per year ($8396 including board) for single students; $6684 per year ($10,908 including board) for married students. *Student services:* Campus employment opportunities, campus safety program, career counseling, free psychological counseling, international student services, low-cost health insurance, multicultural affairs office, services for students with disabilities, teacher training, writing training. *Library facilities:* Bush Library plus 1 other. *Online resources:* library catalog, web page, access to other libraries' catalogs. *Collection:* 413,246 titles, 6,133 serial subscriptions, 6,145 audiovisual materials. *Research affiliation:* Minnesota Women Elected Officials.

Computer facilities: 300 computers available on campus for general student use. A campuswide network can be accessed from student residence rooms and from off campus. Online class registration is available. *Web address:* http://www.hamline.edu/.

General Application Contact: Rae A. Lenway, Director, Graduate Recruitment and Admission, 651-523-2900, Fax: 651-523-3058, E-mail: gradprog@hamline.edu.

GRADUATE UNITS

Graduate School of Liberal Studies Students: 94 full-time (76 women), 119 part-time (85 women); includes 8 minority (6 Black or African American, non-Hispanic/Latino; 1 American Indian or Alaska Native, non-Hispanic/Latino; 1 Hispanic/Latino), 1 international. Average age 37. 73 applicants, 70% accepted, 30 enrolled. *Faculty:* 6 full-time (4 women), 7 part-time/adjunct (5 women). Expenses: Contact institution. *Financial support:* Federal Work-Study and scholarships/grants available. Support available to part-time students. Financial award applicants required to submit FAFSA. In 2010, 60 master's awarded. *Degree program information:* Part-time and evening/weekend programs available. Postbaccalaureate distance learning degree programs offered (minimal on-campus study). Offers liberal studies (MALS, CALS); writing (MFA); writing for children and young adults (MFA). *Application deadline:* For fall admission, 1/5 for domestic and international students; for spring admission, 9/1 for domestic and international students. Applications are processed on a rolling basis. *Application fee:* $0. Electronic applications accepted. *Application Contact:* Rae A. Lenway, Director, Graduate Recruitment and Admission, 651-523-2900, Fax: 651-523-3058, E-mail: rlenway01@gw.hamline.edu. *Dean,* Mary Rockcastle, 651-523-2047, Fax: 651-523-2490, E-mail: mrockcastle@gw.hamline.edu.

School of Business Students: 509 full-time (234 women), 130 part-time (74 women); includes 102 minority (55 Black or African American, non-Hispanic/Latino; 6 American Indian or Alaska Native, non-Hispanic/Latino; 29 Asian, non-Hispanic/Latino; 10 Hispanic/Latino; 2 Two or more races, non-Hispanic/Latino), 66 international. Average age 32. 244 applicants, 73% accepted, 139 enrolled. *Faculty:* 20 full-time (8 women), 42 part-time/adjunct (12 women). Expenses: Contact institution. *Financial support:* Federal Work-Study and scholarships/grants available. Support available to part-time students. Financial award applicants required to submit FAFSA. In 2010, 293 master's, 3 doctorates awarded. *Degree program information:* Part-time and evening/weekend programs available. Offers business (MBA); nonprofit management (MA); public administration (MA, DPA). *Application deadline:* For fall admission, 6/1 for international students; for spring admission, 10/1 for international students. Applications are processed on a rolling basis. *Application fee:* $0. Electronic applications accepted. *Application Contact:* Rae A. Lenway, Director, Graduate Recruitment and Admission, 651-523-2900, Fax: 651-523-3058, E-mail: rlenway@gw.hamline.edu. *Interim Dean,* Nancy Hellerud, 651-523-2284, Fax: 651-523-3098, E-mail: nhellerud@gw.hamline.edu.

School of Education Students: 358 full-time (259 women), 672 part-time (503 women); includes 93 minority (32 Black or African American, non-Hispanic/Latino; 4 American Indian or Alaska Native, non-Hispanic/Latino; 28 Asian, non-Hispanic/Latino; 28 Hispanic/Latino; 1 Two or more races, non-Hispanic/Latino), 17 international. Average age 32. 522 applicants, 81% accepted, 289 enrolled. *Faculty:* 24 full-time (18 women), 109 part-time/adjunct (81 women). Expenses: Contact institution. *Financial support:* Federal Work-Study and scholarships/grants available. Support available to part-time students. Financial award applicants required to submit FAFSA. In 2010, 179 master's, 13 doctorates awarded. *Degree program information:* Part-time and evening/weekend programs available. Postbaccalaureate distance learning degree programs offered (no on-campus study). Offers education (MA Ed, Ed D); English as a second language (MA); literacy education (MA); natural science and environmental education (MA Ed); teaching (MAT). *Application deadline:* Applications are processed on a rolling basis. *Application fee:* $0. Electronic applications accepted. *Application Contact:* Rae A. Lenway, Director, Graduate Recruitment and Admission, 651-523-2900, Fax: 651-523-3058, E-mail: rlenway@gw.hamline.edu. *Acting Dean,* Dr. John Pyle, 651-523-2600, Fax: 651-523-2489, E-mail: jpyle01@gw.hamline.edu.

School of Law Students: 456 full-time (234 women), 196 part-time (105 women); includes 96 minority (22 Black or African American, non-Hispanic/Latino; 5 American Indian or Alaska Native, non-Hispanic/Latino; 41 Asian, non-Hispanic/Latino; 25 Hispanic/Latino; 1 Native Hawaiian or other Pacific Islander, non-Hispanic/Latino; 2 Two or more races, non-Hispanic/Latino), 2 international. Average age 27. 1,350 applicants, 56% accepted, 227 enrolled. *Faculty:* 43 full-time (21 women), 55 part-time/adjunct (25 women). Expenses: Contact institution. *Financial support:* In 2010–11, 617 students received support, including 30 fellowships with full and partial tuition reimbursements available (averaging $2,200 per year); career-related internships or fieldwork, Federal Work-Study, and scholarships/grants also available. Support available to part-time students. Financial award applicants required to submit FAFSA. In 2010, 190 first professional degrees, 2 master's awarded. *Degree program information:* Part-time and evening/weekend programs available. Offers law (JD, LL M). JD/MAOL offered jointly with St. Catherine University. *Application deadline:* For fall admission, 5/1 priority date for domestic and international students. Applications are processed on a rolling basis. *Application fee:* $35. Electronic applications accepted. *Application Contact:* Robin C. Ingli, Director of Admissions, 800-388-3688, Fax: 651-523-3064, E-mail: ringli@hamline.edu. *Dean,* Donald M. Lewis, 651-523-2968, Fax: 651-523-2435, E-mail: dlewis02@hamline.edu.

HAMPTON UNIVERSITY, Hampton, VA 23668

General Information Independent, coed, comprehensive institution. CGS member. *Graduate housing:* Rooms and/or apartments available to single and married students. Housing application deadline: 6/1. *Research affiliation:* NASA–Langley Research Center (physical sciences), Southeastern Universities Research Association (science), Continuous Electron Beam Accelerator Facility (science).

GRADUATE UNITS

Graduate College *Degree program information:* Part-time and evening/weekend programs available. Offers advanced adult nursing (MS); atmospheric physics (MS, PhD); atmospheric sciences (MS, PhD); biology (MS); business administration (MBA, PhD); chemistry (MS); community health nursing (MS); community mental health/psychiatric nursing (MS); computational mathematics (MS); computer science (MS); environmental science (MS); family nursing (MS); gerontological nursing for the nurse practitioner (MS); medical physics (MS, PhD); medical science (MS); nonlinear science (MS); nuclear physics (MS, PhD); optical physics (MS, PhD); pediatric nursing (MS); physical therapy (DPT); planetary sciences (MS, PhD); speech-language pathology (MA); statistics and probability (MS); women's health nursing (MS).

College of Education and Continuing Studies *Degree program information:* Part-time and evening/weekend programs available. Offers college student development (MA); community agency counseling (MA); counseling (MA); early childhood education (MT); educational leadership (MA); elementary education (MA); gifted education (MA); middle school education (MT); Montessori education (MA); music education (MT); pastoral counseling (MA); school counseling (MA); secondary education (MT); special education (MT); teaching (MT).

Hampton U Online

School of Engineering and Technology Offers architecture (M Arch).

School of Pharmacy Offers pharmacy (Pharm D).

HANNIBAL-LAGRANGE UNIVERSITY, Hannibal, MO 63401-1999

General Information Independent-religious, coed, comprehensive institution. *Enrollment:* 1,191 graduate, professional, and undergraduate students; 5 full-time matriculated graduate/professional students (4 women), 10 part-time matriculated graduate/professional students (all women). *Enrollment by degree level:* 15 master's. *Graduate faculty:* 11 part-time/adjunct (10 women). *Tuition:* Part-time $265 per credit. *Required fees:* $168 per semester. One-time fee: $25. *Student services:* Campus safety program, career counseling. *Library facilities:* L. A. Foster Library. *Online resources:* library catalog, web page, access to other libraries' catalogs. *Collection:* 112,378 titles, 395 serial subscriptions, 6,026 audiovisual materials.

Computer facilities: 76 computers available on campus for general student use. A campuswide network can be accessed from student residence rooms and from off campus. Online class registration is available. *Web address:* http://www.hlg.edu/.

General Application Contact: Dr. Jane Schafer, Director of Graduate Studies, 573-629-3108, E-mail: bscha@hlg.edu.

GRADUATE UNITS

Program in Education Students: 5 full-time (4 women), 10 part-time (all women). 5 applicants, 100% accepted, 5 enrolled. *Faculty:* 11 part-time/adjunct (10 women). Expenses: Contact institution. *Financial support:* Tuition concession available. Financial award applicants required to submit FAFSA. In 2010, 8 master's awarded. *Degree program information:* Part-time and evening/weekend programs available. Offers literacy (MS Ed); teaching and learning (MS Ed). *Application deadline:* For fall admission, 9/1 for domestic students; for spring admission, 1/15 for domestic students. *Application fee:* $25. *Application Contact:* Dr. Jane Schafer, Director of Graduate Studies, 573-629-3108, E-mail: bscha@hlg.edu. *Director of Graduate Studies,* Dr. Jane Schafer, 573-629-3108, E-mail: bscha@hlg.edu.

HARDING UNIVERSITY, Searcy, AR 72149-0001

General Information Independent-religious, coed, university. *Enrollment:* 6,748 graduate, professional, and undergraduate students; 511 full-time matriculated graduate/professional students (323 women), 521 part-time matriculated graduate/professional students (302 women). *Enrollment by degree level:* 180 first professional, 790 master's, 33 doctoral, 29 other advanced degrees. *Graduate faculty:* 40 full-time (15 women), 100 part-time/adjunct (42 women). *Tuition:* Full-time $10,098; part-time $561 per credit hour. *Required fees:* $22.50 per credit hour. *Graduate housing:* Rooms and/or apartments available on a first-come, first-served basis to single and married students. Typical cost: $3500 per year for single students; $3500 per year for married students. Room charges vary according to board plan and housing facility selected. *Student services:* Campus employment opportunities, campus safety program, career counseling, exercise/wellness program, free psychological counseling, international student services, services for students with disabilities, writing training. *Library facilities:* Brackett Library plus 1 other. *Online resources:* library catalog, web page, access to other libraries' catalogs. *Collection:* 237,133 titles, 38,495 serial subscriptions, 11,954 audiovisual materials.

Computer facilities: 482 computers available on campus for general student use. A campuswide network can be accessed from student residence rooms and from off campus. Online class registration is available. *Web address:* http://www.harding.edu/.

General Application Contact: Dr. Cheri Yecke, Dean of Graduate Programs, 501-279-4335, Fax: 501-279-5192, E-mail: cyecke@harding.edu.

GRADUATE UNITS

College of Bible and Religion Students: 30 full-time (19 women), 40 part-time (6 women); includes 5 Black or African American, non-Hispanic/Latino; 1 American Indian or Alaska Native, non-Hispanic/Latino; 2 Hispanic/Latino, 3 international. Average age 33. 37 applicants, 78% accepted, 29 enrolled. *Faculty:* 4 full-time (0 women), 8 part-time/adjunct (1 woman). Expenses: Contact institution. *Financial support:* In 2010–11, 42 students received support. Scholarships/grants and unspecified assistantships available. Financial award applicants required to submit FAFSA. In 2010, 18 master's awarded. *Degree program information:* Part-time programs available. Postbaccalaureate distance learning degree programs offered. Offers Bible and religion (M Min, MS); marriage and family therapy (MS); mental health counseling (MS); ministry (M Min). *Application Contact:* Dr. Monte Cox, Dean, 501-279-4448, Fax: 501-279-4042, E-mail: mcox@harding.edu. *Dean,* Dr. Monte Cox, 501-279-4448, Fax: 501-279-4042, E-mail: mcox@harding.edu.

College of Business Administration Students: 85 full-time (49 women), 133 part-time (52 women); includes 35 minority (27 Black or African American, non-Hispanic/Latino; 1 American Indian or Alaska Native, non-Hispanic/Latino; 4 Asian, non-Hispanic/Latino; 1 Hispanic/Latino; 1 Native Hawaiian or other Pacific Islander, non-Hispanic/Latino; 1 Two or more races, non-Hispanic/Latino), 29 international. Average age 30. 52 applicants, 94% accepted, 44 enrolled. *Faculty:* 30 part-time/adjunct (6 women). Expenses: Contact institution. *Financial support:* In 2010–11, 19 students received support. Unspecified assistantships available. Financial award application deadline: 7/30; financial award applicants required to submit FAFSA. In 2010, 100 master's awarded. *Degree program information:* Part-time and evening/weekend programs available. Postbaccalaureate distance learning degree programs offered (no on-campus study). Offers health care management (MBA); information technology management (MBA); international business (MBA); leadership and organizational management (MBA). *Application deadline:* For fall admission, 8/1 priority date for domestic and international students; for spring admission, 12/1 priority date for domestic and international students. Applications are processed on a rolling basis. *Application fee:* $35. *Application Contact:* Melanie Kiihnl, Recruiting Manager/Director of Marketing, 501-279-4523, Fax: 501-279-4805, E-mail: mba@harding.edu. *Director of Graduate Studies,* Glen Metheny, 501-279-5851, Fax: 501-279-4805, E-mail: gmetheny@harding.edu.

Harding University (continued)

College of Communication Students: 33 full-time (all women); includes 2 minority (1 Black or African American, non-Hispanic/Latino; 1 American Indian or Alaska Native, non-Hispanic/Latino). Average age 24. 36 applicants, 56% accepted, 20 enrolled. *Faculty:* 10 part-time/adjunct (8 women). Expenses: Contact institution. *Financial support:* In 2010–11, 11 students received support. Unspecified assistantships available. Financial award applicants required to submit FAFSA. In 2010, 13 master's awarded. Offers speech-language pathology (MS). *Application deadline:* For fall admission, 3/1 for domestic students. *Application fee:* $40. *Application Contact:* Martha Vendetti, Administrative Assistant, 501-279-4648, E-mail: mvendett@harding.edu. *Department Chairman,* Dr. Daniel C. Tullos, 501-279-4633, Fax: 501-279-4325, E-mail: tullos@harding.edu.

College of Education Students: 86 full-time (62 women), 347 part-time (244 women); includes 67 Black or African American, non-Hispanic/Latino; 1 American Indian or Alaska Native, non-Hispanic/Latino; 2 Asian, non-Hispanic/Latino; 5 Hispanic/Latino; 9 Two or more races, non-Hispanic/Latino, 3 international. Average age 36. 93 applicants, 91% accepted, 83 enrolled. *Faculty:* 9 full-time (2 women), 48 part-time/adjunct (26 women). Expenses: Contact institution. *Financial support:* In 2010–11, 37 students received support. Unspecified assistantships available. In 2010, 172 master's, 10 other advanced degrees awarded. *Degree program information:* Part-time and evening/weekend programs available. Offers advanced studies in teaching and learning (M Ed); art (MSE); behavioral science (MSE); counseling (MS, Ed S); early childhood special education (M Ed, MSE); education (MSE); educational leadership (M Ed, Ed S); elementary education (M Ed); English (MSE); French (MSE); history/social science (MSE); kinesiology (MSE); math (MSE); reading (M Ed); secondary education (M Ed); Spanish (MSE); teaching (MAT); teaching English as a second language (MSE). *Application deadline:* For fall admission, 8/1 for domestic and international students; for spring admission, 1/1 for domestic and international students. Applications are processed on a rolling basis. *Application fee:* $35. *Application Contact:* Information Contact, 501-279-4315, E-mail: gradstudiesedu@harding.edu. *Chair,* Dr. Clara Carroll, 501-279-4501, Fax: 501-279-4083, E-mail: ccarroll@harding.edu.

College of Pharmacy Students: 179 full-time (89 women), 1 part-time (0 women); includes 16 Black or African American, non-Hispanic/Latino; 5 American Indian or Alaska Native, non-Hispanic/Latino; 36 Asian, non-Hispanic/Latino; 2 Two or more races, non-Hispanic/Latino, 3 international. Average age 26. 398 applicants, 25% accepted, 64 enrolled. *Faculty:* 24 full-time (11 women), 3 part-time/adjunct (2 women). Expenses: Contact institution. *Financial support:* In 2010–11, 23 students received support. Scholarships/grants available. Financial award applicants required to submit FAFSA. Offers pharmacy (Pharm D). *Application deadline:* For fall admission, 3/1 priority date for domestic and international students. Applications are processed on a rolling basis. *Application fee:* $50. Electronic applications accepted. *Application Contact:* Carol Jones, Director of Admissions, 501-279-5523, Fax: 501-279-5525, E-mail: ccjones@harding.edu. *Dean,* Dr. Julie Ann Hixson-Wallace, 501-279-5205, Fax: 501-279-5525, E-mail: jahixson@harding.edu.

College of Sciences Students: 98 full-time (71 women); includes 1 Black or African American, non-Hispanic/Latino; 4 American Indian or Alaska Native, non-Hispanic/Latino; 5 Asian, non-Hispanic/Latino; 1 Hispanic/Latino. Average age 26. 390 applicants, 10% accepted, 36 enrolled. *Faculty:* 6 full-time (1 woman), 2 part-time/adjunct (1 woman). Expenses: Contact institution. *Financial support:* Applicants required to submit FAFSA. In 2010, 29 master's awarded. Offers physician assistant studies (MS). *Application deadline:* For fall admission, 11/1 for domestic students. Applications are processed on a rolling basis. *Application fee:* $25. Electronic applications accepted. *Application Contact:* Marcia Murphy, Admissions Director, Physician Assistant Program, 501-279-5642, Fax: 501-279-4188, E-mail: paprogram@harding.edu. *Director,* Dr. Michael Murphy, 501-279-5642, E-mail: paprogram@harding.edu.

HARDING UNIVERSITY GRADUATE SCHOOL OF RELIGION, Memphis, TN 38117-5499

General Information Independent-religious, coed, primarily men, graduate-only institution. *Graduate housing:* Rooms and/or apartments available to single and married students.

GRADUATE UNITS

Graduate Programs *Degree program information:* Part-time programs available. Postbaccalaureate distance learning degree programs offered (minimal on-campus study). Offers Christian ministry (MA); counseling (MA); ministry (M Div, D Min); religion (MA). Electronic applications accepted.

HARDIN-SIMMONS UNIVERSITY, Abilene, TX 79698-0001

General Information Independent-religious, coed, comprehensive institution. *Enrollment:* 2,312 graduate, professional, and undergraduate students; 257 full-time matriculated graduate/professional students (140 women), 174 part-time matriculated graduate/professional students (76 women). *Enrollment by degree level:* 84 first professional, 247 master's, 100 doctoral. *Graduate faculty:* 83 full-time (30 women), 21 part-time/adjunct (9 women). *Tuition:* Full-time $12,150; part-time $675 per credit hour. *Required fees:* $650; $110 per semester. Tuition and fees vary according to degree level. *Graduate housing:* Rooms and/or apartments available on a first-come, first-served basis to single and married students. Typical cost: $3123 per year ($6282 including board) for single students; $3780 per year ($5514 including board) for married students. Room and board charges vary according to board plan and housing facility selected. *Student services:* Campus employment opportunities, career counseling, free psychological counseling. *Library facilities:* Richardson Library plus 1 other. *Online resources:* library catalog, web page, access to other libraries' catalogs. *Collection:* 293,464 titles, 37,940 serial subscriptions, 25,370 audiovisual materials.

Computer facilities: 230 computers available on campus for general student use. A campuswide network can be accessed from student residence rooms. *Web address:* http://www.hsutx.edu/.

General Application Contact: Dr. Nancy Kucinski, Dean of Graduate Studies, 325-670-1298, Fax: 325-670-1564, E-mail: gradoff@hsutx.edu.

GRADUATE UNITS

The Acton MBA in Entrepreneurship Expenses: Contact institution. Offers entrepreneurship (MBA). *Application deadline:* For fall admission, 5/1 for domestic students, 2/25 for international students. *Application fee:* $150. *Application Contact:* Jessica Blanchard, Director of Recruiting, 512-703-1231, E-mail: jblanchard@actonmba.org.

Graduate School Students: 257 full-time (140 women), 174 part-time (76 women); includes 19 Black or African American, non-Hispanic/Latino; 5 American Indian or Alaska Native, non-Hispanic/Latino; 4 Asian, non-Hispanic/Latino; 30 Hispanic/Latino, 5 international. Average age 30. 173 applicants, 74% accepted, 111 enrolled. *Faculty:* 83 full-time (30 women), 21 part-time/adjunct (9 women). Expenses: Contact institution. *Financial support:* In 2010–11, 277 students received support, including 40 fellowships (averaging $1,243 per year); career-related internships or fieldwork, scholarships/grants, and recreation assistantships, coaching assistantships also available. Support available to part-time students. Financial award application deadline: 6/30; financial award applicants required to submit FAFSA. In 2010, 17 first professional degrees, 94 master's awarded. *Degree program information:* Part-time programs available. *Application deadline:* For fall admission, 8/15 priority date for domestic students, 4/1 for international students; for spring admission, 1/5 priority date for domestic students, 9/1 for international students. Applications are processed on a rolling basis. *Application fee:* $50. *Application Contact:* Dr. Nancy Kucinski, Dean of Graduate Studies, 325-670-1298, Fax: 325-670-1564, E-mail: gradoff@hsutx.edu. *Dean of Graduate Studies,* Dr. Nancy Kucinski, 325-670-1298, Fax: 325-670-1564, E-mail: gradoff@hsutx.edu.

Cynthia Ann Parker College of Liberal Arts Students: 16 full-time (12 women), 8 part-time (6 women); includes 1 Black or African American, non-Hispanic/Latino; 1 Hispanic/Latino, 1 international. Average age 28. 24 applicants, 46% accepted, 10 enrolled. *Faculty:* 14 full-time (5 women), 1 part-time/adjunct (0 women). Expenses: Contact institution. *Financial support:* In 2010–11, 24 students received support, including 16 fellowships (averaging $600 per year); scholarships/grants also available. Support available to part-time students. Financial award application deadline: 6/30; financial award applicants required to submit FAFSA. In 2010, 12 master's awarded. *Degree program information:* Part-time programs available. Offers English (MA); family psychology (MA); history (MA); liberal arts (MA). *Application deadline:* For fall admission, 8/15 priority date for domestic students, 4/1 for international students; for spring admission, 1/5 priority date for domestic students, 9/1 for international students. Applications are processed on a rolling basis. *Application fee:* $50. *Application Contact:* Dr. Nancy Kucinski, Dean of Graduate Studies, 325-670-1298, Fax: 325-670-1564, E-mail: gradoff@hsutx.edu. *Dean,* Dr. Alan R. Stafford, 325-670-1487, E-mail: stafford@hsutx.edu.

Holland School of Sciences and Mathematics Students: 8 full-time (5 women), 4 part-time (1 woman); includes 1 Hispanic/Latino, 1 international. Average age 27. 4 applicants, 100% accepted, 4 enrolled. *Faculty:* 5 full-time (0 women). Expenses: Contact institution. *Financial support:* In 2010–11, 12 students received support; fellowships, career-related internships or fieldwork and scholarships/grants available. Support available to part-time students. Financial award application deadline: 6/30; financial award applicants required to submit FAFSA. In 2010, 5 master's awarded. *Degree program information:* Part-time programs available. Offers environmental management (MS); physical therapy (DPT); sciences and mathematics (MS, DPT). *Application deadline:* For fall admission, 8/15 priority date for domestic students, 4/1 for international students; for spring admission, 1/5 priority date for domestic students, 9/1 for international students. Applications are processed on a rolling basis. *Application fee:* $50. *Application Contact:* Dr. Nancy Kucinski, Dean of Graduate Studies, 325-670-1298, Fax: 325-670-1564, E-mail: gradoff@hsutx.edu. *Dean,* Dr. Christopher McNair, 325-670-1401, Fax: 325-670-1385, E-mail: cmcnair@hsutx.edu.

Irvin School of Education Students: 49 full-time (40 women), 63 part-time (41 women); includes 6 Black or African American, non-Hispanic/Latino; 1 American Indian or Alaska Native, non-Hispanic/Latino; 14 Hispanic/Latino, 1 international. Average age 31. 56 applicants, 88% accepted, 40 enrolled. *Faculty:* 17 full-time (11 women), 8 part-time/adjunct (5 women). Expenses: Contact institution. *Financial support:* In 2010–11, 100 students received support, including 21 fellowships (averaging $1,373 per year); career-related internships or fieldwork, scholarships/grants, and coaching assistantships also available. Support available to part-time students. Financial award application deadline: 6/30; financial award applicants required to submit FAFSA. In 2010, 36 master's awarded. *Degree program information:* Part-time programs available. Offers counseling and human development (M Ed); education (M Ed); gifted education (M Ed); kinesiology, sport, and recreation (M Ed); reading specialist education (M Ed). *Application deadline:* For fall admission, 8/15 priority date for domestic students, 4/1 for international students; for spring admission, 1/5 priority date for domestic students, 9/1 for international students. Applications are processed on a rolling basis. *Application fee:* $50. *Application Contact:* Dr. Nancy Kucinski, Dean of Graduate Studies, 325-670-1298, Fax: 325-670-1564, E-mail: gradoff@hsutx.edu. *Dean,* Dr. Pam Williford, 325-670-1352, Fax: 325-670-5859, E-mail: pwilliford@hsutx.edu.

Kelley College of Business Students: 11 full-time (6 women), 13 part-time (6 women); includes 2 Black or African American, non-Hispanic/Latino; 1 Hispanic/Latino, 2 international. Average age 25. 20 applicants, 70% accepted, 12 enrolled. *Faculty:* 7 full-time (3 women), 2 part-time/adjunct (0 women). Expenses: Contact institution. *Financial support:* In 2010–11, 23 students received support; fellowships, scholarships/grants available. Support available to part-time students. Financial award application deadline: 6/30; financial award applicants required to submit FAFSA. In 2010, 17 master's awarded. *Degree program information:* Part-time and evening/weekend programs available. Offers business (MBA). *Application deadline:* For fall admission, 8/15 priority date for domestic students, 4/1 for international students; for spring admission, 1/5 priority date for domestic students, 9/1 for international students. Applications are processed on a rolling basis. *Application fee:* $50. *Application Contact:* Dr. Nancy Kucinski, Dean of Graduate Studies, 325-670-1298, Fax: 325-670-1564, E-mail: gradoff@hsutx.edu. *Director,* Dr. Nancy Kucinski, 325-670-1503, Fax: 325-670-1523, E-mail: kucinski@hsutx.edu.

Logsdon School of Theology Students: 57 full-time (15 women), 75 part-time (14 women); includes 8 Black or African American, non-Hispanic/Latino; 2 American Indian or Alaska Native, non-Hispanic/Latino; 1 Asian, non-Hispanic/Latino; 9 Hispanic/Latino. Average age 33. 49 applicants, 80% accepted, 35 enrolled. *Faculty:* 18 full-time (1 woman), 7 part-time/adjunct (2 women). Expenses: Contact institution. *Financial support:* In 2010–11, 102 students received support; fellowships, scholarships/grants available. Support available to part-time students. Financial award application deadline: 6/30; financial award applicants required to submit FAFSA. In 2010, 17 first professional degrees, 5 master's awarded. *Degree program information:* Part-time and evening/weekend programs available. Offers family ministry (MA); ministry (D Min); religion (MA); theology (M Div). *Application deadline:* For fall admission, 8/15 priority date for domestic students, 4/1 for international students; for spring admission, 1/5 priority date for domestic students, 9/1 for international students. Applications are processed on a rolling basis. *Application fee:* $50. *Application Contact:* Dr. Nancy Kucinski, Dean of Graduate Studies, 325-670-1298, Fax: 325-670-1564, E-mail: gradoff@hsutx.edu. *Interim Dean,* Dr. Don Williford, 325-670-1266, Fax: 325-670-1406, E-mail: willifrd@hsutx.edu.

Patty Hanks Shelton School of Nursing Students: 4 full-time (1 woman), 6 part-time (5 women); includes 1 Black or African American, non-Hispanic/Latino; 1 American Indian or Alaska Native, non-Hispanic/Latino. Average age 39. 13 applicants, 54% accepted, 6 enrolled. *Faculty:* 3 full-time (all women), 2 part-time/adjunct (both women). Expenses: Contact institution. *Financial support:* In 2010–11, 8 students received support. Career-related internships or fieldwork and scholarships/grants available. Support available to part-time students. Financial award application deadline: 6/30; financial award applicants required to submit FAFSA. In 2010, 13 master's awarded. *Degree program information:* Part-time programs available. Offers advanced healthcare delivery (MSN); family nurse practitioner (MSN). Programs offered jointly with Abilene Christian University and McMurry University. *Application deadline:* For fall admission, 8/15 priority date for domestic students, 4/1 for international students; for spring admission, 1/5 priority date for domestic students, 9/1 for international students. Applications are processed on a rolling basis. *Application fee:* $50. *Application Contact:* Dr. Nancy Kucinski, Dean of Graduate Studies, 325-670-1298, Fax: 325-670-1564, E-mail: gradoff@hsutx.edu. *Director,* Dr. Amy Toone, 325-671-2361, Fax: 325-671-2386, E-mail: atoone@phssn.edu.

School of Music and Fine Arts Students: 4 full-time (1 woman), 3 part-time (all women). Average age 30. 7 applicants, 57% accepted, 4 enrolled. *Faculty:* 11 full-time (3 women). Expenses: Contact institution. *Financial support:* In 2010–11, 3 fellowships (averaging $1,200 per year) were awarded; career-related internships or fieldwork and scholarships/grants also available. Support available to part-time students. Financial award application deadline: 6/30; financial award applicants required to submit FAFSA. In 2010, 6 master's awarded. *Degree program information:* Part-time programs available. Offers church music (MM); music education (MM); music performance (MM); theory-composition (MM). *Application deadline:* For fall admission, 8/15 priority date for domestic students, 4/1 for international students; for spring admission, 1/5 priority date for domestic students, 9/1 for international students. Applications are processed on a rolling basis. *Application fee:* $50. *Application Contact:* Dr. Nancy Kucinski, Dean of Graduate Studies, 325-670-1298, Fax: 325-670-1564, E-mail: gradoff@hsutx.edu. *Program Director,* Dr. Lynette Chambers, 325-670-1430, Fax: 325-670-5873, E-mail: lborman@hsutx.edu.

HARRINGTON COLLEGE OF DESIGN, Chicago, IL 60605-1496

General Information Proprietary, coed, primarily women, comprehensive institution.

GRADUATE UNITS

Programs in Interior Design Offers interior design (MA, MID).

HARRISBURG UNIVERSITY OF SCIENCE AND TECHNOLOGY, Harrisburg, PA 17101

General Information Independent, coed, comprehensive institution. *Enrollment:* 387 graduate, professional, and undergraduate students; 4 full-time matriculated graduate/professional students (2 women), 65 part-time matriculated graduate/professional students (32 women). *Enrollment by degree level:* 69 master's. *Graduate faculty:* 3 full-time (0 women), 8 part-time/adjunct (3 women). *Tuition:* Full-time $19,500; part-time $700 per credit hour. *Graduate* *housing:* On-campus housing not available. *Student services:* Career counseling. *Library facilities:* Information Commons. *Online resources:* library catalog, web page. *Collection:* 40,000 titles, 45 serial subscriptions.

Computer facilities: Computer purchase and lease plans are available. 10 computers available on campus for general student use. A campuswide network can be accessed from off campus. *Web address:* http://www.HarrisburgU.edu/.

General Application Contact: Timothy Dawson, Information Contact, 717-901-5158, Fax: 717-901-3158, E-mail: admissions@harrisburgu.edu.

GRADUATE UNITS

Program in Information Systems Engineering and Management Students: 4 full-time (2 women), 16 part-time (5 women); includes 5 Black or African American, non-Hispanic/Latino; 2 Hispanic/Latino. Average age 30. 18 applicants, 83% accepted, 11 enrolled. *Faculty:* 1 full-time (0 women), 2 part-time/adjunct (0 women). Expenses: Contact institution. *Financial support:* In 2010–11, 2 students received support. Scholarships/grants available. Financial award applicants required to submit FAFSA. *Degree program information:* Part-time programs available. Offers digital government specialization (MS); digital health specialization (MS); entrepreneurship specialization (MS). *Application deadline:* For fall admission, 8/1 priority date for domestic students, 7/1 priority date for international students. Applications are processed on a rolling basis. *Application fee:* $0. Electronic applications accepted. *Application Contact:* Timothy Dawson, Information Contact, 717-901-5158, Fax: 717-901-3158, E-mail: admissions@harrisburgu.edu. *Director and Professor,* Dr. Amjad Umar, 717-901-5141, Fax: 717-901-3141, E-mail: aumar@harrisburgu.edu.

Program in Learning Technologies Students: 39 part-time (26 women); includes 1 Black or African American, non-Hispanic/Latino. Average age 30. 21 applicants, 67% accepted, 6 enrolled. *Faculty:* 1 full-time (0 women), 4 part-time/adjunct (2 women). Expenses: Contact institution. *Financial support:* In 2010–11, 2 students received support. Scholarships/grants available. Financial award applicants required to submit FAFSA. *Degree program information:* Part-time and evening/weekend programs available. Offers learning technologies (MS). *Application deadline:* For fall admission, 8/1 priority date for domestic students, 7/1 priority date for international students. Applications are processed on a rolling basis. *Application fee:* $0. Electronic applications accepted. *Application Contact:* Timothy Dawson, Information Contact, 717-901-5158, Fax: 717-901-3158, E-mail: admissions@harrisburgu.edu. *Director/Assistant Professor,* Andy Petroski, 717-901-5167, Fax: 717-901-3167, E-mail: apetroski@harrisburgu.edu.

Program in Project Management Students: 11 part-time (2 women); includes 1 Black or African American, non-Hispanic/Latino; 1 Asian, non-Hispanic/Latino; 1 Hispanic/Latino, 1 international. Average age 30. 24 applicants, 75% accepted. *Faculty:* 1 full-time (0 women), 3 part-time/adjunct (0 women). Expenses: Contact institution. *Financial support:* Scholarships/grants available. Financial award applicants required to submit FAFSA. In 2010, 7 master's awarded. *Degree program information:* Part-time and evening/weekend programs available. Offers construction services (MS); governmental services (MS); information technology (MS). *Application deadline:* For fall admission, 8/1 priority date for domestic students, 7/1 priority date for international students. Applications are processed on a rolling basis. *Application fee:* $0. Electronic applications accepted. *Application Contact:* Timothy Dawson, Information Contact, 717-901-5158, Fax: 717-901-3158, E-mail: admissions@harrisburgu.edu. *Director and Professor,* Dr. Amjad Umar, 717-901-5141, Fax: 717-901-3141, E-mail: aumar@harrisburgu.edu.

HARTFORD SEMINARY, Hartford, CT 06105-2279

General Information Independent-religious, coed, graduate-only institution. *Graduate faculty:* 15 full-time (3 women), 19 part-time/adjunct (7 women). *Tuition:* Full-time $10,680; part-time $1780 per course. *Graduate housing:* Rooms and/or apartments available on a first-come, first-served basis to single and married students. Typical cost: $4500 per year for single students; $10,000 per year for married students. Housing application deadline: 7/15. *Student services:* Campus employment opportunities, career counseling, international student services, services for students with disabilities, writing training. *Online resources:* library catalog, web page. *Collection:* 90,000 titles, 311 serial subscriptions, 561 audiovisual materials.

Computer facilities: 7 computers available on campus for general student use. A campuswide network can be accessed from off campus. Online class registration is available. *Web address:* http://www.hartsem.edu/.

General Application Contact: Marcia Pavao, Administrative Assistant, Admissions, 860-509-9512, Fax: 860-509-9509, E-mail: mpavao@hartsem.edu.

GRADUATE UNITS

Graduate Programs Students: 37 full-time (17 women), 121 part-time (68 women); includes 35 minority (27 Black or African American, non-Hispanic/Latino; 5 Asian, non-Hispanic/Latino; 3 Hispanic/Latino), 25 international. *Faculty:* 15 full-time (3 women), 19 part-time/adjunct (7 women). Expenses: Contact institution. *Financial support:* In 2010–11, 74 students received support. Scholarships/grants and tuition waivers (partial) available. Support available to part-time students. Financial award application deadline: 6/1. *Degree program information:* Part-time and evening/weekend programs available. Postbaccalaureate distance learning degree programs offered (no on-campus study). Offers Islamic studies (MA); ministry (D Min); religious studies (MA); spirituality (Certificate). *Application deadline:* For fall admission, 7/15 priority date for domestic students, 5/1 priority date for international students; for winter admission, 12/1 priority date for domestic students, 4/1 priority date for international students; for spring admission, 4/5 priority date for domestic students, 3/1 priority date for international students. Applications are processed on a rolling basis. *Application fee:* $50. *Application Contact:* Dr. Vanessa Avery, Admissions and Recruitment Manager, 860-509-9552, Fax: 860-509-9509, E-mail: vavery@hartsem.edu. *Dean,* Dr. Efrain Agosto, 860-509-9554, E-mail: eagosto@hartsem.edu.

HARVARD UNIVERSITY, Cambridge, MA 02138

General Information Independent, coed, university. CGS member. *Enrollment:* 12,465 full-time matriculated graduate/professional students (5,906 women), 1,509 part-time matriculated graduate/professional students (765 women). *Enrollment by degree level:* 2,745 first professional, 6,311 master's, 4,642 doctoral, 276 other advanced degrees. *Graduate faculty:* 1,867 full-time (580 women), 322 part-time/adjunct (118 women). *Tuition:* Full-time $34,976. *Required fees:* $1166. Full-time tuition and fees vary according to program. *Graduate housing:* Rooms and/or apartments available to single and married students. Housing application deadline: 4/27. *Student services:* Campus employment opportunities, campus safety program, career counseling, child daycare facilities, exercise/wellness program, free psychological counseling, grant writing training, international student services, low-cost health insurance, multicultural affairs office, services for students with disabilities, teacher training, writing training. *Library facilities:* Widener Library plus 73 others. *Online resources:* library catalog, web page, access to other libraries' catalogs. *Collection:* 16.3 million titles, 121,791 serial subscriptions. *Research affiliation:* Woods Hole Oceanographic Institution (biology).

Computer facilities: Computer purchase and lease plans are available. 605 computers available on campus for general student use. A campuswide network can be accessed from student residence rooms and from off campus. Online class registration is available. *Web address:* http://www.harvard.edu/.

General Application Contact: Admissions Office, 617-495-1814, E-mail: gsas@fas.harvard.edu.

GRADUATE UNITS

Cyprus International Institute for the Environment and Public Health in Association with Harvard School of Public Health Offers environmental health (MS). Electronic applications accepted.

Extension School *Degree program information:* Part-time and evening/weekend programs available. Offers applied sciences (CAS); biotechnology (ALM); educational technologies (ALM); educational technology (CET); English for graduate and professional studies (DGP); environmental management (ALM, CEM); information technology (ALM); journalism (ALM); liberal arts (ALM); management (ALM, CM); mathematics for teaching (ALM); museum studies (ALM); premedical studies (Diploma); publication and communication (CPC).

Graduate School of Arts and Sciences Offers African and African American studies (PhD); African history (PhD); Akkadian and Sumerian (AM, PhD); American history (PhD); ancient art (PhD); ancient Near Eastern art (PhD); ancient, medieval, early modern, and modern Europe (PhD); anthropology and Middle Eastern studies (PhD); Arabic (AM, PhD); archaeology (PhD); architecture (PhD); Armenian (AM, PhD); arts and sciences (AM, ME, MFS, SM, PhD); astronomy (PhD); astrophysics (PhD); baroque art (PhD); biblical history (AM, PhD); biochemical chemistry (PhD); biological anthropology (PhD); biological sciences in dental medicine (PhD); biology (PhD); biophysics (PhD); biostatistics (PhD); business economics (PhD); Byzantine art (PhD); Byzantine Greek (PhD); chemical biology (PhD); chemical physics (PhD); Chinese (PhD); Chinese studies (AM); classical archaeology (PhD); classical art (PhD); classical philology (PhD); classical philosophy (PhD); comparative literature (PhD); composition (AM, PhD); critical theory (PhD); descriptive linguistics (PhD); diplomatic history (PhD); earth and planetary sciences (AM, PhD); East Asian history (PhD); economic and social history (PhD); economics (PhD); economics and Middle Eastern studies (PhD); eighteenth-century literature (PhD); experimental physics (PhD); fine arts and Middle Eastern studies (PhD); forest science (MFS); French (AM, PhD); German (PhD); health policy (PhD); Hebrew (AM, PhD); historical linguistics (PhD); history and Middle Eastern studies (PhD); history of American civilization (PhD); history of science (AM, PhD); Indian art (PhD); Indian philosophy (AM, PhD); Indo-Muslim culture (AM, PhD); information, technology and management (PhD); Inner Asian and Altaic studies (PhD); inorganic chemistry (PhD); intellectual history (PhD); Iranian (AM, PhD); Irish (PhD); Islamic art (PhD); Italian (AM, PhD); Japanese (PhD); Japanese and Chinese art (PhD); Japanese studies (AM); Jewish history and literature (AM, PhD); Korean (PhD); Korean studies (AM); landscape architecture (PhD); Latin American history (PhD); legal anthropology (AM); literature: nineteenth-century to the present (PhD); mathematics (PhD); medical anthropology (AM); medical engineering/medical physics (PhD); medieval art (PhD); medieval Latin (PhD); medieval literature and language (PhD); modern art (PhD); modern British and American literature (PhD); molecular and cellular biology (PhD); Mongolian (PhD); Mongolian studies (AM); musicology (AM); musicology and ethnomusicology (PhD); Near Eastern history (PhD); neurobiology (PhD); oceanic history (PhD); oral literature (PhD); organic chemistry (PhD); organizational behavior (PhD); Pali (AM, PhD); Persian (AM, PhD); philosophy (PhD); physical chemistry (PhD); Polish (PhD); political economy and government (PhD); political science (PhD); Portuguese (AM, PhD); psychology (PhD); public policy (PhD); regional studies–Middle East (AM); regional studies-Russia, Eastern Europe, and Central Asia (AM); Renaissance and modern architecture (PhD); Renaissance art (PhD); Renaissance literature (PhD); Russian (PhD); Sanskrit (AM, PhD); Scandinavian (PhD); Semitic philology (AM, PhD); Serbo-Croatian (PhD); Slavic philology (PhD); social anthropology (AM, PhD); social change and development (AM); social policy (PhD); social psychology (PhD); sociology (PhD); Spanish (AM, PhD); statistics (AM, PhD); study of religion (PhD); Syro-Palestinian archaeology (AM, PhD); systems biology (PhD); theoretical linguistics (PhD); theoretical physics (PhD); theory (AM, PhD); Tibetan (AM, PhD); Turkish (AM, PhD); Ukrainian (PhD); urban planning (PhD); Urdu (AM, PhD); Vietnamese (PhD); Vietnamese studies (AM); Welsh (PhD). Electronic applications accepted.

Division of Medical Sciences Offers biological chemistry and molecular pharmacology (PhD); cell biology (PhD); genetics (PhD); microbiology and molecular genetics (PhD); pathology (PhD).

School of Engineering and Applied Sciences *Degree program information:* Part-time programs available. Offers applied mathematics (ME, SM, PhD); applied physics (ME, SM, PhD); computer science (ME, SM, PhD); engineering science (ME); engineering sciences (SM, PhD). Electronic applications accepted.

Graduate School of Design Offers architecture (M Arch); design (M Arch, M Des S, MAUD, MLA, MLAUD, MUP, Dr DES); design studies (M Des S); landscape architecture (MLA); urban planning (MUP); urban planning and design (MAUD, MLAUD). Electronic applications accepted.

Harvard Business School Offers accounting and management (DBA); business (MBA, DBA, PhD); business administration (MBA); business economics (PhD); health policy management (PhD); management (DBA); marketing (DBA); organizational behavior (PhD); science, technology and management (PhD); strategy (DBA); technology and operations management (DBA).

Harvard Divinity School Students: 362 full-time (191 women); includes 24 Black or African American, non-Hispanic/Latino; 2 American Indian or Alaska Native, non-Hispanic/Latino; 19 Asian, non-Hispanic/Latino; 28 Hispanic/Latino; 13 Two or more races, non-Hispanic/Latino, 37 international. Average age 26. 481 applicants, 42% accepted, 130 enrolled. *Faculty:* 45 full-time (19 women), 58 part-time/adjunct (23 women). Expenses: Contact institution. *Financial support:* In 2010–11, 317 students received support, including 317 fellowships with tuition reimbursements available (averaging $26,986 per year); teaching assistantships, career-related internships or fieldwork, Federal Work-Study, and scholarships/grants also available. Support available to part-time students. Financial award application deadline: 2/1; financial award applicants required to submit FAFSA. In 2010, 56 M Divs, 94 master's, 5 doctorates awarded. Offers divinity (M Div, MTS, Th M, Th D). *Application deadline:* For fall admission, 1/11 for domestic and international students. *Application fee:* $75. Electronic applications accepted. *Application Contact:* Loida Feliz, Director of Admissions, 617-495-5796, Fax: 617-495-0345, E-mail: admissions@hds.harvard.edu. *Dean of the Faculty,* William A. Graham, 617-495-4513, Fax: 617-496-8026.

Harvard Graduate School of Education Students: 902 full-time (657 women), 95 part-time (63 women); includes 310 minority (100 Black or African American, non-Hispanic/Latino; 4 American Indian or Alaska Native, non-Hispanic/Latino; 91 Asian, non-Hispanic/Latino; 78 Hispanic/Latino; 3 Native Hawaiian or other Pacific Islander, non-Hispanic/Latino; 34 Two or more races, non-Hispanic/Latino), 109 international. Average age 30. 2,152 applicants, 43% accepted, 662 enrolled. *Faculty:* 79 full-time (42 women), 58 part-time/adjunct (24 women). Expenses: Contact institution. *Financial support:* In 2010–11, 688 students received support, including 123 fellowships with full and partial tuition reimbursements available (averaging $15,098 per year), 44 research assistantships (averaging $9,613 per year), 133 teaching assistantships (averaging $10,500 per year); career-related internships or fieldwork, Federal Work-Study, institutionally sponsored loans, scholarships/grants, health care benefits, tuition waivers (full and partial), and unspecified assistantships also available. Support available to part-time students. Financial award application deadline: 2/1; financial award applicants required to submit FAFSA. In 2010, 634 master's, 54 doctorates awarded. *Degree program information:* Part-time programs available. Offers arts in education (Ed M); culture, communities and education (Ed D); education (Ed M, Ed D, Ed L D); education leadership (Ed L D); education policy and management (Ed M); education policy, leadership and instructional practice (Ed D); higher education (Ed M, Ed D); human development and education (Ed D); human development and psychology (Ed M); international education policy (Ed M); language and literacy (Ed M); learning and teaching (Ed M); mid-career mathematics and science (teaching certificate) (Ed M); mind brain and education (Ed M); prevention science and practice (Ed M); quantitative policy analysis in education (Ed D); school leadership (Ed M); special studies (Ed M); teaching and curriculum (teaching certificate) (Ed M); technology innovation and education (Ed M). *Application deadline:* For fall admission, 1/3 for domestic and international students. *Application fee:* $85. Electronic applications accepted. *Application Contact:* Information Contact, 617-495-3414, Fax: 617-496-3577, E-mail: gseadmissions@harvard.edu. *Dean,* Dr. Kathleen McCartney, 617-495-3401.

Harvard Medical School Offers medicine (MD, M Eng, SM, PhD, Sc D). Electronic applications accepted.

Division of Health Sciences and Technology Students: 334 full-time (122 women); includes 7 Black or African American, non-Hispanic/Latino; 1 American Indian or Alaska Native, non-Hispanic/Latino; 109 Asian, non-Hispanic/Latino; 9 Hispanic/Latino; 13 Two or more races, non-Hispanic/Latino, 46 international. Average age 26. 1,187 applicants, 6% accepted, 53 enrolled. *Faculty:* 68 full-time (6 women), 179 part-time/adjunct (30 women). Expenses: Contact institution. *Financial support:* In 2010–11, 191 students received support, including 89 fellowships with full and partial tuition reimbursements available (averaging $54,804 per year), 101 research assistantships with full and partial tuition reimbursements available (averaging $33,331 per year), 40 teaching assistantships with full and partial tuition reimbursements available (averaging $7,739 per year); career-related internships or fieldwork, scholarships/grants, traineeships, health care benefits, and unspecified assistantships also

Harvard University (continued)

available. Support available to part-time students. Financial award application deadline: 12/15; financial award applicants required to submit FAFSA. In 2010, 28 first professional degrees, 30 doctorates awarded. Offers biomedical engineering (M Eng); biomedical enterprise (SM); biomedical informatics (SM); health sciences and technology (MD, M Eng, SM, PhD, Sc D); medical engineering (PhD); medical engineering/medical physics (Sc D); medical physics (PhD); medical sciences (MD); speech and hearing bioscience and technology (PhD, Sc D). PhD, MD, MD/PhD, and ScD offered jointly with Massachusetts Institute of Technology. *Application Contact:* Dr. David Earl Cohen, Director of Health Sciences and Technology. *Director of Health Sciences and Technology*, Dr. David Earl Cohen.

Harvard School of Public Health Students: 812 full-time, 284 part-time; includes 63 Black or African American, non-Hispanic/Latino; 4 American Indian or Alaska Native, non-Hispanic/Latino; 78 Asian, non-Hispanic/Latino; 34 Hispanic/Latino, 351 international. Average age 31. 2,245 applicants, 37% accepted, 520 enrolled. *Faculty:* 349 full-time (117 women), 117 part-time/adjunct (36 women). Expenses: Contact institution. *Financial support:* Fellowships, research assistantships, teaching assistantships, career-related internships or fieldwork, Federal Work-Study, scholarships/grants, traineeships, tuition waivers (partial), and unspecified assistantships available. Support available to part-time students. Financial award application deadline: 2/8; financial award applicants required to submit FAFSA. In 2010, 483 master's, 60 doctorates awarded. *Degree program information:* Part-time programs available. Offers biological sciences in public health (PhD); biostatistics (SM, PhD); cancer epidemiology (SM, DPH); cardiovascular epidemiology (SM, DPH, SD); clinical effectiveness (MPH); clinical epidemiology (SM, DPH, SD); environmental health (MOH, SM, DPH, PhD, SD); environmental/occupational epidemiology (SM, SD); epidemiologic methods (DPH, SD); epidemiology (SM, DPH, SD); epidemiology of aging (SM, DPH, SD); family and community health (MPH); genetics and complex diseases (PhD); global health (MPH); global health and population (SM, DPH, SD); health care management and policy (MPH); health policy (PhD); health policy and management (SM, SD); immunology and infectious diseases (PhD, SD); infectious diseases (SM, DPH, SD); molecular/genetic epidemiology (DPH, SD); neuroepidemiology (DPH, SD); nutrition (DPH, PhD, SD); nutritional epidemiology (DPH, SD); occupational and environmental health (MPH); occupational health (MOH, SM, DPH, SD); oral and dental health epidemiology (SM, SD); pharmacoepidemiology (SM, DPH, SD); physiology (PhD, SD); psychiatric epidemiology (SM, DPH); public health (MOH, MPH, SM, DPH, PhD, SD); public health nutrition (DPH, SD); quantitative methods (MPH); reproductive epidemiology (SM, SD); society, human development and health (SM, DPH, SD). SM program offered jointly with Simmons College. *Application deadline:* For fall admission, 12/15 for domestic and international students. *Application fee:* $115. Electronic applications accepted. *Application Contact:* Vincent W. James, Director of Admissions, 617-432-1031, Fax: 617-432-7080, E-mail: admissions@hsph.harvard.edu. *Dean of the Faculty*, Dr. Julio Frenk, 617-432-1025, Fax: 617-277-5320, E-mail: deansoff@hsph.harvard.edu.

John F. Kennedy School of Government Students: 880 full-time (367 women), 32 part-time (12 women); includes 32 Black or African American, non-Hispanic/Latino; 7 American Indian or Alaska Native, non-Hispanic/Latino; 61 Asian, non-Hispanic/Latino; 53 Hispanic/Latino; 38 Two or more races, non-Hispanic/Latino, 344 international. Average age 31. 3,129 applicants, 28% accepted, 581 enrolled. Expenses: Contact institution. *Financial support:* Fellowships, research assistantships, teaching assistantships, career-related internships or fieldwork, Federal Work-Study, institutionally sponsored loans, scholarships/grants, and unspecified assistantships available. Support available to part-time students. Financial award applicants required to submit CSS PROFILE or FAFSA. In 2010, 513 master's awarded. Offers government (MPA, MPAID, MPP, PhD); political economy and government (PhD); public administration (MPA); public administration/international development (MPAID); public policy (MPP, PhD). *Application fee:* $100. Electronic applications accepted. *Application Contact:* 617-495-1155, Fax: 617-496-1165, E-mail: hks_admissions@harvard.edu. *Dean*, Dr. David Ellwood, 617-495-1122.

Law School Offers international and comparative law (JD); law (JD, LL M, SJD); law and business (JD); law and government (JD); law and social change (JD); law, science and technology (JD).

School of Dental Medicine Offers advanced general dentistry (Certificate); dental medicine (DMD, M Med Sc, D Med Sc, Certificate); dental public health (Certificate); endodontics (Certificate); general practice residency (Certificate); oral biology (M Med Sc, D Med Sc); oral implantology (Certificate); oral medicine (Certificate); oral pathology (Certificate); oral surgery (Certificate); orthodontics (Certificate); pediatric dentistry (Certificate); periodontics (Certificate); prosthodontics (Certificate).

HASTINGS COLLEGE, Hastings, NE 68901-7696

General Information Independent-religious, coed, comprehensive institution. *Graduate housing:* On-campus housing not available.

GRADUATE UNITS

Department of Teacher Education *Degree program information:* Part-time programs available. Offers teacher education (MAT). Electronic applications accepted.

HAWAI'I PACIFIC UNIVERSITY, Honolulu, HI 96813

General Information Independent, coed, comprehensive institution. *Graduate housing:* Room and/or apartments available on a first-come, first-served basis to single students; on-campus housing not available to married students. *Research affiliation:* Oceanic Institute (marine science).

GRADUATE UNITS

College of Business Administration *Degree program information:* Part-time and evening/weekend programs available. Offers accounting/CPA (MBA); e-business (MBA); economics (MBA); finance (MBA); human resource management (MA); information systems (MBA, MSIS); international business (MBA); knowledge management (MSIS); management (MBA); marketing (MBA); organizational change (MA, MBA); software engineering (MSIS); telecommunications security (MSIS); travel industry management (MBA). Electronic applications accepted.

College of Humanities and Social Sciences *Degree program information:* Part-time and evening/weekend programs available. Offers clinical mental health counseling (MA); communication (MA); diplomacy and military studies (MA); elementary education (M Ed); humanities and social sciences (M Ed, MA, MSW); secondary education (M Ed); social work (MSW); teaching English to speakers of other languages (MA). Electronic applications accepted.

College of Natural and Computational Sciences Offers global leadership and sustainable development (MA); marine science (MS). Electronic applications accepted.

College of Nursing and Health Sciences *Degree program information:* Part-time and evening/weekend programs available. Offers community clinical nurse specialist (MSN); community clinical nurse specialist educator option (MSN); family nurse practitioner (MSN). Electronic applications accepted.

See Close-Up on page 951.

HAZELDEN GRADUATE SCHOOL OF ADDICTION STUDIES, Center City, MN 55012

General Information Independent, coed, graduate-only institution. CGS member. *Graduate housing:* On-campus housing not available.

GRADUATE UNITS

Graduate Programs *Degree program information:* Part-time programs available. Offers addiction counseling (MA, Certificate).

HEBREW COLLEGE, Newton Centre, MA 02459

General Information Independent-religious, coed, comprehensive institution. *Graduate housing:* On-campus housing not available.

GRADUATE UNITS

Cantor Educator Program Offers cantor educator (MJ Ed).

Program in Jewish Studies *Degree program information:* Part-time and evening/weekend programs available. Postbaccalaureate distance learning degree programs offered (minimal on-campus study). Offers Jewish liturgical music (Certificate); Jewish music education (Certificate); Jewish studies (MA).

Rabbinical School

Shoolman Graduate School of Education *Degree program information:* Part-time and evening/weekend programs available. Postbaccalaureate distance learning degree programs offered. Offers early childhood Jewish education (Certificate); Jewish day school education (Certificate); Jewish education (MJ Ed); Jewish family education (Certificate); Jewish special education (Certificate); Jewish youth education, informal education and camping (Certificate).

HEBREW UNION COLLEGE–JEWISH INSTITUTE OF RELIGION, New York, NY 10012-1186

General Information Independent-religious, coed, graduate-only institution. *Graduate housing:* On-campus housing not available.

GRADUATE UNITS

Rabbinical School Offers rabbinical studies (MAHL).

School of Education *Degree program information:* Part-time programs available. Offers education (MARE).

School of Graduate Studies *Degree program information:* Part-time programs available. Offers Hebrew letters (DHL); Judaic studies (MAJS); pastoral counseling (D Min).

School of Jewish Nonprofit Management Offers Jewish nonprofit management (MA).

School of Sacred Music Offers sacred music (MSM).

HEC MONTREAL, Montréal, QC H3T 2A7, Canada

General Information Province-supported, coed, comprehensive institution. *Enrollment:* 12,554 graduate, professional, and undergraduate students; 1,455 full-time matriculated graduate/professional students (662 women), 1,569 part-time matriculated graduate/professional students (796 women). *Enrollment by degree level:* 1,330 master's, 150 doctoral, 1,544 other advanced degrees. *Graduate faculty:* 279 full-time (88 women), 350 part-time/adjunct (108 women). *International tuition:* $17,354 full-time. *Tuition, area resident:* Part-time $68.93 per credit. Tuition, province resident: full-time $2481; part-time $188.92 per credit. Tuition, Canadian resident: full-time $6801; part-time $482.06 per course. *Required fees:* $1310; $30.28 per credit. $93.45 per term. Tuition and fees vary according to degree level and program. *Graduate housing:* Rooms and/or apartments available on a first-come, first-served basis to single and married students. Typical cost: $3530 per year for single students; $5755 per year for married students. *Student services:* Campus employment opportunities, career counseling, child daycare facilities, free psychological counseling, international student services, multicultural affairs office, services for students with disabilities. *Library facilities:* Myriam et J.-Robert Ouimet Library plus 1 other. *Online resources:* library catalog, web page, access to other libraries' catalogs. *Collection:* 361,638 titles, 66,016 serial subscriptions, 3,152 audiovisual materials. *Research affiliation:* Academy of Management (management and business), Association des Sciences Administratives du Canada (ASAC) (management and business), Academy of International Business (finance), International Federation of Operational Research Society (operational research), Centre Francophone de Recherche en Informatisation des Organisations (CEFRIO) (information Systems), The Institute of Finance Mathematics of Montreal (IFM2) (finance).

Computer facilities: Computer purchase and lease plans are available. 250 computers available on campus for general student use. Online class registration, corporate calendar and web site for all the resources available for classes are available. *Web address:* http://www.hec.ca/.

General Application Contact: Manon Vaillant, Registrar, 514-340-6110, Fax: 514-340-5640, E-mail: registraire.info@hec.ca.

GRADUATE UNITS

School of Business Administration Students: 1,455 full-time (662 women), 1,569 part-time (796 women). Average age 29. 2,376 applicants, 56% accepted, 907 enrolled. *Faculty:* 279 full-time (88 women), 350 part-time/adjunct (108 women). Expenses: Contact institution. *Financial support:* In 2010–11, 681 students received support; research assistantships, teaching assistantships, scholarships/grants available. Financial award application deadline: 9/2. In 2010, 513 master's, 23 doctorates, 620 other advanced degrees awarded. *Degree program information:* Part-time and evening/weekend programs available. Offers administration (LL M, M Sc, PhD, Diploma); applied economics (M Sc); applied financial economics (M Sc); business administration (LL M, M Sc, MBA, PhD, Diploma); business administration and management (MBA); business analytics (M Sc); business intelligence (M Sc); e-business (Diploma); electronic commerce (M Sc); finance (M Sc); financial and strategic accounting (M Sc); financial engineering (M Sc); human resources management (M Sc); information technologies (M Sc); international business (M Sc); logistics (M Sc); management (M Sc, Diploma); management and sustainable development (Diploma); management control (M Sc); management of cultural organizations (Diploma); marketing (M Sc); marketing communication (Diploma); organizational development (M Sc); organizational studies (M Sc); production and operations management (M Sc); professional finance (Diploma); public accountancy (Diploma); public accounting (M Sc); strategy (M Sc); supply chain management (Diploma); taxation (LL M, Diploma). Most courses are given in French. *Application fee:* $78 Canadian dollars. Electronic applications accepted. *Application Contact:* Manon Vaillant, Registrar, 514-340-6110, Fax: 514-340-5640, E-mail: registraire.info@hec.ca. *Director*, Dr. Michel Patry, 514-340-6110, Fax: 514-340-5640.

HEIDELBERG UNIVERSITY, Tiffin, OH 44883-2462

General Information Independent-religious, coed, comprehensive institution. *Enrollment:* 23 full-time matriculated graduate/professional students (14 women), 214 part-time matriculated graduate/professional students (155 women). *Enrollment by degree level:* 215 master's. *Graduate faculty:* 3 full-time (2 women), 10 part-time/adjunct (5 women). *Tuition:* Full-time $8910; part-time $495 per credit hour. *Graduate housing:* On-campus housing not available. *Student services:* Campus employment opportunities, career counseling, exercise/wellness program, free psychological counseling, international student services, multicultural affairs office, services for students with disabilities, teacher training, writing training. *Library facilities:* Beeghly Library.

Computer facilities: 125 computers available on campus for general student use. A campuswide network can be accessed from student residence rooms and from off campus. Online class registration is available. *Web address:* http://www.heidelberg.edu/.

General Application Contact: Melissa Nye, Administrative Assistant for Graduate Studies, 419-448-2288, Fax: 419-448-2072, E-mail: mnye@heidelberg.edu.

GRADUATE UNITS

Program in Business Students: 2 full-time (0 women), 43 part-time (23 women); includes 5 minority (all Black or African American, non-Hispanic/Latino). Average age 30. 45 applicants, 42% accepted, 18 enrolled. *Faculty:* 5 full-time (3 women), 4 part-time/adjunct (2 women). Expenses: Contact institution. *Financial support:* In 2010–11, 17 students received support. Federal Work-Study available. Support available to part-time students. Financial award applicants required to submit FAFSA. In 2010, 15 master's awarded. *Degree program information:* Part-time and evening/weekend programs available. Offers business (MBA). *Application deadline:* Applications are processed on a rolling basis. *Application fee:* $25. *Application Contact:* Melissa Nye, Administrative Assistant for Graduate Studies, 419-448-2288, Fax: 419-448-2072, E-mail: mnye@heidelberg.edu. *Director of School of Business*, Dr. Andrew Weiss, 419-448-2036, Fax: 419-448-2072, E-mail: aweiss@heidelberg.edu.

Program in Counseling Students: 14 full-time (10 women), 60 part-time (48 women); includes 2 Black or African American, non-Hispanic/Latino; 1 Asian, non-Hispanic/Latino; 2 Hispanic/Latino, 1 international. Average age 30. 47 applicants, 85% accepted, 31 enrolled.

Faculty: 3 full-time (2 women), 8 part-time/adjunct (4 women). Expenses: Contact institution. *Financial support:* In 2010–11, 51 students received support, including 1 teaching assistantship; Federal Work-Study also available. Support available to part-time students. Financial award applicants required to submit FAFSA. In 2010, 14 master's awarded. *Degree program information:* Part-time and evening/weekend programs available. Offers counseling (MA). *Application deadline:* Applications are processed on a rolling basis. *Application fee:* $25. *Application Contact:* Melissa Nye, Administrative Assistant Graduate Studies Office, 419-448-2288, Fax: 419-448-2072, E-mail: mnye@heidelberg.edu. *Director of Graduate Studies in Counseling,* Dr. Jo-Ann Lipford Sanders, 419-448-2312, Fax: 419-448-2072, E-mail: jsanders@heidelberg.edu.

Program in Education Expenses: Contact institution. *Financial support:* Federal Work-Study available. Support available to part-time students. Financial award applicants required to submit FAFSA. *Degree program information:* Part-time and evening/weekend programs available. Offers education (MAE). *Application deadline:* Applications are processed on a rolling basis. *Application fee:* $25. *Application Contact:* Melissa Nye, Graduate Studies Office, 419-448-2288, Fax: 419-448-2072, E-mail: mnye@heidelberg.edu. *Director of Graduate Studies,* Dr. Diane Armstrong, 419-448-2175, Fax: 419-448-2072, E-mail: darmstro@heidelberg.edu.

Program in Music Education Expenses: Contact institution. *Financial support:* Applicants required to submit FAFSA. *Degree program information:* Part-time programs available. Offers music education (MME). Summer program only. *Application deadline:* Applications are processed on a rolling basis. *Application fee:* $25. *Application Contact:* Melissa Nye, Administrative Assistant for Graduate Studies Office, 419-448-2288, Fax: 419-448-2072, E-mail: mnye@heidelberg.edu. *Director,* Dr. John Owen, 419-448-2085, E-mail: jowen@heidelberg.edu.

HENDERSON STATE UNIVERSITY, Arkadelphia, AR 71999-0001

General Information State-supported, coed, comprehensive institution. CGS member. *Enrollment:* 3,712 graduate, professional, and undergraduate students; 79 full-time matriculated graduate/professional students (47 women), 322 part-time matriculated graduate/professional students (245 women). *Enrollment by degree level:* 388 master's, 12 other advanced degrees. *Graduate faculty:* 55 full-time (22 women), 6 part-time/adjunct (2 women). Tuition, state resident: full-time $3978; part-time $221 per credit hour. Tuition, nonresident: full-time $7956; part-time $442 per credit hour. Tuition and fees vary according to course load. *Graduate housing:* Room and/or apartments available on a first-come, first-served basis to single students; on-campus housing not available to married students. Typical cost: $2014 (including board). Room and board charges vary according to board plan and housing facility selected. *Student services:* Campus employment opportunities, career counseling, free psychological counseling, international student services, services for students with disabilities. *Library facilities:* Huie Library. *Online resources:* library catalog, web page, access to other libraries' catalogs. *Collection:* 26.9 million titles, 277 serial subscriptions, 20,602 audiovisual materials.

Computer facilities: 125 computers available on campus for general student use. A campuswide network can be accessed from student residence rooms and from off campus. Online class registration is available. *Web address:* http://www.hsu.edu/.

General Application Contact: Dr. Ken Taylor, Graduate Dean, 870-230-5126, Fax: 870-230-5479, E-mail: taylorke@hsu.edu.

GRADUATE UNITS

Graduate Studies *Degree program information:* Part-time programs available. Electronic applications accepted.

Ellis College of Arts and Sciences *Degree program information:* Part-time programs available. Offers arts and sciences (MLA). Electronic applications accepted.

School of Business Administration *Degree program information:* Part-time programs available. Offers business administration (MBA). Electronic applications accepted.

School of Education *Degree program information:* Part-time programs available. Offers clinical mental health counseling (MSE); early childhood (P-4) (MSE); education (MAT); educational leadership (Ed S); elementary school counseling (MSE); middle school (MSE); reading (MSE); recreation (MS); school administration (MSE); secondary school counseling (MSE); special education (MSE); sports administration (MS). Electronic applications accepted.

HENDRIX COLLEGE, Conway, AR 72032-3080

General Information Independent-religious, coed, comprehensive institution. *Graduate housing:* Room and/or apartments available on a first-come, first-served basis to single students. Housing application deadline: 6/1.

GRADUATE UNITS

Program in Accounting *Degree program information:* Part-time programs available. Offers accounting (MA).

HENLEY-PUTNAM UNIVERSITY, San Jose, CA 95110

General Information Proprietary, coed, comprehensive institution.

GRADUATE UNITS

Program in Intelligence Management *Degree program information:* Part-time programs available. Postbaccalaureate distance learning degree programs offered. Offers intelligence management (MS).

Program in Management of Personal Protection *Degree program information:* Part-time programs available. Postbaccalaureate distance learning degree programs offered. Offers management of personal protection (MS).

Program in Strategic Security Offers strategic security (PhD).

Program in Terrorism and Counterterrorism Studies *Degree program information:* Part-time programs available. Postbaccalaureate distance learning degree programs offered. Offers terrorism and counterterrorism studies (MS).

HERITAGE BAPTIST COLLEGE AND HERITAGE THEOLOGICAL SEMINARY, Cambridge, ON N3C 3T2, Canada

General Information Independent-religious, coed, comprehensive institution.

GRADUATE UNITS

Program in Theological Studies Offers chaplaincy (M Div); counselling (M Div); general (M Div); ministry (D Min); pastoral (M Div); research (M Div); theological studies (MA, Certificate).

HERITAGE CHRISTIAN UNIVERSITY, Florence, AL 35630

General Information Independent-religious, coed, primarily men, comprehensive institution.

GRADUATE UNITS

Graduate Programs Offers counseling (MM); Greek (MA); ministry (MM); New Testament (MA).

HERITAGE UNIVERSITY, Toppenish, WA 98948-9599

General Information Independent, coed, comprehensive institution. *Graduate housing:* On-campus housing not available.

GRADUATE UNITS

Graduate Programs in Education *Degree program information:* Part-time and evening/weekend programs available. Offers bilingual education/ESL (M Ed); biology (M Ed); counseling (M Ed); educational administration (M Ed); English and literature (M Ed); professional studies (M Ed); reading/literacy (M Ed); special education (M Ed); teaching (MIT).

HERZING UNIVERSITY ONLINE, Milwaukee, WI 53203

General Information Proprietary, coed, comprehensive institution.

GRADUATE UNITS

Program in Business Administration Postbaccalaureate distance learning degree programs offered (no on-campus study). Offers accounting (MBA); business administration (MBA); business management (MBA); healthcare management (MBA); human resources (MBA); marketing (MBA); project management (MBA); technology management (MBA).

Program in Nursing Postbaccalaureate distance learning degree programs offered (no on-campus study). Offers nursing (MSN); nursing education (MSN); nursing management (MSN).

HIGH POINT UNIVERSITY, High Point, NC 27262-3598

General Information Independent-religious, coed, comprehensive institution. CGS member. *Enrollment:* 17 full-time matriculated graduate/professional students (10 women), 292 part-time matriculated graduate/professional students (198 women). *Enrollment by degree level:* 309 master's. *Graduate faculty:* 30 full-time (11 women), 5 part-time/adjunct (1 woman). *Tuition:* Full-time $11,520; part-time $640 per hour. *Required fees:* $90; $150 per semester. Part-time tuition and fees vary according to program. *Graduate housing:* On-campus housing not available. *Student services:* Campus safety program, career counseling, free psychological counseling, low-cost health insurance, services for students with disabilities. *Library facilities:* Smith Library. *Online resources:* library catalog. *Collection:* 163,075 titles, 4,425 serial subscriptions, 10,074 audiovisual materials.

Computer facilities: Computer purchase and lease plans are available. 950 computers available on campus for general student use. A campuswide network can be accessed from student residence rooms and from off campus. Online class registration is available. *Web address:* http://www.highpoint.edu/.

General Application Contact: Graduate School Staff, 336-841-9198, E-mail: graduate@highpoint.edu.

GRADUATE UNITS

Norcross Graduate School Students: 17 full-time (10 women), 292 part-time (198 women); includes 107 minority (100 Black or African American, non-Hispanic/Latino; 1 Asian, non-Hispanic/Latino; 6 Hispanic/Latino), 19 international. 249 applicants, 69% accepted, 141 enrolled. *Faculty:* 30 full-time (11 women), 5 part-time/adjunct (1 woman). Expenses: Contact institution. *Financial support:* Federal Work-Study available. Support available to part-time students. Financial award application deadline: 3/1; financial award applicants required to submit FAFSA. *Degree program information:* Part-time and evening/weekend programs available. Offers business administration (MBA); educational leadership (M Ed); elementary education (M Ed); history (MA); nonprofit management (MA); secondary math (M Ed); special education (M Ed); strategic communication (MA); teaching elementary education k-6 (MAT); teaching secondary mathematics 9-12 (MAT). *Application deadline:* For fall admission, 4/15 priority date for domestic and international students; for spring admission, 10/15 priority date for domestic and international students. Applications are processed on a rolling basis. *Application fee:* $50. Electronic applications accepted. *Application Contact:* Tracy Collum, Associate Dean, 336-767-4840, Fax: 336-841-9024, E-mail: tcollum@highpoint.edu. *Associate Dean,* Tracy Collum, 336-767-4840, Fax: 336-841-9024, E-mail: tcollum@highpoint.edu.

HILLSDALE FREE WILL BAPTIST COLLEGE, Moore, OK 73160-1208

General Information Independent-religious, coed, comprehensive institution. *Graduate housing:* Room and/or apartments available on a first-come, first-served basis to single students.

GRADUATE UNITS

Department of Bible Studies *Degree program information:* Part-time and evening/weekend programs available. Offers ministry (MA).

HIRAM COLLEGE, Hiram, OH 44234-0067

General Information Independent, coed, comprehensive institution. *Enrollment:* 30 part-time matriculated graduate/professional students (23 women). *Graduate faculty:* 12 full-time (6 women), 2 part-time/adjunct (1 woman). *Tuition:* Part-time $450 per semester hour. *Required fees:* $100 per semester. *Student services:* Campus employment opportunities, career counseling, exercise/wellness program, writing training. *Library facilities:* Hiram College Library. *Online resources:* library catalog, web page, access to other libraries' catalogs. *Collection:* 506,792 titles, 8,890 serial subscriptions, 22,786 audiovisual materials.

Computer facilities: Computer purchase and lease plans are available. 100 computers available on campus for general student use. A campuswide network can be accessed from student residence rooms and from off campus. Online class registration is available. *Web address:* http://www.hiram.edu/.

General Application Contact: Terrie Nielsen, Admissions Counselor, 330-569-5180, Fax: 330-569-5003, E-mail: nielsenta@hiram.edu.

GRADUATE UNITS

Graduate Studies Students: 30 part-time (23 women). Average age 40. *Faculty:* 12 full-time (6 women), 2 part-time/adjunct (1 woman). Expenses: Contact institution. *Degree program information:* Part-time and evening/weekend programs available. Offers interdisciplinary studies (MAIS). *Application deadline:* For fall admission, 7/1 for domestic students; for spring admission, 12/1 for domestic students. *Application Contact:* Terrie Nielsen, Admissions Counselor, 330-569-5180, Fax: 330-569-5003, E-mail: nielsenta@hiram.edu. *Dean,* Cathy Mansor, 330-569-6111, Fax: 330-569-5003, E-mail: mansorcn@hiram.edu.

HODGES UNIVERSITY, Naples, FL 34119

General Information Independent, coed, comprehensive institution. *Enrollment:* 27 full-time matriculated graduate/professional students (15 women), 228 part-time matriculated graduate/professional students (146 women). *Enrollment by degree level:* 255 master's. *Graduate faculty:* 25 full-time (9 women), 5 part-time/adjunct (4 women). *Tuition:* Full-time $16,605; part-time $615 per credit hour. *Required fees:* $190 per trimester. *Graduate housing:* On-campus housing not available. *Student services:* Career counseling, services for students with disabilities. *Library facilities:* Information Resource Center plus 1 other. *Online resources:* library catalog, web page, access to other libraries' catalogs. *Collection:* 38,008 titles, 230 serial subscriptions.

Computer facilities: 500 computers available on campus for general student use. A campuswide network can be accessed. *Web address:* http://www.hodges.edu/.

General Application Contact: Rita Lampus, Vice President of Student Enrollment Management, 239-513-1122, Fax: 239-598-6253, E-mail: rlampus@hodges.edu.

GRADUATE UNITS

Graduate Programs Students: 27 full-time (15 women), 228 part-time (146 women); includes 76 minority (35 Black or African American, non-Hispanic/Latino; 5 Asian, non-Hispanic/Latino; 36 Hispanic/Latino). Average age 36. 92 applicants, 91% accepted, 81 enrolled. *Faculty:* 25 full-time (9 women), 5 part-time/adjunct (4 women). Expenses: Contact institution. *Financial support:* In 2010–11, 200 students received support. Federal Work-Study and scholarships/grants available. Financial award application deadline: 7/9; financial award applicants required to submit FAFSA. In 2010, 92 master's awarded. *Degree program information:* Part-time and evening/weekend programs available. Postbaccalaureate distance learning degree programs offered (no on-campus study). Offers business administration (MBA); computer information technology (MS); criminal justice (MCJ); education (MPS); information systems management (MIS); interdisciplinary (MPS); legal studies (MS); management (MSM); mental health counseling (MS); psychology (MPS); public administration (MPA). *Application deadline:* Applications are processed on a rolling basis. *Application fee:* $50. Electronic applications accepted. *Application Contact:* Rita Lampus, Vice President of Student Enrollment Management, 239-513-1122, Fax: 239-598-6253, E-mail: rlampus@hodges.edu. *President,* Terry McMahan, 239-513-1122, Fax: 239-598-6253, E-mail: tmcmahan@hodges.edu.

HOFSTRA UNIVERSITY, Hempstead, NY 11549

General Information Independent, coed, university. CGS member. *Enrollment:* 11,579 graduate, professional, and undergraduate students; 2,554 full-time matriculated graduate/professional students (1,489 women), 1,414 part-time matriculated graduate/professional students (902 women). *Enrollment by degree level:* 1,061 first professional, 2,513 master's, 291 doctoral, 103 other advanced degrees. *Graduate faculty:* 295 full-time (131 women), 191 part-time/adjunct (88 women). *Tuition:* Full-time $18,000; part-time $1000 per credit hour. *Required fees:* $970; $145 per term. Tuition and fees vary according to program. *Graduate housing:* Room and/or apartments available on a first-come, first-served basis to single students; on-campus housing not available to married students. Typical cost: $11,700 per year ($13,200 including board). Room and board charges vary according to board plan and housing facility selected. Housing application deadline: 5/1. *Student services:* Campus employment opportunities, campus safety program, career counseling, child daycare facilities, exercise/wellness program, free psychological counseling, grant writing training, international student services, low-cost health insurance, multicultural affairs office, services for students with disabilities, teacher training, writing training. *Library facilities:* Axinn Library plus 1 other. *Online resources:* library catalog, web page, access to other libraries' catalogs. *Collection:* 1.2 million titles, 11,336 serial subscriptions, 16,616 audiovisual materials.

Computer facilities: Computer purchase and lease plans are available. 1,628 computers available on campus for general student use. A campuswide network can be accessed from student residence rooms and from off campus. Online class registration, Gmail/Google Apps for students; Emergency Notification System; Online course management system; online card services balance update; online e-portfolio are available. *Web address:* http://www.hofstra.edu/.

General Application Contact: Carol Drummer, Dean of Graduate Admissions, 516-463-4876, Fax: 516-463-4664, E-mail: gradstudent@hofstra.edu.

GRADUATE UNITS

College of Liberal Arts and Sciences Students: 382 full-time (282 women), 116 part-time (73 women); includes 83 minority (30 Black or African American, non-Hispanic/Latino; 26 Asian, non-Hispanic/Latino; 26 Hispanic/Latino; 1 Two or more races, non-Hispanic/Latino), 15 international. Average age 27. 771 applicants, 48% accepted, 190 enrolled. *Faculty:* 111 full-time (48 women), 16 part-time/adjunct (6 women). Expenses: Contact institution. *Financial support:* In 2010–11, 229 students received support, including 131 fellowships with full and partial tuition reimbursements available (averaging $6,514 per year), 8 research assistantships with full and partial tuition reimbursements available (averaging $2,346 per year); career-related internships or fieldwork, Federal Work-Study, institutionally sponsored loans, scholarships/grants, tuition waivers (full and partial), unspecified assistantships, and scholarships also available. Support available to part-time students. Financial award applicants required to submit FAFSA. In 2010, 116 master's, 35 doctorates awarded. *Degree program information:* Part-time and evening/weekend programs available. Postbaccalaureate distance learning degree programs offered (minimal on-campus study). Offers applied linguistics (TESOL) (MA); applied organizational psychology (PhD); applied social research and public policy (MA); audiology (Au D); biology (MA, MS); clinical psychology (PhD); computer science (MA, MS); creative writing (MFA); English literature (MA); industrial/organizational psychology (MA); liberal arts and sciences (MA, MFA, MS, Au D, PhD, Psy D); linguistics (MA); school-community psychology (Psy D); speech-language pathology (MA). *Application deadline:* Applications are processed on a rolling basis. *Application fee:* $70 ($75 for international students). Electronic applications accepted. *Application Contact:* Carol Drummer, Dean of Graduate Admissions, 516-463-4876, Fax: 516-463-4664, E-mail: gradstudent@hofstra.edu. *Dean,* Dr. Bernard J. Firestone, 516-463-5411, Fax: 516-463-4861, E-mail: lasbjf@hofstra.edu.

Frank G. Zarb School of Business Students: 449 full-time (194 women), 386 part-time (160 women); includes 127 minority (38 Black or African American, non-Hispanic/Latino; 60 Asian, non-Hispanic/Latino; 29 Hispanic/Latino), 272 international. Average age 29. 959 applicants, 69% accepted, 302 enrolled. *Faculty:* 48 full-time (8 women), 15 part-time/adjunct (2 women). Expenses: Contact institution. *Financial support:* In 2010–11, 112 students received support, including 101 fellowships with full and partial tuition reimbursements available (averaging $9,766 per year), 3 research assistantships with full and partial tuition reimbursements available (averaging $12,631 per year); career-related internships or fieldwork, Federal Work-Study, institutionally sponsored loans, scholarships/grants, tuition waivers (full and partial), and unspecified assistantships also available. Support available to part-time students. Financial award applicants required to submit FAFSA. In 2010, 218 master's awarded. *Degree program information:* Part-time and evening/weekend programs available. Postbaccalaureate distance learning degree programs offered (minimal on-campus study). Offers accounting (MS, Advanced Certificate); banking (Advanced Certificate); business (EMBA, MBA, MS, Advanced Certificate); business administration (MBA); corporate finance (Advanced Certificate); finance (MS); general management (Advanced Certificate); human resource management (MS); information technology (MS, Advanced Certificate); investment management (Advanced Certificate); management (EMBA); marketing (MS); marketing research (MS); quantitative finance (MS); taxation (MS, Advanced Certificate). *Application deadline:* Applications are processed on a rolling basis. *Application fee:* $70 ($75 for international students). Electronic applications accepted. *Application Contact:* Carol Drummer, Dean of Graduate Admissions, 516-463-4876, Fax: 516-463-4664, E-mail: gradstudent@hofstra.edu. *Dean,* Dr. Patrick J. Socci, 516-463-5676, Fax: 516-463-5268, E-mail: bizpjs@hofstra.edu.

School of Communication Students: 37 full-time (25 women), 38 part-time (22 women); includes 23 minority (14 Black or African American, non-Hispanic/Latino; 1 American Indian or Alaska Native, non-Hispanic/Latino; 4 Asian, non-Hispanic/Latino; 4 Hispanic/Latino), 10 international. Average age 28. 79 applicants, 85% accepted, 30 enrolled. *Faculty:* 18 full-time (7 women), 2 part-time/adjunct (1 woman). Expenses: Contact institution. *Financial support:* In 2010–11, 25 students received support, including 10 fellowships with full and partial tuition reimbursements available (averaging $2,450 per year), 2 research assistantships with full and partial tuition reimbursements available (averaging $10,502 per year); Federal Work-Study, institutionally sponsored loans, scholarships/grants, tuition waivers (full and partial), and unspecified assistantships also available. Support available to part-time students. Financial award applicants required to submit FAFSA. In 2010, 16 master's awarded. *Degree program information:* Part-time and evening/weekend programs available. Offers communication (MA, MFA); documentary studies and production (MFA); journalism (MA); speech communication and rhetorical studies (MA). *Application deadline:* Applications are processed on a rolling basis. *Application fee:* $70 ($75 for international students). Electronic applications accepted. *Application Contact:* Carol Drummer, Dean of Graduate Admissions, 516-463-4876, Fax: 516-463-4664, E-mail: gradstudent@hofstra.edu. *Dean,* Dr. Eric W. Cornog, 516-463-5215, Fax: 516-463-4866, E-mail: comewcj@hofstra.edu.

School of Education, Health, and Human Services Students: 738 full-time (542 women), 755 part-time (594 women); includes 291 minority (153 Black or African American, non-Hispanic/Latino; 4 American Indian or Alaska Native, non-Hispanic/Latino; 44 Asian, non-Hispanic/Latino; 82 Hispanic/Latino; 2 Native Hawaiian or other Pacific Islander, non-Hispanic/Latino; 6 Two or more races, non-Hispanic/Latino), 20 international. Average age 30. 1,020 applicants, 79% accepted, 447 enrolled. *Faculty:* 73 full-time (52 women), 112 part-time/adjunct (72 women). Expenses: Contact institution. *Financial support:* In 2010–11, 662 students received support, including 179 fellowships with full and partial tuition reimbursements available (averaging $3,461 per year), 12 research assistantships with full and partial tuition reimbursements available (averaging $9,314 per year); career-related internships or fieldwork, Federal Work-Study, institutionally sponsored loans, scholarships/grants, tuition waivers (full and partial), unspecified assistantships, and scholarships also available. Support available to part-time students. Financial award applicants required to submit FAFSA. In 2010, 559 master's, 7 doctorates, 76 other advanced degrees awarded. *Degree program information:* Part-time and evening/weekend programs available. Postbaccalaureate distance learning degree programs offered (minimal on-campus study). Offers advanced literacy studies (PD); advanced literary studies (PD); adventure education (CAS); bilingual education (MS Ed); bilingual extension (CAS); birth-grade 6 (MS Ed, CAS); business education (MS Ed); community health (MS); counseling (MS Ed, PD); creative arts therapy (MA); early childhood and childhood education (MS Ed); early childhood education (MA, MS Ed); early childhood special education (MS Ed); education, health, and human services (MA, MHA, MS, MS Ed, Ed D, PhD, Advanced Certificate, CAS, PD); educational and policy leadership (MS Ed, Ed D, CAS); educational policy and leadership (MS Ed, CAS); elementary education (MA, MS Ed); English education (MA, MS Ed); family and consumer science (MS Ed); fine art and music education (Advanced Certificate); fine arts education (MA, MS Ed); foreign language and TESOL (MS Ed); foreign language education (MA, MS Ed); foundations of education (MA, CAS); gerontology (MS, Advanced Certificate); grades 5-12 (CAS); health administration (MHA); health education (MS); learning and teaching (Ed D); literacy studies (MS Ed, Ed D, PhD); literacy studies and special education (MS Ed); marriage and family therapy (MA); math specialist (Advanced Certificate); math, science, technology (MA); mathematics education (MA, MS Ed); mental health counseling (MA); middle childhood extension (Advanced Certificate); music education (MA, MS Ed); physical education (MA, MS); rehabilitation counseling (MS Ed, CAS, PD); rehabilitation counseling in mental health (MS Ed, CAS); school counselor-bilingual extension (Advanced Certificate); science education (MA, MS Ed); secondary education (Advanced Certificate); social studies education (MA, MS Ed); special education (MS Ed); sport science (MS); teaching languages other than English and TESOL (MS Ed); teaching of writing (MA); TESOL (MS Ed); wind conducting (MA). *Application deadline:* Applications are processed on a rolling basis. *Application fee:* $70 ($75 for international students). Electronic applications accepted. *Application Contact:* Carol Drummer, Dean of Graduate Admissions, 516-463-4876, Fax: 516-463-4664, E-mail: gradstudent@hofstra.edu. *Interim Dean,* Dr. Nancy E. Halliday, 516-463-5811, Fax: 516-463-6461, E-mail: soedff@hofstra.edu.

School of Law Students: 948 full-time (446 women), 119 part-time (53 women); includes 93 Black or African American, non-Hispanic/Latino; 5 American Indian or Alaska Native, non-Hispanic/Latino; 126 Asian, non-Hispanic/Latino; 79 Hispanic/Latino, 40 international. Average age 25. 5,368 applicants, 38% accepted, 381 enrolled. *Faculty:* 61 full-time (24 women), 34 part-time/adjunct (4 women). Expenses: Contact institution. *Financial support:* In 2010–11, 557 students received support, including 513 fellowships with full and partial tuition reimbursements available (averaging $21,659 per year), 2 research assistantships with full and partial tuition reimbursements available (averaging $17,548 per year); Federal Work-Study, institutionally sponsored loans, scholarships/grants, tuition waivers (full and partial), and unspecified assistantships also available. Support available to part-time students. Financial award applicants required to submit FAFSA. In 2010, 347 first professional degrees, 3 master's awarded. *Degree program information:* Part-time programs available. Offers American legal studies (LL M); family law (LL M); law (JD). *Application deadline:* For fall admission, 4/15 priority date for domestic and international students. Applications are processed on a rolling basis. *Application fee:* $70 ($75 for international students). Electronic applications accepted. *Application Contact:* John Chalmers, Director of Law School Enrollment Operations, 516-463-5791, Fax: 516-463-6264, E-mail: lawadmissions@hofstra.edu. *Dean,* Nora V. Demleitner, 516-463-5854, Fax: 516-463-6264, E-mail: lawnao@hofstra.edu.

School of Medicine Expenses: Contact institution. *Financial support:* Fellowships with full and partial tuition reimbursements, research assistantships with full and partial tuition reimbursements, Federal Work-Study, institutionally sponsored loans, scholarships/grants, and tuition waivers (full and partial) available. Support available to part-time students. Financial award applicants required to submit FAFSA. Offers medicine (MD); molecular basis of medicine (PhD). *Application deadline:* For fall admission, 12/1 priority date for domestic students. *Application fee:* $100. *Application Contact:* Carol Drummer, Dean of Graduate Admissions, 516-463-4876, Fax: 516-463-4664, E-mail: gradstudent@hofstra.edu. *Dean,* Dr. Lawrence Smith, 516-463-7577, Fax: 516-463-5631, E-mail: medlgs@hofstra.edu.

HOLLINS UNIVERSITY, Roanoke, VA 24020-1603

General Information Independent, Undergraduate: women only; graduate: coed, comprehensive institution. *Graduate housing:* Room and/or apartments available on a first-come, first-served basis to single students; on-campus housing not available to married students. Housing application deadline: 8/1.

GRADUATE UNITS

Graduate Programs *Degree program information:* Part-time and evening/weekend programs available. Offers children's literature (MA, MFA); creative writing (MFA); dance (MFA); humanities (MALS); interdisciplinary studies (MALS); justice and legal studies (MALS); liberal studies (CAS); playwriting (MFA); screenwriting and film studies (MA, MFA); social science (MALS); teaching (MAT); visual and performing arts (MALS). Electronic applications accepted.

HOLMES INSTITUTE, Burbank, CA 91505

General Information Independent-religious, coed, graduate-only institution. *Enrollment by degree level:* 72 master's. *Graduate faculty:* 50. *Graduate housing:* On-campus housing not available.

Computer facilities: Online class registration is available. *Web address:* http://www.holmesinstitute.org/.

General Application Contact: Maureen Thurston, Administrative Registrar, 720-279-8992, Fax: 303-526-0913, E-mail: mthurston@religiousscience.org.

GRADUATE UNITS

Graduate Program Students: 72 part-time (51 women). *Faculty:* 50. Expenses: Contact institution. Postbaccalaureate distance learning degree programs offered. Offers consciousness studies (MS). *Application deadline:* Applications are processed on a rolling basis. *Application fee:* $300. *Application Contact:* Maureen Thurston, Administrative Registrar, 720-279-8992, Fax: 303-526-0913, E-mail: mthurston@religiousscience.org. *Director of Education,* Rev. Dr. Lynn Connolly, 720-279-8990, Fax: 303-526-0913, E-mail: lconnolly@religiousscience.org.

HOLY APOSTLES COLLEGE AND SEMINARY, Cromwell, CT 06416-2005

General Information Independent-religious, coed, comprehensive institution. *Graduate housing:* On-campus housing not available.

GRADUATE UNITS

Department of Theology *Degree program information:* Part-time and evening/weekend programs available. Postbaccalaureate distance learning degree programs offered (no on-campus study). Offers bioethics (MA, Certificate, Post Master's Certificate); church history (MA, Certificate, Post Master's Certificate); dogmatic theology (MA, Certificate, Post Master's Certificate); liturgical music (MA, Certificate, Post Master's Certificate); liturgy (MA, Certificate, Post Master's Certificate); moral theology (MA, Certificate, Post Master's Certificate); philosophical theology (MA, Certificate, Post Master's Certificate); religious education (MA, Certificate, Post Master's Certificate); sacred scripture (MA, Post Master's Certificate); sacred scriptures (Certificate); theology (M Div). Electronic applications accepted.

HOLY CROSS GREEK ORTHODOX SCHOOL OF THEOLOGY, Brookline, MA 02445-7496

General Information Independent-religious, coed, primarily men, graduate-only institution. *Enrollment by degree level:* 104 first professional, 43 master's. *Graduate faculty:* 10 full-time (1 woman), 10 part-time/adjunct (2 women). *Tuition:* Full-time $19,136; part-time $797.34 per credit. *Required fees:* $500. *Graduate housing:* Rooms and/or apartments available on a first-come, first-served basis to single and married students. *Student services:* Campus employment opportunities, career counseling, free psychological counseling, international student services, low-cost health insurance. *Library facilities:* Archbishop Iakovos Library and Learning Resource Center. *Online resources:* library catalog, web page, access to other libraries' catalogs. *Collection:* 63,374 titles, 720 serial subscriptions, 3,015 audiovisual materials.

Computer facilities: 35 computers available on campus for general student use. A campuswide network can be accessed from student residence rooms and from off campus. *Web address:* http://www.hchc.edu/.

General Application Contact: Gregory Floor, Director of Admissions, 617-731-3500 Ext. 1285, Fax: 617-850-1460, E-mail: admissions@hchc.edu.

GRADUATE UNITS

Theological Programs Students: 136 full-time (15 women), 11 part-time (2 women); includes 1 Black or African American, non-Hispanic/Latino; 1 Hispanic/Latino, 14 international. Average age 25. 62 applicants, 87% accepted, 46 enrolled. *Faculty:* 10 full-time (1 woman), 10 part-time/adjunct (2 women). Expenses: Contact institution. *Financial support:* In 2010–11, 26 students received support, including 20 teaching assistantships (averaging $525 per year); research assistantships, Federal Work-Study, scholarships/grants, and tuition waivers (partial) also available. Financial award application deadline: 4/1; financial award applicants required to submit FAFSA. In 2010, 22 M Divs, 14 master's awarded. *Degree program information:* Part-time programs available. Offers theology (M Div, MTS, Th M). *Application deadline:* For fall admission, 8/15 for domestic students, 8/1 for international students; for spring admission, 1/3 for domestic students. *Application fee:* $50. *Application Contact:* Gregory Floor, Director of Admissions, 617-731-3500 Ext. 1285, Fax: 617-850-1460, E-mail: gfloor@hchc.edu. *Dean,* Rev. Dr. Thomas FitzGerald, 617-731-3500 Ext. 1213, Fax: 617-850-1460, E-mail: tfitzgerald@hchc.edu.

HOLY FAMILY UNIVERSITY, Philadelphia, PA 19114

General Information Independent-religious, coed, comprehensive institution. *Enrollment:* 3,270 graduate, professional, and undergraduate students; 115 full-time matriculated graduate/professional students (92 women), 979 part-time matriculated graduate/professional students (750 women). *Enrollment by degree level:* 1,094 master's. *Graduate faculty:* 18 full-time (11 women), 51 part-time/adjunct (25 women). *Tuition:* Full-time $14,400; part-time $600 per credit hour. *Required fees:* $85 per term. *Graduate housing:* On-campus housing not available. *Student services:* Campus safety program, career counseling, exercise/wellness program, free psychological counseling, international student services, multicultural affairs office, services for students with disabilities, writing training. *Library facilities:* Holy Family University Library plus 1 other. *Online resources:* library catalog, web page. *Collection:* 145,700 titles, 14,250 serial subscriptions, 4,475 audiovisual materials.

Computer facilities: 900 computers available on campus for general student use. A campuswide network can be accessed from student residence rooms and from off campus. Online class registration is available. *Web address:* http://www.holyfamily.edu/.

General Application Contact: Gidget Marie Montelibano, Graduate Admissions Counselor, 267-341-3358, Fax: 215-637-1478, E-mail: gmontelibano@holyfamily.edu.

GRADUATE UNITS

Division of Extended Learning Students: 116 part-time (71 women); includes 10 Black or African American, non-Hispanic/Latino; 6 Asian, non-Hispanic/Latino; 2 Hispanic/Latino. Average age 35. 46 applicants, 93% accepted, 41 enrolled. *Faculty:* 78 part-time/adjunct (32 women). Expenses: Contact institution. *Financial support:* Applicants required to submit FAFSA. In 2010, 47 master's awarded. *Degree program information:* Part-time and evening/weekend programs available. Offers business administration (MBA); finance (MBA); health care administration (MBA). *Application deadline:* Applications are processed on a rolling basis. *Application fee:* $50. Electronic applications accepted. *Application Contact:* Don Reinmold, Director of Admissions for Division of Extended Learning, 267-341-5001 Ext. 3230, Fax: 215-633-0558, E-mail: dreinmold@holyfamily.edu. *Associate Vice President,* Honour Moore, 267-341-5008, Fax: 215-633-0558, E-mail: hmoore@holyfamily.edu.

Graduate School Students: 115 full-time (92 women), 979 part-time (750 women); includes 52 Black or African American, non-Hispanic/Latino; 15 Asian, non-Hispanic/Latino; 34 Hispanic/Latino, 8 international. Average age 32. 335 applicants, 80% accepted, 225 enrolled. *Faculty:* 17 full-time (10 women), 54 part-time/adjunct (28 women). Expenses: Contact institution. *Financial support:* In 2010–11, 4 research assistantships with partial tuition reimbursements (averaging $8,000 per year) were awarded; Federal Work-Study and unspecified assistantships also available. Support available to part-time students. Financial award application deadline: 2/15; financial award applicants required to submit FAFSA. In 2010, 375 master's awarded. *Degree program information:* Part-time and evening/weekend programs available. *Application deadline:* For fall admission, 7/1 priority date for domestic students; for spring admission, 11/1 priority date for domestic students. Applications are processed on a rolling basis. *Application fee:* $25. Electronic applications accepted. *Application Contact:* Gidget Marie Montelibano, Graduate Admissions Counselor, 267-341-3558, Fax: 215-637-1478, E-mail: gmontelibano@holyfamily.edu. *Director of Graduate Admissions,* Margaret Bacheler, 267-341-3555, Fax: 215-637-1478, E-mail: mbacheler@holyfamily.edu.

School of Arts and Sciences Students: 5 full-time (3 women), 176 part-time (71 women); includes 6 Black or African American, non-Hispanic/Latino; 1 Asian, non-Hispanic/Latino; 2 Hispanic/Latino. Average age 28. 72 applicants, 90% accepted, 36 enrolled. *Faculty:* 6 full-time (5 women), 6 part-time/adjunct (2 women). Expenses: Contact institution. *Financial support:* Application deadline: 5/1. In 2010, 18 master's awarded. *Degree program information:* Part-time and evening/weekend programs available. Offers counseling psychology (MS); criminal justice (MA). *Application deadline:* For fall admission, 8/1 priority date for domestic students; for winter admission, 1/1 for domestic students. Applications are processed on a rolling basis. *Application fee:* $25. Electronic applications accepted. *Application Contact:* Gidget Marie Montelibano, Graduate Admissions Counselor, 267-341-3558, Fax: 215-637-1478, E-mail: gmontelibano@holyfamily.edu. *Dean,* Dr. Michael Markowitz, 267-341-3286, Fax: 215-827-0492, E-mail: mmarkowitz@holyfamily.edu.

School of Business Administration Students: 62 part-time (36 women); includes 3 Black or African American, non-Hispanic/Latino; 1 Asian, non-Hispanic/Latino; 1 Hispanic/Latino. Average age 34. 32 applicants, 75% accepted, 17 enrolled. *Faculty:* 2 full-time (0 women), 10 part-time/adjunct (3 women). Expenses: Contact institution. *Financial support:* Federal Work-Study available. Support available to part-time students. Financial award application deadline: 5/1; financial award applicants required to submit FAFSA. In 2010, 24 master's awarded. *Degree program information:* Part-time and evening/weekend programs available. Offers human resources management (MS); information systems management (MS). *Application deadline:* For fall admission, 8/1 priority date for domestic students; for winter admission, 1/1 priority date for domestic students. Applications are processed on a rolling basis. *Application fee:* $25. Electronic applications accepted. *Application Contact:* Gidget Marie Montelibano, Graduate Admissions Counselor, 267-341-3558, Fax: 215-637-1478, E-mail: gmontelibano@holyfamily.edu. *Dean of the School of Business,* Dr. Jan Duggar, 267-341-3373, Fax: 215-637-5937, E-mail: jduggar@holyfamily.edu.

School of Education Students: 66 full-time (48 women), 625 part-time (504 women); includes 32 Black or African American, non-Hispanic/Latino; 8 Asian, non-Hispanic/Latino; 15 Hispanic/Latino. Average age 31. 205 applicants, 86% accepted, 116 enrolled. *Faculty:* 10 full-time (6 women), 50 part-time/adjunct (30 women). Expenses: Contact institution. *Financial support:* Research assistantships, Federal Work-Study available. Support available to part-time students. Financial award application deadline: 2/15; financial award applicants required to submit FAFSA. In 2010, 287 master's awarded. *Degree program information:* Part-time and evening/weekend programs available. Offers education (M Ed); education leadership (M Ed); elementary education (M Ed); reading specialist (M Ed); secondary education (M Ed); special education (M Ed). *Application deadline:* For fall admission, 7/1 priority date for domestic students; for winter admission, 1/1 priority date for domestic students. Applications are processed on a rolling basis. *Application fee:* $25. Electronic applications accepted. *Application Contact:* Gidget Marie Montelibano, Graduate Admissions Counselor, 267-341-3558, Fax: 215-637-1478, E-mail: gmontelibano@holyfamily.edu. *Dean,* Dr. Leonard Soroka, 267-341-3565, Fax: 215-824-2438, E-mail: lsoroka@holyfamily.edu.

School of Nursing Students: 51 part-time (all women); includes 6 Black or African American, non-Hispanic/Latino; 1 Asian, non-Hispanic/Latino. Average age 40. 20 applicants, 95% accepted, 15 enrolled. *Faculty:* 1 (woman) full-time, 2 part-time/adjunct (both women). Expenses: Contact institution. *Financial support:* Federal Work-Study available. Support available to part-time students. Financial award application deadline: 2/15; financial award applicants required to submit FAFSA. In 2010, 3 master's awarded. *Degree program information:* Part-time and evening/weekend programs available. Offers community health nursing (MSN); nursing administration (MSN); nursing education (MSN). *Application deadline:* For fall admission, 7/1 priority date for domestic students; for winter admission, 1/1 priority date for domestic students. Applications are processed on a rolling basis. *Application fee:* $25. *Application Contact:* Gidget Matie Montelibano, Graduate Admissions Counselor, 267-341-3558, Fax: 215-637-1478, E-mail: gmontelibano@holyfamily.edu. *Dean,* Dr. Christine Rosner, 267-341-3292, Fax: 215-637-6598, E-mail: crosner@holyfamily.edu.

HOLY NAMES UNIVERSITY, Oakland, CA 94619-1699

General Information Independent-religious, coed, primarily women, comprehensive institution. *Enrollment:* 1,216 graduate, professional, and undergraduate students; 128 full-time matriculated graduate/professional students (88 women), 325 part-time matriculated graduate/professional students (249 women). *Enrollment by degree level:* 208 master's, 16 other advanced degrees. *Graduate faculty:* 38 full-time (24 women), 100 part-time/adjunct (61 women). *Tuition:* Full-time $13,788; part-time $766 per credit. *Required fees:* $340; $170 per semester. *Graduate housing:* Room and/or apartments available on a first-come, first-served basis to single students; on-campus housing not available to married students. Typical cost: $5120 per year ($9780 including board). Housing application deadline: 8/15. *Student services:* Campus employment opportunities, campus safety program, career counseling, free psychological counseling, international student services, low-cost health insurance. *Library facilities:* Cushing Library. *Online resources:* library catalog, web page. *Collection:* 86,954 titles, 27,803 serial subscriptions, 75 audiovisual materials.

Computer facilities: 92 computers available on campus for general student use. A campuswide network can be accessed from student residence rooms. Online class registration is available. *Web address:* http://www.hnu.edu/.

General Application Contact: Annie Wenzel, Graduate Admissions Office, 510-436-1642, Fax: 510-436-1325, E-mail: admissions@hnu.edu.

GRADUATE UNITS

Graduate Division Students: 132 full-time (88 women), 325 part-time (249 women); includes 113 Black or African American, non-Hispanic/Latino; 55 Asian, non-Hispanic/Latino; 56 Hispanic/Latino, 7 international. Average age 38. 269 applicants, 67% accepted, 123 enrolled. *Faculty:* 38 full-time (24 women), 100 part-time/adjunct (61 women). Expenses: Contact institution. *Financial support:* In 2010–11, 14 students received support. Scholarships/grants available. Support available to part-time students. Financial award application deadline: 3/2; financial award applicants required to submit FAFSA. In 2010, 117 master's, 29 other advanced degrees awarded. *Degree program information:* Part-time and evening/weekend programs available. Offers administration/management (MS, Certificate); clinical faculty (MS, Certificate); community health nursing/case manager (MS); counseling psychology (MA); creative writing (MA); educational therapy (Certificate); energy and environment management (MBA); family nurse practitioner (MS, Certificate); finance (MBA); forensic psychology (MA, Certificate); Kodaly specialist certificate (Certificate); Kodaly summer certificate (Certificate); level 1 education specialist mild/moderate disabilities (Credential); level 2 education specialist mild/moderate disabilities (Credential); management and leadership (MBA); marketing (MBA); multiple subject teaching credential (Credential); music education with Kodaly emphasis (MM); pastoral counseling (MA, Certificate); pastoral ministries (MA, Certificate); piano pedagogy (MM); piano pedagogy with Suzuki emphasis (MM); single subject teaching credential (Credential); sports management (MBA); teaching English as a second language (TESL) (M Ed); urban education: educational therapy (M Ed); urban education: K-12 education (M Ed); urban education: special education (M Ed); vocal pedagogy (MM). *Application deadline:* For fall admission, 8/1 priority date for domestic students, 8/1 for international students; for spring admission, 12/1 priority date for domestic students, 12/1 for international students. Applications are processed on a rolling basis. *Application fee:* $0. Electronic applications accepted. *Application Contact:* Graduate Admissions Office, 510-436-1321, Fax: 510-436-1325, E-mail: adulted@hnu.edu. *Dean of Admissions,* Brian O'Rouke, 510-436-1430, Fax: 510-436-1325, E-mail: orouke@hnu.edu.

Sophia Center in Culture and Spirituality Offers culture and spirituality (MA, Certificate).

HOOD COLLEGE, Frederick, MD 21701-8575

General Information Independent, coed, comprehensive institution. CGS member. *Enrollment:* 2,447 graduate, professional, and undergraduate students; 74 full-time matriculated graduate/professional students (36 women), 888 part-time matriculated graduate/professional students (613 women). *Enrollment by degree level:* 828 master's, 134 other advanced degrees. *Graduate faculty:* 34 full-time (19 women), 70 part-time/adjunct (31 women). *Tuition:* Full-time $6480; part-time $360 per credit. *Required fees:* $100; $50 per term. *Graduate housing:* On-campus housing not available. *Student services:* Campus employment opportunities, campus safety program, career counseling, international student services, multicultural affairs office, services for students with disabilities, teacher training. *Library facilities:* Beneficial-Hodson Library and Information Technology Center. *Online resources:* library catalog, web page, access to other libraries' catalogs. *Collection:* 205,825 titles, 42,224 serial subscriptions, 5,526 audiovisual materials. *Research affiliation:* NCI (biomedical science), U. S. Department of Agriculture (USDA) (biomedical science and environmental biology), United States Army Medical Research Institute of Infectious Diseases (USAMRID) (biomedical science).

Computer facilities: Computer purchase and lease plans are available. 283 computers available on campus for general student use. A campuswide network can be accessed from student residence rooms and from off campus. Online class registration is available. *Web address:* http://www.hood.edu/.

General Application Contact: Dr. Allen P. Flora, Dean of Graduate School, 301-696-3811, Fax: 301-696-3597, E-mail: gofurther@hood.edu.

GRADUATE UNITS

Graduate School Students: 74 full-time (36 women), 888 part-time (613 women); includes 78 Black or African American, non-Hispanic/Latino; 3 American Indian or Alaska Native, non-Hispanic/Latino; 35 Asian, non-Hispanic/Latino; 23 Hispanic/Latino; 15 Two or more races, non-Hispanic/Latino, 34 international. Average age 33. 400 applicants, 67% accepted, 199 enrolled. *Faculty:* 34 full-time (19 women), 70 part-time/adjunct (31 women). Expenses: Contact institution. *Financial support:* In 2010–11, 7 students received support, including 3 research assistantships with full tuition reimbursements available (averaging $10,609 per year); scholarships/grants and unspecified assistantships also available. Financial award applicants required to submit FAFSA. In 2010, 216 master's, 97 other advanced degrees awarded. *Degree program information:* Part-time and evening/weekend programs available. Offers accounting (MBA); administration and management (MBA); biomedical science (MS); ceramic arts (Certificate); ceramics (MFA); computer and information sciences (MS); computer science (MS); curriculum and instruction (MS); educational leadership (MS, Certificate); environmental biology (MS); finance (MBA); human resource management (MBA); human sciences (MA); humanities (MA); information security (Certificate); information systems (MBA); management of information technology (MS); marketing (MBA); mathematics education (MS); public management (MBA); reading specialization (MS); regulatory compliance (Certificate); secondary mathematics education (Certificate); thanatology (MA, Certificate). *Application deadline:* For fall admission, 7/15 for domestic and international students; for spring admission, 12/15 for domestic and international students. Applications are processed on a rolling basis. *Application fee:* $35. Electronic applications accepted. *Application Contact:* Dr. Allen P. Flora, Dean of Graduate School, 301-696-3811, Fax: 301-696-3597, E-mail: gofurther@hood.edu. *Dean of the Graduate School,* Dr. Allen P. Flora, 301-696-3811, Fax: 301-696-3597, E-mail: gofurther@hood.edu.

HOOD THEOLOGICAL SEMINARY, Salisbury, NC 28144

General Information Independent-religious, coed, graduate-only institution. *Graduate housing:* Rooms and/or apartments guaranteed to single students and available on a first-come, first-served basis to married students. Housing application deadline: 8/15.

GRADUATE UNITS

Graduate and Professional Programs *Degree program information:* Evening/weekend programs available. Offers theology (M Div, MTS, D Min).

HOPE INTERNATIONAL UNIVERSITY, Fullerton, CA 92831-3138

General Information Independent-religious, coed, comprehensive institution. *Graduate housing:* Room and/or apartments available on a first-come, first-served basis to single students; on-campus housing not available to married students. Housing application deadline: 7/1.

Hope International University (continued)

GRADUATE UNITS

School of Graduate and Professional Studies *Degree program information:* Part-time and evening/weekend programs available. Postbaccalaureate distance learning degree programs offered (minimal on-campus study). Offers business administration (MBA); Christian leadership (MCM); church music (MA); church music (Korean track) (MCM); church planting (MCM); education (ME); educational administration (MSM); intercultural studies (MCM); international development (MBA, MSM); management (MBA); marriage and family therapy (MA, MFT); nonprofit management (MBA); worship (MCM). Electronic applications accepted.

HOUGHTON COLLEGE, Houghton, NY 14744

General Information Independent-religious, coed, comprehensive institution. *Graduate housing:* On-campus housing not available.

GRADUATE UNITS

Greatbatch School of Music Offers collaborative performance (MMus); composition (MMus); conducting (MMus); music (MA); performance (MMus); world music with theology and intercultural studies (MA). Electronic applications accepted.

HOUSTON BAPTIST UNIVERSITY, Houston, TX 77074-3298

General Information Independent-religious, coed, comprehensive institution. *Graduate housing:* Room and/or apartments available on a first-come, first-served basis to single students; on-campus housing not available to married students.

GRADUATE UNITS

College of Arts and Humanities *Degree program information:* Part-time and evening/weekend programs available. Offers arts and humanities (MATS, MLA); liberal arts (MLA); theological studies (MATS).

College of Business and Economics *Degree program information:* Part-time and evening/weekend programs available. Offers accounting (MACCT); business administration (MBA, MSM); business and economics (MACCT, MBA, MSHA, MSHRM, MSM); health administration (MSHA); human resources management (MSHRM).

College of Education and Behavioral Sciences *Degree program information:* Part-time and evening/weekend programs available. Offers bilingual education (M Ed); Christian counseling (MACC); counselor education (M Ed); curriculum and instruction (M Ed); education and behavioral sciences (M Ed, MACC, MAP); educational administration (M Ed); educational diagnostician (M Ed); psychology (MAP); reading education (M Ed).

HOUSTON GRADUATE SCHOOL OF THEOLOGY, Houston, TX 77092

General Information Independent-religious, coed, graduate-only institution. *Graduate housing:* On-campus housing not available.

GRADUATE UNITS

Graduate School *Degree program information:* Part-time and evening/weekend programs available. Offers counseling (MA); pastoral ministry (M Div, D Min); theology (MA).

HOWARD PAYNE UNIVERSITY, Brownwood, TX 76801-2715

General Information Independent-religious, coed, comprehensive institution.

GRADUATE UNITS

Program in Instructional Leadership Postbaccalaureate distance learning degree programs offered (no on-campus study). Offers instructional leadership (M Ed).

Program in Youth Ministry Offers youth ministry (MA).

HOWARD UNIVERSITY, Washington, DC 20059-0002

General Information Independent, coed, university. CGS member. *Graduate housing:* Rooms and/or apartments available on a first-come, first-served basis to single and married students. Housing application deadline: 4/1. *Research affiliation:* Ewing Marion Kauffman Foundation (science education), The Tokyo Foundation (women's studies, international affairs), National Oceanic and Atmospheric Administration (NOAA) (atmospheric science and nanotechnology), National Institute of Mental Health (NIMH) (genomic study), Akilu Lamma Institute of Pathobiology (HIV/AIDS infection, water resources development, population movement), Labor Research Laboratories and Medical Center in Benin City, Nigeria (infectious diseases).

GRADUATE UNITS

College of Dentistry Offers advanced education program general dentistry (Certificate); dentistry (DDS); general dentistry (Certificate); oral and maxillofacial surgery (Certificate); orthodontics (Certificate); pediatric dentistry (Certificate).

College of Engineering, Architecture, and Computer Sciences *Degree program information:* Part-time programs available. Offers engineering, architecture, and computer sciences (M Eng, MCS, MS, PhD). Electronic applications accepted.

School of Engineering and Computer Science *Degree program information:* Part-time programs available. Offers chemical engineering (MS); civil engineering (M Eng); electrical engineering (M Eng, PhD); engineering and computer science (M Eng, MCS, MS, PhD); mechanical engineering (M Eng, PhD); systems and computer science (MCS). Electronic applications accepted.

College of Medicine Offers biochemistry and molecular biology (PhD); biotechnology (MS); medicine (MD, MPH, MS, PhD); microbiology (PhD); pharmacology (MS, PhD); public health (MPH).

College of Pharmacy, Nursing and Allied Health Sciences *Degree program information:* Part-time programs available. Offers pharmacy, nursing and allied health sciences (Pharm D, MSN, Certificate). Electronic applications accepted.

Division of Nursing *Degree program information:* Part-time programs available. Offers nurse practitioner (Certificate); primary family health nursing (MSN).

School of Pharmacy Postbaccalaureate distance learning degree programs offered (minimal on-campus study). Offers pharmacy (Pharm D). Electronic applications accepted.

Graduate School *Degree program information:* Part-time and evening/weekend programs available. Offers African diaspora (MA, PhD); African history (MA, PhD); African studies (MA, PhD); analytical chemistry (MS, PhD); anatomy (MS, PhD); applied mathematics (MS, PhD); atmospheric (MS, PhD); atmospheric sciences (MS, PhD); biochemistry (MS, PhD); biology (MS, PhD); biophysics (PhD); clinical psychology (PhD); developmental psychology (PhD); economics (MA, PhD); English (MA, PhD); environmental (MS, PhD); exercise physiology (MS); experimental psychology (PhD); French (MA); health education (MS); inorganic chemistry (MS, PhD); Latin America and the Caribbean (MA, PhD); mathematics (MS, PhD); neuropsychology (PhD); nutrition (MS, PhD); organic chemistry (MS, PhD); personality psychology (PhD); philosophy (MA); physical chemistry (MS, PhD); physics (MS, PhD); physiology (PhD); political science (MA, MAPA, PhD); psychology (MS); public administration (MAPA); public history (MA); social psychology (PhD); sociology (MA, PhD); Spanish (MA); sports studies (MS); United States history (MA, PhD); urban recreation (MS). Electronic applications accepted.

Division of Fine Arts *Degree program information:* Part-time programs available. Offers 3D reality (sculpture and ceramics) (MFA); applied music (MM); art history (MA); design (MFA); electronic studio (MFA); fine arts (MFA); history of art and visual culture (MA); instrument (MM Ed); jazz studies (MM); organ (MM Ed); painting (MFA); photography (MFA); piano (MM Ed); voice (MM Ed).

School of Business *Degree program information:* Part-time and evening/weekend programs available. Postbaccalaureate distance learning degree programs offered (no on-campus study). Offers accounting (MBA); business (MBA); entrepreneurship (MBA); finance (MBA); general management (MBA); human resources management (MBA); information systems (MBA); international business (MBA); marketing (MBA); supply chain management (MBA).

School of Communications *Degree program information:* Part-time and evening/weekend programs available. Offers communication sciences (PhD); communications (MA, MFA, MS, PhD); film (MFA); intercultural communication (MA, PhD); organizational communication (MA, PhD); speech pathology (MS). Electronic applications accepted.

Division of Mass Communication and Media Studies *Degree program information:* Part-time and evening/weekend programs available. Offers mass communication (MA, PhD); media studies (MA, PhD). Electronic applications accepted.

School of Divinity *Degree program information:* Part-time and evening/weekend programs available. Offers theology (M Div, MARS, D Min). Electronic applications accepted.

School of Education Students: 146 full-time (107 women), 94 part-time (71 women); includes 218 Black or African American, non-Hispanic/Latino; 3 Asian, non-Hispanic/Latino, 19 international. Average age 32. 172 applicants, 66% accepted, 77 enrolled. *Faculty:* 30 full-time (18 women), 11 part-time/adjunct (8 women). Expenses: Contact institution. *Financial support:* In 2010–11, 30 students received support, including 8 fellowships with full and partial tuition reimbursements available (averaging $10,000 per year), 22 research assistantships with full and partial tuition reimbursements available (averaging $12,000 per year); career-related internships or fieldwork, Federal Work-Study, institutionally sponsored loans, scholarships/grants, and unspecified assistantships also available. Financial award application deadline: 3/15; financial award applicants required to submit FAFSA. In 2010, 47 master's, 5 doctorates awarded. Postbaccalaureate distance learning degree programs offered (minimal on-campus study). Offers counseling and guidance (M Ed); counseling psychology (M Ed, PhD); early childhood education (MAT); education (M Ed, MAT, Ed D, PhD); educational administration (M Ed, CAGS); educational administration and policy (M Ed, Ed D, CAGS); educational psychology (M Ed, PhD); elementary education (M Ed); school psychology (M Ed, PhD); secondary education (MAT); special education (M Ed). *Application deadline:* For fall admission, 2/15 priority date for domestic students; for spring admission, 11/1 for domestic students. Applications are processed on a rolling basis. *Application fee:* $45. Electronic applications accepted. *Application Contact:* Dr. Melanie Carter, Associate Dean for Academic Programs and Student Affairs, 202-806-7340, Fax: 202-806-5302, E-mail: melcarter@howard.edu. *Head,* Dr. Leslie T. Fenwick, 202-806-7334, Fax: 202-806-5302, E-mail: lfenwick@howard.edu.

School of Law Offers law (JD, LL M). Electronic applications accepted.

School of Social Work *Degree program information:* Part-time programs available. Offers social work (MSW, PhD).

HULT INTERNATIONAL BUSINESS SCHOOL, Cambridge, MA 02141

General Information Independent, coed, primarily men, graduate-only institution. *Graduate housing:* On-campus housing not available.

GRADUATE UNITS

MBA Program Offers business administration (MBA). Electronic applications accepted.

Program in Business Administration—Hult London Campus *Degree program information:* Part-time programs available. Offers entrepreneurship (MBA); international business (MBA); international finance (MBA); marketing (MBA). Electronic applications accepted.

Program in Finance Offers finance (MF).

Program in Finance—Hult Dubai Campus Offers finance (MF).

Program in Finance—Hult London Campus Offers finance (MF). Electronic applications accepted.

Program in International Business Offers international business (MIB).

Program in International Business—Hult Dubai Campus Offers international business (MIB).

Program in International Business—Hult London Campus Offers international business (MIB).

Program in International Business—Hult San Francisco Campus Offers international business (MIB).

Program in International Relations—Hult London Campus *Degree program information:* Part-time programs available. Offers conflict resolution (MA); diplomacy (MA); international public law (MA); international relations (MA); Middle East international security (MA); politics (MA); security studies (MA); terrorism (MA); U.S. foreign policy (MA). Electronic applications accepted.

Program in International Relations—Hult San Francisco Campus Offers international relations (MA).

HUMBOLDT STATE UNIVERSITY, Arcata, CA 95521-8299

General Information State-supported, coed, comprehensive institution. CGS member. *Enrollment:* 7,902 graduate, professional, and undergraduate students; 337 full-time matriculated graduate/professional students (205 women), 130 part-time matriculated graduate/professional students (71 women). *Enrollment by degree level:* 467 master's. *Graduate faculty:* 232 full-time (85 women), 267 part-time/adjunct (163 women). Tuition and fees vary according to program. *Graduate housing:* Room and/or apartments available on a first-come, first-served basis to single students; on-campus housing not available to married students. Typical cost: $5055 per year ($10,055 including board). Housing application deadline: 2/1. *Student services:* Campus employment opportunities, campus safety program, career counseling, child daycare facilities, exercise/wellness program, free psychological counseling, international student services, low-cost health insurance, multicultural affairs office, services for students with disabilities, teacher training. *Library facilities:* Humbolt State University Library. *Online resources:* library catalog, web page, access to other libraries' catalogs. *Collection:* 2 million titles, 864 serial subscriptions, 23,756 audiovisual materials. *Research affiliation:* McIntire-Stennis (forestry), National Sea Grant, U. S. Fish and Wildlife Service–Wildlife Field Station, Redwood Sciences Laboratory of the Pacific Southwest Forest and Range Experiment Station, California Cooperative Fisheries Research Unit.

Computer facilities: Computer purchase and lease plans are available. 1,098 computers available on campus for general student use. A campuswide network can be accessed from student residence rooms and from off campus. Online class registration is available. *Web address:* http://www.humboldt.edu/.

General Application Contact: Cynthia Werner, Admissions Coordinator, 707-826-6250, E-mail: cw7001@humboldt.edu.

GRADUATE UNITS

Academic Programs Students: 337 full-time (205 women), 130 part-time (71 women); includes 79 minority (4 Black or African American, non-Hispanic/Latino; 12 American Indian or Alaska Native, non-Hispanic/Latino; 10 Asian, non-Hispanic/Latino; 38 Hispanic/Latino; 15 Two or more races, non-Hispanic/Latino), 8 international. Average age 31. 541 applicants, 45% accepted, 174 enrolled. *Faculty:* 232 full-time (85 women), 267 part-time/adjunct (163 women). Expenses: Contact institution. *Financial support:* Fellowships, research assistantships, teaching assistantships, career-related internships or fieldwork, Federal Work-Study, and institutionally sponsored loans available. Support available to part-time students. Financial award application deadline: 3/1; financial award applicants required to submit FAFSA. In 2010, 172 master's awarded. *Degree program information:* Part-time and evening/weekend programs available. *Application deadline:* Applications are processed on a rolling basis. *Application fee:* $55. Electronic applications accepted. *Application Contact:* Cynthia Werner, Administrative Support Coordinator, 707-826-6250, Fax: 707-826-6190. *Vice Provost,* Dr. Jena' Burges, 707-826-3511, Fax: 707-826-5480, E-mail: jb139@humboldt.edu.

College of Arts, Humanities, and Social Sciences Students: 84 full-time (60 women), 20 part-time (16 women); includes 21 minority (1 Black or African American, non-Hispanic/Latino; 4 American Indian or Alaska Native, non-Hispanic/Latino; 2 Asian, non-Hispanic/Latino; 8 Hispanic/Latino; 6 Two or more races, non-Hispanic/Latino). Average age 32. 121 applicants, 52% accepted, 58 enrolled. Expenses: Contact institution. *Financial support:* Fellowships, teaching assistantships, career-related internships or fieldwork, Federal Work-

Study, and institutionally sponsored loans available. Support available to part-time students. Financial award application deadline: 3/1; financial award applicants required to submit FAFSA. In 2010, 31 master's awarded. *Degree program information:* Part-time programs available. Offers arts, humanities, and social sciences (MA, MFA); English (MA); environment and community (MA); sociology (MA); theatre arts (MA, MFA). *Application deadline:* Applications are processed on a rolling basis. *Application fee:* $55. Electronic applications accepted. *Application Contact:* Dr. Kenneth Ayoob, Dean, 707-826-4491, Fax: 707-826-4498, E-mail: kpa1@humboldt.edu. *Dean,* Dr. Kenneth Ayoob, 707-826-4491, Fax: 707-826-4498, E-mail: kpa1@humboldt.edu.

College of Natural Resources and Sciences Students: 124 full-time (52 women), 58 part-time (25 women); includes 15 minority (1 American Indian or Alaska Native, non-Hispanic/Latino; 4 Asian, non-Hispanic/Latino; 9 Hispanic/Latino; 1 Two or more races, non-Hispanic/Latino), 5 international. Average age 30. 215 applicants, 51% accepted, 58 enrolled. Expenses: Contact institution. *Financial support:* Fellowships, career-related internships or fieldwork and Federal Work-Study available. Support available to part-time students. Financial award application deadline: 3/1; financial award applicants required to submit FAFSA. In 2010, 53 master's awarded. *Degree program information:* Part-time programs available. Offers biological sciences (MA); environmental systems (MS); natural resources (MS); natural resources and sciences (MA, MS). *Application deadline:* Applications are processed on a rolling basis. *Application fee:* $55. *Application Contact:* Cynthina Werner, Administrative Support Coordinator, 707-826-6250, Fax: 707-826-6190, E-mail: werner@humboldt.edu. *Dean,* Dr. Steven Smith, 707-826-3256, Fax: 707-826-3562, E-mail: ss7006@humboldt.edu.

College of Professional Studies Students: 129 full-time (93 women), 51 part-time (29 women); includes 43 minority (3 Black or African American, non-Hispanic/Latino; 7 American Indian or Alaska Native, non-Hispanic/Latino; 4 Asian, non-Hispanic/Latino; 21 Hispanic/Latino; 8 Two or more races, non-Hispanic/Latino), 3 international. Average age 31. 205 applicants, 74% accepted, 73 enrolled. Expenses: Contact institution. *Financial support:* Fellowships, teaching assistantships, career-related internships or fieldwork, Federal Work-Study, and institutionally sponsored loans available. Support available to part-time students. Financial award application deadline: 3/1; financial award applicants required to submit FAFSA. In 2010, 88 master's awarded. *Degree program information:* Part-time and evening/weekend programs available. Offers athletic training education (MS); business (MBA); education (MA); exercise science/wellness management (MS); pre-physical therapy (MS); psychology (MA); social work (MSW); teaching/coaching (MS). *Application deadline:* Applications are processed on a rolling basis. *Application fee:* $55. *Application Contact:* Cynthia Werner, Research and Graduate Studies, 707-826-6250, Fax: 707-826-6190. *Dean,* Dr. John Lee, 707-826-3961, Fax: 707-826-3963, E-mail: john.lee@humboldt.edu.

HUMPHREYS COLLEGE, Stockton, CA 95207-3896

General Information Independent, coed, comprehensive institution. *Graduate housing:* Room and/or apartments available on a first-come, first-served basis to single students; on-campus housing not available to married students.

GRADUATE UNITS

Laurence Drivon School of Law *Degree program information:* Part-time and evening/weekend programs available. Offers law (JD). Electronic applications accepted.

HUNTER COLLEGE OF THE CITY UNIVERSITY OF NEW YORK, New York, NY 10021-5085

General Information State and locally supported, coed, comprehensive institution. *Enrollment:* 22,407 graduate, professional, and undergraduate students; 1,377 full-time matriculated graduate/professional students (1,115 women), 4,383 part-time matriculated graduate/professional students (3,392 women). *Enrollment by degree level:* 5,539 master's, 221 other advanced degrees. *Graduate faculty:* 307 full-time (159 women), 398 part-time/adjunct (277 women). *Graduate housing:* Room and/or apartments available on a first-come, first-served basis to single students; on-campus housing not available to married students. *Student services:* Campus employment opportunities, campus safety program, career counseling, child daycare facilities, exercise/wellness program, free psychological counseling, international student services, services for students with disabilities, teacher training, writing training. *Library facilities:* Hunter College Library. *Online resources:* library catalog, web page, access to other libraries' catalogs. *Collection:* 873,465 titles, 10,405 serial subscriptions, 20,066 audiovisual materials. *Research affiliation:* Cornell University Medical Center, New York Hospital, The Mount Sinai Medical Center, Bellevue Hospital Center.

Computer facilities: 1,280 computers available on campus for general student use. A campuswide network can be accessed. Online class registration is available. *Web address:* http://www.hunter.cuny.edu/.

General Application Contact: William Zlata, Director for Graduate Admissions, 212-772-4482, Fax: 212-650-3336, E-mail: admissions@hunter.cuny.edu.

GRADUATE UNITS

Graduate School Students: 1,377 full-time (1,115 women), 4,383 part-time (3,392 women); includes 706 Black or African American, non-Hispanic/Latino; 21 American Indian or Alaska Native, non-Hispanic/Latino; 466 Asian, non-Hispanic/Latino; 762 Hispanic/Latino, 213 international. Average age 32. 7,259 applicants, 32% accepted, 1543 enrolled. *Faculty:* 307 full-time (159 women), 398 part-time/adjunct (277 women). Expenses: Contact institution. *Financial support:* Fellowships with full and partial tuition reimbursements, research assistantships with partial tuition reimbursements, teaching assistantships, career-related internships or fieldwork, Federal Work-Study, institutionally sponsored loans, scholarships/grants, traineeships, tuition waivers (full and partial), unspecified assistantships, and lesson stipends available. Support available to part-time students. Financial award applicants required to submit FAFSA. In 2010, 1,577 master's, 88 other advanced degrees awarded. *Degree program information:* Part-time and evening/weekend programs available. *Application deadline:* For fall admission, 4/1 for domestic students; for spring admission, 11/1 for domestic students. *Application fee:* $125. *Application Contact:* Milena Solo, Director for Graduate Admissions, 212-772-4288, Fax: 212-650-3336, E-mail: milena.solo@hunter.cuny.edu. *Director of Admissions,* William Zlata, 212-772-4288, Fax: 212-650-3336, E-mail: bill.zlata@hunter.cuny.edu.

School of Arts and Sciences Students: 231 full-time (152 women), 1,052 part-time (671 women); includes 120 Black or African American, non-Hispanic/Latino; 5 American Indian or Alaska Native, non-Hispanic/Latino; 101 Asian, non-Hispanic/Latino; 128 Hispanic/Latino, 83 international. Average age 30. 2,705 applicants, 23% accepted, 348 enrolled. *Faculty:* 157 full-time (60 women), 38 part-time/adjunct (14 women). Expenses: Contact institution. *Financial support:* Fellowships, research assistantships, teaching assistantships, career-related internships or fieldwork, Federal Work-Study, institutionally sponsored loans, scholarships/grants, tuition waivers (full and partial), unspecified assistantships, and lesson stipends available. Support available to part-time students. In 2010, 321 master's, 6 other advanced degrees awarded. *Degree program information:* Part-time and evening/weekend programs available. Offers accounting (MS); analytical geography (MA); animal behavior and conservation (MA); anthropology (MA); applied and evaluative psychology (MA); applied mathematics (MA); applied social research (MS); art history (MA); arts and sciences (MA, MFA, MS, MUP, PhD, Certificate); biochemistry (MA, PhD); biological sciences (MA, PhD); biopsychology and behavioral neuroscience (PhD); biopsychology and comparative psychology (MA); British and American literature (MA); chemistry (PhD); creative writing (MFA); earth system science (MA); economics (MA); English education (MA); environmental and social issues (MA); fiction (MFA); fine arts (MFA); French (MA); French education (MA); geographic information science (Certificate); geographic information systems (MA); history (MA); integrated media arts (MA, MFA); Italian (MA); Italian education (MA); mathematics for secondary education (MA); music (MA); music education (MA); nonfiction (MFA); physics (MA, PhD); playwriting (MFA); poetry (MFA); pure mathematics (MA); social, cognitive, and developmental psychology (MA); Spanish (MA); Spanish education (MA); studio art (MFA); teaching earth science (MA); teaching Latin (MA); theatre (MA); urban affairs (MS); urban planning (MUP); urban studies/affairs (MS). *Application deadline:* For fall admission, 2/1 for domestic and international students; for spring admission, 11/1 for domestic students, 9/1 for international students. *Application fee:* $125. *Application Contact:* Milena Solo, Director for Graduate Admissions, 212-772-4482, Fax: 212-650-3336, E-mail: milena.solo@hunter.cuny.edu. *Acting Dean,* Dr. Robert D. Greenberg, 212-772-5121, Fax: 212-772-5148, E-mail: robert.greenberg@hunter.cuny.edu.

School of Education Students: 312 full-time (268 women), 1,697 part-time (1,429 women); includes 184 Black or African American, non-Hispanic/Latino; 10 American Indian or Alaska Native, non-Hispanic/Latino; 104 Asian, non-Hispanic/Latino; 290 Hispanic/Latino, 26 international. Average age 31. 2,272 applicants, 36% accepted, 492 enrolled. *Faculty:* 159 full-time (93 women), 443 part-time/adjunct (340 women). Expenses: Contact institution. *Financial support:* Fellowships, career-related internships or fieldwork, Federal Work-Study, institutionally sponsored loans, and tuition waivers (full and partial) available. Support available to part-time students. In 2010, 583 master's, 4 other advanced degrees awarded. Offers bilingual education (MS); biology education (MA); blind or visually impaired (MS Ed); chemistry education (MA); corrective reading (K-12) (MS Ed); deaf or hard of hearing (MS Ed); early childhood education (MS); earth science (MA); education (MA, MS, MS Ed, AC); educational supervision and administration (AC); elementary education (MS); English education (MA); French education (MA); Italian education (MA); literacy education (MS); mathematics education (MA); music education (MA); physics education (MA); rehabilitation counseling (MS Ed); school counseling (MS Ed); school counseling with bilingual extension (MS Ed); school counselor (MS Ed); severe/multiple disabilities (MS Ed); social studies education (MA); Spanish education (MA); special education (MS Ed); teaching English as a second language (MA). *Application deadline:* For fall admission, 4/1 for domestic students, 2/1 for international students; for spring admission, 11/1 for domestic students, 9/1 for international students. Applications are processed on a rolling basis. *Application fee:* $125. *Application Contact:* Milena Solo, Director for Graduate Admissions, 212-772-4482, Fax: 212-650-3336, E-mail: milena.solo@hunter.cuny.edu. *Dean,* Dr. David Steiner, 212-772-4622, E-mail: david.steiner@hunter.cuny.edu.

School of Social Work Students: 700 full-time (582 women), 320 part-time (252 women); includes 225 Black or African American, non-Hispanic/Latino; 1 American Indian or Alaska Native, non-Hispanic/Latino; 40 Asian, non-Hispanic/Latino; 186 Hispanic/Latino, 19 international. Average age 33. 1,376 applicants, 28% accepted, 313 enrolled. *Faculty:* 38 full-time (20 women), 66 part-time/adjunct (46 women). Expenses: Contact institution. *Financial support:* In 2010–11, 120 fellowships (averaging $1,000 per year) were awarded; career-related internships or fieldwork, Federal Work-Study, and tuition waivers (partial) also available. Support available to part-time students. In 2010, 372 master's awarded. Offers social work (MSW, DSW). DSW offered jointly with Graduate School and University Center of the City University of New York. *Application deadline:* For fall admission, 1/15 for domestic and international students. Applications are processed on a rolling basis. *Application fee:* $125. *Application Contact:* Raymond Montero, Coordinator of Admissions, 212-452-7005, E-mail: grad.socworkadvisor@hunter.cuny.edu. *Dean/Professor,* Dr. Jacqueline B. Mondros, 212-452-7085, Fax: 212-452-7150, E-mail: jmondros@hunter.cuny.edu.

Schools of the Health Professions Students: 65 full-time (53 women), 536 part-time (417 women); includes 102 Black or African American, non-Hispanic/Latino; 2 American Indian or Alaska Native, non-Hispanic/Latino; 116 Asian, non-Hispanic/Latino; 47 Hispanic/Latino. Average age 37. 884 applicants, 44% accepted, 289 enrolled. *Faculty:* 40 full-time (28 women), 36 part-time/adjunct (28 women). Expenses: Contact institution. *Financial support:* Federal Work-Study and tuition waivers (partial) available. Support available to part-time students. In 2010, 112 master's, 14 other advanced degrees awarded. *Degree program information:* Part-time and evening/weekend programs available. Offers adult nurse practitioner (MS); community health education (MPH); community health nursing (MS); environmental and occupational health education (MS); epidemiology and biostatistics (MPH); gerontological nurse practitioner (MS); health policy management (MPH); health professions (MPH, MS, AC); health sciences (MPH, MS); nursing (MS, AC); nutrition and public health (MPH); psychiatric nursing (MS, AC); speech-language pathology (MS). *Application deadline:* For fall admission, 4/1 for domestic students, 2/1 for international students; for spring admission, 11/1 for domestic students, 9/1 for international students. *Application fee:* $125. *Application Contact:* Milena Solo, Director for Graduate Admissions, 212-772-4288, Fax: 212-650-3336, E-mail: milena.solo@hunter.cuny.edu. *Dean,* Lauren N. Sherwen, 212-481-4314.

HUNTINGTON COLLEGE OF HEALTH SCIENCES, Knoxville, TN 37919-7736

General Information Proprietary, coed, comprehensive institution.

GRADUATE UNITS

Program in Nutrition *Degree program information:* Part-time and evening/weekend programs available. Postbaccalaureate distance learning degree programs offered (no on-campus study). Offers nutrition (MS).

HUNTINGTON UNIVERSITY, Huntington, IN 46750-1299

General Information Independent-religious, coed, comprehensive institution. *Graduate housing:* On-campus housing not available. *Research affiliation:* Link Institute (youth ministry).

GRADUATE UNITS

Graduate School *Degree program information:* Part-time programs available. Postbaccalaureate distance learning degree programs offered (minimal on-campus study). Offers counseling (MA); education (M Ed); youth ministry leadership (MA). Electronic applications accepted.

HUSSON UNIVERSITY, Bangor, ME 04401-2999

General Information Independent, coed, comprehensive institution. *Graduate housing:* Room and/or apartments available on a first-come, first-served basis to single students; on-campus housing not available to married students. Housing application deadline: 6/1.

GRADUATE UNITS

School of Graduate and Professional Studies *Degree program information:* Part-time and evening/weekend programs available. Offers advanced practice psychiatric nursing (MSN, PMC); counseling psychology (MS); criminal justice administration (MS); family and community nurse practitioner (MSN, PMC); health care management (MSB); nonprofit management (MSB); occupational therapy (MSOT); physical therapy (DPT); school counseling (MS).

ICR GRADUATE SCHOOL, Santee, CA 92071

General Information Independent-religious, coed, graduate-only institution. *Graduate housing:* On-campus housing not available.

GRADUATE UNITS

Graduate Programs *Degree program information:* Part-time programs available. Offers astro/geophysics (MS); biology (MS); geology (MS); science education (MS).

IDAHO STATE UNIVERSITY, Pocatello, ID 83209

General Information State-supported, coed, university. CGS member. *Graduate housing:* Rooms and/or apartments available on a first-come, first-served basis to single and married students. Housing application deadline: 5/1. *Research affiliation:* S. M. Stoller Corporation (ecology, waste management), ON Semiconductor (computer sciences, environmental management), Inland Northwest Research Alliance (INRA) (science), J. R. Simplot Company (plant sciences, environmental studies), Bechtel BWXT Idaho, LLC (environmental management, nuclear sciences), Environmental Science and Research Foundation (waste management, ecology).

GRADUATE UNITS

Office of Graduate Studies *Degree program information:* Part-time programs available. Offers general interdisciplinary (M Ed, MA, MNS); waste management and environmental science (MS). Electronic applications accepted.

College of Arts and Sciences *Degree program information:* Part-time programs available. Offers anthropology (MA, MS); applied physics (PhD); art (MFA); arts and sciences (MA, MFA, MNS, MPA, MS, DA, PhD, Post-Master's Certificate, Postbaccalaureate Certificate); biology (MNS, MS, DA, PhD); chemistry (MNS, MS); clinical laboratory science (MS);

Idaho State University (continued)

clinical psychology (PhD); communication and rhetorical studies (MA); English (MA, DA); English and the teaching of English (PhD); geographic information science (MS); geology (MNS, MS); geology with emphasis in environmental geoscience (MS); geophysics/hydrology/geology (MS); geotechnology (Postbaccalaureate Certificate); health physics (MS); historical resources management (MA); mathematics (MS, DA); mathematics for secondary teachers (MA); microbiology (MS); physics (MNS); political science (MA, DA); psychology (MS); public administration (MPA); sociology (MA); TESOL (Post-Master's Certificate); theatre (MA). Electronic applications accepted.

College of Business *Degree program information:* Part-time programs available. Offers business administration (MBA, Postbaccalaureate Certificate); computer information systems (MS, Postbaccalaureate Certificate). Electronic applications accepted.

College of Education *Degree program information:* Part-time programs available. Offers child and family studies (M Ed); curriculum leadership (M Ed); education (M Ed); educational administration (M Ed, 6th Year Certificate, Ed S); educational foundations (5th Year Certificate); educational leadership (Ed D); educational leadership and instructional design (PhD); elementary education (M Ed); human exceptionality (M Ed); instructional design (PhD); instructional technology (M Ed); physical education (MPE); school psychology (Ed S); special education (Ed S). Electronic applications accepted.

College of Engineering *Degree program information:* Part-time programs available. Offers civil engineering (MS); engineering (MS, PhD, Postbaccalaureate Certificate); engineering and applied science (PhD); environmental engineering (MS); environmental science and management (MS); measurement and control engineering (MS); mechanical engineering (MS); nuclear science and engineering (MS, PhD, Postbaccalaureate Certificate). Electronic applications accepted.

College of Pharmacy *Degree program information:* Part-time programs available. Offers biopharmaceutical analysis (PhD); drug delivery (PhD); medicinal chemistry (PhD); pharmaceutical sciences (MS); pharmacology (PhD); pharmacy (Pharm D, MS, PhD); pharmacy administration (MS, PhD). Electronic applications accepted.

College of Technology *Degree program information:* Part-time and evening/weekend programs available. Offers human resource training and development (MTD); technology (MTD). Electronic applications accepted.

Kasiska College of Health Professions *Degree program information:* Part-time programs available. Offers advanced general dentistry (Post-Doctoral Certificate); audiology (MS, Au D); communication sciences and disorders (Postbaccalaureate Certificate); communication sciences and disorders and education of the deaf (Certificate); counseling (M Coun, Ed S); counselor education and counseling (PhD); deaf education (MS); dental hygiene (MS); dietetics (Certificate); family medicine (Post-Master's Certificate); health education (MHE); health professions (M Coun, MHE, MOT, MPAS, MPH, MS, Au D, DPT, PhD, Certificate, Ed S, Post-Doctoral Certificate, Post-Master's Certificate, Postbaccalaureate Certificate); nursing (MS, Post-Master's Certificate); occupational therapy (MOT); physical therapy (DPT); physician assistant studies (MPAS); public health (MPH); speech language pathology (MS). Electronic applications accepted.

ILIFF SCHOOL OF THEOLOGY, Denver, CO 80210-4798

General Information Independent-religious, coed, graduate-only institution. *Graduate housing:* Rooms and/or apartments available on a first-come, first-served basis to single and married students.

GRADUATE UNITS

Graduate and Professional Programs *Degree program information:* Part-time and evening/weekend programs available. Offers biblical studies (MA); church history (MA); religion (MA); religion and social change (MA); specialized ministry (MASM); theology (M Div, MTS, D Min, PhD); theology/ethics (MA). PhD offered jointly with University of Denver. Electronic applications accepted.

ILLINOIS COLLEGE OF OPTOMETRY, Chicago, IL 60616-3878

General Information Independent, coed, graduate-only institution. *Graduate housing:* Rooms and/or apartments guaranteed to single students and available on a first-come, first-served basis to married students. Housing application deadline: 6/1. *Research affiliation:* University of Chicago (vision science), Rush University (cataract development), Ocular Science (contact lenses), University of Illinois at Chicago (neuropharmacology), Vision Service Plan (pediatric optometry), Ciba Vision (contact lenses).

GRADUATE UNITS

Professional Program Offers optometry (OD). Electronic applications accepted.

ILLINOIS INSTITUTE OF TECHNOLOGY, Chicago, IL 60616-3793

General Information Independent, coed, comprehensive institution. CGS member. *Enrollment:* 7,774 graduate, professional, and undergraduate students; 3,772 full-time matriculated graduate/professional students (1,529 women), 1,229 part-time matriculated graduate/professional students (446 women). *Enrollment by degree level:* 1,096 first professional, 3,175 master's, 616 doctoral, 94 other advanced degrees. *Graduate faculty:* 402 full-time (86 women), 225 part-time/adjunct (62 women). *Tuition:* Full-time $18,576; part-time $1032 per credit hour. *Required fees:* $583 per semester. One-time fee: $150. Tuition and fees vary according to program and student level. *Graduate housing:* Rooms and/or apartments available on a first-come, first-served basis to single and married students. Typical cost: $9984 per year for single students; $15,528 per year for married students. Room charges vary according to board plan and housing facility selected. Housing application deadline: 6/1. *Student services:* Campus employment opportunities, campus safety program, career counseling, free psychological counseling, grant writing training, international student services, low-cost health insurance, multicultural affairs office, services for students with disabilities, teacher training, writing training. *Library facilities:* Paul V. Galvin Library plus 5 others. *Online resources:* library catalog, web page, access to other libraries' catalogs. *Collection:* 1.8 million titles, 34,652 serial subscriptions, 1,162 audiovisual materials.

Computer facilities: 500 computers available on campus for general student use. A campuswide network can be accessed from student residence rooms and from off campus. Online class registration is available. *Web address:* http://www.iit.edu/.

General Application Contact: Deborah Gibson, Director, Graduate Admission, 866-472-3448, Fax: 312-567-3138, E-mail: inquiry.grad@iit.edu.

GRADUATE UNITS

Chicago-Kent College of Law Students: 889 full-time (417 women), 206 part-time (88 women); includes 214 minority (41 Black or African American, non-Hispanic/Latino; 64 Asian, non-Hispanic/Latino; 67 Hispanic/Latino; 26 Native Hawaiian or other Pacific Islander, non-Hispanic/Latino; 16 Two or more races, non-Hispanic/Latino), 112 international. Average age 27. 3,923 applicants, 47% accepted, 374 enrolled. *Faculty:* 70 full-time (24 women), 146 part-time/adjunct (35 women). Expenses: Contact institution. *Financial support:* In 2010–11, 607 students received support. Career-related internships or fieldwork, Federal Work-Study, institutionally sponsored loans, scholarships/grants, and tuition waivers (full) available. Support available to part-time students. Financial award application deadline: 3/15; financial award applicants required to submit FAFSA. In 2010, 297 first professional degrees, 128 master's awarded. *Degree program information:* Part-time and evening/weekend programs available. Offers family law (LL M); financial services (LL M); international intellectual property (LL M); international law (LL M); law (JD); taxation (LL M). *Application deadline:* For fall admission, 3/1 priority date for domestic students, 2/1 priority date for international students. Applications are processed on a rolling basis. *Application fee:* $60 ($75 for international students). Electronic applications accepted. *Application Contact:* Nicole Vilches, Assistant Dean, 312-906-5020, Fax: 312-906-5274, E-mail: admissions@kentlaw.edu. *Dean*, Harold J. Krent, 312-906-5010, Fax: 312-906-5335, E-mail: hkrent@kentlaw.edu.

Graduate College Students: 2,881 full-time (1,111 women), 1,015 part-time (348 women); includes 312 minority (94 Black or African American, non-Hispanic/Latino; 3 American Indian or Alaska Native, non-Hispanic/Latino; 136 Asian, non-Hispanic/Latino; 60 Hispanic/Latino; 2 Native Hawaiian or other Pacific Islander, non-Hispanic/Latino; 17 Two or more races, non-Hispanic/Latino), 2,438 international. Average age 27. 7,636 applicants, 66% accepted, 3896 enrolled. *Faculty:* 343 full-time (64 women), 208 part-time/adjunct (59 women). Expenses: Contact institution. *Financial support:* Fellowships with full and partial tuition reimbursements, research assistantships with full and partial tuition reimbursements, teaching assistantships with full and partial tuition reimbursements, career-related internships or fieldwork, Federal Work-Study, institutionally sponsored loans, scholarships/grants, traineeships, health care benefits, tuition waivers (full and partial), and unspecified assistantships available. Support available to part-time students. Financial award applicants required to submit FAFSA. In 2010, 1,344 master's, 79 doctorates awarded. *Degree program information:* Part-time and evening/weekend programs available. Postbaccalaureate distance learning degree programs offered (no on-campus study). *Application deadline:* Applications are processed on a rolling basis. *Application fee:* $50. Electronic applications accepted. *Application Contact:* Deborah Gibson, Director of Graduate and Professional Admission, 866-472-3448, Fax: 312-567-3138, E-mail: inquiry.grad@iit.edu. *Dean/Vice Provost for Research*, Dr. Ali Cinar, 312-567-3637, Fax: 312-567-7517, E-mail: cinar@iit.edu.

Armour College of Engineering Students: 931 full-time (231 women), 318 part-time (53 women); includes 78 minority (18 Black or African American, non-Hispanic/Latino; 1 American Indian or Alaska Native, non-Hispanic/Latino; 44 Asian, non-Hispanic/Latino; 12 Hispanic/Latino; 3 Two or more races, non-Hispanic/Latino), 884 international. Average age 26. 3,045 applicants, 58% accepted, 448 enrolled. *Faculty:* 93 full-time (8 women), 22 part-time/adjunct (3 women). Expenses: Contact institution. *Financial support:* In 2010–11, 8 fellowships with full and partial tuition reimbursements (averaging $6,850 per year), 160 research assistantships with full and partial tuition reimbursements (averaging $8,568 per year), 69 teaching assistantships with full and partial tuition reimbursements (averaging $6,471 per year) were awarded; career-related internships or fieldwork, Federal Work-Study, institutionally sponsored loans, scholarships/grants, health care benefits, tuition waivers (full and partial), and unspecified assistantships also available. Support available to part-time students. Financial award applicants required to submit FAFSA. In 2010, 380 master's, 37 doctorates awarded. *Degree program information:* Part-time and evening/weekend programs available. Postbaccalaureate distance learning degree programs offered (no on-campus study). Offers architectural engineering (M Arch E); biological engineering (MBE); biomedical engineering (PhD); biomedical imaging and signals (MBMI); chemical engineering (M Ch E, MS, PhD); civil engineering (MS, PhD); computer engineering (MS, PhD); construction engineering and management (MCEM); electrical and computer engineering (MECE); electrical engineering (MS, PhD); electricity markets (MEM); engineering (M Arch E, M Ch E, M Env E, M Geoenv E, M Trans E, MBE, MBMI, MCEM, MECE, MEM, MFPE, MGE, MMAE, MME, MMME, MNE, MPE, MPW, MS, MSE, MTSE, MVM, PhD); environmental engineering (M Env E, PhD); food process engineering (MFPE, MS); geoenvironmental engineering (M Geoenv E); geotechnical engineering (MGE); manufacturing engineering (MME, MS); materials science and engineering (MMME, MS, PhD); mechanical and aerospace engineering (MMAE, MS, PhD); network engineering (MNE); power engineering (MPE); public works (MPW); structural engineering (MSE); telecommunications and software engineering (MTSE); transportation engineering (M Trans E); VLSI and microelectronics (MVM). *Application deadline:* For fall admission, 5/1 for domestic and international students; for spring admission, 10/15 for domestic and international students. Applications are processed on a rolling basis. *Application fee:* $50. Electronic applications accepted. *Application Contact:* Deborah Gibson, Director, Graduate Admission, 866-472-3448, Fax: 312-567-3138, E-mail: inquiry.grad@iit.edu. *Dean*, Dr. Natacha DePaola, 312-567-3009, Fax: 312-567-7961, E-mail: engineering@iit.edu.

College of Architecture Students: 234 full-time (103 women), 14 part-time (7 women); includes 20 minority (3 Black or African American, non-Hispanic/Latino; 7 Asian, non-Hispanic/Latino; 9 Hispanic/Latino; 1 Two or more races, non-Hispanic/Latino), 97 international. Average age 28. 500 applicants, 65% accepted, 114 enrolled. *Faculty:* 39 full-time (5 women), 54 part-time/adjunct (15 women). Expenses: Contact institution. *Financial support:* In 2010–11, 1 research assistantship (averaging $5,000 per year), 39 teaching assistantships with full and partial tuition reimbursements (averaging $1,566 per year) were awarded; fellowships with full and partial tuition reimbursements, career-related internships or fieldwork, Federal Work-Study, institutionally sponsored loans, scholarships/grants, health care benefits, tuition waivers (partial), and unspecified assistantships also available. Support available to part-time students. Financial award applicants required to submit FAFSA. In 2010, 84 master's, 1 doctorate awarded. *Degree program information:* Part-time programs available. Offers architecture (M Arch, M IBD, MLA, MS Arch, PhD). *Application deadline:* For fall admission, 4/15 for domestic and international students; for spring admission, 11/15 for domestic and international students. Applications are processed on a rolling basis. *Application fee:* $50. Electronic applications accepted. *Application Contact:* Katherine Fitzgibbon, Director, Graduate Academic Affairs, 312-567-5858, Fax: 312-567-5820, E-mail: kfitzgib@iit.edu. *Dean*, Donna V. Robertson, 312-567-3230, Fax: 312-567-5820, E-mail: robertson@iit.edu.

College of Psychology Students: 160 full-time (111 women), 39 part-time (33 women); includes 36 minority (8 Black or African American, non-Hispanic/Latino; 1 American Indian or Alaska Native, non-Hispanic/Latino; 15 Asian, non-Hispanic/Latino; 12 Hispanic/Latino), 16 international. Average age 29. 253 applicants, 40% accepted, 43 enrolled. *Faculty:* 21 full-time (7 women), 6 part-time/adjunct (4 women). Expenses: Contact institution. *Financial support:* In 2010–11, 23 research assistantships with full and partial tuition reimbursements (averaging $223 per year) were awarded; fellowships with full and partial tuition reimbursements, career-related internships or fieldwork, Federal Work-Study, institutionally sponsored loans, scholarships/grants, traineeships, health care benefits, tuition waivers (partial), and unspecified assistantships also available. Support available to part-time students. Financial award application deadline: 1/15; financial award applicants required to submit FAFSA. In 2010, 31 master's, 14 doctorates awarded. *Degree program information:* Part-time and evening/weekend programs available. Offers clinical psychology (PhD); industrial/organizational psychology (PhD); personnel/human resource development (MS); rehabilitation (PhD); rehabilitation counseling (MS). *Application deadline:* For fall admission, 1/15 for domestic and international students. *Application fee:* $50. Electronic applications accepted. *Application Contact:* Institute of Psychology Graduate Admissions, 312-567-3500, Fax: 312-567-3493, E-mail: psychology@iit.edu. *Dean*, Dr. M. Ellen Mitchell, 312-567-3362, Fax: 312-567-3493, E-mail: mitchelle@iit.edu.

College of Science and Letters Students: 591 full-time (240 women), 351 part-time (141 women); includes 84 minority (37 Black or African American, non-Hispanic/Latino; 26 Asian, non-Hispanic/Latino; 16 Hispanic/Latino; 5 Two or more races, non-Hispanic/Latino), 569 international. Average age 28. 1,719 applicants, 70% accepted, 332 enrolled. *Faculty:* 134 full-time (36 women), 45 part-time/adjunct (19 women). Expenses: Contact institution. *Financial support:* In 2010–11, 7 fellowships with full and partial tuition reimbursements (averaging $14,605 per year), 71 research assistantships with full and partial tuition reimbursements (averaging $7,581 per year), 82 teaching assistantships with full and partial tuition reimbursements (averaging $8,581 per year) were awarded; career-related internships or fieldwork, Federal Work-Study, institutionally sponsored loans, scholarships/grants, traineeships, health care benefits, tuition waivers (partial), and unspecified assistantships also available. Support available to part-time students. Financial award applicants required to submit FAFSA. In 2010, 284 master's, 19 doctorates awarded. *Degree program information:* Part-time and evening/weekend programs available. Postbaccalaureate distance learning degree programs offered (minimal on-campus study). Offers analytical chemistry (M Ch); applied mathematics (MS, PhD); biochemistry (MBS, MS); biology (MB, MBS, MS, PhD); biotechnology (MBS, MS); business (MCS); cell and molecular biology (MBS, MS); chemistry (M Ch, M Chem, MS, PhD); collegiate mathematics (PhD); collegiate mathematics education (PhD); computer networking and telecommunications (MCS); computer science (MCS, MS, PhD); food safety and technology (MFPE, MFST, MS); health physics (MHP); information architecture (MS); information systems (MCS); materials and chemical synthesis (M Ch); mathematical finance (MMF); mathematics education (MME, MS, PhD); microbiology (MB, MS); molecular biochemistry and biophysics (PhD); molecular biology and biophysics (MS); physics (MHP, MS, PhD); science and letters (M Ch, M Chem, MB, MBS, MCS, MFPE, MFST, MHP, MME, MMF, MS, MSE, MST, PhD); science education (MS, MSE, PhD); software engineering (MCS); teaching (MST); technical communication (PhD); technical communication and information design (MS). *Application deadline:* For fall admission, 5/1 for domestic and international students; for spring admission, 10/15 for domestic and international students. Applications are processed on a rolling basis. *Application fee:* $50. Electronic applications accepted. *Application Contact:* Deborah Gibson, Director, Graduate Admission, 866-472-3448, Fax: 312-567-3138, E-mail: inquiry.grad@iit.edu. *Dean,* Dr. R. Russell Betts, 312-567-3800, Fax: 312-567-3802, E-mail: betts@iit.edu.

Institute of Design Students: 128 full-time (64 women), 18 part-time (8 women); includes 33 minority (5 Black or African American, non-Hispanic/Latino; 1 American Indian or Alaska Native, non-Hispanic/Latino; 21 Asian, non-Hispanic/Latino; 4 Hispanic/Latino; 2 Two or more races, non-Hispanic/Latino), 40 international. Average age 31. 144 applicants, 74% accepted, 51 enrolled. *Faculty:* 13 full-time (2 women), 31 part-time/adjunct (10 women). Expenses: Contact institution. *Financial support:* In 2010–11, 1 research assistantship (averaging $2,000 per year) was awarded; fellowships with full and partial tuition reimbursements, career-related internships or fieldwork, Federal Work-Study, institutionally sponsored loans, scholarships/grants, health care benefits, tuition waivers (partial), and unspecified assistantships also available. Support available to part-time students. Financial award applicants required to submit FAFSA. In 2010, 54 master's, 1 doctorate awarded. *Degree program information:* Part-time programs available. Offers design (M Des, MDM, PhD). *Application deadline:* For fall admission, 2/15 for domestic and international students; for spring admission, 10/15 for domestic students, 9/15 for international students. *Application fee:* $100. Electronic applications accepted. *Application Contact:* Rachel Dean, Director of Admissions and Retention, 312-595-4906, Fax: 312-596-4901, E-mail: rdean@id.iit.edu. *Dean,* Patrick Whitney, 312-595-4900, Fax: 312-595-4901, E-mail: patrick.whitney@iit.edu.

School of Applied Technology Students: 162 full-time (47 women), 90 part-time (24 women); includes 20 minority (6 Black or African American, non-Hispanic/Latino; 10 Asian, non-Hispanic/Latino; 3 Hispanic/Latino; 1 Two or more races, non-Hispanic/Latino), 177 international. Average age 28. 238 applicants, 86% accepted, 88 enrolled. *Faculty:* 6 full-time (2 women), 28 part-time/adjunct (3 women). Expenses: Contact institution. *Financial support:* In 2010–11, 9 teaching assistantships with partial tuition reimbursements (averaging $2,658 per year) were awarded; fellowships with partial tuition reimbursements, career-related internships or fieldwork, Federal Work-Study, institutionally sponsored loans, scholarships/grants, traineeships, health care benefits, tuition waivers (partial), and unspecified assistantships also available. Support available to part-time students. Financial award applicants required to submit FAFSA. In 2010, 139 master's awarded. *Degree program information:* Part-time and evening/weekend programs available. Postbaccalaureate distance learning degree programs offered (no on-campus study). Offers industrial technology and management (MITO); information technology and management (MITM). *Application deadline:* For fall admission, 8/1 for domestic students, 5/1 for international students; for spring admission, 12/15 for domestic students, 10/15 for international students. Applications are processed on a rolling basis. *Application fee:* $50. Electronic applications accepted. *Application Contact:* Deborah Gibson, Director, Graduate Admission, 866-472-3448, Fax: 312-567-3138, E-mail: inquiry.grad@iit.edu. *Director,* C. Robert Carlson, 630-682-6002, Fax: 630-682-6010, E-mail: carlson@iit.edu.

Stuart School of Business Students: 669 full-time (314 women), 185 part-time (82 women); includes 40 minority (17 Black or African American, non-Hispanic/Latino; 13 Asian, non-Hispanic/Latino; 4 Hispanic/Latino; 2 Native Hawaiian or other Pacific Islander, non-Hispanic/Latino; 4 Two or more races, non-Hispanic/Latino), 653 international. Average age 27. 1,737 applicants, 77% accepted, 395 enrolled. *Faculty:* 37 full-time (4 women), 21 part-time/adjunct (5 women). Expenses: Contact institution. *Financial support:* In 2010–11, 1 fellowship with full and partial tuition reimbursement (averaging $4,800 per year), 2 research assistantships with partial tuition reimbursements (averaging $4,850 per year) were awarded; career-related internships or fieldwork, Federal Work-Study, institutionally sponsored loans, scholarships/grants, traineeships, health care benefits, tuition waivers (partial), and unspecified assistantships also available. Support available to part-time students. Financial award applicants required to submit FAFSA. In 2010, 372 master's, 7 doctorates awarded. *Degree program information:* Part-time and evening/weekend programs available. Offers business (MBA, MMF, MPA, MS, PhD); environmental management and sustainability (MS); finance (MS); financial management (MBA); innovation and emerging enterprises (MBA); management science (PhD); marketing (MBA); marketing communication (MS); mathematical finance (MMF); public administration (MPA); sustainability (MBA). *Application deadline:* For fall admission, 8/1 for domestic students, 5/1 for international students; for spring admission, 12/15 for domestic students, 10/15 for international students. Applications are processed on a rolling basis. *Application fee:* $75. Electronic applications accepted. *Application Contact:* Deborah Gibson, Director, Graduate Admission, 866-472-3448, Fax: 312-567-3138, E-mail: inquiry.grad@iit.edu. *Dean,* Dr. Harvey Kahalas, 312-906-6596, Fax: 312-906-6549, E-mail: bizdean@stuart.iit.edu.

ILLINOIS STATE UNIVERSITY, Normal, IL 61790-2200

General Information State-supported, coed, university. CGS member. *Graduate housing:* Rooms and/or apartments available to single and married students. Housing application deadline: 4/1.

GRADUATE UNITS

Graduate School *Degree program information:* Part-time programs available.

College of Applied Science and Technology *Degree program information:* Part-time programs available. Offers agribusiness (MS); applied science and technology (MA, MS); criminal justice sciences (MA, MS); family and consumer sciences (MA, MS); health education (MS); information technology (MS); physical education (MS); technology (MS).

College of Arts and Sciences *Degree program information:* Part-time programs available. Offers animal behavior (MS); arts and sciences (MA, MS, MSW, PhD, SSP); bacteriology (MS); biochemistry (MS); biological sciences (MS); biology (PhD); biophysics (MS); biotechnology (MS); botany (MS, PhD); cell biology (MS); chemistry (MS); communication (MA, MS); communication sciences and disorders (MA, MS); conservation biology (MS); developmental biology (MS); ecology (MS, PhD); economics (MA, MS); English (MA, MS, PhD); English studies (PhD); entomology (MS); evolutionary biology (MS); French (MA); French and German (MA); French and Spanish (MA); genetics (MS, PhD); German (MA); German and Spanish (MA); historical archaeology (MA, MS); history (MA, MS); hydrogeology (MS); immunology (MS); mathematics (MA, MS, PhD); mathematics education (PhD); microbiology (MS, PhD); molecular biology (MS); molecular genetics (MS); neurobiology (MS); neuroscience (MS); parasitology (MS); physiology (MS, PhD); plant biology (MS); plant molecular biology (MS); plant sciences (MS); politics and government (MA, MS); psychology (MA, MS); school psychology (PhD, SSP); social work (MSW); sociology (MA, MS); Spanish (MA, MS); structural biology (MS); writing (MA, MS); zoology (MS, PhD).

College of Business *Degree program information:* Part-time programs available. Offers accounting (MPA, MS); business (MBA, MPA, MS); business administration (MBA).

College of Education *Degree program information:* Part-time programs available. Offers college student personnel administration (MS); curriculum and instruction (MS, MS Ed, Ed D); education (MS, MS Ed, Ed D, PhD); educational administration (MS, MS Ed, Ed D, PhD); educational policies (Ed D); postsecondary education (Ed D); reading (MS Ed); special education (MS, MS Ed, Ed D); supervision (Ed D).

College of Fine Arts *Degree program information:* Part-time programs available. Offers art history (MA, MS); arts technology (MS); ceramics (MFA, MS); drawing (MFA, MS); fibers (MFA, MS); fine arts (MA, MFA, MM, MM Ed, MS); glass (MFA, MS); graphic design (MFA, MS); metals (MFA, MS); music (MM, MM Ed); painting (MFA, MS); photography (MFA, MS); printmaking (MFA, MS); sculpture (MFA, MS); theatre (MA, MFA, MS).

Mennonite College of Nursing Offers family nurse practitioner (PMC); nursing (MSN, PhD).

IMCA–INTERNATIONAL MANAGEMENT CENTRES ASSOCIATION, Buckingham MK18 1BP, United Kingdom

General Information Independent, coed, graduate-only institution.

GRADUATE UNITS

Programs in Business Administration Postbaccalaureate distance learning degree programs offered (no on-campus study). Offers business administration (M Mgt, M Phil, MBA, MS).

IMMACULATA UNIVERSITY, Immaculata, PA 19345

General Information Independent-religious, coed, primarily women, comprehensive institution. CGS member. *Enrollment:* 4,456 graduate, professional, and undergraduate students; 185 full-time matriculated graduate/professional students (150 women), 838 part-time matriculated graduate/professional students (590 women). *Graduate faculty:* 64. *Graduate housing:* On-campus housing not available. *Student services:* Campus employment opportunities, campus safety program, career counseling, exercise/wellness program, international student services, low-cost health insurance, services for students with disabilities, writing training. *Library facilities:* Gabriele Library. *Online resources:* library catalog, web page.

Computer facilities: A campuswide network can be accessed from student residence rooms. *Web address:* http://www.immaculata.edu/.

General Application Contact: Sandra A. Rollison, Director of Graduate Admission, 610-647-4400 Ext. 3215, Fax: 610-993-8550, E-mail: srollison@immaculata.edu.

GRADUATE UNITS

College of Graduate Studies Students: 185 full-time (150 women), 838 part-time (590 women); includes 66 Black or African American, non-Hispanic/Latino; 1 American Indian or Alaska Native, non-Hispanic/Latino; 12 Asian, non-Hispanic/Latino; 33 Hispanic/Latino; 3 Native Hawaiian or other Pacific Islander, non-Hispanic/Latino. Average age 33. 288 applicants, 82% accepted, 177 enrolled. *Faculty:* 64. Expenses: Contact institution. *Financial support:* Career-related internships or fieldwork, Federal Work-Study, and scholarships/grants available. Support available to part-time students. Financial award application deadline: 5/1; financial award applicants required to submit FAFSA. In 2010, 113 master's, 44 doctorates awarded. *Degree program information:* Part-time and evening/weekend programs available. Offers applied communication (MA); clinical psychology (Psy D); counseling psychology (MA, Certificate); cultural and linguistic diversity (MA); educational leadership and administration (MA, Ed D); elementary education (Certificate); music therapy (MA); nursing (MSN); nutrition education (MA); nutrition education/approved pre-professional practice program (MA); organization studies (MA); school principal (Certificate); school superintendent (Certificate); secondary education (Certificate); special education (Certificate). *Application deadline:* Applications are processed on a rolling basis. *Application fee:* $35. Electronic applications accepted. *Application Contact:* Sandra A. Rollison, Director of Graduate Admission, 610-647-4400 Ext. 3215, Fax: 610-993-8550, E-mail: srollison@immaculata.edu. *Dean,* Dr. Janet Kane, 610-647-4400 Ext. 3211, Fax: 610-993-8550.

INDEPENDENCE UNIVERSITY, Salt Lake City, UT 84107

General Information Proprietary, coed, comprehensive institution. *Graduate housing:* On-campus housing not available.

GRADUATE UNITS

Program in Business Administration Offers business administration (MBA).

Program in Business Administration in Health Care *Degree program information:* Part-time and evening/weekend programs available. Postbaccalaureate distance learning degree programs offered (no on-campus study). Offers health care administration (MBA).

Program in Health Care Administration *Degree program information:* Part-time and evening/weekend programs available. Postbaccalaureate distance learning degree programs offered (no on-campus study). Offers health care administration (MSHCA).

Program in Health Services *Degree program information:* Part-time and evening/weekend programs available. Postbaccalaureate distance learning degree programs offered (no on-campus study). Offers community health (MSHS); wellness promotion (MSHS).

Program in Nursing Offers community health (MSN); gerontology (MSN); nursing administration (MSN); wellness promotion (MSN).

Program in Public Health *Degree program information:* Part-time and evening/weekend programs available. Postbaccalaureate distance learning degree programs offered (no on-campus study). Offers public health (MPH).

INDIANA STATE UNIVERSITY, Terre Haute, IN 47809

General Information State-supported, coed, university. CGS member. *Enrollment:* 11,494 graduate, professional, and undergraduate students; 774 full-time matriculated graduate/professional students (474 women), 1,284 part-time matriculated graduate/professional students (800 women). *Graduate faculty:* 272 full-time (90 women), 87 part-time/adjunct (33 women). *Graduate housing:* Rooms and/or apartments available on a first-come, first-served basis to single and married students. *Student services:* Campus employment opportunities, campus safety program, career counseling, child daycare facilities, exercise/wellness program, free psychological counseling, grant writing training, international student services, low-cost health insurance, services for students with disabilities, teacher training, writing training. *Library facilities:* Cunningham Memorial Library plus 2 others. *Online resources:* library catalog, web page, access to other libraries' catalogs. *Research affiliation:* Indiana Space Grant (remote sensing), Indiana University School of Medicine (cancer and Lupus research), Cranberry Lake Biological Station (psychosocial impacts of cancer), Boston Museum of Science (remote sensing, biology), Great Lakes Northern Forest Cooperative Ecosystem Study Unit (biology, life sciences).

Computer facilities: Computer purchase and lease plans are available. 395 computers available on campus for general student use. A campuswide network can be accessed from student residence rooms and from off campus. Online class registration is available. *Web address:* http://www.indstate.edu/.

General Application Contact: Dr. Jay Gatrell, Dean, 800-444-GRAD, Fax: 812-237-8060, E-mail: jay.gatrell@indstate.edu.

GRADUATE UNITS

College of Graduate and Professional Studies *Degree program information:* Part-time and evening/weekend programs available. Postbaccalaureate distance learning degree programs offered (no on-campus study). Offers technology management (PhD). Electronic applications accepted.

College of Arts and Sciences *Degree program information:* Part-time and evening/weekend programs available. Offers arts and sciences (MA, MFA, MM, MPA, MS, PhD, Psy D, CAS); ceramics (MA, MFA); clinical psychology (Psy D); communication studies (MA, MS); criminology and criminal justice (MA, MS); dietetics (MS); drawing (MA, MFA); ecology (PhD); English teaching (MA); family and consumer sciences education (MS); general psychology (MA, MS); geography (MA); geology (MS); graphic design (MA, MFA); history (MA, MS); inter-area option (MS); life sciences (MS); linguistics/teaching English as a second language (MA); literature (MA); math teaching (MA, MS); mathematics and computer science (MA); mathematics and computer sciences (MS); microbiology (PhD); music performance (MM); painting (MA, MFA); photography (MA, MFA); physical geography (PhD); physiology (PhD); political science (MA, MS); printmaking (MA, MFA); public administration (MPA); radio, television and film (MA, MS); science education (MS); sculpture (MA, MFA); TESL/TEFL (CAS). Electronic applications accepted.

College of Business *Degree program information:* Part-time and evening/weekend programs available. Offers business (MBA). Electronic applications accepted.

College of Education *Degree program information:* Part-time and evening/weekend programs available. Offers counseling psychology (MS, PhD); counselor education (PhD); curriculum and instruction (M Ed, PhD); early childhood education (M Ed); education (M Ed, MS, PhD, Ed S); educational administration (PhD); educational technology (MS); elementary education (M Ed); leadership in higher education (PhD); mental health counseling (MS); school administration (Ed S); school administration and supervision (M Ed); school counseling (M Ed); school psychology (PhD, Ed S); student affairs in higher education (MS). Electronic applications accepted.

College of Nursing, Health and Human Services Offers adult fitness (MA, MS); athletic training (MS); coaching (MA, MS); community health promotion (MA, MS); exercise science (MA, MS); health and safety education (MA, MS); nursing (MS); nursing, health and human services (MA, MS); occupational safety management (MA, MS); recreation and sport management (MA, MS). Electronic applications accepted.

Indiana State University (continued)

College of Technology Offers career and technical education (MS); electronics and computer technology (MS); human resource development (MS); industrial technology (MS); technology (MS); technology education (MS). Electronic applications accepted.

See Display below and Close-Up on page 953.

INDIANA TECH, Fort Wayne, IN 46803-1297

General Information Independent, coed, comprehensive institution. *Graduate housing:* On-campus housing not available.

GRADUATE UNITS

Program in Business Administration *Degree program information:* Part-time and evening/weekend programs available. Postbaccalaureate distance learning degree programs offered (no on-campus study). Offers accounting (MBA); health care administration (MBA); human resources (MBA); management (MBA); marketing (MBA). Electronic applications accepted.

Program in Global Leadership *Degree program information:* Part-time and evening/weekend programs available. Postbaccalaureate distance learning degree programs offered (minimal on-campus study). Offers global leadership (PhD). Electronic applications accepted.

Program in Management *Degree program information:* Part-time and evening/weekend programs available. Offers management (MSM). Electronic applications accepted.

Program in Organizational Leadership *Degree program information:* Part-time and evening/weekend programs available. Postbaccalaureate distance learning degree programs offered (minimal on-campus study). Offers organizational leadership (MS). Electronic applications accepted.

Program in Police Administration *Degree program information:* Part-time and evening/weekend programs available. Postbaccalaureate distance learning degree programs offered (no on-campus study). Offers police administration (MS). Electronic applications accepted.

Program in Science *Degree program information:* Part-time and evening/weekend programs available. Offers science (MSE). Electronic applications accepted.

INDIANA UNIVERSITY BLOOMINGTON, Bloomington, IN 47405-7000

General Information State-supported, coed, university. CGS member. *Enrollment:* 42,464 graduate, professional, and undergraduate students; 8,280 full-time matriculated graduate/professional students (4,041 women), 1,341 part-time matriculated graduate/professional students (626 women). *Graduate faculty:* 1,080 full-time (328 women), 4 part-time/adjunct (2 women). *Graduate housing:* Rooms and/or apartments available to single and married students. *Student services:* Campus employment opportunities, campus safety program, career counseling, child daycare facilities, exercise/wellness program, free psychological counseling, international student services, low-cost health insurance, multicultural affairs office, services for students with disabilities, writing training. *Library facilities:* Indiana University Library plus 27 others. *Online resources:* library catalog, web page, access to other libraries' catalogs. *Collection:* 7.8 million titles.

Computer facilities: A campuswide network can be accessed from student residence rooms and from off campus. Online class registration, various software packages are available. *Web address:* http://www.iub.edu/.

General Application Contact: Information Contact, 812-855-0661, Fax: 812-855-5102, E-mail: iuadmit@indiana.edu.

GRADUATE UNITS

Jacobs School of Music Students: 715 full-time (363 women), 184 part-time (94 women); includes 17 Black or African American, non-Hispanic/Latino; 2 American Indian or Alaska Native, non-Hispanic/Latino; 58 Asian, non-Hispanic/Latino; 22 Hispanic/Latino; 9 Two or more races, non-Hispanic/Latino, 237 international. Average age 28. 1,353 applicants, 28% accepted, 240 enrolled. *Faculty:* 139 full-time (35 women), 11 part-time/adjunct (3 women). Expenses: Contact institution. *Financial support:* In 2010–11, 225 students received support, including 6 fellowships with full and partial tuition reimbursements available (averaging $17,000 per year), 85 teaching assistantships with full tuition reimbursements available (averaging $6,000 per year); research assistantships with tuition reimbursements available, Federal Work-Study, institutionally sponsored loans, scholarships/grants, health care benefits, tuition waivers (full and partial), and unspecified assistantships also available. Support available to part-time students. Financial award application deadline: 3/1; financial award applicants required to submit FAFSA. In 2010, 134 master's, 36 doctorates, 59 other advanced degrees awarded. Offers church music (DM); music (MA, MM, MM/MLS, MME, MS, DM, DME, PhD, AD, Performance Diploma, Spec); music literature and performance (DM); performance (MM); performance and church music (MM). *Application deadline:* For fall admission, 12/1 for domestic and international students; for spring admission, 9/1 for domestic and international students. Applications are processed on a rolling basis. *Application fee:* $135 ($145 for international students). Electronic applications accepted. *Application Contact:* Music Admissions, 812-855-7998, Fax: 812-856-6086, E-mail: musicadm@indiana.edu. *Dean,* Gwyn Richards, 812-855-2435, E-mail: jln@indiana.edu.

Kelley School of Business Students: 1,401 full-time (376 women), 452 part-time (101 women); includes 323 minority (61 Black or African American, non-Hispanic/Latino; 1 American Indian or Alaska Native, non-Hispanic/Latino; 200 Asian, non-Hispanic/Latino; 45 Hispanic/Latino; 1 Native Hawaiian or other Pacific Islander, non-Hispanic/Latino; 15 Two or more races, non-Hispanic/Latino), 358 international. Average age 31. 2,746 applicants, 43% accepted, 763 enrolled. *Faculty:* 71 full-time (10 women). Expenses: Contact institution. *Financial support:* Fellowships with full and partial tuition reimbursements, research assistantships, teaching assistantships, career-related internships or fieldwork, Federal Work-Study, institutionally sponsored loans, tuition waivers (full and partial), and unspecified assistantships available. Support available to part-time students. Financial award application deadline: 3/1; financial award applicants required to submit FAFSA. In 2010, 960 master's, 6 doctorates awarded. Offers business (MBA, MPA, MS, DBA, PhD). PhD offered through University Graduate School. *Application deadline:* For fall admission, 1/15 priority date for domestic students, 12/1 priority date for international students; for winter admission, 3/1 priority date for domestic students; for spring admission, 4/15 for domestic students, 9/1 for international students. *Application fee:* $55 ($65 for international students). Electronic applications accepted. *Application Contact:* Director of Admissions and Financial Aid, 812-855-8006, Fax: 812-855-9039. *Dean,* Daniel Smith, 812-855-8100, Fax: 812-855-8679, E-mail: business@indiana.edu.

Maurer School of Law Students: 725 full-time (298 women), 37 part-time (13 women); includes 49 Black or African American, non-Hispanic/Latino; 25 Asian, non-Hispanic/Latino; 32 Hispanic/Latino; 5 Two or more races, non-Hispanic/Latino, 129 international. Average age 26. 1,726 applicants, 49% accepted, 248 enrolled. *Faculty:* 72 full-time (28 women), 14 part-time/adjunct (4 women). Expenses: Contact institution. *Financial support:* In 2010–11, 301 students received support, including 278 fellowships (averaging $16,000 per year), 1 research assistantship (averaging $15,217 per year), 2 teaching assistantships (averaging $14,000 per year); career-related internships or fieldwork, Federal Work-Study, institutionally sponsored loans, scholarships/grants, health care benefits, and unspecified assistantships also available. Financial award application deadline: 3/1; financial award applicants required to submit FAFSA. In 2010, 185 first professional degrees, 44 master's, 10 doctorates, 1 other advanced degree awarded. Offers comparative law (MCL); juridical science (SJD); law (JD, LL M); law and social sciences (PhD); legal studies (Certificate). PhD offered through University Graduate School. *Application deadline:* For fall admission, 3/1 priority date for domestic and international students. Applications are processed on a rolling basis. *Application fee:* $55 ($65 for international students). Electronic applications accepted. *Application Contact:* Kelly M. Compton, Director of Admissions, 812-855-2704, Fax: 812-855-0555, E-mail: kmcompto@indiana.edu. *Dean,* Lauren K. Robel, 812-855-8885, Fax: 812-855-7057, E-mail: lrobel@indiana.edu.

School of Education Expenses: Contact institution. *Financial support:* Fellowships with full and partial tuition reimbursements, research assistantships with tuition reimbursements, teaching assistantships with tuition reimbursements, Federal Work-Study, scholarships/grants, tuition waivers (full and partial), and unspecified assistantships available. Financial award application deadline: 3/1. *Degree program information:* Part-time programs available. Postbaccalaureate distance learning degree programs offered. Offers art education (MS, Ed D, PhD); counseling (MS, PhD, Ed S); counselor education (MS, Ed S); curriculum studies (Ed D, PhD); education (MS, Ed D, PhD, Ed S); education policy studies (PhD); educational leadership (MS, Ed D, Ed S); educational psychology (MS, PhD); elementary education (MS, Ed D, PhD, Ed S); higher education (MS, Ed D, PhD); history and philosophy of education (MS); history of education (PhD); inquiry methodology (PhD); instructional systems technology (MS, PhD); international and comparative education (MS, PhD); learning and developmental sciences (MS, PhD); literacy, culture, and language education (MS, Ed D, PhD, Ed S); mathematics education (MS, Ed D, PhD); philosophy of education (PhD); school psychology (PhD, Ed S); science education (MS, Ed D, PhD); secondary education (MS, Ed D, PhD); social studies education (MS, PhD); special education (PhD, Ed S); student affairs administration (MS). *Application deadline:* For fall admission, 1/15 priority date for domestic students, 12/1 priority date for international students; for spring admission, 11/1 priority date for domestic students, 9/1 priority date for international students. Applications are processed on a rolling basis. *Application fee:* $55 ($65 for international students). Electronic applications accepted. *Application Contact:* Elizabeth Tilghman, Admissions Coordinator, 812-856-8552, Fax: 812-856-8505, E-mail: etilghma@indiana.edu. *Dean,* Dr. Gerardo Gonzalez, 812-856-8001, Fax: 812-856-8088, E-mail: gonzalez@indiana.edu.

School of Health, Physical Education and Recreation Students: 348 full-time (204 women), 84 part-time (49 women); includes 51 Black or African American, non-Hispanic/Latino; 3 American Indian or Alaska Native, non-Hispanic/Latino; 4 Asian, non-Hispanic/Latino; 14 Hispanic/Latino; 6 Two or more races, non-Hispanic/Latino, 76 international. Average age 29. 390 applicants, 68% accepted, 153 enrolled. *Faculty:* 67 full-time (29 women), 2 part-time/adjunct (both women). Expenses: Contact institution. *Financial support:* In 2010–11, 4 fellowships with full and partial tuition reimbursements (averaging $11,900 per year), 8 research assistantships with tuition reimbursements (averaging $12,188 per year), 72 teaching assistantships with tuition reimbursements (averaging $12,239 per year) were awarded; career-related internships or fieldwork, Federal Work-Study, institutionally sponsored loans, scholarships/grants, and tuition waivers (full and partial) also available. Support available to part-time students. Financial award application deadline: 3/1. In 2010, 120 master's, 17 doctorates awarded. *Degree program information:* Part-time programs available. Postbaccalaureate distance learning degree programs offered (no on-campus study). Offers adapted physical education (MS); applied sport science (MS); athletic administration/sport management (MS); athletic training (MS); biomechanics (MS); ergonomics (MS); exercise physiology (MS); fitness management (MS); health behavior (PhD); health promotion (MS); health, physical education and recreation (MPH, MS, PhD, Re Dir); human development/family studies (MS); human performance (PhD); leisure behavior (PhD); motor learning/control (MS); nutrition science (MS); outdoor recreation (MS); public health (MPH); recreation (Re Dir); recreation administration (MS); recreational sports administration (MS); safety management (MS); school and college health programs (MS); therapeutic recreation (MS); tourism management (MS). *Application deadline:* For fall admission, 3/1 for domestic students, 1/1 for international students; for spring admission, 11/1 for domestic students, 9/1 for international students. *Application fee:* $55 ($65 for international students). *Application Contact:* Dr. Robert Goodman, Dean, 812-855-1561, Fax: 812-855-4983, E-mail: rmg@indiana.edu. *Dean,* Dr. Robert Goodman, 812-855-1561, Fax: 812-855-4983, E-mail: rmg@indiana.edu.

School of Informatics and Computing Students: 372 full-time (88 women), 34 part-time (10 women); includes 7 Black or African American, non-Hispanic/Latino; 1 American Indian or Alaska Native, non-Hispanic/Latino; 10 Asian, non-Hispanic/Latino; 3 Hispanic/Latino; 3 Two or more races, non-Hispanic/Latino, 261 international. Average age 27. 746 applicants, 40% accepted, 131 enrolled. *Faculty:* 63 full-time (12 women). Expenses: Contact institution. *Financial support:* In 2010–11, fellowships with full and partial tuition reimbursements (averaging $20,000 per year), research assistantships (averaging $14,000 per year), teaching assistantships (averaging $13,000 per year) were awarded; Federal Work-Study, institutionally sponsored loans, scholarships/grants, health care benefits, tuition waivers (full and partial), and unspecified assistantships also available. Support available to part-time students. In 2010, 117 master's, 20 doctorates awarded. *Degree program information:* Part-time programs available. Postbaccalaureate distance learning degree programs offered (no on-campus study). Offers bioinformatics (MS); chemical informatics (MS); computer science (MS, PhD); health informatics (MS); human computer interaction (MS); informatics (PhD); laboratory informatics (MS); media arts and science (MS); music informatics (MS); security informatics (MS). PhD offered through University Graduate School. *Application deadline:* For fall admission, 1/15 for domestic students, 12/1 for international students. *Application fee:* $55 ($65 for international students). Electronic applications accepted. *Application Contact:* Rachel Lawmaster, Manager of Graduate Admissions and Graduate Studies, 812-856-3622, Fax: 812-856-3825, E-mail: raclee@indiana.edu. *Associate Dean for Graduate Studies,* Dr. David Leake, 812-855-9756, E-mail: leake@cs.indiana.edu.

School of Journalism Students: 62 full-time (37 women), 12 part-time (7 women); includes 2 Black or African American, non-Hispanic/Latino; 1 Asian, non-Hispanic/Latino; 1 Hispanic/Latino; 2 Two or more races, non-Hispanic/Latino, 33 international. Average age 30. 119 applicants, 57% accepted, 26 enrolled. *Faculty:* 11 full-time (5 women). Expenses: Contact institution. *Financial support:* Fellowships, research assistantships with full tuition reimbursements, teaching assistantships with partial tuition reimbursements, career-related internships or fieldwork, Federal Work-Study, institutionally sponsored loans, and tuition waivers (full) available. Financial award application deadline: 1/15. In 2010, 24 master's, 4 doctorates awarded. Offers journalism (MA, MAT); mass communication (PhD). *Application deadline:* For fall admission, 1/15 priority date for domestic students; for spring admission, 9/1 priority date for domestic students. Applications are processed on a rolling basis. *Application fee:* $55 ($65 for international students). *Application Contact:* Amy Reynolds, Associate Dean of Graduate Studies, 812-855-8111. *Dean,* Bradley Hamm, 812-855-9247.

School of Library and Information Science Average age 29. 343 applicants, 86% accepted, 120 enrolled. *Faculty:* 16 full-time (7 women). Expenses: Contact institution. *Financial support:* Fellowships with full and partial tuition reimbursements, research assistantships with full and partial tuition reimbursements, career-related internships or fieldwork, Federal Work-Study, institutionally sponsored loans, scholarships/grants, tuition waivers (partial), and unspecified assistantships available. Support available to part-time students. Financial award application deadline: 1/15. In 2010, 149 master's, 4 doctorates, 3 other advanced degrees awarded. *Degree program information:* Part-time programs available. Offers library and information science (MIS, MLS, PhD, Sp LIS). *Application deadline:* For fall admission, 5/15 priority date for domestic students, 12/1 priority date for international students; for spring admission, 10/15 priority date for domestic students, 9/1 priority date for international students. Applications are processed on a rolling basis. *Application fee:* $55 ($65 for international students). Electronic applications accepted. *Application Contact:* Rhonda Spencer, Director of Admissions, 812-855-2018, Fax: 812-855-6166, E-mail: slis@indiana.edu.

School of Optometry Students: 331 full-time (192 women); includes 13 Black or African American, non-Hispanic/Latino; 3 American Indian or Alaska Native, non-Hispanic/Latino; 25 Asian, non-Hispanic/Latino; 2 Hispanic/Latino; 4 Two or more races, non-Hispanic/Latino, 20 international. Average age 25. 394 applicants, 38% accepted, 81 enrolled. *Faculty:* 36 full-time (11 women), 7 part-time/adjunct (5 women). Expenses: Contact institution. *Financial support:* Fellowships with full tuition reimbursements, research assistantships with full tuition reimbursements, Federal Work-Study, institutionally sponsored loans, scholarships/grants, health care benefits, and research assistantships available. Support available to part-time students. Financial award application deadline: 12/1; financial award applicants required to submit FAFSA. In 2010, 69 first professional degrees, 2 master's, 4 doctorates awarded. Offers optometry (OD, MS, PhD). *Application deadline:* For fall admission, 1/15 for domestic students; for winter admission, 2/1 for domestic and international students; for spring admission, 9/1 for domestic students. Applications are processed on a rolling basis. *Application fee:* $55 ($65 for international students). Electronic applications accepted. *Application Contact:* Patricia Reyes, Associate Director of Student Services, 812-855-1292, Fax: 812-855-4389, E-mail: patreyes@indiana.edu. *Interim Dean,* Dr. P. Sarita Soni, 812-855-4440, Fax: 812-855-8664, E-mail: sonip@indiana.edu.

School of Public and Environmental Affairs Students: 553 full-time (310 women). 729 applicants, 247 enrolled. *Faculty:* 54 full-time, 56 part-time/adjunct. Expenses: Contact institution. *Financial support:* Fellowships with partial tuition reimbursements, research assistantships with partial tuition reimbursements, teaching assistantships with partial tuition reimbursements, Federal Work-Study, scholarships/grants, health care benefits, tuition waivers (partial), unspecified assistantships, and Service Corps Program available. Financial award application deadline: 2/1; financial award applicants required to submit FAFSA. *Degree program information:* Part-time programs available. Offers applied ecology (MSES); arts administration (MAAA); comparative and international affairs (MPA); economic development (MPA); energy (MPA, MSES); environmental chemistry, toxicology, and risk assessment (MSES); environmental policy (PhD); environmental policy and natural resource management (MPA); environmental science (PhD); information systems (MPA); local government management (MPA); nonprofit management (MPA, Certificate); policy analysis (MPA); public and environmental affairs (MAAA, MPA, MSES, PhD, Certificate, MPA/MA); public finance (PhD); public financial administration (MPA); public management (MPA, PhD); public policy analysis (PhD); specialized environmental science (MSES); specialized public affairs (MPA); sustainability and sustainable development (MPA); water resources (MSES). *Application deadline:* For fall admission, 5/1 priority date for domestic students, 12/1 priority date for international students. Applications are processed on a rolling basis. *Application fee:* $55 ($65 for international students). Electronic applications accepted. *Application Contact:* Audrey Whittaker, Admissions Assistant, 812-855-2840, E-mail: speaapps@indiana.edu. *Director of Graduate Student Services,* Jennifer Forney, 812-855-9485, Fax: 812-856-3665, E-mail: speampo@indiana.edu.

University Graduate School Students: 4,107 full-time (2,173 women), 124 part-time (61 women); includes 530 minority (171 Black or African American, non-Hispanic/Latino; 22 American Indian or Alaska Native, non-Hispanic/Latino; 114 Asian, non-Hispanic/Latino; 169 Hispanic/Latino; 2 Native Hawaiian or other Pacific Islander, non-Hispanic/Latino; 52 Two or more races, non-Hispanic/Latino), 1,149 international. Average age 30. 7,338 applicants, 24% accepted, 819 enrolled. Expenses: Contact institution. *Financial support:* Fellowships with full and partial tuition reimbursements, research assistantships, teaching assistantships, career-related internships or fieldwork, Federal Work-Study, institutionally sponsored loans, and tuition waivers (full and partial) available. Support available to part-time students. In 2010, 429 master's, 387 doctorates, 3 other advanced degrees awarded. *Degree program information:* Part-time programs available. *Application deadline:* For fall admission, 1/15 priority date for domestic students, 12/15 for international students; for spring admission, 9/1 for domestic and international students. *Application fee:* $55 ($65 for international students). Electronic applications accepted. *Application Contact:* Graduate School, 812-855-8853, E-mail: grdschl@indiana.edu. *Dean,* Dr. James Wimbush, 812-855-4848.

College of Arts and Sciences Students: 2,841 full-time (1,493 women), 112 part-time (54 women); includes 348 minority (100 Black or African American, non-Hispanic/Latino; 17 American Indian or Alaska Native, non-Hispanic/Latino; 75 Asian, non-Hispanic/Latino; 117 Hispanic/Latino; 2 Native Hawaiian or other Pacific Islander, non-Hispanic/Latino; 37 Two or more races, non-Hispanic/Latino), 689 international. Average age 30. 5,640 applicants, 24% accepted, 590 enrolled. *Faculty:* 620 full-time (184 women). Expenses: Contact institution. *Financial support:* Fellowships with full and partial tuition reimbursements, research assistantships, teaching assistantships, career-related internships or fieldwork, Federal Work-Study, institutionally sponsored loans, and tuition waivers (full and partial) available. Support available to part-time students. In 2010, 369 master's, 269 doctorates, 3 other advanced degrees awarded. *Degree program information:* Part-time programs available. Offers acting (MFA); African American and African diaspora studies (MA); African languages and linguistics (PhD); African studies (MA); analytical chemistry (PhD); anthropology (MA, PhD); applied mathematics-numerical analysis (MA, PhD); arts and sciences (MA, MAT, MFA, MS, Au D, PhD, Certificate); astronomy (MA, PhD); astrophysics (PhD); audiology (Au D); auditory sciences (PhD); biochemistry (PhD); biogeochemistry (MS, PhD); biology and behavior (PhD); biology teaching (MAT); biotechnology (MA); Central Eurasian studies (MA, PhD); chemical biology chemistry (PhD); chemistry (MAT); Chinese (MA, PhD); Chinese language pedagogy (MA); classical studies (MA, MAT, PhD); clinical science (PhD); cognitive psychology (PhD); cognitive science (PhD); comparative literature (MA, MAT, PhD); composition, literacy, and culture (PhD); computational linguistics (MA, PhD); creative writing (MA, MFA); criminal justice (MA, PhD); criminology (MA, PhD); cross-cultural perspectives of crime and justice (MA, PhD); design and technology (MFA); developmental psychology (PhD); directing (MFA); East Asian studies (MA); economic geology (MS, PhD); economics (MA, PhD); evolution, ecology, and behavior (MA, PhD); film and media studies (PhD); fine arts (MA, MFA, PhD); folklore (MA, PhD); French (MA, PhD); gender studies (PhD); genetics (PhD); geobiology (MS, PhD); geography (MA, MAT, MS, PhD); geophysics, structural geology and tectonics (MS, PhD); German philology and linguistics (PhD); German studies (MA, PhD); history (MA, MAT, PhD); history and philosophy of science (MA, PhD); history of art (MA, PhD); hydrogeology (MS, PhD); inorganic chemistry (PhD); Italian (MA, PhD); Japanese (MA, PhD); Japanese language pedagogy (MA); language (MA); language sciences (PhD); Latin American and Caribbean studies (MA); law and society (MA, PhD); linguistics (MA, PhD); literature (MA, PhD); mass communications (PhD); materials chemistry (PhD); mathematics education (MAT); medieval German studies (PhD); microbiology (MA, PhD); mineralogy (MS, PhD); molecular, cellular, and developmental biology (PhD); Near Eastern languages and cultures (MA, PhD); neuroscience (PhD); organic chemistry (PhD); performance and ethnography (PhD); philosophy (MA, PhD); physical chemistry (PhD); physics (MAT, MS, PhD); plant sciences (MA, PhD); playwriting (MFA); political science (MA, PhD); Portuguese (MA, PhD); probability-statistics (MA, PhD); psychological and brain sciences (MA); psychology and the law (MA); pure mathematics (MA); religious studies (MA, PhD); rhetoric and public culture (PhD); Russian and East European studies (MA, Certificate); second language studies (MA, PhD); Slavic languages and literatures (MA, MAT, PhD); social psychology (PhD); sociology (MA, PhD); Spanish (MA, PhD); speech and hearing sciences (MA, PhD); speech and voice sciences (PhD); speech-language pathology (MA); stratigraphy and sedimentology (MS, PhD); teaching German (MAT); telecommunications (MA, MS, PhD); TESOL and applied linguistics (MA); theatre and drama (MAT); theatre history (MA, PhD); theory (MA, PhD); West European studies (MA); writing (MA); zoology (MA, PhD). *Application deadline:* For fall admission, 1/15 priority date for domestic students, 12/15 for international students; for spring admission, 9/1 for domestic and international students. *Application fee:* $55 (for international students). Electronic applications accepted. *Application Contact:* Mitchell Byler, Assistant Dean, 812-855-4871, E-mail: mbyler@indiana.edu. *Dean,* Dr. Bennett Bertenthal, 812-855-2392, E-mail: bbertent@indiana.edu.

INDIANA UNIVERSITY EAST, Richmond, IN 47374-1289

General Information State-supported, coed, comprehensive institution.

GRADUATE UNITS

School of Education Offers education (MS Ed).

School of Social Work Offers social work (MSW).

INDIANA UNIVERSITY KOKOMO, Kokomo, IN 46904-9003

General Information State-supported, coed, comprehensive institution. *Enrollment:* 3,109 graduate, professional, and undergraduate students; 28 full-time matriculated graduate/professional students (16 women), 82 part-time matriculated graduate/professional students (48 women). *Enrollment by degree level:* 90 master's, 20 other advanced degrees. *Graduate faculty:* 22 full-time (8 women). *Graduate housing:* On-campus housing not available. *Student services:* Career counseling, child daycare facilities, multicultural affairs office, services for students with disabilities, teacher training. *Library facilities:* Main library plus 1 other. *Collection:* 132,424 titles, 1,513 serial subscriptions.

Computer facilities: A campuswide network can be accessed. Online class registration is available. *Web address:* http://www.iuk.edu/.

General Application Contact: Admissions Office, 765-455-9357.

GRADUATE UNITS

Division of Education Students: 10 full-time (8 women), 10 part-time (8 women); includes 1 Black or African American, non-Hispanic/Latino. Average age 36. 4 applicants, 100% accepted,

Indiana University Kokomo (continued)

4 enrolled. *Faculty:* 1 full-time (0 women). Expenses: Contact institution. *Financial support:* In 2010–11, 2 fellowships (averaging $375 per year) were awarded; minority teacher scholarships also available. In 2010, 9 master's awarded. *Degree program information:* Part-time and evening/weekend programs available. Offers elementary education (MS Ed). *Application deadline:* For fall admission, 8/1 for domestic students; for spring admission, 12/1 for domestic students. Applications are processed on a rolling basis. *Application fee:* $40 ($50 for international students). *Application Contact:* Charlotte Miller, Coordinator, Educational/Student Resources, 765-455-9367, Fax: 765-455-9503, E-mail: cmiller@iuk.edu. *Dean,* D. Antonio Cantu, 765-455-9441, Fax: 765-455-9503.

School of Arts and Sciences Students: 20 part-time (13 women); includes 2 Hispanic/Latino. Average age 44. 3 applicants, 100% accepted, 3 enrolled. *Faculty:* 32 full-time (10 women). Expenses: Contact institution. In 2010, 3 master's awarded. Offers liberal studies (MALS). *Application deadline:* For fall admission, 4/15 priority date for domestic students; for spring admission, 10/15 priority date for domestic students. Applications are processed on a rolling basis. *Application fee:* $40 ($50 for international students). *Application Contact:* Dr. Susan Sciame-Giesecke, Dean, 765-455-9258, Fax: 765-455-9566, E-mail: sgieseck@iuk.edu. *Dean,* Dr. Susan Sciame-Giesecke, 765-455-9258, Fax: 765-455-9566, E-mail: sgieseck@iuk.edu.

School of Business Students: 7 full-time (2 women), 19 part-time (6 women); includes 4 minority (2 Black or African American, non-Hispanic/Latino; 1 Asian, non-Hispanic/Latino; 1 Two or more races, non-Hispanic/Latino). Average age 35. 13 applicants, 92% accepted, 10 enrolled. *Faculty:* 14 full-time (6 women). Expenses: Contact institution. *Financial support:* In 2010–11, 2 students received support, including 2 fellowships (averaging $500 per year); research assistantships, teaching assistantships, career-related internships or fieldwork and tuition waivers (partial) also available. In 2010, 24 master's awarded. *Degree program information:* Part-time and evening/weekend programs available. Offers business administration (MBA). *Application deadline:* For fall admission, 8/1 priority date for domestic and international students; for spring admission, 12/15 priority date for domestic and international students. Applications are processed on a rolling basis. *Application fee:* $40 ($50 for international students). *Application Contact:* Dr. Linda Ficht, Director of MBA Program, 765-455-9275, Fax: 765-455-9348, E-mail: lficht@iuk.edu. *Dean,* Dr. Niranjan Pati, 756-455-9275, Fax: 756-455-9348, E-mail: npati@iuk.edu.

School of Public and Environmental Affairs Students: 11 full-time (6 women), 33 part-time (21 women); includes 10 minority (6 Black or African American, non-Hispanic/Latino; 1 Asian, non-Hispanic/Latino; 2 Hispanic/Latino; 1 Two or more races, non-Hispanic/Latino), 1 international. Average age 39. 14 applicants, 100% accepted, 12 enrolled. Expenses: Contact institution. In 2010, 19 master's, 5 other advanced degrees awarded. Offers public management (MS, Graduate Certificate). *Application deadline:* For fall admission, 8/1 priority date for domestic students; for spring admission, 12/9 priority date for domestic students. *Application fee:* $40 ($50 for international students). *Application Contact:* Susan Wilson, Information Contact, 765-455-9330. *Assistant Dean,* Dr. Robert Dibie, 765-455-9417, Fax: 765-455-9537, E-mail: iuadmis@iuk.edu.

INDIANA UNIVERSITY NORTHWEST, Gary, IN 46408-1197

General Information State-supported, coed, comprehensive institution. *Enrollment:* 5,969 graduate, professional, and undergraduate students; 131 full-time matriculated graduate/professional students (75 women), 479 part-time matriculated graduate/professional students (343 women). *Graduate faculty:* 44 full-time (15 women). *Graduate housing:* On-campus housing not available. *Student services:* Campus employment opportunities, campus safety program, career counseling, child daycare facilities, free psychological counseling, international student services, low-cost health insurance. *Library facilities:* IUN Library. *Online resources:* library catalog, web page, access to other libraries' catalogs. *Collection:* 251,508 titles, 1,541 serial subscriptions.

Computer facilities: A campuswide network can be accessed from off campus. Online class registration is available. *Web address:* http://www.iun.edu/.

General Application Contact: Admissions Counselor, 219-980-6760, Fax: 219-980-7103.

GRADUATE UNITS

Division of Social Work Students: 21 full-time (17 women), 68 part-time (60 women); includes 37 minority (25 Black or African American, non-Hispanic/Latino; 1 American Indian or Alaska Native, non-Hispanic/Latino; 11 Hispanic/Latino). Average age 37. *Faculty:* 1 full-time (0 women). Expenses: Contact institution. *Financial support:* In 2010–11, 43 students received support. Career-related internships or fieldwork, Federal Work-Study, and tuition waivers (partial) available. Support available to part-time students. Financial award application deadline: 6/1; financial award applicants required to submit FAFSA. In 2010, 43 master's awarded. *Degree program information:* Part-time and evening/weekend programs available. Offers social work (MSW). *Application deadline:* For fall admission, 2/1 for domestic students. *Application fee:* $25. *Application Contact:* Dr. Frank Caucci, Director, 219-985-4286, Fax: 219-981-4264, E-mail: fcaucci@iun.edu. *Director,* Dr. Frank Caucci, 219-985-4286, Fax: 219-981-4264, E-mail: fcaucci@iun.edu.

School of Business and Economics Students: 54 full-time (15 women), 65 part-time (28 women); includes 43 minority (27 Black or African American, non-Hispanic/Latino; 7 Asian, non-Hispanic/Latino; 9 Hispanic/Latino). Average age 34. 64 applicants, 94% accepted, 55 enrolled. *Faculty:* 5 full-time (0 women). Expenses: Contact institution. *Financial support:* In 2010–11, 9 students received support. Federal Work-Study, institutionally sponsored loans, and unspecified assistantships available. Support available to part-time students. Financial award application deadline: 7/15. In 2010, 46 master's, 4 other advanced degrees awarded. *Degree program information:* Part-time and evening/weekend programs available. Offers accountancy (M Acc); accounting (Certificate); business administration (MBA). *Application deadline:* For fall admission, 7/15 priority date for domestic students; for spring admission, 11/15 for domestic students. Applications are processed on a rolling basis. *Application fee:* $25. *Application Contact:* John Gibson, Director of Graduate Program, 219-980-6635, Fax: 219-980-6916, E-mail: jagibson@iun.edu. *Dean,* Anna Rominger, 219-980-6636, Fax: 219-980-6916, E-mail: iunbiz@iun.edu.

School of Education Students: 46 full-time (36 women), 189 part-time (135 women); includes 107 minority (78 Black or African American, non-Hispanic/Latino; 27 Hispanic/Latino; 2 Two or more races, non-Hispanic/Latino). Average age 37. 61 applicants, 100% accepted, 54 enrolled. *Faculty:* 5 full-time (2 women). Expenses: Contact institution. In 2010, 63 master's awarded. *Degree program information:* Part-time and evening/weekend programs available. Offers elementary education (MS Ed); secondary education (MS Ed). *Application deadline:* For fall admission, 7/15 priority date for domestic students; for spring admission, 11/15 for domestic students. *Application fee:* $25. *Application Contact:* Dr. Stanley E. Wigle, Dean, 219-980-6510, Fax: 219-981-4208, E-mail: amsanche@iun.edu. *Dean,* Dr. Stanley E. Wigle, 219-980-6510, Fax: 219-981-4208, E-mail: amsanche@iun.edu.

School of Public and Environmental Affairs Students: 9 full-time (6 women), 127 part-time (96 women); includes 96 minority (81 Black or African American, non-Hispanic/Latino; 1 American Indian or Alaska Native, non-Hispanic/Latino; 2 Asian, non-Hispanic/Latino; 10 Hispanic/Latino; 2 Two or more races, non-Hispanic/Latino). Average age 38. 43 applicants, 95% accepted, 40 enrolled. *Faculty:* 5 full-time (3 women). Expenses: Contact institution. *Financial support:* Career-related internships or fieldwork, Federal Work-Study, and tuition waivers (partial) available. Support available to part-time students. Financial award application deadline: 3/1. In 2010, 37 master's, 24 other advanced degrees awarded. *Degree program information:* Part-time programs available. Offers criminal justice (MPA); environmental affairs (Graduate Certificate); health services administration (MPA); human services administration (MPA); nonprofit management (Graduate Certificate); public management (MPA, Graduate Certificate). *Application deadline:* For fall admission, 8/15 priority date for domestic students. Applications are processed on a rolling basis. *Application fee:* $25. *Application Contact:* Sandra Hall Smith, Secretary, 219-980-6695, Fax: 219-980-6737, E-mail: shsmith@iun.edu. *Interim Dean/Division Director,* George Assibey-Mensah, 219-980-6695, Fax: 219-980-6737.

INDIANA UNIVERSITY OF PENNSYLVANIA, Indiana, PA 15705-1087

General Information State-supported, coed, university. CGS member. *Enrollment:* 15,126 graduate, professional, and undergraduate students; 961 full-time matriculated graduate/professional students (535 women), 1,338 part-time matriculated graduate/professional students (850 women). *Enrollment by degree level:* 1,396 master's, 808 doctoral, 95 other advanced degrees. *Graduate faculty:* 294 full-time (128 women), 8 part-time/adjunct (5 women). *Graduate housing:* Room and/or apartments available on a first-come, first-served basis to single students; on-campus housing not available to married students. Housing application deadline: 4/15. *Student services:* Campus employment opportunities, campus safety program, career counseling, free psychological counseling, international student services, low-cost health insurance, multicultural affairs office, services for students with disabilities. *Library facilities:* Stapleton Library. *Online resources:* library catalog, web page, access to other libraries' catalogs. *Collection:* 875,888 titles, 23,425 serial subscriptions, 58,069 audiovisual materials.

Computer facilities: Computer purchase and lease plans are available. 1,200 computers available on campus for general student use. A campuswide network can be accessed from student residence rooms and from off campus. Online class registration is available. *Web address:* http://www.iup.edu/.

General Application Contact: Donna Griffith, Assistant Dean, 724-357-2222, Fax: 724-357-4862, E-mail: graduate-admissions@iup.edu.

GRADUATE UNITS

School of Graduate Studies and Research Students: 3 full-time (1 woman), 13 part-time (7 women); includes 2 minority (1 Hispanic/Latino; 1 Two or more races, non-Hispanic/Latino). Average age 32. 64 applicants, 81% accepted, 11 enrolled. *Faculty:* 295 full-time (126 women), 7 part-time/adjunct (5 women). Expenses: Contact institution. *Financial support:* Fellowships with full tuition reimbursements, research assistantships with full and partial tuition reimbursements, teaching assistantships with partial tuition reimbursements, career-related internships or fieldwork, Federal Work-Study, scholarships/grants, and tuition waivers (full) available. Support available to part-time students. Financial award application deadline: 3/15; financial award applicants required to submit FAFSA. In 2010, 698 master's, 101 doctorates, 20 other advanced degrees awarded. *Degree program information:* Part-time and evening/weekend programs available. *Application deadline:* Applications are processed on a rolling basis. *Application fee:* $40. *Application Contact:* Donna Griffith, Assistant Dean, 724-357-2222, Fax: 724-357-4862, E-mail: graduate-admissions@iup.edu. *Dean,* Dr. Timothy Mack, 724-357-2222, Fax: 724-357-4862, E-mail: timothy.mack@iup.edu.

College of Education and Educational Technology Students: 240 full-time (189 women), 533 part-time (378 women); includes 50 minority (40 Black or African American, non-Hispanic/Latino; 2 American Indian or Alaska Native, non-Hispanic/Latino; 4 Asian, non-Hispanic/Latino; 4 Hispanic/Latino), 19 international. Average age 33. 1,089 applicants, 43% accepted, 268 enrolled. *Faculty:* 63 full-time (37 women), 4 part-time/adjunct (3 women). Expenses: Contact institution. *Financial support:* In 2010–11, 14 fellowships (averaging $1,500 per year), 123 research assistantships (averaging $4,567 per year), 8 teaching assistantships with partial tuition reimbursements (averaging $19,221 per year) were awarded; career-related internships or fieldwork and Federal Work-Study also available. Support available to part-time students. Financial award application deadline: 3/15; financial award applicants required to submit FAFSA. In 2010, 228 master's, 35 doctorates, 15 other advanced degrees awarded. *Degree program information:* Part-time and evening/weekend programs available. Offers administration and leadership studies (D Ed); adult and community education (MA); adult education and communications technology (MA); communications media and instructional technology (PhD); communications technology (MA); community counseling (MA); counselor education (M Ed); curriculum and instruction (M Ed, D Ed); education (M Ed); education and educational technology (M Ed, MA, MS, D Ed, PhD, Certificate); education of exceptional persons (M Ed); educational psychology (M Ed, Certificate); elementary education (M Ed); literacy (M Ed); principal (Certificate); reading (M Ed); school psychology (D Ed, Certificate); speech-language pathology (MS); student affairs in higher education (MA). *Application deadline:* For fall admission, 7/1 for domestic students; for spring admission, 11/1 for domestic students. Applications are processed on a rolling basis. *Application fee:* $40. *Application Contact:* Dr. Edward Nardi, Associate Dean, 724-357-2480, Fax: 724-357-5595, E-mail: ewnardi@iup.edu. *Dean,* Dr. Mary Ann Rafoth, 724-357-2480, Fax: 724-357-5595.

College of Fine Arts Students: 20 full-time (7 women), 19 part-time (7 women); includes 4 minority (1 Black or African American, non-Hispanic/Latino; 2 Asian, non-Hispanic/Latino; 1 Hispanic/Latino), 4 international. Average age 30. 46 applicants, 30% accepted, 12 enrolled. *Faculty:* 19 full-time (4 women). Expenses: Contact institution. *Financial support:* In 2010–11, 16 research assistantships with full and partial tuition reimbursements (averaging $4,335 per year) were awarded; fellowships, career-related internships or fieldwork and Federal Work-Study also available. Support available to part-time students. Financial award application deadline: 3/15; financial award applicants required to submit FAFSA. In 2010, 17 master's awarded. *Degree program information:* Part-time programs available. Offers art (MA, MFA); fine arts (MA, MFA); music (MA); music education (MA); music history and literature (MA); music theory and composition (MA); performance (MA). *Application deadline:* For fall admission, 7/1 priority date for domestic students; for spring admission, 11/1 for domestic students. Applications are processed on a rolling basis. *Application fee:* $40. *Application Contact:* Dr. Douglas Bish, Associate Dean, 724-357-2397, E-mail: dbish@iup.edu. *Dean,* Michael Hood, 724-357-2397, E-mail: mhood@iup.edu.

College of Health and Human Services Students: 175 full-time (79 women), 277 part-time (166 women); includes 45 minority (30 Black or African American, non-Hispanic/Latino; 1 American Indian or Alaska Native, non-Hispanic/Latino; 5 Asian, non-Hispanic/Latino; 6 Hispanic/Latino; 3 Two or more races, non-Hispanic/Latino), 14 international. Average age 31. 474 applicants, 49% accepted, 188 enrolled. *Faculty:* 43 full-time (28 women), 3 part-time/adjunct (2 women). Expenses: Contact institution. *Financial support:* In 2010–11, 12 fellowships (averaging $750 per year), 58 research assistantships with full and partial tuition reimbursements (averaging $4,344 per year), 5 teaching assistantships (averaging $19,727 per year) were awarded; career-related internships or fieldwork and Federal Work-Study also available. Support available to part-time students. Financial award application deadline: 3/15; financial award applicants required to submit FAFSA. In 2010, 233 master's, 10 doctorates, 22 other advanced degrees awarded. *Degree program information:* Part-time and evening/weekend programs available. Offers aquatics administration and facilities management (MS); criminology (MA, PhD); exercise science (MS); food and nutrition (MS); health and human services (MA, MS, PhD, Certificate); health service administration (MS); industrial and labor relations (MA); nursing (MS, PhD); nursing administration (MS); nursing education (MS); safety sciences (MS); sport management (MS); sport science (MS). *Application deadline:* For fall admission, 7/1 priority date for domestic students; for spring admission, 11/1 for domestic students. Applications are processed on a rolling basis. *Application fee:* $40. *Application Contact:* Dr. Jacqueline Beck, Associate Dean, 724-357-2560, E-mail: jbeck@iup.edu. *Dean,* Dr. Carleen Zoni, 724-357-2555, E-mail: cczoni@iup.edu.

College of Humanities and Social Sciences Students: 223 full-time (124 women), 357 part-time (216 women); includes 47 minority (23 Black or African American, non-Hispanic/Latino; 3 American Indian or Alaska Native, non-Hispanic/Latino; 9 Asian, non-Hispanic/Latino; 8 Hispanic/Latino; 1 Native Hawaiian or other Pacific Islander, non-Hispanic/Latino; 3 Two or more races, non-Hispanic/Latino), 108 international. Average age 35. 545 applicants, 41% accepted, 140 enrolled. *Faculty:* 78 full-time (31 women), 1 part-time/adjunct (0 women). Expenses: Contact institution. *Financial support:* In 2010–11, 11 fellowships (averaging $1,182 per year), 80 research assistantships (averaging $5,211 per year), 21 teaching assistantships (averaging $12,679 per year) were awarded; career-related internships or fieldwork, Federal Work-Study, and tuition waivers (full) also available. Support available to part-time students. Financial award application deadline: 3/15; financial award applicants required to submit FAFSA. In 2010, 61 master's, 46 doctorates awarded. *Degree program information:* Part-time and evening/weekend programs available. Offers administration and leadership studies (PhD); applied archaeology (MA); composition and teaching English to speakers of other languages (MA, MAT, PhD); generalist (MA); geography

(MA, MS); history (MA); humanities and social sciences (MA, MAT, MS, PhD); literature (MA); literature and criticism (MA, PhD); public affairs (MA); rhetoric and linguistics (PhD); sociology (MA); teaching English (MAT); teaching English to speakers of other languages (MA). *Application deadline:* For fall admission, 7/1 priority date for domestic students; for spring admission, 11/1 for domestic students. Applications are processed on a rolling basis. *Application fee:* $40. *Application Contact:* Dr. Yaw Asamoah, Dean, 724-357-5764. *Dean,* Dr. Yaw Asamoah, 724-357-5764.

College of Natural Sciences and Mathematics Students: 106 full-time (63 women), 46 part-time (36 women); includes 11 minority (2 Black or African American, non-Hispanic/Latino; 6 Asian, non-Hispanic/Latino; 2 Hispanic/Latino; 1 Two or more races, non-Hispanic/Latino), 9 international. Average age 28. 249 applicants, 26% accepted, 47 enrolled. *Faculty:* 49 full-time (17 women). Expenses: Contact institution. *Financial support:* In 2010–11, 4 fellowships (averaging $2,000 per year), 69 research assistantships with full and partial tuition reimbursements (averaging $4,296 per year), 2 teaching assistantships (averaging $21,967 per year) were awarded; career-related internships or fieldwork and Federal Work-Study also available. Support available to part-time students. Financial award application deadline: 3/15; financial award applicants required to submit FAFSA. In 2010, 53 master's, 13 doctorates awarded. *Degree program information:* Part-time programs available. Offers applied mathematics (MS); biology (MS); chemistry (MA, MS); clinical psychology (Psy D); elementary and middle school mathematics education (M Ed); mathematics education (M Ed); natural sciences and mathematics (M Ed, MA, MS, Psy D); physics (MA, MS); psychology (MA); science for disaster response (MS). *Application deadline:* Applications are processed on a rolling basis. *Application fee:* $40. *Application Contact:* Dr. Jacqueline Gorman, Dean's Associate, 724-357-2609, E-mail: jgorman@iup.edu. *Interim Dean,* Dr. Gerald Buriok, 724-357-2609.

Eberly College of Business and Information Technology Students: 194 full-time (72 women), 92 part-time (39 women); includes 12 minority (4 Black or African American, non-Hispanic/Latino; 6 Asian, non-Hispanic/Latino; 1 Hispanic/Latino; 1 Two or more races, non-Hispanic/Latino), 172 international. Average age 27. 272 applicants, 62% accepted, 140 enrolled. *Faculty:* 38 full-time (9 women). Expenses: Contact institution. *Financial support:* In 2010–11, 51 research assistantships with full and partial tuition reimbursements (averaging $1,990 per year) were awarded; fellowships, career-related internships or fieldwork and Federal Work-Study also available. Support available to part-time students. Financial award application deadline: 3/15; financial award applicants required to submit FAFSA. In 2010, 205 master's awarded. *Degree program information:* Part-time and evening/weekend programs available. Offers business administration (MBA); business and information technology (M Ed, MBA); business/workforce development (M Ed); executive business administration (MBA). *Application deadline:* For fall admission, 7/1 priority date for domestic students; for spring admission, 11/1 for domestic students. Applications are processed on a rolling basis. *Application fee:* $40. *Application Contact:* Donna Griffith, Assistant Dean, 724-357-2222, Fax: 724-357-4862, E-mail: graduate-admissions@iup.edu. *Dean,* Dr. Robert Camp, 724-357-4783, E-mail: bobcamp@iup.edu.

See Display below and Close-Up on page 955.

INDIANA UNIVERSITY–PURDUE UNIVERSITY FORT WAYNE, Fort Wayne, IN 46805-1499

General Information State-supported, coed, comprehensive institution. CGS member. *Enrollment:* 14,192 graduate, professional, and undergraduate students; 132 full-time matriculated graduate/professional students (64 women), 567 part-time matriculated graduate/professional students (348 women). *Enrollment by degree level:* 689 master's, 10 other advanced degrees. *Graduate faculty:* 209 full-time (83 women), 3 part-time/adjunct (1 woman). Tuition, state resident: full-time $4824; part-time $268 per credit. Tuition, nonresident: full-time $11,625; part-time $646 per credit. *Required fees:* $555; $30.85 per credit. Tuition and fees vary according to course load. *Graduate housing:* Room and/or apartments available on a first-come, first-served basis to single students; on-campus housing not available to married students. Typical cost: $5900 per year. *Student services:* Campus employment opportunities, campus safety program, career counseling, exercise/wellness program, free psychological counseling, international student services, low-cost health insurance, multicultural affairs office, services for students with disabilities, teacher training, writing training. *Library facilities:* Helmke Library. *Online resources:* library catalog, web page, access to other libraries' catalogs. *Collection:* 433,644 titles, 23,130 serial subscriptions, 4,388 audiovisual materials. *Research affiliation:* Earthwatch Institute (biology), Church & Dwight Co. Inc. (health and human services), Northeast Indiana Foundation (education), University Park Research Center (biology), American Chemical Society (geosciences), Johnson & Johnson (health and human services).

Computer facilities: Computer purchase and lease plans are available. 642 computers available on campus for general student use. A campuswide network can be accessed from student residence rooms and from off campus. Online class registration, student academic records are available. *Web address:* http://www.ipfw.edu/.

General Application Contact: Susan Humphrey, Graduate Applications Coordinator, 260-481-6145, Fax: 260-481-6880, E-mail: ask@ipfw.edu.

GRADUATE UNITS

College of Arts and Sciences Students: 42 full-time (23 women), 147 part-time (86 women); includes 24 minority (11 Black or African American, non-Hispanic/Latino; 1 American Indian or Alaska Native, non-Hispanic/Latino; 4 Asian, non-Hispanic/Latino; 4 Hispanic/Latino; 4 Two or more races, non-Hispanic/Latino), 6 international. Average age 33. 90 applicants, 93% accepted, 69 enrolled. *Faculty:* 90 full-time (33 women), 1 (woman) part-time/adjunct. Expenses: Contact institution. *Financial support:* In 2010–11, 4 research assistantships with partial tuition reimbursements (averaging $12,740 per year), 46 teaching assistantships with partial tuition reimbursements (averaging $12,740 per year) were awarded; career-related internships or fieldwork, institutionally sponsored loans, and scholarships/grants also available. Support available to part-time students. Financial award application deadline: 3/1; financial award applicants required to submit FAFSA. In 2010, 37 master's, 7 other advanced degrees awarded. *Degree program information:* Part-time and evening/weekend programs available. Offers applied mathematics (MS); applied statistics (Certificate); arts and sciences (MA, MAT, MLS, MS, Certificate); biology (MS); English (MA, MAT); liberal studies (MLS); mathematics (MS); operations research (MS); professional communication (MA, MS); sociological practice (MA); speech and language pathology (MA); teaching (MAT); TENL (teaching English as a new language) (Certificate). *Application deadline:* Applications are processed on a rolling basis. *Application fee:* $55 ($60 for international students). *Application Contact:* Dr. Carl Drummond, Dean, 260-481-6160, Fax: 260-481-6985, E-mail: drummond@ipfw.edu. *Dean,* Dr. Carl Drummond, 260-481-6160, Fax: 260-481-6985, E-mail: drummond@ipfw.edu.

College of Engineering, Technology, and Computer Science Students: 21 full-time (8 women), 102 part-time (37 women); includes 14 minority (6 Black or African American, non-Hispanic/Latino; 5 Asian, non-Hispanic/Latino; 3 Hispanic/Latino), 12 international. Average age 31. 49 applicants, 92% accepted, 37 enrolled. *Faculty:* 45 full-time (12 women), 2 part-time/adjunct (0 women). Expenses: Contact institution. *Financial support:* In 2010–11, 6 research assistantships with partial tuition reimbursements (averaging $12,740 per year), 7 teaching assistantships with partial tuition reimbursements (averaging $12,740 per year) were awarded; career-related internships or fieldwork, scholarships/grants, and unspecified assistantships also available. Support available to part-time students. Financial award application deadline: 3/1; financial award applicants required to submit FAFSA. In 2010, 20 master's awarded. *Degree program information:* Part-time programs available. Offers applied computer science (MS); computer engineering (MS); electrical engineering (MS); engineering, technology, and computer science (MS, Certificate); facilities and construction management (MS); human resources (MS); industrial technology/manufacturing (MS); information technology/advanced computer applications (MS); leadership (MS); mechanical engineering (MS); organizational leadership and supervision (Certificate); systems engineering (MS). *Application deadline:* For fall admission, 7/15 for domestic students, 5/15 for international students; for spring admission, 12/1 for domestic students, 10/15 for international students. Applications are processed on a rolling basis. *Application fee:* $55 ($60 for international students).

Indiana University–Purdue University Fort Wayne (continued)

Electronic applications accepted. *Application Contact:* Dr. Max Yen, Dean, 260-481-6839, Fax: 260-481-5734, E-mail: yens@ipfw.edu. *Dean,* Dr. Max Yen, 260-481-6839, Fax: 260-481-5734, E-mail: yens@ipfw.edu.

College of Health and Human Services Students: 5 full-time (all women), 36 part-time (34 women); includes 2 minority (1 American Indian or Alaska Native, non-Hispanic/Latino; 1 Hispanic/Latino). Average age 38. 11 applicants, 91% accepted, 9 enrolled. *Faculty:* 8 full-time (all women). Expenses: Contact institution. *Financial support:* In 2010–11, 11 teaching assistantships with partial tuition reimbursements (averaging $12,740 per year) were awarded; scholarships/grants also available. Support available to part-time students. Financial award application deadline: 3/1; financial award applicants required to submit FAFSA. In 2010, 6 master's awarded. *Degree program information:* Part-time programs available. Offers adult nursing practice (MS); health and human services (MS, Certificate); nursing administration (MS, Certificate); nursing education (MS); women's health nursing practice (MS). *Application deadline:* For fall admission, 5/15 priority date for domestic students, 5/1 priority date for international students; for spring admission, 11/15 for domestic students. Applications are processed on a rolling basis. *Application fee:* $55 ($60 for international students). Electronic applications accepted. *Application Contact:* Dr. Carol Sternberger, Chair, 260-481-5798, Fax: 260-481-5767, E-mail: sternber@ipfw.edu. *Dean,* Dr. Linda M. Finke, 260-481-6564, Fax: 260-481-5767, E-mail: finkel@ipfw.edu.

Division of Public and Environmental Affairs Students: 14 full-time (9 women), 33 part-time (21 women); includes 5 minority (3 Black or African American, non-Hispanic/Latino; 1 Hispanic/Latino; 1 Two or more races, non-Hispanic/Latino), 4 international. Average age 31. 21 applicants, 95% accepted, 20 enrolled. *Faculty:* 9 full-time (3 women). Expenses: Contact institution. *Financial support:* In 2010–11, 1 teaching assistantship with partial tuition reimbursement (averaging $12,740 per year) was awarded; career-related internships or fieldwork and scholarships/grants also available. Support available to part-time students. Financial award application deadline: 3/1; financial award applicants required to submit FAFSA. In 2010, 13 master's, 2 Certificates awarded. *Degree program information:* Part-time programs available. Offers public affairs (MPA); public management (MPM, Certificate). *Application deadline:* Applications are processed on a rolling basis. *Application fee:* $55. *Application Contact:* Dr. Brian L. Fife, Director of Graduate Studies, 260-481-6961, Fax: 260-481-6346, E-mail: fifeb@ipfw.edu. *Chair,* Dr. Jane Grant, 260-481-6349, Fax: 260-481-6346, E-mail: grant@ipfw.edu.

Doermer School of Business Students: 43 full-time (12 women), 60 part-time (17 women); includes 12 minority (5 Black or African American, non-Hispanic/Latino; 4 Asian, non-Hispanic/Latino; 3 Hispanic/Latino), 6 international. Average age 32. 108 applicants, 66% accepted, 63 enrolled. *Faculty:* 32 full-time (13 women). Expenses: Contact institution. *Financial support:* In 2010–11, 9 teaching assistantships with partial tuition reimbursements (averaging $12,740 per year) were awarded; scholarships/grants and unspecified assistantships also available. Support available to part-time students. Financial award application deadline: 3/1; financial award applicants required to submit FAFSA. In 2010, 66 master's awarded. *Degree program information:* Part-time programs available. Offers business administration (MBA); business administration-accelerated (MBA). *Application deadline:* For fall admission, 7/15 for domestic students, 5/1 for international students; for spring admission, 11/15 for domestic students, 10/1 for international students. Applications are processed on a rolling basis. *Application fee:* $55. *Application Contact:* Dr. Lyman Lewis, MBA Program Administrator, 260-481-6474, Fax: 260-481-6879, E-mail: lewisl@ipfw.edu. *Dean,* Dr. Otto Chang, 260-481-0219, Fax: 260-481-6879, E-mail: chango@ipfw.edu.

School of Education Students: 7 full-time (all women), 189 part-time (153 women); includes 27 minority (13 Black or African American, non-Hispanic/Latino; 2 American Indian or Alaska Native, non-Hispanic/Latino; 11 Hispanic/Latino; 1 Two or more races, non-Hispanic/Latino), 1 international. Average age 34. 105 applicants, 70% accepted, 63 enrolled. *Faculty:* 25 full-time (14 women). Expenses: Contact institution. *Financial support:* In 2010–11, 2 teaching assistantships with partial tuition reimbursements (averaging $12,740 per year) were awarded; scholarships/grants also available. Support available to part-time students. Financial award application deadline: 3/1; financial award applicants required to submit FAFSA. In 2010, 83 master's awarded. *Degree program information:* Part-time programs available. Offers counselor education (MS Ed); education (MS Ed, Certificate); educational leadership (MS Ed); elementary education (MS Ed); marriage and family therapy (MS Ed); school counseling (MS Ed); secondary education (MS Ed); special education (MS Ed, Certificate). *Application deadline:* For fall admission, 4/1 priority date for domestic and international students. Applications are processed on a rolling basis. *Application fee:* $55. *Application Contact:* Vicky L. Schmidt, Graduate Recorder, 260-481-6450, Fax: 260-481-5408, E-mail: schmidt@ipfw.edu. *Dean,* Dr. Barry Kanpol, 260-481-6456, Fax: 260-481-5408, E-mail: kanpolb@ipfw.edu.

INDIANA UNIVERSITY–PURDUE UNIVERSITY INDIANAPOLIS, Indianapolis, IN 46202-2896

General Information State-supported, coed, university. *Enrollment:* 30,566 graduate, professional, and undergraduate students; 4,760 full-time matriculated graduate/professional students (2,495 women), 2,874 part-time matriculated graduate/professional students (1,826 women). *Enrollment by degree level:* 2,732 first professional, 4,107 master's, 535 doctoral, 260 other advanced degrees. *Graduate faculty:* 599 full-time (195 women), 2 part-time/adjunct (1 woman). *Graduate housing:* Rooms and/or apartments available on a first-come, first-served basis to single and married students. *Student services:* Campus employment opportunities, campus safety program, career counseling, child daycare facilities, exercise/wellness program, free psychological counseling, international student services, low-cost health insurance, multicultural affairs office, services for students with disabilities, writing training. *Library facilities:* University Library plus 4 others. *Online resources:* library catalog, web page, access to other libraries' catalogs. *Collection:* 1.5 million titles, 14,673 serial subscriptions.

Computer facilities: A campuswide network can be accessed from student residence rooms and from off campus. Online class registration is available. *Web address:* http://www.iupui.edu/.

General Application Contact: Dr. Sherry Queener, Director, Graduate Studies and Associate Dean, 317-274-1577, Fax: 317-278-2380.

GRADUATE UNITS

Herron School of Art and Design Students: 32 full-time (18 women), 14 part-time (all women); includes 5 minority (2 Asian, non-Hispanic/Latino; 3 Hispanic/Latino), 6 international. Average age 30. 57 applicants, 42% accepted, 11 enrolled. *Faculty:* 2 full-time (both women). Expenses: Contact institution. *Financial support:* Career-related internships or fieldwork, Federal Work-Study, institutionally sponsored loans, scholarships/grants, and tuition waivers (partial) available. Support available to part-time students. In 2010, 14 master's awarded. *Degree program information:* Part-time and evening/weekend programs available. Offers art education (MAE); furniture design (MFA); printmaking (MFA); sculpture (MFA); visual communication (MFA). *Application deadline:* For fall admission, 6/1 priority date for domestic students, 3/15 priority date for international students; for spring admission, 11/1 priority date for domestic students, 10/15 priority date for international students. Applications are processed on a rolling basis. *Application fee:* $55 ($65 for international students). Electronic applications accepted. *Application Contact:* Herron Student Services Office, 317-378-9400, E-mail: herrart@iupui.edu. *Dean,* Valerie Eickmeier, 317-278-9470, Fax: 317-278-9471, E-mail: herron@iupui.edu.

Indiana University School of Medicine Students: 1,669 full-time (814 women), 135 part-time (98 women); includes 359 minority (107 Black or African American, non-Hispanic/Latino; 6 American Indian or Alaska Native, non-Hispanic/Latino; 173 Asian, non-Hispanic/Latino; 57 Hispanic/Latino; 1 Native Hawaiian or other Pacific Islander, non-Hispanic/Latino; 15 Two or more races, non-Hispanic/Latino), 123 international. Average age 26. 1,699 applicants, 42% accepted, 545 enrolled. *Faculty:* 270 full-time (56 women). Expenses: Contact institution. *Financial support:* Fellowships with full and partial tuition reimbursements, research assistantships with full and partial tuition reimbursements, teaching assistantships with full tuition reimbursements, Federal Work-Study, institutionally sponsored loans, scholarships/grants, tuition waivers (full and partial), and stipends available. Support available to part-time students. In 2010, 255 first professional degrees, 84 master's, 37 doctorates awarded. Offers anatomy and cell biology (MS, PhD); behavioral health science (MPH); biochemistry and molecular biology (PhD); epidemiology (MPH); genetic counseling (MS); health policy and management (MPH); medical and molecular genetics (MS, PhD); medicine (MD, MPH, MS, PhD); microbiology and immunology (MS, PhD); pathology and laboratory medicine (MS, PhD); pharmacology (MS, PhD); toxicology (MS, PhD). *Application deadline:* For fall admission, 8/1 priority date for domestic students. Applications are processed on a rolling basis. *Application fee:* $55 ($65 for international students). *Application Contact:* Robert M. Stump, Director of Admissions, 317-274-3772, E-mail: inmedadm@iupui.edu. *Dean,* Dr. D. Craig Brater, 317-274-5000, Fax: 317-278-5211.

Kelley School of Business Students: 128 full-time (57 women), 409 part-time (148 women); includes 85 minority (29 Black or African American, non-Hispanic/Latino; 40 Asian, non-Hispanic/Latino; 13 Hispanic/Latino; 3 Two or more races, non-Hispanic/Latino), 83 international. Average age 30. 221 applicants, 76% accepted, 113 enrolled. *Faculty:* 20 full-time (4 women), 1 part-time/adjunct (0 women). Expenses: Contact institution. *Financial support:* In 2010–11, 3 fellowships (averaging $16,193 per year), 1 teaching assistantship (averaging $9,000 per year) were awarded; Federal Work-Study, institutionally sponsored loans, and scholarships/grants also available. Support available to part-time students. Financial award application deadline: 3/1; financial award applicants required to submit FAFSA. In 2010, 246 master's awarded. *Degree program information:* Part-time and evening/weekend programs available. Postbaccalaureate distance learning degree programs offered (minimal on-campus study). Offers accounting (MSA); business (MBA). *Application deadline:* For fall admission, 4/15 priority date for domestic and international students; for spring admission, 11/1 priority date for domestic and international students. *Application fee:* $55 ($65 for international students). Electronic applications accepted. *Application Contact:* Julie L. Moore, Recorder/Admission Coordinator, 317-274-4895, Fax: 317-274-2483, E-mail: mbaindy@iupui.edu. *Associate Dean, Indianapolis Programs,* Phil Cochran, 317-274-2481, Fax: 317-274-2483, E-mail: busugrad@iupui.edu.

School of Continuing Studies Students: 1 (woman) full-time, 61 part-time (48 women); includes 6 minority (1 Black or African American, non-Hispanic/Latino; 2 Asian, non-Hispanic/Latino; 2 Hispanic/Latino; 1 Two or more races, non-Hispanic/Latino). Average age 41. 20 applicants, 90% accepted, 18 enrolled. Expenses: Contact institution. In 2010, 18 master's awarded. Offers adult education (MS). *Application Contact:* Dr. Sherry Queener, Director, Graduate Studies and Associate Dean, 317-274-1577, Fax: 317-278-2380.

School of Dentistry Students: 467 full-time (188 women), 49 part-time (15 women); includes 66 minority (4 Black or African American, non-Hispanic/Latino; 44 Asian, non-Hispanic/Latino; 14 Hispanic/Latino; 2 Native Hawaiian or other Pacific Islander, non-Hispanic/Latino; 2 Two or more races, non-Hispanic/Latino), 52 international. Average age 28. 40 applicants, 5% accepted, 2 enrolled. *Faculty:* 96 full-time (28 women). Expenses: Contact institution. *Financial support:* In 2010–11, 43 students received support, including 25 fellowships (averaging $9,864 per year); research assistantships, teaching assistantships, Federal Work-Study, institutionally sponsored loans, and scholarships/grants also available. Financial award application deadline: 3/1; financial award applicants required to submit FAFSA. In 2010, 113 first professional degrees, 34 master's awarded. Offers dentistry (DDS, MS, MSD, PhD, Certificate). *Application fee:* $55 ($65 for international students). *Application Contact:* Robert Kasberg, Associate Dean for Student Affairs and Director of Admissions, 317-274-8173, Fax: 317-274-2419, E-mail: blerner@iupui.edu. *Dean,* Lawrence I. Goldblatt, 317-274-7461.

School of Education Students: 112 full-time (84 women), 368 part-time (292 women); includes 53 minority (29 Black or African American, non-Hispanic/Latino; 2 American Indian or Alaska Native, non-Hispanic/Latino; 7 Asian, non-Hispanic/Latino; 11 Hispanic/Latino; 4 Two or more races, non-Hispanic/Latino), 12 international. Average age 33. 109 applicants, 75% accepted, 58 enrolled. *Faculty:* 41 full-time, 80 part-time/adjunct. Expenses: Contact institution. *Financial support:* In 2010–11, 2 fellowships (averaging $780 per year), 18 teaching assistantships (averaging $9,756 per year) were awarded; research assistantships with partial tuition reimbursements, Federal Work-Study, institutionally sponsored loans, scholarships/grants, and tuition waivers (partial) also available. Support available to part-time students. In 2010, 171 master's awarded. *Degree program information:* Part-time and evening/weekend programs available. Offers computer education (Certificate); curriculum and instruction (MS); early childhood (MS); educational leadership (MS, Certificate); English as a second language (Certificate); higher education and student affairs (MS); kindergarten (Certificate); language education (MS); reading (Certificate); school counseling (MS); special education (MS, Certificate). *Application deadline:* For fall admission, 5/1 priority date for domestic students; for spring admission, 11/1 for domestic students. *Application fee:* $55 ($65 for international students). *Application Contact:* Sarah Brandenburg, Graduate Advisor, 317-274-6801, Fax: 317-274-6864, E-mail: edugrad@iupui.edu. *Interim Executive Associate Dean,* Dr. Chris Leland, 317-274-6801, Fax: 317-274-6864.

School of Engineering and Technology Students: 86 full-time (24 women), 159 part-time (39 women); includes 29 minority (16 Black or African American, non-Hispanic/Latino; 6 Asian, non-Hispanic/Latino; 5 Hispanic/Latino; 2 Two or more races, non-Hispanic/Latino), 85 international. Average age 31. 220 applicants, 60% accepted, 86 enrolled. *Faculty:* 2 full-time (1 woman). Expenses: Contact institution. *Financial support:* In 2010–11, 2 fellowships with tuition reimbursements (averaging $8,700 per year), 19 teaching assistantships (averaging $10,485 per year) were awarded; research assistantships with full and partial tuition reimbursements, Federal Work-Study, institutionally sponsored loans, and tuition waivers (full and partial) also available. Support available to part-time students. Financial award application deadline: 3/1. In 2010, 99 master's awarded. *Degree program information:* Part-time and evening/weekend programs available. Offers biomedical engineering (MS, MS Bm E, PhD); computer-aided mechanical engineering (Certificate); electrical and computer engineering (MS, MSECE, PhD); engineering (interdisciplinary) (MSE); engineering and technology (MS, MS Bm E, MSE, MSECE, MSME, PhD, Certificate); mechanical engineering (MSME, PhD). *Application deadline:* For fall admission, 5/1 for domestic students. *Application fee:* $55 ($65 for international students). *Application Contact:* Valerie Diemer, Graduate Program, 317-278-4960, Fax: 317-278-1671, E-mail: grad@engr.iupui.edu. *Dean,* Dr. H. Oner Yurtseven, 317-274-0802, Fax: 317-274-4567.

School of Music Students: 11 full-time (1 woman), 35 part-time (6 women); includes 5 minority (all Black or African American, non-Hispanic/Latino), 3 international. Average age 32. 31 applicants, 71% accepted, 16 enrolled. Expenses: Contact institution. *Financial support:* Teaching assistantships with full tuition reimbursements, Federal Work-Study, institutionally sponsored loans, and scholarships/grants available. Support available to part-time students. Financial award application deadline: 11/15. In 2010, 18 master's awarded. *Degree program information:* Part-time and evening/weekend programs available. Postbaccalaureate distance learning degree programs offered. Offers music technology (MS). *Application deadline:* For fall admission, 4/15 priority date for domestic students, 3/15 for international students; for spring admission, 11/15 priority date for domestic students, 11/15 for international students. Applications are processed on a rolling basis. *Application fee:* $55 ($65 for international students). *Application Contact:* G. David Peters, Director, 317-278-2594. *Director,* G. David Peters, 317-278-2594.

School of Health and Rehabilitation Sciences Students: 196 full-time (156 women), 8 part-time (7 women); includes 11 minority (4 Asian, non-Hispanic/Latino; 5 Hispanic/Latino; 2 Two or more races, non-Hispanic/Latino), 1 international. Average age 26. 233 applicants, 29% accepted, 61 enrolled. *Faculty:* 8 full-time (5 women). Expenses: Contact institution. *Financial support:* In 2010–11, 10 fellowships (averaging $2,485 per year), 1 teaching assistantship (averaging $3,600 per year) were awarded; research assistantships, Federal Work-Study, institutionally sponsored loans, and scholarships/grants also available. Support available to part-time students. Financial award applicants required to submit FAFSA. In 2010, 36 master's awarded. *Degree program information:* Part-time and evening/weekend programs available. Offers health sciences education (MS); nutrition and dietetics (MS); occupational therapy (MS); physical therapy (DPT). *Application deadline:* For fall admission, 1/15 priority date for domestic students; for spring admission, 10/15 for domestic students. *Application fee:* $55 ($65 for international students). *Application Contact:* Dr. Augustine Agho, Dean, 317-274-4704, E-mail: aagho@iupui.edu. *Dean,* Dr. Augustine Agho, 317-274-4704, E-mail: aagho@iupui.edu.

School of Informatics Students: 43 full-time (15 women), 83 part-time (29 women); includes 21 minority (13 Black or African American, non-Hispanic/Latino; 5 Asian, non-Hispanic/Latino; 3 Hispanic/Latino), 32 international. Average age 34. 87 applicants, 54% accepted, 26 enrolled. *Faculty:* 3 full-time (0 women). Expenses: Contact institution. *Financial support:* In 2010–11, 6 fellowships (averaging $17,447 per year), 13 teaching assistantships (averaging $9,392 per year) were awarded; career-related internships or fieldwork, Federal Work-Study, institutionally sponsored loans, and scholarships/grants also available. Support available to part-time students. In 2010, 39 master's awarded. *Degree program information:* Part-time and evening/weekend programs available. Offers informatics (PhD); media arts and science (MS). *Application deadline:* For fall admission, 3/15 for domestic students; for spring admission, 11/15 for domestic students. *Application fee:* $55 ($65 for international students). *Application Contact:* Dr. Sherry Queener, Director, Graduate Studies and Associate Dean, 317-274-1577, Fax: 317-278-2380. *Executive Associate Dean,* Darrell L. Bailey, 317-278-4636, Fax: 317-278-7769.

School of Law Students: 908 full-time (411 women), 64 part-time (24 women); includes 136 minority (57 Black or African American, non-Hispanic/Latino; 2 American Indian or Alaska Native, non-Hispanic/Latino; 47 Asian, non-Hispanic/Latino; 25 Hispanic/Latino; 5 Two or more races, non-Hispanic/Latino), 54 international. Average age 28. 1,851 applicants, 42% accepted, 298 enrolled. *Faculty:* 1 (woman) full-time. Expenses: Contact institution. *Financial support:* Fellowships, research assistantships with full and partial tuition reimbursements, Federal Work-Study, institutionally sponsored loans, and scholarships/grants also available. Support available to part-time students. Financial award applicants required to submit FAFSA. In 2010, 302 first professional degrees, 52 master's, 2 doctorates awarded. Offers law (JD, LL M, SJD). *Application fee:* $55 ($65 for international students). *Application Contact:* Patricia Kinney, Director of Admissions, 317-274-2459, Fax: 317-278-4780, E-mail: pkkinney@iupui.edu. *Interim Dean,* Susanah M. Mead, 317-274-8523.

School of Liberal Arts Students: 126 full-time (86 women), 164 part-time (116 women); includes 35 minority (19 Black or African American, non-Hispanic/Latino; 1 American Indian or Alaska Native, non-Hispanic/Latino; 6 Asian, non-Hispanic/Latino; 7 Hispanic/Latino; 2 Two or more races, non-Hispanic/Latino), 26 international. Average age 33. 227 applicants, 55% accepted, 92 enrolled. Expenses: Contact institution. In 2010, 126 master's, 7 other advanced degrees awarded. Offers American philosophy (Certificate); bioethics (Certificate); economics (MA); English (MA); family/gender studies (MA); geographic information systems (MS, Certificate); history (MA); liberal arts (MA, MS, XMA, PhD, Certificate); medical sociology (MA); museum studies (MS, Certificate); philanthropic studies (MA, XMA, PhD); philosophy (MA); political science (MA, Certificate); public history (MA); teaching English (MA); work/occupations (MA). *Application fee:* $55 ($65 for international students). *Application Contact:* Director of Research and Graduate Programs, 317-274-8305. *Dean, School of Liberal Arts,* Robert W. White, 317-274-8448.

School of Library and Information Science Students: 81 full-time (53 women), 211 part-time (161 women); includes 39 minority (23 Black or African American, non-Hispanic/Latino; 6 Asian, non-Hispanic/Latino; 7 Hispanic/Latino; 3 Two or more races, non-Hispanic/Latino). Average age 34. 67 applicants, 90% accepted, 40 enrolled. *Faculty:* 3 full-time (2 women). Expenses: Contact institution. *Financial support:* In 2010–11, 2 teaching assistantships (averaging $9,500 per year) were awarded; career-related internships or fieldwork, Federal Work-Study, institutionally sponsored loans, and scholarships/grants also available. Support available to part-time students. In 2010, 133 master's awarded. *Degree program information:* Part-time and evening/weekend programs available. Offers library and information science (MLS). *Application deadline:* For fall admission, 7/15 priority date for domestic students; for spring admission, 11/15 priority date for domestic students. Applications are processed on a rolling basis. *Application fee:* $55 ($65 for international students). *Application Contact:* Dr. Daniel Collison, Executive Associate Dean, 317-278-2375, Fax: 317-278-1807, E-mail: slisindy@iupui.edu. *Executive Associate Dean,* Dr. Daniel Collison, 317-278-2375, Fax: 317-278-1807, E-mail: slisindy@iupui.edu.

School of Nursing Students: 81 full-time (77 women), 352 part-time (336 women); includes 41 minority (28 Black or African American, non-Hispanic/Latino; 7 Asian, non-Hispanic/Latino; 5 Hispanic/Latino; 1 Native Hawaiian or other Pacific Islander, non-Hispanic/Latino), 5 international. Average age 38. 103 applicants, 79% accepted, 51 enrolled. *Faculty:* 85 full-time (82 women), 60 part-time/adjunct (all women). Expenses: Contact institution. *Financial support:* In 2010–11, 93 students received support, including 9 fellowships with full tuition reimbursements available (averaging $7,039 per year), 7 teaching assistantships with full tuition reimbursements available (averaging $5,300 per year); research assistantships with full tuition reimbursements available, Federal Work-Study, institutionally sponsored loans, scholarships/grants, and tuition waivers (full) also available. Support available to part-time students. Financial award application deadline: 5/1. In 2010, 124 master's, 6 doctorates awarded. *Degree program information:* Part-time programs available. Offers acute care nurse practitioner (MSN); adult health clinical nurse specialist (MSN); adult health nursing (MSN); adult nurse practitioner (MSN); adult psychiatric/mental health nursing (MSN); child psychiatric/mental health nursing (MSN); community health nursing (MSN); family nurse practitioner (MSN); neonatal nurse practitioner (MSN); nursing science (PhD); pediatric clinical nurse specialist (MSN); women's health nurse practitioner (MSN). *Application deadline:* For fall admission, 2/15 for domestic students; for spring admission, 9/15 for domestic students. *Application fee:* $55 ($65 for international students). *Application Contact:* Information Contact, 317-274-2806. *Associate Dean for Graduate Programs,* 317-274-2806, E-mail: nursing@iupui.edu.

School of Physical Education and Tourism Management Students: 15 full-time (3 women), 10 part-time (5 women); includes 1 Black or African American, non-Hispanic/Latino, 2 international. Average age 28. 20 applicants, 75% accepted, 11 enrolled. *Faculty:* 4 full-time (2 women). Expenses: Contact institution. *Financial support:* Career-related internships or fieldwork, Federal Work-Study, institutionally sponsored loans, and scholarships/grants available. Support available to part-time students. In 2010, 9 master's awarded. Offers physical education (MS). *Application fee:* $55 ($65 for international students). *Application Contact:* Dr. Sherry Queener, Director, Graduate Studies and Associate Dean, 317-274-1577, Fax: 317-278-2380.

School of Public and Environmental Affairs Students: 81 full-time (47 women), 205 part-time (142 women); includes 30 Black or African American, non-Hispanic/Latino; 6 Asian, non-Hispanic/Latino; 8 Hispanic/Latino, 9 international. Average age 31. 217 applicants, 73% accepted, 136 enrolled. *Faculty:* 23 full-time (7 women). Expenses: Contact institution. *Financial support:* In 2010–11, 1 fellowship with full tuition reimbursement (averaging $14,000 per year), 4 research assistantships with full tuition reimbursements (averaging $12,000 per year) were awarded; teaching assistantships, career-related internships or fieldwork, Federal Work-Study, institutionally sponsored loans, and scholarships/grants also available. Support available to part-time students. Financial award application deadline: 3/1; financial award applicants required to submit FAFSA. In 2010, 77 degrees awarded. *Degree program information:* Part-time and evening/weekend programs available. Postbaccalaureate distance learning degree programs offered (no on-campus study). Offers criminal justice and public safety (MSCJPS); public affairs (MPA); public management (Graduate Certificate). *Application deadline:* For fall admission, 5/15 priority date for domestic students; for spring admission, 2/15 priority date for domestic students. Applications are processed on a rolling basis. *Application fee:* $50 ($65 for international students). Electronic applications accepted. *Executive Associate Dean,* Dr. Terry L. Baumer, 317-274-2016, Fax: 317-274-5153.

School of Science Students: 266 full-time (118 women), 177 part-time (70 women); includes 62 minority (10 Black or African American, non-Hispanic/Latino; 3 American Indian or Alaska Native, non-Hispanic/Latino; 31 Asian, non-Hispanic/Latino; 14 Hispanic/Latino; 4 Two or more races, non-Hispanic/Latino), 124 international. Average age 28. 533 applicants, 50% accepted, 191 enrolled. *Faculty:* 56 full-time (7 women). Expenses: Contact institution. *Financial support:* Fellowships with full and partial tuition reimbursements, research assistantships with full and partial tuition reimbursements, teaching assistantships with full and partial tuition reimbursements, career-related internships or fieldwork, Federal Work-Study, institutionally sponsored loans, scholarships/grants, tuition waivers (full and partial), and cooperative positions available. Support available to part-time students. Financial award applicants required to submit FAFSA. In 2010, 149 master's, 4 doctorates awarded. *Degree program information:* Part-time and evening/weekend programs available. Offers applied earth sciences (PhD); applied mathematics (MS, PhD); applied statistics (MS); biology (MS, PhD); chemistry and chemical biology (MS, PhD); clinical rehabilitation psychology (MS); computer science (MS, PhD); geology (MS); industrial/organizational psychology (MS); math education (MS); mathematics (MS, PhD); physics (MS, PhD); psychobiology of addictions (MS, PhD); science (MS, PhD). *Application fee:* $55 ($65 for international students). Electronic applications accepted. *Application Contact:* Dr. Sherry Queener, Director, Graduate Studies and Associate Dean, 317-274-1577, Fax: 317-278-2380. *Dean,* William Bosran, 317-274-0625, Fax: 317-274-0628, E-mail: science@iupui.edu.

School of Social Work Students: 266 full-time (237 women), 244 part-time (210 women); includes 78 minority (58 Black or African American, non-Hispanic/Latino; 2 American Indian or Alaska Native, non-Hispanic/Latino; 3 Asian, non-Hispanic/Latino; 8 Hispanic/Latino; 1 Native Hawaiian or other Pacific Islander, non-Hispanic/Latino; 6 Two or more races, non-Hispanic/Latino). Average age 32. 222 applicants, 79% accepted, 114 enrolled. *Faculty:* 40 full-time. Expenses: Contact institution. *Financial support:* In 2010–11, 2 fellowships with full tuition reimbursements (averaging $8,313 per year), 10 teaching assistantships (averaging $8,847 per year) were awarded; research assistantships with partial tuition reimbursements, Federal Work-Study, institutionally sponsored loans, scholarships/grants, and tuition waivers (partial) also available. Support available to part-time students. Financial award applicants required to submit FAFSA. In 2010, 183 master's awarded. *Degree program information:* Part-time and evening/weekend programs available. Offers social work (MSW, PhD, Certificate). *Application fee:* $55 ($65 for international students). *Application Contact:* Susan Larimer, Information Contact for MSW, 317-274-6966, Fax: 317-274-8630. *Dean,* Dr. Margaret Adamek, 317-274-6730, Fax: 317-274-8630.

INDIANA UNIVERSITY SOUTH BEND, South Bend, IN 46634-7111

General Information State-supported, coed, comprehensive institution. *Enrollment:* 8,590 graduate, professional, and undergraduate students; 206 full-time matriculated graduate/professional students (127 women), 515 part-time matriculated graduate/professional students (356 women). *Graduate faculty:* 60 full-time (26 women). *Graduate housing:* On-campus housing not available. *Student services:* Campus employment opportunities, campus safety program, career counseling, child daycare facilities, exercise/wellness program, free psychological counseling, international student services, low-cost health insurance, services for students with disabilities. *Library facilities:* Franklin D. Schurz Library plus 1 other. *Collection:* 300,202 titles, 1,937 serial subscriptions.

Computer facilities: A campuswide network can be accessed. Online class registration is available. *Web address:* http://www.iusb.edu/.

General Application Contact: Admissions Counselor, 574-520-4839, Fax: 574-520-4834, E-mail: graduate@iusb.edu.

GRADUATE UNITS

College of Liberal Arts and Sciences Students: 34 full-time (18 women), 100 part-time (69 women); includes 23 minority (15 Black or African American, non-Hispanic/Latino; 2 American Indian or Alaska Native, non-Hispanic/Latino; 3 Asian, non-Hispanic/Latino; 2 Hispanic/Latino; 1 Two or more races, non-Hispanic/Latino), 16 international. Average age 37. 44 applicants, 84% accepted, 27 enrolled. *Faculty:* 79 full-time (33 women). Expenses: Contact institution. *Financial support:* In 2010–11, 5 students received support, including 5 teaching assistantships; Federal Work-Study also available. Support available to part-time students. In 2010, 21 master's awarded. *Degree program information:* Part-time and evening/weekend programs available. Offers applied mathematics and computer science (MS); applied psychology (MA); English (MA); liberal studies (MLS). *Application deadline:* For fall admission, 7/31 priority date for domestic students, 7/1 priority date for international students; for spring admission, 3/31 priority date for domestic students, 11/1 priority date for international students. Applications are processed on a rolling basis. *Application fee:* $50 ($60 for international students). *Application Contact:* Dr. Lynn R. Williams, Dean, 574-520-4322, Fax: 574-520-4528, E-mail: lwilliam@iusb.edu. *Dean,* Dr. Lynn R. Williams, 574-520-4322, Fax: 574-520-4528, E-mail: lwilliam@iusb.edu.

School of Business and Economics Students: 61 full-time (26 women), 100 part-time (32 women); includes 16 minority (6 Black or African American, non-Hispanic/Latino; 1 American Indian or Alaska Native, non-Hispanic/Latino; 4 Asian, non-Hispanic/Latino; 4 Hispanic/Latino; 1 Two or more races, non-Hispanic/Latino), 51 international. Average age 32. 76 applicants, 58% accepted, 28 enrolled. *Faculty:* 17 full-time (2 women), 3 part-time/adjunct (1 woman). Expenses: Contact institution. *Financial support:* In 2010–11, 1 fellowship (averaging $3,846 per year) was awarded; Federal Work-Study and institutionally sponsored loans also available. Support available to part-time students. Financial award applicants required to submit FAFSA. In 2010, 67 master's awarded. *Degree program information:* Part-time and evening/weekend programs available. Offers accounting (MSA); business administration (MBA); management of information technologies (MS). *Application deadline:* For fall admission, 7/1 priority date for domestic and international students; for spring admission, 11/1 priority date for domestic and international students. Applications are processed on a rolling basis. *Application fee:* $50 ($60 for international students). *Application Contact:* Sharon Peterson, Secretary, 574-520-4138, Fax: 574-520-4866, E-mail: speterso@iusb.edu. *Dean,* Robert H. Ducoffe, 574-520-4228, Fax: 574-520-4866.

School of Education Students: 73 full-time (52 women), 197 part-time (149 women); includes 36 minority (21 Black or African American, non-Hispanic/Latino; 3 American Indian or Alaska Native, non-Hispanic/Latino; 1 Asian, non-Hispanic/Latino; 9 Hispanic/Latino; 2 Two or more races, non-Hispanic/Latino), 6 international. Average age 36. 70 applicants, 73% accepted, 42 enrolled. *Faculty:* 21 full-time (11 women), 9 part-time/adjunct (3 women). Expenses: Contact institution. *Financial support:* Career-related internships or fieldwork available. Support available to part-time students. Financial award application deadline: 3/1; financial award applicants required to submit FAFSA. In 2010, 86 master's awarded. *Degree program information:* Part-time and evening/weekend programs available. Offers counseling and human services (MS Ed); elementary education (MS Ed); secondary education (MS Ed); special education (MS Ed). *Application deadline:* For fall admission, 7/1 for domestic students; for spring admission, 11/1 for domestic students. Applications are processed on a rolling basis. *Application fee:* $50 ($60 for international students). Electronic applications accepted. *Application Contact:* Dr. Todd Norris, Director of Education Student Services, 574-520-4845, E-mail: toanorri@iusb.edu. *Professor/Dean,* Dr. Michael Horvath, 574-520-4339, Fax: 574-520-4550.

School of Public and Environmental Affairs Students: 1 full-time (0 women), 9 part-time (7 women); includes 1 minority (Black or African American, non-Hispanic/Latino). Average age 43. 2 applicants, 0% accepted, 0 enrolled. *Faculty:* 4 full-time (1 woman). Expenses: Contact institution. *Financial support:* Fellowships, research assistantships, career-related internships or fieldwork, Federal Work-Study, and institutionally sponsored loans available. Support available to part-time students. Financial award application deadline: 3/1; financial award applicants required to submit FAFSA. In 2010, 11 master's awarded. *Degree program information:* Part-time and evening/weekend programs available. Offers health systems administration and policy (MPA); health systems management (Certificate); nonprofit management (Certificate); public and community services administration and policy (MPA); public management (Certificate); urban affairs (Certificate). *Application deadline:* For fall admission, 7/1 priority date for domestic students; for spring admission, 11/1 for domestic students. Applications are processed on a rolling basis. *Application fee:* $50 ($60 for international students). *Application Contact:* Leda M. Hall, Dean, 574-520-4803. *Dean,* Leda M. Hall, 574-520-4803.

School of Social Work Students: 23 full-time (21 women), 70 part-time (60 women); includes 16 minority (14 Black or African American, non-Hispanic/Latino; 1 Hispanic/Latino; 1 Two or more races, non-Hispanic/Latino). Average age 35. 2 applicants, 100% accepted, 2 enrolled. *Faculty:* 4 full-time (2 women). Expenses: Contact institution. *Financial support:* Career-related internships or fieldwork and Federal Work-Study available. Support available to part-time students. Financial award application deadline: 3/1; financial award applicants required to submit FAFSA. In 2010, 33 master's awarded. *Degree program information:* Part-time and evening/weekend programs available. Offers social work (MSW). *Application deadline:* For fall admission, 2/1 priority date for domestic students. *Application fee:* $50 ($60 for international students). *Application Contact:* Admissions Counselor, 574-520-4839, Fax:

Indiana University South Bend (continued)

574-520-4834, E-mail: graduate@iusb.edu. *Program Director*, Dr. Marilynne Ramsey, 574-520-4880, Fax: 574-520-4876, E-mail: mjramsey@iusb.edu.

School of the Arts Students: 14 full-time (10 women), 3 part-time (all women); includes 1 minority (Black or African American, non-Hispanic/Latino), 14 international. Average age 29. 13 applicants, 62% accepted, 6 enrolled. *Faculty:* 1 full-time (0 women). Expenses: Contact institution. *Financial support:* In 2010–11, 4 fellowships (averaging $2,855 per year), 1 teaching assistantship (averaging $1,320 per year) were awarded; Federal Work-Study also available. Support available to part-time students. Financial award application deadline: 3/1; financial award applicants required to submit FAFSA. In 2010, 3 master's awarded. *Degree program information:* Part-time programs available. Offers music (MM); studio teaching (MM). *Application deadline:* For fall admission, 7/1 priority date for domestic students; for spring admission, 11/1 for domestic students. Applications are processed on a rolling basis. *Application fee:* $50 ($60 for international students). *Application Contact:* Dr. Thomas Miller, Dean, 574-520-4301, Fax: 574-520-4317, E-mail: messelst@iusb.edu. *Dean*, Dr. Thomas Miller, 574-520-4301, Fax: 574-520-4317, E-mail: messelst@iusb.edu.

INDIANA UNIVERSITY SOUTHEAST, New Albany, IN 47150-6405

General Information State-supported, coed, comprehensive institution. *Enrollment:* 7,178 graduate, professional, and undergraduate students; 42 full-time matriculated graduate/professional students (27 women), 704 part-time matriculated graduate/professional students (468 women). *Enrollment by degree level:* 685 master's, 61 other advanced degrees. *Graduate faculty:* 63 full-time (22 women). *Graduate housing:* On-campus housing not available. *Student services:* Campus employment opportunities, campus safety program, career counseling, child daycare facilities, free psychological counseling, low-cost health insurance, multicultural affairs office, services for students with disabilities. *Library facilities:* Main library plus 1 other. *Collection:* 215,429 titles, 962 serial subscriptions.

Computer facilities: A campuswide network can be accessed from off campus. Online class registration is available. *Web address:* http://www.ius.edu/.

General Application Contact: Admissions Counselor, 812-941-2212, Fax: 812-941-2595, E-mail: admissions@ius.edu.

GRADUATE UNITS

Program in Liberal Studies Students: 2 full-time (0 women), 37 part-time (23 women); includes 5 Black or African American, non-Hispanic/Latino; 1 Two or more races, non-Hispanic/Latino. Average age 42. 11 applicants, 73% accepted, 6 enrolled. Expenses: Contact institution. In 2010, 4 master's awarded. Offers liberal studies (MLS). *Application Contact:* Debra Voyles, Administrative Assistant, 812-941-2604, E-mail: davoyles@ius.edu. *Director*, Dr. Sandra S. French, 812-941-2393, E-mail: sfrench@ius.edu.

School of Business Students: 11 full-time (4 women), 222 part-time (88 women); includes 19 minority (4 Black or African American, non-Hispanic/Latino; 8 Asian, non-Hispanic/Latino; 2 Hispanic/Latino; 3 Native Hawaiian or other Pacific Islander, non-Hispanic/Latino; 2 Two or more races, non-Hispanic/Latino), 4 international. Average age 31. 41 applicants, 100% accepted, 37 enrolled. *Faculty:* 11 full-time (2 women). Expenses: Contact institution. *Financial support:* In 2010–11, 2 teaching assistantships (averaging $4,500 per year) were awarded. In 2010, 74 master's awarded. Offers business administration (MBA); strategic finance (MS). *Application fee:* $35. *Application Contact:* Dr. Jay White, Dean, 812-941-2362, Fax: 812-941-2672. *Dean*, Dr. Jay White, 812-941-2362, Fax: 812-941-2672.

School of Education Students: 29 full-time (23 women), 445 part-time (357 women); includes 46 minority (39 Black or African American, non-Hispanic/Latino; 2 American Indian or Alaska Native, non-Hispanic/Latino; 2 Asian, non-Hispanic/Latino; 1 Hispanic/Latino; 1 Native Hawaiian or other Pacific Islander, non-Hispanic/Latino; 1 Two or more races, non-Hispanic/Latino). Average age 33. 92 applicants, 99% accepted, 67 enrolled. Expenses: Contact institution. *Financial support:* In 2010–11, 29 students received support. Career-related internships or fieldwork, Federal Work-Study, and institutionally sponsored loans available. Support available to part-time students. Financial award applicants required to submit FAFSA. In 2010, 159 master's awarded. *Degree program information:* Part-time and evening/weekend programs available. Offers counselor education (MS Ed); elementary education (MS Ed); secondary education (MS Ed). *Application deadline:* Applications are processed on a rolling basis. *Application fee:* $35. *Application Contact:* Dr. Gloria Murray, Dean, 812-941-2169, Fax: 812-941-2667, E-mail: soeinfo@ius.edu. *Dean*, Dr. Gloria Murray, 812-941-2169, Fax: 812-941-2667, E-mail: soeinfo@ius.edu.

INDIANA WESLEYAN UNIVERSITY, Marion, IN 46953-4974

General Information Independent-religious, coed, comprehensive institution. *Enrollment:* 4,499 full-time matriculated graduate/professional students (2,850 women), 450 part-time matriculated graduate/professional students (287 women). *Enrollment by degree level:* 98 first professional, 4,342 master's, 117 doctoral, 392 other advanced degrees. *Graduate faculty:* 64 full-time (28 women), 425 part-time/adjunct (170 women). *Tuition:* Full-time $7902; part-time $439 per credit hour. One-time fee: $290. Tuition and fees vary according to degree level, campus/location and program. *Graduate housing:* On-campus housing not available. *Student services:* Campus employment opportunities, campus safety program, career counseling, free psychological counseling, multicultural affairs office, services for students with disabilities, teacher training, writing training. *Library facilities:* Lewis A. Jackson Library. *Online resources:* library catalog, web page, access to other libraries' catalogs. *Collection:* 175,435 titles, 128,929 serial subscriptions, 13,148 audiovisual materials.

Computer facilities: 691 computers available on campus for general student use. A campuswide network can be accessed from student residence rooms and from off campus. Online class registration is available. *Web address:* http://www.indwes.edu/.

GRADUATE UNITS

College of Adult and Professional Studies *Degree program information:* Part-time and evening/weekend programs available. Postbaccalaureate distance learning degree programs offered (no on-campus study). Offers accounting (MBA); applied management (MBA); business administration (MBA); health care (MBA); human resources (MBA); management (MS); organizational leadership (Ed D). Electronic applications accepted.

School of Educational Leadership *Degree program information:* Part-time and evening/weekend programs available. Postbaccalaureate distance learning degree programs offered (no on-campus study). Offers educational leadership (M Ed, Ed S). Electronic applications accepted.

Graduate School *Degree program information:* Part-time and evening/weekend programs available. Postbaccalaureate distance learning degree programs offered. Electronic applications accepted.

College of Arts and Sciences *Degree program information:* Part-time programs available. Offers addictions counseling (MS); clinical mental health counseling (MS); community counseling (MS); marriage and family therapy (MS); school counseling (MS); student development counseling and administration (MS). Electronic applications accepted.

School of Nursing *Degree program information:* Part-time programs available. Postbaccalaureate distance learning degree programs offered (minimal on-campus study). Offers community health nursing (MS); nursing (Post Master's Certificate); nursing administration (MS); nursing education (MS); primary care nursing (MS).

Wesley Seminary Offers divinity (M Div); ministerial leadership (MA); ministry (MA); youth ministry (MA).

INSTITUTE FOR CHRISTIAN STUDIES, Toronto, ON M5T 1R4, Canada

General Information Independent-religious, coed, graduate-only institution. *Graduate housing:* On-campus housing not available.

GRADUATE UNITS

Graduate Programs *Degree program information:* Part-time programs available. Postbaccalaureate distance learning degree programs offered (minimal on-campus study). Offers education (M Phil F, PhD); history of philosophy (M Phil F, PhD); philosophical aesthetics (M Phil F, PhD); philosophy of religion (M Phil F, PhD); political theory (M Phil F, PhD); systematic philosophy (M Phil F, PhD); theology (M Phil F, PhD); worldview studies (MWS).

INSTITUTE FOR CLINICAL SOCIAL WORK, Chicago, IL 60601

General Information Independent, coed, primarily women, graduate-only institution. CGS member. *Graduate housing:* On-campus housing not available.

GRADUATE UNITS

Graduate Programs *Degree program information:* Part-time programs available. Offers clinical social work (PhD).

INSTITUTE FOR DOCTORAL STUDIES IN THE VISUAL ARTS, Portland, ME 04102

General Information Independent, coed, graduate-only institution. *Enrollment by degree level:* 24 doctoral. *Graduate faculty:* 2 full-time (1 woman), 11 part-time/adjunct (3 women). *Tuition:* Full-time $24,000. *Online resources:* web page. *Web address:* http://www.idsva.org/.

General Application Contact: Diane Einsiedler, Assistant to the Executive Vice President, 207-771-8887, E-mail: info@idsva.org.

GRADUATE UNITS

PhD Program in Visual Art: Philosophy, Aesthetics, and Art Theory Students: 24 full-time (19 women); includes 3 Black or African American, non-Hispanic/Latino; 1 Asian, non-Hispanic/Latino; 1 Hispanic/Latino. Average age 38. *Faculty:* 2 full-time (1 woman), 11 part-time/adjunct (3 women). Expenses: Contact institution. *Financial support:* In 2010–11, 22 students received support, including 1 fellowship (averaging $2,000 per year); scholarships/grants also available. Postbaccalaureate distance learning degree programs offered (minimal on-campus study). Offers aesthetics (PhD); art theory (PhD); philosophy (PhD). *Application deadline:* Applications are processed on a rolling basis. *Application fee:* $50. Electronic applications accepted. *Application Contact:* Diane Einsiedler, Assistant to the Executive Vice President, 207-771-8887, E-mail: info@idsva.org. *Executive Vice President*, Amy Curtis, 207-879-8757, E-mail: acurtis@idsva.org.

THE INSTITUTE FOR THE PSYCHOLOGICAL SCIENCES, Arlington, VA 30327

General Information Independent-religious, coed, graduate-only institution. *Enrollment by degree level:* 40 master's, 33 doctoral. *Graduate faculty:* 9 full-time (2 women), 3 part-time/adjunct (0 women). *Tuition:* Full-time $19,600; part-time $800 per credit hour. *Required fees:* $445. *Student services:* Campus employment opportunities, international student services. *Library facilities:* Mary S. Thelen Library. *Online resources:* library catalog, web page. *Collection:* 12,362 titles, 213 serial subscriptions, 613 audiovisual materials.

Computer facilities: 5 computers available on campus for general student use. *Web address:* http://ipsciences.edu/.

General Application Contact: Anne-Marie Dardis, Director of Admissions, 703-416-1441 Ext. 117, Fax: 703-416-8588, E-mail: amdardis@ipsciences.edu.

GRADUATE UNITS

Program in Clinical Psychology Students: 68 full-time (49 women), 5 part-time (3 women); includes 15 minority (11 Hispanic/Latino; 4 Two or more races, non-Hispanic/Latino), 12 international. 46 applicants, 76% accepted, 24 enrolled. *Faculty:* 9 full-time (2 women), 3 part-time/adjunct (0 women). Expenses: Contact institution. *Financial support:* Scholarships/grants and unspecified assistantships available. Financial award application deadline: 3/15; financial award applicants required to submit FAFSA. In 2010, 19 master's, 2 doctorates awarded. *Degree program information:* Part-time programs available. Offers clinical psychology (MS, Psy D). *Application deadline:* For fall admission, 5/4 for domestic and international students. Applications are processed on a rolling basis. *Application fee:* $50. *Application Contact:* Anne-Marie Dardis, Director of Admissions, 703-416-1441 Ext. 117, Fax: 703-416-8588, E-mail: amdardis@ipsciences.edu. *President*, Fr. Charles Sikorsky, 703-416-1441 Ext. 102, Fax: 703-416-8588, E-mail: csikorsky@ipsciences.edu.

INSTITUTE OF CLINICAL ACUPUNCTURE AND ORIENTAL MEDICINE, Honolulu, HI 96817

General Information Proprietary, coed, graduate-only institution.

GRADUATE UNITS

Program in Oriental Medicine Offers Oriental medicine (MSOM).

INSTITUTE OF PUBLIC ADMINISTRATION, Dublin 4, Ireland

General Information Proprietary, coed, comprehensive institution.

GRADUATE UNITS

Programs in Public Administration Offers healthcare management (MA); local government management (MA); public management (MA, Diploma).

INSTITUTE OF TRANSPERSONAL PSYCHOLOGY, Palo Alto, CA 94303

General Information Independent, coed, graduate-only institution. *Graduate housing:* On-campus housing not available.

GRADUATE UNITS

Global Online Programs Postbaccalaureate distance learning degree programs offered (minimal on-campus study). Offers psychology (PhD); transpersonal psychology (MTP); transpersonal studies (Certificate).

Low-Residency Programs Postbaccalaureate distance learning degree programs offered (minimal on-campus study). Offers counseling psychology (online) (MA); spiritual guidance (MA); women's spirituality (MA).

Residential Programs *Degree program information:* Part-time and evening/weekend programs available. Offers counseling psychology (MA); spiritually oriented clinical psychology (Psy D); transpersonal psychology (MA, PhD).

THE INSTITUTE OF WORLD POLITICS, Washington, DC 20036

General Information Independent, coed, graduate-only institution. *Graduate housing:* On-campus housing not available.

GRADUATE UNITS

Graduate Programs in National Security, Intelligence, and International Affairs *Degree program information:* Part-time and evening/weekend programs available. Offers American foreign policy (Certificate); comparative political culture (Certificate); counterintelligence (Certificate); democracy building (Certificate); intelligence (Certificate); international politics (Certificate); national security affairs (Certificate); public diplomacy and political warfare (Certificate); statecraft and national security affairs (MA); statecraft and world politics (MA); strategic intelligence studies (MA). Electronic applications accepted.

INSTITUT FRANCO-EUROPÉEN DE CHIROPRATIQUE, F-94200 Ivry-sur-Seine, France

General Information Independent, coed, graduate-only institution.

GRADUATE UNITS

Professional Program Offers chiropractic (DC).

INSTITUTO CENTROAMERICANO DE ADMINISTRACIÓN DE EMPRESAS, La Garita, Alajuela, Costa Rica

General Information Independent, coed, graduate-only institution. *Graduate housing:* Rooms and/or apartments guaranteed to single students and available to married students. *Research affiliation:* Tropical Agricultural Research and Higher Education Center (agribusiness), Harvard Institute for International Development (macroeconomics and environment), Earth University (agribusiness), Inter-American Institute for Cooperation on Agriculture (agribusiness), David Rockefeller Center for Latin American Studies (competitiveness), Zamarano (agribusiness).

GRADUATE UNITS

Graduate Programs Offers agribusiness management (MIAM); business administration (EMBA); finance (MBA); real estate management (MGREM); sustainable development (MBA); technology (MBA). Electronic applications accepted.

INSTITUTO TECNOLÓGICO Y DE ESTUDIOS SUPERIORES DE MONTERREY, CAMPUS CENTRAL DE VERACRUZ, 94500 Córdoba, Veracruz, Mexico

General Information Independent, coed, comprehensive institution.

GRADUATE UNITS

Graduate Programs *Degree program information:* Part-time and evening/weekend programs available. Postbaccalaureate distance learning degree programs offered (minimal on-campus study). Electronic applications accepted.

INSTITUTO TECNOLÓGICO Y DE ESTUDIOS SUPERIORES DE MONTERREY, CAMPUS CHIAPAS, 29000 Tuxtla Gutiérrez, Chiapas, Mexico

General Information Independent, coed, comprehensive institution.

INSTITUTO TECNOLÓGICO Y DE ESTUDIOS SUPERIORES DE MONTERREY, CAMPUS CHIHUAHUA, 31300 Chihuahua, Chihuahua, Mexico

General Information Independent, coed, comprehensive institution.

GRADUATE UNITS

Graduate Programs Offers computer systems engineering (Ingeniero); electrical engineering (Ingeniero); electromechanical engineering (Ingeniero); electronic engineering (Ingeniero); engineering administration (MEA); industrial engineering (MIE, Ingeniero); international trade (MIT); mechanical engineering (Ingeniero).

INSTITUTO TECNOLÓGICO Y DE ESTUDIOS SUPERIORES DE MONTERREY, CAMPUS CIUDAD DE MÉXICO, 14380 Ciudad de Mexico, DF, Mexico

General Information Independent, coed, comprehensive institution. *Graduate housing:* On-campus housing not available. *Research affiliation:* McGill University (management), Concordia University (business and management), Eli Lilly S. A. de C. U. (technological development), Ford Motor Company (industrial organization), German Research Center on Artificial Intelligence (informatics), Brent University (telecommunications).

GRADUATE UNITS

Division of Business *Degree program information:* Part-time and evening/weekend programs available. Postbaccalaureate distance learning degree programs offered (minimal on-campus study). Offers business administration (EMBA, MBA, PhD); economy (MBA); finance (MBA). EMBA program offered jointly with The University of Texas at Austin.

Division of Engineering and Architecture *Degree program information:* Part-time and evening/weekend programs available. Postbaccalaureate distance learning degree programs offered (minimal on-campus study). Offers management (MA); telecommunications (MA).

Division of Humanities and Social Sciences *Degree program information:* Part-time and evening/weekend programs available. Offers humanities and social sciences (LL B).

Virtual University Division *Degree program information:* Part-time and evening/weekend programs available. Postbaccalaureate distance learning degree programs offered (minimal on-campus study).

INSTITUTO TECNOLÓGICO Y DE ESTUDIOS SUPERIORES DE MONTERREY, CAMPUS CIUDAD JUÁREZ, 32320 Ciudad Juárez, Chihuahua, Mexico

General Information Independent, coed, comprehensive institution.

GRADUATE UNITS

Program in Administration of Information Technology Offers administration of information technology (MAIT).

Program in Applied Public Management Offers applied public management (MPM).

Program in Business Administration *Degree program information:* Part-time programs available. Postbaccalaureate distance learning degree programs offered. Offers business administration (MBA).

Program in Education Offers education (M Ed).

Program in Educational Administration Offers educational administration (MEA).

Program in Educational Innovation Offers educational innovation (DE).

Program in Educational Technology Offers educational technology (MTE).

Program in Electronic Commerce Offers electronic commerce (MEC).

Program in Humanistic Studies Offers humanistic studies (MEH).

Program in Quality Management Offers quality management (MQM).

INSTITUTO TECNOLÓGICO Y DE ESTUDIOS SUPERIORES DE MONTERREY, CAMPUS CIUDAD OBREGÓN, 85000 Ciudad Obregón, Sonora, Mexico

General Information Independent, coed, comprehensive institution.

GRADUATE UNITS

Program in Administration Offers administration (MA).

Program in Administration of Information Technology Offers administration of information technology (MATI).

Program in Administration of Telecommunications Offers administration of telecommunications (MAT).

Program in Engineering Offers engineering (ME).

Program in Finance Offers finance (MF).

Program in International Relations Offers international relations (MIR).

Program in Marketing Technology Offers marketing technology (MMT).

Programs in Education Offers cognitive development (ME); communications (ME); mathematics (ME).

INSTITUTO TECNOLÓGICO Y DE ESTUDIOS SUPERIORES DE MONTERREY, CAMPUS COLIMA, 28010 Colima, Colima, Mexico

General Information Independent, coed, comprehensive institution.

INSTITUTO TECNOLÓGICO Y DE ESTUDIOS SUPERIORES DE MONTERREY, CAMPUS CUERNAVACA, 62000 Temixco, Morelos, Mexico

General Information Independent, coed, comprehensive institution.

GRADUATE UNITS

Programs in Business Administration Offers finance (MA); human resources management (MA); international business (MA); marketing (MA).

Programs in Information Science Offers administration of information technology (MATI); computer science (MCC, DCC); information technology (MTI).

INSTITUTO TECNOLÓGICO Y DE ESTUDIOS SUPERIORES DE MONTERREY, CAMPUS ESTADO DE MÉXICO, Estado de Mexico 52926, Mexico

General Information Independent, coed, comprehensive institution. *Graduate housing:* On-campus housing not available. *Research affiliation:* Transportadora San Marcos, S. A. de C. V. (quality control), Microsoft Visual Studio (computer science), Trinity (new products), Sony Electronics (new products), Kaltex (quality control), Texas Instruments (semiconductors).

GRADUATE UNITS

Professional and Graduate Division *Degree program information:* Part-time programs available. Postbaccalaureate distance learning degree programs offered (minimal on-campus study). Offers administration of information technologies (MITA); architecture (M Arch); business administration (GMBA, MBA); computer sciences (MCS, PhD); education (M Ed); educational institution administration (MAD); educational technology and innovation (PhD); electronic commerce (MEC); environmental systems (MS); finance (MAF); humanistic studies (MHS); information sciences and knowledge management (MISKM); information systems (MS); manufacturing systems (MS); marketing (MEM); quality systems and productivity (MS); science and materials engineering (PhD); telecommunications management (MTM).

INSTITUTO TECNOLÓGICO Y DE ESTUDIOS SUPERIORES DE MONTERREY, CAMPUS GUADALAJARA, 45140 Zapopan, Jalisco, Mexico

General Information Independent, coed, comprehensive institution. *Graduate housing:* Rooms and/or apartments available to single and married students. Housing application deadline: 8/30.

GRADUATE UNITS

Program in Business Administration *Degree program information:* Part-time and evening/weekend programs available. Postbaccalaureate distance learning degree programs offered. Offers business administration (IEMBA, M Ad).

Program in Finance Offers finance (MF).

INSTITUTO TECNOLÓGICO Y DE ESTUDIOS SUPERIORES DE MONTERREY, CAMPUS HIDALGO, 42090 Pachuca, Hidalgo, Mexico

General Information Independent, coed, comprehensive institution.

INSTITUTO TECNOLÓGICO Y DE ESTUDIOS SUPERIORES DE MONTERREY, CAMPUS IRAPUATO, 36660 Irapuato, Guanajuato, Mexico

General Information Independent, coed, comprehensive institution.

GRADUATE UNITS

Graduate Programs Offers administration (MBA); administration of information technology (MAIT); administration of telecommunications (MAT); architecture (M Arch); computer science (MCS); education (M Ed); educational administration (MEA); educational innovation and technology (DEIT); educational technology (MET); electronic commerce (MBA); environmental administration and planning (MEAP); environmental systems (MES); finances (MBA); humanistic studies (MHS); international management for Latin American executives (MIMLAE); library and information science (MLIS); manufacturing quality management (MMQM); marketing research (MBA).

INSTITUTO TECNOLÓGICO Y DE ESTUDIOS SUPERIORES DE MONTERREY, CAMPUS LAGUNA, 27250 Torreón, Coahuila, Mexico

General Information Independent, coed, comprehensive institution. *Graduate housing:* On-campus housing not available.

GRADUATE UNITS

Graduate School *Degree program information:* Part-time programs available. Offers business administration (MBA); industrial engineering (MIE); management information systems (MS).

INSTITUTO TECNOLÓGICO Y DE ESTUDIOS SUPERIORES DE MONTERREY, CAMPUS LEÓN, 37120 León, Guanajuato, Mexico

General Information Independent, coed, comprehensive institution.

GRADUATE UNITS

Program in Business Administration *Degree program information:* Part-time programs available. Offers business administration (MBA).

INSTITUTO TECNOLÓGICO Y DE ESTUDIOS SUPERIORES DE MONTERREY, CAMPUS MAZATLÁN, 82000 Mazatlán, Sinaloa, Mexico

General Information Independent, coed, comprehensive institution.

INSTITUTO TECNOLÓGICO Y DE ESTUDIOS SUPERIORES DE MONTERREY, CAMPUS MONTERREY, 64849 Monterrey, Nuevo León, Mexico

General Information Independent, coed, comprehensive institution. *Graduate housing:* Room and/or apartments available to single students; on-campus housing not available to married students. *Research affiliation:* IBM de México (computer science), Southwest Research Institute (environment), Hylsa (steel), Vitro (glass products), Cydsa (petrochemicals), Cemex (cement).

GRADUATE UNITS

Graduate and Research Division *Degree program information:* Part-time and evening/weekend programs available. Offers agricultural parasitology (PhD); agricultural sciences (MS); applied statistics (M Eng); artificial intelligence (PhD); automation engineering (M Eng); biotechnology (MS); chemical engineering (M Eng); chemistry (MS, PhD); civil engineering (M Eng); communications (MS); computer science (MS); education (MA); electrical engineering (M Eng); electronic engineering (M Eng); environmental engineering (M Eng); farming productivity (MS); food processing engineering (MS); industrial engineering (M Eng, PhD); informatics (PhD); information systems (MS); information technology (MS); manufacturing engineering (M Eng); mechanical engineering (M Eng); phytopathology (MS); systems and quality engineering (M Eng).

Graduate School of Business Administration and Leadership *Degree program information:* Part-time programs available. Offers business administration (MA, MBA); finance (M Sc); international business (M Sc); management (PhD); management and leadership (M Sc, MA, MBA, PhD); marketing (M Sc).

INSTITUTO TECNOLÓGICO Y DE ESTUDIOS SUPERIORES DE MONTERREY, CAMPUS QUERÉTARO, 76130 Querétaro, Querétaro, Mexico

General Information Independent, coed, comprehensive institution. *Graduate housing:* Room and/or apartments guaranteed to single students; on-campus housing not available to married students. Housing application deadline: 6/15. *Research affiliation:* Transmisiones y Equipos Mecanicos (manufacturing designing).

GRADUATE UNITS

School of Business Offers business (MBA).

INSTITUTO TECNOLÓGICO Y DE ESTUDIOS SUPERIORES DE MONTERREY, CAMPUS SALTILLO, 25270 Saltillo, Coahuila, Mexico

General Information Independent, coed, comprehensive institution.

INSTITUTO TECNOLÓGICO Y DE ESTUDIOS SUPERIORES DE MONTERREY, CAMPUS SAN LUIS POTOSÍ, 78140 San Luis Potosí, SLP, Mexico

General Information Independent, coed, comprehensive institution.

INSTITUTO TECNOLÓGICO Y DE ESTUDIOS SUPERIORES DE MONTERREY, CAMPUS SINALOA, 80800 Culiacán, Sinaloa, Mexico

General Information Independent, coed, comprehensive institution.

INSTITUTO TECNOLÓGICO Y DE ESTUDIOS SUPERIORES DE MONTERREY, CAMPUS SONORA NORTE, 83000 Hermosillo, Sonora, Mexico

General Information Independent, coed, comprehensive institution. *Graduate housing:* On-campus housing not available. *Research affiliation:* National Council for Science and Technology (engineering).

GRADUATE UNITS

Program in Business Offers business (MA).

Program in Education Offers education (MA).

Program in Technological Information Management Offers technological information management (MA).

INSTITUTO TECNOLÓGICO Y DE ESTUDIOS SUPERIORES DE MONTERREY, CAMPUS TAMPICO, 89120 Altimira, Tamaulipas, Mexico

General Information Independent, coed, comprehensive institution.

INSTITUTO TECNOLÓGICO Y DE ESTUDIOS SUPERIORES DE MONTERREY, CAMPUS TOLUCA, 50252 Toluca, Estado de Mexico, Mexico

General Information Independent, coed, comprehensive institution.

GRADUATE UNITS

Graduate Programs *Degree program information:* Part-time and evening/weekend programs available.

INSTITUTO TECNOLÓGICO Y DE ESTUDIOS SUPERIORES DE MONTERREY, CAMPUS ZACATECAS, 98000 Zacatecas, Zacatecas, Mexico

General Information Independent, coed, comprehensive institution.

INTER AMERICAN UNIVERSITY OF PUERTO RICO, AGUADILLA CAMPUS, Aguadilla, PR 00605

General Information Independent, coed, comprehensive institution.

GRADUATE UNITS

Graduate School *Degree program information:* Part-time and evening/weekend programs available. Electronic applications accepted.

INTER AMERICAN UNIVERSITY OF PUERTO RICO, ARECIBO CAMPUS, Arecibo, PR 00614-4050

General Information Independent, coed, comprehensive institution.

GRADUATE UNITS

Program in Anesthesia Offers anesthesia (MS).

Program in Business Administration Offers accounting (MBA); finance (MBA); human resources (MBA).

Program in Nursing Offers critical care nursing (MSN); surgical nursing (MSN).

Programs in Education Offers administration and educational supervision (MA Ed); counseling and guidance (MA Ed); curriculum and teaching (MA Ed); elementary education (MA Ed).

INTER AMERICAN UNIVERSITY OF PUERTO RICO, BARRANQUITAS CAMPUS, Barranquitas, PR 00794

General Information Independent, coed, comprehensive institution. *Graduate housing:* Rooms and/or apartments available to single and married students.

GRADUATE UNITS

Program in Business Administration Offers accounting (IMBA); finance (IMBA).

Program in Education Offers curriculum and teaching (M Ed); educational leadership and management (MA); elementary education (M Ed); information and library service technology (M Ed); special education (MA). Electronic applications accepted.

INTER AMERICAN UNIVERSITY OF PUERTO RICO, BAYAMÓN CAMPUS, Bayamón, PR 00957

General Information Independent, coed, comprehensive institution. *Enrollment:* 5,063 graduate, professional, and undergraduate students; 115 part-time matriculated graduate/professional students (84 women). *Enrollment by degree level:* 115 master's. *Graduate faculty:* 4 full-time (1 woman), 5 part-time/adjunct (4 women). *Tuition:* Full-time $4424; part-time $202 per credit. *Required fees:* $180 per trimester. *Graduate housing:* On-campus housing not available. *Student services:* Campus employment opportunities, child daycare facilities, exercise/wellness program, free psychological counseling. *Library facilities:* Centro de Acceso a la Informacion plus 1 other. *Online resources:* library catalog, web page, access to other libraries' catalogs. *Collection:* 47,549 titles, 700 serial subscriptions, 2,608 audiovisual materials. *Research affiliation:* Central University of Bayamon.

Computer facilities: Computer purchase and lease plans are available. 610 computers available on campus for general student use. A campuswide network can be accessed from student residence rooms and from off campus. Online class registration is available. *Web address:* http://www.bc.inter.edu/.

General Application Contact: Carlos Alicea, Director of Admissions, 787-279-1200, Fax: 787-279-2205, E-mail: calicea@bc.lnter.edu.

GRADUATE UNITS

Graduate School Students: 115 part-time (84 women); includes 49 Hispanic/Latino. Average age 31. *Faculty:* 4 full-time (1 woman), 5 part-time/adjunct (4 women). Expenses: Contact institution. *Degree program information:* Part-time and evening/weekend programs available. Offers biology (MS); electronic commerce (MBA); human resources (MBA). *Application deadline:* For fall admission, 7/1 for domestic students, 5/1 priority date for international students; for winter admission, 11/15 priority date for domestic and international students; for spring admission, 2/15 priority date for domestic and international students. *Application fee:* $31. *Application Contact:* Carlos Alicea, Director of Admission, 787-279-1200 Ext. 2017, Fax: 787-279-2205, E-mail: calicea@bc.inter.edu. *Chancellor,* Prof. Juan F. Martinez, 787-279-1200 Ext. 2295, Fax: 787-279-2205, E-mail: jmartinez@bc.inter.edu.

INTER AMERICAN UNIVERSITY OF PUERTO RICO, GUAYAMA CAMPUS, Guayama, PR 00785

General Information Independent, coed, comprehensive institution.

GRADUATE UNITS

Department of Business Administration Offers marketing (MBA).

Department of Education and Social Sciences *Degree program information:* Part-time programs available. Offers early childhood education (0-4 years) (M Ed); elementary education (M Ed). Electronic applications accepted.

Department of Natural and Applied Sciences Offers computer security and networks (MS); networking and security (MCS).

INTER AMERICAN UNIVERSITY OF PUERTO RICO, METROPOLITAN CAMPUS, San Juan, PR 00919-1293

General Information Independent, coed, comprehensive institution. CGS member. *Graduate housing:* On-campus housing not available. *Research affiliation:* Innovation Technology (electronics).

GRADUATE UNITS

Graduate Programs *Degree program information:* Part-time and evening/weekend programs available. Offers accounting (MBA); administration of clinical laboratories (MS); advanced clinical services (MSW); advanced social work administration (MSW); American history (PhD); Christian education (PhD); clinical services (MSW); commerical education (MA); counseling psychology (MA, PhD); criminal justice (MA); curriculum and instruction (Ed D); educational administration (Ed D); educational computing (MA); elementary education (MA); English (MA); environmental evaluation and protection (MS); finance (MBA); general business (MBA); guidance and counseling (MA, Ed D); higher education administration (MA); history (MA, PhD); history education (MA); human resources (MBA); industrial management (MBA); industrial/organizational psychology (MA, PhD); international business (MIB); interregional and international business (PhD); labor relations (MA); management information systems (MBA); marketing (MBA); molecular microbiology (MS); music education (MM); occupational education (MA); open information systems (MS); pastoral theology (PhD); school psychology (MA, PhD); social work administration (MSW); Spanish (MA); Spanish education (MA); special education (MA); special education administration (Ed D); teaching English as a second language (MA); teaching of math (MA); teaching of physical education (MA); teaching of science (MA); theological studies (PhD); training and sport performance (MA); women's and gender studies (MA). Electronic applications accepted.

INTER AMERICAN UNIVERSITY OF PUERTO RICO, PONCE CAMPUS, Mercedita, PR 00715-1602

General Information Independent, coed, comprehensive institution.

GRADUATE UNITS

Graduate School

INTER AMERICAN UNIVERSITY OF PUERTO RICO, SAN GERMÁN CAMPUS, San Germán, PR 00683-5008

General Information Independent, coed, university. *Enrollment:* 5,380 graduate, professional, and undergraduate students; 560 full-time matriculated graduate/professional students (379 women), 246 part-time matriculated graduate/professional students (173 women). *Enrollment by degree level:* 557 master's, 249 doctoral. *Graduate faculty:* 39 full-time (22 women), 37 part-time/adjunct (19 women). *Tuition:* Part-time $202 per credit. *Required fees:* $258 per semester. *Graduate housing:* Room and/or apartments available on a first-come, first-served basis to single students; on-campus housing not available to married students. Typical cost: $1000 per year ($2500 including board). Housing application deadline: 6/15. *Student services:* Campus employment opportunities, campus safety program, career counseling, child daycare facilities, free psychological counseling, international student services, low-cost health insurance, services for students with disabilities. *Library facilities:* Juan Cancio Ortiz Library. *Online resources:* library catalog, web page, access to other libraries' catalogs. *Collection:* 159,055 titles, 2,306 serial subscriptions, 3,841 audiovisual materials.

Computer facilities: 1,200 computers available on campus for general student use. A campuswide network can be accessed from student residence rooms. Online class registration is available. *Web address:* http://www.sg.inter.edu/.

General Application Contact: Dr. Elba T. Irizarry, Director of Graduate Studies Center, 787-264-1912 Ext. 7357, Fax: 787-892-6350, E-mail: elbatirizarry@sg.inter.edu.

GRADUATE UNITS

Graduate Studies Center *Degree program information:* Part-time and evening/weekend programs available. Offers accounting (MBA); administration and supervision (MA, Ed D); applied mathematics (MA); business education (MA); ceramics (MFA); counseling psychology (MA, PhD); curriculum and instruction (Ed D); drawing (MFA); elementary education (MA); engraving (MFA); environmental biology (MS); environmental chemistry (MS); finance (MBA); financial accounting (M Acc); guidance and counseling (MA, Ed D); human resources (PhD); human resources management (MBA); industrial management (MBA); interregional and international business (PhD); library and information sciences (MLS); management information systems (MBA); managerial accounting (M Acc); marketing management (MBA); music education (MA); painting (MFA); photography (MFA); physical education and scientific analysis of human body movement (MA); school psychology (MA, PhD); science education (MA); sculpture (MFA); special education (MA); teaching English as a second language (MA); water analysis (MS).

INTER AMERICAN UNIVERSITY OF PUERTO RICO SCHOOL OF LAW, San Juan, PR 00936-8351

General Information Independent, coed, graduate-only institution.

GRADUATE UNITS

Professional Program *Degree program information:* Part-time and evening/weekend programs available. Offers law (JD).

INTER AMERICAN UNIVERSITY OF PUERTO RICO SCHOOL OF OPTOMETRY, Bayam¾n, PR 00957

General Information Independent, coed, graduate-only institution. *Enrollment by degree level:* 219 first professional. *Graduate faculty:* 19 full-time (8 women), 20 part-time/adjunct (9 women). *Tuition:* Full-time $25,500. *Graduate housing:* Room and/or apartments available on a first-come, first-served basis to single students; on-campus housing not available to married students. Typical cost: $5000 per year. *Student services:* Campus employment opportunities, career counseling, exercise/wellness program. *Library facilities:* CAI Center for Access to Information (CAI). *Online resources:* library catalog, web page. *Collection:* 10,293 titles, 332 serial subscriptions, 2,124 audiovisual materials.

Computer facilities: 19 computers available on campus for general student use. A campuswide network can be accessed from student residence rooms. Online class registration is available. *Web address:* http://www.optonet.inter.edu/.

General Application Contact: Jose Colon, Admission Officer, 787-765-1915 Ext. 1020, Fax: 787-456-7351, E-mail: jcolon@inter.edu.

GRADUATE UNITS

Professional Program Students: 218 full-time (129 women), 1 (woman) part-time; includes 137 minority (12 Black or African American, non-Hispanic/Latino; 58 Asian, non-Hispanic/Latino; 67 Hispanic/Latino), 18 international. Average age 26. 263 applicants, 53% accepted, 48 enrolled. *Faculty:* 19 full-time (8 women), 20 part-time/adjunct (9 women). Expenses: Contact institution. *Financial support:* In 2010–11, 4 students received support. Scholarships/grants available. Financial award application deadline: 4/30; financial award applicants required to submit FAFSA. In 2010, 36 ODs awarded. Offers optometry (OD). *Application deadline:* For fall admission, 5/31 priority date for domestic and international students. Applications are processed on a rolling basis. *Application fee:* $125. Electronic applications accepted. *Application Contact:* Jose Colon, Admission Officer, 787-765-1915 Ext. 1020, Fax: 787-456-7351, E-mail: jcolon@inter.edu. *Dean,* Dr. Andr??s Pagn Figueroa, 787-765-1915 Ext. 1000, Fax: 787-767-3920, E-mail: apagan@inter.edu.

INTERDENOMINATIONAL THEOLOGICAL CENTER, Atlanta, GA 30314-4112

General Information Independent-religious, coed, graduate-only institution. *Enrollment by degree level:* 358 first professional, 9 master's, 36 doctoral. *Graduate faculty:* 20 full-time (6 women), 26 part-time/adjunct (12 women). *Tuition:* Full-time $11,212; part-time $657 per credit. *Required fees:* $425 per semester. *Graduate housing:* Rooms and/or apartments available on a first-come, first-served basis to single and married students. Typical cost: $4338 per year for single students; $4338 per year for married students. Housing application deadline: 8/1. *Student services:* Campus employment opportunities, campus safety program, exercise/wellness program, free psychological counseling, international student services, low-cost health insurance. *Library facilities:* Robert W. Woodruff Library. *Online resources:* library catalog, access to other libraries' catalogs. *Collection:* 353,745 titles, 1,739 serial subscriptions. *Research affiliation:* Atlanta University Center, Inc., Columbia Theological Seminary Library, Candler School of Theology Library, Emory University Library.

Computer facilities: 50 computers available on campus for general student use. A campuswide network can be accessed. Online class registration is available. *Web address:* http://www.itc.edu/.

General Application Contact: Walter Cabassa, Office of Admission and Recruitment, 404-527-7792, E-mail: wcabassa@itc.edu.

GRADUATE UNITS

Graduate and Professional Programs Students: 236 full-time (96 women), 167 part-time (73 women); includes 388 Black or African American, non-Hispanic/Latino; 1 Asian, non-Hispanic/Latino; 1 Hispanic/Latino; 1 Two or more races, non-Hispanic/Latino, 6 international. 160 applicants, 81% accepted, 104 enrolled. *Faculty:* 20 full-time (6 women), 26 part-time/adjunct (12 women). Expenses: Contact institution. *Financial support:* Research assistantships, career-related internships or fieldwork and Federal Work-Study available. Support available to part-time students. Financial award application deadline: 6/15; financial award applicants required to submit FAFSA. In 2010, 93 first professional degrees, 4 master's awarded. *Degree program information:* Part-time and evening/weekend programs available. Postbaccalaureate distance learning degree programs offered (minimal on-campus study). Offers theology (M Div, MACE, MACM, D Min, Th D). D Min and Th D programs offered jointly with Columbia Theological Seminary and Emory University's Candler School of Theology. *Application deadline:* For fall admission, 7/1 for domestic and international students; for spring admission, 11/1 for domestic and international students. Applications are processed on a rolling basis. *Application fee:* $50. *Application Contact:* Walter Cabassa, Office of Admission and Recruitment, 404-527-7792, E-mail: wcabassa@itc.edu. *President,* Dr. Ronald E. Peters, 404-527-7702, Fax: 404-527-7770, E-mail: rpeters@itc.edu.

INTERIOR DESIGNERS INSTITUTE, Newport Beach, CA 92660

General Information Proprietary, coed, comprehensive institution.

GRADUATE UNITS

Graduate Program Offers interior design (MA).

INTERNATIONAL BAPTIST COLLEGE, Chandler, AZ 85286

General Information Independent-religious, coed, comprehensive institution. *Graduate housing:* Room and/or apartments available on a first-come, first-served basis to single students; on-campus housing not available to married students.

GRADUATE UNITS

Program in Biblical Studies Offers Biblical studies (MA).

Program in Education Offers education (M Ed).

Program in Ministry Offers ministry (M Min, D Min).

INTERNATIONAL COLLEGE OF THE CAYMAN ISLANDS, Newlands, Grand Cayman, Cayman Islands

General Information Independent, coed, comprehensive institution. *Graduate housing:* Room and/or apartments available on a first-come, first-served basis to single students; on-campus housing not available to married students.

GRADUATE UNITS

Graduate Program in Management *Degree program information:* Part-time and evening/weekend programs available. Offers business administration (MBA); management (MS).

INTERNATIONAL TECHNOLOGICAL UNIVERSITY, Santa Clara, CA 95050

General Information Independent, coed, comprehensive institution. *Research affiliation:* Linux Works, Inc. (software), @Channel (software), New Trends Technology, Inc. (hardware), Pico Turbo, Inc. (hardware).

GRADUATE UNITS

Program in Business Administration *Degree program information:* Part-time and evening/weekend programs available. Offers business administration (MBA).

Program in Computer Engineering Offers computer engineering (MSCE).

Program in Computer Science Offers computer science (MS).

Program in Digital Arts Offers digital arts (MA).

Program in Electrical Engineering *Degree program information:* Part-time and evening/weekend programs available. Offers electrical engineering (MSEE, PhD).

Program in Engineering Management Offers engineering management (MEM).

Program in Industrial Management Offers industrial management (MIM).

Program in Software Engineering Offers software engineering (MSSE, PhD).

THE INTERNATIONAL UNIVERSITY OF MONACO, MC-98000 Principality of Monaco, Monaco

General Information Independent, coed, comprehensive institution. *Graduate housing:* Rooms and/or apartments guaranteed to single and married students. *Research affiliation:* Alpstar (hedge funds).

GRADUATE UNITS

Graduate Programs *Degree program information:* Part-time programs available. Offers entrepreneurship (EMBA, MBA); financial engineering (M Sc); hedge fund and private equity (M Sc); international marketing (EMBA, MBA); international wealth management (M Sc); luxury goods and services (EMBA, M Sc, MBA); wealth and asset management (EMBA, MBA). Electronic applications accepted.

IONA COLLEGE, New Rochelle, NY 10801-1890

General Information Independent-religious, coed, comprehensive institution. *Enrollment:* 4,123 graduate, professional, and undergraduate students; 308 full-time matriculated graduate/professional students (214 women), 543 part-time matriculated graduate/professional students (313 women). *Enrollment by degree level:* 843 master's, 8 other advanced degrees. *Graduate faculty:* 120 full-time (44 women), 59 part-time/adjunct (28 women). *Tuition:* Part-time $830 per credit. *Required fees:* $225 per credit. *Graduate housing:* On-campus housing not available. *Student services:* Campus employment opportunities, campus safety program, career counseling, exercise/wellness program, free psychological counseling, international student services, multicultural affairs office, services for students with disabilities. *Library facilities:* Ryan Library plus 3 others. *Online resources:* library catalog, web page, access to other libraries' catalogs. *Collection:* 269,709 titles, 742 serial subscriptions, 3,912 audiovisual materials. *Research affiliation:* IBM (teacher preparation).

Computer facilities: Computer purchase and lease plans are available. 650 computers available on campus for general student use. A campuswide network can be accessed from student residence rooms and from off campus. Online class registration is available. *Web address:* http://www.iona.edu/.

General Application Contact: Kevin Cavanagh, Assistant Vice President for College Admissions, 914-633-2120, Fax: 914-633-2642, E-mail: kcavanagh@iona.edu.

GRADUATE UNITS

Hagan School of Business Students: 115 full-time (58 women), 299 part-time (130 women); includes 71 minority (23 Black or African American, non-Hispanic/Latino; 14 Asian, non-Hispanic/Latino; 33 Hispanic/Latino; 1 Two or more races, non-Hispanic/Latino), 7 international. Average age 32. 152 applicants, 71% accepted, 99 enrolled. *Faculty:* 33 full-time (7 women), 14 part-time/adjunct (3 women). Expenses: Contact institution. *Financial support:* Fellowships with tuition reimbursements, Federal Work-Study, scholarships/grants, tuition waivers (partial), and unspecified assistantships available. Support available to part-time students. Financial award application deadline: 4/15; financial award applicants required to submit FAFSA. In 2010, 179 master's, 139 other advanced degrees awarded. *Degree program information:* Part-time and evening/weekend programs available. Offers accounting (MBA, PMC); business (MBA, Certificate, PMC); business administration (MBA); financial management (MBA, PMC); health care management (MBA); human resource management (MBA, PMC); information systems (MBA, PMC); international business (Certificate, PMC); management (MBA, PMC); marketing (MBA). *Application deadline:* For fall admission, 8/15 priority date for domestic students, 8/1 for international students; for winter admission, 11/15 priority date for domestic students, 11/1 for international students; for spring admission, 2/15 priority date for domestic students, 2/1 for international students. Applications are processed on a rolling basis. *Application fee:* $50. Electronic applications accepted. *Application Contact:* Ben Fan, Director of MBA Admissions, 914-633-2289, Fax: 914-637-2708, E-mail: sfan@iona.edu. *Dean,* Dr. Vincent Calluzo, 914-633-2256, E-mail: vcalluzo@iona.edu.

School of Arts and Science Students: 193 full-time (156 women), 244 part-time (183 women); includes 75 minority (30 Black or African American, non-Hispanic/Latino; 1 American Indian or Alaska Native, non-Hispanic/Latino; 3 Asian, non-Hispanic/Latino; 40 Hispanic/Latino; 1 Native Hawaiian or other Pacific Islander, non-Hispanic/Latino), 7 international. Average age 30. 345 applicants, 72% accepted, 128 enrolled. *Faculty:* 87 full-time (37 women), 45 part-time/adjunct (25 women). Expenses: Contact institution. *Financial support:* Career-related internships or fieldwork, tuition waivers (partial), and unspecified assistantships available. Support available to part-time students. Financial award application deadline: 4/15; financial award applicants required to submit FAFSA. In 2010, 197 master's, 15 other advanced degrees awarded. *Degree program information:* Part-time and evening/weekend programs available. Offers arts and science (MA, MS, MS Ed, MST, Certificate); biology education (MS Ed, MST); computer science (MS); criminal justice (MS); educational leadership (MS Ed); English (MA); English education (MS Ed, MST); experimental psychology (MA); history (MA); industrial-organizational psychology (MA); Italian (MA); journalism (MS); literacy education (MS Ed); marriage and family therapy (MS, Certificate); mathematics education (MS Ed, MST); mental health counseling (MA); psychology (MA); public relations (MA); school psychology (MA); social studies education (MS Ed, MST); Spanish (MA); Spanish education (MS Ed, MST); teaching in childhood education (MST); telecommunications (MS). *Application deadline:* For fall admission, 8/1 priority date for domestic students, 5/1 priority date for international students; for winter admission, 12/1 priority date for domestic students, 8/1 priority date for international students; for spring admission, 1/1 priority date for domestic students, 9/1 priority date for international students. Applications are processed on a rolling basis. *Application fee:* $50. Electronic applications accepted. *Application Contact:* Veronica Jarek-Prinz, Director of Graduate Admissions, 914-633-2420, Fax: 914-633-2277, E-mail: vjarekprinz@iona.edu. *Dean,* Dr. Brian J. Nickerson, 914-633-2112, Fax: 914-633-2023, E-mail: bnickerson@iona.edu.

See Display on next page and Close-Up on page 957.

IOWA STATE UNIVERSITY OF SCIENCE AND TECHNOLOGY, Ames, IA 50011

General Information State-supported, coed, university. CGS member. *Enrollment:* 28,682 graduate, professional, and undergraduate students; 3,180 full-time matriculated graduate/professional students (1,300 women), 1,460 part-time matriculated graduate/professional students (619 women). *Enrollment by degree level:* 2,377 master's, 2,131 doctoral, 132 other advanced degrees. *Graduate faculty:* 1,601 full-time (434 women), 152 part-time/adjunct (67 women). *Graduate housing:* Rooms and/or apartments available on a first-come, first-served basis to single and married students. Housing application deadline: 6/15. *Student services:* Campus employment opportunities, campus safety program, career counseling, child daycare facilities, exercise/wellness program, free psychological counseling, international student services, low-cost health insurance, multicultural affairs office, services for students with disabilities, teacher training. *Library facilities:* University Library plus 1 other. *Online resources:* library catalog, web page, access to other libraries' catalogs. *Collection:* 2.6 million titles, 98,610 serial subscriptions. *Research affiliation:* National Veterinary Services Laboratories, National Animal Disease Center, National Soil Tilth Laboratory, North Central Regional Center for Rural Development, U. S. Department of Energy–Ames Laboratory.

Computer facilities: Computer purchase and lease plans are available. 2,410 computers available on campus for general student use. A campuswide network can be accessed from student residence rooms and from off campus. Online class registration, network services are available. *Web address:* http://www.iastate.edu/.

General Application Contact: Information Contact, 515-294-5836, Fax: 515-294-2592, E-mail: grad_admissions@iastate.edu.

GRADUATE UNITS

College of Veterinary Medicine Students: 634 full-time (436 women), 28 part-time (12 women); includes 1 Black or African American, non-Hispanic/Latino; 1 American Indian or Alaska Native, non-Hispanic/Latino; 7 Asian, non-Hispanic/Latino; 13 Hispanic/Latino, 331 international. *Faculty:* 107 full-time (24 women), 23 part-time/adjunct (5 women). Expenses: Contact institution. *Financial support:* In 2010–11, 52 research assistantships with full and partial tuition reimbursements (averaging $17,020 per year), 6 teaching assistantships with full and partial tuition reimbursements (averaging $13,303 per year) were awarded; career-related internships or fieldwork, Federal Work-Study, institutionally sponsored loans, scholarships/grants, health care benefits, and unspecified assistantships also available. In 2010, 113 first professional degrees, 7 master's, 6 doctorates awarded. *Degree program information:* Part-time programs available. Offers biomedical sciences (MS, PhD); veterinary clinical sciences (MS); veterinary diagnostic and production animal medicine (MS); veterinary medicine (DVM, MS, PhD); veterinary microbiology (MS, PhD); veterinary microbiology and preventive medicine (MS, PhD); veterinary pathology (MS, PhD); veterinary preventative

Iowa State University of Science and Technology (continued)
medicine (MS). Electronic applications accepted. *Application Contact:* Information Contact, 515-294-9348, Fax: 515-294-2592, E-mail: grad_admissions@iastate.edu. *Dean*, Dr. Lisa Nolan, 515-294-9348.

Graduate College Students: 2,962 full-time (1,199 women), 1,332 part-time (585 women); includes 136 Black or African American, non-Hispanic/Latino; 15 American Indian or Alaska Native, non-Hispanic/Latino; 92 Asian, non-Hispanic/Latino; 78 Hispanic/Latino, 1,533 international. 5,597 applicants, 32% accepted, 1169 enrolled. *Faculty:* 1,395 full-time (382 women), 182 part-time/adjunct (74 women). Expenses: Contact institution. *Financial support:* In 2010–11, research assistantships with full and partial tuition reimbursements (averaging $16,000 per year), 737 teaching assistantships with full and partial tuition reimbursements (averaging $16,000 per year) were awarded; fellowships, career-related internships or fieldwork, Federal Work-Study, institutionally sponsored loans, scholarships/grants, traineeships, health care benefits, and unspecified assistantships also available. Support available to part-time students. In 2010, 801 master's, 301 doctorates awarded. *Degree program information:* Part-time and evening/weekend programs available. Postbaccalaureate distance learning degree programs offered (minimal on-campus study). Offers bioinformatics and computational biology (MS, PhD); biorenewable resources and technology (MS, PhD); ecology and evolutionary biology (MS, PhD); environmental sciences (MS, PhD); genetics (MS, PhD); human-computer interaction (MS, PhD); immunobiology (MS, PhD); information assurance (MS); interdisciplinary graduate studies (MA, MS); interdisciplinary studies (MA, MBA, MS, PhD); microbiology (MS, PhD); molecular, cellular, and developmental biology (MS, PhD); neuroscience (MS, PhD); nutritional sciences (MS, PhD); plant biology (MS, PhD); seed technology and business (MS); sustainable agriculture (MS, PhD); toxicology (MS, PhD); transportation (MS). *Application deadline:* Applications are processed on a rolling basis. *Application fee:* $40 ($90 for international students). Electronic applications accepted. *Application Contact:* Information Contact, 515-294-5836, Fax: 515-294-2592, E-mail: grad_admissions@iastate.edu. *Associate Provost for Academic Progress/Dean*, Dr. David K. Holger, 515-294-7184, E-mail: grad_admissions@iastate.edu.

College of Agriculture Students: 439 full-time (193 women), 308 part-time (116 women); includes 17 Black or African American, non-Hispanic/Latino; 2 American Indian or Alaska Native, non-Hispanic/Latino; 11 Asian, non-Hispanic/Latino; 10 Hispanic/Latino, 213 international. 416 applicants, 32% accepted, 88 enrolled. *Faculty:* 271 full-time (47 women), 26 part-time/adjunct (11 women). Expenses: Contact institution. *Financial support:* In 2010–11, 305 research assistantships with full and partial tuition reimbursements (averaging $16,922 per year), 13 teaching assistantships with full and partial tuition reimbursements (averaging $12,294 per year) were awarded; fellowships, Federal Work-Study, scholarships/grants, health care benefits, and unspecified assistantships also available. Support available to part-time students. In 2010, 101 master's, 50 doctorates awarded. *Degree program information:* Part-time programs available. Postbaccalaureate distance learning degree programs offered (no on-campus study). Offers agricultural education and studies (MS, PhD); agricultural meteorology (MS, PhD); agriculture (M Ag, MS, PhD); agronomy (MS); animal breeding and genetics (MS, PhD); animal physiology (MS); animal psychology (PhD); animal science (MS, PhD); biochemistry (MS, PhD); biophysics (MS, PhD); crop production and physiology (MS, PhD); entomology (MS, PhD); forestry (MS, PhD); genetics (MS, PhD); horticulture (MS, PhD); industrial agriculture and technology (MS, PhD); meat science (MS, PhD); molecular, cellular, and developmental biology (MS, PhD); plant breeding (MS, PhD); plant pathology (MS, PhD); soil science (MS, PhD); toxicology (MS, PhD); wildlife ecology (MS). *Application deadline:* Applications are processed on a rolling basis. *Application fee:* $40 ($90 for international students). Electronic applications accepted. *Application Contact:* Information Contact, 515-294-5836, Fax: 515-294-2592, E-mail: grad_admissions@iastate.edu. *Dean*, Dr. Wendy Wintersteen, 515-294-2518, Fax: 515-294-6800.

College of Business Students: 178 full-time (74 women), 130 part-time (41 women); includes 4 Black or African American, non-Hispanic/Latino; 8 Asian, non-Hispanic/Latino; 6 Hispanic/Latino, 85 international. 272 applicants, 44% accepted, 85 enrolled. *Faculty:* 75 full-time (18 women), 1 (woman) part-time/adjunct. Expenses: Contact institution. *Financial support:* In 2010–11, 49 research assistantships with full and partial tuition reimbursements (averaging $5,621 per year), 2 teaching assistantships with full and partial tuition reimbursements (averaging $4,440 per year) were awarded; scholarships/grants, health care benefits, and unspecified assistantships also available. In 2010, 129 master's, 1 doctorate awarded. Offers accounting (M Acc); business (M Acc, MBA, MS, PhD); business administration (MBA, MS); business and technology (PhD); information systems (MS). *Application fee:* $40 ($90 for international students). Electronic applications accepted. *Application Contact:* Dr. Labh S. Hira, Dean, 515-294-2422, E-mail: busgrad@iastate.edu. *Dean*, Dr. Labh S. Hira, 515-294-2422, E-mail: busgrad@iastate.edu.

College of Design Students: 155 full-time (86 women), 63 part-time (29 women); includes 6 Black or African American, non-Hispanic/Latino; 1 American Indian or Alaska Native, non-Hispanic/Latino; 1 Asian, non-Hispanic/Latino; 9 Hispanic/Latino, 45 international. Average age 32. 184 applicants, 63% accepted, 69 enrolled. *Faculty:* 85 full-time (37 women), 5 part-time/adjunct (3 women). Expenses: Contact institution. *Financial support:* In 2010–11, 6 research assistantships with full and partial tuition reimbursements (averaging $1,600 per year), 43 teaching assistantships with full and partial tuition reimbursements (averaging $3,237 per year) were awarded; career-related internships or fieldwork, Federal Work-Study, institutionally sponsored loans, tuition waivers (partial), and unspecified assistantships also available. Support available to part-time students. Financial award applicants required to submit FAFSA. In 2010, 41 master's awarded. *Degree program information:* Part-time programs available. Offers architectural studies (MSAS); architecture (M Arch); art and design (MA); community and regional planning (MCRP); design (M Arch, MA, MCRP, MFA, MLA, MS, MSAS); graphic design (MFA); integrated visual arts (MFA); interior design (MFA); landscape architecture (MLA); transportation (MS). *Application deadline:* Applications are processed on a rolling basis. *Application fee:* $40 ($90 for international students). Electronic applications accepted. *Application Contact:* Dr. Luis Rico-Gutierrez, Dean, 515-294-7427, Fax: 515-294-9755, E-mail: lrico@iastate.edu. *Dean*, Dr. Luis Rico-Gutierrez, 515-294-7427, Fax: 515-294-9755, E-mail: lrico@iastate.edu.

College of Engineering Students: 787 full-time (179 women), 444 part-time (74 women); includes 31 Black or African American, non-Hispanic/Latino; 4 American Indian or Alaska Native, non-Hispanic/Latino; 33 Asian, non-Hispanic/Latino; 17 Hispanic/Latino, 611 international. 2,356 applicants, 16% accepted, 209 enrolled. *Faculty:* 264 full-time (29 women), 16 part-time/adjunct (3 women). Expenses: Contact institution. *Financial support:* In 2010–11, 505 research assistantships with full and partial tuition reimbursements (averaging $10,849 per year), 105 teaching assistantships with full and partial tuition reimbursements (averaging $7,076 per year) were awarded; fellowships, Federal Work-Study, scholarships/grants, health care benefits, and unspecified assistantships also available. Support available to part-time students. In 2010, 199 master's, 73 doctorates awarded. *Degree program information:* Part-time programs available. Offers aerospace engineering (M Eng, MS, PhD); agricultural and biosystems engineering (M Eng, MS, PhD); chemical and biological engineering (M Eng, MS, PhD); civil engineering (MS, PhD); computer engineering (M Eng, MS, PhD); electrical engineering (M Eng, MS, PhD); engineering (M Eng, MS, PhD); engineering mechanics (M Eng, MS, PhD); industrial engineering (M Eng, MS, PhD); materials science and engineering (MS, PhD); mechanical engineering (M Eng, MS, PhD); operations research (MS); systems engineering (M Eng). *Application fee:* $40 ($90 for international students). Electronic applications accepted. *Application Contact:* Dr. Jonathan Wickert, Dean, 515-294-9988. *Dean*, Dr. Jonathan Wickert, 515-294-9988.

College of Human Sciences Students: 384 full-time (270 women), 496 part-time (311 women); includes 64 Black or African American, non-Hispanic/Latino; 4 American Indian or Alaska Native, non-Hispanic/Latino; 11 Asian, non-Hispanic/Latino; 32 Hispanic/Latino, 116 international. 395 applicants, 67% accepted, 128 enrolled. *Faculty:* 160 full-time (93 women), 29 part-time/adjunct (19 women). Expenses: Contact institution. *Financial support:* In 2010–11, 131 research assistantships with full and partial tuition reimbursements (averaging $12,937 per year), 61 teaching assistantships with full and partial tuition reimbursements (averaging $9,836 per year) were awarded; fellowships, career-related internships or fieldwork, Federal Work-Study, scholarships/grants, health care benefits, and unspecified assistantships also available. Support available to part-time students. In 2010, 143 master's, 50 doctorates awarded. *Degree program information:* Part-time programs available. Offers counselor education (M Ed, MS); curriculum and instructional technology (M Ed, MS, PhD); educational administration (M Ed, MS); educational leadership (PhD); elementary education (M Ed, MS); family and consumer sciences (MFCS); family and consumer sciences education and studies (M Ed, MS, PhD); food science and technology (MS, PhD); foodservice and lodging management (MFCS, MS, PhD); higher education (M Ed, MS); historical, philosophical, and comparative studies in education (M Ed, MS); human development and family studies (MFCS, MS, PhD); human sciences (M Ed, MFCS, MS, PhD); kinesiology (MS, PhD); nutrition (MS, PhD); organizational learning and human resource development (M Ed, MS); research and evaluation (MS); special education (M Ed, MS); textiles and clothing (MFCS, MS, PhD). *Application fee:* $40 ($90 for international students). Electronic applications accepted. *Application Contact:* Information Contact, 515-294-5836, Fax: 515-294-2592, E-mail: grad_admissions@iastate.edu. *Dean,* Dr. Pamela White, 515-294-7000.

College of Liberal Arts and Sciences Students: 1,121 full-time (451 women), 358 part-time (158 women); includes 50 Black or African American, non-Hispanic/Latino; 3 American Indian or Alaska Native, non-Hispanic/Latino; 35 Asian, non-Hispanic/Latino; 21 Hispanic/Latino, 602 international. 1,908 applicants, 25% accepted, 242 enrolled. *Faculty:* 607 full-time (179 women), 49 part-time/adjunct (25 women). Expenses: Contact institution. *Financial support:* In 2010–11, 436 research assistantships with full and partial tuition reimbursements (averaging $11,203 per year), 523 teaching assistantships with full and partial tuition reimbursements (averaging $11,789 per year) were awarded; fellowships, Federal Work-Study, institutionally sponsored loans, scholarships/grants, health care benefits, and unspecified assistantships also available. Support available to part-time students. In 2010, 159 master's, 115 doctorates awarded. *Degree program information:* Part-time programs available. Offers agricultural economics (MS, PhD); agricultural history and rural studies (PhD); anthropology (MA); applied mathematics (MS, PhD); applied physics (MS, PhD); astrophysics (MS, PhD); chemistry (MS, PhD); cognitive psychology (PhD); computer science (MS, PhD); condensed matter physics (MS, PhD); counseling psychology (PhD); creative writing (MFA); earth science (MS, PhD); ecology, evolution, and organismal biology (MS, PhD); economics (MS, PhD); English (MA); environmental science (MS, PhD); genetics, developmental and cell biology (MS, PhD); geology (MS, PhD); high energy physics (MS, PhD); history (MA); history of technology and science (MA, PhD); journalism and mass communication (MS); liberal arts and sciences (MA, MFA, MPA, MS, MSM, PhD); mathematics (MS, PhD); meteorology (MS, PhD); nuclear physics (MS, PhD); physics (MS, PhD); political science (MA); public administration (MPA); rhetoric and professional communication (PhD); rural sociology (MS, PhD); school mathematics (MSM); social psychology (PhD); sociology (MS, PhD); statistics (MS, PhD). *Application fee:* $40 ($90 for international students). Electronic applications accepted. *Application Contact:* Information Contact, 515-294-5836, Fax: 515-294-2592, E-mail: grad_admissions@iastate.edu. *Dean,* Dr. Michael Whiteford, 515-294-3220, Fax: 515-294-1303.

ITHACA COLLEGE, Ithaca, NY 14850

General Information Independent, coed, comprehensive institution. CGS member. *Enrollment:* 6,949 graduate, professional, and undergraduate students; 447 full-time matriculated graduate/professional students (300 women), 53 part-time matriculated graduate/professional students (32 women). *Enrollment by degree level:* 345 master's, 155 doctoral. *Graduate faculty:* 171 full-time (77 women), 5 part-time/adjunct (4 women). *Tuition:* Full-time $19,890; part-time $663 per credit hour. *Graduate housing:* On-campus housing not available. *Student services:* Campus employment opportunities, campus safety program, career counseling, exercise/wellness program, free psychological counseling, international student services, low-cost health insurance, multicultural affairs office, services for students with disabilities, writing training. *Library facilities:* Ithaca College Library. *Online resources:* library catalog, web page, access to other libraries' catalogs. *Collection:* 398,000 titles, 44,450 serial subscriptions, 34,660 audiovisual materials. *Research affiliation:* Foundation for HSBC Environmental Education (environmental science), National Science Foundation (physics), National Science Foundation (computer science), Department of Health and Human Services, National Institutes of Health (physical therapy), National Aeronautics and Space Administration (NASA) (astronomy).

Computer facilities: Computer purchase and lease plans are available. 640 computers available on campus for general student use. A campuswide network can be accessed from student residence rooms and from off campus. Online class registration is available. *Web address:* http://www.ithaca.edu/.

General Application Contact: Rob Gearhart, Dean, Graduate and Professional Studies, 607-274-3527, Fax: 607-274-1263, E-mail: gps@ithaca.edu.

GRADUATE UNITS

Division of Graduate and Professional Studies Students: 447 full-time (300 women), 53 part-time (32 women); includes 36 minority (7 Black or African American, non-Hispanic/Latino; 2 American Indian or Alaska Native, non-Hispanic/Latino; 11 Asian, non-Hispanic/Latino; 12 Hispanic/Latino; 4 Two or more races, non-Hispanic/Latino), 30 international. Average age 24. 757 applicants, 62% accepted, 301 enrolled. *Faculty:* 171 full-time (77 women), 5 part-time/adjunct (4 women). Expenses: Contact institution. *Financial support:* In 2010–11, 287 students received support, including 11 fellowships (averaging $7,220 per year), 145 teaching assistantships (averaging $8,783 per year); career-related internships or fieldwork, Federal Work-Study, scholarships/grants, and unspecified assistantships also available. Support available to part-time students. Financial award applicants required to submit CSS PROFILE or FAFSA. In 2010, 206 master's, 55 doctorates awarded. *Degree program information:* Part-time programs available. *Application deadline:* Applications are processed on a rolling basis. *Application fee:* $40. Electronic applications accepted. *Application Contact:* Rob Gearhart, Dean, Graduate and Professional Studies, 607-274-3527, Fax: 607-274-1263, E-mail: gps@ithaca.edu. *Dean, Graduate and Professional Studies,* Rob Gearhart, 607-274-3527, Fax: 607-274-1263, E-mail: gps@ithaca.edu.

Roy H. Park School of Communications Students: 25 full-time (19 women), 16 part-time (10 women); includes 1 minority (American Indian or Alaska Native, non-Hispanic/Latino), 10 international. Average age 27. 45 applicants, 78% accepted, 19 enrolled. *Faculty:* 6 full-time (1 woman). Expenses: Contact institution. *Financial support:* In 2010–11, 17 students received support, including 17 teaching assistantships (averaging $7,741 per year); career-related internships or fieldwork, Federal Work-Study, scholarships/grants, and unspecified assistantships also available. Support available to part-time students. Financial award application deadline: 3/1; financial award applicants required to submit CSS PROFILE or FAFSA. In 2010, 13 master's awarded. *Degree program information:* Part-time programs available. Offers communications (MS). *Application deadline:* For fall admission, 7/5 for domestic and international students; for spring admission, 12/1 for domestic and international students. Applications are processed on a rolling basis. *Application fee:* $40. Electronic applications accepted. *Application Contact:* Rob Gearhart, Dean, Graduate and Professional Studies, 607-274-3527, Fax: 607-274-1263, E-mail: gps@ithaca.edu. *Dean,* Dr. Diane Gayeski, 607-274-1021.

School of Business Students: 34 full-time (10 women), 8 part-time (3 women); includes 4 minority (1 Black or African American, non-Hispanic/Latino; 2 Asian, non-Hispanic/Latino; 1 Hispanic/Latino), 2 international. Average age 25. 62 applicants, 84% accepted, 34 enrolled. *Faculty:* 22 full-time (7 women). Expenses: Contact institution. *Financial support:* In 2010–11, 18 students received support, including 11 fellowships (averaging $7,220 per year), 4 teaching assistantships (averaging $5,516 per year); career-related internships or fieldwork, Federal Work-Study, and scholarships/grants also available. Support available to part-time students. Financial award application deadline: 3/1; financial award applicants required to submit CSS PROFILE or FAFSA. In 2010, 4 master's awarded. *Degree program information:* Part-time programs available. Offers accountancy (MBA); business (MBA); business administration (MBA). *Application deadline:* For fall admission, 6/1 for domestic and international students; for spring admission, 12/1 for domestic and international students. Applications are processed on a rolling basis. *Application fee:* $40. Electronic applications accepted. *Application Contact:* Rob Gearhart, Dean, Graduate and Professional Studies, 607-274-3527, Fax: 607-274-1263, E-mail: gps@ithaca.edu. *Dean,* Dr. Mary Ellen Zuckerman, 607-274-3117.

School of Health Sciences and Human Performance Students: 318 full-time (233 women), 23 part-time (16 women); includes 23 minority (3 Black or African American, non-Hispanic/Latino; 1 American Indian or Alaska Native, non-Hispanic/Latino; 8 Asian, non-Hispanic/Latino; 8 Hispanic/Latino; 3 Two or more races, non-Hispanic/Latino), 15 international. Average age 23. *Faculty:* 61 full-time (40 women), 3 part-time/adjunct (all women). Expenses: Contact institution. *Financial support:* In 2010–11, 198 students received support, including 70 teaching assistantships (averaging $9,624 per year); career-related internships or fieldwork, Federal Work-Study, scholarships/grants, and unspecified assistantships also available. Support available to part-time students. Financial award applicants required to submit CSS PROFILE or FAFSA. In 2010, 155 master's, 55 doctorates awarded. *Degree program information:* Part-time programs available. Offers exercise and sport sciences (MS); health education (MS); health sciences and human performance (MS, DPT); occupational therapy (MS); physical education (MS); physical therapy (MS, DPT); speech pathology (MS); sport management (MS); teacher of students with speech and language disabilities (MS). *Application deadline:* Applications are processed on a rolling basis. *Application fee:* $40. Electronic applications accepted. *Application Contact:* Rob Gearhart, Dean, Graduate and Professional Studies, 607-274-3527, Fax: 607-274-1263, E-mail: gps@ithaca.edu. *Acting Dean,* Dr. John Sigg, 607-274-3237, Fax: 607-274-1263, E-mail: gps@ithaca.edu.

School of Humanities and Sciences Students: 30 full-time (20 women), 1 part-time (0 women); includes 3 minority (1 Black or African American, non-Hispanic/Latino; 2 Hispanic/Latino). Average age 29. 59 applicants, 69% accepted, 29 enrolled. *Faculty:* 25 full-time (9 women). Expenses: Contact institution. *Financial support:* In 2010–11, 18 students received support, including 18 teaching assistantships (averaging $7,228 per year); career-related internships or fieldwork, Federal Work-Study, scholarships/grants, and unspecified assistantships also available. Support available to part-time students. Financial award applicants required to submit CSS PROFILE or FAFSA. In 2010, 2 master's awarded. *Degree program information:* Part-time programs available. Offers biology 7-12 (MAT); chemistry 7-12 (MAT); childhood education (MS); English 7-12 (MAT); French 7-12 (MAT); humanities and sciences (MAT, MS); math 7-12 (MAT); physics 7-12 (MAT); social studies 7-12 (MAT); Spanish (MAT). *Application deadline:* For fall admission, 2/15 for domestic and international students; for spring admission, 12/1 for domestic and international students. Applications are processed on a rolling basis. *Application fee:* $40. Electronic applications accepted. *Application Contact:* Rob Gearhart, Dean, Graduate and Professional Studies, 607-274-3527, Fax: 607-274-1263, E-mail: gps@ithaca.edu. *Dean,* Dr. Leslie Lewis, 607-274-3533.

School of Music Students: 40 full-time (18 women), 5 part-time (3 women); includes 5 minority (2 Black or African American, non-Hispanic/Latino; 1 Asian, non-Hispanic/Latino; 1 Hispanic/Latino; 1 Two or more races, non-Hispanic/Latino), 3 international. Average age 25. 135 applicants, 40% accepted, 17 enrolled. *Faculty:* 57 full-time (20 women), 2 part-time/adjunct (1 woman). Expenses: Contact institution. *Financial support:* In 2010–11, 36 students received support, including 36 teaching assistantships (averaging $8,780 per year); career-related internships or fieldwork, Federal Work-Study, scholarships/grants, and unspecified assistantships also available. Support available to part-time students. Financial award application deadline: 3/1; financial award applicants required to submit CSS PROFILE or FAFSA. In 2010, 32 master's awarded. *Degree program information:* Part-time programs available. Offers composition (MM); conducting (MM); music (MM, MS); music education (MM, MS); performance (MM); Suzuki pedagogy (MM). *Application deadline:* For fall admission, 3/1 for domestic and international students; for spring admission, 12/1 for domestic and international students. Applications are processed on a rolling basis. *Application fee:* $40. Electronic applications accepted. *Application Contact:* Rob Gearhart, Dean, Graduate and Professional Studies, 607-274-3527, Fax: 607-274-1263, E-mail: gps@ithaca.edu. *Interim Dean,* Dr. Steven Mauk, 607-274-3343, E-mail: gps@ithaca.edu.

ITT TECHNICAL INSTITUTE, Indianapolis, IN 46268-1119

General Information Proprietary, coed, comprehensive institution.

GRADUATE UNITS

Online MBA Program Offers business (MBA).

JACKSON STATE UNIVERSITY, Jackson, MS 39217

General Information State-supported, coed, university. CGS member. *Enrollment:* 890 full-time matriculated graduate/professional students (619 women), 1,205 part-time matriculated graduate/professional students (884 women). *Enrollment by degree level:* 1,419 master's, 453 doctoral, 137 other advanced degrees. *Graduate faculty:* 207 full-time (85 women), 27 part-time/adjunct (9 women). Tuition, state resident: full-time $5050; part-time $281 per credit hour. Tuition, nonresident: full-time $12,380; part-time $689 per credit hour. *Graduate housing:* Room and/or apartments available on a first-come, first-served basis to single students; on-campus housing not available to married students. Typical cost: $3820 per year ($6342 including board). Room and board charges vary according to board plan and housing facility selected. Housing application deadline: 7/15. *Student services:* Campus employment opportunities, campus safety program, career counseling, child daycare facilities, exercise/wellness program, grant writing training, international student services, multicultural affairs office, services for students with disabilities, teacher training, writing training. *Library facilities:* H. T. Sampson Library plus 5 others. *Online resources:* library catalog, web page. *Collection:* 749,089 titles, 78,830 serial subscriptions, 2,354 audiovisual materials. *Research affiliation:* Lawrence A. Berkeley Laboratories (biology, chemistry), U. S. Department of Energy (biology), National Science Foundation (biology, chemistry), U. S. Environmental Protection Agency, Oak Ridge Associated Universities (science), Raytheon Systems Company (computer science).

Computer facilities: 300 computers available on campus for general student use. A campuswide network can be accessed from off campus. Online class registration is available. *Web address:* http://www.jsums.edu/.

General Application Contact: Dr. Dorris R. Robinson-Gardner, Dean of the Graduate School, 601-979-2455, Fax: 601-979-4325, E-mail: dgardner@ccaix.jsums.edu.

GRADUATE UNITS

Graduate School Students: 890 full-time (619 women), 1,205 part-time (884 women); includes 1,805 minority (1,775 Black or African American, non-Hispanic/Latino; 18 Asian, non-Hispanic/Latino; 11 Hispanic/Latino; 1 Two or more races, non-Hispanic/Latino), 62 international. Average age 36. *Faculty:* 207 full-time (85 women), 27 part-time/adjunct (9 women). Expenses: Contact institution. *Financial support:* Fellowships, research assistantships, teaching assistantships, career-related internships or fieldwork, Federal Work-Study, institutionally sponsored loans, scholarships/grants, tuition waivers (full and partial), and unspecified assistantships available. Support available to part-time students. Financial award application deadline: 3/1; financial award applicants required to submit FAFSA. In 2010, 395 master's, 70 doctorates, 16 other advanced degrees awarded. *Degree program information:* Part-time and evening/weekend programs available. Postbaccalaureate distance learning degree programs offered (minimal on-campus study). *Application deadline:* For fall admission, 3/1 for domestic students; for spring admission, 10/1 for domestic students. Applications are processed on a rolling basis. *Application fee:* $25. *Application Contact:* Sharlene Wilson, Director of Graduate Admissions, 601-979-2455, Fax: 601-979-4325, E-mail: sharlene.f.wilson@jsums.edu. *Dean,* Dr. Dorris R. Robinson-Gardner, 601-979-2455, Fax: 601-979-4325, E-mail: dgardner@ccaix.jsums.edu.

College of Business Students: 36 full-time (20 women), 37 part-time (21 women); includes 56 Black or African American, non-Hispanic/Latino; 1 Asian, non-Hispanic/Latino, 5 international. Average age 33. *Faculty:* 11 full-time (1 woman), 1 part-time/adjunct (0 women). Expenses: Contact institution. *Financial support:* Fellowships, research assistantships, teaching assistantships, career-related internships or fieldwork, Federal Work-Study, scholarships/grants, tuition waivers (full and partial), and unspecified assistantships available. Support available to part-time students. Financial award application deadline: 3/1; financial award applicants required to submit FAFSA. In 2010, 40 master's, 6 doctorates awarded. *Degree program information:* Part-time and evening/weekend programs available. Offers accounting (MPA); business (MBA, MPA, PhD); business administration (MBA, PhD). *Application deadline:* For fall admission, 3/1 priority date for domestic students, 3/1 for

Jackson State University (continued)

international students; for spring admission, 10/1 for domestic and international students. Applications are processed on a rolling basis. *Application fee:* $25. *Application Contact:* Sharlene Wilson, Director of Graduate Admissions, 601-979-2455, Fax: 601-979-4325, E-mail: sharlene.f.wilson@jsums.edu. *Dean*, Dr. Glenda B. Glover, 601-979-2411, Fax: 601-979-2690, E-mail: gglover@ccaix.jsums.edu.

College of Education and Human Development Students: 271 full-time (179 women), 596 part-time (470 women); includes 802 Black or African American, non-Hispanic/Latino; 2 Asian, non-Hispanic/Latino; 3 Hispanic/Latino, 3 international. Average age 38. *Faculty:* 43 full-time (25 women), 9 part-time/adjunct (2 women). Expenses: Contact institution. *Financial support:* Career-related internships or fieldwork, Federal Work-Study, scholarships/grants, and unspecified assistantships available. Support available to part-time students. Financial award application deadline: 3/1; financial award applicants required to submit FAFSA. In 2010, 126 master's, 33 doctorates, 16 other advanced degrees awarded. *Degree program information:* Part-time and evening/weekend programs available. Offers community and agency counseling (MS); early childhood education (MS Ed, Ed D); education administration (Ed S); education and human development (MS, MS Ed, Ed D, PhD, Ed S); educational administration (MS Ed, PhD); elementary education (MS Ed, Ed S); guidance and counseling (MS, MS Ed); health, physical education and recreation (MS Ed); rehabilitation counseling (MS Ed); secondary education (MS Ed, Ed S); special education (MS Ed, Ed S). *Application deadline:* For fall admission, 3/1 priority date for domestic students, 3/1 for international students; for spring admission, 10/1 for domestic and international students. Applications are processed on a rolling basis. *Application fee:* $25. *Application Contact:* Sharelene Wilson, Director of Graduate Admissions, 601-979-2455, Fax: 601-979-4325, E-mail: sharlene.f.wilson@jsums.edu. *Interim Dean*, Dr. Daniel Watkins, 601-979-2433, E-mail: daniel.watkins@jsums.edu.

College of Liberal Arts Students: 96 full-time (68 women), 152 part-time (108 women); includes 210 Black or African American, non-Hispanic/Latino; 3 Asian, non-Hispanic/Latino; 1 Hispanic/Latino, 1 international. Average age 34. *Faculty:* 49 full-time (26 women), 2 part-time/adjunct (0 women). Expenses: Contact institution. *Financial support:* Fellowships, research assistantships, teaching assistantships, career-related internships or fieldwork, Federal Work-Study, scholarships/grants, tuition waivers (full and partial), and unspecified assistantships available. Support available to part-time students. Financial award application deadline: 3/1; financial award applicants required to submit FAFSA. In 2010, 52 master's, 10 doctorates awarded. *Degree program information:* Part-time and evening/weekend programs available. Offers clinical psychology (PhD); criminology and justice services (MA); English (MA); history (MA); liberal arts (MA, MAT, MM Ed, MS, PhD); mass communications (MS); music education (MM Ed); political science (MA); sociology (MA); teaching English (MAT). *Application deadline:* For fall admission, 3/1 priority date for domestic students, 3/1 for international students; for spring admission, 10/1 for domestic and international students. Applications are processed on a rolling basis. *Application fee:* $25. *Application Contact:* Sharlene Wilson, Director of Graduate Admissions, 601-979-2455, Fax: 601-974-4325, E-mail: sharlene.f.wilson@jsums.edu. *Dean*, Dr. Dollye M. E. Robinson, 601-979-2422, E-mail: dollye.robinson@jsums.edu.

College of Public Service Students: 358 full-time (286 women), 222 part-time (163 women); includes 480 minority (473 Black or African American, non-Hispanic/Latino; 5 Asian, non-Hispanic/Latino; 2 Hispanic/Latino), 18 international. Average age 35. *Faculty:* 45 full-time (23 women), 9 part-time/adjunct (5 women). Expenses: Contact institution. *Financial support:* Career-related internships or fieldwork, Federal Work-Study, scholarships/grants, tuition waivers (full), and unspecified assistantships available. Support available to part-time students. Financial award application deadline: 3/1; financial award applicants required to submit FAFSA. In 2010, 113 master's, 7 doctorates awarded. Offers communicative disorders (MS); public policy and administration (MPPA, PhD); public service (MPPA, MS, PhD); urban and regional planning (MS, PhD). *Application deadline:* For fall admission, 3/1 for domestic and international students; for spring admission, 10/1 for domestic and international students. *Application fee:* $25. *Application Contact:* Sharlene Wilson, Director of Graduate Admissions, 601-979-2455, Fax: 601-979-4325, E-mail: sharlene.f.wilson@jsums.edu. *Interim Dean*, Dr. Mario Azevedo, 601-979-8836, Fax: 601-979-8837, E-mail: deanofcps@jsums.edu.

College of Science, Engineering and Technology Students: 123 full-time (63 women), 118 part-time (68 women); includes 169 Black or African American, non-Hispanic/Latino; 5 Asian, non-Hispanic/Latino; 4 Hispanic/Latino, 35 international. Average age 33. *Faculty:* 58 full-time (10 women), 5 part-time/adjunct (1 woman). Expenses: Contact institution. *Financial support:* Career-related internships or fieldwork, Federal Work-Study, scholarships/grants, and unspecified assistantships available. Support available to part-time students. Financial award application deadline: 3/1; financial award applicants required to submit FAFSA. In 2010, 64 master's, 14 doctorates awarded. *Degree program information:* Part-time and evening/weekend programs available. Offers chemistry and biochemistry (MS, PhD); computer science (MS); environmental science (MS, PhD); hazardous materials management (MS); mathematics (MS); science and mathematics teaching (MST); science, engineering and technology (MS, MS Ed, MST, PhD); technology education (MS Ed). *Application deadline:* For fall admission, 3/1 priority date for domestic students, 3/1 for international students; for spring admission, 10/1 for domestic and international students. Applications are processed on a rolling basis. *Application fee:* $25. *Application Contact:* Sharlene Wilson, Director of Graduate Admissions, 601-979-2455, Fax: 601-977-4325, E-mail: sharlene.f.wilson@jsums.edu. *Interim Dean*, Dr. Mark G. Hardy, 601-979-2513, E-mail: mark.g.hardy@jsums.edu.

School of Social Work Students: 105 full-time (95 women), 63 part-time (51 women); includes 139 Black or African American, non-Hispanic/Latino; 2 Asian, non-Hispanic/Latino; 1 Hispanic/Latino, 1 international. Average age 35. *Faculty:* 19 full-time (14 women), 1 part-time/adjunct (0 women). Expenses: Contact institution. *Financial support:* Career-related internships or fieldwork, Federal Work-Study, scholarships/grants, tuition waivers, and unspecified assistantships available. Support available to part-time students. Financial award application deadline: 3/1; financial award applicants required to submit FAFSA. In 2010, 36 master's, 1 doctorate awarded. *Degree program information:* Evening/weekend programs available. Offers social work (MSW, PhD). *Application deadline:* For fall admission, 3/1 for domestic and international students. *Application fee:* $25. *Application Contact:* Sharlene Wilson, Director of Graduate Admissions, 601-979-2455, Fax: 601-979-4325, E-mail: sharlene.f.wilson@jsums.edu. *Interim Associate Dean*, Dr. Leon Chestang, 601-979-6828, Fax: 601-979-6812, E-mail: schoolofsw@jsums.edu.

JACKSONVILLE STATE UNIVERSITY, Jacksonville, AL 36265-1602

General Information State-supported, coed, comprehensive institution. *Graduate housing:* Rooms and/or apartments available on a first-come, first-served basis to single and married students.

GRADUATE UNITS

College of Graduate Studies and Continuing Education *Degree program information:* Part-time and evening/weekend programs available.

College of Arts and Sciences *Degree program information:* Part-time and evening/weekend programs available. Offers arts and sciences (MA, MPA, MS, D Sc); biology (MS); computer systems and software design (MS); criminal justice (MS); emergency management (MS, D Sc); English (MA); history (MA); liberal studies (MA); mathematics (MS); music (MA); political science (MPA); psychology (MS).

College of Commerce and Business Administration *Degree program information:* Part-time and evening/weekend programs available. Offers commerce and business administration (MBA). Electronic applications accepted.

College of Education and Professional Studies *Degree program information:* Part-time and evening/weekend programs available. Offers early childhood education (MS Ed); education (Ed S); education and professional studies (MS, MS Ed, Ed S); educational administration (MS Ed, Ed S); elementary education (MS Ed); guidance and counseling (MS); instructional media (MS Ed); physical education (MS Ed, Ed S); reading specialist (MS Ed); secondary education (MS Ed); special education (MS Ed). Electronic applications accepted.

College of Nursing *Degree program information:* Part-time and evening/weekend programs available. Offers nursing (MSN). Electronic applications accepted.

JACKSONVILLE UNIVERSITY, Jacksonville, FL 32211

General Information Independent, coed, comprehensive institution. *Graduate housing:* Room and/or apartments available on a first-come, first-served basis to single students; on-campus housing not available to married students. Housing application deadline: 8/1.

GRADUATE UNITS

College of Arts and Sciences *Degree program information:* Part-time and evening/weekend programs available. Offers arts and sciences (MAT, MSN, Certificate).

School of Education *Degree program information:* Part-time and evening/weekend programs available. Offers computer sciences (MAT); early childhood education (Certificate); elementary education (MAT); integrated learning with educational technology (MAT); mathematics education (MAT); music education (MAT); reading education (MAT); second career as a teacher (Certificate); second careers as a teacher (Certificate).

School of Nursing *Degree program information:* Part-time programs available. Offers nursing (MSN).

School of Orthodontics Offers orthodontics (Certificate).

Davis College of Business *Degree program information:* Part-time and evening/weekend programs available. Offers business (Exec MBA, MBA); business administration (Exec MBA, MBA).

JAMES MADISON UNIVERSITY, Harrisonburg, VA 22807

General Information State-supported, coed, comprehensive institution. CGS member. *Enrollment:* 19,434 graduate, professional, and undergraduate students; 1,019 full-time matriculated graduate/professional students (718 women), 435 part-time matriculated graduate/professional students (262 women). *Enrollment by degree level:* 1,309 master's, 102 doctoral, 43 other advanced degrees. *Graduate faculty:* 247 full-time (113 women), 79 part-time/adjunct (47 women). *Graduate housing:* Room and/or apartments available on a first-come, first-served basis to single students; on-campus housing not available to married students. Housing application deadline: 5/1. *Student services:* Campus employment opportunities, campus safety program, career counseling, free psychological counseling, international student services, multicultural affairs office, services for students with disabilities, teacher training. *Library facilities:* Carrier Library plus 2 others. *Online resources:* library catalog, web page. *Collection:* 714,959 titles, 12,339 serial subscriptions, 43,626 audiovisual materials. *Research affiliation:* National Institute of Standards and Technology (NIST) through George Mason University (network risk assessment), National Science Foundation (Science, Technology, Engineering, and Math (STEM)), National Oceanic and Atmospheric Administration (NOAA) (applied metrological research), National Science Foundation (quantitative skills in biology), National Science Foundation (development of a detector array for Compton Scattering using polarized beams and targets).

Computer facilities: Computer purchase and lease plans are available. 600 computers available on campus for general student use. A campuswide network can be accessed from student residence rooms and from off campus. Online class registration is available. *Web address:* http://www.jmu.edu/.

General Application Contact: Dr. Reid Linn, Dean, The Graduate School, 540-568-6131, Fax: 540-568-7860, E-mail: grad@jmu.edu.

GRADUATE UNITS

The Graduate School Students: 1,019 full-time (718 women), 435 part-time (262 women); includes 147 minority (67 Black or African American, non-Hispanic/Latino; 3 American Indian or Alaska Native, non-Hispanic/Latino; 31 Asian, non-Hispanic/Latino; 29 Hispanic/Latino; 3 Native Hawaiian or other Pacific Islander, non-Hispanic/Latino; 14 Two or more races, non-Hispanic/Latino), 40 international. Average age 27. 1,647 applicants, 39% accepted, 422 enrolled. *Faculty:* 256 full-time (121 women), 67 part-time/adjunct (41 women). Expenses: Contact institution. *Financial support:* In 2010–11, 367 students received support, including 35 teaching assistantships with full tuition reimbursements available (averaging $8,664 per year); career-related internships or fieldwork, Federal Work-Study, and 12 athletic assistantships ($8664), 5 service assistantships ($7382), 253 graduate assistantships ($7382), 62 doctoral assistantships ($14,500) also available. Financial award application deadline: 3/1; financial award applicants required to submit FAFSA. In 2010, 629 master's, 23 doctorates, 26 other advanced degrees awarded. *Degree program information:* Part-time and evening/weekend programs available. Postbaccalaureate distance learning degree programs offered (no on-campus study). *Application deadline:* For fall admission, 5/1 priority date for domestic students, 5/1 for international students; for spring admission, 9/1 priority date for domestic students, 9/1 for international students. Applications are processed on a rolling basis. *Application fee:* $55. Electronic applications accepted. *Application Contact:* Lynette M. Bible, Director of Graduate Admissions, 540-568-6395, Fax: 540-568-7860, E-mail: biblelm@jmu.edu. *Dean*, Dr. Reid Linn, 540-568-6131, Fax: 540-568-7860, E-mail: grad@jmu.edu.

College of Arts and Letters Students: 92 full-time (41 women), 45 part-time (25 women); includes 7 minority (4 Black or African American, non-Hispanic/Latino; 1 Asian, non-Hispanic/Latino; 2 Hispanic/Latino), 3 international. Average age 27. *Faculty:* 35 full-time (12 women), 4 part-time/adjunct (3 women). Expenses: Contact institution. *Financial support:* In 2010–11, 40 students received support, including 14 teaching assistantships with full tuition reimbursements available (averaging $8,664 per year); Federal Work-Study, unspecified assistantships, and 26 graduate assistantships ($7382) also available. Financial award application deadline: 3/1; financial award applicants required to submit FAFSA. In 2010, 64 master's awarded. *Degree program information:* Part-time programs available. Offers arts and letters (MA, MPA, MS); English (MA); history (MA); political science (MA, MPA); public administration (MPA); writing, rhetoric, and technical communication (MA, MS). *Application deadline:* For fall admission, 5/1 priority date for domestic students; for spring admission, 9/1 priority date for domestic students. Applications are processed on a rolling basis. *Application fee:* $55. Electronic applications accepted. *Application Contact:* Lynette M. Bible, Director of Graduate Admissions, 540-568-6395, Fax: 540-568-7860, E-mail: biblelm@jmu.edu. *Dean*, Dr. David K. Jeffrey, 540-568-6334.

College of Business Students: 98 full-time (47 women), 43 part-time (12 women); includes 32 minority (9 Black or African American, non-Hispanic/Latino; 11 Asian, non-Hispanic/Latino; 3 Hispanic/Latino; 1 Native Hawaiian or other Pacific Islander, non-Hispanic/Latino; 8 Two or more races, non-Hispanic/Latino), 3 international. Average age 27. *Faculty:* 15 full-time (3 women), 1 part-time/adjunct (0 women). Expenses: Contact institution. *Financial support:* In 2010–11, 20 students received support. Federal Work-Study and 19 graduate assistantships ($7382), 1 athletic assistantship ($8664) available. Financial award application deadline: 3/1; financial award applicants required to submit FAFSA. In 2010, 97 master's awarded. *Degree program information:* Part-time and evening/weekend programs available. Postbaccalaureate distance learning degree programs offered (no on-campus study). Offers accounting (MS); business (MBA, MS); business administration (MBA). *Application deadline:* For fall admission, 5/1 priority date for domestic students, 5/1 for international students; for spring admission, 9/1 priority date for domestic students, 9/1 for international students. Applications are processed on a rolling basis. *Application fee:* $55. Electronic applications accepted. *Application Contact:* Lynette M. Bible, Director of Graduate Admissions, 540-568-6395, Fax: 540-568-7860, E-mail: biblelm@jmu.edu. *Dean*, Dr. Robert D. Reid, 540-568-3254.

College of Education Students: 295 full-time (256 women), 118 part-time (99 women); includes 44 minority (26 Black or African American, non-Hispanic/Latino; 3 Asian, non-Hispanic/Latino; 11 Hispanic/Latino; 4 Two or more races, non-Hispanic/Latino), 2 international. Average age 27. *Faculty:* 42 full-time (33 women), 39 part-time/adjunct (26 women). Expenses: Contact institution. *Financial support:* In 2010–11, 31 students received support. Career-related internships or fieldwork, Federal Work-Study, unspecified assistantships, and 31 graduate assistantships ($7382) available. Financial award application deadline: 3/1; financial award applicants required to submit FAFSA. In 2010, 265 master's awarded. *Degree program information:* Part-time and evening/weekend programs available. Offers adult education/human resource development (MS Ed); early childhood education (M Ed); education (M Ed, MAT, MS Ed); educational leadership (M Ed); elementary education (M Ed); exceptional education (M Ed); middle education (MAT); reading education (M Ed); secondary education (MAT). *Application deadline:* For fall admission, 5/1 priority date for domestic students; for spring admission, 9/1 priority date for domestic students. Applications are processed on a rolling basis. *Application fee:* $55. Electronic applications accepted. *Application Contact:* Lynette M. Bible, Director of Graduate Admissions, 540-568-6395, Fax: 540-568-7860, E-mail: biblelm@jmu.edu. *Dean,* Dr. Phillip M. Wishon, 540-568-6572.

College of Integrated Science and Technology Students: 473 full-time (344 women), 198 part-time (110 women); includes 62 minority (24 Black or African American, non-Hispanic/Latino; 3 American Indian or Alaska Native, non-Hispanic/Latino; 15 Asian, non-Hispanic/Latino; 11 Hispanic/Latino; 2 Native Hawaiian or other Pacific Islander, non-Hispanic/Latino; 7 Two or more races, non-Hispanic/Latino), 27 international. Average age 27. *Faculty:* 104 full-time (47 women), 29 part-time/adjunct (14 women). Expenses: Contact institution. *Financial support:* In 2010–11, 147 students received support, including 18 teaching assistantships with full tuition reimbursements available (averaging $8,664 per year); Federal Work-Study, unspecified assistantships, and 11 athletic assistantships ($8664), 5 service assistantships ($7382), 71 graduate assistantships ($7382), 42 doctoral assistantships ($14,500) also available. Financial award application deadline: 3/1; financial award applicants required to submit FAFSA. In 2010, 194 master's, 23 doctorates, 26 other advanced degrees awarded. *Degree program information:* Part-time programs available. Postbaccalaureate distance learning degree programs offered (no on-campus study). Offers assessment and measurement (PhD); audiology (Au D, PhD); clinical audiology (PhD); clinical mental health counseling (M Ed, MA, Ed S); college student personnel administration (M Ed); combined-integrated clinical and school psychology (Psy D); computer science (MS); health education (MS, MS Ed); integrated science and technology (M Ed, MA, MOT, MPAS, MS, MS Ed, MSN, Au D, PhD, Psy D, Ed S); kinesiology (MS); nursing (MSN); occupational therapy (MOT); physician assistant studies (MPAS); psychological sciences (MA); school counseling (Ed S); school psychology (M Ed, MA, Ed S); speech-language pathology (MS, PhD). *Application deadline:* For fall admission, 2/1 priority date for domestic students; for spring admission, 9/1 priority date for domestic students. Applications are processed on a rolling basis. *Application fee:* $55. Electronic applications accepted. *Application Contact:* Lynette M. Bible, Director of Graduate Admissions, 540-568-6395, Fax: 540-568-7860, E-mail: biblelm@jmu.edu. *Interim Dean,* Dr. Sharon E. Lovell, 540-568-3283.

College of Science and Mathematics Students: 10 full-time (7 women), 8 part-time (4 women); includes 1 minority (Asian, non-Hispanic/Latino). Average age 27. *Faculty:* 11 full-time (4 women), 1 (woman) part-time/adjunct. Expenses: Contact institution. *Financial support:* In 2010–11, 9 students received support. Federal Work-Study and 9 graduate assistantships ($7382) available. Financial award application deadline: 3/1; financial award applicants required to submit FAFSA. In 2010, 7 master's awarded. *Degree program information:* Part-time programs available. Offers biology (MS); mathematics and statistics (M Ed); science and mathematics (M Ed, MS). *Application deadline:* For fall admission, 2/15 priority date for domestic students; for spring admission, 9/1 priority date for domestic students. Applications are processed on a rolling basis. *Application fee:* $55. Electronic applications accepted. *Application Contact:* Lynette M. Bible, Director of Graduate Admissions, 540-568-6395, Fax: 540-568-7860, E-mail: biblelm@jmu.edu. *Dean,* Dr. David F. Brakke, 540-568-3508.

College of Visual and Performing Arts Students: 51 full-time (24 women), 8 part-time (6 women); includes 5 minority (3 Black or African American, non-Hispanic/Latino; 2 Hispanic/Latino), 5 international. Average age 27. *Faculty:* 40 full-time (14 women), 5 part-time/adjunct (3 women). Expenses: Contact institution. *Financial support:* In 2010–11, 40 students received support, including 3 teaching assistantships with full tuition reimbursements available (averaging $8,664 per year); 17 graduate assistantships ($7382), 20 doctoral assistantships ($14,500) also available. Financial award application deadline: 3/1; financial award applicants required to submit FAFSA. In 2010, 13 master's awarded. *Degree program information:* Part-time programs available. Offers art education (MA); art history (MA); ceramics (MFA); conducting (MM); drawing/painting (MFA); metal/jewelry (MFA); music education (MM); musical arts (DMA); performance (MM); photography (MFA); printmaking (MFA); sculpture (MFA); studio art (MA); theory-composition (MM); visual and performing arts (MA, MFA, MM, DMA); weaving/fibers (MFA). *Application deadline:* For fall admission, 2/15 priority date for domestic students; for spring admission, 10/15 priority date for domestic students. Applications are processed on a rolling basis. *Application fee:* $55. Electronic applications accepted. *Application Contact:* Lynette M. Bible, Director of Graduate Admissions, 540-568-6395, Fax: 540-568-7860, E-mail: biblelm@jmu.edu. *Dean,* Dr. George Sparks, 540-568-6247, E-mail: sparksge@jmu.edu.

JEFFERSON COLLEGE OF HEALTH SCIENCES, Roanoke, VA 24031-3186

General Information Independent, coed, comprehensive institution. *Enrollment:* 1,032 graduate, professional, and undergraduate students; 173 full-time matriculated graduate/professional students (144 women), 26 part-time matriculated graduate/professional students (23 women). *Enrollment by degree level:* 199 master's. *Graduate faculty:* 18 full-time (9 women), 5 part-time/adjunct (all women). *Tuition:* Full-time $11,070; part-time $615 per credit hour. *Graduate housing:* Room and/or apartments available on a first-come, first-served basis to single students; on-campus housing not available to married students. Typical cost: $5200 per year. *Student services:* Campus employment opportunities, campus safety program, career counseling, exercise/wellness program, free psychological counseling, grant writing training, low-cost health insurance, services for students with disabilities, writing training. *Library facilities:* JCHS Library. *Online resources:* library catalog, web page. *Collection:* 6,042 titles, 233 serial subscriptions, 424 audiovisual materials. *Research affiliation:* Carilion Clinic (hospital and medical services), Virginia Tech/Carilion Medical School (medical school).

Computer facilities: 72 computers available on campus for general student use. A campuswide network can be accessed from student residence rooms. Online class registration is available. *Web address:* http://www.jchs.edu/.

General Application Contact: Judith McKeon, Director of Admissions, 540-985-9083, Fax: 540-985-9773, E-mail: jomckeon@jchs.edu.

GRADUATE UNITS

Program in Nursing Students: 27 full-time (25 women), 13 part-time (12 women); includes 3 Black or African American, non-Hispanic/Latino; 1 Asian, non-Hispanic/Latino; 1 Hispanic/Latino. Average age 40. 44 applicants, 68% accepted, 20 enrolled. *Faculty:* 10 full-time (5 women), 1 (woman) part-time/adjunct. Expenses: Contact institution. *Financial support:* Career-related internships or fieldwork, Federal Work-Study, scholarships/grants, traineeships, health care benefits, and tuition waivers (full) available. Support available to part-time students. Financial award applicants required to submit FAFSA. In 2010, 21 master's awarded. *Degree program information:* Part-time programs available. Offers nursing education (MSN); nursing management (MSN). *Application deadline:* Applications are processed on a rolling basis. *Application fee:* $35. Electronic applications accepted. *Application Contact:* Judith McKeon, Director of Admissions, 540-985-9083, Fax: 540-985-9773, E-mail: jomckeon@jchs.edu. *Department Chair,* Dr. Ava Porter, 540-985-8531, E-mail: agporter@jchs.edu.

Program in Occupational Therapy Students: 28 full-time (27 women), 13 part-time (11 women); includes 1 Black or African American, non-Hispanic/Latino. Average age 27. 70 applicants, 36% accepted, 14 enrolled. *Faculty:* 11 full-time (3 women), 1 (woman) part-time/adjunct. Expenses: Contact institution. *Financial support:* Career-related internships or fieldwork, Federal Work-Study, scholarships/grants, traineeships, and tuition waivers (full and partial) available. Support available to part-time students. Financial award applicants required to submit FAFSA. In 2010, 13 master's awarded. *Degree program information:* Part-time programs available. Offers occupational therapy (MS). *Application deadline:* Applications are processed on a rolling basis. *Application fee:* $35. Electronic applications accepted. *Application Contact:* Judith McKeon, Director of Admissions, 540-985-9083, Fax: 540-985-9773, E-mail: jomckeon@jchs.edu. *Program Director,* Dr. David Haynes, 540-985-4020, E-mail: dahaynes@jchs.edu.

Program in Physician Assistant Students: 118 full-time (92 women); includes 1 Black or African American, non-Hispanic/Latino; 1 American Indian or Alaska Native, non-Hispanic/Latino; 6 Asian, non-Hispanic/Latino; 6 Hispanic/Latino; 1 Two or more races, non-Hispanic/Latino. Average age 26. 637 applicants, 10% accepted, 40 enrolled. *Faculty:* 15 full-time (7 women), 3 part-time/adjunct (1 woman). Expenses: Contact institution. *Financial support:* Career-related internships or fieldwork, Federal Work-Study, scholarships/grants, traineeships, health care benefits, and tuition waivers (full and partial) available. Support available to part-time students. Financial award applicants required to submit FAFSA. In 2010, 37 master's awarded. Offers physician assistant (MS). *Application deadline:* Applications are processed on a rolling basis. *Application fee:* $35. Electronic applications accepted. *Application Contact:* Judith McKeon, Director of Admissions, 540-985-9083, Fax: 540-985-9773, E-mail: jomckeon@jchs.edu. *Program Director,* Dr. Patricia Airey, 540-985-8376, E-mail: pjairey@jchs.edu.

THE JEWISH THEOLOGICAL SEMINARY, New York, NY 10027-4649

General Information Independent-religious, coed, university. *Graduate housing:* Rooms and/or apartments available on a first-come, first-served basis to single and married students. Housing application deadline: 5/15.

GRADUATE UNITS

The Graduate School *Degree program information:* Part-time programs available. Offers ancient Judaism (MA, DHL, PhD); Bible and ancient Semitic languages (MA, DHL, PhD); interdepartmental studies (MA); Jewish art and visual culture (MA); Jewish gender and women's studies (MA); Jewish history (MA, DHL, PhD); Jewish literature (MA, DHL, PhD); Jewish philosophy (DHL); Jewish thought (MA, PhD); liturgy (MA, DHL, PhD); medieval Jewish studies (MA, DHL, PhD); Midrash (DHL); Midrash and scriptural interpretation (MA, PhD); modern Jewish studies (MA, DHL, PhD); Talmud and rabbinics (MA, DHL, PhD). MA/MSW offered jointly with Columbia University.

H. L. Miller Cantorial School and College of Jewish Music Offers Jewish music (MSM).

The Rabbinical School Offers theology (MA, Rabbi).

William Davidson Graduate School of Jewish Education *Degree program information:* Part-time programs available. Postbaccalaureate distance learning degree programs offered (minimal on-campus study). Offers Jewish education (MA, Ed D). Offered in conjunction with Rabbinical School; H. L. Miller Cantorial School and College of Jewish Music; Teacher's College, Columbia University; and Union Theological Seminary.

JEWISH UNIVERSITY OF AMERICA, Skokie, IL 60077-3248

General Information Independent-religious, men only, graduate-only institution. *Graduate housing:* On-campus housing not available.

GRADUATE UNITS

Graduate School *Degree program information:* Part-time and evening/weekend programs available. Offers Jewish education (MJ Ed, DJ Ed).

Abrams Institute of Pastoral Counseling Offers counseling (MA); pastoral counseling (MPC, DPC).

Graduate Research Division *Degree program information:* Part-time programs available. Offers Bible (MHL, DHL); Hebrew (MHL, DHL); history (MHL, DHL); Jewish studies (MHL, DHL); philosophy (MHL, DHL); rabbinics (MHL, DHL).

JOHN BROWN UNIVERSITY, Siloam Springs, AR 72761-2121

General Information Independent-religious, coed, comprehensive institution. *Graduate housing:* Rooms and/or apartments available on a first-come, first-served basis to single and married students.

GRADUATE UNITS

Graduate Business Programs *Degree program information:* Part-time and evening/weekend programs available. Postbaccalaureate distance learning degree programs offered (minimal on-campus study). Offers business administration (MBA); international community development leadership (MS); leadership and ethics (MS); leadership and higher education (MS). Electronic applications accepted.

Graduate Counseling Programs *Degree program information:* Part-time and evening/weekend programs available. Offers community counseling (MS); marriage and family therapy (MS); school counseling (MS). Electronic applications accepted.

Graduate Ministry Programs *Degree program information:* Part-time and evening/weekend programs available. Offers ministry (MA). Electronic applications accepted.

JOHN CARROLL UNIVERSITY, University Heights, OH 44118-4581

General Information Independent-religious, coed, comprehensive institution. CGS member. *Graduate housing:* On-campus housing not available.

GRADUATE UNITS

Graduate School *Degree program information:* Part-time and evening/weekend programs available. Offers administration (M Ed, MA); biology (MA, MS); clinical counseling (Certificate); communications management (MA); community counseling (MA); educational and school psychology (M Ed, MA); English (MA); history (MA); humanities (MA); integrated science (MA); mathematics (MA, MS); nonprofit administration (MA); professional teacher education (M Ed, MA); religious studies (MA); school based adolescent-young adult education (M Ed); school based early childhood education (M Ed); school based middle childhood education (M Ed); school based multi-age education (M Ed); school counseling (M Ed, MA). Electronic applications accepted.

John M. and Mary Jo Boler School of Business *Degree program information:* Part-time and evening/weekend programs available. Offers accountancy (MS); business (MBA). Electronic applications accepted.

JOHN F. KENNEDY UNIVERSITY, Pleasant Hill, CA 94523-4817

General Information Independent, coed, primarily women, upper-level institution. CGS member. *Graduate housing:* On-campus housing not available.

GRADUATE UNITS

Graduate School of Holistic Studies *Degree program information:* Part-time and evening/weekend programs available. Offers consciousness studies (MA); counseling psychology (MA); dream studies (Certificate); holistic health education (MA); holistic studies (MA, MFA, Certificate); integral psychology (MA, Certificate); life coaching (Certificate); somatic psychology (MA); studio arts (MFA); transformative arts (MA); transpersonal psychology (MA).

Graduate School of Professional Psychology *Degree program information:* Part-time and evening/weekend programs available. Offers counseling psychology (MA); organizational psychology (MA, Certificate); professional psychology (MA, Psy D, Certificate); psychology (Psy D); sport psychology (MA).

School of Education and Liberal Arts *Degree program information:* Part-time and evening/weekend programs available. Offers education (MAT); education and liberal arts (MA, MAT, Certificate); museum studies (MA, Certificate).

School of Law *Degree program information:* Part-time and evening/weekend programs available. Offers law (JD).

School of Management *Degree program information:* Part-time and evening/weekend programs available. Offers business administration (MBA); career coaching (Certificate); career development (MA, Certificate); management (MA, MBA, Certificate); organizational leadership (Certificate).

JOHN JAY COLLEGE OF CRIMINAL JUSTICE OF THE CITY UNIVERSITY OF NEW YORK, New York, NY 10019-1093

General Information State and locally supported, coed, comprehensive institution. *Graduate housing:* On-campus housing not available. *Research affiliation:* Criminal Justice Center,

John Jay College of Criminal Justice of the City University of New York (continued)

Criminal Justice Research and Evaluation Center, Center on Violence and Human Survival, Center for Dispute Resolution, The Fire Science Institute, The Institute For Criminal Justice Ethics.

GRADUATE UNITS

Graduate Studies *Degree program information:* Part-time and evening/weekend programs available. Offers criminal justice (MA, PhD); criminology and deviance (PhD); forensic computing (MS); forensic psychology (PhD); forensic science (PhD); law and philosophy (PhD); organizational behavior (PhD); protection management (MS); public administration (MPA); public policy (PhD).

JOHN MARSHALL LAW SCHOOL, Chicago, IL 60604-3968

General Information Independent, coed, graduate-only institution. *Enrollment by degree level:* 1,440 first professional, 47 master's, 123 other advanced degrees. *Graduate faculty:* 65 full-time (21 women), 152 part-time/adjunct (48 women). *Tuition:* Part-time $1315 per credit. *Required fees:* $50 per semester. *Graduate housing:* On-campus housing not available. *Student services:* Campus employment opportunities, campus safety program, career counseling, free psychological counseling, international student services, low-cost health insurance, multicultural affairs office, services for students with disabilities, writing training. *Library facilities:* The John Marshall Law School Library. *Online resources:* library catalog, web page. *Collection:* 66,226 titles, 2,666 serial subscriptions, 312 audiovisual materials.

Computer facilities: 45 computers available on campus for general student use. A campuswide network can be accessed from off campus. Online class registration is available. *Web address:* http://www.jmls.edu/.

General Application Contact: William B. Powers, Associate Dean of Admission and Student Affairs, 800-537-4280, Fax: 312-427-5136, E-mail: admission@jmls.edu.

GRADUATE UNITS

Graduate and Professional Programs Students: 1,237 full-time (567 women), 373 part-time (181 women); includes 464 minority (138 Black or African American, non-Hispanic/Latino; 12 American Indian or Alaska Native, non-Hispanic/Latino; 96 Asian, non-Hispanic/Latino; 125 Hispanic/Latino; 11 Native Hawaiian or other Pacific Islander, non-Hispanic/Latino; 82 Two or more races, non-Hispanic/Latino), 39 international. Average age 27. 3,523 applicants, 44% accepted, 351 enrolled. *Faculty:* 65 full-time (21 women), 152 part-time/adjunct (48 women). Expenses: Contact institution. *Financial support:* In 2010–11, 1,350 students received support. Scholarships/grants and tuition waivers (full and partial) available. Support available to part-time students. Financial award application deadline: 6/1; financial award applicants required to submit FAFSA. In 2010, 387 first professional degrees, 8 master's awarded. *Degree program information:* Part-time and evening/weekend programs available. Offers comparative legal studies (LL M); employee benefits (LL M, MS); information technology (LL M, MS); intellectual property (LL M); international business and trade (LL M); law (JD); real estate (LL M, MS); taxation (LL M, MS). JD/MBA offered jointly with Dominican University, JD/MA and JD/MPA with Roosevelt University. *Application deadline:* For fall admission, 3/1 priority date for domestic and international students; for spring admission, 10/15 priority date for domestic and international students. Applications are processed on a rolling basis. *Application fee:* $60. Electronic applications accepted. *Application Contact:* William B. Powers, Associate Dean of Admission and Student Affairs, 800-537-4280, Fax: 312-427-5136, E-mail: admission@jmls.edu. *Dean,* John Corkery, 312-427-2737.

THE JOHNS HOPKINS UNIVERSITY, Baltimore, MD 21218-2699

General Information Independent, coed, university. CGS member. *Enrollment:* 6,613 full-time matriculated graduate/professional students (3,494 women), 7,197 part-time matriculated graduate/professional students (3,772 women). *Enrollment by degree level:* 480 first professional, 9,643 master's, 3,074 doctoral, 613 other advanced degrees. *Graduate faculty:* 3,639 full-time (1,413 women), 615 part-time/adjunct (207 women). *Graduate housing:* On-campus housing not available. *Student services:* Campus employment opportunities, campus safety program, career counseling, exercise/wellness program, free psychological counseling, grant writing training, international student services, low-cost health insurance, multicultural affairs office, services for students with disabilities, teacher training, writing training. *Library facilities:* Milton S. Eisenhower Library plus 6 others. *Online resources:* library catalog, web page, access to other libraries' catalogs. *Collection:* 3.7 million titles, 76,000 serial subscriptions, 44,164 audiovisual materials. *Research affiliation:* General Electric Company (GE) (medical technology), Carnegie Institution of Washington (biological sciences), SmithKline Beecham (asthma and allergy), Bristol-Myers Squibb (human nutrition), Howard Hughes Medical Institute (biomedical sciences), Space Telescope Science Institute (astronomy).

Computer facilities: Computer purchase and lease plans are available. 140 computers available on campus for general student use. A campuswide network can be accessed from student residence rooms and from off campus. Online class registration is available. *Web address:* http://www.jhu.edu/.

General Application Contact: Graduate Admissions Office, 410-516-8174.

GRADUATE UNITS

Bloomberg School of Public Health Students: 1,394 full-time (1,019 women), 461 part-time (292 women); includes 522 minority (128 Black or African American, non-Hispanic/Latino; 4 American Indian or Alaska Native, non-Hispanic/Latino; 266 Asian, non-Hispanic/Latino; 68 Hispanic/Latino; 3 Native Hawaiian or other Pacific Islander, non-Hispanic/Latino; 53 Two or more races, non-Hispanic/Latino), 422 international. Average age 30. 3,274 applicants, 51% accepted, 716 enrolled. *Faculty:* 546 full-time (277 women), 680 part-time/adjunct (282 women). Expenses: Contact institution. *Financial support:* In 2010–11, 1,256 students received support, including 38 fellowships (averaging $34,333 per year), 59 research assistantships (averaging $23,525 per year), 11 teaching assistantships (averaging $3,126 per year); career-related internships or fieldwork, Federal Work-Study, institutionally sponsored loans, scholarships/grants, traineeships, health care benefits, and stipends also available. Support available to part-time students. Financial award application deadline: 3/15; financial award applicants required to submit FAFSA. In 2010, 563 master's, 133 doctorates awarded. *Degree program information:* Part-time and evening/weekend programs available. Post-baccalaureate distance learning degree programs offered (minimal on-campus study). Offers biochemistry and molecular biology (MHS, Sc M, PhD); bioethics and policy (PhD); bioinformatics (MHS); biostatistics (MHS, Sc M, PhD); cancer epidemiology (MHS, Sc M, PhD, Sc D); cardiovascular disease epidemiology (MHS, Sc M, PhD, Sc D); child and adolescent health and development (Dr PH, PhD); children's mental health services (PhD); clinical epidemiology (MHS, Sc M, PhD, Sc D); clinical investigation (MHS, Sc M, PhD); clinical trials (PhD, Sc D); demography (MHS); drug dependence epidemiology (PhD); environmental health engineering (PhD); environmental health sciences (MHS, Dr PH); epidemiology (Dr PH); epidemiology (general) (MHS, Sc M, PhD, Sc D); epidemiology of aging (MHS, Sc M, PhD, Sc D); genetic counseling (Sc M); global disease epidemiology and control (MHS, PhD); health and public policy (PhD); health care management and leadership (Dr PH); health economics (MHS); health economics and policy (PhD); health education and health communication (MHS); health finance and management (MHA); health policy (MHS); health services research and policy (PhD); health systems (MHS, PhD); human genetics/genetic epidemiology (MHS, Sc M, PhD, Sc D); human nutrition (MHS, PhD); infectious disease epidemiology (MHS, Sc M, PhD, Sc D); international health (Dr PH); mental health (MHS, Dr PH); molecular microbiology and immunology (MHS, Sc M, PhD); occupational and environmental health (PhD); occupational and environmental hygiene (MHS, MHS); occupational/environmental epidemiology (MHS, Sc M, PhD, Sc D); physiology (PhD); population and health (Dr PH, PhD); population, family and reproductive health (MHS); psychiatric epidemiology (PhD); public health (MHA, MHS, MPH, Sc M, Dr PH, PhD, Sc D); reproductive, perinatal women's health (Dr PH, PhD); social and behavioral interventions (MHS, PhD); social and behavioral sciences (Dr PH, PhD, Sc D); social factors in health (MHS); toxicology (PhD). *Application deadline:* Applications are processed on a rolling basis. *Application fee:* $45. Electronic applications accepted. *Application Contact:* Leslie K. Vink, Director of Recruitment, Communications and Special Projects, 410-955-3543, Fax: 410-955-0464, E-mail: lvink@jhsph.edu. *Dean,* Dr. Michael J. Klag, 410-955-3540, Fax: 410-955-0121, E-mail: mklag@jhsph.edu.

Carey Business School Students: 448 full-time (189 women), 1,181 part-time (468 women); includes 548 minority (237 Black or African American, non-Hispanic/Latino; 5 American Indian or Alaska Native, non-Hispanic/Latino; 217 Asian, non-Hispanic/Latino; 65 Hispanic/Latino; 4 Native Hawaiian or other Pacific Islander, non-Hispanic/Latino; 20 Two or more races, non-Hispanic/Latino), 274 international. Average age 33. 919 applicants, 79% accepted, 472 enrolled. *Faculty:* 29 full-time (6 women), 135 part-time/adjunct (29 women). Expenses: Contact institution. *Financial support:* In 2010–11, 135 students received support. Federal Work-Study and scholarships/grants available. Support available to part-time students. Financial award application deadline: 4/15; financial award applicants required to submit FAFSA. In 2010, 626 master's, 89 other advanced degrees awarded. *Degree program information:* Part-time and evening/weekend programs available. Postbaccalaureate distance learning degree programs offered (minimal on-campus study). Offers business administration (MBA); business of health (MBA, Certificate); business of medicine (Certificate); business of nursing (Certificate); competitive intelligence (Certificate); finance (MS, Certificate); financial management (Certificate); information security management (Certificate); information systems (MS); information technology (MS, Certificate); investments (Certificate); leadership and management in the life sciences (MBA); leadership development (Certificate); management (MS, Certificate); marketing (MS); medical services management (MBA); organization development and human resources (MS); real estate (MS); skilled facilitator (Certificate). *Application deadline:* For fall admission, 4/1 for international students; for spring admission, 9/15 for international students. Applications are processed on a rolling basis. *Application fee:* $100. Electronic applications accepted. *Application Contact:* Robin Greenberg, Admissions Coordinator, 410-234-9227, Fax: 443-529-1554, E-mail: carey.admissions@jhu.edu. *Dean,* Dr. Yash Gupta, 410-234-9210, E-mail: yash.gupta@jhu.edu.

Engineering Program for Professionals Students: 68 full-time (22 women), 2,146 part-time (482 women); includes 690 minority (202 Black or African American, non-Hispanic/Latino; 6 American Indian or Alaska Native, non-Hispanic/Latino; 312 Asian, non-Hispanic/Latino; 127 Hispanic/Latino; 5 Native Hawaiian or other Pacific Islander, non-Hispanic/Latino; 38 Two or more races, non-Hispanic/Latino), 44 international. Average age 31. *Faculty:* 235 part-time/adjunct (30 women). Expenses: Contact institution. In 2010, 580 master's, 31 other advanced degrees awarded. *Degree program information:* Part-time and evening/weekend programs available. Offers applied and computational mathematics (MS, Post-Master's Certificate); applied biomedical engineering (MS, Post-Master's Certificate); applied physics (MS, Post-Master's Certificate); bioinformatics (MS, Post-Master's Certificate); chemical and biomolecular engineering (M Ch E); civil engineering (MCE); computer science (MS, Post-Master's Certificate); electrical and computer engineering (MS, Post-Master's Certificate); engineering (M Ch E, M Mat SE, MCE, MEE, MME, MS, MSE, Graduate Certificate, Post-Master's Certificate); environmental engineering (MS, Graduate Certificate, Post-Master's Certificate); environmental engineering and science (MEE, MS, Graduate Certificate, Post-Master's Certificate); environmental planning and management (MS, Post-Master's Certificate); information assurance (MS); information systems and technology (MS, Post-Master's Certificate); materials science and engineering (M Mat SE, MSE); mechanical engineering (MME); systems engineering (MS, Graduate Certificate, Post-Master's Certificate); technical management (MS, Graduate Certificate, Post-Master's Certificate); telecommunications and networking (MS). *Application deadline:* Applications are processed on a rolling basis. *Application fee:* $75. Electronic applications accepted. *Application Contact:* Priyanka Dwivedi, Admissions Manager, 410-516-2300, Fax: 410-579-8049, E-mail: pdwived1@jhu.edu. *Associate Dean,* Dr. Allan Bjerkaas, 410-516-2300, Fax: 410-579-8049, E-mail: bjerkaas@jhu.edu.

G. W. C. Whiting School of Engineering Students: 777 full-time (209 women), 36 part-time (8 women); includes 111 minority (17 Black or African American, non-Hispanic/Latino; 1 American Indian or Alaska Native, non-Hispanic/Latino; 62 Asian, non-Hispanic/Latino; 21 Hispanic/Latino; 10 Two or more races, non-Hispanic/Latino), 445 international. Average age 26. 2,443 applicants, 37% accepted, 289 enrolled. *Faculty:* 190 full-time (37 women), 94 part-time/adjunct (16 women). Expenses: Contact institution. *Financial support:* In 2010–11, 107 fellowships with full tuition reimbursements (averaging $23,347 per year), 552 research assistantships with full tuition reimbursements (averaging $26,605 per year), 65 teaching assistantships with full tuition reimbursements (averaging $12,624 per year) were awarded; Federal Work-Study, institutionally sponsored loans, scholarships/grants, health care benefits, tuition waivers (full and partial), and unspecified assistantships also available. Support available to part-time students. Financial award applicants required to submit FAFSA. In 2010, 218 master's, 53 doctorates awarded. Offers bioengineering innovation and design (MSE); biomaterials (MSEM); biomedical engineering (MSE, PhD); chemical and biomolecular engineering (MSE, PhD); civil engineering (MCE, MSE, PhD); communications science (MSEM); computational medicine (PhD); computer science (MSE, PhD); discrete mathematics (MA, MSE, PhD); electrical and computer engineering (MSE, PhD); engineering (M Ch E, M Mat SE, MA, MCE, MEE, MME, MS, MSE, MSEM, MSSI, PhD, Certificate, Post-Master's Certificate); financial mathematics (MSE); fluid mechanics (MSEM); geography and environmental engineering (MA, MS, MSE, PhD); materials science and engineering (MSEM); mechanical engineering (MSEM); mechanics and materials (MSEM); nano-biotechnology (MSEM); nanomaterials and nanotechnology (MSEM); operations research/optimization/decision science (MA, MSE, PhD); probability and statistics (MSEM); smart product and device design (MSEM); statistics/probability/stochastic processes (MA, MSE, PhD); systems analysis, management and environmental policy (MSEM). *Application fee:* $75. Electronic applications accepted. *Application Contact:* Dennis McIver, Coordinator of Graduate Admissions, 410-516-8174, Fax: 410-516-0780, E-mail: graduateadmissions@jhu.edu. *Interim Dean,* Dr. Nicholas P. Jones, 410-516-8350 Ext. 3, Fax: 410-516-8627.

Information Security Institute Students: 42 full-time (6 women), 6 part-time (2 women); includes 9 minority (2 Black or African American, non-Hispanic/Latino; 2 Asian, non-Hispanic/Latino; 4 Hispanic/Latino; 1 Two or more races, non-Hispanic/Latino), 28 international. Average age 25. 73 applicants, 92% accepted, 18 enrolled. *Faculty:* 6 part-time/adjunct (0 women). Expenses: Contact institution. *Financial support:* In 2010–11, 28 students received support, including 9 fellowships with full tuition reimbursements available (averaging $18,000 per year); career-related internships or fieldwork, Federal Work-Study, institutionally sponsored loans, scholarships/grants, traineeships, health care benefits, tuition waivers (partial), and unspecified assistantships also available. In 2010, 24 master's awarded. *Degree program information:* Part-time programs available. Offers information security (MSSI). *Application deadline:* For fall admission, 6/15 priority date for domestic students, 3/15 for international students; for spring admission, 11/15 for domestic students, 11/1 for international students. Applications are processed on a rolling basis. *Application fee:* $25. Electronic applications accepted. *Application Contact:* Deborah K. Higgins, Graduate Coordinator, 410-516-8521, Fax: 410-516-3301, E-mail: dhiggins@jhu.edu. *Director,* Dr. Gerald M. Masson, 410-516-7013, Fax: 410-516-3301, E-mail: masson@jhu.edu.

National Institutes of Health Sponsored Programs Offers biology (PhD); cell, molecular, and developmental biology and biophysics (PhD). Electronic applications accepted.

Paul H. Nitze School of Advanced International Studies Students: 627 full-time (305 women), 39 part-time (24 women); includes 127 minority (18 Black or African American, non-Hispanic/Latino; 60 Asian, non-Hispanic/Latino; 32 Hispanic/Latino; 1 Native Hawaiian or other Pacific Islander, non-Hispanic/Latino; 16 Two or more races, non-Hispanic/Latino), 176 international. Average age 27. 1,753 applicants, 42% accepted, 307 enrolled. *Faculty:* 57 full-time (18 women), 125 part-time/adjunct (40 women). Expenses: Contact institution. *Financial support:* In 2010–11, 450 students received support, including 450 fellowships (averaging $12,000 per year), 32 teaching assistantships (averaging $3,906 per year); career-related internships or fieldwork, Federal Work-Study, and scholarships/grants also available. Financial award application deadline: 2/15; financial award applicants required to submit FAFSA. In 2010, 441 master's, 10 doctorates awarded. Offers international development (MA, Certificate); international public policy (MIPP); international relations (PhD); international studies (Certificate); Japan studies (MA); Korea Studies (MA); South Asia studies (MA); Southeast Asia studies (MA). *Application deadline:* For fall admission, 1/7 for domestic and international students. *Application fee:* $85. Electronic applications accepted. *Application Contact:* Admissions,

202-663-5700, Fax: 202-663-7788, E-mail: admissions.sais@jhu.edu. *Director of Admissions*, Sidney Jackson, 202-663-5700, Fax: 202-663-7788.

Peabody Conservatory Students: 332 full-time (188 women), 16 part-time (11 women); includes 62 minority (15 Black or African American, non-Hispanic/Latino; 30 Asian, non-Hispanic/Latino; 12 Hispanic/Latino; 5 Two or more races, non-Hispanic/Latino), 134 international. Average age 25. 763 applicants, 53% accepted, 181 enrolled. *Faculty:* 72 full-time (20 women), 60 part-time/adjunct (22 women). Expenses: Contact institution. *Financial support:* In 2010–11, 293 students received support, including 61 teaching assistantships (averaging $23,738 per year); Federal Work-Study, institutionally sponsored loans, scholarships/grants, and unspecified assistantships also available. Financial award application deadline: 2/1; financial award applicants required to submit FAFSA. In 2010, 100 master's, 5 doctorates, 31 other advanced degrees awarded. Offers music (MA, MM, DMA, AD, GPD). *Application deadline:* For fall admission, 12/1 for domestic students. *Application fee:* $100. *Application Contact:* David Lane, Director of Admissions, 800-368-2521, Fax: 410-659-8102, E-mail: admissions@peabody.jhu.edu. *Director*, Jeffrey Sharkey, 410-234-4700, Fax: 410-659-8131.

School of Education Students: 464 full-time (300 women), 1,386 part-time (1,128 women); includes 537 minority (292 Black or African American, non-Hispanic/Latino; 5 American Indian or Alaska Native, non-Hispanic/Latino; 102 Asian, non-Hispanic/Latino; 96 Hispanic/Latino; 3 Native Hawaiian or other Pacific Islander, non-Hispanic/Latino; 39 Two or more races, non-Hispanic/Latino), 38 international. Average age 32. 764 applicants, 59% accepted, 342 enrolled. *Faculty:* 52 full-time (30 women), 179 part-time/adjunct (111 women). Expenses: Contact institution. *Financial support:* In 2010–11, 752 students received support, including 9 fellowships, 5 research assistantships, 1 teaching assistantship; scholarships/grants also available. Support available to part-time students. Financial award application deadline: 6/1; financial award applicants required to submit FAFSA. In 2010, 638 master's, 5 doctorates, 306 other advanced degrees awarded. *Degree program information:* Part-time and evening/weekend programs available. Postbaccalaureate distance learning degree programs offered (minimal on-campus study). Offers adolescent literacy education (Certificate); advanced methods for differentiated instruction and inclusive education (Certificate); assistive technology (Certificate); clinical community counseling (Certificate); clinical supervision (Certificate); counseling (MS, CAGS); data-based decision making and organizational improvement (Certificate); early intervention/preschool special education specialist (Certificate); earth/space science (Certificate); education (MS); education of students with autism and other pervasive developmental disorders (Certificate); education of students with severe disabilities (Certificate); educational leadership for independent schools (Certificate); effective teaching of reading (Certificate); elementary education (MAT); emergent literacy education (Certificate); English as a second language instruction (Certificate); English for speakers of other languages (MAT); gifted education (Certificate); K-8 mathematics lead-teacher (Certificate); K-8 science lead-teacher (Certificate); leadership for school, family, and community collaboration (Certificate); leadership in technology integration (Certificate); mind, brain, and teaching (Certificate); play therapy (Certificate); school administration and supervision (Certificate); secondary education (MAT); special education (MS, Ed D, CAGS); teacher development and leadership (Ed D); teacher leadership (Certificate); teaching the adult learner (Certificate); technology for educators (MS); urban education (Certificate). *Application deadline:* For fall admission, 5/1 for international students; for spring admission, 10/15 for international students. Applications are processed on a rolling basis. *Application fee:* $80. Electronic applications accepted. *Application Contact:* Jennifer Shaffer, Director of Admissions, 410-516-9797, Fax: 410-516-9799, E-mail: educationinfo@jhu.edu. *Interim Dean*, Dr. Mariale Hardiman, 410-516-7820, Fax: 410-516-6697, E-mail: emayotte@jhu.edu.

Division of Public Safety Leadership Students: 131 full-time (39 women), 12 part-time (1 woman); includes 52 minority (35 Black or African American, non-Hispanic/Latino; 4 Asian, non-Hispanic/Latino; 12 Hispanic/Latino; 1 Two or more races, non-Hispanic/Latino). Average age 40. 81 applicants, 75% accepted, 54 enrolled. *Faculty:* 10 full-time (3 women), 23 part-time/adjunct (7 women). Expenses: Contact institution. *Financial support:* Scholarships/grants available. Support available to part-time students. Financial award application deadline: 6/1; financial award applicants required to submit FAFSA. In 2010, 95 master's awarded. *Degree program information:* Part-time and evening/weekend programs available. Offers intelligence analysis (MS); management (MS). *Application deadline:* For fall admission, 5/1 for international students; for spring admission, 10/15 for international students. Applications are processed on a rolling basis. *Application fee:* $0. Electronic applications accepted. *Application Contact:* Jennifer Shaffer, Director of Admissions, 410-516-9797, Fax: 410-516-9799, E-mail: educationinfo@jhu.edu. *Associate Dean*, Dr. Sheldon Greenberg, 410-516-9900, Fax: 410-290-1061, E-mail: psl@jhu.edu.

School of Medicine Students: 1,377 full-time (689 women); includes 409 minority (79 Black or African American, non-Hispanic/Latino; 2 American Indian or Alaska Native, non-Hispanic/Latino; 259 Asian, non-Hispanic/Latino; 54 Hispanic/Latino; 1 Native Hawaiian or other Pacific Islander, non-Hispanic/Latino; 14 Two or more races, non-Hispanic/Latino), 353 international. 5,064 applicants, 11% accepted, 267 enrolled. *Faculty:* 2,642 full-time (983 women), 1,275 part-time/adjunct (420 women). Expenses: Contact institution. *Financial support:* In 2010–11, fellowships with full tuition reimbursements (averaging $23,000 per year); research assistantships, teaching assistantships, career-related internships or fieldwork, Federal Work-Study, institutionally sponsored loans, and tuition waivers (full) also available. In 2010, 118 first professional degrees, 8 master's, 90 doctorates awarded. Offers medicine (MD, MA, MS, PhD). *Application deadline:* Applications are processed on a rolling basis. *Application fee:* $85. Electronic applications accepted. *Application Contact:* Dr. James Weiss, Associate Dean of Admissions, 410-955-3182. *Dean of Medical Faculty and Chief Executive Officer*, Dr. Edward D. Miller, 410-955-3180.

Division of Health Sciences Informatics Students: 9 full-time (0 women); includes 2 minority (1 Black or African American, non-Hispanic/Latino; 1 Asian, non-Hispanic/Latino), 5 international. 20 applicants, 15% accepted, 1 enrolled. *Faculty:* 40 part-time/adjunct (10 women). Expenses: Contact institution. *Financial support:* In 2010–11, 3 fellowships with full tuition reimbursements (averaging $42,750 per year) were awarded; career-related internships or fieldwork and health care benefits also available. In 2010, 6 master's awarded. Offers applied health sciences informatics (MS); health sciences informatics research (MS). *Application deadline:* For spring admission, 2/15 priority date for domestic students, 2/15 for international students. *Application fee:* $85. Electronic applications accepted. *Application Contact:* Kersti Winny, Academic Program Administrator, 410-502-3768, Fax: 410-614-2064, E-mail: kwinny@jhmi.edu. *Director, Training Program*, Dr. Harold P. Lehmann, 410-502-2569, Fax: 410-614-2064, E-mail: lehmann@jhmi.edu.

Graduate Programs in Medicine Students: 914 full-time (466 women); includes 211 minority (50 Black or African American, non-Hispanic/Latino; 1 American Indian or Alaska Native, non-Hispanic/Latino; 115 Asian, non-Hispanic/Latino; 33 Hispanic/Latino; 12 Two or more races, non-Hispanic/Latino), 320 international. Average age 24. 1,409 applicants, 21% accepted, 147 enrolled. *Faculty:* 258 full-time (77 women), 31 part-time/adjunct (12 women). Expenses: Contact institution. *Financial support:* In 2010–11, fellowships with full tuition reimbursements (averaging $23,000 per year); research assistantships, teaching assistantships with tuition reimbursements, career-related internships or fieldwork, Federal Work-Study, institutionally sponsored loans, and tuition waivers (full) also available. Financial award applicants required to submit FAFSA. In 2010, 18 master's, 90 doctorates awarded. Offers biochemistry, cellular and molecular biology (PhD); biological chemistry (PhD); cellular and molecular medicine (PhD); cellular and molecular physiology (PhD); functional anatomy and evolution (PhD); human genetics (PhD); immunology (PhD); medical and biological illustration (MA); medicine (MA, MS, PhD); molecular biophysics (MS, PhD); neuroscience (PhD); pathobiology (PhD); pharmacology and molecular sciences (PhD); physiology (PhD). *Application deadline:* For fall admission, 1/10 priority date for domestic and international students. Applications are processed on a rolling basis. *Application fee:* $85. Electronic applications accepted. *Application Contact:* Dr. James Weiss, Associate Dean of Admissions, 410-955-3182. *Associate Dean for Graduate Programs*, Dr. Peter Maloney, 410-614-3385.

School of Nursing Students: 131 full-time (123 women), 175 part-time (163 women); includes 32 Black or African American, non-Hispanic/Latino; 6 American Indian or Alaska Native, non-Hispanic/Latino; 32 Asian, non-Hispanic/Latino; 6 Hispanic/Latino, 5 international. Average age 36. 405 applicants, 78% accepted, 94 enrolled. *Faculty:* 31 full-time (27 women), 23 part-time/adjunct (21 women). Expenses: Contact institution. *Financial support:* In 2010–11, 79 students received support, including 6 fellowships with partial tuition reimbursements available (averaging $23,272 per year); research assistantships with full tuition reimbursements available, teaching assistantships with full tuition reimbursements available, career-related internships or fieldwork, Federal Work-Study, scholarships/grants, traineeships, and tuition waivers (partial) also available. Support available to part-time students. Financial award application deadline: 3/1; financial award applicants required to submit FAFSA. In 2010, 80 master's, 3 doctorates awarded. *Degree program information:* Part-time programs available. Offers adult acute/critical care (MSN, Certificate); adult and pediatric primary care (MSN); adult or pediatric primary care (Certificate); business of nursing (Certificate); clinical nurse specialist (MSN); clinical nurse specialist and health systems management (MSN); emergency preparedness/disaster response (Certificate); family primary care (MSN, Certificate); health systems management (MSN); nursing (MSN, DNP, PhD, Certificate); public health nursing (MSN); women's health (Certificate). *Application deadline:* For fall admission, 2/1 priority date for domestic and international students; for winter admission, 7/1 priority date for domestic and international students; for spring admission, 7/1 priority date for domestic and international students. Applications are processed on a rolling basis. *Application fee:* $75. Electronic applications accepted. *Application Contact:* Mary O'Rourke, Director of Admissions/Student Services, 410-955-7548, Fax: 410-614-7086, E-mail: orourke@son.jhmi.edu. *Dean*, Dr. Martha N. Hill, 410-955-7544, Fax: 410-955-4890, E-mail: mnhill@son.jhmi.edu.

Zanvyl Krieger School of Arts and Sciences Students: 1,005 full-time (469 women), 6 part-time (3 women); includes 145 minority (21 Black or African American, non-Hispanic/Latino; 4 American Indian or Alaska Native, non-Hispanic/Latino; 61 Asian, non-Hispanic/Latino; 37 Hispanic/Latino; 22 Two or more races, non-Hispanic/Latino), 319 international. Average age 27. 2,945 applicants, 13% accepted, 309 enrolled. *Faculty:* 357 full-time (128 women), 73 part-time/adjunct (43 women). Expenses: Contact institution. *Financial support:* In 2010–11, 535 students received support, including 180 fellowships with full and partial tuition reimbursements available (averaging $20,213 per year), 164 research assistantships with full and partial tuition reimbursements available (averaging $19,314 per year), 314 teaching assistantships with full and partial tuition reimbursements available (averaging $19,534 per year); career-related internships or fieldwork, Federal Work-Study, institutionally sponsored loans, scholarships/grants, health care benefits, tuition waivers (full and partial), and unspecified assistantships also available. Support available to part-time students. Financial award applicants required to submit FAFSA. In 2010, 164 master's, 123 doctorates awarded. Offers anthropology (PhD); applied economics (MA); arts and sciences (MA, MFA, MS, PhD, Certificate); astronomy (PhD); bioinformatics (MS); biology (PhD); bioscience regulatory affairs (MS); biotechnology (MS); chemistry (PhD); chemistry-biology (PhD); classics (PhD); cognitive science (PhD); communication (MA); earth and planetary sciences (MA, PhD); economics (PhD); energy policy and climate (MS); English and American literature (PhD); environmental sciences and policy (MS); fiction writing (MFA); French (PhD); German (PhD); government (MA, Certificate); history (PhD); history of art (MA, PhD); history of science and technology (MA, PhD); Italian (PhD); liberal arts (MA, Certificate); mathematics (PhD); molecular biophysics (PhD); museum studies (MA); national securities study (Certificate); Near Eastern studies (PhD); philosophy (MA, PhD); physics (PhD); poetry (MFA); political science (MA, PhD); psychological and brain sciences (PhD); romance languages (PhD); science writing (MA); sociology (PhD); Spanish (PhD); writing (MA, MFA). *Application fee:* $75. Electronic applications accepted. *Application Contact:* Dennis McIver, Graduate Admissions Coordinator, 410-516-8174, Fax: 410-516-0780, E-mail: graduateadmissions@jhu.edu. *Dean*, Dr. Michela Gallagher, 410-516-8212, Fax: 410-516-6017.

Humanities Center Students: 11 full-time (5 women); includes 2 minority (1 Hispanic/Latino; 1 Two or more races, non-Hispanic/Latino), 3 international. Average age 28. 52 applicants, 2% accepted, 1 enrolled. *Faculty:* 7 full-time (4 women). Expenses: Contact institution. *Financial support:* In 2010–11, 14 students received support, including 7 fellowships with full tuition reimbursements available (averaging $17,500 per year), 6 teaching assistantships with full tuition reimbursements available (averaging $17,500 per year); Federal Work-Study, institutionally sponsored loans, tuition waivers (full), and unspecified assistantships also available. Financial award application deadline: 12/1. In 2010, 1 doctorate awarded. *Degree program information:* Part-time programs available. Offers humanities (PhD). *Application deadline:* For fall admission, 12/1 for domestic and international students. *Application fee:* $75. Electronic applications accepted. *Application Contact:* Marva Philip, Administrator, 410-516-7619, Fax: 410-516-4897, E-mail: mphilip@jhu.edu. *Chair*, Prof. Hent de Vries, 410-516-0474, Fax: 410-516-4897, E-mail: hentdevries@jhu.edu.

Institute for Policy Studies Students: 83 full-time (54 women); includes 19 minority (4 Black or African American, non-Hispanic/Latino; 1 American Indian or Alaska Native, non-Hispanic/Latino; 8 Asian, non-Hispanic/Latino; 2 Hispanic/Latino; 4 Two or more races, non-Hispanic/Latino), 23 international. Average age 25. 210 applicants, 43% accepted, 45 enrolled. *Faculty:* 7 full-time (4 women), 7 part-time/adjunct (3 women). Expenses: Contact institution. *Financial support:* In 2010–11, 60 students received support. Career-related internships or fieldwork, Federal Work-Study, and unspecified assistantships available. Financial award application deadline: 4/15; financial award applicants required to submit FAFSA. In 2010, 24 master's awarded. Offers public policy (MA). *Application deadline:* For fall admission, 1/15 for domestic and international students. *Application fee:* $75. Electronic applications accepted. *Application Contact:* Dr. Carey Borkoski, Assistant Director, 410-516-4624, Fax: 410-516-8233, E-mail: cborkoski@jhu.edu. *Assistant Director of the Graduate Program*, Dr. Carey C. Borkoski, 410-516-4624, Fax: 410-516-8233, E-mail: cborkoski@jhu.edu.

JOHNSON & WALES UNIVERSITY, Providence, RI 02903-3703

General Information Independent, coed, comprehensive institution. *Enrollment:* 10,974 graduate, professional, and undergraduate students; 828 full-time matriculated graduate/professional students (500 women), 443 part-time matriculated graduate/professional students (286 women). *Enrollment by degree level:* 1,188 master's, 83 doctoral. *Graduate faculty:* 20 full-time (6 women), 20 part-time/adjunct (6 women). *Tuition:* Part-time $1535 per course. Part-time tuition and fees vary according to degree level and program. *Graduate housing:* On-campus housing not available. *Student services:* Campus employment opportunities, campus safety program, career counseling, free psychological counseling, international student services, low-cost health insurance. *Library facilities:* Johnson & Wales University Library. *Online resources:* library catalog, web page, access to other libraries' catalogs. *Research affiliation:* Consortium of Rhode Island Academic and Research Libraries, Association of Institutional Research.

Computer facilities: A campuswide network can be accessed from student residence rooms and from off campus. Online class registration is available. *Web address:* http://www.jwu.edu/.

General Application Contact: Graduate School Admissions, 401-598-1015, Fax: 401-598-1286, E-mail: gradadm@jwu.edu.

GRADUATE UNITS

The Alan Shawn Feinstein Graduate School Students: 828 full-time (500 women), 443 part-time (286 women); includes 26 Black or African American, non-Hispanic/Latino; 7 Asian, non-Hispanic/Latino; 13 Hispanic/Latino, 576 international. 613 applicants, 84% accepted, 348 enrolled. *Faculty:* 20 full-time (6 women), 20 part-time/adjunct (6 women). Expenses: Contact institution. *Financial support:* Career-related internships or fieldwork, institutionally sponsored loans, tuition waivers (partial), and unspecified assistantships available. Support available to part-time students. Financial award application deadline: 5/1. In 2010, 376 master's, 30 doctorates awarded. *Degree program information:* Part-time and evening/weekend programs available. Offers accounting (MBA); business education and secondary special education (MAT); elementary education and elementary special education (MAT); elementary education and elementary/secondary special education (MAT); elementary education and secondary special education (MAT); enhanced accounting (MBA); food service education (MAT); higher education (Ed D); hospitality (MBA); K-12 (Ed D); teaching and learning (M Ed). *Application deadline:* Applications are processed on a rolling basis. *Application fee:* $0. *Application Contact:* Graduate School Admissions, 401-598-1015, Fax: 401-598-1286, E-mail: gradadm@jwu.edu.

JOHNSON STATE COLLEGE, Johnson, VT 05656

General Information State-supported, coed, comprehensive institution. *Enrollment:* 1,949 graduate, professional, and undergraduate students; 62 full-time matriculated graduate/professional students (50 women), 195 part-time matriculated graduate/professional students (132 women). *Enrollment by degree level:* 257 master's. *Graduate faculty:* 11 full-time (6 women), 14 part-time/adjunct (11 women). Tuition, state resident: part-time $437 per credit. Tuition, nonresident: part-time $943 per credit. *Graduate housing:* Rooms and/or apartments available on a first-come, first-served basis to single and married students. Housing application deadline: 5/15. *Student services:* Low-cost health insurance, services for students with disabilities, teacher training. *Library facilities:* Library and Learning Center plus 1 other. *Online resources:* library catalog, access to other libraries' catalogs. *Collection:* 156,818 titles, 522 serial subscriptions, 7,575 audiovisual materials.

Computer facilities: 160 computers available on campus for general student use. A campuswide network can be accessed from student residence rooms and from off campus. Online class registration is available. *Web address:* http://www.jsc.edu/.

General Application Contact: Catherine H. Higley, Program Coordinator, 800-635-2356 Ext. 1244, Fax: 802-635-1248, E-mail: catherine.higley@jsc.edu.

GRADUATE UNITS

Graduate Program in Education *Degree program information:* Part-time programs available. Offers applied behavior analysis (MA Ed); children's mental health (MA Ed); curriculum and instruction (MA Ed); gifted and talented (MA Ed); literacy (MA Ed); science education (MA Ed); secondary education (MA Ed, CAGS); special education (MA Ed).

Program in Counseling *Degree program information:* Part-time programs available. Offers counseling (MA).

Program in Studio Arts *Degree program information:* Part-time programs available. Postbaccalaureate distance learning degree programs offered (minimal on-campus study). Offers drawing (MFA); mixed media (MFA); painting (MFA); sculpture (MFA).

JOHNSON UNIVERSITY, Knoxville, TN 37998-1001

General Information Independent-religious, coed, comprehensive institution. *Enrollment:* 816 graduate, professional, and undergraduate students; 38 full-time matriculated graduate/professional students (30 women), 98 part-time matriculated graduate/professional students (37 women). *Enrollment by degree level:* 136 master's. *Graduate faculty:* 10 full-time (1 woman), 6 part-time/adjunct (1 woman). *Tuition:* Full-time $8300; part-time $320 per credit hour. *Required fees:* $800; $32 per hour. Part-time tuition and fees vary according to course load and program. *Graduate housing:* Rooms and/or apartments available on a first-come, first-served basis to single students and available to married students. Typical cost: $2800 per year ($5800 including board) for single students; $4320 per year for married students. Housing application deadline: 8/1. *Student services:* Campus employment opportunities, career counseling, child daycare facilities, free psychological counseling, low-cost health insurance, services for students with disabilities. *Library facilities:* Glass Memorial Library plus 1 other. *Online resources:* library catalog, web page. *Collection:* 111,776 titles, 310 serial subscriptions, 14,710 audiovisual materials.

Computer facilities: A campuswide network can be accessed from student residence rooms and from off campus. Online class registration is available. *Web address:* http://www.jbc.edu/.

General Application Contact: Dr. Tim W. Wingfield, Dean of Enrollment Management, 865-251-2403, Fax: 865-251-2336, E-mail: twingfield@jbc.edu.

GRADUATE UNITS

Department of Marriage and Family Therapy Offers marriage and family therapy/professional counseling (MA).

Program in New Testament *Degree program information:* Part-time and evening/weekend programs available. Postbaccalaureate distance learning degree programs offered (no on-campus study). Offers preaching (MA); research (MA).

Teacher Education Program *Degree program information:* Part-time programs available. Offers Bible and educational technology (MA); holistic education (MA).

JONES INTERNATIONAL UNIVERSITY, Centennial, CO 80112

General Information Proprietary, coed, university. *Graduate housing:* On-campus housing not available.

GRADUATE UNITS

Graduate School of Education *Degree program information:* Part-time and evening/weekend programs available. Postbaccalaureate distance learning degree programs offered (no on-campus study). Offers adult education (M Ed); corporate training and knowledge management (M Ed); curriculum and instruction (M Ed); e-learning technology and design (M Ed); educational leadership and administration (M Ed); educational leadership and administration: principal and administrator licensure (M Ed); elementary curriculum instruction and assessment (M Ed); higher education leadership and administration (M Ed); K-12 instructional technology (M Ed); K-12 instructional technology: teacher licensure (M Ed); secondary curriculum instruction and assessment (M Ed); technology and design (M Ed). Electronic applications accepted.

School of Business *Degree program information:* Part-time and evening/weekend programs available. Postbaccalaureate distance learning degree programs offered (no on-campus study). Offers accounting (MBA); business communication (MABC); entrepreneurship (MABC, MBA); finance (MBA); global enterprise management (MBA); health care management (MBA); information security management (MBA); information technology management (MBA); leadership and influence (MABC); leading the customer-driven organization (MABC); negotiation and conflict management (MBA); project management (MABC, MBA). Program only offered online. Electronic applications accepted.

THE JUDGE ADVOCATE GENERAL'S SCHOOL, U.S. ARMY, Charlottesville, VA 22903-1781

General Information Federally supported, coed, primarily men, graduate-only institution. *Graduate housing:* On-campus housing not available.

GRADUATE UNITS

Graduate Programs Offers military law (LL M). Only active duty military lawyers attend this school.

JUDSON UNIVERSITY, Elgin, IL 60123-1498

General Information Independent-religious, coed, comprehensive institution. *Enrollment:* 59 full-time matriculated graduate/professional students (38 women), 46 part-time matriculated graduate/professional students (23 women). *Enrollment by degree level:* 105 master's. *Graduate faculty:* 18 full-time (7 women), 27 part-time/adjunct (9 women). *Tuition:* Full-time $18,000; part-time $1000 per credit hour. *Required fees:* $200 per term. Tuition and fees vary according to course load, program and student level. *Graduate housing:* Rooms and/or apartments available on a first-come, first-served basis to single and married students. Typical cost: $5600 per year ($8800 including board) for single students; $5600 per year ($8800 including board) for married students. Room and board charges vary according to board plan and housing facility selected. Housing application deadline: 8/1. *Student services:* Campus employment opportunities, campus safety program, career counseling, exercise/wellness program, international student services, low-cost health insurance, services for students with disabilities, writing training.

Computer facilities: 90 computers available on campus for general student use. A campuswide network can be accessed from student residence rooms and from off campus. *Web address:* http://www.judsonu.edu/.

General Application Contact: Maria Aguirre, Assistant to the Registrar for Graduate Programs, 847-628-1160, E-mail: maguirre@judsonu.edu.

GRADUATE UNITS

Graduate Programs Students: 59 full-time (38 women), 46 part-time (23 women); includes 16 minority (8 Black or African American, non-Hispanic/Latino; 1 Asian, non-Hispanic/Latino; 7 Hispanic/Latino), 2 international. Average age 32. *Faculty:* 18 full-time (7 women), 27 part-time/adjunct (9 women). Expenses: Contact institution. *Financial support:* Applicants required to submit FAFSA. In 2010, 76 master's awarded. *Degree program information:* Part-time and evening/weekend programs available. Postbaccalaureate distance learning degree programs offered (no on-campus study). Offers architecture (M Arch); literacy (M Ed); organizational leadership (MA); teaching (M Ed). *Application deadline:* Applications are processed on a rolling basis. *Application fee:* $40. Electronic applications accepted. *Application Contact:* Maria Aguirre, Assistant to the Registrar for Graduate Programs, 847-628-1160, E-mail: maguirre@judsonu.edu. *Provost and Vice-President for Academic Affairs,* Dr. Dale H. Simmons, 847-628-1000, E-mail: dsimmons@judsonu.edu.

THE JUILLIARD SCHOOL, New York, NY 10023-6588

General Information Independent, coed, comprehensive institution. *Graduate housing:* Room and/or apartments available on a first-come, first-served basis to single students; on-campus housing not available to married students. Housing application deadline: 5/1.

GRADUATE UNITS

Program in Music Offers music (MM, DMA, Artist Diploma, Diploma). Electronic applications accepted.

KANSAS CITY UNIVERSITY OF MEDICINE AND BIOSCIENCES, Kansas City, MO 64106-1453

General Information Independent, coed, graduate-only institution. *Enrollment by degree level:* 985 first professional, 54 master's. *Graduate faculty:* 43 full-time (14 women), 2 part-time/adjunct (0 women). *Tuition:* Full-time $41,013. *Required fees:* $175. *Graduate housing:* On-campus housing not available. *Student services:* Campus employment opportunities, campus safety program, career counseling, free psychological counseling. *Library facilities:* Kansas City University of Medicine and Biosciences Library. *Online resources:* library catalog, web page, access to other libraries' catalogs. *Collection:* 82,302 titles, 892 serial subscriptions, 7,710 audiovisual materials. *Research affiliation:* Boehringer Ingelheim (HIV), Mylanta-Bertek (hypertension), Covance (hypertension), Novartis (hronic obstructive pulmonary disease).

Computer facilities: 98 computers available on campus for general student use. A campuswide network can be accessed. Online class registration is available. *Web address:* http://www.kcumb.edu/.

General Application Contact: Brooke Birdsong, Associate Director of Admissions, 816-654-7160, Fax: 816-654-7161, E-mail: admissions@kcumb.edu.

GRADUATE UNITS

College of Biosciences Students: 51 full-time (29 women); includes 3 Black or African American, non-Hispanic/Latino; 4 Asian, non-Hispanic/Latino; 1 Hispanic/Latino. Average age 25. 138 applicants, 51% accepted, 51 enrolled. Expenses: Contact institution. *Financial support:* Applicants required to submit FAFSA. In 2010, 50 master's awarded. *Degree program information:* Part-time programs available. Offers bioethics (MA); biomedical sciences (MS). *Application deadline:* For fall admission, 1/1 priority date for domestic students. Applications are processed on a rolling basis. *Application fee:* $30. *Application Contact:* Brooke Birdsong, Associate Director of Admissions, 816-654-7160, Fax: 816-654-7161, E-mail: admissions@kcumb.edu. *Dean,* Dr. Douglas Rushing, 816-654-7252.

College of Osteopathic Medicine Students: 985 full-time (458 women). Average age 24. 3,108 applicants, 13% accepted, 245 enrolled. *Faculty:* 44 full-time (13 women), 13 part-time/adjunct (7 women). Expenses: Contact institution. *Financial support:* In 2010–11, 54 students received support. Career-related internships or fieldwork, institutionally sponsored loans, and scholarships/grants available. Financial award application deadline: 4/1; financial award applicants required to submit FAFSA. Offers osteopathic medicine (DO). *Application deadline:* For fall admission, 4/1 for domestic students. Applications are processed on a rolling basis. *Application fee:* $50. *Application Contact:* Ruth Armstrong, Admissions, 816-654-7160, Fax: 816-654-7161, E-mail: admissions@kcumb.edu. *Executive Vice President for Academic and Medical Affairs/Dean,* Dr. Darin Haug, 800-234-4347.

KANSAS STATE UNIVERSITY, Manhattan, KS 66506

General Information State-supported, coed, university. CGS member. *Graduate housing:* Rooms and/or apartments available on a first-come, first-served basis to single and married students. Housing application deadline: 2/1. *Research affiliation:* Visteon Corporation, Midwest Research Institute, NASA–Research Center, U. S. Grain Marketing Research Laboratory.

GRADUATE UNITS

College of Veterinary Medicine Offers biomedical science (MS); clinical sciences (MPH); diagnostic medicine/pathobiology (PhD); physiology (PhD); veterinary medicine (MPH, MS, PhD). Electronic applications accepted.

Graduate School *Degree program information:* Part-time and evening/weekend programs available. Postbaccalaureate distance learning degree programs offered (minimal on-campus study). Electronic applications accepted.

College of Agriculture *Degree program information:* Part-time programs available. Postbaccalaureate distance learning degree programs offered (minimal on-campus study). Offers agricultural economics (MAB, MS, PhD); agriculture (MAB, MS, PhD); animal breeding and genetics (MS, PhD); crop science (MS, PhD); entomology (MS, PhD); food science (MS, PhD); genetics (MS, PhD); grain science and industry (MS, PhD); horticulture (MS, PhD); meat science (MS, PhD); monogastric nutrition (MS, PhD); physiology (MS, PhD); plant pathology (MS, PhD); range management (MS, PhD); ruminant nutrition (MS, PhD); soil science (MS, PhD); weed science (MS, PhD). Electronic applications accepted.

College of Architecture, Planning and Design *Degree program information:* Part-time and evening/weekend programs available. Postbaccalaureate distance learning degree programs offered (minimal on-campus study). Offers architecture (M Arch); architecture, planning and design (M Arch, MLA, MRCP); landscape architecture and regional and community planning (MLA); regional and community planning (MRCP). Electronic applications accepted.

College of Arts and Sciences *Degree program information:* Part-time programs available. Postbaccalaureate distance learning degree programs offered (minimal on-campus study). Offers analytical chemistry (MS); art (MFA); arts and sciences (MA, MFA, MM, MPA, MS, PhD); biochemistry (MS, PhD); biological chemistry (MS); biology (MS, PhD); chemistry (PhD); economics (MA, PhD); English (MA); French (MA); geography (MA, PhD); geology (MS); German (MA); history (MA); inorganic chemistry (MS); kinesiology (MS); mass communications (MS); materials chemistry (MS); mathematics (MS, PhD); microbiology (PhD); music education (MM); music education/band conducting (MM); music history and literature (MM); organic chemistry (MS); performance (MM); performance with pedagogy emphasis (MM); physical chemistry (MS); political science (MA); psychology (MS, PhD); public administration (MPA); rhetoric/communication (MA); security studies (MA, PhD); sociology (MA, PhD); Spanish (MA); statistics (MS, PhD); theatre (MA); theory and composition (MM). Electronic applications accepted.

College of Business Administration *Degree program information:* Part-time programs available. Offers accounting (M Acc); business administration (M Acc, MBA). Electronic applications accepted.

College of Education *Degree program information:* Part-time and evening/weekend programs available. Postbaccalaureate distance learning degree programs offered. Offers academic advising (MS); adult and continuing education (Ed D); adult, occupational and continuing education (MS); college student development (MS); counseling and student development (Ed D); counselor education and supervision (PhD); curriculum and instruction (MS, Ed D, PhD); education (MS, Ed D, PhD); educational administration and leadership (MS, Ed D); school counseling (MS); special education (MS, Ed D); student affairs in higher education (PhD). Electronic applications accepted.

College of Engineering *Degree program information:* Part-time programs available. Postbaccalaureate distance learning degree programs offered (minimal on-campus study). Offers architectural engineering (MS); biological and agricultural engineering (MS, PhD); chemical engineering (MS, PhD); civil engineering (MS, PhD); computer science (MS, PhD); electrical engineering (MS, PhD); engineering (MEM, MS, MSE, PhD); engineering management (MEM); industrial engineering (MS, PhD); mechanical engineering (MS, PhD); nuclear engineering (MS, PhD); operations research (MS); software engineering (MSE). Electronic applications accepted.

College of Human Ecology *Degree program information:* Part-time programs available. Postbaccalaureate distance learning degree programs offered. Offers apparel and textiles (PhD); communication sciences and disorders (MS); design (MS); dietetics (MS); early childhood education (MS); family life education and consultation (PhD); family studies (MS); food service and hospitality management (PhD); food service hospitality management and dietetics administration (MS); general apparel and textile (MS); human ecology (MS, PhD); human nutrition (MS, PhD); life span human development (MS); lifespan and human development (PhD); marketing (MS); marriage and family therapy (MS, PhD); merchandising (MS); personal financial planning (PhD); product development (MS). Electronic applications accepted.

See Display below and Close-Up on page 959.

KANSAS WESLEYAN UNIVERSITY, Salina, KS 67401-6196

General Information Independent-religious, coed, comprehensive institution. *Graduate housing:* Rooms and/or apartments available to single and married students.

GRADUATE UNITS

Program in Business Administration *Degree program information:* Part-time and evening/weekend programs available. Offers business administration (MBA); sports management (MBA).

KAPLAN UNIVERSITY, DAVENPORT CAMPUS, Davenport, IA 52807-2095

General Information Proprietary, coed, comprehensive institution. CGS member.

GRADUATE UNITS

School of Business *Degree program information:* Part-time and evening/weekend programs available. Postbaccalaureate distance learning degree programs offered (no on-campus study). Offers business administration (MBA); change leadership (MS); entrepreneurship (MBA); finance (MBA); health care management (MBA, MS); human resource (MBA); international business (MBA); management (MS); marketing (MBA); project management (MBA, MS); supply chain management and logistics (MBA, MS). Electronic applications accepted.

School of Criminal Justice *Degree program information:* Part-time and evening/weekend programs available. Postbaccalaureate distance learning degree programs offered (no on-campus study). Offers corrections (MSCJ); global issues in criminal justice (MSCJ); law (MSCJ); leadership and executive management (MSCJ); policing (MSCJ). Electronic applications accepted.

School of Higher Education Studies *Degree program information:* Part-time and evening/weekend programs available. Postbaccalaureate distance learning degree programs offered (no on-campus study). Offers college administration and leadership (MS); college teaching and learning (MS); student services (MS).

School of Information Technology *Degree program information:* Part-time and evening/weekend programs available. Postbaccalaureate distance learning degree programs offered (no on-campus study). Offers decision support systems (MS); information security and assurance (MS).

School of Legal Studies *Degree program information:* Part-time and evening/weekend programs available. Postbaccalaureate distance learning degree programs offered (no on-campus study). Offers health care delivery (MS); pathway to paralegal (Postbaccalaureate Certificate); state and local government (MS).

School of Nursing *Degree program information:* Part-time and evening/weekend programs available. Postbaccalaureate distance learning degree programs offered (no on-campus study). Offers nurse administrator (MS); nurse educator (MS).

School of Teacher Education *Degree program information:* Part-time and evening/weekend programs available. Postbaccalaureate distance learning degree programs offered (no on-campus study). Offers education (M Ed); secondary education (M Ed); teaching and learning (MA); teaching literacy and language: grades 6-12 (MA); teaching literacy and language: grades K-6 (MA); teaching mathematics: grades 6-8 (MA); teaching mathematics: grades 9-12 (MA); teaching mathematics: grades K-5 (MA); teaching science: grades 6-12 (MA); teaching science: grades K-6 (MA); teaching students with special needs (MA); teaching with technology (MA).

KEAN UNIVERSITY, Union, NJ 07083

General Information State-supported, coed, comprehensive institution. CGS member. *Enrollment:* 15,939 graduate, professional, and undergraduate students; 828 full-time matriculated graduate/professional students (654 women), 1,574 part-time matriculated graduate/professional students (1,225 women). *Enrollment by degree level:* 2,288 master's, 62 doctoral, 52 other advanced degrees. *Graduate faculty:* 234 full-time (127 women). Tuition, state resident: full-time $10,872; part-time $500 per credit. Tuition, nonresident: full-time $14,736; part-time $614 per credit. *Required fees:* $2741; $125 per credit. Part-time tuition and fees vary according to course load and degree level. *Graduate housing:* On-campus housing not available. *Student services:* Campus employment opportunities, campus safety program, career counseling, child daycare facilities, exercise/wellness program, free psychological counseling, grant writing training, international student services, low-cost health insurance, multicultural affairs office, services for students with disabilities, teacher training, writing training. *Library facilities:* Nancy Thompson Library. *Online resources:* library catalog, web page, access to other libraries' catalogs. *Collection:* 379,905 titles, 34,747 serial subscriptions, 7,087 audiovisual materials. *Research affiliation:* Robert Wood Johnson Foundation (the effect of tobacco control policy), Institute of Vertebrate Paleontology and Paleoanthropology (paleoanthropology), University of Medicine and Dentistry of New Jersey (biochemistry, molecular biology and neuroscience), Shodor Foundation (intelligent Internet search engines for science research and education), New Jersey Institute of Technology (partitioning to support auditing and extending the UMLS), National Bureau of Economic Research (alcoholic advertising and youth).

Computer facilities: 1,700 computers available on campus for general student use. A campuswide network can be accessed from student residence rooms and from off campus. Online class registration is available. *Web address:* http://www.kean.edu/.

General Application Contact: Ann-Marie Kay, Assistant Director of Graduate Admissions, 908-737-4723, Fax: 908-737-5965, E-mail: grad-adm@kean.edu.

GRADUATE UNITS

College of Business and Public Management Students: 93 full-time (61 women), 122 part-time (71 women); includes 68 Black or African American, non-Hispanic/Latino; 12 Asian, non-Hispanic/Latino; 27 Hispanic/Latino, 22 international. Average age 31. 104 applicants, 81% accepted, 56 enrolled. *Faculty:* 23 full-time (8 women). Expenses: Contact institution. *Financial support:* In 2010–11, 11 research assistantships with full tuition reimbursements (averaging $3,263 per year) were awarded; unspecified assistantships also available. Financial award applicants required to submit FAFSA. In 2010, 89 master's awarded. *Degree program information:* Part-time and evening/weekend programs available. Offers accounting (MS); business and public management (MA, MPA, MS); criminal justice (MA); environmental management (MPA); health services administration (MPA); non-profit management (MPA); public administration (MPA). *Application deadline:* For fall admission, 6/1 for domestic students; for spring admission, 11/1 for domestic students. *Application fee:* $75 ($150 for international students). Electronic applications accepted. *Application Contact:* Reenat Hasan, Pre-Admissions Coordinator, 908-737-5923, Fax: 908-737-5925, E-mail: hasanr@kean.edu. *Dean,* Dr. Kathryn Martell, 908-737-4120, Fax: 908-737-4125, E-mail: kmartell@kean.edu.

Kean University (continued)

College of Education Students: 347 full-time (285 women), 819 part-time (704 women); includes 132 Black or African American, non-Hispanic/Latino; 1 American Indian or Alaska Native, non-Hispanic/Latino; 38 Asian, non-Hispanic/Latino; 161 Hispanic/Latino; 5 Two or more races, non-Hispanic/Latino, 10 international. Average age 32. 831 applicants, 70% accepted, 370 enrolled. *Faculty:* 64 full-time (44 women). Expenses: Contact institution. *Financial support:* In 2010–11, 21 research assistantships with full tuition reimbursements (averaging $3,263 per year) were awarded; unspecified assistantships also available. Financial award applicants required to submit FAFSA. In 2010, 276 master's awarded. *Degree program information:* Part-time programs available. Offers administration in early childhood and family studies (MA); adult literacy (MA); advanced curriculum and teaching (MA); alcohol and drug abuse counseling (MA); basic skills (MA); bilingual (MA); classroom instruction (MA); clinical mental heath counseling (MA); education (MA, MS); education for family living (MA); exercise science (MS); high incidence disabilities (MA); low incidence disabilities (MA); mathematics/science/computer education (MA); reading specialization (MA); school counseling (MA); speech language pathology (MA); teaching (MA); teaching English as a second language (MA); teaching physics (MA); world languages (Spanish) (MA). *Application deadline:* For fall admission, 6/1 for domestic students; for spring admission, 11/1 for domestic students. *Application fee:* $75 ($150 for international students). Electronic applications accepted. *Application Contact:* Ann-Marie Kay, Assistant Director of Graduate Admissions, 908-737-5922, Fax: 908-737-5925, E-mail: akay@kean.edu. *Dean,* Dr. Susan Polirstok, 908-737-3750, Fax: 908-737-3760, E-mail: fpolirsts@kean.edu.

College of Humanities and Social Sciences Students: 88 full-time (77 women), 104 part-time (72 women); includes 38 Black or African American, non-Hispanic/Latino; 10 Asian, non-Hispanic/Latino; 32 Hispanic/Latino; 1 Two or more races, non-Hispanic/Latino, 7 international. Average age 28. 139 applicants, 80% accepted, 81 enrolled. *Faculty:* 71 full-time (36 women). Expenses: Contact institution. *Financial support:* In 2010–11, 22 research assistantships with full tuition reimbursements (averaging $3,263 per year) were awarded; unspecified assistantships also available. Financial award applicants required to submit FAFSA. In 2010, 49 master's, 14 other advanced degrees awarded. *Degree program information:* Part-time and evening/weekend programs available. Offers communication studies (MA); English writing (MA); human behavior and organizational psychology (MA); humanities and social sciences (MA, Diploma); marriage and family therapy (Diploma); political science (MA); psychological services (MA); school psychology (Diploma); sociology and social justice (MA). *Application deadline:* For fall admission, 6/1 for domestic students; for spring admission, 11/1 for domestic students. *Application fee:* $75 ($150 for international students). Electronic applications accepted. *Application Contact:* Ann-Marie Kay, Assistant Director of Graduate Admissions, 908-737-5922, Fax: 908-737-5925, E-mail: akay@kean.edu. *Dean,* Dr. Kenneth Dollarhide, 908-737-0430, Fax: 908-737-3914, E-mail: kdollarh@kean.edu.

College of Natural, Applied and Health Sciences Students: 17 full-time (16 women), 103 part-time (88 women); includes 41 Black or African American, non-Hispanic/Latino; 13 Asian, non-Hispanic/Latino; 4 Hispanic/Latino; 2 Native Hawaiian or other Pacific Islander, non-Hispanic/Latino, 3 international. Average age 43. 48 applicants, 98% accepted, 27 enrolled. *Faculty:* 25 full-time (13 women). Expenses: Contact institution. *Financial support:* In 2010–11, 2 research assistantships with full tuition reimbursements (averaging $3,263 per year) were awarded; unspecified assistantships also available. Financial award applicants required to submit FAFSA. In 2010, 39 master's awarded. *Degree program information:* Part-time and evening/weekend programs available. Offers clinical management (MSN); community health nursing (MSN); natural, applied and health sciences (MA, MSN); school nursing (MSN); supervision of math education (MA); teaching of math (MA). *Application deadline:* For fall admission, 6/1 for domestic students; for spring admission, 11/1 for domestic students. *Application fee:* $75 ($150 for international students). Electronic applications accepted. *Application Contact:* Ann-Marie Kay, Assistant Director of Graduate Admissions, 908-737-5922, Fax: 908-737-5925, E-mail: akay@kean.edu. *Dean,* Dr. Jeffrey H. Toney, 908-737-3600, Fax: 908-737-3606, E-mail: jtoney@kean.edu.

College of Visual and Performing Arts Students: 20 full-time (15 women), 54 part-time (41 women); includes 7 Black or African American, non-Hispanic/Latino; 5 Asian, non-Hispanic/Latino; 7 Hispanic/Latino; 1 Two or more races, non-Hispanic/Latino, 4 international. Average age 37. 39 applicants, 97% accepted, 21 enrolled. *Faculty:* 23 full-time (8 women). Expenses: Contact institution. *Financial support:* In 2010–11, 3 research assistantships with full tuition reimbursements (averaging $3,263 per year) were awarded; unspecified assistantships also available. Financial award applicants required to submit FAFSA. In 2010, 30 master's awarded. *Degree program information:* Part-time and evening/weekend programs available. Offers certification (MA); liberal studies (MA); studio/research (general) (MA); supervision (MA); visual and performing arts (MA). *Application deadline:* For fall admission, 6/1 for domestic students; for spring admission, 11/1 for domestic students. *Application fee:* $75 ($150 for international students). Electronic applications accepted. *Application Contact:* Ann-Marie Kay, Assistant Director for Graduate Admissions, 908-737-5922, Fax: 908-737-5925, E-mail: akay@kean.edu. *Dean,* Dr. Holly Logue, 908-737-4376, Fax: 908-737-4377, E-mail: hlogue@kean.edu.

Nathan Weiss Graduate College Students: 243 full-time (192 women), 364 part-time (242 women); includes 265 minority (152 Black or African American, non-Hispanic/Latino; 2 American Indian or Alaska Native, non-Hispanic/Latino; 21 Asian, non-Hispanic/Latino; 85 Hispanic/Latino; 2 Native Hawaiian or other Pacific Islander, non-Hispanic/Latino; 3 Two or more races, non-Hispanic/Latino), 18 international. Average age 33. 451 applicants, 67% accepted, 198 enrolled. *Faculty:* 20 full-time (14 women). Expenses: Contact institution. *Financial support:* In 2010–11, 42 research assistantships with full tuition reimbursements (averaging $3,263 per year) were awarded; unspecified assistantships also available. Financial award applicants required to submit FAFSA. In 2010, 223 master's awarded. *Degree program information:* Part-time and evening/weekend programs available. Offers executive management (MBA); global management (MBA); Holocaust and genocide studies (MA); occupational therapy (MS); school and clinical psychology (Psy D); school business administration (MA); social work (MSW); supervisors and principals (MA); urban leadership (Ed D). *Application deadline:* For fall admission, 6/1 for domestic students; for spring admission, 11/1 for domestic students. *Application fee:* $75 ($150 for international students). Electronic applications accepted. *Application Contact:* Ann-Marie Kay, Assistant Director of Graduate Admissions, 908-737-5922, Fax: 908-737-5925, E-mail: akay@kean.edu. *Dean,* Dr. Steven Lorenzet, 908-737-5900, Fax: 908-737-5905, E-mail: slorenze@kean.edu.

New Jersey Center for Science, Technology and Mathematics Students: 20 full-time (8 women), 8 part-time (7 women); includes 14 minority (1 Black or African American, non-Hispanic/Latino; 7 Asian, non-Hispanic/Latino; 6 Hispanic/Latino), 5 international. Average age 25. 21 applicants, 95% accepted, 14 enrolled. *Faculty:* 8 full-time (4 women). Expenses: Contact institution. *Financial support:* In 2010–11, 7 research assistantships with full tuition reimbursements (averaging $3,263 per year) were awarded; unspecified assistantships also available. Financial award applicants required to submit FAFSA. In 2010, 18 master's awarded. *Degree program information:* Part-time and evening/weekend programs available. Offers biotechnology (MS); science, technology and mathematics (MS). *Application deadline:* For fall admission, 6/1 for domestic students; for spring admission, 11/1 for domestic students. *Application fee:* $75 ($150 for international students). Electronic applications accepted. *Application Contact:* Ann-Marie Kay, Assistant Director of Graduate Admissions, 908-737-5922, Fax: 908-737-5925, E-mail: akay@kean.edu. *Executive Director,* Dr. Laura Lorentzen, 908-737-7200, Fax: 908-737-7205, E-mail: njcste@kean.edu.

KECK GRADUATE INSTITUTE OF APPLIED LIFE SCIENCES, Claremont, CA 91711

General Information Independent, coed, graduate-only institution. CGS member.

GRADUATE UNITS

Bioscience Program Offers applied life science (PhD); bioscience (MBS); bioscience management (Certificate); computational systems biology (PhD). Electronic applications accepted.

KEENE STATE COLLEGE, Keene, NH 03435

General Information State-supported, coed, comprehensive institution. *Enrollment:* 5,340 graduate, professional, and undergraduate students; 25 full-time matriculated graduate/professional students (19 women), 74 part-time matriculated graduate/professional students (56 women). *Enrollment by degree level:* 99 master's. *Graduate faculty:* 11 full-time (7 women), 5 part-time/adjunct (3 women). Tuition, state resident: full-time $7650; part-time $352 per credit. Tuition, nonresident: full-time $15,820; part-time $380 per credit. *Required fees:* $2490; $218 per credit. Tuition and fees vary according to course load. *Graduate housing:* Room and/or apartments available on a first-come, first-served basis to single students; on-campus housing not available to married students. Typical cost: $3040 per year ($8670 including board). Room and board charges vary according to board plan. Housing application deadline: 5/1. *Student services:* Campus employment opportunities, campus safety program, career counseling, child daycare facilities, exercise/wellness program, free psychological counseling, international student services, low-cost health insurance, multicultural affairs office, services for students with disabilities, teacher training, writing training. *Library facilities:* Mason Library. *Online resources:* library catalog, web page, access to other libraries' catalogs. *Collection:* 324,400 titles, 1,306 serial subscriptions, 13,791 audiovisual materials.

Computer facilities: Computer purchase and lease plans are available. 500 computers available on campus for general student use. A campuswide network can be accessed from student residence rooms and from off campus. Online class registration, personal Web pages are available. *Web address:* http://www.keene.edu/.

General Application Contact: Peggy Richmond, Director of Admissions, 603-358-2276, Fax: 603-358-2767, E-mail: admissions@keene.edu.

GRADUATE UNITS

School of Professional and Graduate Studies Students: 25 full-time (19 women), 74 part-time (56 women); includes 1 Asian, non-Hispanic/Latino. Average age 32. 49 applicants, 71% accepted, 25 enrolled. *Faculty:* 11 full-time (7 women), 5 part-time/adjunct (3 women). Expenses: Contact institution. *Financial support:* Research assistantships, career-related internships or fieldwork, Federal Work-Study, institutionally sponsored loans, and unspecified assistantships available. Support available to part-time students. Financial award application deadline: 3/1; financial award applicants required to submit FAFSA. In 2010, 43 master's, 17 other advanced degrees awarded. *Degree program information:* Part-time and evening/weekend programs available. Offers curriculum and instruction (M Ed); education leadership (PMC); educational leadership (M Ed); school counselor (M Ed, PMC); special education (M Ed); teacher certification (Postbaccalaureate Certificate). *Application deadline:* For fall admission, 4/1 for domestic students; for spring admission, 12/1 for domestic students. Applications are processed on a rolling basis. *Application fee:* $40. Electronic applications accepted. *Application Contact:* Peggy Richmond, Director of Admissions, 603-358-2276, Fax: 603-358-2767, E-mail: admissions@keene.edu. *Dean,* Dr. Melinda Treadwell, 603-358-2220.

KEHILATH YAKOV RABBINICAL SEMINARY, Ossining, NY 10562

General Information Independent-religious, men only, comprehensive institution.

GRADUATE UNITS

Graduate Programs

KEISER UNIVERSITY, Fort Lauderdale, FL 33309

General Information Independent, coed, comprehensive institution. *Enrollment by degree level:* 145 master's. *Graduate faculty:* 11 full-time (4 women), 15 part-time/adjunct (8 women). *Graduate housing:* Room and/or apartments available to single students. *Student services:* Campus employment opportunities, campus safety program, career counseling, writing training. *Online resources:* library catalog, web page.

Computer facilities: A campuswide network can be accessed. *Web address:* http://www.keiseruniversity.edu/.

General Application Contact: Graduate School, 888-753-4737, E-mail: graduateschool@keiseruniversity.edu.

GRADUATE UNITS

Doctor of Business Administration Program Offers global business (DBA); global organizational leadership (DBA); marketing (DBA).

MA in Criminal Justice Program Students: 8 full-time (5 women), 14 part-time (9 women); includes 5 Black or African American, non-Hispanic/Latino; 1 American Indian or Alaska Native, non-Hispanic/Latino; 2 Hispanic/Latino. Average age 36. 19 applicants, 89% accepted, 13 enrolled. *Faculty:* 1 (woman) full-time, 5 part-time/adjunct (all women). Expenses: Contact institution. *Financial support:* In 2010–11, 18 students received support. Federal Work-Study available. Financial award applicants required to submit FAFSA. *Degree program information:* Part-time programs available. Postbaccalaureate distance learning degree programs offered (no on-campus study). Offers criminal justice (MA). *Application deadline:* Applications are processed on a rolling basis. *Application fee:* $50. Electronic applications accepted.

Master of Business Administration Program Students: 18 full-time (14 women), 83 part-time (51 women); includes 30 Black or African American, non-Hispanic/Latino; 2 American Indian or Alaska Native, non-Hispanic/Latino; 2 Asian, non-Hispanic/Latino; 17 Hispanic/Latino, 1 international. Average age 42. 30 applicants, 77% accepted, 18 enrolled. *Faculty:* 8 full-time (3 women), 7 part-time/adjunct (2 women). Expenses: Contact institution. *Financial support:* In 2010–11, 95 students received support. Federal Work-Study available. Financial award applicants required to submit FAFSA. In 2010, 21 degrees awarded. *Degree program information:* Part-time programs available. Postbaccalaureate distance learning degree programs offered (minimal on-campus study). Offers accounting (MBA); health services management (MBA); international business (MBA); leadership for managers (MBA); marketing (MBA). Leadership for Managers and International Business concentrations also offered in Spanish. *Application deadline:* Applications are processed on a rolling basis. *Application fee:* $50. Electronic applications accepted.

Master of Science in Education Program Students: 9 full-time (7 women), 13 part-time (11 women); includes 14 Black or African American, non-Hispanic/Latino; 1 American Indian or Alaska Native, non-Hispanic/Latino; 2 Hispanic/Latino. Average age 35. 16 applicants, 88% accepted, 11 enrolled. *Faculty:* 2 full-time (both women), 3 part-time/adjunct (2 women). Expenses: Contact institution. *Financial support:* In 2010–11, 10 students received support. Federal Work-Study available. Financial award applicants required to submit FAFSA. *Degree program information:* Part-time programs available. Postbaccalaureate distance learning degree programs offered (no on-campus study). Offers college administration (MS Ed); leadership (MS Ed); teaching and learning (MS Ed). *Application deadline:* Applications are processed on a rolling basis. *Application fee:* $50. Electronic applications accepted.

Master of Science in Nursing Program Offers nursing (MSN).

MS in Physician Assistant Program Expenses: Contact institution. Offers physician assistant (MS). *Application Contact:* Program Director, 888-7-KEISER. *Program Director,* 888-7-KEISER.

PhD in Educational Leadership Program Expenses: Contact institution. Offers educational leadership (PhD).

PhD in Instructional Design and Technology Program Offers instructional design and technology (PhD).

KENNESAW STATE UNIVERSITY, Kennesaw, GA 30144-5591

General Information State-supported, coed, comprehensive institution. CGS member. *Enrollment:* 23,452 graduate, professional, and undergraduate students; 977 full-time matriculated graduate/professional students (603 women), 892 part-time matriculated graduate/professional students (475 women). *Enrollment by degree level:* 1,720 master's, 149 doctoral. Tuition, state resident: full-time $5500; part-time $225 per credit hour. Tuition, nonresident: full-time $16,100; part-time $813 per credit hour. *Required fees:* $673 per semester. *Gradu-*

ate housing: Room and/or apartments available on a first-come, first-served basis to single students; on-campus housing not available to married students. *Student services:* Campus employment opportunities, campus safety program, career counseling, exercise/wellness program, free psychological counseling, international student services, low-cost health insurance, multicultural affairs office, services for students with disabilities, teacher training, writing training. *Library facilities:* Horace W. Sturgis Library. *Online resources:* library catalog, web page, access to other libraries' catalogs. *Collection:* 573,519 titles, 44,500 serial subscriptions, 9,650 audiovisual materials.

Computer facilities: Computer purchase and lease plans are available. 1,650 computers available on campus for general student use. A campuswide network can be accessed from student residence rooms and from off campus. Online class registration is available. *Web address:* http://www.kennesaw.edu/.

General Application Contact: Tamara Hutto, Admissions Counselor, 770-420-4377, Fax: 770-423-6885, E-mail: ksugrad@kennesaw.edu.

GRADUATE UNITS

College of Health and Human Services Students: 193 full-time (165 women), 27 part-time (17 women); includes 67 minority (37 Black or African American, non-Hispanic/Latino; 1 American Indian or Alaska Native, non-Hispanic/Latino; 13 Asian, non-Hispanic/Latino; 13 Hispanic/Latino; 1 Native Hawaiian or other Pacific Islander, non-Hispanic/Latino; 2 Two or more races, non-Hispanic/Latino), 8 international. Average age 35. 245 applicants, 55% accepted, 94 enrolled. Expenses: Contact institution. *Financial support:* In 2010–11, 2 research assistantships with full tuition reimbursements (averaging $4,000 per year) were awarded; Federal Work-Study also available. Support available to part-time students. Financial award application deadline: 6/15; financial award applicants required to submit FAFSA. In 2010, 91 master's awarded. *Degree program information:* Part-time and evening/weekend programs available. Postbaccalaureate distance learning degree programs offered (no on-campus study). Offers advanced care management and leadership (MSN); applied exercise and health science (MS); health and human services (MS, MSN, MSW, DNS); nursing science (DNS); primary care nurse practitioner (MSN); social work (MSW). *Application deadline:* For fall admission, 6/1 for domestic and international students. *Application fee:* $60. Electronic applications accepted. *Application Contact:* Tamara Hutto, Admissions Counselor, 770-420-4377, Fax: 770-423-6885, E-mail: ksugrad@kennesaw.edu. *Dean,* Dr. Richard Sowell, 770-423-6565, Fax: 770-423-6627, E-mail: rsowell@kennesaw.edu.

College of Humanities and Social Sciences Students: 200 full-time (120 women), 145 part-time (103 women); includes 107 minority (78 Black or African American, non-Hispanic/Latino; 1 American Indian or Alaska Native, non-Hispanic/Latino; 6 Asian, non-Hispanic/Latino; 15 Hispanic/Latino; 1 Native Hawaiian or other Pacific Islander, non-Hispanic/Latino; 6 Two or more races, non-Hispanic/Latino), 21 international. Average age 34. 239 applicants, 67% accepted, 134 enrolled. Expenses: Contact institution. *Financial support:* In 2010–11, 2 research assistantships with full tuition reimbursements (averaging $15,000 per year) were awarded; Federal Work-Study and unspecified assistantships also available. Support available to part-time students. Financial award application deadline: 6/15; financial award applicants required to submit FAFSA. In 2010, 84 master's awarded. *Degree program information:* Part-time and evening/weekend programs available. Offers American studies (MA); conflict management (MSCM); humanities and social sciences (MA, MAPW, MPA, MS, MSCM, PhD); international conflict management (PhD); international policy management (MS); professional writing (MAPW); public administration (MPA). *Application deadline:* For fall admission, 7/1 priority date for domestic and international students; for spring admission, 10/1 priority date for domestic and international students. Applications are processed on a rolling basis. *Application fee:* $60. Electronic applications accepted. *Application Contact:* Tamara Hutto, Admissions Counselor, 770-420-4377, Fax: 770-423-6885, E-mail: ksugrad@kennesaw.edu. *Dean,* Dr. Richard Vengroff, 770-423-6124, E-mail: rvengrof@kennesaw.edu.

College of Science and Mathematics Students: 76 full-time (26 women), 97 part-time (32 women); includes 60 minority (38 Black or African American, non-Hispanic/Latino; 1 American Indian or Alaska Native, non-Hispanic/Latino; 11 Asian, non-Hispanic/Latino; 9 Hispanic/Latino; 1 Two or more races, non-Hispanic/Latino), 26 international. Average age 32. 71 applicants, 85% accepted, 42 enrolled. Expenses: Contact institution. *Financial support:* In 2010–11, 6 research assistantships with full tuition reimbursements (averaging $4,000 per year) were awarded; Federal Work-Study and unspecified assistantships also available. Support available to part-time students. Financial award application deadline: 4/1; financial award applicants required to submit FAFSA. In 2010, 66 master's awarded. *Degree program information:* Part-time programs available. Postbaccalaureate distance learning degree programs offered (minimal on-campus study). Offers applied computer science (MSaCS); applied statistics (MSAS); information systems (MSIS); science and mathematics (MSAS, MSIS, MSaCS). *Application deadline:* For fall admission, 7/1 for domestic and international students; for spring admission, 10/1 for domestic and international students. Applications are processed on a rolling basis. *Application fee:* $60. Electronic applications accepted. *Application Contact:* Tamara Hutto, Admissions Counselor, 770-420-4377, Fax: 770-423-6885, E-mail: ksugrad@kennesaw.edu. *Dean,* Dr. Ron Matson, 770-423-6160, E-mail: rmatson@kennesaw.edu.

Leland and Clarice C. Bagwell College of Education Students: 202 full-time (168 women), 207 part-time (163 women); includes 75 minority (44 Black or African American, non-Hispanic/Latino; 11 Asian, non-Hispanic/Latino; 15 Hispanic/Latino; 5 Two or more races, non-Hispanic/Latino), 4 international. Average age 34. 82 applicants, 76% accepted, 41 enrolled. Expenses: Contact institution. *Financial support:* Federal Work-Study available. Support available to part-time students. Financial award application deadline: 4/1; financial award applicants required to submit FAFSA. In 2010, 164 master's, 15 other advanced degrees awarded. *Degree program information:* Part-time programs available. Offers adolescent education (M Ed); art education (MAT); education (M Ed, MAT, Ed D, Ed S); educational leadership (M Ed); educational leadership technology (M Ed); elementary and early childhood education (M Ed); leadership for learning (Ed D, Ed S); secondary English or mathematics (MAT); secondary science education (MAT); special education (M Ed); teaching English to speakers of other languages (M Ed, MAT). *Application deadline:* For fall admission, 7/1 for domestic and international students; for spring admission, 10/1 for domestic and international students. *Application fee:* $60. Electronic applications accepted. *Application Contact:* Alisha Bello, Administrative Coordinator, 770-423-6043, Fax: 770-420-4435, E-mail: abello2@kennesaw.edu. *Dean,* Dr. Arlinda Eaton, 770-423-6117, Fax: 770-423-6567.

Michael J. Coles College of Business Students: 306 full-time (124 women), 416 part-time (160 women); includes 189 minority (123 Black or African American, non-Hispanic/Latino; 1 American Indian or Alaska Native, non-Hispanic/Latino; 43 Asian, non-Hispanic/Latino; 17 Hispanic/Latino; 1 Native Hawaiian or other Pacific Islander, non-Hispanic/Latino; 4 Two or more races, non-Hispanic/Latino), 49 international. Average age 34. 499 applicants, 50% accepted, 186 enrolled. Expenses: Contact institution. *Financial support:* In 2010–11, 8 research assistantships with tuition reimbursements (averaging $4,000 per year) were awarded; Federal Work-Study also available. Support available to part-time students. Financial award application deadline: 4/1; financial award applicants required to submit FAFSA. In 2010, 375 master's awarded. *Degree program information:* Part-time and evening/weekend programs available. Offers accounting (M Acc); business (M Acc, MBA, DBA); business administration (MBA, DBA). *Application deadline:* For fall admission, 7/1 for domestic and international students; for spring admission, 12/1 for domestic and international students. Applications are processed on a rolling basis. *Application fee:* $60. Electronic applications accepted. *Application Contact:* Tamara Hutto, Admissions Counselor, 770-420-4377, Fax: 770-423-6885, E-mail: ksugrad@kennesaw.edu. *Dean,* Dr. Ken Harmon, 770-423-6425, Fax: 770-423-6141, E-mail: kharmon@kennesaw.edu.

KENRICK-GLENNON SEMINARY, St. Louis, MO 63119-4330

General Information Independent-religious, men only, graduate-only institution. *Graduate housing:* Room and/or apartments available to single students; on-campus housing not available to married students.

GRADUATE UNITS

Graduate and Professional Programs Offers theology (M Div, MA).

KENT STATE UNIVERSITY, Kent, OH 44242-0001

General Information State-supported, coed, university. CGS member. *Enrollment:* 26,589 graduate, professional, and undergraduate students; 2,754 full-time matriculated graduate/professional students (1,703 women), 2,273 part-time matriculated graduate/professional students (1,688 women). *Enrollment by degree level:* 42 first professional, 3,763 master's, 1,105 doctoral, 117 other advanced degrees. *Graduate faculty:* 866. Tuition, state resident: full-time $7866; part-time $437 per credit hour. Tuition, nonresident: full-time $14,022; part-time $779 per credit hour. *Graduate housing:* Rooms and/or apartments available on a first-come, first-served basis to single students and available to married students. *Student services:* Campus employment opportunities, campus safety program, career counseling, child daycare facilities, exercise/wellness program, free psychological counseling, grant writing training, international student services, low-cost health insurance, multicultural affairs office, services for students with disabilities, teacher training, writing training. *Library facilities:* Kent State University Libraries and Media Services plus 7 others. *Online resources:* library catalog, web page, access to other libraries' catalogs. *Collection:* 2.3 million titles, 12,000 serial subscriptions, 15,578 audiovisual materials.

Computer facilities: Computer purchase and lease plans are available. 1,700 computers available on campus for general student use. A campuswide network can be accessed from student residence rooms and from off campus. Online class registration is available. *Web address:* http://www.kent.edu/.

General Application Contact: J. P. Cooney, Division of Graduate Studies, 330-672-2661, Fax: 330-672-2658.

GRADUATE UNITS

College of Architecture and Environmental Design *Degree program information:* Part-time programs available. Offers architecture (M Arch); preservation architecture (Certificate); urban design (M Arch, MUD, Certificate). Electronic applications accepted.

College of Arts and Sciences *Degree program information:* Part-time programs available. Offers analytical chemistry (MS, PhD); anthropology (MA); applied geology (PhD); applied mathematics (MA, MS, PhD); arts and sciences (MA, MFA, MLS, MPA, MS, PhD); biochemistry (MS, PhD); chemical physics (MS, PhD); chemistry (MA); clinical psychology (MA, PhD); comparative literature (MA); computer science (MA, MS, PhD); creative writing (MFA); ecology (MS, PhD); English (PhD); English for teachers (MA); experimental psychology (MA, PhD); French literature (MA); French, Spanish, German and Latin pedagogy (MA); geography (MA, PhD); geology (MS); German literature (MA); history (MA, PhD); inorganic chemistry (MS, PhD); justice studies (MA); liberal studies (MLS); literature and writing (MA); organic chemistry (MS, PhD); philosophy (MA); physical chemistry (MS, PhD); physics (MA, MS, PhD); physiology (MS, PhD); political science (MA); public administration (MPA); public policy (PhD); pure mathematics (MA, MS, PhD); rhetoric and composition (PhD); sociology (MA, PhD); Spanish literature (MA); teaching English as a second language (MA); translation (MA); translation studies (PhD). Electronic applications accepted.

College of Communication and Information Offers communication and information (MA, MFA, MLIS, MS, PhD); information architecture and knowledge management (MS).

School of Communication Studies Offers communication studies (MA, PhD). Electronic applications accepted.

School of Journalism and Mass Communication *Degree program information:* Part-time programs available. Offers journalism and mass communication (MA). Electronic applications accepted.

School of Library and Information Science Offers library and information science (MLIS).

School of Visual Communication Design *Degree program information:* Part-time programs available. Offers visual communication design (MA, MFA).

College of Nursing *Degree program information:* Part-time programs available. Offers adult nurse practitioner (MSN); family nurse practitioner (MSN); geriatric nurse practitioner (MSN); nursing (PhD); nursing and health care management (MSN); nursing of adults (clinical nurse specialist) (MSN); pediatric nurse practitioner (MSN); psychiatric/mental health nursing (MSN); women's health nursing (MSN). PhD program offered jointly with The University of Akron. Electronic applications accepted.

College of Technology *Degree program information:* Part-time programs available. Postbaccalaureate distance learning degree programs offered. Offers technology (MT). Electronic applications accepted.

College of the Arts Offers arts (MA, MFA, MM, PhD). Electronic applications accepted.

Hugh A. Glauser School of Music Offers composition (MA); conducting (MM); ethnomusicology (MA); music education (MM, PhD); musicology (MA); musicology-ethnomusicology (PhD); performance (MM); theory (MA); theory and composition (PhD). Electronic applications accepted.

School of Art Offers art education (MA); art history (MA); crafts (MA, MFA); fine art (MA, MFA). Electronic applications accepted.

School of Theatre and Dance *Degree program information:* Part-time programs available. Offers acting (MFA); design and technology (MFA); theatre (MA, MFA). Electronic applications accepted.

Graduate School of Education, Health, and Human Services Students: 960 full-time (737 women), 796 part-time (629 women); includes 118 Black or African American, non-Hispanic/Latino; 3 American Indian or Alaska Native, non-Hispanic/Latino; 37 Asian, non-Hispanic/Latino; 20 Hispanic/Latino; 1 Native Hawaiian or other Pacific Islander, non-Hispanic/Latino. 1,230 applicants, 52% accepted. *Faculty:* 183 full-time (102 women), 223 part-time/adjunct (162 women). Expenses: Contact institution. *Financial support:* In 2010–11, 37 fellowships with full tuition reimbursements (averaging $11,411 per year), 19 research assistantships with full tuition reimbursements (averaging $9,569 per year), 3 teaching assistantships with full tuition reimbursements (averaging $8,542 per year) were awarded; Federal Work-Study, scholarships/grants, unspecified assistantships, and 101 administrative assistantships (averaging $10,415 per year) also available. Financial award application deadline: 4/1; financial award applicants required to submit FAFSA. In 2010, 522 master's, 35 doctorates, 30 other advanced degrees awarded. *Degree program information:* Part-time and evening/weekend programs available. Postbaccalaureate distance learning degree programs offered. Offers education, health, and human services (M Ed, MA, MAT, MPH, MS, Au D, PhD, Ed S). *Application deadline:* Applications are processed on a rolling basis. *Application fee:* $30 ($60 for international students). Electronic applications accepted. *Application Contact:* Nancy Miller, Academic Program Coordinator, Office of Graduate Student Services, 330-672-2576, Fax: 330-672-9162, E-mail: nmiller1@kent.edu. *Dean,* Dr. Daniel Mahony, 330-672-2202, Fax: 330-672-3407, E-mail: dmahony@kent.edu.

School of Foundations, Leadership and Administration Students: 209 full-time (123 women), 196 part-time (143 women); includes 28 Black or African American, non-Hispanic/Latino; 1 American Indian or Alaska Native, non-Hispanic/Latino; 10 Asian, non-Hispanic/Latino; 9 Hispanic/Latino. 289 applicants, 63% accepted. *Faculty:* 39 full-time (23 women), 42 part-time/adjunct (19 women). Expenses: Contact institution. *Financial support:* In 2010–11, 5 fellowships with full tuition reimbursements (averaging $10,600 per year), 15 research assistantships with full tuition reimbursements (averaging $9,667 per year) were awarded; teaching assistantships with full tuition reimbursements, Federal Work-Study, scholarships/grants, tuition waivers (full), unspecified assistantships, and 20 administrative assistantships (averaging $9,500 per year) also available. Financial award application deadline: 3/15. In 2010, 133 master's, 7 doctorates, 3 other advanced degrees awarded. Offers cultural foundations (M Ed, MA, PhD); evaluation and measurement (M Ed, PhD); exercise, leisure and sport (MA); higher education (PhD, Ed S); higher education and student personnel (M Ed); hospitality and tourism management (MS); K-12 leadership (M Ed, MA, PhD, Ed S); sport and recreation management (MA); sports studies (MA). *Application deadline:* Applications are processed on a rolling basis. *Application fee:* $30 ($60 for international students). Electronic applications accepted. *Application Contact:* Nancy Miller, Academic Program Coordinator, 330-672-2576, Fax: 330-672-9162, E-mail: ogs@kent.edu. *Director,* Dr. Shawn Fitzgerald, 330-672-0583, Fax: 330-672-4106, E-mail: smfitzge@kent.edu.

Kent State University (continued)

School of Health Sciences Students: 202 full-time (174 women), 47 part-time (36 women); includes 9 Black or African American, non-Hispanic/Latino; 9 Asian, non-Hispanic/Latino; 4 Hispanic/Latino. 392 applicants, 35% accepted. *Faculty:* 39 full-time (30 women), 14 part-time/adjunct (12 women). Expenses: Contact institution. *Financial support:* In 2010–11, 8 fellowships with full tuition reimbursements (averaging $10,026 per year), 2 research assistantships with full tuition reimbursements (averaging $8,313 per year), 2 teaching assistantships with full tuition reimbursements (averaging $8,313 per year) were awarded; Federal Work-Study, scholarships/grants, unspecified assistantships, and 32 administrative assistantships (averaging $11,037 per year) also available. Financial award application deadline: 4/1; financial award applicants required to submit FAFSA. In 2010, 65 master's, 5 doctorates awarded. *Degree program information:* Part-time and evening/weekend programs available. Offers athletic training (MA); audiology (Au D, PhD); dietetic (MS); exercise physiology (MS, PhD); health education and promotion (M Ed, MA, PhD); nutrition (MS); speech language pathology (MA, PhD). *Application deadline:* Applications are processed on a rolling basis. *Application fee:* $30 ($60 for international students). Electronic applications accepted. *Application Contact:* Nancy Miller, Academic Program Coordinator, Office of Graduate Student Services, 330-672-2576, Fax: 330-672-9162, E-mail: ogs@kent.edu. *Interim Director,* Dr. Lynne B. Rowan, 330-672-9785, E-mail: lrowan@kent.edu.

School of Lifespan Development and Educational Sciences Students: 392 full-time (322 women), 346 part-time (274 women); includes 61 Black or African American, non-Hispanic/Latino; 2 American Indian or Alaska Native, non-Hispanic/Latino; 12 Asian, non-Hispanic/Latino; 5 Hispanic/Latino; 1 Native Hawaiian or other Pacific Islander, non-Hispanic/Latino. 365 applicants, 54% accepted. *Faculty:* 82 full-time (46 women), 145 part-time/adjunct (112 women). Expenses: Contact institution. *Financial support:* In 2010–11, 14 fellowships with full tuition reimbursements (averaging $11,000 per year), 2 research assistantships with full tuition reimbursements (averaging $9,657 per year), teaching assistantships with full tuition reimbursements (averaging $11,000 per year) were awarded; Federal Work-Study, scholarships/grants, unspecified assistantships, and 33 administrative assistantships (averaging $9,046 per year) also available. Financial award application deadline: 4/1. In 2010, 176 master's, 13 doctorates, 26 other advanced degrees awarded. *Degree program information:* Part-time and evening/weekend programs available. Offers clinical mental health counseling (M Ed); computer technology (M Ed); counseling (Ed S); counseling and human development services (PhD); deaf education (M Ed); early childhood intervention specialist (M Ed); educational interpreter K-12 (M Ed); educational psychology (M Ed, MA, PhD); family studies (MA); general instructional technology (M Ed); general special education (M Ed); gerontology (MA); gifted education (M Ed); human development and family studies (MA); instructional technology (M Ed, MA); intervention specialist (M Ed); library media (M Ed); mild/moderate intervention (M Ed); moderate/intensive intervention (M Ed); rehabilitation counseling (M Ed, Ed S); school counseling (M Ed); school psychology (M Ed, PhD, Ed S); special education (PhD, Ed S); transition to work (M Ed). *Application deadline:* Applications are processed on a rolling basis. *Application fee:* $30 ($60 for international students). Electronic applications accepted. *Application Contact:* Nancy Miller, Academic Program Coordinator, Office of Graduate Student Services, 330-672-2576, Fax: 330-672-9162, E-mail: ogs@kent.edu. *Director,* Dr. Mary Dellmann-Jenkins, 330-672-6958, E-mail: mdellman@kent.edu.

School of Teaching, Learning and Curriculum Studies Students: 157 full-time (118 women), 207 part-time (176 women); includes 20 Black or African American, non-Hispanic/Latino; 6 Asian, non-Hispanic/Latino; 2 Hispanic/Latino. 184 applicants, 69% accepted. *Faculty:* 23 full-time (3 women), 22 part-time/adjunct (19 women). Expenses: Contact institution. *Financial support:* In 2010–11, 10 fellowships with full tuition reimbursements (averaging $13,500 per year), research assistantships with full tuition reimbursements (averaging $9,000 per year), 1 teaching assistantship with full tuition reimbursement (averaging $9,000 per year) were awarded; Federal Work-Study, scholarships/grants, unspecified assistantships, and 16 administrative assistantships (averaging $13,078 per year) also available. Financial award application deadline: 4/1. In 2010, 148 master's, 10 doctorates, 1 other advanced degree awarded. *Degree program information:* Part-time and evening/weekend programs available. Offers career technical teacher education (M Ed); curriculum and instruction (M Ed, PhD, Ed S); early childhood education (M Ed, MA, MAT); junior high/middle school (M Ed, MA); math specialization (M Ed, MA); reading specialization (M Ed, MA); secondary education (MAT). *Application deadline:* Applications are processed on a rolling basis. *Application fee:* $30 ($60 for international students). Electronic applications accepted. *Application Contact:* Nancy Miller, Academic Program Coordinator, Office of Graduate Student Services, 330-672-2576, Fax: 330-672-9162, E-mail: ogs@kent.edu. *Director,* Dr. Alexa Sandmann, 330-672-0652, E-mail: asandman@kent.edu.

Graduate School of Management Students: 271 full-time (130 women), 148 part-time (65 women); includes 10 Black or African American, non-Hispanic/Latino; 11 Asian, non-Hispanic/Latino; 4 Hispanic/Latino, 134 international. Average age 29. 509 applicants, 69% accepted, 142 enrolled. *Faculty:* 57 full-time (15 women), 7 part-time/adjunct (4 women). Expenses: Contact institution. *Financial support:* In 2010–11, 82 students received support, including 42 research assistantships with full tuition reimbursements available (averaging $6,700 per year), 40 teaching assistantships with full tuition reimbursements available (averaging $15,000 per year); fellowships with full tuition reimbursements available, career-related internships or fieldwork, Federal Work-Study, and unspecified assistantships also available. Financial award applicants required to submit FAFSA. In 2010, 161 master's, 6 doctorates awarded. *Degree program information:* Part-time and evening/weekend programs available. Offers accounting (MS, PhD); business administration (MBA); economics (MA); finance (PhD); financial engineering (MSFE); management (MA, MBA, MS, MSFE, PhD); management systems (PhD); marketing (PhD). *Application fee:* $30 ($60 for international students). Electronic applications accepted. *Application Contact:* Louise M. Ditchey, Administrative Director, 330-672-2282, Fax: 330-672-7303, E-mail: gradbus@kent.edu. *Associate Dean,* Dr. Frederick W. Schroath, 330-672-2772, Fax: 330-672-3381, E-mail: fschroat@kent.edu.

School of Biomedical Sciences Offers biological anthropology (PhD); biomedical sciences (MS, PhD); cellular and molecular biology (MS, PhD); neuroscience (MS, PhD); pharmacology (MS, PhD); physiology (MS, PhD). Electronic applications accepted.

KENT STATE UNIVERSITY AT STARK, Canton, OH 44720-7599

General Information State-supported, coed, comprehensive institution.

GRADUATE UNITS

Graduate School of Education

Professional MBA Program Offers business administration (MBA).

KENTUCKY CHRISTIAN UNIVERSITY, Grayson, KY 41143-2205

General Information Independent-religious, coed, comprehensive institution. *Enrollment:* 6 full-time matriculated graduate/professional students (3 women), 36 part-time matriculated graduate/professional students (9 women). *Enrollment by degree level:* 42 master's. *Graduate faculty:* 8 part-time/adjunct (0 women). *Tuition:* Part-time $258.33 per credit. *Graduate housing:* Rooms and/or apartments available on a first-come, first-served basis to single and married students. *Student services:* Exercise/wellness program, international student services, low-cost health insurance. *Library facilities:* Young Library. *Online resources:* library catalog, web page. *Collection:* 103,323 titles, 395 serial subscriptions.

Computer facilities: 50 computers available on campus for general student use. A campuswide network can be accessed from student residence rooms and from off campus. *Web address:* http://www.kcu.edu/.

General Application Contact: Jane Shick, Academic Office Manager, 877-811-6391, Fax: 606-474-3189, E-mail: gradstudies@kcu.edu.

GRADUATE UNITS

Graduate School Students: 6 full-time (3 women), 36 part-time (9 women), 3 international. Average age 33. 14 applicants, 86% accepted, 11 enrolled. *Faculty:* 8 part-time/adjunct (0 women). Expenses: Contact institution. *Financial support:* Teaching assistantships with full tuition reimbursements, scholarships/grants and unspecified assistantships available. Support available to part-time students. *Degree program information:* Part-time programs available. Offers Biblical studies (MA); Christian leadership (MA). *Application deadline:* Applications are processed on a rolling basis. *Application fee:* $35. Electronic applications accepted. *Application Contact:* Jane Shick, Academic Office Manager, 877-811-6391, Fax: 606-474-3189, E-mail: gradstudies@kcu.edu. *Dean,* Dr. David Fiensy, 606-474-3263, Fax: 606-474-3189, E-mail: dfiensy@kcu.edu.

KENTUCKY STATE UNIVERSITY, Frankfort, KY 40601

General Information State-related, coed, comprehensive institution. *Enrollment:* 2,851 graduate, professional, and undergraduate students; 123 full-time matriculated graduate/professional students (73 women), 122 part-time matriculated graduate/professional students (53 women). *Enrollment by degree level:* 245 master's. *Graduate faculty:* 22 full-time (5 women), 3 part-time/adjunct (2 women). Tuition, state resident: full-time $5886; part-time $352 per credit hour. Tuition, nonresident: full-time $9054; part-time $528 per credit hour. *Required fees:* $450; $26 per credit hour. *Graduate housing:* Room and/or apartments available on a first-come, first-served basis to single students; on-campus housing not available to married students. Typical cost: $3240 per year ($6792 including board). Housing application deadline: 6/30. *Student services:* Campus employment opportunities, campus safety program, career counseling, exercise/wellness program, free psychological counseling, grant writing training, international student services, low-cost health insurance, multicultural affairs office, services for students with disabilities, teacher training. *Library facilities:* Paul G. Blazer Library. *Online resources:* library catalog, access to other libraries' catalogs. *Collection:* 326,821 titles, 864 serial subscriptions, 4,653 audiovisual materials.

Computer facilities: 450 computers available on campus for general student use. A campuswide network can be accessed from student residence rooms and from off campus. Online class registration, accepting financial aid awards are available. *Web address:* http://www.kysu.edu/.

General Application Contact: Dr. Titilayo Ufomata, Acting Director of Graduate Studies, 502-597-6443, E-mail: titilayo.ufomata@kysu.edu.

GRADUATE UNITS

College of Mathematics, Sciences, Technology and Health Students: 34 full-time (16 women), 32 part-time (6 women); includes 22 minority (15 Black or African American, non-Hispanic/Latino; 3 Asian, non-Hispanic/Latino; 1 Hispanic/Latino; 1 Native Hawaiian or other Pacific Islander, non-Hispanic/Latino; 2 Two or more races, non-Hispanic/Latino), 12 international. Average age 34. 55 applicants, 51% accepted, 18 enrolled. *Faculty:* 10 full-time (1 woman), 1 part-time/adjunct (0 women). Expenses: Contact institution. *Financial support:* In 2010–11, 41 students received support, including 18 research assistantships (averaging $11,378 per year); career-related internships or fieldwork, scholarships/grants, tuition waivers (partial), and unspecified assistantships also available. Financial award application deadline: 4/15; financial award applicants required to submit FAFSA. In 2010, 16 master's awarded. *Degree program information:* Part-time and evening/weekend programs available. Offers aquaculture (MS); computer science (MS); environmental science (MS). *Application deadline:* Applications are processed on a rolling basis. *Application fee:* $30 ($100 for international students). Electronic applications accepted. *Application Contact:* Dr. Titilayo Ufomata, Acting Director of Graduate Studies, 502-597-6443, E-mail: titilayo.ufomata@kysu.edu. *Dean,* Dr. Charles Bennett, 502-597-6926, E-mail: charles.bennett@kysu.edu.

College of Professional Studies Students: 88 full-time (57 women), 79 part-time (42 women); includes 104 minority (101 Black or African American, non-Hispanic/Latino; 1 Asian, non-Hispanic/Latino; 2 Hispanic/Latino), 2 international. Average age 34. 124 applicants, 62% accepted, 45 enrolled. *Faculty:* 12 full-time (4 women), 2 part-time/adjunct (both women). Expenses: Contact institution. *Financial support:* In 2010–11, 46 students received support, including 4 research assistantships (averaging $10,975 per year); career-related internships or fieldwork, scholarships/grants, tuition waivers (partial), and unspecified assistantships also available. Financial award application deadline: 4/15; financial award applicants required to submit FAFSA. In 2010, 38 master's awarded. *Degree program information:* Part-time and evening/weekend programs available. Postbaccalaureate distance learning degree programs offered (minimal on-campus study). Offers business administration (MBA); public administration (MPA); special education (MA). *Application deadline:* Applications are processed on a rolling basis. *Application fee:* $30 ($100 for international students). Electronic applications accepted. *Application Contact:* Dr. Titilayo Ufomata, Acting Director of Graduate Studies, 502-597-6443, E-mail: titilayo.ufomata@kysu.edu. *Dean,* Dr. Gashaw Lake, 502-597-6105, Fax: 502-597-6715, E-mail: gashaw.lake@kysu.edu.

KETTERING UNIVERSITY, Flint, MI 48504

General Information Independent, coed, primarily men, comprehensive institution. *Enrollment:* 2,187 graduate, professional, and undergraduate students; 11 full-time matriculated graduate/professional students (2 women), 318 part-time matriculated graduate/professional students (99 women). *Enrollment by degree level:* 329 master's. *Graduate faculty:* 27 full-time (6 women), 8 part-time/adjunct (0 women). *Tuition:* Full-time $11,120; part-time $695 per credit hour. *Graduate housing:* Room and/or apartments available on a first-come, first-served basis to single students; on-campus housing not available to married students. Typical cost: $3370 per year ($5810 including board). Housing application deadline: 7/15. *Student services:* Campus employment opportunities, campus safety program, exercise/wellness program, free psychological counseling, international student services, low-cost health insurance, multicultural affairs office, services for students with disabilities. *Library facilities:* Kettering University Library plus 1 other. *Online resources:* library catalog, web page, access to other libraries' catalogs. *Collection:* 148,600 titles, 400 serial subscriptions, 1,200 audiovisual materials. *Research affiliation:* Magna E-Car (battery development), TRW Automotive (automotive seat testing), Delphi Corporation (automotive, fuel cells), Global Testing & Engineering (crash testing and research), McLaren Regional Medical Center (orthopedic testing and research), Ford Motor Company (testing experimental fuel cell stacks).

Computer facilities: 450 computers available on campus for general student use. A campuswide network can be accessed from student residence rooms and from off campus. Online class registration is available. *Web address:* http://www.kettering.edu/.

General Application Contact: Bonnie Switzer, Admissions Representative, 810-762-7953, Fax: 810-762-9935, E-mail: bswitzer@kettering.edu.

GRADUATE UNITS

Graduate School Students: 11 full-time (2 women), 318 part-time (99 women); includes 56 minority (35 Black or African American, non-Hispanic/Latino; 1 American Indian or Alaska Native, non-Hispanic/Latino; 8 Asian, non-Hispanic/Latino; 12 Hispanic/Latino), 16 international. Average age 33. 133 applicants, 70% accepted, 40 enrolled. *Faculty:* 27 full-time (6 women), 8 part-time/adjunct (0 women). Expenses: Contact institution. *Financial support:* In 2010–11, 141 students received support, including fellowships with full tuition reimbursements available (averaging $13,000 per year), research assistantships with full tuition reimbursements available (averaging $13,000 per year), teaching assistantships with full tuition reimbursements available (averaging $13,000 per year); Federal Work-Study, scholarships/grants, and tuition waivers (partial) also available. Support available to part-time students. Financial award application deadline: 7/15; financial award applicants required to submit CSS PROFILE or FAFSA. In 2010, 132 master's awarded. *Degree program information:* Part-time and evening/weekend programs available. Postbaccalaureate distance learning degree programs offered (no on-campus study). Offers business (MBA, MS); engineering (MS). *Application deadline:* For fall admission, 9/15 for domestic students, 6/15 priority date for international students; for winter admission, 12/15 for domestic students, 9/15 for international students; for spring admission, 3/15 for domestic students, 12/15 for international students. Applications are processed on a rolling basis. *Application fee:* $0. Electronic applications accepted. *Application Contact:* Bonnie Switzer, Admissions Representative, 810-762-7953, Fax: 810-762-9935, E-mail: bswitzer@kettering.edu. *Associate Provost, Graduate Studies, Continuing Education and Sponsored Research,* Dr. Tony Hain, 810-762-9616, Fax: 810-762-9935, E-mail: thain@kettering.edu.

KEUKA COLLEGE, Keuka Park, NY 14478-0098

General Information Independent-religious, coed, comprehensive institution. *Enrollment:* 1,867 graduate, professional, and undergraduate students; 127 full-time matriculated graduate/

professional students (93 women), 114 part-time matriculated graduate/professional students (79 women). *Enrollment by degree level:* 241 master's. *Graduate faculty:* 8 full-time (4 women), 26 part-time/adjunct (10 women). *Tuition:* Part-time $585 per credit hour. *Graduate housing:* On-campus housing not available. *Student services:* Career counseling, grant writing training, services for students with disabilities, teacher training, writing training. *Library facilities:* Lightner Library. *Online resources:* library catalog. *Collection:* 112,541 titles, 384 serial subscriptions, 3,551 audiovisual materials.

Computer facilities: 256 computers available on campus for general student use. A campuswide network can be accessed from student residence rooms and from off campus. *Web address:* http://www.keuka.edu/.

General Application Contact: Jack Farrel, Director of Admissions, 315-279-5434, Fax: 315-279-5386, E-mail: admissions@mail.keuka.edu.

GRADUATE UNITS

Program in Childhood Education/Literacy Students: 21 part-time (19 women). 9 applicants, 100% accepted, 9 enrolled. *Faculty:* 5 part-time/adjunct (3 women). Expenses: Contact institution. In 2010, 11 master's awarded. *Degree program information:* Part-time and evening/weekend programs available. Offers childhood education/literacy (MS). *Application deadline:* For fall admission, 8/15 priority date for domestic students; for winter admission, 12/15 priority date for domestic students; for spring admission, 4/15 priority date for domestic students. Applications are processed on a rolling basis. *Application fee:* $30. *Application Contact:* Fred Hoyle, Dean of Enrollment, 315-279-5296. *Director of Graduate Program in Education,* Dr. Andrew Beigel, 315-279-5688.

Program in Criminal Justice Administration Students: 5 full-time (1 woman), 28 part-time (14 women); includes 6 Black or African American, non-Hispanic/Latino; 1 American Indian or Alaska Native, non-Hispanic/Latino; 1 Hispanic/Latino. 89 applicants, 100% accepted. *Faculty:* 6 part-time/adjunct (2 women). Expenses: Contact institution. In 2010, 9 master's awarded. *Degree program information:* Part-time and evening/weekend programs available. Offers criminal justice administration (MS). *Application deadline:* For fall admission, 8/15 for domestic students; for winter admission, 12/15 for domestic students; for spring admission, 4/15 for domestic students. *Application fee:* $30. *Application Contact:* Fred Hoyle, Dean of Enrollment, 315-279-5413, Fax: 315-279-5386, E-mail: admissions@mail.keuka.edu. *Program Director,* Dr. Tom Tremer, 315-279-5672, E-mail: ttremer@mail.keuka.edu.

Program in Management Students: 53 full-time (36 women), 64 part-time (46 women); includes 14 Black or African American, non-Hispanic/Latino; 1 American Indian or Alaska Native, non-Hispanic/Latino; 1 Asian, non-Hispanic/Latino; 4 Hispanic/Latino. 31 applicants, 100% accepted, 31 enrolled. *Faculty:* 3 full-time (1 woman), 15 part-time/adjunct (5 women). Expenses: Contact institution. In 2010, 54 master's awarded. *Degree program information:* Evening/weekend programs available. Offers management (MS). *Application deadline:* For fall admission, 8/15 priority date for domestic students; for winter admission, 12/15 priority date for domestic students; for spring admission, 4/15 priority date for domestic students. Applications are processed on a rolling basis. *Application fee:* $30. *Application Contact:* Jack Ferrel, Director of Admissions, 315-279-5413, Fax: 315-279-5386, E-mail: admissions@mail.keuka.edu. *Chair, Division of Business and Management,* Owen Borda, 315-279-5352, E-mail: gsmith@mail.keuka.edu.

Program in Nursing Students: 23 full-time (21 women). *Faculty:* 2 full-time (both women), 4 part-time/adjunct (all women). Expenses: Contact institution. Offers nursing (MS). *Application Contact:* Jack Farrel, Director of Admissions, 315-279-5434, Fax: 315-279-5386, E-mail: admissions@mail.keuka.edu. *Chair,* Dr. Sparki Mangels, 315-279-5115.

Program in Occupational Therapy Students: 26 full-time (24 women); includes 1 Hispanic/Latino. Average age 23. 15 applicants, 100% accepted. *Faculty:* 5 full-time (3 women). Expenses: Contact institution. In 2010, 21 master's awarded. Offers occupational therapy (MS). *Application deadline:* For fall admission, 8/15 priority date for domestic students; for winter admission, 12/15 priority date for domestic students; for spring admission, 4/15 priority date for domestic students. Applications are processed on a rolling basis. *Application fee:* $30. *Application Contact:* Fred Hoyle, Dean of Enrollment, 315-279-5413, Fax: 315-279-5386, E-mail: admissions@mail.keuka.edu. *Associate Professor and Chair,* Dr. Vicki Smith, 315-279-5666, Fax: 315-279-5439, E-mail: vlsmith@mail.keuka.edu.

KING COLLEGE, Bristol, TN 37620-2699

General Information Independent-religious, coed, comprehensive institution. *Graduate housing:* Room and/or apartments available on a first-come, first-served basis to single students; on-campus housing not available to married students.

GRADUATE UNITS

School of Business and Economics *Degree program information:* Part-time and evening/weekend programs available. Postbaccalaureate distance learning degree programs offered (no on-campus study). Offers business and economics (MBA). Electronic applications accepted.

KING'S COLLEGE, Wilkes-Barre, PA 18711-0801

General Information Independent-religious, coed, comprehensive institution. *Graduate housing:* On-campus housing not available.

GRADUATE UNITS

Program in Physician Assistant Studies Offers physician assistant studies (MSPAS). Electronic applications accepted.

Program in Reading *Degree program information:* Part-time and evening/weekend programs available. Offers reading (M Ed).

William G. McGowan School of Business *Degree program information:* Part-time programs available. Offers health care administration (MS).

KNOWLEDGE SYSTEMS INSTITUTE, Skokie, IL 60076

General Information Independent, coed, graduate-only institution. *Graduate housing:* On-campus housing not available.

GRADUATE UNITS

Program in Computer and Information Sciences *Degree program information:* Part-time and evening/weekend programs available. Postbaccalaureate distance learning degree programs offered (minimal on-campus study). Offers computer and information sciences (MS). Electronic applications accepted.

KNOX COLLEGE, Toronto, ON M5S 2E6, Canada

General Information Independent-religious, coed, graduate-only institution. *Graduate housing:* Room and/or apartments available on a first-come, first-served basis to single students; on-campus housing not available to married students. Housing application deadline: 5/31.

GRADUATE UNITS

College of Theology *Degree program information:* Part-time programs available. Offers theology (M Div, MRE, MTS, Th M, D Min, Th D). Applicants for D Min, Th M, and Th D must apply to Toronto School of Theology; MRE, M Div, MTS, Th D, and Th M programs offered jointly with University of Toronto.

KNOX THEOLOGICAL SEMINARY, Fort Lauderdale, FL 33308

General Information Independent-religious, coed, primarily men, graduate-only institution. *Graduate housing:* On-campus housing not available.

GRADUATE UNITS

Graduate Programs *Degree program information:* Part-time programs available. Offers Biblical studies (CBS); Christianity and culture (MA); divinity (M Div); evangelism (ME); ministry (D Min); New and Old Testament (MBT).

KOL YAAKOV TORAH CENTER, Monsey, NY 10952-2954

General Information Independent-religious, men only, comprehensive institution. *Graduate housing:* Room and/or apartments available to single students; on-campus housing not available to married students.

GRADUATE UNITS

Graduate Program *Degree program information:* Part-time and evening/weekend programs available.

KONA UNIVERSITY, Kailua-Kona, HI 96740

General Information Proprietary, coed, graduate-only institution.

GRADUATE UNITS

Program in Transpersonal Psychology Offers transpersonal psychology (MTP). Electronic applications accepted.

KUTZTOWN UNIVERSITY OF PENNSYLVANIA, Kutztown, PA 19530-0730

General Information State-supported, coed, comprehensive institution. CGS member. *Enrollment:* 10,707 graduate, professional, and undergraduate students; 350 full-time matriculated graduate/professional students (213 women), 550 part-time matriculated graduate/professional students (415 women). *Enrollment by degree level:* 782 master's, 118 other advanced degrees. *Graduate faculty:* 96 full-time (43 women), 1 (woman) part-time/adjunct. Tuition, state resident: full-time $6966; part-time $387 per credit. Tuition, nonresident: full-time $11,146; part-time $619 per credit hour. *Required fees:* $1499; $54 per credit. $68 per year. *Graduate housing:* Rooms and/or apartments available on a first-come, first-served basis to single and married students. Typical cost: $4500 per year for single students; $4500 per year for married students. *Student services:* Campus employment opportunities, campus safety program, career counseling, child daycare facilities, exercise/wellness program, free psychological counseling, international student services, low-cost health insurance, multicultural affairs office, services for students with disabilities. *Library facilities:* Rohrbach Library. *Online resources:* library catalog, web page, access to other libraries' catalogs. *Collection:* 559,934 titles, 48,563 serial subscriptions, 15,953 audiovisual materials.

Computer facilities: Computer purchase and lease plans are available. 1,075 computers available on campus for general student use. A campuswide network can be accessed from student residence rooms. Online class registration is available. *Web address:* http://www.kutztown.edu/.

General Application Contact: Kelly D. Burr, Associate Director, Graduate Admissions, 610-683-4200, Fax: 610-683-1393, E-mail: graduate@kutztown.edu.

GRADUATE UNITS

College of Business Students: 38 full-time (15 women), 43 part-time (18 women); includes 13 minority (2 Black or African American, non-Hispanic/Latino; 2 Asian, non-Hispanic/Latino; 9 Hispanic/Latino), 13 international. Average age 31. 87 applicants, 46% accepted, 26 enrolled. *Faculty:* 10 full-time (2 women). Expenses: Contact institution. *Financial support:* Career-related internships or fieldwork, Federal Work-Study, scholarships/grants, tuition waivers, and unspecified assistantships available. Financial award application deadline: 3/1; financial award applicants required to submit FAFSA. In 2010, 24 master's awarded. *Degree program information:* Part-time and evening/weekend programs available. Offers business (MBA); business administration (MBA). *Application deadline:* For fall admission, 8/15 priority date for domestic and international students; for spring admission, 12/15 priority date for domestic and international students. Applications are processed on a rolling basis. *Application fee:* $35. Electronic applications accepted. *Application Contact:* Kelly D. Burr, Associate Director, Graduate Admissions, 610-683-4200, Fax: 610-683-1393, E-mail: graduate@kutztown.edu. *Dean,* Dr. William Dempsey, 610-683-4575, Fax: 610-683-4573, E-mail: dempsey@kutztown.edu.

College of Education Students: 195 full-time (122 women), 360 part-time (285 women); includes 29 minority (15 Black or African American, non-Hispanic/Latino; 2 American Indian or Alaska Native, non-Hispanic/Latino; 2 Asian, non-Hispanic/Latino; 10 Hispanic/Latino), 2 international. Average age 29. 352 applicants, 68% accepted, 109 enrolled. *Faculty:* 32 full-time (21 women), 1 (woman) part-time/adjunct. Expenses: Contact institution. *Financial support:* Career-related internships or fieldwork, Federal Work-Study, scholarships/grants, and unspecified assistantships available. Financial award application deadline: 3/1; financial award applicants required to submit FAFSA. In 2010, 161 master's awarded. *Degree program information:* Part-time and evening/weekend programs available. Offers agency counseling (MA); biology (M Ed); counselor education (M Ed); curriculum and instruction (M Ed); early childhood education (Certificate); education (M Ed, MA, MLS, Certificate); elementary education (M Ed, Certificate); English (M Ed); instructional technology (M Ed, Certificate); library science (MLS, Certificate); marital and family therapy (MA); mathematics (M Ed); music education (Certificate); reading (M Ed); secondary education (Certificate); social studies (M Ed); special education (Certificate); student affairs in higher education (M Ed). *Application deadline:* For fall admission, 8/15 priority date for domestic and international students; for spring admission, 12/15 priority date for domestic and international students. Applications are processed on a rolling basis. *Application fee:* $35. Electronic applications accepted. *Application Contact:* Kelly D. Burr, Associate Director, Graduate Admissions, 610-683-4200, Fax: 610-683-1393, E-mail: graduate@kutztown.edu. *Dean,* Dr. Darrell Garber, 610-683-4253, Fax: 610-683-4255, E-mail: garber@kutztown.edu.

College of Liberal Arts and Sciences Students: 83 full-time (51 women), 99 part-time (74 women); includes 33 minority (20 Black or African American, non-Hispanic/Latino; 2 American Indian or Alaska Native, non-Hispanic/Latino; 1 Asian, non-Hispanic/Latino; 9 Hispanic/Latino; 1 Two or more races, non-Hispanic/Latino), 8 international. Average age 32. 171 applicants, 67% accepted, 65 enrolled. *Faculty:* 35 full-time (12 women). Expenses: Contact institution. *Financial support:* Career-related internships or fieldwork, Federal Work-Study, scholarships/grants, and unspecified assistantships available. Financial award application deadline: 3/1; financial award applicants required to submit FAFSA. In 2010, 47 master's awarded. *Degree program information:* Part-time and evening/weekend programs available. Offers computer science (MS); electronic media (MS); English (MA); liberal arts and sciences (MA, MPA, MS, MSN, MSW, Certificate); public administration (MPA); school nursing (MSN, Certificate); social work (MSW). *Application deadline:* For fall admission, 8/15 priority date for domestic and international students; for spring admission, 12/15 priority date for domestic and international students. Applications are processed on a rolling basis. *Application fee:* $35. Electronic applications accepted. *Application Contact:* Kelly D. Burr, Associate Director, Graduate Admissions, 610-683-4200, Fax: 610-683-1393, E-mail: graduate@kutztown.edu. *Acting Dean,* Dr. Anne E. Zayaitz, 610-683-4315, Fax: 610-683-4633, E-mail: zayaitz@kutztown.edu.

College of Visual and Performing Arts Students: 34 full-time (25 women), 48 part-time (38 women); includes 2 minority (1 Asian, non-Hispanic/Latino; 1 Hispanic/Latino). Average age 29. 32 applicants, 94% accepted, 24 enrolled. *Faculty:* 19 full-time (8 women). Expenses: Contact institution. *Financial support:* Career-related internships or fieldwork, Federal Work-Study, scholarships/grants, and unspecified assistantships available. Financial award application deadline: 3/1; financial award applicants required to submit FAFSA. In 2010, 14 master's awarded. *Degree program information:* Part-time programs available. Offers art education (M Ed, Certificate); visual and performing arts (M Ed, Certificate). *Application deadline:* For fall admission, 8/15 priority date for domestic and international students; for spring admission, 12/15 priority date for domestic and international students. Applications are processed on a rolling basis. *Application fee:* $35. Electronic applications accepted. *Application Contact:* Kelly D. Burr, Associate Director, Graduate Admissions, 610-683-4200, Fax: 610-683-1393, E-mail: graduate@kutztown.edu. *Dean,* Dr. William Mowder, 610-683-4500, Fax: 610-683-4547, E-mail: mowder@kutztown.edu.

LAGRANGE COLLEGE, LaGrange, GA 30240-2999

General Information Independent-religious, coed, comprehensive institution. *Graduate housing:* Room and/or apartments available on a first-come, first-served basis to single students; on-campus housing not available to married students. Housing application deadline: 5/1.

GRADUATE UNITS

Graduate Programs *Degree program information:* Part-time and evening/weekend programs available. Offers curriculum and instruction (M Ed); middle grades (MAT); organizational leadership (MA); secondary education (MAT). Electronic applications accepted.

LAGUNA COLLEGE OF ART & DESIGN, Laguna Beach, CA 92651-1136

General Information Independent, coed, comprehensive institution.

GRADUATE UNITS

Graduate Program Electronic applications accepted.

LAKE ERIE COLLEGE, Painesville, OH 44077-3389

General Information Independent, coed, comprehensive institution. *Enrollment:* 1,216 graduate, professional, and undergraduate students; 25 full-time matriculated graduate/professional students (8 women), 182 part-time matriculated graduate/professional students (100 women). *Enrollment by degree level:* 207 master's. *Graduate faculty:* 10 full-time (5 women), 4 part-time/adjunct (1 woman). *Tuition:* Full-time $9594; part-time $533 per credit hour. *Required fees:* $51 per credit hour. Tuition and fees vary according to program. *Graduate housing:* Rooms and/or apartments available on a first-come, first-served basis to single and married students. Typical cost: $4054 per year ($8192 including board) for single students. Room and board charges vary according to board plan. *Student services:* Campus employment opportunities, campus safety program, career counseling, exercise/wellness program, international student services, services for students with disabilities, teacher training. *Library facilities:* Lincoln Library. *Online resources:* library catalog, web page. *Collection:* 10,000 serial subscriptions, 1,278 audiovisual materials.

Computer facilities: 75 computers available on campus for general student use. A campuswide network can be accessed from student residence rooms and from off campus. Online class registration is available. *Web address:* http://www.lec.edu/.

General Application Contact: Christopher Harris, Dean of Admissions and Financial Aid, 800-916-0904, Fax: 440-375-7000, E-mail: admissions@lec.edu.

GRADUATE UNITS

Division of Education Students: 2 full-time (0 women), 40 part-time (27 women); includes 1 minority (Black or African American, non-Hispanic/Latino). Average age 36. 63 applicants, 67% accepted, 27 enrolled. *Faculty:* 2 full-time (1 woman), 2 part-time/adjunct (both women). Expenses: Contact institution. *Financial support:* Applicants required to submit FAFSA. In 2010, 3 master's awarded. *Degree program information:* Part-time and evening/weekend programs available. Offers curriculum and instruction (MS Ed); education (MS Ed); educational leadership (MS Ed); reading (MS Ed). *Application deadline:* For fall admission, 8/1 priority date for domestic students, 6/1 for international students; for spring admission, 12/15 for domestic students, 10/1 for international students. Applications are processed on a rolling basis. *Application fee:* $30. Electronic applications accepted. *Application Contact:* Christopher Harris, Dean of Admissions and Financial Aid, 800-916-0904, Fax: 440-375-7000, E-mail: admissions@lec.edu. *Associate Dean,* Dr. Richard Bonde, 440-375-7156, Fax: 440-375-7005, E-mail: rbonde@lec.edu.

Division of Management Studies Students: 23 full-time (8 women), 142 part-time (73 women); includes 17 minority (9 Black or African American, non-Hispanic/Latino; 4 Asian, non-Hispanic/Latino; 1 Hispanic/Latino; 3 Two or more races, non-Hispanic/Latino). Average age 36. 106 applicants, 71% accepted, 56 enrolled. *Faculty:* 7 full-time (3 women), 3 part-time/adjunct (0 women). Expenses: Contact institution. *Financial support:* Career-related internships or fieldwork and unspecified assistantships available. Financial award applicants required to submit FAFSA. In 2010, 79 master's awarded. *Degree program information:* Part-time and evening/weekend programs available. Offers general management (MBA); management healthcare administration (MBA). *Application deadline:* For fall admission, 8/1 priority date for domestic students, 6/1 for international students; for spring admission, 12/15 for domestic students, 10/1 for international students. Applications are processed on a rolling basis. *Application fee:* $30. Electronic applications accepted. *Application Contact:* Christopher Harris, Dean of Admissions and Financial Aid, 800-533-4996, Fax: 440-375-7000, E-mail: admissions@lec.edu. *Associate Dean,* Prof. Robert Trebar, 440-375-7115, Fax: 440-375-7005, E-mail: rtrebar@lec.edu.

LAKE ERIE COLLEGE OF OSTEOPATHIC MEDICINE, Erie, PA 16509-1025

General Information Independent, coed, graduate-only institution. *Graduate housing:* On-campus housing not available. *Research affiliation:* West Virginia University (neurology), Neuro Structural Research Laboratories (neurology), Cornelli Consulting (CORCON) (neurology), University of Maryland (neurology), Duke University (neurology).

GRADUATE UNITS

Professional Programs Offers biomedical sciences (Postbaccalaureate Certificate); medical education (MS); osteopathic medicine (DO); pharmacy (Pharm D). Electronic applications accepted.

LAKE FOREST COLLEGE, Lake Forest, IL 60045

General Information Independent, coed, comprehensive institution. *Enrollment:* 1,443 graduate, professional, and undergraduate students; 4 full-time matriculated graduate/professional students (2 women), 41 part-time matriculated graduate/professional students (22 women). *Enrollment by degree level:* 45 master's. *Graduate faculty:* 16 full-time (7 women). *Tuition:* Part-time $2245 per course. *Graduate housing:* On-campus housing not available. *Student services:* Writing training. *Library facilities:* Donnelley and Lee Library. *Online resources:* library catalog, web page, access to other libraries' catalogs. *Collection:* 287,471 titles, 2,597 serial subscriptions, 8,158 audiovisual materials. *Research affiliation:* Newberry Library (medieval and Renaissance history, American West), Argonne National Laboratory (physics), Merck & Company, Inc. (undergraduate research), Chicago History Museum (Chicago history), Lake Forest Hospital (genomes), Art Institute of Chicago (Asian art).

Computer facilities: Computer purchase and lease plans are available. 130 computers available on campus for general student use. A campuswide network can be accessed from student residence rooms and from off campus. Online class registration, file storage are available. *Web address:* http://www.lakeforest.edu/.

General Application Contact: Prof. Carol Gayle, Associate Director, Graduate Program in Liberal Studies, 847-735-5083, Fax: 847-735-6291, E-mail: gayle@lakeforest.edu.

GRADUATE UNITS

Graduate Program in Liberal Studies Students: 4 full-time (2 women), 41 part-time (22 women), 2 international. Average age 42. 26 applicants, 58% accepted, 12 enrolled. *Faculty:* 16 full-time (7 women). Expenses: Contact institution. *Financial support:* In 2010–11, 9 students received support. Partial tuition waivers for full-time teachers available. Financial award application deadline: 7/1. In 2010, 8 master's awarded. *Degree program information:* Part-time and evening/weekend programs available. Offers liberal studies (MLS). *Application deadline:* For fall admission, 7/1 priority date for domestic students, 6/1 priority date for international students; for winter admission, 12/15 priority date for domestic students, 10/1 priority date for international students. Applications are processed on a rolling basis. *Application fee:* $20. *Application Contact:* Prof. Carol Gayle, Associate Director, 847-735-5083, Fax: 847-735-6291, E-mail: gayle@lakeforest.edu. *Director,* Prof. D. L. LeMahieu, 847-735-5133, Fax: 847-735-6291, E-mail: lemahieu@lakeforest.edu.

Graduate Program in Teaching Expenses: Contact institution. Offers teaching (MAT). *Application Contact:* Kris Sundberg, Admissions Counselor, 847-735-5006, E-mail: ksundberg@lakeforest.edu. *Chair, Department of Education,* Rachel Ragland, 847-735-5198, E-mail: ragland@lakeforest.edu.

LAKE FOREST GRADUATE SCHOOL OF MANAGEMENT, Lake Forest, IL 60045

General Information Independent, coed, graduate-only institution. *Graduate housing:* On-campus housing not available.

GRADUATE UNITS

MBA Program Students: 734 part-time (306 women); includes 156 minority (34 Black or African American, non-Hispanic/Latino; 86 Asian, non-Hispanic/Latino; 14 Hispanic/Latino; 4 Native Hawaiian or other Pacific Islander, non-Hispanic/Latino; 18 Two or more races, non-Hispanic/Latino). Average age 38. *Faculty:* 123 part-time/adjunct (26 women). Expenses: Contact institution. *Financial support:* In 2010–11, 290 students received support. Scholarships/grants available. Support available to part-time students. Financial award applicants required to submit FAFSA. In 2010, 202 master's awarded. *Degree program information:* Part-time and evening/weekend programs available. Offers global business (MBA); healthcare management (MBA); management (MBA); marketing (MBA); organizational behavior (MBA). *Application deadline:* For fall admission, 7/1 for domestic students; for winter admission, 1/5 for domestic students; for spring admission, 3/1 for domestic students. Applications are processed on a rolling basis. *Application fee:* $0. Electronic applications accepted. *Application Contact:* Carolyn Brune, Director of Admissions Operations, 800-737-4MBA, Fax: 847-295-3656, E-mail: admiss@lfgsm.edu. *Vice President and Degree Programs Dean,* Chris Multhauf, 847-574-5270, Fax: 847-295-3656, E-mail: cmulthauf@lfgsm.edu.

LAKEHEAD UNIVERSITY, Thunder Bay, ON P7B 5E1, Canada

General Information Province-supported, coed, comprehensive institution. *Graduate housing:* Rooms and/or apartments available to single students and available on a first-come, first-served basis to married students. Housing application deadline: 3/10. *Research affiliation:* Falcon bridge (biology), Placer Dome (biology), Bowater Inc. (engineering), Centre for Northern Forest Ecosystem Research (biology, forestry, tourism), Thunder Bay Regional Cancer Centre (psychosocial oncology), Bowater Inc. (chemistry).

GRADUATE UNITS

Graduate Studies *Degree program information:* Part-time and evening/weekend programs available. Offers clinical psychology (PhD); experimental psychology (MA); geology (M Sc); gerontology (M Ed, M Sc, MA, MSW); history (MA); physics (M Sc); women's studies (MA).

Faculty of Education *Degree program information:* Part-time and evening/weekend programs available. Offers educational studies (PhD); gerontology (M Ed); women's studies (M Ed).

Faculty of Engineering *Degree program information:* Part-time programs available. Offers control engineering (M Sc Engr); electrical/computer engineering (M Sc Engr); environmental engineering (M Sc Engr).

Faculty of Forestry *Degree program information:* Part-time programs available. Offers forest sciences (PhD); forestry (M Sc F, MF).

Faculty of Social Sciences and Humanities *Degree program information:* Part-time and evening/weekend programs available. Offers biology (M Sc); chemistry (M Sc); economics (MA); English (MA); gerontology (MA); health services and policy research (MA); social sciences and humanities (M Sc, MA, MSW, PhD); sociology (MA); women's studies (MA).

School of Kinesiology *Degree program information:* Part-time programs available. Offers kinesiology (M Sc); kinesiology and gerontology (M Sc).

School of Mathematical Sciences *Degree program information:* Part-time and evening/weekend programs available. Offers computer science (M Sc); mathematical science (MA).

School of Social Work *Degree program information:* Part-time programs available. Offers gerontology (MSW); social work (MSW); women's studies (MSW).

LAKELAND COLLEGE, Sheboygan, WI 53082-0359

General Information Independent-religious, coed, comprehensive institution. *Graduate housing:* On-campus housing not available.

GRADUATE UNITS

Graduate Studies Division *Degree program information:* Part-time and evening/weekend programs available. Offers accounting (MBA); counseling (MA); education (M Ed); finance (MBA); healthcare management (MBA); project management (MBA); theology (MAT).

LAMAR UNIVERSITY, Beaumont, TX 77710

General Information State-supported, coed, university. CGS member. *Enrollment:* 13,826 graduate, professional, and undergraduate students; 602 full-time matriculated graduate/professional students (261 women), 3,281 part-time matriculated graduate/professional students (2,194 women). *Enrollment by degree level:* 3,701 master's, 182 doctoral. *Graduate faculty:* 195 full-time (73 women), 17 part-time/adjunct (4 women). Tuition, state resident: full-time $4160; part-time $208 per credit hour. Tuition, nonresident: full-time $10,360; part-time $518 per credit hour. *Graduate housing:* Room and/or apartments available to single students; on-campus housing not available to married students. Housing application deadline: 9/1. *Student services:* Campus employment opportunities, campus safety program, career counseling, child daycare facilities, exercise/wellness program, free psychological counseling, grant writing training, international student services, low-cost health insurance, multicultural affairs office, services for students with disabilities, teacher training, writing training. *Library facilities:* Mary and John Gray Library. *Online resources:* library catalog, web page. *Collection:* 526,180 titles, 26,618 serial subscriptions, 7,218 audiovisual materials. *Research affiliation:* Grants Resource Center, National Council of Research Administrators, BASF.

Computer facilities: 120 computers available on campus for general student use. A campuswide network can be accessed from student residence rooms and from off campus. *Web address:* http://www.lamar.edu/.

General Application Contact: Sandy Drane, Coordinator of Graduate Admissions, 409-880-8356, Fax: 409-880-8414, E-mail: gradmissions@hal.lamar.edu.

GRADUATE UNITS

College of Graduate Studies Students: 602 full-time (261 women), 3,281 part-time (2,194 women); includes 402 Black or African American, non-Hispanic/Latino; 16 American Indian or Alaska Native, non-Hispanic/Latino; 77 Asian, non-Hispanic/Latino; 389 Hispanic/Latino, 379 international. Average age 34. 2,018 applicants, 69% accepted, 745 enrolled. *Faculty:* 195 full-time (73 women), 17 part-time/adjunct (4 women). Expenses: Contact institution. *Financial support:* Fellowships with partial tuition reimbursements, research assistantships, teaching assistantships, career-related internships or fieldwork, Federal Work-Study, institutionally sponsored loans, scholarships/grants, and tuition waivers (partial) available. Support available to part-time students. Financial award application deadline: 4/1; financial award applicants required to submit FAFSA. In 2010, 2,962 master's, 19 doctorates awarded. *Degree program information:* Part-time and evening/weekend programs available. *Application deadline:* For fall admission, 5/15 for domestic students; for spring admission, 10/1 for domestic students. Applications are processed on a rolling basis. *Application fee:* $25 ($50 for international students). *Application Contact:* Sandy Drane, Coordinator of Graduate Admissions, 409-880-8356, Fax: 409-880-8414, E-mail: gradmissions@hal.lamar.edu.

College of Arts and Sciences Students: 106 full-time (53 women), 98 part-time (55 women); includes 15 Black or African American, non-Hispanic/Latino; 7 Asian, non-Hispanic/Latino; 8 Hispanic/Latino, 67 international. Average age 28. 282 applicants, 68% accepted, 57 enrolled. *Faculty:* 67 full-time (24 women), 4 part-time/adjunct (1 woman). Expenses: Contact institution. *Financial support:* Fellowships, research assistantships, teaching assistantships with tuition reimbursements, career-related internships or fieldwork, Federal Work-Study, institutionally sponsored loans, scholarships/grants, and tuition waivers (partial) available. Support available to part-time students. Financial award application deadline: 4/1. In 2010, 90 master's awarded. *Degree program information:* Part-time and evening/weekend programs available. Offers applied criminology (MS); arts and sciences (MA, MPA, MS, MSN); biology (MS); chemistry (MS); community/clinical psychology (MS); computer science (MS); English (MA); history (MA); industrial/organizational psychology (MS); mathematics (MS); nursing administration (MSN); nursing education (MSN); public administration (MPA). *Application deadline:* For fall admission, 8/1 priority date for domestic students; for spring admission, 12/1 priority date for domestic students. Applications are processed on a rolling basis. *Application fee:* $25 ($50 for international students). *Application Contact:* Dr. James W. Westgate, Assistant Dean, 409-880-7978, E-mail: westgate@hal.lamar.edu. *Dean,* Dr. Brenda S. Nichols, 409-880-8508, Fax: 409-880-8007.

College of Business Students: 79 full-time (37 women), 56 part-time (22 women); includes 14 Black or African American, non-Hispanic/Latino; 8 Asian, non-Hispanic/Latino; 12 Hispanic/Latino, 18 international. Average age 28. 103 applicants, 70% accepted, 40 enrolled. *Faculty:* 17 full-time (4 women), 4 part-time/adjunct (0 women). Expenses: Contact institution. *Financial support:* In 2010–11, 12 students received support, including 4 research assistantships with partial tuition reimbursements available; fellowships with tuition reimbursements available, career-related internships or fieldwork, Federal Work-Study, institutionally sponsored loans, scholarships/grants, and tuition waivers (partial) also available. Support available to part-time students. Financial award application deadline: 4/1; financial award applicants required to submit FAFSA. In 2010, 49 master's awarded. *Degree program information:* Part-time and evening/weekend programs available. Offers accounting (MBA); experiential business and entrepreneurship (MBA); financial management (MBA); healthcare administration (MBA); information systems (MBA); management (MBA). *Application deadline:* For fall admission, 3/15 priority date for domestic students; for spring admission, 10/1 priority date for domestic students. Applications are processed on a rolling basis. *Application fee:* $25 ($50 for international students). *Application Contact:* Dr. Brad Mayer, Professor and Associate Dean, 409-880-2383, Fax: 409-880-8605, E-mail: bradley.mayer@lamar.edu. *Dean,* Dr. Enrique R. Venta, 409-880-8604, Fax: 409-880-8088, E-mail: henry.venta@lamar.edu.

College of Education and Human Development Students: 76 full-time (57 women), 2,922 part-time (2,055 women); includes 353 Black or African American, non-Hispanic/Latino; 15 American Indian or Alaska Native, non-Hispanic/Latino; 39 Asian, non-Hispanic/Latino; 350 Hispanic/Latino, 7 international. Average age 36. 1,075 applicants, 78% accepted, 545 enrolled. *Faculty:* 43 full-time (26 women), 6 part-time/adjunct (3 women). Expenses: Contact institution. *Financial support:* Fellowships, research assistantships, teaching assistantships, career-related internships or fieldwork, Federal Work-Study, institutionally sponsored loans, and scholarships/grants available. Support available to part-time students. Financial award application deadline: 4/1. In 2010, 2,633 master's, 16 doctorates awarded. *Degree program information:* Part-time and evening/weekend programs available. Postbaccalaureate distance learning degree programs offered. Offers counseling and development (M Ed, Certificate); education administration (M Ed); education and human development (M Ed, MS, DE, Ed D, Certificate); educational leadership (DE); family and consumer science (MS); kinesiology (MS); principal (Certificate); professional pedagogy (Ed D); school superintendent (Certificate); supervision (M Ed); technology application (Certificate); vocational home economics (Certificate). *Application deadline:* For fall admission, 8/1 for domestic students; for spring admission, 12/1 for domestic students. Applications are processed on a rolling basis. *Application fee:* $25 ($50 for international students). *Application Contact:* Dr. Lula Henry, Director of Professional Service, 409-880-8218. *Dean,* Dr. H. Lowery-Moore, 409-880-8661.

College of Engineering Students: 244 full-time (37 women), 160 part-time (31 women); includes 6 Black or African American, non-Hispanic/Latino; 21 Asian, non-Hispanic/Latino; 4 Hispanic/Latino, 284 international. Average age 26. 383 applicants, 54% accepted, 46 enrolled. *Faculty:* 39 full-time (3 women). Expenses: Contact institution. *Financial support:* In 2010–11, fellowships with partial tuition reimbursements (averaging $6,000 per year), research assistantships with partial tuition reimbursements (averaging $7,500 per year), teaching assistantships with partial tuition reimbursements (averaging $7,500 per year) were awarded; career-related internships or fieldwork, Federal Work-Study, institutionally sponsored loans, scholarships/grants, tuition waivers (full and partial), and laboratory assistantships also available. Support available to part-time students. Financial award application deadline: 4/1. In 2010, 206 master's, 3 doctorates awarded. *Degree program information:* Part-time and evening/weekend programs available. Offers chemical engineering (ME, MES, DE, PhD); civil engineering (ME, MES, DE); electrical engineering (ME, MES, DE); engineering (ME, MEM, MES, MS, DE, PhD); engineering management (MEM); environmental engineering (MS); environmental studies (MS); industrial engineering (ME, MES, DE); mechanical engineering (ME, MES, DE). *Application deadline:* For fall admission, 5/15 priority date for domestic students; for spring admission, 10/1 priority date for domestic students. Applications are processed on a rolling basis. *Application fee:* $25 ($50 for international students). *Application Contact:* Sandy Drane, Coordinator of Graduate Admissions, 409-880-8356, Fax: 409-880-8414, E-mail: gradmissions@hal.lamar.edu. *Chair,* Dr. Jack Hopper, 409-880-8784, Fax: 409-880-2197, E-mail: che_dept@hal.lamar.edu.

College of Fine Arts and Communication Students: 97 full-time (77 women), 45 part-time (31 women); includes 14 Black or African American, non-Hispanic/Latino; 2 Asian, non-Hispanic/Latino; 15 Hispanic/Latino, 3 international. Average age 31. 173 applicants, 44% accepted, 57 enrolled. *Faculty:* 30 full-time (16 women), 2 part-time/adjunct (0 women). Expenses: Contact institution. *Financial support:* Fellowships, research assistantships, teaching assistantships, career-related internships or fieldwork, Federal Work-Study, institutionally sponsored loans, and tuition waivers (partial) available. Support available to part-time students. Financial award application deadline: 4/1. In 2010, 36 master's, 2 doctorates awarded. *Degree program information:* Part-time and evening/weekend programs available. Offers art history (MA); audiology (MS, Au D); deaf studies and deaf education (MS, Ed D); fine arts and communication (MA, MM, MM Ed, MS, Au D, Ed D); music education (MM Ed); music performance (MM); photography (MA); speech language pathology (MS); studio art (MA); theatre (MS); visual design (MA). *Application deadline:* For fall admission, 8/1 for domestic students; for spring admission, 12/1 for domestic students. Applications are processed on a rolling basis. *Application fee:* $25 ($50 for international students). *Application Contact:* Debbie Piper, Coordinator of Graduate Admissions, 409-880-8356, Fax: 409-880-8414, E-mail: gradmissions@hal.lamar.edu. *Dean,* Dr. Russ A. Schultz, 409-880-8137, Fax: 409-880-2286, E-mail: russ.schultz@lamar.edu.

LANCASTER BIBLE COLLEGE, Lancaster, PA 17601

General Information Independent-religious, coed, comprehensive institution. *Enrollment:* 94 full-time matriculated graduate/professional students (47 women), 89 part-time matriculated graduate/professional students (45 women). *Enrollment by degree level:* 183 master's. *Graduate faculty:* 8 full-time (1 woman), 5 part-time/adjunct (1 woman). *Tuition:* Part-time $1491 per course. *Required fees:* $35 per semester. *Graduate housing:* On-campus housing not available. *Student services:* Campus employment opportunities, career counseling, international student services. *Library facilities:* Lancaster Bible College Library. *Online resources:* library catalog, access to other libraries' catalogs. *Collection:* 132,599 titles, 6,852 serial subscriptions.

Computer facilities: 50 computers available on campus for general student use. A campuswide network can be accessed from student residence rooms. *Web address:* http://www.lbc.edu/.

General Application Contact: Dr. Gary Bredfeldt, Associate Vice President & Dean of iLead Center, 717-560-8297, Fax: 717-560-8236, E-mail: gbredfeldt@lbc.edu.

GRADUATE UNITS

Graduate School Students: 94 full-time (47 women), 89 part-time (45 women); includes 21 minority (15 Black or African American, non-Hispanic/Latino; 5 Asian, non-Hispanic/Latino; 1 Hispanic/Latino). Average age 36. *Faculty:* 8 full-time (1 woman), 5 part-time/adjunct (1 woman). Expenses: Contact institution. *Financial support:* In 2010–11, 31 students received support; teaching assistantships, scholarships/grants and unspecified assistantships available. Support available to part-time students. Financial award application deadline: 6/1; financial award applicants required to submit FAFSA. *Degree program information:* Part-time and evening/weekend programs available. Offers adult ministries (MA); Bible (MA); children and family ministry (MA); consulting resource teacher (M Ed); elementary school counseling (M Ed); leadership (PhD); leadership studies (MA); marriage and family counseling (MA); mental health counseling (MA); pastoral studies (MA); secondary school counseling (M Ed); student ministry (MA). *Application deadline:* Applications are processed on a rolling basis. *Application fee:* $25. *Application Contact:* Mark Wilson, Admissions Counselor, 717-560-8229, E-mail: mwilson@lbc.edu. *Associate Vice President/Dean of iLead Center,* Dr. Gary Bredfeldt, 717-560-8297, Fax: 717-560-8236.

LANCASTER THEOLOGICAL SEMINARY, Lancaster, PA 17603-2812

General Information Independent-religious, coed, graduate-only institution. *Graduate housing:* Rooms and/or apartments available on a first-come, first-served basis to single and married students. Housing application deadline: 8/1.

GRADUATE UNITS

Graduate and Professional Programs Offers biblical studies (MAR); Christian education (MAR); Christianity and the arts (MAR); church history (MAR); congregational life (MAR); lay leadership (Certificate); theological studies (M Div); theology (D Min); theology and ethics (MAR).

LANDER UNIVERSITY, Greenwood, SC 29649-2099

General Information State-supported, coed, comprehensive institution. *Graduate housing:* Room and/or apartments available on a first-come, first-served basis to single students; on-campus housing not available to married students.

GRADUATE UNITS

School of Education *Degree program information:* Part-time programs available. Offers elementary education (M Ed); teaching (MAT). Electronic applications accepted.

LANGSTON UNIVERSITY, Langston, OK 73050

General Information State-supported, coed, comprehensive institution. CGS member. *Graduate housing:* Rooms and/or apartments available on a first-come, first-served basis to single and married students.

GRADUATE UNITS

School of Education and Behavioral Sciences *Degree program information:* Part-time programs available. Offers bilingual/multicultural (M Ed); elementary education (M Ed); English as a second language (M Ed); rehabilitation counseling (M Sc); urban education (M Ed).

School of Physical Therapy Offers physical therapy (DPT).

LA ROCHE COLLEGE, Pittsburgh, PA 15237-5898

General Information Independent-religious, coed, comprehensive institution. *Enrollment:* 1,415 graduate, professional, and undergraduate students; 46 full-time matriculated graduate/professional students (26 women), 78 part-time matriculated graduate/professional students (65 women). *Enrollment by degree level:* 105 master's, 19 other advanced degrees. *Graduate faculty:* 7 full-time (5 women), 10 part-time/adjunct (5 women). *Tuition:* Full-time $10,800; part-time $600 per credit. *Graduate housing:* On-campus housing not available. *Student services:* Campus employment opportunities, career counseling, free psychological counseling, international student services, low-cost health insurance, multicultural affairs office, services for students with disabilities. *Library facilities:* John J. Wright Library. *Online resources:* library catalog, web page. *Collection:* 122,642 titles, 582 serial subscriptions, 1,006 audiovisual materials.

Computer facilities: Computer purchase and lease plans are available. 186 computers available on campus for general student use. A campuswide network can be accessed. Online class registration is available. *Web address:* http://www.laroche.edu/.

General Application Contact: Hope Schiffgens, Director of Graduate Studies and Adult Education, 412-536-1266, Fax: 412-536-1283, E-mail: schombh1@laroche.edu.

GRADUATE UNITS

School of Graduate Studies and Adult Education Students: 46 full-time (26 women), 78 part-time (65 women); includes 5 Black or African American, non-Hispanic/Latino; 2 Asian, non-Hispanic/Latino, 8 international. Average age 32. 37 applicants, 84% accepted, 28 enrolled. *Faculty:* 6 full-time (4 women), 7 part-time/adjunct (3 women). Expenses: Contact institution. *Financial support:* Unspecified assistantships available. Financial award application deadline: 3/31; financial award applicants required to submit FAFSA. In 2010, 52 master's awarded. *Degree program information:* Part-time and evening/weekend programs available. Offers human resources management (MS, Certificate); nurse anesthesia (MS); nursing education (MSN); nursing management (MSN). *Application deadline:* For fall admission, 8/15 for domestic and international students; for spring admission, 12/15 for domestic and international students. Applications are processed on a rolling basis. *Application fee:* $50. Electronic applications accepted. *Application Contact:* Hope Schiffgens, Director of Graduate Studies and Adult Education, 412-536-1266, Fax: 412-536-1283, E-mail: schombh1@laroche.edu. *Dean,* Dr. Rosemary McCarthy, 412-536-1193, Fax: 412-536-1763, E-mail: fortij1@laroche.edu.

LA SALLE UNIVERSITY, Philadelphia, PA 19141-1199

General Information Independent-religious, coed, comprehensive institution. *Graduate housing:* Room and/or apartments available on a first-come, first-served basis to single students; on-campus housing not available to married students. Housing application deadline: 7/1.

GRADUATE UNITS

Program in Instructional Technology Management Offers instructional technology management (MS). Electronic applications accepted.

School of Arts and Sciences *Degree program information:* Part-time and evening/weekend programs available. Offers arts and sciences (MA, MS, Psy D); bilingual/bicultural studies (Spanish) (MA); Central and Eastern European studies (MA); clinical psychology (Psy D); clinical-counseling psychology (MA); computer information science (MS); education (MA); family psychology (Psy D); history (MA); information technology leadership (MS); pastoral studies (MA); professional communication (MA); rehabilitation psychology (Psy D); religion (MA); theological studies (MA).

School of Business *Degree program information:* Part-time and evening/weekend programs available. Offers business (MBA, MS, Certificate). Electronic applications accepted.

School of Nursing and Health Sciences Offers nursing (MSN, Certificate); nursing and health sciences (MS, MSN, Certificate); speech-language-hearing science (MS).

LASELL COLLEGE, Newton, MA 02466-2709

General Information Independent, coed, comprehensive institution. *Enrollment:* 1,798 graduate, professional, and undergraduate students; 36 full-time matriculated graduate/professional students (31 women), 132 part-time matriculated graduate/professional students (89 women). *Enrollment by degree level:* 164 master's, 4 other advanced degrees. *Graduate faculty:* 25 full-time (20 women), 19 part-time/adjunct (15 women). *Tuition:* Part-time $550 per credit hour. *Required fees:* $55 per semester. *Graduate housing:* On-campus housing not available. *Student services:* Campus employment opportunities, campus safety program, career counseling, low-cost health insurance, services for students with disabilities. *Library facilities:* Brennan Library. *Online resources:* library catalog, web page, access to other libraries' catalogs. *Collection:* 53,694 titles, 224 serial subscriptions, 2,736 audiovisual materials. *Research affiliation:* Lasell Village (elder care).

Computer facilities: Computer purchase and lease plans are available. 150 computers available on campus for general student use. A campuswide network can be accessed from student residence rooms and from off campus. Online class registration is available. *Web address:* http://www.lasell.edu/.

General Application Contact: Adrienne Franciosi, Director of Graduate Admission, 617-243-2214, Fax: 617-243-2450, E-mail: gradinfo@lasell.edu.

GRADUATE UNITS

Graduate and Professional Studies in Communication Students: 8 full-time (all women), 25 part-time (22 women); includes 3 minority (all Black or African American, non-Hispanic/Latino), 2 international. Average age 28. 24 applicants, 83% accepted, 13 enrolled. *Faculty:* 2 full-time (both women), 2 part-time/adjunct (both women). Expenses: Contact institution. *Financial support:* In 2010–11, 2 students received support. Available to part-time students. Application deadline: 8/31. In 2010, 10 master's awarded. *Degree program information:* Part-time and evening/weekend programs available. Postbaccalaureate distance learning degree programs offered (minimal on-campus study). Offers integrated marketing communication (MSC, Graduate Certificate); public relations (MSC, Graduate Certificate). *Application deadline:* For fall admission, 8/31 priority date for domestic students, 6/30 priority date for international students; for spring admission, 12/31 priority date for domestic students, 10/31 priority date for international students. Applications are processed on a rolling basis. *Applica-*

Lasell College (continued)

tion fee: $40. Electronic applications accepted. *Application Contact:* Adrienne Franciosi, Director of Graduate Admission, 617-243-2214, Fax: 617-243-2450, E-mail: gradinfo@lasell.edu. *Dean of Graduate and Professional Studies,* Dr. Joan Dolamore, 617-243-2485, Fax: 617-243-2450, E-mail: gradinfo@lasell.edu.

Graduate and Professional Studies in Education Expenses: Contact institution. *Financial support:* Available to part-time students. Application deadline: 8/31. *Degree program information:* Part-time and evening/weekend programs available. Postbaccalaureate distance learning degree programs offered. Offers elementary education—grades 1-6 (M Ed); special education: moderate disabilities (pre-K-8) (M Ed). *Application deadline:* For fall admission, 8/31 priority date for domestic students, 6/30 priority date for international students; for spring admission, 12/31 priority date for domestic students, 10/31 priority date for international students. Applications are processed on a rolling basis. *Application fee:* $40. Electronic applications accepted. *Application Contact:* Adrienne Franciosi, Director of Graduate Admission, 617-243-2214, Fax: 617-243-2450, E-mail: gradinfo@lasell.edu. *Dean of Graduate and Professional Studies,* Dr. Joan Dolamore, 617-243-2485, Fax: 617-243-2450, E-mail: gradinfo@lasell.edu.

Graduate and Professional Studies in Management Students: 25 full-time (21 women), 97 part-time (67 women); includes 16 minority (6 Black or African American, non-Hispanic/Latino; 2 American Indian or Alaska Native, non-Hispanic/Latino; 4 Asian, non-Hispanic/Latino; 4 Hispanic/Latino), 17 international. Average age 33. 56 applicants, 52% accepted, 19 enrolled. *Faculty:* 8 full-time (5 women), 7 part-time/adjunct (5 women). Expenses: Contact institution. *Financial support:* In 2010–11, 40 students received support. Available to part-time students. Application deadline: 8/31. In 2010, 65 master's, 7 other advanced degrees awarded. *Degree program information:* Part-time and evening/weekend programs available. Postbaccalaureate distance learning degree programs offered (no on-campus study). Offers elder care administration (MSM, Graduate Certificate); elder care marketing (MSM, Graduate Certificate); fundraising management (MSM, Graduate Certificate); human resource management (Graduate Certificate); human resources management (MSM); management (MSM, Graduate Certificate); marketing (MSM, Graduate Certificate); non-profit management (MSM, Graduate Certificate); project management (MSM, Graduate Certificate); public relations (MSM). *Application deadline:* For fall admission, 8/31 priority date for domestic students, 6/30 priority date for international students; for spring admission, 12/31 priority date for domestic students, 10/31 priority date for international students. Applications are processed on a rolling basis. *Application fee:* $40. Electronic applications accepted. *Application Contact:* Adrienne Franciosi, Director of Graduate Admission, 617-243-2214, Fax: 617-243-2450, E-mail: gradinfo@lasell.edu. *Dean of Graduate and Professional Studies,* Dr. Joan Dolamore, 617-243-2485, Fax: 617-243-2450, E-mail: gradinfo@lasell.edu.

Graduate and Professional Studies in Sport Management Students: 3 full-time (2 women), 10 part-time (0 women); includes 1 minority (Black or African American, non-Hispanic/Latino). Average age 28. 12 applicants, 58% accepted, 4 enrolled. *Faculty:* 1 full-time (0 women), 4 part-time/adjunct (3 women). Expenses: Contact institution. *Financial support:* In 2010–11, 2 students received support. Available to part-time students. Application deadline: 8/31. *Degree program information:* Part-time programs available. Postbaccalaureate distance learning degree programs offered (no on-campus study). Offers sport hospitality management (MS, Graduate Certificate); sport leadership (MS, Graduate Certificate); sport non-profit management (MS, Graduate Certificate). *Application deadline:* For fall admission, 8/31 priority date for domestic students, 6/30 priority date for international students; for spring admission, 12/31 priority date for domestic students, 10/31 priority date for international students. Applications are processed on a rolling basis. *Application fee:* $40. Electronic applications accepted. *Application Contact:* Adrienne Franciosi, Director of Graduate Admission, 617-243-2214, Fax: 617-243-2450, E-mail: gradinfo@lasell.edu. *Dean of Graduate and Professional Studies,* Dr. Joan Dolamore, 617-243-2485, Fax: 617-243-2450, E-mail: gradinfo@lasell.edu.

LA SIERRA UNIVERSITY, Riverside, CA 92515

General Information Independent-religious, coed, comprehensive institution. CGS member. *Graduate housing:* Rooms and/or apartments available on a first-come, first-served basis to single students and available to married students.

GRADUATE UNITS

College of Arts and Sciences *Degree program information:* Part-time programs available. Offers arts and sciences (MA); communication (MA); English (MA).

School of Business and Management Offers accounting (MBA); finance (MBA); general management (MBA); human resources management (MBA); leadership, values, and ethics for business and management (Certificate); marketing (MBA).

School of Education *Degree program information:* Part-time and evening/weekend programs available. Offers administration and leadership (MA, Ed D, Ed S); counseling (MA); curriculum and instruction (MA, Ed D, Ed S); education (MA, MAT, Ed D, Ed S); educational psychology (Ed S); school psychology (Ed S); teaching (MAT).

School of Religion *Degree program information:* Part-time programs available. Offers pastoral ministry (M Div); religion (MA); religious education (MA); religious studies (MA).

LAURA AND ALVIN SIEGAL COLLEGE OF JUDAIC STUDIES, Beachwood, OH 44122-7116

General Information Independent, coed, comprehensive institution. *Graduate housing:* On-campus housing not available.

GRADUATE UNITS

Graduate Programs *Degree program information:* Part-time and evening/weekend programs available. Postbaccalaureate distance learning degree programs offered (no on-campus study). Offers humanities (MA); Jewish education (MAJS); Judaic studies (MAJS); religious education (MAJS).

LAUREL UNIVERSITY, High Point, NC 27265-3197

General Information Independent-religious, coed, comprehensive institution.

GRADUATE UNITS

School of Management Offers management (MBA).

LAURENTIAN UNIVERSITY, Sudbury, ON P3E 2C6, Canada

General Information Province-supported, coed, comprehensive institution. *Graduate housing:* Rooms and/or apartments available on a first-come, first-served basis to single and married students.

GRADUATE UNITS

School of Graduate Studies and Research *Degree program information:* Part-time and evening/weekend programs available. Offers analytical chemistry (M Sc); applied psychology (MA); applied social research (MA); biochemistry (M Sc); biology (M Sc); boreal ecology (PhD); environmental chemistry (M Sc); European history (MA); experimental psychology (MA); geology (M Sc); history of Northern Ontario (MA); human development (M Sc, MA); humanities: interpretation and values (MA); mineral deposits and precambrian geology (PhD); mineral exploration (M Sc); North American history (MA); nursing (M Sc N); organic chemistry (M Sc); physical/theoretical chemistry (M Sc); physics (M Sc); rural and Northern health (PhD); science communication (G Dip).

School of Commerce and Administration *Degree program information:* Part-time and evening/weekend programs available. Offers commerce and administration (MBA).

School of Engineering *Degree program information:* Part-time programs available. Offers mineral resources engineering (M Eng, MA Sc); natural resources engineering (PhD).

School of Social Work *Degree program information:* Part-time programs available. Offers social work (MSW). Open only to French-speaking students.

LAWRENCE TECHNOLOGICAL UNIVERSITY, Southfield, MI 48075-1058

General Information Independent, coed, university. *Enrollment:* 4,489 graduate, professional, and undergraduate students; 27 full-time matriculated graduate/professional students (8 women), 1,268 part-time matriculated graduate/professional students (461 women). *Enrollment by degree level:* 1,232 master's, 63 doctoral. *Graduate faculty:* 57 full-time (18 women), 91 part-time/adjunct (21 women). *Graduate housing:* Rooms and/or apartments available on a first-come, first-served basis to single and married students. Housing application deadline: 5/1. *Student services:* Campus employment opportunities, career counseling, exercise/wellness program, free psychological counseling, international student services, low-cost health insurance, services for students with disabilities, writing training. *Library facilities:* Lawrence Technological University Library plus 1 other. *Online resources:* library catalog, web page, access to other libraries' catalogs. *Collection:* 155,663 titles, 68,537 serial subscriptions, 592 audiovisual materials. *Research affiliation:* The U. S. Army Tank Automotive Research, Development and Engineering Center (TARDEC) (durability of composite armor structures), Army Research Labs (development of armor structures), U. S. Department of Transportation (development of long-lasting, corrosion-free bridges), Michigan Department of Transportation (use of carbon fiber in box beam highway bridges), National Renewable Energy Laboratory (NREL) (solar design), William Beaumont Hospital (biomedical engineering).

Computer facilities: Computer purchase and lease plans are available. 100 computers available on campus for general student use. A campuswide network can be accessed from student residence rooms and from off campus. Online class registration, degree audit, Blackboard, SCT Banner (student information) are available. *Web address:* http://www.ltu.edu/.

General Application Contact: Jane Rohrback, Director of Admissions, 248-204-3160, Fax: 248-204-2228, E-mail: admissions@ltu.edu.

GRADUATE UNITS

College of Architecture and Design Students: 11 full-time (5 women), 225 part-time (89 women); includes 13 Black or African American, non-Hispanic/Latino; 11 Asian, non-Hispanic/Latino; 7 Hispanic/Latino; 1 Native Hawaiian or other Pacific Islander, non-Hispanic/Latino; 2 Two or more races, non-Hispanic/Latino, 23 international. Average age 31. 174 applicants, 55% accepted, 68 enrolled. *Faculty:* 9 full-time (2 women), 12 part-time/adjunct (3 women). Expenses: Contact institution. *Financial support:* In 2010–11, 83 students received support. Federal Work-Study available. Financial award application deadline: 4/1; financial award applicants required to submit FAFSA. In 2010, 47 master's awarded. *Degree program information:* Part-time and evening/weekend programs available. Offers architecture (M Arch); architecture 3+ (M Arch); interior design (MID); interior design 3+ (MID); urban design (MUD). *Application deadline:* For fall admission, 6/30 priority date for domestic students, 6/30 for international students; for spring admission, 1/15 priority date for domestic students, 1/15 for international students. Applications are processed on a rolling basis. *Application fee:* $50. Electronic applications accepted. *Application Contact:* Jane Rohrback, Director of Admissions, 248-204-3160, Fax: 248-204-2228, E-mail: admissions@ltu.edu. *Dean,* Glen LeRoy, 248-204-2800, Fax: 248-204-2900, E-mail: archdean@ltu.edu.

College of Arts and Sciences Students: 1 full-time (0 women), 93 part-time (54 women); includes 17 Black or African American, non-Hispanic/Latino; 7 Asian, non-Hispanic/Latino; 1 Hispanic/Latino; 4 Two or more races, non-Hispanic/Latino, 10 international. Average age 36. 116 applicants, 61% accepted, 23 enrolled. *Faculty:* 14 full-time (6 women), 14 part-time/adjunct (4 women). Expenses: Contact institution. *Financial support:* In 2010–11, 22 students received support. Federal Work-Study available. Financial award application deadline: 4/1; financial award applicants required to submit FAFSA. In 2010, 40 master's awarded. *Degree program information:* Part-time and evening/weekend programs available. Offers computer science (MS); educational technology (MS); integrated science (MSE); science education (MSE); technical and professional communication (MS). *Application deadline:* For fall admission, 6/30 priority date for domestic students, 6/30 for international students; for spring admission, 11/15 priority date for domestic students, 11/15 for international students. Applications are processed on a rolling basis. *Application fee:* $50. Electronic applications accepted. *Application Contact:* Jane Rohrback, Director of Admissions, 248-204-3160, Fax: 248-204-2228, E-mail: admissions@ltu.edu. *Dean,* Dr. Hsiao-Ping Moore, 248-204-3500, Fax: 248-204-3518, E-mail: scidean@ltu.edu.

College of Engineering Students: 8 full-time (1 woman), 366 part-time (60 women); includes 29 Black or African American, non-Hispanic/Latino; 1 American Indian or Alaska Native, non-Hispanic/Latino; 36 Asian, non-Hispanic/Latino; 9 Hispanic/Latino; 4 Two or more races, non-Hispanic/Latino, 81 international. Average age 32. 398 applicants, 48% accepted, 87 enrolled. *Faculty:* 20 full-time (4 women), 12 part-time/adjunct (0 women). Expenses: Contact institution. *Financial support:* In 2010–11, 72 students received support. Federal Work-Study and institutionally sponsored loans available. Support available to part-time students. Financial award application deadline: 4/1; financial award applicants required to submit FAFSA. In 2010, 121 master's, 5 doctorates awarded. *Degree program information:* Part-time and evening/weekend programs available. Offers architectural engineering (MS); automotive engineering (MS); civil engineering (MS); electrical and computer engineering (MS); engineering management (MEM); industrial engineering (MS); manufacturing systems (ME, DE); mechanical engineering (MS); mechatronic systems engineering (MS). *Application deadline:* For fall admission, 6/30 priority date for domestic students, 6/30 for international students; for spring admission, 11/15 priority date for domestic students, 11/15 for international students. Applications are processed on a rolling basis. *Application fee:* $50. Electronic applications accepted. *Application Contact:* Jane Rohrback, Director of Admissions, 248-204-3160, Fax: 248-204-2228, E-mail: admissions@ltu.edu. *Interim Dean,* Dr. Nabil Grace, 248-204-2500, Fax: 248-204-2509, E-mail: engrdean@ltu.edu.

College of Management Students: 7 full-time (2 women), 584 part-time (258 women); includes 137 Black or African American, non-Hispanic/Latino; 2 American Indian or Alaska Native, non-Hispanic/Latino; 51 Asian, non-Hispanic/Latino; 10 Hispanic/Latino; 8 Two or more races, non-Hispanic/Latino, 48 international. Average age 35. 431 applicants, 54% accepted, 151 enrolled. *Faculty:* 14 full-time (6 women), 53 part-time/adjunct (14 women). Expenses: Contact institution. *Financial support:* In 2010–11, 142 students received support. Federal Work-Study and institutionally sponsored loans available. Support available to part-time students. Financial award application deadline: 4/1; financial award applicants required to submit FAFSA. In 2010, 216 master's, 12 doctorates awarded. *Degree program information:* Part-time and evening/weekend programs available. Offers business administration (MBA, DBA); business administration international (MBA); global leadership and management (MS); global operations and project management (MS); information systems (MS); information technology (DM); operations management (MS). *Application deadline:* For fall admission, 6/30 priority date for domestic students, 6/30 for international students; for spring admission, 11/15 priority date for domestic students, 11/15 for international students. Applications are processed on a rolling basis. *Application fee:* $50. Electronic applications accepted. *Application Contact:* Jane Rohrback, Director of Admissions, 248-204-3160, Fax: 248-204-2228, E-mail: admissions@ltu.edu. *Dean,* Dr. Lou DeGennaro, 248-204-3050, E-mail: degennaro@ltu.edu.

LEBANESE AMERICAN UNIVERSITY, Beirut, Lebanon

General Information Private, coed, comprehensive institution.

GRADUATE UNITS

School of Arts and Sciences Offers computer science (MS); international affairs (MA).

School of Business Offers business (MBA).

School of Pharmacy Offers pharmacy (Pharm D).

LEBANON VALLEY COLLEGE, Annville, PA 17003-1400

General Information Independent-religious, coed, comprehensive institution. *Enrollment:* 2,065 graduate, professional, and undergraduate students; 63 full-time matriculated graduate/professional students (44 women), 183 part-time matriculated graduate/professional students (86 women). *Enrollment by degree level:* 183 master's, 63 doctoral. *Graduate faculty:* 8 full-time (4 women), 25 part-time/adjunct (13 women). *Tuition:* Part-time $420 per credit hour.

Part-time tuition and fees vary according to degree level and program. *Graduate housing:* On-campus housing not available. *Student services:* Career counseling, services for students with disabilities. *Library facilities:* Bishop Library. *Online resources:* library catalog, web page, access to other libraries' catalogs. *Collection:* 202,087 titles, 3,000 serial subscriptions, 17,977 audiovisual materials.

Computer facilities: Computer purchase and lease plans are available. 186 computers available on campus for general student use. A campuswide network can be accessed from student residence rooms and from off campus. Online class registration is available. *Web address:* http://www.lvc.edu/.

General Application Contact: Susan Greenawalt, Assistant for Graduate Studies and Continuing Education, 717-867-6213, Fax: 717-867-6018, E-mail: greenawa@lvc.edu.

GRADUATE UNITS

Graduate Studies and Continuing Education Students: 183 part-time (86 women); includes 11 minority (4 Black or African American, non-Hispanic/Latino; 2 Asian, non-Hispanic/Latino; 5 Hispanic/Latino). Average age 34. *Faculty:* 22 part-time/adjunct (13 women). Expenses: Contact institution. *Financial support:* Application deadline: 5/1. In 2010, 53 master's awarded. *Degree program information:* Part-time and evening/weekend programs available. Offers business administration (MBA); music education (MME); physical therapy (DPT); science education (MSE). *Application deadline:* Applications are processed on a rolling basis. *Application fee:* $30. Electronic applications accepted. *Application Contact:* Hope Witmer, Assistant Dean, Graduate Studies and Continuing Education, 717-867-6213, Fax: 717-867-6018, E-mail: witmer@lvc.edu. *Assistant Dean, Graduate Studies and Continuing Education,* Hope Witmer, 717-867-6213, Fax: 717-867-6018, E-mail: witmer@lvc.edu.

LEE UNIVERSITY, Cleveland, TN 37320-3450

General Information Independent-religious, coed, comprehensive institution. *Enrollment:* 4,377 graduate, professional, and undergraduate students; 163 full-time matriculated graduate/professional students (113 women), 208 part-time matriculated graduate/professional students (131 women). *Enrollment by degree level:* 347 master's, 24 other advanced degrees. *Graduate faculty:* 45 full-time (15 women), 18 part-time/adjunct (9 women). *Tuition:* Full-time $12,120; part-time $506 per credit hour. *Required fees:* $560; $305 per semester. Part-time tuition and fees vary according to course load and campus/location. *Graduate housing:* Rooms and/or apartments available on a first-come, first-served basis to single and married students. Typical cost: $2900 per year ($6010 including board) for single students; $4365 per year for married students. Housing application deadline: 9/1. *Student services:* Campus employment opportunities, campus safety program, career counseling, exercise/wellness program, free psychological counseling, international student services, services for students with disabilities, teacher training, writing training. *Library facilities:* William G. Squires Library plus 3 others. *Online resources:* library catalog, web page, access to other libraries' catalogs. *Collection:* 156,812 titles, 34,881 serial subscriptions, 2,365 audiovisual materials.

Computer facilities: 410 computers available on campus for general student use. A campuswide network can be accessed from student residence rooms and from off campus. Online class registration is available. *Web address:* http://www.leeuniversity.edu/.

General Application Contact: Vicki Glasscock, Director of Graduate Enrollment, 423-614-8059, E-mail: vglasscock@leeuniversity.edu.

GRADUATE UNITS

Graduate Studies in Counseling Students: 74 full-time (64 women), 36 part-time (30 women); includes 2 Black or African American, non-Hispanic/Latino; 2 American Indian or Alaska Native, non-Hispanic/Latino; 1 Asian, non-Hispanic/Latino; 2 Hispanic/Latino; 1 Native Hawaiian or other Pacific Islander, non-Hispanic/Latino, 4 international. Average age 27. 53 applicants, 91% accepted, 34 enrolled. *Faculty:* 7 full-time (3 women), 6 part-time/adjunct (2 women). Expenses: Contact institution. *Financial support:* Teaching assistantships, career-related internships or fieldwork, Federal Work-Study, institutionally sponsored loans, scholarships/grants, and unspecified assistantships available. Financial award application deadline: 3/1; financial award applicants required to submit FAFSA. In 2010, 19 master's awarded. *Degree program information:* Part-time programs available. Offers college student development (MS); holistic child development (MS); marriage and family therapy (MS); school counseling (MS). *Application deadline:* For fall admission, 4/1 priority date for domestic and international students; for spring admission, 10/1 priority date for domestic and international students. Applications are processed on a rolling basis. *Application fee:* $25. *Application Contact:* Vicki Glasscock, Graduate Admissions Director, 423-614-8059, E-mail: vglasscock@leeuniversity.edu. *Director,* Dr. Trevor Milliron, 423-614-8126, Fax: 423-614-8129, E-mail: tmilliron@leeuniversity.edu.

Program in Education Students: 59 full-time (35 women), 139 part-time (86 women); includes 4 Black or African American, non-Hispanic/Latino; 1 American Indian or Alaska Native, non-Hispanic/Latino; 1 Hispanic/Latino; 2 Two or more races, non-Hispanic/Latino, 7 international. Average age 32. 57 applicants, 96% accepted, 44 enrolled. *Faculty:* 10 full-time (4 women), 5 part-time/adjunct (all women). Expenses: Contact institution. *Financial support:* Teaching assistantships, career-related internships or fieldwork, Federal Work-Study, institutionally sponsored loans, scholarships/grants, and unspecified assistantships available. Financial award application deadline: 3/1; financial award applicants required to submit FAFSA. In 2010, 78 master's, 14 other advanced degrees awarded. *Degree program information:* Part-time programs available. Offers classroom teaching (M Ed, Ed S); educational leadership (M Ed, Ed S); elementary/secondary education (MAT); secondary education (MAT); special education (M Ed); special education (secondary) (MAT). *Application deadline:* For fall admission, 4/1 priority date for domestic students; for spring admission, 10/1 priority date for domestic students. Applications are processed on a rolling basis. *Application fee:* $25. *Application Contact:* Vicki Glasscock, Graduate Admissions Director, 423-614-8059, E-mail: vglasscock@leeuniversity.edu. *Director,* Dr. Gary Riggins, 423-614-8193.

Program in Music Students: 17 full-time (9 women), 19 part-time (10 women); includes 1 Black or African American, non-Hispanic/Latino, 4 international. Average age 29. 15 applicants, 100% accepted, 12 enrolled. *Faculty:* 17 full-time (3 women), 9 part-time/adjunct (5 women). Expenses: Contact institution. *Financial support:* Teaching assistantships, career-related internships or fieldwork, Federal Work-Study, institutionally sponsored loans, and scholarships/grants available. Financial award application deadline: 3/1; financial award applicants required to submit FAFSA. In 2010, 8 master's awarded. *Degree program information:* Part-time programs available. Offers church music (MCM); music education (MM); music performance (MM). *Application deadline:* For fall admission, 4/1 for domestic students; for spring admission, 10/1 for domestic students. Applications are processed on a rolling basis. *Application fee:* $25. *Application Contact:* Vicki Glasscock, Graduate Admissions Director, 423-614-8059, E-mail: vglasscock@leeuniversity.edu. *Director,* Dr. Jim W. Burns, 423-614-8240, Fax: 423-614-8242, E-mail: gradmusic@leeuniversity.edu.

Program in Religion Students: 13 full-time (5 women), 14 part-time (5 women); includes 1 Black or African American, non-Hispanic/Latino; 1 Asian, non-Hispanic/Latino; 2 Hispanic/Latino; 1 Two or more races, non-Hispanic/Latino, 1 international. Average age 29. 11 applicants, 100% accepted, 11 enrolled. *Faculty:* 8 full-time (2 women), 1 part-time/adjunct (0 women). Expenses: Contact institution. *Financial support:* Teaching assistantships, career-related internships or fieldwork, Federal Work-Study, institutionally sponsored loans, scholarships/grants, and unspecified assistantships available. Financial award application deadline: 3/1; financial award applicants required to submit FAFSA. In 2010, 5 master's awarded. *Degree program information:* Part-time programs available. Offers biblical studies (MA); ministry studies (MA); theological studies (MA). *Application deadline:* For fall admission, 4/1 priority date for domestic students; for spring admission, 10/1 priority date for domestic students. Applications are processed on a rolling basis. *Application fee:* $25. *Application Contact:* Vicki Glasscock, Graduate Admissions Director, 423-614-8059, E-mail: vglasscock@leeuniversity.edu. *Director,* Dr. Bob Bayles, 423-614-8338, E-mail: bbayles@leeuniversity.edu.

See Display on this page and Close-Up on page 961.

LEHIGH UNIVERSITY, Bethlehem, PA 18015-3094

General Information Independent, coed, university. CGS member. *Enrollment:* 7,051 graduate, professional, and undergraduate students; 1,122 full-time matriculated graduate/

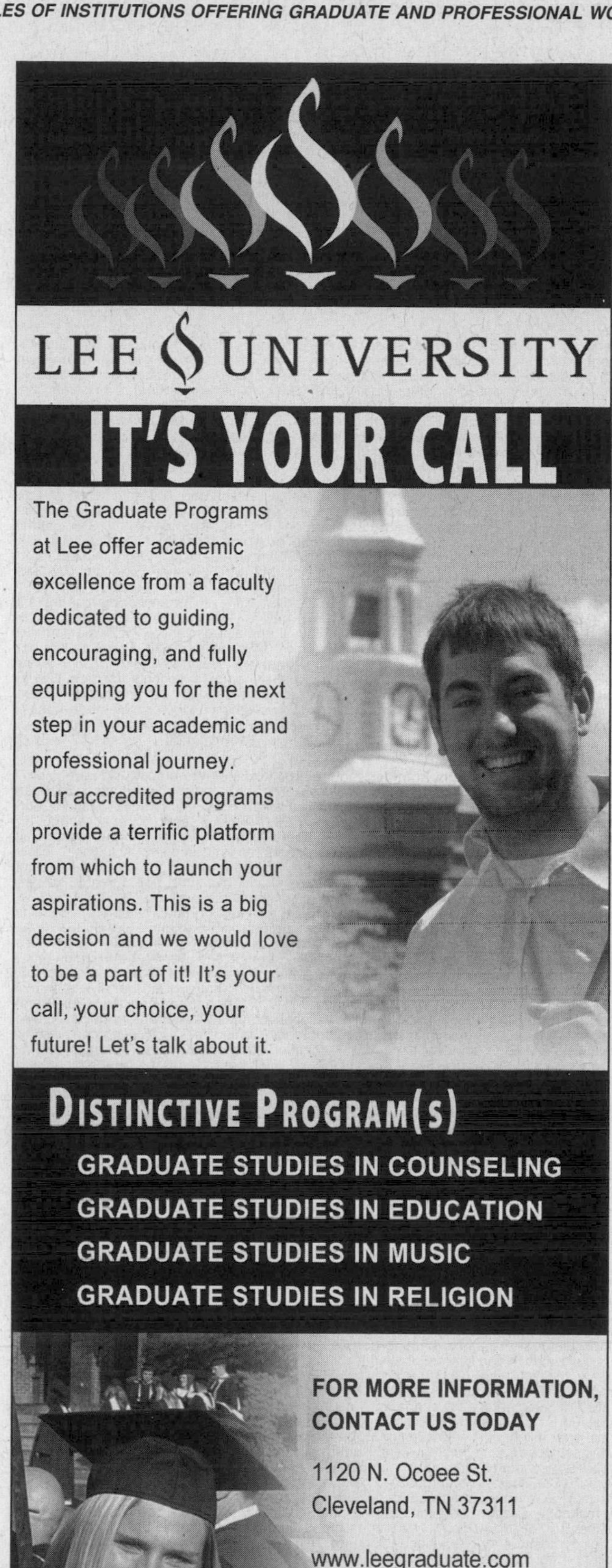

Lehigh University (continued)

professional students (478 women), 968 part-time matriculated graduate/professional students (450 women). *Enrollment by degree level:* 1,343 master's, 733 doctoral, 14 other advanced degrees. *Graduate faculty:* 346 full-time (88 women), 67 part-time/adjunct (30 women). *Graduate housing:* Rooms and/or apartments available on a first-come, first-served basis to single and married students. *Student services:* Campus employment opportunities, campus safety program, career counseling, child daycare facilities, exercise/wellness program, free psychological counseling, international student services, low-cost health insurance, multicultural affairs office, services for students with disabilities, teacher training, writing training. *Library facilities:* E. W. Fairchild-Martindale Library plus 1 other. *Online resources:* library catalog, web page, access to other libraries' catalogs. *Collection:* 1.2 million titles, 55,193 serial subscriptions, 6,705 audiovisual materials.

Computer facilities: Computer purchase and lease plans are available. 638 computers available on campus for general student use. A campuswide network can be accessed from student residence rooms and from off campus. Online class registration is available. *Web address:* http://www.lehigh.edu/.

GRADUATE UNITS

College of Arts and Sciences Students: 290 full-time (150 women), 174 part-time (84 women); includes 27 minority (7 Black or African American, non-Hispanic/Latino; 1 American Indian or Alaska Native, non-Hispanic/Latino; 7 Asian, non-Hispanic/Latino; 10 Hispanic/Latino; 2 Native Hawaiian or other Pacific Islander, non-Hispanic/Latino), 68 international. Average age 29. 610 applicants, 34% accepted, 128 enrolled. *Faculty:* 154 full-time (46 women), 3 part-time/adjunct (2 women). Expenses: Contact institution. *Financial support:* In 2010–11, 27 fellowships with full tuition reimbursements (averaging $22,000 per year), 58 research assistantships with full and partial tuition reimbursements (averaging $18,800 per year), 148 teaching assistantships with full tuition reimbursements (averaging $18,850 per year) were awarded; career-related internships or fieldwork, Federal Work-Study, institutionally sponsored loans, scholarships/grants, traineeships, health care benefits, tuition waivers (full and partial), and unspecified assistantships also available. Support available to part-time students. Financial award application deadline: 1/1. In 2010, 103 master's, 23 doctorates awarded. *Degree program information:* Part-time programs available. Postbaccalaureate distance learning degree programs offered (no on-campus study). Offers American history (PhD); American studies (MA); applied mathematics (MS, PhD); arts and sciences (MA, MS, PhD, Graduate Certificate); biochemistry (PhD); British history (PhD); chemistry (MS, PhD); earth and environmental sciences (MS, PhD); English (MA, PhD); environmental law and policy (Graduate Certificate); environmental policy design (MA); history (MA); human cognition and development (MS, PhD); integrative biology and neuroscience (PhD); mathematics (MS, PhD); molecular biology (MS, PhD); photonics (MS); physics (MS, PhD); politics and policy (MA); polymer science (MS, PhD); sociology (MA); statistics (MS). *Application deadline:* For fall admission, 7/15 for domestic and international students; for spring admission, 12/1 for domestic and international students. Applications are processed on a rolling basis. *Application fee:* $75. Electronic applications accepted. *Application Contact:* Heather Sohara, Administrative Clerk, 610-758-4281, Fax: 610-758-6232, E-mail: incas@lehigh.edu. *Associate Dean of Graduate Studies,* Dr. Michael Stavola, 610-758-4282, Fax: 610-758-6232, E-mail: mjsa@lehigh.edu.

College of Business and Economics Students: 164 full-time (82 women), 242 part-time (72 women); includes 37 minority (6 Black or African American, non-Hispanic/Latino; 25 Asian, non-Hispanic/Latino; 5 Hispanic/Latino; 1 Native Hawaiian or other Pacific Islander, non-Hispanic/Latino), 110 international. Average age 29. 790 applicants, 35% accepted, 158 enrolled. *Faculty:* 43 full-time (10 women), 19 part-time/adjunct (4 women). Expenses: Contact institution. *Financial support:* In 2010–11, 93 students received support, including 2 fellowships with full tuition reimbursements available (averaging $16,000 per year), 39 research assistantships with full and partial tuition reimbursements available (averaging $2,269 per year), 17 teaching assistantships with full tuition reimbursements available (averaging $13,840 per year); career-related internships or fieldwork, scholarships/grants, health care benefits, tuition waivers (full and partial), and unspecified assistantships also available. Support available to part-time students. Financial award application deadline: 1/15. In 2010, 159 master's, 3 doctorates awarded. *Degree program information:* Part-time and evening/weekend programs available. Postbaccalaureate distance learning degree programs offered (minimal on-campus study). Offers accounting (MS); accounting and information analysis (MS); analytical finance (MS); business administration (MBA); economics (MS, PhD); entrepreneurship (Certificate); finance (MS); health and bio-pharmaceutical economics (MS); management (MBA); project management (Certificate); supply chain management (Certificate). *Application deadline:* For fall admission, 7/15 for domestic students, 5/1 for international students; for spring admission, 12/1 for domestic and international students. Applications are processed on a rolling basis. *Application fee:* $100. Electronic applications accepted. *Application Contact:* Corinn McBride, Director of Recruitment and Admissions, 610-758-3418, Fax: 610-758-5283, E-mail: com207@lehigh.edu. *Dean,* Paul R. Brown, 610-758-6725, Fax: 610-758-4499, E-mail: prb207@lehigh.edu.

College of Education Students: 171 full-time (132 women), 404 part-time (261 women); includes 46 minority (18 Black or African American, non-Hispanic/Latino; 15 Asian, non-Hispanic/Latino; 13 Hispanic/Latino), 44 international. Average age 32. 529 applicants, 44% accepted, 180 enrolled. *Faculty:* 29 full-time (17 women), 40 part-time/adjunct (23 women). Expenses: Contact institution. *Financial support:* In 2010–11, 118 students received support, including 6 fellowships with full and partial tuition reimbursements available (averaging $25,000 per year), 36 research assistantships with full and partial tuition reimbursements available (averaging $16,000 per year); teaching assistantships with full and partial tuition reimbursements available, career-related internships or fieldwork, Federal Work-Study, institutionally sponsored loans, scholarships/grants, tuition waivers (full and partial), and unspecified assistantships also available. Financial award application deadline: 3/1; financial award applicants required to submit FAFSA. In 2010, 167 master's, 15 doctorates, 10 other advanced degrees awarded. *Degree program information:* Part-time and evening/weekend programs available. Postbaccalaureate distance learning degree programs offered (minimal on-campus study). Offers comparative and international education (MA); counseling and human services (M Ed); counseling psychology (PhD); education (M Ed, MA, MS, Ed D, PhD, Certificate, Ed S, Graduate Certificate); educational leadership (M Ed, Ed D); elementary counseling with certification (M Ed); elementary education with certification (M Ed); globalization and educational change (M Ed); instructional technology (MS); international counseling (Certificate); international counseling with certification (M Ed); international development in education (Certificate); learning sciences and technology (PhD); principal certification K-12 (Certificate); pupil services (Certificate); school psychology (PhD, Ed S); secondary school counseling (M Ed); special education (Certificate); superintendant certification (Certificate); supervisor of curriculum and instruction (Certificate); supervisor of pupil services (Certificate); teaching and learning (M Ed, MA); technology use in the schools (Graduate Certificate); TESOL (Certificate). *Application deadline:* For fall admission, 1/1 for domestic and international students; for spring admission, 11/1 for domestic and international students. Applications are processed on a rolling basis. *Application fee:* $65. Electronic applications accepted. *Application Contact:* Donna M. Johnson, Manager of Admissions and Recruitment, 610-758-3231, Fax: 610-758-6223, E-mail: dmj4@lehigh.edu. *Dean,* Dr. Gary M. Sasso, 610-758-3221, Fax: 610-758-6223, E-mail: gary.sasso@lehigh.edu.

P. C. Rossin College of Engineering and Applied Science Students: 497 full-time (114 women), 148 part-time (33 women); includes 40 minority (14 Black or African American, non-Hispanic/Latino; 16 Asian, non-Hispanic/Latino; 9 Hispanic/Latino; 1 Native Hawaiian or other Pacific Islander, non-Hispanic/Latino), 345 international. Average age 27. 2,623 applicants, 20% accepted, 262 enrolled. *Faculty:* 120 full-time (15 women), 5 part-time/adjunct (1 woman). Expenses: Contact institution. *Financial support:* In 2010–11, 364 students received support, including 56 fellowships with full and partial tuition reimbursements available (averaging $17,460 per year), 211 research assistantships with full and partial tuition reimbursements available (averaging $21,600 per year), 58 teaching assistantships with full and partial tuition reimbursements available (averaging $18,360 per year); career-related internships or fieldwork, institutionally sponsored loans, scholarships/grants, tuition waivers (full and partial), and unspecified assistantships also available. Support available to part-time students. Financial award application deadline: 1/15. In 2010, 158 master's, 49 doctorates awarded. *Degree program information:* Part-time programs available. Postbaccalaureate distance learning degree programs offered (no on-campus study). Offers analytical finance (MS); biological chemical engineering (M Eng); chemical engineering (M Eng, MS, PhD); civil engineering (M Eng, MS, PhD); computational engineering and mechanics (MS, PhD); computer engineering (M Eng, MS, PhD); computer science (M Eng, MS, PhD); electrical engineering (M Eng, MS, PhD); energy systems engineering (M Eng); engineering and applied science (M Eng, MS, PhD); environmental engineering (MS, PhD); industrial and systems engineering (M Eng, MS); industrial engineering (PhD); management science and engineering (M Eng, MS); manufacturing systems engineering (MS); materials science and engineering (M Eng, MS, PhD); mechanical engineering (M Eng, MS, PhD); photonics (MS); polymer science/engineering (M Eng, MS, PhD); structural engineering (M Eng, MS, PhD); wireless network engineering (MS). *Application deadline:* For fall admission, 7/15 for domestic and international students; for spring admission, 12/1 for domestic and international students. Applications are processed on a rolling basis. *Application fee:* $75. Electronic applications accepted. *Application Contact:* Brianne Lisk, Administrative Coordinator of Graduate Studies and Research, 610-758-6310, Fax: 610-758-5623, E-mail: brc3@lehigh.edu. *Associate Dean of Graduate Studies and Research,* Dr. John P. Coulter, 610-758-6310, Fax: 610-758-5623, E-mail: john.coulter@lehigh.edu.

Center for Polymer Science and Engineering Students: 5 full-time (1 woman), 8 part-time (2 women); includes 1 minority (Hispanic/Latino), 2 international. Average age 33. Expenses: Contact institution. *Financial support:* In 2010–11, 3 students received support, including 5 research assistantships (averaging $24,200 per year), teaching assistantships (averaging $24,200 per year). Financial award application deadline: 1/15. In 2010, 3 master's, 1 doctorate awarded. *Degree program information:* Part-time and evening/weekend programs available. Postbaccalaureate distance learning degree programs offered (no on-campus study). Offers polymer science and engineering (M Eng, MS, PhD). *Application deadline:* For fall admission, 7/15 for domestic students, 1/15 for international students; for spring admission, 12/1 for domestic and international students. Applications are processed on a rolling basis. *Application fee:* $75. Electronic applications accepted. *Application Contact:* James E. Roberts, Chair, Polymer Education Committee, 610-758-4841, Fax: 610-758-6536, E-mail: jer1@lehigh.edu. *Director,* Dr. Raymond A. Pearson, 610-758-3857, Fax: 610-758-3526, E-mail: rp02@lehigh.edu.

LEHMAN COLLEGE OF THE CITY UNIVERSITY OF NEW YORK, Bronx, NY 10468-1589

General Information State and locally supported, coed, comprehensive institution. *Graduate housing:* On-campus housing not available. *Research affiliation:* New York Botanical Gardens, Montefiore Hospital and Medical Center.

GRADUATE UNITS

Division of Arts and Humanities *Degree program information:* Part-time and evening/weekend programs available. Offers art (MA, MFA); arts and humanities (MA, MAT, MFA); English (MA); history (MA); music (MAT); Spanish (MA); speech-language pathology and audiology (MA).

Division of Education *Degree program information:* Part-time and evening/weekend programs available. Offers bilingual special education (MS Ed); business education (MS Ed); early childhood education (MS Ed); early special education (MS Ed); education (MA, MS Ed); elementary education (MS Ed); emotional handicaps (MS Ed); English education (MS Ed); guidance and counseling (MS Ed); learning disabilities (MS Ed); mathematics 7–12 (MS Ed); mental retardation (MS Ed); music education (MS Ed); reading teacher (MS Ed); science education (MS Ed); social studies 7–12 (MA); teachers of special education (MS Ed); teaching English to speakers of other languages (MS Ed).

Division of Natural and Social Sciences *Degree program information:* Part-time and evening/weekend programs available. Offers accounting (MS); adult health nursing (MS); biology (MA); businessclinical nutrition (MS); community nutrition (MS); computer science (MS); dietetic internship (MS); health education and promotion (MA); health N–12 teacher (MS Ed); mathematics (MA); natural and social sciences (MA, MS, MS Ed, PhD); nursing of older adults (MS); nutrition (MS); parent-child nursing (MS); pediatric nurse practitioner (MS); plant sciences (PhD); recreation (MA, MS Ed); recreation education (MA, MS Ed).

LE MOYNE COLLEGE, Syracuse, NY 13214

General Information Independent-religious, coed, comprehensive institution. *Enrollment:* 3,502 graduate, professional, and undergraduate students; 132 full-time matriculated graduate/professional students (81 women), 434 part-time matriculated graduate/professional students (301 women). *Enrollment by degree level:* 512 master's, 54 other advanced degrees. *Graduate faculty:* 37 full-time (18 women), 72 part-time/adjunct (38 women). *Tuition:* Full-time $11,790; part-time $655 per credit hour. *Required fees:* $25 per semester. *Graduate housing:* On-campus housing not available. *Student services:* Campus employment opportunities, campus safety program, career counseling, exercise/wellness program, free psychological counseling, international student services, low-cost health insurance, multicultural affairs office, services for students with disabilities, teacher training. *Library facilities:* Noreen Reale Falcone Library. *Online resources:* library catalog, web page, access to other libraries' catalogs. *Collection:* 259,197 titles, 146,250 serial subscriptions, 10,984 audiovisual materials.

Computer facilities: Computer purchase and lease plans are available. 350 computers available on campus for general student use. A campuswide network can be accessed from student residence rooms and from off campus. Online class registration, ECHO (campuswide portal) are available. *Web address:* http://www.lemoyne.edu/.

General Application Contact: Kristen P. Trapasso, Director of Graduate Admission, 315-445-4265, Fax: 315-445-6027, E-mail: trapaskp@lemoyne.edu.

GRADUATE UNITS

Department of Education Students: 30 full-time (21 women), 330 part-time (239 women); includes 28 minority (13 Black or African American, non-Hispanic/Latino; 3 American Indian or Alaska Native, non-Hispanic/Latino; 4 Asian, non-Hispanic/Latino; 8 Hispanic/Latino). Average age 30. 280 applicants, 86% accepted, 231 enrolled. *Faculty:* 13 full-time (8 women), 54 part-time/adjunct (32 women). Expenses: Contact institution. *Financial support:* In 2010–11, 23 students received support. Career-related internships or fieldwork and health care benefits available. Support available to part-time students. Financial award applicants required to submit FAFSA. In 2010, 155 master's, 19 CASs awarded. *Degree program information:* Part-time and evening/weekend programs available. Offers adolescent education (MS Ed, MST); adolescent education/special education (MS Ed, MST); adolescent English (grades 7-12) (MST); adolescent history (grades 7-12) (MST); childhood education (MS Ed); childhood education/special education (MS Ed); elementary education (MS Ed); general professional education (MS Ed); inclusive childhood education (MST); literacy education (birth to grade 6) (MS Ed); literacy education (grades 5-12) (MS Ed); middle child specialist/special education (MS Ed); middle childhood specialist (MS Ed); school building leadership (MS Ed, CAS); school district business leader (MS Ed, CAS); school district leadership (MS Ed, CAS); secondary education (MS Ed); special education (MS Ed); TESOL (teaching English to speakers of other languages) (MS Ed); urban studies (MS Ed). *Application deadline:* For fall admission, 4/1 priority date for domestic and international students; for spring admission, 10/1 priority date for domestic and international students. Applications are processed on a rolling basis. *Application fee:* $50. *Application Contact:* Kristen P. Trapasso, Director of Graduate Admission, 315-445-4265, Fax: 315-445-6027, E-mail: trapaskp@lemoyne.edu. *Chair/Director of Graduate Programs,* Dr. Suzanne L. Gilmour, 315-445-4376, Fax: 315-445-4744, E-mail: gilmous@lemoyne.edu.

Department of Nursing Students: 25 part-time (all women); includes 2 minority (both Black or African American, non-Hispanic/Latino). Average age 44. 12 applicants, 100% accepted, 12 enrolled. *Faculty:* 3 full-time (all women), 1 (woman) part-time/adjunct. Expenses: Contact institution. *Financial support:* In 2010–11, 11 students received support. Career-related internships or fieldwork, scholarships/grants, health care benefits, unspecified assistantships, and NFLP Federal Loan Program (Nurse Faculty Loan Program) available. Support available to part-time students. Financial award applicants required to submit FAFSA. In 2010, 8 master's awarded. *Degree program information:* Part-time and evening/weekend programs available. Offers nursing administration (MS, CAS); nursing education (MS, CAS). *Application deadline:*

For fall admission, 6/1 priority date for domestic and international students; for spring admission, 11/1 priority date for domestic and international students. Applications are processed on a rolling basis. *Application fee:* $50. *Application Contact:* Kristen P. Trapasso, Director of Graduate Admission, 315-445-4265, Fax: 315-445-6027, E-mail: trapaskp@lemoyne.edu. *Chair/Professor*, Dr. Susan B. Bastable, 315-445-5436, Fax: 315-445-6024, E-mail: bastabsb@lemoyne.edu.

Department of Physician Assistant Studies Students: 79 full-time (51 women), 3 part-time (all women); includes 9 minority (2 Black or African American, non-Hispanic/Latino; 5 Asian, non-Hispanic/Latino; 2 Hispanic/Latino). Average age 26. 415 applicants, 13% accepted, 39 enrolled. *Faculty:* 7 full-time (4 women), 11 part-time/adjunct (4 women). Expenses: Contact institution. *Financial support:* In 2010–11, 2 students received support. Career-related internships or fieldwork, scholarships/grants, and health care benefits available. Financial award applicants required to submit FAFSA. In 2010, 35 master's awarded. Offers physician assistant studies (MS). *Application deadline:* For fall admission, 10/1 priority date for domestic and international students. Electronic applications accepted. *Application Contact:* Kristen P. Trapasso, Director of Graduate Admission, 315-445-4265, Fax: 315-445-6027, E-mail: trapaskp@lemoyne.edu. *Clinical Assistant Professor/Director*, Mary E. Springston, 315-445-4163, Fax: 315-445-4602, E-mail: springme@lemoyne.edu.

Division of Management Students: 23 full-time (9 women), 76 part-time (34 women); includes 6 minority (2 Black or African American, non-Hispanic/Latino; 1 American Indian or Alaska Native, non-Hispanic/Latino; 3 Asian, non-Hispanic/Latino), 1 international. Average age 29. 81 applicants, 77% accepted, 62 enrolled. *Faculty:* 14 full-time (3 women), 6 part-time/adjunct (1 woman). Expenses: Contact institution. *Financial support:* In 2010–11, 8 students received support. Career-related internships or fieldwork, scholarships/grants, health care benefits, and unspecified assistantships available. Support available to part-time students. Financial award applicants required to submit FAFSA. In 2010, 43 master's awarded. *Degree program information:* Part-time and evening/weekend programs available. Offers management (MBA). *Application deadline:* For fall admission, 7/1 priority date for domestic and international students; for spring admission, 11/1 priority date for domestic and international students. Applications are processed on a rolling basis. *Application fee:* $0. *Application Contact:* Kristen P. Trapasso, Director of Graduate Admission, 315-445-4265, Fax: 315-445-6027, E-mail: trapaskp@lemoyne.edu. *Associate Dean*, Dr. George Kulick, 315-445-4786, Fax: 315-445-4787, E-mail: kulick@lemoyne.edu.

LENOIR-RHYNE UNIVERSITY, Hickory, NC 28601

General Information Independent-religious, coed, comprehensive institution. *Graduate housing:* Room and/or apartments available on a first-come, first-served basis to single students; on-campus housing not available to married students.

GRADUATE UNITS

Graduate Programs *Degree program information:* Part-time and evening/weekend programs available. Electronic applications accepted.

Charles M. Snipes School of Business *Degree program information:* Part-time and evening/weekend programs available. Offers accounting (MBA); entrepreneurship (MBA); global leadership (MBA); leadership development (MBA). Electronic applications accepted.

School of Counseling and Human Services *Degree program information:* Part-time and evening/weekend programs available. Offers agency counseling (MA); community counseling (MA); counseling and human services (MA); school counseling (MA). Electronic applications accepted.

School of Education *Degree program information:* Part-time and evening/weekend programs available. Offers birth through kindergarten education (MA); education (MA). Electronic applications accepted.

School of Health, Exercise and Sport Science Offers athletic training (MS).

School of Occupational Therapy Offers occupational therapy (MS).

LESLEY UNIVERSITY, Cambridge, MA 02138-2790

General Information Independent, coed, primarily women, comprehensive institution. *Graduate housing:* On-campus housing not available. *Research affiliation:* TERC (education research and development).

GRADUATE UNITS

Graduate School of Arts and Social Sciences *Degree program information:* Part-time and evening/weekend programs available. Postbaccalaureate distance learning degree programs offered (minimal on-campus study). Offers clinical mental health counseling (MA); counseling psychology (MA, CAGS); creative arts in learning (CAGS); creative writing (MFA); ecological teaching and learning (MS); environmental education (MS); expressive therapies (MA, PhD, CAGS); independent studies (CAGS); independent study (MA); individualized studies (MA); integrative holistic health (MA); intercultural relations (MA, CAGS); interdisciplinary studies (MA); professional counseling (MA); school counseling (MA); urban environmental leadership (MA); visual arts (MFA); women's studies (MA). Electronic applications accepted.

Division of Expressive Therapies Offers art (MA); dance (MA); expressive therapies (MA, PhD, CAGS); music (MA).

School of Education *Degree program information:* Part-time and evening/weekend programs available. Postbaccalaureate distance learning degree programs offered (no on-campus study). Offers curriculum and instruction (M Ed, CAGS); early childhood education (M Ed); educational studies (PhD); elementary education (M Ed); individually designed (M Ed); middle school education (M Ed); moderate special needs (M Ed); reading (M Ed, CAGS); science in education (M Ed); severe special needs (M Ed); special needs (CAGS); technology in education (M Ed, CAGS). Electronic applications accepted.

LETOURNEAU UNIVERSITY, Longview, TX 75607-7001

General Information Independent-religious, coed, comprehensive institution. *Enrollment:* 3,173 graduate, professional, and undergraduate students; 329 full-time matriculated graduate/professional students (233 women). *Enrollment by degree level:* 329 master's. *Graduate faculty:* 9 full-time (1 woman), 62 part-time/adjunct (26 women). *Tuition:* Full-time $13,020; part-time $620 per credit hour. *Graduate housing:* On-campus housing not available. *Student services:* Campus employment opportunities, campus safety program, career counseling, exercise/wellness program, international student services, low-cost health insurance, multicultural affairs office, services for students with disabilities, writing training. *Library facilities:* Margaret Estes Resource Center.

Computer facilities: Computer purchase and lease plans are available. A campuswide network can be accessed from student residence rooms and from off campus. Online class registration is available. *Web address:* http://www.letu.edu/.

General Application Contact: Chris Fontaine, Assistant Vice President for Enrollment Management and Marketing, 903-233-4071, Fax: 903-233-3227, E-mail: chrisfontaine@letu.edu.

GRADUATE UNITS

School of Graduate and Professional Studies Students: 329 full-time (233 women); includes 152 Black or African American, non-Hispanic/Latino; 1 American Indian or Alaska Native, non-Hispanic/Latino; 5 Asian, non-Hispanic/Latino; 23 Hispanic/Latino. Average age 36. 138 applicants, 90% accepted, 120 enrolled. *Faculty:* 9 full-time (1 woman), 62 part-time/adjunct (26 women). Expenses: Contact institution. *Financial support:* Applicants required to submit FAFSA. In 2010, 129 master's awarded. *Degree program information:* Part-time and evening/weekend programs available. Postbaccalaureate distance learning degree programs offered (no on-campus study). Offers business administration (MBA); counseling (MA); curriculum and instruction (M Ed); educational administration (M Ed); engineering (M Sc); psychology (MA); strategic leadership (MSL); teaching and learning (M Ed). *Application deadline:* Applications are processed on a rolling basis. *Application fee:* $0. Electronic applications accepted. *Application Contact:* Chris Fontaine, Assistant Vice President for Enrollment Management and Marketing, 903-233-4071, Fax: 903-233-3227, E-mail: chrisfontaine@letu.edu. *Vice President*, Dr. Carol Green, 903-233-4010, Fax: 903-233-3227, E-mail: carolgreen@letu.edu.

LEWIS & CLARK COLLEGE, Portland, OR 97219-7899

General Information Independent, coed, comprehensive institution. CGS member. *Enrollment:* 3,584 graduate, professional, and undergraduate students; 407 full-time matriculated graduate/professional students (311 women), 165 part-time matriculated graduate/professional students (128 women). *Enrollment by degree level:* 479 master's, 29 doctoral, 64 other advanced degrees. *Graduate faculty:* 33 full-time (24 women), 72 part-time/adjunct (47 women). *Tuition:* Part-time $713 per semester hour. Tuition and fees vary according to course level and campus/location. *Graduate housing:* On-campus housing not available. *Student services:* Campus employment opportunities, campus safety program, career counseling, free psychological counseling, international student services, low-cost health insurance, multicultural affairs office, services for students with disabilities, writing training. *Library facilities:* Aubrey Watzek Library. *Online resources:* library catalog, web page, access to other libraries' catalogs.

Computer facilities: Computer purchase and lease plans are available. A campuswide network can be accessed from student residence rooms and from off campus. Online class registration is available. *Web address:* http://www.lclark.edu/.

General Application Contact: Becky Haas, Director of Admissions, 503-768-6200, Fax: 503-768-6205, E-mail: gseadmit@lclark.edu.

GRADUATE UNITS

Graduate School of Education and Counseling Students: 407 full-time (311 women), 165 part-time (128 women); includes 9 Black or African American, non-Hispanic/Latino; 4 American Indian or Alaska Native, non-Hispanic/Latino; 18 Asian, non-Hispanic/Latino; 28 Hispanic/Latino; 18 Two or more races, non-Hispanic/Latino, 7 international. Average age 32. 630 applicants, 70% accepted, 310 enrolled. *Faculty:* 33 full-time (24 women), 72 part-time/adjunct (47 women). Expenses: Contact institution. *Financial support:* In 2010–11, 70 students received support. Career-related internships or fieldwork, Federal Work-Study, institutionally sponsored loans, scholarships/grants, health care benefits, and tuition waivers (partial) available. Support available to part-time students. Financial award application deadline: 3/1; financial award applicants required to submit FAFSA. In 2010, 245 master's, 3 doctorates awarded. *Degree program information:* Part-time and evening/weekend programs available. Offers addictions treatment (MA, MS); community counseling (MA, MS); curriculum and instruction (M Ed); early childhood/elementary education (MAT); education and counseling (M Ed, MA, MAT, MS, Ed D, Ed S); educational leadership (Ed D, Ed S); educational studies (M Ed); marriage, couple and family therapy (MA, MS); middle level/high school education (MAT); psychological and cultural studies (MA, MS); school counseling (M Ed); school psychology (Ed S); special education (M Ed). *Application deadline:* For fall admission, 2/1 for domestic and international students; for spring admission, 10/1 for domestic and international students. Applications are processed on a rolling basis. *Application fee:* $50. Electronic applications accepted. *Application Contact:* Becky Haas, Director of Admissions, 503-768-6200, Fax: 503-768-6205, E-mail: gseadmit@lclark.edu. *Dean*, Dr. Scott Fletcher, 503-768-6004, Fax: 503-768-6005, E-mail: graddean@lclark.edu.

Lewis & Clark Law School Students: 552 full-time (261 women), 189 part-time (98 women); includes 140 minority (16 Black or African American, non-Hispanic/Latino; 14 American Indian or Alaska Native, non-Hispanic/Latino; 65 Asian, non-Hispanic/Latino; 45 Hispanic/Latino), 17 international. Average age 27. 2,522 applicants, 38% accepted, 237 enrolled. *Faculty:* 52 full-time (22 women), 28 part-time/adjunct (10 women). Expenses: Contact institution. *Financial support:* In 2010–11, 696 students received support, including 40 research assistantships (averaging $1,375 per year), 24 teaching assistantships (averaging $1,788 per year); career-related internships or fieldwork, Federal Work-Study, scholarships/grants, and tuition waivers (partial) also available. Support available to part-time students. Financial award application deadline: 3/1; financial award applicants required to submit FAFSA. In 2010, 226 first professional degrees, 9 master's awarded. *Degree program information:* Part-time and evening/weekend programs available. Offers environmental and natural resources law (LL M); law (JD). *Application deadline:* For fall admission, 3/1 for domestic students, 1/15 priority date for international students. Applications are processed on a rolling basis. *Application fee:* $50. Electronic applications accepted. *Application Contact:* Office of Admissions, 503-768-6613, Fax: 503-768-6793, E-mail: lawadmss@lclark.edu. *Dean*, Robert H. Klonoff, 503-768-6602, Fax: 503-768-6671.

LEWIS UNIVERSITY, Romeoville, IL 60446

General Information Independent-religious, coed, comprehensive institution. CGS member. *Enrollment:* 6,139 graduate, professional, and undergraduate students; 433 full-time matriculated graduate/professional students (274 women), 1,449 part-time matriculated graduate/professional students (1,011 women). *Enrollment by degree level:* 1,817 master's, 50 doctoral, 15 other advanced degrees. *Graduate faculty:* 79 full-time (43 women), 116 part-time/adjunct (52 women). *Tuition:* Full-time $13,320; part-time $740 per credit hour. Tuition and fees vary according to program. *Graduate housing:* Room and/or apartments available on a first-come, first-served basis to single students; on-campus housing not available to married students. Typical cost: $2575 per year ($3675 including board). Room and board charges vary according to board plan and housing facility selected. Housing application deadline: 7/1. *Student services:* Campus employment opportunities, campus safety program, career counseling, exercise/wellness program, free psychological counseling, international student services, low-cost health insurance, multicultural affairs office, services for students with disabilities, teacher training, writing training. *Library facilities:* Lewis University Library. *Online resources:* library catalog, web page, access to other libraries' catalogs. *Collection:* 154,602 titles, 44,925 serial subscriptions, 3,800 audiovisual materials.

Computer facilities: 267 computers available on campus for general student use. A campuswide network can be accessed from student residence rooms and from off campus. Online class registration, online help, online billing, online financial aid, online payments, online application for admission, online housing application, online application for graduation, Blackboard course management system are available. *Web address:* http://www.lewisu.edu/.

General Application Contact: Julie Nickel, Assistant Director, Graduate and Adult Admission, 800-897-9000, Fax: 815-836-5578, E-mail: grad@lewisu.edu.

GRADUATE UNITS

College of Arts and Sciences Students: 162 full-time (115 women), 531 part-time (345 women); includes 145 Black or African American, non-Hispanic/Latino; 2 American Indian or Alaska Native, non-Hispanic/Latino; 11 Asian, non-Hispanic/Latino; 49 Hispanic/Latino, 3 international. Average age 33. Expenses: Contact institution. *Financial support:* Federal Work-Study, scholarships/grants, tuition waivers (partial), and unspecified assistantships available. Financial award application deadline: 5/1; financial award applicants required to submit FAFSA. In 2010, 221 master's awarded. *Degree program information:* Part-time and evening/weekend programs available. Postbaccalaureate distance learning degree programs offered (no on-campus study). Offers administration (MS); arts and sciences (MA, MS); child and adolescent counseling (MA); criminal/social justice (MS); higher education/student services (MA); mental health counseling (MA); organizational management (MA); public administration (MA); public safety administration (MS); safety and security (MS); school counseling and guidance (MA); training and development (MA). *Application deadline:* For fall admission, 5/1 priority date for international students; for spring admission, 11/15 priority date for international students. Applications are processed on a rolling basis. *Application fee:* $40. Electronic applications accepted. *Application Contact:* Julie Nickel, Assistant Director, Graduate and Adult Admission, 800-897-9000, Fax: 815-836-5574, E-mail: grad@lewisu.edu. *Dean*, Dr. Bonnie Bondavalli, 815-838-0500 Ext. 5240, Fax: 815-836-5240, E-mail: bondavbo@lewisu.edu.

College of Business Students: 155 full-time (71 women), 286 part-time (126 women); includes 126 minority (73 Black or African American, non-Hispanic/Latino; 1 American Indian or Alaska Native, non-Hispanic/Latino; 13 Asian, non-Hispanic/Latino; 36 Hispanic/Latino; 2 Native Hawaiian or other Pacific Islander, non-Hispanic/Latino; 1 Two or more races, non-Hispanic/Latino), 19 international. Average age 30. *Faculty:* 18 full-time (2 women), 23 part-time/adjunct (5 women). Expenses: Contact institution. *Financial support:* Career-related internships or fieldwork, Federal Work-Study, scholarships/grants, tuition waivers (full), and unspecified assistantships available. Support available to part-time students. Financial award application deadline: 5/1; financial award applicants required to submit FAFSA. In 2010, 132

Lewis University (continued)

master's awarded. *Degree program information:* Part-time and evening/weekend programs available. Postbaccalaureate distance learning degree programs offered (no on-campus study). Offers business (MBA, MS); information security (MS). *Application deadline:* For fall admission, 5/1 priority date for international students; for spring admission, 11/15 priority date for international students. Applications are processed on a rolling basis. *Application fee:* $40. Electronic applications accepted. *Application Contact:* Michele Ryan, Director of Admission, 815-836-5384, E-mail: gsm@lewisu.edu. *Dean,* Dr. Rami Khasawneh, 800-838-0500 Ext. 5360, E-mail: khasawra@lewisu.edu.

Graduate School of Management Expenses: Contact institution. *Financial support:* Applicants required to submit FAFSA. In 2010, 132 master's awarded. *Degree program information:* Part-time and evening/weekend programs available. Postbaccalaureate distance learning degree programs offered (no on-campus study). Offers accounting (MBA); business administration (MBA); custom elective option (MBA); e-business (MBA); finance (MBA, MS); healthcare management (MBA); human resources management (MBA); information security (MBA); international business (MBA); management (MS); management information systems (MBA); marketing (MBA); project management (MBA); technology and operations management (MBA). *Application fee:* $40. *Application Contact:* Michele Ryan, Director of Admission, 815-836-5384, E-mail: gsm@lewisu.edu.

College of Education Students: 96 full-time (70 women), 362 part-time (276 women); includes 94 minority (49 Black or African American, non-Hispanic/Latino; 8 Asian, non-Hispanic/Latino; 31 Hispanic/Latino; 1 Native Hawaiian or other Pacific Islander, non-Hispanic/Latino; 5 Two or more races, non-Hispanic/Latino), 1 international. Average age 34. *Faculty:* 28 full-time (18 women), 37 part-time/adjunct (22 women). Expenses: Contact institution. *Financial support:* Federal Work-Study, scholarships/grants, tuition waivers (partial), and unspecified assistantships available. Financial award application deadline: 5/1; financial award applicants required to submit FAFSA. In 2010, 145 master's, 1 doctorate awarded. *Degree program information:* Part-time and evening/weekend programs available. Offers advanced study in education (CAS); biology (MA); chemistry (MA); curriculum and instruction: instructional technology (M Ed); curriculum and teacher leadership (M Ed); educational leadership (M Ed, MA); educational leadership for teaching and learning (Ed D); elementary education (MA); English (MA); English as a second language (M Ed); general administrative (CAS); history (MA); instructional technology (M Ed); math (MA); physics (MA); psychology and social science (MA); reading and literacy (M Ed, MA); secondary education (MA); special education (MA); superintendent endorsement (CAS). *Application deadline:* For fall admission, 5/1 priority date for international students; for spring admission, 11/15 priority date for international students. Applications are processed on a rolling basis. *Application fee:* $40. Electronic applications accepted. *Application Contact:* Kelly Lofgren, Graduate Admission Counselor, 815-836-5704, Fax: 815-836-5578, E-mail: lofgreke@lewisu.edu. *Dean,* Dr. Jeanette Mines, 815-838-0500 Ext. 5316, Fax: 815-836-5879, E-mail: minesje@lewisu.edu.

College of Nursing and Health Professions Students: 20 full-time (18 women), 270 part-time (264 women); includes 55 Black or African American, non-Hispanic/Latino; 17 Asian, non-Hispanic/Latino; 16 Hispanic/Latino, 1 international. Average age 41. *Faculty:* 13 full-time (all women), 9 part-time/adjunct (all women). Expenses: Contact institution. *Financial support:* Federal Work-Study, scholarships/grants, tuition waivers (full and partial), and unspecified assistantships available. Financial award application deadline: 5/1; financial award applicants required to submit FAFSA. In 2010, 36 master's awarded. *Degree program information:* Part-time and evening/weekend programs available. Postbaccalaureate distance learning degree programs offered (no on-campus study). Offers adult nurse practitioner (MSN); nursing administration (MSN); nursing and health professions (MSN); nursing education (MSN). *Application deadline:* For fall admission, 5/1 priority date for international students; for spring admission, 11/15 priority date for international students. Applications are processed on a rolling basis. *Application fee:* $40. Electronic applications accepted. *Application Contact:* Nancy Wiksten, Adult Admission Counselor, 815-836-5628, Fax: 815-836-5578, E-mail: wikstena@lewisu.edu. *Dean,* Dr. Peggy Rice, 815-838-0500 Ext. 5245, E-mail: ricema@lewisu.edu.

LEXINGTON THEOLOGICAL SEMINARY, Lexington, KY 40508-3218

General Information Independent-religious, coed, graduate-only institution. *Graduate housing:* Rooms and/or apartments available on a first-come, first-served basis to single and married students. Housing application deadline: 6/15.

GRADUATE UNITS

Graduate and Professional Programs *Degree program information:* Part-time and evening/weekend programs available. Offers theology (M Div, MA, MAPS, D Min). M Div/MSW offered jointly with University of Kentucky.

LIBERTY UNIVERSITY, Lynchburg, VA 24502

General Information Independent-religious, coed, comprehensive institution. *Enrollment:* 7,665 full-time matriculated graduate/professional students (3,965 women), 12,717 part-time matriculated graduate/professional students (7,209 women). *Enrollment by degree level:* 2,747 first professional, 15,504 master's, 2,131 doctoral. *Graduate housing:* Room and/or apartments guaranteed to single students; on-campus housing not available to married students. *Student services:* Campus employment opportunities, career counseling, exercise/wellness program, free psychological counseling, international student services, multicultural affairs office, services for students with disabilities, writing training. *Library facilities:* A. Pierre Guillermin Integrated Learning Resource Center plus 1 other. *Online resources:* library catalog, web page. *Collection:* 372,901 titles, 66,623 serial subscriptions, 52,178 audiovisual materials.

Computer facilities: 1,200 computers available on campus for general student use. A campuswide network can be accessed from student residence rooms and from off campus. Online class registration is available. *Web address:* http://www.liberty.edu/.

General Application Contact: Jay Bridge, Director of Admissions, 800-424-9595, Fax: 800-628-7977, E-mail: gradadmissions@liberty.edu.

GRADUATE UNITS

College of Arts and Sciences Students: 2,021 full-time (1,587 women), 4,301 part-time (3,346 women); includes 1,698 minority (1,424 Black or African American, non-Hispanic/Latino; 20 American Indian or Alaska Native, non-Hispanic/Latino; 59 Asian, non-Hispanic/Latino; 181 Hispanic/Latino; 10 Native Hawaiian or other Pacific Islander, non-Hispanic/Latino; 4 Two or more races, non-Hispanic/Latino), 93 international. Average age 36. Expenses: Contact institution. *Financial support:* Teaching assistantships with tuition reimbursements, Federal Work-Study available. In 2010, 865 master's, 12 doctorates awarded. *Degree program information:* Part-time programs available. Postbaccalaureate distance learning degree programs offered (minimal on-campus study). Offers counseling (MA); human services (MA); nursing (MSN); pastoral care and counseling (PhD); professional counseling (PhD). *Application deadline:* For fall admission, 6/1 priority date for domestic students; for spring admission, 11/1 priority date for domestic students. Applications are processed on a rolling basis. *Application fee:* $50. Electronic applications accepted. *Application Contact:* Jay Bridge, Director of Graduate Admissions, 800-424-9595, Fax: 800-628-7977, E-mail: gradadmissions@liberty.edu. *Dean,* Dr. Ronald E. Hawkins, 434-592-4030, Fax: 434-522-0416, E-mail: rehawkin@liberty.edu.

Liberty Theological Seminary and Graduate School Students: 2,825 full-time (645 women), 3,515 part-time (828 women); includes 1,336 minority (996 Black or African American, non-Hispanic/Latino; 32 American Indian or Alaska Native, non-Hispanic/Latino; 108 Asian, non-Hispanic/Latino; 185 Hispanic/Latino; 11 Native Hawaiian or other Pacific Islander, non-Hispanic/Latino; 4 Two or more races, non-Hispanic/Latino), 258 international. Average age 38. Expenses: Contact institution. *Financial support:* Teaching assistantships with tuition reimbursements, career-related internships or fieldwork and Federal Work-Study available. In 2010, 236 first professional degrees, 1,088 master's, 76 doctorates awarded. *Degree program information:* Part-time programs available. Postbaccalaureate distance learning degree programs offered (minimal on-campus study). Offers religious studies (M Div, MA, MAR, MRE, D Min); theology (Th M). *Application deadline:* For fall admission, 6/1 priority date for domestic students; for spring admission, 11/1 for domestic students. Applications are processed on a rolling basis. *Application fee:* $50. Electronic applications accepted. *Application Contact:* Jay Bridge, Director of Graduate Admissions, 800-424-9595, Fax: 800-628-7977, E-mail: gradadmissions@liberty.edu. *Dean,* Dr. Elmer Towns, 434-582-2169, Fax: 434-582-2766, E-mail: eltowns@liberty.edu.

School of Business Students: 749 full-time (385 women), 2,142 part-time (1,019 women); includes 648 minority (490 Black or African American, non-Hispanic/Latino; 16 American Indian or Alaska Native, non-Hispanic/Latino; 37 Asian, non-Hispanic/Latino; 97 Hispanic/Latino; 7 Native Hawaiian or other Pacific Islander, non-Hispanic/Latino; 1 Two or more races, non-Hispanic/Latino), 60 international. Average age 34. Expenses: Contact institution. In 2010, 559 master's awarded. *Degree program information:* Part-time programs available. Postbaccalaureate distance learning degree programs offered (minimal on-campus study). Offers business (MBA, MS). *Application deadline:* For fall admission, 6/1 for domestic students; for spring admission, 11/1 for domestic students. Applications are processed on a rolling basis. *Application fee:* $50. Electronic applications accepted. *Application Contact:* Jay Bridge, Director of Graduate Admissions, 800-424-9595, Fax: 800-628-7977, E-mail: gradadmissions@liberty.edu. *Dean,* Dr. Bruce K. Bell, 434-592-3863, Fax: 434-582-2366, E-mail: bkbell@liberty.edu.

School of Communications Students: 70 full-time (53 women), 14 part-time (10 women); includes 10 minority (4 Black or African American, non-Hispanic/Latino; 1 American Indian or Alaska Native, non-Hispanic/Latino; 2 Asian, non-Hispanic/Latino; 3 Hispanic/Latino), 9 international. Average age 25. Expenses: Contact institution. *Financial support:* Federal Work-Study and unspecified assistantships available. In 2010, 23 master's awarded. *Degree program information:* Part-time programs available. Offers communications (MA). *Application deadline:* For fall admission, 6/1 priority date for domestic students; for spring admission, 11/1 priority date for domestic students. *Application fee:* $50. Electronic applications accepted. *Application Contact:* Jay Bridge, Director of Graduate Admissions, 800-424-9595, Fax: 800-628-7977, E-mail: gradadmissions@liberty.edu. *Dean,* Dr. William G. Gribbin, 434-582-2466, E-mail: wgribbin@liberty.edu.

School of Education Students: 463 full-time (301 women), 668 part-time (463 women); includes 199 minority (151 Black or African American, non-Hispanic/Latino; 7 American Indian or Alaska Native, non-Hispanic/Latino; 12 Asian, non-Hispanic/Latino; 29 Hispanic/Latino), 10 international. Average age 37. Expenses: Contact institution. *Financial support:* In 2010–11, 226 students received support. Federal Work-Study and tuition waivers (partial) available. In 2010, 485 master's, 43 doctorates, 243 other advanced degrees awarded. *Degree program information:* Part-time programs available. Postbaccalaureate distance learning degree programs offered (minimal on-campus study). Offers administration and supervision (M Ed); curriculum and instruction (M Ed); early childhood education (M Ed); educational leadership (Ed D, Ed S); educational technology and online instruction (M Ed); elementary education (M Ed, MAT); gifted education (M Ed); reading specialist (M Ed); school counseling (M Ed); secondary education (M Ed, MAT); special education (M Ed, MAT); sports administration (MS); teaching and learning (Ed D, Ed S). *Application deadline:* For fall admission, 6/1 priority date for domestic students; for spring admission, 11/1 for domestic students. Applications are processed on a rolling basis. *Application fee:* $50. Electronic applications accepted. *Application Contact:* Jay Bridge, Director of Graduate Admissions, 800-424-9595, Fax: 800-628-7977, E-mail: gradadmissions@liberty.edu. *Dean,* Dr. Karen L. Parker, 434-582-2195, Fax: 434-582-2468, E-mail: kparker@liberty.edu.

School of Law Students: 315 full-time (121 women), 1 part-time (0 women); includes 26 minority (16 Black or African American, non-Hispanic/Latino; 1 American Indian or Alaska Native, non-Hispanic/Latino; 6 Asian, non-Hispanic/Latino; 3 Hispanic/Latino), 7 international. Average age 27. Expenses: Contact institution. In 2010, 57 JDs awarded. Offers law (JD). *Application deadline:* For fall admission, 6/1 for domestic students. *Application fee:* $50. Electronic applications accepted. *Application Contact:* Michelle Crawford Rickert, Assistant Dean, Admissions for the School of Law, 434-592-5471, Fax: 434-522-0404, E-mail: mcrawfordrickert@liberty.edu. *Dean,* Mathew D. Staver, 434-592-5300, Fax: 434-522-0404, E-mail: law@liberty.edu.

LIFE CHIROPRACTIC COLLEGE WEST, Hayward, CA 94545

General Information Independent, coed, graduate-only institution. *Graduate housing:* On-campus housing not available. *Research affiliation:* National Center for Complimentary Medicine (NCCAM), NCCAM/UCRF, Atlas Research Foundation (ARF), University of Illinois at Chicago, Case Western Reserve University, Bay Area Research Roundtable (BAER).

GRADUATE UNITS

Professional Program Offers chiropractic (DC).

LIFE UNIVERSITY, Marietta, GA 30060-2903

General Information Independent, coed, comprehensive institution. *Enrollment:* 2,437 graduate, professional, and undergraduate students; 1,536 full-time matriculated graduate/professional students (661 women), 88 part-time matriculated graduate/professional students (34 women). *Enrollment by degree level:* 1,474 first professional, 100 master's. *Graduate faculty:* 79 full-time (25 women), 24 part-time/adjunct (12 women). *Graduate housing:* Rooms and/or apartments available on a first-come, first-served basis to single and married students. *Student services:* Campus employment opportunities, campus safety program, career counseling, exercise/wellness program, free psychological counseling, international student services, services for students with disabilities. *Library facilities:* Library & Learning Services. *Online resources:* library catalog. *Collection:* 72,480 titles, 29,578 serial subscriptions, 8,139 audiovisual materials.

Computer facilities: 200 computers available on campus for general student use. A campuswide network can be accessed from student residence rooms and from off campus. Online class registration is available. *Web address:* http://www.life.edu/.

General Application Contact: Dr. Mary Flannery, Director of Enrollment Services, 800-543-3202, Fax: 770-426-2895, E-mail: mflannery@life.edu.

GRADUATE UNITS

College of Arts and Sciences Students: 1,302 full-time (496 women), 69 part-time (20 women); includes 158 Black or African American, non-Hispanic/Latino; 8 American Indian or Alaska Native, non-Hispanic/Latino; 70 Asian, non-Hispanic/Latino; 59 Hispanic/Latino. Average age 28. 656 applicants, 47% accepted, 181 enrolled. *Faculty:* 74 full-time (24 women), 21 part-time/adjunct (10 women). Expenses: Contact institution. *Financial support:* Research assistantships, Federal Work-Study, institutionally sponsored loans, scholarships/grants, and tuition waivers (partial) available. Support available to part-time students. Financial award application deadline: 9/1; financial award applicants required to submit FAFSA. In 2010, 9 master's awarded. *Degree program information:* Part-time programs available. Offers chiropractic sport science (MS); exercise and sport science (MS); sport coaching (MS); sport health science (MS); sport injury management (MS). *Application deadline:* Applications are processed on a rolling basis. *Application fee:* $50. Electronic applications accepted. *Application Contact:* Dr. Deborah Heairlston, Director of New Student Development, 770-426-2884, Fax: 770-426-2895, E-mail: drdeb@life.edu. *Academic Dean,* Dr. Jerry Hardee, 770-426-2697, Fax: 770-426-2790, E-mail: jhardee@life.edu.

College of Chiropractic Students: 1,487 full-time (641 women), 35 part-time (13 women). Expenses: Contact institution. *Financial support:* Research assistantships, Federal Work-Study, institutionally sponsored loans, scholarships/grants, and tuition waivers (partial) available. Support available to part-time students. Financial award application deadline: 9/1; financial award applicants required to submit FAFSA. *Degree program information:* Part-time programs available. Offers chiropractic (DC). *Application deadline:* Applications are processed on a rolling basis. *Application fee:* $50. Electronic applications accepted. *Application Contact:* Dr. Deborah Heairlston, Director of New Student Development, 770-426-2884, Fax: 770-426-2895, E-mail: drdeb@life.edu. *Dean of Instruction,* Dr. Leslie King, 770-426-2757, E-mail: lesliek@life.edu.

LIM COLLEGE, New York, NY 10022-5268

General Information Proprietary, coed, primarily women, comprehensive institution.

GRADUATE UNITS

MBA Program Offers entrepreneurship (MBA); fashion management (MBA).

LINCOLN CHRISTIAN SEMINARY, Lincoln, IL 62656-2167

General Information Independent-religious, coed, graduate-only institution. *Graduate housing:* Rooms and/or apartments available on a first-come, first-served basis to single and married students.

GRADUATE UNITS

Graduate and Professional Programs *Degree program information:* Part-time programs available. Offers Bible and theology (MA); Christian ministries (MA); counseling (MA); divinity (M Div); leadership ministry (D Min); religious education (MRE). Electronic applications accepted.

LINCOLN MEMORIAL UNIVERSITY, Harrogate, TN 37752-1901

General Information Independent, coed, comprehensive institution. *Enrollment:* 4,445 graduate, professional, and undergraduate students; 1,202 full-time matriculated graduate/professional students (630 women), 1,457 part-time matriculated graduate/professional students (1,086 women). *Enrollment by degree level:* 782 first professional, 677 master's, 122 doctoral, 1,075 other advanced degrees. *Graduate faculty:* 78. *Graduate housing:* Rooms and/or apartments available on a first-come, first-served basis to single and married students. *Student services:* Campus employment opportunities, career counseling, free psychological counseling, international student services, low-cost health insurance, services for students with disabilities, teacher training. *Library facilities:* Carnegie-Vincent Library. *Online resources:* library catalog, web page. *Collection:* 323,046 titles, 334 serial subscriptions, 4,064 audiovisual materials.

Computer facilities: A campuswide network can be accessed from student residence rooms. Online class registration is available. *Web address:* http://www.lmunet.edu/.

General Application Contact: Sherry McCreary, Dean of Admissions, 423-869-6467, E-mail: sherry.mccreary@lmunet.edu.

GRADUATE UNITS

Carter and Moyers School of Education Students: 169 full-time (132 women), 1,288 part-time (1,004 women); includes 167 Black or African American, non-Hispanic/Latino; 2 American Indian or Alaska Native, non-Hispanic/Latino; 3 Asian, non-Hispanic/Latino; 6 Hispanic/Latino; 4 Two or more races, non-Hispanic/Latino, 2 international. Average age 37. 1,562 applicants, 96% accepted, 1457 enrolled. *Faculty:* 31 full-time (13 women), 22 part-time/adjunct (11 women). Expenses: Contact institution. *Financial support:* In 2010–11, 973 students received support. Career-related internships or fieldwork, health care benefits, and unspecified assistantships available. Support available to part-time students. Financial award application deadline: 4/1; financial award applicants required to submit FAFSA. In 2010, 173 master's, 901 other advanced degrees awarded. *Degree program information:* Part-time and evening/weekend programs available. Postbaccalaureate distance learning degree programs offered. Offers administration and supervision (M Ed, Ed S); counseling and guidance (M Ed); curriculum and instruction (M Ed, Ed D, Ed S); English (M Ed); executive leadership (Ed D); higher education administration (Ed D); human resource development (Ed D); leadership and administration (Ed D). *Application deadline:* For fall admission, 8/1 for domestic students, 8/10 for international students; for spring admission, 1/10 for domestic and international students. *Application fee:* $25. *Application Contact:* Terri Knuckles, Executive Assistant, 423-869-6223, Fax: 423-869-6261, E-mail: terri.knuckles@lmunet.edu. *Dean,* Dr. Michael Clyburn, 423-869-6259, Fax: 423-869-6259, E-mail: michael.clyburn@lmunet.edu.

Caylor School of Nursing Students: 111 full-time (93 women), 7 part-time (5 women); includes 2 Black or African American, non-Hispanic/Latino; 2 Asian, non-Hispanic/Latino; 3 Hispanic/Latino. Average age 30. *Faculty:* 9 full-time (8 women), 1 (woman) part-time/adjunct. Expenses: Contact institution. *Financial support:* Applicants required to submit FAFSA. In 2010, 43 master's awarded. *Degree program information:* Part-time programs available. Offers family nurse practitioner (MSN); nurse anesthesia (MSN); psychiatric mental health nurse practitioner (MSN). *Application deadline:* For fall admission, 2/1 for domestic students. *Application fee:* $25. *Application Contact:* Sherry Pearman, Director of Nursing Recruitment and Advising, 423-869-6283, E-mail: sherry.pearman@lmunet.edu. *Dean,* Dr. Mary Anne Modrcin, 423-869-6319, Fax: 423-869-6244, E-mail: maryanne.modrcin@lmunet.edu.

DeBusk College of Osteopathic Medicine Students: 619 full-time (248 women); includes 15 Black or African American, non-Hispanic/Latino; 1 American Indian or Alaska Native, non-Hispanic/Latino; 36 Asian, non-Hispanic/Latino; 7 Hispanic/Latino; 1 Two or more races, non-Hispanic/Latino, 4 international. Average age 29. 2,849 applicants, 9% accepted, 162 enrolled. *Faculty:* 35 full-time (13 women). Expenses: Contact institution. *Financial support:* In 2010–11, 5 students received support. Applicants required to submit FAFSA. Offers osteopathic medicine (DO). *Application deadline:* For fall admission, 4/1 for domestic students. Applications are processed on a rolling basis. *Application fee:* $50. *Application Contact:* Janette Martin, Director of Admissions, 423-869-7102, Fax: 423-869-7172, E-mail: janette.martin@lmunet.edu. *Vice President and Dean,* Dr. Ray Stowers, 423-869-7077, E-mail: ray.stowers@lmunet.edu.

Duncan School of Law Students: 55 full-time (28 women), 108 part-time (50 women); includes 8 Black or African American, non-Hispanic/Latino; 1 Asian, non-Hispanic/Latino; 2 Hispanic/Latino; 2 Two or more races, non-Hispanic/Latino. Average age 31. 161 applicants, 69% accepted, 55 enrolled. *Faculty:* 10 full-time (4 women). Expenses: Contact institution. *Financial support:* Application deadline: 7/1. *Degree program information:* Part-time programs available. Offers law (JD). *Application deadline:* For fall admission, 1/31 priority date for domestic students. *Application fee:* $50. Electronic applications accepted. *Application Contact:* Terence Cook, Associate Dean for Admissions, 865-545-5304, E-mail: terence.cook@lmunet.edu. *Vice President and Dean,* Dr. Sydney Beckman, 865-545-5302, E-mail: sydney.beckman@lmunet.edu.

School of Business Students: 48 full-time (12 women), 148 part-time (69 women); includes 8 Black or African American, non-Hispanic/Latino; 2 Asian, non-Hispanic/Latino, 21 international. Average age 31. 48 applicants, 94% accepted, 38 enrolled. *Faculty:* 6 full-time (0 women), 1 part-time/adjunct (0 women). Expenses: Contact institution. *Financial support:* Career-related internships or fieldwork, health care benefits, and unspecified assistantships available. Support available to part-time students. Financial award applicants required to submit FAFSA. In 2010, 23 master's awarded. *Degree program information:* Part-time and evening/weekend programs available. Offers business (MBA). *Application deadline:* For fall admission, 7/15 for domestic and international students; for spring admission, 12/1 for domestic and international students. Applications are processed on a rolling basis. *Application fee:* $25. *Application Contact:* Dr. Michael E. Dillon, Director, MBA Program, 423-869-7141, E-mail: michael.dillon@lmunet.edu. *Dean,* Dr. Jack McCann, 423-869-7085, Fax: 423-869-6298, E-mail: jack.mccann@lmunet.edu.

LINCOLN UNIVERSITY, Oakland, CA 94612

General Information Independent, coed, comprehensive institution. *Enrollment:* 297 full-time matriculated graduate/professional students (134 women), 2 part-time matriculated graduate/professional students. *Enrollment by degree level:* 283 master's, 16 doctoral. *Graduate faculty:* 9 full-time (2 women), 11 part-time/adjunct (1 woman). *Tuition:* Full-time $6930. *Required fees:* $195 per semester. *Student services:* Campus employment opportunities, campus safety program, career counseling, international student services, low-cost health insurance, writing training. *Library facilities:* Lincoln University Library. *Collection:* 17,752 titles, 762 serial subscriptions.

Computer facilities: 20 computers available on campus for general student use. A campuswide network can be accessed. *Web address:* http://www.lincolnuca.edu/.

General Application Contact: Peggy Au, Director of Admissions and Records, 510-628-8010, Fax: 510-628-8012, E-mail: admissions@lincolnuca.edu.

GRADUATE UNITS

Graduate Studies Students: 297 full-time (134 women), 2 part-time (0 women). *Faculty:* 9 full-time (2 women), 11 part-time/adjunct (1 woman). Expenses: Contact institution. *Financial support:* In 2010–11, 1 teaching assistantship was awarded; career-related internships or fieldwork and scholarships/grants also available. In 2010, 124 master's awarded. *Degree program information:* Part-time and evening/weekend programs available. Offers finance and investments (DBA); finance management and investment banking (MBA); general business (MBA); human resource management (MBA, DBA); international business (MBA); management information systems (MBA). *Application deadline:* For fall admission, 7/2 priority date for domestic and international students; for spring admission, 11/25 priority date for domestic students, 11/26 priority date for international students. Applications are processed on a rolling basis. *Application fee:* $75. Electronic applications accepted. *Application Contact:* Peggy Au, Director of Admissions and Records, 510-628-8010, Fax: 510-628-8012, E-mail: admissions@lincolnuca.edu. *Director of Graduate Programs,* Dr. Marshall Burak, 510-628-8016, Fax: 510-628-8012, E-mail: mburak@lincolnuca.edu.

LINCOLN UNIVERSITY, Jefferson City, MO 65102

General Information State-supported, coed, comprehensive institution. *Graduate housing:* Room and/or apartments available on a first-come, first-served basis to single students; on-campus housing not available to married students. Housing application deadline: 7/1. *Research affiliation:* U. S. Department of Education (DOE) (defense, government), U. S. Department of Agriculture (USDA) (agriculture, government).

GRADUATE UNITS

School of Graduate Studies and Continuing Education *Degree program information:* Part-time and evening/weekend programs available. Offers business administration (MBA); educational leadership (Ed S); guidance and counseling (M Ed); history (MA); school administration and supervision (M Ed); school teaching (M Ed); social science (MA); sociology (MA); sociology/criminal justice (MA).

LINCOLN UNIVERSITY, Lincoln University, PA 19352

General Information State-related, coed, comprehensive institution. *Graduate housing:* On-campus housing not available.

GRADUATE UNITS

Graduate Center *Degree program information:* Evening/weekend programs available. Offers administration (MSA); early childhood education (M Ed); elementary education (M Ed); human services (M Hum Svcs); reading (MSR).

LINDENWOOD UNIVERSITY, St. Charles, MO 63301-1695

General Information Independent-religious, coed, comprehensive institution. *Enrollment:* 11,345 graduate, professional, and undergraduate students; 1,616 full-time matriculated graduate/professional students (1,025 women), 2,133 part-time matriculated graduate/professional students (1,596 women). *Enrollment by degree level:* 3,463 master's, 151 doctoral, 135 other advanced degrees. *Graduate faculty:* 96 full-time (38 women), 355 part-time/adjunct (155 women). *Tuition:* Full-time $13,260; part-time $380 per credit hour. *Required fees:* $340. One-time fee: $30. Tuition and fees vary according to course level and course load. *Graduate housing:* Rooms and/or apartments available on a first-come, first-served basis to single students and available to married students. Housing application deadline: 8/30. *Student services:* Campus employment opportunities, campus safety program, career counseling, free psychological counseling, international student services, low-cost health insurance, services for students with disabilities, teacher training, writing training. *Library facilities:* Butler Library. *Online resources:* library catalog, web page, access to other libraries' catalogs. *Collection:* 92,946 titles, 268 serial subscriptions, 2,361 audiovisual materials.

Computer facilities: 150 computers available on campus for general student use. A campuswide network can be accessed from student residence rooms and from off campus. Online class registration, Blackboard are available. *Web address:* http://www.lindenwood.edu/.

General Application Contact: Brett Barger, Dean of Evening Admissions and Extension Campuses, 636-949-4934, Fax: 636-949-4109, E-mail: adultadmissions@lindenwood.edu.

GRADUATE UNITS

Graduate Programs Students: 1,616 full-time (1,025 women), 2,133 part-time (1,596 women); includes 835 minority (777 Black or African American, non-Hispanic/Latino; 6 American Indian or Alaska Native, non-Hispanic/Latino; 23 Asian, non-Hispanic/Latino; 28 Hispanic/Latino; 1 Two or more races, non-Hispanic/Latino), 204 international. Average age 35. 634 applicants, 288 enrolled. *Faculty:* 96 full-time (38 women), 355 part-time/adjunct (155 women). Expenses: Contact institution. *Financial support:* In 2010–11, 2,493 students received support. Career-related internships or fieldwork, Federal Work-Study, institutionally sponsored loans, tuition waivers (partial), and unspecified assistantships available. Financial award application deadline: 6/30; financial award applicants required to submit FAFSA. In 2010, 1,347 master's, 81 doctorates, 68 other advanced degrees awarded. *Degree program information:* Part-time and evening/weekend programs available. *Application deadline:* For fall admission, 8/30 priority date for domestic and international students; for winter admission, 12/30 priority date for domestic and international students; for spring admission, 12/30 priority date for domestic and international students. Applications are processed on a rolling basis. *Application fee:* $30 ($100 for international students). Electronic applications accepted. *Application Contact:* Brett Barger, Dean of Evening Admissions and Extension Campuses, 636-949-4934, Fax: 636-949-4109, E-mail: adultadmissions@lindenwood.edu. *Vice President of Academic Affairs and Provost,* Dr. Jann Weitzel, 636-949-4846, Fax: 636-949-4992, E-mail: jweitzel@lindenwood.edu.

College of Individualized Education Students: 828 full-time (527 women), 80 part-time (50 women); includes 284 minority (265 Black or African American, non-Hispanic/Latino; 3 American Indian or Alaska Native, non-Hispanic/Latino; 6 Asian, non-Hispanic/Latino; 10 Hispanic/Latino), 23 international. Average age 35. 223 applicants, 44% accepted, 87 enrolled. *Faculty:* 15 full-time (8 women), 128 part-time/adjunct (53 women). Expenses: Contact institution. *Financial support:* In 2010–11, 631 students received support. Career-related internships or fieldwork, institutionally sponsored loans, tuition waivers (partial), and unspecified assistantships available. Financial award application deadline: 6/30; financial award applicants required to submit FAFSA. In 2010, 478 master's awarded. *Degree program information:* Part-time and evening/weekend programs available. Offers administration (MSA); business administration (MBA); communications (MA); criminal justice and administration (MS); gerontology (MA); health management (MS); human resource management (MS); information technology (MBA, Certificate); managing information technology (MS); writing (MFA). *Application deadline:* For fall admission, 10/2 priority date for domestic and international students; for winter admission, 1/8 priority date for domestic and international students; for spring admission, 4/8 priority date for domestic and international students. Applications are processed on a rolling basis. *Application fee:* $30 ($100 for international students). Electronic applications accepted. *Application Contact:* Brett Barger, Dean of Evening Admissions and Extension Campuses, 636-949-4934, Fax: 636-949-4109, E-mail: adultadmissions@lindenwood.edu. *Dean,* Dan Kemper, 636-949-4501, Fax: 636-949-4505, E-mail: dkemper@lindenwood.edu.

School of American Studies Students: 5 full-time (2 women), 1 international. Average age 33. *Faculty:* 2 full-time (0 women), 9 part-time/adjunct (5 women). Expenses: Contact institution. *Financial support:* In 2010–11, 3 students received support. Career-related internships or fieldwork, Federal Work-Study, institutionally sponsored loans, and tuition waivers (partial) available. Financial award application deadline: 6/30; financial award applicants required to submit FAFSA. *Degree program information:* Part-time and evening/weekend programs available. Offers American studies (MA). *Application deadline:* For fall admission, 8/27 for domestic and international students; for spring admission, 1/28 for domestic and international students. *Application fee:* $30 ($100 for international students). *Application Contact:* Brett Barger, Dean of Evening Admissions and Extension Campuses, 636-949-4934, Fax: 636-949-4109, E-mail: adultadmissions@lindenwood.edu. *Dean,* Dr. David Knotts, 636-798-2166, E-mail: dknotts@lindenwood.edu.

School of Business and Entrepreneurship Students: 179 full-time (73 women), 184 part-time (87 women); includes 27 minority (20 Black or African American, non-Hispanic/Latino; 3 Asian, non-Hispanic/Latino; 4 Hispanic/Latino), 146 international. Average age 28. 149 applicants, 73 enrolled. *Faculty:* 20 full-time (8 women), 17 part-time/adjunct (5 women). Expenses: Contact institution. *Financial support:* In 2010–11, 209 students received support.

Lindenwood University (continued)

Career-related internships or fieldwork, Federal Work-Study, institutionally sponsored loans, and tuition waivers (partial) available. Financial award application deadline: 6/30; financial award applicants required to submit FAFSA. In 2010, 142 master's awarded. *Degree program information:* Part-time and evening/weekend programs available. Offers accounting (MBA, MS); business administration (MBA); entrepreneurial studies (MBA, MS); finance (MBA, MS); human resource management (MBA); human resources (MS); international business (MBA, MS); management (MBA, MS); management information systems (MBA, MS); marketing (MBA, MS); public management (MBA, MS); sport management (MA). *Application deadline:* For fall admission, 7/30 priority date for domestic students, 9/16 priority date for international students; for winter admission, 12/15 priority date for domestic and international students; for spring admission, 2/25 priority date for domestic students, 2/11 priority date for international students. Applications are processed on a rolling basis. *Application fee:* $30 ($100 for international students). Electronic applications accepted. *Application Contact:* Brett Barger, Dean of Evening Admissions and Extension Campuses, 636-949-4934, Fax: 636-949-4109, E-mail: adultadmissions@lindenwood.edu. *Dean,* Roger Ellis, 636-949-4839, E-mail: rellis@lindenwood.edu.

School of Communications Students: 12 full-time (4 women), 2 part-time (1 woman); includes 3 minority (all Black or African American, non-Hispanic/Latino), 1 international. Average age 26. 12 applicants, 5 enrolled. *Faculty:* 5 full-time (0 women), 6 part-time/adjunct (2 women). Expenses: Contact institution. *Financial support:* In 2010–11, 1 student received support. Career-related internships or fieldwork, institutionally sponsored loans, tuition waivers (partial), and unspecified assistantships available. Financial award application deadline: 6/30; financial award applicants required to submit FAFSA. In 2010, 3 master's awarded. *Degree program information:* Part-time and evening/weekend programs available. Offers communications (MA). *Application deadline:* For fall admission, 8/27 priority date for domestic and international students; for spring admission, 1/28 priority date for domestic and international students. Applications are processed on a rolling basis. *Application fee:* $30 ($100 for international students). Electronic applications accepted. *Application Contact:* Brett Barger, Dean of Evening Admissions and Extension Campuses, 636-949-4934, Fax: 636-949-4109, E-mail: adultadmissions@lindenwood.edu. *Dean,* Mike Wall, 636-949-4880.

School of Education Students: 543 full-time (389 women), 1,827 part-time (1,426 women); includes 510 minority (478 Black or African American, non-Hispanic/Latino; 3 American Indian or Alaska Native, non-Hispanic/Latino; 14 Asian, non-Hispanic/Latino; 14 Hispanic/Latino; 1 Two or more races, non-Hispanic/Latino), 20 international. Average age 35. 248 applicants, 120 enrolled. *Faculty:* 33 full-time (13 women), 176 part-time/adjunct (83 women). Expenses: Contact institution. *Financial support:* In 2010–11, 177 students received support. Career-related internships or fieldwork, institutionally sponsored loans, tuition waivers (partial), and unspecified assistantships available. Financial award application deadline: 6/30; financial award applicants required to submit FAFSA. In 2010, 730 master's, 62 doctorates, 67 other advanced degrees awarded. *Degree program information:* Part-time and evening/weekend programs available. Offers education (MA); educational administration (MA, Ed D, Ed S); instructional leadership (Ed D, Ed S); library media (MA); professional and school counseling (MA); professional counseling (MA); school administration (Ed S); school counseling (MA); teaching (MA). *Application deadline:* For fall admission, 8/27 priority date for domestic and international students; for spring admission, 1/28 priority date for domestic and international students. Applications are processed on a rolling basis. *Application fee:* $30 ($100 for international students). Electronic applications accepted. *Application Contact:* Brett Barger, Dean of Evening Admissions and Extension Campuses, 636-949-4934, Fax: 636-949-4109, E-mail: adultadmissions@lindenwood.edu. *Dean,* Dr. Cynthia Bice, 636-949-4618, Fax: 636-949-4197, E-mail: cbice@lindenwood.edu.

School of Fine and Performing Arts Students: 24 full-time (14 women), 16 part-time (12 women); includes 3 minority (all Black or African American, non-Hispanic/Latino), 3 international. Average age 30. 6 applicants, 2 enrolled. *Faculty:* 15 full-time (6 women), 5 part-time/adjunct (2 women). Expenses: Contact institution. *Financial support:* In 2010–11, 10 students received support. Career-related internships or fieldwork, institutionally sponsored loans, tuition waivers (partial), and unspecified assistantships available. Financial award application deadline: 6/30; financial award applicants required to submit FAFSA. In 2010, 9 master's awarded. *Degree program information:* Part-time programs available. Offers arts management (MA); communication arts (MA); studio art (MA, MFA); theatre (MA, MFA). *Application deadline:* For fall admission, 8/27 priority date for domestic and international students; for spring admission, 1/28 priority date for domestic and international students. Applications are processed on a rolling basis. *Application fee:* $30 ($100 for international students). Electronic applications accepted. *Application Contact:* Brett Barger, Dean of Evening Admissions and Extension Campuses, 636-949-4934, Fax: 636-949-4109, E-mail: adultadmissions@lindenwood.edu. *Dean of Fine Arts,* Donnell Walsh, 636-949-4853, Fax: 636-949-4910, E-mail: dwalsh@lindenwood.edu.

School of Humanities Students: 18 full-time (13 women), 2 part-time (1 woman); includes 1 minority (Black or African American, non-Hispanic/Latino), 10 international. Average age 26. 8 applicants, 6 enrolled. *Faculty:* 4 full-time (2 women), 5 part-time/adjunct (1 woman). Expenses: Contact institution. *Financial support:* In 2010–11, 19 students received support. Career-related internships or fieldwork, institutionally sponsored loans, tuition waivers (partial), and unspecified assistantships available. Financial award application deadline: 6/30; financial award applicants required to submit FAFSA. In 2010, 2 master's awarded. *Degree program information:* Part-time programs available. Offers American studies (MA); international studies (MA). *Application deadline:* For fall admission, 8/27 priority date for domestic and international students; for spring admission, 1/28 for domestic students, 1/28 priority date for international students. Applications are processed on a rolling basis. *Application fee:* $30 ($100 for international students). Electronic applications accepted. *Application Contact:* Brett Barger, Dean of Evening Admissions and Extension Campuses, 636-949-4934, Fax: 636-949-4109, E-mail: adultadmissions@lindenwood.edu. *Dean,* Dr. Ana Schnellmann, 636-949-4873, E-mail: aschnellmann@lindenwood.edu.

School of Human Services Students: 7 full-time (3 women), 22 part-time (19 women); includes 7 Black or African American, non-Hispanic/Latino. Average age 33. *Faculty:* 2 full-time (1 woman), 9 part-time/adjunct (4 women). Expenses: Contact institution. *Financial support:* Career-related internships or fieldwork, institutionally sponsored loans, tuition waivers, and unspecified assistantships available. Financial award application deadline: 6/30; financial award applicants required to submit FAFSA. *Degree program information:* Part-time programs available. Offers nonprofit administration (MA); public administration (MPA). *Application deadline:* For fall admission, 8/27 priority date for domestic and international students; for spring admission, 1/28 priority date for domestic and international students. Applications are processed on a rolling basis. *Application fee:* $30 ($100 for international students). Electronic applications accepted. *Application Contact:* Brett Barger, Dean of Evening Admissions and Extension Campuses, 636-949-4934, Fax: 636-949-4109, E-mail: adultadmissions@lindenwood.edu. *Dean,* Carla Mueller, 636-949-4731, E-mail: cmueller@lindenwood.edu.

LINDSEY WILSON COLLEGE, Columbia, KY 42728

General Information Independent-religious, coed, comprehensive institution. *Graduate housing:* Rooms and/or apartments available on a first-come, first-served basis to single and married students.

GRADUATE UNITS

School of Professional Counseling *Degree program information:* Part-time and evening/weekend programs available. Offers counseling and human development (M Ed).

LIPSCOMB UNIVERSITY, Nashville, TN 37204-3951

General Information Independent-religious, coed, comprehensive institution. CGS member. *Enrollment:* 3,742 graduate, professional, and undergraduate students; 755 full-time matriculated graduate/professional students (517 women), 333 part-time matriculated graduate/professional students (165 women). *Enrollment by degree level:* 247 first professional, 841 master's. *Graduate faculty:* 76 full-time (25 women), 52 part-time/adjunct (29 women). *Tuition:* Full-time $18,149; part-time $943 per hour. Tuition and fees vary according to program. *Graduate housing:* Room and/or apartments available on a first-come, first-served basis to single students; on-campus housing not available to married students. Typical cost: $4700 per year ($8360 including board). Housing application deadline: 7/15. *Student services:* Campus employment opportunities, campus safety program, career counseling, exercise/wellness program, free psychological counseling, international student services, multicultural affairs office, services for students with disabilities, teacher training. *Library facilities:* Beaman Library plus 1 other. *Online resources:* library catalog, web page, access to other libraries' catalogs. *Collection:* 253,398 titles, 850 serial subscriptions.

Computer facilities: 185 computers available on campus for general student use. A campuswide network can be accessed from student residence rooms. Online class registration is available. *Web address:* http://www.lipscomb.edu/.

General Application Contact: Dr. Randy Bouldin, Associate Provost for Graduate Studies, 615-966-5711, Fax: 615-966-7619, E-mail: randy.bouldin@lipscomb.edu.

GRADUATE UNITS

Hazelip School of Theology Students: 18 full-time (7 women), 82 part-time (13 women); includes 15 Black or African American, non-Hispanic/Latino; 1 Hispanic/Latino, 1 international. Average age 35. 38 applicants, 97% accepted, 20 enrolled. *Faculty:* 10 full-time (0 women), 2 part-time/adjunct (0 women). Expenses: Contact institution. *Financial support:* Scholarships/grants available. Support available to part-time students. Financial award application deadline: 3/1; financial award applicants required to submit FAFSA. In 2010, 7 first professional degrees, 6 master's awarded. *Degree program information:* Part-time and evening/weekend programs available. Offers biblical studies (MA); Christian studies (MA); divinity (M Div); ministry (MA); New Testament (MA); Old Testament (MA); theological studies (MTS); theology (MA). *Application deadline:* For fall admission, 8/14 priority date for domestic students; for spring admission, 12/31 for domestic students. Applications are processed on a rolling basis. *Application fee:* $0 ($75 for international students). Electronic applications accepted. *Application Contact:* Kellye McCool, Information Contact, 615-966-6051, Fax: 615-966-6052, E-mail: kellye.mccool@lipscomb.edu. *Director,* Dr. Mark Black, 615-966-1000 Ext. 5799, Fax: 615-966-1808, E-mail: mark.black@lipscomb.edu.

Institute for Conflict Management Students: 15 full-time (9 women), 25 part-time (17 women); includes 9 Black or African American, non-Hispanic/Latino; 2 Hispanic/Latino. Average age 40. 16 applicants, 100% accepted, 11 enrolled. *Faculty:* 2 full-time (0 women), 6 part-time/adjunct (3 women). Expenses: Contact institution. In 2010, 12 master's, 3 other advanced degrees awarded. *Degree program information:* Part-time and evening/weekend programs available. Offers conflict management (MA, Certificate). *Application deadline:* Applications are processed on a rolling basis. *Application fee:* $50 ($75 for international students). *Application Contact:* Sherri Guenther, Administrative Assistant, 615-966-7140, Fax: 615-966-7143, E-mail: sherri.guenther@lipscomb.edu. *Executive Director,* Dr. Larry Bridgesmith, 615-966-7145, Fax: 615-966-7143, E-mail: larry.bridgesmith@lipscomb.edu.

Institute for Sustainable Practice Students: 18 full-time (9 women), 10 part-time (6 women); includes 1 Black or African American, non-Hispanic/Latino; 1 Asian, non-Hispanic/Latino; 1 Hispanic/Latino. Average age 31. 17 applicants, 100% accepted, 17 enrolled. *Faculty:* 1 full-time (0 women), 3 part-time/adjunct (2 women). Expenses: Contact institution. In 2010, 10 master's awarded. Offers sustainable practice (MS). *Application Contact:* Aileen Bennett, Program Coordinator, 615-966-1771, E-mail: aileen.bennett@lipscomb.edu. *Executive Director,* G. Dodd Galbreath, 615-966-1771, E-mail: dodd.galbreath@lipscomb.edu.

MBA Program Students: 52 full-time (30 women), 79 part-time (36 women); includes 20 Black or African American, non-Hispanic/Latino; 1 American Indian or Alaska Native, non-Hispanic/Latino; 1 Asian, non-Hispanic/Latino; 7 Hispanic/Latino. Average age 32. 151 applicants, 47% accepted, 45 enrolled. *Faculty:* 17 full-time (5 women), 3 part-time/adjunct (0 women). Expenses: Contact institution. *Financial support:* Career-related internships or fieldwork, Federal Work-Study, scholarships/grants, tuition waivers (partial), and unspecified assistantships available. Support available to part-time students. Financial award application deadline: 7/1; financial award applicants required to submit FAFSA. In 2010, 70 master's awarded. *Degree program information:* Part-time and evening/weekend programs available. Offers accounting (MBA); business administration (general) (MBA); conflict management (MBA); financial services (MBA); healthcare management (MBA); leadership (MBA); nonprofit management (MBA); sports administration (MBA); sustainable practice (MBA). *Application deadline:* For fall admission, 2/1 for international students; for winter admission, 6/1 for international students. Applications are processed on a rolling basis. *Application fee:* $50 ($75 for international students). Electronic applications accepted. *Application Contact:* Emily Landsdell, 615-966-5284, E-mail: emily.lansdell@lipscomb.edu. *Interim Chair of Graduate Business Studies,* Dr. Mike Kendrick, 615-966-1833, Fax: 615-966-1818, E-mail: mikekendrick@lipscomb.edu.

Program in Accountancy Students: 7 full-time (2 women), 13 part-time (7 women); includes 2 Black or African American, non-Hispanic/Latino. Average age 32. 22 applicants, 59% accepted, 5 enrolled. *Faculty:* 2 full-time (0 women), 1 part-time/adjunct (0 women). Expenses: Contact institution. *Financial support:* Career-related internships or fieldwork, Federal Work-Study, scholarships/grants, and tuition waivers available. Support available to part-time students. Financial award application deadline: 7/1. In 2010, 21 master's awarded. *Degree program information:* Part-time and evening/weekend programs available. Offers accountancy (M Acc). *Application fee:* $50 ($75 for international students). *Application Contact:* Emily B. Lansdell, Graduate Business Program Assistant, 615-966-5284, Fax: 615-966-1818, E-mail: emily.lansdell@lipscomb.edu. *Director,* Dr. Perry Moore, 615-966-5795, Fax: 615-966-1818, E-mail: perry.moore@lipscomb.edu.

Program in Education Students: 314 full-time (243 women), 56 part-time (40 women); includes 29 Black or African American, non-Hispanic/Latino; 3 American Indian or Alaska Native, non-Hispanic/Latino; 2 Asian, non-Hispanic/Latino; 10 Hispanic/Latino. Average age 31. 181 applicants, 66% accepted, 85 enrolled. *Faculty:* 10 full-time (5 women), 21 part-time/adjunct (15 women). Expenses: Contact institution. *Financial support:* In 2010–11, 67 students received support. Federal Work-Study, tuition waivers (full), and unspecified assistantships available. Support available to part-time students. Financial award applicants required to submit FAFSA. In 2010, 106 master's awarded. *Degree program information:* Part-time and evening/weekend programs available. Offers English language learners (MAT); instructional leadership (M Ed); instructional technology (M Ed); learning and teaching (MALT); learning organizations and strategic change (Ed D); math specialty (M Ed); school administration and supervision (M Ed); special education instruction, K-12 (MASE). *Application deadline:* For fall admission, 8/29 priority date for domestic students; for spring admission, 1/15 priority date for domestic students. Applications are processed on a rolling basis. *Application fee:* $50. *Application Contact:* Kristin Green, Administrative Assistant, 615-966-7628 Ext. 6081, Fax: 615-966-7628, E-mail: kristin.green@lipscomb.edu. *Director of M Ed Program,* Dr. Deborah Boyd, 615-966-1811.

Program in Exercise and Nutrition Science Students: 18 full-time (13 women), 22 part-time (18 women); includes 4 Black or African American, non-Hispanic/Latino; 1 Asian, non-Hispanic/Latino, 1 international. Average age 26. 33 applicants, 67% accepted, 11 enrolled. *Faculty:* 6 full-time (5 women), 4 part-time/adjunct (2 women). Expenses: Contact institution. In 2010, 3 master's awarded. Offers exercise and nutrition science (MS). *Application deadline:* For fall admission, 6/1 for domestic students; for spring admission, 12/1 for domestic students. *Application Contact:* Dr. Autumn Marshall, Chair, Department of Family and Consumer Sciences, 615-966-6106, E-mail: autumn.marshall@lipscomb.edu. *Chair, Department of Family and Consumer Sciences,* Dr. Autumn Marshall, 615-966-6106, E-mail: autumn.marshall@lipscomb.edu.

Program in Pharmacy Students: 225 full-time (134 women); includes 7 Black or African American, non-Hispanic/Latino; 2 American Indian or Alaska Native, non-Hispanic/Latino; 15 Asian, non-Hispanic/Latino; 3 Hispanic/Latino. Average age 25. 883 applicants, 13% accepted, 75 enrolled. *Faculty:* 23 full-time (9 women). Expenses: Contact institution. *Financial support:* Application deadline: 2/15. Offers pharmacy (Pharm D). *Application deadline:* For fall admission, 2/7 for domestic students. Applications are processed on a rolling basis. *Application fee:* $50. *Application Contact:* Kathryne Chanell, Administrative Assistant, 615-966-7176, E-mail: kathryne.channell@lipscomb.edu. *Dean of College of Pharmacy/Professor of Pharmacy Practice,* Dr. Roger Davis, 615-966-1000.

Programs in Counseling Students: 88 full-time (70 women), 46 part-time (28 women); includes 16 Black or African American, non-Hispanic/Latino; 1 American Indian or Alaska Native, non-Hispanic/Latino; 2 Asian, non-Hispanic/Latino; 3 Hispanic/Latino, 1 international. Average age 30. 101 applicants, 60% accepted, 46 enrolled. *Faculty:* 5 full-time (1 woman), 12 part-time/adjunct (7 women). Expenses: Contact institution. In 2010, 35 master's awarded. *Degree program information:* Part-time and evening/weekend programs available. Postbaccalaureate distance learning degree programs offered (minimal on-campus study). Offers counseling psychology (Certificate); professional counseling (MS); psychology (MS). *Application fee:* $50. Electronic applications accepted. *Application Contact:* Elena Zemmel, Administrative Assistant, 615-966-5906, E-mail: elena.zemmel@lipscomb.edu. *Graduate Program Director and Professor of Psychology,* Dr. Jake Morris, 615-966-5906, E-mail: jake.morris@lipscomb.edu.

LOCK HAVEN UNIVERSITY OF PENNSYLVANIA, Lock Haven, PA 17745-2390

General Information State-supported, coed, comprehensive institution. *Enrollment:* 5,450 graduate, professional, and undergraduate students; 137 full-time matriculated graduate/professional students (103 women), 199 part-time matriculated graduate/professional students (141 women). *Enrollment by degree level:* 336 master's. *Graduate faculty:* 18 full-time (9 women), 2 part-time/adjunct (1 woman). Tuition, state resident: full-time $9073; part-time $599.26 per credit. Tuition, nonresident: full-time $13,400; part-time $894.81 per credit. Tuition and fees vary according to program. *Graduate housing:* Room and/or apartments available on a first-come, first-served basis to single students; on-campus housing not available to married students. Housing application deadline: 6/1. *Student services:* Campus employment opportunities, campus safety program, career counseling, exercise/wellness program, free psychological counseling, international student services, low-cost health insurance, multicultural affairs office, services for students with disabilities, writing training. *Library facilities:* Stevenson Library. *Online resources:* library catalog, web page, access to other libraries' catalogs.

Computer facilities: 290 computers available on campus for general student use. A campuswide network can be accessed from student residence rooms and from off campus. Online class registration is available. *Web address:* http://www.lhup.edu/.

General Application Contact: Jerry Falco, Assistant Director of Admissions, 570-484-3869, Fax: 570-484-2734, E-mail: jfalco@lhup.edu.

GRADUATE UNITS

Department of Education *Degree program information:* Part-time and evening/weekend programs available. Postbaccalaureate distance learning degree programs offered. Offers alternative education (M Ed); teaching and learning (M Ed). Electronic applications accepted.

Department of Health Science Offers physician assistant in rural primary care (MHS). Electronic applications accepted.

Department of Liberal Arts Offers liberal arts (MLA). Electronic applications accepted.

LOGAN UNIVERSITY–COLLEGE OF CHIROPRACTIC, Chesterfield, MO 63006-1065

General Information Independent, coed, upper-level institution. *Enrollment:* 864 full-time matriculated graduate/professional students (323 women), 295 part-time matriculated graduate/professional students (93 women). *Enrollment by degree level:* 956 first professional, 203 master's. *Graduate faculty:* 55 full-time (20 women), 45 part-time/adjunct (18 women). *Tuition:* Full-time $15,842; part-time $495 per credit hour. *Required fees:* $155 per trimester. *Graduate housing:* On-campus housing not available. *Student services:* Campus employment opportunities, career counseling, exercise/wellness program, free psychological counseling, international student services, low-cost health insurance, multicultural affairs office, services for students with disabilities. *Library facilities:* Learning Resources Center. *Online resources:* library catalog, web page, access to other libraries' catalogs. *Collection:* 14,242 titles, 22,632 serial subscriptions, 1,497 audiovisual materials. *Research affiliation:* Biotonix Posture Print (posture analysis), BTE–Multi-Cervical Unit (cervical spine analysis), Cadwell (electrophysiological diagnosis), Standard Process (nutrition and lipid management), Biofreeze (topical analgesic), Foot Levelers, Inc. (orthotics).

Computer facilities: 95 computers available on campus for general student use. A campuswide network can be accessed from off campus. Online class registration, on-line classes, course homepages, wireless technologies, Academic Software Solutions for teaching and learning, library resources, academic records access are available. *Web address:* http://www.logan.edu/.

General Application Contact: Steve Held, Director of Admissions, 636-227-2100 Ext. 1752, Fax: 636-207-2425, E-mail: loganadm@logan.edu.

GRADUATE UNITS

Chiropractic Program Students: 849 full-time (316 women), 107 part-time (40 women); includes 86 minority (34 Black or African American, non-Hispanic/Latino; 3 American Indian or Alaska Native, non-Hispanic/Latino; 21 Asian, non-Hispanic/Latino; 19 Hispanic/Latino; 1 Native Hawaiian or other Pacific Islander, non-Hispanic/Latino; 8 Two or more races, non-Hispanic/Latino), 18 international. Average age 26. 209 applicants, 95% accepted, 129 enrolled. *Faculty:* 55 full-time (20 women), 36 part-time/adjunct (15 women). Expenses: Contact institution. *Financial support:* In 2010–11, 100 students received support. Federal Work-Study and scholarships/grants available. Support available to part-time students. Financial award applicants required to submit FAFSA. In 2010, 264 DCs awarded. Offers chiropractic (DC). *Application deadline:* For fall admission, 7/15 priority date for domestic and international students; for winter admission, 11/15 priority date for domestic and international students; for spring admission, 3/15 priority date for domestic students, 3/15 for international students. Applications are processed on a rolling basis. *Application fee:* $50. Electronic applications accepted. *Application Contact:* Steve Held, Director of Admissions, 636-227-2100 Ext. 1752, Fax: 636-207-2425, E-mail: loganadm@logan.edu. *Acting Vice President, Academic Affairs,* Dr. Carl W. Saubert, IV, 636-227-2100 Ext. 1745, Fax: 636-207-2431, E-mail: carl.saubert@logan.edu.

University Programs Students: 15 full-time (7 women), 188 part-time (53 women); includes 7 Black or African American, non-Hispanic/Latino; 1 American Indian or Alaska Native, non-Hispanic/Latino; 7 Asian, non-Hispanic/Latino; 1 Hispanic/Latino, 2 international. Average age 26. 45 applicants, 98% accepted, 34 enrolled. *Faculty:* 12 full-time (7 women), 10 part-time/adjunct (4 women). Expenses: Contact institution. *Financial support:* Federal Work-Study available. Support available to part-time students. Financial award applicants required to submit FAFSA. In 2010, 51 master's awarded. Offers nutrition and human performance (MS); sports science and rehabilitation (MS). *Application deadline:* For fall admission, 7/15 priority date for domestic and international students; for winter admission, 11/15 priority date for domestic and international students; for spring admission, 3/15 priority date for domestic students, 3/15 for international students. *Application fee:* $50. *Application Contact:* Steve Held, Director of Admissions, 636-227-2100 Ext. 1754, Fax: 636-207-2425, E-mail: loganadm@logan.edu. *Dean,* Dr. Elizabeth A. Goodman, 636-227-2100, Fax: 636-207-2431, E-mail: elizabeth.goodman@logan.edu.

LOGOS EVANGELICAL SEMINARY, El Monte, CA 91731

General Information Independent-religious, coed, graduate-only institution. *Enrollment by degree level:* 43 first professional, 43 master's, 50 doctoral, 9 other advanced degrees. *Graduate faculty:* 11 full-time (2 women), 6 part-time/adjunct (1 woman). *Tuition:* Full-time $8320; part-time $260 per credit. *Graduate housing:* Rooms and/or apartments available on a first-come, first-served basis to single students and guaranteed to married students. Housing application deadline: 7/15. *Student services:* Campus employment opportunities, career counseling, exercise/wellness program, free psychological counseling, international student services, low-cost health insurance. *Library facilities:* Logos Evangelical Seminary Library plus 1 other. *Online resources:* library catalog, web page. *Collection:* 50,212 titles, 1,726 serial subscriptions, 3,468 audiovisual materials.

Computer facilities: 16 computers available on campus for general student use. A campuswide network can be accessed. *Web address:* http://www.logos-seminary.edu/.

General Application Contact: Jane Peng, Administrative Coordinator of Academic Affairs, 626-571-5110 Ext. 128, Fax: 626-571-5119, E-mail: janepeng@les.edu.

GRADUATE UNITS

Graduate Programs Students: 89 full-time (36 women), 61 part-time (41 women); includes 106 Asian, non-Hispanic/Latino, 44 international. Average age 48. 45 applicants, 98% accepted, 37 enrolled. *Faculty:* 10 full-time (2 women), 7 part-time/adjunct (1 woman). Expenses: Contact institution. *Financial support:* Application deadline: 3/1. In 2010, 10 first professional degrees, 4 master's, 3 doctorates awarded. *Degree program information:* Part-time programs available. Offers theology (M Div, MA, Th M, D Min). *Application deadline:* For fall admission, 7/15 for domestic students, 5/15 for international students; for spring admission, 12/15 for domestic students, 10/15 for international students. Applications are processed on a rolling basis. *Application fee:* $25 ($50 for international students). Electronic applications accepted. *Application Contact:* Becky Perng, Admission Officer, 626-571-5110 Ext. 112, Fax: 626-571-5119, E-mail: admission@les.edu. *Academic Dean,* Dr. Jeffrey Lu, 626-571-5110 Ext. 126, Fax: 626-571-5119, E-mail: jefl@les.edu.

LOMA LINDA UNIVERSITY, Loma Linda, CA 92350

General Information Independent-religious, coed, university. CGS member. *Graduate housing:* Room and/or apartments available on a first-come, first-served basis to single students; on-campus housing not available to married students. *Research affiliation:* City of Hope Hospital (cancer research), Children's Hospital Los Angeles (cancer research), Children's Hospital Orange County (cancer research).

GRADUATE UNITS

Department of Graduate Nursing *Degree program information:* Part-time programs available. Offers adult and aging family nursing (MS); growing family nursing (MS); nursing administration (MS). Electronic applications accepted.

Faculty of Religion Offers biomedical and clinical ethics (MA, Certificate); clinical ministry (MA, Certificate); religion (MA, Certificate); religion and science (MA). Electronic applications accepted.

School of Allied Health Professions Offers allied health professions (MHIS, MOT, MPT, MS, D Sc, DPT, DPTSc, OTD); occupational therapy (MOT, OTD); physical therapy (MPT, D Sc, DPT, DPTSc); physician assistant (MS); speech-language pathology and audiology (MS). Electronic applications accepted.

School of Dentistry Offers dentistry (DDS, MS, Certificate); endodontics (MS, Certificate); implant dentistry (MS, Certificate); oral and maxillofacial surgery (MS, Certificate); orthodontics (MS, Certificate); periodontics (MS).

School of Medicine Offers biochemistry/microbiology (MS, PhD); medicine (MD, MS, PhD); pathology and human anatomy (MS, PhD); physiology/pharmacology (MS, PhD).

School of Pharmacy Offers pharmacy (Pharm D).

School of Public Health *Degree program information:* Part-time programs available. Offers environmental and occupational health (MPH, MSPH); epidemiology and biostatistics (MPH, MSPH, Dr PH, Postbaccalaureate Certificate); global health (MPH); health administration (MBA, MHA, MPH); health promotion and education (MPH, Dr PH); public health (MBA, MHA, MPH, MSPH, Dr PH, Postbaccalaureate Certificate); public health nutrition (MPH, Dr PH). Electronic applications accepted.

School of Science and Technology Offers biological and earth sciences (MS, PhD); counseling and family science (MA, MS, DMFT, PhD, Certificate); psychology (PhD, Psy D); science and technology (MA, MS, MSW, DMFT, PhD, Psy D, Certificate); social policy and research (PhD); social work (MSW). Electronic applications accepted.

LONG ISLAND UNIVERSITY AT RIVERHEAD, Riverhead, NY 11901

General Information Independent, coed, graduate-only institution. *Enrollment by degree level:* 205 master's, 4 other advanced degrees. *Graduate faculty:* 3 full-time (1 woman), 40 part-time/adjunct (18 women). *Tuition:* Part-time $982 per credit. *Graduate housing:* On-campus housing not available. *Student services:* Campus employment opportunities, campus safety program, career counseling, low-cost health insurance, services for students with disabilities. *Library facilities:* Long Island University at Riverhead Library plus 1 other. *Online resources:* library catalog, web page. *Collection:* 1.2 million titles.

Computer facilities: 30 computers available on campus for general student use. A campuswide network can be accessed from off campus. Online class registration, Online Bill Pay are available. *Web address:* http://www.southampton.liu.edu/riverhead/.

General Application Contact: Andrea Borra, Admissions Counselor, 631-287-8010 Ext. 8326, Fax: 631-287-8253, E-mail: andrea.borra@liu.edu.

GRADUATE UNITS

Education Division Students: 29 full-time (25 women), 90 part-time (82 women). Average age 30. 48 applicants, 69% accepted, 33 enrolled. *Faculty:* 1 full-time (0 women), 11 part-time/adjunct (7 women). Expenses: Contact institution. *Financial support:* In 2010–11, 105 students received support. Scholarships/grants and tuition waivers (partial) available. Support available to part-time students. Financial award applicants required to submit FAFSA. In 2010, 38 master's awarded. *Degree program information:* Part-time and evening/weekend programs available. Offers applied behavior analysis (Advanced Certificate); childhood education (MS Ed); elementary education (MS Ed); literacy education (MS Ed); teaching students with disabilities (MS Ed). *Application deadline:* Applications are processed on a rolling basis. Electronic applications accepted. *Application Contact:* Andrea Borra, Director of Graduate Admissions and Program Administration, 631-287-8010 Ext. 8326, Fax: 631-287-8253, E-mail: andrea.borra@liu.edu. *Director,* Dr. R. Lawrence McCann, 631-287-8211, E-mail: admissions@southampton.liu.edu.

Homeland Security Management Institute Students: 5 full-time (0 women), 107 part-time (17 women); includes 8 Black or African American, non-Hispanic/Latino; 1 American Indian or Alaska Native, non-Hispanic/Latino; 2 Asian, non-Hispanic/Latino; 5 Hispanic/Latino. 48 applicants, 56% accepted, 23 enrolled. *Faculty:* 2 full-time (0 women), 10 part-time/adjunct (1 woman). Expenses: Contact institution. *Financial support:* In 2010–11, 105 students received support. Career-related internships or fieldwork and scholarships/grants available. Support available to part-time students. Financial award applicants required to submit FAFSA. In 2010, 11 master's, 36 other advanced degrees awarded. *Degree program information:* Part-time programs available. Postbaccalaureate distance learning degree programs offered (no on-campus study). Offers homeland security management (MS, Advanced Certificate). *Application deadline:* Applications are processed on a rolling basis. *Application fee:* $0. Electronic applications accepted. *Application Contact:* Andrea Borra, Admissions Counselor, 631-287-8010 Ext. 8326, Fax: 631-287-8253, E-mail: andrea.borra@liu.edu. *Unit Head,* Dr. Vincent E. Henry, 631-287-8010, Fax: 631-287-8130, E-mail: vincent.henry@liu.edu.

LONG ISLAND UNIVERSITY, BRENTWOOD CAMPUS, Brentwood, NY 11717

General Information Independent, coed, upper-level institution. *Graduate housing:* On-campus housing not available.

GRADUATE UNITS

School of Education *Degree program information:* Part-time and evening/weekend programs available. Offers childhood education (MS); early childhood education (MS); literacy (MS); mental health counseling (MS); school counseling (MS); special education (MS).

School of Public Service *Degree program information:* Part-time and evening/weekend programs available. Offers criminal justice (MS).

LONG ISLAND UNIVERSITY, BROOKLYN CAMPUS, Brooklyn, NY 11201-8423

General Information Independent, coed, university. *Graduate housing:* Rooms and/or apartments available to single and married students. Housing application deadline: 9/1.

Long Island University, Brooklyn Campus (continued)

GRADUATE UNITS

Arnold and Marie Schwartz College of Pharmacy and Health Sciences *Degree program information:* Part-time and evening/weekend programs available. Offers cosmetic science (MS); drug regulatory affairs (MS); industrial pharmacy (MS); pharmaceutical sciences (MS, PhD); pharmaceutics (PhD); pharmacology/toxicology (MS); pharmacy administration (MS); pharmacy and health sciences (MS, PhD); social and administrative sciences (MS).

Richard L. Conolly College of Liberal Arts and Sciences *Degree program information:* Part-time and evening/weekend programs available. Offers biology (MS); chemistry (MS); clinical psychology (PhD); creative writing (MFA); economics (MA); history (MS); liberal arts and sciences (MA, MFA, MS, PhD, Certificate); literature (MA); media arts (MA); political science (MA); professional writing (MA); psychology (MA); speech-language pathology (MS); United Nations studies (Certificate); urban studies (MA); writing and rhetoric (MA). Electronic applications accepted.

School of Business, Public Administration and Information Sciences *Degree program information:* Part-time and evening/weekend programs available. Offers accounting (MS); business administration (MBA); business, public administration and information sciences (MBA, MPA, MS); computer science (MS); human resources management (MS); public administration (MPA); taxation (MS). Electronic applications accepted.

School of Education *Degree program information:* Part-time and evening/weekend programs available. Offers bilingual education (MS Ed); computers in education (MS); counseling and development (MS, MS Ed, Certificate); education (MS, MS Ed, Certificate); elementary education (MS Ed); leadership and policy (MS); mathematics education (MS Ed); reading (MS Ed); school psychology (MS Ed); secondary education (MS Ed); special education (MS Ed); teaching English to speakers of other languages (MS Ed). Electronic applications accepted.

School of Health Professions *Degree program information:* Part-time and evening/weekend programs available. Offers adapted physical education (MS); athletic training and sports sciences (MS); community mental health (MS); exercise physiology (MS); family health (MS); health management (MS); health professions (MS, DPT, TDPT); health sciences (MS); physical therapy (DPT, TDPT). Electronic applications accepted.

School of Nursing Offers adult nurse practitioner (MS, Certificate); nurse executive (MS); nursing (MS, Certificate). Electronic applications accepted.

LONG ISLAND UNIVERSITY, C.W. POST CAMPUS, Brookville, NY 11548-1300

General Information Independent, coed, comprehensive institution. *Graduate housing:* Room and/or apartments available on a first-come, first-served basis to single students; on-campus housing not available to married students. Housing application deadline: 6/1.

GRADUATE UNITS

College of Information and Computer Science *Degree program information:* Part-time and evening/weekend programs available. Postbaccalaureate distance learning degree programs offered. Offers information and computer science (MS, PhD, Certificate); information systems (MS); information technology education (MS); management engineering (MS). Electronic applications accepted.

Palmer School of Library and Information Science *Degree program information:* Part-time and evening/weekend programs available. Postbaccalaureate distance learning degree programs offered (minimal on-campus study). Offers archives and records management (Certificate); information studies (PhD); library and information science (MS); library media specialist (MS); public library management (Certificate). Electronic applications accepted.

College of Liberal Arts and Sciences *Degree program information:* Part-time and evening/weekend programs available. Offers applied mathematics (MS); biology (MS); biology education (MS); clinical psychology (Psy D); earth science (MS); earth science education (MS); English (MA); English for adolescence education (MS); environmental studies (MS); genetic counseling (MS); history (MA); interdisciplinary studies (MA, MS); liberal arts and sciences (MA, MS, Psy D); mathematics education (MS); mathematics for secondary school teachers (MS); political science/international studies (MA); psychology (MA); Spanish (MA); Spanish education (MS). Electronic applications accepted.

College of Management *Degree program information:* Part-time and evening/weekend programs available. Offers criminal justice (MS); fraud examination (MS); gerontology (Certificate); health care administration (MPA); health care administration/gerontology (MPA); management (MBA, MPA, MS, MSW, Certificate); nonprofit management (MPA, Certificate); public administration (MPA); security administration (MS). Electronic applications accepted.

School of Business *Degree program information:* Part-time and evening/weekend programs available. Offers accounting and taxation (Certificate); business administration (Certificate); finance (MBA, Certificate); general business administration (MBA); international business (MBA, Certificate); management (MBA, Certificate); management information systems (MBA, Certificate); marketing (MBA, Certificate). Electronic applications accepted.

School of Professional Accountancy *Degree program information:* Part-time and evening/weekend programs available. Offers accounting (MS); taxation (MS). Electronic applications accepted.

School of Education *Degree program information:* Part-time and evening/weekend programs available. Offers adolescence education (MS); adolescence education: biology (MS); adolescence education: earth science (MS); adolescence education: English (MS); adolescence education: mathematics (MS); adolescence education: social studies (MS); adolescence education: Spanish (MS); art education (MS); bilingual education (MS); childhood education (MS); childhood education/literacy (MS); childhood education/special education (MS); computers in education (MS); early childhood education (MS); education (MA, MS, MS Ed, Ed D, AC); educational leadership (Ed D); literacy (MS Ed); mental health counseling (MS); middle childhood education (MS); music education (MS); school administration and supervision (MS Ed); school building leader (AC); school counseling (MS); school district business leader (AC); school district leader (AC); special education (MS Ed); speech language pathology (MA); teaching and learning (Ed D); teaching English to speakers of other languages (MS). Electronic applications accepted.

School of Health Professions and Nursing *Degree program information:* Part-time and evening/weekend programs available. Postbaccalaureate distance learning degree programs offered. Offers alcohol and substance abuse (MSW); cardiovascular perfusion (MS); child and family welfare (MSW); clinical laboratory management (MS); clinical nurse specialist (MS); dietetic internship (Certificate); family nurse practitioner (MS, Certificate); forensic social work (MSW); gerontology (MSW); health professions and nursing (MS, MSW, Certificate); medical biology (MS); nonprofit management (MSW); nutrition (MS). Electronic applications accepted.

School of Visual and Performing Arts *Degree program information:* Part-time and evening/weekend programs available. Offers art (MA); art education (MS); clinical art therapy (MA); fine art and design (MFA); interactive multimedia (MA); music (MA); music education (MS); theatre (MA); visual and performing arts (MA, MFA, MS). Electronic applications accepted.

LONG ISLAND UNIVERSITY, ROCKLAND GRADUATE CAMPUS, Orangeburg, NY 10962

General Information Independent, coed, graduate-only institution. *Enrollment by degree level:* 435 master's. *Graduate faculty:* 11 full-time (5 women), 35 part-time/adjunct (15 women). *Tuition:* Part-time $1028 per credit. *Required fees:* $340 per semester. *Graduate housing:* On-campus housing not available. *Student services:* Campus employment opportunities, teacher training. *Library facilities:* Long Island University, Rockland Resource Center plus 3 others. *Online resources:* library catalog. *Collection:* 9,200 titles, 550 serial subscriptions, 1,000 audiovisual materials.

Computer facilities: 60 computers available on campus for general student use. A campuswide network can be accessed from off campus. Online class registration is available. *Web address:* http://www.liu.edu/rockland/.

General Application Contact: Peter S. Reiner, Director of Marketing and Recruitment, 845-359-7200, Fax: 845-359-7248, E-mail: peter.reiner@liu.edu.

GRADUATE UNITS

Graduate School *Degree program information:* Part-time and evening/weekend programs available. Offers adolescence education (MS Ed); autism (MS Ed); business administration (Post Master's Certificate); childhood education (MS Ed); childhood/literacy (MS Ed); childhood/special education (MS Ed); cosmetic science (MS); educational leadership (MS Ed, Advanced Certificate); entrepreneurship (MBA); finance (MBA); gerontology (Advanced Certificate); health administration (MPA); healthcare sector management (MBA); industrial pharmacy (MS); literacy (MS Ed); management (MBA); mental health counseling (MS); public administration (MPA); school counselor (MS Ed); special education (MS Ed).

LONG ISLAND UNIVERSITY, WESTCHESTER GRADUATE CAMPUS, Purchase, NY 10577

General Information Independent, coed, graduate-only institution. *Graduate housing:* On-campus housing not available.

GRADUATE UNITS

Program in Business Administration *Degree program information:* Part-time and evening/weekend programs available. Offers business administration (MBA).

Program in Library and Information Science *Degree program information:* Part-time and evening/weekend programs available. Offers library and information science (MS).

Program in Mental Health Counseling Offers mental health counseling (MS).

Programs in Education-School Counselor and School Psychology *Degree program information:* Part-time and evening/weekend programs available. Offers school counselor (MS Ed); school psychologist (MS Ed).

Programs in Education-Teaching *Degree program information:* Part-time and evening/weekend programs available. Offers early childhood education (MS Ed, Advanced Certificate); elementary education (MS Ed, Advanced Certificate); literacy education (MS Ed, Advanced Certificate); second language, TESOL, bilingual education (MS Ed, Advanced Certificate); special education and secondary education (MS Ed, Advanced Certificate).

Program in Second Language, TESOL, Bilingual Education *Degree program information:* Part-time and evening/weekend programs available. Offers second language, TESOL, bilingual education (MS Ed, Advanced Certificate).

LONGWOOD UNIVERSITY, Farmville, VA 23909

General Information State-supported, coed, comprehensive institution. CGS member. *Graduate housing:* On-campus housing not available.

GRADUATE UNITS

Office of Graduate Studies *Degree program information:* Part-time and evening/weekend programs available. Offers 6-12 initial teaching/licensure (MA); creative writing (MA); criminal justice (MS); English education and writing (MA); literature (MA).

College of Business and Economics Offers retail management (MBA).

College of Education and Human Services *Degree program information:* Part-time and evening/weekend programs available. Offers communication sciences and disorders (MS); community and college counseling (MS); curriculum and instruction specialist-elementary (MS); curriculum and instruction specialist-secondary (MS); educational leadership (MS); guidance and counseling (MS); literacy and culture (MS); school library media (MS).

LONGY SCHOOL OF MUSIC, Cambridge, MA 02138

General Information Independent, coed, graduate-only institution. *Enrollment by degree level:* 152 master's, 50 other advanced degrees. *Graduate faculty:* 98 part-time/adjunct (52 women). *Graduate housing:* On-campus housing not available. *Student services:* Campus employment opportunities, career counseling, international student services, low-cost health insurance. *Library facilities:* Bakalar Music Library. *Online resources:* library catalog, web page, access to other libraries' catalogs. *Collection:* 18,034 titles, 32 serial subscriptions, 9,031 audiovisual materials.

Computer facilities: 9 computers available on campus for general student use. A campuswide network can be accessed. *Web address:* http://www.longy.edu/.

General Application Contact: Alex Powell, Director of Admissions and Student Services, 617-876-0956 Ext. 1521, Fax: 617-876-9326, E-mail: admissions@longy.edu.

GRADUATE UNITS

Conservatory at Longy Students: 174 full-time (119 women), 28 part-time (18 women); includes 6 Black or African American, non-Hispanic/Latino; 9 Asian, non-Hispanic/Latino; 1 Hispanic/Latino, 46 international. Average age 28. 231 applicants, 74% accepted, 99 enrolled. *Faculty:* 98 part-time/adjunct (52 women). Expenses: Contact institution. *Financial support:* In 2010–11, 165 students received support, including 12 teaching assistantships (averaging $3,000 per year); scholarships/grants and unspecified assistantships also available. Financial award application deadline: 3/1; financial award applicants required to submit FAFSA. In 2010, 42 master's, 21 GPDs awarded. *Degree program information:* Part-time programs available. Offers chamber ensemble (Artist Diploma); collaborative piano (MM, Artist Diploma, GPD); composition (MM); Dalcroze eurhythmics (MM); early music (MM, Artist Diploma, GPD); instrumental performance (MM, Artist Diploma, GPD); modern American music (MM, GPD); opera performance (MM, GPD); organ performance (MM, Artist Diploma, GPD); piano performance (MM, Artist Diploma, GPD); vocal performance (MM, Artist Diploma, GPD). *Application deadline:* For fall admission, 12/1 priority date for domestic and international students; for spring admission, 11/1 for domestic and international students. *Application fee:* $100. Electronic applications accepted. *Application Contact:* Alex Powell, Director of Admissions and Student Services, 617-876-0956 Ext. 1521, Fax: 617-876-9326, E-mail: admissions@longy.edu. *President*, Karen Zorn, 617-876-0956, Fax: 617-876-9326, E-mail: music@longy.edu.

LORAS COLLEGE, Dubuque, IA 52004-0178

General Information Independent-religious, coed, comprehensive institution. *Graduate housing:* On-campus housing not available.

GRADUATE UNITS

Graduate Division *Degree program information:* Part-time and evening/weekend programs available. Offers applied psychology (MA); educational leadership (MA); instructional strategist I K-6 and 7-12 (MA); ministry (MA); theology (MA).

LOUISIANA STATE UNIVERSITY AND AGRICULTURAL AND MECHANICAL COLLEGE, Baton Rouge, LA 70803

General Information State-supported, coed, university. CGS member. *Enrollment:* 29,451 graduate, professional, and undergraduate students; 3,805 full-time matriculated graduate/professional students (1,889 women), 1,007 part-time matriculated graduate/professional students (579 women). *Enrollment by degree level:* 327 first professional, 2,383 master's, 2,102 doctoral. *Graduate faculty:* 1,231 full-time (327 women), 14 part-time/adjunct (3 women). *Graduate housing:* Rooms and/or apartments available on a first-come, first-served basis to single and married students. Housing application deadline: 3/15. *Student services:* Campus employment opportunities, campus safety program, career counseling, child daycare facilities, exercise/wellness program, free psychological counseling, grant writing training, international student services, low-cost health insurance, multicultural affairs office, services for students with disabilities, teacher training, writing training. *Library facilities:* Troy H. Middleton Library plus 4 others. *Online resources:* library catalog, web page, access to other libraries' catalogs. *Collection:* 4.1 million titles, 107,366 serial subscriptions, 28,799 audiovisual materials. *Research affiliation:* Albert Einstein Institute, Arctic Research Consortium of the U. S., Organization for Tropical Studies, Coalition for Academic Scientific Computing, Inter-University Consortium for Political and Social Research, Laser Interferometer Gravitational Wave Observatory.

Computer facilities: 1,500 computers available on campus for general student use. A campuswide network can be accessed from student residence rooms and from off campus. Online class registration, free software for download, personal Web sites, storage, discounts on hardware, virtual computer lab are available. *Web address:* http://www.lsu.edu/.

General Application Contact: Dr. Renee Renegar, Office of Graduate Admissions, 225-578-1641, Fax: 225-578-1370, E-mail: rreneg1@lsu.edu.

GRADUATE UNITS

Graduate School Students: 3,805 full-time (1,889 women), 1,007 part-time (579 women); includes 653 minority (372 Black or African American, non-Hispanic/Latino; 15 American Indian or Alaska Native, non-Hispanic/Latino; 94 Asian, non-Hispanic/Latino; 140 Hispanic/Latino; 1 Native Hawaiian or other Pacific Islander, non-Hispanic/Latino; 31 Two or more races, non-Hispanic/Latino), 1,145 international. Average age 29. 4,875 applicants, 45% accepted, 852 enrolled. *Faculty:* 1,231 full-time (327 women), 14 part-time/adjunct (3 women). Expenses: Contact institution. *Financial support:* In 2010–11, 3,790 students received support, including 187 fellowships with full tuition reimbursements available (averaging $16,454 per year), 1,134 research assistantships with partial tuition reimbursements available (averaging $17,692 per year), 1,044 teaching assistantships with partial tuition reimbursements available (averaging $14,149 per year); career-related internships or fieldwork, Federal Work-Study, institutionally sponsored loans, scholarships/grants, traineeships, health care benefits, tuition waivers (full and partial), and unspecified assistantships also available. Support available to part-time students. Financial award application deadline: 1/15; financial award applicants required to submit FAFSA. In 2010, 1,063 master's, 278 doctorates awarded. *Degree program information:* Part-time and evening/weekend programs available. Postbaccalaureate distance learning degree programs offered. *Application deadline:* For fall admission, 5/15 priority date for domestic students, 5/15 for international students; for winter admission, 10/15 priority date for domestic students; for spring admission, 10/15 for domestic and international students. Applications are processed on a rolling basis. *Application fee:* $50 ($70 for international students). Electronic applications accepted. *Application Contact:* Dr. Renee Renegar, Director of Graduate Admissions, 225-578-1641, Fax: 225-578-1370. *Dean,* Dr. David Constant, 225-578-3885, Fax: 225-578-1370, E-mail: hscons@lsu.edu.

College of Agriculture Students: 355 full-time (172 women), 149 part-time (88 women); includes 29 Black or African American, non-Hispanic/Latino; 6 Asian, non-Hispanic/Latino; 16 Hispanic/Latino; 2 Two or more races, non-Hispanic/Latino, 167 international. Average age 31. 282 applicants, 50% accepted, 52 enrolled. Expenses: Contact institution. *Financial support:* In 2010–11, 414 students received support, including 8 fellowships with full tuition reimbursements available (averaging $2,030 per year), 233 research assistantships with partial tuition reimbursements available (averaging $17,686 per year), 47 teaching assistantships with partial tuition reimbursements available (averaging $12,661 per year); career-related internships or fieldwork, Federal Work-Study, institutionally sponsored loans, health care benefits, tuition waivers (full), and unspecified assistantships also available. Support available to part-time students. Financial award applicants required to submit FAFSA. In 2010, 95 master's, 42 doctorates awarded. *Degree program information:* Part-time programs available. Offers agricultural economics and agribusiness (MS, PhD); agriculture (M App St, MS, MSBAE, PhD); agriculture and extension education and youth development (MS, PhD); agronomy (MS, PhD); animal sciences (MS, PhD); applied statistics (M App St); biological and agricultural engineering (MSBAE); career and technical education (MS, PhD); comprehensive vocational education (MS, PhD); engineering science (MS, PhD); entomology (MS, PhD); extension and international education (MS, PhD); fisheries (MS); food science (MS, PhD); forestry (MS, PhD); horticulture (MS, PhD); human ecology (MS, PhD); human resource and leadership development (MS, PhD); industrial education (MS); plant health (MS, PhD); plant, environmental and soil science (MS, PhD); vocational agriculture education (MS, PhD); vocational business education (MS); vocational home economics education (MS); wildlife (MS); wildlife and fisheries science (PhD). *Application deadline:* For fall admission, 5/15 for domestic and international students; for spring admission, 10/15 for domestic and international students. Applications are processed on a rolling basis. *Application fee:* $50 ($70 for international students). Electronic applications accepted. *Application Contact:* Paula Beecher, Recruiting Coordinator, 225-578-2468, E-mail: pbeeche@lsu.edu. *Dean,* Dr. Kenneth Koonce, 225-578-2362, Fax: 225-578-2526, E-mail: kkoonce@lsu.edu.

College of Art and Design Students: 129 full-time (71 women), 8 part-time (5 women); includes 4 Asian, non-Hispanic/Latino; 3 Hispanic/Latino; 1 Native Hawaiian or other Pacific Islander, non-Hispanic/Latino, 16 international. Average age 28. 270 applicants, 41% accepted, 49 enrolled. Expenses: Contact institution. *Financial support:* In 2010–11, 114 students received support, including 24 research assistantships with partial tuition reimbursements available (averaging $7,389 per year), 45 teaching assistantships with partial tuition reimbursements available (averaging $7,044 per year); fellowships, career-related internships or fieldwork, Federal Work-Study, institutionally sponsored loans, scholarships/grants, health care benefits, tuition waivers (full and partial), and unspecified assistantships also available. Support available to part-time students. Financial award applicants required to submit FAFSA. In 2010, 42 master's awarded. *Degree program information:* Part-time programs available. Offers architecture (M Arch); art and design (M Arch, MA, MFA, MLA); art history (MA); ceramics (MFA); graphic design (MFA); landscape architecture (MLA); painting and drawing (MFA); photography (MFA); printmaking (MFA); sculpture (MFA); studio art (MFA). *Application deadline:* For fall admission, 1/25 priority date for domestic students, 5/15 for international students; for spring admission, 10/15 for international students. Applications are processed on a rolling basis. *Application fee:* $50 ($70 for international students). Electronic applications accepted. *Application Contact:* Theresa Mooney, Academic Counselor, 225-578-5400, Fax: 225-578-1445, E-mail: deacon1@lsu.edu. *Dean,* Kenneth Carpenter, 225-578-5400, Fax: 225-578-5040, E-mail: dc1@lsu.edu.

College of Basic Sciences Students: 625 full-time (216 women), 52 part-time (16 women); includes 51 Black or African American, non-Hispanic/Latino; 1 American Indian or Alaska Native, non-Hispanic/Latino; 16 Asian, non-Hispanic/Latino; 11 Hispanic/Latino; 3 Two or more races, non-Hispanic/Latino, 297 international. Average age 28. 702 applicants, 40% accepted, 94 enrolled. Expenses: Contact institution. *Financial support:* In 2010–11, 628 students received support, including 81 fellowships with full and partial tuition reimbursements available (averaging $30,612 per year), 235 research assistantships with full and partial tuition reimbursements available (averaging $20,855 per year), 286 teaching assistantships with full and partial tuition reimbursements available (averaging $18,790 per year); career-related internships or fieldwork, Federal Work-Study, institutionally sponsored loans, health care benefits, tuition waivers (full and partial), and unspecified assistantships also available. Support available to part-time students. Financial award applicants required to submit FAFSA. In 2010, 82 master's, 59 doctorates awarded. *Degree program information:* Part-time programs available. Offers astronomy (PhD); astrophysics (PhD); basic sciences (MNS, MS, MSSS, PhD); biochemistry (MS, PhD); biological science (MS, PhD); chemistry (MS, PhD); computer science (MSSS, PhD); geology and geophysics (MS, PhD); mathematics (MS, PhD); medical physics (MS); natural sciences (MNS); physics (MS, PhD); science (MNS); systems science (MSSS). *Application deadline:* For fall admission, 5/15 for international students; for spring admission, 10/15 for international students. Applications are processed on a rolling basis. *Application fee:* $50 ($70 for international students). Electronic applications accepted. *Application Contact:* Dr. Gary Byerly, Associate Dean, 225-578-5318, Fax: 225-578-8826, E-mail: glbyer@lsu.edu. *Dean,* Dr. Kevin Carman, 225-578-8859, Fax: 225-578-8826, E-mail: bascdean@lsu.edu.

College of Education Students: 272 full-time (188 women), 185 part-time (134 women); includes 86 Black or African American, non-Hispanic/Latino; 6 Asian, non-Hispanic/Latino; 12 Hispanic/Latino; 4 Two or more races, non-Hispanic/Latino, 19 international. Average age 31. 229 applicants, 64% accepted, 42 enrolled. Expenses: Contact institution. *Financial support:* In 2010–11, 308 students received support, including 5 fellowships (averaging $16,170 per year), 21 research assistantships with partial tuition reimbursements available (averaging $9,713 per year), 69 teaching assistantships with partial tuition reimbursements available (averaging $11,186 per year); career-related internships or fieldwork, Federal Work-Study, institutionally sponsored loans, health care benefits, tuition waivers (partial), and unspecified assistantships also available. Support available to part-time students. Financial award applicants required to submit FAFSA. In 2010, 140 master's, 18 doctorates, 12 other advanced degrees awarded. *Degree program information:* Part-time and evening/weekend programs available. Offers counseling (M Ed, MA, Ed S); education (M Ed, MA, MAT, MS, PhD, Ed S); educational administration (M Ed, MA, PhD, Ed S); educational technology (MA); elementary education (M Ed, MAT); higher education (PhD); kinesiology (MS, PhD); research methodology (PhD); secondary education (M Ed, MAT). *Application deadline:* For fall admission, 1/25 priority date for domestic students, 5/15 for international students; for spring admission, 10/15 for international students. Applications are processed on a rolling basis. *Application fee:* $50 ($70 for international students). Electronic applications accepted. *Application Contact:* Dr. Patricia Exner, Associate Dean, 225-578-2208, Fax: 225-578-2267, E-mail: pexner@lsu.edu. *Dean,* Dr. Laura F. Lindsay, 225-578-1258, Fax: 225-578-2267, E-mail: aclind@lsu.edu.

College of Engineering Students: 483 full-time (93 women), 74 part-time (12 women); includes 17 Black or African American, non-Hispanic/Latino; 1 American Indian or Alaska Native, non-Hispanic/Latino; 15 Asian, non-Hispanic/Latino; 11 Hispanic/Latino, 383 international. Average age 28. 843 applicants, 45% accepted, 94 enrolled. Expenses: Contact institution. *Financial support:* In 2010–11, 436 students received support, including 29 fellowships with full and partial tuition reimbursements available (averaging $24,803 per year), 316 research assistantships with full and partial tuition reimbursements available (averaging $16,760 per year), 68 teaching assistantships with full and partial tuition reimbursements available (averaging $11,763 per year); career-related internships or fieldwork, Federal Work-Study, institutionally sponsored loans, scholarships/grants, health care benefits, tuition waivers (full and partial), and unspecified assistantships also available. Financial award applicants required to submit FAFSA. In 2010, 84 master's, 32 doctorates awarded. *Degree program information:* Part-time and evening/weekend programs available. Offers chemical engineering (MS Ch E, PhD); electrical and computer engineering (MSEE, PhD); engineering (MS Ch E, MS Pet E, MSCE, MSEE, MSES, MSIE, MSME, PhD); engineering science (MSES, PhD); environmental engineering (MSCE, PhD); geotechnical engineering (MSCE, PhD); industrial engineering (MSIE); mechanical engineering (MSME, PhD); petroleum engineering (MS Pet E, PhD); structural engineering and mechanics (MSCE, PhD); transportation engineering (MSCE, PhD); water resources (MSCE, PhD). *Application deadline:* For fall admission, 1/25 priority date for domestic students, 5/15 for international students; for spring admission, 10/15 for international students. Applications are processed on a rolling basis. *Application fee:* $50 ($70 for international students). Electronic applications accepted. *Application Contact:* Dr. Warren Waggenspack, Associate Dean for Research and Graduate Studies, 225-578-5907, Fax: 225-578-9162, E-mail: mewagg@lsu.edu. *Dean,* Dr. Richard Koubek, 225-578-5701, Fax: 225-578-9162, E-mail: koubek@lsu.edu.

College of Humanities and Social Sciences Students: 537 full-time (310 women), 129 part-time (72 women); includes 29 Black or African American, non-Hispanic/Latino; 3 American Indian or Alaska Native, non-Hispanic/Latino; 7 Asian, non-Hispanic/Latino; 27 Hispanic/Latino; 4 Two or more races, non-Hispanic/Latino, 64 international. Average age 30. 1,065 applicants, 32% accepted, 104 enrolled. Expenses: Contact institution. *Financial support:* In 2010–11, 543 students received support, including 21 fellowships with full tuition reimbursements available (averaging $25,207 per year), 88 research assistantships with full and partial tuition reimbursements available (averaging $16,903 per year), 283 teaching assistantships with full and partial tuition reimbursements available (averaging $13,592 per year); career-related internships or fieldwork, Federal Work-Study, institutionally sponsored loans, scholarships/grants, traineeships, health care benefits, tuition waivers (full), and unspecified assistantships also available. Support available to part-time students. Financial award applicants required to submit FAFSA. In 2010, 132 master's, 71 doctorates awarded. *Degree program information:* Part-time and evening/weekend programs available. Offers anthropology (MA); biological psychology (MA, PhD); clinical psychology (MA, PhD); cognitive psychology (MA, PhD); communication sciences and disorders (MA, PhD); communication studies (MA, PhD); comparative literature (MA, PhD); creative writing (MFA); developmental psychology (MA, PhD); English (MA, PhD); French literature and linguistics (MA, PhD); geography (MA, MS, PhD); Hispanic studies (MA); history (MA, PhD); humanities and social sciences (MA, MALA, MFA, MS, PhD); industrial/organizational psychology (MA, PhD); liberal arts (MALA); linguistics (MA, PhD); philosophy (MA); political science (MA, PhD); school psychology (MA, PhD); sociology (MA, PhD). *Application deadline:* For fall admission, 5/15 priority date for domestic students, 5/15 for international students; for spring admission, 10/15 priority date for domestic students, 10/15 for international students. *Application fee:* $50 ($70 for international students). Electronic applications accepted. *Application Contact:* Dr. Robin Roberts, Associate Dean, 225-578-8273, Fax: 225-578-6447, E-mail: rrobert@lsu.edu. *Dean,* Dr. Gaines Foster, 225-578-8273, Fax: 225-578-6447, E-mail: hyfost@lsu.edu.

College of Music and Dramatic Arts Students: 182 full-time (81 women), 37 part-time (21 women); includes 5 Black or African American, non-Hispanic/Latino; 1 American Indian or Alaska Native, non-Hispanic/Latino; 7 Asian, non-Hispanic/Latino; 9 Hispanic/Latino; 1 Two or more races, non-Hispanic/Latino, 45 international. Average age 30. 232 applicants, 48% accepted, 56 enrolled. Expenses: Contact institution. *Financial support:* In 2010–11, 182 students received support, including 8 fellowships with full and partial tuition reimbursements available (averaging $14,544 per year), 2 research assistantships with full and partial tuition reimbursements available (averaging $12,700 per year), 103 teaching assistantships with full and partial tuition reimbursements available (averaging $11,064 per year); Federal Work-Study, scholarships/grants, health care benefits, tuition waivers (full and partial), and unspecified assistantships also available. Support available to part-time students. Financial award applicants required to submit FAFSA. In 2010, 45 master's, 22 doctorates awarded. *Degree program information:* Part-time programs available. Offers acting (MFA); directing (MFA); music (MM, DMA, PhD); music and dramatic arts (MFA, MM, DMA, PhD); music education (PhD); theatre (PhD); theatre design/technology (MFA). *Application deadline:* For fall admission, 3/15 priority date for domestic students, 5/15 for international students; for spring admission, 10/15 for international students. Applications are processed on a rolling basis. *Application fee:* $50 ($70 for international students). *Application Contact:* Dr. Lawrence Kaptain, Dean, 225-578-3261, Fax: 225-578-2562. *Dean,* Dr. Lawrence Kaptain, 225-578-3261, Fax: 225-578-2562.

E. J. Ourso College of Business Students: 457 full-time (192 women), 177 part-time (75 women); includes 66 Black or African American, non-Hispanic/Latino; 3 American Indian or Alaska Native, non-Hispanic/Latino; 16 Asian, non-Hispanic/Latino; 10 Hispanic/Latino; 10 Two or more races, non-Hispanic/Latino, 98 international. Average age 28. 733 applicants, 44% accepted, 91 enrolled. Expenses: Contact institution. *Financial support:* In 2010–11, 429 students received support, including 2 fellowships (averaging $19,885 per year), 69 research assistantships with full and partial tuition reimbursements available (averaging $15,889 per year), 114 teaching assistantships with full and partial tuition reimbursements available (averaging $13,362 per year); career-related internships or fieldwork, Federal Work-Study, institutionally sponsored loans, scholarships/grants, health care benefits, and unspecified assistantships also available. Support available to part-time students. Financial award applicants required to submit FAFSA. In 2010, 260 master's, 14 doctorates awarded. *Degree program information:* Part-time and evening/weekend programs available. Offers accounting (MS, PhD); business (EMBA, MBA, MPA, MS, PMBA, PhD); business administration (EMBA, MBA, PMBA); economics (MS, PhD); finance (MS); information systems and decision sciences (MS, PhD); public administration (MPA). *Application deadline:* For fall admission, 1/25 priority date for domestic students, 5/15 for international students; for spring admission, 10/15 for international students. Applications are processed on a rolling basis. *Application fee:* $50 ($70 for international students). Electronic applications accepted. *Application Contact:* Dr. Eli Jones, Interim Dean, 225-578-5297, Fax: 225-578-5256. *Interim Dean,* Dr. Eli Jones, 225-578-5297, Fax: 225-578-5256.

Manship School of Mass Communication Students: 53 full-time (32 women), 17 part-time (11 women); includes 10 Black or African American, non-Hispanic/Latino; 2 American Indian or Alaska Native, non-Hispanic/Latino; 2 Hispanic/Latino; 2 Two or more races, non-Hispanic/Latino, 4 international. Average age 30. 77 applicants, 40% accepted, 14 enrolled. *Faculty:* 26 full-time (14 women). Expenses: Contact institution. *Financial support:* In 2010–11, 57 students received support, including 2 fellowships (averaging $23,089 per year), 29 research assistantships with full and partial tuition reimbursements available

Louisiana State University and Agricultural and Mechanical College (continued)

(averaging $16,224 per year), 10 teaching assistantships with full and partial tuition reimbursements available (averaging $18,180 per year); career-related internships or fieldwork, Federal Work-Study, institutionally sponsored loans, scholarships/grants, health care benefits, tuition waivers (full and partial), and unspecified assistantships also available. Support available to part-time students. Financial award application deadline: 3/1; financial award applicants required to submit FAFSA. In 2010, 20 master's, 1 doctorate awarded. *Degree program information:* Part-time programs available. Postbaccalaureate distance learning degree programs offered (minimal on-campus study). Offers mass communication (MMC, PhD). *Application deadline:* For fall admission, 1/25 priority date for domestic students, 5/15 for international students; for spring admission, 10/15 for international students. Applications are processed on a rolling basis. *Application fee:* $50 ($70 for international students). Electronic applications accepted. *Application Contact:* Dr. Amy L. Reynolds, Associate Dean of Graduate Studies and Research, 225-578-9294, Fax: 225-578-2125, E-mail: areynolds@lsu.edu. *Dean,* Dr. John Maxwell Hamilton, 225-578-2002, Fax: 225-578-2125, E-mail: jhamilt@lsu.edu.

School of Library and Information Science Students: 76 full-time (60 women), 113 part-time (94 women); includes 15 Black or African American, non-Hispanic/Latino; 4 Asian, non-Hispanic/Latino; 5 Hispanic/Latino; 1 Two or more races, non-Hispanic/Latino, 1 international. Average age 34. 95 applicants, 85% accepted, 37 enrolled. *Faculty:* 10 full-time (7 women). Expenses: Contact institution. *Financial support:* In 2010–11, 103 students received support, including 5 research assistantships with partial tuition reimbursements available (averaging $12,000 per year), 5 teaching assistantships with partial tuition reimbursements available (averaging $13,104 per year); fellowships, career-related internships or fieldwork, Federal Work-Study, institutionally sponsored loans, scholarships/grants, health care benefits, and unspecified assistantships also available. Support available to part-time students. Financial award applicants required to submit FAFSA. In 2010, 61 master's awarded. *Degree program information:* Part-time and evening/weekend programs available. Postbaccalaureate distance learning degree programs offered (no on-campus study). Offers library and information science (MLIS). *Application deadline:* For fall admission, 1/25 priority date for domestic students, 5/15 for international students; for spring admission, 10/15 for international students. Applications are processed on a rolling basis. *Application fee:* $50 ($70 for international students). Electronic applications accepted. *Application Contact:* LaToya Joseph, Administrative Assistant, 225-578-3150, Fax: 225-578-4581, E-mail: lcjoseph@lsu.edu. *Dean,* Dr. Beth M. Paskoff, 225-578-3158, Fax: 225-578-4581, E-mail: bpaskoff@lsu.edu.

School of Social Work Students: 181 full-time (159 women), 40 part-time (37 women); includes 53 Black or African American, non-Hispanic/Latino; 1 American Indian or Alaska Native, non-Hispanic/Latino; 2 Asian, non-Hispanic/Latino; 8 Hispanic/Latino; 2 Two or more races, non-Hispanic/Latino, 3 international. Average age 29. 165 applicants, 77% accepted, 52 enrolled. *Faculty:* 12 full-time (8 women). Expenses: Contact institution. *Financial support:* In 2010–11, 153 students received support, including 6 research assistantships with partial tuition reimbursements available (averaging $16,267 per year), 12 teaching assistantships with partial tuition reimbursements available (averaging $10,740 per year); fellowships, career-related internships or fieldwork, Federal Work-Study, scholarships/grants, health care benefits, and unspecified assistantships also available. Support available to part-time students. Financial award applicants required to submit FAFSA. In 2010, 86 master's, 2 doctorates awarded. *Degree program information:* Part-time programs available. Offers social work (MSW, PhD). *Application deadline:* For fall admission, 2/15 for domestic and international students. *Application fee:* $50 ($70 for international students). Electronic applications accepted. *Application Contact:* Denise Chiasson, Assistant Dean, 225-578-1234, Fax: 225-578-1357, E-mail: dchiass@lsu.edu. *Dean,* Dr. Christian Molidor, 225-578-5875, Fax: 225-578-1357, E-mail: cmolidor@lsu.edu.

School of the Coast and Environment Students: 77 full-time (47 women), 11 part-time (4 women); includes 5 Black or African American, non-Hispanic/Latino; 2 Asian, non-Hispanic/Latino; 1 Hispanic/Latino, 18 international. Average age 28. 56 applicants, 43% accepted, 17 enrolled. Expenses: Contact institution. *Financial support:* In 2010–11, 81 students received support, including 917,616 fellowships with full tuition reimbursements available (averaging $24,370 per year), 63 research assistantships with full and partial tuition reimbursements available (averaging $18,169 per year), 1 teaching assistantship with full and partial tuition reimbursement available (averaging $15,740 per year); career-related internships or fieldwork, Federal Work-Study, institutionally sponsored loans, health care benefits, and unspecified assistantships also available. Financial award applicants required to submit FAFSA. In 2010, 13 master's, 7 doctorates awarded. *Degree program information:* Part-time programs available. Offers environmental planning and management (MS); environmental toxicology (MS); oceanography and coastal sciences (MS, PhD); the coast and environment (MS, PhD). *Application deadline:* For fall admission, 1/25 priority date for domestic students, 5/15 for international students; for spring admission, 10/15 for international students. Applications are processed on a rolling basis. *Application fee:* $50 ($70 for international students). Electronic applications accepted. *Application Contact:* Dr. Christopher D'Elia, Dean, 225-578-8574, Fax: 225-578-5328, E-mail: cdelia@lsu.edu. *Dean,* Dr. Christopher D'Elia, 225-578-8574, Fax: 225-578-5328, E-mail: cdelia@lsu.edu.

Paul M. Hebert Law Center Students: 627 full-time (260 women), 18 part-time (5 women); includes 111 minority (49 Black or African American, non-Hispanic/Latino; 8 American Indian or Alaska Native, non-Hispanic/Latino; 16 Asian, non-Hispanic/Latino; 32 Hispanic/Latino; 6 Two or more races, non-Hispanic/Latino), 13 international. Average age 26. 1,653 applicants, 35% accepted, 225 enrolled. *Faculty:* 47 full-time (15 women), 49 part-time/adjunct (6 women). Expenses: Contact institution. *Financial support:* Scholarships/grants and tuition waivers (full and partial) available. Financial award applicants required to submit FAFSA. In 2010, 8 master's awarded. Offers law (LL M, JD/CL). *Application deadline:* For fall admission, 3/1 priority date for domestic students, 2/1 priority date for international students. Applications are processed on a rolling basis. *Application fee:* $50. Electronic applications accepted. *Application Contact:* Jake T. Henry, Director of Admissions, 225-578-8646, Fax: 225-578-8647, E-mail: jake.henry@law.lsu.edu. *Chancellor,* Jack M. Weiss, 225-578-8491, Fax: 225-578-8202, E-mail: jack.weiss@law.lsu.edu.

School of Veterinary Medicine Students: 378 full-time (268 women), 15 part-time (10 women); includes 4 Black or African American, non-Hispanic/Latino; 3 American Indian or Alaska Native, non-Hispanic/Latino; 9 Asian, non-Hispanic/Latino; 25 Hispanic/Latino; 2 Two or more races, non-Hispanic/Latino, 30 international. Average age 27. 126 applicants, 83% accepted, 55 enrolled. Expenses: Contact institution. *Financial support:* In 2010–11, 342 students received support, including 9 fellowships with full tuition reimbursements available (averaging $18,086 per year), 43 research assistantships with full and partial tuition reimbursements available (averaging $22,839 per year); teaching assistantships with full and partial tuition reimbursements available, career-related internships or fieldwork, Federal Work-Study, institutionally sponsored loans, scholarships/grants, health care benefits, tuition waivers (full and partial), and unspecified assistantships also available. Financial award applicants required to submit FAFSA. In 2010, 3 master's, 10 doctorates awarded. Offers comparative biomedical sciences (MS, PhD); pathobiological sciences (MS, PhD); veterinary clinical sciences (MS, PhD); veterinary medicine (DVM, MS, PhD). *Application deadline:* For fall admission, 3/1 priority date for domestic students, 5/15 for international students; for spring admission, 10/15 for international students. Applications are processed on a rolling basis. *Application fee:* $50 ($70 for international students). Electronic applications accepted. *Application Contact:* Dr. Peter Haynes, Dean, 225-578-9903, Fax: 225-578-9916, E-mail: pfhaynes@vetmed.lsu.edu. *Dean,* Dr. Peter Haynes, 225-578-9903, Fax: 225-578-9916, E-mail: pfhaynes@vetmed.lsu.edu.

LOUISIANA STATE UNIVERSITY HEALTH SCIENCES CENTER, New Orleans, LA 70112-2223

General Information State-supported, coed, university. CGS member. *Graduate housing:* Rooms and/or apartments available to single and married students. Housing application deadline: 6/1.

GRADUATE UNITS

School of Allied Health Professions Students: 303 full-time (234 women), 10 part-time (9 women); includes 44 minority (21 Black or African American, non-Hispanic/Latino; 9 Asian, non-Hispanic/Latino; 13 Hispanic/Latino; 1 Two or more races, non-Hispanic/Latino). Average age 27. 402 applicants, 34% accepted, 138 enrolled. *Faculty:* 26 full-time (16 women), 7 part-time/adjunct (all women). Expenses: Contact institution. *Financial support:* Fellowships, work assistantships available. Financial award application deadline: 4/15; financial award applicants required to submit FAFSA. In 2010, 62 master's, 35 doctorates awarded. Offers allied health professions (MCD, MHS, MOT, Au D, DPT); audiology (Au D); occupational therapy (MOT); physical therapy (DPT); rehabilitation counseling (MHS); speech pathology (MCD). *Application fee:* $50. *Application Contact:* Yudialys Delgado Stoute, Student Affairs Director, 504-568-4254, Fax: 504-568-3185, E-mail: ydelga@lsuhsc.edu. *Dean,* Dr. Jimmy M. Cairo, 504-568-4246, Fax: 504-568-4249, E-mail: jcairo911@lsuhsc.edu.

School of Dentistry Offers dentistry (DDS).

School of Graduate Studies in New Orleans *Degree program information:* Part-time and evening/weekend programs available. Offers biostatistics (MPH, MS, PhD); cell biology and anatomy (MS, PhD); human genetics (MS, PhD); medicine (MPH, MS, PhD); microbiology and immunology (MS, PhD); neuroscience (MS, PhD); pathology (MS, PhD); pharmacology and experimental therapeutics (MS, PhD); physiology (MS, PhD).

School of Medicine in New Orleans Offers medicine (MD, MPH). Open only to Louisiana residents. Electronic applications accepted.

School of Nursing Students: 162 full-time (96 women), 86 part-time (77 women); includes 80 minority (55 Black or African American, non-Hispanic/Latino; 3 American Indian or Alaska Native, non-Hispanic/Latino; 4 Asian, non-Hispanic/Latino; 18 Hispanic/Latino). Average age 37. 100 applicants, 100% accepted, 100 enrolled. *Faculty:* 19 full-time (17 women), 18 part-time/adjunct (7 women). Expenses: Contact institution. *Financial support:* In 2010–11, 115 students received support. Federal Work-Study, institutionally sponsored loans, scholarships/grants, and traineeships available. Financial award applicants required to submit FAFSA. In 2010, 94 master's, 1 doctorate awarded. *Degree program information:* Part-time programs available. Offers advanced public/community health nursing (MN); clinical nurse specialist (MN); nurse anesthesia (MN); nurse practitioner (MN); nursing (DNS). *Application deadline:* For fall admission, 2/1 for domestic students; for spring admission, 8/15 for domestic students. Applications are processed on a rolling basis. *Application fee:* $100. Electronic applications accepted. *Application Contact:* Dr. Demetrius James Porche, Dean, 504-568-4106, Fax: 504-599-0573, E-mail: dporch@lsuhsc.edu. *Dean,* Dr. Demetrius James Porche, 504-568-4106, Fax: 504-599-0573, E-mail: dporch@lsuhsc.edu.

School of Public Health *Degree program information:* Part-time programs available. Offers behavioral and community health sciences (MPH); biostatistics (MPH, MS, PhD); community health sciences (PhD); environmental and occupational health sciences (MPH); epidemiology (MPH, PhD); health policy and systems management (MPH).

LOUISIANA STATE UNIVERSITY HEALTH SCIENCES CENTER AT SHREVEPORT, Shreveport, LA 71130-3932

General Information State-supported, coed, university.

GRADUATE UNITS

Department of Biochemistry and Molecular Biology Offers biochemistry and molecular biology (MS, PhD).

Department of Cellular Biology and Anatomy Offers cellular biology and anatomy (MS, PhD).

Department of Microbiology and Immunology Offers microbiology and immunology (MS, PhD).

Department of Molecular and Cellular Physiology Offers physiology (MS, PhD).

Department of Pharmacology, Toxicology and Neuroscience Offers pharmacology (PhD).

School of Medicine Offers medicine (MD).

LOUISIANA STATE UNIVERSITY IN SHREVEPORT, Shreveport, LA 71115-2399

General Information State-supported, coed, comprehensive institution. *Enrollment:* 4,504 graduate, professional, and undergraduate students; 116 full-time matriculated graduate/professional students (78 women), 246 part-time matriculated graduate/professional students (142 women). *Enrollment by degree level:* 342 master's, 20 other advanced degrees. Tuition, state resident: full-time $3272; part-time $181.80 per credit hour. Tuition, nonresident: full-time $7902; part-time $471.19 per credit hour. *Required fees:* $850; $47 per credit hour. *Graduate housing:* Rooms and/or apartments available on a first-come, first-served basis to single and married students. *Student services:* Campus employment opportunities, career counseling, exercise/wellness program, free psychological counseling, services for students with disabilities, teacher training. *Library facilities:* Noel Memorial Library. *Online resources:* library catalog, web page, access to other libraries' catalogs. *Research affiliation:* Micromanufacturing Institute (manufacturing technology), Department of Agriculture (crop science), Louisiana Manufacturing Science Center (robotics), Biomedical Research Institute, Cotton, Incorporated (plant physiology).

Computer facilities: A campuswide network can be accessed. Online class registration is available. *Web address:* http://www.lsus.edu/.

General Application Contact: Yvonne Yarbrough, Secretary, Graduate Studies, 318-797-5247, Fax: 318-798-4120, E-mail: yyarbrou@lsus.edu.

GRADUATE UNITS

College of Business Administration Students: 27 full-time (14 women), 103 part-time (43 women); includes 16 minority (14 Black or African American, non-Hispanic/Latino; 2 Hispanic/Latino), 7 international. Average age 32. 66 applicants, 100% accepted, 32 enrolled. Expenses: Contact institution. In 2010, 32 master's awarded. Offers business administration (MBA, MHA); health administration (MHA). *Application fee:* $10. *Application Contact:* Dr. Douglas Bible, Associate Dean, 318-797-5383, Fax: 318-797-5176, E-mail: douglas.bible@lsus.edu. *Associate Dean,* Dr. Douglas Bible, 318-797-5383, Fax: 318-797-5176, E-mail: douglas.bible@lsus.edu.

College of Education and Human Development Students: 65 full-time (48 women), 75 part-time (58 women); includes 36 minority (27 Black or African American, non-Hispanic/Latino; 3 Asian, non-Hispanic/Latino; 6 Hispanic/Latino), 4 international. Average age 32. 83 applicants, 96% accepted, 43 enrolled. Expenses: Contact institution. In 2010, 39 master's, 2 other advanced degrees awarded. Offers counseling psychology (MS); education and human development (M Ed, MPH, MS, SSP); education curriculum and instruction (M Ed); educational leadership (M Ed); kinesiology and wellness (MS); public health (MPH); school counseling (M Ed); school psychology (SSP). *Application deadline:* For fall admission, 6/30 for domestic and international students; for spring admission, 11/30 for domestic and international students. Applications are processed on a rolling basis. *Application fee:* $10 ($20 for international students). *Application Contact:* Yvonne Yarbrough, Secretary, Graduate Studies, 318-797-5247, Fax: 318-798-4120, E-mail: yyarbrou@lsus.edu. *Dean,* Dr. David Gustavson, 318-797-5032, Fax: 318-798-4144, E-mail: dgustavs@pilot.lsus.edu.

College of Liberal Arts Students: 21 full-time (15 women), 54 part-time (38 women); includes 19 minority (16 Black or African American, non-Hispanic/Latino; 1 American Indian or Alaska Native, non-Hispanic/Latino; 2 Hispanic/Latino), 1 international. Average age 35. 38 applicants, 100% accepted, 21 enrolled. Expenses: Contact institution. In 2010, 17 master's awarded. *Degree program information:* Part-time and evening/weekend programs available. Offers human services administration (MS); liberal arts (MA, MS). *Application deadline:* For fall admission, 6/30 for domestic and international students; for spring admission, 11/30 for domestic and international students. Applications are processed on a rolling basis. *Application fee:* $10 ($20 for international students). *Application Contact:* Yvonne Yarbrough,

Secretary, Graduate Studies, 318-797-5247, Fax: 318-798-4120, E-mail: yyarbrou@lsus.edu. *Dean*, Dr. Larry Anderson, 318-797-5371, Fax: 318-797-5358, E-mail: larry.anderson@lsus.edu.

College of Sciences Students: 3 full-time (1 woman), 14 part-time (3 women); includes 2 minority (1 Black or African American, non-Hispanic/Latino; 1 Asian, non-Hispanic/Latino), 3 international. Average age 33. 4 applicants, 75% accepted, 2 enrolled. Expenses: Contact institution. In 2010, 5 master's awarded. Offers computer systems technology (MS); sciences (MS). *Application deadline:* For fall admission, 6/30 for domestic and international students; for spring admission, 11/30 for domestic and international students. Applications are processed on a rolling basis. *Application fee:* $10 ($20 for international students). *Application Contact:* Yvonne Yarbrough, Secretary, Graduate Studies, 318-797-5247, Fax: 318-798-4120, E-mail: yyarbrou@lsus.edu. *Associate Dean*, Dr. Dalton Gossett, 318-797-5231, Fax: 318-797-5230, E-mail: dalton.gossett@lsus.edu.

LOUISIANA TECH UNIVERSITY, Ruston, LA 71272

General Information State-supported, coed, university. *Graduate housing:* Rooms and/or apartments guaranteed to single students and available on a first-come, first-served basis to married students. Housing application deadline: 7/15.

GRADUATE UNITS

Graduate School *Degree program information:* Part-time programs available.

College of Applied and Natural Sciences *Degree program information:* Part-time programs available. Offers applied and natural sciences (MS); biological sciences (MS); dietetics (MS); human ecology (MS).

College of Business *Degree program information:* Part-time programs available. Offers business (MBA, MPA, DBA); business administration (MBA, DBA); business economics (MBA, DBA); finance (MBA, DBA); marketing (MBA, DBA); professional accountancy (MBA, MPA, DBA).

College of Education *Degree program information:* Part-time programs available. Offers counseling (MA); counseling psychology (PhD); curriculum and instruction (MS, Ed D); education (M Ed, MA, MS, Ed D, PhD); educational leadership (Ed D); health and exercise sciences (MS); industrial/organizational psychology (MA); secondary education (M Ed); special education (MA).

College of Engineering and Science *Degree program information:* Part-time programs available. Offers applied computational analysis and modeling (PhD); biomedical engineering (MS, PhD); chemical engineering (MS, PhD); chemistry (MS); civil engineering (MS, PhD); computer science (MS); electrical engineering (MS, PhD); engineering (PhD); engineering and science (MS, PhD); industrial engineering (MS); mathematics and statistics (MS); mechanical engineering (MS, PhD); physics (MS).

College of Liberal Arts *Degree program information:* Part-time programs available. Offers art and graphic design (MFA); English (MA); history (MA); interior design (MFA); liberal arts (MA, MFA); photography (MFA); speech (MA); speech pathology and audiology (MA); studio art (MFA).

LOUISVILLE PRESBYTERIAN THEOLOGICAL SEMINARY, Louisville, KY 40205-1798

General Information Independent-religious, coed, graduate-only institution. *Enrollment by degree level:* 122 first professional, 42 master's, 66 doctoral. *Graduate faculty:* 21 full-time (10 women), 30 part-time/adjunct (11 women). *Tuition:* Full-time $9660; part-time $322 per credit hour. *Required fees:* $143 per semester. *Graduate housing:* Rooms and/or apartments available on a first-come, first-served basis to single and married students. Typical cost: $4419 per year ($6285 including board) for single students; $4914 per year ($8646 including board) for married students. Housing application deadline: 4/15. *Student services:* Campus employment opportunities, career counseling, international student services, low-cost health insurance, services for students with disabilities, writing training. *Library facilities:* Ernest White Library. *Online resources:* library catalog, web page, access to other libraries' catalogs. *Collection:* 185,425 titles, 601 serial subscriptions, 7,205 audiovisual materials. *Research affiliation:* Louisville Institute (American religion).

Computer facilities: 22 computers available on campus for general student use. A campuswide network can be accessed from student residence rooms. *Web address:* http://www.lpts.edu/.

General Application Contact: Cheri Harper, Director of Admissions, 502-895-3411 Ext. 371, Fax: 502-895-1096, E-mail: charper@lpts.edu.

GRADUATE UNITS

Graduate and Professional Programs *Degree program information:* Part-time and evening/weekend programs available. Offers Bible (MAR); divinity (M Div); ministry (D Min); religious thought (MAR); theology (Th M). JD/M Div, M Div/MBA, and M Div/MSW offered jointly with University of Louisville. Electronic applications accepted.

LOURDES COLLEGE, Sylvania, OH 43560-2898

General Information Independent-religious, coed, comprehensive institution. CGS member. *Graduate housing:* On-campus housing not available.

GRADUATE UNITS

School of Graduate and Professional Studies *Degree program information:* Evening/weekend programs available. Offers endorsement in computer technology (M Ed); organizational leadership (MOL).

LOYOLA MARYMOUNT UNIVERSITY, Los Angeles, CA 90045-2659

General Information Independent-religious, coed, comprehensive institution. CGS member. *Enrollment:* 9,224 graduate, professional, and undergraduate students; 2,343 full-time matriculated graduate/professional students (1,401 women), 674 part-time matriculated graduate/professional students (338 women). *Enrollment by degree level:* 1,309 first professional, 1,646 master's, 62 doctoral. *Graduate faculty:* 234 full-time (88 women), 108 part-time/adjunct (60 women). *Graduate housing:* Room and/or apartments available on a first-come, first-served basis to single students; on-campus housing not available to married students. *Student services:* Campus employment opportunities, career counseling, child daycare facilities, exercise/wellness program, free psychological counseling, international student services, low-cost health insurance, multicultural affairs office, services for students with disabilities, teacher training. *Library facilities:* William H. Hannon Library. *Online resources:* library catalog, web page, access to other libraries' catalogs. *Collection:* 561,361 titles, 37,344 serial subscriptions, 26,619 audiovisual materials.

Computer facilities: Computer purchase and lease plans are available. 780 computers available on campus for general student use. A campuswide network can be accessed from student residence rooms and from off campus. Online class registration is available. *Web address:* http://www.lmu.edu/.

General Application Contact: Chake H. Kouyoumjian, Associate Dean of the Graduate Division, 310-338-2721, Fax: 310-338-6086, E-mail: ckouyoum@lmu.edu.

GRADUATE UNITS

College of Business Administration Expenses: Contact institution. Offers business administration (MBA); executive business administration (MBA). *Application Contact:* Dr. Dennis Draper, Dean, 310-338-7504, E-mail: ddraper@lmu.edu. *Dean*, Dr. Dennis Draper, 310-338-7504, E-mail: ddraper@lmu.edu.

College of Fine Arts Expenses: Contact institution. Offers fine arts (MA); marital and family therapy (MA). *Application Contact:* Dr. Barbara J. Busse, Dean, 310-338-7430, E-mail: bbusse@lmu.edu. *Dean*, Dr. Barbara J. Busse, 310-338-7430, E-mail: bbusse@lmu.edu.

College of Liberal Arts Expenses: Contact institution. Offers English (MA); liberal arts (MA); pastoral theology (MA); philosophy (MA); theology (MA). *Application Contact:* Dr. Paul T. Zeleza, Dean, 310-338-2716, E-mail: paul.zeleza@lmu.edu. *Dean*, Dr. Paul T. Zeleza, 310-338-2716, E-mail: paul.zeleza@lmu.edu.

The Bioethics Institute Expenses: Contact institution. Offers bioethics (MA). *Application Contact:* Dr. James J. Walter, Chair, 310-258-8621, Fax: 310-258-8642, E-mail: jwalter@lmu.edu. *Chair*, Dr. James J. Walter, 310-258-8621, Fax: 310-258-8642, E-mail: jwalter@lmu.edu.

College of Science and Engineering Expenses: Contact institution. Offers civil engineering (MSE); computer science (MS); electrical engineering (MSE); environmental science (MS); mechanical engineering (MSE); science and engineering (MAT, MS, MSE); system engineering leadership (MS); systems engineering (MS); teaching in mathematics (MAT). *Application Contact:* Dr. Richard Plumb, Dean, 310-338-2834, E-mail: rplumb@lmu.edu. *Dean*, Dr. Richard Plumb, 310-338-2834, E-mail: rplumb@lmu.edu.

Loyola Law School Los Angeles Students: 1,034 full-time (541 women), 283 part-time (116 women); includes 515 minority (51 Black or African American, non-Hispanic/Latino; 4 American Indian or Alaska Native, non-Hispanic/Latino; 231 Asian, non-Hispanic/Latino; 159 Hispanic/Latino; 2 Native Hawaiian or other Pacific Islander, non-Hispanic/Latino; 68 Two or more races, non-Hispanic/Latino), 15 international. Average age 26. 7,869 applicants, 20% accepted, 403 enrolled. *Faculty:* 74 full-time (35 women), 55 part-time/adjunct (13 women). Expenses: Contact institution. *Financial support:* In 2010–11, 322 students received support; research assistantships, Federal Work-Study and scholarships/grants available. Financial award application deadline: 3/12; financial award applicants required to submit FAFSA. In 2010, 388 first professional degrees, 38 master's awarded. *Degree program information:* Part-time and evening/weekend programs available. Offers law (JD); taxation (LL M). *Application deadline:* For fall admission, 2/1 priority date for domestic and international students. Applications are processed on a rolling basis. *Application fee:* $65. Electronic applications accepted. *Application Contact:* Jannell Lundy Roberts, Assistant Dean, Admissions, 213-736-1074, Fax: 213-736-6523, E-mail: admissions@lls.edu. *Dean*, Victor Gold, 213-736-1062, Fax: 213-487-6736, E-mail: victor.gold@lls.edu.

School of Education Expenses: Contact institution. Offers bilingual elementary education (MA); bilingual secondary education (MA); biliteracy, leadership, and intercultural education (MA); Catholic inclusive education (MA); Catholic school administration (MA); child/adolescent literacy (MA); counseling (MA); early childhood education (MA); education (MA, Ed D); educational leadership in social justice (Ed D); elementary education (MA); general education (MA); guidance and counseling (MA); literacy education (MA); literacy/language arts (MA); school administration (MA); school psychology (MA); secondary education (MA); special education (MA); teaching English as a second language (MA); urban education (MA). *Application Contact:* Dr. Shane Martin, Dean, 310-338-7301, E-mail: smartin@lmu.edu. *Dean*, Dr. Shane Martin, 310-338-7301, E-mail: smartin@lmu.edu.

School of Film and Television Expenses: Contact institution. *Financial support:* Applicants required to submit FAFSA. Offers film and television (MFA); production (film and television) (MFA); screen writing (MFA). Electronic applications accepted. *Application Contact:* Dr. Chake H. Kouyoumjian, Graduate Director, 310-338-2721, E-mail: ckouyoum@lmu.edu. *Dean*, Stephen Ujlaki, 310-338-3033, E-mail: sujlaki@lmu.edu.

LOYOLA UNIVERSITY CHICAGO, Chicago, IL 60660

General Information Independent-religious, coed, university. CGS member. *Enrollment:* 15,951 graduate, professional, and undergraduate students; 4,448 full-time matriculated graduate/professional students (2,675 women), 1,756 part-time matriculated graduate/professional students (1,270 women). *Enrollment by degree level:* 1,438 first professional, 3,611 master's, 894 doctoral, 261 other advanced degrees. *Graduate faculty:* 536 full-time (176 women), 164 part-time/adjunct (93 women). *Tuition:* Full-time $14,940; part-time $830 per credit hour. *Required fees:* $87 per semester. Part-time tuition and fees vary according to course load and program. *Graduate housing:* Room and/or apartments available on a first-come, first-served basis to single students; on-campus housing not available to married students. Typical cost: $11,220 (including board). Housing application deadline: 5/1. *Student services:* Campus employment opportunities, campus safety program, career counseling, free psychological counseling, international student services, low-cost health insurance, services for students with disabilities, teacher training. *Library facilities:* Cudahy Library plus 7 others. *Online resources:* library catalog, web page, access to other libraries' catalogs. *Collection:* 2 million titles, 50,916 serial subscriptions, 16,275 audiovisual materials. *Research affiliation:* Illinois State Board of Education (behavioral intervention), Illinois Positive Behavior Support Network (student behavior), Illinois State Technical Assistance Center (character education—high school), Illinois Children's Mental Health Partnership (children's mental health), Albany Park Community Center (Plan for Early Childcare Providers), McCormick Foundation (professional development of childcare educators).

Computer facilities: Computer purchase and lease plans are available. 1,026 computers available on campus for general student use. A campuswide network can be accessed from student residence rooms and from off campus. Online class registration is available. *Web address:* http://www.luc.edu/.

General Application Contact: Ronald P. Martin, Associate Director, Graduate and Professional Enrollment Management Operations, 312-915-8951, E-mail: rmarti7@luc.edu.

GRADUATE UNITS

Graduate School Students: 1,077 full-time (612 women), 336 part-time (180 women); includes 72 Black or African American, non-Hispanic/Latino; 6 American Indian or Alaska Native, non-Hispanic/Latino; 69 Asian, non-Hispanic/Latino; 55 Hispanic/Latino, 129 international. Average age 32. 2,230 applicants, 32% accepted, 321 enrolled. *Faculty:* 235 full-time (75 women), 33 part-time/adjunct (7 women). Expenses: Contact institution. *Financial support:* In 2010–11, 325 students received support, including 90 fellowships with full tuition reimbursements available (averaging $19,000 per year), 130 research assistantships with full tuition reimbursements available (averaging $18,000 per year), 105 teaching assistantships with full and partial tuition reimbursements available (averaging $13,000 per year); career-related internships or fieldwork, Federal Work-Study, institutionally sponsored loans, scholarships/grants, and unspecified assistantships also available. Support available to part-time students. Financial award application deadline: 2/1; financial award applicants required to submit FAFSA. In 2010, 271 master's, 106 doctorates awarded. *Degree program information:* Part-time and evening/weekend programs available. Postbaccalaureate distance learning degree programs offered (no on-campus study). Offers applied social psychology (MA, PhD); applied statistics (MS); biology (MA, MS); cell and molecular physiology (MS, PhD); cell biology, neurobiology and anatomy (MS, PhD); chemistry (MS, PhD); clinical psychology (MA, PhD); computer science (MS); criminal justice (MA); developmental psychology (MA, PhD); English (MA, PhD); history (MA, PhD); immunology (PhD); infectious disease and immunology (MS); information technology (MS); mathematics and statistics (MS); medical sciences (MA); microbiology (MS); molecular and cellular biochemistry (MS, PhD); molecular biology (MS, PhD); molecular pharmacology and therapeutics (MS, PhD); neuroscience (MS, PhD); philosophy (MA, PhD); political science (MA, PhD); public health (MPH); public history (MA); sociology (MA, PhD); software technology (MS); Spanish (MA); theology (MA, PhD); urban studies (MA). *Application deadline:* Applications are processed on a rolling basis. *Application fee:* $50. Electronic applications accepted. *Application Contact:* Ron Martin, Assistant Director of Enrollment Management, 312-915-8950, Fax: 312-915-8905, E-mail: gradapp@luc.edu. *Dean*, Dr. Samuel Attoh, 773-508-3459, Fax: 773-508-2460, E-mail: sattoh@luc.edu.

Marcella Niehoff School of Nursing Students: 85 full-time (72 women), 342 part-time (323 women); includes 76 minority (23 Black or African American, non-Hispanic/Latino; 34 Asian, non-Hispanic/Latino; 16 Hispanic/Latino; 1 Native Hawaiian or other Pacific Islander, non-Hispanic/Latino; 2 Two or more races, non-Hispanic/Latino), 3 international. Average age 40. 183 applicants, 67% accepted, 106 enrolled. *Faculty:* 26 full-time (25 women), 58 part-time/adjunct (50 women). Expenses: Contact institution. *Financial support:* In 2010–11, 10 students received support, including 1 fellowship with tuition reimbursement available, 4 research assistantships with tuition reimbursements available, 1 teaching assistantship with tuition reimbursement available; career-related internships or fieldwork, Federal Work-Study, institutionally sponsored loans, traineeships, and unspecified assistantships also available. Support available to part-time students. Financial award applicants required to submit FAFSA. In 2010, 67 master's, 4 doctorates awarded. *Degree program information:* Part-time and evening/weekend programs available. Postbaccalaureate distance learning degree programs offered (minimal on-campus study). Offers acute care (Post-Master's

Loyola University Chicago (continued)

Certificate); acute care nurse practitioner (MSN); adult clinical nurse specialist (MSN, Certificate); cardiovascular health (Certificate); cardiovascular health and disease management (Certificate); dietetics (MS, Certificate); emergency nurse practitioner (MSN); family nurse practitioner (MSN); family practice nurse practitioner (Certificate); health systems management (MSN); informatics (Certificate); manager care (Certificate); nursing (MS, MSN, DNP, PhD, Certificate, Post-Master's Certificate); nursing oncology (Certificate); nursing practice (DNP); oncology clinical nurse specialist (MSN); oncology nursing (Certificate); population based infection control (MSN, Certificate); women's health nurse practitioner (MSN). *Application deadline:* For fall admission, 8/1 priority date for domestic and international students; for spring admission, 12/15 priority date for domestic students, 12/1 priority date for international students. Applications are processed on a rolling basis. *Application fee:* $50. Electronic applications accepted. *Application Contact:* Dr. Vicki A. Keough, Associate Professor/Master's Program Director, 708-216-3582, Fax: 708-216-9555, E-mail: vkeough@luc.edu. *Dean*, Dr. Mary K. Walker, 708-216-5448, Fax: 708-216-9555, E-mail: mwalker1@luc.edu.

Graduate School of Business Offers accountancy (MS, MSA); business administration (MBA); finance (MS); healthcare management (MBA); human resources and employee relations (MS, MSHR); information systems and operations management (MS); information systems management (MS); integrated marketing communications (MS); marketing (MS, MSIMC); strategic financial services (MBA).

Institute of Human Resources and Employee Relations *Degree program information:* Part-time programs available. Offers human resources and employee relations (MSHR).

Institute of Pastoral Studies Students: 92 full-time (55 women), 172 part-time (121 women); includes 43 minority (20 Black or African American, non-Hispanic/Latino; 5 Asian, non-Hispanic/Latino; 16 Hispanic/Latino; 2 Two or more races, non-Hispanic/Latino), 16 international. Average age 41. 164 applicants, 76% accepted, 83 enrolled. *Faculty:* 6 full-time (1 woman), 33 part-time/adjunct (16 women). Expenses: Contact institution. *Financial support:* In 2010–11, 84 students received support. Career-related internships or fieldwork, Federal Work-Study, institutionally sponsored loans, scholarships/grants, and tuition waivers (partial) available. Support available to part-time students. Financial award application deadline: 3/1; financial award applicants required to submit FAFSA. In 2010, 6 first professional degrees, 66 master's awarded. *Degree program information:* Part-time and evening/weekend programs available. Offers community development (MA); contemporary spirituality (MA); divinity (M Div); pastoral counseling (MA, Certificate); pastoral studies (M Div, MA, Certificate); religious education (MA, Certificate); social justice (MA); social justice and community development (MA, Certificate); spirituality (MA, Certificate). *Application deadline:* Applications are processed on a rolling basis. *Application fee:* $50. Electronic applications accepted. *Application Contact:* Randy Gibbons, Administrative Assistant, 312-915-7450, Fax: 312-915-7410, E-mail: rgibbon@luc.edu. *Director*, Dr. Robert A. Ludwig, 312-915-7467, Fax: 312-915-7410, E-mail: rludwig@luc.edu.

School of Education Students: 534 full-time (400 women), 307 part-time (215 women); includes 89 Black or African American, non-Hispanic/Latino; 4 American Indian or Alaska Native, non-Hispanic/Latino; 36 Asian, non-Hispanic/Latino; 68 Hispanic/Latino, 28 international. Average age 36. 769 applicants, 56% accepted, 207 enrolled. *Faculty:* 47 full-time (32 women), 53 part-time/adjunct (37 women). Expenses: Contact institution. *Financial support:* In 2010–11, 74 fellowships with full tuition reimbursements (averaging $11,000 per year), 47 research assistantships with full tuition reimbursements (averaging $11,000 per year), 60 teaching assistantships (averaging $2,000 per year) were awarded; career-related internships or fieldwork, Federal Work-Study, institutionally sponsored loans, scholarships/grants, tuition waivers (partial), and unspecified assistantships also available. Support available to part-time students. Financial award application deadline: 2/1; financial award applicants required to submit FAFSA. In 2010, 230 master's, 45 doctorates, 12 other advanced degrees awarded. *Degree program information:* Part-time and evening/weekend programs available. Offers administration and supervision (M Ed, Ed D, Certificate); community counseling (M Ed, MA); counseling psychology (PhD); cultural and educational policy studies (M Ed, MA, Ed D, PhD); curriculum and instruction (M Ed, Ed D); education (M Ed, MA, Ed D, PhD, Certificate, Ed S); educational psychology (M Ed); elementary education (M Ed); English as a second language (Certificate); higher education (M Ed, PhD); instructional leadership (M Ed); math education (M Ed); reading specialist (M Ed); reading teacher endorsement (Certificate); research methods (M Ed, MA, PhD); school counseling (M Ed, Certificate); school psychology (PhD, Ed S); school technology (M Ed); science education (M Ed); secondary education (M Ed); special education (M Ed). *Application fee:* $50. Electronic applications accepted. *Application Contact:* Marie Rosin-Dittmar, Information Contact, 312-915-6800, E-mail: schleduc@luc.edu. *Dean*, Dr. David Prasse, 312-915-6992, Fax: 312-915-6980, E-mail: dprasse@luc.edu.

School of Law Offers business law (LL M, MJ); child and family law (LL M, MJ); health law (LL M, MJ, D Law, SJD); law (JD).

School of Social Work Students: 671 full-time (578 women), 154 part-time (126 women); includes 165 minority (101 Black or African American, non-Hispanic/Latino; 20 Asian, non-Hispanic/Latino; 35 Hispanic/Latino; 9 Two or more races, non-Hispanic/Latino), 11 international. Average age 28. 710 applicants, 92% accepted, 428 enrolled. *Faculty:* 26 full-time (16 women), 80 part-time/adjunct (55 women). Expenses: Contact institution. *Financial support:* In 2010–11, 525 students received support; fellowships, research assistantships, career-related internships or fieldwork, Federal Work-Study, institutionally sponsored loans, scholarships/grants, and unspecified assistantships available. Financial award applicants required to submit FAFSA. In 2010, 280 master's, 8 doctorates awarded. *Degree program information:* Part-time programs available. Offers social work (MSW, PhD, PGC). *Application deadline:* For fall admission, 7/1 for domestic and international students; for winter admission, 11/1 for domestic and international students; for spring admission, 5/1 for domestic and international students. *Application fee:* $0. *Application Contact:* Cara E. Young, Enrollment Advisor, 312-915-7707, Fax: 312-915-7645, E-mail: cyoung@luc.edu. *Associate Dean for Academics*, Dr. James A. Marley, 312-915-7033, Fax: 312-915-7645, E-mail: jmarley@luc.edu.

Stritch School of Medicine Students: 584 full-time (307 women); includes 117 minority (31 Black or African American, non-Hispanic/Latino; 26 Asian, non-Hispanic/Latino; 54 Hispanic/Latino; 1 Native Hawaiian or other Pacific Islander, non-Hispanic/Latino; 5 Two or more races, non-Hispanic/Latino), 1 international. Average age 25. 10,085 applicants, 4% accepted, 150 enrolled. *Faculty:* 109 full-time (37 women), 18 part-time/adjunct (8 women). Expenses: Contact institution. *Financial support:* In 2010–11, 513 students received support. Institutionally sponsored loans and scholarships/grants available. Financial award application deadline: 3/30; financial award applicants required to submit FAFSA. In 2010, 132 MDs awarded. Offers medicine (MD). *Application deadline:* For fall admission, 11/15 for domestic students. Applications are processed on a rolling basis. *Application fee:* $70. *Application Contact:* LaDonna E. Norstrom, Assistant Dean for Admissions, 708-216-3229. *Dean*, Dr. John M. Lee, 708-216-3223, Fax: 708-216-4305.

See Close-Up on page 963.

LOYOLA UNIVERSITY MARYLAND, Baltimore, MD 21210-2699

General Information Independent-religious, coed, university. CGS member. *Graduate housing:* On-campus housing not available.

GRADUATE UNITS

Graduate Programs *Degree program information:* Part-time and evening/weekend programs available.

Loyola College of Arts and Sciences *Degree program information:* Part-time and evening/weekend programs available. Offers arts and sciences (M Ed, MA, MMS, MS, PhD, Psy D, CAS); clinical psychology (MS, Psy D, CAS); computer science (MS); counseling psychology (MS, CAS); liberal studies (MMS); pastoral counseling (MS, PhD, CAS); software engineering (MS); speech-language pathology and audiology (MS, CAS); spiritual and pastoral care (MA).

School of Education *Degree program information:* Part-time and evening/weekend programs available. Offers administration and supervision (M Ed, MA, CAS); curriculum and instruction (M Ed, MA, CAS); educational technology (M Ed); Montessori education (M Ed, CAS); reading (M Ed, CAS); school counseling (M Ed, CAS); special education (M Ed, CAS).

Sellinger School of Business and Management *Degree program information:* Part-time and evening/weekend programs available. Offers accounting (MBA); business and management (MBA, MSF); executive business administration (MBA); finance (MBA); general business (MBA); international business (MBA); management (MBA); management information systems (MBA); marketing (MBA).

LOYOLA UNIVERSITY NEW ORLEANS, New Orleans, LA 70118-6195

General Information Independent-religious, coed, comprehensive institution. *Enrollment:* 4,772 graduate, professional, and undergraduate students; 945 full-time matriculated graduate/professional students (547 women), 976 part-time matriculated graduate/professional students (728 women). *Enrollment by degree level:* 848 first professional, 931 master's, 22 doctoral, 120 other advanced degrees. *Graduate housing:* Room and/or apartments available on a first-come, first-served basis to single students; on-campus housing not available to married students. Housing application deadline: 8/1. *Student services:* Campus employment opportunities, campus safety program, career counseling, child daycare facilities, exercise/wellness program, free psychological counseling, international student services, low-cost health insurance, multicultural affairs office, services for students with disabilities. *Library facilities:* Monroe Library plus 1 other. *Online resources:* library catalog, web page, access to other libraries' catalogs. *Collection:* 623,596 titles, 80,410 serial subscriptions, 17,431 audiovisual materials. *Research affiliation:* New Orleans Museum of Art (communications, history, visual arts).

Computer facilities: Computer purchase and lease plans are available. 525 computers available on campus for general student use. A campuswide network can be accessed from student residence rooms and from off campus. Online class registration is available. *Web address:* http://www.loyno.edu/.

General Application Contact: Salvadore A. Liberto, Vice President for Enrollment Management and Associate Provost, 504-865-3240, Fax: 504-865-3383, E-mail: admit@loyno.edu.

GRADUATE UNITS

College of Law Students: 695 full-time (347 women), 153 part-time (74 women); includes 114 Black or African American, non-Hispanic/Latino; 7 American Indian or Alaska Native, non-Hispanic/Latino; 30 Asian, non-Hispanic/Latino; 76 Hispanic/Latino; 14 Two or more races, non-Hispanic/Latino, 6 international. Average age 27. 2,033 applicants, 42% accepted, 269 enrolled. Expenses: Contact institution. *Financial support:* In 2010–11, 50 research assistantships (averaging $1,428 per year), 22 teaching assistantships (averaging $2,200 per year) were awarded; career-related internships or fieldwork and scholarships/grants also available. Support available to part-time students. Financial award application deadline: 5/1; financial award applicants required to submit FAFSA. In 2010, 282 first professional degrees awarded. *Degree program information:* Part-time and evening/weekend programs available. Offers law (JD, LL M). *Application deadline:* For fall admission, 2/1 priority date for domestic and international students. Applications are processed on a rolling basis. *Application fee:* $40. Electronic applications accepted. *Application Contact:* Michele K. Allison-Davis, Assistant Dean, Admissions, 504-861-5575, Fax: 504-861-5772, E-mail: maldavis@loyno.edu. *Dean*, 504-861-5405, Fax: 504-861-5739.

College of Music and Fine Arts Students: 27 full-time (14 women), 3 part-time (all women); includes 7 Black or African American, non-Hispanic/Latino; 1 Hispanic/Latino, 2 international. Average age 26. 28 applicants, 71% accepted, 11 enrolled. Expenses: Contact institution. *Financial support:* Career-related internships or fieldwork, Federal Work-Study, institutionally sponsored loans, scholarships/grants, and unspecified assistantships available. Support available to part-time students. Financial award application deadline: 5/1; financial award applicants required to submit FAFSA. In 2010, 1 master's awarded. *Degree program information:* Part-time programs available. Offers music therapy (MMT); performance (MM). *Application deadline:* For fall admission, 8/15 priority date for domestic and international students; for spring admission, 1/1 priority date for domestic and international students. Applications are processed on a rolling basis. *Application fee:* $20. Electronic applications accepted. *Application Contact:* Anthony A. Decuir, Associate Dean, 504-865-3037, Fax: 504-865-2852, E-mail: decuir@loyno.edu. *Dean*, Donald R. Boomgaarden, 504-865-3039, Fax: 504-865-2852, E-mail: deancmfa@loyno.edu.

College of Social Sciences Students: 191 full-time (173 women), 779 part-time (630 women); includes 235 minority (148 Black or African American, non-Hispanic/Latino; 10 American Indian or Alaska Native, non-Hispanic/Latino; 17 Asian, non-Hispanic/Latino; 58 Hispanic/Latino; 1 Native Hawaiian or other Pacific Islander, non-Hispanic/Latino; 1 Two or more races, non-Hispanic/Latino), 3 international. Average age 44. 433 applicants, 89% accepted, 264 enrolled. Expenses: Contact institution. *Financial support:* Application deadline: 5/1. In 2010, 316 master's, 40 other advanced degrees awarded. *Degree program information:* Part-time and evening/weekend programs available. Offers counseling (MS); criminal justice (MCJ); criminal justice administration (MS); social sciences (MCJ, MPS, MRE, MS, MSN, DNP, Certificate). *Application deadline:* For fall admission, 8/1 priority date for domestic and international students; for winter admission, 12/15 priority date for international students; for spring admission, 1/5 priority date for domestic and international students. Applications are processed on a rolling basis. *Application fee:* $20. Electronic applications accepted. *Application Contact:* Salvadore A. Liberto, Vice President for Enrollment Management and Associate Provost, 504-865-3240, Fax: 504-865-3383, E-mail: admit@loyno.edu. *Dean*, Dr. Luis F. Miron, 504-865-2497, Fax: 504-865-3883, E-mail: lmiron@loyno.edu.

Loyola Institute for Ministry Students: 5 full-time (3 women), 305 part-time (206 women); includes 19 Black or African American, non-Hispanic/Latino; 4 American Indian or Alaska Native, non-Hispanic/Latino; 2 Asian, non-Hispanic/Latino; 30 Hispanic/Latino, 2 international. Average age 51. 84 applicants, 99% accepted, 56 enrolled. Expenses: Contact institution. *Financial support:* Career-related internships or fieldwork, scholarships/grants, health care benefits, tuition waivers (partial), and room and board assistance available. Support available to part-time students. Financial award application deadline: 5/1; financial award applicants required to submit FAFSA. In 2010, 62 master's, 40 other advanced degrees awarded. *Degree program information:* Part-time and evening/weekend programs available. Postbaccalaureate distance learning degree programs offered (no on-campus study). Offers pastoral studies (MPS); religious education (MRE); theology and ministry (Certificate). *Application deadline:* Applications are processed on a rolling basis. *Application fee:* $20. Electronic applications accepted. *Application Contact:* Cecelia M. Bennett, Associate Director, 504-865-3398, Fax: 504-865-2066, E-mail: abennett@loyno.edu. *Director*, Dr. Tom Ryan, 504-865-2069, Fax: 504-865-2066, E-mail: tfryan@loyno.edu.

School of Nursing Students: 152 full-time (144 women), 429 part-time (392 women); includes 155 minority (112 Black or African American, non-Hispanic/Latino; 6 American Indian or Alaska Native, non-Hispanic/Latino; 14 Asian, non-Hispanic/Latino; 21 Hispanic/Latino; 1 Native Hawaiian or other Pacific Islander, non-Hispanic/Latino; 1 Two or more races, non-Hispanic/Latino), 1 international. Average age 43. 256 applicants, 88% accepted, 177 enrolled. Expenses: Contact institution. *Financial support:* Traineeships and Incumbent Workers Training Program grants available. Financial award application deadline: 5/1; financial award applicants required to submit FAFSA. In 2010, 220 master's awarded. *Degree program information:* Part-time and evening/weekend programs available. Postbaccalaureate distance learning degree programs offered. Offers adult nurse practitioner (MSN); family nurse practitioner (MSN); health care systems management (MSN); nursing (MSN, DNP). *Application deadline:* For fall admission, 8/1 priority date for domestic and international students; for winter admission, 12/15 priority date for domestic and international students; for spring admission, 5/15 priority date for domestic and international students. Applications are processed on a rolling basis. *Application fee:* $20. Electronic applications accepted. *Application Contact:* Deborah Smith, Assistant to the Director, 504-865-2823, Fax: 504-865-3254, E-mail: dhsmith@loyno.edu. *Director*, Dr. Ann H. Cary, 800-488-6257, Fax: 504-865-3254, E-mail: nursing@loyno.edu.

Joseph A. Butt, S. J., College of Business Students: 32 full-time (13 women), 41 part-time (21 women); includes 3 Black or African American, non-Hispanic/Latino; 2 American Indian or

Alaska Native, non-Hispanic/Latino; 2 Asian, non-Hispanic/Latino; 1 Hispanic/Latino; 1 Two or more races, non-Hispanic/Latino. Average age 27. 63 applicants, 79% accepted, 31 enrolled. Expenses: Contact institution. *Financial support:* Research assistantships, scholarships/grants, tuition waivers (partial), and unspecified assistantships available. Financial award application deadline: 5/1; financial award applicants required to submit FAFSA. In 2010, 37 master's awarded. *Degree program information:* Part-time and evening/weekend programs available. Postbaccalaureate distance learning degree programs offered (minimal on-campus study). Offers business (MBA); business administration (MBA). *Application deadline:* For fall admission, 6/15 priority date for domestic and international students; for spring admission, 11/15 priority date for domestic and international students. Applications are processed on a rolling basis. *Application fee:* $50. Electronic applications accepted. *Application Contact:* Stephanie Mansfield, Assistant Director, Graduate Programs, 504-864-7965, Fax: 504-864-7970, E-mail: smans@loyno.edu. *Dean,* Dr. William B. Locander, 504-864-7990, Fax: 504-864-7970, E-mail: locander@loyno.edu.

LUBBOCK CHRISTIAN UNIVERSITY, Lubbock, TX 79407-2099

General Information Independent-religious, coed, comprehensive institution. *Graduate housing:* Rooms and/or apartments available to single and married students. Housing application deadline: 8/15.

GRADUATE UNITS

Graduate Biblical Studies *Degree program information:* Part-time programs available. Offers Bible and ministry (MS); biblical interpretation (MA).

LUTHERAN SCHOOL OF THEOLOGY AT CHICAGO, Chicago, IL 60615-5199

General Information Independent-religious, coed, graduate-only institution. *Enrollment by degree level:* 149 first professional, 44 master's, 73 doctoral, 16 other advanced degrees. *Graduate faculty:* 20 full-time (6 women), 18 part-time/adjunct (5 women). *Tuition:* Full-time $12,294; part-time $1366 per course. *Required fees:* $35 per semester. Tuition and fees vary according to degree level and program. *Graduate housing:* Rooms and/or apartments available on a first-come, first-served basis to single and married students. Typical cost: $2688 per year for single students; $8652 per year for married students. *Student services:* Campus safety program, career counseling, international student services, low-cost health insurance, multicultural affairs office. *Library facilities:* Jesuit-Krauss-McCormick Library. *Online resources:* web page. *Collection:* 334,388 titles. *Research affiliation:* Chicago Center for Public Ministry, Zygon Center for Religion and Science.

Computer facilities: A campuswide network can be accessed from off campus. Online class registration is available. *Web address:* http://www.lstc.edu/.

General Application Contact: Dorothy C. Dominiak, Director of Financial Aid and Admissions, 773-256-0726, Fax: 773-256-0782, E-mail: ddominia@lstc.edu.

GRADUATE UNITS

Graduate and Professional Programs Students: 195 full-time (96 women), 87 part-time (48 women). *Faculty:* 20 full-time (6 women), 18 part-time/adjunct (5 women). Expenses: Contact institution. *Financial support:* Career-related internships or fieldwork and scholarships/grants available. Support available to part-time students. *Degree program information:* Part-time programs available. Offers ministry (MAM, D Min); theological studies (MATS, PhD); theology (M Div, Th M). *Application deadline:* Applications are processed on a rolling basis. *Application fee:* $50. *Application Contact:* Dorothy C. Dominiak, Director of Financial Aid and Admissions, 773-256-0726, Fax: 773-256-0782, E-mail: ddominia@lstc.edu. *Dean,* Michael Shelley, 773-256-0722, Fax: 773-256-0782, E-mail: mshelley@lstc.edu.

LUTHERAN THEOLOGICAL SEMINARY, Saskatoon, SK S7N 0X3, Canada

General Information Independent-religious, coed, graduate-only institution. *Graduate housing:* Room and/or apartments available to single students; on-campus housing not available to married students. Housing application deadline: 4/30.

GRADUATE UNITS

Graduate and Professional Programs *Degree program information:* Part-time programs available. Offers Biblical studies (MTS); church history (MTS); ethics/church and society (MTS); history of Christianity (STM); New Testament (STM); Old Testament (STM); pastoral studies (STM); pastoral theology (MTS); systematic theology (MTS); systematic theology and philosophy of religion (STM); theology (M Div, D Div). STM programs offered jointly with College of Emmanuel and St. Chad and St. Andrew's College.

LUTHERAN THEOLOGICAL SEMINARY AT GETTYSBURG, Gettysburg, PA 17325-1795

General Information Independent-religious, coed, graduate-only institution. *Graduate housing:* Rooms and/or apartments available on a first-come, first-served basis to single and married students. Housing application deadline: 4/1.

GRADUATE UNITS

Graduate and Professional Programs *Degree program information:* Part-time programs available. Postbaccalaureate distance learning degree programs offered (no on-campus study). Offers divinity (M Div); ministerial studies (MAMS); outdoor ministry (MAR); parish ministry (D Min); theology (STM). Electronic applications accepted.

THE LUTHERAN THEOLOGICAL SEMINARY AT PHILADELPHIA, Philadelphia, PA 19119-1794

General Information Independent-religious, coed, graduate-only institution. *Enrollment by degree level:* 134 first professional, 93 master's, 92 doctoral, 6 other advanced degrees. *Graduate faculty:* 18 full-time (5 women), 22 part-time/adjunct (8 women). *Tuition:* Full-time $13,900; part-time $1470 per course. *Required fees:* $2484; $75 per semester. Tuition and fees vary according to degree level. *Graduate housing:* Rooms and/or apartments available on a first-come, first-served basis to single and married students. Typical cost: $9247 (including board) for single students; $7740 per year for married students. Room and board charges vary according to housing facility selected. Housing application deadline: 4/15. *Student services:* Campus employment opportunities, campus safety program, exercise/wellness program, free psychological counseling, multicultural affairs office. *Library facilities:* Krauth Memorial Library. *Online resources:* library catalog, web page, access to other libraries' catalogs. *Collection:* 200,977 titles, 474 serial subscriptions, 5,439 audiovisual materials.

Computer facilities: 3 computers available on campus for general student use. A campuswide network can be accessed from student residence rooms and from off campus. Online class registration is available. *Web address:* http://www.ltsp.edu/.

General Application Contact: Rev. Louise Johnson, Director of Admissions, 800-286-4616 Ext. 6321, Fax: 215-248-7315, E-mail: admissions@ltsp.edu.

GRADUATE UNITS

Graduate School Students: 121 full-time (56 women), 204 part-time (97 women); includes 92 minority (80 Black or African American, non-Hispanic/Latino; 2 Asian, non-Hispanic/Latino; 10 Hispanic/Latino), 14 international. 123 applicants, 86% accepted, 84 enrolled. *Faculty:* 18 full-time (5 women), 22 part-time/adjunct (8 women). Expenses: Contact institution. *Financial support:* In 2010–11, 102 students received support; research assistantships with tuition reimbursements available, teaching assistantships with tuition reimbursements available, career-related internships or fieldwork and Federal Work-Study available. Financial award application deadline: 7/1; financial award applicants required to submit FAFSA. *Degree program information:* Part-time and evening/weekend programs available. Offers divinity (M Div); ministry (D Min); public leadership (MA); religion (MAR); social ministry (Certificate); theology (STM, PhD). *Application deadline:* For fall admission, 6/1 priority date for domestic students. Applications are processed on a rolling basis. *Application fee:* $35. Electronic applications accepted. *Application Contact:* Rev. Louise Johnson, Director of Admissions, 800-286-4616 Ext. 6321, Fax: 215-248-7315, E-mail: admissions@ltsp.edu. *Dean,* Rev. Dr. J. Paul Rajashekar, 215-248-6379, Fax: 215-248-4577, E-mail: rajashekar@ltsp.edu.

LUTHERAN THEOLOGICAL SOUTHERN SEMINARY, Columbia, SC 29203

General Information Independent-religious, coed, graduate-only institution. *Enrollment by degree level:* 136 first professional, 48 master's. *Graduate faculty:* 15 full-time (4 women), 4 part-time/adjunct (3 women). *Graduate housing:* Rooms and/or apartments available on a first-come, first-served basis to single and married students. Housing application deadline: 5/1. *Student services:* Campus employment opportunities, campus safety program, career counseling, exercise/wellness program, international student services, low-cost health insurance, writing training. *Library facilities:* Lineberger Library. *Online resources:* library catalog, web page, access to other libraries' catalogs. *Collection:* 98,202 titles, 391 serial subscriptions, 1,539 audiovisual materials.

Computer facilities: 12 computers available on campus for general student use. A campuswide network can be accessed from student residence rooms and from off campus. *Web address:* http://www.ltss.edu/.

General Application Contact: Jenny Tomalka, Director of Admissions, 800-804-5233, E-mail: jtomalka@ltss.edu.

GRADUATE UNITS

Graduate and Professional Programs Students: 135 full-time (65 women), 49 part-time (22 women); includes 15 minority (all Black or African American, non-Hispanic/Latino), 1 international. Average age 37. 73 applicants, 96% accepted, 45 enrolled. *Faculty:* 15 full-time (4 women), 4 part-time/adjunct (3 women). Expenses: Contact institution. *Financial support:* In 2010–11, 94 students received support; teaching assistantships, career-related internships or fieldwork, institutionally sponsored loans, scholarships/grants, health care benefits, tuition waivers (partial), unspecified assistantships, and on-campus employment available. Support available to part-time students. Financial award application deadline: 3/15; financial award applicants required to submit FAFSA. In 2010, 28 first professional degrees, 12 master's awarded. *Degree program information:* Part-time programs available. Offers theology (M Div, MAR, STM, D Min). *Application deadline:* For fall admission, 5/15 priority date for domestic students, 10/1 for international students; for spring admission, 12/1 priority date for domestic students. Applications are processed on a rolling basis. *Application fee:* $35. *Application Contact:* Jenny Tomalka, Director of Admissions, 800-804-5233, E-mail: jtomalka@ltss.edu. *President,* Rev. Dr. Marcus J. Miller, 803-786-5150, Fax: 803-786-6499, E-mail: mmiller@ltss.edu.

LUTHER RICE UNIVERSITY, Lithonia, GA 30038-2454

General Information Independent-religious, coed, comprehensive institution. *Graduate housing:* On-campus housing not available.

GRADUATE UNITS

Graduate Programs *Degree program information:* Part-time programs available. Postbaccalaureate distance learning degree programs offered (no on-campus study). Offers Bible/theology (M Div); Christian education (M Div); Christian studies (MA); church ministry (D Min); counseling (M Div); discipleship counseling (MA); ministry (M Div, MA); missions/evangelism (M Div).

LUTHER SEMINARY, St. Paul, MN 55108-1445

General Information Independent-religious, coed, graduate-only institution. *Graduate housing:* Rooms and/or apartments available on a first-come, first-served basis to single and married students.

GRADUATE UNITS

Graduate and Professional Programs Offers theology (M Div, M Th, MA, MSM, D Min, PhD). Electronic applications accepted.

LYNCHBURG COLLEGE, Lynchburg, VA 24501-3199

General Information Independent-religious, coed, comprehensive institution. *Enrollment:* 2,643 graduate, professional, and undergraduate students; 133 full-time matriculated graduate/professional students (91 women), 213 part-time matriculated graduate/professional students (145 women). *Enrollment by degree level:* 52 first professional, 267 master's, 27 other advanced degrees. *Graduate faculty:* 43 full-time (25 women), 13 part-time/adjunct (7 women). *Tuition:* Full-time $7200; part-time $400 per credit hour. *Required fees:* $20; $5.10 per credit hour. $15 per term. Tuition and fees vary according to degree level and program. *Graduate housing:* On-campus housing not available. *Student services:* Campus employment opportunities, career counseling, exercise/wellness program, free psychological counseling, international student services, multicultural affairs office, services for students with disabilities, teacher training, writing training. *Library facilities:* Knight-Capron Library. *Online resources:* library catalog, web page. *Collection:* 326,000 titles, 271 serial subscriptions, 8,051 audiovisual materials.

Computer facilities: 300 computers available on campus for general student use. A campuswide network can be accessed from student residence rooms. Online class registration is available. *Web address:* http://www.lynchburg.edu/.

General Application Contact: Dr. Edward Polloway, Vice President for Community Advancement/Dean of Graduate Studies, 434-544-8655, E-mail: polloway@lynchburg.edu.

GRADUATE UNITS

Graduate Studies *Degree program information:* Part-time and evening/weekend programs available. Electronic applications accepted.

School of Business and Economics *Degree program information:* Part-time and evening/weekend programs available. Offers business administration (MBA).

School of Communications and the Arts *Degree program information:* Part-time and evening/weekend programs available. Offers music (MA).

School of Education and Human Development *Degree program information:* Part-time and evening/weekend programs available. Offers clinical mental health counseling (M Ed); community counseling (M Ed); counselor education (M Ed); curriculum and instruction (M Ed); educational leadership (M Ed); leadership studies (Ed D); reading (M Ed); school counseling (M Ed); science education (M Ed); special education (M Ed).

School of Health Sciences and Human Performance Offers nursing (MS); physical therapy (DPT).

School of Humanities and Social Sciences *Degree program information:* Part-time programs available. Offers English (MA); history (MA).

LYNDON STATE COLLEGE, Lyndonville, VT 05851-0919

General Information State-supported, coed, comprehensive institution. *Graduate housing:* On-campus housing not available.

GRADUATE UNITS

Graduate Programs in Education *Degree program information:* Part-time and evening/weekend programs available. Offers curriculum and instruction (M Ed); education (M Ed); natural sciences (MST); reading specialist (M Ed); science education (MST); special education (M Ed); teaching and counseling (M Ed).

LYNN UNIVERSITY, Boca Raton, FL 33431-5598

General Information Independent, coed, comprehensive institution. *Graduate housing:* Room and/or apartments available on a first-come, first-served basis to single students; on-campus housing not available to married students.

GRADUATE UNITS

College of Business and Management *Degree program information:* Part-time and evening/weekend programs available. Postbaccalaureate distance learning degree programs offered. Offers aviation management (MBA); financial valuation and investment management (MBA); hospitality management (MBA); international business (MBA); marketing (MBA); mass communication and media management (MBA); sports and athletics administration (MBA). Electronic applications accepted.

Lynn University (continued)

College of Liberal Education *Degree program information:* Part-time and evening/weekend programs available. Postbaccalaureate distance learning degree programs offered. Offers applied psychology (MS); criminal justice administration (MS); emergency planning and administration (MS, Certificate).

Conservatory of Music *Degree program information:* Part-time and evening/weekend programs available. Offers composition (MM); performance (MM); professional performance (Certificate).

Donald and Helen Ross College of Education *Degree program information:* Part-time and evening/weekend programs available. Offers educational leadership (M Ed, PhD); exceptional student education (M Ed); teacher preparation (PhD). Electronic applications accepted.

Eugene M. and Christine E. Lynn College of International Communication *Degree program information:* Part-time and evening/weekend programs available. Offers communication and media (MS).

MACHZIKEI HADATH RABBINICAL COLLEGE, Brooklyn, NY 11204-1805

General Information Independent-religious, men only, comprehensive institution. *Graduate housing:* Room and/or apartments available to single students; on-campus housing not available to married students.

GRADUATE UNITS

Graduate Programs

MADONNA UNIVERSITY, Livonia, MI 48150-1173

General Information Independent-religious, coed, comprehensive institution. *Graduate housing:* Room and/or apartments available on a first-come, first-served basis to single students; on-campus housing not available to married students. Housing application deadline: 4/29.

GRADUATE UNITS

Department of English *Degree program information:* Part-time and evening/weekend programs available. Offers teaching English to speakers of other languages (MATESOL). Electronic applications accepted.

Department of Psychology *Degree program information:* Part-time and evening/weekend programs available. Offers clinical psychology (MSCP). Electronic applications accepted.

Program in Health Services *Degree program information:* Part-time programs available. Offers health services (MSHS). Electronic applications accepted.

Program in Hospice *Degree program information:* Part-time and evening/weekend programs available. Offers hospice (MSH). Electronic applications accepted.

Program in Liberal Studies Offers liberal studies (MALS).

Program in Nursing *Degree program information:* Part-time programs available. Offers adult health: chronic health conditions (MSN); adult nurse practitioner (MSN); nursing administration (MSN). Electronic applications accepted.

Program in Religious Studies Offers pastoral ministry (MA).

Programs in Education *Degree program information:* Part-time and evening/weekend programs available. Offers Catholic school leadership (MSA); educational leadership (MSA); learning disabilities (MAT); literacy education (MAT); teaching and learning (MAT). Electronic applications accepted.

School of Business *Degree program information:* Part-time and evening/weekend programs available. Postbaccalaureate distance learning degree programs offered (minimal on-campus study). Offers business administration (MBA); international business (MSBA); leadership studies (MSBA); leadership studies in criminal justice (MSBA); quality and operations management (MSBA). Electronic applications accepted.

MAHARISHI UNIVERSITY OF MANAGEMENT, Fairfield, IA 52557

General Information Independent, coed, university. *Graduate housing:* Room and/or apartments guaranteed to single students; on-campus housing not available to married students. Housing application deadline: 8/1.

GRADUATE UNITS

Graduate Studies *Degree program information:* Evening/weekend programs available. Postbaccalaureate distance learning degree programs offered (minimal on-campus study). Offers accounting (MBA); business administration (PhD); computer science (MS); Maharishi Vedic science (MA, PhD); sustainability (MBA); teaching elementary education (MA); teaching secondary education (MA). Electronic applications accepted.

MAINE COLLEGE OF ART, Portland, ME 04101

General Information Independent, coed, comprehensive institution. *Enrollment:* 341 graduate, professional, and undergraduate students; 23 full-time matriculated graduate/professional students (19 women). *Enrollment by degree level:* 23 master's. *Graduate faculty:* 1 (woman) full-time, 26 part-time/adjunct (14 women). *Tuition:* Full-time $27,695. *Required fees:* $250. One-time fee: $50 full-time. *Graduate housing:* Room and/or apartments available on a first-come, first-served basis to single students; on-campus housing not available to married students. Housing application deadline: 4/1. *Student services:* Campus employment opportunities, free psychological counseling, international student services, low-cost health insurance, services for students with disabilities, teacher training. *Library facilities:* Joanne Waxman Library. *Online resources:* library catalog, web page, access to other libraries' catalogs. *Collection:* 33,000 titles, 102 serial subscriptions, 423 audiovisual materials.

Computer facilities: Computer purchase and lease plans are available. 86 computers available on campus for general student use. A campuswide network can be accessed from student residence rooms and from off campus. Online class registration is available. *Web address:* http://www.meca.edu/.

General Application Contact: Rachel A. Katz, Administrative Director, MFA in Studio Art, 207-699-5030, Fax: 207-775-5087, E-mail: rkatz@meca.edu.

GRADUATE UNITS

Program in Studio Arts Students: 23 full-time (19 women). Average age 30. 56 applicants, 12 enrolled. *Faculty:* 1 (woman) full-time, 26 part-time/adjunct (14 women). Expenses: Contact institution. *Financial support:* Application deadline: 3/1. In 2010, 11 master's awarded. Offers studio arts (MFA). *Application deadline:* Applications are processed on a rolling basis. *Application fee:* $40 ($60 for international students). Electronic applications accepted. *Application Contact:* Rachel A. Katz, Administrative Director, MFA in Studio Art, 207-699-5030, Fax: 207-775-5087, E-mail: rkatz@meca.edu. *Administrative Director, MFA in Studio Art,* Rachel A. Katz, 207-699-5030, Fax: 207-775-5087, E-mail: rkatz@meca.edu.

MAINE MARITIME ACADEMY, Castine, ME 04420

General Information State-supported, coed, primarily men, comprehensive institution. *Graduate housing:* Rooms and/or apartments available on a first-come, first-served basis to single and married students. Housing application deadline: 3/15.

GRADUATE UNITS

Department of Graduate Studies *Degree program information:* Part-time and evening/weekend programs available. Postbaccalaureate distance learning degree programs offered (no on-campus study). Offers global supply chain management (MS, Certificate, Diploma); international business (MS, Certificate, Diploma); maritime management (MS, Certificate, Diploma). Electronic applications accepted.

MALONE UNIVERSITY, Canton, OH 44709

General Information Independent-religious, coed, comprehensive institution. *Enrollment:* 2,512 graduate, professional, and undergraduate students; 63 full-time matriculated graduate/professional students (42 women), 361 part-time matriculated graduate/professional students (239 women). *Enrollment by degree level:* 424 master's. *Graduate faculty:* 34 full-time (20 women), 50 part-time/adjunct (26 women). *Tuition:* Part-time $475 per semester hour. Tuition and fees vary according to program. *Graduate housing:* On-campus housing not available. *Student services:* Career counseling, multicultural affairs office, services for students with disabilities, writing training. *Library facilities:* Everett L. Cattell Library. *Online resources:* library catalog, web page, access to other libraries' catalogs. *Collection:* 248,064 titles, 52,231 serial subscriptions, 14,956 audiovisual materials.

Computer facilities: Computer purchase and lease plans are available. 225 computers available on campus for general student use. A campuswide network can be accessed from student residence rooms and from off campus. Online class registration, online advising, online financial aid information, and online credit card payments are available. *Web address:* http://www3.malone.edu/.

General Application Contact: Dr. Brock C. Schroeder, Vice President for Enrollment Management, 330-471-8156, Fax: 330-471-8149, E-mail: bschroeder@malone.edu.

GRADUATE UNITS

Graduate Program in Business Students: 5 full-time (3 women), 93 part-time (36 women); includes 8 Black or African American, non-Hispanic/Latino; 1 Asian, non-Hispanic/Latino; 2 Hispanic/Latino, 1 international. Average age 34. 49 applicants, 61% accepted, 14 enrolled. *Faculty:* 9 full-time (3 women), 7 part-time/adjunct (3 women). Expenses: Contact institution. *Financial support:* Tuition waivers (partial) available. Support available to part-time students. Financial award application deadline: 6/30. In 2010, 61 master's awarded. *Degree program information:* Part-time and evening/weekend programs available. Offers business (MBA). *Application deadline:* Applications are processed on a rolling basis. *Application fee:* $25. *Application Contact:* Mona J. McAuliffe, Corporate Recruiter for Graduate and Professional Studies, 330-471-8623, Fax: 330-471-8343, E-mail: mmcauliffe@malone.edu. *Director,* Dr. Julia A. Frankland, 330-471-8552, Fax: 330-471-8563, E-mail: jfrankland@malone.edu.

Graduate Program in Counseling and Human Development Students: 31 full-time (23 women), 116 part-time (95 women); includes 17 Black or African American, non-Hispanic/Latino; 1 Asian, non-Hispanic/Latino. Average age 33. 75 applicants, 52% accepted, 29 enrolled. *Faculty:* 3 full-time (2 women), 11 part-time/adjunct (6 women). Expenses: Contact institution. *Financial support:* Tuition waivers (partial) available. Support available to part-time students. Financial award application deadline: 6/30. In 2010, 41 master's awarded. *Degree program information:* Part-time and evening/weekend programs available. Offers classroom-based counseling and advocacy (MA); clinical counseling (MA); school counseling (MA). *Application deadline:* Applications are processed on a rolling basis. *Application fee:* $25. *Application Contact:* Dan DePasquale, Senior Recruiter, 330-471-8381, Fax: 330-471-8343, E-mail: depasquale@malone.edu. *Director,* Dr. Susan L. Steiner, 330-471-8510, Fax: 330-471-8343, E-mail: ssteiner@malone.edu.

Graduate Program in Education Students: 2 full-time (1 woman), 44 part-time (32 women); includes 1 Black or African American, non-Hispanic/Latino. Average age 35. 33 applicants, 82% accepted, 10 enrolled. *Faculty:* 7 full-time (5 women), 10 part-time/adjunct (6 women). Expenses: Contact institution. *Financial support:* Tuition waivers (partial) available. Support available to part-time students. Financial award application deadline: 6/30. In 2010, 31 master's awarded. *Degree program information:* Part-time and evening/weekend programs available. Offers curriculum and instruction (MA); curriculum, instruction, and professional development (MA); intervention specialist (MA); reading (MA). *Application deadline:* Applications are processed on a rolling basis. *Application fee:* $25. *Application Contact:* Dan DePasquale, Senior Recruiter, 330-471-8381, Fax: 330-471-8343, E-mail: depasquale@malone.edu. *Director,* Dr. Alice E. Christie, 330-478-8541, Fax: 330-471-8563, E-mail: achristie@malone.edu.

Graduate Program in Nursing Students: 60 part-time (53 women); includes 1 Black or African American, non-Hispanic/Latino; 1 Asian, non-Hispanic/Latino. Average age 37. 77 applicants, 49% accepted, 30 enrolled. *Faculty:* 7 full-time (all women), 15 part-time/adjunct (11 women). Expenses: Contact institution. *Financial support:* Tuition waivers (partial) available. Support available to part-time students. Financial award application deadline: 6/30. In 2010, 15 master's awarded. *Degree program information:* Part-time and evening/weekend programs available. Offers clinical nurse specialist (MSN); family nurse practitioner (MSN). *Application deadline:* Applications are processed on a rolling basis. *Application fee:* $25. *Application Contact:* Heather Pritchard, Recruiter/Adviser, 330-471-8134, Fax: 330-471-8343, E-mail: hpritchard@malone.edu. *Director,* Dr. Kathleen M. Geib Flaherty, 330-471-8330, Fax: 330-471-8607, E-mail: kgeib@malone.edu.

Graduate Program in Organizational Leadership Students: 22 full-time (14 women), 14 part-time (9 women); includes 5 Black or African American, non-Hispanic/Latino. Average age 39. 61 applicants, 77% accepted, 36 enrolled. *Faculty:* 6 full-time (4 women), 3 part-time/adjunct (0 women). Expenses: Contact institution. *Financial support:* Tuition waivers (partial) available. Support available to part-time students. Financial award application deadline: 6/30. *Degree program information:* Part-time and evening/weekend programs available. Offers organizational leadership (MAOL). *Application Contact:* Mona J. McAuliffe, Corporate Recruiter for Graduate and Professional Studies, 330-471-8623, Fax: 330-471-8343, E-mail: mmcauliffe@malone.edu. *Director,* Dr. Mary E. Quinn, 330-471-8556, Fax: 330-471-8343, E-mail: mquinn@malone.edu.

Graduate Program in Theological Studies Students: 3 full-time (1 woman), 34 part-time (14 women); includes 10 Black or African American, non-Hispanic/Latino; 1 Asian, non-Hispanic/Latino. Average age 37. 29 applicants, 69% accepted, 12 enrolled. *Faculty:* 5 full-time (0 women), 4 part-time/adjunct (0 women). Expenses: Contact institution. *Financial support:* Tuition waivers (partial) and unspecified assistantships available. Support available to part-time students. Financial award application deadline: 6/30. In 2010, 8 master's awarded. *Degree program information:* Part-time and evening/weekend programs available. Offers theological studies: general track (MA). *Application deadline:* Applications are processed on a rolling basis. *Application fee:* $25. *Application Contact:* Heather Pritchard, Recruiter/Adviser, 330-471-8134, Fax: 330-471-8343, E-mail: hpritchard@malone.edu. *Director,* Dr. Larry D. Reinhart, 330-471-8198, Fax: 330-471-8477, E-mail: lreinhart@malone.edu.

MANCHESTER COLLEGE, North Manchester, IN 46962-1225

General Information Independent-religious, coed, comprehensive institution. *Enrollment:* 1,278 graduate, professional, and undergraduate students; 3 full-time matriculated graduate/professional students, 1 part-time matriculated graduate/professional student. *Enrollment by degree level:* 4 master's. *Graduate faculty:* 7 full-time (4 women). *Tuition:* Full-time $25,100; part-time $700 per credit hour. *Required fees:* $600. Tuition and fees vary according to course load and program. *Graduate housing:* Rooms and/or apartments available on a first-come, first-served basis to single and married students. Typical cost: $7700 per year ($11,500 including board) for single students. Room and board charges vary according to board plan and housing facility selected. *Student services:* Campus safety program, career counseling, multicultural affairs office. *Library facilities:* Funderburg Library. *Online resources:* library catalog, web page, access to other libraries' catalogs.

Computer facilities: Computer purchase and lease plans are available. 222 computers available on campus for general student use. A campuswide network can be accessed from student residence rooms and from off campus. Online class registration is available. *Web address:* http://www.manchester.edu/.

General Application Contact: Dr. Mark Huntington, Associate Dean for Academic Affairs, 260-982-5033, E-mail: mwhuntington@manchester.edu.

GRADUATE UNITS

Graduate Programs Students: 3 full-time, 1 part-time. Average age 22. 13 applicants, 100% accepted, 4 enrolled. *Faculty:* 7 full-time (4 women). Expenses: Contact institution. *Financial support:* In 2010–11, 2 students received support, including 2 research assistantships (averaging $6,143 per year). Financial award application deadline: 5/1; financial award applicants required to submit FAFSA. *Degree program information:* Part-time and evening/weekend programs available. Postbaccalaureate distance learning degree programs offered (minimal on-campus study). Offers athletic training (MAT); education (M Ed). *Application deadline:* Applications are processed on a rolling basis. Electronic applications accepted. *Application Contact:* Dr. Mark Huntington, Associate Dean for Academic Affairs, 260-982-5033, E-mail:

mwhuntington@manchester.edu. *Associate Dean for Academic Affairs*, Dr. Mark Huntington, 260-982-5033, E-mail: mwhuntington@manchester.edu.

MANHATTAN COLLEGE, Riverdale, NY 10471

General Information Independent-religious, coed, comprehensive institution. *Enrollment:* 3,412 graduate, professional, and undergraduate students; 156 full-time matriculated graduate/professional students (99 women), 254 part-time matriculated graduate/professional students (142 women). *Enrollment by degree level:* 410 master's. *Graduate faculty:* 41 full-time (10 women), 51 part-time/adjunct (28 women). *Graduate housing:* Rooms and/or apartments available on a first-come, first-served basis to single and married students. Typical cost: $11,050 (including board) for single students; $11,050 (including board) for married students. Room and board charges vary according to board plan. *Student services:* Career counseling, free psychological counseling, low-cost health insurance, services for students with disabilities. *Library facilities:* O'Malley Library plus 1 other. *Online resources:* library catalog, web page, access to other libraries' catalogs. *Collection:* 291,420 titles, 742 serial subscriptions, 2,533 audiovisual materials.

Computer facilities: 350 computers available on campus for general student use. A campuswide network can be accessed from student residence rooms and from off campus. Online class registration, course management system are available. *Web address:* http://www.manhattan.edu/.

General Application Contact: William Bisset, Vice President for Enrollment, 718-862-7199, Fax: 718-862-8019, E-mail: william.bisset@manhattan.edu.

GRADUATE UNITS

Graduate Division Students: 156 full-time (99 women), 254 part-time (142 women). Average age 31. 300 applicants, 74% accepted, 187 enrolled. *Faculty:* 41 full-time (12 women), 48 part-time/adjunct (17 women). Expenses: Contact institution. *Financial support:* Fellowships, research assistantships, teaching assistantships, career-related internships or fieldwork, Federal Work-Study, scholarships/grants, tuition waivers (full and partial), and laboratory assistantships available. Support available to part-time students. Financial award application deadline: 2/1. In 2010, 150 master's, 15 other advanced degrees awarded. *Degree program information:* Part-time and evening/weekend programs available. *Application deadline:* For fall admission, 8/10 priority date for domestic and international students; for winter admission, 1/7 priority date for domestic and international students; for spring admission, 1/7 priority date for domestic and international students. Applications are processed on a rolling basis. *Application fee:* $50. *Application Contact:* Dr. Weldon Jackson, Provost, 718-862-7303, Fax: 718-862-8014, E-mail: weldon.jackson@manhattan.edu. *Provost*, Dr. Weldon Jackson, 718-862-7303, Fax: 718-862-8014, E-mail: weldon.jackson@manhattan.edu.

School of Education Students: 95 full-time (77 women), 237 part-time (203 women). Average age 31. 299 applicants, 84% accepted, 148 enrolled. *Faculty:* 12 full-time (8 women), 39 part-time/adjunct (29 women). Expenses: Contact institution. *Financial support:* Federal Work-Study, scholarships/grants, tuition waivers (partial), and unspecified assistantships available. Financial award application deadline: 2/1. In 2010, 72 master's, 21 other advanced degrees awarded. *Degree program information:* Part-time and evening/weekend programs available. Offers bilingual (Certificate); bilingual counseling (Certificate); counseling (MA, MS, Certificate, Diploma); counseling and pupil personnel services (Diploma); dual childhood/special education (MS Ed); mental health counseling (MS); school building leadership (MS, MS Ed, Professional Diploma); school counseling (MA); special education (MS Ed, Certificate). *Application deadline:* For fall admission, 8/10 priority date for domestic students; for spring admission, 1/7 priority date for domestic students. Applications are processed on a rolling basis. *Application Contact:* Dr. William Merriman, Dean, 718-862-7373, Fax: 718-862-8011. *Dean*, Dr. William Merriman, 718-862-7373, Fax: 718-862-8011.

School of Engineering Students: 54 full-time (12 women), 104 part-time (31 women); includes 17 Black or African American, non-Hispanic/Latino; 2 Asian, non-Hispanic/Latino; 15 Hispanic/Latino; 3 Two or more races, non-Hispanic/Latino, 11 international. Average age 28. 126 applicants, 73% accepted, 70 enrolled. *Faculty:* 29 full-time (2 women), 14 part-time/adjunct (0 women). Expenses: Contact institution. *Financial support:* In 2010–11, 29 students received support; fellowships with partial tuition reimbursements available, research assistantships with partial tuition reimbursements available, teaching assistantships with partial tuition reimbursements available, career-related internships or fieldwork, Federal Work-Study, scholarships/grants, and laboratory assistantships available. Support available to part-time students. Financial award application deadline: 2/1. In 2010, 48 master's awarded. *Degree program information:* Part-time and evening/weekend programs available. Offers chemical engineering (MS); civil engineering (MS); computer engineering (MS); electrical engineering (MS); environmental engineering (ME, MS); mechanical engineering (MS). *Application deadline:* For fall admission, 8/10 priority date for domestic students, 8/10 for international students; for spring admission, 1/7 for domestic and international students. Applications are processed on a rolling basis. *Application fee:* $50. *Application Contact:* Sheila M. Halpin, Information Contact, 718-862-7281, Fax: 718-862-8015, E-mail: deanengr@manhattan.edu. *Dean*, Dr. Tim J. Ward, 718-862-7281, Fax: 718-862-8015, E-mail: deanengr@manhattan.edu.

MANHATTAN SCHOOL OF MUSIC, New York, NY 10027-4698

General Information Independent, coed, comprehensive institution. *Graduate housing:* Room and/or apartments available on a first-come, first-served basis to single students; on-campus housing not available to married students. Housing application deadline: 6/15.

GRADUATE UNITS

Graduate Programs Offers composition (MM, DMA); jazz (MM, DMA); music performance (MM, DMA); orchestral performance (MM). Electronic applications accepted.

Professional Studies Certificate Program Offers instrumental music (CPS); vocal music (CPS). Electronic applications accepted.

MANHATTANVILLE COLLEGE, Purchase, NY 10577-2132

General Information Independent, coed, comprehensive institution. *Enrollment:* 2,695 graduate, professional, and undergraduate students; 355 full-time matriculated graduate/professional students (232 women), 677 part-time matriculated graduate/professional students (470 women). *Enrollment by degree level:* 1,032 master's. *Tuition:* Full-time $16,110; part-time $895 per credit. *Required fees:* $50 per semester. *Graduate housing:* Room and/or apartments available to single students. Housing application deadline: 7/1. *Student services:* Campus employment opportunities, campus safety program, career counseling, exercise/wellness program, free psychological counseling, international student services, multicultural affairs office, services for students with disabilities, teacher training, writing training. *Library facilities:* Manhattanville College Library. *Online resources:* library catalog, web page, access to other libraries' catalogs. *Collection:* 250,209 titles, 36,923 serial subscriptions, 5,312 audiovisual materials.

Computer facilities: Computer purchase and lease plans are available. 240 computers available on campus for general student use. A campuswide network can be accessed from student residence rooms and from off campus. Online class registration is available. *Web address:* http://www.manhattanville.edu/.

General Application Contact: Kathy Fitzgerald, Graduate Admissions, 914-694-2200, Fax: 914-694-1732, E-mail: admissions@mville.edu.

GRADUATE UNITS

Graduate Programs Students: 355 full-time (232 women), 677 part-time (470 women); includes 30 Black or African American, non-Hispanic/Latino; 10 Asian, non-Hispanic/Latino; 45 Hispanic/Latino, 8 international. Expenses: Contact institution. *Financial support:* Career-related internships or fieldwork, Federal Work-Study, institutionally sponsored loans, scholarships/grants, tuition waivers (partial), and unspecified assistantships available. Support available to part-time students. Financial award application deadline: 3/1; financial award applicants required to submit FAFSA. In 2010, 407 master's awarded. *Degree program information:* Part-time and evening/weekend programs available. Offers finance (MS); integrated marketing communications (MS); international management (MS); leadership and strategic management (MS); liberal studies (MA); organizational management and human resource development (MS); sport business management (MS); writing (MA). *Application deadline:*

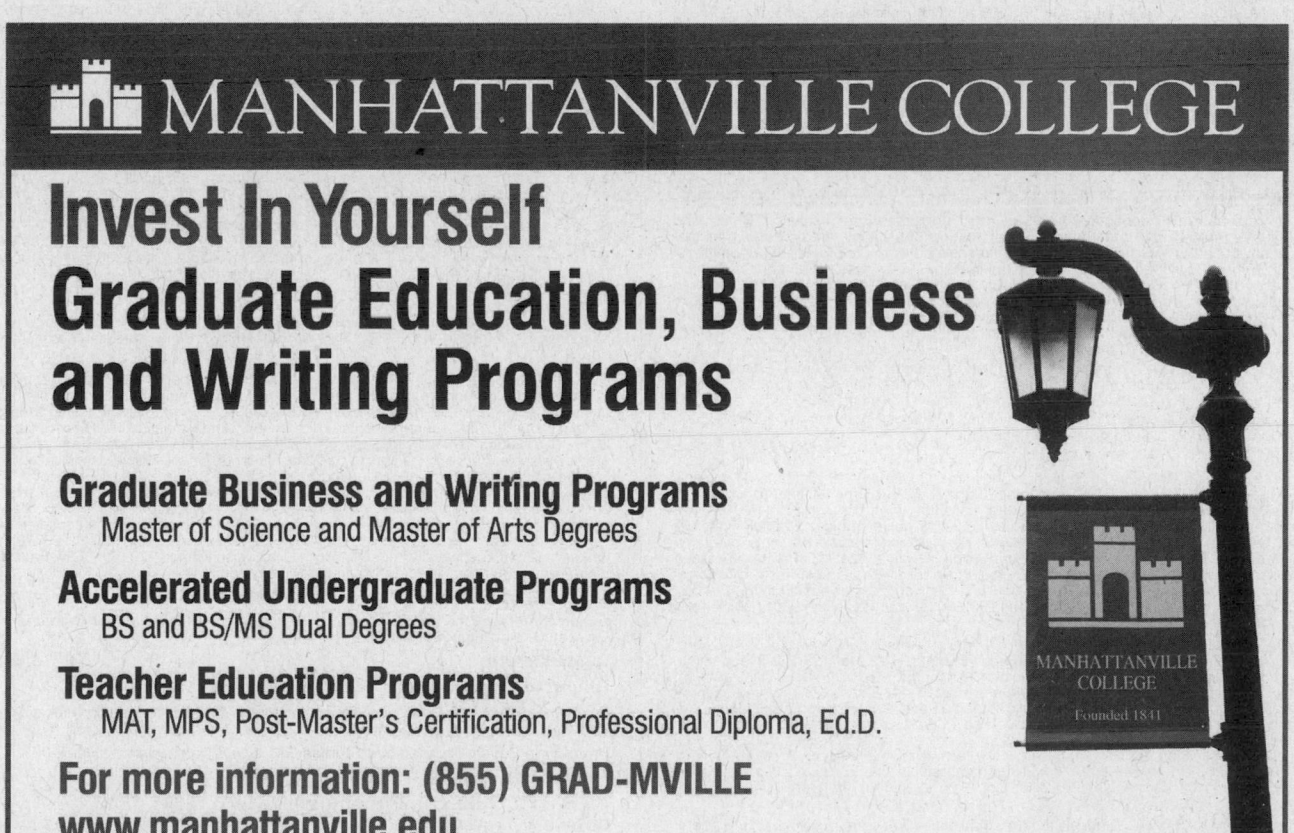

Manhattanville College (continued)

Applications are processed on a rolling basis. *Application fee:* $75. *Application Contact:* Kathy Fitzgerald, Office of Graduate Admissions, 914-323-5464, E-mail: admissions@mville.edu. *Provost,* Dr. Gail Simmons, 914-323-5262, E-mail: provost@mville.edu.

School of Education Students: 321 full-time (225 women), 590 part-time (429 women); includes 26 Black or African American, non-Hispanic/Latino; 9 Asian, non-Hispanic/Latino; 41 Hispanic/Latino, 5 international. Expenses: Contact institution. *Financial support:* Career-related internships or fieldwork, Federal Work-Study, institutionally sponsored loans, and unspecified assistantships available. Financial award application deadline: 3/1; financial award applicants required to submit FAFSA. In 2010, 295 master's awarded. *Degree program information:* Part-time and evening/weekend programs available. Offers biology (MAT); biology and special education (MPS); chemistry (MAT); chemistry and special education (MPS); child and early childhood education (MAT, MPS); childhood and early childhood education (MAT); childhood and special education (MPS); childhood education (MAT); early childhood education (birth-grade 2) (MAT); education (M Ed, MAT, MPS, Ed D); educational leadership (MPS, Ed D); English (MAT); English and special education (MPS); English as a second language (MAT); literacy (MPS); literacy (birth-grade 6) (MPS); literacy (birth-grade 6) and special education (grades 1-6) (MPS); literacy and special education (MPS); math (MAT); math and special education (MPS); music education (MAT); physical education and sport pedagogy (MAT); second language (MAT); social studies (MAT); social studies and special education (MPS); special education (MPS); special education (birth-grade 2) (MPS); special education (birth-grade 6) (MPS); special education childhood (MPS); teaching English as a second language (MPS); visual arts education (MAT). *Application deadline:* Applications are processed on a rolling basis. *Application fee:* $75. Electronic applications accepted. *Application Contact:* Jeanine Pardey-Levine, Director of Admissions, 914-323-3208, Fax: 914-694-1732, E-mail: edschool@mville.edu. *Dean,* Dr. Shelley Wepner, 914-323-5192, Fax: 914-694-2386, E-mail: wepners@mville.edu.

See Display on previous page and Close-Up on page 965.

MANSFIELD UNIVERSITY OF PENNSYLVANIA, Mansfield, PA 16933

General Information State-supported, coed, comprehensive institution. *Enrollment:* 3,411 graduate, professional, and undergraduate students; 86 full-time matriculated graduate/professional students (65 women), 380 part-time matriculated graduate/professional students (329 women). *Enrollment by degree level:* 466 master's. Tuition, state resident: full-time $6966; part-time $387 per credit hour. Tuition, nonresident: full-time $11,146; part-time $619 per credit hour. *Required fees:* $1456; $68 per credit hour. *Graduate housing:* Room and/or apartments available on a first-come, first-served basis to single students; on-campus housing not available to married students. Typical cost: $2600 per year ($6870 including board). Room and board charges vary according to board plan and campus/location. *Student services:* Campus employment opportunities, campus safety program, career counseling, child daycare facilities, exercise/wellness program, free psychological counseling, grant writing training, international student services, low-cost health insurance, multicultural affairs office, services for students with disabilities, teacher training. *Library facilities:* North Hall Library. *Online resources:* library catalog, web page, access to other libraries' catalogs. *Collection:* 246,423 titles, 631 serial subscriptions, 31,369 audiovisual materials.

Computer facilities: 661 computers available on campus for general student use. A campuswide network can be accessed from student residence rooms and from off campus. Online class registration is available. *Web address:* http://www.mansfield.edu/.

General Application Contact: Judith Brayer, Director of Online Programs and Graduate Admissions, 570-662-4818, Fax: 570-662-4121, E-mail: jbrayer@mansfield.edu.

GRADUATE UNITS

Graduate Studies *Degree program information:* Part-time and evening/weekend programs available. Postbaccalaureate distance learning degree programs offered (no on-campus study). Offers art education (M Ed); band conducting (MA); choral conducting (MA); elementary education (M Ed); library science (M Ed); nursing (MSN); organizational leadership (MA); performance (MA); secondary education (MS). Electronic applications accepted.

MAPLE SPRINGS BAPTIST BIBLE COLLEGE AND SEMINARY, Capitol Heights, MD 20743

General Information Independent-religious, coed, comprehensive institution. *Graduate housing:* On-campus housing not available.

GRADUATE UNITS

Graduate and Professional Programs Offers biblical studies (MA, Certificate); Christian counseling (MA); church administration (MA); divinity (M Div); ministry (D Min); religious education (MRE).

MARANATHA BAPTIST BIBLE COLLEGE, Watertown, WI 53094

General Information Independent-religious, coed, comprehensive institution. *Enrollment:* 963 graduate, professional, and undergraduate students; 29 full-time matriculated graduate/professional students (3 women), 55 part-time matriculated graduate/professional students (7 women). *Enrollment by degree level:* 84 master's. *Graduate faculty:* 4 full-time (0 women), 5 part-time/adjunct (0 women). *Tuition:* Full-time $4160; part-time $260 per credit hour. *Required fees:* $350; $23 per credit hour. *Graduate housing:* On-campus housing not available. *Student services:* Campus employment opportunities. *Library facilities:* Cedarholm Library and Resource Center. *Online resources:* library catalog, web page, access to other libraries' catalogs. *Collection:* 124,000 titles, 500 serial subscriptions.

Computer facilities: 120 computers available on campus for general student use. A campuswide network can be accessed from student residence rooms and from off campus. Online class registration is available. *Web address:* http://www.mbbc.edu/.

General Application Contact: Dr. Jim Harrison, Director of Admissions, 920-206-2327, Fax: 920-261-9109, E-mail: admissions@mbbc.edu.

GRADUATE UNITS

Program in Biblical Counseling Students: 6 full-time (3 women), 12 part-time (7 women). Average age 24. 2 applicants, 100% accepted, 2 enrolled. *Faculty:* 4 full-time (0 women), 5 part-time/adjunct (0 women). Expenses: Contact institution. *Financial support:* In 2010–11, 2 students received support. Scholarships/grants and tuition waivers (full and partial) available. Support available to part-time students. *Degree program information:* Part-time programs available. Offers Biblical counseling (MA). *Application deadline:* Applications are processed on a rolling basis. *Application fee:* $50. *Application Contact:* Dr. Jim Harrison, Director of Admissions, 920-206-2327, Fax: 920-261-9109, E-mail: admissions@mbbc.edu. *Dean of Maranatha Baptist Seminary,* Dr. Larry Oats, 920-206-2324, Fax: 920-261-9109, E-mail: loats@mbbc.edu.

Program in Biblical Studies Students: 10 full-time (0 women), 12 part-time (0 women); includes 1 Asian, non-Hispanic/Latino; 1 Hispanic/Latino. Average age 27. 3 applicants, 100% accepted, 3 enrolled. *Faculty:* 4 full-time (0 women), 5 part-time/adjunct (0 women). Expenses: Contact institution. *Financial support:* In 2010–11, 8 students received support. Scholarships/grants and tuition waivers (full and partial) available. Support available to part-time students. In 2010, 8 master's awarded. *Degree program information:* Part-time programs available. Offers biblical studies (MA). *Application deadline:* Applications are processed on a rolling basis. *Application fee:* $50. *Application Contact:* Dr. Jim Harrison, Director of Admissions, 920-206-2327, Fax: 920-261-9109, E-mail: admissions@mbbc.edu. *Dean of Maranatha Baptist Seminary,* Dr. Larry Oats, 920-206-2324, Fax: 920-261-9109, E-mail: loats@mbbc.edu.

Program in Cross-Cultural Studies Students: 1 full-time (0 women), 1 part-time (0 women). Average age 24. 1 applicant, 100% accepted, 1 enrolled. *Faculty:* 4 full-time (0 women), 5 part-time/adjunct (0 women). Expenses: Contact institution. *Financial support:* Scholarships/grants and tuition waivers (full and partial) available. Support available to part-time students. *Degree program information:* Part-time programs available. Offers cross-cultural studies (MA). *Application deadline:* Applications are processed on a rolling basis. *Application fee:* $50. *Application Contact:* Dr. Jim Harrison, Director of Admissions, 920-206-2327, Fax: 920-261-9109, E-mail: admissions@mbbc.edu. *Dean of Maranatha Baptist Seminary,* Dr. Larry Oats, 920-206-2324, Fax: 920-261-9109, E-mail: loats@mbbc.edu.

Program in Divinity Students: 12 full-time (0 women), 10 part-time (0 women); includes 1 Asian, non-Hispanic/Latino; 1 Hispanic/Latino. Average age 25. 4 applicants, 100% accepted, 4 enrolled. *Faculty:* 4 full-time (0 women), 5 part-time/adjunct (0 women). Expenses: Contact institution. *Financial support:* In 2010–11, 4 students received support. Scholarships/grants and tuition waivers (full and partial) available. Support available to part-time students. *Degree program information:* Part-time programs available. Offers divinity (M Div). *Application deadline:* Applications are processed on a rolling basis. *Application fee:* $50. *Application Contact:* Dr. Jim Harrison, Director of Admissions, 920-206-2327, Fax: 920-261-9109, E-mail: admissions@mbbc.edu. *Dean of Maranatha Baptist Seminary,* Dr. Larry Oats, 920-206-2324, Fax: 920-261-9109, E-mail: loats@mbbc.edu.

Program in English Bible Students: 20 part-time (0 women). Average age 28. 10 applicants, 100% accepted, 10 enrolled. *Faculty:* 4 full-time (0 women), 5 part-time/adjunct (0 women). Expenses: Contact institution. *Degree program information:* Part-time programs available. Postbaccalaureate distance learning degree programs offered (no on-campus study). Offers English Bible (MA). *Application fee:* $50. *Application Contact:* Dr. Jim Harrison, Director of Admissions, 920-206-2327, Fax: 920-261-9109, E-mail: admissions@mbbc.edu. *Dean of Maranatha Baptist Seminary,* Dr. Larry Oats, 920-206-2324, Fax: 920-261-9109, E-mail: loats@mbbc.edu.

MARIAN UNIVERSITY, Indianapolis, IN 46222-1997

General Information Independent-religious, coed, comprehensive institution.

GRADUATE UNITS

School of Education *Degree program information:* Part-time and evening/weekend programs available. Offers education (MAT).

MARIAN UNIVERSITY, Fond du Lac, WI 54935-4699

General Information Independent-religious, coed, comprehensive institution. CGS member. *Enrollment:* 2,881 graduate, professional, and undergraduate students; 98 full-time matriculated graduate/professional students (75 women), 755 part-time matriculated graduate/professional students (518 women). *Enrollment by degree level:* 670 master's, 56 doctoral, 127 other advanced degrees. *Graduate faculty:* 22 full-time (13 women), 67 part-time/adjunct (43 women). *Tuition:* Part-time $400 per credit hour. Tuition and fees vary according to degree level and program. *Graduate housing:* On-campus housing not available. *Student services:* Campus employment opportunities, campus safety program, career counseling, child daycare facilities, exercise/wellness program, free psychological counseling, international student services, multicultural affairs office, services for students with disabilities, teacher training, writing training. *Library facilities:* Cardinal Meyer Library. *Online resources:* library catalog, web page, access to other libraries' catalogs. *Collection:* 118,008 titles, 1,503 serial subscriptions, 1,669 audiovisual materials.

Computer facilities: Computer purchase and lease plans are available. 450 computers available on campus for general student use. A campuswide network can be accessed from student residence rooms and from off campus. Online class registration is available. *Web address:* http://www.marianuniversity.edu/.

General Application Contact: Dr. Edward Ogle, Executive Vice President for Academic and Student Affairs, 920-923-7604, E-mail: eogle@marianuniversity.edu.

GRADUATE UNITS

Business Division Students: 11 full-time (6 women), 111 part-time (79 women); includes 7 Black or African American, non-Hispanic/Latino; 3 Asian, non-Hispanic/Latino; 4 Hispanic/Latino. Average age 38. 36 applicants, 92% accepted, 33 enrolled. *Faculty:* 17 part-time/adjunct (1 woman). Expenses: Contact institution. *Financial support:* In 2010–11, 8 students received support. Institutionally sponsored loans available. Support available to part-time students. Financial award application deadline: 3/1; financial award applicants required to submit FAFSA. In 2010, 52 master's awarded. *Degree program information:* Part-time and evening/weekend programs available. Offers organizational leadership and quality (MS). *Application deadline:* Applications are processed on a rolling basis. *Application fee:* $25. Electronic applications accepted. *Application Contact:* Tracy Qualman, Director of Marketing and Admission, 920-923-7159, Fax: 920-923-7167, E-mail: tqualmann@marianuniversity.edu. *Dean of PACE,* Donna Innes, 920-923-8760, Fax: 920-923-7167, E-mail: dinnes@marianuniversity.edu.

School of Education Students: 42 full-time (27 women), 608 part-time (404 women); includes 11 Black or African American, non-Hispanic/Latino; 6 American Indian or Alaska Native, non-Hispanic/Latino; 2 Asian, non-Hispanic/Latino; 10 Hispanic/Latino, 1 international. Average age 36. 105 applicants, 80% accepted, 84 enrolled. *Faculty:* 11 full-time (5 women), 46 part-time/adjunct (25 women). Expenses: Contact institution. *Financial support:* In 2010–11, 33 students received support. Federal Work-Study and institutionally sponsored loans available. Support available to part-time students. Financial award application deadline: 3/1; financial award applicants required to submit FAFSA. In 2010, 307 master's, 5 doctorates awarded. *Degree program information:* Part-time programs available. Offers educational leadership (MAE, PhD); leadership studies (PhD); teacher development (MAE). PhD in leadership studies offered with Business Division. *Application deadline:* Applications are processed on a rolling basis. *Application fee:* $50. *Application Contact:* Robert Bohnsack, Graduate Education Admissions, 920-923-8100, Fax: 920-923-7154, E-mail: bbohnsack@marianuniversity.edu. *Dean,* Sue Stoddart, 920-923-8099, Fax: 920-923-7663, E-mail: sstoddart@marianuniversity.edu.

School of Nursing Students: 45 full-time (42 women), 36 part-time (35 women); includes 2 Black or African American, non-Hispanic/Latino; 4 Asian, non-Hispanic/Latino; 1 Hispanic/Latino. Average age 39. 18 applicants, 83% accepted, 15 enrolled. *Faculty:* 5 full-time (4 women), 4 part-time/adjunct (3 women). Expenses: Contact institution. *Financial support:* In 2010–11, 3 students received support. Institutionally sponsored loans and scholarships/grants available. Support available to part-time students. Financial award application deadline: 3/1; financial award applicants required to submit FAFSA. In 2010, 15 master's awarded. *Degree program information:* Part-time and evening/weekend programs available. Offers adult nurse practitioner (MSN); nurse educator (MSN). *Application deadline:* Applications are processed on a rolling basis. *Application fee:* $50. Electronic applications accepted. *Application Contact:* Dr. Greta Kostac, Director, 920-923-7603, Fax: 920-923-8770, E-mail: gmkostac@marianuniversity.edu. *Dean,* Dr. Julie Luetschwager, 920-923-8094, Fax: 920-923-8770, E-mail: jaluetschwager25@marianuniversity.edu.

MARIETTA COLLEGE, Marietta, OH 45750-4000

General Information Independent, coed, comprehensive institution. *Graduate housing:* On-campus housing not available.

GRADUATE UNITS

Program in Corporate Media Offers corporate media (MCM).

Program in Education *Degree program information:* Part-time and evening/weekend programs available. Offers education (MA).

Program in Physician Assistant Studies Offers physician assistant studies (MS).

Program in Psychology Offers psychology (MAP).

MARIST COLLEGE, Poughkeepsie, NY 12601-1387

General Information Independent, coed, comprehensive institution. *Graduate housing:* On-campus housing not available. *Research affiliation:* Center for Advanced Brain Imaging Psychology (psychology), New York State Office of Technology and Academic Research (NYSTAR) (technology), Hudson Valley Technology Development Corporation (HVTDC) (technology), Hudson River Psychiatric Center (psychology), St. Francis Hospital, Dutchess County Community Mental Health Center (mental health).

GRADUATE UNITS

Graduate Programs *Degree program information:* Part-time and evening/weekend programs available. Postbaccalaureate distance learning degree programs offered (minimal on-campus study). Electronic applications accepted.

School of Communication and the Arts *Degree program information:* Part-time programs available. Postbaccalaureate distance learning degree programs offered (no on-campus study). Offers organizational communication and leadership (MA). Electronic applications accepted.

School of Computer Science and Mathematics *Degree program information:* Part-time and evening/weekend programs available. Postbaccalaureate distance learning degree programs offered (minimal on-campus study). Offers computer science/software development (MS); information systems (MS, Adv C); technology management (MS). Electronic applications accepted.

School of Management *Degree program information:* Part-time and evening/weekend programs available. Postbaccalaureate distance learning degree programs offered (no on-campus study). Offers business administration (MBA, Adv C); executive leadership (Adv C); public administration (MPA); technology management (MS). Electronic applications accepted.

School of Social and Behavioral Sciences *Degree program information:* Part-time and evening/weekend programs available. Offers education (M Ed, MA); mental health counseling (MA); school psychology (MA, Adv C). Electronic applications accepted.

MARLBORO COLLEGE, Marlboro, VT 05344

General Information Independent, coed, comprehensive institution. *Enrollment:* 280 graduate, professional, and undergraduate students; 47 full-time matriculated graduate/professional students (29 women), 60 part-time matriculated graduate/professional students (32 women). *Enrollment by degree level:* 85 master's, 22 other advanced degrees. *Graduate faculty:* 4 full-time (1 woman), 26 part-time/adjunct (17 women). *Tuition:* Full-time $14,280; part-time $680 per credit. Tuition and fees vary according to course load and program. *Graduate housing:* On-campus housing not available. *Student services:* Low-cost health insurance, teacher training. *Library facilities:* Rice-Aron Library. *Online resources:* library catalog. *Collection:* 75,000 titles, 17,000 serial subscriptions.

Computer facilities: 47 computers available on campus for general student use. A campuswide network can be accessed from student residence rooms and from off campus. Online class registration is available. *Web address:* http://www.marlboro.edu/.

General Application Contact: Joe Heslin, Associate Director of Admissions, 802-258-9209, Fax: 802-258-9201, E-mail: jheslin@marlboro.edu.

GRADUATE UNITS

Graduate School Students: 47 full-time (29 women), 60 part-time (32 women); includes 3 Black or African American, non-Hispanic/Latino; 1 American Indian or Alaska Native, non-Hispanic/Latino. Average age 39. 39 applicants, 100% accepted, 36 enrolled. *Faculty:* 4 full-time (1 woman), 26 part-time/adjunct (17 women). Expenses: Contact institution. *Financial support:* Applicants required to submit FAFSA. In 2010, 27 master's awarded. *Degree program information:* Part-time and evening/weekend programs available. Postbaccalaureate distance learning degree programs offered (minimal on-campus study). Offers (management) healthcare administration (MSM); information technologies (MS); managing for sustainability (MBA); open source Web development (Certificate); project management (Certificate); teaching for social justice (MAT); teaching with technology (MAT). *Application deadline:* For fall admission, 7/1 priority date for domestic students; for winter admission, 11/1 priority date for domestic students; for spring admission, 3/1 priority date for domestic students. Applications are processed on a rolling basis. *Application fee:* $0. Electronic applications accepted. *Application Contact:* Joe Heslin, Associate Director of Admissions, 802-258-9209, Fax: 802-258-9201, E-mail: jheslin@gradschool.marlboro.edu. *Associate Dean,* Sean Conley, 802-258-9203, Fax: 802-258-9201, E-mail: sconley@gradschool.marlboro.edu.

MARQUETTE UNIVERSITY, Milwaukee, WI 53201-1881

General Information Independent-religious, coed, university. CGS member. *Enrollment:* 11,806 graduate, professional, and undergraduate students; 2,096 full-time matriculated graduate/professional students (1,039 women), 1,487 part-time matriculated graduate/professional students (758 women). *Enrollment by degree level:* 1,203 first professional, 1,755 master's, 523 doctoral, 102 other advanced degrees. *Graduate faculty:* 659 full-time (261 women), 489 part-time/adjunct (224 women). *Tuition:* Full-time $16,290; part-time $905 per credit hour. Tuition and fees vary according to program. *Graduate housing:* Rooms and/or apartments available on a first-come, first-served basis to single and married students. *Student services:* Campus employment opportunities, campus safety program, career counseling, child daycare facilities, exercise/wellness program, free psychological counseling, grant writing training, international student services, low-cost health insurance, multicultural affairs office, services for students with disabilities, teacher training, writing training. *Library facilities:* Raynor Memorial Libraries plus 1 other. *Online resources:* library catalog, web page, access to other libraries' catalogs. *Collection:* 34,370 serial subscriptions, 21,331 audiovisual materials. *Research affiliation:* Department of Orthopaedic Surgery, Medical College of Wisconsin, Shriners Hospital for Children in Chicago, Rehabilitation Institute of Chicago, Froedtert Memorial Lutheran Hospital, Children???s Hospital of Wisconsin, Blood Center of Wisconsin.

Computer facilities: 1,500 computers available on campus for general student use. A campuswide network can be accessed from student residence rooms and from off campus. Online class registration, AV Software, MATLAB are available. *Web address:* http://www.marquette.edu/.

General Application Contact: Erin Fox, Assistant Director for Recruitment, 414-288-5319, Fax: 414-288-1902, E-mail: erin.fox@marquette.edu.

GRADUATE UNITS

Graduate School Students: 959 full-time (566 women), 910 part-time (549 women); includes 188 minority (69 Black or African American, non-Hispanic/Latino; 5 American Indian or Alaska Native, non-Hispanic/Latino; 40 Asian, non-Hispanic/Latino; 59 Hispanic/Latino; 1 Native Hawaiian or other Pacific Islander, non-Hispanic/Latino; 14 Two or more races, non-Hispanic/Latino), 190 international. Average age 30. 2,331 applicants, 49% accepted, 519 enrolled. *Faculty:* 431 full-time (178 women), 386 part-time/adjunct (169 women). Expenses: Contact institution. *Financial support:* In 2010–11, 60 fellowships, 96 research assistantships with full tuition reimbursements, 289 teaching assistantships with full tuition reimbursements were awarded; career-related internships or fieldwork, Federal Work-Study, institutionally sponsored loans, scholarships/grants, and tuition waivers (full and partial) also available. Support available to part-time students. Financial award application deadline: 2/15. In 2010, 294 master's, 42 doctorates, 35 other advanced degrees awarded. *Degree program information:* Part-time and evening/weekend programs available. Postbaccalaureate distance learning degree programs offered (minimal on-campus study). Offers criminal justice administration (MLS); dispute resolution (MDR, MLS); engineering (MLS); health care administration (MLS); interdisciplinary studies (PhD); law enforcement leadership and management (Certificate); leadership studies (Certificate); non-profit sector (MLS); public service (MAPS, MLS); sports leadership (MLS); transfusion medicine (MS). *Application deadline:* Applications are processed on a rolling basis. *Application fee:* $50. Electronic applications accepted. *Application Contact:* Erin Fox, Assistant Director for Recruitment, 414-288-5319, Fax: 414-288-1902, E-mail: erin.fox@marquette.edu. *Vice Provost for Research/Dean,* Dr. Jeanne Hossenlopp, 414-288-1532, Fax: 414-288-1578.

College of Arts and Sciences Students: 334 full-time (137 women), 189 part-time (66 women); includes 33 minority (8 Black or African American, non-Hispanic/Latino; 11 Asian, non-Hispanic/Latino; 12 Hispanic/Latino; 2 Two or more races, non-Hispanic/Latino), 98 international. Average age 31. 784 applicants, 41% accepted, 114 enrolled. *Faculty:* 260 full-time (96 women), 81 part-time/adjunct (34 women). Expenses: Contact institution. *Financial support:* In 2010–11, 28 fellowships, 43 research assistantships, 79 teaching assistantships were awarded; career-related internships or fieldwork, Federal Work-Study, institutionally sponsored loans, scholarships/grants, and tuition waivers (full and partial) also available. Support available to part-time students. Financial award application deadline: 2/15. In 2010, 55 master's, 23 doctorates awarded. *Degree program information:* Part-time programs available. Offers American literature (PhD); analytical chemistry (MS, PhD); ancient philosophy (PhD); arts and sciences (MA, MACD, MS, PhD); bioanalytical chemistry (MS, PhD); bioinformatics (MS); biophysical chemistry (MS, PhD); British and American literature (MA); British empiricism and analytic philosophy (PhD); British literature (PhD); cell biology (MS, PhD); chemical physics (MS, PhD); Christian philosophy (PhD); computational sciences (MS, PhD); computing (MS); developmental biology (MS, PhD); early modern European philosophy (PhD); ecology (MS, PhD); epithelial physiology (MS, PhD); ethics (PhD); European history (MA, PhD); genetics (MS, PhD); German philosophy (PhD); global studies (MA); historical theology (MA, PhD); history of philosophy (MA); inorganic chemistry (MS, PhD); international affairs (MA); Judaism and Christianity in antiquity (MA, PhD); mathematics education (MS); medieval philosophy (PhD); microbiology (MS, PhD); molecular biology (MS, PhD); muscle and exercise physiology (MS, PhD); neuroscience (PhD); organic chemistry (MS, PhD); phenomenology and existentialism (PhD); philosophy of religion (PhD); physical chemistry (MS, PhD); political science (MA); political science/communication (MA); psychology (PhD); social and applied philosophy (MA); Spanish (MA); systematic theology (MA, PhD); theological ethics (PhD); theology (MACD); theology and society (PhD); United States history (MA, PhD). *Application deadline:* Applications are processed on a rolling basis. *Application fee:* $50. Electronic applications accepted. *Application Contact:* Erin Fox, Assistant Director for Recruitment, 414-288-5319, Fax: 414-288-1902, E-mail: erin.fox@marquette.edu. *Interim Dean,* Rev. Philip Rossi, SJ, 414-288-7472.

College of Communication Students: 35 full-time (20 women), 31 part-time (25 women); includes 5 minority (2 Black or African American, non-Hispanic/Latino; 1 Hispanic/Latino; 2 Two or more races, non-Hispanic/Latino), 4 international. Average age 28. 97 applicants, 52% accepted, 21 enrolled. *Faculty:* 33 full-time (18 women), 30 part-time/adjunct (16 women). Expenses: Contact institution. *Financial support:* In 2010–11, 2 fellowships, 7 research assistantships, 12 teaching assistantships were awarded; career-related internships or fieldwork, Federal Work-Study, institutionally sponsored loans, scholarships/grants, and tuition waivers (full and partial) also available. Support available to part-time students. Financial award application deadline: 2/15. In 2010, 16 master's, 5 other advanced degrees awarded. *Degree program information:* Part-time and evening/weekend programs available. Offers advertising and public relations (MA); broadcasting and electronic communications (MA); communications studies (MA); digital storytelling (Certificate); health, environment, science and sustainability (MA); journalism (MA); mass communications (MA). *Application deadline:* Applications are processed on a rolling basis. *Application fee:* $50. Electronic applications accepted. *Application Contact:* Erin Fox, Assistant Director for Recruitment, 414-288-5319, Fax: 414-288-1902, E-mail: erin.fox@marquette.edu. *Dean,* Dr. Lori Bergen, 414-288-7133, Fax: 414-288-1578.

College of Education Students: 91 full-time (66 women), 208 part-time (133 women); includes 47 minority (21 Black or African American, non-Hispanic/Latino; 2 American Indian or Alaska Native, non-Hispanic/Latino; 7 Asian, non-Hispanic/Latino; 14 Hispanic/Latino; 3 Two or more races, non-Hispanic/Latino), 3 international. Average age 31. 326 applicants, 58% accepted, 99 enrolled. *Faculty:* 24 full-time (15 women), 35 part-time/adjunct (27 women). Expenses: Contact institution. *Financial support:* In 2010–11, 3 fellowships, 17 research assistantships, 17 teaching assistantships were awarded; Federal Work-Study, institutionally sponsored loans, scholarships/grants, and tuition waivers (full and partial) also available. Support available to part-time students. Financial award application deadline: 2/15. In 2010, 62 master's, 9 doctorates, 4 other advanced degrees awarded. *Degree program information:* Part-time programs available. Offers clinical mental health counseling (MS); college student personnel administration (M Ed); counseling (MA); counseling psychology (PhD); curriculum and instruction (MA); education (PhD); educational administration (M Ed); educational policy and foundations (MA); educational psychology (MA); elementary education (Certificate); literacy (MA); principal (Certificate); reading specialist (Certificate); reading teacher (Certificate); secondary education (Certificate); superintendent (Certificate). *Application deadline:* For fall admission, 1/15 for domestic and international students. *Application fee:* $50. *Application Contact:* Erin Fox, Director of Graduate Admissions, 414-288-7182, Fax: 414-288-1902. *Dean,* Dr. Bill Henk, 414-288-7376.

College of Engineering Students: 129 full-time (33 women), 106 part-time (17 women); includes 17 minority (4 Black or African American, non-Hispanic/Latino; 1 American Indian or Alaska Native, non-Hispanic/Latino; 8 Asian, non-Hispanic/Latino; 3 Hispanic/Latino; 1 Native Hawaiian or other Pacific Islander, non-Hispanic/Latino), 77 international. Average age 28. 327 applicants, 51% accepted, 50 enrolled. *Faculty:* 58 full-time (7 women), 15 part-time/adjunct (2 women). Expenses: Contact institution. *Financial support:* In 2010–11, 115 students received support, including 12 fellowships with tuition reimbursements available, 23 research assistantships with tuition reimbursements available, 43 teaching assistantships with tuition reimbursements available; Federal Work-Study, institutionally sponsored loans, scholarships/grants, and tuition waivers (full and partial) also available. Support available to part-time students. Financial award application deadline: 2/15. In 2010, 30 master's, 2 doctorates awarded. *Degree program information:* Part-time and evening/weekend programs available. Offers biocomputing (ME); bioimaging (ME); bioinstrumentation (ME); bioinstrumentation/computers (MS, PhD); biomechanics (ME); biomechanics/biomaterials (MS, PhD); biorehabilitation (ME); construction and public works management (MS, PhD); construction engineering and management (Certificate); digital signal processing (Certificate); electric machines, drives, and controls (Certificate); electrical and computer engineering (MS, PhD); engineering (ME, MS, MSEM, PhD, Certificate); engineering innovation (Certificate); engineering management (MSEM); environmental/water resources engineering (MS, PhD); functional imaging (PhD); healthcare technologies management (MS); mechanical engineering (MS, PhD); microwaves and antennas (Certificate); new product and process development (Certificate); rehabilitation bioengineering (PhD); sensors and smart systems (Certificate); structural design (Certificate); structural/geotechnical engineering (MS, PhD); systems physiology (MS, PhD); transportation planning and engineering (MS, PhD); waste and wastewater treatment processes (Certificate). *Application deadline:* Applications are processed on a rolling basis. *Application fee:* $40. Electronic applications accepted. *Application Contact:* Erin Fox, Director of Graduate Admissions, 414-288-7182, Fax: 414-288-1902, E-mail: erin.fox@marquette.edu. *Dean,* Dr. Robert Bishop, 414-288-6591, Fax: 414-288-7082, E-mail: robert.bishop@marquette.edu.

College of Health Sciences Students: 230 full-time (201 women), 5 part-time (all women); includes 27 minority (3 Black or African American, non-Hispanic/Latino; 1 American Indian or Alaska Native, non-Hispanic/Latino; 6 Asian, non-Hispanic/Latino; 14 Hispanic/Latino; 3 Two or more races, non-Hispanic/Latino), 1 international. Average age 24. 402 applicants, 40% accepted, 99 enrolled. *Faculty:* 32 full-time (19 women), 35 part-time/adjunct (26 women). Expenses: Contact institution. *Financial support:* In 2010–11, 2 fellowships, 7 teaching assistantships were awarded; research assistantships. In 2010, 72 master's, 6 other advanced degrees awarded. Offers bilingual English/Spanish (Certificate); health sciences (MPAS, MS, DPT, Certificate); physical therapy (DPT); physician assistant studies (MPAS); speech-language pathology (MS). Electronic applications accepted. *Application Contact:* Erin Fox, Assistant Director for Recruitment, 414-288-5319, Fax: 414-288-1902, E-mail: erin.fox@marquette.edu. *Dean,* Dr. William C. Cullinan, 414-288-5053, E-mail: jack.brooks@mu.edu.

College of Nursing Students: 109 full-time (95 women), 228 part-time (213 women); includes 28 minority (9 Black or African American, non-Hispanic/Latino; 7 Asian, non-Hispanic/Latino; 8 Hispanic/Latino; 4 Two or more races, non-Hispanic/Latino), 2 international. Average age 31. 282 applicants, 58% accepted, 98 enrolled. *Faculty:* 29 full-time (28 women), 48 part-time/adjunct (47 women). Expenses: Contact institution. *Financial support:* In 2010–11, 1 fellowship, 6 research assistantships, 10 teaching assistantships were awarded; career-related internships or fieldwork, Federal Work-Study, institutionally sponsored loans, scholarships/grants, and tuition waivers (full and partial) also available. Support available to part-time students. Financial award application deadline: 2/15. In 2010, 48 master's, 10 doctorates, 7 other advanced degrees awarded. *Degree program information:* Part-time and evening/weekend programs available. Offers acute care nurse practitioner (Certificate); adult clinical nurse specialist (Certificate); adult nurse practitioner (Certificate); advanced practice nursing (MSN, DNP); clinical nurse leader (MSN); gerontologic clinical nurse specialist (Certificate); gerontologic nurse practitioner (Certificate); health care systems leadership (MSN, DNP); nurse-midwifery (Certificate); nursing (PhD);

Marquette University (continued)

pediatrics acute care (Certificate); pediatrics primary care (Certificate). *Application deadline:* For fall admission, 2/15 for domestic and international students. *Application fee:* $50. Electronic applications accepted. *Application Contact:* Karen Nest, Graduate Program Coordinator, 414-288-3810, Fax: 414-288-1578. *Dean,* Dr. Margaret Callahan, 414-288-3800, Fax: 414-288-1578.

Graduate School of Management Students: 174 full-time (76 women), 431 part-time (133 women); includes 51 minority (9 Black or African American, non-Hispanic/Latino; 2 American Indian or Alaska Native, non-Hispanic/Latino; 27 Asian, non-Hispanic/Latino; 12 Hispanic/Latino; 1 Two or more races, non-Hispanic/Latino), 96 international. Average age 30. 665 applicants, 57% accepted, 202 enrolled. *Faculty:* 69 full-time (20 women), 30 part-time/adjunct (6 women). Expenses: Contact institution. *Financial support:* In 2010–11, 6 fellowships, 24 teaching assistantships were awarded; research assistantships, Federal Work-Study, institutionally sponsored loans, scholarships/grants, and tuition waivers (full and partial) also available. Support available to part-time students. Financial award application deadline: 2/15. In 2010, 143 master's awarded. *Degree program information:* Part-time and evening/weekend programs available. Offers accounting (MSA); business administration (MBA); business economics (MSAE); economics (MBA); entrepreneurship (Graduate Certificate); finance (MBA); financial economics (MSAE); human resources (MBA); international business (MBA); international economics (MSAE); management (MBA, MSA, MSAE, MSHR, Graduate Certificate); management information systems (MBA); marketing (MBA); marketing research (MSAE); operations and supply chain management (MBA); real estate economics (MSAE); sports business (MBA). *Application deadline:* Applications are processed on a rolling basis. *Application fee:* $50. Electronic applications accepted. *Application Contact:* Dr. Jeanne Simmons, Associate Dean, 414-288-5126, Fax: 414-288-1902, E-mail: jeanne.simmons@marquette.edu. *Dean,* Dr. Linda Salchenberger, 414-288-7141, Fax: 414-288-1578.

Law School Students: 614 full-time (251 women), 143 part-time (74 women); includes 115 minority (30 Black or African American, non-Hispanic/Latino; 4 American Indian or Alaska Native, non-Hispanic/Latino; 20 Asian, non-Hispanic/Latino; 47 Hispanic/Latino; 1 Native Hawaiian or other Pacific Islander, non-Hispanic/Latino; 13 Two or more races, non-Hispanic/Latino). Average age 27. 2,282 applicants, 42% accepted, 247 enrolled. *Faculty:* 41 full-time (19 women), 20 part-time/adjunct (10 women). Expenses: Contact institution. *Financial support:* In 2010–11, 302 students received support. Career-related internships or fieldwork, Federal Work-Study, and scholarships/grants available. Support available to part-time students. Financial award application deadline: 3/1; financial award applicants required to submit FAFSA. In 2010, 214 first professional degrees awarded. *Degree program information:* Part-time and evening/weekend programs available. Offers law (JD). *Application deadline:* For fall admission, 4/1 for domestic students. Applications are processed on a rolling basis. *Application fee:* $50. Electronic applications accepted. *Application Contact:* Sean Reilly, Assistant Dean for Admissions, 414-288-6767, Fax: 414-288-0676, E-mail: sean.reilly@marquette.edu. *Dean,* Joseph D. Kearney, 414-288-7090, Fax: 414-288-6403, E-mail: joseph.kearney@marquette.edu.

School of Dentistry Offers advanced training in general dentistry (MS); dental biomaterials (MS); dentistry (DDS, MS); endodontics (MS); orthodontics (MS); prosthodontics (MS).

MARSHALL UNIVERSITY, Huntington, WV 25755

General Information State-supported, coed, university. CGS member. *Enrollment:* 14,192 graduate, professional, and undergraduate students; 1,790 full-time matriculated graduate/professional students (1,009 women), 1,537 part-time matriculated graduate/professional students (1,159 women). *Enrollment by degree level:* 301 first professional, 2,683 master's, 266 doctoral, 77 other advanced degrees. *Graduate faculty:* 338 full-time (134 women), 50 part-time/adjunct (27 women). *Graduate housing:* Rooms and/or apartments available on a first-come, first-served basis to single and married students. *Student services:* Campus employment opportunities, campus safety program, career counseling, child daycare facilities, exercise/wellness program, free psychological counseling, grant writing training, international student services, low-cost health insurance, multicultural affairs office, services for students with disabilities, teacher training, writing training. *Library facilities:* John Deaver Drinko Library plus 2 others. *Online resources:* library catalog, web page. *Collection:* 1.5 million titles, 41,118 serial subscriptions, 33,760 audiovisual materials. *Research affiliation:* Bayer Corporation (field research), Kanawha Valley Local Port District (field research), Greenbrier County Commission (field research), Dominion Power (field research), Wyeth-Ayerst (clinical pharmaceutical study).

Computer facilities: Computer purchase and lease plans are available. 1,461 computers available on campus for general student use. A campuswide network can be accessed from student residence rooms and from off campus. Online class registration, Virtual Computer Lab—MU Remote and Web Conferencing are available. *Web address:* http://www.marshall.edu/.

General Application Contact: Dr. Tammy Johnson, Graduate Admissions, 304-746-1900, Fax: 304-746-1902, E-mail: services@marshall.edu.

GRADUATE UNITS

Academic Affairs Division Students: 1,790 full-time (1,009 women), 1,537 part-time (1,159 women); includes 107 Black or African American, non-Hispanic/Latino; 10 American Indian or Alaska Native, non-Hispanic/Latino; 76 Asian, non-Hispanic/Latino; 28 Hispanic/Latino; 1 Native Hawaiian or other Pacific Islander, non-Hispanic/Latino, 176 international. Average age 32. *Faculty:* 338 full-time (134 women), 50 part-time/adjunct (27 women). Expenses: Contact institution. *Financial support:* Fellowships, research assistantships, teaching assistantships, career-related internships or fieldwork, Federal Work-Study, tuition waivers (full and partial), and unspecified assistantships available. Support available to part-time students. In 2010, 867 master's, 21 doctorates, 26 other advanced degrees awarded. *Degree program information:* Part-time and evening/weekend programs available. *Application deadline:* Applications are processed on a rolling basis. *Application fee:* $40 ($100 for international students). *Application Contact:* Information Contact, Graduate Admissions, 304-746-1900, Fax: 304-746-1902, E-mail: services@marshall.edu. *Provost/Senior Vice President,* Dr. Gayle Ormiston, 304-696-3716, E-mail: ormiston@marshall.edu.

College of Education and Human Services Students: 146 full-time (88 women), 167 part-time (124 women); includes 21 Black or African American, non-Hispanic/Latino; 5 Asian, non-Hispanic/Latino, 21 international. Average age 34. *Faculty:* 29 full-time (16 women), 8 part-time/adjunct (7 women). Expenses: Contact institution. *Financial support:* Career-related internships or fieldwork, Federal Work-Study, tuition waivers (full and partial), and unspecified assistantships available. Support available to part-time students. In 2010, 103 master's awarded. *Degree program information:* Evening/weekend programs available. Offers adult and technical education (MS); education (MAT); education and human services (MA, MAT, MS); family and consumer sciences (MA); human development and allied technology (MA, MS). *Application deadline:* Applications are processed on a rolling basis. *Application fee:* $40 ($100 for international students). *Application Contact:* Graduate Admissions, 304-746-1900, Fax: 304-746-1902, E-mail: services@marshall.edu. *Interim Dean,* Dr. Robert Bookwalter, 304-696-3131, E-mail: bookwalter@marshall.edu.

College of Fine Arts Students: 17 full-time (7 women), 10 part-time (6 women); includes 1 Black or African American, non-Hispanic/Latino, 3 international. Average age 29. *Faculty:* 29 full-time (11 women), 1 (woman) part-time/adjunct. Expenses: Contact institution. In 2010, 9 master's awarded. *Degree program information:* Evening/weekend programs available. Offers art (MA); fine arts (MA); music (MA). *Application fee:* $40. *Application Contact:* Information Contact, 304-746-1900, Fax: 304-746-1902, E-mail: services@marshall.edu. *Dean,* Dr. Donald Van Horn, 304-696-2964, E-mail: vanhorn@marshall.edu.

College of Health Professions Students: 163 full-time (119 women), 167 part-time (143 women); includes 8 Black or African American, non-Hispanic/Latino; 1 American Indian or Alaska Native, non-Hispanic/Latino; 4 Asian, non-Hispanic/Latino; 3 Hispanic/Latino, 7 international. Average age 30. *Faculty:* 25 full-time (17 women), 1 (woman) part-time/adjunct. Expenses: Contact institution. In 2010, 93 master's awarded. Offers communication disorders (MA); dietetics (MS); exercise science (MS); health professions (MA, MS, MSN); kinesiology (MS); nursing (MSN); sport administration (MS). *Application fee:* $40. *Application Contact:* Information Contact, 304-746-1900, Fax: 304-746-1902, E-mail: services@marshall.edu. *Dean,* Dr. Michael Prewitt, 304-696-3765, E-mail: prewittm@marshall.edu.

College of Information Technology and Engineering Students: 78 full-time (12 women), 96 part-time (16 women); includes 6 Black or African American, non-Hispanic/Latino; 2 Asian, non-Hispanic/Latino; 3 Hispanic/Latino, 41 international. Average age 32. *Faculty:* 16 full-time (2 women), 4 part-time/adjunct (0 women). Expenses: Contact institution. *Financial support:* Fellowships, tuition waivers (full) available. Support available to part-time students. Financial award application deadline: 8/1; financial award applicants required to submit FAFSA. In 2010, 45 master's awarded. *Degree program information:* Part-time and evening/weekend programs available. Offers applied science and technology (MS); engineering (MSE); environmental science (MS); information systems (MS); information technology and engineering (MS, MSE); safety (MS); technology management (MS). *Application fee:* $40. *Application Contact:* Information Contact, 304-746-1900, Fax: 304-746-1902, E-mail: services@marshall.edu. *Dean,* Dr. Betsy Dulin, 304-746-2087, E-mail: bdulin@marshall.edu.

College of Liberal Arts Students: 234 full-time (135 women), 79 part-time (55 women); includes 11 Black or African American, non-Hispanic/Latino; 1 American Indian or Alaska Native, non-Hispanic/Latino; 1 Asian, non-Hispanic/Latino; 2 Hispanic/Latino; 1 Native Hawaiian or other Pacific Islander, non-Hispanic/Latino, 19 international. Average age 28. *Faculty:* 102 full-time (43 women), 6 part-time/adjunct (2 women). Expenses: Contact institution. *Financial support:* Fellowships, teaching assistantships with tuition reimbursements available. In 2010, 106 master's, 4 doctorates awarded. *Degree program information:* Evening/weekend programs available. Offers clinical psychology (MA); communication studies (MA); criminal justice (MS); English (MA); general psychology (MA); geography (MA, MS); history (MA); humanities (MA); industrial and organizational psychology (MA); Latin (MA); liberal arts (MA, MS, Psy D); political science (MA); psychology (Psy D); sociology (MA); Spanish (MA). *Application fee:* $40. *Application Contact:* Graduate Admissions, 304-746-1900, Fax: 304-746-1902, E-mail: services@marshall.edu. *Dean,* Dr. David J. Pittenger, 304-696-2731, E-mail: pittengerd@marshell.edu.

College of Science Students: 73 full-time (29 women), 12 part-time (5 women); includes 7 Black or African American, non-Hispanic/Latino; 2 American Indian or Alaska Native, non-Hispanic/Latino; 4 Asian, non-Hispanic/Latino; 1 Hispanic/Latino, 16 international. Average age 27. *Faculty:* 64 full-time (16 women), 1 part-time/adjunct (0 women). Expenses: Contact institution. *Financial support:* Career-related internships or fieldwork available. In 2010, 30 master's awarded. Offers biological science (MA, MS); chemistry (MS); mathematics (MA, MS); physical science (MS); science (MA, MS). *Application fee:* $40. *Application Contact:* Information Contact, Graduate Admissions, 304-746-1900, Fax: 304-746-1902, E-mail: services@marshall.edu. *Dean,* Dr. Charles Somerville, 304-696-2424, E-mail: somervil@marshall.edu.

Graduate School of Education and Professional Development Students: 335 full-time (259 women), 845 part-time (704 women); includes 31 Black or African American, non-Hispanic/Latino; 2 American Indian or Alaska Native, non-Hispanic/Latino; 8 Asian, non-Hispanic/Latino; 6 Hispanic/Latino, 2 international. Average age 35. *Faculty:* 36 full-time (20 women), 27 part-time/adjunct (15 women). Expenses: Contact institution. *Financial support:* Career-related internships or fieldwork, Federal Work-Study, tuition waivers (full and partial), and unspecified assistantships available. Support available to part-time students. Financial award applicants required to submit FAFSA. In 2010, 239 master's, 10 doctorates, 26 other advanced degrees awarded. *Degree program information:* Part-time and evening/weekend programs available. Offers counseling (MA, Ed S); early childhood education (MA); education and professional development (MA, Ed D, Ed S); elementary education (MA); leadership studies (MA, Ed D, Ed S); reading education (MA, Ed S); school psychology (Ed S); secondary education (MA); special education (MA). *Application deadline:* Applications are processed on a rolling basis. *Application fee:* $40. *Application Contact:* Information Contact, 304-746-1900, Fax: 304-746-1902, E-mail: services@marshall.edu. *Dean,* Dr. Teresa Eagle, 304-746-8924, E-mail: thardman@marshall.edu.

Lewis College of Business Students: 314 full-time (138 women), 90 part-time (51 women); includes 17 Black or African American, non-Hispanic/Latino; 1 American Indian or Alaska Native, non-Hispanic/Latino; 6 Asian, non-Hispanic/Latino; 2 Hispanic/Latino, 52 international. Average age 29. *Faculty:* 32 full-time (7 women), 2 part-time/adjunct (1 woman). Expenses: Contact institution. *Financial support:* Career-related internships or fieldwork and tuition waivers (full) available. Support available to part-time students. Financial award applicants required to submit FAFSA. In 2010, 215 master's awarded. *Degree program information:* Part-time and evening/weekend programs available. Offers business (IMBA, MBA, MS, DMPNA, Graduate Certificate); business administration (IMBA, MBA); business management foundations (Graduate Certificate); health care administration (MS, DMPNA); human resource management (MS); management (IMBA, MBA, MS, DMPNA, Graduate Certificate). *Application deadline:* Applications are processed on a rolling basis. *Application fee:* $40. *Application Contact:* Dr. Uday Tate, Information Contact, 304-696-2672, Fax: 304-746-1902, E-mail: tate@marshall.edu. *Dean,* Dr. Chong Kim, 304-696-2862, Fax: 304-696-4344, E-mail: kim@marshall.edu.

School of Journalism and Mass Communications Students: 24 full-time (18 women), 6 part-time (4 women); includes 1 Black or African American, non-Hispanic/Latino, 6 international. Average age 26. *Faculty:* 5 full-time (2 women). Expenses: Contact institution. In 2010, 10 master's awarded. Offers journalism and mass communications (MAJ). *Application fee:* $40. *Application Contact:* Janet Dooley, Assistant Dean, 304-696-2734, Fax: 304-746-1902, E-mail: dooley@marshall.edu. *Dean,* Dr. Corley F. Dennison, 304-696-2809, E-mail: dennisoc@marshall.edu.

Joan C. Edwards School of Medicine Offers biomedical sciences (MS, PhD); medicine (MD, MS, PhD). Electronic applications accepted.

MARS HILL GRADUATE SCHOOL, Seattle, WA 98121

General Information Independent-religious, coed, graduate-only institution.

GRADUATE UNITS

Graduate Programs *Degree program information:* Part-time programs available.

MARTIN LUTHER COLLEGE, New Ulm, MN 56073

General Information Independent-religious, coed, comprehensive institution.

GRADUATE UNITS

Graduate Studies *Degree program information:* Part-time programs available. Postbaccalaureate distance learning degree programs offered. Offers instruction (MS Ed); leadership (MS Ed); special education (MS Ed). Electronic applications accepted.

MARTIN UNIVERSITY, Indianapolis, IN 46218-3867

General Information Independent, coed, comprehensive institution. *Graduate housing:* On-campus housing not available.

GRADUATE UNITS

Division of Psychology *Degree program information:* Part-time and evening/weekend programs available. Offers community psychology (MS).

Graduate School of Urban Ministry *Degree program information:* Part-time and evening/weekend programs available. Offers urban ministry studies (MA).

MARY BALDWIN COLLEGE, Staunton, VA 24401-3610

General Information Independent, coed, primarily women, comprehensive institution. *Graduate housing:* On-campus housing not available.

GRADUATE UNITS

Graduate Studies *Degree program information:* Part-time and evening/weekend programs available. Postbaccalaureate distance learning degree programs offered (minimal on-campus study). Offers acting (M Litt); directing (M Litt); elementary education (MAT); middle grades education (MAT); Shakespeare and Renaissance literature in performance (M Litt, MFA); teaching (M Litt, MAT).

MARYGROVE COLLEGE, Detroit, MI 48221-2599

General Information Independent-religious, coed, primarily women, comprehensive institution. *Graduate housing:* Room and/or apartments available to single students; on-campus housing not available to married students.

GRADUATE UNITS

Graduate Division *Degree program information:* Part-time and evening/weekend programs available. Postbaccalaureate distance learning degree programs offered (no on-campus study). Offers art of teaching (MAT); educational leadership (MA); English (MA); Griot (M Ed); human resource management (MA); modern language translation (Certificate); reading and literacy (M Ed); Sage (M Ed); social justice (MA). Electronic applications accepted.

MARYLAND INSTITUTE COLLEGE OF ART, Baltimore, MD 21217

General Information Independent, coed, comprehensive institution. *Enrollment:* 1,975 graduate, professional, and undergraduate students; 166 full-time matriculated graduate/professional students (105 women), 72 part-time matriculated graduate/professional students (51 women). *Enrollment by degree level:* 214 master's, 24 other advanced degrees. *Graduate faculty:* 21 full-time (15 women), 30 part-time/adjunct (16 women). *Tuition:* Full-time $34,550; part-time $1440 per credit hour. *Required fees:* $1140; $570 per term. *Graduate housing:* Room and/or apartments available on a first-come, first-served basis to single students; on-campus housing not available to married students. Typical cost: $5850 per year ($8260 including board). Room and board charges vary according to board plan. Housing application deadline: 5/1. *Student services:* Campus employment opportunities, campus safety program, career counseling, exercise/wellness program, free psychological counseling, grant writing training, international student services, low-cost health insurance, multicultural affairs office, services for students with disabilities, teacher training, writing training. *Library facilities:* Decker Library plus 1 other. *Online resources:* library catalog, web page, access to other libraries' catalogs. *Collection:* 89,500 titles, 324 serial subscriptions, 5,880 audiovisual materials.

Computer facilities: 650 computers available on campus for general student use. A campuswide network can be accessed from student residence rooms and from off campus. Online class registration, campus Portal, online gallery space, network storage space, personal Web sites, online software training tutorials (Lynda.com), and Learning management system (Moodle) are available. *Web address:* http://www.mica.edu/.

General Application Contact: Scott G. Kelly, Associate Dean of Graduate Admission, 410-225-2256, Fax: 410-225-2408, E-mail: graduate@mica.edu.

GRADUATE UNITS

Graduate Studies Students: 166 full-time (105 women), 72 part-time (51 women); includes 30 minority (3 Black or African American, non-Hispanic/Latino; 1 American Indian or Alaska Native, non-Hispanic/Latino; 12 Asian, non-Hispanic/Latino; 9 Hispanic/Latino; 5 Two or more races, non-Hispanic/Latino), 24 international. Average age 29. *Faculty:* 21 full-time (15 women), 30 part-time/adjunct (16 women). Expenses: Contact institution. *Financial support:* In 2010–11, 226 students received support, including 226 fellowships (averaging $10,000 per year), 91 teaching assistantships (averaging $1,800 per year); career-related internships or fieldwork and scholarships/grants also available. Financial award application deadline: 3/1; financial award applicants required to submit FAFSA. In 2010, 95 master's, 20 other advanced degrees awarded. *Degree program information:* Part-time programs available. Offers art education (MA, MAT); community arts (MA, MFA); curatorial practice (MFA); fine arts (Certificate); graphic design (MFA); illustration practice (MFA); photographic and electronic media (MFA); studio art (MFA); the business of art and design (MPS). *Application deadline:* For fall admission, 1/15 for domestic and international students. *Application fee:* $60. *Application Contact:* Scott G. Kelly, Associate Dean of Graduate Admission, 410-225-2256, Fax: 410-225-2408, E-mail: graduate@mica.edu. *Vice Provost for Research/Dean*, Guna Nadarajan, 410-225-5273, Fax: 410-225-5275, E-mail: graduate@mica.edu.

Hoffberger School of Painting Students: 16 full-time (8 women); includes 2 minority (1 Asian, non-Hispanic/Latino; 1 Hispanic/Latino), 2 international. Average age 27. *Faculty:* 1 (woman) full-time, 1 part-time/adjunct (0 women). Expenses: Contact institution. *Financial support:* In 2010–11, 16 students received support, including 16 fellowships with partial tuition reimbursements available (averaging $16,000 per year), 8 teaching assistantships (averaging $1,800 per year); career-related internships or fieldwork and scholarships/grants also available. Financial award application deadline: 3/1; financial award applicants required to submit FAFSA. In 2010, 6 master's awarded. Offers painting (MFA). *Application deadline:* For fall admission, 1/15 for domestic and international students. *Application fee:* $60. *Application Contact:* Scott G. Kelly, Associate Dean of Graduate Admission, 410-225-2256, Fax: 410-225-2408, E-mail: graduate@mica.edu. *Director*, Joan Waltemath, 410-225-2255, Fax: 410-225-2408, E-mail: graduate@mica.edu.

Mount Royal School of Art Students: 25 full-time (16 women); includes 2 minority (1 Asian, non-Hispanic/Latino; 1 Two or more races, non-Hispanic/Latino), 3 international. Average age 27. *Faculty:* 1 (woman) full-time, 4 part-time/adjunct (1 woman). Expenses: Contact institution. *Financial support:* In 2010–11, 15 students received support, including 15 fellowships with partial tuition reimbursements available (averaging $10,000 per year), 1 teaching assistantship (averaging $1,800 per year); career-related internships or fieldwork and scholarships/grants also available. Financial award application deadline: 3/1; financial award applicants required to submit FAFSA. In 2010, 15 master's awarded. Offers painting (MFA). *Application deadline:* For fall admission, 1/15 for domestic and international students. *Application fee:* $60. *Application Contact:* Scott G. Kelly, Associate Dean of Graduate Admission, 410-225-2256, Fax: 410-225-2408, E-mail: graduate@mica.edu. *Director*, Frances Barth, 410-225-2347, Fax: 410-225-5275, E-mail: graduate@mica.edu.

Rinehart School of Sculpture Students: 9 full-time (5 women), 1 part-time (0 women); includes 1 minority (Asian, non-Hispanic/Latino), 3 international. Average age 31. *Faculty:* 2 full-time (1 woman), 1 (woman) part-time/adjunct. Expenses: Contact institution. *Financial support:* In 2010–11, 10 students received support, including 10 fellowships with partial tuition reimbursements available (averaging $10,000 per year), 9 teaching assistantships (averaging $1,800 per year); career-related internships or fieldwork and scholarships/grants also available. Financial award application deadline: 3/1; financial award applicants required to submit FAFSA. In 2010, 6 master's awarded. Offers sculpture (MFA). *Application deadline:* For fall admission, 1/15 for domestic and international students. *Application fee:* $60. *Application Contact:* Scott G. Kelly, Associate Dean of Graduate Admission, 410-225-2256, Fax: 410-225-2408, E-mail: graduate@mica.edu. *Director*, Maren Hassinger, 410-225-2271, Fax: 410-225-2408.

MARYLHURST UNIVERSITY, Marylhurst, OR 97036-0261

General Information Independent-religious, coed, primarily women, comprehensive institution. *Enrollment:* 1,917 graduate, professional, and undergraduate students; 147 full-time matriculated graduate/professional students (107 women), 830 part-time matriculated graduate/professional students (452 women). *Enrollment by degree level:* 35 first professional, 941 master's. *Graduate faculty:* 15 full-time (8 women), 72 part-time/adjunct (35 women). *Tuition:* Full-time $13,932; part-time $516 per credit. Tuition and fees vary according to course load and program. *Graduate housing:* On-campus housing not available. *Student services:* Career counseling, international student services, low-cost health insurance, services for students with disabilities, writing training. *Library facilities:* Shoen Library. *Online resources:* library catalog, web page, access to other libraries' catalogs. *Collection:* 109,963 titles, 23,286 serial subscriptions, 4,425 audiovisual materials.

Computer facilities: 50 computers available on campus for general student use. A campuswide network can be accessed from off campus. Online class registration is available. *Web address:* http://www.marylhurst.edu/.

General Application Contact: Office of Admissions, 503-699-6268, Fax: 503-699-6320, E-mail: admissions@marylhurst.edu.

GRADUATE UNITS

Department of Art Therapy Counseling Students: 5 full-time (3 women), 25 part-time (20 women); includes 1 American Indian or Alaska Native, non-Hispanic/Latino; 1 Asian, non-Hispanic/Latino; 4 Hispanic/Latino; 1 Two or more races, non-Hispanic/Latino. Average age 34. 30 applicants, 83% accepted, 18 enrolled. *Faculty:* 3 full-time (all women), 4 part-time/adjunct (all women). Expenses: Contact institution. *Financial support:* Scholarships/grants available. Support available to part-time students. Financial award applicants required to submit FAFSA. In 2010, 18 master's awarded. *Degree program information:* Part-time programs available. Offers art therapy (PGC); art therapy counseling (MA); counseling (PGC). *Application deadline:* For fall admission, 1/31 priority date for domestic and international students. Applications are processed on a rolling basis. *Application fee:* $50. Electronic applications accepted. *Application Contact:* Maruska Lynch, Graduate Admissions Specialist, 800-634-9982 Ext. 6322, Fax: 503-699-6320, E-mail: admissions@marylhurst.edu. *Chair*, Christine Turner, 503-636-8141, Fax: 503-636-9526, E-mail: cturner@marylhurst.edu.

Department of Business Administration Students: 27 full-time (13 women), 727 part-time (373 women); includes 167 minority (47 Black or African American, non-Hispanic/Latino; 6 American Indian or Alaska Native, non-Hispanic/Latino; 36 Asian, non-Hispanic/Latino; 51 Hispanic/Latino; 6 Native Hawaiian or other Pacific Islander, non-Hispanic/Latino; 21 Two or more races, non-Hispanic/Latino), 7 international. Average age 38. 262 applicants, 91% accepted, 194 enrolled. *Faculty:* 3 full-time (0 women), 36 part-time/adjunct (6 women). Expenses: Contact institution. *Financial support:* Scholarships/grants available. Support available to part-time students. Financial award applicants required to submit FAFSA. In 2010, 289 master's awarded. *Degree program information:* Part-time and evening/weekend programs available. Postbaccalaureate distance learning degree programs offered (no on-campus study). Offers finance (MBA); general management (MBA); government policy and administration (MBA); green development (MBA); health care management (MBA); marketing (MBA); natural and organic resources (MBA); nonprofit management (MBA); organizational behavior (MBA); real estate (MBA); renewable energy (MBA); sustainable business (MBA). *Application deadline:* For fall admission, 9/11 priority date for domestic and international students; for winter admission, 12/15 priority date for domestic and international students; for spring admission, 3/15 priority date for domestic students, 3/17 priority date for international students. Applications are processed on a rolling basis. *Application fee:* $50. Electronic applications accepted. *Application Contact:* Maruska Lynch, Graduate Admissions Specialist, 800-634-9982 Ext. 6322, Fax: 503-699-6320, E-mail: admissions@marylhurst.edu. *Director of Business and Real Estate Programs*, Bob Hanks, 503-636-8141, Fax: 503-697-5597, E-mail: mba@marylhurst.edu.

Department of Education Students: 67 full-time (47 women), 29 part-time (23 women); includes 1 Black or African American, non-Hispanic/Latino; 1 American Indian or Alaska Native, non-Hispanic/Latino; 3 Asian, non-Hispanic/Latino; 6 Hispanic/Latino; 5 Two or more races, non-Hispanic/Latino. Average age 34. 58 applicants, 81% accepted, 40 enrolled. *Faculty:* 5 full-time (3 women), 25 part-time/adjunct (20 women). Expenses: Contact institution. *Financial support:* Federal Work-Study and scholarships/grants available. Support available to part-time students. Financial award applicants required to submit FAFSA. In 2010, 45 master's awarded. *Degree program information:* Part-time programs available. Offers education (M Ed, MA). *Application deadline:* For fall admission, 3/1 priority date for domestic and international students. Applications are processed on a rolling basis. *Application fee:* $50. *Application Contact:* Maruska Lynch, Graduate Admissions Specialist, 800-634-9982 Ext. 6322, Fax: 503-699-6320, E-mail: admissions@marylhurst.edu. *Chair*, Dr. Thomas Ruhl, 503-636-8141, Fax: 503-636-9526, E-mail: truhl@marylhurst.edu.

Department of Interdisciplinary Studies Students: 3 full-time (2 women), 33 part-time (27 women); includes 2 Hispanic/Latino; 1 Two or more races, non-Hispanic/Latino. Average age 50. 12 applicants, 83% accepted, 7 enrolled. *Faculty:* 2 full-time (both women), 1 part-time/adjunct (0 women). Expenses: Contact institution. *Financial support:* Federal Work-Study and scholarships/grants available. Support available to part-time students. Financial award applicants required to submit FAFSA. In 2010, 4 master's awarded. *Degree program information:* Part-time and evening/weekend programs available. Offers interdisciplinary studies (MA). *Application deadline:* Applications are processed on a rolling basis. *Application fee:* $50. Electronic applications accepted. *Application Contact:* Maruska Lynch, Graduate Admissions Specialist, 800-634-9982 Ext. 6322, Fax: 503-699-6320, E-mail: admissions@marylhurst.edu. *Chair*, Dr. Debrah B. Bokowski, 503-636-8141, Fax: 503-697-5597, E-mail: dbokowski@marylhurst.edu.

Department of Religious Studies–Applied Theology Program Students: 15 part-time (12 women). Average age 48. 4 applicants, 50% accepted, 2 enrolled. *Faculty:* 2 full-time (1 woman), 8 part-time/adjunct (3 women). Expenses: Contact institution. *Financial support:* Fellowships, research assistantships, teaching assistantships, scholarships/grants available. Support available to part-time students. Financial award applicants required to submit FAFSA. In 2010, 2 master's awarded. *Degree program information:* Part-time and evening/weekend programs available. Offers applied theology (MA). *Application deadline:* For fall admission, 6/30 priority date for domestic students, 6/30 for international students; for winter admission, 11/30 priority date for domestic students, 11/30 for international students; for spring admission, 3/30 priority date for domestic students, 3/30 for international students. Applications are processed on a rolling basis. *Application fee:* $50. Electronic applications accepted. *Application Contact:* Maruksa Lynch, Graduate Admissions Specialist, 800-634-9982 Ext. 6322, Fax: 503-699-6320, E-mail: admissions@marylhurst.edu. *Chair*, Dr. Jerry Roussell, 503-636-8141, Fax: 503-697-5597, E-mail: jroussell@marylhurst.edu.

Department of Religious Studies–Divinity Program Students: 12 full-time (9 women), 23 part-time (15 women); includes 1 Hispanic/Latino; 1 Two or more races, non-Hispanic/Latino. Average age 47. 8 applicants, 88% accepted, 7 enrolled. *Faculty:* 2 full-time (1 woman), 8 part-time/adjunct (3 women). Expenses: Contact institution. *Financial support:* Fellowships, research assistantships, teaching assistantships, scholarships/grants available. Support available to part-time students. Financial award applicants required to submit FAFSA. *Degree program information:* Part-time and evening/weekend programs available. Offers divinity (M Div). *Application deadline:* For fall admission, 6/30 for domestic students; for winter admission, 11/30 for domestic students; for spring admission, 3/30 for domestic students. Applications are processed on a rolling basis. *Application fee:* $50. Electronic applications accepted. *Application Contact:* Maruska Lynch, Graduate Admissions Specialist, 800-634-9982 Ext. 6322, Fax: 503-699-6320, E-mail: admissions@marylhurst.edu. *Chair*, Dr. Jerry Roussell, 503-636-8141, Fax: 503-697-5597, E-mail: jroussell@marylhurst.edu.

MARYMOUNT UNIVERSITY, Arlington, VA 22207-4299

General Information Independent-religious, coed, comprehensive institution. CGS member. *Graduate housing:* On-campus housing not available.

GRADUATE UNITS

Educational Partnerships Program *Degree program information:* Part-time and evening/weekend programs available. Offers business administration (MBA); health care management (MS); management studies (Certificate); organization development (Certificate). Electronic applications accepted.

School of Arts and Sciences *Degree program information:* Part-time and evening/weekend programs available. Offers arts and sciences (MA); humanities (MA); interior design (MA); literature and languages (MA). Electronic applications accepted.

School of Business Administration *Degree program information:* Part-time and evening/weekend programs available. Offers business administration (MA, MBA, MS, Certificate); computer security and information assurance (Certificate); health care informatics (Certificate); health care management (MS); human resource management (MA, Certificate); information technology (MS, Certificate); information technology project management: technology leadership (Certificate); instructional design (Certificate); leadership (Certificate); legal administration (MA); management (MS); organization development (Certificate); paralegal studies (Certificate); project management (Certificate). Electronic applications accepted.

School of Education and Human Services *Degree program information:* Part-time and evening/weekend programs available. Postbaccalaureate distance learning degree programs offered (minimal on-campus study). Offers Catholic school leadership (M Ed, Certificate); community counseling (MA, Certificate); education and human services (M Ed, MA, Certificate); elementary education (M Ed); English as a second language (M Ed); forensic psychology (MA); pastoral and spiritual care (MA); pastoral counseling (MA, Certificate); professional studies (M Ed); school counseling (MA); secondary education (M Ed); special education, general curriculum (M Ed). Electronic applications accepted.

Marymount University (continued)

School of Health Professions *Degree program information:* Part-time and evening/weekend programs available. Offers family nurse practitioner (MSN, Certificate); health professions (MS, MSN, DNP, DPT, Certificate); health promotion management (MS); nursing (DNP); nursing education (MSN, Certificate); physical therapy (DPT); RN to MSN (MSN). Electronic applications accepted.

MARYVILLE UNIVERSITY OF SAINT LOUIS, St. Louis, MO 63141-7299

General Information Independent, coed, comprehensive institution. *Enrollment:* 3,676 graduate, professional, and undergraduate students; 191 full-time matriculated graduate/professional students (147 women), 517 part-time matriculated graduate/professional students (379 women). *Enrollment by degree level:* 519 master's, 189 doctoral. *Graduate faculty:* 47 full-time (33 women), 40 part-time/adjunct (27 women). *Tuition:* Full-time $21,100; part-time $633.50 per credit hour. *Required fees:* $150 per semester. *Graduate housing:* Room and/or apartments available on a first-come, first-served basis to single students; on-campus housing not available to married students. Typical cost: $8500 (including board). Room and board charges vary according to board plan and housing facility selected. Housing application deadline: 5/1. *Student services:* Campus employment opportunities, campus safety program, career counseling, exercise/wellness program, free psychological counseling, international student services, low-cost health insurance, multicultural affairs office, services for students with disabilities, teacher training, writing training. *Library facilities:* Maryville University Library. *Online resources:* library catalog, web page, access to other libraries' catalogs. *Collection:* 159,788 titles, 42,500 serial subscriptions, 10,016 audiovisual materials. *Research affiliation:* Southwestern Bell Foundation (secondary education curriculum and teacher education), Monsanto Fund (early childhood, science, mathematics curriculum development and teacher enrichment).

Computer facilities: Computer purchase and lease plans are available. 450 computers available on campus for general student use. A campuswide network can be accessed from student residence rooms and from off campus. Online class registration, specialized software, university catalog are available. *Web address:* http://www.maryville.edu/.

General Application Contact: Denise Evans, Assistant Vice President, Adult and Continuing Education, 314-529-9676, Fax: 314-529-9927, E-mail: devans1@maryville.edu.

GRADUATE UNITS

College of Arts and Sciences Students: 13 full-time (7 women), 13 part-time (10 women); includes 2 Black or African American, non-Hispanic/Latino; 1 Asian, non-Hispanic/Latino; 1 Two or more races, non-Hispanic/Latino, 3 international. Average age 31. *Faculty:* 6 full-time (all women), 1 part-time/adjunct (0 women). Expenses: Contact institution. *Financial support:* Application deadline: 3/1. In 2010, 7 master's awarded. *Degree program information:* Part-time and evening/weekend programs available. Offers actuarial science (MS); organizational leadership (MA). *Application deadline:* Applications are processed on a rolling basis. *Application fee:* $40 ($60 for international students). Electronic applications accepted. *Application Contact:* Denise Evans, Assistant Vice President, Adult and Continuing Education, 314-529-9676, Fax: 314-529-9927, E-mail: devans1@maryville.edu. *Dean*, Dr. Dan Sparling, 314-529-9436, Fax: 314-529-9965, E-mail: dsparling@maryville.edu.

The John E. Simon School of Business Students: 16 full-time (8 women), 119 part-time (57 women); includes 15 minority (9 Black or African American, non-Hispanic/Latino; 3 Asian, non-Hispanic/Latino; 3 Hispanic/Latino), 5 international. Average age 31. *Faculty:* 7 full-time (4 women), 13 part-time/adjunct (5 women). Expenses: Contact institution. *Financial support:* Career-related internships or fieldwork, Federal Work-Study, tuition waivers (partial), and campus employment available. Financial award application deadline: 3/1; financial award applicants required to submit FAFSA. In 2010, 60 master's awarded. *Degree program information:* Part-time and evening/weekend programs available. Offers accounting (MBA, PGC); business studies (PGC); management (MBA, PGC); marketing (MBA, PGC); process and project management (MBA, PGC); sport and entertainment management (MBA, PGC). *Application deadline:* Applications are processed on a rolling basis. *Application fee:* $40 ($60 for international students). Electronic applications accepted. *Application Contact:* Kathy Dougherty, Director of MBA Programs, 314-529-9382, Fax: 314-529-9975, E-mail: business@maryville.edu. *Dean*, Dr. Pamela Horwitz, 314-529-9418, Fax: 314-529-9975, E-mail: horwitz@maryville.edu.

School of Education Students: 33 full-time (29 women), 253 part-time (195 women); includes 43 Black or African American, non-Hispanic/Latino; 1 American Indian or Alaska Native, non-Hispanic/Latino; 2 Asian, non-Hispanic/Latino; 1 Hispanic/Latino; 1 Two or more races, non-Hispanic/Latino. Average age 37. *Faculty:* 11 full-time (6 women), 14 part-time/adjunct (12 women). Expenses: Contact institution. *Financial support:* Career-related internships or fieldwork, Federal Work-Study, tuition waivers (partial), and professional educator discounts available. Financial award application deadline: 3/1; financial award applicants required to submit FAFSA. In 2010, 63 master's, 24 doctorates awarded. *Degree program information:* Part-time and evening/weekend programs available. Offers art education (MA Ed); early childhood education (MA Ed); educational leadership (Ed D); educational leadership: principal certification (MA Ed); elementary education (MA Ed); gifted education (MA Ed); higher education leadership (Ed D); literacy specialist (MA Ed); middle grades education (MA Ed); secondary teaching and inquiry (MA Ed); teacher as leader (MA Ed). *Application deadline:* Applications are processed on a rolling basis. *Application fee:* $40 ($60 for international students). Electronic applications accepted. *Application Contact:* Holly Stanwich, Graduate Admissions Coordinator, 314-529-9542, Fax: 314-529-9921, E-mail: teachered@maryville.edu. *Dean*, Dr. Sam Hausfather, 314-529-9466, Fax: 314-529-9921, E-mail: shausfather@maryville.edu.

School of Health Professions Students: 129 full-time (103 women), 128 part-time (114 women); includes 28 minority (19 Black or African American, non-Hispanic/Latino; 8 Asian, non-Hispanic/Latino; 1 Hispanic/Latino), 3 international. Average age 31. *Faculty:* 23 full-time (17 women), 12 part-time/adjunct (10 women). Expenses: Contact institution. *Financial support:* Career-related internships or fieldwork, Federal Work-Study, and campus employment available. Financial award application deadline: 3/1; financial award applicants required to submit FAFSA. In 2010, 113 master's awarded. *Degree program information:* Part-time and evening/weekend programs available. Offers accelerated RN to MSN (MSN); adult nurse practitioner (MSN); advanced practice nursing (DNP); family nurse practitioner (MSN); geriatric nurse practitioner (MSN); health professions (MARC, MMT, MOT, MSN, DNP, DPT, CAGS); marriage and family therapy (MARC); music therapy (MARC); nursing education (MSN); occupational therapy (MOT); physical therapy (DPT); rehabilitation counseling (CAGS); substance abuse (MARC). *Application deadline:* Applications are processed on a rolling basis. *Application fee:* $40 ($60 for international students). Electronic applications accepted. *Application Contact:* Denise Evans, Assistant Vice President, Adult and Continuing Education, 314-529-9342, Fax: 314-529-9927, E-mail: devans1@maryville.edu. *Dean*, Dr. Charles Gulas, 314-529-9625, Fax: 314-529-9495, E-mail: hlthprofessions@maryville.edu.

MARYWOOD UNIVERSITY, Scranton, PA 18509-1598

General Information Independent-religious, coed, comprehensive institution. CGS member. *Enrollment:* 3,479 graduate, professional, and undergraduate students; 595 full-time matriculated graduate/professional students (487 women), 525 part-time matriculated graduate/professional students (403 women). *Enrollment by degree level:* 953 master's, 126 doctoral, 41 other advanced degrees. *Tuition:* Part-time $735 per credit. *Required fees:* $470 per semester. Tuition and fees vary according to degree level and campus/location. *Student services:* Campus employment opportunities, campus safety program, career counseling, child daycare facilities, exercise/wellness program, free psychological counseling, grant writing training, international student services, low-cost health insurance, multicultural affairs office, services for students with disabilities, teacher training, writing training. *Library facilities:* Learning Resources Center plus 1 other. *Online resources:* library catalog, web page, access to other libraries' catalogs. *Collection:* 220,530 titles, 28,091 serial subscriptions, 53,850 audiovisual materials.

Computer facilities: 460 computers available on campus for general student use. A campuswide network can be accessed from student residence rooms and from off campus. Online class registration is available. *Web address:* http://www.marywood.edu/.

General Application Contact: Christian DiGregorio, Director of University Admissions, 866-279-9663, Fax: 570-961-4763, E-mail: gograd@marywood.edu.

GRADUATE UNITS

Academic Affairs Electronic applications accepted.

College of Health and Human Services Offers clinical physician assistant (MS); dietetic internship (Certificate); gerontology (MS); health and human services (MHSA, MPA, MS, MSW, Certificate); health services administration (MHSA); kinesiology (MS); nonprofit management (MPA); nursing administration (MS); nutrition (MS); physician assistant studies (MS); public administration (MPA); social work (MSW); sports nutrition and exercise science (MS).

College of Liberal Arts and Sciences Offers biotechnology (MS); criminal justice (MS); finance and investments (MBA); financial information systems (MS); general management (MBA); liberal arts and sciences (MBA, MS); management information systems (MBA, MS). Electronic applications accepted.

Insalaco College of Creative and Performing Arts Offers advertising design (MA, MFA); art (Post Master's Certificate); art education (MA); art therapy (MA, Post Master's Certificate); ceramics (MA); clay (MA, MFA); communication arts (MA); corporate communication (Certificate); creative and performing arts (MA, MFA, MMT, MS, Certificate, Post Master's Certificate); e-business (Certificate); graphic design (MA, MFA); health communication (Certificate); illustration (MA, MFA); information sciences (MS, Certificate); instructional technology (Certificate); interdisciplinary (MA); media management (MA); metals (MFA); music education (MA); music therapy (MMT, Certificate); painting (MA, MFA); photography (MA, MFA); printmaking (MA, MFA); production (MA); sculpture (MA); studio art (MA); visual arts (MFA); vocal pedagogy (Post Master's Certificate); weaving (MA). Electronic applications accepted.

Reap College of Education and Human Development Offers clinical psychology (Psy D); clinical services (MA); counseling (Post-Master's Certificate); counselor education–elementary (MS); counselor education–secondary (MS); early childhood intervention (MS); education and human development (M Ed, MA, MAT, MS, PhD, Psy D, Ed S, Post-Master's Certificate); educational administration (PhD); elementary education (MAT); general theoretical (MA); health promotion (PhD); higher education administration (MS, PhD); human development (PhD); instructional leadership (M Ed, PhD); mental health counseling (MA); psychology (MA); reading education (MS); school leadership (MS); school psychology (Ed S); secondary/k-12 education (MAT); social work (PhD); special education (MS); special education administration and supervision (MS); speech-language pathology (MS).

School of Architecture Offers architecture (M Arch); studio art (MA).

MASSACHUSETTS COLLEGE OF ART AND DESIGN, Boston, MA 02115-5882

General Information State-supported, coed, comprehensive institution. *Enrollment:* 2,446 graduate, professional, and undergraduate students; 159 full-time matriculated graduate/professional students (99 women), 9 part-time matriculated graduate/professional students (5 women). *Enrollment by degree level:* 168 master's. *Graduate faculty:* 23 full-time (11 women), 40 part-time/adjunct (21 women). Tuition, state resident: part-time $665 per credit. Tuition, nonresident: part-time $665 per credit. *Graduate housing:* Room and/or apartments available on a first-come, first-served basis to single students; on-campus housing not available to married students. Housing application deadline: 2/1. *Student services:* Campus employment opportunities, campus safety program, career counseling, free psychological counseling, international student services, low-cost health insurance, multicultural affairs office, services for students with disabilities, teacher training, writing training. *Library facilities:* Morton R. Godine Library. *Online resources:* library catalog, web page, access to other libraries' catalogs. *Collection:* 258,675 titles, 557 serial subscriptions.

Computer facilities: Computer purchase and lease plans are available. 370 computers available on campus for general student use. A campuswide network can be accessed from student residence rooms and from off campus. *Web address:* http://www.massart.edu/.

General Application Contact: Graduate Programs, 617-879-7166, E-mail: gradinfo@massart.edu.

GRADUATE UNITS

Graduate Programs Students: 159 full-time (99 women), 9 part-time (5 women); includes 1 Asian, non-Hispanic/Latino; 7 Hispanic/Latino; 6 Two or more races, non-Hispanic/Latino, 22 international. Average age 34. 419 applicants, 37% accepted, 83 enrolled. *Faculty:* 23 full-time (11 women), 40 part-time/adjunct (21 women). Expenses: Contact institution. *Financial support:* In 2010–11, 19 fellowships (averaging $5,000 per year) were awarded; research assistantships, teaching assistantships, career-related internships or fieldwork and Federal Work-Study also available. Support available to part-time students. Financial award application deadline: 3/1; financial award applicants required to submit FAFSA. In 2010, 55 master's awarded. *Degree program information:* Part-time programs available. Postbaccalaureate distance learning degree programs offered (minimal on-campus study). Offers architecture (M Arch); art education (MSAE); ceramics (MFA); design (MFA); fibers (MFA); film/video (MFA); glass (MFA); media and performing arts (MFA); metals/jewelry (MFA); painting (MFA); photography (MFA); printmaking (MFA); sculpture (MFA); teaching (MAT). *Application deadline:* For fall admission, 1/15 for domestic and international students. *Application fee:* $85. Electronic applications accepted. *Application Contact:* George Creamer, Dean of Graduate Programs, 617-879-7163, Fax: 617-879-7171, E-mail: creamer@massart.edu. *Dean of Graduate Programs*, George Creamer, 617-879-7163, Fax: 617-879-7171, E-mail: creamer@massart.edu.

MASSACHUSETTS COLLEGE OF LIBERAL ARTS, North Adams, MA 01247-4100

General Information State-supported, coed, comprehensive institution. *Enrollment:* 1,974 graduate, professional, and undergraduate students; 51 full-time matriculated graduate/professional students (29 women), 202 part-time matriculated graduate/professional students (122 women). *Enrollment by degree level:* 253 master's. Tuition and fees vary according to program. *Graduate housing:* On-campus housing not available. *Student services:* Campus safety program, career counseling, low-cost health insurance. *Library facilities:* Eugene L. Freel Library. *Online resources:* library catalog, web page, access to other libraries' catalogs. *Collection:* 211,000 titles, 19,000 serial subscriptions, 7,000 audiovisual materials.

Computer facilities: Computer purchase and lease plans are available. 140 computers available on campus for general student use. A campuswide network can be accessed from student residence rooms and from off campus. Online class registration is available. *Web address:* http://www.mcla.edu/.

General Application Contact: Joshua Mendel, Associate Director of Admissions, 413-662-5409.

GRADUATE UNITS

Program in Education Students: 51 full-time (29 women), 202 part-time (122 women). Expenses: Contact institution. *Financial support:* Career-related internships or fieldwork available. Financial award application deadline: 5/1; financial award applicants required to submit FAFSA. In 2010, 15 master's awarded. *Degree program information:* Part-time and evening/weekend programs available. Offers curriculum (M Ed); educational administration (M Ed); reading (M Ed); special education (M Ed). *Application deadline:* Applications are processed on a rolling basis. *Application Contact:* Dr. Susan Edgerton, Chair, 413-662-5381. *Chair*, Dr. Susan Edgerton, 413-662-5381.

MASSACHUSETTS COLLEGE OF PHARMACY AND HEALTH SCIENCES, Boston, MA 02115-5896

General Information Independent, coed, university. *Graduate housing:* Room and/or apartments available on a first-come, first-served basis to single students; on-campus housing not available to married students. Housing application deadline: 5/1. *Research affiliation:* Cephrim Biosciences, Inc. (pharmaceutics), Center for Analytical Science (analytical medicinal chemistry).

GRADUATE UNITS

Graduate Studies Students: 2,895 full-time (1,836 women), 151 part-time (109 women); includes 955 minority (133 Black or African American, non-Hispanic/Latino; 4 American Indian or Alaska Native, non-Hispanic/Latino; 758 Asian, non-Hispanic/Latino; 43 Hispanic/Latino; 6 Native Hawaiian or other Pacific Islander, non-Hispanic/Latino; 11 Two or more races, non-Hispanic/Latino), 199 international. Average age 30. 5,553 applicants, 28% accepted, 760 enrolled. Expenses: Contact institution. *Financial support:* Fellowships with partial tuition reimbursements, research assistantships with partial tuition reimbursements, teaching assistantships with partial tuition reimbursements, scholarships/grants, tuition waivers (partial), and unspecified assistantships available. Financial award application deadline: 3/15. In 2010, 438 first professional degrees, 2 master's, 2 doctorates awarded. *Degree program information:* Part-time programs available. Offers applied natural products (MANP); community oral health (MS); drug regulatory affairs and health policy (MS); medicinal chemistry (MS, PhD); nursing (MS); pharmaceutics (MS, PhD); pharmacology (MS, PhD); pharmacy and health sciences (Pharm D, MANP, MPAS, MS, PhD). *Application Contact:* Brian Barilone, Associate Director of Graduate and Transfer Admission, 617-879-5032, E-mail: admissions@mcphs.edu. *Assistant Dean of Graduate Studies,* Dr. Barbara LeDuc, 617-732-2757, E-mail: barbara.leduc@mcphs.edu.

School of Pharmacy–Boston Offers pharmacy (Pharm D, MANP).

School of Physician Assistant Studies Offers physician assistant studies (MPAS). Electronic applications accepted.

School of Pharmacy–Worcester/Manchester Offers pharmacy (Pharm D).

MASSACHUSETTS INSTITUTE OF TECHNOLOGY, Cambridge, MA 02139-4307

General Information Independent, coed, university. CGS member. *Enrollment:* 10,566 graduate, professional, and undergraduate students; 6,094 full-time matriculated graduate/professional students (1,893 women), 34 part-time matriculated graduate/professional students (17 women). *Enrollment by degree level:* 2,472 master's, 3,656 doctoral. *Graduate faculty:* 1,007 full-time (215 women), 10 part-time/adjunct (1 woman). *Tuition:* Full-time $38,940; part-time $605 per unit. *Required fees:* $272. *Graduate housing:* Rooms and/or apartments available to single and married students. Housing application deadline: 5/15. *Student services:* Campus employment opportunities, campus safety program, career counseling, child daycare facilities, exercise/wellness program, free psychological counseling, grant writing training, international student services, low-cost health insurance, services for students with disabilities, teacher training, writing training. *Library facilities:* MIT Libraries plus 7 others. *Online resources:* library catalog, web page. *Collection:* 3.1 million titles, 53,155 serial subscriptions, 44,011 audiovisual materials. *Research affiliation:* Novartis (pharmaceutical manufacturing), Singapore National Research Foundation (infectious diseases, environmental sensing, biosystems, urban transportation), Woods Hole Oceanographic Institution (applied ocean science and engineering), Broad Institute (genomics and biomedical research), Whitehead Institute for Biomedical Research (developmental biology), Eni S.p.A (renewable energy).

Computer facilities: Computer purchase and lease plans are available. 1,100 computers available on campus for general student use. A campuswide network can be accessed from student residence rooms and from off campus. Online class registration is available. *Web address:* http://web.mit.edu/.

General Application Contact: Stuart Schmill, Dean of Admissions, 617-253-2917, Fax: 617-687-9174, E-mail: mitgrad@mit.edu.

GRADUATE UNITS

MIT Sloan School of Management Offers management (M Fin, MBA, MS, SM, PhD). Electronic applications accepted.

Operations Research Center Students: 52 full-time (11 women); includes 5 minority (4 Asian, non-Hispanic/Latino; 1 Hispanic/Latino), 26 international. Average age 26. 224 applicants, 9% accepted, 9 enrolled. *Faculty:* 45 full-time (8 women). Expenses: Contact institution. *Financial support:* In 2010–11, 51 students received support, including 5 fellowships (averaging $23,821 per year), 35 research assistantships (averaging $28,777 per year), 11 teaching assistantships (averaging $31,352 per year); Federal Work-Study, institutionally sponsored loans, scholarships/grants, health care benefits, tuition waivers, and unspecified assistantships also available. Financial award application deadline: 12/15. In 2010, 13 master's, 5 doctorates awarded. Offers operations research (SM, PhD). *Application deadline:* For fall admission, 12/15 for domestic and international students. *Application fee:* $75. Electronic applications accepted. *Application Contact:* Laura A. Rose, Admissions Coordinator, 617-253-9303, Fax: 617-258-9214, E-mail: lrose@mit.edu. *Co-Director,* Dr. Dimitris J. Bertsimas, 617-253-3601, Fax: 617-258-9214, E-mail: orc-www@mit.edu.

School of Architecture and Planning Students: 601 full-time (262 women), 4 part-time (2 women); includes 130 minority (19 Black or African American, non-Hispanic/Latino; 6 American Indian or Alaska Native, non-Hispanic/Latino; 67 Asian, non-Hispanic/Latino; 27 Hispanic/Latino; 11 Two or more races, non-Hispanic/Latino), 197 international. Average age 29. 2,534 applicants, 15% accepted, 265 enrolled. *Faculty:* 77 full-time (22 women). Expenses: Contact institution. *Financial support:* In 2010–11, 506 students received support, including 248 fellowships with tuition reimbursements available (averaging $20,023 per year), 211 research assistantships with tuition reimbursements available (averaging $25,918 per year), 47 teaching assistantships with tuition reimbursements available (averaging $29,117 per year); Federal Work-Study, institutionally sponsored loans, scholarships/grants, health care benefits, and unspecified assistantships also available. In 2010, 197 master's, 21 doctorates awarded. Offers architecture (M Arch, PhD); architecture and planning (M Arch, MCP, MSRED, SM, SM Arch S, SM Vis S, SMBT, PhD); architecture studies (SM Arch S); building technology (SMBT); city planning (MCP); media arts and sciences (SM, PhD); media technology (SM); real estate development (MSRED); urban and regional planning (PhD); urban and regional studies (PhD); urban studies and planning (SM); visual studies (SM Vis S). *Application fee:* $75. Electronic applications accepted. *Application Contact:* Graduate Admissions, 617-253-2917, Fax: 617-687-9174, E-mail: mitgrad@mit.edu. *Dean,* Prof. Adele Naude Santos, 617-253-4401, Fax: 617-253-9417, E-mail: sap-info@mit.edu.

School of Engineering Students: 2,672 full-time (645 women), 5 part-time (1 woman); includes 456 minority (45 Black or African American, non-Hispanic/Latino; 5 American Indian or Alaska Native, non-Hispanic/Latino; 285 Asian, non-Hispanic/Latino; 97 Hispanic/Latino; 24 Two or more races, non-Hispanic/Latino), 1,145 international. Average age 27. 7,549 applicants, 18% accepted, 898 enrolled. *Faculty:* 369 full-time (59 women), 1 part-time/adjunct (0 women). Expenses: Contact institution. *Financial support:* In 2010–11, 2,382 students received support, including 624 fellowships with tuition reimbursements available (averaging $28,558 per year), 1,531 research assistantships with tuition reimbursements available (averaging $28,814 per year), 236 teaching assistantships with tuition reimbursements available (averaging $30,032 per year); career-related internships or fieldwork, Federal Work-Study, institutionally sponsored loans, scholarships/grants, traineeships, health care benefits, and unspecified assistantships also available. In 2010, 771 master's, 297 doctorates, 17 other advanced degrees awarded. Offers aeronautics and astronautics (SM, PhD, Sc D, EAA); aerospace computational engineering (PhD, Sc D); air transportation systems (PhD, Sc D); air-breathing propulsion (PhD, Sc D); aircraft systems engineering (PhD, Sc D); applied biosciences (PhD, Sc D); archaeological materials (PhD, Sc D); autonomous systems (PhD, Sc D); bio- and polymeric materials (PhD, Sc D); bioengineering (PhD, Sc D); biological engineering (PhD, Sc D); biological oceanography (PhD, Sc D); biomedical engineering (M Eng); chemical engineering (SM, PhD, Sc D); chemical engineering practice (SM, PhD); chemical oceanography (PhD, Sc D); civil and environmental engineering (M Eng, SM, PhD, Sc D); civil and environmental systems (PhD, Sc D); civil engineering (PhD, Sc D, CE); coastal engineering (PhD, Sc D); communications and networks (PhD, Sc D); computation for design and optimization (SM); computational and systems biology (PhD); computer science (PhD, Sc D, ECS); computer science and engineering (PhD, Sc D); construction engineering and management (PhD, Sc D); controls (PhD, Sc D); electrical engineering (PhD, Sc D, EE); electrical engineering and computer science (M Eng, SM, PhD, Sc D); electronic, photonic and magnetic materials (PhD, Sc D); emerging, fundamental and computational studies in materials science (Sc D); emerging, fundamental, and computational studies in materials science (PhD); engineering (M Eng, SM, PhD, Sc D, CE, EAA, ECS, EE, Mat E, Mech E, Met E, NE, Naval E); engineering and management (SM); engineering systems (SM, PhD); environmental biology (PhD, Sc D); environmental chemistry (PhD, Sc D); environmental engineering (PhD, Sc D); environmental fluid mechanics (PhD, Sc D); geotechnical and geoenvironmental engineering (PhD, Sc D); humans in aerospace (PhD, Sc D); hydrology (PhD, Sc D); information technology (PhD, Sc D); logistics (M Eng); manufacturing (M Eng); materials and structures (PhD, Sc D); materials engineering (Mat E); materials science and engineering (M Eng, SM, PhD, Sc D); mechanical engineering (SM, PhD, Sc D, Mech E); metallurgical engineering (Met E); naval architecture and marine engineering (SM, PhD, Sc D); naval engineering (Naval E); nuclear science and engineering (SM, PhD, Sc D, NE); ocean engineering (SM, PhD, Sc D); oceanographic engineering (SM, PhD, Sc D); space propulsion (PhD, Sc D); space systems (PhD, Sc D); structural and environmental materials (PhD, Sc D); structures and materials (PhD, Sc D); technology and policy (SM); technology, management and policy (PhD); toxicology (SM); transportation (PhD, Sc D). *Application fee:* $75. Electronic applications accepted. *Application Contact:* Graduate Admissions, 617-253-2917, Fax: 617-687-9174, E-mail: mitgrad@mit.edu. *Dean,* Prof. Ian A. Waitz, 617-253-3291, Fax: 617-253-8549.

School of Humanities, Arts, and Social Sciences Students: 277 full-time (104 women), 1 (woman) part-time; includes 29 minority (4 Black or African American, non-Hispanic/Latino; 2 American Indian or Alaska Native, non-Hispanic/Latino; 14 Asian, non-Hispanic/Latino; 3 Hispanic/Latino; 6 Two or more races, non-Hispanic/Latino), 113 international. Average age 27. 1,849 applicants, 7% accepted, 70 enrolled. *Faculty:* 162 full-time (50 women), 4 part-time/adjunct (1 woman). Expenses: Contact institution. *Financial support:* In 2010–11, 261 students received support, including 124 fellowships with tuition reimbursements available (averaging $31,562 per year), 39 research assistantships with tuition reimbursements available (averaging $31,480 per year), 64 teaching assistantships with tuition reimbursements available (averaging $35,607 per year); Federal Work-Study, institutionally sponsored loans, scholarships/grants, health care benefits, and unspecified assistantships also available. In 2010, 28 master's, 40 doctorates awarded. Offers comparative media studies (SM); economics (SM, PhD); history, anthropology, and science, technology and society (PhD); humanities, arts, and social sciences (SM, PhD); linguistics (PhD); philosophy (PhD); political science (SM, PhD); science writing (SM). *Application fee:* $75. Electronic applications accepted. *Application Contact:* Graduate Admissions Office, 617-253-2917, Fax: 617-687-9174, E-mail: mitgrad@mit.edu. *Dean,* Prof. Deborah Fitzgerald, 617-253-3450, Fax: 617-253-3451, E-mail: shass-www@mit.edu.

School of Science Students: 1,078 full-time (395 women); includes 193 minority (15 Black or African American, non-Hispanic/Latino; 5 American Indian or Alaska Native, non-Hispanic/Latino; 90 Asian, non-Hispanic/Latino; 68 Hispanic/Latino; 15 Two or more races, non-Hispanic/Latino), 334 international. Average age 26. 2,890 applicants, 17% accepted, 225 enrolled. *Faculty:* 274 full-time (52 women), 2 part-time/adjunct (0 women). Expenses: Contact institution. *Financial support:* In 2010–11, 964 students received support, including 424 fellowships with tuition reimbursements available (averaging $31,373 per year), 510 research assistantships with tuition reimbursements available (averaging $30,730 per year), 131 teaching assistantships with tuition reimbursements available (averaging $31,247 per year); Federal Work-Study, institutionally sponsored loans, scholarships/grants, health care benefits, and unspecified assistantships also available. In 2010, 26 master's, 180 doctorates awarded. Offers atmospheric chemistry (PhD, Sc D); atmospheric science (SM, PhD, Sc D); biochemistry (PhD); biological chemistry (PhD, Sc D); biological oceanography (PhD); biology (PhD); biophysical chemistry and molecular structure (PhD); cell biology (PhD); chemical oceanography (SM, PhD, Sc D); climate physics and chemistry (SM, PhD, Sc D); cognitive science (PhD); computational and systems biology (PhD); developmental biology (PhD); earth and planetary sciences (SM); genetics (PhD); geochemistry (PhD, Sc D); geology (PhD, Sc D); geophysics (PhD, Sc D); immunology (PhD); inorganic chemistry (PhD, Sc D); marine geology and geophysics (SM, PhD, Sc D); mathematics (PhD); microbiology (PhD); molecular biology (PhD); neurobiology (PhD); neuroscience (PhD); organic chemistry (PhD, Sc D); physical chemistry (PhD, Sc D); physical oceanography (SM, PhD, Sc D); physics (SM, PhD); planetary sciences (PhD, Sc D); science (SM, PhD, Sc D). *Application fee:* $75. Electronic applications accepted. *Application Contact:* Graduate Admissions Office, 617-253-2917, Fax: 617-687-9174, E-mail: mitgrad@mit.edu. *Dean,* Prof. Marc A. Kastner, 617-253-8900, Fax: 617-253-8901, E-mail: scnc@mit.edu.

MASSACHUSETTS MARITIME ACADEMY, Buzzards Bay, MA 02532-1803

General Information State-supported, coed, primarily men, comprehensive institution.

GRADUATE UNITS

Program in Emergency Management Offers emergency management (MS).

Program in Facilities Management *Degree program information:* Part-time and evening/weekend programs available. Offers facilities management (MS).

MASSACHUSETTS SCHOOL OF LAW AT ANDOVER, Andover, MA 01810

General Information Independent, coed, graduate-only institution. *Graduate housing:* On-campus housing not available.

GRADUATE UNITS

Professional Program *Degree program information:* Part-time and evening/weekend programs available. Offers law (JD). Electronic applications accepted.

MASSACHUSETTS SCHOOL OF PROFESSIONAL PSYCHOLOGY, Boston, MA 02132

General Information Independent, coed, primarily women, graduate-only institution. *Tuition:* Full-time $32,352; part-time $1011 per credit. Full-time tuition and fees vary according to degree level. *Graduate housing:* On-campus housing not available. *Student services:* Campus employment opportunities, career counseling, international student services, low-cost health insurance, multicultural affairs office, writing training. *Library facilities:* Mintz Library plus 1 other. *Online resources:* library catalog. *Collection:* 6,500 titles, 59 serial subscriptions, 132 audiovisual materials.

Computer facilities: 12 computers available on campus for general student use. A campuswide network can be accessed. Online class registration is available. *Web address:* http://www.mspp.edu/.

General Application Contact: Elizabeth Sweeney, Admissions Coordinator, 617-327-6777 Ext. 210, Fax: 617-327-4447, E-mail: admissions@mspp.edu.

GRADUATE UNITS

Graduate Programs Students: 515. Average age 28. *Faculty:* 24 full-time (11 women), 13 part-time/adjunct (9 women). Expenses: Contact institution. *Financial support:* Teaching assistantships, career-related internships or fieldwork available. Financial award applicants required to submit FAFSA. Offers applied psychology in higher education student personnel administration (MA); clinical psychology (Psy D); counseling psychology (MA); counseling psychology and community mental health (MA); counseling psychology and global mental health (MA); executive coaching (Graduate Certificate); forensic and counseling psychology (MA); leadership psychology (Psy D); organizational psychology (MA); primary care psychology (MA); respecialization in clinical psychology (Certificate); school psychology (Psy D). *Application fee:* $50. Electronic applications accepted. *Application Contact:* Admissions and Marketing, 617-327-6777 Ext. 210, Fax: 617-327-4447, E-mail: admissions@mspp.edu. *President,* Dr. Nicholas A. Covino, 617-327-6777, Fax: 617-327-4447.

THE MASTER'S COLLEGE AND SEMINARY, Santa Clarita, CA 91321-1200

General Information Independent-religious, coed, comprehensive institution. *Graduate housing:* On-campus housing not available.

The Master's College and Seminary (continued)

GRADUATE UNITS

The Master's Seminary *Degree program information:* Part-time programs available. Offers biblical counseling (MABC); New Testament (Th D); Old Testament (Th D); preaching (D Min); theology (M Div, M Th, Th D).

MAYO GRADUATE SCHOOL, Rochester, MN 55905

General Information Independent, coed, graduate-only institution. *Graduate housing:* On-campus housing not available.

GRADUATE UNITS

Graduate Programs in Biomedical Sciences Offers biochemistry and structural biology (PhD); biomedical engineering (PhD); biomedical sciences (PhD); cell biology and genetics (PhD); immunology (PhD); molecular biology (PhD); molecular neuroscience (PhD); molecular pharmacology and experimental therapeutics (PhD); tumor biology (PhD); virology and gene therapy (PhD). Electronic applications accepted.

MAYO MEDICAL SCHOOL, Rochester, MN 55905

General Information Independent, coed, graduate-only institution. *Graduate housing:* On-campus housing not available.

GRADUATE UNITS

Professional Program Offers medicine (MD). MD offered through the Mayo Foundation's Division of Education; MD/PhD, MD/Certificate with Mayo Graduate School. Electronic applications accepted.

MAYO SCHOOL OF HEALTH SCIENCES, Rochester, MN 55905

General Information Independent, coed, graduate-only institution.

GRADUATE UNITS

Program in Nurse Anesthesia Offers nurse anesthesia (MNA). Electronic applications accepted.

Program in Physical Therapy Offers physical therapy (DPT). Electronic applications accepted.

McCORMICK THEOLOGICAL SEMINARY, Chicago, IL 60615

General Information Independent-religious, coed, graduate-only institution. *Graduate housing:* Rooms and/or apartments available on a first-come, first-served basis to single and married students. Housing application deadline: 7/1.

GRADUATE UNITS

Graduate and Professional Programs *Degree program information:* Part-time and evening/weekend programs available. Offers ministry (D Min); theological studies (MATS, Certificate); theology (M Div). M Div/MSW offered jointly with Loyola University Chicago, University of Chicago, and University of Illinois at Chicago.

McDANIEL COLLEGE, Westminster, MD 21157-4390

General Information Independent, coed, comprehensive institution. *Graduate housing:* On-campus housing not available.

GRADUATE UNITS

Graduate and Professional Studies *Degree program information:* Part-time and evening/weekend programs available. Offers curriculum and instruction (MS); education of the deaf (MS); educational administration (MS); elementary education (MS); guidance and counseling (MS); human resources development (MS); human services management in special education (MS); liberal studies (MLA); media/library science (MS); physical education (MS); reading education (MS); secondary education (MS); special education (MS). Electronic applications accepted.

McGILL UNIVERSITY, Montréal, QC H3A 2T5, Canada

General Information Province-supported, coed, university. CGS member. *Graduate housing:* Room and/or apartments available to married students; on-campus housing not available to single students.

GRADUATE UNITS

Faculty of Graduate and Postdoctoral Studies

Desautels Faculty of Management Offers administration (PhD); entrepreneurial studies (MBA); finance (MBA); general management (Post Master's Certificate); information systems (MBA); international business (exchange program) (MBA); international Master's program in practicing management (MM); management (MBA); management for development (MBA); manufacturing management (MMM); marketing (MBA); operations management (MBA); public accountancy (Diploma); strategic management (MBA). MMM offered jointly with Faculty of Engineering; PhD with Concordia University, HEC Montreal, Université de Montréal, Université du Québec à Montréal.

Faculty of Agricultural and Environmental Sciences Offers agricultural and environmental sciences (M Sc, M Sc A, PhD, Certificate, Graduate Diploma); agricultural economics (M Sc); animal science (M Sc, M Sc A, PhD); biotechnology (M Sc A, Certificate); computer applications (M Sc, M Sc A, PhD); dietetics (M Sc A, Graduate Diploma); entomology (M Sc, PhD); environmental assessment (M Sc); food engineering (M Sc, M Sc A, PhD); food science and agricultural chemistry (M Sc, PhD); forest science (M Sc, PhD); grain drying (M Sc, M Sc A, PhD); human nutrition (M Sc, M Sc A, PhD); irrigation and drainage (M Sc, M Sc A, PhD); machinery (M Sc, M Sc A, PhD); microbiology (M Sc, PhD); micrometeorology (M Sc, PhD); neotropical environment (M Sc, PhD); parasitology (M Sc, PhD); plant science (M Sc, M Sc A, PhD, Certificate); pollution control (M Sc, M Sc A, PhD); post-harvest technology (M Sc, M Sc A, PhD); soil dynamics (M Sc, M Sc A, PhD); soil science (M Sc, PhD); structure and environment (M Sc, M Sc A, PhD); vegetable and fruit storage (M Sc, M Sc A, PhD); wildlife biology (M Sc, PhD).

Faculty of Arts Offers anthropology (MA, PhD); art history and communication studies (MA, PhD); arts (MA, MSW, PhD, Diploma); bioethics (MA); East Asian studies (MA, PhD); economics (MA, PhD); English (MA, PhD); French language and literature (MA, PhD); German studies (MA, PhD); Hispanic studies (MA, PhD); history (MA, PhD); history of medicine (MA); Islamic studies (MA, PhD, Diploma); Italian studies (MA, PhD); Jewish studies (MA); language acquisition (PhD); linguistics (MA, PhD); medical anthropology (MA); medical sociology (MA); neo-tropical environment (MA); philosophy (PhD); political science (MA, PhD); Russian literature (MA, PhD); social statistics (MA); social work (MSW, PhD, Diploma); sociology (MA, PhD, Diploma).

Faculty of Dentistry Offers forensic dentistry (Certificate); oral and maxillofacial surgery (M Sc, PhD).

Faculty of Education Offers counseling psychology (MA, PhD); culture and values in education (MA, PhD); curriculum studies (MA); education (M Ed, M Sc, MA, MLIS, PhD, Certificate, Diploma); educational leadership (MA, Certificate); educational psychology (M Ed, MA, PhD); educational studies (PhD); information studies (MLIS, PhD, Certificate, Diploma); integrated studies in education (M Ed); kinesiology and physical education (M Sc, MA, PhD, Certificate, Diploma); school/applied child psychology and applied developmental psychology (M Ed, MA, PhD, Diploma); second language education (MA, PhD).

Faculty of Engineering Offers aerospace (M Eng); affordable homes (M Arch II, Diploma); architectural history and theory (M Arch II); architecture (PhD); chemical engineering (M Eng, PhD); domestic environment (M Arch II); domestic environments (Diploma); electrical and computer engineering (M Eng, PhD); engineering (M Arch I, M Arch II, M Eng, M Sc, MMM, MUP, PhD, Diploma); environmental engineering (M Eng, M Sc, PhD); environmental planning (MUP); fluid mechanics (M Sc); fluid mechanics and hydraulic engineering (M Eng, PhD); housing (MUP); manufacturing management (MMM); materials engineering (M Eng, PhD); mechanical engineering (M Eng, M Sc, PhD); minimum cost housing in developing countries (M Arch II, Diploma); mining engineering (M Eng, M Sc, PhD, Diploma); professional architecture (M Arch I); rehabilitation of urban infrastructure (M Eng, PhD); soil behavior (M Eng, PhD); soil mechanics and foundations (M Eng, PhD); structures and structural mechanics (M Eng, PhD); transportation (MUP); urban design (MUP); urban planning, policy and design (PhD); water resources (M Sc); water resources engineering (M Eng, PhD).

Faculty of Law Offers air and space law (LL M, DCL, Graduate Certificate); bioethics (LL M); comparative law (LL M, DCL, Graduate Certificate); law (LL M, DCL). Applications for LL M with specialization in bioethics are made initially through the Biomedical Ethics Unit in the Faculty of Medicine.

Faculty of Medicine Offers anatomy and cell biology (M Sc, PhD); assessing driving capability (PGC); biochemistry (M Sc, PhD); biomedical engineering (M Eng, PhD); communication science and disorders (M Sc); communication sciences and disorders (PhD); community health (M Sc); environmental health (M Sc); epidemiology and biostatistics (M Sc, PhD, Diploma); experimental medicine (M Sc, PhD); genetic counseling (M Sc); health care evaluation (M Sc); human genetics (M Sc, PhD); medical anthropology (MA, PhD); medical history (MA, PhD); medical physics (M Sc, PhD); medical sociology (MA, PhD); medical statistics (M Sc); medicine (M Eng, M Sc, M Sc A, MA, PhD, Diploma, Graduate Diploma, PGC); microbiology and immunology (M Sc, M Sc A, PhD); neurology and neurosurgery (M Sc, PhD); nurse practitioner (Graduate Diploma); nursing (M Sc A, PhD); occupational health (M Sc, PhD); otolaryngology (M Sc); pathology (M Sc, PhD); pharmacology and therapeutics (M Sc, PhD); physiology (M Sc, PhD); psychiatry (M Sc); rehabilitation science (M Sc, PhD); speech-language pathology (M Sc A); surgery (M Sc, PhD).

Faculty of Religious Studies Offers religious studies (MA, STM, PhD).

Faculty of Science Offers atmospheric science (M Sc, PhD); bioinformatics (M Sc, PhD); chemical biology (M Sc, PhD); chemistry (M Sc, PhD); clinical psychology (PhD); computational science and engineering (M Sc); computer science (M Sc, PhD); earth and planetary sciences (M Sc, PhD); environment (M Sc, PhD); experimental psychology (M Sc, MA, PhD); geography (M Sc, MA, PhD); mathematics and statistics (M Sc, MA, PhD); neo-tropical environment (M Sc, MA, PhD); physical oceanography (M Sc, PhD); physics (M Sc, PhD); science (M Sc, MA, PhD); social statistics (MA).

Schulich School of Music Offers composition (M Mus, D Mus, PhD); music education (MA, PhD); music technology (MA, PhD); musicology (MA, PhD); performance (M Mus); performance studies (D Mus); sound recording (M Mus, PhD); theory (MA, PhD).

Professional Program in Dentistry Offers dentistry (DMD). Electronic applications accepted.

Professional Program in Law Offers law (JD).

Professional Program in Medicine Offers medicine.

McKENDREE UNIVERSITY, Lebanon, IL 62254-1299

General Information Independent-religious, coed, comprehensive institution. *Enrollment:* 3,299 graduate, professional, and undergraduate students; 247 full-time matriculated graduate/professional students (168 women), 725 part-time matriculated graduate/professional students (493 women). *Enrollment by degree level:* 972 master's. *Graduate faculty:* 31 full-time (15 women), 66 part-time/adjunct (30 women). *Tuition:* Full-time $6750; part-time $375 per credit hour. One-time fee: $100. Tuition and fees vary according to program. *Graduate housing:* On-campus housing not available. *Student services:* Campus safety program, career counseling, exercise/wellness program, free psychological counseling, international student services, multicultural affairs office, services for students with disabilities, teacher training, writing training. *Library facilities:* Holman Library. *Online resources:* library catalog, web page, access to other libraries' catalogs. *Collection:* 109,000 titles, 450 serial subscriptions, 6,637 audiovisual materials.

Computer facilities: Computer purchase and lease plans are available. 140 computers available on campus for general student use. A campuswide network can be accessed from student residence rooms and from off campus. Online class registration is available. *Web address:* http://www.mckendree.edu/.

General Application Contact: Sabrina K. Storner, Director of Graduate Admission, 618-537-6477, Fax: 618-537-6410, E-mail: skstorner@mckendree.edu.

GRADUATE UNITS

Graduate Programs Students: 247 full-time (168 women), 725 part-time (493 women); includes 75 Black or African American, non-Hispanic/Latino; 4 American Indian or Alaska Native, non-Hispanic/Latino; 4 Asian, non-Hispanic/Latino; 14 Hispanic/Latino, 2 international. Average age 36. *Faculty:* 31 full-time (15 women), 66 part-time/adjunct (30 women). Expenses: Contact institution. *Financial support:* Application deadline: 6/30. In 2010, 300 master's awarded. *Degree program information:* Part-time and evening/weekend programs available. Offers business administration (MBA); certification (MA Ed); educational administration and leadership (MA Ed); educational studies (MA Ed); higher education administrative services (MA Ed); human resource management (MBA); international business (MBA); music education (MA Ed); nursing education (MSN); nursing management/administration (MSN); professional counseling (MAPC); special education (MA Ed); teacher leadership (MA Ed); transition to teaching (MA Ed). *Application deadline:* Applications are processed on a rolling basis. *Application fee:* $0. Electronic applications accepted. *Application Contact:* Sabrina K. Storner, Director of Graduate Admission, 618-537-6477, Fax: 618-537-6410, E-mail: skstorner@mckendree.edu. *Provost and Dean of the University,* Dr. Christine Bahr, 618-537-6810, E-mail: cmbahr@mckendree.edu.

McMASTER UNIVERSITY, Hamilton, ON L8S 4M2, Canada

General Information Province-supported, coed, university. CGS member. *Graduate housing:* Room and/or apartments available to single students; on-campus housing not available to married students. Housing application deadline: 6/30. *Research affiliation:* Commonwealth Development (telecommunications), Canadian Centre for Inland Waters (chemical and civil engineering).

GRADUATE UNITS

Faculty of Health Sciences *Degree program information:* Part-time programs available. Postbaccalaureate distance learning degree programs offered (minimal on-campus study). Offers biochemistry and biomedical sciences (M Sc, PhD); blood and vascular (M Sc, PhD); genetics and cancer (M Sc, PhD); health research methodology (course-based) (M Sc); health research methodology (thesis) (M Sc, PhD); health sciences (M Sc, PhD); immunity and infection (M Sc, PhD); metabolism and nutrition (M Sc, PhD); neurosciences and behavioral sciences (M Sc, PhD); nursing (M Sc, PhD); occupational therapy (M Sc); physiology/pharmacology (M Sc, PhD); physiotherapy (M Sc); rehabilitation science (M Sc, PhD); rehabilitation science (course-based) (M Sc).

McMaster Divinity College *Degree program information:* Part-time programs available. Offers Biblical studies (MA, MTS, Diploma); biblical studies (M Div); Christian interpretation/history (M Div, MA, MTS, Diploma); Christian ministry (M Div, MA, MTS, Diploma); Christian Studies (Certificate); Christian theology (PhD). Affiliated with the Toronto School of Theology.

School of Graduate Studies *Degree program information:* Part-time programs available.

Faculty of Business *Degree program information:* Part-time programs available. Offers business (MBA, PhD); human resources and management (MBA, PhD); information systems (PhD).

Faculty of Engineering *Degree program information:* Part-time programs available. Offers chemical engineering (M Eng, MA Sc, PhD); civil engineering (M Eng, MA Sc, PhD); computer science (M Sc, PhD); electrical engineering (M Eng, MA Sc, PhD); engineering (M Eng, M Sc, MA Sc, PhD); engineering physics (M Eng, MA Sc, PhD); materials engineering (M Eng, MA Sc, PhD); materials science (M Eng, PhD); mechanical engineering (M Eng, MA Sc, PhD); nuclear engineering (PhD); software engineering (M Eng, MA Sc, PhD).

Faculty of Humanities *Degree program information:* Part-time and evening/weekend programs available. Offers classics (MA, PhD); cultural studies and critical theory (MA); English (MA, PhD); French (MA); globalization studies (MA); history (MA, PhD); humanities (MA, PhD); philosophy (MA, PhD).

Faculty of Science *Degree program information:* Part-time and evening/weekend programs available. Offers analytical chemistry (M Sc, PhD); applied statistics (M Sc); astrophysics (PhD); biology (M Sc, PhD); chemical physics (M Sc, PhD); chemistry (M Sc, PhD); geochemistry (PhD); geology (M Sc, PhD); health and radiation physics (M Sc); human geography (MA, PhD); inorganic chemistry (M Sc, PhD); mathematics (M Sc, PhD); medical physics (M Sc, PhD); medical statistics (M Sc); organic chemistry (M Sc, PhD); physical chemistry (M Sc, PhD); physical geography (M Sc, PhD); physics (PhD); polymer chemistry (M Sc, PhD); psychology (M Sc, PhD); science (M Sc, MA, PhD); statistical theory (M Sc); statistics (M Sc).

Faculty of Social Sciences *Degree program information:* Part-time and evening/weekend programs available. Offers analysis of social welfare policy (MSW); analysis of social work practice (MSW); anthropology (MA, PhD); economics (MA, PhD); human biodynamics (M Sc, PhD); international relations (PhD); political science (MA); public and the global economy (MA); public policy (PhD); public policy and administration (MA); religious studies (MA, PhD); social sciences (M Sc, MA, MSW, PhD); sociology (MA, PhD); work and society (MA).

McNEESE STATE UNIVERSITY, Lake Charles, LA 70609

General Information State-supported, coed, comprehensive institution. *Enrollment:* 355 full-time matriculated graduate/professional students (213 women), 485 part-time matriculated graduate/professional students (344 women). *Enrollment by degree level:* 829 master's, 11 other advanced degrees. *Graduate faculty:* 130 full-time (39 women), 2 part-time/adjunct (1 woman). Tuition and fees vary according to course load. *Graduate housing:* Room and/or apartments available on a first-come, first-served basis to single students. Housing application deadline: 8/15. *Student services:* Campus employment opportunities, campus safety program, career counseling, exercise/wellness program, free psychological counseling, grant writing training, international student services, low-cost health insurance, multicultural affairs office, services for students with disabilities, teacher training, writing training. *Library facilities:* Frazer Memorial Library plus 2 others.

Computer facilities: 700 computers available on campus for general student use. A campuswide network can be accessed from student residence rooms and from off campus. Online class registration is available. *Web address:* http://www.mcneese.edu/.

General Application Contact: Dr. George F. Mead, Interim Dean of Dore' School of Graduate Studies, 337-475-5396, Fax: 337-475-5397, E-mail: admissions@mcneese.edu.

GRADUATE UNITS

Doré School of Graduate Studies Students: 355 full-time (213 women), 485 part-time (344 women); includes 148 minority (111 Black or African American, non-Hispanic/Latino; 2 American Indian or Alaska Native, non-Hispanic/Latino; 9 Asian, non-Hispanic/Latino; 18 Hispanic/Latino; 8 Two or more races, non-Hispanic/Latino), 127 international. Average age 30. *Faculty:* 130 full-time (39 women), 2 part-time/adjunct (1 woman). Expenses: Contact institution. *Financial support:* Fellowships, research assistantships, teaching assistantships, career-related internships or fieldwork, Federal Work-Study, institutionally sponsored loans, and unspecified assistantships available. Support available to part-time students. Financial award application deadline: 5/1. In 2010, 327 master's, 2 other advanced degrees awarded. *Degree program information:* Part-time and evening/weekend programs available. *Application deadline:* For fall admission, 5/15 priority date for domestic and international students; for spring admission, 10/15 priority date for domestic and international students. Applications are processed on a rolling basis. *Application fee:* $20 ($30 for international students). *Application Contact:* Dr. George F. Mead, Interim Dean of Dore' School of Graduate Studies, 337-475-5396, Fax: 337-475-5397, E-mail: admissions@mcneese.edu. *Interim Dean,* Dr. George F. Mead, 337-475-5394, Fax: 337-475-5397, E-mail: mead@mcneese.edu.

Burton College of Education Students: 173 full-time (132 women), 320 part-time (247 women); includes 103 minority (81 Black or African American, non-Hispanic/Latino; 3 Asian, non-Hispanic/Latino; 13 Hispanic/Latino; 6 Two or more races, non-Hispanic/Latino), 14 international. *Faculty:* 34 full-time (15 women), 1 (woman) part-time/adjunct. Expenses: Contact institution. *Financial support:* Fellowships, research assistantships, teaching assistantships, Federal Work-Study available. Support available to part-time students. Financial award application deadline: 5/1. In 2010, 188 master's, 2 other advanced degrees awarded. *Degree program information:* Part-time and evening/weekend programs available. Offers addiction treatment (MA); advanced professional (M Ed); applied behavior analysis (MA); autism (M Ed); counseling psychology (MA); curriculum and instruction (M Ed); early childhood education (M Ed); early childhood education grades PK-3 (Postbaccalaureate Certificate); early intervention birth-5 (Postbaccalaureate Certificate); education (M Ed, MA, MAT, MS, Ed S, Postbaccalaureate Certificate); educational diagnostician (M Ed, Postbaccalaureate Certificate); educational leadership (M Ed, Ed S); educational technology (Ed S); educational technology leadership (M Ed); elementary education (M Ed); elementary education grades 1-5 (MAT, Postbaccalaureate Certificate); exercise physiology (MS); general/experimental psychology (MA); grades K-12 (Postbaccalaureate Certificate); health promotion (MS); instructional technology (MS); middle school education grades 4-8 (Postbaccalaureate Certificate); mild/moderate grades 6-12 (MAT); multiple levels grades K-12 (Postbaccalaureate Certificate); nutrition and wellness (MS); reading (M Ed); school counseling (M Ed, Postbaccalaureate Certificate); school librarian (Postbaccalaureate Certificate); secondary education (M Ed); secondary education grades 6-12 (MAT, Postbaccalaureate Certificate); special education mild/moderate grades 1-12 (M Ed, MAT, Postbaccalaureate Certificate); teaching (MAT, Postbaccalaureate Certificate). *Application deadline:* For fall admission, 5/15 priority date for domestic and international students; for spring admission, 10/15 priority date for domestic and international students. Applications are processed on a rolling basis. *Application fee:* $20 ($30 for international students). *Application Contact:* Dr. George F. Mead, Interim Dean of Dore' School of Graduate Studies, 337-475-5396, Fax: 337-475-5397, E-mail: admissions@mcneese.edu. *Dean,* Dr. Wayne R. Fetter, 337-475-5432, Fax: 337-475-5467, E-mail: wfetter@mcneese.edu.

College of Business Students: 54 full-time (28 women), 33 part-time (17 women); includes 5 minority (3 Black or African American, non-Hispanic/Latino; 1 Asian, non-Hispanic/Latino; 1 Hispanic/Latino), 33 international. *Faculty:* 17 full-time (1 woman). Expenses: Contact institution. *Financial support:* Research assistantships, teaching assistantships, Federal Work-Study available. Support available to part-time students. Financial award application deadline: 5/1. In 2010, 38 master's awarded. *Degree program information:* Part-time and evening/weekend programs available. Offers accounting (MBA); business (MBA); business administration (MBA). *Application deadline:* For fall admission, 5/15 priority date for domestic and international students; for spring admission, 10/15 priority date for domestic and international students. Applications are processed on a rolling basis. *Application fee:* $20 ($30 for international students). *Application Contact:* Dr. Akm Rahman, MBA Director, 337-475-5576, Fax: 337-475-5986, E-mail: mrahman@mcneese.edu. *Dean,* Dr. Mitchell Adrian, 337-475-5514, Fax: 337-475-5010, E-mail: madrian@mcneese.edu.

College of Engineering and Engineering Technology Students: 37 full-time (10 women), 18 part-time (1 woman); includes 5 minority (3 Black or African American, non-Hispanic/Latino; 1 American Indian or Alaska Native, non-Hispanic/Latino; 1 Two or more races, non-Hispanic/Latino), 43 international. *Faculty:* 15 full-time (1 woman). Expenses: Contact institution. *Financial support:* Federal Work-Study available. Support available to part-time students. Financial award application deadline: 5/1. In 2010, 28 master's awarded. *Degree program information:* Part-time and evening/weekend programs available. Offers chemical engineering (M Eng); civil engineering (M Eng); electrical engineering (M Eng); engineering management (M Eng); mechanical engineering (M Eng). *Application deadline:* For fall admission, 5/15 priority date for domestic and international students; for spring admission, 10/15 priority date for domestic and international students. Applications are processed on a rolling basis. *Application fee:* $20 ($30 for international students). *Dean,* Dr. Nikos Kiritsis, 337-475-5875, Fax: 337-475-5237, E-mail: nikosk@mcneese.edu.

College of Liberal Arts Students: 25 full-time (12 women), 10 part-time (7 women); includes 5 minority (2 Black or African American, non-Hispanic/Latino; 2 Asian, non-Hispanic/Latino; 1 Hispanic/Latino). *Faculty:* 29 full-time (13 women). Expenses: Contact institution. *Financial support:* Teaching assistantships, Federal Work-Study available. Support available to part-time students. Financial award application deadline: 5/1. In 2010, 25 master's awarded. *Degree program information:* Part-time and evening/weekend programs available. Offers creative writing (MFA); English (MA); instrumental (MM Ed); Kodaly studies (Postbaccalaureate Certificate); liberal arts (MA, MFA, MM Ed, Postbaccalaureate Certificate); music education (MM Ed, Postbaccalaureate Certificate); vocal (MM Ed). *Application deadline:* For fall admission, 5/15 priority date for domestic and international students; for spring admission, 10/15 priority date for domestic and international students. Applications are processed on a rolling basis. *Application fee:* $20 ($30 for international students). *Application Contact:* Dr. George F. Mead, Interim Dean of Dore' School of Graduate Studies, 337-475-5396, Fax: 337-475-5397, E-mail: admissions@mcneese.edu. *Dean,* Dr. Ray Miles, 337-475-5192, Fax: 337-475-5594, E-mail: rmiles@mcneese.edu.

College of Nursing Students: 8 full-time (7 women), 76 part-time (57 women); includes 22 minority (17 Black or African American, non-Hispanic/Latino; 2 Asian, non-Hispanic/Latino; 2 Hispanic/Latino; 1 Two or more races, non-Hispanic/Latino). *Faculty:* 4 full-time (all women), 1 part-time/adjunct (0 women). Expenses: Contact institution. *Financial support:* Application deadline: 5/1. In 2010, 16 master's awarded. Offers clinical nurse specialist (MSN); nurse educator (MSN); nurse practitioner (MSN); nursing leadership and administration (MSN). Program offered jointly with Southeastern Louisiana University, Southern University and Agricultural and Mechanical College. *Application deadline:* For fall admission, 5/15 priority date for domestic and international students; for spring admission, 10/15 priority date for domestic and international students. Applications are processed on a rolling basis. *Application fee:* $20 ($30 for international students). *Application Contact:* Valarie Waldmeier, Coordinator, 337-475-5285, Fax: 337-475-5702, E-mail: vwaldmeier@mcneese.edu. *Dean,* Dr. Peggy L. Wolfe, 337-475-5820, Fax: 337-475-5924, E-mail: pwolfe@mcneese.edu.

College of Science Students: 58 full-time (24 women), 28 part-time (15 women); includes 8 minority (5 Black or African American, non-Hispanic/Latino; 1 American Indian or Alaska Native, non-Hispanic/Latino; 1 Asian, non-Hispanic/Latino; 1 Hispanic/Latino), 37 international. *Faculty:* 31 full-time (5 women). Expenses: Contact institution. *Financial support:* Teaching assistantships, Federal Work-Study available. Support available to part-time students. Financial award application deadline: 5/1. In 2010, 32 master's awarded. *Degree program information:* Part-time and evening/weekend programs available. Offers agricultural sciences (MS); chemistry (MS); chemistry/environmental science education (MS); computer science (MS); environmental and chemical sciences (MS); environmental science (MS); mathematics (MS); science (MS); statistics (MS). *Application deadline:* For fall admission, 5/15 priority date for domestic and international students; for spring admission, 10/15 priority date for domestic and international students. Applications are processed on a rolling basis. *Application fee:* $20 ($30 for international students). *Application Contact:* Dr. George F. Mead, Interim Dean of Dore' School of Graduate Studies, 337-475-5396, Fax: 337-475-5397, E-mail: admissions@mcneese.edu. *Dean,* Dr. George F. Mead, 337-475-5785, Fax: 337-475-5249, E-mail: mead@mcneese.edu.

MEADVILLE LOMBARD THEOLOGICAL SCHOOL, Chicago, IL 60637-1602

General Information Independent-religious, coed, graduate-only institution. *Graduate housing:* Rooms and/or apartments available on a first-come, first-served basis to single and married students. Housing application deadline: 3/15.

GRADUATE UNITS

Graduate and Professional Programs *Degree program information:* Part-time programs available. Postbaccalaureate distance learning degree programs offered (minimal on-campus study). Offers divinity (M Div); ministry (D Min); religion (MA). M Div/MSW offered jointly with University of Chicago.

MEDAILLE COLLEGE, Buffalo, NY 14214-2695

General Information Independent, coed, comprehensive institution. *Enrollment:* 2,736 graduate, professional, and undergraduate students; 889 full-time matriculated graduate/professional students (677 women), 2 part-time matriculated graduate/professional students (both women). *Enrollment by degree level:* 891 master's. *Graduate faculty:* 34 full-time (20 women), 61 part-time/adjunct (36 women). *Graduate housing:* Rooms and/or apartments available on a first-come, first-served basis to single and married students. Housing application deadline: 8/15. *Student services:* Campus employment opportunities, campus safety program, career counseling, exercise/wellness program, free psychological counseling, low-cost health insurance, multicultural affairs office, services for students with disabilities, teacher training, writing training. *Library facilities:* Medaille College Library. *Online resources:* library catalog, web page, access to other libraries' catalogs. *Collection:* 55,690 titles, 236 serial subscriptions, 1,411 audiovisual materials.

Computer facilities: 120 computers available on campus for general student use. A campuswide network can be accessed from student residence rooms and from off campus. Online class registration is available. *Web address:* http://www.medaille.edu/.

General Application Contact: Jacqueline Matheny, Executive Director of Marketing and Enrollment, 716-932-2541, Fax: 716-632-1811, E-mail: jmatheny@medaille.edu.

GRADUATE UNITS

Program in Business Administration—Amherst Students: 222 full-time (126 women), 1 (woman) part-time; includes 24 Black or African American, non-Hispanic/Latino; 3 Asian, non-Hispanic/Latino; 6 Hispanic/Latino; 1 Two or more races, non-Hispanic/Latino. Average age 31. *Faculty:* 8 full-time (3 women), 14 part-time/adjunct (4 women). Expenses: Contact institution. *Financial support:* In 2010–11, 180 students received support. Federal Work-Study available. Financial award applicants required to submit FAFSA. In 2010, 143 master's awarded. *Degree program information:* Evening/weekend programs available. Offers business administration (MBA); organizational leadership (MA). *Application deadline:* Applications are processed on a rolling basis. *Application fee:* $100. *Application Contact:* Jacqueline Matheny, Executive Director of Marketing and Enrollment, 716-932-2541, Fax: 716-632-1811, E-mail: jmatheny@medaille.edu. *Associate Dean for Special Programs,* Jennifer Bavifard, 716-631-1061 Ext. 150, Fax: 716-631-1380, E-mail: jbavifar@medaille.edu.

Program in Business Administration—Rochester Students: 37 full-time (26 women); includes 9 Black or African American, non-Hispanic/Latino; 5 Hispanic/Latino. Average age 36. 31 applicants, 90% accepted, 25 enrolled. *Faculty:* 3 full-time (2 women), 40 part-time/adjunct (20 women). Expenses: Contact institution. *Financial support:* In 2010–11, 37 students received support. Federal Work-Study available. Financial award applicants required to submit FAFSA. In 2010, 27 master's awarded. *Degree program information:* Evening/weekend programs available. Offers business administration (MBA); organizational leadership (MA). *Application deadline:* Applications are processed on a rolling basis. *Application fee:* $100. *Application Contact:* Jane Rowlands, Marketing Support, 585-272-0030, Fax: 585-272-0057, E-mail: jrowlands@medaille.edu. *Branch Campus Director,* Jennifer Bavifard, 716-932-2591, Fax: 716-631-1380, E-mail: jbavifard@medaille.edu.

Program in Education Students: 458 full-time (365 women), 1 (woman) part-time; includes 6 Black or African American, non-Hispanic/Latino, 293 international. Average age 29. *Faculty:* 17 full-time (11 women), 37 part-time/adjunct (26 women). Expenses: Contact institution. *Financial support:* Federal Work-Study available. Financial award applicants required to submit FAFSA. In 2010, 624 master's awarded. *Degree program information:* Part-time and evening/weekend programs available. Offers adolescent education (MS Ed); curriculum and instruction (MS Ed); education preparation (MS Ed); literacy (MS Ed); special education (MS). *Application deadline:* For fall admission, 8/15 priority date for domestic students; for spring admission, 1/15 priority date for domestic students. Applications are processed on a rolling basis. *Application fee:* $35. Electronic applications accepted. *Application Contact:* Jacqueline Matheny, Executive Director of Marketing and Enrollment, 716-932-2541, Fax: 716-632-1811, E-mail: jmatheny@medaille.edu. *Director of Graduate Programs,* Dr. Robert DiSibio, 716-932-2548, Fax: 716-631-1380, E-mail: rdisibio@medaille.edu.

Programs in Psychology Students: 186 full-time (165 women); includes 22 Black or African American, non-Hispanic/Latino; 3 Asian, non-Hispanic/Latino; 2 Hispanic/Latino; 2 Two or more races, non-Hispanic/Latino. Average age 31. *Faculty:* 9 full-time (6 women), 9 part-time/adjunct (6 women). Expenses: Contact institution. *Financial support:* In 2010–11, 90 students received support. Federal Work-Study available. Financial award applicants required to submit FAFSA. In 2010, 69 master's awarded. *Degree program information:* Part-time and evening/weekend programs available. Offers mental health counseling (MA); psychology (MA). *Application deadline:* Applications are processed on a rolling basis. *Application fee:* $35. Electronic applications accepted. *Application Contact:* Jacqueline Matheny, Executive Director of Marketing and Enrollment, 716-932-2541, Fax: 716-632-1811, E-mail: jmatheny@

Medaille College (continued)

medaille.edu. *Dean of Adult and Graduate Studies,* Dr. Judith Horowitz, 716-880-2229, Fax: 716-884-0291, E-mail: jhorowitz@medaille.edu.

MEDICAL COLLEGE OF WISCONSIN, Milwaukee, WI 53226-0509

General Information Independent, coed, graduate-only institution. CGS member. *Enrollment by degree level:* 256 master's, 210 doctoral. *Tuition:* Full-time $30,000; part-time $710 per credit. *Required fees:* $150. *Graduate housing:* On-campus housing not available. *Student services:* Campus employment opportunities, campus safety program, career counseling, exercise/wellness program, free psychological counseling, international student services, low-cost health insurance, multicultural affairs office, services for students with disabilities. *Library facilities:* Todd Wehr Library plus 2 others. *Online resources:* library catalog, web page. *Collection:* 236,700 titles, 1,550 serial subscriptions, 1,692 audiovisual materials. *Research affiliation:* General Electric Medical Systems (biophysics, radiology).

Computer facilities: 250 computers available on campus for general student use. A campuswide network can be accessed from off campus. Online class registration, multimedia resources, i.e., CDROM books are available. *Web address:* http://www.mcw.edu/.

General Application Contact: Susan K. Barnes, Director of Enrollment, 414-955-8218, Fax: 414-955-6555, E-mail: sbarnes@mcw.edu.

GRADUATE UNITS

Graduate School of Biomedical Sciences *Degree program information:* Part-time and evening/weekend programs available. Postbaccalaureate distance learning degree programs offered (minimal on-campus study). Offers AMA and MCW professionalism and bioethics (Graduate Certificate); basic and translational science (PhD); biochemistry (PhD); bioethics (MA, Graduate Certificate); bioinformatics (MS); biomedical sciences (MA, MPH, MS, PhD, Graduate Certificate); biophysics (PhD); biostatistics (PhD); clinical and translational science (MS); clinical bioethics (Graduate Certificate); epidemiology (MS); functional imaging (PhD); health care technologies management (MS); medical informatics (MS); microbiology and molecular genetics (MS, PhD); neuroscience (PhD); pharmacology and toxicology (PhD); physiology (PhD); public and community health (PhD); public health (MPH, PhD, Graduate Certificate); research bioethics (Graduate Certificate). Electronic applications accepted.

Interdisciplinary Program in Biomedical Sciences Offers biomedical sciences (PhD).

Medical School *Degree program information:* Part-time programs available. Postbaccalaureate distance learning degree programs offered (no on-campus study). Offers medicine (MD, MPH); occupational health and medicine (MPH); public and community health (MPH).

MEDICAL UNIVERSITY OF SOUTH CAROLINA, Charleston, SC 29425

General Information State-supported, coed, upper-level institution. CGS member. *Enrollment:* 2,560 graduate, professional, and undergraduate students; 2,157 full-time matriculated graduate/professional students (1,273 women), 145 part-time matriculated graduate/professional students (117 women). *Enrollment by degree level:* 1,255 first professional, 505 master's, 536 doctoral, 6 other advanced degrees. *Graduate faculty:* 1,291 full-time (529 women), 214 part-time/adjunct (102 women). *Student services:* Campus employment opportunities, campus safety program, exercise/wellness program, free psychological counseling, grant writing training, international student services, low-cost health insurance, multicultural affairs office, services for students with disabilities, teacher training, writing training. *Library facilities:* Medical University of South Carolina Library plus 1 other. *Online resources:* library catalog, web page, access to other libraries' catalogs. *Collection:* 151,763 titles, 20,173 serial subscriptions, 1,819 audiovisual materials. *Research affiliation:* Novartis (cancer), Boston Scientific Corporation (cardiovascular diseases), Genentech (Alzheimer's disease), AstraZeneca (cancer/cardiovascular diseases), Merck & Company, Inc. (neuroscience), Eli Lilly and Company (substance abuse).

Computer facilities: 200 computers available on campus for general student use. A campuswide network can be accessed from off campus. Online class registration is available. *Web address:* http://www.musc.edu/.

General Application Contact: Lyla E. Hudson, Director of Admissions, 843-792-3281, Fax: 843-792-6615, E-mail: oesadmis@musc.edu.

GRADUATE UNITS

College of Dental Medicine Students: 239 full-time (97 women); includes 7 Black or African American, non-Hispanic/Latino; 2 American Indian or Alaska Native, non-Hispanic/Latino; 12 Asian, non-Hispanic/Latino; 2 Hispanic/Latino. Average age 26. 793 applicants, 9% accepted, 70 enrolled. *Faculty:* 51 full-time (14 women), 35 part-time/adjunct (8 women). Expenses: Contact institution. *Financial support:* In 2010–11, 52 students received support. Federal Work-Study, scholarships/grants, and tuition waivers (partial) available. Support available to part-time students. Financial award application deadline: 3/10; financial award applicants required to submit FAFSA. In 2010, 56 DMDs awarded. Offers dental medicine (DMD). *Application deadline:* For spring admission, 1/15 for domestic and international students. *Application fee:* $95. Electronic applications accepted. *Application Contact:* William H. Liner, Dental Admissions Counselor, 843-792-4892, Fax: 843-792-6615, E-mail: linerw@musc.edu. *Dean,* Dr. John J. Sanders, 843-792-3811, Fax: 843-792-1376, E-mail: sandersjj@musc.edu.

College of Graduate Studies Students: 161 full-time (106 women), 41 part-time (33 women); includes 14 Black or African American, non-Hispanic/Latino; 1 American Indian or Alaska Native, non-Hispanic/Latino; 2 Asian, non-Hispanic/Latino; 6 Hispanic/Latino, 27 international. Average age 33. 272 applicants, 28% accepted, 44 enrolled. *Faculty:* 268 full-time (79 women), 20 part-time/adjunct (3 women). Expenses: Contact institution. *Financial support:* In 2010–11, 114 students received support, including 114 research assistantships with partial tuition reimbursements available (averaging $23,000 per year); Federal Work-Study and scholarships/grants also available. Support available to part-time students. Financial award application deadline: 3/10; financial award applicants required to submit FAFSA. In 2010, 31 master's, 47 doctorates awarded. Offers biochemistry and molecular biology (MS, PhD); cancer biology (PhD); cardiovascular biology (PhD); cardiovascular imaging (PhD); cell and molecular pharmacology and experimental therapeutics (MS, PhD); cell injury and repair (PhD); cell regulation (PhD); craniofacial biology (PhD); drug discovery (PhD); genetics and development (PhD); marine biomedicine (PhD); medicinal chemistry (PhD); microbiology and immunology (MS, PhD); neurosciences (MS, PhD); pathology and laboratory medicine (MS, PhD); toxicology (PhD). *Application deadline:* For fall admission, 1/15 priority date for domestic and international students. Applications are processed on a rolling basis. *Application fee:* $85 for international students. Electronic applications accepted. *Application Contact:* Dr. Cynthia F. Wright, Associate Dean for Career Development and Admissions, 843-792-2564, Fax: 843-792-6590, E-mail: wrightcf@musc.edu. *Dean,* Dr. Perry V. Halushka, 843-792-3012, Fax: 843-792-6590, E-mail: halushpv@musc.edu.

Division of Biostatistics and Epidemiology Students: 21 full-time (16 women); includes 3 Black or African American, non-Hispanic/Latino; 1 Hispanic/Latino, 4 international. Average age 29. 36 applicants, 31% accepted, 5 enrolled. *Faculty:* 21 full-time (14 women), 1 part-time/adjunct (0 women). Expenses: Contact institution. *Financial support:* In 2010–11, 18 students received support, including 18 research assistantships with partial tuition reimbursements available (averaging $23,000 per year); Federal Work-Study and scholarships/grants also available. Support available to part-time students. Financial award application deadline: 3/10; financial award applicants required to submit FAFSA. In 2010, 4 doctorates awarded. Offers biostatistics (MS, PhD); epidemiology (MS, PhD). *Application deadline:* For fall admission, 1/15 priority date for domestic and international students. Applications are processed on a rolling basis. *Application fee:* $0 ($85 for international students). Electronic applications accepted. *Application Contact:* Dr. Ramesh Ramakrishnan, Associate Professor, 843-876-1140, Fax: 843-876-1126, E-mail: ramakris@musc.edu. *Professor/Director,* Dr. Yuko Y. Palesch, 843-876-1917, Fax: 843-792-6590, E-mail: paleschy@musc.edu.

College of Health Professions Students: 636 full-time (485 women), 42 part-time (28 women); includes 57 Black or African American, non-Hispanic/Latino; 3 American Indian or Alaska Native, non-Hispanic/Latino; 11 Asian, non-Hispanic/Latino; 19 Hispanic/Latino, 2 international. Average age 28. 1,158 applicants, 33% accepted, 292 enrolled. *Faculty:* 39 full-time (17 women), 6 part-time/adjunct (4 women). Expenses: Contact institution. *Financial support:* In 2010–11, 20 students received support. Career-related internships or fieldwork, Federal Work-Study, scholarships/grants, and tuition waivers (partial) available. Support available to part-time students. Financial award application deadline: 3/10; financial award applicants required to submit FAFSA. In 2010, 209 master's, 70 doctorates awarded. *Degree program information:* Part-time programs available. Offers anesthesia for nurses (MSNA); health administration (DHA); health administration-executive (MHA); health administration-global (MHA); health administration-residential (MHA); health and rehabilitation science (PhD); health professions (MHA, MRA, MS, MSNA, MSRS, DHA, DPT, PhD); occupational therapy (MSRS); physical therapy (DPT); physician assistant studies (MS); research administration (MRA). *Application fee:* $85. Electronic applications accepted. *Application Contact:* Melissa Freeland, Recruitment and Student Affairs Coordinator, 843-792-8510, Fax: 843-792-3327, E-mail: freelan@musc.edu. *Interim Dean,* Dr. Lisa Saladin, 843-792-3328, Fax: 843-792-3322, E-mail: sothmann@musc.edu.

College of Medicine Students: 697 full-time (287 women); includes 87 Black or African American, non-Hispanic/Latino; 6 American Indian or Alaska Native, non-Hispanic/Latino; 63 Asian, non-Hispanic/Latino; 15 Hispanic/Latino, 7 international. Average age 26. 3,188 applicants, 6% accepted, 158 enrolled. *Faculty:* 1,110 full-time (429 women), 182 part-time/adjunct (76 women). Expenses: Contact institution. *Financial support:* In 2010–11, 676 students received support. Federal Work-Study and scholarships/grants available. Financial award application deadline: 3/10; financial award applicants required to submit FAFSA. In 2010, 136 first professional degrees awarded. Offers medicine (MD). *Application deadline:* For fall admission, 12/1 for domestic students. Applications are processed on a rolling basis. *Application fee:* $85. Electronic applications accepted. *Application Contact:* Joan M. Graesch, Admissions Counselor, 843-792-3283, Fax: 843-792-0204, E-mail: jmg26@musc.edu. *Dean,* Dr. Etta D. Pisano, 843-792-2842, Fax: 843-792-2967, E-mail: pisanoe@musc.edu.

College of Nursing Students: 90 full-time (86 women), 60 part-time (55 women); includes 20 Black or African American, non-Hispanic/Latino; 1 American Indian or Alaska Native, non-Hispanic/Latino; 1 Asian, non-Hispanic/Latino; 4 Hispanic/Latino. Average age 33. 348 applicants, 47% accepted, 112 enrolled. *Faculty:* 33 full-time (32 women), 7 part-time/adjunct (5 women). Expenses: Contact institution. *Financial support:* Federal Work-Study, scholarships/grants, and traineeships available. Support available to part-time students. Financial award application deadline: 3/10; financial award applicants required to submit FAFSA. In 2010, 36 master's, 3 doctorates awarded. *Degree program information:* Part-time programs available. Postbaccalaureate distance learning degree programs offered (minimal on-campus study). Offers adult nurse practitioner (MSN); advanced practice nursing (DNP); family nurse practitioner (MSN); nurse administrator (MSN); nurse educator (MSN); nursing (MSN, DNP, PhD); pediatric nurse practitioner (MSN). *Application deadline:* For fall admission, 2/1 priority date for domestic and international students. *Application fee:* $85. Electronic applications accepted. *Application Contact:* Carolyn F. Page, Director, Student Services, 843-792-3844, Fax: 843-792-5395, E-mail: pagecf@musc.edu. *Dean,* Dr. Gail W. Stuart, 843-792-3941, Fax: 843-792-0504, E-mail: stuartg@musc.edu.

South Carolina Clinical and Translational Research Institute Students: 8 full-time (3 women), 7 part-time (5 women); includes 1 Black or African American, non-Hispanic/Latino, 4 international. Average age 32. 18 applicants, 83% accepted, 13 enrolled. *Faculty:* 7 full-time (2 women), 1 part-time/adjunct (0 women). Expenses: Contact institution. *Financial support:* In 2010–11, 9 students received support. Federal Work-Study, scholarships/grants, and unspecified assistantships available. Support available to part-time students. Financial award application deadline: 3/10; financial award applicants required to submit FAFSA. In 2010, 15 master's awarded. Postbaccalaureate distance learning degree programs offered (no on-campus study). Offers clinical and translational research (MS). *Application deadline:* For fall admission, 5/19 priority date for domestic students, 12/31 priority date for international students. Applications are processed on a rolling basis. *Application fee:* $95. Electronic applications accepted. *Application Contact:* Lisa E. Frawley, Program Coordinator, 843-792-8449, Fax: 843-792-0227, E-mail: frawleyl@musc.edu. *Director,* Dr. Thomas C. Hulsey, 843-792-9907, Fax: 843-792-0227, E-mail: hulseytc@musc.edu.

South Carolina College of Pharmacy Students: 318 full-time (208 women), 2 part-time (1 woman); includes 18 Black or African American, non-Hispanic/Latino; 2 American Indian or Alaska Native, non-Hispanic/Latino; 20 Asian, non-Hispanic/Latino; 10 Hispanic/Latino, 1 international. Average age 25. 526 applicants, 43% accepted, 192 enrolled. *Faculty:* 36 full-time (15 women), 3 part-time/adjunct (2 women). Expenses: Contact institution. *Financial support:* Career-related internships or fieldwork, Federal Work-Study, institutionally sponsored loans, and scholarships/grants available. Financial award application deadline: 3/10; financial award applicants required to submit FAFSA. In 2010, 78 Pharm Ds awarded. Offers pharmacy (Pharm D). *Application deadline:* For fall admission, 1/1 for domestic and international students. *Application fee:* $85. Electronic applications accepted. *Application Contact:* Dr. Philip D. Hall, Associate Dean, 843-792-8979, Fax: 843-792-9081, E-mail: hallpd@sccp.sc.edu. *Executive Dean,* Dr. Joseph T. DiPiro, 843-792-8452, Fax: 843-792-9081, E-mail: jdipiro@sccp.sc.edu.

MEHARRY MEDICAL COLLEGE, Nashville, TN 37208-9989

General Information Independent-religious, coed, graduate-only institution. CGS member. *Graduate housing:* Rooms and/or apartments available on a first-come, first-served basis to single and married students.

GRADUATE UNITS

School of Dentistry Offers dentistry (DDS).

School of Graduate Studies Postbaccalaureate distance learning degree programs offered (minimal on-campus study). Offers cancer biology (PhD); interdisciplinary studiesmicrobiology and immunology (PhD); neuroscience (PhD); occupational medicine (MSPH); pharmacology (PhD); public health administration (MSPH).

School of Medicine Offers medicine (MD). Electronic applications accepted.

MEMORIAL UNIVERSITY OF NEWFOUNDLAND, St. John's, NL A1C 5S7, Canada

General Information Province-supported, coed, university. CGS member. *Graduate housing:* Rooms and/or apartments available on a first-come, first-served basis to single and married students. *Research affiliation:* Eastern Regional Health Authority (health research).

GRADUATE UNITS

Faculty of Medicine *Degree program information:* Part-time programs available. Postbaccalaureate distance learning degree programs offered (no on-campus study). Offers medicine (M Sc, PhD, Diploma). Electronic applications accepted.

Graduate Programs in Medicine *Degree program information:* Part-time programs available. Offers applied health services research (M Sc); cancer (M Sc, PhD); cardiovascular (M Sc, PhD); clinical epidemiology (M Sc, PhD, Diploma); community health (M Sc, PhD, Diploma); human genetics (M Sc, PhD); immunology (M Sc, PhD); medicine (M Sc, PhD, Diploma); neuroscience (M Sc, PhD). Electronic applications accepted.

School of Graduate Studies *Degree program information:* Part-time and evening/weekend programs available. Postbaccalaureate distance learning degree programs offered (minimal on-campus study). Offers applied social psychology (MASP); aquaculture (M Sc); archaeology and physical anthropology (MA, PhD); atomic and molecular physics (M Sc, PhD); biochemistry (M Sc, PhD); biology (M Sc, PhD); chemistry (M Sc, PhD); classics (MA); cognitive and behavioral ecology (M Sc, PhD); computational science (M Sc); computational science (cooperative) (M Sc); computer engineering (MA Sc); computer science (M Sc, PhD); condensed matter physics (M Sc, PhD); economics (MA); employment relations (MER); English language and literature (MA, PhD); environmental science (M Env Sc, M Sc); environmental systems engineering and management (MA Sc); ethnomusicology (MA, PhD); experimental psychology (M Sc, PhD); fisheries resource management (MMS, Advanced Diploma); folklore (MA, PhD); food science (M Sc, PhD); French studies (MA); gender (PhD); geography (M Sc, MA, PhD); geology (M Sc, PhD); geophysics (M Sc, PhD); German language and literature (M Phil, MA); history (MA, PhD); humanities (M Phil); instrumental analysis (M Sc); linguistics (MA, PhD); marine biology (M Sc, PhD); maritime sociology (PhD); mathematics (M Sc, PhD); philosophy (MA); physical oceanography (M Sc, PhD); physics (M Sc); political science (MA); religious studies (MA); social and cultural anthropology (MA, PhD); sociology (M Phil, MA); statistics (M Sc, MAS, PhD); women's studies (MWS); work and development (PhD). Electronic applications accepted.

Faculty of Business Administration *Degree program information:* Part-time programs available. Offers business administration (EMBA, MBA). Electronic applications accepted.

Faculty of Education *Degree program information:* Part-time programs available. Offers counseling psychology (M Ed); curriculum, teaching, and learning studies (M Ed); education (PhD); educational leadership studies (M Ed); information technology (M Ed); post-secondary studies (M Ed, Diploma). Electronic applications accepted.

Faculty of Engineering and Applied Science *Degree program information:* Part-time programs available. Offers civil engineering (M Eng, PhD); electrical and computer engineering (M Eng, PhD); mechanical engineering (M Eng, PhD); ocean and naval architecture engineering (M Eng, PhD). Electronic applications accepted.

School of Human Kinetics and Recreation *Degree program information:* Part-time programs available. Offers administration, curriculum and supervision (MPE); biomechanics/ergonomics (MS Kin); exercise and work physiology (MS Kin); sport psychology (MS Kin). Electronic applications accepted.

School of Music Offers conducting (MMus); performance pedagogy (MMus); performing (MMus). Electronic applications accepted.

School of Nursing *Degree program information:* Part-time programs available. Offers nursing (MN, PMD). Electronic applications accepted.

School of Pharmacy *Degree program information:* Part-time programs available. Offers pharmacy (MSCPharm, PhD). Electronic applications accepted.

School of Social Work *Degree program information:* Part-time and evening/weekend programs available. Offers social work (MSW). Electronic applications accepted.

MEMPHIS COLLEGE OF ART, Memphis, TN 38104-2764

General Information Independent, coed, comprehensive institution. *Enrollment:* 28 full-time matriculated graduate/professional students (18 women), 42 part-time matriculated graduate/professional students (27 women). *Enrollment by degree level:* 70 master's. *Graduate faculty:* 26 full-time (15 women), 13 part-time/adjunct (8 women). *Tuition:* Full-time $24,300; part-time $1012 per credit hour. *Required fees:* $650; $325 per semester. Tuition and fees vary according to course load. *Graduate housing:* Room and/or apartments available on a first-come, first-served basis to single students; on-campus housing not available to married students. Typical cost: $6500 per year ($8500 including board). Room and board charges vary according to housing facility selected. Housing application deadline: 8/15. *Student services:* Campus employment opportunities, campus safety program, career counseling, international student services, services for students with disabilities. *Library facilities:* Main library plus 1 other.

Computer facilities: Computer purchase and lease plans are available. 100 computers available on campus for general student use. *Web address:* http://www.mca.edu/.

General Application Contact: Annette Moore, Dean of Admissions, 901-272-5153, Fax: 901-272-5158, E-mail: amoore@mca.edu.

GRADUATE UNITS

Graduate Programs Students: 28 full-time (18 women), 42 part-time (27 women); includes 13 minority (11 Black or African American, non-Hispanic/Latino; 1 Asian, non-Hispanic/Latino; 1 Hispanic/Latino), 2 international. Average age 28. 68 applicants, 56% accepted, 22 enrolled. *Faculty:* 26 full-time (15 women), 13 part-time/adjunct (8 women). Expenses: Contact institution. *Financial support:* Application deadline: 8/1. In 2010, 28 master's awarded. *Degree program information:* Part-time and evening/weekend programs available. Offers art education (MA, MAT); studio art (MFA). *Application deadline:* For fall admission, 3/1 for domestic and international students; for spring admission, 11/1 for domestic and international students. Applications are processed on a rolling basis. *Application fee:* $50. Electronic applications accepted. *Application Contact:* Annette Moore, Dean of Admissions, 901-272-5153, Fax: 901-272-5158, E-mail: amoore@mca.edu. *Vice President for Academic Affairs,* Ken Strickland, 901-272-5107, Fax: 901-272-5158, E-mail: kstrickland@mca.edu.

MEMPHIS THEOLOGICAL SEMINARY, Memphis, TN 38104-4395

General Information Independent-religious, coed, graduate-only institution. *Enrollment by degree level:* 200 first professional, 36 master's, 29 doctoral, 17 other advanced degrees. *Graduate faculty:* 11 full-time (4 women), 7 part-time/adjunct (0 women). *Tuition:* Part-time $400 per semester hour. *Graduate housing:* Rooms and/or apartments available on a first-come, first-served basis to single and married students. Housing application deadline: 7/15. *Student services:* Campus employment opportunities, career counseling, international student services. *Library facilities:* Memphis Theological Seminary Library. *Online resources:* library catalog, access to other libraries' catalogs. *Collection:* 93,367 titles, 428 serial subscriptions, 425 audiovisual materials. *Research affiliation:* Lilly Foundation (technology, religion), Wabash Center for Teaching and Learning (theology, religion).

Computer facilities: 12 computers available on campus for general student use. A campuswide network can be accessed. Online class registration is available. *Web address:* http://www.mtscampus.edu/.

General Application Contact: Barry L. Anderson, Director of Admissions, 901-458-8232 Ext. 109, Fax: 901-452-4501, E-mail: banderson@memphisseminary.edu.

GRADUATE UNITS

Graduate and Professional Programs Students: 163 full-time (76 women), 119 part-time (60 women); includes 96 minority (94 Black or African American, non-Hispanic/Latino; 1 American Indian or Alaska Native, non-Hispanic/Latino; 1 Asian, non-Hispanic/Latino), 1 international. Average age 43. *Faculty:* 11 full-time (4 women), 7 part-time/adjunct (0 women). Expenses: Contact institution. *Financial support:* Career-related internships or fieldwork and scholarships/grants available. Support available to part-time students. Financial award application deadline: 4/15. *Degree program information:* Part-time programs available. Offers theology (M Div, MAR, D Min). *Application deadline:* For fall admission, 8/10 for domestic students; for spring admission, 1/10 for domestic students. Applications are processed on a rolling basis. *Application fee:* $35. *Application Contact:* Barry L. Anderson, Director of Admissions, 901-458-8232 Ext. 109, Fax: 901-452-4501, E-mail: banderson@memphisseminary.edu. *President,* Dr. Daniel J. Earheart-Brown, 901-458-8232, Fax: 901-452-4501, E-mail: jebrown@memphisseminary.edu.

MERCER UNIVERSITY, Macon, GA 31207-0003

General Information Independent-religious, coed, university. *Enrollment:* 6,071 graduate, professional, and undergraduate students; 2,460 full-time matriculated graduate/professional students (1,509 women), 1,218 part-time matriculated graduate/professional students (855 women). *Enrollment by degree level:* 1,634 first professional, 1,698 master's, 259 doctoral, 87 other advanced degrees. *Graduate faculty:* 150 full-time (72 women), 25 part-time/adjunct (11 women). *Graduate housing:* Rooms and/or apartments available on a first-come, first-served basis to single and married students. *Student services:* Campus employment opportunities, campus safety program, career counseling, free psychological counseling, international student services, low-cost health insurance, services for students with disabilities. *Library facilities:* Jack Tarver Library plus 3 others. *Online resources:* library catalog, web page. *Collection:* 796,693 titles, 25,037 serial subscriptions, 68,619 audiovisual materials. *Research affiliation:* Piedmont (medical research), Total Therapeutic Management (Pharmaceutical Research), The Coca Cola Company (pharmaceutical research), Georgia Neurological Institute (medical research), Medical Center of Central Georgia (medical research), Memorial Health Care (medical research).

Computer facilities: A campuswide network can be accessed from student residence rooms and from off campus. Online class registration is available. *Web address:* http://www.mercer.edu/.

General Application Contact: 478-301-2700.

GRADUATE UNITS

Graduate Studies, Cecil B. Day Campus Students: 1,395 full-time (948 women), 958 part-time (716 women); includes 990 minority (775 Black or African American, non-Hispanic/Latino; 4 American Indian or Alaska Native, non-Hispanic/Latino; 173 Asian, non-Hispanic/Latino; 34 Hispanic/Latino; 4 Two or more races, non-Hispanic/Latino), 69 international. Average age 32. *Faculty:* 102 full-time (54 women), 22 part-time/adjunct (10 women). Expenses: Contact institution. *Financial support:* Teaching assistantships, career-related internships or fieldwork, Federal Work-Study, and scholarships/grants available. Support available to part-time students. In 2010, 184 first professional degrees, 434 master's, 29 doctorates, 54 other advanced degrees awarded. *Degree program information:* Part-time and evening/weekend programs available. Postbaccalaureate distance learning degree programs offered (no on-campus study). *Application Contact:* Andrew I. Horn, Director of Admissions and Marketing, 678-547-6206, E-mail: horn_ai@mercer.edu. *Senior Vice President,* Richard V. Swindle, 678-547-6397, E-mail: swindle_rv@mercer.edu.

College of Pharmacy and Health Sciences Students: 703 full-time (466 women), 6 part-time (4 women); includes 219 minority (76 Black or African American, non-Hispanic/Latino; 132 Asian, non-Hispanic/Latino; 9 Hispanic/Latino; 2 Two or more races, non-Hispanic/Latino), 44 international. Average age 26. 1,895 applicants, 18% accepted, 176 enrolled. *Faculty:* 28 full-time (18 women), 6 part-time/adjunct (4 women). Expenses: Contact institution. *Financial support:* In 2010–11, 350 students received support; teaching assistantships with tuition reimbursements available, career-related internships or fieldwork, Federal Work-Study, institutionally sponsored loans, scholarships/grants, tuition waivers, and unspecified assistantships available. Support available to part-time students. Financial award application deadline: 5/1; financial award applicants required to submit FAFSA. In 2010, 144 first professional degrees, 26 master's, 8 doctorates awarded. Offers medical sciences/physician assistant studies (MM Sc); pharmaceutical sciences (PhD); pharmacy (Pharm D); physical therapy (DPT). *Application deadline:* Applications are processed on a rolling basis. Electronic applications accepted. *Application Contact:* Dr. James W. Bartling, Associate Dean for Student Affairs and Admissions, 678-547-6181, Fax: 678-547-6518, E-mail: bartling_jw@mercer.edu. *Dean,* Dr. Hewitt W. Matthews, 678-547-6306, Fax: 678-547-6315, E-mail: matthews_h@mercer.edu.

Eugene W. Stetson School of Business and Economics (Atlanta) Students: 146 full-time (63 women), 91 part-time (43 women); includes 67 minority (44 Black or African American, non-Hispanic/Latino; 17 Asian, non-Hispanic/Latino; 6 Hispanic/Latino), 15 international. Average age 32. 169 applicants, 54% accepted, 64 enrolled. *Faculty:* 18 full-time (6 women), 4 part-time/adjunct (0 women). Expenses: Contact institution. *Financial support:* Federal Work-Study available. Financial award application deadline: 5/1; financial award applicants required to submit FAFSA. In 2010, 154 master's awarded. *Degree program information:* Part-time and evening/weekend programs available. Offers business administration (MBA, XMBA). *Application deadline:* For fall admission, 7/1 priority date for domestic students, 7/1 for international students; for spring admission, 11/1 priority date for domestic students, 11/1 for international students. Applications are processed on a rolling basis. *Application fee:* $50 ($100 for international students). Electronic applications accepted. *Application Contact:* Jamie Thomas, Graduate Enrollment Associate, 678-547-6177, Fax: 678-547-6337, E-mail: atlbusadm@mercer.edu. *Associate Dean,* Dr. Gina L. Miller, 678-547-6177, Fax: 678-547-6337, E-mail: miller_gl@mercer.edu.

Georgia Baptist College of Nursing Students: 21 full-time (all women), 15 part-time (14 women); includes 11 minority (9 Black or African American, non-Hispanic/Latino; 2 Hispanic/Latino). Average age 44. *Faculty:* 11 full-time (10 women). Expenses: Contact institution. *Financial support:* Institutionally sponsored loans, scholarships/grants, and traineeships available. Support available to part-time students. Financial award application deadline: 5/1; financial award applicants required to submit FAFSA. In 2010, 10 master's awarded. *Degree program information:* Part-time programs available. Offers nurse education (Certificate); nursing (MSN, PhD). *Application deadline:* For fall admission, 6/1 for domestic students, 4/1 for international students; for winter admission, 11/1 for domestic students, 9/1 for international students; for spring admission, 4/1 for domestic students, 2/1 for international students. Applications are processed on a rolling basis. *Application fee:* $50. *Application Contact:* Lynn Vines, Director of Admissions, 678-547-6700, Fax: 678-547-6794, E-mail: vines_ml@mercer.edu. *Dean/Professor,* Dr. Linda Streit, 678-547-6793, Fax: 678-547-6796, E-mail: gunby_ss@mercer.edu.

James and Carolyn McAfee School of Theology Students: 173 full-time (94 women), 92 part-time (45 women); includes 127 minority (121 Black or African American, non-Hispanic/Latino; 1 American Indian or Alaska Native, non-Hispanic/Latino; 1 Asian, non-Hispanic/Latino; 3 Hispanic/Latino; 1 Two or more races, non-Hispanic/Latino), 3 international. Average age 35. 140 applicants, 70% accepted, 60 enrolled. *Faculty:* 13 full-time (3 women), 7 part-time/adjunct (2 women). Expenses: Contact institution. *Financial support:* In 2010–11, 30 students received support. Career-related internships or fieldwork, Federal Work-Study, institutionally sponsored loans, and merit-based scholarships available. Support available to part-time students. Financial award applicants required to submit FAFSA. In 2010, 40 first professional degrees, 5 master's, 5 doctorates awarded. *Degree program information:* Part-time programs available. Offers theology (M Div, MACM, D Min). *Application deadline:* For fall admission, 7/1 for domestic students, 2/1 for international students; for spring admission, 1/4 for domestic students. Applications are processed on a rolling basis. *Application fee:* $35. *Application Contact:* Dr. Ryan A. Clark, Director of Admissions, 678-547-6451, Fax: 678-547-6478, E-mail: clark_ra@mercer.edu. *Dean,* Dr. R. Alan Culpepper, 678-547-6470, Fax: 678-547-6478, E-mail: culpepper_ra@mercer.edu.

Tift College of Education (Atlanta) Students: 243 full-time (206 women), 550 part-time (441 women); includes 376 Black or African American, non-Hispanic/Latino; 3 American Indian or Alaska Native, non-Hispanic/Latino; 18 Asian, non-Hispanic/Latino; 6 Hispanic/Latino; 3 Two or more races, non-Hispanic/Latino, 6 international. Average age 34. *Faculty:* 28 full-time (14 women), 2 part-time/adjunct (both women). Expenses: Contact institution. *Financial support:* Federal Work-Study available. Support available to part-time students. Financial award application deadline: 5/1. In 2010, 206 master's, 16 doctorates, 54 other advanced degrees awarded. *Degree program information:* Part-time and evening/weekend programs available. Offers curriculum and instruction (PhD); early childhood education (M Ed, MAT); educational leadership (PhD, Ed S); middle grades education (M Ed, MAT); reading education (M Ed); secondary education (M Ed, MAT); teacher leadership (Ed S). *Application deadline:* For fall admission, 8/1 for domestic and international students; for spring admission, 12/1 for domestic and international students. Applications are processed on a rolling basis. *Application fee:* $25. *Application Contact:* Dr. Allison Gilmore, Associate Dean for Graduate Teacher Education, 678-547-6330, Fax: 678-547-6055, E-mail: gilmore_a@mercer.edu. *Dean,* Dr. Carl R. Martray, 478-301-5397, Fax: 478-301-2280, E-mail: martray_cr@mercer.edu.

Graduate Studies, Macon Campus Students: 98 full-time (67 women), 247 part-time (131 women); includes 112 minority (92 Black or African American, non-Hispanic/Latino; 13 Asian, non-Hispanic/Latino; 7 Hispanic/Latino), 3 international. Average age 34. *Faculty:* 44 full-time (17 women), 1 part-time/adjunct (0 women). Expenses: Contact institution. *Financial support:* Career-related internships or fieldwork, Federal Work-Study, and institutionally sponsored loans available. Support available to part-time students. In 2010, 136 master's, 8 doctorates, 34 other advanced degrees awarded. *Degree program information:* Part-time and evening/weekend programs available. *Application Contact:* Director, 912-301-2700.

Eugene W. Stetson School of Business and Economics (Macon) Students: 8 full-time (1 woman), 29 part-time (12 women); includes 3 minority (all Black or African American, non-Hispanic/Latino). Average age 26. 15 applicants, 93% accepted, 14 enrolled. *Faculty:* 10 full-time (5 women). Expenses: Contact institution. In 2010, 18 master's awarded. *Degree program information:* Part-time and evening/weekend programs available. Offers business and economics (MBA). *Application deadline:* For fall admission, 8/1 for domestic students; for spring admission, 12/1 for domestic students. Applications are processed on a rolling basis. *Application fee:* $50 ($100 for international students). *Application Contact:* Robert Holland, Director/Academic Administrator, 478-301-2835, Fax: 478-301-2635, E-mail: holland_r@mercer.edu. *Dean,* Dr. David Scott Davis, 478-301-2990, Fax: 478-301-2635, E-mail: davis_ds@mercer.edu.

Mercer University (continued)

School of Engineering Students: 11 full-time (2 women), 100 part-time (22 women); includes 26 minority (13 Black or African American, non-Hispanic/Latino; 12 Asian, non-Hispanic/Latino; 1 Hispanic/Latino), 3 international. Average age 32. *Faculty:* 18 full-time (4 women), 1 part-time/adjunct (0 women). Expenses: Contact institution. *Financial support:* Federal Work-Study available. In 2010, 46 master's awarded. *Degree program information:* Part-time and evening/weekend programs available. Postbaccalaureate distance learning degree programs offered (no on-campus study). Offers biomedical engineering (MSE); computer engineering (MSE); electrical engineering (MSE); engineering management (MSE); environmental engineering (MSE); environmental systems (MS); mechanical engineering (MSE); software engineering (MSE); software systems (MS); technical communications management (MS); technical management (MS). *Application deadline:* For fall admission, 7/1 for domestic students; for spring admission, 11/15 for domestic students. Applications are processed on a rolling basis. *Application fee:* $35 ($50 for international students). Electronic applications accepted. *Application Contact:* Greg Lofton, Graduate Program Coordinator, 478-301-5480, Fax: 478-301-5434, E-mail: lofton_g@mercer.edu. *Dean,* Dr. Wade H. Shaw, 478-301-2459, Fax: 478-301-5593, E-mail: shaw_wh@mercer.edu.

School of Music Students: 16 full-time (6 women); includes 4 minority (3 Black or African American, non-Hispanic/Latino; 1 Asian, non-Hispanic/Latino). Average age 28. 5 applicants, 100% accepted, 5 enrolled. *Faculty:* 2 full-time (0 women). Expenses: Contact institution. *Financial support:* In 2010–11, 14 students received support. Tuition waivers and unspecified assistantships available. Financial award applicants required to submit FAFSA. In 2010, 8 master's awarded. *Degree program information:* Part-time programs available. Offers choral conducting (MM); church music (M Div, MM); collaborative piano (MM); instrumental conducting (MM); performance (MM). *Application deadline:* Applications are processed on a rolling basis. *Application fee:* $100. Electronic applications accepted. *Application Contact:* Kimberly T. Beach, Enrollment Associate, 478-301-2570, Fax: 478-301-2650, E-mail: beach_kt@mercer.edu. *Director of Graduate Studies,* Dr. Charles David Keith, 478-301-4012, Fax: 478-301-5633, E-mail: keith_cd@mercer.edu.

Tift College of Education (Macon) Students: 63 full-time (58 women), 118 part-time (97 women); includes 79 minority (73 Black or African American, non-Hispanic/Latino; 6 Hispanic/Latino). Average age 33. *Faculty:* 14 full-time (8 women). Expenses: Contact institution. *Financial support:* Federal Work-Study and institutionally sponsored loans available. Support available to part-time students. Financial award application deadline: 5/1. In 2010, 68 master's, 8 doctorates, 34 other advanced degrees awarded. *Degree program information:* Part-time and evening/weekend programs available. Offers collaborative education (M Ed); curriculum and instruction (PhD); educational leadership (PhD, Ed S). *Application deadline:* For fall admission, 8/1 for domestic students; for spring admission, 12/1 for domestic students. Applications are processed on a rolling basis. *Application fee:* $25. *Application Contact:* Dr. Penny Elkins, Associate Dean, 678-547-6556, Fax: 678-547-6389, E-mail: elkins_pl@mercer.edu. *Dean,* Dr. Carl R. Martray, 478-301-5397, Fax: 478-301-2280, E-mail: martray_cr@mercer.edu.

School of Medicine Offers medicine (MD, MFT, MPH, MSA).

Walter F. George School of Law *Degree program information:* Part-time programs available. Offers law (JD). Electronic applications accepted.

MERCY COLLEGE, Dobbs Ferry, NY 10522-1189

General Information Independent, coed, comprehensive institution. CGS member. *Enrollment:* 10,851 graduate, professional, and undergraduate students; 1,583 full-time matriculated graduate/professional students (1,267 women), 2,215 part-time matriculated graduate/professional students (1,814 women). *Enrollment by degree level:* 3,289 master's, 109 doctoral, 52 other advanced degrees. *Tuition:* Full-time $13,572; part-time $754 per credit hour. *Required fees:* $130 per term. *Student services:* Campus employment opportunities, campus safety program, career counseling, exercise/wellness program, free psychological counseling, international student services, low-cost health insurance, services for students with disabilities, teacher training, writing training. *Library facilities:* Mercy College Library. *Online resources:* library catalog, web page, access to other libraries' catalogs. *Collection:* 249,571 titles, 736 serial subscriptions, 7,421 audiovisual materials.

Computer facilities: Computer purchase and lease plans are available. 186 computers available on campus for general student use. A campuswide network can be accessed from student residence rooms and from off campus. Online class registration is available. *Web address:* http://www.mercy.edu/.

General Application Contact: Allison Gurdineer, Senior Associate Director of Recruitment, 877-MERCY-GO, Fax: 914-674-7608, E-mail: admissions@mercy.edu.

GRADUATE UNITS

School of Business Students: 279 full-time (190 women), 79 part-time (61 women); includes 134 Black or African American, non-Hispanic/Latino; 14 Asian, non-Hispanic/Latino; 73 Hispanic/Latino; 4 Two or more races, non-Hispanic/Latino, 20 international. Average age 33. 366 applicants, 64% accepted, 155 enrolled. Expenses: Contact institution. *Financial support:* In 2010–11, 27 students received support. Career-related internships or fieldwork, Federal Work-Study, scholarships/grants, and unspecified assistantships available. Support available to part-time students. Financial award applicants required to submit FAFSA. In 2010, 118 master's awarded. *Degree program information:* Part-time and evening/weekend programs available. Postbaccalaureate distance learning degree programs offered (minimal on-campus study). Offers business administration (MBA); human resource management (MS, AC); organizational leadership (MS); public accounting (MS). *Application deadline:* For fall admission, 8/1 for international students. Applications are processed on a rolling basis. *Application fee:* $40. Electronic applications accepted. *Application Contact:* Allison Gurdineer, Senior Associate Director of Recruitment, 914-674-7601, E-mail: agurdineer@mercy.edu. *Interim Dean,* Dr. Lucretia Mann, 914-674-7490, E-mail: lmann@mercy.edu.

School of Education Students: 636 full-time (547 women), 1,160 part-time (934 women); includes 380 Black or African American, non-Hispanic/Latino; 5 American Indian or Alaska Native, non-Hispanic/Latino; 23 Asian, non-Hispanic/Latino; 338 Hispanic/Latino; 11 Two or more races, non-Hispanic/Latino, 3 international. Average age 32. 919 applicants, 79% accepted, 577 enrolled. Expenses: Contact institution. *Financial support:* In 2010–11, 206 students received support. Career-related internships or fieldwork, Federal Work-Study, scholarships/grants, and unspecified assistantships available. Support available to part-time students. Financial award applicants required to submit FAFSA. In 2010, 813 master's, 2 other advanced degrees awarded. Postbaccalaureate distance learning degree programs offered (minimal on-campus study). Offers adolescence education, grades 7-12 (MS); applied behavior analysis (Post Master's Certificate); bilingual education (MS); childhood education, grade 1-6 (MS); early childhood education, birth-grade 2 (MS); early childhood education/students with disabilities (MS); individualized certification plan for teachers (ICPT) (MS); middle childhood education, grades 5-9 (MS); school building leadership (MS, Advanced Certificate); teaching English to speakers of other languages (TESOL) (MS, Advanced Certificate); teaching literacy, birth-6 (MS); teaching literacy/birth-grade 12 (MS); teaching literacy/grades 5-12 (MS); urban education (MS). *Application deadline:* For fall admission, 8/1 for international students. Applications are processed on a rolling basis. *Application fee:* $40. Electronic applications accepted. *Application Contact:* Mary Ellen Hoffman, Interim Associate Dean, 914-674-7334, E-mail: mehoffman@mercy.edu. *Interim Dean for the School of Education,* Dr. Andrew Peiser, 914-674-7489, E-mail: apeiser@mercy.edu.

School of Health and Natural Sciences Students: 337 full-time (267 women), 198 part-time (172 women); includes 89 Black or African American, non-Hispanic/Latino; 1 American Indian or Alaska Native, non-Hispanic/Latino; 61 Asian, non-Hispanic/Latino; 59 Hispanic/Latino; 1 Two or more races, non-Hispanic/Latino, 10 international. Average age 34. 807 applicants, 28% accepted, 160 enrolled. Expenses: Contact institution. *Financial support:* In 2010–11, 6 students received support. Career-related internships or fieldwork, Federal Work-Study, scholarships/grants, and unspecified assistantships available. Support available to part-time students. Financial award applicants required to submit FAFSA. In 2010, 173 master's, 16 doctorates, 3 other advanced degrees awarded. *Degree program information:* Part-time and evening/weekend programs available. Postbaccalaureate distance learning degree programs offered (minimal on-campus study). Offers communication disorders (MS); nursing (MS, Certificate); nursing administration (MS, Certificate); nursing education (MS, Certificate); occupational therapy (MS); physical therapy (DPT); physician assistant (MS); physician assistant studies (MS). *Application deadline:* For fall admission, 8/1 for international students. Applications are processed on a rolling basis. *Application fee:* $62. Electronic applications accepted. *Application Contact:* Allison Gurdineer, Senior Associate Director of Recruitment, 914-674-7601, E-mail: agurdineer@mercy.edu. *Interim Dean,* Dr. William Susman, 914-674-7746, E-mail: wsusman@mercy.edu.

School of Liberal Arts Students: 29 full-time (12 women), 74 part-time (57 women); includes 17 Black or African American, non-Hispanic/Latino; 2 Asian, non-Hispanic/Latino; 9 Hispanic/Latino; 2 Two or more races, non-Hispanic/Latino, 5 international. Average age 35. 97 applicants, 52% accepted, 35 enrolled. Expenses: Contact institution. *Financial support:* Career-related internships or fieldwork, Federal Work-Study, scholarships/grants, and unspecified assistantships available. Support available to part-time students. Financial award applicants required to submit FAFSA. In 2010, 20 master's awarded. *Degree program information:* Part-time and evening/weekend programs available. Postbaccalaureate distance learning degree programs offered (minimal on-campus study). Offers cybersecurity (MS); English literature (MA); information assurance and security (MS); Internet business systems (MS, Certificate); Web strategy and design (MS, Certificate). *Application deadline:* For fall admission, 8/1 for international students. Applications are processed on a rolling basis. *Application fee:* $40. Electronic applications accepted. *Application Contact:* Allison Gurdineer, 914-674-7481, E-mail: agurdineer@mercy.edu. *Interim Dean,* Dr. Sean Dugan, 914-674-7356, E-mail: sdugan@mercy.edu.

School of Social and Behavioral Sciences Students: 285 full-time (238 women), 372 part-time (324 women); includes 440 minority (212 Black or African American, non-Hispanic/Latino; 1 American Indian or Alaska Native, non-Hispanic/Latino; 10 Asian, non-Hispanic/Latino; 208 Hispanic/Latino; 1 Native Hawaiian or other Pacific Islander, non-Hispanic/Latino; 8 Two or more races, non-Hispanic/Latino), 9 international. Average age 34. 572 applicants, 46% accepted, 193 enrolled. Expenses: Contact institution. *Financial support:* Career-related internships or fieldwork, Federal Work-Study, scholarships/grants, and unspecified assistantships available. Support available to part-time students. Financial award applicants required to submit FAFSA. In 2010, 151 master's, 17 other advanced degrees awarded. *Degree program information:* Part-time and evening/weekend programs available. Postbaccalaureate distance learning degree programs offered (minimal on-campus study). Offers alcohol and substance abuse counseling (Certificate); counseling (MS, Certificate); family counseling (Certificate); health services management (MPA, MS); marriage and family therapy (MS); mental health counseling (MS); psychology (MS); school counseling (Certificate); school counseling and bilingual extension (Certificate); school psychology (MS). *Application deadline:* For fall admission, 8/1 for international students. Applications are processed on a rolling basis. *Application fee:* $40. Electronic applications accepted. *Application Contact:* Allison Gurdineer, Senior Associate Director of Recruitment, 914-674-7601, E-mail: agurdineer@mercy.edu. *Interim Dean,* Hind Rassam Culhane, 914-674-7376, E-mail: hculhane@mercy.edu.

MERCYHURST COLLEGE, Erie, PA 16546

General Information Independent-religious, coed, comprehensive institution. *Graduate housing:* Room and/or apartments available on a first-come, first-served basis to single students; on-campus housing not available to married students. Housing application deadline: 8/15.

GRADUATE UNITS

Graduate Program *Degree program information:* Part-time and evening/weekend programs available. Offers administration of justice (MS); applied intelligence (MS, Certificate); bilingual/bicultural special education (MS); educational leadership (Certificate); forensic and biological anthropology (MS); organizational leadership (MS, Certificate); special education (MS). Electronic applications accepted.

MEREDITH COLLEGE, Raleigh, NC 27607-5298

General Information Independent, Undergraduate: women only; graduate: coed, comprehensive institution. *Enrollment:* 69 full-time matriculated graduate/professional students (65 women), 236 part-time matriculated graduate/professional students (201 women). *Enrollment by degree level:* 292 master's, 13 other advanced degrees. *Graduate faculty:* 21 full-time (17 women), 7 part-time/adjunct (5 women). *Graduate housing:* On-campus housing not available. *Student services:* Campus safety program, career counseling, free psychological counseling, international student services, services for students with disabilities. *Library facilities:* Carlyle Campbell Library. *Online resources:* library catalog. *Collection:* 155,165 titles, 2,867 serial subscriptions, 14,671 audiovisual materials.

Computer facilities: 140 computers available on campus for general student use. A campuswide network can be accessed from student residence rooms. Online class registration, laptop computers for full-time students are available. *Web address:* http://www.meredith.edu/.

General Application Contact: Sylvia Horton, Admissions Coordinator, 919-760-8423, Fax: 919-760-2898, E-mail: hortons@meredith.edu.

GRADUATE UNITS

John E. Weems Graduate School Students: 69 full-time (65 women), 236 part-time (201 women); includes 47 minority (29 Black or African American, non-Hispanic/Latino; 10 Asian, non-Hispanic/Latino; 5 Hispanic/Latino; 1 Native Hawaiian or other Pacific Islander, non-Hispanic/Latino; 2 Two or more races, non-Hispanic/Latino). Average age 32. 387 applicants, 40% accepted, 115 enrolled. *Faculty:* 21 full-time (17 women), 7 part-time/adjunct (6 women). Expenses: Contact institution. *Financial support:* Career-related internships or fieldwork, institutionally sponsored loans, scholarships/grants, and tuition waivers (partial) available. Support available to part-time students. Financial award application deadline: 2/15; financial award applicants required to submit FAFSA. In 2010, 58 master's, 13 other advanced degrees awarded. *Degree program information:* Part-time and evening/weekend programs available. Offers dietetic internship (Postbaccalaureate Certificate); nutrition (MS). *Application deadline:* For fall admission, 7/1 priority date for domestic and international students; for spring admission, 11/1 priority date for domestic and international students. Applications are processed on a rolling basis. *Application fee:* $50. Electronic applications accepted. *Application Contact:* Director of Graduate Admissions, 919-760-8423, Fax: 919-760-2898. *Director,* 919-760-8423, Fax: 919-760-2898.

School of Business Students: 2 full-time (0 women), 90 part-time (64 women); includes 11 Black or African American, non-Hispanic/Latino; 6 Asian, non-Hispanic/Latino; 2 Hispanic/Latino. Average age 34. 48 applicants, 83% accepted, 34 enrolled. *Faculty:* 8 full-time (5 women), 1 part-time/adjunct (0 women). Expenses: Contact institution. *Financial support:* Career-related internships or fieldwork, institutionally sponsored loans, scholarships/grants, and tuition waivers (partial) available. Support available to part-time students. Financial award application deadline: 2/15; financial award applicants required to submit FAFSA. In 2010, 21 master's awarded. *Degree program information:* Part-time and evening/weekend programs available. Offers business administration (MBA). *Application deadline:* For fall admission, 7/1 priority date for domestic and international students; for spring admission, 11/1 priority date for domestic and international students. Applications are processed on a rolling basis. *Application fee:* $50. Electronic applications accepted. *Application Contact:* Page Midyette, Coordinator, 919-760-2281, Fax: 919-760-2898, E-mail: midyette@meredith.edu. *Dean,* Dr. Denise Rotundo, 919-760-8471, Fax: 919-760-8470.

School of Education Students: 39 full-time (37 women), 102 part-time (96 women); includes 13 Black or African American, non-Hispanic/Latino; 4 Asian, non-Hispanic/Latino; 2 Hispanic/Latino; 1 Native Hawaiian or other Pacific Islander, non-Hispanic/Latino. Average age 33. 87 applicants, 66% accepted, 39 enrolled. *Faculty:* 10 full-time (all women), 4 part-time/adjunct (all women). Expenses: Contact institution. *Financial support:* Career-related internships or fieldwork, institutionally sponsored loans, and tuition waivers (partial) available. Support available to part-time students. Financial award application deadline: 2/15; financial award applicants required to submit FAFSA. In 2010, 24 master's awarded. *Degree program information:* Part-time and evening/weekend programs available. Offers education (M Ed, MAT). *Application deadline:* For fall admission, 7/1 priority date for domestic students; for spring admission, 11/1 priority date for domestic students. Applications are processed on a rolling basis. *Application fee:* $50. Electronic applications accepted. *Application Contact:* Dr. Ellen Graden, Coordinator, 919-760-8077, Fax: 919-760-2303, E-mail: gradene@meredith.edu. *Graduate Program Manager*, Erin Barrow, 919-760-8316, Fax: 919-760-2303, E-mail: barrower@meredith.edu.

MERRIMACK COLLEGE, North Andover, MA 01845-5800

General Information Independent-religious, coed, comprehensive institution. *Enrollment:* 2,169 graduate, professional, and undergraduate students; 24 full-time matriculated graduate/professional students (21 women), 53 part-time matriculated graduate/professional students (48 women). *Enrollment by degree level:* 77 master's. *Graduate faculty:* 4 full-time (3 women), 16 part-time/adjunct (12 women). *Tuition:* Part-time $450 per credit hour. *Graduate housing:* On-campus housing not available. *Student services:* Campus employment opportunities, campus safety program, career counseling, exercise/wellness program, international student services, low-cost health insurance, multicultural affairs office, services for students with disabilities, teacher training, writing training. *Library facilities:* McQuade Library. *Online resources:* library catalog, web page, access to other libraries' catalogs. *Collection:* 114,219 titles, 4,393 serial subscriptions, 2,629 audiovisual materials.

Computer facilities: Computer purchase and lease plans are available. A campuswide network can be accessed from student residence rooms and from off campus. Online class registration is available. *Web address:* http://www.merrimack.edu/.

General Application Contact: Dr. Theresa Kirk, Chair, 978-837-5436, E-mail: kirkt@merrimack.edu.

GRADUATE UNITS

School of Education Students: 24 full-time (21 women), 53 part-time (48 women), 1 international. Average age 30. 58 applicants, 86% accepted, 50 enrolled. *Faculty:* 4 full-time (3 women), 16 part-time/adjunct (12 women). Expenses: Contact institution. *Financial support:* In 2010–11, 17 fellowships (averaging $17,000 per year) were awarded; career-related internships or fieldwork, scholarships/grants, and discounts for local school district teachers also available. In 2010, 13 master's awarded. *Degree program information:* Part-time and evening/weekend programs available. Offers community engagement (M Ed); early childhood education (M Ed); elementary education (M Ed); elementary education plus moderate disabilities-dual license (M Ed); English as a second language (M Ed); general studies (M Ed); high education (M Ed); middle (M Ed); moderate disabilities (preK-8) (M Ed); reading specialist (M Ed); secondary (M Ed); teacher leadership (CAGS). *Application deadline:* Applications are processed on a rolling basis. *Application fee:* $50. Electronic applications accepted. *Application Contact:* Jessica McCarthy, Program Coordinator, 978-837-5443, E-mail: mccarthyj@merrimack.edu. *Chair*, Dr. Theresa Kirk, 978-837-5436, E-mail: kirkt@merrimack.edu.

MESA STATE COLLEGE, Grand Junction, CO 81501-3122

General Information State-supported, coed, comprehensive institution. *Enrollment:* 8,130 graduate, professional, and undergraduate students; 17 full-time matriculated graduate/professional students (10 women), 67 part-time matriculated graduate/professional students (46 women). *Enrollment by degree level:* 84 master's. *Graduate faculty:* 18 full-time (4 women), 9 part-time/adjunct (3 women). Tuition, state resident: full-time $5400; part-time $300 per credit hour. Tuition, nonresident: full-time $16,200; part-time $900 per credit hour. *Required fees:* $461; $25.61 per credit hour. Tuition and fees vary according to course load and program. *Graduate housing:* Room and/or apartments available on a first-come, first-served basis to single students; on-campus housing not available to married students. Typical cost: $8298 (including board). Room and board charges vary according to board plan and housing facility selected. Housing application deadline: 6/1. *Student services:* Campus safety program, child daycare facilities, exercise/wellness program, free psychological counseling, international student services, low-cost health insurance, multicultural affairs office, services for students with disabilities, teacher training. *Library facilities:* John U. Tomlinson Library. *Online resources:* library catalog, web page. *Collection:* 392,679 titles, 31,992 serial subscriptions, 18,606 audiovisual materials.

Computer facilities: 525 computers available on campus for general student use. A campuswide network can be accessed from student residence rooms and from off campus. Online class registration is available. *Web address:* http://www.mesastate.edu/.

General Application Contact: Office of Graduate Admissions, 970-248-1020.

GRADUATE UNITS

Center for Teacher Education Students: 40 part-time (31 women); includes 5 Hispanic/Latino. Average age 39. 66 applicants, 79% accepted, 38 enrolled. *Faculty:* 6 full-time (3 women), 8 part-time/adjunct (3 women). Expenses: Contact institution. *Financial support:* Applicants required to submit FAFSA. In 2010, 38 master's awarded. *Degree program information:* Part-time programs available. Postbaccalaureate distance learning degree programs offered (minimal on-campus study). Offers educational leadership (MAEd); English for speakers of other languages (MAEd). *Application deadline:* For fall admission, 4/1 for domestic students; for spring admission, 3/31 for domestic students. Applications are processed on a rolling basis. *Application fee:* $50. Electronic applications accepted. *Application Contact:* Becky Gibb, Administrative Assistant, 970-248-1618, Fax: 970-248-1112, E-mail: rgibb@mesastate.edu. *Director*, Valerie J. Dobbs, 970-248-1953, Fax: 970-248-1112, E-mail: vjdobbs@mesastate.edu.

Department of Business Students: 17 full-time (10 women), 27 part-time (15 women); includes 3 Hispanic/Latino; 1 Native Hawaiian or other Pacific Islander, non-Hispanic/Latino. Average age 32. 32 applicants, 81% accepted, 19 enrolled. *Faculty:* 12 full-time (1 woman), 1 part-time/adjunct (0 women). Expenses: Contact institution. *Financial support:* In 2010–11, 3 students received support. Scholarships/grants available. Financial award applicants required to submit FAFSA. In 2010, 10 master's awarded. *Degree program information:* Part-time and evening/weekend programs available. Offers business (MBA). *Application deadline:* For fall admission, 7/15 priority date for domestic students; for spring admission, 12/22 priority date for domestic students. Applications are processed on a rolling basis. *Application fee:* $50. Electronic applications accepted. *Application Contact:* Jane Sandoval, MBA Coordinator, 970-248-1778, Fax: 970-248-1730, E-mail: jsandova@mesastate.edu. *Department Head*, Dr. Morgan Bridge, 970-248-1169, Fax: 970-248-1730, E-mail: mbridge@mesastate.edu.

MESIVTA OF EASTERN PARKWAY–YESHIVA ZICHRON MEILECH, Brooklyn, NY 11218-5559

General Information Independent-religious, men only, comprehensive institution.

GRADUATE UNITS

Graduate Programs

MESIVTA TIFERETH JERUSALEM OF AMERICA, New York, NY 10002-6301

General Information Independent-religious, men only, comprehensive institution.

GRADUATE UNITS

Graduate Programs

MESIVTA TORAH VODAATH RABBINICAL SEMINARY, Brooklyn, NY 11218-5299

General Information Independent-religious, men only, comprehensive institution.

GRADUATE UNITS

Graduate Programs

MESSIAH COLLEGE, Grantham, PA 17027

General Information Independent-religious, coed, comprehensive institution. *Library facilities:* Murray Library. *Online resources:* library catalog, web page, access to other libraries' catalogs. *Collection:* 292,272 titles, 50,751 serial subscriptions, 20,328 audiovisual materials.

Computer facilities: Computer purchase and lease plans are available. 571 computers available on campus for general student use. A campuswide network can be accessed from student residence rooms and from off campus. Online class registration, access to software are available. *Web address:* http://www.messiah.edu/.

General Application Contact: Tonya L. Baker, Graduate Programs Manager, 717-796-5061, Fax: 717-691-2386, E-mail: tbaker@messiah.edu.

GRADUATE UNITS

Program in Art Education Expenses: Contact institution. *Financial support:* Applicants required to submit FAFSA. *Degree program information:* Part-time programs available. Offers art education (MA). *Application deadline:* Applications are processed on a rolling basis. *Application fee:* $30. Electronic applications accepted. *Application Contact:* Dr. Gene VanDyke, Program Coordinator, 717-796-1800 Ext. 6726, Fax: 717-691-2386, E-mail: gvandyke@messiah.edu. *Program Coordinator*, Dr. Gene VanDyke, 717-796-1800 Ext. 6726, Fax: 717-691-2386, E-mail: gvandyke@messiah.edu.

Program in Conducting Expenses: Contact institution. *Financial support:* Applicants required to submit FAFSA. *Degree program information:* Part-time programs available. Offers choral conducting (MM); orchestral conducting (MM); wind conducting (MM). *Application deadline:* Applications are processed on a rolling basis. *Application fee:* $30. Electronic applications accepted. *Application Contact:* Dr. Bradley Genevro, Program Coordinator, 717-796-1800 Ext. 2750, Fax: 717-691-2386, E-mail: bgenevro@messiah.edu. *Program Coordinator*, Dr. Bradley Genevro, 717-796-1800 Ext. 2750, Fax: 717-691-2386, E-mail: bgenevro@messiah.edu.

Program in Counseling Expenses: Contact institution. *Financial support:* Applicants required to submit FAFSA. *Degree program information:* Part-time programs available. Offers clinical mental health counseling (MAC); counseling (CAGS); marriage, couple, and family counseling (MAC); school counseling (MAC). *Application deadline:* Applications are processed on a rolling basis. *Application fee:* $30. Electronic applications accepted. *Application Contact:* Dr. John Addleman, Director, 717-796-1800 Ext. 2980, Fax: 717-691-2386, E-mail: jaddlemn@messiah.edu. *Director*, Dr. John Addleman, 717-796-1800 Ext. 2980, Fax: 717-691-2386, E-mail: jaddlemn@messiah.edu.

Program in Youth and Young Adult Ministries Offers youth and young adult ministries (MA).

METHODIST THEOLOGICAL SCHOOL IN OHIO, Delaware, OH 43015-8004

General Information Independent-religious, coed, graduate-only institution. *Graduate housing:* Rooms and/or apartments available on a first-come, first-served basis to single students and available to married students. Housing application deadline: 8/15.

GRADUATE UNITS

Graduate and Professional Programs *Degree program information:* Part-time programs available. Offers theology (M Div, MACE, MACM, MTS, D Min).

METHODIST UNIVERSITY, Fayetteville, NC 28311-1498

General Information Independent-religious, coed, comprehensive institution. *Graduate housing:* Room and/or apartments available on a first-come, first-served basis to single students; on-campus housing not available to married students. Housing application deadline: 6/1.

GRADUATE UNITS

School of Graduate Studies *Degree program information:* Part-time and evening/weekend programs available. Offers business administration (MBA); justice administration (MJA); physician assistant studies (MMS). Electronic applications accepted.

METROPOLITAN COLLEGE OF NEW YORK, New York, NY 10013

General Information Independent, coed, primarily women, comprehensive institution. *Graduate housing:* On-campus housing not available. *Research affiliation:* U. S. Department of Homeland Security (homeland security), U. S. Federal Emergency Management Administration (higher education).

GRADUATE UNITS

Program in Childhood Education Offers childhood education (MS).

Program in General Management *Degree program information:* Evening/weekend programs available. Offers general management (MBA). Electronic applications accepted.

Program in Media Management *Degree program information:* Evening/weekend programs available. Offers media management (MBA). Electronic applications accepted.

Program in Public Administration *Degree program information:* Evening/weekend programs available. Offers public administration (MPA). Electronic applications accepted.

METROPOLITAN STATE UNIVERSITY, St. Paul, MN 55106-5000

General Information State-supported, coed, comprehensive institution. *Enrollment:* 7,787 graduate, professional, and undergraduate students; 288 full-time matriculated graduate/professional students (163 women), 428 part-time matriculated graduate/professional students (284 women). *Enrollment by degree level:* 621 master's, 30 doctoral, 65 other advanced degrees. Tuition, state resident: full-time $5827; part-time $291 per credit hour. Tuition, nonresident: full-time $11,654; part-time $583 per credit hour. *Required fees:* $10 per credit hour. Tuition and fees vary according to degree level. *Graduate housing:* On-campus housing not available. *Student services:* Campus employment opportunities, career counseling, free psychological counseling, international student services, low-cost health insurance, multicultural affairs office, services for students with disabilities, writing training. *Library facilities:* Library and Learning Center. *Online resources:* library catalog, web page, access to other libraries' catalogs. *Collection:* 77,378 titles, 43,014 serial subscriptions, 7,218 audiovisual materials.

Computer facilities: 375 computers available on campus for general student use. A campuswide network can be accessed from off campus. Online class registration is available. *Web address:* http://www.metrostate.edu/.

General Application Contact: Lucille Maghrak, Graduate Studies Coordinator, 651-793-1932, E-mail: lucille.maghrak@metrostate.edu.

GRADUATE UNITS

College of Arts and Sciences Students: 38 full-time (16 women), 72 part-time (49 women); includes 4 Black or African American, non-Hispanic/Latino; 8 Asian, non-Hispanic/Latino; 3 Hispanic/Latino, 13 international. Average age 38. Expenses: Contact institution. *Financial support:* Research assistantships available. Financial award applicants required to submit FAFSA. In 2010, 22 master's awarded. *Degree program information:* Part-time and evening/weekend programs available. Offers computer science (MS); liberal studies (MA); technical communication (MS). *Application deadline:* For fall admission, 8/1 priority date for domestic students, 3/15 for international students; for winter admission, 10/15 for international students; for spring admission, 12/1 priority date for domestic students, 3/15 for international students. Applications are processed on a rolling basis. *Application fee:* $20. Electronic applications accepted. *Application Contact:* Lucille Maghrak, Graduate Studies Coordinator, 651-793-1932, E-mail: lucille.maghrak@metrostate.edu. *Dean*, Dr. Becky Omdahl, 651-793-1443, Fax: 651-793-1446, E-mail: becky.omdahl1@metrostate.edu.

College of Management Students: 158 full-time (74 women), 217 part-time (114 women); includes 31 Black or African American, non-Hispanic/Latino; 26 Asian, non-Hispanic/Latino; 10 Hispanic/Latino; 6 Two or more races, non-Hispanic/Latino, 47 international. Average age 35. Expenses: Contact institution. *Financial support:* Research assistantships with partial tuition reimbursements, career-related internships or fieldwork and Federal Work-Study available. Support available to part-time students. Financial award applicants required to submit FAFSA. In 2010, 100 master's, 7 other advanced degrees awarded. *Degree program information:* Part-time and evening/weekend programs available. Offers business administra-

Metropolitan State University (continued)

tion (MBA, DBA); information assurance security (Graduate Certificate); management information systems (MMIS); MIS generalist (Graduate Certificate); MIS systems analysis and design (Graduate Certificate); nonprofit management (MPNA); project management (Graduate Certificate); public administration (MPNA). *Application deadline:* For fall admission, 7/15 for international students; for winter admission, 11/15 for international students; for spring admission, 3/15 for international students. Applications are processed on a rolling basis. *Application fee:* $20. Electronic applications accepted. *Application Contact:* Gloria B. Marcus, Recruiter/Admissions Adviser, 612-659-7258, Fax: 612-659-7268, E-mail: gloria.marcus@metrostate.edu. *Graduate Director,* Dr. Paul Huo, 612-659-7271, Fax: 612-659-7268, E-mail: carol.bormann.young@metrostate.edu.

College of Nursing and Health Sciences Students: 52 full-time (43 women), 104 part-time (95 women); includes 6 Black or African American, non-Hispanic/Latino; 1 American Indian or Alaska Native, non-Hispanic/Latino; 2 Asian, non-Hispanic/Latino; 2 Hispanic/Latino; 7 Two or more races, non-Hispanic/Latino, 7 international. Average age 36. Expenses: Contact institution. *Financial support:* In 2010–11, fellowships (averaging $800 per year); career-related internships or fieldwork, Federal Work-Study, institutionally sponsored loans, and traineeships also available. Financial award applicants required to submit FAFSA. In 2010, 30 master's, 2 doctorates awarded. *Degree program information:* Part-time programs available. Offers leadership and management (MSN); nurse educator (MSN); nursing (DNP); oral health care practitioner (MS); public health nursing leadership (MSN); women's health care nurse practitioner (MSN). *Application deadline:* For fall admission, 1/15 for domestic students; for winter admission, 1/15 for international students. *Application fee:* $20. *Application Contact:* Lynda Zimmerman, Graduate Student Adviser/Recruiter, 651-793-1378, Fax: 651-793-1382, E-mail: lynda.zimmerman@metrostate.edu. *Dean,* Ann Leja, 651-793-1402, Fax: 651-793-1382, E-mail: ann.leja@metrostate.edu.

College of Professional Studies Students: 40 full-time (29 women), 37 part-time (28 women); includes 11 Black or African American, non-Hispanic/Latino; 4 Asian, non-Hispanic/Latino; 2 Hispanic/Latino; 5 Two or more races, non-Hispanic/Latino. Average age 36. Expenses: Contact institution. *Financial support:* Applicants required to submit FAFSA. In 2010, 2 master's awarded. *Degree program information:* Part-time and evening/weekend programs available. Offers psychology (MA); urban secondary education (Certificate). *Application deadline:* For fall admission, 8/1 priority date for domestic students; for spring admission, 12/1 priority date for domestic students. Electronic applications accepted. *Application Contact:* Lucille Maghrak, Graduate Studies Coordinator, 651-793-1932, E-mail: lucille.maghrak@metrostate.edu. *Interim Dean,* Dr. Daniel Abebe, 651-793-1333, Fax: 651-793-1355, E-mail: daniel.abebe@metrostate.edu.

MGH INSTITUTE OF HEALTH PROFESSIONS, Boston, MA 02129

General Information Independent, coed, primarily women, graduate-only institution. *Enrollment by degree level:* 460 master's, 253 doctoral, 177 other advanced degrees. *Graduate faculty:* 69 full-time (58 women), 22 part-time/adjunct (20 women). *Tuition:* Full-time $11,652; part-time $971 per credit. *Required fees:* $275 per semester. One-time fee: $300. Tuition and fees vary according to program. *Graduate housing:* On-campus housing not available. *Student services:* Campus employment opportunities, campus safety program, career counseling, child daycare facilities, exercise/wellness program, free psychological counseling, international student services, low-cost health insurance, multicultural affairs office, services for students with disabilities, teacher training, writing training. *Library facilities:* Treadwell Library. *Online resources:* library catalog, web page, access to other libraries' catalogs. *Collection:* 50,000 titles, 1,600 serial subscriptions, 200 audiovisual materials. *Research affiliation:* Brigham and Women's Hospital, Partners Health Care System, Inc., McLean Psychiatric Hospital, Spaulding Rehabilitation Hospital, Massachusetts General Hospital.

Computer facilities: 50 computers available on campus for general student use. A campuswide network can be accessed from off campus. Online class registration, online billing are available. *Web address:* http://www.mghihp.edu/.

General Application Contact: Maureen Rika Judd, Manager of Admissions, 617-726-6069, Fax: 617-726-8010, E-mail: admissions@mghihp.edu.

GRADUATE UNITS

School of Health and Rehabilitation Sciences Students: 267 full-time (231 women), 176 part-time (137 women); includes 69 minority (5 Black or African American, non-Hispanic/Latino; 2 American Indian or Alaska Native, non-Hispanic/Latino; 58 Asian, non-Hispanic/Latino; 4 Hispanic/Latino). Average age 31. 956 applicants, 41% accepted, 213 enrolled. *Faculty:* 42 full-time (33 women), 14 part-time/adjunct (13 women). Expenses: Contact institution. *Financial support:* In 2010–11, 90 students received support, including 20 research assistantships (averaging $1,200 per year), 13 teaching assistantships (averaging $1,200 per year); career-related internships or fieldwork, scholarships/grants, and unspecified assistantships also available. Support available to part-time students. Financial award application deadline: 4/1; financial award applicants required to submit FAFSA. In 2010, 49 master's, 104 doctorates, 3 other advanced degrees awarded. *Degree program information:* Part-time programs available. Offers health and rehabilitation sciences (MS, DPT, Certificate); medical imaging (Certificate); physical therapy (MS, DPT, Certificate); reading (Certificate); speech-language pathology (MS). *Application fee:* $65. Electronic applications accepted. *Application Contact:* Maureen Rika Judd, Director of Admissions, 617-726-6069, Fax: 617-726-8010, E-mail: admissions@mghihp.edu. *President,* Dr. Janis P. Bellack, 617-726-8002, Fax: 617-726-3716, E-mail: jbellack@mghihp.edu.

School of Nursing Students: 359 full-time (317 women), 87 part-time (75 women); includes 49 minority (20 Black or African American, non-Hispanic/Latino; 22 Asian, non-Hispanic/Latino; 7 Hispanic/Latino). Average age 32. 917 applicants, 43% accepted, 233 enrolled. *Faculty:* 41 full-time (36 women), 14 part-time/adjunct (13 women). Expenses: Contact institution. *Financial support:* In 2010–11, 75 students received support, including 4 research assistantships (averaging $1,200 per year), 17 teaching assistantships (averaging $1,200 per year); career-related internships or fieldwork, scholarships/grants, traineeships, and unspecified assistantships also available. Support available to part-time students. Financial award application deadline: 4/1; financial award applicants required to submit FAFSA. In 2010, 75 master's, 12 doctorates, 87 other advanced degrees awarded. Offers advanced practice nursing (MSN); gerontological nursing (MSN); nursing (DNP); pediatric nursing (MSN); psychiatric nursing (MSN); teaching and learning for health care education (Certificate); women's health nursing (MSN). *Application deadline:* For fall admission, 1/10 for domestic and international students; for spring admission, 11/1 for domestic and international students. *Application fee:* $65. Electronic applications accepted. *Application Contact:* Maureen Rika Judd, Director of Admissions, 617-726-6069, Fax: 617-726-8010, E-mail: admissions@mghihp.edu. *Dean,* Dr. Laurie Lauzon-Clabo, 617-643-0605, Fax: 617-726-8022, E-mail: llauzonclabo@mghihp.edu.

MIAMI INTERNATIONAL UNIVERSITY OF ART & DESIGN, Miami, FL 33132-1418

General Information Proprietary, coed, comprehensive institution. CGS member. *Web address:* http://www.artinstitutes.edu/miami/.

General Application Contact: Office of Graduate Admissions, 305-428-5700.

GRADUATE UNITS

Program in Computer Animation Expenses: Contact institution. Postbaccalaureate distance learning degree programs offered. Offers computer animation (MA). *Application Contact:* Office of Graduate Admissions, 305-428-5700.

Program in Film Expenses: Contact institution. Postbaccalaureate distance learning degree programs offered. Offers film (MFA). *Application Contact:* Office of Graduate Admissions, 305-428-5700.

Program in Graphic Design Expenses: Contact institution. Postbaccalaureate distance learning degree programs offered. Offers graphic design (MFA). *Application Contact:* Office of Graduate Admissions, 305-428-5700.

Program in Interior Design Expenses: Contact institution. Offers interior design (MFA). *Application Contact:* Office of Graduate Admissions, 305-428-5700.

Program in Visual Arts Expenses: Contact institution. Postbaccalaureate distance learning degree programs offered. Offers visual arts (MFA). *Application Contact:* Office of Graduate Admissions, 305-428-5700.

MIAMI UNIVERSITY, Oxford, OH 45056

General Information State-related, coed, university. CGS member. *Enrollment:* 17,472 graduate, professional, and undergraduate students; 1,028 full-time matriculated graduate/professional students (574 women), 534 part-time matriculated graduate/professional students (409 women). *Enrollment by degree level:* 1,170 master's, 375 doctoral, 17 other advanced degrees. *Graduate faculty:* 659 full-time (255 women). Tuition, state resident: full-time $11,616; part-time $484 per credit hour. Tuition, nonresident: full-time $25,656; part-time $1069 per credit hour. *Required fees:* $528. *Graduate housing:* Rooms and/or apartments available on a first-come, first-served basis to single and married students. Typical cost: $4952 per year ($9786 including board) for single students. Room and board charges vary according to board plan, campus/location and housing facility selected. *Student services:* Campus employment opportunities, campus safety program, career counseling, child daycare facilities, exercise/wellness program, free psychological counseling, grant writing training, international student services, low-cost health insurance, multicultural affairs office, services for students with disabilities, teacher training, writing training. *Library facilities:* King Library plus 3 others. *Online resources:* library catalog, web page, access to other libraries' catalogs. *Collection:* 4.1 million titles, 93,225 serial subscriptions, 718,656 audiovisual materials.

Computer facilities: Computer purchase and lease plans are available. 400 computers available on campus for general student use. A campuswide network can be accessed from student residence rooms and from off campus. Online class registration is available. *Web address:* http://www.muohio.edu/.

General Application Contact: Graduate Admission Coordinator, 513-529-3734, Fax: 513-529-3762, E-mail: gradschool@muohio.edu.

GRADUATE UNITS

Graduate School Students: 1,028 full-time (574 women), 534 part-time (409 women); includes 159 minority (70 Black or African American, non-Hispanic/Latino; 2 American Indian or Alaska Native, non-Hispanic/Latino; 45 Asian, non-Hispanic/Latino; 23 Hispanic/Latino; 2 Native Hawaiian or other Pacific Islander, non-Hispanic/Latino; 17 Two or more races, non-Hispanic/Latino), 217 international. Average age 30. *Faculty:* 659 full-time (255 women). Expenses: Contact institution. *Financial support:* Fellowships with full tuition reimbursements, research assistantships with full tuition reimbursements, teaching assistantships with full tuition reimbursements, career-related internships or fieldwork, Federal Work-Study, scholarships/grants, health care benefits, and unspecified assistantships available. Financial award application deadline: 3/1; financial award applicants required to submit FAFSA. In 2010, 519 master's, 60 doctorates awarded. *Degree program information:* Part-time and evening/weekend programs available. *Application deadline:* Applications are processed on a rolling basis. *Application fee:* $50. Electronic applications accepted. *Application Contact:* Admission, 513-529-3734, Fax: 513-529-3762, E-mail: gradschool@muohio.edu. *Associate Provost for Research and Scholarship/Dean,* Dr. Bruce J. Cochrane, 513-529-3734, Fax: 513-529-3762, E-mail: cochrabj@muohio.edu.

College of Arts and Science Students: 620 full-time (348 women), 373 part-time (295 women); includes 74 minority (22 Black or African American, non-Hispanic/Latino; 2 American Indian or Alaska Native, non-Hispanic/Latino; 29 Asian, non-Hispanic/Latino; 10 Hispanic/Latino; 1 Native Hawaiian or other Pacific Islander, non-Hispanic/Latino; 10 Two or more races, non-Hispanic/Latino), 137 international. Average age 30. Expenses: Contact institution. *Financial support:* Fellowships with full tuition reimbursements, research assistantships with full tuition reimbursements, teaching assistantships with full tuition reimbursements, career-related internships or fieldwork, Federal Work-Study, scholarships/grants, health care benefits, tuition waivers (full), and unspecified assistantships available. Financial award application deadline: 3/1. In 2010, 242 master's, 45 doctorates awarded. *Degree program information:* Part-time programs available. Offers arts and science (MA, MAT, MGS, MS, MTSC, PhD); biological sciences (MAT); botany (MA, MAT, MS, PhD); chemistry and biochemistry (MS, PhD); comparative religion (MA); English (MA, MAT, MTSC, PhD); French (MA); geography (MA); geology (MA, MS, PhD); gerontology (MGS); history (MA); mathematics (MA, MAT, MS); microbiology (MS, PhD); philosophy (MA); physics (MAT); political science (MA); psychology (PhD); social gerontology (PhD); speech pathology and audiology (MA, MS); statistics (MS); zoology (MS, PhD). *Application fee:* $50. *Application Contact:* Admission Coordinator, 513-529-3734, Fax: 513-529-3762, E-mail: gradschool@muohio.edu. *Interim Dean,* Dr. Phyllis Callahan, 513-529-1234, Fax: 513-529-5026, E-mail: cas@muohio.edu.

Farmer School of Business Students: 66 full-time (21 women), 1 part-time (0 women); includes 10 minority (2 Black or African American, non-Hispanic/Latino; 4 Asian, non-Hispanic/Latino; 2 Hispanic/Latino; 2 Two or more races, non-Hispanic/Latino), 16 international. Average age 26. Expenses: Contact institution. *Financial support:* Fellowships with tuition reimbursements, research assistantships, Federal Work-Study, tuition waivers (full), and unspecified assistantships available. Financial award application deadline: 3/1; financial award applicants required to submit FAFSA. In 2010, 69 master's awarded. *Degree program information:* Part-time and evening/weekend programs available. Offers accountancy (M Acc); business administration (MBA); economics (MA). *Application deadline:* For fall admission, 4/15 for domestic students, 2/15 for international students. *Application fee:* $50. *Application Contact:* MBA Program Office, 513-529-6643, E-mail: miamimba@muohio.edu. *Dean,* Dr. Roger Jenkins, 513-529-3631, Fax: 513-529-6992, E-mail: deanofbusiness@muohio.edu.

Institute of Environmental Sciences Students: 53 full-time (33 women), 6 part-time (3 women); includes 4 minority (1 Black or African American, non-Hispanic/Latino; 1 American Indian or Alaska Native, non-Hispanic/Latino; 1 Asian, non-Hispanic/Latino; 1 Two or more races, non-Hispanic/Latino), 5 international. Average age 29. Expenses: Contact institution. *Financial support:* Fellowships with tuition reimbursements, research assistantships, teaching assistantships, career-related internships or fieldwork, Federal Work-Study, health care benefits, tuition waivers (full), and unspecified assistantships available. Financial award application deadline: 3/1; financial award applicants required to submit FAFSA. In 2010, 14 master's awarded. *Degree program information:* Part-time programs available. Offers environmental sciences (M En). *Application fee:* $50. *Application Contact:* Dr. Doug Miekle, Co-Director, 513-529-5811, Fax: 513-529-5814, E-mail: ies@muohio.edu. *Co-Director,* Dr. Doug Miekle, 513-529-5811, Fax: 513-529-5814, E-mail: ies@muohio.edu.

School of Education and Allied Professions Students: 221 full-time (156 women), 139 part-time (100 women); includes 51 minority (37 Black or African American, non-Hispanic/Latino; 10 Asian, non-Hispanic/Latino; 4 Hispanic/Latino), 31 international. Average age 30. Expenses: Contact institution. *Financial support:* Fellowships with full tuition reimbursements, research assistantships with full tuition reimbursements, teaching assistantships with full tuition reimbursements, career-related internships or fieldwork, Federal Work-Study, health care benefits, tuition waivers (full), and unspecified assistantships available. Financial award application deadline: 3/1; financial award applicants required to submit FAFSA. In 2010, 155 master's, 15 doctorates awarded. *Degree program information:* Part-time programs available. Offers child and family studies (MS); curriculum and teacher leadership (M Ed); education and allied professions (M Ed, MA, MAT, MS, Ed D, PhD, Ed S); educational administration (Ed D, PhD); educational psychology (M Ed); elementary education (M Ed, MAT); exercise and health studies (MS); instructional design and technology (M Ed, MA); reading education (M Ed); school leadership (MS); school psychology (MS, Ed S); secondary education (M Ed, MAT); special education (M Ed); sport studies (MS); student affairs in higher education (MS, PhD). *Application fee:* $50. *Application Contact:* Graduate Admission Coordinator, 513-529-3734, Fax: 513-529-3762, E-mail: gradschool@muohio.edu. *Dean,* Dr. Carine M. Feyten, 513-529-6317, Fax: 513-529-7270.

School of Engineering and Applied Science Students: 40 full-time (11 women), 4 part-time (1 woman); includes 1 Black or African American, non-Hispanic/Latino; 1 Asian, non-Hispanic/Latino; 1 Hispanic/Latino, 23 international. Average age 25. Expenses: Contact institution. *Financial support:* Fellowships with full tuition reimbursements, research assistantships, teaching assistantships, Federal Work-Study, health care benefits, tuition waivers (full), and unspecified assistantships available. Financial award application deadline: 3/1. In 2010, 14 master's awarded. Offers chemical and paper engineering (MS); computational science and engineering (MS); computer science (MCS); computer science and software engineering (MCS); software development (Certificate). *Application fee:* $50. *Application Contact:* Graduate Admission Coordinator, 513-529-3734, Fax: 513-529-3734, E-mail: gradschool@muohio.edu. *Dean*, Dr. Marek Dollar, 513-529-0700, E-mail: seasfyi@muohio.edu.

School of Fine Arts Students: 80 full-time (37 women), 6 part-time (3 women); includes 15 minority (8 Black or African American, non-Hispanic/Latino; 1 Asian, non-Hispanic/Latino; 5 Hispanic/Latino; 1 Native Hawaiian or other Pacific Islander, non-Hispanic/Latino), 9 international. Average age 27. Expenses: Contact institution. *Financial support:* Fellowships, research assistantships, teaching assistantships, career-related internships or fieldwork, Federal Work-Study, health care benefits, tuition waivers (full), and unspecified assistantships available. Financial award application deadline: 3/1. In 2010, 39 master's awarded. *Degree program information:* Part-time programs available. Offers architecture (M Arch); art education (MA); fine arts (M Arch, MA, MFA, MM); music education (MM); music performance (MM); studio art (MFA); theatre (MA). *Application fee:* $50. *Application Contact:* Admission Coordinator, 513-529-3734, Fax: 513-529-3762, E-mail: gradschool@muohio.edu. *Dean*, Dr. James Lentini, 513-529-6010, E-mail: sfa@muohio.edu.

MICHIGAN SCHOOL OF PROFESSIONAL PSYCHOLOGY, Farmington Hills, MI 48334

General Information Independent, coed, graduate-only institution. *Enrollment by degree level:* 53 master's, 85 doctoral. *Graduate faculty:* 7 full-time (3 women), 20 part-time/adjunct (11 women). Tuition and fees vary according to course load and degree level. *Graduate housing:* On-campus housing not available. *Student services:* Campus employment opportunities, international student services, services for students with disabilities, writing training. *Library facilities:* The Moustakas Johnson Library. *Online resources:* library catalog, web page. *Collection:* 10,521 titles, 580 serial subscriptions, 334 audiovisual materials.

Computer facilities: 16 computers available on campus for general student use. A campuswide network can be accessed from off campus. *Web address:* http://www.mispp.edu/.

General Application Contact: Amanda Ming, Admissions and Recruitment Coordinator, 248-476-1122 Ext. 117, Fax: 248-476-1125, E-mail: aming@mispp.edu.

GRADUATE UNITS

MA and PsyD Programs in Clinical Psychology Students: 120 full-time (92 women), 18 part-time (16 women); includes 29 minority (22 Black or African American, non-Hispanic/Latino; 4 Asian, non-Hispanic/Latino; 3 Hispanic/Latino). 126 applicants, 75% accepted, 77 enrolled. *Faculty:* 7 full-time (3 women), 20 part-time/adjunct (11 women). Expenses: Contact institution. *Financial support:* In 2010–11, 6 students received support, including 3 research assistantships (averaging $12,000 per year), 1 teaching assistantship (averaging $12,000 per year); career-related internships or fieldwork, institutionally sponsored loans, and scholarships/grants also available. Financial award application deadline: 6/30; financial award applicants required to submit FAFSA. In 2010, 41 master's, 20 doctorates awarded. *Degree program information:* Part-time programs available. Offers clinical psychology (MA, Psy D). *Application deadline:* Applications are processed on a rolling basis. *Application fee:* $75. *Application Contact:* Amanda Ming, Admissions and Recruitment Coordinator, 248-476-1122 Ext. 117, Fax: 248-476-1125, E-mail: aming@mispp.edu. *President*, Dr. Kerry Moustakas, 248-476-1122, Fax: 248-476-1125.

MICHIGAN STATE UNIVERSITY, East Lansing, MI 48824

General Information State-supported, coed, university. CGS member. *Graduate housing:* Rooms and/or apartments available on a first-come, first-served basis to single and married students. *Research affiliation:* Argonne National Laboratory (high-energy physics and structural biology), Association of Sea Grant Programs (fresh water ecosystems), Fraunhofer Center (manufacturing), Michigan Economic Development Corporation (life sciences, homeland security, automotive technologies), Oak Ridge Associated Universities (scientific research and education), Southern Astrophysical Research (SOAR) Telescope (astronomy).

GRADUATE UNITS

College of Human Medicine Offers biochemistry and molecular biology (MS, PhD); epidemiology (MS, PhD); human medicine (MD, MPH, MS, PhD); human medicine/medical scientist training program (MD); microbiology (MS); microbiology and molecular genetics (PhD); pharmacology and toxicology (MS, PhD); physiology (MS, PhD); public health (MPH).

College of Osteopathic Medicine Offers biochemistry and molecular biology (MS, PhD); integrative pharmacology (MS); microbiology (MS); microbiology and molecular genetics (PhD); osteopathic medicine (DO, MS, PhD); pharmacology and toxicology (MS, PhD); pharmacology and toxicology-environmental toxicology (PhD); physiology (MS, PhD).

College of Veterinary Medicine Offers animal science–environmental toxicology (PhD); biochemistry and molecular biology–environmental toxicology (PhD); chemistry–environmental toxicology (PhD); comparative medicine and integrative biology (MS, PhD); comparative medicine and integrative biology–environmental toxicology (PhD); crop and soil sciences–environmental toxicology (PhD); environmental engineering–environmental toxicology (PhD); environmental geosciences–environmental toxicology (PhD); fisheries and wildlife-environmental toxicology (PhD); food safety (MS); food safety and toxicology (MS); food science–environmental toxicology (PhD); forestry–environmental toxicology (PhD); genetics–environmental toxicology (PhD); human nutrition–environmental toxicology (PhD); industrial microbiology (MS, PhD); integrative toxicology (PhD); large animal clinical sciences (MS, PhD); microbiology (MS, PhD); microbiology and molecular genetics (MS, PhD); microbiology–environmental toxicology (PhD); pathobiology and diagnostic investigation (MS, PhD); pathology (MS, PhD); pathology–environmental toxicology (PhD); pharmacology and toxicology (MS, PhD); pharmacology and toxicology–environmental toxicology (PhD); physiology (MS, PhD); small animal clinical sciences (MS); veterinary medicine (DVM, MS, PhD); veterinary medicine/medical scientist training program (DVM); zoology–environmental toxicology (PhD).

The Graduate School *Degree program information:* Part-time and evening/weekend programs available. Postbaccalaureate distance learning degree programs offered. Electronic applications accepted.

College of Agriculture and Natural Resources Offers agricultural economics (MS, PhD); agricultural, food, and resource economics (MS, PhD); agriculture and natural resources (MA, MIPS, MS, MURP, PhD); animal science (MS, PhD); animal science-environmental toxicology (PhD); biochemistry and molecular biology (PhD); biosystems engineering (MS, PhD); cellular and molecular biology (PhD); community, agriculture, recreation, and resource studies (MS, PhD); construction management (MS, PhD); crop and soil sciences (MS, PhD); crop and soil sciences-environmental toxicology (PhD); entomology (MS, PhD); environmental design (MA); fisheries and wildlife (MS, PhD); fisheries and wildlife—environmental toxicology (PhD); food science (MS, PhD); food science—environmental toxicology (PhD); forestry (MS, PhD); forestry-environmental toxicology (PhD); genetics (PhD); horticulture (MS, PhD); human nutrition (MS, PhD); human nutrition-environmental toxicology (PhD); integrated pest management (MS); interior design and facilities management (MA); international planning studies (MIPS); microbiology and molecular genetics (PhD); packaging (MS, PhD); plant biology (PhD); plant breeding and genetics (MS, PhD); plant breeding and genetics-crop and soil sciences (MS); plant breeding, genetics and biotechnology-crop and soil sciences (PhD); plant breeding, genetics and biotechnology-forestry (MS, PhD); plant breeding, genetics and biotechnology-horticulture (MS, PhD); plant pathology (MS, PhD); plant physiology (PhD); urban and regional planning (MURP).

College of Arts and Letters Offers African American and African studies (MA, PhD); American studies (MA, PhD); applied Spanish linguistics (MA); arts and letters (MA, MFA, PhD); critical studies in literacy and pedagogy (MA); digital rhetoric and professional writing (MA); English (PhD); French (MA); French language and literature (PhD); German studies (MA, PhD); Hispanic cultural studies (PhD); Hispanic literatures (MA); linguistics (MA, PhD); literature in English (MA); philosophy (MA, PhD); rhetoric and writing (PhD); second language studies (PhD); studio art (MFA); teaching English to speakers of other languages (MA); theatre (MA, MFA). Electronic applications accepted.

College of Communication Arts and Sciences Offers advertising (MA); communication (MA, PhD); communication arts and sciences (MA, MS, PhD); communication arts and sciences–media and information studies (PhD); communicative sciences and disorders (MA, PhD); digital media arts and technology (MA); health communication (MA); information and telecommunication management (MA); information, policy and society (MA); journalism (MA); public relations (MA); retailing (MS, PhD); serious game design (MA).

College of Education Offers counseling (MA); curriculum, instruction and teacher education (PhD, Ed S); education (MA, MS, PhD, Ed S); educational policy (PhD); educational psychology and educational technology (PhD); educational technology (MA); higher, adult and lifelong education (MA, PhD); K–12 educational administration (MA, PhD, Ed S); kinesiology (MS, PhD); literacy instruction (MA); measurement and quantitative methods (PhD); rehabilitation counseling (MA); rehabilitation counselor education (PhD); school psychology (MA, PhD, Ed S); special education (MA, PhD); student affairs administration (MA); teaching and curriculum (MA). Electronic applications accepted.

College of Engineering *Degree program information:* Part-time programs available. Offers chemical engineering (MS, PhD); civil engineering (MS, PhD); computer science (MS, PhD); electrical engineering (MS, PhD); engineering (MS, PhD); engineering mechanics (MS, PhD); environmental engineering (MS, PhD); environmental engineering-environmental toxicology (PhD); materials science and engineering (MS, PhD); mechanical engineering (MS, PhD). Electronic applications accepted.

College of Music Offers collaborative piano (M Mus); jazz studies (M Mus); music (PhD); music composition (M Mus, DMA); music conducting (M Mus, DMA); music education (M Mus); music performance (M Mus, DMA); music theory (M Mus); music therapy (M Mus); musicology (MA); piano pedagogy (M Mus). Electronic applications accepted.

College of Natural Science Offers applied mathematics (MS, PhD); applied statistics (MS); astrophysics and astronomy (MS, PhD); biochemistry and molecular biology (MS, PhD); biochemistry and molecular biology/environmental toxicology (PhD); biological, physical and general science for teachers (MAT, MS); biomedical laboratory operations (MS); cell and molecular biology (MS, PhD); cell and molecular biology/environmental toxicology (PhD); chemical physics (PhD); chemistry (MS, PhD); chemistry-environmental toxicology (PhD); clinical laboratory sciences (MS); computational chemistry (MS); ecology, evolutionary biology and behavior (PhD); environmental geosciences (MS, PhD); environmental geosciences-environmental toxicology (PhD); genetics (MS, PhD); genetics–environmental toxicology (PhD); geological sciences (MS, PhD); industrial mathematics (MS); mathematics (MAT, MS, PhD); mathematics education (MS, PhD); natural science (MAT, MS, PhD); neuroscience (MS, PhD); physics (MS, PhD); physiology (MS, PhD); plant biology (MS, PhD); plant breeding, genetics and biotechnology—plant biology (MS, PhD); quantitative biology (PhD); statistics (MS, PhD); zoo and aquarium management (MS); zoology (MS, PhD); zoology-environmental toxicology (PhD). Electronic applications accepted.

College of Nursing *Degree program information:* Part-time programs available. Postbaccalaureate distance learning degree programs offered (no on-campus study). Offers nursing (MSN, PhD). Electronic applications accepted.

College of Social Science Offers anthropology (MA, PhD); Chicano/Latino studies (PhD); child development (MA); clinical social work (MSW); community services (MS); criminal justice (MS, PhD); economics (MA, PhD); family and child ecology (PhD); family studies (MA); forensic science (MS); geographic information science (MS); geography (MS, PhD); history (MA, PhD); history-secondary school teaching (MA); human resources and labor relations (MLRHR); industrial relations and human resources (PhD); law enforcement intelligence and analysis (MS); marriage and family therapy (MA); organizational and community practice (MSW); political science (MA, PhD); professional applications in anthropology (MA); psychology (MA, PhD); public policy (MPP); social science (MA, MIPS, MLRHR, MPP, MS, MSW, MURP, PhD); social work (PhD); sociology (MA, PhD); youth development (MA). Electronic applications accepted.

Eli Broad Graduate School of Management *Degree program information:* Evening/weekend programs available. Offers accounting (MS); business administration (MBA, PhD); business research (MBA); corporate business administration (MBA); finance (MS); foodservice business management (MS); hospitality business management (MS); integrative management (MBA); management (MBA, MS, PhD); marketing (MBA, PhD); supply chain management (MS). Electronic applications accepted.

National Superconducting Cyclotron Laboratory Offers chemistry (PhD); physics (PhD).

MICHIGAN STATE UNIVERSITY COLLEGE OF LAW, East Lansing, MI 48824-1300

General Information Independent, coed, graduate-only institution. *Enrollment by degree level:* 882 first professional, 54 other advanced degrees. *Graduate faculty:* 57 full-time (28 women), 85 part-time/adjunct (19 women). *Tuition:* Full-time $33,785; part-time $1165 per credit. *Required fees:* $226; $226 $13 per year. One-time fee: $200. *Graduate housing:* Rooms and/or apartments available on a first-come, first-served basis to single and married students. Housing application deadline: 4/1. *Student services:* Campus employment opportunities, campus safety program, career counseling, exercise/wellness program, international student services, low-cost health insurance, multicultural affairs office, services for students with disabilities, writing training. *Library facilities:* Michigan State University College of Law Library plus 5 others. *Online resources:* library catalog, access to other libraries' catalogs. *Collection:* 156,669 titles, 15,067 serial subscriptions, 1,031 audiovisual materials.

Computer facilities: 72 computers available on campus for general student use. A campuswide network can be accessed from student residence rooms and from off campus. Online class registration is available. *Web address:* http://www.law.msu.edu/.

General Application Contact: Charles Roboski, Assistant Dean of Admissions, 517-432-0222, Fax: 517-432-0098, E-mail: roboski@law.msu.edu.

GRADUATE UNITS

Professional Program Students: 853 full-time (362 women), 83 part-time (39 women); includes 136 minority (61 Black or African American, non-Hispanic/Latino; 12 American Indian or Alaska Native, non-Hispanic/Latino; 25 Asian, non-Hispanic/Latino; 30 Hispanic/Latino; 1 Native Hawaiian or other Pacific Islander, non-Hispanic/Latino; 7 Two or more races, non-Hispanic/Latino), 100 international. Average age 26. 3,471 applicants, 35% accepted, 299 enrolled. *Faculty:* 57 full-time (28 women), 85 part-time/adjunct (19 women). Expenses: Contact institution. *Financial support:* In 2010–11, 351 students received support, including 346 fellowships (averaging $24,370 per year); career-related internships or fieldwork, Federal Work-Study, institutionally sponsored loans, scholarships/grants, and tuition waivers (full) also available. Support available to part-time students. Financial award application deadline: 4/15; financial award applicants required to submit FAFSA. In 2010, 348 first professional degrees, 8 master's awarded. *Degree program information:* Part-time programs available. Offers American legal system (LL M); intellectual property (LL M); jurisprudence (MJ); law (JD). *Application deadline:* For fall admission, 3/15 priority date for domestic students, 7/1 priority date for international students. Applications are processed on a rolling basis. *Application fee:* $60. Electronic applications accepted. *Application Contact:* Charles Roboski, Assistant Dean of Admissions, 517-432-0222, Fax: 517-432-0098, E-mail: roboski@law.msu.edu. *Dean and Professor of Law*, Joan W. Howarth, 517-432-6993, Fax: 517-432-6801, E-mail: howarth@law.msu.edu.

MICHIGAN TECHNOLOGICAL UNIVERSITY, Houghton, MI 49931

General Information State-supported, coed, university. CGS member. *Graduate housing:* Rooms and/or apartments available on a first-come, first-served basis to single and married students.

GRADUATE UNITS

Graduate School *Degree program information:* Part-time programs available. Postbaccalaureate distance learning degree programs offered (minimal on-campus study). Electronic applications accepted.

Michigan Technological University (continued)

College of Engineering *Degree program information:* Part-time programs available. Postbaccalaureate distance learning degree programs offered (minimal on-campus study). Offers biomedical engineering (PhD); chemical engineering (MS, PhD); civil engineering (ME, MS, PhD); computational science and engineering (PhD); electrical engineering (MS, PhD); engineering (ME, MS, PhD); engineering mechanics (MS); environmental engineering (ME, MS, PhD); environmental engineering science (MS); geological engineering (MS, PhD); geology (MS, PhD); geophysics (MS); materials science and engineering (MS, PhD); mechanical engineering (MS, PhD); mechanical engineering-engineering mechanics (PhD); mining engineering (MS, PhD). Electronic applications accepted.

College of Sciences and Arts *Degree program information:* Part-time programs available. Offers applied science education (MS); atmospheric sciences (PhD); biological sciences (MS, PhD); chemistry (MS, PhD); computational science and engineering (PhD); computer science (MS, PhD); engineering physics (PhD); environmental and energy policy (PhD); environmental policy (MS); industrial archaeology (MS); industrial heritage and archeology (PhD); mathematical sciences (MS, PhD); physics (MS, PhD); rhetoric and technical communication (MS, PhD); sciences and arts (MS, PhD). Electronic applications accepted.

School of Business and Economics *Degree program information:* Part-time programs available. Offers applied natural resource economics (MS); business administration (MBA); business and economics (MBA, MS). Electronic applications accepted.

School of Forest Resources and Environmental Science *Degree program information:* Part-time programs available. Offers applied ecology (MS); forest ecology and management (MS); forest molecular genetics and biotechnology (MS, PhD); forest resources and environmental science (MF, MS, PhD); forest science (PhD); forestry (MF, MS). Electronic applications accepted.

Sustainable Futures Institute *Degree program information:* Part-time programs available. Offers sustainability (Certificate).

MICHIGAN THEOLOGICAL SEMINARY, Plymouth, MI 48170

General Information Independent-religious, coed, graduate-only institution. *Graduate housing:* On-campus housing not available.

GRADUATE UNITS

Graduate Programs *Degree program information:* Part-time and evening/weekend programs available. Offers Bible (Graduate Certificate); Christian education (MA); counseling psychology (MA); divinity (M Div); theological studies (MA).

MID-AMERICA BAPTIST THEOLOGICAL SEMINARY, Cordova, TN 38016

General Information Independent-religious, men only, comprehensive institution. *Graduate housing:* Rooms and/or apartments available on a first-come, first-served basis to single and married students.

GRADUATE UNITS

Graduate and Professional Programs Offers theology (M Div, MACE, MCE, MM, D Min, PhD). Electronic applications accepted.

MID-AMERICA BAPTIST THEOLOGICAL SEMINARY NORTHEAST BRANCH, Schenectady, NY 12303-3463

General Information Independent-religious, coed, primarily men, graduate-only institution. *Graduate housing:* Rooms and/or apartments available on a first-come, first-served basis to single and married students.

GRADUATE UNITS

Program in Theology *Degree program information:* Part-time and evening/weekend programs available. Offers theology (M Div). Electronic applications accepted.

MID-AMERICA CHRISTIAN UNIVERSITY, Oklahoma City, OK 73170-4504

General Information Independent-religious, coed, comprehensive institution.

GRADUATE UNITS

Program in Business Administration Offers business administration (MBA).

Program in Counseling Offers marital and family therapy (MS); pastoral/spiritual direction (MS); professional counselor (MS).

Program in Leadership Offers leadership (MA).

Program in Public Administration Offers public administration (MA).

MIDAMERICA NAZARENE UNIVERSITY, Olathe, KS 66062-1899

General Information Independent-religious, coed, comprehensive institution. *Graduate housing:* On-campus housing not available.

GRADUATE UNITS

Graduate Studies in Counseling *Degree program information:* Evening/weekend programs available. Offers counseling (MAC); play therapy (PMC).

Graduate Studies in Education *Degree program information:* Part-time and evening/weekend programs available. Postbaccalaureate distance learning degree programs offered (no on-campus study). Offers ESOL (M Ed); professional teaching (M Ed); special education (MA); technology enhanced teaching (M Ed).

Graduate Studies in Management *Degree program information:* Evening/weekend programs available. Offers management (MBA); organizational administration (MA). Electronic applications accepted.

MID-AMERICA REFORMED SEMINARY, Dyer, IN 46311

General Information Independent-religious, men only, graduate-only institution.

GRADUATE UNITS

Graduate Programs Offers theology (M Div, MTS).

MIDDLEBURY COLLEGE, Middlebury, VT 05753-6002

General Information Independent, coed, comprehensive institution. *Enrollment:* 2,532 graduate, professional, and undergraduate students; 866 full-time matriculated graduate/professional students. *Graduate housing:* Room and/or apartments guaranteed to single students; on-campus housing not available to married students. *Student services:* Campus safety program, career counseling, free psychological counseling, international student services, services for students with disabilities, teacher training. *Library facilities:* Main Library plus 3 others. *Online resources:* library catalog, web page, access to other libraries' catalogs. *Collection:* 729,660 titles, 48,033 serial subscriptions, 44,873 audiovisual materials.

Computer facilities: 494 computers available on campus for general student use. A campuswide network can be accessed from student residence rooms and from off campus. Online class registration, help-line, personal Web pages, file servers are available. *Web address:* http://www.middlebury.edu/.

General Application Contact: Admissions Office, 802-443-3000, Fax: 802-443-2056, E-mail: admissions@middlebury.edu.

GRADUATE UNITS

Bread Loaf School of English Offers English (M Litt, MA). Offered during summer only. Electronic applications accepted.

Language Schools Students: 393 full-time (280 women); includes 93 minority (9 Black or African American, non-Hispanic/Latino; 1 American Indian or Alaska Native, non-Hispanic/Latino; 27 Asian, non-Hispanic/Latino; 56 Hispanic/Latino). Average age 30. 734 applicants, 78% accepted. *Faculty:* 87 full-time (37 women). Expenses: Contact institution. *Financial support:* Fellowships, scholarships/grants available. Financial award applicants required to submit FAFSA. In 2010, 134 master's, 5 doctorates awarded. Offers French (MA, DML); German (MA, DML); Italian (MA, DML); language (MA, DML); Russian (MA, DML); Spanish (MA, DML). *Application deadline:* Applications are processed on a rolling basis. *Application fee:* $65. Electronic applications accepted. *Application Contact:* Kara Gennarelli, Technical and Lead Coordinator, Language Schools Office, 802-443-5727, Fax: 802-443-2075, E-mail: languages@middlebury.edu. *Vice President for Language Schools, Schools Abroad and Graduate Programs,* Dr. Michael E. Geisler, 802-443-5508, Fax: 802-443-2075.

Chinese School Students: 29 full-time (23 women); includes 21 minority (all Asian, non-Hispanic/Latino). Average age 34. 49 applicants, 82% accepted, 29 enrolled. *Faculty:* 4 full-time (3 women). Expenses: Contact institution. *Financial support:* In 2010–11, 2 fellowships with full tuition reimbursements (averaging $7,000 per year) were awarded; scholarships/grants also available. Financial award applicants required to submit FAFSA. In 2010, 8 master's awarded. Offers Chinese (MA). *Application deadline:* Applications are processed on a rolling basis. *Application fee:* $65. Electronic applications accepted. *Application Contact:* Anna Sun, Coordinator, 802-443-5520, Fax: 802-443-2075, E-mail: sun@middlebury.edu. *Director,* Dr. Jianhua Bai, 802-443-5520, Fax: 802-443-2075, E-mail: jbai@middlebury.edu.

MIDDLE TENNESSEE SCHOOL OF ANESTHESIA, Madison, TN 37116

General Information Independent-religious, coed, graduate-only institution. *Enrollment by degree level:* 209 master's. *Graduate faculty:* 6 full-time (2 women), 13 part-time/adjunct (4 women). *Tuition:* Full-time $20,742. *Required fees:* $8117. *Graduate housing:* On-campus housing not available. *Student services:* Career counseling. *Library facilities:* Nelda Ackerman Learning Resource Center. *Online resources:* library catalog, web page. *Collection:* 1,500 titles, 25 serial subscriptions.

Computer facilities: 10 computers available on campus for general student use. A campuswide network can be accessed from off campus. *Web address:* http://www.mtsa.edu/.

General Application Contact: Dr. Mary E. DeVasher, Vice President and Dean, 615-732-7677, Fax: 615-868-9885, E-mail: ikey@mtsa.edu.

GRADUATE UNITS

Program in Nurse Anesthesia Expenses: Contact institution. *Financial support:* Traineeships available. Offers nurse anesthesia (MS). *Application deadline:* For fall admission, 10/31 for domestic students. Applications are processed on a rolling basis. *Application Contact:* Pam Gann, Admissions/Financial Aid Assistant, 615-868-6503, Fax: 615-868-9885, E-mail: pam@mtsa.edu. *Vice President and Dean,* Dr. Mary E. DeVasher, 615-868-6503, Fax: 615-868-9885, E-mail: ikey@mtsa.edu.

MIDDLE TENNESSEE STATE UNIVERSITY, Murfreesboro, TN 37132

General Information State-supported, coed, university. CGS member. *Enrollment:* 26,430 graduate, professional, and undergraduate students; 253 full-time matriculated graduate/professional students (136 women), 2,460 part-time matriculated graduate/professional students (1,557 women). *Graduate faculty:* 416 full-time (175 women), 10 part-time/adjunct (3 women). Tuition, state resident: full-time $4632. Tuition, nonresident: full-time $11,520. *Graduate housing:* Rooms and/or apartments available on a first-come, first-served basis to single and married students. Typical cost: $10,147 (including board) for single students. *Student services:* Campus employment opportunities, campus safety program, career counseling, exercise/wellness program, free psychological counseling, international student services, low-cost health insurance, multicultural affairs office, services for students with disabilities. *Library facilities:* James E. Walker Library. *Online resources:* library catalog, web page, access to other libraries' catalogs.

Computer facilities: A campuswide network can be accessed from student residence rooms and from off campus. Online class registration is available. *Web address:* http://www.mtsu.edu/.

General Application Contact: Dr. Michael Allen, Dean and Vice Provost for Research, 615-898-2840, Fax: 615-904-8020, E-mail: mallen@mtsu.edu.

GRADUATE UNITS

College of Graduate Studies Students: 253 full-time (136 women), 2,460 part-time (1,557 women); includes 368 Black or African American, non-Hispanic/Latino; 6 American Indian or Alaska Native, non-Hispanic/Latino; 169 Asian, non-Hispanic/Latino; 55 Hispanic/Latino; 43 Two or more races, non-Hispanic/Latino. Average age 29. 2,173 applicants, 69% accepted, 1493 enrolled. *Faculty:* 416 full-time (175 women), 10 part-time/adjunct (3 women). Expenses: Contact institution. *Financial support:* In 2010–11, 348 students received support. Career-related internships or fieldwork and institutionally sponsored loans available. Support available to part-time students. Financial award application deadline: 5/1; financial award applicants required to submit FAFSA. In 2010, 695 master's, 20 doctorates, 142 other advanced degrees awarded. *Degree program information:* Part-time and evening/weekend programs available. Postbaccalaureate distance learning degree programs offered. *Application deadline:* For fall admission, 6/1 for domestic and international students. Applications are processed on a rolling basis. *Application fee:* $25 ($30 for international students). Electronic applications accepted. *Application Contact:* Dr. Michael Allen, Dean and Vice Provost for Research, 615-898-2840, Fax: 615-904-8020, E-mail: mallen@mtsu.edu. *Dean and Vice Provost for Research,* Dr. Michael Allen, 615-898-2840, Fax: 615-904-8020, E-mail: mallen@mtsu.edu.

College of Basic and Applied Sciences Students: 31 full-time (7 women), 307 part-time (140 women); includes 46 Black or African American, non-Hispanic/Latino; 1 American Indian or Alaska Native, non-Hispanic/Latino; 55 Asian, non-Hispanic/Latino; 7 Hispanic/Latino; 3 Two or more races, non-Hispanic/Latino. Average age 30. 298 applicants, 58% accepted, 172 enrolled. *Faculty:* 102 full-time (44 women). Expenses: Contact institution. *Financial support:* In 2010–11, 98 students received support. Institutionally sponsored loans available. Support available to part-time students. Financial award application deadline: 5/1; financial award applicants required to submit FAFSA. In 2010, 76 master's, 1 doctorate awarded. *Degree program information:* Part-time and evening/weekend programs available. Postbaccalaureate distance learning degree programs offered. Offers aerospace education (M Ed); aviation administration (MS); basic and applied sciences (M Ed, MS, MSN, MST, DA, PhD, Graduate Certificate); biology (MS); biostatistics (MS); chemistry (MS, DA); computer science (MS); engineering technology (MS); health care informatics (MS); health care management (Graduate Certificate); mathematics (MS, MST, PhD). *Application deadline:* For fall admission, 6/1 for domestic and international students. Applications are processed on a rolling basis. *Application fee:* $25 ($30 for international students). Electronic applications accepted. *Application Contact:* Dr. Michael Allen, Dean and Vice Provost for Research, 615-898-2840, Fax: 615-904-8020, E-mail: mallen@mtsu.edu. *Dean,* Dr. Thomas Cheatham, 615-898-5508, Fax: 615-898-2615.

College of Behavioral and Health Sciences Students: 62 full-time (51 women), 305 part-time (189 women); includes 83 Black or African American, non-Hispanic/Latino; 16 Asian, non-Hispanic/Latino; 5 Hispanic/Latino; 1 Two or more races, non-Hispanic/Latino. Expenses: Contact institution. Offers behavioral and health sciences (MA, MCJ, MS, MSW, PhD, Ed S); child development and family studies (MS); clinical psychology (MA); criminal justice administration (MCJ); exercise science (MS); experimental psychology (MA); health, physical education and recreation (MS); human performance (PhD); industrial/organizational psychology (MA); nutrition and food science (MS); psychology (MA); quantitative psychology (MA); school psychology (MA, Ed S); social work (MSW). *Application Contact:* Dr. Michael Allen, Dean and Vice Provost for Research, 615-898-2840, Fax: 615-904-8020, E-mail: mallen@mtsu.edu. *Dean and Vice Provost for Research,* Dr. Michael Allen, 615-898-2840, Fax: 615-904-8020, E-mail: mallen@mtsu.edu.

College of Education Students: 50 full-time (39 women), 775 part-time (644 women); includes 92 Black or African American, non-Hispanic/Latino; 1 American Indian or Alaska Native, non-Hispanic/Latino; 13 Asian, non-Hispanic/Latino; 9 Hispanic/Latino; 11 Two or more races, non-Hispanic/Latino. Average age 31. 715 applicants. *Faculty:* 109 full-time (56 women), 7 part-time/adjunct (2 women). Expenses: Contact institution. *Financial support:* In 2010–11, 79 students received support. Career-related internships or fieldwork and institutionally sponsored loans available. Support available to part-time students. Financial award application deadline: 5/1; financial award applicants required to submit FAFSA. In 2010, 214 master's, 128 other advanced degrees awarded. *Degree program information:* Part-time and evening/weekend programs available. Postbaccalaureate distance learning degree programs offered. Offers administration and supervision (M Ed, Ed S); curriculum and instruction (M Ed, Ed S); dyslexic studies (Graduate Certificate); early childhood education (M Ed); education (M Ed, PhD, Ed S, Graduate Certificate); elementary education (M Ed, Ed S); English as a second language (M Ed, Ed S); literacy studies (PhD); mental health counseling (M Ed); middle school education (M Ed); professional counseling (M Ed, Ed S); reading (M Ed); school counseling (M Ed); secondary education (M Ed); special education (M Ed); technology and curriculum design (Ed S). *Application deadline:* For fall admission, 6/1 for domestic and international students. Applications are processed on a rolling basis. *Application fee:* $25 ($30 for international students). Electronic applications accepted. *Application Contact:* Dr. Michael Allen, Dean and Vice Provost for Research, 615-898-2840, Fax: 615-904-8020, E-mail: mallen@mtsu.edu. *Dean,* Dr. Lana Seivers, 615-898-2874, Fax: 615-898-2530, E-mail: lseivers@mtsu.edu.

College of Liberal Arts Students: 19 full-time (15 women), 246 part-time (165 women); includes 12 Black or African American, non-Hispanic/Latino; 7 Asian, non-Hispanic/Latino; 10 Hispanic/Latino; 7 Two or more races, non-Hispanic/Latino. Average age 34. 162 applicants, 76% accepted, 123 enrolled. *Faculty:* 106 full-time (55 women), 3 part-time/adjunct (1 woman). Expenses: Contact institution. *Financial support:* In 2010–11, 99 students received support. Career-related internships or fieldwork and institutionally sponsored loans available. Support available to part-time students. Financial award application deadline: 5/1; financial award applicants required to submit FAFSA. In 2010, 46 master's, 10 doctorates, 2 other advanced degrees awarded. *Degree program information:* Part-time and evening/weekend programs available. Postbaccalaureate distance learning degree programs offered. Offers English (MA, PhD); English as a second language (M Ed); foreign language (MAT); geosciences (Graduate Certificate); gerontology (Graduate Certificate); history (MA); liberal arts (M Ed, MA, MAT, MSW, PhD, Graduate Certificate); music (MA); public history (MA, PhD); sociology (MA). *Application deadline:* For fall admission, 6/1 for domestic and international students. Applications are processed on a rolling basis. *Application fee:* $25 ($30 for international students). Electronic applications accepted. *Application Contact:* Dr. Michael Allen, Dean and Vice Provost for Research, 615-898-2840, Fax: 615-904-8020, E-mail: mallen@mtsu.edu. *Interim Dean,* Dr. Mark E. Byrnes, 615-898-2534, Fax: 615-904-8279, E-mail: mbyrnes@mtsu.edu.

College of Mass Communication Students: 13 full-time (3 women), 71 part-time (39 women); includes 10 Black or African American, non-Hispanic/Latino; 1 American Indian or Alaska Native, non-Hispanic/Latino; 5 Asian, non-Hispanic/Latino; 3 Hispanic/Latino; 1 Two or more races, non-Hispanic/Latino. Average age 27. 75 applicants, 56% accepted, 42 enrolled. *Faculty:* 32 full-time (3 women). Expenses: Contact institution. *Financial support:* In 2010–11, 12 students received support. Institutionally sponsored loans available. Support available to part-time students. Financial award application deadline: 5/1; financial award applicants required to submit FAFSA. In 2010, 18 master's awarded. *Degree program information:* Part-time and evening/weekend programs available. Postbaccalaureate distance learning degree programs offered. Offers mass communication (MFA, MS); recording arts and technologies (MFA). *Application deadline:* For fall admission, 6/1 for domestic and international students. Applications are processed on a rolling basis. *Application fee:* $25 ($30 for international students). Electronic applications accepted. *Application Contact:* Dr. Michael Allen, Dean and Vice Provost for Research, 615-898-2840, Fax: 615-904-8020, E-mail: mallen@mtsu.edu. *Dean,* Dr. Roy L. Moore, 615-898-5171, Fax: 615-898-5682, E-mail: rlmoore@mtsu.edu.

Jennings A. Jones College of Business Students: 77 full-time (20 women), 572 part-time (236 women); includes 97 Black or African American, non-Hispanic/Latino; 2 American Indian or Alaska Native, non-Hispanic/Latino; 73 Asian, non-Hispanic/Latino; 18 Hispanic/Latino; 8 Two or more races, non-Hispanic/Latino. Average age 29. 326 applicants, 67% accepted, 217 enrolled. *Faculty:* 67 full-time (17 women). Expenses: Contact institution. *Financial support:* In 2010–11, 57 students received support. Institutionally sponsored loans available. Support available to part-time students. Financial award application deadline: 5/1; financial award applicants required to submit FAFSA. In 2010, 198 master's, 5 doctorates awarded. *Degree program information:* Part-time and evening/weekend programs available. Postbaccalaureate distance learning degree programs offered. Offers accounting (MS); business (MA, MBA, MBE, MS, PhD); business education (MBE); computer information systems (MS); economics (MA, PhD); management and marketing (MBA). *Application deadline:* For fall admission, 6/1 for domestic and international students. Applications are processed on a rolling basis. *Application fee:* $25 ($30 for international students). Electronic applications accepted. *Application Contact:* Dr. Michael Allen, Dean and Vice Provost for Research, 615-898-2840, Fax: 615-904-8020, E-mail: mallen@mtsu.edu. *Dean,* Dr. E. James Burton, 615-898-2764, Fax: 615-898-4736, E-mail: eburton@mtsu.edu.

University College Students: 1 (woman) full-time, 184 part-time (144 women); includes 28 Black or African American, non-Hispanic/Latino; 1 American Indian or Alaska Native, non-Hispanic/Latino; 3 Hispanic/Latino; 5 Two or more races, non-Hispanic/Latino. Average age 38. 41 applicants, 78% accepted, 32 enrolled. Expenses: Contact institution. *Financial support:* In 2010–11, 4 students received support. Application deadline: 5/1. In 2010, 38 master's, 1 other advanced degree awarded. *Degree program information:* Part-time and evening/weekend programs available. Postbaccalaureate distance learning degree programs offered. Offers family nurse practitioner (MSN, Graduate Certificate); nursing (MSN, Graduate Certificate); social sciences (M Ed, MPS, MSN, Graduate Certificate); teaching and learning (M Ed). *Application deadline:* For fall admission, 6/1 for domestic and international students. Applications are processed on a rolling basis. *Application fee:* $25 ($30 for international students). *Application Contact:* Dr. Michael Allen, Dean and Vice Provost for Research, 615-898-2840, Fax: 615-904-8020, E-mail: mallen@mtsu.edu. *Dean,* Dr. Mike Boyle, 615-898-2177, Fax: 615-896-7925, E-mail: mboyle@mtsu.edu.

MIDWAY COLLEGE, Midway, KY 40347-1120

General Information Independent-religious, coed, primarily women, comprehensive institution. *Graduate housing:* On-campus housing not available.

GRADUATE UNITS

Leadership MBA Program Offers leadership (MBA).

MIDWEST COLLEGE OF ORIENTAL MEDICINE, Racine, WI 53403-9747

General Information Proprietary, coed, graduate-only institution. *Graduate housing:* On-campus housing not available. *Research affiliation:* Guangzhou University of Traditional Chinese Medicine (pharmacology).

GRADUATE UNITS

Graduate Programs *Degree program information:* Part-time and evening/weekend programs available. Offers acupuncture (Certificate); oriental medicine (MSOM).

Graduate Programs-Chicago *Degree program information:* Part-time and evening/weekend programs available.

MIDWESTERN BAPTIST THEOLOGICAL SEMINARY, Kansas City, MO 64118-4697

General Information Independent-religious, coed, graduate-only institution. *Graduate housing:* Rooms and/or apartments guaranteed to single and married students.

GRADUATE UNITS

Graduate and Professional Programs *Degree program information:* Part-time programs available. Postbaccalaureate distance learning degree programs offered (minimal on-campus study). Offers Biblical archaeology (MA); Biblical languages (MA); Christian education (M Div, MACE); Christian foundations—lay ministry (Graduate Certificate); collegiate ministries (M Div); counseling (MA); educational ministry (D Ed Min); international church planting (M Div); ministry (M Div, D Min); North American church planting (M Div); sacred music (MCM); urban ministry (M Div); worship leadership (M Div); youth ministry (M Div). Electronic applications accepted.

MIDWESTERN STATE UNIVERSITY, Wichita Falls, TX 76308

General Information State-supported, coed, comprehensive institution. *Enrollment:* 6,426 graduate, professional, and undergraduate students; 161 full-time matriculated graduate/professional students (94 women), 553 part-time matriculated graduate/professional students (386 women). *Enrollment by degree level:* 714 master's. *Graduate faculty:* 80 full-time (30 women), 10 part-time/adjunct (7 women). *International tuition:* $7200 full-time. Tuition, state resident: full-time $1620; part-time $90 per credit hour. Tuition, nonresident: full-time $2160; part-time $120 per credit hour. *Graduate housing:* Rooms and/or apartments available on a first-come, first-served basis to single and married students. Typical cost: $2840 per year ($5940 including board) for single students. Room and board charges vary according to board plan and housing facility selected. *Student services:* Campus employment opportunities, career counseling, exercise/wellness program, free psychological counseling, international student services, low-cost health insurance, services for students with disabilities, teacher training. *Library facilities:* Moffett Library. *Online resources:* library catalog, web page, access to other libraries' catalogs. *Collection:* 462,657 titles, 884 serial subscriptions, 10,476 audiovisual materials.

Computer facilities: 405 computers available on campus for general student use. A campuswide network can be accessed from student residence rooms and from off campus. Online class registration is available. *Web address:* http://www.mwsu.edu/.

General Application Contact: Barbara Ramos Merkle, Director of Admissions, 800-842-1922, Fax: 940-397-4672, E-mail: admissions@mwsu.edu.

GRADUATE UNITS

Graduate Studies Students: 107 full-time (68 women), 427 part-time (277 women); includes 24 Black or African American, non-Hispanic/Latino; 9 American Indian or Alaska Native, non-Hispanic/Latino; 13 Asian, non-Hispanic/Latino; 23 Hispanic/Latino, 61 international. Average age 34. 250 applicants, 83% accepted, 101 enrolled. *Faculty:* 78 full-time (29 women), 13 part-time/adjunct (8 women). Expenses: Contact institution. *Financial support:* In 2010–11, 414 students received support, including 106 teaching assistantships with partial tuition reimbursements available (averaging $6,557 per year); career-related internships or fieldwork, Federal Work-Study, institutionally sponsored loans, scholarships/grants, tuition waivers (partial), and unspecified assistantships also available. Support available to part-time students. Financial award application deadline: 5/1; financial award applicants required to submit FAFSA. In 2010, 160 master's awarded. *Degree program information:* Part-time and evening/weekend programs available. *Application deadline:* For fall admission, 7/1 for domestic students, 4/1 for international students; for spring admission, 11/1 for domestic students, 8/1 for international students. Applications are processed on a rolling basis. *Application fee:* $35 ($50 for international students). Electronic applications accepted. *Application Contact:* Barbara Ramos Merkle, Director of Admissions, 800-842-1922, Fax: 940-397-4672, E-mail: admissions@mwsu.edu. *Dean and Associate Provost,* Dr. Emerson Capps, 940-397-4315, Fax: 940-397-4042, E-mail: emerson.capps@mwsu.edu.

College of Business Administration Students: 37 full-time (10 women), 44 part-time (20 women); includes 11 minority (2 Black or African American, non-Hispanic/Latino; 1 American Indian or Alaska Native, non-Hispanic/Latino; 1 Asian, non-Hispanic/Latino; 7 Hispanic/Latino), 27 international. Average age 29. 22 applicants, 77% accepted, 17 enrolled. *Faculty:* 13 full-time (3 women). Expenses: Contact institution. *Financial support:* In 2010–11, 32 students received support, including 1 teaching assistantship with partial tuition reimbursement available (averaging $2,667 per year); career-related internships or fieldwork, Federal Work-Study, institutionally sponsored loans, tuition waivers (partial), and unspecified assistantships also available. Support available to part-time students. Financial award application deadline: 3/1; financial award applicants required to submit FAFSA. In 2010, 27 master's awarded. *Degree program information:* Part-time and evening/weekend programs available. Offers business administration (MBA). *Application deadline:* For fall admission, 7/1 priority date for domestic students, 4/1 for international students; for spring admission, 11/1 priority date for domestic students, 8/1 for international students. Applications are processed on a rolling basis. *Application fee:* $35 ($50 for international students). Electronic applications accepted. *Application Contact:* Dr. Chris Shao, Director of Graduate Programs, 940-397-4366, Fax: 940-397-4280, E-mail: chris.shao@mwsu.edu. *Dean,* Dr. Barbara Nemecek, 940-397-4088, Fax: 940-397-4280, E-mail: barbar.nemecek@mwsu.edu.

College of Education Students: 35 full-time (31 women), 203 part-time (173 women); includes 20 Black or African American, non-Hispanic/Latino; 1 American Indian or Alaska Native, non-Hispanic/Latino; 19 Hispanic/Latino; 3 Two or more races, non-Hispanic/Latino, 14 international. Average age 36. 65 applicants, 80% accepted, 40 enrolled. *Faculty:* 15 full-time (10 women), 4 part-time/adjunct (all women). Expenses: Contact institution. *Financial support:* In 2010–11, 64 students received support, including 7 teaching assistantships with partial tuition reimbursements available (averaging $6,412 per year); career-related internships or fieldwork, Federal Work-Study, institutionally sponsored loans, tuition waivers (partial), and unspecified assistantships also available. Support available to part-time students. Financial award application deadline: 3/1; financial award applicants required to submit FAFSA. In 2010, 57 master's awarded. *Degree program information:* Part-time and evening/weekend programs available. Offers curriculum and instruction (ME); education (M Ed, MA, ME); educational leadership and technology (ME); general counseling (MA); human resource development (MA); reading education (M Ed); school counseling (M Ed); special education (M Ed); training and development (MA). *Application deadline:* For fall admission, 7/1 priority date for domestic students, 4/1 for international students; for spring admission, 11/1 priority date for domestic students, 8/1 for international students. Applications are processed on a rolling basis. *Application fee:* $35 ($50 for international students). Electronic applications accepted. *Application Contact:* Chair. *Dean,* Dr. Matthew Capps, 940-397-4138, Fax: 940-397-4694, E-mail: matthew.capps@mwsu.edu.

College of Health Sciences and Human Services Students: 33 full-time (20 women), 210 part-time (140 women); includes 49 minority (20 Black or African American, non-Hispanic/Latino; 5 American Indian or Alaska Native, non-Hispanic/Latino; 7 Asian, non-Hispanic/Latino; 13 Hispanic/Latino; 4 Two or more races, non-Hispanic/Latino), 34 international. Average age 34. *Faculty:* 18 full-time (13 women), 4 part-time/adjunct (3 women). Expenses: Contact institution. *Financial support:* In 2010–11, 106 students received support; teaching assistantships with partial tuition reimbursements available, career-related internships or fieldwork, Federal Work-Study, institutionally sponsored loans, scholarships/grants, tuition waivers (partial), and unspecified assistantships available. Support available to part-time students. Financial award application deadline: 3/1; financial award applicants required to submit FAFSA. In 2010, 60 master's awarded. *Degree program information:* Part-time and evening/weekend programs available. Offers family nurse practitioner (MSN); family psychiatric mental health nurse practitioner (MSN); health sciences and human services (MHA, MPA, MSK, MSN, MSR); health services administration (MHA, MSN); kinesiology (MSK); nurse educator (MSN); public administration (MPA); public administration (administrative justice) (MPA); public administration (health services administration) with certificate (MPA); public administration (health services) (MPA); radiologic administration (MSR); radiologic education (MSR); radiologic sciences (MSR); radiologist assistant (MSR). *Application deadline:* For fall admission, 7/1 priority date for domestic students, 4/1 for international students; for spring admission, 11/1 priority date for domestic students, 8/1 for international students. Applications are processed on a rolling basis. *Application fee:* $35 ($50 for international students). Electronic applications accepted. *Application Contact:* 800-842-1922, Fax: 940-397-4672, E-mail: admissions@mwsu.edu. *Director,* Dr. Susan Sportsman, 940-397-4597.

College of Humanities and Social Sciences Students: 32 full-time (22 women), 44 part-time (24 women); includes 3 Black or African American, non-Hispanic/Latino; 1 American Indian or Alaska Native, non-Hispanic/Latino; 1 Asian, non-Hispanic/Latino; 5 Hispanic/Latino, 2 international. Average age 31. 42 applicants, 69% accepted, 21 enrolled. *Faculty:* 17 full-time (1 woman), 1 part-time/adjunct (0 women). Expenses: Contact institution. *Financial support:* In 2010–11, 47 students received support; teaching assistantships with partial tuition reimbursements available, career-related internships or fieldwork, Federal Work-Study, institutionally sponsored loans, scholarships/grants, tuition waivers (partial), and unspecified assistantships available. Support available to part-time students. Financial award application deadline: 3/1; financial award applicants required to submit FAFSA. In 2010, 17 master's awarded. *Degree program information:* Part-time and evening/weekend

Midwestern State University (continued)

programs available. Offers English (MA); history (MA); humanities and social sciences (MA); political science (MA); psychology (MA). *Application deadline:* For fall admission, 7/1 priority date for domestic students, 4/1 for international students; for spring admission, 11/1 priority date for domestic students, 8/1 for international students. Applications are processed on a rolling basis. *Application fee:* $35 ($50 for international students). Electronic applications accepted. *Application Contact:* 800-842-1922, Fax: 940-397-4672, E-mail: admissions@mwsu.edu. *Dean*, Dr. Samuel E. Watson, 940-397-4746, Fax: 940-397-4929, E-mail: samuel.watson@mwsu.edu.

College of Science and Mathematics Students: 15 full-time (4 women), 33 part-time (20 women); includes 2 Black or African American, non-Hispanic/Latino; 1 American Indian or Alaska Native, non-Hispanic/Latino; 2 Asian, non-Hispanic/Latino, 22 international. Average age 27. *Faculty:* 11 full-time (2 women), 1 part-time/adjunct (0 women). Expenses: Contact institution. *Financial support:* In 2010–11, 29 students received support; teaching assistantships with partial tuition reimbursements available, career-related internships or fieldwork, Federal Work-Study, institutionally sponsored loans, scholarships/grants, and unspecified assistantships available. Support available to part-time students. Financial award application deadline: 3/1; financial award applicants required to submit FAFSA. In 2010, 19 master's awarded. *Degree program information:* Part-time and evening/weekend programs available. Offers biology (MS); computer science (MS); science and mathematics (MS). *Application deadline:* For fall admission, 7/1 priority date for domestic students, 4/1 for international students; for spring admission, 11/1 priority date for domestic students, 8/1 for international students. Applications are processed on a rolling basis. *Application fee:* $35 ($50 for international students). Electronic applications accepted. *Application Contact:* Dr. Rodney L. Cate, Interim Dean, 940-397-4198, Fax: 940-397-4299, E-mail: rodney.cate@mwsu.edu. *Interim Dean*, Dr. Rodney L. Cate, 940-397-4198, Fax: 940-397-4299, E-mail: rodney.cate@mwsu.edu.

MIDWESTERN UNIVERSITY, DOWNERS GROVE CAMPUS, Downers Grove, IL 60515-1235

General Information Independent, coed, graduate-only institution. *Enrollment by degree level:* 1,572 first professional, 338 master's, 221 doctoral. *Graduate faculty:* 357 full-time (252 women), 34 part-time/adjunct (15 women). *Graduate housing:* Rooms and/or apartments available on a first-come, first-served basis to single and married students. *Student services:* Campus employment opportunities, campus safety program, career counseling, exercise/wellness program, free psychological counseling, low-cost health insurance. *Library facilities:* Alumni Memorial Library plus 2 others. *Online resources:* web page. *Collection:* 84,097 titles, 1,450 serial subscriptions.

Computer facilities: 190 computers available on campus for general student use. A campuswide network can be accessed from student residence rooms and from off campus. Black Board Learning Software available. *Web address:* http://www.midwestern.edu/.

General Application Contact: Michael Laken, Director of Admissions, 630-515-6171, Fax: 630-971-6086, E-mail: admissil@midwestern.edu.

GRADUATE UNITS

Chicago College of Osteopathic Medicine Students: 751 full-time (353 women), 3 part-time (2 women); includes 3 Black or African American, non-Hispanic/Latino; 96 Asian, non-Hispanic/Latino; 2 Hispanic/Latino, 1 international. Average age 26. 4,930 applicants, 8% accepted, 176 enrolled. *Faculty:* 37 full-time (15 women), 30 part-time/adjunct (11 women). Expenses: Contact institution. *Financial support:* In 2010–11, 568 students received support; fellowships with partial tuition reimbursements available, career-related internships or fieldwork, Federal Work-Study, institutionally sponsored loans, and tuition waivers (full and partial) available. Financial award application deadline: 6/1; financial award applicants required to submit FAFSA. In 2010, 178 DOs awarded. Offers osteopathic medicine (DO). *Application deadline:* For fall admission, 1/1 for domestic students. Applications are processed on a rolling basis. *Application fee:* $50. *Application Contact:* Michael Laken, Director of Admissions, 630-515-6171, Fax: 630-971-6086, E-mail: admissil@midwestern.edu. *Dean*, Dr. Karen J. Nichols, 630-515-6159, E-mail: knicho@midwestern.edu.

Chicago College of Pharmacy Students: 808 full-time (473 women), 10 part-time (6 women); includes 9 Black or African American, non-Hispanic/Latino; 1 American Indian or Alaska Native, non-Hispanic/Latino; 229 Asian, non-Hispanic/Latino; 16 Hispanic/Latino, 11 international. Average age 25. 2,499 applicants, 19% accepted, 201 enrolled. *Faculty:* 50 full-time (35 women). Expenses: Contact institution. *Financial support:* Federal Work-Study and institutionally sponsored loans available. Support available to part-time students. Financial award applicants required to submit FAFSA. In 2010, 217 Pharm Ds awarded. *Degree program information:* Part-time programs available. Postbaccalaureate distance learning degree programs offered (minimal on-campus study). Offers pharmacy (Pharm D). *Application deadline:* For fall admission, 2/3 for domestic students. *Application fee:* $50. *Application Contact:* Michael Laken, Director of Admissions, 630-515-6171, Fax: 630-971-6086, E-mail: admissil@midwestern.edu. *Dean*, Dr. Nancy Fjortoft, 630-971-6408.

College of Health Sciences, Illinois Campus Students: 521 full-time (410 women), 38 part-time (28 women); includes 10 Black or African American, non-Hispanic/Latino; 33 Asian, non-Hispanic/Latino; 17 Hispanic/Latino, 4 international. Average age 25. 1,425 applicants, 33% accepted, 221 enrolled. *Faculty:* 37 full-time (28 women). Expenses: Contact institution. *Financial support:* In 2010–11, 229 students received support. Federal Work-Study, institutionally sponsored loans, and scholarships/grants available. Financial award applicants required to submit FAFSA. In 2010, 96 master's, 28 doctorates awarded. Offers biomedical sciences (MBS); clinical psychology (MA, Psy D); health sciences (MA, MBS, MMS, MOT, DPT, Psy D); occupational therapy (MOT); physical therapy (DPT); physician assistant studies (MMS). *Application deadline:* Applications are processed on a rolling basis. *Application fee:* $50. *Application Contact:* Michael Laken, Director of Admissions, 630-515-6171, Fax: 630-971-6086, E-mail: admissil@midwestern.edu. *Dean*, Dr. Jacquelyn J. Smith, 630-515-6388.

MIDWESTERN UNIVERSITY, GLENDALE CAMPUS, Glendale, AZ 85308

General Information Independent, coed, graduate-only institution. *Enrollment:* 2,422 full-time matriculated graduate/professional students (1,121 women), 28 part-time matriculated graduate/professional students (14 women). *Enrollment by degree level:* 1,877 first professional, 536 master's, 37 doctoral. *Graduate faculty:* 101 full-time (45 women), 903 part-time/adjunct (161 women). *Graduate housing:* Rooms and/or apartments available on a first-come, first-served basis to single and married students. *Student services:* Exercise/wellness program. *Web address:* http://www.midwestern.edu/.

General Application Contact: James Walter, Director of Admissions, 888-247-9277, Fax: 623-572-3229, E-mail: admissaz@midwestern.edu.

GRADUATE UNITS

Arizona College of Optometry Students: 100 full-time (39 women); includes 2 Black or African American, non-Hispanic/Latino; 1 American Indian or Alaska Native, non-Hispanic/Latino; 10 Asian, non-Hispanic/Latino; 3 Hispanic/Latino. Average age 25. 178 applicants, 39% accepted, 52 enrolled. *Faculty:* 4 full-time (0 women). Expenses: Contact institution. Offers optometry (OD). *Application Contact:* James Walter, Director of Admissions, 888-247-9277, Fax: 623-572-3229, E-mail: admissaz@midwestern.edu. *Dean*, Hector Santiago, 623-572-3901, Fax: 623-572-3911, E-mail: azoptometry@midwestern.edu.

Arizona College of Osteopathic Medicine Students: 904 full-time (344 women), 9 part-time (5 women); includes 2 Black or African American, non-Hispanic/Latino; 3 American Indian or Alaska Native, non-Hispanic/Latino; 21 Asian, non-Hispanic/Latino; 3 Hispanic/Latino, 7 international. Average age 27. 3,211 applicants, 19% accepted, 255 enrolled. *Faculty:* 43 full-time (14 women), 12 part-time/adjunct (5 women). Expenses: Contact institution. *Financial support:* Fellowships with partial tuition reimbursements, career-related internships or fieldwork, Federal Work-Study, institutionally sponsored loans, and tuition waivers (full and partial) available. Financial award application deadline: 6/12; financial award applicants required to submit FAFSA. In 2010, 135 DOs awarded. Offers osteopathic medicine (DO). *Application deadline:* For fall admission, 11/1 priority date for domestic students; for winter admission, 2/1 for domestic students. Applications are processed on a rolling basis. *Application fee:* $50. Electronic applications accepted. *Application Contact:* James Walter, Director of Admissions, 888-247-9277, Fax: 623-572-3229, E-mail: admissaz@midwestern.edu. *Dean*, Dr. Lori Kemper, 623-572-3202.

College of Dental Medicine Students: 332 full-time (147 women). Average age 27. 2,328 applicants, 9% accepted, 112 enrolled. *Faculty:* 18 full-time (6 women), 2 part-time/adjunct (0 women). Expenses: Contact institution. Offers dental medicine (DMD). *Application Contact:* James Walter, Director of Admissions, 888-247-9277, Fax: 623-572-3229, E-mail: admissaz@midwestern.edu. *Dean*, Dr. Richard Simonsen, 623-572-3801.

College of Health Sciences, Arizona Campus Students: 690 full-time (405 women), 8 part-time (2 women); includes 20 Black or African American, non-Hispanic/Latino; 4 American Indian or Alaska Native, non-Hispanic/Latino; 48 Asian, non-Hispanic/Latino; 26 Hispanic/Latino. Average age 27. 1,349 applicants, 31% accepted, 230 enrolled. *Faculty:* 44 full-time (21 women), 4 part-time/adjunct (3 women). Expenses: Contact institution. *Financial support:* Federal Work-Study available. In 2010, 107 master's awarded. *Degree program information:* Part-time programs available. Offers bioethics (MA, Certificate); biomedical sciences (MA, MBS); cardiovascular science (MCVS); clinical psychology (Psy D); health professions education (MHPE); health sciences (DPM, MA, MBS, MCVS, MHPE, MMS, MOT, MS, DPT, Psy D, Certificate); nurse anesthesia (MS); occupational therapy (MOT); physical therapy (DPT); physician assistant studies (MMS); podiatric medicine (DPM). *Application deadline:* For fall admission, 6/4 for domestic students. Applications are processed on a rolling basis. *Application fee:* $50. *Application Contact:* James Walter, Director of Admissions, 888-247-9277, Fax: 623-572-3229, E-mail: admissaz@midwestern.edu. *Dean*, Dr. Jacquelyn Smith, 623-572-3601, Fax: 623-572-3601.

College of Pharmacy-Glendale Students: 396 full-time (186 women), 11 part-time (7 women); includes 4 Black or African American, non-Hispanic/Latino; 1 American Indian or Alaska Native, non-Hispanic/Latino; 101 Asian, non-Hispanic/Latino; 23 Hispanic/Latino, 11 international. Average age 28. 1,550 applicants, 15% accepted, 134 enrolled. *Faculty:* 36 full-time (27 women), 1 (woman) part-time/adjunct. Expenses: Contact institution. *Financial support:* Applicants required to submit FAFSA. In 2010, 133 Pharm Ds awarded. Offers pharmacy (Pharm D). *Application deadline:* For fall admission, 2/1 for domestic students. *Application fee:* $50. *Application Contact:* James Walter, Director of Admissions, 888-247-9277, Fax: 623-572-3229, E-mail: admissaz@midwestern.edu. *Interim Dean*, Dr. Dennis McCallian, 623-572-3501.

MIDWEST UNIVERSITY, Wentzville, MO 63385

General Information Independent-religious, coed, university. *Graduate housing:* Rooms and/or apartments available on a first-come, first-served basis to single and married students. Housing application deadline: 1/21.

GRADUATE UNITS

Graduate Programs *Degree program information:* Part-time programs available. Postbaccalaureate distance learning degree programs offered (minimal on-campus study). Offers social work (DSW); teaching English to speakers of other languages (MA); theology (M Div, MA, D Min).

MIDWIVES COLLEGE OF UTAH, Salt Lake City, UT 84106

General Information Independent, women only, comprehensive institution.

GRADUATE UNITS

Graduate Program Offers midwifery (MS).

MILLERSVILLE UNIVERSITY OF PENNSYLVANIA, Millersville, PA 17551-0302

General Information State-supported, coed, comprehensive institution. CGS member. *Enrollment:* 8,729 graduate, professional, and undergraduate students; 172 full-time matriculated graduate/professional students (131 women), 505 part-time matriculated graduate/professional students (383 women). *Enrollment by degree level:* 677 master's. *Graduate faculty:* 194 full-time (102 women), 84 part-time/adjunct (48 women). Tuition, state resident: full-time $6966; part-time $387 per credit. Tuition, nonresident: full-time $11,146; part-time $619 per credit. *Required fees:* $1830; $88 per credit. One-time fee: $60 part-time. Tuition and fees vary according to course load. *Graduate housing:* On-campus housing not available. *Student services:* Campus employment opportunities, campus safety program, career counseling, exercise/wellness program, free psychological counseling, international student services, low-cost health insurance, services for students with disabilities, teacher training, writing training. *Library facilities:* Helen A. Ganser Library. *Online resources:* library catalog, web page, access to other libraries' catalogs. *Collection:* 451,740 titles, 9,710 serial subscriptions, 11,839 audiovisual materials. *Research affiliation:* Marine Science Consortium at Wallops Island, Virginia (biology).

Computer facilities: 712 computers available on campus for general student use. A campuswide network can be accessed from student residence rooms and from off campus. Online class registration is available. *Web address:* http://www.millersville.edu/.

General Application Contact: Dr. Victor S. DeSantis, Dean of Graduate and Professional Studies, 717-872-3099, Fax: 717-872-3453, E-mail: victor.desantis@millersville.edu.

GRADUATE UNITS

College of Graduate and Professional Studies Students: 172 full-time (131 women), 505 part-time (383 women); includes 18 Black or African American, non-Hispanic/Latino; 1 American Indian or Alaska Native, non-Hispanic/Latino; 11 Asian, non-Hispanic/Latino; 18 Hispanic/Latino, 5 international. Average age 31. 278 applicants, 86% accepted, 180 enrolled. *Faculty:* 194 full-time (102 women), 84 part-time/adjunct (48 women). Expenses: Contact institution. *Financial support:* In 2010–11, 101 students received support, including 101 research assistantships with full and partial tuition reimbursements available (averaging $4,763 per year); institutionally sponsored loans and unspecified assistantships also available. Support available to part-time students. Financial award application deadline: 3/15; financial award applicants required to submit FAFSA. In 2010, 250 master's awarded. *Degree program information:* Part-time and evening/weekend programs available. Postbaccalaureate distance learning degree programs offered (no on-campus study). *Application deadline:* For fall admission, 1/15 priority date for domestic and international students; for winter admission, 10/1 priority date for domestic and international students; for spring admission, 10/1 priority date for domestic and international students. Applications are processed on a rolling basis. *Application fee:* $40 ($50 for international students). Electronic applications accepted. *Application Contact:* Dr. Victor S. DeSantis, Dean of Graduate and Professional Studies, 717-872-3099, Fax: 717-872-3453, E-mail: victor.desantis@millersville.edu. *Dean of Graduate and Professional Studies*, Dr. Victor S. DeSantis, 717-872-3099, Fax: 717-872-3453, E-mail: victor.desantis@millersville.edu.

School of Education Students: 98 full-time (75 women), 279 part-time (213 women); includes 7 Black or African American, non-Hispanic/Latino; 5 Asian, non-Hispanic/Latino; 5 Hispanic/Latino, 3 international. Average age 29. 148 applicants, 78% accepted, 74 enrolled. *Faculty:* 84 full-time (45 women), 39 part-time/adjunct (18 women). Expenses: Contact institution. *Financial support:* In 2010–11, 66 students received support, including 66 research assistantships with full and partial tuition reimbursements available (averaging $4,798 per year); institutionally sponsored loans and unspecified assistantships also available. Support available to part-time students. Financial award application deadline: 3/15; financial award applicants required to submit FAFSA. In 2010, 136 master's awarded. *Degree program information:* Part-time and evening/weekend programs available. Offers athletic coaching (M Ed); athletic management (M Ed); clinical psychology (MS); early childhood education (M Ed); education (M Ed, MS); elementary education (M Ed); gifted education (M Ed); language and literacy education (M Ed); leadership for teaching and learning (M Ed); school counseling (M Ed); school psychology (MS); special education (M Ed); sport management (M Ed); technology education (M Ed). *Application deadline:* For fall admission, 1/15 priority date for domestic and international students; for winter admission, 10/1 priority date for domestic and international students; for spring admission, 10/1 priority date for domestic and international students. Applications are processed on a rolling basis. *Application fee:*

$40 ($50 for international students). Electronic applications accepted. *Application Contact:* Dr. Victor S. DeSantis, Dean of Graduate and Professional Studies, 717-872-3099, Fax: 717-872-3453, E-mail: victor.desantis@millersville.edu. *Dean,* Dr. Jane S. Bray, 717-872-3379, Fax: 717-872-3856, E-mail: jane.bray@millersville.edu.

School of Humanities and Social Sciences Students: 65 full-time (48 women), 146 part-time (101 women); includes 5 Black or African American, non-Hispanic/Latino; 1 American Indian or Alaska Native, non-Hispanic/Latino; 4 Asian, non-Hispanic/Latino; 9 Hispanic/Latino, 2 international. Average age 31. 100 applicants, 94% accepted, 81 enrolled. *Faculty:* 66 full-time (38 women), 31 part-time/adjunct (19 women). Expenses: Contact institution. *Financial support:* In 2010–11, 31 students received support, including 31 research assistantships with full and partial tuition reimbursements available (averaging $5,115 per year); institutionally sponsored loans and unspecified assistantships also available. Support available to part-time students. Financial award application deadline: 3/15; financial award applicants required to submit FAFSA. In 2010, 88 master's awarded. *Degree program information:* Part-time and evening/weekend programs available. Postbaccalaureate distance learning degree programs offered (no on-campus study). Offers art (M Ed); emergency management (MS); English (MA); English education (M Ed); French (M Ed, MA); German (M Ed, MA); history (MA); humanities and social sciences (M Ed, MA, MS, MSW); social work (MSW); Spanish (M Ed, MA). *Application deadline:* For fall admission, 1/15 priority date for domestic and international students; for winter admission, 10/1 priority date for domestic and international students; for spring admission, 10/1 priority date for domestic and international students. Applications are processed on a rolling basis. *Application fee:* $40 ($50 for international students). Electronic applications accepted. *Application Contact:* Dr. Victor S. DeSantis, Dean of Graduate and Professional Studies, 717-872-3099, Fax: 717-872-3453, E-mail: victor.desantis@millersville.edu. *Dean,* Dr. Diane Umble, 717-872-3553, Fax: 717-871-2003, E-mail: diane.umble@millersville.edu.

School of Science and Mathematics Students: 9 full-time (8 women), 80 part-time (69 women); includes 1 Black or African American, non-Hispanic/Latino; 2 Asian, non-Hispanic/Latino; 4 Hispanic/Latino. Average age 37. 30 applicants, 93% accepted, 25 enrolled. *Faculty:* 44 full-time (19 women), 14 part-time/adjunct (11 women). Expenses: Contact institution. *Financial support:* In 2010–11, 5 students received support, including 5 research assistantships with full and partial tuition reimbursements available (averaging $2,736 per year); institutionally sponsored loans and unspecified assistantships also available. Support available to part-time students. Financial award application deadline: 3/15; financial award applicants required to submit FAFSA. In 2010, 26 master's awarded. *Degree program information:* Part-time and evening/weekend programs available. Offers mathematics (M Ed); nursing (MSN); science and mathematics (M Ed, MSN). *Application deadline:* For fall admission, 1/15 priority date for domestic and international students; for winter admission, 10/1 priority date for domestic and international students; for spring admission, 10/1 priority date for domestic and international students. Applications are processed on a rolling basis. *Application fee:* $40 ($50 for international students). Electronic applications accepted. *Application Contact:* Dr. Victor S. DeSantis, Dean of Graduate and Professional Studies, 717-872-3099, Fax: 717-872-3453, E-mail: victor.desantis@millersville.edu. *Dean,* Dr. Robert T. Smith, 717-872-3407, Fax: 717-872-3985, E-mail: robert.smith@millersville.edu.

MILLIGAN COLLEGE, Milligan College, TN 37682

General Information Independent-religious, coed, comprehensive institution. *Graduate housing:* Rooms and/or apartments available on a first-come, first-served basis to single and married students. Housing application deadline: 4/1.

GRADUATE UNITS

Area of Teacher Education *Degree program information:* Part-time programs available. Offers teacher education (M Ed). Electronic applications accepted.

Program in Business Administration Postbaccalaureate distance learning degree programs offered (minimal on-campus study). Offers business administration (MBA). Electronic applications accepted.

Program in Occupational Therapy Students: 75 full-time (66 women), 3 part-time (all women). Average age 28. 110 applicants, 30% accepted, 32 enrolled. *Faculty:* 5 full-time (3 women), 5 part-time/adjunct (4 women). Expenses: Contact institution. *Financial support:* Career-related internships or fieldwork and institutionally sponsored loans available. Financial award application deadline: 4/15; financial award applicants required to submit FAFSA. In 2010, 28 master's awarded. Offers occupational therapy (MSOT). *Application deadline:* For spring admission, 1/15 priority date for domestic and international students. *Application fee:* $30. Electronic applications accepted. *Application Contact:* Kristia Brown, Office Manager and Admissions Representative, 423-975-8010, Fax: 423-975-8019, E-mail: kngarland@milligan.edu. *Program Director and Associate Professor,* Dr. Jeff Snodgrass, 423-975-8010, Fax: 423-975-8019, E-mail: jsnodgrass@milligan.edu.

MILLIKIN UNIVERSITY, Decatur, IL 62522-2084

General Information Independent-religious, coed, comprehensive institution. *Enrollment:* 2,326 graduate, professional, and undergraduate students; 25 full-time matriculated graduate/professional students (17 women), 8 part-time matriculated graduate/professional students (7 women). *Enrollment by degree level:* 33 master's. *Graduate faculty:* 16 full-time (10 women), 5 part-time/adjunct (0 women). *Tuition:* Full-time $24,890; part-time $681 per credit hour. *Student services:* Campus employment opportunities, career counseling, exercise/wellness program, international student services, multicultural affairs office, services for students with disabilities, writing training. *Library facilities:* Staley Library. *Online resources:* library catalog, web page, access to other libraries' catalogs. *Collection:* 218,110 titles, 365 serial subscriptions, 9,762 audiovisual materials.

Computer facilities: 280 computers available on campus for general student use. A campuswide network can be accessed from student residence rooms. Online class registration, online degree audit; online financials (view and pay bills; view financial aid) are available. *Web address:* http://www.millikin.edu/.

GRADUATE UNITS

School of Nursing Students: 12 full-time (11 women), 8 part-time (7 women); includes 3 minority (2 Black or African American, non-Hispanic/Latino; 1 Two or more races, non-Hispanic/Latino). Average age 36. 20 applicants, 100% accepted, 20 enrolled. *Faculty:* 9 full-time (8 women). Expenses: Contact institution. *Financial support:* In 2010–11, 1 student received support. Institutionally sponsored loans available. Financial award applicants required to submit FAFSA. In 2010, 6 master's awarded. *Degree program information:* Part-time programs available. Offers clinical nurse leader (MSN); entry into nursing practice: pre-licensure (MSN); nurse anesthesia (MSN); nurse educator (MSN). *Application deadline:* For spring admission, 11/1 priority date for domestic students. Applications are processed on a rolling basis. *Application fee:* $0. Electronic applications accepted. *Application Contact:* Marianne Taylor, Administrative Assistant, 800-373-7733 Ext. 5034, Fax: 217-420-6677, E-mail: mgtaylor@millikin.edu. *Director,* Dr. Deborah Slayton, 217-424-6348, Fax: 217-420-6731, E-mail: dslayton@millikin.edu.

Tabor School of Business Students: 13 full-time (6 women). Average age 36. 14 applicants, 100% accepted, 13 enrolled. *Faculty:* 6 full-time (1 woman), 5 part-time/adjunct (0 women). Expenses: Contact institution. *Financial support:* Applicants required to submit FAFSA. In 2010, 20 master's awarded. *Degree program information:* Evening/weekend programs available. Offers business (MBA). *Application deadline:* For spring admission, 11/1 priority date for domestic students, 8/1 priority date for international students. Applications are processed on a rolling basis. *Application fee:* $0. Electronic applications accepted. *Application Contact:* Dr. Anthony Liberatore, Director of MBA Program, 217-424-6338, E-mail: aliberatore@millikin.edu. *Dean,* Dr. James G. Dahl, 217-420-6634, Fax: 217-424-6286, E-mail: jdahl@millikin.edu.

MILLSAPS COLLEGE, Jackson, MS 39210-0001

General Information Independent-religious, coed, comprehensive institution. *Graduate housing:* Room and/or apartments available to single students; on-campus housing not available to married students. Housing application deadline: 6/1.

GRADUATE UNITS

Else School of Management *Degree program information:* Part-time programs available. Offers accounting (M Acc); business administration (MBA). Electronic applications accepted.

MILLS COLLEGE, Oakland, CA 94613-1000

General Information Independent, Undergraduate: women only; graduate: coed, comprehensive institution. *Enrollment:* 1,589 graduate, professional, and undergraduate students; 591 full-time matriculated graduate/professional students (485 women), 43 part-time matriculated graduate/professional students (34 women). *Enrollment by degree level:* 506 master's, 46 doctoral, 79 other advanced degrees. *Graduate faculty:* 102 full-time (68 women), 98 part-time/adjunct (63 women). *Tuition:* Full-time $28,280; part-time $7070 per course. *Required fees:* $1058; $1058 per year. Tuition and fees vary according to program. *Graduate housing:* Rooms and/or apartments available on a first-come, first-served basis to single and married students. Typical cost: $6242 per year ($12,052 including board) for single students. Room and board charges vary according to board plan and housing facility selected. Housing application deadline: 6/15. *Student services:* Campus employment opportunities, campus safety program, career counseling, exercise/wellness program, free psychological counseling, international student services, low-cost health insurance, multicultural affairs office, services for students with disabilities, teacher training, writing training. *Library facilities:* F. W. Olin Library plus 1 other. *Online resources:* library catalog, web page. *Collection:* 228,425 titles, 43,560 serial subscriptions, 13,641 audiovisual materials.

Computer facilities: Computer purchase and lease plans are available. 345 computers available on campus for general student use. A campuswide network can be accessed from student residence rooms and from off campus. Online class registration, online degree audit are available. *Web address:* http://www.mills.edu/.

General Application Contact: Jessica King, Graduate Admission Specialist, 510-430-3305, Fax: 510-430-2159, E-mail: grad-studies@mills.edu.

GRADUATE UNITS

Graduate Studies Students: 592 full-time (486 women), 43 part-time (34 women); includes 194 minority (64 Black or African American, non-Hispanic/Latino; 3 American Indian or Alaska Native, non-Hispanic/Latino; 42 Asian, non-Hispanic/Latino; 67 Hispanic/Latino; 2 Native Hawaiian or other Pacific Islander, non-Hispanic/Latino; 16 Two or more races, non-Hispanic/Latino). Average age 32. 972 applicants, 68% accepted, 302 enrolled. *Faculty:* 102 full-time (68 women), 98 part-time/adjunct (63 women). Expenses: Contact institution. *Financial support:* In 2010–11, 616 students received support, including 616 fellowships (averaging $5,861 per year), 147 teaching assistantships with partial tuition reimbursements available (averaging $5,462 per year); career-related internships or fieldwork, institutionally sponsored loans, and scholarships/grants also available. Support available to part-time students. Financial award application deadline: 2/1; financial award applicants required to submit FAFSA. In 2010, 174 master's, 15 doctorates, 75 other advanced degrees awarded. *Degree program information:* Part-time and evening/weekend programs available. Offers book art and creative writing (MFA); ceramics (MFA); composition (MA); computer science (Certificate); creative writing, poetry (MFA); creative writing, prose (MFA); dance (MA, MFA); electronic music and recording media (MFA); English and American literature (MA); infant mental health (MA); interdisciplinary computer science (MA); intermedia (MFA); music performance and literature (MFA); painting (MFA); photography (MFA); pre-medical studies (Certificate); public policy (MPP); sculpture (MFA). *Application deadline:* For fall admission, 12/15 priority date for domestic students, 12/15 for international students; for spring admission, 11/1 priority date for domestic students, 11/1 for international students. Applications are processed on a rolling basis. *Application fee:* $50. Electronic applications accepted. *Application Contact:* Jessica King, Graduate Admission Specialist, 510-430-3305, Fax: 510-430-2159, E-mail: grad-studies@mills.edu. *Administrative Dean for Graduate Recruitment and Enrollment,* Carol Langlois, 510-430-3118, Fax: 510-430-2159, E-mail: clangloi@mills.edu.

Lori I. Lokey Graduate School of Business Students: 98 full-time (92 women), 11 part-time (10 women); includes 17 Black or African American, non-Hispanic/Latino; 2 American Indian or Alaska Native, non-Hispanic/Latino; 8 Asian, non-Hispanic/Latino; 17 Hispanic/Latino; 3 Two or more races, non-Hispanic/Latino. Average age 33. 62 applicants, 97% accepted, 39 enrolled. *Faculty:* 1 full-time (0 women), 9 part-time/adjunct (4 women). Expenses: Contact institution. *Financial support:* In 2010–11, 97 students received support, including 97 fellowships (averaging $7,106 per year); scholarships/grants also available. Support available to part-time students. Financial award applicants required to submit FAFSA. In 2010, 28 master's awarded. Offers management (MBA). *Application deadline:* For fall admission, 2/1 priority date for domestic students, 12/15 for international students. *Application fee:* $50. *Application Contact:* Jessica King, Graduate Admission Specialist, 510-430-3305, Fax: 510-430-2159, E-mail: grad-studies@mills.edu. *Dean,* Nancy Thornborrow, 510-430-2344, Fax: 510-430-3314, E-mail: nancy@mills.edu.

School of Education Students: 184 full-time (171 women), 18 part-time (15 women); includes 80 minority (36 Black or African American, non-Hispanic/Latino; 2 American Indian or Alaska Native, non-Hispanic/Latino; 14 Asian, non-Hispanic/Latino; 23 Hispanic/Latino; 1 Native Hawaiian or other Pacific Islander, non-Hispanic/Latino; 4 Two or more races, non-Hispanic/Latino). Average age 34. 270 applicants, 72% accepted, 109 enrolled. *Faculty:* 13 full-time (10 women), 16 part-time/adjunct (13 women). Expenses: Contact institution. *Financial support:* In 2010–11, 203 fellowships (averaging $4,898 per year), 36 teaching assistantships with partial tuition reimbursements (averaging $3,396 per year) were awarded; career-related internships or fieldwork and scholarships/grants also available. Support available to part-time students. Financial award application deadline: 2/1; financial award applicants required to submit FAFSA. In 2010, 39 master's, 7 doctorates awarded. *Degree program information:* Part-time and evening/weekend programs available. Offers child life in hospitals (MA); early childhood education (MA); education (MA); educational leadership (MA, Ed D). *Application deadline:* For fall admission, 12/15 priority date for domestic students, 12/15 for international students. Applications are processed on a rolling basis. *Application fee:* $50. Electronic applications accepted. *Application Contact:* Jessica King, Graduate Admission Specialist, 510-430-3305, Fax: 510-430-2159, E-mail: grad-studies@mills.edu. *Chairperson,* Katherine Schultz, 510-430-3170, Fax: 510-430-3379, E-mail: grad-studies@mills.edu.

MILWAUKEE SCHOOL OF ENGINEERING, Milwaukee, WI 53202-3109

General Information Independent, coed, primarily men, comprehensive institution. *Enrollment:* 2,589 graduate, professional, and undergraduate students; 24 full-time matriculated graduate/professional students (6 women), 172 part-time matriculated graduate/professional students (41 women). *Enrollment by degree level:* 196 master's. *Graduate faculty:* 17 full-time (2 women), 29 part-time/adjunct (6 women). *Tuition:* Full-time $17,550; part-time $650 per credit. One-time fee: $75. *Graduate housing:* Room and/or apartments available on a first-come, first-served basis to single students; on-campus housing not available to married students. Typical cost: $7794 (including board). Housing application deadline: 7/1. *Student services:* Campus employment opportunities, campus safety program, career counseling, exercise/wellness program, free psychological counseling, international student services, low-cost health insurance, multicultural affairs office, services for students with disabilities, writing training. *Library facilities:* Walter Schroeder Library. *Online resources:* library catalog, web page, access to other libraries' catalogs. *Collection:* 85,409 titles, 362 serial subscriptions, 1,643 audiovisual materials. *Research affiliation:* Kern Foundation (entrepreneurship), National Fluid Power Association (hydraulics and pneumatics), 3DMD (biomolecular modeling), The Procter & Gamble Company (rapid tooling), Caterpillar, Inc. (electrohydraulics), Medical College of Wisconsin (physics).

Computer facilities: Computer purchase and lease plans are available. 125 computers available on campus for general student use. A campuswide network can be accessed from student residence rooms and from off campus. Online class registration is available. *Web address:* http://www.msoe.edu/.

General Application Contact: Sarah K. Winchowky, Director of Graduate Admissions, 800-331-6763, Fax: 414-277-7475, E-mail: winchowky@msoe.edu.

Milwaukee School of Engineering (continued)

GRADUATE UNITS

Civil and Architectural Engineering and Construction Management Department Students: 2 full-time (1 woman), 15 part-time (2 women). Average age 22. 38 applicants, 74% accepted, 6 enrolled. *Faculty:* 6 full-time (1 woman), 5 part-time/adjunct (1 woman). Expenses: Contact institution. *Financial support:* In 2010–11, 7 students received support; research assistantships, career-related internships or fieldwork available. Support available to part-time students. Financial award applicants required to submit FAFSA. In 2010, 21 master's awarded. *Degree program information:* Part-time and evening/weekend programs available. Offers civil engineering (MS); environmental engineering (MS); structural engineering (MS). *Application deadline:* Applications are processed on a rolling basis. *Application fee:* $30. Electronic applications accepted. *Application Contact:* Sarah K. Winchowky, Graduate Admissions Director, 800-321-6763, Fax: 414-277-7475, E-mail: wp@msoe.edu. *Chair,* Dr. Deborah J. Jackman, 414-277-7472, Fax: 414-277-7479, E-mail: jackman@msoe.edu.

Department of Electrical Engineering and Computer Science Students: 14 full-time (4 women), 42 part-time (3 women); includes 2 Black or African American, non-Hispanic/Latino; 4 Asian, non-Hispanic/Latino, 1 international. Average age 27. 54 applicants, 50% accepted, 16 enrolled. *Faculty:* 5 full-time (0 women), 8 part-time/adjunct (2 women). Expenses: Contact institution. *Financial support:* In 2010–11, 27 students received support, including 4 research assistantships (averaging $15,000 per year); career-related internships or fieldwork also available. Support available to part-time students. Financial award applicants required to submit FAFSA. In 2010, 7 master's awarded. *Degree program information:* Part-time and evening/weekend programs available. Offers cardiovascular studies (MS); engineering (MS); perfusion (MS). *Application deadline:* Applications are processed on a rolling basis. *Application fee:* $30. Electronic applications accepted. *Application Contact:* David E. Tietyen, Graduate Admissions Director, 800-332-6763, Fax: 414-277-7475, E-mail: wp@msoe.edu. *Chairman,* Dr. Owe Petersen, 414-277-7114, Fax: 414-277-7465, E-mail: petersen@msoe.edu.

Rader School of Business Students: 8 full-time (1 woman), 106 part-time (32 women); includes 2 Black or African American, non-Hispanic/Latino; 1 American Indian or Alaska Native, non-Hispanic/Latino; 6 Asian, non-Hispanic/Latino; 4 Hispanic/Latino; 1 Two or more races, non-Hispanic/Latino, 10 international. Average age 25. 35 applicants, 69% accepted, 18 enrolled. *Faculty:* 6 full-time (1 woman), 16 part-time/adjunct (3 women). Expenses: Contact institution. *Financial support:* In 2010–11, 36 students received support, including 2 research assistantships (averaging $15,000 per year); career-related internships or fieldwork also available. Support available to part-time students. Financial award applicants required to submit FAFSA. In 2010, 32 master's awarded. *Degree program information:* Part-time and evening/weekend programs available. Offers engineering management (MS); marketing and export management (MS); medical informatics (MS); new product management (MS). *Application deadline:* Applications are processed on a rolling basis. *Application fee:* $30. Electronic applications accepted. *Application Contact:* Sarah K. Winchowky, 800-321-6763, Fax: 414-277-7475, E-mail: wp@msoe.edu. *Chairman,* Dr. Steven Bialek, 414-277-7364, Fax: 414-277-7479, E-mail: bialek@msoe.edu.

MINNEAPOLIS COLLEGE OF ART AND DESIGN, Minneapolis, MN 55404-4347

General Information Independent, coed, comprehensive institution. *Graduate housing:* On-campus housing not available.

GRADUATE UNITS

Certificate Programs *Degree program information:* Part-time programs available. Postbaccalaureate distance learning degree programs offered. Offers design (Certificate); fine arts (Certificate); graphic design (Certificate); media (Certificate); sustainable design (Certificate). Electronic applications accepted.

Program in Visual Studies *Degree program information:* Part-time programs available. Offers animation (MFA); comic art (MFA); drawing (MFA); filmmaking (MFA); fine arts (MFA); furniture design (MFA); graphic design (MFA); illustration (MFA); interactive media (MFA); painting (MFA); photography (MFA); printmaking (MFA); sculpture (MFA). Electronic applications accepted.

MINNESOTA STATE UNIVERSITY MANKATO, Mankato, MN 56001

General Information State-supported, coed, university. CGS member. *Enrollment:* 15,306 graduate, professional, and undergraduate students; 639 full-time matriculated graduate/professional students (403 women), 1,368 part-time matriculated graduate/professional students (823 women). *Enrollment by degree level:* 1,883 master's, 29 doctoral. *Graduate housing:* Room and/or apartments available on a first-come, first-served basis to single students; on-campus housing not available to married students. *Student services:* Campus employment opportunities, campus safety program, career counseling, child daycare facilities, exercise/wellness program, free psychological counseling, international student services, low-cost health insurance, multicultural affairs office, services for students with disabilities, teacher training, writing training. *Library facilities:* Memorial Library. *Online resources:* library catalog, web page. *Collection:* 1.2 million titles, 20,000 serial subscriptions.

Computer facilities: Computer purchase and lease plans are available. 900 computers available on campus for general student use. A campuswide network can be accessed from student residence rooms and from off campus. Online class registration is available. *Web address:* http://www.mnsu.edu/.

General Application Contact: Information Contact, 507-389-2321, E-mail: grad@mnsu.edu.

GRADUATE UNITS

College of Graduate Studies Students: 639 full-time (403 women), 1,368 part-time (823 women). Average age 32. Expenses: Contact institution. *Financial support:* In 2010–11, research assistantships with full and partial tuition reimbursements (averaging $9,000 per year), teaching assistantships with full and partial tuition reimbursements (averaging $10,800 per year) were awarded; fellowships with full tuition reimbursements, career-related internships or fieldwork, Federal Work-Study, institutionally sponsored loans, scholarships/grants, and unspecified assistantships also available. Support available to part-time students. Financial award application deadline: 3/15; financial award applicants required to submit FAFSA. *Degree program information:* Part-time programs available. Postbaccalaureate distance learning degree programs offered. Offers cross-disciplinary studies (MS). *Application deadline:* For fall admission, 7/1 for domestic students, 5/1 for international students; for spring admission, 11/1 for domestic students, 10/1 for international students. Applications are processed on a rolling basis. *Application fee:* $40. Electronic applications accepted. *Application Contact:* 507-389-2321, E-mail: grad@mnsu.edu. *Interim Dean,* Terrance Flaherty, 507-389-2321.

College of Allied Health and Nursing Students: 122 full-time (90 women), 183 part-time (127 women). Expenses: Contact institution. *Financial support:* Research assistantships with full tuition reimbursements, teaching assistantships with full tuition reimbursements, career-related internships or fieldwork, Federal Work-Study, institutionally sponsored loans, and unspecified assistantships available. Support available to part-time students. Financial award application deadline: 3/15; financial award applicants required to submit FAFSA. *Degree program information:* Part-time programs available. Offers allied health and nursing (MA, MS, MSN, DNP, Postbaccalaureate Certificate); communication disorders (MS); community health education (MS); family nursing (MSN); human performance (MA, MS); nursing (DNP); rehabilitation counseling (MS); school health education (MS, Postbaccalaureate Certificate). *Application deadline:* Applications are processed on a rolling basis. *Application fee:* $40. Electronic applications accepted. *Application Contact:* 507-389-2321, E-mail: grad@mnsu.edu. *Interim Dean,* Dr. Harry Krampf, 507-389-6315.

College of Arts and Humanities Students: 100 full-time (57 women), 193 part-time (115 women). Expenses: Contact institution. *Financial support:* Research assistantships with full tuition reimbursements, teaching assistantships with full tuition reimbursements, career-related internships or fieldwork, Federal Work-Study, institutionally sponsored loans, and unspecified assistantships available. Support available to part-time students. Financial award application deadline: 3/15; financial award applicants required to submit FAFSA. *Degree program information:* Part-time and evening/weekend programs available. Offers arts and humanities (MA, MAT, MFA, MM, MS, Certificate); communication education (Certificate); communication studies (MA, MS); creative writing (MFA); English (MAT); English studies (MA); forensics (MFA); French (MAT, MS); music (MAT, MM); professional communication (Certificate); Spanish (MAT, MS); studio art (MA); teaching art (MAT); teaching English as a second language (MA, Certificate); technical communication (MA, Certificate); theatre arts (MA, MFA). *Application deadline:* For fall admission, 7/1 for domestic students, 5/1 for international students; for spring admission, 11/1 for domestic students, 10/1 for international students. Applications are processed on a rolling basis. *Application fee:* $40. *Application Contact:* 507-389-2321, E-mail: grad@mnsu.edu. *Dean,* Dr. Walter Zakahi, 507-389-2117.

College of Business Students: 11 full-time (3 women), 71 part-time (21 women). Expenses: Contact institution. Offers business (MBA). *Application deadline:* For fall admission, 7/1 for domestic students, 5/1 for international students; for spring admission, 11/1 for domestic students, 10/1 for international students. Electronic applications accepted. *Application Contact:* Dr. Kevin Elliott, Graduate Coordinator, 507-389-5420. *Graduate Coordinator,* Dr. Kevin Elliott, 507-389-5420.

College of Education Students: 170 full-time (125 women), 505 part-time (344 women). Expenses: Contact institution. *Financial support:* Fellowships with partial tuition reimbursements, research assistantships with full tuition reimbursements, teaching assistantships with full tuition reimbursements, career-related internships or fieldwork, Federal Work-Study, institutionally sponsored loans, and unspecified assistantships available. Support available to part-time students. Financial award application deadline: 3/15; financial award applicants required to submit FAFSA. In 2010, 46 other advanced degrees awarded. *Degree program information:* Part-time and evening/weekend programs available. Offers college student affairs (MS); counselor education and supervision (Ed D); curriculum and instruction (SP); education (MAT, MS, Ed D, Certificate, SP); educational leadership (MS, Ed D, SP); educational technology (MS); elementary and early childhood education (MS, Certificate); emotional/behavioral disorders (MS, Certificate); experiential education (MS); learning disabilities (MS, Certificate); library media education (MS, Certificate); marriage and family counseling (Certificate); mental health counseling (MS); professional school counseling (MS); teacher licensure program (MAT); teaching and learning (MS, Certificate). *Application deadline:* Applications are processed on a rolling basis. *Application fee:* $40. Electronic applications accepted. *Application Contact:* 507-389-2321, E-mail: grad@mnsu.edu. *Interim Dean,* Dr. Jean Haar, 507-389-5445.

College of Science, Engineering and Technology Students: 60 full-time (19 women), 98 part-time (27 women). Expenses: Contact institution. *Financial support:* Research assistantships with full tuition reimbursements, teaching assistantships with full tuition reimbursements, career-related internships or fieldwork, Federal Work-Study, institutionally sponsored loans, and unspecified assistantships available. Support available to part-time students. Financial award application deadline: 3/15; financial award applicants required to submit FAFSA. *Degree program information:* Part-time programs available. Offers biology (MS); biology education (MS); database technologies (Certificate); electrical and computer engineering and technology (MSE); environmental sciences (MS); information technology (MS); manufacturing engineering technology (MS); mathematics (MA, MS); mathematics education (MS); physics and astronomy (MS); science, engineering and technology (MA, MAT, MS, MSE, Certificate); statistics (MS). *Application deadline:* For fall admission, 7/1 priority date for domestic students; for spring admission, 11/1 for domestic students. Applications are processed on a rolling basis. *Application fee:* $40. Electronic applications accepted. *Application Contact:* 507-389-2321, E-mail: grad@mnsu.edu. *Dean,* John Knox, 507-389-5998.

College of Social and Behavioral Sciences Students: 163 full-time (102 women), 195 part-time (108 women). Expenses: Contact institution. *Financial support:* Fellowships with partial tuition reimbursements, research assistantships with full tuition reimbursements, teaching assistantships with full tuition reimbursements, career-related internships or fieldwork, Federal Work-Study, institutionally sponsored loans, and unspecified assistantships available. Support available to part-time students. Financial award application deadline: 3/15; financial award applicants required to submit FAFSA. *Degree program information:* Part-time programs available. Offers anthropology (MS); clinical psychology (MA); ethnic studies (MS, Certificate); gender and women's studies (MS, Certificate); geography (MS); gerontology (MS, Certificate); GIS (Certificate); history (MA, MS); industrial/organizational psychology (MA); local government management (Certificate); public administration (MPA); school psychology (Psy D); social and behavioral sciences (MA, MAT, MPA, MS, MSW, Psy D, Certificate); social studies (MAT); social work (MSW); sociology (MA); sociology: college teaching option (MA); sociology: corrections (MS); sociology: human services planning and administration (MS); urban and regional studies (MA); urban planning (MA, Certificate). *Application deadline:* Applications are processed on a rolling basis. *Application fee:* $40. Electronic applications accepted. *Application Contact:* 507-389-2321, E-mail: grad@mnsu.edu. *Dean,* Dr. John Alessio, 507-389-6307.

MINNESOTA STATE UNIVERSITY MOORHEAD, Moorhead, MN 56563-0002

General Information State-supported, coed, comprehensive institution. *Graduate housing:* Room and/or apartments available to single students; on-campus housing not available to married students. Housing application deadline: 3/1. *Research affiliation:* West Central Minnesota Business Innovation Center.

GRADUATE UNITS

Graduate Studies *Degree program information:* Part-time and evening/weekend programs available. Postbaccalaureate distance learning degree programs offered (minimal on-campus study). Electronic applications accepted.

College of Arts and Humanities *Degree program information:* Part-time programs available. Offers arts and humanities (MFA, MLA); creative writing (MFA); liberal studies (MLA). Electronic applications accepted.

College of Education and Human Services *Degree program information:* Part-time and evening/weekend programs available. Offers counseling and student affairs (MS); curriculum and instruction (MS); educational leadership (MS, Ed S); nursing (MS); reading (MS); special education (MS); speech-language pathology (MS). Electronic applications accepted.

College of Social and Natural Sciences *Degree program information:* Part-time and evening/weekend programs available. Offers public, human services, and health administration (MS); school psychology (MS, Psy S); social and natural sciences (MS, Psy S). Electronic applications accepted.

MINOT STATE UNIVERSITY, Minot, ND 58707-0002

General Information State-supported, coed, comprehensive institution. *Graduate housing:* Rooms and/or apartments available on a first-come, first-served basis to single and married students. Housing application deadline: 6/30. *Research affiliation:* Rural Crime and Justice Center (criminal justice research), North Dakota Center for Persons with Disabilities (NDCPD) (research and aid).

GRADUATE UNITS

Graduate School Postbaccalaureate distance learning degree programs offered. Offers audiology (MS); criminal justice (MS); education of the deaf (MS); elementary education (M Ed); information systems (MSIS); learning disabilities (MS); management (MS); mathematics (MAT); school psychology (Ed Sp); science (MAT); special education strategist (MS); speech-language pathology (MS).

Division of Music Offers music education (MME). Program offered during summer only.

MIRRER YESHIVA, Brooklyn, NY 11223-2010

General Information Independent-religious, men only, comprehensive institution.

MISERICORDIA UNIVERSITY, Dallas, PA 18612-1098

General Information Independent-religious, coed, primarily women, comprehensive institution. *Enrollment:* 2,812 graduate, professional, and undergraduate students; 78 full-time matriculated graduate/professional students (64 women), 304 part-time matriculated graduate/professional students (221 women). *Enrollment by degree level:* 334 master's, 48 doctoral. *Graduate faculty:* 35 full-time (24 women), 38 part-time/adjunct (15 women). *Tuition:* Full-time $23,750; part-time $525 per credit. *Required fees:* $1240. *Graduate housing:* On-campus housing not available. *Student services:* Campus employment opportunities, campus safety program, career counseling, exercise/wellness program, free psychological counseling, international student services, low-cost health insurance, multicultural affairs office, services for students with disabilities, writing training. *Library facilities:* Mary Kintz Bevevino Library. *Online resources:* library catalog, web page, access to other libraries' catalogs. *Collection:* 81,966 titles, 26,263 serial subscriptions, 10,898 audiovisual materials.

Computer facilities: Computer purchase and lease plans are available. 100 computers available on campus for general student use. A campuswide network can be accessed from student residence rooms and from off campus. Online class registration, student leadership transcript are available. *Web address:* http://www.misericordia.edu/.

General Application Contact: Larree Brown, Assistant Director of Admissions, Part-Time Undergraduate and Graduate Programs, 570-674-6451, Fax: 570-674-6232, E-mail: lbrown@misericordia.edu.

GRADUATE UNITS

College of Health Sciences Students: 78 full-time (64 women), 102 part-time (89 women); includes 1 minority (Hispanic/Latino). Average age 29. *Faculty:* 25 full-time (19 women), 13 part-time/adjunct (9 women). Expenses: Contact institution. *Financial support:* In 2010–11, 106 students received support; teaching assistantships, career-related internships or fieldwork, Federal Work-Study, scholarships/grants, traineeships, and tuition waivers (partial) available. Support available to part-time students. Financial award application deadline: 6/30; financial award applicants required to submit FAFSA. In 2010, 111 master's, 32 doctorates awarded. *Degree program information:* Part-time and evening/weekend programs available. Offers health sciences (MSN, MSOT, MSPT, MSSLP, DPT, OTD); nursing (MSN); occupational therapy (MSOT, OTD); physical therapy (MSPT, DPT); speech-language pathology (MSSLP). *Application deadline:* Applications are processed on a rolling basis. *Application fee:* $25. Electronic applications accepted. *Application Contact:* Larree Brown, Assistant Director of Admissions, Part-Time Undergraduate and Graduate Programs, 570-674-6451, Fax: 570-674-6232, E-mail: lbrown@misericordia.edu. *Dean,* Dr. Jean A. Dyer, 570-674-8152, E-mail: jdyer@misericordia.edu.

College of Professional Studies and Social Sciences Students: 202 part-time (132 women); includes 5 minority (2 Black or African American, non-Hispanic/Latino; 2 Hispanic/Latino; 1 Two or more races, non-Hispanic/Latino), 1 international. Average age 33. 52 applicants, 81% accepted, 37 enrolled. *Faculty:* 10 full-time (5 women), 25 part-time/adjunct (6 women). Expenses: Contact institution. *Financial support:* In 2010–11, 106 students received support. Career-related internships or fieldwork and scholarships/grants available. Support available to part-time students. Financial award application deadline: 6/30; financial award applicants required to submit FAFSA. In 2010, 55 master's awarded. *Degree program information:* Part-time and evening/weekend programs available. Offers business administration (MBA); education/curriculum (MS); organizational management (MS). *Application deadline:* Applications are processed on a rolling basis. *Application fee:* $25. Electronic applications accepted. *Application Contact:* Larree Brown, Coordinator of Part-Time Undergraduate and Graduate Programs, 570-674-6451, Fax: 570-674-6232, E-mail: lbrown@misericordia.edu. *Dean,* Fred Croop, 570-674-6327, E-mail: fcroop@misericordia.edu.

MISSISSIPPI COLLEGE, Clinton, MS 39058

General Information Independent-religious, coed, comprehensive institution. *Graduate housing:* Room and/or apartments available on a first-come, first-served basis to single students; on-campus housing not available to married students. Housing application deadline: 8/15. *Research affiliation:* Gulf Coast Research Laboratory (marine biology).

GRADUATE UNITS

Graduate School *Degree program information:* Part-time and evening/weekend programs available. Postbaccalaureate distance learning degree programs offered (no on-campus study). Offers health services administration (MHSA); liberal studies (MLS). Electronic applications accepted.

College of Arts and Sciences *Degree program information:* Part-time and evening/weekend programs available. Offers administration of justice (MSS); applied communication (MSC); applied music performance (MM); art (M Ed, MA, MFA); arts and sciences (M Ed, MA, MCS, MFA, MM, MS, MSC, MSS, Certificate); biological science (M Ed); biology (MCS); biology-biological sciences (MS); biology-medical sciences (MS); chemistry and biochemistry (MCS, MS); Christian studies and the arts (M Ed, MA, MFA, MM, MSC); computer science (M Ed, MS); conducting (MM); English (M Ed, MA); history (M Ed, MA, MSS); humanities and social sciences (M Ed, MA, MS, MSS, Certificate); mathematics (M Ed, MCS, MS); music education (MM); music performance: organ (MM); paralegal studies (Certificate); political science (MSS); public relations and corporate communication (MSC); science and mathematics (M Ed, MCS, MS); social sciences (M Ed, MSS); teaching English to speakers of other languages (MA, MS); vocal pedagogy (MM). Electronic applications accepted.

School of Business *Degree program information:* Part-time and evening/weekend programs available. Offers accounting (Certificate); business administration (MBA); business education (M Ed); finance (MBA, Certificate). Electronic applications accepted.

School of Education *Degree program information:* Part-time and evening/weekend programs available. Postbaccalaureate distance learning degree programs offered (no on-campus study). Offers art (M Ed); athletic administration (MS); biological science (M Ed); business education (M Ed); computer science (M Ed); counseling (Ed S); dyslexia therapy (M Ed); education (M Ed, MS, Ed D, Ed S); educational leadership (M Ed, Ed D, Ed S); elementary education (M Ed, Ed S); English (M Ed); higher education administration (MS); marriage and family counseling (MS); mathematics (M Ed); mental health counseling (MS); school counseling (M Ed); secondary education (M Ed); social studies (history) (M Ed); teaching arts (M Ed). Electronic applications accepted.

School of Law Offers civil law studies (Certificate); law (JD). Electronic applications accepted.

MISSISSIPPI STATE UNIVERSITY, Mississippi State, MS 39762

General Information State-supported, coed, university. CGS member. *Enrollment:* 19,644 graduate, professional, and undergraduate students; 2,009 full-time matriculated graduate/professional students (960 women), 1,712 part-time matriculated graduate/professional students (925 women). *Enrollment by degree level:* 316 first professional, 2,201 master's, 1,133 doctoral, 71 other advanced degrees. *Graduate faculty:* 632 full-time (164 women), 27 part-time/adjunct (2 women). Tuition, state resident: full-time $2731; part-time $304 per credit hour. Tuition, nonresident: full-time $6901; part-time $767 per credit hour. *Graduate housing:* Rooms and/or apartments available on a first-come, first-served basis to single and married students. Typical cost: $5234 per year for single students; $3843 per year for married students. Housing application deadline: 8/1. *Student services:* Campus employment opportunities, campus safety program, career counseling, child daycare facilities, exercise/wellness program, free psychological counseling, grant writing training, international student services, low-cost health insurance, multicultural affairs office, services for students with disabilities, teacher training, writing training. *Library facilities:* Mitchell Memorial Library plus 2 others. *Online resources:* library catalog, web page, access to other libraries' catalogs. *Collection:* 2.3 million titles, 143,314 serial subscriptions, 24,511 audiovisual materials. *Research affiliation:* Southeastern Universities Research Association (interdisciplinary research), Oak Ridge Associated Universities (energy related research–interdisciplinary), Mississippi Research and Technology Park (engineering–interdisciplinary), Mississippi Mineral Resources Institute (geology–sciences and engineering), NASA John C. Stennis Space Center (interdisciplinary research), Mississippi Research Consortium (interdisciplinary research).

Computer facilities: 1,000 computers available on campus for general student use. A campuswide network can be accessed from student residence rooms and from off campus. Online class registration, campus-wide wireless Internet access are available. *Web address:* http://www.msstate.edu/.

General Application Contact: Karin Lee, Manager, Graduate Programs, 662-325-8095, Fax: 662-325-1967, E-mail: grad@grad.msstate.edu.

GRADUATE UNITS

Bagley College of Engineering Students: 387 full-time (78 women), 220 part-time (42 women); includes 71 minority (39 Black or African American, non-Hispanic/Latino; 17 Asian, non-Hispanic/Latino; 12 Hispanic/Latino; 1 Native Hawaiian or other Pacific Islander, non-Hispanic/Latino; 2 Two or more races, non-Hispanic/Latino), 230 international. Average age 29. 813 applicants, 32% accepted, 171 enrolled. *Faculty:* 101 full-time (14 women), 10 part-time/adjunct (1 woman). Expenses: Contact institution. *Financial support:* In 2010–11, 130 research assistantships with full tuition reimbursements (averaging $14,505 per year), 41 teaching assistantships with full tuition reimbursements (averaging $13,061 per year) were awarded; Federal Work-Study, institutionally sponsored loans, scholarships/grants, and unspecified assistantships also available. Financial award application deadline: 4/1; financial award applicants required to submit FAFSA. In 2010, 101 master's, 41 doctorates awarded. *Degree program information:* Part-time programs available. Postbaccalaureate distance learning degree programs offered (no on-campus study). Offers aerospace engineering (MS); civil engineering (MS); computer engineering (MS, PhD); computer science (MS, PhD); electrical engineering (MS, PhD); engineering (PhD); industrial and systems engineering (PhD); industrial engineering (MS); mechanical engineering (MS). *Application deadline:* For fall admission, 7/1 for domestic students, 5/1 for international students; for spring admission, 11/1 for domestic students, 9/1 for international students. Applications are processed on a rolling basis. *Application fee:* $40. Electronic applications accepted. *Application Contact:* Rita Burrell, Manager, Graduate and Distance Education, 662-325-5923, Fax: 662-325-8573, E-mail: rburrell@bagley.msstate.edu. *Dean,* Dr. Sarah A. Rajala, 662-325-2270, Fax: 662-325-8573, E-mail: rajala@bagley.msstate.edu.

David C. Swalm School of Chemical Engineering Students: 11 full-time (3 women), 16 part-time (4 women); includes 3 minority (2 Black or African American, non-Hispanic/Latino; 1 Asian, non-Hispanic/Latino), 11 international. Average age 29. 29 applicants, 21% accepted, 4 enrolled. *Faculty:* 10 full-time (3 women), 1 part-time/adjunct (0 women). Expenses: Contact institution. *Financial support:* In 2010–11, 9 research assistantships with full tuition reimbursements (averaging $15,969 per year) were awarded; Federal Work-Study, institutionally sponsored loans, and unspecified assistantships also available. Financial award application deadline: 4/1; financial award applicants required to submit FAFSA. In 2010, 3 master's, 4 doctorates awarded. Offers chemical engineering (MS); engineering (PhD). *Application deadline:* For fall admission, 4/1 priority date for domestic students, 5/1 for international students; for spring admission, 8/1 priority date for domestic students, 9/1 for international students. Applications are processed on a rolling basis. *Application fee:* $40. Electronic applications accepted. *Application Contact:* Dr. Rafael Hernandez, Associate Professor and Graduate Coordinator, 662-325-0790, Fax: 662-325-2482, E-mail: rhernandez@che.msstate.edu. *Interim Director and Associate Professor,* Dr. Bill Elmore, 662-325-7206, Fax: 662-325-2482, E-mail: elmore@che.msstate.edu.

College of Agriculture and Life Sciences Students: 214 full-time (90 women), 142 part-time (83 women); includes 40 minority (29 Black or African American, non-Hispanic/Latino; 2 American Indian or Alaska Native, non-Hispanic/Latino; 2 Asian, non-Hispanic/Latino; 5 Hispanic/Latino; 1 Native Hawaiian or other Pacific Islander, non-Hispanic/Latino; 1 Two or more races, non-Hispanic/Latino), 72 international. Average age 31. 253 applicants, 51% accepted, 90 enrolled. *Faculty:* 130 full-time (20 women), 2 part-time/adjunct (0 women). Expenses: Contact institution. *Financial support:* In 2010–11, 145 research assistantships with full tuition reimbursements (averaging $14,299 per year), 18 teaching assistantships with full tuition reimbursements (averaging $11,343 per year) were awarded; career-related internships or fieldwork, Federal Work-Study, institutionally sponsored loans, scholarships/grants, tuition waivers (partial), and unspecified assistantships also available. Financial award application deadline: 4/1; financial award applicants required to submit FAFSA. In 2010, 74 master's, 22 doctorates awarded. Postbaccalaureate distance learning degree programs offered (no on-campus study). Offers agribusiness management (MABM); agricultural life sciences (MS); agricultural science (PhD); agricultural sciences (PhD); agriculture (MS); agriculture and life sciences (MABM, MLA, MS, PhD); agriculture life sciences (MS); agriculture sciences (PhD); biological engineering (MS); biomedical engineering (MS, PhD); engineering (PhD); food science and technology (MS, PhD); health promotion (MS); landscape architecture (MLA); life sciences (PhD); molecular biology (PhD); nutrition (MS, PhD). *Application deadline:* For fall admission, 7/1 for domestic students, 5/1 for international students; for spring admission, 11/1 for domestic students, 9/1 for international students. Applications are processed on a rolling basis. *Application fee:* $40. Electronic applications accepted. *Application Contact:* Forest Sparks, Admissions Manager, 662-325-7400, Fax: 662-325-1967, E-mail: grad@grad.msstate.edu. *Interim Dean/Vice President for Agriculture, Forestry and Veterinary Medicine,* Dr. George Hopper, 662-325-2953, E-mail: ghopper@cfr.msstate.edu.

School of Human Sciences Students: 9 full-time (4 women), 51 part-time (35 women); includes 14 minority (all Black or African American, non-Hispanic/Latino), 1 international. Average age 37. 20 applicants, 85% accepted, 15 enrolled. *Faculty:* 15 full-time (8 women). Expenses: Contact institution. *Financial support:* In 2010–11, 1 research assistantship (averaging $9,872 per year), 5 teaching assistantships with full tuition reimbursements (averaging $12,126 per year) were awarded; Federal Work-Study, institutionally sponsored loans, and unspecified assistantships also available. Financial award application deadline: 4/1; financial award applicants required to submit FAFSA. In 2010, 18 degrees awarded. *Degree program information:* Part-time programs available. Offers agricultural sciences (PhD); agriculture and extension education (MS). *Application deadline:* For fall admission, 7/1 for domestic students, 5/1 for international students; for spring admission, 11/1 for domestic students, 9/1 for international students. Applications are processed on a rolling basis. *Application fee:* $40. Electronic applications accepted. *Application Contact:* Dr. Jacquelyn Deeds, Professor and Graduate Coordinator, 662-325-7834, E-mail: jdeeds@ais.msstate.edu. *Interim Director,* Dr. Walter Taylor, 662-325-8593, E-mail: wntaylor@ais.msstate.edu.

College of Architecture, Art and Design Students: 4 full-time (all women), 1 (woman) part-time; includes 2 minority (both Black or African American, non-Hispanic/Latino), 1 international. Average age 30. 8 applicants, 25% accepted, 2 enrolled. *Faculty:* 18 full-time (6 women). Expenses: Contact institution. *Financial support:* Career-related internships or fieldwork, Federal Work-Study, institutionally sponsored loans, and unspecified assistantships available. Financial award application deadline: 4/1; financial award applicants required to submit FAFSA. In 2010, 2 master's awarded. Offers architecture, art and design (MS). *Application deadline:* For fall admission, 7/1 for domestic students, 5/1 for international students; for spring admission, 11/1 for domestic students, 9/1 for international students. Applications are processed on a rolling basis. *Application fee:* $40. Electronic applications accepted. *Application Contact:* Dr. David C. Lewis, Associate Dean and Graduate Coordinator, 662-325-2202, Fax: 662-325-8872, E-mail: dlewis@caad.msstate.edu. *Dean/Professor,* Jim West, 662-325-2202, Fax: 662-325-8872, E-mail: jwest@caad.msstate.edu.

School of Architecture Students: 4 full-time (all women), 1 (woman) part-time; includes 2 minority (both Black or African American, non-Hispanic/Latino), 1 international. Average age 30. 8 applicants, 25% accepted, 2 enrolled. *Faculty:* 10 full-time (2 women). Expenses: Contact institution. *Financial support:* Federal Work-Study, institutionally sponsored loans, scholarships/grants, and unspecified assistantships available. Financial award application deadline: 4/1; financial award applicants required to submit FAFSA. In 2010, 2 master's awarded. Offers architecture (MS). *Application deadline:* For fall admission, 7/1 for domestic students, 5/1 for international students; for spring admission, 11/1 for domestic students, 9/1 for international students. Applications are processed on a rolling basis. *Application fee:* $40. Electronic applications accepted. *Application Contact:* Dr. Michael Berk, Director/Professor, 662-325-2202, Fax: 662-325-8872, E-mail: mberk@caad.msstate.edu. *Director/Professor,* Dr. Michael Berk, 662-325-2202, Fax: 662-325-8872, E-mail: mberk@caad.msstate.edu.

Mississippi State University (continued)

College of Arts and Sciences Students: 419 full-time (206 women), 500 part-time (298 women); includes 130 minority (80 Black or African American, non-Hispanic/Latino; 10 American Indian or Alaska Native, non-Hispanic/Latino; 12 Asian, non-Hispanic/Latino; 18 Hispanic/Latino; 10 Two or more races, non-Hispanic/Latino), 111 international. Average age 32. 775 applicants, 60% accepted, 350 enrolled. *Faculty:* 190 full-time (56 women), 5 part-time/adjunct (0 women). Expenses: Contact institution. *Financial support:* In 2010–11, 54 research assistantships with full tuition reimbursements (averaging $15,106 per year), 252 teaching assistantships with full tuition reimbursements (averaging $12,641 per year) were awarded; Federal Work-Study, institutionally sponsored loans, scholarships/grants, tuition waivers (partial), and unspecified assistantships also available. Financial award application deadline: 4/1; financial award applicants required to submit FAFSA. In 2010, 220 master's, 16 doctorates awarded. *Degree program information:* Part-time and evening/weekend programs available. Offers applied anthropology (MA); arts and sciences (MA, MPPA, MS, PhD); biological sciences (MS, PhD); chemistry (MS, PhD); cognitive science (PhD); earth and atmospheric science (PhD); engineering (PhD); English (MA); foreign language (MA); general biology (MS); geoscience (MS); history (PhD); interdisciplinary sciences (MA); mathematical sciences (PhD); mathematics (MS); physics (MS); political science (MA); psychology (MS); public policy and administration (MPPA, PhD); sociology (MS, PhD); statistics (MS); U. S. and European history (MA). *Application deadline:* For fall admission, 7/1 for domestic students, 5/1 for international students; for spring admission, 11/1 for domestic students, 9/1 for international students. Applications are processed on a rolling basis. *Application fee:* $40. Electronic applications accepted. *Application Contact:* Forest Sparks, Admissions Manager, 662-325-7403, Fax: 662-325-1967, E-mail: grad@grad.msstate.edu. *Dean/Professor,* Dr. Gary Myers, 662-325-2646, Fax: 662-325-8740, E-mail: gmyers@deanas.msstate.edu.

College of Business Students: 190 full-time (78 women), 268 part-time (92 women); includes 47 minority (23 Black or African American, non-Hispanic/Latino; 4 American Indian or Alaska Native, non-Hispanic/Latino; 4 Asian, non-Hispanic/Latino; 10 Hispanic/Latino; 1 Native Hawaiian or other Pacific Islander, non-Hispanic/Latino; 5 Two or more races, non-Hispanic/Latino), 40 international. Average age 29. 411 applicants, 47% accepted, 146 enrolled. *Faculty:* 40 full-time (10 women), 2 part-time/adjunct (0 women). Expenses: Contact institution. *Financial support:* In 2010–11, 1 research assistantship with full tuition reimbursement (averaging $11,779 per year), 44 teaching assistantships with full tuition reimbursements (averaging $10,792 per year) were awarded; career-related internships or fieldwork, Federal Work-Study, institutionally sponsored loans, scholarships/grants, and unspecified assistantships also available. Financial award application deadline: 4/1; financial award applicants required to submit FAFSA. In 2010, 194 master's, 4 doctorates awarded. *Degree program information:* Part-time and evening/weekend programs available. Postbaccalaureate distance learning degree programs offered (no on-campus study). Offers applied economics (PhD); business (MA, MBA, MPA, MSBA, MSIS, MTX, PhD); business administration (MBA, PhD); economics (MA); finance (MSBA); information systems (MSIS); project management (MBA). *Application deadline:* For fall admission, 3/1 priority date for domestic students, 5/1 for international students; for spring admission, 11/1 for domestic students, 9/1 for international students. Applications are processed on a rolling basis. *Application fee:* $40. Electronic applications accepted. *Application Contact:* Dr. Barbara Spencer, Associate Dean for Research and Outreach, 662-325-1891, Fax: 662-325-7360, E-mail: gsbi@cobilan.msstate.edu. *Interim Dean and Professor,* Dr. Louis Dawkins, 662-325-2580, Fax: 662-325-2410, E-mail: ldawkins@cobilan.msstate.edu.

School of Accountancy Students: 53 full-time (27 women), 13 part-time (10 women); includes 8 minority (3 Black or African American, non-Hispanic/Latino; 3 Asian, non-Hispanic/Latino; 2 Two or more races, non-Hispanic/Latino), 2 international. Average age 26. 59 applicants, 47% accepted, 21 enrolled. *Faculty:* 6 full-time (2 women), 2 part-time/adjunct (0 women). Expenses: Contact institution. *Financial support:* Career-related internships or fieldwork, Federal Work-Study, institutionally sponsored loans, scholarships/grants, and unspecified assistantships available. Support available to part-time students. Financial award application deadline: 4/1; financial award applicants required to submit FAFSA. In 2010, 33 master's awarded. Offers accounting (MBA); business administration (PhD); systems (MPA); taxation (MTX). MBA (accounting) only offered at the Meridian campus. *Application deadline:* For fall admission, 7/1 for domestic students, 5/1 for international students; for spring admission, 11/1 for domestic students, 9/1 for international students. Applications are processed on a rolling basis. *Application fee:* $40. Electronic applications accepted. *Application Contact:* Dr. Barbara Spencer, Graduate Coordinator, 662-325-3710, Fax: 662-325-1646, E-mail: sac@cobilan.msstate.edu. *Director,* Dr. Jim Scheiner, 662-325-1633, Fax: 662-325-1646, E-mail: jscheiner@cobilan.msstate.edu.

College of Education Students: 317 full-time (217 women), 497 part-time (381 women); includes 341 minority (321 Black or African American, non-Hispanic/Latino; 2 American Indian or Alaska Native, non-Hispanic/Latino; 5 Asian, non-Hispanic/Latino; 8 Hispanic/Latino; 2 Native Hawaiian or other Pacific Islander, non-Hispanic/Latino; 3 Two or more races, non-Hispanic/Latino), 10 international. Average age 35. 403 applicants, 66% accepted, 193 enrolled. *Faculty:* 49 full-time (32 women), 2 part-time/adjunct (1 woman). Expenses: Contact institution. *Financial support:* In 2010–11, 8 research assistantships (averaging $9,438 per year), 25 teaching assistantships (averaging $9,517 per year) were awarded; career-related internships or fieldwork, Federal Work-Study, institutionally sponsored loans, scholarships/grants, and unspecified assistantships also available. Financial award applicants required to submit FAFSA. In 2010, 186 master's, 31 doctorates, 30 other advanced degrees awarded. *Degree program information:* Part-time and evening/weekend programs available. Postbaccalaureate distance learning degree programs offered (minimal on-campus study). Offers college/postsecondary student counseling and personnel services (PhD); community college education (MAT); community college leadership (PhD); counselor education (MS); counselor education/student counseling and guidance services (PhD); curriculum and instruction (PhD); education (MAT, MS, MSIT, Ed D, PhD, Ed S); educational psychology (MS, PhD); elementary education (MS, PhD); elementary, middle school, and secondary education administration (PhD); instructional systems and workforce development (PhD); instructional technology (MSIT); physical education (MS); school administration (MS); secondary education (MS, PhD); secondary teacher alternate route (MAT); special education (MS); technology (MS); workforce educational leadership (MS). *Application deadline:* For fall admission, 7/1 for domestic students, 5/1 for international students; for spring admission, 11/1 for domestic students, 9/1 for international students. Applications are processed on a rolling basis. *Application fee:* $40. Electronic applications accepted. *Application Contact:* Forest Sparks, Admissions Manager, 662-325-7403, Fax: 662-325-1967, E-mail: grad@grad.msstate.edu. *Dean,* Dr. Richard Blackbourn, 662-325-3717, Fax: 662-325-8784, E-mail: rlb277@msstate.edu.

College of Forest Resources Students: 125 full-time (34 women), 47 part-time (10 women); includes 10 minority (2 Black or African American, non-Hispanic/Latino; 1 American Indian or Alaska Native, non-Hispanic/Latino; 1 Asian, non-Hispanic/Latino; 4 Hispanic/Latino; 1 Native Hawaiian or other Pacific Islander, non-Hispanic/Latino; 1 Two or more races, non-Hispanic/Latino), 36 international. Average age 30. 96 applicants, 58% accepted, 49 enrolled. *Faculty:* 51 full-time (6 women), 4 part-time/adjunct (0 women). Expenses: Contact institution. *Financial support:* In 2010–11, 102 research assistantships with full tuition reimbursements (averaging $14,293 per year), 4 teaching assistantships with full tuition reimbursements (averaging $13,395 per year) were awarded; career-related internships or fieldwork, Federal Work-Study, institutionally sponsored loans, and unspecified assistantships also available. Financial award application deadline: 4/1; financial award applicants required to submit FAFSA. In 2010, 28 master's, 11 doctorates awarded. *Degree program information:* Part-time programs available. Offers forest products (MS); forest resources (MS, PhD); forestry (MS); wildlife and fisheries science (MS). *Application deadline:* For fall admission, 7/1 for domestic students, 5/1 for international students; for spring admission, 11/1 for domestic students, 9/1 for international students. Applications are processed on a rolling basis. *Application fee:* $40. Electronic applications accepted. *Application Contact:* Tedrick Ratcliff, Admissions Coordinator, 662-325-2624, Fax: 662-325-8726, E-mail: tratcliff@cfr.msstate.edu. *Dean,* Dr. George M. Hopper, 662-325-2696, Fax: 662-325-8726, E-mail: ghopper@cfr.msstate.edu.

College of Veterinary Medicine Students: 353 full-time (253 women), 37 part-time (18 women); includes 30 minority (11 Black or African American, non-Hispanic/Latino; 1 American Indian or Alaska Native, non-Hispanic/Latino; 4 Asian, non-Hispanic/Latino; 11 Hispanic/Latino; 1 Native Hawaiian or other Pacific Islander, non-Hispanic/Latino; 2 Two or more races, non-Hispanic/Latino), 26 international. Average age 27. 121 applicants, 82% accepted, 95 enrolled. *Faculty:* 53 full-time (20 women), 2 part-time/adjunct (0 women). Expenses: Contact institution. *Financial support:* In 2010–11, 35 research assistantships with full tuition reimbursements (averaging $15,682 per year) were awarded; career-related internships or fieldwork, Federal Work-Study, and institutionally sponsored loans also available. Financial award application deadline: 6/30; financial award applicants required to submit FAFSA. In 2010, 73 first professional degrees, 7 master's, 2 doctorates awarded. Offers environmental toxicology (PhD); veterinary medical sciences (MS, PhD); veterinary medicine (DVM, MS, PhD). *Application deadline:* For fall admission, 7/1 for domestic students, 5/1 for international students; for spring admission, 11/1 for domestic students, 9/1 for international students. *Application fee:* $40. Electronic applications accepted. *Application Contact:* Missy Hadaway, Admission Coordinator, 662-325-9065, Fax: 662-325-1498, E-mail: hadaway@cvm.msstate.edu. *Dean,* Dr. Kent Hoblet, 662-325-1131, Fax: 662-325-1498, E-mail: hoblet@cvm.msstate.edu.

MISSISSIPPI UNIVERSITY FOR WOMEN, Columbus, MS 39701-9998

General Information State-supported, coed, primarily women, comprehensive institution. *Graduate housing:* Rooms and/or apartments available on a first-come, first-served basis to single and married students.

GRADUATE UNITS

Graduate School *Degree program information:* Part-time programs available. Offers health education (MS).

College of Education and Human Sciences *Degree program information:* Part-time programs available. Offers differentiated instruction (M Ed); educational leadership (M Ed); gifted studies (M Ed); reading/literacy (M Ed); teaching (MAT).

College of Nursing and Speech Language Pathology *Degree program information:* Part-time programs available. Offers nursing (MSN, PMC); speech-language pathology (MS).

MISSISSIPPI VALLEY STATE UNIVERSITY, Itta Bena, MS 38941-1400

General Information State-supported, coed, comprehensive institution. *Graduate housing:* Room and/or apartments available to single students; on-campus housing not available to married students. Housing application deadline: 8/1.

GRADUATE UNITS

Department of Criminal Justice and Social Work *Degree program information:* Part-time and evening/weekend programs available. Offers criminal justice (MS). Electronic applications accepted.

Department of Education Offers education (MAT); elementary education (MA).

Department of Natural Science and Environmental Health *Degree program information:* Part-time and evening/weekend programs available. Offers bioinformatics (MS); environmental health (MS).

MISSOURI BAPTIST UNIVERSITY, St. Louis, MO 63141-8660

General Information Independent-religious, coed, comprehensive institution.

GRADUATE UNITS

Graduate Programs

MISSOURI SOUTHERN STATE UNIVERSITY, Joplin, MO 64801-1595

General Information State-supported, coed, comprehensive institution.

GRADUATE UNITS

Program in Business Administration Postbaccalaureate distance learning degree programs offered. Offers business administration (MBA). Program offered jointly with Northwest Missouri State University.

Program in Criminal Justice Administration Postbaccalaureate distance learning degree programs offered. Offers criminal justice administration (MS). Program offered jointly with Southeast Missouri State University.

Program in Dental Hygiene *Degree program information:* Part-time programs available. Offers dental hygiene (MS). Program offered jointly with University of Missouri–Kansas City. Electronic applications accepted.

Program in Early Childhood Education Offers early childhood education (MS Ed). Program offered jointly with Northwest Missouri State University.

Program in Instructional Technology Offers instructional technology (MS Ed). Program offered jointly with Northwest Missouri State University.

Program in Nursing *Degree program information:* Part-time programs available. Offers nursing (MSN). Program offered jointly with University of Missouri–Kansas City. Electronic applications accepted.

Program in Teaching Offers teaching (MAT). Program offered jointly with Missouri State University.

MISSOURI STATE UNIVERSITY, Springfield, MO 65897

General Information State-supported, coed, comprehensive institution. CGS member. *Enrollment:* 20,472 graduate, professional, and undergraduate students; 1,424 full-time matriculated graduate/professional students (798 women), 1,395 part-time matriculated graduate/professional students (830 women). *Enrollment by degree level:* 2,614 master's, 127 doctoral, 78 other advanced degrees. *Graduate faculty:* 456 full-time (163 women), 152 part-time/adjunct (49 women). Tuition, state resident: full-time $3348; part-time $186 per credit hour. Tuition, nonresident: full-time $6696; part-time $372 per credit hour. *Required fees:* $238 per semester. Tuition and fees vary according to course level, course load and program. *Graduate housing:* Rooms and/or apartments available on a first-come, first-served basis to single and married students. Typical cost: $7680 (including board) for single students; $8774 per year for married students. Room and board charges vary according to board plan and housing facility selected. Housing application deadline: 7/1. *Student services:* Campus employment opportunities, campus safety program, career counseling, child daycare facilities, exercise/wellness program, free psychological counseling, grant writing training, international student services, low-cost health insurance, multicultural affairs office, services for students with disabilities, teacher training, writing training. *Library facilities:* Meyer Library plus 3 others. *Online resources:* library catalog, web page, access to other libraries' catalogs. *Collection:* 1.6 million titles, 3,314 serial subscriptions, 23,275 audiovisual materials.

Computer facilities: 1,800 computers available on campus for general student use. A campuswide network can be accessed from student residence rooms and from off campus. Online class registration is available. *Web address:* http://www.missouristate.edu/.

General Application Contact: Graduate Admissions, 417-836-5331, Fax: 417-836-6200, E-mail: graduateadmissions@missouristate.edu.

GRADUATE UNITS

Graduate College *Degree program information:* Part-time programs available. Postbaccalaureate distance learning degree programs offered. Offers applied communication (MS); criminal justice (MS); environmental management (MS); project management (MS); sports management (MS). Electronic applications accepted.

College of Arts and Letters *Degree program information:* Part-time and evening/weekend programs available. Offers arts and letters (MA, MM, MS Ed); communication and mass media (MA); English and writing (MA); music (MM); secondary education (MS Ed); theatre (MA). Electronic applications accepted.

College of Business Administration *Degree program information:* Part-time and evening/weekend programs available. Postbaccalaureate distance learning degree programs offered.

Offers accountancy (M Acc); business administration (M Acc, MBA, MHA, MS, MS Ed); computer information systems (MS); health administration (MHA); secondary education (MS Ed); technology and construction management (MS). Electronic applications accepted.

College of Education *Degree program information:* Part-time programs available. Offers counseling (MS); early childhood and family development (MS); education (MAT, MS, MS Ed, Ed S); educational administration (MS Ed, Ed S); elementary education (MS Ed); elementary principal (Ed S); instructional media technology (MS Ed); reading (MS Ed); reading education (MS Ed); secondary education (MS Ed); secondary principal (Ed S); special education (MS Ed); student affairs (MS); superintendent (Ed S); teaching (MAT). Electronic applications accepted.

College of Health and Human Services *Degree program information:* Part-time programs available. Offers audiology (Au D); cell and molecular biology (MS); communication sciences and disorders (MS); health and human services (MPH, MS, MS Ed, MSN, MSW, Au D, DPT); health promotion and wellness management (MS); nurse anesthesia (MS); nursing (MSN); physical therapy (DPT); physician assistant studies (MS); psychology (MS); public health (MPH); secondary education (MS Ed); social work (MSW). Electronic applications accepted.

College of Humanities and Public Affairs *Degree program information:* Part-time programs available. Offers applied anthropology (MS); criminology (MS); defense and strategic studies (MS); global studies (MGS); history (MA); humanities and public affairs (MA, MGS, MIAA, MPA, MS, MS Ed); public administration (MPA); religious studies (MA); secondary education (MS Ed). Electronic applications accepted.

College of Natural and Applied Sciences *Degree program information:* Part-time and evening/weekend programs available. Offers biology (MS); chemistry (MS); computer science (MNAS); geospatial sciences (MS); materials science (MS); mathematics (MS); natural and applied science (MNAS); natural and applied sciences (MNAS, MS, MS Ed); physics, astronomy, and materials science (MNAS); plant science (MS); secondary education (MS Ed). Electronic applications accepted.

See Display below and Close-Up on page 967.

MISSOURI UNIVERSITY OF SCIENCE AND TECHNOLOGY, Rolla, MO 65409

General Information State-supported, coed, primarily men, university. CGS member. *Graduate housing:* Rooms and/or apartments available on a first-come, first-served basis to single and married students.

GRADUATE UNITS

Graduate School *Degree program information:* Part-time and evening/weekend programs available. Offers aerospace engineering (MS, PhD); applied and environmental biology (MS); applied mathematics (MS); business and information technology (MBA); ceramic engineering (MS, DE, PhD); chemical engineering (MS, DE, PhD); chemistry (MS, MST, PhD); civil engineering (MS, DE, PhD); computer science (MS, PhD); construction engineering (MS, DE, PhD); engineering management (MS, DE, PhD); environmental engineering (MS); fluid mechanics (MS, DE, PhD); geological engineering (MS, DE, PhD); geology and geophysics (MS, PhD); geotechnical engineering (MS, DE, PhD); hydrology and hydraulic engineering (MS, DE, PhD); information science and technology (MS); manufacturing engineering (M Eng, MS); mathematics (MST, PhD); mechanical engineering (MS, DE, PhD); metallurgical engineering (MS, PhD); mining engineering (MS, DE, PhD); nuclear engineering (MS, DE, PhD); petroleum engineering (MS, DE, PhD); physics (MS, MST, PhD); systems engineering (MS, PhD). Electronic applications accepted.

School of Engineering *Degree program information:* Part-time and evening/weekend programs available. Offers computer engineering (MS, DE, PhD); electrical engineering (MS, DE, PhD); engineering (M Eng, MS, DE, PhD). Electronic applications accepted.

MISSOURI WESTERN STATE UNIVERSITY, St. Joseph, MO 64507-2294

General Information State-supported, coed, comprehensive institution. *Enrollment:* 45 full-time matriculated graduate/professional students (24 women), 73 part-time matriculated graduate/professional students (57 women). *Enrollment by degree level:* 89 master's, 29 other advanced degrees. *Graduate faculty:* 75 full-time (30 women), 8 part-time/adjunct (5 women). Tuition, state resident: full-time $5544; part-time $308 per credit hour. Tuition, nonresident: full-time $10,206; part-time $567 per credit hour. *Required fees:* $30 per semester. One-time fee: $45 full-time. *Graduate housing:* Room and/or apartments available on a first-come, first-served basis to single students. *Student services:* Campus employment opportunities, campus safety program, career counseling, child daycare facilities, exercise/wellness program, international student services, low-cost health insurance, multicultural affairs office, services for students with disabilities. *Library facilities:* Warren E. Hearnes Library. *Online resources:* library catalog, web page, access to other libraries' catalogs. *Collection:* 147,509 titles, 1,068 serial subscriptions.

Computer facilities: 400 computers available on campus for general student use. A campuswide network can be accessed from student residence rooms and from off campus. Online class registration is available. *Web address:* http://www.missouriwestern.edu/.

General Application Contact: Dr. Brian C. Cronk, Dean of the Graduate School, 816-271-4394, E-mail: graduate@missouriwestern.edu.

GRADUATE UNITS

Program in Applied Science Offers chemistry (MAS); engineering technology management (MAS); human factors and usability testing (MAS); information technology management (MAS).

Program in Assessment Offers autism spectrum disorders (MAS); learning improvement (MAS); TESOL (MAS); writing (MAS).

Program in Forensic Investigations Offers forensic investigations (MAS).

Program in Health Care Leadership Offers health care leadership (MSN).

Program in Integrated Media Offers applied integrated media (MAS); convergent media (MAS).

Program in Written Communication Offers technical communication (MAS); writing studies (MAS).

MOLLOY COLLEGE, Rockville Centre, NY 11571-5002

General Information Independent, coed, comprehensive institution. *Enrollment:* 4,188 graduate, professional, and undergraduate students; 203 full-time matriculated graduate/professional students (151 women), 751 part-time matriculated graduate/professional students (637 women). *Enrollment by degree level:* 930 master's, 24 other advanced degrees. *Graduate faculty:* 47 full-time (32 women), 33 part-time/adjunct (20 women). *Graduate housing:* On-campus housing not available. *Student services:* Campus employment opportunities, campus safety program, career counseling, free psychological counseling, low-cost health insurance, services for students with disabilities, teacher training, writing training. *Library facilities:* James Edward Tobin Library. *Online resources:* library catalog, web page, access to other libraries' catalogs. *Collection:* 110,000 titles, 720 serial subscriptions, 3,170 audiovisual materials.

Computer facilities: 328 computers available on campus for general student use. A campuswide network can be accessed from off campus. Online class registration is available. *Web address:* http://www.molloy.edu/.

General Application Contact: Alina Haitz, Assistant Director of Graduate Admissions, 516-678-5000 Ext. 6399, Fax: 516-256-2247, E-mail: ahaitz@molloy.edu.

GRADUATE UNITS

Criminal Justice Program Students: 16 full-time (11 women), 20 part-time (10 women); includes 5 Black or African American, non-Hispanic/Latino; 5 Hispanic/Latino. Average age

Molloy College (continued)

32. *Faculty:* 3 full-time (1 woman), 1 part-time/adjunct (0 women). Expenses: Contact institution. In 2010, 11 master's awarded. Offers criminal justice (MS). *Application Contact:* Alina Haitz, Interim Associate Dean/Director, 516-678-5000 Ext. 6399, Fax: 516-256-2247, E-mail: ahaitz@molloy.edu. *Associate Dean/Director*, Dr. John Eterno, 516-678-5000 Ext. 6135.

Division of Nursing Students: 19 full-time (16 women), 435 part-time (407 women); includes 225 minority (124 Black or African American, non-Hispanic/Latino; 1 American Indian or Alaska Native, non-Hispanic/Latino; 66 Asian, non-Hispanic/Latino; 30 Hispanic/Latino; 3 Native Hawaiian or other Pacific Islander, non-Hispanic/Latino; 1 Two or more races, non-Hispanic/Latino), 1 international. Average age 39. *Faculty:* 23 full-time (22 women), 5 part-time/adjunct (4 women). Expenses: Contact institution. *Financial support:* Research assistantships with partial tuition reimbursements, teaching assistantships with partial tuition reimbursements, institutionally sponsored loans, scholarships/grants, and unspecified assistantships available. Support available to part-time students. Financial award application deadline: 4/1; financial award applicants required to submit FAFSA. In 2010, 79 master's awarded. *Degree program information:* Part-time and evening/weekend programs available. Offers adult nurse practitioner (Advanced Certificate); clinical nurse specialist: adult health (Advanced Certificate); family nurse practitioner (Advanced Certificate); nurse practitioner psychiatry (Advanced Certificate); nursing (MS); nursing administration (Advanced Certificate); nursing administration with informatics (Advanced Certificate); nursing education (Advanced Certificate); nursing informatics (Advanced Certificate); pediatric nurse practitioner (Advanced Certificate). *Application deadline:* For fall admission, 9/2 priority date for domestic students; for spring admission, 1/20 priority date for domestic students. Applications are processed on a rolling basis. *Application fee:* $60. *Application Contact:* Alina Haitz, Assistant Director of Graduate Admissions, 516-678-5000 Ext. 6399, Fax: 516-256-2247, E-mail: ahaitz@molloy.edu. *Acting Director, Graduate Nursing Program*, Dr. Mary T. O'Shaughnessy, 516-678-5000, Fax: 516-678-9718, E-mail: moshaughnessy@molloy.edu.

Graduate Business Program Students: 26 full-time (15 women), 69 part-time (35 women); includes 19 Black or African American, non-Hispanic/Latino; 1 American Indian or Alaska Native, non-Hispanic/Latino; 7 Asian, non-Hispanic/Latino; 9 Hispanic/Latino. Average age 33. *Faculty:* 5 full-time (0 women), 8 part-time/adjunct (2 women). Expenses: Contact institution. In 2010, 28 master's awarded. *Degree program information:* Part-time programs available. Offers accounting (MBA); accounting and management (MBA); management (MBA); personal financial planning and accounting (MBA); personal financial planning and management (MBA). *Application deadline:* Applications are processed on a rolling basis. *Application Contact:* Alina Haitz, Assistant Director of Graduate Admissions, 516-678-5000 Ext. 6399, Fax: 516-256-2247, E-mail: ahaitz@molloy.edu.

Graduate Education Program Students: 129 full-time (98 women), 207 part-time (170 women); includes 14 Black or African American, non-Hispanic/Latino; 5 Asian, non-Hispanic/Latino; 22 Hispanic/Latino. Average age 30. *Faculty:* 20 full-time (15 women), 24 part-time/adjunct (15 women). Expenses: Contact institution. In 2010, 113 master's awarded. Offers education (MS Ed, Certificate). *Application deadline:* Applications are processed on a rolling basis. *Application Contact:* Alina Haitz, Assistant Director of Graduate Admissions, 516-678-5000 Ext. 6399, Fax: 516-256-2247, E-mail: ahaitz@molloy.edu. *Associate Dean/Director*, Joanne O'Brien, 516-678-5000 Ext. 6280.

Graduate Music Therapy Program Students: 13 full-time (11 women), 20 part-time (15 women); includes 2 Black or African American, non-Hispanic/Latino; 7 Asian, non-Hispanic/Latino; 2 Hispanic/Latino. Average age 32. *Faculty:* 2 full-time (1 woman), 2 part-time/adjunct (both women). Expenses: Contact institution. In 2010, 1 master's awarded. Offers music therapy (MS). *Application deadline:* Applications are processed on a rolling basis. *Application Contact:* Dr. Mary O'Shaughnessy, Interim Associate Dean/Director, 516-678-5000 Ext. 6838, Fax: 516-256-2267, E-mail: moshaughnessy@molloy.edu.

Graduate Social Work Program Expenses: Contact institution. Offers social work (MSW). *Application Contact:* Jennifer S. McKinnon, Coordinator, 516-678-5000 Ext. 6957, E-mail: jmckinnon@molloy.edu. *Coordinator*, Jennifer S. McKinnon, 516-678-5000 Ext. 6957, E-mail: jmckinnon@molloy.edu.

MONMOUTH UNIVERSITY, West Long Branch, NJ 07764-1898

General Information Independent, coed, comprehensive institution. *Enrollment:* 6,506 graduate, professional, and undergraduate students; 723 full-time matriculated graduate/professional students (528 women), 1,102 part-time matriculated graduate/professional students (841 women). *Enrollment by degree level:* 1,825 master's. *Graduate faculty:* 138 full-time (71 women), 77 part-time/adjunct (48 women). *Tuition:* Full-time $19,572; part-time $816 per credit. *Required fees:* $628; $157 per semester. *Graduate housing:* On-campus housing not available. *Student services:* Campus employment opportunities, campus safety program, career counseling, exercise/wellness program, free psychological counseling, international student services, low-cost health insurance, multicultural affairs office, services for students with disabilities, writing training. *Library facilities:* Monmouth University Library. *Online resources:* library catalog, web page. *Collection:* 286,000 titles, 43,200 serial subscriptions. *Research affiliation:* The U.S. Army Edgewood Chemical Biological Center, The U.S. Army Northeast Regional Response Center, NJ Business Force (NJBF) at New Jersey Institute of Technology, PSU-EOC (Penn State University Electro-Optics Center, Saint Francis University, CERMUSA (Center of Excellence for Remote & Medically Under Served Areas), Stevens Institute of Technology, The National Center for Secure & Resilient Maritime Commerce, (U. S. Department of Homeland Security National Center of Excellence).

Computer facilities: 467 computers available on campus for general student use. A campuswide network can be accessed from student residence rooms and from off campus. Online class registration is available. *Web address:* http://www.monmouth.edu/.

General Application Contact: Kevin Roane, Director, Office of Graduate Admission, 732-571-3452, Fax: 732-263-5123, E-mail: gradadm@monmouth.edu.

GRADUATE UNITS

The Graduate School Students: 723 full-time (528 women), 1,102 part-time (841 women); includes 97 Black or African American, non-Hispanic/Latino; 4 American Indian or Alaska Native, non-Hispanic/Latino; 73 Asian, non-Hispanic/Latino; 95 Hispanic/Latino; 18 Two or more races, non-Hispanic/Latino, 68 international. Average age 31. 1,302 applicants, 90% accepted, 712 enrolled. *Faculty:* 138 full-time (71 women), 77 part-time/adjunct (48 women). Expenses: Contact institution. *Financial support:* In 2010–11, 1,150 students received support, including 1,122 fellowships (averaging $1,961 per year), 115 research assistantships (averaging $7,341 per year); career-related internships or fieldwork, scholarships/grants, and unspecified assistantships also available. Support available to part-time students. Financial award applicants required to submit FAFSA. In 2010, 584 master's awarded. *Degree program information:* Part-time and evening/weekend programs available. Offers computer science (MS); corporate and public communication (MA); creative writing (MA); criminal justice administration (MA, Certificate); European specialization (MA); financial mathematics (MS); homeland security (MA, Certificate); human resources communication (Certificate); liberal arts (MA); mental health counseling (MS); New Jersey studies (MA); psychological counseling (MA, PMC); public policy (MA); public relations (Certificate); public service communication specialist (Certificate); rhetoric and writing (MA); software design and development (Certificate); software development (Certificate); software engineering (MS, Certificate); U. S. specialization (MA); world specialization (MA). *Application deadline:* For fall admission, 7/15 priority date for domestic students, 6/1 for international students; for spring admission, 11/15 priority date for domestic students, 11/1 for international students. Applications are processed on a rolling basis. *Application fee:* $50. Electronic applications accepted. *Application Contact:* Kevin Roane, Director, Office of Graduate Admission, 732-571-3452, Fax: 732-263-5123, E-mail: gradadm@monmouth.edu. *Dean*, Dr. Datta V. Naik, 732-571-7550, Fax: 732-263-5142.

Leon Hess Business School Students: 87 full-time (31 women), 144 part-time (69 women); includes 6 Black or African American, non-Hispanic/Latino; 14 Asian, non-Hispanic/Latino; 8 Hispanic/Latino; 2 Two or more races, non-Hispanic/Latino, 17 international. Average age 29. 181 applicants, 78% accepted, 81 enrolled. *Faculty:* 27 full-time (9 women), 7 part-time/adjunct (1 woman). Expenses: Contact institution. *Financial support:* In 2010–11, 166 students received support, including 161 fellowships (averaging $1,741 per year), 17 research assistantships (averaging $10,505 per year); career-related internships or fieldwork, scholarships/grants, and unspecified assistantships also available. Support available to part-time students. Financial award applicants required to submit FAFSA. In 2010, 88 master's awarded. *Degree program information:* Part-time and evening/weekend programs available. Offers accounting (MBA, Post-Master's Certificate); business (MBA); finance (MBA); healthcare management (MBA, Post-Master's Certificate); real estate (MBA). *Application deadline:* For fall admission, 7/15 priority date for domestic students, 6/1 for international students; for spring admission, 11/15 priority date for domestic students, 11/1 for international students. Applications are processed on a rolling basis. *Application fee:* $50. Electronic applications accepted. *Application Contact:* Kevin Roane, Director, Office of Graduate Admission, 732-571-3452, Fax: 732-263-5123, E-mail: gradadm@monmouth.edu. *MBA Program Director*, Douglas Stives, 732-263-5894, Fax: 732-263-5517, E-mail: dstives@monmouth.edu.

The Marjorie K. Unterberg School of Nursing and Health Studies Students: 18 full-time (16 women), 213 part-time (206 women); includes 16 Black or African American, non-Hispanic/Latino; 1 American Indian or Alaska Native, non-Hispanic/Latino; 32 Asian, non-Hispanic/Latino; 8 Hispanic/Latino; 1 Two or more races, non-Hispanic/Latino, 2 international. Average age 41. 154 applicants, 87% accepted, 86 enrolled. *Faculty:* 12 full-time (all women). Expenses: Contact institution. *Financial support:* In 2010–11, 147 students received support, including 144 fellowships (averaging $1,472 per year), 5 research assistantships (averaging $4,020 per year); career-related internships or fieldwork, scholarships/grants, and unspecified assistantships also available. Support available to part-time students. Financial award applicants required to submit FAFSA. In 2010, 36 master's awarded. *Degree program information:* Part-time and evening/weekend programs available. Offers adult nurse practitioner (MSN); adult psychiatric and mental health advanced practice nursing (MSN, Post-Master's Certificate); advanced practice nursing (Post-Master's Certificate); family nurse practitioner (MSN, Post-Master's Certificate); forensic nursing (MSN, Certificate); nursing (MSN); nursing administration (MSN, Post-Master's Certificate); nursing education (MSN, Post-Master's Certificate); nursing practice (DNP); school nursing (MSN, Certificate). *Application deadline:* For fall admission, 7/15 priority date for domestic students, 6/1 for international students; for spring admission, 11/15 priority date for domestic students, 11/1 for international students. Applications are processed on a rolling basis. *Application fee:* $50. Electronic applications accepted. *Application Contact:* Kevin Roane, Director, Office of Graduate Admission, 732-571-3452, Fax: 732-263-5123, E-mail: gradadm@monmouth.edu. *Dean*, Dr. Janet Mahoney, 732-571-3443, Fax: 732-263-5131, E-mail: jmahoney@monmouth.edu.

School of Education Students: 180 full-time (144 women), 316 part-time (261 women); includes 13 Black or African American, non-Hispanic/Latino; 5 Asian, non-Hispanic/Latino; 17 Hispanic/Latino; 5 Two or more races, non-Hispanic/Latino, 2 international. Average age 29. 347 applicants, 91% accepted, 207 enrolled. *Faculty:* 19 full-time (12 women), 29 part-time/adjunct (23 women). Expenses: Contact institution. *Financial support:* In 2010–11, 281 students received support, including 275 fellowships (averaging $1,863 per year), 21 research assistantships (averaging $8,710 per year); career-related internships or fieldwork, scholarships/grants, and unspecified assistantships also available. Support available to part-time students. Financial award applicants required to submit FAFSA. In 2010, 188 master's awarded. *Degree program information:* Part-time and evening/weekend programs available. Offers education (M Ed); initial certification (MAT); learning disabilities-teacher consultant (Certificate); principal (MS Ed); principal/school administrator (MS Ed); reading specialist (MS Ed, Certificate); school counseling (MS Ed); special education (MS Ed); supervisor (Certificate); teacher of the handicapped (Certificate); teaching English to speakers of other languages (TESOL) (Certificate). *Application deadline:* For fall admission, 7/15 priority date for domestic students, 7/1 for international students; for spring admission, 11/15 priority date for domestic students, 11/1 for international students. Applications are processed on a rolling basis. *Application fee:* $50. Electronic applications accepted. *Application Contact:* Kevin Roane, Director, Office of Graduate Admission, 732-571-3452, Fax: 732-263-5123, E-mail: gradadm@monmouth.edu. *Associate Dean*, Dr. Terri Rothman, 732-571-7507, Fax: 732-263-5277, E-mail: trothman@monmouth.edu.

School of Social Work Students: 160 full-time (149 women), 89 part-time (78 women); includes 29 Black or African American, non-Hispanic/Latino; 3 Asian, non-Hispanic/Latino; 21 Hispanic/Latino; 1 Two or more races, non-Hispanic/Latino. Average age 32. 235 applicants, 97% accepted, 124 enrolled. *Faculty:* 12 full-time (10 women), 21 part-time/adjunct (14 women). Expenses: Contact institution. *Financial support:* In 2010–11, 116 students received support, including 116 fellowships (averaging $3,193 per year), 5 research assistantships (averaging $10,975 per year); career-related internships or fieldwork, scholarships/grants, and unspecified assistantships also available. Support available to part-time students. Financial award applicants required to submit FAFSA. In 2010, 101 master's awarded. *Degree program information:* Part-time and evening/weekend programs available. Offers clinical practice with families and children (MSW); international and community development (MSW); play therapy (Post-Master's Certificate). *Application deadline:* For fall admission, 3/15 priority date for domestic students, 3/15 for international students. Applications are processed on a rolling basis. *Application fee:* $50. Electronic applications accepted. *Application Contact:* Kevin Roane, Director, Office of Graduate Admission, 732-571-3452, Fax: 732-263-5123, E-mail: gradadm@monmouth.edu. *Program Director*, Dr. Nora Smith, 732-263-5372, Fax: 732-263-5217, E-mail: swdept@monmouth.edu.

See Close-Up on page 969.

MONROE COLLEGE, Bronx, NY 10468-5407

General Information Proprietary, coed, comprehensive institution.

GRADUATE UNITS

King School of Business Postbaccalaureate distance learning degree programs offered. Offers business management (MBA). Program also offered in New Rochelle, NY.

MONTANA STATE UNIVERSITY, Bozeman, MT 59717

General Information State-supported, coed, university. CGS member. *Enrollment:* 13,559 graduate, professional, and undergraduate students; 477 full-time matriculated graduate/professional students (248 women), 1,170 part-time matriculated graduate/professional students (614 women). *Enrollment by degree level:* 1,251 master's, 396 doctoral. *Graduate faculty:* 545 full-time (206 women), 212 part-time/adjunct (110 women). Tuition, state resident: full-time $5554. Tuition, nonresident: full-time $14,646. *Required fees:* $1233. *Graduate housing:* Rooms and/or apartments available on a first-come, first-served basis to single and married students. *Student services:* Campus employment opportunities, campus safety program, career counseling, child daycare facilities, exercise/wellness program, free psychological counseling, international student services, low-cost health insurance, multicultural affairs office, services for students with disabilities, teacher training, writing training. *Library facilities:* Renne Library plus 2 others. *Online resources:* library catalog, web page, access to other libraries' catalogs. *Collection:* 744,989 titles, 10,131 serial subscriptions, 13,446 audiovisual materials. *Research affiliation:* Phillips Environmental (microbial technology), Microvision (information transmission system), LigoCyte Pharmaceuticals, Inc. (pharmaceuticals), Eli Lilly and Company (antifungal technology), S2 Corporation (instrumentation), ILX Lightwave (laser diodes, electro-optical test equipment).

Computer facilities: 850 computers available on campus for general student use. A campuswide network can be accessed from student residence rooms and from off campus. Online class registration is available. *Web address:* http://www.montana.edu/.

General Application Contact: Dr. Carl A. Fox, Vice Provost for Graduate Education, 406-994-4145, Fax: 406-994-7433, E-mail: gradstudy@montana.edu.

GRADUATE UNITS

College of Graduate Studies Students: 22 full-time (9 women), 253 part-time (167 women); includes 12 minority (2 Black or African American, non-Hispanic/Latino; 3 American Indian or Alaska Native, non-Hispanic/Latino; 2 Asian, non-Hispanic/Latino; 3 Hispanic/Latino; 2 Two or more races, non-Hispanic/Latino), 1 international. Average age 36. 137 applicants, 73% accepted, 70 enrolled. *Faculty:* 2 full-time (1 woman), 3 part-time/adjunct (2 women). Expenses: Contact institution. *Financial support:* Fellowships with full and partial tuition reimbursements, research assistantships with full and partial tuition reimbursements, teaching assistantships with full and partial tuition reimbursements, career-related internships or fieldwork, Federal Work-Study, institutionally sponsored loans, scholarships/grants, traineeships, tuition waivers (full and partial), and unspecified assistantships available. Support available to part-time students. Financial award application deadline: 3/1; financial award applicants required to submit FAFSA. In 2010, 71 master's awarded. *Degree program information:* Part-time programs available. Postbaccalaureate distance learning degree programs offered (minimal on-campus study). *Application deadline:* For fall admission, 7/15 priority date for domestic students, 5/15 priority date for international students; for spring admission, 12/1 priority date for domestic students, 10/1 priority date for international students. Applications are processed on a rolling basis. *Application fee:* $30. Electronic applications accepted. *Application Contact:* Dr. Carl A. Fox, Vice Provost for Graduate Education, 406-994-4145, Fax: 406-994-7433, E-mail: gradstudy@montana.edu. *Vice Provost for Graduate Education,* Dr. Carl A. Fox, 406-994-4145, Fax: 406-994-7433, E-mail: gradstudy@montana.edu.

College of Agriculture Students: 26 full-time (7 women), 95 part-time (45 women); includes 9 minority (3 American Indian or Alaska Native, non-Hispanic/Latino; 1 Asian, non-Hispanic/Latino; 4 Hispanic/Latino; 1 Two or more races, non-Hispanic/Latino), 12 international. Average age 30. 88 applicants, 42% accepted, 30 enrolled. *Faculty:* 90 full-time (21 women), 15 part-time/adjunct (4 women). Expenses: Contact institution. *Financial support:* Application deadline: 3/1. In 2010, 28 master's, 7 doctorates awarded. *Degree program information:* Part-time programs available. Postbaccalaureate distance learning degree programs offered (minimal on-campus study). Offers agricultural education (MS); agriculture (MS, PhD); animal and range sciences (MS, PhD); immunology and infectious diseases (MS, PhD); land rehabilitation (interdisciplinary) (MS); land resources and environmental sciences (MS); plant pathology (MS); plant sciences (MS, PhD). *Application deadline:* For fall admission, 7/15 priority date for domestic students, 5/15 priority date for international students; for spring admission, 12/1 priority date for domestic students, 10/1 priority date for international students. Applications are processed on a rolling basis. *Application fee:* $30. Electronic applications accepted. *Application Contact:* Dr. Carl A. Fox, Vice Provost for Graduate Education, 406-994-4145, Fax: 406-994-7433, E-mail: gradstudy@montana.edu. *Dean,* Dr. Jeffrey S. Jacobsen, 406-994-7060, Fax: 406-994-3933, E-mail: jefj@montana.edu.

College of Arts and Architecture Students: 102 full-time (45 women), 40 part-time (17 women); includes 12 minority (5 Black or African American, non-Hispanic/Latino; 1 American Indian or Alaska Native, non-Hispanic/Latino; 2 Hispanic/Latino; 1 Native Hawaiian or other Pacific Islander, non-Hispanic/Latino; 3 Two or more races, non-Hispanic/Latino), 6 international. Average age 27. 127 applicants, 34% accepted, 36 enrolled. *Faculty:* 66 full-time (21 women), 31 part-time/adjunct (14 women). Expenses: Contact institution. *Financial support:* Application deadline: 3/1. In 2010, 79 master's awarded. *Degree program information:* Part-time programs available. Offers architecture (M Arch); art (MFA); art history (MA); arts and architecture (M Arch, MA, MFA); science and natural history filmmaking (MFA). *Application deadline:* For fall admission, 7/15 priority date for domestic students, 5/15 priority date for international students; for spring admission, 12/1 priority date for domestic students, 10/1 priority date for international students. Applications are processed on a rolling basis. *Application fee:* $30. Electronic applications accepted. *Application Contact:* Dr. Carl A. Fox, Vice Provost for Graduate Education, 406-994-4145, Fax: 406-994-7433, E-mail: gradstudy@montana.edu. *Dean,* Susan Agre-Kippenhan, 406-994-4405, Fax: 406-994-3680, E-mail: susanak@montana.edu.

College of Business Students: 41 full-time (25 women), 7 part-time (all women); includes 3 minority (1 Asian, non-Hispanic/Latino; 2 Hispanic/Latino). Average age 25. 27 applicants, 78% accepted, 18 enrolled. *Faculty:* 25 full-time (8 women), 28 part-time/adjunct (12 women). Expenses: Contact institution. *Financial support:* In 2010–11, 6 students received support, including 6 teaching assistantships with partial tuition reimbursements available (averaging $3,800 per year); career-related internships or fieldwork and tuition waivers (partial) also available. Financial award application deadline: 3/1; financial award applicants required to submit FAFSA. In 2010, 43 master's awarded. *Degree program information:* Part-time programs available. Offers professional accountancy (MP Ac). *Application deadline:* For fall admission, 7/15 priority date for domestic students, 5/15 priority date for international students; for spring admission, 12/1 priority date for domestic students, 10/1 priority date for international students. Applications are processed on a rolling basis. *Application fee:* $30. Electronic applications accepted. *Application Contact:* Dr. Carl A. Fox, Vice Provost for Graduate Education, 406-994-4145, Fax: 406-994-7433, E-mail: gradstudy@montana.edu. *Dean,* Dr. Dan Moshavi, 406-994-4423, Fax: 406-994-6206, E-mail: dmoshavi@montana.edu.

College of Education, Health, and Human Development Students: 75 full-time (63 women), 262 part-time (157 women); includes 28 minority (13 American Indian or Alaska Native, non-Hispanic/Latino; 3 Asian, non-Hispanic/Latino; 5 Hispanic/Latino; 7 Two or more races, non-Hispanic/Latino), 3 international. Average age 35. 137 applicants, 66% accepted, 82 enrolled. *Faculty:* 51 full-time (36 women), 18 part-time/adjunct (12 women). Expenses: Contact institution. *Financial support:* Application deadline: 3/1. In 2010, 101 master's, 9 doctorates, 3 other advanced degrees awarded. *Degree program information:* Part-time programs available. Postbaccalaureate distance learning degree programs offered (minimal on-campus study). Offers adult and higher education (Ed D); curriculum and instruction (M Ed, Ed D); education (M Ed); education, health, and human development (M Ed, MS, Ed D, Ed S); educational leadership (Ed D, Ed S); family and consumer sciences (MS). *Application deadline:* For fall admission, 7/15 priority date for domestic students, 5/15 priority date for international students; for spring admission, 12/1 priority date for domestic students, 10/1 priority date for international students. Applications are processed on a rolling basis. *Application fee:* $30. Electronic applications accepted. *Application Contact:* Dr. Carl A. Fox, Vice Provost for Graduate Education, 406-994-4145, Fax: 406-994-7433, E-mail: gradstudy@montana.edu. *Dean,* Dr. Larry Baker, 406-994-6752, Fax: 406-994-1854, E-mail: lbaker@montana.edu.

College of Engineering Students: 76 full-time (10 women), 112 part-time (27 women); includes 13 minority (3 American Indian or Alaska Native, non-Hispanic/Latino; 7 Asian, non-Hispanic/Latino; 1 Hispanic/Latino; 2 Two or more races, non-Hispanic/Latino), 27 international. Average age 27. 165 applicants, 39% accepted, 48 enrolled. *Faculty:* 68 full-time (6 women), 20 part-time/adjunct (3 women). Expenses: Contact institution. *Financial support:* Application deadline: 3/1. In 2010, 56 master's, 11 doctorates awarded. *Degree program information:* Part-time programs available. Offers chemical engineering (MS); civil engineering (MS); computer science (MS, PhD); construction engineering management (MCEM); electrical engineering (MS); engineering (PhD); environmental engineering (MS); industrial and management engineering (MS); mechanical engineering (MS). *Application deadline:* For fall admission, 7/15 priority date for domestic students, 5/15 priority date for international students; for spring admission, 12/1 priority date for domestic students, 10/1 priority date for international students. Applications are processed on a rolling basis. *Application fee:* $30. Electronic applications accepted. *Application Contact:* Dr. Carl A. Fox, Vice Provost for Graduate Education, 406-994-4145, Fax: 406-994-7433, E-mail: gradstudy@montana.edu. *Dean,* Dr. Robert Marley, 406-994-2272, Fax: 406-994-6665, E-mail: rmarley@coe.montana.edu.

College of Letters and Science Students: 86 full-time (42 women), 363 part-time (159 women); includes 32 minority (2 Black or African American, non-Hispanic/Latino; 9 American Indian or Alaska Native, non-Hispanic/Latino; 4 Asian, non-Hispanic/Latino; 8 Hispanic/Latino; 9 Two or more races, non-Hispanic/Latino), 43 international. Average age 27. 338 applicants, 40% accepted, 101 enrolled. *Faculty:* 190 full-time (63 women), 70 part-time/adjunct (38 women). Expenses: Contact institution. *Financial support:* Application deadline: 3/1. In 2010, 77 master's, 18 doctorates awarded. *Degree program information:* Part-time programs available. Postbaccalaureate distance learning degree programs offered (minimal on-campus study). Offers biochemistry (MS, PhD); biological sciences (PhD); chemistry (MS, PhD); earth sciences (MS, PhD); ecological and environmental statistics (MS); ecology and environmental sciences (PhD); English (MA); fish and wildlife biology (PhD); fish and wildlife management (MS); history (MA, PhD); letters and science (MA, MPA, MS, PhD); mathematics (MS, PhD); microbiology (MS, PhD); Native American studies (MA); neuroscience (MS, PhD); physics (MS, PhD); psychology (MS); public administration (MPA); statistics (MS, PhD). *Application deadline:* For fall admission, 7/15 priority date for domestic students, 5/15 priority date for international students; for spring admission, 12/1 priority date for domestic students, 10/1 priority date for international students. Applications are processed on a rolling basis. *Application fee:* $30. Electronic applications accepted. *Application Contact:* Dr. Carl A. Fox, Vice Provost for Graduate Education, 406-994-4145, Fax: 406-994-7433, E-mail: gradstudy@montana.edu. *Interim Dean,* Dr. Paula Lutz, 406-994-4288, Fax: 406-994-6879, E-mail: plutz@montana.edu.

College of Nursing Students: 47 full-time (46 women), 29 part-time (28 women); includes 7 minority (5 American Indian or Alaska Native, non-Hispanic/Latino; 2 Two or more races, non-Hispanic/Latino). Average age 37. 64 applicants, 50% accepted, 28 enrolled. *Faculty:* 53 full-time (50 women), 27 part-time/adjunct (25 women). Expenses: Contact institution. *Financial support:* In 2010–11, 18 students received support, including 8 teaching assistantships with partial tuition reimbursements available (averaging $7,050 per year); scholarships/grants, traineeships, and tuition waivers (partial) also available. Financial award application deadline: 3/1; financial award applicants required to submit FAFSA. In 2010, 15 master's awarded. *Degree program information:* Part-time programs available. Postbaccalaureate distance learning degree programs offered (minimal on-campus study). Offers clinical nurse leader (MN); family nurse practitioner (MN, Post-Master's Certificate); nursing education (Certificate, Post-Master's Certificate); psychiatric mental health nurse practitioner (MN). *Application deadline:* For fall admission, 7/15 priority date for domestic students, 5/15 priority date for international students; for spring admission, 12/1 priority date for domestic students, 10/1 priority date for international students. Applications are processed on a rolling basis. *Application fee:* $30. Electronic applications accepted. *Application Contact:* Dr. Carl A. Fox, Vice Provost for Graduate Education, 406-994-4145, Fax: 406-994-7433, E-mail: gradstudy@montana.edu. *Dean,* Dr. Elizabeth Kinion, 406-994-2725, Fax: 406-994-6020, E-mail: ekinion@montana.edu.

MONTANA STATE UNIVERSITY BILLINGS, Billings, MT 59101-0298

General Information State-supported, coed, comprehensive institution. *Graduate housing:* Rooms and/or apartments available on a first-come, first-served basis to single and married students.

GRADUATE UNITS

College of Allied Health Professions *Degree program information:* Part-time and evening/weekend programs available. Postbaccalaureate distance learning degree programs offered (minimal on-campus study). Offers allied health professions (MHA, MS, MSRC); athletic training (MS); health administration (MHA); rehabilitation and human services (MSRC); sport management (MS).

College of Arts and Sciences *Degree program information:* Part-time programs available. Postbaccalaureate distance learning degree programs offered. Offers arts and sciences (MPA, MS); psychology (MS); public administration (MPA); public relations (MS).

College of Education *Degree program information:* Part-time programs available. Postbaccalaureate distance learning degree programs offered (minimal on-campus study). Offers advanced studies (MS Sp Ed); early childhood education (M Ed); education (M Ed, MS Sp Ed, Certificate); educational technology (M Ed); general curriculum (M Ed); interdisciplinary studies (M Ed); reading (M Ed); school counseling (M Ed); secondary education (M Ed); special education (MS Sp Ed); special education generalist (MS Sp Ed); teaching (Certificate).

MONTANA STATE UNIVERSITY–NORTHERN, Havre, MT 59501-7751

General Information State-supported, coed, comprehensive institution. *Enrollment:* 71 part-time matriculated graduate/professional students (52 women). *Enrollment by degree level:* 71 master's. *Graduate faculty:* 3 full-time (1 woman), 6 part-time/adjunct (3 women). *Graduate housing:* Rooms and/or apartments available on a first-come, first-served basis to single students and available to married students. Housing application deadline: 8/22. *Student services:* Campus employment opportunities, career counseling, child daycare facilities, exercise/wellness program, low-cost health insurance, multicultural affairs office, teacher training. *Library facilities:* Vande Bogart Libraries. *Online resources:* library catalog, web page, access to other libraries' catalogs. *Collection:* 128,000 titles, 1,729 serial subscriptions.

Computer facilities: A campuswide network can be accessed from student residence rooms and from off campus. Online class registration is available. *Web address:* http://www.msun.edu/.

General Application Contact: Norton Pease, Chair, College of Education, Arts and Sciences, and Nursing, 406-265-3735, E-mail: norton.pease@msun.edu.

GRADUATE UNITS

Graduate Programs *Degree program information:* Part-time and evening/weekend programs available. Postbaccalaureate distance learning degree programs offered (minimal on-campus study). Offers counselor education (M Ed); learning development (M Ed). Electronic applications accepted.

MONTANA TECH OF THE UNIVERSITY OF MONTANA, Butte, MT 59701-8997

General Information State-supported, coed, comprehensive institution. *Enrollment:* 2,864 graduate, professional, and undergraduate students; 69 full-time matriculated graduate/professional students (27 women), 82 part-time matriculated graduate/professional students (32 women). *Enrollment by degree level:* 151 master's. *Graduate faculty:* 134 full-time (46 women), 80 part-time/adjunct (35 women). Tuition, state resident: full-time $5084. Tuition, nonresident: full-time $15,104. *Graduate housing:* Rooms and/or apartments available on a first-come, first-served basis to single and married students. Typical cost: $3084 per year ($6924 including board) for married students. *Student services:* Campus employment opportunities, campus safety program, career counseling, exercise/wellness program, grant writing training, international student services, low-cost health insurance, multicultural affairs office, services for students with disabilities. *Library facilities:* Montana Tech Library. *Online resources:* library catalog, web page, access to other libraries' catalogs. *Collection:* 139,398 titles, 50,693 serial subscriptions, 4,355 audiovisual materials. *Research affiliation:* Newmont Mining (mining and mineral processing), Stillwater Mining (mineral production and training), NorthWestern Energy (electric efficiency), Edison Welding Institute (fuel cell design), Montana Resources, Inc. (mine reclamation and revegetation), QualTech, Inc. (battery monitor technology).

Computer facilities: 522 computers available on campus for general student use. A campuswide network can be accessed from student residence rooms and from off campus. Online class registration is available. *Web address:* http://www.mtech.edu/.

General Application Contact: Fred Sullivan, Administrator, Graduate School, 406-496-4304, Fax: 406-496-4710, E-mail: fsullivan@mtech.edu.

GRADUATE UNITS

Graduate School Students: 69 full-time (27 women), 82 part-time (32 women); includes 3 Black or African American, non-Hispanic/Latino; 5 American Indian or Alaska Native, non-Hispanic/Latino; 1 Asian, non-Hispanic/Latino; 5 Hispanic/Latino, 7 international. 108 applicants, 37% accepted, 38 enrolled. *Faculty:* 134 full-time (46 women), 80 part-time/adjunct (35 women). Expenses: Contact institution. *Financial support:* In 2010–11, 70 students received support, including 55 teaching assistantships with partial tuition reimbursements available (averaging $4,980 per year); research assistantships with full tuition reimbursements available, career-related internships or fieldwork, tuition waivers (full and partial), and unspecified assistantships also available. Financial award application deadline: 4/1; financial award applicants required to submit FAFSA. In 2010, 18 master's awarded. *Degree program information:* Part-time and evening/weekend programs available. Postbaccalaureate distance learning degree programs offered (no on-campus study). Offers electrical engineering (MS); environmental engineering (MS); general engineering (MS); geochemistry (MS); geological engineering (MS); geology (MS); geophysical engineering (MS); hydrogeological engineering (MS); hydrogeology (MS); industrial hygiene (MS); interdisciplinary studies (MS); metallurgical/mineral processing engineering (MS); mining engineering (MS); petroleum engineering (MS);

Montana Tech of The University of Montana (continued)

project engineering and management (MPEM); technical communication (MS). *Application deadline:* For fall admission, 4/1 priority date for domestic students, 3/1 priority date for international students; for spring admission, 10/1 priority date for domestic students, 7/1 priority date for international students. Applications are processed on a rolling basis. *Application fee:* $30. Electronic applications accepted. *Application Contact:* Fred Sullivan, Administrator, Graduate School, 406-496-4304, Fax: 406-496-4710, E-mail: fsullivan@mtech.edu. *Associate Vice Chancellor, Research and Graduate Studies*, Dr. Joseph Figueira, 406-496-4102, Fax: 406-496-4334.

MONTCLAIR STATE UNIVERSITY, Montclair, NJ 07043-1624

General Information State-supported, coed, comprehensive institution. CGS member. *Enrollment:* 18,171 graduate, professional, and undergraduate students; 1,062 full-time matriculated graduate/professional students (734 women), 2,040 part-time matriculated graduate/professional students (1,437 women). *Enrollment by degree level:* 2,695 master's, 137 doctoral, 270 other advanced degrees. *Graduate faculty:* 569 full-time (276 women), 961 part-time/adjunct (539 women). Tuition, state resident: part-time $501.34 per credit. Tuition, nonresident: part-time $773.88 per credit. *Required fees:* $71.15 per credit. *Graduate housing:* Room and/or apartments available on a first-come, first-served basis to single students. Typical cost: $11,478 (including board). Housing application deadline: 3/1. *Student services:* Campus employment opportunities, campus safety program, career counseling, child daycare facilities, exercise/wellness program, free psychological counseling, international student services, low-cost health insurance, services for students with disabilities, teacher training. *Library facilities:* Sprague Library. *Online resources:* library catalog, web page, access to other libraries' catalogs. *Collection:* 521,826 titles, 35,000 serial subscriptions, 27,007 audiovisual materials. *Research affiliation:* Spencer Foundation (education improvement), The International Society for Optical Engineering (optics and photonics), Deafness Research Foundation (heating science).

Computer facilities: Computer purchase and lease plans are available. 218 computers available on campus for general student use. A campuswide network can be accessed from student residence rooms and from off campus. Online class registration is available. *Web address:* http://www.montclair.edu/.

General Application Contact: Amy Aiello, Director of Graduate Admissions and Operations, 973-655-5147, Fax: 973-655-7869, E-mail: aielloa@mail.montclair.edu.

GRADUATE UNITS

The Graduate School Students: 1,062 full-time (734 women), 2,040 part-time (1,437 women); includes 665 minority (255 Black or African American, non-Hispanic/Latino; 2 American Indian or Alaska Native, non-Hispanic/Latino; 131 Asian, non-Hispanic/Latino; 265 Hispanic/Latino; 3 Native Hawaiian or other Pacific Islander, non-Hispanic/Latino; 9 Two or more races, non-Hispanic/Latino), 110 international. Average age 31. 1,843 applicants, 51% accepted, 661 enrolled. *Faculty:* 569 full-time (276 women), 961 part-time/adjunct (539 women). Expenses: Contact institution. *Financial support:* In 2010–11, 3 fellowships with full tuition reimbursements, 198 research assistantships with full tuition reimbursements, 38 teaching assistantships with full tuition reimbursements were awarded; Federal Work-Study, institutionally sponsored loans, scholarships/grants, and unspecified assistantships also available. Support available to part-time students. Financial award application deadline: 3/1; financial award applicants required to submit FAFSA. In 2010, 997 master's, 10 doctorates, 118 other advanced degrees awarded. *Degree program information:* Part-time and evening/weekend programs available. *Application deadline:* For fall admission, 6/1 for international students; for spring admission, 10/1 for international students. Applications are processed on a rolling basis. *Application fee:* $60. Electronic applications accepted. *Application Contact:* Amy Aiello, Director of Graduate Admissions and Operations, 973-655-5147, Fax: 973-655-7869, E-mail: graduate.school@montclair.edu. *Dean*, Dr. Joan C. Ficke, 973-655-5147, Fax: 973-655-7869, E-mail: graduate.school@montclair.edu.

College of Education and Human Services Students: 550 full-time (393 women), 982 part-time (777 women); includes 123 Black or African American, non-Hispanic/Latino; 51 Asian, non-Hispanic/Latino; 120 Hispanic/Latino; 3 Native Hawaiian or other Pacific Islander, non-Hispanic/Latino; 4 Two or more races, non-Hispanic/Latino, 22 international. Average age 31. 727 applicants, 37% accepted, 263 enrolled. *Faculty:* 203 full-time (114 women), 312 part-time/adjunct (171 women). Expenses: Contact institution. *Financial support:* In 2010–11, 80 research assistantships with full tuition reimbursements (averaging $7,000 per year), 18 teaching assistantships with full tuition reimbursements (averaging $15,000 per year) were awarded; Federal Work-Study, scholarships/grants, and unspecified assistantships also available. Support available to part-time students. Financial award application deadline: 3/1; financial award applicants required to submit FAFSA. In 2010, 501 master's, 27 other advanced degrees awarded. *Degree program information:* Part-time and evening/weekend programs available. Offers advanced counseling (Certificate); American Dietetic Association (Certificate); certified alcohol and drug counselor (Certificate); counseling (MA); counselor education (PhD); director of school counseling services (Certificate); early childhood education (MAT); early childhood education and teaching students with disabilities (MAT); early childhood/elementary education (M Ed); education (M Ed); education and human services (M Ed, MA, MAT, MPH, MS, Ed D, PhD, Certificate); educational leadership (MA); educational technology (M Ed); elementary education (MAT); elementary education with disabilities (MAT); elementary school teacher (Certificate); exercise science (MA); food safety instructor (Certificate); health and physical education (Certificate); health education (MA); inclusive early childhood education (M Ed); learning disabilities teacher consultant (Certificate); new literacies, digital technologies and learning (Certificate); nutrition and exercise science (Certificate); nutrition and food science (MS); pedagogy and philosophy (Ed D); philosophy for children (Certificate); physical education (Certificate); principal (Certificate); public health (MPH); reading (MA); reading specialist (Certificate); school business administrator (Certificate); school counselor (Certificate); sports administration and coach (MA); substance awareness coordinator (Certificate); supervisor (Certificate); teacher of pre-school through grade 3 (Certificate); teacher of students with disabilities (P-3) (Certificate); teaching (MAT); teaching and supervision: physical education (MA). *Application deadline:* For fall admission, 6/1 for international students; for spring admission, 10/1 for international students. Applications are processed on a rolling basis. *Application fee:* $60. Electronic applications accepted. *Application Contact:* Amy Aiello, Director of Graduate Admissions and Operations, 973-655-5147, E-mail: graduate.school@montclair.edu. *Dean*, Dr. Ada Beth Cutler, 973-655-5167, E-mail: cutler@mail.montclair.edu.

College of Humanities and Social Sciences Students: 218 full-time (178 women), 367 part-time (284 women); includes 156 minority (73 Black or African American, non-Hispanic/Latino; 2 American Indian or Alaska Native, non-Hispanic/Latino; 20 Asian, non-Hispanic/Latino; 61 Hispanic/Latino), 12 international. Average age 31. 727 applicants, 36% accepted, 186 enrolled. *Faculty:* 203 full-time (114 women), 312 part-time/adjunct (171 women). Expenses: Contact institution. *Financial support:* In 2010–11, 43 research assistantships with full tuition reimbursements (averaging $7,000 per year), 6 teaching assistantships with full tuition reimbursements (averaging $7,000 per year) were awarded; Federal Work-Study, scholarships/grants, and unspecified assistantships also available. Support available to part-time students. Financial award application deadline: 3/1; financial award applicants required to submit FAFSA. In 2010, 121 master's, 74 doctorates, 74 other advanced degrees awarded. *Degree program information:* Part-time and evening/weekend programs available. Offers applied linguistics (MA); applied sociology (MA); audiology (Au D, Sc D); child advocacy (MA, Certificate); community development (Certificate); educational psychology (MA); elementary school specialization: language arts/literature 5-9 (Certificate); English (MA); French (MA, Certificate); history (MA); humanities and social sciences (MA, Au D, Sc D, Certificate); Italian (Certificate); law and governance (MA); paralegal studies (Certificate); psychology (MA); public child welfare (MA); school psychology (Certificate); social studies (Certificate); Spanish (MA, Certificate); speech-language specialist (Certificate); speech/language pathology (MA); teaching English as a second language (Certificate); teaching writing (Certificate); translation and interpretation in Spanish (Certificate). *Application deadline:* For fall admission, 6/1 for international students; for spring admission, 10/1 for international students. Applications are processed on a rolling basis. *Application fee:* $60. Electronic applications accepted. *Application Contact:* Amy Aiello, Director of Graduate Admissions and Operations, 973-655-5147, Fax: 973-655-7869, E-mail: graduate.school@montclair.edu. *Dean*, Dr. Marietta Morrissey, 973-655-4314, E-mail: morrisseym@mail.montclair.edu.

College of Science and Mathematics Students: 115 full-time (61 women), 287 part-time (184 women); includes 20 Black or African American, non-Hispanic/Latino; 17 Asian, non-Hispanic/Latino; 43 Hispanic/Latino; 2 Two or more races, non-Hispanic/Latino, 33 international. Average age 31. 166 applicants, 72% accepted, 82 enrolled. *Faculty:* 102 full-time (26 women), 98 part-time/adjunct (44 women). Expenses: Contact institution. *Financial support:* In 2010–11, 3 fellowships with full tuition reimbursements, 41 research assistantships with full tuition reimbursements (averaging $7,000 per year), 14 teaching assistantships with full tuition reimbursements (averaging $15,000 per year) were awarded; Federal Work-Study, scholarships/grants, and unspecified assistantships also available. Support available to part-time students. Financial award application deadline: 3/1; financial award applicants required to submit FAFSA. In 2010, 87 master's, 3 doctorates, 9 other advanced degrees awarded. *Degree program information:* Part-time and evening/weekend programs available. Offers biological science (Certificate); biology (MS); chemistry (MS, Certificate); CISCO (Certificate); earth science (Certificate); environmental management (MA, PhD); environmental studies (MS); geographic information science (Certificate); geoscience (MS); informatics (MS); math education (Ed D); mathematics (Certificate); molecular biology (MS, Certificate); object oriented computing (Certificate); pharmaceutical biochemistry (MS); physical science (Certificate); science and mathematics (MA, MS, Ed D, Certificate); statistics (MS); teaching middle grades math (MA, Certificate). *Application deadline:* For fall admission, 6/1 for international students; for spring admission, 10/1 for international students. Applications are processed on a rolling basis. *Application fee:* $60. Electronic applications accepted. *Application Contact:* Amy Aiello, Director of Graduate Admissions and Operations, 973-655-5147, Fax: 973-655-7869, E-mail: graduate.school@montclair.edu. *Dean*, Dr. Robert Prezant, 973-655-5108.

School of Business Students: 92 full-time (45 women), 296 part-time (124 women); includes 31 Black or African American, non-Hispanic/Latino; 35 Asian, non-Hispanic/Latino; 27 Hispanic/Latino; 1 Two or more races, non-Hispanic/Latino, 30 international. Average age 29. 209 applicants, 58% accepted, 65 enrolled. *Faculty:* 77 full-time (26 women), 39 part-time/adjunct (10 women). Expenses: Contact institution. *Financial support:* In 2010–11, 28 students received support, including 21 research assistantships with full tuition reimbursements available (averaging $7,000 per year); Federal Work-Study, scholarships/grants, and unspecified assistantships also available. Support available to part-time students. Financial award application deadline: 3/1; financial award applicants required to submit FAFSA. In 2010, 110 master's, 1 other advanced degree awarded. *Degree program information:* Part-time and evening/weekend programs available. Offers accounting (MBA, MS, Certificate); business (MBA, MS, Certificate); finance (MBA, Certificate); international business (MBA, Certificate); management (MBA, Certificate); management information systems (MBA, Certificate); marketing (MBA). *Application deadline:* For fall admission, 6/1 for international students; for spring admission, 10/1 for international students. Applications are processed on a rolling basis. *Application fee:* $60. Electronic applications accepted. *Application Contact:* Amy Aiello, Director of Graduate Admissions and Operations, 973-655-5147, Fax: 973-655-7869, E-mail: graduate.school@montclair.edu. *Dean*, Dr. E. LeBrent Chrite, 973-655-4304, E-mail: chritee@mail.montclair.edu.

School of the Arts Students: 87 full-time (57 women), 108 part-time (68 women); includes 8 Black or African American, non-Hispanic/Latino; 8 Asian, non-Hispanic/Latino; 14 Hispanic/Latino; 2 Two or more races, non-Hispanic/Latino, 13 international. Average age 31. 140 applicants, 63% accepted, 58 enrolled. *Faculty:* 73 full-time (30 women), 274 part-time/adjunct (148 women). Expenses: Contact institution. *Financial support:* In 2010–11, 13 research assistantships with full tuition reimbursements (averaging $7,000 per year) were awarded; Federal Work-Study, scholarships/grants, and unspecified assistantships also available. Support available to part-time students. Financial award application deadline: 3/1; financial award applicants required to submit FAFSA. In 2010, 57 master's, 7 other advanced degrees awarded. *Degree program information:* Part-time and evening/weekend programs available. Offers art (Certificate); arts (MA, MFA, AD, Certificate); fine arts (MA); music (AD, Certificate); music education (MA); music therapy (MA, Certificate); performance (MA, Certificate); public and organizational relations (MA); studio art (MFA); theatre (MA); theory/composition (MA). *Application deadline:* For fall admission, 2/1 for domestic students, 6/1 for international students; for spring admission, 10/1 for international students. Applications are processed on a rolling basis. *Application fee:* $60. Electronic applications accepted. *Application Contact:* Amy Aiello, Director of Graduate Admissions and Operations, 973-655-5147, Fax: 973-655-7869, E-mail: graduate.school@montclair.edu. *Dean*, Dr. Geoffrey Newman, 973-655-5104, E-mail: newmang@mail.montclair.edu.

MONTEREY INSTITUTE OF INTERNATIONAL STUDIES, Monterey, CA 93940-2691

General Information Independent, coed, graduate-only institution. *Enrollment:* 650 full-time matriculated graduate/professional students (392 women), 65 part-time matriculated graduate/professional students (44 women). *Enrollment by degree level:* 709 master's, 6 other advanced degrees. *Graduate faculty:* 61 full-time (30 women), 73 part-time/adjunct (53 women). *Tuition:* Full-time $32,000; part-time $1525 per credit hour. *Required fees:* $56. *Graduate housing:* On-campus housing not available. *Student services:* Campus employment opportunities, career counseling, exercise/wellness program, international student services, low-cost health insurance, services for students with disabilities, writing training. *Library facilities:* William Tell Coleman Library. *Online resources:* library catalog, web page, access to other libraries' catalogs. *Collection:* 105,684 titles, 519 serial subscriptions, 367 audiovisual materials.

Computer facilities: 55 computers available on campus for general student use. A campuswide network can be accessed from off campus. Online class registration is available. *Web address:* http://www.miis.edu/.

General Application Contact: Admissions Office, 831-647-4123, Fax: 831-647-6405, E-mail: admit@miis.edu.

GRADUATE UNITS

Graduate School of International Policy and Management Offers international business administration (MBA); international environmental policy (MA); international policy and management (MA, MBA, MPA); international policy studies (MA); international public administration (MPA); international trade policy (MA). Electronic applications accepted.

Graduate School of Translation, Interpretation and Language Education Offers conference interpretation (MA); teaching English to speakers of other languages (MATESOL); teaching foreign language (MATFL); translation (MA); translation and interpretation (MA); translation and localization management (MA); translation, interpretation and language education (MA, MATESOL, MATFL). Electronic applications accepted.

MONTREAT COLLEGE, Montreat, NC 28757-1267

General Information Independent-religious, coed, comprehensive institution. *Enrollment:* 1,082 graduate, professional, and undergraduate students; 231 full-time matriculated graduate/professional students (163 women), 1 part-time matriculated graduate/professional student. *Enrollment by degree level:* 232 master's. *Graduate faculty:* 5 full-time (1 woman). *Graduate housing:* On-campus housing not available. *Library facilities:* L. Nelson Bell Library. *Online resources:* library catalog, web page, access to other libraries' catalogs. *Collection:* 500,000 titles, 18,000 serial subscriptions, 2,648 audiovisual materials.

Computer facilities: 40 computers available on campus for general student use. A campuswide network can be accessed from student residence rooms and from off campus. *Web address:* http://www.montreat.edu/.

General Application Contact: Joey Higgins, Director of Enrollment Marketing and Communication, 828-669-8012 Ext. 3782, Fax: 828-669-0120, E-mail: jhiggins@montreat.edu.

GRADUATE UNITS

School of Professional and Adult Studies Students: 231 full-time (163 women), 1 part-time (0 women). Average age 34. Expenses: Contact institution. *Financial support:* Available to part-time students. Applicants required to submit FAFSA. In 2010, 117 degrees awarded. *Degree program information:* Evening/weekend programs available. Postbaccalaureate distance learning degree programs offered. Offers business administration (MBA); environmental education (MS); K-6 education (MA Ed); management and leadership (MS). *Application deadline:* Applications are processed on a rolling basis. *Application Contact:* Joey Higgins, Director of Enrollment Marketing and Communication, 828-669-8012 Ext. 3782, Fax: 818-669-0120, E-mail: jhiggins@montreat.edu.

MOODY BIBLE INSTITUTE, Chicago, IL 60610-3284

General Information Independent-religious, coed, comprehensive institution. *Graduate housing:* Rooms and/or apartments guaranteed to single students and available on a first-come, first-served basis to married students. Housing application deadline: 6/1.

GRADUATE UNITS

Graduate School *Degree program information:* Part-time programs available. Offers biblical studies (MABS, Graduate Certificate); intercultural studies (MAIS, Graduate Certificate); ministry (M Div, M Min); spiritual formation and discipleship (MASF, Graduate Certificate); urban studies (MA, Graduate Certificate).

MOORE COLLEGE OF ART & DESIGN, Philadelphia, PA 19103

General Information Independent, women only, comprehensive institution.

GRADUATE UNITS

Program in Art Education *Degree program information:* Part-time programs available. Offers art education (MA).

Program in Interior Design *Degree program information:* Evening/weekend programs available. Offers interior design (MFA).

Program in Studio Art Offers studio art (MFA).

MORAVIAN COLLEGE, Bethlehem, PA 18018-6650

General Information Independent-religious, coed, comprehensive institution. *Enrollment:* 2,034 graduate, professional, and undergraduate students; 206 part-time matriculated graduate/professional students (158 women). *Enrollment by degree level:* 206 master's. *Graduate faculty:* 12 full-time (6 women), 21 part-time/adjunct (9 women). *Tuition:* Part-time $1986 per course. Part-time tuition and fees vary according to program. *Graduate housing:* On-campus housing not available. *Student services:* Career counseling, international student services, multicultural affairs office, services for students with disabilities, teacher training, writing training. *Library facilities:* Reeves Library. *Online resources:* library catalog, web page, access to other libraries' catalogs. *Collection:* 249,308 titles, 22,946 serial subscriptions, 6,940 audiovisual materials.

Computer facilities: Computer purchase and lease plans are available. 180 computers available on campus for general student use. A campuswide network can be accessed from student residence rooms and from off campus. *Web address:* http://www.moravian.edu/.

General Application Contact: Dr. William A. Kleintop, Associate Dean for Business and Management Programs, 610-625-7704, Fax: 610-861-1466, E-mail: comenius@moravian.edu.

GRADUATE UNITS

Moravian College Comenius Center Students: 206 part-time (158 women). 81 applicants, 73% accepted, 56 enrolled. *Faculty:* 12 full-time (6 women), 21 part-time/adjunct (9 women). Expenses: Contact institution. *Financial support:* In 2010–11, 1 fellowship with full tuition reimbursement was awarded. In 2010, 25 master's awarded. *Degree program information:* Part-time and evening/weekend programs available. Offers accounting (MBA); business and management (MBA, MSHRM); curriculum and instruction (M Ed); education (M Ed); general management (MBA); health care management (MBA); human resource management (MBA); leadership (MSHRM); learning and performance management (MSHRM); nursing (MS); supply chain management (MBA). *Application deadline:* Applications are processed on a rolling basis. *Application fee:* $40. *Application Contact:* Dr. Donna G. Smith, Dean, 610-861-1400, Fax: 610-861-1466, E-mail: comenius@moravian.edu. *Dean,* Dr. Donna G. Smith, 610-861-1400, Fax: 610-861-1466, E-mail: comenius@moravian.edu.

St. Luke's School of Nursing Students: 56 part-time (55 women); includes 2 minority (1 Black or African American, non-Hispanic/Latino; 1 Asian, non-Hispanic/Latino). Average age 45. 34 applicants, 94% accepted, 31 enrolled. *Faculty:* 2 full-time (both women). Expenses: Contact institution. *Degree program information:* Part-time and evening/weekend programs available. Offers nurse administrator (MS); nurse educator (MS); nurse leadership (MS). *Application deadline:* Applications are processed on a rolling basis. *Application fee:* $40. *Application Contact:* Dr. Lori Hoffman, Director, Master of Science Program in Nursing, 610-861-1400, Fax: 610-861-1466, E-mail: comenius@moravian.edu. *Director, Master of Science Program in Nursing,* Dr. Lori Hoffman, 610-861-1400, Fax: 610-861-1466, E-mail: comenius@moravian.edu.

MORAVIAN THEOLOGICAL SEMINARY, Bethlehem, PA 18018-6614

General Information Independent-religious, coed, graduate-only institution. *Enrollment by degree level:* 36 first professional, 35 master's, 5 other advanced degrees. *Graduate faculty:* 7 full-time (3 women), 11 part-time/adjunct (5 women). *Tuition:* Full-time $13,800; part-time $3078 per semester. *Required fees:* $90 per semester. *Graduate housing:* Rooms and/or apartments available on a first-come, first-served basis to single and married students. Housing application deadline: 2/15. *Student services:* Campus employment opportunities, campus safety program, exercise/wellness program, international student services, low-cost health insurance, multicultural affairs office, services for students with disabilities, writing training. *Library facilities:* Reeves Library. *Online resources:* library catalog, web page, access to other libraries' catalogs. *Collection:* 258,693 titles, 37,875 serial subscriptions, 5,987 audiovisual materials.

Computer facilities: 170 computers available on campus for general student use. A campuswide network can be accessed from student residence rooms and from off campus. Online class registration is available. *Web address:* http://www.moravianseminary.edu/.

General Application Contact: Ann Gibson, Director of Enrollment, 610-861-1512, Fax: 610-861-1569, E-mail: agibson@moravian.edu.

GRADUATE UNITS

Graduate and Professional Programs Students: 27 full-time (12 women), 49 part-time (34 women); includes 14 minority (5 Black or African American, non-Hispanic/Latino; 1 Asian, non-Hispanic/Latino; 8 Hispanic/Latino), 2 international. Average age 45. 44 applicants, 86% accepted, 36 enrolled. *Faculty:* 7 full-time (3 women), 11 part-time/adjunct (5 women). Expenses: Contact institution. *Financial support:* In 2010–11, 72 students received support. Career-related internships or fieldwork, Federal Work-Study, and scholarships/grants available. Support available to part-time students. Financial award application deadline: 5/1; financial award applicants required to submit FAFSA. In 2010, 6 M Divs, 16 master's awarded. *Degree program information:* Part-time programs available. Offers divinity (M Div); formative spirituality (M Div, MAPC, MATS); pastoral counseling (MAPC); theological studies (MATS). *Application deadline:* For fall admission, 4/1 priority date for international students; for spring admission, 9/1 priority date for international students. Applications are processed on a rolling basis. *Application fee:* $35. *Application Contact:* Ann Gibson, Director of Enrollment, 610-861-1512, Fax: 610-861-1569, E-mail: agibson@moravian.edu. *Dean and Vice President,* Rev. Dr. Frank L. Crouch, 610-861-1516.

MOREHEAD STATE UNIVERSITY, Morehead, KY 40351

General Information State-supported, coed, comprehensive institution. *Graduate housing:* Room and/or apartments available on a first-come, first-served basis to single students; on-campus housing not available to married students. Housing application deadline: 3/12.

GRADUATE UNITS

Graduate Programs *Degree program information:* Part-time and evening/weekend programs available. Postbaccalaureate distance learning degree programs offered (minimal on-campus study). Electronic applications accepted.

Caudill College of Arts, Humanities and Social Sciences *Degree program information:* Part-time and evening/weekend programs available. Postbaccalaureate distance learning degree programs offered. Offers art education (MA); arts, humanities and social sciences (MA, MM); communication (MA); criminology (MA); English (MA); general sociology (MA); gerontology (MA); graphic design (MA); music education (MM); music performance (MM); sociology regional analysis (MA); sociology/chemical dependency (MA); studio art (MA). Electronic applications accepted.

College of Business and Public Affairs *Degree program information:* Part-time and evening/weekend programs available. Postbaccalaureate distance learning degree programs offered (minimal on-campus study). Offers business administration (MA, MBA, MSIS); business and public affairs (MA, MBA, MPA, MSIS); information systems (MSIS); public policy (MPA); sport management (MA). Electronic applications accepted.

College of Education *Degree program information:* Part-time and evening/weekend programs available. Offers adult and higher education (MA, Ed S); business and marketing education (MAT); certified professional counselor (Ed S); counseling P-12 (MA); curriculum and instruction (Ed S); education (MA, MA Ed, MAT, Ed S); educational technology (MA Ed); elementary education (MA Ed); English/language arts 5-9 (MAT); French (MAT); health P-12 (MAT); instructional leadership (Ed S); learning and behavioral disorders P-12 (MAT); mathematics 5-9 (MAT); moderate and severe disabilities P-12 (MAT); physical education P-12 (MAT); school administration (MA); school counseling (Ed S); science 5-9 (MAT); secondary biology (MAT); secondary chemistry (MAT); secondary earth science (MAT); secondary education (MA Ed); secondary English (MAT); secondary math (MAT); secondary physics (MAT); secondary social studies (MAT); social studies 5-9 (MAT); Spanish (MAT); special education (MA Ed); teacher leader business and marketing content (MA Ed); teacher leader business and marketing technology (MA Ed); teacher leader educational technology (MA Ed); teacher leader English (MA Ed); teacher leader gifted education (MA Ed); teacher leader IECE certification (MA Ed); teacher leader interdisciplinary education P-5 (MA Ed); teacher leader middle grades (MA Ed); teacher leader non IECE certification (MA Ed); teacher leader reading/writing—non-certification (MA Ed); teacher leader reading/writing certification (MA Ed); teacher leader school communication—certification (MA Ed); teacher leader school communication—non-certification (MA Ed); teacher leader social studies (MA Ed); teacher leader special education (MA Ed); teaching (MAT). Electronic applications accepted.

College of Science and Technology *Degree program information:* Part-time and evening/weekend programs available. Offers biology (MS); biology regional analysis (MS); career and technical agricultural education (MS); career and technical education (MS); clinical/counseling psychology (MS); engineering technology (MS); general/experimental psychology (MS); health/physical education (MA); science and technology (MA, MS). Electronic applications accepted.

Institute for Regional Analysis and Public Policy Offers public administration (MPA). Electronic applications accepted.

MOREHOUSE SCHOOL OF MEDICINE, Atlanta, GA 30310-1495

General Information Independent, coed, graduate-only institution. CGS member. *Enrollment by degree level:* 217 first professional, 68 master's, 31 doctoral. *Graduate faculty:* 219 full-time (109 women), 47 part-time/adjunct (22 women). *Tuition:* Full-time $33,022; part-time $600 per credit hour. *Required fees:* $4500. Tuition and fees vary according to course load, degree level, program and student level. *Graduate housing:* On-campus housing not available. *Student services:* Campus employment opportunities, career counseling, exercise/wellness program, free psychological counseling, international student services. *Library facilities:* MSM Library. *Online resources:* library catalog. *Collection:* 40,000 titles, 362 serial subscriptions, 490 audiovisual materials. *Research affiliation:* Merck & Company, Inc. (hypotension), CareStat (renal insufficiency), Wyeth (helicobacter pylori study), Bristol Myers Squibb (pharmacokinetics), Parke-Davis (cardiovascular risk factors), NitroMel, Inc. (heart failure).

Computer facilities: 160 computers available on campus for general student use. A campuswide network can be accessed from off campus. Online class registration is available. *Web address:* http://www.msm.edu/.

General Application Contact: Dr. Sterling Roaf, Director of Admissions, 404-752-1650, Fax: 404-752-1512, E-mail: sroaf@msm.edu.

GRADUATE UNITS

Graduate Programs in Biomedical Sciences Students: 31 full-time (19 women); includes 18 Black or African American, non-Hispanic/Latino. Average age 28. 21 applicants, 38% accepted, 6 enrolled. *Faculty:* 52 full-time (17 women), 7 part-time/adjunct (2 women). Expenses: Contact institution. *Financial support:* Fellowships with full and partial tuition reimbursements, career-related internships or fieldwork, institutionally sponsored loans, scholarships/grants, traineeships, health care benefits, and tuition waivers (full) available. Financial award application deadline: 5/1; financial award applicants required to submit FAFSA. In 2010, 3 doctorates awarded. Offers biomedical research (MS); biomedical sciences (PhD); biomedical technology (MS). *Application deadline:* For fall admission, 10/1 for domestic and international students; for spring admission, 2/1 for domestic and international students. *Application fee:* $50. Electronic applications accepted. *Application Contact:* Dr. Sterling Roaf, Director of Admissions, 404-752-1650, Fax: 404-752-1512, E-mail: phdadmissions@msm.edu. *Director,* Dr. Douglas Paulsen, 404-752-1559.

Master of Public Health Program Students: 54 full-time (37 women), 3 part-time (2 women); includes 33 Black or African American, non-Hispanic/Latino; 1 American Indian or Alaska Native, non-Hispanic/Latino. Average age 28. 62 applicants, 48% accepted, 29 enrolled. *Faculty:* 4 full-time (1 woman), 36 part-time/adjunct (21 women). Expenses: Contact institution. *Financial support:* In 2010–11, 32 students received support, including 6 research assistantships with partial tuition reimbursements available (averaging $10,000 per year); fellowships, teaching assistantships, career-related internships or fieldwork, Federal Work-Study, institutionally sponsored loans, scholarships/grants, and unspecified assistantships also available. Support available to part-time students. Financial award application deadline: 5/1; financial award applicants required to submit FAFSA. In 2010, 13 master's awarded. *Degree program information:* Part-time programs available. Offers epidemiology (MPH); health administration, management and policy (MPH); health education/health promotion (MPH); international health (MPH). *Application deadline:* For fall admission, 3/1 for domestic and international students. *Application fee:* $50. Electronic applications accepted. *Application Contact:* Dr. Sterling Roaf, Director of Admissions, 404-752-1650, Fax: 404-752-1512, E-mail: mphadmissions@msm.edu. *Director/Assistant Dean for Public Health Education,* Dr. Patricia Rodney, 404-752-1944, Fax: 404-752-1051, E-mail: prodney@msm.edu.

Master of Science in Clinical Research Program Students: 11 full-time (10 women); includes 9 Black or African American, non-Hispanic/Latino; 2 Asian, non-Hispanic/Latino. Average age 32. 5 applicants, 60% accepted, 3 enrolled. *Faculty:* 15 full-time (3 women), 10 part-time/adjunct (2 women). Expenses: Contact institution. *Financial support:* Applicants required to submit FAFSA. In 2010, 3 master's awarded. *Degree program information:* Part-time programs available. Offers clinical research (MS). *Application deadline:* For fall admission, 4/6 for domestic students, 4/6 priority date for international students. *Application fee:* $0. Electronic applications accepted. *Application Contact:* Dr. Sterling Roaf, Director of Admissions, 404-752-1650, Fax: 404-752-1512, E-mail: sroaf@msm.edu. *Director,* Dr. Elizabeth Ofili, 404-752-1192, E-mail: ofilie@msm.edu.

Professional Program Students: 217 full-time (133 women); includes 156 Black or African American, non-Hispanic/Latino; 22 American Indian or Alaska Native, non-Hispanic/Latino; 11 Asian, non-Hispanic/Latino; 7 Hispanic/Latino. Average age 26. 3,753 applicants, 4% accepted, 56 enrolled. *Faculty:* 220 full-time (105 women), 41 part-time/adjunct (16 women). Expenses: Contact institution. *Financial support:* In 2010–11, 200 students received support. Career-related internships or fieldwork, Federal Work-Study, institutionally sponsored loans, and scholarships/grants available. Financial award application deadline: 5/1; financial award applicants required to submit FAFSA. In 2010, 56 first professional degrees awarded. Offers medicine (MD). *Application deadline:* For fall admission, 12/1 for domestic students. Applications are processed on a rolling basis. *Application fee:* $50. Electronic applications accepted. *Application Contact:* Dr. Sterling Roaf, Director of Admissions, 404-752-1650, Fax: 404-752-

Morehouse School of Medicine (continued)

1512, E-mail: mdadmission@msm.edu. *Senior Associate Dean for Education and Faculty Affairs*, Dr. Martha Elks, 404-752-1881, Fax: 404-752-1594, E-mail: melks@msm.edu.

MORGAN STATE UNIVERSITY, Baltimore, MD 21251

General Information State-supported, coed, university. CGS member. *Graduate housing:* Rooms and/or apartments available on a first-come, first-served basis to single and married students.

GRADUATE UNITS

School of Graduate Studies *Degree program information:* Part-time and evening/weekend programs available.

Clarence M. Mitchell, Jr. School of Engineering *Degree program information:* Part-time and evening/weekend programs available. Offers civil engineering (M Eng, D Eng); electrical engineering (M Eng, D Eng); industrial engineering (M Eng, D Eng); transportation (MS).

College of Liberal Arts *Degree program information:* Part-time programs available. Offers African-American studies (MA); economics (MA); English (MA, PhD); history (MA, PhD); international studies (MA); liberal arts (MA, MS, PhD); music (MA); psychometrics (MS, PhD); sociology (MA, MS); telecommunications management (MS).

Earl G. Graves School of Business and Management *Degree program information:* Part-time and evening/weekend programs available. Offers business administration (MBA, PhD); business and management (MBA, PhD).

Institute of Architecture and Planning Offers architecture (M Arch); city and regional planning (MCRP); landscape architecture (MLA, MSLA).

School of Community Health and Policy Offers nursing (MS, PhD); public health (MPH, Dr PH).

School of Computer, Mathematical, and Natural Sciences Offers bioenvironmental science (PhD); bioinformatics (MS); biology (MS); chemistry (MS); computer, mathematical, and natural sciences (MA, MS, PhD); mathematics (MA).

School of Education and Urban Studies *Degree program information:* Part-time programs available. Offers education and urban studies (MAT, MS, MSW, Ed D, PhD); educational administration and supervision (MS); elementary and middle school education (MS); elementary education (MAT, MS); high school education (MAT); higher education administration (PhD); higher education-community college leadership (Ed D); mathematics education (MS, Ed D); middle school education (MAT); science education (MS, Ed D); social work (MSW, PhD); urban educational leadership (Ed D).

MORNINGSIDE COLLEGE, Sioux City, IA 51106

General Information Independent-religious, coed, comprehensive institution. *Graduate housing:* Rooms and/or apartments available to single and married students. Housing application deadline: 7/1. *Research affiliation:* Iowa Public Service Company (biology, chemistry, physics).

GRADUATE UNITS

Graduate Division *Degree program information:* Part-time and evening/weekend programs available. Offers professional educator (MAT); special education: instructional strategist I: mild/moderate elementary (K-6) (MAT); special education: instructional strategist II-mild/moderate secondary (7-12) (MAT); special education: K-12 instructional strategist II-behavior disorders/learning disabilities (MAT); special education: K-12 instructional strategist II-mental disabilities (MAT).

MORRISON UNIVERSITY, Reno, NV 89521

General Information Proprietary, coed, comprehensive institution. *Graduate housing:* On-campus housing not available.

GRADUATE UNITS

Graduate School *Degree program information:* Part-time and evening/weekend programs available. Electronic applications accepted.

MOUNTAIN STATE UNIVERSITY, Beckley, WV 25802-9003

General Information Independent, coed, comprehensive institution. CGS member. *Enrollment:* 5,550 graduate, professional, and undergraduate students; 611 full-time matriculated graduate/professional students (384 women), 53 part-time matriculated graduate/professional students (41 women). *Enrollment by degree level:* 629 master's, 35 doctoral. *Graduate faculty:* 26 full-time (16 women), 30 part-time/adjunct (11 women). *Tuition:* Full-time $4800; part-time $400 per credit hour. *Required fees:* $2250; $2250 per credit hour. Tuition and fees vary according to degree level and program. *Graduate housing:* Room and/or apartments available on a first-come, first-served basis to single students; on-campus housing not available to married students. Typical cost: $4750 per year ($7990 including board). Room and board charges vary according to board plan and housing facility selected. *Student services:* Campus employment opportunities, campus safety program, career counseling, exercise/wellness program, grant writing training, international student services, multicultural affairs office, services for students with disabilities, writing training. *Library facilities:* Mountain State University Library. *Online resources:* library catalog. *Collection:* 133,365 titles, 157 serial subscriptions, 4,913 audiovisual materials.

Computer facilities: Computer purchase and lease plans are available. 230 computers available on campus for general student use. A campuswide network can be accessed from student residence rooms and from off campus. Online class registration is available. *Web address:* http://www.mountainstate.edu/.

General Application Contact: Anita Diaz, Coordinator of Graduate Academic Services, 304-929-1731, Fax: 304-929-1710, E-mail: adiaz@mountainstate.edu.

GRADUATE UNITS

Program in Nursing Students: 99 full-time (93 women), 17 part-time (16 women); includes 12 minority (7 Black or African American, non-Hispanic/Latino; 1 American Indian or Alaska Native, non-Hispanic/Latino; 4 Asian, non-Hispanic/Latino), 3 international. Average age 38. 128 applicants, 32% accepted, 40 enrolled. *Faculty:* 5 full-time (all women), 4 part-time/adjunct (all women). Expenses: Contact institution. *Financial support:* Federal Work-Study, scholarships/grants, and unspecified assistantships available. Support available to part-time students. Financial award applicants required to submit FAFSA. In 2010, 31 master's awarded. *Degree program information:* Part-time programs available. Postbaccalaureate distance learning degree programs offered (minimal on-campus study). Offers administration/education (MSN); family nurse practitioner (MSN). *Application deadline:* For spring admission, 6/30 for domestic and international students. Applications are processed on a rolling basis. *Application fee:* $25 ($50 for international students). Electronic applications accepted. *Application Contact:* Misty Okes, Program Specialist, 304-461-3495, Fax: 304-929-1601, E-mail: mokes@mountainstate.edu. *Dean, School of Health Sciences*, Dr. Sheila Garland, 304-929-1516, Fax: 304-929-1601, E-mail: sgarland@mountainstate.edu.

School of Graduate Studies Students: 611 full-time (384 women), 53 part-time (41 women); includes 76 Black or African American, non-Hispanic/Latino; 3 American Indian or Alaska Native, non-Hispanic/Latino; 12 Asian, non-Hispanic/Latino; 24 Hispanic/Latino, 14 international. Average age 37. 911 applicants, 36% accepted, 243 enrolled. *Faculty:* 26 full-time (16 women), 30 part-time/adjunct (11 women). Expenses: Contact institution. *Financial support:* Career-related internships or fieldwork, Federal Work-Study, scholarships/grants, tuition waivers (partial), and unspecified assistantships available. Support available to part-time students. Financial award applicants required to submit FAFSA. In 2010, 372 master's awarded. *Degree program information:* Part-time and evening/weekend programs available. Postbaccalaureate distance learning degree programs offered (no on-campus study). Offers criminal justice administration (MCJA); executive leadership (DEL); health science (MHS); interdisciplinary studies (MA, MS); physician assistant (MSPA); psychology (MA); strategic leadership (MSSL). *Application deadline:* For fall admission, 5/31 priority date for domestic and international students. Applications are processed on a rolling basis. *Application fee:* $25 ($50 for international students). Electronic applications accepted. *Application Contact:* Anita Diaz, Enrollment Coordinator of Graduate Studies, 304-929-1731, Fax: 304-929-1710, E-mail: adiaz@mountainstate.edu. *Interim Dean, School of Graduate Studies/Dean, School of Leadership and Professional Development*, Dr. William White, 304-929-1658, Fax: 304-929-1637, E-mail: wwhite@mountainstate.edu.

MOUNT ALLISON UNIVERSITY, Sackville, NB E4L 1E4, Canada

General Information Province-supported, coed, comprehensive institution. *Graduate housing:* Room and/or apartments available to single students; on-campus housing not available to married students. Housing application deadline: 5/15. *Research affiliation:* Huntsman Marine Science Centre (marine biology), Atlantic Cancer Institute (medical research), Moncton Hospital (medical research).

GRADUATE UNITS

Department of Biology Offers biology (M Sc).

Department of Chemistry Offers chemistry (M Sc).

MOUNT ALOYSIUS COLLEGE, Cresson, PA 16630-1999

General Information Independent-religious, coed, comprehensive institution.

GRADUATE UNITS

Criminal Justice Management in Correctional Administration Program Offers criminal justice management in correctional administration (MA). Electronic applications accepted.

Masters in Business Administration Program *Degree program information:* Part-time and evening/weekend programs available. Offers business administration (MBA). Electronic applications accepted.

Program in Community Counseling *Degree program information:* Part-time programs available. Offers community counseling (MS).

Program in Education *Degree program information:* Part-time programs available. Offers education (MS).

Program in Psychology Offers psychology (MS).

MOUNT ANGEL SEMINARY, Saint Benedict, OR 97373

General Information Independent-religious, Undergraduate: men only; graduate: coed, comprehensive institution. *Graduate housing:* Room and/or apartments guaranteed to single students; on-campus housing not available to married students.

GRADUATE UNITS

Program in Theology *Degree program information:* Part-time programs available. Offers theology (M Div, MA).

MOUNT CARMEL COLLEGE OF NURSING, Columbus, OH 43222

General Information Independent, coed, primarily women, comprehensive institution. *Enrollment:* 818 graduate, professional, and undergraduate students; 15 full-time matriculated graduate/professional students (all women), 57 part-time matriculated graduate/professional students (54 women). *Enrollment by degree level:* 20 first professional, 50 master's, 2 other advanced degrees. *Graduate faculty:* 10 full-time (all women), 7 part-time/adjunct (5 women). *Tuition:* Full-time $6435; part-time $390 per credit. *Graduate housing:* Room and/or apartments available on a first-come, first-served basis to single students; on-campus housing not available to married students. Typical cost: $4500 per year. Housing application deadline: 4/1. *Student services:* Free psychological counseling, grant writing training, multicultural affairs office, teacher training, writing training. *Library facilities:* The Mount Carmel Health Sciences Library. *Online resources:* library catalog, web page, access to other libraries' catalogs. *Collection:* 31,850 titles, 781 serial subscriptions, 596 audiovisual materials.

Computer facilities: 70 computers available on campus for general student use. A campuswide network can be accessed from off campus. Online class registration is available. *Web address:* http://www.mccn.edu/.

General Application Contact: Elsie Sexton, Program Coordinator, 614-234-5169, Fax: 614-234-2875, E-mail: ksexton@mccn.edu.

GRADUATE UNITS

Nursing Program Students: 15 full-time (all women), 57 part-time (54 women); includes 7 minority (5 Black or African American, non-Hispanic/Latino; 1 Asian, non-Hispanic/Latino; 1 Native Hawaiian or other Pacific Islander, non-Hispanic/Latino). Average age 40. 20 applicants, 100% accepted, 20 enrolled. *Faculty:* 10 full-time (all women), 7 part-time/adjunct (5 women). Expenses: Contact institution. *Financial support:* In 2010–11, 3 students received support. Institutionally sponsored loans and scholarships/grants available. Financial award application deadline: 7/1; financial award applicants required to submit FAFSA. In 2010, 11 master's awarded. *Degree program information:* Part-time programs available. Offers adult health CNS (clinical nurse specialist) (MS); family nurse practitioner (MS); nursing administration (MS); nursing education (MS). *Application deadline:* For fall admission, 6/15 priority date for domestic students; for winter admission, 11/1 priority date for domestic students. Applications are processed on a rolling basis. *Application fee:* $30. *Application Contact:* Elsie Sexton, Program Coordinator, 614-234-5169, Fax: 614-234-2875, E-mail: ksexton@mccn.edu. *Associate Dean*, Dr. Angela Phillips-Lowe, 614-234-5717, Fax: 614-234-2875, E-mail: aphillips-lowe@mccn.edu.

MOUNT HOLYOKE COLLEGE, South Hadley, MA 01075

General Information Independent, women only, comprehensive institution.

GRADUATE UNITS

Department of Psychology and Education Offers psychology and education (MA).

MOUNT IDA COLLEGE, Newton, MA 02459-3310

General Information Independent, coed, comprehensive institution. *Graduate housing:* On-campus housing not available.

GRADUATE UNITS

Program in Interior Design *Degree program information:* Part-time and evening/weekend programs available. Postbaccalaureate distance learning degree programs offered (minimal on-campus study). Offers interior design (MSM). Electronic applications accepted.

Program in Management *Degree program information:* Part-time and evening/weekend programs available. Postbaccalaureate distance learning degree programs offered (minimal on-campus study). Offers management (MSM). Electronic applications accepted.

MOUNT MARTY COLLEGE, Yankton, SD 57078-3724

General Information Independent-religious, coed, comprehensive institution. *Graduate housing:* On-campus housing not available.

GRADUATE UNITS

Graduate Studies Division Offers business administration (MBA); nurse anesthesia (MS); nursing (MSN); pastoral ministries (MPM). Electronic applications accepted.

MOUNT MARY COLLEGE, Milwaukee, WI 53222-4597

General Information Independent-religious, Undergraduate: women only; graduate: coed, comprehensive institution. CGS member. *Graduate housing:* Room and/or apartments available on a first-come, first-served basis to single students; on-campus housing not available to married students.

GRADUATE UNITS

Graduate Programs *Degree program information:* Part-time and evening/weekend programs available. Offers administrative dietetics (MS); art therapy (MS); business administration (MBA); clinical dietetics (MS); community counseling (MS); education (MA); English (MA); nutrition education (MS); occupational therapy (MS); pastoral counseling (MS); professional development (MA); school counseling (MS). Electronic applications accepted.

MOUNT MERCY UNIVERSITY, Cedar Rapids, IA 52402-4797

General Information Independent-religious, coed, comprehensive institution.

GRADUATE UNITS

Program in Business Administration *Degree program information:* Evening/weekend programs available. Offers business administration (MBA). Electronic applications accepted.

Program in Education Offers reading (MA Ed); special education (MA Ed). Electronic applications accepted.

MOUNT SAINT MARY COLLEGE, Newburgh, NY 12550-3494

General Information Independent, coed, comprehensive institution. *Enrollment:* 2,700 graduate, professional, and undergraduate students; 98 full-time matriculated graduate/professional students (68 women), 289 part-time matriculated graduate/professional students (227 women). *Enrollment by degree level:* 383 master's, 4 other advanced degrees. *Graduate faculty:* 24 full-time (18 women), 20 part-time/adjunct (12 women). *Tuition:* Full-time $13,356; part-time $742 per credit. *Required fees:* $70 per semester. *Graduate housing:* On-campus housing not available. *Student services:* Campus employment opportunities, campus safety program, career counseling, free psychological counseling, international student services. *Library facilities:* Curtin Memorial Library plus 1 other. *Online resources:* library catalog, web page, access to other libraries' catalogs. *Collection:* 125,362 titles, 63,941 serial subscriptions, 8,344 audiovisual materials.

Computer facilities: Computer purchase and lease plans are available. 586 computers available on campus for general student use. A campuswide network can be accessed from student residence rooms and from off campus. Online class registration, Intranet are available. *Web address:* http://www.msmc.edu/.

General Application Contact: Courtney McDermott, Graduate Recruiter, 845-569-3402, Fax: 845-569-3450, E-mail: courtney.mcdermott@msmc.edu.

GRADUATE UNITS

Division of Business Students: 35 full-time (21 women), 52 part-time (31 women); includes 20 minority (4 Black or African American, non-Hispanic/Latino; 4 Asian, non-Hispanic/Latino; 10 Hispanic/Latino; 2 Two or more races, non-Hispanic/Latino), 20 international. Average age 30. 22 applicants, 95% accepted, 10 enrolled. *Faculty:* 5 full-time (1 woman), 6 part-time/adjunct (2 women). Expenses: Contact institution. *Financial support:* In 2010–11, 25 students received support. Unspecified assistantships available. Financial award application deadline: 4/15; financial award applicants required to submit FAFSA. In 2010, 45 master's awarded. *Degree program information:* Part-time and evening/weekend programs available. Offers business (MBA); financial planning (MBA). *Application deadline:* Applications are processed on a rolling basis. *Application fee:* $45. *Application Contact:* Kathryn Sharp, Secretary, 845-569-3582, Fax: 845-569-3885, E-mail: ksharp@msmc.edu. *Graduate Coordinator*, Dr. James Gearity, 845-569-3121, Fax: 845-562-6762, E-mail: james.gearity@msmc.edu.

Division of Education Students: 63 full-time (47 women), 193 part-time (156 women); includes 25 minority (6 Black or African American, non-Hispanic/Latino; 1 Asian, non-Hispanic/Latino; 18 Hispanic/Latino). Average age 30. 91 applicants, 55% accepted, 33 enrolled. *Faculty:* 16 full-time (14 women), 12 part-time/adjunct (8 women). Expenses: Contact institution. *Financial support:* In 2010–11, 140 students received support. Unspecified assistantships available. Financial award application deadline: 4/15; financial award applicants required to submit FAFSA. In 2010, 131 master's awarded. *Degree program information:* Part-time and evening/weekend programs available. Offers adolescence and special education (MS Ed); adolescence education (MS Ed); childhood and special education (MS Ed); childhood education (MS Ed); literacy (5-12) (Advanced Certificate); literacy (birth-6) (Advanced Certificate); literacy and special education (MS Ed); literacy/childhood (MS Ed); middle school (5-6) (MS Ed); middle school (7-9) (MS Ed); special education (1-6) (MS Ed); special education (7-12) (MS Ed). *Application deadline:* Applications are processed on a rolling basis. *Application fee:* $45. *Application Contact:* Theresa Brundage, 845-569-3525, Fax: 845-569-3551, E-mail: theresa@msmc.edu. *Coordinator*, Dr. Theresa Lewis, 845-569-3149, Fax: 845-569-3535, E-mail: tlewis@msmc.edu.

Division of Nursing Students: 44 part-time (40 women); includes 12 minority (6 Black or African American, non-Hispanic/Latino; 2 Asian, non-Hispanic/Latino; 4 Hispanic/Latino). Average age 39. 19 applicants, 100% accepted, 9 enrolled. *Faculty:* 3 full-time (all women), 2 part-time/adjunct (both women). Expenses: Contact institution. *Financial support:* In 2010–11, 12 students received support. Unspecified assistantships available. Financial award application deadline: 4/15; financial award applicants required to submit FAFSA. In 2010, 13 master's, 2 other advanced degrees awarded. *Degree program information:* Part-time and evening/weekend programs available. Offers adult nurse practitioner (MS, Advanced Certificate); clinical nurse specialist-adult health (MS); family nurse practitioner (Advanced Certificate). *Application deadline:* For fall admission, 6/3 priority date for domestic students; for spring admission, 10/31 priority date for domestic students. Applications are processed on a rolling basis. *Application fee:* $45. *Application Contact:* Graduate Coordinator, 845-561-0800, Fax: 845-562-6762. *Coordinator*, Dr. Karen Baldwin, 845-569-3512, Fax: 845-562-6762, E-mail: baldwin@msmc.edu.

MOUNT ST. MARY'S COLLEGE, Los Angeles, CA 90049-1599

General Information Independent-religious, coed, primarily women, comprehensive institution. *Graduate housing:* On-campus housing not available.

GRADUATE UNITS

Graduate Division *Degree program information:* Part-time and evening/weekend programs available. Offers administrative services (MS); business administration (MBA); clinical nurse specialist/adult health (MS); community health (MS); counseling psychology (MS); educator (MS); elementary education (MS); humanities (MA); instructional leadership (MS); leadership and administration (MS); marriage and family therapy (MS); nursing (MS); physical therapy (DPT); psychology (MS); religious studies (MA); secondary education (MS); special education (MS). Electronic applications accepted.

MOUNT ST. MARY'S UNIVERSITY, Emmitsburg, MD 21727-7799

General Information Independent-religious, coed, comprehensive institution. *Enrollment:* 2,112 graduate, professional, and undergraduate students; 231 full-time matriculated graduate/professional students (48 women), 246 part-time matriculated graduate/professional students (122 women). *Enrollment by degree level:* 117 first professional, 356 master's, 4 other advanced degrees. *Graduate faculty:* 32 full-time (8 women), 17 part-time/adjunct (10 women). *Tuition:* Full-time $8640; part-time $480 per credit hour. Tuition and fees vary according to program. *Graduate housing:* Room and/or apartments available on a first-come, first-served basis to single students; on-campus housing not available to married students. Typical cost: $5044 per year ($10,308 including board). Room and board charges vary according to board plan. *Student services:* Campus employment opportunities, campus safety program, career counseling, exercise/wellness program, free psychological counseling, international student services, low-cost health insurance, multicultural affairs office, services for students with disabilities, teacher training, writing training. *Library facilities:* Phillips Library. *Online resources:* library catalog, web page, access to other libraries' catalogs. *Collection:* 218,264 titles, 510 serial subscriptions, 3,816 audiovisual materials.

Computer facilities: 100 computers available on campus for general student use. A campuswide network can be accessed from student residence rooms. Online class registration, tuition payment, course management system are available. *Web address:* http://www.msmary.edu/.

General Application Contact: Joseph Lebherz, Director, Center for Professional and Continuing Studies, 301-682-8315, Fax: 301-682-5247, E-mail: lebherz@msmary.edu.

GRADUATE UNITS

Graduate Seminary Students: 148 full-time (0 women), 3 part-time (1 woman); includes 9 minority (1 Black or African American, non-Hispanic/Latino; 3 Asian, non-Hispanic/Latino; 5 Hispanic/Latino), 18 international. Average age 29. 67 applicants, 97% accepted, 54 enrolled. *Faculty:* 12 full-time (0 women), 5 part-time/adjunct (3 women). Expenses: Contact institution. *Financial support:* Career-related internships or fieldwork and scholarships/grants available. Financial award applicants required to submit FAFSA. In 2010, 26 first professional degrees, 12 master's awarded. Offers theology (M Div, MA). *Application deadline:* For fall admission, 8/1 for domestic and international students. *Application fee:* $0. *Application Contact:* Susan Nield, Seminary Admissions, 301-447-7423, Fax: 301-447-7402, E-mail: nield@msmary.edu. *Vice President/Rector*, Rev. Steven P. Rohlfs, 301-447-5295, Fax: 301-447-5636, E-mail: rohlfs@msmary.edu.

Program in Business Administration Students: 45 full-time (21 women), 182 part-time (76 women); includes 31 minority (15 Black or African American, non-Hispanic/Latino; 6 Asian, non-Hispanic/Latino; 8 Hispanic/Latino; 2 Two or more races, non-Hispanic/Latino), 9 international. Average age 31. 101 applicants, 78% accepted, 79 enrolled. *Faculty:* 12 full-time (4 women), 7 part-time/adjunct (2 women). Expenses: Contact institution. *Financial support:* Career-related internships or fieldwork and unspecified assistantships available. Financial award applicants required to submit FAFSA. In 2010, 107 master's awarded. *Degree program information:* Part-time and evening/weekend programs available. Offers business administration (MBA). *Application deadline:* Applications are processed on a rolling basis. *Application fee:* $35. *Application Contact:* Dr. William Forgang, Dean, School of Business, 301-447-5326, Fax: 301-447-5335, E-mail: mbareq@msmary.edu. *Dean, School of Business*, Dr. William Forgang, 301-447-5326, Fax: 301-447-5335, E-mail: mbareq@msmary.edu.

Program in Education Students: 37 full-time (27 women), 58 part-time (45 women); includes 3 minority (1 Black or African American, non-Hispanic/Latino; 1 Asian, non-Hispanic/Latino; 1 Hispanic/Latino), 1 international. Average age 34. 22 applicants, 100% accepted, 22 enrolled. *Faculty:* 5 full-time (3 women), 5 part-time/adjunct (all women). Expenses: Contact institution. *Financial support:* Career-related internships or fieldwork and unspecified assistantships available. Financial award applicants required to submit FAFSA. In 2010, 23 master's awarded. *Degree program information:* Part-time and evening/weekend programs available. Offers education (M Ed, MAT). *Application deadline:* For fall admission, 8/15 for domestic and international students. Applications are processed on a rolling basis. *Application fee:* $35. *Application Contact:* Dr. Barbara Martin-Palmer, Dean of School of Education and Human Services, 301-447-5371, Fax: 301-447-5250, E-mail: gradeducation@msmary.edu. *Dean of School of Education and Human Services*, Dr. Barbara Martin-Palmer, 301-447-5371, Fax: 301-447-5250, E-mail: gradeducation@msmary.edu.

Program in Philosophical Studies Students: 1 full-time (0 women), 3 part-time (0 women). Average age 30. *Faculty:* 4 full-time (1 woman). Expenses: Contact institution. *Financial support:* Unspecified assistantships available. Financial award applicants required to submit FAFSA. In 2010, 3 master's awarded. *Degree program information:* Part-time programs available. Offers philosophical studies (MA). *Application Contact:* Dr. Christopher Anadale, Director, 301-447-5368 Ext. 4307, E-mail: anadale@msmary.edu. *Director*, Dr. Christopher Anadale, 301-447-5368 Ext. 4307, E-mail: anadale@msmary.edu.

MOUNT SAINT VINCENT UNIVERSITY, Halifax, NS B3M 2J6, Canada

General Information Province-supported, coed, primarily women, comprehensive institution. *Graduate housing:* Room and/or apartments available on a first-come, first-served basis to single students; on-campus housing not available to married students. Housing application deadline: 5/15.

GRADUATE UNITS

Graduate Programs *Degree program information:* Part-time and evening/weekend programs available. Postbaccalaureate distance learning degree programs offered (minimal on-campus study). Offers applied human nutrition (M Sc AHN, MAHN); child and youth study (MA); family studies and gerontology (MA); women's studies (MA). Electronic applications accepted.

Faculty of Education *Degree program information:* Part-time and evening/weekend programs available. Postbaccalaureate distance learning degree programs offered (minimal on-campus study). Offers adult education (M Ed, MA Ed, MA-R); curriculum studies (M Ed, MA Ed, MA-R); education of the blind or visually impaired (M Ed, MA Ed); education of the deaf or hard of hearing (M Ed, MA Ed); education of young adolescents (M Ed, MA Ed, MA-R); educational foundations (M Ed, MA Ed, MA-R); educational psychology (M Ed, MA Ed, MA-R); elementary education (M Ed, MA Ed, MA-R); general studies (M Ed, MA Ed, MA-R); human relations (M Ed, MA Ed); literacy education (M Ed, MA Ed, MA-R); school psychology (MASP); teaching English as a second language (M Ed, MA Ed, MA-R). Electronic applications accepted.

MOUNT SINAI SCHOOL OF MEDICINE, New York, NY 10029-6504

General Information Independent, coed, graduate-only institution. *Enrollment by degree level:* 588 first professional, 185 master's, 253 doctoral. *Graduate faculty:* 1,843 full-time. *Tuition:* Full-time $25,600; part-time $800 per credit hour. *Required fees:* $1600. Full-time tuition and fees vary according to program. *Graduate housing:* Rooms and/or apartments guaranteed to single and married students. Typical cost: $6936 per year for single students; $13,210 per year for married students. Housing application deadline: 6/1. *Student services:* Campus employment opportunities, campus safety program, career counseling, exercise/wellness program, free psychological counseling, grant writing training, international student services, low-cost health insurance, multicultural affairs office, services for students with disabilities, teacher training, writing training. *Library facilities:* Levy Library. *Online resources:* library catalog, web page. *Collection:* 156,000 titles, 2,600 serial subscriptions.

Computer facilities: 120 computers available on campus for general student use. A campuswide network can be accessed from student residence rooms and from off campus. Online class registration is available. *Web address:* http://www.mssm.edu/.

General Application Contact: Jessica Maysonet, Assistant Director, Admissions, 212-241-6696, Fax: 212-876-4658, E-mail: admissions@mssm.edu.

GRADUATE UNITS

The Bioethics Program Expenses: Contact institution. Offers bioethics (MS). Program offered jointly with Union Graduate College. *Application Contact:* Dr. Rosamond Rhodes, Director, 212-241-3757, E-mail: rosamond.rhodes@mssm.edu. *Director*, Dr. Rosamond Rhodes, 212-241-3757, E-mail: rosamond.rhodes@mssm.edu.

Department of Medical Education Students: 588 full-time (290 women); includes 241 minority (34 Black or African American, non-Hispanic/Latino; 6 American Indian or Alaska Native, non-Hispanic/Latino; 122 Asian, non-Hispanic/Latino; 67 Hispanic/Latino; 2 Native Hawaiian or other Pacific Islander, non-Hispanic/Latino; 10 Two or more races, non-Hispanic/Latino), 21 international. Average age 24. 6,814 applicants, 5% accepted, 140 enrolled. *Faculty:* 1,843 full-time. Expenses: Contact institution. *Financial support:* In 2010–11, 403 students received support. Career-related internships or fieldwork, Federal Work-Study, institutionally sponsored loans, and scholarships/grants available. Financial award application deadline: 4/30; financial award applicants required to submit FAFSA. In 2010, 127 first professional degrees awarded. Offers medical education (MD). *Application deadline:* For fall admission, 11/15 for domestic and international students. *Application fee:* $105. Electronic applications accepted. *Application Contact:* Jessica Maysonet, Assistant Director of Admissions, 212-241-2260, Fax: 212-828-4135, E-mail: jessica.maysonet@mssm.edu. *Dean*, Dr. David Muller, 212-241-8716, Fax: 212-369-6013, E-mail: david.muller@mssm.edu.

Graduate School of Biological Sciences Students: 438 full-time (260 women); includes 29 Black or African American, non-Hispanic/Latino; 3 American Indian or Alaska Native, non-Hispanic/Latino; 86 Asian, non-Hispanic/Latino; 18 Hispanic/Latino, 99 international. 924 applicants, 29% accepted, 104 enrolled. *Faculty:* 126 full-time (40 women). Expenses: Contact institution. *Financial support:* In 2010–11, fellowships with full tuition reimbursements (averaging $32,000 per year), research assistantships with full tuition reimbursements (averaging $32,000 per year) were awarded; Federal Work-Study, institutionally sponsored loans, scholarships/grants, health care benefits, and unspecified assistantships also available. Financial award application deadline: 4/30; financial award applicants required to submit FAFSA. In 2010, 58 master's, 36 doctorates awarded. Offers biomedical sciences (MS, PhD); clinical research education (MS, PhD); community medicine (MPH); genetic counseling (MS); neurosciences (PhD). *Application deadline:* For fall admission, 12/15 for domestic and inter-

Mount Sinai School of Medicine (continued)

national students. Applications are processed on a rolling basis. *Application fee:* $80. Electronic applications accepted. *Application Contact:* Lily Recanati, Manager, 212-241-2793, Fax: 212-241-0651, E-mail: lily.recantati@mssm.edu. *Dean*, Dr. John Morrison, 212-241-6546, Fax: 212-241-0651, E-mail: john.morrison@mssm.edu.

MOUNT VERNON NAZARENE UNIVERSITY, Mount Vernon, OH 43050-9500

General Information Independent-religious, coed, comprehensive institution. *Graduate housing:* On-campus housing not available.

GRADUATE UNITS

Department of Education *Degree program information:* Part-time and evening/weekend programs available. Offers education (MA Ed); professional educator's license (MA Ed).

Program in Management *Degree program information:* Part-time and evening/weekend programs available. Offers management (MSM).

Program in Ministry *Degree program information:* Part-time and evening/weekend programs available. Offers ministry (M Min).

MULTNOMAH UNIVERSITY, Portland, OR 97220-5898

General Information Independent-religious, coed, comprehensive institution. *Enrollment:* 907 graduate, professional, and undergraduate students; 226 full-time matriculated graduate/professional students (93 women), 83 part-time matriculated graduate/professional students (32 women). *Enrollment by degree level:* 141 first professional, 139 master's, 29 other advanced degrees. *Graduate faculty:* 13 full-time (7 women), 32 part-time/adjunct (11 women). *Tuition:* Part-time $485 per credit. *Graduate housing:* Rooms and/or apartments available on a first-come, first-served basis to single and married students. Housing application deadline: 7/15. *Student services:* Campus employment opportunities, career counseling, free psychological counseling, international student services. *Library facilities:* John Mitchell Library. *Online resources:* library catalog, access to other libraries' catalogs. *Collection:* 110,838 titles, 347 serial subscriptions, 7,116 audiovisual materials.

Computer facilities: 44 computers available on campus for general student use. A campuswide network can be accessed from student residence rooms and from off campus. Online class registration is available. *Web address:* http://www.multnomah.edu/.

General Application Contact: Jennifer Hancock, Graduate Studies and Seminary Admissions Counselor, 503-251-6485, Fax: 503-254-1268, E-mail: admiss@multnomah.edu.

GRADUATE UNITS

Multnomah Bible College Graduate Degree Programs Students: 77 full-time (54 women), 24 part-time (16 women); includes 10 minority (1 Black or African American, non-Hispanic/Latino; 1 American Indian or Alaska Native, non-Hispanic/Latino; 5 Asian, non-Hispanic/Latino; 3 Hispanic/Latino). Average age 35. 58 applicants, 42 enrolled. *Faculty:* 5 full-time (all women), 19 part-time/adjunct (9 women). Expenses: Contact institution. *Financial support:* Career-related internships or fieldwork and scholarships/grants available. Support available to part-time students. Financial award application deadline: 7/1; financial award applicants required to submit FAFSA. In 2010, 14 master's awarded. Offers counseling (MA); teaching (MA); TESOL (MA). *Application deadline:* For fall admission, 7/15 for domestic and international students; for spring admission, 11/15 for domestic and international students. *Application fee:* $40. *Application Contact:* Jennifer Hancock, Seminary Admissions Counselor, 503-251-6481, Fax: 503-254-1268, E-mail: admiss@multnomah.edu. *Academic Dean*, Dr. Wayne Strickland, 503-251-6401.

Multnomah Biblical Seminary Students: 149 full-time (39 women), 59 part-time (16 women); includes 31 minority (10 Black or African American, non-Hispanic/Latino; 1 American Indian or Alaska Native, non-Hispanic/Latino; 10 Asian, non-Hispanic/Latino; 8 Hispanic/Latino; 1 Native Hawaiian or other Pacific Islander, non-Hispanic/Latino; 1 Two or more races, non-Hispanic/Latino), 11 international. Average age 35. 120 applicants, 76 enrolled. *Faculty:* 8 full-time (2 women), 13 part-time/adjunct (2 women). Expenses: Contact institution. *Financial support:* In 2010–11, 153 students received support. Career-related internships or fieldwork and scholarships/grants available. Support available to part-time students. Financial award application deadline: 7/1; financial award applicants required to submit FAFSA. In 2010, 31 first professional degrees, 19 master's, 31 other advanced degrees awarded. *Degree program information:* Part-time programs available. Offers theology (M Div, MABS, MAPS, Th M, Certificate). *Application deadline:* For fall admission, 7/15 priority date for domestic and international students; for spring admission, 11/15 priority date for domestic and international students. Applications are processed on a rolling basis. *Application fee:* $40. *Application Contact:* Jeffrey Mattson, Seminary Admissions Counselor, 503-251-6485, Fax: 503-254-1268, E-mail: admiss@multnomah.edu. *Dean*, Dr. Robert R. Redman, 503-255-0332, Fax: 503-251-6444, E-mail: rredman@multnomah.edu.

MURRAY STATE UNIVERSITY, Murray, KY 42071

General Information State-supported, coed, comprehensive institution. *Graduate housing:* Rooms and/or apartments available on a first-come, first-served basis to single and married students.

GRADUATE UNITS

College of Business and Public Affairs *Degree program information:* Part-time and evening/weekend programs available. Offers business administration (MBA); business and public affairs (MA, MBA, MPAC, MS); economics (MS); mass communications (MA, MS); organizational communication (MA, MS); professional accountancy (MPAC); telecommunications systems management (MS).

College of Education *Degree program information:* Part-time programs available. Offers advanced learning behavior disorders (MA Ed); community and agency counseling (Ed S); early childhood education (MA Ed); education (MA Ed, MS, Ed D, PhD, Ed S); elementary education (MA Ed, Ed S); elementary education/reading and writing (MA Ed, Ed S); health, physical education, and recreation (MA); human development and leadership (MS); industrial and technical education (MS); learning disabilities (MA Ed); middle school education (MA Ed, Ed S); moderate/severe disorders (MA Ed); reading and writing (MA Ed); school administration (MA Ed, Ed S); school guidance and counseling (MA Ed, Ed S); secondary education (MA Ed, Ed S); special education (MA Ed). PhD, Ed D offered jointly with University of Kentucky.

College of Health Sciences and Human Services *Degree program information:* Part-time programs available. Offers clinical nurse specialist (MSN); environmental science (MS); exercise and leisure studies (MS); family nurse practitioner (MSN); health sciences and human services (MS, MSN); industrial hygiene (MS); nurse anesthesia (MSN); safety management (MS); speech-language pathology (MS).

College of Humanities and Fine Arts *Degree program information:* Part-time programs available. Offers clinical psychology (MA, MS); creative writing (MFA); English (MA); history (MA); humanities and fine arts (MA, MFA, MME, MPA, MS); music education (MME); psychology (MA, MS); public administration (MPA); public affairs (MPA); teaching English to speakers of other languages (MA).

College of Science, Engineering and Technology *Degree program information:* Part-time programs available. Offers biological sciences (MAT, MS, PhD); chemistry (MS); geosciences (MS); management of technology (MS); mathematics (MA, MAT, MS); science, engineering and technology (MA, MAT, MS, PhD); water science (MS).

School of Agriculture *Degree program information:* Evening/weekend programs available. Postbaccalaureate distance learning degree programs offered (minimal on-campus study). Offers agriculture (MS); agriculture education (MS).

MUSKINGUM UNIVERSITY, New Concord, OH 43762

General Information Independent-religious, coed, comprehensive institution. *Graduate housing:* On-campus housing not available.

GRADUATE UNITS

Graduate Programs in Education *Degree program information:* Part-time programs available. Offers education (MAE, MAT).

NAROPA UNIVERSITY, Boulder, CO 80302-6697

General Information Independent, coed, comprehensive institution. *Enrollment:* 1,082 graduate, professional, and undergraduate students; 437 full-time matriculated graduate/professional students (289 women), 181 part-time matriculated graduate/professional students (132 women). *Enrollment by degree level:* 618 master's. *Graduate faculty:* 34 full-time (17 women), 71 part-time/adjunct (47 women). *Tuition:* Full-time $17,820; part-time $810 per credit. *Required fees:* $305 per semester. Tuition and fees vary according to course load, program and reciprocity agreements. *Graduate housing:* Rooms and/or apartments available on a first-come, first-served basis to single and married students. Typical cost: $8010 per year for single students; $8010 per year for married students. Room charges vary according to housing facility selected. Housing application deadline: 6/15. *Student services:* Campus employment opportunities, campus safety program, career counseling, free psychological counseling, international student services, low-cost health insurance, multicultural affairs office, services for students with disabilities, writing training. *Library facilities:* Allen Ginsberg Library. *Online resources:* library catalog, web page. *Collection:* 28,655 titles, 80 serial subscriptions, 5,784 audiovisual materials.

Computer facilities: 77 computers available on campus for general student use. A campuswide network can be accessed from student residence rooms and from off campus. Online class registration is available. *Web address:* http://www.naropa.edu/.

General Application Contact: Office of Admissions, 303-546-3572, Fax: 303-546-3583, E-mail: admissions@naropa.edu.

GRADUATE UNITS

Graduate Programs Students: 437 full-time (289 women), 181 part-time (132 women); includes 80 minority (12 Black or African American, non-Hispanic/Latino; 2 American Indian or Alaska Native, non-Hispanic/Latino; 3 Asian, non-Hispanic/Latino; 25 Hispanic/Latino; 5 Native Hawaiian or other Pacific Islander, non-Hispanic/Latino; 33 Two or more races, non-Hispanic/Latino), 21 international. Average age 32. 702 applicants, 65% accepted, 246 enrolled. *Faculty:* 34 full-time (17 women), 71 part-time/adjunct (47 women). Expenses: Contact institution. *Financial support:* In 2010–11, 194 students received support, including 39 research assistantships with partial tuition reimbursements available (averaging $2,320 per year), 16 teaching assistantships with partial tuition reimbursements available (averaging $2,361 per year); career-related internships or fieldwork, scholarships/grants, tuition waivers (partial), and unspecified assistantships also available. Support available to part-time students. Financial award application deadline: 3/1; financial award applicants required to submit FAFSA. In 2010, 188 master's awarded. *Degree program information:* Part-time and evening/weekend programs available. Postbaccalaureate distance learning degree programs offered (minimal on-campus study). Offers art therapy (MA); body psychotherapy (MA); contemplative education (MA); contemplative psychotherapy (MA); counseling psychology (MA); creative writing (MFA); dance/movement therapy (MA); divinity (M Div); ecopsychology (MA); environmental leadership (MA); Indo-Tibetan Buddhism (MA); Indo-Tibetan Buddhism with language (MA); religious studies (MA); religious studies with language (MA); theater: contemporary performance (MFA); transpersonal psychology (MA); wilderness therapy (MA); writing and poetics (MFA). *Application deadline:* For fall admission, 1/15 priority date for domestic and international students; for spring admission, 10/15 priority date for domestic and international students. Applications are processed on a rolling basis. *Application fee:* $60. Electronic applications accepted. *Application Contact:* Office of Admissions, 303-546-3572, Fax: 303-546-3583, E-mail: admissions@naropa.edu. *Dean of Admissions*, Susan Boyle, 303-546-3517, Fax: 303-546-3583, E-mail: sboyle@naropa.edu.

NASHOTAH HOUSE, Nashotah, WI 53058-9793

General Information Independent-religious, coed, primarily men, graduate-only institution. *Graduate housing:* Rooms and/or apartments available on a first-come, first-served basis to single and married students. Housing application deadline: 8/15.

GRADUATE UNITS

School of Theology *Degree program information:* Part-time programs available. Offers theology (M Div, MTS, STM, Certificate).

NATIONAL AMERICAN UNIVERSITY, Rapid City, SD 57701

General Information Proprietary, coed, comprehensive institution. *Graduate housing:* Room and/or apartments available on a first-come, first-served basis to single students. Housing application deadline: 6/1.

GRADUATE UNITS

Graduate Programs *Degree program information:* Part-time and evening/weekend programs available. Postbaccalaureate distance learning degree programs offered. Offers business (MBA, MM). Programs also offered in Wichita, KS; Albuquerque, NM; Bloomington, MN; Brooklyn Center, MN; Colorado Springs, CO; Denver, CO; Independence, MO; Overland Park, KS; Rio Rancho, NM; Roseville, MN; Zona Rosa, MO. Electronic applications accepted.

NATIONAL COLLEGE OF MIDWIFERY, Taos, NM 87571

General Information Independent, women only, comprehensive institution.

GRADUATE UNITS

Graduate Programs *Degree program information:* Part-time and evening/weekend programs available. Postbaccalaureate distance learning degree programs offered (no on-campus study). Offers midwifery (MS, PhD). Electronic applications accepted.

NATIONAL COLLEGE OF NATURAL MEDICINE, Portland, OR 97201

General Information Independent, coed, primarily women, graduate-only institution. *Enrollment by degree level:* 430 first professional, 99 master's. *Graduate faculty:* 35 full-time (14 women), 74 part-time/adjunct (46 women). *Tuition:* Full-time $24,795. *Required fees:* $3708. *Graduate housing:* On-campus housing not available. *Student services:* Campus employment opportunities, campus safety program, career counseling, free psychological counseling, grant writing training, low-cost health insurance, services for students with disabilities, writing training. *Library facilities:* Natural College of Natural Medicine Library. *Online resources:* web page. *Collection:* 16,000 titles, 125 serial subscriptions. *Research affiliation:* Oregon College of Oriental Medicine, Kaiser Center for Health Research, Oregon Health and Science University, Bob's Red Mill.

Computer facilities: 25 computers available on campus for general student use. A campuswide network can be accessed. Online class registration, VRS Software Programs, WIFI are available. *Web address:* http://www.ncnm.edu/.

General Application Contact: Hang Nguyen, Admissions Coordinator, 503-552-1660, Fax: 503-499-0027, E-mail: admissions@ncmn.edu.

GRADUATE UNITS

School of Classical Chinese Medicine Students: 86 full-time (54 women), 13 part-time (10 women); includes 1 Black or African American, non-Hispanic/Latino; 5 Asian, non-Hispanic/Latino; 2 Hispanic/Latino. Average age 29. 30 applicants, 93% accepted, 16 enrolled. *Faculty:* 12 full-time (3 women), 15 part-time/adjunct (6 women). Expenses: Contact institution. *Financial support:* In 2010–11, 77 students received support. Federal Work-Study and scholarships/grants available. Financial award application deadline: 4/30; financial award applicants required to submit FAFSA. In 2010, 25 master's awarded. Offers classical Chinese medicine (M Ac, MSOM). *Application deadline:* For fall admission, 11/1 priority date for domestic and international students; for winter admission, 2/1 priority date for domestic and international students. Applications are processed on a rolling basis. *Application fee:* $75. *Application Contact:* Hang Nguyen, Admissions Coordinator, 503-552-1660, Fax: 503-499-0027, E-mail: admissions@ncmn.edu. *Dean*, Dr. Laurie Regan, 503-552-1775, Fax: 503-499-0027, E-mail: admissions@ncnm.edu.

School of Naturopathic Medicine Students: 414 full-time (340 women), 15 part-time (13 women); includes 7 Black or African American, non-Hispanic/Latino; 3 American Indian or Alaska Native, non-Hispanic/Latino; 25 Asian, non-Hispanic/Latino; 11 Hispanic/Latino, 8 international. Average age 29. 183 applicants, 90% accepted, 98 enrolled. *Faculty:* 22 full-time (10 women), 59 part-time/adjunct (40 women). Expenses: Contact institution. *Financial support:* In 2010–11, 308 students received support. Federal Work-Study and scholarships/grants available. Financial award application deadline: 4/30; financial award applicants required to submit FAFSA. In 2010, 60 doctorates awarded. Offers natural medicine research (MS); naturopathic medicine (ND). *Application deadline:* For fall admission, 11/1 priority date for domestic and international students; for winter admission, 2/1 priority date for domestic and international students. Applications are processed on a rolling basis. *Application fee:* $75. *Application Contact:* Hang Nguyen, Admissions Coordinator, 503-552-1660, Fax: 503-499-0027, E-mail: admissions@ncmn.edu. *Dean,* Dr. Margot Longenecker, 503-552-1697, Fax: 503-499-0022, E-mail: mlongenecker@ncnm.edu.

NATIONAL DEFENSE INTELLIGENCE COLLEGE, Washington, DC 20340-5100

General Information Federally supported, coed, graduate-only institution. *Graduate housing:* On-campus housing not available.

GRADUATE UNITS

Graduate Program *Degree program information:* Part-time and evening/weekend programs available. Offers strategic intelligence (MSSI). Open only to federal government employees.

NATIONAL DEFENSE UNIVERSITY, Washington, DC 20319-5066

General Information Federally supported, coed, graduate-only institution. *Graduate housing:* On-campus housing not available.

GRADUATE UNITS

College of International Security Affairs *Degree program information:* Part-time and evening/weekend programs available. Offers strategic security studies (MA).

Industrial College of the Armed Forces Offers national resource strategy (MS). Open only to Department of Defense employees and specific federal agencies.

Joint Advanced Warfighting School Offers joint campaign planning and strategy (MS). Open only to Department of Defense employees and specific federal agencies.

National War College Offers national security strategy (MS). Open only to Department of Defense employees and specific federal agencies.

THE NATIONAL GRADUATE SCHOOL OF QUALITY MANAGEMENT, Falmouth, MA 02541

General Information Independent, coed, graduate-only institution.

GRADUATE UNITS

Program in Quality Systems Management Offers e-commerce (MS); management (MS); six sigma (MS).

NATIONAL-LOUIS UNIVERSITY, Chicago, IL 60603

General Information Independent, coed, university. *Enrollment:* 6,475 graduate, professional, and undergraduate students; 655 full-time matriculated graduate/professional students (472 women), 3,147 part-time matriculated graduate/professional students (2,421 women). *Enrollment by degree level:* 3,224 master's, 388 doctoral, 190 other advanced degrees. *Graduate faculty:* 252 full-time (167 women), 260 part-time/adjunct (176 women). *Student services:* Campus employment opportunities, career counseling, international student services, low-cost health insurance, services for students with disabilities, teacher training, writing training. *Library facilities:* NLU Library plus 5 others. *Online resources:* library catalog. *Collection:* 4,857 audiovisual materials.

Computer facilities: 165 computers available on campus for general student use. A campuswide network can be accessed from off campus. Online class registration is available. *Web address:* http://www.nl.edu/.

GRADUATE UNITS

College of Arts and Sciences Students: 29 full-time (22 women), 489 part-time (405 women); includes 186 minority (137 Black or African American, non-Hispanic/Latino; 8 Asian, non-Hispanic/Latino; 32 Hispanic/Latino; 9 Two or more races, non-Hispanic/Latino), 2 international. Average age 38. Expenses: Contact institution. *Financial support:* Career-related internships or fieldwork, Federal Work-Study, institutionally sponsored loans, scholarships/grants, and tuition waivers available. Support available to part-time students. Financial award applicants required to submit FAFSA. In 2010, 245 master's, 9 doctorates, 24 other advanced degrees awarded. *Degree program information:* Part-time and evening/weekend programs available. Postbaccalaureate distance learning degree programs offered (minimal on-campus study). Offers counseling and human services (MS); language and academic development (M Ed, Certificate); psychology (MA, PhD, Certificate); public policy (MA); written communication (MS, Certificate). *Application deadline:* Applications are processed on a rolling basis. *Application fee:* $40. Electronic applications accepted. *Application Contact:* Dr. George Valcourt, Vice President of Enrollment and Student Services, 888-658-8632, Fax: 312-261-3550, E-mail: george.valcourt@nl.edu. *Interim Dean,* Dr. Stephen Thompson, 224-233-2539, Fax: 224-233-2539, E-mail: sthompson@nl.edu.

College of Management and Business Students: 125 full-time (80 women), 8 part-time (5 women); includes 59 minority (28 Black or African American, non-Hispanic/Latino; 1 American Indian or Alaska Native, non-Hispanic/Latino; 3 Asian, non-Hispanic/Latino; 26 Hispanic/Latino; 1 Two or more races, non-Hispanic/Latino). Average age 37. Expenses: Contact institution. *Financial support:* Federal Work-Study, institutionally sponsored loans, and scholarships/grants available. Support available to part-time students. Financial award applicants required to submit FAFSA. In 2010, 173 master's awarded. *Degree program information:* Part-time and evening/weekend programs available. Offers business administration (MBA); human resource management and development (MS); management (MS). *Application deadline:* Applications are processed on a rolling basis. *Application fee:* $40. *Application Contact:* Dr. Larry Poselli, Vice President of Enrollment and Student Services, 800-443-5522 Ext. 5718, Fax: 312-261-3550, E-mail: larry.polselli@nl.edu. *Executive Dean,* Walter Roetlger, 312-261-3073, Fax: 312-261-3073, E-mail: chris.multhauf@nl.edu.

National College of Education Students: 501 full-time (370 women), 2,650 part-time (2,011 women); includes 572 minority (258 Black or African American, non-Hispanic/Latino; 2 American Indian or Alaska Native, non-Hispanic/Latino; 60 Asian, non-Hispanic/Latino; 210 Hispanic/Latino; 6 Native Hawaiian or other Pacific Islander, non-Hispanic/Latino; 36 Two or more races, non-Hispanic/Latino), 4 international. Average age 34. Expenses: Contact institution. *Financial support:* Fellowships, research assistantships, teaching assistantships, career-related internships or fieldwork, Federal Work-Study, institutionally sponsored loans, and scholarships/grants available. Support available to part-time students. Financial award applicants required to submit FAFSA. In 2010, 1,711 master's, 76 doctorates, 86 other advanced degrees awarded. *Degree program information:* Part-time and evening/weekend programs available. Offers administration and supervision (M Ed, Ed D, CAS, Ed S); curriculum and instruction (M Ed, MS Ed, CAS); early childhood administration (M Ed, CAS); early childhood education (M Ed, MAT, MS Ed, CAS); education (Ed D); educational psychology/human learning and development (M Ed, MS Ed, CAS, Ed S); elementary education (MAT); interdisciplinary curriculum and instruction (M Ed); mathematics education (M Ed, MS Ed, CAS); reading and language (M Ed, MS Ed, CAS); school psychology (M Ed, Ed S); science education (M Ed, MS Ed, CAS); secondary education (MAT); special education (M Ed, MAT, CAS); technology in education (M Ed, CAS). *Application deadline:* Applications are processed on a rolling basis. *Application fee:* $40. *Application Contact:* Dr. George Valcourt, Vice President of Enrollment and Student Services, 312-261-3550, Fax: 312-261-3550, E-mail: george.valcourt@nl.edu. *Dean,* Dr. Alison Hilsabeck, 312-361-3580, Fax: 312-261-2580, E-mail: ahilsabeck@nl.edu.

NATIONAL THEATRE CONSERVATORY, Denver, CO 80204-2157

General Information Independent, coed, graduate-only institution. *Graduate housing:* On-campus housing not available.

GRADUATE UNITS

Department of Acting Offers acting (MFA, Certificate).

NATIONAL UNIVERSITY, La Jolla, CA 92037-1011

General Information Independent, coed, comprehensive institution. CGS member. *Enrollment:* 6,119 full-time matriculated graduate/professional students (4,152 women), 11,625 part-time matriculated graduate/professional students (7,551 women). *Enrollment by degree level:* 17,744 master's. *Graduate faculty:* 237 full-time (115 women), 2,637 part-time/adjunct (1,357 women). *Tuition:* Full-time $9450; part-time $350 per unit. *Required fees:* $350 per unit. One-time fee: $60. *Graduate housing:* On-campus housing not available. *Student services:* Campus employment opportunities, campus safety program, career counseling, international student services, multicultural affairs office, services for students with disabilities, teacher training, writing training. *Library facilities:* National University Library. *Online resources:* library catalog, web page. *Collection:* 303,000 titles, 22,700 serial subscriptions, 9,700 audiovisual materials.

Computer facilities: Computer purchase and lease plans are available. 3,100 computers available on campus for general student use. A campuswide network can be accessed from off campus. Online class registration is available. *Web address:* http://www.nu.edu/.

General Application Contact: Dominick Giovanniello, Associate Regional Dean—San Diego, 800-NAT-UNIV, Fax: 858-541-7792, E-mail: dgiovann@nu.edu.

GRADUATE UNITS

Academic Affairs Students: 6,119 full-time (4,152 women), 11,625 part-time (7,551 women); includes 6,253 minority (1,690 Black or African American, non-Hispanic/Latino; 102 American Indian or Alaska Native, non-Hispanic/Latino; 1,063 Asian, non-Hispanic/Latino; 3,055 Hispanic/Latino; 93 Native Hawaiian or other Pacific Islander, non-Hispanic/Latino; 250 Two or more races, non-Hispanic/Latino), 517 international. Average age 36. 10,481 applicants, 100% accepted, 7621 enrolled. *Faculty:* 237 full-time (115 women), 2,637 part-time/adjunct (1,357 women). Expenses: Contact institution. *Financial support:* Career-related internships or fieldwork, institutionally sponsored loans, scholarships/grants, and tuition waivers (partial) available. Support available to part-time students. Financial award application deadline: 6/30; financial award applicants required to submit FAFSA. In 2010, 3,451 master's awarded. *Degree program information:* Part-time and evening/weekend programs available. Postbaccalaureate distance learning degree programs offered (no on-campus study). *Application deadline:* Applications are processed on a rolling basis. *Application fee:* $60 ($65 for international students). Electronic applications accepted. *Application Contact:* Dominick Giovanniello, Associate Regional Dean—San Diego, 800-NAT-UNIV, Fax: 858-541-7792, E-mail: dgiovann@nu.edu. *Provost,* Dr. Eileen Heveron, 858-642-8130, Fax: 858-642-8719, E-mail: officeoftheprovost@nu.edu.

College of Letters and Sciences Students: 974 full-time (721 women), 1,713 part-time (1,190 women); includes 1,038 minority (389 Black or African American, non-Hispanic/Latino; 21 American Indian or Alaska Native, non-Hispanic/Latino; 122 Asian, non-Hispanic/Latino; 449 Hispanic/Latino; 13 Native Hawaiian or other Pacific Islander, non-Hispanic/Latino; 44 Two or more races, non-Hispanic/Latino), 4 international. Average age 36. 1,912 applicants, 100% accepted, 1218 enrolled. *Faculty:* 68 full-time (27 women), 747 part-time/adjunct (345 women). Expenses: Contact institution. *Financial support:* Career-related internships or fieldwork, institutionally sponsored loans, scholarships/grants, and tuition waivers (partial) available. Support available to part-time students. Financial award application deadline: 6/30; financial award applicants required to submit FAFSA. In 2010, 563 master's awarded. *Degree program information:* Part-time and evening/weekend programs available. Postbaccalaureate distance learning degree programs offered (no on-campus study). Offers counseling psychology (MA); creative writing (MFA); English (MA); forensic science (MFS); forensic sciences (MFS); history (MA); human behavior (MA); letters and sciences (MA, MFA, MFS, MPA); public administration (MPA). *Application deadline:* Applications are processed on a rolling basis. *Application fee:* $60 ($65 for international students). Electronic applications accepted. *Application Contact:* Dominick Giovanniello, Associate Regional Dean—San Diego, 800-NAT-UNIV, Fax: 858-541-7792, E-mail: dgiovann@nu.edu. *Dean,* Dr. Michael Mcanear, 858-642-8450, Fax: 858-642-8715, E-mail: mcanear@nu.edu.

School of Business and Management Students: 654 full-time (322 women), 1,102 part-time (550 women); includes 658 minority (194 Black or African American, non-Hispanic/Latino; 6 American Indian or Alaska Native, non-Hispanic/Latino; 197 Asian, non-Hispanic/Latino; 230 Hispanic/Latino; 9 Native Hawaiian or other Pacific Islander, non-Hispanic/Latino; 22 Two or more races, non-Hispanic/Latino), 345 international. Average age 35. 1,108 applicants, 100% accepted, 764 enrolled. *Faculty:* 31 full-time (6 women), 282 part-time/adjunct (82 women). Expenses: Contact institution. *Financial support:* Career-related internships or fieldwork, scholarships/grants, and tuition waivers (partial) available. Support available to part-time students. Financial award application deadline: 6/30; financial award applicants required to submit FAFSA. In 2010, 474 master's awarded. *Degree program information:* Part-time and evening/weekend programs available. Postbaccalaureate distance learning degree programs offered (no on-campus study). Offers accountancy (MS); alternative dispute resolution (MBA); business and management (MA, MBA, MS); corporate and international finance (MS); e-business (MBA, MS); financial management (MBA); human resource management (MBA); human resources management (MA); international business (MBA); knowledge management (MS); management (MA); marketing (MBA); organizational leadership (MBA, MS); technology management (MBA). *Application deadline:* Applications are processed on a rolling basis. *Application fee:* $60 ($65 for international students). Electronic applications accepted. *Application Contact:* Dominick Giovanniello, Associate Regional Dean—San Diego, 800-NAT-UNIV, Fax: 858-541-7792, E-mail: dgiovann@nu.edu. *Interim Dean,* Dr. Ronald Uhlig, 858-642-8400, Fax: 858-642-8740, E-mail: ruhlig@nu.edu.

School of Education Students: 4,200 full-time (3,003 women), 8,090 part-time (5,481 women); includes 4,221 minority (1,004 Black or African American, non-Hispanic/Latino; 72 American Indian or Alaska Native, non-Hispanic/Latino; 654 Asian, non-Hispanic/Latino; 2,267 Hispanic/Latino; 62 Native Hawaiian or other Pacific Islander, non-Hispanic/Latino; 162 Two or more races, non-Hispanic/Latino), 20 international. Average age 36. 6,796 applicants, 100% accepted, 5219 enrolled. *Faculty:* 82 full-time (51 women), 1,155 part-time/adjunct (710 women). Expenses: Contact institution. *Financial support:* Career-related internships or fieldwork, institutionally sponsored loans, scholarships/grants, and tuition waivers (partial) available. Support available to part-time students. Financial award application deadline: 6/30. In 2010, 2,020 master's awarded. *Degree program information:* Part-time and evening/weekend programs available. Postbaccalaureate distance learning degree programs offered (no on-campus study). Offers applied school leadership (MS); best practices (MA); cross-cultural teaching (M Ed); deaf and hard-of-hearing education (MS); education (M Ed, MA, MS); educational administration (MS); educational counseling (MS); juvenile justice special education (MS); school psychology (MS); special education (MS); teacher leadership (MA); teaching (MA); teaching/learning in global society (MA). *Application deadline:* Applications are processed on a rolling basis. *Application fee:* $60 ($65 for international students). Electronic applications accepted. *Application Contact:* Dominick Giovanniello, Associate Regional Dean—San Diego, 800-NAT-UNIV, Fax: 858-541-7792, E-mail: dgiovann@nu.edu. *Interim Dean,* Dr. Kenneth Fawson, 858-642-8320, Fax: 858-642-8724, E-mail: kfawson@nu.edu.

School of Engineering and Technology Students: 142 full-time (28 women), 301 part-time (75 women); includes 153 minority (43 Black or African American, non-Hispanic/Latino; 1 American Indian or Alaska Native, non-Hispanic/Latino; 56 Asian, non-Hispanic/Latino; 42 Hispanic/Latino; 4 Native Hawaiian or other Pacific Islander, non-Hispanic/Latino; 7 Two or more races, non-Hispanic/Latino), 114 international. Average age 32. 307 applicants, 100% accepted, 187 enrolled. *Faculty:* 14 full-time (2 women), 159 part-time/adjunct (25 women). Expenses: Contact institution. *Financial support:* Career-related internships or fieldwork, institutionally sponsored loans, scholarships/grants, and tuition waivers (partial) available.

National University (continued)

Support available to part-time students. Financial award application deadline: 6/30; financial award applicants required to submit FAFSA. In 2010, 158 master's awarded. *Degree program information:* Part-time and evening/weekend programs available. Postbaccalaureate distance learning degree programs offered (no on-campus study). Offers computer science (MS); database administration (MS); engineering and technology (MS); engineering management (MS); environmental engineering (MS); homeland security and safety engineering (MS); information systems (MS); software engineering (MS); system engineering (MS); technology management (MS); wireless communications (MS). *Application deadline:* Applications are processed on a rolling basis. *Application fee:* $60 ($65 for international students). Electronic applications accepted. *Application Contact:* Dominick Giovanniello, Associate Regional Dean—San Diego, 800-NAT-UNIV, Fax: 858-642-8709, E-mail: dgiovann@nu.edu. *Dean,* Dr. George E. Beckwith, 909-806-3347, E-mail: ebeckwit@nu.edu.

School of Health and Human Services Students: 51 full-time (38 women), 42 part-time (26 women); includes 44 minority (12 Black or African American, non-Hispanic/Latino; 17 Asian, non-Hispanic/Latino; 12 Hispanic/Latino; 2 Native Hawaiian or other Pacific Islander, non-Hispanic/Latino; 1 Two or more races, non-Hispanic/Latino), 24 international. Average age 31. 89 applicants, 100% accepted, 49 enrolled. *Faculty:* 28 full-time (23 women), 205 part-time/adjunct (164 women). Expenses: Contact institution. *Financial support:* Career-related internships or fieldwork, institutionally sponsored loans, and scholarships/grants available. Support available to part-time students. Financial award application deadline: 6/30; financial award applicants required to submit FAFSA. In 2010, 16 master's awarded. *Degree program information:* Part-time and evening/weekend programs available. Postbaccalaureate distance learning degree programs offered (no on-campus study). Offers health and human services (MHA, MHCA, MIH, MPH, MS); health informatics (MS); healthcare administration (MHA); integrative health (MIH); public health (MPH). *Application deadline:* Applications are processed on a rolling basis. *Application fee:* $60 ($65 for international students). Electronic applications accepted. *Application Contact:* Dominick Giovanniello, Associate Regional Dean—San Diego, 800-NAT-UNIV, Fax: 858-541-7792, E-mail: dgiovann@nu.edu. *Dean,* Dr. Michael Lacourse, 858-309-3472, Fax: 858-309-3480, E-mail: mlacourse@nu.edu.

School of Media and Communication Students: 97 full-time (39 women), 173 part-time (85 women); includes 93 minority (42 Black or African American, non-Hispanic/Latino; 1 American Indian or Alaska Native, non-Hispanic/Latino; 8 Asian, non-Hispanic/Latino; 30 Hispanic/Latino; 2 Native Hawaiian or other Pacific Islander, non-Hispanic/Latino; 10 Two or more races, non-Hispanic/Latino), 10 international. Average age 39. 172 applicants, 100% accepted, 104 enrolled. *Faculty:* 14 full-time (6 women), 89 part-time/adjunct (31 women). Expenses: Contact institution. *Financial support:* Career-related internships or fieldwork, institutionally sponsored loans, scholarships/grants, and tuition waivers (partial) available. Support available to part-time students. Financial award application deadline: 6/30; financial award applicants required to submit FAFSA. In 2010, 60 master's awarded. *Degree program information:* Part-time and evening/weekend programs available. Postbaccalaureate distance learning degree programs offered (no on-campus study). Offers digital cinema (MFA); educational and instructional technology (MS); media and communication (MA, MFA, MS); strategic communication (MA); video game production and design (MFA). *Application deadline:* Applications are processed on a rolling basis. *Application fee:* $60 ($65 for international students). Electronic applications accepted. *Application Contact:* Dominick Giovanniello, Associate Regional Dean—San Diego, 800-NAT-UNIV, Fax: 858-541-7792, E-mail: dgiovann@nu.edu. *Dean,* Karla Berry, 858-309-3442, Fax: 858-309-3450, E-mail: kberry@nu.edu.

NATIONAL UNIVERSITY OF HEALTH SCIENCES, Lombard, IL 60148-4583

General Information Independent, coed, graduate-only institution. *Enrollment:* 713 full-time matriculated graduate/professional students (362 women), 23 part-time matriculated graduate/professional students (11 women). *Enrollment by degree level:* 658 first professional, 78 master's. *Graduate faculty:* 59 full-time (26 women), 57 part-time/adjunct (27 women). *Graduate housing:* Rooms and/or apartments available on a first-come, first-served basis to single and married students. Typical cost: $9780 per year for single students; $9780 per year for married students. Room charges vary according to housing facility selected. *Student services:* Campus employment opportunities, campus safety program, career counseling, international student services, services for students with disabilities. *Library facilities:* NUHS—Learning Resource Center. *Online resources:* library catalog. *Collection:* 29,892 titles, 163 serial subscriptions, 2,259 audiovisual materials. *Research affiliation:* University of Illinois at Chicago (evidence-based practice), Canadian Memorial Chiropractic College (mechanisms of CAM), Miami University of Ohio (evidence-based practice), Palmer College of Chiropractic (mechanisms of CAM), Foot Levelers, Inc. (orthotics/biomechanics), Auburn University (mechanisms of CAM).

Computer facilities: 48 computers available on campus for general student use. A campuswide network can be accessed from student residence rooms. Online class registration, student email, course documents are available. *Web address:* http://www.nuhs.edu/.

General Application Contact: Teri Hatfield, Assistant Director of Admissions, 800-826-6285, Fax: 630-889-6566, E-mail: thatfield@nuhs.edu.

GRADUATE UNITS

Chiropractic Program in Florida Students: 33 full-time (18 women); includes 4 Black or African American, non-Hispanic/Latino; 4 Asian, non-Hispanic/Latino; 2 Hispanic/Latino. Average age 26. 48 applicants, 58% accepted, 14 enrolled. *Faculty:* 7 full-time (4 women), 4 part-time/adjunct (0 women). Expenses: Contact institution. *Financial support:* In 2010–11, 18 students received support; fellowships, research assistantships, teaching assistantships, Federal Work-Study and scholarships/grants available. Support available to part-time students. Financial award applicants required to submit FAFSA. Offers chiropractic (DC). *Application deadline:* For fall admission, 8/15 for domestic students, 8/1 for international students; for winter admission, 12/10 for domestic students, 12/1 for international students; for spring admission, 4/15 for domestic students, 4/1 for international students. Applications are processed on a rolling basis. *Application fee:* $55. Electronic applications accepted. *Application Contact:* Teri Hatfield, Assistant Director of Admissions, 800-826-6285, Fax: 630-889-6566, E-mail: thatfield@nuhs.edu. *Dean, College of Professional Studies—Florida,* Dr. Joseph Stiefel, 727-394-6058, Fax: 727-394-6210, E-mail: jstiefel@nuhs.edu.

College of Professional Studies Students: 680 full-time (344 women), 23 part-time (11 women); includes 56 Black or African American, non-Hispanic/Latino; 73 Asian, non-Hispanic/Latino; 36 Hispanic/Latino; 1 Native Hawaiian or other Pacific Islander, non-Hispanic/Latino; 7 Two or more races, non-Hispanic/Latino, 23 international. Average age 25. 190 applicants, 76% accepted, 76 enrolled. *Faculty:* 52 full-time (22 women), 53 part-time/adjunct (27 women). Expenses: Contact institution. *Financial support:* In 2010–11, 174 students received support, including 10 fellowships (averaging $4,000 per year), 15 research assistantships (averaging $2,500 per year); teaching assistantships, Federal Work-Study, scholarships/grants, and tuition waivers (partial) also available. Support available to part-time students. Financial award applicants required to submit FAFSA. In 2010, 129 DCs, 18 master's awarded. Offers acupuncture (MSAC); chiropractic medicine (DC); naturopathic medicine (ND); Oriental medicine (MSOM). *Application deadline:* For fall admission, 8/13 for domestic students, 8/1 for international students; for winter admission, 12/10 for domestic students, 12/1 for international students; for spring admission, 4/6 for domestic students, 4/1 for international students. Applications are processed on a rolling basis. *Application fee:* $55. Electronic applications accepted. *Application Contact:* Teri Hatfield, Assistant Director of Admissions, 800-826-6285, Fax: 630-889-6566, E-mail: thatfield@nuhs.edu. *Dean,* Dr. Nicholas A. Trongale, 630-889-6673, Fax: 630-889-6499, E-mail: ntrongale@nuhs.edu.

Lincoln College of Postprofessional, Graduate and Continuing Education Students: 18 full-time (16 women), 16 part-time (all women); includes 4 minority (3 Asian, non-Hispanic/Latino; 1 Hispanic/Latino), 1 international. Average age 37. 35 applicants, 69% accepted, 23 enrolled. Expenses: Contact institution. *Financial support:* Applicants required to submit FAFSA. In 2010, 1 master's awarded. *Degree program information:* Evening/weekend programs available. Offers advanced clinical practice (MS); diagnostic imaging (MS). *Application deadline:* For fall admission, 7/1 for domestic students. *Application fee:* $55. Electronic applications accepted. *Dean,* Dr. Jonathan Soltys, 630-889-6622, E-mail: jsoltys@nuhs.edu.

NAVAL POSTGRADUATE SCHOOL, Monterey, CA 93943

General Information Federally supported, coed, graduate-only institution. CGS member. *Enrollment by degree level:* 2,417 master's, 86 doctoral, 321 other advanced degrees. *Graduate faculty:* 600 full-time (119 women), 115 part-time/adjunct (31 women). *Graduate housing:* Rooms and/or apartments available to single and married students. *Student services:* Career counseling, child daycare facilities, exercise/wellness program, international student services, multicultural affairs office. *Library facilities:* Dudley Knox Library. *Online resources:* library catalog, web page. *Collection:* 560,863 titles, 24,600 serial subscriptions, 1,597 audiovisual materials. *Research affiliation:* Dept. of Transportation, National Intelligence Council, National Oceanographic & Atmospheric Administration, NASA, National Science Foundation.

Computer facilities: 260 computers available on campus for general student use. A campuswide network can be accessed from student residence rooms and from off campus. Online class registration is available. *Web address:* http://www.nps.navy.mil/.

General Application Contact: Per Andersen, Registrar/Director, 831-656-1062, E-mail: panderse@nps.edu.

GRADUATE UNITS

Graduate Programs *Degree program information:* Part-time programs available. Postbaccalaureate distance learning degree programs offered (minimal on-campus study). Offers applied mathematics (MS, PhD); applied physics (MS); applied science (MS); computer science (MS, PhD); defense analysis (MS); electrical and computer engineering (MS, PhD, Eng); electrical engineering (MS); engineering acoustics (MS); information sciences (MS); intelligence (MA); international relations (MA); joint information operations (MS); knowledge superiority (MS, Certificate); mechanical and astronautical engineering (MS, D Eng, PhD, Eng); meteorology (MS, PhD); modeling of virtual environments and simulations (MS, PhD); oceanography (MS, PhD); operations research (MS, PhD); physical oceanography (MS); physics (MS, PhD); political science (MA); regional security education (MA); security building (MA); security studies (MA); software engineering (MS, PhD); space systems operations (MS); special operations (MS); systems engineering (MS, PhD, Certificate); systems engineering and analysis (MS); systems engineering management (MS). Programs only open to commissioned officers of the United States and friendly nations and selected United States federal civilian employees.

School of Business and Public Policy *Degree program information:* Part-time programs available. Postbaccalaureate distance learning degree programs offered (minimal on-campus study). Offers contract management (MS); defense-focused business administration (MBA); executive business administration (MBA); leadership and human resource development (MS); management (MS); program management (MS); systems engineering management (MS). Program only open to commissioned officers of the United States and friendly nations and selected United States federal civilian employees.

NAVAL WAR COLLEGE, Newport, RI 02841-1207

General Information Federally supported, coed, primarily men, graduate-only institution.

GRADUATE UNITS

Program in National Security and Strategic Studies Offers national security and strategic studies (MA). Program open only to full-time military personnel.

NAZARENE THEOLOGICAL SEMINARY, Kansas City, MO 64131-1263

General Information Independent-religious, coed, graduate-only institution. *Graduate housing:* Rooms and/or apartments available on a first-come, first-served basis to single and married students. *Research affiliation:* University of Missouri–Kansas City (religious studies).

GRADUATE UNITS

Graduate and Professional Programs *Degree program information:* Part-time programs available. Offers Christian education (MA); intercultural studies (MA); theological studies (MA); theology (M Div, D Min). Electronic applications accepted.

NAZARETH COLLEGE OF ROCHESTER, Rochester, NY 14618-3790

General Information Independent, coed, comprehensive institution. *Graduate housing:* Room and/or apartments available on a first-come, first-served basis to single students; on-campus housing not available to married students. Housing application deadline: 5/15.

GRADUATE UNITS

Graduate Studies *Degree program information:* Part-time and evening/weekend programs available. Postbaccalaureate distance learning degree programs offered. Offers art education (MS Ed); art therapy (MS); business education (MS Ed); communication sciences and disorders (MS); educational technology/computer education (MS Ed); gerontological nurse practitioner (MS); human resource management (MS); inclusive education-adolescence level (MS Ed); inclusive education-childhood level (MS Ed); inclusive education-early childhood level (MS Ed); liberal studies (MA); literacy education (MS Ed); management (MS); music education (MS Ed); music therapy (MS); physical therapy (MS, DPT); social work (MSW); teaching English to speakers of other languages (MS Ed).

NEBRASKA METHODIST COLLEGE, Omaha, NE 68114

General Information Independent-religious, coed, primarily women, comprehensive institution. *Enrollment:* 89 full-time matriculated graduate/professional students (75 women), 20 part-time matriculated graduate/professional students (19 women). *Enrollment by degree level:* 109 master's. *Graduate faculty:* 1 (woman) full-time, 24 part-time/adjunct (15 women). *Tuition:* Full-time $6768; part-time $564 per credit hour. *Graduate housing:* Room and/or apartments available on a first-come, first-served basis to single students; on-campus housing not available to married students. Typical cost: $6710 per year. Housing application deadline: 4/1. *Student services:* Campus employment opportunities, campus safety program, career counseling, exercise/wellness program, free psychological counseling, international student services, low-cost health insurance, services for students with disabilities, teacher training, writing training. *Library facilities:* John Moritz Library. *Online resources:* library catalog. *Collection:* 10,300 titles, 164 serial subscriptions.

Computer facilities: 47 computers available on campus for general student use. A campuswide network can be accessed. Online class registration is available. *Web address:* http://www.methodistcollege.edu/.

General Application Contact: Sara Hanson, Director of Admissions, 402-354-7111, Fax: 402-354-7020, E-mail: admissions@methodistcollege.edu.

GRADUATE UNITS

Program in Health Promotion Management Students: 39 full-time (32 women), 2 part-time (1 woman); includes 3 minority (2 Black or African American, non-Hispanic/Latino; 1 American Indian or Alaska Native, non-Hispanic/Latino). Average age 24. *Faculty:* 8 part-time/adjunct (6 women). Expenses: Contact institution. *Financial support:* In 2010–11, 8 students received support; research assistantships with full and partial tuition reimbursements available, scholarships/grants available. Support available to part-time students. Financial award applicants required to submit FAFSA. In 2010, 13 master's awarded. *Degree program information:* Evening/weekend programs available. Postbaccalaureate distance learning degree programs offered (no on-campus study). Offers health promotion management (MS). *Application deadline:* Applications are processed on a rolling basis. *Application fee:* $25. *Application Contact:* Sara Hanson, Director of Admissions, 402-354-7111, Fax: 402-354-7020, E-mail: admissions@methodistcollege.edu. *Program Development Officer,* Beth Pernie, 402-354-7138, Fax: 402-354-7020, E-mail: beth.pirnie@methodistcollege.edu.

Program in Medical Group Administration Students: 12 full-time (5 women); includes 1 minority (Asian, non-Hispanic/Latino). Average age 39. 8 applicants, 75% accepted, 6 enrolled. *Faculty:* 9 part-time/adjunct (2 women). Expenses: Contact institution. *Financial support:* Scholarships/grants available. Financial award applicants required to submit FAFSA. *Degree* *program information:* Evening/weekend programs available. Postbaccalaureate distance learning degree programs offered (no on-campus study). Offers medical group administration (MS). *Application fee:* $25. *Application Contact:* Sara Hanson, Director of Admissions, 402-354-7111, Fax: 402-354-7020, E-mail: admissions@methodistcollege.edu. *Program Development Officer,* Beth Pernie, 402-354-7138, Fax: 402-354-7020, E-mail: beth.pernie@methodistcollege.edu.

Program in Nursing Students: 38 full-time (all women), 18 part-time (all women); includes 3 minority (all Black or African American, non-Hispanic/Latino). Average age 41. 17 applicants, 41% accepted, 7 enrolled. *Faculty:* 1 (woman) full-time, 5 part-time/adjunct (all women). Expenses: Contact institution. *Financial support:* Research assistantships with full and partial tuition reimbursements, scholarships/grants available. Support available to part-time students. Financial award applicants required to submit FAFSA. *Degree program information:* Evening/weekend programs available. Postbaccalaureate distance learning degree programs offered (no on-campus study). Offers nurse educator (MSN); nurse executive (MSN). *Application deadline:* For spring admission, 11/1 for domestic and international students. Applications are processed on a rolling basis. *Application fee:* $25. *Application Contact:* Sara Hanson, Director of Admissions, 402-354-7111, Fax: 402-354-7020, E-mail: admissions@methodistcollege.edu. *Coordinator,* Linda Foley, 402-354-7050, Fax: 402-354-7020, E-mail: linda.foley@methodistcollege.edu.

NEBRASKA WESLEYAN UNIVERSITY, Lincoln, NE 68504-2796

General Information Independent-religious, coed, comprehensive institution.

GRADUATE UNITS

University College *Degree program information:* Part-time programs available. Offers forensic science (MFS); historical studies (MA); nursing (MSN).

NER ISRAEL RABBINICAL COLLEGE, Baltimore, MD 21208

General Information Independent-religious, men only, comprehensive institution. *Graduate housing:* Rooms and/or apartments guaranteed to single students and available on a first-come, first-served basis to married students.

GRADUATE UNITS

Graduate Programs Offers rabbinics (MTL, DTL, Professional Certificate).

NER ISRAEL YESHIVA COLLEGE OF TORONTO, Thornhill, ON L4J 8A7, Canada

General Information Independent-religious, men only, comprehensive institution.

GRADUATE UNITS

Graduate Programs

NEUMANN UNIVERSITY, Aston, PA 19014-1298

General Information Independent-religious, coed, comprehensive institution. *Graduate housing:* On-campus housing not available.

GRADUATE UNITS

Program in Education *Degree program information:* Part-time programs available. Offers education (MS).

Program in Educational Leadership Offers educational leadership (Ed D).

Program in Nursing and Health Sciences *Degree program information:* Part-time programs available. Offers nursing and health sciences (MS).

Program in Pastoral Counseling *Degree program information:* Part-time and evening/weekend programs available. Offers pastoral counseling (MS, CAS); spiritual direction (CSD). Electronic applications accepted.

Program in Physical Therapy *Degree program information:* Evening/weekend programs available. Offers physical therapy (DPT). Electronic applications accepted.

Program in Sports Management *Degree program information:* Part-time programs available. Offers sports management (MS). Electronic applications accepted.

Program in Strategic Leadership Offers strategic leadership (MS). Electronic applications accepted.

NEW BRUNSWICK THEOLOGICAL SEMINARY, New Brunswick, NJ 08901-1196

General Information Independent-religious, coed, graduate-only institution. *Graduate housing:* Rooms and/or apartments available on a first-come, first-served basis to single students and available to married students.

GRADUATE UNITS

Graduate and Professional Programs *Degree program information:* Part-time and evening/weekend programs available. Offers metro-urban ministry (D Min); theological studies (M Div, MA, D Min). Electronic applications accepted.

NEW ENGLAND COLLEGE, Henniker, NH 03242-3293

General Information Independent, coed, comprehensive institution. *Graduate housing:* Room and/or apartments available on a first-come, first-served basis to single students; on-campus housing not available to married students. Housing application deadline: 5/1.

GRADUATE UNITS

Program in Community Mental Health Counseling *Degree program information:* Part-time and evening/weekend programs available. Offers human services (MS); mental health counseling (MS).

Program in Education *Degree program information:* Part-time and evening/weekend programs available. Offers higher education administration (MS); literacy and language arts (M Ed); meeting the needs of all learners/special education (M Ed); teacher leadership/school reform (M Ed).

Program in Management *Degree program information:* Part-time and evening/weekend programs available. Offers accounting (MSA); healthcare administration (MS); international relations (MA); marketing management (MS); nonprofit leadership (MS); project management (MS); strategic leadership (MS). Electronic applications accepted.

Program in Public Policy *Degree program information:* Part-time and evening/weekend programs available. Postbaccalaureate distance learning degree programs offered (no on-campus study). Offers public policy (MA). Electronic applications accepted.

Program in Sports and Recreation Management: Coaching Offers sports and recreation management: coaching (MS).

Programs in Writing *Degree program information:* Part-time and evening/weekend programs available. Offers poetry (MFA); professional writing (MA). Electronic applications accepted.

NEW ENGLAND COLLEGE OF BUSINESS AND FINANCE, Boston, MA 02111-2645

General Information Independent, coed, primarily women, comprehensive institution.

GRADUATE UNITS

Program in Business Ethics and Compliance Postbaccalaureate distance learning degree programs offered (no on-campus study). Offers business ethics and compliance (MS).

Program in Finance Postbaccalaureate distance learning degree programs offered (no on-campus study). Offers finance (MSF).

THE NEW ENGLAND COLLEGE OF OPTOMETRY, Boston, MA 02115-1100

General Information Independent, coed, graduate-only institution. *Enrollment by degree level:* 464 first professional. *Graduate faculty:* 37 full-time (18 women), 28 part-time/adjunct (13 women). *Graduate housing:* On-campus housing not available. *Student services:* Campus employment opportunities, career counseling, free psychological counseling, international student services, low-cost health insurance. *Online resources:* library catalog, web page. *Collection:* 18,537 titles, 239 serial subscriptions, 12,229 audiovisual materials. *Research affiliation:* Vistakon-Johnson & Johnson (contact lens study), Boston University School of Medicine (vision science).

Computer facilities: 31 computers available on campus for general student use. A campuswide network can be accessed from off campus. *Web address:* http://www.neco.edu/.

General Application Contact: Dr. Taline Farra, Assistant Dean and Director of Admissions, 617-587-5580, Fax: 617-587-5550, E-mail: farrat@neco.edu.

GRADUATE UNITS

Professional Program Students: 456 full-time (321 women), 8 part-time (all women); includes 4 Black or African American, non-Hispanic/Latino; 122 Asian, non-Hispanic/Latino; 9 Hispanic/Latino, 104 international. Average age 25. 899 applicants, 117 enrolled. Expenses: Contact institution. *Financial support:* In 2010–11, 357 students received support, including 12 research assistantships (averaging $5,193 per year); career-related internships or fieldwork, Federal Work-Study, institutionally sponsored loans, and scholarships/grants also available. Financial award application deadline: 4/1; financial award applicants required to submit FAFSA. In 2010, 115 first professional degrees awarded. Offers optometry (OD); vision science (MS). *Application deadline:* For fall admission, 3/15 for domestic students. Applications are processed on a rolling basis. *Application fee:* $65. Electronic applications accepted. *Application Contact:* Dr. Taline Farra, Director of Admissions, 617-587-5580, Fax: 617-587-5550, E-mail: farrat@neco.edu.

NEW ENGLAND CONSERVATORY OF MUSIC, Boston, MA 02115-5000

General Information Independent, coed, comprehensive institution. *Enrollment:* 798 graduate, professional, and undergraduate students; 359 full-time matriculated graduate/professional students (181 women), 26 part-time matriculated graduate/professional students (14 women). *Enrollment by degree level:* 298 master's, 30 doctoral, 57 other advanced degrees. *Graduate faculty:* 92 full-time (30 women), 115 part-time/adjunct (32 women). *Tuition:* Full-time $34,500; part-time $2200 per credit hour. *Required fees:* $450; $450 per year. *Graduate housing:* Room and/or apartments available on a first-come, first-served basis to single students; on-campus housing not available to married students. Typical cost: $12,100 (including board). Room and board charges vary according to board plan and housing facility selected. Housing application deadline: 6/15. *Student services:* Campus employment opportunities, career counseling, free psychological counseling, international student services, low-cost health insurance, services for students with disabilities. *Library facilities:* Spaulding Library plus 3 others. *Online resources:* library catalog, web page, access to other libraries' catalogs. *Collection:* 95,000 titles, 300 serial subscriptions, 65,000 audiovisual materials.

Computer facilities: 70 computers available on campus for general student use. A campuswide network can be accessed. Online class registration, online activity effective Fall 2010 are available. *Web address:* http://necmusic.edu/.

General Application Contact: Christina Daly, Director of Admissions, 617-585-1101, Fax: 617-585-1115, E-mail: christina.daly@newenglandconservatory.edu.

GRADUATE UNITS

Graduate Program in Music Students: 359 full-time (181 women), 26 part-time (14 women); includes 51 minority (4 Black or African American, non-Hispanic/Latino; 24 Asian, non-Hispanic/Latino; 12 Hispanic/Latino; 1 Native Hawaiian or other Pacific Islander, non-Hispanic/Latino; 10 Two or more races, non-Hispanic/Latino), 133 international. Average age 25. 1,622 applicants, 26% accepted, 172 enrolled. *Faculty:* 92 full-time (30 women), 115 part-time/adjunct (32 women). Expenses: Contact institution. *Financial support:* In 2010–11, 347 students received support, including 339 fellowships with partial tuition reimbursements available (averaging $16,232 per year); teaching assistantships, Federal Work-Study, scholarships/grants, and tuition waivers (partial) also available. Support available to part-time students. Financial award application deadline: 12/1; financial award applicants required to submit FAFSA. In 2010, 150 master's, 5 doctorates, 33 Diplomas awarded. Offers music (MM, DMA, Diploma). *Application deadline:* For fall admission, 12/1 priority date for domestic and international students; for spring admission, 11/1 for domestic and international students. Applications are processed on a rolling basis. *Application fee:* $115. *Application Contact:* Christina Daly, Director of Admissions, 617-585-1101, Fax: 617-585-1115, E-mail: christina.daly@newenglandconservatory.edu. *Dean of the College,* Tom Novak, 617-585-1304, Fax: 617-585-1303, E-mail: tnovak@newenglandconservatory.edu.

NEW ENGLAND LAWÛBOSTON, Boston, MA 02116-5687

General Information Independent, coed, graduate-only institution. *Enrollment by degree level:* 1,132 first professional. *Graduate faculty:* 34 full-time (10 women), 72 part-time/adjunct (27 women). *Tuition:* Full-time $39,910; part-time $29,910 per year. *Required fees:* $80. One-time fee: $80 part-time. Tuition and fees vary according to course load. *Graduate housing:* On-campus housing not available. *Student services:* Campus employment opportunities, career counseling, low-cost health insurance, services for students with disabilities, writing training. *Library facilities:* New England Law [B]oston Law Library. *Online resources:* library catalog, web page. *Collection:* 84,167 titles, 1,114 serial subscriptions, 1,174 audiovisual materials.

Computer facilities: 74 computers available on campus for general student use. A campuswide network can be accessed from off campus. Online class registration is available. *Web address:* http://www.nesl.edu/.

General Application Contact: Michelle L'Etoile, Director of Admissions, 617-422-7210, Fax: 617-422-7201, E-mail: admit@nesl.edu.

GRADUATE UNITS

Professional Program Students: 796 full-time (468 women), 336 part-time (165 women); includes 16 Black or African American, non-Hispanic/Latino; 49 Asian, non-Hispanic/Latino; 26 Hispanic/Latino; 22 Two or more races, non-Hispanic/Latino, 7 international. Average age 27. 3,210 applicants, 60% accepted, 393 enrolled. *Faculty:* 34 full-time (10 women), 72 part-time/adjunct (27 women). Expenses: Contact institution. *Financial support:* In 2010–11, 709 students received support. Federal Work-Study, scholarships/grants, and tuition waivers (full and partial) available. Support available to part-time students. Financial award application deadline: 4/7; financial award applicants required to submit FAFSA. *Degree program information:* Part-time and evening/weekend programs available. Offers law (JD, LL M). *Application deadline:* For fall admission, 3/15 for domestic students. Applications are processed on a rolling basis. *Application fee:* $65. Electronic applications accepted. *Application Contact:* Michelle L'Etoile, Director of Admissions, 617-422-7210, Fax: 617-422-7201, E-mail: admit@nesl.edu. *Dean,* John F. O'Brien, 617-422-7221, Fax: 617-422-7333, E-mail: plamonica@nesl.edu.

NEW ENGLAND SCHOOL OF ACUPUNCTURE, Newton, MA 02458

General Information Independent, coed, graduate-only institution. *Graduate housing:* On-campus housing not available.

GRADUATE UNITS

Program in Acupuncture and Oriental Medicine *Degree program information:* Part-time programs available. Offers acupuncture (M Ac); acupuncture and Oriental medicine (MAOM).

NEW JERSEY CITY UNIVERSITY, Jersey City, NJ 07305-1597

General Information State-supported, coed, comprehensive institution. *Graduate housing:* On-campus housing not available.

GRADUATE UNITS

Graduate Studies and Continuing Education *Degree program information:* Part-time and evening/weekend programs available.

New Jersey City University (continued)

College of Professional Studies *Degree program information:* Part-time and evening/weekend programs available. Offers accounting (MS); community health education (MS); criminal justice (MS); finance (MBA, MS); health administration (MS); law enforcement (MS); marketing (MBA); organizational management and leadership (MBA); school health education (MS).

Debra Cannon Partridge Wolfe College of Education *Degree program information:* Part-time and evening/weekend programs available. Offers basics and urban studies (MA); bilingual/bicultural education and English as a second language (MA); counseling (MA); early childhood education (MA); education (MA, MAT); educational administration and supervision (MA); educational technology (MA); elementary education (MAT); elementary school reading (MA); reading specialist (MA); secondary education (MAT); secondary school reading (MA); special education (MA).

William J. Maxwell College of Arts and Sciences *Degree program information:* Part-time and evening/weekend programs available. Offers art (MFA); art education (MA); arts and sciences (MA, MFA, MM, PD); educational psychology (MA); mathematics education (MA); music education (MA); performance (MM); school psychology (PD); studio art (MFA).

NEW JERSEY INSTITUTE OF TECHNOLOGY, Newark, NJ 07102

General Information State-supported, coed, university. CGS member. *Enrollment:* 8,934 graduate, professional, and undergraduate students; 1,619 full-time matriculated graduate/professional students (510 women), 1,080 part-time matriculated graduate/professional students (318 women). *Enrollment by degree level:* 2,159 master's, 439 doctoral, 101 other advanced degrees. *Graduate faculty:* 408 full-time (75 women), 246 part-time/adjunct (50 women). Tuition, state resident: full-time $14,724; part-time $818 per credit. Tuition, nonresident: full-time $20,304; part-time $1128 per credit. *Required fees:* $2272; $209 per credit. $103 per semester. One-time fee: $312 full-time; $212 part-time. *Graduate housing:* Room and/or apartments available on a first-come, first-served basis to single students; on-campus housing not available to married students. Typical cost: $11,736 (including board). Housing application deadline: 3/31. *Student services:* Campus employment opportunities, campus safety program, career counseling, child daycare facilities, exercise/wellness program, free psychological counseling, international student services, low-cost health insurance, services for students with disabilities, teacher training, writing training. *Library facilities:* Van Houten Library plus 1 other. *Online resources:* library catalog, web page, access to other libraries' catalogs. *Collection:* 160,000 titles, 1,100 serial subscriptions.

Computer facilities: Computer purchase and lease plans are available. 1,938 computers available on campus for general student use. A campuswide network can be accessed from student residence rooms and from off campus. Online class registration is available. *Web address:* http://www.njit.edu/.

General Application Contact: Kathryn Kelly, Director of Admissions, 973-596-3300, Fax: 973-596-3461, E-mail: admissions@njit.edu.

GRADUATE UNITS

Office of Graduate Studies Students: 1,619 full-time (510 women), 1,080 part-time (318 women); includes 222 Black or African American, non-Hispanic/Latino; 10 American Indian or Alaska Native, non-Hispanic/Latino; 376 Asian, non-Hispanic/Latino; 202 Hispanic/Latino, 1,120 international. Average age 29. 5,003 applicants, 85% accepted, 1078 enrolled. *Faculty:* 408 full-time (75 women), 246 part-time/adjunct (50 women). Expenses: Contact institution. *Financial support:* Fellowships with full and partial tuition reimbursements, research assistantships with full and partial tuition reimbursements, teaching assistantships with full and partial tuition reimbursements, career-related internships or fieldwork, Federal Work-Study, institutionally sponsored loans, and unspecified assistantships available. Financial award application deadline: 3/15. In 2010, 959 master's, 67 doctorates awarded. *Degree program information:* Part-time and evening/weekend programs available. *Application deadline:* For fall admission, 6/5 priority date for domestic students, 4/1 for international students; for spring admission, 11/15 for domestic and international students. Applications are processed on a rolling basis. *Application fee:* $65. Electronic applications accepted. *Application Contact:* Kathryn Kelly, Director of Admissions, 973-596-3300, Fax: 973-596-3461, E-mail: admissions@njit.edu. *Associate Provost*, Dr. Marino Xanthos, 973-596-3462, E-mail: marinos.xanthos@njit.edu.

College of Computing Science Students: 337 full-time (104 women), 298 part-time (59 women); includes 55 Black or African American, non-Hispanic/Latino; 3 American Indian or Alaska Native, non-Hispanic/Latino; 94 Asian, non-Hispanic/Latino; 46 Hispanic/Latino, 261 international. Average age 29. 1,328 applicants, 44% accepted, 245 enrolled. *Faculty:* 51 full-time (7 women), 15 part-time/adjunct (2 women). Expenses: Contact institution. *Financial support:* Fellowships with full and partial tuition reimbursements, research assistantships with full and partial tuition reimbursements, teaching assistantships with full and partial tuition reimbursements, career-related internships or fieldwork, Federal Work-Study, institutionally sponsored loans, and unspecified assistantships available. Financial award application deadline: 3/15. In 2010, 268 master's, 11 doctorates awarded. *Degree program information:* Part-time and evening/weekend programs available. Offers bioinformatics (MS); business and information systems (MS); computer science (MS, PhD); computing and business (MS); computing science (MS, PhD); emergency management and business continuity (MS); information systems (MS, PhD); software engineering (MS). *Application deadline:* For fall admission, 6/5 priority date for domestic students, 4/1 for international students; for spring admission, 11/15 for domestic and international students. Applications are processed on a rolling basis. *Application fee:* $65. Electronic applications accepted. *Application Contact:* Kathryn Kelly, Director of Admissions, 973-596-3300, Fax: 973-596-3461, E-mail: admissions@njit.edu. *Dean*, Dr. Narain Gehani, 973-542-5488, Fax: 973-596-5777, E-mail: narain.gehani@njit.edu.

College of Science and Liberal Arts Students: 238 full-time (97 women), 113 part-time (56 women); includes 25 Black or African American, non-Hispanic/Latino; 2 American Indian or Alaska Native, non-Hispanic/Latino; 48 Asian, non-Hispanic/Latino; 11 Hispanic/Latino, 162 international. Average age 30. 622 applicants, 36% accepted, 107 enrolled. *Faculty:* 160 full-time (36 women), 62 part-time/adjunct (19 women). Expenses: Contact institution. *Financial support:* Fellowships with full tuition reimbursements, research assistantships with full tuition reimbursements, teaching assistantships with full tuition reimbursements available. Financial award application deadline: 3/15. In 2010, 65 master's, 16 doctorates awarded. *Degree program information:* Part-time and evening/weekend programs available. Offers applied mathematics (MS); applied physics (MS, PhD); applied statistics (MS); biology (MS, PhD); biostatistics (MS); chemistry (MS, PhD); computational biology (MS); computing biology (MS); environmental policy studies (MS); environmental science (MS, PhD); history (MA, MAT); material science and engineering (MS); materials science and engineering (PhD); mathematics science (PhD); professional and technical communication (MS); science and liberal arts (MA, MAT, MS, PhD). *Application deadline:* For fall admission, 6/5 priority date for domestic students, 4/1 for international students; for spring admission, 11/15 for domestic and international students. Applications are processed on a rolling basis. *Application fee:* $65. Electronic applications accepted. *Application Contact:* Kathryn Kelly, Director of Admissions, 973-596-3300, Fax: 973-596-3461, E-mail: admissions@njit.edu. *Dean*, Dr. Fadi P. Deek, 973-596-3676, Fax: 973-565-0586, E-mail: fadi.deek@njit.edu.

Newark College of Engineering Students: 783 full-time (207 women), 475 part-time (123 women); includes 94 Black or African American, non-Hispanic/Latino; 3 American Indian or Alaska Native, non-Hispanic/Latino; 159 Asian, non-Hispanic/Latino; 99 Hispanic/Latino, 587 international. Average age 28. 2,442 applicants, 44% accepted, 390 enrolled. *Faculty:* 135 full-time (14 women), 97 part-time/adjunct (6 women). Expenses: Contact institution. *Financial support:* Fellowships with full and partial tuition reimbursements, research assistantships with full and partial tuition reimbursements, teaching assistantships with full and partial tuition reimbursements available. Financial award application deadline: 3/15. In 2010, 545 master's, 31 doctorates awarded. *Degree program information:* Part-time and evening/weekend programs available. Offers biomedical engineering (MS, PhD); chemical engineering (MS, PhD); civil engineering (MS, PhD); computer engineering (MS, PhD); electrical engineering (MS, PhD); engineering (MS, PhD, Engineer); engineering management (MS); engineering science (MS); environmental engineering (MS, PhD); industrial engineering (MS, PhD); Internet engineering (MS); manufacturing engineering (MS); mechanical engineering (MS, PhD, Engineer); occupational safety and health engineering (MS); pharmaceutical engineering (MS); power and energy systems (MS); transportation (MS, PhD). *Application deadline:* For fall admission, 6/5 priority date for domestic students, 4/1 for international students; for spring admission, 11/15 for domestic and international students. Applications are processed on a rolling basis. *Application fee:* $65. Electronic applications accepted. *Application Contact:* Kathryn Kelly, Director of Admissions, 973-596-3300, Fax: 973-596-3461, E-mail: admissions@njit.edu. *Dean*, Dr. Sunil Saigal, 973-596-5443, E-mail: sunil.saigal@njit.edu.

School of Architecture Students: 91 full-time (44 women), 20 part-time (12 women); includes 28 minority (7 Black or African American, non-Hispanic/Latino; 1 American Indian or Alaska Native, non-Hispanic/Latino; 8 Asian, non-Hispanic/Latino; 12 Hispanic/Latino), 28 international. Average age 31. 215 applicants, 42% accepted, 42 enrolled. *Faculty:* 33 full-time (6 women), 51 part-time/adjunct (22 women). Expenses: Contact institution. *Financial support:* Fellowships with full and partial tuition reimbursements, research assistantships with full and partial tuition reimbursements, teaching assistantships with full and partial tuition reimbursements, career-related internships or fieldwork, Federal Work-Study, institutionally sponsored loans, scholarships/grants, and unspecified assistantships available. Financial award application deadline: 3/15. In 2010, 29 master's, 3 doctorates awarded. *Degree program information:* Part-time and evening/weekend programs available. Offers architecture (M Arch, MIP, MS, PhD); infrastructure planning (MIP); urban systems (PhD). *Application deadline:* For fall admission, 6/5 priority date for domestic students, 4/1 for international students; for spring admission, 11/15 for domestic and international students. Applications are processed on a rolling basis. *Application fee:* $65. Electronic applications accepted. *Application Contact:* Kathryn Kelly, Director of Admissions, 973-596-3300, Fax: 973-596-3461, E-mail: admissions@njit.edu. *Dean*, Urs P. Gauchat, 973-596-3079, E-mail: urs.p.gauchat@njit.edu.

School of Management Students: 161 full-time (56 women), 82 part-time (27 women); includes 29 Black or African American, non-Hispanic/Latino; 1 American Indian or Alaska Native, non-Hispanic/Latino; 50 Asian, non-Hispanic/Latino; 26 Hispanic/Latino, 76 international. Average age 30. 393 applicants, 47% accepted, 93 enrolled. *Faculty:* 29 full-time (12 women), 16 part-time/adjunct (2 women). Expenses: Contact institution. *Financial support:* Fellowships with full and partial tuition reimbursements, research assistantships with full and partial tuition reimbursements, teaching assistantships with full and partial tuition reimbursements, career-related internships or fieldwork, Federal Work-Study, institutionally sponsored loans, and unspecified assistantships available. Financial award application deadline: 3/15. In 2010, 110 master's awarded. *Degree program information:* Part-time and evening/weekend programs available. Offers management of business administration (MBA); management of technology (MS). *Application deadline:* For fall admission, 6/5 priority date for domestic students, 4/1 for international students; for spring admission, 11/15 for domestic and international students. Applications are processed on a rolling basis. *Application fee:* $65. Electronic applications accepted. *Application Contact:* Kathryn Kelly, Director of Admissions, 973-596-3300, Fax: 973-596-3461, E-mail: admissions@njit.edu. *Interim Dean*, Dr. Robert English, 973-596-3224, Fax: 973-596-3074, E-mail: robert.english@njit.edu.

NEW LIFE THEOLOGICAL SEMINARY, Charlotte, NC 28206-7901

General Information Independent-religious, coed, comprehensive institution.

GRADUATE UNITS

Graduate Program *Degree program information:* Part-time and evening/weekend programs available. Offers urban Christian ministry (MA). Electronic applications accepted.

NEWMAN THEOLOGICAL COLLEGE, Edmonton, AB T6V 1H3, Canada

General Information Independent-religious, coed, graduate-only institution. *Enrollment:* 27 full-time matriculated graduate/professional students (4 women), 139 part-time matriculated graduate/professional students (73 women). *Enrollment by degree level:* 53 first professional, 29 master's, 84 other advanced degrees. *Graduate faculty:* 6 full-time (1 woman), 36 part-time/adjunct (12 women). *Graduate tuition:* Tuition and fees charges are reported in Canadian dollars. *Tuition:* Full-time $5700 Canadian dollars; part-time $570 Canadian dollars per course. *Required fees:* $55 Canadian dollars per semester. Tuition and fees vary according to course load and campus/location. *Graduate housing:* On-campus housing not available. *Student services:* Campus employment opportunities, career counseling, free psychological counseling, services for students with disabilities. *Library facilities:* Newman Library. *Online resources:* library catalog, web page, access to other libraries' catalogs. *Collection:* 58,800 titles, 222 serial subscriptions, 2,000 audiovisual materials.

Computer facilities: 6 computers available on campus for general student use. A campuswide network can be accessed. *Web address:* http://www.newman.edu/.

General Application Contact: Patricia Johnson, Assistant to the Registrar, 780-392-2450 Ext. 5228, Fax: 780-462-4013, E-mail: registrar.assistant@newman.edu.

GRADUATE UNITS

Religious Education Programs Students: 1 (woman) full-time, 105 part-time (57 women). Average age 44. 12 applicants, 100% accepted, 12 enrolled. *Faculty:* 12 part-time/adjunct (5 women). Expenses: Contact institution. *Financial support:* Tuition bursaries available. Support available to part-time students. Financial award application deadline: 5/30. In 2010, 4 master's, 8 other advanced degrees awarded. *Degree program information:* Part-time programs available. Postbaccalaureate distance learning degree programs offered (no on-campus study). Offers Catholic school administration (CCSA); religious education (MRE, GDRE). *Application deadline:* For fall admission, 8/7 priority date for domestic students; for winter admission, 1/2 priority date for domestic students; for spring admission, 5/1 priority date for domestic students. *Application fee:* $45 ($250 for international students). *Application Contact:* Maria Saulnier, Registrar, 780-392-2450 Ext. 5227, Fax: 780-462-4013, E-mail: registrar@newman.edu. *Director*, Sandra Talarico, 780-392-2450 Ext. 5239, Fax: 780-462-4013, E-mail: sandra.talarico@newman.edu.

Theology Programs Students: 27 full-time (4 women), 31 part-time (13 women). Average age 39. 8 applicants, 100% accepted, 7 enrolled. *Faculty:* 13 full-time (3 women), 23 part-time/adjunct (8 women). Expenses: Contact institution. *Financial support:* In 2010–11, 14 students received support. Tuition bursaries available. Support available to part-time students. Financial award application deadline: 5/31. In 2010, 10 first professional degrees, 1 master's awarded. *Degree program information:* Part-time programs available. Offers theology (M Div, M Th, MTS). *Application deadline:* For fall admission, 8/7 priority date for domestic students; for winter admission, 1/3 priority date for domestic students; for spring admission, 5/1 priority date for domestic students. Applications are processed on a rolling basis. *Application fee:* $45 ($250 for international students). *Application Contact:* Maria Saulnier, Registrar, 780-392-2450 Ext. 5227, Fax: 780-462-4013, E-mail: registrar@newman.edu. *Dean*, Fr. Stefano Penna, 780-392-2450 Ext. 5223, Fax: 780-462-4013, E-mail: stefano.penna@newman.edu.

NEWMAN UNIVERSITY, Wichita, KS 67213-2097

General Information Independent-religious, coed, comprehensive institution. *Enrollment:* 2,746 graduate, professional, and undergraduate students; 160 full-time matriculated graduate/professional students (110 women), 583 part-time matriculated graduate/professional students (408 women). *Enrollment by degree level:* 428 master's, 315 other advanced degrees. *Graduate faculty:* 20 full-time (8 women), 35 part-time/adjunct (25 women). Tuition and fees vary according to course load, campus/location and program. *Graduate housing:* Rooms and/or apartments available on a first-come, first-served basis to single and married students. Typical cost: $7558 (including board) for single students; $6900 per year for married students. Housing application deadline: 8/1. *Student services:* Campus employment opportunities, campus safety program, career counseling, exercise/wellness program, free psychological counseling, international student services, low-cost health insurance, services for students with disabilities, teacher training, writing training. *Library facilities:* Dungan Library and Campus Center. *Online resources:* library catalog, web page, access to other libraries' catalogs. *Collection:* 110,167 titles, 122 serial subscriptions, 2,061 audiovisual materials.

Computer facilities: 90 computers available on campus for general student use. A campuswide network can be accessed from student residence rooms. Online class registration is available. *Web address:* http://www.newmanu.edu/.

General Application Contact: Linda Kay Sabala, Director of Graduate Admissions, 316-942-4291 Ext. 2230, Fax: 316-942-4483, E-mail: sabalal@newmanu.edu.

GRADUATE UNITS

Master of Education Program Students: 16 full-time (10 women), 348 part-time (265 women); includes 9 Black or African American, non-Hispanic/Latino; 2 American Indian or Alaska Native, non-Hispanic/Latino; 10 Asian, non-Hispanic/Latino; 26 Hispanic/Latino; 2 Two or more races, non-Hispanic/Latino, 4 international. Average age 37. 39 applicants, 87% accepted, 30 enrolled. *Faculty:* 2 full-time (0 women), 24 part-time/adjunct (22 women). Expenses: Contact institution. *Financial support:* In 2010–11, 20 students received support. Federal Work-Study available. Financial award application deadline: 8/15; financial award applicants required to submit FAFSA. In 2010, 45 master's awarded. *Degree program information:* Part-time programs available. Postbaccalaureate distance learning degree programs offered (no on-campus study). Offers building leadership (MS Ed); curriculum and instruction (MS Ed). *Application deadline:* For fall admission, 8/15 priority date for domestic students, 7/15 priority date for international students; for spring admission, 1/10 priority date for domestic students, 11/15 priority date for international students. Applications are processed on a rolling basis. *Application fee:* $25 ($40 for international students). Electronic applications accepted. *Application Contact:* Linda Kay Sabala, Director of Graduate Admissions, 316-942-4291 Ext. 2230, Fax: 316-942-4483, E-mail: sabalal@newmanu.edu. *Director,* Dr. Guy Glidden, 316-942-4291 Ext. 2331, Fax: 316-942-4483, E-mail: gliddeng@newmanu.edu.

MBA Program Students: 33 full-time (14 women), 92 part-time (37 women); includes 28 minority (7 Black or African American, non-Hispanic/Latino; 6 Asian, non-Hispanic/Latino; 12 Hispanic/Latino; 1 Native Hawaiian or other Pacific Islander, non-Hispanic/Latino; 2 Two or more races, non-Hispanic/Latino), 24 international. Average age 32. 80 applicants, 83% accepted, 45 enrolled. *Faculty:* 4 full-time (2 women), 7 part-time/adjunct (2 women). Expenses: Contact institution. *Financial support:* In 2010–11, 29 students received support. Federal Work-Study available. Financial award application deadline: 8/15; financial award applicants required to submit FAFSA. In 2010, 72 master's awarded. *Degree program information:* Part-time programs available. Offers finance (MBA); international business (MBA); leadership (MBA); management (MBA); technology (MBA). *Application deadline:* For fall admission, 8/1 priority date for domestic students, 7/15 priority date for international students; for winter admission, 1/1 priority date for domestic students; for spring admission, 1/1 priority date for domestic students, 11/15 priority date for international students. Applications are processed on a rolling basis. *Application fee:* $25 ($40 for international students). Electronic applications accepted. *Application Contact:* Linda Kay Sabala, Director of Graduate Admissions, 316-942-4291 Ext. 2230, Fax: 316-942-4483, E-mail: sabalal@newmanu.edu. *Dean of the College of Professional Studies/Director,* Dr. George Goetz, 316-942-4291 Ext. 2205, Fax: 316-942-4483, E-mail: smithge@newmanu.edu.

School of Arts and Humanities Students: 56 part-time (31 women); includes 1 Black or African American, non-Hispanic/Latino; 1 Asian, non-Hispanic/Latino; 5 Hispanic/Latino, 1 international. Average age 45. 25 applicants, 92% accepted, 19 enrolled. *Faculty:* 3 full-time (0 women). Expenses: Contact institution. *Financial support:* In 2010–11, 55 students received support. Federal Work-Study available. Financial award application deadline: 8/15; financial award applicants required to submit FAFSA. *Degree program information:* Part-time programs available. Postbaccalaureate distance learning degree programs offered (minimal on-campus study). Offers theological studies (MTS); theology (MA). *Application deadline:* For fall admission, 8/1 priority date for domestic students. *Application fee:* $25 ($40 for international students). *Application Contact:* Linda Kay Sabala, Director of Graduate Admissions, 316-942-4291 Ext. 2230, E-mail: sabalal@newmanu.edu. *Assistant Professor of Theology and Graduate Theology Director,* Fr. Gile Joseph, 316-942-4291 Ext. 2861, Fax: 316-942-4483, E-mail: gilej@newmanu.edu.

School of Nursing and Allied Health Students: 38 full-time (24 women), 3 part-time (2 women); includes 1 Black or African American, non-Hispanic/Latino; 1 American Indian or Alaska Native, non-Hispanic/Latino; 1 Asian, non-Hispanic/Latino; 1 Hispanic/Latino. Average age 31. 132 applicants, 17% accepted, 22 enrolled. *Faculty:* 4 full-time (2 women), 1 part-time/adjunct (0 women). Expenses: Contact institution. *Financial support:* In 2010–11, 1 student received support. Federal Work-Study available. Financial award application deadline: 8/15; financial award applicants required to submit FAFSA. In 2010, 18 master's awarded. Offers nurse anesthesia (MS). *Application deadline:* For fall admission, 11/15 for domestic and international students. Applications are processed on a rolling basis. *Application fee:* $25 ($40 for international students). Electronic applications accepted. *Application Contact:* Linda Kay Sabala, Director of Graduate Admissions, 316-942-4291 Ext. 2230, Fax: 316-942-4483. *Director,* Prof. Sharon Niemann, 316-942-4291 Ext. 2272, Fax: 316-942-4483, E-mail: niemanns@newmanu.edu.

School of Social Work Students: 71 full-time (62 women), 73 part-time (65 women); includes 10 Black or African American, non-Hispanic/Latino; 3 American Indian or Alaska Native, non-Hispanic/Latino; 3 Asian, non-Hispanic/Latino; 14 Hispanic/Latino; 6 Two or more races, non-Hispanic/Latino, 1 international. Average age 36. 135 applicants, 60% accepted, 59 enrolled. *Faculty:* 7 full-time (4 women), 3 part-time/adjunct (1 woman). Expenses: Contact institution. *Financial support:* In 2010–11, 2 students received support. Federal Work-Study and scholarships/grants available. Financial award application deadline: 8/15; financial award applicants required to submit FAFSA. In 2010, 51 master's awarded. Postbaccalaureate distance learning degree programs offered (no on-campus study). Offers social work (MSW). *Application deadline:* For fall admission, 8/15 for domestic students, 7/15 priority date for international students. Applications are processed on a rolling basis. *Application fee:* $25 ($40 for international students). *Application Contact:* Linda Kay Sabala, Director of Graduate Admissions, 316-942-4291 Ext. 2230, Fax: 316-942-4483, E-mail: sabalal@newmanu.edu. *Director,* Dr. Kevin Brown, 316-942-4291 Ext. 2458, Fax: 316-942-4483.

NEW MEXICO HIGHLANDS UNIVERSITY, Las Vegas, NM 87701

General Information State-supported, coed, comprehensive institution. CGS member. *Enrollment:* 3,764 graduate, professional, and undergraduate students; 590 full-time matriculated graduate/professional students (420 women), 591 part-time matriculated graduate/professional students (412 women). *Enrollment by degree level:* 1,181 master's. *Graduate faculty:* 109 full-time (47 women). Tuition, state resident: full-time $2544. *Required fees:* $624; $132 per credit hour. *Graduate housing:* Rooms and/or apartments guaranteed to single and married students. *Student services:* Career counseling, child daycare facilities, exercise/wellness program, free psychological counseling, international student services, low-cost health insurance, services for students with disabilities, teacher training, writing training. *Library facilities:* Donnelly Library. *Online resources:* library catalog, web page, access to other libraries' catalogs. *Collection:* 440,165 titles, 41,363 serial subscriptions, 1,098 audiovisual materials. *Research affiliation:* Spectra Gases, Inc. (chemistry), Los Alamos National Laboratory (chemistry), Sigma Aldrich (chemistry).

Computer facilities: 500 computers available on campus for general student use. A campuswide network can be accessed from student residence rooms and from off campus. Online class registration is available. *Web address:* http://www.nmhu.edu/.

General Application Contact: Diane Trujillo, Administrative Assistant, Graduate Studies, 505-454-3266, Fax: 505-426-2117, E-mail: dtrujillo@nmhu.edu.

GRADUATE UNITS

Graduate Studies Students: 590 full-time (420 women), 591 part-time (412 women); includes 658 minority (39 Black or African American, non-Hispanic/Latino; 70 American Indian or Alaska Native, non-Hispanic/Latino; 7 Asian, non-Hispanic/Latino; 529 Hispanic/Latino; 1 Native Hawaiian or other Pacific Islander, non-Hispanic/Latino; 12 Two or more races, non-Hispanic/Latino), 88 international. Average age 36. 508 applicants, 98% accepted, 365 enrolled. *Faculty:* 109 full-time (47 women). Expenses: Contact institution. *Financial support:* In 2010–11, 149 students received support; fellowships, research assistantships with full and partial tuition reimbursements available, teaching assistantships with full and partial tuition reimbursements available, career-related internships or fieldwork, Federal Work-Study, institutionally sponsored loans, scholarships/grants, tuition waivers (full and partial), and unspecified assistantships available. Support available to part-time students. Financial award application deadline: 3/1. In 2010, 335 master's awarded. *Degree program information:* Part-time programs available. *Application deadline:* For fall admission, 8/1 priority date for domestic students. Applications are processed on a rolling basis. *Application fee:* $15. *Application Contact:* Diane Trujillo, Administrative Assistant, Graduate Studies, 505-454-3266, Fax: 505-426-2117, E-mail: dtrujillo@nmhu.edu. *Vice President for Academic Affairs,* Dr. Gilbert Rivera, 505-426-2250, Fax: 505-454-3558, E-mail: gilbertrivera@nmhu.edu.

College of Arts and Sciences Students: 121 full-time (53 women), 94 part-time (45 women); includes 11 Black or African American, non-Hispanic/Latino; 3 American Indian or Alaska Native, non-Hispanic/Latino; 1 Asian, non-Hispanic/Latino; 98 Hispanic/Latino; 3 Two or more races, non-Hispanic/Latino, 35 international. Average age 31. 77 applicants, 99% accepted, 56 enrolled. *Faculty:* 56 full-time (22 women). Expenses: Contact institution. *Financial support:* In 2010–11, 91 students received support, including research assistantships with full and partial tuition reimbursements available (averaging $6,500 per year), teaching assistantships with full and partial tuition reimbursements available (averaging $6,500 per year); career-related internships or fieldwork, Federal Work-Study, institutionally sponsored loans, scholarships/grants, tuition waivers (full and partial), and unspecified assistantships also available. Support available to part-time students. Financial award application deadline: 3/1. In 2010, 44 master's awarded. *Degree program information:* Part-time programs available. Offers arts and sciences (MA, MS); chemistry (MS); English (MA); history, political science, and languages and culture (MA); life science (MS); media arts and computer science (MS); psychology (MS); Southwest studies (MA, MS). *Application deadline:* For fall admission, 8/1 priority date for domestic students. Applications are processed on a rolling basis. *Application fee:* $15. Electronic applications accepted. *Application Contact:* Diane Trujillo, Administrative Assistant, Graduate Studies, 505-454-3266, Fax: 505-454-3558, E-mail: dtrujillo@nmhu.edu. *Dean,* Dr. Roy Lujan, 505-454-3080, Fax: 505-454-3389, E-mail: rlujana@nmhu.edu.

School of Business Students: 71 full-time (44 women), 124 part-time (68 women); includes 119 minority (8 Black or African American, non-Hispanic/Latino; 18 American Indian or Alaska Native, non-Hispanic/Latino; 1 Asian, non-Hispanic/Latino; 89 Hispanic/Latino; 1 Native Hawaiian or other Pacific Islander, non-Hispanic/Latino; 2 Two or more races, non-Hispanic/Latino), 34 international. Average age 34. 128 applicants, 98% accepted, 34 enrolled. *Faculty:* 14 full-time (3 women). Expenses: Contact institution. *Financial support:* In 2010–11, 29 students received support. Career-related internships or fieldwork, Federal Work-Study, institutionally sponsored loans, scholarships/grants, tuition waivers (full and partial), and unspecified assistantships available. Support available to part-time students. Financial award application deadline: 3/1; financial award applicants required to submit FAFSA. In 2010, 48 master's awarded. Offers business administration (MBA). *Application deadline:* For fall admission, 8/1 priority date for domestic students. Applications are processed on a rolling basis. *Application fee:* $15. *Application Contact:* Diane Trujillo, Administrative Assistant, Graduate Studies, 505-454-3266, Fax: 505-426-2117, E-mail: dtrujillo@nmhu.edu. *Dean,* Dr. Margaret Young, 505-454-3522, Fax: 505-454-3354, E-mail: young_m@nmhu.edu.

School of Education Students: 129 full-time (100 women), 254 part-time (202 women); includes 6 Black or African American, non-Hispanic/Latino; 25 American Indian or Alaska Native, non-Hispanic/Latino; 2 Asian, non-Hispanic/Latino; 197 Hispanic/Latino; 3 Two or more races, non-Hispanic/Latino, 9 international. Average age 38. 128 applicants, 98% accepted, 109 enrolled. *Faculty:* 23 full-time (16 women). Expenses: Contact institution. *Financial support:* In 2010–11, 12 students received support. Career-related internships or fieldwork, Federal Work-Study, institutionally sponsored loans, scholarships/grants, traineeships, tuition waivers (partial), and unspecified assistantships available. Support available to part-time students. Financial award application deadline: 3/1; financial award applicants required to submit FAFSA. In 2010, 110 master's awarded. *Degree program information:* Part-time programs available. Offers curriculum and instruction (MA); education (MA); educational leadership (MA); exercise and sport sciences (MA); guidance and counseling (MA); human performance and sport (MA); special education (MA); sports administration (MA); teacher education (MA). *Application deadline:* For fall admission, 8/1 priority date for domestic students. Applications are processed on a rolling basis. *Application fee:* $15. *Application Contact:* Diane Trujillo, Administrative Assistant for Graduate Studies, 505-454-3266, Fax: 505-426-2117, E-mail: dtrujillo@nmhu.edu. *Interim Dean,* Dr. Michael Anderson, 505-454-3213, E-mail: mfanderson@nmhu.edu.

School of Social Work Students: 260 full-time (216 women), 102 part-time (88 women); includes 13 Black or African American, non-Hispanic/Latino; 22 American Indian or Alaska Native, non-Hispanic/Latino; 3 Asian, non-Hispanic/Latino; 142 Hispanic/Latino; 4 Two or more races, non-Hispanic/Latino, 8 international. Average age 36. 222 applicants, 99% accepted, 164 enrolled. *Faculty:* 11 full-time (3 women). Expenses: Contact institution. *Financial support:* In 2010–11, 17 students received support. Career-related internships or fieldwork, Federal Work-Study, institutionally sponsored loans, scholarships/grants, tuition waivers (partial), and unspecified assistantships available. Support available to part-time students. Financial award application deadline: 3/1; financial award applicants required to submit FAFSA. In 2010, 133 master's awarded. *Degree program information:* Part-time programs available. Offers bilingual/bicultural social work practice (MSW); clinical practice (MSW); government non-profit management (MSW). *Application deadline:* For fall admission, 8/1 priority date for domestic students. Applications are processed on a rolling basis. *Application fee:* $15. *Application Contact:* LouAnn Romero, Administrative Assistant, Graduate Studies, 505-454-3087, E-mail: laromero@nmhu.edu. *Dean,* Dr. Alfredo Garcia, 505-891-9053, Fax: 505-454-3290, E-mail: a_garcia@nmhu.edu.

NEW MEXICO INSTITUTE OF MINING AND TECHNOLOGY, Socorro, NM 87801

General Information State-supported, coed, university. *Graduate housing:* Rooms and/or apartments available on a first-come, first-served basis to single and married students. Housing application deadline: 6/1. *Research affiliation:* National Center for Atmospheric Research (atmosphere research), National Radio Astronomy Observatory (astronomy), Joint Center for Materials Research (materials engineering, metallurgy), Gas Technology Institute (natural gas recovery), Optical Surface Technologies LLC (custom optical components).

GRADUATE UNITS

Graduate Studies Offers advanced mechanics (MS); applied math (PhD); astrophysics (MS, PhD); atmospheric physics (MS, PhD); biochemistry (MS); biology (MS); chemistry (MS); computer science (MS, PhD); electrical engineering (MS); engineering management (MEM); environmental chemistry (PhD); environmental engineering (MS); explosives engineering (MS); explosives technology and atmospheric chemistry (PhD); geochemistry (MS, PhD); geology (MS, PhD); geology and geochemistry (MS, PhD); geophysics (MS, PhD); hydrology (MS, PhD); instrumentation (MS); materials engineering (MS, PhD); mathematical physics (PhD); mathematics (MS); mining and mineral engineering (MS); operations research (MS); petroleum engineering (MS, PhD); science teaching (MST). Electronic applications accepted.

See Display on next page and Close-Up on page 973.

NEW MEXICO STATE UNIVERSITY, Las Cruces, NM 88003-8001

General Information State-supported, coed, university. CGS member. *Enrollment:* 18,552 graduate, professional, and undergraduate students; 1,957 full-time matriculated graduate/professional students (1,013 women), 1,730 part-time matriculated graduate/professional students (1,074 women). *Enrollment by degree level:* 2,853 master's, 779 doctoral, 55 other advanced degrees. *Graduate faculty:* 461 full-time (178 women), 62 part-time/adjunct (37 women). Tuition, state resident: full-time $4536; part-time $242 per credit. Tuition, nonresident: full-time $15,816; part-time $712 per credit. *Required fees:* $636 per term. *Graduate housing:* Rooms and/or apartments available on a first-come, first-served basis to single students and available to married students. Typical cost: $2790 per year ($6526 including board) for single students; $5535 per year for married students. *Student services:* Campus employment opportunities, campus safety program, career counseling, child daycare facilities, free psychological counseling, grant writing training, international student services, low-cost health insurance, multicultural affairs office, services for students with disabilities, teacher training, writing training. *Library facilities:* New Mexico State University Library plus 1 other. *Online*

New Mexico State University (continued)

resources: library catalog, web page, access to other libraries' catalogs. *Collection:* 1.8 million titles, 55,896 serial subscriptions, 16,369 audiovisual materials. *Research affiliation:* Los Alamos National Laboratory (energy research, environmental sciences, information sciences), Sandia National Laboratories (energy research, information sciences), General Electric Company (GE) (water resources research), United States Army Research Laboratories (information sciences), Northrop Grumman Corporation (aerospace), Sapphire Energy (biofuel research).

Computer facilities: Computer purchase and lease plans are available. 740 computers available on campus for general student use. A campuswide network can be accessed from student residence rooms and from off campus. Online class registration, online financial aid, wireless is available in many areas are available. *Web address:* http://www.nmsu.edu/.

General Application Contact: Dr. Linda Lacey, Dean, 575-646-5745, Fax: 575-646-7721, E-mail: gradinfo@nmsu.edu.

GRADUATE UNITS

Graduate School Students: 1,957 full-time (1,013 women), 1,730 part-time (1,074 women); includes 1,387 minority (101 Black or African American, non-Hispanic/Latino; 92 American Indian or Alaska Native, non-Hispanic/Latino; 52 Asian, non-Hispanic/Latino; 1,119 Hispanic/Latino; 1 Native Hawaiian or other Pacific Islander, non-Hispanic/Latino; 22 Two or more races, non-Hispanic/Latino), 637 international. Average age 33. 3,248 applicants, 88% accepted, 1411 enrolled. *Faculty:* 461 full-time (178 women), 62 part-time/adjunct (37 women). Expenses: Contact institution. *Financial support:* In 2010–11, 362 research assistantships (averaging $12,655 per year), 687 teaching assistantships (averaging $10,338 per year) were awarded; career-related internships or fieldwork, Federal Work-Study, scholarships/grants, traineeships, health care benefits, and unspecified assistantships also available. Support available to part-time students. In 2010, 971 master's, 99 doctorates, 27 other advanced degrees awarded. *Degree program information:* Part-time and evening/weekend programs available. Postbaccalaureate distance learning degree programs offered (no on-campus study). Offers interdisciplinary studies (MA, MS, PhD); molecular biology (MS, PhD). *Application fee:* $30 ($50 for international students). Electronic applications accepted. *Application Contact:* Coordinator, 575-646-2736, Fax: 575-646-7721, E-mail: gradinfo@nmsu.edu. *Dean,* Dr. Linda Lacey, 575-646-5746, Fax: 575-646-7721, E-mail: lacey@nmsu.edu.

College of Agricultural, Consumer and Environmental Sciences Students: 170 full-time (95 women), 89 part-time (53 women); includes 66 minority (1 Black or African American, non-Hispanic/Latino; 7 American Indian or Alaska Native, non-Hispanic/Latino; 3 Asian, non-Hispanic/Latino; 52 Hispanic/Latino; 3 Two or more races, non-Hispanic/Latino), 47 international. Average age 30. 161 applicants, 88% accepted, 99 enrolled. *Faculty:* 59 full-time (21 women), 1 (woman) part-time/adjunct. Expenses: Contact institution. *Financial support:* In 2010–11, 64 research assistantships (averaging $19,208 per year), 59 teaching assistantships (averaging $15,241 per year) were awarded; career-related internships or fieldwork, Federal Work-Study, and health care benefits also available. Support available to part-time students. Financial award application deadline: 3/1. In 2010, 75 master's, 6 doctorates awarded. *Degree program information:* Part-time and evening/weekend programs available. Offers agribusiness (M Ag, MBA); agricultural and extension education (MA); agricultural biology (MS); agricultural economics (MS); agricultural, consumer and environmental sciences (M Ag, MA, MBA, MS, DED, PhD); animal science (MS, PhD); domestic animal biology (M Ag); economics (MA); family and consumer sciences (MS); horticulture (MS); plant and environmental sciences (MS, PhD); range science (M Ag, MS, PhD); wildlife science (MS). *Application deadline:* For fall admission, 7/1 priority date for domestic students; for spring admission, 11/1 for domestic students. Applications are processed on a rolling basis. *Application fee:* $30 ($50 for international students). Electronic applications accepted. *Application Contact:* Dr. Lowell Catlett, Dean, 575-646-1806, Fax: 575-646-5975, E-mail: agdean@nmsu.edu. *Dean,* Dr. Lowell Catlett, 575-646-1806, Fax: 575-646-5975, E-mail: agdean@nmsu.edu.

College of Arts and Sciences Students: 678 full-time (310 women), 357 part-time (187 women); includes 270 minority (24 Black or African American, non-Hispanic/Latino; 24 American Indian or Alaska Native, non-Hispanic/Latino; 14 Asian, non-Hispanic/Latino; 204 Hispanic/Latino; 4 Two or more races, non-Hispanic/Latino), 241 international. Average age 31. 1,080 applicants, 86% accepted, 371 enrolled. *Faculty:* 212 full-time (79 women), 21 part-time/adjunct (8 women). Expenses: Contact institution. *Financial support:* In 2010–11, 117 research assistantships (averaging $12,382 per year), 341 teaching assistantships (averaging $11,052 per year) were awarded; career-related internships or fieldwork, Federal Work-Study, scholarships/grants, and health care benefits also available. Support available to part-time students. In 2010, 249 master's, 40 doctorates awarded. *Degree program information:* Part-time programs available. Postbaccalaureate distance learning degree programs offered. Offers anthropology (MA); art history (MA); arts and sciences (MA, MAG, MCJ, MFA, MM, MPA, MS, PhD); astronomy (MS, PhD); bioinformatics (MS); biology (MS, PhD); biotechnology and business (MS); ceramics (MA, MFA); chemistry (MS, PhD); communication studies (MA); computer science (MS, PhD); conducting (MM); creative writing (MFA); criminal justice (MCJ); design (MA, MFA); drawing (MFA); English (MA); geography (MAG); geological sciences (MS); government (MA, MPA); history (MA); mathematical sciences (MS, PhD); metals (MA, MFA); music education (MM); painting (MFA); performance (MM); photography (MFA); physics (MS, PhD); psychology (MA, PhD); public history (MA); rhetoric and professional communication (PhD); sculpture (MA, MFA); Spanish (MA). *Application fee:* $30 ($50 for international students). Electronic applications accepted. *Application Contact:* Dr. Christa Slaton, Dean, 575-646-2001, Fax: 575-646-6096, E-mail: slatocd@nmsu.edu. *Dean,* Dr. Christa Slaton, 575-646-2001, Fax: 575-646-6096, E-mail: slatocd@nmsu.edu.

College of Business Students: 208 full-time (89 women), 163 part-time (75 women); includes 136 minority (9 Black or African American, non-Hispanic/Latino; 3 American Indian or Alaska Native, non-Hispanic/Latino; 7 Asian, non-Hispanic/Latino; 114 Hispanic/Latino; 3 Two or more races, non-Hispanic/Latino), 82 international. Average age 31. 300 applicants, 82% accepted, 135 enrolled. *Faculty:* 37 full-time (7 women), 2 part-time/adjunct (1 woman). Expenses: Contact institution. *Financial support:* In 2010–11, 29 research assistantships (averaging $11,075 per year), 84 teaching assistantships (averaging $9,492 per year) were awarded; fellowships, career-related internships or fieldwork, Federal Work-Study, institutionally sponsored loans, scholarships/grants, health care benefits, and unspecified assistantships also available. Support available to part-time students. Financial award application deadline: 3/1. In 2010, 162 master's, 4 doctorates awarded. *Degree program information:* Part-time programs available. Offers accounting and information systems (M Acct); applied statistics (MS); business (M Acct, MA, MBA, MS, DED, PhD); business administration (MBA, PhD); economic development (DED); economics (MA). *Application deadline:* For fall admission, 7/1 priority date for domestic students; for spring admission, 11/1 for domestic students. Applications are processed on a rolling basis. *Application fee:* $30 ($50 for international students). Electronic applications accepted. *Application Contact:* Dr. Garrey Carruthers, Dean, 575-646-2821, Fax: 575-646-6155, E-mail: garrey@nmsu.edu. *Dean,* Dr. Garrey Carruthers, 575-646-2821, Fax: 575-646-6155, E-mail: garrey@nmsu.edu.

College of Education Students: 318 full-time (249 women), 575 part-time (441 women); includes 449 minority (22 Black or African American, non-Hispanic/Latino; 25 American Indian or Alaska Native, non-Hispanic/Latino; 11 Asian, non-Hispanic/Latino; 386 Hispanic/Latino; 5 Two or more races, non-Hispanic/Latino), 37 international. Average age 36. 682 applicants, 84% accepted, 340 enrolled. *Faculty:* 61 full-time (39 women), 25 part-time/adjunct (20 women). Expenses: Contact institution. *Financial support:* In 2010–11, 37 research assistantships (averaging $10,937 per year), 74 teaching assistantships (averaging $9,841 per year) were awarded; fellowships, career-related internships or fieldwork, Federal Work-Study, and health care benefits also available. Support available to part-time students. Financial award application deadline: 3/1. In 2010, 123 master's, 28 doctorates, 9 other advanced degrees awarded. *Degree program information:* Part-time and evening/weekend programs available. Postbaccalaureate distance learning degree programs offered (minimal on-campus study). Offers bilingual/multicultural special education (Ed D, PhD); communication disorders (MA); counseling and guidance (MA); counseling psychology (PhD); curriculum and instruction (MAT, Ed D, PhD); education (MA, MAT, Ed D, PhD, Ed S); educational administration (MA, PhD); educational management and development

(Ed D); general education (MA); school psychology (Ed S); special education (MA, Ed D, PhD). *Application deadline:* Applications are processed on a rolling basis. *Application fee:* $30 ($50 for international students). Electronic applications accepted. *Application Contact:* Dr. Michael Morehead, Dean, 575-646-3404, Fax: 575-646-6032, E-mail: mmorehea@nmsu.edu. *Dean*, Dr. Michael Morehead, 575-646-3404, Fax: 575-646-6032, E-mail: mmorehea@nmsu.edu.

College of Engineering Students: 280 full-time (58 women), 156 part-time (35 women); includes 105 minority (8 Black or African American, non-Hispanic/Latino; 4 American Indian or Alaska Native, non-Hispanic/Latino; 5 Asian, non-Hispanic/Latino; 86 Hispanic/Latino; 2 Two or more races, non-Hispanic/Latino), 210 international. Average age 29. 510 applicants, 79% accepted, 146 enrolled. *Faculty:* 59 full-time (9 women), 3 part-time/adjunct (1 woman). Expenses: Contact institution. *Financial support:* In 2010–11, 98 research assistantships (averaging $9,276 per year), 103 teaching assistantships (averaging $7,551 per year) were awarded; fellowships, career-related internships or fieldwork, Federal Work-Study, and health care benefits also available. Support available to part-time students. Financial award application deadline: 3/1. In 2010, 128 master's, 13 doctorates awarded. *Degree program information:* Part-time programs available. Offers chemical engineering (MS Ch E, PhD); civil engineering (MSCE, PhD); electrical and computer engineering (MSEE, PhD); engineering (MS Ch E, MS Env E, MSCE, MSEE, MSIE, MSME, PhD); environmental engineering (MS Env E); industrial engineering (MSIE, PhD); mechanical engineering (MSME, PhD). *Application deadline:* For fall admission, 7/1 priority date for domestic students; for spring admission, 11/1 for domestic students. Applications are processed on a rolling basis. *Application fee:* $30 ($50 for international students). Electronic applications accepted. *Application Contact:* Dr. Ricardo Jacquez, Dean, 575-646-7234, Fax: 575-646-3549, E-mail: rjaquez@nmsu.edu. *Dean*, Dr. Ricardo Jacquez, 575-646-7234, Fax: 575-646-3549, E-mail: rjaquez@nmsu.edu.

College of Health and Social Services Students: 206 full-time (166 women), 138 part-time (109 women); includes 168 minority (19 Black or African American, non-Hispanic/Latino; 23 American Indian or Alaska Native, non-Hispanic/Latino; 6 Asian, non-Hispanic/Latino; 115 Hispanic/Latino; 1 Native Hawaiian or other Pacific Islander, non-Hispanic/Latino; 4 Two or more races, non-Hispanic/Latino), 9 international. Average age 38. 267 applicants, 92% accepted, 127 enrolled. *Faculty:* 28 full-time (19 women), 10 part-time/adjunct (6 women). Expenses: Contact institution. *Financial support:* In 2010–11, 8 research assistantships (averaging $13,138 per year), 28 teaching assistantships (averaging $6,613 per year) were awarded; fellowships, career-related internships or fieldwork, Federal Work-Study, scholarships/grants, traineeships, and health care benefits also available. Financial award application deadline: 3/1. In 2010, 127 master's, 1 doctorate awarded. *Degree program information:* Part-time and evening/weekend programs available. Postbaccalaureate distance learning degree programs offered. Offers community health education (MPH); community/public health (MSN); health and social services (MPH, MSN, MSW, PhD); medical-surgical (adult health) (MSN); nursing (PhD); nursing administration (MSN); psychiatric/mental health (MSN); social work (MSW). *Application deadline:* For fall admission, 7/1 priority date for domestic students. Applications are processed on a rolling basis. *Application fee:* $30 ($50 for international students). Electronic applications accepted. *Application Contact:* Dr. Tilahun Adera, Dean, 575-646-3526, Fax: 575-646-6166, E-mail: tadera@nmsu.edu. *Dean*, Dr. Tilahun Adera, 575-646-3526, Fax: 575-646-6166, E-mail: tadera@nmsu.edu.

NEW ORLEANS BAPTIST THEOLOGICAL SEMINARY, New Orleans, LA 70126-4858

General Information Independent-religious, coed, primarily men, comprehensive institution. *Enrollment:* 987 full-time matriculated graduate/professional students (189 women), 586 part-time matriculated graduate/professional students (119 women). *Enrollment by degree level:* 995 first professional, 247 master's, 316 doctoral, 15 other advanced degrees. *Graduate faculty:* 60 full-time (8 women), 54 part-time/adjunct (5 women). *Tuition:* Full-time $3040. *Required fees:* $160 per credit hour. $80 per semester. One-time fee: $80 full-time. Tuition and fees vary according to course load and student's religious affiliation. *Graduate housing:* Rooms and/or apartments available to single and married students. Typical cost: $3150 per year for single students; $4650 per year for married students. *Student services:* Campus employment opportunities, campus safety program, career counseling, child daycare facilities, free psychological counseling, international student services. *Library facilities:* John Christian Library plus 1 other. *Collection:* 206,321 titles. *Web address:* http://www.nobts.edu/.

General Application Contact: Dr. Paul E. Gregoire, Director of Admissions and Registrar, 504-282-4455 Ext. 3337, Fax: 504-286-3591, E-mail: registrar@nobts.edu.

GRADUATE UNITS

Graduate and Professional Programs Students: 1,291. *Faculty:* 60 full-time (8 women), 54 part-time/adjunct (5 women). Expenses: Contact institution. *Financial support:* Institutionally sponsored loans available. Support available to part-time students. In 2010, 151 first professional degrees, 70 master's, 29 doctorates awarded. *Degree program information:* Evening/weekend programs available. Offers biblical studies (M Div, MA, PhD); Christian education (M Div, MACE, D Min, DEM, PhD); church music ministries (M Div, MMCM, DMA); pastoral ministries (M Div, MAMFC, D Min, PhD); theological and historical studies (M Div, MA, D Min, PhD); theology (M Div, MA, MACE, MAMFC, MMCM, D Min, DEM, DMA, PhD). *Application deadline:* For fall admission, 8/1 priority date for domestic students. Applications are processed on a rolling basis. *Application fee:* $25. *Application Contact:* Dr. Paul E. Gregoire, Director of Admissions and Registrar, 504-282-4455 Ext. 3337, Fax: 504-286-3591, E-mail: registrar@nobts.edu. *President*, Dr. Charles S. Kelly, 504-282-4455.

NEW SAINT ANDREWS COLLEGE, Moscow, ID 83843

General Information Independent-religious, coed, comprehensive institution.

GRADUATE UNITS

Graduate Studies *Degree program information:* Part-time programs available. Offers classical Christian studies (Graduate Certificate); Trinitarian theology and culture (MA). Electronic applications accepted.

THE NEW SCHOOL: A UNIVERSITY, New York, NY 10011

General Information Independent, coed, university. *Graduate housing:* Room and/or apartments available on a first-come, first-served basis to single students; on-campus housing not available to married students. Housing application deadline: 7/1. *Research affiliation:* The Goldman Sachs Group, Inc., Siemens, Raytheon Corporation, National Geospatial-Intelligence Agency, Environmental Systems Research Institute, Dow Jones & Company, Inc.

GRADUATE UNITS

Mannes College The New School for Music Offers music performance and composition (MM). Electronic applications accepted.

Milano The New School for Management and Urban Policy *Degree program information:* Part-time and evening/weekend programs available. Postbaccalaureate distance learning degree programs offered (minimal on-campus study). Offers environmental policy and sustainability management (MS); management and urban policy (MS, PhD, Adv C); nonprofit management (MS); organizational change management (MS); public and urban policy (PhD); urban policy analysis and management (MS). Electronic applications accepted.

The New School for Drama Offers acting (MFA); directing (MFA); playwriting (MFA). Electronic applications accepted.

The New School for General Studies *Degree program information:* Part-time and evening/weekend programs available. Postbaccalaureate distance learning degree programs offered (minimal on-campus study). Offers creative writing (MFA); documentary media studies (Graduate Certificate); general studies (MA, MFA, MS, Graduate Certificate); international affairs (MA, MS); media management (Graduate Certificate); media studies (MA); teaching English to speakers of other languages (MA). Electronic applications accepted.

The New School for Social Research *Degree program information:* Part-time and evening/weekend programs available. Offers anthropology (M Phil, MA, DS Sc, PhD); clinical psychology (PhD); cognitive, social and developmental psychology (PhD); economics (M Phil, MA, MS, DS Sc, PhD); general psychology (MA); global finance (MS); global political economy and finance (MA); historical studies (MA, PhD); liberal studies (MA); philosophy (MA, DS Sc, PhD); political science (M Phil, MA, DS Sc, PhD); social research (M Phil, MA, MS, DS Sc, PhD); sociology (MA, DS Sc, PhD); sociology and historical studies (MA, PhD). Electronic applications accepted.

Parsons The New School for Design Offers architecture (M Arch); design (M Arch, MA, MFA, MS); design and technology (MFA); design and urban ecologies (MS); design studies (MA); fashion design and society (MFA); fashion studies (MA); fine arts (MFA); history of decorative arts and design (MA); interior design (MFA); lighting design (MFA); photography (MFA); theories of urban practice (MA); transdisciplinary design (MFA). Electronic applications accepted.

NEWSCHOOL OF ARCHITECTURE & DESIGN, San Diego, CA 92101-6634

General Information Proprietary, coed, primarily men, comprehensive institution. *Graduate housing:* On-campus housing not available. *Research affiliation:* Center City Development Corporation.

GRADUATE UNITS

Program in Architecture *Degree program information:* Part-time and evening/weekend programs available. Offers architecture (M Arch, MS).

NEW YORK ACADEMY OF ART, New York, NY 10013-2911

General Information Independent, coed, graduate-only institution. *Graduate housing:* On-campus housing not available.

GRADUATE UNITS

Program in Figurative Art Offers figurative art (MFA).

NEW YORK CHIROPRACTIC COLLEGE, Seneca Falls, NY 13148-0800

General Information Independent, coed, graduate-only institution. *Enrollment by degree level:* 672 first professional, 169 master's. *Graduate faculty:* 64 full-time (30 women), 33 part-time/adjunct (16 women). *Tuition:* Full-time $19,050; part-time $443 per credit hour. *Required fees:* $680; $340 per term. Part-time tuition and fees vary according to program. *Graduate housing:* Rooms and/or apartments available on a first-come, first-served basis to single and married students. Typical cost: $2235 per year for single students; $3185 per year for married students. *Student services:* Campus employment opportunities, campus safety program, career counseling, exercise/wellness program, free psychological counseling, services for students with disabilities. *Library facilities:* New York Chiropractic College Library. *Online resources:* library catalog, web page. *Collection:* 17,368 titles, 500 serial subscriptions, 39,223 audiovisual materials. *Research affiliation:* Foot Levelers, Inc. (orthotics research), Atrium Innovations (nutrition), Nimmo Education Foundation (muscle physiology).

Computer facilities: 152 computers available on campus for general student use. A campuswide network can be accessed from student residence rooms and from off campus. Online class registration is available. *Web address:* http://www.nycc.edu/.

General Application Contact: Michael Lynch, Director of Admissions, 315-568-3040, Fax: 315-568-3087, E-mail: mlynch@nycc.edu.

GRADUATE UNITS

Acupuncture and Oriental Medicine Programs Students: 51 full-time (43 women), 24 part-time (15 women); includes 5 minority (1 Black or African American, non-Hispanic/Latino; 3 Asian, non-Hispanic/Latino; 1 Hispanic/Latino), 1 international. Average age 32. 60 applicants, 80% accepted, 25 enrolled. *Faculty:* 8 full-time (6 women), 7 part-time/adjunct (6 women). Expenses: Contact institution. *Financial support:* In 2010–11, 23 students received support; fellowships with tuition reimbursements available, Federal Work-Study and scholarships/grants available. Financial award applicants required to submit FAFSA. In 2010, 24 master's awarded. Offers acupuncture (MS); acupuncture and oriental medicine (MS). *Application deadline:* Applications are processed on a rolling basis. *Application fee:* $60. Electronic applications accepted. *Application Contact:* Michael Lynch, Director of Admissions, 315-568-3040, Fax: 315-568-3087, E-mail: mlynch@nycc.edu. *Dean of Finger Lakes School of Acupuncture and Oriental Medicine*, Jason Wright, 315-568-3268, E-mail: jwright@nycc.edu.

Doctor of Chiropractic Program Students: 672 full-time (265 women); includes 80 minority (14 Black or African American, non-Hispanic/Latino; 4 American Indian or Alaska Native, non-Hispanic/Latino; 36 Asian, non-Hispanic/Latino; 24 Hispanic/Latino; 2 Native Hawaiian or other Pacific Islander, non-Hispanic/Latino), 94 international. Average age 26. 219 applicants, 82% accepted, 133 enrolled. *Faculty:* 56 full-time (24 women), 25 part-time/adjunct (11 women). Expenses: Contact institution. *Financial support:* In 2010–11, 294 students received support, including 1 fellowship with full tuition reimbursement available (averaging $34,500 per year); research assistantships, Federal Work-Study and scholarships/grants also available. Financial award applicants required to submit FAFSA. In 2010, 177 DCs awarded. Offers chiropractic (DC). *Application deadline:* Applications are processed on a rolling basis. *Application fee:* $60. Electronic applications accepted. *Application Contact:* Michael Lynch, Director of Admissions, 315-568-3040, Fax: 315-568-3087, E-mail: mlynch@nycc.edu. *Dean*, Dr. Karen A. Bobak, 315-568-3864, Fax: 315-568-3087.

Program in Applied Clinical Nutrition Students: 59 part-time (40 women); includes 5 minority (4 Black or African American, non-Hispanic/Latino; 1 Hispanic/Latino), 5 international. Average age 34. 53 applicants, 87% accepted, 30 enrolled. *Faculty:* 4 part-time/adjunct (2 women). Expenses: Contact institution. *Financial support:* In 2010–11, 3 students received support. Federal Work-Study and scholarships/grants available. Financial award applicants required to submit FAFSA. In 2010, 34 master's awarded. *Degree program information:* Part-time and evening/weekend programs available. Offers applied clinical nutrition (MS). *Application deadline:* Applications are processed on a rolling basis. *Application fee:* $60. Electronic applications accepted. *Application Contact:* Michael Lynch, Director of Admissions, 315-568-3040, Fax: 315-568-3087, E-mail: mlynch@nycc.edu. *Director*, Dr. Anna R. Kelles, 315-568-3310.

Program in Clinical Anatomy Students: 1 part-time (0 women). 6 applicants, 0% accepted, 0 enrolled. *Faculty:* 2 full-time (0 women). Expenses: Contact institution. *Financial support:* In 2010–11, 1 fellowship with full tuition reimbursement (averaging $33,500 per year) was awarded. Financial award applicants required to submit FAFSA. Offers clinical anatomy (MS). *Application deadline:* Applications are processed on a rolling basis. *Application fee:* $0. *Application Contact:* Dr. Karen Gana, Director, 315-568-3184, E-mail: kgana@nycc.edu. *Director*, Dr. Karen Gana, 315-568-3184, E-mail: kgana@nycc.edu.

Program in Diagnostic Imaging Students: 4 part-time (3 women); includes 2 Black or African American, non-Hispanic/Latino. Average age 32. 2 applicants, 50% accepted, 1 enrolled. *Faculty:* 1 full-time (0 women). Expenses: Contact institution. *Financial support:* In 2010–11, 3 fellowships with full tuition reimbursements (averaging $33,000 per year) were awarded. Financial award applicants required to submit FAFSA. In 2010, 1 master's awarded. Offers diagnostic imaging (MS). *Application deadline:* Applications are processed on a rolling basis. *Application fee:* $0. *Application Contact:* Dr. Jean-Nicolas Poirier, Director, 315-568-3197, E-mail: npoirier@nycc.edu. *Director*, Dr. Jean-Nicolas Poirier, 315-568-3197, E-mail: npoirier@nycc.edu.

Program in Human Anatomy and Physiology Instruction Students: 30 part-time (11 women); includes 1 Hispanic/Latino, 1 international. Average age 43. *Faculty:* 1 part-time/adjunct (0 women). Expenses: Contact institution. *Financial support:* In 2010–11, 1 student received support. Applicants required to submit FAFSA. Postbaccalaureate distance learning degree programs offered. Offers human anatomy and physiology (MS). *Application Contact:* Michael Lynch, Director of Admissions, 315-568-3040, Fax: 315-568-3087, E-mail: mlynch@nycc.edu. *Director*, Dr. Robert A. Crocker, 516-796-4800, E-mail: rcrocker@nycc.edu.

NEW YORK COLLEGE OF HEALTH PROFESSIONS, Syosset, NY 11791-4413

General Information Independent, coed, comprehensive institution. *Graduate housing:* On-campus housing not available. *Research affiliation:* North Shore Hospital (acupuncture).

New York College of Health Professions (continued)

GRADUATE UNITS

Graduate School of Oriental Medicine *Degree program information:* Part-time programs available. Offers acupuncture (MS); Oriental medicine (MS).

NEW YORK COLLEGE OF PODIATRIC MEDICINE, New York, NY 10035

General Information Independent, coed, graduate-only institution. *Graduate housing:* Rooms and/or apartments available on a first-come, first-served basis to single and married students. Housing application deadline: 8/15. *Research affiliation:* Cyberlogics (ultrasound use), Novartis (fungal diseases of nail), Prescription Dispensing Laboratories (topical verapamil), Anodyne Corporation (light energy applications).

GRADUATE UNITS

Professional Program Offers podiatric medicine (DPM).

NEW YORK COLLEGE OF TRADITIONAL CHINESE MEDICINE, Mineola, NY 11501

General Information Independent, coed, graduate-only institution.

GRADUATE UNITS

Graduate Programs

NEW YORK FILM ACADEMY, Los Angeles, CA 90068

General Information Independent, coed, comprehensive institution.

GRADUATE UNITS

Program in Filmmaking–Hollywood Offers acting for film (MFA); cinematography (MFA); filmmaking (MFA); photography (MFA); producing (MFA); screenwriting (MFA).

Program in Filmmaking–New York Offers acting for film (MFA); filmmaking (MFA); producing (MFA); screenwriting (MFA).

Program in Filmmaking–United Arab Emirates Offers acting for film (MFA); filmmaking (MFA); producing (MFA); screenwriting (MFA).

NEW YORK INSTITUTE OF TECHNOLOGY, Old Westbury, NY 11568-8000

General Information Independent, coed, university. CGS member. *Enrollment:* 11,471 graduate, professional, and undergraduate students; 2,569 full-time matriculated graduate/professional students (1,288 women), 1,303 part-time matriculated graduate/professional students (585 women). *Enrollment by degree level:* 1,185 first professional, 2,555 master's, 110 doctoral, 22 other advanced degrees. *Tuition:* Part-time $835 per credit. *Graduate housing:* Room and/or apartments available on a first-come, first-served basis to single students; on-campus housing not available to married students. *Student services:* Campus employment opportunities, career counseling, exercise/wellness program, free psychological counseling, international student services, low-cost health insurance, multicultural affairs office, services for students with disabilities, teacher training, writing training. *Library facilities:* George and Gertrude Wisser Memorial Library plus 4 others. *Online resources:* library catalog, web page. *Collection:* 152,397 titles, 1,002 serial subscriptions, 2,246 audiovisual materials.

Computer facilities: 1,250 computers available on campus for general student use. A campuswide network can be accessed from student residence rooms and from off campus. E-mail available. *Web address:* http://www.nyit.edu/.

General Application Contact: Dr. Jacquelyn Nealon, Vice President for Enrollment Services, 516-686-7925, Fax: 516-686-7597, E-mail: jnealon@nyit.edu.

GRADUATE UNITS

Graduate Division Students: 1,384 full-time (662 women), 1,303 part-time (585 women); includes 411 minority (150 Black or African American, non-Hispanic/Latino; 5 American Indian or Alaska Native, non-Hispanic/Latino; 146 Asian, non-Hispanic/Latino; 107 Hispanic/Latino; 3 Two or more races, non-Hispanic/Latino), 725 international. Average age 30. Expenses: Contact institution. *Financial support:* Fellowships with partial tuition reimbursements, research assistantships with partial tuition reimbursements, career-related internships or fieldwork, Federal Work-Study, institutionally sponsored loans, tuition waivers (full and partial), and unspecified assistantships available. Support available to part-time students. Financial award applicants required to submit FAFSA. In 2010, 1,012 master's, 30 doctorates, 56 other advanced degrees awarded. *Degree program information:* Part-time and evening/weekend programs available. Postbaccalaureate distance learning degree programs offered (minimal on-campus study). *Application deadline:* For fall admission, 7/1 priority date for domestic students; for spring admission, 12/1 priority date for domestic students. Applications are processed on a rolling basis. *Application fee:* $50. Electronic applications accepted. *Application Contact:* Dr. Jacquelyn Nealon, Vice President for Enrollment Services, 516-686-7925, Fax: 516-686-7597, E-mail: jnealon@nyit.edu. *Provost and Vice President for Academic Affairs,* Dr. Richard Pizer, 516-686-7630, Fax: 516-686-7631, E-mail: rpizer@nyit.edu.

School of Architecture and Design Students: 24 full-time (11 women), 3 part-time (all women); includes 6 minority (3 Asian, non-Hispanic/Latino; 3 Hispanic/Latino), 16 international. Average age 27. Expenses: Contact institution. *Financial support:* Research assistantships with partial tuition reimbursements, institutionally sponsored loans and tuition waivers (full and partial) available. Support available to part-time students. Financial award applicants required to submit FAFSA. In 2010, 12 master's awarded. *Degree program information:* Part-time programs available. Offers urban and regional design (M Arch). *Application deadline:* For fall admission, 7/1 priority date for domestic students; for spring admission, 12/1 priority date for domestic students. Applications are processed on a rolling basis. *Application fee:* $50. Electronic applications accepted. *Application Contact:* Dr. Jacquelyn Nealon, Vice President for Enrollment Services, 516-686-7925, Fax: 516-686-7597, E-mail: jnealon@nyit.edu. *Dean,* Judith DiMaio, 516-686-7594, Fax: 516-686-7921, E-mail: jdimaio@nyit.edu.

School of Arts and Sciences Students: 132 full-time (91 women), 89 part-time (55 women); includes 60 minority (31 Black or African American, non-Hispanic/Latino; 9 Asian, non-Hispanic/Latino; 19 Hispanic/Latino; 1 Two or more races, non-Hispanic/Latino), 73 international. Average age 27. Expenses: Contact institution. *Financial support:* Research assistantships with partial tuition reimbursements, career-related internships or fieldwork, Federal Work-Study, institutionally sponsored loans, tuition waivers (partial), and unspecified assistantships available. Support available to part-time students. Financial award applicants required to submit FAFSA. In 2010, 105 master's awarded. *Degree program information:* Part-time and evening/weekend programs available. Offers arts and sciences (MA, MFA); communication arts (MA); computer graphics and animation (MFA); fine arts and technology (MFA); graphic design (MFA). *Application deadline:* For fall admission, 7/1 priority date for domestic students; for spring admission, 12/1 priority date for domestic students. Applications are processed on a rolling basis. *Application fee:* $50. Electronic applications accepted. *Application Contact:* Dr. Jacquelyn Nealon, Vice President for Enrollment Services, 516-686-7925, Fax: 516-686-7597, E-mail: jnealon@nyit.edu. *Dean,* Dr. Roger Yu, 516-686-7700, Fax: 516-686-1192, E-mail: ryu@nyit.edu.

School of Education Students: 30 full-time (21 women), 304 part-time (186 women); includes 63 minority (25 Black or African American, non-Hispanic/Latino; 1 American Indian or Alaska Native, non-Hispanic/Latino; 15 Asian, non-Hispanic/Latino; 22 Hispanic/Latino), 6 international. Average age 32. Expenses: Contact institution. *Financial support:* Research assistantships with partial tuition reimbursements, career-related internships or fieldwork, institutionally sponsored loans, and tuition waivers (full and partial) available. Support available to part-time students. Financial award applicants required to submit FAFSA. In 2010, 110 master's, 18 other advanced degrees awarded. *Degree program information:* Part-time and evening/weekend programs available. Postbaccalaureate distance learning degree programs offered. Offers childhood education (MS); distance learning (Advanced Certificate); education (MS, Advanced Certificate, Professional Diploma); instructional technology (MS); multimedia (Advanced Certificate); school counseling (MS); school leadership and technology (Professional Diploma). *Application deadline:* For fall admission, 7/1 priority date for domestic students; for spring admission, 12/1 priority date for domestic students. Applications are processed on a rolling basis. *Application fee:* $50. Electronic applications accepted. *Application Contact:* Dr. Jacquelyn Nealon, Vice President for Enrollment Services, 516-686-7925, Fax: 516-686-7597, E-mail: jnealon@nyit.edu. *Dean,* Dr. Michael Uttendorfer, 516-686-7706, Fax: 516-686-7655, E-mail: muttendo@nyit.edu.

School of Engineering and Computing Sciences Students: 356 full-time (87 women), 284 part-time (54 women); includes 97 minority (40 Black or African American, non-Hispanic/Latino; 3 American Indian or Alaska Native, non-Hispanic/Latino; 32 Asian, non-Hispanic/Latino; 21 Hispanic/Latino; 1 Two or more races, non-Hispanic/Latino), 331 international. Average age 28. Expenses: Contact institution. *Financial support:* Fellowships, research assistantships with partial tuition reimbursements, career-related internships or fieldwork, institutionally sponsored loans, tuition waivers (full and partial), and unspecified assistantships available. Support available to part-time students. Financial award applicants required to submit FAFSA. In 2010, 244 master's, 34 other advanced degrees awarded. *Degree program information:* Part-time and evening/weekend programs available. Postbaccalaureate distance learning degree programs offered. Offers computer science (MS); electrical engineering and computer engineering (MS); energy management (MS); energy technology (Advanced Certificate); engineering and computing sciences (MS, Advanced Certificate); environmental management (Advanced Certificate); environmental technology (MS); facilities management (Advanced Certificate); information, network, and computer security (MS). *Application deadline:* For fall admission, 7/1 priority date for domestic students; for spring admission, 12/1 priority date for domestic students. Applications are processed on a rolling basis. *Application fee:* $50. Electronic applications accepted. *Application Contact:* Dr. Jacquelyn Nealon, Vice President for Enrollment Services, 516-686-7925, Fax: 516-686-7597, E-mail: jnealon@nyit.edu. *Dean,* Dr. Nada Anid, 516-686-7931, Fax: 516-625-7933, E-mail: nanid@nyit.edu.

School of Health Professions Students: 347 full-time (236 women), 48 part-time (39 women); includes 106 minority (23 Black or African American, non-Hispanic/Latino; 1 American Indian or Alaska Native, non-Hispanic/Latino; 59 Asian, non-Hispanic/Latino; 22 Hispanic/Latino; 1 Two or more races, non-Hispanic/Latino), 3 international. Average age 26. Expenses: Contact institution. *Financial support:* Fellowships, research assistantships with partial tuition reimbursements, career-related internships or fieldwork, institutionally sponsored loans, tuition waivers (full and partial), and unspecified assistantships available. Support available to part-time students. Financial award applicants required to submit FAFSA. In 2010, 79 master's, 30 doctorates awarded. *Degree program information:* Part-time and evening/weekend programs available. Postbaccalaureate distance learning degree programs offered. Offers clinical nutrition (MS); health professions (MS, DPT); mental health counseling (MS); occupational therapy (MS); physical therapy (DPT); physician assistant (MS). *Application deadline:* For fall admission, 7/1 priority date for domestic students; for spring admission, 12/1 priority date for domestic students. Applications are processed on a rolling basis. *Application fee:* $50. Electronic applications accepted. *Application Contact:* Dr. Jacquelyn Nealon, Vice President for Enrollment Services, 516-686-7925, Fax: 516-686-7597, E-mail: jnealon@nyit.edu. *Dean,* Dr. Patricia Chute, 516-686-3939, Fax: 516-686-3854, E-mail: pchute@nyit.edu.

School of Management Students: 495 full-time (216 women), 575 part-time (248 women); includes 79 minority (31 Black or African American, non-Hispanic/Latino; 28 Asian, non-Hispanic/Latino; 20 Hispanic/Latino), 296 international. Average age 29. Expenses: Contact institution. *Financial support:* Fellowships, research assistantships with partial tuition reimbursements, career-related internships or fieldwork, institutionally sponsored loans, tuition waivers (full and partial), and unspecified assistantships available. Support available to part-time students. Financial award applicants required to submit FAFSA. In 2010, 462 master's, 4 other advanced degrees awarded. *Degree program information:* Part-time and evening/weekend programs available. Postbaccalaureate distance learning degree programs offered. Offers accounting (Advanced Certificate); business administration (MBA); finance (Advanced Certificate); human resources administration (Advanced Certificate); human resources management and labor relations (MS); international business (Advanced Certificate); labor relations (Advanced Certificate); management (MBA, MS, Advanced Certificate); management of information systems (Advanced Certificate); marketing (Advanced Certificate). *Application deadline:* For fall admission, 7/1 priority date for domestic students; for spring admission, 12/1 priority date for domestic students. Applications are processed on a rolling basis. *Application fee:* $50. Electronic applications accepted. *Application Contact:* Dr. Jacquelyn Nealon, Vice President for Enrollment Services, 516-686-7925, Fax: 516-686-7597, E-mail: jnealon@nyit.edu. *Dean,* Dr. Jess Boronico, 516-686-7838, Fax: 516-686-7430, E-mail: jboronic@nyit.edu.

New York College of Osteopathic Medicine Students: 1,185 full-time (626 women); includes 525 minority (57 Black or African American, non-Hispanic/Latino; 410 Asian, non-Hispanic/Latino; 56 Hispanic/Latino; 1 Native Hawaiian or other Pacific Islander, non-Hispanic/Latino; 1 Two or more races, non-Hispanic/Latino). Average age 26. Expenses: Contact institution. *Financial support:* Fellowships with partial tuition reimbursements, tuition waivers (full and partial) available. Financial award application deadline: 4/1; financial award applicants required to submit FAFSA. In 2010, 275 DOs awarded. Offers osteopathic medicine (DO). *Application deadline:* For fall admission, 2/1 for domestic students. *Application fee:* $60. *Application Contact:* Rodika Zaika, Director of NYCOM Admissions, 516-686-3792, Fax: 516-686-3831, E-mail: rzaika@nyit.edu. *Dean,* Dr. Thomas Scandalis, 516-686-3722, Fax: 516-686-3830, E-mail: tscandal@nyit.edu.

NEW YORK LAW SCHOOL, New York, NY 10013

General Information Independent, coed, graduate-only institution. *Enrollment by degree level:* 1,923 first professional, 115 master's. *Graduate faculty:* 86 full-time (33 women), 111 part-time/adjunct (40 women). *Tuition:* Full-time $44,860; part-time $34,500 per year. *Required fees:* $1600. *Graduate housing:* Room and/or apartments available on a first-come, first-served basis to single students; on-campus housing not available to married students. Typical cost: $22,680 per year. Housing application deadline: 6/1. *Student services:* Campus employment opportunities, campus safety program, career counseling, free psychological counseling, international student services, low-cost health insurance, services for students with disabilities, writing training. *Library facilities:* Mendik Library. *Online resources:* library catalog, web page, access to other libraries' catalogs. *Collection:* 522,118 titles, 5,379 serial subscriptions.

Computer facilities: 120 computers available on campus for general student use. A campuswide network can be accessed from student residence rooms and from off campus. Online class registration is available. *Web address:* http://www.nyls.edu/.

General Application Contact: William D. Perez, Assistant Dean for Admissions and Financial Aid, 212-431-2888, Fax: 212-966-1522, E-mail: wperez@nyls.edu.

GRADUATE UNITS

Graduate Programs Students: 1,547 full-time (824 women), 491 part-time (214 women); includes 488 minority (145 Black or African American, non-Hispanic/Latino; 11 American Indian or Alaska Native, non-Hispanic/Latino; 67 Asian, non-Hispanic/Latino; 233 Hispanic/Latino; 1 Native Hawaiian or other Pacific Islander, non-Hispanic/Latino; 31 Two or more races, non-Hispanic/Latino). Average age 28. 5,405 applicants, 45% accepted, 550 enrolled. *Faculty:* 75 full-time (26 women), 100 part-time/adjunct (40 women). Expenses: Contact institution. *Financial support:* In 2010–11, 682 students received support, including 202 research assistantships (averaging $3,920 per year), 5 teaching assistantships (averaging $1,000 per year); career-related internships or fieldwork, Federal Work-Study, institutionally sponsored loans, and scholarships/grants also available. Support available to part-time students. Financial award application deadline: 4/2; financial award applicants required to submit FAFSA. In 2010, 539 first professional degrees, 9 master's awarded. *Degree program information:* Part-time and evening/weekend programs available. Postbaccalaureate distance learning degree programs offered. Offers financial services (LL M); law (JD); mental disability law (MA); real estate (LL M); taxation (LL M). JD/MBA offered jointly with Bernard M. Baruch College of the City University of New York. *Application deadline:* For fall admission, 4/1 priority date for domestic and international students. Applications are processed on a rolling basis. *Application fee:* $65. Electronic applications accepted. *Application Contact:* William D. Perez, Assistant Dean for Admissions and Financial Aid, 212-431-2888, Fax: 212-966-1522, E-mail: wperez@nyls.edu. *President and Dean,* Richard A. Matasar, 212-431-2840, Fax: 212-219-3752, E-mail: rmatasar@nyls.edu.

NEW YORK MEDICAL COLLEGE, Valhalla, NY 10595-1691

General Information Independent, coed, graduate-only institution. CGS member. *Graduate housing:* Rooms and/or apartments available on a first-come, first-served basis to single and married students. *Research affiliation:* Westchester Medical Center (disaster medicine), Danbury Hospital (behavioral sciences and epidemiology), Westchester Institute for Human Development (disability and human development).

GRADUATE UNITS

Graduate School of Basic Medical Sciences Students: 170 full-time (90 women), 6 part-time (4 women); includes 92 minority (13 Black or African American, non-Hispanic/Latino; 1 American Indian or Alaska Native, non-Hispanic/Latino; 67 Asian, non-Hispanic/Latino; 11 Hispanic/Latino). Average age 26. 500 applicants, 47% accepted, 77 enrolled. *Faculty:* 91 full-time (18 women), 5 part-time/adjunct (4 women). Expenses: Contact institution. *Financial support:* In 2010–11, 53 research assistantships with full tuition reimbursements (averaging $24,000 per year) were awarded; Federal Work-Study, institutionally sponsored loans, scholarships/grants, tuition waivers (full), and health benefits (for PhD candidates only) also available. Financial award applicants required to submit FAFSA. In 2010, 50 master's, 8 doctorates awarded. *Degree program information:* Part-time and evening/weekend programs available. Offers basic medical sciences (MS, PhD); biochemistry and molecular biology (MS, PhD); cell biology and neuroscience (MS, PhD); experimental pathology (MS, PhD); microbiology and immunology (MS, PhD); pharmacology (MS, PhD); physiology (MS, PhD). *Application deadline:* For fall admission, 7/1 priority date for domestic students, 5/1 priority date for international students; for spring admission, 12/1 priority date for domestic students, 10/1 priority date for international students. Applications are processed on a rolling basis. *Application fee:* $50 ($75 for international students). Electronic applications accepted. *Application Contact:* Valerie Romeo-Messana, Admission Coordinator, 914-594-4110, Fax: 914-594-4944, E-mail: v_romeomessana@nymc.edu. *Dean,* Dr. Francis L. Belloni, 914-594-4110, Fax: 914-594-4944, E-mail: francis_belloni@nymc.edu.

Professional Program Offers medicine (MD). Electronic applications accepted.

School of Health Sciences and Practice *Degree program information:* Part-time and evening/weekend programs available. Postbaccalaureate distance learning degree programs offered (no on-campus study). Offers behavioral sciences and health promotion (MPH); emergency preparedness (Graduate Certificate); environmental health science (MPH); epidemiology (MPH); global health (Graduate Certificate); health education (Graduate Certificate); health policy and management (MPH, Dr PH); health sciences and practice (MPH, MS, DPT, Dr PH, Graduate Certificate); industrial hygiene (Graduate Certificate); physical therapy (DPT); speech-language pathology (MS). Electronic applications accepted.

NEW YORK SCHOOL OF INTERIOR DESIGN, New York, NY 10021-5110

General Information Independent, coed, primarily women, comprehensive institution. *Enrollment:* 714 graduate, professional, and undergraduate students; 102 full-time matriculated graduate/professional students (81 women). *Enrollment by degree level:* 102 master's. *Graduate faculty:* 24 part-time/adjunct (10 women). *Tuition:* Full-time $26,500. *Required fees:* $335. One-time fee: $60 full-time. *Graduate housing:* Room and/or apartments available to single students; on-campus housing not available to married students. Housing application deadline: 5/1. *Student services:* Campus employment opportunities, career counseling, free psychological counseling, international student services, low-cost health insurance. *Research affiliation:* Metropolitan New York Library Council–Research Consortium.

Computer facilities: 135 computers available on campus for general student use. A campuswide network can be accessed from student residence rooms and from off campus. Online class registration is available. *Web address:* http://www.nysid.edu/.

General Application Contact: Scott Ageloff, Dean, 212-472-1500 Ext. 301, Fax: 212-288-6577, E-mail: sageloff@nysid.edu.

GRADUATE UNITS

Program in Interior Design Students: 68 full-time (56 women); includes 22 minority (3 Black or African American, non-Hispanic/Latino; 18 Asian, non-Hispanic/Latino; 1 Hispanic/Latino). Average age 30. 128 applicants, 77% accepted, 36 enrolled. *Faculty:* 24 part-time/adjunct (10 women). Expenses: Contact institution. *Financial support:* In 2010–11, 2 research assistantships (averaging $10,000 per year) were awarded; career-related internships or fieldwork, Federal Work-Study, institutionally sponsored loans, and scholarships/grants also available. Financial award application deadline: 8/1; financial award applicants required to submit FAFSA. In 2010, 1 master's awarded. Offers interior design (MFA). *Application deadline:* For fall admission, 2/1 for domestic and international students. *Application fee:* $60 ($100 for international students). Electronic applications accepted. *Application Contact:* David T. Sprouls, Director of Admissions, 212-472-1500 Ext. 202, Fax: 212-472-1867, E-mail: dsprouls@nysid.edu. *Dean,* Scott Ageloff, 212-472-1500 Ext. 301, Fax: 212-288-6577, E-mail: sageloff@nysid.edu.

Program in Interior Design (Post-Professional Level) Students: 25 full-time (18 women); includes 13 minority (12 Asian, non-Hispanic/Latino; 1 Hispanic/Latino). Average age 27. 47 applicants, 68% accepted, 14 enrolled. *Faculty:* 24 part-time/adjunct (10 women). Expenses: Contact institution. *Financial support:* In 2010–11, 3 research assistantships (averaging $10,000 per year) were awarded; career-related internships or fieldwork, Federal Work-Study, institutionally sponsored loans, and scholarships/grants also available. Financial award application deadline: 8/1; financial award applicants required to submit FAFSA. In 2010, 1 master's awarded. Offers interior design (MFA). *Application deadline:* For fall admission, 2/1 priority date for domestic and international students. *Application fee:* $60 ($100 for international students). Electronic applications accepted. *Application Contact:* Scott Ageloff, Dean, 212-472-1500 Ext. 301, Fax: 212-288-6577, E-mail: sageloff@nysid.edu.

Program in Interior Lighting Design Expenses: Contact institution. *Financial support:* Fellowships available. Financial award application deadline: 8/1; financial award applicants required to submit FAFSA. In 2010, 1 master's awarded. Offers interior lighting design (MPS). *Application deadline:* For fall admission, 2/1 for domestic and international students. *Application fee:* $60 ($100 for international students). Electronic applications accepted. *Application Contact:* Scott Ageloff, Dean, 212-472-1500 Ext. 301, Fax: 212-288-6577, E-mail: sageloff@nysid.edu.

Program in Sustainable Interior Environments Students: 9 full-time (7 women); includes 4 minority (2 Asian, non-Hispanic/Latino; 2 Hispanic/Latino). Average age 27. *Faculty:* 24 part-time/adjunct (10 women). Expenses: Contact institution. *Financial support:* Research assistantships, Federal Work-Study available. Financial award applicants required to submit FAFSA. In 2010, 1 master's awarded. Offers sustainable interior environments (MPS). *Application deadline:* For fall admission, 2/1 priority date for domestic and international students. Applications are processed on a rolling basis. *Application fee:* $60 ($100 for international students). Electronic applications accepted. *Application Contact:* Scott Ageloff, Dean, 212-472-1500 Ext. 301, Fax: 212-288-6577, E-mail: sageloff@nysid.edu.

NEW YORK STUDIO SCHOOL OF DRAWING, PAINTING AND SCULPTURE, New York, NY 10011

General Information Independent, coed, comprehensive institution.

GRADUATE UNITS

Certificate Program Offers studio art (Certificate).

MFA Program Offers painting (MFA); sculpture (MFA).

NEW YORK THEOLOGICAL SEMINARY, New York, NY 10115

General Information Independent-religious, coed, graduate-only institution. *Graduate housing:* On-campus housing not available. *Research affiliation:* Bellevue Hospital Center, Goldwater Memorial Hospital, Institutes of Religion and Health, Lutheran Medical Center, Postgraduate Center for Mental Health.

GRADUATE UNITS

Graduate and Professional Programs *Degree program information:* Part-time programs available. Offers theology (M Div, MPS, MSW, D Min). MSW offered jointly with Fordham University.

NEW YORK UNIVERSITY, New York, NY 10012-1019

General Information Independent, coed, university. CGS member. *Graduate housing:* Room and/or apartments available on a first-come, first-served basis to single students; on-campus housing not available to married students. Housing application deadline: 5/1. *Research affiliation:* Smithsonian Institution, Metropolitan Museum of Art, Inter-University Doctoral Consortium, American Museum of Natural History, Center for American Archaeology, New York Botanical Gardens.

GRADUATE UNITS

College of Dentistry Students: 1,413 full-time (687 women), 10 part-time (6 women); includes 49 Black or African American, non-Hispanic/Latino; 3 American Indian or Alaska Native, non-Hispanic/Latino; 755 Asian, non-Hispanic/Latino; 71 Hispanic/Latino. Average age 27. 6,168 applicants, 14% accepted, 421 enrolled. *Faculty:* 242 full-time (85 women), 689 part-time/adjunct (186 women). Expenses: Contact institution. *Financial support:* In 2010–11, 106 students received support. Application deadline: 3/1. In 2010, 359 first professional degrees, 11 master's, 41 other advanced degrees awarded. Offers clinical research (MS); dentistry (DDS, MS, Advanced Certificate); endodontics (Advanced Certificate); oral and maxillofacial surgery (Advanced Certificate); orthodontics (Advanced Certificate); pediatric dentistry (Advanced Certificate); periodontics (Advanced Certificate); prosthodontics (Advanced Certificate); prosthodontics (implantology) (Advanced Certificate). *Application deadline:* For fall admission, 1/4 priority date for domestic students, 12/1 priority date for international students. Applications are processed on a rolling basis. *Application fee:* $75. Electronic applications accepted. *Application Contact:* Dr. Anthony M. Palatta, Assistant Dean for Student Affairs and Admissions, 212-998-9918, Fax: 212-995-4240, E-mail: ap16@nyu.edu. *Dean,* Dr. Charles Bertolami, 212-998-9898, Fax: 212-995-4240, E-mail: charles.bertolami@nyu.edu.

College of Nursing Students: 62 full-time (51 women), 530 part-time (500 women); includes 75 Black or African American, non-Hispanic/Latino; 54 Asian, non-Hispanic/Latino; 27 Hispanic/Latino. Average age 41. 294 applicants, 82% accepted, 175 enrolled. *Faculty:* 31 full-time (30 women), 30 part-time/adjunct (24 women). Expenses: Contact institution. *Financial support:* In 2010–11, 148 students received support, including 2 research assistantships with full and partial tuition reimbursements available (averaging $23,000 per year); fellowships with full and partial tuition reimbursements available, career-related internships or fieldwork, institutionally sponsored loans, scholarships/grants, and tuition waivers (partial) also available. Support available to part-time students. Financial award application deadline: 2/1; financial award applicants required to submit FAFSA. In 2010, 114 master's, 1 doctorate, 5 other advanced degrees awarded. *Degree program information:* Part-time and evening/weekend programs available. Offers advanced practice nursing (DNP); advanced practice nursing: adult acute care (MS, Advanced Certificate); advanced practice nursing: adult nurse practitioner/holistic nurse practitioner (Advanced Certificate); advanced practice nursing: adult nurse practitioner/holistic nursing (MS); advanced practice nursing: adult nurse practitioner/palliative care nurse practitioner (Advanced Certificate); advanced practice nursing: adult nurse practitioner/palliative care nursing (MS); advanced practice nursing: adult primary care (MS, Advanced Certificate); advanced practice nursing: adult primary care and geriatrics (Advanced Certificate); advanced practice nursing: adult primary care/geriatrics (MS); advanced practice nursing: geriatrics (MS, Advanced Certificate); advanced practice nursing: mental health (MS); advanced practice nursing: mental health nursing (Advanced Certificate); advanced practice nursing: pediatrics (MS, Advanced Certificate); nurse midwifery (MS, Advanced Certificate); nursing (MS, DNP, PhD, Advanced Certificate); nursing administration (MS, Advanced Certificate); nursing education (MS, Advanced Certificate); nursing informatics (MS, Advanced Certificate); research and theory development in nursing science (PhD). *Application deadline:* Applications are processed on a rolling basis. *Application fee:* $75. *Application Contact:* Amy Knowles, Assistant Dean for Student Affairs and Admissions, 212-998-5333, Fax: 212-995-4302, E-mail: ak96@nyu.edu. *Dean,* Dr. Terry Fulmer, 212-998-5303, Fax: 212-995-3143.

Gallatin School of Individualized Study Students: 64 full-time (52 women), 135 part-time (94 women); includes 15 Black or African American, non-Hispanic/Latino; 1 American Indian or Alaska Native, non-Hispanic/Latino; 13 Asian, non-Hispanic/Latino; 10 Hispanic/Latino. Average age 34. 330 applicants, 41% accepted, 56 enrolled. *Faculty:* 52 full-time (28 women), 102 part-time/adjunct (44 women). Expenses: Contact institution. *Financial support:* In 2010–11, 88 students received support, including 3 fellowships with tuition reimbursements available (averaging $25,000 per year), 4 research assistantships with full tuition reimbursements available (averaging $17,284 per year); Federal Work-Study, scholarships/grants, and unspecified assistantships also available. Support available to part-time students. Financial award application deadline: 2/1; financial award applicants required to submit FAFSA. In 2010, 58 degrees awarded. *Degree program information:* Part-time programs available. Offers individualized study (MA). *Application deadline:* For fall admission, 1/15 priority date for domestic and international students; for spring admission, 11/1 for domestic and international students. Applications are processed on a rolling basis. *Application fee:* $50. Electronic applications accepted. *Application Contact:* John Bradley, Assistant to the Director of Enrollment, 212-998-7364, E-mail: gallatin.gradadmissions@nyu.edu. *Director of Enrollment,* Frances R. Levin, 212-998-7370, Fax: 212-995-4150.

Graduate School of Arts and Science Students: 3,585 full-time (1,941 women), 1,145 part-time (641 women); includes 128 Black or African American, non-Hispanic/Latino; 9 American Indian or Alaska Native, non-Hispanic/Latino; 301 Asian, non-Hispanic/Latino; 219 Hispanic/Latino, 1,568 international. Average age 29. 13,440 applicants, 27% accepted, 1468 enrolled. *Faculty:* 597 full-time (159 women). Expenses: Contact institution. *Financial support:* Fellowships with tuition reimbursements, research assistantships with tuition reimbursements, teaching assistantships with tuition reimbursements, career-related internships or fieldwork, Federal Work-Study, institutionally sponsored loans, scholarships/grants, health care benefits, tuition waivers (partial), unspecified assistantships, and instructorships available. Financial award applicants required to submit FAFSA. In 2010, 1,036 master's, 261 doctorates awarded. *Degree program information:* Part-time and evening/weekend programs available. Offers African diaspora (PhD); African history (PhD); Africana studies (MA); American studies (MA, PhD); anthropology (MA, PhD); anthropology and French studies (PhD); applied economic analysis (Advanced Certificate); archival management and historical editing (Advanced Certificate); arts and science (MA, MFA, MS, PhD, Advanced Certificate); Atlantic history (PhD); bioethics (MA); biology (PhD); biomaterials science (MS); biomedical journalism (MS); cancer and molecular biology (PhD); chemistry (MS, PhD); classics (MA, PhD); cognition and perception (PhD); community psychology (PhD); comparative literature (MA, PhD); composition and theory (MA, PhD); computational biology (PhD); computers in biological research (MS); creative writing (MA, MFA); developmental genetics (PhD); early music performance (Advanced Certificate); East Asian studies (MA, PhD); economics (MA, PhD); English and American literature (MA, PhD); environmental health sciences (MS, PhD); ethnomusicology (MA, PhD); French studies and sociology (PhD); French studies/history (PhD); general biology (MS); general psychology (MA); German studies and critical thought (MA, PhD); Hebrew and Judaic studies (MA, PhD); Hebrew and Judaic studies/history (PhD); Hebrew and Judaic studies/museum studies (MA); history (MA, PhD); humanities and social thought (MA); immunology and microbiology (PhD); industrial/organizational psychology (MA); Irish and Irish American studies (MA); Italian (MA, PhD); Italian studies (MA); linguistics (MA, PhD); Middle Eastern history (MA); Middle Eastern studies/history (PhD); molecular genetics (PhD); museum studies (MA, Advanced Certificate); neurobiology (PhD); oral biology (MS); philosophy (MA, PhD); physics (MS, PhD); plant biology (PhD); poetics and theory (Advanced Certificate); political campaign management (MA); politics (MA, PhD); Portuguese (MA,

New York University (continued)

PhD); psychotherapy and psychoanalysis (Advanced Certificate); public history (Advanced Certificate); recombinant DNA technology (MS); religion (Advanced Certificate); religious studies (MA); Russian literature (MA); Slavic literature (MA); social theory (Advanced Certificate); social/personality psychology (PhD); sociology (MA, PhD); Spanish (PhD); Spanish and Latin American literatures and cultures (MA); Spanish language and translation (MA); trauma and violence transdisciplinary studies (MA, Advanced Certificate); world history (MA). *Application fee:* $90. Electronic applications accepted. *Application Contact:* Roberta Popik, Associate Dean of Enrollment, 212-998-8050, Fax: 212-995-4557, E-mail: gsas.admissions@nyu.edu. *Acting Dean,* Malcolm Semple, 212-998-8040.

Arthur L. Carter Journalism Institute Students: 215 full-time (156 women), 41 part-time (28 women); includes 16 Black or African American, non-Hispanic/Latino; 1 American Indian or Alaska Native, non-Hispanic/Latino; 16 Asian, non-Hispanic/Latino; 14 Hispanic/Latino, 55 international. Average age 27. 490 applicants, 53% accepted, 135 enrolled.. Expenses: Contact institution. *Financial support:* Fellowships with tuition reimbursements, teaching assistantships with tuition reimbursements, Federal Work-Study, institutionally sponsored loans, scholarships/grants, and tuition waivers (partial) available. Financial award application deadline: 1/4; financial award applicants required to submit FAFSA. In 2010, 109 master's, 23 other advanced degrees awarded. *Degree program information:* Part-time programs available. Offers biomedical journalism (MS); cultural reporting and criticism (MA); French studies/journalism (MA); journalism (MA); Latin American and Caribbean studies/journalism (MA); Near Eastern studies/journalism (MA); science and environmental reporting (Advanced Certificate). *Application deadline:* For fall admission, 1/4 priority date for domestic students. *Application fee:* $90. *Application Contact:* Perri Klass, Director of Graduate Studies, 212-998-7980, Fax: 212-995-4148, E-mail: graduate.journalism@nyu.edu. *Chair,* Brooke Kroeger, 212-998-7980, Fax: 212-995-4148, E-mail: graduate.journalism@nyu.edu.

Center for European Studies Students: 16 full-time (10 women), 7 part-time (5 women), 5 international. Average age 25. 28 applicants, 86% accepted, 13 enrolled. *Faculty:* 4 full-time (0 women). Expenses: Contact institution. *Financial support:* Fellowships with tuition reimbursements, teaching assistantships with tuition reimbursements, career-related internships or fieldwork, Federal Work-Study, institutionally sponsored loans, and scholarships/grants available. Financial award application deadline: 1/4; financial award applicants required to submit FAFSA. In 2010, 9 master's awarded. Offers European studies (MA). *Application deadline:* For fall admission, 1/1 priority date for domestic students. *Application fee:* $90. Electronic applications accepted. *Application Contact:* Jennifer Denbo, Department Graduate Administrator, 212-998-3838, Fax: 212-995-4188, E-mail: european.studies@nyu.edu. *Director,* Larry Wolff, 212-998-3838, Fax: 212-995-4188, E-mail: european.studies@nyu.edu.

Center for French Civilization and Culture Students: 106 full-time (76 women), 13 part-time (8 women); includes 2 Black or African American, non-Hispanic/Latino; 5 Asian, non-Hispanic/Latino; 5 Hispanic/Latino, 26 international. Average age 30. 123 applicants, 59% accepted, 36 enrolled. Expenses: Contact institution. *Financial support:* Fellowships with tuition reimbursements, research assistantships with tuition reimbursements, teaching assistantships with tuition reimbursements, Federal Work-Study, institutionally sponsored loans, scholarships/grants, traineeships, unspecified assistantships, and instructorships available. Financial award application deadline: 1/4; financial award applicants required to submit FAFSA. In 2010, 11 master's, 4 doctorates awarded. *Degree program information:* Part-time and evening/weekend programs available. Offers French (PhD); French civilization (PhD); French civilization and culture (MA, PhD, Advanced Certificate); French language and civilization (MA); French literature (MA); French studies (MA, PhD, Advanced Certificate); French studies and anthropology (PhD); French studies and history (PhD); French studies and journalism (MA); French studies and sociology (PhD); Romance languages and literatures (MA). *Application deadline:* For fall admission, 1/4 for domestic students. *Application fee:* $90. *Application Contact:* Brett Underhill, Graduate Secretary, 212-998-8700, Fax: 212-995-3539, E-mail: french.grad@nyu.edu. *Chair,* Judith Miller, 212-998-8700, Fax: 212-995-3539, E-mail: french.grad@nyu.edu.

Center for Latin American and Caribbean Studies Students: 23 full-time (15 women), 13 part-time (9 women); includes 12 Hispanic/Latino, 4 international. Average age 27. 57 applicants, 82% accepted, 20 enrolled. Expenses: Contact institution. *Financial support:* Fellowships with tuition reimbursements, teaching assistantships with tuition reimbursements, Federal Work-Study, institutionally sponsored loans, scholarships/grants, health care benefits, and unspecified assistantships available. Financial award application deadline: 1/4; financial award applicants required to submit FAFSA. In 2010, 20 master's awarded. *Degree program information:* Part-time programs available. Offers Latin American and Caribbean studies (MA). *Application deadline:* For fall admission, 1/4 priority date for domestic students. *Application fee:* $90. *Application Contact:* Jennifer Lewis, Assistant Director, 212-998-8686, Fax: 212-995-4163, E-mail: clacs.info@nyu.edu. *Director,* Ada Ferrer, 212-998-8686, Fax: 212-995-4163, E-mail: clacs.info@nyu.edu.

Center for Neural Science Students: 40 full-time (23 women); includes 2 Black or African American, non-Hispanic/Latino; 7 Asian, non-Hispanic/Latino; 2 Hispanic/Latino, 6 international. Average age 27. 162 applicants, 15% accepted, 12 enrolled. *Faculty:* 15 full-time (3 women). Expenses: Contact institution. *Financial support:* Fellowships with tuition reimbursements, research assistantships with tuition reimbursements, career-related internships or fieldwork, Federal Work-Study, institutionally sponsored loans, scholarships/grants, health care benefits, and unspecified assistantships available. Financial award application deadline: 12/15; financial award applicants required to submit FAFSA. In 2010, 5 doctorates awarded. Offers neural science (PhD). *Application deadline:* For fall admission, 12/12 for domestic students. *Application fee:* $90. *Application Contact:* Alex Reyes, Director of Graduate Studies, 212-998-7780, Fax: 212-995-4011, E-mail: cns@nyu.edu. *Chair,* J. Anthony Movshon, 212-998-7780, Fax: 212-995-4011, E-mail: cns@nyu.edu.

Courant Institute of Mathematical Sciences Students: 436 full-time (89 women), 212 part-time (46 women); includes 5 Black or African American, non-Hispanic/Latino; 1 American Indian or Alaska Native, non-Hispanic/Latino; 64 Asian, non-Hispanic/Latino; 7 Hispanic/Latino, 395 international. Average age 28. 2,109 applicants, 34% accepted, 254 enrolled. *Faculty:* 76 full-time (1 woman). Expenses: Contact institution. *Financial support:* Fellowships with tuition reimbursements, research assistantships with tuition reimbursements, teaching assistantships with tuition reimbursements, career-related internships or fieldwork, Federal Work-Study, institutionally sponsored loans, scholarships/grants, health care benefits, tuition waivers (full and partial), and unspecified assistantships available. Financial award application deadline: 1/4; financial award applicants required to submit FAFSA. In 2010, 157 master's, 29 doctorates awarded. *Degree program information:* Part-time and evening/weekend programs available. Offers atmosphere ocean science and mathematics (PhD); computer science (MS, PhD); information systems (MS); mathematics (MS, PhD); mathematics and statistics/operations research (MS); mathematics in finance (MS); scientific computing (MS). *Application deadline:* For fall admission, 1/4 for domestic students. *Application fee:* $90. *Application Contact:* Tamar Arnon, Program Administrator, 212-998-3238, Fax: 212-995-4121, E-mail: admissions@math.nyu.edu. *Director of Graduate Studies,* Fedor Bogomolov, 212-998-3238, Fax: 212-995-4121, E-mail: admissions@math.nyu.edu.

Hagop Kevorkian Center for Near Eastern Studies Students: 72 full-time (42 women), 8 part-time (4 women); includes 7 Asian, non-Hispanic/Latino; 1 Hispanic/Latino, 21 international. Average age 28. 242 applicants, 29% accepted, 29 enrolled. *Faculty:* 32 full-time (11 women). Expenses: Contact institution. *Financial support:* Fellowships with tuition reimbursements, teaching assistantships with tuition reimbursements, Federal Work-Study and institutionally sponsored loans available. Financial award application deadline: 1/4; financial award applicants required to submit FAFSA. In 2010, 15 master's, 3 doctorates awarded. *Degree program information:* Part-time and evening/weekend programs available. Offers Middle Eastern and Islamic studies (MA, PhD); Middle Eastern and Islamic studies/history (PhD); Near Eastern studies (MA, PhD); Near Eastern studies (museum studies) (MA); Near Eastern studies/journalism (MA). *Application deadline:* For fall admission, 1/4 for domestic students. *Application fee:* $90. *Application Contact:* Nadia Guessous, Director of Graduate Studies, 212-998-8877, Fax: 212-995-4144, E-mail: kevorkian.center@nyu.edu. *Director,* Michael Gilsenan, 212-998-8877, Fax: 212-995-4144, E-mail: kevorkian.center@nyu.edu.

Institute for Law and Society Students: 14 full-time (8 women); includes 1 Black or African American, non-Hispanic/Latino; 1 Hispanic/Latino, 1 international. Average age 31. *Faculty:* 3 full-time (1 woman). Expenses: Contact institution. *Financial support:* Fellowships with tuition reimbursements, teaching assistantships with tuition reimbursements, career-related internships or fieldwork, Federal Work-Study, institutionally sponsored loans, scholarships/grants, health care benefits, and unspecified assistantships available. Financial award applicants required to submit FAFSA. In 2010, 1 master's, 5 doctorates awarded. Offers law and society (MA, PhD). *Application fee:* $90.

Institute for the Study of the Ancient World Students: 5 full-time (2 women), 3 international. Average age 30. 25 applicants, 16% accepted, 2 enrolled. Expenses: Contact institution. *Financial support:* Fellowships covering tuition, fees, and twelve-month stipend (about $33,000) available. Financial award application deadline: 1/4. Offers study of the ancient world (PhD). *Application deadline:* For fall admission, 1/4 for domestic students. *Application fee:* $90. Electronic applications accepted. *Application Contact:* Alexander Lawson, Director of Graduate Studies, 212-992-7833, Fax: 212-995-4014, E-mail: isaw@nyu.edu. *Director,* Dr. Roger Bagnall, 212-992-7833, Fax: 212-995-4014, E-mail: isaw@nyu.edu.

Institute of Fine Arts Students: 243 full-time (192 women), 59 part-time (47 women); includes 2 Black or African American, non-Hispanic/Latino; 20 Asian, non-Hispanic/Latino; 8 Hispanic/Latino, 29 international. Average age 32. 394 applicants, 27% accepted, 57 enrolled. *Faculty:* 19 full-time (5 women). Expenses: Contact institution. *Financial support:* Fellowships with tuition reimbursements, research assistantships with tuition reimbursements, teaching assistantships with tuition reimbursements, career-related internships or fieldwork, Federal Work-Study, institutionally sponsored loans, and tuition waivers (partial) available. Financial award application deadline: 12/15; financial award applicants required to submit FAFSA. In 2010, 29 master's, 12 doctorates awarded. *Degree program information:* Part-time programs available. Offers architectural studies (PhD); art history and archaeology (MA, PhD); classical art and archaeology (PhD); conservation trainingcuratorial studies (PhD); East and South Asian art (PhD); Near Eastern art and archaeology (PhD). *Application deadline:* For fall admission, 12/15 for domestic students. *Application fee:* $90. *Application Contact:* Priscilla Saucek, Director of Graduate Studies, 212-992-5800, Fax: 212-992-5807, E-mail: ifa.program@nyu.edu. *Chair,* Patricia Rubin, 212-992-5800, Fax: 212-992-5807, E-mail: ifa.program@nyu.edu.

Leonard N. Stern School of Business *Degree program information:* Part-time and evening/weekend programs available. Offers accounting (MBA, PhD); economics (MBA, PhD); entertainment, media and technology (MBA); finance (MBA, PhD); general marketing (MBA); information systems (MBA, PhD); information, operations and management sciences (MBA, PhD); management and organizations (MBA, PhD, APC); management organizations (MBA); marketing (MBA, PhD); operations management (MBA, PhD); organization theory (PhD); organizational behavior (PhD); product management (MBA); statistics (MBA, PhD); strategy (PhD). Electronic applications accepted.

NYU in Madrid Offers creative writing in Spanish (MFA); Spanish (PhD); Spanish and Latin American literatures and cultures (MA); Spanish language and translation (MA).

NYU in Paris Offers teaching French as a foreign language (MA).

Robert F. Wagner Graduate School of Public Service Students: 581 full-time (414 women), 424 part-time (303 women); includes 70 Black or African American, non-Hispanic/Latino; 106 Asian, non-Hispanic/Latino; 59 Hispanic/Latino, 90 international. Average age 30. 2,103 applicants, 49% accepted, 388 enrolled. *Faculty:* 34 full-time (13 women), 60 part-time/adjunct (31 women). Expenses: Contact institution. *Financial support:* In 2010–11, 245 students received support, including 240 fellowships (averaging $12,588 per year), 7 research assistantships with full tuition reimbursements available (averaging $22,440 per year); career-related internships or fieldwork, Federal Work-Study, institutionally sponsored loans, scholarships/grants, health care benefits, and unspecified assistantships also available. Support available to part-time students. Financial award application deadline: 1/5; financial award applicants required to submit FAFSA. In 2010, 359 master's, 5 doctorates awarded. *Degree program information:* Part-time and evening/weekend programs available. Offers health finance (MPA); health policy analysis (MPA); health policy and management (Advanced Certificate); health services management (MPA); housing (Advanced Certificate); international health (MPA); nurse leader (EMPA); public administration (EMPA, PhD); public and nonprofit management and policy (MPA, Advanced Certificate); public economics (Advanced Certificate); public service (EMPA, MPA, MUP, PhD, Advanced Certificate); quantitative analysis and computer applications for policy and planning (Advanced Certificate); urban planning (MUP). *Application deadline:* For fall admission, 5/15 for domestic students, 1/4 for international students; for spring admission, 11/15 for domestic students, 10/1 for international students. Applications are processed on a rolling basis. *Application fee:* $80. Electronic applications accepted. *Application Contact:* Christopher Alexander, Administrative Aide, Enrollment, 212-998-7414, Fax: 212-995-4611, E-mail: wagner.admissions@nyu.edu. *Dean,* Prof. Ellen Schall, 212-998-7400, Fax: 212-995-4161.

School of Continuing and Professional Studies Students: 426 full-time (245 women), 1,045 part-time (525 women); includes 103 Black or African American, non-Hispanic/Latino; 8 American Indian or Alaska Native, non-Hispanic/Latino; 113 Asian, non-Hispanic/Latino; 103 Hispanic/Latino, 277 international. Average age 30. 1,951 applicants, 50% accepted, 462 enrolled. *Faculty:* 48 full-time (16 women), 367 part-time/adjunct (111 women). Expenses: Contact institution. *Financial support:* In 2010–11, 917 students received support, including 917 fellowships (averaging $2,460 per year), 8 research assistantships with partial tuition reimbursements available (averaging $8,500 per year); career-related internships or fieldwork, Federal Work-Study, institutionally sponsored loans, scholarships/grants, and tuition waivers (partial) also available. Support available to part-time students. Financial award application deadline: 3/1; financial award applicants required to submit FAFSA. In 2010, 692 master's, 158 other advanced degrees awarded. *Degree program information:* Part-time and evening/weekend programs available. Postbaccalaureate distance learning degree programs offered (no on-campus study). *Application deadline:* For fall admission, 2/1 priority date for domestic and international students; for spring admission, 10/15 priority date for domestic students, 8/15 priority date for international students. Applications are processed on a rolling basis. *Application fee:* $75. Electronic applications accepted. *Application Contact:* Office of Admissions, 212-998-7100, Fax: 212-995-4674. *Dean,* Robert Lapiner, 212-998-7000, Fax: 212-995-4130.

Center for Global Affairs Students: 92 full-time (62 women), 119 part-time (90 women); includes 12 Black or African American, non-Hispanic/Latino; 1 American Indian or Alaska Native, non-Hispanic/Latino; 14 Asian, non-Hispanic/Latino; 10 Hispanic/Latino, 32 international. Average age 30. 419 applicants, 58% accepted, 81 enrolled. *Faculty:* 10 full-time (3 women), 29 part-time/adjunct (14 women). Expenses: Contact institution. *Financial support:* In 2010–11, 163 students received support, including 163 fellowships (averaging $2,554 per year); institutionally sponsored loans, scholarships/grants, and tuition waivers (partial) also available. Support available to part-time students. Financial award application deadline: 3/1; financial award applicants required to submit FAFSA. In 2010, 113 master's awarded. *Degree program information:* Part-time and evening/weekend programs available. Offers global affairs (MS). *Application deadline:* For fall admission, 2/1 priority date for domestic and international students; for spring admission, 10/15 priority date for domestic students, 8/15 priority date for international students. Applications are processed on a rolling basis. *Application fee:* $75. Electronic applications accepted. *Application Contact:* Cori Epstein, Associate Director, 212-992-8380, Fax: 212-995-4597, E-mail: graduate.global.affairs@nyu.edu. *Divisional Dean and Clinical Associate Professor,* Dr. Vera Jelinek, 212-992-8380, Fax: 212-995-4597, E-mail: vera.jelinek@nyu.edu.

Division for Media Industry Studies and Design Students: 67 full-time (45 women), 97 part-time (61 women); includes 11 Black or African American, non-Hispanic/Latino; 9 Asian, non-Hispanic/Latino; 11 Hispanic/Latino, 30 international. Average age 30. 193 applicants, 56% accepted, 65 enrolled. *Faculty:* 4 full-time (3 women), 82 part-time/adjunct (30 women). Expenses: Contact institution. *Financial support:* In 2010–11, 143 students received support, including 143 fellowships (averaging $2,371 per year). Financial award application deadline: 3/1; financial award applicants required to submit FAFSA. In 2010, 107 master's awarded. *Degree program information:* Part-time and evening/weekend programs available. Offers advanced digital applications (MS); digital imaging and design (MS); graphic communications management and technology (MA); publishing (MS). *Application deadline:* For fall admission, 2/1 priority date for domestic and international students; for spring admission, 10/15 priority date for domestic students, 8/15 priority date for international students. Applications are processed on a rolling basis. *Application fee:* $75. Electronic applications accepted. *Application Contact:* Office of Admissions, 212-998-7100, Fax: 212-995-4674. *Academic Director*, Bonnie Blake, 212-998-7000, Fax: 212-995-4130.

Division of Liberal Studies and Allied Arts Offers translation (MS).

Division of Programs in Business Students: 116 full-time (87 women), 414 part-time (263 women); includes 53 Black or African American, non-Hispanic/Latino; 3 American Indian or Alaska Native, non-Hispanic/Latino; 47 Asian, non-Hispanic/Latino; 55 Hispanic/Latino, 112 international. Average age 31. 678 applicants, 42% accepted, 141 enrolled. *Faculty:* 5 full-time (1 woman), 126 part-time/adjunct (46 women). Expenses: Contact institution. *Financial support:* In 2010–11, 308 students received support, including 308 fellowships (averaging $2,154 per year); career-related internships or fieldwork, institutionally sponsored loans, and scholarships/grants also available. Support available to part-time students. Financial award application deadline: 3/1; financial award applicants required to submit FAFSA. In 2010, 221 master's, 43 other advanced degrees awarded. *Degree program information:* Part-time and evening/weekend programs available. Postbaccalaureate distance learning degree programs offered (minimal on-campus study). Offers benefits and compensation (Advanced Certificate); brand management (MS); core business competencies (Advanced Certificate); corporate and organizational communications (MS); database technologies (MS); digital marketing (MS); enterprise and risk management (Advanced Certificate); enterprise risk management (MS); human resource development (MS); human resource management (MS, Advanced Certificate); information technologies (Advanced Certificate); integrated marketing (MS); leadership and human capital management (MS, Advanced Certificate); management and systems (MS, Advanced Certificate); marketing analytics (MS); organizational and executive coaching (Advanced Certificate); organizational effectiveness (MS); public relations and corporate communication (MS); public relations management (MS); strategy and leadership (MS, Advanced Certificate); systems management (MS). *Application deadline:* For fall admission, 2/1 priority date for domestic and international students; for spring admission, 10/15 priority date for domestic students, 8/15 priority date for international students. Applications are processed on a rolling basis. *Application fee:* $75. Electronic applications accepted. *Application Contact:* James Stuckey, Divisional Dean, 212-992-3600, Fax: 212-995-3650, E-mail: james.stuckey@nyu.edu. *Divisional Dean*, James Stuckey, 212-992-3600, Fax: 212-995-3650, E-mail: james.stuckey@nyu.edu.

The George Heyman Jr. Center for Philanthropy and Fundraising Students: 8 full-time (all women), 20 part-time (13 women); includes 4 Black or African American, non-Hispanic/Latino; 2 Asian, non-Hispanic/Latino, 4 international. Average age 33. 24 applicants, 63% accepted, 12 enrolled. *Faculty:* 1 full-time (0 women), 17 part-time/adjunct (9 women). Expenses: Contact institution. *Financial support:* In 2010–11, 23 students received support, including 23 fellowships (averaging $2,443 per year); scholarships/grants also available. Financial award application deadline: 3/1; financial award applicants required to submit FAFSA. In 2010, 12 master's awarded. *Degree program information:* Part-time and evening/weekend programs available. Offers fundraising (MS). *Application deadline:* For fall admission, 2/1 priority date for domestic and international students; for spring admission, 10/15 priority date for domestic students, 8/15 priority date for international students. Applications are processed on a rolling basis. *Application fee:* $75. Electronic applications accepted. *Application Contact:* Mayelly Moreno, 212-998-6777, Fax: 212-995-4784, E-mail: mm172@nyu.edu. *Chair and Executive Director*, Levine Naomi, 212-998-6770, Fax: 212-995-4784.

The Preston Robert Tisch Center for Hospitality, Tourism, and Sports Management Students: 34 full-time (22 women), 68 part-time (27 women); includes 5 Black or African American, non-Hispanic/Latino; 1 American Indian or Alaska Native, non-Hispanic/Latino; 8 Asian, non-Hispanic/Latino; 7 Hispanic/Latino, 25 international. Average age 29. 286 applicants, 28% accepted, 37 enrolled. *Faculty:* 12 full-time (5 women), 29 part-time/adjunct (5 women). Expenses: Contact institution. *Financial support:* In 2010–11, 58 students received support, including 58 fellowships (averaging $3,036 per year), 8 research assistantships with partial tuition reimbursements available (averaging $8,500 per year); career-related internships or fieldwork, Federal Work-Study, institutionally sponsored loans, and scholarships/grants also available. Support available to part-time students. Financial award application deadline: 3/1; financial award applicants required to submit FAFSA. In 2010, 59 master's, 15 other advanced degrees awarded. *Degree program information:* Part-time and evening/weekend programs available. Offers brand strategy (MS); collegiate and professional sports operations (MS); hospitality industry studies (MS, Advanced Certificate); hotel finance (MS); marketing and media (MS); sports business (MS, Advanced Certificate); tourism management (MS, Advanced Certificate). *Application deadline:* For fall admission, 2/1 priority date for domestic and international students; for spring admission, 10/15 priority date for domestic students, 8/15 priority date for international students. Applications are processed on a rolling basis. *Application fee:* $75. Electronic applications accepted. *Application Contact:* Office of Admissions, 212-998-7100, Fax: 212-995-4674. *Divisional Dean, Clinical Professor, HVS Chair*, Bjorn Hanson, 212-998-9100, Fax: 212-995-4676.

Schack Institute of Real Estate Students: 109 full-time (21 women), 327 part-time (71 women); includes 18 Black or African American, non-Hispanic/Latino; 3 American Indian or Alaska Native, non-Hispanic/Latino; 33 Asian, non-Hispanic/Latino; 20 Hispanic/Latino, 74 international. Average age 31. 351 applicants, 67% accepted, 126 enrolled. *Faculty:* 16 full-time (4 women), 93 part-time/adjunct (10 women). Expenses: Contact institution. *Financial support:* In 2010–11, 222 students received support, including 222 fellowships (averaging $2,202 per year); scholarships/grants also available. Support available to part-time students. Financial award application deadline: 3/1; financial award applicants required to submit FAFSA. In 2010, 216 master's, 64 other advanced degrees awarded. *Degree program information:* Part-time and evening/weekend programs available. Offers business of development (MS); construction management (MS, Advanced Certificate); construction management for the development process (MS); finance and investment (MS); global real estate (MS); project management (MS); real estate (MS, Advanced Certificate); strategic real estate management (MS); sustainable development (MS). *Application deadline:* For fall admission, 2/1 priority date for domestic and international students; for spring admission, 10/15 priority date for domestic students, 8/15 priority date for international students. Applications are processed on a rolling basis. *Application fee:* $75. Electronic applications accepted. *Application Contact:* Jennifer Monahan, Director of Administration and Student Services, 212-992-3335, Fax: 212-992-3686, E-mail: jm189@nyu.edu. *Divisional Dean*, James Stuckey, 212-992-3335, Fax: 212-992-3686, E-mail: james.stuckey@nyu.edu.

School of Law Students: 1,427 full-time (628 women); includes 88 Black or African American, non-Hispanic/Latino; 3 American Indian or Alaska Native, non-Hispanic/Latino; 150 Asian, non-Hispanic/Latino; 91 Hispanic/Latino, 44 international. 7,272 applicants, 450 enrolled. *Faculty:* 125 full-time (36 women), 70 part-time/adjunct (23 women). Expenses: Contact institution. *Financial support:* Fellowships, research assistantships, teaching assistantships, career-related internships or fieldwork, Federal Work-Study, institutionally sponsored loans, scholarships/grants, tuition waivers (partial), and loan repayment assistance available. Financial award application deadline: 4/15; financial award applicants required to submit FAFSA. In 2010, 471 first professional degrees, 534 master's, 3 doctorates awarded. *Degree program information:* Part-time programs available. Offers law (JD, LL M, JSD); law and business (Advanced Certificate); taxation (Advanced Certificate). *Application deadline:* For fall admission, 2/1 for domestic students. *Application fee:* $75. Electronic applications accepted. *Application Contact:* Kenneth J. Kleinrock, Assistant Dean for Admissions, 212-998-6060, Fax: 212-995-4527. *Dean*, Richard L. Revesz, 212-998-6000, Fax: 212-995-3150.

School of Medicine Offers biomedical sciences (PhD); clinical investigation (MS); medicine (MD, MS, PhD).

Sackler Institute of Graduate Biomedical Sciences Offers cellular and molecular biology (PhD); computational biology (PhD); developmental genetics (PhD); immunology (PhD); medical and molecular parasitology (PhD); microbiology (PhD); molecular oncology (PhD); molecular oncology and immunology (PhD); molecular pharmacology (PhD); neuroscience and physiology (PhD); pathobiology (PhD); pharmacology (PhD); structural biology (PhD). Electronic applications accepted.

Silver School of Social Work Students: 784 full-time (674 women), 321 part-time (285 women); includes 81 Black or African American, non-Hispanic/Latino; 68 Asian, non-Hispanic/Latino; 151 Hispanic/Latino. Average age 27. 1,671 applicants, 78% accepted, 508 enrolled. *Faculty:* 42 full-time (32 women), 115 part-time/adjunct (79 women). Expenses: Contact institution. *Financial support:* In 2010–11, 950 students received support. Career-related internships or fieldwork, Federal Work-Study, scholarships/grants, health care benefits, tuition waivers (partial), and unspecified assistantships available. Support available to part-time students. Financial award application deadline: 3/1; financial award applicants required to submit FAFSA. In 2010, 420 master's, 10 doctorates awarded. *Degree program information:* Part-time and evening/weekend programs available. Offers social work (MSW, PhD). *Application deadline:* For fall admission, 2/1 priority date for domestic and international students; for spring admission, 11/1 priority date for domestic and international students. Applications are processed on a rolling basis. *Application fee:* $60. Electronic applications accepted. *Application Contact:* Robert W. Sommo, Assistant Dean for Enrollment Services, 212-998-5910, Fax: 212-995-4171, E-mail: ssw.admissions@nyu.edu. *Dean*, Dr. Lynn Videka, 212-998-5959, Fax: 212-995-4172.

Steinhardt School of Culture, Education, and Human Development Students: 2,305 full-time (1,758 women), 1,385 part-time (1,059 women); includes 253 Black or African American, non-Hispanic/Latino; 4 American Indian or Alaska Native, non-Hispanic/Latino; 312 Asian, non-Hispanic/Latino; 187 Hispanic/Latino, 536 international. Average age 30. 5,812 applicants, 49% accepted, 1293 enrolled. *Faculty:* 262 full-time (154 women), 644 part-time/adjunct (524 women). Expenses: Contact institution. *Financial support:* Fellowships with full and partial tuition reimbursements, research assistantships with full and partial tuition reimbursements, teaching assistantships with full and partial tuition reimbursements, career-related internships or fieldwork, Federal Work-Study, institutionally sponsored loans, scholarships/grants, traineeships, tuition waivers (partial), and unspecified assistantships available. Support available to part-time students. Financial award application deadline: 2/1; financial award applicants required to submit FAFSA. In 2010, 1,225 master's, 101 doctorates, 21 other advanced degrees awarded. *Degree program information:* Part-time programs available. Offers advanced occupational therapy (MA); art education (MA); art therapy (MA); bilingual education (MA, PhD, Advanced Certificate); biology grades 7-12 (MA); business education (MA, Advanced Certificate); business education in higher education (MA); chemistry grades 7-12 (MA); childhood (MA); childhood education (MA); childhood education/special education: childhood (MA); communication sciences and disorders (MS, PhD); community public health (PhD); costume studies (MA); counseling and guidance (MA, Advanced Certificate); counseling for mental health and wellness (MA); counseling psychology (PhD); counselor education (MA, PhD, Advanced Certificate); culture, education, and human development (MA, MFA, MM, MS, DPS, DPT, Ed D, PhD, Advanced Certificate); dance education (MA, Ed D, PhD); drama therapy (MA); dual certification: childhood education/childhood special education (MA); dual certification: early childhood education/early childhood special education (MA); dual certification: educational theatre and English 7-12 (MA); dual certification: educational theatre and social studies (MA); early childhood (MA); early childhood and childhood education (MA, PhD); early childhood education (MA); education and Jewish studies (MA, PhD); education and social policy (MA); educational and developmental psychology (MA, PhD); educational communication and technology (MA, PhD, Advanced Certificate); educational leadership (MA, Ed D, PhD, Advanced Certificate); educational leadership, politics and advocacy (MA); educational psychology (MA); educational theatre (MA, Ed D, PhD, Advanced Certificate); educational theatre for colleges and communities (MA); English education (MA, PhD, Advanced Certificate); environmental conservation education (MA); food studies (MA); food studies and food management (MA, PhD); for-profit sector (MA); foreign language education (MA, Advanced Certificate); foreign language education/TESOL (MA); higher and postsecondary education (PhD); higher education (MA, Ed D, PhD); higher education administration (Ed D); history of education (MA, PhD); human development and social intervention (MA); instrumental performance (MM); international education (MA, PhD, Advanced Certificate); literacy education (MA); mathematics education (MA); media, culture, and communication (MA, PhD); multilingual/multicultural studies (MA, PhD, Advanced Certificate); music business (MA); music education (MA, Ed D, PhD, Advanced Certificate); music performance and composition (MA, MM, PhD, Advanced Certificate); music technology (MM, PhD); music theory and composition (MM, PhD); music therapy (MA); not-for-profit sector (MA); nutrition and dietetics (MS, PhD); occupational therapy (MS, DPS); orthopedic physical therapy (Advanced Certificate); performing arts administration (MA); physical therapy (MA, DPT); physical therapy for practicing physical therapists (DPT); physics grades 7-12 (MA); piano performance (MM); positions of leadership: early childhood and elementary education (PhD); psychological development (PhD); psychology and social intervention (PhD); research in occupational therapy (PhD); research in physical therapy (PhD); school building leader (MA); school district leader (Advanced Certificate); science education (MA); secondary and college (PhD); social studies education (MA); sociology of education (MA, PhD); special education (MA); student personnel administration in higher education (MA); studio art (MA, MFA, Advanced Certificate); teachers of English 7-12 (MA); teachers of English language and literature in college (Advanced Certificate); teaching and learning (Ed D, PhD); teaching dance in higher education and the professions (MA); teaching educational theatre, all grades (MA); teaching English to speakers of other languages (MA, PhD, Advanced Certificate); teaching French as a foreign language (MA); teaching music (MA); visual arts administration (MA); visual culture (MA); vocal pedagogy (Advanced Certificate); vocal performance (MM); vocal performance/vocal pedagogy (MM); workplace learning (Advanced Certificate). *Application deadline:* For fall admission, 12/1 priority date for domestic students, 12/1 for international students; for spring admission, 1/1 for domestic and international students. Applications are processed on a rolling basis. *Application fee:* $75. Electronic applications accepted. *Application Contact:* John Myers, Director of Enrollment Management, 212-998-5030, Fax: 212-995-4328, E-mail: steinhardt.gradadmissions@nyu.edu. *Dean*, Dr. Mary Brabeck, 212-998-5000.

Tisch School of the Arts Students: 784 full-time (397 women), 27 part-time (16 women); includes 50 Black or African American, non-Hispanic/Latino; 2 American Indian or Alaska Native, non-Hispanic/Latino; 89 Asian, non-Hispanic/Latino; 40 Hispanic/Latino. Average age 25. 2,907 applicants, 27% accepted, 428 enrolled. *Faculty:* 95 full-time (39 women), 149 part-time/adjunct (63 women). Expenses: Contact institution. *Financial support:* In 2010–11, 542 students received support, including 162 fellowships with full and partial tuition reimbursements available (averaging $39,884 per year); career-related internships or fieldwork, Federal Work-Study, and scholarships ($11,904 average), partial awards also available. Support available to part-time students. Financial award application deadline: 2/15; financial award applicants required to submit FAFSA. In 2010, 286 master's, 15 doctorates awarded. Offers acting (MFA); arts (MA, MFA, MPS, PhD); arts politics (MA); cinema studies (MA, PhD); dance (MFA); design for stage and film (MFA); dramatic writing (MFA); interactive telecommunications (MPS); moving image archiving and preservation (MA); musical theatre writing (MFA); performance studies (MA, PhD). *Application fee:* $60. Electronic applications accepted. *Application Contact:* Dan Sandford, Director of Graduate Admissions, 212-998-1918, Fax: 212-995-4060, E-mail: tisch.gradadmissions@nyu.edu. *Dean*, Dr. Mary Schmidt Campbell, 212-998-1800.

Tisch School of the Arts Asia Offers animation and digital arts (MFA); dramatic writing (MFA); film production (MFA). Electronic applications accepted.

Kanbar Institute of Film and Television Students: 111 full-time (53 women), 76 part-time (35 women); includes 23 Black or African American, non-Hispanic/Latino; 2 American Indian or Alaska Native, non-Hispanic/Latino; 36 Asian, non-Hispanic/Latino; 6 Hispanic/Latino. Average age 25. 630 applicants, 9% accepted, 37 enrolled. *Faculty:* 19 full-time, 20 part-time/adjunct. Expenses: Contact institution. *Financial support:* In 2010–11, 60 students received support, including 16 fellowships with full and partial tuition reimbursements available, 6 teaching assistantships with tuition reimbursements available; Federal Work-Study, institutionally sponsored loans, scholarships/grants, tuition waivers (full and partial), and unspecified assistantships also available. Financial award application deadline: 2/15; financial award applicants required to submit FAFSA. In 2010, 30 master's awarded. Offers film and television (MFA). *Application deadline:* For fall admission, 12/1 for domestic and international students. *Application fee:* $60. Electronic applications accepted. *Application*

New York University (continued)

Contact: Dan Sandford, Director of Graduate Admissions, 212-998-1918, Fax: 212-995-4060, E-mail: tisch.gradadmissions@nyu.edu. *Chair,* John Tintori, 212-998-1780, E-mail: jt42@nyu.edu.

NIAGARA UNIVERSITY, Niagara Falls, Niagara University, NY 14109

General Information Independent-religious, coed, comprehensive institution. *Enrollment:* 4,273 graduate, professional, and undergraduate students; 607 full-time matriculated graduate/professional students (391 women), 358 part-time matriculated graduate/professional students (241 women). *Enrollment by degree level:* 913 master's, 52 other advanced degrees. *Graduate faculty:* 36 full-time (16 women), 44 part-time/adjunct (20 women). *Tuition:* Full-time $13,230; part-time $735 per credit hour. *Required fees:* $50. One-time fee: $120 full-time. *Graduate housing:* Room and/or apartments available to single students; on-campus housing not available to married students. Typical cost: $10,650 (including board). Housing application deadline: 8/1. *Student services:* Campus employment opportunities, campus safety program, career counseling, free psychological counseling, international student services, low-cost health insurance, multicultural affairs office, services for students with disabilities. *Library facilities:* Our Lady of Angels. *Online resources:* library catalog. *Collection:* 297,813 titles, 164 serial subscriptions. *Research affiliation:* Roswell Park Memorial Institute.

Computer facilities: 175 computers available on campus for general student use. A campuswide network can be accessed from student residence rooms. Online class registration is available. *Web address:* http://www.niagara.edu/.

General Application Contact: Carlos Tejada, Associate Dean for Graduate Recruitment, 716-286-8769, Fax: 716-286-8170.

GRADUATE UNITS

Graduate Division of Arts and Sciences Students: 27 full-time (17 women), 29 part-time (19 women); includes 5 Black or African American, non-Hispanic/Latino; 1 Hispanic/Latino, 2 international. Average age 29. *Faculty:* 7 full-time (2 women). Expenses: Contact institution. *Financial support:* Fellowships, career-related internships or fieldwork and Federal Work-Study available. Support available to part-time students. In 2010, 28 master's awarded. *Degree program information:* Part-time and evening/weekend programs available. Offers arts and sciences (MA, MS); criminal justice administration (MS); interdisciplinary studies (MA). *Application deadline:* For fall admission, 8/1 for domestic students. Applications are processed on a rolling basis. *Application fee:* $30. *Application Contact:* Ronald Winkley, Director, 716-286-8089, Fax: 716-286-8061, E-mail: rwinkley@niagara.edu. *Dean,* Dr. Nancy McGlen, 716-286-8060, Fax: 716-286-8061, E-mail: nmcglen@niagara.edu.

Graduate Division of Business Administration Students: 156 full-time (67 women), 64 part-time (25 women); includes 9 Black or African American, non-Hispanic/Latino; 7 Asian, non-Hispanic/Latino; 3 Hispanic/Latino, 22 international. Average age 33. 89 applicants, 73% accepted. *Faculty:* 6 full-time (1 woman), 7 part-time/adjunct (1 woman). Expenses: Contact institution. *Financial support:* In 2010–11, 3 fellowships, 2 research assistantships were awarded; career-related internships or fieldwork and Federal Work-Study also available. Support available to part-time students. Financial award application deadline: 8/1; financial award applicants required to submit FAFSA. In 2010, 74 master's awarded. *Degree program information:* Part-time and evening/weekend programs available. Offers business (MBA); commerce (MBA). *Application deadline:* For fall admission, 8/1 for domestic students; for spring admission, 11/1 for domestic students. Applications are processed on a rolling basis. *Application fee:* $30. *Application Contact:* Carlos Tejada, Associate Dean for Graduate Recruitment, 716-286-8769, Fax: 716-286-8170. *Director,* Dr. Peggy Choong, 716-286-8178, Fax: 716-286-8206.

Graduate Division of Education Students: 424 full-time (307 women), 265 part-time (197 women); includes 5 Black or African American, non-Hispanic/Latino; 2 American Indian or Alaska Native, non-Hispanic/Latino; 2 Asian, non-Hispanic/Latino; 4 Hispanic/Latino, 101 international. Average age 28. 382 applicants, 75% accepted. *Faculty:* 26 full-time (16 women), 36 part-time/adjunct (17 women). Expenses: Contact institution. *Financial support:* In 2010–11, 2 fellowships, 3 research assistantships were awarded; career-related internships or fieldwork, Federal Work-Study, scholarships/grants, and unspecified assistantships also available. Support available to part-time students. Financial award application deadline: 3/15; financial award applicants required to submit FAFSA. In 2010, 344 master's, 18 other advanced degrees awarded. *Degree program information:* Part-time and evening/weekend programs available. Offers administration/supervision (Certificate); early childhood and childhood education (MS Ed); educational administration/supervision (MS Ed); educational leadership (MS Ed, Certificate); educational leadership school district building (MS Ed); foundations of teaching (MA, MS Ed); literacy instruction (MS Ed); mental health counseling (MS, Certificate); middle and adolescence education (MS Ed); school business administration (Certificate); school business leadership (MS Ed); school counseling (MS Ed, Certificate); school district administration (Certificate); school psychology (MS, Certificate); special education (grades 1-12) (MS Ed); teacher education (Certificate). *Application deadline:* For fall admission, 8/1 for domestic students. Applications are processed on a rolling basis. *Application fee:* $30. *Application Contact:* Carlos Tejada, Associate Dean for Graduate Recruitment, 716-286-8769, Fax: 716-286-8170. *Dean,* Dr. Debra A. Colley, 716-286-8560, Fax: 716-286-8561, E-mail: dcolley@niagara.edu.

NICHOLLS STATE UNIVERSITY, Thibodaux, LA 70310

General Information State-supported, coed, comprehensive institution. *Graduate housing:* Rooms and/or apartments available on a first-come, first-served basis to single and married students. Housing application deadline: 4/13.

GRADUATE UNITS

Graduate Studies *Degree program information:* Part-time and evening/weekend programs available. Postbaccalaureate distance learning degree programs offered (minimal on-campus study).

College of Arts and Sciences *Degree program information:* Part-time and evening/weekend programs available. Offers arts and sciences (MS); community/technical college mathematics (MS); marine and environmental biology (MS). Electronic applications accepted.

College of Business Administration *Degree program information:* Part-time and evening/weekend programs available. Offers business administration (MBA). Electronic applications accepted.

College of Education *Degree program information:* Part-time and evening/weekend programs available. Offers administration and supervision (M Ed); counselor education (M Ed); curriculum and instruction (M Ed); education (M Ed, MA, SSP); psychological counseling (MA); school psychology (SSP). Electronic applications accepted.

NICHOLS COLLEGE, Dudley, MA 01571-5000

General Information Independent, coed, comprehensive institution. *Graduate housing:* On-campus housing not available.

GRADUATE UNITS

Graduate Program in Business Administration *Degree program information:* Part-time and evening/weekend programs available. Postbaccalaureate distance learning degree programs offered (no on-campus study). Offers business administration (MBA, MOL); security management (MBA); sport management (MBA). Electronic applications accepted.

THE NIGERIAN BAPTIST THEOLOGICAL SEMINARY, Ogbomoso, Oyo, Nigeria

General Information Independent-religious, coed, primarily men, comprehensive institution. *Graduate housing:* Rooms and/or apartments available to single and married students.

GRADUATE UNITS

Graduate Studies *Degree program information:* Part-time programs available. Offers church music (M Div, M Th, Diploma); divinity (M Div); ministry (D Min); religious education (M Div, M Th, PhD); theological studies (MATS); theology (M Th, PhD).

NIPISSING UNIVERSITY, North Bay, ON P1B 8L7, Canada

General Information Province-supported, coed, comprehensive institution. *Graduate housing:* Room and/or apartments available to single students; on-campus housing not available to married students. Housing application deadline: 6/13. *Research affiliation:* Metals in the Human Environment Research Network (MITHE-RN) (assessing environmental pollutants on aquatic ecosystems), Canada Space Agency (CSA) and MacDonald, Dettwiler and Associates Ltd. (MDA–RADARSAT-2) (remote sensing), Education Quality and Accountability Office (EQAO) (assessing educational quality), Ontario Association of Deans of Education (OADE) (assessing pre-service practicum processes), Tembec (forestry restoration).

GRADUATE UNITS

Faculty of Education *Degree program information:* Part-time and evening/weekend programs available. Offers education (M Ed, Certificate).

NORFOLK STATE UNIVERSITY, Norfolk, VA 23504

General Information State-supported, coed, comprehensive institution. CGS member. *Graduate housing:* Room and/or apartments available to single students; on-campus housing not available to married students. Housing application deadline: 3/1. *Research affiliation:* Department of Energy NASA, National Science (fundamental and applied research studies), NASA Langley Research Center (NASA interests, aerospace applications, lidan application), National Science Foundation (fundamental and aerospace research studies), Department of Education (Title III projects, no child left behind initiative), University of Virginia's Integrative Graduate Education and Research Traineeship (IGERT) (science and engineering interactions with matter), Applied Research Center (technology transfer).

GRADUATE UNITS

School of Graduate Studies *Degree program information:* Part-time programs available. Electronic applications accepted.

School of Education *Degree program information:* Part-time programs available. Offers early childhood education (MAT); education (MA, MAT); pre-elementary education (MA); principal preparation (MA); secondary education (MAT); severe disabilities (MA); teaching (MA); urban education/administration (MA).

School of Liberal Arts *Degree program information:* Part-time programs available. Offers applied sociology (MS); community/clinical psychology (MA); criminal justice (MA); liberal arts (MA, MFA, MM, MS, Psy D); media and communication (MA); music (MM); music education (MM); performance (MM); psychology (Psy D); theory and composition (MM); urban affairs (MA); visual studies (MA, MFA).

School of Science and Technology Offers computer science (MS); electronics engineering (MS); materials science (MS); optical engineering (MS); science and technology (MS).

School of Social Work *Degree program information:* Part-time programs available. Offers social work (MSW, PhD).

NORTH CAROLINA AGRICULTURAL AND TECHNICAL STATE UNIVERSITY, Greensboro, NC 27411

General Information State-supported, coed, university. CGS member. *Graduate housing:* Room and/or apartments available on a first-come, first-served basis to single students; on-campus housing not available to married students. Housing application deadline: 5/8. *Research affiliation:* North Carolina Biotechnology Research Center (biotechnology research), The Boeing Company (aerospace engineering), Northrop Grumman Corporation (high performance computing), Research Triangle Institute (environmental protection, advanced technology), Rockwell, Inc. (avionics technology, communications technology), Honeywell (industrial automation control).

GRADUATE UNITS

Graduate School *Degree program information:* Part-time and evening/weekend programs available.

College of Arts and Sciences *Degree program information:* Part-time and evening/weekend programs available. Offers art education (MS); arts and sciences (MA, MAT, MS, MSW); biology (MS); biology education (MAT); chemistry (MS); English (MA); English and Afro-American literature (MA); English education (MS); history education (MAT, MS); mathematics education (MS); social studies education (MS); sociology and social work (MSW).

College of Engineering *Degree program information:* Part-time programs available. Offers bioengineering (MS); biological engineering (MS); chemical engineering (MS, MS Ch E); civil engineering (MSCE); computer science (MSCS); electrical engineering (MSEE, PhD); engineering (MS Ch E, MSCE, MSCS, MSE, MSEE, MSIE, MSME, PhD); industrial engineering (MSIE, PhD); mechanical engineering (MSME, PhD).

School of Agriculture and Environmental Sciences *Degree program information:* Part-time and evening/weekend programs available. Offers agricultural economics (MS); agricultural education (MS); agriculture and environmental sciences (MS); animal health science (MS); food and nutrition (MS); plant, soil and environmental science (MS).

School of Education *Degree program information:* Part-time and evening/weekend programs available. Offers adult education (MS); counselor education (MS); education (MA Ed, MAT, MS); elementary education (MA Ed); human resources-agency counseling (MS); human resources-rehabilitation counseling (MS); instructional technology (MS); leadership studies (PhD); physical education (MAT, MS); reading (MA Ed); school administration (MS); teaching (MAT).

School of Technology *Degree program information:* Part-time and evening/weekend programs available. Offers construction management (MSIT); electronics and computer technology (MSIT); industrial arts education (MS); industrial technology (MS, MSIT); occupational safety and health (MSIT); safety and driver education (MS); technology (MS, MSIT, PhD); technology education (MS); technology management (PhD); vocational-industrial education (MS); workforce development director (MS).

NORTH CAROLINA CENTRAL UNIVERSITY, Durham, NC 27707-3129

General Information State-supported, coed, comprehensive institution. CGS member. *Graduate housing:* Room and/or apartments available to single students; on-campus housing not available to married students. Housing application deadline: 7/1.

GRADUATE UNITS

Division of Academic Affairs *Degree program information:* Part-time and evening/weekend programs available.

College of Behavioral and Social Sciences Offers athletic administration (MS); behavioral and social sciences (MA, MPA, MS); criminal justice (MS); family and consumer sciences (MS); physical education (MS); psychology (MA); public administration (MPA); recreation administration (MS); sociology (MA); therapeutic recreation (MS).

College of Liberal Arts *Degree program information:* Part-time and evening/weekend programs available. Offers English (MA); history (MA); jazz studies (MM); liberal arts (MA, MM).

College of Science and Technology Offers applied mathematics (MS); biology (MS); chemistry (MS); earth sciences (MS); mathematics education (MS); physics (MS); pure mathematics (MS); science and technology (MS).

School of Business *Degree program information:* Part-time and evening/weekend programs available. Offers business (MBA).

School of Education *Degree program information:* Part-time and evening/weekend programs available. Offers career counseling (MA); communication disorders (M Ed); community agency counseling (MA); curriculum and instruction (MA); education (M Ed, MA, MAT, MSA); educational technology (MA); instructional technology (M Ed); school administration (MSA); school counseling (MA); special education (M Ed, MAT).

School of Law *Degree program information:* Part-time and evening/weekend programs available. Offers law (JD).

School of Library and Information Sciences *Degree program information:* Part-time and evening/weekend programs available. Offers library and information sciences (MIS, MLS).

NORTH CAROLINA STATE UNIVERSITY, Raleigh, NC 27695

General Information State-supported, coed, university. CGS member. *Graduate housing:* Rooms and/or apartments available on a first-come, first-served basis to single and married students. *Research affiliation:* Triangle Universities Nuclear Laboratory, Research Triangle Institute, Highlands Biological Station, National Humanities Center, Microelectronics Center of North Carolina, North Carolina–Japan Center.

GRADUATE UNITS

College of Veterinary Medicine *Degree program information:* Part-time programs available. Offers cell biology (MS, PhD); infectious disease (MS, PhD); pathology (MS, PhD); pharmacology (MS, PhD); population medicine (MS, PhD); specialized veterinary medicine (MSpVM); veterinary medicine (DVM, MS, MSpVM, MVPH, PhD); veterinary public health (MVPH). Electronic applications accepted.

Graduate School *Degree program information:* Part-time and evening/weekend programs available. Postbaccalaureate distance learning degree programs offered. Electronic applications accepted.

College of Agriculture and Life Sciences *Degree program information:* Part-time programs available. Offers agricultural and extension education (Ed D); agricultural and resource economics (MS); agricultural education (MAE, MS, Certificate); agriculture and life sciences (M Tox, MAE, MB, MBAE, MFG, MFM, MFS, MG, MMB, MN, MP, MS, MZS, Ed D, PhD, Certificate); animal and poultry science (PhD); animal science (MS); biochemistry (PhD); bioinformatics (MB, PhD); biological and agricultural engineering (MBAE, MS, PhD, Certificate); crop science (MS, PhD); entomology (MS, PhD); environmental and molecular toxicology (M Tox, MS, PhD); extension education (MS); financial mathematics (MFM); food science (MFS, MS, PhD); functional genomics (MFG, MS, PhD); genetics (MG, MS, PhD); genomic sciences (MS, PhD); horticultural science (MS, PhD, Certificate); immunology (MS, PhD); microbial biotechnology (MMB); microbiology (MMB, MS, PhD); nutrition (MN, MS, PhD); physiology (MP, MS, PhD); plant biology (MS, PhD); plant pathology (MS, PhD); poultry science (MS); soil science (MS, PhD); zoology (MS, MZS, PhD). Electronic applications accepted.

College of Design *Degree program information:* Part-time programs available. Offers architecture (M Arch); art and design (MAD); design (M Arch, MAD, MGD, MID, MLA, PhD); graphic design (MGD); industrial design (MID); landscape architecture (MLA). Electronic applications accepted.

College of Education *Degree program information:* Part-time programs available. Offers adult and community college education (M Ed, MS, Ed D); agency counseling (M Ed, MS); business and marketing education (M Ed, MS); counselor education (M Ed, MS, PhD); curriculum and instruction (M Ed, MS, MS Ed, PhD); education (M Ed, MS, MS Ed, MSA, Ed D, PhD, Certificate); educational administration and supervision (Ed D); educational research and policy analysis (PhD); elementary education (M Ed); higher education administration (M Ed, MS, Ed D); human resource development (MS); instructional technology (M Ed, MS); mathematics education (M Ed, MS, PhD); middle grades education (M Ed, MS); school administration (MSA); science education (M Ed, MS, PhD); secondary English education (M Ed, MS Ed); social studies education (M Ed); special education (M Ed, MS); technology education (M Ed, MS, Ed D); training and development (M Ed, Ed D, Certificate). Electronic applications accepted.

College of Engineering *Degree program information:* Part-time programs available. Offers aerospace engineering (MS, PhD); biomedical engineering (MS, PhD); chemical engineering (M Ch E, MS, PhD); civil engineering (MCE, MS, PhD); computer engineering (MS, PhD); computer networking (MS); computer science (MC Sc, MS, PhD); electrical engineering (MS, PhD); engineering (M Ch E, M Eng, MC Sc, MCE, MIE, MIMS, MMSE, MNE, MOR, MS, PhD); industrial engineering (MIE, MS, PhD); integrated manufacturing systems engineering (MIMS); materials science and engineering (MMSE, MS, PhD); mechanical engineering (MS, PhD); nuclear engineering (MNE, MS, PhD); operations research (MOR, MS, PhD). Electronic applications accepted.

College of Humanities and Social Sciences *Degree program information:* Part-time and evening/weekend programs available. Offers anthropology (MA); bioarchaeology (MA); communication (MS); communication, rhetoric, and digital media (PhD); creative writing (MFA); cultural anthropology (MA); developmental psychology (PhD); English (MA, MFA, MS); environmental anthropology (MA); ergonomics and experimental psychology (PhD); French language and literature (MA); history (MA); humanities and social sciences (M Soc, MA, MFA, MIS, MPA, MS, MSW, PhD, Certificate); industrial/organizational psychology (PhD); international studies (MIS); liberal studies (MA); nonprofit management (Certificate); psychology in the public interest (PhD); public administration (MPA, PhD); public history (MA); school psychology (PhD); social work (MSW); sociology (M Soc, MS, PhD); Spanish language and literature (MA); technical communication (MS). Electronic applications accepted.

College of Management *Degree program information:* Part-time programs available. Offers accounting (MAC); analytics (MS); biosciences management (MBA); economics (M Econ, MA, PhD); entrepreneurship and technology commercialization (MBA); financial management (MBA); innovation management (MBA); management (M Econ, MA, MAC, MBA, MS, PhD); marketing management (MBA); services management and consulting (MBA); supply chain management (MBA). Electronic applications accepted.

College of Natural Resources *Degree program information:* Part-time programs available. Offers fisheries and wildlife sciences (MFWS, MS, PhD); forestry and environmental resources (MF, MS, PhD); natural resource management (MPRTM, MS); natural resources (MF, MFWS, MNR, MPRTM, MS, MWPS, PhD); park and recreation management (MPRTM, MS); parks, recreation and tourism management (PhD); recreational sport management (MPRTM, MS); spatial information science (MPRTM, MS); tourism policy and development (MPRTM, MS); wood and paper science (MS, MWPS, PhD). Electronic applications accepted.

College of Physical and Mathematical Sciences *Degree program information:* Part-time programs available. Offers applied mathematics (MS, PhD); biomathematics (M Biomath, MS, PhD); chemistry (MS, PhD); marine, earth, and atmospheric sciences (MS, PhD); mathematics (MS, PhD); meteorology (MS, PhD); oceanography (MS, PhD); physical and mathematical sciences (M Biomath, M Stat, MS, PhD); physics (MS, PhD); statistics (M Stat, MS, PhD). Electronic applications accepted.

College of Textiles *Degree program information:* Part-time and evening/weekend programs available. Postbaccalaureate distance learning degree programs offered. Offers fiber and polymer science (PhD); textile and apparel technology and management (MS, MT); textile chemistry (MS); textile engineering (MS); textile technology management (PhD); textiles (MS, MT, PhD). Electronic applications accepted.

NORTH CENTRAL COLLEGE, Naperville, IL 60566-7063

General Information Independent-religious, coed, comprehensive institution. *Enrollment:* 2,902 graduate, professional, and undergraduate students; 117 full-time matriculated graduate/professional students (61 women), 171 part-time matriculated graduate/professional students (89 women). *Enrollment by degree level:* 288 master's. *Graduate faculty:* 36 full-time (12 women), 18 part-time/adjunct (1 woman). *Graduate housing:* Room and/or apartments available on a first-come, first-served basis to single students; on-campus housing not available to married students. *Student services:* Campus employment opportunities, campus safety program, career counseling, free psychological counseling, international student services, multicultural affairs office, teacher training, writing training. *Library facilities:* Oesterle Library. *Online resources:* library catalog, web page, access to other libraries' catalogs. *Collection:* 148,904 titles, 5,113 serial subscriptions, 3,928 audiovisual materials.

Computer facilities: 351 computers available on campus for general student use. A campuswide network can be accessed from student residence rooms and from off campus. Online class registration, software packages are available. *Web address:* http://www.northcentralcollege.edu/.

General Application Contact: Wendy Kulpinski, Graduate Admissions Counselor, 630-637-5808, Fax: 630-637-5819, E-mail: wekulpinski@noctrl.edu.

GRADUATE UNITS

Graduate and Continuing Education Programs Students: 117 full-time (61 women), 171 part-time (89 women); includes 12 Black or African American, non-Hispanic/Latino; 2 American Indian or Alaska Native, non-Hispanic/Latino; 8 Asian, non-Hispanic/Latino; 13 Hispanic/Latino; 1 Two or more races, non-Hispanic/Latino, 10 international. Average age 29. 189 applicants, 79% accepted, 95 enrolled. *Faculty:* 36 full-time (12 women), 18 part-time/adjunct (1 woman). Expenses: Contact institution. *Financial support:* In 2010–11, 2 students received support. Unspecified assistantships available. Support available to part-time students. In 2010, 88 master's awarded. *Degree program information:* Part-time and evening/weekend programs available. Offers business administration (MBA); change management (MBA); curriculum and instruction (MA Ed); finance (MBA); higher education leadership (MLS); human resource management (MBA); leadership and administration (MA Ed); liberal studies (MALS); management (MBA); management information systems (MS); marketing (MBA); professional leadership (MLS); social entrepreneurship (MLS); sports leadership (MLS); Web and Internet applications (MS). *Application deadline:* For fall admission, 8/15 for domestic students, 7/15 for international students; for winter admission, 12/1 for domestic students, 11/1 for international students; for spring admission, 2/1 for domestic students, 12/1 for international students. Applications are processed on a rolling basis. *Application fee:* $25. Electronic applications accepted. *Application Contact:* Wendy Kulpinski, Director of Graduate and Continuing Education Admission, 630-637-5808, Fax: 630-637-5819, E-mail: wekulpinski@noctrl.edu. Dr. Peter Barger, 630-637-5362, Fax: 630-637-5844.

NORTHCENTRAL UNIVERSITY, Prescott Valley, AZ 86314

General Information Proprietary, coed, comprehensive institution. *Enrollment:* 9,085 graduate, professional, and undergraduate students; 8,363 full-time matriculated graduate/professional students (4,501 women). *Enrollment by degree level:* 1,608 master's, 6,685 doctoral, 70 other advanced degrees. *Library facilities:* Northcentral University Library. *Online resources:* web page.

Computer facilities: A campuswide network can be accessed from off campus. Online class registration is available. *Web address:* http://www.ncu.edu/.

General Application Contact: Kevin Lustig, Vice President, Enrollment Services, 480-478-7490, Fax: 928-759-6285, E-mail: admissions@ncu.edu.

GRADUATE UNITS

Graduate Studies Students: 8,363 full-time (4,501 women); includes 896 minority (606 Black or African American, non-Hispanic/Latino; 35 American Indian or Alaska Native, non-Hispanic/Latino; 92 Asian, non-Hispanic/Latino; 142 Hispanic/Latino; 13 Native Hawaiian or other Pacific Islander, non-Hispanic/Latino; 8 Two or more races, non-Hispanic/Latino). Average age 43. *Faculty:* 18 full-time (7 women), 449 part-time/adjunct (199 women). Expenses: Contact institution. *Financial support:* Scholarships/grants available. In 2010, 367 master's, 150 doctorates, 33 other advanced degrees awarded. *Degree program information:* Evening/weekend programs available. Postbaccalaureate distance learning degree programs offered (no on-campus study). Offers business (MBA, DBA, PhD, CAGS); education (M Ed, Ed D, PhD, CAGS); marriage and family therapy (MA, PhD); psychology (MA, PhD, CAGS). *Application deadline:* Applications are processed on a rolling basis. *Application fee:* $75. *Application Contact:* Kevin Lustig, Vice President, Enrollment Services, 480-478-7490, Fax: 928-759-6285, E-mail: klustig@ncu.edu. *President and Provost,* Dr. Clinton D. Gardner, 888-327-2877, Fax: 928-759-6381, E-mail: president@ncu.edu.

NORTH DAKOTA STATE UNIVERSITY, Fargo, ND 58108

General Information State-supported, coed, university. CGS member. *Enrollment:* 14,407 graduate, professional, and undergraduate students; 1,204 full-time matriculated graduate/professional students (531 women), 617 part-time matriculated graduate/professional students (284 women). *Enrollment by degree level:* 1,204 master's, 617 doctoral. *Graduate faculty:* 510 full-time (140 women), 21 part-time/adjunct (6 women). *Graduate housing:* Rooms and/or apartments available on a first-come, first-served basis to single and married students. *Student services:* Campus employment opportunities, career counseling, child daycare facilities, exercise/wellness program, free psychological counseling, international student services, low-cost health insurance, multicultural affairs office, services for students with disabilities. *Library facilities:* North Dakota State University Library plus 3 others. *Online resources:* library catalog, web page, access to other libraries' catalogs. *Research affiliation:* U. S. Department of Agriculture (USDA)–Metabolism and Radiation Laboratory.

Computer facilities: Computer purchase and lease plans are available. 500 computers available on campus for general student use. A campuswide network can be accessed from student residence rooms. Online class registration is available. *Web address:* http://www.ndsu.edu/.

General Application Contact: Sonya Goergen, Marketing, Recruitment, and Public Relations Coordinator, 701-231-7033, Fax: 701-231-6524.

GRADUATE UNITS

College of Graduate and Interdisciplinary Studies Students: 1,204 full-time (531 women), 617 part-time (284 women). Average age 25. 1,081 applicants, 65% accepted, 399 enrolled. *Faculty:* 510 full-time (140 women), 21 part-time/adjunct (6 women). Expenses: Contact institution. *Financial support:* Fellowships with full tuition reimbursements, research assistantships with full tuition reimbursements, teaching assistantships with full tuition reimbursements, career-related internships or fieldwork, Federal Work-Study, institutionally sponsored loans, scholarships/grants, traineeships, tuition waivers (full and partial), and unspecified assistantships available. Support available to part-time students. Financial award applicants required to submit FAFSA. In 2010, 281 master's, 59 doctorates, 8 other advanced degrees awarded. *Degree program information:* Part-time and evening/weekend programs available. Postbaccalaureate distance learning degree programs offered (minimal on-campus study). Offers cellular and molecular biology (PhD); environmental and conservation sciences (MS, PhD); food safety (MS, PhD); genomics and bioinformatics (MS, PhD); materials and nanotechnology (PhD); natural resources management (MS, PhD); transportation and logistics (PhD). *Application deadline:* For fall admission, 7/31 priority date for domestic students, 5/1 priority date for international students; for spring admission, 12/15 priority date for domestic students, 8/1 priority date for international students. *Application fee:* $45 ($60 for international students). Electronic applications accepted. *Application Contact:* Dr. David A. Wittrock, Dean, 701-231-7033, Fax: 701-231-6524. *Dean,* Dr. David A. Wittrock, 701-231-7033, Fax: 701-231-6524.

College of Agriculture, Food Systems, and Natural Resources Students: 110 full-time (50 women), 45 part-time (20 women); includes 4 Black or African American, non-Hispanic/Latino; 1 American Indian or Alaska Native, non-Hispanic/Latino; 17 Asian, non-Hispanic/Latino; 9 Hispanic/Latino, 30 international. Expenses: Contact institution. *Financial support:* Fellowships with full tuition reimbursements, research assistantships with full tuition reimbursements, teaching assistantships with full tuition reimbursements, career-related internships or fieldwork, Federal Work-Study, and institutionally sponsored loans available. Support available to part-time students. *Degree program information:* Part-time programs available. Offers agribusiness and applied economics (MS); agriculture, food systems, and natural resources (MS, PhD); animal science (MS, PhD); cereal science (MS, PhD); crop and weed sciences (MS); entomology (MS, PhD); environment and conservation science (MS, PhD); environmental and conservation science (PhD); environmental conservation science (MS); food safety (MS); horticulture (MS); international agribusiness (MS); microbiology (MS); molecular pathogenesis (PhD); natural resource management (MS, PhD); plant pathology (MS, PhD); plant sciences (PhD); range sciences (MS, PhD); soil sciences (MS, PhD). *Application deadline:* Applications are processed on a rolling basis. *Application fee:* $45 ($60 for international students). Electronic applications accepted. *Application Contact:* Dr. Kenneth F. Grafton, Dean, 701-231-8790, Fax: 701-231-8520, E-mail: k.grafton@ndsu.edu. *Dean,* Dr. Kenneth F. Grafton, 701-231-8790, Fax: 701-231-8520, E-mail: k.grafton@ndsu.edu.

College of Arts, Humanities and Social Sciences Students: 109 full-time (58 women), 84 part-time (48 women). *Faculty:* 77 full-time (26 women). Expenses: Contact institution. *Financial support:* In 2010–11, 3 fellowships with full tuition reimbursements (averaging $12,150 per year), 93 teaching assistantships with full tuition reimbursements (averaging

North Dakota State University (continued)

$8,000 per year) were awarded; research assistantships with full tuition reimbursements, career-related internships or fieldwork, Federal Work-Study, institutionally sponsored loans, scholarships/grants, and tuition waivers (full) also available. Support available to part-time students. In 2010, 20 master's, 5 doctorates awarded. *Degree program information:* Part-time and evening/weekend programs available. Offers arts, humanities and social sciences (M Ed, MA, MM, MS, DMA, PhD); communication (PhD); criminal justice (MS, PhD); emergency management (MS, PhD); English (MA, MS); history (MA, MS, PhD); mass communication (MA, MS); music (M Ed, MM, DMA); social science (MA, MS); sociology (MS); speech communication (MA, MS). *Application deadline:* Applications are processed on a rolling basis. *Application fee:* $45 ($60 for international students). *Application Contact:* Dr. Thomas J. Riley, Dean, 701-231-9588, Fax: 701-231-1047, E-mail: thomas.riley@ndsu.edu. *Dean,* Dr. Thomas J. Riley, 701-231-9588, Fax: 701-231-1047, E-mail: thomas.riley@ndsu.edu.

College of Business Students: 64 full-time (22 women), 30 part-time (9 women); includes 1 Black or African American, non-Hispanic/Latino; 2 Asian, non-Hispanic/Latino; 1 Hispanic/Latino, 18 international. Average age 29. 55 applicants, 76% accepted, 38 enrolled. *Faculty:* 25 full-time (5 women). Expenses: Contact institution. *Financial support:* In 2010–11, 14 students received support, including 13 research assistantships, 1 teaching assistantship; institutionally sponsored loans and tuition waivers (partial) also available. Support available to part-time students. Financial award application deadline: 5/15; financial award applicants required to submit FAFSA. In 2010, 26 master's awarded. *Degree program information:* Part-time and evening/weekend programs available. Offers business (MBA). *Application deadline:* For fall admission, 7/15 priority date for domestic students; for spring admission, 11/15 for domestic students. Applications are processed on a rolling basis. *Application fee:* $45 ($60 for international students). *Application Contact:* Paul R. Brown, Director, 701-231-7681, Fax: 701-231-7508, E-mail: paul.brown@ndsu.edu. *Dean,* Dr. Ron Johnson, 701-231-8805.

College of Engineering and Architecture Students: 197 full-time (44 women), 108 part-time (20 women). Average age 27. 297 applicants, 43% accepted. *Faculty:* 72 full-time (9 women), 11 part-time/adjunct (0 women). Expenses: Contact institution. *Financial support:* In 2010–11, 150 students received support, including fellowships with full tuition reimbursements available (averaging $15,000 per year), research assistantships with full tuition reimbursements available (averaging $9,000 per year), teaching assistantships with full tuition reimbursements available (averaging $8,000 per year); career-related internships or fieldwork, Federal Work-Study, institutionally sponsored loans, scholarships/grants, and tuition waivers (full) also available. Support available to part-time students. Financial award application deadline: 4/15. In 2010, 32 master's, 5 doctorates awarded. *Degree program information:* Part-time programs available. Offers agricultural and biosystems engineering (MS, PhD); civil engineering (MS, PhD); construction management (MS); electrical and computer engineering (MS, PhD); engineering (PhD); engineering and architecture (MS, PhD); environmental engineering (MS, PhD); industrial and manufacturing engineering (PhD); industrial engineering and management (MS); manufacturing engineering (MS); mechanical engineering and applied mechanics (MS, PhD); natural resource management (MS); natural resources management (PhD); transportation and logistics (PhD). *Application deadline:* For fall admission, 4/1 priority date for domestic and international students; for spring admission, 10/1 priority date for domestic and international students. Applications are processed on a rolling basis. *Application fee:* $45 ($60 for international students). *Application Contact:* Dr. David A. Wittrock, Dean, 701-231-7033, Fax: 701-231-6524. *Dean,* Dr. Gary R. Smith, 701-231-7494, Fax: 701-231-8957, E-mail: gary.smith@ndsu.edu.

College of Human Development and Education Students: 22 full-time (14 women), 16 part-time (12 women); includes 1 Black or African American, non-Hispanic/Latino; 5 American Indian or Alaska Native, non-Hispanic/Latino; 1 Asian, non-Hispanic/Latino; 1 Hispanic/Latino, 1 international. Average age 32. Expenses: Contact institution. *Financial support:* Fellowships, research assistantships, teaching assistantships, career-related internships or fieldwork, Federal Work-Study, institutionally sponsored loans, and tuition waivers (full) available. Support available to part-time students. In 2010, 6 master's, 9 doctorates awarded. *Degree program information:* Part-time and evening/weekend programs available. Post-baccalaureate distance learning degree programs offered (minimal on-campus study). Offers agricultural education (M Ed, MS); agricultural extension education (MS); child development and family science (MS); counseling (M Ed, MS, PhD); couple and family therapy (MS); curriculum and instruction (M Ed, MS); dietetics (MS); education (PhD); educational leadership (M Ed, MS, Ed S); entry level athletic training (MS); exercise science (MS); family and consumer sciences education (M Ed, MS); family financial planning (MS); gerontology (MS, PhD); history education (M Ed, MS); human development (PhD); human development and education (M Ed, MS, Ed D, PhD, Ed S); institutional analysis (Ed D); mathematics education (M Ed, MS); music education (M Ed, MS); nutrition science (MS); occupational and adult education (Ed D); pedagogy (M Ed, MS); physical education and athletic administration (M Ed, MS); public health (MS); science education (M Ed, MS); sport pedagogy (MS); sports recreation management (MS). *Application deadline:* Applications are processed on a rolling basis. *Application fee:* $45 ($60 for international students). *Application Contact:* Dr. Virginia Clark Johnson, Dean, 701-231-8211, Fax: 701-231-7174, E-mail: virginia.clark@ndsu.edu. *Dean,* Dr. Virginia Clark Johnson, 701-231-8211, Fax: 701-231-7174, E-mail: virginia.clark@ndsu.edu.

College of Pharmacy, Nursing and Allied Sciences Students: 25 full-time (17 women), 12 part-time (9 women). Expenses: Contact institution. *Financial support:* Research assistantships with full tuition reimbursements, career-related internships or fieldwork, Federal Work-Study, institutionally sponsored loans, and scholarships/grants available. Financial award application deadline: 4/1. In 2010, 3 master's, 13 doctorates awarded. *Degree program information:* Part-time programs available. Offers nursing (MS, DNP); pharmaceutical sciences (MS, PhD); pharmacy, nursing and allied sciences (MS, DNP, PhD). *Application deadline:* For fall admission, 4/1 for domestic students. Applications are processed on a rolling basis. *Application fee:* $45 ($60 for international students). *Application Contact:* Dr. Jonathan Sheng, Assistant Professor, 701-231-6140, Fax: 701-231-8333, E-mail: jonathan.sheng@ndsu.edu. *Dean,* Dr. Charles D. Peterson, 701-231-7609, Fax: 701-231-7606.

College of Science and Mathematics Students: 236 full-time (69 women), 140 part-time (44 women). Expenses: Contact institution. *Financial support:* Fellowships with full tuition reimbursements, research assistantships with full tuition reimbursements, teaching assistantships with full tuition reimbursements, career-related internships or fieldwork, Federal Work-Study, institutionally sponsored loans, scholarships/grants, traineeships, tuition waivers (full and partial), and unspecified assistantships available. Support available to part-time students. Financial award applicants required to submit FAFSA. *Degree program information:* Part-time programs available. Offers applied mathematics (MS, PhD); applied statistics (MS, Certificate); biochemistry (MS, PhD); biology (MS); botany (MS, PhD); cellular and molecular biology (PhD); chemistry (MS, PhD); clinical psychology (MS); coatings and polymeric materials (MS, PhD); cognitive and visual neuroscience (PhD); computer science (MS, PhD); environmental and conservation sciences (MS, PhD); genomics (PhD); health and social psychology (PhD); mathematics (MS, PhD); natural resources management (MS, PhD); operations research (MS); physics (MS, PhD); psychology (MS); science and mathematics (MS, PhD, Certificate); software engineering (MS, PhD, Certificate); statistics (PhD); zoology (MS, PhD). *Application deadline:* Applications are processed on a rolling basis. *Application fee:* $45 ($60 for international students). Electronic applications accepted. *Application Contact:* Dr. Kevin McCaul, Dean, 701-231-7411, E-mail: kevin.mccaul@ndsu.edu. *Dean,* Dr. Kevin McCaul, 701-231-7411, E-mail: kevin.mccaul@ndsu.edu.

See Display below and Close-Up on page 973.

NORTHEASTERN ILLINOIS UNIVERSITY, Chicago, IL 60625-4699

General Information State-supported, coed, comprehensive institution. CGS member. *Enrollment:* 11,746 graduate, professional, and undergraduate students; 373 full-time matriculated graduate/professional students (221 women), 1,462 part-time matriculated graduate/professional students (975 women). *Enrollment by degree level:* 1,835 master's. *Graduate faculty:* 259 full-time (110 women), 170 part-time/adjunct (85 women). *Graduate housing:* On-campus housing not available. *Student services:* Campus employment opportunities, campus safety program, career counseling, child daycare facilities, exercise/wellness program, free psychological counseling, grant writing training, international student services, low-cost health insurance, services for students with disabilities, teacher training. *Library facilities:* Ronald Williams Library. *Online resources:* library catalog, web page, access to other libraries' catalogs. *Collection:* 705,949 titles, 18,923 serial subscriptions, 8,638 audiovisual materials. *Research affiliation:* Advocate Health Care Network (health care cost containment), Lutheran General Hospital (clinical cardiology), Advocate Medical Group (health care outcomes research).

Computer facilities: 520 computers available on campus for general student use. A campuswide network can be accessed from off campus. Online class registration, productivity software are available. *Web address:* http://www.neiu.edu/.

General Application Contact: Ada Umeh, Admission Director, Graduate College, 773-442-6008, Fax: 773-442-6040, E-mail: a-umeh@neiu.edu.

GRADUATE UNITS

Graduate College Students: 373 full-time (221 women), 1,463 part-time (976 women); includes 469 minority (143 Black or African American, non-Hispanic/Latino; 7 American Indian or Alaska Native, non-Hispanic/Latino; 90 Asian, non-Hispanic/Latino; 216 Hispanic/Latino; 4 Native Hawaiian or other Pacific Islander, non-Hispanic/Latino; 9 Two or more races, non-Hispanic/Latino), 86 international. Average age 34. 577 applicants, 82% accepted. *Faculty:* 259 full-time (110 women), 173 part-time/adjunct (85 women). Expenses: Contact institution. *Financial support:* In 2010–11, 510 students received support, including 90 research assistantships with full tuition reimbursements available (averaging $6,600 per year); career-related internships or fieldwork, Federal Work-Study, institutionally sponsored loans, scholarships/grants, tuition waivers (full and partial), and unspecified assistantships also available. Support available to part-time students. Financial award applicants required to submit FAFSA. In 2010, 500 master's awarded. *Degree program information:* Part-time and evening/weekend programs available. *Application deadline:* For fall admission, 4/1 priority date for domestic students; for spring admission, 8/15 for domestic students. Applications are processed on a rolling basis. *Application fee:* $25. Electronic applications accepted. *Application Contact:* Dr. Janet P. Fredericks, Dean, 773-442-6010, Fax: 773-442-6020, E-mail: j-fredericks@neiu.edu. *Dean,* Dr. Janet P. Fredericks, 773-442-6010, Fax: 773-442-6020, E-mail: j-fredericks@neiu.edu.

College of Arts and Sciences Students: 141 full-time (66 women), 456 part-time (271 women); includes 147 minority (34 Black or African American, non-Hispanic/Latino; 51 Asian, non-Hispanic/Latino; 57 Hispanic/Latino; 5 Two or more races, non-Hispanic/Latino), 51 international. Average age 32. 376 applicants, 79% accepted. *Faculty:* 139 full-time (47 women), 65 part-time/adjunct (23 women). Expenses: Contact institution. *Financial support:* In 2010–11, 270 students received support, including 58 research assistantships with full tuition reimbursements available (averaging $6,600 per year); career-related internships or fieldwork, Federal Work-Study, institutionally sponsored loans, scholarships/grants, tuition waivers (full and partial), and unspecified assistantships also available. Support available to part-time students. Financial award applicants required to submit FAFSA. In 2010, 152 master's awarded. *Degree program information:* Part-time and evening/weekend programs available. Offers arts and sciences (MA, MS); biology (MS); chemistry (MS); communication, media and theatre (MA); composition/writing (MA); computer science (MS); English (MA); geography and environmental studies (MA); gerontology (MA); history (MA); linguistics (MA); literature (MA); mathematics (MA, MS); mathematics for elementary school teachers (MA); music (MA); political science (MA); TESL (MA). *Application deadline:* For fall admission, 4/1 priority date for domestic students; for spring admission, 8/15 for domestic students. Applications are processed on a rolling basis. *Application fee:* $25. Electronic applications accepted. *Application Contact:* Dr. Wamucii Njogu, Dean, 773-442-5700. *Dean,* Dr. Wamucii Njogu, 773-442-5700.

College of Business and Management Students: 41 full-time (19 women), 69 part-time (32 women); includes 23 minority (4 Black or African American, non-Hispanic/Latino; 1 American Indian or Alaska Native, non-Hispanic/Latino; 11 Asian, non-Hispanic/Latino; 6 Hispanic/Latino; 1 Two or more races, non-Hispanic/Latino), 21 international. Average age 31. 112 applicants, 75% accepted, 80 enrolled. *Faculty:* 24 full-time (3 women), 13 part-time/adjunct (4 women). Expenses: Contact institution. *Financial support:* In 2010–11, 20 students received support, including 6 research assistantships with full and partial tuition reimbursements available (averaging $6,600 per year); career-related internships or fieldwork, Federal Work-Study, institutionally sponsored loans, scholarships/grants, tuition waivers (full and partial), and unspecified assistantships also available. Support available to part-time students. In 2010, 34 master's awarded. *Degree program information:* Part-time and evening/weekend programs available. Offers accounting (MSA); finance (MBA); management (MBA); marketing (MBA). *Application deadline:* For fall admission, 4/1 priority date for domestic students; for spring admission, 8/15 for domestic students. Applications are processed on a rolling basis. *Application fee:* $30. Electronic applications accepted. *Application Contact:* Dr. Amy B. Hietapelto, Dean, 773-442-6105. *Dean,* Dr. Amy B. Hietapelto, 773-442-6105.

College of Education Students: 200 full-time (144 women), 938 part-time (673 women); includes 300 minority (105 Black or African American, non-Hispanic/Latino; 6 American Indian or Alaska Native, non-Hispanic/Latino; 28 Asian, non-Hispanic/Latino; 154 Hispanic/Latino; 4 Native Hawaiian or other Pacific Islander, non-Hispanic/Latino; 3 Two or more races, non-Hispanic/Latino), 15 international. Average age 35. 670 applicants, 82% accepted, 417 enrolled. *Faculty:* 83 full-time (47 women), 64 part-time/adjunct (40 women). Expenses: Contact institution. *Financial support:* In 2010–11, 219 students received support, including 21 research assistantships with full and partial tuition reimbursements available (averaging $6,600 per year); career-related internships or fieldwork, Federal Work-Study, institutionally sponsored loans, scholarships/grants, tuition waivers (full and partial), and unspecified assistantships also available. Support available to part-time students. Financial award applicants required to submit FAFSA. In 2010, 420 master's awarded. *Degree program information:* Part-time and evening/weekend programs available. Offers bilingual/bicultural education (MAT, MSI); early childhood special education (MA); educating children with behavior disorders (MA); educating individuals with mental retardation (MA); education (MA, MAT, MS, MSI); educational administration and supervision (MA); educational leadership (MA); gifted education (MA); guidance and counseling (MA); human resource development (MA); inner city studies (MA); instruction (MSI); language arts (MAT, MSI); reading (MA); special education (MA, MS); teaching (MAT); teaching children with learning disabilities (MA). *Application deadline:* For fall admission, 4/1 priority date for domestic students; for spring admission, 8/15 for domestic students. Applications are processed on a rolling basis. *Application fee:* $30. Electronic applications accepted. *Application Contact:* Dr. Maureen D. Gillette, Dean, 773-442-5500. *Dean,* Dr. Maureen D. Gillette, 773-442-5500.

NORTHEASTERN OHIO UNIVERSITIES COLLEGES OF MEDICINE AND PHARMACY, Rootstown, OH 44272-0095

General Information State-supported, coed, graduate-only institution. *Enrollment by degree level:* 767 first professional. *Graduate faculty:* 423 full-time (139 women), 2,011 part-time/adjunct (539 women). *Graduate housing:* On-campus housing not available. *Student services:* Campus employment opportunities, campus safety program, career counseling, free psychological counseling, low-cost health insurance, multicultural affairs office, services for students with disabilities. *Library facilities:* Oliver Ocasek Regional Medical Information Center. *Online resources:* library catalog, web page, access to other libraries' catalogs. *Collection:* 56,952 titles, 7,900 serial subscriptions, 1,247 audiovisual materials. *Research affiliation:* Austen BioInnovation Institute in Akron (pharmacology, drug delivery, biotechnology, community health), American Heart Association (physiology, biochemistry), National Science Foundation (anatomy), National Institutes of Health (anatomy, biochemistry, immunology, neurobiology, microbiology), Summa Health Systems (orthopaedics, anatomy), Margaret Clark Morgan Foundation (schizophrenia, mental illness).

Computer facilities: 50 computers available on campus for general student use. A campuswide network can be accessed from student residence rooms and from off campus. Online class registration is available. *Web address:* http://www.neoucom.edu/.

General Application Contact: Michelle Cassetty Collins, Director, Admissions and Student Services, 330-325-6270, E-mail: admission@neoucom.edu.

GRADUATE UNITS

College of Medicine Students: 492 full-time (229 women); includes 10 Black or African American, non-Hispanic/Latino; 1 American Indian or Alaska Native, non-Hispanic/Latino; 166 Asian, non-Hispanic/Latino; 18 Hispanic/Latino. Average age 24. 2,344 applicants, 13% accepted, 132 enrolled. *Faculty:* 371 full-time (119 women), 1,798 part-time/adjunct (437 women). Expenses: Contact institution. *Financial support:* In 2010–11, 264 students received support. Institutionally sponsored loans and scholarships/grants available. Financial award application deadline: 4/15; financial award applicants required to submit FAFSA. In 2010, 110 MDs awarded. Offers medicine (MD). *Application deadline:* For fall admission, 8/1 priority date for domestic students; for winter admission, 10/1 for domestic students. Applications are processed on a rolling basis. *Application fee:* $40. Electronic applications accepted. *Application Contact:* Luke Gloeckner, Enrollment Services Specialist, 330-325-6274, E-mail: lgloeckner@neoucom.edu. *Dean,* Dr. Jeffrey L. Susman, 330-325-6254.

College of Pharmacy Students: 275 full-time (152 women); includes 14 Black or African American, non-Hispanic/Latino; 1 American Indian or Alaska Native, non-Hispanic/Latino; 37 Asian, non-Hispanic/Latino; 3 Hispanic/Latino. Average age 26. 420 applicants, 27% accepted, 66 enrolled. *Faculty:* 52 full-time (20 women), 213 part-time/adjunct (102 women). Expenses: Contact institution. *Financial support:* In 2010–11, 112 students received support. Scholarships/grants available. Financial award application deadline: 4/15; financial award applicants required to submit FAFSA. Offers pharmacy (Pharm D). *Application deadline:* For fall admission, 9/1 priority date for domestic students; for winter admission, 1/5 for domestic students. Applications are processed on a rolling basis. *Application fee:* $50. Electronic applications accepted. *Application Contact:* Luke Gloeckner, Enrollment Services Specialist, 330-325-6274, E-mail: lgloeckner@neoucom.edu. *Dean,* Dr. David D. Allen, 330-325-6467, Fax: 330-325-5930.

NORTHEASTERN SEMINARY AT ROBERTS WESLEYAN COLLEGE, Rochester, NY 14624

General Information Independent-religious, coed, graduate-only institution. *Graduate housing:* On-campus housing not available.

GRADUATE UNITS

Graduate and Professional Programs *Degree program information:* Evening/weekend programs available. Offers ministry (D Min); theological studies (MA); theology (M Div). M Div/MSW offered jointly with Roberts Wesleyan College. Electronic applications accepted.

NORTHEASTERN STATE UNIVERSITY, Tahlequah, OK 74464-2399

General Information State-supported, coed, comprehensive institution. *Enrollment:* 9,588 graduate, professional, and undergraduate students; 444 full-time matriculated graduate/professional students (304 women), 681 part-time matriculated graduate/professional students (478 women). *Enrollment by degree level:* 140 first professional, 985 master's. *Graduate faculty:* 231 full-time (88 women), 11 part-time/adjunct (6 women). Tuition, state resident: part-time $144 per credit hour. Tuition, nonresident: part-time $384.05 per credit hour. *Required fees:* $34.90 per credit hour. Tuition and fees vary according to program. *Graduate housing:* Rooms and/or apartments available to single and married students. Housing application deadline: 6/1. *Student services:* Campus employment opportunities, career counseling, free psychological counseling, international student services, low-cost health insurance, multicultural affairs office, services for students with disabilities, teacher training. *Library facilities:* John Vaughn Library. *Online resources:* library catalog, web page. *Collection:* 418,643 titles, 25,100 serial subscriptions, 8,991 audiovisual materials.

Computer facilities: Computer purchase and lease plans are available. 1,172 computers available on campus for general student use. A campuswide network can be accessed from student residence rooms and from off campus. *Web address:* http://www.nsuok.edu/.

General Application Contact: Donna Trout, Graduate Program Coordinator, 918-449-6123, Fax: 918-449-6120, E-mail: troutdk@nsuok.edu.

GRADUATE UNITS

College of Optometry Students: 111 full-time (54 women); includes 3 Black or African American, non-Hispanic/Latino; 6 American Indian or Alaska Native, non-Hispanic/Latino; 8 Asian, non-Hispanic/Latino; 4 Hispanic/Latino. Average age 26. 112 applicants, 35% accepted, 28 enrolled. *Faculty:* 110 full-time (53 women), 1 (woman) part-time/adjunct. Expenses: Contact institution. *Financial support:* In 2010–11, 83 students received support. Federal Work-Study, institutionally sponsored loans, scholarships/grants, tuition waivers (partial), and residencies available. Financial award application deadline: 5/1; financial award applicants required to submit FAFSA. In 2010, 26 ODs awarded. Offers optometry (OD). Applicants must be a resident of Oklahoma, Arkansas, Kansas, Colorado, New Mexico, Missouri, Texas, or Nebraska. *Application deadline:* For fall admission, 2/1 for domestic students. Applications are processed on a rolling basis. *Application fee:* $45. *Application Contact:* Natalie Batt, Student and Alumni Affairs, 918-456-5511 Ext. 4036, Fax: 918-458-2104, E-mail: batt@nsuok.edu. Natalie Batt.

Graduate College Students: 333 full-time (250 women), 681 part-time (478 women); includes 283 minority (39 Black or African American, non-Hispanic/Latino; 216 American Indian or Alaska Native, non-Hispanic/Latino; 7 Asian, non-Hispanic/Latino; 21 Hispanic/Latino), 26 international. Average age 35. *Faculty:* 121 full-time (35 women), 10 part-time/adjunct (5 women). Expenses: Contact institution. *Financial support:* Research assistantships, teaching assistantships, career-related internships or fieldwork, Federal Work-Study, scholarships/grants, and tuition waivers (partial) available. Financial award application deadline: 3/1. In 2010, 285 master's awarded. *Degree program information:* Part-time and evening/weekend programs available. *Application deadline:* Applications are processed on a rolling basis. *Application fee:* $0. Electronic applications accepted. *Application Contact:* Margie Railey, Administrative Assistant, 918-456-5511 Ext. 2093, Fax: 918-458-2061, E-mail: railey@nsuok.edu. *Dean,* Dr. Thomas L. Jackson, 918-456-5511 Ext. 2220, Fax: 918-458-2061, E-mail: jacks009@nsuok.edu.

College of Business and Technology Students: 36 full-time (15 women), 153 part-time (78 women); includes 7 Black or African American, non-Hispanic/Latino; 51 American Indian or Alaska Native, non-Hispanic/Latino; 3 Asian, non-Hispanic/Latino; 5 Hispanic/Latino, 11 international. *Faculty:* 12 full-time (2 women). Expenses: Contact institution. *Financial support:* Teaching assistantships, Federal Work-Study available. Financial award application deadline: 3/1. In 2010, 30 master's awarded. *Degree program information:* Part-time and evening/weekend programs available. Offers accounting and financial analysis (MS); business administration (MBA); business and technology (MBA, MS); industrial management (MS). *Application deadline:* For fall admission, 6/1 priority date for domestic students. Applications are processed on a rolling basis. *Application fee:* $0 ($25 for international students). *Application Contact:* Dr. John Schleede, Dean, 918-456-5511 Ext. 2910, Fax: 918-458-2337, E-mail: schleede@nsuok.edu. *Dean,* Dr. John Schleede, 918-456-5511 Ext. 2910, Fax: 918-458-2337, E-mail: schleede@nsuok.edu.

College of Education Students: 178 full-time (139 women), 433 part-time (340 women); includes 154 minority (20 Black or African American, non-Hispanic/Latino; 118 American Indian or Alaska Native, non-Hispanic/Latino; 3 Asian, non-Hispanic/Latino; 13 Hispanic/Latino), 9 international. *Faculty:* 26 full-time (11 women). Expenses: Contact institution. *Financial support:* Teaching assistantships, career-related internships or fieldwork and Federal Work-Study available. Financial award application deadline: 3/1. In 2010, 207 master's awarded. *Degree program information:* Part-time and evening/weekend programs available. Offers collegiate scholarship and services (MS); counseling psychology (MS); early childhood education (M Ed); education (M Ed, MS, MS Ed); health and kinesiology

Northeastern State University (continued)

(MS Ed); higher education administration and services (MS); library media and information technology (MS Ed); mathematics education (M Ed); nursing education (MS); reading (M Ed); school administration (M Ed); school counseling (M Ed); substance abuse counseling (MS); teaching (M Ed). *Application deadline:* For fall admission, 6/1 priority date for domestic students. Applications are processed on a rolling basis. *Application fee:* $0 ($25 for international students). Electronic applications accepted. *Application Contact:* Margie Railey, Administrative Assistant, 918-456-5511 Ext. 2093, Fax: 918-458-2061, E-mail: railey@nsouk.edu. *Head*, Dr. Kay Grant, 918-456-5511 Ext. 3700.

College of Liberal Arts Students: 61 full-time (38 women), 78 part-time (49 women); includes 44 minority (10 Black or African American, non-Hispanic/Latino; 32 American Indian or Alaska Native, non-Hispanic/Latino; 1 Asian, non-Hispanic/Latino; 1 Hispanic/Latino), 2 international. *Faculty:* 26 full-time (6 women). Expenses: Contact institution. *Financial support:* Teaching assistantships, Federal Work-Study available. Financial award application deadline: 3/1. In 2010, 29 master's awarded. *Degree program information:* Part-time and evening/weekend programs available. Offers American studies (MA); communication (MA); criminal justice (MS); English (MA); liberal arts (MA, MS). *Application deadline:* For fall admission, 6/1 priority date for domestic students. Applications are processed on a rolling basis. *Application fee:* $0 ($25 for international students). Electronic applications accepted. *Application Contact:* Margie Railey, Administrative Assistant, 918-456-5511 Ext. 2093, Fax: 918-458-2061, E-mail: railey@nsouk.edu. *Interim Dean*, Dr. Paul Westbrook, 918-456-5511 Ext. 3600, Fax: 918-458-2348, E-mail: westbroo@nsuok.edu.

College of Science and Health Professions Students: 58 full-time (all women), 17 part-time (11 women); includes 19 minority (2 Black or African American, non-Hispanic/Latino; 15 American Indian or Alaska Native, non-Hispanic/Latino; 2 Hispanic/Latino), 4 international. Expenses: Contact institution. In 2010, 19 master's awarded. Offers science and health professions (M Ed, MS); science education (M Ed); speech-language pathology (MS). *Application Contact:* Margie Railey, Administrative Assistant, 918-456-5511 Ext. 2093, Fax: 918-458-2061, E-mail: railey@nsouk.edu. *Interim Dean*, Dr. Doug Penisten, 918-456-5511 Ext. 3800.

NORTHEASTERN UNIVERSITY, Boston, MA 02115-5096

General Information Independent, coed, university. CGS member. *Enrollment:* 22,863 graduate, professional, and undergraduate students; 4,625 full-time matriculated graduate/professional students (2,412 women), 2,333 part-time matriculated graduate/professional students (995 women). *Enrollment by degree level:* 968 first professional, 4,770 master's, 1,104 doctoral, 116 other advanced degrees. *Graduate faculty:* 1,033 full-time (407 women), 415 part-time/adjunct (218 women). *Graduate housing:* Room and/or apartments available on a first-come, first-served basis to single students; on-campus housing not available to married students. *Student services:* Campus employment opportunities, campus safety program, career counseling, child daycare facilities, exercise/wellness program, free psychological counseling, international student services, low-cost health insurance, multicultural affairs office, services for students with disabilities, teacher training. *Library facilities:* Snell Library plus 3 others. *Online resources:* library catalog, web page, access to other libraries' catalogs. *Collection:* 1.3 million titles, 94,520 serial subscriptions, 19,363 audiovisual materials. *Research affiliation:* Analog Devices, Inc. (electronics), General Electric Company (GE) (engineering), Jobs for America's Graduates (labor studies), Cytyc Corporation (medical technology), BBN Technologies (information technology).

Computer facilities: Computer purchase and lease plans are available. 1,993 computers available on campus for general student use. A campuswide network can be accessed from student residence rooms and from off campus. Online class registration is available. *Web address:* http://www.northeastern.edu/.

General Application Contact: Information Contact, 617-373-2000.

GRADUATE UNITS

Bouvé College of Health Sciences Graduate School Students: 1,132 full-time (834 women), 213 part-time (172 women). 1,778 applicants, 36% accepted, 259 enrolled. *Faculty:* 162 full-time (100 women), 117 part-time/adjunct (86 women). Expenses: Contact institution. *Financial support:* Fellowships, research assistantships with full tuition reimbursements, teaching assistantships with full tuition reimbursements, career-related internships or fieldwork, Federal Work-Study, institutionally sponsored loans, scholarships/grants, traineeships, tuition waivers (full and partial), and administrative assistantships available. Support available to part-time students. Financial award application deadline: 3/1; financial award applicants required to submit FAFSA. In 2010, 418 master's, 125 doctorates awarded. *Degree program information:* Part-time and evening/weekend programs available. Offers applied behavior analysis (MS); audiology (Au D); clinical exercise physiology (MS); college student development and counseling (MS, CAGS); counseling psychology (MS, PhD, CAGS); health sciences (Pharm D, MPH, MS, MS Ed, Au D, DPT, PhD, CAGS, CAS); physical therapy (DPT); physician assistant (MS); school psychology (MS, PhD, CAGS); speech-language pathology (MS); urban health (MPH). *Application fee:* $50. Electronic applications accepted. *Application Contact:* Margaret Schnabel, Director of Graduate Admissions, 617-373-2708, E-mail: bouvegrad@neu.edu. *Director*, Suzanne B. Greenberg, 617-373-3195, E-mail: s.greenberg@neu.edu.

School of Nursing Students: 308 full-time (219 women), 108 part-time (93 women). 510 applicants, 32% accepted, 115 enrolled. *Faculty:* 25 full-time (24 women), 4 part-time/adjunct (all women). Expenses: Contact institution. *Financial support:* In 2010–11, 34 students received support; fellowships, research assistantships with full tuition reimbursements available, teaching assistantships with full tuition reimbursements available, career-related internships or fieldwork, institutionally sponsored loans, scholarships/grants, traineeships, tuition waivers (full and partial), and unspecified assistantships available. Support available to part-time students. Financial award application deadline: 7/1; financial award applicants required to submit FAFSA. In 2010, 95 master's awarded. *Degree program information:* Part-time programs available. Offers critical care-acute care nurse practitioner (MS, CAGS, CAS); critical care-neonatal nurse practitioner (MS, CAS); nurse anesthesia (MS, CAGS); nursing (MS, DNP, PhD, CAGS, CAS); nursing administration (MS); pediatric nurse practitioner (MS, CAGS); primary care nursing (MS, CAGS, CAS); psychiatric-mental health nursing (MS, CAGS, CAS). *Application deadline:* For fall admission, 8/1 for domestic students, 6/1 for international students; for winter admission, 12/1 for domestic students. Applications are processed on a rolling basis. *Application fee:* $50. Electronic applications accepted. *Application Contact:* Margaret Schnabel, Director of Graduate Admissions, 617-373-2708, E-mail: bouvegrad@neu.edu. *Director of Graduate Programs*, Dr. Susan Roberts, 617-373-3130, E-mail: s.roberts@neu.edu.

School of Pharmacy Students: 125 full-time (57 women), 10 part-time (8 women). 304 applicants, 34% accepted, 56 enrolled. Expenses: Contact institution. *Financial support:* In 2010–11, 17 research assistantships, 18 teaching assistantships were awarded; scholarships/grants also available. In 2010, 39 master's, 19 doctorates awarded. Offers pharmacy (Pharm D, MS, PhD). Students enter program as undergraduates. *Application deadline:* For fall admission, 3/1 for domestic students, 6/1 for international students. Electronic applications accepted. *Application Contact:* Margaret Schnabel, Director of Graduate Admission, 617-373-2708, Fax: 617-373-8780, E-mail: admissions@neu.edu. *Professor*, Ralph Loring, 617-373-3216, Fax: 617-373-7655, E-mail: r.loring@neu.edu.

College of Arts, Media and Design Students: 44 full-time (26 women), 9 part-time (5 women). 234 applicants, 53% accepted, 40 enrolled. *Faculty:* 65 full-time (28 women), 56 part-time/adjunct (27 women). Expenses: Contact institution. *Financial support:* In 2010–11, 1 fellowship (averaging $17,040 per year) was awarded; career-related internships or fieldwork, Federal Work-Study, institutionally sponsored loans, scholarships/grants, tuition waivers (partial), and unspecified assistantships also available. Financial award application deadline: 3/1; financial award applicants required to submit FAFSA. In 2010, 43 master's awarded. Offers arts, media and design (M Arch, MA, MFA); communication, media, and cultural studies (MA); studio art (MFA). *Application deadline:* For fall admission, 2/1 priority date for domestic students. Applications are processed on a rolling basis. *Application fee:* $50. Electronic applications accepted. *Application Contact:* Jo-Anne Dickinson, Information Contact, 617-373-5990, Fax: 617-373-7281, E-mail: gsas@neu.edu.

School of Architecture Students: 39 full-time (17 women). 138 applicants, 47% accepted, 36 enrolled. *Faculty:* 12 full-time (4 women), 26 part-time/adjunct (10 women). Expenses: Contact institution. *Financial support:* Federal Work-Study and scholarships/grants available. Support available to part-time students. Financial award application deadline: 3/1; financial award applicants required to submit FAFSA. In 2010, 27 master's awarded. Offers architecture (M Arch). *Application deadline:* For fall admission, 2/1 priority date for domestic and international students. Applications are processed on a rolling basis. *Application fee:* $50. Electronic applications accepted. *Application Contact:* Jo-Anne Dickinson, Administrative Assistant, 617-373-5990, Fax: 617-373-7281, E-mail: gsas@neu.edu. *Chair*, Peter Wiederspahn, 617-373-4637, Fax: 617-373-7080, E-mail: p.wiederspahn@neu.edu.

School of Journalism Students: 12 full-time (8 women), 3 part-time (2 women). 58 applicants, 72% accepted, 11 enrolled. *Faculty:* 12 full-time (4 women), 6 part-time/adjunct (4 women). Expenses: Contact institution. *Financial support:* Career-related internships or fieldwork, Federal Work-Study, institutionally sponsored loans, scholarships/grants, tuition waivers (partial), and unspecified assistantships available. Financial award application deadline: 3/1; financial award applicants required to submit FAFSA. In 2010, 14 master's awarded. *Degree program information:* Part-time and evening/weekend programs available. Offers journalism (MA). *Application deadline:* For fall admission, 2/1 priority date for domestic students, 2/1 for international students. Applications are processed on a rolling basis. *Application fee:* $50. Electronic applications accepted. *Application Contact:* Jo-Anne Dickinson, Graduate Assistant, 617-373-5990, Fax: 617-373-7281, E-mail: gsas@neu.edu. *Graduate Coordinator*, Prof. Belle Adler, 617-373-3238, Fax: 617-373-8773, E-mail: b.adler@neu.edu.

College of Computer and Information Science Students: 337 full-time (91 women), 90 part-time (52 women). 1,045 applicants, 56% accepted, 150 enrolled. *Faculty:* 28 full-time (3 women), 3 part-time/adjunct (all women). Expenses: Contact institution. *Financial support:* In 2010–11, 59 students received support, including 1 fellowship, 40 research assistantships with full tuition reimbursements available (averaging $18,260 per year), 33 teaching assistantships with full tuition reimbursements available (averaging $18,260 per year); career-related internships or fieldwork, Federal Work-Study, institutionally sponsored loans, scholarships/grants, and unspecified assistantships also available. Financial award application deadline: 1/15. In 2010, 88 master's, 7 doctorates awarded. *Degree program information:* Part-time and evening/weekend programs available. Offers computer and information science (PhD); computer science (MS); health informatics (MS); information assurance (MS). *Application deadline:* For fall admission, 7/15 for domestic students, 5/1 for international students; for spring admission, 10/15 for domestic students, 9/1 for international students. Applications are processed on a rolling basis. *Application fee:* $50. Electronic applications accepted. *Application Contact:* Dr. Agnes Chan, Associate Dean and Director of Graduate Program, 617-373-2462, Fax: 617-373-5121, E-mail: gradschool@ccs.neu.edu. *Dean*, Dr. Larry A. Finkelstein, 617-373-2462, Fax: 617-373-5121.

College of Engineering Students: 1,069 full-time (289 women), 298 part-time (51 women). 2,648 applicants, 62% accepted, 496 enrolled. *Faculty:* 120 full-time (23 women), 25 part-time/adjunct (1 woman). Expenses: Contact institution. *Financial support:* In 2010–11, 268 students received support, including 4 fellowships with full tuition reimbursements available, 146 research assistantships with full tuition reimbursements available (averaging $18,320 per year), 117 teaching assistantships with full tuition reimbursements available (averaging $18,320 per year); career-related internships or fieldwork, Federal Work-Study, scholarships/grants, tuition waivers (full), and unspecified assistantships also available. Support available to part-time students. Financial award application deadline: 1/15; financial award applicants required to submit FAFSA. In 2010, 360 master's, 27 doctorates awarded. *Degree program information:* Part-time programs available. Offers chemical engineering (MS, PhD); civil and environmental engineering (MS, PhD); computer engineering (PhD); electrical engineering (MS, PhD); energy systems (MS); engineering (MS, PhD, Certificate); engineering leadership (MS); engineering management (MS); industrial engineering (MS, PhD); information systems (MS, Certificate); mechanical engineering (MS, PhD); operations research (MS); telecommunication systems management (MS). *Application deadline:* For fall admission, 1/15 priority date for domestic and international students. Applications are processed on a rolling basis. *Application fee:* $50. Electronic applications accepted. *Application Contact:* Jeffery Hengel, Admissions Specialist, 617-373-2711, Fax: 617-373-2501, E-mail: grad-eng@coe.neu.edu. *Associate Dean of Engineering for Research and Graduate Studies*, Dr. Yaman Yener, 617-373-2711, Fax: 617-373-2501.

College of Science Students: 421 full-time (215 women), 40 part-time (19 women). 871 applicants, 34% accepted, 108 enrolled. *Faculty:* 162 full-time (39 women), 46 part-time/adjunct (22 women). Expenses: Contact institution. *Financial support:* In 2010–11, 1 fellowship, 80 research assistantships, 161 teaching assistantships were awarded; career-related internships or fieldwork, Federal Work-Study, institutionally sponsored loans, tuition waivers (full and partial), and unspecified assistantships also available. Support available to part-time students. Financial award application deadline: 3/1. In 2010, 74 master's, 30 doctorates awarded. Offers analytical chemistry (PhD); applied mathematics (MS); bioinformatics (PMS); biology (MS, PhD); biotechnology (MS, PSM); chemistry (MS, PhD); experimental psychology (MA, PhD); inorganic chemistry (PhD); marine biology (MS); mathematics (MS, PhD); operations research (MSOR); organic chemistry (PhD); physical chemistry (PhD); physics (MS, PhD); science (MA, MS, MSOR, PMS, PSM, PhD). *Application deadline:* For fall admission, 2/1 for domestic and international students. Applications are processed on a rolling basis. *Application fee:* $50. Electronic applications accepted. *Application Contact:* Information Contact, 617-373-2000.

College of Social Sciences and Humanities Students: 461 full-time (291 women), 107 part-time (66 women). 834 applicants, 48% accepted, 174 enrolled. *Faculty:* 176 full-time (74 women), 79 part-time/adjunct (50 women). Expenses: Contact institution. *Financial support:* In 2010–11, 2 research assistantships, 39 teaching assistantships were awarded; career-related internships or fieldwork, Federal Work-Study, institutionally sponsored loans, scholarships/grants, tuition waivers (full and partial), and unspecified assistantships also available. Support available to part-time students. Financial award application deadline: 2/1; financial award applicants required to submit FAFSA. In 2010, 119 master's, 17 doctorates awarded. Offers economics (MA, PhD); English (MA, PhD); history (MA); political science (MA); public administration (MPA, Certificate); public and international affairs (PhD); public history (MA); social sciences and humanities (MA, MPA, MS, MURP, PhD, Certificate); sociology (MA, PhD); world history (PhD). *Application fee:* $50. *Application Contact:* Information Contact, 617-373-2000.

School of Criminology and Criminal Justice Students: 77 full-time (52 women), 14 part-time (5 women); includes 7 Black or African American, non-Hispanic/Latino; 1 American Indian or Alaska Native, non-Hispanic/Latino; 1 Asian, non-Hispanic/Latino, 10 international. 108 applicants, 63% accepted, 29 enrolled. *Faculty:* 17 full-time (6 women), 11 part-time/adjunct (5 women). Expenses: Contact institution. *Financial support:* In 2010–11, 2 research assistantships with full and partial tuition reimbursements, 13 teaching assistantships with full tuition reimbursements (averaging $13,654 per year) were awarded; career-related internships or fieldwork, Federal Work-Study, and institutionally sponsored loans also available. Support available to part-time students. Financial award application deadline: 3/31; financial award applicants required to submit FAFSA. In 2010, 22 master's awarded. *Degree program information:* Part-time and evening/weekend programs available. Offers criminology and criminal justice (MS, PhD). *Application deadline:* For fall admission, 3/1 for domestic students; for spring admission, 10/1 for domestic students. Applications are processed on a rolling basis. *Application fee:* $50. Electronic applications accepted. *Application Contact:* Laurie A. Mastone, Assistant to the Director, 617-373-2813, Fax: 617-373-8723, E-mail: l.mastone@neu.edu. *Associate Dean*, Jack McDevitt, 617-373-2813, Fax: 617-373-8723.

School of Public Policy and Urban Affairs Students: 22 full-time (14 women), 12 part-time (7 women). Average age 27. 51 applicants, 57% accepted, 18 enrolled. *Faculty:* 8 full-time (3 women), 4 part-time/adjunct (3 women). Expenses: Contact institution. *Financial support:* Federal Work-Study, scholarships/grants, and tuition waivers available. Financial award application deadline: 2/1; financial award applicants required to submit FAFSA. *Degree program information:* Part-time and evening/weekend programs available. Offers development administration (MPA); health administration and policy (MPA); law and public policy

(PhD); public administration (MPA, Certificate); state and local government (MPA); urban and regional policy (MURP); urban studies (Certificate). *Application deadline:* For fall admission, 2/1 priority date for domestic and international students. Applications are processed on a rolling basis. *Application fee:* $50. Electronic applications accepted. *Application Contact:* Jo-Anne Dickinson, Graduate Admissions Contact, 617-373-5990, Fax: 617-373-7281, E-mail: gsas@neu.edu. *Graduate Coordinator,* Dr. Laurie Dopkins, 617-373-2889, E-mail: murp@neu.edu.

Graduate School of Business Administration Students: 200 full-time (80 women), 483 part-time (174 women). 955 applicants, 43% accepted, 259 enrolled. *Faculty:* 46 full-time (7 women), 5 part-time/adjunct (0 women). Expenses: Contact institution. *Financial support:* Federal Work-Study, institutionally sponsored loans, and scholarships/grants available. Support available to part-time students. Financial award application deadline: 3/1; financial award applicants required to submit FAFSA. In 2010, 285 master's awarded. *Degree program information:* Part-time and evening/weekend programs available. Postbaccalaureate distance learning degree programs offered (no on-campus study). Offers business administration (EMBA, MBA, MS, CAGS). *Application deadline:* For fall admission, 11/30 for domestic and international students; for winter admission, 2/1 for domestic and international students; for spring admission, 4/15 for domestic students. *Application fee:* $100. Electronic applications accepted. *Application Contact:* Evelyn Tate, Director, Graduate Admissions, 617-373-5992, Fax: 617-373-8564, E-mail: e.tate@neu.edu. *Associate Dean, Graduate Business Programs,* Kate Klepper, 617-373-5417, Fax: 617-373-8564, E-mail: k.klepper@neu.edu.

Graduate School of Professional Accounting Students: 100 full-time (47 women), 77 part-time (31 women). Average age 26. 284 applicants, 58% accepted, 116 enrolled. *Faculty:* 8 full-time (2 women), 6 part-time/adjunct (0 women). Expenses: Contact institution. *Financial support:* In 2010–11, 58 fellowships (averaging $8,295 per year) were awarded; career-related internships or fieldwork, Federal Work-Study, institutionally sponsored loans, and scholarships/grants also available. Support available to part-time students. Financial award application deadline: 3/1; financial award applicants required to submit FAFSA. In 2010, 127 master's awarded. Postbaccalaureate distance learning degree programs offered (no on-campus study). Offers professional accounting (MS, MST). *Application deadline:* For fall admission, 8/1 for domestic students, 2/1 for international students; for winter admission, 11/15 for domestic and international students; for spring admission, 3/15 for domestic students. *Application fee:* $100. Electronic applications accepted. *Application Contact:* Annarita Meeker, Director, Graduate Accounting and Tax Programs, 617-373-4621, Fax: 617-373-8564, E-mail: a.meeker@neu.edu. *Associate Dean, Graduate Business Programs,* Kate Klepper, 617-373-5417, Fax: 617-373-8564, E-mail: k.klepper@neu.edu.

School of Law Students: 629 full-time (375 women). Average age 26. 4,316 applicants, 32% accepted, 220 enrolled. *Faculty:* 35 full-time (18 women), 33 part-time/adjunct (15 women). Expenses: Contact institution. *Financial support:* In 2010–11, 534 students received support, including 48 fellowships (averaging $3,000 per year), 18 research assistantships (averaging $869 per year), 18 teaching assistantships (averaging $565 per year); career-related internships or fieldwork, Federal Work-Study, institutionally sponsored loans, scholarships/grants, and tuition waivers (full and partial) also available. Financial award application deadline: 2/15; financial award applicants required to submit FAFSA. In 2010, 192 first professional degrees awarded. Offers law (JD). JD/MPH offered jointly with Tufts University, JD/MS/MBA with Graduate School of Professional Accounting, JD/PhD with Program in Law, Policy, and Society, JD offered jointly with Vermont Law School and Brandeis University. *Application deadline:* For fall admission, 3/1 for domestic and international students. Applications are processed on a rolling basis. *Application fee:* $75. Electronic applications accepted. *Application Contact:* Information Contact, 617-373-2395, Fax: 617-373-8865, E-mail: lawadmissions@neu.edu. *Dean,* Emily A. Spieler, 617-373-3307, Fax: 617-373-8793, E-mail: e.spieler@neu.edu.

School of Technological Entrepreneurship Students: 22 full-time (10 women), 1 part-time (0 women). 38 applicants, 87% accepted, 22 enrolled. *Faculty:* 7 full-time (2 women), 3 part-time/adjunct (0 women). Expenses: Contact institution. In 2010, 13 master's awarded. *Degree program information:* Part-time programs available. Offers technological entrepreneurship (MS). *Application deadline:* For fall admission, 7/1 for international students. Applications are processed on a rolling basis. *Application fee:* $50. Electronic applications accepted. *Application Contact:* Information Contact, 617-373-2788, Fax: 617-373-7490, E-mail: ste@neu.edu. *Dean,* Dr. Paul M. Zavracky, 617-373-2788, Fax: 617-373-7490, E-mail: ste@neu.edu.

NORTHERN ARIZONA UNIVERSITY, Flagstaff, AZ 86011

General Information State-supported, coed, university. CGS member. *Enrollment:* 25,204 graduate, professional, and undergraduate students; 2,080 full-time matriculated graduate/professional students (1,388 women), 2,664 part-time matriculated graduate/professional students (1,914 women). *Enrollment by degree level:* 4,007 master's, 485 doctoral, 252 other advanced degrees. *Graduate faculty:* 836 full-time (409 women). *Graduate housing:* Rooms and/or apartments available to single students and available on a first-come, first-served basis to married students. *Student services:* Campus employment opportunities, campus safety program, career counseling, child daycare facilities, exercise/wellness program, free psychological counseling, grant writing training, international student services, low-cost health insurance, multicultural affairs office, services for students with disabilities, teacher training, writing training. *Library facilities:* Cline Library. *Online resources:* library catalog, web page, access to other libraries' catalogs. *Collection:* 929,089 titles, 53,775 serial subscriptions, 37,039 audiovisual materials. *Research affiliation:* Museum of Northern Arizona, Lowell Observatory, Rocky Mountain Forest and Range Experiment Station, U. S. Naval Observatory, U. S. Geological Survey (USGS), W. L. Gore and Associates, Inc.

Computer facilities: Computer purchase and lease plans are available. 400 computers available on campus for general student use. A campuswide network can be accessed from student residence rooms and from off campus. Online class registration is available. *Web address:* http://www.nau.edu/.

General Application Contact: Director of Graduate Admissions, 928-523-4348, Fax: 928-523-8950, E-mail: graduate@nau.edu.

GRADUATE UNITS

Graduate College Students: 2,080 full-time (1,388 women), 2,664 part-time (1,914 women); includes 1,204 minority (163 Black or African American, non-Hispanic/Latino; 207 American Indian or Alaska Native, non-Hispanic/Latino; 81 Asian, non-Hispanic/Latino; 669 Hispanic/Latino; 8 Native Hawaiian or other Pacific Islander, non-Hispanic/Latino; 76 Two or more races, non-Hispanic/Latino), 91 international. Average age 36. 2,874 applicants, 53% accepted, 1068 enrolled. *Faculty:* 836 full-time (409 women). Expenses: Contact institution. *Financial support:* In 2010–11, 32 fellowships, 84 research assistantships with partial tuition reimbursements (averaging $13,000 per year), 287 teaching assistantships with partial tuition reimbursements (averaging $10,000 per year) were awarded; career-related internships or fieldwork, Federal Work-Study, institutionally sponsored loans, scholarships/grants, traineeships, health care benefits, tuition waivers (full and partial), and unspecified assistantships also available. Support available to part-time students. Financial award applicants required to submit FAFSA. In 2010, 1,697 master's, 45 doctorates, 153 other advanced degrees awarded. *Degree program information:* Part-time programs available. Postbaccalaureate distance learning degree programs offered (minimal on-campus study). *Application deadline:* Applications are processed on a rolling basis. *Application fee:* $65. Electronic applications accepted. *Application Contact:* Shirley Robinson, Coordinator, 928-523-4348, Fax: 928-523-8950, E-mail: shirley.robinson@nau.edu. *Dean,* Dr. Ramona Mellott, 928-523-6534, Fax: 928-523-8950, E-mail: ramona.mellott@nau.edu.

College of Arts and Letters Students: 233 full-time (138 women), 130 part-time (100 women); includes 55 minority (13 Black or African American, non-Hispanic/Latino; 7 American Indian or Alaska Native, non-Hispanic/Latino; 3 Asian, non-Hispanic/Latino; 24 Hispanic/Latino; 8 Two or more races, non-Hispanic/Latino), 31 international. Average age 32. 308 applicants, 68% accepted, 116 enrolled. *Faculty:* 175 full-time (93 women). Expenses: Contact institution. *Financial support:* In 2010–11, 6 fellowships, 94 teaching assistantships were awarded; research assistantships, Federal Work-Study, scholarships/grants, health care benefits, tuition waivers (full and partial), and unspecified assistantships also available. Financial award applicants required to submit FAFSA. In 2010, 110 master's, 3 doctorates, 20 other advanced degrees awarded. *Degree program information:* Part-time programs available. Offers applied linguistics (PhD); arts and letters (MA, MAT, MM, PhD, Certificate); choral conducting (MM); English (MA); history (MA, PhD); instrumental conducting (MM); instrumental performance (MM); musicology (MM); performance (Certificate); piano accompanying and chamber music (MM); professional writing (Certificate); Spanish teaching (MAT); Spanish teaching/Spanish education (MAT); Suzuki violin/viola (MM); teaching English as a second language (MA, Certificate); theory or composition (MM); vocal performance (MM). *Application deadline:* Applications are processed on a rolling basis. *Application fee:* $65. Electronic applications accepted. *Application Contact:* Dr. Michael Vincent, Dean, 928-523-8632, E-mail: michael.vincent@nau.edu. *Dean,* Dr. Michael Vincent, 928-523-8632, E-mail: michael.vincent@nau.edu.

College of Education Students: 1,005 full-time (759 women), 1,762 part-time (1,323 women); includes 804 minority (107 Black or African American, non-Hispanic/Latino; 146 American Indian or Alaska Native, non-Hispanic/Latino; 43 Asian, non-Hispanic/Latino; 465 Hispanic/Latino; 5 Native Hawaiian or other Pacific Islander, non-Hispanic/Latino; 38 Two or more races, non-Hispanic/Latino), 15 international. Average age 36. 736 applicants, 84% accepted, 451 enrolled. *Faculty:* 102 full-time (63 women). Expenses: Contact institution. *Financial support:* In 2010–11, 2 research assistantships with partial tuition reimbursements (averaging $10,000 per year), 15 teaching assistantships with partial tuition reimbursements (averaging $10,000 per year) were awarded; career-related internships or fieldwork, Federal Work-Study, scholarships/grants, health care benefits, tuition waivers (full and partial), and unspecified assistantships also available. Financial award applicants required to submit FAFSA. In 2010, 1,195 master's, 27 doctorates, 87 other advanced degrees awarded. *Degree program information:* Part-time and evening/weekend programs available. Postbaccalaureate distance learning degree programs offered (minimal on-campus study). Offers autism spectrum disorders (Certificate); bilingual/multicultural education (M Ed); career and technical education (M Ed, Certificate); community college/higher education (M Ed); counseling (MA); curriculum and instruction (Ed D); early childhood education (M Ed); early childhood special education (M Ed); early intervention (Certificate); education (M Ed, MA, Ed D, PhD, Certificate); educational foundations (M Ed); educational leadership (M Ed, Ed D); educational psychology (PhD); educational technology (M Ed, Certificate); elementary education—certification (M Ed); elementary education—continuing professional (M Ed); human relations (M Ed); principal (Certificate); principal K-12 (M Ed); school counseling (M Ed); school leadership K-12 (M Ed); school psychology (MA, Certificate); secondary education—certification (M Ed); secondary education—continuing professional (M Ed); special education (M Ed); student affairs (M Ed); superintendent (Certificate). *Application deadline:* Applications are processed on a rolling basis. *Application fee:* $65. Electronic applications accepted. *Application Contact:* Dr. Gypsy Denzine, Dean, 928-523-9211, Fax: 928-523-1929, E-mail: gypsy.denzine@nau.edu. *Dean,* Dr. Gypsy Denzine, 928-523-9211, Fax: 928-523-1929, E-mail: gypsy.denzine@nau.edu.

College of Engineering, Forestry and Natural Sciences Students: 272 full-time (134 women), 91 part-time (45 women); includes 45 minority (3 Black or African American, non-Hispanic/Latino; 11 American Indian or Alaska Native, non-Hispanic/Latino; 5 Asian, non-Hispanic/Latino; 22 Hispanic/Latino; 4 Two or more races, non-Hispanic/Latino), 22 international. 291 applicants, 41% accepted, 88 enrolled. *Faculty:* 195 full-time (62 women). Expenses: Contact institution. *Financial support:* In 2010–11, 32 students received support, including 23 fellowships, 62 research assistantships, 113 teaching assistantships. Financial award applicants required to submit FAFSA. In 2010, 97 master's, 9 doctorates, 1 other advanced degree awarded. Offers applied physics (MS); applied statistics (Certificate); biological sciences (MS, PhD); chemistry (MS); civil and environmental engineering (M Eng); civil engineering (MSE); climate science and solutions (MS); computer science (MSE); earth science (MS); electrical engineering (M Eng, MSE); engineering (M Eng, MSE); engineering, forestry and natural sciences (M Ed, M Eng, MAST, MAT, MF, MS, MSE, MSF, PhD, Certificate); environmental engineering (M Eng, MSE); environmental sciences and policy (MS); forest science (MF, MSF); forestry (PhD); geology (MS); mathematics (MAT, MS); mathematics or science teaching (Certificate); mechanical engineering (M Eng, MSE); science teaching and learning (M Ed, MAST); statistics (MS). *Application fee:* $65. *Application Contact:* Paul W. Jagodzinski, Dean, 928-523-2701, Fax: 928-523-2300, E-mail: paul.jagodzinski@nau.edu. *Dean,* Paul W. Jagodzinski, 928-523-2701, Fax: 928-523-2300, E-mail: paul.jagodzinski@nau.edu.

College of Health and Human Services Students: 225 full-time (169 women), 141 part-time (125 women); includes 66 minority (7 Black or African American, non-Hispanic/Latino; 3 American Indian or Alaska Native, non-Hispanic/Latino; 9 Asian, non-Hispanic/Latino; 42 Hispanic/Latino; 5 Two or more races, non-Hispanic/Latino). Average age 31. 886 applicants, 11% accepted, 85 enrolled. *Faculty:* 79 full-time (65 women). Expenses: Contact institution. *Financial support:* Tuition waivers (full and partial) available. Financial award applicants required to submit FAFSA. In 2010, 43 master's, 46 doctorates awarded. *Degree program information:* Part-time programs available. Offers clinical and translational sciences (Certificate); clinical speech pathology (MS); family nurse practitioner (MSN, Certificate); health and human services (M Ad, MPH, MS, MSN, DPT, Certificate, PPDPT); interdisciplinary health policy (Certificate); nurse educator (MSN); nurse generalist (MSN); nursing (MSN); physical therapy (DPT, PPDPT). *Application fee:* $65. *Application Contact:* Leslie Schulz, Executive Dean, 928-523-4331, E-mail: leslie.schulz@nau.edu. *Executive Dean,* Leslie Schulz, 928-523-4331, E-mail: leslie.schulz@nau.edu.

College of Social and Behavioral Sciences Students: 233 full-time (132 women), 181 part-time (127 women); includes 78 minority (6 Black or African American, non-Hispanic/Latino; 19 American Indian or Alaska Native, non-Hispanic/Latino; 10 Asian, non-Hispanic/Latino; 35 Hispanic/Latino; 1 Native Hawaiian or other Pacific Islander, non-Hispanic/Latino; 7 Two or more races, non-Hispanic/Latino), 20 international. Average age 32. 312 applicants, 62% accepted, 146 enrolled. *Faculty:* 156 full-time (74 women). Expenses: Contact institution. *Financial support:* Applicants required to submit FAFSA. In 2010, 90 master's, 6 doctorates, 45 other advanced degrees awarded. *Degree program information:* Part-time programs available. Offers applied communication (MA); applied criminology (MS); applied geospatial sciences (MS); applied sociology (MA); archaeology (MA); assistive technology (Certificate); clinical health psychology (MA); cultural anthropology (MA); disability policy and practice (Certificate); ethnic studies (Graduate Certificate); general psychology (MA); geographic information systems (Certificate); linguistic anthropology (MA); political science (MA, PhD); positive behavior support (Certificate); public administration (MPA); public management (Certificate); social and behavioral sciences (MA, MPA, MS, PhD, Certificate, Graduate Certificate); sustainable communities (MA); teaching psychology (MA); women's and gender studies (Graduate Certificate). *Application deadline:* Applications are processed on a rolling basis. *Application fee:* $65. Electronic applications accepted. *Application Contact:* Dr. Michael Stevenson, Dean, 928-523-6540, Fax: 928-523-7185, E-mail: michael.stevenson@nau.edu. *Dean,* Dr. Michael Stevenson, 928-523-6540, Fax: 928-523-7185, E-mail: michael.stevenson@nau.edu.

NAU-Yuma Students: 85 full-time (45 women), 357 part-time (194 women); includes 146 minority (26 Black or African American, non-Hispanic/Latino; 22 American Indian or Alaska Native, non-Hispanic/Latino; 8 Asian, non-Hispanic/Latino; 82 Hispanic/Latino; 2 Native Hawaiian or other Pacific Islander, non-Hispanic/Latino; 6 Two or more races, non-Hispanic/Latino), 1 international. 116 applicants, 94% accepted, 83 enrolled. *Faculty:* 31 full-time (13 women). Expenses: Contact institution. *Financial support:* Applicants required to submit FAFSA. In 2010, 131 master's awarded. Offers administration (M Adm). *Application deadline:* Applications are processed on a rolling basis. *Application fee:* $65. Electronic applications accepted. *Application Contact:* Dr. Larry Gould, Associate Vice President/Campus Executive Officer, 928-317-6475, E-mail: larry.gould@nau.edu. *Associate Vice President/Campus Executive Officer,* Dr. Larry Gould, 928-317-6475, E-mail: larry.gould@nau.edu.

The W. A. Franke College of Business Students: 25 full-time (9 women), 3 part-time (1 woman); includes 5 minority (1 Black or African American, non-Hispanic/Latino; 2 Asian, non-Hispanic/Latino; 2 Two or more races, non-Hispanic/Latino), 2 international. Average age 32. 59 applicants, 27% accepted, 9 enrolled. *Faculty:* 52 full-time (33 women). Expenses: Contact institution. *Financial support:* In 2010–11, 6 research assistantships (averaging $9,479 per year) were awarded; Federal Work-Study, institutionally sponsored loans, scholarships/grants, health care benefits, tuition waivers (partial), and unspecified assistant-

Northern Arizona University (continued)

ships also available. Support available to part-time students. Financial award applicants required to submit FAFSA. In 2010, 31 master's awarded. *Degree program information:* Part-time programs available. Offers business (MBA). *Application deadline:* For fall admission, 5/15 priority date for domestic students, 3/1 priority date for international students. Applications are processed on a rolling basis. *Application fee:* $65. Electronic applications accepted. *Application Contact:* Katie Poindexter, Coordinator, 928-523-7342, Fax: 928-523-6559, E-mail: mba@nau.edu. *Dean*, Dr. Marc Chopin, 928-523-3657, Fax: 928-523-7331, E-mail: marc.chopin@nau.edu.

NORTHERN BAPTIST THEOLOGICAL SEMINARY, Lombard, IL 60148-5698

General Information Independent-religious, coed, primarily men, graduate-only institution. *Enrollment by degree level:* 120 master's, 11 doctoral, 6 other advanced degrees. *Graduate faculty:* 5 full-time (0 women), 30 part-time/adjunct (5 women). *Tuition:* Full-time $15,840. *Required fees:* $115 per quarter. *Graduate housing:* Rooms and/or apartments available on a first-come, first-served basis to single and married students. Typical cost: $8100 per year for single students; $8100 per year for married students. Room charges vary according to housing facility selected. Housing application deadline: 7/30. *Student services:* Campus employment opportunities, low-cost health insurance. *Library facilities:* Brimsom-Grow Library. *Online resources:* library catalog, web page, access to other libraries' catalogs. *Collection:* 53,200 titles, 282 serial subscriptions, 1,397 audiovisual materials.

Computer facilities: 18 computers available on campus for general student use. A campuswide network can be accessed from student residence rooms and from off campus. Online class registration, wireless internet connection are available. *Web address:* http://www.seminary.edu/.

General Application Contact: Greg Henson, Executive Director of External Relations, 630-620-2180, Fax: 630-620-2190, E-mail: admissions@seminary.edu.

GRADUATE UNITS

Graduate and Professional Programs Students: 78 full-time (29 women), 79 part-time (37 women); includes 69 minority (55 Black or African American, non-Hispanic/Latino; 8 Asian, non-Hispanic/Latino; 6 Hispanic/Latino), 4 international. Average age 40. 100 applicants, 70% accepted, 50 enrolled. *Faculty:* 7 full-time (0 women), 24 part-time/adjunct (3 women). Expenses: Contact institution. *Financial support:* In 2010–11, 69 students received support. Career-related internships or fieldwork and scholarships/grants available. Support available to part-time students. Financial award application deadline: 9/1; financial award applicants required to submit FAFSA. In 2010, 18 master's, 5 doctorates awarded. *Degree program information:* Part-time programs available. Offers Biblical studies (M Div); Christian ministries (MACM); ministry (D Min); theology (M Div). *Application deadline:* For fall admission, 8/25 for domestic students, 2/1 for international students; for winter admission, 12/10 for domestic students, 2/1 for international students; for spring admission, 3/15 for domestic students, 2/1 for international students. Applications are processed on a rolling basis. *Application fee:* $35. Electronic applications accepted. *Application Contact:* Greg Henson, Executive Director of External Relations, 630-620-2180, Fax: 630-620-2190, E-mail: admissions@seminary.edu. *Chief Academic Officer*, Dr. J. Alistair Brown, 630-620-2101, Fax: 630-620-2190.

NORTHERN ILLINOIS UNIVERSITY, De Kalb, IL 60115-2854

General Information State-supported, coed, university. CGS member. *Enrollment:* 23,850 graduate, professional, and undergraduate students; 2,209 full-time matriculated graduate/professional students (1,084 women), 2,794 part-time matriculated graduate/professional students (1,655 women). *Enrollment by degree level:* 326 first professional, 3,581 master's, 1,041 doctoral, 55 other advanced degrees. *Graduate faculty:* 672 full-time (248 women), 66 part-time/adjunct (17 women). Tuition, state resident: full-time $7200; part-time $300 per credit hour. Tuition, nonresident: full-time $14,400; part-time $600 per credit hour. *Required fees:* $79 per credit hour. *Graduate housing:* Rooms and/or apartments available on a first-come, first-served basis to single and married students. *Student services:* Campus employment opportunities, campus safety program, career counseling, child daycare facilities, exercise/wellness program, free psychological counseling, grant writing training, international student services, low-cost health insurance, services for students with disabilities, teacher training, writing training. *Library facilities:* Founders Memorial Library plus 6 others. *Online resources:* library catalog, web page, access to other libraries' catalogs. *Collection:* 3.1 million titles, 27,911 serial subscriptions, 58,140 audiovisual materials. *Research affiliation:* Field Museum of Natural History, Burpee Museum of Natural History, Argonne National Laboratory, Fermi National Accelerator Laboratory.

Computer facilities: 1,500 computers available on campus for general student use. A campuswide network can be accessed from student residence rooms and from off campus. Online class registration is available. *Web address:* http://www.niu.edu/.

General Application Contact: Dr. Bradley G. Bond, Associate Dean, Graduate School, 815-753-0395, Fax: 815-753-6366, E-mail: gradsch@niu.edu.

GRADUATE UNITS

College of Law Students: 324 full-time (137 women), 3 part-time (1 woman); includes 67 minority (24 Black or African American, non-Hispanic/Latino; 1 American Indian or Alaska Native, non-Hispanic/Latino; 12 Asian, non-Hispanic/Latino; 26 Hispanic/Latino; 2 Native Hawaiian or other Pacific Islander, non-Hispanic/Latino; 2 Two or more races, non-Hispanic/Latino), 1 international. Average age 26. 1,514 applicants, 26% accepted, 105 enrolled. *Faculty:* 22 full-time (11 women). Expenses: Contact institution. *Financial support:* In 2010–11, 9 teaching assistantships were awarded; research assistantships, career-related internships or fieldwork, Federal Work-Study, tuition waivers (full and partial), and unspecified assistantships also available. Support available to part-time students. Financial award application deadline: 3/1; financial award applicants required to submit FAFSA. In 2010, 99 JDs awarded. *Degree program information:* Part-time programs available. Offers law (JD). *Application deadline:* For fall admission, 5/15 priority date for domestic and international students. Applications are processed on a rolling basis. *Application fee:* $35 ($50 for international students). Electronic applications accepted. *Application Contact:* Judith L. Malen, Director of Admissions and Financial Aid, 815-753-1420, E-mail: jmalen@niu.edu. *Dean*, Jennifer L. Rosato, 815-753-1380, Fax: 815-753-8552, E-mail: jrosato@niu.edu.

Graduate School Students: 2,209 full-time (1,084 women), 2,794 part-time (1,655 women); includes 870 minority (318 Black or African American, non-Hispanic/Latino; 11 American Indian or Alaska Native, non-Hispanic/Latino; 218 Asian, non-Hispanic/Latino; 275 Hispanic/Latino; 4 Native Hawaiian or other Pacific Islander, non-Hispanic/Latino; 44 Two or more races, non-Hispanic/Latino), 556 international. Average age 35. 3,919 applicants, 48% accepted, 1017 enrolled. *Faculty:* 672 full-time (248 women), 66 part-time/adjunct (17 women). Expenses: Contact institution. *Financial support:* In 2010–11, 24 fellowships with full tuition reimbursements, 319 research assistantships with full tuition reimbursements, 678 teaching assistantships with full tuition reimbursements were awarded; career-related internships or fieldwork, Federal Work-Study, scholarships/grants, tuition waivers (full), and staff assistantships also available. Support available to part-time students. Financial award applicants required to submit FAFSA. In 2010, 1,626 master's, 88 doctorates, 21 other advanced degrees awarded. *Degree program information:* Part-time and evening/weekend programs available. Postbaccalaureate distance learning degree programs offered (minimal on-campus study). *Application deadline:* For fall admission, 6/1 for domestic students, 5/1 for international students; for spring admission, 11/1 for domestic students, 10/1 for international students. Applications are processed on a rolling basis. *Application fee:* $30. Electronic applications accepted. *Application Contact:* Graduate School Office, 815-753-0395, E-mail: gradsch@niu.edu. *Dean/Vice President for Research*, Dr. Bradley G. Bond, 815-753-9403, Fax: 815-753-6366, E-mail: bbond@niu.edu.

College of Business Students: 285 full-time (84 women), 538 part-time (186 women); includes 163 minority (32 Black or African American, non-Hispanic/Latino; 93 Asian, non-Hispanic/Latino; 28 Hispanic/Latino; 1 Native Hawaiian or other Pacific Islander, non-Hispanic/Latino; 9 Two or more races, non-Hispanic/Latino), 87 international. Average age 30. 404 applicants, 62% accepted, 164 enrolled. *Faculty:* 53 full-time (17 women), 3 part-time/adjunct (0 women). Expenses: Contact institution. *Financial support:* In 2010–11, 3 research assistantships with full tuition reimbursements, 1 teaching assistantship with full tuition reimbursement were awarded; fellowships with full tuition reimbursements, career-related internships or fieldwork, Federal Work-Study, scholarships/grants, tuition waivers (full), and unspecified assistantships also available. Support available to part-time students. Financial award applicants required to submit FAFSA. In 2010, 393 master's awarded. *Degree program information:* Part-time and evening/weekend programs available. Offers accountancy (MAS, MST); business (MAS, MBA, MS, MST); business administration (MBA); management information systems (MS). *Application deadline:* For fall admission, 6/1 for domestic students, 5/1 for international students; for spring admission, 11/1 for domestic students, 10/1 for international students. Applications are processed on a rolling basis. *Application fee:* $30. Electronic applications accepted. *Application Contact:* Office of Graduate Studies in Business, 815-753-6301. *Dean*, Dr. Denise Schoenbachler, 815-753-6225, Fax: 815-753-5305, E-mail: denises@niu.edu.

College of Education Students: 319 full-time (198 women), 1,315 part-time (928 women); includes 184 Black or African American, non-Hispanic/Latino; 5 American Indian or Alaska Native, non-Hispanic/Latino; 32 Asian, non-Hispanic/Latino; 117 Hispanic/Latino; 9 Two or more races, non-Hispanic/Latino, 56 international. Average age 36. 545 applicants, 58% accepted, 221 enrolled. *Faculty:* 110 full-time (66 women), 5 part-time/adjunct (3 women). Expenses: Contact institution. *Financial support:* In 2010–11, 6 teaching assistantships with full tuition reimbursements were awarded; fellowships with full tuition reimbursements, research assistantships with full tuition reimbursements, career-related internships or fieldwork, Federal Work-Study, scholarships/grants, tuition waivers (full), and staff assistantships also available. Support available to part-time students. Financial award applicants required to submit FAFSA. In 2010, 565 master's, 40 doctorates, 12 other advanced degrees awarded. *Degree program information:* Part-time and evening/weekend programs available. Postbaccalaureate distance learning degree programs offered (minimal on-campus study). Offers adult and higher education (MS Ed, Ed D); counseling (MS Ed, Ed D); curriculum and instruction (MS Ed, Ed D); early childhood education (MS Ed); education (MS, MS Ed, Ed D, Ed S); educational administration (MS Ed, Ed D, Ed S); educational psychology (MS Ed, Ed D); educational research and evaluation (MS); elementary education (MS Ed); foundations of education (MS Ed); instructional technology (MS Ed, Ed D); literacy education (MS Ed); physical education (MS Ed); school business management (MS Ed); special education (MS Ed); sport management (MS). *Application deadline:* For fall admission, 6/1 for domestic students, 5/1 for international students; for spring admission, 11/1 for domestic students, 10/1 for international students. Applications are processed on a rolling basis. *Application fee:* $30. Electronic applications accepted. *Application Contact:* Graduate School Office, 815-753-0395, E-mail: gradsch@niu.edu. *Dean*, Dr. Lemuel W. Watson, 815-753-9055, Fax: 851-753-2100, E-mail: watson@niu.edu.

College of Engineering and Engineering Technology Students: 111 full-time (17 women), 146 part-time (35 women); includes 5 Black or African American, non-Hispanic/Latino; 8 Asian, non-Hispanic/Latino; 7 Hispanic/Latino; 5 Two or more races, non-Hispanic/Latino, 131 international. Average age 27. 551 applicants, 42% accepted, 76 enrolled. *Faculty:* 36 full-time (2 women), 2 part-time/adjunct (0 women). Expenses: Contact institution. *Financial support:* In 2010–11, 42 research assistantships with full tuition reimbursements, 10 teaching assistantships with full tuition reimbursements were awarded; fellowships with full tuition reimbursements, career-related internships or fieldwork, Federal Work-Study, scholarships/grants, tuition waivers (full), and unspecified assistantships also available. Support available to part-time students. Financial award applicants required to submit FAFSA. In 2010, 78 master's awarded. *Degree program information:* Part-time and evening/weekend programs available. Offers electrical engineering (MS); engineering and engineering technology (MS); industrial engineering (MS); industrial management (MS); mechanical engineering (MS). *Application deadline:* For fall admission, 6/1 for domestic students, 5/1 for international students; for spring admission, 11/1 for domestic students, 10/1 for international students. Applications are processed on a rolling basis. *Application fee:* $30. Electronic applications accepted. *Application Contact:* Graduate School Office, 815-753-0395, E-mail: gradsch@niu.edu. *Dean*, Dr. Promod Vohra, 815-753-1281, Fax: 815-753-1310, E-mail: pvohra@niu.edu.

College of Health and Human Sciences Students: 293 full-time (240 women), 248 part-time (227 women); includes 29 Black or African American, non-Hispanic/Latino; 40 Asian, non-Hispanic/Latino; 33 Hispanic/Latino; 7 Two or more races, non-Hispanic/Latino, 17 international. Average age 29. 570 applicants, 46% accepted, 111 enrolled. *Faculty:* 46 full-time (37 women), 5 part-time/adjunct (3 women). Expenses: Contact institution. *Financial support:* In 2010–11, 6 teaching assistantships with full tuition reimbursements were awarded; fellowships with full tuition reimbursements, research assistantships with full tuition reimbursements, career-related internships or fieldwork, Federal Work-Study, scholarships/grants, tuition waivers (full), and staff assistantships also available. Support available to part-time students. Financial award applicants required to submit FAFSA. In 2010, 159 master's, 2 doctorates awarded. *Degree program information:* Part-time and evening/weekend programs available. Offers allied health and communicative disorders (MA, MPT, Au D); applied family and child studies (MS); communicative disorders (MA, Au D); health and human sciences (MA, MPH, MPT, MS, Au D); nursing (MS); nutrition and dietetics (MS); physical therapy (MPT); public health (MPH). *Application deadline:* For fall admission, 6/1 for domestic students, 5/1 for international students; for spring admission, 11/1 for domestic students, 10/1 for international students. Applications are processed on a rolling basis. *Application fee:* $30. Electronic applications accepted. *Application Contact:* Graduate School Office, 815-753-0395, E-mail: gradsch@niu.edu. *Dean*, Dr. Shirley Richmond, 815-753-6155, E-mail: srichmond@niu.edu.

College of Liberal Arts and Sciences Students: 723 full-time (331 women), 471 part-time (229 women); includes 123 minority (35 Black or African American, non-Hispanic/Latino; 4 American Indian or Alaska Native, non-Hispanic/Latino; 24 Asian, non-Hispanic/Latino; 50 Hispanic/Latino; 1 Native Hawaiian or other Pacific Islander, non-Hispanic/Latino; 9 Two or more races, non-Hispanic/Latino), 237 international. Average age 29. 1,649 applicants, 45% accepted, 377 enrolled. *Faculty:* 342 full-time (99 women), 36 part-time/adjunct (7 women). Expenses: Contact institution. *Financial support:* In 2010–11, 2 teaching assistantships with full tuition reimbursements were awarded; fellowships with full tuition reimbursements, research assistantships with full tuition reimbursements, career-related internships or fieldwork, Federal Work-Study, scholarships/grants, tuition waivers (full), and unspecified assistantships also available. Support available to part-time students. Financial award applicants required to submit FAFSA. In 2010, 336 master's, 48 doctorates awarded. *Degree program information:* Part-time and evening/weekend programs available. Offers anthropology (MA); biological sciences (MS, PhD); chemistry (MS, PhD); communication studies (MA); computer science (MS); economics (MA, PhD); English (MA, PhD); French (MA); geography (MS, PhD); geology (MS, PhD); history (MA, PhD); liberal arts and sciences (MA, MPA, MS, PhD); mathematical sciences (PhD); mathematics (MS); philosophy (MA); physics (MS, PhD); political science (MA, PhD); psychology (MA, PhD); public administration (MPA); sociology (MA); Spanish (MA); statistics (MS). *Application deadline:* For fall admission, 6/1 for domestic students, 5/1 for international students; for spring admission, 11/1 for domestic students, 10/1 for international students. Applications are processed on a rolling basis. *Application fee:* $30. Electronic applications accepted. *Application Contact:* Graduate School Office, 815-753-0395, E-mail: gradsch@niu.edu. *Acting Dean*, Dr. Christopher McCord, 815-753-1061, Fax: 815-753-7950, E-mail: mccord@niu.edu.

College of Visual and Performing Arts Students: 154 full-time (77 women), 73 part-time (49 women); includes 9 Black or African American, non-Hispanic/Latino; 1 American Indian or Alaska Native, non-Hispanic/Latino; 9 Asian, non-Hispanic/Latino; 14 Hispanic/Latino; 3 Two or more races, non-Hispanic/Latino, 27 international. Average age 29. 200 applicants, 52% accepted, 68 enrolled. *Faculty:* 85 full-time (27 women), 15 part-time/adjunct (4 women). Expenses: Contact institution. *Financial support:* Fellowships with full tuition reimbursements, research assistantships with full tuition reimbursements, teaching assistantships with full tuition reimbursements, career-related internships or fieldwork, Federal Work-Study, scholarships/grants, tuition waivers (full), and staff assistantships available. Support available to part-time students. Financial award applicants required to submit FAFSA. In 2010, 83 master's, 20 other advanced degrees awarded. *Degree program information:* Part-time and evening/weekend programs available. Offers art (MA, MFA,

MS); music (MM, Performer's Certificate); theatre and dance (MFA); visual and performing arts (MA, MFA, MM, MS, Performer's Certificate). *Application deadline:* For fall admission, 5/1 for international students; for spring admission, 10/1 for international students. Applications are processed on a rolling basis. *Application fee:* $30. Electronic applications accepted. *Application Contact:* Graduate School Office, 815-753-0395, E-mail: gradsch@niu.edu. *Dean,* Dr. Rich Holly, 815-753-1138, Fax: 815-753-8372, E-mail: rhollyr@niu.edu.

NORTHERN KENTUCKY UNIVERSITY, Highland Heights, KY 41099

General Information State-supported, coed, comprehensive institution. CGS member. *Enrollment:* 15,716 graduate, professional, and undergraduate students; 615 full-time matriculated graduate/professional students (307 women), 1,458 part-time matriculated graduate/professional students (946 women). *Enrollment by degree level:* 595 first professional, 1,323 master's, 46 doctoral, 109 other advanced degrees. *Graduate faculty:* 135 full-time (64 women), 37 part-time/adjunct (18 women). Tuition, state resident: full-time $7254; part-time $403 per credit hour. Tuition, nonresident: full-time $12,492; part-time $694 per credit hour. Tuition and fees vary according to degree level and program. *Graduate housing:* Room and/or apartments available on a first-come, first-served basis to single students; on-campus housing not available to married students. Typical cost: $4136 per year ($6976 including board). Housing application deadline: 5/1. *Student services:* Campus employment opportunities, campus safety program, career counseling, child daycare facilities, exercise/wellness program, free psychological counseling, international student services, low-cost health insurance, multicultural affairs office, services for students with disabilities. *Library facilities:* W. Frank Steely Library plus 1 other. *Online resources:* library catalog, web page, access to other libraries' catalogs. *Collection:* 892,212 titles, 813 serial subscriptions, 14,983 audiovisual materials.

Computer facilities: Computer purchase and lease plans are available. 250 computers available on campus for general student use. A campuswide network can be accessed from student residence rooms and from off campus. Online class registration is available. *Web address:* http://www.nku.edu/.

General Application Contact: Dr. Peg Griffin, Director of Graduate Programs, 859-572-5224, Fax: 859-572-6670, E-mail: griffinp@nku.edu.

GRADUATE UNITS

Chase College of Law Students: 377 full-time (161 women), 236 part-time (106 women); includes 54 minority (27 Black or African American, non-Hispanic/Latino; 1 American Indian or Alaska Native, non-Hispanic/Latino; 12 Asian, non-Hispanic/Latino; 11 Hispanic/Latino; 1 Native Hawaiian or other Pacific Islander, non-Hispanic/Latino; 2 Two or more races, non-Hispanic/Latino). Average age 24. 1,145 applicants, 48% accepted, 200 enrolled. *Faculty:* 38 full-time (15 women), 24 part-time/adjunct (11 women). Expenses: Contact institution. *Financial support:* In 2010–11, 301 students received support, including 12 fellowships (averaging $3,500 per year), 36 research assistantships (averaging $1,000 per year); career-related internships or fieldwork, Federal Work-Study, scholarships/grants, and unspecified assistantships also available. Support available to part-time students. Financial award application deadline: 3/1; financial award applicants required to submit FAFSA. In 2010, 148 first professional degrees awarded. *Degree program information:* Part-time and evening/weekend programs available. Offers law (JD). *Application deadline:* For fall admission, 4/1 priority date for domestic and international students. Applications are processed on a rolling basis. *Application fee:* $40. Electronic applications accepted. *Application Contact:* Ashley Folger Gray, Director of Admissions, 859-572-5841, Fax: 859-572-6081, E-mail: graya4@nku.edu. *Dean,* Dennis R. Honabach, 859-572-6406, Fax: 859-572-6183, E-mail: honabachd1@nku.edu.

Office of Graduate Programs Students: 169 full-time (114 women), 1,260 part-time (849 women); includes 67 Black or African American, non-Hispanic/Latino; 3 American Indian or Alaska Native, non-Hispanic/Latino; 24 Asian, non-Hispanic/Latino; 15 Hispanic/Latino, 25 international. Average age 34. 993 applicants, 60% accepted, 456 enrolled. *Faculty:* 103 full-time (51 women), 69 part-time/adjunct (31 women). Expenses: Contact institution. *Financial support:* In 2010–11, 244 students received support. Unspecified assistantships available. Financial award application deadline: 5/1; financial award applicants required to submit FAFSA. In 2010, 493 master's, 132 other advanced degrees awarded. *Degree program information:* Part-time and evening/weekend programs available. Postbaccalaureate distance learning degree programs offered (no on-campus study). *Application deadline:* For fall admission, 6/1 for international students; for spring admission, 10/1 for international students. *Application fee:* $40. Electronic applications accepted. *Application Contact:* Dr. Peg Griffin, Director of Graduate Programs, 859-572-6934, Fax: 859-572-6670, E-mail: griffinp@nku.edu. *Director of Graduate Programs,* Dr. Peg Griffin, 859-572-6934, Fax: 859-572-6670, E-mail: griffin@nku.edu.

College of Arts and Sciences Students: 56 full-time (28 women), 237 part-time (160 women); includes 40 minority (30 Black or African American, non-Hispanic/Latino; 1 American Indian or Alaska Native, non-Hispanic/Latino; 4 Asian, non-Hispanic/Latino; 3 Hispanic/Latino; 2 Two or more races, non-Hispanic/Latino), 5 international. Average age 34. 184 applicants, 66% accepted, 100 enrolled. *Faculty:* 14 full-time (1 woman), 15 part-time/adjunct (14 women). Expenses: Contact institution. *Financial support:* Unspecified assistantships available. Financial award applicants required to submit FAFSA. In 2010, 43 master's, 9 other advanced degrees awarded. *Degree program information:* Part-time and evening/weekend programs available. Postbaccalaureate distance learning degree programs offered (no on-campus study). Offers arts and sciences (MA, MPA, MS, Certificate); civic engagement (Certificate); composition and rhetoric (Certificate); creative writing (Certificate); cultural studies (Certificate); English (MA); industrial psychology (Certificate); industrial-organizational psychology (MS); integrative studies (MA); non-profit management (Certificate); occupational health psychology (Certificate); organizational psychology (Certificate); professional writing (Certificate); public administration (MPA); public history (MA, Certificate). *Application deadline:* For fall admission, 8/1 for domestic students, 6/1 for international students; for spring admission, 12/1 for domestic students, 10/1 for international students. *Application fee:* $40. Electronic applications accepted. *Application Contact:* Dr. Peg Griffin, Director of Graduate Programs, 859-572-6934, Fax: 859-572-6670, E-mail: griffinp@nku.edu. *Dean,* Dr. Samuel Zachary, 859-572-5495, Fax: 859-572-6185, E-mail: zachary@nku.edu.

College of Business Students: 35 full-time (14 women), 203 part-time (91 women); includes 20 minority (8 Black or African American, non-Hispanic/Latino; 1 American Indian or Alaska Native, non-Hispanic/Latino; 7 Asian, non-Hispanic/Latino; 3 Hispanic/Latino; 1 Two or more races, non-Hispanic/Latino), 10 international. Average age 33. 214 applicants, 52% accepted, 75 enrolled. *Faculty:* 17 full-time (7 women), 5 part-time/adjunct (0 women). Expenses: Contact institution. *Financial support:* Unspecified assistantships available. Financial award applicants required to submit FAFSA. In 2010, 93 master's, 3 other advanced degrees awarded. *Degree program information:* Part-time and evening/weekend programs available. Offers accountancy (M Acc); advanced taxation (Certificate); business (M Acc, MBA, MS, Certificate); business administration (MBA, Certificate); executive leadership and organizational change (MS). *Application deadline:* For fall admission, 6/1 priority date for international students; for spring admission, 10/1 priority date for international students. *Application fee:* $40. Electronic applications accepted. *Application Contact:* Dr. Carol Cornell, Director, 859-442-4281, Fax: 859-572-6177, E-mail: cornellc1@nku.edu. *Dean,* Dr. John Beehler, 859-572-5551, Fax: 859-572-6177, E-mail: beehlerj1@nku.edu.

College of Education and Human Services Students: 87 full-time (69 women), 377 part-time (276 women); includes 24 minority (16 Black or African American, non-Hispanic/Latino; 1 American Indian or Alaska Native, non-Hispanic/Latino; 5 Asian, non-Hispanic/Latino; 2 Hispanic/Latino). Average age 34. 323 applicants, 57% accepted, 154 enrolled. *Faculty:* 28 full-time (16 women), 3 part-time/adjunct (0 women). Expenses: Contact institution. *Financial support:* Unspecified assistantships available. Financial award applicants required to submit FAFSA. In 2010, 213 master's, 6 other advanced degrees awarded. *Degree program information:* Part-time and evening/weekend programs available. Offers clinical mental health counseling (MA); college student development administration (Certificate); community counseling (Certificate); education and human services (MA, MSW, Ed D, Certificate); educational leadership (Ed D); instructional leadership (MA); rank 1 (Certificate); rank 1 supervisor of instruction (Certificate); school counseling (MA); school superintendent (Certificate); social work (MSW); special education (MA, Certificate); teacher as a leader (MA); teaching (MA); temporary school counseling provision (Certificate). *Application deadline:* For fall admission, 6/1 for international students; for spring admission, 10/1 for international students. *Application fee:* $40. Electronic applications accepted. *Application Contact:* Dr. Peg Griffin, Director of Graduate Programs, 859-572-6934, Fax: 859-572-6670, E-mail: griffinp@nku.edu. *Dean,* Dr. Mark Wasicsko, 859-572-5229, Fax: 859-572-6623, E-mail: wasicskom1@nku.edu.

College of Informatics Students: 44 full-time (14 women), 178 part-time (84 women); includes 30 minority (15 Black or African American, non-Hispanic/Latino; 8 Asian, non-Hispanic/Latino; 7 Hispanic/Latino), 13 international. Average age 35. 190 applicants, 68% accepted, 82 enrolled. *Faculty:* 22 full-time (6 women), 2 part-time/adjunct (0 women). Expenses: Contact institution. *Financial support:* Unspecified assistantships available. Financial award applicants required to submit FAFSA. In 2010, 42 master's, 22 other advanced degrees awarded. *Degree program information:* Part-time and evening/weekend programs available. Offers business informatics (MS, Certificate); communication (MA); communication teaching (Certificate); computer information technology (MSCIT); computer science (MSCS); corporate information security (Certificate); documentary studies (Certificate); enterprise resource planning (Certificate); geographic information systems (Certificate); health informatics (MS, Certificate); informatics (MA, MS, MSCIT, MSCS, Certificate); public relations (Certificate); relationships (Certificate); secure software engineering (Certificate). *Application deadline:* For fall admission, 6/1 priority date for international students; for spring admission, 10/1 priority date for international students. Applications are processed on a rolling basis. *Application fee:* $40. Electronic applications accepted. *Application Contact:* Dr. Peg Griffin, Director of Graduate Programs, 859-572-6934, Fax: 859-572-6670, E-mail: griffinp@nku.edu.

School of Nursing and Health Professions Students: 13 full-time (11 women), 240 part-time (222 women); includes 18 minority (8 Black or African American, non-Hispanic/Latino; 1 American Indian or Alaska Native, non-Hispanic/Latino; 5 Asian, non-Hispanic/Latino; 2 Hispanic/Latino; 2 Two or more races, non-Hispanic/Latino). Average age 39. 174 applicants, 37% accepted, 58 enrolled. *Faculty:* 12 full-time (11 women), 9 part-time/adjunct (all women). Expenses: Contact institution. *Financial support:* Unspecified assistantships available. Financial award applicants required to submit FAFSA. In 2010, 70 master's, 22 other advanced degrees awarded. *Degree program information:* Part-time and evening/weekend programs available. Postbaccalaureate distance learning degree programs offered (no on-campus study). Offers nursing (MSN, Certificate, Post-Master's Certificate); nursing and health professions (MSN, Certificate, Post-Master's Certificate). *Application deadline:* For fall admission, 2/1 for domestic and international students; for spring admission, 10/15 for domestic and international students. Applications are processed on a rolling basis. *Application fee:* $40. Electronic applications accepted. *Application Contact:* Dr. Peg Griffin, Director of Graduate Programs, 859-572-6934, Fax: 859-572-6670, E-mail: griffinp@nku.edu. *Program Director,* Dr. Marilyn C. Schleyer, 859-572-5240, Fax: 859-572-1934, E-mail: schleyerm1@nku.edu.

NORTHERN MICHIGAN UNIVERSITY, Marquette, MI 49855-5301

General Information State-supported, coed, comprehensive institution. CGS member. *Graduate housing:* Rooms and/or apartments available to single and married students.

GRADUATE UNITS

College of Graduate Studies *Degree program information:* Part-time and evening/weekend programs available. Postbaccalaureate distance learning degree programs offered. Electronic applications accepted.

College of Arts and Sciences *Degree program information:* Part-time programs available. Postbaccalaureate distance learning degree programs offered (minimal on-campus study). Offers arts and sciences (MA, MFA, MPA, MS); biology (MS); creative writing (MFA); literature (MA); pedagogy (MA); psychology (MS); public administration (MPA); writing (MA).

College of Professional Studies *Degree program information:* Part-time programs available. Offers administration and supervision (MA Ed, Ed S); criminal justice (MS); elementary education (MA Ed); exercise science (MS); learning disabilities (MA Ed); literacy leadership (Ed S); nursing (MSN); reading (MA Ed); reading education (MA Ed, Ed S); reading specialist (MA Ed); school guidance counseling (MA Ed); science education (MS); secondary education (MA Ed).

NORTHERN STATE UNIVERSITY, Aberdeen, SD 57401-7198

General Information State-supported, coed, comprehensive institution. *Enrollment:* 3,200 graduate, professional, and undergraduate students; 51 full-time matriculated graduate/professional students (38 women), 90 part-time matriculated graduate/professional students (62 women). *Enrollment by degree level:* 141 master's. *Graduate faculty:* 63 full-time (22 women), 10 part-time/adjunct (4 women). Tuition, state resident: full-time $1400; part-time $152 per credit. Tuition, nonresident: full-time $2900; part-time $320 per credit. *Required fees:* $1000; $111 per credit. Tuition and fees vary according to course load, degree level and reciprocity agreements. *Graduate housing:* Room and/or apartments available on a first-come, first-served basis to single students; on-campus housing not available to married students. Typical cost: $1306 per year ($2756 including board). Room and board charges vary according to board plan. Housing application deadline: 8/1. *Student services:* Campus employment opportunities, campus safety program, career counseling, child daycare facilities, exercise/wellness program, free psychological counseling, international student services, low-cost health insurance, multicultural affairs office, services for students with disabilities, writing training. *Library facilities:* Beulah Williams Library. *Online resources:* library catalog, web page, access to other libraries' catalogs. *Collection:* 216,773 titles, 170 serial subscriptions, 4,000 audiovisual materials. *Research affiliation:* AASCU–Grants Resource Center.

Computer facilities: 135 computers available on campus for general student use. A campuswide network can be accessed from student residence rooms and from off campus. Online class registration is available. *Web address:* http://www.northern.edu/.

General Application Contact: Tammy K. Griffith, Program Assistant, 605-626-2558, Fax: 605-626-7190, E-mail: griffith@northern.edu.

GRADUATE UNITS

Division of Graduate Studies in Education Students: 51 full-time (38 women), 90 part-time (62 women); includes 1 Black or African American, non-Hispanic/Latino; 4 American Indian or Alaska Native, non-Hispanic/Latino; 3 Asian, non-Hispanic/Latino; 1 Hispanic/Latino. Average age 32. 98 applicants, 83% accepted, 73 enrolled. *Faculty:* 63 full-time (22 women), 10 part-time/adjunct (4 women). Expenses: Contact institution. *Financial support:* In 2010–11, 51 students received support, including 47 teaching assistantships with partial tuition reimbursements available (averaging $5,558 per year); career-related internships or fieldwork, Federal Work-Study, institutionally sponsored loans, scholarships/grants, and unspecified assistantships also available. Support available to part-time students. Financial award application deadline: 3/1; financial award applicants required to submit FAFSA. In 2010, 70 master's awarded. *Degree program information:* Part-time and evening/weekend programs available. Offers counseling (MS Ed); education (MS, MS Ed); educational studies (MS Ed); elementary classroom teaching (MS Ed); elementary school administration (MS Ed); health, physical education, and coaching (MS Ed); secondary classroom teaching (MS Ed); secondary school administration (MS Ed). *Application deadline:* For fall admission, 8/15 priority date for domestic and international students; for spring admission, 12/15 for domestic students, 12/15 priority date for international students. Applications are processed on a rolling basis. *Application fee:* $35. Electronic applications accepted. *Application Contact:* Tammy K. Griffith, Program Assistant, 605-626-2558, Fax: 605-626-7190, E-mail: griffith@northern.edu. *Director of Graduate Studies,* Dr. Constance Geier, 605-626-2558, Fax: 605-626-7190, E-mail: geierc@northern.edu.

Center for Statewide E-Learning Students: 8 full-time (5 women); includes 6 Asian, non-Hispanic/Latino. Average age 25. 7 applicants, 71% accepted, 5 enrolled. *Faculty:* 1 full-time (0 women), 1 (woman) part-time/adjunct. Expenses: Contact institution. *Financial support:* In 2010–11, 7 teaching assistantships with partial tuition reimbursements (averaging $5,558 per year) were awarded; career-related internships or fieldwork, Federal Work-Study, institutionally sponsored loans, scholarships/grants, and unspecified assistantships

Northern State University (continued)

also available. Support available to part-time students. Financial award application deadline: 3/1; financial award applicants required to submit FAFSA. In 2010, 2 master's awarded. *Degree program information:* Part-time and evening/weekend programs available. Offers e-learning design and instruction (MS Ed); e-learning technology and administration (MS). *Application deadline:* For fall admission, 8/15 priority date for domestic students, 8/15 for international students; for spring admission, 12/15 for domestic and international students. Applications are processed on a rolling basis. *Application fee:* $35. Electronic applications accepted. *Application Contact:* Tammy K. Griffith, Program Assistant, 605-626-2558, Fax: 605-626-7190, E-mail: griffith@northern.edu. *Head,* Dr. Mark Zaidel, 605-626-3397, E-mail: zaidel@northern.edu.

NORTH GEORGIA COLLEGE & STATE UNIVERSITY, Dahlonega, GA 30597

General Information State-supported, coed, comprehensive institution. *Enrollment:* 5,912 graduate, professional, and undergraduate students; 178 full-time matriculated graduate/professional students (122 women), 381 part-time matriculated graduate/professional students (274 women). *Enrollment by degree level:* 79 first professional, 389 master's, 36 other advanced degrees. *Graduate faculty:* 83 full-time (48 women), 15 part-time/adjunct (9 women). Tuition, state resident: full-time $4704; part-time $196 per credit hour. Tuition, nonresident: full-time $18,770; part-time $783 per credit hour. *Required fees:* $1718; $671 per semester. Tuition and fees vary according to course load, degree level and program. *Graduate housing:* Room and/or apartments available on a first-come, first-served basis to single students; on-campus housing not available to married students. Housing application deadline: 1/1. *Student services:* Campus employment opportunities, campus safety program, career counseling, exercise/wellness program, free psychological counseling, international student services, low-cost health insurance, multicultural affairs office, services for students with disabilities, teacher training, writing training. *Library facilities:* Library Technology Center. *Online resources:* library catalog, web page, access to other libraries' catalogs. *Collection:* 176,693 titles, 8,050 serial subscriptions, 1,826 audiovisual materials. *Research affiliation:* Northeast Georgia Medical Center, Morehouse School of Medicine, St. Joseph's Hospital, Mettler Electronic Corporation.

Computer facilities: 850 computers available on campus for general student use. A campuswide network can be accessed from student residence rooms and from off campus. Online class registration is available. *Web address:* http://www.northgeorgia.edu/.

General Application Contact: Susan Perry, 706-864-1543, E-mail: slperry@northgeorgia.edu.

GRADUATE UNITS

Graduate Studies *Degree program information:* Part-time and evening/weekend programs available. Postbaccalaureate distance learning degree programs offered. Offers community counseling (MS); early childhood education (M Ed); educational leadership (Ed S); family nurse practitioner (MSN); middle grades education (M Ed); nursing education (MSN); physical therapy (DPT); public administration (MPA); secondary education (M Ed); special education (M Ed). Electronic applications accepted.

NORTH GREENVILLE UNIVERSITY, Tigerville, SC 29688-1892

General Information Independent-religious, coed, comprehensive institution. *Enrollment:* 2,318 graduate, professional, and undergraduate students; 80 full-time matriculated graduate/professional students (33 women), 148 part-time matriculated graduate/professional students (53 women). *Enrollment by degree level:* 228 master's. *Graduate faculty:* 4 full-time (1 woman), 16 part-time/adjunct (1 woman). *Required fees:* $280 per credit hour. One-time fee: $30. *Graduate housing:* Room and/or apartments available on a first-come, first-served basis to single students; on-campus housing not available to married students. Housing application deadline: 8/1. *Student services:* Campus employment opportunities, campus safety program, career counseling, exercise/wellness program, free psychological counseling, international student services, low-cost health insurance, services for students with disabilities, writing training. *Library facilities:* Hester Memorial Library. *Online resources:* library catalog, web page, access to other libraries' catalogs. *Collection:* 50,000 titles, 536 serial subscriptions, 5,644 audiovisual materials.

Computer facilities: 95 computers available on campus for general student use. A campuswide network can be accessed from student residence rooms and from off campus. Online class registration is available. *Web address:* http://www.ngu.edu/.

General Application Contact: Tawana P. Scott, Director of Graduate Enrollment, 864-877-1598, Fax: 864-877-1653, E-mail: tawana.scott@ngu.edu.

GRADUATE UNITS

T. Walter Brashier Graduate School Students: 80 full-time (33 women), 148 part-time (53 women); includes 48 minority (37 Black or African American, non-Hispanic/Latino; 1 American Indian or Alaska Native, non-Hispanic/Latino; 3 Asian, non-Hispanic/Latino; 5 Hispanic/Latino; 2 Two or more races, non-Hispanic/Latino). Average age 32. 180 applicants, 98% accepted, 170 enrolled. *Faculty:* 4 full-time (1 woman), 16 part-time/adjunct (1 woman). Expenses: Contact institution. *Financial support:* In 2010–11, 112 students received support. Federal Work-Study, institutionally sponsored loans, scholarships/grants, and tuition waivers (partial) available. Support available to part-time students. Financial award applicants required to submit FAFSA. In 2010, 29 master's awarded. *Degree program information:* Part-time and evening/weekend programs available. Postbaccalaureate distance learning degree programs offered (no on-campus study). Offers Christian ministry (MCM); human resources (MBA). *Application deadline:* For fall admission, 8/1 for domestic students, 6/1 for international students; for winter admission, 1/1 for domestic students, 10/1 for international students; for spring admission, 3/1 for domestic students, 1/1 for international students. Applications are processed on a rolling basis. *Application fee:* $30. Electronic applications accepted. *Application Contact:* Tawana P. Scott, Director of Graduate Enrollment, 864-877-1598, Fax: 864-877-1653, E-mail: tscott@ngu.edu. *Vice President for Graduate Studies,* Dr. Joseph Samuel Isgett, 864-877-3052, Fax: 864-877-1653, E-mail: sisgett@ngu.edu.

NORTH PARK THEOLOGICAL SEMINARY, Chicago, IL 60625-4895

General Information Independent-religious, coed, graduate-only institution. *Graduate housing:* Rooms and/or apartments available to single and married students. Housing application deadline: 9/1. *Research affiliation:* Northside Chicago Theological Institute, Covenant Archives and Historical Society, American Theological Library Association.

GRADUATE UNITS

Graduate and Professional Programs *Degree program information:* Part-time programs available. Offers adult ministry (Certificate); camping and retreat ministry (Certificate); children and family ministry (Certificate); Christian formation (Certificate); Christian ministry (MACM); faith and health (Certificate); intercultural studies (Certificate); justice ministry (Certificate); leadership and administration (Certificate); preaching (D Min); spiritual direction (Certificate); theological studies (MATS); theology (M Div); youth ministry (Certificate).

NORTH PARK UNIVERSITY, Chicago, IL 60625-4895

General Information Independent-religious, coed, comprehensive institution. *Graduate housing:* Rooms and/or apartments available to single and married students.

GRADUATE UNITS

School of Business and Nonprofit Management Students: 12 full-time (5 women), 338 part-time (185 women). Average age 34. 130 applicants, 77% accepted, 87 enrolled. *Faculty:* 12 full-time (5 women), 40 part-time/adjunct (22 women). Expenses: Contact institution. *Financial support:* In 2010–11, 98 students received support. Scholarships/grants available. Support available to part-time students. Financial award application deadline: 8/15; financial award applicants required to submit FAFSA. In 2010, 85 master's awarded. *Degree program information:* Part-time and evening/weekend programs available. Postbaccalaureate distance learning degree programs offered (no on-campus study). Offers business and nonprofit management (MBA, MHEA, MHRM, MM, MNA). *Application deadline:* For fall admission, 8/1 priority date for domestic students, 7/1 for international students; for spring admission, 12/15 for domestic students, 12/1 for international students. Applications are processed on a rolling basis. *Application fee:* $30. *Application Contact:* Dr. Christopher Nicholson, Director of Admissions for Graduate and Continuing Education, 773-244-5518, Fax: 773-255-4953, E-mail: cnicholson@northpark.edu. *Dean,* Dr. Wesley E. Lindahl, 773-784-3000.

School of Education Offers education (MA).

School of Music Offers vocal performance (MM).

School of Nursing *Degree program information:* Part-time and evening/weekend programs available. Offers advanced practice nursing (MS); leadership and management (MS).

NORTH SHORE–LIJ GRADUATE SCHOOL OF MOLECULAR MEDICINE, Manhasset, NY 11030

General Information Independent, coed, graduate-only institution. *Enrollment by degree level:* 12 doctoral. *Graduate faculty:* 39 full-time (15 women). *Graduate housing:* On-campus housing not available. *Student services:* Campus employment opportunities, campus safety program, career counseling, child daycare facilities, exercise/wellness program, free psychological counseling, grant writing training, low-cost health insurance. *Library facilities:* North Shore University Hospital Library plus 3 others. *Online resources:* library catalog. *Collection:* 30,000 titles, 5,800 serial subscriptions. *Research affiliation:* Feinstein Institute for Medical Research (biomedical research), North Shore Long Island Jewish Health System (medicine).

Computer facilities: 20 computers available on campus for general student use. A campuswide network can be accessed from student residence rooms and from off campus. *Web address:* http://www.elmezzigraduateschool.org/.

General Application Contact: Emilia C. Hristis, Education Coordinator, 516-562-3405, Fax: 516-562-1022, E-mail: ehristis@nshs.edu.

GRADUATE UNITS

Graduate Program Students: 12 full-time (4 women), 11 international. Average age 30. 8 applicants, 25% accepted, 2 enrolled. *Faculty:* 38 full-time (14 women). Expenses: Contact institution. *Financial support:* In 2010–11, 12 students received support, including 12 fellowships with full tuition reimbursements available (averaging $55,000 per year); health care benefits and tuition waivers (full) also available. In 2010, 1 doctorate awarded. Offers molecular medicine (PhD). *Application deadline:* Applications are processed on a rolling basis. *Application fee:* $25. *Application Contact:* Emilia C. Hristis, Education Coordinator, 516-562-3405, Fax: 516-562-1022, E-mail: ehristis@nshs.edu. *Dean,* Dr. Bettie M. Steinberg, 516-562-1159, Fax: 516-562-1022, E-mail: bsteinbe@lij.edu.

NORTHWEST BAPTIST SEMINARY, Tacoma, WA 98407

General Information Independent-religious, coed, primarily men, graduate-only institution. *Graduate housing:* On-campus housing not available.

GRADUATE UNITS

Programs in Theology *Degree program information:* Part-time and evening/weekend programs available. Offers theology (M Div, M Min, MTS, STM, Th M, D Min, Certificate).

NORTHWEST CHRISTIAN UNIVERSITY, Eugene, OR 97401-3745

General Information Independent-religious, coed, comprehensive institution. *Enrollment:* 623 graduate, professional, and undergraduate students; 131 full-time matriculated graduate/professional students (90 women), 12 part-time matriculated graduate/professional students (9 women). *Enrollment by degree level:* 144 master's. *Graduate faculty:* 7 full-time (3 women). *Student services:* Campus employment opportunities, career counseling, free psychological counseling, low-cost health insurance, services for students with disabilities, teacher training, writing training. *Library facilities:* Edward P. Kellenberger Library. *Online resources:* library catalog, web page, access to other libraries' catalogs. *Collection:* 70,163 titles.

Computer facilities: 60 computers available on campus for general student use. A campuswide network can be accessed from student residence rooms and from off campus. *Web address:* http://www.northwestchristian.edu/.

General Application Contact: Kathy Wilson, Assistant Director of Admission, Graduate and Professional Studies, 541-684-7326, Fax: 541-684-7333, E-mail: kwilson@nwcu.edu.

GRADUATE UNITS

School of Business and Management Students: 39 full-time (23 women), 2 part-time (1 woman); includes 1 Black or African American, non-Hispanic/Latino; 2 Hispanic/Latino; 1 Native Hawaiian or other Pacific Islander, non-Hispanic/Latino, 1 international. 30 applicants, 73% accepted, 16 enrolled. *Faculty:* 1 full-time (0 women). Expenses: Contact institution. In 2010, 10 master's awarded. *Degree program information:* Part-time and evening/weekend programs available. Offers business and management (MBA). *Application deadline:* For fall admission, 3/15 priority date for domestic students. Applications are processed on a rolling basis. *Application fee:* $50. Electronic applications accepted. *Application Contact:* Kathy Wilson, Assistant Director of Admission, Graduate and Professional Studies, 541-684-7326, Fax: 541-684-7333, E-mail: kwilson@nwcu.edu. *Professor,* Dr. Michael Kennedy, 541-684-7243, Fax: 541-684-7333, E-mail: mkennedy@nwcu.edu.edu.

School of Education and Counseling Students: 89 full-time (65 women), 8 part-time (6 women); includes 7 minority (2 Black or African American, non-Hispanic/Latino; 1 American Indian or Alaska Native, non-Hispanic/Latino; 2 Hispanic/Latino; 2 Native Hawaiian or other Pacific Islander, non-Hispanic/Latino). 90 applicants, 72% accepted, 53 enrolled. *Faculty:* 6 full-time (3 women). Expenses: Contact institution. *Financial support:* Scholarships/grants available. In 2010, 35 master's awarded. *Degree program information:* Part-time and evening/weekend programs available. Offers community counseling (MA); education (M Ed); school counseling (MA). *Application deadline:* For fall admission, 3/15 priority date for domestic students. Applications are processed on a rolling basis. *Application fee:* $50. Electronic applications accepted. *Application Contact:* Kathy Wilson, Assistant Director of Admission, Graduate and Professional Studies, 541-684-7326, Fax: 541-684-7333, E-mail: kwilson@northwestchristian.edu. *Dean,* Jim Howard, 541-684-7262, Fax: 541-684-7310, E-mail: jhoward@northwestchristian.edu.

NORTHWESTERN COLLEGE, St. Paul, MN 55113-1598

General Information Independent-religious, coed, comprehensive institution.

GRADUATE UNITS

Program in Organizational Leadership *Degree program information:* Evening/weekend programs available. Offers organizational leadership (MOL).

Program in Theological Studies *Degree program information:* Evening/weekend programs available. Offers theological studies (MATS).

NORTHWESTERN HEALTH SCIENCES UNIVERSITY, Bloomington, MN 55431-1599

General Information Independent, coed, graduate-only institution. *Enrollment by degree level:* 611 first professional, 114 master's. *Graduate housing:* On-campus housing not available. *Student services:* Campus employment opportunities, campus safety program, career counseling, exercise/wellness program, free psychological counseling, international student services, low-cost health insurance, services for students with disabilities. *Library facilities:* Greenwalt Library. *Online resources:* library catalog, web page. *Collection:* 12,000 titles, 400 serial subscriptions, 450 audiovisual materials. *Research affiliation:* University of Minnesota, School of Medicine (orthopedic surgery), Pain Assessment and Rehabilitation Center (pain management), Berman Center for Outcomes and Clinical Research (outcomes and clinical research).

Computer facilities: 76 computers available on campus for general student use. A campuswide network can be accessed from off campus. Online class registration is available. *Web address:* http://www.nwhealth.edu/.

General Application Contact: Lynn Heieie, Associate Director of Admissions, 952-888-4777 Ext. 409, Fax: 952-888-6713, E-mail: admit@nwhealth.edu.

GRADUATE UNITS

Minnesota College of Acupuncture and Oriental Medicine Offers acupuncture (M Ac); oriental medicine (MOM). Electronic applications accepted.

Northwestern College of Chiropractic Offers chiropractic (DC). Electronic applications accepted.

School of Massage Therapy Offers massage therapy (Professional Certificate).

NORTHWESTERN OKLAHOMA STATE UNIVERSITY, Alva, OK 73717-2799

General Information State-supported, coed, comprehensive institution. *Enrollment:* 2,302 graduate, professional, and undergraduate students; 35 full-time matriculated graduate/professional students (23 women), 88 part-time matriculated graduate/professional students (58 women). *Enrollment by degree level:* 123 master's. *Graduate faculty:* 36 full-time (16 women), 24 part-time/adjunct (17 women). *Graduate housing:* Room and/or apartments available to single students; on-campus housing not available to married students. *Student services:* Campus employment opportunities, career counseling, exercise/wellness program, free psychological counseling, international student services, services for students with disabilities. *Library facilities:* J. W. Martin Library plus 1 other. *Online resources:* library catalog, web page, access to other libraries' catalogs. *Collection:* 238,658 titles, 16,259 serial subscriptions, 1,607 audiovisual materials.

Computer facilities: Computer purchase and lease plans are available. 260 computers available on campus for general student use. A campuswide network can be accessed. Online class registration is available. *Web address:* http://www.nwosu.edu/.

General Application Contact: Sabrina Watson, Coordinator of Graduate Studies, 580-327-8410, E-mail: sdwatson@nwosu.edu.

GRADUATE UNITS

School of Professional Studies Students: 35 full-time (23 women), 88 part-time (58 women); includes 7 Black or African American, non-Hispanic/Latino; 5 American Indian or Alaska Native, non-Hispanic/Latino; 3 Hispanic/Latino, 1 international. Average age 31. 43 applicants, 100% accepted, 37 enrolled. *Faculty:* 48 full-time (25 women), 24 part-time/adjunct (17 women). Expenses: Contact institution. *Financial support:* Federal Work-Study available. Support available to part-time students. Financial award application deadline: 5/1; financial award applicants required to submit FAFSA. In 2010, 66 master's awarded. *Degree program information:* Part-time programs available. Offers adult education management and administration (M Ed); counseling psychology (MCP); curriculum and instruction (M Ed); educational leadership (M Ed); elementary education (M Ed); reading specialist (M Ed); school counseling (M Ed); secondary education (M Ed). *Application deadline:* Applications are processed on a rolling basis. *Application fee:* $15. *Application Contact:* Sabrina Watson, Coordinator of Graduate Studies, 580-327-8410, E-mail: sdwatson@nwosu.edu. *Associate Dean of Graduate Studies,* Dr. Shawn Holliday, 580-327-8451, E-mail: spholliday@nwosu.edu.

NORTHWESTERN POLYTECHNIC UNIVERSITY, Fremont, CA 94539-7482

General Information Independent, coed, comprehensive institution. *Graduate housing:* Room and/or apartments available on a first-come, first-served basis to single students; on-campus housing not available to married students. Housing application deadline: 7/15.

GRADUATE UNITS

School of Business and Information Technology *Degree program information:* Part-time and evening/weekend programs available. Offers business and information technology (MBA).

School of Engineering *Degree program information:* Part-time and evening/weekend programs available. Offers computer science (MS); computer systems engineering (MS); electrical engineering (MS).

NORTHWESTERN STATE UNIVERSITY OF LOUISIANA, Natchitoches, LA 71497

General Information State-supported, coed, comprehensive institution. CGS member. *Graduate housing:* Rooms and/or apartments available on a first-come, first-served basis to single and married students. Housing application deadline: 7/30. *Research affiliation:* National Aeronautics and Space Administration (NASA) (strategic defense initiative), Central State Hospital, Federal Records and Archives Services.

GRADUATE UNITS

Graduate Studies and Research *Degree program information:* Part-time and evening/weekend programs available. Postbaccalaureate distance learning degree programs offered (no on-campus study). Offers clinical psychology (MS); English (MA); health and human performance (MS); heritage resources (MA). Electronic applications accepted.

College of Education Offers adult and continuing education (M Ed); business and distributive education (M Ed); counseling (M Ed, Ed S); counseling and guidance (M Ed, Ed S); curriculum and instruction (M Ed); early childhood education (M Ed); early childhood education and teaching (M Ed); education (M Ed, MA, MAT, Ed S); education leadership (M Ed); educational leadership (Ed S); educational technology (M Ed, Ed S); educational technology leadership (M Ed); elementary education (MAT); elementary teaching (M Ed, Ed S); English education (M Ed); home economics education (M Ed); mathematics education (M Ed); middle school education (MAT); reading (M Ed, Ed S); school counseling (MA); science education (M Ed); secondary education (MAT); secondary teaching (M Ed, Ed S); social sciences education (M Ed); special education (MA); student personnel services (MA); teacher education and professional development, specific levels and methods (M Ed).

College of Nursing *Degree program information:* Part-time programs available. Offers nursing (MSN).

School of Creative and Performing Arts Offers art (MA); fine and graphic arts (MA); music (MM).

NORTHWESTERN UNIVERSITY, Evanston, IL 60208

General Information Independent, coed, university. CGS member. *Graduate housing:* Rooms and/or apartments available on a first-come, first-served basis to single students and available to married students. Housing application deadline: 9/1. *Research affiliation:* Amoco Oil Company (materials science and engineering), Dow Chemical Company (materials science and engineering), E. I. du Pont de Nemours and Company (physics), Exxon Chemical Company (chemical engineering), Ford Motor Company (mechanical engineering), Medtronics, Inc. (cardiology).

GRADUATE UNITS

The Graduate School *Degree program information:* Part-time and evening/weekend programs available. Offers African studies (Certificate); biochemistry, molecular biology, and cell biology (PhD); biotechnology (PhD); cell and molecular biology (PhD); clinical investigation (MSCI, Certificate); clinical psychology (PhD); counseling psychology (MA); developmental biology and genetics (PhD); genetic counseling (MS); hormone action and signal transduction (PhD); law and social science (Certificate); liberal studies (MA); literature (MA); management and organizations and sociology (PhD); marital and family therapy (MS); mathematical methods in social science (MS); neuroscience (PhD); public health (MPH); structural biology, biochemistry, and biophysics (PhD). DPT offered through the Medical School; MSC offered through the School of Speech. Electronic applications accepted.

Center for International and Comparative Studies Offers international and comparative studies (Certificate).

Institute for Neuroscience Offers neuroscience (PhD). Admissions and degree offered through The Graduate School.

Judd A. and Marjorie Weinberg College of Arts and Sciences *Degree program information:* Part-time and evening/weekend programs available. Offers African American studies (PhD); anthropology (PhD); art history (PhD); arts and sciences (MA, MFA, MS, PhD, Certificate); astrophysics (PhD); brain, behavior and cognition (PhD); chemistry (PhD); clinical psychology (PhD); cognitive psychology (PhD); comparative literary studies (PhD); economics (MA, PhD); eighteenth-century studies (Certificate); English (MA, PhD); French (PhD); French and comparative literature (PhD); geological sciences (MS, PhD); German literature and critical thought (PhD); history (PhD); Italian studies (Certificate); linguistics (MA, PhD); mathematics (PhD); neurobiology and physiology (MS); personality (PhD); philosophy (PhD); physics (MS, PhD); political science (MA, PhD); Slavic languages and literature (PhD); social psychology (PhD); sociology (PhD); statistics (MS, PhD); visual arts (MFA).

Kellogg School of Management *Degree program information:* Part-time and evening/weekend programs available. Offers accounting (PhD); business administration (MBA); finance (PhD); management (MBA, PhD); management and organizations (PhD); managerial economics and strategy (PhD); marketing (PhD). PhD admissions and degree offered through The Graduate School. Electronic applications accepted.

School of Communication *Degree program information:* Part-time programs available. Offers audiology and hearing sciences (MA, PhD); clinical audiology (Au D); communication (MA, MFA, MSC, Au D, PhD); communication studies (MA, PhD); communication systems strategy and management (MSC); directing (MFA); learning disabilities (MA, PhD); managerial communication (MSC); performance studies (MA, PhD); radio/television/film (MA, MFA, PhD); speech and language pathology (MA, PhD); speech and language pathology and learning disabilities (MA); stage design (MFA); theatre (MA); theatre and drama (PhD). MA, MFA, and PhD admissions and degrees offered through The Graduate School; MSC admissions and degrees offered through the School of Speech.

School of Education and Social Policy *Degree program information:* Part-time and evening/weekend programs available. Offers advanced teaching (MS); education and social policy (MS); elementary education and policy (MS); higher education administration (MS); human development and social policy (PhD); learning and organizational change (MS); learning sciences (MA, PhD); secondary teaching (MS). MA and PhD admissions and degrees offered through The Graduate School. Electronic applications accepted.

Henry and Leigh Bienen School of Music Offers collaborative arts (DM); conducting (MM, DM); jazz (MM); music (MM, DM, PhD, CP); music composition (DM); music education (MM, PhD); music theory (MM, PhD); musicology (MM, PhD); performance (MM); piano performance (MM, DM, CP); piano performance and collaborative arts (MM); piano performance and pedagogy (MM); string performance and pedagogy (MM); strings (MM, DM); strings, winds and percussion (CP); voice (MM, DM, CP); winds and percussion (MM, DM). PhD admissions and degree offered through The Graduate School. Electronic applications accepted.

Law School Offers executive (LL M); international human rights (LL M); law (JD, LL M); tax (LL M in Tax); two-year accelerated (JD). Electronic applications accepted.

McCormick School of Engineering and Applied Science Students: 1,179 full-time (342 women), 260 part-time (52 women); includes 240 minority (30 Black or African American, non-Hispanic/Latino; 3 American Indian or Alaska Native, non-Hispanic/Latino; 143 Asian, non-Hispanic/Latino; 52 Hispanic/Latino; 1 Native Hawaiian or other Pacific Islander, non-Hispanic/Latino; 11 Two or more races, non-Hispanic/Latino), 542 international. Average age 26. 3,516 applicants, 28% accepted, 476 enrolled. *Faculty:* 173 full-time (20 women). Expenses: Contact institution. *Financial support:* Fellowships with tuition reimbursements, research assistantships with tuition reimbursements, teaching assistantships with tuition reimbursements, career-related internships or fieldwork, Federal Work-Study, institutionally sponsored loans, traineeships, health care benefits, and unspecified assistantships available. Financial award application deadline: 1/15; financial award applicants required to submit FAFSA. In 2010, 370 master's, 121 doctorates awarded. *Degree program information:* Part-time and evening/weekend programs available. Offers biomedical engineering (MS, PhD); chemical engineering (MS, PhD); computer science (MS, PhD); electrical and computer engineering (MS, PhD); electronic materials (MS, PhD, Certificate); engineering and applied science (MEM, MIT, MME, MMM, MPD, MS, PhD, Certificate); engineering management (MEM); engineering sciences and applied mathematics (MS, PhD); environmental engineering and science (MS, PhD); fluid mechanics (MS, PhD); geotechnical engineering (MS, PhD); industrial engineering and management science (MS, PhD); information technology (MS); integrated computational materials engineering (Certificate); materials science and engineering (MS, PhD); mechanical engineering (MS, PhD); mechanics of materials and solids (MS, PhD); project management (MS); solid mechanics (MS, PhD); structural engineering and materials (MS, PhD); theoretical and applied mechanics (MS, PhD); transportation systems analysis and planning (MS, PhD). MS and PhD admissions and degrees offered through The Graduate School. *Application deadline:* 12/31 for domestic and international students. *Application fee:* $75. Electronic applications accepted. *Application Contact:* Dr. Bruce Alan Lindvall, Assistant Dean for Graduate Studies, 847-491-4547, Fax: 847-491-5341, E-mail: b-lindvall@northwestern.edu. *Dean,* Dr. Julio Ottino, 847-491-3558, Fax: 847-491-5220, E-mail: jm-ottino@northwestern.edu.

Segal Design Institute Expenses: Contact institution. Offers engineering design and innovation (MS). *Application Contact:* Joseph Holtgreive, Admission Officer, 847-491-3332, Fax: 847-491-8539, E-mail: jjh@northwestern.edu. *Co-Director,* J. Edward Colgate, 847-491-4264, E-mail: colgate@northwestern.edu.

Medill School of Journalism Offers advertising/sales promotion (MSIMC); broadcast journalism (MSJ); direct database and e-commerce marketing (MSIMC); general studies (MSIMC); integrated marketing communications (MSIMC); magazine publishing (MSJ); new media (MSJ); public relations (MSIMC); reporting and writing (MSJ). Electronic applications accepted.

Northwestern University Feinberg School of Medicine Offers cancer biology (PhD); cell biology (PhD); clinical investigation (MSCI); developmental biology (PhD); evolutionary biology (PhD); immunology and microbial pathogenesis (PhD); medicine (MD, MS, MSCI, DPT, PhD); molecular biology and genetics (PhD); movement and rehabilitation science (PhD); neurobiology (PhD); pharmacology and toxicology (PhD); physical therapy (DPT); structural biology and biochemistry (PhD). Electronic applications accepted.

School of Continuing Studies Offers American literature (MA); American studies (MA); British literature (MA); clinical research and regulatory administration (MS); comparative and world literature (MA); creative writing (MA, MFA); database and Internet technologies (MS); history (MA); information systems management (MS); information systems security (MS); medical informatics (MS); predictive analytics (MS); public policy and administration (MA); quality assurance and regulatory science (MS); religious and ethical studies (MA); software project management and development (MS); sports management (MA); sports marketing and public relations (MA).

NORTHWEST MISSOURI STATE UNIVERSITY, Maryville, MO 64468-6001

General Information State-supported, coed, comprehensive institution. *Enrollment:* 7,142 graduate, professional, and undergraduate students; 290 full-time matriculated graduate/professional students (127 women), 542 part-time matriculated graduate/professional students (324 women). *Enrollment by degree level:* 747 master's, 85 other advanced degrees. *Graduate faculty:* 193 full-time (76 women). *Graduate housing:* Room and/or apartments available on a first-come, first-served basis to single students; on-campus housing not available to married students. Housing application deadline: 7/1. *Student services:* Campus employment opportunities, campus safety program, career counseling, free psychological counseling, international student services, low-cost health insurance, multicultural affairs office, services for students with disabilities, writing training. *Library facilities:* Owens Library. *Online resources:* library catalog, web page, access to other libraries' catalogs. *Collection:* 361,614 titles, 28,896 serial subscriptions, 8,868 audiovisual materials.

Computer facilities: Computer purchase and lease plans are available. 7,550 computers available on campus for general student use. A campuswide network can be accessed from student residence rooms and from off campus. Online class registration, online courses with library and databases are available. *Web address:* http://www.nwmissouri.edu/.

General Application Contact: Dr. Gregory Haddock, Dean of Graduate School, 660-562-1145, Fax: 660-562-1096, E-mail: gradsch@nwmissouri.edu.

GRADUATE UNITS

Graduate School Students: 290 full-time (127 women), 542 part-time (324 women); includes 60 minority (20 Black or African American, non-Hispanic/Latino; 2 American Indian or Alaska Native, non-Hispanic/Latino; 9 Asian, non-Hispanic/Latino; 14 Hispanic/Latino; 1 Native Hawai-

Northwest Missouri State University (continued)

ian or other Pacific Islander, non-Hispanic/Latino; 14 Two or more races, non-Hispanic/Latino), 123 international. Average age 25. 472 applicants, 72% accepted, 203 enrolled. *Faculty:* 193 full-time (76 women). Expenses: Contact institution. *Financial support:* In 2010–11, 540 students received support, including 69 research assistantships with full tuition reimbursements available (averaging $6,000 per year), 66 teaching assistantships with full tuition reimbursements available (averaging $6,000 per year); career-related internships or fieldwork, Federal Work-Study, institutionally sponsored loans, scholarships/grants, and administrative assistantships, tutorial assistantships also available. Financial award application deadline: 4/1; financial award applicants required to submit FAFSA. In 2010, 309 master's, 25 other advanced degrees awarded. *Degree program information:* Part-time programs available. *Application deadline:* For fall admission, 7/1 for domestic and international students; for spring admission, 11/15 for domestic and international students. Applications are processed on a rolling basis. *Application fee:* $0 ($50 for international students). Electronic applications accepted. *Application Contact:* Nina Nickerson, Office Manager, 660-562-1145, Fax: 660-562-1096, E-mail: gradsch@nwmissouri.edu. *Dean of Graduate School,* Dr. Gregory Haddock, 660-562-1145, Fax: 660-562-1096, E-mail: gradsch@nwmissouri.edu.

College of Arts and Sciences Students: 43 full-time (21 women), 118 part-time (42 women); includes 1 Black or African American, non-Hispanic/Latino; 4 Asian, non-Hispanic/Latino; 1 Hispanic/Latino; 3 Two or more races, non-Hispanic/Latino), 2 international. 58 applicants, 67% accepted, 30 enrolled. *Faculty:* 91 full-time (25 women). Expenses: Contact institution. *Financial support:* In 2010–11, 10 research assistantships with full tuition reimbursements (averaging $6,000 per year), 16 teaching assistantships with full tuition reimbursements (averaging $6,000 per year) were awarded; administrative assistantships, tutorial assistantships also available. Financial award application deadline: 4/1; financial award applicants required to submit FAFSA. In 2010, 29 master's awarded. *Degree program information:* Part-time programs available. Offers arts and sciences (MA, MS, MS Ed, Certificate); biology (MS); English (MA); English with speech emphasis (MA); geographic information sciences (MS, Certificate); history (MA); teaching English (option 1) (MS Ed); teaching English with speech emphasis (MS Ed); teaching history (MS Ed); teaching mathematics (MS Ed); teaching music (MS Ed); teaching: science (MS Ed). *Application deadline:* For fall admission, 7/1 for domestic and international students; for spring admission, 11/15 for domestic and international students. Applications are processed on a rolling basis. *Application fee:* $0 ($50 for international students). Electronic applications accepted. *Application Contact:* Dr. Gregory Haddock, Dean of Graduate School, 660-562-1145, Fax: 660-562-1096, E-mail: gradsch@nwmissouri.edu. *Dean,* Dr. Charles McAdams, 660-562-1197.

College of Education and Human Services Students: 90 full-time (51 women), 294 part-time (215 women); includes 15 Black or African American, non-Hispanic/Latino; 1 Asian, non-Hispanic/Latino; 11 Hispanic/Latino; 6 Two or more races, non-Hispanic/Latino, 4 international. 148 applicants, 76% accepted, 81 enrolled. *Faculty:* 55 full-time (37 women). Expenses: Contact institution. *Financial support:* In 2010–11, 14 research assistantships with full tuition reimbursements (averaging $6,000 per year), 30 teaching assistantships with full tuition reimbursements (averaging $6,000 per year) were awarded; unspecified assistantships also available. Financial award application deadline: 4/1; financial award applicants required to submit FAFSA. In 2010, 174 master's, 15 other advanced degrees awarded. *Degree program information:* Part-time programs available. Offers applied health science (MS); education and human services (MS, MS Ed, Certificate, Ed S); educational leadership (MS Ed, Ed S); educational leadership: elementary (MS Ed); educational leadership: secondary (MS Ed); elementary principalship (Ed S); English language learners (Certificate); guidance and counseling (MS Ed); health and physical education (MS Ed); higher education leadership (MS); reading (MS Ed); recreation (MS); secondary individualized prescribed programs (MS Ed); secondary principalship (Ed S); special education (MS Ed); superintendency (Ed S); teaching secondary (MS Ed); teaching: early childhood (MS Ed); teaching: elementary self contained (MS Ed); teaching: English language learners (MS Ed); teaching: middle school (MS Ed). *Application deadline:* For fall admission, 7/1 for domestic and international students; for spring admission, 11/15 for domestic and international students. *Application fee:* $0 ($50 for international students). Electronic applications accepted. *Application Contact:* Dr. Gregory Haddock, Dean of Graduate School, 660-562-1145, Fax: 660-562-1096, E-mail: gradsch@nwmissouri.edu. *Dean,* Dr. Joyce Piveral, 660-562-1778.

Melvin and Valorie Booth College of Business and Professional Studies Students: 157 full-time (55 women), 130 part-time (67 women); includes 18 minority (4 Black or African American, non-Hispanic/Latino; 2 American Indian or Alaska Native, non-Hispanic/Latino; 4 Asian, non-Hispanic/Latino; 2 Hispanic/Latino; 1 Native Hawaiian or other Pacific Islander, non-Hispanic/Latino; 5 Two or more races, non-Hispanic/Latino), 117 international. 266 applicants, 70% accepted, 92 enrolled. *Faculty:* 47 full-time (14 women). Expenses: Contact institution. *Financial support:* In 2010–11, 26 research assistantships with full tuition reimbursements (averaging $6,000 per year), 6 teaching assistantships with full tuition reimbursements (averaging $6,000 per year) were awarded; career-related internships or fieldwork and administrative assistantships, tutorial assistantships also available. Financial award application deadline: 4/1; financial award applicants required to submit FAFSA. In 2010, 106 master's awarded. *Degree program information:* Part-time programs available. Offers accounting (MBA); agricultural economics (MBA); agriculture (MS); applied computer science (MS); business administration (MBA); business and professional studies (MBA, MS, MS Ed, Certificate); information technology management (MBA); instructional technology (Certificate); teaching agriculture (MS Ed); teaching instructional technology (MS Ed). *Application deadline:* For fall admission, 7/1 for domestic and international students; for spring admission, 11/15 for domestic and international students. Applications are processed on a rolling basis. *Application fee:* $0 ($50 for international students). Electronic applications accepted. *Application Contact:* Dr. Gregory Haddock, Dean of Graduate School, 660-562-1145, Fax: 660-562-1096, E-mail: gradsch@nwmissouri.edu. *Dean,* Dr. Thomas Billesbach, 660-562-1277.

NORTHWEST NAZARENE UNIVERSITY, Nampa, ID 83686-5897

General Information Independent-religious, coed, comprehensive institution. *Enrollment:* 2,020 graduate, professional, and undergraduate students; 497 full-time matriculated graduate/professional students (282 women), 189 part-time matriculated graduate/professional students (139 women). *Enrollment by degree level:* 65 first professional, 560 master's. *Graduate faculty:* 44 full-time (22 women), 52 part-time/adjunct (26 women). *Graduate housing:* Rooms and/or apartments available on a first-come, first-served basis to single students and available to married students. Housing application deadline: 4/1. *Student services:* Career counseling, free psychological counseling, multicultural affairs office, teacher training. *Library facilities:* John E. Riley Library. *Online resources:* library catalog, web page, access to other libraries' catalogs.

Computer facilities: Computer purchase and lease plans are available. 78 computers available on campus for general student use. A campuswide network can be accessed from student residence rooms. Online class registration, various software packages are available. *Web address:* http://www.nnu.edu/.

General Application Contact: Dr. Mark Maddix, Director, Graduate Studies, 208-467-8817, Fax: 208-467-8252, E-mail: mamaddix@nnu.edu.

GRADUATE UNITS

Graduate Studies Students: 497 full-time (282 women), 189 part-time (139 women); includes 48 minority (7 Black or African American, non-Hispanic/Latino; 3 American Indian or Alaska Native, non-Hispanic/Latino; 7 Asian, non-Hispanic/Latino; 28 Hispanic/Latino; 2 Native Hawaiian or other Pacific Islander, non-Hispanic/Latino; 1 Two or more races, non-Hispanic/Latino), 9 international. Average age 34. *Faculty:* 44 full-time (22 women), 52 part-time/adjunct (26 women). Expenses: Contact institution. *Financial support:* In 2010–11, 193 students received support. Career-related internships or fieldwork available. In 2010, 209 master's awarded. *Degree program information:* Part-time and evening/weekend programs available. Offers business administration (MBA); Christian education (MA); community counseling (MS); curriculum and instruction (M Ed); educational leadership (M Ed); exceptional child (M Ed); marriage and family counseling (MS); missional leadership (MA); nursing (MSN); pastoral ministry (MA); reading education (M Ed); religion (M Div); school counseling (M Ed, MS); social work (MSW); spiritual formation (MA). *Application deadline:* Applications are processed on a rolling basis. *Application fee:* $50. Electronic applications accepted. *Application Contact:* Jill Jones, Program Assistant, 208-467-8368, Fax: 208-467-8252, E-mail: jdjones@nnu.edu. *Director, Graduate Studies,* Dr. Mark Maddix, 208-467-8817, Fax: 208-467-8252, E-mail: mamaddix@nnu.edu.

NORTHWEST UNIVERSITY, Kirkland, WA 98033

General Information Independent-religious, coed, comprehensive institution. *Enrollment:* 1,422 graduate, professional, and undergraduate students; 165 full-time matriculated graduate/professional students (107 women), 109 part-time matriculated graduate/professional students (61 women). *Enrollment by degree level:* 242 master's, 32 doctoral. *Graduate faculty:* 22 full-time (4 women), 62 part-time/adjunct (19 women). Tuition and fees vary according to program. *Graduate housing:* Rooms and/or apartments available on a first-come, first-served basis to single and married students. *Student services:* Campus employment opportunities, campus safety program, career counseling, free psychological counseling, international student services, low-cost health insurance, services for students with disabilities, writing training. *Library facilities:* Hurst Library. *Online resources:* library catalog, web page, access to other libraries' catalogs. *Collection:* 100,356 titles, 13,443 serial subscriptions, 1,053 audiovisual materials.

Computer facilities: 134 computers available on campus for general student use. A campuswide network can be accessed from student residence rooms and from off campus. Online class registration, online classes are available. *Web address:* http://www.northwestu.edu/.

General Application Contact: Aaron Oosterwyk, Director of Graduate and Professional Studies Enrollment, 425-889-7799, Fax: 425-803-3059, E-mail: gpse@northwestu.edu.

GRADUATE UNITS

College of Ministry Students: 17 full-time (3 women), 43 part-time (9 women); includes 7 minority (5 Black or African American, non-Hispanic/Latino; 1 Asian, non-Hispanic/Latino; 1 Hispanic/Latino), 2 international. 32 applicants, 97% accepted, 29 enrolled. *Faculty:* 9 full-time (1 woman), 21 part-time/adjunct (2 women). Expenses: Contact institution. In 2010, 6 master's awarded. *Degree program information:* Evening/weekend programs available. Offers ministry (MA); missional leadership (MA); theology and culture (MA). *Application fee:* $75. *Application Contact:* Aaron Oosterwyk, Director of Graduate and Professional Studies Enrollment, 425-889-7799, Fax: 425-803-3059, E-mail: gpse@northwestu.edu. *Dean,* Dr. Wayde Goodall, 425-889-5253, E-mail: wayde.goodall@northwestu.edu.

College of Social and Behavioral Sciences Students: 82 full-time (64 women), 10 part-time (8 women); includes 18 minority (3 Black or African American, non-Hispanic/Latino; 8 Asian, non-Hispanic/Latino; 7 Hispanic/Latino), 1 international. 114 applicants, 68% accepted, 58 enrolled. *Faculty:* 5 full-time (2 women), 11 part-time/adjunct (5 women). Expenses: Contact institution. *Financial support:* Career-related internships or fieldwork, health care benefits, and international student scholarships available. Financial award application deadline: 6/30. In 2010, 39 master's awarded. *Degree program information:* Evening/weekend programs available. Offers counseling psychology (MA, Psy D); international care and community development (MA). *Application deadline:* For fall admission, 12/1 priority date for domestic and international students; for spring admission, 4/1 priority date for domestic and international students. Applications are processed on a rolling basis. *Application fee:* $75. *Application Contact:* Shoshana Weed, Director of Student Services, 425-889-5249, Fax: 425-739-4602, E-mail: shoshana.weed@northwestu.edu. *Dean,* Dr. Matt Nelson, 425-889-5328, Fax: 425-739-4602, E-mail: matt.nelson@northwestu.edu.

School of Business and Management Students: 41 full-time (20 women), 3 part-time (1 woman); includes 10 minority (5 Black or African American, non-Hispanic/Latino; 3 Asian, non-Hispanic/Latino; 2 Hispanic/Latino), 9 international. Average age 34. 21 applicants, 86% accepted, 18 enrolled. *Faculty:* 6 full-time (1 woman), 7 part-time/adjunct (3 women). Expenses: Contact institution. *Financial support:* Federal Work-Study, scholarships/grants, health care benefits, and tuition waivers (full) available. Financial award applicants required to submit FAFSA. In 2010, 11 master's awarded. *Degree program information:* Evening/weekend programs available. Offers business administration (MBA); social entrepreneurship (MA). *Application deadline:* For fall admission, 8/1 for domestic and international students; for spring admission, 12/1 for domestic and international students. Applications are processed on a rolling basis. *Application fee:* $75. Electronic applications accepted. *Application Contact:* Aaron Oosterwyk, Director of Graduate and Professional Studies Enrollment, 425-889-7799, Fax: 425-803-3059, E-mail: aaron.oosterwyk@northwestu.edu. *Dean,* Dr. Teresa Gillespie, 425-889-5290, E-mail: teresa.gillespie@northwestu.edu.

School of Education Students: 24 full-time (19 women), 18 part-time (14 women); includes 4 minority (1 Black or African American, non-Hispanic/Latino; 3 Asian, non-Hispanic/Latino). 38 applicants, 100% accepted, 30 enrolled. *Faculty:* 6 full-time (3 women), 6 part-time/adjunct (3 women). Expenses: Contact institution. *Financial support:* Federal Work-Study and health care benefits available. In 2010, 41 master's awarded. *Degree program information:* Part-time and evening/weekend programs available. Offers education (M Ed); teaching (MIT). *Application deadline:* For fall admission, 3/1 priority date for domestic students. Applications are processed on a rolling basis. *Application fee:* $75. *Application Contact:* Pam Skolrud, Coordinator/Certification Specialist, 425-889-5299, Fax: 425-889-6332, E-mail: pam.skolrud@northwestu.edu. *Dean,* Dr. Gary Newbill, 425-889-5272, E-mail: gary.newbill@northwestu.edu.

NORTHWOOD UNIVERSITY, Midland, MI 48640-2398

General Information Independent, coed, comprehensive institution. *Graduate housing:* Room and/or apartments available on a first-come, first-served basis to single students. Housing application deadline: 8/30. *Research affiliation:* Motor & Equipment Manufacturers Association (automotive), Specialized Equipment Manufacturers Association (automotive), Automotive Aftermarket Industry Association (automotive), Automotive Warehouse Distributors Association (automotive).

GRADUATE UNITS

Richard DeVos Graduate School of Management *Degree program information:* Part-time and evening/weekend programs available. Offers management (EMBA, MBA, MMBA). Electronic applications accepted.

NORWICH UNIVERSITY, Northfield, VT 05663

General Information Independent, coed, primarily men, comprehensive institution. *Enrollment:* 2,660 full-time matriculated graduate/professional students (767 women), 5 part-time matriculated graduate/professional students. *Enrollment by degree level:* 2,665 master's. *Graduate faculty:* 250 part-time/adjunct (52 women). *Tuition:* Full-time $17,380; part-time $645 per credit. Tuition and fees vary according to program. *Graduate housing:* On-campus housing not available. *Student services:* Services for students with disabilities. *Library facilities:* Kreitzberg Library. *Online resources:* library catalog, web page, access to other libraries' catalogs. *Collection:* 280,000 titles, 904 serial subscriptions, 1,501 audiovisual materials.

Computer facilities: 200 computers available on campus for general student use. A campuswide network can be accessed from student residence rooms and from off campus. *Web address:* http://www.norwich.edu/.

General Application Contact: Sally Burkart, Administrative Assistant, 802-485-2096, Fax: 802-485-2533, E-mail: sburkart@norwich.edu.

GRADUATE UNITS

School of Graduate and Continuing Studies Students: 2,660 full-time (767 women), 5 part-time (0 women); includes 131 Black or African American, non-Hispanic/Latino; 19 American Indian or Alaska Native, non-Hispanic/Latino; 44 Asian, non-Hispanic/Latino; 105 Hispanic/Latino, 24 international. Average age 37. 628 applicants, 90% accepted, 507 enrolled. *Faculty:* 250 part-time/adjunct (52 women). Expenses: Contact institution. *Financial support:* Scholarships/grants available. Financial award application deadline: 9/1; financial award applicants required to submit FAFSA. In 2010, 741 master's awarded. *Degree program information:* Part-time and evening/weekend programs available. Offers business continuity management (MS); construction management (MCE); consultancy project (MS); continuity of government operations (MPA, MS); criminal justice (MPA); finance (MBA); fiscal management (MPA); geo-technical (MCE); international commerce (MA); international conflict management (MA); international terrorism (MA); leadership (MPA); managing cyber crime and digital incidents (MS); nursing administration (MSN); nursing education (MSN); organizational leadership (MBA, MPA); private sector continuity of operations (MS); project management (MBA); public works administration (MPA); race and gender in military history (MA); structural (MCE); total war (MA); U. S. military history (MA); water/environmental (MCE). *Application deadline:* For fall admission, 8/10 for domestic and international students; for winter admission, 11/7 for domestic and international students; for spring admission, 2/6 for domestic and international students. *Application fee:* $50. Electronic applications accepted. *Application Contact:* Allison Crownson, Director of Admissions and Retention, 802-485-2720, Fax: 802-485-2533. *Vice President of Academic Affairs/Dean,* Dr. William Clements, 802-485-2730.

NOTRE DAME COLLEGE, South Euclid, OH 44121-4293

General Information Independent-religious, coed, comprehensive institution. *Graduate housing:* On-campus housing not available.

GRADUATE UNITS

Graduate Studies *Degree program information:* Part-time and evening/weekend programs available. Offers accounting (Certificate); creative critical thinking (M Ed); financial services management (Certificate); information systems (Certificate); learning disabilities (M Ed); management (Certificate); paralegal (Certificate); pastoral ministry (Certificate); reading (M Ed); security policy studies (MA); teacher education (Certificate).

NOTRE DAME DE NAMUR UNIVERSITY, Belmont, CA 94002-1908

General Information Independent-religious, coed, comprehensive institution. *Enrollment:* 1,790 graduate, professional, and undergraduate students; 252 full-time matriculated graduate/professional students (192 women), 536 part-time matriculated graduate/professional students (418 women). *Enrollment by degree level:* 533 master's, 255 other advanced degrees. *Graduate faculty:* 28 full-time (13 women), 63 part-time/adjunct (44 women). *Tuition:* Full-time $14,220; part-time $790 per credit. *Required fees:* $35 per semester. Tuition and fees vary according to program. *Graduate housing:* Room and/or apartments available on a first-come, first-served basis to single students; on-campus housing not available to married students. Typical cost: $7610 per year ($11,680 including board). Room and board charges vary according to board plan and housing facility selected. Housing application deadline: 7/1. *Student services:* Campus employment opportunities, campus safety program, career counseling, free psychological counseling, international student services, low-cost health insurance, multicultural affairs office, services for students with disabilities, teacher training, writing training. *Library facilities:* The Carl Gellert and Celia Berta Gellert Library. *Online resources:* library catalog, web page, access to other libraries' catalogs. *Collection:* 91,389 titles, 14,000 serial subscriptions, 9,122 audiovisual materials.

Computer facilities: 80 computers available on campus for general student use. A campuswide network can be accessed from student residence rooms and from off campus. Online class registration is available. *Web address:* http://www.ndnu.edu/.

General Application Contact: Candace Hallmark, Associate Director of Admissions, 650-508-3600, Fax: 650-508-3426, E-mail: grad.admit@ndnu.edu.

GRADUATE UNITS

Division of Academic Affairs Students: 252 full-time (192 women), 536 part-time (418 women); includes 224 minority (13 Black or African American, non-Hispanic/Latino; 4 American Indian or Alaska Native, non-Hispanic/Latino; 81 Asian, non-Hispanic/Latino; 95 Hispanic/Latino; 24 Native Hawaiian or other Pacific Islander, non-Hispanic/Latino; 7 Two or more races, non-Hispanic/Latino), 53 international. Average age 34. 567 applicants, 55% accepted, 230 enrolled. *Faculty:* 28 full-time (13 women), 63 part-time/adjunct (44 women). Expenses: Contact institution. *Financial support:* Career-related internships or fieldwork, scholarships/grants, and unspecified assistantships available. Support available to part-time students. Financial award applicants required to submit FAFSA. In 2010, 173 master's awarded. *Degree program information:* Part-time and evening/weekend programs available. *Application deadline:* For fall admission, 8/1 priority date for domestic students; for spring admission, 12/1 priority date for domestic students. Applications are processed on a rolling basis. *Application fee:* $60. Electronic applications accepted. *Application Contact:* Candace Hallmark, Associate Director of Admissions, 650-508-3600, Fax: 650-508-3426, E-mail: grad.admit@ndnu.edu. *Provost,* Dr. Diana Demetrulias, 650-508-3494, Fax: 650-508-3495, E-mail: ddemetrulias@ndnu.edu.

College of Arts and Sciences Students: 76 full-time (69 women), 181 part-time (159 women); includes 80 minority (9 Black or African American, non-Hispanic/Latino; 2 American Indian or Alaska Native, non-Hispanic/Latino; 24 Asian, non-Hispanic/Latino; 37 Hispanic/Latino; 5 Native Hawaiian or other Pacific Islander, non-Hispanic/Latino; 3 Two or more races, non-Hispanic/Latino), 13 international. Average age 34. 195 applicants, 49% accepted, 77 enrolled. *Faculty:* 11 full-time (8 women), 16 part-time/adjunct (12 women). Expenses: Contact institution. *Financial support:* Available to part-time students. Applicants required to submit FAFSA. In 2010, 55 master's awarded. *Degree program information:* Part-time programs available. Offers art therapy (MA); arts and sciences (MA, MFA, MS, Certificate); clinical psychology (MS); clinical psychology: marital and family therapy (MS); English (MA); marriage and family therapy (MA); musical performance (MFA, Certificate); premedical studies (Certificate); teaching English to speakers of other languages (Certificate). *Application deadline:* For fall admission, 8/1 for domestic students; for spring admission, 12/1 for domestic students. *Application fee:* $60. *Application Contact:* Candace Hallmark, Associate Director of Admissions, 650-508-3600, Fax: 650-508-3426, E-mail: grad.admit@ndnu.edu. *Interim Dean,* Dr. Lisa Bjerknes, 650-508-3771, E-mail: lbjerknes@ndnu.edu.

School of Business and Management Students: 66 full-time (38 women), 134 part-time (95 women); includes 82 minority (8 Black or African American, non-Hispanic/Latino; 37 Asian, non-Hispanic/Latino; 33 Hispanic/Latino; 3 Native Hawaiian or other Pacific Islander, non-Hispanic/Latino; 1 Two or more races, non-Hispanic/Latino), 36 international. Average age 33. 175 applicants, 52% accepted, 55 enrolled. *Faculty:* 8 full-time (1 woman), 8 part-time/adjunct (2 women). Expenses: Contact institution. *Financial support:* Scholarships/grants available. Support available to part-time students. Financial award applicants required to submit FAFSA. In 2010, 60 master's awarded. *Degree program information:* Part-time programs available. Offers business administration (MBA); business and management (MBA, MPA, MSM); finance (MBA); human resource management (MBA, MPA); management (MSM); marketing (MBA); public administration (MPA); public affairs administration (MPA). *Application deadline:* For fall admission, 8/1 for domestic students; for spring admission, 12/1 for domestic students. *Application fee:* $60. *Application Contact:* Candace Hallmark, Associate Director of Admissions, 650-508-3600, Fax: 650-508-3426, E-mail: grad.admit@ndnu.edu. *Dean,* Barbara Caulley, 650-508-3684, E-mail: bcaulley@ndnu.edu.

School of Education and Leadership Students: 109 full-time (85 women), 206 part-time (153 women); includes 59 minority (6 Black or African American, non-Hispanic/Latino; 2 American Indian or Alaska Native, non-Hispanic/Latino; 18 Asian, non-Hispanic/Latino; 25 Hispanic/Latino; 5 Native Hawaiian or other Pacific Islander, non-Hispanic/Latino; 3 Two or more races, non-Hispanic/Latino), 3 international. Average age 35. 184 applicants, 67% accepted, 97 enrolled. *Faculty:* 9 full-time (7 women), 16 part-time/adjunct (13 women). Expenses: Contact institution. *Financial support:* Available to part-time students. Applicants required to submit FAFSA. In 2010, 78 master's awarded. *Degree program information:* Part-time and evening/weekend programs available. Offers administrative services credential (Certificate); education (MA); education and leadership (MA, Certificate); education specialist level I credential (Certificate); education specialist level II credential (Certificate); multiple subject teaching credential (Certificate); reading (MA, Certificate); school administration (MA); single subject teaching credential (Certificate); special education (MA). *Application deadline:* For fall admission, 8/1 for domestic students; for spring admission, 12/1 for domestic students. *Application fee:* $60. *Application Contact:* Candace Hallmark, Associate Director of Admissions, 650-508-3600, Fax: 650-508-3426, E-mail: grad.admit@ndnu.edu. *Dean,* Dr. Joanne Rossi, 650-508-3701, E-mail: jrossi@ndnu.edu.

NOTRE DAME SEMINARY, New Orleans, LA 70118-4391

General Information Independent-religious, coed, primarily men, graduate-only institution. *Graduate housing:* Room and/or apartments guaranteed to single students; on-campus housing not available to married students. Housing application deadline: 7/31.

GRADUATE UNITS

Graduate School of Theology *Degree program information:* Part-time programs available. Offers theology (M Div, MA).

NOVA SCOTIA AGRICULTURAL COLLEGE, Truro, NS B2N 5E3, Canada

General Information Province-supported, coed, comprehensive institution. *Graduate housing:* Room and/or apartments available on a first-come, first-served basis to single students; on-campus housing not available to married students. Housing application deadline: 6/30. *Research affiliation:* Atlantic BioVenture Centre (bio-products, bio-resources, value-added), Bio-Environmental Engineering Centre (resource and environmental sciences), Performance Genomics, Inc. (animal genomics), Organic Agriculture Centre of Canada (organic agriculture), Atlantic Poultry Research Institute (poultry), Crop Development Institute (crop physiology, horticulture).

GRADUATE UNITS

Research and Graduate Studies *Degree program information:* Part-time programs available. Offers agriculture (M Sc). Program offered jointly with Dalhousie University.

NOVA SOUTHEASTERN UNIVERSITY, Fort Lauderdale, FL 33314-7796

General Information Independent, coed, university. CGS member. *Enrollment:* 28,741 graduate, professional, and undergraduate students; 10,889 full-time matriculated graduate/professional students (7,444 women), 11,678 part-time matriculated graduate/professional students (8,114 women). *Enrollment by degree level:* 3,948 first professional, 10,973 master's, 6,345 doctoral, 1,301 other advanced degrees. *Graduate housing:* Rooms and/or apartments guaranteed to single and married students. Typical cost: $6486 per year ($9086 including board) for single students. *Student services:* Campus employment opportunities, campus safety program, career counseling, exercise/wellness program, free psychological counseling, international student services, low-cost health insurance, services for students with disabilities, teacher training. *Library facilities:* Alvin Sherman Library, Research, and Information Technology Center plus 4 others. *Online resources:* library catalog, web page, access to other libraries' catalogs. *Collection:* 986,227 titles, 86,612 serial subscriptions, 48,855 audiovisual materials,

Computer facilities: 3,144 computers available on campus for general student use. A campuswide network can be accessed from student residence rooms and from off campus. Online class registration is available. *Web address:* http://www.nova.edu/.

General Application Contact: Information Contact, 800-541-6682, E-mail: nsuinfo@nsu.nova.edu.

GRADUATE UNITS

Center for Psychological Studies Students: 915 full-time (771 women), 771 part-time (694 women); includes 723 minority (278 Black or African American, non-Hispanic/Latino; 2 American Indian or Alaska Native, non-Hispanic/Latino; 42 Asian, non-Hispanic/Latino; 382 Hispanic/Latino; 2 Native Hawaiian or other Pacific Islander, non-Hispanic/Latino; 17 Two or more races, non-Hispanic/Latino), 39 international. Average age 30. 1,433 applicants, 49% accepted, 520 enrolled. *Faculty:* 34 full-time (11 women), 68 part-time/adjunct (32 women). Expenses: Contact institution. *Financial support:* In 2010–11, 5 research assistantships, 34 teaching assistantships (averaging $1,000 per year) were awarded; career-related internships or fieldwork, Federal Work-Study, institutionally sponsored loans, scholarships/grants, and unspecified assistantships also available. Support available to part-time students. Financial award application deadline: 4/1. In 2010, 382 master's, 83 doctorates, 34 other advanced degrees awarded. Postbaccalaureate distance learning degree programs offered. Offers clinical pharmacology (MS); clinical psychology (PhD, Psy D, SPS); mental health counseling (MS); psychological studies (MS, PhD, Psy D, Psy S, SPS); school guidance and counseling (MS); school psychology (Psy S). *Application deadline:* Applications are processed on a rolling basis. *Application fee:* $50. Electronic applications accepted. *Application Contact:* Carlos Perez, Enrollment Management, 954-262-5790, Fax: 954-262-3893, E-mail: cpsinfo@cps.nova.edu. *Dean,* Karen Grosby, 954-262-5701, Fax: 954-262-3859, E-mail: grosby@nova.edu.

Criminal Justice Institute Students: 72 full-time (60 women), 210 part-time (160 women); includes 195 minority (140 Black or African American, non-Hispanic/Latino; 3 American Indian or Alaska Native, non-Hispanic/Latino; 2 Asian, non-Hispanic/Latino; 48 Hispanic/Latino; 1 Native Hawaiian or other Pacific Islander, non-Hispanic/Latino; 1 Two or more races, non-Hispanic/Latino). Average age 33. 41 applicants, 73% accepted, 30 enrolled. *Faculty:* 41 part-time/adjunct (7 women). Expenses: Contact Institution. *Financial support:* Applicants required to submit FAFSA. In 2010, 65 master's awarded. *Degree program information:* Part-time programs available. Postbaccalaureate distance learning degree programs offered (no on-campus study). Offers child protection services (MHS); criminal justice (MHS, MS). *Application deadline:* For fall admission, 8/4 for domestic and international students; for winter admission, 12/1 for domestic and international students; for spring admission, 4/15 for domestic students, 4/14 for international students. Applications are processed on a rolling basis. *Application fee:* $50. Electronic applications accepted. *Application Contact:* Russell Garner, Program Coordinator, 954-262-7001, E-mail: cjl@nova.edu. *Executive Associate Dean,* Dr. Tammy Kushner, 954-262-7001, Fax: 954-262-7005, E-mail: kushner@nova.edu.

Fischler School of Education and Human Services Students: 3,949 full-time (3,156 women), 4,756 part-time (3,874 women); includes 5,150 minority (3,503 Black or African American, non-Hispanic/Latino; 29 American Indian or Alaska Native, non-Hispanic/Latino; 120 Asian, non-Hispanic/Latino; 1,443 Hispanic/Latino; 16 Native Hawaiian or other Pacific Islander, non-Hispanic/Latino; 39 Two or more races, non-Hispanic/Latino), 55 international. Average age 40. 4,354 applicants, 65% accepted, 2078 enrolled. *Faculty:* 105 full-time (55 women), 438 part-time/adjunct (266 women). Expenses: Contact institution. *Financial support:* In 2010–11, 6,903 students received support, including 2 fellowships with full tuition reimbursements available (averaging $30,000 per year); career-related internships or fieldwork, Federal Work-Study, and tuition waivers (full) also available. Support available to part-time students. Financial award application deadline: 4/15; financial award applicants required to submit FAFSA. In 2010, 1,927 master's, 471 doctorates, 686 other advanced degrees awarded. *Degree program information:* Part-time and evening/weekend programs available. Offers adult education (Ed D); athletic administration (MS); brain research (MS, Ed S); charter school education/leadership (MS); child and youth studies (Ed D); child protection (MHS); cognitive and behavioral disabilities (MS); computer science education (Ed S); computer science education (K-12) (MS); computing and information technology (Ed D); curriculum and teaching (Ed S); curriculum, instruction and technology (MS); curriculum, instruction, management and administration (Ed S); early childhood education (MS); early literacy and reading (Ed S); early literacy education (MS); education (MS); education and human services (MA, MHS, MS, Ed D, SLPD, Ed S); education technology (MS); educational leaders (Ed D); educational leadership (Ed D); educational leadership (administration K-12) (MS, Ed S); educational media (Ed S); educational media (K-12) (MS); elementary education (MS, Ed S); English education (MS, Ed S); environmental education (MS); exceptional student education (MS); gifted education (MS, Ed S); health care education (Ed D); health professions education (MS); higher education (Ed D); higher education leadership (Ed D); human services administration (Ed D); instructional leadership (Ed D); instructional technology and distance education (MS, Ed D); interdisciplinary arts education (MS); leadership (MS); management and administration of educational programs (MS); mathematics (MS); mathematics education (Ed S); multicultural early intervention (MS); organizational leadership (Ed D); pre-kindergarten/primary (MS); preschool education (MS); reading (MS); reading and TESOL (MS); reading education (Ed S); science (MS); science education (Ed S); secondary education (MS); social studies (MS, Ed S); Spanish language (MS); special education (Ed D); special education and reading (MS); speech language pathology (Ed D); speech-language pathology (MS, SLPD); substance abuse counseling and education (MS); teaching and learning (MA, MS); teaching

Nova Southeastern University (continued)

English to speakers of other languages (MS, Ed S); technology management and administration (Ed S); urban studies education (MS); vocational, occupational and technical education (Ed D). *Application deadline:* Applications are processed on a rolling basis. *Application fee:* $50. Electronic applications accepted. *Application Contact:* Dr. Jennifer Quinones Nottingham, Dean of Student Affairs, 800-986-3223 Ext. 8500, E-mail: jlquinon@nova.edu. *Provost/Dean,* Dr. H. Wells Singleton, 954-262-8730, Fax: 954-262-3894, E-mail: singlew@nova.edu.

Graduate School of Computer and Information Sciences Students: 142 full-time (35 women), 1,000 part-time (283 women); includes 219 Black or African American, non-Hispanic/Latino; 8 American Indian or Alaska Native, non-Hispanic/Latino; 88 Asian, non-Hispanic/Latino; 163 Hispanic/Latino; 8 Two or more races, non-Hispanic/Latino, 44 international. Average age 41. 486 applicants, 45% accepted. *Faculty:* 20 full-time (5 women), 21 part-time/adjunct (3 women). Expenses: Contact institution. *Financial support:* Federal Work-Study, scholarships/grants, and unspecified assistantships available. Support available to part-time students. Financial award application deadline: 5/1. In 2010, 128 master's, 44 doctorates awarded. *Degree program information:* Part-time and evening/weekend programs available. Postbaccalaureate distance learning degree programs offered (no on-campus study). Offers computer information systems (MS, PhD); computer science (MS, PhD); computing technology in education (PhD); information security (MS); information systems (MS, PhD); management information systems (MS). *Application deadline:* Applications are processed on a rolling basis. *Application fee:* $50. Electronic applications accepted. *Application Contact:* 954-262-2000, Fax: 954-262-2752, E-mail: scisinfo@nova.edu. *Interim Dean,* Dr. Amon Seagull, 954-262-7300.

Graduate School of Humanities and Social Sciences Students: 434 full-time (315 women), 336 part-time (251 women); includes 228 Black or African American, non-Hispanic/Latino; 2 American Indian or Alaska Native, non-Hispanic/Latino; 18 Asian, non-Hispanic/Latino; 120 Hispanic/Latino; 9 Two or more races, non-Hispanic/Latino, 62 international. Average age 36. 407 applicants, 58% accepted, 147 enrolled. *Faculty:* 21 full-time (11 women), 33 part-time/adjunct (22 women). Expenses: Contact institution. *Financial support:* In 2010–11, 393 students received support, including 20 research assistantships (averaging $15,600 per year); teaching assistantships, career-related internships or fieldwork, Federal Work-Study, and scholarships/grants also available. Financial award application deadline: 4/1; financial award applicants required to submit CSS PROFILE. In 2010, 87 master's, 17 doctorates awarded. *Degree program information:* Part-time and evening/weekend programs available. Postbaccalaureate distance learning degree programs offered (minimal on-campus study). Offers advanced family systems (Certificate); college student affairs (MS); college student personnel administration (Certificate); conflict analysis and resolution (MS, PhD); conflict analysis and resolution studies (Certificate); cross-disciplinary studies (MA); family studies (Certificate); family systems healthcare (Certificate); family therapy (MS, DMFT, PhD, Certificate); health care conflict resolution (Certificate); humanities and social sciences (MA, MS, DMFT, PhD, Certificate); marriage and family therapy (DMFT); national security affairs (MS); peace studies (Certificate); qualitative methods (Certificate). *Application deadline:* For fall admission, 6/1 priority date for domestic and international students; for winter admission, 10/1 priority date for domestic and international students; for spring admission, 3/1 priority date for domestic and international students. Applications are processed on a rolling basis. *Application fee:* $50. Electronic applications accepted. *Application Contact:* Marcia Arango, Student Recruitment Coordinator, 954-262-3006, Fax: 954-262-3968, E-mail: marango@nsu.nova.edu. *Dean,* Dr. Honggang Yang, 954-262-3016, Fax: 954-262-3968, E-mail: yangh@nova.edu.

Health Professions Division Students: 3,811 full-time (2,262 women), 800 part-time (578 women); includes 1,956 minority (351 Black or African American, non-Hispanic/Latino; 13 American Indian or Alaska Native, non-Hispanic/Latino; 717 Asian, non-Hispanic/Latino; 815 Hispanic/Latino; 15 Native Hawaiian or other Pacific Islander, non-Hispanic/Latino; 45 Two or more races, non-Hispanic/Latino), 213 international. Average age 29. Expenses: Contact institution. *Financial support:* Fellowships, teaching assistantships, career-related internships or fieldwork, Federal Work-Study, institutionally sponsored loans, scholarships/grants, and unspecified assistantships available. Support available to part-time students. In 2010, 702 first professional degrees, 365 master's, 158 doctorates awarded. Postbaccalaureate distance learning degree programs offered (minimal on-campus study). Offers health professions (DMD, DO, OD, Pharm D, MBS, MH Sc, MMS, MOT, MPH, MS, MSN, Au D, DHSc, DPT, Dr OT, PhD, TDPT, Graduate Certificate). *Application deadline:* Applications are processed on a rolling basis. *Application fee:* $50. *Application Contact:* Information Contact, 800-541-6682, E-mail: nsuinfo@nsu.nova.edu. *Chancellor,* Dr. Frederick Lippman, 954-262-1100 Ext. 1507.

College of Allied Health and Nursing Students: 965 full-time (693 women), 603 part-time (435 women); includes 498 minority (183 Black or African American, non-Hispanic/Latino; 5 American Indian or Alaska Native, non-Hispanic/Latino; 106 Asian, non-Hispanic/Latino; 179 Hispanic/Latino; 6 Native Hawaiian or other Pacific Islander, non-Hispanic/Latino; 19 Two or more races, non-Hispanic/Latino), 13 international. Average age 32. *Faculty:* 43 full-time (25 women), 8 part-time/adjunct (4 women). Expenses: Contact institution. *Financial support:* Teaching assistantships, institutionally sponsored loans and unspecified assistantships available. In 2010, 304 master's, 158 doctorates awarded. Postbaccalaureate distance learning degree programs offered (minimal on-campus study). Offers allied health and nursing (MH Sc, MMS, MOT, MSN, Au D, DHSc, DPT, Dr OT, PhD, TDPT); audiology (Au D); health science (MH Sc, DHSc); medical science/physician assistant (MMS); nursing (MSN, PhD); occupational therapy (MOT, Dr OT, PhD); physical therapy (DPT, PhD, TDPT). *Application deadline:* Applications are processed on a rolling basis. *Application fee:* $50. *Application Contact:* Marla Frolinger, Admissions Counselor, 954-262-1100, E-mail: marlaf@nova.edu. *Dean,* Dr. Richard Davis, 954-262-1203, E-mail: redavis@nova.edu.

College of Dental Medicine Students: 491 full-time (273 women); includes 192 minority (7 Black or African American, non-Hispanic/Latino; 79 Asian, non-Hispanic/Latino; 97 Hispanic/Latino; 5 Native Hawaiian or other Pacific Islander, non-Hispanic/Latino; 4 Two or more races, non-Hispanic/Latino), 42 international. Average age 27. 2,774 applicants, 6% accepted, 105 enrolled. *Faculty:* 83 full-time (23 women), 200 part-time/adjunct (44 women). Expenses: Contact institution. *Financial support:* In 2010–11, 372 students received support, including 1 fellowship with full tuition reimbursement available, 11 teaching assistantships with full tuition reimbursements available. Financial award application deadline: 4/1; financial award applicants required to submit FAFSA. In 2010, 146 first professional degrees, 3 master's awarded. Offers dental medicine (DMD); dentistry (MS). *Application deadline:* For fall admission, 1/15 for domestic students, 2/15 for international students. Applications are processed on a rolling basis. *Application fee:* $50. *Application Contact:* Su-Ann Zarrett, Associate Director, 954-262-1108, Fax: 954-262-2282, E-mail: zarrett@nova.edu. *Dean,* Dr. Robert A. Uchin, 954-262-7312, Fax: 954-262-1782, E-mail: ruchin@nova.edu.

College of Medical Sciences Students: 28 full-time (14 women), 1 (woman) part-time; includes 1 Black or African American, non-Hispanic/Latino; 5 Asian, non-Hispanic/Latino; 4 Hispanic/Latino; 2 Two or more races, non-Hispanic/Latino. Average age 25. 108 applicants, 23% accepted. *Faculty:* 32 full-time (13 women), 4 part-time/adjunct (1 woman). Expenses: Contact institution. *Financial support:* Applicants required to submit FAFSA. In 2010, 11 master's awarded. Offers biomedical sciences (MBS). *Application deadline:* For spring admission, 4/15 for domestic students. Applications are processed on a rolling basis. *Application fee:* $50. *Application Contact:* Richard Wilson, Admissions Counselor, 954-262-1111, Fax: 954-262-1802, E-mail: rwilson@nsu.nova.edu. *Dean,* Dr. Harold E. Laubach, 954-262-1303, Fax: 954-262-1802, E-mail: harold@nsu.nova.edu.

College of Optometry Students: 431 full-time (280 women), 3 part-time (0 women); includes 189 minority (12 Black or African American, non-Hispanic/Latino; 1 American Indian or Alaska Native, non-Hispanic/Latino; 121 Asian, non-Hispanic/Latino; 50 Hispanic/Latino; 1 Native Hawaiian or other Pacific Islander, non-Hispanic/Latino; 4 Two or more races, non-Hispanic/Latino), 32 international. Average age 26. 746 applicants, 25% accepted, 106 enrolled. *Faculty:* 48 full-time (32 women), 11 part-time/adjunct (10 women). Expenses: Contact institution. *Financial support:* In 2010–11, 393 students received support. Federal Work-Study, institutionally sponsored loans, and scholarships/grants available. Financial award applicants required to submit FAFSA. In 2010, 109 first professional degrees awarded. Postbaccalaureate distance learning degree programs offered (no on-campus study). Offers clinical vision research (MS); optometry (OD). *Application deadline:* For fall admission, 4/1 for domestic and international students. Applications are processed on a rolling basis. *Application fee:* $50. Electronic applications accepted. *Application Contact:* Fran Franconeri, Admissions Counselor, 954-262-1132, Fax: 954-262-2282. *Dean,* Dr. David Loshin, 954-262-1404, Fax: 954-262-1818.

College of Osteopathic Medicine Students: 1,001 full-time (436 women), 121 part-time (86 women); includes 452 minority (81 Black or African American, non-Hispanic/Latino; 5 American Indian or Alaska Native, non-Hispanic/Latino; 227 Asian, non-Hispanic/Latino; 124 Hispanic/Latino; 3 Native Hawaiian or other Pacific Islander, non-Hispanic/Latino; 12 Two or more races, non-Hispanic/Latino), 28 international. Average age 27. 3,427 applicants, 11% accepted, 232 enrolled. *Faculty:* 82 full-time (33 women), 983 part-time/adjunct (212 women). Expenses: Contact institution. *Financial support:* In 2010–11, 815 students received support, including 18 fellowships with full tuition reimbursements available (averaging $13,000 per year); research assistantships, teaching assistantships, career-related internships or fieldwork, Federal Work-Study, institutionally sponsored loans, and scholarships/grants also available. Financial award application deadline: 6/1; financial award applicants required to submit FAFSA. In 2010, 206 first professional degrees, 45 master's awarded. Offers biomedical informatics (MS, Graduate Certificate); clinical informatics (Graduate Certificate); osteopathic medicine (DO); public health (MPH); public health informatics (Graduate Certificate). *Application deadline:* For fall admission, 1/15 for domestic students. Applications are processed on a rolling basis. *Application fee:* $50. Electronic applications accepted. *Application Contact:* Ellen Rondino, COM Admissions Counselor, 866-817-4068. *Dean,* Dr. Anthony J. Silvagni, 954-262-1407, E-mail: silvagni@hpd.nova.edu.

College of Pharmacy Students: 897 full-time (568 women), 67 part-time (51 women); includes 67 Black or African American, non-Hispanic/Latino; 2 American Indian or Alaska Native, non-Hispanic/Latino; 179 Asian, non-Hispanic/Latino; 360 Hispanic/Latino; 4 Two or more races, non-Hispanic/Latino, 98 international. Average age 27. 1,177 applicants, 22% accepted, 189 enrolled. *Faculty:* 52 full-time (32 women), 9 part-time/adjunct (3 women). Expenses: Contact institution. *Financial support:* Career-related internships or fieldwork, Federal Work-Study, institutionally sponsored loans, and scholarships/grants available. Financial award application deadline: 4/15; financial award applicants required to submit FAFSA. In 2010, 241 first professional degrees awarded. Postbaccalaureate distance learning degree programs offered (minimal on-campus study). Offers pharmacy (Pharm D, PhD). *Application deadline:* For fall admission, 3/1 for domestic students, 2/1 for international students. Applications are processed on a rolling basis. *Application fee:* $50. Electronic applications accepted. *Application Contact:* Tracy Templin, Admissions Counselor, 954-262-1112, Fax: 954-262-2282, E-mail: dpetracy@nsu.nova.edu. *Dean,* Dr. Andres Malave, 954-262-1300, Fax: 954-262-2278.

H. Wayne Huizenga School of Business and Entrepreneurship Students: 346 full-time (194 women), 3,508 part-time (2,055 women); includes 2,496 minority (1,215 Black or African American, non-Hispanic/Latino; 6 American Indian or Alaska Native, non-Hispanic/Latino; 141 Asian, non-Hispanic/Latino; 1,099 Hispanic/Latino; 3 Native Hawaiian or other Pacific Islander, non-Hispanic/Latino; 32 Two or more races, non-Hispanic/Latino), 213 international. Average age 33. 1,634 applicants, 66% accepted, 734 enrolled. *Faculty:* 75 full-time (25 women), 124 part-time/adjunct (29 women). Expenses: Contact institution. *Financial support:* In 2010–11, 2 students received support. Federal Work-Study and scholarships/grants available. Support available to part-time students. Financial award applicants required to submit FAFSA. In 2010, 1,230 master's, 33 doctorates awarded. *Degree program information:* Part-time and evening/weekend programs available. Postbaccalaureate distance learning degree programs offered (minimal on-campus study). Offers accounting (DBA); business administration (MBA); business and entrepreneurship (M Acc, M Tax, MBA, MIBA, MPA, MS, MSHRM, DBA); decision sciences (DBA); finance (DBA); human resource management (DBA); human resources management (MSHRM); international business (DBA); international business administration (MIBA); leadership (MS); management (DBA); marketing (DBA); public administration (MPA); real estate development (MS); taxation (M Tax). *Application deadline:* Applications are processed on a rolling basis. *Application fee:* $50. Electronic applications accepted. *Application Contact:* Karen Goldberg, Associate Director of Recruitment and Special Events, 954-262-5039, Fax: 954-262-3822, E-mail: karen@nova.edu. *Dean,* Dr. D. Michael Fields, 954-262-5005, E-mail: fieldsm@nova.edu.

Oceanographic Center Students: 126 full-time (79 women), 109 part-time (77 women); includes 4 Black or African American, non-Hispanic/Latino; 1 American Indian or Alaska Native, non-Hispanic/Latino; 4 Asian, non-Hispanic/Latino; 21 Hispanic/Latino; 1 Two or more races, non-Hispanic/Latino, 6 international. Average age 29. 98 applicants, 82% accepted, 67 enrolled. *Faculty:* 15 full-time (1 woman), 5 part-time/adjunct (0 women). Expenses: Contact institution. *Financial support:* In 2010–11, 25 research assistantships (averaging $4,000 per year), 3 teaching assistantships (averaging $3,500 per year) were awarded; career-related internships or fieldwork, Federal Work-Study, scholarships/grants, tuition waivers (partial), and unspecified assistantships also available. Support available to part-time students. Financial award applicants required to submit FAFSA. In 2010, 40 master's, 3 doctorates awarded. *Degree program information:* Part-time and evening/weekend programs available. Offers biological sciences (MS); coastal zone management (MS); marine biology (MS, PhD); marine biology and oceanography (PhD); marine environmental science (MS); oceanography (PhD); physical oceanography (MS). *Application deadline:* Applications are processed on a rolling basis. *Application fee:* $50. *Application Contact:* Dr. Richard Spieler, Director of Academic Programs, 954-262-3600, Fax: 954-262-4020, E-mail: spieler@nova.edu. *Dean,* Dr. Richard Dodge, 954-262-3600, Fax: 954-262-4020, E-mail: dodge@nsu.nova.edu.

Shepard Broad Law Center Students: 1,093 full-time (572 women), 170 part-time (126 women); includes 423 minority (105 Black or African American, non-Hispanic/Latino; 6 American Indian or Alaska Native, non-Hispanic/Latino; 46 Asian, non-Hispanic/Latino; 245 Hispanic/Latino; 12 Native Hawaiian or other Pacific Islander, non-Hispanic/Latino; 9 Two or more races, non-Hispanic/Latino), 31 international. Average age 28. 2,855 applicants, 45% accepted, 384 enrolled. *Faculty:* 63 full-time (35 women), 48 part-time/adjunct (18 women). Expenses: Contact institution. *Financial support:* In 2010–11, 58 fellowships were awarded; research assistantships, teaching assistantships, Federal Work-Study, scholarships/grants, tuition waivers (full and partial), and unspecified assistantships also available. Support available to part-time students. Financial award application deadline: 4/15; financial award applicants required to submit FAFSA. In 2010, 295 first professional degrees, 41 master's awarded. *Degree program information:* Part-time and evening/weekend programs available. Postbaccalaureate distance learning degree programs offered (minimal on-campus study). Offers education law (MS, Certificate); employment law (MS); health law (MS); law (JD). JD/MURP offered jointly with Florida Atlantic University. *Application deadline:* For fall admission, 3/1 priority date for domestic students. Applications are processed on a rolling basis. *Application fee:* $50. Electronic applications accepted. *Application Contact:* Beth Hall, Assistant Dean of Admissions, 954-262-6121, Fax: 954-262-3844, E-mail: hallb@nsu.law.nova.edu. *Dean,* Joseph D. Harbaugh, 954-262-6105, Fax: 954-262-3834, E-mail: harbaughj@nsu.law.nova.edu.

NSCAD UNIVERSITY, Halifax, NS B3J 3J6, Canada

General Information Province-supported, coed, comprehensive institution. *Graduate housing:* On-campus housing not available.

GRADUATE UNITS

Program in Fine Arts Offers craft (MFA); design (M Des); fine and media arts (MFA).

NYACK COLLEGE, Nyack, NY 10960-3698

General Information Independent-religious, coed, comprehensive institution. *Enrollment:* 3,320 graduate, professional, and undergraduate students; 435 full-time matriculated graduate/professional students (227 women), 706 part-time matriculated graduate/professional students (432 women). *Enrollment by degree level:* 464 first professional, 677 master's. *Graduate faculty:* 25 full-time (10 women), 33 part-time/adjunct (13 women). Tuition and fees vary according to program. *Graduate housing:* Rooms and/or apartments available on a first-come, first-served basis to single and married students. Housing application deadline: 9/1. *Student services:* Campus employment opportunities, career counseling, international student services, low-cost health insurance, services for students with disabilities, writing training. *Library facilities:* Bailey Library plus 3 others. *Online resources:* library catalog, web page. *Collection:* 156,340 titles, 437 serial subscriptions, 7,624 audiovisual materials.

Computer facilities: 124 computers available on campus for general student use. A campuswide network can be accessed from student residence rooms and from off campus. Online class registration is available. *Web address:* http://www.nyack.edu/.

General Application Contact: Traci Piescki, Director of Admissions, 800-541-6891, Fax: 845-348-3912, E-mail: admissions.grad@nyack.edu.

GRADUATE UNITS

Alliance Graduate School of Counseling Students: 66 full-time (59 women), 190 part-time (154 women); includes 182 minority (103 Black or African American, non-Hispanic/Latino; 30 Asian, non-Hispanic/Latino; 40 Hispanic/Latino; 9 Two or more races, non-Hispanic/Latino), 7 international. Average age 40. Expenses: Contact institution. In 2010, 50 master's awarded. *Degree program information:* Part-time programs available. Offers marriage and family therapy (MA); mental health counseling (MA). *Application deadline:* Applications are processed on a rolling basis. *Application fee:* $35. Electronic applications accepted. *Application Contact:* Traci Piescki, Director of Admissions, 800-541-6891, Fax: 845-348-3912, E-mail: admissions.grad@nyack.edu. *Director*, Dr. Carol Robles, 845-770-5730, Fax: 845-348-3923.

Alliance Theological Seminary Students: 256 full-time (96 women), 482 part-time (251 women); includes 231 Black or African American, non-Hispanic/Latino; 2 American Indian or Alaska Native, non-Hispanic/Latino; 123 Asian, non-Hispanic/Latino; 187 Hispanic/Latino; 12 Two or more races, non-Hispanic/Latino, 80 international. Average age 40. Expenses: Contact institution. *Financial support:* Teaching assistantships, career-related internships or fieldwork, Federal Work-Study, and scholarships/grants available. Financial award applicants required to submit FAFSA. In 2010, 47 first professional degrees, 45 master's awarded. *Degree program information:* Part-time programs available. Offers Biblical literature (MA); Christian ministry (MPS); intercultural studies (MA); ministry (D Min); theology (M Div); urban ministry (MPS). *Application deadline:* Applications are processed on a rolling basis. *Application fee:* $30. Electronic applications accepted. *Application Contact:* Traci Piescki, Director of Admissions, 845-770-5701, Fax: 845-348-3912, E-mail: admissions.ats@nyack.edu. *Dean*, Dr. Ron Walborn, 845-770-5715, Fax: 845-358-1663.

School of Business and Leadership Students: 112 full-time (72 women), 7 part-time (5 women); includes 96 minority (83 Black or African American, non-Hispanic/Latino; 3 Asian, non-Hispanic/Latino; 7 Hispanic/Latino; 3 Two or more races, non-Hispanic/Latino), 6 international. Average age 40. Expenses: Contact institution. In 2010, 53 master's awarded. *Degree program information:* Evening/weekend programs available. Offers business administration (MBA); organizational leadership (MS). *Application deadline:* Applications are processed on a rolling basis. *Application fee:* $50. Electronic applications accepted. *Application Contact:* Traci Piescki, Director of Admissions, 800-541-6891, Fax: 845-348-3912, E-mail: admissions.grad@nyack.edu. *Dean*, Dr. Anita Underwood, 845-675-4511, Fax: 845-353-5812.

School of Education Students: 1 full-time (0 women), 27 part-time (22 women); includes 15 minority (6 Black or African American, non-Hispanic/Latino; 3 Asian, non-Hispanic/Latino; 4 Hispanic/Latino; 2 Two or more races, non-Hispanic/Latino), 1 international. Average age 34. Expenses: Contact institution. *Financial support:* State aid for N. Y. residents available. In 2010, 8 master's awarded. *Degree program information:* Part-time and evening/weekend programs available. Offers childhood education (MS); childhood special education (MS); inclusive education (MS). *Application deadline:* Applications are processed on a rolling basis. *Application fee:* $30. *Application Contact:* Traci Piescki, Director of Admissions, 800-541-6891, Fax: 845-348-3912, E-mail: admissions.grad@nyack.edu. *Dean*, Dr. JoAnn Looney, 845-675-4538, Fax: 845-358-0874.

OAKLAND CITY UNIVERSITY, Oakland City, IN 47660-1099

General Information Independent-religious, coed, comprehensive institution. *Enrollment:* 46 full-time matriculated graduate/professional students (24 women), 110 part-time matriculated graduate/professional students (53 women). *Enrollment by degree level:* 12 first professional, 108 master's, 36 doctoral. *Graduate faculty:* 8 full-time (1 woman), 41 part-time/adjunct (11 women). *Graduate housing:* Rooms and/or apartments guaranteed to single students and available on a first-come, first-served basis to married students. Housing application deadline: 7/1. *Student services:* Campus employment opportunities, career counseling, free psychological counseling. *Library facilities:* Barger-Richardson Library. *Online resources:* library catalog, web page, access to other libraries' catalogs. *Collection:* 87,724 titles, 222 serial subscriptions, 2,570 audiovisual materials.

Computer facilities: 92 computers available on campus for general student use. A campuswide network can be accessed from student residence rooms and from off campus. *Web address:* http://www.oak.edu/.

General Application Contact: Kim Heldt, Director of Admissions, 812-749-1218, E-mail: kheldt@oak.edu.

GRADUATE UNITS

Chapman Seminary Students: 7 full-time (1 woman), 5 part-time (1 woman); includes 1 minority (Black or African American, non-Hispanic/Latino). Average age 33. 11 applicants, 100% accepted, 8 enrolled. *Faculty:* 5 full-time (0 women), 5 part-time/adjunct (1 woman). Expenses: Contact institution. *Financial support:* In 2010–11, 10 students received support. Career-related internships or fieldwork and Federal Work-Study available. Support available to part-time students. Financial award applicants required to submit FAFSA. In 2010, 2 M Divs awarded. *Degree program information:* Part-time programs available. Offers religious studies (M Div, D Min). *Application deadline:* Applications are processed on a rolling basis. *Application fee:* $35. *Application Contact:* Dr. Douglas Low, Dean, 812-749-1280, Fax: 812-749-1308, E-mail: dlow@oak.edu. *Dean*, Dr. Douglas Low, 812-749-1280, Fax: 812-749-1308, E-mail: dlow@oak.edu.

School of Adult and Extended Learning Students: 40 part-time (14 women); includes 8 minority (7 Black or African American, non-Hispanic/Latino; 1 Two or more races, non-Hispanic/Latino). Average age 35. 23 applicants, 87% accepted, 18 enrolled. *Faculty:* 23 part-time/adjunct (2 women). Expenses: Contact institution. *Financial support:* Institutionally sponsored loans available. Financial award application deadline: 3/10; financial award applicants required to submit FAFSA. In 2010, 44 master's awarded. *Degree program information:* Part-time and evening/weekend programs available. Offers management (MBA). *Application deadline:* Applications are processed on a rolling basis. *Application fee:* $35. *Dean*, Dr. Michael Pelt, 812-749-1542, Fax: 812-749-1511, E-mail: mpelt@oak.edu.

School of Education Students: 39 full-time (23 women), 65 part-time (38 women); includes 9 Black or African American, non-Hispanic/Latino. Average age 32. 46 applicants, 91% accepted, 40 enrolled. *Faculty:* 4 full-time (1 woman), 16 part-time/adjunct (8 women). Expenses: Contact institution. *Financial support:* Unspecified assistantships available. Financial award applicants required to submit FAFSA. In 2010, 64 master's, 8 doctorates awarded. Offers educational leadership (Ed D); teaching (MA). *Application deadline:* For spring admission, 5/1 for domestic students. Applications are processed on a rolling basis. *Application fee:* $35. *Dean*, Dr. Mary Jo Beauchamp, 812-749-1399, Fax: 812-749-1511, E-mail: mbeauchamp@oak.edu.

OAKLAND UNIVERSITY, Rochester, MI 48309-4401

General Information State-supported, coed, university. CGS member. *Graduate housing:* Rooms and/or apartments available on a first-come, first-served basis to single and married students. Housing application deadline: 9/1. *Research affiliation:* Beaumont Hospital Corporation (eye research, nursing), Henry Ford Health Systems (medical physics).

GRADUATE UNITS

Graduate Study and Lifelong Learning *Degree program information:* Part-time and evening/weekend programs available. Electronic applications accepted.

College of Arts and Sciences *Degree program information:* Part-time and evening/weekend programs available. Offers applied mathematical sciences (PhD); applied statistics (MS); arts and sciences (MA, MM, MPA, MS, PhD, Certificate); biological sciences (MA, MS); biological sciences: health and environmental chemistry (PhD); biomedical sciences: biological communications (PhD); chemistry (MS); English (MA); history (MA); industrial applied mathematics (MS); liberal studies (MA); linguistics (MA); mathematics (MA); medical physics (PhD); music (MM); music education (PhD); physics (MS); public administration (MPA); statistical methods (Certificate); teaching English as a second language (Certificate). Electronic applications accepted.

School of Business Administration *Degree program information:* Part-time and evening/weekend programs available. Offers accounting (M Acc, Certificate); business administration (M Acc, MBA, MS, Certificate); economics (Certificate); entrepreneurship (Certificate); finance (Certificate); general management (Certificate); human resource management (Certificate); information technology management (MS); international business (Certificate); management information systems (Certificate); marketing (Certificate); production and operations management (Certificate). Electronic applications accepted.

School of Education and Human Services *Degree program information:* Part-time and evening/weekend programs available. Offers advanced microcomputer applications (Certificate); counseling (MA, PhD, Certificate); early childhood education (M Ed, PhD, Certificate); early mathematics education (Certificate); education and human services (M Ed, MA, MAT, MTD, PhD, Certificate, Ed S); education studies (M Ed); educational leadership (M Ed, PhD); higher education (Certificate); higher education administration (Certificate); human resource development (MTD); microcomputer applications (Certificate); reading (Certificate); reading and language arts (MAT); reading education (PhD); reading, language arts and literature (Certificate); school administration (Ed S); secondary education (MAT); special education (M Ed, Certificate). Electronic applications accepted.

School of Engineering and Computer Science *Degree program information:* Part-time and evening/weekend programs available. Offers computer science (MS); electrical and computer engineering (MS); embedded systems (MS); engineering and computer science (MS, PhD); engineering management (MS); information systems engineering (MS); mechanical engineering (MS, PhD); software engineering (MS); systems engineering (MS, PhD). Electronic applications accepted.

School of Health Sciences Offers complimentary medicine and wellness (Certificate); exercise science (MS, Certificate); health sciences (MS, MSPT, DPT, Dr Sc PT, Certificate); neurological rehabilitation (Certificate); orthopedic manual physical therapy (Certificate); orthopedic physical therapy (Certificate); pediatric rehabilitation (Certificate); physical therapy (MSPT, DPT, Dr Sc PT); safety management (MS); teaching and learning for rehabilitation professionals (Certificate). Electronic applications accepted.

School of Nursing *Degree program information:* Part-time and evening/weekend programs available. Offers adult gerontological nurse practitioner (MSN, Certificate); adult health (MSN); family nurse practitioner (MSN, Certificate); nurse anesthetist (MSN, Certificate); nursing (MSN, DNP, Certificate); nursing education (MSN, Certificate); nursing practice (DNP). Electronic applications accepted.

OAKWOOD UNIVERSITY, Huntsville, AL 35896

General Information Independent-religious, coed, comprehensive institution.

GRADUATE UNITS

Program in Pastoral Studies Offers pastoral studies (MA).

OBERLIN COLLEGE, Oberlin, OH 44074

General Information Independent, coed, comprehensive institution. *Graduate housing:* Room and/or apartments available on a first-come, first-served basis to single students; on-campus housing not available to married students. Housing application deadline: 6/15.

GRADUATE UNITS

Conservatory of Music Offers music (MM, MMT, AD). Electronic applications accepted.

Graduate Teacher Education Program Offers early childhood education (M Ed); middle childhood education (M Ed).

OBLATE SCHOOL OF THEOLOGY, San Antonio, TX 78216-6693

General Information Independent-religious, coed, graduate-only institution. *Enrollment by degree level:* 77 first professional, 42 master's, 25 doctoral, 6 other advanced degrees. *Graduate faculty:* 19 full-time (6 women), 2 part-time/adjunct (0 women). *Tuition:* Full-time $12,350; part-time $475 per credit hour. *Required fees:* $175 per semester. One-time fee: $90. Tuition and fees vary according to course level, course load and degree level. *Graduate housing:* On-campus housing not available. *Student services:* Campus employment opportunities, international student services, writing training. *Library facilities:* Donald E. O'Shaughnessey Library. *Online resources:* library catalog. *Collection:* 90,000 titles, 360 serial subscriptions.

Computer facilities: 10 computers available on campus for general student use. A campuswide network can be accessed from student residence rooms and from off campus. *Web address:* http://www.ost.edu/.

General Application Contact: James Oberhausen, Registrar, 210-341-1366 Ext. 212, Fax: 210-341-4519, E-mail: registrar@ost.edu.

GRADUATE UNITS

Graduate and Professional Programs Students: 91 full-time (7 women), 59 part-time (34 women); includes 4 Black or African American, non-Hispanic/Latino; 1 American Indian or Alaska Native, non-Hispanic/Latino; 18 Asian, non-Hispanic/Latino; 30 Hispanic/Latino, 36 international. 24 applicants, 100% accepted, 24 enrolled. *Faculty:* 19 full-time (6 women), 2 part-time/adjunct (0 women). Expenses: Contact institution. *Financial support:* Scholarships/grants available. Support available to part-time students. Financial award application deadline: 8/1; financial award applicants required to submit FAFSA. In 2010, 13 first professional degrees, 17 master's, 4 doctorates awarded. *Degree program information:* Part-time programs available. Offers divinity (M Div); Hispanic ministry (D Min); pastoral ministry (MAP Min); pastoral studies (Certificate); spirituality (MA Sp); supervision (D Min); theology (MA Th). *Application deadline:* For fall admission, 6/15 priority date for domestic and international students; for spring admission, 11/30 for domestic and international students. Applications are processed on a rolling basis. *Application fee:* $50. *Application Contact:* James Oberhausen, Director of Admission/Registrar, 210-341-1366 Ext. 212, Fax: 210-341-4519, E-mail: registrar@ost.edu. *Academic Dean*, Dr. Scott Woodward, 210-341-1366, Fax: 210-341-4519, E-mail: swoodward@ost.edu.

OCCIDENTAL COLLEGE, Los Angeles, CA 90041-3314

General Information Independent, coed, comprehensive institution. *Graduate housing:* On-campus housing not available.

GRADUATE UNITS

Graduate Studies *Degree program information:* Part-time programs available. Offers biology (MA); elementary education (MAT); English and comparative literary studies (MAT); history (MAT); liberal studies (MAT); life science (MAT); mathematics (MAT); physical science (MAT); secondary education (MAT); social science (MAT); Spanish (MAT).

OGI SCHOOL OF SCIENCE & ENGINEERING AT OREGON HEALTH & SCIENCE UNIVERSITY, Beaverton, OR 97006-8921

General Information State-related, coed, graduate-only institution. *Graduate housing:* On-campus housing not available. *Research affiliation:* BioSpeech, Inc. (center for spoken language), GeoSyntech (environmental and biomolecular systems), Intel Corporation (computer science), Calpine Corporation (coastal land), HemCon, Inc. (biomedical), Medical Research Foundation (biomedical spoken language, environmental and biomolecular).

GRADUATE UNITS

Graduate Studies *Degree program information:* Part-time and evening/weekend programs available. Offers biochemistry and molecular biology (MS, PhD); biomedical engineering (MS, PhD); computer science (PhD); computer science and engineering (MS, PhD); electrical engineering (MS, PhD); environmental health systems (MS); environmental information technology (MS, PhD); environmental science and engineering (MS, PhD); health care management (Certificate); management in science and technology (MS, Certificate). Electronic applications accepted.

OGI School of Science & Engineering at Oregon Health & Science University (continued)

Science and Technology Center for Coastal and Land Margin Research *Degree program information:* Part-time programs available. Offers coastal and land margin research (M Sc, PhD). Electronic applications accepted.

OGLALA LAKOTA COLLEGE, Kyle, SD 57752-0490

General Information State and locally supported, coed, comprehensive institution. *Graduate housing:* On-campus housing not available.

GRADUATE UNITS

Graduate Studies *Degree program information:* Part-time and evening/weekend programs available. Offers educational administration (MA); Lakota leadership and management (MA).

OGLETHORPE UNIVERSITY, Atlanta, GA 30319-2797

General Information Independent, coed, comprehensive institution. *Graduate housing:* On-campus housing not available.

GRADUATE UNITS

Division of Education *Degree program information:* Part-time programs available. Offers early childhood education (MAT).

OHIO COLLEGE OF PODIATRIC MEDICINE, Independence, OH 44131

General Information Independent, coed, graduate-only institution. *Enrollment by degree level:* 415 first professional. *Graduate faculty:* 17 full-time (7 women), 11 part-time/adjunct (4 women). *Tuition:* Full-time $28,750; part-time $1437 per credit hour. *Required fees:* $2748. *Graduate housing:* On-campus housing not available. *Student services:* Campus employment opportunities, campus safety program, career counseling, exercise/wellness program, free psychological counseling, international student services, low-cost health insurance, services for students with disabilities. *Library facilities:* Morton and Norma Seidman Memorial Medical Library. *Online resources:* library catalog, web page. *Collection:* 19,092 titles, 394 serial subscriptions, 788 audiovisual materials.

Computer facilities: 55 computers available on campus for general student use. A campuswide network can be accessed from off campus. Academic catalog, student handbook available. *Web address:* http://www.ocpm.edu/.

General Application Contact: Lois Lott, Dean of Student Affairs, 216-231-3300 Ext. 7486, Fax: 216-447-0210, E-mail: llott@ocpm.edu.

GRADUATE UNITS

Professional Program Students: 414 full-time (166 women), 1 part-time (0 women); includes 82 minority (37 Black or African American, non-Hispanic/Latino; 4 American Indian or Alaska Native, non-Hispanic/Latino; 26 Asian, non-Hispanic/Latino; 15 Hispanic/Latino), 8 international. Average age 27. 468 applicants, 44% accepted, 113 enrolled. *Faculty:* 26 full-time (7 women), 11 part-time/adjunct (4 women). Expenses: Contact institution. *Financial support:* In 2010–11, 86 students received support. Career-related internships or fieldwork, Federal Work-Study, institutionally sponsored loans, and scholarships/grants available. Financial award applicants required to submit FAFSA. In 2010, 88 DPMs awarded. Offers podiatric medicine (DPM). *Application deadline:* For fall admission, 4/1 priority date for domestic students. Applications are processed on a rolling basis. *Application fee:* $50. Electronic applications accepted. *Application Contact:* Lois Lott, Dean of Student Affairs, 216-231-3300 Ext. 7486, Fax: 216-447-0210, E-mail: llott@ocpm.edu. *President,* Dr. Thomas Melillo, 216-231-3300.

OHIO DOMINICAN UNIVERSITY, Columbus, OH 43219-2099

General Information Independent-religious, coed, comprehensive institution. *Enrollment:* 633 full-time matriculated graduate/professional students (414 women), 115 part-time matriculated graduate/professional students (75 women). *Enrollment by degree level:* 748 master's. *Tuition:* Part-time $485 per credit hour. *Graduate housing:* Room and/or apartments available on a first-come, first-served basis to single students; on-campus housing not available to married students. *Student services:* Campus employment opportunities, campus safety program, career counseling, free psychological counseling, international student services, services for students with disabilities, writing training. *Library facilities:* Spangler Library plus 1 other. *Online resources:* library catalog, web page, access to other libraries' catalogs. *Collection:* 128,788 titles, 9,161 serial subscriptions, 4,173 audiovisual materials.

Computer facilities: 198 computers available on campus for general student use. A campuswide network can be accessed from student residence rooms and from off campus. Online class registration is available. *Web address:* http://www.ohiodominican.edu/.

General Application Contact: Jill M. Westerfeld, Assistant Director for Graduate Admissions, 614-251-4725, Fax: 614-251-6654, E-mail: westerfj@ohiodominican.edu.

GRADUATE UNITS

Graduate Programs Students: 633 full-time (414 women), 115 part-time (75 women); includes 167 minority (139 Black or African American, non-Hispanic/Latino; 1 American Indian or Alaska Native, non-Hispanic/Latino; 8 Asian, non-Hispanic/Latino; 13 Hispanic/Latino; 1 Native Hawaiian or other Pacific Islander, non-Hispanic/Latino; 5 Two or more races, non-Hispanic/Latino), 2 international. Average age 34. Expenses: Contact institution. *Financial support:* Applicants required to submit FAFSA. In 2010, 321 master's awarded. *Degree program information:* Part-time and evening/weekend programs available. Offers liberal studies (MA); TESOL (MA). *Application deadline:* For fall admission, 7/15 priority date for domestic students, 7/18 priority date for international students; for spring admission, 12/18 priority date for domestic and international students. Applications are processed on a rolling basis. *Application fee:* $25. *Application Contact:* Jill M. Westerfeld, Assistant Director for Graduate Admissions, 614-251-4725, Fax: 614-251-6654, E-mail: westerfj@ohiodominican.edu. *Dean of Graduate and Professional Studies,* Dr. Linda Schoen, 614-251-4715, Fax: 614-253-3656, E-mail: schoenl@ohiodominican.edu.

Division of Business Students: 354 full-time (185 women), 33 part-time (14 women); includes 128 minority (113 Black or African American, non-Hispanic/Latino; 1 American Indian or Alaska Native, non-Hispanic/Latino; 3 Asian, non-Hispanic/Latino; 7 Hispanic/Latino; 1 Native Hawaiian or other Pacific Islander, non-Hispanic/Latino; 3 Two or more races, non-Hispanic/Latino), 1 international. Average age 33. Expenses: Contact institution. *Financial support:* Applicants required to submit FAFSA. In 2010, 387 master's awarded. *Degree program information:* Part-time and evening/weekend programs available. Post-baccalaureate distance learning degree programs offered (no on-campus study). Offers business (MBA, MS). Program also offered in Dayton, OH. *Application deadline:* For fall admission, 7/15 priority date for domestic students, 7/18 priority date for international students; for spring admission, 12/18 priority date for domestic and international students. Applications are processed on a rolling basis. *Application fee:* $25. *Application Contact:* Jill M. Westerfeld, Assistant Director Graduate Admissions, 614-251-4725, Fax: 614-251-6654, E-mail: westerfj@ohiodominican.edu. *Director of Graduate Business Programs,* Antonio R. Emanuel, 614-251-4559, E-mail: emanu@ohiodominican.edu.

Division of Education Students: 218 full-time (183 women), 42 part-time (33 women); includes 22 minority (18 Black or African American, non-Hispanic/Latino; 1 Asian, non-Hispanic/Latino; 2 Hispanic/Latino; 1 Two or more races, non-Hispanic/Latino). Average age 35. Expenses: Contact institution. *Financial support:* Tuition waivers and tuition discount for Diocesan teachers available. Financial award applicants required to submit FAFSA. In 2010, 135 master's awarded. *Degree program information:* Part-time and evening/weekend programs available. Postbaccalaureate distance learning degree programs offered. Offers education (M Ed). *Application deadline:* For fall admission, 7/15 priority date for domestic students, 7/18 priority date for international students; for spring admission, 12/18 priority date for domestic and international students. Applications are processed on a rolling basis. *Application fee:* $25. *Application Contact:* Jill M. Westerfeld, Assistant Director Graduate Admissions, 614-251-4725, Fax: 614-251-6654, E-mail: westerfj@ohiodominican.edu. *Dean,* Dr. JoAnn Hohenbrink, 614-251-4759, E-mail: hohenbrj@ohiodominican.edu.

Division of Theology, Arts and Ideas Students: 10 full-time (4 women), 8 part-time (6 women); includes 1 minority (Hispanic/Latino), 1 international. Average age 38. Expenses: Contact institution. *Financial support:* Applicants required to submit FAFSA. In 2010, 9 master's awarded. *Degree program information:* Part-time and evening/weekend programs available. Offers theology (MA). *Application deadline:* For fall admission, 7/15 priority date for domestic students, 7/18 priority date for international students; for spring admission, 12/18 priority date for domestic and international students. Applications are processed on a rolling basis. *Application fee:* $25. *Application Contact:* Jill M. Westerfeld, Assistant Director Graduate Admissions, 614-251-4725, Fax: 614-251-6654, E-mail: westerfj@ohiodominican.edu. *Program Director,* Dr. Leo Madden, 614-251-4720, E-mail: maddenl@ohiodominican.edu.

OHIO NORTHERN UNIVERSITY, Ada, OH 45810-1599

General Information Independent-religious, coed, comprehensive institution. *Enrollment:* 1,307 full-time matriculated graduate/professional students (733 women), 16 part-time matriculated graduate/professional students (5 women). *Enrollment by degree level:* 1,318 first professional, 5 master's. *Graduate faculty:* 54 full-time (20 women), 12 part-time/adjunct (3 women). *Graduate housing:* Room and/or apartments available on a first-come, first-served basis to single students; on-campus housing not available to married students. *Student services:* Campus employment opportunities, campus safety program, career counseling, child daycare facilities, exercise/wellness program, free psychological counseling, international student services, multicultural affairs office, services for students with disabilities. *Library facilities:* Heterick Memorial Library plus 1 other. *Online resources:* library catalog, web page, access to other libraries' catalogs.

Computer facilities: 533 computers available on campus for general student use. A campuswide network can be accessed from student residence rooms and from off campus. Online class registration is available. *Web address:* http://www.onu.edu/.

General Application Contact: Amanda Sheets, Assistant Director of Law Admissions, 419-772-2211.

GRADUATE UNITS

Claude W. Pettit College of Law Students: 316 full-time (122 women), 2 part-time (0 women); includes 35 minority (22 Black or African American, non-Hispanic/Latino; 1 American Indian or Alaska Native, non-Hispanic/Latino; 5 Asian, non-Hispanic/Latino; 4 Hispanic/Latino; 3 Two or more races, non-Hispanic/Latino), 5 international. Average age 25. 1,291 applicants, 37% accepted, 126 enrolled. *Faculty:* 26 full-time (9 women), 11 part-time/adjunct (3 women). Expenses: Contact institution. *Financial support:* Career-related internships or fieldwork, Federal Work-Study, institutionally sponsored loans, and scholarships/grants available. Financial award applicants required to submit FAFSA. In 2010, 11 master's awarded. Offers law (JD, LL M). *Application deadline:* Applications are processed on a rolling basis. Electronic applications accepted. *Application Contact:* Linda English, Assistant Dean and Director of Law Admissions, 419-772-2210, Fax: 419-772-3042, E-mail: l-english@onu.edu. *Dean,* Dr. David C. Crago, 419-772-2205, Fax: 419-772-1875, E-mail: c-crago@onu.edu.

Raabe College of Pharmacy Students: 991 full-time (611 women), 14 part-time (5 women); includes 70 minority (18 Black or African American, non-Hispanic/Latino; 1 American Indian or Alaska Native, non-Hispanic/Latino; 35 Asian, non-Hispanic/Latino; 2 Hispanic/Latino; 14 Two or more races, non-Hispanic/Latino), 30 international. Average age 21. 968 applicants, 33% accepted, 186 enrolled. *Faculty:* 28 full-time (11 women), 1 part-time/adjunct (0 women). Expenses: Contact institution. *Financial support:* Federal Work-Study, institutionally sponsored loans, and scholarships/grants available. Financial award applicants required to submit FAFSA. Offers pharmacy (Pharm D). Students enter the program as undergraduates. *Application Contact:* Dr. Robert McCurdy, Assistant Dean and Director of Pharmacy Student Services, 419-772-2278, Fax: 419-772-3554, E-mail: r-mccurdy@onu.edu. *Dean,* Dr. Jon E. Sprague, 419-772-2275, Fax: 419-772-3554, E-mail: j-sprague@onu.edu.

THE OHIO STATE UNIVERSITY, Columbus, OH 43210

General Information State-supported, coed, university. CGS member. *Enrollment:* 56,064 graduate, professional, and undergraduate students; 9,639 full-time matriculated graduate/professional students (5,043 women), 4,343 part-time matriculated graduate/professional students (2,415 women). *Enrollment by degree level:* 3,317 first professional, 5,973 master's, 4,666 doctoral, 26 other advanced degrees. *Graduate faculty:* 3,608. Tuition, state resident: full-time $10,605. Tuition, nonresident: full-time $26,535. Tuition and fees vary according to course load and program. *Graduate housing:* Rooms and/or apartments available on a first-come, first-served basis to single and married students. *Student services:* Campus employment opportunities, campus safety program, career counseling, child daycare facilities, exercise/wellness program, free psychological counseling, grant writing training, international student services, low-cost health insurance, multicultural affairs office, services for students with disabilities, teacher training, writing training. *Library facilities:* Thompson Library plus 12 others. *Online resources:* library catalog, web page, access to other libraries' catalogs. *Collection:* 6.2 million titles, 75,963 serial subscriptions, 87,485 audiovisual materials. *Research affiliation:* Children's Hospital (pediatrics), Transportation Research Center, Midwest Universities Consortium for International Activities, Science and Technology Campus, Ohio Learning Network (education).

Computer facilities: 675 computers available on campus for general student use. A campuswide network can be accessed from student residence rooms and from off campus. Online class registration, students can apply for admission, register, check grades, pay fees and obtain library resources, including books, online are available. *Web address:* http://www.osu.edu/.

General Application Contact: Graduate School Admissions, 614-292-9444, Fax: 614-292-3895, E-mail: domestic.grad@osu.edu.

GRADUATE UNITS

College of Dentistry Students: 516 full-time (223 women), 7 part-time (4 women); includes 22 Black or African American, non-Hispanic/Latino; 5 American Indian or Alaska Native, non-Hispanic/Latino; 43 Asian, non-Hispanic/Latino; 20 Hispanic/Latino; 1 Two or more races, non-Hispanic/Latino, 22 international. Average age 27. *Faculty:* 148 full-time (51 women), 150 part-time/adjunct (30 women). Expenses: Contact institution. *Financial support:* In 2010–11, 7 fellowships with tuition reimbursements, 13 research assistantships with tuition reimbursements (averaging $11,000 per year), 78 teaching assistantships with tuition reimbursements (averaging $12,000 per year) were awarded; Federal Work-Study and institutionally sponsored loans also available. Financial award application deadline: 3/1. In 2010, 101 first professional degrees, 25 master's, 4 doctorates awarded. Offers dentistry (DDS, MS); oral biology (PhD). *Application deadline:* Applications are processed on a rolling basis. Electronic applications accepted. *Application Contact:* Graduate Admissions, 614-292-9444, Fax: 614-292-3895, E-mail: domestic.grad@osu.edu. *Dean,* Dr. Patrick M. Lloyd, 614-292-9755, Fax: 614-292-7619.

College of Medicine Offers experimental pathobiology (MS); medicine (MD, MOT, MPT, MS, PhD); pathology assistant (MS). Electronic applications accepted.

School of Allied Medical Professions *Degree program information:* Part-time programs available. Offers allied health (MS); health and rehabilitation sciences (PhD); occupational therapy (MOT); physical therapy (DPT). Electronic applications accepted.

School of Biomedical Science Offers anatomy (MS, PhD); biomedical science (MD, MS, PhD); immunology (PhD); medical genetics (PhD); medicine (MD); molecular virology (PhD); pharmacology (PhD). Electronic applications accepted.

College of Optometry Students: 259 full-time (138 women), 5 part-time (2 women); includes 2 Black or African American, non-Hispanic/Latino; 1 American Indian or Alaska Native, non-Hispanic/Latino; 16 Asian, non-Hispanic/Latino; 4 Hispanic/Latino, 4 international. Average age 27. Expenses: Contact institution. *Financial support:* Research assistantships with full tuition reimbursements, teaching assistantships with full tuition reimbursements, Federal Work-Study, institutionally sponsored loans, and scholarships/grants available. Financial award application deadline: 2/1; financial award applicants required to submit FAFSA. In 2010, 62 first professional degrees, 12 master's, 1 doctorate awarded. Offers optometry (OD); vision science (MS, PhD). *Application deadline:* For fall admission, 8/15 priority date for domestic students, 7/1 priority date for international students; for winter admission, 12/1 priority date for domestic students, 11/1 priority date for international students; for spring admission, 3/1 priority date for domestic students, 2/1 priority date for international students. Applications are processed on a rolling basis. Electronic applications accepted. *Application Contact:* 614-292-9444, Fax: 614-292-3895, E-mail: domestic.grad@osu.edu. *Dean*, Dr. Melvin Shipp, 614-292-3246, Fax: 614-292-7493, E-mail: shipp.25@osu.edu.

College of Pharmacy Students: 572 full-time (343 women), 27 part-time (11 women); includes 21 Black or African American, non-Hispanic/Latino; 1 American Indian or Alaska Native, non-Hispanic/Latino; 101 Asian, non-Hispanic/Latino; 13 Hispanic/Latino; 2 Two or more races, non-Hispanic/Latino, 59 international. Average age 28. Expenses: Contact institution. *Financial support:* Fellowships with full tuition reimbursements, research assistantships with full tuition reimbursements, teaching assistantships with full tuition reimbursements, career-related internships or fieldwork, Federal Work-Study, institutionally sponsored loans, scholarships/grants, and traineeships available. In 2010, 131 first professional degrees, 9 master's, 11 doctorates awarded. *Degree program information:* Part-time programs available. Offers pharmacy (Pharm D, MS, PhD). *Application deadline:* For fall admission, 1/1 priority date for domestic students. *Application fee:* $40 ($50 for international students). Electronic applications accepted. *Application Contact:* Kathy I. Brooks, Graduate Program Coordinator, 614-292-6822, Fax: 614-292-2588, E-mail: brooks@pharmacy.ohio-state.edu. *Dean*, Dr. Robert W. Brueggemeier, 614-292-5711, Fax: 614-292-2435, E-mail: brueggemeier@pharmacy.ohio-state.edu.

College of Public Health Students: 191 full-time (133 women), 97 part-time (63 women); includes 18 Black or African American, non-Hispanic/Latino; 20 Asian, non-Hispanic/Latino; 6 Hispanic/Latino; 5 Two or more races, non-Hispanic/Latino, 21 international. Average age 30. Expenses: Contact institution. *Financial support:* Fellowships, research assistantships available. In 2010, 118 master's, 4 doctorates awarded. Offers public health (MHA, MPH, MS, PhD). *Application deadline:* Applications are processed on a rolling basis. *Application fee:* $40 ($50 for international students). Electronic applications accepted. *Application Contact:* Graduate Admissions, 614-292-9444, Fax: 614-292-3895, E-mail: domestic.grad@osu.edu. *Dean*, Stanley Lemeshow, 614-293-3913, Fax: 614-293-3937, E-mail: lemeshow.1@osu.edu.

College of Veterinary Medicine Students: 631 full-time (482 women), 37 part-time (27 women); includes 4 Black or African American, non-Hispanic/Latino; 4 American Indian or Alaska Native, non-Hispanic/Latino; 23 Asian, non-Hispanic/Latino; 14 Hispanic/Latino; 2 Two or more races, non-Hispanic/Latino, 45 international. Average age 26. *Faculty:* 133. Expenses: Contact institution. In 2010, 142 first professional degrees, 13 master's, 10 doctorates awarded. Offers anatomy and cellular biology (MS, PhD); comparative and veterinary medicine (MS, PhD); pathobiology (MS, PhD); pharmacology (MS, PhD); toxicology (MS, PhD); veterinary clinical sciences (MS, PhD); veterinary medicine (DVM, MS, PhD); veterinary physiology (MS, PhD); veterinary preventive medicine (MS, PhD). *Application deadline:* For fall admission, 8/15 priority date for domestic students, 7/1 priority date for international students; for winter admission, 12/1 priority date for domestic students, 11/1 priority date for international students; for spring admission, 3/1 priority date for domestic students, 2/1 priority date for international students. Applications are processed on a rolling basis. *Application fee:* $40 ($50 for international students). Electronic applications accepted. *Application Contact:* 614-292-9444, Fax: 614-292-3895, E-mail: domestic.grad@osu.edu. *Dean*, Lonnie King, 614-688-8749, Fax: 614-292-3544, E-mail: king.1518@osu.edu.

Graduate School Students: 6,344 full-time (3,311 women), 4,321 part-time (2,403 women); includes 1,171 minority (455 Black or African American, non-Hispanic/Latino; 23 American Indian or Alaska Native, non-Hispanic/Latino; 354 Asian, non-Hispanic/Latino; 267 Hispanic/Latino; 1 Native Hawaiian or other Pacific Islander, non-Hispanic/Latino; 71 Two or more races, non-Hispanic/Latino), 2,635 international. Average age 30. *Faculty:* 2,876. Expenses: Contact institution. *Financial support:* Fellowships, research assistantships, teaching assistantships, career-related internships or fieldwork, Federal Work-Study, institutionally sponsored loans, and unspecified assistantships available. Support available to part-time students. In 2010, 2,686 master's, 757 doctorates awarded. *Degree program information:* Part-time and evening/weekend programs available. *Application deadline:* For fall admission, 8/12 priority date for domestic students, 7/1 priority date for international students; for winter admission, 12/1 priority date for domestic students, 11/1 priority date for international students; for spring admission, 3/1 priority date for domestic students, 2/1 priority date for international students. Applications are processed on a rolling basis. *Application fee:* $40 ($50 for international students). Electronic applications accepted. *Application Contact:* 614-292-9444, Fax: 614-292-3895, E-mail: domestic.grad@osu.edu. *Dean*, Patrick S. Osmer, 614-292-6031, Fax: 614-292-3656, E-mail: osmer.1@osu.edu.

College of Arts and Sciences Students: 1,864 full-time (998 women), 1,284 part-time (589 women); includes 323 minority (90 Black or African American, non-Hispanic/Latino; 9 American Indian or Alaska Native, non-Hispanic/Latino; 96 Asian, non-Hispanic/Latino; 103 Hispanic/Latino; 1 Native Hawaiian or other Pacific Islander, non-Hispanic/Latino; 24 Two or more races, non-Hispanic/Latino), 868 international. Average age 29. *Faculty:* 193. Expenses: Contact institution. *Financial support:* Fellowships, research assistantships, teaching assistantships, career-related internships or fieldwork, Federal Work-Study, institutionally sponsored loans, and unspecified assistantships available. Support available to part-time students. Financial award applicants required to submit FAFSA. In 2010, 552 master's, 371 doctorates awarded. *Degree program information:* Part-time programs available. Offers African-American and African studies (MA); ancient Greek (MA); anthropology (MA, PhD); art (MFA); art education (MA, PhD); arts and humanities (MA, MFA, MM, DMA, PhD); arts and sciences (M Mus, MA, MFA, MS, DMA, PhD); arts policy and administration (MA); astronomy (MS, PhD); atmospheric sciences (MS, PhD); audiology (Au D, PhD); behavioral neuroscience (PhD); biochemistry (MS, PhD); biophysics (MS, PhD); biostatistics (PhD); cell and developmental biology (MS, PhD); chemical physics (MS, PhD); chemistry (MS, PhD); Chinese (MA, PhD); choreography (MFA); clinical psychology (PhD); cognitive psychology (PhD); communication (MA, PhD); comparative studies (MA, PhD); dance (MA, MFA, PhD); dance and technology (MFA); dance studies (PhD); developmental psychology (PhD); economics (MA, PhD); English (MA, MFA, PhD); evolution, ecology, and organismal biology (MS, PhD); French (MA, PhD); genetics (MS, PhD); geodetic science (MS); geography (MA, PhD); geological sciences (MS, PhD); Germanic languages and literatures (MA, PhD); Greek studies (MA, PhD); hearing science (PhD); history (MA, PhD); history of art (MA, PhD); industrial, interior, and visual communication design (MA, MFA); Italian (MA); Japanese (MA, PhD); Labanotation (MFA); Latin studies (MA, PhD); lighting (MFA); linguistics (MA, PhD); literature (MA); mathematics (MA, MS, PhD); mental retardation and developmental disabilities (PhD); microbiology (MS, PhD); modern Greek (MA, PhD); molecular biology (MS, PhD); molecular, cellular and developmental biology (MS, PhD); music (MA, MM, DMA, PhD); natural and mathematical sciences (M Appl Stat, MA, MS, PhD); Near Eastern languages and cultures (MA, PhD); neuroscience (PhD); performance (MFA); philosophy (MA, PhD); physics (MS, PhD); political science (MA, PhD); psychology (MA); quantitative psychology (PhD); Russian literature (PhD); Slavic linguistics (PhD); social and behavioral sciences (MA, MS, Au D, PhD); social psychology (PhD); sociology (MA, PhD); Spanish and Portuguese (MA, PhD); speech hearing science (MA); speech-language pathology (MA, PhD); speech-language science (PhD); statistics (M Appl Stat, MS, PhD); theatre (MA, MFA, PhD); women's studies (MA, PhD). *Application deadline:* For fall admission, 8/15 priority date for domestic students, 7/1 priority date for international students; for winter admission, 12/1 priority date for domestic students, 11/1 priority date for international students; for spring admission, 3/1 priority date for domestic students, 2/1 priority date for international students. Applications are processed on a rolling basis. *Application fee:* $40 ($50 for international students). Electronic applications accepted. *Application Contact:* 614-292-9444, Fax: 614-292-3895, E-mail: domestic.grad@osu.edu. *Executive Dean and Vice Provost*, Joseph Steinmetz, 614-292-3236, E-mail: steinmetz.53@osu.edu.

College of Education and Human Ecology Students: 702 full-time (506 women), 562 part-time (418 women); includes 93 Black or African American, non-Hispanic/Latino; 5 American Indian or Alaska Native, non-Hispanic/Latino; 23 Asian, non-Hispanic/Latino; 29 Hispanic/Latino; 6 Two or more races, non-Hispanic/Latino, 209 international. Average age 33. *Faculty:* 178. Expenses: Contact institution. *Financial support:* Fellowships with tuition reimbursements, research assistantships with tuition reimbursements, teaching assistantships with tuition reimbursements, career-related internships or fieldwork, Federal Work-Study, institutionally sponsored loans, scholarships/grants, traineeships, health care benefits, and unspecified assistantships available. Support available to part-time students. In 2010, 595 master's, 84 doctorates awarded. Offers education and human ecology (M Ed, MA, MS, PhD); educational policy and leadership (M Ed, MA, PhD); family resource management (MS, PhD); fashion and retail studies (MS, PhD); food service management (MS, PhD); foods (MS, PhD); hospitality management (MS, PhD); human development and family science (M Ed, MS, PhD); nutrition (PhD); physical activity and educational services (M Ed, MA, PhD); teaching and learning (M Ed, MA, PhD). *Application deadline:* For fall admission, 8/15 priority date for domestic students, 7/1 priority date for international students; for winter admission, 12/1 priority date for domestic students, 11/1 priority date for international students; for spring admission, 3/1 priority date for domestic students, 2/1 priority date for international students. Applications are processed on a rolling basis. *Application fee:* $40 ($50 for international students). Electronic applications accepted. *Application Contact:* 614-292-9444, Fax: 614-292-3895, E-mail: domestic.grad@osu.edu. *Dean*, Cheryl Achterberg, 614-292-2461, Fax: 614-292-8052, E-mail: cachterberg@ehe.osu.edu.

College of Engineering Students: 1,309 full-time (297 women), 459 part-time (96 women); includes 24 Black or African American, non-Hispanic/Latino; 1 American Indian or Alaska Native, non-Hispanic/Latino; 56 Asian, non-Hispanic/Latino; 32 Hispanic/Latino; 5 Two or more races, non-Hispanic/Latino, 895 international. Average age 27. *Faculty:* 475. Expenses: Contact institution. *Financial support:* Fellowships, research assistantships, teaching assistantships, career-related internships or fieldwork, Federal Work-Study, institutionally sponsored loans, and unspecified assistantships available. Support available to part-time students. In 2010, 296 master's, 128 doctorates awarded. *Degree program information:* Part-time and evening/weekend programs available. Offers architecture (M Arch); biomedical engineering (MS, PhD); chemical engineering (MS, PhD); city and regional planning (MCRP, PhD); civil engineering (MS, PhD); computer and information science (MS, PhD); computer science and engineering (MS); electrical engineering (MS, PhD); engineering (M Arch, M Land Arch, MCRP, MS, MWE, PhD); geodetic science and surveying (MS, PhD); industrial and systems engineering (MS, PhD); landscape architecture (M Land Arch); materials science and engineering (MS, PhD); mechanical engineering (MS, PhD); nuclear engineering (MS, PhD); welding engineering (MS, MWE, PhD). *Application deadline:* For fall admission, 8/15 priority date for domestic students, 7/1 priority date for international students; for winter admission, 12/1 priority date for domestic students, 11/1 priority date for international students; for spring admission, 3/1 priority date for domestic students, 2/1 priority date for international students. Applications are processed on a rolling basis. *Application fee:* $40 ($50 for international students). Electronic applications accepted. *Application Contact:* 614-292-9444, Fax: 614-292-3895, E-mail: domestic.grad@osu.edu. *Dean*, Dr. David B. Williams, 614-292-2836, Fax: 614-292-9379, E-mail: williams.4219@osu.edu.

College of Food, Agricultural, and Environmental Sciences Students: 407 full-time (232 women), 138 part-time (64 women); includes 12 Black or African American, non-Hispanic/Latino; 16 Asian, non-Hispanic/Latino; 15 Hispanic/Latino; 1 Two or more races, non-Hispanic/Latino, 203 international. Average age 28. *Faculty:* 313. Expenses: Contact institution. *Financial support:* Fellowships, research assistantships, teaching assistantships, career-related internships or fieldwork, Federal Work-Study, institutionally sponsored loans, and unspecified assistantships available. Support available to part-time students. In 2010, 93 master's, 49 doctorates awarded. *Degree program information:* Part-time programs available. Offers agricultural and extension education (M Ed, MS, PhD); agricultural economics and rural sociology (MS, PhD); animal sciences (MS, PhD); entomology (MS, PhD); environment and natural resources (MS, PhD); food science (MS, PhD); food, agricultural, and biological engineering (MS, PhD); food, agricultural, and environmental sciences (M Ed, MS, PhD); horticulture and crop science (MS, PhD); human and community resource development (M Ed, MS, PhD); plant pathology (MS, PhD); rural sociology (MS, PhD); soil science (MS, PhD). *Application deadline:* For fall admission, 8/15 priority date for domestic students, 7/1 priority date for international students; for winter admission, 12/1 priority date for domestic students, 11/1 priority date for international students; for spring admission, 3/1 priority date for domestic students, 2/1 priority date for international students. Applications are processed on a rolling basis. *Application fee:* $40 ($50 for international students). Electronic applications accepted. *Application Contact:* Graduate Admissions, 614-292-9444, Fax: 614-292-3895, E-mail: domestic.grad@osu.edu. *Dean*, Dr. Bobby Moser, 614-292-6891, Fax: 614-292-1218, E-mail: moser.2@osu.edu.

College of Nursing Students: 234 full-time (201 women), 148 part-time (134 women); includes 19 Black or African American, non-Hispanic/Latino; 1 American Indian or Alaska Native, non-Hispanic/Latino; 11 Asian, non-Hispanic/Latino; 7 Hispanic/Latino; 6 Two or more races, non-Hispanic/Latino, 3 international. Average age 33. *Faculty:* 31. Expenses: Contact institution. *Financial support:* Fellowships, research assistantships, teaching assistantships, Federal Work-Study, institutionally sponsored loans, and unspecified assistantships available. Support available to part-time students. In 2010, 102 master's, 2 doctorates awarded. *Degree program information:* Part-time programs available. Offers nursing (MS, DNP, PhD). *Application deadline:* For fall admission, 8/15 priority date for domestic students, 7/1 priority date for international students; for winter admission, 12/1 priority date for domestic students, 11/1 priority date for international students; for spring admission, 3/1 priority date for domestic students, 2/1 priority date for international students. Applications are processed on a rolling basis. *Application fee:* $40 ($50 for international students). Electronic applications accepted. *Application Contact:* 614-292-9444, Fax: 614-292-3895, E-mail: domestic.grad@osu.edu. *Dean*, Dr. Elizabeth R. Lenz, 614-292-8900, Fax: 614-292-4535, E-mail: lenz.23@osu.edu.

College of Social Work Students: 325 full-time (288 women), 218 part-time (185 women); includes 53 Black or African American, non-Hispanic/Latino; 2 American Indian or Alaska Native, non-Hispanic/Latino; 7 Asian, non-Hispanic/Latino; 17 Hispanic/Latino; 3 Two or more races, non-Hispanic/Latino, 6 international. Average age 35. *Faculty:* 31. Expenses: Contact institution. *Financial support:* Fellowships, research assistantships, teaching assistantships, Federal Work-Study, institutionally sponsored loans, and unspecified assistantships available. Support available to part-time students. In 2010, 210 master's, 9 doctorates awarded. *Degree program information:* Part-time programs available. Offers social work (MSW, PhD). *Application deadline:* For fall admission, 8/15 priority date for domestic students, 7/1 priority date for international students; for winter admission, 12/1 priority date for domestic students, 11/1 priority date for international students; for spring admission, 3/1 priority date for domestic students, 2/1 priority date for international students. Applications are processed on a rolling basis. *Application fee:* $40 ($50 for international students). Electronic applications accepted. *Application Contact:* 614-292-9444, Fax: 614-292-3895, E-mail: domestic.grad@osu.edu. *Interim Dean*, Tom Gregoire, 614-292-6288, Fax: 614-292-6940, E-mail: gregoire.5@osu.edu.

John Glenn School of Public Affairs Students: 82 full-time (37 women), 114 part-time (72 women); includes 13 Black or African American, non-Hispanic/Latino; 7 Asian, non-Hispanic/Latino; 5 Hispanic/Latino; 4 Two or more races, non-Hispanic/Latino, 15 international. Average age 32. *Faculty:* 14. Expenses: Contact institution. *Financial support:* Fellowships, research assistantships, teaching assistantships, Federal Work-Study, institutionally sponsored loans, and unspecified assistantships available. Support available to part-time students. In 2010, 55 master's, 1 doctorate awarded. *Degree program information:* Part-time programs available. Offers public administration (MA, MPA); public policy and management (PhD). *Application deadline:* For fall admission, 8/15 priority date for domestic students, 7/1 priority date for international students; for winter admission, 12/1 priority date for domestic students, 11/1 priority date for international students; for spring admission, 3/1 priority date for domestic students, 2/1 priority date for international students. Applications are processed on a rolling basis. *Application fee:* $40 ($50 for international students). Electronic applications accepted. *Application Contact:* 614-292-9444, Fax: 614-292-3895, E-mail: domestic.grad@osu.edu. *Graduate Studies Committee Chair*, Charles R. Wise, 614-292-8696, Fax: 614-292-4868, E-mail: wise.983@osu.edu.

Max M. Fisher College of Business Students: 636 full-time (249 women), 347 part-time (128 women); includes 42 Black or African American, non-Hispanic/Latino; 3 American Indian or Alaska Native, non-Hispanic/Latino; 64 Asian, non-Hispanic/Latino; 19 Hispanic/Latino; 7 Two or more races, non-Hispanic/Latino, 247 international. Average age 30.

The Ohio State University (continued)

Faculty: 128. Expenses: Contact institution. *Financial support:* Fellowships, research assistantships, teaching assistantships, career-related internships or fieldwork, Federal Work-Study, institutionally sponsored loans, and unspecified assistantships available. Support available to part-time students. In 2010, 482 master's, 15 doctorates awarded. *Degree program information:* Part-time programs available. Offers accounting (M Acc, MA, MS); accounting and management information systems (M Acc, MA, MS, PhD); business (M Acc, MA, MBA, MBLE, MBOE, MLHR, MS, PhD); business administration (MA, MBA, PhD); business logistics engineering (MBLE); business operational excellence (MBOE); labor and human resources (MLHR, PhD); marketing (MBA, MS, PhD). *Application deadline:* For fall admission, 8/15 priority date for domestic students, 7/1 priority date for international students; for winter admission, 12/1 priority date for domestic students, 11/1 priority date for international students; for spring admission, 3/1 priority date for domestic students, 2/1 priority date for international students. Applications are processed on a rolling basis. *Application fee:* $40 ($50 for international students). Electronic applications accepted. *Application Contact:* Graduate Admissions, 614-292-9444, Fax: 614-292-3895, E-mail: domestic.grad@osu.edu. *Dean,* Christine A. Poon, 614-292-2666, E-mail: poon.36@osu.edu.

Moritz College of Law Offers law (JD, LL M, MSL). Electronic applications accepted.

THE OHIO STATE UNIVERSITY AT LIMA, Lima, OH 45804

General Information State-supported, coed, comprehensive institution. *Enrollment:* 1,530 graduate, professional, and undergraduate students; 34 full-time matriculated graduate/professional students (29 women), 66 part-time matriculated graduate/professional students (55 women). *Enrollment by degree level:* 99 master's, 1 doctoral. *Graduate faculty:* 41. Tuition, state resident: full-time $10,605. Tuition, nonresident: full-time $26,535. *Graduate housing:* On-campus housing not available. *Student services:* Campus safety program, career counseling, child daycare facilities, exercise/wellness program, free psychological counseling, grant writing training, international student services, low-cost health insurance, multicultural affairs office, services for students with disabilities, teacher training, writing training. *Library facilities:* Lima Campus Library. *Online resources:* library catalog, web page, access to other libraries' catalogs. *Collection:* 6.2 million titles, 75,963 serial subscriptions, 800 audiovisual materials.

Computer facilities: Computer purchase and lease plans are available. 150 computers available on campus for general student use. A campuswide network can be accessed. Online class registration is available. *Web address:* http://lima.osu.edu/.

General Application Contact: Graduate Admissions, 614-292-9444, Fax: 614-292-3985, E-mail: domestic.grad@osu.edu.

GRADUATE UNITS

Graduate Programs Students: 34 full-time (29 women), 66 part-time (55 women); includes 5 Black or African American, non-Hispanic/Latino; 1 Asian, non-Hispanic/Latino; 1 Two or more races, non-Hispanic/Latino. Average age 34. *Faculty:* 41. Expenses: Contact institution. *Degree program information:* Part-time programs available. Offers early childhood education (M Ed); education (MA); middle childhood education (M Ed); social work (MSW). *Application deadline:* For fall admission, 7/1 priority date for domestic and international students; for winter admission, 10/15 priority date for domestic and international students; for spring admission, 2/1 priority date for domestic and international students. Applications are processed on a rolling basis. *Application fee:* $40 ($50 for international students). Electronic applications accepted. *Application Contact:* Graduate Admissions, 614-292-9444, Fax: 614-292-3895, E-mail: domestic.grad@osu.edu. *Dean/Director,* Dr. John Snyder, 419-995-8481, E-mail: snyder.4@osu.edu.

THE OHIO STATE UNIVERSITY AT MARION, Marion, OH 43302-5695

General Information State-supported, coed, comprehensive institution. *Enrollment:* 1,816 graduate, professional, and undergraduate students; 57 full-time matriculated graduate/professional students (41 women), 10 part-time matriculated graduate/professional students (8 women). *Enrollment by degree level:* 67 master's. *Graduate faculty:* 39. Tuition, state resident: full-time $10,605. Tuition, nonresident: full-time $26,535. *Graduate housing:* On-campus housing not available. *Student services:* Campus employment opportunities, campus safety program, career counseling, child daycare facilities, exercise/wellness program, free psychological counseling, grant writing training, international student services, low-cost health insurance, multicultural affairs office, services for students with disabilities, teacher training, writing training. *Library facilities:* Marion Campus Library. *Online resources:* library catalog, web page, access to other libraries' catalogs. *Collection:* 6.2 million titles, 75,963 serial subscriptions, 1,576 audiovisual materials.

Computer facilities: Computer purchase and lease plans are available. 163 computers available on campus for general student use. A campuswide network can be accessed. Online class registration is available. *Web address:* http://osumarion.osu.edu/.

General Application Contact: Graduate Admissions, 614-292-9444, Fax: 614-292-3985, E-mail: domestic.grad@osu.edu.

GRADUATE UNITS

Graduate Programs Students: 57 full-time (41 women), 10 part-time (8 women); includes 1 Black or African American, non-Hispanic/Latino; 1 American Indian or Alaska Native, non-Hispanic/Latino. Average age 30. *Faculty:* 39. Expenses: Contact institution. *Degree program information:* Part-time programs available. Offers early childhood education (pre-K to grade 3) (M Ed); education—teaching and learning (MA); middle childhood education (grades 4-9) (M Ed). *Application deadline:* For fall admission, 7/1 priority date for domestic and international students; for winter admission, 10/15 priority date for domestic and international students; for spring admission, 2/1 priority date for domestic and international students. Applications are processed on a rolling basis. *Application fee:* $40 ($50 for international students). Electronic applications accepted. *Application Contact:* Graduate Admissions, 614-292-9444, Fax: 614-292-3895, E-mail: domestic.grad@osu.edu. *Dean/Director,* Dr. Gregory S. Rose, 740-389-6786 Ext. 6218, E-mail: rose.9@osu.edu.

THE OHIO STATE UNIVERSITY–MANSFIELD CAMPUS, Mansfield, OH 44906-1599

General Information State-supported, coed, comprehensive institution. *Enrollment:* 1,405 graduate, professional, and undergraduate students; 23 full-time matriculated graduate/professional students (22 women), 41 part-time matriculated graduate/professional students (37 women). *Enrollment by degree level:* 62 master's, 2 doctoral. *Graduate faculty:* 46 full-time (20 women). Tuition, state resident: full-time $10,605. Tuition, nonresident: full-time $26,535. *Graduate housing:* On-campus housing not available. *Student services:* Campus employment opportunities, campus safety program, career counseling, child daycare facilities, exercise/wellness program, free psychological counseling, grant writing training, international student services, low-cost health insurance, multicultural affairs office, services for students with disabilities, teacher training, writing training. *Library facilities:* Bromfield Library. *Online resources:* library catalog, web page, access to other libraries' catalogs. *Collection:* 6.2 million titles, 75,963 serial subscriptions.

Computer facilities: Computer purchase and lease plans are available. 260 computers available on campus for general student use. A campuswide network can be accessed. Online class registration is available. *Web address:* http://www.mansfield.osu.edu/.

General Application Contact: Graduate Admissions, 614-292-9444, Fax: 914-292-3895, E-mail: domestic.grad@osu.edu.

GRADUATE UNITS

Graduate Programs Students: 23 full-time (22 women), 41 part-time (37 women); includes 2 Black or African American, non-Hispanic/Latino; 1 Asian, non-Hispanic/Latino; 1 Hispanic/Latino; 2 Two or more races, non-Hispanic/Latino. Average age 33. *Faculty:* 46. Expenses: Contact institution. *Financial support:* Teaching assistantships with full tuition reimbursements, Federal Work-Study and scholarships/grants available. Support available to part-time students. Financial award application deadline: 7/1. *Degree program information:* Part-time programs available. Offers early childhood education (M Ed); education (MA); middle childhood education (M Ed); social work (MSW). *Application deadline:* For fall admission, 7/1 priority date for domestic and international students; for winter admission, 10/15 priority date for domestic and international students; for spring admission, 2/1 priority date for domestic and international students. Applications are processed on a rolling basis. *Application fee:* $40 ($50 for international students). Electronic applications accepted. *Application Contact:* Graduate Admissions, 614-292-9444, Fax: 614-292-3895, E-mail: domestic.grad@osu.edu. *Dean and Director,* Dr. Stephen M. Gavazzi, 419-755-4011, E-mail: gavazzi.1@osu.edu.

THE OHIO STATE UNIVERSITY–NEWARK CAMPUS, Newark, OH 43055-1797

General Information State-supported, coed, comprehensive institution. *Enrollment:* 2,562 graduate, professional, and undergraduate students; 42 full-time matriculated graduate/professional students (36 women), 53 part-time matriculated graduate/professional students (50 women). *Enrollment by degree level:* 94 master's, 1 doctoral. *Graduate faculty:* 55. Tuition, state resident: full-time $10,605. Tuition, nonresident: full-time $26,535. *Graduate housing:* Rooms and/or apartments available on a first-come, first-served basis to single and married students. *Student services:* Campus safety program, career counseling, child daycare facilities, exercise/wellness program, free psychological counseling, grant writing training, international student services, low-cost health insurance, multicultural affairs office, services for students with disabilities, teacher training, writing training. *Library facilities:* Newark Campus Library. *Online resources:* library catalog, web page, access to other libraries' catalogs. *Collection:* 6.2 million titles, 75,963 serial subscriptions, 1,000 audiovisual materials.

Computer facilities: Computer purchase and lease plans are available. 1,100 computers available on campus for general student use. A campuswide network can be accessed from student residence rooms. Online class registration is available. *Web address:* http://www.newark.osu.edu/.

General Application Contact: Graduate Admissions, 614-292-9444, Fax: 614-292-3985, E-mail: domestic.grad@osu.edu.

GRADUATE UNITS

Graduate Programs Students: 42 full-time (36 women), 53 part-time (50 women); includes 2 Black or African American, non-Hispanic/Latino; 1 Asian, non-Hispanic/Latino; 2 Hispanic/Latino, 1 international. Average age 33. *Faculty:* 55. Expenses: Contact institution. *Degree program information:* Part-time programs available. Offers early/middle childhood education (M Ed); education—teaching and learning (MA); social work (MSW). *Application deadline:* For fall admission, 7/1 priority date for domestic and international students; for winter admission, 10/15 priority date for domestic students, 10/1 priority date for international students; for spring admission, 2/1 priority date for domestic and international students. Applications are processed on a rolling basis. *Application fee:* $40 ($50 for international students). Electronic applications accepted. *Application Contact:* Graduate Admissions, 614-292-9444, Fax: 614-292-3985, E-mail: domestic.grad@osu.edu. *Dean/Director,* Dr. William L. MacDonald, 740-366-9333 Ext. 330, E-mail: macdonald.24@osu.edu.

OHIO UNIVERSITY, Athens, OH 45701-2979

General Information State-supported, coed, university. CGS member. *Enrollment:* 25,108 graduate, professional, and undergraduate students; 2,887 full-time matriculated graduate/professional students (1,496 women), 1,225 part-time matriculated graduate/professional students (709 women). *Enrollment by degree level:* 467 first professional, 2,737 master's, 908 doctoral. *Graduate faculty:* 961 full-time (361 women), 326 part-time/adjunct (151 women). *Graduate housing:* Rooms and/or apartments available on a first-come, first-served basis to single and married students. Housing application deadline: 5/1. *Student services:* Campus employment opportunities, campus safety program, career counseling, child daycare facilities, exercise/wellness program, free psychological counseling, grant writing training, international student services, low-cost health insurance, multicultural affairs office, services for students with disabilities, teacher training, writing training. *Library facilities:* Alden Library plus 3 others. *Online resources:* library catalog, web page, access to other libraries' catalogs. *Collection:* 3 million titles, 52,206 serial subscriptions, 78,291 audiovisual materials.

Computer facilities: Computer purchase and lease plans are available. 1,000 computers available on campus for general student use. A campuswide network can be accessed from student residence rooms and from off campus. Online class registration is available. *Web address:* http://www.ohio.edu/.

General Application Contact: Graduate College, 740-593-2800, Fax: 740-593-4625, E-mail: graduate@ohio.edu.

GRADUATE UNITS

College of Osteopathic Medicine Students: 466 full-time (262 women); includes 48 Black or African American, non-Hispanic/Latino; 9 American Indian or Alaska Native, non-Hispanic/Latino; 45 Asian, non-Hispanic/Latino; 20 Hispanic/Latino. Average age 25. 3,651 applicants, 5% accepted, 120 enrolled. *Faculty:* 80 full-time (33 women), 29 part-time/adjunct (9 women). Expenses: Contact institution. *Financial support:* In 2010–11, 171 students received support, including 7 fellowships with full tuition reimbursements available (averaging $44,864 per year); career-related internships or fieldwork, Federal Work-Study, institutionally sponsored loans, scholarships/grants, and tuition waivers (partial) also available. Financial award applicants required to submit FAFSA. In 2010, 110 DOs awarded. Offers osteopathic medicine (DO). *Application deadline:* For fall admission, 2/1 for domestic students. Applications are processed on a rolling basis. *Application fee:* $50. Electronic applications accepted. *Application Contact:* Dr. John D. Schriner, Director of Admissions, 740-593-4313, Fax: 740-593-2256, E-mail: admissions@exchange.oucom.ohiou.edu. *Dean,* Dr. John A. Brose, 740-593-9350, Fax: 740-593-0761, E-mail: wilcox@ohio.edu.

Graduate College Students: 2,889 full-time (1,496 women), 1,225 part-time (709 women); includes 353 minority (174 Black or African American, non-Hispanic/Latino; 11 American Indian or Alaska Native, non-Hispanic/Latino; 40 Asian, non-Hispanic/Latino; 74 Hispanic/Latino; 1 Native Hawaiian or other Pacific Islander, non-Hispanic/Latino; 53 Two or more races, non-Hispanic/Latino), 749 international. 4,029 applicants, 42% accepted, 1242 enrolled. *Faculty:* 898 full-time (339 women), 283 part-time/adjunct (132 women). Expenses: Contact institution. *Financial support:* Fellowships with full tuition reimbursements, research assistantships with full and partial tuition reimbursements, teaching assistantships with full and partial tuition reimbursements, career-related internships or fieldwork, Federal Work-Study, institutionally sponsored loans, scholarships/grants, traineeships, tuition waivers (full and partial), and unspecified assistantships available. Financial award applicants required to submit FAFSA. In 2010, 1,202 master's, 166 doctorates awarded. *Degree program information:* Part-time and evening/weekend programs available. Postbaccalaureate distance learning degree programs offered (minimal on-campus study). *Application fee:* $50 ($55 for international students). Electronic applications accepted. *Application Contact:* Marnie Miller, Student Services Coordinator, 740-593-2800, Fax: 740-593-4625, E-mail: graduate@ohio.edu. *Vice President for Research and Creative Activity/Dean,* Dr. Rathindra Bose, 740-593-2800, Fax: 740-593-4625, E-mail: graduate@ohio.edu.

Center for International Studies Students: 105 full-time (64 women), 9 part-time (6 women); includes 17 minority (12 Black or African American, non-Hispanic/Latino; 4 Hispanic/Latino; 1 Two or more races, non-Hispanic/Latino), 60 international. 234 applicants, 60% accepted, 54 enrolled. *Faculty:* 1 full-time (0 women). Expenses: Contact institution. *Financial support:* Fellowships with full tuition reimbursements, research assistantships with full and partial tuition reimbursements, teaching assistantships with full and partial tuition reimbursements, career-related internships or fieldwork, Federal Work-Study, institutionally sponsored loans, scholarships/grants, tuition waivers (partial), and unspecified assistantships available. Financial award application deadline: 1/1. In 2010, 78 master's awarded. *Degree program information:* Part-time programs available. Offers African studies (MA); communications and development studies (MA); international development studies (MA); international studies (MA); Latin American studies (MA); Southeast Asian studies (MA). *Application deadline:* For fall admission, 1/1 for domestic and international students. *Application fee:* $50 ($55 for international students). Electronic applications accepted. *Application Contact:* Joan

Kraynanski, Administrative Assistant, 740-593-1840, Fax: 740-593-1837, E-mail: kraynans@ohio.edu. *Director*, Dr. Daniel Weiner, 740-593-1889, Fax: 740-593-1837, E-mail: weinerd1@ohio.edu.

College of Arts and Sciences Students: 714 full-time (317 women), 132 part-time (69 women); includes 63 minority (22 Black or African American, non-Hispanic/Latino; 3 American Indian or Alaska Native, non-Hispanic/Latino; 9 Asian, non-Hispanic/Latino; 16 Hispanic/Latino; 13 Two or more races, non-Hispanic/Latino), 282 international. 1,343 applicants, 33% accepted, 255 enrolled. *Faculty:* 425 full-time (166 women), 121 part-time/adjunct (58 women). Expenses: Contact institution. *Financial support:* Fellowships with full tuition reimbursements, research assistantships with full tuition reimbursements, teaching assistantships with full tuition reimbursements, career-related internships or fieldwork, Federal Work-Study, institutionally sponsored loans, scholarships/grants, traineeships, tuition waivers (full and partial), and unspecified assistantships available. In 2010, 254 master's, 63 doctorates awarded. *Degree program information:* Part-time and evening/weekend programs available. Offers applied economics (MA); applied linguistics/TESOL (MA); arts and sciences (MA, MFE, MS, MSS, MSW, PhD); astronomy (MS, PhD); biological sciences (MS, PhD); cell biology and physiology (MS, PhD); chemistry and biochemistry (MS, PhD); clinical psychology (PhD); ecology and evolutionary biology (MS, PhD); English language and literature (MA, PhD); environmental and plant biology (MS, PhD); environmental geochemistry (MS); environmental geology (MS); environmental studies (MS); environmental/hydrology (MS); exercise physiology and muscle biology (MS, PhD); experimental psychology (PhD); financial economics (MFE); French (MA); geography (MA); geology (MS); geology education (MS); geomorphology/surficial processes (MS); geophysics (MS); history (MA, PhD); hydrogeology (MS); mathematics (MS, PhD); microbiology (MS, PhD); molecular and cellular biology (MS, PhD); neuroscience (MS, PhD); organizational psychology (PhD); philosophy (MA); physics (MS, PhD); political science (MA); sedimentology (MS); social sciences (MSS); social work (MSW); sociology (MA); Spanish (MA); structure/tectonics (MS). *Application fee:* $50 ($55 for international students). Electronic applications accepted. *Application Contact:* Dr. Ben M. Ogles, Dean, 740-593-2850, Fax: 740-593-0053, E-mail: ogles@ohio.edu. *Dean*, Dr. Ben M. Ogles, 740-593-2850, Fax: 740-593-0053, E-mail: ogles@ohio.edu.

College of Business Students: 162 full-time (51 women), 91 part-time (23 women); includes 42 minority (23 Black or African American, non-Hispanic/Latino; 1 American Indian or Alaska Native, non-Hispanic/Latino; 5 Asian, non-Hispanic/Latino; 8 Hispanic/Latino; 5 Two or more races, non-Hispanic/Latino), 9 international. 193 applicants, 55% accepted, 55 enrolled. *Faculty:* 64 full-time (22 women), 22 part-time/adjunct (8 women). Expenses: Contact institution. *Financial support:* Research assistantships with full and partial tuition reimbursements, career-related internships or fieldwork, Federal Work-Study, institutionally sponsored loans, and unspecified assistantships available. Financial award application deadline: 2/1. In 2010, 233 master's awarded. *Degree program information:* Part-time and evening/weekend programs available. Offers business (EMBA, MBA, MS, MSA); business administration (EMBA, MBA); recreation and sport sciences (MS); sports administration (MSA). *Application deadline:* For fall admission, 2/1 priority date for domestic and international students. *Application fee:* $50 ($55 for international students). Electronic applications accepted. *Application Contact:* Jan Ross, Assistant Dean, 740-593-2007, Fax: 740-593-1388, E-mail: rossj@ohio.edu. *Dean*, Dr. Hugh Sherman, 740-593-2001, Fax: 740-593-1388, E-mail: shermanh@ohio.edu.

College of Fine Arts Students: 227 full-time (113 women), 27 part-time (11 women); includes 27 minority (7 Black or African American, non-Hispanic/Latino; 2 American Indian or Alaska Native, non-Hispanic/Latino; 5 Asian, non-Hispanic/Latino; 9 Hispanic/Latino; 4 Two or more races, non-Hispanic/Latino), 41 international. 465 applicants, 27% accepted, 89 enrolled. *Faculty:* 98 full-time (41 women), 30 part-time/adjunct (14 women). Expenses: Contact institution. *Financial support:* Research assistantships with full and partial tuition reimbursements, teaching assistantships with full and partial tuition reimbursements, career-related internships or fieldwork, Federal Work-Study, institutionally sponsored loans, scholarships/grants, tuition waivers (full and partial), and unspecified assistantships available. In 2010, 59 master's, 1 doctorate awarded. *Degree program information:* Part-time and evening/weekend programs available. Postbaccalaureate distance learning degree programs offered (minimal on-campus study). Offers accompanying (MM); art history (MA); ceramics (MFA); composition (MM); conducting (MM); film (MFA); film studies (MA); fine arts (MA, MFA, MM, PhD, Certificate); graphic design (MFA); history/literature (MM); interdisciplinary arts (PhD); music education (MM); music therapy (MM); painting (MFA); performance (MM, Certificate); performance/pedagogy (MM); photography (MFA); printmaking (MFA); sculpture (MFA); theater (MA, MFA); theory (MM). *Application fee:* $50 ($55 for international students). Electronic applications accepted. *Application Contact:* Jody Lamb, Graduate Admissions, 740-593-1811, E-mail: lambj@ohio.edu. *Dean*, Charles A. McWeeney, 740-593-1808, Fax: 740-593-0570, E-mail: mcweeny@ohio.edu.

College of Health Sciences and Professions Students: 282 full-time (204 women), 377 part-time (276 women); includes 67 minority (33 Black or African American, non-Hispanic/Latino; 1 American Indian or Alaska Native, non-Hispanic/Latino; 14 Asian, non-Hispanic/Latino; 11 Hispanic/Latino; 8 Two or more races, non-Hispanic/Latino), 37 international. 465 applicants, 43% accepted, 149 enrolled. *Faculty:* 58 full-time (29 women), 27 part-time/adjunct (16 women). Expenses: Contact institution. *Financial support:* Fellowships with tuition reimbursements, research assistantships with full and partial tuition reimbursements, teaching assistantships with full and partial tuition reimbursements, career-related internships or fieldwork, Federal Work-Study, institutionally sponsored loans, scholarships/grants, tuition waivers (partial), unspecified assistantships, and stipends available. In 2010, 181 master's, 43 doctorates awarded. *Degree program information:* Part-time and evening/weekend programs available. Postbaccalaureate distance learning degree programs offered (no on-campus study). Offers athletic training (MS); clinical audiology (Au D); communication sciences and disorders (MA, Au D, PhD); early child development and family life (MS); family nurse practitioner (MSN); family studies (MS); food and nutrition (MS); health administration (MHA); health sciences and professions (MA, MHA, MPH, MS, MSN, Au D, DPT, PhD); hearing science (PhD); nurse administrator (MSN); nurse administrator and family nurse practitioner (MSN); nurse educator (MSN); nurse educator and family nurse practitioner (MSN); nurse educator and nurse administrator (MSN); physical therapy (DPT); physiology of exercise (MS); public health (MPH); speech language pathology (MA); speech language science (PhD). *Application deadline:* Applications are processed on a rolling basis. *Application fee:* $50 ($55 for international students). Electronic applications accepted. *Application Contact:* Dr. Randy Leite, Interim Dean, 740-593-4756, Fax: 740-593-0285, E-mail: leite@ohio.edu. *Interim Dean*, Dr. Randy Leite, 740-593-4756, Fax: 740-593-0285, E-mail: leite@ohio.edu.

Gladys W. and David H. Patton College of Education and Human Services Students: 462 full-time (296 women), 340 part-time (189 women); includes 93 minority (55 Black or African American, non-Hispanic/Latino; 3 American Indian or Alaska Native, non-Hispanic/Latino; 3 Asian, non-Hispanic/Latino; 15 Hispanic/Latino; 1 Native Hawaiian or other Pacific Islander, non-Hispanic/Latino; 16 Two or more races, non-Hispanic/Latino), 73 international. 570 applicants, 72% accepted, 264 enrolled. *Faculty:* 65 full-time (36 women), 44 part-time/adjunct (24 women). Expenses: Contact institution. *Financial support:* Research assistantships with full and partial tuition reimbursements, teaching assistantships with full and partial tuition reimbursements, Federal Work-Study, institutionally sponsored loans, tuition waivers (full and partial), and unspecified assistantships available. Financial award application deadline: 3/15. In 2010, 281 master's, 24 doctorates awarded. *Degree program information:* Part-time and evening/weekend programs available. Offers adolescent to young adult education (M Ed); apparel, textiles, and merchandising (MS); coaching education (MS); college student personnel (M Ed); community/agency counseling (M Ed); computer education and technology (M Ed); counselor education (PhD); cultural studies (M Ed); curriculum and instruction (M Ed, PhD); early childhood/special education (M Ed); education and human services (M Ed, MS, MSA, Ed D, PhD); educational administration (M Ed, Ed D); educational research and evaluation (M Ed, PhD); higher education (PhD); instructional technology (PhD); intervention specialist/mild-moderate needs (M Ed); intervention specialist/moderate-intensive needs (M Ed); mathematics education (PhD); middle child education (M Ed); reading education (M Ed); recreation studies (MS); rehabilitation counseling (M Ed); school counseling (M Ed); social studies education (PhD). *Application deadline:* Applications are processed on a rolling basis. *Application fee:* $50 ($55 for international students). Electronic applications accepted. *Application Contact:* Floyd J. Doney, Director of Student Affairs, 740-593-4400, Fax: 740-593-9310, E-mail: doney@ohio.edu. *Dean*, Dr. Renee A. Middleton, 740-593-4403, E-mail: middletonr@ohio.edu.

Russ College of Engineering and Technology Students: 236 full-time (60 women), 77 part-time (9 women); includes 11 minority (2 Black or African American, non-Hispanic/Latino; 1 Asian, non-Hispanic/Latino; 5 Hispanic/Latino; 3 Two or more races, non-Hispanic/Latino), 185 international. 355 applicants, 54% accepted, 62 enrolled. *Faculty:* 90 full-time (10 women), 13 part-time/adjunct (2 women). Expenses: Contact institution. *Financial support:* Fellowships with full tuition reimbursements, research assistantships with full tuition reimbursements, teaching assistantships with full tuition reimbursements, career-related internships or fieldwork, Federal Work-Study, institutionally sponsored loans, and unspecified assistantships available. Financial award application deadline: 3/15. In 2010, 51 master's, 12 doctorates awarded. *Degree program information:* Part-time programs available. Offers biomedical engineering (MS); chemical engineering (MS, PhD); civil engineering (PhD); computer science (MS); construction (MS); electrical engineering (MS); electrical engineering and computer science (PhD); engineering and technology (M Eng Mgt, MS, PhD); environmental (MS); geotechnical and geoenvironmental (MS); industrial and systems engineering (M Eng Mgt, MS); industrial engineering (PhD); mechanical engineering (MS, PhD); mechanics (MS); structures (MS); transportation (MS); water resources and structures (MS). *Application deadline:* Applications are processed on a rolling basis. *Application fee:* $50 ($55 for international students). Electronic applications accepted. *Application Contact:* Dr. Shawn Ostermann, Associate Dean, 740-593-1482, Fax: 740-593-0659, E-mail: ostermann@ohio.edu. *Dean*, Dr. Dennis Irwin, 740-593-1482, Fax: 740-593-0659, E-mail: irwind@ohio.edu.

Scripps College of Communication Students: 160 full-time (92 women), 74 part-time (50 women); includes 19 minority (11 Black or African American, non-Hispanic/Latino; 1 American Indian or Alaska Native, non-Hispanic/Latino; 2 Asian, non-Hispanic/Latino; 4 Hispanic/Latino; 1 Two or more races, non-Hispanic/Latino), 57 international. 362 applicants, 49% accepted, 100 enrolled. *Faculty:* 90 full-time (30 women), 10 part-time/adjunct (4 women). Expenses: Contact institution. *Financial support:* Fellowships with tuition reimbursements, research assistantships with full and partial tuition reimbursements, teaching assistantships with full tuition reimbursements, career-related internships or fieldwork, Federal Work-Study, institutionally sponsored loans, tuition waivers (full and partial), and unspecified assistantships available. Financial award applicants required to submit FAFSA. In 2010, 65 master's, 23 doctorates awarded. *Degree program information:* Part-time programs available. Offers communication (MA, MCTP, MS, PhD); health communication (PhD); information and telecommunication systems (MCTP); journalism (MS, PhD); mass communication (PhD); media arts and studies (MA); organizational communication (MA); relating and organizing (PhD); rhetoric and public culture (PhD); visual communication (MA). *Application fee:* $50 ($55 for international students). Electronic applications accepted. *Application Contact:* Dr. Eric Rothenbuhler, Associate Dean, 740-593-4885, Fax: 740-593-0459. *Dean*, Dr. Gregory J. Shepherd, 740-593-4883, Fax: 740-593-0459, E-mail: shepherg@ohio.edu.

Voinovich School of Leadership and Public Affairs Students: 33 full-time (17 women), 1 (woman) part-time; includes 3 minority (1 Black or African American, non-Hispanic/Latino; 1 Hispanic/Latino; 1 Two or more races, non-Hispanic/Latino), 1 international. 65 applicants, 83% accepted, 12 enrolled. *Faculty:* 7 full-time (5 women), 1 part-time/adjunct (0 women). Expenses: Contact institution. Offers public administration (MPA). *Application fee:* $50 ($55 for international students). Electronic applications accepted. *Application Contact:* Dr. Judith Millesen, MPA Director, 740-593-4381, E-mail: millesen@ohio.edu. *Head*, Dr. Mark Weinberg, 740-593-4390, Fax: 740-593-9758, E-mail: weinberm@ohio.edu.

OHIO VALLEY UNIVERSITY, Vienna, WV 26105-8000

General Information Independent-religious, coed, comprehensive institution. *Enrollment:* 483 graduate, professional, and undergraduate students; 10 full-time matriculated graduate/professional students (6 women), 30 part-time matriculated graduate/professional students (24 women). *Enrollment by degree level:* 40 master's. *Graduate faculty:* 2 full-time (1 woman), 4 part-time/adjunct (2 women). *Tuition:* Full-time $9450; part-time $350 per credit hour. *Required fees:* $50 per course. *Library facilities:* Icy Belle Library. *Online resources:* library catalog, access to other libraries' catalogs. *Collection:* 34,000 titles, 455 serial subscriptions.

Computer facilities: 30 computers available on campus for general student use. A campuswide network can be accessed from student residence rooms. Online class registration is available. *Web address:* http://www.ovu.edu/.

General Application Contact: Brad Wilson, Coordinator of Recruiting and Retention, 304-865-6177, E-mail: brad.wilson@ovu.edu.

GRADUATE UNITS

School of Graduate Education Students: 10 full-time (6 women), 30 part-time (24 women). *Faculty:* 2 full-time (1 woman), 4 part-time/adjunct (2 women). Expenses: Contact institution. Postbaccalaureate distance learning degree programs offered. Offers education (M Ed). *Application fee:* $30. *Application Contact:* Dr. Daniel C. Doak, Chair, 304-865-6162, E-mail: daniel.doak@ovu.edu. *Chair*, Dr. Daniel C. Doak, 304-865-6162, E-mail: daniel.doak@ovu.edu.

OHR HAMEIR THEOLOGICAL SEMINARY, Cortlandt Manor, NY 10567

General Information Independent-religious, men only, comprehensive institution.

GRADUATE UNITS

Graduate Programs

OKLAHOMA CHRISTIAN UNIVERSITY, Oklahoma City, OK 73136-1100

General Information Independent-religious, coed, comprehensive institution. *Graduate housing:* Rooms and/or apartments available on a first-come, first-served basis to single and married students.

GRADUATE UNITS

Graduate School of Theology *Degree program information:* Part-time programs available. Postbaccalaureate distance learning degree programs offered (minimal on-campus study). Offers family life ministry (MA); ministry (M Div, MA); youth ministry (MA). Electronic applications accepted.

OKLAHOMA CITY UNIVERSITY, Oklahoma City, OK 73106-1402

General Information Independent-religious, coed, comprehensive institution. *Graduate housing:* Rooms and/or apartments available on a first-come, first-served basis to single and married students. Housing application deadline: 8/15.

GRADUATE UNITS

Kramer School of Nursing Offers nursing (MSN, DNP, PhD).

Margaret E. Petree College of Performing Arts Offers performing arts (MA, MFA, MM).

Ann Lacy School of American Dance and Arts Management Offers dance (MFA).

School of Theatre *Degree program information:* Part-time programs available. Offers costume design (MA); technical theater (MA); theater (MA); theater for young audiences (MA).

Wanda L. Bass School of Music *Degree program information:* Part-time programs available. Offers composition (MM); conducting (MM); musical theatre (MM); opera performance (MM); performance (MM).

Meinders School of Business *Degree program information:* Part-time and evening/weekend programs available. Offers accounting (MSA); business (MBA, MS, MSA); finance (MBA); health administration (MBA); information technology (MBA); integrated marketing communications (MBA); international business (MBA); marketing (MBA).

Oklahoma City University (continued)

Division of Computer Science *Degree program information:* Part-time and evening/weekend programs available. Offers computer science (MS).

Petree College of Arts and Sciences *Degree program information:* Part-time and evening/weekend programs available. Offers art (MLA); arts and sciences (M Ed, M Rel, MA, MCJ, MLA); general studies (MLA); leadership/management (MLA); literature (MLA); mass communications (MLA); philosophy (MLA); teaching English to speakers of other languages (MA); writing (MLA).

Division of Education and Kinesiology Exercise Studies *Degree program information:* Part-time and evening/weekend programs available. Offers applied behavioral studies (M Ed); early childhood education (M Ed); education and kinesiology exercise studies (M Ed); elementary education (M Ed).

Division of Sociology and Justice Studies *Degree program information:* Part-time and evening/weekend programs available. Offers applied sociology (MA); criminal justice (MCJ).

Wimberly School of Religion and Graduate Theological Center *Degree program information:* Part-time and evening/weekend programs available. Offers religion and theology (M Rel).

School of Law *Degree program information:* Part-time and evening/weekend programs available. Offers law (JD). Electronic applications accepted.

OKLAHOMA STATE UNIVERSITY, Stillwater, OK 74078

General Information State-supported, coed, university. CGS member. *Enrollment:* 23,522 graduate, professional, and undergraduate students; 2,075 full-time matriculated graduate/professional students (1,042 women), 2,879 part-time matriculated graduate/professional students (1,239 women). *Enrollment by degree level:* 344 first professional, 2,990 master's, 1,586 doctoral, 34 other advanced degrees. *Graduate faculty:* 1,157 full-time (385 women), 221 part-time/adjunct (100 women). Tuition, state resident: full-time $3716; part-time $154.85 per credit hour. Tuition, nonresident: full-time $14,892; part-time $621 per credit hour. *Required fees:* $2044; $85.20 per credit hour. One-time fee: $50. Tuition and fees vary according to course load and campus/location. *Graduate housing:* Rooms and/or apartments available on a first-come, first-served basis to single and married students. Typical cost: $3600 per year ($6800 including board) for single students; $9060 per year for married students. Room and board charges vary according to board plan and housing facility selected. *Student services:* Campus employment opportunities, campus safety program, career counseling, child daycare facilities, exercise/wellness program, free psychological counseling, grant writing training, international student services, low-cost health insurance, multicultural affairs office, services for students with disabilities, teacher training, writing training. *Library facilities:* Edmon Low Library plus 3 others. *Online resources:* library catalog, web page, access to other libraries' catalogs. *Research affiliation:* NextGen Aeronautics, Inc. (mechanical engineering), American Heart Association (physiological sciences), U.S. Golf Association (USGA) (plant and soil sciences), National Cattlemen's Beef Association (animal science), Cotton, Incorporated (plant and soil sciences), Howard Hughes Foundation (biological sciences).

Computer facilities: Computer purchase and lease plans are available. A campuswide network can be accessed from student residence rooms and from off campus. Online class registration is available. *Web address:* http://www.okstate.edu/.

General Application Contact: Dr. Gordon Emslie, Dean, 405-744-6368, Fax: 405-744-0355, E-mail: grad-i@okstate.edu.

GRADUATE UNITS

Center for Veterinary Health Sciences Expenses: Contact institution. *Financial support:* Fellowships, research assistantships, teaching assistantships, career-related internships or fieldwork, Federal Work-Study, and tuition waivers (partial) available. Support available to part-time students. Financial award application deadline: 3/1; financial award applicants required to submit FAFSA. Postbaccalaureate distance learning degree programs offered. Offers veterinary biomedical sciences (MS, PhD); veterinary health sciences (DVM, MS, PhD); veterinary medicine (DVM). *Application deadline:* Applications are processed on a rolling basis. *Application fee:* $50. *Application Contact:* Dr. Jerry R. Malayer, Associate Dean, Research and Graduate Education, 405-744-8085, Fax: 405-744-8263, E-mail: jerry.malayer@okstate.edu. *Associate Dean, Research and Graduate Education,* Dr. Jerry R. Malayer, 405-744-8085, Fax: 405-744-8263, E-mail: jerry.malayer@okstate.edu.

College of Agricultural Science and Natural Resources Students: 175 full-time (86 women), 317 part-time (150 women); includes 7 Black or African American, non-Hispanic/Latino; 18 American Indian or Alaska Native, non-Hispanic/Latino; 6 Asian, non-Hispanic/Latino; 7 Hispanic/Latino, 196 international. Average age 29. 516 applicants, 35% accepted, 104 enrolled. *Faculty:* 244 full-time (57 women), 18 part-time/adjunct (2 women). Expenses: Contact institution. *Financial support:* In 2010–11, 299 research assistantships (averaging $15,727 per year), 20 teaching assistantships (averaging $15,655 per year) were awarded; fellowships, career-related internships or fieldwork, Federal Work-Study, scholarships/grants, health care benefits, tuition waivers (partial), and unspecified assistantships also available. Support available to part-time students. Financial award application deadline: 3/1; financial award applicants required to submit FAFSA. In 2010, 103 master's, 32 doctorates awarded. Postbaccalaureate distance learning degree programs offered. Offers agricultural economics (M Ag, MS, PhD); agricultural education, communications and leadership (M Ag, MS, PhD); agricultural science and natural resources (M Ag, MS, PhD); agriculture (M Ag); animal sciences (M Ag, MS); biochemistry and molecular biology (MS, PhD); biosystems engineering (MS, PhD); crop science (PhD); entomology (PhD); entomology and plant pathology (MS); environmental and natural resources (MS, PhD); environmental science (PhD); food science (MS, PhD); horticulture (MS); international agriculture (M Ag); natural resource ecology and management (M Ag, MS, PhD); plant and soil sciences (MS); plant pathology (PhD); plant science (PhD); soil science (M Ag, PhD). *Application deadline:* For fall admission, 3/1 priority date for international students; for spring admission, 8/1 priority date for international students. Applications are processed on a rolling basis. *Application fee:* $40 ($75 for international students). Electronic applications accepted. *Application Contact:* Dr. Gordon Emslie, Dean, 405-744-6368, Fax: 405-744-0355, E-mail: grad-i@okstate.edu. *Dean,* Dr. Robert E. Whitson, 405-744-5398, Fax: 405-744-2480.

College of Arts and Sciences Students: 326 full-time (148 women), 659 part-time (255 women); includes 18 Black or African American, non-Hispanic/Latino; 37 American Indian or Alaska Native, non-Hispanic/Latino; 15 Asian, non-Hispanic/Latino; 22 Hispanic/Latino, 259 international. Average age 31. 1,478 applicants, 30% accepted, 220 enrolled. *Faculty:* 409 full-time (132 women), 60 part-time/adjunct (33 women). Expenses: Contact institution. *Financial support:* In 2010–11, 120 research assistantships (averaging $15,850 per year), 509 teaching assistantships (averaging $14,211 per year) were awarded; career-related internships or fieldwork, Federal Work-Study, scholarships/grants, health care benefits, tuition waivers (partial), and unspecified assistantships also available. Support available to part-time students. Financial award application deadline: 3/1; financial award applicants required to submit FAFSA. In 2010, 149 master's, 49 doctorates awarded. Offers applied mathematics (MS, PhD); arts and sciences (MA, MFA, MM, MS, PhD); botany (MS); chemistry (MS, PhD); clinical psychology (PhD); communications sciences and disorders (MS); computer science (MS, PhD); creative writing (MFA); English (MA, PhD); environmental science (MS, PhD); fire and emergency management administration (MS, PhD); general psychology (MS); geography (MS, PhD); history (MA, PhD); lifespan development psychology (PhD); mathematics education (MS, PhD); microbiology and molecular genetics (MS, PhD); pedagogy and performance (MM); philosophy (MA); photonics (MS, PhD); physics (MS, PhD); plant science (PhD); political science (MA); pure mathematics (MS, PhD); sociology (MS, PhD); statistics (MS, PhD); theatre (MA); zoology (MS, PhD). *Application deadline:* For fall admission, 3/1 priority date for international students; for spring admission, 8/1 priority date for international students. Applications are processed on a rolling basis. *Application fee:* $40 ($75 for international students). Electronic applications accepted. *Application Contact:* Dr. Gordon Emslie, Dean, 405-744-6368, Fax: 405-744-0355, E-mail: grad-i@okstate.edu. *Dean,* Dr. Peter M. A. Sherwood, 405-744-5663, Fax: 405-744-1797.

School of Geology Students: 35 full-time (8 women), 23 part-time (9 women); includes 1 American Indian or Alaska Native, non-Hispanic/Latino; 1 Hispanic/Latino, 14 international. Average age 29. 73 applicants, 40% accepted, 16 enrolled. *Faculty:* 11 full-time (3 women), 2 part-time/adjunct (1 woman). Expenses: Contact institution. *Financial support:* In 2010–11, 8 research assistantships (averaging $10,418 per year), 20 teaching assistantships (averaging $8,053 per year) were awarded; career-related internships or fieldwork, Federal Work-Study, scholarships/grants, health care benefits, tuition waivers (partial), and unspecified assistantships also available. Support available to part-time students. Financial award application deadline: 3/1; financial award applicants required to submit FAFSA. In 2010, 9 master's, 2 doctorates awarded. Offers geology (MS, PhD). *Application deadline:* For fall admission, 3/1 priority date for international students; for spring admission, 8/1 priority date for international students. Applications are processed on a rolling basis. *Application fee:* $40 ($75 for international students). Electronic applications accepted. *Application Contact:* Dr. Gordon Emslie, Dean, 405-744-6368, Fax: 405-744-0355, E-mail: grad-i@okstate.edu. *Head,* Dr. Jay Gregg, 405-744-6358, Fax: 405-744-7841.

School of Media and Strategic Communications Students: 14 full-time (9 women), 21 part-time (11 women); includes 2 Black or African American, non-Hispanic/Latino; 3 American Indian or Alaska Native, non-Hispanic/Latino; 1 Hispanic/Latino, 4 international. Average age 30. 27 applicants, 30% accepted, 8 enrolled. *Faculty:* 19 full-time (7 women), 5 part-time/adjunct (1 woman). Expenses: Contact institution. *Financial support:* In 2010–11, 1 research assistantship (averaging $5,550 per year), 5 teaching assistantships (averaging $10,301 per year) were awarded; career-related internships or fieldwork, Federal Work-Study, scholarships/grants, health care benefits, tuition waivers (partial), and unspecified assistantships also available. Support available to part-time students. Financial award application deadline: 3/1; financial award applicants required to submit FAFSA. In 2010, 8 master's awarded. Offers mass communication (MS). *Application deadline:* For fall admission, 3/1 priority date for international students; for spring admission, 8/1 priority date for international students. Applications are processed on a rolling basis. *Application fee:* $40 ($75 for international students). Electronic applications accepted. *Application Contact:* Dr. Gordon Emslie, Dean, 405-744-6368, Fax: 405-744-0355, E-mail: grad-i@okstate.edu. *Director,* Dr. Derina Holtzhausen, 405-744-6354, Fax: 405-744-7104.

College of Education Students: 313 full-time (216 women), 660 part-time (445 women); includes 64 Black or African American, non-Hispanic/Latino; 85 American Indian or Alaska Native, non-Hispanic/Latino; 15 Asian, non-Hispanic/Latino; 24 Hispanic/Latino, 56 international. Average age 36. 506 applicants, 42% accepted, 167 enrolled. *Faculty:* 104 full-time (60 women), 67 part-time/adjunct (33 women). Expenses: Contact institution. *Financial support:* In 2010–11, 60 research assistantships (averaging $8,812 per year), 85 teaching assistantships (averaging $8,707 per year) were awarded; career-related internships or fieldwork, Federal Work-Study, scholarships/grants, health care benefits, tuition waivers (partial), and unspecified assistantships also available. Support available to part-time students. Financial award application deadline: 3/1; financial award applicants required to submit FAFSA. In 2010, 155 master's, 44 doctorates awarded. *Degree program information:* Part-time programs available. Postbaccalaureate distance learning degree programs offered. Offers education (MS, Ed D, PhD, Ed S). *Application deadline:* For fall admission, 3/1 priority date for international students; for spring admission, 8/1 priority date for international students. Applications are processed on a rolling basis. *Application fee:* $40 ($75 for international students). Electronic applications accepted. *Application Contact:* Dr. Gordon Emslie, Dean, 405-744-6368, Fax: 405-744-0355, E-mail: grad-i@okstate.edu. *Dean,* Dr. Pamela Fry, 405-744-3373, Fax: 405-744-6399.

School of Applied Health and Educational Psychology Students: 199 full-time (144 women), 146 part-time (104 women); includes 25 Black or African American, non-Hispanic/Latino; 27 American Indian or Alaska Native, non-Hispanic/Latino; 12 Asian, non-Hispanic/Latino; 12 Hispanic/Latino, 13 international. Average age 31. 247 applicants, 35% accepted, 65 enrolled. *Faculty:* 38 full-time (17 women), 19 part-time/adjunct (11 women). Expenses: Contact institution. *Financial support:* In 2010–11, 30 research assistantships (averaging $6,839 per year), 64 teaching assistantships (averaging $8,416 per year) were awarded; career-related internships or fieldwork, Federal Work-Study, scholarships/grants, health care benefits, tuition waivers (partial), and unspecified assistantships also available. Support available to part-time students. Financial award application deadline: 3/1; financial award applicants required to submit FAFSA. In 2010, 72 master's, 16 doctorates awarded. *Degree program information:* Part-time programs available. Offers applied behavioral studies (Ed D); applied health and educational psychology (MS, PhD, Ed S). *Application deadline:* For fall admission, 3/1 priority date for international students; for spring admission, 8/1 priority date for international students. Applications are processed on a rolling basis. *Application fee:* $40 ($75 for international students). Electronic applications accepted. *Application Contact:* Dr. Gordon Emslie, Dean, 405-744-6368, Fax: 405-744-0355, E-mail: grad-i@okstate.edu. *Head,* Dr. John Romans, 405-744-6040, Fax: 405-744-6779.

School of Educational Studies Students: 62 full-time (32 women), 270 part-time (155 women); includes 21 Black or African American, non-Hispanic/Latino; 33 American Indian or Alaska Native, non-Hispanic/Latino; 1 Asian, non-Hispanic/Latino; 5 Hispanic/Latino, 30 international. Average age 38. 134 applicants, 47% accepted, 48 enrolled. *Faculty:* 30 full-time (13 women), 27 part-time/adjunct (5 women). Expenses: Contact institution. *Financial support:* In 2010–11, 16 research assistantships (averaging $10,822 per year), 11 teaching assistantships (averaging $8,468 per year) were awarded; career-related internships or fieldwork, Federal Work-Study, scholarships/grants, health care benefits, tuition waivers (partial), and unspecified assistantships also available. Support available to part-time students. Financial award application deadline: 3/1; financial award applicants required to submit FAFSA. In 2010, 37 master's, 16 doctorates awarded. *Degree program information:* Part-time programs available. Offers higher education (Ed D). *Application deadline:* For fall admission, 3/1 priority date for international students; for spring admission, 8/1 priority date for international students. Applications are processed on a rolling basis. *Application fee:* $40 ($75 for international students). Electronic applications accepted. *Application Contact:* Dr. Gordon Emslie, Dean, 405-744-6368, Fax: 405-744-0355, E-mail: grad-i@okstate.edu. *Head,* Dr. Bert Jacobson, 405-744-6275, Fax: 405-744-7758.

School of Teaching and Curriculum Leadership Students: 52 full-time (40 women), 244 part-time (186 women); includes 18 Black or African American, non-Hispanic/Latino; 25 American Indian or Alaska Native, non-Hispanic/Latino; 2 Asian, non-Hispanic/Latino; 7 Hispanic/Latino, 13 international. Average age 38. 125 applicants, 51% accepted, 54 enrolled. *Faculty:* 35 full-time (29 women), 21 part-time/adjunct (17 women). Expenses: Contact institution. *Financial support:* In 2010–11, 13 research assistantships (averaging $10,705 per year), 10 teaching assistantships (averaging $10,839 per year) were awarded; career-related internships or fieldwork, Federal Work-Study, scholarships/grants, health care benefits, tuition waivers (partial), and unspecified assistantships also available. Support available to part-time students. Financial award application deadline: 3/1; financial award applicants required to submit FAFSA. In 2010, 46 master's, 12 doctorates awarded. *Degree program information:* Part-time programs available. Offers teaching and curriculum leadership (MS, PhD). *Application deadline:* For fall admission, 3/1 priority date for international students; for spring admission, 8/1 priority date for international students. Applications are processed on a rolling basis. *Application fee:* $40 ($75 for international students). Electronic applications accepted. *Application Contact:* Dr. Gordon Emslie, Dean, 405-744-6368, Fax: 405-744-0355, E-mail: grad-i@okstate.edu. *Head,* Dr. Christine Ormsbee, 405-744-7125, Fax: 405-744-6290.

College of Engineering, Architecture and Technology Students: 361 full-time (68 women), 448 part-time (69 women); includes 8 Black or African American, non-Hispanic/Latino; 15 American Indian or Alaska Native, non-Hispanic/Latino; 16 Asian, non-Hispanic/Latino; 10 Hispanic/Latino, 515 international. Average age 28. 1,174 applicants, 38% accepted, 193 enrolled. *Faculty:* 112 full-time (12 women), 6 part-time/adjunct (1 woman). Expenses: Contact institution. *Financial support:* In 2010–11, 250 research assistantships (averaging $11,510 per year), 170 teaching assistantships (averaging $8,002 per year) were awarded; career-related internships or fieldwork, Federal Work-Study, scholarships/grants, health care benefits, tuition waivers (partial), and unspecified assistantships also available. Support available to part-time students. Financial award application deadline: 3/1; financial award applicants required to submit FAFSA. In 2010, 209 master's, 21 doctorates awarded. Postbaccalaureate distance learning degree programs offered. Offers engineering, architecture and technology (MS, PhD). *Application deadline:* For fall admission, 3/1 priority date for international students; for spring admission, 8/1 priority date for international students. Applications are processed on a rolling basis. *Application fee:* $40 ($75 for international students). Electronic applications accepted. *Application Contact:* Dr. Gordon Emslie, Dean, 405-744-6368, Fax: 405-744-0355, E-mail: grad-i@okstate.edu. *Dean*, Dr. Karl N. Reid, 405-744-5140.

School of Chemical Engineering Students: 27 full-time (8 women), 25 part-time (7 women); includes 2 American Indian or Alaska Native, non-Hispanic/Latino; 1 Asian, non-Hispanic/Latino, 47 international. Average age 27. 110 applicants, 23% accepted, 10 enrolled. *Faculty:* 14 full-time (2 women), 1 part-time/adjunct (0 women). Expenses: Contact institution. *Financial support:* In 2010–11, 23 research assistantships (averaging $13,151 per year), 27 teaching assistantships (averaging $8,625 per year) were awarded; fellowships, career-related internships or fieldwork, Federal Work-Study, scholarships/grants, health care benefits, tuition waivers (partial), and unspecified assistantships also available. Support available to part-time students. Financial award application deadline: 3/1; financial award applicants required to submit FAFSA. In 2010, 13 master's, 8 doctorates awarded. Offers chemical engineering (MS, PhD). *Application deadline:* For fall admission, 3/1 priority date for international students; for spring admission, 8/1 priority date for international students. Applications are processed on a rolling basis. *Application fee:* $40 ($75 for international students). Electronic applications accepted. *Application Contact:* Dr. Gordon Emslie, Dean, 405-744-6368, Fax: 405-744-0355, E-mail: grad-i@okstate.edu. *Head*, Dr. Khaled A. M. Gasem, 405-744-5280, Fax: 405-744-6338.

School of Civil and Environmental Engineering Students: 40 full-time (11 women), 45 part-time (7 women); includes 1 Black or African American, non-Hispanic/Latino; 3 American Indian or Alaska Native, non-Hispanic/Latino; 2 Asian, non-Hispanic/Latino; 1 Hispanic/Latino, 46 international. Average age 28. 100 applicants, 36% accepted, 15 enrolled. *Faculty:* 15 full-time (1 woman), 3 part-time/adjunct (0 women). Expenses: Contact institution. *Financial support:* In 2010–11, 24 research assistantships (averaging $13,245 per year), 16 teaching assistantships (averaging $10,681 per year) were awarded; career-related internships or fieldwork, Federal Work-Study, scholarships/grants, health care benefits, tuition waivers (partial), and unspecified assistantships also available. Support available to part-time students. Financial award application deadline: 3/1; financial award applicants required to submit FAFSA. In 2010, 25 master's, 1 doctorate awarded. Offers civil engineering (MS); environmental engineering (PhD). *Application deadline:* For fall admission, 3/1 priority date for international students; for spring admission, 8/1 priority date for international students. Applications are processed on a rolling basis. *Application fee:* $40 ($75 for international students). Electronic applications accepted. *Application Contact:* Dr. Gordon Emslie, Dean, 405-744-6368, Fax: 405-744-0355, E-mail: grad-i@okstate.edu. *Head*, Dr. John Veenstra, 405-744-5190, Fax: 405-744-7554.

School of Electrical and Computer Engineering Students: 99 full-time (23 women), 107 part-time (20 women); includes 1 Black or African American, non-Hispanic/Latino; 2 American Indian or Alaska Native, non-Hispanic/Latino; 4 Asian, non-Hispanic/Latino; 3 Hispanic/Latino, 157 international. Average age 28. 393 applicants, 45% accepted, 48 enrolled. *Faculty:* 26 full-time (2 women). Expenses: Contact institution. *Financial support:* In 2010–11, 70 research assistantships (averaging $12,214 per year), 30 teaching assistantships (averaging $8,654 per year) were awarded; career-related internships or fieldwork, Federal Work-Study, scholarships/grants, health care benefits, tuition waivers (partial), and unspecified assistantships also available. Support available to part-time students. Financial award application deadline: 3/1; financial award applicants required to submit FAFSA. In 2010, 47 master's, 6 doctorates awarded. Postbaccalaureate distance learning degree programs offered. Offers electrical and computer engineering (MS, PhD). *Application deadline:* For fall admission, 3/1 priority date for international students; for spring admission, 8/1 priority date for international students. Applications are processed on a rolling basis. *Application fee:* $40 ($75 for international students). Electronic applications accepted. *Application Contact:* Dr. Gordon Emslie, Dean, 405-744-6368, Fax: 405-744-0355, E-mail: grad-i@okstate.edu. *Head*, Dr. Keith Teague, 405-744-5151, Fax: 405-744-9198.

School of Industrial Engineering and Management Students: 99 full-time (23 women), 107 part-time (20 women); includes 1 Black or African American, non-Hispanic/Latino; 2 American Indian or Alaska Native, non-Hispanic/Latino; 4 Asian, non-Hispanic/Latino; 3 Hispanic/Latino, 157 international. Average age 28. 393 applicants, 45% accepted, 48 enrolled. *Faculty:* 26 full-time (2 women). Expenses: Contact institution. *Financial support:* In 2010–11, 70 research assistantships (averaging $12,214 per year), 30 teaching assistantships (averaging $8,654 per year) were awarded; career-related internships or fieldwork, Federal Work-Study, scholarships/grants, health care benefits, tuition waivers (partial), and unspecified assistantships also available. Support available to part-time students. Financial award application deadline: 3/1; financial award applicants required to submit FAFSA. In 2010, 47 master's, 6 doctorates awarded. Postbaccalaureate distance learning degree programs offered. Offers industrial engineering and management (MS, PhD). *Application deadline:* For fall admission, 3/1 priority date for international students; for spring admission, 8/1 priority date for international students. Applications are processed on a rolling basis. *Application fee:* $40 ($75 for international students). Electronic applications accepted. *Application Contact:* Dr. Gordon Emslie, Dean, 405-744-6368, Fax: 405-744-0355, E-mail: grad-i@okstate.edu. *Head*, Dr. William J. Kolarik, 405-744-6055, Fax: 405-744-4654.

School of Mechanical and Aerospace Engineering Students: 89 full-time (10 women), 92 part-time (8 women); includes 1 American Indian or Alaska Native, non-Hispanic/Latino; 1 Asian, non-Hispanic/Latino; 1 Hispanic/Latino, 146 international. Average age 26. 297 applicants, 30% accepted, 48 enrolled. *Faculty:* 25 full-time (2 women), 1 part-time/adjunct (0 women). Expenses: Contact institution. *Financial support:* In 2010–11, 92 research assistantships (averaging $10,986 per year), 69 teaching assistantships (averaging $7,403 per year) were awarded; career-related internships or fieldwork, Federal Work-Study, scholarships/grants, health care benefits, tuition waivers (partial), and unspecified assistantships also available. Support available to part-time students. Financial award application deadline: 3/1; financial award applicants required to submit FAFSA. In 2010, 54 master's, 3 doctorates awarded. Postbaccalaureate distance learning degree programs offered. Offers mechanical and aerospace engineering (MS, PhD); mechanical engineering (MS, PhD). *Application deadline:* For fall admission, 3/1 priority date for international students; for spring admission, 8/1 priority date for international students. Applications are processed on a rolling basis. *Application fee:* $40 ($75 for international students). Electronic applications accepted. *Application Contact:* Dr. Gordon Emslie, Dean, 405-744-6368, Fax: 405-744-0355, E-mail: grad-i@okstate.edu. *Head*, Dr. Lawrence L. Hoberock, 405-744-5900, Fax: 405-744-7873.

College of Human Sciences Students: 109 full-time (95 women), 124 part-time (93 women); includes 13 Black or African American, non-Hispanic/Latino; 6 American Indian or Alaska Native, non-Hispanic/Latino; 4 Asian, non-Hispanic/Latino; 6 Hispanic/Latino, 64 international. Average age 32. 221 applicants, 36% accepted, 56 enrolled. *Faculty:* 75 full-time (51 women), 7 part-time/adjunct (4 women). Expenses: Contact institution. *Financial support:* In 2010–11, 66 research assistantships (averaging $9,462 per year), 60 teaching assistantships (averaging $9,516 per year) were awarded; career-related internships or fieldwork, Federal Work-Study, scholarships/grants, health care benefits, tuition waivers (partial), and unspecified assistantships also available. Support available to part-time students. Financial award application deadline: 3/1; financial award applicants required to submit FAFSA. In 2010, 39 master's, 16 doctorates awarded. Postbaccalaureate distance learning degree programs offered. Offers design, housing and merchandising (MS, PhD); family financial planning (MS); human development and family science (MS, PhD); human environmental sciences (PhD); human sciences (MS, PhD); marriage and family therapy (MS); nutritional sciences (MS, PhD). *Application deadline:* For fall admission, 3/1 priority date for international students; for spring admission, 8/1 priority date for international students. Applications are processed on a rolling basis. *Application fee:* $40 ($75 for international students). Electronic applications accepted. *Application Contact:* Dr. Gordon Emslie, Dean, 405-744-6368, Fax: 405-744-0355, E-mail: grad-i@okstate.edu. *Dean*, Dr. Stephan Wilson, 405-744-5053, Fax: 405-744-7113.

School of Hotel and Restaurant Administration Students: 21 full-time (15 women), 34 part-time (22 women); includes 3 Black or African American, non-Hispanic/Latino; 1 Asian, non-Hispanic/Latino; 3 Hispanic/Latino, 35 international. Average age 37. 30 applicants, 20% accepted, 3 enrolled. *Faculty:* 10 full-time (3 women), 3 part-time/adjunct (0 women). Expenses: Contact institution. *Financial support:* In 2010–11, 5 research assistantships (averaging $7,974 per year), 14 teaching assistantships (averaging $10,881 per year) were awarded; career-related internships or fieldwork, Federal Work-Study, scholarships/grants, health care benefits, tuition waivers (partial), and unspecified assistantships also available. Support available to part-time students. Financial award application deadline: 3/1; financial award applicants required to submit FAFSA. In 2010, 4 master's, 5 doctorates awarded. Offers hotel and restaurant administration (MS, PhD). *Application deadline:* For fall admission, 3/1 priority date for international students; for spring admission, 8/1 priority date for international students. Applications are processed on a rolling basis. *Application fee:* $40 ($75 for international students). Electronic applications accepted. *Application Contact:* Dr. Gordon Emslie, Dean, 405-744-6368, Fax: 405-744-0355, E-mail: grad-i@okstate.edu. *Director*, Dr. Bill Ryan, 405-744-6713, Fax: 405-744-6299.

Graduate College Students: 69 full-time (40 women), 131 part-time (68 women); includes 13 Black or African American, non-Hispanic/Latino; 15 American Indian or Alaska Native, non-Hispanic/Latino; 8 Asian, non-Hispanic/Latino; 8 Hispanic/Latino, 70 international. Average age 30. 690 applicants, 74% accepted, 75 enrolled. *Faculty:* 2 full-time (1 woman). Expenses: Contact institution. *Financial support:* In 2010–11, 2 research assistantships (averaging $12,900 per year) were awarded; career-related internships or fieldwork, Federal Work-Study, scholarships/grants, health care benefits, tuition waivers (partial), and unspecified assistantships also available. Support available to part-time students. Financial award application deadline: 3/1; financial award applicants required to submit FAFSA. In 2010, 66 master's, 7 doctorates awarded. Offers environmental science (MS); international studies (MS); natural and applied science (MS); photonics (PhD); plant science (PhD). Programs are interdisciplinary. *Application deadline:* For fall admission, 3/1 priority date for international students; for spring admission, 8/1 priority date for international students. Applications are processed on a rolling basis. *Application fee:* $40 ($75 for international students). Electronic applications accepted. *Application Contact:* Dr. Susan Mathew, Coordinator of Admissions, 405-744-6368, Fax: 405-744-0355, E-mail: grad-i@okstate.edu. *Dean*, Dr. Gordon Emslie, 405-744-6368, Fax: 405-744-0355, E-mail: grad-i@okstate.edu.

Spears School of Business Students: 377 full-time (123 women), 502 part-time (140 women); includes 19 Black or African American, non-Hispanic/Latino; 41 American Indian or Alaska Native, non-Hispanic/Latino; 14 Asian, non-Hispanic/Latino; 13 Hispanic/Latino, 168 international. Average age 29. 1,075 applicants, 36% accepted, 255 enrolled. *Faculty:* 118 full-time (29 women), 35 part-time/adjunct (9 women). Expenses: Contact institution. *Financial support:* In 2010–11, 39 research assistantships (averaging $11,833 per year), 80 teaching assistantships (averaging $14,124 per year) were awarded; career-related internships or fieldwork, Federal Work-Study, scholarships/grants, health care benefits, tuition waivers (partial), and unspecified assistantships also available. Support available to part-time students. Financial award application deadline: 3/1; financial award applicants required to submit FAFSA. In 2010, 283 master's, 10 doctorates awarded. *Degree program information:* Part-time programs available. Postbaccalaureate distance learning degree programs offered. Offers business (MBA, MS, PhD); business administration (MBA, PhD); economics and legal studies in business (MS, PhD); finance (PhD); management (MBA, MS, PhD); management information systems (MS); management science and information systems (PhD); marketing (MBA); quantitative financial economics (MS); telecommunications management (MS). *Application deadline:* For fall admission, 3/1 priority date for international students; for spring admission, 8/1 priority date for international students. Applications are processed on a rolling basis. *Application fee:* $40 ($75 for international students). Electronic applications accepted. *Application Contact:* Jan Analla, Assistant Director, 405-744-2951, E-mail: jan.analla@okstate.edu. *Dean*, Dr. Sara M. Freedman, 405-744-5064, Fax: 405-744-8956.

School of Accounting Students: 81 full-time (35 women), 33 part-time (17 women); includes 5 American Indian or Alaska Native, non-Hispanic/Latino, 14 international. Average age 26. 75 applicants, 44% accepted, 24 enrolled. *Faculty:* 17 full-time (6 women), 2 part-time/adjunct (0 women). Expenses: Contact institution. *Financial support:* In 2010–11, 5 research assistantships (averaging $18,984 per year), 28 teaching assistantships (averaging $9,314 per year) were awarded; career-related internships or fieldwork, Federal Work-Study, scholarships/grants, health care benefits, tuition waivers (partial), and unspecified assistantships also available. Support available to part-time students. Financial award application deadline: 3/1; financial award applicants required to submit FAFSA. In 2010, 44 master's, 1 doctorate awarded. *Degree program information:* Part-time programs available. Offers accounting (MS, PhD). *Application deadline:* For fall admission, 3/1 priority date for international students; for spring admission, 8/1 priority date for international students. Applications are processed on a rolling basis. *Application fee:* $40 ($75 for international students). Electronic applications accepted. *Application Contact:* Dr. Gordon Emslie, Dean, 405-744-6368, Fax: 405-744-0355, E-mail: grad-i@okstate.edu. *Head*, Dr. Don Hansen, 405-744-5123, Fax: 405-744-1680.

OKLAHOMA STATE UNIVERSITY CENTER FOR HEALTH SCIENCES, Tulsa, OK 74107-1898

General Information State-supported, coed, graduate-only institution. *Enrollment by degree level:* 368 first professional, 40 master's, 15 doctoral, 3 other advanced degrees. *Graduate housing:* On-campus housing not available. *Student services:* Campus safety program, career counseling, free psychological counseling, low-cost health insurance, services for students with disabilities. *Library facilities:* Oklahoma State University Center for Health Sciences Medical Library plus 1 other. *Online resources:* library catalog, web page, access to other libraries' catalogs. *Collection:* 53,994 titles, 12,573 serial subscriptions, 119,076 audiovisual materials. *Research affiliation:* Sun River, Inc. (cognitive rehabilitation), Merck & Company, Inc. (pharmaceutical sciences), Viropharma, Inc. (pharmaceutical sciences), Ingenex (pharmaceutical sciences), The Procter & Gamble Company (pharmaceutical sciences), Glaxo-Smith Kline (pharmaceutical sciences).

Computer facilities: 56 computers available on campus for general student use. A campuswide network can be accessed from off campus. Online class registration is available. *Web address:* http://www.healthsciences.okstate.edu/.

General Application Contact: Lindsey Kirkpatrick, Assistant Director of Admissions and Recruitment, 800-677-1972, Fax: 918-561-8243, E-mail: lindsey.kirkpatrick@okstate.edu.

GRADUATE UNITS

College of Osteopathic Medicine Students: 368 full-time (176 women); includes 106 minority (16 Black or African American, non-Hispanic/Latino; 37 American Indian or Alaska Native, non-Hispanic/Latino; 32 Asian, non-Hispanic/Latino; 21 Hispanic/Latino). Average age 28. 1,860 applicants, 8% accepted, 92 enrolled. *Faculty:* 25 full-time (6 women), 2 part-time/adjunct (1 woman). Expenses: Contact institution. *Financial support:* In 2010–11, 328 students received support. Federal Work-Study, institutionally sponsored loans, scholarships/grants, and tuition waivers available. Financial award application deadline: 3/31; financial award applicants required to submit FAFSA. In 2010, 80 DOs awarded. *Degree program information:* Part-time programs available. Offers osteopathic medicine (DO). *Application deadline:* For fall admission, 2/1 for domestic students. Applications are processed on a rolling basis. *Application fee:* $40. *Application Contact:* Lindsey Kirkpatrick, Assistant Director of Admissions and Recruitment, 800-677-1972, Fax: 918-561-8243, E-mail: lindsey.kirkpatrick@okstate.edu. *Provost and Dean, Center for Health Sciences*, Dr. Kayse Shrum, 918-561-8201, Fax: 918-561-8413, E-mail: lana.rusch@okstate.edu.

Graduate Program in Forensic Sciences Students: 7 full-time (6 women), 21 part-time (12 women); includes 5 minority (2 Black or African American, non-Hispanic/Latino; 2 Asian, non-Hispanic/Latino; 1 Hispanic/Latino). Average age 34. 21 applicants, 57% accepted, 7 enrolled. *Faculty:* 2 full-time (0 women), 14 part-time/adjunct (5 women). Expenses: Contact institution. *Financial support:* In 2010–11, 10 students received support, including 10 research assistantships (averaging $29,000 per year); career-related internships or fieldwork, Federal Work-Study, and tuition waivers (partial) also available. Support available to part-time students. Financial award application deadline: 4/1; financial award applicants required to submit FAFSA. In 2010, 6 master's awarded. *Degree program information:* Part-time and evening/weekend programs available. Postbaccalaureate distance learning degree programs offered (no on-campus study). Offers forensic DNA/molecular biology (MS); forensic examination of questioned documents (Certificate); forensic pathology (MS); forensic psychology (MS); forensic toxicology (MS). *Application deadline:* For fall admission, 3/1 for domestic and international students; for spring admission, 10/1 for domestic and international students. *Application fee:*

Oklahoma State University Center for Health Sciences (continued)

$40 ($75 for international students). *Application Contact:* Cathy Newsome, Coordinator, 918-561-1108, Fax: 918-561-8414, E-mail: cathy.newsome@okstate.edu. *Director*, Dr. Robert T. Allen, 918-561-1108, Fax: 918-561-8414.

Program in Biomedical Sciences Students: 20 full-time (13 women), 10 part-time (6 women); includes 11 minority (2 Black or African American, non-Hispanic/Latino; 4 American Indian or Alaska Native, non-Hispanic/Latino; 5 Asian, non-Hispanic/Latino), 5 international. Average age 31. 36 applicants, 61% accepted, 18 enrolled. *Faculty:* 25 full-time (6 women), 2 part-time/adjunct (1 woman). Expenses: Contact institution. *Financial support:* In 2010–11, 9 students received support, including 1 research assistantship with partial tuition reimbursement available (averaging $21,180 per year); scholarships/grants and tuition waivers (partial) also available. Financial award application deadline: 4/10; financial award applicants required to submit FAFSA. In 2010, 3 master's, 1 doctorate awarded. Offers biomedical sciences (MS, PhD). *Application deadline:* For fall admission, 2/15 for domestic students, 2/18 for international students; for winter admission, 9/15 for domestic and international students. *Application fee:* $40 ($75 for international students). *Application Contact:* Patrick Anderson, Coordinator of Graduate Admissions, 800-677-1972, Fax: 918-561-8243, E-mail: patrick.anderson@okstate.edu. *Director*, Dr. Greg L. Sawyer, 918-561-1221, Fax: 918-561-8276.

Program in Health Care Administration Expenses: Contact institution. Offers health care administration (MS). *Application deadline:* For fall admission, 7/1 for domestic students; for spring admission, 12/1 for domestic students. *Application Contact:* Leah Haines, Associate Director of Admissions and Registrar, 800-677-1972, Fax: 918-561-8243, E-mail: leah.haines@okstate.edu. *Director*, Dr. Leigh Goodson, 918-561-1406, Fax: 918-561-1416, E-mail: leigh.goodson@okstate.edu.

OLD DOMINION UNIVERSITY, Norfolk, VA 23529

General Information State-supported, coed, university. CGS member. *Enrollment:* 24,466 graduate, professional, and undergraduate students; 1,743 full-time matriculated graduate/professional students (1,056 women), 2,334 part-time matriculated graduate/professional students (1,264 women). *Enrollment by degree level:* 2,860 master's, 1,163 doctoral, 54 other advanced degrees. *Graduate faculty:* 616 full-time (216 women), 124 part-time/adjunct (66 women). Tuition, state resident: full-time $8592; part-time $358 per credit. Tuition, nonresident: full-time $21,672; part-time $903 per credit. *Required fees:* $119 per semester. One-time fee: $50. *Graduate housing:* Room and/or apartments available on a first-come, first-served basis to single students; on-campus housing not available to married students. Typical cost: $4840 per year ($8322 including board). Room and board charges vary according to board plan and housing facility selected. Housing application deadline: 5/1. *Student services:* Campus employment opportunities, campus safety program, career counseling, exercise/wellness program, free psychological counseling, grant writing training, international student services, low-cost health insurance, multicultural affairs office, services for students with disabilities, teacher training. *Library facilities:* Patricia W. and Douglas Perry Library plus 3 others. *Online resources:* library catalog, web page, access to other libraries' catalogs. *Collection:* 1.4 million titles, 42,205 serial subscriptions, 51,834 audiovisual materials. *Research affiliation:* Virginia Commercial Space Flight Authority (aerospace engineering), Joint Forces Command (modeling, simulation, and technology development), Thomas Jefferson National Accelerator Facility (high energy physics and laser processing), NASA–Langley Research Center (aerodynamic testing and evaluation), Eastern Virginia Medical Center (medicine), Mid-Atlantic Institute for Space and Technology (aerospace engineering).

Computer facilities: Computer purchase and lease plans are available. 1,130 computers available on campus for general student use. A campuswide network can be accessed from student residence rooms and from off campus. Online class registration, online courses are available. *Web address:* http://www.odu.edu/.

General Application Contact: William Heffelfinger, Director of Graduate Admissions, 757-683-5554, Fax: 757-683-3255, E-mail: gradadmit@odu.edu.

GRADUATE UNITS

College of Arts and Letters Students: 184 full-time (103 women), 202 part-time (118 women); includes 58 minority (27 Black or African American, non-Hispanic/Latino; 1 American Indian or Alaska Native, non-Hispanic/Latino; 6 Asian, non-Hispanic/Latino; 14 Hispanic/Latino; 2 Native Hawaiian or other Pacific Islander, non-Hispanic/Latino; 8 Two or more races, non-Hispanic/Latino), 40 international. Average age 32. 276 applicants, 66% accepted, 117 enrolled. *Faculty:* 135 full-time (61 women), 11 part-time/adjunct (4 women). Expenses: Contact institution. *Financial support:* In 2010–11, 214 students received support, including 6 fellowships with full and partial tuition reimbursements available (averaging $15,000 per year), 16 research assistantships with full and partial tuition reimbursements available (averaging $11,000 per year), 58 teaching assistantships with full and partial tuition reimbursements available (averaging $10,000 per year); career-related internships or fieldwork, institutionally sponsored loans, scholarships/grants, tuition waivers (partial), and unspecified assistantships also available. Support available to part-time students. Financial award application deadline: 2/15; financial award applicants required to submit CSS PROFILE or FAFSA. In 2010, 90 master's, 7 doctorates awarded. *Degree program information:* Part-time and evening/weekend programs available. Offers applied linguistics (MA); applied sociology (MA); arts and letters (MA, MFA, MME, PhD); creative writing (MFA); criminology and criminal justice (PhD); English (MA, PhD); history (MA); humanities (MA); lifespan and digital communication (MA); modeling and simulation (MA); music education (MME); women's studies (PhD). *Application deadline:* For fall admission, 6/1 priority date for domestic students, 2/15 for international students; for spring admission, 11/1 priority date for domestic students, 10/1 for international students. *Application fee:* $40. Electronic applications accepted. *Application Contact:* Dr. Robert Wojtowicz, Associate Dean, 757-683-6077, Fax: 757-683-5746, E-mail: rwojtowi@odu.edu. *Dean*, Dr. Chandra deSilva, 757-683-3925, Fax: 757-683-5746, E-mail: cdesilva@odu.edu.

College of Business and Public Administration Students: 200 full-time (101 women), 337 part-time (142 women); includes 122 minority (71 Black or African American, non-Hispanic/Latino; 3 American Indian or Alaska Native, non-Hispanic/Latino; 18 Asian, non-Hispanic/Latino; 21 Hispanic/Latino; 2 Native Hawaiian or other Pacific Islander, non-Hispanic/Latino; 7 Two or more races, non-Hispanic/Latino), 71 international. Average age 32. 356 applicants, 58% accepted, 128 enrolled. *Faculty:* 73 full-time (16 women), 12 part-time/adjunct (6 women). Expenses: Contact institution. *Financial support:* In 2010–11, 94 students received support, including 3 fellowships with partial tuition reimbursements available (averaging $15,000 per year), 133 research assistantships with full and partial tuition reimbursements available (averaging $9,150 per year), 8 teaching assistantships with full and partial tuition reimbursements available (averaging $15,000 per year); career-related internships or fieldwork, Federal Work-Study, scholarships/grants, tuition waivers (partial), and unspecified assistantships also available. Financial award application deadline: 2/15; financial award applicants required to submit FAFSA. In 2010, 165 master's, 7 doctorates awarded. *Degree program information:* Part-time and evening/weekend programs available. Postbaccalaureate distance learning degree programs offered (no on-campus study). Offers accounting (MS); business and economic forecasting (MBA); business and public administration (MA, MBA, MPA, MS, PhD); economics (MA); finance (PhD); financial analysis and valuation (MBA); information technology (PhD); information technology and enterprise integration (MBA); international business (MBA); maritime and port management (MBA); marketing (PhD); public administration (MPA); public administration and urban policy (PhD); strategic management (PhD). *Application deadline:* For fall admission, 6/1 priority date for domestic and international students; for winter admission, 11/1 priority date for domestic and international students. Applications are processed on a rolling basis. *Application fee:* $50. Electronic applications accepted. *Application Contact:* Dr. Ali Ardalan, Associate Dean, 757-683-3520, Fax: 757-683-4076, E-mail: aardalan@odu.edu. *Dean*, Dr. Gilbert Yochum, 757-683-3520, Fax: 757-683-4076, E-mail: gyochum@odu.edu.

College of Health Sciences Students: 265 full-time (209 women), 207 part-time (185 women); includes 112 minority (59 Black or African American, non-Hispanic/Latino; 1 American Indian or Alaska Native, non-Hispanic/Latino; 22 Asian, non-Hispanic/Latino; 16 Hispanic/Latino; 6 Native Hawaiian or other Pacific Islander, non-Hispanic/Latino; 8 Two or more races, non-Hispanic/Latino), 12 international. Average age 33. 688 applicants, 48% accepted, 258 enrolled. *Faculty:* 42 full-time (31 women), 17 part-time/adjunct (14 women). Expenses: Contact institution. *Financial support:* In 2010–11, 210 students received support, including 6 fellowships with full tuition reimbursements available (averaging $15,000 per year), 9 research assistantships with tuition reimbursements available (averaging $10,000 per year), 9 teaching assistantships with tuition reimbursements available (averaging $10,000 per year); career-related internships or fieldwork, institutionally sponsored loans, scholarships/grants, traineeships, tuition waivers (partial), and unspecified assistantships also available. Support available to part-time students. Financial award application deadline: 2/15; financial award applicants required to submit FAFSA. In 2010, 103 master's, 61 doctorates awarded. *Degree program information:* Part-time and evening/weekend programs available. Postbaccalaureate distance learning degree programs offered (minimal on-campus study). Offers community health and environmental health (MS); environmental health (MPH); health promotion (MPH); health sciences (MPH, MS, MSN, DNP, DPT, PhD); health services research (PhD); nursing practice (DNP). *Application deadline:* Applications are processed on a rolling basis. *Application fee:* $40. Electronic applications accepted. *Application Contact:* Dr. Deanne Shuman, Dean, 757-683-4960, Fax: 757-683-3674, E-mail: dshuman@odu.edu. *Dean*, Dr. Deanne Shuman, 757-683-4960, Fax: 757-683-3674, E-mail: dshuman@odu.edu.

School of Dental Hygiene Students: 7 full-time (5 women), 15 part-time (all women); includes 4 minority (3 Black or African American, non-Hispanic/Latino; 1 Asian, non-Hispanic/Latino), 4 international. Average age 31. 5 applicants, 80% accepted, 4 enrolled. *Faculty:* 7 full-time (all women). Expenses: Contact institution. *Financial support:* In 2010–11, 4 students received support, including 3 teaching assistantships with partial tuition reimbursements available (averaging $10,000 per year); fellowships, research assistantships, career-related internships or fieldwork, scholarships/grants, tuition waivers, and unspecified assistantships also available. Support available to part-time students. Financial award application deadline: 2/15; financial award applicants required to submit CSS PROFILE or FAFSA. In 2010, 5 master's awarded. *Degree program information:* Part-time programs available. Offers dental hygiene (MS). *Application deadline:* For fall admission, 7/1 for domestic students, 4/15 for international students; for spring admission, 12/1 for domestic students, 10/1 for international students. Applications are processed on a rolling basis. *Application fee:* $40. Electronic applications accepted. *Application Contact:* Prof. Gayle B. McCombs, Graduate Program Director, 757-683-3338, Fax: 757-683-5329, E-mail: smccombs@odu.edu. *Graduate Program Director*, Prof. Gayle B. McCombs, 757-683-3338, Fax: 757-683-5329, E-mail: smccombs@odu.edu.

School of Nursing Students: 84 full-time (76 women), 127 part-time (121 women); includes 51 minority (23 Black or African American, non-Hispanic/Latino; 1 American Indian or Alaska Native, non-Hispanic/Latino; 13 Asian, non-Hispanic/Latino; 7 Hispanic/Latino; 7 Native Hawaiian or other Pacific Islander, non-Hispanic/Latino). Average age 36. 163 applicants, 57% accepted, 80 enrolled. *Faculty:* 11 full-time (10 women), 15 part-time/adjunct (14 women). Expenses: Contact institution. *Financial support:* In 2010–11, 18 students received support, including 2 research assistantships with partial tuition reimbursements available (averaging $10,000 per year); teaching assistantships, career-related internships or fieldwork, scholarships/grants, traineeships, and tuition waivers (partial) also available. Support available to part-time students. Financial award application deadline: 2/15; financial award applicants required to submit FAFSA. In 2010, 80 master's awarded. *Degree program information:* Part-time programs available. Postbaccalaureate distance learning degree programs offered (no on-campus study). Offers family nurse practitioner (MSN); nurse administrator (MSN); nurse anesthesia (MSN); nurse educator (MSN); nurse midwifery (MSN); women's health nurse practitioner (MSN). *Application deadline:* For fall admission, 5/1 for domestic students, 4/15 for international students. Applications are processed on a rolling basis. *Application fee:* $50. Electronic applications accepted. *Application Contact:* Sue Parker, Coordinator, Graduate Student Services, 757-683-4298, Fax: 757-683-5253, E-mail: sparker@odu.edu. *Chair*, Dr. Karen Karlowicz, 757-683-5262, Fax: 757-683-5253, E-mail: nursgpd@odu.edu.

School of Physical Therapy Students: 127 full-time (93 women), 3 part-time (all women); includes 23 minority (12 Black or African American, non-Hispanic/Latino; 2 Asian, non-Hispanic/Latino; 3 Hispanic/Latino; 3 Native Hawaiian or other Pacific Islander, non-Hispanic/Latino; 3 Two or more races, non-Hispanic/Latino), 1 international. Average age 25. 475 applicants, 17% accepted, 45 enrolled. *Faculty:* 9 full-time (6 women), 6 part-time/adjunct (4 women). Expenses: Contact institution. *Financial support:* In 2010–11, 4 students received support, including 1 fellowship (averaging $15,000 per year), 4 teaching assistantships with partial tuition reimbursements available (averaging $7,500 per year); career-related internships or fieldwork and unspecified assistantships also available. Financial award applicants required to submit FAFSA. In 2010, 40 doctorates awarded. Offers physical therapy (DPT). *Application deadline:* For fall admission, 11/1 for domestic and international students. *Application fee:* $50. Electronic applications accepted. *Application Contact:* Dr. Martha Walker, Graduate Program Director, 757-683-4519, Fax: 757-683-4410, E-mail: ptgpd@odu.edu. *Graduate Program Director*, Dr. Martha Walker, 757-683-4519, Fax: 757-683-4410, E-mail: ptgpd@odu.edu.

College of Sciences Students: 281 full-time (143 women), 208 part-time (87 women); includes 30 minority (10 Black or African American, non-Hispanic/Latino; 10 Asian, non-Hispanic/Latino; 6 Hispanic/Latino; 1 Native Hawaiian or other Pacific Islander, non-Hispanic/Latino; 3 Two or more races, non-Hispanic/Latino), 193 international. Average age 29. *Faculty:* 136 full-time (34 women), 3 part-time/adjunct (0 women). Expenses: Contact institution. *Financial support:* In 2010–11, 3 fellowships (averaging $5,000 per year), 158 research assistantships with tuition reimbursements (averaging $18,000 per year), 101 teaching assistantships with tuition reimbursements (averaging $16,000 per year) were awarded; career-related internships or fieldwork, scholarships/grants, and tuition waivers (partial) also available. Support available to part-time students. Financial award application deadline: 2/15; financial award applicants required to submit FAFSA. In 2010, 93 master's, 32 doctorates awarded. *Degree program information:* Part-time and evening/weekend programs available. Offers analytical chemistry (MS); applied experimental psychology (PhD); biochemistry (MS); biology (MS); biomedical sciences (PhD); chemistry (PhD); clinical psychology (Psy D); computational and applied mathematics (MS, PhD); computer science (MS, PhD); ecological sciences (PhD); environmental chemistry (MS); human factors psychology (PhD); industrial/organizational psychology (PhD); ocean and earth sciences (MS); oceanography (PhD); organic chemistry (MS); physical chemistry (MS); physics (MS, PhD); psychology (MS, PhD); sciences (MS, PhD, Psy D). *Application fee:* $40. Electronic applications accepted. *Application Contact:* Dr. Chris Platsoucas, Dean, 757-683-3274, Fax: 757-683-3034, E-mail: cplatsoucas@odu.edu. *Dean*, Dr. Chris Platsoucas, 757-683-3274, Fax: 757-683-3034, E-mail: cplatsoucas@odu.edu.

Darden College of Education Students: 619 full-time (475 women), 850 part-time (640 women); includes 318 minority (210 Black or African American, non-Hispanic/Latino; 4 American Indian or Alaska Native, non-Hispanic/Latino; 22 Asian, non-Hispanic/Latino; 42 Hispanic/Latino; 6 Native Hawaiian or other Pacific Islander, non-Hispanic/Latino; 34 Two or more races, non-Hispanic/Latino), 14 international. Average age 33. 1,125 applicants, 72% accepted. *Faculty:* 94 full-time (55 women), 62 part-time/adjunct (40 women). Expenses: Contact institution. *Financial support:* In 2010–11, 141 students received support, including 4 fellowships with full and partial tuition reimbursements available (averaging $15,000 per year), 60 research assistantships with full and partial tuition reimbursements available (averaging $15,000 per year), 72 teaching assistantships with full and partial tuition reimbursements available (averaging $15,000 per year); career-related internships or fieldwork, Federal Work-Study, institutionally sponsored loans, scholarships/grants, tuition waivers (partial), and unspecified assistantships also available. Support available to part-time students. Financial award application deadline: 2/15; financial award applicants required to submit CSS PROFILE or FAFSA. In 2010, 608 master's, 49 doctorates, 31 other advanced degrees awarded. *Degree program information:* Part-time and evening/weekend programs available. Postbaccalaureate distance learning degree programs offered (no on-campus study). Offers athletic training (MS Ed); biology (MS Ed); business and industry training (MS); career and technical education (MS, PhD); chemistry (MS Ed); community college leadership (PhD); community college teaching (MS); counseling (MS Ed, PhD, Ed S); curriculum and instruction (MS Ed, PhD); early childhood education (MS Ed, PhD); education (MS, MS Ed, PhD, Ed S); educational leadership (MS Ed, PhD, Ed S); educational training (MS Ed); elementary education (MS Ed); English (MS Ed); exercise and wellness (MS Ed); higher education (MS Ed, PhD, Ed S);

human movement science (PhD); human resources training (PhD); instructional design and technology (PhD); instructional technology (MS Ed); library science (MS Ed); literacy leadership (PhD); middle school education (MS Ed); physical education (MS Ed); principal preparation (MS Ed); reading education (MS Ed); recreation and tourism studies (MS Ed); secondary education (MS Ed); special education (MS Ed, PhD); speech-language pathology (MS Ed); sport management (MS Ed); technology education (PhD). *Application deadline:* For fall admission, 6/1 priority date for domestic and international students; for spring admission, 11/1 priority date for domestic and international students. Applications are processed on a rolling basis. *Application fee:* $40. Electronic applications accepted. *Application Contact:* Nechell Bonds, Director of Admissions, 757-683-3685, Fax: 757-683-3255, E-mail: gradadmit@odu.edu. *Dean*, Dr. Linda Irwin-DeVitis, 757-683-3938, Fax: 757-683-5083, E-mail: ldevitis@odu.edu.

Frank Batten College of Engineering and Technology Students: 216 full-time (40 women), 530 part-time (92 women); includes 120 minority (57 Black or African American, non-Hispanic/Latino; 2 American Indian or Alaska Native, non-Hispanic/Latino; 23 Asian, non-Hispanic/Latino; 23 Hispanic/Latino; 2 Native Hawaiian or other Pacific Islander, non-Hispanic/Latino; 13 Two or more races, non-Hispanic/Latino), 205 international. Average age 32. 558 applicants, 63% accepted, 144 enrolled. *Faculty:* 93 full-time (12 women), 32 part-time/adjunct (5 women). Expenses: Contact institution. *Financial support:* In 2010–11, 168 students received support, including 8 fellowships with full and partial tuition reimbursements available (averaging $15,000 per year), 92 research assistantships with full and partial tuition reimbursements available (averaging $15,000 per year), 68 teaching assistantships with full and partial tuition reimbursements available (averaging $15,000 per year); career-related internships or fieldwork, Federal Work-Study, institutionally sponsored loans, scholarships/grants, and unspecified assistantships also available. Support available to part-time students. Financial award applicants required to submit FAFSA. In 2010, 220 master's, 31 doctorates awarded. *Degree program information:* Part-time and evening/weekend programs available. Postbaccalaureate distance learning degree programs offered. Offers aerospace engineering (ME, MS, D Eng, PhD); civil and environmental engineering (D Eng, PhD); civil engineering (ME, MS); electrical and computer engineering (ME, MS, PhD); engineering and technology (ME, MEM, MS, D Eng, PhD); engineering management (MEM, MS, PhD); engineering management and systems engineering (D Eng); environmental engineering (ME, MS); mechanical engineering (ME, MS, D Eng, PhD); modeling and simulation (ME, MS, D Eng, PhD); systems engineering (ME). *Application deadline:* For fall admission, 6/1 for domestic students, 2/15 priority date for international students; for spring admission, 11/1 for domestic students, 10/1 for international students. Applications are processed on a rolling basis. *Application fee:* $40. Electronic applications accepted. *Application Contact:* Dr. Linda Vahala, Associate Dean, 757-683-3789, Fax: 757-683-4898, E-mail: lvahala@odu.edu. *Dean*, Dr. Oktay Baysal, 757-683-3789, Fax: 757-683-4898, E-mail: obaysal@odu.edu.

OLIVET COLLEGE, Olivet, MI 49076-9701

General Information Independent-religious, coed, comprehensive institution.

GRADUATE UNITS

Program in Education Offers education (MAT). Electronic applications accepted.

OLIVET NAZARENE UNIVERSITY, Bourbonnais, IL 60914

General Information Independent-religious, coed, comprehensive institution. *Graduate housing:* Room and/or apartments available to single students; on-campus housing not available to married students. Housing application deadline: 8/15.

GRADUATE UNITS

Graduate School *Degree program information:* Part-time and evening/weekend programs available. Offers business administration (MBA); practical ministries (MPM).

Division of Education *Degree program information:* Evening/weekend programs available. Offers curriculum and instruction (MAE); elementary education (MAT); library information specialist (MAE); reading specialist (MAE); school leadership (MAE); secondary education (MAT).

Division of Religion *Degree program information:* Part-time programs available. Offers biblical literature (MA); religion (MA); theology (MA).

Program in Organizational Leadership Offers organizational leadership (MOL).

ORAL ROBERTS UNIVERSITY, Tulsa, OK 74171

General Information Independent-religious, coed, comprehensive institution. *Graduate housing:* Room and/or apartments available on a first-come, first-served basis to single students; on-campus housing not available to married students.

GRADUATE UNITS

School of Business *Degree program information:* Part-time programs available. Postbaccalaureate distance learning degree programs offered (minimal on-campus study). Offers accounting (MBA); entrepreneurship (MBA); finance (MBA); international business (MBA); management (MBA); marketing (MBA); non-profit management (MBA); not for profit management (MNM). Electronic applications accepted.

School of Education *Degree program information:* Part-time programs available. Postbaccalaureate distance learning degree programs offered (minimal on-campus study). Offers Christian school administration (K-12) (MA Ed, Ed D); Christian school curriculum development (MA Ed); college and higher education administration (Ed D); public school administration (K-12) (MA Ed, Ed D); public school teaching (MA Ed).

School of Theology and Missions *Degree program information:* Part-time programs available. Postbaccalaureate distance learning degree programs offered (minimal on-campus study). Offers biblical literature (MA); Christian counseling (MA); divinity (M Div); missions (MA); practical theology (MA); theological/historical studies (MA); theology (D Min). Electronic applications accepted.

OREGON COLLEGE OF ORIENTAL MEDICINE, Portland, OR 97216

General Information Independent, coed, graduate-only institution. *Graduate housing:* On-campus housing not available.

GRADUATE UNITS

Graduate Program in Acupuncture and Oriental Medicine *Degree program information:* Part-time programs available. Offers acupuncture and Oriental medicine (M Ac OM, MAcOM, DAOM).

OREGON HEALTH & SCIENCE UNIVERSITY, Portland, OR 97239-3098

General Information State-related, coed, upper-level institution. *Enrollment:* 1,367 full-time matriculated graduate/professional students (720 women), 453 part-time matriculated graduate/professional students (250 women). *Enrollment by degree level:* 803 first professional, 421 master's, 305 doctoral, 291 other advanced degrees. *Graduate faculty:* 820. *Graduate housing:* On-campus housing not available. *Student services:* Campus safety program, career counseling, exercise/wellness program, free psychological counseling, low-cost health insurance, multicultural affairs office, services for students with disabilities. *Library facilities:* OHSU Main Library plus 7 others. *Online resources:* library catalog, web page, access to other libraries' catalogs. *Collection:* 272,853 titles, 12,888 serial subscriptions, 861 audiovisual materials. *Research affiliation:* Oregon Regional Primate Research Center.

Computer facilities: 45 computers available on campus for general student use. A campuswide network can be accessed from student residence rooms and from off campus. *Web address:* http://www.ohsu.edu/.

General Application Contact: Registrar's Office, 503-494-7800.

GRADUATE UNITS

School of Dentistry Offers biomaterials and biomechanics (MS); dentistry (DMD); endodontics (Certificate); oral and maxillofacial surgery (Certificate); oral molecular biology (MS); orthodontics (MS, Certificate); pediatric dentistry (Certificate); periodontology (MS, Certificate); restorative dentistry (MS). Electronic applications accepted.

School of Medicine Students: 961 full-time (555 women), 479 part-time (243 women); includes 278 minority (22 Black or African American, non-Hispanic/Latino; 7 American Indian or Alaska Native, non-Hispanic/Latino; 161 Asian, non-Hispanic/Latino; 55 Hispanic/Latino; 4 Native Hawaiian or other Pacific Islander, non-Hispanic/Latino; 29 Two or more races, non-Hispanic/Latino), 73 international. Average age 30. 5,137 applicants, 9% accepted, 256 enrolled. *Faculty:* 1,578. Expenses: Contact institution. *Financial support:* Fellowships, research assistantships, teaching assistantships, career-related internships or fieldwork, Federal Work-Study, institutionally sponsored loans, scholarships/grants, health care benefits, and tuition waivers (full) available. Support available to part-time students. Financial award application deadline: 3/1; financial award applicants required to submit FAFSA. In 2010, 215 first professional degrees, 107 master's, 41 doctorates awarded. *Degree program information:* Part-time programs available. Postbaccalaureate distance learning degree programs offered. Offers medicine (MD, MBA, MCR, MPAS, MPH, MS, MSCNU, PhD, Certificate). *Application deadline:* Applications are processed on a rolling basis. Electronic applications accepted. *Application Contact:* Dr. Mark Richardson, Dean, 503-494-8220, Fax: 503-494-3400. *Dean*, Dr. Mark Richardson, 503-494-8220, Fax: 503-494-3400.

Graduate Programs in Medicine Students: 646 (342 women); includes 13 Black or African American, non-Hispanic/Latino; 8 American Indian or Alaska Native, non-Hispanic/Latino; 43 Asian, non-Hispanic/Latino; 21 Hispanic/Latino; 11 Native Hawaiian or other Pacific Islander, non-Hispanic/Latino, 88 international. Average age 33. 589 applicants, 38% accepted, 132 enrolled. *Faculty:* 344 full-time (120 women), 205 part-time/adjunct (91 women). Expenses: Contact institution. *Financial support:* Fellowships, research assistantships, teaching assistantships, scholarships/grants, health care benefits, and full tuition and stipends available. In 2010, 71 master's, 36 doctorates awarded. Postbaccalaureate distance learning degree programs offered (minimal on-campus study). Offers behavioral neuroscience (PhD); biochemistry and molecular biology (PhD); biomedical engineering (MS, PhD); cancer biology (PhD); cell and developmental biology (PhD); clinical dietetics (MS); clinical dietetics and nutrition (MSCNU); clinical informatics (MS, PhD, Certificate); clinical research (MCR, Certificate); computational biology (MS, PhD); computer science and engineering (MS, PhD); dietetic internship (Certificate); electrical engineering (MS, PhD); environmental science and engineering (MS, PhD); epidemiology and biostatistics (MPH); health information management (Certificate); healthcare management (MBA, MS); medicine (MBA, MCR, MPAS, MPH, MS, MSCNU, PhD, Certificate); molecular and cellular biosciences (PhD); molecular and medical genetics (PhD); molecular microbiology and immunology (PhD); neuroscience (PhD); physician assistant education (MPAS); physiology and pharmacology (PhD). *Application fee:* $65. Electronic applications accepted. *Application Contact:* Lorie Gookin, Admissions Coordinator, 503-494-6222, Fax: 503-494-3400, E-mail: somgrad@ohsu.edu. *Associate Dean for Graduate Studies*, Dr. Allison Fryer, 503-494-6222, Fax: 503-494-3400, E-mail: somgrad@ohsu.edu.

School of Nursing *Degree program information:* Part-time programs available. Offers gerontological nursing (Post Master's Certificate); mental health nursing (MN, MS, Post Master's Certificate); nurse anesthesia (MN, MS); nurse midwifery (MN, MS, Post Master's Certificate); nurse practitioner (MN, MS, Post Master's Certificate); nursing (MN, MPH, MS, DNP, PhD, Post Master's Certificate); nursing education (MN, MS, Post Master's Certificate); primary care and disparities (MPH); public health (MPH, Post Master's Certificate). Electronic applications accepted.

OREGON STATE UNIVERSITY, Corvallis, OR 97331

General Information State-supported, coed, university. CGS member. *Graduate housing:* Rooms and/or apartments available on a first-come, first-served basis to single and married students. Housing application deadline: 9/10. *Research affiliation:* David and Lucille Packard Foundation (science, environmental science), W. M. Keck Foundation (science, engineering), William and Flora Hewlett Foundation (science, engineering), George and Betty Moore Foundation (medical research, science education), Comer Science and Educational Foundation (science).

GRADUATE UNITS

College of Pharmacy *Degree program information:* Part-time programs available. Offers pharmacy (Pharm D, MS, PhD).

College of Veterinary Medicine *Degree program information:* Part-time programs available. Offers comparative veterinary medicine (PhD); veterinary medicine (DVM, MS, PhD). DVM admissions open only to residents of Oregon and other states participating in the Western Interstate Commission for Higher Education.

Graduate School *Degree program information:* Part-time programs available. Offers environmental sciences (MA, MS, PhD); interdisciplinary studies (MAIS); molecular and cellular biology (MS, PhD); plant physiology (MS, PhD); water resources engineering (MS, PhD).

College of Agricultural Sciences *Degree program information:* Part-time programs available. Offers agricultural and resource economics (M Agr, MAIS, MS, PhD); agricultural education (M Agr, MAIS, MAT, MS); agricultural sciences (M Ag, M Agr, MA, MAIS, MAT, MS, PhD); animal science (M Agr, MAIS, MS, PhD); crop science (M Agr, MAIS, MS, PhD); economics (MS, PhD); fisheries science (M Agr, MAIS, MS, PhD); food science and technology (M Agr, MAIS, MS, PhD); genetics (MA, MAIS, MS, PhD); horticulture (M Ag, MAIS, MS, PhD); poultry science (M Agr, MAIS, MS, PhD); rangeland ecology and management (M Agr, MAIS, MS, PhD); soil science (M Agr, MAIS, MS, PhD); toxicology (MS, PhD); wildlife science (MAIS, MS, PhD).

College of Business *Degree program information:* Part-time programs available. Offers business (MAIS, MBA, Certificate).

College of Education *Degree program information:* Part-time programs available. Offers adult education and higher education leadership (Ed M, MAIS); college student service administration (Ed M, MS); counseling (MS, PhD); education (Ed M, MAIS, MAT, MS, Ed D, PhD); elementary education (MAT); family and consumer sciences education (MAT, MS); general education (Ed M, MAIS, MS, Ed D, PhD); language arts education (MAT); music education (MAT).

College of Engineering *Degree program information:* Part-time programs available. Offers biological and ecological engineering (M Eng, MS, PhD); chemical engineering (M Eng, MS, PhD); chemical, biological and environmental engineering (M Eng, MS, PhD); civil engineering (MS, PhD); coastal and ocean engineering (M Oc E, PhD); coastal engineering (MS); computer science (M Eng, MAIS, MS, PhD); construction engineering management (MBE, PhD); electrical and computer engineering (M Eng, MS, PhD); engineering (M Eng, M Engr, M Oc E, MA, MAIS, MBE, MHP, MS, PhD); geotechnical engineering (MS, PhD); human systems engineering (MS, PhD); industrial engineering (MS, PhD); information systems engineering (MS, PhD); manufacturing engineering (M Engr); manufacturing systems engineering (MS, PhD); materials science (MAIS, MS, PhD); mechanical engineering (MS, PhD); nano/micro fabrication (MS, PhD); nuclear engineering (M Eng, MS, PhD); radiation health physics (MA, MHP, MS, PhD); structural engineering (MS, PhD); transportation engineering (MS, PhD); water engineering (MS, PhD).

College of Forestry *Degree program information:* Part-time programs available. Offers forest ecosystems and society (MAIS, MF, MS, PhD); forest engineering (MF, MS); forest hydrology (MF, MS, PhD); forest operations (MF); forest products (MAIS, MF, MS, PhD); forest soil science (MF, MS, PhD); forestry (MAIS, MF, MS, PhD); timber harvesting (PhD); wood science and technology (MF, MS, PhD).

College of Health and Human Sciences Offers design and human environment (MA, MAIS, MS, PhD); environmental health and occupational safety management (MAIS, MS); exercise and sport science (MS, PhD); gerontology (MAIS); health and human sciences (MA, MAIS, MPH, MS, PhD); health management and policy (MS, PhD); health promotion and health behavior (MS, PhD); human development and family studies (MS, PhD); movement studies in disabilities (MAIS, MS); nutrition and exercise sciences (MAIS); nutrition and food management (MS); public health (MPH, PhD).

College of Liberal Arts *Degree program information:* Part-time programs available. Offers anthropology (MAIS); applied anthropology (MA); economics (MA, MS, PhD); English (MA, MAIS, MFA); history of science (MA, PhD); liberal arts (MA, MAIS, MFA, MS, PhD).

Oregon State University (continued)

College of Oceanic and Atmospheric Sciences Offers atmospheric sciences (MA, MS, PhD); geophysics (MA, MS, PhD); marine resource management (MA, MS); oceanic and atmospheric sciences (MA, MS, PhD); oceanography (MA, MS, PhD).

College of Science *Degree program information:* Part-time programs available. Offers analytical chemistry (MS, PhD); applied physics (MS); biochemistry and biophysics (MA, MAIS, MS, PhD); biology education (MS); chemistry (MA, MAIS); chemistry education (MS); ecology (MA, MAIS, MS, PhD); genetics (MA, MAIS, MS, PhD); geography (MA, MAIS, MS, PhD); geology (MA, MAIS, MS, PhD); inorganic chemistry (MS, PhD); integrated science education (MS); mathematics (MA, MAIS, MS, PhD); mathematics education (MA, MS, PhD); microbiology (MA, MAIS, MS, PhD); molecular and cellular biology (MA, MAIS, MS, PhD); mycology (MA, MAIS, MS, PhD); nuclear and radiation chemistry (MS, PhD); operations research (MA, MS); organic chemistry (MS, PhD); physical chemistry (MS, PhD); physics (MA, MS, PhD); physics education (MS); plant pathology (MA, MAIS, MS, PhD); plant physiology (MA, MAIS, MS, PhD); science (MA, MAIS, MAT, MS, PhD); science education (MA, MS, PhD); statistics (MA, MS, PhD); structural botany (MA, MAIS, MS, PhD); systematics (MA, MAIS, MS, PhD); zoology (MA, MAIS, MS, PhD).

OREGON STATE UNIVERSITY–CASCADES, Bend, OR 97701

General Information State-supported, coed, comprehensive institution.

GRADUATE UNITS

Program in Counseling Offers community counseling (MS); school counseling (MS).

Program in Education Offers education (MAT).

OTIS COLLEGE OF ART AND DESIGN, Los Angeles, CA 90045-9785

General Information Independent, coed, comprehensive institution. *Enrollment:* 1,226 graduate, professional, and undergraduate students; 53 full-time matriculated graduate/professional students (38 women), 15 part-time matriculated graduate/professional students (13 women). *Enrollment by degree level:* 68 master's. *Graduate faculty:* 2 full-time (1 woman), 22 part-time/adjunct (11 women). *Tuition:* Full-time $33,900; part-time $1107 per unit. *Required fees:* $700. *Graduate housing:* On-campus housing not available. *Student services:* Campus employment opportunities, campus safety program, career counseling, free psychological counseling, international student services, low-cost health insurance, writing training. *Library facilities:* Milliard Sheets Library. *Online resources:* library catalog, web page, access to other libraries' catalogs. *Collection:* 42,000 titles, 150 serial subscriptions.

Computer facilities: 300 computers available on campus for general student use. A campuswide network can be accessed. Online class registration is available. *Web address:* http://www.otis.edu/.

General Application Contact: Graduate Studies, 310-665-6820, E-mail: admissions@otis.edu.

GRADUATE UNITS

Program in Fine Arts Students: 23 full-time (14 women); includes 2 minority (1 Asian, non-Hispanic/Latino; 1 Hispanic/Latino), 3 international. Average age 32. 140 applicants, 26% accepted, 15 enrolled. *Faculty:* 1 (woman) full-time, 6 part-time/adjunct (3 women). Expenses: Contact institution. *Financial support:* Career-related internships or fieldwork, Federal Work-Study, scholarships/grants, and tuition waivers (partial) available. Financial award applicants required to submit FAFSA. In 2010, 7 master's awarded. Offers new genres (MFA); painting (MFA); photography (MFA); sculpture (MFA). *Application deadline:* For fall admission, 1/15 for domestic and international students; for spring admission, 11/15 for domestic and international students. *Application fee:* $60. Electronic applications accepted. *Application Contact:* Information Contact, 310-665-6820, Fax: 310-665-6821, E-mail: admissions@otis.edu. *Chair,* Roy Dowell, 310-665-6893, Fax: 310-665-6998, E-mail: grads@otis.edu.

Program in Graphic Design Students: 19 full-time (8 women), 6 part-time (5 women); includes 9 minority (2 Black or African American, non-Hispanic/Latino; 2 Asian, non-Hispanic/Latino; 5 Hispanic/Latino), 6 international. 75 applicants, 29% accepted, 14 enrolled. *Faculty:* 3 part-time/adjunct (2 women). Expenses: Contact institution. In 2010, 9 master's awarded. Offers graphic design (MFA). *Application deadline:* For fall admission, 1/15 for domestic students. *Application fee:* $60. Electronic applications accepted. *Application Contact:* Information Contact, 310-665-6820, Fax: 310-665-6821, E-mail: admissions@otis.edu. *Chair, Graduate Studies,* Kali Nikitas, 310-665-6820, Fax: 310-665-6843, E-mail: jhayes@otis.edu.

Program in Public Practice Students: 15 full-time (12 women), 1 (woman) part-time; includes 4 minority (all Hispanic/Latino), 4 international. 23 applicants, 74% accepted, 7 enrolled. *Faculty:* 12 part-time/adjunct (7 women). Expenses: Contact institution. In 2010, 5 master's awarded. Offers public practice (MFA). *Application deadline:* For fall admission, 1/15 for domestic and international students; for spring admission, 11/1 for domestic and international students. *Application fee:* $60. Electronic applications accepted. *Application Contact:* Information Contact, 310-665-6820, Fax: 310-665-6821, E-mail: admissions@otis.edu. *Chair, Graduate Studies,* Suzanne Lacy, 310-665-6820, Fax: 310-846-2612, E-mail: cvelasco@otis.edu.

Program in Writing Students: 15 full-time (12 women), 14 part-time (11 women); includes 11 minority (3 Black or African American, non-Hispanic/Latino; 2 Asian, non-Hispanic/Latino; 5 Hispanic/Latino; 1 Two or more races, non-Hispanic/Latino), 3 international. Average age 34. 40 applicants, 55% accepted, 6 enrolled. *Faculty:* 1 full-time (0 women), 7 part-time/adjunct (1 woman). Expenses: Contact institution. *Financial support:* Federal Work-Study, scholarships/grants, and tuition waivers (partial) available. Financial award applicants required to submit FAFSA. In 2010, 8 master's awarded. Offers writing (MFA). *Application deadline:* For fall admission, 1/15 for domestic and international students; for spring admission, 11/1 for domestic and international students. *Application fee:* $60. Electronic applications accepted. *Application Contact:* Information Contact, 310-665-6820, Fax: 310-665-6821, E-mail: admissions@otis.edu. *Chair,* Paul Vangelisti, 310-665-6891, Fax: 310-665-6890, E-mail: pvangel@otis.edu.

OTTAWA UNIVERSITY, Ottawa, KS 66067-3399

General Information Independent-religious, coed, comprehensive institution. *Graduate housing:* On-campus housing not available.

GRADUATE UNITS

Graduate Studies-Arizona *Degree program information:* Part-time and evening/weekend programs available. Postbaccalaureate distance learning degree programs offered. Offers business administration (MBA); Christian counseling (MA); community college counseling (MA); curriculum and instruction (MA); early childhood (MA); education intervention (MA); education leadership (MA); education technology (MA); expressive arts therapy (MA); finance (MBA); human resources (MA, MBA); leadership (MBA); marketing (MBA); marriage and family therapy (MA); Montessori early childhood education (MA); Montessori elementary education (MA); professional development (MA); school guidance counseling (MA); special education—cross categorical (MA); treatment of trauma, abuse and deprivation (MA). Electronic applications accepted.

Graduate Studies-International Postbaccalaureate distance learning degree programs offered (minimal on-campus study). Offers business administration (MBA). Electronic applications accepted.

Graduate Studies-Kansas City *Degree program information:* Part-time and evening/weekend programs available. Postbaccalaureate distance learning degree programs offered (minimal on-campus study). Offers business administration (MBA); human resources (MA). Electronic applications accepted.

Graduate Studies-Wisconsin *Degree program information:* Part-time and evening/weekend programs available. Postbaccalaureate distance learning degree programs offered. Offers business administration (MBA). Electronic applications accepted.

OTTERBEIN UNIVERSITY, Westerville, OH 43081

General Information Independent-religious, coed, comprehensive institution. *Graduate housing:* On-campus housing not available.

GRADUATE UNITS

Department of Business, Accounting and Economics *Degree program information:* Part-time and evening/weekend programs available. Offers business, accounting and economics (MBA).

Department of Education Offers education (MAE, MAT).

Department of Nursing *Degree program information:* Part-time and evening/weekend programs available. Postbaccalaureate distance learning degree programs offered (minimal on-campus study). Offers adult nurse practitioner (MSN, Certificate); clinical nurse leader (MSN); family nurse practitioner (MSN, Certificate); nurse service administration (MSN).

OUR LADY OF HOLY CROSS COLLEGE, New Orleans, LA 70131-7399

General Information Independent-religious, coed, comprehensive institution. *Graduate housing:* On-campus housing not available.

GRADUATE UNITS

Program in Education and Counseling *Degree program information:* Part-time and evening/weekend programs available. Offers administration and supervision (M Ed); curriculum and instruction (M Ed); marriage and family counseling (MA); school counseling (M Ed, MA).

OUR LADY OF THE LAKE COLLEGE, Baton Rouge, LA 70808

General Information Independent-religious, coed, primarily women, comprehensive institution.

GRADUATE UNITS

School of Arts, Sciences and Health Professions Offers physician associate studies (MMS).

School of Nursing Offers administration (MS); education (MS); nurse anesthesia (MS); nursing (MS).

OUR LADY OF THE LAKE UNIVERSITY OF SAN ANTONIO, San Antonio, TX 78207-4689

General Information Independent-religious, coed, comprehensive institution. *Enrollment:* 2,751 graduate, professional, and undergraduate students; 282 full-time matriculated graduate/professional students (230 women), 869 part-time matriculated graduate/professional students (613 women). *Enrollment by degree level:* 893 master's, 249 doctoral, 9 other advanced degrees. *Tuition:* Full-time $13,500; part-time $750 per contact hour. *Required fees:* $330. Tuition and fees vary according to course level, degree level and campus/location. *Graduate housing:* Room and/or apartments available on a first-come, first-served basis to single students; on-campus housing not available to married students. Typical cost: $6838 (including board). Housing application deadline: 7/15. *Student services:* Campus employment opportunities, career counseling, exercise/wellness program, free psychological counseling, international student services, low-cost health insurance, services for students with disabilities, teacher training. *Library facilities:* The Sueltenfuss Library. *Online resources:* library catalog, web page. *Collection:* 93,551 titles, 600 serial subscriptions, 7,140 audiovisual materials.

Computer facilities: 230 computers available on campus for general student use. A campuswide network can be accessed from student residence rooms and from off campus. Online class registration is available. *Web address:* http://www.ollusa.edu/.

General Application Contact: Graduate Admissions Counselor, 210-434-6711 Ext. 2314, Fax: 210-431-4036, E-mail: gradadm@lake.ollusa.edu.

GRADUATE UNITS

College of Arts and Sciences Students: 6 full-time (5 women), 18 part-time (14 women); includes 1 Black or African American, non-Hispanic/Latino; 1 American Indian or Alaska Native, non-Hispanic/Latino; 15 Hispanic/Latino. Average age 35. Expenses: Contact institution. *Financial support:* Research assistantships, teaching assistantships, career-related internships or fieldwork, Federal Work-Study, institutionally sponsored loans, and tuition waivers (partial) available. Support available to part-time students. Financial award application deadline: 4/15. In 2010, 8 master's awarded. *Degree program information:* Part-time and evening/weekend programs available. Offers arts and sciences (MA); communication arts (MA); English and literature (MA); English education (MA); writing (MA). *Application deadline:* Applications are processed on a rolling basis. *Application fee:* $25 ($50 for international students). Electronic applications accepted. *Application Contact:* 210-434-6711, Fax: 210-431-4036, E-mail: gradadm@lake.ollusa.edu. *Dean,* Dr. Mary Francine Danis, 210-434-6711 Ext. 2240.

School of Business and Leadership Students: 54 full-time (30 women), 537 part-time (322 women); includes 335 minority (64 Black or African American, non-Hispanic/Latino; 2 American Indian or Alaska Native, non-Hispanic/Latino; 4 Asian, non-Hispanic/Latino; 255 Hispanic/Latino; 4 Native Hawaiian or other Pacific Islander, non-Hispanic/Latino; 6 Two or more races, non-Hispanic/Latino), 4 international. Average age 35. Expenses: Contact institution. *Financial support:* In 2010–11, 40 students received support; fellowships available. Financial award application deadline: 4/15. In 2010, 128 master's, 12 doctorates awarded. *Degree program information:* Part-time and evening/weekend programs available. Offers accounting/finance (MBA); business administration (MBA); healthcare management (MBA); information systems and security (MS); leadership studies (PhD); management (MBA); nonprofit management (MS); organizational leadership (MS). *Application deadline:* Applications are processed on a rolling basis. *Application fee:* $25 ($50 for international students). Electronic applications accepted. *Application Contact:* 210-434-6711, Fax: 210-436-2314. *Dean,* Dr. Robert Bisking, 210-434-6711, Fax: 210-434-0821.

School of Professional Studies Students: 181 full-time (157 women), 297 part-time (266 women); includes 270 minority (44 Black or African American, non-Hispanic/Latino; 1 American Indian or Alaska Native, non-Hispanic/Latino; 3 Asian, non-Hispanic/Latino; 211 Hispanic/Latino; 3 Native Hawaiian or other Pacific Islander, non-Hispanic/Latino; 8 Two or more races, non-Hispanic/Latino), 7 international. Average age 36. Expenses: Contact institution. *Financial support:* Research assistantships, teaching assistantships, career-related internships or fieldwork, Federal Work-Study, institutionally sponsored loans, scholarships/grants, and tuition waivers (partial) available. Support available to part-time students. In 2010, 154 master's, 4 doctorates awarded. *Degree program information:* Part-time and evening/weekend programs available. Offers bilingual (M Ed); communication and learning disorders (MA); counseling psychology (MS, Psy D); curriculum and instruction (M Ed); early childhood education (M Ed); early elementary education (M Ed); elementary education (M Ed); English as a second language (M Ed); generic special education (M Ed); human sciences (MA); integrated math teaching (M Ed); integrated science teaching (M Ed); intermediate education (M Ed); learning resources specialist (M Ed); marriage and family therapy (MS); master reading teacher (M Ed); master technology teacher (M Ed); math/science education (M Ed); principal (M Ed); professional studies (M Ed); psychology (MS, Psy D); reading specialist (M Ed); school counseling (M Ed); school psychology (MS); secondary education (M Ed). *Application deadline:* Applications are processed on a rolling basis. *Application fee:* $25 ($50 for international students). Electronic applications accepted. *Application Contact:* 210-434-6711 Ext. 2314, Fax: 210-431-4036, E-mail: gradadm@lake.ollusa.edu. *Dean,* Dr. Teresita Aguilar, 210-434-6711 Ext. 2291, Fax: 210-431-3927, E-mail: secs@lake.ollusa.edu.

Worden School of Social Service Students: 41 full-time (38 women), 17 part-time (11 women); includes 31 minority (9 Black or African American, non-Hispanic/Latino; 1 Asian, non-Hispanic/Latino; 16 Hispanic/Latino; 5 Two or more races, non-Hispanic/Latino), 2 international. Average age 36. Expenses: Contact institution. *Financial support:* In 2010–11, 11 research assistantships were awarded; career-related internships or fieldwork, Federal Work-Study, institutionally sponsored loans, and tuition waivers (partial) also available. Financial award application deadline: 4/15. In 2010, 15 master's awarded. *Degree program information:* Part-time programs available. Offers social service (MSW). *Application deadline:* For fall admission, 4/2 priority date for domestic and international students; for spring admission, 11/1 priority date for domestic and international students. Applications are processed on a rolling basis. *Application fee:* $25 ($50 for international students). Electronic applications accepted. *Application Contact:* 210-434-6711 Ext. 2314, Fax: 210-431-4036, E-mail: gradadm@lake.ollusa.edu. *Director,* Dr. Walter Calvo, 210-431-3969, Fax: 210-431-4028, E-mail: wecalvo@lake.ollusa.edu.

OXFORD GRADUATE SCHOOL, Dayton, TN 37321-6736

General Information Independent-religious, coed, graduate-only institution. *Enrollment by degree level:* 20 master's, 85 doctoral. *Graduate faculty:* 10 full-time (2 women), 22 part-time/adjunct (7 women). *Graduate housing:* Rooms and/or apartments guaranteed to single students and available to married students. *Student services:* Campus employment opportunities, campus safety program, international student services, services for students with disabilities, teacher training, writing training. *Online resources:* library catalog, web page, access to other libraries' catalogs. *Collection:* 117,309 titles, 4,541 serial subscriptions, 2,117 audiovisual materials.

Computer facilities: 15 computers available on campus for general student use. A campuswide network can be accessed from student residence rooms and from off campus. Online class registration, extensive research databases are available. *Web address:* http://www.oxnetedu.org/.

General Application Contact: Joanne Phillips, Information Contact, 423-775-6596, Fax: 423-775-6599, E-mail: oxfordgraduateschool@ogs.edu.

GRADUATE UNITS

Graduate Programs Students: 105 full-time (40 women). *Faculty:* 10 full-time (2 women), 22 part-time/adjunct (7 women). Expenses: Contact institution. Offers family life education (M Litt); organizational leadership (M Litt); sociological integration of religion and society (D Phil). *Application Contact:* Joanne Phillips, Information Contact, 423-775-6596, Fax: 423-775-6599, E-mail: oxfordgraduateschool@ogs.edu.

PACE UNIVERSITY, New York, NY 10038

General Information Independent, coed, university. *Graduate housing:* Room and/or apartments available on a first-come, first-served basis to single students; on-campus housing not available to married students.

GRADUATE UNITS

Dyson College of Arts and Sciences *Degree program information:* Part-time and evening/weekend programs available. Offers acting (MFA); arts and sciences (MA, MFA, MPA, MS, MS Ed, Psy D, Certificate); book publishing (Certificate); business side of publishing (Certificate); counseling-substance abuse (MS); directing (MFA); environmental management (MPA); environmental science (MS); forensic science (MS); government management (MPA); health care administration (MPA); loss and grief (MS); magazine publishing (Certificate); management for public safety and homeland security (MA); mental health (MS); nonprofit management (MPA); physician assistant (MS); playwriting (MFA); psychology (MA); publishing (MS); school psychology (MS Ed); school-clinical child psychology (MS Ed, Psy D); school-clinical psychology (Psy D); substance abuse (MS). Electronic applications accepted.

Lienhard School of Nursing *Degree program information:* Part-time and evening/weekend programs available. Offers family nurse practitioner (MS); nursing education (MA); nursing leadership (Advanced Certificate); nursing practice (DNP). Electronic applications accepted.

Lubin School of Business *Degree program information:* Part-time and evening/weekend programs available. Postbaccalaureate distance learning degree programs offered (minimal on-campus study). Offers banking and finance (MBA); business (MBA, MS, DPS, APC); corporate economic planning (MBA); corporate financial management (MBA); financial economics (MBA); financial management (MBA); information systems (MBA); international business (MBA); international economics (MBA); investment management (MBA, MS); management (MBA); management science (MBA); managerial accounting (MBA); marketing management (MBA); marketing research (MBA); operations management (MBA); professional studies (DPS); public accounting (MBA, MS); taxation (MBA, MS). Electronic applications accepted.

Pace Law School Students: 582 full-time (326 women), 230 part-time (145 women); includes 33 Black or African American, non-Hispanic/Latino; 1 American Indian or Alaska Native, non-Hispanic/Latino; 53 Asian, non-Hispanic/Latino; 49 Hispanic/Latino, 17 international. Average age 26. 3,082 applicants, 38% accepted, 263 enrolled. *Faculty:* 41 full-time (18 women), 52 part-time/adjunct (23 women). Expenses: Contact institution. *Financial support:* Career-related internships or fieldwork, Federal Work-Study, institutionally sponsored loans, scholarships/grants, and unspecified assistantships available. Support available to part-time students. Financial award application deadline: 2/1; financial award applicants required to submit FAFSA. In 2010, 216 first professional degrees, 20 master's, 1 doctorate awarded. *Degree program information:* Part-time programs available. Offers comparative legal studies (LL M); environmental law (LL M, SJD); law (JD). JD/MA offered jointly with Sarah Lawrence College; JD/MEM offered jointly with Yale University School of Forestry and Environmental Studies. *Application deadline:* For fall admission, 3/1 priority date for domestic students; for winter admission, 11/15 priority date for domestic students. Applications are processed on a rolling basis. *Application fee:* $65. Electronic applications accepted. *Application Contact:* Cathy Alexander, Assistant Dean, 914-422-4210, Fax: 914-989-8714, E-mail: calexander@law.pace.edu. *Dean,* Michelle S. Simon, 914-422-4407, E-mail: msimon@law.pace.edu.

School of Education *Degree program information:* Part-time and evening/weekend programs available. Offers administration and supervision (MS Ed); adolescent education (MST); childhood education (MST); curriculum and instruction (MS); education (MST); literacy (MSE); school business management (Certificate); teaching students with disabilities (MSE); teaching visual arts (MST). Electronic applications accepted.

Seidenberg School of Computer Science and Information Systems *Degree program information:* Part-time and evening/weekend programs available. Offers computer communications and networks (Certificate); computer science (MS); computing studies (DPS); information systems (MS); Internet technologies for e-commerce (MS); Internet technology (MS); object-oriented programming (Certificate); security and information assurance (Certificate); software development and engineering (MS); telecommunications (MS, Certificate). Electronic applications accepted.

PACIFICA GRADUATE INSTITUTE, Carpinteria, CA 93013

General Information Proprietary, coed, graduate-only institution. *Graduate housing:* Rooms and/or apartments guaranteed to single and married students. Housing application deadline: 8/15. *Research affiliation:* Elton B. Stevens Company (EBSCO) (journal management), American Psychological Association (psychology–research), North California consortium of Psychology Libraries (psychology).

GRADUATE UNITS

Graduate Programs Offers clinical psychology (PhD); counseling psychology (MA); depth psychology (MA, PhD); mythological studies (MA, PhD).

PACIFIC COLLEGE OF ORIENTAL MEDICINE, San Diego, CA 92108

General Information Proprietary, coed, graduate-only institution. *Graduate housing:* On-campus housing not available. *Research affiliation:* National Institutes of Health (complementary and alternative medicine).

GRADUATE UNITS

Graduate Program *Degree program information:* Part-time and evening/weekend programs available. Offers Oriental medicine (MSTOM, DAOM).

PACIFIC COLLEGE OF ORIENTAL MEDICINE-CHICAGO, Chicago, IL 60613

General Information Proprietary, coed, graduate-only institution. *Graduate housing:* On-campus housing not available. *Research affiliation:* Children's Memorial Hospital of Chicago (pediatric research).

GRADUATE UNITS

Graduate Program *Degree program information:* Part-time and evening/weekend programs available. Offers oriental medicine (MTOM).

PACIFIC COLLEGE OF ORIENTAL MEDICINE-NEW YORK, New York, NY 10010

General Information Proprietary, coed, graduate-only institution. *Graduate housing:* On-campus housing not available.

GRADUATE UNITS

Graduate Program *Degree program information:* Part-time and evening/weekend programs available. Offers Oriental medicine (MSTOM).

PACIFIC LUTHERAN THEOLOGICAL SEMINARY, Berkeley, CA 94708-1597

General Information Independent-religious, coed, graduate-only institution. *Graduate housing:* Rooms and/or apartments available on a first-come, first-served basis to single and married students. Housing application deadline: 8/1.

GRADUATE UNITS

Graduate and Professional Programs *Degree program information:* Part-time programs available. Offers theology (M Div, MA, MCM, MTS, PhD, Th D, Certificate). MA, Th D, PhD offered jointly with Graduate Theological Union; PhD with University of California, Berkeley.

PACIFIC LUTHERAN UNIVERSITY, Tacoma, WA 98447

General Information Independent-religious, coed, comprehensive institution. *Graduate housing:* Rooms and/or apartments available on a first-come, first-served basis to single and married students. Housing application deadline: 5/1.

GRADUATE UNITS

Division of Graduate Studies *Degree program information:* Part-time and evening/weekend programs available. Electronic applications accepted.

Division of Humanities *Degree program information:* Part-time programs available. Offers creative writing (MFA). Offered during summer only. Electronic applications accepted.

Division of Social Sciences Offers marriage and family therapy (MA); social sciences (MA). Electronic applications accepted.

School of Business *Degree program information:* Part-time and evening/weekend programs available. Offers business administration (MBA).

School of Education *Degree program information:* Part-time and evening/weekend programs available. Offers education (MAE); educational leadership (MAE); initial teaching certification (MAE); principal certification (MAE).

School of Nursing *Degree program information:* Part-time and evening/weekend programs available. Offers client systems management (MSN); entry level nursing (MSN); family nurse practitioner (MSN); health care systems management (MSN); nursing (MSN).

PACIFIC NORTHWEST COLLEGE OF ART, Portland, OR 97209

General Information Independent, coed, comprehensive institution.

GRADUATE UNITS

Program in Applied Craft and Design Offers applied craft and design (MFA). Program offered in collaboration with Oregon College of Art & Craft.

Program in Visual Studies Offers visual studies (MFA).

PACIFIC OAKS COLLEGE, Pasadena, CA 91103

General Information Independent, coed, primarily women, upper-level institution. *Graduate housing:* Room and/or apartments available to single students; on-campus housing not available to married students.

GRADUATE UNITS

Graduate School *Degree program information:* Part-time and evening/weekend programs available. Postbaccalaureate distance learning degree programs offered (minimal on-campus study). Offers human development (MA); marriage, family and child counseling (MA).

PACIFIC SCHOOL OF RELIGION, Berkeley, CA 94709-1323

General Information Independent, coed, graduate-only institution. *Graduate housing:* Rooms and/or apartments guaranteed to single and married students. Housing application deadline: 4/1. *Research affiliation:* Center for Women and Religion (women's studies), Center for Ethics and Social Policy (business ethics), Disciples Seminary Foundation (theology), Swedenborgean House of Studies (theology), Bay Area Faith and Health Consortium (public health).

GRADUATE UNITS

Graduate and Professional Programs *Degree program information:* Part-time programs available. Offers religion (M Div, MA, MTS, D Min, PhD, Th D, CAPS, CMS, CSS, CTS). MA, PhD, Th D offered jointly with Graduate Theological Union; D Min with Church Divinity School of the Pacific. Electronic applications accepted.

PACIFIC STATES UNIVERSITY, Los Angeles, CA 90006

General Information Independent, coed, comprehensive institution. *Enrollment:* 196 graduate, professional, and undergraduate students; 146 full-time matriculated graduate/professional students (69 women). *Graduate faculty:* 4 full-time (1 woman), 17 part-time/adjunct (0 women). *Tuition:* Full-time $8280; part-time $345 per credit hour. *Required fees:* $150 per quarter. *Graduate housing:* Room and/or apartments available on a first-come, first-served basis to single students; on-campus housing not available to married students. Typical cost: $7200 per year. *Student services:* Campus employment opportunities, career counseling, international student services, low-cost health insurance. *Library facilities:* University Library plus 1 other. *Online resources:* library catalog, web page.

Computer facilities: 50 computers available on campus for general student use. A campuswide network can be accessed. *Web address:* http://www.psuca.edu/.

General Application Contact: Zolzaya Enkhbayar, Admission Advisor, 323-731-2383, Fax: 323-731-7276, E-mail: admissions@psuca.edu.

GRADUATE UNITS

College of Business Students: 130 full-time (55 women); includes 1 Black or African American, non-Hispanic/Latino; 7 Asian, non-Hispanic/Latino; 3 Native Hawaiian or other Pacific Islander, non-Hispanic/Latino, 115 international. Average age 31. 42 applicants, 83% accepted, 33 enrolled. *Faculty:* 4 full-time (1 woman), 13 part-time/adjunct (0 women). Expenses: Contact institution. *Financial support:* Scholarships/grants available. Financial award applicants required to submit FAFSA. In 2010, 67 master's awarded. *Degree program information:* Part-time and evening/weekend programs available. Postbaccalaureate distance learning degree programs offered (no on-campus study). Offers accounting (MBA); business administration (DBA); finance (MBA); international business (MBA); management of information technology (MBA); real estate management (MBA). *Application deadline:* For fall admission, 8/15 priority date for domestic students; for winter admission, 10/15 priority date for domestic students; for spring admission, 1/15 priority date for domestic students. Applications are processed on a rolling basis. *Application fee:* $100. *Application Contact:* Zolzaya Enkhbayar, Assistant Director of Admissions, 323-731-2383, Fax: 323-731-7276, E-mail: admissions@psuca.edu. *Director,* Dr. Chase C. Lee, 888-200-0383, Fax: 323-731-2383, E-mail: admission@psuca.edu.

College of Computer Science Students: 16 full-time (2 women); includes 1 Asian, non-Hispanic/Latino, 14 international. Average age 27. 9 applicants, 78% accepted, 6 enrolled. *Faculty:* 4 part-time/adjunct (0 women). Expenses: Contact institution. *Financial support:* Scholarships/grants available. Financial award applicants required to submit FAFSA. In 2010, 7 master's awarded. *Degree program information:* Part-time and evening/weekend programs available. Offers computer science (MSCS); information systems (MSCS). *Application deadline:*

Pacific States University (continued)

For fall admission, 8/15 priority date for domestic students; for winter admission, 10/15 priority date for domestic students; for spring admission, 1/15 priority date for domestic students. Applications are processed on a rolling basis. *Application fee:* $100. *Application Contact:* Namyoung Chah, Registrar, 323-731-2383, Fax: 323-731-7276, E-mail: registrar@psuca.edu. *Director,* John Ma, 888-200-0383, Fax: 323-731-7276, E-mail: admission@psuca.edu.

PACIFIC UNION COLLEGE, Angwin, CA 94508-9707

General Information Independent-religious, coed, comprehensive institution. *Enrollment:* 1,527 graduate, professional, and undergraduate students; 34 part-time matriculated graduate/professional students (24 women). *Enrollment by degree level:* 14 master's, 20 other advanced degrees. *Graduate faculty:* 3 full-time (1 woman). *Tuition:* Part-time $370 per quarter hour. *Required fees:* $370 per quarter hour. Part-time tuition and fees vary according to student's religious affiliation. *Graduate housing:* Rooms and/or apartments available on a first-come, first-served basis to single and married students. *Student services:* Child daycare facilities, teacher training. *Library facilities:* W.E. Nelson Memorial Library. *Online resources:* library catalog, web page, access to other libraries' catalogs. *Collection:* 185,668 titles, 36,988 serial subscriptions, 5,630 audiovisual materials.

Computer facilities: 150 computers available on campus for general student use. A campuswide network can be accessed from student residence rooms and from off campus. Online class registration, student financial information are available. *Web address:* http://www.puc.edu/.

General Application Contact: Marsha Crow, Assistant Chair/Accreditation and Certification Specialist, 707-965-6643, Fax: 707-965-6645, E-mail: mcrow@puc.edu.

GRADUATE UNITS

Education Department Students: 34 part-time (24 women); includes 2 Asian, non-Hispanic/Latino; 2 Hispanic/Latino; 2 Native Hawaiian or other Pacific Islander, non-Hispanic/Latino. Average age 30. *Faculty:* 3 full-time (1 woman). Expenses: Contact institution. *Financial support:* Available to part-time students. *Degree program information:* Part-time programs available. Offers education (M Ed). Summer only program; not available during the regular school year. *Application deadline:* For spring admission, 6/1 priority date for domestic students. Applications are processed on a rolling basis. *Application fee:* $0. *Application Contact:* Marsha Crow, Assistant Chair/Accreditation and Certification Specialist, 707-965-6643, Fax: 707-965-6645, E-mail: mcrow@puc.edu. *Chair,* Prof. Thomas Lee, 707-965-6646, Fax: 707-965-6645, E-mail: tdlee@puc.edu.

PACIFIC UNIVERSITY, Forest Grove, OR 97116-1797

General Information Independent, coed, comprehensive institution. *Graduate housing:* On-campus housing not available. *Research affiliation:* Jacob Lieberman, O. D. (contact lens, vision research, sports vision), NEI/PEDIG–JAEB Center of Health Research (amblyopia treatment study), BSK (student thesis projects), CIBA Vision (contact lens), Cooper Vision (contact lens), Ohio State University/Vistakon-Johnson & Johnson (achieve study, adolescent and child vision care).

GRADUATE UNITS

College of Education *Degree program information:* Part-time and evening/weekend programs available. Offers early childhood education (MAT); education (MAE); elementary education (MAT); high school education (MAT); middle school education (MAT); special education (MAT); visual function in learning (M Ed). Electronic applications accepted.

College of Optometry Offers optometry (OD, MS). Electronic applications accepted.

Healthcare Administration Program Offers healthcare administration (MHA).

Program in Writing *Degree program information:* Part-time programs available. Offers writing (MFA).

School of Occupational Therapy Offers occupational therapy (MOT). Electronic applications accepted.

School of Pharmacy Offers pharmacy (Pharm D). Electronic applications accepted.

School of Physical Therapy Offers entry level (DPT); post-professional (DPT). Electronic applications accepted.

School of Physician Assistant Studies Offers physician assistant studies (MHS, MS).

School of Professional Psychology *Degree program information:* Part-time programs available. Offers clinical psychology (MS, Psy D); counseling psychology (MA). Electronic applications accepted.

PALM BEACH ATLANTIC UNIVERSITY, West Palm Beach, FL 33416-4708

General Information Independent-religious, coed, comprehensive institution. *Enrollment:* 3,659 graduate, professional, and undergraduate students; 579 full-time matriculated graduate/professional students (395 women), 239 part-time matriculated graduate/professional students (158 women). *Enrollment by degree level:* 301 first professional, 517 master's. *Graduate faculty:* 47 full-time (21 women), 18 part-time/adjunct (7 women). *Tuition:* Full-time $8280; part-time $460 per credit hour. *Required fees:* $99 per semester. Tuition and fees vary according to course load, degree level and campus/location. *Graduate housing:* On-campus housing not available. *Student services:* Campus safety program, career counseling, exercise/wellness program, free psychological counseling, international student services, low-cost health insurance, multicultural affairs office, services for students with disabilities, writing training. *Library facilities:* Warren Library. *Online resources:* library catalog, web page. *Collection:* 198,396 titles, 25,098 serial subscriptions, 5,800 audiovisual materials.

Computer facilities: 465 computers available on campus for general student use. A campuswide network can be accessed from student residence rooms and from off campus. Online class registration is available. *Web address:* http://www.pba.edu/.

General Application Contact: Joe Sharp, Dean of Admissions, 888-468-6722, E-mail: grad@pba.edu.

GRADUATE UNITS

Gregory School of Pharmacy Students: 291 full-time (170 women), 10 part-time (8 women); includes 18 Black or African American, non-Hispanic/Latino; 1 American Indian or Alaska Native, non-Hispanic/Latino; 58 Asian, non-Hispanic/Latino; 34 Hispanic/Latino; 2 Native Hawaiian or other Pacific Islander, non-Hispanic/Latino, 11 international. Average age 25. 546 applicants, 33% accepted, 79 enrolled. *Faculty:* 17 full-time (13 women), 2 part-time/adjunct (1 woman). Expenses: Contact institution. *Financial support:* Unspecified assistantships available. Financial award applicants required to submit FAFSA. In 2010, 85 Pharm Ds awarded. Offers pharmacy (Pharm D). *Application deadline:* For fall admission, 5/31 priority date for domestic and international students. Applications are processed on a rolling basis. *Application fee:* $85. Electronic applications accepted. *Application Contact:* Lucas Whittaker, Director of Pharmacy Admissions, 561-803-2750. *Dean,* Dr. Mary Ferrill, 561-803-2700, E-mail: mary_ferrill@pba.edu.

MacArthur School of Leadership Students: 5 full-time (all women), 83 part-time (56 women); includes 34 minority (20 Black or African American, non-Hispanic/Latino; 1 American Indian or Alaska Native, non-Hispanic/Latino; 1 Asian, non-Hispanic/Latino; 12 Hispanic/Latino), 1 international. Average age 37. 46 applicants, 91% accepted, 35 enrolled. *Faculty:* 5 full-time (2 women), 3 part-time/adjunct (0 women). Expenses: Contact institution. *Financial support:* Tuition waivers (partial) available. Financial award applicants required to submit FAFSA. In 2010, 32 master's awarded. *Degree program information:* Part-time and evening/weekend programs available. Offers organizational leadership (MS). *Application deadline:* For fall admission, 7/15 priority date for domestic students; for spring admission, 11/15 priority date for domestic students. Applications are processed on a rolling basis. *Application fee:* $45. Electronic applications accepted. *Application Contact:* Graduate Admissions, 888-468-6722, E-mail: grad@pba.edu. *Dean,* Dr. Jim Laub, 561-803-2302, E-mail: jim_laub@pba.edu.

Rinker School of Business Students: 33 full-time (11 women), 80 part-time (43 women); includes 26 minority (15 Black or African American, non-Hispanic/Latino; 3 Asian, non-Hispanic/Latino; 8 Hispanic/Latino), 16 international. Average age 32. 48 applicants, 92% accepted, 40 enrolled. *Faculty:* 10 full-time (3 women), 3 part-time/adjunct (1 woman). Expenses: Contact institution. *Financial support:* Applicants required to submit FAFSA. In 2010, 54 master's awarded. *Degree program information:* Part-time and evening/weekend programs available. Offers business (MBA). *Application deadline:* For fall admission, 7/15 priority date for domestic students; for spring admission, 11/15 priority date for domestic students. Applications are processed on a rolling basis. *Application fee:* $45. Electronic applications accepted. *Application Contact:* Graduate Admissions, 888-468-6722, Fax: 561-803-2115, E-mail: grad@pba.edu. *MBA Program Director,* Dr. Edgar Langlois, 561-803-2456, E-mail: edgar_langlois@pba.edu.

School of Education and Behavioral Studies Students: 250 full-time (209 women), 61 part-time (47 women); includes 63 Black or African American, non-Hispanic/Latino; 2 Asian, non-Hispanic/Latino; 37 Hispanic/Latino; 1 Native Hawaiian or other Pacific Islander, non-Hispanic/Latino, 7 international. Average age 35. 108 applicants, 92% accepted, 83 enrolled. *Faculty:* 13 full-time (3 women), 10 part-time/adjunct (5 women). Expenses: Contact institution. *Financial support:* Applicants required to submit FAFSA. In 2010, 96 master's awarded. *Degree program information:* Part-time and evening/weekend programs available. Offers counseling psychology (MSCP). *Application deadline:* For fall admission, 7/15 priority date for domestic students; for spring admission, 11/15 priority date for domestic students. Applications are processed on a rolling basis. *Application fee:* $45. Electronic applications accepted. *Application Contact:* Graduate Admissions, 888-468-6722, E-mail: grad@pba.edu. *Program Director,* Dr. Lisa Stubbs, 561-803-2286.

PALMER COLLEGE OF CHIROPRACTIC, Davenport, IA 52803-5287

General Information Independent, coed, comprehensive institution. *Enrollment:* 2,310 graduate, professional, and undergraduate students; 2,225 full-time matriculated graduate/professional students (797 women), 18 part-time matriculated graduate/professional students (5 women). *Enrollment by degree level:* 2,229 first professional, 14 master's. *Graduate faculty:* 149 full-time (57 women), 35 part-time/adjunct (15 women). *Tuition:* Full-time $28,650; part-time $368 per credit hour. *Required fees:* $85 per trimester. One-time fee: $150. *Student services:* Campus employment opportunities, campus safety program, career counseling, child daycare facilities, exercise/wellness program, free psychological counseling, international student services, low-cost health insurance, services for students with disabilities. *Library facilities:* David D. Palmer Health Sciences Library. *Online resources:* library catalog, web page. *Collection:* 72,918 titles, 24,697 serial subscriptions, 1,200 audiovisual materials.

Computer facilities: 94 computers available on campus for general student use. A campuswide network can be accessed. *Web address:* http://www.palmer.edu/.

General Application Contact: Karen Eden, Director of Admissions, 563-884-5656, Fax: 563-884-5414, E-mail: pcadmit@palmer.edu.

GRADUATE UNITS

Division of Graduate Studies Students: 7 full-time (2 women), 1 (woman) part-time; includes 1 Black or African American, non-Hispanic/Latino. 3 applicants, 100% accepted, 3 enrolled. *Faculty:* 8 full-time (3 women), 3 part-time/adjunct (2 women). Expenses: Contact institution. *Financial support:* In 2010–11, 7 students received support, including 7 research assistantships with full tuition reimbursements available (averaging $30,000 per year), teaching assistantships with full and partial tuition reimbursements available (averaging $6,269 per year); tuition waivers (full) and unspecified assistantships also available. Financial award application deadline: 8/1; financial award applicants required to submit FAFSA. In 2010, 5 master's awarded. Offers clinical research (MS). *Application deadline:* For fall admission, 8/1 for domestic and international students; for spring admission, 5/28 for domestic students. Applications are processed on a rolling basis. *Application fee:* $50. Electronic applications accepted. *Application Contact:* Lori Byrd, Program Coordinator, 563-884-5198, Fax: 563-884-5227, E-mail: lori.byrd@plamer.edu. *Interim Vice President for Academic Affairs,* Dr. Dan Weinert, 563-884-5761, Fax: 563-884-5624, E-mail: weinert_d@palmer.edu.

Professional Program Students: 1,170 full-time (397 women), 8 part-time (2 women); includes 133 minority (16 Black or African American, non-Hispanic/Latino; 5 American Indian or Alaska Native, non-Hispanic/Latino; 73 Asian, non-Hispanic/Latino; 31 Hispanic/Latino; 1 Native Hawaiian or other Pacific Islander, non-Hispanic/Latino; 7 Two or more races, non-Hispanic/Latino), 2 international. Average age 24. 380 applicants, 36% accepted, 134 enrolled. *Faculty:* 71 full-time (23 women), 7 part-time/adjunct (2 women). Expenses: Contact institution. *Financial support:* Career-related internships or fieldwork, Federal Work-Study, and scholarships/grants available. Support available to part-time students. Financial award application deadline: 4/1; financial award applicants required to submit FAFSA. In 2010, 574 DCs awarded. *Degree program information:* Part-time programs available. Offers chiropractic (DC). *Application deadline:* Applications are processed on a rolling basis. *Application fee:* $50. Electronic applications accepted. *Application Contact:* Karen Eden, Director of Admissions, 563-884-5656, Fax: 563-884-5414, E-mail: pcadmit@palmer.edu. *Chancellor,* Dr. Dennis Marchiori, 563-884-5466, Fax: 563-884-5624, E-mail: marchiori_d@palmer.edu.

Professional Program–Florida Campus Students: 740 full-time (284 women); includes 40 Black or African American, non-Hispanic/Latino; 2 American Indian or Alaska Native, non-Hispanic/Latino; 23 Asian, non-Hispanic/Latino; 63 Hispanic/Latino; 8 Two or more races, non-Hispanic/Latino. Average age 25. *Faculty:* 47 full-time (12 women), 4 part-time/adjunct (2 women). Expenses: Contact institution. *Financial support:* Career-related internships or fieldwork, Federal Work-Study, and scholarships/grants available. Support available to part-time students. Financial award application deadline: 4/1; financial award applicants required to submit FAFSA. In 2010, 152 DCs awarded. *Degree program information:* Part-time programs available. Offers chiropractic (DC). *Application fee:* $50. *Application Contact:* Admissions Representative, 866-585-9677, Fax: 386-763-2620, E-mail: pcaf_admiss@palmer.edu. *Chancellor,* Dr. Dennis Marchiori, 563-884-5511, Fax: 563-884-5409, E-mail: marchiori_d@palmer.edu.

Professional Program–West Campus Students: 308 full-time (112 women), 6 part-time (2 women); includes 4 Black or African American, non-Hispanic/Latino; 3 American Indian or Alaska Native, non-Hispanic/Latino; 64 Asian, non-Hispanic/Latino; 28 Hispanic/Latino, 3 international. Average age 28. 73 applicants, 60% accepted, 35 enrolled. *Faculty:* 21 full-time (6 women), 16 part-time/adjunct (7 women). Expenses: Contact institution. *Financial support:* Career-related internships or fieldwork, Federal Work-Study, and scholarships/grants available. Support available to part-time students. Financial award application deadline: 4/1; financial award applicants required to submit FAFSA. In 2010, 117 DCs awarded. *Degree program information:* Part-time programs available. Offers chiropractic (DC). *Application deadline:* Applications are processed on a rolling basis. *Application fee:* $50. Electronic applications accepted. *Application Contact:* Julie Behn, Campus Enrollment Director, 408-944-6121, Fax: 408-944-6032, E-mail: julie.behn@palmer.edu. *Campus Enrollment Director,* Julie Behn, 408-944-6121, Fax: 908-944-6032, E-mail: julie.behn@palmer.edu.

PALO ALTO UNIVERSITY, Palo Alto, CA 94303-4232

General Information Independent, coed, graduate-only institution. *Graduate housing:* On-campus housing not available.

GRADUATE UNITS

Distance Learning Program in Psychology Postbaccalaureate distance learning degree programs offered (no on-campus study). Offers psychology (MS). Electronic applications accepted.

PGSP-Stanford Psy D Consortium Program Offers psychology (Psy D). Program offered jointly with Stanford University. Electronic applications accepted.

Program in Clinical Psychology Offers clinical psychology (PhD). JD/PhD offered jointly with Golden Gate University; MBA/PhD with Masagung Graduate School of Management. Electronic applications accepted.

PARKER COLLEGE OF CHIROPRACTIC, Dallas, TX 75229-5668

General Information Independent, coed, graduate-only institution. *Graduate housing:* On-campus housing not available.

GRADUATE UNITS

Doctor of Chiropractic Program *Degree program information:* Part-time programs available. Offers chiropractic (DC). Electronic applications accepted.

PARK UNIVERSITY, Parkville, MO 64152-3795

General Information Independent, coed, comprehensive institution. *Graduate housing:* Room and/or apartments available on a first-come, first-served basis to single students; on-campus housing not available to married students.

GRADUATE UNITS

College of Graduate and Professional Studies *Degree program information:* Part-time and evening/weekend programs available. Postbaccalaureate distance learning degree programs offered (no on-campus study). Offers adult education (M Ed); at-risk students (M Ed); disaster and emergency management (MPA); educational administration (M Ed); entrepreneurship (MBA); general business (MBA); general education (M Ed); government/business relations (MPA); healthcare/services management (MBA, MPA); international business (MBA); K-12 certification (MAT); management information systems (MBA); management of information systems (MPA); middle school certification (MAT); multi-cultural education (M Ed); nonprofit management (MPA); public management (MPA); school law (M Ed); secondary school certification (MAT); special education (M Ed). Electronic applications accepted.

PAYNE THEOLOGICAL SEMINARY, Wilberforce, OH 45384-3474

General Information Independent-religious, coed, graduate-only institution. *Graduate housing:* Rooms and/or apartments available on a first-come, first-served basis to single and married students. Housing application deadline: 8/15.

GRADUATE UNITS

Program in Theology *Degree program information:* Part-time and evening/weekend programs available. Postbaccalaureate distance learning degree programs offered (minimal on-campus study). Offers theology (M Div).

PENN STATE DICKINSON SCHOOL OF LAW, Carlisle, PA 17013-2899

General Information State-related, coed, graduate-only institution. *Graduate housing:* On-campus housing not available. *Student services:* Campus employment opportunities, campus safety program, career counseling, international student services, low-cost health insurance, services for students with disabilities, teacher training, writing training. *Library facilities:* The H. Laddie Montague, Jr. Law Library of The Dickinson School of Law. *Online resources:* library catalog, web page, access to other libraries' catalogs.

Computer facilities: A campuswide network can be accessed from student residence rooms and from off campus. Online class registration is available. *Web address:* http://www.dsl.psu.edu/.

General Application Contact: Barbara W. Guillaume, Director, Law Admissions, 717-240-5207, Fax: 717-241-3503, E-mail: bwg1@psu.edu.

GRADUATE UNITS

Graduate and Professional Programs Students: 586 full-time (234 women), 11 part-time (5 women). Average age 25. Expenses: Contact institution. *Financial support:* Research assistantships, Federal Work-Study, institutionally sponsored loans, and scholarships/grants available. Support available to part-time students. Financial award application deadline: 3/1; financial award applicants required to submit FAFSA. In 2010, 202 first professional degrees, 12 master's awarded. *Degree program information:* Part-time programs available. Offers comparative law (LL M); law (JD). *Application deadline:* For fall admission, 3/1 priority date for domestic students. Applications are processed on a rolling basis. *Application fee:* $60. Electronic applications accepted. *Application Contact:* Barbara W. Guillaume, Director, Law Admissions, 717-240-5207, Fax: 717-241-3503, E-mail: bwg1@psu.edu. *Dean*, Philip J. McConnaughay, 814-863-1521, E-mail: pjm30@psu.edu.

PENN STATE ERIE, THE BEHREND COLLEGE, Erie, PA 16563-0001

General Information State-related, coed, comprehensive institution. *Graduate housing:* Room and/or apartments available on a first-come, first-served basis to single students; on-campus housing not available to married students. *Student services:* Campus employment opportunities, campus safety program, career counseling, child daycare facilities, exercise/wellness program, free psychological counseling, grant writing training, international student services, low-cost health insurance, multicultural affairs office, services for students with disabilities. *Library facilities:* John M. Lilley Library. *Online resources:* library catalog, web page, access to other libraries' catalogs.

Computer facilities: Computer purchase and lease plans are available. A campuswide network can be accessed from student residence rooms and from off campus. Online class registration is available. *Web address:* http://www.pserie.psu.edu/.

General Application Contact: Ann M. Burbules, Graduate Admissions Counselor, 814-898-7255, Fax: 814-898-6044, E-mail: amb29@psu.edu.

GRADUATE UNITS

Graduate School Students: 48 full-time (9 women), 59 part-time (17 women). Average age 28. 70 applicants, 70% accepted, 35 enrolled. Expenses: Contact institution. *Financial support:* Federal Work-Study available. Financial award application deadline: 2/15; financial award applicants required to submit FAFSA. In 2010, 123 master's awarded. *Degree program information:* Part-time programs available. Offers business administration (MBA); engineering (M Eng). *Application deadline:* Applications are processed on a rolling basis. *Application fee:* $65. Electronic applications accepted. *Application Contact:* Ann M. Burbules, Graduate Admissions Counselor, 814-898-7255, Fax: 814-898-6044, E-mail: amb29@psu.edu. *Chief Executive Officer/Dean*, Dr. John D. Burke, 814-898-6160, Fax: 814-898-6461, E-mail: jdb1@psu.edu.

PENN STATE GREAT VALLEY, Malvern, PA 19355-1488

General Information State-related, coed, graduate-only institution. *Graduate housing:* On-campus housing not available. *Student services:* Campus employment opportunities, campus safety program, career counseling, grant writing training, international student services, low-cost health insurance, multicultural affairs office, services for students with disabilities. *Library facilities:* Great Valley Library. *Online resources:* library catalog, web page, access to other libraries' catalogs.

Computer facilities: A campuswide network can be accessed from off campus. Online class registration is available. *Web address:* http://www.gv.psu.edu/.

General Application Contact: Dr. Kathy Mingioni, Assistant Director of Admissions, 610-648-3315, Fax: 610-725-5296, E-mail: kgm2@psu.edu.

GRADUATE UNITS

Graduate Studies Students: 80 full-time (33 women), 868 part-time (377 women). Average age 33. 391 applicants, 78% accepted, 225 enrolled. Expenses: Contact institution. *Financial support:* Fellowships, research assistantships, teaching assistantships, Federal Work-Study, scholarships/grants, health care benefits, and unspecified assistantships available. Support available to part-time students. Financial award application deadline: 2/15; financial award applicants required to submit FAFSA. In 2010, 375 master's awarded. *Degree program information:* Evening/weekend programs available. *Application deadline:* Applications are processed on a rolling basis. *Application fee:* $65. Electronic applications accepted. *Application Contact:* 610-648-3242, Fax: 610-889-1334. *Chancellor*, Dr. Craig Edelbrock, 610-648-3202, E-mail: cse1@psu.edu.

Education Division Expenses: Contact institution. Offers education (M Ed, MS). *Application Contact:* Dr. Roy Clariana, Division Head, 610-648-3253, Fax: 610-725-5253, E-mail: rbc4@psu.edu. *Division Head*, Dr. Roy Clariana, 610-648-3253, Fax: 610-725-5253, E-mail: rbc4@psu.edu.

Engineering Division Expenses: Contact institution. Offers engineering (ME, MEM, MS, MSE). *Application Contact:* Dr. James A. Nemes, Division Head, 610-648-3335 Ext. 610, Fax: 648-648-3377, E-mail: jan16@psu.edu. *Division Head*, Dr. James A. Nemes, 610-648-3335 Ext. 610, Fax: 648-648-3377, E-mail: jan16@psu.edu.

Management Division Expenses: Contact institution. Offers management (M Fin, MBA, MLD). *Application Contact:* Dr. Daniel Indro, Division Head, 610-725-5283, Fax: 610-725-5224, E-mail: dci1@psu.edu. *Division Head*, Dr. Daniel Indro, 610-725-5283, Fax: 610-725-5224, E-mail: dci1@psu.edu.

PENN STATE HARRISBURG, Middletown, PA 17057-4898

General Information State-related, coed, comprehensive institution. *Graduate housing:* Room and/or apartments available on a first-come, first-served basis to single students; on-campus housing not available to married students. *Student services:* Campus employment opportunities, campus safety program, career counseling, child daycare facilities, exercise/wellness program, free psychological counseling, grant writing training, international student services, low-cost health insurance, multicultural affairs office, services for students with disabilities, writing training. *Library facilities:* Penn State Harrisburg Library. *Online resources:* library catalog, web page, access to other libraries' catalogs.

Computer facilities: Computer purchase and lease plans are available. A campuswide network can be accessed from student residence rooms and from off campus. Online class registration is available. *Web address:* http://www.hbg.psu.edu/.

General Application Contact: Robert Coffman, Director of Admissions, 717-948-6250, Fax: 717-948-6325, E-mail: ric1@psu.edu.

GRADUATE UNITS

Graduate School Students: 190 full-time (104 women), 1,114 part-time (706 women). Average age 31. 736 applicants, 75% accepted, 367 enrolled. Expenses: Contact institution. *Financial support:* Fellowships, research assistantships, teaching assistantships, career-related internships or fieldwork, Federal Work-Study, and unspecified assistantships available. Support available to part-time students. Financial award application deadline: 2/15; financial award applicants required to submit FAFSA. In 2010, 496 master's, 15 doctorates awarded. *Degree program information:* Part-time and evening/weekend programs available. *Application deadline:* Applications are processed on a rolling basis. *Application fee:* $65. Electronic applications accepted. *Application Contact:* Robert Coffman, Director of Admissions, 717-948-6250, Fax: 717-948-6325, E-mail: ric1@psu.edu. *Interim Chancellor*, Dr. Mukund Kulkarni, 717-948-6000, Fax: 717-948-6100, E-mail: msk5@psu.edu.

School of Behavioral Sciences and Education Expenses: Contact institution. *Financial support:* Career-related internships or fieldwork available. *Degree program information:* Part-time and evening/weekend programs available. Offers behavioral sciences and education (M Ed, MA, D Ed). *Application Contact:* Robert Coffman, Director of Admissions, 717-948-6214, E-mail: rwc11@psu.edu. *Director*, Dr. William D. Milheim, 717-948-6205, Fax: 717-948-6209, E-mail: wdm2@psu.edu.

School of Business Administration Expenses: Contact institution. Offers business administration (MBA, MS). *Application Contact:* Dr. Stephen P. Schappe, Acting Director, 717-948-6141, E-mail: sxs28@psu.edu. *Acting Director*, Dr. Stephen P. Schappe, 717-948-6141, E-mail: sxs28@psu.edu.

School of Humanities Expenses: Contact institution. *Degree program information:* Evening/weekend programs available. Offers American studies (MA). *Application Contact:* Robert Coffman, Director of Admissions, 717-948-6250, Fax: 717-948-6325, E-mail: ric1@psu.edu. *Director*, Dr. Kathryn Robinson, 717-948-6470, E-mail: kdr12@psu.edu.

School of Public Affairs Expenses: Contact institution. Offers public affairs (MA, MHA, MPA, PhD). *Application Contact:* Robert Coffman, Director of Admissions, 717-948-6250, Fax: 717-948-6325, E-mail: ric1@psu.edu. *Director*, Dr. Steven A. Peterson, 717-948-6154, E-mail: sap12@psu.edu.

School of Science, Engineering and Technology Expenses: Contact institution. *Degree program information:* Evening/weekend programs available. Offers science, engineering and technology (M Eng, MEPC, MPS, MS). *Application Contact:* Robert Coffman, Director of Admissions, 717-948-6250, Fax: 717-948-6325, E-mail: ric1@psu.edu. *Director*, Dr. Omid Ansary, 717-948-6353, E-mail: axa8@psu.edu.

PENN STATE HERSHEY MEDICAL CENTER, Hershey, PA 17033-2360

General Information State-related, coed, graduate-only institution. *Enrollment by degree level:* 31 master's, 146 doctoral, 22 other advanced degrees. *Graduate faculty:* 209 full-time (47 women), 7 part-time/adjunct (3 women). *Graduate housing:* Rooms and/or apartments available on a first-come, first-served basis to single and married students. Typical cost: $5952 per year for single students; $11,904 per year for married students. *Student services:* Campus safety program, career counseling, child daycare facilities, exercise/wellness program, free psychological counseling, grant writing training, international student services, low-cost health insurance, multicultural affairs office, services for students with disabilities, teacher training, writing training. *Library facilities:* George T. Harrell Library. *Online resources:* library catalog, web page, access to other libraries' catalogs. *Collection:* 40 titles, 5 serial subscriptions.

Computer facilities: A campuswide network can be accessed from student residence rooms and from off campus. Online class registration is available. *Web address:* http://www.hmc.psu.edu/college/.

General Application Contact: Dr. Michael F. Verderame, Associate Dean of Graduate Studies, 717-531-8892, Fax: 717-531-0786, E-mail: grad-hmc@psu.edu.

GRADUATE UNITS

College of Medicine Expenses: Contact institution. *Financial support:* In 2010–11, 99 students received support, including research assistantships with full tuition reimbursements available (averaging $22,260 per year); fellowships with full tuition reimbursements available, career-related internships or fieldwork, scholarships/grants, health care benefits, and unspecified assistantships also available. Offers medicine (MD, MS, PhD). *Application deadline:* Applications are processed on a rolling basis. *Application fee:* $65. Electronic applications accepted. *Application Contact:* Dr. Michael Verderame, Assistant Dean for Graduate Studies, 717-531-8892, Fax: 717-531-0786, E-mail: grad-hmc@psu.edu. *Assistant Dean for Graduate Studies*, Dr. Michael Verderame, 717-531-8892, Fax: 717-531-0786, E-mail: grad-hmc@psu.edu.

Graduate School Programs in the Biomedical Sciences Average age 24. Expenses: Contact institution. *Financial support:* In 2010–11, 3 fellowships with full tuition reimbursements (averaging $26,500 per year), 37 research assistantships with full tuition reimbursements (averaging $22,250 per year) were awarded; career-related internships or fieldwork, scholarships/grants, health care benefits, tuition waivers (full), and unspecified assistantships also available. Financial award applicants required to submit FAFSA. Offers anatomy (MS, PhD); biochemistry and molecular biology (MS, PhD); bioengineering (MS, PhD); biomedical sciences (MS, PhD); cell and molecular biology (MS, PhD); genetics (PhD); immunology (MS, PhD); integrative biosciences (MS, PhD); laboratory animal medicine (MS); life sciences (MS, PhD); microbiology (MS); microbiology/virology (PhD); molecular biology (PhD); molecular medicine (MS, PhD); molecular toxicology (MS, PhD); neuroscience (MS, PhD); pharmacology (MS, PhD); physiology (MS, PhD); public health sciences (MS). *Application deadline:* For fall admission, 1/31 priority date for domestic students, 2/1 priority date for international students. Applications are processed on a rolling basis. *Application fee:* $65. Electronic applications accepted. *Application Contact:* Kathleen M. Simon, Administrative Assistant, 717-531-8892, Fax: 717-531-0786, E-mail: grad-hmc@psu.edu. *Associate Dean of Graduate Studies*, Dr. Michael F. Verderame, 717-531-8892, Fax: 717-531-0786, E-mail: grad-hmc@psu.edu.

PENN STATE UNIVERSITY PARK, State College, University Park, PA 16802-1503

General Information State-related, coed, university. CGS member. *Graduate housing:* Rooms and/or apartments available on a first-come, first-served basis to single and married students. *Student services:* Campus employment opportunities, campus safety program, career counseling, child daycare facilities, exercise/wellness program, free psychological counseling, grant writing training, international student services, low-cost health insurance, multicultural affairs office, services for students with disabilities, teacher training, writing training. *Library facilities:* Pattee Library plus 16 others. *Online resources:* library catalog, web page, access to other libraries' catalogs. *Collection:* 5.4 million titles, 109,132 serial subscriptions, 127,834 audiovisual materials.

Computer facilities: Computer purchase and lease plans are available. 6,150 computers available on campus for general student use. A campuswide network can be accessed from student residence rooms and from off campus. Online class registration is available. *Web address:* http://www.psu.edu/.

General Application Contact: Cynthia E. Nicosia, Director, Graduate Enrollment Services, 814-865-1834, E-mail: cey1@psu.edu.

GRADUATE UNITS

Graduate School Students: 5,347 full-time (2,346 women), 876 part-time (462 women). Average age 30. 14,442 applicants, 23% accepted, 1618 enrolled. Expenses: Contact institution. *Financial support:* Fellowships, research assistantships, teaching assistantships, Federal Work-Study, traineeships, health care benefits, tuition waivers (full), and unspecified assistantships available. Support available to part-time students. Financial award application deadline: 2/15; financial award applicants required to submit FAFSA. In 2010, 1,218 master's, 598 doctorates awarded. *Degree program information:* Part-time programs available. Postbaccalaureate distance learning degree programs offered. *Application deadline:* Applications are processed on a rolling basis. *Application fee:* $65. Electronic applications accepted. *Application Contact:* Cynthia E. Nicosia, Director, Graduate Enrollment Services, 814-865-1795, Fax: 814-865-4627, E-mail: cey1@psu.edu. *Vice President, Research/Dean,* Dr. Henry C. Foley, 814-863-9580, Fax: 814-863-9659, E-mail: hcf2@psu.edu.

College of Agricultural Sciences Students: 336 full-time (192 women), 31 part-time (16 women). Average age 29. 528 applicants, 30% accepted, 91 enrolled. Expenses: Contact institution. *Financial support:* Fellowships, research assistantships, teaching assistantships available. Financial award applicants required to submit FAFSA. In 2010, 65 master's, 40 doctorates awarded. Offers agricultural and biological engineering (MS, PhD); agricultural and extension education (M Ed, MS, PhD); agricultural economics and rural sociology (MS, PhD); agricultural sciences (M Agr, M Ed, MFR, MPS, MS, PhD); crop and soil sciences (MS, PhD); dairy and animal science (MPS, MS, PhD); entomology (MS, PhD); food science (MS, PhD); forest resources (M Agr, MFR, MS, PhD); horticulture (M Agr, MS, PhD); pathobiology (PhD); plant pathology (MS, PhD). *Application deadline:* Applications are processed on a rolling basis. *Application fee:* $65. Electronic applications accepted. *Application Contact:* Cynthia E. Nicosia, Director of Graduate Enrollment Services, 814-865-1834, E-mail: cey1@psu.edu. *Dean,* Dr. Bruce A. McPheron, 814-865-2541, Fax: 814-865-3103, E-mail: bam10@psu.edu.

College of Arts and Architecture Students: 199 full-time (119 women), 19 part-time (13 women). Average age 29. 407 applicants, 40% accepted, 84 enrolled. Expenses: Contact institution. *Financial support:* Fellowships, research assistantships, teaching assistantships available. Financial award applicants required to submit FAFSA. In 2010, 82 master's, 12 doctorates awarded. Offers architecture (M Arch, PhD); art history (MA, PhD); arts and architecture (M Arch, M Ed, M Mus, MA, MFA, MLA, MME, MPS, MS, DMA, PhD); landscape architecture (MLA, MS); music (M Mus, MA, MME, DMA, PhD); theatre (MFA); visual arts (M Ed, MFA, MPS, MS, PhD). *Application deadline:* Applications are processed on a rolling basis. *Application fee:* $65. Electronic applications accepted. *Application Contact:* Cynthia E. Nicosia, Director, Graduate Enrollment Services, 814-865-1834, E-mail: cey1@psu.edu. *Dean,* Dr. Barbara O. Korner, 814-865-2591, Fax: 814-865-2018, E-mail: bok2@psu.edu.

College of Communications Students: 71 full-time (44 women), 14 part-time (11 women). Average age 31. 201 applicants, 29% accepted, 18 enrolled. Expenses: Contact institution. *Financial support:* Fellowships, research assistantships, teaching assistantships available. Financial award applicants required to submit FAFSA. In 2010, 6 master's, 13 doctorates awarded. Offers communications (MA, PhD). *Application deadline:* Applications are processed on a rolling basis. *Application fee:* $65. Electronic applications accepted. *Application Contact:* Cynthia E. Nicosia, Director, Graduate Enrollment Services, 814-865-1834, E-mail: cey1@psu.edu. *Dean,* Dr. Douglas A. Anderson, 814-863-1484, Fax: 814-863-8044, E-mail: douganderson@psu.edu.

College of Earth and Mineral Sciences Students: 362 full-time (131 women), 33 part-time (10 women). Average age 28. 634 applicants, 37% accepted, 110 enrolled. Expenses: Contact institution. *Financial support:* Fellowships, research assistantships, teaching assistantships available. Financial award applicants required to submit FAFSA. In 2010, 73 master's, 51 doctorates awarded. Offers earth and mineral sciences (MS, PhD); energy and mineral engineering (MS, PhD); geography (MS, PhD); geosciences (MS, PhD); materials science and engineering (MS, PhD); meteorology (MS, PhD). *Application deadline:* Applications are processed on a rolling basis. *Application fee:* $65. Electronic applications accepted. *Application Contact:* Cynthia E. Nicosia, Director of Graduate Enrollment Services, 814-865-1834, E-mail: cey1@psu.edu. *Dean,* Dr. William E. Easterling, 814-865-6546, Fax: 814-863-7708, E-mail: wee2@psu.edu.

College of Education Students: 513 full-time (363 women), 288 part-time (181 women). Average age 35. 854 applicants, 42% accepted, 194 enrolled. Expenses: Contact institution. *Financial support:* Fellowships, research assistantships, teaching assistantships available. Financial award applicants required to submit FAFSA. In 2010, 199 master's, 97 doctorates awarded. Offers counselor education, counseling psychology and rehabilitation services (M Ed, MS, PhD); curriculum and instruction (M Ed, MS, D Ed, PhD); education (M Ed, MA, MS, D Ed, PhD); education policy studies (MA, PhD); educational and school psychology and special education (M Ed, MS, PhD); learning and performance systems (M Ed, MS, D Ed, PhD). *Application deadline:* Applications are processed on a rolling basis. *Application fee:* $65. Electronic applications accepted. *Application Contact:* Cynthia E. Nicosia, Director, Graduate Enrollment Services, 814-865-1834, E-mail: cey1@psu.edu. *Dean,* Dr. David H. Monk, 814-865-2526, Fax: 814-865-0555, E-mail: dhm6@psu.edu.

College of Engineering Students: 1,169 full-time (235 women), 133 part-time (16 women). Average age 27. 3,916 applicants, 26% accepted, 369 enrolled. Expenses: Contact institution. *Financial support:* Fellowships, research assistantships, teaching assistantships available. Financial award applicants required to submit FAFSA. In 2010, 310 master's, 131 doctorates awarded. Offers aerospace engineering (M Eng, MS, PhD); architectural engineering (M Eng, MAE, MS, PhD); chemical engineering (MS, PhD); civil and environmental engineering (M Eng, MS, PhD); computer science and engineering (M Eng, MS, PhD); electrical engineering (MS, PhD); engineering (M Eng, MAE, MS, PhD); engineering science and mechanics (M Eng, MS, PhD); industrial and manufacturing engineering (M Eng, MS, PhD); mechanical and nuclear engineering (M Eng, MS, PhD). *Application deadline:* Applications are processed on a rolling basis. *Application fee:* $65. Electronic applications accepted. *Application Contact:* Cynthia E. Nicosia, Director, Graduate Enrollment Services, 814-865-1834, E-mail: cey1@psu.edu. *Dean,* Dr. David N. Wormley, 814-865-7537, Fax: 814-865-8767, E-mail: dnw2@engr.psu.edu.

College of Health and Human Development Students: 318 full-time (236 women), 21 part-time (8 women). Average age 28. 612 applicants, 32% accepted, 108 enrolled. Expenses: Contact institution. *Financial support:* Fellowships, research assistantships, teaching assistantships available. Financial award applicants required to submit FAFSA. In 2010, 70 master's, 35 doctorates awarded. Offers biobehavioral health (PhD); communication sciences and disorders (MS, PhD); health and human development (M Ed, MBA, MHA, MS, PhD); health policy and administration (MBA, MHA, MS, PhD); hospitality management (MS, PhD); human development and family studies (MS, PhD); kinesiology (MS, PhD); nursing (MS, PhD); nutritional sciences (M Ed, MS, PhD); recreation, park and tourism management (MS, PhD). *Application deadline:* Applications are processed on a rolling basis. *Application fee:* $65. Electronic applications accepted. *Application Contact:* Cynthia E. Nicosia, Director, Graduate Enrollment Services, 814-865-1795, Fax: 814-865-4627, E-mail: cey1@psu.edu. *Dean,* Dr. Ann C. Crouter, 814-865-1428, Fax: 814-865-3282, E-mail: ac1@psu.edu.

College of Information Sciences and Technology Students: 95 full-time (39 women), 9 part-time (2 women). Average age 29. 183 applicants, 17% accepted, 24 enrolled. Expenses: Contact institution. *Financial support:* Fellowships, research assistantships, teaching assistantships available. Financial award applicants required to submit FAFSA. In 2010, 9 master's, 14 doctorates awarded. Offers information sciences and technology (MPS, MS, PhD). *Application deadline:* Applications are processed on a rolling basis. *Application fee:* $65. Electronic applications accepted. *Application Contact:* Cynthia E. Nicosia, Director, Graduate Enrollment Services, 814-865-1795, Fax: 814-865-4627, E-mail: cey1@psu.edu. *Interim Dean,* Dr. David L. Hall, 814-863-3528, Fax: 814-865-5604, E-mail: dlh28@psu.edu.

College of the Liberal Arts Students: 725 full-time (379 women), 51 part-time (33 women). Average age 28. 3,361 applicants, 12% accepted, 201 enrolled. Expenses: Contact institution. *Financial support:* Fellowships, research assistantships, teaching assistantships available. Financial award applicants required to submit FAFSA. In 2010, 157 master's, 88 doctorates awarded. Offers anthropology (MA, PhD); communication arts and sciences (MA, PhD); economics (MA, PhD); English (MA, MFA, PhD); French and Francophone studies (MA, PhD); German (MA, PhD); history (MA, PhD); labor studies and employment relations (MPS, MS); languages and literatures (MA, PhD); liberal arts (MA, MFA, MPS, MS, PhD); linguistics and applied language studies (MA, PhD); philosophy (MA, PhD); political science (MA, PhD); psychology (MS, PhD); sociology (MA, PhD); Spanish, Italian, and Portuguese (MA, PhD). *Application fee:* $65. *Application Contact:* Cynthia E. Nicosia, Director, Graduate Enrollment Services, 814-865-1795, Fax: 814-865-4627, E-mail: cey1@psu.edu. *Dean,* Dr. Susan Welch, 814-865-7691, Fax: 814-863-2085, E-mail: swelch@psu.edu.

Eberly College of Science Students: 686 full-time (242 women), 17 part-time (6 women). Average age 26. 1,365 applicants, 16% accepted, 131 enrolled. Expenses: Contact institution. *Financial support:* Fellowships, research assistantships, teaching assistantships available. Financial award applicants required to submit FAFSA. In 2010, 54 master's, 102 doctorates awarded. Offers astronomy and astrophysics (MS, PhD); biochemistry and molecular biology (MS, PhD); biochemistry, microbiology, and molecular biology (MS, PhD); biology (MS, PhD); chemistry (MS, PhD); mathematics (MA); physics (M Ed, MS, PhD); science (M Ed, MA, MAS, MS, D Ed, PhD); statistics (MA, MAS, MS, PhD). *Application deadline:* Applications are processed on a rolling basis. *Application fee:* $65. Electronic applications accepted. *Application Contact:* Cynthia E. Nicosia, Director, Graduate Enrollment Services, 814-865-1795, Fax: 814-865-4627, E-mail: cey1@psu.edu. *Dean,* Dr. Daniel J. Larson, 814-865-9591, Fax: 814-863-0491, E-mail: sciencedean@psu.edu.

Intercollege Graduate Programs Students: 402 full-time (167 women), 15 part-time (2 women). Average age 27. 1,221 applicants, 14% accepted, 114 enrolled. Expenses: Contact institution. *Financial support:* Fellowships, research assistantships, teaching assistantships available. Financial award applicants required to submit FAFSA. Offers acoustics (M Eng, MS, PhD); bioengineering (MS, PhD); ecology (MS, PhD); environmental pollution control (MEPC, MS); genetics (MS, PhD); integrative biosciences (PhD); physiology (MS, PhD); plant physiology (MS, PhD); quality and manufacturing management (MMM). *Application deadline:* Applications are processed on a rolling basis. *Application fee:* $45. Electronic applications accepted. *Application Contact:* Cynthia E. Nicosia, Director, Graduate Enrollment Services, 814-865-1795, Fax: 814-865-4627, E-mail: cey1@psu.edu. *Senior Associate Dean,* Dr. Regina Vasilatos-Younken, 814-865-2516, Fax: 814-863-4627, E-mail: rxv@psu.edu.

The Mary Jean and Frank P. Smeal College of Business Administration Students: 256 full-time (91 women), 2 part-time (0 women). Average age 31. 1,130 applicants, 28% accepted, 160 enrolled. Expenses: Contact institution. *Financial support:* Fellowships, research assistantships, teaching assistantships available. Financial award applicants required to submit FAFSA. In 2010, 171 master's, 9 doctorates awarded. Offers business administration (MBA, PhD). *Application deadline:* Applications are processed on a rolling basis. *Application fee:* $65. Electronic applications accepted. *Application Contact:* Cynthia E. Nicosia, Director, Graduate Enrollment Services, 814-865-1795, Fax: 814-865-4627, E-mail: cey1@psu.edu. *Dean,* Dr. James B. Thomas, 814-863-0448, Fax: 814-865-7064, E-mail: j2t@psu.edu.

PENNSYLVANIA ACADEMY OF THE FINE ARTS, Philadelphia, PA 19102

General Information Independent, coed, graduate-only institution. *Graduate faculty:* 9 full-time (4 women), 19 part-time/adjunct (9 women). *Tuition:* Full-time $31,000. *Graduate housing:* On-campus housing not available. *Student services:* Campus employment opportunities, campus safety program, career counseling, free psychological counseling, international student services, low-cost health insurance. *Library facilities:* Arcadia Fine Arts Library. *Online resources:* library catalog, web page. *Collection:* 26,383 titles, 2,414 serial subscriptions, 20,966 audiovisual materials.

Computer facilities: 27 computers available on campus for general student use. A campuswide network can be accessed. *Web address:* http://www.pafa.edu/.

General Application Contact: Stan Greidus, Vice President of Admissions and Financial Aid, 215-972-2047, Fax: 215-569-0153, E-mail: sgreidus@pafa.edu.

GRADUATE UNITS

Graduate School Students: 104 full-time (61 women); includes 9 minority (8 Asian, non-Hispanic/Latino; 1 Hispanic/Latino). Average age 26. 115 applicants, 52% accepted, 34 enrolled. *Faculty:* 9 full-time (4 women), 19 part-time/adjunct (9 women). Expenses: Contact institution. *Financial support:* Federal Work-Study, institutionally sponsored loans, and scholarships/grants available. Financial award application deadline: 3/1; financial award applicants required to submit FAFSA. In 2010, 33 master's, 12 other advanced degrees awarded. Offers drawing (MFA, Postbaccalaureate Certificate); painting (MFA, Postbaccalaureate Certificate); printmaking (MFA, Postbaccalaureate Certificate); sculpture (MFA, Postbaccalaureate Certificate). *Application deadline:* For fall admission, 2/1 for domestic and international students. *Application fee:* $50. Electronic applications accepted. *Application Contact:* Stan Greidus, Vice President of Admissions and Financial Aid, 215-972-2047, Fax: 215-569-0153, E-mail: sgreidus@pafa.edu. *Graduate Program Coordinator,* Steven Connell, 215-972-2027, Fax: 215-569-0153, E-mail: sconnell@pafa.edu.

PENTECOSTAL THEOLOGICAL SEMINARY, Cleveland, TN 37320-3330

General Information Independent-religious, coed, graduate-only institution. *Graduate housing:* Rooms and/or apartments available to single and married students.

GRADUATE UNITS

Graduate and Professional Programs *Degree program information:* Part-time programs available. Offers counseling (MA); discipleship and Christian formations (MA); ministry (D Min); theology (M Div).

PEPPERDINE UNIVERSITY, Malibu, CA 90263

General Information Independent-religious, coed, university. CGS member. *Enrollment:* 7,604 graduate, professional, and undergraduate students; 2,376 full-time matriculated graduate/professional students (1,346 women), 1,781 part-time matriculated graduate/professional students (1,116 women). *Enrollment by degree level:* 813 first professional, 2,883 master's, 461 doctoral. *Graduate housing:* Rooms and/or apartments available on a first-come, first-served basis to single and married students. *Student services:* Campus employment opportunities, campus safety program, career counseling, exercise/wellness program, free psychological counseling, international student services, low-cost health insurance, multicultural affairs office, services for students with disabilities, teacher training. *Library facilities:* Payson Library plus 2 others. *Online resources:* library catalog, web page, access to other libraries' catalogs.

Computer facilities: Computer purchase and lease plans are available. 292 computers available on campus for general student use. A campuswide network can be accessed from student residence rooms and from off campus. Online class registration is available. *Web address:* http://www.pepperdine.edu/.

General Application Contact: Michael E. Truschke, Dean of Admission and Enrollment Management, Seaver College, 310-506-4392, Fax: 310-506-4861, E-mail: admission-seaver@pepperdine.edu.

GRADUATE UNITS

Graduate School of Education and Psychology Students: 707 full-time (571 women), 938 part-time (718 women); includes 523 minority (188 Black or African American, non-Hispanic/Latino; 12 American Indian or Alaska Native, non-Hispanic/Latino; 125 Asian, non-Hispanic/Latino; 186 Hispanic/Latino; 10 Native Hawaiian or other Pacific Islander, non-Hispanic/Latino; 2 Two or more races, non-Hispanic/Latino), 17 international. *Faculty:* 50 full-time (29 women), 114 part-time/adjunct (68 women). Expenses: Contact institution. *Financial support:* Research assistantships, teaching assistantships, career-related internships or fieldwork, Federal Work-Study, institutionally sponsored loans, scholarships/grants, and unspecified assistantships available. Support available to part-time students. Financial award applicants required to submit FAFSA. In 2010, 563 master's awarded. Offers education and psychology (MA, MS, Ed D, Psy D). *Application deadline:* Applications are processed on a rolling basis. *Application fee:* $55. *Application Contact:* Lucinda Glossop, Director, Recruitment and Admissions, 310-258-2850, E-mail: cindi.glossop@pepperdine.edu. *Dean*, Dr. Margaret J. Weber, 310-568-5600, E-mail: margaret.weber@pepperdine.edu.

Division of Education Students: 267 full-time (203 women), 439 part-time (281 women); includes 104 Black or African American, non-Hispanic/Latino; 7 American Indian or Alaska Native, non-Hispanic/Latino; 64 Asian, non-Hispanic/Latino; 89 Hispanic/Latino, 17 international. *Faculty:* 25 full-time (15 women), 11 part-time/adjunct (4 women). Expenses: Contact institution. *Financial support:* Research assistantships, teaching assistantships, career-related internships or fieldwork, institutionally sponsored loans, and scholarships/grants available. Support available to part-time students. Financial award application deadline: 7/1; financial award applicants required to submit FAFSA. In 2010, 330 master's, 68 doctorates awarded. *Degree program information:* Part-time and evening/weekend programs available. Postbaccalaureate distance learning degree programs offered (minimal on-campus study). Offers administration and preliminary administrative services credential (MS); education (MA); educational leadership, administration, and policy (Ed D); learning technologies (MA, Ed D); organization change (Ed D); organizational leadership (Ed D); social entrepreneurship and change (MA). *Application deadline:* Applications are processed on a rolling basis. *Application fee:* $45. *Application Contact:* Brenden Wysocki, Admissions Manager, 310-568-5786. *Associate Dean*, Dr. Chester McCall, 310-568-2323, E-mail: chester.mccall@pepperdine.edu.

Division of Psychology Students: 409 full-time (342 women), 523 part-time (449 women); includes 75 Black or African American, non-Hispanic/Latino; 7 American Indian or Alaska Native, non-Hispanic/Latino; 81 Asian, non-Hispanic/Latino; 100 Hispanic/Latino, 20 international. *Faculty:* 26 full-time (14 women), 78 part-time/adjunct (51 women). Expenses: Contact institution. *Financial support:* Research assistantships, teaching assistantships, career-related internships or fieldwork and scholarships/grants available. Support available to part-time students. Financial award application deadline: 7/1; financial award applicants required to submit FAFSA. *Degree program information:* Part-time and evening/weekend programs available. Offers clinical psychology (MA); marriage and family therapy (MA); psychology (MA, Psy D). *Application deadline:* For fall admission, 2/1 for domestic students. Applications are processed on a rolling basis. *Application fee:* $55. *Application Contact:* Brenden Wysocki, Admissions Manager, 310-568-5786. *Associate Dean*, Dr. Robert deMayo, 310-568-5747, E-mail: robert.demayo@pepperdine.edu.

Graziadio School of Business and Management Students: 827 full-time (346 women), 704 part-time (308 women); includes 464 minority (82 Black or African American, non-Hispanic/Latino; 10 American Indian or Alaska Native, non-Hispanic/Latino; 258 Asian, non-Hispanic/Latino; 107 Hispanic/Latino; 5 Native Hawaiian or other Pacific Islander, non-Hispanic/Latino; 2 Two or more races, non-Hispanic/Latino), 190 international. 1,356 applicants, 59% accepted, 557 enrolled. *Faculty:* 88 full-time (19 women), 46 part-time/adjunct (16 women). Expenses: Contact institution. *Financial support:* Career-related internships or fieldwork, institutionally sponsored loans, scholarships/grants, and unspecified assistantships available. Support available to part-time students. Financial award applicants required to submit FAFSA. In 2010, 815 master's awarded. *Degree program information:* Part-time programs available. Offers applied finance (MS); business administration (MBA); business and management (Exec MBA, IMBA, MBA, MS, MSOD); executive business administration (Exec MBA); global business (MS); international business administration (IMBA); management and leadership (MS); organization development (MSOD). *Application fee:* $75. Electronic applications accepted. *Application Contact:* Darrell Eriksen, Director of Admission and Student Accounts, 310-568-5525, E-mail: darrell.eriksen@pepperdine.edu. *Dean*, Dr. Linda A. Livingstone, 310-568-5689, Fax: 310-568-5766, E-mail: linda.livingstone@pepperdine.edu.

School of Law Students: 700 full-time (347 women), 48 part-time (30 women); includes 131 minority (25 Black or African American, non-Hispanic/Latino; 2 American Indian or Alaska Native, non-Hispanic/Latino; 50 Asian, non-Hispanic/Latino; 38 Hispanic/Latino; 16 Two or more races, non-Hispanic/Latino), 20 international. 3,482 applicants, 29% accepted, 240 enrolled. *Faculty:* 35 full-time (12 women), 40 part-time/adjunct (5 women). Expenses: Contact institution. *Financial support:* Fellowships, research assistantships, teaching assistantships, career-related internships or fieldwork, Federal Work-Study, institutionally sponsored loans, and scholarships/grants available. Support available to part-time students. Financial award application deadline: 4/1; financial award applicants required to submit FAFSA. In 2010, 202 first professional degrees awarded. Offers dispute resolution (LL M, MDR); law (JD, LL M, MDR). *Application deadline:* For fall admission, 3/1 priority date for domestic students, 3/1 for international students. Applications are processed on a rolling basis. *Application fee:* $60. Electronic applications accepted. *Application Contact:* Shannon Phillips, Director of Admissions and Records, 310-506-4631, Fax: 310-506-4266, E-mail: shannon.phillips@pepperdine.edu. *Vice Dean*, Timothy L. Perrin, 310-506-4662, Fax: 310-506-4266, E-mail: timothy.perrin@pepperdine.edu.

School of Public Policy Students: 123 full-time (72 women), 4 part-time (all women); includes 36 minority (11 Black or African American, non-Hispanic/Latino; 2 American Indian or Alaska Native, non-Hispanic/Latino; 11 Asian, non-Hispanic/Latino; 9 Hispanic/Latino; 3 Two or more races, non-Hispanic/Latino), 13 international. 168 applicants, 93% accepted, 66 enrolled. *Faculty:* 7 full-time (2 women), 10 part-time/adjunct (0 women). Expenses: Contact institution. *Financial support:* Institutionally sponsored loans and scholarships/grants available. Financial award application deadline: 5/1; financial award applicants required to submit FAFSA. In 2010, 50 master's awarded. Offers American politics (MPP); economics (MPP); international relations (MPP); public policy (MPP); state and local policy (MPP). *Application deadline:* For fall admission, 5/1 for domestic students. Applications are processed on a rolling basis. *Application fee:* $50. Electronic applications accepted. *Application Contact:* Melinda E. van Hemert, Director of Recruitment and Career Services, 310-506-7492, Fax: 310-506-7494, E-mail: melinda.vanhemert@pepperdine.edu. *Dean*, Dr. James R. Wilburn, 310-506-7490, Fax: 310-506-7494, E-mail: james.wilburn@pepperdine.edu.

Seaver College Expenses: Contact institution. *Financial support:* Fellowships, research assistantships, teaching assistantships, career-related internships or fieldwork, Federal Work-Study, institutionally sponsored loans, scholarships/grants, and tuition waivers (partial) available. Support available to part-time students. Financial award application deadline: 2/15; financial award applicants required to submit FAFSA. *Degree program information:* Part-time and evening/weekend programs available. Offers American studies (MA); communication (MA, MS); divinity (M Div); history (MA); ministry (MS); religion (MA); writing for screen and television (MFA). *Application deadline:* For fall admission, 5/1 for domestic students. Applications are processed on a rolling basis. *Application fee:* $55. *Application Contact:* Michael Truschke, Dean of Admission and Enrollment Management, 310-506-6165, Fax: 310-506-4861, E-mail: admission-seaver@pepperdine.edu. *Dean*, Rick Marrs, 310-506-6108, E-mail: rick.marrs@pepperdine.edu.

PERELANDRA COLLEGE, La Mesa, CA 91941

General Information Independent-religious, coed, comprehensive institution.

GRADUATE UNITS

Program in Counseling Offers counseling (MA).

Program in Creative Writing Offers creative writing (MA).

PERU STATE COLLEGE, Peru, NE 68421

General Information State-supported, coed, comprehensive institution. *Graduate housing:* Rooms and/or apartments available to single and married students.

GRADUATE UNITS

Graduate Programs *Degree program information:* Part-time programs available. Postbaccalaureate distance learning degree programs offered. Offers curriculum and instruction (MS Ed); organizational management (MS).

PFEIFFER UNIVERSITY, Misenheimer, NC 28109-0960

General Information Independent-religious, coed, comprehensive institution. *Graduate housing:* On-campus housing not available.

GRADUATE UNITS

Program in Business Administration *Degree program information:* Part-time and evening/weekend programs available. Postbaccalaureate distance learning degree programs offered (minimal on-campus study). Offers business administration (MBA).

Program in Elementary Education Offers elementary education (MAT, MS).

Program in Health Administration Offers health administration (MHA).

Program in Leadership and Organizational Change Offers leadership and organizational change (MS).

Program in Practical Theology *Degree program information:* Part-time and evening/weekend programs available. Offers practical theology (MA).

PHILADELPHIA BIBLICAL UNIVERSITY, Langhorne, PA 19047-2990

General Information Independent-religious, coed, comprehensive institution. *Enrollment:* 1,296 graduate, professional, and undergraduate students; 36 full-time matriculated graduate/professional students (20 women), 255 part-time matriculated graduate/professional students (146 women). *Enrollment by degree level:* 39 first professional, 252 master's. *Graduate faculty:* 15 full-time (3 women), 13 part-time/adjunct (10 women). *Tuition:* Full-time $10,710; part-time $595 per credit. Tuition and fees vary according to program. *Graduate housing:* Rooms and/or apartments available on a first-come, first-served basis to single and married students. Typical cost: $4162 per year for single students. *Student services:* Campus employment opportunities, campus safety program, career counseling, exercise/wellness program, international student services, low-cost health insurance, services for students with disabilities, teacher training. *Library facilities:* Masland Learning Resource Center. *Online resources:* library catalog, web page. *Collection:* 132,778 titles, 18,748 serial subscriptions, 9,540 audiovisual materials.

Computer facilities: Computer purchase and lease plans are available. 79 computers available on campus for general student use. A campuswide network can be accessed from student residence rooms and from off campus. Online class registration is available. *Web address:* http://www.pbu.edu/.

General Application Contact: Binu Abraham, Assistant Director, Graduate Admissions, 800-572-2472, Fax: 215-702-4248, E-mail: babraham@pbu.edu.

GRADUATE UNITS

Department of Christian Counseling Students: 1 (woman) full-time, 120 part-time (86 women); includes 48 minority (37 Black or African American, non-Hispanic/Latino; 5 Asian, non-Hispanic/Latino; 5 Hispanic/Latino; 1 Two or more races, non-Hispanic/Latino), 4 international. Average age 37. 78 applicants, 54% accepted, 38 enrolled. *Faculty:* 2 full-time (0 women), 10 part-time/adjunct (8 women). Expenses: Contact institution. *Financial support:* In 2010–11, 23 students received support. Scholarships/grants available. Support available to part-time students. Financial award applicants required to submit FAFSA. In 2010, 37 master's awarded. *Degree program information:* Part-time and evening/weekend programs available. Offers Christian counseling (MSCC). *Application deadline:* Applications are processed on a rolling basis. *Application fee:* $25. Electronic applications accepted. *Application Contact:* Gwen Dorsey, Enrollment Counselor, Graduate Counseling, 800-572-2472, Fax: 215-702-4248, E-mail: gdorsey@pbu.edu. *Chair*, Dr. Jeff Black, 215-702-4347, E-mail: jblack@pbu.edu.

School of Biblical Studies Students: 17 full-time (7 women), 66 part-time (17 women); includes 40 minority (35 Black or African American, non-Hispanic/Latino; 4 Asian, non-Hispanic/Latino; 1 Hispanic/Latino), 2 international. Average age 39. 38 applicants, 47% accepted, 9 enrolled. *Faculty:* 8 full-time (0 women), 1 part-time/adjunct (0 women). Expenses: Contact institution. *Financial support:* In 2010–11, 15 students received support. Scholarships/grants available. Support available to part-time students. Financial award applicants required to submit FAFSA. In 2010, 6 M Divs, 3 master's awarded. *Degree program information:* Part-time and evening/weekend programs available. Offers Biblical studies (M Div, MSB). *Application deadline:* Applications are processed on a rolling basis. *Application fee:* $25. Electronic applications accepted. *Application Contact:* Timothy Nessler, Assistant Director, Graduate Admissions, 800-572-2472, Fax: 215-702-4248, E-mail: tnessler@pbu.edu. *Dean*, Dr. O. Herbert Hirt, 215-702-4354, Fax: 215-702-4359, E-mail: bible@pbu.edu.

School of Business and Leadership Students: 3 full-time (1 woman), 26 part-time (10 women); includes 11 Black or African American, non-Hispanic/Latino; 1 Asian, non-Hispanic/Latino; 1 Hispanic/Latino, 2 international. Average age 42. 18 applicants, 78% accepted, 12 enrolled. *Faculty:* 2 full-time (0 women). Expenses: Contact institution. *Financial support:* In 2010–11, 2 students received support. Scholarships/grants available. Support available to part-time students. Financial award applicants required to submit FAFSA. In 2010, 14 master's awarded. *Degree program information:* Part-time and evening/weekend programs available. Offers organizational leadership (MSOL). *Application deadline:* Applications are processed on a rolling basis. *Application fee:* $25. Electronic applications accepted. *Application Contact:* Timothy Nessler, Assistant Director, Graduate Admissions, 800-572-2472, Fax: 215-702-4248, E-mail: tnessler@pbu.edu. *Chair, Graduate Programs*, Dr. William Bowles, 215-702-4871, Fax: 215-702-4248, E-mail: wbowles@pbu.edu.

School of Education Students: 15 full-time (11 women), 43 part-time (33 women); includes 14 minority (12 Black or African American, non-Hispanic/Latino; 1 Asian, non-Hispanic/Latino; 1 Native Hawaiian or other Pacific Islander, non-Hispanic/Latino), 4 international. Average age 36. 34 applicants, 76% accepted, 22 enrolled. *Faculty:* 3 full-time (all women), 2 part-time/adjunct (both women). Expenses: Contact institution. *Financial support:* In 2010–11, 28 students received support. Scholarships/grants available. Support available to part-time students. Financial award applicants required to submit FAFSA. In 2010, 42 master's awarded. *Degree program information:* Part-time and evening/weekend programs available. Offers educational leadership and administration (MS El); teacher education (MS Ed). *Application deadline:* Applications are processed on a rolling basis. *Application fee:* $25. Electronic applications accepted. *Application Contact:* Katerina Penkova, Enrollment Counselor, Graduate Education, 800-572-2472, Fax: 215-702-4248, E-mail: kpenkova@pbu.edu. *Dean*, Dr. Deborah MacCullough, 215-702-4360, E-mail: teacher.ed@pbu.edu.

PHILADELPHIA COLLEGE OF OSTEOPATHIC MEDICINE, Philadelphia, PA 19131-1694

General Information Independent, coed, graduate-only institution. *Graduate housing:* On-campus housing not available. *Research affiliation:* Mount Sinai School of Medicine (joint and bone disease), Neuromuscular Engineering (exercise), Medical College of Georgia (coronary artery disease), Lankenau Institute for Medical Research (cell differentiation), Albert Einstein Medical Center (clinical pain studies, chronic inflammation).

Philadelphia College of Osteopathic Medicine (continued)

GRADUATE UNITS

Graduate and Professional Programs Offers biomedical sciences (MS, Certificate); clinical psychology (Psy D); counseling and clinical health psychology (MS); forensic medicine (MS); health sciences (MS); organizational leadership and development (MS); osteopathic medicine (DO); psychology (Certificate, Post-Doctoral Certificate); school psychology (MS, Psy D, Ed S).

PHILADELPHIA UNIVERSITY, Philadelphia, PA 19144

General Information Independent, coed, comprehensive institution. *Graduate housing:* On-campus housing not available.

GRADUATE UNITS

School of Architecture Offers architecture (MS); construction management (MS); sustainable design (MS).

School of Business Administration *Degree program information:* Part-time and evening/weekend programs available. Postbaccalaureate distance learning degree programs offered (no on-campus study).. Offers business (MBA, MS, PhD); business administration (MBA); finance (MBA); health care management (MBA); international business (MBA); marketing (MBA); taxation (MS). Electronic applications accepted.

School of Design and Media *Degree program information:* Part-time and evening/weekend programs available. Offers design and media (MS); digital design (MS).

School of Engineering and Textiles *Degree program information:* Part-time programs available. Offers engineering and textiles (MS, PhD); fashion apparel studies (MS); textile design (MS); textile engineering (MS, PhD). Electronic applications accepted.

School of Science and Health *Degree program information:* Part-time and evening/weekend programs available. Postbaccalaureate distance learning degree programs offered (minimal on-campus study). Offers disaster medicine and management (MS); midwifery (MS); nurse midwifery (Postbaccalaureate Certificate); occupational therapy (MS); physician assistant studies (MS); science and health (MS, Postbaccalaureate Certificate). Electronic applications accepted.

PHILLIPS GRADUATE INSTITUTE, Encino, CA 91316-1509

General Information Independent, coed, graduate-only institution. *Graduate housing:* On-campus housing not available.

GRADUATE UNITS

Program in Organizational Management and Consulting *Degree program information:* Evening/weekend programs available. Offers organizational management and consulting (Psy D).

Programs in Marriage and Family Therapy, School Counseling and School Psychology *Degree program information:* Evening/weekend programs available. Offers marriage and family therapy (MA); school counseling (MA); school psychology (MA).

PHILLIPS THEOLOGICAL SEMINARY, Tulsa, OK 74116

General Information Independent-religious, coed, graduate-only institution. *Graduate housing:* On-campus housing not available.

GRADUATE UNITS

Programs in Theology *Degree program information:* Part-time programs available. Postbaccalaureate distance learning degree programs offered (minimal on-campus study). Offers administration of church agencies (M Div); campus ministry (M Div); church-related social work (M Div); college and seminary teaching (M Div); global mission work (M Div); institutional chaplaincy (M Div); ministerial vocations in Christian education (M Div); ministry (D Min); ministry and culture (MAMC); ministry of music (M Div); parish ministry (D Min); pastoral care and counseling (M Div); pastoral counseling (D Min); pastoral ministry (M Div); practices of ministry (D Min); theological studies (MTS).

PHOENIX SEMINARY, Phoenix, AZ 85018

General Information Independent-religious, coed, graduate-only institution. *Enrollment by degree level:* 184 master's, 6 doctoral. *Graduate faculty:* 6 full-time (0 women), 7 part-time/adjunct (0 women). *Tuition:* Full-time $10,105; part-time $430 per semester hour. *Required fees:* $430 per semester hour. $60 per semester. One-time fee: $160. *Student services:* Campus employment opportunities, campus safety program, career counseling, services for students with disabilities, writing training. *Library facilities:* Phoenix Seminary Library. *Online resources:* library catalog, web page, access to other libraries' catalogs. *Collection:* 80,617 titles, 152 serial subscriptions, 1,351 audiovisual materials.

Computer facilities: 3 computers available on campus for general student use. A campuswide network can be accessed. *Web address:* http://www.phoenixseminary.edu/.

General Application Contact: Eric Channing, Director of Enrollment, 602-850-8000 Ext. 128, Fax: 602-850-8080, E-mail: enrollment@ps.edu.

GRADUATE UNITS

Graduate Programs Students: 30 full-time (4 women), 160 part-time (50 women); includes 40 minority (18 Black or African American, non-Hispanic/Latino; 8 Asian, non-Hispanic/Latino; 12 Hispanic/Latino; 2 Two or more races, non-Hispanic/Latino). Average age 37. 49 applicants, 96% accepted, 37 enrolled. *Faculty:* 6 full-time (0 women), 7 part-time/adjunct (0 women). Expenses: Contact institution. *Financial support:* In 2010–11, 123 students received support. Institutionally sponsored loans and scholarships/grants available. Support available to part-time students. Financial award application deadline: 6/1; financial award applicants required to submit FAFSA. In 2010, 21 master's, 5 doctorates, 8 other advanced degrees awarded. *Degree program information:* Part-time and evening/weekend programs available. Offers Biblical and theological studies (Graduate Diploma); Biblical communication (M Div); Biblical leadership (MA); Christian counseling (Graduate Diploma); counseling and family (M Div); leadership development (M Div); ministry (D Min); professional counseling (MA). *Application deadline:* For fall admission, 6/1 for domestic students; for spring admission, 11/1 for domestic students. Applications are processed on a rolling basis. *Application fee:* $90. *Application Contact:* Roma Royer, Director of Admissions and Academic Services, 602-850-8000 Ext. 111, Fax: 602-850-8080, E-mail: rroyer@ps.edu.

PIEDMONT BAPTIST COLLEGE AND GRADUATE SCHOOL, Winston-Salem, NC 27101-5197

General Information Independent-religious, coed, comprehensive institution. *Graduate housing:* Rooms and/or apartments available on a first-come, first-served basis to single and married students. Housing application deadline: 5/1.

GRADUATE UNITS

Piedmont Baptist Graduate School *Degree program information:* Part-time programs available. Postbaccalaureate distance learning degree programs offered (no on-campus study). Offers chaplaincy track (MABS); non-language track (MABS); PhD preparation track (MABS); theology (M Min, PhD). Electronic applications accepted.

PIEDMONT COLLEGE, Demorest, GA 30535-0010

General Information Independent-religious, coed, comprehensive institution. CGS member. *Enrollment:* 2,676 graduate, professional, and undergraduate students; 443 full-time matriculated graduate/professional students (338 women), 977 part-time matriculated graduate/professional students (839 women). *Enrollment by degree level:* 520 first professional, 840 master's, 60 doctoral. *Graduate faculty:* 40 full-time (17 women), 9 part-time/adjunct (7 women). *Graduate housing:* On-campus housing not available. *Student services:* Campus employment opportunities, campus safety program, career counseling, exercise/wellness program, free psychological counseling, services for students with disabilities, teacher training, writing training. *Library facilities:* Arrendale Library plus 1 other. *Online resources:* library catalog, web page, access to other libraries' catalogs. *Collection:* 311,722 titles, 290 serial subscriptions, 2,677 audiovisual materials.

Computer facilities: 150 computers available on campus for general student use. A campuswide network can be accessed from student residence rooms and from off campus. *Web address:* http://www.piedmont.edu/.

General Application Contact: Anthony J. Cox, Director of Graduate Admissions, 706-778-8500 Ext. 1118, Fax: 706-776-6635, E-mail: acox@piedmont.edu.

GRADUATE UNITS

School of Business Students: 26 full-time (12 women), 76 part-time (42 women); includes 8 Black or African American, non-Hispanic/Latino; 1 American Indian or Alaska Native, non-Hispanic/Latino; 3 Hispanic/Latino, 2 international. 33 applicants, 79% accepted, 24 enrolled. *Faculty:* 9 full-time (1 woman). Expenses: Contact institution. *Financial support:* Federal Work-Study and unspecified assistantships available. Financial award applicants required to submit FAFSA. In 2010, 50 master's awarded. *Degree program information:* Part-time and evening/weekend programs available. Offers business (MBA). *Application deadline:* For fall admission, 7/15 for domestic students; for spring admission, 12/1 for domestic students. Applications are processed on a rolling basis. Electronic applications accepted. *Application Contact:* Anthony J. Cox, Director of Graduate Admissions, 706-778-8500 Ext. 1118, Fax: 706-776-6635, E-mail: acox@piedmont.edu. *Dean,* Dr. John Misner, 706-778-3000 Ext. 1349, Fax: 706-778-0701, E-mail: jmisner@piedmont.edu.

School of Education Students: 417 full-time (326 women), 901 part-time (797 women); includes 125 Black or African American, non-Hispanic/Latino; 1 American Indian or Alaska Native, non-Hispanic/Latino; 14 Asian, non-Hispanic/Latino; 19 Hispanic/Latino, 15 international. 377 applicants, 87% accepted, 279 enrolled. *Faculty:* 31 full-time (16 women), 9 part-time/adjunct (7 women). Expenses: Contact institution. *Financial support:* Career-related internships or fieldwork, Federal Work-Study, and unspecified assistantships available. Support available to part-time students. Financial award applicants required to submit FAFSA. In 2010, 444 master's, 510 other advanced degrees awarded. *Degree program information:* Part-time and evening/weekend programs available. Offers early childhood education (MA, MAT); middle grades education (MA); secondary education (MA, MAT); special education (MA, MAT); teacher leadership (Ed S). *Application deadline:* For fall admission, 7/15 for domestic students; for spring admission, 12/1 for domestic students. Applications are processed on a rolling basis. Electronic applications accepted. *Application Contact:* Anthony J. Cox, Director of Graduate Admissions, 706-778-8500 Ext. 1118, Fax: 706-776-6635, E-mail: acox@piedmont.edu. *Dean,* Dr. Bob Cummings, 706-778-3000 Ext. 1201, Fax: 706-776-9608, E-mail: bcummings@piedmont.edu.

PIKEVILLE COLLEGE, Pikeville, KY 41501

General Information Independent-religious, coed, comprehensive institution. *Graduate housing:* Room and/or apartments available on a first-come, first-served basis to married students; on-campus housing not available to single students.

GRADUATE UNITS

School of Osteopathic Medicine Offers osteopathic medicine (DO).

PITTSBURGH THEOLOGICAL SEMINARY, Pittsburgh, PA 15206-2596

General Information Independent-religious, coed, graduate-only institution. *Enrollment by degree level:* 183 first professional, 26 master's, 96 doctoral. *Graduate faculty:* 17 full-time (3 women), 9 part-time/adjunct (3 women). *Tuition:* Full-time $2574; part-time $303 per credit hour. *Required fees:* $51 per term. Tuition and fees vary according to course load. *Graduate housing:* Rooms and/or apartments available on a first-come, first-served basis to single and married students. Typical cost: $3735 per year for single students; $6069 per year for married students. Housing application deadline: 6/1. *Student services:* Campus employment opportunities, campus safety program, career counseling, child daycare facilities, exercise/wellness program, free psychological counseling, international student services, low-cost health insurance, services for students with disabilities, writing training. *Library facilities:* Clifford E. Barbour Library. *Online resources:* library catalog, web page. *Collection:* 292,340 titles, 862 serial subscriptions, 19,104 audiovisual materials.

Computer facilities: 15 computers available on campus for general student use. A campuswide network can be accessed from student residence rooms. Online class registration is available. *Web address:* http://www.pts.edu/.

General Application Contact: Sherry Sparks, Associate Dean for Admissions and Vocations, 412-924-1382, Fax: 412-924-1782, E-mail: ssparks@pts.edu.

GRADUATE UNITS

Graduate and Professional Programs Students: 248 full-time (87 women), 57 part-time (29 women); includes 38 Black or African American, non-Hispanic/Latino; 4 Asian, non-Hispanic/Latino; 2 Hispanic/Latino, 9 international. Average age 36. 123 applicants, 80% accepted, 68 enrolled. *Faculty:* 17 full-time (3 women), 9 part-time/adjunct (3 women). Expenses: Contact institution. *Financial support:* In 2010–11, 104 students received support. Career-related internships or fieldwork, scholarships/grants, and institutional work-study available. Financial award application deadline: 3/30; financial award applicants required to submit FAFSA. In 2010, 37 first professional degrees, 17 master's, 23 doctorates awarded. *Degree program information:* Part-time and evening/weekend programs available. Offers divinity (M Div); ministry (D Min); theology (MA, STM). M Div/MSW offered jointly with University of Pittsburgh; JD/M Div with Duquesne University; M Div/MS with Carnegie Mellon University. *Application deadline:* For fall admission, 6/30 priority date for domestic students, 12/1 for international students; for winter admission, 10/15 priority date for domestic students; for spring admission, 1/15 priority date for domestic students. Applications are processed on a rolling basis. *Application fee:* $40. *Application Contact:* Sherry Sparks, Associate Dean of Admissions, 412-924-1382, Fax: 412-924-1782, E-mail: ssparks@pts.edu. *Dean of Faculty and Vice President for Academic Affairs,* Dr. Byron H. Jackson, 412-924-1374, Fax: 412-924-1774, E-mail: bjackson@pts.edu.

PITTSBURG STATE UNIVERSITY, Pittsburg, KS 66762

General Information State-supported, coed, comprehensive institution. CGS member. *Graduate housing:* Rooms and/or apartments available on a first-come, first-served basis to single students and available to married students. Housing application deadline: 8/15. *Research affiliation:* Cargill, Inc. (vegetable oil).

GRADUATE UNITS

Graduate School *Degree program information:* Part-time and evening/weekend programs available. Postbaccalaureate distance learning degree programs offered (no on-campus study). Electronic applications accepted.

College of Arts and Sciences Offers applied communication (MA); applied physics (MS); art education (MA); arts and sciences (MA, MM, MS, MSN); biology (MS); chemistry (MS); communication education (MA); English (MA); history (MA); instrumental music education (MM); mathematics (MS); music history/music literature (MM); nursing (MSN); performance (MM); physics (MS); professional physics (MS); studio art (MA); theatre (MA); theory and composition (MM); vocal music education (MM).

College of Education Offers behavioral disorders (MS); classroom reading teacher (MS); community college and higher education (Ed S); community counseling (MS); counselor education (MS); early childhood education (MS); education (MAT, MS, Ed S); educational leadership (MS); educational technology (MS); elementary education (MS); general school administration (Ed S); learning disabilities (MS); mentally retarded (MS); physical education (MS); psychology (MS); reading (MS); reading specialist (MS); school counseling (MS); school psychology (Ed S); secondary education (MS); special education (MS); teaching (MAT).

College of Technology Offers career and technical education (MS); commercial graphics (MST); construction (MET); engineering technology (MET); human resource development (MS); printing management (MST); technology (MET, MS, MST, Ed S); workforce development and education (Ed S).

Kelce College of Business Offers accounting (MBA); business (MBA); general administration (MBA).

PLYMOUTH STATE UNIVERSITY, Plymouth, NH 03264-1595

General Information State-supported, coed, comprehensive institution. *Graduate housing:* Rooms and/or apartments available on a first-come, first-served basis to single students and guaranteed to married students. Housing application deadline: 5/1. *Research affiliation:* Hubbard Brook Experimental Forest (science), New Hampshire Department of Environmental Services (science), White Mountain National Forest (science), National Oceanic and Atmospheric Administration (NOAA) (science).

GRADUATE UNITS

College of Graduate Studies *Degree program information:* Part-time and evening/weekend programs available. Postbaccalaureate distance learning degree programs offered (minimal on-campus study). Offers business (MBA).

Graduate Studies in Education *Degree program information:* Part-time and evening/weekend programs available. Postbaccalaureate distance learning degree programs offered (minimal on-campus study). Offers applied meteorology (MS); athletic training (M Ed, MS); counselor education (M Ed); education (M Ed, MAT, MS, Ed D, CAGS); educational leadership (M Ed); elementary education (M Ed); English education (M Ed); environmental science and policy (MS); health education (M Ed); k-12 education (M Ed); learning, leadership and community (Ed D); mathematics education (M Ed); reading and writing specialist (M Ed); science (MS); science education (MS); secondary education (M Ed); special education administration (M Ed); special education k-12 (M Ed); teaching (MAT).

POINT LOMA NAZARENE UNIVERSITY, San Diego, CA 92106-2899

General Information Independent-religious, coed, comprehensive institution. *Graduate housing:* On-campus housing not available.

GRADUATE UNITS

Program in Biology *Degree program information:* Part-time programs available. Offers biology (MA, MS).

Program in Business Administration *Degree program information:* Part-time and evening/weekend programs available. Offers business administration (MBA).

Program in Education *Degree program information:* Part-time and evening/weekend programs available. Offers education (MA, MAT, Ed S).

Program in Nursing *Degree program information:* Part-time programs available. Offers nursing (MSN, Post-MSN Certificate).

Program in Religion *Degree program information:* Part-time programs available. Offers religion (M Min, MA).

POINT PARK UNIVERSITY, Pittsburgh, PA 15222-1984

General Information Independent, coed, comprehensive institution. *Enrollment:* 4,077 graduate, professional, and undergraduate students; 209 full-time matriculated graduate/professional students (136 women), 375 part-time matriculated graduate/professional students (210 women). *Enrollment by degree level:* 584 master's. *Graduate faculty:* 31 full-time, 41 part-time/adjunct. *Tuition:* Full-time $12,456; part-time $692 per credit. *Required fees:* $630; $35 per credit. *Graduate housing:* Room and/or apartments available on a first-come, first-served basis to single students; on-campus housing not available to married students. Typical cost: $4520 per year ($9480 including board). Room and board charges vary according to board plan and housing facility selected. Housing application deadline: 7/31. *Student services:* Campus employment opportunities, career counseling, child daycare facilities, free psychological counseling, international student services, low-cost health insurance, services for students with disabilities. *Library facilities:* Point Park University Library. *Online resources:* library catalog, web page, access to other libraries' catalogs. *Collection:* 125,000 titles, 171 serial subscriptions, 5,352 audiovisual materials.

Computer facilities: Computer purchase and lease plans are available. 247 computers available on campus for general student use. A campuswide network can be accessed from student residence rooms. Online class registration is available. *Web address:* http://www.pointpark.edu/.

General Application Contact: Kathy Ballas, Director, Graduate and Adult Enrollment, 412-392-3812, Fax: 412-392-6164, E-mail: kballas@pointpark.edu.

GRADUATE UNITS

Conservatory of Performing Arts Students: 6 full-time (3 women), 1 international. Average age 42. 6 applicants, 0% accepted, 0 enrolled. *Faculty:* 3 full-time, 1 part-time/adjunct. Expenses: Contact institution. *Financial support:* In 2010–11, 6 students received support, including 5 teaching assistantships with full tuition reimbursements available (averaging $6,400 per year); scholarships/grants also available. Financial award application deadline: 4/15; financial award applicants required to submit FAFSA. Offers theatre arts-acting (MFA). *Application deadline:* Applications are processed on a rolling basis. *Application fee:* $30. Electronic applications accepted. *Application Contact:* Lynn C. Ribar, Associate Director, Adult and Graduate Enrollment, 412-392-3908, Fax: 412-392-6164, E-mail: lribar@pointpark.edu. *Dean/Artistic Producing Director*, Ronald Allan-Lindblom, 412-392-3454, Fax: 412-392-2424, E-mail: rlindblom@pointpark.edu.

School of Arts and Sciences Students: 51 full-time (41 women), 67 part-time (46 women); includes 31 Black or African American, non-Hispanic/Latino; 4 Asian, non-Hispanic/Latino; 5 Hispanic/Latino; 1 Two or more races, non-Hispanic/Latino, 3 international. Average age 33. 120 applicants, 68% accepted, 57 enrolled. *Faculty:* 11 full-time, 16 part-time/adjunct. Expenses: Contact institution. *Financial support:* In 2010–11, 95 students received support, including 7 teaching assistantships with full tuition reimbursements available (averaging $6,400 per year); scholarships/grants also available. Financial award application deadline: 4/15; financial award applicants required to submit FAFSA. In 2010, 50 master's awarded. *Degree program information:* Part-time and evening/weekend programs available. Offers arts and sciences (M Ed, MA, MS); criminal justice administration (MS); curriculum and instruction (MA); educational administration (MA); engineering management (MS); environmental studies (MS); teaching and leadership (M Ed). *Application deadline:* Applications are processed on a rolling basis. *Application fee:* $30. Electronic applications accepted. *Application Contact:* Dr. Charles Fox, Dean, 412-392-8084, E-mail: cfox@pointpark.edu. *Dean*, Dr. Charles Fox, 412-392-8084, E-mail: cfox@pointpark.edu.

School of Business Students: 121 full-time (69 women), 272 part-time (137 women); includes 107 minority (86 Black or African American, non-Hispanic/Latino; 1 American Indian or Alaska Native, non-Hispanic/Latino; 9 Asian, non-Hispanic/Latino; 5 Hispanic/Latino; 6 Two or more races, non-Hispanic/Latino), 23 international. Average age 32. 356 applicants, 73% accepted, 166 enrolled. *Faculty:* 11 full-time, 14 part-time/adjunct. Expenses: Contact institution. *Financial support:* In 2010–11, 48 students received support, including 5 teaching assistantships with full tuition reimbursements available (averaging $6,400 per year); scholarships/grants also available. Financial award application deadline: 4/15; financial award applicants required to submit FAFSA. In 2010, 168 master's awarded. *Degree program information:* Part-time and evening/weekend programs available. Offers business (MBA); organizational leadership (MA). *Application deadline:* Applications are processed on a rolling basis. *Application fee:* $30. Electronic applications accepted. *Application Contact:* Marty M. Paonessa, Associate Director, Graduate and Adult Enrollment, 412-392-3915, Fax: 412-392-6164, E-mail: mpaonessa@pointpark.edu. *Dean*, Dr. Angela Isaac, 412-392-8011, Fax: 412-392-8048, E-mail: aisaac@pointpark.edu.

School of Communication Students: 31 full-time (23 women), 33 part-time (25 women); includes 8 minority (5 Black or African American, non-Hispanic/Latino; 1 Asian, non-Hispanic/Latino; 2 Two or more races, non-Hispanic/Latino), 2 international. Average age 27. 103 applicants, 67% accepted, 32 enrolled. *Faculty:* 6 full-time, 10 part-time/adjunct. Expenses: Contact institution. *Financial support:* In 2010–11, 6 teaching assistantships with full tuition reimbursements (averaging $6,400 per year) were awarded; scholarships/grants and unspecified assistantships also available. Financial award application deadline: 4/15; financial award applicants required to submit FAFSA. In 2010, 21 master's awarded. *Degree program information:* Part-time and evening/weekend programs available. Offers communication (MA). *Application deadline:* Applications are processed on a rolling basis. *Application fee:* $30. Electronic applications accepted. *Application Contact:* Marty M. Paonessa, Recruiter/Counselor, 412-392-3915, Fax: 412-392-6164, E-mail: mpaonessa@pointpark.edu. *Chair*, Dr. Tim Hudson, 412-392-4748, E-mail: thudson@pointpark.edu.

POLYTECHNIC INSTITUTE OF NYU, Brooklyn, NY 11201-2990

General Information Independent, coed, university. CGS member. *Enrollment:* 4,432 graduate, professional, and undergraduate students; 1,555 full-time matriculated graduate/professional students (463 women), 880 part-time matriculated graduate/professional students (208 women). *Enrollment by degree level:* 2,126 master's, 206 doctoral, 103 other advanced degrees. *Graduate faculty:* 101 full-time (14 women), 121 part-time/adjunct (17 women). *Tuition:* Full-time $21,492; part-time $1194 per credit. *Required fees:* $385 per semester. Tuition and fees vary according to course load. *Graduate housing:* Room and/or apartments available on a first-come, first-served basis to single students; on-campus housing not available to married students. Typical cost: $10,080 (including board). Room and board charges vary according to housing facility selected. Housing application deadline: 6/30. *Student services:* Campus employment opportunities, campus safety program, career counseling, free psychological counseling, international student services, low-cost health insurance. *Library facilities:* Bern Dibner Library plus 1 other. *Online resources:* library catalog, web page, access to other libraries' catalogs. *Collection:* 140,000 titles, 1,621 serial subscriptions.

Computer facilities: Computer purchase and lease plans are available. 1,334 computers available on campus for general student use. A campuswide network can be accessed from student residence rooms and from off campus. Online class registration is available. *Web address:* http://www.poly.edu/.

General Application Contact: JeanCarlo Bonilla, Director of Graduate Enrollment Management, 718-260-3182, Fax: 718-260-3624, E-mail: gradinfo@poly.edu.

GRADUATE UNITS

Department of Applied Physics Students: 1 full-time (0 women), all international. Average age 29. *Faculty:* 3 full-time (0 women). Expenses: Contact institution. *Financial support:* Fellowships, research assistantships, teaching assistantships, institutionally sponsored loans available. Support available to part-time students. Financial award applicants required to submit FAFSA. *Degree program information:* Part-time and evening/weekend programs available. Offers applied physics (MS, PhD). *Application deadline:* For fall admission, 7/31 priority date for domestic students, 4/30 priority date for international students; for spring admission, 12/31 priority date for domestic students, 11/30 priority date for international students. Applications are processed on a rolling basis. *Application fee:* $75. Electronic applications accepted. *Application Contact:* JeanCarlo Bonilla, Director of Graduate Enrollment Management, 718-260-3182, Fax: 718-260-3624, E-mail: gradinfo@poly.edu. *Head*, Dr. Lorcan M. Folan, 718-260-3072, E-mail: lfolan@poly.edu.

Department of Chemical and Biological Engineering Students: 24 full-time (11 women), 18 part-time (8 women); includes 6 Black or African American, non-Hispanic/Latino; 5 Asian, non-Hispanic/Latino; 1 Hispanic/Latino, 21 international. Average age 26. 106 applicants, 42% accepted, 16 enrolled. *Faculty:* 3 full-time (0 women), 1 part-time/adjunct (0 women). Expenses: Contact institution. *Financial support:* In 2010–11, 29 fellowships with partial tuition reimbursements (averaging $24,228 per year), 3 research assistantships with partial tuition reimbursements (averaging $26,400 per year), 6 teaching assistantships (averaging $12,324 per year) were awarded; institutionally sponsored loans, scholarships/grants, and unspecified assistantships also available. Support available to part-time students. Financial award applicants required to submit FAFSA. In 2010, 19 master's, 10 doctorates awarded. *Degree program information:* Part-time and evening/weekend programs available. Offers chemical engineering (MS, PhD); polymer science and engineering (MS). *Application deadline:* For fall admission, 7/31 priority date for domestic students, 4/30 priority date for international students; for spring admission, 12/31 priority date for domestic students, 11/30 priority date for international students. Applications are processed on a rolling basis. *Application fee:* $75. Electronic applications accepted. *Application Contact:* JeanCarlo Bonilla, Dir. Graduate Enrollment Management, 718-260-3182, Fax: 718-260-3624, E-mail: gradinfo@poly.edu. *Head*, Dr. Walter Zurawsky, 718-260-3725, Fax: 718-260-3125, E-mail: zurawsky@poly.edu.

Department of Chemical and Biological Sciences Students: 156 full-time (66 women), 75 part-time (28 women); includes 4 Black or African American, non-Hispanic/Latino; 15 Asian, non-Hispanic/Latino; 4 Hispanic/Latino, 167 international. Average age 25. 395 applicants, 53% accepted, 78 enrolled. *Faculty:* 13 full-time (3 women), 1 (woman) part-time/adjunct. Expenses: Contact institution. *Financial support:* In 2010–11, 19 fellowships with tuition reimbursements (averaging $36,020 per year), 3 research assistantships with tuition reimbursements (averaging $6,600 per year), 5 teaching assistantships with tuition reimbursements (averaging $5,295 per year) were awarded; institutionally sponsored loans, scholarships/grants, and unspecified assistantships also available. Support available to part-time students. In 2010, 93 master's, 3 doctorates awarded. Offers biomedical engineering (MS, PhD); biotechnology (MS); biotechnology and entrepreneurship (MS); chemistry (MS); materials chemistry (PhD). *Application deadline:* For fall admission, 7/31 priority date for domestic students, 4/30 priority date for international students; for spring admission, 12/31 priority date for domestic students, 11/30 priority date for international students. Applications are processed on a rolling basis. *Application fee:* $75. Electronic applications accepted. *Application Contact:* JeanCarlo Bonilla, Director, Graduate Enrollment Management, 718-260-3182, Fax: 718-260-3624, E-mail: gradinfo@poly.edu. *Department Head*, Dr. Bruce Garetz, 718-260-3287.

Department of Civil Engineering Students: 122 full-time (43 women), 182 part-time (41 women); includes 39 Black or African American, non-Hispanic/Latino; 1 American Indian or Alaska Native, non-Hispanic/Latino; 34 Asian, non-Hispanic/Latino; 11 Hispanic/Latino, 94 international. Average age 30. 310 applicants, 63% accepted, 108 enrolled. *Faculty:* 10 full-time (1 woman), 15 part-time/adjunct (0 women). Expenses: Contact institution. *Financial support:* In 2010–11, 6 fellowships with partial tuition reimbursements (averaging $24,300 per year) were awarded; research assistantships, teaching assistantships, institutionally sponsored loans, scholarships/grants, and unspecified assistantships also available. Support available to part-time students. Financial award applicants required to submit FAFSA. In 2010, 93 master's, 2 doctorates awarded. *Degree program information:* Part-time and evening/weekend programs available. Offers civil engineering (MS, PhD); construction management (MS); environmental engineering (MS); environmental science (MS); transportation management (MS); transportation planning and engineering (MS, PhD); urban systems engineering and management (MS). *Application deadline:* For fall admission, 7/31 priority date for domestic students, 4/30 priority date for international students; for spring admission, 12/31 priority date for domestic students, 10/30 priority date for international students. Applications are processed on a rolling basis. *Application fee:* $75. Electronic applications accepted. *Application Contact:* JeanCarlo Bonilla, Director of Graduate Enrollment Management, 718-260-3182, Fax: 718-260-3624, E-mail: gradinfo@poly.edu. *Head*, Dr. Lawrence Chiarelli, 718-260-4040, Fax: 718-260-3433, E-mail: lchiarel@poly.edu.

Department of Computer Science and Engineering Students: 272 full-time (57 women), 134 part-time (17 women); includes 10 Black or African American, non-Hispanic/Latino; 26 Asian, non-Hispanic/Latino; 10 Hispanic/Latino, 261 international. Average age 27. 818 applicants, 52% accepted, 190 enrolled. *Faculty:* 18 full-time (1 woman), 12 part-time/adjunct (2 women). Expenses: Contact institution. *Financial support:* In 2010–11, 6 fellowships with partial tuition reimbursements (averaging $25,617 per year), 22 research assistantships with tuition reimbursements (averaging $26,693 per year), 1 teaching assistantship with tuition reimbursement (averaging $26,572 per year) were awarded; institutionally sponsored loans, scholarships/grants, and unspecified assistantships also available. Support available to part-time students. Financial award applicants required to submit FAFSA. In 2010, 121 master's, 3 doctorates awarded. *Degree program information:* Part-time and evening/weekend programs available. Offers computer science (MS, PhD); cyber security (Graduate Certificate); software engineering (Graduate Certificate). *Application deadline:* For fall admission, 7/31 priority date for domestic students, 4/30 priority date for international students; for spring admission, 12/31 priority date for domestic students, 10/30 priority date for international students. Applications are processed on a rolling basis. *Application fee:* $75. Electronic applications accepted.

Polytechnic Institute of NYU (continued)

Application Contact: JeanCarlo Bonilla, Director, Graduate Center, 718-260-3182, Fax: 718-260-3624, E-mail: gradinfo@poly.edu. *Head,* Dr. Keith W. Ross, 718-260-3859, Fax: 718-260-3609, E-mail: ross@poly.edu.

Department of Electrical and Computer Engineering Students: 476 full-time (98 women), 214 part-time (28 women); includes 25 Black or African American, non-Hispanic/Latino; 58 Asian, non-Hispanic/Latino; 17 Hispanic/Latino, 486 international. Average age 26. 1,234 applicants, 51% accepted, 261 enrolled. *Faculty:* 25 full-time (4 women), 15 part-time/adjunct (0 women). Expenses: Contact institution. *Financial support:* In 2010–11, 15 fellowships with partial tuition reimbursements (averaging $22,178 per year), 33 research assistantships with partial tuition reimbursements (averaging $23,144 per year), 11 teaching assistantships (averaging $52,614 per year) were awarded; institutionally sponsored loans, scholarships/grants, and unspecified assistantships also available. Support available to part-time students. Financial award applicants required to submit FAFSA. In 2010, 266 master's, 6 doctorates awarded. *Degree program information:* Part-time and evening/weekend programs available. Offers computer engineering (MS, Certificate); electrical engineering (MS, PhD); electrophysics (MS); image processing (Certificate); systems engineering (MS); telecommunication networks (MS); wireless communications (Certificate). *Application deadline:* For fall admission, 7/31 priority date for domestic students, 4/30 priority date for international students; for spring admission, 12/31 priority date for domestic students, 11/30 priority date for international students. Applications are processed on a rolling basis. *Application fee:* $75. Electronic applications accepted. *Application Contact:* JeanCarlo Bonilla, Director of Graduate Enrollment Management, 718-260-3182, Fax: 718-260-3624, E-mail: gradinfo@poly.edu. *Head,* Dr. Jonathan Chao, 718-860-3478, Fax: 718-260-3302, E-mail: chao@poly.edu.

Department of Finance and Risk Engineering Students: 126 full-time (45 women), 61 part-time (15 women); includes 4 Black or African American, non-Hispanic/Latino; 17 Asian, non-Hispanic/Latino; 1 Hispanic/Latino, 130 international. Average age 27. 528 applicants, 44% accepted, 67 enrolled. *Faculty:* 6 full-time (1 woman), 24 part-time/adjunct (5 women). Expenses: Contact institution. *Financial support:* Institutionally sponsored loans, scholarships/grants, and unspecified assistantships available. Support available to part-time students. Financial award applicants required to submit FAFSA. In 2010, 154 master's awarded. *Degree program information:* Part-time and evening/weekend programs available. Offers financial engineering (MS, Advanced Certificate); financial technology management (Advanced Certificate); organizational behavior (Advanced Certificate); risk management (Advanced Certificate); technology management (Advanced Certificate). *Application deadline:* For fall admission, 7/31 priority date for domestic students, 4/30 priority date for international students; for spring admission, 12/31 priority date for domestic students, 11/30 priority date for international students. Applications are processed on a rolling basis. *Application fee:* $75. Electronic applications accepted. *Application Contact:* JeanCarlo Bonilla, Director, Graduate Enrollment Management, 718-260-3182, Fax: 718-260-3624. *Academic Director,* Prof. Charles S. Tapiero, 718-260-3653, Fax: 718-260-3874, E-mail: ctapiero@poly.edu.

Department of Humanities and Social Sciences Students: 31 full-time (15 women), 4 part-time (3 women); includes 4 Black or African American, non-Hispanic/Latino; 1 American Indian or Alaska Native, non-Hispanic/Latino; 1 Asian, non-Hispanic/Latino, 19 international. Average age 28. 37 applicants, 68% accepted, 15 enrolled. *Faculty:* 5 full-time (2 women), 6 part-time/adjunct (3 women). Expenses: Contact institution. *Financial support:* Fellowships, research assistantships, teaching assistantships, career-related internships or fieldwork, institutionally sponsored loans, scholarships/grants, and unspecified assistantships available. Support available to part-time students. Financial award applicants required to submit FAFSA. In 2010, 22 master's awarded. *Degree program information:* Part-time and evening/weekend programs available. Offers environment—behavior studies (Graduate Certificate); environment-behavior studies (MS); history of science (MS); integrated digital media (MS, Graduate Certificate); technical writing and specialized journalism (MS). *Application deadline:* For fall admission, 7/31 priority date for domestic students, 4/30 priority date for international students; for spring admission, 12/31 priority date for domestic students, 11/30 priority date for international students. Applications are processed on a rolling basis. *Application fee:* $75. Electronic applications accepted. *Application Contact:* JeanCarlo Bonilla, Director, Graduate Enrollment Management, 718-260-3182, Fax: 718-260-3624, E-mail: gradinfo@poly.edu. *Head,* Prof. Kristen Day, 718-260-3999, E-mail: kday@poly.edu.

Department of Interdisciplinary Studies Students: 62 full-time (24 women), 42 part-time (20 women); includes 4 Black or African American, non-Hispanic/Latino; 5 Asian, non-Hispanic/Latino; 3 Hispanic/Latino, 50 international. Average age 29. 127 applicants, 47% accepted, 28 enrolled. *Faculty:* 3 full-time (0 women), 14 part-time/adjunct (2 women). Expenses: Contact institution. *Financial support:* Institutionally sponsored loans, scholarships/grants, and unspecified assistantships available. Support available to part-time students. In 2010, 41 master's awarded. *Degree program information:* Part-time programs available. Offers bioinformatics (MS); industrial engineering (MS); manufacturing engineering (MS). *Application deadline:* For fall admission, 7/31 priority date for domestic students, 4/30 priority date for international students; for spring admission, 12/31 priority date for domestic students, 11/30 priority date for international students. Applications are processed on a rolling basis. *Application fee:* $75. Electronic applications accepted. *Application Contact:* JeanCarlo Bonilla, Dir. Graduate Enrollment Management, 718-260-3182, Fax: 718-260-3624, E-mail: gradinfo@poly.edu. *Department Head,* Prof. Michael Greenstein, 718-260-3835, E-mail: mgreenst@poly.edu.

Department of Mathematics Students: 16 full-time (6 women), 13 part-time (2 women); includes 1 Asian, non-Hispanic/Latino; 2 Hispanic/Latino, 14 international. Average age 32. 58 applicants, 57% accepted, 9 enrolled. *Faculty:* 3 full-time (0 women), 1 part-time/adjunct (0 women). Expenses: Contact institution. *Financial support:* In 2010–11, 5 fellowships (averaging $35,280 per year), 5 teaching assistantships (averaging $47,554 per year) were awarded; research assistantships, institutionally sponsored loans, scholarships/grants, and unspecified assistantships also available. Support available to part-time students. Financial award applicants required to submit FAFSA. In 2010, 5 master's, 2 doctorates awarded. *Degree program information:* Part-time and evening/weekend programs available. Offers mathematics (MS, PhD). *Application deadline:* For fall admission, 7/31 priority date for domestic students, 4/30 priority date for international students; for spring admission, 12/31 priority date for domestic students, 11/30 priority date for international students. Applications are processed on a rolling basis. *Application fee:* $75. Electronic applications accepted. *Application Contact:* JeanCarlo Bonilla, Director of Graduate Enrollment Management, 718-260-3182, Fax: 718-260-3624, E-mail: gradinfo@poly.edu. *Head,* Dr. Erwin Lutwak, 718-260-3366, Fax: 718-260-3139, E-mail: lutwak@magnus.poly.edu.

Department of Mechanical and Aerospace Engineering Students: 45 full-time (5 women), 19 part-time (6 women); includes 9 Asian, non-Hispanic/Latino; 2 Hispanic/Latino, 36 international. Average age 25. 168 applicants, 54% accepted, 34 enrolled. *Faculty:* 5 full-time (0 women), 4 part-time/adjunct (0 women). Expenses: Contact institution. *Financial support:* In 2010–11, 16 fellowships with partial tuition reimbursements (averaging $28,163 per year), 4 research assistantships with partial tuition reimbursements (averaging $24,600 per year) were awarded; teaching assistantships, career-related internships or fieldwork, institutionally sponsored loans, scholarships/grants, and unspecified assistantships also available. Support available to part-time students. Financial award applicants required to submit FAFSA. In 2010, 14 master's awarded. *Degree program information:* Part-time and evening/weekend programs available. Offers mechanical engineering (MS, PhD). *Application deadline:* For fall admission, 7/31 priority date for domestic students, 4/30 priority date for international students; for spring admission, 12/31 priority date for domestic students, 11/30 priority date for international students. Applications are processed on a rolling basis. *Application fee:* $75. Electronic applications accepted. *Application Contact:* JeanCarlo Bonilla, Director, Graduate Enrollment Management, 718-260-3182, Fax: 718-260-3624, E-mail: gradinfo@poly.edu. *Head,* Dr. George Vradis, 718-260-3875, Fax: 718-260-3532, E-mail: gvradis@poly.edu.

Department of Technology Management Students: 224 full-time (93 women), 106 part-time (38 women); includes 15 Black or African American, non-Hispanic/Latino; 41 Asian, non-Hispanic/Latino; 10 Hispanic/Latino, 158 international. Average age 30. 370 applicants, 60% accepted, 120 enrolled. *Faculty:* 7 full-time (2 women), 28 part-time/adjunct (4 women). Expenses: Contact institution. *Financial support:* In 2010–11, 1 fellowship (averaging $26,400 per year) was awarded; research assistantships, teaching assistantships, institutionally sponsored loans, scholarships/grants, and unspecified assistantships also available. Support available to part-time students. In 2010, 173 master's, 1 doctorate awarded. *Degree program information:* Part-time and evening/weekend programs available. Offers construction management (Advanced Certificate); electronic business management (Advanced Certificate); entrepreneurship (Advanced Certificate); human resources management (Advanced Certificate); information management (Advanced Certificate); management (MS); management of technology (MS); organizational behavior (MS, Advanced Certificate); project management (Advanced Certificate); technology management (MBA, MS, PhD, Advanced Certificate); telecommunications and information management (MS); telecommunications management (Advanced Certificate). *Application deadline:* For fall admission, 7/31 priority date for domestic students, 4/30 priority date for international students; for spring admission, 12/31 priority date for domestic students, 11/30 priority date for international students. Applications are processed on a rolling basis. *Application fee:* $75. Electronic applications accepted. *Application Contact:* JeanCarlo Bonilla, Director of Graduate Enrollment Management, 718-260-3182, Fax: 718-260-3624, E-mail: gradinfo@poly.edu. *Head,* Prof. Bharadwaj Rao, 718-260-3617, Fax: 718-260-3874, E-mail: brao@poly.edu.

POLYTECHNIC INSTITUTE OF NYU, LONG ISLAND GRADUATE CENTER, Melville, NY 11747

General Information Independent, coed, graduate-only institution. *Enrollment:* 16 full-time matriculated graduate/professional students (4 women), 119 part-time matriculated graduate/professional students (15 women). *Enrollment by degree level:* 97 master's, 34 other advanced degrees. *Graduate faculty:* 4 full-time (0 women), 12 part-time/adjunct (0 women). *Tuition:* Full-time $21,492; part-time $1194 per credit. *Required fees:* $385 per semester. Tuition and fees vary according to course load. *Graduate housing:* On-campus housing not available. *Student services:* Campus employment opportunities, career counseling, international student services. *Library facilities:* Dibner Library. *Online resources:* library catalog, web page, access to other libraries' catalogs. *Collection:* 120,514 titles, 43,500 serial subscriptions, 460 audiovisual materials.

Computer facilities: 12 computers available on campus for general student use. A campuswide network can be accessed from off campus. Online class registration is available. *Web address:* http://www.poly.edu/li/.

General Application Contact: JeanCarlo Bonilla, Director of Graduate Enrollment Management, 718-260-3182, Fax: 718-260-3624, E-mail: gradinfo@poly.edu.

GRADUATE UNITS

Graduate Programs Students: 16 full-time (4 women), 119 part-time (15 women); includes 12 Black or African American, non-Hispanic/Latino; 21 Asian, non-Hispanic/Latino; 6 Hispanic/Latino, 15 international. Average age 31. 163 applicants, 60% accepted, 58 enrolled. *Faculty:* 4 full-time (0 women), 12 part-time/adjunct (0 women). Expenses: Contact institution. *Financial support:* Institutionally sponsored loans, scholarships/grants, and unspecified assistantships available. Support available to part-time students. Financial award applicants required to submit FAFSA. In 2010, 51 master's awarded. *Degree program information:* Part-time and evening/weekend programs available. Offers aeronautics and astronautics (MS); bioinformatics (MS); chemical and biological sciences (MS); chemical engineering (MS); chemistry (MS); civil engineering (MS); computer engineering (MS); computer science (MS); construction management (MS); electrical engineering (MS); electrophysics (MS); environmental engineering (MS); financial engineering (MS, AC); industrial engineering (MS); information systems engineering (MS); management (MS); management of technology (MS); manufacturing engineering (MS); mechanical engineering (MS); systems engineering (MS); telecommunication networks (MS); transportation planning and engineering (MS); wireless innovations (M Engr). *Application deadline:* For fall admission, 7/31 priority date for domestic students, 4/30 priority date for international students; for spring admission, 12/31 priority date for domestic students, 11/30 priority date for international students. Applications are processed on a rolling basis. *Application fee:* $75. Electronic applications accepted. *Application Contact:* JeanCarlo Bonilla, Director of Graduate Enrollment Management, 718-260-3182, Fax: 718-260-3624, E-mail: gradinfo@poly.edu. *Director, Long Island Graduate Center,* Dr. Frank Cassara, 631-755-4360, Fax: 516-755-4404, E-mail: cassara@poly.edu.

POLYTECHNIC INSTITUTE OF NYU, WESTCHESTER GRADUATE CENTER, Hawthorne, NY 10532-1507

General Information Independent, coed, graduate-only institution. *Enrollment by degree level:* 82 master's, 12 other advanced degrees. *Graduate faculty:* 1 full-time (0 women), 17 part-time/adjunct (2 women). *Tuition:* Full-time $21,492; part-time $1194 per credit. *Required fees:* $385 per semester. Tuition and fees vary according to course load. *Graduate housing:* Room and/or apartments available to single students; on-campus housing not available to married students. *Student services:* Campus employment opportunities, career counseling, international student services, low-cost health insurance. *Library facilities:* Dibner Library. *Online resources:* library catalog, web page, access to other libraries' catalogs. *Collection:* 120,514 titles, 43,500 serial subscriptions, 460 audiovisual materials.

Computer facilities: 12 computers available on campus for general student use. A campuswide network can be accessed from student residence rooms and from off campus. Online class registration is available. *Web address:* http://www.poly.edu/west/.

General Application Contact: JeanCarlo Bonilla, Director of Graduate Enrollment Management, 718-260-3182, Fax: 718-260-3624, E-mail: gradinfo@poly.edu.

GRADUATE UNITS

Graduate Programs Students: 11 full-time (1 woman), 83 part-time (12 women); includes 5 Black or African American, non-Hispanic/Latino; 6 Asian, non-Hispanic/Latino; 6 Hispanic/Latino, 10 international. Average age 34. 48 applicants, 71% accepted, 21 enrolled. *Faculty:* 1 full-time (0 women), 17 part-time/adjunct (2 women). Expenses: Contact institution. *Financial support:* Fellowships, research assistantships, teaching assistantships, institutionally sponsored loans, scholarships/grants, and unspecified assistantships available. Support available to part-time students. Financial award applicants required to submit FAFSA. In 2010, 82 master's awarded. *Degree program information:* Part-time and evening/weekend programs available. Offers bioinformatics (MS); capital markets (MS); chemistry (MS); computational finance (MS); computer engineering (MS); computer science (MS); cyber security (MS); electrical engineering (MS); financial engineering (MS, AC); financial technology (MS); financial technology management (AC); industrial engineering (MS); information management (AC); information systems engineering (MS); management (MS); management of technology (MS); manufacturing engineering (MS); telecommunication networks (MS); wireless innovation (ME, Certificate). *Application deadline:* For fall admission, 7/31 priority date for domestic students, 4/30 priority date for international students; for spring admission, 12/31 priority date for domestic students, 11/30 priority date for international students. Applications are processed on a rolling basis. *Application fee:* $75. Electronic applications accepted. *Application Contact:* JeanCarlo Bonilla, Director of Graduate Enrollment Management, 718-260-3182, Fax: 718-260-3624, E-mail: gradinfo@poly.edu.

POLYTECHNIC UNIVERSITY OF PUERTO RICO, Hato Rey, PR 00919

General Information Independent, coed, primarily men, comprehensive institution. CGS member. *Graduate housing:* On-campus housing not available. *Research affiliation:* University of Missouri–Columbia (engineering, mathematics and science), University of Puerto Rico, Mayagüez Campus (electrical engineering), Virginia Polytechnic Institute (mechanical/electrical engineering), Navy Research Laboratories (mechanical/electrical engineering), Department of Energy Laboratories (electrical engineering).

GRADUATE UNITS

Graduate School *Degree program information:* Part-time and evening/weekend programs available.

POLYTECHNIC UNIVERSITY OF PUERTO RICO, MIAMI CAMPUS, Miami, FL 33166

General Information Independent, coed, comprehensive institution.

GRADUATE UNITS

Graduate School *Degree program information:* Part-time and evening/weekend programs available. Postbaccalaureate distance learning degree programs offered (no on-campus study). Electronic applications accepted.

POLYTECHNIC UNIVERSITY OF PUERTO RICO, ORLANDO CAMPUS, Winter Park, FL 32792

General Information Independent, coed, comprehensive institution. *Graduate housing:* On-campus housing not available.

GRADUATE UNITS

Graduate School *Degree program information:* Part-time and evening/weekend programs available. Postbaccalaureate distance learning degree programs offered (no on-campus study). Electronic applications accepted.

PONCE SCHOOL OF MEDICINE, Ponce, PR 00732-7004

General Information Independent, coed, graduate-only institution. *Enrollment by degree level:* 426 first professional, 47 master's, 134 doctoral. *Graduate faculty:* 170 full-time (70 women), 227 part-time/adjunct (56 women). *Tuition:* Full-time $22,984; part-time $200 per credit. *Required fees:* $2729. Full-time tuition and fees vary according to course level. *Student services:* Career counseling, free psychological counseling, grant writing training, low-cost health insurance, writing training. *Library facilities:* Fundación Angel Ramos Library. *Online resources:* library catalog, access to other libraries' catalogs. *Collection:* 69,364 titles, 948 serial subscriptions, 774 audiovisual materials. *Research affiliation:* H. L. Moffitt Cancer Center, Tampa Florida (cancer biology, oncology), University of Kentucky (biomedical sciences), University of Puerto Rico, Mayagüez Campus (cancer biology, molecular genetics), University of Puerto Rico, Medical Sciences Campus (translational research), University of Maryland –Institute of Virology (HIV/AIDS research).

Computer facilities: 60 computers available on campus for general student use. A campuswide network can be accessed from off campus. *Web address:* http://www.psm.edu/.

General Application Contact: Maria Colon, Admissions Officer, 787-840-2575 Ext. 2143, E-mail: mcolon@psm.edu.

GRADUATE UNITS

Professional Program Students: 259 full-time (129 women); includes 4 Asian, non-Hispanic/Latino; 241 Hispanic/Latino; 1 Native Hawaiian or other Pacific Islander, non-Hispanic/Latino. Average age 25. 1,248 applicants, 13% accepted, 66 enrolled. *Faculty:* 130 full-time (47 women), 208 part-time/adjunct (48 women). Expenses: Contact institution. *Financial support:* In 2010–11, 37 students received support; fellowships, scholarships/grants available. Financial award application deadline: 4/30; financial award applicants required to submit FAFSA. In 2010, 60 MDs awarded. Offers medicine (MD). *Application deadline:* For fall admission, 12/15 for domestic and international students. Applications are processed on a rolling basis. *Application fee:* $100. Electronic applications accepted. *Application Contact:* Maria Colon, Admissions Officer, 787-840-2575 Ext. 2143, E-mail: mcolon@psm.edu. *President and Dean,* Dr. Joxel Garcia, 787-844-3710, Fax: 787-840-9756, E-mail: jgarcia@psm.edu.

Program in Biomedical Sciences Students: 33 full-time (26 women); includes 29 Hispanic/Latino. Average age 29. 9 applicants, 67% accepted, 5 enrolled. *Faculty:* 6 full-time (1 woman). Expenses: Contact institution. *Financial support:* In 2010–11, 19 students received support, including 16 fellowships with full tuition reimbursements available (averaging $145,928 per year), research assistantships with full tuition reimbursements available (averaging $47,612 per year); scholarships/grants also available. Financial award application deadline: 4/30; financial award applicants required to submit FAFSA. In 2010, 5 doctorates awarded. Offers biomedical sciences (PhD). *Application deadline:* For fall admission, 1/15 for domestic and international students. *Application fee:* $100. *Application Contact:* Dr. Jose Torres, Associate Dean for Graduate Studies and Research, 787-840-2158, E-mail: jtorres@psm.edu. *Associate Dean for Graduate Studies and Research,* Dr. Jose Torres, 787-840-2158, E-mail: jtorres@psm.edu.

Program in Clinical Psychology Students: 215 full-time (189 women); includes 192 Hispanic/Latino. Average age 27. 133 applicants, 45% accepted, 48 enrolled. *Faculty:* 13 full-time (5 women), 5 part-time/adjunct (4 women). Expenses: Contact institution. *Financial support:* In 2010–11, 14 students received support; fellowships, scholarships/grants available. Financial award application deadline: 4/30; financial award applicants required to submit FAFSA. In 2010, 27 doctorates awarded. Offers clinical psychology (PhD, Psy D). *Application deadline:* For fall admission, 3/15 for domestic and international students. *Application fee:* $100. *Application Contact:* Maria Colon, Admissions Officer, 787-840-2575 Ext. 2143, E-mail: mcolon@psm.edu. *Head,* Dr. Jose Pons, 787-840-2575, E-mail: jpons@psm.edu.

Program in Public Health Students: 100 full-time (82 women); includes 90 Hispanic/Latino. Average age 32. 48 applicants, 71% accepted, 25 enrolled. *Faculty:* 10 full-time (6 women), 14 part-time/adjunct (4 women). Expenses: Contact institution. *Financial support:* In 2010–11, 6 students received support. Scholarships/grants available. Financial award application deadline: 5/30; financial award applicants required to submit FAFSA. In 2010, 13 master's awarded. Offers epidemiology (Dr PH); public health (MPH). *Application deadline:* For fall admission, 5/15 for domestic students. *Application fee:* $100. *Application Contact:* Maria Colon, Admissions Officer, 787-840-2575 Ext. 2143, E-mail: mcolon@psm.edu. *Head,* Dr. Manuel Bayona, 787-840-2575 Ext. 2232, E-mail: mbayona@psm.edu.

PONTIFICAL CATHOLIC UNIVERSITY OF PUERTO RICO, Ponce, PR 00717-0777

General Information Independent-religious, coed, university. *Graduate housing:* Room and/or apartments available to single students; on-campus housing not available to married students. Housing application deadline: 7/15.

GRADUATE UNITS

College of Arts and Humanities *Degree program information:* Part-time and evening/weekend programs available. Offers arts and humanities (MA, Professional Certificate); grammar and writing (Professional Certificate); Hispanic studies (MA); history (MA); painting and drawing (MA); theology and philosophy (M Div).

College of Business Administration *Degree program information:* Part-time and evening/weekend programs available. Offers accounting (MBA); business administration (MBA, DBA, PhD, Professional Certificate); finance (MBA); general business (MBA, Professional Certificate); human resources (MBA, Professional Certificate); international business (MBA); management (MBA); management and accounting (Professional Certificate); management information systems (MBA, Professional Certificate); maritime logistics and transportation (Professional Certificate); marketing (MBA); office administration (MBA, MS).

College of Education *Degree program information:* Part-time and evening/weekend programs available. Offers business teacher education (M Ed, PhD); counselor education (M Ed); curriculum and instruction (M Ed, PhD); education (M Ed, MA Ed, MRE, PhD); education-general (M Ed, MA Ed); educational leadership and administration (PhD); educational psychology (M Ed); English as a second language (M Ed).

College of Graduate Studies in Behavioral Science and Community Affairs *Degree program information:* Part-time and evening/weekend programs available. Offers clinical psychology (PhD, Psy D); clinical social work (MSW); criminology (MA); industrial psychology (PhD); psychology (PhD); public administration (MSS); rehabilitation counseling (MA).

College of Sciences *Degree program information:* Part-time and evening/weekend programs available. Offers chemistry (MS); environmental sciences (MS); medical-surgical nursing (MSN); mental health and psychiatric nursing (MSN); sciences (MS, Certificate).

School of Medical Technology Offers medical technology (Certificate).

School of Law *Degree program information:* Part-time and evening/weekend programs available. Offers law (JD).

PONTIFICAL COLLEGE JOSEPHINUM, Columbus, OH 43235

General Information Independent-religious, men only, comprehensive institution. *Graduate housing:* Room and/or apartments guaranteed to single students; on-campus housing not available to married students. Housing application deadline: 8/15.

GRADUATE UNITS

School of Theology *Degree program information:* Part-time programs available. Offers theology (M Div, MA).

PORTLAND STATE UNIVERSITY, Portland, OR 97207-0751

General Information State-supported, coed, university. CGS member. *Enrollment:* 28,035 graduate, professional, and undergraduate students; 2,538 full-time matriculated graduate/professional students (1,523 women), 2,441 part-time matriculated graduate/professional students (1,424 women). *Enrollment by degree level:* 4,187 master's, 635 doctoral, 157 other advanced degrees. *Graduate faculty:* 739 full-time (333 women), 587 part-time/adjunct (304 women). Tuition, state resident: full-time $8505; part-time $315 per credit. Tuition, nonresident: full-time $13,284; part-time $492 per credit. *Required fees:* $1482; $21 per credit. $99 per term. One-time fee: $120. Part-time tuition and fees vary according to course load and program. *Graduate housing:* Rooms and/or apartments available on a first-come, first-served basis to single and married students. Typical cost: $7098 per year ($10,065 including board) for single students; $7098 per year ($10,065 including board) for married students. Room and board charges vary according to housing facility selected. Housing application deadline: 8/30. *Student services:* Campus employment opportunities, campus safety program, career counseling, child daycare facilities, exercise/wellness program, free psychological counseling, international student services, low-cost health insurance, multicultural affairs office, services for students with disabilities, teacher training, writing training. *Library facilities:* Branford P. Millar Library plus 1 other. *Online resources:* library catalog, web page, access to other libraries' catalogs. *Collection:* 1.8 million titles, 18,083 serial subscriptions, 90,288 audiovisual materials. *Research affiliation:* Bonneville Power Administration (civil and mechanical engineering, geology, urban studies), Battelle Pacific Northwest Laboratories (computer science, geographic information systems, mechanical engineering, science education), Intel Corporation (electronic cooling, engineering), City of Portland (civil engineering, urban planning), Tri-County Metropolitan Transportation District of Oregon, Tektronix (electrical engineering).

Computer facilities: 1,000 computers available on campus for general student use. A campuswide network can be accessed from student residence rooms and from off campus. Online class registration is available. *Web address:* http://www.pdx.edu/.

General Application Contact: Information Contact, 503-725-3511, Fax: 503-725-5525, E-mail: admissions@pdx.edu.

GRADUATE UNITS

Graduate Studies Students: 2,538 full-time (1,523 women), 2,441 part-time (1,424 women); includes 659 minority (102 Black or African American, non-Hispanic/Latino; 48 American Indian or Alaska Native, non-Hispanic/Latino; 233 Asian, non-Hispanic/Latino; 216 Hispanic/Latino; 12 Native Hawaiian or other Pacific Islander, non-Hispanic/Latino; 48 Two or more races, non-Hispanic/Latino), 537 international. Average age 33. 3,526 applicants, 62% accepted, 1431 enrolled. *Faculty:* 739 full-time (333 women), 587 part-time/adjunct (304 women). Expenses: Contact institution. *Financial support:* In 2010–11, 124 research assistantships with full tuition reimbursements (averaging $10,918 per year), 164 teaching assistantships with full tuition reimbursements (averaging $9,912 per year) were awarded; fellowships, career-related internships or fieldwork, Federal Work-Study, scholarships/grants, tuition waivers (partial), and unspecified assistantships also available. Support available to part-time students. Financial award application deadline: 3/1; financial award applicants required to submit FAFSA. In 2010, 1,625 master's, 50 doctorates awarded. *Degree program information:* Part-time and evening/weekend programs available. Postbaccalaureate distance learning degree programs offered (minimal on-campus study). Offers computational intelligence (Certificate); computer modeling and simulation (Certificate); systems science (MS); systems science/anthropology (PhD); systems science/business administration (PhD); systems science/civil engineering (PhD); systems science/economics (PhD); systems science/engineering management (PhD); systems science/general (PhD); systems science/mathematical sciences (PhD); systems science/mechanical engineering (PhD); systems science/psychology (PhD); systems science/sociology (PhD). *Application deadline:* For fall admission, 6/1 for domestic students, 3/1 for international students; for winter admission, 10/1 for domestic students, 7/1 for international students; for spring admission, 2/1 for domestic students, 11/1 for international students. Applications are processed on a rolling basis. *Application fee:* $50. *Application Contact:* 503-725-3511, Fax: 503-725-5525. *Interim Dean,* Dr. DeLys Ostlund, 503-725-5258, Fax: 503-725-3416, E-mail: ostlundd@pdx.edu.

College of Liberal Arts and Sciences Students: 769 full-time (476 women), 507 part-time (286 women); includes 130 minority (17 Black or African American, non-Hispanic/Latino; 10 American Indian or Alaska Native, non-Hispanic/Latino; 41 Asian, non-Hispanic/Latino; 46 Hispanic/Latino; 2 Native Hawaiian or other Pacific Islander, non-Hispanic/Latino; 14 Two or more races, non-Hispanic/Latino), 110 international. Average age 32. 1,212 applicants, 51% accepted, 409 enrolled. *Faculty:* 361 full-time (167 women), 216 part-time/adjunct (122 women). Expenses: Contact institution. *Financial support:* In 2010–11, 37 research assistantships with full tuition reimbursements (averaging $11,535 per year), 145 teaching assistantships with full tuition reimbursements (averaging $9,905 per year) were awarded; career-related internships or fieldwork, Federal Work-Study, scholarships/grants, and tuition waivers (partial) also available. Support available to part-time students. Financial award application deadline: 3/1; financial award applicants required to submit FAFSA. In 2010, 301 master's, 16 doctorates awarded. *Degree program information:* Part-time and evening/weekend programs available. Offers anthropology (MA); applied economics (MA, MS); biology (MA, MS, PhD); chemistry (MA, MS, PhD); conflict resolution (MA, MS); economics (PhD); English (MA); environmental management (MEM); environmental sciences and resources (PhD); environmental sciences/biology (PhD); environmental sciences/chemistry (PhD); environmental sciences/civil engineering (PhD); environmental sciences/geography (PhD); environmental sciences/geology (PhD); environmental sciences/physics (PhD); environmental studies (MS); foreign literature and language (MA); French (MA); general arts and letters education (MAT, MST); general economics (MA, MS); general science education (MAT, MST); general social science education (MAT, MST); general speech communication (MA, MS, Certificate); geography (MA, MAT, MS, MST, PhD); geology (MA, MS); German (MA); history (MA); Japanese (MA); liberal arts and sciences (MA, MAT, MEM, MS, MST, MST, PhD, Certificate); mathematical sciences (PhD); mathematics education (PhD); physics (MA, MS, PhD); psychology (MA, MS, PhD); science/environmental science (MST); science/geology (MAT, MST); sociology (MA, MS, PhD); Spanish (MA); speech-language pathology (MA, MS); statistics (MS); teaching English to speakers of other languages (MA). *Application deadline:* Applications are processed on a rolling basis. *Application fee:* $50. *Application Contact:* Richard Knight, Interim Dean, 503-725-3514, Fax: 503-725-3693. *Interim Dean,* Richard Knight, 503-725-3514, Fax: 503-725-3693.

College of Urban and Public Affairs Students: 301 full-time (182 women), 310 part-time (195 women); includes 71 minority (11 Black or African American, non-Hispanic/Latino; 6 American Indian or Alaska Native, non-Hispanic/Latino; 27 Asian, non-Hispanic/Latino; 18 Hispanic/Latino; 1 Native Hawaiian or other Pacific Islander, non-Hispanic/Latino; 8 Two or more races, non-Hispanic/Latino), 27 international. Average age 32. 583 applicants, 61% accepted, 197 enrolled. *Faculty:* 73 full-time (33 women), 73 part-time/adjunct (37 women). Expenses: Contact institution. *Financial support:* In 2010–11, 22 research assistantships with full tuition reimbursements (averaging $9,050 per year), 5 teaching assistantships with full tuition reimbursements (averaging $8,445 per year) were awarded; fellowships, career-related internships or fieldwork, Federal Work-Study, scholarships/grants, tuition waivers (partial), and unspecified assistantships also available. Support available to part-time students. Financial award application deadline: 3/1; financial award applicants required to submit FAFSA. In 2010, 191 master's, 10 doctorates awarded. *Degree program information:* Part-time and evening/weekend programs available. Offers aging (Certificate); criminology and criminal justice (MS, PhD); government (MA, MAT, MPA, MS, MST, PhD); health administration (MPA, MPH); health education (MA, MS); health education and health promotion (MPH); health studies (MPA, MPH); political science (MA, MAT, MS, MST, PhD);

Portland State University (continued)

public administration (MPA); public administration and policy (PhD); urban and public affairs (MA, MAT, MPA, MPH, MS, MST, MURP, MUS, PhD, Certificate); urban and regional planning (MURP); urban studies (MUS, PhD); urban studies and planning (MURP, MUS, PhD). *Application fee:* $50. *Application Contact:* Rod Johnson, Admissions Officer, 503-725-4044, Fax: 503-725-5199, E-mail: rod@pdx.edu. *Dean,* Dr. Lawrence Wallack, 503-725-4043, Fax: 503-725-5199, E-mail: wallackl@pdx.edu.

Maseeh College of Engineering and Computer Science Students: 299 full-time (69 women), 349 part-time (80 women); includes 85 minority (9 Black or African American, non-Hispanic/Latino; 52 Asian, non-Hispanic/Latino; 20 Hispanic/Latino; 2 Native Hawaiian or other Pacific Islander, non-Hispanic/Latino; 2 Two or more races, non-Hispanic/Latino), 269 international. Average age 31. 458 applicants, 62% accepted, 139 enrolled. *Faculty:* 79 full-time (13 women), 18 part-time/adjunct (5 women). Expenses: Contact institution. *Financial support:* In 2010–11, 32 research assistantships with full tuition reimbursements (averaging $14,238 per year), 4 teaching assistantships with full tuition reimbursements (averaging $11,440 per year) were awarded; career-related internships or fieldwork, Federal Work-Study, scholarships/grants, and unspecified assistantships also available. Support available to part-time students. Financial award application deadline: 3/1; financial award applicants required to submit FAFSA. In 2010, 187 master's, 9 doctorates awarded. *Degree program information:* Part-time and evening/weekend programs available. Offers civil and environmental engineering (M Eng, MS, PhD); civil and environmental engineering management (M Eng); computer science (MS, PhD); electrical and computer engineering (M Eng, MS, PhD); engineering and computer science (M Eng, ME, MS, MSE, PhD, Certificate); engineering and technology management (M Eng); engineering management (MS); environmental sciences and resources (PhD); manufacturing engineering (ME); manufacturing management (M Eng); mechanical engineering (M Eng, MS, PhD); software engineering (MSE); systems engineering (M Eng); systems engineering fundamentals (Certificate); systems science (PhD); systems science/engineering management (PhD). *Application deadline:* For fall admission, 4/1 for domestic students, 3/1 for international students; for winter admission, 9/1 for domestic and international students; for spring admission, 2/1 for domestic and international students. Applications are processed on a rolling basis. *Application fee:* $50. *Application Contact:* Marcia Fischer, Assistant Dean for Enrollment, 503-725-4289, Fax: 503-725-4298, E-mail: fischerm@cecs.pdx.edu. *Dean,* Dr. Renjeng Su, 503-725-8393, Fax: 503-725-2825, E-mail: renjengs@pdx.edu.

School of Business Administration Students: 218 full-time (91 women), 302 part-time (123 women); includes 71 minority (6 Black or African American, non-Hispanic/Latino; 4 American Indian or Alaska Native, non-Hispanic/Latino; 48 Asian, non-Hispanic/Latino; 12 Hispanic/Latino; 1 Two or more races, non-Hispanic/Latino), 96 international. Average age 31. 229 applicants, 86% accepted, 188 enrolled. *Faculty:* 60 full-time (26 women), 54 part-time/adjunct (16 women). Expenses: Contact institution. *Financial support:* Research assistantships with full tuition reimbursements, teaching assistantships with full tuition reimbursements, career-related internships or fieldwork, Federal Work-Study, scholarships/grants, tuition waivers (partial), and unspecified assistantships available. Support available to part-time students. Financial award application deadline: 3/1; financial award applicants required to submit FAFSA. In 2010, 234 master's awarded. *Degree program information:* Part-time and evening/weekend programs available. Offers business administration (MBA, MIM, MSFA, PhD); financial analysis (MSFA); international management (MIM). *Application deadline:* For fall admission, 4/1 priority date for domestic students, 3/1 priority date for international students. Applications are processed on a rolling basis. *Application fee:* $50. *Application Contact:* Pam Mitchell, Administrator, 503-725-3730, Fax: 503-725-5850, E-mail: pamm@sba.pdx.edu. *Dean,* Dr. Scott Dawson, 503-725-3714, Fax: 503-725-5850, E-mail: scottd@sba.pdx.edu.

School of Education Students: 475 full-time (357 women), 735 part-time (576 women); includes 163 minority (29 Black or African American, non-Hispanic/Latino; 12 American Indian or Alaska Native, non-Hispanic/Latino; 35 Asian, non-Hispanic/Latino; 73 Hispanic/Latino; 5 Native Hawaiian or other Pacific Islander, non-Hispanic/Latino; 9 Two or more races, non-Hispanic/Latino), 21 international. Average age 35. 367 applicants, 86% accepted, 216 enrolled. *Faculty:* 62 full-time (41 women), 84 part-time/adjunct (57 women). Expenses: Contact institution. *Financial support:* In 2010–11, 19 research assistantships with full tuition reimbursements (averaging $6,342 per year), 1 teaching assistantship with full tuition reimbursement (averaging $10,408 per year) were awarded; career-related internships or fieldwork, Federal Work-Study, institutionally sponsored loans, scholarships/grants, and unspecified assistantships also available. Support available to part-time students. Financial award application deadline: 3/1; financial award applicants required to submit FAFSA. In 2010, 449 master's, 8 doctorates awarded. *Degree program information:* Part-time and evening/weekend programs available. Offers counselor education (MA, MS); early childhood education (MA, MS); education (M Ed, MA, MS); educational leadership (MA, MS, Ed D); educational leadership: curriculum and instruction (Ed D); educational media/school librarianship (MA, MS); elementary education (M Ed, MAT, MST); postsecondary, adult and continuing education (Ed D); reading (MA, MS); secondary education (M Ed, MAT, MST); special and counselor education (Ed D); special education (MA, MS). *Application deadline:* For fall admission, 4/1 for domestic and international students; for winter admission, 9/1 for domestic and international students; for spring admission, 11/1 for domestic and international students. *Application fee:* $50. *Application Contact:* Tasa Lehman, Information Contact, 503-725-4619, Fax: 503-725-5599, E-mail: lehmant@pdx.edu. *Dean,* Dr. Randy Hitz, 503-725-4619, Fax: 503-725-5399.

School of Fine and Performing Arts Students: 68 full-time (31 women), 35 part-time (22 women); includes 12 minority (1 Black or African American, non-Hispanic/Latino; 2 American Indian or Alaska Native, non-Hispanic/Latino; 5 Asian, non-Hispanic/Latino; 4 Hispanic/Latino), 6 international. Average age 30. 60 applicants, 95% accepted, 42 enrolled. *Faculty:* 65 full-time (29 women), 119 part-time/adjunct (52 women). Expenses: Contact institution. *Financial support:* In 2010–11, 1 research assistantship with full tuition reimbursement (averaging $9,437 per year) was awarded; teaching assistantships with full tuition reimbursements, career-related internships or fieldwork, Federal Work-Study, scholarships/grants, tuition waivers (partial), and unspecified assistantships also available. Support available to part-time students. Financial award application deadline: 3/1; financial award applicants required to submit FAFSA. In 2010, 47 master's awarded. *Degree program information:* Part-time programs available. Offers conducting (MMC); drawing (MFA); fine and performing arts (MA, MAT, MFA, MMC, MMP, MS, MST); mixed media (MFA); music education (MAT, MST); painting (MFA); performance (MMP); printmaking (MFA); sculpture (MFA); theater arts (MA, MS). *Application deadline:* For fall admission, 3/1 for domestic and international students. Applications are processed on a rolling basis. *Application fee:* $50. *Application Contact:* Dr. Barbara Sestak, Dean, 503-725-3105, Fax: 503-725-3351. *Dean,* Dr. Barbara Sestak, 503-725-3105, Fax: 503-725-3351.

School of Social Work Students: 393 full-time (313 women), 168 part-time (131 women); includes 124 minority (29 Black or African American, non-Hispanic/Latino; 13 American Indian or Alaska Native, non-Hispanic/Latino; 24 Asian, non-Hispanic/Latino; 43 Hispanic/Latino; 2 Native Hawaiian or other Pacific Islander, non-Hispanic/Latino; 13 Two or more races, non-Hispanic/Latino), 4 international. Average age 35. 598 applicants, 54% accepted, 235 enrolled. *Faculty:* 35 full-time (24 women), 22 part-time/adjunct (15 women). Expenses: Contact institution. *Financial support:* In 2010–11, 10 research assistantships with full tuition reimbursements (averaging $11,972 per year), 1 teaching assistantship with full tuition reimbursement (averaging $13,692 per year) were awarded; career-related internships or fieldwork, Federal Work-Study, scholarships/grants, tuition waivers (partial), and unspecified assistantships also available. Support available to part-time students. Financial award application deadline: 3/1; financial award applicants required to submit FAFSA. In 2010, 158 master's, 4 doctorates awarded. *Degree program information:* Part-time programs available. Offers social work (MSW); social work and social research (PhD). *Application deadline:* For fall admission, 2/1 for domestic and international students. *Application fee:* $50. *Application Contact:* Janet Putnam, Director of Student Affairs, 503-725-4712, Fax: 503-725-5545, E-mail: putnamj@pdx.edu. *Dean,* Dr. Kristine E. Nelson, 503-725-4712, Fax: 503-725-5545, E-mail: nelsonk@pdx.edu.

POST UNIVERSITY, Waterbury, CT 06723-2540

General Information Independent, coed, comprehensive institution.

GRADUATE UNITS

Program in Business Administration Postbaccalaureate distance learning degree programs offered. Offers business administration (MBA); corporate innovation (MBA); entrepreneurship (MBA); finance (MBA); leadership (MBA); marketing (MBA).

Program in Education Postbaccalaureate distance learning degree programs offered. Offers education (M Ed); instructional design and technology (M Ed); teaching and learning (M Ed).

Program in Human Services *Degree program information:* Part-time programs available. Postbaccalaureate distance learning degree programs offered. Offers human services (MS); human services/clinical (MS); human services/management (MS).

PRAIRIE VIEW A&M UNIVERSITY, Prairie View, TX 77446-0519

General Information State-supported, coed, university. *Enrollment:* 8,781 graduate, professional, and undergraduate students; 580 full-time matriculated graduate/professional students (366 women), 1,269 part-time matriculated graduate/professional students (946 women). *Enrollment by degree level:* 1,680 master's, 128 doctoral, 41 other advanced degrees. *Graduate faculty:* 151 full-time (45 women), 37 part-time/adjunct (21 women). Tuition, state resident: part-time $119.06 per credit hour. Tuition, nonresident: part-time $511.23 per credit hour. *Graduate housing:* Room and/or apartments available on a first-come, first-served basis to single students; on-campus housing not available to married students. Typical cost: $4752 per year ($7064 including board). Room and board charges vary according to board plan and housing facility selected. Housing application deadline: 4/16. *Student services:* Campus employment opportunities, campus safety program, career counseling, exercise/wellness program, free psychological counseling, grant writing training, international student services, low-cost health insurance, multicultural affairs office, services for students with disabilities, teacher training, writing training. *Library facilities:* John B. Coleman Library plus 1 other. *Online resources:* library catalog, web page, access to other libraries' catalogs. *Collection:* 1.2 million titles, 42,660 serial subscriptions, 3,242 audiovisual materials. *Research affiliation:* U. S. Department of Education (DOE) (engineering), U. S. Department of Energy (engineering and sciences), Science and Engineering Alliance, National Aeronautics and Space Administration (NASA) (space radiation on material systems and devices), Lawrence Livermore National Laboratory (engineering and sciences), Sandia National Laboratories (engineering and chemistry).

Computer facilities: 4,400 computers available on campus for general student use. A campuswide network can be accessed from student residence rooms and from off campus. Online class registration is available. *Web address:* http://www.pvamu.edu/.

General Application Contact: Dr. William H. Parker, Office of Graduate Admissions, 936-261-3500, Fax: 936-261-3529, E-mail: whparker@pvamu.edu.

GRADUATE UNITS

College of Agriculture and Human Sciences Students: 47 full-time (33 women), 34 part-time (26 women); includes 62 Black or African American, non-Hispanic/Latino; 2 Asian, non-Hispanic/Latino; 2 Hispanic/Latino, 5 international. Average age 30. 147 applicants, 100% accepted. *Faculty:* 11 full-time (2 women). Expenses: Contact institution. *Financial support:* In 2010–11, 57 students received support, including 8 fellowships with tuition reimbursements available (averaging $12,000 per year), 10 research assistantships with tuition reimbursements available (averaging $15,000 per year); career-related internships or fieldwork, Federal Work-Study, institutionally sponsored loans, scholarships/grants, tuition waivers (partial), and unspecified assistantships also available. Support available to part-time students. Financial award application deadline: 4/1; financial award applicants required to submit FAFSA. In 2010, 21 master's awarded. *Degree program information:* Part-time and evening/weekend programs available. Offers agricultural economics (MS); animal sciences (MS); interdisciplinary human sciences (MS); soil science (MS). *Application deadline:* For fall admission, 6/1 for domestic and international students; for spring admission, 10/1 for domestic and international students. Applications are processed on a rolling basis. *Application fee:* $50. *Application Contact:* Dr. Richard W. Griffin, Interim Department Head, 936-261-5019, Fax: 936-261-5148, E-mail: rwgriffin@pvamu.edu. *Dean,* Dr. Freddie Richards, 936-261-2528, Fax: 936-261-5143, E-mail: flrichards@pvamu.edu.

College of Arts and Sciences Students: 22 full-time (15 women), 42 part-time (28 women); includes 48 Black or African American, non-Hispanic/Latino; 1 Asian, non-Hispanic/Latino; 3 Hispanic/Latino, 3 international. Average age 30. 14 applicants, 93% accepted, 12 enrolled. *Faculty:* 22 full-time (4 women). Expenses: Contact institution. *Financial support:* In 2010–11, 1 research assistantship with partial tuition reimbursement (averaging $14,400 per year), 8 teaching assistantships with partial tuition reimbursements were awarded; fellowships with partial tuition reimbursements, career-related internships or fieldwork, Federal Work-Study, institutionally sponsored loans, and tuition waivers (full and partial) also available. Support available to part-time students. Financial award application deadline: 4/1; financial award applicants required to submit FAFSA. In 2010, 4 master's awarded. *Degree program information:* Part-time and evening/weekend programs available. Offers arts and sciences (MA, MS); bio- environmental toxicology (MS); biology (MS); chemistry (MS); English (MA); mathematics (MS). *Application deadline:* For fall admission, 10/1 priority date for domestic students; for spring admission, 2/15 for domestic students. Applications are processed on a rolling basis. *Application fee:* $50. Electronic applications accepted. *Application Contact:* Dr. Danny R. Kelley, Dean, 936-261-3180, Fax: 936-261-3188, E-mail: drkelley@pvamu.edu. *Dean,* Dr. Danny R. Kelley, 936-261-3180, Fax: 936-261-3188, E-mail: drkelley@pvamu.edu.

Division of Social Work, Behavioral and Political Science Students: 4 full-time (3 women), 17 part-time (15 women); includes 17 Black or African American, non-Hispanic/Latino; 1 Asian, non-Hispanic/Latino; 2 Hispanic/Latino, 1 international. Average age 30. 5 applicants, 100% accepted, 5 enrolled. *Faculty:* 3 full-time (2 women), 1 part-time/adjunct (0 women). Expenses: Contact institution. *Financial support:* Federal Work-Study and institutionally sponsored loans available. Financial award application deadline: 4/1; financial award applicants required to submit FAFSA. In 2010, 1 master's awarded. *Degree program information:* Part-time and evening/weekend programs available. Offers sociology (MA). *Application deadline:* Applications are processed on a rolling basis. *Application fee:* $50. *Application Contact:* Dr. Walle Engedayehu, Division Head, 936-261-3200, Fax: 936-261-3229, E-mail: waengedayehu@pvamu.edu. *Division Head,* Dr. Walle Engedayehu, 936-261-3200, Fax: 936-261-3229, E-mail: waengedayehu@pvamu.edu.

College of Business Students: 55 full-time (33 women), 158 part-time (99 women); includes 166 Black or African American, non-Hispanic/Latino; 6 Asian, non-Hispanic/Latino; 8 Hispanic/Latino, 20 international. Average age 31. *Faculty:* 14 full-time (5 women). Expenses: Contact institution. *Financial support:* In 2010–11, 9 research assistantships (averaging $6,240 per year), 7 teaching assistantships (averaging $6,240 per year) were awarded; career-related internships or fieldwork, Federal Work-Study, institutionally sponsored loans, and tuition waivers (partial) also available. Support available to part-time students. Financial award application deadline: 4/1; financial award applicants required to submit FAFSA. In 2010, 48 master's awarded. *Degree program information:* Part-time and evening/weekend programs available. Offers accounting (MS); general business administration (MBA). *Application deadline:* For fall admission, 7/1 for domestic students, 6/1 priority date for international students; for spring admission, 11/1 for domestic students, 10/1 priority date for international students. Applications are processed on a rolling basis. *Application fee:* $50. Electronic applications accepted. *Application Contact:* Dr. John Dyck, Director, Graduate Programs in Business, 936-261-9217, Fax: 936-261-9232, E-mail: jwdyck@pvamu.edu. *Dean,* Dr. Munir Quddus, 936-261-9217, Fax: 936-261-9241, E-mail: muquddus@pvamu.edu.

College of Education Students: 266 full-time (201 women), 849 part-time (668 women); includes 956 Black or African American, non-Hispanic/Latino; 2 American Indian or Alaska Native, non-Hispanic/Latino; 5 Asian, non-Hispanic/Latino; 33 Hispanic/Latino, 11 international. Average age 35. 1,093 applicants, 95% accepted, 1003 enrolled. *Faculty:* 31 full-time (12 women), 33 part-time/adjunct (14 women). Expenses: Contact institution. *Financial support:* In 2010–11, 1,050 students received support, including 7 research assistantships with tuition reimbursements available (averaging $24,000 per year); fellowships with tuition reimbursements available, teaching assistantships, career-related internships or fieldwork, institutionally sponsored loans, scholarships/grants, and unspecified assistantships also available. Support available to part-time students. Financial award application deadline: 4/1; financial award applicants required to submit FAFSA. In 2010, 372 master's, 5 doctorates awarded. *Degree program information:* Part-time and evening/weekend programs available. Postbaccalaureate distance learning degree programs offered (no on-campus study). Offers counseling (MA, MS Ed); curriculum and instruction (M Ed, MS Ed); education (M Ed, MA, MS, MS Ed, PhD); educational administration (M Ed, MS Ed); educational leadership (PhD); health education (M Ed, MS); physical education (M Ed, MS); special education (M Ed, MS Ed). *Application deadline:* For fall admission, 7/1 priority date for domestic students, 6/1 for international students; for spring admission, 11/1 priority date for domestic students, 10/1 for international students. Applications are processed on a rolling basis. *Application fee:* $50. Electronic applications accepted. *Application Contact:* Head. *Dean,* Dr. Lucian Yates, 936-261-3600, Fax: 936-261-2911, E-mail: luyates@pvamu.edu.

College of Engineering Students: 89 full-time (26 women), 34 part-time (5 women); includes 45 Black or African American, non-Hispanic/Latino; 1 American Indian or Alaska Native, non-Hispanic/Latino; 13 Asian, non-Hispanic/Latino; 3 Hispanic/Latino, 53 international. Average age 32. 50 applicants, 84% accepted, 33 enrolled. *Faculty:* 19 full-time (0 women). Expenses: Contact institution. *Financial support:* In 2010–11, 80 students received support, including 14 fellowships (averaging $1,050 per year), 16 research assistantships (averaging $16,150 per year), 13 teaching assistantships (averaging $14,000 per year); career-related internships or fieldwork, institutionally sponsored loans, scholarships/grants, health care benefits, tuition waivers (partial), and unspecified assistantships also available. Financial award application deadline: 3/1; financial award applicants required to submit FAFSA. In 2010, 8 master's, 2 doctorates awarded. *Degree program information:* Part-time and evening/weekend programs available. Offers computer information systems (MSCIS); computer science (MSCS); electrical engineering (MSEE, PhDEE); engineering (MS Engr). *Application deadline:* For fall admission, 7/1 priority date for domestic and international students; for spring admission, 11/1 priority date for domestic and international students. *Application fee:* $50. Electronic applications accepted. *Application Contact:* Barbara A. Thompson, Administrative Assistant, 936-261-9896, Fax: 936-261-9869, E-mail: bathompson@pvamu.edu. *Dean,* Dr. Kendall T. Harris, 936-261-9956, Fax: 936-261-9869, E-mail: tharris@pvamu.edu.

College of Juvenile Justice and Psychology Students: 48 full-time (35 women), 30 part-time (22 women); includes 64 Black or African American, non-Hispanic/Latino; 3 Hispanic/Latino, 4 international. Average age 26. 55 applicants, 60% accepted, 33 enrolled. *Faculty:* 12 full-time (7 women). Expenses: Contact institution. *Financial support:* In 2010–11, 23 students received support, including 12 research assistantships (averaging $15,000 per year), 11 teaching assistantships (averaging $20,000 per year); career-related internships or fieldwork, Federal Work-Study, institutionally sponsored loans, tuition waivers (full and partial), and unspecified assistantships also available. Support available to part-time students. Financial award application deadline: 3/1; financial award applicants required to submit FAFSA. In 2010, 20 master's, 1 doctorate awarded. *Degree program information:* Part-time and evening/weekend programs available. Offers clinical adolescent psychology (PhD); juvenile forensic psychology (MSJFP); juvenile justice (MSJJ, PhD). *Application deadline:* For fall admission, 3/1 for domestic and international students; for spring admission, 10/1 for domestic and international students. Applications are processed on a rolling basis. *Application fee:* $50. *Application Contact:* Sandy Siegmund, Executive Secretary, Graduate Program, 936-261-5234, Fax: 936-261-5249, E-mail: sisiegmund@pvamu.edu. *Interim Dean,* Dr. Dennis E. Daniels, 936-261-5205, Fax: 936-261-5252, E-mail: dedaniels@pvamu.edu.

College of Nursing Students: 22 full-time (17 women), 84 part-time (80 women); includes 69 Black or African American, non-Hispanic/Latino; 18 Asian, non-Hispanic/Latino; 5 Hispanic/Latino, 7 international. Average age 37. 37 applicants, 100% accepted, 32 enrolled. *Faculty:* 6 full-time (all women), 6 part-time/adjunct (all women). Expenses: Contact institution. *Financial support:* In 2010–11, 17 students received support. Career-related internships or fieldwork, Federal Work-Study, institutionally sponsored loans, scholarships/grants, and traineeships available. Support available to part-time students. Financial award application deadline: 4/1; financial award applicants required to submit FAFSA. In 2010, 35 master's awarded. *Degree program information:* Part-time programs available. Offers family nurse practitioner (MSN); nursing administration (MSN); nursing education (MSN). *Application deadline:* For fall admission, 6/1 priority date for domestic students; for spring admission, 11/1 priority date for domestic students. Applications are processed on a rolling basis. *Application fee:* $50. *Application Contact:* Dr. Forest Smith, Director of Student Services and Admissions, 713-797-7031, Fax: 713-797-7012, E-mail: fdsmith@pvamu.edu. *Dean,* Dr. Betty N. Adams, 713-797-7009, Fax: 713-797-7013, E-mail: bnadams@pvamu.edu.

School of Architecture Students: 31 full-time (6 women), 38 part-time (18 women); includes 55 Black or African American, non-Hispanic/Latino; 1 Asian, non-Hispanic/Latino; 6 Hispanic/Latino, 5 international. Average age 31. 63 applicants, 100% accepted. *Faculty:* 4 full-time (1 woman), 6 part-time/adjunct (2 women). Expenses: Contact institution. *Financial support:* In 2010–11, 1 research assistantship (averaging $6,792 per year) was awarded; career-related internships or fieldwork, Federal Work-Study, institutionally sponsored loans, scholarships/grants, tuition waivers (full and partial), and unspecified assistantships also available. Support available to part-time students. Financial award application deadline: 3/1; financial award applicants required to submit FAFSA. In 2010, 35 master's awarded. *Degree program information:* Part-time and evening/weekend programs available. Offers architecture (M Arch); community development (MCD). *Application deadline:* For fall admission, 6/1 priority date for domestic and international students; for spring admission, 11/1 priority date for domestic students, 10/1 priority date for international students. Applications are processed on a rolling basis. *Application fee:* $50. Electronic applications accepted. *Application Contact:* Dr. Ikhlas Sabouni, Dean, 936-261-9800, Fax: 936-261-2350, E-mail: isabouni@pvamu.edu. *Dean,* Dr. Ikhlas Sabouni, 936-261-9800, Fax: 936-261-2350, E-mail: isabouni@pvamu.edu.

PRATT INSTITUTE, Brooklyn, NY 11205-3899

General Information Independent, coed, comprehensive institution. *Enrollment:* 4,733 graduate, professional, and undergraduate students; 1,456 full-time matriculated graduate/professional students (1,014 women), 261 part-time matriculated graduate/professional students (205 women). *Enrollment by degree level:* 1,710 master's, 7 other advanced degrees. *Graduate faculty:* 57 full-time (22 women), 362 part-time/adjunct (164 women). *Tuition:* Full-time $22,734; part-time $1263 per credit. *Required fees:* $1280. *Graduate housing:* Rooms and/or apartments available on a first-come, first-served basis to single and married students. Typical cost: $13,128 per year ($16,808 including board) for single students; $13,128 per year ($16,808 including board) for married students. Housing application deadline: 5/1. *Student services:* Campus employment opportunities, campus safety program, career counseling, exercise/wellness program, free psychological counseling, grant writing training, international student services, low-cost health insurance, multicultural affairs office, services for students with disabilities, teacher training, writing training. *Library facilities:* Pratt Institute Library. *Online resources:* library catalog, web page, access to other libraries' catalogs. *Research affiliation:* General Motors Corporation (transportation), The Procter & Gamble Company (product design), Ford Motor Company (transportation).

Computer facilities: A campuswide network can be accessed from student residence rooms and from off campus. Online class registration is available. *Web address:* http://www.pratt.edu/.

General Application Contact: Young Hah, Director of Graduate Admissions, 718-636-3683, Fax: 718-399-4242, E-mail: yhah@pratt.edu.

GRADUATE UNITS

School of Architecture Students: 362 full-time (173 women), 31 part-time (22 women); includes 24 Black or African American, non-Hispanic/Latino; 22 Asian, non-Hispanic/Latino; 34 Hispanic/Latino; 3 Two or more races, non-Hispanic/Latino, 80 international. Average age 28. 942 applicants, 53% accepted, 134 enrolled. *Faculty:* 13 full-time (5 women), 74 part-time/adjunct (27 women). Expenses: Contact institution. *Financial support:* Career-related internships or fieldwork, Federal Work-Study, institutionally sponsored loans, scholarships/grants, health care benefits, and unspecified assistantships available. Support available to part-time students. Financial award application deadline: 2/1; financial award applicants required to submit FAFSA. In 2010, 107 master's awarded. Offers architecture (M Arch, MS, MS Arch, MSCRP); architecture (first-professional) (M Arch); architecture (post-professional) (MS Arch); architecture and urban design (post-profession) (MS); city and regional planning (MSCRP); environmental systems management (MS); facilities management (MS); historic preservation (MS). *Application deadline:* For fall admission, 1/5 for domestic and international students; for spring admission, 10/1 for domestic and international students. Applications are processed on a rolling basis. *Application fee:* $50 ($90 for international students). Electronic applications accepted. *Application Contact:* Young Hah, Director of Graduate Admissions, 718-636-3683, Fax: 718-399-4242, E-mail: yhah@pratt.edu. *Dean,* Thomas Hanrahan, 718-399-4304, Fax: 718-399-4315, E-mail: hanrahan@pratt.edu.

School of Art and Design Students: 952 full-time (728 women), 47 part-time (36 women); includes 34 Black or African American, non-Hispanic/Latino; 82 Asian, non-Hispanic/Latino; 61 Hispanic/Latino; 14 Two or more races, non-Hispanic/Latino, 288 international. Average age 28. 1,882 applicants, 47% accepted, 394 enrolled. *Faculty:* 41 full-time (17 women), 200 part-time/adjunct (99 women). Expenses: Contact institution. *Financial support:* Career-related internships or fieldwork, Federal Work-Study, institutionally sponsored loans, scholarships/grants, health care benefits, and unspecified assistantships available. Support available to part-time students. Financial award application deadline: 2/1; financial award applicants required to submit FAFSA. In 2010, 347 master's awarded. *Degree program information:* Part-time programs available. Offers art and design (MFA, MID, MPS, MS, Adv C); art and design education (MS, Adv C); art history (MS); art history theory and criticism (MS); art therapy and creativity development (MPS); art therapy-special education (MPS); arts and cultural management (MPS); communications design (MFA, MS); dance/movement therapy (MS); design management (MPS); digital arts (MFA); industrial design (MID); interior design (MS); new forms (MFA); package design (MS); painting and drawing (MFA); photography (MFA); printmaking (MFA); sculpture (MFA). *Application deadline:* For fall admission, 1/5 for domestic and international students; for spring admission, 10/1 for domestic and international students. *Application fee:* $50 ($90 for international students). Electronic applications accepted. *Application Contact:* Young Hah, Director of Graduate Admissions, 718-636-3683, Fax: 718-399-4242, E-mail: yhah@pratt.edu. *Dean,* Concetta Stewart, 718-636-3619.

School of Information and Library Science Students: 142 full-time (113 women), 183 part-time (147 women); includes 16 Black or African American, non-Hispanic/Latino; 16 Asian, non-Hispanic/Latino; 10 Hispanic/Latino; 5 Two or more races, non-Hispanic/Latino, 4 international. Average age 31. 233 applicants, 94% accepted, 94 enrolled. *Faculty:* 9 full-time (6 women), 27 part-time/adjunct (15 women). Expenses: Contact institution. *Financial support:* Career-related internships or fieldwork, Federal Work-Study, institutionally sponsored loans, scholarships/grants, health care benefits, and unspecified assistantships available. Support available to part-time students. Financial award application deadline: 2/1; financial award applicants required to submit FAFSA. In 2010, 126 master's, 30 other advanced degrees awarded. *Degree program information:* Part-time programs available. Offers archives (Adv C); library and information science (MS, Adv C); library and information science media specialist (MS); library media specialist (Adv C); museum libraries (Adv C). *Application deadline:* For fall admission, 1/5 for domestic and international students; for spring admission, 10/1 for domestic and international students. *Application fee:* $50 ($90 for international students). Electronic applications accepted. *Application Contact:* Young Hah, Director of Graduate Admissions, 718-636-3683, Fax: 718-399-4242, E-mail: yhah@pratt.edu. *Dean,* Dr. Tula Giannini, 212-647-7682, E-mail: giannini@pratt.edu.

PRESCOTT COLLEGE, Prescott, AZ 86301

General Information Independent, coed, comprehensive institution. *Enrollment:* 1,156 graduate, professional, and undergraduate students; 165 full-time matriculated graduate/professional students (116 women), 188 part-time matriculated graduate/professional students (135 women). *Enrollment by degree level:* 292 master's, 48 doctoral, 13 other advanced degrees. *Graduate faculty:* 9 full-time (6 women), 232 part-time/adjunct (128 women). *Tuition:* Full-time $15,600; part-time $650 per credit. *Required fees:* $50 per term. One-time fee: $190. Tuition and fees vary according to course load and degree level. *Graduate housing:* On-campus housing not available. *Student services:* Campus employment opportunities, career counseling, free psychological counseling, international student services, low-cost health insurance, services for students with disabilities. *Library facilities:* Prescott College Library. *Online resources:* library catalog, web page, access to other libraries' catalogs. *Collection:* 80,322 titles, 22,311 serial subscriptions, 1,664 audiovisual materials. *Research affiliation:* Packard Foundation (Kino Bay research), Marshall Foundation (youth and wilderness), U. S. Department of Agriculture (USDA) (agro-ecology), National Park Service (forest health).

Computer facilities: 50 computers available on campus for general student use. A campuswide network can be accessed from student residence rooms and from off campus. *Web address:* http://www.prescott.edu/.

General Application Contact: Kirsten Alicki, Admissions Counselor, 928-277-1546, Fax: 928-277-4695, E-mail: admissions@prescott.edu.

GRADUATE UNITS

Graduate Programs Students: 165 full-time (116 women), 188 part-time (135 women); includes 55 minority (16 Black or African American, non-Hispanic/Latino; 6 American Indian or Alaska Native, non-Hispanic/Latino; 3 Asian, non-Hispanic/Latino; 13 Hispanic/Latino; 1 Native Hawaiian or other Pacific Islander, non-Hispanic/Latino; 16 Two or more races, non-Hispanic/Latino), 17 international. Average age 38. 246 applicants, 74% accepted, 116 enrolled. *Faculty:* 9 full-time (6 women), 232 part-time/adjunct (128 women). Expenses: Contact institution. *Financial support:* Career-related internships or fieldwork, Federal Work-Study, and scholarships/grants available. Financial award applicants required to submit FAFSA. In 2010, 58 master's, 6 doctorates awarded. *Degree program information:* Part-time programs available. Postbaccalaureate distance learning degree programs offered (minimal on-campus study). Offers adventure education (MA); adventure-based environmental education (MA); adventure-based psychotherapy (MA); counseling psychology (MA); early childhood education (MA); early childhood special education (MA); ecopsychology (MA); ecotherapy (MA); education (MA); elementary education (MA); environmental education leadership and administration (MA); environmental studies (MA); equine-assisted experiential learning (MA); equine-assisted mental health (MA); expressive arts therapy (MA); humanities (MA); school guidance counseling (MA); secondary education (MA); somatic psychology (MA); special education, learning disability (MA); special education, mental retardation (MA); special education, serious emotional disability (MA); student-directed concentrations (MA); student-directed independent study (MA); sustainability education (PhD). *Application deadline:* For fall admission, 4/15 priority date for domestic and international students; for spring admission, 9/15 priority date for domestic and international students. Applications are processed on a rolling basis. *Application fee:* $40. Electronic applications accepted. *Application Contact:* Kerstin Alicki, Admissions Counselor, 877-412-8705, Fax: 928-277-4695, E-mail: admissions@prescott.edu. *Interim Dean,* Dr. Joan Clingan, 928-350-3208, Fax: 928-776-5151, E-mail: jclingan@prescott.edu.

PRINCETON THEOLOGICAL SEMINARY, Princeton, NJ 08542-0803

General Information Independent-religious, coed, graduate-only institution. *Graduate housing:* Rooms and/or apartments available on a first-come, first-served basis to single and married students. *Research affiliation:* Center of Theological Inquiry.

GRADUATE UNITS

Graduate and Professional Programs *Degree program information:* Part-time programs available. Offers theology (M Div, MA, Th M, D Min, PhD). Electronic applications accepted.

PRINCETON UNIVERSITY, Princeton, NJ 08544-1019

General Information Independent, coed, university. CGS member. *Graduate housing:* Rooms and/or apartments available to single and married students. Housing application deadline: 4/15. *Research affiliation:* Institute for Advanced Study (physics and mathematics), Brookhaven National Laboratory (experimental physics), Textile Research Institute (polymer research), National Oceanic and Atmospheric Administration (NOAA)–GFD Laboratory (weather prediction).

Princeton University (continued)

GRADUATE UNITS

Graduate School Offers anthropology (PhD); applied and computational mathematics (PhD); astronomy (PhD); atmospheric and oceanic sciences (PhD); chemistry (PhD); classical and hellenic studies (PhD); classical art and archaeology (PhD); classical philosophy (PhD); comparative literature (PhD); composition (PhD); demography (PhD, Certificate); East Asian art and archaeology (PhD); East Asian studies (PhD); ecology and evolutionary biology (PhD); economics (PhD); economics and demography (PhD); English (PhD); French language and literature (PhD); geosciences (PhD); German (PhD); history (PhD); history (the ancient world) (PhD); history of science (PhD); industrial chemistry (MS); literature and philology (PhD); mathematics (PhD); molecular biology (PhD); musicology (PhD); Near Eastern studies (MA, PhD); neuroscience (PhD); ocean sciences and marine biology (PhD); philosophy (PhD); philosophy of science (PhD); physics (PhD); plasma physics (PhD); political philosophy (PhD); politics (PhD); psychology (PhD); public affairs and demography (PhD); religion (PhD); Russian and Slavic linguistics (PhD); Russian literature (PhD); sociology (PhD); sociology and demography (PhD); Spanish and Portuguese languages and cultures (PhD). Electronic applications accepted.

Bendheim Center for Finance Offers finance (M Fin). Electronic applications accepted.

School of Architecture Offers architecture (M Arch, PhD). Electronic applications accepted.

School of Engineering and Applied Science Offers chemical engineering (M Eng, MSE, PhD); civil and environmental engineering (MSE); computer science (MSE, PhD); electrical engineering (M Eng, PhD); engineering and applied science (M Eng, MSE, PhD); mechanical and aerospace engineering (M Eng, MSE, PhD); operations research and financial engineering (M Eng, MSE, PhD). Electronic applications accepted.

Woodrow Wilson School of Public and International Affairs Offers public affairs (MPA, PhD); public policy (MPP). JD/MPA offered jointly with Columbia University, New York University, Stanford University. Electronic applications accepted.

Princeton Institute for the Science and Technology of Materials (PRISM) Offers materials (PhD).

Princeton Neuroscience Institute Offers neuroscience (PhD). Electronic applications accepted.

PROVIDENCE COLLEGE, Providence, RI 02918

General Information Independent-religious, coed, comprehensive institution. *Enrollment:* 4,592 graduate, professional, and undergraduate students; 180 full-time matriculated graduate/professional students (102 women), 335 part-time matriculated graduate/professional students (194 women). *Enrollment by degree level:* 515 master's. *Graduate faculty:* 36 full-time (18 women), 98 part-time/adjunct (50 women). *Tuition:* Part-time $367 per credit. *Required fees:* $367. *Graduate housing:* On-campus housing not available. *Student services:* Campus employment opportunities, career counseling, exercise/wellness program, international student services, low-cost health insurance, multicultural affairs office, services for students with disabilities, teacher training, writing training. *Library facilities:* Phillips Memorial Library. *Online resources:* library catalog, web page, access to other libraries' catalogs. *Collection:* 961,909 titles, 45,645 serial subscriptions.

Computer facilities: Computer purchase and lease plans are available. 350 computers available on campus for general student use. A campuswide network can be accessed from student residence rooms and from off campus. Online class registration is available. *Web address:* http://www.providence.edu/.

General Application Contact: Rev. Mark D. Nowel, Dean of Undergraduate and Graduate Studies, 401-865-2649, Fax: 401-865-1496, E-mail: mnowel@providence.edu.

GRADUATE UNITS

Graduate Studies Students: 81 full-time (30 women), 145 part-time (58 women); includes 9 minority (3 Black or African American, non-Hispanic/Latino; 1 Asian, non-Hispanic/Latino; 1 Hispanic/Latino; 4 Two or more races, non-Hispanic/Latino), 6 international. Average age 33. 108 applicants, 84% accepted. *Faculty:* 30 full-time (14 women), 31 part-time/adjunct (11 women). Expenses: Contact institution. *Financial support:* In 2010–11, 62 research assistantships with full tuition reimbursements (averaging $8,400 per year) were awarded; career-related internships or fieldwork, Federal Work-Study, institutionally sponsored loans, and unspecified assistantships also available. Support available to part-time students. Financial award application deadline: 8/1; financial award applicants required to submit FAFSA. In 2010, 105 master's awarded. *Degree program information:* Part-time and evening/weekend programs available. Offers administration (M Ed); American history (MA); Biblical studies (MA); counseling (M Ed); elementary administration (M Ed); elementary special education (M Ed); European history (MA); literacy (M Ed); secondary administration (M Ed); secondary education (M Ed); special education (M Ed); teaching (M Ed); teaching mathematics (MA); theology (MA, MTS). *Application deadline:* For fall admission, 8/1 priority date for domestic and international students; for spring admission, 12/1 priority date for domestic and international students. Applications are processed on a rolling basis. *Application fee:* $55. *Application Contact:* Carol A. Daniels, Coordinator of Graduate Faculty and Administrative Services, 401-865-2247, Fax: 401-865-1147, E-mail: daniels@providence.edu. *Dean of Undergraduate and Graduate Studies,* Rev. Mark D. Nowel, 401-865-2649, Fax: 401-865-1496, E-mail: mnowel@providence.edu.

School of Business Students: 53 full-time (20 women), 57 part-time (22 women); includes 4 minority (1 Black or African American, non-Hispanic/Latino; 1 Asian, non-Hispanic/Latino; 2 Two or more races, non-Hispanic/Latino), 6 international. Average age 26. 72 applicants, 81% accepted. *Faculty:* 17 full-time (9 women), 10 part-time/adjunct (2 women). Expenses: Contact institution. *Financial support:* In 2010–11, 34 research assistantships with full tuition reimbursements (averaging $8,400 per year) were awarded; Federal Work-Study, institutionally sponsored loans, and unspecified assistantships also available. Support available to part-time students. Financial award application deadline: 8/1; financial award applicants required to submit FAFSA. In 2010, 56 master's awarded. *Degree program information:* Part-time and evening/weekend programs available. Offers accounting (MBA); entrepreneurship (MBA); finance (MBA); international business (MBA); management (MBA); marketing (MBA); not-for-profit organizations (MBA). *Application deadline:* For fall admission, 8/1 priority date for domestic and international students; for spring admission, 12/1 priority date for domestic and international students. Applications are processed on a rolling basis. *Application fee:* $55. *Application Contact:* Katherine A. Follett, Administrative Coordinator, 401-865-2333, Fax: 401-865-2978, E-mail: kfollett@providence.edu. *Director, MBA Program,* Dr. MaryJane Lenon, 401-865-2566, Fax: 401-865-2978, E-mail: mjlenon@providence.edu.

PROVIDENCE COLLEGE AND THEOLOGICAL SEMINARY, Otterburne, MB R0A 1G0, Canada

General Information Independent-religious, coed, comprehensive institution. *Graduate housing:* Rooms and/or apartments guaranteed to single students and available on a first-come, first-served basis to married students. Housing application deadline: 8/15.

GRADUATE UNITS

Theological Seminary *Degree program information:* Part-time programs available. Offers children's ministry (Certificate); Christian studies (MA, Certificate); counseling (MA); cross-cultural discipleship (Certificate); divinity (M Div); educational studies (MA); global studies (MA); lay counseling (Diploma); ministry (D Min); teaching English to speakers of other languages (Certificate); theological studies (MA); training teacher of English to speakers of other languages (Certificate); youth ministry (Certificate).

PURCHASE COLLEGE, STATE UNIVERSITY OF NEW YORK, Purchase, NY 10577-1400

General Information State-supported, coed, comprehensive institution. *Graduate housing:* Rooms and/or apartments available on a first-come, first-served basis to single and married students.

GRADUATE UNITS

Conservatory of Dance Offers dance (MFA). Electronic applications accepted.

Conservatory of Music Offers composition (MM); instrumental performance (MM); jazz studies (MM); studio composition (MM); voice and opera studies (MM). Electronic applications accepted.

Conservatory of Theatre Arts Offers theatre design/stage technology (MFA). Electronic applications accepted.

School of Art and Design Offers art and design (MFA). Electronic applications accepted.

School of Humanities Offers art history (MA).

PURDUE UNIVERSITY, West Lafayette, IN 47907

General Information State-supported, coed, university. CGS member. *Graduate housing:* Rooms and/or apartments available on a first-come, first-served basis to single and married students. Housing application deadline: 3/1.

GRADUATE UNITS

College of Engineering *Degree program information:* Part-time programs available. Postbaccalaureate distance learning degree programs offered (no on-campus study). Offers agricultural and biological engineering (MS, MSABE, MSE, PhD); biomedical engineering (MSBME, PhD); engineering (MS, MSAAE, MSABE, MSBME, MSCE, MSChE, MSE, MSECE, MSIE, MSME, MSMSE, MSNE, PhD, Certificate); engineering professional education (MS, MSE). Electronic applications accepted.

School of Aeronautics and Astronautics Engineering *Degree program information:* Part-time programs available. Postbaccalaureate distance learning degree programs offered (no on-campus study). Offers aeronautics and astronautics engineering (MS, MSAAE, MSE, PhD). Electronic applications accepted.

School of Chemical Engineering Offers chemical engineering (MSChE, PhD). Electronic applications accepted.

School of Civil Engineering *Degree program information:* Part-time programs available. Offers civil engineering (MS, MSCE, MSE, PhD). Electronic applications accepted.

School of Electrical and Computer Engineering *Degree program information:* Part-time programs available. Postbaccalaureate distance learning degree programs offered (no on-campus study). Offers electrical and computer engineering (MS, MSE, MSECE, PhD). MS and PhD degree programs in biomedical engineering offered jointly with School of Mechanical Engineering and School of Chemical Engineering. Electronic applications accepted.

School of Engineering Education Offers engineering education (PhD). Electronic applications accepted.

School of Industrial Engineering *Degree program information:* Part-time programs available. Postbaccalaureate distance learning degree programs offered (no on-campus study). Offers industrial engineering (MS, MSIE, PhD). Electronic applications accepted.

School of Materials Engineering *Degree program information:* Part-time programs available. Offers materials engineering (MSMSE, PhD). Electronic applications accepted.

School of Mechanical Engineering *Degree program information:* Part-time programs available. Postbaccalaureate distance learning degree programs offered (no on-campus study). Offers mechanical engineering (MS, MSE, MSME, PhD, Certificate). MS and PhD degree programs in biomedical engineering offered jointly with School of Electrical and Computer Engineering and School of Chemical Engineering. Electronic applications accepted.

School of Nuclear Engineering *Degree program information:* Part-time programs available. Offers nuclear engineering (MS, MSNE, PhD). Electronic applications accepted.

College of Pharmacy and Pharmacal Sciences *Degree program information:* Part-time programs available. Offers pharmacy and pharmacal sciences (Pharm D, MS, PhD, Certificate). Electronic applications accepted.

Graduate Programs in Pharmacy and Pharmacal Sciences *Degree program information:* Part-time programs available. Offers analytical medicinal chemistry (PhD); clinical pharmacy (MS, PhD); computational and biophysical medicinal chemistry (PhD); industrial and physical pharmacy (MS, PhD, Certificate); medicinal and bioorganic chemistry (PhD); medicinal biochemistry and molecular biology (PhD); medicinal chemistry and molecular pharmacology (MS, PhD); molecular pharmacology and toxicology (PhD); natural products and pharmacognosy (PhD); nuclear pharmacy (MS); pharmaceutics (PhD); pharmacy administration (MS, PhD); pharmacy practice (MS, PhD); radiopharmaceutical chemistry and nuclear pharmacy (PhD); regulatory quality compliance (MS, Certificate). Electronic applications accepted.

Graduate School *Degree program information:* Part-time and evening/weekend programs available. Postbaccalaureate distance learning degree programs offered (no on-campus study). Offers life sciences (PhD). MD/PhD offered jointly with Indiana University–Purdue University Indianapolis. Electronic applications accepted.

Center for Education and Research in Information Assurance and Security (CERIAS) Offers information security (MS).

College of Agriculture *Degree program information:* Part-time programs available. Offers agricultural economics (MS, PhD); agriculture (EMBA, M Agr, MA, MS, MSF, PhD); agronomy (MS, PhD); animal sciences (MS, PhD); aquaculture, fisheries, aquatic science (MSF); aquaculture, fisheries, aquatic sciences (MS, PhD); biochemistry (MS, PhD); botany and plant pathology (MS, PhD); entomology (MS, PhD); food and agricultural business (EMBA); food science (MS, PhD); forest biology (MS, MSF, PhD); horticulture (M Agr, MS, PhD); natural resources and environmental policy (MS, MSF); natural resources environmental policy (PhD); quantitative resource analysis (MS, MSF, PhD); wildlife science (MS, MSF, PhD); wood science and technology (MS, MSF, PhD); youth development and agricultural education (MA, PhD). Electronic applications accepted.

College of Consumer and Family Sciences *Degree program information:* Part-time programs available. Offers consumer and family sciences (MS, PhD); consumer behavior (MS, PhD); developmental studies (MS, PhD); family and consumer economics (MS, PhD); family studies (MS, PhD); hospitality and tourism management (MS, PhD); marriage and family therapy (MS, PhD); nutrition (MS, PhD); retail management (MS, PhD); textile science (MS, PhD). Electronic applications accepted.

College of Liberal Arts *Degree program information:* Part-time and evening/weekend programs available. Offers American studies (MA, PhD); anthropology (MS, PhD); art and design (MA); audiology (MS, Au D, PhD); communication (MA, MS, PhD); comparative literature (MA, PhD); creative writing (MFA); exercise, human physiology of movement and sport (PhD); French (MA, MAT, PhD); German (MA, MAT, PhD); health and fitness (MS); health promotion (MS); health promotion and disease prevention (PhD); history (MA, PhD); liberal arts (MA, MAT, MFA, MS, Au D, PhD); linguistics (MS, PhD); literature (MA, PhD); movement and sport science (MS); pedagogy and administration (MS); pedagogy of physical activity and health (PhD); philosophy (MA, PhD); political science (MA, PhD); psychological sciences (PhD); psychology of sport and exercise, and motor behavior (PhD); sociology (MS, PhD); Spanish (MA, MAT, PhD); speech and hearing science (MS, PhD); speech-language pathology (MS, PhD); theatre (MA, MFA). Electronic applications accepted.

College of Science *Degree program information:* Part-time programs available. Offers analytical chemistry (MS, PhD); biochemistry (MS, PhD); biophysics (PhD); cell and developmental biology (PhD); chemical education (MS, PhD); computer sciences (MS, PhD); earth and atmospheric sciences (MS, PhD); ecology, evolutionary and population biology (MS, PhD); genetics (MS, PhD); inorganic chemistry (MS, PhD); mathematics (MS, PhD); microbiology (MS, PhD); molecular biology (PhD); neurobiology (MS, PhD); organic chemistry (MS, PhD); physical chemistry (MS, PhD); physics (MS, PhD); plant physiology (PhD); science (MS, PhD, Certificate); statistics (MS, PhD, Certificate). Electronic applications accepted.

College of Technology Postbaccalaureate distance learning degree programs offered. Offers industrial technology (MS); technology (MS). Electronic applications accepted.

Krannert School of Management Offers business administration (MBA); economics (PhD); finance (MSF); general business (MBA); human resource management (MSHRM); industrial administration (MSIA); international management (MBA); management (EMBA, MBA, MS, MSF, MSHRM, MSIA, PhD); organizational behavior and human resource management (PhD). Electronic applications accepted.

School of Education *Degree program information:* Part-time and evening/weekend programs available. Offers administration (MS Ed, PhD, Ed S); agricultural and extension education (PhD, Ed S); agriculture and extension education (MS, MS Ed); art education (PhD); consumer and family sciences and extension education (MS Ed, PhD, Ed S); counseling and development (MS Ed, PhD); curriculum studies (MS Ed, PhD, Ed S); education (MS, MS Ed, PhD, Ed S); education of the gifted (MS Ed); educational psychology (MS Ed, PhD); educational technology (MS Ed, PhD, Ed S); elementary education (MS Ed); foreign language education (MS Ed, PhD, Ed S); foundations of education (MS Ed, PhD); higher education administration (MS Ed, PhD); industrial technology (PhD, Ed S); language arts (MS Ed, PhD, Ed S); literacy (MS Ed, PhD, Ed S); mathematics/science education (MS, MS Ed, PhD, Ed S); social studies (MS Ed, PhD); social studies education (Ed S); special education (MS Ed, PhD); vocational/industrial education (MS Ed, PhD, Ed S); vocational/technical education (MS Ed, PhD, Ed S). Electronic applications accepted.

School of Health Sciences *Degree program information:* Part-time programs available. Offers health sciences (MS, PhD). Electronic applications accepted.

School of Veterinary Medicine *Degree program information:* Part-time and evening/weekend programs available. Offers anatomy (MS, PhD); basic medical sciences (MS, PhD); comparative epidemiology and public health (MS); comparative epidemiology and public heath (PhD); comparative microbiology and immunology (MS, PhD); comparative pathobiology (MS, PhD); interdisciplinary studies (PhD); lab animal medicine (MS); pharmacology (MS, PhD); physiology (MS, PhD); veterinary anatomic pathology (MS); veterinary clinical pathology (MS); veterinary clinical sciences (MS, PhD); veterinary medicine (DVM, MS, PhD).

PURDUE UNIVERSITY CALUMET, Hammond, IN 46323-2094

General Information State-supported, coed, comprehensive institution. *Enrollment:* 9,807 graduate, professional, and undergraduate students; 1,143 matriculated graduate/professional students (689 women). *Enrollment by degree level:* 1,143 master's. *Graduate faculty:* 140. Tuition, state resident: full-time $6867. Tuition, nonresident: full-time $14,157. *Graduate housing:* Room and/or apartments available on a first-come, first-served basis to single students; on-campus housing not available to married students. *Student services:* Campus employment opportunities, campus safety program, career counseling, child daycare facilities, exercise/wellness program, free psychological counseling, international student services, services for students with disabilities, teacher training, writing training. *Library facilities:* Purdue University Calumet Library. *Online resources:* library catalog, web page.

Computer facilities: A campuswide network can be accessed from student residence rooms and from off campus. Online class registration, student Web page publishing are available. *Web address:* http://www.purduecal.edu/.

General Application Contact: Margaret R. Greer, Coordinator of Graduate Admissions and Records, 219-989-2257, Fax: 219-989-4130, E-mail: margaret.greer@purduecal.edu.

GRADUATE UNITS

Graduate Studies Office Students: 1,143 (689 women); includes 132 Black or African American, non-Hispanic/Latino; 3 American Indian or Alaska Native, non-Hispanic/Latino; 31 Asian, non-Hispanic/Latino; 80 Hispanic/Latino; 11 Two or more races, non-Hispanic/Latino, 227 international. Average age 27. *Faculty:* 140. Expenses: Contact institution. *Financial support:* Research assistantships, teaching assistantships, career-related internships or fieldwork, Federal Work-Study, and tuition waivers (partial) available. Support available to part-time students. Financial award application deadline: 3/1; financial award applicants required to submit FAFSA. In 2010, 261 master's awarded. *Degree program information:* Part-time and evening/weekend programs available. Postbaccalaureate distance learning degree programs offered (no on-campus study). *Application deadline:* Applications are processed on a rolling basis. *Application fee:* $55. Electronic applications accepted. *Application Contact:* Margaret Greer, Coordinator of Admissions and Records, 219-989-2257, Fax: 219-989-4130, E-mail: margaret.greer@purduecal.edu. *Director of Graduate Studies,* Dr. Joy L. Colwell, 219-989-2545, Fax: 219-989-4130, E-mail: colwell@purduecal.edu.

School of Education Students: 308. Expenses: Contact institution. *Financial support:* Application deadline: 3/1. Offers counseling (MS Ed); educational administration (MS Ed); human services (MS Ed); instructional technology (MS Ed); mental health counseling (MS Ed); school counseling (MS Ed); special education (MS Ed). *Application fee:* $30. *Application Contact:* Margaret Greer, Coordinator of Admissions and Records, 219-989-2257, Fax: 219-989-4130, E-mail: margaret.greer@purduecal.edu. *Director, Graduate Studies in Education,* Dr. Robert Colon, 219-989-2867, E-mail: colon2@purduecal.edu.

School of Engineering, Mathematics, and Science Students: 39 full-time (3 women), 16 part-time (6 women); includes 3 Black or African American, non-Hispanic/Latino; 6 Asian, non-Hispanic/Latino; 3 Hispanic/Latino. Average age 21. 19 applicants, 84% accepted, 16 enrolled. *Faculty:* 14 full-time (1 woman). Expenses: Contact institution. *Financial support:* In 2010–11, research assistantships with full tuition reimbursements (averaging $8,000 per year), teaching assistantships with full tuition reimbursements (averaging $8,000 per year) were awarded. Financial award application deadline: 3/1. In 2010, 7 master's awarded. *Degree program information:* Part-time and evening/weekend programs available. Postbaccalaureate distance learning degree programs offered (minimal on-campus study). Offers biology (MS); biology teaching (MS); biotechnology (MS); computer engineering (MSE); computer science (MS); electrical engineering (MSE); engineering (MS); engineering, mathematics, and science (MAT, MS, MSE); mathematics (MAT, MS); mechanical engineering (MSE). *Application deadline:* For fall admission, 8/1 priority date for domestic students; for winter admission, 6/1 priority date for domestic students; for spring admission, 12/1 priority date for domestic students. Applications are processed on a rolling basis. *Application fee:* $30. Electronic applications accepted. *Application Contact:* Janice Novosel, Engineering Graduate Program Secretary, 219-989-3106, E-mail: janice.novosel@purduecal.edu. *Graduate Director,* Dr. Kaliappan Gopalan, 219-989-2685, E-mail: gopalan@purduecal.edu.

School of Liberal Arts and Social Sciences Expenses: Contact institution. *Financial support:* Teaching assistantships available. Support available to part-time students. Financial award application deadline: 3/1. *Degree program information:* Part-time programs available. Offers child development and family studies (MS); communication (MA); English (MA); history (MA); liberal arts and social sciences (MA, MS); marriage and family therapy (MS). *Application fee:* $30. *Application Contact:* Coordinator for Graduate Admissions and Records, 219-989-2257, Fax: 219-989-4130. *Interim Dean,* Dr. John Rowan, 219-989-2255, E-mail: jrowan@purduecal.edu.

School of Management Students: 180 full-time, 15 part-time. *Faculty:* 25 full-time (7 women). Expenses: Contact institution. *Financial support:* In 2010–11, 2 research assistantships with full tuition reimbursements (averaging $8,000 per year) were awarded. Financial award application deadline: 3/1. In 2010, 80 master's awarded. *Degree program information:* Part-time and evening/weekend programs available. Offers accountancy (M Acc); business administration (MBA); business administration for executives (EMBA). *Application deadline:* For fall admission, 8/20 priority date for domestic students; for spring admission, 1/15 priority date for domestic students. Applications are processed on a rolling basis. *Application fee:* $55. Electronic applications accepted. *Application Contact:* Kimberly Uhll, Graduate Adviser, 219-989-3150, E-mail: kuhll@purduecal.edu. *Dean,* Dr. Martine SuChatelet, 219-989-2606, E-mail: duchatel@purduecal.edu.

School of Nursing Students: 133. Average age 38. *Faculty:* 6 full-time (5 women), 6 part-time/adjunct (all women). Expenses: Contact institution. *Financial support:* In 2010–11, 31 students received support, including 4 research assistantships with partial tuition reimbursements available (averaging $4,270 per year); traineeships also available. Financial award application deadline: 3/1. In 2010, 27 master's awarded. *Degree program information:* Part-time programs available. Postbaccalaureate distance learning degree programs offered (minimal on-campus study). Offers adult health clinical nurse specialist (MS); critical care clinical nurse specialist (MS); family nurse practitioner (MS); nurse executive (MS). *Application deadline:* For fall admission, 5/1 priority date for domestic students; for spring admission, 10/1 priority date for domestic students. Applications are processed on a rolling basis. *Application fee:* $55. Electronic applications accepted. *Application Contact:* Dr. Jane Walker, Coordinator, 219-989-2815, E-mail: walkerj@purduecal.edu. *Dean,* Dr. Peggy Gerard, 219-989-2818, E-mail: psgerard@purduecal.edu.

School of Technology Expenses: Contact institution. Offers technology (MS). *Application Contact:* Margaret Greer, Coordinator of Admissions and Records, 219-989-2257, Fax: 219-989-4130, E-mail: margaret.greer@purduecal.edu. *Dean,* Niaz Latif, 219-989-8320, E-mail: nlatif@purduecal.edu.

PURDUE UNIVERSITY NORTH CENTRAL, Westville, IN 46391-9542

General Information State-supported, coed, comprehensive institution. *Graduate housing:* On-campus housing not available.

GRADUATE UNITS

Program in Education *Degree program information:* Part-time and evening/weekend programs available. Offers elementary education (MS Ed). Electronic applications accepted.

QUEENS COLLEGE OF THE CITY UNIVERSITY OF NEW YORK, Flushing, NY 11367-1597

General Information State and locally supported, coed, comprehensive institution. CGS member. *Enrollment:* 20,906 graduate, professional, and undergraduate students; 524 full-time matriculated graduate/professional students (367 women), 3,848 part-time matriculated graduate/professional students (2,720 women). *Enrollment by degree level:* 4,372 master's. *Graduate faculty:* 641 full-time (293 women), 895 part-time/adjunct (461 women). *Graduate housing:* Room and/or apartments available on a first-come, first-served basis to single students; on-campus housing not available to married students. Housing application deadline: 6/1. *Student services:* Campus employment opportunities, career counseling, child daycare facilities, free psychological counseling, international student services, low-cost health insurance, multicultural affairs office, services for students with disabilities, teacher training, writing training. *Library facilities:* The Benjamin S. Rosenthal Library plus 1 other. *Online resources:* library catalog, web page, access to other libraries' catalogs. *Collection:* 1.1 million titles, 42,000 serial subscriptions, 40,426 audiovisual materials. *Research affiliation:* The New York Times (sociology), Brookhaven National Laboratory/Stony Brook University (SUNY) (physics).

Computer facilities: Computer purchase and lease plans are available. 2,500 computers available on campus for general student use. A campuswide network can be accessed from student residence rooms and from off campus. Online class registration is available. *Web address:* http://www.qc.cuny.edu/.

General Application Contact: Mario Caruso, Director of Graduate Admissions, 718-997-5200, Fax: 718-997-5193, E-mail: graduate_admissions@qc.edu.

GRADUATE UNITS

Division of Graduate Studies Students: 524 full-time (367 women), 3,848 part-time (2,720 women); includes 329 Black or African American, non-Hispanic/Latino; 1 American Indian or Alaska Native, non-Hispanic/Latino; 497 Asian, non-Hispanic/Latino; 519 Hispanic/Latino, 209 international. Average age 26. 3,645 applicants, 52% accepted, 1440 enrolled. *Faculty:* 641 full-time (293 women), 895 part-time/adjunct (461 women). Expenses: Contact institution. *Financial support:* Career-related internships or fieldwork, Federal Work-Study, institutionally sponsored loans, tuition waivers (partial), and unspecified assistantships available. Support available to part-time students. Financial award application deadline: 4/1; financial award applicants required to submit FAFSA. In 2010, 1,205 master's, 61 other advanced degrees awarded. *Degree program information:* Part-time and evening/weekend programs available. *Application deadline:* For fall admission, 4/1 priority date for domestic students, 3/1 priority date for international students; for winter admission, 11/1 priority date for domestic students, 10/1 priority date for international students; for spring admission, 11/1 priority date for domestic students, 10/1 priority date for international students. Applications are processed on a rolling basis. *Application fee:* $125. *Application Contact:* Mario Caruso, Director of Graduate Admissions, 718-997-5200, Fax: 718-997-5193, E-mail: graduate_admissions@qc.edu. *Acting Dean of Research and Graduate Services,* Dr. Richard Bodnar, 718-997-5190, Fax: 718-997-5493, E-mail: richard.bodnar@qc.cuny.edu.

Arts and Humanities Division Students: 85 full-time (60 women), 450 part-time (293 women); includes 23 Black or African American, non-Hispanic/Latino; 37 Asian, non-Hispanic/Latino; 81 Hispanic/Latino, 83 international. Average age 26. 809 applicants, 32% accepted, 175 enrolled. *Faculty:* 136 full-time (61 women). Expenses: Contact institution. *Financial support:* Career-related internships or fieldwork, Federal Work-Study, institutionally sponsored loans, and tuition waivers (partial) available. Support available to part-time students. Financial award application deadline: 4/1; financial award applicants required to submit FAFSA. In 2010, 147 master's awarded. *Degree program information:* Part-time and evening/weekend programs available. Offers applied linguistics (MA); art history (MA); arts and humanities (MA, MFA, MS Ed); creative writing (MA); English language and literature (MA); fine arts (MFA); French (MA); Italian (MA); music (MA); Spanish (MA); speech pathology (MA); teaching English to speakers of other languages (MS Ed). *Application deadline:* Applications are processed on a rolling basis. *Application fee:* $125. *Application Contact:* Mario Caruso, Director of Graduate Admissions, 718-997-5200, Fax: 718-997-5193, E-mail: graduate_admissions@qc.edu. *Dean,* Dr. Tamara Evans, 718-997-5790, E-mail: tamara_evans@qc.edu.

Division of Education Students: 294 full-time (221 women), 2,058 part-time (1,583 women); includes 142 Black or African American, non-Hispanic/Latino; 211 Asian, non-Hispanic/Latino; 285 Hispanic/Latino, 11 international. 1,603 applicants, 58% accepted, 709 enrolled. *Faculty:* 73 full-time (50 women). Expenses: Contact institution. *Financial support:* Career-related internships or fieldwork, Federal Work-Study, institutionally sponsored loans, and tuition waivers (partial) available. Support available to part-time students. Financial award application deadline: 4/1; financial award applicants required to submit FAFSA. In 2010, 612 master's, 124 other advanced degrees awarded. *Degree program information:* Part-time and evening/weekend programs available. Offers art (MS Ed); bilingual education (MS Ed); biology (MS Ed, AC); chemistry (MS Ed, AC); childhood education (MA); counselor education (MS Ed); early childhood education (MA); earth sciences (MS Ed, AC); education (MA, MS Ed, AC); educational leadership (AC); elementary education (MS Ed, AC); English (MS Ed, AC); French (MS Ed, AC); Italian (MS Ed, AC); literacy (MS Ed); mathematics (MS Ed, AC); music (MS Ed, AC); physics (MS Ed, AC); school psychology (MS Ed, AC); social studies (MS Ed, AC); Spanish (MS Ed, AC); special education (MS Ed). *Application deadline:* For fall admission, 4/1 for domestic students; for spring admission, 11/1 for domestic students. Applications are processed on a rolling basis. *Application fee:* $125. *Application Contact:* Mario Caruso, Director of Graduate Admissions, 718-997-5200, Fax: 718-997-5193, E-mail: graduate_admissions@qc.edu. *Dean,* Dr. Penny Hammrich, 718-997-5220.

Mathematics and Natural Sciences Division Students: 48 full-time (27 women), 328 part-time (193 women); includes 24 Black or African American, non-Hispanic/Latino; 1 American Indian or Alaska Native, non-Hispanic/Latino; 86 Asian, non-Hispanic/Latino; 38 Hispanic/Latino, 53 international. Average age 26. 385 applicants, 55% accepted, 135 enrolled. *Faculty:* 149 full-time (46 women). Expenses: Contact institution. *Financial support:* Career-related internships or fieldwork, Federal Work-Study, institutionally sponsored loans, tuition waivers (partial), and unspecified assistantships available. Support available to part-time students. Financial award application deadline: 4/1; financial award applicants required to submit FAFSA. In 2010, 141 master's awarded. *Degree program information:* Part-time and evening/weekend programs available. Offers biochemistry (MA); biology (MA); chemistry (MA); clinical behavioral applications in mental health settings (MA); computer science (MA); earth and environmental sciences (MA); home economics (MS Ed); mathematics (MA); mathematics and natural sciences (MA, MS Ed, PhD); physical education and exercise sciences (MS Ed); physics (MA, PhD); psychology (MA). *Application deadline:* For fall admission, 4/1 for domestic students; for spring admission, 11/1 for domestic students. Applications are processed on a rolling basis. *Application fee:* $125. *Application Contact:*

Queens College of the City University of New York (continued)

Mario Caruso, Director of Graduate Admissions, 718-997-5200, Fax: 718-997-5193, E-mail: graduate_admissions@qc.edu. *Dean*, Dr. Thomas Strekas, 718-997-4105, E-mail: thomas_strekas@qc.edu.

Social Science Division Students: 97 full-time (59 women), 1,012 part-time (651 women); includes 140 Black or African American, non-Hispanic/Latino; 163 Asian, non-Hispanic/Latino; 115 Hispanic/Latino, 62 international. 848 applicants, 60% accepted, 395 enrolled. *Faculty:* 98 full-time (37 women). Expenses: Contact institution. *Financial support:* Career-related internships or fieldwork, Federal Work-Study, institutionally sponsored loans, and tuition waivers (partial) available. Support available to part-time students. Financial award application deadline: 4/1; financial award applicants required to submit FAFSA. In 2010, 239 master's awarded. *Degree program information:* Part-time and evening/weekend programs available. Offers accounting (MS); history (MA); liberal studies (MALS); library and information studies (MLS, AC); social science (MA, MALS, MASS, MLS, MS, AC); social sciences (MASS); sociology (MA); urban studies (MA). *Application deadline:* For fall admission, 4/1 for domestic students; for spring admission, 11/1 for domestic students. Applications are processed on a rolling basis. *Application fee:* $125. *Application Contact:* Mario Caruso, Director of Graduate Admissions, 718-997-5200, Fax: 718-997-5193, E-mail: graduate_admissions@qc.edu. *Dean*, Dr. Elizabeth Hendrey, 718-997-5210.

See Display below and Close-Up on page 975.

QUEEN'S UNIVERSITY AT KINGSTON, Kingston, ON K7L 3N6, Canada

General Information Province-supported, coed, university. CGS member. *Graduate housing:* Rooms and/or apartments available to single students and available on a first-come, first-served basis to married students. Housing application deadline: 6/15.

GRADUATE UNITS

Faculty of Law *Degree program information:* Part-time programs available. Offers law (JD, LL M).

Queens School of Business Offers business (M Sc, MBA, PhD); consulting and project management (MBA); finance (MBA); innovation and entrepreneurship (MBA); marketing (MBA).

Queen's Theological College *Degree program information:* Part-time programs available. Offers theology (M Div, MTS, Certificate).

School of Graduate Studies and Research *Degree program information:* Part-time programs available.

Faculty of Applied Science *Degree program information:* Part-time programs available. Offers applied science (M Eng, M Sc, M Sc Eng, PhD); chemical engineering (M Sc, PhD); civil engineering (M Eng, M Sc Eng, PhD); electrical and computer engineering (M Eng, M Sc, M Sc Eng, PhD); mechanical and materials engineering (M Eng, M Sc, M Sc Eng, PhD); mining engineering (M Eng, M Sc, M Sc Eng, PhD). Electronic applications accepted.

Faculty of Arts and Sciences *Degree program information:* Part-time programs available. Offers arts and sciences (M Sc, M Sc Eng, MA, PhD); biology (M Sc, PhD); brain behavior and cognitive science (MA, PhD); Canadian politics (PhD); chemistry (M Sc, PhD); classics, Greek, Latin (MA); clinical psychology (MA, PhD); communication and Information technology (MA, PhD); comparative politics (PhD); computing (M Sc, PhD); developmental psychology (MA, PhD); English language and literature (MA, PhD); feminist sociology (MA, PhD); French studies (MA, PhD); gender and politics (PhD); geography (M Sc, MA, PhD); geological sciences and geological engineering (M Sc, M Sc Eng, PhD); German language and literature (MA, PhD); international relations (PhD); mathematics (M Sc, M Sc Eng, PhD); philosophy (MA, PhD); physics (M Sc, M Sc Eng, PhD); political theory (PhD); religious studies (MA); social personality psychology (MA, PhD); socio-legal studies (MA, PhD); sociological theory (MA, PhD); Spanish language and literature (MA); statistics (M Sc, M Sc Eng, PhD). Electronic applications accepted.

Faculty of Education *Degree program information:* Part-time programs available. Offers education (M Ed, PhD).

Faculty of Health Sciences *Degree program information:* Part-time programs available. Offers biochemistry (M Sc, PhD); biology of reproduction (M Sc, PhD); cancer (M Sc, PhD); cardiovascular pathophysiology (M Sc, PhD); cell and molecular biology (M Sc, PhD); drug metabolism (M Sc, PhD); endocrinology (M Sc, PhD); epidemiology (PhD); epidemiology and population health (M Sc); health and chronic illness (M Sc); health sciences (M Sc, M Sc OT, M Sc PT, MPH, PhD, Certificate); health services (M Sc); microbiology and immunology (M Sc, PhD); motor control (M Sc, PhD); neural regeneration (M Sc, PhD); neurophysiology (M Sc, PhD); nurse scientist (PhD); occupational therapy (M Sc OT); pathology and molecular medicine (M Sc, PhD); pharmacology and toxicology (M Sc, PhD); physical therapy (M Sc PT); physiology (M Sc, PhD); policy research and clinical epidemiology (M Sc); primary health care nurse practitioner (Certificate); public health (MPH); rehabilitation science (M Sc, PhD); women's and children's health (M Sc). Electronic applications accepted.

School of Industrial Relations *Degree program information:* Part-time programs available. Offers industrial relations (MIR).

School of Kinesiology and Health Studies *Degree program information:* Part-time programs available. Offers applied exercise science (PhD); biomechanics/ergonomics (M Sc); exercise physiology (M Sc); social psychology of sport and exercise rehabilitation (MA); sociology of sport (MA). Electronic applications accepted.

School of Policy Studies *Degree program information:* Part-time programs available. Offers policy studies (MIR, MPA).

School of Urban and Regional Planning *Degree program information:* Part-time programs available. Offers urban and regional planning (M Pl).

School of Medicine Offers medicine (MD). Electronic applications accepted.

QUEENS UNIVERSITY OF CHARLOTTE, Charlotte, NC 28274-0002

General Information Independent-religious, coed, comprehensive institution. *Graduate housing:* On-campus housing not available.

GRADUATE UNITS

College of Arts and Sciences *Degree program information:* Part-time programs available. Postbaccalaureate distance learning degree programs offered (minimal on-campus study). Offers creative writing (MFA). Electronic applications accepted.

McColl School of Business *Degree program information:* Part-time and evening/weekend programs available. Offers business administration (EMBA, MBA). Electronic applications accepted.

Presbyterian School of Nursing Offers nursing management (MSN). Electronic applications accepted.

School of Communication *Degree program information:* Part-time and evening/weekend programs available. Offers organizational and strategic communication (MA).

Wayland H. Cato, Jr. School of Education *Degree program information:* Part-time and evening/weekend programs available. Offers education in literacy (M Ed); elementary education (MAT); school administration (MSA).

QUINCY UNIVERSITY, Quincy, IL 62301-2699

General Information Independent-religious, coed, comprehensive institution. *Enrollment:* 1,907 graduate, professional, and undergraduate students; 380 full-time matriculated graduate/professional students (266 women), 161 part-time matriculated graduate/professional students (109 women). *Enrollment by degree level:* 541 master's. *Graduate faculty:* 16 full-time (9 women), 25 part-time/adjunct (20 women). *Tuition:* Full-time $8880; part-time $370 per semester hour. *Required fees:* $360; $15 per semester hour. Tuition and fees vary according to course load, campus/location and program. *Graduate housing:* Room and/or apartments available to single students; on-campus housing not available to married students. *Student services:* Campus employment opportunities, campus safety program, career counseling, exercise/wellness program, free psychological counseling, international student services, low-cost health insurance, services for students with disabilities, teacher training, writing training. *Library facilities:* Brenner Library. *Online resources:* library catalog, web page, access to other libraries' catalogs. *Collection:* 217,382 titles, 311 serial subscriptions, 8,827 audiovisual materials.

Computer facilities: 160 computers available on campus for general student use. A campuswide network can be accessed from student residence rooms and from off campus. Online class registration is available. *Web address:* http://www.quincy.edu/.

General Application Contact: Jennifer Bang, Coordinator of Adult Studies, 217-228-5404, Fax: 217-228-5479, E-mail: admissions@quincy.edu.

GRADUATE UNITS

Program in Business Administration Students: 8 full-time (6 women), 17 part-time (8 women); includes 1 Black or African American, non-Hispanic/Latino; 1 Hispanic/Latino. *Faculty:* 5 full-time (3 women). Expenses: Contact institution. *Financial support:* Available to part-time students. Applicants required to submit FAFSA. In 2010, 21 master's awarded. *Degree program information:* Part-time and evening/weekend programs available. Offers business administration (MBA); human resource management (MBA). *Application deadline:* Applications are processed on a rolling basis. *Application fee:* $25. Electronic applications accepted. *Application Contact:* Jennifer Bang, Coordinator of Adult Studies, 217-228-5404, Fax: 217-228-5479, E-mail: admissions@quincy.edu. *Director,* Dr. John Palmer, 217-228-5432 Ext. 3070, E-mail: palmejo@quincy.edu.

Program in Counseling Students: 2 full-time (both women), 17 part-time (15 women); includes 1 Black or African American, non-Hispanic/Latino; 1 Two or more races, non-Hispanic/Latino. *Faculty:* 2 full-time (1 woman). Expenses: Contact institution. *Financial support:* Available to part-time students. Applicants required to submit FAFSA. In 2010, 17 master's awarded. *Degree program information:* Part-time and evening/weekend programs available. Offers education (MS Ed). *Application deadline:* Applications are processed on a rolling basis. *Application fee:* $25. Electronic applications accepted. *Application Contact:* Jennifer Bang, Coordinator of Adult Studies, 217-228-5404, Fax: 217-228-5479, E-mail: admissions@quincy.edu. *Director,* Dr. Kenneth Oliver, 217-228-5432 Ext. 3113, E-mail: oliveke@quincy.edu.

Program in Education Students: 370 full-time (258 women), 123 part-time (85 women); includes 52 Black or African American, non-Hispanic/Latino; 6 Asian, non-Hispanic/Latino; 46 Hispanic/Latino; 3 Two or more races, non-Hispanic/Latino. *Faculty:* 7 full-time (5 women), 25 part-time/adjunct (20 women). Expenses: Contact institution. *Financial support:* Available to part-time students. Applicants required to submit FAFSA. In 2010, 30 master's awarded. *Degree program information:* Part-time programs available. Postbaccalaureate distance learning degree programs offered. Offers alternative certification (MS Ed); curriculum and instruction (MS Ed); leadership (MRS); reading education (MS Ed); school administration (MS Ed); special education (MS Ed); teacher leader in reading (MS Ed); teaching certification (MS Ed). *Application deadline:* Applications are processed on a rolling basis. *Application fee:* $25. Electronic applications accepted. *Application Contact:* Jennifer Bang, Coordinator of Adult Studies, 217-228-5404, Fax: 217-228-5479, E-mail: admissions@quincy.edu. *Director,* Kristen Anguiano, 217-228-5432 Ext. 3119, E-mail: anguikr@quincy.edu.

Program in Theological Studies Students: 4 part-time (1 woman); includes 1 Black or African American, non-Hispanic/Latino. *Faculty:* 2 full-time (0 women). Expenses: Contact institution. *Financial support:* Applicants required to submit FAFSA. *Degree program information:* Part-time and evening/weekend programs available. Offers theological studies (MTS). *Application deadline:* Applications are processed on a rolling basis. *Application fee:* $25. Electronic applications accepted. *Application Contact:* Jennifer Bang, Coordinator of Adult Studies, 217-228-5404, Fax: 217-228-5479, E-mail: admissions@quincy.edu. *Director,* Dr. Daniel Strudwick, 217-228-5432 Ext. 3202, E-mail: strudda@quincy.edu.

QUINNIPIAC UNIVERSITY, Hamden, CT 06518-1940

General Information Independent, coed, comprehensive institution. *Enrollment:* 8,166 graduate, professional, and undergraduate students; 829 full-time matriculated graduate/professional students (592 women), 749 part-time matriculated graduate/professional students (455 women). *Enrollment by degree level:* 1,410 master's, 168 doctoral. *Graduate faculty:* 101 full-time (46 women), 139 part-time/adjunct (68 women). *Tuition:* Part-time $810 per credit. *Required fees:* $35 per credit. *Graduate housing:* On-campus housing not available. *Student services:* Campus employment opportunities, campus safety program, career counseling, exercise/wellness program, free psychological counseling, international student services, low-cost health insurance, multicultural affairs office. *Library facilities:* Arnold Bernhard Library plus 1 other. *Online resources:* library catalog, web page, access to other libraries' catalogs. *Collection:* 311,000 titles, 44,700 serial subscriptions, 6,000 audiovisual materials.

Computer facilities: Computer purchase and lease plans are available. 600 computers available on campus for general student use. A campuswide network can be accessed from student residence rooms and from off campus. Online class registration, e-commerce 'Q' card for local merchants, food service, dorm card access are available. *Web address:* http://www.quinnipiac.edu/.

General Application Contact: Information Contact, 800-462-1944, Fax: 203-582-3443, E-mail: graduate@quinnipiac.edu.

GRADUATE UNITS

School of Business Students: 113 full-time (40 women), 345 part-time (175 women); includes 38 minority (12 Black or African American, non-Hispanic/Latino; 12 Asian, non-Hispanic/Latino; 13 Hispanic/Latino; 1 Two or more races, non-Hispanic/Latino), 18 international. 242 applicants, 86% accepted, 172 enrolled. *Faculty:* 29 full-time (3 women), 6 part-time/adjunct (4 women). Expenses: Contact institution. *Financial support:* Career-related internships or fieldwork, Federal Work-Study, tuition waivers (partial), and unspecified assistantships available. Support available to part-time students. Financial award application deadline: 4/15; financial award applicants required to submit FAFSA. In 2010, 119 master's awarded. *Degree program information:* Part-time and evening/weekend programs available. Offers business (MBA, MS); chartered financial analyst (MBA); finance (MBA); health care management (MBA); healthcare management (MBA); information systems management (MBA); information technology (MS); marketing (MBA); organizational leadership (MS); supply chain management (MBA). *Application deadline:* For fall admission, 7/30 priority date for domestic students, 4/30 priority date for international students; for spring admission, 12/15 priority date for domestic students, 9/15 priority date for international students. Applications are processed on a rolling basis. *Application fee:* $45. Electronic applications accepted. *Application Contact:* Jennifer Boutin, Associate Director of Graduate Admissions, 800-462-1944, Fax: 203-582-3443, E-mail: jennifer.boutin@quinnipiac.edu. *MBA Program Director,* Lisa Braiewa, 203-582-3710, Fax: 203-582-8664, E-mail: lisa.eraiewa@quinnipiac.edu.

School of Communications Students: 53 full-time (34 women), 101 part-time (63 women); includes 21 minority (14 Black or African American, non-Hispanic/Latino; 4 Asian, non-Hispanic/Latino; 3 Hispanic/Latino), 5 international. 79 applicants, 87% accepted, 49 enrolled. *Faculty:* 10 full-time (5 women), 23 part-time/adjunct (11 women). Expenses: Contact institution. *Financial support:* In 2010–11, 1 fellowship with full tuition reimbursement was awarded; career-related internships or fieldwork, tuition waivers (partial), and unspecified assistantships also available. Support available to part-time students. Financial award application deadline: 4/30; financial award applicants required to submit FAFSA. In 2010, 39 master's awarded. *Degree program information:* Part-time and evening/weekend programs available. Offers communications (MS); interactive communications (MS); journalism (MS); public relations (MS). *Application deadline:* For fall admission, 7/30 priority date for domestic students, 4/30 priority date for international students; for spring admission, 12/15 priority date for domestic students, 9/15 priority date for international students. Applications are processed on a rolling basis. *Application fee:* $45. Electronic applications accepted. *Application Contact:* Scott Farber, Information Contact, 203-582-8672, Fax: 203-582-3443, E-mail: graduate@quinnipiac.edu. *Graduate Admissions Office,* 800-462-1944, Fax: 203-582-3443, E-mail: graduate@quinnipiac.edu.

School of Education Students: 135 full-time (110 women), 55 part-time (39 women); includes 11 minority (5 Black or African American, non-Hispanic/Latino; 3 Asian, non-Hispanic/Latino; 3 Hispanic/Latino). Average age 24. 146 applicants, 92% accepted, 117 enrolled. *Faculty:* 8 full-time (4 women), 45 part-time/adjunct (28 women). Expenses: Contact institution. *Financial support:* Career-related internships or fieldwork, Federal Work-Study, scholarships/grants, tuition waivers (partial), and unspecified assistantships available. Financial award application deadline: 4/30; financial award applicants required to submit FAFSA. In 2010, 129 master's awarded. Offers biology (MAT); education (MAT); elementary education (MAT); English (MAT); history/social studies (MAT); mathematics (MAT); Spanish (MAT). *Application deadline:* For fall admission, 3/31 priority date for domestic students. Applications are processed on a rolling basis. *Application fee:* $45. Electronic applications accepted. *Application Contact:* Jennifer Boutin, Associate Director of Graduate Admissions, 800-462-1944, Fax: 203-582-3443, E-mail: jennifer.boutin@quinnipiac.edu. *Dean,* Dr. Cynthia Dubea, 203-582-8730, Fax: 203-582-8709, E-mail: cynthia.dubea@quinnipiac.edu.

School of Health Sciences Students: 512 full-time (397 women), 200 part-time (144 women); includes 35 Black or African American, non-Hispanic/Latino; 32 Asian, non-Hispanic/Latino; 29 Hispanic/Latino, 29 international. 1,430 applicants, 24% accepted, 285 enrolled. *Faculty:* 44 full-time (30 women), 53 part-time/adjunct (20 women). Expenses: Contact institution. *Financial support:* Career-related internships or fieldwork, traineeships, tuition waivers (partial), and unspecified assistantships available. Support available to part-time students. Financial award application deadline: 4/15; financial award applicants required to submit FAFSA. In 2010, 170 master's, 52 doctorates awarded. Offers biomedical sciences (MHS); cardiovascular perfusion (MHS); health sciences (MHS, MHS, MOT, MPT, MS, MSN, DPT); laboratory management (MHS); microbiology (MHS); molecular and cell biology (MS); occupational therapy (MOT); pathologists' assistant (MHS); physical therapy (MPT, DPT); physician assistant (MHS); radiologist assistant (MHS). *Application deadline:* For fall admission, 4/30 priority date for international students; for spring admission, 9/15 priority date for international students. Applications are processed on a rolling basis. *Application fee:* $45. Electronic applications accepted. *Application Contact:* Kristin Parent, Assistant Director of Graduate Health Sciences Admissions, 800-462-1944, Fax: 203-582-3443, E-mail: kristin.parent@quinnipiac.edu. *Dean,* Dr. Edward O'Connor, 203-582-8710, Fax: 203-582-8706.

School of Law Students: 344 full-time (169 women), 128 part-time (56 women); includes 11 Black or African American, non-Hispanic/Latino; 2 American Indian or Alaska Native, non-Hispanic/Latino; 22 Asian, non-Hispanic/Latino; 17 Hispanic/Latino; 2 Two or more races, non-Hispanic/Latino, 11 international. Average age 24. 2,490 applicants, 44% accepted, 163 enrolled. *Faculty:* 34 full-time (12 women), 39 part-time/adjunct (19 women). Expenses: Contact institution. *Financial support:* In 2010–11, 291 students received support, including 27 fellowships (averaging $1,560 per year), 44 research assistantships (averaging $680 per year); career-related internships or fieldwork, Federal Work-Study, and scholarships/grants also available. Support available to part-time students. Financial award application deadline: 4/15; financial award applicants required to submit FAFSA. In 2010, 100 first professional degrees awarded. *Degree program information:* Part-time and evening/weekend programs available. Offers health law (LL M); law (JD). *Application deadline:* For fall admission, 3/1 priority date for domestic students. Applications are processed on a rolling basis. *Application fee:* $65. Electronic applications accepted. *Application Contact:* Edwin Wilkes, Executive Dean of Law School Admissions, 203-582-3400, Fax: 203-582-3339, E-mail: ladm@quinnipiac.edu. *Dean,* Brad Saxton, 203-582-3200, Fax: 203-582-3209, E-mail: ladm@quinnipiac.edu.

School of Nursing Students: 41 full-time (38 women), 107 part-time (98 women); includes 32 minority (18 Black or African American, non-Hispanic/Latino; 9 Asian, non-Hispanic/Latino; 5 Hispanic/Latino), 1 international. 106 applicants, 62% accepted, 54 enrolled. *Faculty:* 7 full-time (5 women), 8 part-time/adjunct (3 women). Expenses: Contact institution. *Financial support:* Traineeships, tuition waivers (partial), and unspecified assistantships available. Support available to part-time students. Financial award application deadline: 4/15; financial award applicants required to submit FAFSA. *Degree program information:* Part-time programs available. Offers adult nurse practitioner (DNP); care of populations (DNP); care of the individual (DNP); family nurse practitioner (DNP); nursing (DNP); women's health nurse practitioner (DNP). *Application deadline:* For fall admission, 6/1 priority date for domestic students, 4/30 priority date for international students. Applications are processed on a rolling basis. *Application fee:* $45. Electronic applications accepted. *Application Contact:* Kristin Parent, Assistant Director of Graduate Health Sciences Admissions, 800-462-1944, Fax: 203-582-3443, E-mail: kristin.parent@quinnipiac.edu. *Director of Graduate Admissions,* Dr. Jeanne LeVasseur, 203-582-3484, Fax: 203-582-3230, E-mail: jeanne.levasseur@quinnipiac.edu.

RABBI ISAAC ELCHANAN THEOLOGICAL SEMINARY, New York, NY 10033-2807

General Information Independent-religious, men only, graduate-only institution. *Graduate housing:* Rooms and/or apartments guaranteed to single students and available on a first-come, first-served basis to married students. Housing application deadline: 6/1.

GRADUATE UNITS

Graduate Program Offers theology (Certificate of Advanced Ordination, Certificate of Ordination).

RABBINICAL ACADEMY MESIVTA RABBI CHAIM BERLIN, Brooklyn, NY 11230-4715

General Information Independent-religious, men only, comprehensive institution. *Graduate housing:* Room and/or apartments available to single students; on-campus housing not available to married students. Housing application deadline: 9/30.

GRADUATE UNITS

Graduate Program Offers Talmudic law and rabbinics (Advanced Talmudic Degree, Second Talmudic Degree).

RABBINICAL COLLEGE BETH SHRAGA, Monsey, NY 10952-3035

General Information Independent-religious, men only, comprehensive institution.

GRADUATE UNITS

Graduate Programs Offers theology.

RABBINICAL COLLEGE BOBOVER YESHIVA B'NEI ZION, Brooklyn, NY 11219

General Information Independent-religious, men only, comprehensive institution. *Graduate housing:* Room and/or apartments available to single students; on-campus housing not available to married students.

GRADUATE UNITS

Graduate Programs Offers theology.

RABBINICAL COLLEGE CH'SAN SOFER, Brooklyn, NY 11204

General Information Independent-religious, men only, comprehensive institution.

GRADUATE UNITS

Graduate Programs Offers theology.

RABBINICAL COLLEGE OF LONG ISLAND, Long Beach, NY 11561-3305

General Information Independent-religious, men only, comprehensive institution.

Rabbinical College of Long Island (continued)

GRADUATE UNITS

Graduate Programs Offers theology.

RABBINICAL SEMINARY M'KOR CHAIM, Brooklyn, NY 11219

General Information Independent-religious, men only, comprehensive institution.

GRADUATE UNITS

Graduate Programs Offers theology.

RABBINICAL SEMINARY OF AMERICA, Flushing, NY 11367

General Information Independent-religious, men only, comprehensive institution. *Graduate housing:* Room and/or apartments available to single students; on-campus housing not available to married students. Housing application deadline: 6/15.

GRADUATE UNITS

Graduate Programs School offers a master's and first professional degree.

RADFORD UNIVERSITY, Radford, VA 24142

General Information State-supported, coed, comprehensive institution. CGS member. *Enrollment:* 9,007 graduate, professional, and undergraduate students; 533 full-time matriculated graduate/professional students (394 women), 450 part-time matriculated graduate/professional students (338 women). *Enrollment by degree level:* 885 master's, 36 doctoral, 62 other advanced degrees. *Graduate faculty:* 203 full-time (100 women), 119 part-time/adjunct (76 women). Tuition, state resident: full-time $5746; part-time $239 per credit hour. Tuition, nonresident: full-time $14,174; part-time $591 per credit hour. *Required fees:* $2634; $111 per credit hour. *Graduate housing:* Room and/or apartments guaranteed to single students; on-campus housing not available to married students. Housing application deadline: 5/1. *Student services:* Campus employment opportunities, campus safety program, career counseling, exercise/wellness program, free psychological counseling, grant writing training, international student services, low-cost health insurance, multicultural affairs office, services for students with disabilities, teacher training, writing training. *Library facilities:* McConnell Library. *Online resources:* library catalog, web page, access to other libraries' catalogs. *Collection:* 312,003 titles, 10,089 serial subscriptions, 18,157 audiovisual materials. *Research affiliation:* National Science Foundation (communication sciences and disorders, nursing, criminal justice, psychology, mathematics, biology, computer science), U. S. Department of Health and Human Services (nursing), Virginia Department of Social Services (social work), Virginia Department of Education (teacher education and leadership), Verizon Foundation (communication sciences and disorders), U. S. Department of Education (DOE) (teacher education and leadership).

Computer facilities: 772 computers available on campus for general student use. A campuswide network can be accessed from student residence rooms and from off campus. Online class registration, online financial aid status and student accounts payable are available. *Web address:* http://www.radford.edu/.

General Application Contact: Graduate Admissions, 540-831-5431, Fax: 540-831-6061, E-mail: gradcollege@radford.edu.

GRADUATE UNITS

College of Graduate and Professional Studies Students: 533 full-time (394 women), 450 part-time (338 women); includes 90 minority (58 Black or African American, non-Hispanic/Latino; 3 American Indian or Alaska Native, non-Hispanic/Latino; 9 Asian, non-Hispanic/Latino; 18 Hispanic/Latino; 1 Native Hawaiian or other Pacific Islander, non-Hispanic/Latino; 1 Two or more races, non-Hispanic/Latino), 21 international. Average age 30. 740 applicants, 76% accepted, 329 enrolled. *Faculty:* 203 full-time (100 women), 119 part-time/adjunct (76 women). Expenses: Contact institution. *Financial support:* In 2010–11, 320 students received support, including 149 research assistantships with partial tuition reimbursements available (averaging $8,000 per year), 80 teaching assistantships with partial tuition reimbursements available (averaging $8,700 per year); career-related internships or fieldwork, Federal Work-Study, institutionally sponsored loans, scholarships/grants, and unspecified assistantships also available. Financial award application deadline: 3/1; financial award applicants required to submit FAFSA. In 2010, 384 master's, 6 other advanced degrees awarded. *Degree program information:* Part-time and evening/weekend programs available. *Application deadline:* For fall admission, 2/15 priority date for domestic students, 12/1 for international students; for spring admission, 7/1 for international students. Applications are processed on a rolling basis. *Application fee:* $50. Electronic applications accepted. *Application Contact:* Rebecca Conner, Graduate Admissions, 540-831-5431, Fax: 540-831-6061, E-mail: gradcollege@radford.edu. *Dean,* Dr. Dennis Grady, 540-831-7163, Fax: 540-831-6061, E-mail: dgrady4@radford.edu.

College of Business and Economics Students: 39 full-time (15 women), 44 part-time (15 women); includes 11 minority (6 Black or African American, non-Hispanic/Latino; 1 American Indian or Alaska Native, non-Hispanic/Latino; 1 Asian, non-Hispanic/Latino; 3 Hispanic/Latino), 9 international. Average age 30. 70 applicants, 67% accepted, 33 enrolled. *Faculty:* 38 full-time (6 women), 4 part-time/adjunct (1 woman). Expenses: Contact institution. *Financial support:* In 2010–11, 21 students received support, including 14 research assistantships with partial tuition reimbursements available (averaging $8,000 per year), 4 teaching assistantships with partial tuition reimbursements available (averaging $8,700 per year); career-related internships or fieldwork, Federal Work-Study, institutionally sponsored loans, scholarships/grants, and unspecified assistantships also available. Financial award application deadline: 3/1; financial award applicants required to submit FAFSA. In 2010, 50 master's awarded. *Degree program information:* Part-time and evening/weekend programs available. Offers business administration (MBA); business and economics (MBA). *Application deadline:* For fall admission, 2/15 priority date for domestic students, 12/1 for international students; for spring admission, 7/1 for international students. Applications are processed on a rolling basis. *Application fee:* $50. Electronic applications accepted. *Application Contact:* Rebecca Conner, Graduate Admissions, 540-831-5431, Fax: 540-831-6061, E-mail: gradcollege@radford.edu. *Director of MBA,* Dr. Elizabeth Jamison, 540-831-6712, Fax: 540-831-6655, E-mail: rumba@radford.edu.

College of Education and Human Development Students: 160 full-time (120 women), 287 part-time (224 women); includes 24 minority (19 Black or African American, non-Hispanic/Latino; 1 American Indian or Alaska Native, non-Hispanic/Latino; 2 Asian, non-Hispanic/Latino; 2 Hispanic/Latino), 4 international. Average age 32. 168 applicants, 88% accepted, 101 enrolled. *Faculty:* 36 full-time (24 women), 55 part-time/adjunct (37 women). Expenses: Contact institution. *Financial support:* In 2010–11, 95 students received support, including 30 research assistantships with partial tuition reimbursements available (averaging $8,000 per year), 8 teaching assistantships with partial tuition reimbursements available (averaging $8,700 per year); career-related internships or fieldwork, Federal Work-Study, institutionally sponsored loans, scholarships/grants, and unspecified assistantships also available. Financial award application deadline: 3/1; financial award applicants required to submit FAFSA. In 2010, 184 master's awarded. *Degree program information:* Part-time programs available. Offers adapted curriculum (MS); community counseling (MS); content area studies (MS); curriculum and instruction (MS); early childhood education (MS); early childhood special education (MS); education (MS); education and human development (MS); educational leadership (MS); educational technology (MS); general curriculum (MS); hearing impairments (MS); licensure option (MS); literacy education (MS); non-licensure option (MS); school counseling (MS); special education (MS); student affairs—administration (MS); student affairs—counseling (MS); visual impairment (MS). *Application deadline:* For fall admission, 2/15 priority date for domestic students, 12/1 for international students; for spring admission, 7/1 for international students. Applications are processed on a rolling basis. *Application fee:* $50. Electronic applications accepted. *Application Contact:* Rebecca Conner, Graduate Admissions, 540-831-5431, Fax: 540-831-6061, E-mail: gradcollege@radford.edu. *Dean,* Dr. Patricia Shoemaker, 540-831-5439, Fax: 540-831-5440, E-mail: pshoemak@radford.edu.

College of Humanities and Behavioral Sciences Students: 151 full-time (107 women), 30 part-time (17 women); includes 25 minority (15 Black or African American, non-Hispanic/Latino; 1 American Indian or Alaska Native, non-Hispanic/Latino; 3 Asian, non-Hispanic/Latino; 5 Hispanic/Latino; 1 Two or more races, non-Hispanic/Latino), 4 international. Average age 26. 222 applicants, 77% accepted, 76 enrolled. *Faculty:* 63 full-time (29 women), 8 part-time/adjunct (4 women). Expenses: Contact institution. *Financial support:* In 2010–11, 107 students received support, including 52 research assistantships with partial tuition reimbursements available (averaging $8,000 per year), 47 teaching assistantships with partial tuition reimbursements available (averaging $8,700 per year); career-related internships or fieldwork, Federal Work-Study, institutionally sponsored loans, scholarships/grants, and unspecified assistantships also available. Financial award application deadline: 3/1; financial award applicants required to submit FAFSA. In 2010, 68 master's, 6 other advanced degrees awarded. *Degree program information:* Part-time and evening/weekend programs available. Offers clinical psychology (MA, MS); corporate and professional communication (MS); counseling psychology (Psy D); criminal justice (MA, MS); English (MA, MS); experimental psychology (MA, MS); general psychology (MS); humanities and behavioral sciences (MA, MS, Psy D, Ed S); industrial/organizational psychology (MA, MS); school psychology (Ed S). *Application deadline:* For fall admission, 2/15 priority date for domestic students, 12/1 for international students; for spring admission, 7/1 for international students. Applications are processed on a rolling basis. *Application fee:* $50. Electronic applications accepted. *Application Contact:* Rebecca Conner, Graduate Admissions, 540-831-5431, Fax: 540-831-6061, E-mail: gradcollege@radford.edu. *Dean,* Dr. Katherine Hawkins, 540-831-5149, Fax: 540-831-5970, E-mail: chbs@radford.edu.

College of Visual and Performing Arts Students: 33 full-time (16 women), 3 part-time (2 women); includes 6 minority (2 Black or African American, non-Hispanic/Latino; 2 Asian, non-Hispanic/Latino; 1 Hispanic/Latino; 1 Native Hawaiian or other Pacific Islander, non-Hispanic/Latino), 2 international. Average age 27. 30 applicants, 80% accepted, 17 enrolled. *Faculty:* 34 full-time (13 women), 18 part-time/adjunct (10 women). Expenses: Contact institution. *Financial support:* In 2010–11, 28 students received support, including 8 research assistantships with partial tuition reimbursements available (averaging $8,000 per year), 14 teaching assistantships with partial tuition reimbursements available (averaging $8,700 per year); career-related internships or fieldwork, Federal Work-Study, institutionally sponsored loans, scholarships/grants, and unspecified assistantships also available. Financial award application deadline: 3/1; financial award applicants required to submit FAFSA. In 2010, 16 master's awarded. *Degree program information:* Part-time programs available. Offers art (MFA); music (MA); music education (MS); music therapy (MS); visual and performing arts (MA, MFA, MS). *Application deadline:* For fall admission, 2/15 priority date for domestic students, 12/1 for international students; for spring admission, 7/1 for international students. Applications are processed on a rolling basis. *Application fee:* $50. Electronic applications accepted. *Application Contact:* Rebecca Conner, Graduate Admissions, 540-831-5431, Fax: 540-831-6061, E-mail: gradcollege@radford.edu. *Dean,* Dr. Joseph P. Scartelli, 540-831-5265, Fax: 540-831-6313, E-mail: jscartel@radford.edu.

Waldron College of Health and Human Services Students: 150 full-time (136 women), 85 part-time (79 women); includes 24 minority (16 Black or African American, non-Hispanic/Latino; 1 Asian, non-Hispanic/Latino; 7 Hispanic/Latino), 2 international. Average age 32. 250 applicants, 71% accepted, 102 enrolled. *Faculty:* 32 full-time (28 women), 34 part-time/adjunct (24 women). Expenses: Contact institution. *Financial support:* In 2010–11, 67 students received support, including 45 research assistantships with partial tuition reimbursements available (averaging $8,000 per year), 7 teaching assistantships with partial tuition reimbursements available (averaging $8,700 per year); career-related internships or fieldwork, Federal Work-Study, institutionally sponsored loans, scholarships/grants, and unspecified assistantships also available. Financial award application deadline: 3/1; financial award applicants required to submit FAFSA. In 2010, 77 master's awarded. *Degree program information:* Part-time and evening/weekend programs available. Offers health and human services (MA, MOT, MS, MSN, MSW, DNP); nursing (MSN, DNP); occupational therapy (MOT); social work (MSW); speech-language pathology (MS). *Application deadline:* For fall admission, 2/15 priority date for domestic students, 12/1 for international students; for spring admission, 7/1 for international students. Applications are processed on a rolling basis. *Application fee:* $50. Electronic applications accepted. *Application Contact:* Rebecca Conner, Graduate Admissions Office, 540-831-5431, Fax: 540-831-6061, E-mail: gradcollege@radford.edu. *Dean,* Dr. Raymond Linville, 540-831-7600, Fax: 540-831-7604, E-mail: rlinvill@radford.edu.

RAMAPO COLLEGE OF NEW JERSEY, Mahwah, NJ 07430-1680

General Information State-supported, coed, comprehensive institution. *Enrollment:* 6,008 graduate, professional, and undergraduate students; 7 full-time matriculated graduate/professional students (6 women), 179 part-time matriculated graduate/professional students (136 women). *Enrollment by degree level:* 186 master's. *Graduate faculty:* 23 part-time/adjunct (13 women). Tuition, state resident: part-time $525.30 per credit. Tuition, nonresident: part-time $675.20 per credit. *Required fees:* $107.70 per credit. *Graduate housing:* On-campus housing not available. *Student services:* Campus safety program, career counseling, exercise/wellness program, free psychological counseling, international student services, low-cost health insurance, services for students with disabilities. *Library facilities:* George T. Potter Library. *Online resources:* library catalog, web page, access to other libraries' catalogs. *Collection:* 294,811 titles, 488 serial subscriptions, 9,890 audiovisual materials. *Research affiliation:* New Jersey Meadowlands Commission (environment), The Valley Hospital (nursing), New Jersey Association of State Colleges and Universities (veterans' issues).

Computer facilities: 1,058 computers available on campus for general student use. A campuswide network can be accessed from student residence rooms and from off campus. Online class registration is available. *Web address:* http://www.ramapo.edu/.

General Application Contact: Dr. Beth E. Barnett, Vice President of Academic Affairs/Provost, 201-684-7529, E-mail: bbarnett@ramapo.edu.

GRADUATE UNITS

Master of Arts in Liberal Studies Program Students: 29 part-time (16 women); includes 7 minority (4 Black or African American, non-Hispanic/Latino; 3 Hispanic/Latino). Average age 40. 5 applicants, 100% accepted, 4 enrolled. *Faculty:* 5 part-time/adjunct (4 women). Expenses: Contact institution. *Financial support:* Tuition waivers (full) available. Financial award applicants required to submit FAFSA. In 2010, 7 master's awarded. *Degree program information:* Part-time and evening/weekend programs available. Offers liberal studies (MALS). *Application deadline:* For fall admission, 9/1 priority date for domestic and international students; for spring admission, 1/30 priority date for domestic and international students. Applications are processed on a rolling basis. *Application fee:* $60. Electronic applications accepted. *Application Contact:* Melissa C. Kupfer, MALS Secretary, 201-684-7709, Fax: 201-684-7973, E-mail: mkupfer@ramapo.edu. *Director,* Dr. Anthony T. Padovano, 201-684-7430, Fax: 201-684-7973, E-mail: apadovan@ramapo.edu.

Master of Arts in Sustainability Studies Program Students: 17 part-time (10 women). Average age 36. 29 applicants, 76% accepted, 17 enrolled. *Faculty:* 4 part-time/adjunct (1 woman). Expenses: Contact institution. *Financial support:* In 2010–11, 1 research assistantship was awarded; career-related internships or fieldwork and tuition waivers (full) also available. *Degree program information:* Evening/weekend programs available. Offers sustainability studies (MA). *Application deadline:* For fall admission, 5/1 priority date for domestic and international students. Applications are processed on a rolling basis. *Application fee:* $60. Electronic applications accepted. *Application Contact:* Dr. Ashwani Vasishth, Director, 201-684-6616, E-mail: vasishth@ramapo.edu. *Director,* Dr. Ashwani Vasishth, 201-684-6616, E-mail: vasishth@ramapo.edu.

Master of Science in Educational Technology Program Students: 2 full-time (1 woman), 92 part-time (72 women); includes 10 minority (1 Black or African American, non-Hispanic/Latino; 1 American Indian or Alaska Native, non-Hispanic/Latino; 2 Asian, non-Hispanic/Latino; 6 Hispanic/Latino). Average age 33. 40 applicants, 95% accepted, 32 enrolled. *Faculty:* 11 part-time/adjunct (6 women). Expenses: Contact institution. *Financial support:* Scholarships/grants available. Financial award application deadline: 3/1; financial award applicants required to submit FAFSA. In 2010, 69 master's awarded. *Degree program information:* Part-time programs available. Offers educational technology (MS). *Application deadline:* Applications are processed on a rolling basis. *Application fee:* $60. *Application Contact:* Joyce Wilson, Administrative Assistant, 201-684-7721, Fax: 201-684-6699, E-mail:

mlafayet@ramapo.edu. *Dean/Executive Director of Special Programs, Office Of The Provost,* Dr. Angela Cristini, 201-684-7721, Fax: 201-684-6699, E-mail: acristin@ramapo.edu.

Master of Science in Nursing Program Students: 5 full-time (all women), 41 part-time (38 women); includes 7 minority (3 Black or African American, non-Hispanic/Latino; 3 Asian, non-Hispanic/Latino; 1 Two or more races, non-Hispanic/Latino). Average age 41. 21 applicants, 100% accepted, 15 enrolled. *Faculty:* 3 part-time/adjunct (2 women). Expenses: Contact institution. *Financial support:* In 2010–11, 10 students received support, including 10 fellowships with partial tuition reimbursements available (averaging $1,992 per year); traineeships also available. Financial award applicants required to submit FAFSA. In 2010, 13 master's awarded. *Degree program information:* Part-time programs available. Postbaccalaureate distance learning degree programs offered (minimal on-campus study). Offers nursing education (MSN). *Application deadline:* Applications are processed on a rolling basis. *Application fee:* $60. *Application Contact:* Ulysses Simpkins, Program Assistant, 201-684-7749, E-mail: usimpkin@ramapo.edu. *Assistant Dean,* Dr. Kathleen M. Burke, 201-684-7737, E-mail: kmburke@ramapo.edu.

RANDOLPH COLLEGE, Lynchburg, VA 24503

General Information Independent-religious, coed, comprehensive institution.

GRADUATE UNITS

Programs in Education Offers curriculum and instruction (MAT); special education-learning disabilities (M Ed, MAT).

RECONSTRUCTIONIST RABBINICAL COLLEGE, Wyncote, PA 19095-1898

General Information Independent-religious, coed, graduate-only institution. *Enrollment by degree level:* 59 first professional. *Graduate faculty:* 8 full-time (4 women), 25 part-time/adjunct (14 women). *Graduate housing:* On-campus housing not available. *Student services:* Campus employment opportunities, career counseling, international student services, low-cost health insurance, services for students with disabilities, writing training. *Library facilities:* Mordecai M. Kaplan Library. *Online resources:* library catalog, access to other libraries' catalogs. *Collection:* 50,800 titles, 125 serial subscriptions, 80 audiovisual materials.

Computer facilities: 20 computers available on campus for general student use. A campuswide network can be accessed from off campus. Class materials available. *Web address:* http://www.rrc.edu/.

General Application Contact: Rabbi Amber Powers, Dean of Recruitment and Admissions, 215-576-0800 Ext. 145, Fax: 215-576-6143, E-mail: apowers@rrc.edu.

GRADUATE UNITS

Graduate Programs Students: 52 full-time (37 women), 7 part-time (4 women). 25 applicants, 52% accepted, 11 enrolled. *Faculty:* 8 full-time (4 women), 25 part-time/adjunct (14 women). Expenses: Contact institution. *Financial support:* In 2010–11, 46 students received support, including 4 fellowships with full tuition reimbursements available (averaging $11,000 per year), 1 research assistantship with partial tuition reimbursement available (averaging $5,500 per year), 5 teaching assistantships (averaging $5,500 per year); career-related internships or fieldwork, institutionally sponsored loans, and scholarships/grants also available. Financial award application deadline: 4/15. *Degree program information:* Part-time programs available. Offers Jewish studies (MAJS); rabbinics (MAHL, DHL); women's studies (Certificate). Certificate offered jointly with Temple University. *Application deadline:* Applications are processed on a rolling basis. *Application fee:* $50. *Application Contact:* Rabbi Amber Powers, Dean of Recruitment and Admissions, 215-576-0800 Ext. 145, Fax: 215-576-6143, E-mail: apowers@rrc.edu. *President,* Rabbi Dan Ehrenkrantz, 215-576-0800 Ext. 129, Fax: 215-576-6143, E-mail: dehrenkrantz@rrc.edu.

REED COLLEGE, Portland, OR 97202-8199

General Information Independent, coed, comprehensive institution. *Enrollment:* 1,477 graduate, professional, and undergraduate students; 36 part-time matriculated graduate/professional students (20 women). *Enrollment by degree level:* 36 master's. *Graduate faculty:* 14 part-time/adjunct (6 women). *Tuition:* Part-time $3710 per unit. Part-time tuition and fees vary according to course load. *Graduate housing:* On-campus housing not available. *Student services:* Campus employment opportunities, campus safety program, career counseling, exercise/wellness program, free psychological counseling, low-cost health insurance, multicultural affairs office, services for students with disabilities, writing training. *Library facilities:* Erik V. Hauser Memorial Library. *Online resources:* library catalog, web page, access to other libraries' catalogs. *Collection:* 614,393 titles, 9,046 serial subscriptions, 24,974 audiovisual materials.

Computer facilities: Computer purchase and lease plans are available. 434 computers available on campus for general student use. A campuswide network can be accessed from student residence rooms and from off campus. Online class registration is available. *Web address:* http://www.reed.edu/.

General Application Contact: Barbara A. Amen, Director, Graduate Studies, 503-777-7259, Fax: 503-517-7345, E-mail: bamen@reed.edu.

GRADUATE UNITS

Graduate Program in Liberal Studies Students: 36 part-time (20 women); includes 2 Asian, non-Hispanic/Latino; 1 Hispanic/Latino. Average age 40. 12 applicants, 58% accepted, 4 enrolled. *Faculty:* 14 part-time/adjunct (6 women). Expenses: Contact institution. *Financial support:* In 2010–11, 7 students received support. Scholarships/grants, health care benefits, and institutional scholarship available. Support available to part-time students. Financial award application deadline: 5/1; financial award applicants required to submit CSS PROFILE or FAFSA. In 2010, 5 master's awarded. *Degree program information:* Part-time and evening/weekend programs available. Offers liberal studies (MALS). *Application deadline:* For fall admission, 7/1 priority date for domestic students; for spring admission, 12/1 priority date for domestic students. Applications are processed on a rolling basis. *Application fee:* $60. *Application Contact:* Barbara A. Amen, Director, Graduate Studies, 503-777-7259, Fax: 503-517-7345, E-mail: bamen@reed.edu. *Director, Graduate Studies,* Barbara A. Amen, 503-777-7259, Fax: 503-517-7345, E-mail: bamen@reed.edu.

REFORMED PRESBYTERIAN THEOLOGICAL SEMINARY, Pittsburgh, PA 15208-2594

General Information Independent-religious, coed, primarily men, graduate-only institution. *Graduate housing:* Rooms and/or apartments available on a first-come, first-served basis to single and married students.

GRADUATE UNITS

Graduate and Professional Programs *Degree program information:* Part-time and evening/weekend programs available. Offers theology (M Div, MTS, D Min). Electronic applications accepted.

REFORMED THEOLOGICAL SEMINARY–ATLANTA CAMPUS, Atlanta, GA 30327

General Information Independent-religious, coed, primarily men, graduate-only institution.

GRADUATE UNITS

Graduate Programs Offers theology (M Div, MABS, MAR, D Min, Certificate).

REFORMED THEOLOGICAL SEMINARY–CHARLOTTE CAMPUS, Charlotte, NC 28226-6318

General Information Independent-religious, coed, primarily men, graduate-only institution. *Graduate housing:* On-campus housing not available.

GRADUATE UNITS

Graduate and Professional Programs *Degree program information:* Part-time programs available. Offers biblical studies (MA); ministry (D Min); pastoral ministry (M Div); theological studies (MA). Electronic applications accepted.

REFORMED THEOLOGICAL SEMINARY–JACKSON CAMPUS, Jackson, MS 39209-3099

General Information Independent-religious, coed, primarily men, graduate-only institution. *Graduate housing:* Rooms and/or apartments available on a first-come, first-served basis to single and married students.

GRADUATE UNITS

Graduate and Professional Programs Offers Bible, theology, and missions (Certificate); biblical studies (MA); Christian education (M Div, MA); counseling (M Div); divinity (M Div, Diploma); marriage and family therapy (MA); ministry (D Min); missions (M Div, MA, D Min); New Testament (Th M); Old Testament (Th M); theological studies (MA); theology (Th M).

REFORMED THEOLOGICAL SEMINARY–ORLANDO CAMPUS, Oviedo, FL 32765-7197

General Information Independent-religious, coed, primarily men, graduate-only institution. *Graduate housing:* On-campus housing not available.

GRADUATE UNITS

Graduate Program *Degree program information:* Part-time programs available. Postbaccalaureate distance learning degree programs offered (minimal on-campus study). Offers biblical studies (MA); counseling (MA); ministry (D Min); reformation studies (Th M); theological studies (MA); theology (M Div). Ma/Certificate offered jointly with University of Central Florida. Electronic applications accepted.

REFORMED THEOLOGICAL SEMINARY–WASHINGTON D.C., McLean, VA 22101

General Information Independent-religious, coed; primarily men, graduate-only institution. *Enrollment by degree level:* 86 master's, 2 other advanced degrees. *Graduate faculty:* 2 full-time (0 women), 5 part-time/adjunct (0 women). *Tuition:* Full-time $7020; part-time $1755 per semester. Tuition and fees vary according to course load. *Graduate housing:* On-campus housing not available. *Student services:* Campus employment opportunities, career counseling, international student services, low-cost health insurance, writing training. *Library facilities:* Library Consortium plus 1 other. *Collection:* 400,000 titles, 100 serial subscriptions, 10,000 audiovisual materials.

Computer facilities: Online class registration is available. *Web address:* http://www.rts.edu/.

General Application Contact: Geoff M. Sackett, Director of Admissions, 703-448-3393, Fax: 703-738-7389, E-mail: gsackett@rts.edu.

GRADUATE UNITS

Graduate and Professional Programs Students: 13 full-time (1 woman), 69 part-time (7 women); includes 4 Black or African American, non-Hispanic/Latino; 20 Asian, non-Hispanic/Latino; 2 Hispanic/Latino, 1 international. Average age 35. 30 applicants, 77% accepted, 15 enrolled. *Faculty:* 2 full-time (0 women), 5 part-time/adjunct (0 women). Expenses: Contact institution. *Financial support:* In 2010–11, 76 students received support, including 7 fellowships (averaging $1,000 per year); institutionally sponsored loans, scholarships/grants, tuition waivers (partial), and unspecified assistantships also available. Support available to part-time students. Financial award application deadline: 6/1. In 2010, 11 master's awarded. *Degree program information:* Part-time and evening/weekend programs available. Offers Bible (M Div); practical theology (M Div); religion (MA); theology (M Div). *Application deadline:* Applications are processed on a rolling basis. *Application fee:* $75. Electronic applications accepted. *Application Contact:* Geoff M. Sackett, Director of Admissions, 703-448-3393, Fax: 703-738-7389, E-mail: gsackett@rts.edu. *Executive Director,* Hugh C. Whelchel, 703-448-3393, Fax: 703-738-7389, E-mail: hwhelchel@rts.edu.

REGENT COLLEGE, Vancouver, BC V6T 2E4, Canada

General Information Independent-religious, coed, graduate-only institution. *Enrollment by degree level:* 146 first professional, 237 master's, 70 other advanced degrees. *Graduate faculty:* 16 full-time (3 women), 16 part-time/adjunct (6 women). *Graduate housing:* On-campus housing not available. *Student services:* Campus employment opportunities, campus safety program, career counseling, international student services, low-cost health insurance, services for students with disabilities, writing training. *Library facilities:* The John Richard Allison Library plus 3 others. *Online resources:* library catalog, web page, access to other libraries' catalogs. *Collection:* 122,280 titles, 360 serial subscriptions, 10,446 audiovisual materials.

Computer facilities: 8 computers available on campus for general student use. A campuswide network can be accessed. *Web address:* http://www.regent-college.edu/.

General Application Contact: Amy Petroelje, Housing and Inquiries Coordinator, 604-224-3245 Ext. 355, Fax: 604-224-3097, E-mail: admissions@regent-college.edu.

GRADUATE UNITS

Program in Theology Students: 220 full-time (76 women), 233 part-time (94 women); includes 2 Black or African American, non-Hispanic/Latino; 1 American Indian or Alaska Native, non-Hispanic/Latino; 113 Asian, non-Hispanic/Latino; 7 Hispanic/Latino. Average age 33. 220 applicants, 88% accepted, 133 enrolled. *Faculty:* 16 full-time (3 women), 16 part-time/adjunct (6 women). Expenses: Contact institution. *Financial support:* In 2010–11, 130 students received support, including 112 teaching assistantships (averaging $2,365 per year); career-related internships or fieldwork, scholarships/grants, and health care benefits also available. Financial award application deadline: 3/1. In 2010, 51 M Divs, 81 master's, 64 other advanced degrees awarded. *Degree program information:* Part-time programs available. Offers theology (M Div, MCS, Th M, Dip CS). *Application deadline:* For fall admission, 2/1 priority date for domestic students, 1/1 priority date for international students; for winter admission, 7/1 priority date for domestic and international students; for spring admission, 2/1 priority date for domestic students, 1/1 priority date for international students. Applications are processed on a rolling basis. *Application fee:* $60 Canadian dollars. Electronic applications accepted. *Application Contact:* Amy Petroelje, Housing and Inquiries Coordinator, 604-224-3245 Ext. 355, Fax: 604-224-3097, E-mail: admissions@regent-college.edu. *President,* Dr. Rod Wilson, 604-221-3318, Fax: 604-224-3097, E-mail: presidentsoffice@regent-college.edu.

REGENT'S AMERICAN COLLEGE LONDON, London NW1 4NS, United Kingdom

General Information Independent, coed, comprehensive institution.

GRADUATE UNITS

Webster Graduate School *Degree program information:* Part-time programs available. Offers business (MBA); finance (MS); human resources (MA); information technology management (MA); international business (MA); international non-governmental organizations (MA); international relations (MA); management and leadership (MA); marketing (MA).

REGENT UNIVERSITY, Virginia Beach, VA 23464-9800

General Information Independent-religious, coed, comprehensive institution. CGS member. *Enrollment:* 5,555 graduate, professional, and undergraduate students; 1,115 full-time matriculated graduate/professional students (659 women), 2,198 part-time matriculated graduate/professional students (1,268 women). *Enrollment by degree level:* 704 first professional, 1,739 master's, 870 doctoral. *Graduate faculty:* 177 full-time (58 women), 411 part-time/adjunct (172 women). *Tuition:* Full-time $14,400; part-time $800 per credit hour. *Required fees:* $230 per semester. Tuition and fees vary according to course load, degree level and program. *Graduate housing:* Rooms and/or apartments available on a first-come, first-served basis to single and married students. Typical cost: $7920 per year for single students; $7920 per year for married students. Room charges vary according to housing facility selected. Housing application deadline: 8/30. *Student services:* Campus employment opportunities, campus safety program, career counseling, free psychological counseling, international student services, low-cost health insurance, services for students with disabilities, teacher training, writing training. *Library facilities:* Regent University Library plus 1 other. *Online resources:*

Regent University (continued)

library catalog, web page, access to other libraries' catalogs. *Collection:* 410,014 titles, 3,329 serial subscriptions, 18,937 audiovisual materials.

Computer facilities: 123 computers available on campus for general student use. A campuswide network can be accessed from student residence rooms and from off campus. Online class registration is available. *Web address:* http://www.regent.edu/.

General Application Contact: Matthew Chadwick, Director of Enrollment Support Services, 800-373-5504, Fax: 757-352-4381, E-mail: admissions@regent.edu.

GRADUATE UNITS

Graduate School Students: 1,115 full-time (659 women), 2,198 part-time (1,268 women); includes 804 Black or African American, non-Hispanic/Latino; 25 American Indian or Alaska Native, non-Hispanic/Latino; 75 Asian, non-Hispanic/Latino; 102 Hispanic/Latino, 185 international. Average age 37. 2,753 applicants, 54% accepted, 751 enrolled. *Faculty:* 177 full-time (58 women), 411 part-time/adjunct (172 women). Expenses: Contact institution. *Financial support:* Fellowships with full and partial tuition reimbursements, research assistantships with full and partial tuition reimbursements, teaching assistantships with full and partial tuition reimbursements, career-related internships or fieldwork, scholarships/grants, and tuition waivers (full and partial) available. Support available to part-time students. Financial award application deadline: 9/1; financial award applicants required to submit FAFSA. In 2010, 154 first professional degrees, 515 master's, 142 doctorates awarded. *Degree program information:* Part-time and evening/weekend programs available. Postbaccalaureate distance learning degree programs offered (minimal on-campus study). *Application deadline:* Applications are processed on a rolling basis. *Application fee:* $50. Electronic applications accepted. *Application Contact:* Matthew Chadwick, Director of Enrollment Support Services, 800-373-5504, Fax: 757-352-4381, E-mail: admissions@regent.edu. *President,* Dr. Carlos Campo, 757-352-4015, Fax: 757-352-4037, E-mail: ccampo@regent.edu.

Robertson School of Government Students: 91 full-time (57 women), 62 part-time (37 women); includes 41 Black or African American, non-Hispanic/Latino; 3 Asian, non-Hispanic/Latino; 7 Hispanic/Latino, 1 international. Average age 30. 149 applicants, 61% accepted, 40 enrolled. *Faculty:* 6 full-time (1 woman), 11 part-time/adjunct (2 women). Expenses: Contact institution. *Financial support:* Career-related internships or fieldwork, scholarships/grants, tuition waivers (full and partial), and unspecified assistantships available. Support available to part-time students. Financial award application deadline: 9/1; financial award applicants required to submit FAFSA. In 2010, 59 master's awarded. *Degree program information:* Part-time and evening/weekend programs available. Postbaccalaureate distance learning degree programs offered (minimal on-campus study). Offers American government (MA); international politics (MA); political theory (MA); public administration (MA). *Application deadline:* For fall admission, 5/1 priority date for domestic students; for spring admission, 11/1 priority date for domestic students. Applications are processed on a rolling basis. *Application fee:* $50. Electronic applications accepted. *Application Contact:* Matthew Chadwick, Director of Enrollment Support Services, 800-373-5504, Fax: 757-352-4381, E-mail: admissions@regent.edu. *Interim Dean,* Dr. Gary Roberts, 757-352-4962, Fax: 757-352-4735, E-mail: garyrob@regent.edu.

School of Communication and the Arts Students: 93 full-time (48 women), 167 part-time (80 women); includes 45 Black or African American, non-Hispanic/Latino; 2 American Indian or Alaska Native, non-Hispanic/Latino; 3 Asian, non-Hispanic/Latino; 9 Hispanic/Latino, 11 international. Average age 32. 247 applicants, 45% accepted, 65 enrolled. *Faculty:* 29 full-time (4 women), 25 part-time/adjunct (5 women). Expenses: Contact institution. *Financial support:* Fellowships with full and partial tuition reimbursements, career-related internships or fieldwork, scholarships/grants, tuition waivers (full and partial), and unspecified assistantships available. Support available to part-time students. Financial award application deadline: 9/1; financial award applicants required to submit FAFSA. In 2010, 82 master's, 17 doctorates awarded. *Degree program information:* Part-time programs available. Postbaccalaureate distance learning degree programs offered (minimal on-campus study). Offers acting (MFA); cinema arts/television arts (MA); communication (MA, PhD); digital media (MA); directing for cinema/television (MA, MFA); editing for cinema/television (MA); journalism (MA); producing for cinema/television (MA, MFA); script and screenwriting (MFA); theatre (MA). *Application deadline:* For fall admission, 3/1 priority date for domestic students; for spring admission, 10/1 priority date for domestic students. Applications are processed on a rolling basis. *Application fee:* $50. Electronic applications accepted. *Application Contact:* Matthew Chadwick, Director of Enrollment Support Services, 800-373-5504, Fax: 757-352-4381, E-mail: admissions@regent.edu. *Interim Dean,* Dr. Emmanuel Ayee, 757-352-4945, Fax: 757-352-4291, E-mail: eayee@regent.edu.

School of Divinity Students: 128 full-time (60 women), 524 part-time (225 women); includes 278 Black or African American, non-Hispanic/Latino; 4 American Indian or Alaska Native, non-Hispanic/Latino; 16 Asian, non-Hispanic/Latino; 24 Hispanic/Latino, 20 international. Average age 41. 361 applicants, 64% accepted, 154 enrolled. *Faculty:* 20 full-time (4 women), 26 part-time/adjunct (5 women). Expenses: Contact institution. *Financial support:* Fellowships with full and partial tuition reimbursements, career-related internships or fieldwork, scholarships/grants, tuition waivers (full and partial), and unspecified assistantships available. Support available to part-time students. Financial award application deadline: 9/1; financial award applicants required to submit FAFSA. In 2010, 32 first professional degrees, 61 master's, 9 doctorates awarded. *Degree program information:* Part-time programs available. Postbaccalaureate distance learning degree programs offered (minimal on-campus study). Offers Biblical studies (MA); leadership and renewal (D Min); missiology (M Div, MA); practical theology (M Div, MA); renewal studies (PhD). *Application deadline:* For fall admission, 5/1 priority date for domestic students. Applications are processed on a rolling basis. *Application fee:* $50. Electronic applications accepted. *Application Contact:* Matthew Chadwick, Director of Enrollment Support Services, 800-373-5504, Fax: 757-352-4381, E-mail: admissions@regent.edu. *Dean,* Dr. Michael Palmer, 757-352-4406, Fax: 757-352-4597, E-mail: mpalmer@regent.edu.

School of Education Students: 116 full-time (93 women), 695 part-time (558 women); includes 186 Black or African American, non-Hispanic/Latino; 3 American Indian or Alaska Native, non-Hispanic/Latino; 9 Asian, non-Hispanic/Latino; 18 Hispanic/Latino, 6 international. Average age 40. 645 applicants, 60% accepted, 220 enrolled. *Faculty:* 25 full-time (13 women), 93 part-time/adjunct (70 women). Expenses: Contact institution. *Financial support:* Fellowships, career-related internships or fieldwork, scholarships/grants, tuition waivers (full and partial), and unspecified assistantships available. Support available to part-time students. Financial award application deadline: 4/1; financial award applicants required to submit FAFSA. In 2010, 145 master's, 29 doctorates awarded. *Degree program information:* Part-time and evening/weekend programs available. Postbaccalaureate distance learning degree programs offered (minimal on-campus study). Offers career switcher (M Ed); Christian school program (M Ed); cross-categorical special education (M Ed); education (M Ed, Ed D, PhD); education licensure (M Ed); educational leadership (M Ed); elementary education (M Ed); individualized degree plan (M Ed); leadership in character education (M Ed); master teacher (M Ed); mathematics education (M Ed); special education leadership (Ed S); student affairs (M Ed); TESOL (M Ed). *Application deadline:* For fall admission, 4/1 priority date for domestic students; for spring admission, 10/15 priority date for domestic students. Applications are processed on a rolling basis. *Application fee:* $50. Electronic applications accepted. *Application Contact:* Matthew Chadwick, Director of Enrollment Support Services, 800-373-5504, Fax: 757-352-4381, E-mail: admissions@regent.edu. *Dean,* Dr. Alan A. Arroyo, 757-352-4261, Fax: 757-352-4318, E-mail: alanarr@regent.edu.

School of Global Leadership and Entrepreneurship Students: 30 full-time (11 women), 499 part-time (184 women); includes 125 Black or African American, non-Hispanic/Latino; 4 American Indian or Alaska Native, non-Hispanic/Latino; 10 Asian, non-Hispanic/Latino; 15 Hispanic/Latino, 93 international. Average age 41. 157 applicants, 66% accepted, 64 enrolled. *Faculty:* 13 full-time (3 women), 9 part-time/adjunct (3 women). Expenses: Contact institution. *Financial support:* Career-related internships or fieldwork, scholarships/grants, and tuition waivers (full and partial) available. Support available to part-time students. Financial award application deadline: 9/1. In 2010, 86 master's, 30 doctorates awarded. *Degree program information:* Part-time and evening/weekend programs available. Postbaccalaureate distance learning degree programs offered (minimal on-campus study). Offers business administration (MBA); management (MA); organizational leadership (MA, PhD, Certificate); strategic foresight (MA); strategic leadership (DSL). *Application deadline:* For fall admission, 5/1 priority date for domestic students; for spring admission, 10/1 priority date for domestic students. Applications are processed on a rolling basis. *Application fee:* $50. Electronic applications accepted. *Application Contact:* Matthew Chadwick, Director of Enrollment Support Services, 800-373-5504, Fax: 757-352-4381, E-mail: admissions@regent.edu. *Dean,* Dr. Bruce Winston, 757-352-4306, Fax: 757-352-4634, E-mail: brucwin@regent.edu.

School of Law Students: 422 full-time (200 women), 48 part-time (26 women); includes 25 Black or African American, non-Hispanic/Latino; 12 American Indian or Alaska Native, non-Hispanic/Latino; 27 Asian, non-Hispanic/Latino; 18 Hispanic/Latino, 41 international. Average age 27. 758 applicants, 44% accepted, 97 enrolled. *Faculty:* 26 full-time (8 women), 53 part-time/adjunct (9 women). Expenses: Contact institution. *Financial support:* Career-related internships or fieldwork, scholarships/grants, and tuition waivers (full and partial) available. Support available to part-time students. Financial award application deadline: 2/1; financial award applicants required to submit FAFSA. In 2010, 122 first professional degrees awarded. *Degree program information:* Part-time programs available. Offers American legal studies (LL M); law (JD). *Application deadline:* For fall admission, 3/1 for domestic students. Applications are processed on a rolling basis. *Application fee:* $50. Electronic applications accepted. *Application Contact:* Matthew Chadwick, Director of Enrollment Support Services, 800-373-5504, Fax: 757-352-4381, E-mail: admissions@regent.edu. *Dean,* Jeffrey Brauch, 757-352-4040, Fax: 757-352-4595, E-mail: jeffbra@regent.edu.

School of Psychology and Counseling Students: 235 full-time (190 women), 203 part-time (158 women); includes 104 Black or African American, non-Hispanic/Latino; 7 Asian, non-Hispanic/Latino; 11 Hispanic/Latino, 13 international. Average age 35. 436 applicants, 49% accepted, 111 enrolled. *Faculty:* 31 full-time (16 women), 23 part-time/adjunct (14 women). Expenses: Contact institution. *Financial support:* Research assistantships with full and partial tuition reimbursements, teaching assistantships with full and partial tuition reimbursements, career-related internships or fieldwork, scholarships/grants, and tuition waivers (full and partial) available. Support available to part-time students. Financial award application deadline: 9/1; financial award applicants required to submit FAFSA. In 2010, 82 master's, 57 doctorates awarded. *Degree program information:* Part-time and evening/weekend programs available. Postbaccalaureate distance learning degree programs offered (minimal on-campus study). Offers clinical psychology (MA, Psy D); counseling studies (CAGS); counselor education and supervision (PhD); human services counseling (MA). PhD program offered online only. *Application deadline:* For fall admission, 4/1 priority date for domestic students; for spring admission, 11/1 priority date for domestic students. Applications are processed on a rolling basis. *Application fee:* $50. Electronic applications accepted. *Application Contact:* Matthew Chadwick, Director of Enrollment Support Services, 800-373-5504, Fax: 757-352-4381, E-mail: admissions@regent.edu. *Acting Dean,* Dr. William Hathaway, 757-352-4294, Fax: 757-352-4282, E-mail: willhat@regent.edu.

REGIS COLLEGE, Toronto, ON M5S 2Z5, Canada

General Information Independent-religious, coed, graduate-only institution. *Graduate housing:* Room and/or apartments available on a first-come, first-served basis to single students; on-campus housing not available to married students. *Research affiliation:* Lonergan Research Institute (theology/philosophy), Lupina Foundation (research and innovation related to health/society issues).

GRADUATE UNITS

Graduate and Professional Programs Offers eastern Christian studies (Certificate); Ignatian studies (Diploma); Lonergan studies (Diploma); ministry (D Min); ministry and spirituality (MAMS); philosophical studies (Diploma); retreat direction (Certificate); sacred theology (STB, STM, STD, STL); spiritual direction (Diploma); spiritual theology (Diploma); theological studies (MTS, Diploma); theology (M Div, MA, Th M, PhD, Th D).

REGIS COLLEGE, Weston, MA 02493

General Information Independent-religious, coed, comprehensive institution. *Enrollment:* 1,737 graduate, professional, and undergraduate students; 215 full-time matriculated graduate/professional students (195 women), 656 part-time matriculated graduate/professional students (620 women). *Enrollment by degree level:* 803 master's, 68 doctoral. *Tuition:* Part-time $765 per credit. Tuition and fees vary according to course load and degree level. *Graduate housing:* Room and/or apartments available on a first-come, first-served basis to single students; on-campus housing not available to married students. *Student services:* Campus employment opportunities, campus safety program, career counseling, exercise/wellness program, low-cost health insurance, multicultural affairs office, teacher training. *Library facilities:* Regis College Library. *Online resources:* library catalog, web page, access to other libraries' catalogs. *Collection:* 134,109 titles, 424 serial subscriptions, 8,031 audiovisual materials. *Research affiliation:* Beth Israel Deaconess Medical Center (nursing), Caritas Norwood Hospital (nursing), Boston Medical Center (nursing), Lahey Clinic Medical Center (nursing).

Computer facilities: 196 computers available on campus for general student use. A campuswide network can be accessed from student residence rooms and from off campus. Online class registration, online bills, financial aid award letters and check-in requirements are available. *Web address:* http://www.regiscollege.edu/.

General Application Contact: Christine Petherick, Administrative Coordinator, Planning and Enrollment, 866-438-7330, Fax: 781-768-7071, E-mail: christine.petherick@regiscollege.edu.

GRADUATE UNITS

Department of Education Students: 83 part-time (77 women); includes 1 Black or African American, non-Hispanic/Latino; 1 Asian, non-Hispanic/Latino. Average age 36. 7 applicants, 100% accepted, 6 enrolled. *Faculty:* 2 full-time (both women), 5 part-time/adjunct (all women). Expenses: Contact institution. *Financial support:* In 2010–11, 1 student received support, including 1 fellowship with full tuition reimbursement available (averaging $11,970 per year); Federal Work-Study and scholarships/grants also available. Financial award applicants required to submit FAFSA. In 2010, 9 master's awarded. *Degree program information:* Part-time and evening/weekend programs available. Offers elementary teacher (MAT); reading (MAT); special education (MAT). *Application deadline:* Applications are processed on a rolling basis. *Application fee:* $60. Electronic applications accepted. *Application Contact:* Christine Petherick, Administrative Coordinator, Graduate Admission, 866-438-7344, Fax: 781-768-7071, E-mail: christine.petherick@regiscollege.edu. *Program Director,* Dr. Leona McCaughey-Oreszak, 781-768-7421, Fax: 781-768-7159, E-mail: leona.mccaughey-oreszak@regiscollege.edu.

Department of Health Product Regulation and Clinical Research *Degree program information:* Part-time and evening/weekend programs available. Offers health product regulation and clinical research (MS).

Department of Organizational and Professional Communication *Degree program information:* Part-time and evening/weekend programs available. Offers organizational and professional communication (MS).

School of Nursing and Health Professions *Degree program information:* Part-time and evening/weekend programs available. Offers health administration (MS); nurse educator (Certificate); nurse practitioner (Certificate); nursing (MS, DNP). Electronic applications accepted.

REGIS UNIVERSITY, Denver, CO 80221-1099

General Information Independent-religious, coed, comprehensive institution. *Graduate housing:* On-campus housing not available. *Research affiliation:* Learning Anytime Anywhere Partnership (Internet-based technology), Commission for Accelerated Programs (accelerated advit programs), Transparency by Design (online programs, best practices).

GRADUATE UNITS

College for Professional Studies *Degree program information:* Part-time and evening/weekend programs available. Postbaccalaureate distance learning degree programs offered (no on-campus study). Offers emerging markets (MBA). Electronic applications accepted.

School of Computer and Information Sciences *Degree program information:* Part-time and evening/weekend programs available. Postbaccalaureate distance learning degree programs offered (no on-campus study). Offers database administration with Oracle (Certificate); database development (Certificate); database technologies (M Sc); enterprise Java software development (Certificate); enterprise resource planning (Certificate); executive information technologies (Certificate); information assurance (M Sc, Certificate); information technology management (M Sc); software engineering (M Sc, Certificate); software engineering and database technologies (M Sc); storage area networks (Certificate); systems engineering (M Sc, Certificate). Offered at Boulder Campus, Northwest Denver Campus, Southeast Denver Campus, Fort Collins Campus, Colorado Springs Campus, and Broomfield Campus. Electronic applications accepted.

School of Education and Counseling Offers adult learning, training, and development (M Ed, Certificate); autism (Certificate); community counseling (MAC); counseling children and adolescents (Post-Graduate Certificate); curriculum, instruction, and assessment (M Ed); education and counseling (M Ed, MA, MAC, Certificate, Post-Graduate Certificate); educational leadership (Certificate); educational technology (Certificate); instructional technology (M Ed); literacy (Certificate); marriage and family therapy (MA, Post-Graduate Certificate); professional leadership (M Ed); reading (M Ed); self-designed (M Ed); space studies (M Ed); transformative counseling (Post-Graduate Certificate).

School of Humanities and Social Sciences Offers communication (MA); criminology (M Sc); fine arts (Certificate); humanities and social sciences (M Sc, MA, MNM, Certificate); interdisciplinary studies (MA); leadership (Certificate); mediation and conflict resolution (Certificate); nonprofit management (MNM); psychology (MA).

School of Management *Degree program information:* Part-time and evening/weekend programs available. Postbaccalaureate distance learning degree programs offered (no on-campus study). Offers accounting (MS, Certificate); executive international management (Certificate); executive leadership (Certificate); executive project management (Certificate); finance and accounting (MBA); general business administration (MBA); health care management (MBA); human resource management and leadership (MSOL); information technology leadership and management (MSOL); international business (MBA); marketing (MBA); operations management (MBA); organizational leadership and management (MSOL); project leadership and management (MSOL); project management (Certificate); strategic business management (Certificate); strategic human resource management (Certificate); strategic management (MBA). Offered at Colorado Springs Campus, Northwest Denver Campus, Southeast Denver Campus, Fort Collins Campus, Broomfield Campus, Henderson (Nevada) Campus, and Summerlin (Nevada) Campus and online. Electronic applications accepted.

Regis College *Degree program information:* Part-time and evening/weekend programs available. Offers education (MA). Offered at Northwest Denver Campus.

Rueckert-Hartman College for Health Professions Offers family nurse practitioner (MSN); health informatics (Postbaccalaureate Certificate); health services administration (MS); leadership in healthcare systems (MSN); neonatal nurse practitioner (MSN); nursing (MSN); pharmacy (Pharm D); physical therapy (DPT, TDPT). Electronic applications accepted.

REINHARDT UNIVERSITY, Waleska, GA 30183-2981

General Information Independent-religious, coed, comprehensive institution. *Enrollment:* 1,219 graduate, professional, and undergraduate students; 105 full-time matriculated graduate/professional students (83 women), 12 part-time matriculated graduate/professional students (7 women). *Enrollment by degree level:* 117 master's. *Graduate faculty:* 13 full-time (8 women), 8 part-time/adjunct (4 women). *Tuition:* Full-time $8400; part-time $350 per credit hour. *Required fees:* $125 per semester. *Graduate housing:* On-campus housing not available. *Student services:* Career counseling, exercise/wellness program, free psychological counseling, international student services, low-cost health insurance, services for students with disabilities, writing training. *Library facilities:* Hill Freeman Library/Spruill Learning Center plus 1 other. *Online resources:* library catalog, web page, access to other libraries' catalogs. *Collection:* 60,278 titles, 117,200 serial subscriptions, 12,000 audiovisual materials.

Computer facilities: Computer purchase and lease plans are available. 164 computers available on campus for general student use. A campuswide network can be accessed from student residence rooms and from off campus. Online class registration is available. *Web address:* http://www.reinhardt.edu/.

General Application Contact: Ray Schumacher, Admissions Counselor, 770-993-6971, Fax: 770-475-0263, E-mail: res@reinhardt.edu.

GRADUATE UNITS

Program in Business Administration Students: 2 full-time (1 woman), 32 part-time (16 women); includes 4 Black or African American, non-Hispanic/Latino; 2 Asian, non-Hispanic/Latino. Average age 38. 57 applicants, 47% accepted, 23 enrolled. *Faculty:* 5 full-time (3 women). Expenses: Contact institution. *Financial support:* Application deadline: 5/1. In 2010, 12 master's awarded. *Degree program information:* Part-time and evening/weekend programs available. Offers business administration (MBA). Program offered on the Alpharetta Campus. *Application deadline:* For fall admission, 5/7 for domestic and international students; for spring admission, 8/9 for domestic and international students. Applications are processed on a rolling basis. *Application fee:* $25. Electronic applications accepted. *Application Contact:* Ray Schumacher, Admissions Counselor, 770-993-6971, Fax: 770-475-0263, E-mail: res@reinhardt.edu. *Admissions Counselor*, Ray Schumacher, 770-993-6971, Fax: 770-475-0263, E-mail: res@reinhardt.edu.

Program in Early Childhood Education Students: 72 full-time (66 women), 2 part-time (0 women); includes 8 Black or African American, non-Hispanic/Latino; 1 Asian, non-Hispanic/Latino; 1 Hispanic/Latino. Average age 35. 62 applicants, 79% accepted, 41 enrolled. *Faculty:* 12 full-time (8 women), 6 part-time/adjunct (5 women). Expenses: Contact institution. *Financial support:* Application deadline: 5/1. *Degree program information:* Part-time and evening/weekend programs available. Postbaccalaureate distance learning degree programs offered. Offers early childhood education (MAT). *Application deadline:* For fall admission, 5/7 for domestic and international students. Applications are processed on a rolling basis. *Application fee:* $25. Electronic applications accepted. *Application Contact:* Ray Schumacher, Admissions Counselor, 770-993-6971, Fax: 770-475-0263, E-mail: res@reinhardt.edu. *Coordinator*, Nancy Carter, 770-720-5948, Fax: 770-720-9173, E-mail: ntc@reinhardt.edu.

Program in Music Students: 9 part-time (6 women). Average age 33. 11 applicants, 82% accepted, 9 enrolled. *Faculty:* 3 full-time (1 woman), 6 part-time/adjunct (2 women). Expenses: Contact institution. *Financial support:* Application deadline: 5/1. *Degree program information:* Part-time and evening/weekend programs available. Postbaccalaureate distance learning degree programs offered. Offers conducting (MM); music education (MM); piano pedagogy (MM). *Application deadline:* For fall admission, 5/7 for domestic and international students. Applications are processed on a rolling basis. *Application fee:* $25. Electronic applications accepted. *Application Contact:* Ray Schumacher, Admissions Counselor, 770-993-6971, Fax: 770-475-0263, E-mail: res@reinhardt.edu. *Coordinator*, Dr. Paula Thomas-Lee, 770-720-5658, E-mail: ptl@reinhardt.edu.

RENSSELAER AT HARTFORD, Hartford, CT 06120-2991

General Information Independent, coed, graduate-only institution. *Graduate housing:* On-campus housing not available.

GRADUATE UNITS

Department of Computer and Information Science *Degree program information:* Part-time and evening/weekend programs available. Offers computer science (MS); information technology (MS). Electronic applications accepted.

Department of Engineering *Degree program information:* Part-time and evening/weekend programs available. Offers computer and systems engineering (ME); electrical engineering (ME, MS); engineering (ME, MS); engineering science (MS); mechanical engineering (ME, MS). Electronic applications accepted.

Lally School of Management and Technology *Degree program information:* Part-time and evening/weekend programs available. Postbaccalaureate distance learning degree programs offered (no on-campus study). Offers management and technology (MBA, MS). Electronic applications accepted.

RENSSELAER POLYTECHNIC INSTITUTE, Troy, NY 12180-3590

General Information Independent, coed, university. CGS member. *Enrollment:* 7,144 graduate, professional, and undergraduate students; 1,081 full-time matriculated graduate/professional students (308 women), 164 part-time matriculated graduate/professional students (50 women). *Enrollment by degree level:* 364 master's, 881 doctoral. *Graduate faculty:* 386 full-time (79 women), 89 part-time/adjunct (19 women). *Tuition:* Full-time $39,600; part-time $1650 per credit. *Required fees:* $1896. *Graduate housing:* Rooms and/or apartments available on a first-come, first-served basis to single and married students. Typical cost: $10,850 (including board) for single students; $10,850 (including board) for married students. *Student services:* Campus employment opportunities, campus safety program, career counseling, exercise/wellness program, free psychological counseling, grant writing training, international student services, low-cost health insurance, multicultural affairs office, services for students with disabilities, teacher training, writing training. *Library facilities:* Folsom Library plus 2 others. *Online resources:* library catalog, web page, access to other libraries' catalogs. *Collection:* 438,802 titles, 65,000 serial subscriptions, 12,662 audiovisual materials. *Research affiliation:* New York State Energy Research and Development Authority (fuel cells, polymer membranes, renewable energy sources), Cleveland Clinic Foundation (tissue engineering and regenerative medicine, imaging, bio-nano materials), Semiconductor Research Corporation (high density magnetic storage devices), Lockheed Martin Corporation (advanced sensors systems, THz detection technologies), IBM (broadband technologies, modeling and simulation of complex systems).

Computer facilities: Computer purchase and lease plans are available. A campuswide network can be accessed from student residence rooms and from off campus. Online class registration, billing, downloadable software, web pages are available. *Web address:* http://www.rpi.edu/.

General Application Contact: James G. Nondorf, Vice President for Enrollment, 518-276-6216, Fax: 518-276-4072, E-mail: admissions@rpi.edu.

GRADUATE UNITS

Graduate School Students: 1,081 full-time (308 women), 164 part-time (50 women); includes 137 minority (30 Black or African American, non-Hispanic/Latino; 8 American Indian or Alaska Native, non-Hispanic/Latino; 44 Asian, non-Hispanic/Latino; 32 Hispanic/Latino; 4 Native Hawaiian or other Pacific Islander, non-Hispanic/Latino; 19 Two or more races, non-Hispanic/Latino), 567 international. Average age 28. 3,985 applicants, 27% accepted, 512 enrolled. *Faculty:* 386 full-time (79 women), 89 part-time/adjunct (19 women). Expenses: Contact institution. *Financial support:* In 2010–11, 867 students received support, including 103 fellowships with full tuition reimbursements available (averaging $23,300 per year), 446 research assistantships with full tuition reimbursements available (averaging $22,480 per year), 331 teaching assistantships with full tuition reimbursements available (averaging $17,500 per year); career-related internships or fieldwork, institutionally sponsored loans, scholarships/grants, health care benefits, tuition waivers (partial), and unspecified assistantships also available. Financial award application deadline: 1/15. In 2010, 374 master's, 151 doctorates awarded. *Degree program information:* Part-time and evening/weekend programs available. *Application deadline:* For fall admission, 1/1 priority date for domestic and international students; for spring admission, 8/15 priority date for domestic and international students. Applications are processed on a rolling basis. *Application fee:* $75. Electronic applications accepted. *Application Contact:* Paul Marthers, 518-276-6216, Fax: 518-276-4072, E-mail: admissions@rpi.edu. *Vice Provost and Dean of Graduate Education*, Dr. Stanley M. Dunn, 518-276-8433, Fax: 518-276-2256, E-mail: dunns6@rpi.edu.

Lally School of Management and Technology Students: 189 full-time (82 women), 162 part-time (40 women); includes 65 minority (22 Black or African American, non-Hispanic/Latino; 34 Asian, non-Hispanic/Latino; 9 Hispanic/Latino), 92 international. Average age 28. 507 applicants, 56% accepted, 150 enrolled. *Faculty:* 44 full-time (10 women), 19 part-time/adjunct (0 women). Expenses: Contact institution. *Financial support:* Fellowships with partial tuition reimbursements, career-related internships or fieldwork, institutionally sponsored loans, scholarships/grants, and assistantships are for Ph D students only available. Financial award application deadline: 3/15; financial award applicants required to submit FAFSA. In 2010, 263 master's, 7 doctorates awarded. *Degree program information:* Part-time and evening/weekend programs available. Offers business (MBA); financial engineering and risk analysis (MS); management (MS, PhD); technology, commercialization, and entrepreneurship (MS). *Application deadline:* For fall admission, 3/15 priority date for domestic and international students. Applications are processed on a rolling basis. *Application fee:* $75. Electronic applications accepted. *Application Contact:* Michele M. Martens, Manager of Graduate Programs, 518-276-6586, Fax: 518-276-8190, E-mail: lallymba@rpi.edu. *Acting Dean/Professor*, Dr. Iftekhar Hasan, 518-276-6586, Fax: 518-276-2665, E-mail: lallymba@rpi.edu.

School of Architecture Students: 57 full-time (25 women), 11 part-time (1 woman); includes 2 Black or African American, non-Hispanic/Latino; 3 Asian, non-Hispanic/Latino; 2 Hispanic/Latino; 1 Two or more races, non-Hispanic/Latino, 19 international. Average age 28. 165 applicants, 40% accepted, 29 enrolled. *Faculty:* 16 full-time (4 women), 16 part-time/adjunct (5 women). Expenses: Contact institution. *Financial support:* In 2010–11, 36 students received support, including 5 fellowships with full tuition reimbursements available (averaging $23,500 per year), 19 research assistantships with full tuition reimbursements available (averaging $17,500 per year), 1 teaching assistantship with full tuition reimbursement available (averaging $17,500 per year); career-related internships or fieldwork, institutionally sponsored loans, scholarships/grants, tuition waivers (partial), and unspecified assistantships also available. Financial award application deadline: 1/1. In 2010, 16 master's, 4 doctorates awarded. Offers acoustics (PhD); architectural acoustics (MS); architecture (M Arch, MS, PhD); built ecologies (PhD); lighting (MS). *Application deadline:* For fall admission, 1/1 priority date for domestic and international students. Applications are processed on a rolling basis. *Application fee:* $75. Electronic applications accepted. *Application Contact:* Erin Bermingham, Senior Program Administrator, 518-276-3986, Fax: 518-276-3034, E-mail: bermie@rpi.edu. *Head, Graduate Programs*, Prof. Ted Krueger, 518-276-2562, Fax: 518-276-3034, E-mail: krueger@rpi.edu.

School of Engineering Students: 473 full-time (99 women), 63 part-time (7 women); includes 33 minority (3 Black or African American, non-Hispanic/Latino; 18 Asian, non-Hispanic/Latino; 12 Hispanic/Latino), 271 international. Average age 26. 1,941 applicants, 21% accepted, 126 enrolled. *Faculty:* 131 full-time (15 women), 15 part-time/adjunct (0 women). Expenses: Contact institution. *Financial support:* In 2010–11, 38 fellowships with full tuition reimbursements (averaging $22,442 per year), 267 research assistantships with full and partial tuition reimbursements (averaging $19,068 per year), 135 teaching assistantships with full and partial tuition reimbursements (averaging $17,166 per year) were awarded; career-related internships or fieldwork, institutionally sponsored loans, scholarships/grants, tuition waivers (full and partial), and unspecified assistantships also available. Financial award application deadline: 2/1. In 2010, 114 master's, 71 doctorates awarded. *Degree program information:* Part-time and evening/weekend programs available. Postbaccalaureate distance learning degree programs offered (no on-campus study). Offers aerospace engineering (M Eng, MS, PhD); biomedical engineering (MS, D Eng, PhD); ceramics and glass science (M Eng, MS, PhD); chemical engineering (M Eng, MS, PhD); composites (M Eng, MS, PhD); computer and systems engineering (M Eng, MS, PhD); electrical engineering (M Eng, MS, PhD); electronic materials (M Eng, MS, PhD); engineering (M Eng, MS, D Eng, PhD); engineering physics (MS, PhD); environmental engineering (M Eng, MS, PhD); geotechnical engineering (M Eng, MS, PhD); industrial and management engineering (M Eng, MS); industrial and systems engineering (PhD); mechanical engineering (M Eng, MS, PhD); mechanics of composite materials and structures (M Eng, MS, PhD); metallurgy (M Eng, MS, PhD); nuclear engineering (M Eng, MS); nuclear engineering and science (PhD); polymers (M Eng, MS, PhD); structural engineering (M Eng, MS, PhD); systems engineering and technology management (M Eng); transportation engineering (M Eng, MS, PhD). *Application deadline:* For fall admission, 1/1 priority date for domestic and

Rensselaer Polytechnic Institute (continued)

international students; for spring admission, 8/15 priority date for domestic and international students. Applications are processed on a rolling basis. *Application fee:* $75. Electronic applications accepted. *Application Contact:* James G. Nondorf, Vice President for Enrollment, 518-276-6216, Fax: 518-276-4072, E-mail: admissions@rpi.edu. *Acting Dean*, Dr. Joe Chow, 518-276-6374, Fax: 518-276-6261, E-mail: chowj@rpi.edu.

School of Humanities, Arts, and Social Sciences Students: 93 full-time (33 women), 17 part-time (11 women); includes 18 minority (4 Black or African American, non-Hispanic/Latino; 1 American Indian or Alaska Native, non-Hispanic/Latino; 8 Asian, non-Hispanic/Latino; 4 Hispanic/Latino; 1 Two or more races, non-Hispanic/Latino), 11 international. Average age 26. 238 applicants, 28% accepted, 26 enrolled. *Faculty:* 58 full-time (20 women), 2 part-time/adjunct (0 women). Expenses: Contact institution. *Financial support:* In 2010–11, 66 students received support, including 16 fellowships with full tuition reimbursements available (averaging $21,830 per year), 20 research assistantships with full tuition reimbursements available (averaging $18,075 per year), 35 teaching assistantships with full tuition reimbursements available (averaging $17,883 per year); career-related internships or fieldwork, institutionally sponsored loans, and tuition waivers (full and partial) also available. Financial award application deadline: 2/1. In 2010, 30 master's, 10 doctorates awarded. *Degree program information:* Part-time and evening/weekend programs available. Postbaccalaureate distance learning degree programs offered (no on-campus study). Offers cognitive science (MS, PhD); communication and rhetoric (MS, PhD); design studies (MS, PhD); ecological economics (PhD); electronic arts (MFA, PhD); human-computer interaction (MS); humanities, arts, and social sciences (MFA, MS, PhD); policy studies (MS, PhD); science studies (MS, PhD); sustainability studies (MS, PhD); technical communication (MS); technology studies (MS, PhD). *Application deadline:* For fall admission, 1/1 priority date for domestic students, 1/15 priority date for international students; for spring admission, 8/15 priority date for domestic and international students. Applications are processed on a rolling basis. *Application fee:* $75. Electronic applications accepted. *Application Contact:* Paul Marthers, Vice President for Enrollment, 518-276-6216, Fax: 518-276-4072, E-mail: admissions@rpi.edu. *Acting Dean*, Dr. Wayne D. Gray, 518-276-6575, Fax: 518-276-4871, E-mail: grayw@rpi.edu.

School of Science Students: 327 full-time (99 women), 16 part-time (6 women); includes 41 minority (40 Asian, non-Hispanic/Latino; 1 Two or more races, non-Hispanic/Latino), 80 international. Average age 25. 1,083 applicants, 23% accepted, 89 enrolled. *Faculty:* 109 full-time (24 women). Expenses: Contact institution. *Financial support:* In 2010–11, 171 students received support, including 13 fellowships with full tuition reimbursements available (averaging $22,500 per year), 125 research assistantships with full tuition reimbursements available (averaging $19,246 per year), 138 teaching assistantships with full tuition reimbursements available (averaging $17,656 per year); career-related internships or fieldwork, institutionally sponsored loans, and tuition waivers (full) also available. Financial award application deadline: 2/1. In 2010, 54 master's, 47 doctorates awarded. *Degree program information:* Part-time and evening/weekend programs available. Postbaccalaureate distance learning degree programs offered (no on-campus study). Offers analytical chemistry (MS, PhD); applied mathematics (MS); biochemistry (MS, PhD); biochemistry and biophysics (MS, PhD); biology (MS, PhD); computer science (MS, PhD); geology (MS, PhD); information technology and Web science (MS); inorganic chemistry (MS, PhD); mathematics (MS, PhD); multi-disciplinary science (MS, PhD); organic chemistry (MS, PhD); physical chemistry (MS, PhD); physics, applied physics, and astronomy (MS, PhD); polymer chemistry (MS, PhD); science (MS, PhD). *Application deadline:* For fall admission, 1/1 priority date for domestic students, 1/15 priority date for international students. Applications are processed on a rolling basis. *Application fee:* $75. Electronic applications accepted. *Application Contact:* James G. Nondorf, Vice President for Enrollment, 518-276-6216, Fax: 518-276-4072, E-mail: admissions@rpi.edu. *Acting Dean*, Dr. David L. Spooner, 518-276-6890, Fax: 518-276-2825, E-mail: spoond@rpi.edu.

RESEARCH COLLEGE OF NURSING, Kansas City, MO 64132

General Information Independent, coed, primarily women, comprehensive institution. *Enrollment:* 444 graduate, professional, and undergraduate students; 7 full-time matriculated graduate/professional students (6 women), 117 part-time matriculated graduate/professional students (110 women). *Enrollment by degree level:* 124 master's. *Graduate faculty:* 8 full-time (all women), 1 (woman) part-time/adjunct. *Tuition:* Part-time $400 per credit hour. *Required fees:* $25 per contact hour. $50 per semester. *Graduate housing:* Rooms and/or apartments available on a first-come, first-served basis to single and married students. *Student services:* Campus safety program, child daycare facilities. *Library facilities:* Greenlease Library. *Online resources:* library catalog, web page, access to other libraries' catalogs. *Collection:* 150,000 titles, 675 serial subscriptions.

Computer facilities: 125 computers available on campus for general student use. A campuswide network can be accessed from student residence rooms and from off campus. Online class registration is available. *Web address:* http://www.researchcollege.edu/.

General Application Contact: Leslie Mendenhall, Director of Transfer and Graduate Recruitment, 816-995-2820, Fax: 816-995-2813, E-mail: leslie.mendenhall@researchcollege.edu.

GRADUATE UNITS

Nursing Program Students: 7 full-time (6 women), 117 part-time (110 women). Average age 30. *Faculty:* 8 full-time (all women), 1 (woman) part-time/adjunct. Expenses: Contact institution. *Financial support:* Applicants required to submit FAFSA. In 2010, 23 master's awarded. *Degree program information:* Part-time programs available. Postbaccalaureate distance learning degree programs offered (no on-campus study). Offers clinical nurse leader (MSN); executive nurse practitioner (MSN); family nurse practitioner (MSN); nurse educator (MSN). *Application deadline:* Applications are processed on a rolling basis. *Application fee:* $50. *Application Contact:* Leslie Mendenhall, Director of Transfer and Graduate Recruitment, 816-995-2820, Fax: 816-995-2813, E-mail: leslie.mendenhall@researchcollege.edu. *President and Dean*, Dr. Nancy O. De Basio, 816-995-2815, Fax: 816-995-2817, E-mail: nancy.debasio@researchcollege.edu.

RESURRECTION UNIVERSITY, Oak Park, IL 60302

General Information Independent, coed, primarily women, upper-level institution.

GRADUATE UNITS

Nursing Program Offers nursing (MSN).

RHODE ISLAND COLLEGE, Providence, RI 02908-1991

General Information State-supported, coed, comprehensive institution. *Enrollment:* 9,155 graduate, professional, and undergraduate students; 204 full-time matriculated graduate/professional students (179 women), 580 part-time matriculated graduate/professional students (461 women). *Enrollment by degree level:* 653 master's, 61 doctoral, 70 other advanced degrees. *Graduate faculty:* 113 full-time (59 women), 61 part-time/adjunct (36 women). Tuition, state resident: full-time $8208; part-time $342 per credit hour. Tuition, nonresident: full-time $16,080; part-time $670 per credit hour. *Required fees:* $554; $20 per credit. $72 per term. *Graduate housing:* On-campus housing not available. *Student services:* Campus employment opportunities, career counseling, free psychological counseling, international student services, low-cost health insurance, multicultural affairs office, services for students with disabilities. *Library facilities:* Adams Library. *Online resources:* library catalog, web page, access to other libraries' catalogs. *Collection:* 701,201 titles, 1.3 million serial subscriptions, 7,070 audiovisual materials.

Computer facilities: Computer purchase and lease plans are available. 267 computers available on campus for general student use. A campuswide network can be accessed from student residence rooms and from off campus. Online class registration is available. *Web address:* http://www.ric.edu/.

General Application Contact: Dr. Leslie Schuster, Interim Dean of Graduate Studies, 401-456-9723, E-mail: graduatestudies@ric.edu.

GRADUATE UNITS

School of Graduate Studies Students: 204 full-time (179 women), 580 part-time (461 women); includes 73 minority (42 Black or African American, non-Hispanic/Latino; 3 American Indian or Alaska Native, non-Hispanic/Latino; 9 Asian, non-Hispanic/Latino; 18 Hispanic/Latino; 1 Two or more races, non-Hispanic/Latino), 2 international. Average age 35. *Faculty:* 113 full-time (59 women), 61 part-time/adjunct (36 women). Expenses: Contact institution. *Financial support:* In 2010–11, 11 teaching assistantships with full tuition reimbursements (averaging $4,550 per year) were awarded; research assistantships with partial tuition reimbursements, career-related internships or fieldwork, Federal Work-Study, traineeships, health care benefits, tuition waivers (partial), and unspecified assistantships also available. Support available to part-time students. Financial award application deadline: 5/15; financial award applicants required to submit FAFSA. In 2010, 268 master's, 7 doctorates, 21 other advanced degrees awarded. *Degree program information:* Part-time and evening/weekend programs available. *Application deadline:* For fall admission, 3/1 priority date for domestic students; for spring admission, 11/1 for domestic students. Applications are processed on a rolling basis. *Application fee:* $50. *Application Contact:* Graduate Studies, 401-456-8700. *Interim Dean of Graduate Studies*, Dr. Leslie Schuster, 401-456-9723, E-mail: graduatestudies@ric.edu.

Faculty of Arts and Sciences Students: 15 full-time (12 women), 68 part-time (39 women); includes 6 minority (2 Black or African American, non-Hispanic/Latino; 1 American Indian or Alaska Native, non-Hispanic/Latino; 2 Hispanic/Latino; 1 Two or more races, non-Hispanic/Latino). Average age 35. *Faculty:* 54 full-time (22 women), 14 part-time/adjunct (6 women). Expenses: Contact institution. *Financial support:* In 2010–11, 9 teaching assistantships with full tuition reimbursements (averaging $4,550 per year) were awarded; research assistantships with tuition reimbursements, career-related internships or fieldwork, Federal Work-Study, scholarships/grants, health care benefits, and unspecified assistantships also available. Support available to part-time students. Financial award application deadline: 5/15; financial award applicants required to submit FAFSA. In 2010, 40 master's awarded. *Degree program information:* Part-time and evening/weekend programs available. Offers art education (MA, MAT); arts and sciences (MA, MAT, MM Ed, MPA, CGS); biology (MA); creative writing (MA, CGS); English (MA); health psychology (CGS); history (MA); literature (CGS); mathematics (MA); mathematics content specialist (CGS); media studies (MA); modern biological sciences (CGS); music education (MAT, MM Ed); psychology (MA); public administration (MPA). *Application deadline:* For fall admission, 3/1 for domestic students; for spring admission, 11/1 for domestic students. Applications are processed on a rolling basis. *Application fee:* $50. *Application Contact:* Graduate Studies, 401-456-8700. *Dean*, Dr. Earl Simson, 401-456-8107, E-mail: esimson@ric.edu.

Feinstein School of Education and Human Development Students: 80 full-time (67 women), 383 part-time (311 women); includes 27 minority (13 Black or African American, non-Hispanic/Latino; 1 American Indian or Alaska Native, non-Hispanic/Latino; 7 Asian, non-Hispanic/Latino; 6 Hispanic/Latino). Average age 34. *Faculty:* 45 full-time (25 women), 37 part-time/adjunct (24 women). Expenses: Contact institution. *Financial support:* Teaching assistantships with full tuition reimbursements, career-related internships or fieldwork, Federal Work-Study, scholarships/grants, health care benefits, and unspecified assistantships available. Support available to part-time students. Financial award application deadline: 5/15; financial award applicants required to submit FAFSA. In 2010, 126 master's, 7 doctorates, 21 other advanced degrees awarded. *Degree program information:* Part-time and evening/weekend programs available. Offers advanced studies in teaching and learning (M Ed); agency counseling (MA); autism education (CGS); co-occurring disorders (MA, CGS); early childhood education (M Ed); education (PhD); education and human development (M Ed, MA, MAT, PhD, CAGS, CGS); educational leadership (M Ed); educational psychology (MA); elementary education (M Ed, MAT); English (MAT); French (MAT); health education (M Ed); history (MAT); math (MAT); mental health counseling (CAGS); middle-secondary level special education (CGS); physical education (CGS); reading (M Ed); school counseling (MA, CAGS); school psychology (CAGS); secondary education (MAT); Spanish (MAT); special education (M Ed); teaching English as a second language (M Ed); technology education (M Ed). *Application deadline:* For fall admission, 3/1 for domestic students; for spring admission, 11/1 for domestic students. Applications are processed on a rolling basis. *Application fee:* $50. *Application Contact:* Graduate Studies, 401-456-8700. *Dean*, Dr. Alexander Sidorkin, 401-456-8110, E-mail: asidorkin@ric.edu.

School of Management Students: 2 full-time (1 woman), 10 part-time (8 women); includes 1 minority (Asian, non-Hispanic/Latino), 1 international. Average age 29. *Faculty:* 1 (woman) full-time. Expenses: Contact institution. *Financial support:* Federal Work-Study, scholarships/grants, health care benefits, and unspecified assistantships available. Support available to part-time students. Financial award application deadline: 5/15; financial award applicants required to submit FAFSA. In 2010, 5 master's awarded. *Degree program information:* Part-time and evening/weekend programs available. Offers accounting (MP Ac); financial planning (CGS); management (MP Ac, CGS). *Application deadline:* For fall admission, 3/1 for domestic students. Applications are processed on a rolling basis. *Application fee:* $50. *Application Contact:* Graduate Studies, 401-456-8700. *Dean*, Dr. David Blanchette, 401-456-8009, E-mail: dblanchette@ric.edu.

School of Nursing Students: 1 (woman) full-time, 42 part-time (41 women); includes 3 minority (2 Black or African American, non-Hispanic/Latino; 1 Hispanic/Latino), 1 international. Average age 45. *Faculty:* 6 full-time (all women). Expenses: Contact institution. *Financial support:* In 2010–11, 2 teaching assistantships with full tuition reimbursements (averaging $4,550 per year) were awarded; Federal Work-Study, scholarships/grants, health care benefits, and unspecified assistantships also available. Support available to part-time students. Financial award application deadline: 5/15; financial award applicants required to submit FAFSA. In 2010, 7 master's awarded. *Degree program information:* Part-time programs available. Offers nursing (MSN). *Application deadline:* For fall admission, 2/15 for domestic students. Applications are processed on a rolling basis. *Application fee:* $50. *Application Contact:* Graduate Studies, 401-456-8700. *Dean*, Dr. Jane Williams, 401-456-8013, Fax: 401-456-9608, E-mail: jwilliams@ric.edu.

School of Social Work Students: 106 full-time (98 women), 77 part-time (62 women); includes 36 minority (25 Black or African American, non-Hispanic/Latino; 1 American Indian or Alaska Native, non-Hispanic/Latino; 1 Asian, non-Hispanic/Latino; 9 Hispanic/Latino). Average age 33. *Faculty:* 7 full-time (5 women), 10 part-time/adjunct (6 women). Expenses: Contact institution. *Financial support:* Career-related internships or fieldwork, Federal Work-Study, scholarships/grants, health care benefits, and unspecified assistantships available. Support available to part-time students. Financial award application deadline: 5/15; financial award applicants required to submit FAFSA. In 2010, 90 master's awarded. *Degree program information:* Part-time programs available. Offers social work (MSW). *Application deadline:* For fall admission, 2/1 for domestic students. Applications are processed on a rolling basis. *Application fee:* $50. *Application Contact:* Graduate Studies, 401-456-8700. *Dean*, Dr. Sue Pearlmutter, 401-456-8042, E-mail: spearlmutter@ric.edu.

RHODE ISLAND SCHOOL OF DESIGN, Providence, RI 02903-2784

General Information Independent, coed, comprehensive institution. *Graduate housing:* Room and/or apartments available on a first-come, first-served basis to single students; on-campus housing not available to married students.

GRADUATE UNITS

Graduate Studies Offers art education (MA, MAT); digital media (MFA). Electronic applications accepted.

Division of Architecture and Design Offers architecture (M Arch); architecture and design (M Arch, MFA, MIA, MID, MLA); furniture design (MFA); graphic design (MFA); industrial design (MID); interior architecture (MIA); landscape architecture (MLA).

Division of Fine Arts Offers ceramics (MFA); glass (MFA); jewelry and light metals (MFA); painting (MFA); photography (MFA); printmaking (MFA); sculpture (MFA); textiles (MFA).

RHODES COLLEGE, Memphis, TN 38112-1690

General Information Independent, coed, comprehensive institution. *Enrollment:* 1,730 graduate, professional, and undergraduate students; 18 full-time matriculated graduate/professional students (5 women). *Enrollment by degree level:* 18 master's. *Graduate faculty:* 5 full-time (3 women), 2 part-time/adjunct (0 women). *Tuition:* Full-time $34,270; part-time $1440 per credit. *Required fees:* $310. *Graduate housing:* Room and/or apartments available on a first-come, first-served basis to single students; on-campus housing not available to married students. Housing application deadline: 3/1. *Student services:* Campus employment opportunities, campus safety program, career counseling, free psychological counseling, international student services, multicultural affairs office, services for students with disabilities. *Library facilities:* Burrow Library. *Online resources:* library catalog, web page, access to other libraries' catalogs.

Computer facilities: A campuswide network can be accessed from student residence rooms and from off campus. Online class registration is available. *Web address:* http://www.rhodes.edu/.

General Application Contact: Dr. Pamela H. Church, Program Director, 901-843-3863, Fax: 901-843-3736, E-mail: church@rhodes.edu.

GRADUATE UNITS

Department of Economics and Business Administration Students: 18 full-time (5 women). Average age 22. *Faculty:* 5 full-time (3 women), 2 part-time/adjunct (0 women). Expenses: Contact institution. *Financial support:* Career-related internships or fieldwork and scholarships/grants available. Financial award application deadline: 3/1; financial award applicants required to submit FAFSA. In 2010, 10 master's awarded. *Degree program information:* Part-time programs available. Offers accounting (MS). *Application deadline:* For fall admission, 3/1 for domestic students. *Application fee:* $25. *Application Contact:* Dr. Pamela H. Church, Program Director, 901-843-3863, Fax: 901-843-3798, E-mail: church@rhodes.edu. *Program Director,* Dr. Pamela H. Church, 901-843-3863, Fax: 901-843-3798, E-mail: church@rhodes.edu.

RICE UNIVERSITY, Houston, TX 77251-1892

General Information Independent, coed, university. CGS member. *Graduate housing:* Rooms and/or apartments available on a first-come, first-served basis to single and married students. Housing application deadline: 7/15. *Research affiliation:* Fermi National Accelerator Laboratory, Los Alamos National Laboratory, Brookhaven National Laboratory, Arecibo Observatory, Houston Area Research Center.

GRADUATE UNITS

Graduate Programs *Degree program information:* Part-time programs available. Offers education (MAT). Electronic applications accepted.

George R. Brown School of Engineering *Degree program information:* Part-time programs available. Offers bioengineering (MS, PhD); bioinformatics (PhD); biostatistics (PhD); chemical and biomolecular engineering (MS, PhD); chemical engineering (M Ch E); circuits, controls, and communication systems (MS, PhD); civil engineering (MCE, MS, PhD); computational and applied mathematics (MA, MCAM, PhD); computational finance (PhD); computational science and engineering (MCSE); computer science (MCS, MS, PhD); computer science and engineering (MS, PhD); electrical engineering (MEE); engineering (M Ch E, M Stat, MA, MBE, MCAM, MCE, MCS, MEE, MEE, MES, MME, MMS, MS, PhD); environmental engineering (MEE, MES, MS, PhD); environmental science (MEE, MES, MS, PhD); general statistics (PhD); lasers, microwaves, and solid-state electronics (MS, PhD); materials science (MMS, MS, PhD); mechanical engineering (MME, MS, PhD); statistics (M Stat, MA). MD/PhD offered jointly with Baylor College of Medicine, The University of Texas Health Science Center at Houston. Electronic applications accepted.

Jesse H. Jones Graduate School of Management *Degree program information:* Evening/weekend programs available. Offers business administration (EMBA, MBA, PMBA). Electronic applications accepted.

School of Architecture Offers architecture (M Arch, D Arch); urban design (M Arch). Electronic applications accepted.

School of Humanities Offers African religions (PhD); African-American religions (PhD); art history (PhD); contemplative studies (PhD); English (MA, PhD); gnosticism, esotericism, mysticism (PhD); history (MA, PhD); humanities (MA, PhD); Islam (PhD); Jewish thought and philosophy (PhD); linguistics (MA, PhD); modern Christianity in thought and popular culture (PhD); philosophy (MA, PhD); psychology of religion (PhD); the Bible and beyond (PhD).

School of Social Sciences Offers archaeology (MA, PhD); cognitive sciences (MA, PhD); economics (MA, PhD); industrial-organizational/social psychology (MA, PhD); political science (PhD); psychology (MA, PhD); social sciences (MA, PhD); social-cultural anthropology (MA, PhD); sociology (PhD).

Shepherd School of Music Offers composition (MM, DMA); conducting (MM); musicology (MM); performance (MM, DMA); theory (MM).

Susanne M. Glasscock School of Continuing Studies *Degree program information:* Part-time and evening/weekend programs available. Offers liberal studies (MLS).

Wiess School of Natural Sciences *Degree program information:* Part-time programs available. Offers biochemistry and cell biology (MA, PhD); chemistry (MA); earth science (MS, PhD); ecology and evolutionary biology (MA, MS, PhD); inorganic chemistry (PhD); mathematics (PhD); nanoscale physics (MS); natural sciences (MA, MS, MST, PhD); organic chemistry (PhD); physical chemistry (PhD); physics and astronomy (PhD); science teaching (MST). Electronic applications accepted.

Wiess School–Professional Science Master's Programs Offers bioscience research and health policy (MS); environmental analysis and decision making (MS); geophysics (MS); nanoscale physics (MS); professional science (MS).

Rice Quantum Institute Offers quantum physics (MS, PhD). Electronic applications accepted.

THE RICHARD STOCKTON COLLEGE OF NEW JERSEY, Pomona, NJ 08240-0195

General Information State-supported, coed, comprehensive institution. CGS member. *Enrollment:* 7,879 graduate, professional, and undergraduate students; 191 full-time matriculated graduate/professional students (142 women), 408 part-time matriculated graduate/professional students (292 women). *Enrollment by degree level:* 494 master's, 105 doctoral. *Graduate faculty:* 62 full-time (35 women), 25 part-time/adjunct (15 women). Tuition, state resident: full-time $9310; part-time $517.25 per credit. Tuition, nonresident: full-time $14,332; part-time $796.23 per credit. *Required fees:* $2600; $144 per credit. $70 per semester. Tuition and fees vary according to degree level. *Graduate housing:* Room and/or apartments available on a first-come, first-served basis to single students; on-campus housing not available to married students. Typical cost: $7165 per year ($10,380 including board). Room and board charges vary according to board plan and housing facility selected. Housing application deadline: 4/1. *Student services:* Campus employment opportunities, campus safety program, career counseling, child daycare facilities, exercise/wellness program, free psychological counseling, grant writing training, international student services, low-cost health insurance, services for students with disabilities, teacher training, writing training. *Library facilities:* The Richard Stockton College of New Jersey Library. *Online resources:* library catalog, web page. *Collection:* 303,785 titles, 41,241 serial subscriptions, 12,811 audiovisual materials. *Research affiliation:* Aviation Research and Technology Park (aviation research), Nature Conservancy of New Jersey (environmental studies), Association of State Colleges (civic engagement), Jewish Foundation (Holocaust studies), Wetlands Institute (marine biology).

Computer facilities: 865 computers available on campus for general student use. A campuswide network can be accessed from student residence rooms and from off campus. Online class registration is available. *Web address:* http://www.stockton.edu/.

General Application Contact: Tara Williams, Assistant Director of Graduate Enrollment Management, 609-626-3640, E-mail: gradschool@stockton.edu.

GRADUATE UNITS

School of Graduate and Continuing Studies Students: 191 full-time (142 women), 408 part-time (292 women); includes 99 minority (30 Black or African American, non-Hispanic/Latino; 5 American Indian or Alaska Native, non-Hispanic/Latino; 32 Asian, non-Hispanic/Latino; 20 Hispanic/Latino; 1 Native Hawaiian or other Pacific Islander, non-Hispanic/Latino; 11 Two or more races, non-Hispanic/Latino), 4 international. Average age 33. 472 applicants, 48% accepted, 163 enrolled. *Faculty:* 62 full-time (35 women), 25 part-time/adjunct (15 women). Expenses: Contact institution. *Financial support:* In 2010–11, 115 students received support, including 23 fellowships, 92 research assistantships; career-related internships or fieldwork, Federal Work-Study, scholarships/grants, and unspecified assistantships also available. Support available to part-time students. Financial award application deadline: 3/1; financial award applicants required to submit FAFSA. In 2010, 120 master's, 29 doctorates awarded. *Degree program information:* Part-time programs available. Offers business administration (MBA); computational science (MS); criminal justice (MA); education (MA); educational leadership (MA); environmental science (PSM); Holocaust and genocide studies (MA); instructional technology (MA); nursing (MSN); occupational therapy (MSOT); physical therapy (DPT); social work (MSW). *Application deadline:* For fall admission, 7/1 for domestic and international students. Applications are processed on a rolling basis. *Application fee:* $50. Electronic applications accepted. *Application Contact:* Tara Williams, Assistant Director of Enrollment Management, 609-626-3640, Fax: 609-626-6050, E-mail: gradschool@stockton.edu. *Interim Dean,* Dr. Lewis Leitner, 609-652-4298, E-mail: graduatestudies@stockton.edu.

RICHMOND, THE AMERICAN INTERNATIONAL UNIVERSITY IN LONDON, Richmond, Surrey TW10 6JP, United Kingdom

General Information Independent, coed, comprehensive institution. *Graduate housing:* Room and/or apartments available on a first-come, first-served basis to single students; on-campus housing not available to married students. Housing application deadline: 8/1.

GRADUATE UNITS

MA in Art History Program *Degree program information:* Part-time programs available. Offers art history (MA). Electronic applications accepted.

MA in International Relations Program *Degree program information:* Part-time programs available. Offers international relations (MA). Electronic applications accepted.

RICHMONT GRADUATE UNIVERSITY, Atlanta, GA 30327

General Information Independent-religious, coed, graduate-only institution.

GRADUATE UNITS

Graduate Programs

RIDER UNIVERSITY, Lawrenceville, NJ 08648-3001

General Information Independent, coed, comprehensive institution. *Enrollment:* 5,816 graduate, professional, and undergraduate students; 301 full-time matriculated graduate/professional students (191 women), 536 part-time matriculated graduate/professional students (362 women). *Enrollment by degree level:* 837 master's. *Graduate faculty:* 79 full-time (36 women), 83 part-time/adjunct (41 women). *Tuition:* Full-time $29,870; part-time $667.34 per credit. *Required fees:* $350; $11.60 per credit. Part-time tuition and fees vary according to program. *Graduate housing:* On-campus housing not available. *Student services:* Campus employment opportunities, campus safety program, career counseling, exercise/wellness program, free psychological counseling, international student services, multicultural affairs office, services for students with disabilities. *Library facilities:* Franklin F. Moore Library plus 1 other. *Online resources:* library catalog, web page, access to other libraries' catalogs. *Collection:* 481,958 titles, 42,085 serial subscriptions, 4,485 audiovisual materials.

Computer facilities: Computer purchase and lease plans are available. 300 computers available on campus for general student use. A campuswide network can be accessed from student residence rooms and from off campus. Online class registration is available. *Web address:* http://www.rider.edu/.

General Application Contact: Jamie L. Mitchell, Director of Graduate Admissions, 609-896-5036, Fax: 609-895-5680, E-mail: jmitchell@rider.edu.

GRADUATE UNITS

College of Business Administration Students: 123 full-time (61 women), 185 part-time (88 women); includes 12 Black or African American, non-Hispanic/Latino; 28 Asian, non-Hispanic/Latino; 8 Hispanic/Latino, 59 international. Average age 29. *Faculty:* 18 full-time (5 women), 9 part-time/adjunct (3 women). Expenses: Contact institution. *Financial support:* Career-related internships or fieldwork, Federal Work-Study, institutionally sponsored loans, unspecified assistantships, and institutional work-study available. Support available to part-time students. Financial award applicants required to submit FAFSA. In 2010, 122 master's awarded. *Degree program information:* Part-time and evening/weekend programs available. Offers accountancy (M Acc); business administration (M Acc, MBA). *Application deadline:* For fall admission, 8/1 priority date for domestic students, 3/15 priority date for international students; for spring admission, 12/1 priority date for domestic students, 11/1 priority date for international students. Applications are processed on a rolling basis. *Application fee:* $50. Electronic applications accepted. *Application Contact:* Jamie L. Mitchell, Director of Graduate Admissions, 609-896-5036, Fax: 609-895-5680, E-mail: jmitchell@rider.edu. *MBA Program Director,* Dr. John Farrell, 609-895-5776, Fax: 609-896-5304.

Department of Graduate Education, Leadership and Counseling Students: 74 full-time (63 women), 338 part-time (266 women); includes 45 Black or African American, non-Hispanic/Latino; 14 Asian, non-Hispanic/Latino; 16 Hispanic/Latino, 5 international. Average age 32. *Faculty:* 24 full-time (16 women), 34 part-time/adjunct (17 women). Expenses: Contact institution. *Financial support:* In 2010–11, 316 students received support. Career-related internships or fieldwork, Federal Work-Study, institutionally sponsored loans, and unspecified assistantships available. Support available to part-time students. Financial award applicants required to submit FAFSA. In 2010, 148 master's, 18 other advanced degrees awarded. *Degree program information:* Part-time and evening/weekend programs available. Offers alternative route in special education (Certificate); business education (Certificate); counseling services (MA, Certificate, Ed S); curriculum, instruction and supervision (MA, Certificate); director of school counseling (Certificate); educational administration (MA, Certificate); elementary education (Certificate); English as a second language (Certificate); English education (Certificate); mathematics education (Certificate); organizational leadership (MA); preschool to grade 3 (Certificate); principal (Certificate); reading specialist (Certificate); reading/language arts (MA, Certificate); school administrator (Certificate); school counseling services (Certificate); school psychology (Certificate, Ed S); science education (Certificate); social studies education (Certificate); special education (MA, Certificate); supervisor (Certificate); teacher certification (Certificate); teacher of students with disabilities (Certificate); teacher of the handicapped (Certificate); teaching (MA); world languages (Certificate). *Application deadline:* For fall admission, 5/1 priority date for domestic students, 3/15 priority date for international students; for spring admission, 11/1 priority date for domestic and international students. Applications are processed on a rolling basis. *Application fee:* $50. Electronic applications accepted. *Application Contact:* Jamie L. Mitchell, Director of Graduate Admissions, 609-896-5036, Fax: 609-895-5680, E-mail: jmitchell@rider.edu. *Chair,* Dr. Kathleen M. Pierce, 609-895-5478, Fax: 609-896-5362, E-mail: kpierce@rider.edu.

Westminster Choir College Students: 104 full-time (67 women), 13 part-time (8 women); includes 3 Black or African American, non-Hispanic/Latino; 10 Asian, non-Hispanic/Latino; 3 Hispanic/Latino, 13 international. Average age 26. *Faculty:* 32 full-time (11 women), 38 part-time/adjunct (21 women). Expenses: Contact institution. In 2010, 45 master's awarded. Offers choral conducting (MM); composition (MM); music (MAT, MM, MME, MVP); music education (MAT, MM, MME); organ performance (MM); piano accompanying and coaching (MM); piano pedagogy and performance (MM); piano performance (MM); sacred music (MM); vocal pedagogy and performance (MM); vocal training (MVP). *Application deadline:* For fall admission, 5/1 priority date for domestic students, 3/15 priority date for international students; for spring admission, 11/1 priority date for domestic and international students. Applications are processed on a rolling basis. *Application fee:* $50. Electronic applications accepted. *Application Contact:* Kate Shields, Director of Admissions, 609-921-7100 Ext. 8103, Fax: 609-921-2538, E-mail: wccadmission@rider.edu.

RIVIER COLLEGE, Nashua, NH 03060

General Information Independent-religious, coed, comprehensive institution. *Enrollment:* 2,357 graduate, professional, and undergraduate students; 198 full-time matriculated graduate/professional students (152 women), 677 part-time matriculated graduate/professional students (521 women). *Enrollment by degree level:* 835 master's, 40 doctoral. *Graduate faculty:* 35 full-time (20 women), 57 part-time/adjunct (32 women). *Tuition:* Part-time $456 per credit. *Graduate housing:* On-campus housing not available. *Student services:* Campus safety

Rivier College (continued)

program, career counseling, free psychological counseling, international student services, low-cost health insurance, multicultural affairs office, services for students with disabilities, teacher training. *Library facilities:* Regina Library plus 1 other. *Online resources:* web page. *Collection:* 150,902 titles, 315 serial subscriptions, 315 audiovisual materials.

Computer facilities: 189 computers available on campus for general student use. A campuswide network can be accessed from student residence rooms and from off campus. Online class registration is available. *Web address:* http://www.rivier.edu/.

General Application Contact: Mathew Kittredge, Director of Graduate Admissions, 603-897-8229, Fax: 603-897-8810, E-mail: gadmissions@rivier.edu.

GRADUATE UNITS

School of Graduate Studies Students: 198 full-time (152 women), 677 part-time (521 women); includes 13 Black or African American, non-Hispanic/Latino; 44 Asian, non-Hispanic/Latino; 19 Hispanic/Latino, 1 international. Average age 36. 595 applicants, 82% accepted, 330 enrolled. *Faculty:* 34 full-time (18 women), 33 part-time/adjunct (16 women). Expenses: Contact institution. *Financial support:* Available to part-time students. Application deadline: 2/1. In 2010, 239 master's, 7 other advanced degrees awarded. *Degree program information:* Part-time programs available. Offers business administration (MBA); clinical psychology (MS); computer information systems (MS); computer science (MS); curriculum and instruction (M Ed); early childhood education (M Ed); educational administration (M Ed); educational studies (M Ed); elementary education (M Ed); elementary education and general special education (M Ed); emotional and behavioral disorders (M Ed); English (MAT); experimental psychology (MS); general social education (M Ed); leadership and learning (Ed D, CAGS); learning disabilities (M Ed); learning disabilities and reading (M Ed); mathematics (MAT); mental health counseling (MA); reading (M Ed); school counseling (M Ed); social studies education (MAT); Spanish (MAT); writing and literature (MA). *Application deadline:* Applications are processed on a rolling basis. *Application fee:* $25. Electronic applications accepted. *Application Contact:* Mathew Kittredge, Director of Graduate Admissions, 603-897-8229, Fax: 603-897-8810, E-mail: mkittredge@rivier.edu. *Vice President of Academic Affairs,* Sr. Therese LaRochelle, 603-888-1311.

Division of Nursing Students: 11 full-time (9 women), 56 part-time (53 women); includes 1 Black or African American, non-Hispanic/Latino; 2 Asian, non-Hispanic/Latino; 1 Hispanic/Latino. Average age 41. 79 applicants, 15% accepted, 9 enrolled. *Faculty:* 4 full-time (3 women). Expenses: Contact institution. *Financial support:* Available to part-time students. Application deadline: 2/1. In 2010, 12 master's awarded. *Degree program information:* Part-time and evening/weekend programs available. Offers adult psychiatric/mental health practitioner (MS); family nurse practitioner (MS); nursing education (MS). *Application deadline:* Applications are processed on a rolling basis. *Application fee:* $25. Electronic applications accepted. *Application Contact:* Mathew Kittredge, Director of Graduate Admissions, 603-897-8229, Fax: 603-897-8810, E-mail: mkittredge@rivier.edu. *Head,* Dr. Paula Williams, 603-897-8529.

THE ROBERT E. WEBBER INSTITUTE FOR WORSHIP STUDIES, Orange Park, FL 32073

General Information Graduate-only institution. *Graduate faculty:* 18 part-time/adjunct (5 women). *Web address:* http://www.iws.edu/IWS/.

General Application Contact: Mark Murray, Director of Admissions, 800-282-2977 Ext. 105, Fax: 904-278-2878, E-mail: admissions@iws.edu.

GRADUATE UNITS

Doctor of Worship Studies Program Offers worship studies (DWS).

Master of Worship Studies Program Offers worship studies (MWS).

ROBERT MORRIS UNIVERSITY, Moon Township, PA 15108-1189

General Information Independent, coed, university. *Enrollment:* 4,967 graduate, professional, and undergraduate students; 1,164 part-time matriculated graduate/professional students (609 women). *Enrollment by degree level:* 847 master's, 261 doctoral, 56 other advanced degrees. *Graduate faculty:* 80 full-time (29 women), 34 part-time/adjunct (14 women). *Tuition:* Part-time $795 per credit. Part-time tuition and fees vary according to course load, degree level and program. *Graduate housing:* Room and/or apartments available on a first-come, first-served basis to single students; on-campus housing not available to married students. Typical cost: $5240 per year ($11,030 including board). Room and board charges vary according to board plan and housing facility selected. Housing application deadline: 5/1. *Student services:* Campus employment opportunities, campus safety program, career counseling, exercise/wellness program, international student services, multicultural affairs office, services for students with disabilities. *Library facilities:* Robert Morris University Library. *Online resources:* library catalog, access to other libraries' catalogs. *Collection:* 126,886 titles, 766 serial subscriptions, 3,664 audiovisual materials.

Computer facilities: Computer purchase and lease plans are available. 300 computers available on campus for general student use. A campuswide network can be accessed from student residence rooms and from off campus. Online class registration, online payment are available. *Web address:* http://www.rmu.edu/.

General Application Contact: Debra Roach, Assistant Dean, Graduate Admissions, 412-397-5200, Fax: 412-397-2425, E-mail: graduateadmissions@rmu.edu.

GRADUATE UNITS

Graduate Studies *Degree program information:* Part-time and evening/weekend programs available. Electronic applications accepted.

School of Business *Degree program information:* Part-time and evening/weekend programs available. Offers business administration and management (MBA); human resource management (MS); nonprofit management (MS); taxation (MS). Electronic applications accepted.

School of Communications and Information Systems *Degree program information:* Part-time and evening/weekend programs available. Offers communication and information systems (MS); competitive intelligence systems (MS); information security and assurance (MS); information systems and communications (D Sc); information systems management (MS); information technology project management (MS); Internet information systems (MS); organizational studies (MS). Electronic applications accepted.

School of Education and Social Sciences *Degree program information:* Part-time and evening/weekend programs available. Offers business education (MS); education (Post-baccalaureate Certificate); instructional leadership (MS); instructional management and leadership (PhD). Electronic applications accepted.

School of Engineering, Mathematics and Science *Degree program information:* Part-time and evening/weekend programs available. Offers engineering management (MS). Electronic applications accepted.

School of Nursing and Health Sciences *Degree program information:* Part-time and evening/weekend programs available. Offers nursing (MS, DNP). Electronic applications accepted.

See Display below and Close-Up on page 977.

ROBERT MORRIS UNIVERSITY ILLINOIS, Chicago, IL 60605

General Information Independent, coed, comprehensive institution. *Enrollment:* 4,558 graduate, professional, and undergraduate students; 275 full-time matriculated graduate/professional students (151 women), 212 part-time matriculated graduate/professional students (138 women). *Enrollment by degree level:* 487 master's. *Graduate faculty:* 9 full-time (2 women), 21 part-time/adjunct (6 women). *Tuition:* Full-time $13,200; part-time $2200 per course. *Graduate housing:* Rooms and/or apartments available on a first-come, first-served basis to single and married students. Typical cost: $8100 per year ($10,422 including board) for single students; $8100 per year ($10,422 including board) for married students. Room and board charges vary according to housing facility selected. Housing application deadline: 5/1. *Student services:* Campus employment opportunities, career counseling, exercise/wellness program, free psychological counseling, international student services, services for students with disabilities, writing training. *Library facilities:* Information Technology Library. *Online resources:* library catalog, web page, access to other libraries' catalogs. *Collection:* 153,728 titles, 42 serial subscriptions, 32,045 audiovisual materials.

Computer facilities: 1,830 computers available on campus for general student use. A campuswide network can be accessed from student residence rooms and from off campus. Online credentials, online payments, online student accounts, online degree audit available. *Web address:* http://www.robertmorris.edu/.

General Application Contact: Courtney A. Kohn Sanders, Dean of Graduate Admissions, 312-935-4810, Fax: 312-935-6020, E-mail: ckohn@robertmorris.edu.

GRADUATE UNITS

Morris Graduate School of Management Students: 275 full-time (151 women), 212 part-time (138 women); includes 170 Black or African American, non-Hispanic/Latino; 1 American Indian or Alaska Native, non-Hispanic/Latino; 21 Asian, non-Hispanic/Latino; 73 Hispanic/Latino; 2 Native Hawaiian or other Pacific Islander, non-Hispanic/Latino, 23 international. Average age 32. 172 applicants, 87% accepted, 105 enrolled. *Faculty:* 9 full-time (2 women), 21 part-time/adjunct (6 women). Expenses: Contact institution. *Financial support:* Federal Work-Study, scholarships/grants, and tuition waivers available. Support available to part-time students. In 2010, 174 master's awarded. *Degree program information:* Part-time and evening/weekend programs available. Offers accounting (MBA); accounting/finance (MBA); health care administration (MM); higher education administration (MM); human resource management (MBA); information systems (MIS); leadership (MBA); management/finance (MIS); management/human resource management (MBA). *Application deadline:* Applications are processed on a rolling basis. *Application fee:* $50 ($100 for international students). Electronic applications accepted. *Application Contact:* Courtney A. Kohn Sanders, Dean of Graduate Admissions, 312-935-4810, Fax: 312-935-6020, E-mail: ckohn@robertmorris.edu. *Dean,* Kayed Akkawi, 312-935-6025, Fax: 312-935-6020, E-mail: kakkawi@robertmorris.edu.

ROBERTS WESLEYAN COLLEGE, Rochester, NY 14624-1997

General Information Independent-religious, coed, comprehensive institution. *Graduate housing:* Room and/or apartments available on a first-come, first-served basis to single students; on-campus housing not available to married students.

GRADUATE UNITS

Division of Adult Professional Studies *Degree program information:* Evening/weekend programs available. Offers health administration (MS).

Division of Business *Degree program information:* Evening/weekend programs available. Offers nonprofit leadership (Certificate); strategic leadership (MS); strategic marketing (MS).

Division of Nursing Offers nursing administration (MSN); nursing education (MSN).

Division of Social Sciences Offers counseling in ministry (MA); school counseling (MS); school psychology (MS).

Division of Social Work Offers child and family practice (MSW); congregational and community practice (MSW); mental health practice (MSW).

Division of Teacher Education *Degree program information:* Part-time and evening/weekend programs available. Offers adolescence education (M Ed); childhood and special education (M Ed); literacy education (M Ed); urban education (M Ed).

ROCHESTER COLLEGE, Rochester Hills, MI 48307-2764

General Information Independent-religious, coed, comprehensive institution.

GRADUATE UNITS

Center for Missional Leadership Offers missional leadership (MRE).

ROCHESTER INSTITUTE OF TECHNOLOGY, Rochester, NY 14623-5603

General Information Independent, coed, comprehensive institution. CGS member. *Enrollment:* 1,680 full-time matriculated graduate/professional students (583 women), 1,194 part-time matriculated graduate/professional students (407 women). *Enrollment by degree level:* 2,689 master's, 154 doctoral, 31 other advanced degrees. *Tuition:* Full-time $33,234; part-time $924 per credit hour. *Required fees:* $219. *Graduate housing:* Rooms and/or apartments available on a first-come, first-served basis to single and married students. Typical cost: $5862 per year ($10,551 including board) for single students; $5862 per year ($10,551 including board) for married students. Room and board charges vary according to board plan, campus/location and housing facility selected. *Student services:* Campus employment opportunities, campus safety program, career counseling, child daycare facilities, exercise/wellness program, free psychological counseling, grant writing training, international student services, low-cost health insurance, multicultural affairs office, services for students with disabilities, teacher training, writing training. *Library facilities:* Wallace Memorial Library. *Online resources:* library catalog, web page, access to other libraries' catalogs. *Collection:* 452,355 titles, 23,325 serial subscriptions, 9,719 audiovisual materials.

Computer facilities: Computer purchase and lease plans are available. 2,500 computers available on campus for general student use. A campuswide network can be accessed from student residence rooms and from off campus. Online class registration, student account information are available. *Web address:* http://www.rit.edu/.

General Application Contact: Diane Ellison, Assistant Vice President, Graduate Enrollment Services, 585-475-2229, Fax: 585-475-7164, E-mail: gradinfo@rit.edu.

GRADUATE UNITS

Graduate Enrollment Services Students: 1,680 full-time (583 women), 1,194 part-time (407 women); includes 243 minority (81 Black or African American, non-Hispanic/Latino; 10 American Indian or Alaska Native, non-Hispanic/Latino; 80 Asian, non-Hispanic/Latino; 66 Hispanic/Latino; 1 Native Hawaiian or other Pacific Islander, non-Hispanic/Latino; 5 Two or more races, non-Hispanic/Latino), 1,065 international. Average age 30. 3,990 applicants, 53% accepted, 973 enrolled. Expenses: Contact institution. *Financial support:* Fellowships, research assistantships, teaching assistantships, career-related internships or fieldwork, Federal Work-Study, scholarships/grants, and unspecified assistantships available. Support available to part-time students. Financial award applicants required to submit FAFSA. In 2010, 883 master's, 15 doctorates, 42 other advanced degrees awarded. *Degree program information:* Part-time and evening/weekend programs available. Postbaccalaureate distance learning degree programs offered (no on-campus study). *Application deadline:* Applications are processed on a rolling basis. *Application fee:* $50. Electronic applications accepted. *Application Contact:* Diane Ellison, Assistant Vice President, Graduate Enrollment Services, 585-475-2229, Fax: 585-475-7164, E-mail: gradinfo@rit.edu. *Assistant Vice President, Graduate Enrollment Services,* Diane Ellison, 585-475-2229, Fax: 585-475-7164, E-mail: gradinfo@rit.edu.

B. Thomas Golisano College of Computing and Information Sciences Students: 376 full-time (67 women), 259 part-time (50 women); includes 13 Black or African American, non-Hispanic/Latino; 3 American Indian or Alaska Native, non-Hispanic/Latino; 17 Asian, non-Hispanic/Latino; 16 Hispanic/Latino, 336 international. Average age 28. 825 applicants, 64% accepted, 203 enrolled. Expenses: Contact institution. *Financial support:* In 2010–11, 458 students received support; research assistantships with partial tuition reimbursements available, teaching assistantships with partial tuition reimbursements available, career-related internships or fieldwork, scholarships/grants, health care benefits, and unspecified assistantships available. Support available to part-time students. Financial award applicants required to submit FAFSA. In 2010, 160 master's, 11 other advanced degrees awarded. *Degree program information:* Part-time and evening/weekend programs available. Postbaccalaureate distance learning degree programs offered (no on-campus study). Offers computer science (MS); computing and information sciences (MS, PhD, AC); database administration (AC); game design and development (MS); human computer interaction (MS); information assurance (AC); information technology (MS, AC); interactive multimedia development (AC); medical informatics (MS); network planning and design (AC); networking and systems administration (MS, AC); security and information assurance (MS); software development and management (MS); software engineering (MS). *Application deadline:* For fall admission, 2/1 priority date for domestic and international students; for winter admission, 11/1 for domestic and international students; for spring admission, 2/1 for domestic and international students. Applications are processed on a rolling basis. Electronic applications accepted. *Application Contact:* Diane Ellison, Assistant Vice President, Graduate Enrollment Services, 585-475-2229, Fax: 585-475-7164, E-mail: gradinfo@rit.edu. *Dean,* Andrew Sears, 585-475-4786, Fax: 585-475-4775.

Center for Multidisciplinary Studies Students: 43 full-time (18 women), 139 part-time (79 women); includes 13 Black or African American, non-Hispanic/Latino; 2 Asian, non-Hispanic/Latino; 6 Hispanic/Latino, 19 international. Average age 35. 116 applicants, 42% accepted, 44 enrolled. Expenses: Contact institution. *Financial support:* In 2010–11, 48 students received support. Career-related internships or fieldwork and scholarships/grants available. Support available to part-time students. Financial award application deadline: 2/15; financial award applicants required to submit FAFSA. In 2010, 28 master's, 20 other advanced degrees awarded. *Degree program information:* Part-time and evening/weekend programs available. Postbaccalaureate distance learning degree programs offered (no on-campus study). Offers multidisciplinary studies (MS, AC); professional studies (MS); technical information design (AC). *Application deadline:* For fall admission, 2/15 priority date for domestic and international students; for winter admission, 11/1 for domestic and international students; for spring admission, 2/1 for domestic and international students. Applications are processed on a rolling basis. *Application Contact:* Diane Ellison, Assistant Vice President, Graduate Enrollment Services, 585-475-2229, Fax: 585-475-7164, E-mail: gradinfo@rit.edu. *Director,* Dr. James Myers, 585-475-2234, Fax: 585-475-6292, E-mail: cms@rit.edu.

College of Applied Science and Technology Students: 165 full-time (71 women), 215 part-time (89 women); includes 20 Black or African American, non-Hispanic/Latino; 2 American Indian or Alaska Native, non-Hispanic/Latino; 8 Asian, non-Hispanic/Latino; 8 Hispanic/Latino; 1 Two or more races, non-Hispanic/Latino, 132 international. Average age 33. 387 applicants, 58% accepted, 115 enrolled. Expenses: Contact institution. *Financial support:* In 2010–11, 266 students received support; research assistantships with partial tuition reimbursements available, teaching assistantships with partial tuition reimbursements available, career-related internships or fieldwork, scholarships/grants, and unspecified assistantships available. Support available to part-time students. Financial award applicants required to submit FAFSA. In 2010, 125 master's, 2 other advanced degrees awarded. *Degree program information:* Part-time and evening/weekend programs available. Postbaccalaureate distance learning degree programs offered (no on-campus study). Offers applied science and technology (MS, AC); civil engineering technology, environmental management and safety (MS); elements of health care leadership (AC); facility management (MS); health information resources (AC); health systems administration (MS, AC); health systems administration executive leader (MS); health systems-finance (AC); hospitality-tourism management (MS); human resources development (MS); manufacturing and mechanical engineering technology/packaging science (MS); manufacturing and mechanical systems integration (MS); service leadership and innovation (MS); telecommunications engineering technology (MS). *Application deadline:* For fall admission, 2/15 priority date for domestic and international students; for winter admission, 11/1 priority date for domestic students, 10/1 priority date for international students; for spring admission, 2/1 priority date for domestic students, 1/1 priority date for international students. Applications are processed on a rolling basis. Electronic applications accepted. *Application Contact:* Diane Ellison, Assistant Vice President, Graduate Enrollment Services, 585-475-2229, Fax: 585-475-7164, E-mail: gradinfo@rit.edu. *Dean,* Dr. H. Fred Walker, 585-475-6349, Fax: 585-475-7080, E-mail: cast@rit.edu.

College of Imaging Arts and Sciences Students: 254 full-time (134 women), 80 part-time (45 women); includes 34 minority (6 Black or African American, non-Hispanic/Latino; 3 American Indian or Alaska Native, non-Hispanic/Latino; 13 Asian, non-Hispanic/Latino; 9 Hispanic/Latino; 1 Native Hawaiian or other Pacific Islander, non-Hispanic/Latino; 2 Two or more races, non-Hispanic/Latino), 145 international. Average age 29. 619 applicants, 42% accepted, 129 enrolled. Expenses: Contact institution. *Financial support:* In 2010–11, 199 students received support; fellowships with partial tuition reimbursements available, research assistantships with partial tuition reimbursements available, teaching assistantships with partial tuition reimbursements available, career-related internships or fieldwork, institutionally sponsored loans, scholarships/grants, and unspecified assistantships available. Support available to part-time students. Financial award application deadline: 8/30; financial award applicants required to submit FAFSA. In 2010, 85 master's awarded. *Degree program information:* Part-time programs available. Offers ceramics (MFA); computer graphics design (MFA); fine arts (MFA, MST); fine arts studio (MST); glass (MFA); graphic design (MFA); imaging arts (MFA); imaging arts and sciences (MFA, MS, MST); industrial design (MFA); medical illustration (MFA); metal crafts and jewelry (MFA); painting (MFA); print media (MS); printmaking (MFA); visual art (MST); woodworking and furniture design (MFA). *Application deadline:* For fall admission, 2/15 priority date for domestic and international students. Applications are processed on a rolling basis. *Application fee:* $50. Electronic applications accepted. *Application Contact:* Diane Ellison, Assistant Vice President, Graduate Enrollment Services, 585-475-2229, Fax: 585-475-7164, E-mail: gradinfo@rit.edu. *Interim Dean,* Frank Cost, 585-475-5436, E-mail: frank.cost@rit.edu.

College of Liberal Arts Students: 79 full-time (56 women), 42 part-time (33 women); includes 5 Black or African American, non-Hispanic/Latino; 3 Asian, non-Hispanic/Latino; 1 Hispanic/Latino; 2 Two or more races, non-Hispanic/Latino, 10 international. Average age 28. 132 applicants, 61% accepted, 47 enrolled. Expenses: Contact institution. *Financial support:* In 2010–11, 71 students received support; research assistantships with partial tuition reimbursements available, teaching assistantships with partial tuition reimbursements available, career-related internships or fieldwork, scholarships/grants, and unspecified assistantships available. Support available to part-time students. Financial award applicants required to submit FAFSA. In 2010, 30 master's awarded. *Degree program information:* Part-time programs available. Offers communication and media technologies (MS); criminal justice (MS); liberal arts (MS); psychology (MS); science, technology and public policy (MS). *Application deadline:* For fall admission, 2/1 priority date for domestic and international students; for winter admission, 11/1 for domestic and international students; for spring admission, 2/1 for domestic and international students. Applications are processed on a rolling basis. Electronic applications accepted. *Application Contact:* Diane Ellison, Assistant Vice President, Graduate Enrollment Services, 585-475-2229, Fax: 585-475-7164, E-mail: gradinfo@rit.edu. *Dean,* Dr. James Winebrake, 585-475-2929, Fax: 585-475-7120, E-mail: libarts@rit.edu.

College of Science, Health Sciences and Sustainability Students: 150 full-time (50 women), 78 part-time (29 women); includes 2 Black or African American, non-Hispanic/Latino; 4 Asian, non-Hispanic/Latino; 5 Hispanic/Latino, 94 international. Average age 29. 309 applicants, 49% accepted, 82 enrolled. Expenses: Contact institution. *Financial support:* In 2010–11, 149 students received support; fellowships with full and partial tuition reimbursements available, research assistantships with full and partial tuition reimbursements available, teaching assistantships with full and partial tuition reimbursements available, career-related internships or fieldwork, scholarships/grants, and unspecified assistantships available. Support available to part-time students. Financial award applicants required to submit FAFSA. In 2010, 36 master's, 12 doctorates awarded. *Degree program information:* Part-time and evening/weekend programs available. Postbaccalaureate distance learning degree programs offered (no on-campus study). Offers astrophysical sciences and technology (MS, PhD); bioinformatics (MS); chemistry (MS); clinical chemistry (MS); color science (MS, PhD); environmental science (MS); imaging science (MS, PhD); industrial and applied mathematics (MS); materials science and engineering (MS); science, health sciences and sustainability (MS, PhD). *Application deadline:* For fall admission, 2/15 priority date for domestic and international students. Applications are processed on a rolling basis. *Application fee:* $50. Electronic applications accepted. *Application Contact:* Diane Ellison, Assistant Vice President, Graduate Enrollment Services, 585-475-2229, Fax: 585-475-7164, E-mail: gradinfo@rit.edu. *Dean,* Dr. Sophia Maggelakis, 585-475-5127, E-mail: sxmsma@rit.edu.

E. Philip Saunders College of Business Students: 239 full-time (78 women), 107 part-time (37 women); includes 32 minority (14 Black or African American, non-Hispanic/Latino; 1 American Indian or Alaska Native, non-Hispanic/Latino; 11 Asian, non-Hispanic/Latino; 6 Hispanic/Latino), 101 international. Average age 31. 622 applicants, 46% accepted, 137

Rochester Institute of Technology (continued)

enrolled. Expenses: Contact institution. *Financial support:* In 2010–11, 198 students received support; research assistantships with partial tuition reimbursements available, teaching assistantships with partial tuition reimbursements available, career-related internships or fieldwork, scholarships/grants, and unspecified assistantships available. Support available to part-time students. Financial award applicants required to submit FAFSA. In 2010, 165 master's awarded. *Degree program information:* Part-time and evening/weekend programs available. Postbaccalaureate distance learning degree programs offered (minimal on-campus study). Offers accounting (MBA); business (Exec MBA, MBA, MS); business administration (MBA); executive business administration (Exec MBA); finance (MS); innovation management (MS); management (MS). *Application deadline:* For fall admission, 2/15 priority date for domestic and international students; for winter admission, 11/1 priority date for domestic students, 10/1 priority date for international students; for spring admission, 2/1 priority date for domestic students, 1/1 priority date for international students. Applications are processed on a rolling basis. *Application fee:* $50. *Application Contact:* Diane Ellison, Assistant Vice President, 585-475-2229, Fax: 585-475-7164, E-mail: gradinfo@rit.edu. *Dean*, Dr. Ashok Rao, 585-475-7181, Fax: 585-475-7055, E-mail: arao@saunders.rit.edu.

Golisano Institute for Sustainability Students: 11 full-time (7 women), 1 part-time (0 women); includes 1 Black or African American, non-Hispanic/Latino; 1 Hispanic/Latino, 5 international. Average age 31. 45 applicants, 24% accepted, 6 enrolled. Expenses: Contact institution. *Financial support:* In 2010–11, 12 students received support. Offers architecture (M Arch); sustainability (M Arch, PhD). *Application deadline:* For fall admission, 1/15 priority date for domestic and international students. *Application fee:* $50. *Application Contact:* Diane Ellison, Assistant Vice President, Graduate Enrollment Services, 585-475-2229, Fax: 585-475-7164, E-mail: gradinfo@rit.edu. *Assistant Provost and Director*, Dr. Nabil Nasr, 585-475-2602, E-mail: info@sustainability.rit.edu.

Kate Gleason College of Engineering Students: 306 full-time (59 women), 264 part-time (37 women); includes 5 Black or African American, non-Hispanic/Latino; 1 American Indian or Alaska Native, non-Hispanic/Latino; 20 Asian, non-Hispanic/Latino; 12 Hispanic/Latino, 223 international. Average age 28. 887 applicants, 56% accepted, 181 enrolled. Expenses: Contact institution. *Financial support:* In 2010–11, 346 students received support; fellowships with partial tuition reimbursements available, research assistantships with partial tuition reimbursements available, teaching assistantships with partial tuition reimbursements available, career-related internships or fieldwork, institutionally sponsored loans, scholarships/grants, tuition waivers (partial), and unspecified assistantships available. Support available to part-time students. Financial award applicants required to submit FAFSA. In 2010, 236 master's, 3 doctorates, 1 other advanced degree awarded. *Degree program information:* Part-time and evening/weekend programs available. Postbaccalaureate distance learning degree programs offered (no on-campus study). Offers applied statistics (MS); computer engineering (MS); electrical engineering (MSEE); engineering (ME, MS, MSEE, PhD, AC); engineering management (ME); industrial engineering (ME, MS); manufacturing engineering (ME, MS); manufacturing leadership (MS); mechanical engineering (ME, MS); microelectronic engineering (MS); microelectronic manufacturing engineering (ME); microsystems engineering (PhD); product development (MS); statistical quality (AC); systems engineering (ME). *Application deadline:* For fall admission, 2/15 priority date for domestic and international students. Applications are processed on a rolling basis. *Application fee:* $50. Electronic applications accepted. *Application Contact:* Diane Ellison, Assistant Vice President, Graduate Enrollment Services, 585-475-2229, Fax: 585-475-7164, E-mail: gradinfo@rit.edu. *Dean*, Dr. Harvey Palmer, 585-475-2145, Fax: 585-475-6879, E-mail: coe@rit.edu.

National Technical Institute for the Deaf Students: 57 full-time (43 women), 9 part-time (8 women); includes 2 Black or African American, non-Hispanic/Latino; 2 Asian, non-Hispanic/Latino; 2 Hispanic/Latino. Average age 28. 48 applicants, 69% accepted, 29 enrolled. Expenses: Contact institution. *Financial support:* In 2010–11, 46 students received support; fellowships with partial tuition reimbursements available, research assistantships with partial tuition reimbursements available, teaching assistantships with partial tuition reimbursements available, career-related internships or fieldwork, scholarships/grants, and unspecified assistantships available. Support available to part-time students. Financial award applicants required to submit FAFSA. In 2010, 18 master's awarded. Offers deaf studies (MS); research and teacher education (MS). *Application deadline:* For fall admission, 2/15 priority date for domestic and international students. Applications are processed on a rolling basis. *Application fee:* $50. *Application Contact:* Diane Ellison, Assistant Vice President, Graduate Enrollment Services, 585-475-2229, Fax: 585-475-7164, E-mail: gradinfo@rit.edu. *President*, Dr. Gerard J. Buckley, 585-475-6400, Fax: 585-475-5978, E-mail: gbuckley@ntid.rit.edu.

THE ROCKEFELLER UNIVERSITY, New York, NY 10021-6399

General Information Independent, coed, graduate-only institution. CGS member. *Enrollment by degree level:* 13 master's, 180 doctoral. *Graduate faculty:* 97 full-time (21 women), 152 part-time/adjunct (39 women). *Graduate housing:* Rooms and/or apartments guaranteed to single and married students. Typical cost: $8060 per year for single students. Housing application deadline: 6/1. *Student services:* Campus safety program, career counseling, child daycare facilities, exercise/wellness program, free psychological counseling, grant writing training, low-cost health insurance. *Library facilities:* Rita and Frits Markus Library and Scientific Information Center. *Online resources:* library catalog, web page, access to other libraries' catalogs. *Collection:* 40,306 titles, 4,230 serial subscriptions, 145 audiovisual materials.

Computer facilities: 15 computers available on campus for general student use. A campuswide network can be accessed from student residence rooms and from off campus. Online class registration is available. *Web address:* http://www.rockefeller.edu/.

General Application Contact: Dr. Sidney Strickland, Dean of Graduate Studies, 212-327-8086, Fax: 212-327-8505, E-mail: phd@rockefeller.edu.

GRADUATE UNITS

Graduate Program in Biomedical Sciences Students: 193 full-time (90 women); includes 27 minority (8 Black or African American, non-Hispanic/Latino; 15 Asian, non-Hispanic/Latino; 4 Hispanic/Latino), 78 international. Average age 28. 732 applicants, 10% accepted, 30 enrolled. *Faculty:* 97 full-time (21 women), 152 part-time/adjunct (39 women). Expenses: Contact institution. *Financial support:* In 2010–11, 193 students received support, including 193 fellowships with full tuition reimbursements available (averaging $31,600 per year); institutionally sponsored loans, scholarships/grants, traineeships, and health care benefits also available. In 2010, 10 master's, 37 doctorates awarded. Offers biomedical sciences (MA, PhD). *Application deadline:* For winter admission, 12/5 for domestic and international students. *Application fee:* $80. Electronic applications accepted. *Application Contact:* Kristen Cullen, Graduate Admissions Administrator and Registrar, 212-327-8088, Fax: 212-327-8505, E-mail: cullenk@rockefeller.edu. *Dean of Graduate Studies*, Dr. Sidney Strickland, 212-327-8086, Fax: 212-327-8505, E-mail: phd@rockefeller.edu.

ROCKFORD COLLEGE, Rockford, IL 61108-2393

General Information Independent, coed, comprehensive institution. *Enrollment:* 1,424 graduate, professional, and undergraduate students; 53 full-time matriculated graduate/professional students (29 women), 189 part-time matriculated graduate/professional students (121 women). *Enrollment by degree level:* 242 master's. *Graduate faculty:* 23 full-time (6 women), 35 part-time/adjunct (17 women). *Tuition:* Full-time $16,280; part-time $675 per hour. *Required fees:* $40 per semester. *Student services:* Campus employment opportunities, campus safety program, career counseling, free psychological counseling, grant writing training, international student services, low-cost health insurance, multicultural affairs office, services for students with disabilities, teacher training, writing training. *Library facilities:* Howard Colman Library. *Online resources:* library catalog, web page. *Collection:* 140,000 titles, 831 serial subscriptions.

Computer facilities: 75 computers available on campus for general student use. A campuswide network can be accessed from student residence rooms and from off campus. Online class registration, online bill payment are available. *Web address:* http://www.rockford.edu/.

General Application Contact: Michele Mehren, Office Manager for Graduate Studies, 815-226-4041, Fax: 815-394-3706, E-mail: mmehren@rockford.edu.

GRADUATE UNITS

Graduate Studies Students: 53 full-time (29 women), 189 part-time (121 women); includes 4 Black or African American, non-Hispanic/Latino; 6 Asian, non-Hispanic/Latino; 12 Hispanic/Latino; 3 Two or more races, non-Hispanic/Latino, 2 international. Average age 33. *Faculty:* 23 full-time (6 women), 35 part-time/adjunct (17 women). Expenses: Contact institution. *Financial support:* Scholarships/grants and unspecified assistantships available. Support available to part-time students. Financial award application deadline: 3/1; financial award applicants required to submit FAFSA. In 2010, 120 master's awarded. *Degree program information:* Part-time and evening/weekend programs available. Offers business administration (MBA); education (MAT, Certificate); elementary education (MAT); instructional strategies (MAT); reading (MAT); secondary education (MAT); special education (MAT, Certificate). *Application deadline:* Applications are processed on a rolling basis. *Application fee:* $50. Electronic applications accepted. *Application Contact:* Michele Mehren, Office Manager for Graduate Studies, 815-226-4041, Fax: 815-394-3706, E-mail: mmehren@rockford.edu. *MAT Director*, Dr. Michelle M. McReynolds, 815-226-3390, Fax: 815-394-3706, E-mail: mmcreynolds@rockford.edu.

ROCKHURST UNIVERSITY, Kansas City, MO 64110-2561

General Information Independent-religious, coed, comprehensive institution. CGS member. *Enrollment:* 2,895 graduate, professional, and undergraduate students; 306 full-time matriculated graduate/professional students (149 women), 482 part-time matriculated graduate/professional students (191 women). *Enrollment by degree level:* 651 master's, 137 doctoral. *Graduate faculty:* 55 full-time (30 women), 36 part-time/adjunct (22 women). Tuition and fees vary according to program. *Graduate housing:* Room and/or apartments available on a first-come, first-served basis to single students; on-campus housing not available to married students. Typical cost: $4590 per year ($7490 including board). Room and board charges vary according to board plan and housing facility selected. Housing application deadline: 5/6. *Student services:* Campus employment opportunities, campus safety program, career counseling, free psychological counseling, international student services, multicultural affairs office, services for students with disabilities, teacher training. *Library facilities:* Greenlease Library. *Online resources:* library catalog, access to other libraries' catalogs. *Collection:* 202,352 titles, 34,894 serial subscriptions, 1,368 audiovisual materials.

Computer facilities: Computer purchase and lease plans are available. 1,200 computers available on campus for general student use. A campuswide network can be accessed from student residence rooms and from off campus. Online class registration is available. *Web address:* http://www.rockhurst.edu/.

General Application Contact: Cheryl Hooper, Director of Graduate Recruitment, 816-501-4097, Fax: 816-501-4241, E-mail: graduate.admission@rockhurst.edu.

GRADUATE UNITS

Helzberg School of Management Students: 116 full-time (35 women), 111 part-time (32 women); includes 25 minority (10 Black or African American, non-Hispanic/Latino; 10 Asian, non-Hispanic/Latino; 5 Hispanic/Latino), 3 international. Average age 30. 104 applicants, 51% accepted, 40 enrolled. *Faculty:* 24 full-time (5 women), 9 part-time/adjunct (4 women). Expenses: Contact institution. *Financial support:* Career-related internships or fieldwork available. Support available to part-time students. Financial award application deadline: 4/1; financial award applicants required to submit FAFSA. In 2010, 197 master's awarded. *Degree program information:* Part-time and evening/weekend programs available. Offers management (MBA). *Application deadline:* For fall admission, 7/25 priority date for domestic students; for spring admission, 12/15 priority date for domestic students. Applications are processed on a rolling basis. *Application fee:* $0. Electronic applications accepted. *Application Contact:* Michele Haggerty, Director of MBA Advising, 816-501-4823, E-mail: michele.haggerty@rockhurst.edu. *Dean*, Dr. James Daley, 816-501-4201, Fax: 816-501-4650, E-mail: james.daley@rockhurst.edu.

School of Graduate and Professional Studies Students: 332 full-time (256 women), 229 part-time (159 women); includes 63 minority (20 Black or African American, non-Hispanic/Latino; 2 American Indian or Alaska Native, non-Hispanic/Latino; 10 Asian, non-Hispanic/Latino; 25 Hispanic/Latino; 2 Native Hawaiian or other Pacific Islander, non-Hispanic/Latino; 4 Two or more races, non-Hispanic/Latino). Average age 28. 373 applicants, 91% accepted, 171 enrolled. *Faculty:* 31 full-time (25 women), 27 part-time/adjunct (18 women). Expenses: Contact institution. *Financial support:* In 2010–11, 10 research assistantships, 20 teaching assistantships were awarded; career-related internships or fieldwork, institutionally sponsored loans, and unspecified assistantships also available. Financial award applicants required to submit FAFSA. In 2010, 145 master's, 38 doctorates awarded. *Degree program information:* Part-time and evening/weekend programs available. Offers arts and sciences (M Ed, MOT, MS, DPT); communication sciences and disorders (MS); education (M Ed); occupational therapy (MOT); physical therapy (DPT). *Application deadline:* Applications are processed on a rolling basis. *Application fee:* $25. Electronic applications accepted. *Application Contact:* Cheryl Hooper, Director of Graduate Admission, 816-501-4097, Fax: 816-501-4241, E-mail: cheryl.hooper@rockhurst.edu. *Dean*, Dr. Jeffrey Breese, 816-501-4767, E-mail: donna.calvert@rockhurst.edu.

ROCKY MOUNTAIN COLLEGE, Billings, MT 59102-1796

General Information Independent-religious, coed, comprehensive institution. *Enrollment:* 994 graduate, professional, and undergraduate students; 69 full-time matriculated graduate/professional students (43 women). *Enrollment by degree level:* 69 master's. *Graduate faculty:* 10 full-time (5 women), 13 part-time/adjunct (5 women). *Tuition:* Part-time $860 per credit. *Required fees:* $94 per semester. Part-time tuition and fees vary according to course load and program. *Graduate housing:* Rooms and/or apartments available on a first-come, first-served basis to single and married students. Typical cost: $4120 per year ($7630 including board) for single students; $4120 per year ($7630 including board) for married students. *Student services:* Campus employment opportunities, campus safety program, career counseling, child daycare facilities, free psychological counseling, international student services, services for students with disabilities, teacher training. *Library facilities:* Paul M. Adams Memorial Library. *Online resources:* library catalog, web page, access to other libraries' catalogs. *Collection:* 102,028 titles, 398 serial subscriptions, 1,496 audiovisual materials.

Computer facilities: 129 computers available on campus for general student use. A campuswide network can be accessed from student residence rooms and from off campus. Online class registration is available. *Web address:* http://www.rocky.edu/.

General Application Contact: Kelly Edwards, Director of Admissions, 406-657-1026, Fax: 406-657-1189, E-mail: admissions@rocky.edu.

GRADUATE UNITS

Program in Accountancy Students: 8 full-time (6 women), 1 international. *Faculty:* 2 full-time (1 woman), 1 part-time/adjunct (0 women). Expenses: Contact institution. *Financial support:* Federal Work-Study and scholarships/grants available. Financial award applicants required to submit FAFSA. In 2010, 6 master's awarded. *Degree program information:* Part-time programs available. Offers accountancy (M Acc). *Application deadline:* Applications are processed on a rolling basis. *Application fee:* $35 ($40 for international students). Electronic applications accepted. *Application Contact:* Kelly Edwards, Director of Admissions, 406-657-1026, Fax: 406-657-1189, E-mail: admissions@rocky.edu. *Academic Vice President*, Anthony Piltz, 406-657-1020, Fax: 406-259-9751, E-mail: piltza@rocky.edu.

Program in Educational Leadership Students: 11 full-time (4 women). Average age 35. 89 applicants, 25% accepted, 11 enrolled. *Faculty:* 10 full-time (5 women), 1 (woman) part-time/adjunct. Expenses: Contact institution. *Financial support:* Applicants required to submit FAFSA. In 2010, 15 master's awarded. Offers educational leadership (M Ed). *Application deadline:* Applications are processed on a rolling basis. Electronic applications accepted. *Application Contact:* Kelly Edwards, Director of Admissions, 406-657-1026, Fax: 406-657-1189, E-mail: admissions@rocky.edu. *Director*, Dr. Stevie Schmitz, 406-238-7366, E-mail: schmitzs@rocky.edu.

Program in Physician Assistant Studies Students: 51 full-time (34 women). Average age 27. 306 applicants, 11% accepted, 30 enrolled. *Faculty:* 7 full-time (3 women), 2 part-time/adjunct (0 women). Expenses: Contact institution. *Financial support:* Applicants required to submit FAFSA. In 2010, 26 master's awarded. Offers physician assistant studies (MPAS). *Application deadline:* For fall admission, 10/1 for domestic and international students. Applications are processed on a rolling basis. *Application fee:* $35 ($40 for international students). Electronic applications accepted. *Application Contact:* Kelly Edwards, Director of Admissions, 406-657-1026, Fax: 406-657-1189, E-mail: admissions@rocky.edu. *Program Director,* Bob Wilmouth, 406-657-1190, Fax: 406-657-1194, E-mail: bob.wilmouth@rocky.edu.

ROCKY MOUNTAIN UNIVERSITY OF HEALTH PROFESSIONS, Provo, UT 84606

General Information Proprietary, coed, graduate-only institution. *Enrollment by degree level:* 353 doctoral. *Graduate faculty:* 10 full-time (4 women), 120 part-time/adjunct (48 women). *Tuition:* Full-time $15,600; part-time $650 per credit. *Required fees:* $50 per course. *Student services:* Campus safety program. *Library facilities:* Rocky Mountain University Learning Center. *Research affiliation:* Aegis Corporation.

Computer facilities: 20 computers available on campus for general student use. A campuswide network can be accessed from off campus. *Web address:* http://www.rmuohp.edu/.

General Application Contact: Bryce Greenberg, Director of Admissions, 801-734-6832, Fax: 801-734-6833, E-mail: bgreenberg@rmuohp.edu.

GRADUATE UNITS

Doctor of Nursing Practice Program Students: 60 full-time (52 women); includes 5 Black or African American, non-Hispanic/Latino; 2 Asian, non-Hispanic/Latino; 3 Hispanic/Latino; 1 Two or more races, non-Hispanic/Latino. Average age 52. Expenses: Contact institution. Offers nursing practice (DNP). *Application Contact:* Bryce Greenberg, Director of Admissions, 801-734-6832, Fax: 801-734-6833, E-mail: bgreenberg@rmuohp.edu. *Program Director,* Dr. Marie-Eileen Onieal, 801-375-5125, E-mail: monieal@rmuohp.edu.

Doctor of Science Program in Clinical Electrophysiology Students: 14 part-time (1 woman); includes 1 Black or African American, non-Hispanic/Latino. Average age 43. Expenses: Contact institution. Offers clinical electrophysiology (D Sc). *Application deadline:* For fall admission, 7/26 for domestic students. *Application Contact:* Bryce Greenberg, Director of Admissions, 801-734-6832, Fax: 801-734-6833, E-mail: bgreenberg@rmuohp.edu. *Co-Director,* Dr. Lisa DePasquale, 801-375-5125, E-mail: ldepasquale@rmuohp.edu.

MSN Program in Nursing Expenses: Contact institution. Offers nursing (MSN). *Application Contact:* Dr. Sandra L. Pennington, Program Director, 801-375-5125. *Program Director,* Dr. Sandra L. Pennington, 801-375-5125.

PhD Program in Athletic Training Students: 14 full-time (8 women), 18 part-time (7 women); includes 2 Black or African American, non-Hispanic/Latino; 4 Hispanic/Latino. Average age 39. Expenses: Contact institution. Offers athletic training (PhD). *Application deadline:* For fall admission, 3/28 for domestic students. *Application Contact:* Dr. Malissa Martin, Program Director, 801-375-5125, E-mail: mmartin@rmuohp.edu. *Program Director,* Dr. Malissa Martin, 801-375-5125, E-mail: mmartin@rmuohp.edu.

PhD Program in Health Promotion and Wellness Students: 7 full-time (4 women), 10 part-time (8 women); includes 3 Black or African American, non-Hispanic/Latino. Average age 46. Expenses: Contact institution. Offers health promotion and wellness (PhD). *Application deadline:* For fall admission, 3/28 for domestic students. *Application Contact:* Bryce Greenberg, Director of Admissions, 801-734-6832, Fax: 801-734-6833, E-mail: bgreenberg@rmuohp.edu. *Co-Director,* Dr. Andrea White Gorman, 801-375-5125, E-mail: agorman@rmuohp.edu.

PhD Program in Nursing Students: 4 full-time (all women), 12 part-time (11 women). Average age 54. Expenses: Contact institution. Offers nursing (PhD). *Application deadline:* For fall admission, 7/26 for domestic students. *Application Contact:* Bryce Greenberg, Director of Admissions, 801-734-6832, Fax: 801-734-6833, E-mail: bgreenberg@rmuohp.edu. *Co-Director,* Dr. Susan S. Gardner, 801-375-5125, E-mail: sgardner@rmuohp.edu.

Program in Occupational Therapy Students: 62 full-time (54 women); includes 11 Black or African American, non-Hispanic/Latino; 3 Asian, non-Hispanic/Latino; 2 Hispanic/Latino; 2 Two or more races, non-Hispanic/Latino. Expenses: Contact institution. Offers occupational therapy (OTD). *Application deadline:* For fall admission, 3/28 for domestic students. *Application Contact:* Bryce Greenberg, Director of Admissions, 801-734-6832, Fax: 801-734-6833, E-mail: bgreenberg@rmuohp.edu. *Program Director,* Dr. Elysa Roberts, 801-375-5125, E-mail: eroberts@rmuohp.edu.

Program in Orthopaedic and Sports Science Students: 8 full-time (3 women), 14 part-time (5 women); includes 1 Native Hawaiian or other Pacific Islander, non-Hispanic/Latino. Average age 42. Expenses: Contact institution. Offers orthopaedic and sports science (PhD). *Application deadline:* For fall admission, 3/28 for domestic students. *Application Contact:* Bryce Greenberg, Director of Admissions, 801-734-6832, Fax: 801-734-6833, E-mail: bgreenberg@rmuohp.edu. *Program Director,* Dr. Lori Thein Brody, 801-375-5125, E-mail: ltbrody@rmuohp.edu.

Program in Pediatric Science Students: 6 full-time (all women), 14 part-time (all women); includes 1 Black or African American, non-Hispanic/Latino; 2 Asian, non-Hispanic/Latino; 1 Hispanic/Latino. Average age 51. Expenses: Contact institution. Offers pediatric science (PhD). *Application Contact:* Bryce Greenberg, Director of Admissions, 801-734-6832, Fax: 801-734-6833, E-mail: bgreenberg@rmuohp.edu. *Program Director,* Dr. Jane K. Sweeney, 801-375-5125, E-mail: jsweeney@rmuohp.edu.

Programs in Physical Therapy Students: 106 full-time (54 women); includes 4 Black or African American, non-Hispanic/Latino; 1 American Indian or Alaska Native, non-Hispanic/Latino; 2 Asian, non-Hispanic/Latino; 6 Hispanic/Latino; 3 Two or more races, non-Hispanic/Latino. Average age 39. Expenses: Contact institution. Offers physical therapy (DPT, TDPT). *Application deadline:* For fall admission, 2/1 priority date for domestic students. Applications are processed on a rolling basis. *Application Contact:* Bryce Greenberg, Director of Admissions, 801-734-6832, Fax: 801-734-6833, E-mail: bgreenberg@rmuohp.edu. *Director,* Dr. J. Wesley McWhorter, 801-375-5125, E-mail: wmcwhorter@rmuohp.edu.

ROGER WILLIAMS UNIVERSITY, Bristol, RI 02809

General Information Independent, coed, comprehensive institution. *Graduate housing:* Room and/or apartments available on a first-come, first-served basis to single students; on-campus housing not available to married students.

GRADUATE UNITS

Feinstein College of Arts and Sciences *Degree program information:* Part-time and evening/weekend programs available. Postbaccalaureate distance learning degree programs offered (minimal on-campus study). Offers arts and sciences (MA, MPA); forensic psychology (MA); public administration (MPA). Electronic applications accepted.

School of Architecture, Art and Historic Preservation Offers architecture (M Arch). Students often begin 5-6 year dual degree sequence as undergraduates. Electronic applications accepted.

School of Education *Degree program information:* Part-time and evening/weekend programs available. Offers education (MA, MAT); elementary education (MAT); literacy (MA). Electronic applications accepted.

School of Engineering, Computing and Construction Management Offers construction management (MSCM).

School of Justice Studies *Degree program information:* Part-time and evening/weekend programs available. Offers criminal justice (MS). Electronic applications accepted.

School of Law Offers law (JD). JD/MMA, JD/MLRHR offered jointly with University of Rhode Island; JD/MSCJ with School of Justice Studies. Electronic applications accepted.

ROLLINS COLLEGE, Winter Park, FL 32789-4499

General Information Independent, coed, comprehensive institution. *Enrollment:* 2,451 graduate, professional, and undergraduate students; 362 full-time matriculated graduate/professional students (165 women), 359 part-time matriculated graduate/professional students (224 women). *Enrollment by degree level:* 721 master's. *Graduate faculty:* 48 full-time (14 women), 20 part-time/adjunct (11 women). *Graduate housing:* Room and/or apartments available on a first-come, first-served basis to single students; on-campus housing not available to married students. *Student services:* Campus employment opportunities, campus safety program, career counseling, exercise/wellness program, free psychological counseling, international student services, low-cost health insurance, multicultural affairs office, services for students with disabilities. *Library facilities:* Olin Library. *Online resources:* library catalog, web page, access to other libraries' catalogs. *Collection:* 321,022 titles, 53,590 serial subscriptions, 7,194 audiovisual materials.

Computer facilities: Computer purchase and lease plans are available. 240 computers available on campus for general student use. A campuswide network can be accessed from student residence rooms and from off campus. Online class registration is available. *Web address:* http://www.rollins.edu/.

General Application Contact: Information Contact, 407-646-2000.

GRADUATE UNITS

Crummer Graduate School of Business Students: 303 full-time (117 women), 130 part-time (49 women); includes 111 minority (30 Black or African American, non-Hispanic/Latino; 1 American Indian or Alaska Native, non-Hispanic/Latino; 29 Asian, non-Hispanic/Latino; 50 Hispanic/Latino; 1 Two or more races, non-Hispanic/Latino), 29 international. Average age 32. 484 applicants, 42% accepted, 131 enrolled. *Faculty:* 22 full-time (3 women), 5 part-time/adjunct (3 women). Expenses: Contact institution. *Financial support:* In 2010–11, 112 students received support, including 95 fellowships, 56 research assistantships (averaging $2,400 per year); career-related internships or fieldwork, scholarships/grants, and unspecified assistantships also available. Support available to part-time students. Financial award applicants required to submit FAFSA. In 2010, 223 master's awarded. *Degree program information:* Part-time and evening/weekend programs available. Postbaccalaureate distance learning degree programs offered (minimal on-campus study). Offers entrepreneurship (MBA); finance (MBA); international business (MBA); management (MBA); marketing (MBA); operations and technology management (MBA). *Application deadline:* Applications are processed on a rolling basis. *Application fee:* $50. Electronic applications accepted. *Application Contact:* Linda Puritz, Student Admissions Office, 407-646-2405, Fax: 407-646-1550, E-mail: mbaadmissions@rollins.edu. *Dean,* Dr. Craig M. McAllaster, 407-646-2249, Fax: 407-646-1550, E-mail: cmcallaster@rollins.edu.

Hamilton Holt School Students: 59 full-time (48 women), 229 part-time (175 women); includes 69 minority (24 Black or African American, non-Hispanic/Latino; 7 Asian, non-Hispanic/Latino; 35 Hispanic/Latino; 3 Two or more races, non-Hispanic/Latino), 7 international. Average age 33. 231 applicants, 75% accepted, 119 enrolled. *Faculty:* 26 full-time (11 women), 15 part-time/adjunct (8 women). Expenses: Contact institution. *Financial support:* Career-related internships or fieldwork, scholarships/grants, and unspecified assistantships available. Support available to part-time students. Financial award applicants required to submit FAFSA. In 2010, 72 master's awarded. *Degree program information:* Part-time and evening/weekend programs available. Offers civic urbanism (M Pl); elementary education (M Ed, MAT); human resources (MA); liberal studies (MLS); mental health counseling (MA); secondary education (MAT). *Application fee:* $50. *Application Contact:* Graduate Program Admission, 407-646-2232, Fax: 407-646-1551. *Dean,* Dr. Debra K. Wellman, 407-646-2292, Fax: 407-646-1551, E-mail: dwellman@rollins.edu.

ROOSEVELT UNIVERSITY, Chicago, IL 60605

General Information Independent, coed, comprehensive institution. CGS member. *Graduate housing:* Room and/or apartments available on a first-come, first-served basis to single students; on-campus housing not available to married students. Housing application deadline: 7/1.

GRADUATE UNITS

Graduate Division *Degree program information:* Part-time and evening/weekend programs available. Electronic applications accepted.

Chicago College of Performing Arts *Degree program information:* Part-time and evening/weekend programs available. Offers directing and dramaturgy (MFA); music (MM); musical theatre (MFA); performing arts (MA, MFA, MM, Diploma); piano pedagogy (Diploma); theatre (MA, MFA); theatre-directing (MA); theatre-performance (MFA).

College of Arts and Sciences *Degree program information:* Part-time and evening/weekend programs available. Offers anthropology (MA); applied economics (MA); arts and sciences (MA, MFA, MPA, MS, MSC, MSIMC, MSJ, MST, PhD, Psy D, Certificate); biotechnology and chemical science (MS); clinical professional psychology (MA); clinical psychology (MA, Psy D); computer science (MSC); creative writing (MFA); economics (MA); English (MA); history (MA); industrial/organizational psychology (MA, PhD); integrated marketing communications (MSIMC); journalism (MSJ); mathematical sciences (MS); mathematics (MS); political science (MA); public administration (MPA); sociology (MA); Spanish (MA); telecommunications (MST); women's and gender studies (MA, Certificate).

College of Education *Degree program information:* Part-time and evening/weekend programs available. Offers counseling and human services (MA); early childhood education (MA); education (MA, Ed D); educational leadership (MA, Ed D); elementary education (MA); reading teacher education (MA); secondary education (MA); special education (MA); teacher leadership (MA).

College of Pharmacy Offers pharmacy (Pharm D).

College of Professional Studies *Degree program information:* Part-time and evening/weekend programs available. Offers hospitality management (MS); training and development (MA).

Walter E. Heller College of Business Administration *Degree program information:* Part-time and evening/weekend programs available. Offers accounting (MSA); business administration (MBA, MS, MSA, MSHRM, MSIB, MSIS, Certificate); commercial real estate development (Certificate); human resource management (MSHRM); information systems (MSIS); international business (MSIB); real estate (MBA, MS).

ROSALIND FRANKLIN UNIVERSITY OF MEDICINE AND SCIENCE, North Chicago, IL 60064-3095

General Information Independent, coed, graduate-only institution. *Graduate housing:* Rooms and/or apartments available on a first-come, first-served basis to single and married students. Housing application deadline: 3/13. *Research affiliation:* Argonne National Laboratory (medical physics), Veterans Administration Hospital (pulmonary medicine).

GRADUATE UNITS

The Chicago Medical School Offers medicine (MD).

College of Health Professions *Degree program information:* Part-time programs available. Postbaccalaureate distance learning degree programs offered (minimal on-campus study). Offers biomedical sciences (MS); clinical counseling (MS); clinical nutrition (MS); health professions (MS, D Sc, DPT, PhD, TDPT, Certificate); healthcare administration and management (MS, Certificate); interprofessional healthcare (D Sc, PhD); interprofessional studies (D Sc); medical radiation physics (MS); nurse anesthesia (MS); nutrition education (MS); pathologists' assistant (MS); physical therapy (MS, DPT, TDPT); physician assistant (MS); psychology (MS, PhD); women's healthcare studies (MS, Certificate).

The Dr. William M. Scholl College of Podiatric Medicine Offers podiatric medicine (DPM).

School of Graduate and Postdoctoral Studies—Interdisciplinary Graduate Program in Biomedical Sciences Offers biochemistry and molecular biology (MS, PhD); cell biology and anatomy (MS, PhD); cellular and molecular pharmacology (MS, PhD); microbiology and immunology (MS, PhD); neuroscience (PhD); physiology and biophysics (MS, PhD).

ROSE-HULMAN INSTITUTE OF TECHNOLOGY, Terre Haute, IN 47803-3999

General Information Independent, coed, primarily men, comprehensive institution. *Enrollment:* 1,980 graduate, professional, and undergraduate students; 59 full-time matriculated graduate/professional students (13 women), 46 part-time matriculated graduate/professional students (8 women). *Enrollment by degree level:* 105 master's. *Graduate faculty:* 88 full-time (20 women), 5 part-time/adjunct (2 women). *Tuition:* Full-time $35,595; part-time $1038 per credit hour. *Graduate housing:* On-campus housing not available. *Student services:* Campus employment opportunities, career counseling, exercise/wellness program, free psychological counseling, international student services, low-cost health insurance, services for students with disabilities. *Library facilities:* John A. Logan Library. *Online resources:* library catalog, web page, access to other libraries' catalogs. *Collection:* 49,908 titles, 68,663 serial subscriptions, 719 audiovisual materials.

Computer facilities: Computer purchase and lease plans are available. 45 computers available on campus for general student use. A campuswide network can be accessed from student residence rooms and from off campus. Online class registration is available. *Web address:* http://www.rose-hulman.edu/.

General Application Contact: Dr. Daniel J. Moore, Associate Dean of the Faculty, 812-877-8110, Fax: 812-877-8061, E-mail: daniel.j.moore@rose-hulman.edu.

GRADUATE UNITS

Faculty of Engineering and Applied Sciences Students: 59 full-time (13 women), 46 part-time (8 women); includes 4 minority (all Asian, non-Hispanic/Latino), 27 international. Average age 25. 77 applicants, 90% accepted, 42 enrolled. *Faculty:* 88 full-time (20 women), 5 part-time/adjunct (2 women). Expenses: Contact institution. *Financial support:* In 2010–11, 59 students received support; fellowships with full and partial tuition reimbursements available, research assistantships with full and partial tuition reimbursements available, institutionally sponsored loans, scholarships/grants, and tuition waivers (full and partial) available. In 2010, 56 master's awarded. *Degree program information:* Part-time and evening/weekend programs available. Postbaccalaureate distance learning degree programs offered (minimal on-campus study). Offers biomedical engineering (MS); chemical engineering (MS); civil engineering (MS); electrical and computer engineering (M Eng); electrical engineering (MS); engineering and applied sciences (M Eng, MS); engineering management (MS); environmental engineering (MS); mechanical engineering (MS); optical engineering (MS); software engineering (MS). *Application deadline:* For fall admission, 2/1 priority date for domestic students. Applications are processed on a rolling basis. *Application fee:* $0. *Application Contact:* Dr. Daniel J. Moore, Associate Dean of the Faculty, 812-877-8110, Fax: 812-877-8061, E-mail: daniel.j.moore@rose-hulman.edu. *Associate Dean of the Faculty*, Dr. Daniel J. Moore, 812-877-8110, Fax: 812-877-8061, E-mail: daniel.j.moore@rose-hulman.edu.

ROSEMAN UNIVERSITY OF HEALTH SCIENCES, Henderson, NV 89014

General Information Private, coed, graduate-only institution. *Enrollment by degree level:* 670 first professional, 11 master's, 29 other advanced degrees. *Graduate faculty:* 64 full-time (29 women), 39 part-time/adjunct (11 women). *Tuition:* Full-time $39,800. *Required fees:* $625. *Graduate housing:* On-campus housing not available. *Student services:* Campus safety program, international student services, low-cost health insurance, services for students with disabilities. *Library facilities:* Library and Learning Resources Center plus 1 other. *Online resources:* library catalog, web page. *Collection:* 14,356 titles, 384 serial subscriptions, 1,336 audiovisual materials.

Computer facilities: 31 computers available on campus for general student use. A campuswide network can be accessed. SharePoint LMS available. *Web address:* http://www.usn.edu/.

General Application Contact: Dr. Okeleke Nzeogwu, Director, MBA Program, 702-968-1659, E-mail: onzeogwu@usn.edu.

GRADUATE UNITS

College of Dental Medicine Students: 29 full-time (7 women); includes 2 Black or African American, non-Hispanic/Latino; 1 American Indian or Alaska Native, non-Hispanic/Latino; 12 Asian, non-Hispanic/Latino, 1 international. Average age 28. 105 applicants, 10% accepted, 10 enrolled. *Faculty:* 3 full-time (1 woman), 9 part-time/adjunct (0 women). Expenses: Contact institution. *Financial support:* In 2010–11, 1 student received support. Scholarships/grants, health care benefits, and stipends available. Financial award application deadline: 3/2; financial award applicants required to submit FAFSA. Offers advanced education in orthodontics and dentofacial orthopedics (MAIA). *Application deadline:* For fall admission, 9/15 for domestic students. Applications are processed on a rolling basis. *Application fee:* $50. *Application Contact:* Lore Loiacono, Administrative Assistant to the Program Director, 702-968-1682, Fax: 702-968-5277, E-mail: lloiacano@usn.edu. *Program Director, AEODO/MBA Residency Program/Associate Professor of Dental Medicine*, Dr. Jaleh Pourhamidi, 702-968-1652, Fax: 702-968-5277, E-mail: jpourhamidi@usn.edu.

College of Pharmacy Students: 670 full-time (361 women); includes 45 Black or African American, non-Hispanic/Latino; 4 American Indian or Alaska Native, non-Hispanic/Latino; 215 Asian, non-Hispanic/Latino; 18 Hispanic/Latino, 21 international. Average age 27. 730 applicants, 47% accepted, 249 enrolled. *Faculty:* 59 full-time (28 women), 11 part-time/adjunct (5 women). Expenses: Contact institution. *Financial support:* In 2010–11, 82 students received support. Scholarships/grants available. Financial award application deadline: 3/2; financial award applicants required to submit FAFSA. In 2010, 207 Pharm Ds awarded. Offers pharmacy (Pharm D). *Application deadline:* For fall admission, 12/1 for domestic students, 12/8 for international students. Applications are processed on a rolling basis. *Application fee:* $150. *Application Contact:* Dr. Michael DeYoung, Associate Dean for Admissions, 702-968-2006, Fax: 702-968-1644, E-mail: mdeyoung@usn.edu. *Dean*, Dr. Renee Coffman, 702-968-2017, Fax: 702-990-4435, E-mail: rcoffman@usn.edu.

MBA Program Students: 11 full-time (7 women); includes 1 American Indian or Alaska Native, non-Hispanic/Latino; 2 Asian, non-Hispanic/Latino; 1 Native Hawaiian or other Pacific Islander, non-Hispanic/Latino. Average age 38. 5 applicants, 0% accepted, 0 enrolled. *Faculty:* 3 full-time (0 women), 19 part-time/adjunct (6 women). Expenses: Contact institution. *Financial support:* Scholarships/grants available. Financial award application deadline: 3/1; financial award applicants required to submit FAFSA. In 2010, 5 master's awarded. *Degree program information:* Evening/weekend programs available. Offers business administration (MBA). *Application deadline:* Applications are processed on a rolling basis. *Application fee:* $100. *Application Contact:* Dr. Okeleke Nzeogwu, Program Director, 702-968-1659, Fax: 702-968-1685, E-mail: onzeogwu@usn.edu. *Program Director*, Dr. Okeleke Nzeogwu, 702-968-1659, Fax: 702-968-1685, E-mail: onzeogwu@usn.edu.

ROSEMONT COLLEGE, Rosemont, PA 19010-1699

General Information Independent-religious, coed, comprehensive institution. *Enrollment:* 863 graduate, professional, and undergraduate students; 97 full-time matriculated graduate/professional students (85 women), 265 part-time matriculated graduate/professional students (206 women). *Enrollment by degree level:* 362 master's. *Graduate faculty:* 2 full-time (both women), 51 part-time/adjunct (27 women). *Tuition:* Full-time $11,700; part-time $650 per credit. *Graduate housing:* Room and/or apartments available on a first-come, first-served basis to single students; on-campus housing not available to married students. Typical cost: $11,000 (including board). Housing application deadline: 8/1. *Student services:* Campus employment opportunities, career counseling, exercise/wellness program, free psychological counseling, international student services, teacher training, writing training. *Library facilities:* Kistler Library plus 1 other. *Online resources:* library catalog, web page, access to other libraries' catalogs. *Collection:* 166,349 titles, 5,949 serial subscriptions, 3,362 audiovisual materials.

Computer facilities: 100 computers available on campus for general student use. A campuswide network can be accessed from student residence rooms and from off campus. Online class registration is available. *Web address:* http://www.rosemont.edu/.

General Application Contact: Megan Mellinger, Admissions Counselor, Graduate and Professional Studies, 610-527-0200 Ext. 2187, Fax: 610-526-2964, E-mail: gradstudies@rosemont.edu.

GRADUATE UNITS

Schools of Graduate and Professional Studies *Degree program information:* Part-time and evening/weekend programs available. Offers business administration (MBA); creative writing (MFA); elementary certification (MA); English and publishing (MA); English literature (MA); human services (MA); management (MSM); school counseling (MA). Electronic applications accepted.

ROWAN UNIVERSITY, Glassboro, NJ 08028-1701

General Information State-supported, coed, comprehensive institution. CGS member. *Enrollment:* 11,392 graduate, professional, and undergraduate students; 358 full-time matriculated graduate/professional students (243 women), 779 part-time matriculated graduate/professional students (545 women). *Enrollment by degree level:* 883 master's, 190 doctoral, 64 other advanced degrees. *Graduate faculty:* 117 full-time (56 women), 91 part-time/adjunct (39 women). *Tuition, area resident:* Part-time $602 per semester hour. Tuition, nonresident: part-time $602 per semester hour. *Required fees:* $100 per semester hour. One-time fee: $10 part-time. *Graduate housing:* Room and/or apartments available on a first-come, first-served basis to single students; on-campus housing not available to married students. Typical cost: $7598 per year ($11,448 including board). Housing application deadline: 5/1. *Student services:* Campus employment opportunities, campus safety program, career counseling, child daycare facilities, exercise/wellness program, free psychological counseling, international student services, low-cost health insurance, multicultural affairs office, services for students with disabilities, teacher training, writing training. *Library facilities:* Keith and Shirley Campbell Library plus 1 other. *Online resources:* library catalog, web page, access to other libraries' catalogs. *Collection:* 379,481 titles, 25,947 serial subscriptions, 13,412 audiovisual materials.

Computer facilities: 1,200 computers available on campus for general student use. A campuswide network can be accessed from student residence rooms and from off campus. Online class registration, online library are available. *Web address:* http://www.rowan.edu/.

General Application Contact: Dr. Horacio Sosa, Dean, College of Graduate and Continuing Education, 856-256-4747, Fax: 856-256-5638, E-mail: sosa@rowan.edu.

GRADUATE UNITS

Graduate School Students: 358 full-time (243 women), 779 part-time (545 women); includes 112 Black or African American, non-Hispanic/Latino; 128 Asian, non-Hispanic/Latino; 59 Hispanic/Latino; 2 Native Hawaiian or other Pacific Islander, non-Hispanic/Latino. Average age 32. 433 applicants, 61% accepted, 198 enrolled. *Faculty:* 117 full-time (56 women), 91 part-time/adjunct (39 women). Expenses: Contact institution. *Financial support:* In 2010–11, 80 students received support, including 80 research assistantships with full and partial tuition reimbursements available (averaging $10,000 per year); career-related internships or fieldwork, Federal Work-Study, scholarships/grants, traineeships, health care benefits, tuition waivers, and unspecified assistantships also available. Support available to part-time students. Financial award applicants required to submit FAFSA. In 2010, 317 master's, 28 doctorates awarded. *Degree program information:* Part-time and evening/weekend programs available. *Application deadline:* For fall admission, 10/15 for domestic and international students; for spring admission, 2/15 for domestic and international students. Applications are processed on a rolling basis. *Application fee:* $65 ($200 for international students). Electronic applications accepted. *Application Contact:* Karen Haynes, Director of Graduate Admissions, 856-256-4052, Fax: 856-256-4436, E-mail: haynesk@rowan.edu. *Dean, College of Graduate and Continuing Education*, Dr. Horacio Sosa, 856-256-4747, Fax: 856-256-5638, E-mail: sosa@rowan.edu.

College of Communication Students: 27 full-time (22 women), 24 part-time (16 women); includes 2 Black or African American, non-Hispanic/Latino; 3 Asian, non-Hispanic/Latino; 3 Hispanic/Latino. Average age 29. 34 applicants, 88% accepted, 21 enrolled. *Faculty:* 4 full-time (2 women), 3 part-time/adjunct (2 women). Expenses: Contact institution. *Financial support:* Career-related internships or fieldwork and unspecified assistantships available. Support available to part-time students. In 2010, 21 master's awarded. *Degree program information:* Part-time and evening/weekend programs available. Offers communication (MA); public relations (MA); writing (MA). *Application deadline:* Applications are processed on a rolling basis. *Application fee:* $65 ($200 for international students). Electronic applications accepted. *Application Contact:* Karen Haynes, Adviser, 856-256-4052, E-mail: haynesk@rowan.edu. *Dean, College of Graduate and Continuing Education*, Dr. Horacio Sosa, 856-256-4747, Fax: 856-256-5638, E-mail: sosa@rowan.edu.

College of Education Students: 254 full-time (197 women), 580 part-time (461 women); includes 95 Black or African American, non-Hispanic/Latino; 105 Asian, non-Hispanic/Latino; 46 Hispanic/Latino; 2 Native Hawaiian or other Pacific Islander, non-Hispanic/Latino. Average age 42. 242 applicants, 94% accepted, 192 enrolled. *Faculty:* 30 full-time (23 women), 44 part-time/adjunct (23 women). Expenses: Contact institution. *Financial support:* Career-related internships or fieldwork, Federal Work-Study, scholarships/grants, health care benefits, and unspecified assistantships available. Support available to part-time students. In 2010, 198 master's, 28 doctorates awarded. *Degree program information:* Part-time and evening/weekend programs available. Offers business administration (MA); collaborative teaching (MST); counseling in educational settings (MA); education (M Ed, MA, MST, MST, Ed D, Ed S); educational leadership (Ed D); elementary education (MST); elementary school teaching (MA); ESL/bilingual education (Graduate Certificate); foreign language education (MST); health promotion management (MA); higher education administration (MA); learning disabilities (MA); music education (MA); principal preparation (MA, CAGS); reading education (MA); school administration (MA); school and public librarianship (MA); school business administration (MA); school psychology (MA, Ed S); secondary education (MST); special education (MA); standards-based practice (M Ed); subject matter teaching (MA); supervision and curriculum development (MA); teacher leadership (M Ed). *Application deadline:* Applications are processed on a rolling basis. *Application fee:* $65 ($200 for international students). Electronic applications accepted. *Application Contact:* Karen Haynes, Graduate Coordinator, 856-256-4052, Fax: 856-256-4436, E-mail: haynes@rowan.edu. *Dean, College of Graduate and Continuing Education*, Dr. Horacio Sosa, 856-256-4747, Fax: 856-256-5638, E-mail: sosa@rowan.edu.

College of Engineering Students: 42 full-time (26 women), 59 part-time (13 women); includes 26 Black or African American, non-Hispanic/Latino; 7 Asian, non-Hispanic/Latino; 3 Hispanic/Latino. Average age 27. 39 applicants, 92% accepted, 25 enrolled. *Faculty:* 32 full-time (10 women), 9 part-time/adjunct (1 woman). Expenses: Contact institution. *Financial support:* Career-related internships or fieldwork, Federal Work-Study, and unspecified assistantships available. Support available to part-time students. In 2010, 15 master's awarded. *Degree program information:* Part-time and evening/weekend programs available. Offers chemical engineering (MS); civil engineering (MS); construction management (MS); electrical engineering (MS); engineering (MEM, MS); engineering management (MEM); mechanical engineering (MS); project management (MS). *Application deadline:* Applications are processed on a rolling basis. *Application fee:* $65 ($200 for international students). Electronic applications accepted. *Application Contact:* Dr. Ralph Dusseau, Program Adviser, 856-256-5332. *Dean*, Dr. Steve Chin, 856-256-5301.

College of Fine and Performing Arts Students: 6 full-time (3 women), 14 part-time (9 women); includes 3 Asian, non-Hispanic/Latino; 1 Hispanic/Latino. Average age 30. 5 applicants, 60% accepted, 3 enrolled. *Faculty:* 19 full-time (6 women), 33 part-time/adjunct (12 women). Expenses: Contact institution. *Financial support:* Career-related internships or fieldwork, scholarships/grants, health care benefits, and unspecified assistantships available. In 2010, 4 master's awarded. *Degree program information:* Part-time and evening/weekend programs available. Offers fine and performing arts (MA, MM, MST); performance (MM); theatre (MA); theatre education (MST). *Application deadline:* Applications are processed on a rolling basis. *Application fee:* $65 ($200 for international students). Electronic applications accepted. *Application Contact:* Karen Haynes, Graduate Coordinator, 856-256-4052, Fax: 856-256-4436, E-mail: haynes@rowan.edu. *Dean, College of Graduate and Continuing Education*, Dr. Horacio Sosa, 856-256-4747, Fax: 856-256-5638, E-mail: sosa@rowan.edu.

College of Liberal Arts and Sciences Students: 6 full-time (0 women), 18 part-time (7 women); includes 4 Black or African American, non-Hispanic/Latino; 2 Hispanic/Latino. Average age 41. 93 applicants, 60% accepted. *Faculty:* 11 full-time (5 women), 8 part-time/adjunct (2 women). Expenses: Contact institution. *Financial support:* Career-related internships or fieldwork, Federal Work-Study, scholarships/grants, health care benefits, and unspecified assistantships available. Support available to part-time students. In 2010, 10 master's awarded. *Degree program information:* Part-time and evening/weekend programs available. Offers applied behavioral analysis (MA); clinical mental health counseling (MA); criminal justice (MA); liberal arts and sciences (MA); mathematics (MA); mental health counseling (MA); mental health counseling and applied psychology (MA). *Application deadline:* Applications are processed on a rolling basis. *Application fee:* $65 ($200 for international students). Electronic applications accepted. *Application Contact:* Karen Haynes, Graduate Coordinator, 856-256-4052, Fax: 856-256-4436, E-mail: haynes@rowan.edu. *Dean, College of Graduate and Continuing Education,* Dr. Horacio Sosa, 856-256-4747, Fax: 856-256-5638, E-mail: sosa@rowan.edu.

William G. Rohrer College of Business Students: 47 full-time (19 women), 114 part-time (69 women); includes 9 Black or African American, non-Hispanic/Latino; 10 Asian, non-Hispanic/Latino; 4 Hispanic/Latino. Average age 28. 63 applicants, 67% accepted, 33 enrolled. *Faculty:* 13 full-time (5 women), 4 part-time/adjunct (3 women). Expenses: Contact institution. *Financial support:* Career-related internships or fieldwork, scholarships/grants, health care benefits, and unspecified assistantships available. In 2010, 29 master's awarded. *Degree program information:* Part-time and evening/weekend programs available. Offers accounting (MBA); business (MBA); business administration (MBA); entrepreneurship (MBA); finance (MBA); management (MBA); marketing and business information systems (MBA). *Application deadline:* Applications are processed on a rolling basis. *Application fee:* $65 ($200 for international students). Electronic applications accepted. *Application Contact:* Karen Haynes, Graduate Coordinator, 856-256-4052, E-mail: haynes@rowan.edu. *Dean, College of Graduate and Continuing Education,* Dr. Horacio Sosa, 856-256-4747, E-mail: sosa@rowan.edu.

ROYAL MILITARY COLLEGE OF CANADA, Kingston, ON K7K 7B4, Canada

General Information Federally supported, coed, comprehensive institution.

GRADUATE UNITS

Division of Graduate Studies and Research *Degree program information:* Part-time programs available. Postbaccalaureate distance learning degree programs offered (minimal on-campus study). Electronic applications accepted.

Continuing Studies Offers business administration (MBA); defense management and policy (MA); history (PhD); war studies (MA). Electronic applications accepted.

Engineering Division Offers chemical and materials (M Eng); chemical and materials science (M Sc, PhD); chemistry (M Eng); civil engineering (M Eng, MA Sc, PhD); computer engineering (M Eng, PhD); electrical engineering (M Eng, PhD); engineering (M Eng, M Sc, MA Sc, PhD); environmental (PhD); environmental engineering (M Eng, PhD); environmental science (M Sc, PhD); mechanical engineering (M Eng, MA Sc, PhD); nuclear (PhD); nuclear engineering (M Eng, MA Sc, PhD); nuclear science (M Sc, PhD); software engineering (M Eng, PhD). Electronic applications accepted.

Science Division Offers chemical engineering (M Eng, MA Sc, PhD); chemistry (M Sc, PhD); computer science (M Sc); mathematics (M Sc); physics (M Sc); science (M Eng, M Sc, MA Sc, PhD). Electronic applications accepted.

ROYAL ROADS UNIVERSITY, Victoria, BC V9B 5Y2, Canada

General Information Province-supported, coed, upper-level institution. *Graduate housing:* Room and/or apartments available on a first-come, first-served basis to single students; on-campus housing not available to married students.

GRADUATE UNITS

Graduate Studies Postbaccalaureate distance learning degree programs offered (minimal on-campus study). Offers conflict analysis (G Dip); conflict analysis and management (MA); destination development (Graduate Certificate); disaster and emergency management (MA); environment and management (M Sc, MA); environmental education and communication (MA, G Dip, Graduate Certificate); executive coaching (Graduate Certificate); health systems leadership (Graduate Certificate); human security and peacebuilding (MA); international hotel management (MA); project management (Graduate Certificate); public relations management (Graduate Certificate); strategic human resources management (Graduate Certificate); sustainable tourism (Graduate Certificate); tourism leadership (Graduate Certificate); tourism management (MA). Electronic applications accepted.

Faculty of Management Postbaccalaureate distance learning degree programs offered (minimal on-campus study). Offers digital technologies management (MBA); executive management (MBA); human resources management (MBA). Electronic applications accepted.

RUSH UNIVERSITY, Chicago, IL 60612-3832

General Information Independent, coed, upper-level institution. CGS member. *Graduate housing:* Rooms and/or apartments available on a first-come, first-served basis to single and married students. Housing application deadline: 6/1.

GRADUATE UNITS

College of Health Sciences *Degree program information:* Part-time and evening/weekend programs available. Offers audiology (Au D); clinical laboratory management (MS); clinical laboratory science (MS); clinical nutrition (MS); health sciences (MA, MS, Au D, DHSc, Graduate Certificate); health systems management (MS, DHSc); healthcare ethics (MA, Graduate Certificate); occupational therapy (MS); physician assistant studies (MS); speech-language pathology (MS). Electronic applications accepted.

College of Nursing *Degree program information:* Part-time programs available. Postbaccalaureate distance learning degree programs offered (minimal on-campus study). Offers acute care nurse practitioner (MSN, Post-Master's Certificate); adult health nursing (DNP, PhD); adult nurse practitioner (MSN, Post-Master's Certificate); adult/gerontological nurse practitioner (MSN); anesthesia nurse practitioner (MSN, Post-Master's Certificate); community and mental health nursing (DNP, PhD); critical care clinical specialist (MSN); family nurse practitioner (MSN, Post-Master's Certificate); gerontological nurse practitioner (MSN, Post-Master's Certificate); medical surgical clinical specialist (MSN); neonatal nurse practitioner (MSN, Post-Master's Certificate); nursing (MSN, DNP, PhD, Post-Master's Certificate); pediatric acute/chronic care nurse practitioner (MSN); pediatric clinical nurse specialist (MSN); pediatric nurse practitioner (MSN, Post-Master's Certificate); psychiatric clinical specialist (MSN); psychiatric nurse practitioner—adult (MSN); psychiatric nurse practitioner—family (MSN); psychiatric-mental health clinical specialist (Post-Master's Certificate); psychiatric-mental health nurse practitioner (Post-Master's Certificate); public health nursing (MSN); women's and children's health nursing (DNP, PhD). Electronic applications accepted.

Graduate College *Degree program information:* Part-time programs available. Offers anatomy and cell biology (MS, PhD); biochemistry (PhD); clinical research (MS); immunology (MS, PhD); medical physics (MS, PhD); microbiology (PhD); pharmacology (MS, PhD); physiology (PhD); virology (MS, PhD). Electronic applications accepted.

Division of Neuroscience Offers neuroscience (MS, PhD). Electronic applications accepted.

Rush Medical College Offers medicine (MD). Electronic applications accepted.

RUTGERS, THE STATE UNIVERSITY OF NEW JERSEY, CAMDEN, Camden, NJ 08102-1401

General Information State-supported, coed, university. *Enrollment:* 6,158 graduate, professional, and undergraduate students; 903 full-time matriculated graduate/professional students (389 women), 758 part-time matriculated graduate/professional students (347 women). *Enrollment by degree level:* 803 first professional. *Graduate faculty:* 244 full-time (94 women), 245 part-time/adjunct (90 women). Tuition, state resident: full-time $4963; part-time $319 per credit. Tuition, nonresident: full-time $10,493; part-time $680 per credit. *Graduate housing:* Rooms and/or apartments available to single and married students. *Student services:* Campus employment opportunities, campus safety program, career counseling, child daycare facilities, free psychological counseling, low-cost health insurance, multicultural affairs office, services for students with disabilities, teacher training. *Library facilities:* Paul Robeson Library plus 2 others. *Collection:* 729,987 titles, 15,013 serial subscriptions, 591 audiovisual materials.

Computer facilities: Computer purchase and lease plans are available. 184 computers available on campus for general student use. A campuswide network can be accessed from student residence rooms and from off campus. Online class registration, online grade reports are available. *Web address:* http://www.rutgers.edu/.

General Application Contact: Information Contact, 856-225-6149, Fax: 856-225-6498, E-mail: camden@ugadm.rutgers.edu.

GRADUATE UNITS

Graduate School of Arts and Sciences Students: 235 full-time (129 women), 286 part-time (157 women); includes 75 Black or African American, non-Hispanic/Latino; 2 American Indian or Alaska Native, non-Hispanic/Latino; 25 Asian, non-Hispanic/Latino; 26 Hispanic/Latino, 19 international. Average age 31. 737 applicants, 61% accepted, 213 enrolled. *Faculty:* 179 full-time (71 women), 23 part-time/adjunct (10 women). Expenses: Contact institution. *Financial support:* In 2010–11, 374 students received support, including 99 fellowships with partial tuition reimbursements available (averaging $177 per year), 1 research assistantship with full tuition reimbursement available (averaging $26,000 per year), 18 teaching assistantships with full tuition reimbursements available (averaging $26,000 per year); career-related internships or fieldwork, Federal Work-Study, institutionally sponsored loans, scholarships/grants, tuition waivers (partial), and unspecified assistantships also available. Support available to part-time students. Financial award application deadline: 3/15; financial award applicants required to submit FAFSA. In 2010, 107 master's, 14 doctorates awarded. *Degree program information:* Part-time and evening/weekend programs available. Offers American and public history (MA); biology (MS); chemistry (MS); childhood studies (MA, PhD); computer science (MS); creative writing (MFA); criminal justice (MA); education policy and leadership (MPA); English (MA); international public service and development (MPA); liberal studies (MALS); mathematics (MS); physical therapy (DPT); psychology (MA); public management (MPA). *Application deadline:* For fall admission, 4/15 priority date for domestic and international students; for spring admission, 11/15 priority date for domestic and international students. Applications are processed on a rolling basis. *Application fee:* $65. Electronic applications accepted. *Application Contact:* Dr. Michael Palis, Interim Dean, 856-225-6097, Fax: 856-225-6603, E-mail: palis@camden.rutgers.edu. *Interim Dean,* Dr. Michael Palis, 856-225-6097, Fax: 856-225-6603, E-mail: palis@camden.rutgers.edu.

School of Business Students: 39 full-time (13 women), 212 part-time (70 women). Average age 28. 212 applicants, 61% accepted, 57 enrolled. *Faculty:* 34 full-time, 5 part-time/adjunct. Expenses: Contact institution. *Financial support:* Research assistantships, career-related internships or fieldwork, Federal Work-Study, institutionally sponsored loans, and scholarships/grants available. Support available to part-time students. Financial award application deadline: 8/1; financial award applicants required to submit FAFSA. *Degree program information:* Part-time and evening/weekend programs available. Offers business (MBA). *Application deadline:* For fall admission, 7/1 priority date for domestic students, 2/1 for international students; for spring admission, 11/1 priority date for domestic students, 9/1 for international students. Applications are processed on a rolling basis. *Application fee:* $60. Electronic applications accepted. *Application Contact:* Dr. Rakesh B. Sambharya, Associate Dean, MBA Program, 856-225-6712, Fax: 856-225-6231, E-mail: sambhary@camden.rutgers.edu. *Dean,* Dr. Jaishankar Ganesh, 856-225-6217, Fax: 856-225-6231, E-mail: jganesh@camden.rutgers.edu.

School of Law Students: 589 full-time (223 women), 214 part-time (96 women); includes 42 Black or African American, non-Hispanic/Latino; 3 American Indian or Alaska Native, non-Hispanic/Latino; 77 Asian, non-Hispanic/Latino; 44 Hispanic/Latino. Average age 25. 2,013 applicants, 31% accepted, 274 enrolled. *Faculty:* 70 full-time (30 women), 56 part-time/adjunct (22 women). Expenses: Contact institution. *Financial support:* In 2010–11, 662 students received support. Career-related internships or fieldwork, Federal Work-Study, and scholarships/grants available. Support available to part-time students. Financial award application deadline: 4/1; financial award applicants required to submit FAFSA. In 2010, 244 first professional degrees awarded. *Degree program information:* Part-time and evening/weekend programs available. Offers law (JD). JD/MCRP, JD/MA, JD/MPA, JD/MSW, JD/MS offered jointly with Rutgers, The State University of New Jersey, New Brunswick; JD/MPA, JD/MD, JD/DO with University of Medicine and Dentistry of New Jersey. *Application deadline:* For fall admission, 3/1 priority date for domestic and international students. Applications are processed on a rolling basis. *Application fee:* $65. Electronic applications accepted. *Application Contact:* Camille Spinello Andrews, Associate Dean of Enrollment, 856-225-6102, Fax: 856-225-6537, E-mail: csa@camlaw.rutgers.edu. *Dean,* Rayman L. Solomon, 856-225-6191, Fax: 856-225-6487, E-mail: raysol@camlaw.rutgers.edu.

RUTGERS, THE STATE UNIVERSITY OF NEW JERSEY, NEWARK, Newark, NJ 07102

General Information State-supported, coed, university. CGS member. *Enrollment:* 11,798 graduate, professional, and undergraduate students; 1,812 full-time matriculated graduate/professional students (849 women), 2,507 part-time matriculated graduate/professional students (1,233 women). *Enrollment by degree level:* 839 first professional. *Graduate faculty:* 461 full-time (178 women), 253 part-time/adjunct (119 women). Tuition, state resident: part-time $600 per credit. Tuition, nonresident: full-time $10,694. *Graduate housing:* Room and/or apartments available to single students; on-campus housing not available to married students. Housing application deadline: 5/15. *Student services:* Career counseling, free psychological counseling, low-cost health insurance. *Library facilities:* John Cotton Dana Library plus 4 others. *Collection:* 1.1 million titles, 14,321 serial subscriptions, 43,210 audiovisual materials.

Computer facilities: Computer purchase and lease plans are available. 708 computers available on campus for general student use. A campuswide network can be accessed from student residence rooms and from off campus. Online grade reports are available. *Web address:* http://www.rutgers.edu/.

General Application Contact: Information Contact, 973-353-5205, Fax: 973-353-1191, E-mail: gradnwk@andromeda.rutgers.edu.

GRADUATE UNITS

Graduate School Students: 474 full-time (245 women), 703 part-time (457 women); includes 155 Black or African American, non-Hispanic/Latino; 2 American Indian or Alaska Native, non-Hispanic/Latino; 237 Asian, non-Hispanic/Latino; 84 Hispanic/Latino. 1,768 applicants, 47% accepted, 457 enrolled. *Faculty:* 379 full-time (104 women), 32 part-time/adjunct (14 women). Expenses: Contact institution. *Financial support:* In 2010–11, 36 fellowships (averaging $18,000 per year), 15 research assistantships with full and partial tuition reimbursements (averaging $23,112 per year), 181 teaching assistantships with full and partial tuition reimbursements (averaging $23,112 per year) were awarded; career-related internships or fieldwork, Federal Work-Study, tuition waivers (full and partial), and unspecified assistantships also available. Support available to part-time students. In 2010, 176 master's, 55 doctorates awarded. *Degree program information:* Part-time and evening/weekend programs available. Offers accounting (PhD); accounting information systems (PhD); American political system (MA); American studies (MA, PhD); analytical chemistry (MS, PhD); applied physics (MS, PhD); biochemistry (MS, PhD); biology (MS, PhD); cognitive neuroscience (PhD); cognitive science (PhD); computational biology (MS); computer information systems (PhD); creative writing (MFA); economics (MA); English (MA); environmental geology (MS); environmental science (MS, PhD); finance (PhD); health care administration (MPA); history (MA, MAT); human resources administration (MPA); information technology (PhD); inorganic chemistry (MS, PhD); integrative neuroscience (PhD); international business (PhD); international relations (MA); jazz history and research (MA); management science (PhD); marketing (PhD); mathematical sciences (PhD); nursing (MS); organic chemistry (MS, PhD); organization management (PhD); perception (PhD); physical chemistry (MS, PhD); psychobiology (PhD); public administration (PhD); public management (MPA); public policy analysis (MPA); social cognition (PhD); urban systems (PhD); urban systems and issues (MPA). *Application deadline:*

Rutgers, The State University of New Jersey, Newark (continued)

Applications are processed on a rolling basis. *Application fee:* $60. Electronic applications accepted. *Application Contact:* Jason Hand, Director of Admissions, 973-353-5205, Fax: 973-353-1440. *Associate Dean*, Dr. Barry R. Komisaruk, 973-353-5834 Ext. 10, Fax: 973-353-1191, E-mail: brk@psychology.rutgers.edu.

Division of Global Affairs Students: 62 full-time (30 women), 92 part-time (46 women); includes 24 Black or African American, non-Hispanic/Latino; 22 Asian, non-Hispanic/Latino; 11 Hispanic/Latino. 199 applicants, 62% accepted, 50 enrolled. *Faculty:* 35 full-time (7 women). Expenses: Contact institution. *Financial support:* In 2010–11, 2 fellowships (averaging $18,000 per year), 9 teaching assistantships with full and partial tuition reimbursements (averaging $23,112 per year) were awarded; research assistantships, career-related internships or fieldwork, Federal Work-Study, institutionally sponsored loans, and tuition waivers (full and partial) also available. Support available to part-time students. Financial award application deadline: 3/7; financial award applicants required to submit FAFSA. In 2010, 23 master's, 9 doctorates awarded. *Degree program information:* Part-time and evening/weekend programs available. Offers global affairs (MS, PhD). *Application deadline:* Applications are processed on a rolling basis. *Application fee:* $60. Electronic applications accepted. *Application Contact:* Jason Hand, Director of Admissions, 973-353-5205, Fax: 973-353-1440. *Director*, Dr. Alex Motyl, 973-353-3285, Fax: 973-353-5074, E-mail: ajmotyl@andromeda.rutgers.edu.

School of Criminal Justice Students: 92 full-time (55 women), 42 part-time (25 women); includes 12 Black or African American, non-Hispanic/Latino; 22 Asian, non-Hispanic/Latino; 12 Hispanic/Latino. Average age 27. 151 applicants, 45% accepted, 33 enrolled. *Faculty:* 16 full-time (3 women). Expenses: Contact institution. *Financial support:* In 2010–11, 1 fellowship with full tuition reimbursement (averaging $18,000 per year), 10 teaching assistantships with full tuition reimbursements (averaging $18,347 per year) were awarded; career-related internships or fieldwork, Federal Work-Study, institutionally sponsored loans, scholarships/grants, and tuition waivers (partial) also available. Support available to part-time students. Financial award applicants required to submit FAFSA. In 2010, 17 master's, 7 doctorates awarded. Offers criminal justice (MA, PhD). *Application deadline:* For fall admission, 4/1 for domestic students, 3/1 for international students. *Application fee:* $50. Electronic applications accepted. *Application Contact:* Teresa Fontanez, Graduate Enrollment Coordinator, 973-353-3029, Fax: 973-353-1228, E-mail: tfontane@andromeda.rutgers.edu. *Program Director*, Dr. Marcus Felson, 973-353-5237, E-mail: felson@andromeda.rutgers.edu.

Rutgers Business School–Newark and New Brunswick Students: 208 full-time (86 women), 1,004 part-time (343 women); includes 68 Black or African American, non-Hispanic/Latino; 2 American Indian or Alaska Native, non-Hispanic/Latino; 248 Asian, non-Hispanic/Latino; 64 Hispanic/Latino, 79 international. Average age 28. 635 applicants, 72% accepted, 313 enrolled. *Faculty:* 148 full-time (27 women), 124 part-time/adjunct (36 women). Expenses: Contact institution. *Financial support:* Fellowships with tuition reimbursements, teaching assistantships, career-related internships or fieldwork, Federal Work-Study, institutionally sponsored loans, and scholarships/grants available. Financial award application deadline: 3/15; financial award applicants required to submit FAFSA. In 2010, 400 master's awarded. *Degree program information:* Part-time and evening/weekend programs available. Offers accounting (PhD); accounting information systems (PhD); business (MBA); economics (PhD); finance (PhD); individualized study (PhD); information technology (PhD); international business (PhD); management science (PhD); marketing science (PhD); organizational management (PhD); science, technology and management (PhD); supply chain management (PhD). *Application deadline:* For fall admission, 5/1 for domestic students, 3/15 for international students; for spring admission, 11/15 for domestic students. Applications are processed on a rolling basis. *Application fee:* $73. Electronic applications accepted. *Application Contact:* Rita Galen, Assistant Dean of Admissions, 973-353-1234, Fax: 973-353-1592, E-mail: admit@business.rutgers.edu. *Dean*, Dr. Michael Cooper, 973-353-5128, Fax: 973-353-1345.

School of Law Students: 558 full-time (248 women), 258 part-time (107 women). Average age 27. *Faculty:* 54 full-time (24 women), 46 part-time/adjunct (12 women). Expenses: Contact institution. *Financial support:* In 2010–11, 585 students received support; fellowships, research assistantships with partial tuition reimbursements available, teaching assistantships, career-related internships or fieldwork, Federal Work-Study, institutionally sponsored loans, and scholarships/grants available. Support available to part-time students. Financial award application deadline: 3/1; financial award applicants required to submit FAFSA. In 2010, 221 first professional degrees awarded. *Degree program information:* Part-time and evening/weekend programs available. Offers law (JD). JD/MCRP, JD/PhD offered jointly with Rutgers, The State University of New Jersey, New Brunswick. *Application deadline:* For fall admission, 3/15 for domestic and international students. Applications are processed on a rolling basis. *Application fee:* $50. *Application Contact:* Anita T. Walton, Assistant Dean for Admissions, 973-353-3077, Fax: 973-353-3459, E-mail: awalton@kinoy.rutgers.edu. *Dean*, John J. Farmer, 973-353-5551, Fax: 973-353-1248, E-mail: jfarmer@kinoy.rutgers.edu.

RUTGERS, THE STATE UNIVERSITY OF NEW JERSEY, NEW BRUNSWICK, Piscataway, NJ 08854-8097

General Information State-supported, coed, university. CGS member. *Enrollment:* 38,912 graduate, professional, and undergraduate students; 4,951 full-time matriculated graduate/professional students (2,945 women), 3,610 part-time matriculated graduate/professional students (2,311 women). *Enrollment by degree level:* 413 first professional. *Graduate faculty:* 1,626 full-time (603 women), 831 part-time/adjunct (426 women). Tuition, state resident: full-time $7200; part-time $600 per credit. Tuition, nonresident: full-time $11,124; part-time $927 per credit. *Graduate housing:* Rooms and/or apartments available to single and married students. *Student services:* Campus employment opportunities, career counseling, child daycare facilities, free psychological counseling, international student services, low-cost health insurance. *Library facilities:* Archibald S. Alexander Library plus 12 others. *Online resources:* library catalog, web page, access to other libraries' catalogs. *Collection:* 5.1 million titles, 87,902 serial subscriptions, 112,656 audiovisual materials.

Computer facilities: 1,450 computers available on campus for general student use. A campuswide network can be accessed from student residence rooms and from off campus. Online grade reports available. *Web address:* http://www.rutgers.edu/.

General Application Contact: Information Contact, 732-932-7711, Fax: 732-932-7407, E-mail: gradadm@rci.rutgers.edu.

GRADUATE UNITS

Edward J. Bloustein School of Planning and Public Policy Students: 572 (260 women); includes 71 Black or African American, non-Hispanic/Latino; 2 American Indian or Alaska Native, non-Hispanic/Latino; 72 Asian, non-Hispanic/Latino; 24 Hispanic/Latino, 8 international. Average age 27. 705 applicants, 50% accepted, 183 enrolled. *Faculty:* 35 full-time (11 women), 41 part-time/adjunct (16 women). Expenses: Contact institution. *Financial support:* In 2010–11, 60 students received support, including 60 fellowships with full and partial tuition reimbursements available (averaging $10,000 per year), 28 research assistantships with full and partial tuition reimbursements available (averaging $18,347 per year), 48 teaching assistantships with full and partial tuition reimbursements available (averaging $18,347 per year); career-related internships or fieldwork, Federal Work-Study, institutionally sponsored loans, scholarships/grants, tuition waivers (full and partial), and unspecified assistantships also available. Financial award application deadline: 1/15; financial award applicants required to submit FAFSA. In 2010, 152 master's, 6 doctorates awarded. *Degree program information:* Part-time and evening/weekend programs available. Postbaccalaureate distance learning degree programs offered. Offers planning and public policy (MCRP, MCRS, MPAP, MPH, MPP, Dr PH, PhD); public health (MPH, Dr PH, PhD); public policy (MPAP, MPP); urban planning and policy development (MCRP, MCRS). *Application deadline:* For fall admission, 1/15 for domestic students; for spring admission, 11/1 for domestic students. *Application fee:* $65. Electronic applications accepted. *Application Contact:* James W. Hughes, Dean, 732-932-5475. *Dean*, James W. Hughes, 732-932-5475.

Ernest Mario School of Pharmacy Students: 1,336 full-time (812 women), 15 part-time (7 women); includes 73 Black or African American, non-Hispanic/Latino; 748 Asian, non-Hispanic/Latino; 68 Hispanic/Latino, 32 international. Average age 21. 3,871 applicants, 18% accepted, 208 enrolled. *Faculty:* 72 full-time (34 women), 9 part-time/adjunct (5 women). Expenses: Contact institution. *Financial support:* Career-related internships or fieldwork, Federal Work-Study, scholarships/grants, and tuition waivers (partial) available. Financial award application deadline: 2/1; financial award applicants required to submit FAFSA. In 2010, 245 first professional degrees awarded. Offers medicinal chemistry (MS, PhD); pharmaceutical science (MS, PhD); pharmacy (Pharm D). *Application deadline:* For fall admission, 12/1 priority date for domestic and international students. Applications are processed on a rolling basis. *Application fee:* $65. Electronic applications accepted. *Application Contact:* Donald K. Woodward, Associate Dean, 732-445-2675 Ext. 605, E-mail: donald.woodward@rutgers.edu. *Dean*, Christopher J. Molloy, 732-445-2675.

Graduate School-New Brunswick Students: 1,997 full-time (957 women), 1,437 part-time (643 women). Expenses: Contact institution. *Financial support:* Fellowships with full tuition reimbursements, research assistantships with full tuition reimbursements, teaching assistantships with full tuition reimbursements, career-related internships or fieldwork, Federal Work-Study, institutionally sponsored loans, scholarships/grants, traineeships, tuition waivers (full and partial), and unspecified assistantships available. Support available to part-time students. Financial award applicants required to submit FAFSA. *Degree program information:* Part-time and evening/weekend programs available. Postbaccalaureate distance learning degree programs offered. Offers African-American history (PhD); air pollution and resources (MS, PhD); American politics (PhD); anthropology (MA, PhD); applied mathematics (MS, PhD); applied microbiology (MS, PhD); applied statistics (MS); aquatic biology (MS, PhD); aquatic chemistry (MS, PhD); art history (MA, PhD); astronomy (MS, PhD); atmospheric science (MS, PhD); behavioral neuroscience (PhD); bilingualism and second language acquisition (MA, PhD); biochemistry (PhD); biological chemistry (MS, PhD); biomedical engineering (MS, PhD); biophysics (PhD); biostatistics (MS); cell and developmental biology (MS, PhD); cellular and molecular pharmacology (PhD); chemical and biochemical engineering (MS, PhD); chemistry and physics of aerosol and hydrosol systems (MS, PhD); civil and environmental engineering (MS, PhD); classics (MA, MAT, PhD); clinical microbiology (MS, PhD); clinical psychology (PhD); cognitive psychology (PhD); communications and solid-state electronics (MS, PhD); comparative literature (MA, PhD); comparative politics (PhD); computational biology and molecular biophysics (PhD); computational molecular biology (PhD); computer engineering (MS, PhD); computer science (MS, PhD); condensed matter physics (MS, PhD); control systems (MS, PhD); curatorial studies (Certificate); data mining (MS); design and control (MS, PhD); digital signal processing (MS, PhD); early American history (PhD); early modern European history (PhD); east Asian history (PhD); ecology and evolution (MS, PhD); economics (MA, PhD); elementary particle physics (MS, PhD); endocrinology and animal biosciences (MS, PhD); entomology (MS, PhD); environmental chemistry (MS, PhD); environmental microbiology (MS, PhD); environmental toxicology (MS, PhD); exposure assessment (PhD); fate and effects of pollutants (MS, PhD); fluid mechanics (MS, PhD); food and business economics (MS); food science (M Phil, MS, PhD); French (MA, PhD); French studies (MAT); geography (MA, MS, PhD); geological sciences (MS, PhD); German (MAT, PhD); German literature (MA, PhD); global and comparative history (PhD); historic preservation (Certificate); history (PhD); history of diplomacy and foreign relations (PhD); history of technology, environment and health (PhD); history of the Atlantic cultures and African diaspora (PhD); horticulture and plant technology (MS, PhD); immunology (MS, PhD); industrial and systems engineering (MS, PhD); industrial-occupational toxicology (MS, PhD); information technology (MS); inorganic chemistry (MS, PhD); interdisciplinary classical studies and ancient history (MA, PhD); interdisciplinary health psychology (PhD); intermediate energy nuclear physics (MS); international relations (PhD); Italian (MA, PhD); Italian literature and literary criticism (MA); language, literature and culture (MAT); Latin American history (PhD); linguistics (PhD); literatures in English (PhD); manufacturing systems engineering (MS); materials science and engineering (MS, PhD); mathematics (MS, PhD); mechanics (MS, PhD); medieval history (PhD); microbial biochemistry (MS, PhD); microbiology and molecular genetics (MS, PhD); modern European history (PhD); molecular and cellular biology (MS, PhD); molecular genetics (MS, PhD); neuroscience (PhD); nineteenth and twentieth century American history (PhD); nuclear physics (MS, PhD); nutritional sciences (MS, PhD); nutritional toxicology (MS, PhD); oceanography (MS, PhD); operations research (PhD); organic chemistry (MS, PhD); organismal and population biology (MS, PhD); pharmaceutical toxicology (MS, PhD); philosophy (PhD); physical chemistry (MS, PhD); physics (MST); plant pathology (MS, PhD); political theory (PhD); pollution prevention and control (MS, PhD); public law (PhD); quality and productivity management (MS); quality and reliability engineering (MS); social psychology (PhD); sociology (MA, PhD); solid mechanics (MS, PhD); Spanish (MA, MAT, PhD); Spanish literature (MA, PhD); statistics (MS, PhD); surface science (PhD); theoretical physics (MS, PhD); thermal sciences (MS, PhD); translation (MA); virology (MS, PhD); water and wastewater treatment (MS, PhD); water resources (MS, PhD); women and politics (PhD); women's and gender history (PhD); women's and gender studies (MA, PhD). *Application deadline:* Applications are processed on a rolling basis. *Application Contact:* Dr. Judy McCarthy, Director of Graduate Admissions, 732-932-7711, Fax: 732-932-8231, E-mail: kdc@rci.rutgers.edu. *Interim Dean*, Dr. Jerome J. Kukor, 732-932-7896.

Graduate School of Applied and Professional Psychology Students: 187 full-time (141 women), 8 part-time (all women); includes 17 Black or African American, non-Hispanic/Latino; 13 Asian, non-Hispanic/Latino; 14 Hispanic/Latino, 1 international. Average age 31. 505 applicants, 10% accepted, 35 enrolled. *Faculty:* 20 full-time (11 women), 14 part-time/adjunct (11 women). Expenses: Contact institution. *Financial support:* In 2010–11, 32 students received support, including 43 fellowships with partial tuition reimbursements available (averaging $10,000 per year), 1 research assistantship with full tuition reimbursement available (averaging $16,988 per year), 8 teaching assistantships with full tuition reimbursements available (averaging $16,988 per year); career-related internships or fieldwork, Federal Work-Study, institutionally sponsored loans, scholarships/grants, traineeships, and unspecified assistantships also available. Support available to part-time students. Financial award application deadline: 3/15; financial award applicants required to submit FAFSA. In 2010, 37 master's, 27 doctorates awarded. Offers applied and professional psychology (Psy M, Psy D); clinical psychology (Psy M, Psy D); school psychology (Psy M, Psy D). *Application deadline:* For fall admission, 1/5 for domestic and international students. *Application fee:* $65. Electronic applications accepted. *Application Contact:* Jennifer Leon, Associate Dean, 732-445-2000 Ext. 113, Fax: 732-445-4888, E-mail: j.leon@rutgers.edu. *Dean*, Dr. Stanley B. Messer, 732-445-2000 Ext. 110, Fax: 732-445-4888, E-mail: smesser@rci.rutgers.edu.

Graduate School of Education Students: 333 full-time (241 women), 434 part-time (304 women); includes 43 Black or African American, non-Hispanic/Latino; 1 American Indian or Alaska Native, non-Hispanic/Latino; 56 Asian, non-Hispanic/Latino; 36 Hispanic/Latino, 29 international. 860 applicants, 62% accepted, 339 enrolled. *Faculty:* 54 full-time (30 women), 59 part-time/adjunct (41 women). Expenses: Contact institution. *Financial support:* In 2010–11, 315 students received support, including 5 fellowships with full and partial tuition reimbursements available, 4 research assistantships with full tuition reimbursements available (averaging $23,112 per year), 14 teaching assistantships with full tuition reimbursements available (averaging $23,112 per year); career-related internships or fieldwork, Federal Work-Study, institutionally sponsored loans, and scholarships/grants also available. Support available to part-time students. Financial award application deadline: 2/1; financial award applicants required to submit FAFSA. In 2010, 313 master's, 32 doctorates awarded. *Degree program information:* Part-time and evening/weekend programs available. Offers college student affairs (Ed M); early childhood/elementary education (Ed M, Ed D); education (Ed M, Ed D, PhD); educational administration and supervision (Ed M, Ed D); educational policy (PhD); educational psychology (PhD); educational statistics, measurement and evaluation (Ed M); English as a second language education (Ed M); English education (Ed M); language education (Ed M, Ed D); learning, cognition and development (Ed M); literacy education (Ed M, Ed D); mathematics education (Ed M, Ed D, PhD); reading education (Ed M); school counseling and counseling psychology (Ed M); science education (Ed M, Ed D); social and philosophical foundations of education (Ed M, Ed D); social studies education (Ed M, Ed D); special education (Ed M, Ed D). *Application fee:* $65. Electronic applications accepted. *Application Contact:* Dr. William Firestone, Associate Dean for Academic Affairs, 732-932-7496 Ext. 8102, Fax: 732-932-8206, E-mail: william.firestone@gse.rutgers.edu. *Dean*, Dr. Richard DeLisi, 732-932-7496 Ext. 8117, Fax: 732-932-8206, E-mail: delisi@rci.rutgers.edu.

Mason Gross School of the Arts Students: 180 full-time (99 women), 141 part-time (81 women); includes 19 Black or African American, non-Hispanic/Latino; 23 Asian, non-Hispanic/

Latino; 8 Hispanic/Latino. Average age 28. 703 applicants, 21% accepted, 104 enrolled. *Faculty:* 60 full-time (27 women), 51 part-time/adjunct (15 women). Expenses: Contact institution. *Financial support:* Fellowships, teaching assistantships, career-related internships or fieldwork, Federal Work-Study, institutionally sponsored loans, and tuition waivers (full and partial) available. Support available to part-time students. Financial award applicants required to submit FAFSA. In 2010, 67 master's, 21 doctorates awarded. *Degree program information:* Part-time programs available. Offers acting (MFA); arts (MFA, MM, DMA, AD); collaborative piano (MM, DMA); conducting: choral (MM, DMA); conducting: instrumental (MM, DMA); conducting: orchestral (MM, DMA); design (MFA); directing (MFA); drawing (MFA); jazz studies (MM); music (DMA, AD); music education (MM, DMA); music performance (MM); painting (MFA); playwriting (MFA); sculpture (MFA); stage management (MFA); visual arts (MFA). *Application deadline:* For fall admission, 2/1 for domestic and international students; for spring admission, 11/1 for domestic and international students. Applications are processed on a rolling basis. *Application fee:* $65. *Application Contact:* Mandy R. Feiler, Admissions Officer, 732-932-9360 Ext. 517, Fax: 732-932-8497, E-mail: mfeiler@masongross.rutgers.edu. *Dean,* George B. Stauffer, 732-932-9360 Ext. 507, Fax: 732-932-8794.

School of Communication, Information and Library Studies Students: 132 full-time (94 women), 243 part-time (192 women). Average age 32. 409 applicants, 61% accepted, 92 enrolled. *Faculty:* 92 full-time (46 women), 27 part-time/adjunct (18 women). Expenses: Contact institution. *Financial support:* Fellowships with full tuition reimbursements, research assistantships, teaching assistantships, career-related internships or fieldwork, Federal Work-Study, institutionally sponsored loans, scholarships/grants, and tuition waivers available. Support available to part-time students. Financial award application deadline: 4/2; financial award applicants required to submit FAFSA. In 2010, 128 master's, 11 doctorates awarded. *Degree program information:* Part-time programs available. Postbaccalaureate distance learning degree programs offered (no on-campus study). Offers communication and information studies (MCIS); communication, information and library studies (MCIS, MLS, PhD); communication, library and information science and media studies (PhD); library and information science (MLS). *Application deadline:* For fall admission, 5/17 priority date for domestic students, 5/15 for international students. Applications are processed on a rolling basis. *Application fee:* $50. Electronic applications accepted. *Application Contact:* Linda J. Costa, Director of Graduate Admissions, 732-932-7711, Fax: 732-932-8231, E-mail: smeds@rci.rutgers.edu. *Dean,* Dr. Jorge Reina Schement, 732-932-7500 Ext. 8018, Fax: 732-932-6919, E-mail: comminfo.dean@rutgers.edu.

School of Management and Labor Relations Students: 142 full-time (99 women), 187 part-time (136 women); includes 30 Black or African American, non-Hispanic/Latino; 1 American Indian or Alaska Native, non-Hispanic/Latino; 62 Asian, non-Hispanic/Latino; 6 Hispanic/Latino, 71 international. Average age 32. 320 applicants, 49% accepted, 88 enrolled. *Faculty:* 48 full-time (20 women), 7 part-time/adjunct (2 women). Expenses: Contact institution. *Financial support:* In 2010–11, 30 students received support, including 28 fellowships (averaging $1,500 per year), teaching assistantships with tuition reimbursements available (averaging $23,842 per year); research assistantships, career-related internships or fieldwork, Federal Work-Study, scholarships/grants, tuition waivers (full and partial), and unspecified assistantships also available. Support available to part-time students. Financial award applicants required to submit FAFSA. In 2010, 114 master's awarded. *Degree program information:* Part-time and evening/weekend programs available. Offers human resource management (MHRM); industrial relations and human resources (PhD); labor and employment relations (MLER). *Application deadline:* Applications are processed on a rolling basis. Electronic applications accepted. *Application Contact:* Information Contact, 732-445-5973, Fax: 732-445-2830. *Dean,* Prof. David Finegold, 732-445-5993, Fax: 732-445-5188, E-mail: dfinegold@smlr.rutgers.edu.

School of Social Work Students: 688 full-time (591 women), 303 part-time (244 women). Average age 30. 862 applicants, 39% accepted, 332 enrolled. *Faculty:* 32 full-time (19 women), 70 part-time/adjunct (39 women). Expenses: Contact institution. *Financial support:* In 2010–11, 65 students received support; fellowships, research assistantships, teaching assistantships with full and partial tuition reimbursements available, scholarships/grants and traineeships available. Financial award applicants required to submit FAFSA. In 2010, 323 master's, 6 doctorates awarded. *Degree program information:* Part-time programs available. Offers social work (MSW, PhD). *Application deadline:* For fall admission, 3/1 priority date for domestic students. Applications are processed on a rolling basis. *Application fee:* $60. Electronic applications accepted. *Application Contact:* Arlene M. Hunter, Associate Dean for Student Services/Director of Admissions, 732-932-7126, Fax: 732-932-6822, E-mail: amhunter@ssw.rutgers.edu. *Dean,* Dr. Richard L. Edwards, 732-932-7253, Fax: 732-932-8181, E-mail: redwards@ssw.rutgers.edu.

RYERSON UNIVERSITY, Toronto, ON M5B 2K3, Canada

General Information Province-supported, coed, comprehensive institution. CGS member.

GRADUATE UNITS

School of Graduate Studies Offers photographic preservation and collections management (MA).

SACRED HEART MAJOR SEMINARY, Detroit, MI 48206-1799

General Information Independent-religious, coed, comprehensive institution. *Graduate housing:* Room and/or apartments guaranteed to single students; on-campus housing not available to married students. Housing application deadline: 8/1.

GRADUATE UNITS

School of Theology *Degree program information:* Part-time and evening/weekend programs available. Offers pastoral studies (MAPS); theology (M Div, MA).

SACRED HEART SCHOOL OF THEOLOGY, Hales Corners, WI 53130-0429

General Information Independent-religious, coed, primarily men, graduate-only institution. *Enrollment by degree level:* 88 first professional, 15 master's, 4 other advanced degrees. *Graduate faculty:* 29 full-time (6 women), 14 part-time/adjunct (6 women). *Tuition:* Full-time $14,100; part-time $480 per credit. *Required fees:* $25 per term. *Graduate housing:* Room and/or apartments guaranteed to single students; on-campus housing not available to married students. Typical cost: $9500 (including board). *Student services:* Campus employment opportunities, career counseling, exercise/wellness program, free psychological counseling, international student services, multicultural affairs office, services for students with disabilities, writing training. *Library facilities:* Leo Dehon Library. *Online resources:* library catalog, access to other libraries' catalogs. *Collection:* 99,562 titles, 430 serial subscriptions, 18,021 audiovisual materials.

Computer facilities: 5 computers available on campus for general student use. A campuswide network can be accessed from student residence rooms and from off campus. Intranet available. *Web address:* http://www.shst.edu/.

General Application Contact: Rev. Thomas L. Knoebel, Director of Admissions, 414-425-8300 Ext. 6984, Fax: 414-529-6999, E-mail: tknoebel@shst.edu.

GRADUATE UNITS

Graduate and Professional Programs Students: 89 full-time (0 women), 18 part-time (8 women); includes 11 minority (4 Black or African American, non-Hispanic/Latino; 2 American Indian or Alaska Native, non-Hispanic/Latino; 2 Asian, non-Hispanic/Latino; 1 Hispanic/Latino; 2 Native Hawaiian or other Pacific Islander, non-Hispanic/Latino), 18 international. Average age 47. 39 applicants, 100% accepted, 39 enrolled. *Faculty:* 29 full-time (6 women), 14 part-time/adjunct (6 women). Expenses: Contact institution. *Financial support:* In 2010–11, 5 students received support. Career-related internships or fieldwork and scholarships/grants available. Financial award application deadline: 9/30; financial award applicants required to submit FAFSA. In 2010, 11 first professional degrees, 5 master's awarded. *Degree program information:* Part-time programs available. Offers theology (M Div, MA). *Application deadline:* For fall admission, 8/1 for domestic students; for spring admission, 12/1 for domestic students. Applications are processed on a rolling basis. *Application fee:* $50. *Application Contact:* Rev. Thomas L. Knoebel, Director of Admissions, 414-425-8300 Ext. 6984, Fax: 414-529-6999, E-mail: tknoebel@shst.edu. *President-Rector,* Very Rev. Jan de Jong, 414-425-8300 Ext. 6972, Fax: 414-529-6999, E-mail: jdejong@shst.edu.

SACRED HEART UNIVERSITY, Fairfield, CT 06825-1000

General Information Independent-religious, coed, comprehensive institution. *Graduate housing:* On-campus housing not available.

GRADUATE UNITS

Graduate Programs *Degree program information:* Part-time and evening/weekend programs available. Postbaccalaureate distance learning degree programs offered (no on-campus study). Electronic applications accepted.

College of Arts and Sciences *Degree program information:* Part-time and evening/weekend programs available. Offers arts and sciences (MA, MS, CPS); chemistry (MS); computer science (MS); criminal justice (MA); database (CPS); information technology (MS, CPS); information technology and network security (CPS); interactive multimedia (CPS); religious studies (MA); Web development (CPS). Electronic applications accepted.

College of Education and Health Professions *Degree program information:* Part-time and evening/weekend programs available. Postbaccalaureate distance learning degree programs offered (minimal on-campus study). Offers administration (CAS); clinical nurse leader (MSN); clinical practice in health care (DNP); education and health professions (MAT, MS, MSN, MSOT, DN Sc, DNP, DPT, CAS); educational technology (MAT); elementary education (MAT); exercise science and nutrition (MS); family nurse practitioner (MSN); geriatric health and wellness (MS); leadership in health care (DNP); nursing (DN Sc); occupational therapy (MSOT); patient care services administration (MSN); physical therapy (DPT); reading (CAS); secondary education (MAT); teaching (CAS). Electronic applications accepted.

John F. Welch College of Business *Degree program information:* Part-time and evening/weekend programs available. Postbaccalaureate distance learning degree programs offered. Offers accounting (MBA); finance (MBA); management (MBA); marketing (MBA). Electronic applications accepted.

SAGE GRADUATE SCHOOL, Troy, NY 12180-4115

General Information Independent, coed, graduate-only institution. *Enrollment by degree level:* 979 master's, 196 doctoral, 23 other advanced degrees. *Graduate faculty:* 44 full-time (38 women), 63 part-time/adjunct (50 women). *Tuition:* Full-time $10,980; part-time $610 per credit hour. Tuition and fees vary according to course load, degree level and program. *Graduate housing:* Room and/or apartments available on a first-come, first-served basis to single students; on-campus housing not available to married students. Typical cost: $5350 per year ($10,150 including board). Housing application deadline: 5/1. *Student services:* Career counseling, low-cost health insurance. *Library facilities:* James Wheelock Clark Library plus 1 other. *Online resources:* library catalog, web page. *Collection:* 228,045 titles, 353 serial subscriptions, 35,695 audiovisual materials. *Research affiliation:* St. Peter's Hospital (health care services), Ellis Hospital (nursing), Samaritan Hospital (nursing), Albany Medical College (occupational therapy), Enlarged City School District of Troy (education).

Computer facilities: 360 computers available on campus for general student use. A campuswide network can be accessed from student residence rooms and from off campus. Online class registration is available. *Web address:* http://www.sage.edu/.

General Application Contact: Wendy D. Diefendorf, Director of Graduate and Adult Admission, 518-244-2443, Fax: 518-244-6880, E-mail: sgsadm@sage.edu.

GRADUATE UNITS

Graduate School Students: 456 full-time (385 women), 742 part-time (625 women); includes 124 minority (62 Black or African American, non-Hispanic/Latino; 2 American Indian or Alaska Native, non-Hispanic/Latino; 28 Asian, non-Hispanic/Latino; 28 Hispanic/Latino; 4 Two or more races, non-Hispanic/Latino), 9 international. Average age 30. 913 applicants, 51% accepted, 303 enrolled. *Faculty:* 44 full-time (38 women), 63 part-time/adjunct (50 women). Expenses: Contact institution. *Financial support:* Fellowships, research assistantships, Federal Work-Study, scholarships/grants, tuition waivers (partial), and unspecified assistantships available. Support available to part-time students. Financial award application deadline: 3/1; financial award applicants required to submit FAFSA. In 2010, 273 master's, 61 doctorates, 38 other advanced degrees awarded. *Degree program information:* Part-time and evening/weekend programs available. *Application deadline:* Applications are processed on a rolling basis. *Application fee:* $40. *Application Contact:* Wendy D. Diefendorf, Director of Graduate and Adult Admission, 518-244-2443, Fax: 518-244-6880, E-mail: diefew@sage.edu.

School of Education Students: 133 full-time (108 women), 309 part-time (249 women); includes 33 minority (11 Black or African American, non-Hispanic/Latino; 2 American Indian or Alaska Native, non-Hispanic/Latino; 6 Asian, non-Hispanic/Latino; 13 Hispanic/Latino; 1 Two or more races, non-Hispanic/Latino). Average age 29. 481 applicants, 45% accepted, 139 enrolled. *Faculty:* 12 full-time (8 women), 27 part-time/adjunct (23 women). Expenses: Contact institution. *Financial support:* Fellowships, research assistantships, Federal Work-Study, scholarships/grants, tuition waivers (partial), and unspecified assistantships available. Support available to part-time students. Financial award application deadline: 3/1; financial award applicants required to submit FAFSA. In 2010, 142 master's, 18 doctorates, 10 other advanced degrees awarded. *Degree program information:* Part-time and evening/weekend programs available. Offers applied behavior analysis and autism (MS, Post Master's Certificate); art education (MAT); childhood education (MS Ed); childhood education/literacy (MS); childhood special education (MS Ed); community health education (MS); education (MAT, MS, MS Ed, Ed D, Post Master's Certificate); educational leadership (Ed D); English (MAT); guidance and counseling (MS, Post Master's Certificate); literacy (MS Ed); literacy/childhood special education (MS Ed); mathematics (MAT); school health education (MS); social studies (MAT). *Application deadline:* Applications are processed on a rolling basis. *Application fee:* $40. *Application Contact:* Wendy D. Diefendorf, Director of Graduate and Adult Admission, 518-244-2443, Fax: 518-244-6880, E-mail: diefew@sage.edu. *Dean, School of Education,* Dr. Lori Quigley, 518-244-2326, Fax: 518-244-4571, E-mail: l.quigley@sage.edu.

School of Health Sciences Students: 299 full-time (262 women), 299 part-time (284 women); includes 55 minority (25 Black or African American, non-Hispanic/Latino; 18 Asian, non-Hispanic/Latino; 9 Hispanic/Latino; 3 Two or more races, non-Hispanic/Latino), 8 international. Average age 31. 293 applicants, 57% accepted, 129 enrolled. *Faculty:* 29 full-time (28 women), 32 part-time/adjunct (28 women). Expenses: Contact institution. *Financial support:* Fellowships, research assistantships, Federal Work-Study, scholarships/grants, and unspecified assistantships available. Support available to part-time students. Financial award application deadline: 3/1; financial award applicants required to submit FAFSA. In 2010, 80 master's, 43 doctorates, 20 other advanced degrees awarded. Offers adult health (MS); adult nurse practitioner (MS, Post Master's Certificate); applied nutrition (MS); child care and children's services (MA); clinical nurse leader/specialist (Post Master's Certificate); community health (MS, Post Master's Certificate); community psychology (MA); counseling and community psychology (MA); dietetic internship (Certificate); education and leadership (DNS); family nurse practitioner (MS, Post Master's Certificate); forensic mental health (MS, Certificate); gerontological nurse practitioner (Post Master's Certificate); health sciences (MA, MS, DNS, DPT, Certificate, Post Master's Certificate); nurse administrator/executive (Post Master's Certificate); nursing (Post Master's Certificate); occupational therapy (MS); physical therapy (DPT); psychiatric mental health (MS, Post Master's Certificate); psychiatric mental health nurse practitioner (MS, Post Master's Certificate). *Application deadline:* Applications are processed on a rolling basis. *Application fee:* $40. *Application Contact:* Wendy D. Diefendorf, Director of Graduate and Adult Admission, 518-244-2443, Fax: 518-244-6880, E-mail: diefew@sage.edu. *Interim Dean, School of Health Sciences,* Dr. Esther Haskevitz, 518-244-2296, Fax: 518-244-4571, E-mail: haskve@sage.edu.

School of Management Students: 24 full-time (15 women), 134 part-time (92 women); includes 26 Black or African American, non-Hispanic/Latino; 4 Asian, non-Hispanic/Latino; 6 Hispanic/Latino, 1 international. Average age 31. 89 applicants, 61% accepted, 37 enrolled. *Faculty:* 4 full-time (2 women), 8 part-time/adjunct (3 women). Expenses: Contact institution. *Financial support:* Fellowships, research assistantships, Federal Work-Study, scholarships/grants, and unspecified assistantships available. Support available to part-

Sage Graduate School (continued)

time students. Financial award application deadline: 3/1; financial award applicants required to submit FAFSA. In 2010, 47 master's, 2 other advanced degrees awarded. *Degree program information:* Part-time and evening/weekend programs available. Offers business strategy (MBA); dietetic internship (Certificate); finance (MBA); gerontology (MS); human resources (MBA); management (MBA, MS, Certificate); marketing (MBA); organization management (MS); public administration (MS). *Application deadline:* Applications are processed on a rolling basis. *Application fee:* $40. *Application Contact:* Wendy D. Diefendorf, Director of Graduate and Adult Admission, 518-244-2443, Fax: 518-244-6880, E-mail: diefew@sage.edu. *Dean, School of Management,* Dr. Daniel Robeson, 518-292-8637, Fax: 518-292-1964, E-mail: robesd@sage.edu.

SAGINAW VALLEY STATE UNIVERSITY, University Center, MI 48710

General Information State-supported, coed, comprehensive institution. *Enrollment:* 10,656 graduate, professional, and undergraduate students; 292 full-time matriculated graduate/professional students (191 women), 1,248 part-time matriculated graduate/professional students (953 women). *Enrollment by degree level:* 1,465 master's, 75 other advanced degrees. *Graduate faculty:* 154 full-time (92 women), 74 part-time/adjunct (47 women). Tuition, state resident: full-time $7902. *Graduate housing:* Room and/or apartments available on a first-come, first-served basis to single students; on-campus housing not available to married students. Typical cost: $5650 per year ($9000 including board). Housing application deadline: 6/5. *Student services:* Campus employment opportunities, career counseling, exercise/wellness program, free psychological counseling, international student services, multicultural affairs office, services for students with disabilities, writing training. *Library facilities:* Zahnow Library plus 1 other. *Online resources:* library catalog, web page, access to other libraries' catalogs. *Collection:* 241,661 titles, 23,741 serial subscriptions, 25,099 audiovisual materials.

Computer facilities: 1,033 computers available on campus for general student use. A campuswide network can be accessed from student residence rooms and from off campus. Online class registration is available. *Web address:* http://www.svsu.edu/.

General Application Contact: P. Laine Blasch, Graduate Recruitment Coordinator, 989-964-2182, Fax: 989-790-0180, E-mail: blasch@svsu.edu.

GRADUATE UNITS

College of Arts and Behavioral Sciences Students: 43 full-time (24 women), 68 part-time (45 women); includes 16 Black or African American, non-Hispanic/Latino; 1 American Indian or Alaska Native, non-Hispanic/Latino; 2 Asian, non-Hispanic/Latino; 6 Hispanic/Latino, 14 international. Average age 33. 51 applicants, 86% accepted, 28 enrolled. *Faculty:* 9 full-time (2 women), 8 part-time/adjunct (3 women). Expenses: Contact institution. *Financial support:* Federal Work-Study available. Support available to part-time students. Financial award applicants required to submit FAFSA. In 2010, 32 master's awarded. *Degree program information:* Part-time and evening/weekend programs available. Offers administrative science (MA); arts and behavioral sciences (MA); communication and digital media design (MA). *Application deadline:* Applications are processed on a rolling basis. *Application fee:* $25. Electronic applications accepted. *Application Contact:* Dr. Mary Hedberg, Dean, 989-964-4062, Fax: 989-964-7232, E-mail: hedberg@svsu.edu. *Dean,* Dr. Mary Hedberg, 989-964-4062, Fax: 989-964-7232, E-mail: hedberg@svsu.edu.

College of Business and Management *Degree program information:* Part-time and evening/weekend programs available. Offers business administration (MBA); business and management (MBA). Electronic applications accepted.

College of Education *Degree program information:* Part-time and evening/weekend programs available. Offers adapted physical activity (MAT); chief business officers (M Ed); e-learning (MA); early childhood education (MAT); education (M Ed, MA, MAT, Ed S); education leadership (Ed S); educational administration and supervision (M Ed); elementary (MAT); elementary classroom teaching (MAT); instructional technology (MAT); learning and behavioral disorders (MAT); middle school (MAT); middle school classroom teaching (MAT); principalship (M Ed); reading education (MAT); secondary classroom teaching (MAT); secondary school (MAT); special education (MAT); superintendency (M Ed). Electronic applications accepted.

Crystal M. Lange College of Nursing and Health Sciences *Degree program information:* Part-time and evening/weekend programs available. Offers clinical nurse specialist (MSN); health leadership (MS); health system nurse specialist (MSN); nurse practitioner (MSN); nursing (MSN); nursing and health sciences (MS, MSN, MSOT); occupational therapy (MSOT). Electronic applications accepted.

ST. AMBROSE UNIVERSITY, Davenport, IA 52803-2898

General Information Independent-religious, coed, comprehensive institution. *Enrollment:* 3,663 graduate, professional, and undergraduate students; 333 full-time matriculated graduate/professional students (249 women), 507 part-time matriculated graduate/professional students (308 women). *Enrollment by degree level:* 713 master's, 127 doctoral. *Graduate faculty:* 67 full-time (29 women), 32 part-time/adjunct (10 women). *Tuition:* Full-time $13,230; part-time $735 per credit hour. *Required fees:* $60 per semester. Tuition and fees vary according to degree level, program and reciprocity agreements. *Graduate housing:* Room and/or apartments available on a first-come, first-served basis to single students; on-campus housing not available to married students. Housing application deadline: 3/1. *Student services:* Campus employment opportunities, campus safety program, career counseling, free psychological counseling, international student services, multicultural affairs office, services for students with disabilities, teacher training, writing training. *Library facilities:* SAU Library plus 1 other. *Online resources:* library catalog, web page, access to other libraries' catalogs. *Collection:* 156,303 titles, 679 serial subscriptions, 3,865 audiovisual materials.

Computer facilities: 276 computers available on campus for general student use. A campuswide network can be accessed from student residence rooms and from off campus. Online class registration, online course syllabi, online class listings, and online payments are available. *Web address:* http://www.sau.edu/.

General Application Contact: Elizabeth Loveless, Director of Graduate Student Recruitment, 563-333-6271, Fax: 563-333-6268, E-mail: lovelesselizabethb@sau.edu.

GRADUATE UNITS

College of Arts and Sciences Students: 70 full-time (58 women), 68 part-time (44 women); includes 14 minority (4 Black or African American, non-Hispanic/Latino; 3 American Indian or Alaska Native, non-Hispanic/Latino; 1 Asian, non-Hispanic/Latino; 6 Hispanic/Latino). Average age 34. 64 applicants, 92% accepted, 50 enrolled. *Faculty:* 13 full-time (7 women), 6 part-time/adjunct (2 women). Expenses: Contact institution. *Financial support:* In 2010–11, 101 students received support, including 13 research assistantships with partial tuition reimbursements available (averaging $3,346 per year); career-related internships or fieldwork, scholarships/grants, tuition waivers (partial), and unspecified assistantships also available. Financial award application deadline: 8/15; financial award applicants required to submit FAFSA. In 2010, 48 master's awarded. *Degree program information:* Part-time and evening/weekend programs available. Offers arts and sciences (MCJ, MP Th, MSW); criminal justice (MCJ); juvenile justice education (MCJ); pastoral theology (MP Th); social work (MSW). *Application deadline:* For fall admission, 8/1 priority date for domestic students; for winter admission, 12/15 priority date for domestic students; for spring admission, 1/1 priority date for domestic students. Applications are processed on a rolling basis. *Application fee:* $25. Electronic applications accepted. *Application Contact:* Elizabeth Loveless, Director of Graduate Student Recruitment, 563-333-6271, Fax: 563-333-6268, E-mail: lovelesselizabethb@sau.edu. *Dean,* Dr. Aron R. Aji, 563-333-6053, Fax: 563-333-6052, E-mail: aronajir@sau.edu.

College of Business Students: 97 full-time (45 women), 341 part-time (188 women); includes 35 minority (17 Black or African American, non-Hispanic/Latino; 2 American Indian or Alaska Native, non-Hispanic/Latino; 5 Asian, non-Hispanic/Latino; 10 Hispanic/Latino; 1 Two or more races, non-Hispanic/Latino), 7 international. Average age 33. 142 applicants, 84% accepted, 109 enrolled. *Faculty:* 28 full-time (5 women), 14 part-time/adjunct (3 women). Expenses: Contact institution. *Financial support:* In 2010–11, 132 students received support, including 16 research assistantships with partial tuition reimbursements available (averaging $3,450 per year); career-related internships or fieldwork, scholarships/grants, tuition waivers (partial), and unspecified assistantships also available. Financial award application deadline: 3/15; financial award applicants required to submit FAFSA. In 2010, 159 master's, 5 doctorates awarded. *Degree program information:* Part-time and evening/weekend programs available. Offers accounting (MAC); business (MAC, MBA, MOL, MSITM, DBA); business administration (DBA); health care (MBA); human resources (MBA); information technology management (MSITM); organizational leadership (MOL). *Application deadline:* For fall admission, 8/15 priority date for domestic students; for winter admission, 12/15 for domestic students; for spring admission, 1/1 for domestic students. Applications are processed on a rolling basis. *Application fee:* $25. Electronic applications accepted. *Application Contact:* Elizabeth Loveless, Director of Graduate Student Recruitment, 563-333-6271, Fax: 563-333-6268, E-mail: lovelesselizabethb@sau.edu. *Dean,* Dr. David J. O'Connell, 563-333-6092, Fax: 563-333-6268, E-mail: oconnelldavidj@sau.edu.

College of Education and Health Sciences Students: 166 full-time (146 women), 98 part-time (76 women); includes 11 minority (1 Black or African American, non-Hispanic/Latino; 1 American Indian or Alaska Native, non-Hispanic/Latino; 5 Asian, non-Hispanic/Latino; 2 Hispanic/Latino; 2 Two or more races, non-Hispanic/Latino), 2 international. Average age 28. 528 applicants, 22% accepted, 115 enrolled. *Faculty:* 26 full-time (17 women), 12 part-time/adjunct (5 women). Expenses: Contact institution. *Financial support:* In 2010–11, 192 students received support, including 22 research assistantships with partial tuition reimbursements available (averaging $3,555 per year); career-related internships or fieldwork, scholarships/grants, tuition waivers (full and partial), and unspecified assistantships also available. Financial award application deadline: 3/15; financial award applicants required to submit FAFSA. In 2010, 67 master's, 47 doctorates awarded. *Degree program information:* Part-time and evening/weekend programs available. Postbaccalaureate distance learning degree programs offered (no on-campus study). Offers education and health sciences (M Ed, MEA, MOT, MSLP, MSN, DPT); educational administration (MEA); nursing (MSN); occupational therapy (MOT); physical therapy (DPT); special education (M Ed); speech-language pathology (MSLP); teaching (M Ed). *Application deadline:* For fall admission, 8/15 priority date for domestic students; for winter admission, 12/15 priority date for domestic students; for spring admission, 1/1 priority date for domestic students. Applications are processed on a rolling basis. *Application fee:* $25. Electronic applications accepted. *Application Contact:* Elizabeth Loveless, Director of Graduate Student Recruitment, 563-333-6271, Fax: 563-333-6268, E-mail: lovelesselizabethb@sau.edu. *Dean,* Dr. Sandra Cassady, 563-333-6409, Fax: 563-333-6297, E-mail: cassadysandral@sau.edu.

ST. ANDREW'S COLLEGE, Saskatoon, SK S7N 0W3, Canada

General Information Independent-religious, coed, graduate-only institution. *Enrollment by degree level:* 10 first professional, 15 master's, 1 other advanced degree. *Graduate faculty:* 4 full-time (3 women), 2 part-time/adjunct (both women). *Graduate tuition:* Tuition and fees charges are reported in Canadian dollars. *Tuition:* Full-time $6500 Canadian dollars; part-time $650 Canadian dollars per course. *Required fees:* $150 Canadian dollars. One-time fee: $150 Canadian dollars part-time. Tuition and fees vary according to course level and degree level. *Library facilities:* St. Andrew's Library. *Web address:* http://www.usask.ca/stu/standrews/.

General Application Contact: Colleen Walker, Registrar, 306-966-5244, Fax: 306-966-8981, E-mail: standrews.registrar@usask.ca.

GRADUATE UNITS

Graduate Programs in Theology Students: 10 full-time (4 women), 16 part-time (12 women). *Faculty:* 4 full-time (3 women), 2 part-time/adjunct (both women). Expenses: Contact institution. Offers theology (M Div, MTS, STM).

ST. ANDREW'S COLLEGE IN WINNIPEG, Winnipeg, MB R3T 2M7, Canada

General Information Independent-religious, coed, primarily men, graduate-only institution. *Graduate housing:* Rooms and/or apartments available to single and married students. Housing application deadline: 7/31.

GRADUATE UNITS

Graduate Programs Offers theology (M Div).

SAINT ANTHONY COLLEGE OF NURSING, Rockford, IL 61108-2468

General Information Independent-religious, coed, primarily women, upper-level institution.

GRADUATE UNITS

Graduate Program *Degree program information:* Part-time programs available. Offers nursing (MSN).

ST. AUGUSTINE'S SEMINARY OF TORONTO, Scarborough, ON M1M 1M3, Canada

General Information Independent-religious, coed, primarily men, graduate-only institution. *Graduate housing:* On-campus housing not available.

GRADUATE UNITS

Graduate and Professional Programs *Degree program information:* Part-time and evening/weekend programs available. Offers divinity (M Div); lay ministry (Diploma); religious education (MRE); theological studies (MTS, Diploma).

SAINT BERNARD'S SCHOOL OF THEOLOGY AND MINISTRY, Rochester, NY 14618

General Information Independent-religious, coed, graduate-only institution. *Enrollment by degree level:* 20 first professional, 80 master's, 13 other advanced degrees. *Graduate faculty:* 3 full-time (all women), 8 part-time/adjunct (4 women). *Tuition:* Full-time $9144; part-time $1524 per course. *Required fees:* $30 per semester. *Graduate housing:* On-campus housing not available. *Student services:* Writing training. *Library facilities:* Rush Rhees Library at University of Rochester. *Online resources:* library catalog, access to other libraries' catalogs. *Collection:* 68,025 titles, 329 serial subscriptions. *Research affiliation:* Colgate Rochester Crozer Divinity School.

Computer facilities: 2 computers available on campus for general student use. Word processing, scanning, image editing, chat utilities available. *Web address:* http://www.stbernards.edu/.

General Application Contact: Laura Smith, Director of Admissions and Financial Aid, 585-271-3657 Ext. 289, Fax: 585-271-2045, E-mail: admissions@stbernards.edu.

GRADUATE UNITS

Graduate and Professional Programs Students: 7 full-time (2 women), 106 part-time (50 women); includes 1 Black or African American, non-Hispanic/Latino; 1 Asian, non-Hispanic/Latino; 2 Hispanic/Latino. Average age 50. 17 applicants, 94% accepted, 16 enrolled. *Faculty:* 3 full-time (all women), 8 part-time/adjunct (4 women). Expenses: Contact institution. *Financial support:* In 2010–11, 31 students received support; fellowships, research assistantships, teaching assistantships, career-related internships or fieldwork, scholarships/grants, and tuition waivers (partial) available. Support available to part-time students. Financial award application deadline: 4/15; financial award applicants required to submit FAFSA. In 2010, 3 first professional degrees, 14 master's awarded. *Degree program information:* Part-time and evening/weekend programs available. Offers pastoral studies (MA, Certificate); theological studies (MA); theology (M Div). *Application deadline:* Applications are processed on a rolling basis. *Application fee:* $75. *Application Contact:* Laura Smith, Director of Admissions and Financial Aid, 585-271-3657 Ext. 289, Fax: 585-271-2045, E-mail: admissions@stbernards.edu. *President,* Dr. Patricia Schoelles, 585-271-3657 Ext. 276, Fax: 585-271-2045, E-mail: pschoelles@stbernards.edu.

ST. BONAVENTURE UNIVERSITY, St. Bonaventure, NY 14778-2284

General Information Independent-religious, coed, comprehensive institution. CGS member. *Enrollment:* 2,514 graduate, professional, and undergraduate students; 319 full-time matriculated graduate/professional students (217 women), 184 part-time matriculated graduate/professional students (108 women). *Enrollment by degree level:* 472 master's, 31 other advanced degrees. *Graduate faculty:* 49 full-time (16 women), 16 part-time/adjunct (9 women). *Tuition:* Part-time $670 per credit hour. *Graduate housing:* Room and/or apartments available on a first-come, first-served basis to single students; on-campus housing not available to married students. Housing application deadline: 3/19. *Student services:* Campus employment opportunities, campus safety program, career counseling, free psychological counseling, international student services, low-cost health insurance, teacher training. *Library facilities:* Friedsam Library. *Online resources:* library catalog, web page, access to other libraries' catalogs. *Collection:* 342,443 titles, 20,780 serial subscriptions, 14,808 audiovisual materials.

Computer facilities: 180 computers available on campus for general student use. A campuswide network can be accessed from student residence rooms and from off campus. Online class registration is available. *Web address:* http://www.sbu.edu/.

General Application Contact: Bruce Campbell, Director of Graduate Admissions, 716-375-2429, Fax: 716-375-4005, E-mail: gradsch@sbu.edu.

GRADUATE UNITS

School of Graduate Studies Students: 323 full-time (219 women), 200 part-time (120 women); includes 24 minority (9 Black or African American, non-Hispanic/Latino; 5 American Indian or Alaska Native, non-Hispanic/Latino; 1 Asian, non-Hispanic/Latino; 8 Hispanic/Latino; 1 Native Hawaiian or other Pacific Islander, non-Hispanic/Latino), 12 international. Average age 30. 401 applicants, 69% accepted, 200 enrolled. *Faculty:* 49 full-time (16 women), 16 part-time/adjunct (9 women). Expenses: Contact institution. *Financial support:* Research assistantships with full and partial tuition reimbursements, career-related internships or fieldwork, Federal Work-Study, scholarships/grants, health care benefits, tuition waivers (full and partial), and unspecified assistantships available. Support available to part-time students. Financial award application deadline: 4/15. In 2010, 261 master's, 9 other advanced degrees awarded. *Degree program information:* Part-time and evening/weekend programs available. Offers English (MA). *Application deadline:* For fall admission, 3/15 priority date for domestic students, 2/1 priority date for international students; for spring admission, 10/15 priority date for domestic students, 7/1 priority date for international students. Applications are processed on a rolling basis. *Application fee:* $30. Electronic applications accepted. *Application Contact:* Bruce Campbell, Director of Graduate Admissions, 716-375-2429, E-mail: gradsch@sbu.edu. *Dean,* Dr. Peggy Y. Burke, 716-375-2394, E-mail: pyburke@sbu.edu.

Russell J. Jandoli School of Journalism and Mass Communication Students: 37 full-time (24 women), 7 part-time (3 women); includes 3 minority (2 Black or African American, non-Hispanic/Latino; 1 American Indian or Alaska Native, non-Hispanic/Latino). Average age 26. 42 applicants, 69% accepted, 20 enrolled. *Faculty:* 4 full-time (2 women). Expenses: Contact institution. *Financial support:* In 2010–11, 1 research assistantship with full and partial tuition reimbursement was awarded; Federal Work-Study, scholarships/grants, health care benefits, tuition waivers (partial), and unspecified assistantships also available. Support available to part-time students. Financial award application deadline: 4/15; financial award applicants required to submit FAFSA. In 2010, 34 master's awarded. *Degree program information:* Evening/weekend programs available. Offers integrated marketing communications (MA). *Application deadline:* For fall admission, 3/15 priority date for domestic students, 2/1 priority date for international students; for spring admission, 10/15 priority date for domestic students, 7/1 priority date for international students. Applications are processed on a rolling basis. *Application fee:* $30. Electronic applications accepted. *Application Contact:* Dr. Pauline Hoffmann, Program Director, 716-375-2578, E-mail: hoffmann@sbu.edu. *Program Director,* Dr. Pauline Hoffmann, 716-375-2578, E-mail: hoffmann@sbu.edu.

School of Business Students: 76 full-time (30 women), 68 part-time (25 women); includes 8 minority (2 Black or African American, non-Hispanic/Latino; 2 American Indian or Alaska Native, non-Hispanic/Latino; 1 Asian, non-Hispanic/Latino; 2 Hispanic/Latino; 1 Native Hawaiian or other Pacific Islander, non-Hispanic/Latino), 7 international. Average age 31. 71 applicants, 96% accepted, 52 enrolled. *Faculty:* 22 full-time (5 women), 1 part-time/adjunct (0 women). Expenses: Contact institution. *Financial support:* In 2010–11, 12 research assistantships with full and partial tuition reimbursements were awarded; career-related internships or fieldwork, Federal Work-Study, scholarships/grants, health care benefits, and unspecified assistantships also available. Support available to part-time students. Financial award application deadline: 4/15; financial award applicants required to submit FAFSA. In 2010, 102 master's awarded. *Degree program information:* Part-time and evening/weekend programs available. Offers general business (MBA). *Application deadline:* For fall admission, 3/15 priority date for domestic students, 2/1 priority date for international students; for spring admission, 10/1 priority date for domestic students, 7/1 priority date for international students. Applications are processed on a rolling basis. *Application fee:* $30. Electronic applications accepted. *Application Contact:* John B. Stevens, MBA Director, 716-375-7662, Fax: 716-375-2191, E-mail: jstevens@sbu.edu. *MBA Director,* John B. Stevens, 716-375-7662, Fax: 716-375-2191, E-mail: jstevens@sbu.edu.

School of Education Students: 195 full-time (156 women), 103 part-time (76 women); includes 12 minority (5 Black or African American, non-Hispanic/Latino; 1 American Indian or Alaska Native, non-Hispanic/Latino; 6 Hispanic/Latino), 2 international. Average age 29. 226 applicants, 75% accepted, 121 enrolled. *Faculty:* 13 full-time (7 women), 14 part-time/adjunct (8 women). Expenses: Contact institution. *Financial support:* In 2010–11, 12 research assistantships with full and partial tuition reimbursements were awarded; career-related internships or fieldwork, Federal Work-Study, scholarships/grants, health care benefits, tuition waivers (partial), and unspecified assistantships also available. Support available to part-time students. Financial award application deadline: 4/15; financial award applicants required to submit FAFSA. In 2010, 104 master's, 8 Adv Cs awarded. *Degree program information:* Part-time and evening/weekend programs available. Offers adolescence education (MS Ed); adolescent literacy 5-12 (MS Ed); advanced inclusive processes (MS Ed); childhood literacy B-6 (MS Ed); community mental health counseling (MS Ed); education (MS Ed, Adv C); educational leadership (MS Ed); school building leader (Adv C); school counseling (MS Ed); school counselor (Adv C); school district leader (Adv C). *Application deadline:* For fall admission, 3/15 priority date for domestic students, 2/1 priority date for international students; for spring admission, 10/15 priority date for domestic students, 7/1 priority date for international students. Applications are processed on a rolling basis. *Application fee:* $30. Electronic applications accepted. *Application Contact:* Bruce Campbell, Director of Graduate Admissions, 716-375-2429, E-mail: gradsch@sbu.edu. *Dean,* Dr. Peggy Yehl Burke, 716-375-2394, E-mail: pyburke@sbu.edu.

School of Franciscan Studies Students: 5 part-time (3 women), 2 international. Average age 48. 12 applicants, 83% accepted. *Faculty:* 2 full-time (0 women). Expenses: Contact institution. *Financial support:* In 2010–11, 1 research assistantship with full and partial tuition reimbursement was awarded; Federal Work-Study, scholarships/grants, health care benefits, tuition waivers (full and partial), and unspecified assistantships also available. Support available to part-time students. Financial award application deadline: 4/15; financial award applicants required to submit FAFSA. In 2010, 8 master's awarded. *Degree program information:* Part-time programs available. Offers Franciscan studies (MA). *Application deadline:* For fall admission, 3/15 priority date for domestic students, 2/1 priority date for international students. Applications are processed on a rolling basis. *Application fee:* $30. Electronic applications accepted. *Application Contact:* Bruce E. Campbell, Director, Graduate Admissions, 716-375-2429, Fax: 716-375-7834, E-mail: gradsch@sbu.edu. *Interim Dean,* Fr. Edward Coughlin, 716-375-2032, E-mail: coughlin@sbu.edu.

ST. CATHERINE UNIVERSITY, St. Paul, MN 55105

General Information Independent-religious, Undergraduate: women only; graduate: coed, comprehensive institution. CGS member. *Enrollment:* 5,328 graduate, professional, and undergraduate students; 985 full-time matriculated graduate/professional students (897 women), 513 part-time matriculated graduate/professional students (473 women). *Enrollment by degree level:* 1,356 master's, 124 doctoral. *Graduate faculty:* 93 full-time (74 women). *Tuition:* Part-time $763 per credit. Part-time tuition and fees vary according to degree level and program. *Graduate housing:* Rooms and/or apartments available on a first-come, first-served basis to single and married students. Housing application deadline: 5/1. *Student services:* Campus employment opportunities, campus safety program, career counseling, free psychological counseling, international student services, low-cost health insurance, multicultural affairs office, writing training. *Library facilities:* St. Catherine Library plus 1 other. *Online resources:* library catalog, web page, access to other libraries' catalogs. *Collection:* 250,865 titles, 55,053 serial subscriptions, 7,844 audiovisual materials.

Computer facilities: Computer purchase and lease plans are available. 150 computers available on campus for general student use. A campuswide network can be accessed from student residence rooms and from off campus. Online class registration, transcript are available. *Web address:* http://www.stkate.edu/.

General Application Contact: Sylvia Alexander-Sedey, Senior Admissions Counselor, 651-690-6933, Fax: 651-690-6064, E-mail: graduate_study@stkate.edu.

GRADUATE UNITS

Graduate Programs Students: 985 full-time (897 women), 513 part-time (473 women); includes 126 minority (32 Black or African American, non-Hispanic/Latino; 2 American Indian or Alaska Native, non-Hispanic/Latino; 42 Asian, non-Hispanic/Latino; 21 Hispanic/Latino; 29 Two or more races, non-Hispanic/Latino), 12 international. Average age 37. 1,037 applicants, 59% accepted, 449 enrolled. *Faculty:* 94 full-time (74 women). Expenses: Contact institution. *Financial support:* In 2010–11, 609 students received support; research assistantships with tuition reimbursements available, career-related internships or fieldwork and institutionally sponsored loans available. Support available to part-time students. Financial award application deadline: 4/1; financial award applicants required to submit FAFSA. In 2010, 346 master's, 25 doctorates awarded. *Degree program information:* Part-time and evening/weekend programs available. Offers adult-gerontological nurse practitioner (MA); catechetical ministry (Certificate); education—initial licensure (MA); education–curriculum and instruction (MA); holistic health studies (MA); library and information science (MLIS); neonatal nurse practitioner (MA); nurse educator (MA); nursing (DNP); occupational therapy (MA); organizational leadership (MA); pastoral ministry (Certificate); pediatric nurse practitioner (MA); physical therapy (DPT); social work (MSW); spiritual direction (Certificate); theology (MA). *Application fee:* $35. *Application Contact:* 651-690-6933, Fax: 651-690-6064. *Dean of the School of Professional Studies and Graduate College,* Dr. MaryAnn Janosik, 651-690-6020, Fax: 651-690-6024.

ST. CHARLES BORROMEO SEMINARY, OVERBROOK, Wynnewood, PA 19096

General Information Independent-religious, coed, primarily men, comprehensive institution. *Enrollment:* 242 graduate, professional, and undergraduate students; 59 full-time matriculated graduate/professional students, 46 part-time matriculated graduate/professional students (26 women). *Enrollment by degree level:* 48 first professional, 57 master's. *Graduate faculty:* 12 full-time (3 women), 12 part-time/adjunct (3 women). *Tuition:* Full-time $18,888; part-time $1548 per course. *Required fees:* $1140. *Graduate housing:* Room and/or apartments guaranteed to single students; on-campus housing not available to married students. Housing application deadline: 7/15. *Student services:* Campus employment opportunities, career counseling. *Library facilities:* Ryan Memorial Library. *Online resources:* web page. *Collection:* 143,546 titles, 320 serial subscriptions, 17,736 audiovisual materials.

Computer facilities: 60 computers available on campus for general student use. A campuswide network can be accessed. *Web address:* http://www.scs.edu/.

General Application Contact: Rev. Joseph W. Bongard, Vice Rector, 610-785-6271, Fax: 610-617-9267, E-mail: frjbongard@adphila.org.

GRADUATE UNITS

Graduate and Professional Programs Students: 59 full-time (0 women), 46 part-time (26 women); includes 11 minority (4 Black or African American, non-Hispanic/Latino; 4 Asian, non-Hispanic/Latino; 2 Hispanic/Latino; 1 Two or more races, non-Hispanic/Latino), 1 international. Average age 39. 53 applicants, 100% accepted, 51 enrolled. *Faculty:* 12 full-time (3 women), 12 part-time/adjunct (3 women). Expenses: Contact institution. *Financial support:* In 2010–11, 74 students received support. Federal Work-Study and scholarships/grants available. Financial award application deadline: 7/15; financial award applicants required to submit CSS PROFILE. In 2010, 13 first professional degrees, 26 master's awarded. *Degree program information:* Part-time programs available. Offers religious studies (MA); theology (M Div, MA). *Application deadline:* For fall admission, 7/15 for domestic students, 3/15 priority date for international students. Applications are processed on a rolling basis. *Application fee:* $0. *Application Contact:* Rev. Joseph W. Bongard, Vice Rector, 610-785-6271, Fax: 610-617-9267, E-mail: frjbongard@adphila.org. *Rector and President,* Rev. Shaun L. Mahoney, 610-785-6200, Fax: 610-667-7635, E-mail: frsmahon@adphila.org.

ST. CLOUD STATE UNIVERSITY, St. Cloud, MN 56301-4498

General Information State-supported, coed, comprehensive institution. CGS member. *Graduate housing:* Room and/or apartments available on a first-come, first-served basis to single students; on-campus housing not available to married students. Housing application deadline: 4/15.

GRADUATE UNITS

School of Graduate Studies *Degree program information:* Part-time and evening/weekend programs available. Postbaccalaureate distance learning degree programs offered (no on-campus study).

College of Education *Degree program information:* Part-time and evening/weekend programs available. Postbaccalaureate distance learning degree programs offered (no on-campus study). Offers applied behavior analysis (MS); child and family studies (MS); college counseling and student development (MS); community counseling (MS); curriculum and instruction (MS); educable mentally handicapped (MS); education (MS, Ed D, Spt); educational administration and leadership (MS); educational leadership and community psychology (Spt); emotionally disturbed (MS); exercise science (MS); gifted and talented (MS); higher education administration (MS, Ed D); information media (MS); learning disabled (MS); marriage and family therapy (MS); physical education (MS); rehabilitation counseling (MS); school counseling (MS); social responsibility (MS); special education (MS); sports management (MS); trainable mentally retarded (MS).

College of Fine Arts and Humanities Offers communication sciences and disorders (MS); conducting and literature (MM); English (MA, MS); fine arts and humanities (MA, MM, MS); mass communication (MS); music education (MM); piano pedagogy (MM); teaching English as a second language (MA).

College of Science and Engineering Offers applied statistics (MS); biological sciences (MA, MS); computer science (MS); electrical engineering (MS); engineering management (MEM); environmental and technological studies (MS); information assurance (MS); mathematics (MS); mechanical engineering (MS); regulatory affairs and services (MS); science and engineering (MA, MEM, MS). Electronic applications accepted.

College of Social Sciences *Degree program information:* Part-time programs available. Offers applied economics (MS); criminal justice (MS); criminal justice administration (MS); cultural resource management archeology (MS); geography (MS); gerontology (MS); history (MA, MS); industrial-organizational psychology (MS); public and nonprofit institutions (MS); public safety executive leadership (MS); social sciences (MA, MS, MSW); social work (MSW). Electronic applications accepted.

G.R. Herberger College of Business *Degree program information:* Part-time and evening/weekend programs available. Offers business (MBA, MS); business administration (MBA); information assurance (MS). Electronic applications accepted.

ST. EDWARD'S UNIVERSITY, Austin, TX 78704

General Information Independent-religious, coed, comprehensive institution. *Enrollment:* 5,454 graduate, professional, and undergraduate students; 209 full-time matriculated graduate/professional students (133 women), 701 part-time matriculated graduate/professional students (433 women). *Enrollment by degree level:* 910 master's. *Graduate faculty:* 44 full-time (18

St. Edward's University (continued)

women), 66 part-time/adjunct (29 women). *Tuition:* Full-time $16,200; part-time $900 per credit hour. *Required fees:* $50 per trimester. Full-time tuition and fees vary according to course load and program. *Graduate housing:* On-campus housing not available. *Student services:* Campus employment opportunities, campus safety program, career counseling, exercise/wellness program, free psychological counseling, international student services, low-cost health insurance, services for students with disabilities, writing training. *Library facilities:* Scarborough-Phillips Library. *Online resources:* library catalog, web page. *Collection:* 190,640 titles, 2,030 serial subscriptions, 4,194 audiovisual materials.

Computer facilities: 790 computers available on campus for general student use. A campuswide network can be accessed from student residence rooms. Online class registration, online library, ability to change address and biographical data, look at transcripts, pull up statements of account, grades, online progress reports and degree audit, campus job postings, student timesheets, financial aid information are available. *Web address:* http://www.gotostedwards.com/.

General Application Contact: Bridget S. Davidson, Director, Center for Academic Progress, 512-428-1061, Fax: 512-428-1032, E-mail: bridgets@stedwards.edu.

GRADUATE UNITS

New College Students: 103 full-time (85 women), 267 part-time (207 women); includes 98 minority (20 Black or African American, non-Hispanic/Latino; 1 American Indian or Alaska Native, non-Hispanic/Latino; 3 Asian, non-Hispanic/Latino; 67 Hispanic/Latino; 1 Native Hawaiian or other Pacific Islander, non-Hispanic/Latino; 6 Two or more races, non-Hispanic/Latino), 1 international. Average age 33. 173 applicants, 69% accepted, 92 enrolled. *Faculty:* 16 full-time (9 women), 33 part-time/adjunct (20 women). Expenses: Contact institution. *Financial support:* In 2010–11, 7 students received support. Scholarships/grants available. In 2010, 104 master's awarded. *Degree program information:* Part-time and evening/weekend programs available. Offers college student development (MA); counseling (MA); global issues (MLA); humanities (MLA); liberal arts (Certificate); social sciences (MLA). *Application deadline:* For fall admission, 7/1 for domestic and international students; for spring admission, 11/1 for domestic and international students. Applications are processed on a rolling basis. *Application fee:* $45 ($50 for international students). Electronic applications accepted. *Application Contact:* Bridget S. Davidson, Director, Center for Academic Progress, 512-428-1061, Fax: 512-428-1032, E-mail: bridgets@stedwards.edu. *Interim Dean*, Dr. Helene L. Caudill, 512-448-8648, Fax: 512-448-8492, E-mail: helenec@stedwards.edu.

School of Education Students: 7 full-time (6 women), 38 part-time (28 women); includes 13 minority (2 Black or African American, non-Hispanic/Latino; 10 Hispanic/Latino; 1 Two or more races, non-Hispanic/Latino). Average age 29. 25 applicants, 80% accepted, 17 enrolled. *Faculty:* 4 full-time (1 woman), 3 part-time/adjunct (0 women). Expenses: Contact institution. *Financial support:* In 2010–11, 4 students received support. Scholarships/grants available. In 2010, 14 master's awarded. *Degree program information:* Part-time and evening/weekend programs available. Offers curriculum leadership (Certificate); education (MA, Certificate); instructional technology (Certificate); mediation (Certificate); mentoring and supervision (Certificate); special education (Certificate); sports management (Certificate); teaching (MA). *Application deadline:* For fall admission, 7/1 for domestic and international students; for spring admission, 11/1 for domestic and international students. Applications are processed on a rolling basis. *Application fee:* $45 ($50 for international students). Electronic applications accepted. *Application Contact:* Carrie Martin, Graduate Admission Coordinator, 512-233-1694, Fax: 512-428-1032, E-mail: carriem@stedwards.edu. *Dean*, Dr. Grant Simpson, 512-448-8655, Fax: 512-428-1372, E-mail: grants@stedwards.edu.

School of Management and Business Students: 99 full-time (42 women), 396 part-time (198 women); includes 182 minority (33 Black or African American, non-Hispanic/Latino; 3 American Indian or Alaska Native, non-Hispanic/Latino; 14 Asian, non-Hispanic/Latino; 125 Hispanic/Latino; 1 Native Hawaiian or other Pacific Islander, non-Hispanic/Latino; 6 Two or more races, non-Hispanic/Latino), 15 international. Average age 33. 221 applicants, 78% accepted, 118 enrolled. *Faculty:* 24 full-time (8 women), 30 part-time/adjunct (9 women). Expenses: Contact institution. *Financial support:* In 2010–11, 19 students received support. Scholarships/grants available. In 2010, 183 master's awarded. *Degree program information:* Part-time and evening/weekend programs available. Offers accounting (M Ac); business management (MBA); computer information systems (MS); corporate finance (MBA, Certificate); digital media management (MBA); global entrepreneurship (MBA); human resource management (Certificate); management and business (M Ac, MA, MBA, MS, Certificate); management information systems (MBA, Certificate); marketing (MBA, Certificate); operations management (MBA, Certificate); organization development (MA); organizational leadership and ethics (MS); project management (MS). *Application deadline:* For fall admission, 7/1 for domestic and international students; for spring admission, 11/1 for domestic and international students. Applications are processed on a rolling basis. *Application fee:* $45 ($50 for international students). Electronic applications accepted. *Application Contact:* Kelly Luna, Graduate Admissions Coordinator, 512-233-1697, Fax: 512-428-1032, E-mail: kellyl@stedwards.edu. *Dean*, Marsha Kelliher, 512-448-8588, Fax: 512-448-8492, E-mail: marshak@stedwards.edu.

ST. FRANCIS COLLEGE, Brooklyn Heights, NY 11201-4398

General Information Independent-religious, coed, comprehensive institution.

GRADUATE UNITS

Program in Professional Accountancy Offers professional accountancy (MS).

SAINT FRANCIS MEDICAL CENTER COLLEGE OF NURSING, Peoria, IL 61603-3783

General Information Independent-religious, coed, primarily women, upper-level institution. *Enrollment:* 490 graduate, professional, and undergraduate students; 6 full-time matriculated graduate/professional students (all women), 144 part-time matriculated graduate/professional students (133 women). *Enrollment by degree level:* 139 master's, 7 doctoral, 4 other advanced degrees. *Graduate faculty:* 3 full-time (all women), 9 part-time/adjunct (all women). *Graduate housing:* Room and/or apartments available on a first-come, first-served basis to single students; on-campus housing not available to married students. Housing application deadline: 3/14. *Student services:* Campus safety program, exercise/wellness program, free psychological counseling. *Library facilities:* Sister Mary Ludgera Pieperbeck Learning and Resource Center plus 1 other. *Online resources:* library catalog, web page, access to other libraries' catalogs. *Collection:* 6,790 titles, 139 serial subscriptions, 782 audiovisual materials.

Computer facilities: 49 computers available on campus for general student use. A campuswide network can be accessed from student residence rooms and from off campus. Online class registration is available. *Web address:* http://www.sfmccon.edu/.

General Application Contact: Dr. Janice F. Boundy, Associate Dean, 309-655-2230, Fax: 309-624-8973, E-mail: jan.f.boundy@osfhealthcare.org.

GRADUATE UNITS

Graduate Program Students: 6 full-time (all women), 144 part-time (133 women); includes 9 minority (1 Black or African American, non-Hispanic/Latino; 1 American Indian or Alaska Native, non-Hispanic/Latino; 3 Asian, non-Hispanic/Latino; 4 Hispanic/Latino). Average age 28. 19 applicants, 100% accepted, 19 enrolled. *Faculty:* 3 full-time (all women), 8 part-time/adjunct (all women). Expenses: Contact institution. *Financial support:* In 2010–11, 3 students received support. Scholarships/grants and tuition waivers (partial) available. Support available to part-time students. Financial award application deadline: 6/15; financial award applicants required to submit FAFSA. In 2010, 29 master's awarded. *Degree program information:* Part-time programs available. Postbaccalaureate distance learning degree programs offered (minimal on-campus study). Offers child and family nursing (MSN); clinical nurse leader (MSN); medical-surgical nursing (MSN); neonatal nurse practitioner (MSN); nurse clinician (Post-Graduate Certificate); nurse educator (Post-Graduate Certificate); nursing (DNP). *Application deadline:* For fall admission, 6/1 priority date for domestic and international students; for spring admission, 11/15 priority date for domestic and international students. Applications are processed on a rolling basis. *Application fee:* $50. Electronic applications accepted. *Application Contact:* Dr. Janice F. Boundy, Associate Dean, 309-655-2230, Fax: 309-624-8973, E-mail: jan.f.boundy@osfhealthcare.org. *Dean*, Dr. Lois J. Hamilton, 309-655-2201, Fax: 309-624-8973, E-mail: lois.j.hamilton@osfhealthcare.org.

SAINT FRANCIS SEMINARY, St. Francis, WI 53235-3795

General Information Independent-religious, coed, graduate-only institution. *Graduate housing:* Room and/or apartments available to single students; on-campus housing not available to married students. Housing application deadline: 7/15.

GRADUATE UNITS

Graduate and Professional Programs *Degree program information:* Part-time programs available. Offers theology (M Div, MAPS).

SAINT FRANCIS UNIVERSITY, Loretto, PA 15940-0600

General Information Independent-religious, coed, comprehensive institution. *Enrollment:* 2,449 graduate, professional, and undergraduate students; 281 full-time matriculated graduate/professional students (204 women), 436 part-time matriculated graduate/professional students (281 women). *Enrollment by degree level:* 592 master's, 125 doctoral. *Graduate faculty:* 36 full-time (22 women), 68 part-time/adjunct (24 women). *Graduate housing:* Rooms and/or apartments available on a first-come, first-served basis to single and married students. *Student services:* Campus employment opportunities, campus safety program, career counseling, exercise/wellness program, free psychological counseling, low-cost health insurance, multicultural affairs office, services for students with disabilities, writing training. *Library facilities:* Pasquerilla Library. *Online resources:* library catalog, web page, access to other libraries' catalogs. *Collection:* 126,201 titles, 30,143 serial subscriptions, 5,318 audiovisual materials.

Computer facilities: Computer purchase and lease plans are available. 75 computers available on campus for general student use. A campuswide network can be accessed from student residence rooms and from off campus. Online class registration, wireless access throughout all of campus are available. *Web address:* http://www.francis.edu/.

General Application Contact: Dr. Peter Raymond Skoner, Associate Provost, 814-472-3085, Fax: 814-472-3365, E-mail: pskoner@francis.edu.

GRADUATE UNITS

Department of Occupational Therapy Students: 33 full-time (29 women). Average age 22. 33 applicants, 100% accepted, 33 enrolled. *Faculty:* 6 full-time (4 women). Expenses: Contact institution. In 2010, 23 master's awarded. Offers occupational therapy (MOT). *Application Contact:* Dr. Peter Raymond Skoner, Associate Vice President for Academic Affairs, 814-472-3085, Fax: 814-472-3365, E-mail: pskoner@francis.edu. *Chair*, Dr. Donald Walkovich, 814-472-3899, Fax: 814-472-3950, E-mail: dwalkovich@francis.edu.

Department of Physical Therapy Students: 125 full-time (82 women); includes 2 Black or African American, non-Hispanic/Latino; 1 Asian, non-Hispanic/Latino; 1 Two or more races, non-Hispanic/Latino. Average age 23. 50 applicants, 44% accepted, 15 enrolled. *Faculty:* 8 full-time (4 women), 10 part-time/adjunct (3 women). Expenses: Contact institution. *Financial support:* In 2010–11, 8 students received support, including 8 teaching assistantships with partial tuition reimbursements available; unspecified assistantships also available. Offers physical therapy (DPT). *Application deadline:* For winter admission, 1/15 for domestic and international students. *Application fee:* $30. Electronic applications accepted. *Application Contact:* Dr. Kay Malek, Chair/Associate Professor, 814-472-3123, Fax: 814-472-3140, E-mail: kmalek@francis.edu. *Chair/Associate Professor*, Dr. Kay Malek, 814-472-3123, Fax: 814-472-3140, E-mail: kmalek@francis.edu.

Department of Physician Assistant Sciences Students: 107 full-time (85 women); includes 1 Black or African American, non-Hispanic/Latino; 3 Asian, non-Hispanic/Latino; 1 Hispanic/Latino. Average age 25. 1,061 applicants, 5% accepted, 15 enrolled. *Faculty:* 11 full-time (9 women), 3 part-time/adjunct (0 women). Expenses: Contact institution. *Financial support:* Applicants required to submit FAFSA. In 2010, 53 master's awarded. Offers health science (MHS); medical science (MMS); physician assistant sciences (MPAS). *Application deadline:* For fall admission, 10/1 for domestic and international students. Applications are processed on a rolling basis. *Application fee:* $170. Electronic applications accepted. *Application Contact:* Marie S. Link, Director of Research and MPAS Graduate Admission, 814-472-3138, Fax: 814-472-3137, E-mail: mlink@francis.edu. *Director*, Donna L. Yeisley, 814-472-3131, Fax: 814-472-3137, E-mail: dyeisley@francis.edu.

Graduate Education Program Students: 172 part-time (127 women). Average age 30. 26 applicants, 100% accepted, 26 enrolled. *Faculty:* 20 part-time/adjunct (7 women). Expenses: Contact institution. *Financial support:* Applicants required to submit FAFSA. In 2010, 44 master's awarded. *Degree program information:* Part-time and evening/weekend programs available. Offers education (M Ed); leadership (M Ed); reading (M Ed). *Application deadline:* Applications are processed on a rolling basis. *Application fee:* $30. *Application Contact:* Sherri L. Toth, Coordinator, 814-472-3058, Fax: 814-472-3864, E-mail: stoth@francis.edu. *Director*, Dr. Janette D. Kelly, 814-472-3068, Fax: 814-472-3864, E-mail: jkelly@francis.edu.

Graduate School of Business and Human Resource Management Students: 16 full-time (8 women), 141 part-time (66 women); includes 2 Black or African American, non-Hispanic/Latino. Average age 32. 40 applicants, 88% accepted, 25 enrolled. *Faculty:* 8 full-time (2 women), 25 part-time/adjunct (12 women). Expenses: Contact institution. *Financial support:* Fellowships with partial tuition reimbursements, career-related internships or fieldwork and unspecified assistantships available. In 2010, 67 master's awarded. *Degree program information:* Part-time and evening/weekend programs available. Offers business administration (MBA); human resource management (MHRM). *Application deadline:* For fall admission, 8/1 priority date for domestic and international students; for spring admission, 12/1 priority date for domestic students, 12/1 for international students. Applications are processed on a rolling basis. *Application fee:* $30. *Application Contact:* Dr. Peter Raymond Skoner, Associate Vice President for Academic Affairs, 814-472-3085, Fax: 814-472-3365, E-mail: pskoner@francis.edu. *Director*, Dr. Randy Frye, 814-472-3041, Fax: 814-472-3174, E-mail: rfrye@francis.edu.

ST. FRANCIS XAVIER UNIVERSITY, Antigonish, NS B2G 2W5, Canada

General Information Independent-religious, coed, comprehensive institution. *Graduate housing:* Room and/or apartments available on a first-come, first-served basis to single students; on-campus housing not available to married students. Housing application deadline: 7/1.

GRADUATE UNITS

Graduate Studies *Degree program information:* Part-time programs available. Postbaccalaureate distance learning degree programs offered (minimal on-campus study). Offers adult education (M Ad Ed); biology (M Sc); Celtic studies (MA); chemistry (M Sc); computer science (M Sc); curriculum and instruction (M Ed); earth sciences (M Sc); educational administration and leadership (M Ed); physics (M Sc).

ST. JOHN FISHER COLLEGE, Rochester, NY 14618-3597

General Information Independent-religious, coed, comprehensive institution. *Enrollment:* 4,020 graduate, professional, and undergraduate students; 630 full-time matriculated graduate/professional students (395 women), 478 part-time matriculated graduate/professional students (356 women). *Enrollment by degree level:* 303 first professional, 700 master's, 105 doctoral. *Graduate faculty:* 79 full-time (38 women), 41 part-time/adjunct (20 women). *Tuition:* Part-time $705 per credit hour. *Required fees:* $25 per semester. *Graduate housing:* On-campus housing not available. *Student services:* Campus employment opportunities, campus safety program, career counseling, child daycare facilities, exercise/wellness program, free psychological counseling, international student services, low-cost health insurance, multicultural affairs office, services for students with disabilities, teacher training, writing training. *Library facilities:* Charles J. Lavery Library. *Online resources:* library catalog, web page, access to other libraries' catalogs. *Collection:* 229,031 titles, 48,558 serial subscriptions, 7,641 audiovisual materials.

Computer facilities: 550 computers available on campus for general student use. A campuswide network can be accessed from student residence rooms and from off campus. Online class registration is available. *Web address:* http://www.sjfc.edu/.

General Application Contact: Jose Perales, Director of Transfer and Graduate Admissions, 585-385-8161, Fax: 585-385-8344, E-mail: jperales@sjfc.edu.

GRADUATE UNITS

Ralph C. Wilson Jr. School of Education Students: 214 full-time (154 women), 170 part-time (132 women); includes 64 Black or African American, non-Hispanic/Latino; 3 Asian, non-Hispanic/Latino; 16 Hispanic/Latino; 1 Two or more races, non-Hispanic/Latino. Average age 33. 332 applicants, 78% accepted, 175 enrolled. *Faculty:* 25 full-time (14 women), 22 part-time/adjunct (15 women). Expenses: Contact institution. *Financial support:* In 2010–11, 308 students received support. Scholarships/grants available. Financial award applicants required to submit FAFSA. In 2010, 149 master's, 21 doctorates, 6 other advanced degrees awarded. *Degree program information:* Part-time and evening/weekend programs available. Offers adolescence English (MS Ed); adolescence French (MS Ed); adolescence social studies (MS Ed); adolescence Spanish (MS Ed); childhood education/special education (MS); education (MS, MS Ed, Ed D, Certificate); educational leadership (MS Ed); executive leadership (Ed D); literacy birth to grade 6 (MS); literacy grades 5 to 12 (MS); special education (MS, Certificate). *Application deadline:* Applications are processed on a rolling basis. *Application fee:* $30. Electronic applications accepted. *Application Contact:* Jose Perales, Director of Graduate Admissions, 585-385-8067, E-mail: jperales@sjfc.edu. *Dean,* Dr. Wendy A. Paterson, 585-385-3813, E-mail: jadams@sjfc.edu.

Ronald L. Bittner School of Business Students: 50 full-time (27 women), 117 part-time (69 women); includes 22 minority (9 Black or African American, non-Hispanic/Latino; 1 American Indian or Alaska Native, non-Hispanic/Latino; 8 Asian, non-Hispanic/Latino; 2 Hispanic/Latino; 2 Two or more races, non-Hispanic/Latino). Average age 28. 129 applicants, 79% accepted, 73 enrolled. *Faculty:* 13 full-time (3 women), 9 part-time/adjunct (2 women). Expenses: Contact institution. *Financial support:* In 2010–11, 99 students received support. Scholarships/grants available. Financial award applicants required to submit FAFSA. In 2010, 44 master's awarded. *Degree program information:* Part-time and evening/weekend programs available. Offers business (MBA, MS); business administration (MBA); organizational learning and human resource development (MS). *Application deadline:* Applications are processed on a rolling basis. *Application fee:* $30. Electronic applications accepted. *Application Contact:* Jose Perales, Interim Director of Graduate Admissions, 585-385-8067, E-mail: jperales@sjfc.edu. *Dean,* Dr. David Martin, 585-385-8082, Fax: 585-385-8094, E-mail: dmartin@sjfc.edu.

School of Arts and Sciences Students: 25 full-time (16 women), 69 part-time (40 women); includes 7 minority (4 Black or African American, non-Hispanic/Latino; 2 Asian, non-Hispanic/Latino; 1 Hispanic/Latino). Average age 29. 33 applicants, 76% accepted, 17 enrolled. *Faculty:* 9 full-time (2 women), 8 part-time/adjunct (2 women). Expenses: Contact institution. *Financial support:* In 2010–11, 63 students received support. Scholarships/grants available. Financial award applicants required to submit FAFSA. In 2010, 32 master's awarded. *Degree program information:* Part-time and evening/weekend programs available. Offers arts and sciences (MS); international studies (MS); mathematics/science/technology education (MS). *Application deadline:* Applications are processed on a rolling basis. *Application fee:* $30. Electronic applications accepted. *Application Contact:* Jose Perales, Director of Graduate Admissions, 585-385-8067, E-mail: jperales@sjfc.edu. *Dean,* Dr. David Pate, 585-385-8034, E-mail: dpate@sjfc.edu.

Wegmans School of Nursing Students: 57 full-time (49 women), 120 part-time (115 women); includes 27 minority (14 Black or African American, non-Hispanic/Latino; 2 American Indian or Alaska Native, non-Hispanic/Latino; 10 Hispanic/Latino; 1 Two or more races, non-Hispanic/Latino), 2 international. Average age 34. 137 applicants, 72% accepted, 66 enrolled. *Faculty:* 15 full-time (11 women), 2 part-time/adjunct (1 woman). Expenses: Contact institution. *Financial support:* In 2010–11, 131 students received support. Scholarships/grants available. Financial award applicants required to submit FAFSA. In 2010, 46 master's awarded. *Degree program information:* Part-time and evening/weekend programs available. Offers advanced practice nursing (MS); clinical nurse specialist (Certificate); family nurse practitioner (Certificate); mental health counseling (MS); nurse educator (Certificate); nursing (MS, DNP, Certificate); nursing practice (DNP). *Application deadline:* Applications are processed on a rolling basis. Electronic applications accepted. *Application Contact:* Jose Perales, Director of Graduate Admissions, 585-385-8067, E-mail: jperales@sjfc.edu. *Dean,* Dr. Diane Cooney-Miner, 585-385-8241, Fax: 585-385-8466, E-mail: dcooney-miner@sjfc.edu.

Wegmans School of Pharmacy Students: 284 full-time (149 women), 2 part-time (0 women); includes 51 minority (7 Black or African American, non-Hispanic/Latino; 38 Asian, non-Hispanic/Latino; 6 Hispanic/Latino), 9 international. Average age 25. 1,019 applicants, 15% accepted, 78 enrolled. *Faculty:* 18 full-time (9 women). Expenses: Contact institution. *Financial support:* In 2010–11, 256 students received support. Scholarships/grants available. Financial award applicants required to submit FAFSA. In 2010, 52 Pharm Ds awarded. Offers pharmacy (Pharm D). *Application deadline:* For fall admission, 3/1 for domestic students. Applications are processed on a rolling basis. *Application fee:* $50. Electronic applications accepted. *Application Contact:* Jose Perales, Director of Graduate Admissions, 585-385-8067, E-mail: jperales@sjfc.edu. *Dean,* Dr. Scott A. Swigart, 585-385-8201, Fax: 585-385-8453, E-mail: sswigart@sjfc.edu.

ST. JOHN'S COLLEGE, Annapolis, MD 21404

General Information Independent, coed, comprehensive institution. *Graduate housing:* On-campus housing not available.

GRADUATE UNITS

Graduate Institute in Liberal Education *Degree program information:* Evening/weekend programs available. Offers liberal arts (MALA).

ST. JOHN'S COLLEGE, Santa Fe, NM 87505

General Information Independent, coed, comprehensive institution. *Graduate housing:* Rooms and/or apartments available on a first-come, first-served basis to single and married students. Housing application deadline: 4/1.

GRADUATE UNITS

Graduate Institute in Liberal Education *Degree program information:* Evening/weekend programs available. Offers Eastern classics (MA); liberal arts (MA); liberal education (MA).

ST. JOHN'S SEMINARY, Camarillo, CA 93012-2598

General Information Independent-religious, coed, primarily men, graduate-only institution. *Enrollment by degree level:* 67 first professional, 22 master's. *Graduate faculty:* 23 full-time (5 women), 7 part-time/adjunct (1 woman). *Tuition:* Full-time $14,000; part-time $467 per unit. One-time fee: $5201.96 full-time; $105 part-time. Full-time tuition and fees vary according to course load and program. *Graduate housing:* Room and/or apartments guaranteed to single students; on-campus housing not available to married students. Typical cost: $11,500 (including board). *Student services:* Campus employment opportunities, career counseling, free psychological counseling, international student services, low-cost health insurance, writing training. *Library facilities:* Edward Laurence Doheny Memorial Library plus 1 other. *Online resources:* library catalog, web page. *Collection:* 57,827 titles, 250 serial subscriptions, 5,888 audiovisual materials.

Computer facilities: 23 computers available on campus for general student use. A campuswide network can be accessed from student residence rooms and from off campus. Class schedules by e-mail available. *Web address:* http://www.stjohnsem.edu/.

General Application Contact: Dr. Mark F. Fischer, Director of Admissions, 805-482-2755 Ext. 2042, Fax: 805-482-3470, E-mail: fischer@stjohnsem.edu.

GRADUATE UNITS

Graduate and Professional Programs Students: 77 full-time (5 women), 12 part-time (6 women); includes 14 Asian, non-Hispanic/Latino; 32 Hispanic/Latino; 1 Native Hawaiian or other Pacific Islander, non-Hispanic/Latino, 19 international. Average age 34. 19 applicants, 100% accepted, 16 enrolled. *Faculty:* 23 full-time (5 women), 7 part-time/adjunct (1 woman). Expenses: Contact institution. In 2010, 6 first professional degrees, 1 master's awarded. *Degree program information:* Part-time programs available. Offers divinity (M Div); pastoral ministry (MAPM); theology (MA). *Application deadline:* For fall admission, 7/15 priority date for domestic students. Applications are processed on a rolling basis. *Application fee:* $0. Electronic applications accepted. *Application Contact:* Esme M. Takahashi, Registrar, 805-482-2755 Ext. 1014, Fax: 805-482-3470, E-mail: esme@stjohnsem.edu. *Interim Academic Dean,* Rev. Kevin McCracken, CM, 805-482-2755 Ext. 1012, Fax: 805-482-3470, E-mail: kmccracken@stjohnsem.edu.

SAINT JOHN'S SEMINARY, Brighton, MA 02135

General Information Independent-religious, coed, graduate-only institution. *Graduate housing:* Room and/or apartments available to single students; on-campus housing not available to married students. Housing application deadline: 8/1.

GRADUATE UNITS

Graduate Programs Offers theology (M Div, MA Th, MAM).

SAINT JOHN'S UNIVERSITY, Collegeville, MN 56321

General Information Independent-religious, men only, comprehensive institution. *Graduate housing:* Rooms and/or apartments available on a first-come, first-served basis to single and married students. *Research affiliation:* Hill Monastic Manuscript Library (monastic studies, liturgy, spirituality), Center for Ecumenical and Cultural Research, Arca Artium (visual and book arts).

GRADUATE UNITS

Saint John's School of Theology and Seminary *Degree program information:* Part-time programs available. Postbaccalaureate distance learning degree programs offered (no on-campus study). Offers divinity (M Div); liturgical music (MA); liturgical studies (MA); pastoral ministry (MA); theology (MA). Electronic applications accepted.

ST. JOHN'S UNIVERSITY, Queens, NY 11439

General Information Independent-religious, coed, university. CGS member. *Enrollment:* 21,354 graduate, professional, and undergraduate students; 3,139 full-time matriculated graduate/professional students (1,820 women), 2,495 part-time matriculated graduate/professional students (1,665 women). *Enrollment by degree level:* 1,448 first professional, 3,502 master's, 597 doctoral, 87 other advanced degrees. *Graduate faculty:* 648 full-time (280 women), 794 part-time/adjunct (318 women). *Tuition:* Full-time $17,100; part-time $950 per credit. *Required fees:* $340; $170 per semester. Tuition and fees vary according to program. *Graduate housing:* Room and/or apartments available to single students; on-campus housing not available to married students. *Student services:* Campus employment opportunities, campus safety program, career counseling, exercise/wellness program, free psychological counseling, international student services, low-cost health insurance, services for students with disabilities, teacher training, writing training. *Library facilities:* St. John's University Library plus 1 other. *Online resources:* library catalog, web page, access to other libraries' catalogs. *Collection:* 397,602 titles, 43,654 serial subscriptions, 10,985 audiovisual materials. *Research affiliation:* Hoffman LaRoche Inc. (pharmaceutical research), Edwin Gould Service for Children and Families (social science), Ray Biotech Inc. (pharmaceutical research), American Speech-Language-Hearing Association (communications and science disorders research), New York University School of Medicine (psychology), Merck & Co., Inc. (pharmaceutical research).

Computer facilities: Computer purchase and lease plans are available. 12,959 computers available on campus for general student use. A campuswide network can be accessed from student residence rooms and from off campus. Online class registration, various software packages are available. *Web address:* http://www.stjohns.edu/.

General Application Contact: Kathleen Davis, Director of Graduate Admissions, 718-990-1601, E-mail: gradhelp@stjohns.edu.

GRADUATE UNITS

College of Pharmacy and Allied Health Professions Students: 626 full-time (332 women), 133 part-time (72 women); includes 393 minority (9 Black or African American, non-Hispanic/Latino; 345 Asian, non-Hispanic/Latino; 18 Hispanic/Latino; 9 Native Hawaiian or other Pacific Islander, non-Hispanic/Latino; 12 Two or more races, non-Hispanic/Latino), 215 international. Average age 24. 538 applicants, 42% accepted, 73 enrolled. *Faculty:* 84 full-time (43 women), 22 part-time/adjunct (8 women). Expenses: Contact institution. *Financial support:* In 2010–11, 155 students received support, including 32 fellowships with full and partial tuition reimbursements available (averaging $10,555 per year), 3 research assistantships with full and partial tuition reimbursements available (averaging $16,245 per year), 32 teaching assistantships with full and partial tuition reimbursements available (averaging $13,749 per year); career-related internships or fieldwork, scholarships/grants, and unspecified assistantships also available. Support available to part-time students. Financial award application deadline: 3/1; financial award applicants required to submit FAFSA. In 2010, 250 first professional degrees, 82 master's, 4 doctorates awarded. *Degree program information:* Part-time and evening/weekend programs available. Offers pharmaceutical sciences (MS, PhD); pharmacy (Pharm D, MS, PhD); pharmacy administration (MS); pharmacy and allied health professions (Pharm D, MS, PhD); toxicology (MS). *Application deadline:* For fall admission, 3/1 for domestic students, 5/1 priority date for international students; for spring admission, 11/1 for domestic students, 11/1 priority date for international students. Applications are processed on a rolling basis. *Application fee:* $70. Electronic applications accepted. *Application Contact:* Kathleen Davis, Director of Graduate Admission, 718-990-2790, E-mail: gradhelp@stjohns.edu. *Dean,* Dr. Robert Mangione, 718-990-6411, Fax: 718-990-1871, E-mail: mangionr@stjohns.edu.

College of Professional Studies Students: 93 full-time (42 women), 73 part-time (38 women); includes 80 minority (30 Black or African American, non-Hispanic/Latino; 1 American Indian or Alaska Native, non-Hispanic/Latino; 11 Asian, non-Hispanic/Latino; 37 Hispanic/Latino; 1 Two or more races, non-Hispanic/Latino), 10 international. Average age 27. 153 applicants, 67% accepted, 58 enrolled. *Faculty:* 87 full-time (30 women), 210 part-time/adjunct (68 women). Expenses: Contact institution. *Financial support:* In 2010–11, 86 students received support, including 1 teaching assistantship (averaging $19,950 per year); research assistantships. Financial award application deadline: 3/1; financial award applicants required to submit FAFSA. In 2010, 37 master's awarded. Offers criminal justice and legal studies (MPS); international communications (MS); sport management (MPS). *Application deadline:* For fall admission, 5/1 priority date for domestic and international students; for spring admission, 11/1 priority date for domestic and international students. Applications are processed on a rolling basis. *Application fee:* $70. Electronic applications accepted. *Application Contact:* Kathleen Davis, Director of Graduate Admission, 718-990-2790, Fax: 718-990-5686, E-mail: gradhelp@stjohns.edu. *Dean,* Dr. Kathleen Voute MacDonald, 718-990-6435, Fax: 718-990-1882, E-mail: macdonak@stjohns.edu.

Institute for Biotechnology Students: 8 full-time (4 women), 12 part-time (7 women); includes 6 minority (5 Asian, non-Hispanic/Latino; 1 Hispanic/Latino), 12 international. Average age 25. 65 applicants, 38% accepted, 5 enrolled. Expenses: Contact institution. *Financial support:* In 2010–11, 3 students received support, including 2 teaching assistantships with full tuition reimbursements available (averaging $7,612 per year). Financial award application deadline: 3/1; financial award applicants required to submit FAFSA. In 2010, 4 master's awarded. Offers biological/pharmaceutical biotechnology (MS). *Application deadline:* For fall admission, 5/1 priority date for domestic and international students; for spring admission, 11/1 priority date for domestic and international students. Applications are processed on a rolling basis. *Application fee:* $70. Electronic applications accepted. *Application Contact:* Kathleen Davis, Director of Graduate Admission, 718-990-1601, E-mail: gradhelp@stjohns.edu. *Director,* Dr. Vijaya L. Korlipara, 718-990-5396, E-mail: korlipav@stjohns.edu.

The Peter J. Tobin College of Business Students: 629 full-time (337 women), 272 part-time (115 women); includes 202 minority (54 Black or African American, non-Hispanic/Latino; 1 American Indian or Alaska Native, non-Hispanic/Latino; 87 Asian, non-Hispanic/Latino; 49 Hispanic/Latino; 1 Native Hawaiian or other Pacific Islander, non-Hispanic/Latino; 10 Two or more races, non-Hispanic/Latino), 383 international. Average age 26. 1,105 applicants, 68% accepted, 384 enrolled. *Faculty:* 94 full-time (22 women), 32 part-time/adjunct (5 women).

St. John's University (continued)

Expenses: Contact institution. *Financial support:* In 2010–11, 214 students received support, including 1 fellowship (averaging $23,115 per year), 55 research assistantships with full and partial tuition reimbursements available (averaging $16,637 per year), 2 teaching assistantships (averaging $11,870 per year); scholarships/grants also available. Support available to part-time students. Financial award application deadline: 3/1; financial award applicants required to submit FAFSA. In 2010, 368 master's, 1 other advanced degree awarded. *Degree program information:* Part-time and evening/weekend programs available. Offers accounting (MBA, MS, Adv C); business (MBA, MS, Adv C); computer information systems and decision sciences (MBA, Adv C); finance (MBA, Adv C); international business (MBA, Adv C); investment management (MS); management (MBA, Adv C); marketing (MBA, Adv C); taxation (MBA, MS, Adv C). *Application deadline:* For fall admission, 5/1 priority date for domestic and international students; for spring admission, 11/1 priority date for domestic and international students. Applications are processed on a rolling basis. *Application fee:* $70. Electronic applications accepted. *Application Contact:* Carol Swanberg, Assistant Dean/Director of Graduate Admissions, 718-990-1345, Fax: 718-990-5242, E-mail: tobingradnyc@stjohns.edu. *Dean,* Dr. Victoria Shoaf, 718-990-6458, E-mail: shoafv@stjohns.edu.

School of Risk Management and Actuarial Science Students: 67 full-time (30 women), 31 part-time (10 women); includes 23 minority (6 Black or African American, non-Hispanic/Latino; 6 Asian, non-Hispanic/Latino; 7 Hispanic/Latino; 4 Two or more races, non-Hispanic/Latino), 51 international. Average age 25. 155 applicants, 68% accepted, 54 enrolled. Expenses: Contact institution. *Financial support:* Research assistantships available. In 2010, 43 master's awarded. Offers risk management and actuarial science (MBA, MS). *Application deadline:* For fall admission, 5/1 priority date for domestic and international students; for spring admission, 11/1 priority date for domestic and international students. Applications are processed on a rolling basis. *Application fee:* $70. Electronic applications accepted. *Application Contact:* Carol Swanberg, Assistant Dean/Director of Graduate Admissions, 718-990-1345, Fax: 718-990-5242, E-mail: tobingradnyc@stjohns.edu. *Chair,* Dr. W Jean Kwon, 212-277-5196, E-mail: kwonw@stjohns.edu.

St. John's College of Liberal Arts and Sciences Students: 522 full-time (383 women), 604 part-time (429 women); includes 341 minority (115 Black or African American, non-Hispanic/Latino; 2 American Indian or Alaska Native, non-Hispanic/Latino; 76 Asian, non-Hispanic/Latino; 130 Hispanic/Latino; 4 Native Hawaiian or other Pacific Islander, non-Hispanic/Latino; 14 Two or more races, non-Hispanic/Latino), 92 international. Average age 30. 1,689 applicants, 36% accepted, 296 enrolled. *Faculty:* 267 full-time (117 women), 344 part-time/adjunct (159 women). Expenses: Contact institution. *Financial support:* In 2010–11, 581 students received support, including 92 fellowships with full and partial tuition reimbursements available (averaging $19,643 per year), 92 research assistantships with full and partial tuition reimbursements available (averaging $17,071 per year), 36 teaching assistantships with full and partial tuition reimbursements available (averaging $16,085 per year); career-related internships or fieldwork, scholarships/grants, and unspecified assistantships also available. Support available to part-time students. Financial award application deadline: 3/1; financial award applicants required to submit FAFSA. In 2010, 316 master's, 50 doctorates, 31 other advanced degrees awarded. *Degree program information:* Part-time and evening/weekend programs available. Offers algebra (MA); analysis (MA); applied mathematics (MA); biological sciences (MS, PhD); chemistry (MS); clinical psychology (MA, PhD); clinical psychology-child (PhD); clinical psychology-general (PhD); communication sciences and disorders (MA, Au D); computer science (MA); criminology and justice (MA); English (MA, DA); general experimental psychology (MA); geometry-topology (MA); global development and social justice (MA); government and politics (MA, Adv C); government information specialisthistory (MA); international law and diplomacy (Adv C); liberal arts and sciences (M Div, MA, MLS, MS, Au D, DA, PhD, Psy D, Adv C, Certificate); liberal studies (MA); library and information science (MLS, Adv C); logic and foundations (MA); modern world history (DA); pastoral ministry (Certificate); philosophy (MA); priestly studies (M Div); probability and statistics (MA); school psychology (MS, Psy D); sociology (MA); Spanish (MA); theology (MA, Certificate). *Application deadline:* For fall admission, 5/1 priority date for domestic and international students; for spring admission, 11/1 priority date for domestic and international students. Applications are processed on a rolling basis. *Application fee:* $70. Electronic applications accepted. *Application Contact:* Kathleen Davis, Associate Vice President and Executive Director, Enrollment Management, 718-990-1601, Fax: 718-990-5686, E-mail: gradhelp@stjohns.edu. *Dean,* Dr. Jeffrey Fagen, 718-990-6068, Fax: 718-990-6593, E-mail: fagenj@stjohns.edu.

Institute of Asian Studies Students: 8 full-time (6 women), 6 part-time (4 women); includes 7 minority (1 Black or African American, non-Hispanic/Latino; 4 Asian, non-Hispanic/Latino; 2 Hispanic/Latino), 7 international. Average age 32. 15 applicants, 73% accepted, 1 enrolled. Expenses: Contact institution. *Financial support:* Research assistantships, scholarships/grants available. Support available to part-time students. Financial award application deadline: 3/1; financial award applicants required to submit FAFSA. In 2010, 3 master's awarded. *Degree program information:* Part-time and evening/weekend programs available. Offers Asian and African cultural studies (Adv C); Asian studies (Adv C); Chinese studies (MA, Adv C); East Asian culture studies (Adv C); East Asian studies (MA). *Application deadline:* For fall admission, 5/1 priority date for domestic and international students; for spring admission, 11/1 priority date for domestic and international students. Applications are processed on a rolling basis. *Application fee:* $70. Electronic applications accepted. *Application Contact:* Kathleen Davis, Director of Graduate Admission, 718-990-1601, Fax: 718-990-5686, E-mail: gradhelp@stjohns.edu. *Chair,* Dr. Bernadette Li, 718-990-1657, Fax: 718-990-1881, E-mail: lib@stjohns.edu.

The School of Education Students: 461 full-time (373 women), 1,205 part-time (915 women); includes 529 minority (189 Black or African American, non-Hispanic/Latino; 65 Asian, non-Hispanic/Latino; 255 Hispanic/Latino; 5 Native Hawaiian or other Pacific Islander, non-Hispanic/Latino; 15 Two or more races, non-Hispanic/Latino), 50 international. Average age 32. 983 applicants, 78% accepted, 457 enrolled. *Faculty:* 43 full-time (31 women), 118 part-time/adjunct (60 women). Expenses: Contact institution. *Financial support:* In 2010–11, 923 students received support, including 70 fellowships with full and partial tuition reimbursements available (averaging $18,913 per year), 6 research assistantships with full and partial tuition reimbursements available (averaging $11,685 per year), 7 teaching assistantships with full and partial tuition reimbursements available (averaging $15,797 per year); career-related internships or fieldwork, scholarships/grants, and unspecified assistantships also available. Support available to part-time students. Financial award application deadline: 3/1; financial award applicants required to submit FAFSA. In 2010, 442 master's, 35 doctorates, 19 other advanced degrees awarded. *Degree program information:* Part-time and evening/weekend programs available. Postbaccalaureate distance learning degree programs offered (no on-campus study). Offers administration and supervision (Ed D); adolescent education (MS Ed); bilingual school counseling (MS Ed); bilingual/multicultural education/teaching English to speakers of other languages (MS Ed); childhood education (MS Ed); early childhood (MS Ed); early childhood and teaching students with disabilities (MS Ed); early childhood education (MS Ed); education (MS Ed, Ed D, PhD, Adv C); educational administration and supervision (Ed D, Adv C); instructional leadership (Ed D, Adv C); literacy (MS Ed, PhD, Adv C); literacy B-6 or 5-12 (Adv C); mental health counseling (MS Ed); middle school education (Adv C); school building leadership (MS Ed, Adv C); school counseling (MS Ed); school district leadership (Adv C); teaching children with disabilities in childhood education (MS Ed); teaching literacy 5-12 (MS Ed); teaching literacy B-12 (MS Ed); teaching literacy B-6 (MS Ed). *Application deadline:* For fall admission, 4/1 priority date for domestic students, 5/1 priority date for international students; for spring admission, 11/1 priority date for domestic and international students. Applications are processed on a rolling basis. *Application fee:* $70. Electronic applications accepted. *Application Contact:* Dr. Kelly K. Ronayne, Associate Dean for Graduate Admissions, 718-990-2303, Fax: 718-990-2343, E-mail: graded@stjohns.edu. *Dean,* Dr. Jerrold Ross, 718-990-1305, Fax: 718-990-6096, E-mail: rossj@stjohns.edu.

School of Law Students: 800 full-time (349 women), 196 part-time (89 women); includes 243 minority (55 Black or African American, non-Hispanic/Latino; 81 Asian, non-Hispanic/Latino; 82 Hispanic/Latino; 2 Native Hawaiian or other Pacific Islander, non-Hispanic/Latino; 23 Two or more races, non-Hispanic/Latino), 16 international. Average age 25. 4,583 applicants, 36% accepted, 367 enrolled. *Faculty:* 53 full-time (25 women), 64 part-time/adjunct (15 women). Expenses: Contact institution. *Financial support:* In 2010–11, 463 students received support; research assistantships, career-related internships or fieldwork and scholarships/grants available. Support available to part-time students. Financial award application deadline: 3/1; financial award applicants required to submit FAFSA. In 2010, 293 first professional degrees, 22 master's awarded. *Degree program information:* Part-time and evening/weekend programs available. Offers bankruptcy (LL M); law (JD, LL M); U.S. legal studies (LL M). *Application deadline:* For fall admission, 4/1 priority date for domestic and international students. Applications are processed on a rolling basis. *Application fee:* $60. Electronic applications accepted. *Application Contact:* Robert Harrison, Assistant Dean and Director of Admissions, 718-990-6474, Fax: 718-990-6699, E-mail: lawinfo@stjohns.edu. *Dean,* Michael A. Simons, 718-990-6601, Fax: 718-990-6694, E-mail: simonsm@stjohns.edu.

SAINT JOSEPH COLLEGE, West Hartford, CT 06117-2700

General Information Independent-religious, Undergraduate: women only; graduate: coed, comprehensive institution. *Enrollment:* 2,326 graduate, professional, and undergraduate students; 207 full-time matriculated graduate/professional students (186 women), 1,060 part-time matriculated graduate/professional students (928 women). *Enrollment by degree level:* 1,157 master's, 110 other advanced degrees. *Tuition:* Full-time $11,340; part-time $630 per credit. *Required fees:* $540; $30 per credit. Tuition and fees vary according to course load, campus/location and program. *Graduate housing:* On-campus housing not available. *Student services:* Campus safety program, career counseling, exercise/wellness program, free psychological counseling, services for students with disabilities, teacher training. *Library facilities:* Pope Pius XII Library. *Online resources:* library catalog, web page, access to other libraries' catalogs.

Computer facilities: A campuswide network can be accessed from student residence rooms and from off campus. Online class registration is available. *Web address:* http://www.sjc.edu/.

General Application Contact: Graduate Admissions Office, 860-231-5261, E-mail: graduate@sjc.edu.

GRADUATE UNITS

Department of Biology Students: 4 full-time (3 women), 88 part-time (70 women); includes 4 Black or African American, non-Hispanic/Latino; 2 Asian, non-Hispanic/Latino. Expenses: Contact institution. *Financial support:* Unspecified assistantships available. Support available to part-time students. Financial award applicants required to submit FAFSA. *Degree program information:* Part-time and evening/weekend programs available. Postbaccalaureate distance learning degree programs offered (no on-campus study). Offers biology (MS). *Application deadline:* Applications are processed on a rolling basis. *Application fee:* $50. Electronic applications accepted. *Application Contact:* Graduate Admissions Office, 860-231-5261, E-mail: graduate@sjc.edu.

Department of Business Students: 28 full-time (25 women), 30 part-time (22 women); includes 9 Black or African American, non-Hispanic/Latino; 2 Asian, non-Hispanic/Latino; 4 Hispanic/Latino; 1 Two or more races, non-Hispanic/Latino, 1 international. Expenses: Contact institution. *Financial support:* Career-related internships or fieldwork and unspecified assistantships available. Support available to part-time students. Financial award applicants required to submit FAFSA. *Degree program information:* Part-time and evening/weekend programs available. Offers management (MS). *Application deadline:* Applications are processed on a rolling basis. *Application fee:* $50. Electronic applications accepted. *Application Contact:* Graduate Admissions Assistant, 860-231-5261, E-mail: graduate@sjc.edu.

Department of Chemistry Students: 2 full-time (1 woman), 30 part-time (18 women); includes 3 Black or African American, non-Hispanic/Latino; 2 Asian, non-Hispanic/Latino; 2 Hispanic/Latino. Expenses: Contact institution. *Financial support:* Career-related internships or fieldwork and unspecified assistantships available. Support available to part-time students. Financial award applicants required to submit FAFSA. *Degree program information:* Part-time and evening/weekend programs available. Postbaccalaureate distance learning degree programs offered. Offers biochemistry (MS); chemistry (MS). *Application deadline:* Applications are processed on a rolling basis. *Application fee:* $50. Electronic applications accepted. *Application Contact:* Graduate Admissions Office, 860-231-5261, E-mail: graduate@sjc.edu.

Department of Counselor Education Students: 57 full-time (54 women), 80 part-time (70 women); includes 1 Black or African American, non-Hispanic/Latino; 4 Hispanic/Latino; 1 Two or more races, non-Hispanic/Latino. Expenses: Contact institution. *Financial support:* Career-related internships or fieldwork and unspecified assistantships available. Support available to part-time students. Financial award applicants required to submit FAFSA. *Degree program information:* Part-time and evening/weekend programs available. Offers community counseling (MA); school counseling (MA). *Application deadline:* Applications are processed on a rolling basis. *Application fee:* $50. Electronic applications accepted. *Application Contact:* Graduate Admissions Office, 860-231-5261, E-mail: graduate@sjc.edu.

Department of Education Students: 75 full-time (64 women), 584 part-time (516 women); includes 14 Black or African American, non-Hispanic/Latino; 3 Asian, non-Hispanic/Latino; 18 Hispanic/Latino; 1 Two or more races, non-Hispanic/Latino, 1 international. Expenses: Contact institution. *Financial support:* Career-related internships or fieldwork and unspecified assistantships available. Support available to part-time students. Financial award applicants required to submit FAFSA. *Degree program information:* Part-time and evening/weekend programs available. Offers education (MA); special education (MA). *Application deadline:* Applications are processed on a rolling basis. *Application fee:* $50. Electronic applications accepted. *Application Contact:* Graduate Admissions Office, 860-231-5261, E-mail: graduate@sjc.edu.

Department of Gerontology Students: 17 part-time (all women). Expenses: Contact institution. *Financial support:* Career-related internships or fieldwork and unspecified assistantships available. Support available to part-time students. Financial award applicants required to submit FAFSA. *Degree program information:* Part-time and evening/weekend programs available. Offers human development/gerontology (MA, Certificate). *Application deadline:* Applications are processed on a rolling basis. *Application fee:* $50. Electronic applications accepted. *Application Contact:* Graduate Admissions Office, 860-231-5261, E-mail: graduate@sjc.edu.

Department of Marriage and Family Therapy Students: 9 full-time (8 women), 37 part-time (35 women); includes 3 Black or African American, non-Hispanic/Latino. Expenses: Contact institution. *Financial support:* Career-related internships or fieldwork and unspecified assistantships available. Support available to part-time students. Financial award applicants required to submit FAFSA. *Degree program information:* Part-time and evening/weekend programs available. Offers marriage and family therapy (MA). *Application deadline:* Applications are processed on a rolling basis. *Application fee:* $50. Electronic applications accepted. *Application Contact:* Graduate Admissions Office, 860-231-5261, E-mail: graduate@sjc.edu.

Department of Nursing Students: 10 full-time (9 women), 77 part-time (71 women); includes 9 Black or African American, non-Hispanic/Latino; 1 Asian, non-Hispanic/Latino; 4 Hispanic/Latino, 2 international. Expenses: Contact institution. *Financial support:* Career-related internships or fieldwork and unspecified assistantships available. Support available to part-time students. Financial award applicants required to submit FAFSA. *Degree program information:* Part-time and evening/weekend programs available. Offers nursing (MS). *Application deadline:* Applications are processed on a rolling basis. *Application fee:* $50. Electronic applications accepted. *Application Contact:* Graduate Admissions Office, 860-231-5261, E-mail: graduate@sjc.edu.

Department of Nutrition Students: 18 full-time (all women), 59 part-time (56 women). Expenses: Contact institution. *Financial support:* Career-related internships or fieldwork and unspecified assistantships available. Support available to part-time students. Financial award applicants required to submit FAFSA. *Degree program information:* Part-time and evening/weekend programs available. Postbaccalaureate distance learning degree programs offered. Offers nutrition (MS). *Application deadline:* Applications are processed on a rolling basis. *Application fee:* $50. Electronic applications accepted. *Application Contact:* Graduate Admissions Office, 860-231-5261, E-mail: graduate@sjc.edu.

SAINT JOSEPH'S COLLEGE, Rensselaer, IN 47978

General Information Independent-religious, coed, comprehensive institution. *Graduate housing:* Rooms and/or apartments available on a first-come, first-served basis to single students and available to married students. Housing application deadline: 6/20.

GRADUATE UNITS

Rensselaer Program of Church Music and Liturgy *Degree program information:* Part-time programs available. Offers church music and liturgy (MA); pastoral liturgy and music (Diploma). Offered during summer only.

ST. JOSEPH'S COLLEGE, LONG ISLAND CAMPUS, Patchogue, NY 11772-2399

General Information Independent, coed, comprehensive institution. *Graduate housing:* On-campus housing not available.

GRADUATE UNITS

Executive MBA Program Offers business administration (EMBA).

Program in Accounting Offers accounting (MBA).

Program in Infant/Toddler Early Childhood Special Education *Degree program information:* Part-time and evening/weekend programs available. Offers infant/toddler early childhood special education (MA).

Program in Literacy and Cognition Offers literacy and cognition (MA).

Program in Management Offers health care (AC); health care management (MS); human resource management (AC); human resources management (MS); organizational management (MS).

Program in Nursing Offers nursing (MS).

ST. JOSEPH'S COLLEGE, NEW YORK, Brooklyn, NY 11205-3688

General Information Independent, coed, comprehensive institution.

GRADUATE UNITS

Graduate Programs Offers accounting (MBA); executive business administration (EMBA); health care management (MBA); human services management and leadership (MS); infant/toddler early childhood special education (MA); literacy and cognition (MA); management (MS); nursing (MS); severe and multiple disabilities (MA); special education (MA).

SAINT JOSEPH'S COLLEGE OF MAINE, Standish, ME 04084

General Information Independent-religious, coed, comprehensive institution. *Graduate housing:* On-campus housing not available.

GRADUATE UNITS

Department of Nursing *Degree program information:* Part-time programs available. Postbaccalaureate distance learning degree programs offered (minimal on-campus study). Offers nursing (MS); nursing administration and leadership (Certificate); nursing and health care education (Certificate). MS degree offered only through faculty-directed independent study. Electronic applications accepted.

Program in Business Administration *Degree program information:* Part-time programs available. Offers quality leadership (MBA).

Program in Health Services Administration *Degree program information:* Part-time programs available. Postbaccalaureate distance learning degree programs offered (minimal on-campus study). Offers health services administration (MHSA). Degree program is external; available only by correspondence and online. Electronic applications accepted.

Program in Teacher Education *Degree program information:* Part-time programs available. Postbaccalaureate distance learning degree programs offered (minimal on-campus study). Offers teacher education (MS). Program available by correspondence. Electronic applications accepted.

ST. JOSEPH'S SEMINARY, Yonkers, NY 10704

General Information Independent-religious, coed, graduate-only institution. *Graduate housing:* Room and/or apartments guaranteed to single students; on-campus housing not available to married students.

GRADUATE UNITS

Institute of Religious Studies *Degree program information:* Part-time and evening/weekend programs available. Offers religious studies (MA). Electronic applications accepted.

Professional Program Offers divinity (M Div); theology (MA).

SAINT JOSEPH'S UNIVERSITY, Philadelphia, PA 19131-1395

General Information Independent-religious, coed, comprehensive institution. *Enrollment:* 8,916 graduate, professional, and undergraduate students; 629 full-time matriculated graduate/professional students (367 women), 2,727 part-time matriculated graduate/professional students (1,664 women). *Enrollment by degree level:* 3,045 master's, 56 doctoral, 255 other advanced degrees. *Graduate faculty:* 158 full-time (57 women), 197 part-time/adjunct (94 women). *Tuition:* Part-time $729 per credit. Tuition and fees vary according to course load, degree level and program. *Graduate housing:* On-campus housing not available. *Student services:* Campus employment opportunities, campus safety program, career counseling, free psychological counseling, international student services, low-cost health insurance, multicultural affairs office, services for students with disabilities, teacher training, writing training. *Library facilities:* Francis A. Drexel Library plus 1 other. *Online resources:* library catalog, web page, access to other libraries' catalogs. *Collection:* 355,000 titles, 49,400 serial subscriptions, 5,100 audiovisual materials.

Computer facilities: Computer purchase and lease plans are available. 720 computers available on campus for general student use. A campuswide network can be accessed from student residence rooms and from off campus. Online class registration is available. *Web address:* http://www.sju.edu/.

General Application Contact: Eileen Conroy, Coordinator, Graduate Admissions, 610-660-1101, Fax: 610-660-1224, E-mail: graduate@sju.edu.

GRADUATE UNITS

College of Arts and Sciences Students: 368 full-time (245 women), 1,842 part-time (1,302 women); includes 504 minority (363 Black or African American, non-Hispanic/Latino; 9 American Indian or Alaska Native, non-Hispanic/Latino; 42 Asian, non-Hispanic/Latino; 70 Hispanic/Latino; 2 Native Hawaiian or other Pacific Islander, non-Hispanic/Latino; 18 Two or more races, non-Hispanic/Latino), 93 international. Average age 33. 852 applicants, 83% accepted, 577 enrolled. *Faculty:* 83 full-time (45 women), 143 part-time/adjunct (75 women). Expenses: Contact institution. *Financial support:* In 2010–11, 91 students received support; fellowships, research assistantships, teaching assistantships, scholarships/grants and unspecified assistantships available. Financial award applicants required to submit FAFSA. In 2010, 499 master's, 8 doctorates awarded. *Degree program information:* Part-time and evening/weekend programs available. Postbaccalaureate distance learning degree programs offered. Offers administration/police executive (MS); adult learning and training (MS, Certificate); arts and sciences (MA, MS, Ed D, Certificate, Post-Master's Certificate); behavior analysis (MS, Post-Master's Certificate); biology (MA, MS); computer science (MS); criminal justice (MS, Post-Master's Certificate); criminology (MS); educational leadership (Ed D); elementary education (MS); environmental protection and safety management (MS, Post-Master's Certificate); federal law (MS); gerontological counseling (MS); gerontological services (Post-Master's Certificate); health administration (MS, Post-Master's Certificate); health care ethics (Post-Master's Certificate); health education (MS, Post-Master's Certificate); health informatics (Post-Master's Certificate); healthcare ethics (MS); homeland security (MS, Certificate); human services administration (MS); instructional technology (MS); intelligence and crime (MS); mathematics and computer science (Post-Master's Certificate); nurse anesthesia (MS); organization dynamics and leadership (MS, Certificate); organizational development and leadership (MS); organizational psychology and development (MS, Certificate); probation, parole, and corrections (MS); professional education (MS); psychology (MS); public safety management (MS, Certificate); reading specialist (MS); school nurse certification (MS); secondary education (MS); special education (MS); writing studies (MA). *Application deadline:* For fall admission, 7/15 priority date for domestic students, 4/15 for international students; for winter admission, 4/15 for domestic students, 1/15 for international students; for spring admission, 11/15 priority date for domestic students, 10/15 for international students. Applications are processed on a rolling basis. *Application fee:* $35. Electronic applications accepted. *Application Contact:* Kate McConnell, Director, Graduate College of Arts and Sciences Admissions and Retention, 610-660-3184, Fax: 610-660-3230, E-mail: kate.mcconnell@sju.edu. *Associate Dean/Executive Director of Graduate Programs*, Dr. Sabrina DeTurk, 610-660-1289, Fax: 610-660-3230, E-mail: sdeturk@sju.edu.

Erivan K. Haub School of Business Students: 181 full-time (101 women), 932 part-time (374 women); includes 182 minority (90 Black or African American, non-Hispanic/Latino; 1 American Indian or Alaska Native, non-Hispanic/Latino; 59 Asian, non-Hispanic/Latino; 25 Hispanic/Latino; 1 Native Hawaiian or other Pacific Islander, non-Hispanic/Latino; 6 Two or more races, non-Hispanic/Latino), 111 international. Average age 32. *Faculty:* 75 full-time (12 women), 41 part-time/adjunct (10 women). Expenses: Contact institution. *Financial support:* In 2010–11, research assistantships with full and partial tuition reimbursements (averaging $4,000 per year), teaching assistantships with full and partial tuition reimbursements (averaging $4,000 per year) were awarded; fellowships, scholarships/grants and unspecified assistantships also available. Financial award application deadline: 5/1; financial award applicants required to submit FAFSA. In 2010, 307 master's awarded. *Degree program information:* Part-time and evening/weekend programs available. Postbaccalaureate distance learning degree programs offered (no on-campus study). Offers accounting (MBA); business (MBA, MS, Post Master's Certificate); business intelligence (MS); executive business administration (MBA); executive pharmaceutical marketing (Post Master's Certificate); finance (MBA); financial services (MS); food marketing (MBA, MS); general business (MBA); health and medical services administration (MBA); human resource management (MBA, MS); international business (MBA); international marketing (MS); management (MBA); marketing (MBA); pharmaceutical marketing (MBA). *Application deadline:* For fall admission, 7/15 priority date for domestic students, 4/15 priority date for international students; for spring admission, 11/15 priority date for domestic students, 10/15 priority date for international students. Applications are processed on a rolling basis. *Application fee:* $35. Electronic applications accepted. *Application Contact:* Janine N. Guerra, Assistant Director, MBA Program, 610-660-1695, Fax: 610-660-1599, E-mail: jguerra@sju.edu. *Dean*, Dr. Joseph A. DiAngelo, 610-660-1645, Fax: 610-660-1649, E-mail: jodiange@sju.edu.

ST. LAWRENCE UNIVERSITY, Canton, NY 13617-1455

General Information Independent, coed, comprehensive institution. *Graduate housing:* Room and/or apartments available on a first-come, first-served basis to single students; on-campus housing not available to married students. Housing application deadline: 4/1.

GRADUATE UNITS

Department of Education *Degree program information:* Part-time and evening/weekend programs available. Offers combined school building leadership/school district leadership (CAS); counseling and human development (M Ed, MS, CAS); educational leadership (M Ed, CAS); general studies in education (M Ed); mental health counseling (MS); school building leadership (M Ed); school counseling (M Ed, CAS); school district leadership (CAS).

SAINT LEO UNIVERSITY, Saint Leo, FL 33574-6665

General Information Independent-religious, coed, comprehensive institution. *Enrollment:* 4,665 graduate, professional, and undergraduate students; 2,757 full-time matriculated graduate/professional students (1,726 women), 46 part-time matriculated graduate/professional students (28 women). *Enrollment by degree level:* 2,756 master's, 47 other advanced degrees. *Graduate faculty:* 61 full-time (18 women), 88 part-time/adjunct (44 women). *Tuition:* Part-time $609 per semester hour. *Required fees:* $115 per course. Tuition and fees vary according to campus/location and program. *Graduate housing:* Room and/or apartments available on a first-come, first-served basis to single students; on-campus housing not available to married students. *Student services:* Campus employment opportunities, career counseling, exercise/wellness program, free psychological counseling, international student services, low-cost health insurance, multicultural affairs office, services for students with disabilities, teacher training, writing training. *Library facilities:* Cannon Memorial Library. *Online resources:* library catalog, web page. *Collection:* 222,532 titles, 79,655 serial subscriptions, 3,072 audiovisual materials. *Research affiliation:* American Jewish Committee (religion).

Computer facilities: Computer purchase and lease plans are available. 130 computers available on campus for general student use. A campuswide network can be accessed from student residence rooms and from off campus. Online class registration, campus residents are issued a laptop for their personal use are available. *Web address:* http://www.saintleo.edu/.

General Application Contact: Jared Welling, Director, Graduate/Weekend and Evening Admission, 800-707-8846, Fax: 352-588-7873, E-mail: grad.admissions@saintleo.edu.

GRADUATE UNITS

Graduate Business Studies Students: 1,498 full-time (890 women), 10 part-time (6 women); includes 593 minority (465 Black or African American, non-Hispanic/Latino; 5 American Indian or Alaska Native, non-Hispanic/Latino; 23 Asian, non-Hispanic/Latino; 84 Hispanic/Latino; 2 Native Hawaiian or other Pacific Islander, non-Hispanic/Latino; 14 Two or more races, non-Hispanic/Latino), 14 international. Average age 38. *Faculty:* 32 full-time (4 women), 53 part-time/adjunct (21 women). Expenses: Contact institution. *Financial support:* In 2010–11, 51 students received support. Career-related internships or fieldwork, Federal Work-Study, scholarships/grants, and health care benefits available. Financial award application deadline: 3/1; financial award applicants required to submit FAFSA. In 2010, 557 master's awarded. *Degree program information:* Part-time and evening/weekend programs available. Postbaccalaureate distance learning degree programs offered (no on-campus study). Offers accounting (MBA); business (MBA); health services management (MBA); human resource management (MBA); information security management (MBA); marketing (MBA); sport business (MBA). *Application deadline:* For fall admission, 7/1 priority date for domestic and international students; for spring admission, 11/12 priority date for domestic students, 11/1 for international students. Applications are processed on a rolling basis. *Application fee:* $75. Electronic applications accepted. *Application Contact:* Jared Welling, Director, Graduate/Weekend and Evening Admission, 800-707-8846, Fax: 352-588-7873, E-mail: grad.admissions@saintleo.edu. *Director*, Dr. Lorrie McGovern, 352-588-7390, Fax: 352-588-8585, E-mail: mbaslu@saintleo.edu.

Graduate Studies in Criminal Justice Students: 432 full-time (261 women), 5 part-time (1 woman); includes 195 minority (160 Black or African American, non-Hispanic/Latino; 4 American Indian or Alaska Native, non-Hispanic/Latino; 6 Asian, non-Hispanic/Latino; 20 Hispanic/Latino; 1 Native Hawaiian or other Pacific Islander, non-Hispanic/Latino; 4 Two or more races, non-Hispanic/Latino). Average age 38. *Faculty:* 4 full-time (0 women), 11 part-time/adjunct (3 women). Expenses: Contact institution. *Financial support:* In 2010–11, 17 students received support. Federal Work-Study, scholarships/grants, and health care benefits available. In 2010, 75 master's awarded. *Degree program information:* Part-time and evening/weekend programs available. Postbaccalaureate distance learning degree programs offered (minimal on-campus study). Offers criminal justice (MS); critical incident management (MS); forensic studies (MS). *Application deadline:* For fall admission, 7/1 priority date for domestic and international students; for spring admission, 11/1 priority date for domestic and international students. Applications are processed on a rolling basis. *Application fee:* $75. Electronic applications accepted. *Application Contact:* Jared Welling, Director, Graduate/Weekend and Evening Admission, 800-707-8846, Fax: 352-588-7873, E-mail: grad.admissions@saintleo.edu. *Director*, Dr. Robert Diemer, 352-588-8974, Fax: 352-588-8289, E-mail: robert.diemer@saintleo.edu.

Graduate Studies in Education Students: 589 full-time (493 women), 30 part-time (21 women); includes 53 minority (42 Black or African American, non-Hispanic/Latino; 1 American Indian or Alaska Native, non-Hispanic/Latino; 10 Hispanic/Latino), 2 international. Average age 37. *Faculty:* 14 full-time (11 women), 20 part-time/adjunct (16 women). Expenses:

Saint Leo University (continued)

Contact institution. *Financial support:* In 2010–11, 18 students received support. Career-related internships or fieldwork, Federal Work-Study, scholarships/grants, and health care benefits available. Financial award application deadline: 3/1; financial award applicants required to submit FAFSA. In 2010, 96 master's, 1 other advanced degree awarded. *Degree program information:* Part-time and evening/weekend programs available. Postbaccalaureate distance learning degree programs offered (minimal on-campus study). Offers educational leadership (M Ed); exceptional student education (M Ed); higher education leadership (Ed S); instructional design (MS); instructional leadership (M Ed); reading (M Ed); school leadership (Ed S). *Application deadline:* For fall admission, 7/1 priority date for domestic students, 7/1 for international students; for winter admission, 7/1 for international students; for spring admission, 11/1 priority date for domestic students. Applications are processed on a rolling basis. *Application fee:* $75. Electronic applications accepted. *Application Contact:* Jared Welling, Director, Graduate/Weekend and Evening Admission, 800-707-8846, Fax: 352-588-7873, E-mail: grad.admissions@saintleo.edu. *Director,* Dr. Karen Hahn, 352-588-8309, Fax: 352-588-8861, E-mail: med@saintleo.edu.

Graduate Studies in Social Work Students: 54 full-time (45 women); includes 25 minority (20 Black or African American, non-Hispanic/Latino; 4 Hispanic/Latino; 1 Two or more races, non-Hispanic/Latino). Average age 37. *Faculty:* 4 full-time (3 women), 5 part-time/adjunct (4 women). Expenses: Contact institution. *Financial support:* Career-related internships or fieldwork, Federal Work-Study, and health care benefits available. Postbaccalaureate distance learning degree programs offered (minimal on-campus study). Offers advanced clinical practice (MSW); management (MSW). *Application deadline:* For fall admission, 3/15 for domestic and international students. *Application fee:* $75. Electronic applications accepted. *Application Contact:* Jared Welling, Director, Graduate/Weekend and Evening Admission, 800-707-8846, Fax: 352-588-7873, E-mail: grad.admissions@saintleo.edu. *Director,* Dr. Cindy Lee, 352-588-8869, Fax: 352-588-8289, E-mail: cindy.lee@saintleo.edu.

Graduate Studies in Theology Students: 184 full-time (37 women), 1 part-time (0 women); includes 20 minority (10 Black or African American, non-Hispanic/Latino; 1 American Indian or Alaska Native, non-Hispanic/Latino; 2 Asian, non-Hispanic/Latino; 7 Hispanic/Latino). Average age 52. *Faculty:* 8 full-time (0 women), 1 part-time/adjunct (0 women). Expenses: Contact institution. *Financial support:* In 2010–11, 4 students received support. Federal Work-Study, scholarships/grants, and health care benefits available. Financial award applicants required to submit FAFSA. In 2010, 6 master's awarded. *Degree program information:* Part-time and evening/weekend programs available. Offers theology (MA). *Application deadline:* For fall admission, 7/1 priority date for domestic and international students; for spring admission, 11/1 priority date for domestic and international students. Applications are processed on a rolling basis. *Application fee:* $75. Electronic applications accepted. *Application Contact:* Jared Welling, Director, Graduate/Weekend and Evening Admission, 800-707-8846, Fax: 352-588-7873, E-mail: grad.admissions@saintleo.edu. *Director,* Fr. Anthony Kissel, 352-588-7297, Fax: 352-588-8404, E-mail: anthony.kissel@saintleo.edu.

ST. LOUIS COLLEGE OF PHARMACY, St. Louis, MO 63110-1088

General Information Independent, coed, comprehensive institution. *Enrollment:* 1,215 graduate, professional, and undergraduate students; 551 full-time matriculated graduate/professional students (311 women), 4 part-time matriculated graduate/professional students (1 woman). *Enrollment by degree level:* 555 first professional. *Graduate faculty:* 78 full-time (47 women), 51 part-time/adjunct (25 women). *Tuition:* Full-time $24,600; part-time $825 per credit hour. *Required fees:* $250. Tuition and fees vary according to student level. *Graduate housing:* Room and/or apartments available on a first-come, first-served basis to single students; on-campus housing not available to married students. Typical cost: $8338 (including board). Housing application deadline: 5/1. *Student services:* Campus safety program, career counseling, exercise/wellness program, free psychological counseling, low-cost health insurance, multicultural affairs office, services for students with disabilities, writing training. *Library facilities:* O. J. Cloughly Alumni Library. *Online resources:* library catalog, web page, access to other libraries' catalogs. *Collection:* 71,104 titles, 201 serial subscriptions, 1,887 audiovisual materials.

Computer facilities: Computer purchase and lease plans are available. 6 computers available on campus for general student use. A campuswide network can be accessed from student residence rooms and from off campus. Online class registration is available. *Web address:* http://www.stlcop.edu/.

General Application Contact: Penny Bryant, Director of Admissions/Registrar, 314-446-8313, Fax: 314-446-8310, E-mail: pbryant@stlcop.edu.

GRADUATE UNITS

Professional Program Students: 551 full-time (311 women), 4 part-time (1 woman); includes 72 minority (8 Black or African American, non-Hispanic/Latino; 1 American Indian or Alaska Native, non-Hispanic/Latino; 58 Asian, non-Hispanic/Latino; 5 Hispanic/Latino), 2 international. Average age 22. 100 applicants, 5% accepted, 5 enrolled. *Faculty:* 78 full-time (47 women), 51 part-time/adjunct (25 women). Expenses: Contact institution. *Financial support:* In 2010–11, 482 students received support. Federal Work-Study and scholarships/grants available. Financial award application deadline: 12/15; financial award applicants required to submit FAFSA. In 2010, 143 Pharm Ds awarded. Offers pharmacy (Pharm D). *Application fee:* $50. Electronic applications accepted. *Application Contact:* Penny Bryant, Director of Admissions/Registrar, 314-446-8313, Fax: 314-446-8310, E-mail: pbryant@stlcop.edu. *Director of Admissions/Registrar,* Penny Bryant, 314-446-8313, Fax: 314-446-8310, E-mail: pbryant@stlcop.edu.

SAINT LOUIS UNIVERSITY, St. Louis, MO 63103-2097

General Information Independent-religious, coed, university. CGS member. *Graduate housing:* Rooms and/or apartments available to single and married students. Housing application deadline: 5/1. *Research affiliation:* National Center for Atmospheric Research (earth and atmospheric sciences), Argonne National Laboratory (energy, physics, chemistry, mathematics and computer science), Small Business Administration (business, administration and entrepreneurship), Monsanto Chemical Corporation (chemistry), Missouri Botanical Garden (biology, plant science), AT&T Foundation (communication).

GRADUATE UNITS

Graduate Education *Degree program information:* Part-time and evening/weekend programs available. Postbaccalaureate distance learning degree programs offered (minimal on-campus study). Offers anatomy (MS-R, PhD); biochemistry and molecular biology (PhD); biomedical sciences (MS-R, PhD); molecular microbiology and immunology (PhD); pathology (PhD); pharmacological and physiological science (PhD). Electronic applications accepted.

Center for Advanced Dental Education Offers endodontics (MSD); orthodontics (MSD); periodontics (MSD). Electronic applications accepted.

Center for Health Care Ethics Offers clinical health care ethics (Certificate); health care ethics (PhD). Electronic applications accepted.

College of Arts and Sciences *Degree program information:* Part-time and evening/weekend programs available. Offers American studies (MA, MA-R, PhD); arts and sciences (M Pr Met, MA, MA-R, MS, MS-R, PhD); biology (MS, MS-R, PhD); chemistry (MS, MS-R, PhD); clinical psychology (MS-R, PhD); communication (MA, MA-R); communication sciences and disorders (MA, MA-R); English (MA, MA-R, PhD); experimental psychology (MS-R, PhD); French (MA); geophysics (PhD); geoscience (MS); historical theology (MA, PhD); history (MA, MA-R, PhD); industrial-organizational psychology (PhD); mathematics (MA, MA-R, PhD); meteorology (M Pr Met, MS-R, PhD); philosophy (MA, MA-R, PhD); political science (MA); psychology (PhD); Spanish (MA); theology (MA). Electronic applications accepted.

College of Education and Public Service *Degree program information:* Part-time programs available. Offers Catholic school leadership (MA); counseling and family therapy (PhD); curriculum and instruction (MA, Ed D, PhD); education and public service (MA, MA-R, MAPA, MAT, MAUA, MSW, MUPRED, Ed D, PhD, Certificate, Ed S); educational administration (MA, Ed D, PhD, Ed S); educational foundations (MA, Ed D, PhD); geographic information systems (Certificate); higher education (MA, Ed D, PhD); human development counseling (MA); marriage and family therapy (Certificate); organizational development (Certificate); public administration (MAPA); public policy analysis (PhD); school counseling (MA, MA-R); social work (MSW); special education (MA); student personnel administration (MA); teaching (MAT); urban affairs (MAUA); urban planning and real estate development (MUPRED). Electronic applications accepted.

Doisy College of Health Sciences *Degree program information:* Part-time programs available. Offers athletic training (MAT); health sciences (MAT, MMS, MOT, MS, MSN, MSN-R, DNP, DPT, PhD, Certificate); medical dietetics (MS); nursing (MSN, MSN-R, DNP, PhD, Certificate); nutrition and physical performance (MS); occupational science and occupational therapy (MOT); physical therapy (DPT); physician assistant education (MMS).

John Cook School of Business *Degree program information:* Part-time and evening/weekend programs available. Offers accounting (M Acct, MBA); business (EMIB, M Acct, MBA, MSF, PhD); business administration (MBA); executive international business (EMIB); finance (MBA, MSF); international business (MBA). Electronic applications accepted.

Parks College of Engineering, Aviation, and Technology *Degree program information:* Part-time programs available. Postbaccalaureate distance learning degree programs offered (minimal on-campus study). Offers biomedical engineering (MS, MS-R, PhD); engineering, aviation, and technology (MS, MS-R, PhD).

School of Medicine Offers medicine (MD). Electronic applications accepted.

School of Public Health *Degree program information:* Part-time programs available. Offers biosecurity (Certificate); community health (MPH, MS, MSPH); health administration (MHA); health management and policy (MHA, MPH, PhD); health policy (MPH); public health (PhD); public health studies (PhD).

School of Law *Degree program information:* Part-time and evening/weekend programs available. Offers law (JD, LL M). Electronic applications accepted.

SAINT LOUIS UNIVERSITY–MADRID CAMPUS, 28003 Madrid, Spain

General Information Independent-religious, coed, comprehensive institution. *Graduate housing:* Room and/or apartments guaranteed to single students. *Research affiliation:* Universidad Autonoma de Madrid (English philology).

GRADUATE UNITS

Graduate Programs *Degree program information:* Part-time programs available. Offers English (MA); Spanish (MA); Spanish language and literature (MA).

SAINT MARTIN'S UNIVERSITY, Lacey, WA 98503

General Information Independent-religious, coed, comprehensive institution. *Enrollment:* 1,687 graduate, professional, and undergraduate students; 180 full-time matriculated graduate/professional students (124 women), 94 part-time matriculated graduate/professional students (68 women). *Enrollment by degree level:* 274 master's. *Graduate faculty:* 24 full-time (12 women), 21 part-time/adjunct (10 women). *Graduate housing:* Room and/or apartments available on a first-come, first-served basis to single students; on-campus housing not available to married students. Housing application deadline: 3/15. *Student services:* Campus employment opportunities, campus safety program, career counseling, exercise/wellness program, free psychological counseling, international student services, low-cost health insurance, services for students with disabilities, writing training. *Library facilities:* O'Grady Library. *Online resources:* library catalog, web page, access to other libraries' catalogs. *Collection:* 110,726 titles, 2,927 serial subscriptions, 2,242 audiovisual materials.

Computer facilities: 80 computers available on campus for general student use. A campuswide network can be accessed from student residence rooms. Online class registration is available. *Web address:* http://www.stmartin.edu/.

General Application Contact: Information Contact, 360-438-4311.

GRADUATE UNITS

Graduate Programs Students: 180 full-time (124 women), 94 part-time (68 women); includes 51 minority (14 Black or African American, non-Hispanic/Latino; 6 American Indian or Alaska Native, non-Hispanic/Latino; 18 Asian, non-Hispanic/Latino; 8 Hispanic/Latino; 3 Native Hawaiian or other Pacific Islander, non-Hispanic/Latino; 2 Two or more races, non-Hispanic/Latino), 23 international. Average age 34. 88 applicants, 89% accepted, 70 enrolled. *Faculty:* 20 full-time (11 women), 25 part-time/adjunct (12 women). Expenses: Contact institution. *Financial support:* In 2010–11, 191 students received support. Career-related internships or fieldwork, institutionally sponsored loans, and scholarships/grants available. Support available to part-time students. Financial award application deadline: 3/1; financial award applicants required to submit FAFSA. In 2010, 57 master's awarded. *Degree program information:* Part-time and evening/weekend programs available. Offers civil engineering (MCE); counseling psychology (MAC); engineering management (M Eng Mgt). *Application deadline:* For fall admission, 7/1 for domestic students. Applications are processed on a rolling basis. *Application fee:* $35. *Application Contact:* Dr. Joseph Bessie, Provost and Vice President of Academic Affairs, 360-438-4310, Fax: 360-438-4591, E-mail: jbessie@stmartin.edu. *Provost and Vice President of Academic Affairs,* Dr. Joseph Bessie, 360-438-4310, Fax: 360-438-4591, E-mail: jbessie@stmartin.edu.

College of Education Students: 61 full-time (42 women), 23 part-time (17 women); includes 9 minority (2 Black or African American, non-Hispanic/Latino; 1 American Indian or Alaska Native, non-Hispanic/Latino; 3 Asian, non-Hispanic/Latino; 1 Hispanic/Latino; 1 Native Hawaiian or other Pacific Islander, non-Hispanic/Latino; 1 Two or more races, non-Hispanic/Latino), 3 international. Average age 35. 26 applicants, 92% accepted, 22 enrolled. *Faculty:* 13 full-time (9 women), 11 part-time/adjunct (7 women). Expenses: Contact institution. *Financial support:* In 2010–11, 62 students received support. Career-related internships or fieldwork, Federal Work-Study, institutionally sponsored loans, and unspecified assistantships available. Support available to part-time students. Financial award application deadline: 3/1; financial award applicants required to submit FAFSA. In 2010, 12 master's awarded. *Degree program information:* Part-time and evening/weekend programs available. Offers administration (M Ed); English as a second language (M Ed); guidance and counseling (M Ed); reading (M Ed); special education (M Ed); teaching (MIT); technology in education (M Ed). *Application deadline:* For fall admission, 6/1 priority date for domestic and international students; for spring admission, 10/1 priority date for domestic and international students. Applications are processed on a rolling basis. *Application fee:* $35. *Application Contact:* Ryan M. Smith, Administrative Assistant, 360-438-4333, Fax: 360-438-4486, E-mail: ryan.smith@stmartin.edu. *Director,* Dr. Joyce Westgard, 360-438-4509, Fax: 360-438-4486, E-mail: westgard@stmartin.edu.

School of Business Students: 45 full-time (29 women), 29 part-time (18 women); includes 8 Black or African American, non-Hispanic/Latino; 1 American Indian or Alaska Native, non-Hispanic/Latino; 6 Asian, non-Hispanic/Latino; 1 Hispanic/Latino; 2 Native Hawaiian or other Pacific Islander, non-Hispanic/Latino, 12 international. Average age 33. 34 applicants, 94% accepted, 28 enrolled. *Faculty:* 5 full-time (0 women), 5 part-time/adjunct (0 women). Expenses: Contact institution. *Financial support:* In 2010–11, 29 students received support. Career-related internships or fieldwork and scholarships/grants available. Support available to part-time students. Financial award application deadline: 3/1; financial award applicants required to submit FAFSA. In 2010, 21 master's awarded. *Degree program information:* Part-time and evening/weekend programs available. Offers business (MBA). *Application deadline:* Applications are processed on a rolling basis. *Application fee:* $35. *Application Contact:* Keri Olsen, Administrative Assistant, 360-438-4512, Fax: 360-438-4522, E-mail: kolsen@stmartin.edu. *Director,* Dr. Heather Grob, 360-438-4292, Fax: 360-438-4522, E-mail: hgrob@stmartin.edu.

SAINT MARY-OF-THE-WOODS COLLEGE, Saint Mary-of-the-Woods, IN 47876

General Information Independent-religious, coed, primarily women, comprehensive institution. *Graduate housing:* Rooms and/or apartments guaranteed to single students and available to married students.

GRADUATE UNITS

Program in Art Therapy *Degree program information:* Part-time and evening/weekend programs available. Postbaccalaureate distance learning degree programs offered (minimal on-campus study). Offers art therapy (MA, Post-Master's Certificate). Electronic applications accepted.

Program in Earth Literacy *Degree program information:* Part-time programs available. Postbaccalaureate distance learning degree programs offered (minimal on-campus study). Offers earth literacy (MA). Electronic applications accepted.

Program in Leadership Development Offers leadership development (MLD).

Program in Music Therapy *Degree program information:* Part-time programs available. Postbaccalaureate distance learning degree programs offered (minimal on-campus study). Offers music therapy (MA). Electronic applications accepted.

Program in Pastoral Theology *Degree program information:* Part-time and evening/weekend programs available. Postbaccalaureate distance learning degree programs offered (minimal on-campus study). Offers pastoral theology (MA); youth ministry (Graduate Certificate).

SAINT MARY'S COLLEGE OF CALIFORNIA, Moraga, CA 94556

General Information Independent-religious, coed, comprehensive institution. CGS member. *Enrollment:* 3,917 graduate, professional, and undergraduate students; 592 full-time matriculated graduate/professional students (351 women), 526 part-time matriculated graduate/professional students (386 women). *Enrollment by degree level:* 1,057 master's, 61 doctoral. *Graduate faculty:* 189 full-time (99 women), 271 part-time/adjunct (175 women). *Graduate housing:* Room and/or apartments available on a first-come, first-served basis to single students; on-campus housing not available to married students. Typical cost: $6770 per year ($12,350 including board). Room and board charges vary according to board plan and housing facility selected. Housing application deadline: 6/1. *Student services:* Campus employment opportunities, campus safety program, career counseling, international student services, low-cost health insurance, multicultural affairs office, services for students with disabilities, teacher training. *Library facilities:* St. Albert Hall Library. *Online resources:* library catalog, web page, access to other libraries' catalogs. *Collection:* 233,566 titles, 44,000 serial subscriptions, 8,225 audiovisual materials.

Computer facilities: 325 computers available on campus for general student use. A campuswide network can be accessed from student residence rooms and from off campus. Online class registration, student accounts are available. *Web address:* http://www.stmarys-ca.edu/.

General Application Contact: Michael Beseda, Vice Provost for Enrollment, 925-631-4277, Fax: 925-376-8339, E-mail: mbeseda@stmarys-ca.edu.

GRADUATE UNITS

Graduate Business Programs Students: 278 full-time (108 women), 37 part-time (13 women); includes 81 minority (14 Black or African American, non-Hispanic/Latino; 37 Asian, non-Hispanic/Latino; 30 Hispanic/Latino), 3 international. Average age 33. 105 applicants, 90% accepted, 69 enrolled. Expenses: Contact institution. *Financial support:* Career-related internships or fieldwork available. Support available to part-time students. Financial award applicants required to submit FAFSA. In 2010, 119 master's awarded. *Degree program information:* Part-time and evening/weekend programs available. Offers business (MBA); business administration (MBA); executive business administration (MBA). *Application deadline:* Applications are processed on a rolling basis. *Application fee:* $50. *Application Contact:* Bob Peterson, Director of Admissions, 925-631-4505, Fax: 925-376-6521, E-mail: bpeterso@stmarys-ca.edu. *Associate Dean/Director*, Dr. Guido Krickx, 925-631-4514, Fax: 925-376-6521, E-mail: gakl@stmarys-ca.edu.

Kalmanovitz School of Education Students: 251 full-time (207 women), 365 part-time (297 women); includes 135 minority (28 Black or African American, non-Hispanic/Latino; 1 American Indian or Alaska Native, non-Hispanic/Latino; 33 Asian, non-Hispanic/Latino; 59 Hispanic/Latino; 10 Native Hawaiian or other Pacific Islander, non-Hispanic/Latino; 4 Two or more races, non-Hispanic/Latino), 8 international. Average age 35. *Faculty:* 28 full-time (25 women), 45 part-time/adjunct (38 women). Expenses: Contact institution. *Financial support:* Career-related internships or fieldwork and tuition waivers (partial) available. Support available to part-time students. Financial award application deadline: 2/15; financial award applicants required to submit FAFSA. In 2010, 60 master's awarded. *Degree program information:* Part-time and evening/weekend programs available. Offers early childhood education and Montessori teacher training (M Ed, MA); education (M Ed, MA, MAT); educational leadership (M Ed, MA); general counseling (MA); instruction (M Ed); marital and family therapy (MA); reading leadership (MA); school counseling (MA); special education (M Ed, MA); teaching (MAT); teaching leadership (MA). *Application deadline:* Applications are processed on a rolling basis. *Application fee:* $50. *Application Contact:* Jane Joyce, Coordinator, Recruitment and Admissions, 925-631-4700, Fax: 925-376-8379, E-mail: soereq@stmarys-ca.edu. *Dean*, Dr. Phyllis Metcalf-Turner, 925-631-4309, Fax: 925-376-8379.

School of Liberal Arts Students: 63 full-time (36 women), 63 part-time (35 women); includes 15 Black or African American, non-Hispanic/Latino; 13 Asian, non-Hispanic/Latino; 16 Hispanic/Latino. Average age 34. *Faculty:* 13 full-time (6 women), 39 part-time/adjunct (18 women). Expenses: Contact institution. *Financial support:* Fellowships, teaching assistantships, career-related internships or fieldwork, institutionally sponsored loans, and tuition waivers (partial) available. Support available to part-time students. Financial award applicants required to submit FAFSA. In 2010, 79 master's awarded. *Degree program information:* Part-time programs available. Offers creative writing (MFA); leadership (MA); liberal arts (MA, MFA); sport management (MA); sport studies (MA). *Application Contact:* Michael Beseda, Vice Provost for Enrollment, 925-631-4277, Fax: 925-376-8339, E-mail: mbeseda@stmarys-ca.edu. *Dean*, Stephen Woolpert, 925-631-4609, Fax: 925-631-4490, E-mail: woolpert@stmarys-ca.edu.

ST. MARY'S COLLEGE OF MARYLAND, St. Mary's City, MD 20686-3001

General Information State-supported, coed, comprehensive institution. *Enrollment:* 2,017 graduate, professional, and undergraduate students; 35 full-time matriculated graduate/professional students (23 women). *Enrollment by degree level:* 35 master's. *Graduate faculty:* 8 full-time (7 women). *Graduate housing:* On-campus housing not available. *Student services:* Career counseling, exercise/wellness program, free psychological counseling, multicultural affairs office, services for students with disabilities, teacher training. *Library facilities:* The Library. *Online resources:* library catalog, web page, access to other libraries' catalogs. *Collection:* 162,043 titles, 21,103 serial subscriptions, 16,927 audiovisual materials.

Computer facilities: Computer purchase and lease plans are available. 390 computers available on campus for general student use. A campuswide network can be accessed from student residence rooms and from off campus. Online class registration, Blackboard are available. *Web address:* http://www.smcm.edu/.

General Application Contact: Dr. Lois T. Stover, Chair of Educational Studies and Director of Teacher Education, 240-895-2187, Fax: 240-895-4436, E-mail: ltstover@smcm.edu.

GRADUATE UNITS

Department of Educational Studies Students: 35 full-time (23 women); includes 1 Asian, non-Hispanic/Latino; 2 Hispanic/Latino; 1 Two or more races, non-Hispanic/Latino. Average age 25. 42 applicants, 95% accepted, 35 enrolled. *Faculty:* 8 full-time (7 women). Expenses: Contact institution. *Financial support:* Application deadline: 3/1. In 2010, 38 master's awarded. Offers educational studies (MAT). *Application deadline:* For fall admission, 10/1 for domestic students. *Application fee:* $50. Electronic applications accepted. *Application Contact:* Dr. Lois Thomas Stover, Chair, 240-895-2187, E-mail: ltstover@smcm.edu. *Chair*, Dr. Lois Thomas Stover, 240-895-2187, E-mail: ltstover@smcm.edu.

SAINT MARY SEMINARY AND GRADUATE SCHOOL OF THEOLOGY, Wickliffe, OH 44092-2527

General Information Independent-religious, coed, primarily men, graduate-only institution. *Graduate housing:* Room and/or apartments available to single students; on-campus housing not available to married students.

GRADUATE UNITS

School of Theology *Degree program information:* Part-time programs available. Offers theology (M Div, MA, D Min).

ST. MARY'S SEMINARY AND UNIVERSITY, Baltimore, MD 21210-1994

General Information Independent-religious, coed, primarily men, graduate-only institution. *Graduate housing:* Room and/or apartments guaranteed to single students; on-campus housing not available to married students. Housing application deadline: 8/15.

GRADUATE UNITS

Ecumenical Institute of Theology *Degree program information:* Part-time and evening/weekend programs available. Offers church ministries (MA); theology (MA Th, Certificate).

School of Theology *Degree program information:* Part-time programs available. Offers theology (M Div, STB, MA Th, STD, STL).

SAINT MARY'S UNIVERSITY, Halifax, NS B3H 3C3, Canada

General Information Province-supported, coed, comprehensive institution. *Graduate housing:* Rooms and/or apartments available on a first-come, first-served basis to single students and available to married students.

GRADUATE UNITS

Faculty of Arts *Degree program information:* Part-time and evening/weekend programs available. Offers arts (MA, Certificate, Graduate Diploma); Atlantic Canada studies (MA, Certificate); criminology (MA); history (MA); international development studies (MA, Graduate Diploma); philosophy (MA); theology and religious studies (MA); women and gender studies (MA).

Faculty of Commerce *Degree program information:* Part-time and evening/weekend programs available. Offers commerce (MBA, MF, PhD).

Faculty of Science *Degree program information:* Part-time programs available. Offers applied psychology (M Sc, PhD); applied science (M Sc); astronomy (M Sc, PhD); science (M Sc, PhD).

ST. MARY'S UNIVERSITY, San Antonio, TX 78228-8507

General Information Independent-religious, coed, comprehensive institution. *Enrollment:* 1,198 full-time matriculated graduate/professional students (545 women), 470 part-time matriculated graduate/professional students (269 women). *Enrollment by degree level:* 903 first professional, 681 master's, 84 doctoral. *Graduate faculty:* 46 full-time (19 women), 43 part-time/adjunct (19 women). *Graduate housing:* Room and/or apartments available on a first-come, first-served basis to single students; on-campus housing not available to married students. Housing application deadline: 5/1. *Student services:* Campus employment opportunities, career counseling, exercise/wellness program, free psychological counseling, international student services, low-cost health insurance, services for students with disabilities. *Library facilities:* Louis J. Blume Library plus 1 other. *Online resources:* library catalog, web page, access to other libraries' catalogs. *Collection:* 601,478 titles, 20,562 serial subscriptions, 5,742 audiovisual materials. *Research affiliation:* Southeast Research Consortium (behavioral science, biomedical engineering, social science).

Computer facilities: Computer purchase and lease plans are available. 100 computers available on campus for general student use. A campuswide network can be accessed from student residence rooms and from off campus. Online class registration is available. *Web address:* http://www.stmarytx.edu/.

General Application Contact: Dr. Henry Flores, Dean of the Graduate School, 210-436-3101, Fax: 210-431-2220, E-mail: hflores@stmarytx.edu.

GRADUATE UNITS

Graduate School *Degree program information:* Part-time and evening/weekend programs available. Postbaccalaureate distance learning degree programs offered (minimal on-campus study). Offers Catholic principalship (Certificate); Catholic school administrators (Certificate); Catholic school leadership (MA, Certificate); Catholic school teachers (Certificate); clinical psychology (MA, MS); communication studies (MA); community counseling (MA); computer information systems (MS); computer science (MS); counseling (Sp C); counseling education and supervision (PhD); educational leadership (MA, Certificate); electrical engineering (MS); electrical/computer engineering (MS); engineering administration (MS); engineering computer applications (MS); engineering management (MS); engineering systems management (MS); English literature and language (MA); industrial engineering (MS); industrial/organizational psychology (MA, MS); inter-American administration (MPA); international relations (MA); marriage and family relations (Certificate); marriage and family therapy (MA, PhD); mental health (MA); mental health and substance abuse counseling (Certificate); operations research (MS); pastoral ministry (MA); political communications and applied science (MA); political science (MA); principalship (mid-management) (Certificate); public administration (MPA); public management (MPA); reading (MA); software engineering (MS); substance abuse (MA); theology (MA). Electronic applications accepted.

Bill Greehey School of Business *Degree program information:* Part-time and evening/weekend programs available. Postbaccalaureate distance learning degree programs offered (minimal on-campus study). Offers accountingbusiness administration (MBA); finance (MBA); international business (MBA); management (MBA). Electronic applications accepted.

School of Law Offers law (JD). Electronic applications accepted.

SAINT MARY'S UNIVERSITY OF MINNESOTA, Winona, MN 55987-1399

General Information Independent-religious, coed, comprehensive institution. *Enrollment:* 6,058 graduate, professional, and undergraduate students; 699 full-time matriculated graduate/professional students (471 women), 2,846 part-time matriculated graduate/professional students (1,896 women). *Enrollment by degree level:* 3,002 master's, 241 doctoral, 302 other advanced degrees. *Graduate faculty:* 9 full-time (3 women), 399 part-time/adjunct (224 women). *Student services:* Campus safety program, services for students with disabilities, teacher training, writing training. *Library facilities:* Fitzgerald Library plus 1 other. *Online resources:* library catalog, web page, access to other libraries' catalogs. *Collection:* 241,470 titles, 39,650 serial subscriptions, 10,087 audiovisual materials.

Computer facilities: 200 computers available on campus for general student use. A campuswide network can be accessed from student residence rooms and from off campus. Online class registration is available. *Web address:* http://www.smumn.edu/.

General Application Contact: Yasin Alsaidi, Director of Admissions for Graduate and Professional Programs, 612-728-5207, Fax: 612-728-5121, E-mail: yalsaidi@smumn.edu.

GRADUATE UNITS

Schools of Graduate and Professional Programs Students: 699 full-time (471 women), 2,846 part-time (1,896 women); includes 360 minority (206 Black or African American, non-Hispanic/Latino; 12 American Indian or Alaska Native, non-Hispanic/Latino; 76 Asian, non-Hispanic/Latino; 59 Hispanic/Latino; 1 Native Hawaiian or other Pacific Islander, non-Hispanic/Latino; 6 Two or more races, non-Hispanic/Latino), 104 international. Average age 36. *Faculty:* 9 full-time (3 women), 399 part-time/adjunct (224 women). Expenses: Contact institution. *Application Contact:* Yasin Alsaidi, Director of Admissions for Graduate and Professional Programs, 612-728-5207, Fax: 612-728-5121, E-mail: yalsaidi@smumn.edu. *Vice President*, Dr. Marcel Dumestre, 612-728-5201, Fax: 612-728-5169, E-mail: mdumestr@smumn.edu.

Graduate School of Business and Technology Expenses: Contact institution. Offers arts and cultural management (MA); business administration (MBA); business and technology (MA, MBA, MS, Certificate); geographic information science (MS, Certificate); human development (MA); human resource management (MA); information technology management (MS); international business (MA); management (MA); organizational leadership (MA); philanthropy and development (MA); project management (MS, Certificate); public safety administration (MA). *Application Contact:* Yasin Alsaidi, Director of Admissions for

Saint Mary's University of Minnesota (continued)

Graduate and Professional Programs, 612-728-5207, Fax: 612-728-5121, E-mail: yalsaidi@smumn.edu. *Dean,* Dushan G. Knezevich, 612-728-5156, E-mail: dknezevi@smumn.edu.

Graduate School of Education Expenses: Contact institution. Offers behavioral disorders (Certificate); Catholic school leadership (MA); education (MA); education-Wisconsin (MA); educational administration (Certificate, Ed S); educational leadership (MA, Ed D); gifted and talented instruction (Certificate); instruction (MA, Certificate); K-12 reading teacher (Certificate); LaSallian leadership (MA); LaSallian studies (MA); learning disabilities (Certificate); literacy education (MA); special education (MA); teaching and learning (M Ed). *Application Contact:* Yasin Alsaidi, Director of Admissions for Graduate and Professional Programs, 612-728-5207, Fax: 612-728-5121, E-mail: yalsaidi@smumn.edu. *Dean,* Rebecca Hopkins, 507-457-6620, E-mail: rhopkins@smumn.edu.

Graduate School of Health and Human Services Expenses: Contact institution. Offers Canon law (Certificate); counseling and psychological services (MA); counseling psychology (Psy D); health and human services (MA, MS, Psy D, Certificate); health and human services administration (MA); marriage and family therapy (MA, Certificate); nurse anesthesia (MS); pastoral administration (MA); pastoral ministries (MA); play therapy (Certificate). *Application Contact:* Yasin Alsaidi, Director of Admissions for Graduate and Professional Programs, 612-728-5207, Fax: 612-728-5121, E-mail: yalsaidi@smumn.edu. *Dean,* Merri Moody, 612-728-5133, E-mail: mmoody@smumn.edu.

SAINT MEINRAD SCHOOL OF THEOLOGY, Saint Meinrad, IN 47577

General Information Independent-religious, coed, primarily men, graduate-only institution. *Enrollment by degree level:* 121 first professional, 85 master's. *Graduate faculty:* 21 full-time (2 women), 11 part-time/adjunct (1 woman). *Graduate housing:* Room and/or apartments guaranteed to single students; on-campus housing not available to married students. Housing application deadline: 7/15. *Student services:* Campus employment opportunities, campus safety program, exercise/wellness program, free psychological counseling, low-cost health insurance, writing training. *Library facilities:* Archabbey Library. *Online resources:* library catalog. *Collection:* 177,019 titles, 325 serial subscriptions, 6,782 audiovisual materials.

Computer facilities: 30 computers available on campus for general student use. A campuswide network can be accessed from student residence rooms and from off campus. *Web address:* http://www.saintmeinrad.edu/.

General Application Contact: Rev. Brendan Moss, Director of Enrollment, 812-357-6422, Fax: 812-357-6462, E-mail: apply@saintmeinrad.edu.

GRADUATE UNITS

Professional Program Offers theology (M Div).

Program in Catholic Thought and Life *Degree program information:* Part-time and evening/weekend programs available. Offers Catholic thought and life (MA).

Program in Theological Studies *Degree program information:* Part-time and evening/weekend programs available. Offers theological studies (MTS).

SAINT MICHAEL'S COLLEGE, Colchester, VT 05439

General Information Independent-religious, coed, comprehensive institution. *Graduate housing:* On-campus housing not available.

GRADUATE UNITS

Graduate Programs *Degree program information:* Part-time and evening/weekend programs available. Offers administration (M Ed, CAGS); administration and management (MSA, CAMS); arts in education (CAGS); clinical psychology (MA); curriculum and instruction (M Ed, CAGS); information technology (CAGS); reading (M Ed); special education (M Ed, CAGS); teaching English as a second language (MATESL, Certificate); technology (M Ed); theology (MA, CAS, Certificate). Electronic applications accepted.

ST. NORBERT COLLEGE, De Pere, WI 54115-2099

General Information Independent-religious, coed, comprehensive institution. *Enrollment:* 2,241 graduate, professional, and undergraduate students; 87 part-time matriculated graduate/professional students (63 women). *Enrollment by degree level:* 87 master's. *Graduate faculty:* 16 part-time/adjunct (5 women). *Tuition:* Part-time $390 per credit hour. *Graduate housing:* On-campus housing not available. *Student services:* Campus safety program, career counseling, child daycare facilities, exercise/wellness program, free psychological counseling, international student services, multicultural affairs office, services for students with disabilities, teacher training, writing training. *Library facilities:* Miriam B. and James J. Mulva Library. *Online resources:* library catalog, web page, access to other libraries' catalogs. *Collection:* 230,639 titles, 328 serial subscriptions, 3,682 audiovisual materials.

Computer facilities: Computer purchase and lease plans are available. 247 computers available on campus for general student use. A campuswide network can be accessed from student residence rooms and from off campus. Online class registration is available. *Web address:* http://www.snc.edu/.

General Application Contact: Dinah Grassel, Program Coordinator, 920-403-3957, Fax: 920-403-4086.

GRADUATE UNITS

Program in Education Students: 9 part-time (8 women). 12 applicants, 100% accepted, 8 enrolled. *Faculty:* 2 part-time/adjunct (1 woman). Expenses: Contact institution. In 2010, 15 master's awarded. *Degree program information:* Part-time and evening/weekend programs available. Offers education (MS). *Application fee:* $35. Electronic applications accepted. *Application Contact:* Dr. Susan M. Landt, Director/Professor, 920-403-1328, Fax: 920-403-4078, E-mail: susan.landt@snc.edu. *Director/Professor,* Dr. Susan M. Landt, 920-403-1328, Fax: 920-403-4078, E-mail: susan.landt@snc.edu.

Program in Liberal Studies Students: 21 part-time (12 women); includes 1 American Indian or Alaska Native, non-Hispanic/Latino; 2 Hispanic/Latino. Average age 33. 5 applicants, 100% accepted, 5 enrolled. *Faculty:* 5 part-time/adjunct (1 woman). Expenses: Contact institution. *Degree program information:* Part-time programs available. Offers liberal studies (MA). *Application deadline:* Applications are processed on a rolling basis. *Application fee:* $50. Electronic applications accepted. *Application Contact:* Program Coordinator, 920-403-3155, Fax: 920-403-4086, E-mail: deette.radant@snc.edu. *Director,* Dr. Howard Ebert, 920-403-3956, Fax: 920-403-4086, E-mail: howard.ebert@snc.edu.

Program in Theological Studies Students: 57 part-time (43 women); includes 1 Asian, non-Hispanic/Latino; 6 Hispanic/Latino. 2 applicants, 100% accepted, 2 enrolled. *Faculty:* 9 part-time/adjunct (3 women). Expenses: Contact institution. *Financial support:* In 2010–11, 13 students received support. Scholarships/grants available. Support available to part-time students. In 2010, 5 master's awarded. *Degree program information:* Part-time programs available. Offers theological studies (MTS). *Application deadline:* Applications are processed on a rolling basis. *Application fee:* $50. Electronic applications accepted. *Application Contact:* Dinah Grassel, Program Coordinator, 920-403-3957, Fax: 920-403-4086, E-mail: dinah.grassel@snc.edu. *Director,* Dr. Howard Ebert, 920-403-3956, Fax: 920-403-4086, E-mail: howard.ebert@snc.edu.

ST. PATRICK'S SEMINARY & UNIVERSITY, Menlo Park, CA 94025-3596

General Information Independent-religious, coed, primarily men, graduate-only institution. *Graduate housing:* Room and/or apartments guaranteed to single students; on-campus housing not available to married students. Housing application deadline: 8/15.

GRADUATE UNITS

School of Theology *Degree program information:* Part-time programs available. Offers theology (M Div, STB, MA). STB offered jointly with St. Mary's Seminary and University.

SAINT PAUL SCHOOL OF THEOLOGY, Kansas City, MO 64127-2440

General Information Independent-religious, coed, graduate-only institution. *Graduate housing:* Rooms and/or apartments available to single and married students. Housing application deadline: 5/31.

GRADUATE UNITS

Graduate and Professional Programs *Degree program information:* Part-time programs available. Offers theology (M Div, MA, MTS, D Min).

SAINT PAUL UNIVERSITY, Ottawa, ON K1S 1C4, Canada

General Information Province-supported, coed, university. *Graduate housing:* Room and/or apartments available to single students; on-campus housing not available to married students.

GRADUATE UNITS

Faculty of Canon Law Students: 58 full-time (9 women), 14 part-time (8 women); includes 17 Black or African American, non-Hispanic/Latino; 15 Asian, non-Hispanic/Latino; 1 Hispanic/Latino. Average age 40. 78 applicants, 92% accepted, 72 enrolled. *Faculty:* 9 full-time (1 woman), 7 part-time/adjunct (1 woman). Expenses: Contact institution. *Financial support:* Scholarships/grants and bursaries available. In 2010, 15 master's, 3 doctorates, 33 other advanced degrees awarded. *Degree program information:* Part-time programs available. Offers canon law (MCL, JCD, PhD, Graduate Certificate, JCL); canonical practice (Graduate Certificate); ecclesiastical administration (Graduate Certificate). *Application deadline:* For fall admission, 8/15 priority date for domestic students, 3/1 priority date for international students. Applications are processed on a rolling basis. *Application fee:* $75 Canadian dollars. *Application Contact:* Beverly Ruth Kavanaugh, Administrative Assistant, 613-751-4018, Fax: 613-751-4036, E-mail: bkavanaugh@ustpaul.ca. *Dean,* Dr. Anne Asselin, 613-751-4018, Fax: 613-751-4036, E-mail: canonlaw@ustpaul.ca.

Faculty of Human Sciences Offers conflict studies (MA); counseling and spirituality (MA); individual and/or marital/couple counseling (MA Past St); individual or marital/couple counseling (MA); mission and interreligious studies (MA); pastoral care in health care services (MA Past St); spiritual care (MA). Programs offered in French and English.

Faculty of Theology Offers theology (MA Th, MP Th, MRE, D Min, D Th, PhD, L Th).

SAINT PETER'S COLLEGE, Jersey City, NJ 07306-5997

General Information Independent-religious, coed, comprehensive institution. *Enrollment:* 255 full-time matriculated graduate/professional students, 373 part-time matriculated graduate/professional students. *Enrollment by degree level:* 545 master's, 18 doctoral, 65 other advanced degrees. *Graduate housing:* On-campus housing not available. *Student services:* Campus employment opportunities, campus safety program, career counseling, exercise/wellness program, free psychological counseling, international student services, low-cost health insurance, multicultural affairs office, services for students with disabilities. *Library facilities:* Theresa and Edward O'Toole Library plus 1 other. *Online resources:* library catalog, web page, access to other libraries' catalogs. *Collection:* 178,587 titles, 1,741 serial subscriptions, 330 audiovisual materials.

Computer facilities: 150 computers available on campus for general student use. A campuswide network can be accessed from student residence rooms and from off campus. *Web address:* http://www.spc.edu/.

General Application Contact: Stephanie Autenrieth, Director, Graduate and Professional Studies Admission, 201-761-6474, Fax: 201-435-5270, E-mail: sautenrieth@spc.edu.

GRADUATE UNITS

Graduate Business Programs 154 applicants, 77% accepted, 80 enrolled. Expenses: Contact institution. *Financial support:* Applicants required to submit FAFSA. *Degree program information:* Part-time and evening/weekend programs available. Offers accountancy (MS); business (MBA, MS); finance (MBA); health care administration (MBA); human resource management (MBA); international business (MBA); management (MBA); management information systems (MBA); marketing (MBA); risk management (MBA). *Application deadline:* Applications are processed on a rolling basis. Electronic applications accepted. *Application Contact:* Stephanie Autenrieth, Director, Graduate and Professional Studies Admission, 201-761-6474, Fax: 201-435-5270, E-mail: sautenrieth@spc.edu.

Graduate Programs in Education 132 applicants, 70% accepted, 63 enrolled. Expenses: Contact institution. *Financial support:* Applicants required to submit FAFSA. *Degree program information:* Part-time and evening/weekend programs available. Offers 6-8 middle school education (MA Ed, Certificate); director of school counseling services (Certificate); educational leadership (MA Ed, Ed D); K-12 secondary education (MA Ed, Certificate); K-5 elementary education (MA Ed, Certificate); literacy (MA Ed); middle school mathematics (Certificate); professional/associate counselor (Certificate); reading (MA Ed); school business administrator (Certificate); school counseling (MA, Certificate); special education (MA Ed, Certificate); teaching (MA Ed, Certificate). *Application deadline:* Applications are processed on a rolling basis. Electronic applications accepted. *Application Contact:* Stephanie Autenrieth, Director, Graduate and Professional Studies Admission, 201-761-6474, Fax: 201-435-5270, E-mail: sautenrieth@spc.edu. *Chairperson,* Dr. Anthony Sciarrillo.

Program in Criminal Justice Administration Expenses: Contact institution. *Financial support:* Applicants required to submit FAFSA. *Degree program information:* Part-time and evening/weekend programs available. Offers federal law enforcement administration (MA); police administration (MA). *Application deadline:* Applications are processed on a rolling basis. Electronic applications accepted. *Application Contact:* Stephanie Autenrieth, Director, Graduate and Professional Studies Admission, 201-761-6474, Fax: 201-435-5270, E-mail: sautenrieth@spc.edu. *Graduate Director,* Dr. Richard Cosgrove, 201-761-6160, E-mail: rcosgrove@spc.edu.

School of Nursing 33 applicants, 48% accepted, 13 enrolled. Expenses: Contact institution. *Financial support:* Applicants required to submit FAFSA. *Degree program information:* Part-time and evening/weekend programs available. Offers adult nurse practitioner (MSN, Certificate); advanced practice (DNP); case management (MSN, DNP); nursing (MSN, DNP, Certificate). *Application deadline:* Applications are processed on a rolling basis. Electronic applications accepted. *Application Contact:* Stephanie Autenrieth, Director, Graduate and Professional Studies Admission, 201-761-6474, Fax: 201-435-5270, E-mail: sautenrieth@spc.edu. *Dean,* Ann Tritak, 201-761-6270.

ST. PETER'S SEMINARY, London, ON N6A 3Y1, Canada

General Information Independent-religious, coed, primarily men, graduate-only institution.

GRADUATE UNITS

Department of Theology Offers theology (M Div, MTS).

SAINTS CYRIL AND METHODIUS SEMINARY, Orchard Lake, MI 48324

General Information Independent-religious, coed, graduate-only institution. *Graduate housing:* Room and/or apartments guaranteed to single students; on-campus housing not available to married students. Housing application deadline: 7/1.

GRADUATE UNITS

Graduate and Professional Programs *Degree program information:* Part-time programs available. Offers pastoral ministry (MAPM); religious education (MARE); theology (M Div, MA).

ST. STEPHEN'S COLLEGE, Edmonton, AB T6G 2J6, Canada

General Information Independent-religious, coed, graduate-only institution. *Graduate housing:* On-campus housing not available.

GRADUATE UNITS

Programs in Theology *Degree program information:* Part-time and evening/weekend programs available. Postbaccalaureate distance learning degree programs offered (minimal on-campus study). Offers ministry (D Min); pastoral counseling (MA); social transformation ministry (MA); spirituality and liturgy (MA); theological studies (MTS); theology (M Th). Electronic applications accepted.

ST. THOMAS AQUINAS COLLEGE, Sparkill, NY 10976

General Information Independent, coed, comprehensive institution. *Graduate housing:* On-campus housing not available. *Research affiliation:* Lederle Laboratories (science education), Lamont Doherty Laboratories (science education).

GRADUATE UNITS

Division of Business Administration *Degree program information:* Part-time and evening/weekend programs available. Offers business administration (MBA); finance (MBA); management (MBA); marketing (MBA). Electronic applications accepted.

Division of Teacher Education *Degree program information:* Part-time and evening/weekend programs available. Offers adolescence education (MST); childhood and special education (MST); childhood education (MST); educational leadership (MS Ed); reading (MS Ed, PMC); special education (MS Ed, PMC); teaching (MS Ed). Electronic applications accepted.

ST. THOMAS UNIVERSITY, Miami Gardens, FL 33054-6459

General Information Independent-religious, coed, comprehensive institution. *Graduate housing:* Room and/or apartments available on a first-come, first-served basis to single students; on-campus housing not available to married students. Housing application deadline: 7/1.

GRADUATE UNITS

Biscayne College Offers guidance and counseling (MS, Post-Master's Certificate); marriage and family therapy (MS, Post-Master's Certificate); mental health counseling (MS).

School of Business Offers accounting (MBA); business (M Acc, MBA, MIB, MS, MSM, Certificate); business administration (M Acc, MBA, Certificate); general management (MSM, Certificate); health management (MBA, MSM, Certificate); human resource management (MBA, MSM, Certificate); international business (MBA, MIB, MSM, Certificate); justice administration (MSM, Certificate); management accounting (MSM, Certificate); public management (MSM, Certificate); sports administration (MS).

School of Law Postbaccalaureate distance learning degree programs offered (no on-campus study). Offers international human rights (LL M); international taxation (LL M); law (JD). Electronic applications accepted.

School of Leadership Studies *Degree program information:* Part-time and evening/weekend programs available. Offers art management (MA); electronic media (MA); executive management (MPS); Hispanic media (MA, Certificate); leadership studies (MA, MPS, MS, Ed D, Certificate).

Institute for Education *Degree program information:* Part-time and evening/weekend programs available. Offers earth/space science (Certificate); educational administration (MS, Certificate); educational leadership (Ed D); elementary education (MS); ESOL (Certificate); gifted education (Certificate); instructional technology (MS, Certificate); professional/studies (Certificate); reading (MS, Certificate); special education (MS). Electronic applications accepted.

School of Theology and Ministry Offers theology and ministry (MA, PhD, Certificate).

Institute for Pastoral Ministries *Degree program information:* Part-time and evening/weekend programs available. Offers pastoral ministries (MA, Certificate); practical theology (PhD). Electronic applications accepted.

ST. TIKHON'S ORTHODOX THEOLOGICAL SEMINARY, South Canaan, PA 18459

General Information Independent-religious, men only, graduate-only institution. *Enrollment by degree level:* 57 first professional. *Graduate faculty:* 8 full-time (1 woman), 6 part-time/adjunct (0 women). *Tuition:* Full-time $2100. *Required fees:* $400. One-time fee: $30 full-time. *Graduate housing:* Room and/or apartments guaranteed to single students; on-campus housing not available to married students. Typical cost: $3000 (including board). Room and board charges vary according to campus/location. *Student services:* Career counseling. *Library facilities:* St. Tikhon's Seminary Library. *Online resources:* library catalog, web page, access to other libraries' catalogs. *Collection:* 49,000 titles, 250 serial subscriptions, 550 audiovisual materials.

Computer facilities: 25 computers available on campus for general student use. A campuswide network can be accessed from student residence rooms and from off campus. *Web address:* http://www.stots.edu/.

General Application Contact: Fr. Alexander Atty, Dean and Director of Admissions, 570-561-1818 Ext. 101, E-mail: father.alexander@stots.edu.

GRADUATE UNITS

Divinity Program Students: 51 full-time (1 woman), 6 part-time (0 women); includes 1 Black or African American, non-Hispanic/Latino, 4 international. 35 applicants, 80% accepted, 28 enrolled. *Faculty:* 8 full-time (1 woman), 6 part-time/adjunct (0 women). Expenses: Contact institution. *Financial support:* Fellowships with partial tuition reimbursements, career-related internships or fieldwork, institutionally sponsored loans, scholarships/grants, and tuition waivers (partial) available. Offers divinity (M Div). *Application deadline:* For fall admission, 7/30 for domestic students, 6/30 for international students. Applications are processed on a rolling basis. *Application fee:* $28. *Application Contact:* Fr. Alexander Atty, Dean and Director of Admissions, 570-561-1818 Ext. 191, E-mail: father.alexander@stots.edu. *Rector,* Bp. Tikhon Mollard, 570-937-9331, Fax: 570-937-4139, E-mail: bp.tikhon@stots.edu.

SAINT VINCENT COLLEGE, Latrobe, PA 15650-2690

General Information Independent-religious, coed, comprehensive institution. *Graduate housing:* Room and/or apartments available on a first-come, first-served basis to single students; on-campus housing not available to married students.

GRADUATE UNITS

Program in Education *Degree program information:* Part-time and evening/weekend programs available. Offers curriculum and instruction (MS); educational media and technology (MS); environmental education (MS); school administration and supervision (MS); special education (MS).

Program in Health Services Offers nurse anesthesia (MS).

Program in Health Services Leadership Offers health services leadership (MS).

SAINT VINCENT DE PAUL REGIONAL SEMINARY, Boynton Beach, FL 33436-4899

General Information Independent-religious, coed, primarily men, graduate-only institution. *Graduate housing:* Room and/or apartments guaranteed to single students; on-campus housing not available to married students.

GRADUATE UNITS

Graduate and Professional Programs *Degree program information:* Part-time programs available. Offers theology (M Div, MA Th).

SAINT VINCENT SEMINARY, Latrobe, PA 15650-2690

General Information Independent-religious, coed, primarily men, graduate-only institution. *Graduate housing:* Room and/or apartments guaranteed to single students; on-campus housing not available to married students. Housing application deadline: 8/1.

GRADUATE UNITS

School of Theology *Degree program information:* Part-time programs available. Offers theology (M Div, MA). Electronic applications accepted.

ST. VLADIMIR'S ORTHODOX THEOLOGICAL SEMINARY, Crestwood, NY 10707-1699

General Information Independent-religious, coed, primarily men, graduate-only institution. *Graduate housing:* Rooms and/or apartments available on a first-come, first-served basis to single and married students. Housing application deadline: 5/1.

GRADUATE UNITS

Graduate School of Theology *Degree program information:* Part-time programs available. Offers general theological studies (MA); liturgical music (MA); religious education (MA); theology (M Div, M Th, D Min). MA in general theological studies, M Div offered jointly with St. Nersess Seminary.

SAINT XAVIER UNIVERSITY, Chicago, IL 60655-3105

General Information Independent-religious, coed, comprehensive institution. *Graduate housing:* Room and/or apartments available on a first-come, first-served basis to single students; on-campus housing not available to married students. Housing application deadline: 8/15. *Research affiliation:* Alexian Brothers Hospital, Holy Cross Hospital, Little Company of Mary Hospital, Mercy Center for Health Care Services.

GRADUATE UNITS

Graduate Studies *Degree program information:* Part-time and evening/weekend programs available. Electronic applications accepted.

Graham School of Management *Degree program information:* Part-time and evening/weekend programs available. Offers e-commerce (MBA); employee health benefits (Certificate); finance (MBA, MS); financial analysis and investments (MBA); financial planning (MBA, Certificate); financial trading and practice (MBA, Certificate); generalist/administration (MBA); health administration (MBA, MS); managed care (Certificate); management (MBA, MS); marketing (MBA); public and non-profit management (MBA); public health (MPH); service management (MBA); training and performance management (MBA). Electronic applications accepted.

School of Arts and Sciences *Degree program information:* Part-time and evening/weekend programs available. Offers adult counseling (Certificate); applied computer science in Internet information systems (MS); arts and sciences (MA, MS, CAS, Certificate); child/adolescent counseling (Certificate); core counseling (Certificate); counseling psychology (MA); English (CAS); literary studies (MA); mathematics and computer science (MA); speech-language pathology (MS); teaching of writing (MA); writing pedagogy (CAS).

School of Education *Degree program information:* Part-time and evening/weekend programs available. Offers counseling (MA); counselor education (MA); curriculum and instruction (MA); early childhood education (MA); education (CAS); educational administration (MA); elementary education (MA); field-based education (MA); general educational studies (MA); individualized program (MA); learning disabilities (MA); reading (MA); secondary education (MA).

School of Nursing *Degree program information:* Part-time and evening/weekend programs available. Offers adult health clinical nurse specialist (MS); family nurse practitioner (MS, PMC); leadership in community health nursing (MS); psychiatric-mental health clinical nurse specialist (MS); psychiatric-mental health clinical specialist (PMC).

SALEM COLLEGE, Winston-Salem, NC 27101

General Information Independent-religious, coed, primarily women, comprehensive institution. *Graduate housing:* On-campus housing not available.

GRADUATE UNITS

Department of Education *Degree program information:* Part-time and evening/weekend programs available. Offers early education and leadership (MAT); elementary education (MAT); English as a second language (MAT); language and literacy (M Ed); middle school education (MAT); secondary education (MAT); special education (MAT).

SALEM INTERNATIONAL UNIVERSITY, Salem, WV 26426-0500

General Information Independent, coed, comprehensive institution. *Graduate housing:* Rooms and/or apartments available on a first-come, first-served basis to single students and available to married students.

GRADUATE UNITS

School of Business *Degree program information:* Part-time programs available. Postbaccalaureate distance learning degree programs offered (no on-campus study). Offers information security (MBA); international business (MBA). Electronic applications accepted.

School of Education *Degree program information:* Part-time and evening/weekend programs available. Postbaccalaureate distance learning degree programs offered. Offers curriculum and instruction (M Ed); educational leadership (M Ed). Electronic applications accepted.

SALEM STATE UNIVERSITY, Salem, MA 01970-5353

General Information State-supported, coed, comprehensive institution. CGS member. *Enrollment:* 9,993 graduate, professional, and undergraduate students; 303 full-time matriculated graduate/professional students (239 women), 1,064 part-time matriculated graduate/professional students (790 women). *Enrollment by degree level:* 1,367 master's. Tuition, state resident: full-time $2520; part-time $290 per credit hour. Tuition, nonresident: full-time $4140; part-time $380 per credit hour. *Required fees:* $2700. *Graduate housing:* On-campus housing not available. *Student services:* Campus employment opportunities, campus safety program, career counseling, child daycare facilities, exercise/wellness program, free psychological counseling, international student services, low-cost health insurance, multicultural affairs office, services for students with disabilities, teacher training, writing training. *Library facilities:* Salem State University Library. *Online resources:* library catalog, web page, access to other libraries' catalogs. *Collection:* 297,889 titles, 58,079 serial subscriptions, 10,931 audiovisual materials.

Computer facilities: Computer purchase and lease plans are available. 160 computers available on campus for general student use. A campuswide network can be accessed from student residence rooms and from off campus. Online class registration is available. *Web address:* http://www.salemstate.edu/.

General Application Contact: Dr. Carol Glod, Dean of School of Graduate Studies, 978-542-6323, E-mail: cglod@salemstate.edu.

GRADUATE UNITS

School of Graduate Studies Students: 303 full-time (239 women), 1,064 part-time (790 women); includes 32 Black or African American, non-Hispanic/Latino; 1 American Indian or Alaska Native, non-Hispanic/Latino; 23 Asian, non-Hispanic/Latino; 32 Hispanic/Latino; 10 Two or more races, non-Hispanic/Latino, 33 international. Average age 34. Expenses: Contact institution. *Financial support:* Career-related internships or fieldwork, Federal Work-Study, scholarships/grants, and unspecified assistantships available. Support available to part-time students. Financial award applicants required to submit FAFSA. In 2010, 556 master's, 55 other advanced degrees awarded. *Degree program information:* Part-time and evening/weekend programs available. Offers advanced professional studies in counseling (Graduate Certificate); art (MAT); biology (MAT); business administration (MBA); chemistry (MAT); counseling and psychological services (MS, Graduate Certificate); criminal justice (MS); direct entry nursing (MSN); early childhood education (M Ed); education (CAGS); educational leadership (M Ed); elementary education (M Ed); English (MA, MAT); geo-information science (MS); higher education in student affairs (M Ed); history (MA, MAT); humanities (M Ed); library media studies (M Ed); math/science (MAT); mathematics (MAT, MS); middle school general science (MAT); middle school math (MAT); occupational therapy (MS); physical education (M Ed); reading (M Ed); school counseling (M Ed); secondary education (M Ed); social work (MSW); Spanish (MAT); special education (M Ed); teaching English as a second language (MAT); technology in education (M Ed). *Application deadline:* For fall admission, 5/1 for domestic students; for spring admission, 10/1 for domestic students. Applications are processed on a rolling basis. *Application fee:* $50. *Application Contact:* Dr. Lee A. Brossoit,

Salem State University (continued)

Assistant Dean of Graduate Admissions, 978-542-6673, E-mail: lbrossoit@salemstate.edu. *Dean*, Dr. Carol Glod, 978-542-6323, E-mail: cglod@salemstate.edu.

SALISBURY UNIVERSITY, Salisbury, MD 21801-6837

General Information State-supported, coed, comprehensive institution. CGS member. *Enrollment:* 8,397 graduate, professional, and undergraduate students; 272 full-time matriculated graduate/professional students (191 women), 419 part-time matriculated graduate/professional students (286 women). *Enrollment by degree level:* 691 master's. *Graduate faculty:* 91 full-time (44 women), 22 part-time/adjunct (17 women). *Graduate housing:* On-campus housing not available. *Student services:* Campus employment opportunities, campus safety program, career counseling, exercise/wellness program, free psychological counseling, international student services, multicultural affairs office, services for students with disabilities, writing training. *Library facilities:* Blackwell Library plus 1 other. *Online resources:* library catalog, web page, access to other libraries' catalogs. *Collection:* 279,080 titles, 1,186 serial subscriptions, 1,541 audiovisual materials. *Research affiliation:* National Aeronautics and Space Administration (NASA) (mathematics, physics).

Computer facilities: Computer purchase and lease plans are available. 298 computers available on campus for general student use. A campuswide network can be accessed from student residence rooms and from off campus. Online class registration, accounts for all students are available. *Web address:* http://www.salisbury.edu/.

General Application Contact: Melissa Boog, Associate Director of Admissions, 410-543-6161, Fax: 410-546-6016, E-mail: admissions@salisbury.edu.

GRADUATE UNITS

Graduate Division Students: 272 full-time (191 women), 419 part-time (286 women); includes 59 Black or African American, non-Hispanic/Latino; 2 American Indian or Alaska Native, non-Hispanic/Latino; 6 Asian, non-Hispanic/Latino; 4 Hispanic/Latino; 16 Two or more races, non-Hispanic/Latino, 16 international. Average age 30. 392 applicants, 63% accepted, 133 enrolled. *Faculty:* 91 full-time (44 women), 22 part-time/adjunct (17 women). Expenses: Contact institution. *Financial support:* In 2010–11, 201 students received support. Career-related internships or fieldwork, institutionally sponsored loans, scholarships/grants, and unspecified assistantships available. Support available to part-time students. Financial award application deadline: 2/1; financial award applicants required to submit FAFSA. In 2010, 213 master's awarded. *Degree program information:* Part-time and evening/weekend programs available. Postbaccalaureate distance learning degree programs offered (minimal on-campus study). Offers accounting track (MBA); applied health physiology (MS); composition, language and rhetoric (MA); conflict analysis and dispute resolution (MA); education (M Ed); educational leadership (M Ed); general track (MBA); geographic information systems management (MS); history (MA); literature (MA); mathematics education (MSME); nursing (MS); reading specialist (M Ed); social work (MSW); teaching (MAT); teaching English to speakers of other languages (MA). *Application deadline:* Applications are processed on a rolling basis. *Application fee:* $45. Electronic applications accepted. *Application Contact:* Melissa Boog, Associate Director of Admissions, 410-543-6161, Fax: 410-546-6016, E-mail: admissions@salisbury.edu. *Associate Director of Admissions*, Melissa Boog, 410-543-6161, Fax: 410-546-6016, E-mail: admissions@salisbury.edu.

SALUS UNIVERSITY, Elkins Park, PA 19027-1598

General Information Independent, coed, graduate-only institution. *Graduate housing:* On-campus housing not available. *Research affiliation:* Dynamis Pharmaceuticals (diabetes research), DakDak (photobiology).

GRADUATE UNITS

College of Health Sciences Offers health sciences (MS). Electronic applications accepted.

George S. Osborne College of Audiology Offers audiology (Au D). Electronic applications accepted.

Graduate Studies in Vision Impairment and Audiology *Degree program information:* Part-time programs available. Postbaccalaureate distance learning degree programs offered. Offers education of children and youth with visual and multiple impairments (M Ed, Certificate); low vision rehabilitation (MS, Certificate); orientation and mobility therapy (MS, Certificate); vision rehabilitation therapy (MS, Certificate).

Professional Program Offers optometry (OD). Electronic applications accepted.

SALVE REGINA UNIVERSITY, Newport, RI 02840-4192

General Information Independent-religious, coed, comprehensive institution. *Enrollment:* 2,618 graduate, professional, and undergraduate students; 135 full-time matriculated graduate/professional students (83 women), 459 part-time matriculated graduate/professional students (244 women). *Enrollment by degree level:* 518 master's, 76 doctoral. *Graduate faculty:* 20 full-time (9 women), 47 part-time/adjunct (15 women). *Tuition:* Full-time $7740; part-time $430 per credit. *Required fees:* $40 per semester. Tuition and fees vary according to course level and degree level. *Graduate housing:* On-campus housing not available. *Student services:* Campus employment opportunities, campus safety program, career counseling, international student services, multicultural affairs office, services for students with disabilities, writing training. *Library facilities:* McKillop Library. *Online resources:* library catalog, web page, access to other libraries' catalogs.

Computer facilities: Computer purchase and lease plans are available. 163 computers available on campus for general student use. A campuswide network can be accessed from student residence rooms and from off campus. Online class registration is available. *Web address:* http://www.salve.edu/.

General Application Contact: Kelly Alverson, Associate Director of Graduate Admissions, 401-341-2153, Fax: 401-341-2973, E-mail: kelly.alverson@salve.edu.

GRADUATE UNITS

Graduate Studies *Degree program information:* Part-time and evening/weekend programs available. Postbaccalaureate distance learning degree programs offered (minimal on-campus study). Offers business administration (MBA); business studies (Certificate); expressive and creative arts (CAGS); healthcare administration and management (MS, Certificate); holistic counseling (MA); holistic leadership (MA, CAGS); homeland security (Certificate); human resources management (Certificate); humanities (MA, PhD, CAGS); international relations (MA, Certificate); justice and homeland security (MS); law enforcement leadership (MS); management (Certificate); mental health (CAGS); mental health counseling (CAGS); organizational development (Certificate); rehabilitation counseling (MA). Electronic applications accepted.

SAMFORD UNIVERSITY, Birmingham, AL 35229

General Information Independent-religious, coed, university. *Enrollment:* 4,715 graduate, professional, and undergraduate students; 1,498 full-time matriculated graduate/professional students (744 women), 262 part-time matriculated graduate/professional students (162 women). *Enrollment by degree level:* 487 first professional, 599 master's, 658 doctoral, 16 other advanced degrees. *Graduate faculty:* 128 full-time (61 women), 35 part-time/adjunct (13 women). *Tuition:* Part-time $622 per credit. *Required fees:* $110 per semester. *Graduate housing:* Room and/or apartments available on a first-come, first-served basis to single students; on-campus housing not available to married students. Typical cost: $7024 (including board). Room and board charges vary according to board plan, campus/location and housing facility selected. Housing application deadline: 5/1. *Student services:* Campus employment opportunities, campus safety program, career counseling, child daycare facilities, exercise/wellness program, free psychological counseling, grant writing training, international student services, low-cost health insurance, services for students with disabilities. *Library facilities:* Samford University Library plus 4 others. *Online resources:* library catalog, web page, access to other libraries' catalogs. *Collection:* 737,129 titles, 11,812 audiovisual materials. *Research affiliation:* Vulcan Materials Company (risk science and management), Southern Research Institute (SRI) of Birmingham, University of Alabama at Birmingham Medical School, University of Alabama at Birmingham Medical School, Vulcan Materials Center (risk science and management), Clinical Research Institute, Wallace Memorial Baptist Hospital.

Computer facilities: 330 computers available on campus for general student use. A campuswide network can be accessed from student residence rooms and from off campus. Online class registration, free online storage and tech support are available. *Web address:* http://www.samford.edu/.

General Application Contact: Brian E. Willett, Director of Admissions, 205-726-2902, Fax: 205-726-2171, E-mail: bewillet@samford.edu.

GRADUATE UNITS

Beeson School of Divinity Students: 176 full-time (26 women), 8 part-time (4 women); includes 24 minority (21 Black or African American, non-Hispanic/Latino; 3 Hispanic/Latino), 2 international. Average age 30. 55 applicants, 76% accepted, 31 enrolled. *Faculty:* 14 full-time (3 women), 2 part-time/adjunct (1 woman). Expenses: Contact institution. *Financial support:* In 2010–11, 135 students received support. Scholarships/grants and tuition waivers (full and partial) available. Financial award applicants required to submit FAFSA. In 2010, 13 first professional degrees, 34 master's awarded. Offers divinity (M Div, MATS, D Min). *Application deadline:* For fall admission, 3/1 for domestic and international students; for spring admission, 10/1 for domestic and international students. *Application fee:* $25. Electronic applications accepted. *Application Contact:* Sherri Spurling Brown, Director of Admission, 205-726-2066, Fax: 205-726-4120, E-mail: sbrown5@samford.edu. *Dean*, Dr. Timothy George, 205-726-2632, E-mail: tfgeorge@samford.edu.

Brock School of Business Students: 88 full-time (36 women), 21 part-time (7 women); includes 13 minority (9 Black or African American, non-Hispanic/Latino; 3 Asian, non-Hispanic/Latino; 1 Two or more races, non-Hispanic/Latino), 3 international. Average age 27. 109 applicants, 69% accepted, 66 enrolled. *Faculty:* 12 full-time (3 women). Expenses: Contact institution. *Financial support:* In 2010–11, 32 students received support. Career-related internships or fieldwork, institutionally sponsored loans, scholarships/grants, and tuition waivers (partial) available. Support available to part-time students. Financial award applicants required to submit FAFSA. In 2010, 66 master's awarded. *Degree program information:* Part-time and evening/weekend programs available. Offers business (M Acc, MBA). *Application deadline:* For fall admission, 7/31 priority date for domestic students, 6/1 for international students; for spring admission, 12/1 priority date for domestic students, 10/1 for international students. Applications are processed on a rolling basis. *Application fee:* $25. *Application Contact:* Larron Harper, Director of Graduate Programs, 205-726-2931, Fax: 205-726-4555, E-mail: lcharper@samford.edu. *Acting Dean*, Dr. Jim Reburn, 205-726-2364, Fax: 205-726-2464, E-mail: jpreburn@samford.edu.

Cumberland School of Law Students: 481 full-time (209 women), 6 part-time (2 women); includes 59 minority (28 Black or African American, non-Hispanic/Latino; 5 American Indian or Alaska Native, non-Hispanic/Latino; 5 Asian, non-Hispanic/Latino; 9 Hispanic/Latino; 1 Native Hawaiian or other Pacific Islander, non-Hispanic/Latino; 11 Two or more races, non-Hispanic/Latino). Average age 25. 980 applicants, 52% accepted, 178 enrolled. *Faculty:* 22 full-time (6 women), 15 part-time/adjunct (7 women). Expenses: Contact institution. *Financial support:* In 2010–11, 173 students received support. Career-related internships or fieldwork, Federal Work-Study, institutionally sponsored loans, and scholarships/grants available. Financial award application deadline: 3/1; financial award applicants required to submit FAFSA. In 2010, 155 first professional degrees, 2 master's awarded. *Degree program information:* Part-time programs available. Offers law (JD, MCL). JD/MPH, JD/MPA offered jointly with The University of Alabama at Birmingham. *Application deadline:* For fall admission, 2/28 priority date for domestic and international students. Applications are processed on a rolling basis. *Application fee:* $50. Electronic applications accepted. *Application Contact:* Jennifer Y. Sims, Assistant Dean of Admissions, 205-726-2702, Fax: 205-726-2057, E-mail: law.admissions@samford.edu. *Dean*, John L. Carroll, 205-726-2704, Fax: 205-726-4107, E-mail: jlcarrol@samford.edu.

Howard College of Arts and Sciences Students: 21 full-time (10 women), 13 part-time (8 women); includes 7 minority (4 Black or African American, non-Hispanic/Latino; 1 American Indian or Alaska Native, non-Hispanic/Latino; 2 Asian, non-Hispanic/Latino), 9 international. Average age 31. 26 applicants, 96% accepted, 22 enrolled. *Faculty:* 6 full-time (1 woman), 6 part-time/adjunct (0 women). Expenses: Contact institution. *Financial support:* In 2010–11, 1 student received support. In 2010, 14 master's awarded. *Degree program information:* Part-time and evening/weekend programs available. Offers arts and sciences (MSEM). *Application deadline:* For fall admission, 8/1 for domestic and international students; for winter admission, 2/1 for domestic students; for spring admission, 1/2 for domestic students, 12/14 for international students. Applications are processed on a rolling basis. *Application fee:* $35. *Application Contact:* Dr. Ronald N. Hunsinger, Professor/Chair, 205-726-2944, Fax: 205-726-2479, E-mail: rnhunsin@samford.edu. *Dean*, David W. Chapman, 205-726-2771, Fax: 205-726-2279.

Ida V. Moffett School of Nursing Students: 214 full-time (133 women), 44 part-time (22 women); includes 35 minority (15 Black or African American, non-Hispanic/Latino; 4 American Indian or Alaska Native, non-Hispanic/Latino; 6 Asian, non-Hispanic/Latino; 7 Hispanic/Latino; 1 Native Hawaiian or other Pacific Islander, non-Hispanic/Latino; 2 Two or more races, non-Hispanic/Latino), 1 international. Average age 38. 75 applicants, 93% accepted, 50 enrolled. *Faculty:* 14 full-time (all women), 1 part-time/adjunct (0 women). Expenses: Contact institution. *Financial support:* In 2010–11, 3 students received support. Institutionally sponsored loans, scholarships/grants, and traineeships available. Financial award application deadline: 3/1; financial award applicants required to submit FAFSA. In 2010, 54 master's, 17 doctorates awarded. *Degree program information:* Part-time programs available. Postbaccalaureate distance learning degree programs offered (minimal on-campus study). Offers advance practice (DNP); anesthesia (MSN); family nurse practitioner (MSN); nurse educator (MSN); nurse executive (DNP); nurse manager (MSN). *Application deadline:* For fall admission, 7/1 priority date for domestic and international students; for spring admission, 10/1 priority date for domestic and international students. *Application fee:* $35. *Application Contact:* Dr. Marian Carter, Director of Graduate Student Services, 205-726-2047, Fax: 205-726-4269, E-mail: mwcarter@samford.edu. *Dean*, Dr. Nena F. Sanders, 205-726-2629, E-mail: nfsander@samford.edu.

McWhorter School of Pharmacy Students: 498 full-time (309 women), 3 part-time (2 women); includes 18 Black or African American, non-Hispanic/Latino; 3 American Indian or Alaska Native, non-Hispanic/Latino; 21 Asian, non-Hispanic/Latino; 8 Hispanic/Latino, 7 international. Average age 23. 910 applicants, 20% accepted, 128 enrolled. *Faculty:* 38 full-time (23 women), 1 part-time/adjunct (0 women). Expenses: Contact institution. *Financial support:* In 2010–11, 109 students received support. Career-related internships or fieldwork, Federal Work-Study, and institutionally sponsored loans available. Financial award application deadline: 5/2; financial award applicants required to submit FAFSA. In 2010, 125 Pharm Ds awarded. Offers pharmacy (Pharm D). *Application deadline:* For fall admission, 2/1 for domestic students. Applications are processed on a rolling basis. *Application fee:* $50. Electronic applications accepted. *Application Contact:* C. Bruce Foster, Director of External Relations and Pharmacy Admissions, 205-726-2982, Fax: 205-726-4141, E-mail: cbfoster@samford.edu. *Dean*, Dr. Charles D. Sands, 205-726-2820, Fax: 205-726-2759, E-mail: ccsands@samford.edu.

Orlean Bullard Beeson School of Education and Professional Studies Students: 6 full-time (all women), 164 part-time (117 women); includes 38 minority (34 Black or African American, non-Hispanic/Latino; 2 American Indian or Alaska Native, non-Hispanic/Latino; 1 Asian, non-Hispanic/Latino; 1 Hispanic/Latino), 1 international. Average age 40. 21 applicants, 100% accepted, 17 enrolled. *Faculty:* 11 full-time (7 women), 5 part-time/adjunct (4 women). Expenses: Contact institution. *Financial support:* In 2010–11, 81 students received support; research assistantships, career-related internships or fieldwork, Federal Work-Study, scholarships/grants, and tuition waivers (partial) available. Support available to part-time students. Financial award applicants required to submit FAFSA. In 2010, 36 master's, 15 doctorates, 11 other advanced degrees awarded. *Degree program information:* Part-time programs available. Offers early childhood education (Ed S); early childhood/elementary education (MS Ed); educational administration (Ed S); educational leadership (Ed D); elementary education (Ed S); gifted education (MS Ed); instructional leadership (MS Ed); secondary collaboration (MS Ed). *Application deadline:* For fall admission, 7/15 for domestic students; for winter admission, 4/5 for domestic students; for spring admission, 12/4 for domestic students. Applications are processed on a rolling basis. *Application fee:* $25.

Application Contact: Dr. Maurice Persall, Director, Graduate Office, 205-726-2019, E-mail: jmpersal@samford.edu. *Dean*, Dr. Jean Ann Box, 205-726-2559, E-mail: jabox@samford.edu.

School of the Arts Students: 11 full-time (6 women), 3 part-time (1 woman), 1 international. Average age 28. 13 applicants, 77% accepted, 10 enrolled. *Faculty:* 10 full-time (4 women), 5 part-time/adjunct (1 woman). Expenses: Contact institution. *Financial support:* In 2010–11, 11 students received support, including research assistantships (averaging $4,000 per year); Federal Work-Study, scholarships/grants, tuition waivers (partial), and unspecified assistantships also available. Financial award application deadline: 9/1. In 2010, 7 master's awarded. *Degree program information:* Part-time programs available. Offers church music (MM); music (MME); piano pedagogy (MM). *Application deadline:* For fall admission, 5/1 priority date for domestic students; for spring admission, 12/1 priority date for domestic students. Applications are processed on a rolling basis. *Application fee:* $35. *Application Contact:* Dr. Moya Nordlund, Director, Graduate Studies, 205-726-2651, Fax: 205-726-2165, E-mail: mlnordlu@samford.edu. *Associate Dean*, Dr. Billy J. Strickland, 205-726-4363, E-mail: bjstrick@samford.edu.

SAM HOUSTON STATE UNIVERSITY, Huntsville, TX 77341

General Information State-supported, coed, university. CGS member. *Enrollment:* 17,291 graduate, professional, and undergraduate students; 623 full-time matriculated graduate/professional students (363 women), 1,788 part-time matriculated graduate/professional students (1,250 women). *Enrollment by degree level:* 2,112 master's, 299 doctoral. *Graduate faculty:* 4 full-time (1 woman), 3 part-time/adjunct (2 women). Tuition, state resident: full-time $1363; part-time $163 per credit hour. Tuition, nonresident: full-time $3856; part-time $473 per credit hour. *Graduate housing:* Room and/or apartments available on a first-come, first-served basis to single students; on-campus housing not available to married students. Typical cost: $3914 per year ($7022 including board). Housing application deadline: 8/20. *Student services:* Campus employment opportunities, campus safety program, career counseling, child daycare facilities, exercise/wellness program, free psychological counseling, grant writing training, international student services, multicultural affairs office, services for students with disabilities, writing training. *Library facilities:* Newton Gresham Library plus 1 other. *Online resources:* library catalog, web page, access to other libraries' catalogs. *Collection:* 1.3 million titles, 13,946 serial subscriptions, 14,751 audiovisual materials. *Research affiliation:* Texas Criminal Justice Division, Texas Department of Corrections, Research Division.

Computer facilities: 607 computers available on campus for general student use. A campuswide network can be accessed from student residence rooms and from off campus. Online class registration is available. *Web address:* http://www.shsu.edu/.

General Application Contact: Dr. Kandi Tayebi, Dean of Graduate Studies and Associate Vice President for Academic Affairs, 936-294-1971, Fax: 936-294-1271, E-mail: graduate@shsu.edu.

GRADUATE UNITS

College of Arts and Sciences Students: 116 full-time (46 women), 98 part-time (45 women); includes 4 Black or African American, non-Hispanic/Latino; 3 Asian, non-Hispanic/Latino; 10 Hispanic/Latino, 48 international. Average age 24. 110 applicants, 84% accepted, 68 enrolled. *Faculty:* 1 (woman) part-time/adjunct. Expenses: Contact institution. *Financial support:* Research assistantships, teaching assistantships, career-related internships or fieldwork, Federal Work-Study, institutionally sponsored loans, scholarships/grants, and tuition waivers (partial) available. Support available to part-time students. Financial award application deadline: 5/31; financial award applicants required to submit FAFSA. In 2010, 53 master's awarded. *Degree program information:* Part-time and evening/weekend programs available. Offers agriculture (MS); arts and sciences (MA, MFA, MM, MS); biology (MA, MS); chemistry (MS); computing and information science (MS); dance (MFA); industrial technology (MA); mathematics (MA, MS); statistics (MS). *Application deadline:* For fall admission, 8/1 for domestic and international students; for spring admission, 12/1 for domestic and international students. Applications are processed on a rolling basis. *Application fee:* $20. Electronic applications accepted. *Application Contact:* Tammy Gray, Advisor, 936-294-1230, E-mail: dca_tag@shsu.edu. *Dean*, Dr. Jaimie Hebert, 936-294-1401, Fax: 936-294-1598, E-mail: mth_jlh@shsu.edu.

School of Music Students: 9 full-time (5 women), 10 part-time (5 women); includes 1 Black or African American, non-Hispanic/Latino; 1 Asian, non-Hispanic/Latino, 2 international. Average age 34. 11 applicants, 91% accepted, 9 enrolled. *Faculty:* 14 full-time (3 women), 1 part-time/adjunct (0 women). Expenses: Contact institution. *Financial support:* Teaching assistantships, Federal Work-Study and scholarships/grants available. Financial award application deadline: 5/31; financial award applicants required to submit FAFSA. In 2010, 13 master's awarded. *Degree program information:* Part-time programs available. Offers music (MM); music education (MM). *Application deadline:* For fall admission, 8/1 for domestic and international students; for spring admission, 12/1 for domestic and international students. Applications are processed on a rolling basis. *Application fee:* $20. *Application Contact:* Scott Plugge, Advisor, 936-294-1393, E-mail: plugge@shsu.edu. *Director*, Dr. James Bankhead, 936-294-3808, Fax: 936-294-3765, E-mail: bankhead@shsu.edu.

College of Business Administration Students: 146 full-time (63 women), 150 part-time (71 women); includes 20 Black or African American, non-Hispanic/Latino; 2 American Indian or Alaska Native, non-Hispanic/Latino; 8 Asian, non-Hispanic/Latino; 24 Hispanic/Latino, 29 international. Average age 29. 141 applicants, 83% accepted, 78 enrolled. *Faculty:* 31 full-time (8 women). Expenses: Contact institution. *Financial support:* Research assistantships, Federal Work-Study, institutionally sponsored loans, and unspecified assistantships available. Financial award application deadline: 5/31; financial award applicants required to submit FAFSA. In 2010, 97 master's awarded. *Degree program information:* Part-time and evening/weekend programs available. Offers accounting (MS); business administration (MBA); finance (MS); general business and finance (MS). *Application deadline:* For fall admission, 8/1 for domestic students; for spring admission, 12/1 for domestic students. Applications are processed on a rolling basis. *Application fee:* $20. *Application Contact:* Dr. Leroy Ashorn, Advisor, 936-294-1246, Fax: 936-294-3612, E-mail: busgrad@shsu.edu. *Dean*, Dr. Mitchell J. Muehsam, 936-294-1254, Fax: 936-294-3612, E-mail: mmuehsam@shsu.edu.

College of Criminal Justice Students: 91 full-time (55 women), 238 part-time (83 women); includes 25 Black or African American, non-Hispanic/Latino; 1 American Indian or Alaska Native, non-Hispanic/Latino; 6 Asian, non-Hispanic/Latino; 35 Hispanic/Latino, 33 international. Average age 34. 148 applicants, 88% accepted, 114 enrolled. *Faculty:* 22 full-time (4 women). Expenses: Contact institution. *Financial support:* Fellowships, research assistantships, teaching assistantships, career-related internships or fieldwork, Federal Work-Study, institutionally sponsored loans, and unspecified assistantships available. Support available to part-time students. Financial award application deadline: 5/31; financial award applicants required to submit FAFSA. In 2010, 46 master's, 6 doctorates awarded. Offers criminal justice (MS, PhD); criminal justice and criminology (MA); criminal justice management (MS); forensic science (MS); security studies (MS); victim services management (MS). *Application deadline:* For fall admission, 8/1 for domestic students; for spring admission, 12/1 for domestic students. Applications are processed on a rolling basis. *Application fee:* $20. *Application Contact:* Doris Powell-Pratt, Advisor, 936-294-3637, Fax: 936-294-4055, E-mail: icc_dcp@shsu.edu. *Dean*, Dr. Vincent Webb, 936-294-1632, Fax: 936-294-1653, E-mail: vwebb@shsu.edu.

College of Education and Applied Science Students: 147 full-time (107 women), 1,133 part-time (954 women); includes 150 Black or African American, non-Hispanic/Latino; 8 American Indian or Alaska Native, non-Hispanic/Latino; 11 Asian, non-Hispanic/Latino; 176 Hispanic/Latino, 17 international. Average age 35. 494 applicants, 94% accepted, 353 enrolled. *Faculty:* 70 full-time (46 women), 12 part-time/adjunct (10 women). Expenses: Contact institution. *Financial support:* Research assistantships, teaching assistantships, career-related internships or fieldwork, Federal Work-Study, institutionally sponsored loans, and tuition waivers (partial) available. Support available to part-time students. Financial award application deadline: 5/31; financial award applicants required to submit FAFSA. In 2010, 466 master's, 17 doctorates awarded. *Degree program information:* Part-time and evening/weekend programs available. Offers administration (M Ed, MA); counseling (M Ed, MA); counselor education (MA, PhD); curriculum and instruction (M Ed, MA); education and applied science (M Ed, MA, MLS, Ed D, PhD); educational leadership (Ed D); health (M Ed, MA); instructional leadership (M Ed, MA); instructional technology (M Ed); kinesiology (M Ed, MA); library science (MLS); reading (M Ed, MA, Ed D); special education (M Ed, MA). *Application deadline:* For fall admission, 8/1 for domestic students; for spring admission, 12/1 for domestic students. *Application fee:* $20. *Application Contact:* Molly Doughtie, Advisor, 936-294-1105, E-mail: edu_mxd@shsu.edu. *Dean*, Dr. Genevieve Brown, 936-294-1101, Fax: 936-294-1102, E-mail: edu_gxb@shsu.edu.

College of Humanities and Social Sciences Students: 123 full-time (92 women), 169 part-time (97 women); includes 12 Black or African American, non-Hispanic/Latino; 3 Asian, non-Hispanic/Latino; 16 Hispanic/Latino, 10 international. Average age 30. 216 applicants, 56% accepted, 96 enrolled. *Faculty:* 60 full-time (30 women), 1 part-time/adjunct (0 women). Expenses: Contact institution. In 2010, 67 master's, 4 doctorates awarded. Offers clinical psychology (PhD); dietetics (MS); English (MA); English and foreign languages (MA); family and consumer sciences (MS); history (MA); political science (MA, MPA); psychology (MA); psychology and philosophy (MA, PhD); public administration (MPA); sociology (MA); speech communication (MA). *Application deadline:* For fall admission, 8/1 for domestic students; for spring admission, 12/1 for domestic students. *Application fee:* $20. *Application Contact:* Dr. Kandi Tayebi, Dean of Graduate Studies and Associate Vice President for Academic Affairs, 936-294-1971, Fax: 936-294-1271, E-mail: graduate@shsu.edu. *Dean*, Dr. John deCastro, 936-294-2200, Fax: 936-294-2207, E-mail: jmd018@shsu.edu.

SAMRA UNIVERSITY OF ORIENTAL MEDICINE, Los Angeles, CA 90015

General Information Independent, coed, graduate-only institution. *Graduate housing:* On-campus housing not available.

GRADUATE UNITS

Program in Oriental Medicine *Degree program information:* Part-time and evening/weekend programs available. Offers Oriental medicine (MS, DAOM).

SAMUEL MERRITT UNIVERSITY, Oakland, CA 94609-3108

General Information Independent, coed, primarily women, upper-level institution. *Graduate housing:* Room and/or apartments available to single students; on-campus housing not available to married students. *Research affiliation:* Summit Medical Center (nursing).

GRADUATE UNITS

Department of Occupational Therapy Offers occupational therapy (MOT).

Department of Physical Therapy Offers physical therapy (DPT).

Department of Physician Assistant Studies Offers physician assistant studies (MPA).

School of Nursing *Degree program information:* Part-time and evening/weekend programs available. Offers case management (MSN); family nurse practitioner (MSN, Certificate); nurse anesthetist (MSN, Certificate); nursing (MSN).

SAN DIEGO STATE UNIVERSITY, San Diego, CA 92182

General Information State-supported, coed, university. CGS member. *Graduate housing:* Room and/or apartments available on a first-come, first-served basis to single students; on-campus housing not available to married students. Housing application deadline: 5/1. *Research affiliation:* Children's Hospital and Research Center (children's health), Qualcomm (wireless and telecommunications), Robert Wood Johnson Foundation (public health), General Atomics (technical student services), William and Flora Hewlett Foundation (teacher education), American Heart Association (biology).

GRADUATE UNITS

Graduate and Research Affairs *Degree program information:* Part-time and evening/weekend programs available. Offers interdisciplinary studies (MA, MS). Electronic applications accepted.

College of Arts and Letters *Degree program information:* Part-time and evening/weekend programs available. Offers anthropology (MA); applied linguistics and English as a second language (CAL); arts and letters (MA, MFA, PhD, CAL); Asian studies (MA); computational linguistics (MA); creative writing (MFA); economics (MA); English (MA); English as a second language/applied linguistics (MA); European studies (MA); general linguistics (MA); geography (MA, PhD); history (MA); Latin American studies (MA); liberal arts and sciences (MA); philosophy (MA); political science (MA); rhetoric and writing (MA); sociology (MA); Spanish (MA); women's studies (MA). Electronic applications accepted.

College of Business Administration *Degree program information:* Part-time and evening/weekend programs available. Offers accountancy (MS); business administration (MBA, MS); entrepreneurship (MS); finance (MS); human resources management (MS); information and decision systems (MS); international business (MS); management science (MS); marketing (MS); production and operations management (MS); sports business management (MBA). Electronic applications accepted.

College of Education *Degree program information:* Part-time and evening/weekend programs available. Offers child development (MS); counseling and school psychology (MS); education (MA, MS, Ed D, PhD); educational leadership (MA); educational leadership in postsecondary education (MA); educational technology (MA); educational technology and teaching and learning (Ed D); elementary curriculum and instruction (MA); multi-cultural emphasis (PhD); policy studies in language and cross cultural education (MA); reading education (MA); rehabilitation counseling (MS); secondary curriculum and instruction (MA); special education (MA). Electronic applications accepted.

College of Engineering *Degree program information:* Part-time and evening/weekend programs available. Offers aerospace engineering (MS); civil engineering (MS); electrical engineering (MS); engineering (MS, PhD); engineering mechanics (MS); engineering sciences and applied mechanics (PhD); flight dynamics (MS); fluid dynamics (MS); manufacture and design (MS); mechanical engineering (MS). Electronic applications accepted.

College of Health and Human Services *Degree program information:* Part-time and evening/weekend programs available. Offers audiology (Au D); biometry (MPH); communicative disorders (MA); environmental health (MPH); epidemiology (MPH, PhD); gerontology (MS); global emergency preparedness and response (MS); global health (PhD); health and human services (MA, MPH, MS, MSW, Au D, PhD); health behavior (PhD); health promotion (MPH); health services administration (MPH); language and communicative disorders (PhD); nursing (MS); social work (MSW); toxicology (MS). Electronic applications accepted.

College of Professional Studies and Fine Arts *Degree program information:* Part-time programs available. Offers advertising and public relations (MA); art history (MA); city planning (MCP); composition (acoustic and electronic) (MM); conducting (MM); criminal justice administration (MPA); criminal justice and criminology (MS); critical-cultural studies (MA); ethnomusicology (MA); exercise physiology (MS); interaction studies (MA); intercultural and international studies (MA); jazz studies (MM); musicology (MA); new media studies (MA); news and information studies (MA); nutritional science (MS); nutritional sciences (MS); performance (MM); physical education/kinesiology (MS); piano pedagogy (MA); professional studies and fine arts (MA, MCP, MFA, MM, MPA, MS); public administration (MPA); studio arts (MA, MFA); telecommunications and media management (MA); television, film, and new media production (MA); theatre arts (MA, MFA); theory (MA).

College of Sciences *Degree program information:* Part-time programs available. Offers applied mathematics (MS); astronomy (MS); biology (MA, MS); cell and molecular biology (PhD); chemistry (MA, MS, PhD); clinical psychology (MS, PhD); computational science (MS, PhD); computer science (MS); ecology (MS, PhD); geological sciences (MS); industrial and organizational psychology (MS); mathematics (MA); mathematics and science education (PhD); microbiology (MS); molecular biology (MA, MS); physics (MA, MS); program evaluation (MS); psychology (MA); radiological physics (MS); regulatory affairs (MS); sciences (MA, MS, PhD); statistics (MS). Electronic applications accepted.

SAN FRANCISCO ART INSTITUTE, San Francisco, CA 94133

General Information Independent, coed, comprehensive institution. *Graduate housing:* Room and/or apartments available on a first-come, first-served basis to single students;

San Francisco Art Institute (continued)

on-campus housing not available to married students. *Research affiliation:* Exploratorium (museum of science, art, and human perception).

GRADUATE UNITS

Graduate Program *Degree program information:* Part-time programs available. Offers design and technology (MFA, Certificate); exhibition and museum studies (MA); film (MFA, Certificate); fine arts (MA, MFA, Certificate); history and theory of contemporary art (MA); new genres (Certificate); painting (MFA, Certificate); performance/video (MFA); photography (MFA, Certificate); printmaking (MFA, Certificate); sculpture (MFA, Certificate); urban studies (MA). Electronic applications accepted.

SAN FRANCISCO CONSERVATORY OF MUSIC, San Francisco, CA 94102

General Information Independent, coed, comprehensive institution. *Graduate housing:* Rooms and/or apartments available on a first-come, first-served basis to single and married students.

GRADUATE UNITS

Graduate Division Offers chamber music (MM); classical guitar (MM); composition (MM); conducting (MM); keyboards (MM); orchestral instruments (MM); voice (MM). Electronic applications accepted.

SAN FRANCISCO STATE UNIVERSITY, San Francisco, CA 94132-1722

General Information State-supported, coed, university. *Enrollment:* 29,718 graduate, professional, and undergraduate students; 2,716 full-time matriculated graduate/professional students (1,780 women), 1,832 part-time matriculated graduate/professional students (1,144 women). *Graduate faculty:* 818 full-time (375 women). *Graduate housing:* Room and/or apartments available on a first-come, first-served basis to single students; on-campus housing not available to married students. *Student services:* Campus employment opportunities, campus safety program, career counseling, child daycare facilities, exercise/wellness program, free psychological counseling, international student services, low-cost health insurance, multicultural affairs office, services for students with disabilities, teacher training. *Library facilities:* J. Paul Leonard Library. *Online resources:* library catalog, web page, access to other libraries' catalogs. *Collection:* 915,408 titles, 65,459 serial subscriptions, 134,460 audiovisual materials.

Computer facilities: Computer purchase and lease plans are available. 2,800 computers available on campus for general student use. A campuswide network can be accessed from student residence rooms and from off campus. Online class registration is available. *Web address:* http://www.sfsu.edu/.

General Application Contact: Brian J. Gallagher, Director of Graduate Admissions, 415-338-2234, Fax: 415-338-0942, E-mail: gadstdy@sfsu.edu.

GRADUATE UNITS

Division of Graduate Studies Expenses: Contact institution. *Financial support:* Fellowships, research assistantships, teaching assistantships, career-related internships or fieldwork, Federal Work-Study, institutionally sponsored loans, tuition waivers (partial), and unspecified assistantships available. Support available to part-time students. Financial award application deadline: 3/1; financial award applicants required to submit FAFSA. *Degree program information:* Part-time and evening/weekend programs available. *Application fee:* $55. *Application Contact:* Maria Conrad, Special Assistant to Dean, 415-405-4391, Fax: 415-338-0942, E-mail: mashac@sfsu.edu. *Dean,* Dr. Ann Hallum, 415-338-2234, Fax: 415-338-0942, E-mail: glider@sfsu.edu.

College of Behavioral and Social Sciences Expenses: Contact institution. *Financial support:* Fellowships, research assistantships, teaching assistantships available. *Degree program information:* Part-time and evening/weekend programs available. Offers archaeology (MA); behavioral and social sciences (MA, MPA, MS); biological/physical anthropology (MA); clinical psychology (MS); developmental psychology (MA); economics (MA); geographic information science (MS); geography (MA); history (MA); human sexuality studies (MA); industrial/organizational psychology (MS); international relations (MA); nonprofit administration (MPA); policy making and analysis (MPA); political science (MA); psychological research (MA); public management (MPA); school psychology (MS); social psychology (MA); social/cultural anthropology (MA); urban administration (MPA); visual anthropology (MA). *Application Contact:* Sylvia Leng, Curriculum Coordinator, 415-338-7692. *Dean,* Dr. Joel Kassiola, 415-338-1846, E-mail: kassiola@sfsu.edu.

College of Business Expenses: Contact institution. Offers accountancy (MSA); business administration (MBA). *Application Contact:* Armaan Moattari, Assistant Director, Graduate Programs, 415-817-4314, E-mail: amoatt@sfsu.edu. *Dean,* Dr. Caran Colvin, 415-405-3752.

College of Creative Arts Expenses: Contact institution. Offers art (MFA); broadcast and electronic communication arts (MA); chamber music (MM); cinema (MFA); cinema studies (MA); classical performance (MM); composition (MM); conducting (MM); creative arts (MA, MFA, MM); drama (MA); industrial arts (MA); music education (MA); music history (MA); theatre arts (MFA). *Application Contact:* Dr. Ronald Caltabiano, Associate Dean, 415-338-1471. *Dean,* Dr. Kurt Daw, 415-338-7618.

College of Education Expenses: Contact institution. Offers adult education (MA Ed, AC); autism spectrum (AC); communicative disorders (MS); early childhood education (MA); early childhood special education (AC); education (MA, MA Ed, MS, Ed D, PhD, AC, Credential); educational administration (MA, AC); educational leadership (Ed D); elementary education (MA); equity and social justice (AC); equity and social justice in education (MA Ed); guide dog mobility (AC); language and literacy education (MA); mathematics education (MA); orientation and mobility (MA, Credential); secondary education (MA Ed); special education (MA, PhD); special interest (MA Ed); training systems development (AC). *Application Contact:* Dr. David Hemphill, Associate Dean, 415-338-2689, E-mail: hemphill@sfsu.edu. *Dean,* Dr. Jacob Perea, 415-338-2687, E-mail: pjoost@sfsu.edu.

College of Ethnic Studies Expenses: Contact institution. *Degree program information:* Part-time programs available. Offers Asian American studies (MA); ethnic studies (MA). *Application Contact:* Dr. Laureen Chew, Associate Dean, 415-338-1693, E-mail: ethnicst@sfsu.edu. *Dean,* Dr. Kenneth P. Montiero, 415-338-1693.

College of Health and Human Services Expenses: Contact institution. *Financial support:* Fellowships, research assistantships, teaching assistantships, career-related internships or fieldwork, Federal Work-Study, institutionally sponsored loans, and unspecified assistantships available. *Degree program information:* Part-time programs available. Offers case management (MS); counseling (MS); exercise physiology (MS); family and consumer sciences (MA); geriatric care management (MA); health and human services (MA, MPH, MS, MSC, MSW, DPT, Dr Sc PT); health education (MPH); health, wellness and aging (MA); kinesiology (MS); long-term care administration (MA); marriage, family, and child counseling (MSC); movement science (MS); nursing administration (MS); nursing education (MS); physical activity: social scientific perspectives (MS); physical therapy (MS, DPT, Dr Sc PT); recreation (MS); rehabilitation counseling (MS); social work (MSW). *Application Contact:* Christina Alcantara, Office Manager, 415-338-3326. *Dean,* Dr. Don Taylor, 415-338-3326, E-mail: dtaylor@sfsu.edu.

College of Humanities Expenses: Contact institution. *Financial support:* Teaching assistantships, career-related internships or fieldwork and Federal Work-Study available. *Degree program information:* Part-time and evening/weekend programs available. Offers Chinese (MA); classics (MA); communication studies (MA); comparative literature (MA); composition (MA); creative writing (MA, MFA); French (MA); German (MA); humanities (MA, MFA, Certificate); Italian (MA); Japanese (MA); linguistics (MA); literature (MA); museum studies (MA); philosophy (MA); Spanish (MA); teaching critical thinking (Certificate); teaching English to speakers of other languages (MA); teaching of composition (Certificate); teaching post-secondary reading (Certificate); women and gender studies (MA). *Application Contact:* Margaret Boehm, Assistant to Graduate Dean, 415-338-1541, Fax: 415-338-7030, E-mail: mboehm@sfsu.edu. *Dean,* Dr. Paul Sherwin, 415-338-1541, Fax: 415-338-7030, E-mail: psherwin@sfsu.edu.

College of Science and Engineering Expenses: Contact institution. *Degree program information:* Part-time programs available. Offers biomedical science (MS); biotechnology (PSM); cell and molecular biology (MS); chemistry (MS); computer science (MS); computer science: computing and business (MS); computer science: computing for life sciences (MS); computer science: software and engineering (MS); conservation biology (MS); ecology and systematic biology (MS); embedded electrical and computer systems (MS); geosciences (MS); marine biology (MS); marine science (MS); mathematics (MA); microbiology (MS); physics (MS); physiology and behavioral biology (MS); science (PSM); science and engineering (MA, MS, PSM); stem cell science (PSM); structural/earthquake engineering (MS). *Application deadline:* Applications are processed on a rolling basis. Electronic applications accepted. *Application Contact:* Ruth MacKay-Shea, Assistant to Dean, 415-338-1571, E-mail: ramackay@sfsu.edu. *Dean,* Dr. Sheldon Axler, 415-338-1571, Fax: 415-338-6136, E-mail: axler@sfsu.edu.

SAN FRANCISCO THEOLOGICAL SEMINARY, San Anselmo, CA 94960-2997

General Information Independent-religious, coed, graduate-only institution. *Graduate housing:* Rooms and/or apartments available on a first-come, first-served basis to single and married students. Housing application deadline: 5/1.

GRADUATE UNITS

Graduate and Professional Programs *Degree program information:* Part-time programs available. Offers theology (M Div, MA, MATS, D Min, PhD, Th D). MA, Th D, PhD, M Div/MA offered jointly with Graduate Theological Union.

SAN JOAQUIN COLLEGE OF LAW, Clovis, CA 93612-1312

General Information Independent, coed, graduate-only institution. *Graduate housing:* On-campus housing not available.

GRADUATE UNITS

Law Program *Degree program information:* Part-time and evening/weekend programs available. Offers law (JD).

SAN JOSE STATE UNIVERSITY, San Jose, CA 95192-0001

General Information State-supported, coed, comprehensive institution. CGS member. *Graduate housing:* Room and/or apartments available on a first-come, first-served basis to single students; on-campus housing not available to married students. *Research affiliation:* Moss Landing Marine Laboratories.

GRADUATE UNITS

Graduate Studies and Research *Degree program information:* Part-time and evening/weekend programs available. Postbaccalaureate distance learning degree programs offered (minimal on-campus study). Offers interdisciplinary studies (MA, MS). Electronic applications accepted.

Charles W. Davidson College of Engineering *Degree program information:* Part-time programs available. Offers aerospace engineering (MS); chemical engineering (MS); civil engineering (MS); computer engineering (MS); electrical engineering (MS); engineering (MS); general engineering (MS); industrial and systems engineering (MS); materials engineering (MS); mechanical engineering (MS); quality assurance (MS); software engineering (MS). Electronic applications accepted.

College of Applied Sciences and Arts *Degree program information:* Part-time and evening/weekend programs available. Offers applied sciences and arts (MA, MLIS, MPH, MS, MSW, PhD, Certificate); applied social gerontology (Certificate); community health education (MPH); gerontology nurse practitioner (MS); justice studies (MS); kinesiology (MA); library and information science (MLIS, PhD); mass communications (MS); nursing (Certificate); nursing administration (MS); nursing education (MS); nutritional science (MS); occupational therapy (MS); recreation (MS); social work (MSW, Certificate). Electronic applications accepted.

College of Humanities and the Arts Offers animation/illustration (MA); art history (MA); computational linguistics (Certificate); digital media arts (MFA); English (MFA); English literature (MA); French (MA); humanities and the arts (MA, MFA, Certificate); linguistics (MA); music (MA); philosophy (MA); photography (MFA); pictorial arts (MFA); Spanish (MA); spatial arts (MFA); teaching English to speakers of other languages (MA, Certificate); theatre arts (MA). Electronic applications accepted.

College of Science *Degree program information:* Part-time and evening/weekend programs available. Offers applied mathematics (MS); biological sciences (MA, MS); chemistry (MA, MS); computational physics (MS); computer science (MS); geology (MS); marine science (MS); mathematics (MA, MS); mathematics education (MA); meteorology (MS); molecular biology and microbiology (MS); natural science (MA); organismal biology, conservation and ecology (MS); physics (MS); physiology (MS); science (MA, MBT, MS); statistics (MA). Electronic applications accepted.

College of Social Sciences *Degree program information:* Part-time and evening/weekend programs available. Offers applied anthropology (MA); applied economics (MA); clinical psychology (MS); communication studies (MA); economics (MA); environmental studies (MS); experimental psychology (MA); geographic information science (Certificate); geography (MA); history (MA); history education (MA); industrial/organizational psychology (MS); Mexican American studies (MA); psychology (MA); public administration (MPA); social sciences (MA, MPA, MS, MUP, Certificate); sociology (MA); urban and regional planning (MUP, Certificate). Electronic applications accepted.

Connie L. Lurie College of Education *Degree program information:* Evening/weekend programs available. Offers child and adolescent development (MA); counselor education (MA); curriculum and instruction (MA); education (MA, Certificate); educational administration (K-12) (MA); higher education administration (MA); reading (Certificate); secondary education (Certificate); special education (MA); speech-language pathology (MA). Electronic applications accepted.

Lucas Graduate School of Business *Degree program information:* Part-time and evening/weekend programs available. Postbaccalaureate distance learning degree programs offered (minimal on-campus study). Offers accounting (MS); business (MBA, MS); business administration (MBA); taxation (MS); transportation management (MS). Electronic applications accepted.

SAN JUAN BAUTISTA SCHOOL OF MEDICINE, Caguas, PR 00726-4968

General Information Independent, coed, graduate-only institution. *Enrollment by degree level:* 257 first professional. *Graduate faculty:* 35 full-time (19 women), 20 part-time/adjunct (4 women). *Graduate housing:* On-campus housing not available. *Student services:* Campus employment opportunities, career counseling, exercise/wellness program, grant writing training, low-cost health insurance, multicultural affairs office, services for students with disabilities, writing training. *Library facilities:* San Juan Bautista School of Medicine Library. *Online resources:* library catalog, web page. *Collection:* 7,447 titles, 1,288 serial subscriptions, 8,659 audiovisual materials. *Research affiliation:* University of Puerto Rico, Medical Science Campus (molecular biology, microbiology, neurosciences, pediatrics, public health), Ponce School of Medicine (virology, immunology), Veteran Affairs (clinical research).

Computer facilities: 50 computers available on campus for general student use. A campuswide network can be accessed from off campus. *Web address:* http://www.sanjuanbautista.edu/.

General Application Contact: Jaymi Sanchez, Admissions, 787-743-3038 Ext. 236, Fax: 787-746-3093, E-mail: jsanchez@sanjuanbautista.edu.

GRADUATE UNITS

Professional Program Students: 272 full-time (143 women); includes 255 minority (5 Black or African American, non-Hispanic/Latino; 4 Asian, non-Hispanic/Latino; 238 Hispanic/Latino; 8 Native Hawaiian or other Pacific Islander, non-Hispanic/Latino). Average age 25. 924 applicants, 14% accepted, 64 enrolled. *Faculty:* 35 full-time (19 women), 20 part-time/adjunct (4 women). Expenses: Contact institution. *Financial support:* Applicants required to submit FAFSA. In 2010, 59 MDs awarded. Offers medicine (MD). *Application deadline:* For fall admission, 12/15 priority date for domestic students. Applications are processed on a rolling basis. *Application fee:* $75. *Application Contact:* Jaymi Sanchez, Admissions Officer, 787-743-3038 Ext. 236, Fax: 787-746-3093, E-mail: jsanchez@sanjuanbautista.edu. *President/Dean*, Dr. Yocasta Brugal, 787-743-3038, Fax: 787-746-3093, E-mail: xbrugal@sanjuanbautista.edu.

SANTA CLARA UNIVERSITY, Santa Clara, CA 95053

General Information Independent-religious, coed, university. CGS member. *Enrollment:* 8,831 graduate, professional, and undergraduate students; 1,830 full-time matriculated graduate/professional students (825 women), 1,768 part-time matriculated graduate/professional students (714 women). *Enrollment by degree level:* 984 first professional, 2,333 master's, 72 doctoral, 209 other advanced degrees. *Graduate faculty:* 226 full-time (82 women), 212 part-time/adjunct (69 women). Tuition and fees vary according to course load and program. *Graduate housing:* Rooms and/or apartments available on a first-come, first-served basis to single and married students. Typical cost: $11,742 (including board) for single students; $11,742 (including board) for married students. Room and board charges vary according to board plan, campus/location and housing facility selected. Housing application deadline: 5/1. *Student services:* Campus employment opportunities, campus safety program, career counseling, child daycare facilities, exercise/wellness program, free psychological counseling, international student services, low-cost health insurance, multicultural affairs office. *Library facilities:* University Library plus 1 other. *Online resources:* library catalog, web page, access to other libraries' catalogs. *Collection:* 1.2 million titles, 8,811 serial subscriptions, 26,325 audiovisual materials.

Computer facilities: Computer purchase and lease plans are available. 782 computers available on campus for general student use. A campuswide network can be accessed from student residence rooms and from off campus. Online class registration is available. *Web address:* http://www.scu.edu/.

GRADUATE UNITS

College of Arts and Sciences Students: 9 full-time (6 women), 22 part-time (16 women); includes 8 minority (4 Asian, non-Hispanic/Latino; 3 Hispanic/Latino; 1 Native Hawaiian or other Pacific Islander, non-Hispanic/Latino), 2 international. Average age 43. 15 applicants, 73% accepted, 7 enrolled. *Faculty:* 5 full-time (2 women), 5 part-time/adjunct (4 women). Expenses: Contact institution. *Financial support:* Fellowships, research assistantships, career-related internships or fieldwork, Federal Work-Study, institutionally sponsored loans, and scholarships/grants available. Support available to part-time students. Financial award applicants required to submit FAFSA. In 2010, 13 master's awarded. *Degree program information:* Part-time and evening/weekend programs available. Offers arts and sciences (MA); pastoral ministries (MA). *Application deadline:* Applications are processed on a rolling basis. *Application fee:* $50. Electronic applications accepted.

Jesuit School of Theology Students: 98 full-time (29 women), 46 part-time (19 women); includes 21 minority (1 Black or African American, non-Hispanic/Latino; 13 Asian, non-Hispanic/Latino; 6 Hispanic/Latino; 1 Native Hawaiian or other Pacific Islander, non-Hispanic/Latino), 65 international. Average age 37. 102 applicants, 82% accepted, 64 enrolled. *Faculty:* 15 full-time (3 women), 5 part-time/adjunct (3 women). Expenses: Contact institution. *Financial support:* Application deadline: 3/2. In 2010, 26 master's, 4 doctorates, 10 other advanced degrees awarded. *Degree program information:* Part-time and evening/weekend programs available. Offers theology (M Div, STB, MA, MTS, Th M, STD, STL). *Application deadline:* For fall admission, 8/15 priority date for domestic and international students; for spring admission, 1/10 priority date for domestic and international students. Applications are processed on a rolling basis. *Application fee:* $50. Electronic applications accepted. *Application Contact:* Grace Hogan, Associate Director of Enrollment Management, 510-549-5013, Fax: 510-841-8536, E-mail: ghogan@jstb.edu. *Dean*, Kevin F. Burke, SJ, 510-549-5040, E-mail: kburke@jstb.edu.

Leavey School of Business Students: 254 full-time (91 women), 793 part-time (255 women); includes 367 minority (14 Black or African American, non-Hispanic/Latino; 1 American Indian or Alaska Native, non-Hispanic/Latino; 298 Asian, non-Hispanic/Latino; 43 Hispanic/Latino; 6 Native Hawaiian or other Pacific Islander, non-Hispanic/Latino; 5 Two or more races, non-Hispanic/Latino), 242 international. Average age 32. 372 applicants, 74% accepted, 200 enrolled. *Faculty:* 75 full-time (18 women), 63 part-time/adjunct (14 women). Expenses: Contact institution. *Financial support:* In 2010–11, 20 fellowships with partial tuition reimbursements (averaging $8,000 per year), 20 research assistantships with partial tuition reimbursements (averaging $8,000 per year) were awarded; career-related internships or fieldwork, Federal Work-Study, institutionally sponsored loans, scholarships/grants, health care benefits, and unspecified assistantships also available. Support available to part-time students. Financial award applicants required to submit FAFSA. In 2010, 320 master's awarded. *Degree program information:* Part-time and evening/weekend programs available. Offers accounting (MBA); business (EMBA, MBA, MS); entrepreneurship (MBA); executive business administration (EMBA); finance (MBA); food and agribusiness (MBA); information systems (MS); international business (MBA); leading people and organizations (MBA); managing technology and innovation (MBA); marketing management (MBA); supply chain management (MBA). *Application deadline:* For fall admission, 6/1 for domestic and international students; for spring admission, 1/19 for domestic and international students. Applications are processed on a rolling basis. *Application fee:* $75 ($100 for international students). Electronic applications accepted. *Application Contact:* Jennifer W. Taylor, Senior Director, 408-554-4539, Fax: 408-554-4571, E-mail: mbaadmissions@scu.edu. *Senior Assistant Dean*, Elizabeth B. Ford, 408-554-2752, Fax: 408-554-4571, E-mail: eford@scu.edu.

School of Education and Counseling Psychology Students: 183 full-time (143 women), 355 part-time (283 women); includes 154 minority (13 Black or African American, non-Hispanic/Latino; 2 American Indian or Alaska Native, non-Hispanic/Latino; 68 Asian, non-Hispanic/Latino; 64 Hispanic/Latino; 2 Native Hawaiian or other Pacific Islander, non-Hispanic/Latino; 5 Two or more races, non-Hispanic/Latino), 17 international. Average age 33. 337 applicants, 73% accepted, 153 enrolled. *Faculty:* 19 full-time (11 women), 36 part-time/adjunct (16 women). Expenses: Contact institution. *Financial support:* In 2010–11, 118 students received support, including 118 fellowships (averaging $1,300 per year); Federal Work-Study, institutionally sponsored loans, and scholarships/grants also available. Support available to part-time students. Financial award application deadline: 5/15; financial award applicants required to submit FAFSA. In 2010, 191 master's, 165 other advanced degrees awarded. *Degree program information:* Part-time and evening/weekend programs available. Offers counseling (MA); counseling psychology (MA); education and counseling psychology (MA, Certificate); educational administration (MA, Certificate); interdisciplinary education (MA); teacher education (Certificate). *Application deadline:* For fall admission, 6/15 for domestic and international students; for winter admission, 10/15 for domestic and international students; for spring admission, 1/31 for domestic and international students. Applications are processed on a rolling basis. *Application fee:* $50. Electronic applications accepted. *Application Contact:* Paul Somoff, Admissions and Financial Aid Coordinator, 408-554-7884, Fax: 408-554-4367, E-mail: psomoff@scu.edu. *Interim Dean*, Dr. Atom Yee, 408-554-4455, Fax: 408-554-5038, E-mail: ayee@scu.edu.

School of Engineering Students: 332 full-time (103 women), 475 part-time (108 women); includes 242 minority (14 Black or African American, non-Hispanic/Latino; 192 Asian, non-Hispanic/Latino; 24 Hispanic/Latino; 4 Native Hawaiian or other Pacific Islander, non-Hispanic/Latino; 8 Two or more races, non-Hispanic/Latino), 334 international. Average age 29. 737 applicants, 67% accepted, 269 enrolled. *Faculty:* 45 full-time (14 women), 59 part-time/adjunct (8 women). Expenses: Contact institution. *Financial support:* Research assistantships, teaching assistantships available. Financial award application deadline: 3/2; financial award applicants required to submit FAFSA. In 2010, 223 master's, 9 doctorates, 6 other advanced degrees awarded. *Degree program information:* Part-time and evening/weekend programs available. Offers analog circuit design (Certificate); applied mathematics (MS); ASIC design and test (Certificate); civil engineering (MS); computer science and engineering (MS, PhD, Engineer); controls (Certificate); digital signal processing (Certificate); dynamics (Certificate); electrical engineering (MS, PhD, Engineer); engineering (MS, PhD, Certificate, Engineer); engineering management (MS); fundamentals of electrical engineering (Certificate); information assurance (Certificate); materials engineering (Certificate); mathematical finance (MS); mechanical design analysis (Certificate); mechanical engineering (MS, PhD, Engineer); mechatronics systems engineering (Certificate); microwave and antennas (Certificate); networking (Certificate); renewable energy (Certificate); software engineering (MS, Certificate); technology jump-start (Certificate); thermofluids (Certificate). *Application deadline:* For fall admission, 8/1 for domestic students, 7/15 for international students; for winter admission, 10/28 for domestic students, 9/23 for international students; for spring admission, 2/25 for domestic students, 1/21 for international students. Applications are processed on a rolling basis. *Application fee:* $60. Electronic applications accepted. *Application Contact:* Stacey Tinker, Director of Enrollment Management, 408-554-4748, Fax: 408-554-4323, E-mail: stinker@scu.edu. *Associate Dean for Graduate Studies*, Dr. Alex Zecevic, 408-554-2394, E-mail: azecevic@scu.edu.

School of Law Students: 954 full-time (453 women), 77 part-time (33 women); includes 397 minority (27 Black or African American, non-Hispanic/Latino; 9 American Indian or Alaska Native, non-Hispanic/Latino; 242 Asian, non-Hispanic/Latino; 85 Hispanic/Latino; 8 Native Hawaiian or other Pacific Islander, non-Hispanic/Latino; 26 Two or more races, non-Hispanic/Latino), 56 international. Average age 28. 5,158 applicants, 43% accepted, 375 enrolled. *Faculty:* 66 full-time (32 women), 46 part-time/adjunct (24 women). Expenses: Contact institution. *Financial support:* In 2010–11, 454 students received support; fellowships with full and partial tuition reimbursements available, Federal Work-Study and scholarships/grants available. Financial award application deadline: 2/1; financial award applicants required to submit FAFSA. In 2010, 304 first professional degrees, 32 master's awarded. *Degree program information:* Part-time and evening/weekend programs available. Offers high technology law (Certificate); intellectual property law (LL M); international and comparative law (LL M); international high tech law (Certificate); international law (Certificate); law (JD); public interest and social justice law (Certificate); U. S. law for foreign lawyers (LL M). *Application deadline:* For fall admission, 2/1 priority date for domestic and international students. Applications are processed on a rolling basis. *Application fee:* $75. Electronic applications accepted. *Application Contact:* Jeannette Leach, Director of Admissions, 408-554-5048. *Dean*, Donald Polden, 408-554-4362.

SANTA FE UNIVERSITY OF ART AND DESIGN, Santa Fe, NM 87505-7634

General Information Independent, coed. *Graduate housing:* Room and/or apartments available on a first-come, first-served basis to single students; on-campus housing not available to married students.

GRADUATE UNITS

Program in Education *Degree program information:* Part-time and evening/weekend programs available. Offers education (MA).

SARAH LAWRENCE COLLEGE, Bronxville, NY 10708-5999

General Information Independent, coed, comprehensive institution. CGS member. *Graduate housing:* On-campus housing not available. *Research affiliation:* Westchester/New York Medical College, New York Hospital–Cornell Medical Center, Albert Einstein College of Medicine of Yeshiva University, New York University Medical Center, Columbia University Medical Center.

GRADUATE UNITS

Graduate Studies *Degree program information:* Part-time programs available. Offers art of teaching (MS Ed); child development (MA); creative non-fiction (MFA); dance (MFA); fiction (MFA); health advocacy (MA); human genetics (MS); individualized study (MA); poetry (MFA); theater (MFA); women's history (MA). Electronic applications accepted.

See Display on next page and Close-Up on page 979.

SAVANNAH COLLEGE OF ART AND DESIGN, Savannah, GA 31402-3146

General Information Independent, coed, comprehensive institution. CGS member. *Enrollment:* 10,461 graduate, professional, and undergraduate students; 1,576 full-time matriculated graduate/professional students (898 women), 407 part-time matriculated graduate/professional students (240 women). *Enrollment by degree level:* 1,983 master's. *Graduate faculty:* 521 full-time (218 women), 199 part-time/adjunct (104 women). *Tuition:* Full-time $29,520; part-time $3280 per quarter. Tuition and fees vary according to campus/location. *Graduate housing:* Room and/or apartments available on a first-come, first-served basis to single students; on-campus housing not available to married students. Typical cost: $23,010 per year. Room charges vary according to board plan, campus/location and housing facility selected. Housing application deadline: 4/1. *Student services:* Campus employment opportunities, campus safety program, career counseling, exercise/wellness program, free psychological counseling, international student services, multicultural affairs office, services for students with disabilities, teacher training, writing training. *Library facilities:* Jen Library plus 1 other. *Online resources:* library catalog, web page. *Collection:* 198,402 titles, 1,214 serial subscriptions, 6,280 audiovisual materials.

Computer facilities: Computer purchase and lease plans are available. 3,400 computers available on campus for general student use. A campuswide network can be accessed from student residence rooms and from off campus. Online class registration is available. *Web address:* http://www.scad.edu/.

General Application Contact: Elizabeth Mathis, Director of Graduate Recruitment, 912-525-5965, Fax: 912-525-5985, E-mail: admission@scad.edu.

GRADUATE UNITS

Graduate School Students: 1,576 full-time (898 women), 407 part-time (240 women); includes 208 minority (115 Black or African American, non-Hispanic/Latino; 8 American Indian or Alaska Native, non-Hispanic/Latino; 29 Asian, non-Hispanic/Latino; 45 Hispanic/Latino; 2 Native Hawaiian or other Pacific Islander, non-Hispanic/Latino; 9 Two or more races, non-Hispanic/Latino), 435 international. Average age 28. 2,826 applicants, 36% accepted, 642 enrolled. Expenses: Contact institution. *Financial support:* Fellowships, career-related internships or fieldwork, Federal Work-Study, and scholarships/grants available. Financial award application deadline: 4/1; financial award applicants required to submit FAFSA. In 2010, 534 master's, 8 other advanced degrees awarded. *Degree program information:* Part-time programs available. Postbaccalaureate distance learning degree programs offered (no on-campus study). Offers accessory design (MA, MFA); advertising design (MA, MFA); animation (MA, MFA); architectural history (MA, MFA); architecture (M Arch); art (MAT); art history (MA); arts administration (MA); broadcast design (MA, MFA); cinema studies (MA); commercial photography (MA); digital photography (MA); documentary photography (MA); drama (MAT); fashion (MA, MFA); fibers (MA, MFA); film and television (MA, MFA); furniture design (MA, MFA); graphic design (MA, MFA); historic preservation (MA, MFA, Graduate Certificate); illustration (MA, MFA); illustration design (MA); industrial design (MA, MFA); interactive design and game development (MA, MFA, Graduate Certificate); interior design (MA, MFA); international preservation (MA); luxury and fashion management (MA, MFA); metals and jewelry (MA, MFA); painting (MA, MFA); performing arts (MFA); photography (MA, MFA); printmaking (MA, MFA); production design (MA, MFA); professional education (MAT); professional writing (MFA); sculpture (MA, MFA); sequential art (MA, MFA); service design (MFA); sound design (MA, MFA); urban design and development (MUD); visual effects (MA, MFA). *Application deadline:* For fall admission, 4/1 priority date for domestic and international students. Applications are processed on a rolling basis. *Application fee:* $35. Electronic applications accepted. *Application Contact:* Elizabeth Mathis, Director of Graduate Recruitment, 912-525-5965, Fax: 912-525-5985, E-mail: emathis@scad.edu. *Dean of Graduate Studies*, Edward Dupuy, 912-525-5838, E-mail: edupuy@scad.edu.

SAVANNAH STATE UNIVERSITY, Savannah, GA 31404

General Information State-supported, coed, comprehensive institution. *Enrollment:* 4,080 graduate, professional, and undergraduate students; 89 full-time matriculated graduate/professional students (70 women), 50 part-time matriculated graduate/professional students (34 women). *Enrollment by degree level:* 139 master's. *Graduate faculty:* 21 full-time (11 women), 1 (woman) part-time/adjunct. Tuition, state resident: full-time $4042. Tuition, nonresident: full-time $15,028. *Required fees:* $1350. *Graduate housing:* Room and/or apartments available on a first-come, first-served basis to single students; on-campus housing not available to married students. Housing application deadline: 5/1. *Student services:* Campus employment opportunities, career counseling, exercise/wellness program, free psychological counseling, international student services, multicultural affairs office, services for students with disabilities. *Library facilities:* Asa H. Gordon Library. *Online resources:* library catalog, web page, access to other libraries' catalogs. *Collection:* 278,141 titles, 586,933 serial subscriptions, 3,725 audiovisual materials.

Computer facilities: 420 computers available on campus for general student use. A campuswide network can be accessed from student residence rooms. Online class registration is available. *Web address:* http://www.savannahstate.edu/.

General Application Contact: Dr. Emily Crawford, Interim Dean of Graduate Studies, 912-358-4182, Fax: 912-356-2256, E-mail: crawford@savannahstate.edu.

GRADUATE UNITS

Master of Business Administration Program Students: 11 full-time (6 women), 8 part-time (6 women); includes 16 Black or African American, non-Hispanic/Latino, 2 international. Average age 28. Expenses: Contact institution. *Financial support:* Career-related internships or fieldwork, Federal Work-Study, institutionally sponsored loans, scholarships/grants, and unspecified assistantships available. Financial award applicants required to submit FAFSA. In 2010, 8 master's awarded. *Degree program information:* Part-time programs available. Offers business administration (MBA). *Application deadline:* For fall admission, 7/1 for domestic students, 5/15 for international students; for spring admission, 10/31 for domestic students, 10/1 for international students. Applications are processed on a rolling basis. *Application fee:* $25. Electronic applications accepted. *Application Contact:* Emily Crawford, Interim Dean of Graduate Studies, 912-358-4183, E-mail: crawford@savannahstate.edu. *Dean,* Dr. Mostafa Sarhan, 912-358-3388, E-mail: sarhanm@savannahstate.edu.

Master of Public Administration Program Students: 15 full-time (11 women), 15 part-time (10 women); includes 28 minority (all Black or African American, non-Hispanic/Latino). Average age 29. *Faculty:* 5 full-time (2 women). Expenses: Contact institution. *Financial support:* Career-related internships or fieldwork, Federal Work-Study, institutionally sponsored loans, scholarships/grants, and unspecified assistantships available. Financial award applicants required to submit FAFSA. In 2010, 7 master's awarded. *Degree program information:* Part-time programs available. Offers public administration (MPA). *Application deadline:* For fall admission, 7/1 priority date for domestic students, 7/1 for international students; for spring admission, 10/31 priority date for domestic students, 10/1 for international students. Applications are processed on a rolling basis. *Application fee:* $25. *Application Contact:* Dr. Emily Crawford, Interim Dean of Graduate Studies, 912-358-4182, Fax: 912-356-2299, E-mail: crawford@savannahstate.edu. *Interim Chair,* Dr. Ronald Bailey, 912-358-2331, E-mail: baileyr@savannahstate.edu.

Master of Science in Marine Sciences Program Students: 12 full-time (5 women), 9 part-time (7 women); includes 7 Black or African American, non-Hispanic/Latino; 2 Asian, non-Hispanic/Latino. Average age 29. Expenses: Contact institution. *Financial support:* Career-related internships or fieldwork, Federal Work-Study, institutionally sponsored loans, scholarships/grants, and unspecified assistantships available. Financial award applicants required to submit FAFSA. In 2010, 8 master's awarded. *Degree program information:* Part-time programs available. Offers marine sciences (MS). *Application deadline:* For fall admission, 7/1 for domestic students, 5/15 for international students; for spring admission, 10/31 for domestic students, 10/1 for international students. Applications are processed on a rolling basis. *Application fee:* $20. Electronic applications accepted. *Application Contact:* Emily Crawford, Interim Dean of Graduate Studies, 912-358-4182, Fax: 912-356-2299, E-mail: crawford@savnnahstate.edu. *Coordinator,* Dr. Matthew Gilligan, 912-358-4098, E-mail: gilliganm@savannahstate.edu.

Master of Science in Urban Studies and Planning Program Students: 9 full-time (7 women), 3 part-time (0 women); includes 8 Black or African American, non-Hispanic/Latino; 1 Asian, non-Hispanic/Latino. Average age 34. *Faculty:* 1 (woman) full-time, 5 part-time/adjunct (0 women). Expenses: Contact institution. *Financial support:* In 2010–11, 5 students received support, including 1 fellowship (averaging $1,000 per year), 2 research assistantships (averaging $2,000 per year); career-related internships or fieldwork, Federal Work-Study, institutionally sponsored loans, and scholarships/grants also available. Support available to part-time students. Financial award applicants required to submit FAFSA. In 2010, 8 master's awarded. *Degree program information:* Part-time programs available. Offers urban studies and planning (MS). *Application deadline:* For fall admission, 7/1 priority date for domestic students, 5/15 for international students; for spring admission, 10/31 priority date for domestic students, 10/1 for international students. Applications are processed on a rolling basis. *Application fee:* $25. *Application Contact:* Dr. Rukmana Deden, Graduate Coordinator, 912-356-2982, E-mail: rukmanad@savannahstate.edu.

Master of Social Work Program Students: 42 full-time (41 women), 13 part-time (11 women); includes 41 Black or African American, non-Hispanic/Latino; 2 Hispanic/Latino. Average age 31. *Faculty:* 11 full-time (7 women). Expenses: Contact institution. *Financial support:* Career-related internships or fieldwork, Federal Work-Study, institutionally sponsored loans, scholarships/grants, and unspecified assistantships available. Financial award applicants required to submit FAFSA. In 2010, 17 master's awarded. Offers social work (MSW). *Application deadline:* For fall admission, 7/1 for domestic students, 7/15 for international students; for spring admission, 10/31 for domestic students, 10/1 for international students. Applications are processed on a rolling basis. *Application fee:* $25. *Application Contact:* Dr. Emily Crawford, Interim Dean of Graduate Studies, 912-358-4182, Fax: 912-356-2299, E-mail: crawford@savannahstate.edu. *Chair,* Dr. Roenia Deloach, 912-358-3247, E-mail: deloachr@savannahstate.edu.

SAYBROOK UNIVERSITY, San Francisco, CA 94111-1920

General Information Independent, coed, graduate-only institution. *Enrollment by degree level:* 235 master's, 407 doctoral. *Graduate faculty:* 20 full-time (8 women), 167 part-time/adjunct (77 women). *Student services:* Campus employment opportunities, career counseling. *Library facilities:* Library and Information Services plus 1 other. *Online resources:* library catalog, web page. *Collection:* 20,000 titles, 10,000 serial subscriptions, 20 audiovisual materials. *Research affiliation:* Rollo May Center for Humanistic Studies.

Computer facilities: A campuswide network can be accessed from off campus. Online class registration is available. *Web address:* http://www.saybrook.edu/.

General Application Contact: Admissions Specialist, 800-825-4480, Fax: 415-433-9271, E-mail: admissions@saybrook.edu.

GRADUATE UNITS

Graduate College of Mind-Body Medicine Expenses: Contact institution. Offers mind-body medicine (MS, PhD, Certificate). *Application deadline:* For fall admission, 5/1 priority date for domestic students, 5/1 for international students; for spring admission, 10/1 priority date for domestic students, 10/1 for international students. Applications are processed on a rolling basis. Electronic applications accepted. *Application Contact:* Admissions Specialist, 800-825-4480, Fax: 415-433-9271, E-mail: admissions@saybrook.edu.

Graduate College of Psychology and Humanistic Studies Students: 479 full-time (333 women); includes 30 Black or African American, non-Hispanic/Latino; 1 American Indian or Alaska Native, non-Hispanic/Latino; 13 Asian, non-Hispanic/Latino; 18 Hispanic/Latino, 18 international. Average age 43. 280 applicants, 52% accepted, 105 enrolled. *Faculty:* 15 full-time (5 women), 83 part-time/adjunct (34 women). Expenses: Contact institution. *Financial support:* In 2010–11, 335 students received support. Scholarships/grants available. Financial award applicants required to submit FAFSA. In 2010, 28 master's, 43 doctorates awarded.

Postbaccalaureate distance learning degree programs offered (minimal on-campus study). Offers clinical psychology (Psy D); human science (MA, PhD); organizational systems (MA, PhD); psychology (MA, PhD). *Application deadline:* For fall admission, 6/1 priority date for domestic students; for spring admission, 12/16 priority date for domestic students. *Application fee:* $50. Electronic applications accepted. *Application Contact:* Director of Admissions, 800-825-4480, Fax: 415-433-9271, E-mail: admissions@saybrook.edu. *President,* Mark Schulman, 800-825-4480, Fax: 415-433-9271.

LIOS Graduate College Students: 108 full-time (87 women); includes 16 minority (4 Black or African American, non-Hispanic/Latino; 1 American Indian or Alaska Native, non-Hispanic/Latino; 3 Asian, non-Hispanic/Latino; 3 Hispanic/Latino; 1 Native Hawaiian or other Pacific Islander, non-Hispanic/Latino; 4 Two or more races, non-Hispanic/Latino), 3 international. Average age 35. 55 applicants, 69% accepted, 34 enrolled. *Faculty:* 10 full-time (5 women), 5 part-time/adjunct (2 women). Expenses: Contact institution. *Financial support:* In 2010–11, 101 students received support. Federal Work-Study and scholarships/grants available. Financial award application deadline: 6/1; financial award applicants required to submit FAFSA. In 2010, 45 master's awarded. Offers leadership and organization development (MA); systems counseling (MA). *Application deadline:* For fall admission, 6/1 priority date for domestic and international students; for winter admission, 12/2 priority date for domestic and international students. Applications are processed on a rolling basis. *Application fee:* $50. *Application Contact:* Jennifer Herron, Director, Academic Admissions, 425-968-3400, Fax: 425-968-4306, E-mail: jherron@lios.saybrook.edu. *Dean,* Dr. Judy Heinrich, 425-968-3400, Fax: 425-968-3406, E-mail: jheinrich@lios.saybrook.edu.

SCHILLER INTERNATIONAL UNIVERSITY, D-69121 Heidelberg, Germany

General Information Independent, coed, comprehensive institution. *Graduate housing:* Room and/or apartments available on a first-come, first-served basis to single students; on-campus housing not available to married students.

GRADUATE UNITS

MBA Programs, Heidelberg, Germany *Degree program information:* Part-time and evening/weekend programs available. Offers international business (MBA, MIM); management of information technology (MBA).

SCHILLER INTERNATIONAL UNIVERSITY, F-75015 Paris, France

General Information Independent, coed, comprehensive institution. *Graduate housing:* On-campus housing not available.

GRADUATE UNITS

MBA Program Paris, France *Degree program information:* Part-time and evening/weekend programs available. Postbaccalaureate distance learning degree programs offered (no on-campus study). Offers international business (MBA). Bilingual French/English MBA available for native French speakers.

Program in International Relations and Diplomacy *Degree program information:* Part-time and evening/weekend programs available. Offers international relations and diplomacy (MA).

SCHILLER INTERNATIONAL UNIVERSITY, 28015 Madrid, Spain

General Information Independent, coed, comprehensive institution. *Graduate housing:* On-campus housing not available.

GRADUATE UNITS

MBA Program, Madrid, Spain *Degree program information:* Part-time programs available. Offers international business (MBA).

SCHILLER INTERNATIONAL UNIVERSITY, F-67000 Strasbourg, France

General Information Independent, coed, graduate-only institution. *Graduate housing:* Rooms and/or apartments available to single and married students. Housing application deadline: 8/1.

GRADUATE UNITS

MBA Program, Strasbourg, France Campus *Degree program information:* Part-time and evening/weekend programs available. Postbaccalaureate distance learning degree programs offered (no on-campus study). Offers international business (MBA).

SCHILLER INTERNATIONAL UNIVERSITY, London SE1 8TX, United Kingdom

General Information Independent, coed, comprehensive institution. *Graduate housing:* Room and/or apartments available on a first-come, first-served basis to single students; on-campus housing not available to married students. Housing application deadline: 8/1.

GRADUATE UNITS

Graduate Programs, London *Degree program information:* Part-time and evening/weekend programs available. Postbaccalaureate distance learning degree programs offered (no on-campus study). Offers business communication (MA); international business (MBA); international hotel and tourism management (MA, MBA); international management (MIM); international relations and diplomacy (MA); management of information technology (MBA).

SCHILLER INTERNATIONAL UNIVERSITY, Largo, FL 33770

General Information Independent, coed, comprehensive institution. *Graduate housing:* Room and/or apartments available on a first-come, first-served basis to single students; on-campus housing not available to married students. Housing application deadline: 8/1.

GRADUATE UNITS

MBA Programs, Florida *Degree program information:* Part-time and evening/weekend programs available. Postbaccalaureate distance learning degree programs offered (no on-campus study). Offers financial planning (MBA); information technology (MBA); international business (MBA); international hotel and tourism management (MBA).

SCHOOL OF ADVANCED AIR AND SPACE STUDIES, Maxwell AFB, AL 36112-6424

General Information Federally supported, coed, primarily men, graduate-only institution.

GRADUATE UNITS

Program in Airpower Art and Science Offers airpower art and science (MA). Available to active duty military officers only.

THE SCHOOL OF PROFESSIONAL PSYCHOLOGY AT FOREST INSTITUTE, Springfield, MO 65807

General Information Independent, coed, graduate-only institution. *Enrollment by degree level:* 34 master's, 226 doctoral. *Graduate faculty:* 17 full-time (8 women), 18 part-time/adjunct (10 women). *Graduate housing:* Rooms and/or apartments available on a first-come, first-served basis to single and married students. *Student services:* Campus employment opportunities, international student services, services for students with disabilities, writing training. *Library facilities:* Francis D. Jones Library and Information Commons. *Online resources:* library catalog, web page, access to other libraries' catalogs. *Collection:* 8,774 titles, 7 serial subscriptions, 420 audiovisual materials.

Computer facilities: 56 computers available on campus for general student use. A campuswide network can be accessed from student residence rooms and from off campus. Digital clinical supervision system available. *Web address:* http://www.forest.edu/.

General Application Contact: Dawn Medley, Vice President of Enrollment Services, 417-823-3434, Fax: 417-823-3442, E-mail: dmedley@forest.edu.

GRADUATE UNITS

Graduate Programs Students: 214 full-time (144 women), 46 part-time (35 women); includes 35 minority (11 Black or African American, non-Hispanic/Latino; 9 American Indian or Alaska Native, non-Hispanic/Latino; 5 Asian, non-Hispanic/Latino; 10 Hispanic/Latino), 3 international. Average age 28. 176 applicants, 69% accepted, 45 enrolled. *Faculty:* 17 full-time (8 women), 18 part-time/adjunct (10 women). Expenses: Contact institution. *Financial support:* In 2010–11, 59 students received support; fellowships with partial tuition reimbursements available, teaching assistantships, career-related internships or fieldwork, Federal Work-Study, scholarships/grants, tuition waivers (partial), and unspecified assistantships available. Financial award applicants required to submit FAFSA. In 2010, 35 master's, 31 doctorates awarded. Offers applied behavior analysis (MS); clinical psychology (MA, Psy D); counseling psychology (MA); marriage and family therapy (MA, PGC). *Application deadline:* For fall admission, 1/15 priority date for domestic and international students; for spring admission, 8/1 priority date for domestic and international students. Applications are processed on a rolling basis. *Application fee:* $50. Electronic applications accepted. *Application Contact:* Bethany Ritter, Admissions Counselor, 417-823-3477, Fax: 417-823-3442, E-mail: britter@forest.edu. *President,* Dr. Mark E. Skrade, 417-823-3477, Fax: 417-823-3442, E-mail: mskrade@forest.edu.

SCHOOL OF THE ART INSTITUTE OF CHICAGO, Chicago, IL 60603-3103

General Information Independent, coed, comprehensive institution. *Graduate housing:* Room and/or apartments available on a first-come, first-served basis to single students; on-campus housing not available to married students. Housing application deadline: 3/21.

GRADUATE UNITS

Graduate Division *Degree program information:* Part-time programs available. Offers architecture (M Arc); art and technology studies (MFA); art education and art teaching (MAAE, MAT); art therapy (MAAT); arts administration (MAAAP); ceramics (MFA); design for emerging technologies (MFA); designed objects (M Des); fashion, body, and garment (M Des, Certificate); fiber and material studies (MFA); film, video, and new media (MFA); historic preservation (MSHP); interior architecture (M Arc); modern art history, theory, and criticism (MA); new arts journalism (MA); painting and drawing (MFA); performance (MFA); photography (MFA); printmaking (MFA); sculpture (MFA); sound (MFA); visual and critical studies (MA); visual communication (MFA); writing (MFA, Certificate).

SCHOOL OF THE MUSEUM OF FINE ARTS, BOSTON, Boston, MA 02115

General Information Independent, coed, comprehensive institution. *Enrollment:* 758 graduate, professional, and undergraduate students; 118 full-time matriculated graduate/professional students (82 women). *Enrollment by degree level:* 118 master's. *Graduate faculty:* 48 full-time (24 women), 47 part-time/adjunct (27 women). *Graduate housing:* On-campus housing not available. *Student services:* Campus employment opportunities, campus safety program, career counseling, free psychological counseling, international student services, low-cost health insurance, teacher training, writing training. *Library facilities:* W. Van Alan Clark, Jr. Library plus 1 other. *Online resources:* library catalog, web page, access to other libraries' catalogs. *Collection:* 1 million titles, 523 serial subscriptions, 408 audiovisual materials.

Computer facilities: Computer purchase and lease plans are available. 170 computers available on campus for general student use. A campuswide network can be accessed from student residence rooms. Online class registration is available. *Web address:* http://www.smfa.edu/.

General Application Contact: Eric Thompson, Dean of Admissions, 617-369-3626, Fax: 617-369-4264, E-mail: admissions@smfa.edu.

GRADUATE UNITS

Graduate Programs Students: 118 full-time (82 women); includes 22 minority (5 Black or African American, non-Hispanic/Latino; 10 Asian, non-Hispanic/Latino; 4 Hispanic/Latino; 3 Two or more races, non-Hispanic/Latino), 7 international. Average age 30. 227 applicants, 51% accepted, 51 enrolled. *Faculty:* 48 full-time (24 women), 47 part-time/adjunct (27 women). Expenses: Contact institution. *Financial support:* In 2010–11, 9 fellowships (averaging $2,400 per year), 20 teaching assistantships (averaging $2,000 per year) were awarded; career-related internships or fieldwork, Federal Work-Study, scholarships/grants, tuition waivers (partial), and unspecified assistantships also available. Support available to part-time students. Financial award application deadline: 2/15; financial award applicants required to submit FAFSA. In 2010, 31 master's awarded. Offers fine arts (MAT, MFA). MFA, MAT offered jointly with Tufts University. *Application deadline:* For fall admission, 1/15 priority date for domestic and international students. *Application fee:* $65. Electronic applications accepted. *Application Contact:* Admissions Representative, 617-369-3626, Fax: 617-369-4264, E-mail: admissions@smfa.edu. *Associate Dean of Academic Affairs,* David L. Brown, 617-369-3870, E-mail: dbrown@smfa.edu.

SCHOOL OF VISUAL ARTS, New York, NY 10010-3994

General Information Proprietary, coed, comprehensive institution. *Graduate housing:* Room and/or apartments available on a first-come, first-served basis to single students; on-campus housing not available to married students.

GRADUATE UNITS

Graduate Programs Offers art criticism and writing (MFA); art education (MAT); art therapy (MPS); branding (MPS); computer art (MFA); design (MFA); design criticism (MFA); digital photography (MPS); illustration (MFA); painting (MFA); photography, video and related media (MFA); printmaking (MFA); sculpture (MFA). Electronic applications accepted.

SCHREINER UNIVERSITY, Kerrville, TX 78028-5697

General Information Independent-religious, coed, comprehensive institution. *Enrollment:* 1,076 graduate, professional, and undergraduate students; 33 full-time matriculated graduate/professional students (24 women). *Enrollment by degree level:* 33 master's. *Graduate faculty:* 3 full-time (2 women), 1 (woman) part-time/adjunct. *Tuition:* Full-time $16,200; part-time $450 per credit hour. *Required fees:* $75 per semester. *Graduate housing:* Room and/or apartments available to single students. Typical cost: $4560 (including board). *Student services:* Campus employment opportunities, campus safety program, career counseling, exercise/wellness program, free psychological counseling, services for students with disabilities, teacher training. *Library facilities:* W. M. Logan Library. *Online resources:* library catalog, web page, access to other libraries' catalogs. *Collection:* 110,300 titles, 225 serial subscriptions, 720 audiovisual materials.

Computer facilities: Computer purchase and lease plans are available. 120 computers available on campus for general student use. A campuswide network can be accessed from student residence rooms and from off campus. Online class registration is available. *Web address:* http://www.schreiner.edu/.

General Application Contact: Betty Lavonne Miller, Administrative Assistant, 830-792-7455, Fax: 830-792-7382, E-mail: lmiller@schreiner.edu.

GRADUATE UNITS

Department of Education Students: 33 full-time (24 women); includes 8 minority (1 Black or African American, non-Hispanic/Latino; 7 Hispanic/Latino). Average age 35. 24 applicants, 92% accepted, 22 enrolled. *Faculty:* 3 full-time (2 women), 1 (woman) part-time/adjunct. Expenses: Contact institution. *Financial support:* Institutionally sponsored loans available. Financial award application deadline: 8/1; financial award applicants required to submit FAFSA. In 2010, 17 master's awarded. *Degree program information:* Evening/weekend programs available. Offers education (M Ed). *Application deadline:* For fall admission, 7/1 priority date for domestic students. Applications are processed on a rolling basis. *Application fee:* $25. Electronic applications accepted. *Application Contact:* Betty Lavonne Miller, Administrative Assistant, 830-792-7455, Fax: 830-792-7382, E-mail: lmiller@schreiner.edu. *Director, Teacher Education,* Dr. Neva Cramer, 830-792-7266, Fax: 830-792-7382, E-mail: nvcramer@schreiner.edu.

THE SCRIPPS RESEARCH INSTITUTE, La Jolla, CA 92037

General Information Independent, coed, graduate-only institution. *Enrollment by degree level:* 222 doctoral. *Graduate faculty:* 163 full-time (35 women). *Tuition:* Full-time $5000. *Graduate housing:* On-campus housing not available. *Student services:* Campus employment opportunities, campus safety program, career counseling, exercise/wellness program, free psychological counseling, grant writing training, international student services, low-cost health insurance, multicultural affairs office, services for students with disabilities, teacher training, writing training. *Library facilities:* Kresge Library. *Online resources:* library catalog, web page, access to other libraries' catalogs. *Collection:* 45,865 titles, 765 serial subscriptions, 255 audiovisual materials.

Computer facilities: 257 computers available on campus for general student use. A campuswide network can be accessed from student residence rooms and from off campus. Online evaluation forms available. *Web address:* http://www.scripps.edu/.

General Application Contact: Marylyn Rinaldi, Administrative Director, 858-784-8469, Fax: 858-784-2802, E-mail: mrinaldi@scripps.edu.

GRADUATE UNITS

Kellogg School of Science and Technology Students: 222 full-time (78 women). 494 applicants, 20% accepted, 32 enrolled. *Faculty:* 163 full-time (35 women). Expenses: Contact institution. *Financial support:* Fellowships, institutionally sponsored loans, tuition waivers (full), and annual stipends available. Offers chemical and biological sciences (PhD). *Application deadline:* For fall admission, 12/1 for domestic and international students. *Application fee:* $0. Electronic applications accepted. *Application Contact:* Marylyn Rinaldi, Administrative Director, 858-784-8469, Fax: 858-784-2802, E-mail: mrinaldi@scripps.edu. *Dean of Graduate and Postdoctoral Studies,* Dr. James R. Williamson, 858-784-8469, Fax: 858-784-2802, E-mail: gradprgm@scripps.edu.

SEABURY-WESTERN THEOLOGICAL SEMINARY, Evanston, IL 60201-2976

General Information Independent-religious, coed, graduate-only institution. *Graduate housing:* Rooms and/or apartments available to single students and available on a first-come, first-served basis to married students. Housing application deadline: 5/30.

GRADUATE UNITS

School of Theology *Degree program information:* Part-time programs available. Offers advanced theological studies (Certificate); church music and liturgy (MTS); congregational development (D Min); preaching (D Min); theological studies (MA); theology (M Div, L Th). D Min in congregational development offered in summer only; D Min in preaching offered jointly with Chicago Theological Seminary, Lutheran School of Theology at Chicago, McCormick Theological Seminary, and Northern Baptist Theological Seminary.

SEATTLE INSTITUTE OF ORIENTAL MEDICINE, Seattle, WA 98115

General Information Proprietary, coed, primarily women, graduate-only institution. *Graduate housing:* On-campus housing not available.

GRADUATE UNITS

Graduate Program Offers Oriental medicine (M Ac OM).

SEATTLE PACIFIC UNIVERSITY, Seattle, WA 98119-1997

General Information Independent-religious, coed, comprehensive institution. *Enrollment:* 4,117 graduate, professional, and undergraduate students; 310 full-time matriculated graduate/professional students (223 women), 609 part-time matriculated graduate/professional students (421 women). *Enrollment by degree level:* 762 master's, 157 doctoral. *Graduate faculty:* 107 full-time (37 women), 68 part-time/adjunct (38 women). *Graduate housing:* Rooms and/or apartments available on a first-come, first-served basis to single and married students. Housing application deadline: 8/1. *Student services:* Campus employment opportunities, campus safety program, career counseling, exercise/wellness program, free psychological counseling, international student services, low-cost health insurance, multicultural affairs office, services for students with disabilities, teacher training, writing training. *Library facilities:* Seattle Pacific University Library. *Online resources:* library catalog, web page, access to other libraries' catalogs. *Collection:* 211,210 titles, 2,125 serial subscriptions, 7,109 audiovisual materials. *Research affiliation:* Battelle Research Center (business marketing), Washington Research Center/Gates Foundation (education effectiveness), Fred Hutchinson Cancer Research Center (cancer and tumors).

Computer facilities: 150 computers available on campus for general student use. A campuswide network can be accessed from student residence rooms and from off campus. Online class registration is available. *Web address:* http://www.spu.edu/.

General Application Contact: John Glancy, Director, Graduate Admissions and Marketing, 206-281-2325, Fax: 206-281-2877, E-mail: jglancy@spu.edu.

GRADUATE UNITS

Educational Leadership Program Students: 1 full-time (0 women), 58 part-time (44 women); includes 5 minority (1 Black or African American, non-Hispanic/Latino; 2 Asian, non-Hispanic/Latino; 2 Hispanic/Latino). Average age 40. 5 applicants, 40% accepted, 2 enrolled. *Faculty:* 3 full-time (0 women), 4 part-time/adjunct (2 women). Expenses: Contact institution. *Financial support:* In 2010–11, 35 students received support. Career-related internships or fieldwork available. Financial award applicants required to submit FAFSA. In 2010, 10 master's awarded. *Degree program information:* Part-time and evening/weekend programs available. Offers educational leadership (M Ed, Ed D); principal (Certificate); program administrator (Certificate); superintendent (Certificate). *Application deadline:* For fall admission, 8/15 priority date for domestic students; for winter admission, 11/15 for domestic students; for spring admission, 2/15 priority date for domestic students. Applications are processed on a rolling basis. *Application fee:* $50. Electronic applications accepted. *Application Contact:* The Graduate Center, 206-281-2091. *Chair,* Dr. William Prenevost, 206-281-2370, Fax: 206-281-2756, E-mail: prenew@spu.edu.

Industrial Organizational Psychology Program Students: 44 full-time (35 women), 30 part-time (24 women); includes 19 minority (5 Black or African American, non-Hispanic/Latino; 8 Asian, non-Hispanic/Latino; 1 Hispanic/Latino; 5 Two or more races, non-Hispanic/Latino), 2 international. Average age 29. 74 applicants, 39% accepted, 29 enrolled. *Faculty:* 7 full-time (2 women), 2 part-time/adjunct (0 women). Expenses: Contact institution. *Financial support:* In 2010–11, 44 students received support. Applicants required to submit FAFSA. In 2010, 16 master's awarded. Offers industrial organizational psychology (MA, PhD). *Application deadline:* For fall admission, 2/15 for domestic and international students. *Application fee:* $50. Electronic applications accepted. *Application Contact:* The Graduate Center, 206-281-2091. *Chair,* Dr. Robert B. McKenna, 206-281-2629, E-mail: rmckenna@spu.edu.

MA in Teaching English to Speakers of Other Languages Program Students: 16 full-time (12 women), 12 part-time (9 women); includes 2 minority (1 Black or African American, non-Hispanic/Latino; 1 Two or more races, non-Hispanic/Latino), 8 international. Average age 34. 24 applicants, 46% accepted, 11 enrolled. *Faculty:* 2 full-time (both women), 3 part-time/adjunct (2 women). Expenses: Contact institution. *Financial support:* In 2010–11, 12 students received support. Career-related internships or fieldwork available. Financial award applicants required to submit FAFSA. In 2010, 11 master's awarded. *Degree program information:* Part-time programs available. Offers K-12 certification (MA); teaching English to speakers of other languages (MA). *Application deadline:* For fall admission, 8/1 priority date for domestic students; for winter admission, 12/1 for domestic students; for spring admission, 3/1 for domestic students. Applications are processed on a rolling basis. *Application fee:* $50. Electronic applications accepted. *Application Contact:* Dr. Kathryn Bartholomew, Program Director, 206-281-3533, Fax: 206-281-2500, E-mail: kbarthol@spu.edu. *Program Director,* Dr. Kathryn Bartholomew, 206-281-3533, Fax: 206-281-2500, E-mail: kbarthol@spu.edu.

Master of Arts in Teaching Program Students: 64 full-time (42 women), 80 part-time (49 women); includes 18 minority (5 Black or African American, non-Hispanic/Latino; 1 American Indian or Alaska Native, non-Hispanic/Latino; 4 Asian, non-Hispanic/Latino; 3 Hispanic/Latino; 5 Two or more races, non-Hispanic/Latino). Average age 32. 89 applicants, 30% accepted, 27 enrolled. *Faculty:* 7 full-time (2 women), 3 part-time/adjunct (2 women). Expenses: Contact institution. *Financial support:* In 2010–11, 108 students received support. Scholarships/grants available. Financial award applicants required to submit FAFSA. In 2010, 74 master's awarded. *Degree program information:* Part-time and evening/weekend programs available. Offers alternate routes to certification (Certificate); teaching (MAT). *Application deadline:* For fall admission, 3/15 for domestic students. *Application fee:* $50. Electronic applications accepted. *Application Contact:* The Graduate Center, 206-281-2091. *Chair,* Dr. Richard Schuerman, 206-281-2186, Fax: 206-281-2756, E-mail: scheur@spu.edu.

Master of Arts in Theology Program Students: 7 full-time (3 women), 7 part-time (3 women); includes 3 minority (1 Black or African American, non-Hispanic/Latino; 2 Asian, non-Hispanic/Latino). Average age 37. 15 applicants, 33% accepted, 5 enrolled. *Faculty:* 6 full-time (1 woman), 1 (woman) part-time/adjunct. Expenses: Contact institution. *Financial support:* In 2010–11, 8 students received support. Application deadline: 4/1. Offers theology (MA). *Application deadline:* For fall admission, 6/15 for domestic and international students. Applications are processed on a rolling basis. *Application fee:* $50. Electronic applications accepted. *Application Contact:* John Glancy, Director, Graduate Admissions and Marketing, 206-281-2325, Fax: 206-281-2877, E-mail: jglancy@spu.edu. *Dean,* Dr. Douglas Strong, 206-281-2473, E-mail: dstrong@spu.edu.

The Master of Divinity Program Students: 21 full-time (9 women), 8 part-time (0 women); includes 7 minority (1 American Indian or Alaska Native, non-Hispanic/Latino; 4 Asian, non-Hispanic/Latino; 1 Hispanic/Latino; 1 Two or more races, non-Hispanic/Latino). Average age 30. 22 applicants, 64% accepted, 14 enrolled. *Faculty:* 5 full-time (1 woman), 2 part-time/adjunct (1 woman). Expenses: Contact institution. *Financial support:* In 2010–11, 11 students received support. Scholarships/grants available. Financial award applicants required to submit FAFSA. Offers divinity (M Div). *Application deadline:* For fall admission, 6/15 for domestic students. *Application fee:* $50. *Application Contact:* John Glancy, Director, Graduate Admissions and Marketing, 206-281-2325, Fax: 206-281-2877, E-mail: jglancy@spu.edu. *Dean,* Douglas Strong, 206-281-2473, E-mail: dstrong@spu.edu.

Master's Degree in Business Administration (MBA) Program Students: 17 full-time (6 women), 80 part-time (31 women); includes 24 minority (3 Black or African American, non-Hispanic/Latino; 18 Asian, non-Hispanic/Latino; 2 Hispanic/Latino; 1 Two or more races, non-Hispanic/Latino), 15 international. Average age 31. 42 applicants, 26% accepted, 11 enrolled. *Faculty:* 15 full-time (5 women), 1 part-time/adjunct (0 women). Expenses: Contact institution. *Financial support:* In 2010–11, 28 students received support. Scholarships/grants available. Financial award applicants required to submit FAFSA. In 2010, 38 master's awarded. *Degree program information:* Part-time programs available. Offers business administration (MBA). *Application deadline:* For fall admission, 8/1 for domestic and international students; for winter admission, 11/1 for domestic and international students; for spring admission, 2/1 for domestic and international students. Applications are processed on a rolling basis. *Application fee:* $50. Electronic applications accepted. *Application Contact:* Gary Karns, Associate Dean for Graduate Studies, 206-281-2948, Fax: 206-281-2733. *Associate Dean for Graduate Studies,* Gary Karns, 206-281-2948, Fax: 206-281-2733.

Master's Degree in Information Systems Management (MS-ISM) Program Students: 2 full-time (0 women), 16 part-time (5 women); includes 4 minority (3 Black or African American, non-Hispanic/Latino; 1 Asian, non-Hispanic/Latino), 4 international. Average age 30. 15 applicants, 33% accepted, 5 enrolled. *Faculty:* 1 full-time (0 women). Expenses: Contact institution. *Financial support:* In 2010–11, 4 students received support. Applicants required to submit FAFSA. In 2010, 7 master's awarded. *Degree program information:* Part-time programs available. Offers information systems management (MS). *Application deadline:* For fall admission, 8/1 for domestic students, 6/1 for international students; for winter admission, 11/1 for domestic and international students; for spring admission, 2/1 for domestic students, 12/1 for international students. Applications are processed on a rolling basis. *Application fee:* $50. Electronic applications accepted. *Application Contact:* Gary Karns, Associate Dean for Graduate Studies, 206-281-2948, Fax: 206-281-2733. *Associate Dean for Graduate Studies,* Gary Karns, 206-281-2948, Fax: 206-281-2733.

Masters of Fine Arts in Creative Writing Program Students: 25 part-time (14 women); includes 1 minority (Two or more races, non-Hispanic/Latino), 1 international. Average age 37. 1 applicant, 0% accepted, 0 enrolled. *Faculty:* 1 full-time (0 women), 6 part-time/adjunct (4 women). Expenses: Contact institution. *Financial support:* In 2010–11, 14 students received support. Applicants required to submit FAFSA. In 2010, 5 master's awarded. *Degree program information:* Part-time programs available. Offers creative writing (MFA). *Application deadline:* For winter admission, 10/1 for domestic students. *Application fee:* $50. Electronic applications accepted. *Application Contact:* The Graduate Center, 206-281-2091. *Director,* Dr. Gregory Wolfe, 206-281-2109, E-mail: gwolfe@spu.edu.

M Ed in Curriculum and Instruction Program Students: 2 full-time (both women), 78 part-time (67 women); includes 5 minority (1 Black or African American, non-Hispanic/Latino; 1 Asian, non-Hispanic/Latino; 2 Hispanic/Latino; 1 Two or more races, non-Hispanic/Latino). Average age 33. 24 applicants, 46% accepted, 11 enrolled. *Faculty:* 3 full-time (2 women), 5 part-time/adjunct (3 women). Expenses: Contact institution. *Financial support:* In 2010–11, 61 students received support. Applicants required to submit FAFSA. In 2010, 34 master's awarded. *Degree program information:* Part-time and evening/weekend programs available. Offers reading/language arts education (M Ed). *Application deadline:* For fall admission, 8/15 priority date for domestic students, 7/1 for international students; for winter admission, 11/15 for domestic students; for spring admission, 2/15 priority date for domestic students, 3/1 for international students. Applications are processed on a rolling basis. *Application fee:* $50. Electronic applications accepted. *Application Contact:* The Graduate Center, 206-281-2091. *Chair,* Dr. Andrew Lumpe, 206-281-2369.

M Ed in Literacy Program Students: 4 full-time (3 women), 19 part-time (17 women); includes 2 minority (1 American Indian or Alaska Native, non-Hispanic/Latino; 1 Hispanic/Latino). Average age 34. 10 applicants, 80% accepted, 7 enrolled. *Faculty:* 2 full-time (0 women), 1 (woman) part-time/adjunct. Expenses: Contact institution. *Financial support:* In 2010–11, 8 students received support. Scholarships/grants available. Financial award applicants required to submit FAFSA. In 2010, 7 master's awarded. *Degree program information:* Part-time programs available. Offers literacy (M Ed). *Application deadline:* For fall admission, 8/15 for domestic students; for winter admission, 11/15 for domestic students; for spring admission, 2/15 for domestic students. Applications are processed on a rolling basis. *Application fee:* $50. Electronic applications accepted. *Application Contact:* The Graduate Center, 206-281-2091. *Chair,* Dr. Scott F. Beers, 206-281-2707, E-mail: sbeers@spu.edu.

M Ed/PhD School Counseling Program Students: 19 full-time (17 women), 31 part-time (29 women); includes 8 minority (1 Black or African American, non-Hispanic/Latino; 4 Asian, non-Hispanic/Latino; 1 Hispanic/Latino; 2 Two or more races, non-Hispanic/Latino), 1 international. Average age 29. 54 applicants, 17% accepted, 9 enrolled. *Faculty:* 3 full-time (2 women), 1 part-time/adjunct (0 women). Expenses: Contact institution. *Financial support:* In 2010–11, 50 students received support. Scholarships/grants available. Financial award applicants required to submit FAFSA. In 2010, 15 master's awarded. *Degree program information:* Part-time programs available. Offers school counseling (M Ed, PhD, Certificate). *Application deadline:* For fall admission, 4/1 priority date for domestic students. *Application fee:* $50. Electronic applications accepted. *Application Contact:* Dr. Cher Edwards, Chair, 206-281-2286, Fax: 206-281-2756. *Chair,* Dr. Cher Edwards, 206-281-2286, Fax: 206-281-2756.

MS in Marriage and Family Therapy Program Students: 54 full-time (44 women), 23 part-time (19 women); includes 6 minority (2 Asian, non-Hispanic/Latino; 1 Hispanic/Latino; 3 Two or more races, non-Hispanic/Latino). Average age 31. 118 applicants, 31% accepted, 36 enrolled. *Faculty:* 6 full-time (4 women), 6 part-time/adjunct (4 women). Expenses: Contact institution. *Financial support:* In 2010–11, 51 students received support; fellowships, Federal Work-Study available. Financial award applicants required to submit FAFSA. In 2010, 28 master's awarded. *Degree program information:* Part-time programs available. Offers marriage and family therapy (MS); medical family therapy (Certificate). *Application deadline:* For fall admission, 1/15 for domestic students, 2/1 for international students. Applications are processed on a rolling basis. *Application fee:* $50. Electronic applications accepted. *Applica-*

tion Contact: Dr. Claudia Grauf-Grounds, Chair, 206-281-2632, Fax: 206-281-2695, E-mail: claudiagg@spu.edu. *Chair,* Dr. Claudia Grauf-Grounds, 206-281-2632, Fax: 206-281-2695, E-mail: claudiagg@spu.edu.

MS in Nursing Program Students: 8 full-time (all women), 64 part-time (58 women); includes 14 minority (4 Black or African American, non-Hispanic/Latino; 8 Asian, non-Hispanic/Latino; 1 Hispanic/Latino; 1 Two or more races, non-Hispanic/Latino), 2 international. Average age 40. 56 applicants, 50% accepted, 27 enrolled. *Faculty:* 2 full-time (both women), 6 part-time/adjunct (4 women). Expenses: Contact institution. *Financial support:* In 2010–11, 41 students received support; fellowships, scholarships/grants available. Financial award applicants required to submit FAFSA. In 2010, 14 master's awarded. *Degree program information:* Part-time programs available. Offers administration (MSN); adult/gerontology nurse practitioner (MSN); clinical nurse specialist (MSN); family nurse practitioner (MSN, Certificate); informatics (MSN); nurse educator (MSN). *Application deadline:* For fall admission, 5/1 priority date for domestic students; for spring admission, 1/15 for domestic students. Applications are processed on a rolling basis. *Application fee:* $50. Electronic applications accepted. *Application Contact:* Dr. Susan Casey, Associate Dean, 206-281-2769, Fax: 206-281-2767, E-mail: caseys@spu.edu. *Associate Dean,* Dr. Susan Casey, 206-281-2769, Fax: 206-281-2767, E-mail: caseys@spu.edu.

PhD in Clinical Psychology Program Students: 44 full-time (36 women), 29 part-time (23 women); includes 12 minority (5 Asian, non-Hispanic/Latino; 3 Hispanic/Latino; 4 Two or more races, non-Hispanic/Latino). Average age 29. 127 applicants, 8% accepted, 10 enrolled. *Faculty:* 8 full-time (5 women), 3 part-time/adjunct (0 women). Expenses: Contact institution. *Financial support:* In 2010–11, 65 students received support; fellowships, scholarships/grants available. Financial award applicants required to submit FAFSA. In 2010, 13 doctorates awarded. Offers clinical psychology (PhD). *Application deadline:* For fall admission, 12/15 for domestic and international students. Electronic applications accepted. *Application Contact:* Dr. Jay Skidmore, Chair, 206-281-2916. *Chair,* Dr. Jay Skidmore, 206-281-2916.

SEATTLE UNIVERSITY, Seattle, WA 98122-1090

General Information Independent-religious, coed, comprehensive institution. *Graduate housing:* Room and/or apartments available on a first-come, first-served basis to single students; on-campus housing not available to married students. *Research affiliation:* Swedish Medical Centers (nursing).

GRADUATE UNITS

Albers School of Business and Economics *Degree program information:* Part-time and evening/weekend programs available. Offers business administration (MBA, MIB, Certificate); business and economics (EMBA, MBA, MIB, MPAC, MSF, Certificate); finance (MSF, Certificate); professional accounting (MPAC).

Center for Leadership Formation Offers leadership formation (EMBA, Certificate).

College of Arts and Sciences Offers arts and sciences (MA Psych, MACJ, MNPL, MPA, MSAL); criminal justice (MACJ); existential and phenomenological therapeutic psychology (MA Psych).

The Center for Nonprofit and Social Enterprise Management Offers nonprofit and social enterprise management (MNPL).

Center for the Study of Sport and Exercise Offers sport and exercise (MSAL).

Institute of Public Service Offers public service (MPA).

College of Education *Degree program information:* Part-time and evening/weekend programs available. Offers adult education and training (M Ed, MA, Certificate); counseling and school psychology (MA, Certificate, Ed S); curriculum and instruction (M Ed, MA, Certificate); education (M Ed, MA, MIT, Ed D, Certificate, Ed S, Post-Master's Certificate); educational administration (M Ed, MA, Certificate, Ed S); educational leadership (Ed D); literacy (M Ed, Post-Master's Certificate); special education (M Ed, MA, Certificate); student development administration (M Ed, MA); teacher education (MIT); teaching English to speakers of other languages (M Ed, MA, Certificate).

College of Nursing *Degree program information:* Part-time and evening/weekend programs available. Offers advanced practice nursing immersion (MSN); leadership in community nursing (MSN); nursing (MSN); primary care nurse practitioner (MSN).

College of Science and Engineering *Degree program information:* Part-time and evening/weekend programs available. Offers science and engineering (MSE); software engineering (MSE).

School of Law Students: 806 full-time (408 women), 202 part-time (105 women); includes 32 Black or African American, non-Hispanic/Latino; 10 American Indian or Alaska Native, non-Hispanic/Latino; 95 Asian, non-Hispanic/Latino; 60 Hispanic/Latino, 9 international. Average age 27. 2,892 applicants, 35% accepted, 324 enrolled. *Faculty:* 65 full-time (28 women), 59 part-time/adjunct (15 women). Expenses: Contact institution. *Financial support:* In 2010–11, 527 students received support. Career-related internships or fieldwork, Federal Work-Study, institutionally sponsored loans, and scholarships/grants available. Support available to part-time students. Financial award application deadline: 2/15; financial award applicants required to submit FAFSA. In 2010, 320 first professional degrees awarded. *Degree program information:* Part-time programs available. Offers law (JD, JD/MATL). *Application deadline:* For fall admission, 3/1 priority date for domestic and international students. Applications are processed on a rolling basis. *Application fee:* $60. Electronic applications accepted. *Application Contact:* Carol T. Cochran, Assistant Dean for Admission, 206-398-4206, Fax: 206-398-4058, E-mail: ccochran@seattleu.edu. *Dean,* Mark C. Niles, 206-398-4300, Fax: 206-398-4310, E-mail: nilesm@seattleu.edu.

School of Theology and Ministry *Degree program information:* Part-time and evening/weekend programs available. Offers divinity (M Div); pastoral counseling (MA); pastoral studies (MAPS); theology and ministry (M Div, MA, MAPS, MATS, Certificate); transforming spirituality (MATS, Certificate).

SEMINARY OF THE IMMACULATE CONCEPTION, Huntington, NY 11743-1696

General Information Independent-religious, coed, graduate-only institution. *Enrollment by degree level:* 38 first professional, 89 master's, 1 other advanced degree. *Graduate faculty:* 9 full-time (2 women), 15 part-time/adjunct (2 women). *Tuition:* Full-time $12,000; part-time $450 per credit. *Required fees:* $300; $50 per semester. One-time fee: $200 part-time. *Graduate housing:* Room and/or apartments guaranteed to single students; on-campus housing not available to married students. Typical cost: $8000 (including board). Housing application deadline: 8/30. *Student services:* Campus employment opportunities, low-cost health insurance, writing training. *Library facilities:* Seminary of the Immaculate Conception Library. *Online resources:* library catalog, web page. *Collection:* 61,631 titles, 225 serial subscriptions, 705 audiovisual materials.

Computer facilities: 17 computers available on campus for general student use. A campuswide network can be accessed from student residence rooms. *Web address:* http://www.icseminary.edu/.

General Application Contact: Sr. Mary Louise Brink, Academic Dean, 631-423-0483 Ext. 130, Fax: 631-432-2346, E-mail: mlbrink@icseminary.edu.

GRADUATE UNITS

School of Theology Students: 39 full-time (1 woman), 89 part-time (40 women); includes 24 minority (8 Black or African American, non-Hispanic/Latino; 7 Asian, non-Hispanic/Latino; 9 Hispanic/Latino), 6 international. Average age 49. 19 applicants, 100% accepted, 19 enrolled. *Faculty:* 9 full-time (2 women), 15 part-time/adjunct (2 women). Expenses: Contact institution. *Financial support:* In 2010–11, 19 students received support. Scholarships/grants available. In 2010, 6 first professional degrees, 37 master's awarded. *Degree program information:* Part-time and evening/weekend programs available. Offers pastoral studies (MA); theology (M Div, MA, D Min, Certificate). *Application deadline:* For fall admission, 8/30 priority date for domestic students; for spring admission, 1/20 priority date for domestic students. Applications are processed on a rolling basis. *Application fee:* $75. *Application Contact:* Kathryn L. Zahner, Registrar, 631-423-0483 Ext. 147, Fax: 631-423-2346, E-mail: kzahner@icseminary.edu. *Academic Dean,* Sr. Mary Louise Brink, SC, 631-423-0483 Ext. 130, Fax: 631-432-2346, E-mail: mlbrink@icseminary.edu.

SEMINARY OF THE SOUTHWEST, Austin, TX 78768-2247

General Information Independent-religious, coed, graduate-only institution. *Enrollment by degree level:* 43 first professional, 61 master's, 7 other advanced degrees. *Graduate faculty:* 11 full-time (3 women), 26 part-time/adjunct (7 women). *Tuition:* Full-time $13,152; part-time $548 per credit hour. *Required fees:* $75. One-time fee: $20 part-time. *Graduate housing:* Rooms and/or apartments available on a first-come, first-served basis to single and married students. Housing application deadline: 8/1. *Student services:* Campus employment opportunities, international student services, low-cost health insurance, writing training. *Library facilities:* Harold H. and Patricia M. Booher Library plus 1 other. *Online resources:* library catalog, web page, access to other libraries' catalogs. *Collection:* 143,725 titles, 288 serial subscriptions, 2,732 audiovisual materials.

Computer facilities: 8 computers available on campus for general student use. A campuswide network can be accessed from student residence rooms. *Web address:* http://www.ssw.edu/.

General Application Contact: Jennielle Strother, Director of Admissions, 512-472-4133 Ext. 375, Fax: 512-472-3098, E-mail: jstrother@ssw.edu.

GRADUATE UNITS

Graduate and Professional Programs Students: 69 full-time (40 women), 47 part-time (34 women); includes 11 minority (4 Black or African American, non-Hispanic/Latino; 4 Hispanic/Latino; 3 Two or more races, non-Hispanic/Latino), 3 international. Average age 45. 57 applicants, 93% accepted, 46 enrolled. *Faculty:* 11 full-time (3 women), 26 part-time/adjunct (7 women). Expenses: Contact institution. *Financial support:* Career-related internships or fieldwork and scholarships/grants available. Support available to part-time students. Financial award application deadline: 6/15. In 2010, 13 first professional degrees, 8 master's, 6 other advanced degrees awarded. *Degree program information:* Part-time and evening/weekend programs available. Offers Anglican studies (Advanced Diploma); chaplaincy (MCPC); counseling (MAC); divinity (M Div); religion (MAR); spiritual formation (MAPM, MSF); theological studies (Advanced Diploma). *Application deadline:* For fall admission, 7/1 for domestic students; for spring admission, 11/1 for domestic students. Applications are processed on a rolling basis. *Application fee:* $50. *Application Contact:* Jennielle Strother, Director of Admissions, 512-472-4133 Ext. 375, Fax: 512-472-3098, E-mail: jstrother@ssw.edu. *Dean and President,* Very Rev. Douglas Travis, 512-472-4133 Ext. 307, Fax: 512-472-3098, E-mail: dtravis@ssw.edu.

SETON HALL UNIVERSITY, South Orange, NJ 07079-2697

General Information Independent-religious, coed, university. CGS member. *Graduate housing:* On-campus housing not available.

GRADUATE UNITS

College of Arts and Sciences *Degree program information:* Part-time and evening/weekend programs available. Postbaccalaureate distance learning degree programs offered (minimal on-campus study). Offers analytical chemistry (MS, PhD); arts and sciences (MA, MHA, MPA, MS, PhD, Graduate Certificate); Asian languages (MA); Asian studies (MA); biochemistry (MS, PhD); biology (MS); biology/business administration (MS); chemistry (MS); corporate and professional communication (MA); English (MA); experimental psychology (MS); healthcare administration (MHA, Graduate Certificate); history (MA); Holocaust studies (MA); inorganic chemistry (MS, PhD); intercultural communication (MA); Jewish-Christian Studies (MA); microbiology (MS); molecular bioscience (PhD); molecular bioscience/neuroscience (PhD); museum professions (MA); nonprofit organization management (MPA); organic chemistry (MS, PhD); organizational communication (MA); physical chemistry (MS, PhD); public administration (MPA, Graduate Certificate); public relations (MA); strategic communication and leadership (MA); strategic communication planning (MA); teaching Chinese language and culture (MA). Electronic applications accepted.

College of Education and Human Services Students: 204 full-time (122 women), 444 part-time (292 women); includes 108 Black or African American, non-Hispanic/Latino; 9 Asian, non-Hispanic/Latino; 29 Hispanic/Latino, 12 international. Average age 35. 432 applicants, 66% accepted, 199 enrolled. *Faculty:* 39 full-time (21 women), 116 part-time/adjunct (32 women). Expenses: Contact institution. *Financial support:* In 2010–11, 13 students received support; fellowships, research assistantships, career-related internships or fieldwork, institutionally sponsored loans, and unspecified assistantships available. Financial award application deadline: 2/1; financial award applicants required to submit FAFSA. In 2010, 282 master's, 41 doctorates, 80 other advanced degrees awarded. *Degree program information:* Part-time and evening/weekend programs available. Offers bilingual education (Ed S); Catholic school teaching EPICS (MA); college student personnel administration (MA); counseling psychology (MA, PhD); education and human services (MA, MS, Ed D, Exec Ed D, PhD, Ed S); education media specialist (MA); education research, assessment and program evaluation (PhD); higher education administration (Ed D, PhD); human resource training and development (MA); instructional design (MA); K–12 administration and supervision (Ed D, Exec Ed D, Ed S); K–12 leadership, management and policy (Ed D, Exec Ed D, Ed S); marriage and family therapy (MS, PhD, Ed S); professional development (MA); psychological studies (MA); school psychology (Ed S). *Application deadline:* Applications are processed on a rolling basis. *Application fee:* $50. Electronic applications accepted. *Application Contact:* Dr. Manina Urgolo Huckvale, Associate Dean, 973-761-9668, Fax: 973-275-2187, E-mail: manina.urgolo-huckvale@shu.edu. *Dean,* Dr. Joseph V. De Pierro, 973-761-9025, E-mail: joseph.depierro@shu.edu.

College of Nursing *Degree program information:* Part-time programs available. Postbaccalaureate distance learning degree programs offered (minimal on-campus study). Offers advanced practice in primary health care (MSN); entry into practice (MSN); health systems administration (MSN, DNP); nursing (PhD); nursing case management (MSN); nursing education (MA); school nurse (MSN). Electronic applications accepted.

Immaculate Conception Seminary School of Theology Students: 105 full-time (7 women), 112 part-time (43 women); includes 4 Black or African American, non-Hispanic/Latino; 9 Asian, non-Hispanic/Latino; 31 Hispanic/Latino, 72 international. Average age 39. 74 applicants, 100% accepted, 69 enrolled. *Faculty:* 13 full-time (2 women), 12 part-time/adjunct (1 woman). Expenses: Contact institution. *Financial support:* In 2010–11, 217 students received support. Career-related internships or fieldwork, Federal Work-Study, scholarships/grants, tuition waivers (partial), and unspecified assistantships available. Support available to part-time students. Financial award application deadline: 8/1; financial award applicants required to submit FAFSA. In 2010, 16 first professional degrees, 32 master's, 6 other advanced degrees awarded. *Degree program information:* Part-time and evening/weekend programs available. Offers Christian spirituality (Certificate); great spiritual books (Certificate); pastoral ministry (M Div, MA, Certificate); scripture studies (Certificate); Seminary's Theological Education for Parish Services (STEPS) (Certificate); theology (MA); youth ministry (Certificate). *Application deadline:* For fall admission, 8/1 priority date for domestic and international students; for spring admission, 12/15 priority date for domestic and international students. Applications are processed on a rolling basis. *Application fee:* $50. Electronic applications accepted. *Application Contact:* Rev. Msgr. Joseph R. Chapel, Associate Dean, 973-761-9633, Fax: 973-761-9577, E-mail: theology@shu.edu. *Rector and Dean,* Rev. Msgr. Robert F. Coleman, 973-761-9016, Fax: 973-761-9577, E-mail: robert.coleman@shu.edu.

School of Health and Medical Sciences *Degree program information:* Part-time and evening/weekend programs available. Offers athletic training (MS); health and medical sciences (MS, DPT, PhD); health sciences (MS, PhD); occupational therapy (MS); physician assistant (MS); professional physical therapy (DPT); speech-language pathology (MS). Electronic applications accepted.

School of Law *Degree program information:* Part-time and evening/weekend programs available. Offers health law (JD, LL M); intellectual property (JD, LL M); law (MSJ). MD/JD, MD/MSJ offered jointly with University of Medicine and Dentistry of New Jersey. Electronic applications accepted.

Seton Hall University (continued)

Stillman School of Business Students: 93 full-time (33 women), 165 part-time (76 women); includes 26 Black or African American, non-Hispanic/Latino; 39 Asian, non-Hispanic/Latino; 8 Hispanic/Latino. Average age 28. 404 applicants, 74% accepted, 258 enrolled. *Faculty:* 35 full-time (8 women), 11 part-time/adjunct (1 woman). Expenses: Contact institution. *Financial support:* In 2010–11, 16 students received support, including research assistantships with full tuition reimbursements available (averaging $34,404 per year); career-related internships or fieldwork, Federal Work-Study, scholarships/grants, and unspecified assistantships also available. Support available to part-time students. Financial award application deadline: 6/30; financial award applicants required to submit FAFSA. In 2010, 203 master's awarded. *Degree program information:* Part-time and evening/weekend programs available. Offers accounting (MBA, MS); business (MBA, MS, Certificate); finance (MBA); information technology management (MBA); international business (MBA, Certificate); management (MBA); marketing (MBA); professional accounting (MS); sport management (MBA); supply chain management (MBA); taxation (MS). *Application deadline:* For fall admission, 5/31 priority date for domestic students, 3/31 priority date for international students; for spring admission, 10/31 priority date for domestic students, 9/30 priority date for international students. Applications are processed on a rolling basis. *Application fee:* $75. Electronic applications accepted. *Application Contact:* Catherine Bianchi, Director of Graduate Admissions, 973-761-9262, Fax: 973-761-9208, E-mail: catherine.bianchi@shu.edu. *Acting Dean*, Dr. Joyce Strawser, 973-761-9013, Fax: 973-275-2465, E-mail: joyce.strawser@shu.edu.

Whitehead School of Diplomacy and International Relations Students: 250. Average age 26. *Faculty:* 16 full-time (5 women), 16 part-time/adjunct (5 women). Expenses: Contact institution. *Financial support:* Research assistantships with full and partial tuition reimbursements, career-related internships or fieldwork, scholarships/grants, tuition waivers (full and partial), and unspecified assistantships available. In 2010, 80 master's awarded. *Degree program information:* Part-time and evening/weekend programs available. Offers diplomacy and international relations (MA). *Application deadline:* For fall admission, 5/1 priority date for domestic students. Applications are processed on a rolling basis. *Application fee:* $50. Electronic applications accepted. *Application Contact:* Dr. Catherine Ruby, Director of Graduate Admissions, 973-275-2142, Fax: 973-275-2519, E-mail: catherine.ruby@shu.edu. *Associate Dean*, Dr. Ursula Sanjamino, 973-313-6210, Fax: 973-275-2519, E-mail: ursula.sanjamino@shu.edu.

SETON HILL UNIVERSITY, Greensburg, PA 15601

General Information Independent-religious, coed, comprehensive institution. *Enrollment:* 2,232 graduate, professional, and undergraduate students; 283 full-time matriculated graduate/professional students (210 women), 140 part-time matriculated graduate/professional students (103 women). *Enrollment by degree level:* 411 master's, 12 other advanced degrees. *Graduate faculty:* 40 full-time (23 women), 85 part-time/adjunct (41 women). *Tuition:* Full-time $13,050; part-time $725 per credit. *Required fees:* $700; $34 per credit. $50 per semester. Tuition and fees vary according to course load and program. *Graduate housing:* Room and/or apartments available on a first-come, first-served basis to single students; on-campus housing not available to married students. Typical cost: $8810 (including board). Room and board charges vary according to board plan and housing facility selected. Housing application deadline: 8/15. *Student services:* Campus employment opportunities, campus safety program, career counseling, exercise/wellness program, free psychological counseling, international student services, multicultural affairs office, services for students with disabilities, teacher training, writing training. *Library facilities:* Reeves Memorial Library. *Online resources:* library catalog, web page, access to other libraries' catalogs. *Collection:* 100,408 titles, 295 serial subscriptions, 4,802 audiovisual materials.

Computer facilities: Computer purchase and lease plans are available. 450 computers available on campus for general student use. A campuswide network can be accessed from student residence rooms and from off campus. Online class registration is available. *Web address:* http://www.setonhill.edu/.

General Application Contact: Tracey Bartos, Director of Graduate and Adult Studies, 724-838-4283, Fax: 724-830-1891, E-mail: bartos@setonhill.edu.

GRADUATE UNITS

Orthodontics Certificate Program Students: 8 full-time (2 women); includes 1 Asian, non-Hispanic/Latino. Average age 29. 50 applicants, 16% accepted, 8 enrolled. *Faculty:* 2 full-time (0 women), 7 part-time/adjunct (0 women). Expenses: Contact institution. *Financial support:* Application deadline: 6/1. Offers orthodontics (Certificate). *Application deadline:* For fall admission, 9/15 for domestic and international students. Electronic applications accepted. *Application Contact:* Laurel Komarny, Program Advisor, 724-838-4209, Fax: 724-830-1891, E-mail: 1komarny@setonhill.edu. *Program Director*, Dr. Donald Rinchuse, 724-552-2950, E-mail: rinchuse@setonhill.edu.

Program in Art Therapy Students: 39 full-time (38 women), 18 part-time (16 women). Average age 31. 58 applicants, 45% accepted, 18 enrolled. *Faculty:* 2 full-time (both women), 6 part-time/adjunct (all women). Expenses: Contact institution. *Financial support:* Federal Work-Study, scholarships/grants, tuition waivers (partial), and unspecified assistantships available. Support available to part-time students. Financial award application deadline: 8/15; financial award applicants required to submit FAFSA. In 2010, 12 master's awarded. *Degree program information:* Part-time programs available. Offers art therapy (MA). *Application deadline:* For fall admission, 8/15 priority date for domestic students; for spring admission, 12/15 for domestic students. Applications are processed on a rolling basis. *Application fee:* $35. Electronic applications accepted. *Application Contact:* Laurel Komarny, Program Counselor, 724-838-4209, Fax: 724-830-1891, E-mail: 1komarny@setonhill.edu. *Director*, Nina Denninger, 724-830-1047, Fax: 724-830-1294, E-mail: denninger@setonhill.edu.

Program in Business Administration Students: 25 full-time (14 women), 48 part-time (22 women); includes 6 minority (3 Black or African American, non-Hispanic/Latino; 1 American Indian or Alaska Native, non-Hispanic/Latino; 1 Asian, non-Hispanic/Latino; 1 Hispanic/Latino), 1 international. Average age 32. 107 applicants, 38% accepted, 31 enrolled. *Faculty:* 5 full-time (3 women), 6 part-time/adjunct (0 women). Expenses: Contact institution. *Financial support:* Federal Work-Study, scholarships/grants, tuition waivers (partial), and unspecified assistantships available. Support available to part-time students. Financial award application deadline: 8/15; financial award applicants required to submit FAFSA. In 2010, 50 degrees awarded. *Degree program information:* Part-time and evening/weekend programs available. Offers entrepreneurship (MBA, Certificate); management (MBA). *Application deadline:* For fall admission, 8/15 priority date for domestic students; for spring admission, 12/15 for domestic students. Applications are processed on a rolling basis. *Application fee:* $35. Electronic applications accepted. *Application Contact:* Laurel Komarny, Program Counselor, 724-838-4209, Fax: 724-830-1891, E-mail: 1komarny@setonhill.edu. *Director*, Dr. Douglas Nelson, 724-830-4738, E-mail: dnelson@setonhill.edu.

Program in Elementary Education Students: 20 full-time (16 women), 8 part-time (7 women). Average age 30. 30 applicants, 50% accepted, 13 enrolled. *Faculty:* 6 full-time (3 women), 4 part-time/adjunct (3 women). Expenses: Contact institution. *Financial support:* Scholarships/grants, tuition waivers (partial), and unspecified assistantships available. Support available to part-time students. Financial award application deadline: 8/15; financial award applicants required to submit FAFSA. In 2010, 8 master's awarded. *Degree program information:* Part-time and evening/weekend programs available. Offers elementary education (MA, Certificate). *Application deadline:* For fall admission, 8/15 priority date for domestic students; for spring admission, 12/15 for domestic students. Applications are processed on a rolling basis. *Application fee:* $35. Electronic applications accepted. *Application Contact:* Laurel Komarny, Program Counselor, 724-838-4209, Fax: 724-830-1891, E-mail: 1komarny@setonhill.edu. *Director*, Dr. Audrey Quinlan, 724-830-4734, Fax: 724-830-1294, E-mail: quinlan@setonhill.edu.

Program in Genocide and Holocaust Studies Students: 4 part-time (3 women). Average age 42. 14 applicants, 57% accepted, 4 enrolled. *Faculty:* 2 full-time (1 woman), 3 part-time/adjunct (1 woman). Expenses: Contact institution. *Financial support:* Scholarships/grants available. Financial award application deadline: 8/15; financial award applicants required to submit FAFSA. *Degree program information:* Part-time programs available. Postbaccalaureate distance learning degree programs offered (no on-campus study). Offers genocide and Holocaust studies (Certificate). *Application fee:* $35. *Application Contact:* Laurel Komarny, Program Counselor, 724-838-4209, Fax: 724-830-1891, E-mail: 1komarny@setonhill.edu. *Program Advisor*, Dr. James Paharik, 724-838-1073, E-mail: jpaharik@setonhill.edu.

Program in Inclusive Education Students: 3 full-time (all women), 12 part-time (11 women). Average age 28. 19 applicants, 47% accepted, 8 enrolled. *Faculty:* 5 full-time (2 women), 5 part-time/adjunct (4 women). Expenses: Contact institution. *Financial support:* Scholarships/grants, tuition waivers (partial), and unspecified assistantships available. Support available to part-time students. Financial award application deadline: 8/15; financial award applicants required to submit FAFSA. In 2010, 17 master's awarded. *Degree program information:* Part-time and evening/weekend programs available. Postbaccalaureate distance learning degree programs offered (no on-campus study). Offers inclusive education (MA). *Application fee:* $35. *Application Contact:* Laurel Komarny, Program Counselor, 724-838-4209, Fax: 724-830-1891, E-mail: 1komarny@setonhill.edu. *Director*, Dr. Sondra Lettrich, 724-830-1010, Fax: 724-830-1294, E-mail: lettrich@setonhill.edu.

Program in Marriage and Family Therapy Students: 32 full-time (23 women), 14 part-time (13 women); includes 1 Black or African American, non-Hispanic/Latino. Average age 30. 83 applicants, 41% accepted, 17 enrolled. *Faculty:* 3 full-time (2 women), 10 part-time/adjunct (7 women). Expenses: Contact institution. *Financial support:* Scholarships/grants, tuition waivers (partial), and unspecified assistantships available. Support available to part-time students. Financial award application deadline: 8/15; financial award applicants required to submit FAFSA. In 2010, 11 master's awarded. *Degree program information:* Part-time and evening/weekend programs available. Offers marriage and family therapy (MA). *Application deadline:* For fall admission, 8/15 priority date for domestic students; for spring admission, 12/15 for domestic students. Applications are processed on a rolling basis. *Application fee:* $35. Electronic applications accepted. *Application Contact:* Laurel Komarny, Program Counselor, 724-838-4209, Fax: 724-830-1891, E-mail: 1komarny@setonhill.edu. *Director*, Dr. Rebecca Harvey, 724-552-0339, E-mail: harvey@setonhill.edu.

Program in Physician Assistant Students: 52 full-time (41 women), 1 (woman) part-time; includes 2 Black or African American, non-Hispanic/Latino; 2 Hispanic/Latino. Average age 25. 392 applicants, 18% accepted, 36 enrolled. *Faculty:* 6 full-time (3 women), 19 part-time/adjunct (7 women). Expenses: Contact institution. *Financial support:* Application deadline: 8/15. In 2010, 27 master's awarded. Offers physician assistant (MS). *Application deadline:* For spring admission, 3/1 for domestic and international students. *Application fee:* $110. Electronic applications accepted. *Application Contact:* Laurel Komarny, Program Counselor, 724-838-4209, Fax: 724-830-1891, E-mail: 1komarny@setonhill.edu. *Director*, Dr. James France, 724-838-2455, Fax: 724-838-7843, E-mail: france@setonhill.edu.

Program in Special Education Students: 23 full-time (14 women), 12 part-time (all women); includes 1 Black or African American, non-Hispanic/Latino; 1 Asian, non-Hispanic/Latino, 1 international. Average age 32. 30 applicants, 57% accepted, 8 enrolled. *Faculty:* 7 full-time (5 women), 4 part-time/adjunct (3 women). Expenses: Contact institution. *Financial support:* Scholarships/grants, tuition waivers (partial), and unspecified assistantships available. Support available to part-time students. Financial award application deadline: 8/15; financial award applicants required to submit FAFSA. In 2010, 16 master's awarded. *Degree program information:* Part-time and evening/weekend programs available. Offers special education (MA, Certificate). *Application deadline:* For fall admission, 8/15 priority date for domestic students; for spring admission, 12/15 for domestic students. Applications are processed on a rolling basis. *Application fee:* $35. Electronic applications accepted. *Application Contact:* Laurel Komarny, Program Counselor, 724-838-4209, Fax: 724-830-1891, E-mail: 1komarny@setonhill.edu. *Director*, Dr. Sondra Lettrich, 724-830-1010, Fax: 724-830-1294, E-mail: lettrich@setonhill.edu.

Program in Writing Popular Fiction Students: 81 full-time (59 women), 20 part-time (16 women); includes 4 Black or African American, non-Hispanic/Latino; 1 American Indian or Alaska Native, non-Hispanic/Latino; 8 Hispanic/Latino, 3 international. Average age 40. 95 applicants, 36% accepted, 19 enrolled. *Faculty:* 4 full-time (2 women), 22 part-time/adjunct (11 women). Expenses: Contact institution. *Financial support:* Scholarships/grants, tuition waivers (partial), and unspecified assistantships available. Support available to part-time students. Financial award application deadline: 8/15; financial award applicants required to submit FAFSA. In 2010, 3 master's awarded. *Degree program information:* Part-time programs available. Postbaccalaureate distance learning degree programs offered (minimal on-campus study). Offers writing popular fiction (MFA, Certificate). *Application deadline:* For fall admission, 6/1 for domestic students; for spring admission, 12/15 for domestic students. Applications are processed on a rolling basis. *Application fee:* $35. Electronic applications accepted. *Application Contact:* Laurel Komarny, Program Counselor, 724-838-4209, Fax: 724-830-1891, E-mail: 1komarny@setonhill.edu. *Director*, Dr. Albert Wendland, 724-830-1019, Fax: 724-830-1294, E-mail: wendland@setonhill.edu.

SEWANEE: THE UNIVERSITY OF THE SOUTH, Sewanee, TN 37383-1000

General Information Independent-religious, coed, comprehensive institution. *Graduate housing:* Rooms and/or apartments available on a first-come, first-served basis to single and married students. Housing application deadline: 4/1.

GRADUATE UNITS

School of Theology *Degree program information:* Part-time programs available. Offers theology (M Div, MA, STM, D Min).

Sewanee School of Letters *Degree program information:* Part-time programs available. Offers American and English literature (MA); creative writing (MFA). Programs offered only during the summer. Electronic applications accepted.

SHASTA BIBLE COLLEGE, Redding, CA 96002

General Information Independent-religious, coed, comprehensive institution. *Graduate housing:* Rooms and/or apartments available on a first-come, first-served basis to single and married students.

GRADUATE UNITS

Program in Biblical Counseling *Degree program information:* Part-time programs available. Offers biblical counseling and Christian family life education (MA).

Program in Christian Ministry *Degree program information:* Part-time programs available. Postbaccalaureate distance learning degree programs offered (minimal on-campus study). Offers Christian ministry (MA).

Program in School and Church Administration *Degree program information:* Part-time and evening/weekend programs available. Offers school and church administration (MS).

SHAWNEE STATE UNIVERSITY, Portsmouth, OH 45662-4344

General Information State-supported, coed, comprehensive institution.

GRADUATE UNITS

Program in Curriculum and Instruction Offers curriculum and instruction (M Ed).

Program in Occupational Therapy Offers occupational therapy (MOT).

SHAW UNIVERSITY, Raleigh, NC 27601-2399

General Information Independent-religious, coed, comprehensive institution. *Graduate housing:* Room and/or apartments available on a first-come, first-served basis to single students; on-campus housing not available to married students. *Research affiliation:* Old North State Medical Society (health and spirituality), The University of North Carolina at Chapel Hill (health disparities in the African American community), General Baptist State Convention (domestic violence prevention), Wabash Center (philosophy of religious education), UNC (end of life in African American community).

GRADUATE UNITS

Department of Education *Degree program information:* Part-time and evening/weekend programs available. Offers curriculum and instruction (MS). Electronic applications accepted.

Divinity School *Degree program information:* Part-time and evening/weekend programs available. Offers divinity (M Div, MRE). Electronic applications accepted.

SHENANDOAH UNIVERSITY, Winchester, VA 22601-5195

General Information Independent-religious, coed, comprehensive institution. *Enrollment:* 3,679 graduate, professional, and undergraduate students; 766 full-time matriculated graduate/professional students (490 women), 903 part-time matriculated graduate/professional students (639 women). *Enrollment by degree level:* 463 first professional, 694 master's, 408 doctoral, 104 other advanced degrees. *Graduate faculty:* 124 full-time (67 women), 51 part-time/adjunct (34 women). *Tuition:* Full-time $17,352; part-time $723 per credit. Tuition and fees vary according to course load and program. *Graduate housing:* Room and/or apartments available on a first-come, first-served basis to single students; on-campus housing not available to married students. Typical cost: $8870 (including board). Room and board charges vary according to board plan and housing facility selected. Housing application deadline: 7/1. *Student services:* Campus employment opportunities, campus safety program, career counseling, child daycare facilities, exercise/wellness program, free psychological counseling, international student services, low-cost health insurance, multicultural affairs office, services for students with disabilities, writing training. *Library facilities:* Alson H. Smith Jr. Library plus 1 other. *Online resources:* library catalog, web page, access to other libraries' catalogs. *Collection:* 210,461 titles, 57,209 serial subscriptions, 68,102 audiovisual materials.

Computer facilities: Computer purchase and lease plans are available. 142 computers available on campus for general student use. A campuswide network can be accessed from student residence rooms and from off campus. Online class registration, online student account information are available. *Web address:* http://www.su.edu/.

General Application Contact: David Anthony, Dean of Admissions, 540-665-4581, Fax: 540-665-4627, E-mail: admit@su.edu.

GRADUATE UNITS

Byrd School of Business Students: 47 full-time (26 women), 22 part-time (9 women); includes 7 minority (4 Black or African American, non-Hispanic/Latino; 2 American Indian or Alaska Native, non-Hispanic/Latino; 1 Asian, non-Hispanic/Latino), 29 international. Average age 30. 112 applicants, 43% accepted, 25 enrolled. *Faculty:* 11 full-time (1 woman), 1 part-time/adjunct (0 women). Expenses: Contact institution. *Financial support:* Career-related internships or fieldwork, institutionally sponsored loans, and unspecified assistantships available. Support available to part-time students. Financial award application deadline: 3/15; financial award applicants required to submit FAFSA. In 2010, 35 master's, 7 other advanced degrees awarded. *Degree program information:* Part-time and evening/weekend programs available. Offers business administration (MBA); business administration essentials (Certificate). *Application deadline:* Applications are processed on a rolling basis. *Application fee:* $30. Electronic applications accepted. *Application Contact:* David Anthony, Dean of Admissions, 540-665-4581, Fax: 540-665-4627, E-mail: admit@su.edu. *Dean,* Dr. Randy Boxx, 540-665-4572, Fax: 540-665-5437, E-mail: rboxx@su.edu.

School of Education and Human Development Students: 22 full-time (14 women), 369 part-time (267 women); includes 27 minority (12 Black or African American, non-Hispanic/Latino; 4 Asian, non-Hispanic/Latino; 10 Hispanic/Latino; 1 Two or more races, non-Hispanic/Latino), 13 international. Average age 38. 270 applicants, 91% accepted, 187 enrolled. *Faculty:* 14 full-time (8 women), 25 part-time/adjunct (20 women). Expenses: Contact institution. *Financial support:* Application deadline: 3/15. In 2010, 111 master's, 7 doctorates, 45 other advanced degrees awarded. *Degree program information:* Part-time and evening/weekend programs available. Postbaccalaureate distance learning degree programs offered (minimal on-campus study). Offers administrative leadership (D Ed); advanced professional teaching English to speakers of other languages (Certificate); education (MSE); elementary education (Certificate); middle school education (Certificate); organizational leadership (MS, D Prof); professional studies (Certificate); professional teaching English to speakers of other languages (Certificate); public management (Certificate); school reform (Certificate); secondary education (Certificate). *Application deadline:* For fall admission, 7/1 for domestic and international students; for spring admission, 10/15 for domestic and international students. *Application fee:* $30. Electronic applications accepted. *Application Contact:* David Anthony, Dean of Admissions, 540-665-4581, Fax: 540-665-4627, E-mail: admit@su.edu. *Director,* Dr. Steven E. Humphries, 540-535-3574, E-mail: shumphri@su.edu.

School of Health Professions Students: 315 full-time (243 women), 249 part-time (206 women); includes 71 minority (28 Black or African American, non-Hispanic/Latino; 2 American Indian or Alaska Native, non-Hispanic/Latino; 26 Asian, non-Hispanic/Latino; 13 Hispanic/Latino; 2 Two or more races, non-Hispanic/Latino), 11 international. Average age 32. 1,404 applicants, 27% accepted, 220 enrolled. *Faculty:* 37 full-time (30 women), 9 part-time/adjunct (7 women). Expenses: Contact institution. *Financial support:* Application deadline: 3/15. In 2010, 86 master's, 105 doctorates, 8 other advanced degrees awarded. *Degree program information:* Part-time programs available. Postbaccalaureate distance learning degree programs offered. Offers health professions (MS, MSN, DNP, DPT, Certificate). *Application deadline:* Applications are processed on a rolling basis. *Application fee:* $30. Electronic applications accepted. *Application Contact:* David Anthony, Dean of Admissions, 540-665-4581, Fax: 540-665-4627, E-mail: admit@su.edu.

Division of Athletic Training Students: 20 full-time (9 women), 4 part-time (all women); includes 5 minority (2 Black or African American, non-Hispanic/Latino; 1 American Indian or Alaska Native, non-Hispanic/Latino; 2 Hispanic/Latino), 1 international. Average age 25. 19 applicants, 100% accepted, 13 enrolled. *Faculty:* 4 full-time (3 women). Expenses: Contact institution. *Financial support:* Application deadline: 3/15. In 2010, 11 master's awarded. Offers athletic training (MS); performing arts medicine (Certificate). *Application deadline:* Applications are processed on a rolling basis. *Application fee:* $30. Electronic applications accepted. *Application Contact:* David Anthony, Dean of Admissions, 540-665-4581, Fax: 540-665-4627, E-mail: admit@su.edu. *Director,* Dr. Rose A. Schmieg, 540-545-7385, Fax: 540-545-7387, E-mail: rschmieg@su.edu.

Division of Nursing Students: 25 full-time (22 women), 93 part-time (91 women); includes 22 minority (15 Black or African American, non-Hispanic/Latino; 1 American Indian or Alaska Native, non-Hispanic/Latino; 4 Asian, non-Hispanic/Latino; 2 Hispanic/Latino), 2 international. Average age 38. 70 applicants, 91% accepted, 47 enrolled. *Faculty:* 12 full-time (all women), 3 part-time/adjunct (all women). Expenses: Contact institution. *Financial support:* Application deadline: 3/15. In 2010, 16 master's, 4 doctorates, 8 other advanced degrees awarded. *Degree program information:* Part-time programs available. Offers family nurse practitioner (Certificate); nurse-midwifery (Certificate); nurse-midwifery endorsement (Certificate); nursing (MSN, DNP); post-master's in nursing education (Certificate); psychiatric mental health nurse practitioner (Certificate). *Application deadline:* For fall admission, 6/15 priority date for domestic and international students. Applications are processed on a rolling basis. *Application fee:* $30. Electronic applications accepted. *Application Contact:* David Anthony, Dean of Admissions, 540-665-4581, Fax: 540-665-4627, E-mail: admit@su.edu. *Director,* Dr. Kathryn Ganske, 540-678-4374, Fax: 540-665-5519, E-mail: kganske@su.edu.

Division of Occupational Therapy Students: 50 full-time (46 women), 27 part-time (24 women); includes 5 minority (1 Black or African American, non-Hispanic/Latino; 2 Asian, non-Hispanic/Latino; 1 Hispanic/Latino; 1 Two or more races, non-Hispanic/Latino). Average age 29. 72 applicants, 58% accepted, 25 enrolled. *Faculty:* 4 full-time (3 women), 3 part-time/adjunct (all women). Expenses: Contact institution. *Financial support:* Application deadline: 3/15. In 2010, 24 master's awarded. Offers occupational therapy (MS). *Application deadline:* For fall admission, 7/1 for domestic students. Applications are processed on a rolling basis. *Application fee:* $30. Electronic applications accepted. *Application Contact:* David Anthony, Dean of Admissions, 540-665-4581, Fax: 540-665-4627, E-mail: admit@su.edu. *Director,* Dr. Deborah A. Marr, 540-665-5440, Fax: 540-665-5564, E-mail: dmarr@su.edu.

Division of Physical Therapy Students: 111 full-time (77 women), 124 part-time (86 women); includes 28 minority (8 Black or African American, non-Hispanic/Latino; 13 Asian, non-Hispanic/Latino; 7 Hispanic/Latino), 7 international. Average age 33. 545 applicants, 36% accepted, 99 enrolled. *Faculty:* 8 full-time (5 women), 3 part-time/adjunct (1 woman). Expenses: Contact institution. *Financial support:* Application deadline: 3/15. In 2010, 101 doctorates awarded. *Degree program information:* Part-time programs available. Postbaccalaureate distance learning degree programs offered. Offers physical therapy and non-traditional physical therapy (DPT). *Application deadline:* For fall admission, 7/31 for domestic students; for spring admission, 5/15 for domestic students. Applications are processed on a rolling basis. *Application fee:* $30. Electronic applications accepted. *Application Contact:* David Anthony, Dean of Admissions, 540-665-4581, Fax: 540-665-4627, E-mail: admit@su.edu. *Director,* Dr. Karen Abraham-Justice, 540-665-5520, Fax: 540-545-7387, E-mail: kabraham@su.edu.

Division of Physician Assistant Studies Students: 109 full-time (89 women), 1 (woman) part-time; includes 11 minority (2 Black or African American, non-Hispanic/Latino; 7 Asian, non-Hispanic/Latino; 1 Hispanic/Latino; 1 Two or more races, non-Hispanic/Latino), 1 international. Average age 26. 698 applicants, 8% accepted, 36 enrolled. *Faculty:* 9 full-time (7 women). Expenses: Contact institution. *Financial support:* Application deadline: 3/15. In 2010, 35 master's awarded. Offers physician assistant studies (MS). *Application deadline:* For fall admission, 1/15 for domestic students. Applications are processed on a rolling basis. *Application fee:* $30. Electronic applications accepted. *Application Contact:* David Anthony, Dean of Admissions, 540-665-4581, Fax: 540-665-4627, E-mail: admit@su.edu. *Director,* Anthony A. Miller, 540-542-6208, Fax: 540-542-6210, E-mail: amiller@su.edu.

School of Pharmacy Students: 319 full-time (169 women), 144 part-time (81 women); includes 138 minority (23 Black or African American, non-Hispanic/Latino; 2 American Indian or Alaska Native, non-Hispanic/Latino; 109 Asian, non-Hispanic/Latino; 3 Hispanic/Latino; 1 Two or more races, non-Hispanic/Latino), 18 international. Average age 31. 1,108 applicants, 28% accepted, 118 enrolled. *Faculty:* 24 full-time (13 women), 2 part-time/adjunct (both women). Expenses: Contact institution. *Financial support:* Application deadline: 3/15. In 2010, 140 Pharm Ds awarded. *Degree program information:* Part-time programs available. Postbaccalaureate distance learning degree programs offered (minimal on-campus study). Offers pharmacy and non-traditional pharmacy (Pharm D). *Application deadline:* For fall admission, 2/1 for domestic and international students. Applications are processed on a rolling basis. *Application fee:* $30. Electronic applications accepted. *Application Contact:* David Anthony, Dean of Admissions, 540-665-4581, Fax: 540-665-4627, E-mail: admit@su.edu. *Dean,* Dr. Alan McKay, 540-665-1282, Fax: 540-665-1283, E-mail: amckay@su.edu.

Shenandoah Conservatory Students: 63 full-time (38 women), 119 part-time (76 women); includes 18 minority (7 Black or African American, non-Hispanic/Latino; 5 Asian, non-Hispanic/Latino; 5 Hispanic/Latino; 1 Two or more races, non-Hispanic/Latino), 40 international. Average age 34. 109 applicants, 75% accepted, 51 enrolled. *Faculty:* 38 full-time (15 women), 14 part-time/adjunct (5 women). Expenses: Contact institution. *Financial support:* Application deadline: 3/15. In 2010, 29 master's, 12 doctorates, 14 other advanced degrees awarded. Offers arts management (MS); church music (MM, Certificate); collaborative piano (MM); composition (MM); conducting (MM); music education (MME, DMA); music therapy (MMT, Certificate); pedagogy (MM, DMA); performance (MM, DMA, Artist Diploma). *Application deadline:* Applications are processed on a rolling basis. *Application fee:* $30. Electronic applications accepted. *Application Contact:* David Anthony, Dean of Admissions, 540-665-4581, Fax: 540-665-4627, E-mail: admit@su.edu. *Dean,* Dr. Michael J. Stepniak, 540-665-4600, Fax: 540-665-5402, E-mail: mstepnia@su.edu.

SHEPHERD UNIVERSITY, Shepherdstown, WV 25443

General Information State-supported, coed, comprehensive institution. CGS member.

GRADUATE UNITS

Program in Curriculum and Instruction Offers curriculum and instruction (MA).

SHERMAN COLLEGE OF CHIROPRACTIC, Spartanburg, SC 29304-1452

General Information Independent, coed, graduate-only institution. *Graduate housing:* On-campus housing not available. *Research affiliation:* Foundation for Chiropractic Education and Research, American Public Health Service (chiropractic research).

GRADUATE UNITS

Professional Program Offers chiropractic (DC). Electronic applications accepted.

SHIPPENSBURG UNIVERSITY OF PENNSYLVANIA, Shippensburg, PA 17257-2299

General Information State-supported, coed, comprehensive institution. CGS member. *Enrollment:* 8,326 graduate, professional, and undergraduate students; 274 full-time matriculated graduate/professional students (180 women), 737 part-time matriculated graduate/professional students (497 women). *Enrollment by degree level:* 1,011 master's. *Graduate faculty:* 148 full-time (70 women), 31 part-time/adjunct (20 women). Tuition, state resident: full-time $6966. Tuition, nonresident: full-time $11,146. *Required fees:* $1802. *Graduate housing:* On-campus housing not available. *Student services:* Campus employment opportunities, campus safety program, career counseling, child daycare facilities, exercise/wellness program, free psychological counseling, grant writing training, international student services, low-cost health insurance, multicultural affairs office, services for students with disabilities, teacher training, writing training. *Library facilities:* Ezra Lehman Memorial Library plus 1 other. *Online resources:* library catalog, web page, access to other libraries' catalogs. *Collection:* 373,678 titles, 1,011 serial subscriptions, 72,940 audiovisual materials.

Computer facilities: 1,100 computers available on campus for general student use. A campuswide network can be accessed from student residence rooms and from off campus. Online class registration, personal Web pages are available. *Web address:* http://www.ship.edu/.

General Application Contact: Jeremy R. Goshorn, Associate Dean of Graduate Admissions, 717-477-1231, Fax: 717-477-4016, E-mail: jrgoshorn@ship.edu.

GRADUATE UNITS

School of Graduate Studies Students: 274 full-time (180 women), 737 part-time (497 women); includes 116 minority (76 Black or African American, non-Hispanic/Latino; 1 American Indian or Alaska Native, non-Hispanic/Latino; 17 Asian, non-Hispanic/Latino; 15 Hispanic/Latino; 7 Two or more races, non-Hispanic/Latino), 18 international. Average age 30. 768 applicants, 59% accepted, 276 enrolled. *Faculty:* 148 full-time (70 women), 31 part-time/adjunct (20 women). Expenses: Contact institution. *Financial support:* In 2010–11, 126 research assistantships with full tuition reimbursements (averaging $5,000 per year) were awarded; career-related internships or fieldwork, scholarships/grants, unspecified assistantships, and resident hall director and student payroll positions also available. Support available to part-time students. Financial award application deadline: 3/1; financial award applicants required to submit FAFSA. In 2010, 389 master's awarded. *Degree program information:* Part-time and evening/weekend programs available. Postbaccalaureate distance learning degree programs offered (minimal on-campus study). *Application deadline:* For fall admission, 3/1 for international students; for spring admission, 7/1 for international students. Applications are processed on a rolling basis. *Application fee:* $30. Electronic applications accepted. *Application Contact:* Jeremy R. Goshorn, Associate Dean of Graduate Admissions, 717-477-1231, Fax: 717-477-4016, E-mail: jrgoshorn@ship.edu. *Dean/Associate Provost,* Dr. Tracy Schoolcraft, 717-477-1148, Fax: 717-477-4038, E-mail: tascho@ship.edu.

College of Arts and Sciences Students: 118 full-time (63 women), 148 part-time (78 women); includes 38 minority (23 Black or African American, non-Hispanic/Latino; 9 Asian, non-Hispanic/Latino; 4 Hispanic/Latino; 2 Two or more races, non-Hispanic/Latino), 13 international. Average age 30. 256 applicants, 64% accepted, 86 enrolled. *Faculty:* 84 full-time (32 women), 2 part-time/adjunct (1 woman). Expenses: Contact institution. *Financial support:* In 2010–11, 55 research assistantships with full tuition reimbursements (averaging $5,000 per year) were awarded; career-related internships or fieldwork, scholarships/grants, unspecified assistantships, and resident hall director and student payroll positions also available. Support available to part-time students. Financial award application deadline: 3/1; financial award applicants required to submit FAFSA. In 2010, 138 master's awarded. *Degree program information:* Part-time and evening/weekend programs available. Offers applied history (MA, Certificate); applied track (MS); arts and sciences (MA, MPA, MS, Certificate); biology (MS); communication studies (MS); computer science (MS); general/

Shippensburg University of Pennsylvania (continued)

reading track (MS); geoenvironmental studies (MS); organizational development and leadership (MS); public administration (MPA); research track (MS). *Application deadline:* For fall admission, 3/1 for international students; for spring admission, 7/1 for international students. Applications are processed on a rolling basis. *Application fee:* $30. Electronic applications accepted. *Application Contact:* Jeremy R. Goshorn, Associate Dean of Graduate Admissions, 717-477-1231, Fax: 717-477-4016, E-mail: jrgoshorn@ship.edu. *Dean*, Dr. James Mike, 717-477-1151, Fax: 717-477-4026, E-mail: jhmike@ship.edu.

College of Education and Human Services Students: 145 full-time (112 women), 483 part-time (379 women); includes 68 minority (49 Black or African American, non-Hispanic/Latino; 4 Asian, non-Hispanic/Latino; 10 Hispanic/Latino; 5 Two or more races, non-Hispanic/Latino), 4 international. Average age 30. 380 applicants, 61% accepted, 154 enrolled. *Faculty:* 44 full-time (27 women), 28 part-time/adjunct (18 women). Expenses: Contact institution. *Financial support:* In 2010–11, 64 research assistantships with full tuition reimbursements (averaging $5,000 per year) were awarded; career-related internships or fieldwork, scholarships/grants, unspecified assistantships, and resident hall director and student payroll positions also available. Support available to part-time students. Financial award application deadline: 3/1; financial award applicants required to submit FAFSA. In 2010, 193 master's awarded. *Degree program information:* Part-time and evening/weekend programs available. Offers Adlerian studies (Certificate); administration of justice (MS); advanced study in counseling (Certificate); aging (Certificate); alcohol and drug counseling (Certificate); counseling (M Ed, MS); couple and family counseling (Certificate); curriculum and instruction (M Ed); education and human services (M Ed, MS, MSW, Certificate); reading (M Ed); school administration principal K-12 (M Ed); social work (MSW); special education (M Ed). *Application deadline:* For fall admission, 3/1 for international students; for spring admission, 7/1 for international students. Applications are processed on a rolling basis. *Application fee:* $30. Electronic applications accepted. *Application Contact:* Jeremy R. Goshorn, Associate Dean of Graduate Admissions, 717-477-1231, Fax: 717-477-4016, E-mail: jrgoshorn@ship.edu. *Dean*, Dr. James R. Johnson, 717-477-1373, Fax: 717-477-4012, E-mail: jrjohnson@ship.edu.

John L. Grove College of Business Students: 11 full-time (5 women), 106 part-time (40 women); includes 10 minority (4 Black or African American, non-Hispanic/Latino; 1 American Indian or Alaska Native, non-Hispanic/Latino; 4 Asian, non-Hispanic/Latino; 1 Hispanic/Latino), 1 international. Average age 32. 132 applicants, 43% accepted, 36 enrolled. *Faculty:* 20 full-time (11 women), 1 (woman) part-time/adjunct. Expenses: Contact institution. *Financial support:* In 2010–11, 7 research assistantships with full tuition reimbursements (averaging $5,000 per year) were awarded; career-related internships or fieldwork, scholarships/grants, unspecified assistantships, and resident hall director and student payroll positions also available. Support available to part-time students. Financial award application deadline: 3/1; financial award applicants required to submit FAFSA. In 2010, 58 master's awarded. *Degree program information:* Part-time and evening/weekend programs available. Postbaccalaureate distance learning degree programs offered (minimal on-campus study). Offers advanced studies in business (Certificate); business administration (MBA). *Application deadline:* For fall admission, 3/1 for international students; for spring admission, 7/1 for international students. Applications are processed on a rolling basis. *Application fee:* $30. Electronic applications accepted. *Application Contact:* Jeremy R. Goshorn, Associate Dean of Graduate Admissions, 717-477-1231, Fax: 717-477-4016, E-mail: jrgoshorn@ship.edu. *Director of MBA Program*, Dr. Robert Stephens, 717-477-1684, Fax: 717-477-4003, E-mail: rdstep@ship.edu.

SHORTER UNIVERSITY, Rome, GA 30165

General Information Independent-religious, coed, comprehensive institution. *Enrollment:* 1,555 graduate, professional, and undergraduate students; 330 full-time matriculated graduate/professional students (212 women). *Enrollment by degree level:* 330 master's. *Graduate faculty:* 9 full-time (3 women), 25 part-time/adjunct (9 women). *Tuition:* Full-time $9840. *Required fees:* $360. One-time fee: $225 full-time. Tuition and fees vary according to course load and program. *Graduate housing:* Room and/or apartments available on a first-come, first-served basis to single students; on-campus housing not available to married students. Typical cost: $8200 (including board). Room and board charges vary according to board plan and housing facility selected. Housing application deadline: 3/30. *Student services:* Campus employment opportunities, career counseling. *Library facilities:* Livingston Library. *Online resources:* library catalog, web page, access to other libraries' catalogs. *Collection:* 144,475 titles, 8,511 serial subscriptions, 12,134 audiovisual materials.

Computer facilities: 100 computers available on campus for general student use. A campuswide network can be accessed from student residence rooms. Online class registration is available. *Web address:* http://www.shorter.edu/.

General Application Contact: Patrick McElhaney, Director of Admissions, 800-868-6980, E-mail: pmcelhaney@shorter.edu.

GRADUATE UNITS

Professional Studies Students: 330 full-time (212 women); includes 168 Black or African American, non-Hispanic/Latino; 5 American Indian or Alaska Native, non-Hispanic/Latino; 4 Asian, non-Hispanic/Latino; 5 Hispanic/Latino, 3 international. Average age 39. *Faculty:* 9 full-time (3 women), 25 part-time/adjunct (9 women). Expenses: Contact institution. *Financial support:* Institutionally sponsored loans and scholarships/grants available. Financial award applicants required to submit FAFSA. In 2010, 177 master's awarded. *Degree program information:* Evening/weekend programs available. Offers accountancy (MAC); business administration (MBA); curriculum and instruction (M Ed); leadership (MA). *Application deadline:* Applications are processed on a rolling basis. *Application fee:* $50. *Application Contact:* Irene Barassa, Admissions Specialist, 678-260-3531, E-mail: ibarassa@shorter.edu. *Dean of Students*, Jacqueline Avant, 678-260-3538, E-mail: javant@shorter.edu.

SH'OR YOSHUV RABBINICAL COLLEGE, Lawrence, NY 11559-1714

General Information Independent-religious, men only, comprehensive institution.

GRADUATE UNITS

Graduate Programs

SIENA HEIGHTS UNIVERSITY, Adrian, MI 49221-1796

General Information Independent-religious, coed, comprehensive institution. *Graduate housing:* Room and/or apartments available on a first-come, first-served basis to single students; on-campus housing not available to married students. Housing application deadline: 4/1.

GRADUATE UNITS

Graduate College *Degree program information:* Part-time and evening/weekend programs available. Offers early childhood education (MA); educational leadership (MA); elementary education (MA); elementary education/reading (MA); mathematics education (MA); middle school education (MA); Montessori education (MA); secondary education (MA); secondary education/reading (MA).

SIERRA NEVADA COLLEGE, Incline Village, NV 89451

General Information Independent, coed, comprehensive institution. *Enrollment:* 992 graduate, professional, and undergraduate students; 247 full-time matriculated graduate/professional students (192 women), 240 part-time matriculated graduate/professional students (162 women). *Enrollment by degree level:* 487 master's. *Graduate faculty:* 2 full-time (both women), 26 part-time/adjunct (16 women). *Tuition:* Part-time $385 per credit. *Graduate housing:* On-campus housing not available. *Student services:* Campus employment opportunities, career counseling, free psychological counseling, low-cost health insurance, services for students with disabilities, teacher training, writing training. *Library facilities:* Prim Library. *Online resources:* library catalog, web page, access to other libraries' catalogs. *Collection:* 40,845 titles, 224 serial subscriptions.

Computer facilities: 50 computers available on campus for general student use. A campuswide network can be accessed from student residence rooms and from off campus. *Web address:* http://www.sierranevada.edu/.

General Application Contact: Katrina Midgley, Director of Graduate Admission, 775-831-1314 Ext. 7517, Fax: 775-832-1686, E-mail: kmidgley@sierranevada.edu.

GRADUATE UNITS

Teacher Education Program Students: 247 full-time (192 women), 240 part-time (162 women); includes 234 minority (44 Black or African American, non-Hispanic/Latino; 8 American Indian or Alaska Native, non-Hispanic/Latino; 132 Asian, non-Hispanic/Latino; 38 Hispanic/Latino; 12 Native Hawaiian or other Pacific Islander, non-Hispanic/Latino). Average age 35. *Faculty:* 2 full-time (both women), 26 part-time/adjunct (16 women). Expenses: Contact institution. *Financial support:* In 2010–11, 230 students received support. Federal Work-Study available. Support available to part-time students. Financial award application deadline: 8/15; financial award applicants required to submit FAFSA. In 2010, 161 master's awarded. *Degree program information:* Part-time and evening/weekend programs available. Postbaccalaureate distance learning degree programs offered (minimal on-campus study). Offers advanced teaching and leadership (M Ed); elementary education (MAT); secondary education (MAT). *Application deadline:* For fall admission, 8/15 priority date for domestic students; for winter admission, 1/10 priority date for domestic students; for spring admission, 5/25 priority date for domestic students. Applications are processed on a rolling basis. *Application fee:* $50. *Application Contact:* Katrina Midgley, Director of Graduate Admission, 775-831-1314 Ext. 7517, Fax: 775-832-1686, E-mail: kmidgley@sierranevada.edu. *Chair of Education Department*, Beth Bouchard, 775-831-1314, Fax: 775-832-1686, E-mail: bbouchard@sierranevada.edu.

SILICON VALLEY UNIVERSITY, San Jose, CA 95131

General Information Proprietary, coed, comprehensive institution.

GRADUATE UNITS

Graduate Programs

SILVER LAKE COLLEGE, Manitowoc, WI 54220-9319

General Information Independent-religious, coed, comprehensive institution. *Enrollment:* 720 graduate, professional, and undergraduate students; 16 full-time matriculated graduate/professional students (14 women), 139 part-time matriculated graduate/professional students (95 women). *Enrollment by degree level:* 155 master's. *Graduate faculty:* 5 full-time (all women), 44 part-time/adjunct (24 women). *Tuition:* Part-time $425 per credit. *Required fees:* $10 per semester. *Graduate housing:* Room and/or apartments guaranteed to single students. Typical cost: $4900 per year ($8500 including board). Room and board charges vary according to board plan. Housing application deadline: 6/1. *Student services:* Campus employment opportunities, campus safety program, career counseling, international student services, services for students with disabilities, teacher training, writing training. *Library facilities:* The Erma M. and Theodore M. Zigmunt Library. *Online resources:* library catalog, access to other libraries' catalogs. *Collection:* 62,418 titles, 259 serial subscriptions, 11,005 audiovisual materials.

Computer facilities: 88 computers available on campus for general student use. A campuswide network can be accessed. Online class registration is available. *Web address:* http://www.sl.edu/.

General Application Contact: Cindy St. John, Director of Admissions, 800-236-4752 Ext. 350, Fax: 920-686-6322, E-mail: cynthia.st.john@sl.edu.

GRADUATE UNITS

Division of Graduate Studies Students: 16 full-time (14 women), 139 part-time (95 women); includes 12 minority (4 Black or African American, non-Hispanic/Latino; 6 American Indian or Alaska Native, non-Hispanic/Latino; 2 Asian, non-Hispanic/Latino). Average age 36. 88 applicants, 95% accepted, 40 enrolled. *Faculty:* 5 full-time (all women), 44 part-time/adjunct (24 women). Expenses: Contact institution. *Financial support:* Career-related internships or fieldwork, Federal Work-Study, and scholarships/grants available. Support available to part-time students. Financial award application deadline: 6/30; financial award applicants required to submit FAFSA. In 2010, 57 master's awarded. *Degree program information:* Part-time and evening/weekend programs available. Postbaccalaureate distance learning degree programs offered (minimal on-campus study). Offers administrative leadership (MA Ed); management and organizational behavior (MS); music education-Kodaly emphasis (MM); special education (MASE); teacher leadership (MA Ed). *Application deadline:* For fall admission, 8/1 priority date for domestic students, 8/1 for international students; for spring admission, 12/1 priority date for domestic students, 12/1 for international students. Applications are processed on a rolling basis. Electronic applications accepted. *Application Contact:* Cindy St. John, Interim Director of Admissions, 800-236-4752 Ext. 350, Fax: 920-686-6322, E-mail: cynthia.st.john@sl.edu. *Graduate Education*, Sr. Michaela Melko, 920-686-6371 Ext. 371, E-mail: michaela.melko@sl.edu.

SIMMONS COLLEGE, Boston, MA 02115

General Information Independent, Undergraduate: women only; graduate: coed, university. CGS member. *Graduate housing:* Room and/or apartments available on a first-come, first-served basis to single students; on-campus housing not available to married students. Housing application deadline: 7/15.

GRADUATE UNITS

College of Arts and Sciences Graduate Studies Offers applied behavior analysis (PhD); arts and sciences (MA, MAT, MFA, MS, MS Ed, PhD, CAGS, Ed S); assistive technology (MS Ed, Ed S); behavior analysis (MS, PhD); behavioral education (MS Ed, Ed S); children's literature (MA); communications management (MS); educational leadership (MS Ed, PhD, CAGS); elementary education (MAT); English (MA); gender/cultural studies (MA); general education (CAGS); general purposes (MS); health professions education (PhD); history (MA); language and literacy (MS Ed, Ed S); middle school education (MAT); moderate disabilities (Ed S); moderate special needs (MS Ed); professional license (CAGS); professional license: elementary (MS Ed); professional license: middle/high (MS Ed); secondary education (MAT); severe disabilities (Ed S); severe special needs (MS Ed); Spanish (MA); special education (MS Ed, PhD, Ed S); special education administration (MS Ed, PhD, Ed S); teacher preparation (MAT, MS, MS Ed, CAGS); teaching English as a second language (MAT, CAGS); urban education (MS Ed, CAGS); writing for children (MFA).

Graduate School of Library and Information Science *Degree program information:* Part-time and evening/weekend programs available. Offers history and archives data (Certificate); history and archives management (Certificate); library and information science (MS, PhD); school library teacher (MS, Certificate). Electronic applications accepted.

School of Health Sciences Offers didactic program in dietetics (Certificate); health professions education (PhD, CAGS); health sciences (MS, MSN, DNP, DPT, PhD, CAGS, Certificate); nursing (MSN, DNP); nursing practice (PhD); nutrition (dietetic internship) (Certificate); nutrition and health promotion (MS); physical therapy (DPT); primary health care nursing (MS, CAGS); sports nutrition (Certificate).

School of Management *Degree program information:* Part-time and evening/weekend programs available. Offers health care administration (MHA, CAGS); management (MBA). Electronic applications accepted.

School of Social Work *Degree program information:* Part-time programs available. Offers clinical social work (MSW, PhD); social work (CAGS). Electronic applications accepted.

SIMON FRASER UNIVERSITY, Burnaby, BC V5A 1S6, Canada

General Information Province-supported, coed, university. CGS member. *Graduate housing:* Rooms and/or apartments available on a first-come, first-served basis to single and married students. Housing application deadline: 1/2. *Research affiliation:* Bamfield Marine Research Station.

GRADUATE UNITS

Graduate Studies *Degree program information:* Part-time and evening/weekend programs available.

Faculty of Applied Sciences Offers applied sciences (M Eng, M Sc, MA, MA Sc, MRM, PhD); communication (MA, PhD); computing science (M Sc, PhD); engineering science (M Eng, MA Sc, PhD); information technology (M Sc, PhD); interactive arts (M Sc, PhD); kinesiology (M Sc, PhD); resource and environmental management (MRM, PhD).

Faculty of Arts and Social Sciences *Degree program information:* Part-time and evening/weekend programs available. Offers anthropology (MA, PhD); archaeology (MA, PhD); arts and social sciences (M Pub, M Sc, MA, MALS, MFA, MPP, MUS, PhD, Graduate Diploma); contemporary arts (MFA); criminology (MA, PhD); economics (MA, PhD); English (MA, PhD); French (MA); geography (M Sc, MA, PhD); gerontology (MA, PhD); history (MA, PhD); Latin American studies (MA); liberal studies (MALS); linguistics (MA, PhD); philosophy (MA, PhD); political science (MA, PhD); psychology (MA, PhD); public policy (MPP); publishing (M Pub); sociology (MA, PhD); urban studies (MUS, Graduate Diploma); women's studies (MA, PhD).

Faculty of Business Administration Postbaccalaureate distance learning degree programs offered. Offers business administration (EMBA, PhD); financial management (MA); general business (MBA); global asset and wealth management (MBA); management of technology/biotechnology (MBA).

Faculty of Education Offers arts education (M Ed, MA, PhD); counseling psychology (M Ed, MA); curriculum theory and implementation (PhD); education (M Ed, M Sc, MA, Ed D, PhD); educational leadership (M Ed, MA, Ed D); educational psychology (M Ed, MA, PhD); educational technology and learning design (M Ed, MA, PhD); foundations (M Ed, MA); mathematics education (M Ed, M Sc, PhD); philosophy of education (PhD); teaching English as a second/foreign language (M Ed).

Faculty of Health Sciences Offers population and public health (M Sc).

Faculty of Science *Degree program information:* Part-time programs available. Offers applied and computational mathematics (M Sc, PhD); biological sciences (M Sc, PhD); biophysics (M Sc, PhD); chemical physics (M Sc, PhD); chemistry (PhD); earth sciences (M Sc, PhD); environmental toxicology (MET); mathematics (M Sc, PhD); molecular biology and biochemistry (M Sc, PhD); pest management (MPM); physics (M Sc, PhD); science (M Sc, MET, MPM, PhD); statistics and actuarial science (M Sc, PhD).

SIMPSON COLLEGE, Indianola, IA 50125-1297

General Information Independent-religious, coed, comprehensive institution.

GRADUATE UNITS

Department of Education Offers secondary education (MAT).

Department of Social Sciences *Degree program information:* Evening/weekend programs available. Offers criminal justice (MACJ).

SIMPSON UNIVERSITY, Redding, CA 96003-8606

General Information Independent-religious, coed, comprehensive institution. *Graduate housing:* On-campus housing not available.

GRADUATE UNITS

A.W. Tozer Theological Seminary *Degree program information:* Part-time and evening/weekend programs available. Postbaccalaureate distance learning degree programs offered (minimal on-campus study). Offers intellectual leadership (MA); ministry (M Div). Electronic applications accepted.

MA in Counseling Psychology Program *Degree program information:* Evening/weekend programs available. Offers counseling psychology (MA). Electronic applications accepted.

School of Education *Degree program information:* Part-time and evening/weekend programs available. Offers education (MA); education and preliminary administrative services (MA); education and preliminary teaching (MA); teaching (MA). Electronic applications accepted.

SINTE GLESKA UNIVERSITY, Mission, SD 57555

General Information Independent, coed, comprehensive institution. *Graduate housing:* Rooms and/or apartments available on a first-come, first-served basis to single and married students.

GRADUATE UNITS

Graduate Education Program *Degree program information:* Part-time and evening/weekend programs available. Offers elementary education (M Ed).

SIOUX FALLS SEMINARY, Sioux Falls, SD 57105-1599

General Information Independent-religious, coed, graduate-only institution. *Graduate faculty:* 8 full-time (2 women), 6 part-time/adjunct (1 woman). *Graduate housing:* On-campus housing not available. *Student services:* Campus employment opportunities, career counseling, free psychological counseling, international student services, low-cost health insurance. *Library facilities:* Mikelsen Library. *Collection:* 66,978 titles, 590 serial subscriptions, 9,128 audiovisual materials. *Web address:* http://sfseminary.edu/.

General Application Contact: Nathan M. Helling, Director of Enrollment Development, 605-336-6588, Fax: 605-335-9090, E-mail: nhelling@sfseminary.edu.

GRADUATE UNITS

Graduate and Professional Programs *Degree program information:* Part-time programs available. Offers Bible and theology (MA); Christian leadership (MA); counseling (MA); marriage and family therapy (MA); ministry (D Min); pastoral ministry (M Div); theological studies (Certificate).

SIT GRADUATE INSTITUTE, Brattleboro, VT 05302-0676

General Information Independent, coed, graduate-only institution. *Enrollment by degree level:* 623 master's. *Graduate faculty:* 27 full-time (12 women), 19 part-time/adjunct (8 women). *Tuition:* Full-time $35,260; part-time $14,876 per year. *Required fees:* $1495; $1495 per year. Tuition and fees vary according to class time and campus/location. *Graduate housing:* Rooms and/or apartments available on a first-come, first-served basis to single and married students. Typical cost: $4025 per year ($8315 including board) for single students; $8050 per year ($16,630 including board) for married students. Housing application deadline: 7/1. *Student services:* Campus employment opportunities, campus safety program, career counseling, exercise/wellness program, free psychological counseling, international student services, low-cost health insurance, multicultural affairs office, services for students with disabilities, teacher training, writing training. *Library facilities:* Donald B. Watt Library. *Online resources:* library catalog, web page. *Collection:* 120,000 titles, 12,000 serial subscriptions, 2,000 audiovisual materials.

Computer facilities: 55 computers available on campus for general student use. A campuswide network can be accessed from student residence rooms and from off campus. Online class registration is available. *Web address:* http://www.sit.edu/.

General Application Contact: Information Contact, 800-336-1616, Fax: 802-258-3500, E-mail: admissions@sit.edu.

GRADUATE UNITS

Graduate Programs *Degree program information:* Part-time programs available. Postbaccalaureate distance learning degree programs offered (minimal on-campus study). Offers conflict transformation (MA); English for speakers of other languages (MAT); intercultural service, leadership, and management (MA); international education (MA); sustainable development (MA). Electronic applications accepted.

SKIDMORE COLLEGE, Saratoga Springs, NY 12866

General Information Independent, coed, comprehensive institution. *Graduate housing:* On-campus housing not available.

GRADUATE UNITS

Liberal Studies Program *Degree program information:* Part-time programs available. Postbaccalaureate distance learning degree programs offered (minimal on-campus study). Offers liberal studies (MA). Electronic applications accepted.

SLIPPERY ROCK UNIVERSITY OF PENNSYLVANIA, Slippery Rock, PA 16057-1383

General Information State-supported, coed, comprehensive institution. *Enrollment:* 8,852 graduate, professional, and undergraduate students; 443 full-time matriculated graduate/professional students (291 women), 376 part-time matriculated graduate/professional students (265 women). *Enrollment by degree level:* 636 master's, 136 doctoral, 47 other advanced degrees. *Graduate faculty:* 69 full-time (34 women), 8 part-time/adjunct (6 women). Tuition, state resident: full-time $6966; part-time $387 per credit. Tuition, nonresident: full-time $11,146; part-time $619 per credit. *Required fees:* $2388; $202 per credit. *Graduate housing:* Room and/or apartments available on a first-come, first-served basis to single students; on-campus housing not available to married students. Typical cost: $5964 per year ($8884 including board). Room and board charges vary according to board plan, campus/location and housing facility selected. *Student services:* Campus employment opportunities, campus safety program, career counseling, child daycare facilities, exercise/wellness program, free psychological counseling, international student services, multicultural affairs office, services for students with disabilities, writing training. *Library facilities:* Bailey Library. *Online resources:* library catalog, web page, access to other libraries' catalogs. *Collection:* 688,461 titles, 501 serial subscriptions, 10,958 audiovisual materials.

Computer facilities: Computer purchase and lease plans are available. 1,323 computers available on campus for general student use. A campuswide network can be accessed from student residence rooms and from off campus. Online class registration is available. *Web address:* http://www.sru.edu/.

General Application Contact: Angela Piverotto, Director of Graduate Admissions, 724-738-2051, Fax: 724-738-2146, E-mail: graduate.admissions@sru.edu.

GRADUATE UNITS

Graduate Studies (Recruitment) Students: 443 full-time (291 women), 376 part-time (265 women); includes 34 minority (14 Black or African American, non-Hispanic/Latino; 5 American Indian or Alaska Native, non-Hispanic/Latino; 5 Asian, non-Hispanic/Latino; 8 Hispanic/Latino; 2 Two or more races, non-Hispanic/Latino), 4 international. Average age 28. 779 applicants, 65% accepted, 361 enrolled. *Faculty:* 69 full-time (34 women), 8 part-time/adjunct (6 women). Expenses: Contact institution. *Financial support:* In 2010–11, 152 students received support. Career-related internships or fieldwork, Federal Work-Study, institutionally sponsored loans, scholarships/grants, tuition waivers (partial), and unspecified assistantships available. Support available to part-time students. Financial award application deadline: 5/1; financial award applicants required to submit FAFSA. In 2010, 248 master's, 46 doctorates awarded. *Degree program information:* Part-time and evening/weekend programs available. Postbaccalaureate distance learning degree programs offered. *Application deadline:* For fall admission, 3/1 priority date for domestic students, 5/1 priority date for international students; for spring admission, 11/1 priority date for domestic students, 9/1 priority date for international students. Applications are processed on a rolling basis. *Application fee:* $25 ($30 for international students). Electronic applications accepted. *Application Contact:* Angela Piverotto, Director of Graduate Studies, 724-738-2051, Fax: 724-738-2146, E-mail: graduate.admissions@sru.edu. *Director of Graduate Studies,* Angela Piverotto, 724-738-2051, Fax: 724-738-2146, E-mail: graduate.admissions@sru.edu.

College of Business, Information and Social Sciences Students: 20 full-time (12 women), 4 part-time (1 woman); includes 4 minority (all Black or African American, non-Hispanic/Latino). Average age 26. 41 applicants, 66% accepted, 24 enrolled. *Faculty:* 3 full-time (2 women). Expenses: Contact institution. *Financial support:* Career-related internships or fieldwork, scholarships/grants, and tuition waivers (partial) available. Support available to part-time students. Financial award application deadline: 5/1; financial award applicants required to submit FAFSA. *Degree program information:* Part-time and evening/weekend programs available. Postbaccalaureate distance learning degree programs offered. Offers business, information and social sciences (MA); criminal justice (MA). *Application deadline:* For fall admission, 3/1 priority date for domestic students, 5/1 priority date for international students; for spring admission, 11/1 priority date for domestic students, 9/1 priority date for international students. Applications are processed on a rolling basis. *Application fee:* $25 ($30 for international students). Electronic applications accepted. *Application Contact:* Angela Piverotto, Interim Director of Graduate Studies, 724-738-2051, Fax: 724-738-2146, E-mail: graduate.admissions@sru.edu. *Interim Dean,* Dr. David Valentine, 724-738-2008, E-mail: david.valentine@sru.edu.

College of Education Students: 232 full-time (161 women), 279 part-time (224 women); includes 21 minority (8 Black or African American, non-Hispanic/Latino; 3 American Indian or Alaska Native, non-Hispanic/Latino; 5 Asian, non-Hispanic/Latino; 3 Hispanic/Latino; 2 Two or more races, non-Hispanic/Latino), 4 international. Average age 28. 432 applicants, 69% accepted, 226 enrolled. *Faculty:* 39 full-time (19 women), 4 part-time/adjunct (all women). Expenses: Contact institution. *Financial support:* Career-related internships or fieldwork, Federal Work-Study, institutionally sponsored loans, scholarships/grants, tuition waivers (partial), and unspecified assistantships available. Support available to part-time students. Financial award application deadline: 5/1; financial award applicants required to submit FAFSA. In 2010, 189 master's awarded. *Degree program information:* Part-time and evening/weekend programs available. Postbaccalaureate distance learning degree programs offered. Offers adapted physical activity (MS); community counseling (MA); education (M Ed, MA, MS); educational leadership (M Ed); elementary guidance and counseling (M Ed); master teacher (M Ed); math/science (K-8) (M Ed); physical education (M Ed); reading (M Ed); secondary education in English (M Ed); secondary education in history (M Ed); secondary education in math/science (M Ed); secondary guidance and counseling (M Ed); student affairs (MA); supervision (M Ed). *Application deadline:* For fall admission, 3/1 priority date for domestic students, 5/1 priority date for international students; for spring admission, 11/1 priority date for domestic students, 9/1 priority date for international students. Applications are processed on a rolling basis. *Application fee:* $25 ($30 for international students). Electronic applications accepted. *Application Contact:* Angela Piverotto, Director of Graduate Admissions, 724-738-2051, Fax: 724-738-2146, E-mail: graduate.admissions@sru.edu. *Interim Dean,* Dr. Kathleen Strickland, 724-738-2007, Fax: 724-738-2880, E-mail: kathleen.strickland@sru.edu.

College of Health, Environment, and Science Students: 167 full-time (112 women), 78 part-time (34 women); includes 8 minority (2 Black or African American, non-Hispanic/Latino; 1 American Indian or Alaska Native, non-Hispanic/Latino; 5 Hispanic/Latino). Average age 26. 285 applicants, 58% accepted, 100 enrolled. *Faculty:* 16 full-time (9 women), 3 part-time/adjunct (2 women). Expenses: Contact institution. *Financial support:* Career-related internships or fieldwork, Federal Work-Study, institutionally sponsored loans, scholarships/grants, tuition waivers (partial), and unspecified assistantships available. Support available to part-time students. Financial award application deadline: 5/1; financial award applicants required to submit FAFSA. In 2010, 33 master's, 46 doctorates awarded. *Degree program information:* Part-time and evening/weekend programs available. Postbaccalaureate distance learning degree programs offered. Offers environmental education (M Ed); health, environment, and science (M Ed, MS, DPT); physical therapy (DPT); resource management (MS); sustainable systems (MS). *Application deadline:* For fall admission, 3/1 priority date for domestic students, 5/1 priority date for international students; for spring admission, 11/1 priority date for domestic students, 9/1 priority date for international students. Applications are processed on a rolling basis. *Application fee:* $25 ($30 for international students). Electronic applications accepted. *Application Contact:* Angela Piverotto, Director of Graduate Admissions, 724-738-2051, Fax: 724-738-2146, E-mail: graduate.admissions@sru.edu. *Dean,* Dr. Susan Hannam, 724-738-4862, Fax: 724-738-2881, E-mail: susan.hannam@sru.edu.

College of Humanities, Fine and Performing Arts Students: 24 full-time (6 women), 15 part-time (6 women); includes 1 minority (American Indian or Alaska Native, non-Hispanic/Latino). Average age 29. 21 applicants, 76% accepted, 11 enrolled. *Faculty:* 11 full-time (4 women), 1 part-time/adjunct (0 women). Expenses: Contact institution. *Financial support:*

Slippery Rock University of Pennsylvania (continued)

Career-related internships or fieldwork, Federal Work-Study, institutionally sponsored loans, scholarships/grants, tuition waivers (partial), and unspecified assistantships available. Support available to part-time students. Financial award application deadline: 5/1; financial award applicants required to submit FAFSA. In 2010, 26 master's awarded. *Degree program information:* Part-time and evening/weekend programs available. Offers history (MA); humanities, fine and performing arts (MA). *Application deadline:* For fall admission, 3/1 priority date for domestic students, 5/1 priority date for international students; for spring admission, 11/1 priority date for domestic students, 9/1 priority date for international students. Applications are processed on a rolling basis. *Application fee:* $25 ($30 for international students). Electronic applications accepted. *Application Contact:* Angela Piverotto, Director of Graduate Admissions, 724-738-2051, Fax: 724-738-2146, E-mail: graduate.admissions@sru.edu. *Interim Dean,* Dr. Eva Tsuquiashi-Daddesio, 724-738-2400, Fax: 724-738-2188, E-mail: eva.tsuquiash@sru.edu.

SMITH COLLEGE, Northampton, MA 01063

General Information Independent, Undergraduate: women only; graduate: coed, comprehensive institution. *Enrollment:* 3,113 graduate, professional, and undergraduate students; 449 full-time matriculated graduate/professional students (387 women), 76 part-time matriculated graduate/professional students (66 women). *Enrollment by degree level:* 428 master's, 71 doctoral, 26 other advanced degrees. *Graduate faculty:* 273 full-time (149 women), 23 part-time/adjunct (12 women). *Tuition:* Full-time $14,520; part-time $1210 per credit. *Graduate housing:* Room and/or apartments available on a first-come, first-served basis to single students; on-campus housing not available to married students. Typical cost: $6500 per year ($13,000 including board). Housing application deadline: 5/1. *Student services:* Campus employment opportunities, campus safety program, career counseling, child daycare facilities, exercise/wellness program, international student services, low-cost health insurance, multicultural affairs office, services for students with disabilities, teacher training, writing training. *Library facilities:* Neilson Library plus 4 others. *Online resources:* library catalog, web page, access to other libraries' catalogs. *Collection:* 1.5 million titles, 60,916 serial subscriptions, 76,662 audiovisual materials.

Computer facilities: Computer purchase and lease plans are available. 582 computers available on campus for general student use. A campuswide network can be accessed from student residence rooms and from off campus. Online class registration is available. *Web address:* http://www.smith.edu/.

General Application Contact: Danielle Ramdath, Director of Graduate Programs, 413-585-3050, Fax: 413-585-3054, E-mail: dramdath@smith.edu.

GRADUATE UNITS

Graduate and Special Programs Students: 76 full-time (66 women), 24 part-time (22 women); includes 13 minority (4 Black or African American, non-Hispanic/Latino; 6 Asian, non-Hispanic/Latino; 3 Hispanic/Latino), 14 international. Average age 26. 181 applicants, 53% accepted, 62 enrolled. *Faculty:* 273 full-time (149 women), 23 part-time/adjunct (12 women). Expenses: Contact institution. *Financial support:* In 2010–11, 78 students received support, including 7 fellowships with full tuition reimbursements available, 3 research assistantships with full tuition reimbursements available (averaging $11,910 per year), 19 teaching assistantships with full tuition reimbursements available (averaging $11,910 per year); career-related internships or fieldwork, institutionally sponsored loans, scholarships/grants, and tuition waivers (full and partial) also available. Support available to part-time students. Financial award application deadline: 1/15; financial award applicants required to submit CSS PROFILE or FAFSA. In 2010, 61 master's, 10 other advanced degrees awarded. *Degree program information:* Part-time programs available. Offers biological sciences (MAT, MS); biological sciences education (MAT); chemistry (MAT); chemistry education (MAT); dance (MFA); education of the deaf (MED); elementary education (MAT); English education (MAT); English language and literature (MAT); exercise and sport studies (MS); French education (MAT); French language and literature (MAT); geology education (MAT); government education (MAT); history (MAT); history education (MAT); mathematics (MAT); mathematics education (MAT); middle school education (MAT); physics education (MAT); playwriting (MFA); secondary education (MAT); Spanish (MAT); Spanish education (MAT); women in mathematics (Postbaccalaureate Certificate). *Application deadline:* For fall admission, 1/15 for domestic and international students; for spring admission, 12/1 for domestic students. *Application fee:* $60. *Application Contact:* Ruth Morgan, Administrative Assistant, 413-585-3050, Fax: 413-585-3054, E-mail: gradstdy@smith.edu. *Director,* Danielle Ramdath, 413-585-3050, Fax: 413-585-3054, E-mail: dramdath@smith.edu.

School for Social Work Students: 373 full-time (321 women), 52 part-time (44 women); includes 93 minority (25 Black or African American, non-Hispanic/Latino; 2 American Indian or Alaska Native, non-Hispanic/Latino; 15 Asian, non-Hispanic/Latino; 29 Hispanic/Latino; 22 Two or more races, non-Hispanic/Latino), 10 international. Average age 34. 476 applicants, 58% accepted, 148 enrolled. *Faculty:* 15 full-time (11 women), 145 part-time/adjunct (107 women). Expenses: Contact institution. *Financial support:* In 2010–11, 225 students received support. Career-related internships or fieldwork, institutionally sponsored loans, and scholarships/grants available. Financial award application deadline: 3/20; financial award applicants required to submit FAFSA. In 2010, 102 master's, 2 doctorates awarded. Offers social work (MSW, PhD). *Application deadline:* For fall admission, 2/21 for domestic students. Applications are processed on a rolling basis. *Application fee:* $60. *Application Contact:* Irene Rodriguez Martin, Director of Enrollment Management and Continuing Education, 413-585-7960, Fax: 413-585-7994, E-mail: imartin@smith.edu. *Dean/Professor,* Dr. Carolyn Jacobs, 413-585-7977, E-mail: cjacobs@smith.edu.

SOJOURNER-DOUGLASS COLLEGE, Baltimore, MD 21205-1814

General Information Independent, coed, primarily women, comprehensive institution.

GRADUATE UNITS

Graduate Program *Degree program information:* Part-time and evening/weekend programs available.

SOKA UNIVERSITY OF AMERICA, Aliso Viejo, CA 92656

General Information Independent, coed, comprehensive institution.

GRADUATE UNITS

Graduate School *Degree program information:* Evening/weekend programs available.

SONOMA STATE UNIVERSITY, Rohnert Park, CA 94928-3609

General Information State-supported, coed, comprehensive institution. *Enrollment:* 8,395 graduate, professional, and undergraduate students; 386 full-time matriculated graduate/professional students (299 women), 577 part-time matriculated graduate/professional students (413 women). *Enrollment by degree level:* 644 master's, 319 other advanced degrees. *Graduate faculty:* 67 full-time (44 women), 19 part-time/adjunct (13 women). *Graduate housing:* Room and/or apartments available on a first-come, first-served basis to single students; on-campus housing not available to married students. Typical cost: $6774 per year ($10,522 including board). Housing application deadline: 1/1. *Student services:* Campus employment opportunities, career counseling, child daycare facilities, exercise/wellness program, free psychological counseling, international student services, multicultural affairs office, services for students with disabilities. *Library facilities:* Jean and Charles Schultz Information Center. *Online resources:* library catalog, web page, access to other libraries' catalogs. *Collection:* 577,031 titles, 32,357 serial subscriptions, 38,727 audiovisual materials. *Research affiliation:* Kenwood Vineyards (science), Bimimetica Shantee CA (bioacoustics, metabolic flux modeling), Gallo Family Vineyards (science), Natural Industries, Inc. (Sudden Oak Death research), Clean Filtration Technologies (environmental microbiology fund).

Computer facilities: 400 computers available on campus for general student use. A campuswide network can be accessed from student residence rooms and from off campus. Online class registration is available. *Web address:* http://www.sonoma.edu/.

General Application Contact: Elaine Sundberg, Associate Vice Provost, Academic Programs/Graduate Studies, 707-664-2215, Fax: 707-664-4060, E-mail: elaine.sundberg@sonoma.edu.

GRADUATE UNITS

Department of English Students: 24 full-time (16 women), 17 part-time (11 women); includes 4 minority (all Two or more races, non-Hispanic/Latino), 1 international. Average age 31. 27 applicants, 78% accepted, 9 enrolled. *Faculty:* 6 full-time (4 women), 1 part-time/adjunct (0 women). Expenses: Contact institution. *Financial support:* Teaching assistantships, career-related internships or fieldwork and Federal Work-Study available. Financial award application deadline: 3/2; financial award applicants required to submit FAFSA. In 2010, 7 master's awarded. *Degree program information:* Part-time and evening/weekend programs available. Offers American literature (MA); creative writing (MA); English literature (MA); world literature (MA). *Application deadline:* For fall admission, 11/30 priority date for domestic students. *Application fee:* $55. *Application Contact:* Dr. Sherril Jaffe, 707-664-2508, E-mail: sherril.jaffe@sonoma.edu. *Chair of Graduate Studies,* Dr. Thaine Stearns, 707-661-2882, E-mail: thaine.stearns@sonoma.edu.

Institute of Interdisciplinary Studies Students: 4 full-time (2 women), 29 part-time (18 women); includes 1 Hispanic/Latino; 3 Two or more races, non-Hispanic/Latino. Average age 38. 17 applicants, 76% accepted, 8 enrolled. *Faculty:* 2 full-time (1 woman). Expenses: Contact institution. *Financial support:* Career-related internships or fieldwork, Federal Work-Study, and institutionally sponsored loans available. Support available to part-time students. Financial award applicants required to submit FAFSA. In 2010, 12 master's awarded. *Degree program information:* Part-time programs available. Offers interdisciplinary studies (MA, MS). *Application deadline:* For fall admission, 1/31 for domestic students; for spring admission, 10/31 for domestic students. *Application fee:* $55. *Application Contact:* Elaine Sundberg, Associate Vice Provost, Academic Programs/Graduate Studies, 707-664-2215, Fax: 707-664-4060, E-mail: elaine.sundberg@sonoma.edu. *Coordinator,* Dr. Ellen Carlton, 707-664-3918, E-mail: ellen.carlton@sonoma.edu.

School of Business and Economics Students: 7 full-time (6 women), 37 part-time (19 women); includes 1 American Indian or Alaska Native, non-Hispanic/Latino; 1 Asian, non-Hispanic/Latino; 8 Hispanic/Latino; 2 Two or more races, non-Hispanic/Latino. Average age 30. 38 applicants, 68% accepted, 12 enrolled. *Faculty:* 6 full-time (2 women). Expenses: Contact institution. *Financial support:* Career-related internships or fieldwork, Federal Work-Study, institutionally sponsored loans, and scholarships/grants available. Support available to part-time students. Financial award application deadline: 3/2; financial award applicants required to submit FAFSA. In 2010, 25 master's awarded. *Degree program information:* Part-time and evening/weekend programs available. Offers business and economics (MBA). *Application deadline:* For fall admission, 1/31 priority date for domestic students; for spring admission, 8/31 for domestic students. Applications are processed on a rolling basis. *Application fee:* $55. *Application Contact:* Dr. Kris Wright, Associate Vice Provost, Academic Programs/Graduate Studies, 707-664-3954, E-mail: wright@sonoma.edu. *Coordinator,* Dr. William Silver, 707-664-2220, E-mail: silver@sonoma.edu.

School of Education Students: 245 full-time (189 women), 212 part-time (165 women); includes 90 minority (6 Black or African American, non-Hispanic/Latino; 3 American Indian or Alaska Native, non-Hispanic/Latino; 15 Asian, non-Hispanic/Latino; 34 Hispanic/Latino; 3 Native Hawaiian or other Pacific Islander, non-Hispanic/Latino; 29 Two or more races, non-Hispanic/Latino), 5 international. Average age 38. 321 applicants, 74% accepted, 87 enrolled. *Faculty:* 12 full-time (9 women), 4 part-time/adjunct (1 woman). Expenses: Contact institution. *Financial support:* Fellowships, career-related internships or fieldwork and Federal Work-Study available. Support available to part-time students. Financial award application deadline: 3/2; financial award applicants required to submit FAFSA. In 2010, 36 master's, 512 doctorates awarded. *Degree program information:* Part-time and evening/weekend programs available. Offers early childhood (MA); education (MA, Ed D); education—curriculum, teaching and learning (MA); educational administration (MA); educational leadership (Ed D); reading and language (MA); special education (MA). *Application fee:* $55. *Application Contact:* Dr. Chiara Baciqalupa, Coordinator of Graduate Studies, 707-664-2104, E-mail: chiara.baciqalupa@sonoma.edu. *Dean,* Dr. Carlos Ayala, 707-664-4412, E-mail: carlos.ayala@sonoma.edu.

School of Science and Technology Students: 2 part-time (1 woman); includes 1 minority (Asian, non-Hispanic/Latino). Average age 32. 10 applicants, 10% accepted, 1 enrolled. *Faculty:* 1 (woman) full-time. Expenses: Contact institution. *Financial support:* Fellowships, research assistantships, teaching assistantships, career-related internships or fieldwork, Federal Work-Study, and tuition waivers (full) available. Support available to part-time students. Financial award application deadline: 3/2; financial award applicants required to submit FAFSA. In 2010, 3 master's awarded. *Degree program information:* Part-time programs available. Offers environmental biology (MA); family nurse practitioner (MS); general biology (MA); kinesiology (MA); science and technology (MA, MS). *Application deadline:* For fall admission, 11/30 for domestic students. *Application fee:* $55. *Application Contact:* Dr. Jagan Agrawal, Coordinator of Graduate Studies, 707-664-2030, E-mail: jagan.agrawal@sonoma.edu. *Dean,* Dr. Lynn Stauffer, 707-664-2171, E-mail: stauffer@sonoma.edu.

School of Social Sciences Students: 71 full-time (45 women), 118 part-time (83 women); includes 1 Black or African American, non-Hispanic/Latino; 1 American Indian or Alaska Native, non-Hispanic/Latino; 6 Asian, non-Hispanic/Latino; 10 Hispanic/Latino, 2 international. Average age 33. 212 applicants, 38% accepted, 28 enrolled. *Faculty:* 13 full-time (6 women), 9 part-time/adjunct (6 women). Expenses: Contact institution. *Financial support:* Research assistantships, teaching assistantships, career-related internships or fieldwork and Federal Work-Study available. Support available to part-time students. Financial award application deadline: 3/2. In 2010, 59 master's awarded. *Degree program information:* Part-time and evening/weekend programs available. Offers counseling (MA); cultural resources management (MA); history (MA); marriage, family, and child counseling (MA); public administration (MPA); pupil personnel services (MA); social sciences (MA, MPA). *Application deadline:* For fall admission, 11/30 for domestic students. *Application fee:* $55. *Application Contact:* Elaine Sundberg, Associate Vice Provost, Academic Programs/Graduate Studies, 707-664-2215, Fax: 707-664-4060, E-mail: elaine.sundberg@sonoma.edu. *Dean,* Dr. Elaine Leeder, 707-664-2112, E-mail: elaine.leeder@sonoma.edu.

SOTHEBY'S INSTITUTE OF ART–LONDON, London WC1B 3EE, United Kingdom

General Information Private, coed, graduate-only institution.

GRADUATE UNITS

Graduate Programs Offers art business (MA); contemporary art (MA); contemporary design (MA); East Asian art (MA); fine and decorative art (MA); photography (MA).

SOTHEBY'S INSTITUTE OF ART–NEW YORK, New York, NY 10021

General Information Proprietary, coed, graduate-only institution.

GRADUATE UNITS

Graduate Programs Offers American fine and decorative art (MA); art business (MA); contemporary art (MA).

SOUTH BAYLO UNIVERSITY, Anaheim, CA 92801-1701

General Information Independent, coed, graduate-only institution. *Graduate housing:* On-campus housing not available. *Research affiliation:* University of California Irvine College of Medicine (complimentary and alternative medicine), National Nutritional Foods Association (herbs and nutritional supplements), Henan College of Traditional Chinese Medicine (herbology and acupuncture), Kaiser Permanente (patient care: acupuncture and oriental medicine), University of Illinois at Chicago (testing of herbal formulations).

GRADUATE UNITS

Program in Oriental Medicine and Acupuncture *Degree program information:* Evening/weekend programs available. Offers Oriental medicine and acupuncture (MS). Electronic applications accepted.

SOUTH CAROLINA STATE UNIVERSITY, Orangeburg, SC 29117-0001

General Information State-supported, coed, comprehensive institution. CGS member. *Graduate housing:* On-campus housing not available.

GRADUATE UNITS

School of Graduate Studies *Degree program information:* Part-time and evening/weekend programs available. Offers agribusiness (MS); agribusiness and entrepreneurship (MBA); counseling education (M Ed); early childhood and special education (M Ed); early childhood education (MAT); educational leadership (Ed D, Ed S); elementary education (M Ed, MAT); engineering (MAT); general science (MAT); individual and family development (MS); mathematics (MAT); nutritional sciences (MS); rehabilitation counseling (MA); secondary education (M Ed); special education (M Ed); speech pathology and audiology (MA); transportation (MS). Electronic applications accepted.

SOUTH COLLEGE, Knoxville, TN 37917

General Information Proprietary, coed, primarily women, comprehensive institution.

GRADUATE UNITS

Program in Physician Assistant Studies Offers physician assistant studies (MHS).

SOUTH DAKOTA SCHOOL OF MINES AND TECHNOLOGY, Rapid City, SD 57701-3995

General Information State-supported, coed, university. CGS member. *Graduate housing:* Room and/or apartments available on a first-come, first-served basis to single students; on-campus housing not available to married students. *Research affiliation:* CEA USA, Inc. (radium/nickel extraction), Black Hills Corporation (wind power), EG & G Idaho, Inc. (ground-probing radar), RE/SPEC, Inc. (preparation of new plant growth regulators), Horizons, Inc. (interferometric synthetic aperture radar).

GRADUATE UNITS

Graduate Division *Degree program information:* Part-time programs available. Offers atmospheric and environmental sciences (PhD); atmospheric sciences (MS); biomedical engineering (MS, PhD); chemical and biological engineering (PhD); chemical engineering (MS); civil engineering (MS); construction management (MS); electrical engineering (MS); engineering (MS, PhD); engineering management (MS); geology and geological engineering (MS, PhD); materials engineering and science (MS, PhD); mechanical engineering (MS, PhD); nanoscience and nanoengineering (PhD); paleontology (MS); physics (MS, PhD); robotics and intelligent autonomous systems (MS). Electronic applications accepted.
College of Science and Letters Offers science and letters (MS, PhD).

SOUTH DAKOTA STATE UNIVERSITY, Brookings, SD 57007

General Information State-supported, coed, university. CGS member. *Graduate housing:* Rooms and/or apartments available to single and married students.

GRADUATE UNITS

Graduate School *Degree program information:* Part-time and evening/weekend programs available. Postbaccalaureate distance learning degree programs offered (no on-campus study).

College of Agriculture and Biological Sciences *Degree program information:* Part-time programs available. Offers agriculture and biological sciences (MS, PhD); agriculture and biosystems engineering (MS, PhD); agronomy (PhD); animal science (MS, PhD); animal sciences (MS, PhD); biological sciences (MS, PhD); economics (MS); plant science (MS); rural sociology (MS); sociology (PhD); wildlife and fisheries sciences (MS, PhD).

College of Arts and Science *Degree program information:* Part-time programs available. Offers arts and science (MA, MS, PhD); chemistry (MS, PhD); communication studies and journalism (MS); English (MA); geography (MS).

College of Education and Human Sciences Offers apparel merchandising and interior design (MFCS); counseling and human resource development (MS); curriculum and instruction (M Ed); dietetics (MS); education and human sciences (M Ed, MFCS, MS, PhD); educational administration (M Ed); health, physical education and recreation (MS); human development, consumer and family sciences (MFCS); nutrition, food science and hospitality (MFCS); nutritional sciences (MS, PhD).

College of Engineering *Degree program information:* Part-time programs available. Offers biological sciences (MS, PhD); computational science and statistics (PhD); electrical engineering (PhD); engineering (MS); geospatial science and engineering (PhD); industrial management (MS); mathematics (MS); statistics (MS).

College of Nursing *Degree program information:* Part-time and evening/weekend programs available. Postbaccalaureate distance learning degree programs offered. Offers nursing (MS, PhD).

College of Pharmacy Offers biological science (MS); pharmaceutical sciences (PhD); pharmacy (Pharm D, MS, PhD).

SOUTHEASTERN BAPTIST THEOLOGICAL SEMINARY, Wake Forest, NC 27588-1889

General Information Independent-religious, coed, comprehensive institution. *Graduate housing:* Rooms and/or apartments available on a first-come, first-served basis to single and married students.

GRADUATE UNITS

Graduate and Professional Programs Offers advanced biblical studies (M Div); Christian education (M Div, MACE); Christian ethics (PhD); Christian ministry (M Div); Christian planting (M Div); church music (MACM); counseling (MACO); evangelism (PhD); language (M Div); ministry (D Min); New Testament (PhD); Old Testament (PhD); philosophy (PhD); theology (Th M, PhD); women's studies (M Div).

SOUTHEASTERN LOUISIANA UNIVERSITY, Hammond, LA 70402

General Information State-supported, coed, comprehensive institution. CGS member. *Enrollment:* 15,351 graduate, professional, and undergraduate students; 373 full-time matriculated graduate/professional students (281 women), 741 part-time matriculated graduate/professional students (565 women). *Enrollment by degree level:* 1,043 master's, 71 doctoral. *Graduate faculty:* 157 full-time (70 women), 13 part-time/adjunct (8 women). Tuition, state resident: full-time $3533. Tuition, nonresident: full-time $12,002. *Required fees:* $907. Tuition and fees vary according to degree level. *Graduate housing:* Room and/or apartments available on a first-come, first-served basis to single students; on-campus housing not available to married students. Typical cost: $4140 per year ($6590 including board). Room and board charges vary according to board plan and housing facility selected. Housing application deadline: 6/15. *Student services:* Campus employment opportunities, campus safety program, career counseling, exercise/wellness program, free psychological counseling, international student services, low-cost health insurance, multicultural affairs office, services for students with disabilities, teacher training, writing training. *Library facilities:* Sims Memorial Library. *Online resources:* library catalog, web page, access to other libraries' catalogs. *Collection:* 719,386 titles, 3,526 serial subscriptions, 11,347 audiovisual materials. *Research affiliation:* Laser Interferometer for Gravitational-Wave Observatory (LIGO) (physics), National Center for Technology Innovation (NCTI) (educational technology), Entergy (biology), Lake Ponchartrain Basin Foundation (water quality and wetland ecology), Petroleum Research Fund (chemistry).

Computer facilities: 1,440 computers available on campus for general student use. A campuswide network can be accessed from student residence rooms and from off campus. Online class registration, campus Webmail, student newspaper, transcripts, bookstore are available. *Web address:* http://www.selu.edu/.

General Application Contact: Sandra Meyers, Graduate Admissions Analyst, 985-549-5620, Fax: 985-549-5882, E-mail: admissions@selu.edu.

GRADUATE UNITS

College of Arts, Humanities and Social Sciences Students: 96 full-time (62 women), 114 part-time (76 women); includes 27 minority (21 Black or African American, non-Hispanic/Latino; 1 American Indian or Alaska Native, non-Hispanic/Latino; 2 Asian, non-Hispanic/Latino; 2 Hispanic/Latino; 1 Native Hawaiian or other Pacific Islander, non-Hispanic/Latino), 7 international. Average age 29. 154 applicants, 57% accepted, 64 enrolled. *Faculty:* 53 full-time (19 women), 5 part-time/adjunct (4 women). Expenses: Contact institution. *Financial support:* In 2010–11, 70 students received support, including 2 fellowships (averaging $11,700 per year), 31 research assistantships (averaging $9,603 per year), 22 teaching assistantships (averaging $9,450 per year); career-related internships or fieldwork, Federal Work-Study, institutionally sponsored loans, scholarships/grants, and administrative assistantships also available. Support available to part-time students. Financial award application deadline: 5/1; financial award applicants required to submit FAFSA. In 2010, 53 master's awarded. *Degree program information:* Part-time programs available. Offers applied sociology (MS); arts, humanities and social sciences (M Mus, MA, MS); creative writing (MA); history (MA); language and theory (MA); music (M Mus); music (M Mus); organizational communication (MA); professional writing (MA); psychology (MA). *Application deadline:* For fall admission, 7/15 priority date for domestic students, 6/1 priority date for international students; for spring admission, 12/1 priority date for domestic students, 10/1 priority date for international students. Applications are processed on a rolling basis. *Application fee:* $20 ($30 for international students). Electronic applications accepted. *Application Contact:* Sandra Meyers, Graduate Admissions Analyst, 985-549-5620, Fax: 985-549-5632, E-mail: admissions@selu.edu. *Interim Dean,* Dr. Karen Fontenot, 985-549-2101, Fax: 985-549-5014, E-mail: kfontenot@selu.edu.

College of Business Students: 52 full-time (29 women), 56 part-time (21 women); includes 12 minority (8 Black or African American, non-Hispanic/Latino; 1 Asian, non-Hispanic/Latino; 2 Hispanic/Latino; 1 Two or more races, non-Hispanic/Latino), 8 international. Average age 28. 109 applicants, 40% accepted, 25 enrolled. *Faculty:* 15 full-time (1 woman), 1 part-time/adjunct (0 women). Expenses: Contact institution. *Financial support:* In 2010–11, 21 students received support, including 1 research assistantship (averaging $9,000 per year); career-related internships or fieldwork, Federal Work-Study, institutionally sponsored loans, scholarships/grants, and administrative assistantships, graduate professional services assistants also available. Support available to part-time students. Financial award application deadline: 5/1; financial award applicants required to submit FAFSA. In 2010, 62 master's awarded. *Degree program information:* Part-time and evening/weekend programs available. Offers accounting (MBA); general (MBA); information systems for supply chain management (MBA). *Application deadline:* For fall admission, 7/15 priority date for domestic students, 6/1 priority date for international students; for spring admission, 12/1 priority date for domestic students, 10/1 priority date for international students. Applications are processed on a rolling basis. *Application fee:* $20 ($30 for international students). Electronic applications accepted. *Application Contact:* Sandra Meyers, Graduate Admissions Analyst, 985-549-5620, Fax: 985-549-5882, E-mail: admissions@selu.edu. *Dean,* Dr. Randy Settoon, 985-549-2258, Fax: 985-549-5038, E-mail: rsettoon@selu.edu.

College of Education and Human Development Students: 113 full-time (108 women), 412 part-time (351 women); includes 117 minority (101 Black or African American, non-Hispanic/Latino; 1 American Indian or Alaska Native, non-Hispanic/Latino; 2 Asian, non-Hispanic/Latino; 9 Hispanic/Latino; 4 Two or more races, non-Hispanic/Latino), 2 international. Average age 35. 159 applicants, 58% accepted, 70 enrolled. *Faculty:* 34 full-time (20 women). Expenses: Contact institution. *Financial support:* In 2010–11, 26 students received support, including 2 research assistantships (averaging $10,100 per year); career-related internships or fieldwork, Federal Work-Study, institutionally sponsored loans, scholarships/grants, and administrative assistantships also available. Support available to part-time students. Financial award application deadline: 5/1; financial award applicants required to submit FAFSA. In 2010, 169 master's, 8 doctorates awarded. *Degree program information:* Part-time programs available. Offers counselor education (M Ed); curriculum and instruction (M Ed); education and human development (M Ed, MAT, Ed D); educational leadership (M Ed, Ed D); educational technology leadership (M Ed); elementary education (MAT); special education (M Ed); special education: early interventionist (MAT). *Application deadline:* For fall admission, 7/15 priority date for domestic students, 6/1 priority date for international students; for spring admission, 12/1 priority date for domestic students, 10/1 priority date for international students. Applications are processed on a rolling basis. *Application fee:* $20 ($30 for international students). Electronic applications accepted. *Application Contact:* Sandra Meyers, Graduate Admissions Analyst, 985-549-5620, Fax: 985-549-5632, E-mail: admissions@selu.edu. *Interim Dean,* Dr. Bill Neal, 985-549-2217, Fax: 985-549-2070, E-mail: bill.neal@selu.edu.

College of Nursing and Health Sciences Students: 85 full-time (68 women), 134 part-time (108 women); includes 32 minority (21 Black or African American, non-Hispanic/Latino; 4 Asian, non-Hispanic/Latino; 4 Hispanic/Latino; 3 Two or more races, non-Hispanic/Latino), 6 international. Average age 32. 198 applicants, 65% accepted, 49 enrolled. *Faculty:* 29 full-time (22 women), 7 part-time/adjunct (4 women). Expenses: Contact institution. *Financial support:* In 2010–11, 26 students received support, including 2 fellowships (averaging $11,700 per year), 9 research assistantships (averaging $9,244 per year), 4 teaching assistantships (averaging $9,275 per year); career-related internships or fieldwork, Federal Work-Study, institutionally sponsored loans, scholarships/grants, unspecified assistantships, and administrative assistantships also available. Support available to part-time students. Financial award application deadline: 5/1; financial award applicants required to submit FAFSA. In 2010, 61 master's awarded. *Degree program information:* Part-time programs available. Offers communication sciences and disorders (MS); health and kinesiology (MA); nursing and health sciences (MA, MS, MSN). *Application deadline:* For fall admission, 7/15 priority date for domestic students, 6/1 priority date for international students; for spring admission, 12/1 priority date for domestic students, 10/1 priority date for international students. Applications are processed on a rolling basis. *Application fee:* $20 ($30 for international students). Electronic applications accepted. *Application Contact:* Sandra Meyers, Graduate Admissions Analyst, 985-549-5620, Fax: 985-549-5632, E-mail: admissions@selu.edu. *Interim Dean,* Dr. Ann Carruth, 985-549-3772, Fax: 985-549-5179, E-mail: acarruth@selu.edu.

School of Nursing Students: 10 full-time (9 women), 93 part-time (77 women); includes 10 minority (7 Black or African American, non-Hispanic/Latino; 2 Asian, non-Hispanic/Latino; 1 Two or more races, non-Hispanic/Latino). Average age 37. 54 applicants, 54% accepted, 15 enrolled. *Faculty:* 11 full-time (10 women), 5 part-time/adjunct (2 women). Expenses: Contact institution. *Financial support:* In 2010–11, 8 students received support, including 1 fellowship (averaging $10,800 per year), 1 teaching assistantship (averaging $9,000 per year); career-related internships or fieldwork, Federal Work-Study, institutionally sponsored loans, scholarships/grants, unspecified assistantships, and administrative assistantships also available. Support available to part-time students. Financial award application deadline: 5/1; financial award applicants required to submit FAFSA. In 2010, 18 master's awarded. *Degree program information:* Part-time programs available. Offers adult psychiatric/mental health nurse practitioner/clinical nurse specialist (MSN); education (MSN); nurse executive (MSN); nurse practitioner (MSN). *Application deadline:* For fall admission, 7/15 priority date for domestic students, 6/1 priority date for international students; for spring admission, 12/1 priority date for domestic students, 10/1 priority date for international students. Applications are processed on a rolling basis. *Application fee:* $20 ($30 for international students). Electronic applications accepted. *Application Contact:* Sandra Meyers, Graduate Admissions Analyst, 985-549-5620, Fax: 985-549-5632, E-mail: admissions@selu.edu. *Interim Department Head,* Dr. Susan Pryor, 985-549-2156, Fax: 985-549-2869, E-mail: spryor@selu.edu.

College of Science and Technology Students: 27 full-time (14 women), 25 part-time (9 women); includes 2 minority (1 Black or African American, non-Hispanic/Latino; 1 Asian, non-Hispanic/Latino), 8 international. Average age 28. 38 applicants, 61% accepted, 12 enrolled. *Faculty:* 25 full-time (7 women). Expenses: Contact institution. *Financial support:* In

Southeastern Louisiana University (continued)

2010–11, 32 students received support, including 4 fellowships (averaging $10,800 per year), 15 research assistantships (averaging $10,769 per year), 11 teaching assistantships (averaging $10,000 per year); career-related internships or fieldwork, Federal Work-Study, institutionally sponsored loans, unspecified assistantships, and administrative assistantships also available. Support available to part-time students. Financial award application deadline: 5/1; financial award applicants required to submit FAFSA. In 2010, 16 master's awarded. *Degree program information:* Part-time programs available. Offers biology (MS); chemistry (MS); computer science (MS); information technology (MS); mathematics (MS); physics (MS); science and technology (MS). *Application deadline:* For fall admission, 7/15 priority date for domestic students, 6/1 priority date for international students; for spring admission, 12/1 priority date for domestic students, 10/1 priority date for international students. Applications are processed on a rolling basis. *Application fee:* $20 ($30 for international students). Electronic applications accepted. *Application Contact:* Sandra Meyers, Graduate Admissions Analyst, 985-549-5620, Fax: 985-549-5632, E-mail: admissions@selu.edu. *Dean*, Dr. Daniel McCarthy, 985-549-2055, Fax: 985-549-3396, E-mail: dmccarthy@selu.edu.

SOUTHEASTERN OKLAHOMA STATE UNIVERSITY, Durant, OK 74701-0609

General Information State-supported, coed, comprehensive institution. *Enrollment:* 4,181 graduate, professional, and undergraduate students; 137 full-time matriculated graduate/professional students (59 women), 208 part-time matriculated graduate/professional students (99 women). *Enrollment by degree level:* 345 master's. *Graduate faculty:* 97 full-time (33 women), 8 part-time/adjunct (3 women). *Graduate housing:* Room and/or apartments available on a first-come, first-served basis to single students; on-campus housing not available to married students. Housing application deadline: 8/1. *Student services:* Campus employment opportunities, campus safety program, career counseling, exercise/wellness program, free psychological counseling, international student services, low-cost health insurance, multicultural affairs office, services for students with disabilities. *Library facilities:* Henry G. Bennett Memorial Library. *Online resources:* library catalog, web page, access to other libraries' catalogs. *Collection:* 316,193 titles, 1,415 serial subscriptions, 10,138 audiovisual materials. *Research affiliation:* Virginia Polytechnic Institute (physical sciences), United States Department of Agriculture (biological sciences), J. J. Keller Foundation (occupational safety research), Oklahoma Small Business Development Center (business development).

Computer facilities: 598 computers available on campus for general student use. A campuswide network can be accessed from student residence rooms. Online class registration, campus Blackboard classes are available. *Web address:* http://www.se.edu/.

General Application Contact: Carrie Williamson, Administrative Assistant, Graduate Office, 580-745-2200, Fax: 580-745-7474, E-mail: cwilliamson@se.edu.

GRADUATE UNITS

Department of Aviation Science Students: 51 full-time (8 women), 65 part-time (12 women); includes 9 Black or African American, non-Hispanic/Latino; 6 American Indian or Alaska Native, non-Hispanic/Latino; 7 Asian, non-Hispanic/Latino; 12 Hispanic/Latino, 2 international. Average age 30. 117 applicants, 99% accepted, 116 enrolled. Expenses: Contact institution. *Financial support:* Federal Work-Study and institutionally sponsored loans available. Support available to part-time students. Financial award application deadline: 6/15. *Degree program information:* Part-time and evening/weekend programs available. Offers aerospace administration and logistics (MS). *Application deadline:* For fall admission, 8/1 for domestic students, 6/1 for international students; for spring admission, 1/5 for domestic students, 11/1 for international students. *Application fee:* $20 ($55 for international students). Electronic applications accepted. *Application Contact:* Carrie Williamson, Administrative Assistant, Graduate Office, 580-745-2200, Fax: 580-745-7474, E-mail: cwilliamson@se.edu. *Director*, Dr. David Conway, 580-745-3240, Fax: 580-924-0741, E-mail: dconway@se.edu.

School of Arts and Sciences Students: 19 full-time (4 women), 39 part-time (6 women); includes 13 American Indian or Alaska Native, non-Hispanic/Latino; 2 Hispanic/Latino. Average age 28. 10 applicants, 100% accepted, 10 enrolled. *Faculty:* 12 full-time (4 women), 1 part-time/adjunct (0 women). Expenses: Contact institution. *Financial support:* In 2010–11, 8 students received support; fellowships, research assistantships, teaching assistantships, Federal Work-Study and institutionally sponsored loans available. Support available to part-time students. Financial award application deadline: 6/15; financial award applicants required to submit FAFSA. *Degree program information:* Part-time and evening/weekend programs available. Offers biology (MT); computer information systems (MT). *Application deadline:* For fall admission, 8/1 for domestic students, 6/1 for international students; for spring admission, 1/5 for domestic students, 11/1 for international students. *Application fee:* $20 ($55 for international students). Electronic applications accepted. *Application Contact:* Carrie Williamson, Graduate Secretary, 580-745-2200, Fax: 580-745-7474, E-mail: cwilliamson@se.edu. *Graduate Coordinator*, Dr. Teresa Golden, 580-745-2286, E-mail: tgolden@se.edu.

School of Behavioral Sciences Students: 29 full-time (23 women), 14 part-time (12 women); includes 2 Black or African American, non-Hispanic/Latino; 12 American Indian or Alaska Native, non-Hispanic/Latino; 1 Asian, non-Hispanic/Latino; 1 Hispanic/Latino, 2 international. Average age 35. 12 applicants, 100% accepted, 12 enrolled. *Faculty:* 10 full-time (3 women). Expenses: Contact institution. *Financial support:* Fellowships, research assistantships, teaching assistantships, Federal Work-Study available. Support available to part-time students. Financial award application deadline: 6/15. *Degree program information:* Part-time and evening/weekend programs available. Offers clinical mental health counseling (MS). *Application deadline:* For fall admission, 8/1 for domestic students, 6/1 for international students; for spring admission, 1/5 for domestic students, 11/1 for international students. *Application fee:* $20 ($55 for international students). Electronic applications accepted. *Application Contact:* Carrie Williamson, Graduate Secretary, 580-745-2200, Fax: 580-745-7474, E-mail: cwilliamson@se.edu. *Program Coordinator*, Dr. Kimberly Donovan, 580-745-2312, E-mail: kdonovan@se.edu.

School of Business Students: 11 full-time (5 women), 22 part-time (13 women); includes 9 American Indian or Alaska Native, non-Hispanic/Latino; 2 Asian, non-Hispanic/Latino, 4 international. Average age 32. 8 applicants, 100% accepted, 8 enrolled. *Faculty:* 13 full-time (6 women), 5 part-time/adjunct (0 women). Expenses: Contact institution. *Financial support:* In 2010–11, 30 students received support, including 3 teaching assistantships with full tuition reimbursements available (averaging $5,000 per year); Federal Work-Study, institutionally sponsored loans, and tuition waivers (partial) also available. Support available to part-time students. Financial award application deadline: 6/15; financial award applicants required to submit FAFSA. *Degree program information:* Part-time and evening/weekend programs available. Offers business (MBA). *Application deadline:* For fall admission, 8/1 for domestic students, 6/1 for international students; for spring admission, 1/5 for domestic students, 11/1 for international students. *Application fee:* $20 ($55 for international students). Electronic applications accepted. *Application Contact:* Carrie Williamson, Graduate Secretary, 580-745-2200, Fax: 580-745-7474, E-mail: cwilliamson@se.edu. *Dean*, Dr. Buddy Gaster, 580-745-2030, Fax: 580-970-7479, E-mail: bgaster@se.edu.

School of Education Students: 27 full-time (19 women), 68 part-time (56 women); includes 3 Black or African American, non-Hispanic/Latino; 17 American Indian or Alaska Native, non-Hispanic/Latino; 4 Hispanic/Latino. Average age 34. 23 applicants, 91% accepted, 21 enrolled. *Faculty:* 52 full-time (19 women), 1 (woman) part-time/adjunct. Expenses: Contact institution. *Financial support:* In 2010–11, 1 teaching assistantship with full tuition reimbursement (averaging $5,000 per year) was awarded; Federal Work-Study, institutionally sponsored loans, and tuition waivers (partial) also available. Support available to part-time students. Financial award application deadline: 6/15; financial award applicants required to submit FAFSA. *Degree program information:* Part-time and evening/weekend programs available. Offers math specialist (M Ed); reading specialist (M Ed); school administration (M Ed); school counseling (M Ed); special education (M Ed). *Application deadline:* For fall admission, 8/1 for domestic students, 6/1 for international students; for spring admission, 1/5 for domestic students, 11/1 for international students. *Application fee:* $20 ($55 for international students). Electronic applications accepted. *Application Contact:* Carrie Williamson, Graduate Secretary, 580-745-2200, Fax: 580-745-7474, E-mail: cwilliamson@se.edu. *Chair*, Dr. Melanie Price, 580-745-2602, Fax: 580-745-7474, E-mail: mprice@se.edu.

SOUTHEASTERN UNIVERSITY, Lakeland, FL 33801-6099

General Information Independent-religious, coed, comprehensive institution.

GRADUATE UNITS

College of Business and Legal Studies *Degree program information:* Evening/weekend programs available. Postbaccalaureate distance learning degree programs offered. Offers business administration (MBA). Electronic applications accepted.

College of Christian Ministries and Religion *Degree program information:* Evening/weekend programs available. Postbaccalaureate distance learning degree programs offered. Offers ministerial leadership (MA).

College of Education Offers educational leadership (M Ed); elementary education (M Ed); teaching and learning (M Ed).

Department of Behavioral and Social Sciences *Degree program information:* Evening/weekend programs available. Offers human services (MA); professional counseling (MS); school counseling (MS).

SOUTHEAST MISSOURI STATE UNIVERSITY, Cape Girardeau, MO 63701-4799

General Information State-supported, coed, comprehensive institution. CGS member. *Enrollment:* 11,112 graduate, professional, and undergraduate students; 287 full-time matriculated graduate/professional students (170 women), 622 part-time matriculated graduate/professional students (434 women). *Enrollment by degree level:* 841 master's, 13 doctoral, 55 other advanced degrees. *Graduate faculty:* 217 full-time (93 women), 3 part-time/adjunct (1 woman). Tuition, state resident: full-time $4698; part-time $261 per credit hour. Tuition, nonresident: full-time $8379; part-time $465.50 per credit hour. *Graduate housing:* Room and/or apartments available on a first-come, first-served basis to single students; on-campus housing not available to married students. Typical cost: $4872 per year ($7342 including board). Room and board charges vary according to board plan and housing facility selected. Housing application deadline: 12/15. *Student services:* Campus employment opportunities, campus safety program, career counseling, child daycare facilities, exercise/wellness program, free psychological counseling, international student services, multicultural affairs office, services for students with disabilities, teacher training, writing training. *Library facilities:* Kent Library. *Online resources:* library catalog, web page, access to other libraries' catalogs. *Collection:* 433,851 titles, 57,313 serial subscriptions, 15,343 audiovisual materials.

Computer facilities: 1,311 computers available on campus for general student use. A campuswide network can be accessed from student residence rooms. Online class registration is available. *Web address:* http://www.semo.edu/.

General Application Contact: Dr. Chris McGowan, Interim Dean, School of Graduate Studies, 573-651-2192, Fax: 573-651-2001, E-mail: graduateschool@semo.edu.

GRADUATE UNITS

School of Graduate Studies Students: 287 full-time (170 women), 622 part-time (434 women); includes 62 minority (37 Black or African American, non-Hispanic/Latino; 12 American Indian or Alaska Native, non-Hispanic/Latino; 9 Asian, non-Hispanic/Latino; 3 Hispanic/Latino; 1 Native Hawaiian or other Pacific Islander, non-Hispanic/Latino), 110 international. Average age 31. 621 applicants, 81% accepted, 317 enrolled. *Faculty:* 217 full-time (93 women), 3 part-time/adjunct (1 woman). Expenses: Contact institution. *Financial support:* In 2010–11, 262 students received support, including 105 teaching assistantships with full tuition reimbursements available (averaging $7,600 per year); career-related internships or fieldwork, Federal Work-Study, institutionally sponsored loans, scholarships/grants, tuition waivers (full), and unspecified assistantships also available. Financial award application deadline: 6/30; financial award applicants required to submit FAFSA. In 2010, 204 master's, 20 other advanced degrees awarded. Offers applied chemistry (MNS); biology (MNS); career counseling (MA); communication disorders (MA); community counseling (MA); community wellness and leisure (MPA); counseling (MA, Ed S); counseling education (Ed S); criminal justice (MS); educational administration (MA, Ed S); educational leadership development (Ed S); elementary administration and supervision (MA); elementary education (MA); English (MA); environmental science (MS); exceptional child education (MA); heritage education (Certificate); higher education administration (MA); historic preservation (Certificate); history (MA); human environmental studies (MA); industrial management (MS); mathematics (MNS); mental health counseling (MA); nursing (MSN); nutrition and exercise science (MS); public administration (MPA); public history (MA); school counseling (MA); secondary administration and supervision (MA); secondary education (MA); teacher leadership (MA); teaching English to speakers of other languages (MA); technology management (MS). *Application deadline:* For fall admission, 8/1 for domestic students, 6/1 for international students; for spring admission, 11/21 for domestic students, 10/1 for international students. Applications are processed on a rolling basis. *Application fee:* $25 ($35 for international students). Electronic applications accepted. *Application Contact:* Gail Amick, Administrative Secretary, 573-651-2049, Fax: 573-651-2001, E-mail: gamick@semo.edu. *Interim Dean*, Dr. Chris McGowan, 573-651-2163, E-mail: graduateschool@semo.edu.

Godwin Center for Science and Mathematics Education Students: 5 part-time (all women). Average age 39. 2 applicants, 100% accepted, 2 enrolled. *Faculty:* 4 full-time (3 women). Expenses: Contact institution. *Financial support:* Career-related internships or fieldwork, Federal Work-Study, institutionally sponsored loans, scholarships/grants, tuition waivers (full), and unspecified assistantships available. Financial award application deadline: 6/30; financial award applicants required to submit FAFSA. In 2010, 3 master's awarded. *Degree program information:* Part-time programs available. Offers science education (MNS). *Application deadline:* For fall admission, 8/1 for domestic students, 6/1 for international students; for spring admission, 11/21 for domestic students, 10/1 for international students. Applications are processed on a rolling basis. *Application fee:* $25 ($35 for international students). Electronic applications accepted. *Application Contact:* Gail Amick, Administrative Secretary, 573-651-2049, Fax: 573-651-2001, E-mail: gamick@semo.edu. *Director of Graduate Program*, Dr. Rachel Morgan Theall, 573-651-2372, Fax: 573-986-6792, E-mail: rmtheall@semo.edu.

Harrison College of Business Students: 51 full-time (24 women), 72 part-time (34 women); includes 4 minority (1 American Indian or Alaska Native, non-Hispanic/Latino; 3 Asian, non-Hispanic/Latino), 32 international. Average age 28. 71 applicants, 83% accepted, 33 enrolled. *Faculty:* 31 full-time (10 women). Expenses: Contact institution. *Financial support:* In 2010–11, 52 students received support, including 10 teaching assistantships with full tuition reimbursements available (averaging $7,600 per year); career-related internships or fieldwork, Federal Work-Study, institutionally sponsored loans, scholarships/grants, tuition waivers (full), and unspecified assistantships also available. Financial award application deadline: 6/30; financial award applicants required to submit FAFSA. In 2010, 46 master's awarded. *Degree program information:* Part-time and evening/weekend programs available. Postbaccalaureate distance learning degree programs offered (no on-campus study). Offers accounting (MBA); entrepreneurship (MBA); environmental management (MBA); financial management (MBA); general management (MBA); health administration (MBA); industrial management (MBA); international business (MBA); sport management (MBA). *Application deadline:* For fall admission, 8/1 for domestic students, 6/1 for international students; for spring admission, 11/21 for domestic students, 10/1 for international students. Applications are processed on a rolling basis. *Application fee:* $25 ($35 for international students). Electronic applications accepted. *Application Contact:* Gail Amick, Administrative Secretary, 573-651-2049, Fax: 573-651-2001, E-mail: gamick@semo.edu. *Director, Graduate Programs*, Dr. Kenneth A. Heischmidt, 573-651-5116, Fax: 573-651-5032, E-mail: kheischmidt@semo.edu.

SOUTHERN ADVENTIST UNIVERSITY, Collegedale, TN 37315-0370

General Information Independent-religious, coed, comprehensive institution. *Graduate housing:* Rooms and/or apartments available on a first-come, first-served basis to single and married students. Housing application deadline: 7/1.

GRADUATE UNITS

School of Business and Management *Degree program information:* Part-time and evening/weekend programs available. Postbaccalaureate distance learning degree programs offered (no on-campus study). Offers accounting (MBA); church administration (MSA); church and nonprofit leadership (MBA); financial management (MBA, MSA); healthcare administration (MBA); management (MBA); marketing management (MBA); outdoor education (MSA). Electronic applications accepted.

School of Education and Psychology *Degree program information:* Part-time and evening/weekend programs available. Offers clinical mental health counseling (MS); inclusive education (MS Ed); instructional leadership (MS Ed); literacy education (MS Ed); outdoor teacher education (MS Ed); school counseling (MS). Electronic applications accepted.

School of Nursing *Degree program information:* Part-time programs available. Offers acute care nurse practitioner (MSN); adult nurse practitioner (MSN); family nurse practitioner (MSN); nurse educator (MSN). Electronic applications accepted.

School of Religion *Degree program information:* Part-time programs available. Offers Biblical and theological studies (MA); church leadership and management (M Min); church ministry and homiletics (M Min); evangelism and world mission (M Min); religious studies (MA).

School of Social Work Postbaccalaureate distance learning degree programs offered. Offers social work (MSW).

SOUTHERN ARKANSAS UNIVERSITY–MAGNOLIA, Magnolia, AR 71753

General Information State-supported, coed, comprehensive institution. *Enrollment:* 3,379 graduate, professional, and undergraduate students; 71 full-time matriculated graduate/professional students (43 women), 364 part-time matriculated graduate/professional students (275 women). *Enrollment by degree level:* 435 master's. *Graduate faculty:* 32 full-time (16 women), 6 part-time/adjunct (5 women). Tuition, state resident: part-time $221 per hour. Tuition, nonresident: part-time $325 per hour. *Graduate housing:* Rooms and/or apartments available on a first-come, first-served basis to single and married students. Housing application deadline: 6/1. *Student services:* Campus employment opportunities, campus safety program, career counseling, exercise/wellness program, free psychological counseling, international student services, low-cost health insurance, multicultural affairs office, services for students with disabilities. *Library facilities:* Magale Library. *Online resources:* library catalog, web page. *Collection:* 151,166 titles, 1,065 serial subscriptions.

Computer facilities: 194 computers available on campus for general student use. A campuswide network can be accessed from student residence rooms and from off campus. Online class registration is available. *Web address:* http://www.saumag.edu/.

General Application Contact: Dr. Kim Bloss, Dean, Graduate Studies, 870-235-4150, Fax: 870-235-5227, E-mail: kkbloss@saumag.edu.

GRADUATE UNITS

Graduate Programs Students: 71 full-time (43 women), 364 part-time (275 women); includes 109 Black or African American, non-Hispanic/Latino; 1 American Indian or Alaska Native, non-Hispanic/Latino; 3 Asian, non-Hispanic/Latino, 19 international. Average age 33. 107 applicants, 71% accepted, 69 enrolled. *Faculty:* 32 full-time (16 women), 6 part-time/adjunct (5 women). Expenses: Contact institution. *Financial support:* Career-related internships or fieldwork, Federal Work-Study, scholarships/grants, tuition waivers (full), and unspecified assistantships available. Financial award applicants required to submit FAFSA. In 2010, 157 master's awarded. *Degree program information:* Part-time and evening/weekend programs available. Offers agriculture (MS); business administration (MBA); computer and information sciences (MS); education (M Ed); kinesiology (M Ed); library media and information specialist (M Ed); mental health and clinical counseling (MS); public administration (MPA); school counseling (M Ed); teaching (MAT). *Application deadline:* For fall admission, 7/31 for domestic students; for winter admission, 12/1 for domestic students; for spring admission, 12/1 for domestic students. Applications are processed on a rolling basis. *Application fee:* $25. *Application Contact:* Dr. Kim Bloss, Dean, Graduate Studies, 870-235-4150, Fax: 870-235-5227, E-mail: kkbloss@saumag.edu. *Dean, Graduate Studies,* Dr. Kim Bloss, 870-235-4150, Fax: 870-235-5227, E-mail: kkbloss@saumag.edu.

SOUTHERN BAPTIST THEOLOGICAL SEMINARY, Louisville, KY 40280-0004

General Information Independent-religious, coed, comprehensive institution. *Graduate housing:* Rooms and/or apartments available on a first-come, first-served basis to single and married students.

GRADUATE UNITS

Billy Graham School of Missions, Evangelism and Church Growth *Degree program information:* Part-time and evening/weekend programs available. Postbaccalaureate distance learning degree programs offered (minimal on-campus study). Offers Christian mission/world religion (PhD); evangelism/church growth (PhD); ministry (D Min); missiology (MA, D Miss); missions, evangelism and church growth (M Div); religion (Th M); theological studies (MA).

School of Church Ministries *Degree program information:* Part-time programs available. Postbaccalaureate distance learning degree programs offered (minimal on-campus study). Offers children's and family ministry (M Div, MA); church music (M Div, MA, MCM); college ministry (M Div, MA); discipleship and family ministry (M Div, MA); family ministry (PhD); higher education (PhD); leadership (M Div, MA, PhD); ministry (D Ed Min, D Min); women's leadership (M Div, MA); worship leadership (M Div, MA); youth and family ministry (M Div, MA).

School of Theology *Degree program information:* Part-time and evening/weekend programs available. Postbaccalaureate distance learning degree programs offered (minimal on-campus study). Offers applied theology (D Min); biblical and theological studies (M Div); biblical counseling (M Div, MA, D Min); biblical spirituality (D Min); Christian ministry (M Div); expository preaching (D Min); pastoral studies (M Div); theological studies (MA); theology (Th M, PhD); worldview and apologetics (M Div).

SOUTHERN CALIFORNIA COLLEGE OF OPTOMETRY, Fullerton, CA 92831-1615

General Information Independent, coed, graduate-only institution. *Graduate housing:* On-campus housing not available. *Research affiliation:* Alcon Laboratories (ophthalmic products), Essilor (spectacle lenses), Allergan (ophthalmic products).

GRADUATE UNITS

Professional Program Offers optometry (OD). Electronic applications accepted.

SOUTHERN CALIFORNIA INSTITUTE OF ARCHITECTURE, Los Angeles, CA 90013

General Information Independent, coed, comprehensive institution. *Enrollment:* 485 graduate, professional, and undergraduate students; 230 full-time matriculated graduate/professional students (81 women). *Enrollment by degree level:* 230 master's. *Graduate faculty:* 43 full-time (12 women), 43 part-time/adjunct (15 women). *Tuition:* Full-time $13,750; part-time $764 per credit hour. *Required fees:* $350. *Graduate housing:* On-campus housing not available. *Student services:* Campus employment opportunities, campus safety program, career counseling, free psychological counseling, international student services. *Library facilities:* Kappe Library. *Online resources:* library catalog, access to other libraries' catalogs. *Collection:* 30,000 titles, 109 serial subscriptions.

Computer facilities: 60 computers available on campus for general student use. A campuswide network can be accessed from off campus. Online class registration is available. *Web address:* http://www.sciarc.edu/.

General Application Contact: J. J. Jackman, Director of Admissions, 213-356-5321, Fax: 213-613-2260, E-mail: jj@sciarc.edu.

GRADUATE UNITS

Graduate Program In Architecture Students: 230 full-time (81 women); includes 86 minority (8 Black or African American, non-Hispanic/Latino; 4 American Indian or Alaska Native, non-Hispanic/Latino; 34 Asian, non-Hispanic/Latino; 38 Hispanic/Latino; 2 Native Hawaiian or other Pacific Islander, non-Hispanic/Latino), 85 international. Average age 27. 506 applicants, 63% accepted, 103 enrolled. *Faculty:* 43 full-time (12 women), 43 part-time/adjunct (15 women). Expenses: Contact institution. *Financial support:* In 2010–11, 32 students received support; teaching assistantships, Federal Work-Study and scholarships/grants available. Financial award application deadline: 2/15. In 2010, 93 master's awarded. Offers architecture (M Arch). *Application deadline:* For fall admission, 12/15 for domestic students. *Application fee:* $75. Electronic applications accepted. *Application Contact:* J. J. Jackman, Director of Admissions, 213-356-5321, Fax: 213-613-2260, E-mail: jj@sciarc.edu. *Graduate Program Chair,* Hernan Diaz Alonso, 213-613-2200, Fax: 213-613-2260, E-mail: hernan@sciarc.edu.

SOUTHERN CALIFORNIA SEMINARY, El Cajon, CA 92019

General Information Independent-religious, coed, comprehensive institution. *Enrollment:* 37 full-time matriculated graduate/professional students (8 women), 80 part-time matriculated graduate/professional students (37 women). *Enrollment by degree level:* 43 first professional, 63 master's, 11 doctoral. *Tuition:* Part-time $339 per unit. Part-time tuition and fees vary according to degree level, campus/location and program. *Graduate housing:* Rooms and/or apartments available on a first-come, first-served basis to single and married students. *Student services:* Campus employment opportunities, career counseling, international student services, teacher training, writing training.

Computer facilities: 12 computers available on campus for general student use. A campuswide network can be accessed from off campus. Online class registration is available. *Web address:* http://www.socalsem.edu/.

General Application Contact: Thomas Pittman, Admissions Officer/Director of Student Services, 888-389-7244, Fax: 619-201-8975, E-mail: thpittman@socalsem.edu.

GRADUATE UNITS

Graduate and Professional Programs Students: 37 full-time (8 women), 80 part-time (37 women); includes 55 minority (20 Black or African American, non-Hispanic/Latino; 14 Asian, non-Hispanic/Latino; 16 Hispanic/Latino; 1 Native Hawaiian or other Pacific Islander, non-Hispanic/Latino; 4 Two or more races, non-Hispanic/Latino), 5 international. Average age 41. Expenses: Contact institution. *Financial support:* In 2010–11, 14 students received support. Federal Work-Study, scholarships/grants, and tuition waivers (partial) available. Financial award application deadline: 3/1; financial award applicants required to submit FAFSA. In 2010, 7 first professional degrees, 50 master's, 4 doctorates awarded. *Degree program information:* Part-time and evening/weekend programs available. Postbaccalaureate distance learning degree programs offered (minimal on-campus study). Offers Biblical studies (MABS); counseling psychology (MACP); marriage and family therapy (MAMFT); psychology (Psy D); religious studies (MRS); theology (M Div). *Application deadline:* For fall admission, 8/13 for domestic and international students; for spring admission, 12/11 for domestic students, 12/15 for international students. Applications are processed on a rolling basis. *Application fee:* $31 ($126 for international students). Electronic applications accepted. *Application Contact:* Thomas Pittman, Admissions Officer and Director of Student Services, 888-389-7244, Fax: 619-201-8975, E-mail: thpittman@socalsem.edu. *Vice-President of Academics,* Dr. Chuck Emert, 619-201-8995, Fax: 619-201-8975.

SOUTHERN CALIFORNIA UNIVERSITY OF HEALTH SCIENCES, Whittier, CA 90609-1166

General Information Independent, coed, graduate-only institution. *Enrollment by degree level:* 380 first professional, 160 master's. *Graduate faculty:* 34 full-time (16 women), 40 part-time/adjunct (13 women). *Tuition:* Full-time $12,748; part-time $443 per unit. *Required fees:* $200 per term. Tuition and fees vary according to course load, degree level and program. *Graduate housing:* On-campus housing not available. *Student services:* Campus employment opportunities, campus safety program, career counseling, international student services, low-cost health insurance, multicultural affairs office, services for students with disabilities. *Library facilities:* Learning Resource Center. *Collection:* 27,227 titles, 527 serial subscriptions, 1,077 audiovisual materials. *Research affiliation:* Anton B. Burg Foundation (alternative health care), Samueli Institute (alternative health care).

Computer facilities: 50 computers available on campus for general student use. A campuswide network can be accessed. Online class registration is available. *Web address:* http://www.scuhs.edu/.

General Application Contact: Peter Hanna, Executive Director of Enrollment Management, 562-902-3384, E-mail: peterhanna@scuhs.edu.

GRADUATE UNITS

College of Acupuncture and Oriental Medicine Students: 2 full-time (1 woman), 158 part-time (88 women); includes 89 minority (1 Black or African American, non-Hispanic/Latino; 67 Asian, non-Hispanic/Latino; 15 Hispanic/Latino; 6 Native Hawaiian or other Pacific Islander, non-Hispanic/Latino). Average age 30. 177 applicants, 65% accepted, 86 enrolled. *Faculty:* 11 full-time (6 women), 13 part-time/adjunct (4 women). Expenses: Contact institution. *Financial support:* In 2010–11, 2 students received support. Federal Work-Study, scholarships/grants, and International Student Work Program available. Financial award applicants required to submit FAFSA. In 2010, 25 master's awarded. *Degree program information:* Part-time and evening/weekend programs available. Offers acupuncture and Oriental medicine (MAOM). *Application deadline:* Applications are processed on a rolling basis. *Application fee:* $50. Electronic applications accepted. *Application Contact:* Tracy Nieto, Assistant Director of Admissions, 562-902-3319, Fax: 562-902-3321, E-mail: tracynieto@scuhs.edu. *Dean,* Dr. Wen-Shuo Wu, 562-947-8755 Ext. 7028, E-mail: wen-shuowu@scuhs.edu.

Los Angeles College of Chiropractic Students: 137 full-time (55 women), 243 part-time (95 women); includes 164 minority (14 Black or African American, non-Hispanic/Latino; 2 American Indian or Alaska Native, non-Hispanic/Latino; 95 Asian, non-Hispanic/Latino; 39 Hispanic/Latino; 12 Native Hawaiian or other Pacific Islander, non-Hispanic/Latino; 2 Two or more races, non-Hispanic/Latino). Average age 28. 285 applicants, 62% accepted, 127 enrolled. *Faculty:* 22 full-time (8 women), 17 part-time/adjunct (5 women). Expenses: Contact institution. *Financial support:* In 2010–11, 48 students received support. Career-related internships or fieldwork, Federal Work-Study, scholarships/grants, and International Student Work Program available. Financial award applicants required to submit FAFSA. In 2010, 76 DCs awarded. Offers chiropractic (DC). *Application deadline:* Applications are processed on a rolling basis. *Application fee:* $50. Electronic applications accepted. *Application Contact:* Tracy Nieto, Assistant Director of Admissions, 562-947-8755 Ext. 319, Fax: 562-902-3321, E-mail: tracynieto@scuhs.edu. *Dean,* Dr. Michael Sackett, 562-947-8755 Ext. 522, Fax: 562-947-5724, E-mail: mikesackett@scuhs.edu.

SOUTHERN COLLEGE OF OPTOMETRY, Memphis, TN 38104-2222

General Information Independent, coed, graduate-only institution. *Graduate housing:* On-campus housing not available.

GRADUATE UNITS

Professional Program Offers optometry (OD).

SOUTHERN CONNECTICUT STATE UNIVERSITY, New Haven, CT 06515-1355

General Information State-supported, coed, comprehensive institution. CGS member. *Enrollment:* 11,964 graduate, professional, and undergraduate students; 1,000 full-time matriculated graduate/professional students, 2,188 part-time matriculated graduate/professional students. *Graduate faculty:* 424 full-time (210 women). Tuition, state resident: full-time $5137; part-time $518 per credit. Tuition, nonresident: part-time $542 per credit. *Required fees:* $4008; $55 per semester. Tuition and fees vary according to program. *Graduate housing:* Room and/or apartments available on a first-come, first-served basis to single students; on-campus housing not available to married students. Typical cost: $4552 per year ($6851

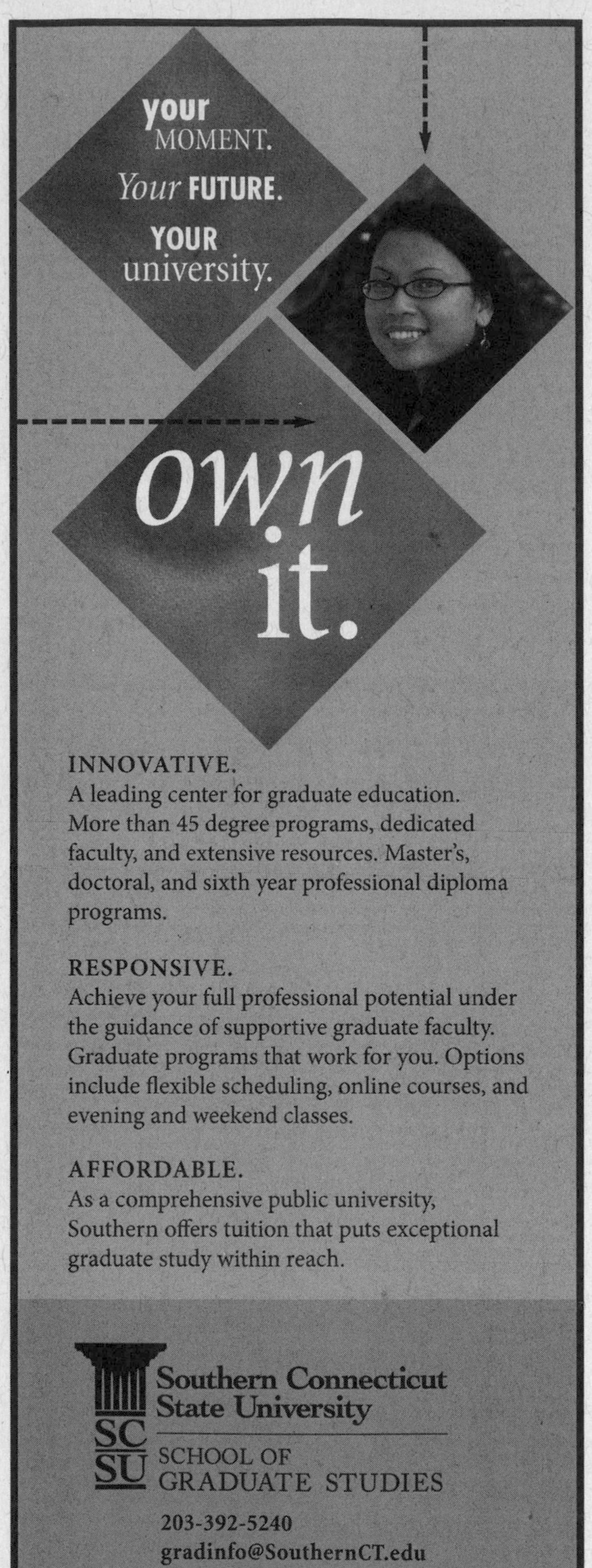

including board). *Student services:* Campus employment opportunities, campus safety program, career counseling, child daycare facilities, exercise/wellness program, free psychological counseling, grant writing training, international student services, low-cost health insurance, multicultural affairs office, services for students with disabilities, teacher training, writing training. *Library facilities:* Hilton C. Buley Library. *Online resources:* library catalog, web page, access to other libraries' catalogs. *Collection:* 484,468 titles, 3,786 serial subscriptions, 9,840 audiovisual materials.

Computer facilities: 800 computers available on campus for general student use. A campuswide network can be accessed from student residence rooms and from off campus. Online class registration is available. *Web address:* http://www.southernct.edu/.

General Application Contact: Lisa Galvin, Assistant Dean, 203-392-5240, Fax: 203-392-5235, E-mail: gradinfo@southernct.edu.

GRADUATE UNITS

School of Graduate Studies Students: 1,000 full-time (778 women), 2,188 part-time (1,643 women); includes 479 minority (228 Black or African American, non-Hispanic/Latino; 3 American Indian or Alaska Native, non-Hispanic/Latino; 66 Asian, non-Hispanic/Latino; 151 Hispanic/Latino; 31 Two or more races, non-Hispanic/Latino), 28 international. Average age 34. 4,096 applicants, 21% accepted, 747 enrolled. *Faculty:* 424 full-time (210 women). Expenses: Contact institution. *Financial support:* Fellowships, research assistantships, teaching assistantships, career-related internships or fieldwork, Federal Work-Study, scholarships/grants, and unspecified assistantships available. Support available to part-time students. Financial award application deadline: 4/15; financial award applicants required to submit FAFSA. In 2010, 692 master's, 6 doctorates, 169 other advanced degrees awarded. *Degree program information:* Part-time and evening/weekend programs available. Postbaccalaureate distance learning degree programs offered (no on-campus study). *Application deadline:* Applications are processed on a rolling basis. *Application fee:* $50. Electronic applications accepted. *Application Contact:* Lisa Galvin, Assistant Dean of Graduate Studies, 203-392-5240, Fax: 203-392-5235, E-mail: galvinl1@southernct.edu. *Dean,* Dr. Holly Crawford, 203-392-5240, Fax: 203-392-5235, E-mail: crawfordh1@southernct.edu.

School of Arts and Sciences Students: 209 full-time (136 women), 302 part-time (200 women); includes 35 Black or African American, non-Hispanic/Latino; 11 Asian, non-Hispanic/Latino; 20 Hispanic/Latino; 7 Two or more races, non-Hispanic/Latino, 7 international. 655 applicants, 23% accepted, 126 enrolled. *Faculty:* 246 full-time (108 women). Expenses: Contact institution. *Financial support:* Teaching assistantships, career-related internships or fieldwork available. In 2010, 114 master's awarded. Offers art education (MS); arts and sciences (MA, MFA, MS, Diploma); biology (MS); chemistry (MS); computer science (MS); English (MA, MS); environmental education (MS); history (MA, MS); mathematics (MS); multicultural-bilingual education/teaching English to speakers of other languages (MS); political science (MS); psychology (MA); science education (MS, Diploma); sociology (MS); urban studies (MS); women's studies (MA). *Application deadline:* Applications are processed on a rolling basis. *Application fee:* $50. Electronic applications accepted. *Application Contact:* Lisa Galvin, Assistant Dean of Graduate Studies, 203-392-5240, Fax: 203-392-5235, E-mail: galvinl1@southernct.edu. *Dean,* Dr. Donna Jean Fredeen, 203-392-5468, Fax: 203-392-6807, E-mail: fredeend1@southernct.edu.

School of Business Students: 83 full-time (40 women), 109 part-time (54 women); includes 24 Black or African American, non-Hispanic/Latino; 2 American Indian or Alaska Native, non-Hispanic/Latino; 17 Asian, non-Hispanic/Latino; 11 Hispanic/Latino; 2 Two or more races, non-Hispanic/Latino, 8 international. 185 applicants, 30% accepted, 48 enrolled. *Faculty:* 34 full-time (8 women). Expenses: Contact institution. *Financial support:* Application deadline: 4/15. In 2010, 57 master's awarded. *Degree program information:* Part-time and evening/weekend programs available. Offers business (MBA); business administration (MBA). *Application deadline:* For fall admission, 7/1 priority date for domestic students. Applications are processed on a rolling basis. *Application fee:* $50. Electronic applications accepted. *Application Contact:* Dr. Wafeek Abdelsayed, Director, 203-392-5873, Fax: 203-392-5988, E-mail: abdelsayedw1@southernct.edu. *Dean,* Dr. Ellen D. Durnin, 203-392-5631, Fax: 203-392-5674, E-mail: durnine1@southernct.edu.

School of Education Students: 404 full-time (336 women), 1,001 part-time (804 women); includes 68 Black or African American, non-Hispanic/Latino; 17 Asian, non-Hispanic/Latino; 57 Hispanic/Latino; 11 Two or more races, non-Hispanic/Latino, 5 international. 2,206 applicants, 20% accepted, 368 enrolled. *Faculty:* 77 full-time (47 women). Expenses: Contact institution. *Financial support:* Research assistantships, teaching assistantships, career-related internships or fieldwork available. In 2010, 386 master's, 6 doctorates, 169 other advanced degrees awarded. *Degree program information:* Part-time programs available. Offers classroom teacher specialist (Diploma); community counseling (MS); counseling (Diploma); education (MLS, MS, MS Ed, Ed D, Diploma); educational foundations (Diploma); educational leadership (Ed D, Diploma); elementary education (MS); human performance (MS); library science (MLS); library/information studies (Diploma); physical education (MS); reading (MS, Diploma); research, statistics, and measurement (MS); school counseling (MS); school health education (MS); school psychology (MS, Diploma); special education (MS Ed, Diploma); sport psychology (MS). *Application fee:* $50. Electronic applications accepted. *Application Contact:* Lisa Galvin, Assistant Dean of Graduate Studies, 203-392-5240, Fax: 203-392-5235, E-mail: galvinl1@southernct.edu. *Dean,* Dr. Michael R. Sampson, 203-392-5900, E-mail: misasis1@southernct.edu.

School of Health and Human Services Students: 304 full-time (266 women), 140 part-time (113 women); includes 66 Black or African American, non-Hispanic/Latino; 6 Asian, non-Hispanic/Latino; 30 Hispanic/Latino; 5 Two or more races, non-Hispanic/Latino, 6 international. 1,049 applicants, 18% accepted, 166 enrolled. *Faculty:* 64 full-time (45 women). Expenses: Contact institution. *Financial support:* Teaching assistantships, career-related internships or fieldwork available. Financial award application deadline: 4/15; financial award applicants required to submit FAFSA. In 2010, 135 master's awarded. *Degree program information:* Part-time and evening/weekend programs available. Offers health and human services (MPH, MS, MSN, MSW); nursing administration (MSN); nursing education (MSN); public health (MPH); recreation and leisure studies (MS); social work (MSW); speech pathology (MS). *Application fee:* $50. Electronic applications accepted. *Application Contact:* Lisa Galvin, Assistant Dean of Graduate Studies, 203-392-5240, Fax: 203-392-5235, E-mail: galvinl1@southernct.edu. *Dean,* Dr. Gregory J. Paveza, 203-392-6905, E-mail: pavezag1@southernct.edu.

See Display on this page and Close-Up on page 981.

SOUTHERN EVANGELICAL SEMINARY, Matthews, NC 28105

General Information Independent-religious, coed, primarily men, graduate-only institution. *Enrollment by degree level:* 167 master's, 23 doctoral. *Graduate faculty:* 5 full-time (0 women), 11 part-time/adjunct (0 women). *Tuition:* Full-time $9405; part-time $313.50 per credit hour. *Required fees:* $150; $50 per semester. *Graduate housing:* On-campus housing not available. *Student services:* Campus employment opportunities, career counseling, international student services, writing training. *Library facilities:* Jamison Library. *Online resources:* library catalog. *Collection:* 75,000 titles, 103 serial subscriptions, 318 audiovisual materials.

Computer facilities: 10 computers available on campus for general student use. A campuswide network can be accessed. Online class registration is available. *Web address:* http://www.ses.edu/.

General Application Contact: Duke Hale, Director of Recruitment, 704-847-5600 Ext. 216, Fax: 704-845-1747, E-mail: dhale@ses.edu.

GRADUATE UNITS

Graduate Programs Expenses: Contact institution. *Financial support:* Scholarships/grants available. *Degree program information:* Part-time and evening/weekend programs available. Postbaccalaureate distance learning degree programs offered. Offers apologetics (MA, Certificate); Christian education (MA); church ministry (MA, Certificate); divinity (Certificate); Islamic studies (MA, Certificate); Jewish studies (MA); philosophy (MA); religion (MA); theology (M Div); youth ministry (MA). *Application deadline:* For fall admission, 8/15 priority date for domestic students, 8/5 priority date for international students; for winter admission, 12/15 priority date for domestic and international students; for spring admission, 1/15 priority date for domestic and international students. Applications are processed on a rolling basis. *Applica-*

tion fee: $25. *Application Contact:* Duke Hale, Director of Recruitment, 704-847-5600 Ext. 216, Fax: 704-845-1747, E-mail: dhale@ses.edu. *Dean,* Dr. Barry R. Leventhal, 704-847-5600 Ext. 204, Fax: 704-845-1747, E-mail: dean@ses.edu.

SOUTHERN ILLINOIS UNIVERSITY CARBONDALE, Carbondale, IL 62901-4701

General Information State-supported, coed, university. CGS member. *Graduate housing:* Rooms and/or apartments available on a first-come, first-served basis to single and married students. *Research affiliation:* Argonne National Laboratory, NASA–Ames Research Center.

GRADUATE UNITS

Graduate School *Degree program information:* Part-time programs available. Offers molecular, cellular and systemic physiology (MS); pharmacology (MS, PhD); physiology (MS, PhD).

College of Agriculture *Degree program information:* Part-time programs available. Offers agribusiness economics (MS); agriculture (MS); animal science (MS); food and nutrition (MS); forestry (MS); horticultural science (MS); plant and soil science (MS).

College of Applied Science Offers applied science (M Arch, MSPA); architecture (M Arch); physician assistant studies (MSPA).

College of Business and Administration *Degree program information:* Part-time programs available. Offers accountancy (M Acc, PhD); business administration (MBA, PhD); business and administration (M Acc, MBA, PhD).

College of Education *Degree program information:* Part-time programs available. Offers behavior analysis and therapy (MS); behavioral analysis and therapy (MS); communication disorders and sciences (MS); community health education (MPH); counselor education (MS Ed, PhD); curriculum and instruction (MS Ed, PhD); education (MPH, MS, MS Ed, MSW, PhD, Rh D); educational administration (MS Ed, PhD); educational psychology (MS Ed, PhD); health education (MS Ed, PhD); higher education (MS Ed); human learning and development (MS Ed); measurement and statistics (PhD); physical education (MS Ed); recreation (MS Ed); rehabilitation (Rh D); rehabilitation administration and services (MS); rehabilitation counseling (MS); social work (MSW); special education (MS Ed); workforce education and development (MS Ed, PhD).

College of Engineering Offers biomedical engineering (ME, MS); civil engineering (MS); electrical and computer engineering (MS, PhD); electrical systems (PhD); engineering (ME, MS, PhD); fossil energy (PhD); manufacturing systems (MS); mechanical engineering and energy processes (MS); mechanics (PhD); mining engineering (MS).

College of Liberal Arts *Degree program information:* Part-time programs available. Offers administration of justice (MA); anthropology (MA, PhD); applied linguistics (MA); ceramics (MFA); clinical psychology (MA, MS, PhD); composition (MA, PhD); composition and theory (MM); counseling psychology (MA, MS, PhD); creative writing (MFA); drawing (MFA); economics (MA, MS, PhD); experimental psychology (MA, MS, PhD); fiber/weaving (MFA); foreign languages and literatures (MA); geography (MS, PhD); glass (MFA); history (MA, PhD); history and literature (MM); jewelry (MFA); liberal arts (MA, MFA, MM, MPA, MS, PhD); metalsmithing/blacksmithing (MFA); music education (MM); opera/music theater (MM); painting (MFA); performance (MM); philosophy (MA, PhD); piano pedagogy (MM); political science (MA, PhD); printmaking (MFA); public administration (MPA); sculpture (MFA); sociology (MA, PhD); speech communication (MA, MS, PhD); speech/theater (PhD); teaching English to speakers of other languages (MA); theater (MFA).

College of Mass Communication and Media Arts *Degree program information:* Part-time programs available. Offers journalism (PhD); mass communication and media arts (MA, MFA, PhD); media theory and research (MA); professional media and media management studies (MA).

College of Science *Degree program information:* Part-time programs available. Offers biological sciences (MS); chemistry and biochemistry (MS, PhD); computer science (MS, PhD); environmental resources and policy (PhD); geology (MS, PhD); mathematics (MA, MS, PhD); molecular biology, microbiology, and biochemistry (MS, PhD); physics (MS, PhD); plant biology (MS, PhD); science (MA, MS, PhD); statistics (MS); zoology (MS, PhD).

School of Law *Degree program information:* Part-time programs available. Offers general law (LL M, MLS); health law and policy (LL M, MLS); law (JD); legal studies (MLS). Electronic applications accepted.

SOUTHERN ILLINOIS UNIVERSITY EDWARDSVILLE, Edwardsville, IL 62026-0001

General Information State-supported, coed, comprehensive institution. CGS member. *Enrollment:* 14,133 graduate, professional, and undergraduate students; 1,252 full-time matriculated graduate/professional students (686 women), 1,422 part-time matriculated graduate/professional students (903 women). *Enrollment by degree level:* 517 first professional, 2,031 master's, 126 other advanced degrees. *Graduate faculty:* 484 full-time (192 women). Tuition, state resident: full-time $6012; part-time $1503 per semester. Tuition, nonresident: full-time $15,030; part-time $3758 per semester. *Required fees:* $1711; $675 per semester. *Graduate housing:* Rooms and/or apartments available on a first-come, first-served basis to single and married students. Typical cost: $4800 per year for single students; $7600 per year for married students. Room charges vary according to board plan, campus/location and housing facility selected. Housing application deadline: 5/1. *Student services:* Campus employment opportunities, campus safety program, career counseling, child daycare facilities, exercise/wellness program, free psychological counseling, grant writing training, international student services, low-cost health insurance, multicultural affairs office, services for students with disabilities, teacher training, writing training. *Library facilities:* Lovejoy Library. *Online resources:* library catalog, web page, access to other libraries' catalogs. *Collection:* 1.4 million titles, 25,811 serial subscriptions, 32,653 audiovisual materials. *Research affiliation:* Metastable Instruments, Inc. (physics), Streamline Automation, LLC (computer science), Long Island Veterinary Specialists (electrical engineering), Amsted Rail (mechanical and industrial engineering), Mallinckrodt (pharmacy), Covidien (management and marketing).

Computer facilities: Computer purchase and lease plans are available. 600 computers available on campus for general student use. A campuswide network can be accessed from student residence rooms and from off campus. Online class registration, online job finder are available. *Web address:* http://www.siue.edu/.

General Application Contact: Michelle Robinson, Coordinator of Graduate Recruitment, 618-650-2811, Fax: 618-650-3523, E-mail: michero@siue.edu.

GRADUATE UNITS

Graduate School Students: 735 full-time (422 women), 1,422 part-time (903 women); includes 284 minority (171 Black or African American, non-Hispanic/Latino; 5 American Indian or Alaska Native, non-Hispanic/Latino; 35 Asian, non-Hispanic/Latino; 42 Hispanic/Latino; 4 Native Hawaiian or other Pacific Islander, non-Hispanic/Latino; 27 Two or more races, non-Hispanic/Latino), 228 international. Average age 26. 1,941 applicants, 54% accepted. *Faculty:* 445 full-time (185 women). Expenses: Contact institution. *Financial support:* In 2010–11, 19 fellowships with full tuition reimbursements (averaging $8,370 per year), 61 research assistantships with full tuition reimbursements (averaging $8,064 per year), 500 teaching assistantships with full tuition reimbursements (averaging $8,064 per year) were awarded; career-related internships or fieldwork, Federal Work-Study, institutionally sponsored loans, scholarships/grants, traineeships, tuition waivers (full), and unspecified assistantships also available. Support available to part-time students. Financial award application deadline: 3/1; financial award applicants required to submit FAFSA. In 2010, 765 master's, 44 other advanced degrees awarded. *Degree program information:* Part-time and evening/weekend programs available. Postbaccalaureate distance learning degree programs offered (minimal on-campus study). *Application deadline:* For fall admission, 7/22 for domestic students, 6/1 for international students; for spring admission, 12/9 for domestic students, 10/1 for international students. Applications are processed on a rolling basis. *Application fee:* $30. Electronic applications accepted. *Application Contact:* Michelle Robinson, Coordinator of Graduate Recruitment, 618-650-2811, Fax: 618-650-3523, E-mail: michero@siue.edu. *Acting Associate Provost for Research/Dean,* Dr. Jerry Weinberg, 618-650-3010, Fax: 618-650-3523, E-mail: gradsch@siue.edu.

College of Arts and Sciences Students: 305 full-time (199 women), 410 part-time (269 women); includes 124 minority (81 Black or African American, non-Hispanic/Latino; 3 American Indian or Alaska Native, non-Hispanic/Latino; 9 Asian, non-Hispanic/Latino; 19 Hispanic/Latino; 3 Native Hawaiian or other Pacific Islander, non-Hispanic/Latino; 9 Two or more races, non-Hispanic/Latino), 57 international. Average age 26. 687 applicants, 55% accepted. *Faculty:* 242 full-time (96 women). Expenses: Contact institution. *Financial support:* In 2010–11, 8 fellowships with full tuition reimbursements (averaging $8,370 per year), 15 research assistantships with full tuition reimbursements (averaging $8,064 per year), 268 teaching assistantships with full tuition reimbursements (averaging $8,064 per year) were awarded; career-related internships or fieldwork, Federal Work-Study, institutionally sponsored loans, scholarships/grants, traineeships, and unspecified assistantships also available. Support available to part-time students. Financial award application deadline: 3/1; financial award applicants required to submit FAFSA. In 2010, 241 master's, 14 other advanced degrees awarded. *Degree program information:* Part-time and evening/weekend programs available. Postbaccalaureate distance learning degree programs offered (minimal on-campus study). Offers American and English literature (MA, Postbaccalaureate Certificate); art therapy counseling (MA); arts and sciences (MA, MFA, MM, MPA, MS, MSW, Postbaccalaureate Certificate); biology (MA, MS); biotechnology management (MS); chemistry (MS); corporate and organizational communication (Postbaccalaureate Certificate); creative writing (MA); environmental science management (MS); environmental sciences (MS); geography (MS); health communication (MA); history (MA); interpersonal communication (MA); mass communications (MS, Postbaccalaureate Certificate); mathematics (MS); media literacy (Postbaccalaureate Certificate); museum studies (Postbaccalaureate Certificate); music education (MM); music performance (MM); organizational communication (MA); piano pedagogy (Postbaccalaureate Certificate); public administration (MPA); school social work (MSW); social work (MSW); sociology (MA); speech communication (MA, Postbaccalaureate Certificate); studio art (MFA); teaching English as a second language (MA, Postbaccalaureate Certificate); teaching of writing (MA, Postbaccalaureate Certificate); vocal pedagogy (Postbaccalaureate Certificate). *Application deadline:* For fall admission, 7/22 for domestic students, 6/1 for international students; for spring admission, 12/9 for domestic students, 10/1 for international students. Applications are processed on a rolling basis. *Application fee:* $30. Electronic applications accepted. *Application Contact:* Michelle Robinson, Coordinator of Graduate Recruitment, 618-650-2811, Fax: 618-650-3523, E-mail: michero@siue.edu. *Dean,* Dr. Aldemaro Romero, 618-650-5044, E-mail: college_arts_sciences@siue.edu.

School of Business Students: 87 full-time (33 women), 196 part-time (68 women); includes 25 minority (11 Black or African American, non-Hispanic/Latino; 4 Asian, non-Hispanic/Latino; 5 Hispanic/Latino; 1 Native Hawaiian or other Pacific Islander, non-Hispanic/Latino; 4 Two or more races, non-Hispanic/Latino), 42 international. Average age 26. 214 applicants, 58% accepted. *Faculty:* 43 full-time (15 women). Expenses: Contact institution. *Financial support:* In 2010–11, 2 fellowships with full tuition reimbursements (averaging $8,370 per year), 6 research assistantships with full tuition reimbursements (averaging $8,064 per year), 78 teaching assistantships with full tuition reimbursements (averaging $8,064 per year) were awarded; career-related internships or fieldwork, Federal Work-Study, institutionally sponsored loans, scholarships/grants, traineeships, and unspecified assistantships also available. Support available to part-time students. Financial award application deadline: 3/1; financial award applicants required to submit FAFSA. In 2010, 119 master's awarded. *Degree program information:* Part-time programs available. Offers accountancy (MSA); business (MA, MBA, MMR, MS, MSA); computer management and information systems (MS); economics and finance (MA, MS); management information systems (MBA); marketing research (MMR); project management (MBA); taxation (MSA). *Application deadline:* For fall admission, 7/22 for domestic students, 6/1 for international students; for spring admission, 12/10 for domestic students, 10/1 for international students. Applications are processed on a rolling basis. *Application fee:* $30. Electronic applications accepted. *Application Contact:* Michelle Robinson, Coordinator of Graduate Recruitment, 618-650-2811, Fax: 618-650-3523, E-mail: michero@siue.edu. *Dean,* Dr. Gary Giamartino, 618-650-3822, E-mail: ggiamar@siue.edu.

School of Education Students: 168 full-time (123 women), 542 part-time (406 women); includes 94 minority (63 Black or African American, non-Hispanic/Latino; 5 Asian, non-Hispanic/Latino; 16 Hispanic/Latino; 10 Two or more races, non-Hispanic/Latino), 8 international. Average age 26. 534 applicants, 44% accepted. *Faculty:* 82 full-time (42 women). Expenses: Contact institution. *Financial support:* In 2010–11, 3 fellowships with full tuition reimbursements (averaging $8,370 per year), 6 research assistantships with full tuition reimbursements (averaging $8,064 per year), 74 teaching assistantships with full tuition reimbursements (averaging $8,064 per year) were awarded; career-related internships or fieldwork, Federal Work-Study, institutionally sponsored loans, scholarships/grants, traineeships, and unspecified assistantships also available. Support available to part-time students. Financial award application deadline: 3/1; financial award applicants required to submit FAFSA. In 2010, 281 master's, 21 other advanced degrees awarded. *Degree program information:* Part-time programs available. Offers art (MS Ed); biology (MS Ed); chemistry (MS Ed); clinical child and school psychology (MS); clinical-adult psychology (MA); curriculum and instruction (MS Ed); earth and space sciences (MS Ed); education (MA, MAT, MS, MS Ed, Ed D, Ed S, Post-Master's Certificate, Postbaccalaureate Certificate, SD); educational administration (MS Ed, Ed S); educational leadership (MS Ed, Ed D, Ed S, Postbaccalaureate Certificate); English/language arts (MS Ed); foreign languages (MS Ed); history (MS Ed); industrial-organizational psychology (MA); instructional technology (MS Ed); kinesiology (MS Ed); learning, culture, and society (MS Ed); literacy education (MS Ed); literacy specialist (Post-Master's Certificate); mathematics (MS Ed); physics (MS Ed); school psychology (SD); secondary education (MS Ed); special education (MS Ed, Post-Master's Certificate); speech-language pathology (MS); teaching (MAT); web-based learning (Postbaccalaureate Certificate). *Application deadline:* For fall admission, 7/22 for domestic students, 6/1 for international students; for spring admission, 12/10 for domestic students, 10/1 for international students. Applications are processed on a rolling basis. *Application fee:* $30. Electronic applications accepted. *Application Contact:* Dr. Bill Searcy, Associate Dean, 618-650-2373, E-mail: lsearcy@siue.edu. *Interim Dean,* Dr. Bette Bergeron, 618-650-3350, E-mail: bberger@siue.edu.

School of Engineering Students: 103 full-time (22 women), 127 part-time (25 women); includes 20 minority (9 Black or African American, non-Hispanic/Latino; 1 American Indian or Alaska Native, non-Hispanic/Latino; 7 Asian, non-Hispanic/Latino; 1 Hispanic/Latino; 2 Two or more races, non-Hispanic/Latino), 119 international. Average age 26. 375 applicants, 65% accepted. *Faculty:* 43 full-time (3 women). Expenses: Contact institution. *Financial support:* In 2010–11, 4 fellowships with full tuition reimbursements (averaging $8,370 per year), 34 research assistantships with full tuition reimbursements (averaging $8,064 per year), 77 teaching assistantships with full tuition reimbursements (averaging $8,064 per year) were awarded; career-related internships or fieldwork, Federal Work-Study, institutionally sponsored loans, scholarships/grants, traineeships, and unspecified assistantships also available. Support available to part-time students. Financial award application deadline: 3/1; financial award applicants required to submit FAFSA. In 2010, 88 master's awarded. *Degree program information:* Part-time programs available. Offers civil engineering (MS); computer science (MS); electrical engineering (MS); engineering (MS); industrial engineering (MS); mechanical engineering (MS). *Application deadline:* For fall admission, 7/22 for domestic students, 6/1 for international students; for spring admission, 12/9 for domestic students, 10/1 for international students. Applications are processed on a rolling basis. *Application fee:* $30. Electronic applications accepted. *Application Contact:* Michelle Robinson, Coordinator of Graduate Recruitment, 618-650-2811, Fax: 618-650-3523, E-mail: michero@siue.edu. *Dean,* Dr. Hasan Sevim, 618-650-2541, E-mail: hsevim@siue.edu.

School of Nursing Students: 72 full-time (45 women), 145 part-time (135 women); includes 21 minority (7 Black or African American, non-Hispanic/Latino; 1 American Indian or Alaska Native, non-Hispanic/Latino; 10 Asian, non-Hispanic/Latino; 1 Hispanic/Latino; 2 Two or more races, non-Hispanic/Latino), 2 international. Average age 26. 131 applicants, 44% accepted. *Faculty:* 28 full-time (26 women). Expenses: Contact institution. *Financial support:* In 2010–11, 2 fellowships with full tuition reimbursements (averaging $8,370 per year), 3 teaching assistantships with full tuition reimbursements (averaging $8,064 per year) were awarded; research assistantships, career-related internships or fieldwork, Federal Work-

Southern Illinois University Edwardsville (continued)

Study, institutionally sponsored loans, scholarships/grants, traineeships, and unspecified assistantships also available. Support available to part-time students. Financial award application deadline: 3/1; financial award applicants required to submit FAFSA. In 2010, 59 master's, 6 other advanced degrees awarded. Offers family nurse practitioner (MS, Post-Master's Certificate); health care and nursing administration (MS, Post-Master's Certificate); nurse anesthesia (MS, Post-Master's Certificate); nurse educator (MS, Post-Master's Certificate); nursing (MS, DNP, Post-Master's Certificate); nursing doctoral practice (DNP). *Application deadline:* For fall admission, 3/1 for domestic and international students. *Application fee:* $30. Electronic applications accepted. *Application Contact:* Dr. Kathy Ketchum, Director, 618-650-3936, E-mail: kketchu@siue.edu. *Dean*, Dr. Marcia Maurer, 618-650-3959, E-mail: mamaure@siue.edu.

School of Dental Medicine Students: 198 full-time (78 women); includes 26 minority (6 Black or African American, non-Hispanic/Latino; 1 American Indian or Alaska Native, non-Hispanic/Latino; 5 Asian, non-Hispanic/Latino; 9 Hispanic/Latino; 2 Native Hawaiian or other Pacific Islander, non-Hispanic/Latino; 3 Two or more races, non-Hispanic/Latino), 1 international. Average age 25. *Faculty:* 20 full-time (2 women). Expenses: Contact institution. *Financial support:* Application deadline: 3/1. In 2010, 44 DMDs awarded. Offers dental medicine (DMD). *Application deadline:* For fall admission, 6/1 priority date for domestic students, 6/1 for international students. *Application fee:* $20. Electronic applications accepted. *Application Contact:* Dr. Ann Boyle, Dean, 618-474-7249, E-mail: sdmapps@siue.edu. *Dean*, Dr. Ann Boyle, 618-474-7249, E-mail: sdmapps@siue.edu.

School of Pharmacy Students: 319 full-time (186 women); includes 37 minority (7 Black or African American, non-Hispanic/Latino; 13 Asian, non-Hispanic/Latino; 13 Hispanic/Latino; 4 Two or more races, non-Hispanic/Latino), 1 international. Average age 26. *Faculty:* 19 full-time (5 women). Expenses: Contact institution. *Financial support:* Career-related internships or fieldwork, Federal Work-Study, institutionally sponsored loans, scholarships/grants, and traineeships available. Support available to part-time students. Financial award application deadline: 3/1; financial award applicants required to submit FAFSA. Offers pharmacy (Pharm D). *Application deadline:* For fall admission, 12/1 for domestic and international students. *Application fee:* $40. Electronic applications accepted. *Application Contact:* Dr. Gireesh V. Gupchup, Dean, 618-650-5150, E-mail: pharmacy@siue.edu. *Dean*, Dr. Gireesh V. Gupchup, 618-650-5150, E-mail: pharmacy@siue.edu.

SOUTHERN METHODIST UNIVERSITY, Dallas, TX 75275

General Information Independent-religious, coed, university. CGS member. *Enrollment:* 10,938 graduate, professional, and undergraduate students; 2,309 full-time matriculated graduate/professional students (931 women), 2,269 part-time matriculated graduate/professional students (1,091 women). *Enrollment by degree level:* 1,132 first professional, 2,885 master's, 500 doctoral, 61 other advanced degrees. *Graduate faculty:* 668 full-time (247 women), 372 part-time/adjunct (152 women). *Graduate housing:* Rooms and/or apartments available on a first-come, first-served basis to single and married students. Housing application deadline: 5/31. *Student services:* Campus employment opportunities, campus safety program, career counseling, child daycare facilities, exercise/wellness program, free psychological counseling, grant writing training, international student services, low-cost health insurance, multicultural affairs office, services for students with disabilities, teacher training. *Library facilities:* Central University Library plus 7 others. *Online resources:* library catalog, web page, access to other libraries' catalogs. *Collection:* 2.8 million titles, 11,701 serial subscriptions, 45,168 audiovisual materials.

Computer facilities: 758 computers available on campus for general student use. A campuswide network can be accessed from student residence rooms and from off campus. Online class registration, online billing/payment processing are available. *Web address:* http://www.smu.edu/.

General Application Contact: Dr. James E. Quick, Associate Vice President for Research and Dean of Graduate Studies, 214-768-4345.

GRADUATE UNITS

Annette Caldwell Simmons School of Education and Human Development Students: 61 full-time (43 women), 794 part-time (668 women); includes 226 minority (87 Black or African American, non-Hispanic/Latino; 10 American Indian or Alaska Native, non-Hispanic/Latino; 29 Asian, non-Hispanic/Latino; 93 Hispanic/Latino; 1 Native Hawaiian or other Pacific Islander, non-Hispanic/Latino; 6 Two or more races, non-Hispanic/Latino), 26 international. Average age 36. *Faculty:* 44 full-time (26 women), 67 part-time/adjunct (43 women). Expenses: Contact institution. In 2010, 251 master's, 2 doctorates, 40 other advanced degrees awarded. Offers bilingual/ESL education (MBE); counseling (MS); dispute resolution (MA, Certificate); education (M Ed, PhD); education and human development (M Ed, MA, MBE, MLS, MS, PhD, Certificate); educational preparation (Certificate); gifted and talented focus (MBE); learning therapist (Certificate); liberal studies (MLS). *Application fee:* $75. *Application Contact:* Associate Vice President for Research and Dean of Graduate Studies. *Dean*, Dr. David J. Chard, 214-768-7587, Fax: 214-768-1797.

Bobby B. Lyle School of Engineering Students: 203 full-time (52 women), 669 part-time (144 women); includes 208 minority (57 Black or African American, non-Hispanic/Latino; 4 American Indian or Alaska Native, non-Hispanic/Latino; 76 Asian, non-Hispanic/Latino; 68 Hispanic/Latino; 2 Native Hawaiian or other Pacific Islander, non-Hispanic/Latino; 1 Two or more races, non-Hispanic/Latino), 216 international. Average age 32. 672 applicants, 54% accepted, 226 enrolled. *Faculty:* 55 full-time (10 women), 61 part-time/adjunct (5 women). Expenses: Contact institution. *Financial support:* In 2010–11, 72 students received support, including 35 research assistantships with full tuition reimbursements available (averaging $16,800 per year), 33 teaching assistantships with full tuition reimbursements available (averaging $12,600 per year); fellowships, career-related internships or fieldwork, Federal Work-Study, institutionally sponsored loans, scholarships/grants, and tuition waivers (full and partial) also available. Financial award applicants required to submit FAFSA. In 2010, 315 master's, 16 doctorates awarded. *Degree program information:* Part-time and evening/weekend programs available. Postbaccalaureate distance learning degree programs offered (no on-campus study). Offers applied science (MS, PhD); civil and environmental engineering (PhD); civil engineering (MS); computer engineering (MS Cp E, PhD); computer science (MS, PhD); electrical engineering (MSEE, PhD); electronic and optical packaging (MS); engineering (MS, MS Cp E, MSEE, MSEM, MSIEM, MSME, DE, PhD); engineering management (MSEM, DE); environmental engineering (MS); environmental science (MS); information engineering and management (MSIEM); manufacturing systems management (MS); mechanical engineering (MSME, PhD); operations research (MS, PhD); security engineering (MS); software engineering (MS); systems engineering (MS, PhD); telecommunications (MS). *Application deadline:* For fall admission, 7/1 for domestic students, 5/15 for international students; for spring admission, 11/15 for domestic students, 9/1 for international students. Applications are processed on a rolling basis. *Application fee:* $75. *Application Contact:* Marc Valerin, Director of Graduate and Executive Admissions, 214-768-3042, E-mail: valerin@engr.smu.edu. *Dean*, Dr. Geoffrey Orsak, 214-768-3050, Fax: 214-768-3845.

Cox School of Business Students: 359 full-time (116 women), 592 part-time (154 women); includes 215 minority (44 Black or African American, non-Hispanic/Latino; 10 American Indian or Alaska Native, non-Hispanic/Latino; 118 Asian, non-Hispanic/Latino; 39 Hispanic/Latino; 2 Native Hawaiian or other Pacific Islander, non-Hispanic/Latino; 2 Two or more races, non-Hispanic/Latino), 92 international. Average age 30. *Faculty:* 59 full-time (13 women), 30 part-time/adjunct (7 women). Expenses: Contact institution. *Financial support:* Research assistantships available. Financial award application deadline: 3/1; financial award applicants required to submit FAFSA. In 2010, 486 master's awarded. *Degree program information:* Part-time and evening/weekend programs available. Offers accounting (MBA, MSA); business (Exec MBA); business administration (MBA); entrepreneurship (MS); finance (MBA); financial consulting (MBA); general business (MBA); information technology and operations management (MBA); management (MBA, MSM); marketing (MBA); real estate (MBA); strategy and entrepreneurship (MBA). *Application deadline:* Applications are processed on a rolling basis. Electronic applications accepted. *Application Contact:* Patti Cudney, Director of MBA Admissions, 214-768-3001, Fax: 214-768-3956, E-mail: pcudney@cox.smu.edu. *Dean*, Dr. Albert W. Niemi, 214-768-3012, Fax: 214-768-3713, E-mail: aniemi@mail.cox.smu.edu.

Dedman College Students: 188 full-time (91 women), 165 part-time (82 women); includes 6 Black or African American, non-Hispanic/Latino; 3 American Indian or Alaska Native, non-Hispanic/Latino; 16 Asian, non-Hispanic/Latino; 22 Hispanic/Latino; 1 Two or more races, non-Hispanic/Latino, 103 international. Average age 29. 555 applicants, 37% accepted, 90 enrolled. *Faculty:* 195 full-time (69 women), 66 part-time/adjunct (42 women). Expenses: Contact institution. *Financial support:* In 2010–11, 194 students received support, including research assistantships with full tuition reimbursements available (averaging $16,000 per year), teaching assistantships with full tuition reimbursements available (averaging $16,000 per year); fellowships, career-related internships or fieldwork, Federal Work-Study, institutionally sponsored loans, scholarships/grants, tuition waivers (full and partial), and unspecified assistantships also available. Support available to part-time students. Financial award applicants required to submit FAFSA. In 2010, 61 master's, 34 doctorates awarded. *Degree program information:* Part-time and evening/weekend programs available. Offers anthropology (PhD); applied economics (MA); applied geophysics (MS); biological sciences (MA, MS, PhD); chemistry (MS, PhD); clinical psychology (PhD); computational and applied mathematics (MS, PhD); economics (MA, PhD); English (MA, PhD); geology (MS, PhD); geophysics (MS, PhD); history (MA, PhD); medical anthropology (MA); medieval studies (MA); physics (MS, PhD); religious studies (MA, PhD); statistical science (MS, PhD). *Application deadline:* For fall admission, 2/1 priority date for domestic and international students; for winter admission, 11/30 priority date for domestic and international students. Applications are processed on a rolling basis. *Application fee:* $75. Electronic applications accepted. *Application Contact:* Barbara Phillips, Assistant Dean, 214-768-4202, Fax: 214-768-4235, E-mail: bphillips@smu.edu. *Dean*, Dr. William Tsutsui, 214-768-4485.

Dedman School of Law Students: 963 full-time (433 women), 58 part-time (26 women); includes 50 Black or African American, non-Hispanic/Latino; 12 American Indian or Alaska Native, non-Hispanic/Latino; 76 Asian, non-Hispanic/Latino; 80 Hispanic/Latino; 1 Two or more races, non-Hispanic/Latino, 79 international. Average age 27. 3,015 applicants, 26% accepted, 309 enrolled. *Faculty:* 40 full-time (17 women), 50 part-time/adjunct (11 women). Expenses: Contact institution. *Financial support:* Career-related internships or fieldwork, Federal Work-Study, and scholarships/grants available. Financial award application deadline: 2/15; financial award applicants required to submit FAFSA. In 2010, 270 first professional degrees, 58 master's awarded. *Degree program information:* Part-time and evening/weekend programs available. Offers foreign law school graduates (LL M); law (JD, SJD); law-general (LL M); taxation (LL M). *Application deadline:* For fall admission, 2/15 priority date for domestic students. Applications are processed on a rolling basis. *Application fee:* $75. Electronic applications accepted. *Application Contact:* Virginia Keehan, Assistant Dean for Admissions, 214-768-2550, Fax: 214-768-2549, E-mail: lawadmit@smu.edu. *Dean*, John B. Attanasio, 214-768-8999, Fax: 214-768-2182, E-mail: jba@mail.smu.edu.

Meadows School of the Arts Students: 120 full-time (82 women), 104 part-time (54 women); includes 42 minority (14 Black or African American, non-Hispanic/Latino; 1 American Indian or Alaska Native, non-Hispanic/Latino; 5 Asian, non-Hispanic/Latino; 17 Hispanic/Latino; 3 Native Hawaiian or other Pacific Islander, non-Hispanic/Latino; 2 Two or more races, non-Hispanic/Latino), 36 international. Average age 27. 219 applicants, 62% accepted, 89 enrolled. *Faculty:* 112 full-time (46 women), 63 part-time/adjunct (28 women). Expenses: Contact institution. *Financial support:* In 2010–11, 138 students received support, including 136 teaching assistantships (averaging $4,400 per year); research assistantships, scholarships/grants and unspecified assistantships also available. Financial award application deadline: 3/1; financial award applicants required to submit FAFSA. In 2010, 79 master's, 9 other advanced degrees awarded. *Degree program information:* Evening/weekend programs available. Offers acting (MFA); advertising (MA); art history (MA); arts (MA, MFA, MM, MSM, Diploma); arts administrationcinema and television (MA, MFA); communication arts (MA); conducting (MM); dance (MFA); design (MFA); music composition (MM); music education (MM); music history (MM); music theory (MM); performance (MM); piano performance and pedagogy (MM); sacred music (MSM); studio art (MFA). *Application deadline:* For fall admission, 2/15 for domestic students; for spring admission, 11/1 for domestic students. *Application fee:* $75. Electronic applications accepted. *Application Contact:* Joe S. Hoselton, Graduate Admissions and Records Coordinator, 214-768-3765, Fax: 214-768-3272, E-mail: hoselton@smu.edu. *Dean*, Jose Antonio Bowen, 214-768-2880.

Perkins School of Theology Students: 180 full-time (91 women), 173 part-time (89 women); includes 92 minority (64 Black or African American, non-Hispanic/Latino; 1 American Indian or Alaska Native, non-Hispanic/Latino; 6 Asian, non-Hispanic/Latino; 18 Hispanic/Latino; 1 Native Hawaiian or other Pacific Islander, non-Hispanic/Latino; 2 Two or more races, non-Hispanic/Latino), 17 international. Average age 39. 162 applicants, 80% accepted, 92 enrolled. *Faculty:* 27 full-time (11 women), 8 part-time/adjunct (4 women). Expenses: Contact institution. *Financial support:* In 2010–11, 188 students received support, including 3 fellowships with full tuition reimbursements available (averaging $5,000 per year); career-related internships or fieldwork, Federal Work-Study, scholarships/grants, and minister's family tuition awards also available. Support available to part-time students. Financial award application deadline: 3/1; financial award applicants required to submit FAFSA. In 2010, 56 M Divs, 25 master's, 4 doctorates awarded. *Degree program information:* Part-time programs available. Offers theology (M Div, CMM, MSM, MTS, D Min). *Application deadline:* For fall admission, 5/1 for domestic students, 12/15 for international students; for spring admission, 11/1 for domestic students. Applications are processed on a rolling basis. *Application fee:* $50. *Application Contact:* Rev. Herbert S. Coleman, Director, Recruitment and Admissions, 214-768-2139, Fax: 214-768-4245, E-mail: theology@smu.edu. *Dean*, Dr. William B. Lawrence, 214-768-2534, Fax: 214-768-2966.

SOUTHERN NAZARENE UNIVERSITY, Bethany, OK 73008

General Information Independent-religious, coed, comprehensive institution. *Enrollment:* 2,051 graduate, professional, and undergraduate students; 432 full-time matriculated graduate/professional students (255 women), 11 part-time matriculated graduate/professional students (6 women). *Enrollment by degree level:* 443 master's. *Tuition:* Part-time $575 per credit hour. *Graduate housing:* Rooms and/or apartments available on a first-come, first-served basis to single and married students. Housing application deadline: 8/1. *Student services:* Campus employment opportunities, campus safety program, career counseling, international student services, low-cost health insurance, multicultural affairs office, services for students with disabilities. *Library facilities:* R. T. Williams Learning Resources Center. *Online resources:* library catalog, web page. *Collection:* 101,117 titles, 41,048 serial subscriptions, 8,033 audiovisual materials.

Computer facilities: Computer purchase and lease plans are available. 120 computers available on campus for general student use. A campuswide network can be accessed from student residence rooms and from off campus. *Web address:* http://www.snu.edu/.

General Application Contact: Dr. W. Davis Berryman, Dean of Graduate College, 405-491-6316, Fax: 405-491-6302, E-mail: dberryma@snu.edu.

GRADUATE UNITS

Graduate College *Degree program information:* Part-time and evening/weekend programs available. Offers theology (MA). Electronic applications accepted.

School of Business *Degree program information:* Part-time and evening/weekend programs available. Offers business (MBA, MS Mgt). Electronic applications accepted.

School of Education *Degree program information:* Part-time and evening/weekend programs available. Offers curriculum and instruction (MA); educational leadership (MA).

School of Nursing *Degree program information:* Part-time and evening/weekend programs available. Offers nursing education (MS); nursing leadership (MS).

School of Psychology Offers counseling psychology (MSCP); marriage and family therapy (MA).

SOUTHERN NEW HAMPSHIRE UNIVERSITY, Manchester, NH 03106-1045

General Information Independent, coed, comprehensive institution. *Graduate housing:* Room and/or apartments available on a first-come, first-served basis to single students; on-campus housing not available to married students.

GRADUATE UNITS

School of Business *Degree program information:* Part-time and evening/weekend programs available. Postbaccalaureate distance learning degree programs offered (no on-campus study). Offers accounting (MS); business administration (MBA, Certificate); finance (MS); hospitality and tourism leadership (Certificate); information technology (MS, Certificate); information technology/international business (Certificate); integrated marketing communications (Certificate); international business (MS, DBA); marketing (MS); operations and project management (MS); organizational leadership (MS); project management (Certificate); sport management (MS). Electronic applications accepted.

School of Community Economic Development *Degree program information:* Part-time and evening/weekend programs available. Offers community economic development (MA, MBA, MS, PhD). Electronic applications accepted.

School of Education *Degree program information:* Part-time and evening/weekend programs available. Postbaccalaureate distance learning degree programs offered (no on-campus study). Offers business education (MS); child development (M Ed); computer technology education (Certificate); curriculum and instruction (M Ed); education (M Ed, CAS); elementary education (M Ed); general special education (Certificate); school business administrator (Certificate); secondary education (M Ed); training and development (Certificate). Electronic applications accepted.

School of Liberal Arts *Degree program information:* Part-time and evening/weekend programs available. Offers clinical services for adults psychiatric disabilities (Certificate); clinical services for children and adolescents with psychiatric disabilities (Certificate); clinical services for persons with co-occurring substance abuse and psychiatric disabilities (Certificate); community mental health (MS); fiction writing (MFA); non-fiction writing (MFA); teaching English as a foreign language (MS). Electronic applications accepted.

SOUTHERN OREGON UNIVERSITY, Ashland, OR 97520

General Information State-supported, coed, comprehensive institution. *Enrollment:* 6,512 graduate, professional, and undergraduate students; 218 full-time matriculated graduate/professional students (143 women), 214 part-time matriculated graduate/professional students (124 women). *Enrollment by degree level:* 432 master's. *Graduate faculty:* 186 full-time (76 women), 152 part-time/adjunct (78 women). Tuition, state resident: full-time $9450; part-time $350 per credit. Tuition, nonresident: full-time $15,000; part-time $350 per credit. *Required fees:* $400 per quarter. *Graduate housing:* Rooms and/or apartments available on a first-come, first-served basis to single and married students. Typical cost: $8508 (including board) for single students; $7980 per year for married students. *Student services:* Campus employment opportunities, campus safety program, career counseling, child daycare facilities, exercise/wellness program, free psychological counseling, international student services, low-cost health insurance, multicultural affairs office, services for students with disabilities, teacher training, writing training. *Library facilities:* Lenn and Dixie Hannon Library. *Online resources:* library catalog, web page, access to other libraries' catalogs. *Collection:* 315,000 titles, 1,949 serial subscriptions, 7,800 audiovisual materials. *Research affiliation:* U. S. Forest Service (biology, ecology studies), U. S. Fish and Wildlife Service (forensics), Oregon Shakespeare Festival, Crater Lake National Park (scientific studies), Bureau of Land Management (ecological studies), Bear Creek Corporation (environmental studies).

Computer facilities: 750 computers available on campus for general student use. A campuswide network can be accessed from student residence rooms and from off campus. Online class registration is available. *Web address:* http://www.sou.edu/.

General Application Contact: Mark Bottorff, Director of Admissions, 541-552-6411, Fax: 541-552-8403, E-mail: admissions@sou.edu.

GRADUATE UNITS

Graduate Studies Students: 238 full-time (162 women), 220 part-time (125 women); includes 62 minority (7 Black or African American, non-Hispanic/Latino; 7 American Indian or Alaska Native, non-Hispanic/Latino; 11 Asian, non-Hispanic/Latino; 23 Hispanic/Latino; 4 Native Hawaiian or other Pacific Islander, non-Hispanic/Latino; 10 Two or more races, non-Hispanic/Latino), 25 international. Average age 36. 382 applicants, 66% accepted, 227 enrolled. *Faculty:* 205 full-time (79 women), 48 part-time/adjunct (24 women). Expenses: Contact institution. *Financial support:* Career-related internships or fieldwork, Federal Work-Study, institutionally sponsored loans, scholarships/grants, and unspecified assistantships available. Support available to part-time students. In 2010, 231 master's awarded. *Degree program information:* Part-time programs available. Postbaccalaureate distance learning degree programs offered (minimal on-campus study). Offers environmental education (MS). *Application deadline:* Applications are processed on a rolling basis. *Application fee:* $50. Electronic applications accepted. *Application Contact:* Mark Bottorff, Director of Admissions, 541-552-6411, Fax: 541-552-8403, E-mail: admissions@sou.edu. *Dean*, Dr. Sue Walsh, 541-552-6122, E-mail: walsh@sou.edu.

College of Arts and Sciences Students: 64 full-time (45 women), 16 part-time (6 women); includes 9 minority (1 Black or African American, non-Hispanic/Latino; 4 Asian, non-Hispanic/Latino; 4 Hispanic/Latino), 2 international. Average age 35. 92 applicants, 48% accepted, 33 enrolled. *Faculty:* 144 full-time (55 women), 27 part-time/adjunct (11 women). Expenses: Contact institution. In 2010, 57 master's awarded. *Degree program information:* Part-time programs available. Postbaccalaureate distance learning degree programs offered (no on-campus study). Offers applied computer science (PSM); arts and sciences (MA, MAP, MIS, MS, PSM); interdisciplinary studies (MIS); mental health counseling (MAP); Spanish language teaching (MA). *Application deadline:* Applications are processed on a rolling basis. *Application fee:* $50. *Application Contact:* Mark Bottorff, Director of Admissions, 541-552-6411, Fax: 541-552-8403, E-mail: admissions@sou.edu. *Dean*, Dr. Alissa Arp, 541-552-6424, E-mail: cas@sou.edu.

School of Business Students: 36 full-time (14 women), 99 part-time (41 women); includes 14 minority (2 Black or African American, non-Hispanic/Latino; 2 American Indian or Alaska Native, non-Hispanic/Latino; 3 Asian, non-Hispanic/Latino; 3 Hispanic/Latino; 2 Native Hawaiian or other Pacific Islander, non-Hispanic/Latino; 2 Two or more races, non-Hispanic/Latino), 20 international. Average age 36. 106 applicants, 82% accepted, 81 enrolled. *Faculty:* 15 full-time (4 women), 5 part-time/adjunct (1 woman). Expenses: Contact institution. *Financial support:* Career-related internships or fieldwork, Federal Work-Study, institutionally sponsored loans, scholarships/grants, and unspecified assistantships available. Support available to part-time students. In 2010, 43 master's awarded. *Degree program information:* Part-time and evening/weekend programs available. Postbaccalaureate distance learning degree programs offered (minimal on-campus study). Offers business (MBA, MIM). *Application deadline:* Applications are processed on a rolling basis. *Application fee:* $50. Electronic applications accepted. *Application Contact:* Mark Bottorff, Director of Admissions, 541-552-6411, Fax: 541-552-8403, E-mail: admissions@sou.edu. *Dean*, Rajeev Parikh, 541-552-6483, E-mail: parikhr@sou.edu.

School of Education Students: 101 full-time (74 women), 95 part-time (67 women); includes 23 minority (1 Black or African American, non-Hispanic/Latino; 4 American Indian or Alaska Native, non-Hispanic/Latino; 3 Asian, non-Hispanic/Latino; 6 Hispanic/Latino; 2 Native Hawaiian or other Pacific Islander, non-Hispanic/Latino; 7 Two or more races, non-Hispanic/Latino), 2 international. Average age 35. 164 applicants, 63% accepted, 95 enrolled. *Faculty:* 16 full-time (8 women), 10 part-time/adjunct (all women). Expenses: Contact institution. In 2010, 147 master's awarded. Offers elementary education (MA Ed, MS Ed); secondary education (MA Ed, MS Ed); teaching (MAT). *Application deadline:* For fall admission, 2/1 for domestic students. *Application fee:* $50. Electronic applications accepted. *Application Contact:* Mark Bottorff, Director of Admissions, 541-552-6411, Fax: 541-552-8403, E-mail: admissions@sou.edu. *Dean*, Dr. Geoff Mills, 541-552-6920, E-mail: mills@sou.edu.

SOUTHERN POLYTECHNIC STATE UNIVERSITY, Marietta, GA 30060-2896

General Information State-supported, coed, comprehensive institution. *Enrollment:* 5,514 graduate, professional, and undergraduate students; 270 full-time matriculated graduate/professional students (110 women), 432 part-time matriculated graduate/professional students (170 women). *Enrollment by degree level:* 633 master's, 69 other advanced degrees. *Graduate faculty:* 52 full-time (13 women), 25 part-time/adjunct (11 women). Tuition, state resident: full-time $3690; part-time $205 per semester hour. Tuition, nonresident: full-time $13,428; part-time $746 per semester hour. *Required fees:* $598 per semester. *Graduate housing:* Room and/or apartments available on a first-come, first-served basis to single students; on-campus housing not available to married students. Typical cost: $3650 per year ($6604 including board). Housing application deadline: 8/1. *Student services:* Campus employment opportunities, campus safety program, career counseling, exercise/wellness program, free psychological counseling, international student services, low-cost health insurance, multicultural affairs office, services for students with disabilities. *Library facilities:* Lawrence V. Johnson Library. *Online resources:* library catalog, web page, access to other libraries' catalogs. *Collection:* 129,954 titles, 994 serial subscriptions, 330 audiovisual materials. *Research affiliation:* Cyber Object (information technology), Eagle Hospital Physician's Group (health care information technology), Technical Laboratory Associates, Inc. (engineering design), Siemens Corporation (mechatronics engineering), PowerBlock Industrial Supplies, Inc. (construction safety), Intercontinental Hotel Group (usability testing).

Computer facilities: 1,400 computers available on campus for general student use. A campuswide network can be accessed from student residence rooms and from off campus. Online class registration is available. *Web address:* http://www.spsu.edu/.

General Application Contact: Nikki Palamiotis, Director of Graduate Studies, 678-915-4276, Fax: 678-915-7292, E-mail: npalamio@spsu.edu.

GRADUATE UNITS

Division of Engineering Students: 8 full-time (0 women), 42 part-time (9 women); includes 12 Black or African American, non-Hispanic/Latino; 2 Asian, non-Hispanic/Latino; 3 Hispanic/Latino, 2 international. Average age 39. 15 applicants, 93% accepted, 11 enrolled. *Faculty:* 3 full-time (1 woman), 4 part-time/adjunct (3 women). Expenses: Contact institution. In 2010, 12 master's awarded. *Degree program information:* Part-time and evening/weekend programs available. Offers systems engineering (MS, Advanced Certificate, Graduate Certificate). *Application deadline:* For fall admission, 7/1 priority date for domestic students, 5/1 priority date for international students; for spring admission, 11/1 priority date for domestic students, 9/1 priority date for international students. Applications are processed on a rolling basis. *Application fee:* $20. Electronic applications accepted. *Application Contact:* Nikki Palamiotis, Director of Graduate Studies, 678-915-4276, Fax: 678-915-7292, E-mail: npalamio@spsu.edu. *Associate Dean*, Dr. Tom Currin, 678-915-7482, Fax: 678-915-5527, E-mail: tcurrin@spsu.edu.

School of Architecture, Civil Engineering Technology and Construction Students: 24 full-time (6 women), 7 part-time (0 women); includes 10 Black or African American, non-Hispanic/Latino; 1 Hispanic/Latino, 5 international. Average age 35. 21 applicants, 76% accepted, 9 enrolled. *Faculty:* 8 full-time (1 woman), 2 part-time/adjunct (0 women). Expenses: Contact institution. *Financial support:* Research assistantships with tuition reimbursements, career-related internships or fieldwork, scholarships/grants, and unspecified assistantships available. Support available to part-time students. Financial award application deadline: 5/1; financial award applicants required to submit FAFSA. In 2010, 15 master's awarded. *Degree program information:* Part-time and evening/weekend programs available. Offers architecture, civil engineering technology and construction (MS); construction management (MS). *Application deadline:* For fall admission, 7/1 priority date for domestic students, 5/1 priority date for international students; for spring admission, 11/1 priority date for domestic students, 9/1 priority date for international students. Applications are processed on a rolling basis. *Application fee:* $20. Electronic applications accepted. *Application Contact:* Nikki Palamiotis, Director of Graduate Studies, 678-915-4276, Fax: 678-915-7292, E-mail: npalamio@spsu.edu. *Dean*, Dr. Wilson Barnes, 678-915-5481, Fax: 678-915-3945, E-mail: wbarnes@spsu.edu.

School of Arts and Sciences Students: 2 full-time (both women), 61 part-time (40 women); includes 19 Black or African American, non-Hispanic/Latino; 1 Two or more races, non-Hispanic/Latino, 3 international. Average age 38. 37 applicants, 100% accepted, 29 enrolled. *Faculty:* 4 full-time (3 women), 1 (woman) part-time/adjunct. Expenses: Contact institution. *Financial support:* Research assistantships with tuition reimbursements, teaching assistantships with tuition reimbursements, career-related internships or fieldwork, Federal Work-Study, scholarships/grants, and unspecified assistantships available. Support available to part-time students. Financial award application deadline: 5/1; financial award applicants required to submit FAFSA. In 2010, 6 master's, 5 other advanced degrees awarded. *Degree program information:* Part-time and evening/weekend programs available. Postbaccalaureate distance learning degree programs offered (no on-campus study). Offers arts and sciences (MS, MSIID, AGC, Graduate Certificate); communications management (AGC); content development (AGC); information and instructional design (MSIID); information design and communication (MS); instructional design (AGC); technical communication (Graduate Certificate); visual communication and graphics (AGC). *Application deadline:* For fall admission, 7/1 priority date for domestic students, 5/1 priority date for international students; for spring admission, 11/1 priority date for domestic students, 9/1 priority date for international students. Applications are processed on a rolling basis. *Application fee:* $20. Electronic applications accepted. *Application Contact:* Nikki Palamiotis, Director of Graduate Studies, 678-915-4276, Fax: 678-915-7292, E-mail: npalamio@spsu.edu. *Dean*, Dr. Alan Gabrielli, 678-915-7464, Fax: 678-915-7292, E-mail: agabriel@spsu.edu.

School of Computing and Software Engineering Students: 119 full-time (43 women), 134 part-time (37 women); includes 71 Black or African American, non-Hispanic/Latino; 24 Asian, non-Hispanic/Latino; 6 Hispanic/Latino; 2 Two or more races, non-Hispanic/Latino, 65 international. Average age 33. 167 applicants, 91% accepted, 86 enrolled. *Faculty:* 19 full-time (4 women), 6 part-time/adjunct (1 woman). Expenses: Contact institution. *Financial support:* Research assistantships with tuition reimbursements, teaching assistantships with tuition reimbursements, career-related internships or fieldwork, scholarships/grants, and unspecified assistantships available. Support available to part-time students. Financial award application deadline: 5/1; financial award applicants required to submit FAFSA. In 2010, 59 master's, 6 other advanced degrees awarded. *Degree program information:* Part-time and evening/weekend programs available. Postbaccalaureate distance learning degree programs offered. Offers business continuity (Graduate Certificate); computer science (MS, Graduate Certificate, Graduate Transition Certificate); computing and software engineering (MS, MSIT, MSSWE, Graduate Certificate, Graduate Transition Certificate); information security and assurance (Graduate Certificate); information technology (MSIT, Graduate Certificate, Graduate Transition Certificate); software engineering (MSSWE, Graduate Certificate). *Application deadline:* For fall admission, 7/1 priority date for domestic students, 5/1 priority date for international students; for spring admission, 11/1 priority date for domestic students, 9/1 priority date for international students. Applications are processed on a rolling basis. *Application fee:* $20. Electronic applications accepted. *Application Contact:* Nikki Palamiotis, Director of Graduate Studies, 678-915-4276, Fax: 678-915-7292, E-mail: npalamio@spsu.edu. *Dean*, Dr. Han Reichgelt, 678-915-7399, Fax: 678-915-5577, E-mail: hreichge@spsu.edu.

School of Engineering Technology and Management Students: 117 full-time (59 women), 188 part-time (84 women); includes 91 Black or African American, non-Hispanic/Latino; 26 Asian, non-Hispanic/Latino; 9 Hispanic/Latino; 2 Two or more races, non-Hispanic/Latino, 62 international. Average age 34. 173 applicants, 93% accepted, 119 enrolled. *Faculty:* 18 full-time (4 women), 12 part-time/adjunct (6 women). Expenses: Contact institution. *Financial support:* Research assistantships with tuition reimbursements, teaching assistantships with tuition reimbursements, career-related internships or fieldwork, scholarships/grants, and unspecified assistantships available. Support available to part-time students. Financial award application deadline: 5/1; financial award applicants required to submit FAFSA. In 2010, 91 master's, 1 other advanced degree awarded. *Degree program information:* Part-time and evening/weekend programs available. Postbaccalaureate distance learning degree programs offered. Offers accounting (MSA); business administration (MBA, Graduate Transition Certificate); engineering technology and management (MBA, MS, MSA, Graduate Certificate, Graduate Transition Certificate); engineering technology/electrical (MS); quality assurance (MS, Graduate Certificate). *Application deadline:* For fall admission, 7/1 priority date for domestic students, 5/1 priority date for international students; for spring admission, 11/1 priority date for domestic students, 9/1 priority date for international students. Applications are processed on a rolling basis. *Application fee:* $20. Electronic applications accepted. *Applica-*

Southern Polytechnic State University (continued)

tion Contact: Nikki Palamiotis, Director of Graduate Studies, 678-915-4276, Fax: 678-915-7292, E-mail: npalamio@spsu.edu. *Dean,* Dr. Jeff Ray, 678-915-7205, Fax: 678-915-7134, E-mail: jray@spsu.edu.

SOUTHERN UNIVERSITY AND AGRICULTURAL AND MECHANICAL COLLEGE, Baton Rouge, LA 70813

General Information State-supported, coed, university. CGS member. *Graduate housing:* Room and/or apartments available on a first-come, first-served basis to single students; on-campus housing not available to married students. Housing application deadline: 6/30. *Research affiliation:* Livingston Observatory (gravitational waves, cosmic gravity waves, black waves), National Aeronautics and Space Administration (NASA) (mechanical engineering), Michigan State University (language screening of African-Americans), University of Georgia at Athens (substance abuse prevention), University of Alabama (diabetes), National Aeronautics and Space Administration (NASA) (drinking water remote sensing).

GRADUATE UNITS

College of Business Offers business (MBA).

Graduate School *Degree program information:* Part-time programs available. Offers science/mathematics education (PhD); special education (M Ed, PhD).

College of Agricultural, Family and Consumer Sciences Offers urban forestry (MS).

College of Arts and Humanities Offers arts and humanities (MA); mass communications (MA); social sciences (MA).

College of Education Offers administration and supervision (M Ed); counselor education (MA); education (M Ed, MA, MS, PhD); educational leadership (M Ed); elementary education (M Ed); media (M Ed); mental health counseling (MA); secondary education (M Ed); therapeutic recreation (MS).

College of Engineering Offers engineering (ME).

College of Sciences *Degree program information:* Part-time programs available. Offers analytical chemistry (MS); biochemistry (MS); biology (MS); environmental sciences (MS); information systems (MS); inorganic chemistry (MS); mathematics (MS); micro/minicomputer architecture (MS); operating systems (MS); organic chemistry (MS); physical chemistry (MS); physics (MS); rehabilitation counseling (MS); sciences (MA, MS).

Nelson Mandela School of Public Policy and Urban Affairs Offers criminal justice (MS); public administration (MPA); public policy (PhD); public policy and urban affairs (MA, MPA, MS, PhD); social sciences (MA).

School of Nursing *Degree program information:* Part-time programs available. Offers educator/administrator (PhD); family health nursing (MSN); family nurse practitioner (Post Master's Certificate); geriatric nurse practitioner/gerontology (PhD).

Southern University Law Center *Degree program information:* Part-time and evening/weekend programs available. Offers law (JD). Electronic applications accepted.

SOUTHERN UNIVERSITY AT NEW ORLEANS, New Orleans, LA 70126-1009

General Information State-supported, coed, primarily women, comprehensive institution. *Graduate housing:* On-campus housing not available.

GRADUATE UNITS

School of Social Work *Degree program information:* Part-time and evening/weekend programs available. Offers social work (MSW).

SOUTHERN UTAH UNIVERSITY, Cedar City, UT 84720-2498

General Information State-supported, coed, comprehensive institution. *Enrollment:* 8,019 graduate, professional, and undergraduate students; 89 full-time matriculated graduate/professional students (22 women), 699 part-time matriculated graduate/professional students (409 women). *Enrollment by degree level:* 788 master's. *Graduate faculty:* 46 full-time (9 women), 10 part-time/adjunct (3 women). *Graduate housing:* Room and/or apartments available on a first-come, first-served basis to single students; on-campus housing not available to married students. *Student services:* Campus employment opportunities, campus safety program, career counseling, exercise/wellness program, free psychological counseling, international student services, low-cost health insurance, multicultural affairs office, services for students with disabilities, teacher training. *Library facilities:* Southern Utah University Library. *Online resources:* library catalog, web page, access to other libraries' catalogs.

Computer facilities: A campuswide network can be accessed from student residence rooms and from off campus. *Web address:* http://www.suu.edu/.

General Application Contact: Nicole Funderburk, Graduate Recruitment Coordinator, 435-865-8602, Fax: 435-865-8223, E-mail: funderburk@suu.edu.

GRADUATE UNITS

College of Education Average age 39. Expenses: Contact institution. *Financial support:* Scholarships/grants available. In 2010, 222 master's awarded. *Degree program information:* Part-time programs available. Offers education (M Ed, MS); sports conditioning (MS). *Application Contact:* Suzanne Brinkerhoff, Administrative Assistant, 435-865-8320, Fax: 435-865-8046, E-mail: brinkerhoffs@suu.edu. *Dean,* Dr. David Lund, 435-586-7803, Fax: 435-865-8485, E-mail: lundd@suu.edu.

College of Humanities and Social Sciences Expenses: Contact institution. In 2010, 20 master's awarded. Offers communication (MA); humanities and social sciences (MA, MS); public administration (MS). *Application Contact:* Kristine Frost, Administrative Assistant, 435-586-7898, Fax: 435-586-7813, E-mail: frost@suu.edu. *Dean,* Dr. James McDonald, 435-586-7898, Fax: 435-865-8193, E-mail: mcdonaldj@suu.edu.

College of Performing and Visual Arts Expenses: Contact institution. In 2010, 6 master's awarded. Offers arts administration (MFA); performing and visual arts (MFA). *Application Contact:* Matt Neves, Director, 435-586-7873, Fax: 435-865-8657, E-mail: neves@suu.edu. *Interim Dean,* Shauna Mendini, 435-865-8554, Fax: 435-865-8580, E-mail: mendini_s@suu.edu.

College of Science Expenses: Contact institution. In 2010, 4 master's awarded. Offers forensic science (MS); science (MS). *Application Contact:* Barbara Rodriguez, Administrative Assistant, 435-586-7920, Fax: 435-865-8550, E-mail: rodriguez@suu.edu. *Dean,* Dr. Robert Eves, 435-586-7920, Fax: 435-865-8550, E-mail: eves@suu.edu.

School of Business Expenses: Contact institution. *Financial support:* Career-related internships or fieldwork, institutionally sponsored loans, tuition waivers (full and partial), and unspecified assistantships available. In 2010, 101 master's awarded. *Degree program information:* Part-time programs available. Offers accounting (M Acc); business (M Acc, MBA); business administration (MBA). *Application deadline:* For fall admission, 8/1 priority date for domestic students. Applications are processed on a rolling basis. *Application Contact:* Vicki Meier, Administrative Assistant, 435-586-5401, Fax: 435-586-5493, E-mail: meier@suu.edu. *Dean,* Dr. Carl Templin, 435-586-7704, Fax: 435-586-5475, E-mail: templin@suu.edu.

SOUTHERN WESLEYAN UNIVERSITY, Central, SC 29630-1020

General Information Independent-religious, coed, comprehensive institution. *Enrollment:* 1,883 graduate, professional, and undergraduate students; 423 full-time matriculated graduate/professional students (281 women). *Enrollment by degree level:* 423 master's. *Graduate faculty:* 17 full-time (6 women), 38 part-time/adjunct (14 women). *Tuition:* Full-time $8925; part-time $425 per credit hour. *Required fees:* $1659; $230 per course. *Graduate housing:* On-campus housing not available. *Student services:* Career counseling, free psychological counseling, services for students with disabilities, writing training. *Library facilities:* Rickman Library. *Online resources:* library catalog, web page, access to other libraries' catalogs. *Collection:* 116,475 titles, 278 serial subscriptions, 5,730 audiovisual materials.

Computer facilities: 95 computers available on campus for general student use. A campuswide network can be accessed from student residence rooms and from off campus. Online class registration is available. *Web address:* http://www.swu.edu/.

General Application Contact: Corrie Creasman, Enrollment Services Coordinator, 877-644-5577, Fax: 864-644-5972, E-mail: ccreasman@swu.edu.

GRADUATE UNITS

Program in Business Administration Students: 197 full-time (92 women); includes 78 minority (71 Black or African American, non-Hispanic/Latino; 1 American Indian or Alaska Native, non-Hispanic/Latino; 2 Asian, non-Hispanic/Latino; 4 Hispanic/Latino), 1 international. Average age 39. 37 applicants, 86% accepted, 16 enrolled. *Faculty:* 6 full-time (1 woman), 13 part-time/adjunct (3 women). Expenses: Contact institution. In 2010, 67 master's awarded. *Degree program information:* Evening/weekend programs available. Offers business administration (MBA). *Application deadline:* Applications are processed on a rolling basis. *Application fee:* $50. *Application Contact:* Corrie Creasman, Enrollment Services Coordinator, 877-644-5557, Fax: 864-644-5972, E-mail: ccreasman@swu.edu. *Dean, School of Business,* Dr. Royce Caines, 864-644-5349, Fax: 864-644-5958, E-mail: rcaines@swu.edu.

Program in Christian Ministries Students: 5 full-time (2 women); includes 2 minority (both Black or African American, non-Hispanic/Latino). Average age 45. *Faculty:* 3 full-time (2 women). Expenses: Contact institution. *Degree program information:* Part-time and evening/weekend programs available. Offers Christian ministries (M Min). *Application deadline:* Applications are processed on a rolling basis. *Application fee:* $50. *Application Contact:* Corrie Creasman, Enrollment Services Coordinator, 877-644-5577, Fax: 864-644-5972, E-mail: ccreasman@swu.edu. *Chair, Religion Division,* Dr. Christina Accornero, 864-644-5226, Fax: 864-644-5902, E-mail: caccornero@swu.edu.

Program in Education Students: 178 full-time (157 women); includes 36 minority (33 Black or African American, non-Hispanic/Latino; 3 Hispanic/Latino), 1 international. Average age 33. 42 applicants, 90% accepted, 25 enrolled. *Faculty:* 6 full-time (3 women), 19 part-time/adjunct (11 women). Expenses: Contact institution. In 2010, 315 master's awarded. *Degree program information:* Evening/weekend programs available. Offers education (M Ed). Program also offered at Greenville, S. C. site. *Application deadline:* Applications are processed on a rolling basis. *Application fee:* $50. *Application Contact:* Corrie Creasman, Enrollment Services Coordinator, 877-644-5557, Fax: 864-644-5972, E-mail: ccreasman@swu.edu. *Assistant Professor/Associate Dean,* Dr. Sandra McLendon, 864-644-5353, Fax: 864-644-5974, E-mail: smclendon@swu.edu.

Program in Management Students: 43 full-time (30 women); includes 34 Black or African American, non-Hispanic/Latino. Average age 42. 22 applicants, 95% accepted, 21 enrolled. *Faculty:* 5 full-time (1 woman), 7 part-time/adjunct (1 woman). Expenses: Contact institution. In 2010, 98 master's awarded. *Degree program information:* Evening/weekend programs available. Offers management (MSM). *Application deadline:* Applications are processed on a rolling basis. *Application fee:* $50. *Application Contact:* Corrie Creasman, Enrollment Services Coordinator, 877-644-5557, Fax: 864-644-5972, E-mail: ccreasman@swu.edu. *Dean,* Dr. Royce Caines, 864-644-5349, Fax: 864-644-5958, E-mail: rcaines@swu.edu.

SOUTH TEXAS COLLEGE OF LAW, Houston, TX 77002-7000

General Information Independent, coed, graduate-only institution. *Enrollment by degree level:* 1,305 first professional. *Graduate faculty:* 55 full-time (20 women), 41 part-time/adjunct (14 women). *Tuition:* Full-time $25,740; part-time $17,160 per year. *Required fees:* $600; $600 per year. *Student services:* Campus employment opportunities, campus safety program, career counseling, international student services, services for students with disabilities. *Library facilities:* The Fred Parks Law Library. *Online resources:* library catalog, web page, access to other libraries' catalogs.

Computer facilities: A campuswide network can be accessed from off campus. *Web address:* http://www.stcl.edu/.

General Application Contact: Alicia K. Cramer, Assistant Dean of Admissions, 713-646-1810, Fax: 713-646-2906, E-mail: admissions@stcl.edu.

GRADUATE UNITS

Professional Program Students: 1,009 full-time (472 women), 296 part-time (138 women); includes 378 minority (45 Black or African American, non-Hispanic/Latino; 7 American Indian or Alaska Native, non-Hispanic/Latino; 113 Asian, non-Hispanic/Latino; 175 Hispanic/Latino; 3 Native Hawaiian or other Pacific Islander, non-Hispanic/Latino; 35 Two or more races, non-Hispanic/Latino), 4 international. Average age 28. 2,436 applicants, 45% accepted, 461 enrolled. *Faculty:* 55 full-time (20 women), 41 part-time/adjunct (14 women). Expenses: Contact institution. *Financial support:* In 2010–11, 1,135 students received support. Federal Work-Study, scholarships/grants, and tuition waivers (full and partial) available. Support available to part-time students. Financial award application deadline: 5/1; financial award applicants required to submit FAFSA. In 2010, 373 JDs awarded. *Degree program information:* Part-time and evening/weekend programs available. Offers law (JD). *Application deadline:* For fall admission, 2/15 for domestic and international students; for spring admission, 10/1 for domestic and international students. *Application fee:* $55. Electronic applications accepted. *Application Contact:* Alicia K. Cramer, Assistant Dean of Admissions, 713-646-1810, Fax: 713-646-2906, E-mail: admissions@stcl.edu. *President and Dean,* Donald J. Guter, 713-646-1819, Fax: 713-646-2909, E-mail: dguter@stcl.edu.

SOUTH UNIVERSITY, Montgomery, AL 36116-1120

General Information Proprietary, coed, comprehensive institution.

GRADUATE UNITS

Program in Business Administration Offers business administration (MBA).

Program in Healthcare Administration Offers healthcare administration (MBA).

Program in Professional Counseling Offers professional counseling (MA).

SOUTH UNIVERSITY, Royal Palm Beach, FL 33411

General Information Proprietary, coed, comprehensive institution.

GRADUATE UNITS

Program in Business Administration Offers business administration (MBA); healthcare administration (MBA).

Program in Professional Counseling Offers professional counseling (MA).

SOUTH UNIVERSITY, Tampa, FL 33614

General Information Proprietary, coed, comprehensive institution.

GRADUATE UNITS

Program in Healthcare Administration Offers healthcare administration (MBA).

Program in Physician Assistant Studies Offers physician assistant studies (MS).

SOUTH UNIVERSITY, Savannah, GA 31406

General Information Proprietary, coed, comprehensive institution.

GRADUATE UNITS

Graduate Programs

College of Arts and Sciences Offers arts and sciences (MA); professional counseling (MA).

College of Business Offers corrections (MBA); entrepreneurship and small business (MBA); hospitality management (MBA); sustainability (MBA).

College of Health Professions Offers anesthesiologist assistant (MM Sc); health professions (MM Sc, MS); physician assistant studies (MS).

School of Pharmacy Offers pharmacy (Pharm D).

SOUTH UNIVERSITY, Novi, MI 48377

General Information Proprietary, coed, comprehensive institution.

GRADUATE UNITS

Program in Business Administration Offers business administration (MBA).

Program in Professional Counseling Offers professional counseling (MA).

SOUTH UNIVERSITY, Columbia, SC 29203

General Information Proprietary, coed, comprehensive institution.

GRADUATE UNITS

Program in Business Administration Offers business administration (MBA).

Program in Criminal Justice Offers criminal justice (MS).

Program in Healthcare Administration Offers healthcare administration (MBA).

Program in Pharmacy Offers pharmacy (Pharm D).

Program in Professional Counseling Offers professional counseling (MA).

SOUTH UNIVERSITY, Austin, TX 78681

General Information Comprehensive institution.

GRADUATE UNITS

Program in Business Administration Offers business administration (MBA).

SOUTH UNIVERSITY, Glen Allen, VA 23060

General Information Proprietary, coed, comprehensive institution.

GRADUATE UNITS

Program in Business Administration Offers business administration (MBA).

Program in Professional Counseling Offers professional counseling (MA).

SOUTH UNIVERSITY, Virginia Beach, VA 23452

General Information Proprietary, coed, comprehensive institution.

GRADUATE UNITS

Program in Business Administration Offers business administration (MBA).

Program in Professional Counseling Offers professional counseling (MA).

SOUTHWEST ACUPUNCTURE COLLEGE, Santa Fe, NM 87505

General Information Private, coed, primarily women, graduate-only institution. *Graduate housing:* On-campus housing not available.

GRADUATE UNITS

Program in Oriental Medicine, Albuquerque Campus *Degree program information:* Part-time programs available. Offers Oriental medicine (MS). Electronic applications accepted.

Program in Oriental Medicine, Boulder Campus *Degree program information:* Part-time programs available. Offers Oriental medicine (MS).

Program in Oriental Medicine, Santa Fe Campus *Degree program information:* Part-time programs available. Offers Oriental medicine (MS). Electronic applications accepted.

SOUTHWEST BAPTIST UNIVERSITY, Bolivar, MO 65613-2597

General Information Independent-religious, coed, comprehensive institution. *Graduate housing:* Room and/or apartments available on a first-come, first-served basis to single students; on-campus housing not available to married students.

GRADUATE UNITS

Program in Business *Degree program information:* Part-time programs available. Postbaccalaureate distance learning degree programs offered (no on-campus study). Offers business administration (MBA); health administration (MBA).

Program in Education *Degree program information:* Part-time programs available. Offers education (MS); educational administration (MS, Ed S).

Program in Physical Therapy Offers physical therapy (DPT).

SOUTHWEST COLLEGE OF NATUROPATHIC MEDICINE AND HEALTH SCIENCES, Tempe, AZ 85282

General Information Independent, coed, graduate-only institution. *Enrollment by degree level:* 355 doctoral. *Graduate faculty:* 28 full-time (16 women), 50 part-time/adjunct (31 women). *Tuition:* Full-time $29,282. *Required fees:* $983. One-time fee: $815 full-time. *Graduate housing:* On-campus housing not available. *Student services:* Campus employment opportunities, career counseling, free psychological counseling, low-cost health insurance. *Library facilities:* SCNM Library plus 1 other. *Online resources:* library catalog, web page, access to other libraries' catalogs. *Collection:* 7,965 titles, 88 serial subscriptions, 660 audiovisual materials. *Research affiliation:* University of Arizona (biochemistry, herbal medicine), Translational Genomics Research Institute (genomics, herbal medicine), Arizona State University, Biodesign Institute (genomics, herbal medicine).

Computer facilities: 16 computers available on campus for general student use. A campuswide network can be accessed from off campus. Online class registration is available. *Web address:* http://www.scnm.edu/.

General Application Contact: Gary Parker, Assistant Director of Admissions, 480-858-9100 Ext. 213, Fax: 480-222-9413, E-mail: g.parker@scnm.edu.

GRADUATE UNITS

Program in Naturopathic Medicine Students: 346 full-time (255 women), 9 part-time (6 women); includes 73 minority (36 Black or African American, non-Hispanic/Latino; 4 American Indian or Alaska Native, non-Hispanic/Latino; 18 Asian, non-Hispanic/Latino; 15 Hispanic/Latino), 13 international. Average age 31. 227 applicants, 65% accepted, 73 enrolled. *Faculty:* 28 full-time (16 women), 50 part-time/adjunct (31 women). Expenses: Contact institution. *Financial support:* Federal Work-Study and scholarships/grants available. Support available to part-time students. Financial award application deadline: 7/1; financial award applicants required to submit FAFSA. In 2010, 69 doctorates awarded. Offers naturopathic medicine (ND). *Application deadline:* For fall admission, 2/1 priority date for domestic students; for spring admission, 11/1 priority date for domestic students. Applications are processed on a rolling basis. *Application fee:* $65 ($90 for international students). *Application Contact:* Gary Parker, Assistant Director of Admissions, 480-858-9100 Ext. 213, Fax: 480-222-9413, E-mail: g.parker@scnm.edu. *Executive Vice President of Academic and Clinical Affairs,* Dr. Christine Girard, 480-858-9100 Ext. 114, Fax: 480-222-9860, E-mail: c.girard@scnm.edu.

SOUTHWESTERN ADVENTIST UNIVERSITY, Keene, TX 76059

General Information Independent-religious, coed, comprehensive institution. *Graduate housing:* Rooms and/or apartments available on a first-come, first-served basis to single and married students. Housing application deadline: 8/31.

GRADUATE UNITS

Business Administration Department *Degree program information:* Part-time and evening/weekend programs available. Offers accounting (MBA); finance (MBA); management/leadership (MBA).

Education Department *Degree program information:* Part-time and evening/weekend programs available. Offers curriculum and instruction with reading emphasis (M Ed); educational leadership (M Ed).

SOUTHWESTERN ASSEMBLIES OF GOD UNIVERSITY, Waxahachie, TX 75165-5735

General Information Independent-religious, coed, comprehensive institution. *Graduate housing:* Room and/or apartments guaranteed to single students.

GRADUATE UNITS

Thomas F. Harrison School of Graduate Studies *Degree program information:* Part-time and evening/weekend programs available. Postbaccalaureate distance learning degree programs offered (minimal on-campus study). Offers Bible and theology (MS); Biblical studies (M Div); Christian school administration (MS); counseling (M Div); counseling psychology (clinical) (MCP); cross cultural missions (M Div); curriculum development (MS); early education administration (M Ed); history (MA); human services counseling (MS); middle and secondary education (M Ed); practical theology (M Div); theological studies (M Div). Electronic applications accepted.

SOUTHWESTERN BAPTIST THEOLOGICAL SEMINARY, Fort Worth, TX 76122-0000

General Information Independent-religious, coed, primarily men, graduate-only institution. *Graduate housing:* Rooms and/or apartments available on a first-come, first-served basis to single and married students. *Research affiliation:* Campus Crusade for Christ/Jesus Film Project (evangelical missions), DAWN: Discipling A Whole Nation (evangelical missions).

GRADUATE UNITS

School of Church Music *Degree program information:* Part-time programs available. Offers church music (MACM, MAWSHP, MM, DMA, PhD, SPCM). Electronic applications accepted.

School of Educational Ministries *Degree program information:* Part-time and evening/weekend programs available. Offers educational ministries (MA Comm, MACC, MACCM, MACE, MACSE, MAMFC, DEM, PhD, SPEM). Electronic applications accepted.

School of Theology *Degree program information:* Part-time and evening/weekend programs available. Offers theology (M Div, MA Islamic, MA Miss, MA Th, Th M, D Min, PhD, SPTH). Electronic applications accepted.

SOUTHWESTERN CHRISTIAN UNIVERSITY, Bethany, OK 73008-0340

General Information Independent-religious, coed, comprehensive institution.

GRADUATE UNITS

Program in Ministry *Degree program information:* Part-time programs available. Offers church planting (M Min); church revitalization and renewal (M Min); intercultural studies (M Min); leadership (M Min); life coaching (M Min); pastoral ministries (M Min); work place ministries (M Min). Electronic applications accepted.

SOUTHWESTERN COLLEGE, Winfield, KS 67156-2499

General Information Independent-religious, coed, comprehensive institution. *Enrollment:* 1,791 graduate, professional, and undergraduate students; 10 full-time matriculated graduate/professional students (4 women), 249 part-time matriculated graduate/professional students (125 women). *Enrollment by degree level:* 259 master's. *Graduate faculty:* 11 full-time (2 women), 49 part-time/adjunct (25 women). *Tuition:* Full-time $7470; part-time $415 per credit hour. Tuition and fees vary according to program. *Graduate housing:* Rooms and/or apartments available on a first-come, first-served basis to single and married students. Typical cost: $2910 per year ($6322 including board) for single students. Room and board charges vary according to board plan and housing facility selected. Housing application deadline: 6/1. *Student services:* Campus employment opportunities, career counseling, services for students with disabilities, teacher training. *Library facilities:* Harold and Mary Ellen Deets Library plus 1 other. *Online resources:* library catalog, web page. *Collection:* 111,398 titles, 142 serial subscriptions, 13,308 audiovisual materials.

Computer facilities: 30 computers available on campus for general student use. A campuswide network can be accessed from student residence rooms and from off campus. Online class registration is available. *Web address:* http://www.sckans.edu/.

General Application Contact: Marla Sexson, Director of Admissions, 620-229-6364, Fax: 620-229-6344, E-mail: marla.sexson@sckans.edu.

GRADUATE UNITS

Education Programs Students: 1 (woman) full-time, 87 part-time (60 women); includes 12 minority (4 Black or African American, non-Hispanic/Latino; 1 American Indian or Alaska Native, non-Hispanic/Latino; 1 Asian, non-Hispanic/Latino; 3 Hispanic/Latino; 1 Native Hawaiian or other Pacific Islander, non-Hispanic/Latino; 2 Two or more races, non-Hispanic/Latino), 1 international. Average age 35. 86 applicants, 71% accepted, 44 enrolled. *Faculty:* 2 full-time (0 women), 7 part-time/adjunct (6 women). Expenses: Contact institution. *Financial support:* In 2010–11, 5 students received support. Federal Work-Study, tuition waivers (partial), and unspecified assistantships available. Financial award application deadline: 4/1; financial award applicants required to submit FAFSA. In 2010, 90 master's awarded. *Degree program information:* Part-time and evening/weekend programs available. Postbaccalaureate distance learning degree programs offered (minimal on-campus study). Offers curriculum and instruction (M Ed); special education (M Ed); teaching (MA). *Application deadline:* For fall admission, 8/1 for domestic students; for spring admission, 12/1 for domestic students. Applications are processed on a rolling basis. *Application fee:* $0. Electronic applications accepted. *Application Contact:* Lindy Kralicek, Program Representative, 888-684-5335 Ext. 130, Fax: 316-688-5218, E-mail: lindy.kralicek@sckans.edu. *Director of Teacher Education,* Dr. David Hofmeister, 800-846-1543 Ext. 6115, Fax: 620-229-6341, E-mail: david.hofmeister@sckans.edu.

Fifth-Year Graduate Programs Students: 9 full-time (3 women), 8 part-time (3 women), 6 international. Average age 25. 10 applicants, 90% accepted, 9 enrolled. *Faculty:* 9 full-time (1 woman), 8 part-time/adjunct (2 women). Expenses: Contact institution. *Financial support:* In 2010–11, 6 students received support. Federal Work-Study, tuition waivers (partial), and unspecified assistantships available. Financial award application deadline: 4/1; financial award applicants required to submit FAFSA. In 2010, 26 master's awarded. *Degree program information:* Part-time programs available. Offers leadership (MS); management (MBA); music (MA). *Application deadline:* For fall admission, 4/1 priority date for domestic students; for spring admission, 12/1 priority date for domestic students. Applications are processed on a rolling basis. Electronic applications accepted. *Application Contact:* Marla Sexson, Director of Admissions, 800-846-1543 Ext. 6364, Fax: 620-229-6344, E-mail: marla.sexson@sckans.edu. *Vice President for Academic Affairs,* Dr. James Sheppard, 620-229-6227, Fax: 620-229-6224, E-mail: james.sheppard@sckans.edu.

Professional Studies Programs Students: 154 part-time (62 women); includes 29 minority (20 Black or African American, non-Hispanic/Latino; 1 American Indian or Alaska Native, non-Hispanic/Latino; 4 Hispanic/Latino; 4 Two or more races, non-Hispanic/Latino). Average age 35. 91 applicants, 66% accepted, 52 enrolled. *Faculty:* 12 part-time/adjunct (5 women). Expenses: Contact institution. *Financial support:* In 2010–11, 6 students received support. Federal Work-Study, tuition waivers (partial), and unspecified assistantships available. Financial award application deadline: 4/1; financial award applicants required to submit FAFSA. In 2010, 112 master's awarded. *Degree program information:* Part-time and evening/weekend programs available. Postbaccalaureate distance learning degree programs offered (minimal on-campus study). Offers business administration (MBA); leadership (MS); management (MS); security administration (MS); specialized ministries (MA); theological studies (MA). *Application deadline:* For fall admission, 8/1 for domestic students; for spring admission, 12/1 for domestic students. Applications are processed on a rolling basis. *Application fee:* $0. Electronic applications accepted. *Application Contact:* Gail Cullen, Director of Academic Affairs, 888-684-5335 Ext. 203, Fax: 316-688-5218, E-mail: gail.cullen@sckans.edu. *Director of Academic Affairs,* Gail Cullen, 888-684-5335 Ext. 203, Fax: 316-688-5218, E-mail: gail.cullen@sckans.edu.

SOUTHWESTERN COLLEGE, Santa Fe, NM 87502-4788

General Information Independent, coed, primarily women, graduate-only institution. *Graduate housing:* On-campus housing not available.

GRADUATE UNITS

Program in Art Therapy/Counseling *Degree program information:* Part-time and evening/weekend programs available. Offers art therapy/counseling (MA).

Program in Counseling *Degree program information:* Part-time and evening/weekend programs available. Offers counseling (MA).

Southwestern College (continued)

Program in Grief, Loss and Trauma Counseling *Degree program information:* Part-time and evening/weekend programs available. Postbaccalaureate distance learning degree programs offered (minimal on-campus study). Offers grief, loss and trauma counseling (MA, Certificate).

Program in Integral Somatic Psychology Offers integral somatic psychology (Certificate).

Program in Psychodrama and Action Methods Offers psychodrama and action methods (Certificate).

Program in Transformational Ecopsychology Offers transformational ecopsychology (Certificate).

SOUTHWESTERN LAW SCHOOL, Los Angeles, CA 90010

General Information Independent, coed, graduate-only institution. *Graduate housing:* On-campus housing not available.

GRADUATE UNITS

Graduate Program *Degree program information:* Part-time and evening/weekend programs available. Offers entertainment and media law (LL M); general studies (LL M); law (JD). Electronic applications accepted.

SOUTHWESTERN OKLAHOMA STATE UNIVERSITY, Weatherford, OK 73096-3098

General Information State-supported, coed, comprehensive institution. *Graduate housing:* Rooms and/or apartments available on a first-come, first-served basis to single and married students. Housing application deadline: 8/19. *Research affiliation:* Gulf Coast Research Laboratory.

GRADUATE UNITS

College of Arts and Sciences *Degree program information:* Part-time programs available. Offers art education (M Ed); arts and sciences (M Ed, MM); English (M Ed); mathematics (M Ed); music education (MM); natural sciences (M Ed); performance (MM); social sciences (M Ed).

College of Pharmacy Offers pharmacy (Pharm D).

College of Professional and Graduate Studies *Degree program information:* Part-time and evening/weekend programs available. Postbaccalaureate distance learning degree programs offered (minimal on-campus study).

School of Behavioral Sciences and Education *Degree program information:* Part-time and evening/weekend programs available. Postbaccalaureate distance learning degree programs offered (minimal on-campus study). Offers community counseling (M Ed); early childhood education (M Ed); educational administration (M Ed); elementary education (M Ed); health sciences and microbiology (M Ed); kinesiology (M Ed); parks and recreation management (M Ed); school counseling (M Ed); school psychology (MS); school psychometry (M Ed); secondary education (M Ed); special education (M Ed).

School of Business and Technology *Degree program information:* Part-time and evening/weekend programs available. Postbaccalaureate distance learning degree programs offered (minimal on-campus study). Offers business and technology (MBA). MBA distance learning degree program offered to Oklahoma residents only.

SOUTHWEST MINNESOTA STATE UNIVERSITY, Marshall, MN 56258

General Information State-supported, coed, comprehensive institution. *Enrollment:* 6,611 graduate, professional, and undergraduate students; 300 full-time matriculated graduate/professional students (217 women), 148 part-time matriculated graduate/professional students (84 women). *Enrollment by degree level:* 448 master's. *Graduate faculty:* 23 full-time (11 women), 12 part-time/adjunct (6 women). *Graduate housing:* Room and/or apartments available to single students; on-campus housing not available to married students. *Student services:* Campus employment opportunities, campus safety program, career counseling, child daycare facilities, exercise/wellness program, free psychological counseling, international student services, low-cost health insurance, multicultural affairs office, services for students with disabilities, teacher training, writing training. *Library facilities:* Southwest Minnesota State University. *Online resources:* library catalog, web page, access to other libraries' catalogs. *Collection:* 404,784 titles, 45,569 serial subscriptions, 12,465 audiovisual materials.

Computer facilities: 420 computers available on campus for general student use. A campuswide network can be accessed from student residence rooms and from off campus. Online class registration is available. *Web address:* http://www.smsu.edu/.

General Application Contact: Senior Office and Administrative Specialist for Admission, 507-537-6286.

GRADUATE UNITS

Department of Business and Public Affairs Students: 27 full-time (15 women), 82 part-time (38 women); includes 7 minority (3 Black or African American, non-Hispanic/Latino; 1 Asian, non-Hispanic/Latino; 2 Hispanic/Latino; 1 Two or more races, non-Hispanic/Latino), 21 international. Average age 30. 49 applicants, 55% accepted, 18 enrolled. *Faculty:* 11 full-time (3 women), 1 (woman) part-time/adjunct. Expenses: Contact institution. *Financial support:* Institutionally sponsored loans and unspecified assistantships available. Support available to part-time students. Financial award application deadline: 3/1; financial award applicants required to submit FAFSA. In 2010, 20 master's awarded. *Degree program information:* Part-time and evening/weekend programs available. Postbaccalaureate distance learning degree programs offered (no on-campus study). Offers leadership (MBA); management (MBA); marketing (MBA). *Application deadline:* For fall admission, 8/28 for domestic students, 6/15 for international students; for spring admission, 1/15 for domestic students, 12/15 for international students. Applications are processed on a rolling basis. *Application fee:* $30. Electronic applications accepted. *Application Contact:* Cori Ann Dahlager, Graduate Office Coordinator, 507-537-6819, Fax: 507-537-6227, E-mail: coriann.dahlager@smsu.edu. *Dean of Professional Studies*, Dr. Daniel Campagna, 507-537-6251, E-mail: daniel.campagna@smsu.edu.

Department of Education Students: 273 full-time (202 women), 66 part-time (46 women); includes 8 minority (1 Black or African American, non-Hispanic/Latino; 1 Asian, non-Hispanic/Latino; 4 Hispanic/Latino; 2 Two or more races, non-Hispanic/Latino). Average age 30. 165 applicants, 91% accepted, 130 enrolled. *Faculty:* 12 full-time (8 women), 11 part-time/adjunct (5 women). Expenses: Contact institution. *Financial support:* Institutionally sponsored loans and unspecified assistantships available. Support available to part-time students. Financial award application deadline: 3/1; financial award applicants required to submit FAFSA. In 2010, 101 master's awarded. *Degree program information:* Part-time and evening/weekend programs available. Postbaccalaureate distance learning degree programs offered (no on-campus study). Offers ESL (MS); math (MS); reading (MS); special education (MS); teaching, learning and leadership (MS). *Application deadline:* For fall admission, 8/28 for domestic students, 6/15 for international students; for spring admission, 1/15 for domestic students, 12/15 for international students. Applications are processed on a rolling basis. *Application fee:* $30. *Application Contact:* Cori Ann Dahlager, Graduate Office Coordinator, 507-537-6819, E-mail: coriann.dahlager@smsu.edu. *Dean of Business, Education and Professional Studies*, Dr. Daniel Campagna, 507-537-6218, E-mail: daniel.campagna@smsu.edu.

SOUTHWEST UNIVERSITY, Kenner, LA 70062

General Information Proprietary, coed, comprehensive institution.

GRADUATE UNITS

MBA Program Offers business administration (MBA); management (MBA); organizational management (MBA).

Program in Criminal Justice Offers criminal justice (MS).

Program in Management Offers management (MA).

Program in Organizational Management Offers organizational management (MA).

SPALDING UNIVERSITY, Louisville, KY 40203-2188

General Information Independent-religious, coed, comprehensive institution. CGS member. *Enrollment:* 2,346 graduate, professional, and undergraduate students; 714 full-time matriculated graduate/professional students (570 women), 295 part-time matriculated graduate/professional students (222 women). *Enrollment by degree level:* 791 master's, 218 doctoral. *Graduate faculty:* 42 full-time (25 women), 85 part-time/adjunct (47 women). *Graduate housing:* Room and/or apartments available on a first-come, first-served basis to single students; on-campus housing not available to married students. Typical cost: $5400 per year ($10,856 including board). Room and board charges vary according to board plan. Housing application deadline: 5/1. *Student services:* Campus employment opportunities, campus safety program, career counseling, exercise/wellness program, free psychological counseling, international student services, low-cost health insurance, services for students with disabilities, teacher training, writing training. *Library facilities:* Spalding Library. *Online resources:* library catalog, web page. *Collection:* 101,266 titles, 102 serial subscriptions, 2,330 audiovisual materials.

Computer facilities: 250 computers available on campus for general student use. A campuswide network can be accessed from student residence rooms and from off campus. Online class registration is available. *Web address:* http://www.spalding.edu/.

General Application Contact: Admissions Office, 502-585-7111, E-mail: admissions@spalding.edu.

GRADUATE UNITS

Graduate Studies Students: 714 full-time (570 women), 295 part-time (222 women); includes 237 minority (175 Black or African American, non-Hispanic/Latino; 2 American Indian or Alaska Native, non-Hispanic/Latino; 16 Asian, non-Hispanic/Latino; 23 Hispanic/Latino; 21 Two or more races, non-Hispanic/Latino), 19 international. Average age 35. 545 applicants, 53% accepted, 270 enrolled. *Faculty:* 42 full-time (25 women), 85 part-time/adjunct (47 women). Expenses: Contact institution. *Financial support:* In 2010–11, 353 students received support, including 67 research assistantships with partial tuition reimbursements available (averaging $4,055 per year); career-related internships or fieldwork, Federal Work-Study, scholarships/grants, traineeships, and unspecified assistantships also available. Support available to part-time students. Financial award application deadline: 3/15; financial award applicants required to submit FAFSA. In 2010, 259 master's, 44 doctorates awarded. *Degree program information:* Part-time and evening/weekend programs available. *Application fee:* $30. *Application Contact:* Admissions Office, 502-585-7111, E-mail: admissions@spalding.edu. *Provost*, Dr. Randy Strickland, 502-585-9911 Ext. 2101, E-mail: rstrickland@spalding.edu.

College of Business and Communication Students: 44 full-time (35 women), 41 part-time (32 women); includes 38 minority (27 Black or African American, non-Hispanic/Latino; 1 Asian, non-Hispanic/Latino; 1 Hispanic/Latino; 9 Two or more races, non-Hispanic/Latino). Average age 37. 41 applicants, 78% accepted, 31 enrolled. *Faculty:* 6 full-time (2 women), 7 part-time/adjunct (2 women). Expenses: Contact institution. *Financial support:* In 2010–11, 26 students received support. Application deadline: 3/15. In 2010, 29 master's awarded. *Degree program information:* Part-time and evening/weekend programs available. Offers business communication (MS). *Application deadline:* Applications are processed on a rolling basis. *Application fee:* $30. *Application Contact:* Claire Rayburn, Administrative Assistant, 502-585-9911 Ext. 2120, E-mail: cbc@spalding.edu. *Program Director*, Dr. Orville Blackman, 502-585-9911 Ext. 2630, E-mail: cbc@spalding.edu.

College of Education Students: 175 full-time (129 women), 111 part-time (71 women); includes 108 minority (88 Black or African American, non-Hispanic/Latino; 2 American Indian or Alaska Native, non-Hispanic/Latino; 6 Asian, non-Hispanic/Latino; 7 Hispanic/Latino; 5 Two or more races, non-Hispanic/Latino), 13 international. Average age 37. 89 applicants, 73% accepted, 59 enrolled. *Faculty:* 9 full-time (6 women), 38 part-time/adjunct (23 women). Expenses: Contact institution. *Financial support:* In 2010–11, 91 students received support, including 7 research assistantships with partial tuition reimbursements available (averaging $3,847 per year); scholarships/grants, traineeships, and unspecified assistantships also available. Financial award application deadline: 3/15; financial award applicants required to submit FAFSA. In 2010, 75 master's, 29 doctorates awarded. *Degree program information:* Part-time and evening/weekend programs available. Offers education (MA, MAT, Ed D); elementary school education (MAT); general education (MA); high school education (MAT); leadership education (Ed D); middle school education (MAT); school administration (MA); special education (learning and behavioral disorders) (MAT); student guidance counselor (MA). *Application deadline:* Applications are processed on a rolling basis. *Application fee:* $30. Electronic applications accepted. *Application Contact:* Bonnie Caughron, Admissions Office, 502-585-9911 Ext. 2267, E-mail: bcaughron@spalding.edu. *Dean*, Dr. Beverly Keepers, 502-588-7121, Fax: 502-585-7123, E-mail: bkeepers@spalding.edu.

College of Health and Natural Sciences Students: 156 full-time (140 women), 74 part-time (69 women); includes 27 minority (18 Black or African American, non-Hispanic/Latino; 4 Asian, non-Hispanic/Latino; 2 Hispanic/Latino; 3 Two or more races, non-Hispanic/Latino), 3 international. Average age 32. 114 applicants, 74% accepted, 72 enrolled. *Faculty:* 10 full-time (8 women), 11 part-time/adjunct (10 women). Expenses: Contact institution. *Financial support:* In 2010–11, 69 students received support, including 6 research assistantships with partial tuition reimbursements available (averaging $3,225 per year); career-related internships or fieldwork, scholarships/grants, traineeships, and unspecified assistantships also available. Support available to part-time students. Financial award application deadline: 3/15; financial award applicants required to submit FAFSA. In 2010, 75 master's awarded. *Degree program information:* Part-time and evening/weekend programs available. Offers adult nurse practitioner (MSN); family nurse practitioner (MSN); health and natural sciences (MS, MSN); leadership in nursing and healthcare (MSN); occupational therapy (advanced-level) (MS); occupational therapy (entry-level) (MS); pediatric nurse practitioner (MSN). *Application deadline:* For winter admission, 2/1 for domestic students. Applications are processed on a rolling basis. *Application Contact:* Admissions Office, 502-585-7111, E-mail: admissions@spalding.edu. *Dean*, Dr. Joanne Berryman, 502-585-9911 Ext. 2270, E-mail: jberryman@spalding.edu.

College of Social Sciences and Humanities Students: 339 full-time (266 women), 69 part-time (50 women); includes 42 Black or African American, non-Hispanic/Latino; 5 Asian, non-Hispanic/Latino; 13 Hispanic/Latino; 13 Two or more races, non-Hispanic/Latino, 3 international. Average age 35. 210 applicants, 52% accepted, 108 enrolled. *Faculty:* 18 full-time (10 women), 26 part-time/adjunct (11 women). Expenses: Contact institution. *Financial support:* In 2010–11, 167 students received support, including 54 research assistantships with partial tuition reimbursements available (averaging $4,748 per year); career-related internships or fieldwork, Federal Work-Study, scholarships/grants, and unspecified assistantships also available. Financial award application deadline: 3/15; financial award applicants required to submit FAFSA. *Degree program information:* Part-time and evening/weekend programs available. Postbaccalaureate distance learning degree programs offered (minimal on-campus study). Offers applied behavior analysis (MA); clinical psychology (MA, Psy D); social sciences and humanities (MA, MFA, MSW, Psy D); social work (MSW); writing (MFA). *Application fee:* $30. *Application Contact:* Deborah Pierce, Administrative Assistant, 502-585-9911, E-mail: dpierce@spalding.edu. *Dean*, Dr. John James, 502-585-9911 Ext. 2434, E-mail: jjames@spalding.edu.

SPERTUS INSTITUTE OF JEWISH STUDIES, Chicago, IL 60605-1901

General Information Independent, coed, graduate-only institution. *Enrollment by degree level:* 270 master's, 52 doctoral. *Graduate faculty:* 35 part-time/adjunct (12 women). Part-time tuition and fees vary according to degree level and program. *Graduate housing:* On-campus housing not available. *Student services:* Career counseling, grant writing training, international student services, writing training. *Library facilities:* Asher Library. *Online resources:* web page. *Collection:* 110,000 titles, 200 serial subscriptions.

Computer facilities: 10 computers available on campus for general student use. *Web address:* http://www.spertus.edu/.

General Application Contact: Dr. Dean Bell, Assistant Director of Recruitment and Alumni Affairs, 312-322-1707, Fax: 312-994-5360, E-mail: nwhiteside@spertus.edu.

GRADUATE UNITS

Graduate Programs *Degree program information:* Part-time and evening/weekend programs available. Postbaccalaureate distance learning degree programs offered (minimal on-campus study). Offers Jewish education (MAJ Ed); Jewish studies (MAJS, MSJE, MSJS, DJS, DSJS); nonprofit management (MSNM).

SPRING ARBOR UNIVERSITY, Spring Arbor, MI 49283-9799

General Information Independent-religious, coed, comprehensive institution. *Enrollment:* 4,195 graduate, professional, and undergraduate students; 616 full-time matriculated graduate/professional students (456 women), 578 part-time matriculated graduate/professional students (470 women). *Enrollment by degree level:* 1,194 master's. *Graduate faculty:* 32 full-time (11 women), 123 part-time/adjunct (69 women). *Tuition:* Full-time $6300; part-time $525 per credit hour. *Required fees:* $240; $120 per semester. Tuition and fees vary according to course load and program. *Graduate housing:* Rooms and/or apartments available on a first-come, first-served basis to single and married students. Housing application deadline: 5/1. *Student services:* Campus employment opportunities, campus safety program, career counseling, multicultural affairs office, services for students with disabilities. *Library facilities:* Hugh A. White Library. *Online resources:* library catalog, web page, access to other libraries' catalogs. *Collection:* 115,987 titles, 523 serial subscriptions, 3,999 audiovisual materials.

Computer facilities: 251 computers available on campus for general student use. A campuswide network can be accessed from student residence rooms and from off campus. Online class registration is available. *Web address:* http://www.arbor.edu/.

General Application Contact: Dale Glinz, Lead Recruitment Specialist, Graduate and Professional Studies, 517-750-1703, E-mail: dglinz@arbor.edu.

GRADUATE UNITS

Gainey School of Business Students: 84 full-time (41 women), 5 part-time (3 women); includes 16 Black or African American, non-Hispanic/Latino; 1 American Indian or Alaska Native, non-Hispanic/Latino; 3 Asian, non-Hispanic/Latino. Average age 36. *Faculty:* 7 full-time (2 women), 4 part-time/adjunct (1 woman). Expenses: Contact institution. *Financial support:* Career-related internships or fieldwork, scholarships/grants, and tuition waivers (partial) available. Support available to part-time students. Financial award application deadline: 8/25; financial award applicants required to submit FAFSA. In 2010, 30 master's awarded. *Degree program information:* Part-time and evening/weekend programs available. Postbaccalaureate distance learning degree programs offered. Offers business (MBA). *Application deadline:* Applications are processed on a rolling basis. *Application fee:* $40. *Application Contact:* Greg Bentle, Coordinator of Graduate Recruitment, 517-750-6763, Fax: 517-750-6624, E-mail: gbentle@arbor.edu. *Dean,* Dr. James Coe, 517-750-1200 Ext. 1569, Fax: 517-750-6624, E-mail: jcoe@arbor.edu.

School of Arts and Sciences Students: 92 full-time (60 women), 75 part-time (57 women); includes 6 Black or African American, non-Hispanic/Latino; 1 Asian, non-Hispanic/Latino; 1 Hispanic/Latino. Average age 39. *Faculty:* 6 full-time (1 woman), 9 part-time/adjunct (6 women). Expenses: Contact institution. *Financial support:* Applicants required to submit FAFSA. In 2010, 37 master's awarded. *Degree program information:* Part-time programs available. Postbaccalaureate distance learning degree programs offered (no on-campus study). Offers communication (MA); spiritual formation and leadership (MA). *Application fee:* $40. *Application Contact:* Dale Glinz, Lead Recruitment Specialist/Trainer, Graduate and Professional Studies, 517-750-6703, E-mail: dglinz@arbor.edu. *Chair of the Department of Communication,* Dr. Wally Metts, 517-750-1200 Ext. 1491, E-mail: wmetts@arbor.edu.

School of Education Students: 33 full-time (31 women), 141 part-time (117 women); includes 5 Black or African American, non-Hispanic/Latino; 2 American Indian or Alaska Native, non-Hispanic/Latino; 1 Asian, non-Hispanic/Latino; 1 Hispanic/Latino, 1 international. Average age 35. *Faculty:* 4 full-time (2 women), 11 part-time/adjunct (7 women). Expenses: Contact institution. *Financial support:* Applicants required to submit FAFSA. In 2010, 56 master's awarded. *Degree program information:* Part-time and evening/weekend programs available. Postbaccalaureate distance learning degree programs offered (minimal on-campus study). Offers education (MAE); special education (MSE). *Application deadline:* For fall admission, 9/1 priority date for domestic students; for winter admission, 2/1 priority date for domestic students; for spring admission, 2/1 priority date for domestic students. Applications are processed on a rolling basis. *Application fee:* $40. Electronic applications accepted. *Application Contact:* Terri Reeves, Coordinator of Graduate Recruitment, 517-750-6554, Fax: 517-750-6629, E-mail: treeves@arbor.edu. *Dean,* Dr. Linda Sherrill, 517-750-1200 Ext. 1562, Fax: 517-750-6629, E-mail: lsherril@arbor.edu.

School of Graduate and Professional Studies Students: 407 full-time (324 women), 357 part-time (293 women); includes 171 Black or African American, non-Hispanic/Latino; 3 American Indian or Alaska Native, non-Hispanic/Latino; 9 Asian, non-Hispanic/Latino; 19 Hispanic/Latino, 2 international. Average age 39. *Faculty:* 16 full-time (7 women), 100 part-time/adjunct (56 women). Expenses: Contact institution. *Financial support:* Scholarships/grants available. Support available to part-time students. Financial award applicants required to submit FAFSA. In 2010, 279 master's awarded. *Degree program information:* Part-time and evening/weekend programs available. Postbaccalaureate distance learning degree programs offered (no on-campus study). Offers counseling (MAC); family studies (MAFS); nursing (MSN); organizational management (MAOM). *Application deadline:* Applications are processed on a rolling basis. *Application fee:* $40. Electronic applications accepted. *Application Contact:* Greg Bentle, Coordinator of Graduate Recruitment, 517-750-6763, Fax: 517-750-6624, E-mail: gbentle@arbor.edu. *Dean,* Natalie Gianetti, 517-750-1200 Ext. 1343, Fax: 517-750-6602, E-mail: gianetti@arbor.edu.

SPRINGFIELD COLLEGE, Springfield, MA 01109-3797

General Information Independent, coed, comprehensive institution. *Graduate housing:* Rooms and/or apartments available on a first-come, first-served basis to single and married students. Housing application deadline: 5/1.

GRADUATE UNITS

Graduate Programs *Degree program information:* Part-time and evening/weekend programs available. Offers adapted physical education (M Ed, MPE, MS); advanced level coaching (M Ed, MPE, MS); alcohol rehabilitation/substance abuse counseling (M Ed, MS); art therapy (M Ed, MS, CAGS); athletic administration (M Ed, MPE, MS); athletic counseling (M Ed, MS, CAGS); athletic training (MS); counseling and secondary education (M Ed, MS); deaf counseling (M Ed, MS); developmental disabilities (M Ed, MS); early childhood education (M Ed, MS); education (M Ed, MS); educational administration (M Ed, MS); educational studies (M Ed, MS); elementary education (M Ed, MS); exercise physiology (MS); exercise science and sport studies (PhD); general counseling and casework (M Ed, MS); general physical education (PhD, CAGS); health care management (M Ed, MS); health education licensure (MPE, MS); health education licensure program (M Ed); health promotion and disease prevention (MS); human services (MS); industrial/organizational psychology (M Ed, MS, CAGS); marriage and family therapy (M Ed, MS, CAGS); mental health counseling (M Ed, MS, CAGS); occupational therapy (M Ed, MS, CAGS); physical education licensure (MPE, MS); physical education licensure program (M Ed); physical therapy (DPT); physician assistant (MS); psychiatric rehabilitation/mental health counseling (M Ed, MS); recreational management (M Ed, MS); school guidance and counseling (M Ed, MS, CAGS); secondary education (M Ed, MS); special education (M Ed, MS); special services (M Ed, MS); sport management (M Ed, MS); sport psychology (MS); student personnel in higher education (M Ed, MS, CAGS); teaching and administration (MS); therapeutic recreational management (M Ed, MS). Electronic applications accepted.

School of Social Work *Degree program information:* Part-time programs available. Offers advanced generalist (weekday and weekend) (MSW); advanced standing (MSW). Electronic applications accepted.

SPRING HILL COLLEGE, Mobile, AL 36608-1791

General Information Independent-religious, coed, comprehensive institution. *Enrollment:* 1,601 graduate, professional, and undergraduate students; 19 full-time matriculated graduate/professional students (12 women), 158 part-time matriculated graduate/professional students (102 women). *Enrollment by degree level:* 177 master's. *Graduate faculty:* 19 full-time (9 women), 13 part-time/adjunct (8 women). *Tuition:* Full-time $5364; part-time $298 per credit hour. Tuition and fees vary according to program. *Graduate housing:* On-campus housing not available. *Student services:* Campus safety program, career counseling, exercise/wellness program, writing training. *Library facilities:* Marnie and John Burke Memorial Library plus 1 other. *Online resources:* library catalog, web page, access to other libraries' catalogs.

Computer facilities: 194 computers available on campus for general student use. A campuswide network can be accessed from student residence rooms and from off campus. Online class registration is available. *Web address:* http://www.shc.edu/.

General Application Contact: Donna B. Tarasavage, Director of Admissions, Graduate and Continuing Studies, 251-380-3067, Fax: 251-460-2190, E-mail: dtarasavage@shc.edu.

GRADUATE UNITS

Graduate Programs Students: 19 full-time (12 women), 158 part-time (102 women); includes 41 minority (33 Black or African American, non-Hispanic/Latino; 1 American Indian or Alaska Native, non-Hispanic/Latino; 4 Asian, non-Hispanic/Latino; 3 Hispanic/Latino), 2 international. Average age 39. *Faculty:* 19 full-time (9 women), 13 part-time/adjunct (8 women). Expenses: Contact institution. *Financial support:* Applicants required to submit FAFSA. In 2010, 52 master's awarded. *Degree program information:* Part-time and evening/weekend programs available. Offers business administration (MBA); clinical nurse leader (MSN); early childhood education (MAT, MS Ed); educational theory (MS Ed); elementary education (MAT, MS Ed); fine arts (MLA); history and social science (MLA); leadership and ethics (MLA); literature (MLA); pastoral studies (MPS); secondary education (MAT, MS Ed); theological studies (MTS); theology (MA). *Application deadline:* For fall admission, 8/1 priority date for domestic and international students; for spring admission, 12/1 priority date for domestic and international students. Applications are processed on a rolling basis. *Application fee:* $25 ($35 for international students). Electronic applications accepted. *Application Contact:* Donna B. Tarasavage, Director of Admissions, Graduate and Continuing Studies, 251-380-3067, Fax: 251-460-2190, E-mail: dtarasavage@shc.edu. *Vice President for Enrollment Management,* Ramona Marsalis Hill, 251-380-3092, Fax: 251-460-2111, E-mail: rhill@shc.edu.

STANFORD UNIVERSITY, Stanford, CA 94305-9991

General Information Independent, coed, university. CGS member. *Enrollment:* 19,535 graduate, professional, and undergraduate students; 8,302 full-time matriculated graduate/professional students (3,086 women), 477 part-time matriculated graduate/professional students (146 women). *Enrollment by degree level:* 997 first professional, 3,357 master's, 4,425 doctoral. *Graduate faculty:* 1,903 full-time (499 women). *Tuition:* Full-time $38,700; part-time $860 per unit. One-time fee: $200 full-time. *Graduate housing:* Rooms and/or apartments guaranteed to single and married students. Typical cost: $12,501 per year for single students; $15,341 per year for married students. Room charges vary according to housing facility selected. Housing application deadline: 5/6. *Student services:* Campus employment opportunities, campus safety program, career counseling, child daycare facilities, exercise/wellness program, free psychological counseling, international student services, low-cost health insurance, multicultural affairs office, services for students with disabilities, teacher training. *Library facilities:* Green Library plus 17 others. *Online resources:* library catalog, web page, access to other libraries' catalogs. *Collection:* 8.5 million titles, 75,000 serial subscriptions, 1.5 million audiovisual materials.

Computer facilities: Computer purchase and lease plans are available. 1,000 computers available on campus for general student use. A campuswide network can be accessed from student residence rooms and from off campus. Online class registration is available. *Web address:* http://www.stanford.edu/.

General Application Contact: Graduate Admissions, 866-432-7472, Fax: 650-723-8371, E-mail: gradadmissions@stanford.edu.

GRADUATE UNITS

Graduate School of Business Offers business (MBA, PhD). Electronic applications accepted.

Law School Offers law (JD, JSM, MLS, JSD). Electronic applications accepted.

School of Earth Sciences Offers earth sciences (MS, PhD, Eng); earth systems (MS); geological and environmental sciences (MS, PhD, Eng); geophysics (MS, PhD); petroleum engineering (MS, PhD, Eng). Electronic applications accepted.

School of Education Offers administration and policy analysis (Ed D, PhD); anthropology of education (PhD); art education (MA, PhD); child and adolescent development (PhD); counseling psychology (PhD); dance education (MA); economics of education (PhD); education (MA, Ed D, PhD); educational linguistics (PhD); educational psychology (PhD); English education (MA, PhD); evaluation (MA); general curriculum studies (MA, PhD); higher education (PhD); history of education (PhD); interdisciplinary studies (PhD); international comparative education (MA, PhD); international education administration and policy analysis (MA); languages education (MA); learning, design, and technology (MA, PhD); mathematics education (MA, PhD); philosophy of education (PhD); policy analysis (MA); prospective principal's program (MA); science education (MA, PhD); social studies education (MA, PhD); sociology of education (PhD); symbolic systems in education (PhD); teacher education (MA, PhD). Electronic applications accepted.

School of Engineering Offers aeronautics and astronautics (MS, PhD, Eng); biomechanical engineering (MS); chemical engineering (MS, PhD, Eng); civil and environmental engineering (MS, PhD, Eng); computer science (MS, PhD); electrical engineering (MS, PhD, Eng); engineering (MS, PhD, Eng); management science and engineering (MS, PhD); materials science and engineering (MS, PhD, Eng); mechanical engineering (MS, PhD, Eng); product design (MS); scientific computing and computational mathematics (MS, PhD). Electronic applications accepted.

School of Humanities and Sciences Offers anthropological sciences (MA, MS, PhD); applied physics (MS, PhD); art history (PhD); art practice (MFA); biological sciences (MS, PhD); biophysics (PhD); chemistry (PhD); Chinese (MA, PhD); classics (MA, PhD); communication (journalism specialization) (MA); communication theory and research (PhD); comparative literature (PhD); computer-based music theory and acoustics (MA, PhD); cultural and social anthropology (MA, PhD); drama (PhD); economics (PhD); English (MA, PhD); financial mathematics (MS); French (MA, PhD); German studies (MA, PhD); history (MA, PhD); humanities (MA); humanities and sciences (MA, MFA, MS, DMA, PhD); international policy studies (MA); Italian (MA, PhD); Japanese (MA, PhD); linguistics (MA, PhD); mathematics (MS, PhD); modern thought and literature (PhD); music composition (MA, DMA); music history (MA); music, science, and technology (MA); musicology (PhD); philosophy (MA, PhD); physics (PhD); political science (MA, PhD); psychology (PhD); religious studies (MA, PhD); Russian (MA); Slavic languages and literatures (PhD); sociology (PhD); Spanish (MA, PhD); statistics (MS, PhD). Electronic applications accepted.

Center for East Asian Studies Offers East Asian studies (MA). Electronic applications accepted.

Center for Russian and East European Studies Offers Russian and East European studies (MA). Electronic applications accepted.

School of Medicine Offers bioengineering (MS, PhD); medicine (MD, MS, PhD). Electronic applications accepted.

Graduate Programs in Medicine Offers biochemistry (PhD); biomedical informatics (MS, PhD); cancer biology (PhD); developmental biology (PhD); epidemiology (MS, PhD); genetics (PhD); health services research (MS); immunology (PhD); medicine (MS, PhD); microbiology and immunology (PhD); molecular and cellular physiology (PhD); molecular pharmacology (PhD); neurosciences (PhD); structural biology (PhD). Electronic applications accepted.

STARR KING SCHOOL FOR THE MINISTRY, Berkeley, CA 94709-1209

General Information Independent-religious, coed, graduate-only institution. *Graduate housing:* On-campus housing not available.

GRADUATE UNITS

Professional Program Offers theology (M Div).

STATE UNIVERSITY OF NEW YORK AT BINGHAMTON, Binghamton, NY 13902-6000

General Information State-supported, coed, university. CGS member. *Enrollment:* 14,895 graduate, professional, and undergraduate students; 1,664 full-time matriculated graduate/professional students (789 women), 1,313 part-time matriculated graduate/professional students (651 women). *Enrollment by degree level:* 1,682 master's, 1,259 doctoral, 36 other advanced degrees. *Graduate faculty:* 561 full-time (222 women), 233 part-time/adjunct (108 women). *Graduate housing:* On-campus housing not available. *Student services:* Campus employment opportunities, campus safety program, career counseling, child daycare facilities, exercise/wellness program, free psychological counseling, grant writing training, international student services, low-cost health insurance, multicultural affairs office, services for students with disabilities, teacher training, writing training. *Library facilities:* Glenn G. Bartle Library plus 2 others. *Online resources:* library catalog, web page, access to other libraries' catalogs. *Collection:* 2.4 million titles, 81,959 serial subscriptions, 123,131 audiovisual materials. *Research affiliation:* Universal Instruments (engineering), Lockheed Martin Corporation (engineering, management, mathematics), Matco Company (engineering), IBM (engineering).

Computer facilities: 1,116 computers available on campus for general student use. A campuswide network can be accessed from student residence rooms and from off campus. Online class registration, course management system, personal Web space, wiki, virtual desktop are available. *Web address:* http://www.binghamton.edu/.

General Application Contact: Dr. Nancy E. Stamp, Vice Provost and Dean of the Graduate School, 607-777-2070, Fax: 607-777-2501, E-mail: nstamp@binghamton.edu.

GRADUATE UNITS

Graduate School Students: 1,664 full-time (789 women), 1,313 part-time (651 women); includes 85 Black or African American, non-Hispanic/Latino; 9 American Indian or Alaska Native, non-Hispanic/Latino; 161 Asian, non-Hispanic/Latino; 107 Hispanic/Latino, 951 international. Average age 30. 3,563 applicants, 43% accepted, 919 enrolled. *Faculty:* 561 full-time (222 women), 233 part-time/adjunct (108 women). Expenses: Contact institution. *Financial support:* In 2010–11, 938 students received support, including 84 fellowships with full tuition reimbursements available (averaging $10,000 per year), 201 research assistantships with full tuition reimbursements available (averaging $10,000 per year), 521 teaching assistantships with full tuition reimbursements available (averaging $10,000 per year); career-related internships or fieldwork, Federal Work-Study, institutionally sponsored loans, scholarships/grants, traineeships, health care benefits, tuition waivers (full and partial), and unspecified assistantships also available. Support available to part-time students. Financial award application deadline: 2/15; financial award applicants required to submit FAFSA. In 2010, 820 master's, 136 doctorates, 43 other advanced degrees awarded. *Degree program information:* Part-time and evening/weekend programs available. *Application deadline:* Applications are processed on a rolling basis. *Application fee:* $60. Electronic applications accepted. *Application Contact:* Catherine Smith, Recruiting and Admissions Coordinator, 607-777-2151, Fax: 607-777-2501, E-mail: cmsmith@binghamton.edu. *Vice Provost and Dean of the Graduate School*, Dr. Nancy E. Stamp, 607-777-2070, Fax: 607-777-2501, E-mail: nstamp@binghamton.edu.

College of Community and Public Affairs Students: 159 full-time (110 women), 113 part-time (85 women); includes 27 Black or African American, non-Hispanic/Latino; 8 Asian, non-Hispanic/Latino; 13 Hispanic/Latino, 12 international. Average age 31. 245 applicants, 60% accepted, 102 enrolled. *Faculty:* 23 full-time (15 women), 14 part-time/adjunct (10 women). Expenses: Contact institution. *Financial support:* In 2010–11, 33 students received support, including 3 fellowships with partial tuition reimbursements available (averaging $2,500 per year), 1 research assistantship with full tuition reimbursement available (averaging $10,000 per year), 2 teaching assistantships with full tuition reimbursements available (averaging $10,000 per year); career-related internships or fieldwork, Federal Work-Study, institutionally sponsored loans, scholarships/grants, health care benefits, and unspecified assistantships also available. Financial award application deadline: 2/15; financial award applicants required to submit FAFSA. In 2010, 95 master's awarded. *Degree program information:* Part-time and evening/weekend programs available. Offers community and public affairs (MPA, MS, MSW); public administration (MPA); social work (MSW); student affairs administration (MS). *Application deadline:* Applications are processed on a rolling basis. *Application fee:* $60. Electronic applications accepted. *Application Contact:* Catherine Smith, Recruiting and Admissions Coordinator, 607-777-2151, Fax: 607-777-2501, E-mail: cmsmith@binghamton.edu. *Dean*, Dr. Patricia Ingraham, 607-777-5572, Fax: 607-777-2406, E-mail: pingraham@binghamton.edu.

Decker School of Nursing Students: 68 full-time (60 women), 87 part-time (81 women); includes 6 Black or African American, non-Hispanic/Latino; 7 Asian, non-Hispanic/Latino; 3 Hispanic/Latino, 2 international. Average age 38. 79 applicants, 89% accepted, 64 enrolled. *Faculty:* 42 full-time (39 women), 15 part-time/adjunct (12 women). Expenses: Contact institution. *Financial support:* In 2010–11, 18 students received support, including 4 fellowships with partial tuition reimbursements available (averaging $8,250 per year), 1 research assistantship with full tuition reimbursement available (averaging $10,000 per year), 5 teaching assistantships with full tuition reimbursements available (averaging $10,000 per year); career-related internships or fieldwork, Federal Work-Study, institutionally sponsored loans, traineeships, health care benefits, tuition waivers (full and partial), and unspecified assistantships also available. Financial award application deadline: 2/15; financial award applicants required to submit FAFSA. In 2010, 32 master's, 3 doctorates, 33 other advanced degrees awarded. *Degree program information:* Part-time and evening/weekend programs available. Offers nursing (MS, PhD, Certificate). *Application deadline:* For fall admission, 4/15 priority date for domestic students, 1/15 priority date for international students; for spring admission, 11/1 for domestic students, 10/1 priority date for international students. Applications are processed on a rolling basis. *Application fee:* $60. Electronic applications accepted. *Application Contact:* Catherine Smith, Director of Graduate Studies, 607-777-2151, Fax: 607-777-2501, E-mail: cmsmith@binghamton.edu. *Dean*, Dr. Joyce Ferrario, 607-777-2311, Fax: 607-777-4440, E-mail: jferrari@binghamton.edu.

School of Arts and Sciences Students: 592 full-time (292 women), 544 part-time (301 women); includes 32 Black or African American, non-Hispanic/Latino; 5 American Indian or Alaska Native, non-Hispanic/Latino; 44 Asian, non-Hispanic/Latino; 62 Hispanic/Latino, 327 international. Average age 31. 1,328 applicants, 36% accepted, 245 enrolled. *Faculty:* 311 full-time (111 women), 132 part-time/adjunct (58 women). Expenses: Contact institution. *Financial support:* In 2010–11, 545 students received support, including 60 fellowships with full tuition reimbursements available (averaging $14,100 per year), 47 research assistantships with full tuition reimbursements available (averaging $14,100 per year), 412 teaching assistantships with full tuition reimbursements available (averaging $14,100 per year); career-related internships or fieldwork, Federal Work-Study, institutionally sponsored loans, scholarships/grants, health care benefits, tuition waivers (full and partial), and unspecified assistantships also available. Financial award application deadline: 2/15; financial award applicants required to submit FAFSA. In 2010, 178 master's, 97 doctorates, 2 other advanced degrees awarded. *Degree program information:* Part-time and evening/weekend programs available. Offers analytical chemistry (PhD); anthropology (MA, PhD); applied physics (MS); art history (MA, PhD); arts and sciences (MA, MM, MS, PhD, Certificate); behavioral neuroscience (MA, PhD); biological sciences (MA, PhD); chemistry (MA, MS); clinical psychology (MA, PhD); cognitive and behavioral science (MA, PhD); comparative literature (MA, PhD); computer science (MA, PhD); economics (MA, PhD); economics and finance (MA, PhD); English (MA, PhD); French (MA); geography (MA); geological sciences (MA, PhD); history (MA, PhD); inorganic chemistry (PhD); Italian (MA); music (MA, MM); organic chemistry (PhD); philosophy (MA, PhD); philosophy, interpretation and culture (MA, PhD); physical chemistry (PhD); physics (MA, MS, PhD); political science (MA, PhD); probability and statistics (MA, PhD); public policy (MA, PhD); social, political, ethical and legal philosophy (MA, PhD); sociology (MA, PhD); Spanish (MA, Certificate); theater (MA); translation (Certificate); translation research and instruction (Certificate). *Application deadline:* Applications are processed on a rolling basis. *Application fee:* $60. Electronic applications accepted. *Application Contact:* Catherine Smith, Recruiting and Admissions Coordinator, 607-777-2151, Fax: 607-777-2501, E-mail: cmsmith@binghamton.edu. *Dean*, Dr. Donald Nieman, 607-777-2144, E-mail: dnieman@binghamton.edu.

School of Education Students: 167 full-time (114 women), 137 part-time (106 women); includes 5 Black or African American, non-Hispanic/Latino; 2 American Indian or Alaska Native, non-Hispanic/Latino; 4 Asian, non-Hispanic/Latino; 7 Hispanic/Latino, 4 international. Average age 31. 164 applicants, 71% accepted, 90 enrolled. *Faculty:* 19 full-time (13 women), 14 part-time/adjunct (8 women). Expenses: Contact institution. *Financial support:* In 2010–11, 28 students received support, including 8 fellowships with full tuition reimbursements available (averaging $12,000 per year), 2 research assistantships with full tuition reimbursements available (averaging $12,000 per year), 2 teaching assistantships with full tuition reimbursements available (averaging $12,000 per year); career-related internships or fieldwork, Federal Work-Study, institutionally sponsored loans, scholarships/grants, health care benefits, tuition waivers (full and partial), and unspecified assistantships also available. Financial award application deadline: 2/15; financial award applicants required to submit FAFSA. In 2010, 113 master's, 1 doctorate awarded. *Degree program information:* Part-time and evening/weekend programs available. Offers biology education (MAT, MS Ed, MST); childhood education (MS Ed); earth science education (MAT, MS Ed, MST); education (MAT, MS Ed, MST, Ed D); educational theory and practice (Ed D); English education (MAT, MS Ed, MST); French education (MAT, MST); literacy education (MS Ed); mathematical sciences education (MAT, MS Ed, MST); physics (MAT, MS Ed, MST); social studies (MAT, MS Ed, MST); Spanish education (MAT, MST); special education (MS Ed). *Application deadline:* For fall admission, 2/1 priority date for domestic and international students; for spring admission, 10/15 priority date for domestic and international students. Applications are processed on a rolling basis. *Application fee:* $60. Electronic applications accepted. *Application Contact:* Catherine Smith, Recruiting and Admissions Coordinator, 607-777-2151, Fax: 607-777-2501, E-mail: cmsmith@binghamton.edu. *Dean*, Dr. S. S. Grant, 607-777-7329, E-mail: ssgrant@binghamton.edu.

School of Management Students: 290 full-time (129 women), 40 part-time (18 women); includes 4 Black or African American, non-Hispanic/Latino; 52 Asian, non-Hispanic/Latino; 13 Hispanic/Latino, 118 international. Average age 25. 864 applicants, 30% accepted, 208 enrolled. *Faculty:* 40 full-time (8 women), 26 part-time/adjunct (6 women). Expenses: Contact institution. *Financial support:* In 2010–11, 30 students received support, including 3 fellowships with full tuition reimbursements available (averaging $17,000 per year), 2 research assistantships, 16 teaching assistantships with full tuition reimbursements available (averaging $17,000 per year); career-related internships or fieldwork, Federal Work-Study, institutionally sponsored loans, scholarships/grants, health care benefits, tuition waivers (partial), and unspecified assistantships also available. Financial award application deadline: 2/15; financial award applicants required to submit FAFSA. In 2010, 196 master's, 2 doctorates awarded. *Degree program information:* Part-time and evening/weekend programs available. Offers accounting (MS, PhD); business administration (MBA, PhD); health care professional executive (MBA); management (MBA, MS, PhD). *Application deadline:* Applications are processed on a rolling basis. *Application fee:* $60. Electronic applications accepted. *Application Contact:* Catherine Smith, Recruiting and Admissions Coordinator, 607-777-2151, Fax: 607-777-2501, E-mail: cmsmith@binghamton.edu. *Dean*, Dr. Upinder S. Dhillon, 607-777-2314, E-mail: dhillon@binghamton.edu.

Thomas J. Watson School of Engineering and Applied Science Students: 388 full-time (84 women), 392 part-time (60 women); includes 11 Black or African American, non-Hispanic/Latino; 2 American Indian or Alaska Native, non-Hispanic/Latino; 46 Asian, non-Hispanic/Latino; 9 Hispanic/Latino, 488 international. Average age 27. 883 applicants, 54% accepted, 210 enrolled. *Faculty:* 74 full-time (11 women), 13 part-time/adjunct (3 women). Expenses: Contact institution. *Financial support:* In 2010–11, 272 students received support, including 6 fellowships with full tuition reimbursements available (averaging $16,500 per year), 148 research assistantships with full tuition reimbursements available (averaging $16,500 per year), 84 teaching assistantships with full tuition reimbursements available (averaging $16,500 per year); career-related internships or fieldwork, Federal Work-Study, institutionally sponsored loans, scholarships/grants, health care benefits, tuition waivers (full and partial), and unspecified assistantships also available. Financial award application deadline: 2/15; financial award applicants required to submit FAFSA. In 2010, 205 master's, 33 doctorates awarded. *Degree program information:* Part-time and evening/weekend programs available. Offers biomedical engineering (MS, PhD); computer science (M Eng, MS, PhD); electrical and computer engineering (M Eng, MS, PhD); engineering and applied science (M Eng, MS, MSAT, PhD); materials science and engineering (MS, PhD); mechanical engineering (M Eng, MS, PhD); systems science and industrial engineering (M Eng, MS, MSAT, PhD). *Application deadline:* Applications are processed on a rolling basis. *Application fee:* $60. Electronic applications accepted. *Application Contact:* Catherine Smith, Recruiting and Admissions Coordinator, 607-777-2151, Fax: 607-777-2501, E-mail: cmsmith@binghamton.edu. *Dean*, Dr. Hari Srihari, 607-777-2871, E-mail: hsrihari@binghamton.edu.

STATE UNIVERSITY OF NEW YORK AT FREDONIA, Fredonia, NY 14063-1136

General Information State-supported, coed, comprehensive institution. CGS member. *Enrollment:* 5,769 graduate, professional, and undergraduate students; 201 full-time matriculated graduate/professional students (145 women), 180 part-time matriculated graduate/professional students (123 women). *Enrollment by degree level:* 335 master's, 29 other advanced degrees. *Graduate faculty:* 81 full-time (44 women), 12 part-time/adjunct (7 women). Tuition, state resident: full-time $8370; part-time $349 per credit hour. Tuition, nonresident: full-time $13,250; part-time $552 per credit hour. *Required fees:* $1328; $55.15 per credit hour. *Graduate housing:* Room and/or apartments available on a first-come, first-served basis to single students; on-campus housing not available to married students. Typical cost: $8600 per year ($10,530 including board). Room and board charges vary according to board plan. Housing application deadline: 7/15. *Student services:* Campus employment opportunities, campus safety program, career counseling, child daycare facilities, exercise/wellness program, free psychological counseling, grant writing training, international student services, low-cost health insurance, multicultural affairs office, services for students with disabilities, teacher training, writing training. *Library facilities:* Daniel A. Reed Library. *Online resources:* library catalog, web page, access to other libraries' catalogs. *Collection:* 514,608 titles, 48,000 serial subscriptions, 26,726 audiovisual materials.

Computer facilities: Computer purchase and lease plans are available. 500 computers available on campus for general student use. A campuswide network can be accessed from student residence rooms and from off campus. Online class registration is available. *Web address:* http://www.fredonia.edu/.

General Application Contact: Dr. Kevin P. Kearns, Associate Vice President of Graduate Studies and Research, 716-673-3808, Fax: 716-673-3338, E-mail: kevin.kearns@fredonia.edu.

GRADUATE UNITS

Graduate Studies *Degree program information:* Part-time and evening/weekend programs available. Offers biology (MS, MS Ed); chemistry (MS); curriculum and instruction science education (MS Ed); English (MA, MS Ed); interdisciplinary studies (MA, MS); mathematical sciences (MS Ed); speech pathology and audiology (MS, MS Ed). Electronic applications accepted.

College of Education *Degree program information:* Part-time and evening/weekend programs available. Offers educational administration (CAS); elementary education (MS Ed); literacy (MS Ed); secondary education (MS Ed); teaching English to speakers of other languages (MS Ed).

School of Music *Degree program information:* Part-time and evening/weekend programs available. Offers music (MM); music education (MM).

STATE UNIVERSITY OF NEW YORK AT NEW PALTZ, New Paltz, NY 12561

General Information State-supported, coed, comprehensive institution. *Enrollment:* 7,885 graduate, professional, and undergraduate students; 522 full-time matriculated graduate/professional students (342 women), 780 part-time matriculated graduate/professional students (554 women). *Enrollment by degree level:* 1,023 master's, 113 other advanced degrees. *Graduate faculty:* 136 full-time (78 women), 51 part-time/adjunct (38 women). Tuition, state resident: full-time $8370; part-time $349 per credit hour. Tuition, nonresident: full-time $13,780; part-time $574 per credit hour. *Required fees:* $1165; $33.80 per credit hour. $175 per term. Tuition and fees vary according to program. *Graduate housing:* On-campus housing not available. *Student services:* Campus employment opportunities, campus safety program, career counseling, child daycare facilities, free psychological counseling, international student services, low-cost health insurance, services for students with disabilities, teacher training. *Library facilities:* Sojourner Truth Library plus 1 other. *Online resources:* library catalog, web page. *Collection:* 525,476 titles, 106,269 serial subscriptions, 6,585 audiovisual materials.

Computer facilities: 950 computers available on campus for general student use. A campuswide network can be accessed from student residence rooms and from off campus. Online class registration is available. *Web address:* http://www.newpaltz.edu/.

General Application Contact: Caroline Murphy, Graduate Admissions Advisor, 845-257-3285, Fax: 845-257-3284, E-mail: gradschool@newpaltz.edu.

GRADUATE UNITS

Graduate School Students: 522 full-time (342 women), 780 part-time (554 women); includes 139 minority (26 Black or African American, non-Hispanic/Latino; 3 American Indian or Alaska Native, non-Hispanic/Latino; 30 Asian, non-Hispanic/Latino; 68 Hispanic/Latino; 1 Native Hawaiian or other Pacific Islander, non-Hispanic/Latino; 11 Two or more races, non-Hispanic/Latino), 152 international. Average age 31. 1,098 applicants, 57% accepted, 416 enrolled. *Faculty:* 136 full-time (78 women), 51 part-time/adjunct (38 women). Expenses: Contact institution. *Financial support:* In 2010–11, 92 students received support, including 9 fellowships (averaging $9,000 per year), 18 research assistantships with partial tuition reimbursements available (averaging $5,000 per year), 44 teaching assistantships with partial tuition reimbursements available (averaging $5,000 per year); career-related internships or fieldwork, Federal Work-Study, institutionally sponsored loans, scholarships/grants, traineeships, health care benefits, tuition waivers (full and partial), and unspecified assistantships also available. Support available to part-time students. Financial award application deadline: 8/1; financial award applicants required to submit FAFSA. In 2010, 526 master's, 61 other advanced degrees awarded. *Degree program information:* Part-time and evening/weekend programs available. *Application deadline:* For fall admission, 5/15 priority date for domestic students, 5/15 for international students; for spring admission, 11/15 priority date for domestic students, 11/15 for international students. Applications are processed on a rolling basis. *Application fee:* $50. Electronic applications accepted. *Application Contact:* Vika F. Shock, Director of Graduate Admissions, 845-257-3285, Fax: 845-257-3284, E-mail: gradschool@newpaltz.edu. *Associate Provost for Academic Affairs/Dean,* Dr. Laurel M. Garrick Duhaney, 845-257-3947.

School of Business Students: 45 full-time (19 women), 41 part-time (25 women); includes 2 Black or African American, non-Hispanic/Latino; 6 Asian, non-Hispanic/Latino; 6 Hispanic/Latino, 20 international. Average age 28. 64 applicants, 58% accepted, 31 enrolled. *Faculty:* 11 full-time (4 women), 3 part-time/adjunct (2 women). Expenses: Contact institution. *Financial support:* In 2010–11, 8 students received support, including 1 fellowship (averaging $2,500 per year), 6 research assistantships with partial tuition reimbursements available (averaging $5,000 per year), 1 teaching assistantship with partial tuition reimbursement available (averaging $5,000 per year); career-related internships or fieldwork, scholarships/grants, traineeships, and unspecified assistantships also available. Financial award application deadline: 8/1; financial award applicants required to submit FAFSA. In 2010, 41 master's awarded. *Degree program information:* Part-time and evening/weekend programs available. Offers business administration (MBA); public accountancy (MBA). *Application deadline:* For fall admission, 5/15 priority date for domestic students, 5/15 for international students; for spring admission, 11/15 for domestic and international students. Applications are processed on a rolling basis. *Application fee:* $50. Electronic applications accepted. *Application Contact:* Aaron Hines, Coordinator, 845-257-2968, E-mail: mba@newpaltz.edu. *Dean,* Dr. Hadi Salavitabar, 845-257-2930, E-mail: mba@newpaltz.edu.

School of Education Students: 208 full-time (158 women), 407 part-time (310 women); includes 71 minority (15 Black or African American, non-Hispanic/Latino; 1 American Indian or Alaska Native, non-Hispanic/Latino; 10 Asian, non-Hispanic/Latino; 38 Hispanic/Latino; 1 Native Hawaiian or other Pacific Islander, non-Hispanic/Latino; 6 Two or more races, non-Hispanic/Latino), 3 international. Average age 32. 438 applicants, 64% accepted, 225 enrolled. *Faculty:* 33 full-time (24 women), 22 part-time/adjunct (19 women). Expenses: Contact institution. *Financial support:* In 2010–11, 12 students received support, including 4 fellowships (averaging $5,000 per year); career-related internships or fieldwork, Federal Work-Study, institutionally sponsored loans, scholarships/grants, and tuition waivers (full) also available. Financial award application deadline: 8/1; financial award applicants required to submit FAFSA. In 2010, 279 master's, 61 other advanced degrees awarded. *Degree program information:* Part-time and evening/weekend programs available. Offers adolescence (7-12) (MS Ed); adolescence education: biology (MAT, MS Ed); adolescence education: chemistry (MAT, MS Ed); adolescence education: earth science (MAT, MS Ed); adolescence education: English (MAT, MS Ed); adolescence education: French (MAT, MS Ed); adolescence education: social studies (MAT, MS Ed); adolescence education: Spanish (MAT, MS Ed); adolescence special education and literacy education (MS Ed); alternative certificate: school district leader (transition D) (CAS); childhood (1-6) (MS Ed); childhood education (MS Ed); childhood education (1-6) (MST); childhood special education and literacy education (MS Ed); early childhood (B-2) (MS Ed); education (MAT, MPS, MS Ed, MST, CAS); humanistic/multicultural education (MPS); literacy education (5-12) (MS Ed); literacy education (B-6) (MS Ed); literacy education and adolescence special education (MS Ed); literacy education and childhood education and childhood special education (MS Ed); school business leadership (CAS); school leadership (MS Ed, CAS); second language education (MS Ed); special education (MS Ed). *Application deadline:* For fall admission, 3/1 priority date for domestic and international students; for spring admission, 10/1 priority date for domestic and international students. Applications are processed on a rolling basis. *Application fee:* $50. Electronic applications accepted. *Application Contact:* Caroline Murphy, Graduate Admissions Advisor, 845-257-3285, Fax: 845-257-3284, E-mail: gradschool@newpaltz.edu. *Dean,* Dr. Robert Michael, 845-257-2800, E-mail: michaelr@newpaltz.edu.

School of Fine and Performing Arts Students: 66 full-time (48 women), 50 part-time (41 women); includes 5 Asian, non-Hispanic/Latino; 1 Hispanic/Latino; 1 Two or more races, non-Hispanic/Latino, 11 international. Average age 30. 115 applicants, 57% accepted, 46 enrolled. *Faculty:* 28 full-time (21 women), 9 part-time/adjunct (3 women). Expenses: Contact institution. *Financial support:* In 2010–11, 14 students received support, including 3 research assistantships with partial tuition reimbursements available (averaging $5,000 per year), 10 teaching assistantships with partial tuition reimbursements available (averaging $5,000 per year); Federal Work-Study, institutionally sponsored loans, scholarships/grants, traineeships, tuition waivers (full), and unspecified assistantships also available. Financial award application deadline: 8/1; financial award applicants required to submit FAFSA. In 2010, 60 master's awarded. *Degree program information:* Part-time and evening/weekend programs available. Offers art studio (MA); ceramics (MFA); fine and performing arts (MA, MFA, MS, MS Ed); metal (MFA); music therapy (MS); painting/drawing (MFA); printmaking (MFA); sculpture (MFA); visual arts education (MS Ed). *Application deadline:* For fall admission, 2/15 priority date for domestic students, 2/15 for international students. Applications are processed on a rolling basis. *Application fee:* $50. Electronic applications accepted. *Application Contact:* Matthew Friday, Graduate Coordinator, 845-257-2609. *Dean,* Dr. Mary Hafeli, 845-257-3860, E-mail: hafelim@newpaltz.edu.

School of Liberal Arts and Sciences Students: 105 full-time (88 women), 70 part-time (51 women); includes 4 Black or African American, non-Hispanic/Latino; 1 American Indian or Alaska Native, non-Hispanic/Latino; 2 Asian, non-Hispanic/Latino; 7 Hispanic/Latino; 3 Two or more races, non-Hispanic/Latino, 3 international. Average age 28. 290 applicants, 42% accepted, 71 enrolled. *Faculty:* 44 full-time (26 women), 11 part-time/adjunct (10 women). Expenses: Contact institution. *Financial support:* In 2010–11, 32 students received support, including 1 fellowship (averaging $11,000 per year), 3 research assistantships with partial tuition reimbursements available (averaging $5,000 per year), 26 teaching assistantships with partial tuition reimbursements available (averaging $5,000 per year); career-related internships or fieldwork, Federal Work-Study, institutionally sponsored loans, scholarships/grants, traineeships, tuition waivers (full), and unspecified assistantships also available. Financial award application deadline: 8/1; financial award applicants required to submit FAFSA. In 2010, 62 master's awarded. *Degree program information:* Part-time and evening/weekend programs available. Offers communication disorders (MS); English (MA); liberal arts and sciences (MA, MS); mental health counseling (MS); psychology (MA); school counseling (MS). *Application deadline:* For fall admission, 5/15 for domestic and international students; for spring admission, 11/15 for domestic and international students. Applications are processed on a rolling basis. *Application fee:* $50. Electronic applications accepted. *Application Contact:* Caroline Murphy, Graduate Admissions Advisor, 845-257-3285, E-mail: gradschool@newpaltz.edu. *Dean,* Dr. James Schiffer, 845-257-3520, E-mail: schiffej@newpaltz.edu.

School of Science and Engineering Students: 85 full-time (20 women), 59 part-time (13 women); includes 2 Black or African American, non-Hispanic/Latino; 1 American Indian or Alaska Native, non-Hispanic/Latino; 3 Asian, non-Hispanic/Latino; 5 Hispanic/Latino, 113 international. Average age 25. 208 applicants, 57% accepted, 42 enrolled. *Faculty:* 22 full-time (5 women), 6 part-time/adjunct (1 woman). Expenses: Contact institution. *Financial support:* In 2010–11, 17 students received support, including 6 teaching assistantships with partial tuition reimbursements available (averaging $5,000 per year); traineeships, tuition waivers (partial), and unspecified assistantships also available. Financial award application deadline: 8/1; financial award applicants required to submit FAFSA. In 2010, 84 master's awarded. *Degree program information:* Part-time and evening/weekend programs available. Offers biology (MA); computer science (MS); electrical engineering (MS); science and engineering (MA, MS). *Application deadline:* For fall admission, 5/15 priority date for domestic and international students; for spring admission, 11/15 for domestic students, 11/15 priority date for international students. Applications are processed on a rolling basis. *Application fee:* $50. Electronic applications accepted. *Application Contact:* Caroline Murphy, Graduate Admissions Advisor, 845-257-3285, E-mail: gradschool@newpaltz.edu. *Dean,* Dr. Daniel Jelski, 845-257-3728, E-mail: jelskid@newpaltz.edu.

STATE UNIVERSITY OF NEW YORK AT OSWEGO, Oswego, NY 13126

General Information State-supported, coed, comprehensive institution. CGS member. *Enrollment:* 8,297 graduate, professional, and undergraduate students; 391 full-time matriculated graduate/professional students (263 women), 342 part-time matriculated graduate/professional students (231 women). *Enrollment by degree level:* 602 master's, 131 other advanced degrees. *Graduate faculty:* 94 full-time (45 women), 57 part-time/adjunct (30 women). Tuition, state resident: full-time $8370; part-time $349 per credit hour. Tuition, nonresident: full-time $13,780; part-time $574 per credit hour. *Required fees:* $853; $22.59 per credit hour. *Graduate housing:* Room and/or apartments available on a first-come, first-served basis to single students; on-campus housing not available to married students. Typical cost: $7390 per year ($11,610 including board). Room and board charges vary according to board plan. Housing application deadline: 4/1. *Student services:* Campus employment opportunities, career counseling, child daycare facilities, exercise/wellness program, free psychological counseling, grant writing training, international student services, low-cost health insurance, services for students with disabilities. *Library facilities:* Penfield Library. *Online resources:* library catalog, web page. *Collection:* 554,480 titles, 2,710 serial subscriptions, 33,142 audiovisual materials. *Research affiliation:* Alcan (research and education), MACTEC (research and education), IBM (research and education), Entergy (research and education), Intel Corporation (research and education), IBM (research and education).

Computer facilities: 750 computers available on campus for general student use. A campuswide network can be accessed from student residence rooms and from off campus. Online class registration is available. *Web address:* http://www.oswego.edu/.

General Application Contact: Dr. David W. King, Dean of Graduate Studies, 315-312-3692, Fax: 315-312-3228, E-mail: david.king@oswego.edu.

GRADUATE UNITS

Graduate Studies Students: 391 full-time (263 women), 342 part-time (231 women); includes 41 minority (10 Black or African American, non-Hispanic/Latino; 3 American Indian or Alaska Native, non-Hispanic/Latino; 10 Asian, non-Hispanic/Latino; 14 Hispanic/Latino; 4 Two or more races, non-Hispanic/Latino), 11 international. Average age 30. 658 applicants, 84% accepted. *Faculty:* 94 full-time (45 women), 57 part-time/adjunct (30 women). Expenses: Contact institution. *Financial support:* In 2010–11, 131 students received support, including 9 fellowships with full tuition reimbursements available (averaging $5,100 per year), 122 teaching assistantships with full and partial tuition reimbursements available (averaging $7,000 per year); research assistantships with full tuition reimbursements available, career-related internships or fieldwork, Federal Work-Study, institutionally sponsored loans, scholarships/grants, health care benefits, tuition waivers (partial), and unspecified assistantships also available. Support available to part-time students. Financial award application deadline: 4/1; financial award applicants required to submit FAFSA. In 2010, 349 master's, 72 other advanced degrees awarded. *Degree program information:* Part-time programs available. Offers art (MA). *Application deadline:* For fall admission, 2/1 for domestic students, 4/15 for international students; for spring admission, 10/1 for domestic students, 11/1 for international students. Applications are processed on a rolling basis. *Application fee:* $50. *Application Contact:* Dr. David W. King, Dean of Graduate Studies, 315-312-3692, Fax: 315-312-3228, E-mail: david.king@oswego.edu. *Dean of Graduate Studies,* Dr. David W. King, 315-312-3692, Fax: 315-312-3228, E-mail: david.king@oswego.edu.

College of Liberal Arts and Sciences Students: 27 full-time (14 women), 21 part-time (11 women); includes 3 Hispanic/Latino, 1 international. Average age 25. 42 applicants, 86% accepted. *Faculty:* 32 full-time (8 women), 3 part-time/adjunct (1 woman). Expenses: Contact institution. *Financial support:* In 2010–11, 24 students received support, including 1 fellowship (averaging $5,100 per year), 23 research assistantships with partial tuition reimbursements available (averaging $3,800 per year); teaching assistantships with full and partial tuition reimbursements available, career-related internships or fieldwork, Federal Work-Study, institutionally sponsored loans, scholarships/grants, health care benefits, tuition waivers (partial), and unspecified assistantships also available. Support available to part-time students. Financial award application deadline: 4/1; financial award applicants required to submit FAFSA. In 2010, 17 master's awarded. *Degree program information:* Part-time programs available. Offers chemistry (MS); English (MA); history (MA); human computer interaction (MA); liberal arts and sciences (MA, MS). *Application deadline:* For fall admission, 4/1 priority date for domestic students, 4/1 for international students; for spring admission, 10/1 priority date for domestic students, 10/1 for international students. Applications are processed on a rolling basis. *Application fee:* $50. *Application Contact:* Dr. David W. King, Dean of Graduate Studies, 315-312-3152, Fax: 315-312-3228, E-mail: david.king@oswego.edu. *Interim Dean,* Dr. Rhonda Mandel, 315-312-2285, E-mail: rhonda.mandel@oswego.edu.

School of Business Students: 72 full-time (32 women), 39 part-time (20 women); includes 2 Black or African American, non-Hispanic/Latino; 6 Asian, non-Hispanic/Latino; 2 Hispanic/Latino, 9 international. Average age 27. 101 applicants, 99% accepted. *Faculty:* 8 full-time (3 women), 7 part-time/adjunct (1 woman). Expenses: Contact institution. *Financial support:* In 2010–11, 21 students received support, including 3 fellowships with full tuition reimbursements available (averaging $5,100 per year), 18 teaching assistantships with partial tuition reimbursements available (averaging $2,400 per year); career-related internships or fieldwork, Federal Work-Study, institutionally sponsored loans, scholarships/grants, health care benefits, tuition waivers (partial), and unspecified assistantships also available. Support available to part-time students. Financial award application deadline: 4/1; financial award applicants required to submit FAFSA. In 2010, 39 master's awarded. *Degree program information:* Part-time and evening/weekend programs available. Offers business (MBA); business administration (MBA). *Application deadline:* For fall admission, 4/15 for domestic and international students; for spring admission, 10/1 for domestic students, 11/1 for inter-

State University of New York at Oswego (continued)

national students. Applications are processed on a rolling basis. *Application fee:* $50. *Application Contact:* Dr. David W. King, Director, 315-312-3152, Fax: 315-312-3228, E-mail: david.king@oswego.edu. *Dean*, Dr. Richard Skolnik, 315-312-3168, E-mail: richard.skolnik@oswego.edu.

School of Education Students: 288 full-time (215 women), 277 part-time (197 women); includes 28 minority (8 Black or African American, non-Hispanic/Latino; 3 American Indian or Alaska Native, non-Hispanic/Latino; 4 Asian, non-Hispanic/Latino; 9 Hispanic/Latino; 4 Two or more races, non-Hispanic/Latino). Average age 29. 505 applicants, 88% accepted. *Faculty:* 32 full-time (24 women), 38 part-time/adjunct (23 women). Expenses: Contact institution. *Financial support:* In 2010–11, 74 students received support, including 5 fellowships with full tuition reimbursements available (averaging $5,100 per year), 69 teaching assistantships with full and partial tuition reimbursements available (averaging $3,800 per year); research assistantships, career-related internships or fieldwork, Federal Work-Study, institutionally sponsored loans, scholarships/grants, health care benefits, and unspecified assistantships also available. Support available to part-time students. Financial award application deadline: 4/1; financial award applicants required to submit FAFSA. In 2010, 304 master's, 51 other advanced degrees awarded. *Degree program information:* Part-time programs available. Offers adolescence education (MST); agriculture (MS Ed); art education (MAT); business and marketing (MS Ed); childhood education (MST); counseling services (MS, CAS); education (MAT, MS, MS Ed, MST, CAS); educational administration and supervision (CAS); elementary education (MS Ed); family and consumer sciences (MS Ed); health careers (MS Ed); literacy education (MS Ed); mental health counseling (MS); school building leadership (CAS); school psychology (MS, CAS); secondary education (MS Ed); special education (MS Ed); technical education (MS Ed); technology (MS Ed); trade education (MS Ed). *Application deadline:* For fall admission, 1/15 for domestic and international students; for spring admission, 10/1 for domestic and international students. *Application fee:* $50. *Application Contact:* Dr. David W. King, Dean of Graduate Studies, 315-312-3152, Fax: 315-312-3228, E-mail: dking@oswego.edu. *Dean*, Dr. Pamela Michel, 315-312-2102.

STATE UNIVERSITY OF NEW YORK AT PLATTSBURGH, Plattsburgh, NY 12901-2681

General Information State-supported, coed, comprehensive institution. *Graduate housing:* Room and/or apartments available on a first-come, first-served basis to single students; on-campus housing not available to married students. Housing application deadline: 5/1. *Research affiliation:* New York State Sea Grant (environmental science), Miner Agricultural Research Institute (environmental science).

GRADUATE UNITS

Division of Education, Health, and Human Services *Degree program information:* Part-time programs available. Offers adolescence education (MST); biology 7-12 (MST); birth to grade 2 (MS Ed); birth-grade 6 (MS Ed); chemistry 7-12 (MST); childhood education (grades 1-6) (MST); college/agency counseling (MS); earth science 7-12 (MST); education, health, and human services (MA, MS, MS Ed, MST, CAS); educational leadership (CAS); English 7-12 (MST); French 7-12 (MST); grades 1 to 6 (MS Ed); grades 5-12 (MS Ed); grades 7 to 12 (MS Ed); mathematics 7-12 (MST); physics 7-12 (MST); school counselor (MS Ed, CAS); social studies 7-12 (MST); Spanish 7-12 (MST); speech-language pathology (MA); teacher education: curriculum and instruction (MS Ed).

Faculty of Arts and Science *Degree program information:* Part-time programs available. Offers arts and science (MA, MS, CAS); natural science (MS); school psychology (MA, CAS).

School of Business and Economics *Degree program information:* Part-time and evening/weekend programs available. Offers business and economics (MA, MS); leadership (MS); liberal studies (MA).

STATE UNIVERSITY OF NEW YORK COLLEGE AT CORTLAND, Cortland, NY 13045

General Information State-supported, coed, comprehensive institution. *Graduate housing:* On-campus housing not available.

GRADUATE UNITS

Graduate Studies *Degree program information:* Part-time and evening/weekend programs available.

School of Arts and Sciences *Degree program information:* Part-time and evening/weekend programs available. Offers American civilization and culture (CAS); arts and sciences (MA, MAT, MS Ed, CAS); biology (MAT, MS Ed); chemistry (MAT, MS Ed); earth science (MAT, MS Ed); English (MA, MAT, MS Ed); French (MS Ed); history (MA, MS Ed); mathematics (MAT, MS Ed); physics (MAT, MS Ed); second language education (MS Ed); social studies (MS Ed); Spanish (MS Ed).

School of Education *Degree program information:* Part-time and evening/weekend programs available. Offers childhood/early child education (MS Ed, MST); educational leadership (CAS); literacy (MS Ed); teaching students with disabilities (MS Ed).

School of Professional Studies *Degree program information:* Part-time and evening/weekend programs available. Offers exercise science and sport studies (MS); health education (MS Ed, MST); international sport management (MS); physical education (MS Ed); professional studies (MS, MS Ed, MST); recreation and leisure studies (MS, MS Ed); sport management (MS).

STATE UNIVERSITY OF NEW YORK COLLEGE AT GENESEO, Geneseo, NY 14454-1401

General Information State-supported, coed, comprehensive institution. *Enrollment:* 5,695 graduate, professional, and undergraduate students; 73 full-time matriculated graduate/professional students (55 women), 137 part-time matriculated graduate/professional students (119 women). *Enrollment by degree level:* 210 master's. *Graduate faculty:* 74 full-time (41 women), 11 part-time/adjunct (5 women). Tuition, state resident: full-time $8370; part-time $349 per credit hour. Tuition, nonresident: full-time $13,780; part-time $574 per credit hour. *Required fees:* $726; $60.08 per credit hour. Tuition and fees vary according to program. *Graduate housing:* On-campus housing not available. *Student services:* Campus employment opportunities, campus safety program, career counseling, exercise/wellness program, free psychological counseling, international student services, low-cost health insurance, multicultural affairs office, services for students with disabilities, teacher training. *Library facilities:* Milne Library. *Online resources:* library catalog, web page, access to other libraries' catalogs. *Collection:* 647,902 titles, 67,247 serial subscriptions, 24,263 audiovisual materials. *Research affiliation:* Mt. Hope Family Center (psychology), Center for Nanomaterials and Nanoelectronics (chemistry), Rochester National Technical Institute for the Deaf (communicative disorders), Great Lakes Research Consortium (biology), Rochester Laboratory for Laser Energetics (nuclear physics), Genesee Valley Health Partnership (health).

Computer facilities: Computer purchase and lease plans are available. 640 computers available on campus for general student use. A campuswide network can be accessed from student residence rooms and from off campus. Online class registration is available. *Web address:* http://www.geneseo.edu/.

General Application Contact: Dr. Savi Iyer, Director of Graduate Studies, 585-245-5855, Fax: 585-245-5032, E-mail: iyer@geneseo.edu.

GRADUATE UNITS

Graduate Studies Students: 73 full-time (55 women), 137 part-time (119 women); includes 2 Asian, non-Hispanic/Latino; 3 Hispanic/Latino; 1 Two or more races, non-Hispanic/Latino. Average age 25. 206 applicants, 73% accepted, 100 enrolled. *Faculty:* 74 full-time (41 women), 11 part-time/adjunct (5 women). Expenses: Contact institution. *Financial support:* Career-related internships or fieldwork, institutionally sponsored loans, scholarships/grants, health care benefits, tuition waivers (full), and unspecified assistantships available. Support available to part-time students. Financial award application deadline: 4/1; financial award applicants required to submit FAFSA. In 2010, 71 master's awarded. *Degree program information:* Part-time and evening/weekend programs available. *Application deadline:* For fall admission, 3/1 for domestic students; for spring admission, 10/1 for domestic students. *Application fee:* $50. *Application Contact:* Dr. Savi Iyer, Associate Dean of the College/Director, 585-245-5855, Fax: 585-245-5032, E-mail: iyer@geneseo.edu. *Dean of the College*, Dr. Mary Radosh, 585-245-5541, Fax: 585-245-5032, E-mail: radosh@geneseo.edu.

School of Business Students: 16 full-time (3 women). Average age 23. 33 applicants, 88% accepted, 16 enrolled. *Faculty:* 3 full-time (1 woman), 1 part-time/adjunct (0 women). Expenses: Contact institution. *Financial support:* Application deadline: 4/1. In 2010, 9 master's awarded. Offers accounting (MS). *Application deadline:* For fall admission, 2/1 priority date for domestic students; for spring admission, 9/1 for domestic students. *Application fee:* $50. *Application Contact:* Dr. Harry Howe, Director, Graduate Program, 585-245-5465, Fax: 585-245-5467, E-mail: howeh@geneseo.edu. *Interim Dean*, Dr. Michael Schinski, 585-245-5367, Fax: 585-245-5467, E-mail: schinski@geneseo.edu.

School of Education Students: 26 full-time (24 women), 79 part-time (67 women); includes 1 Black or African American, non-Hispanic/Latino; 2 Asian, non-Hispanic/Latino. Average age 26. 92 applicants, 99% accepted, 73 enrolled. *Faculty:* 31 full-time (18 women), 3 part-time/adjunct (0 women). Expenses: Contact institution. *Financial support:* In 2010–11, 6 students received support. Scholarships/grants, health care benefits, tuition waivers (full), and unspecified assistantships available. Support available to part-time students. Financial award application deadline: 4/1; financial award applicants required to submit FAFSA. In 2010, 46 master's awarded. *Degree program information:* Part-time and evening/weekend programs available. Offers childhood multicultural education (1-6) (MS Ed); early childhood education (MS Ed); elementary education (MS Ed); reading (MS Ed); secondary education (MS Ed). *Application deadline:* For fall admission, 3/1 priority date for domestic students; for spring admission, 10/1 for domestic students. *Application fee:* $50. *Application Contact:* Dr. Susan Salmon, Assistant to the Dean/Graduate Liaison, 585-245-5560, Fax: 585-245-5220, E-mail: salmon@geneseo.edu. *Dean/Chairperson*, Dr. Osman Alawiye, 585-245-5560, Fax: 585-245-5220, E-mail: alawiyeo@geneseo.edu.

STATE UNIVERSITY OF NEW YORK COLLEGE AT OLD WESTBURY, Old Westbury, NY 11568-0210

General Information State-supported, coed, comprehensive institution. *Graduate housing:* Room and/or apartments available on a first-come, first-served basis to single students; on-campus housing not available to married students.

GRADUATE UNITS

Program in Accounting *Degree program information:* Part-time and evening/weekend programs available. Offers accounting (MS). Electronic applications accepted.

STATE UNIVERSITY OF NEW YORK COLLEGE AT ONEONTA, Oneonta, NY 13820-4015

General Information State-supported, coed, comprehensive institution. *Enrollment:* 6,014 graduate, professional, and undergraduate students; 83 full-time matriculated graduate/professional students (74 women), 84 part-time matriculated graduate/professional students (59 women). *Enrollment by degree level:* 148 master's, 19 other advanced degrees. Tuition, state resident: full-time $8370; part-time $349 per credit hour. Tuition, nonresident: full-time $13,780; part-time $558 per credit hour. *Required fees:* $899; $22 per credit hour. *Graduate housing:* Room and/or apartments available on a first-come, first-served basis to single students; on-campus housing not available to married students. Housing application deadline: 5/1. *Student services:* Campus employment opportunities, campus safety program, career counseling, child daycare facilities, exercise/wellness program, free psychological counseling, grant writing training, international student services, low-cost health insurance, multicultural affairs office, services for students with disabilities, teacher training, writing training. *Library facilities:* Milne Library. *Online resources:* library catalog, web page, access to other libraries' catalogs. *Collection:* 456,868 titles, 50,000 serial subscriptions, 9,790 audiovisual materials. *Research affiliation:* New York State Historical Association (history museum studies).

Computer facilities: Computer purchase and lease plans are available. 700 computers available on campus for general student use. A campuswide network can be accessed from student residence rooms and from off campus. Online class registration is available. *Web address:* http://www.oneonta.edu/.

General Application Contact: Patrick J. Mente, Graduate Office, 607-436-2523, Fax: 607-436-3084, E-mail: gradstudies@oneonta.edu.

GRADUATE UNITS

Graduate Education Students: 83 full-time (74 women), 84 part-time (59 women); includes 2 Black or African American, non-Hispanic/Latino; 2 Asian, non-Hispanic/Latino; 3 Hispanic/Latino. Average age 27. 42 applicants, 100% accepted, 42 enrolled. Expenses: Contact institution. *Financial support:* In 2010–11, 14 students received support; fellowships, teaching assistantships, Federal Work-Study and scholarships/grants available. Financial award applicants required to submit FAFSA. In 2010, 49 master's, 9 other advanced degrees awarded. *Degree program information:* Part-time and evening/weekend programs available. Postbaccalaureate distance learning degree programs offered (no on-campus study). Offers biology (MA); earth sciences (MA); history museum studies (MA); nutrition and dietetics (MS). *Application deadline:* Applications are processed on a rolling basis. *Application fee:* $50. *Application Contact:* Patrick J. Mente, Director of Graduate Studies, 607-436-2523, Fax: 607-436-3084, E-mail: gradstudies@oneonta.edu. *Director of Graduate Studies*, Patrick J. Mente, 607-436-2523, Fax: 607-436-3084, E-mail: gradstudies@oneonta.edu.

Division of Education Students: 26 full-time (20 women), 42 part-time (32 women). Average age 25. 73 applicants, 85% accepted, 57 enrolled. Expenses: Contact institution. In 2010, 17 master's awarded. *Degree program information:* Part-time and evening/weekend programs available. Offers adolescence education (MS Ed); childhood education (MS Ed); educational psychology and counseling (MS Ed, CAS); educational technology specialist (MS Ed); elementary education and reading (MS Ed); family and consumer science education (MS Ed); literacy education (MS Ed); school counselor K-12 (MS Ed, CAS); secondary education (MS Ed); special education (MS Ed). *Application deadline:* For fall admission, 3/25 priority date for domestic students; for spring admission, 10/1 priority date for domestic students. Applications are processed on a rolling basis. *Application fee:* $50. *Application Contact:* Patrick J. Mente, Director of Graduate Studies, 607-436-2523, Fax: 607-436-3084, E-mail: gradstudies@oneonta.edu. *Associate Dean*, Dr. Joanne Curran, 607-436-2541, Fax: 607-436-2554, E-mail: curranjm@oneonta.edu.

STATE UNIVERSITY OF NEW YORK COLLEGE AT POTSDAM, Potsdam, NY 13676

General Information State-supported, coed, comprehensive institution. *Enrollment:* 4,413 graduate, professional, and undergraduate students; 290 full-time matriculated graduate/professional students (195 women), 203 part-time matriculated graduate/professional students (157 women). *Enrollment by degree level:* 493 master's. *Graduate faculty:* 71 full-time (34 women), 32 part-time/adjunct (21 women). *Graduate housing:* Room and/or apartments available on a first-come, first-served basis to single students; on-campus housing not available to married students. *Student services:* Campus employment opportunities, campus safety program, career counseling, child daycare facilities, exercise/wellness program, free psychological counseling, grant writing training, international student services, low-cost health insurance, multicultural affairs office, services for students with disabilities, teacher training, writing training. *Library facilities:* F. W. Crumb Memorial Library plus 1 other. *Online resources:* library catalog, web page, access to other libraries' catalogs. *Collection:* 467,382 titles, 15,570 serial subscriptions, 20,455 audiovisual materials.

Computer facilities: Computer purchase and lease plans are available. 690 computers available on campus for general student use. A campuswide network can be accessed from student residence rooms and from off campus. Online class registration, online access to financial aid status, unofficial transcripts, billing, meal plan and housing sign ups are available. *Web address:* http://www.potsdam.edu/.

General Application Contact: Peter Cutler, Graduate Admissions Counselor, 315-267-3154, Fax: 315-267-4802, E-mail: cutlerpj@potsdam.edu.

GRADUATE UNITS

Crane School of Music Students: 10 full-time (5 women), 11 part-time (2 women); includes 2 minority (1 Black or African American, non-Hispanic/Latino; 1 Asian, non-Hispanic/Latino). 28 applicants, 61% accepted, 13 enrolled. *Faculty:* 25 full-time (9 women), 5 part-time/adjunct (1 woman). Expenses: Contact institution. *Financial support:* In 2010–11, 2 students received support; teaching assistantships with full tuition reimbursements available, career-related internships or fieldwork, Federal Work-Study, scholarships/grants, and unspecified assistantships available. Support available to part-time students. Financial award application deadline: 3/1; financial award applicants required to submit FAFSA. In 2010, 21 master's awarded. *Degree program information:* Part-time programs available. Offers music composition (MM); music education (MM); music performance (MM). *Application deadline:* For fall admission, 4/1 for domestic and international students; for winter admission, 10/15 for domestic and international students; for spring admission, 3/1 for domestic and international students. Applications are processed on a rolling basis. *Application fee:* $50. *Application Contact:* Karen Miller, Secretary, 315-267-3418, Fax: 315-267-2413, E-mail: millerkl@potsdam.edu. *Dean*, Dr. Michael R. Sitton, 315-267-2415, Fax: 315-267-2413, E-mail: sittonmr@potsdam.edu.

School of Arts and Sciences Students: 2 full-time (0 women), 14 part-time (9 women); includes 4 minority (3 Black or African American, non-Hispanic/Latino; 1 American Indian or Alaska Native, non-Hispanic/Latino). 7 applicants, 100% accepted, 6 enrolled. *Faculty:* 11 full-time (5 women). Expenses: Contact institution. *Financial support:* In 2010–11, 2 students received support; teaching assistantships with full tuition reimbursements available, Federal Work-Study and unspecified assistantships available. Support available to part-time students. Financial award application deadline: 3/1; financial award applicants required to submit FAFSA. In 2010, 8 master's awarded. *Degree program information:* Part-time and evening/weekend programs available. Offers arts and sciences (MA); English and communication (MA); mathematics (MA). *Application deadline:* For fall admission, 4/1 for domestic and international students; for winter admission, 10/15 for domestic and international students; for spring admission, 3/1 for domestic and international students. Applications are processed on a rolling basis. *Application fee:* $50. *Application Contact:* Peter Cutler, Graduate Admissions Counselor, 315-267-3154, Fax: 315-267-4802, E-mail: cutlerpj@potsdam.edu. *Interim Dean*, Dr. Steven J. Marqusee, 315-267-3186, Fax: 315-267-3176, E-mail: marqussj@potsdam.edu.

School of Education and Professional Studies Students: 278 full-time (190 women), 179 part-time (146 women); includes 14 minority (8 Black or African American, non-Hispanic/Latino; 3 American Indian or Alaska Native, non-Hispanic/Latino; 3 Hispanic/Latino), 106 international. 238 applicants, 92% accepted, 205 enrolled. *Faculty:* 35 full-time (20 women), 27 part-time/adjunct (20 women). Expenses: Contact institution. *Financial support:* In 2010–11, 3 students received support; fellowships, teaching assistantships with full tuition reimbursements available, career-related internships or fieldwork, Federal Work-Study, scholarships/grants, tuition waivers (full), and unspecified assistantships available. Support available to part-time students. Financial award application deadline: 3/1; financial award applicants required to submit FAFSA. In 2010, 326 master's awarded. *Degree program information:* Part-time programs available. Postbaccalaureate distance learning degree programs offered (minimal on-campus study). Offers birth—grade 2 (MS Ed); childhood education (MST); curriculum and instruction (MS Ed); education and professional studies (MS Ed, MST); educational technology specialist (MS Ed); English (MST); grades 1-6 (MS Ed); grades 7-12 (MS Ed); literacy educator (MS Ed); literacy specialist (MS Ed); mathematics (with grades 5-6 extension) (MST); organizational performance, leadership and technology (MS Ed); science (MST); Social Studies (with grades 5-6 extension) (MST). *Application deadline:* For fall admission, 4/1 for domestic and international students; for winter admission, 10/15 for domestic and international students; for spring admission, 3/1 for domestic and international students. Applications are processed on a rolling basis. *Application fee:* $50. *Application Contact:* Peter Cutler, Graduate Admissions Counselor, 315-267-3154, Fax: 315-267-4802, E-mail: cutlerpj@potsdam.edu. *Interim Dean*, Dr. Peter S. Brouwer, 315-267-2515, Fax: 315-267-4802, E-mail: brouweps@potsdam.edu.

STATE UNIVERSITY OF NEW YORK COLLEGE OF ENVIRONMENTAL SCIENCE AND FORESTRY, Syracuse, NY 13210-2779

General Information State-supported, coed, university. CGS member. *Enrollment:* 2,343 graduate, professional, and undergraduate students; 313 full-time matriculated graduate/professional students (170 women), 174 part-time matriculated graduate/professional students (71 women). *Enrollment by degree level:* 289 master's, 194 doctoral, 4 other advanced degrees. *Graduate faculty:* 119 full-time (25 women), 18 part-time/adjunct (9 women). Tuition, state resident: full-time $8370; part-time $349 per credit hour. Tuition, nonresident: full-time $13,780. *Required fees:* $30.30 per credit hour. $20 per year. *Graduate housing:* On-campus housing not available. *Student services:* Campus employment opportunities, campus safety program, career counseling, exercise/wellness program, free psychological counseling, grant writing training, international student services, low-cost health insurance, multicultural affairs office, services for students with disabilities, teacher training, writing training. *Library facilities:* F. Franklin Moon Library plus 1 other. *Online resources:* library catalog, web page, access to other libraries' catalogs. *Collection:* 135,596 titles, 1,984 serial subscriptions, 726 audiovisual materials. *Research affiliation:* U. S. Department of Agriculture (USDA) (forest and natural resources management), National Aeronautics and Space Administration (NASA) (remote sensing and GIS), New York State Department of Agriculture & Markets (green infrastructure and food systems), New York State Department of Environmental Conservation (environmental conservation and wildlife management), Honeywell International (brownfields remediation), Department of Commerce (Great Lakes water research).

Computer facilities: Computer purchase and lease plans are available. 150 computers available on campus for general student use. A campuswide network can be accessed from student residence rooms and from off campus. Online class registration is available. *Web address:* http://www.esf.edu/.

General Application Contact: Scott S. Shannon, Dean, Instruction and Graduate Studies, 315-470-6599, Fax: 315-470-6978, E-mail: esfgrad@esf.edu.

GRADUATE UNITS

Department of Chemistry Offers biochemistry (MPS, MS, PhD); environmental and forest chemistry (MPS, MS, PhD); organic chemistry (MPS); organic chemistry of natural products (MS, PhD); polymer chemistry (MPS, MS, PhD). Electronic applications accepted.

Department of Environmental and Forest Biology Offers applied ecology (MPS); chemical ecology (MPS, MS, PhD); conservation biology (MPS, MS, PhD); ecology (MPS, MS, PhD); entomology (MPS, MS, PhD); environmental interpretation (MPS, MS, PhD); environmental physiology (MPS, MS, PhD); fish and wildlife biology and management (MPS, MS, PhD); forest pathology and mycology (MPS, MS, PhD); plant biotechnology (MPS); plant science and biotechnology (MPS, MS, PhD).

Department of Environmental Resources Engineering Offers ecological engineering (MS, PhD); environmental and resources engineering (MPS, MS, PhD); environmental management (MPS); geospatial information science and engineering (MS, PhD); mapping sciences (MPS); water resources engineering (MS, PhD).

Department of Environmental Studies Offers environmental studies (MPS, MS).

Department of Forest and Natural Resources Management Offers ecology and ecosystems (MPS, MS, PhD); economics, governance and human dimensions (MPS, MS, PhD); environmental and natural resource policy (PhD); forest resources management (MF); monitoring, analysis and modeling (MPS, MS, PhD); natural resources management (MPS, MS, PhD).

Department of Landscape Architecture Offers community design and planning (MLA, MS); cultural landscape conservation (MLA, MS); landscape and urban ecology (MLA, MS).

Department of Paper and Bioprocess Engineering Offers environmental and resource engineering (MPS, MS, PhD).

Department of Sustainable Construction Management and Engineering Offers construction management (MPS, MS, PhD); engineered wood products and structures (MPS, MS, PhD); tropical timbers wood science and technology (MPS, MS, PhD); wood anatomy and ultrastructure (MPS, MS, PhD); wood treatments (MPS, MS, PhD).

Program in Environmental Science *Degree program information:* Part-time programs available. Offers environmental and community land planning (MPS, MS, PhD); environmental and natural resources policy (PhD); environmental communication and participatory processes (MPS, MS, PhD); environmental policy and democratic processes (MPS, MS, PhD); environmental systems and risk management (MPS, MS, PhD); water and wetland resource studies (MPS, MS, PhD).

STATE UNIVERSITY OF NEW YORK COLLEGE OF OPTOMETRY, New York, NY 10036

General Information State-supported, coed, graduate-only institution. *Enrollment by degree level:* 278 first professional, 4 doctoral. *Graduate faculty:* 90 full-time (32 women), 75 part-time/adjunct (35 women). Tuition, state resident: full-time $17,380. Tuition, nonresident: full-time $33,370. *Required fees:* $395. *Graduate housing:* On-campus housing not available. *Student services:* Campus employment opportunities, campus safety program, career counseling, international student services, low-cost health insurance. *Library facilities:* Harold Kohn Visual Science Library. *Collection:* 3,600 titles, 400 serial subscriptions. *Research affiliation:* Schnurmacher Institute for Vision Research (vision science).

Computer facilities: 32 computers available on campus for general student use. A campuswide network can be accessed from off campus. Online class registration is available. *Web address:* http://www.sunyopt.edu/.

General Application Contact: Guilherme Albieri, Director of Admissions and Marketing, 212-938-5500, Fax: 212-938-5504, E-mail: admissions@sunyopt.edu.

GRADUATE UNITS

Graduate Programs Students: 11 full-time (6 women), 4 part-time (2 women); includes 11 Asian, non-Hispanic/Latino. 11 applicants, 45% accepted, 1 enrolled. *Faculty:* 23 full-time (2 women). Expenses: Contact institution. *Financial support:* In 2010–11, 9 students received support, including 7 teaching assistantships with full tuition reimbursements available (averaging $18,000 per year); fellowships, research assistantships, Federal Work-Study, tuition waivers (full and partial), and unspecified assistantships also available. Financial award application deadline: 3/1. In 2010, 1 doctorate awarded. *Degree program information:* Part-time programs available. Offers vision science (PhD). *Application deadline:* For fall admission, 3/1 priority date for domestic and international students. Applications are processed on a rolling basis. *Application fee:* $75. *Application Contact:* Debra Berger, Assistant to Associate Dean, 212-938-5544, Fax: 212-938-5537, E-mail: dberger@sunyopt.edu. *Associate Dean*, Dr. Jerry Feldman, 212-938-5541, Fax: 212-938-5537, E-mail: jfeldman@sunyopt.edu.

Professional Program Students: 278 full-time (207 women); includes 5 Black or African American, non-Hispanic/Latino; 104 Asian, non-Hispanic/Latino; 5 Hispanic/Latino, 24 international. Average age 24. 499 applicants, 28% accepted, 74 enrolled. *Faculty:* 67 full-time (30 women), 75 part-time/adjunct (35 women). Expenses: Contact institution. *Financial support:* In 2010–11, 234 students received support; fellowships, career-related internships or fieldwork, Federal Work-Study, and tuition waivers (full and partial) available. Financial award application deadline: 4/15; financial award applicants required to submit FAFSA. In 2010, 73 ODs awarded. Offers optometry (OD). *Application deadline:* For fall admission, 2/15 priority date for domestic and international students. Applications are processed on a rolling basis. *Application fee:* $75. Electronic applications accepted. *Application Contact:* Guilherme Albieri, Director of Admissions and Marketing, 212-938-5500, Fax: 212-938-5504, E-mail: admissions@sunyopt.edu. *Vice President of Student Affairs*, Dr. Jeffrey L. Philpott, 212-938-5500, Fax: 212-938-5504, E-mail: jphilpott@sunyopt.edu.

STATE UNIVERSITY OF NEW YORK DOWNSTATE MEDICAL CENTER, Brooklyn, NY 11203-2098

General Information State-supported, coed, upper-level institution. *Graduate housing:* Rooms and/or apartments available on a first-come, first-served basis to single and married students. Housing application deadline: 5/29. *Research affiliation:* Brooklyn Veterans Administration Medical Center, Polytechnic University Brooklyn (biomedical engineering).

GRADUATE UNITS

College of Medicine Offers medicine (MD, MPH); urban and immigrant health (MPH).

College of Nursing *Degree program information:* Part-time and evening/weekend programs available. Offers clinical nurse specialist (MS, Post Master's Certificate); nurse anesthesia (MS); nurse midwifery (MS, Post Master's Certificate); nurse practitioner (MS, Post Master's Certificate); nursing (MS, Post Master's Certificate).

School of Graduate Studies Offers bioimaging and neuroengineering (PhD); biomedical engineering (MS); molecular and cellular biology (PhD); neural and behavioral science (PhD).

STATE UNIVERSITY OF NEW YORK EMPIRE STATE COLLEGE, Saratoga Springs, NY 12866-4391

General Information State-supported, coed, comprehensive institution. *Graduate housing:* On-campus housing not available.

GRADUATE UNITS

Graduate Studies *Degree program information:* Part-time and evening/weekend programs available. Postbaccalaureate distance learning degree programs offered (minimal on-campus study). Offers business administration (MBA); business and policy studies (MA); labor and policy studies (MA); liberal studies (MA); social policy (MA); teaching (MA). Electronic applications accepted.

STATE UNIVERSITY OF NEW YORK INSTITUTE OF TECHNOLOGY, Utica, NY 13504-3050

General Information State-supported, coed, comprehensive institution. *Graduate housing:* Room and/or apartments available on a first-come, first-served basis to single students; on-campus housing not available to married students. *Research affiliation:* Wyle Laboratories–Reliability Information Analysis Center (reliability analysis and information).

GRADUATE UNITS

School of Arts and Sciences *Degree program information:* Part-time and evening/weekend programs available. Offers applied sociology (MS); information design and technology (MS).

School of Business *Degree program information:* Part-time and evening/weekend programs available. Postbaccalaureate distance learning degree programs offered (no on-campus study). Offers accountancy (MS); business administration in technology management (MBA); health services administration (MS); technology management (MBA).

School of Information Systems and Engineering Technology *Degree program information:* Part-time and evening/weekend programs available. Offers advanced technology (MS); computer and information science (MS); telecommunications (MS).

School of Nursing and Health Systems *Degree program information:* Part-time programs available. Offers adult nurse practitioner (MS, CAS); family nurse practitioner (MS, CAS); gerontological nurse practitioner (MS, CAS); nursing administration (MS, CAS); nursing education (MS, CAS).

STATE UNIVERSITY OF NEW YORK MARITIME COLLEGE, Throggs Neck, NY 10465-4198

General Information State-supported, coed, primarily men, comprehensive institution. *Graduate housing:* Room and/or apartments available to single students; on-campus housing not available to married students. *Research affiliation:* Port Authority of New York and New Jersey (transportation), Transportation Infrastructure Research Consortium, Transportation Research Board (maritime transportation).

State University of New York Maritime College (continued)

GRADUATE UNITS

Program in International Transportation Management *Degree program information:* Part-time and evening/weekend programs available. Offers international transportation management (MS).

STATE UNIVERSITY OF NEW YORK UPSTATE MEDICAL UNIVERSITY, Syracuse, NY 13210-2334

General Information State-supported, coed, upper-level institution. CGS member. *Graduate housing:* Rooms and/or apartments available on a first-come, first-served basis to single and married students. Housing application deadline: 8/1.

GRADUATE UNITS

College of Graduate Studies Offers anatomy (MS, PhD); biochemistry (MS); biochemistry and molecular biology (PhD); microbiology (MS); microbiology and immunology (PhD); neuroscience (PhD); pharmacology (PhD); physiology (MS, PhD). Electronic applications accepted.

College of Medicine Offers medicine (MD). Electronic applications accepted.

College of Nursing Students: 23 full-time (14 women), 203 part-time (190 women); includes 7 Black or African American, non-Hispanic/Latino; 1 American Indian or Alaska Native, non-Hispanic/Latino; 7 Asian, non-Hispanic/Latino; 5 Hispanic/Latino, 2 international. Average age 39. 165 applicants, 73% accepted, 99 enrolled. *Faculty:* 15 full-time (all women), 4 part-time/adjunct (all women). Expenses: Contact institution. *Financial support:* In 2010–11, 110 students received support. Federal Work-Study, institutionally sponsored loans, scholarships/grants, and traineeships available. Support available to part-time students. Financial award application deadline: 3/1; financial award applicants required to submit FAFSA. In 2010, 40 master's, 14 other advanced degrees awarded. *Degree program information:* Part-time programs available. Postbaccalaureate distance learning degree programs offered (no on-campus study). Offers nurse practitioner (Post Master's Certificate); nursing (MS). *Application deadline:* For fall admission, 3/15 priority date for domestic and international students; for spring admission, 9/15 priority date for domestic and international students. Applications are processed on a rolling basis. *Application fee:* $40. Electronic applications accepted. *Application Contact:* Donna Vavonese, Associate Director of Admissions, 315-464-4570, Fax: 315-464-8867, E-mail: vavonesd@upstate.edu. *Dean,* Dr. Elvira Szigeti, 315-464-4276, Fax: 315-464-5168.

Department of Physical Therapy *Degree program information:* Part-time and evening/weekend programs available. Postbaccalaureate distance learning degree programs offered (minimal on-campus study). Offers physical therapy (DPT). Electronic applications accepted.

Program in Medical Technology Offers medical technology (MS).

STEPHEN F. AUSTIN STATE UNIVERSITY, Nacogdoches, TX 75962

General Information State-supported, coed, comprehensive institution. *Graduate housing:* Rooms and/or apartments available on a first-come, first-served basis to single students and available to married students. Housing application deadline: 6/1. *Research affiliation:* University Health Center at Tyler (biotechnology, environmental science).

GRADUATE UNITS

Graduate School *Degree program information:* Part-time and evening/weekend programs available. Postbaccalaureate distance learning degree programs offered. Electronic applications accepted.

College of Applied Arts and Science *Degree program information:* Part-time programs available. Offers applied arts and science (MA, MIS, MSW); communication (MA); interdisciplinary studies (MIS); mass communication (MA); social work (MSW).

College of Business *Degree program information:* Part-time and evening/weekend programs available. Offers business (MBA, MPAC, MS); computer science (MS); management and marketing (MBA); professional accountancy (MPAC).

College of Education *Degree program information:* Part-time and evening/weekend programs available. Offers athletic training (MS); counseling (MA); early childhood education (M Ed); education (M Ed, MA, MS, Ed D); educational leadership (Ed D); elementary education (M Ed); human sciences (MS); kinesiology (M Ed); school psychology (MA); secondary education (M Ed); special education (M Ed); speech pathology (MS).

College of Fine Arts *Degree program information:* Part-time programs available. Offers art (MA); design (MFA); drawing (MFA); fine arts (MA, MFA, MM); music (MA, MM); painting (MFA); sculpture (MFA).

College of Forestry and Agriculture Offers agriculture (MS); forestry (MF, MS, PhD); forestry and agriculture (MF, MS, PhD).

College of Liberal Arts *Degree program information:* Part-time and evening/weekend programs available. Offers English (MA); history (MA); liberal arts (MA, MPA); psychology (MA); public administration (MPA).

College of Sciences and Mathematics *Degree program information:* Part-time programs available. Offers biology (MS); biotechnology (MS); chemistry (MS); environmental science (MS); geology (MS, MSNS); mathematics (MS); mathematics education (MS); physics (MS); sciences and mathematics (MS, MSNS); statistics (MS).

STEPHENS COLLEGE, Columbia, MO 65215-0002

General Information Independent, coed, primarily women, comprehensive institution. *Enrollment:* 1,122 graduate, professional, and undergraduate students; 190 full-time matriculated graduate/professional students (168 women), 41 part-time matriculated graduate/professional students (40 women). *Enrollment by degree level:* 231 master's. *Graduate faculty:* 5 full-time (all women), 41 part-time/adjunct (31 women). *Graduate housing:* On-campus housing not available. *Student services:* Campus employment opportunities, teacher training. *Library facilities:* Hugh Stephens Library. *Online resources:* library catalog, web page, access to other libraries' catalogs. *Collection:* 135,389 titles, 21,500 serial subscriptions, 1,761 audiovisual materials.

Computer facilities: Computer purchase and lease plans are available. 107 computers available on campus for general student use. A campuswide network can be accessed from student residence rooms and from off campus. *Web address:* http://www.stephens.edu/.

General Application Contact: Jennifer Deaver, Director of Recruitment for Graduate and Continuing Studies, 800-388-7579, E-mail: online@stephens.edu.

GRADUATE UNITS

Division of Graduate and Continuing Studies Students: 203 full-time (177 women), 60 part-time (54 women); includes 41 minority (25 Black or African American, non-Hispanic/Latino; 1 American Indian or Alaska Native, non-Hispanic/Latino; 7 Asian, non-Hispanic/Latino; 7 Hispanic/Latino; 1 Two or more races, non-Hispanic/Latino). Average age 35. 89 applicants, 46% accepted, 39 enrolled. *Faculty:* 2 full-time (both women), 27 part-time/adjunct (18 women). Expenses: Contact institution. *Financial support:* In 2010–11, 143 students received support, including 5 fellowships with full tuition reimbursements available (averaging $5,067 per year); scholarships/grants and unspecified assistantships also available. Financial award applicants required to submit FAFSA. In 2010, 94 master's awarded. *Degree program information:* Part-time and evening/weekend programs available. Postbaccalaureate distance learning degree programs offered (minimal on-campus study). Offers business (MBA, MSL); counseling (M Ed); curriculum and instruction (M Ed); health information administration (Post-baccalaureate Certificate). *Application deadline:* For fall admission, 7/25 priority date for domestic and international students; for winter admission, 12/1 priority date for domestic and international students; for spring admission, 4/25 priority date for domestic and international students. Applications are processed on a rolling basis. *Application fee:* $40. Electronic applications accepted. *Application Contact:* Jennifer Deaver, Director of Marketing and Recruitment, 800-388-7579, E-mail: online@stephens.edu. *Dean,* Suzanne Sharp, 573-876-7123, Fax: 573-876-7237, E-mail: online@stephens.edu.

STETSON UNIVERSITY, DeLand, FL 32723

General Information Independent, coed, comprehensive institution. *Enrollment:* 3,756 graduate, professional, and undergraduate students; 1,184 full-time matriculated graduate/professional students (640 women), 383 part-time matriculated graduate/professional students (208 women). *Enrollment by degree level:* 1,122 first professional, 445 master's. *Graduate faculty:* 91 full-time (44 women), 59 part-time/adjunct (19 women). *Graduate housing:* Rooms and/or apartments available to single and married students. *Student services:* Campus employment opportunities, campus safety program, career counseling, free psychological counseling, international student services, multicultural affairs office, teacher training. *Library facilities:* DuPont-Ball Library plus 1 other. *Online resources:* library catalog, web page. *Collection:* 395,365 titles, 88,887 serial subscriptions, 20,364 audiovisual materials.

Computer facilities: 487 computers available on campus for general student use. A campuswide network can be accessed from student residence rooms and from off campus. Online class registration is available. *Web address:* http://www.stetson.edu/.

General Application Contact: Office of Graduate Studies, 386-822-7075, Fax: 386-822-7388.

GRADUATE UNITS

College of Arts and Sciences Students: 126 full-time (97 women), 26 part-time (21 women); includes 14 Black or African American, non-Hispanic/Latino; 2 Asian, non-Hispanic/Latino; 18 Hispanic/Latino; 4 Two or more races, non-Hispanic/Latino, 3 international. Average age 33. Expenses: Contact institution. *Financial support:* Career-related internships or fieldwork, Federal Work-Study, institutionally sponsored loans, scholarships/grants, and tuition waivers (partial) available. Support available to part-time students. In 2010, 89 master's awarded. *Degree program information:* Part-time and evening/weekend programs available. Offers arts and sciences (M Ed, MA, MS, Ed S); education (M Ed, MS, Ed S); educational leadership (M Ed, Ed S); marriage and family therapy (MS); mental health counseling (MS); reading education (M Ed); school guidance and family consultation (MS). *Application deadline:* For fall admission, 3/1 priority date for domestic students; for spring admission, 11/1 for domestic students. Applications are processed on a rolling basis. *Application fee:* $25. *Application Contact:* Diana Belian, Office of Graduate Studies, 386-822-7075, Fax: 386-822-7388, E-mail: dbelian@stetson.edu. *Dean,* Dr. Grady Ballenger, 386-822-7515.

Division of Humanities Students: 12 part-time (9 women). Average age 27. Expenses: Contact institution. In 2010, 2 master's awarded. Offers English (MA); humanities (MA). *Application deadline:* For fall admission, 3/1 priority date for domestic students; for spring admission, 11/1 for domestic students. Applications are processed on a rolling basis. *Application fee:* $25. *Application Contact:* Diana Belian, Office of Graduate Studies, 386-822-7075, Fax: 386-822-7388, E-mail: dbelian@stetson.edu. *Dean,* Dr. Grady Ballenger, 386-822-7515.

College of Law Students: 948 full-time (496 women), 174 part-time (96 women); includes 221 minority (60 Black or African American, non-Hispanic/Latino; 10 American Indian or Alaska Native, non-Hispanic/Latino; 26 Asian, non-Hispanic/Latino; 97 Hispanic/Latino; 2 Native Hawaiian or other Pacific Islander, non-Hispanic/Latino; 26 Two or more races, non-Hispanic/Latino), 30 international. Average age 27. Expenses: Contact institution. *Financial support:* Research assistantships, teaching assistantships, career-related internships or fieldwork, institutionally sponsored loans, and scholarships/grants available. Financial award application deadline: 4/1; financial award applicants required to submit FAFSA. In 2010, 346 first professional degrees awarded. Offers law (JD, LL M). *Application deadline:* For fall admission, 3/1 priority date for domestic students; for spring admission, 9/1 for domestic students. *Application fee:* $50. *Application Contact:* Laura Zuppo, Executive Director of Admissions and Financial Aid, 727-562-7802, E-mail: lawadmit@law.stetson.edu. *Dean,* Dr. Darby Dickerson, 727-562-7810.

School of Business Administration Students: 110 full-time (47 women), 183 part-time (91 women); includes 14 Black or African American, non-Hispanic/Latino; 1 American Indian or Alaska Native, non-Hispanic/Latino; 6 Asian, non-Hispanic/Latino; 22 Hispanic/Latino; 4 Two or more races, non-Hispanic/Latino, 18 international. Average age 31. Expenses: Contact institution. *Financial support:* In 2010–11, 3 research assistantships were awarded; Federal Work-Study and institutionally sponsored loans also available. Support available to part-time students. Financial award application deadline: 3/15. In 2010, 161 master's awarded. *Degree program information:* Part-time and evening/weekend programs available. Offers accounting (M Acc); business administration (M Acc, MBA). *Application deadline:* For fall admission, 7/1 for domestic students. *Application fee:* $25. *Application Contact:* Kathryn Hannon, Assistant Director of Graduate Business Programs, 386-822-7410, Fax: 386-822-7413, E-mail: khannon@stetson.edu. *Dean,* Dr. Stuart Michelson, 386-822-7415.

STEVENS INSTITUTE OF TECHNOLOGY, Hoboken, NJ 07030

General Information Independent, coed, university. CGS member. *Enrollment:* 1,259 full-time matriculated graduate/professional students (343 women), 1,570 part-time matriculated graduate/professional students (361 women). *Enrollment by degree level:* 2,345 master's, 415 doctoral, 69 other advanced degrees. *Graduate faculty:* 249 full-time (48 women), 212 part-time/adjunct (36 women). *Graduate housing:* Room and/or apartments available on a first-come, first-served basis to single students; on-campus housing not available to married students. *Student services:* Campus employment opportunities, campus safety program, career counseling, exercise/wellness program, free psychological counseling, grant writing training, international student services, low-cost health insurance, multicultural affairs office, services for students with disabilities, teacher training, writing training. *Library facilities:* Samuel Williams plus 1 other. *Online resources:* library catalog, web page. *Collection:* 123,063 titles, 39,500 serial subscriptions. *Research affiliation:* Homeland Security (secure maritime systems), Department of Defense (systems engineering), National Science Foundation (nanotechnology and multi-scale systems), AT&T (intelligent networked systems), National Science Foundation (secure systems and information assurance).

Computer facilities: 500 computers available on campus for general student use. A campuswide network can be accessed from student residence rooms and from off campus. Online class registration, online account information, debit dining program, laundry status are available. *Web address:* http://www.stevens.edu/.

General Application Contact: Dean Daniel G. Gallagher, Graduate Admissions, 800-496-4935, Fax: 201-216-8044, E-mail: gradadmissions@stevens.edu.

GRADUATE UNITS

Graduate School Students: 1,259 full-time (343 women), 1,570 part-time (361 women); includes 85 Black or African American, non-Hispanic/Latino; 313 Asian, non-Hispanic/Latino; 143 Hispanic/Latino, 1,005 international. Average age 30. 2,011 applicants, 77% accepted. *Faculty:* 104 full-time (8 women), 80 part-time/adjunct (9 women). Expenses: Contact institution. *Financial support:* Fellowships, research assistantships, teaching assistantships, career-related internships or fieldwork, Federal Work-Study, institutionally sponsored loans, tuition waivers (partial), and unspecified assistantships available. In 2010, 447 master's, 32 doctorates awarded. *Degree program information:* Part-time and evening/weekend programs available. Postbaccalaureate distance learning degree programs offered (no on-campus study). *Application deadline:* Applications are processed on a rolling basis. *Application fee:* $50. Electronic applications accepted. *Application Contact:* Graduate Admissions, 800-496-4935, Fax: 201-216-8044, E-mail: gradadmissions@stevens.edu. *Dean of the Graduate School,* Dr. Charles L. Suffel, 201-216-5234, Fax: 201-216-8044, E-mail: csuffel@stevens-tech.edu.

Charles V. Schaefer Jr. School of Engineering Students: 940 full-time (237 women), 499 part-time (88 women); includes 24 Black or African American, non-Hispanic/Latino; 150 Asian, non-Hispanic/Latino; 54 Hispanic/Latino, 722 international. Average age 27. 664 applicants, 76% accepted. Expenses: Contact institution. *Financial support:* Fellowships, research assistantships, teaching assistantships, career-related internships or fieldwork, Federal Work-Study, institutionally sponsored loans, tuition waivers (partial), and unspecified assistantships available. *Degree program information:* Part-time and evening/weekend programs available. Postbaccalaureate distance learning degree programs offered. Offers advanced manufacturing (Certificate); air pollution technology (Certificate); analytical chemistry (PhD, Certificate); applied mathematics (MS); applied optics (Certificate); applied statistics (Certificate); armament engineering (M Eng); bioinformatics (PhD, Certificate); biomedical chemistry (Certificate); biomedical engineering (M Eng, Certificate); chemical biology (MS, PhD, Certificate); chemical engineering (M Eng, PhD, Engr); chemical physiology (Certificate); chemistry (MS, PhD); civil engineering (M Eng, PhD, Certificate, Engr); computational fluid mechanics and heat transfer (Certificate); computer and electrical engineering (M Eng); computer architecture and digital systems (M Eng); computer engineering (M Eng, PhD, Certificate); computer graphics (Certificate); computer science (MS, PhD, Certificate); computer systems (M Eng, Certificate); construction accounting/estimating (Certificate); construction engineering (Certificate); construction law/disputes (Certificate); construction management (MS, Certificate); construction/quality management (Certificate); data communications and networks (M Eng); database management systems (Certificate); design and production management (Certificate); digital signal processing (Certificate); digital systems design (M Eng); distributed systems (Certificate); electrical engineering (M Eng, PhD, Certificate); elements of computer science (Certificate); engineered software systems (M Eng); engineering (M Eng, MS, PhD, Certificate, Engr); engineering physics (M Eng); enterprise computing (Certificate); enterprise security and information assurance (Certificate); environmental compatibility in engineering (Certificate); environmental engineering (M Eng, PhD, Certificate); environmental processes (M Eng, Certificate); geotechnical engineering (Certificate); geotechnical/geoenvironmental engineering (M Eng, Engr); groundwater and soil pollution control (M Eng, Certificate); health informatics (Certificate); hydrologic modeling (M Eng); image processing and multimedia (M Eng); information system security (M Eng); information systems (M Eng); inland and coastal environmental hydrodynamics (M Eng, Certificate); integrated product development (M Eng); manufacturing technologies (M Eng); maritime systems (MS); materials science (M Eng, PhD); mathematics (MS, PhD); mechanical engineering (M Eng, PhD); microdevices and microsystems (Certificate); microelectronics and photonics (Certificate); microelectronics and photonics science and technology (M Eng); multimedia experience and management (Certificate); networks and systems administration (Certificate); ocean engineering (M Eng, PhD); organic chemistry (PhD); pharmaceutical manufacturing (M Eng, MS, Certificate); physical chemistry (PhD); physics (MS, PhD); plasma and surface physics (Certificate); polymer chemistry (PhD, Certificate); power generation (Certificate); product architecture and engineering (M Eng); real-time and embedded systems (Certificate); robotics and control (Certificate); security and privacy (Certificate); service oriented computing (Certificate); signal processing for communications (M Eng); software design (Certificate); stochastic systems (MS, Certificate); stormwater management (M Eng); structural analysis and design (Certificate); structural engineering (M Eng, Engr); systems reliability and design (M Eng); telecommunications systems engineering (M Eng); theoretical computer science (Certificate); vibration and noise control (Certificate); water quality control (Certificate); water resources engineering (M Eng); wireless communications (M Eng, Certificate). *Application deadline:* Applications are processed on a rolling basis. *Application fee:* $50. Electronic applications accepted. *Application Contact:* Graduate Admissions, 800-496-4935, Fax: 201-216-8044, E-mail: gradadmissions@stevens.edu. *Dean*, Dr. George Korfiatis, 201-216-5263.

School of Systems and Enterprises Students: 149 full-time (45 women), 328 part-time (71 women); includes 22 Black or African American, non-Hispanic/Latino; 50 Asian, non-Hispanic/Latino; 23 Hispanic/Latino, 114 international. Average age 32. Expenses: Contact institution. Offers agile systems and enterprises (Certificate); engineering management (M Eng, PhD); enterprise systems (MS, PhD); financial engineering (MS); software engineering (MS); space systems engineering (M Eng, Certificate); systems and enterprises (M Eng, MS, PhD, Certificate); systems and supportability engineering (Certificate); systems design and operational effectiveness (M Eng); systems engineering (M Eng, PhD); systems engineering management (Certificate). *Application Contact:* Graduate Admissions, 800-496-4935, Fax: 201-216-8044, E-mail: gradadmissions@stevens.edu. *Dean of the Graduate School*, Dr. Charles L. Suffel, 201-216-5234, Fax: 201-216-8044, E-mail: csuffel@stevens-tech.edu.

Wesley J. Howe School of Technology Management Students: 170 full-time (61 women), 743 part-time (202 women); includes 39 Black or African American, non-Hispanic/Latino; 113 Asian, non-Hispanic/Latino; 66 Hispanic/Latino, 169 international. Average age 34. 841 applicants, 84% accepted. Expenses: Contact institution. *Financial support:* Fellowships, research assistantships, teaching assistantships, Federal Work-Study, institutionally sponsored loans, and unspecified assistantships available. *Degree program information:* Part-time and evening/weekend programs available. Postbaccalaureate distance learning degree programs offered. Offers business (MS); computer science (MS); e-commerce (MS); engineering management (MBA); enterprise systems (MS); entrepreneurial information technology (MS); financial engineering (MBA); general management (MS); global innovation management (MS); human resource management (MS); information architecture (MS); information management (MBA, MS, PhD, Certificate); information security (MS); information technology in financial services (MBA); information technology in financial services industry (MS); information technology in the pharmaceutical industry (MBA, MS); information technology outsourcing (MBA); information technology outsourcing management (MS); management of wireless networks (MS); online security, technology and business (MS); pharmaceutical management (MBA); professional communications (Certificate); project management (MBA, MS, Certificate); software engineering (MS); technical management (MS); technology commercialization (MS); technology management (EMBA, MBA, MS, PhD); technology management for experienced professionals (EMTM, MS, Certificate); telecommunications (MS); telecommunications management (MBA, PhD, Certificate). *Application deadline:* Applications are processed on a rolling basis. *Application fee:* $50. Electronic applications accepted. *Application Contact:* Graduate Admissions, 800-496-4935, Fax: 201-216-8044, E-mail: gradadmissions@stevens.edu. *Dean*, Dr. Lex McCusker, 201-216-8119.

STEVENSON UNIVERSITY, Stevenson, MD 21153

General Information Independent, coed, comprehensive institution. *Enrollment:* 3,941 graduate, professional, and undergraduate students; 74 full-time matriculated graduate/professional students (58 women), 292 part-time matriculated graduate/professional students (206 women). *Enrollment by degree level:* 366 master's. *Graduate faculty:* 4 full-time (2 women), 4 part-time/adjunct (2 women). *Tuition:* Part-time $560 per credit. *Required fees:* $100 per semester. Part-time tuition and fees vary according to program. *Graduate housing:* On-campus housing not available. *Student services:* Campus employment opportunities, campus safety program, career counseling, exercise/wellness program, international student services, multicultural affairs office, services for students with disabilities. *Library facilities:* Stevenson University Learning Resource Center-Greenspring Campus plus 1 other. *Online resources:* library catalog, web page, access to other libraries' catalogs. *Collection:* 81,802 titles, 1,058 serial subscriptions, 2,727 audiovisual materials.

Computer facilities: Computer purchase and lease plans are available. 300 computers available on campus for general student use. A campuswide network can be accessed from student residence rooms and from off campus. Online class registration is available. *Web address:* http://www.stevenson.edu/.

General Application Contact: Angela Scagliola, Director, Recruitment and Admissions, 443-352-4414, Fax: 443-352-4440, E-mail: ascagliola@stevenson.edu.

GRADUATE UNITS

Program in Business and Technology Management Students: 20 full-time (15 women), 53 part-time (27 women); includes 17 Black or African American, non-Hispanic/Latino; 3 Asian, non-Hispanic/Latino, 2 international. Expenses: Contact institution. In 2010, 24 master's awarded. Offers business and technology management (MS). *Application Contact:* Angela Scagliola, Director, Recruitment and Admissions, 443-352-4414, Fax: 443-352-4440, E-mail: ascagliola@stevenson.edu. *Coordinator*, Steve Engorn, 443-352-4220, Fax: 443-394-0538, E-mail: sengorn@stevenson.edu.

Program in Forensic Science Students: 18 full-time (17 women), 9 part-time (8 women); includes 3 Black or African American, non-Hispanic/Latino; 1 Asian, non-Hispanic/Latino, 1 international. Expenses: Contact institution. In 2010, 7 master's awarded. Offers forensic science (MS). Partnership program with Maryland State Police Forensic Sciences Division. *Application Contact:* Angela Scagliola, Director, Recruitment and Admissions, 443-352-4414, Fax: 443-352-4440, E-mail: ascagliola@stevenson.edu. *Coordinator*, John Tobin, 443-352-4142, Fax: 443-392-0538, E-mail: jtobin@stevenson.edu.

Program in Forensic Studies Students: 36 full-time (26 women), 186 part-time (130 women); includes 76 Black or African American, non-Hispanic/Latino; 2 American Indian or Alaska Native, non-Hispanic/Latino; 4 Asian, non-Hispanic/Latino; 3 Hispanic/Latino; 1 Two or more races, non-Hispanic/Latino, 1 international. Expenses: Contact institution. In 2010, 55 master's awarded. Postbaccalaureate distance learning degree programs offered (minimal on-campus study). Offers forensic accounting (MS); forensic legal professional (MS); information technology (MS); interdisciplinary track (MS); investigations (MS). *Application Contact:* Angela Scagliola, Director, Recruitment and Admissions, 443-352-4414, Fax: 443-352-4440, E-mail: ascagliola@stevenson.edu. *Coordinator*, Thomas Coogan, 443-352-4075, Fax: 443-394-0538.

Program in Nursing Offers nursing (MS).

STONY BROOK UNIVERSITY, STATE UNIVERSITY OF NEW YORK, Stony Brook, NY 11794

General Information State-supported, coed, university. CGS member. *Enrollment:* 24,594 graduate, professional, and undergraduate students; 4,861 full-time matriculated graduate/professional students (2,455 women), 2,413 part-time matriculated graduate/professional students (1,638 women). *Enrollment by degree level:* 661 first professional, 3,558 master's, 2,504 doctoral, 551 other advanced degrees. *Graduate faculty:* 1,343 full-time (472 women), 476 part-time/adjunct (203 women). Tuition, state resident: full-time $8370; part-time $349 per credit. Tuition, nonresident: full-time $13,780; part-time $574 per credit. *Required fees:* $994. *Graduate housing:* Rooms and/or apartments available to single and married students. *Student services:* Campus employment opportunities, campus safety program, career counseling, child daycare facilities, exercise/wellness program, free psychological counseling, grant writing training, international student services, low-cost health insurance, multicultural affairs office, services for students with disabilities, teacher training, writing training. *Library facilities:* Frank Melville, Jr. Building Library plus 7 others. *Online resources:* library catalog, web page, access to other libraries' catalogs. *Collection:* 2.5 million titles, 64,803 serial subscriptions, 52,872 audiovisual materials. *Research affiliation:* Veterans Affairs Medical Center, Nassau University Medical Center, Winthrop University Hospital, Cold Spring Harbor Laboratory, Brookhaven National Laboratory.

Computer facilities: Computer purchase and lease plans are available. 2,600 computers available on campus for general student use. A campuswide network can be accessed from student residence rooms and from off campus. Online class registration is available. *Web address:* http://www.sunysb.edu/.

General Application Contact: Barbara Byrne, Assistant Dean for Finance and Budget, Admissions and Records, 631-632-7039, Fax: 631-632-4723, E-mail: barbara.byrne@stonybrook.edu.

GRADUATE UNITS

Graduate School Students: 3,162 full-time (1,393 women), 597 part-time (298 women); includes 100 Black or African American, non-Hispanic/Latino; 5 American Indian or Alaska Native, non-Hispanic/Latino; 258 Asian, non-Hispanic/Latino; 158 Hispanic/Latino; 13 Two or more races, non-Hispanic/Latino, 1,666 international. Expenses: Contact institution. *Financial support:* Fellowships, research assistantships, teaching assistantships, career-related internships or fieldwork, Federal Work-Study, institutionally sponsored loans, scholarships/grants, traineeships, health care benefits, tuition waivers (full), and unspecified assistantships available. *Degree program information:* Part-time and evening/weekend programs available. *Application deadline:* For fall admission, 1/15 for domestic and international students; for spring admission, 10/1 for domestic and international students. *Application fee:* $100. *Application Contact:* Barbara Byrne, Assistant Dean for Finance and Budget, Admissions and Records, 631-632-4723, Fax: 631-632-7039, E-mail: barbara.byrne@stonybrook.edu. *Dean*, Dr. Lawrence B. Martin, 631-632-7035, Fax: 631-632-7243, E-mail: lori.carron@stonybrook.edu.

College of Arts and Sciences Students: 1,714 full-time (852 women), 214 part-time (143 women); includes 52 Black or African American, non-Hispanic/Latino; 4 American Indian or Alaska Native, non-Hispanic/Latino; 104 Asian, non-Hispanic/Latino; 103 Hispanic/Latino; 8 Two or more races, non-Hispanic/Latino, 672 international. 4,338 applicants, 26% accepted, 508 enrolled. *Faculty:* 479 full-time (148 women), 88 part-time/adjunct (41 women). Expenses: Contact institution. *Financial support:* In 2010–11, 367 research assistantships, 721 teaching assistantships were awarded; fellowships, career-related internships or fieldwork, Federal Work-Study, scholarships/grants, traineeships, health care benefits, and unspecified assistantships also available. In 2010, 271 master's, 196 doctorates, 17 other advanced degrees awarded. *Degree program information:* Part-time and evening/weekend programs available. Offers Africana studies (MA); anthropology (MA, PhD); applied ecology (MA); art history and criticism (MA, PhD); arts and sciences (MA, MAPP, MAT, MFA, MM, MS, DMA, PhD, Certificate); astronomy (PhD); biochemistry and molecular biology (PhD); biochemistry and structural biology (PhD); biological sciences (MA); biopsychology (PhD); cellular and developmental biology (PhD); chemistry (MS, PhD); clinical psychology (PhD); cognitive/experimental psychology (PhD); comparative literature (MA, PhD); composition studies (Certificate); cultural studies (PhD); dramaturgy (MFA); earth science (MAT); ecology and evolution (PhD); economics (MA, PhD); English (MA, PhD); English education (MAT); ethnomusicology (MA, PhD); French (MA); genetics (PhD); geosciences (MS, PhD); Hispanic languages and literature (MA, PhD); history (MA, PhD); immunology and pathology (PhD); Italian (MA); linguistics (MA, PhD); mathematics (MA, MAT, PhD); modern research instrumentation (MS); molecular and cellular biology (MA, PhD); music history/theory (MA, PhD); music performance (MM, DMA); neuroscience (PhD); philosophy (MA, PhD); physics (MA, MAT, MS, PhD); physics education (MAT); political science (MA, PhD); public policy (MAPP); public policy and urban development (MA); Romance languages (MA); science education (PhD); social and health psychology (PhD); sociology (MA, PhD); studio art (MFA); teaching English to speakers of other languages (MA); theatre arts (MA, MFA); women's studies (Certificate). *Application deadline:* For fall admission, 1/15 for domestic students. *Application fee:* $100. *Application Contact:* Barbara Byrne, Assistant Dean for Finance and Budget, Admissions and Records, 631-632-4723, Fax: 631-632-7243, E-mail: barbara.byrne@stonybrook.edu. *Dean*, Dr. Nancy Squires, 631-632-6999, Fax: 631-632-6900.

College of Business Students: 182 full-time (103 women), 117 part-time (35 women); includes 11 Black or African American, non-Hispanic/Latino; 35 Asian, non-Hispanic/Latino; 10 Hispanic/Latino; 2 Two or more races, non-Hispanic/Latino, 88 international. Average age 29. 281 applicants, 60% accepted, 102 enrolled. *Faculty:* 14 full-time (2 women), 27 part-time/adjunct (6 women). Expenses: Contact institution. *Financial support:* In 2010–11, 1 teaching assistantship was awarded; research assistantships. In 2010, 95 master's, 1 other advanced degree awarded. Offers business (MBA, MS, Certificate); finance (MBA, Certificate); health care management (MBA, Certificate); human resource management (Certificate); human resources (MBA); information systems management (MBA, Certificate); management (MBA); marketing (MBA); technology management (MS). *Application deadline:* For fall admission, 3/1 for domestic students, 1/15 for international students; for spring admission, 10/1 for domestic and international students. *Application fee:* $100. *Application Contact:* Aristotle Lekacos, Director, Graduate Programs, 631-632-7171, E-mail: aristotle.lekacost@notes.cc.sunysb.edu. *Interim Dean*, Dr. Manuel London, 631-632-7171, Fax: 631-632-8181.

College of Engineering and Applied Sciences Students: 982 full-time (269 women), 193 part-time (67 women); includes 19 Black or African American, non-Hispanic/Latino; 93 Asian, non-Hispanic/Latino; 22 Hispanic/Latino; 2 Two or more races, non-Hispanic/Latino, 844 international. 3,541 applicants, 40% accepted, 417 enrolled. *Faculty:* 135 full-time (21 women), 33 part-time/adjunct (5 women). Expenses: Contact institution. *Financial support:* In 2010–11, 263 research assistantships, 171 teaching assistantships were awarded; fellowships, career-related internships or fieldwork also available. In 2010, 332 master's, 57 doctorates awarded. *Degree program information:* Part-time and evening/weekend programs available. Offers applied mathematics and statistics (MS, PhD); biomedical engineering (MS, PhD, Certificate); computer engineering (MS, PhD); computer science (MS, PhD); educational technology (MS); electrical engineering (MS, PhD); energy and

Stony Brook University, State University of New York (continued)

environmental systems (MS, Advanced Certificate); engineering and applied sciences (MS, PhD, Advanced Certificate, Certificate); global operations management (MS); information systems (Certificate); information systems engineering (MS); materials science and engineering (MS, PhD); mechanical engineering (MS, PhD); medical physics (MS, PhD); software engineering (Certificate); technology, policy, and innovation (PhD). *Application deadline:* For fall admission, 1/15 for domestic students. *Application fee:* $100. *Application Contact:* Barbara Byrne, Assistant Dean for Finance and Budget in Admissions and Records, 631-632-4723, Fax: 631-632-7039, E-mail: barbara.byrne@stonybrook.edu. *Dean*, Dr. Yacov Shamash, 631-632-8380.

School of Marine and Atmospheric Sciences Students: 114 full-time (66 women), 12 part-time (7 women); includes 1 Black or African American, non-Hispanic/Latino; 2 Asian, non-Hispanic/Latino; 6 Hispanic/Latino, 37 international. Average age 28. 166 applicants, 38% accepted, 28 enrolled. *Faculty:* 40 full-time (8 women), 3 part-time/adjunct (all women). Expenses: Contact institution. *Financial support:* In 2010–11, 45 research assistantships, 32 teaching assistantships were awarded; fellowships, career-related internships or fieldwork and tuition waivers (full) also available. In 2010, 16 master's, 10 doctorates awarded. *Degree program information:* Evening/weekend programs available. Offers atmospheric sciences (MS, PhD); marine and atmospheric sciences (MA, MS, PhD); marine conservation and policy (MA); marine sciences (MS, PhD). *Application fee:* $100. *Application Contact:* Dr. Anne McElroy, Assistant Director, 631-632-8488, Fax: 631-632-8200, E-mail: amcelroy@notes.cc.sunysb.edu. *Interim Dean*, Dr. Minghua Zhang, 631-632-8700, Fax: 631-632-8200, E-mail: somas@stonybrook.edu.

School of Professional Development Students: 360 full-time (228 women), 1,097 part-time (729 women); includes 180 minority (65 Black or African American, non-Hispanic/Latino; 2 American Indian or Alaska Native, non-Hispanic/Latino; 30 Asian, non-Hispanic/Latino; 81 Hispanic/Latino; 1 Native Hawaiian or other Pacific Islander, non-Hispanic/Latino; 1 Two or more races, non-Hispanic/Latino), 10 international. Average age 28. *Faculty:* 25 full-time (10 women), 105 part-time/adjunct (40 women). Expenses: Contact institution. *Financial support:* In 2010–11, 1 teaching assistantship was awarded; fellowships, research assistantships, career-related internships or fieldwork also available. Support available to part-time students. In 2010, 505 master's, 187 other advanced degrees awarded. *Degree program information:* Part-time and evening/weekend programs available. Postbaccalaureate distance learning degree programs offered. Offers biology-grade 7-12 (MAT); chemistry-grade 7-12 (MAT); coaching (Graduate Certificate); coaching online (Graduate Certificate); computer integrated engineering (Graduate Certificate); earth science-grade 7-12 (MAT); educational computing (Graduate Certificate); educational leadership (Advanced Certificate); English-grade 7-12 (MAT); environmental management (Graduate Certificate); environmental/occupational health and safety (Graduate Certificate); French-grade 7-12 (MAT); German-grade 7-12 (MAT); human resource management (Graduate Certificate); human resource management online (Graduate Certificate); information systems management (Graduate Certificate); Italian-grade 7-12 (MAT); liberal studies (MA); liberal studies online (MAT); mathematics-grade 7-12 (MAT); operation research (Graduate Certificate); physics-grade 7-12 (MAT); professional studies online (MPS); school administration and supervision (Graduate Certificate); school building leadership (Graduate Certificate); school district administration (Graduate Certificate); school district business leadership (Advanced Certificate); school district leadership (Graduate Certificate); social science and the professions (MPS); social studies-grade 7-12 (MAT); Spanish-grade 7-12 (MAT); waste management (Graduate Certificate). *Application deadline:* Applications are processed on a rolling basis. *Application fee:* $100. *Application Contact:* Dr. Paul J. Edelson, Dean, 631-632-7052, Fax: 631-632-9046, E-mail: paul.edelson@stonybrook.edu. *Dean*, Dr. Paul J. Edelson, 631-632-7052, Fax: 631-632-9046, E-mail: paul.edelson@stonybrook.edu.

Stony Brook Southampton Students: 22 full-time (14 women), 56 part-time (42 women); includes 5 Black or African American, non-Hispanic/Latino; 1 American Indian or Alaska Native, non-Hispanic/Latino; 2 Asian, non-Hispanic/Latino; 5 Hispanic/Latino. *Faculty:* 2 full-time (both women), 21 part-time/adjunct (9 women). Expenses: Contact institution. *Financial support:* Teaching assistantships available. In 2010, 4 master's awarded. Offers fiction (MFA); poetry (MFA); scientific writing (MFA); scriptwriting (MFA). *Application fee:* $100. *Application Contact:* Dr. Robert Reeves, Director, 631-632-5030, Fax: 631-632-2576, E-mail: southamptonwriters@notes.cc.sunysb.edu. *Director*, Dr. Robert Reeves, 631-632-5030, Fax: 631-632-2576, E-mail: southamptonwriters@notes.cc.sunysb.edu.

Stony Brook University Medical Center Expenses: Contact institution. *Application Contact:* Barbara Byrne, Assistant Dean for Finance and Budget in Admissions and Records, 631-632-4723, Fax: 631-632-7039, E-mail: barbara.byrne@stonybrook.edu. *Chief Executive Officer*, Dr. Steven L. Strongwater, 631-444-4000.

Health Sciences Center Students: 1,485 full-time (921 women), 726 part-time (617 women); includes 209 Black or African American, non-Hispanic/Latino; 4 American Indian or Alaska Native, non-Hispanic/Latino; 370 Asian, non-Hispanic/Latino; 120 Hispanic/Latino; 7 Two or more races, non-Hispanic/Latino, 54 international. 7,232 applicants, 15% accepted. *Faculty:* 717 full-time (305 women), 262 part-time/adjunct (128 women). Expenses: Contact institution. *Financial support:* In 2010–11, 54 research assistantships, 18 teaching assistantships were awarded; fellowships, career-related internships or fieldwork, Federal Work-Study, institutionally sponsored loans, traineeships, and tuition waivers (full) also available. Financial award applicants required to submit FAFSA. In 2010, 150 first professional degrees, 464 master's, 112 doctorates, 51 other advanced degrees awarded. *Degree program information:* Part-time programs available. Offers adult health nurse practitioner (Certificate); adult health/primary care nursing (MS); child health nurse practitioner (Certificate); child health nursing (MS); dental medicine (DDS, MS, PhD, Certificate); endodontics (Certificate); family nurse practitioner (MS, Certificate); health care management (Advanced Certificate); health care policy and management (MS); health sciences (DDS, MD, MS, MSW, DNP, DPT, PhD, Advanced Certificate, Certificate); mental health/psychiatric nursing (MS, Certificate); neonatal nurse practitioner (Certificate); neonatal nursing (MS); nurse midwifery (MS, Certificate); nursing (MS, DNP, Certificate); nursing practice (DNP); occupational therapy (MS); oral biology and pathology (MS, PhD); orthodontics (Certificate); perinatal women's health nursing (MS, Certificate); periodontics (Certificate); physical therapy (DPT); physician assistant (MS); social welfare (PhD); social work (MSW). *Application fee:* $100. *Application Contact:* Barbara Byrne, Assistant Dean for Finance and Budget in Admissions and Records, 631-632-4723, Fax: 631-632-7039, E-mail: kmarks@notes.cc.sunysb.edu. *Dean and Senior Vice President of Health Sciences*, Dr. Kenneth Kaushansky, 631-444-2121, Fax: 631-444-2113.

School of Medicine Students: 616 full-time (300 women), 10 part-time (5 women); includes 38 Black or African American, non-Hispanic/Latino; 1 American Indian or Alaska Native, non-Hispanic/Latino; 180 Asian, non-Hispanic/Latino; 26 Hispanic/Latino, 22 international. 4,226 applicants, 8% accepted. *Faculty:* 587 full-time (218 women), 89 part-time/adjunct (50 women). Expenses: Contact institution. *Financial support:* In 2010–11, 52 research assistantships, 5 teaching assistantships were awarded; fellowships, career-related internships or fieldwork, Federal Work-Study, and tuition waivers (full) also available. In 2010, 111 first professional degrees, 29 master's, 16 doctorates awarded. Offers anatomical sciences (PhD); community health (MPH); evaluation sciences (MPH); family violence (MPH); health economics (MPH); medical scientistmedicine (MD, MPH, PhD); molecular and cellular pharmacology (PhD); molecular microbiology (PhD); physiology and biophysics (PhD); population health (MPH); population health and clinical outcomes research (PhD); substance abuse (MPH). *Application deadline:* For fall admission, 1/15 for domestic students. *Application fee:* $100. *Application Contact:* Dr. Jack Fuhrer, 631-444-2113, Fax: 631-444-6032, E-mail: somadmissions@stonybrook.edu. *Dean and Senior Vice President of Health Sciences*, Dr. Kenneth Kaushansky, 631-444-2113, Fax: 631-444-6032.

STRATFORD UNIVERSITY, Falls Church, VA 22043

General Information Proprietary, coed, comprehensive institution. *Graduate housing:* On-campus housing not available.

GRADUATE UNITS

School of Graduate Studies *Degree program information:* Part-time and evening/weekend programs available. Postbaccalaureate distance learning degree programs offered (no on-campus study). Offers accounting (MS); business administration (IMBA, MBA); enterprise business management (MS); entrepreneurial management (MS); information assurance (MS); information systems (MS); software engineering (MS); telecommunications (MS). Electronic applications accepted.

STRAYER UNIVERSITY, Washington, DC 20005-2603

General Information Proprietary, coed, comprehensive institution. *Graduate housing:* On-campus housing not available.

GRADUATE UNITS

Graduate Studies *Degree program information:* Part-time and evening/weekend programs available. Postbaccalaureate distance learning degree programs offered (minimal on-campus study). Offers accounting (MS); acquisition (MBA); business administration (MBA); communications technology (MS); educational management (M Ed); finance (MBA); health services administration (MHSA); hospitality and tourism management (MBA); human resource management (MBA); information systems (MS); management (MBA); management information systems (MS); marketing (MBA); professional accounting (MS); public administration (MPA); supply chain management (MBA); technology in education (M Ed). Programs also offered at campus locations in Birmingham, AL; Chamblee, GA; Cobb County, GA; Morrow, GA; White Marsh, MD; Charleston, SC; Columbia, SC; Greensboro, NC; Greenville, SC; Lexington, KY; Louisville, KY; Nashville, TN; North Raleigh, NC; Washington, DC. Electronic applications accepted.

SUFFOLK UNIVERSITY, Boston, MA 02108-2770

General Information Independent, coed, comprehensive institution. *Enrollment:* 9,312 graduate, professional, and undergraduate students; 1,715 full-time matriculated graduate/professional students (893 women), 1,727 part-time matriculated graduate/professional students (930 women). *Enrollment by degree level:* 1,716 first professional, 1,551 master's, 90 doctoral, 85 other advanced degrees. *Graduate faculty:* 241 full-time (99 women), 60 part-time/adjunct (25 women). *Graduate housing:* On-campus housing not available. *Student services:* Campus employment opportunities, campus safety program, career counseling, exercise/wellness program, free psychological counseling, grant writing training, international student services, low-cost health insurance, multicultural affairs office, services for students with disabilities, teacher training, writing training. *Library facilities:* Mildred Sawyer Library plus 2 others. *Online resources:* library catalog, web page, access to other libraries' catalogs. *Collection:* 208,365 titles, 26,198 serial subscriptions, 743 audiovisual materials.

Computer facilities: Computer purchase and lease plans are available. 539 computers available on campus for general student use. A campuswide network can be accessed from student residence rooms and from off campus. Online class registration is available. *Web address:* http://www.suffolk.edu/.

General Application Contact: Judith Reynolds, Director of Graduate Admissions, 617-573-8302, Fax: 617-305-1733, E-mail: grad.admission@suffolk.edu.

GRADUATE UNITS

College of Arts and Sciences Students: 296 full-time (211 women), 393 part-time (294 women); includes 27 Black or African American, non-Hispanic/Latino; 1 American Indian or Alaska Native, non-Hispanic/Latino; 20 Asian, non-Hispanic/Latino; 20 Hispanic/Latino; 1 Two or more races, non-Hispanic/Latino, 72 international. Average age 28. 1,051 applicants, 52% accepted, 254 enrolled. *Faculty:* 107 full-time (53 women), 37 part-time/adjunct (17 women). Expenses: Contact institution. *Financial support:* In 2010–11, 457 students received support, including 280 fellowships with full and partial tuition reimbursements available (averaging $9,599 per year); career-related internships or fieldwork, Federal Work-Study, institutionally sponsored loans, scholarships/grants, and unspecified assistantships also available. Support available to part-time students. Financial award application deadline: 4/1; financial award applicants required to submit FAFSA. In 2010, 252 master's, 10 doctorates, 2 other advanced degrees awarded. *Degree program information:* Part-time and evening/weekend programs available. Offers administration of higher education (M Ed, CAGS); arts and sciences (M Ed, MA, MAC, MS, MSCJS, MSCS, MSE, MSEP, MSIE, MSPS, PhD, CAGS, Graduate Certificate); clinical psychology (PhD); communication studies (MAC); crime and justice studies (MSCJS); economic policy (MSEP); economics (MSE, PhD); ethics and public policy (MS); human resource, learning and performance (MS, CAGS, Graduate Certificate); integrated marketing communication (MAC); international economics (MSIE); international relations (MSPS); mental health counseling (MS, CAGS); organizational communication (MAC); political science (MSPS); professional politics (MSPS, CAGS); public relations and advertising (MAC); school counseling (M Ed, CAGS); school teaching (M Ed, CAGS); software engineering and databases (MSCS); women's health (MA). *Application deadline:* For fall admission, 6/15 priority date for domestic students, 6/15 for international students; for spring admission, 11/1 priority date for domestic students, 11/1 for international students. Applications are processed on a rolling basis. *Application fee:* $50. Electronic applications accepted. *Application Contact:* Judith Reynolds, Director of Graduate Admissions, 617-573-8302, Fax: 617-305-1733, E-mail: grad.admission@suffolk.edu. *Dean*, Dr. Kenneth S. Greenberg, 617-573-8265, Fax: 617-573-8513, E-mail: kgreenbe@suffolk.edu.

Law School Expenses: Contact institution. *Financial support:* Career-related internships or fieldwork, Federal Work-Study, institutionally sponsored loans, and scholarships/grants available. Support available to part-time students. Financial award application deadline: 3/1; financial award applicants required to submit FAFSA. *Degree program information:* Part-time and evening/weekend programs available. Offers business law and financial services (JD); civil litigation (JD); global law and technology (LL M); health and biomedical law (JD); intellectual property law (JD); international law (JD). *Application deadline:* For fall admission, 3/1 priority date for domestic and international students. Applications are processed on a rolling basis. *Application fee:* $60. Electronic applications accepted. *Application Contact:* Ian A. Menchini, Director of Electronic Marketing and Enrollment Management, 617-573-8144, Fax: 617-523-1367, E-mail: imenchin@suffolk.edu. *Dean of Admissions*, Gail N. Ellis, 617-573-8144, Fax: 617-523-1367, E-mail: gellis@suffolk.edu.

New England School of Art and Design Students: 56 full-time (45 women), 76 part-time (65 women); includes 2 Black or African American, non-Hispanic/Latino; 5 Asian, non-Hispanic/Latino; 5 Hispanic/Latino, 13 international. Average age 30. 113 applicants, 67% accepted, 48 enrolled. *Faculty:* 21 full-time (12 women), 7 part-time/adjunct (2 women). Expenses: Contact institution. *Financial support:* In 2010–11, 83 students received support, including 39 fellowships with partial tuition reimbursements available (averaging $7,001 per year). Financial award application deadline: 4/1. In 2010, 30 master's awarded. *Degree program information:* Part-time and evening/weekend programs available. Offers graphic design (MA); interior architecture (MFA); interior design (MA). *Application deadline:* For fall admission, 6/15 priority date for domestic students, 6/15 for international students; for spring admission, 11/1 priority date for domestic students, 11/1 for international students. Applications are processed on a rolling basis. *Application fee:* $50. Electronic applications accepted. *Application Contact:* Judith Reynolds, Director of Graduate Admissions, 617-573-8302, Fax: 617-305-1733, E-mail: grad.admission@suffolk.edu. *Director*, William Davis, 617-994-4264, Fax: 617-994-4250, E-mail: wdavis@suffolk.edu.

Sawyer Business School Students: 309 full-time (147 women), 728 part-time (365 women); includes 121 minority (44 Black or African American, non-Hispanic/Latino; 4 American Indian or Alaska Native, non-Hispanic/Latino; 46 Asian, non-Hispanic/Latino; 23 Hispanic/Latino; 1 Native Hawaiian or other Pacific Islander, non-Hispanic/Latino; 3 Two or more races, non-Hispanic/Latino), 186 international. Average age 30. 1,190 applicants, 64% accepted, 299 enrolled. *Faculty:* 109 full-time (35 women), 23 part-time/adjunct (8 women). Expenses: Contact institution. *Financial support:* In 2010–11, 988 students received support, including 508 fellowships with partial tuition reimbursements available (averaging $11,076 per year); career-related internships or fieldwork, Federal Work-Study, and institutionally sponsored loans also available. Support available to part-time students. Financial award application deadline: 4/1; financial award applicants required to submit FAFSA. In 2010, 480 master's, 5 other advanced degrees awarded. *Degree program information:* Part-time and evening/weekend programs available. Postbaccalaureate distance learning degree programs offered (no on-campus study). Offers accounting (MBA, MSA, GDPA); business (EMBA, GMBA, MBA, MBAH, MHA, MPA, MSA, MSF, MSFSB, MST, APC, CASPA, CPASF, GDPA); business administration (APC); corporate financial executive track (MBA); entrepreneurship (MBA);

executive business administration (EMBA); finance (MBA); global business administration (GMBA); health administration (MBAH, MHA); international business (MBA); marketing (MBA); nonprofit management (MPA); organizational behavior (MBA); public administration (CASPA); state and local government (MPA); strategic management (MBA); taxation (MBA, MST). *Application deadline:* For fall admission, 6/15 priority date for domestic students, 6/15 for international students; for spring admission, 11/1 for domestic and international students. Applications are processed on a rolling basis. *Application fee:* $50. Electronic applications accepted. *Application Contact:* Judith Reynolds, Director of Graduate Admissions, 617-573-8302, Fax: 617-305-1733, E-mail: grad.admission@suffolk.edu. *Dean,* Dr. William J. O'Neill, 617-573-2665, Fax: 617-573-8704, E-mail: woneill@suffolk.edu.

SULLIVAN UNIVERSITY, Louisville, KY 40205

General Information Proprietary, coed, comprehensive institution. *Enrollment:* 429 full-time matriculated graduate/professional students (239 women), 322 part-time matriculated graduate/professional students (198 women). *Graduate faculty:* 13 full-time (7 women), 11 part-time/adjunct (4 women). *Graduate housing:* On-campus housing not available. *Student services:* Campus employment opportunities, campus safety program, career counseling, exercise/wellness program, international student services, services for students with disabilities. *Library facilities:* McWhorter Library. *Online resources:* library catalog, web page, access to other libraries' catalogs. *Collection:* 22,500 titles, 16,500 serial subscriptions.

Computer facilities: 225 computers available on campus for general student use. A campuswide network can be accessed from student residence rooms and from off campus. *Web address:* http://www.sullivan.edu/.

General Application Contact: Beverly Horsley, Admissions Officer, 502-456-6505, Fax: 502-456-0040, E-mail: bhorsley@sullivan.edu.

GRADUATE UNITS

School of Business Students: 429 full-time (239 women), 322 part-time (198 women); includes 244 minority (152 Black or African American, non-Hispanic/Latino; 5 American Indian or Alaska Native, non-Hispanic/Latino; 5 Hispanic/Latino; 56 Native Hawaiian or other Pacific Islander, non-Hispanic/Latino; 26 Two or more races, non-Hispanic/Latino), 15 international. *Faculty:* 13 full-time (7 women), 11 part-time/adjunct (4 women). Expenses: Contact institution. In 2010, 133 master's awarded. *Degree program information:* Part-time programs available. Postbaccalaureate distance learning degree programs offered (no on-campus study). Offers business administration (MBA); collaborative leadership (MSCL); conflict management (MSCM); dispute resolution (MSDR); executive business administration (EMBA); human resource leadership (MSHRL); information technology (MSMIT); management (PhD); management and information technology (MBIT); pharmacy (Pharm D). *Application deadline:* Applications are processed on a rolling basis. *Application fee:* $100. *Application Contact:* Beverly Horsley, Admissions Officer, 502-456-6505, Fax: 502-456-0040, E-mail: bhorsley@sullivan.edu. *Dean of Graduate School,* Dr. Eric S. Harter, 502-456-6504, Fax: 502-456-0040, E-mail: eharter@sullivan.edu.

SUL ROSS STATE UNIVERSITY, Alpine, TX 79832

General Information State-supported, coed, comprehensive institution. *Graduate housing:* Rooms and/or apartments available to single and married students. *Research affiliation:* Chihuahuan Desert Research Institute (biology, geology), Big Bend National Park (biology, geology).

GRADUATE UNITS

Division of Agricultural and Natural Resource Science *Degree program information:* Part-time programs available. Offers agricultural and natural resource science (M Ag, MS); animal science (M Ag, MS); range and wildlife management (M Ag, MS).

Rio Grande College of Sul Ross State University *Degree program information:* Part-time and evening/weekend programs available. Offers business administration (MBA); teacher education (M Ed).

School of Arts and Sciences *Degree program information:* Part-time and evening/weekend programs available. Offers art education (M Ed); art history (M Ed); arts and sciences (M Ed, MA, MS); biology (MS); Earth and physical sciences (MS); English (MA); history (MA); political science (MA); psychology (MA); public administration (MA); studio art (M Ed).

School of Professional Studies *Degree program information:* Part-time and evening/weekend programs available. Offers bilingual education (M Ed); business administration (MBA); counseling (M Ed); criminal justice (MS); educational diagnostics (M Ed); elementary education (M Ed); physical education (M Ed); professional studies (M Ed, MBA, MS); reading specialist (M Ed); school administration (M Ed); secondary education (M Ed); supervision (M Ed).

SWEDISH INSTITUTE, COLLEGE OF HEALTH SCIENCES, New York, NY 10001-6700

General Information Proprietary, coed, comprehensive institution. *Graduate housing:* On-campus housing not available.

GRADUATE UNITS

Graduate Program *Degree program information:* Part-time and evening/weekend programs available.

SWEET BRIAR COLLEGE, Sweet Briar, VA 24595

General Information Independent, women only, comprehensive institution. *Enrollment:* 760 graduate, professional, and undergraduate students; 10 full-time matriculated graduate/professional students (9 women), 2 part-time matriculated graduate/professional students (both women). *Enrollment by degree level:* 12 master's. *Graduate faculty:* 3 full-time (2 women), 4 part-time/adjunct (all women). *Tuition:* Full-time $13,950; part-time $465 per credit. *Graduate housing:* Room and/or apartments available on a first-come, first-served basis to single students; on-campus housing not available to married students. Typical cost: $4320 per year. *Student services:* Campus employment opportunities, campus safety program, career counseling, exercise/wellness program, free psychological counseling, international student services, low-cost health insurance, services for students with disabilities, teacher training, writing training. *Library facilities:* Mary Helen Cochran Library plus 3 others. *Online resources:* library catalog, web page, access to other libraries' catalogs. *Collection:* 377,648 titles, 56,403 serial subscriptions, 9,395 audiovisual materials.

Computer facilities: Computer purchase and lease plans are available. 128 computers available on campus for general student use. A campuswide network can be accessed from student residence rooms and from off campus. Online class registration is available. *Web address:* http://www.sbc.edu/.

General Application Contact: David J. Moss, Associate Director of Admissions, 434-381-6710, Fax: 434-381-6152, E-mail: dmoss@sbc.edu.

GRADUATE UNITS

Department of Education Students: 10 full-time (9 women), 2 part-time (both women). Average age 30. 10 applicants, 90% accepted, 5 enrolled. *Faculty:* 3 full-time (2 women), 4 part-time/adjunct (all women). Expenses: Contact institution. *Financial support:* Available to part-time students. Applicants required to submit FAFSA. In 2010, 7 master's awarded. *Degree program information:* Part-time programs available. Offers education (M Ed, MAT). *Application deadline:* For fall admission, 2/1 for domestic and international students. *Application fee:* $40. Electronic applications accepted. *Application Contact:* David J. Moss, Associate Director of Admissions, 434-381-6710, Fax: 434-381-6152, E-mail: dmoss@sbc.edu. *Director of Graduate Program,* Dr. James L. Alouf, 434-381-6130, E-mail: alouf@sbc.edu.

SYRACUSE UNIVERSITY, Syracuse, NY 13244

General Information Independent, coed, university. CGS member. *Enrollment:* 20,407 graduate, professional, and undergraduate students; 4,365 full-time matriculated graduate/professional students (2,229 women), 1,450 part-time matriculated graduate/professional students (766 women). *Enrollment by degree level:* 638 first professional, 3,630 master's, 1,419 doctoral, 128 other advanced degrees. *Graduate faculty:* 1,002 full-time (372 women), 538 part-time/adjunct (279 women). *Tuition:* Part-time $1162 per credit. *Graduate housing:* Rooms and/or apartments available on a first-come, first-served basis to single and married students. Typical cost: $12,230 (including board) for single students; $12,230 (including board) for married students. Room and board charges vary according to housing facility selected. Housing application deadline: 6/1. *Student services:* Campus employment opportunities, campus safety program, career counseling, child daycare facilities, exercise/wellness program, free psychological counseling, grant writing training, international student services, low-cost health insurance, multicultural affairs office, services for students with disabilities, teacher training, writing training. *Library facilities:* E. S. Bird Library plus 5 others. *Online resources:* library catalog, web page, access to other libraries' catalogs. *Collection:* 3.3 million titles, 49,405 serial subscriptions, 1.1 million audiovisual materials. *Research affiliation:* Center of Excellence (environmental and energy systems), Say Yes to Education, Inc. (high school support for higher education).

Computer facilities: Computer purchase and lease plans are available. 3,427 computers available on campus for general student use. A campuswide network can be accessed from student residence rooms and from off campus. Online class registration, online services, networked client and server computing are available. *Web address:* http://www.syr.edu.

General Application Contact: Diana Hahn, Associate Director, Graduate Recruitment and Retention, 315-443-4492, Fax: 315-443-3423, E-mail: grad@syr.edu.

GRADUATE UNITS

College of Arts and Sciences Students: 653 full-time (383 women), 65 part-time (28 women); includes 67 minority (23 Black or African American, non-Hispanic/Latino; 18 Asian, non-Hispanic/Latino; 20 Hispanic/Latino; 2 Native Hawaiian or other Pacific Islander, non-Hispanic/Latino; 4 Two or more races, non-Hispanic/Latino), 171 international. Average age 28. 1,997 applicants, 23% accepted, 195 enrolled. *Faculty:* 305 full-time (113 women), 139 part-time/adjunct (93 women). Expenses: Contact institution. *Financial support:* Fellowships with full and partial tuition reimbursements, research assistantships with full and partial tuition reimbursements, teaching assistantships with full and partial tuition reimbursements, career-related internships or fieldwork, Federal Work-Study, scholarships/grants, health care benefits, tuition waivers (full and partial), and unspecified assistantships available. Support available to part-time students. Financial award application deadline: 1/1. In 2010, 94 master's, 57 doctorates, 25 other advanced degrees awarded. *Degree program information:* Part-time programs available. Offers applied statistics (MS); art history (MA); arts and sciences (MA, MFA, MS, Au D, PhD, CAS); audiology (Au D, PhD); biology (MS, PhD); chemistry (MS, PhD); clinical psychology (PhD); college science teaching (PhD); composition and cultural rhetoric (PhD); creative writing (MFA); earth sciences (MA, MS, PhD); English (MA, PhD); experimental psychology (PhD); forensic science (MS); French and Francophone studies (MA); language teaching: TESOL/TLOTE (CAS); linguistic studies (MA); mathematics (MS, PhD); Middle Eastern studies (CAS); Pan-African studies (MA); philosophy (MA, PhD); physics (MS, PhD); religion (MA, PhD); school psychology (PhD); social psychology (PhD); Spanish language, literature and culture (MA); speech language pathology (MS, PhD); structural biology, biochemistry and biophysics (PhD); women's and gender studies (CAS). *Application deadline:* For fall admission, 1/10 priority date for domestic and international students. Applications are processed on a rolling basis. *Application fee:* $75. Electronic applications accepted. *Application Contact:* Dr. George M. Langford, Dean, 315-443-2201, E-mail: dean@cas.syr.edu. *Dean,* Dr. George M. Langford, 315-443-2201, E-mail: dean@cas.syr.edu.

College of Human Ecology Students: 228 full-time (204 women), 122 part-time (110 women); includes 68 minority (37 Black or African American, non-Hispanic/Latino; 5 American Indian or Alaska Native, non-Hispanic/Latino; 6 Asian, non-Hispanic/Latino; 15 Hispanic/Latino; 1 Native Hawaiian or other Pacific Islander, non-Hispanic/Latino; 4 Two or more races, non-Hispanic/Latino), 29 international. Average age 31. 163 applicants, 67% accepted, 64 enrolled. *Faculty:* 53 full-time (32 women), 21 part-time/adjunct (15 women). Expenses: Contact institution. *Financial support:* Fellowships with full tuition reimbursements, research assistantships with full and partial tuition reimbursements, teaching assistantships with full and partial tuition reimbursements, career-related internships or fieldwork, Federal Work-Study, institutionally sponsored loans, scholarships/grants, health care benefits, tuition waivers (full and partial), and unspecified assistantships available. Support available to part-time students. Financial award application deadline: 1/1; financial award applicants required to submit FAFSA. In 2010, 95 master's, 6 doctorates awarded. *Degree program information:* Part-time and evening/weekend programs available. Offers addiction studies (CAS); child and family health in the global community (MS); child and family studies (MA, MS, PhD); human ecology (MA, MS, MSW, PhD, CAS); marriage and family therapy (MA); nutrition science (MA, MS); social work (MSW). *Application deadline:* For fall admission, 3/15 priority date for domestic and international students. *Application fee:* $75. Electronic applications accepted. *Application Contact:* Felecia Otero, Director of College Admissions, 315-443-5555, Fax: 315-443-2562, E-mail: inquire@hshp.syr.edu. *Dean,* Dr. Diane Lyden Murphy, 315-443-5582, Fax: 315-443-2562.

College of Law *Degree program information:* Part-time programs available. Offers law (JD). Electronic applications accepted.

College of Visual and Performing Arts Students: 118 full-time (69 women), 8 part-time (5 women); includes 8 minority (1 Black or African American, non-Hispanic/Latino; 5 Asian, non-Hispanic/Latino; 1 Hispanic/Latino; 1 Two or more races, non-Hispanic/Latino), 30 international. Average age 27. 337 applicants, 34% accepted, 48 enrolled. *Faculty:* 120 full-time (48 women), 108 part-time/adjunct (60 women). Expenses: Contact institution. *Financial support:* Fellowships with full tuition reimbursements, teaching assistantships with full and partial tuition reimbursements, Federal Work-Study, institutionally sponsored loans, health care benefits, tuition waivers (full and partial), and unspecified assistantships available. Financial award application deadline: 1/1; financial award applicants required to submit FAFSA. In 2010, 44 master's awarded. Offers art photography (MFA); art video (MFA); ceramics (MFA); collaborative design (MFA); communication and rhetorical studies (MA); computer art (MFA); conducting (M Mu); film (MFA); illustration (MFA); jewelry and metalsmithing (MFA); museum studies (MA); music composition (M Mus); organ (M Mus); painting (MFA); percussion (M Mus); piano (M Mus); printmaking (MFA); sculpture (MFA); strings (M Mus); visual and performing arts (M Mu, M Mus, MA, MFA, MS); voice (M Mus); wind instruments (M Mus). *Application deadline:* For fall admission, 2/1 priority date for domestic and international students; for spring admission, 3/1 priority date for domestic students. *Application fee:* $75. Electronic applications accepted. *Application Contact:* Harriett Conti, Assistant Dean for Recruitment and Admissions, 315-443-5755, E-mail: hmconti@syr.edu. *Chair,* Dr. Ann Clarke, 315-443-5889.

L. C. Smith College of Engineering and Computer Science Students: 669 full-time (180 women), 153 part-time (24 women); includes 42 minority (8 Black or African American, non-Hispanic/Latino; 27 Asian, non-Hispanic/Latino; 7 Hispanic/Latino), 611 international. Average age 26. 1,815 applicants, 44% accepted, 270 enrolled. *Faculty:* 72 full-time (7 women), 22 part-time/adjunct (1 woman). Expenses: Contact institution. *Financial support:* Fellowships with full tuition reimbursements, research assistantships with full and partial tuition reimbursements, teaching assistantships with full and partial tuition reimbursements, scholarships/grants and tuition waivers (partial) available. Financial award application deadline: 1/1; financial award applicants required to submit FAFSA. In 2010, 218 master's, 27 doctorates awarded. *Degree program information:* Part-time and evening/weekend programs available. Offers bioengineering (MS, PhD); chemical engineering (MS, PhD); civil engineering (MS, PhD); computer and information science and engineering (PhD); computer engineering (MS, CE); computer science (MS); electrical and computer engineering (PhD); electrical engineering (MS, EE); engineering and computer science (MS, PhD, CAS, CE, EE); engineering management (MS); environmental engineering (MS); environmental engineering science (MS); mechanical and aerospace engineering (MS, PhD); microwave engineering (CAS). *Application deadline:* For fall admission, 7/1 priority date for domestic students, 6/1 priority date for international students. Applications are processed on a rolling basis. *Application fee:* $75. Electronic applications accepted. *Application Contact:* Kathleen Joyce, Assistant Dean, 314-443-2219, E-mail: topgrads@syr.edu. *Dean,* Dr. Laura J. Steinberg, 315-443-2545, E-mail: ljs@syr.edu.

Martin J. Whitman School of Management *Degree program information:* Part-time programs available. Postbaccalaureate distance learning degree programs offered (minimal on-campus study). Offers accounting (MS Acct); entrepreneurship (MBA); entrepreneurship and emerg-

Syracuse University (continued)

ing enterprises (MS); finance (MSF); management (MBA, MS Acct, MSF, PhD); management information systems (PhD); managerial statistics (PhD); marketing (MBA, PhD); operations management (PhD); organizational behavior (PhD); professional accounting (MS); strategy and human resources (PhD); supply chain management (MBA, PhD); sustainable enterprise (CAS). Electronic applications accepted.

Maxwell School of Citizenship and Public Affairs Students: 600 full-time (316 women), 142 part-time (70 women); includes 94 minority (34 Black or African American, non-Hispanic/Latino; 1 American Indian or Alaska Native, non-Hispanic/Latino; 27 Asian, non-Hispanic/Latino; 25 Hispanic/Latino; 7 Two or more races, non-Hispanic/Latino), 254 international. Average age 31. 1,883 applicants, 41% accepted, 248 enrolled. *Faculty:* 145 full-time (51 women), 30 part-time/adjunct (7 women). Expenses: Contact institution. *Financial support:* Fellowships with full tuition reimbursements, research assistantships with full and partial tuition reimbursements, teaching assistantships with full and partial tuition reimbursements available. Financial award application deadline: 1/1. In 2010, 231 master's, 32 doctorates, 66 other advanced degrees awarded. *Degree program information:* Part-time and evening/weekend programs available. Postbaccalaureate distance learning degree programs offered. Offers anthropology (MA, PhD); citizenship and public affairs (EMPA, MA, MPA, MS Sc, PhD, CAS); conflict resolution (CAS); e-government management and leadership (CAS); econometrics (CAS); economics (MA, PhD); European Union and contemporary Europe (CAS); geography (MA, PhD); health services management and policy (CAS); history (MA, PhD); international relations (MA); Latin American studies (CAS); leadership of international and non-governmental organizations (CAS); political science (MA, PhD); post conflict reconstruction (CAS); public administration (EMPA, MPA, PhD, CAS); public management and policy (CAS); social sciences (MS Sc, PhD); sociology (MA, PhD). *Application deadline:* For fall admission, 2/1 priority date for domestic and international students. Applications are processed on a rolling basis. *Application fee:* $75. Electronic applications accepted. *Application Contact:* Dr. Michael Wasylenko, Interim Dean, 315-443-4000, Fax: 315-443-3385. *Interim Dean,* Dr. Michael Wasylenko, 315-443-4000, Fax: 315-443-3385.

School of Architecture Students: 112 full-time (42 women), 4 part-time (3 women); includes 23 minority (6 Black or African American, non-Hispanic/Latino; 8 Asian, non-Hispanic/Latino; 8 Hispanic/Latino; 1 Two or more races, non-Hispanic/Latino), 17 international. Average age 26. 256 applicants, 42% accepted, 44 enrolled. *Faculty:* 37 full-time (12 women), 7 part-time/adjunct (3 women). Expenses: Contact institution. *Financial support:* Fellowships with full tuition reimbursements, research assistantships with full and partial tuition reimbursements, teaching assistantships with full and partial tuition reimbursements available. Financial award application deadline: 1/1. In 2010, 17 degrees awarded. Offers architecture (M Arch I, M Arch II). *Application deadline:* For fall admission, 2/1 priority date for domestic and international students. *Application fee:* $75. Electronic applications accepted. *Application Contact:* Prof. Francisco Sanin, Graduate Director, 315-443-1041, Fax: 315-443-5082, E-mail: fesanin@syr.edu. *Dean,* Mark Robbins, 315-443-1041, Fax: 315-443-5082.

School of Education Students: 377 full-time (276 women), 318 part-time (234 women); includes 90 minority (43 Black or African American, non-Hispanic/Latino; 3 American Indian or Alaska Native, non-Hispanic/Latino; 15 Asian, non-Hispanic/Latino; 18 Hispanic/Latino; 2 Native Hawaiian or other Pacific Islander, non-Hispanic/Latino; 9 Two or more races, non-Hispanic/Latino), 80 international. Average age 33. 486 applicants, 70% accepted, 161 enrolled. *Faculty:* 53 full-time (34 women), 64 part-time/adjunct (46 women). Expenses: Contact institution. *Financial support:* Fellowships with full tuition reimbursements, research assistantships with full and partial tuition reimbursements, teaching assistantships with full and partial tuition reimbursements, career-related internships or fieldwork, institutionally sponsored loans, scholarships/grants, health care benefits, tuition waivers (partial), and unspecified assistantships available. Support available to part-time students. Financial award application deadline: 1/1; financial award applicants required to submit FAFSA. In 2010, 134 master's, 15 doctorates, 13 other advanced degrees awarded. *Degree program information:* Part-time programs available. Offers art education (CAS); art education/professional certification (MS); art education: preparation (MS); biology education (MS); chemistry education (MS); childhood education: (1-6) preparation (MS); clinical mental health counseling (MS); counselor education (PhD); cultural foundations of education (MS, PhD); disability studies (CAS); early childhood special education (MS); earth science education (MS); education (M Mus, MS, Ed D, PhD, CAS); educational leadership (MS, Ed D, CAS); educational technology (CAS); English education (PhD); English education: preparation 7-12 (MS); exercise science (MS); higher education (MS, PhD); inclusive special education (grades 1-6) (MS); inclusive special education (grades 7-12) (MS); inclusive special education: severe/multiple disabilities (MS); instructional design, development, and evaluation (MS, PhD, CAS); instructional technology (MS); literacy education (MS); literacy education: grades 5-12 (MS); mathematics education (PhD); mathematics education: preparation 7-12 (MS); music education/professional certification (M Mus, MS); music education: teacher preparation (MS); physics education (MS); reading education (PhD); school counseling (MS, CAS); school district business leadership (CAS); science education (PhD); social studies education (MS); special education (PhD); student affairs counseling (MS); teaching and curriculum (MS, PhD); teaching English language learners (MS). *Application deadline:* For fall admission, 2/1 priority date for domestic and international students; for spring admission, 10/15 priority date for domestic and international students. Applications are processed on a rolling basis. *Application fee:* $75. Electronic applications accepted. *Application Contact:* Liza Rochelson, Graduate Recruiter, School of Education, 315-443-2505, E-mail: e-gradrcrt@syr.edu. *Dean,* Dr. Douglas Biklen, 315-443-4751.

School of Information Studies Students: 373 full-time (175 women), 343 part-time (173 women); includes 113 minority (41 Black or African American, non-Hispanic/Latino; 4 American Indian or Alaska Native, non-Hispanic/Latino; 28 Asian, non-Hispanic/Latino; 32 Hispanic/Latino; 2 Native Hawaiian or other Pacific Islander, non-Hispanic/Latino; 6 Two or more races, non-Hispanic/Latino), 202 international. Average age 32. 936 applicants, 67% accepted, 273 enrolled. *Faculty:* 34 full-time (12 women), 31 part-time/adjunct (8 women). Expenses: Contact institution. *Financial support:* Fellowships with full tuition reimbursements, research assistantships with partial tuition reimbursements, teaching assistantships with partial tuition reimbursements, scholarships/grants available. Financial award application deadline: 1/1; financial award applicants required to submit FAFSA. In 2010, 216 master's, 3 doctorates, 58 other advanced degrees awarded. *Degree program information:* Part-time and evening/weekend programs available. Postbaccalaureate distance learning degree programs offered (minimal on-campus study). Offers cultural heritage preservation (CAS); digital libraries (CAS); eScience (CAS); global enterprise technology (CAS); information innovation (CAS); information management (MS, DPS); information science and technology (PhD); information security management (CAS); information studies (MS, DPS, PhD, CAS); information systems and telecommunications management (CAS); library and information science (MS); library and information science: school media (MS); school media (CAS); telecommunications and network management (MS). *Application deadline:* For fall admission, 2/1 priority date for domestic and international students; for spring admission, 10/15 priority date for domestic and international students. *Application fee:* $75. Electronic applications accepted. *Application Contact:* Susan Corieri, Director of Enrollment Management, 315-443-2575, E-mail: ist@syr.edu. *Dean,* Elizabeth Liddy, 315-443-2736.

S. I. Newhouse School of Public Communications Students: 271 full-time (185 women), 73 part-time (42 women); includes 83 minority (51 Black or African American, non-Hispanic/Latino; 1 American Indian or Alaska Native, non-Hispanic/Latino; 13 Asian, non-Hispanic/Latino; 15 Hispanic/Latino; 3 Two or more races, non-Hispanic/Latino), 67 international. Average age 28. 889 applicants, 55% accepted, 230 enrolled. *Faculty:* 65 full-time (23 women), 45 part-time/adjunct (18 women). Expenses: Contact institution. *Financial support:* Fellowships with full tuition reimbursements, research assistantships with partial tuition reimbursements, teaching assistantships with partial tuition reimbursements, career-related internships or fieldwork, Federal Work-Study, scholarships/grants, and tuition waivers (partial) available. Support available to part-time students. Financial award application deadline: 2/1; financial award applicants required to submit FAFSA. In 2010, 161 master's, 3 doctorates awarded. Postbaccalaureate distance learning degree programs offered (minimal on-campus study). Offers advertising (MA); arts journalism (MA); broadcast and digital journalism (MS); communications management (MS); documentary film and history (MA); magazine, newspaper and online journalism (MA); mass communications (PhD); media management (MS); media studies (MA); photography (MS); public communications (MA, MS, PhD); public relations (MS); television, radio, and film (MA). *Application deadline:* For fall admission, 2/1 priority date for domestic and international students. *Application fee:* $45. Electronic applications accepted. *Application Contact:* Martha Coria, Graduate Records Office, 315-443-5749, Fax: 315-443-1834, E-mail: pcgrad@syr.edu. *Dean,* Dr. Lorraine Branham, 315-443-3627, Fax: 315-443-3946.

TABOR COLLEGE, Hillsboro, KS 67063

General Information Independent-religious, coed, comprehensive institution.

GRADUATE UNITS

Graduate Program Offers accounting (MBA). Program offered at the Wichita campus only.

TAFT LAW SCHOOL, Santa Ana, CA 92704-6954

General Information Graduate-only institution.

GRADUATE UNITS

Graduate Programs Offers American jurisprudence (LL M); law (JD); taxation (LL M).

TAI SOPHIA INSTITUTE, Laurel, MD 20723

General Information Independent, coed, primarily women, graduate-only institution. *Graduate housing:* On-campus housing not available. *Research affiliation:* Maryland State Department of Public Safety and Corrections (acupuncture detoxification services).

GRADUATE UNITS

Chinese Herb Certificate Program *Degree program information:* Part-time and evening/weekend programs available. Offers Chinese herb (Certificate).

Program in Acupuncture Offers acupuncture (M Ac).

Program in Applied Healing Arts Offers applied healing arts (MA).

Program in Herbal Medicine Offers herbal medicine (MS).

TALMUDICAL ACADEMY OF NEW JERSEY, Adelphia, NJ 07710

General Information Independent-religious, men only, comprehensive institution.

GRADUATE UNITS

Graduate Program

TALMUDIC COLLEGE OF FLORIDA, Miami Beach, FL 33139

General Information Independent-religious, men only, comprehensive institution. *Graduate housing:* Rooms and/or apartments available on a first-come, first-served basis to single and married students.

GRADUATE UNITS

Program in Talmudic Law Offers Talmudic law (MRE).

TARLETON STATE UNIVERSITY, Stephenville, TX 76402

General Information State-supported, coed, comprehensive institution. *Graduate housing:* Rooms and/or apartments available on a first-come, first-served basis to single and married students. Housing application deadline: 8/1.

GRADUATE UNITS

College of Graduate Studies *Degree program information:* Part-time and evening/weekend programs available. Postbaccalaureate distance learning degree programs offered (minimal on-campus study). Offers liberal studies (MS). Electronic applications accepted.

College of Agriculture and Human Sciences *Degree program information:* Part-time and evening/weekend programs available. Postbaccalaureate distance learning degree programs offered (minimal on-campus study). Offers agriculture (MS); agriculture and human sciences (MS); agriculture education (MS). Electronic applications accepted.

College of Business Administration *Degree program information:* Part-time and evening/weekend programs available. Postbaccalaureate distance learning degree programs offered (minimal on-campus study). Offers business administration (MBA, MS); human resource management (MS); information systems (MS); management and leadership (MS). Electronic applications accepted.

College of Education *Degree program information:* Part-time and evening/weekend programs available. Postbaccalaureate distance learning degree programs offered (minimal on-campus study). Offers counseling and psychology (M Ed); curriculum and instruction (M Ed); education (M Ed, Ed D, Certificate); educational administration (M Ed); educational leadership (Ed D, Certificate); physical education (M Ed); secondary education (Certificate); special education (Certificate). Electronic applications accepted.

College of Liberal and Fine Arts *Degree program information:* Part-time and evening/weekend programs available. Offers criminal justice (MCJ); English (MA); history (MA); liberal and fine arts (MA, MCJ, MM); music education (MM); political science (MA). Electronic applications accepted.

College of Science and Technology *Degree program information:* Part-time and evening/weekend programs available. Postbaccalaureate distance learning degree programs offered (minimal on-campus study). Offers biology (MS); environmental science (MS); mathematics (MS); science and technology (MS). Electronic applications accepted.

TAYLOR COLLEGE AND SEMINARY, Edmonton, AB T6J 4T3, Canada

General Information Independent-religious, coed, comprehensive institution. *Graduate housing:* Room and/or apartments available on a first-come, first-served basis to single students; on-campus housing not available to married students. Housing application deadline: 8/1.

GRADUATE UNITS

Graduate and Professional Programs *Degree program information:* Part-time programs available. Postbaccalaureate distance learning degree programs offered (minimal on-campus study). Offers Christian studies (Diploma); intercultural studies (MA, Diploma); theology (M Div, MTS).

TAYLOR UNIVERSITY, Upland, IN 46989-1001

General Information Independent-religious, coed, comprehensive institution. *Enrollment:* 2,589 graduate, professional, and undergraduate students; 111 full-time matriculated graduate/professional students (43 women), 12 part-time matriculated graduate/professional students (5 women). *Enrollment by degree level:* 123 master's. *Graduate faculty:* 3 full-time (1 woman), 20 part-time/adjunct (0 women). *Tuition:* Full-time $10,260; part-time $570 per credit hour. *Required fees:* $72 per semester. One-time fee: $100. *Graduate housing:* On-campus housing not available. *Student services:* Campus employment opportunities, campus safety program, career counseling, exercise/wellness program, free psychological counseling, international student services, low-cost health insurance, multicultural affairs office, services for students with disabilities, writing training. *Library facilities:* Zondervan Library. *Online resources:* library catalog, web page, access to other libraries' catalogs. *Collection:* 207,425 titles, 35,004 serial subscriptions, 15,004 audiovisual materials.

Computer facilities: Computer purchase and lease plans are available. 340 computers available on campus for general student use. A campuswide network can be accessed from student residence rooms and from off campus. Online class registration is available. *Web address:* http://www.taylor.edu/.

General Application Contact: Sherri Blair, Assistant to the Dean of Professional and Graduate Studies, 765-998-5108, Fax: 765-998-4389, E-mail: shblair@taylor.edu.

GRADUATE UNITS

Master of Arts in Higher Education Program Students: 34 full-time (19 women), 2 part-time (1 woman); includes 1 Black or African American, non-Hispanic/Latino; 2 Asian, non-Hispanic/

Latino; 1 Hispanic/Latino, 1 international. Average age 27. 30 applicants, 83% accepted, 19 enrolled. *Faculty:* 1 full-time (0 women), 7 part-time/adjunct (0 women). Expenses: Contact institution. *Financial support:* In 2010–11, 11 students received support, including 30 fellowships (averaging $5,000 per year). Financial award applicants required to submit FAFSA. In 2010, 16 master's awarded. *Degree program information:* Part-time programs available. Offers higher education (MA). *Application deadline:* For fall admission, 2/1 for domestic students, 1/1 for international students. Applications are processed on a rolling basis. *Application fee:* $100. *Application Contact:* Cindi Carder, Program Assistant, 765-998-5373, Fax: 765-998-4577, E-mail: jccarder@taylor.edu. *Chair*, Dr. Tim Herrmann, 765-998-5142, E-mail: tmherrmann@taylor.edu.

Master of Arts in Religious Studies Program Students: 2 full-time (1 woman), 4 part-time (1 woman); includes 1 Black or African American, non-Hispanic/Latino. Average age 31. *Faculty:* 1 (woman) full-time, 2 part-time/adjunct (0 women). Expenses: Contact institution. *Financial support:* In 2010–11, 1 student received support, including 2 fellowships (averaging $1,500 per year). Financial award applicants required to submit FAFSA. In 2010, 1 master's awarded. *Degree program information:* Part-time programs available. Offers biblical studies (MA); world religions (MA). *Application deadline:* Applications are processed on a rolling basis. *Application fee:* $100. *Application Contact:* Kari Manganello, Program Assistant, 765-998-5148, Fax: 765-998-4930, E-mail: krmangane@taylor.edu. *Chair*, Dr. Sheri Klouda, 765-998-4786, Fax: 765-998-4930, E-mail: shklouda@taylor.edu.

Master of Business Administration Program Students: 59 full-time (15 women), 4 part-time (1 woman); includes 2 Black or African American, non-Hispanic/Latino; 2 Hispanic/Latino; 1 Two or more races, non-Hispanic/Latino, 1 international. Average age 35. 28 applicants, 79% accepted, 17 enrolled. *Faculty:* 1 full-time (0 women), 8 part-time/adjunct (0 women). Expenses: Contact institution. *Financial support:* Applicants required to submit FAFSA. In 2010, 37 master's awarded. *Degree program information:* Part-time programs available. Offers emerging business strategies (MBA); global leadership (MBA). *Application deadline:* Applications are processed on a rolling basis. *Application fee:* $100. *Application Contact:* Wendy Speakman, Program Director, 866-471-6062, Fax: 260-492-0452, E-mail: wnspeakman@taylor.edu. *Interim Chair*, Dr. Evan Wood, 260-627-9663, E-mail: evwood@taylor.edu.

Master of Environmental Science Program Students: 16 full-time (8 women), 2 part-time (both women), 1 international. Average age 26. 35 applicants, 31% accepted, 8 enrolled. *Faculty:* 3 part-time/adjunct (0 women). Expenses: Contact institution. *Financial support:* In 2010–11, 18 fellowships (averaging $10,000 per year), 5 teaching assistantships (averaging $6,000 per year) were awarded; scholarships/grants also available. Financial award applicants required to submit FAFSA. In 2010, 8 master's awarded. Offers environmental science (MES). *Application deadline:* Applications are processed on a rolling basis. *Application fee:* $0. *Application Contact:* Becky Taylor, Program Assistant, 765-998-4960, Fax: 765-998-4976, E-mail: mes@taylor.edu. *Chair*, Dr. Edwin Richard Squiers, 765-998-5386, Fax: 765-998-4976, E-mail: rcsquiers@taylor.edu.

TEACHER EDUCATION UNIVERSITY, Winter Park, FL 32789

General Information Proprietary, coed, graduate-only institution.

GRADUATE UNITS

Graduate Programs Offers educational leadership (MA); educational technology (MA); elementary education K-6 (MA); instructional strategies (MA Ed); school guidance and counseling (MA).

TEACHERS COLLEGE, COLUMBIA UNIVERSITY, New York, NY 10027-6696

General Information Independent, coed, graduate-only institution. *Enrollment by degree level:* 3,617 master's, 1,470 doctoral. *Tuition:* Full-time $28,272; part-time $1178 per credit. *Required fees:* $756; $378 per semester. *Graduate housing:* Rooms and/or apartments available on a first-come, first-served basis to single and married students. Housing application deadline: 2/1. *Student services:* Campus employment opportunities, campus safety program, career counseling, child daycare facilities, exercise/wellness program, free psychological counseling, grant writing training, international student services, low-cost health insurance, multicultural affairs office, services for students with disabilities, teacher training, writing training. *Library facilities:* Milbank Memorial Library. *Online resources:* library catalog, web page, access to other libraries' catalogs. *Collection:* 585,901 titles, 2,095 serial subscriptions, 3,987 audiovisual materials.

Computer facilities: 482 computers available on campus for general student use. A campuswide network can be accessed from student residence rooms and from off campus. Online class registration is available. *Web address:* http://www.tc.columbia.edu/.

General Application Contact: Thomas P. Rock, Director of Admissions, 212-678-3083, Fax: 212-678-4171, E-mail: rock@tc.edu.

GRADUATE UNITS

Graduate Faculty of Education Students: 1,803 full-time (1,388 women), 3,284 part-time (2,520 women); includes 1,593 minority (447 Black or African American, non-Hispanic/Latino; 8 American Indian or Alaska Native, non-Hispanic/Latino; 527 Asian, non-Hispanic/Latino; 431 Hispanic/Latino; 13 Native Hawaiian or other Pacific Islander, non-Hispanic/Latino; 167 Two or more races, non-Hispanic/Latino), 774 international. Average age 31. 5,206 applicants, 56% accepted, 1352 enrolled. Expenses: Contact institution. *Financial support:* Fellowships, research assistantships, teaching assistantships, career-related internships or fieldwork, Federal Work-Study, institutionally sponsored loans, traineeships, tuition waivers (full and partial), and unspecified assistantships available. Support available to part-time students. Financial award application deadline: 2/1. In 2010, 1,726 master's, 254 doctorates awarded. *Degree program information:* Part-time and evening/weekend programs available. Offers administration and supervision in special education (Ed M, MA, Ed D, PhD); administration studies (MA); adult education guided intensive study (Ed D); adult learning and leadership (Ed M, MA, Ed D); anthropology (Ed M, MA, Ed D, PhD); applied behavior analysis (MA, Ed D, PhD); applied educational psychology–school psychology (Ed M, MA, Ed D, PhD); applied linguistics (Ed M, MA, Ed D); applied physiology (Ed M, MA, Ed D); art and art education (Ed M, MA, Ed D, Ed DCT); arts administration (MA); bilingual and bicultural education (MA); blind and visual impairment (MA, Ed D); change leadership (MA); childhood/disabilities (Certificate); clinical psychology (PhD); communication (Ed M, MA, Ed D); comparative and international education (Ed M, MA, Ed D, PhD); computing in education (MA); counseling psychology (Ed M, Ed D, PhD); curriculum and teaching (Ed M, MA, Ed D, Certificate); curriculum and teaching in physical education (Ed M, MA, Ed D); developmental psychology (MA, Ed D, PhD); early childhood education (Ed M, MA, Ed D); early childhood special education (Ed M, MA); economics and education (Ed M, MA, PhD); education (Ed M, MA, MS, Ed D, Ed DCT, PhD, Certificate); education leadership (Ed M, MA, Ed D, PhD); education leadership studies (Ed M, MA, Ed D); educational administration (Ed M, MA, Ed D, PhD); educational psychology-human cognition and learning (Ed M, MA, Ed D, PhD); elementary/childhood education, preservice (MA); English education (Ed M, MA, Ed D, PhD); giftedness (MA, Ed D); guidance and rehabilitation (MA); health education (MA, MS, Ed D); hearing impairment (MA, Ed D); higher education (Ed M, MA, Ed D); history and education (Ed M, MA, Ed D, PhD); inquiry in education leadership (Ed D); instructional technology and media (Ed M, MA, Ed D); interdisciplinary studies (Ed M, MA, Ed D); international educational development (Ed M, MA, Ed D, PhD); kinesiology (PhD); leadership, policy and politics (Ed M, MA, Ed D, PhD); learning disabilities (Ed M, MA, Ed D); literacy specialist (MA); mathematics education (Ed M, MA, MS, Ed D, Ed DCT, PhD); measurement, evaluation, and statistics (MA, MS, Ed D, PhD); mental retardation (MA, Ed D, PhD); motor learning/movement science (Ed M, MA, Ed D); music and music education (Ed M, MA, Ed D, Ed DCT); neuroscience and education (MA); nurse executive (MA, Ed D); nursing, professional role (Ed M, MA, Ed D); nutrition and education (Ed M, MS, Ed D); nutrition and public health (MS, Ed D); nutrition education (Ed M, MS, Ed D); nutrition education and public health nutrition (Ed M, MS, Ed D); philosophy and education (Ed M, MA, Ed D, PhD); physical disabilities (Ed D, PhD); politics and education (Ed M, MA, Ed D, PhD); private school leadership (Ed M, MA, Ed D); professorial studies (MA); public school and school district leadership (Ed M, MA, Ed D); reading specialist (MA); research in special education (Ed D); science education (Ed M, MA, MS, Ed D, Ed DCT, PhD); severe or multiple disabilities (MA); social and organizational psychology (MA); social studies education (Ed M, MA, Ed D, PhD); social-organizational psychology (MA); sociology and education (Ed M, MA, Ed D, PhD); special education (Ed M, MA, Ed D); speech-language pathology (Ed M, MS, Ed D, PhD); student personnel administration (Ed M, MA, Ed D); teaching English to speakers of other languages (Ed M, MA, Ed D); teaching of sign language (MA); technology specialist (MA); urban education leadership (Ed D). *Application fee:* $65. Electronic applications accepted. *Application Contact:* Thomas P. Rock, Director of Admissions, 212-678-3083, Fax: 212-678-4171, E-mail: rock@tc.edu. *President*, Susan Furhman, 212-678-3050.

TÉLÉ-UNIVERSITÉ, Québec, QC G1K 9H5, Canada

General Information Province-supported, coed, comprehensive institution. *Graduate housing:* On-campus housing not available.

GRADUATE UNITS

Graduate Programs *Degree program information:* Part-time programs available. Offers computer science (PhD); corporate finance (MS); distance learning (MS).

TELSHE YESHIVA–CHICAGO, Chicago, IL 60625-5598

General Information Independent-religious, men only, comprehensive institution.

GRADUATE UNITS

Graduate Program

TEMPLE BAPTIST SEMINARY, Chattanooga, TN 37404-3530

General Information Independent-religious, coed, primarily men, graduate-only institution. *Graduate housing:* On-campus housing not available.

GRADUATE UNITS

Program in Theology *Degree program information:* Part-time and evening/weekend programs available. Postbaccalaureate distance learning degree programs offered (minimal on-campus study). Offers biblical languages (M Div); Biblical studies (MABS); Christian education (MACE); English Bible û language tools (M Div); theology (MM, D Min).

TEMPLE UNIVERSITY, Philadelphia, PA 19122-6096

General Information State-related, coed, university. CGS member. *Enrollment:* 37,367 graduate, professional, and undergraduate students; 6,504 full-time matriculated graduate/professional students (3,442 women), 1,899 part-time matriculated graduate/professional students (1,127 women). *Enrollment by degree level:* 3,599 first professional, 3,152 master's, 1,652 doctoral. *Graduate faculty:* 915 full-time (310 women). *Graduate housing:* Rooms and/or apartments available on a first-come, first-served basis to single and married students. Housing application deadline: 5/1. *Student services:* Campus employment opportunities, campus safety program, career counseling, exercise/wellness program, free psychological counseling, grant writing training, international student services, low-cost health insurance, multicultural affairs office, services for students with disabilities, teacher training, writing training. *Library facilities:* Paley Library plus 14 others. *Online resources:* library catalog, web page, access to other libraries' catalogs. *Collection:* 62,173 serial subscriptions, 37,856 audiovisual materials.

Computer facilities: Computer purchase and lease plans are available. 3,670 computers available on campus for general student use. A campuswide network can be accessed from student residence rooms and from off campus. Online class registration, student accounts, Web hosting are available. *Web address:* http://www.temple.edu/.

General Application Contact: Tara Schumacher, Coordinator of Outreach, 215-204-6575, Fax: 215-204-8781, E-mail: tara.schumacher@temple.edu.

GRADUATE UNITS

College of Education Students: 263 full-time (189 women), 400 part-time (272 women); includes 92 Black or African American, non-Hispanic/Latino; 1 American Indian or Alaska Native, non-Hispanic/Latino; 17 Asian, non-Hispanic/Latino; 15 Hispanic/Latino; 3 Two or more races, non-Hispanic/Latino, 18 international. Average age 33. 550 applicants, 53% accepted, 184 enrolled. *Faculty:* 53 full-time (29 women). Expenses: Contact institution. *Financial support:* Fellowships, research assistantships, teaching assistantships, career-related internships or fieldwork and Federal Work-Study available. Financial award application deadline: 1/15; financial award applicants required to submit FAFSA. In 2010, 211 master's, 34 doctorates awarded. *Degree program information:* Part-time and evening/weekend programs available. Offers adult and organizational development (Ed M); applied behavioral analysis (MS Ed); career and technical education (MS Ed); counseling psychology (Ed M, PhD); early childhood education and elementary education (MS Ed); education (Ed M, MS Ed, Ed D, PhD); educational administration (Ed M, Ed D); educational psychology (Ed M, PhD); English education (MS Ed); language arts education (Ed D); math/science education (Ed D); mathematics education (MS Ed); school psychology (Ed M, PhD); science education (MS Ed); second and foreign language education (MS Ed); special education (MS Ed); teaching English as a second language (MS Ed); urban education (Ed M, Ed D). *Application deadline:* For fall admission, 12/15 for international students; for spring admission, 8/1 for international students. Applications are processed on a rolling basis. *Application fee:* $50. Electronic applications accepted. *Application Contact:* Dr. James Earl Davis, Interim Dean, 215-204-8017, Fax: 215-204-5622, E-mail: dean.ed@temple.edu. *Interim Dean*, Dr. James Earl Davis, 215-204-8017, Fax: 215-204-5622, E-mail: dean.ed@temple.edu.

College of Engineering Students: 80 full-time (23 women), 36 part-time (7 women); includes 3 Black or African American, non-Hispanic/Latino; 2 American Indian or Alaska Native, non-Hispanic/Latino; 11 Asian, non-Hispanic/Latino; 1 Hispanic/Latino, 68 international. Average age 29. 176 applicants, 49% accepted, 30 enrolled. *Faculty:* 38 full-time (5 women). Expenses: Contact institution. *Financial support:* Fellowships with full tuition reimbursements, research assistantships with full tuition reimbursements, teaching assistantships with full tuition reimbursements, career-related internships or fieldwork, Federal Work-Study, and institutionally sponsored loans available. Financial award application deadline: 1/15. In 2010, 46 master's, 2 doctorates awarded. *Degree program information:* Part-time programs available. Offers civil engineering (MSE); electrical engineering (MSE); engineering (MS, MSE, PhD); mechanical engineering (MSE). *Application deadline:* For fall admission, 7/1 priority date for domestic students, 12/15 for international students; for spring admission, 11/1 priority date for domestic students, 8/1 for international students. Applications are processed on a rolling basis. *Application fee:* $50. Electronic applications accepted. *Application Contact:* Tara Schumacher, Coordinator of Outreach, 215-204-6575, Fax: 215-204-8781, E-mail: tara.schumacher@temple.edu. *Dean*, Dr. Keyanoush Sadeghipour, 215-204-5285, Fax: 215-204-6936, E-mail: keya@temple.edu.

College of Liberal Arts Students: 698 full-time (358 women), 164 part-time (87 women); includes 91 Black or African American, non-Hispanic/Latino; 7 American Indian or Alaska Native, non-Hispanic/Latino; 27 Asian, non-Hispanic/Latino; 39 Hispanic/Latino; 6 Two or more races, non-Hispanic/Latino, 56 international. Average age 32. 1,620 applicants, 34% accepted, 213 enrolled. *Faculty:* 260 full-time (102 women). Expenses: Contact institution. *Financial support:* Fellowships, research assistantships, teaching assistantships, career-related internships or fieldwork, Federal Work-Study, institutionally sponsored loans, scholarships/grants, and tuition waivers (full and partial) available. Support available to part-time students. Financial award application deadline: 1/15; financial award applicants required to submit FAFSA. In 2010, 115 master's, 57 doctorates awarded. *Degree program information:* Part-time and evening/weekend programs available. Offers African American studies (MA, PhD); anthropology (PhD); brain and cognitive sciences (PhD); clinical psychology (PhD); creative writing (MA, MFA); criminal justice (MA, PhD); developmental psychology (PhD); economics (MA, PhD); English (MA, PhD); geography (MA); geography and urban studies (MA); history (MA, PhD); liberal arts (MA, MFA, MLA, PhD); philosophy (MA, PhD); political science (MA, PhD); psychology (MA, PhD); religion (MA, PhD); social psychology (PhD); sociology (MA, PhD); Spanish (MA, PhD); urban studies (MA, PhD). *Application deadline:* For fall admission, 12/15 for international students; for spring admission, 8/1 for international

Temple University (continued)

students. *Application fee:* $50. Electronic applications accepted. *Application Contact:* Dr. Teresa Scott Soufas, Dean, 215-204-7743, Fax: 215-204-3731. *Dean*, Dr. Teresa Scott Soufas, 215-204-7743, Fax: 215-204-3731.

College of Science and Technology Students: 213 full-time (64 women), 78 part-time (24 women); includes 10 Black or African American, non-Hispanic/Latino; 13 Asian, non-Hispanic/Latino; 2 Hispanic/Latino; 1 Two or more races, non-Hispanic/Latino, 149 international. Average age 28. 356 applicants, 42% accepted, 66 enrolled. *Faculty:* 102 full-time (17 women). Expenses: Contact institution. *Financial support:* Fellowships, research assistantships, teaching assistantships, career-related internships or fieldwork, Federal Work-Study, institutionally sponsored loans, scholarships/grants, tuition waivers (full and partial), and laboratory assistantships available. Financial award application deadline: 1/15; financial award applicants required to submit FAFSA. In 2010, 39 master's, 16 doctorates awarded. *Degree program information:* Part-time and evening/weekend programs available. Offers applied mathematics (MA); biology (MS, PhD); chemistry (MA, PhD); computer and information sciences (MS, PhD); earth and environmental science (MS); mathematics (PhD); physics (MA, PhD); pure mathematics (MA); science and technology (MA, MS, PhD). *Application deadline:* For fall admission, 12/15 for international students; for spring admission, 8/1 for international students. *Application fee:* $50. Electronic applications accepted. *Application Contact:* Dr. Hai-Lung Dai, Dean, 215-204-2888, Fax: 215-204-1255, E-mail: cst@temple.edu. *Dean*, Dr. Hai-Lung Dai, 215-204-2888, Fax: 215-204-1255, E-mail: cst@temple.edu.

Esther Boyer College of Music and Dance Students: 211 full-time (137 women), 64 part-time (38 women); includes 10 Black or African American, non-Hispanic/Latino; 18 Asian, non-Hispanic/Latino; 11 Hispanic/Latino; 1 Native Hawaiian or other Pacific Islander, non-Hispanic/Latino, 52 international. Average age 29. 418 applicants, 36% accepted, 89 enrolled. *Faculty:* 41 full-time (16 women). Expenses: Contact institution. *Financial support:* Fellowships with full and partial tuition reimbursements, research assistantships with full and partial tuition reimbursements, teaching assistantships with full and partial tuition reimbursements, career-related internships or fieldwork, Federal Work-Study, and scholarships/grants available. Financial award application deadline: 1/15; financial award applicants required to submit FAFSA. In 2010, 61 master's, 3 doctorates awarded. *Degree program information:* Part-time and evening/weekend programs available. Offers dance (Ed M, MFA, PhD); music (MM, MMT, DMA, PhD); music and dance (Ed M, MFA, MM, MMT, DMA, PhD). *Application deadline:* For fall admission, 12/15 for international students; for spring admission, 8/1 for international students. Applications are processed on a rolling basis. *Application fee:* $50. Electronic applications accepted. *Application Contact:* Dr. Robert T. Stroker, Dean, 215-204-5527, Fax: 215-204-4957, E-mail: rstroker@temple.edu. *Dean*, Dr. Robert T. Stroker, 215-204-5527, Fax: 215-204-4957, E-mail: rstroker@temple.edu.

Fox School of Business *Degree program information:* Part-time and evening/weekend programs available. Postbaccalaureate distance learning degree programs offered (minimal on-campus study). Offers accountancy (MS); accounting (MBA, PhD); actuarial science (MS); business (EMBA, IMBA, MBA, MHM, MS, PhD); business management (MBA); entrepreneurship (PhD); finance (MS, PhD); financial engineering (MS); financial management (MBA); healthcare and life sciences innovation (MBA); human resource management (MBA, MS); international business (IMBA, PhD); IT management (MBA); management information systems (PhD); marketing (MS, PhD); marketing management (MBA); pharmaceutical management (MBA); risk management and insurance (PhD); statistics (MS, PhD); strategic management (EMBA, MBA, PhD); tourism and sport (PhD). Electronic applications accepted.

Health Sciences Center Students: 2,881 full-time (1,517 women), 450 part-time (334 women); includes 248 Black or African American, non-Hispanic/Latino; 45 American Indian or Alaska Native, non-Hispanic/Latino; 610 Asian, non-Hispanic/Latino; 170 Hispanic/Latino; 6 Two or more races, non-Hispanic/Latino, 163 international. Average age 27. 1,334 applicants, 34% accepted, 272 enrolled. *Faculty:* 178 full-time (57 women). Expenses: Contact institution. *Financial support:* Fellowships, research assistantships, teaching assistantships, career-related internships or fieldwork, Federal Work-Study, institutionally sponsored loans, scholarships/grants, traineeships, and tuition waivers (full and partial) available. Support available to part-time students. Financial award application deadline: 1/15; financial award applicants required to submit FAFSA. In 2010, 687 first professional degrees, 222 master's, 28 doctorates, 54 other advanced degrees awarded. *Degree program information:* Part-time and evening/weekend programs available. Offers health sciences (DMD, DPM, MD, Pharm D, Ed M, MA, MOT, MPH, MS, MSN, DOT, DPT, PhD, Certificate). *Application fee:* $50. Electronic applications accepted. *Application Contact:* Tara Schumacher, Coordinator of Outreach, 215-204-6575, Fax: 215-204-8781, E-mail: tara.schumacher@temple.edu.

College of Health Professions Students: 430 full-time (324 women), 302 part-time (231 women); includes 62 Black or African American, non-Hispanic/Latino; 51 Asian, non-Hispanic/Latino; 17 Hispanic/Latino; 1 Two or more races, non-Hispanic/Latino, 29 international. Average age 31. 975 applicants, 37% accepted, 212 enrolled. *Faculty:* 53 full-time (27 women). Expenses: Contact institution. *Financial support:* Fellowships, research assistantships, teaching assistantships with full tuition reimbursements, career-related internships or fieldwork, Federal Work-Study, institutionally sponsored loans, traineeships, and tuition waivers (partial) available. Support available to part-time students. Financial award application deadline: 1/15. In 2010, 98 master's, 8 doctorates awarded. *Degree program information:* Part-time and evening/weekend programs available. Postbaccalaureate distance learning degree programs offered (minimal on-campus study). Offers communication sciences (PhD); environmental health (MS); epidemiology (MS); health informatics (MS); health professions (Ed M, MA, MOT, MPH, MS, MSN, DOT, DPT, PhD); kinesiology (Ed M, PhD); linguistics (MA); nursing (MSN); occupational therapy (MOT, MS, DOT); physical therapy (DPT, PhD); public health (MPH, PhD); school health education (Ed M); speech-language-hearing (MA); therapeutic recreation (Ed M). *Application fee:* $50. *Application Contact:* Tara Schumacher, Coordinator of Outreach, 215-204-6575, Fax: 215-204-8781, E-mail: tara.schumacher@temple.edu. *Interim Dean*, Dr. Michael Sitler, 215-707-4800, Fax: 215-707-7819, E-mail: sitler@temple.edu.

Kornberg School of Dentistry Offers advanced education in general dentistry (Certificate); dentistry (DMD, MS, Certificate); endodontology (Certificate); oral biology (MS); orthodontics (Certificate); periodontology (Certificate). Electronic applications accepted.

School of Medicine Students: 886 full-time (420 women), 4 part-time (3 women); includes 66 Black or African American, non-Hispanic/Latino; 15 American Indian or Alaska Native, non-Hispanic/Latino; 146 Asian, non-Hispanic/Latino; 65 Hispanic/Latino; 2 Two or more races, non-Hispanic/Latino, 53 international. Average age 26. *Faculty:* 95 full-time (27 women). Expenses: Contact institution. *Financial support:* Fellowships, research assistantships, career-related internships or fieldwork, Federal Work-Study, institutionally sponsored loans, scholarships/grants, and tuition waivers (full and partial) available. Support available to part-time students. Financial award application deadline: 1/15; financial award applicants required to submit FAFSA. In 2010, 159 first professional degrees, 5 master's, 20 doctorates awarded. Offers anatomy and cell biology (MS, PhD); biochemistry (MS, PhD); medicine (MD, MS, PhD); microbiology and immunology (MS, PhD); molecular biology and genetics (MS, PhD); neuroscience (MS, PhD); pathology and laboratory medicine (PhD); pharmacology (PhD); physiology (PhD). *Application fee:* $50. Electronic applications accepted. *Application Contact:* Dr. Larry R. Kaiser, Dean, 215-707-7000, Fax: 215-707-8431, E-mail: kaiser@temple.edu. *Dean*, Dr. Larry R. Kaiser, 215-707-7000, Fax: 215-707-8431, E-mail: kaiser@temple.edu.

School of Pharmacy Students: 644 full-time (395 women), 144 part-time (100 women); includes 71 Black or African American, non-Hispanic/Latino; 2 American Indian or Alaska Native, non-Hispanic/Latino; 234 Asian, non-Hispanic/Latino; 15 Hispanic/Latino; 1 Two or more races, non-Hispanic/Latino, 64 international. Average age 28. Expenses: Contact institution. *Financial support:* Fellowships with tuition reimbursements, research assistantships with tuition reimbursements, teaching assistantships with tuition reimbursements, career-related internships or fieldwork, Federal Work-Study, and institutionally sponsored loans available. Financial award application deadline: 1/15; financial award applicants required to submit FAFSA. In 2010, 140 first professional degrees, 113 master's awarded. *Degree program information:* Part-time and evening/weekend programs available. Postbaccalaureate distance learning degree programs offered (minimal on-campus study). Offers medicinal chemistry (MS, PhD); pharmaceutics (MS, PhD); pharmacodynamics (MS, PhD); pharmacy (Pharm D, MS, PhD); quality assurance/regulatory affairs (MS). *Application fee:* $50. Electronic applications accepted. *Application Contact:* Dr. Peter H. Doukas, Dean, 215-707-4990, Fax: 215-707-5620, E-mail: pdoukas@temple.edu. *Dean*, Dr. Peter H. Doukas, 215-707-4990, Fax: 215-707-5620, E-mail: pdoukas@temple.edu.

School of Podiatric Medicine Offers podiatric medicine (DPM). DPM/PhD offered jointly with Drexel University, University of Pennsylvania.

James E. Beasley School of Law Students: 798 full-time (351 women), 186 part-time (76 women); includes 246 minority (71 Black or African American, non-Hispanic/Latino; 9 American Indian or Alaska Native, non-Hispanic/Latino; 85 Asian, non-Hispanic/Latino; 74 Hispanic/Latino; 7 Two or more races, non-Hispanic/Latino), 4 international. Average age 25. 4,682 applicants, 39% accepted, 326 enrolled. *Faculty:* 61 full-time (25 women), 94 part-time/adjunct (35 women). Expenses: Contact institution. *Financial support:* In 2010–11, 680 students received support, including research assistantships (averaging $5,500 per year), teaching assistantships (averaging $5,500 per year); Federal Work-Study, scholarships/grants, tuition waivers (full and partial), and unspecified assistantships also available. Support available to part-time students. Financial award application deadline: 3/1; financial award applicants required to submit FAFSA. In 2010, 295 first professional degrees awarded. *Degree program information:* Part-time and evening/weekend programs available. Offers law (JD); legal education (SJD); taxation (LL M); transnational law (LL M); trial advocacy (LL M). *Application deadline:* For fall admission, 3/1 for domestic and international students. Applications are processed on a rolling basis. *Application fee:* $60. Electronic applications accepted. *Application Contact:* Johanne L. Johnston, Assistant Dean for Admissions and Financial Aid, 800-560-1428, Fax: 215-204-9319, E-mail: lawadmis@temple.edu. *Dean*, JoAnne A. Epps, 215-204-7863, Fax: 215-204-1185, E-mail: law@temple.edu.

School of Communications and Theater Students: 146 full-time (83 women), 53 part-time (33 women); includes 15 Black or African American, non-Hispanic/Latino; 1 American Indian or Alaska Native, non-Hispanic/Latino; 4 Asian, non-Hispanic/Latino; 3 Hispanic/Latino; 2 Two or more races, non-Hispanic/Latino, 35 international. Average age 31. 314 applicants, 44% accepted, 54 enrolled. *Faculty:* 61 full-time (24 women). Expenses: Contact institution. *Financial support:* Fellowships, research assistantships with partial tuition reimbursements, teaching assistantships with partial tuition reimbursements, career-related internships or fieldwork, Federal Work-Study, institutionally sponsored loans, and tuition waivers (partial) available. Financial award application deadline: 1/15; financial award applicants required to submit FAFSA. In 2010, 36 master's, 5 doctorates awarded. *Degree program information:* Part-time and evening/weekend programs available. Offers acting (MFA); broadcasting, telecommunications and mass media (MA); communication management (MS); communications and theater (MA, MFA, MJ, MS, PhD); design (MFA); directing (MFA); film and media arts (MFA); journalism (MJ); mass media and communication (PhD). *Application deadline:* For fall admission, 12/15 for international students. *Application fee:* $50. Electronic applications accepted. *Application Contact:* Nicole McKenna, Director, Office of Research and Graduate Studies, 215-204-1497, Fax: 215-204-0310, E-mail: nmckenna@temple.edu. *Interim Dean*, Dr. Thomas Jacobson, 215-204-8422, Fax: 215-204-4811, E-mail: sct@temple.edu.

School of Environmental Design Students: 49 full-time (27 women), 28 part-time (14 women); includes 1 Black or African American, non-Hispanic/Latino; 2 Asian, non-Hispanic/Latino, 3 international. Average age 33. 73 applicants, 79% accepted, 45 enrolled. *Faculty:* 11 full-time (4 women). Expenses: Contact institution. *Financial support:* Application deadline: 1/15. In 2010, 13 master's awarded. Offers community and regional planning (MS); environmental design (ML Arch, MS); landscape architecture (ML Arch). *Application fee:* $50. Electronic applications accepted. *Application Contact:* Tara Schumacher, Coordinator of Outreach, 215-204-6575, Fax: 215-204-8781, E-mail: tara.schumacher@temple.edu. *Interim Dean*, Dr. James Hilty, 267-468-8020, E-mail: jhilty@temple.edu.

School of Social Administration Students: 342 full-time (297 women), 138 part-time (118 women); includes 110 Black or African American, non-Hispanic/Latino; 4 American Indian or Alaska Native, non-Hispanic/Latino; 11 Asian, non-Hispanic/Latino; 22 Hispanic/Latino; 4 Two or more races, non-Hispanic/Latino, 7 international. Average age 32. 469 applicants, 61% accepted, 140 enrolled. *Faculty:* 12 full-time (6 women). Expenses: Contact institution. *Financial support:* Fellowships with tuition reimbursements, research assistantships with tuition reimbursements, teaching assistantships with tuition reimbursements, career-related internships or fieldwork, Federal Work-Study, institutionally sponsored loans, scholarships/grants, traineeships, tuition waivers (partial), unspecified assistantships, and field assistantships available. Financial award application deadline: 1/15; financial award applicants required to submit FAFSA. In 2010, 191 master's awarded. *Degree program information:* Part-time and evening/weekend programs available. Offers social administration (MSW). *Application deadline:* For fall admission, 2/15 priority date for domestic students, 12/15 for international students; for spring admission, 11/1 priority date for domestic students, 8/1 for international students. Applications are processed on a rolling basis. *Application fee:* $50. Electronic applications accepted. *Application Contact:* Dr. Bernie Sue Newman, Chair, 215-204-1205, Fax: 215-204-9606, E-mail: bernie.newman@temple.edu. *Chair*, Dr. Bernie Sue Newman, 215-204-1205, Fax: 215-204-9606, E-mail: bernie.newman@temple.edu.

School of Tourism and Hospitality Management Students: 40 full-time (22 women), 22 part-time (12 women); includes 4 Black or African American, non-Hispanic/Latino; 1 American Indian or Alaska Native, non-Hispanic/Latino; 3 Asian, non-Hispanic/Latino, 1 international. Average age 26. 143 applicants, 37% accepted, 22 enrolled. *Faculty:* 18 full-time (7 women). Expenses: Contact institution. *Financial support:* Teaching assistantships available. Financial award application deadline: 1/15; financial award applicants required to submit FAFSA. In 2010, 32 master's awarded. *Degree program information:* Part-time and evening/weekend programs available. Offers sport and recreation administration (Ed M); tourism and hospitality management (Ed M, MTHM). *Application deadline:* For fall admission, 12/15 for international students; for spring admission, 8/1 for international students. *Application fee:* $50. Electronic applications accepted. *Application Contact:* Dr. Elizabeth H. Barber, Associate Dean, 215-204-6294, E-mail: elizabeth.barber@temple.edu. *Associate Dean*, Dr. Elizabeth H. Barber, 215-204-6294, E-mail: elizabeth.barber@temple.edu.

Tyler School of Art Students: 137 full-time (101 women), 15 part-time (all women); includes 3 Black or African American, non-Hispanic/Latino; 1 American Indian or Alaska Native, non-Hispanic/Latino; 4 Asian, non-Hispanic/Latino; 2 Hispanic/Latino, 10 international. Average age 29. 628 applicants, 19% accepted, 72 enrolled. *Faculty:* 49 full-time (24 women). Expenses: Contact institution. *Financial support:* Fellowships with full tuition reimbursements, research assistantships with full tuition reimbursements, teaching assistantships with full tuition reimbursements, career-related internships or fieldwork, Federal Work-Study, and institutionally sponsored loans available. Support available to part-time students. Financial award application deadline: 1/15; financial award applicants required to submit FAFSA. In 2010, 58 master's, 1 doctorate awarded. *Degree program information:* Part-time and evening/weekend programs available. Offers architecture (M Arch); art (Ed M, M Arch, MA, MFA, PhD); art and art education (Ed M); art history (MA, PhD); ceramics/glass (MFA); fibers and fabric design (MFA); graphic and interactive design (MFA); metals/jewelry/CAD-CAM (MFA); painting (MFA); photography (MFA); printmaking (MFA); sculpture (MFA). *Application fee:* $50. Electronic applications accepted. *Application Contact:* Carmina Cianciulli, Assistant Dean for Admissions, 215-782-2875, Fax: 215-782-2711, E-mail: tylerart@temple.edu. *Interim Dean*, Dr. Robert Stroker, 215-777-9000, E-mail: tyler@temple.edu.

TENNESSEE STATE UNIVERSITY, Nashville, TN 37209-1561

General Information State-supported, coed, comprehensive institution. CGS member. *Graduate housing:* Rooms and/or apartments available on a first-come, first-served basis to single and married students. Housing application deadline: 8/1.

GRADUATE UNITS

The School of Graduate Studies and Research

College of Arts and Sciences *Degree program information:* Part-time and evening/weekend programs available. Offers arts and sciences (MA, MCJ, MS, PhD); biological sciences (MS, PhD); chemistry (MS); criminal justice (MCJ); English (MA); mathematical sciences (MS); music education (MS). Electronic applications accepted.

College of Business *Degree program information:* Part-time and evening/weekend programs available. Postbaccalaureate distance learning degree programs offered. Offers business (MBA). Electronic applications accepted.

College of Education *Degree program information:* Part-time and evening/weekend programs available. Offers administration and supervision (M Ed, Ed D, Ed S); counseling and guidance (MS); counseling psychology (PhD); curriculum and instruction (M Ed, Ed D); education (M Ed, MA Ed, MS, Ed D, PhD, Ed S); elementary education (M Ed, MA Ed, Ed D); human performance and sports science (MA Ed); psychology (MS, PhD); school psychology (MS, PhD); special education (M Ed, MA Ed, Ed D).

College of Engineering, Technology, and Computer Science *Degree program information:* Part-time and evening/weekend programs available. Offers computer and information systems engineering (MS, PhD); engineering (ME).

College of Health Sciences *Degree program information:* Part-time and evening/weekend programs available. Offers health sciences (MPT, MS, DPT); physical therapy (MPT, DPT); speech and hearing science (MS). Electronic applications accepted.

Institute of Government *Degree program information:* Part-time and evening/weekend programs available. Offers public administration (MPA, PhD).

School of Agriculture and Consumer Sciences *Degree program information:* Part-time and evening/weekend programs available. Offers agricultural sciences (MS).

School of Nursing Offers family nurse practitioner (MSN); holistic nursing (MSN); nursing administration (MSN); nursing education (MSN); nursing informatics (MSN).

TENNESSEE TECHNOLOGICAL UNIVERSITY, Cookeville, TN 38505

General Information State-supported, coed, university. CGS member. *Enrollment:* 11,538 graduate, professional, and undergraduate students; 452 full-time matriculated graduate/professional students (230 women), 848 part-time matriculated graduate/professional students (539 women). *Enrollment by degree level:* 1,042 master's, 90 doctoral, 168 other advanced degrees. *Graduate faculty:* 341 full-time (62 women). Tuition, state resident: full-time $7934; part-time $388 per credit hour. Tuition, nonresident: full-time $19,758; part-time $962 per credit hour. *Graduate housing:* Rooms and/or apartments available on a first-come, first-served basis to single students and available to married students. Housing application deadline: 6/1. *Student services:* Campus employment opportunities, campus safety program, career counseling, child daycare facilities, exercise/wellness program, free psychological counseling, international student services, low-cost health insurance, services for students with disabilities, teacher training. *Library facilities:* Angelo and Jennette Volpe Library and Media Center. *Online resources:* library catalog, web page, access to other libraries' catalogs. *Collection:* 704,377 titles, 1,636 serial subscriptions, 19,784 audiovisual materials. *Research affiliation:* Center for Excellence in Teacher Evaluation, Appalachian Center for Crafts, Center of Excellence in Water Resources, Center of Excellence in Manufacturing Resources, Center of Excellence in Energy Systems Research.

Computer facilities: 227 computers available on campus for general student use. A campuswide network can be accessed from student residence rooms. Online class registration, 590 additional computers are available for student use in individual departmental labs are available. *Web address:* http://www.tntech.edu/.

General Application Contact: Shelia K. Kendrick, Coordinator of Graduate Admissions, 931-372-3808, Fax: 931-372-3497, E-mail: skendrick@tntech.edu.

GRADUATE UNITS

Graduate School Students: 452 full-time (230 women), 848 part-time (539 women); includes 78 Black or African American, non-Hispanic/Latino; 7 American Indian or Alaska Native, non-Hispanic/Latino; 80 Asian, non-Hispanic/Latino; 25 Hispanic/Latino; 1 Native Hawaiian or other Pacific Islander, non-Hispanic/Latino. Average age 27. 1,008 applicants, 60% accepted, 344 enrolled. *Faculty:* 341 full-time (62 women). Expenses: Contact institution. *Financial support:* In 2010–11, 50 fellowships (averaging $8,000 per year), 152 research assistantships (averaging $6,973 per year), 103 teaching assistantships (averaging $6,213 per year) were awarded; career-related internships or fieldwork and Federal Work-Study also available. Support available to part-time students. Financial award application deadline: 4/1. In 2010, 467 master's, 22 doctorates, 153 other advanced degrees awarded. *Degree program information:* Part-time and evening/weekend programs available. Offers human resources leadership (MPS); strategic leadership (MPS); training and development (MPS). *Application deadline:* For fall admission, 8/1 for domestic students, 5/1 for international students; for spring admission, 12/1 for domestic students, 10/1 for international students. *Application fee:* $25 ($30 for international students). Electronic applications accepted. *Application Contact:* Shelia K. Kendrick, Coordinator of Graduate Admissions, 931-372-3808, Fax: 931-372-3497, E-mail: skendrick@tntech.edu. *Associate Vice President for Research and Graduate Studies,* Dr. Francis O. Otuonye, 931-372-3233, Fax: 931-372-3497, E-mail: fotuonye@tntech.edu.

College of Arts and Sciences Students: 43 full-time (16 women), 34 part-time (17 women); includes 5 Black or African American, non-Hispanic/Latino; 11 Asian, non-Hispanic/Latino; 3 Hispanic/Latino. Average age 27. 66 applicants, 44% accepted, 15 enrolled. *Faculty:* 78 full-time (15 women). Expenses: Contact institution. *Financial support:* In 2010–11, 30 research assistantships (averaging $7,600 per year), 36 teaching assistantships (averaging $6,630 per year) were awarded; fellowships, career-related internships or fieldwork also available. Support available to part-time students. Financial award application deadline: 4/1. In 2010, 18 master's, 4 doctorates awarded. *Degree program information:* Part-time programs available. Offers arts and sciences (MA, MS, PhD); biology (PhD); chemistry (MS); English (MA); fish, game, and wildlife management (MS); mathematics (MS). *Application deadline:* For fall admission, 8/1 for domestic students, 5/1 for international students; for spring admission, 12/1 for domestic students, 10/1 for international students. *Application fee:* $25 ($30 for international students). Electronic applications accepted. *Application Contact:* Shelia K. Kendrick, Coordinator of Graduate Admissions, 931-372-3808, Fax: 931-372-3497, E-mail: skendrick@tntech.edu. *Interim Dean,* Dr. Paul Semmes, 931-372-3118, Fax: 931-372-6142.

College of Business Students: 58 full-time (18 women), 139 part-time (49 women); includes 10 Black or African American, non-Hispanic/Latino; 7 Asian, non-Hispanic/Latino; 7 Hispanic/Latino; 1 Native Hawaiian or other Pacific Islander, non-Hispanic/Latino. Average age 25. 211 applicants, 51% accepted, 59 enrolled. *Faculty:* 28 full-time (5 women). Expenses: Contact institution. *Financial support:* In 2010–11, 5 fellowships (averaging $10,000 per year), 18 research assistantships (averaging $4,000 per year), teaching assistantships (averaging $4,000 per year) were awarded. Support available to part-time students. Financial award application deadline: 4/1. In 2010, 116 master's awarded. *Degree program information:* Part-time and evening/weekend programs available. Offers accounting (MBA); finance (MBA); human resource management (MBA); international business (MBA); management information systems (MBA); risk management & insurance (MBA). *Application deadline:* For fall admission, 8/1 for domestic and international students; for spring admission, 12/1 for domestic students, 10/1 for international students. *Application fee:* $25 ($30 for international students). Electronic applications accepted. *Application Contact:* Shelia K. Kendrick, Coordinator of Graduate Admissions, 931-372-3808, Fax: 931-372-3497, E-mail: skendrick@tntech.edu. *Director,* Dr. Tom Timmerman, 931-372-3600, Fax: 931-372-6249.

College of Education Students: 247 full-time (172 women), 548 part-time (424 women); includes 40 Black or African American, non-Hispanic/Latino; 6 American Indian or Alaska Native, non-Hispanic/Latino; 3 Asian, non-Hispanic/Latino; 9 Hispanic/Latino. Average age 27. 394 applicants, 77% accepted, 215 enrolled. *Faculty:* 58 full-time (16 women). Expenses: Contact institution. *Financial support:* In 2010–11, 42 fellowships (averaging $8,000 per year), 33 research assistantships (averaging $4,000 per year), 26 teaching assistantships (averaging $4,000 per year) were awarded; career-related internships or fieldwork also available. Support available to part-time students. Financial award application deadline: 4/1. In 2010, 273 master's, 5 doctorates, 153 other advanced degrees awarded. *Degree program information:* Part-time and evening/weekend programs available. Offers advanced studies in teaching and learning (M Ed); applied behavior and learning (PhD); curriculum (MA, Ed S); early childhood education (MA, Ed S); education (M Ed, MA, PhD, Ed S); educational psychology (MA, Ed S); educational psychology and student personnel (MA, Ed S); elementary education (MA, Ed S); exceptional learning (PhD); exercise science, physical education and wellness (MA); instructional leadership (MA, Ed S); library science (MA); literacy (PhD); program planning and evaluation (PhD); reading (MA, Ed S); secondary education (MA, Ed S); special education (MA, Ed S). *Application deadline:* For fall admission, 8/1 for domestic students, 5/1 for international students; for spring admission, 12/1 for domestic students, 10/1 for international students. *Application fee:* $25 ($30 for international students). Electronic applications accepted. *Application Contact:* Shelia K. Kendrick, Coordinator of Graduate Admissions, 931-372-3808, Fax: 931-372-3497, E-mail: skendrick@tntech.edu. *Interim Dean,* Dr. Larry Peach, 931-372-3124, Fax: 931-372-6319, E-mail: lpeach@tntech.edu.

College of Engineering Students: 87 full-time (9 women), 72 part-time (9 women); includes 19 Black or African American, non-Hispanic/Latino; 59 Asian, non-Hispanic/Latino; 3 Hispanic/Latino. Average age 28. 279 applicants, 52% accepted, 38 enrolled. *Faculty:* 76 full-time (2 women). Expenses: Contact institution. *Financial support:* In 2010–11, 3 fellowships (averaging $8,000 per year), 71 research assistantships (averaging $9,293 per year), 41 teaching assistantships (averaging $7,223 per year) were awarded; career-related internships or fieldwork also available. Support available to part-time students. Financial award application deadline: 4/1. In 2010, 38 master's, 13 doctorates awarded. *Degree program information:* Part-time programs available. Offers chemical engineering (MS, PhD); civil engineering (MS, PhD); computer science (MS); electrical engineering (MS, PhD); engineering (MS, PhD); mechanical engineering (MS, PhD). *Application deadline:* For fall admission, 8/1 for domestic students, 5/1 for international students; for spring admission, 12/1 for domestic students, 10/1 for international students. *Application fee:* $25 ($30 for international students). Electronic applications accepted. *Application Contact:* Shelia K. Kendrick, Coordinator of Graduate Admissions, 931-372-3808, Fax: 931-372-3497, E-mail: skendrick@tntech.edu. *Interim Dean,* Dr. David Huddleston.

School of Nursing Students: 11 full-time (all women), 30 part-time (26 women); includes 2 Hispanic/Latino. 42 applicants, 40% accepted, 11 enrolled. Expenses: Contact institution. *Financial support:* Application deadline: 4/1. In 2010, 11 master's awarded. Offers family nurse practitioner (MSN); informatics (MSN); nursing administration (MSN); nursing education (MSN). *Application deadline:* For fall admission, 8/1 for domestic students, 5/1 for international students; for spring admission, 12/1 for domestic students, 10/1 for international students. *Application fee:* $25 ($30 for international students). Electronic applications accepted. *Application Contact:* Shelia K. Kendrick, Coordinator of Graduate Admissions, 931-372-3808, Fax: 931-372-3497, E-mail: skendrick@tntech.edu. *Interim Dean,* Dr. Sheila Green, 931-372-3203, Fax: 931-372-6244, E-mail: sgreen@tntech.edu.

TENNESSEE TEMPLE UNIVERSITY, Chattanooga, TN 37404-3587

General Information Independent-religious, coed, comprehensive institution. *Graduate housing:* Rooms and/or apartments available to single students and available on a first-come, first-served basis to married students. Housing application deadline: 6/1.

GRADUATE UNITS

Graduate Studies in Education *Degree program information:* Part-time programs available. Offers education (M Ed); educational leadership (M Ed); instructional effectiveness (M Ed).

TEXAS A&M HEALTH SCIENCE CENTER, College Station, TX 77840

General Information State-supported, coed, upper-level institution. *Graduate housing:* On-campus housing not available.

GRADUATE UNITS

Baylor College of Dentistry Offers dentistry (DDS, MD, MS, PhD, Certificate).

Graduate Division *Degree program information:* Part-time programs available. Offers biomaterials science (MS); biomedical sciences (MS, PhD); dental hygiene (MS); endodontics (MS, PhD, Certificate); health professions education (MS); oral and maxillofacial pathology (MS, PhD, Certificate); oral and maxillofacial surgery (MD, Certificate); oral biology (MS, PhD); orthodontics (MS, Certificate); pediatric dentistry (MS, Certificate); periodontics (MS, Certificate); prosthodontics (MS, Certificate).

College of Medicine Offers medicine (MD, PhD). Electronic applications accepted.

Graduate School of Biomedical Sciences Offers cell and molecular biology (PhD); immunology (PhD); microbial and molecular pathogenesis (PhD); microbiology (PhD); molecular and cellular medicine (PhD); molecular biology (PhD); neuroscience and experimental therapeutics (PhD); systems biology and translational medicine (PhD); virology (PhD).

Institute of Biosciences and Technology Offers medical sciences (PhD). Degree awarded by the Graduate School for Biomedical Sciences.

School of Rural Public Health *Degree program information:* Part-time programs available. Postbaccalaureate distance learning degree programs offered (no on-campus study). Offers environmental/occupational health (MPH); epidemiology/biostatistics (MPH); health policy/management (MPH); social and behavioral health (MPH). Electronic applications accepted.

TEXAS A&M INTERNATIONAL UNIVERSITY, Laredo, TX 78041-1900

General Information State-supported, coed, comprehensive institution. CGS member. *Enrollment:* 6,853 graduate, professional, and undergraduate students; 164 full-time matriculated graduate/professional students (80 women), 869 part-time matriculated graduate/professional students (556 women). *Enrollment by degree level:* 999 master's, 34 doctoral. *Graduate faculty:* 83 full-time (25 women), 10 part-time/adjunct (4 women). *Graduate housing:* Rooms and/or apartments available on a first-come, first-served basis to single and married students. *Student services:* Campus employment opportunities, campus safety program, career counseling, exercise/wellness program, free psychological counseling, grant writing training, international student services, low-cost health insurance, multicultural affairs office, services for students with disabilities, teacher training, writing training. *Library facilities:* Sue and Radcliff Killam Library. *Online resources:* library catalog, web page, access to other libraries' catalogs. *Collection:* 378,730 titles, 33,587 serial subscriptions, 5,997 audiovisual materials.

Computer facilities: 410 computers available on campus for general student use. A campuswide network can be accessed from student residence rooms and from off campus. Online class registration is available. *Web address:* http://www.tamiu.edu/.

General Application Contact: Dr. Jeff Brown, Dean, Office of Graduate Studies, 956-326-2596, Fax: 956-326-3021, E-mail: jbrown@tamiu.edu.

GRADUATE UNITS

Office of Graduate Studies and Research Students: 164 full-time (80 women), 869 part-time (556 women); includes 8 Black or African American, non-Hispanic/Latino; 1 American Indian or Alaska Native, non-Hispanic/Latino; 6 Asian, non-Hispanic/Latino; 844 Hispanic/Latino, 127 international. Average age 32. 704 applicants, 71% accepted, 335 enrolled. *Faculty:* 83 full-time (25 women), 10 part-time/adjunct (4 women). Expenses: Contact institution. *Financial support:* In 2010–11, 227 students received support, including 6 fellowships with partial tuition reimbursements available, 39 research assistantships, 3 teaching assistantships; Federal Work-Study, institutionally sponsored loans, and scholarships/grants also available. Support available to part-time students. Financial award application deadline: 11/1; financial award applicants required to submit FAFSA. In 2010, 282 master's, 4 doctorates awarded. *Degree program information:* Part-time and evening/weekend programs available. *Application deadline:* For fall admission, 4/30 priority date for domestic students, 4/30 for international students; for spring admission, 11/30 priority date for domestic students, 10/1 for international students. Applications are processed on a rolling basis. *Application fee:* $25. *Application Contact:* Suzanne Hansen-Alford, Director of Graduate Recruiting, 956-326-3023, Fax: 956-326-3021, E-mail: graduateschool@tamiu.edu. *Dean,* Dr. Jeff Brown, 956-326-2596, Fax: 956-326-3021, E-mail: jbrown@tamiu.edu.

College of Arts and Sciences Students: 34 full-time (18 women), 242 part-time (150 women); includes 1 Black or African American, non-Hispanic/Latino; 3 Asian, non-Hispanic/

Texas A&M International University (continued)

Latino; 246 Hispanic/Latino, 10 international. Average age 30. 171 applicants, 81% accepted, 102 enrolled. *Faculty:* 30 full-time (11 women), 2 part-time/adjunct (1 woman). Expenses: Contact institution. *Financial support:* In 2010–11, 51 students received support, including 5 fellowships with tuition reimbursements available, 27 research assistantships (averaging $9,100 per year), 3 teaching assistantships (averaging $9,100 per year); Federal Work-Study, institutionally sponsored loans, and scholarships/grants also available. Support available to part-time students. Financial award application deadline: 11/1; financial award applicants required to submit FAFSA. In 2010, 46 master's awarded. *Degree program information:* Part-time and evening/weekend programs available. Postbaccalaureate distance learning degree programs offered (no on-campus study). Offers arts and sciences (MA, MACP, MPA, MS, PhD); biology (MS); counseling psychology (MACP); criminal justice (MS); English (MA); Hispanic studies (PhD); history (MA); mathematics (MS); political science (MA); psychology (MS); public administration (MPA); sociology (MA); Spanish (MA). *Application deadline:* For fall admission, 4/30 priority date for domestic students, 4/30 for international students; for spring admission, 11/30 for domestic students, 10/1 for international students. Applications are processed on a rolling basis. *Application fee:* $25. *Application Contact:* Suzanne Hansen-Alford, Director of Graduate Recruiting, 956-326-3023, Fax: 956-326-3021, E-mail: graduateschool@tamiu.edu. *Dean,* Dr. Thomas R. Mitchell, 956-326-2633, Fax: 956-326-2459, E-mail: tmitchell@tamiu.edu.

College of Business Administration Students: 91 full-time (35 women), 232 part-time (101 women); includes 5 Black or African American, non-Hispanic/Latino; 2 Asian, non-Hispanic/Latino; 190 Hispanic/Latino, 115 international. Average age 29. 236 applicants, 48% accepted, 84 enrolled. *Faculty:* 29 full-time (2 women), 2 part-time/adjunct (0 women). Expenses: Contact institution. *Financial support:* In 2010–11, 27 students received support, including 8 research assistantships; Federal Work-Study, institutionally sponsored loans, and scholarships/grants also available. Support available to part-time students. Financial award application deadline: 11/1; financial award applicants required to submit FAFSA. In 2010, 136 master's awarded. *Degree program information:* Part-time and evening/weekend programs available. Offers accounting (MP Acc); business administration (MBA, MP Acc, MSIS); information systems (MSIS); international banking (MBA); international trade (MBA). *Application deadline:* For fall admission, 4/30 priority date for domestic students; for spring admission, 11/30 for domestic students, 10/1 for international students. Applications are processed on a rolling basis. *Application fee:* $25. *Application Contact:* Imelda Lopez, Graduate Admissions Counselor, 956-326-2485, Fax: 956-326-2459, E-mail: lopez@tamiu.edu. *Dean,* Dr. Stephen R. Sears, 956-326-2480, E-mail: steve.sears@tamiu.edu.

College of Education Students: 39 full-time (27 women), 369 part-time (286 women); includes 2 Black or African American, non-Hispanic/Latino; 385 Hispanic/Latino, 2 international. Average age 34. 257 applicants, 88% accepted, 135 enrolled. *Faculty:* 21 full-time (9 women), 6 part-time/adjunct (3 women). Expenses: Contact institution. *Financial support:* In 2010–11, 101 students received support, including 1 fellowship; Federal Work-Study and institutionally sponsored loans also available. Support available to part-time students. Financial award application deadline: 11/1; financial award applicants required to submit FAFSA. In 2010, 88 degrees awarded. *Degree program information:* Part-time and evening/weekend programs available. Offers curriculum and instruction (MS); early childhood education (MS Ed); education (MS, MS Ed); educational administration (MS Ed); generic special education (MS Ed); reading (MS Ed); school counseling (MS). *Application deadline:* For fall admission, 4/30 priority date for domestic students; for spring admission, 11/30 for domestic students, 10/1 for international students. Applications are processed on a rolling basis. *Application fee:* $25. *Application Contact:* Suzanne Hansen-Alford, Director of Graduate Recruiting, 956-326-3023, Fax: 956-326-3021, E-mail: graduateschool@tamiu.edu. *Interim Dean,* Dr. Juan Lira, 956-326-2601, E-mail: jlira@tamiu.edu.

College of Nursing and Health Sciences Students: 26 part-time (19 women); includes 1 Asian, non-Hispanic/Latino; 23 Hispanic/Latino. Average age 32. 37 applicants, 68% accepted, 14 enrolled. *Faculty:* 3 full-time (all women). Expenses: Contact institution. *Financial support:* In 2010–11, 12 students received support. In 2010, 12 master's awarded. Offers family nurse practitioner (MSN). *Application fee:* $25. *Application Contact:* Suzanne Hansen-Alford, Director of Graduate Recruiting, 956-326-3023, Fax: 956-326-3021, E-mail: enroll@tamiu.edu. *Dean,* Regina Aune, 956-326-2574, E-mail: regina.aune@tamiu.edu.

TEXAS A&M UNIVERSITY, College Station, TX 77843

General Information State-supported, coed, university. CGS member. *Enrollment:* 49,129 graduate, professional, and undergraduate students; 7,267 full-time matriculated graduate/professional students (2,936 women), 1,864 part-time matriculated graduate/professional students (918 women). *Enrollment by degree level:* 482 first professional, 5,456 master's, 3,193 doctoral. *Graduate faculty:* 1,583. *Graduate housing:* Rooms and/or apartments available on a first-come, first-served basis to single and married students. *Student services:* Campus employment opportunities, campus safety program, career counseling, child daycare facilities, exercise/wellness program, free psychological counseling, grant writing training, international student services, low-cost health insurance, multicultural affairs office, services for students with disabilities, teacher training, writing training. *Library facilities:* Sterling C. Evans Library plus 6 others. *Online resources:* library catalog, web page, access to other libraries' catalogs. *Collection:* 4.6 million titles, 108,064 serial subscriptions, 75,973 audiovisual materials. *Research affiliation:* Texas Department of Transportation (transportation), U. S. Department of Agriculture (USDA) (agriculture), National Science Foundation (geosciences), Joint Oceanographic Institutions, Inc. (geosciences).

Computer facilities: 1,840 computers available on campus for general student use. A campuswide network can be accessed from student residence rooms and from off campus. Online class registration is available. *Web address:* http://www.tamu.edu/.

General Application Contact: Graduate Admissions, 979-458-0427, E-mail: admissions@tamu.edu.

GRADUATE UNITS

Bush School of Government and Public Service Students: 215 full-time (98 women), 93 part-time (32 women); includes 20 Black or African American, non-Hispanic/Latino; 2 American Indian or Alaska Native, non-Hispanic/Latino; 14 Asian, non-Hispanic/Latino; 30 Hispanic/Latino, 15 international. Average age 24. *Faculty:* 45. Expenses: Contact institution. *Financial support:* In 2010–11, fellowships (averaging $11,000 per year), research assistantships (averaging $11,250 per year) were awarded; career-related internships or fieldwork, Federal Work-Study, and institutionally sponsored loans also available. Financial award application deadline: 2/1; financial award applicants required to submit FAFSA. In 2010, 93 master's awarded. Offers advanced international affairs (Certificate); China studies (Certificate); homeland security (Certificate); international affairs (MPIA); national security affairs (Certificate); nonprofit management (Certificate); public service and administration (MPSA). *Application deadline:* For fall admission, 1/24 for domestic and international students. *Application fee:* $50 ($75 for international students). Electronic applications accepted. *Application Contact:* Kathryn Meyer, Director of Recruiting, 979-458-4767, Fax: 979-845-4155, E-mail: kmeyer@bushschool.tamu.edu. *Dean,* Ryan C. Crocker, 979-862-8007, E-mail: rcrocker@bushschool.tamu.edu.

College of Agriculture and Life Sciences Students: 1,103 full-time (550 women), 299 part-time (134 women); includes 188 minority (43 Black or African American, non-Hispanic/Latino; 6 American Indian or Alaska Native, non-Hispanic/Latino; 25 Asian, non-Hispanic/Latino; 114 Hispanic/Latino), 432 international. Average age 29. *Faculty:* 326. Expenses: Contact institution. *Financial support:* Fellowships, research assistantships, teaching assistantships, career-related internships or fieldwork, Federal Work-Study, institutionally sponsored loans, scholarships/grants, tuition waivers (partial), and unspecified assistantships available. Support available to part-time students. Financial award applicants required to submit FAFSA. In 2010, 157 master's, 78 doctorates awarded. *Degree program information:* Part-time programs available. Postbaccalaureate distance learning degree programs offered (minimal on-campus study). Offers agribusiness (MAB); agribusiness and managerial economics (PhD); agricultural and life sciences (MS); agricultural development (M Agr); agricultural economics (MS, PhD); agricultural education (M Ed, Ed D, PhD); agriculture and life sciences (M Agr, M Ed, M Eng, MAB, MS, DE, Ed D, PhD); agronomy (M Agr, MS, PhD); animal science (M Agr, MS, PhD); biochemistry (MS, PhD); biological and agricultural engineering (M Agr, M Eng, MS, DE, PhD); biophysics (MS); entomology (M Agr, MS, PhD); food science and technology (M Agr, MS, PhD); forestry (MS, PhD); genetics (PhD); horticultural sciences (M Agr, MS, PhD); molecular and environmental plant sciences (MS, PhD); natural resources development (M Agr); nutrition (MS, PhD); plant breeding (MS, PhD); plant pathology and microbiology (M Agr, MS, PhD); poultry science (M Agr, MS, PhD); rangeland ecology and management (M Agr, MS, PhD); recreation resources development (M Agr); recreation, park, and tourism sciences (MS, PhD); soil science (MS, PhD); wildlife and fisheries sciences (MS, PhD). *Application deadline:* For fall admission, 7/21 priority date for domestic students, 6/1 priority date for international students; for spring admission, 12/1 priority date for domestic students, 10/1 priority date for international students. Applications are processed on a rolling basis. *Application fee:* $50 ($75 for international students). Electronic applications accepted. *Application Contact:* Graduate Admissions, 979-845-1044, E-mail: admissions@tamu.edu. *Vice Chancellor/Dean,* Dr. Mark Hussey, 979-845-4747, Fax: 979-845-9938, E-mail: mhussey@tamu.edu.

College of Architecture Students: 423 full-time (173 women), 60 part-time (17 women); includes 68 minority (9 Black or African American, non-Hispanic/Latino; 3 American Indian or Alaska Native, non-Hispanic/Latino; 19 Asian, non-Hispanic/Latino; 37 Hispanic/Latino), 216 international. Average age 29. *Faculty:* 92. Expenses: Contact institution. *Financial support:* In 2010–11, fellowships with partial tuition reimbursements (averaging $1,000 per year), research assistantships with partial tuition reimbursements (averaging $8,139 per year), teaching assistantships with partial tuition reimbursements (averaging $7,650 per year) were awarded; career-related internships or fieldwork, Federal Work-Study, institutionally sponsored loans, scholarships/grants, and unspecified assistantships also available. Financial award application deadline: 1/15; financial award applicants required to submit FAFSA. In 2010, 151 master's, 12 doctorates awarded. Offers architecture (M Arch, MLA, MS, MS Arch, MSLD, MUP, PhD); construction management (MS); land development (MSLD); landscape architecture (MLA); urban and regional science (PhD); urban planning (MUP); visualization (MS, PhD). *Application deadline:* For fall admission, 1/15 priority date for domestic and international students. Applications are processed on a rolling basis. *Application fee:* $50 ($75 for international students). Electronic applications accepted. *Dean,* Jorge Vanegas, 979-845-1222, Fax: 979-845-4491, E-mail: jvanegas@tamu.edu.

College of Education and Human Development Students: 609 full-time (421 women), 714 part-time (500 women); includes 417 minority (178 Black or African American, non-Hispanic/Latino; 8 American Indian or Alaska Native, non-Hispanic/Latino; 45 Asian, non-Hispanic/Latino; 186 Hispanic/Latino), 156 international. Average age 36. *Faculty:* 146. Expenses: Contact institution. *Financial support:* In 2010–11, fellowships with partial tuition reimbursements (averaging $12,000 per year), research assistantships with partial tuition reimbursements (averaging $10,000 per year), teaching assistantships with partial tuition reimbursements (averaging $10,000 per year) were awarded; career-related internships or fieldwork, Federal Work-Study, institutionally sponsored loans, scholarships/grants, tuition waivers (partial), and unspecified assistantships also available. Financial award applicants required to submit FAFSA. In 2010, 226 master's, 102 doctorates awarded. *Degree program information:* Part-time and evening/weekend programs available. Postbaccalaureate distance learning degree programs offered (no on-campus study). Offers adult education (PhD); bilingual education (M Ed, PhD); cognition, creativity, instruction and development (MS, PhD); counseling psychology (PhD); culture and curriculum (M Ed, MS); curriculum and instruction (PhD); education and human development (M Ed, MS, Ed D, PhD); educational psychology (PhD); educational technology (PhD); English as a second language (M Ed, MS, PhD); health education (MS, PhD); higher education administration (MS, PhD); human resource development (MS, PhD); kinesiology (MS, PhD); mathematics education (M Ed, MS, PhD); physical education (M Ed); public school administration (M Ed, Ed D, PhD); reading and language arts education (M Ed, MS, PhD); research, measurement and statistics (MS); research, measurement, and statistics (PhD); school psychology (PhD); science education (M Ed, MS, PhD); special education (M Ed, PhD); sport management (MS); urban education (M Ed, MS, PhD). *Application fee:* $50 ($75 for international students). Electronic applications accepted. *Application Contact:* Dr. Becky Carr, Assistant Dean for Administrative Services, 979-862-1342, Fax: 979-845-6129, E-mail: bcarr@tamu.edu. *Dean,* Doug Palmer, 979-862-6649, E-mail: dpalmer@tamu.edu.

College of Engineering Students: 2,591 full-time (528 women), 310 part-time (50 women); includes 52 Black or African American, non-Hispanic/Latino; 5 American Indian or Alaska Native, non-Hispanic/Latino; 116 Asian, non-Hispanic/Latino; 133 Hispanic/Latino, 1,891 international. *Faculty:* 373. Expenses: Contact institution. *Financial support:* Fellowships, research assistantships, teaching assistantships, career-related internships or fieldwork, institutionally sponsored loans, scholarships/grants, and unspecified assistantships available. Financial award applicants required to submit FAFSA. In 2010, 600 master's, 155 doctorates awarded. *Degree program information:* Part-time programs available. Postbaccalaureate distance learning degree programs offered (minimal on-campus study). Offers aerospace engineering (M Eng, MS, PhD); biomedical engineering (M Eng, MS, D Eng, PhD); chemical engineering (M Eng, MS, PhD); coastal and ocean engineering (M Eng, MS, D Eng, PhD); computer engineering (M En, M Eng, MS, PhD); computer science (MCS); computer science and engineering (MS, PhD); construction engineering and management (M Eng, MS, D Eng, PhD); electrical engineering (MS, PhD); engineering (M En, M Eng, MCS, MID, MS, D Eng, PhD); environmental engineering (M Eng, MS, D Eng, PhD); geotechnical engineering (M Eng, MS, D Eng, PhD); health physics (MS, PhD); industrial and systems engineering (M Eng, MS); industrial distribution (MID); industrial engineering (D Eng, PhD); materials engineering (M Eng, MS, D Eng, PhD); mechanical engineering (M Eng, MS, D Eng, PhD); nuclear engineering (M Eng, MS, PhD); petroleum engineering (M Eng, MS, PhD); structural engineering (M Eng, MS, D Eng, PhD); transportation engineering (M Eng, MS, D Eng, PhD); water resources engineering (M Eng, MS, D Eng, PhD). *Application fee:* $50 ($75 for international students). Electronic applications accepted. *Application Contact:* Dr. G. Kemble Bennett, Dean, 979-845-7203, Fax: 979-845-8986, E-mail: kem-bennett@tamu.edu. *Dean,* Dr. G. Kemble Bennett, 979-845-7203, Fax: 979-845-8986, E-mail: kem-bennett@tamu.edu.

College of Geosciences Students: 306 full-time (135 women), 48 part-time (14 women); includes 29 minority (2 Black or African American, non-Hispanic/Latino; 13 Asian, non-Hispanic/Latino; 14 Hispanic/Latino), 127 international. Average age 30. *Faculty:* 95. Expenses: Contact institution. *Financial support:* Fellowships with partial tuition reimbursements, research assistantships, teaching assistantships, career-related internships or fieldwork, Federal Work-Study, institutionally sponsored loans, scholarships/grants, tuition waivers (partial), and unspecified assistantships available. Financial award application deadline: 3/1; financial award applicants required to submit FAFSA. In 2010, 33 master's, 21 doctorates awarded. *Degree program information:* Part-time programs available. Offers atmospheric sciences (MS, PhD); geography (MS, PhD); geology (MS, PhD); geophysics (MS, PhD); geosciences (MS, PhD); oceanography (MS, PhD). *Application deadline:* For fall admission, 3/1 priority date for domestic students; for spring admission, 12/1 for domestic students. Applications are processed on a rolling basis. *Application fee:* $50 ($75 for international students). Electronic applications accepted. *Application Contact:* Graduate Admissions, 979-845-1044, E-mail: admissions@tamu.edu. *Dean,* Dr. Kate C. Miller, 979-845-3651, E-mail: kcmiller@tamu.edu.

College of Liberal Arts Students: 622 full-time (313 women), 185 part-time (95 women); includes 174 minority (48 Black or African American, non-Hispanic/Latino; 3 American Indian or Alaska Native, non-Hispanic/Latino; 19 Asian, non-Hispanic/Latino; 104 Hispanic/Latino), 180 international. *Faculty:* 220. Expenses: Contact institution. *Financial support:* Fellowships, research assistantships with partial tuition reimbursements, teaching assistantships with partial tuition reimbursements, career-related internships or fieldwork, Federal Work-Study, institutionally sponsored loans, unspecified assistantships, and assistant lecturer positions available. Financial award applicants required to submit FAFSA. In 2010, 78 master's, 74 doctorates awarded. *Degree program information:* Part-time programs available. Offers anthropology (MA, PhD); behavioral and cellular neuroscience (PhD); clinical psychology (PhD); cognitive psychology (PhD); communication (MA, PhD); developmental psychology (PhD); economics (MS, PhD); English (MA, PhD); Hispanic studies (MA, PhD); history (MA, PhD); industrial/organizational psychology (PhD); liberal arts (MA, MS, PhD); philosophy (MA, PhD); political science (PhD); social psychology (PhD); sociology (MS, PhD). *Application fee:* $50 ($75 for international students). Electronic applications accepted. *Application Contact:* Dr. Larry J. Oliver, Associate Dean, 979-845-1520, Fax: 979-845-5164, E-mail: l-oliver@tamu.edu. *Dean,* Jose Luis Bermudez, 979-862-6797, Fax: 979-845-5164, E-mail: jbermudez@tamu.edu.

College of Science Students: 763 full-time (262 women), 121 part-time (52 women); includes 111 minority (17 Black or African American, non-Hispanic/Latino; 3 American Indian or Alaska Native, non-Hispanic/Latino; 48 Asian, non-Hispanic/Latino; 43 Hispanic/Latino), 405 international. *Faculty:* 215. Expenses: Contact institution. *Financial support:* Fellowships, research assistantships, teaching assistantships, career-related internships or fieldwork, institutionally sponsored loans, and scholarships/grants available. Financial award applicants required to submit FAFSA. In 2010, 65 master's, 82 doctorates awarded. *Degree program information:* Part-time programs available. Offers applied physics (PhD); biology (MS, PhD); botany (MS, PhD); chemistry (MS, PhD); mathematics (MS, PhD); microbiology (MS, PhD); molecular and cell biology (PhD); neuroscience (MS, PhD); physics (MS, PhD); science (MS, PhD); statistics (MS, PhD); zoology (MS, PhD). *Application Contact:* Mark Zoran, Associate Dean for Graduate Studies, 979-862-2819, Fax: 979-845-6077, E-mail: zoran@mail.bio.tamu.edu. *Dean,* H. Joseph Newton, 979-845-8817, Fax: 979-845-6077, E-mail: jnewton@stat.tamu.edu.

College of Veterinary Medicine and Biomedical Sciences Students: 635 full-time (456 women), 34 part-time (24 women); includes 168 minority (87 Black or African American, non-Hispanic/Latino; 2 American Indian or Alaska Native, non-Hispanic/Latino; 24 Asian, non-Hispanic/Latino; 55 Hispanic/Latino), 53 international. *Faculty:* 71. Expenses: Contact institution. *Financial support:* Fellowships, research assistantships, teaching assistantships, career-related internships or fieldwork, Federal Work-Study, institutionally sponsored loans, tuition waivers (partial), and clinical associateships available. Support available to part-time students. Financial award applicants required to submit FAFSA. In 2010, 125 first professional degrees, 18 master's, 9 doctorates awarded. *Degree program information:* Part-time programs available. Offers biomedical science (MS, PhD); epidemiology (MS); food safety/toxicology/environmental health (MS); genetics (MS, PhD); large animal clinical sciences (MS); science and technology journalism (MS); toxicology (PhD); veterinary medicine (DVM); veterinary medicine and biomedical sciences (DVM, MS, PhD); veterinary microbiology (MS, PhD); veterinary parasitology (MS, PhD); veterinary pathology (MS, PhD); veterinary public health (MS); veterinary small animal medicine and surgery (MS). *Application Contact:* Graduate Admissions, 979-845-1044, E-mail: admissions@tamu.edu. *Dean,* Dr. Eleanor Green, 979-845-5051, Fax: 979-845-5088, E-mail: emgreen@tamu.edu.

Mays Business School Students: 790 full-time (312 women), 23 part-time (10 women); includes 23 Black or African American, non-Hispanic/Latino; 6 American Indian or Alaska Native, non-Hispanic/Latino; 47 Asian, non-Hispanic/Latino; 53 Hispanic/Latino, 170 international. Average age 28. 850 applicants, 59% accepted, 202 enrolled. *Faculty:* 94. Expenses: Contact institution. *Financial support:* In 2010–11, 235 students received support; fellowships, research assistantships, teaching assistantships, career-related internships or fieldwork, Federal Work-Study, and institutionally sponsored loans available. Financial award application deadline: 2/1. In 2010, 536 master's, 8 doctorates awarded. Offers accounting (MS, PhD); business (EMBA, MBA, MRE, MS, PhD); business administration (EMBA, MBA); finance (MS, PhD); human resource management (MS); management (PhD); management information systems (MS, PhD); management science (PhD); marketing (MS, PhD); production and operations management (PhD); real estate (MRE). *Application deadline:* Applications are processed on a rolling basis. *Application fee:* $50 ($75 for international students). Electronic applications accepted. *Application Contact:* Wendy Flynn, Director, MBA Program, 979-845-4714, Fax: 979-862-2393, E-mail: maysmba@tamu.edu. *Dean,* Dr. Ricky W. Griffin, 979-845-4711, E-mail: rgriffin@tamu.edu.

TEXAS A&M UNIVERSITY AT GALVESTON, Galveston, TX 77553-1675

General Information State-supported, coed, comprehensive institution. CGS member. *Enrollment:* 34 full-time matriculated graduate/professional students (20 women), 28 part-time matriculated graduate/professional students (18 women). *Enrollment by degree level:* 50 master's, 12 doctoral. *Graduate faculty:* 33 full-time (7 women). *Graduate housing:* Room and/or apartments available on a first-come, first-served basis to single students; on-campus housing not available to married students. *Student services:* Campus employment opportunities, career counseling, international student services, services for students with disabilities. *Library facilities:* Jack K. Williams Library. *Online resources:* library catalog, web page, access to other libraries' catalogs. *Collection:* 56,589 titles, 640 serial subscriptions.

Computer facilities: 122 computers available on campus for general student use. A campuswide network can be accessed from student residence rooms and from off campus. Online class registration, degree plan progress, billing statement are available. *Web address:* http://www.tamug.edu/.

General Application Contact: Nicole Wilkins, Administrative Coordinator for Graduate Studies, 409-740-4937, Fax: 409-740-4754, E-mail: wilkinsn@tamug.edu.

GRADUATE UNITS

Department of Marine Biology Students: 16 full-time (10 women), 2 part-time (both women); includes 5 minority (1 Asian, non-Hispanic/Latino; 2 Hispanic/Latino; 2 Two or more races, non-Hispanic/Latino), 1 international. Average age 23. 17 applicants, 35% accepted, 5 enrolled. *Faculty:* 33 full-time (7 women). Expenses: Contact institution. *Financial support:* In 2010–11, 16 students received support, including 4 research assistantships, 12 teaching assistantships; scholarships/grants, health care benefits, and unspecified assistantships also available. Financial award applicants required to submit FAFSA. Offers marine biology (MS, PhD). *Application deadline:* For fall admission, 12/15 priority date for domestic students; for spring admission, 5/15 priority date for domestic students. Applications are processed on a rolling basis. *Application fee:* $50 ($75 for international students). Electronic applications accepted. *Application Contact:* Nicole Wilkins, Administrative Coordinator for Graduate Studies, 409-740-4937, Fax: 409-740-4754, E-mail: wilkinsn@tamug.edu. *Associate Professor/Chair of Marine Biology Interdisciplinary Program,* Dr. Christopher D. Marshall, 409-740-4884, E-mail: marshalc@tamug.edu.

Department of Marine Sciences Students: 20 full-time (11 women), 11 part-time (8 women); includes 2 minority (1 Asian, non-Hispanic/Latino; 1 Hispanic/Latino), 1 international. Average age 23. 17 applicants, 82% accepted, 12 enrolled. *Faculty:* 33 full-time (7 women). Expenses: Contact institution. *Financial support:* In 2010–11, 10 students received support, including 10 teaching assistantships; research assistantships, scholarships/grants, health care benefits, and unspecified assistantships also available. Financial award application deadline: 4/1; financial award applicants required to submit FAFSA. In 2010, 12 master's awarded. Offers marine resources management (MMRM). *Application deadline:* Applications are processed on a rolling basis. *Application fee:* $50 ($75 for international students). Electronic applications accepted. *Application Contact:* Dr. Frederick C. Schlemmer, Associate Professor/Graduate Advisor, 409-740-4518, Fax: 409-740-4429, E-mail: schlemme@tamug.edu. *Professor/Head,* Dr. Patrick Louchouarn, 409-740-4710.

TEXAS A&M UNIVERSITY–COMMERCE, Commerce, TX 75429-3011

General Information State-supported, coed, university. CGS member. *Graduate housing:* Rooms and/or apartments available on a first-come, first-served basis to single and married students. *Research affiliation:* Texas A&M University–Commerce Regional Division of Texas Engineering Experiment Station.

GRADUATE UNITS

Graduate School *Degree program information:* Part-time programs available. Electronic applications accepted.

College of Arts and Sciences *Degree program information:* Part-time programs available. Offers agricultural education (M Ed, MS); agricultural sciences (M Ed, MS); art (MA, MS); art history (MA); arts and sciences (M Ed, MA, MFA, MM, MS, PhD); biological and earth sciences (M Ed, MS); chemistry (M Ed, MS); college teaching of English (PhD); computer science (MS); English (MA, MS); fine arts (MFA); history (MA, MS); mathematics (MA, MS); music (MA, MS); music composition (MA, MM); music education (MA, MM, MS); music literature (MA); music performance (MA, MM); music theory (MA, MM); physics (M Ed, MS); social sciences (M Ed, MS); sociology (MA, MS); Spanish (MA); studio art (MA); theatre (MA, MS). Electronic applications accepted.

College of Business and Technology *Degree program information:* Part-time programs available. Offers business administration (MBA); business and technology (MA, MBA, MS); economics (MA, MS); industrial technology (MS); technology management (MS). Electronic applications accepted.

College of Education and Human Services *Degree program information:* Part-time programs available. Offers bilingual/ESL education (M Ed, MS); cognition and instruction (PhD); counseling (M Ed, MS, PhD); early childhood education (M Ed, MS); education and human services (M Ed, MA, MS, MSW, Ed D, PhD); educational administration (M Ed, Ed D); educational technology (M Ed, MS); elementary education (M Ed, MS); exercise physiology (MS); health and human performance (M Ed); health promotion (MS); health, kinesiology and sports studies (Ed D); higher education (MS, Ed D); learning technology and information systems (M Ed, MS); motor performance (MS); psychology (MA, MS); reading (M Ed, MS); secondary education (M Ed, MS); social work (MSW); special education (M Ed, MA, MS); sport studies (MS); supervision, curriculum and instruction: elementary education (Ed D); supervision, curriculum, and instruction (Ed D); training and development (MS). Electronic applications accepted.

TEXAS A&M UNIVERSITY–CORPUS CHRISTI, Corpus Christi, TX 78412-5503

General Information State-supported, coed, university. CGS member. *Graduate housing:* Room and/or apartments available on a first-come, first-served basis to single students; on-campus housing not available to married students. Housing application deadline: 5/1.

GRADUATE UNITS

Graduate Studies and Research *Degree program information:* Part-time and evening/weekend programs available. Postbaccalaureate distance learning degree programs offered (minimal on-campus study). Electronic applications accepted.

College of Business *Degree program information:* Part-time and evening/weekend programs available. Offers accounting (M Acc); health care administration (MBA); international business (MBA). Electronic applications accepted.

College of Education *Degree program information:* Part-time and evening/weekend programs available. Offers counseling (MS, PhD); counselor education (PhD); curriculum and instruction (MS, Ed D); early childhood education (MS); educational administration (MS); educational leadership (Ed D); educational technology (MS); elementary education (MS); kinesiology (MS); reading (MS); secondary education (MS); special education (MS). Electronic applications accepted.

College of Liberal Arts *Degree program information:* Part-time and evening/weekend programs available. Offers English (MA); history (MA); psychology (MA); public administration (MPA); studio arts (MA, MFA). Electronic applications accepted.

College of Nursing and Health Sciences *Degree program information:* Part-time and evening/weekend programs available. Offers clinical nurse specialist (MSN); family nurse practitioner (MSN); health care administration (MSN); leadership in nursing systems (MSN). Electronic applications accepted.

College of Science and Technology *Degree program information:* Part-time and evening/weekend programs available. Offers applied and computational mathematics (MS); biology (MS); coastal and marine system science (PhD); computer science (MS); curriculum content (MS); environmental science (MS); mariculture (MS); science and technology (MS, PhD). Electronic applications accepted.

TEXAS A&M UNIVERSITY–KINGSVILLE, Kingsville, TX 78363

General Information State-supported, coed, university. *Graduate housing:* Rooms and/or apartments available on a first-come, first-served basis to single and married students. Housing application deadline: 8/1. *Research affiliation:* Gas Research Institute (engineering), U. S. Filters (engineering), Texas A&M University (biology), University of Texas Health Science Center–Houston (biology), University of Texas Health Science Center–San Antonio (biology), Institute of Biosciences and Technology (biology).

GRADUATE UNITS

College of Graduate Studies *Degree program information:* Part-time and evening/weekend programs available. Postbaccalaureate distance learning degree programs offered (minimal on-campus study).

College of Agriculture and Home Economics *Degree program information:* Part-time and evening/weekend programs available. Offers agribusiness (MS); agricultural education (MS); agriculture and home economics (MS, PhD); animal sciences (MS); human sciences (MS); plant and soil sciences (MS, PhD); range and wildlife management (MS); wildlife science (PhD).

College of Arts and Sciences *Degree program information:* Part-time and evening/weekend programs available. Offers applied geology (MS); art (MA, MS); arts and sciences (MA, MM, MS); biology (MS); chemistry (MS); communication (MS); English (MA, MS); gerontology (MS); history and political science (MA, MS); mathematics (MS); music education (MM); psychology (MA, MS); sociology (MA, MS); Spanish (MA).

College of Business Administration *Degree program information:* Part-time and evening/weekend programs available. Offers business administration (MBA, MS).

College of Education *Degree program information:* Part-time and evening/weekend programs available. Offers adult education (M Ed); bilingual education (MA, MS, Ed D); early childhood education (M Ed); education (M Ed, MA, MS, Ed D, PhD); elementary education (MA, MS); English as a second language (M Ed); guidance and counseling (MA, MS); health and kinesiology (MA, MS); higher education administration leadership (PhD); reading (MS); school administration (MA, MS, Ed D); secondary education (MA, MS); special education (M Ed); supervision (MA, MS).

College of Engineering *Degree program information:* Part-time and evening/weekend programs available. Offers chemical engineering (ME, MS); civil engineering (ME, MS); computer science (MS); electrical engineering (ME, MS); engineering (ME, MS, PhD); environmental engineering (ME, MS, PhD); industrial engineering (ME, MS); mechanical engineering (ME, MS); natural gas engineering (ME, MS).

TEXAS A&M UNIVERSITY–SAN ANTONIO, San Antonio, TX 78224

General Information State-supported, coed, comprehensive institution. *Enrollment by degree level:* 796 master's. *Graduate faculty:* 42 full-time (21 women), 12 part-time/adjunct (9 women). Tuition, state resident: full-time $2899; part-time $161 per credit hour. Tuition, nonresident: full-time $8479; part-time $471 per credit hour. *Required fees:* $1056; $61 per credit hour. $368 per semester. *Student services:* Campus employment opportunities, campus safety program, career counseling, free psychological counseling, international student services, low-cost health insurance, services for students with disabilities, teacher training. *Web address:* http://www.tamuk.edu/sanantonio/.

General Application Contact: Melissa A. Villanueva, Graduate Admissions Specialist, 210-932-6200, E-mail: melissa.villanueva@tamusa.tamus.edu.

GRADUATE UNITS

Department of Curriculum and Kinesiology *Faculty:* 14 full-time (10 women), 5 part-time/adjunct (4 women). Expenses: Contact institution. *Financial support:* Application deadline: 3/31. In 2010, 46 master's awarded. *Degree program information:* Part-time and evening/weekend programs available. Offers bilingual education (MA); early childhood education (M Ed); kinesiology (MS); reading (MS); special education (M Ed). *Application deadline:* For fall admission, 8/15 priority date for domestic students, 6/1 priority date for international students; for spring admission, 12/15 priority date for domestic students, 10/1 priority date for international students. Applications are processed on a rolling basis. *Application fee:* $35 ($50 for international students). Electronic applications accepted. *Application Contact:* Melissa Villanueva, Graduate Admissions Specialist, 210-932-6200, E-mail: admissions@tamusa.tamus.edu. *Department Chair,* Dr. Samuel Garcia, 210-932-7862, E-mail: samuel.garcia@tamusa.tamus.edu.

Texas A&M University–San Antonio (continued)

Department of Leadership and Counseling *Faculty:* 12 full-time (7 women), 7 part-time/adjunct (5 women). Expenses: Contact institution. *Financial support:* Application deadline: 3/31. In 2010, 70 master's awarded. *Degree program information:* Part-time and evening/weekend programs available. Offers counseling and guidance (MA); educational leadership (MA). *Application deadline:* For fall admission, 8/15 priority date for domestic students, 6/1 priority date for international students; for spring admission, 12/15 priority date for domestic students, 10/1 priority date for international students. Applications are processed on a rolling basis. *Application fee:* $35 ($50 for international students). Electronic applications accepted. *Application Contact:* Melissa Villanueva, Graduate Admissions Specialist, 210-932-6200, E-mail: admissions@tamusa.tamus.edu. *Department Chair*, Dr. Albert Valadez, 210-932-7843, E-mail: albert.valadez@tamusa.tamus.edu.

School of Arts and Sciences Students: 10 full-time (9 women), 2 part-time (1 woman); includes 1 Black or African American, non-Hispanic/Latino; 7 Hispanic/Latino. Average age 32. 5 applicants, 100% accepted, 5 enrolled. *Faculty:* 2 full-time (both women), 1 (woman) part-time/adjunct. Expenses: Contact institution. *Financial support:* Application deadline: 3/31. *Degree program information:* Part-time and evening/weekend programs available. Offers English (MA). *Application deadline:* For fall admission, 8/15 for domestic students, 6/1 priority date for international students; for spring admission, 12/15 for domestic students, 10/1 priority date for international students. Applications are processed on a rolling basis. *Application fee:* $35 ($50 for international students). Electronic applications accepted. *Application Contact:* Melissa A. Villanueva, Graduate Admissions Specialist, 210-931-6200, E-mail: melissa.villanueva@tamus.tamus.edu. *Head*, Dr. William Bush, 210-932-6276, E-mail: william.bush@tamusa.tamus.edu.

School of Business Students: 49 full-time (21 women), 195 part-time (107 women). *Faculty:* 18 full-time (6 women), 1 part-time/adjunct (0 women). Expenses: Contact institution. *Financial support:* Application deadline: 3/31. In 2010, 20 master's awarded. *Degree program information:* Part-time and evening/weekend programs available. Offers business administration (MBA); enterprise resource planning systems (MBA); finance (MBA); healthcare management (MBA); human resources management (MBA); information assurance and security (MBA); international business (MBA); project management (MBA); supply chain management (MBA). *Application deadline:* For fall admission, 7/1 priority date for domestic students, 6/1 priority date for international students; for spring admission, 11/15 priority date for domestic students, 10/1 priority date for international students. Applications are processed on a rolling basis. *Application fee:* $35 ($50 for international students). Electronic applications accepted. *Application Contact:* Melissa A. Villanueva, Graduate Admissions Specialist, 210-932-6200, Fax: 210-932-6209, E-mail: melissa.villanueva@tamusa.tamus.edu. *MBA Coordinator*, Dr. Tracy Hurley, 210-932-6200, E-mail: tracy.hurley@tamusa.tamus.edu.

TEXAS A&M UNIVERSITY–TEXARKANA, Texarkana, TX 75505-5518

General Information State-supported, coed, upper-level institution. *Graduate housing:* On-campus housing not available.

GRADUATE UNITS

Graduate Studies and Research *Degree program information:* Part-time and evening/weekend programs available. Electronic applications accepted.

College of Business *Degree program information:* Part-time and evening/weekend programs available. Offers accounting (MSA); business administration (MBA, MS). Electronic applications accepted.

College of Education and Liberal Arts *Degree program information:* Part-time and evening/weekend programs available. Offers adult education (MS); curriculum and instruction (M Ed); education (MS); educational administration (M Ed); English (MA); instructional technology (MS); interdisciplinary studies (MA, MS); special education (MS). Electronic applications accepted.

College of Health and Behavioral Sciences *Degree program information:* Part-time and evening/weekend programs available. Offers counseling psychology (MS). Electronic applications accepted.

TEXAS CHIROPRACTIC COLLEGE, Pasadena, TX 77505-1699

General Information Independent, coed, graduate-only institution. *Enrollment by degree level:* 291 first professional. *Graduate faculty:* 29 full-time, 4 part-time/adjunct. *Tuition:* Full-time $26,700; part-time $742 per credit hour. *Graduate housing:* On-campus housing not available. *Student services:* Campus employment opportunities, career counseling, exercise/wellness program, free psychological counseling, international student services, low-cost health insurance. *Library facilities:* Mae Hilty Memorial Library. *Online resources:* library catalog. *Collection:* 16,923 titles, 167 serial subscriptions, 1,103 audiovisual materials.

Computer facilities: A campuswide network can be accessed. Online class registration is available. *Web address:* http://www.txchiro.edu/.

General Application Contact: Dr. David Anderson, Director of Enrollment Management, 281-998-6098.

GRADUATE UNITS

Professional Program Students: 274 full-time (119 women), 17 part-time (10 women). *Faculty:* 29 full-time, 4 part-time/adjunct. Expenses: Contact institution. *Financial support:* Career-related internships or fieldwork, Federal Work-Study, institutionally sponsored loans, and tuition waivers available. Support available to part-time students. Financial award application deadline: 4/15; financial award applicants required to submit FAFSA. *Degree program information:* Part-time programs available. Offers chiropractic (DC). *Application deadline:* For fall admission, 9/1 priority date for domestic students; for spring admission, 12/1 priority date for domestic students. Applications are processed on a rolling basis. *Application fee:* $50. *Application Contact:* Dr. David Anderson, Director of Enrollment Management, 281-998-6098. *President*, Dr. Richard G. Brassard, 281-998-6070.

TEXAS CHRISTIAN UNIVERSITY, Fort Worth, TX 76129-0002

General Information Independent-religious, coed, university. CGS member. *Enrollment:* 9,142 graduate, professional, and undergraduate students; 536 full-time matriculated graduate/professional students (278 women), 732 part-time matriculated graduate/professional students (391 women). *Enrollment by degree level:* 972 master's, 296 doctoral. *Graduate faculty:* 296 full-time (103 women), 24 part-time/adjunct (10 women). *Tuition:* Full-time $18,720; part-time $1040 per credit hour. Tuition and fees vary according to course load and program. *Graduate housing:* Rooms and/or apartments available on a first-come, first-served basis to single and married students. Housing application deadline: 5/1. *Student services:* Campus employment opportunities, campus safety program, career counseling, exercise/wellness program, free psychological counseling, international student services, low-cost health insurance, multicultural affairs office, services for students with disabilities, teacher training, writing training. *Library facilities:* Mary Couts Burnett Library. *Online resources:* library catalog, web page, access to other libraries' catalogs. *Collection:* 1.4 million titles, 69,078 serial subscriptions, 67,898 audiovisual materials. *Research affiliation:* Bell Helicopter (engineering), Lockheed Martin Corporation (business), Botanical Research Institute of Texas, Inc. (biology, environmental science, ranch management), Next Era Energy (environmental science, geology, biology), Accurate Conceptions (chemistry), UNT—Health Science Center (physics, biology).

Computer facilities: 1,200 computers available on campus for general student use. A campuswide network can be accessed from student residence rooms and from off campus. Online class registration is available. *Web address:* http://www.tcu.edu/.

General Application Contact: Anita Unger, Admissions, TCU Graduate Studies Office, 817-257-7515, Fax: 817-257-7484, E-mail: frogmail@tcu.edu.

GRADUATE UNITS

AddRan College of Liberal Arts Expenses: Contact institution. *Financial support:* In 2010–11, 5 fellowships with full tuition reimbursements (averaging $17,500 per year), 44 teaching assistantships with full tuition reimbursements (averaging $15,000 per year) were awarded; unspecified assistantships also available. Financial award application deadline: 3/1. *Degree program information:* Part-time and evening/weekend programs available. Offers composition (MA); English (PhD); history (MA, PhD); liberal arts (MA, PhD); literature (MA); rhetoric (MA); rhetoric/composition (PhD). *Application deadline:* For fall admission, 3/1 for domestic students; for spring admission, 12/1 for domestic students. Applications are processed on a rolling basis. *Application fee:* $60. Electronic applications accepted. *Application Contact:* Admissions, TCU Graduate Studies Office, 817-257-7515, Fax: 817-257-7484, E-mail: frogmail@tcu.edu. *Dean*, Dr. Andrew Schoolmaster, 817-257-7160, E-mail: a.schoolmaster@tcu.edu.

College of Communication Expenses: Contact institution. *Financial support:* In 2010–11, 5 research assistantships with full and partial tuition reimbursements (averaging $3,500 per year), 11 teaching assistantships with full and partial tuition reimbursements (averaging $8,000 per year) were awarded; tuition waivers (full and partial) and unspecified assistantships also available. Financial award application deadline: 3/1. *Degree program information:* Part-time and evening/weekend programs available. Offers communication (MS); communication studies (MS). *Application deadline:* For fall admission, 3/1 for domestic students; for spring admission, 12/1 for domestic students. Applications are processed on a rolling basis. *Application fee:* $50. *Application Contact:* Dr. Melissa Schroeder, Director of Graduate Studies/Associate Dean, 817-257-5918, Fax: 817-257-5921, E-mail: m.y.schroeder@tcu.edu. *Dean*, Dr. David Whillock, 817-257-5918, E-mail: d.whillock@tcu.edu.

Schieffer School of Journalism Expenses: Contact institution. *Financial support:* Tuition waivers (full and partial) and unspecified assistantships available. Financial award application deadline: 3/1. *Degree program information:* Part-time and evening/weekend programs available. Offers advertising/public relations (MS); news-editorial (MS). *Application deadline:* For fall admission, 3/1 for domestic and international students; for spring admission, 10/1 for domestic and international students. Applications are processed on a rolling basis. *Application fee:* $50. *Application Contact:* Dr. John Tisdale, Associate Director, 817-257-7425, E-mail: j.tisdale@tcu.edu. *Director*, John Lumpkin, 817-257-4908, E-mail: j.lumpkin@tcu.edu.

College of Education Expenses: Contact institution. *Financial support:* Teaching assistantships with full tuition reimbursements, career-related internships or fieldwork, scholarships/grants, and unspecified assistantships available. Financial award application deadline: 3/15. *Degree program information:* Part-time and evening/weekend programs available. Offers counseling (M Ed); curriculum studies (M Ed); education (M Ed, Ed D, Certificate); educational administration (M Ed); educational leadership (Ed D); educational studies: science education (M Ed); elementary (M Ed); elementary education (M Ed); LPC (Certificate); middle school education (M Ed); principal (Certificate); school counseling (Certificate); science education (M Ed); secondary education (M Ed); special education (M Ed). *Application deadline:* For fall admission, 11/16 for domestic and international students; for spring admission, 3/15 for domestic and international students. *Application fee:* $50. Electronic applications accepted. *Application Contact:* Patricia Chairez, Academic Program Specialist, 817-257-7661, E-mail: p.chairez@tcu.edu. *Associate Dean*, Dr. Jan Lacina, 817-257-6786, E-mail: j.lacina@tcu.edu.

College of Fine Arts Students: 47 full-time (19 women); includes 21 minority (1 Black or African American, non-Hispanic/Latino; 6 Asian, non-Hispanic/Latino; 12 Hispanic/Latino; 2 Two or more races, non-Hispanic/Latino). *Faculty:* 113 full-time (31 women), 16 part-time/adjunct (7 women). Expenses: Contact institution. *Financial support:* In 2010–11, 70 fellowships with full tuition reimbursements (averaging $6,000 per year) were awarded. Financial award application deadline: 1/15. Offers art history (MA); fine arts (M Mus, MA, MFA, MM Ed, DMA, Artist Diploma); studio art (MFA). *Application deadline:* For fall admission, 1/15 for domestic and international students; for spring admission, 10/1 for domestic and international students. *Application fee:* $0. *Application Contact:* Dr. Joseph Butler, TCU College of Fine Arts Graduate Office, 817-257-7603, Fax: 817-257-5672, E-mail: cfagradinfol@tcu.edu. *Dean*, Dr. Scott Sullivan, 817-257-7601, E-mail: s.sullivan@tcu.edu.

School of Music Students: 47 full-time (19 women); includes 21 minority (1 Black or African American, non-Hispanic/Latino; 6 Asian, non-Hispanic/Latino; 12 Hispanic/Latino; 2 Two or more races, non-Hispanic/Latino). Expenses: Contact institution. *Financial support:* Application deadline: 1/15. Offers composition (DMA); conducting (M Mus, DMA); music education (MM Ed); musicology (M Mus); organ performance (M Mus); pedagogy (DMA); performance (DMA); piano (Artist Diploma); piano pedagogy (M Mus); piano performance (M Mus); string performance (M Mus); theory/composition (M Mus); vocal performance (M Mus); voice pedagogy (M Mus); wind and percussion performance (M Mus). *Application deadline:* For fall admission, 1/15 for domestic and international students; for spring admission, 10/1 for domestic and international students. *Application fee:* $0. *Application Contact:* Dr. Joseph Butler, Associate Dean, College of Fine Arts, 817-257-6629, E-mail: j.butler@tcu.edu. *Director*, Dr. Richard Gipson, 817-257-7602.

College of Science and Engineering Expenses: Contact institution. *Financial support:* In 2010–11, 116 students received support, including 7 fellowships with full tuition reimbursements available (averaging $19,000 per year), 4 research assistantships with full tuition reimbursements available (averaging $19,000 per year), 77 teaching assistantships with full tuition reimbursements available (averaging $16,000 per year); tuition waivers (partial) and unspecified assistantships also available. Financial award application deadline: 3/1. *Degree program information:* Part-time programs available. Offers biochemistry (MS, PhD); biology (MA, MS); chemistry (MA); environmental science (MA, MEM, MS); experimental psychology (PhD); geology (MS); inorganic (MS, PhD); mathematics (MAT, MS, PhD); organic (MS, PhD); physical (MS, PhD); physics (MA, MS, PhD); psychology (MA, MS); science and engineering (MA, MAT, MEM, MS, PhD). *Application deadline:* For fall admission, 3/1 priority date for domestic and international students; for spring admission, 11/1 priority date for domestic and international students. Applications are processed on a rolling basis. *Application fee:* $60. Electronic applications accepted. *Application Contact:* Dr. Magnus Rittby, Associate Dean for Administration and Graduate Programs, 817-257-7729, Fax: 817-257-7736, E-mail: m.rittby@tcu.edu. *Dean*, Dr. Demitris Kouris, 817-257-7727, E-mail: d.kouris@tcu.edu.

School of Geology, Energy and the Environment Expenses: Contact institution. Offers environmental science (MS); geology (MS). *Application Contact:* Dr. Magnus Rittby, Associate Dean for Administration and Graduate Programs, 817-257-7729, Fax: 817-257-7736, E-mail: m.rittby@tcu.edu. *Dean*, Dr. Demitris Kouris, 817-257-7727, E-mail: d.kouris@tcu.edu.

Graduate Studies Expenses: Contact institution. *Financial support:* Applicants required to submit FAFSA. *Degree program information:* Part-time and evening/weekend programs available. Postbaccalaureate distance learning degree programs offered (no on-campus study). Offers liberal arts (MLA). *Application deadline:* For fall admission, 8/1 for domestic students; for spring admission, 1/1 for domestic students. Applications are processed on a rolling basis. *Application fee:* $50. *Application Contact:* Anita Unger, Graduate Program Coordinator, 817-257-7515, E-mail: a.unger@tcu.edu. *Associate Provost for Academic Affairs*, Dr. Bonnie Melhart, 817-257-7104, E-mail: b.melhart@tcu.edu.

Harris College of Nursing and Health Sciences Expenses: Contact institution. *Financial support:* Teaching assistantships, Tuition discount for all MSN students available. Financial award application deadline: 2/1; financial award applicants required to submit FAFSA. *Degree program information:* Part-time programs available. Postbaccalaureate distance learning degree programs offered (no on-campus study). Offers adult/gerontological nursing (CNS) (MSN); advanced practice registered nurse (DNP); clinical nurse leader (MSN); kinesiology (MS); nurse anesthesia (DNP); nurse educator (MSN); nursing administration (DNP); nursing and health sciences (MS, MSN, MSNA, DNP); pediatric nursing (CNS) (MSN); speech-language pathology (MS). *Application deadline:* For fall admission, 2/1 for domestic students. *Application fee:* $0. *Application Contact:* Sybil J. White, Assistant to the Dean of Graduate Studies, 817-257-6750, Fax: 817-257-6751, E-mail: s.white@tcu.edu. *Dean*, Dr. Paulette Burns, 817-257-6742, Fax: 817-257-6751, E-mail: p.burns@tcu.edu.

School of Nurse Anesthesia Expenses: Contact institution. *Financial support:* Applicants required to submit FAFSA. Postbaccalaureate distance learning degree programs offered (minimal on-campus study). Offers nurse anesthesia (MSNA, DNP). *Application deadline:* For fall admission, 10/1 for domestic and international students. *Application fee:* $50.

Application Contact: Admissions, TCU Graduate Studies Office, 817-257-7515, Fax: 817-257-7484, E-mail: frogmail@tcu.edu. *Director*, Dr. Kay K. Sanders, 817-257-7887, E-mail: k.sanders@tcu.edu.

The Neeley School of Business at TCU Expenses: Contact institution. *Financial support:* Career-related internships or fieldwork, Federal Work-Study, institutionally sponsored loans, scholarships/grants, and unspecified assistantships available. Support available to part-time students. Financial award application deadline: 5/1; financial award applicants required to submit FAFSA. *Degree program information:* Part-time and evening/weekend programs available. Offers accounting (M Ac); business (M Ac, MBA); business administration (MBA); international management (MBA). *Application deadline:* For fall admission, 4/15 priority date for domestic students, 3/1 priority date for international students. Applications are processed on a rolling basis. *Application fee:* $100. Electronic applications accepted. *Application Contact:* Peggy Conway, Director, MBA Admissions, 817-257-7531, Fax: 817-257-6431, E-mail: mbainfo@tcu.edu. *Dean*, Dr. Homer Erekson, 817-257-7526, Fax: 817-257-7227, E-mail: h.erekson@tcu.edu.

TEXAS COLLEGE OF TRADITIONAL CHINESE MEDICINE, Austin, TX 78702

General Information Private, coed, graduate-only institution.

GRADUATE UNITS

Program in Acupuncture and Oriental Medicine Offers acupuncture and Oriental medicine (MAOM). Electronic applications accepted.

TEXAS SOUTHERN UNIVERSITY, Houston, TX 77004-4584

General Information State-supported, coed, university. CGS member. *Enrollment:* 9,557 graduate, professional, and undergraduate students; 1,578 full-time matriculated graduate/professional students (917 women), 920 part-time matriculated graduate/professional students (599 women). *Enrollment by degree level:* 1,055 first professional, 1,214 master's, 229 doctoral. *Graduate faculty:* 166 full-time (78 women), 46 part-time/adjunct (14 women). Tuition, state resident: full-time $1875; part-time $100 per credit hour. Tuition, nonresident: full-time $6641; part-time $343 per credit hour. Tuition and fees vary according to course level, course load and degree level. *Graduate housing:* Room and/or apartments available on a first-come, first-served basis to single students; on-campus housing not available to married students. Housing application deadline: 7/15. *Student services:* Campus employment opportunities, campus safety program, career counseling, child daycare facilities, exercise/wellness program, free psychological counseling, international student services, multicultural affairs office, services for students with disabilities, teacher training. *Library facilities:* Robert J. Terry Library plus 2 others. *Online resources:* library catalog, access to other libraries' catalogs. *Collection:* 264,254 titles, 1,774 serial subscriptions. *Research affiliation:* Gerald B. Smith Center for Entrepreneurship & Executive Development (business, urban planning and environmental policy), Environmental Research & Technology Transfer Center (chemistry and environmental toxicology), Institute for International & Immigration Law; Center on Legal Pedagogy (law), Innovative Transportation Research Institute (transportation planning and management), NASA University Research Biotechnology & Environmental Health (biology), Economic Development Center; JP Chase Center for Financial Education (business).

Computer facilities: A campuswide network can be accessed from student residence rooms and from off campus. Online class registration, Blackboard Learning and Community Portal System (E-education) are available. *Web address:* http://www.tsu.edu/.

General Application Contact: Dr. Gregory Maddox, Dean of the Graduate School, 713-313-7011 Ext. 4410, Fax: 713-639-1876, E-mail: maddox_gh@tsu.edu.

GRADUATE UNITS

College of Education Students: 149 full-time (124 women), 259 part-time (203 women); includes 375 Black or African American, non-Hispanic/Latino; 5 Asian, non-Hispanic/Latino; 11 Hispanic/Latino, 2 international. Average age 36. 113 applicants, 98% accepted, 88 enrolled. *Faculty:* 22 full-time (11 women), 3 part-time/adjunct (0 women). Expenses: Contact institution. *Financial support:* In 2010–11, 1 research assistantship (averaging $6,000 per year), 11 teaching assistantships (averaging $7,724 per year) were awarded; fellowships, scholarships/grants and unspecified assistantships also available. Support available to part-time students. Financial award application deadline: 5/1. In 2010, 53 master's, 17 doctorates awarded. *Degree program information:* Part-time and evening/weekend programs available. Offers bilingual education (M Ed); counseling (M Ed); counselor education (Ed D); curriculum and instruction (Ed D); education (M Ed, MS, Ed D); educational administration (M Ed, Ed D); health education (MS); human performance (MS); secondary education (M Ed). *Application deadline:* For fall admission, 7/1 for domestic and international students; for spring admission, 11/1 for domestic and international students. Applications are processed on a rolling basis. *Application fee:* $50 ($75 for international students). Electronic applications accepted. *Application Contact:* Dr. Gregory Maddox, Dean of the Graduate School, 713-313-7011 Ext. 4410, Fax: 713-639-1876, E-mail: maddox_gh@tsu.edu. *Interim Dean*, Dr. Lillian Poats, 713-313-7978, E-mail: poats_lb@tsu.edu.

College of Liberal Arts and Behavioral Sciences Students: 75 full-time (52 women), 102 part-time (75 women); includes 164 Black or African American, non-Hispanic/Latino; 4 Asian, non-Hispanic/Latino; 3 Hispanic/Latino. Average age 35. 67 applicants, 96% accepted, 52 enrolled. *Faculty:* 27 full-time (16 women), 4 part-time/adjunct (2 women). Expenses: Contact institution. *Financial support:* In 2010–11, 1 research assistantship (averaging $8,000 per year), 11 teaching assistantships (averaging $8,182 per year) were awarded; scholarships/grants and unspecified assistantships also available. Support available to part-time students. Financial award application deadline: 5/1. In 2010, 26 master's awarded. *Degree program information:* Part-time and evening/weekend programs available. Offers English (MA); fine arts (MA); history (MA); human services and consumer sciences (MS); liberal arts and behavioral sciences (MA, MS); music (MA); psychology (MA); sociology (MA). *Application deadline:* For fall admission, 7/1 for domestic and international students; for spring admission, 11/1 for domestic and international students. Applications are processed on a rolling basis. *Application fee:* $50 ($75 for international students). Electronic applications accepted. *Application Contact:* Dr. Gregory Maddox, Dean of the Graduate School, 713-313-7011 Ext. 4410, Fax: 713-639-1876, E-mail: maddox_gh@tsu.edu. *Dean*, Dr. Danille Taylor, 713-313-7662, E-mail: ctaylordk@tsu.edu.

College of Pharmacy and Health Sciences Students: 340 full-time (205 women), 196 part-time (107 women); includes 255 Black or African American, non-Hispanic/Latino; 185 Asian, non-Hispanic/Latino; 16 Hispanic/Latino, 48 international. Average age 29. 124 applicants, 100% accepted, 122 enrolled. *Faculty:* 15 full-time (8 women), 4 part-time/adjunct (2 women). Expenses: Contact institution. *Financial support:* In 2010–11, 10 fellowships (averaging $28,000 per year), 2 research assistantships (averaging $28,000 per year), 6 teaching assistantships (averaging $25,700 per year) were awarded; career-related internships or fieldwork, scholarships/grants, and tuition waivers (partial) also available. Financial award application deadline: 5/1; financial award applicants required to submit FAFSA. In 2010, 91 first professional degrees, 5 master's awarded. Postbaccalaureate distance learning degree programs offered. Offers pharmacy and health sciences (Pharm D, MS, PhD). *Application deadline:* For fall admission, 2/15 for domestic and international students. Applications are processed on a rolling basis. *Application fee:* $50 ($75 for international students). Electronic applications accepted. *Application Contact:* LaJoy Kay, Director, 713-313-1880, E-mail: kay_lj@tsu.edu. *Dean*, Dr. Barbara Hayes, 713-313-7164, Fax: 713-313-1091, E-mail: hayes_bc@tsu.edu.

Jesse H. Jones School of Business Students: 108 full-time (56 women), 146 part-time (74 women); includes 220 Black or African American, non-Hispanic/Latino; 13 Asian, non-Hispanic/Latino; 6 Hispanic/Latino, 8 international. Average age 32. 103 applicants, 99% accepted, 86 enrolled. *Faculty:* 14 full-time (4 women), 2 part-time/adjunct (0 women). Expenses: Contact institution. *Financial support:* In 2010–11, 3 research assistantships (averaging $3,167 per year), 10 teaching assistantships (averaging $2,464 per year) were awarded; fellowships, career-related internships or fieldwork, scholarships/grants, tuition waivers (partial), and unspecified assistantships also available. Financial award application deadline: 5/1. In 2010, 216 master's awarded. *Degree program information:* Part-time and evening/weekend programs available. Offers business (MBA, MS); business administration (MBA); management information systems (MS). *Application deadline:* For fall admission, 7/1 for domestic and international students; for spring admission, 11/1 for domestic and international students. Applications are processed on a rolling basis. *Application fee:* $50 ($75 for international students). Electronic applications accepted. *Application Contact:* Bobbie J. Richardson, Executive Secretary, 713-313-7309, Fax: 713-313-7705, E-mail: richardson_bj@tsu.edu. *Dean*, Dr. Joseph Boyd, 713-313-7215, Fax: 713-313-7701, E-mail: boyd_jl@tsu.edu.

School of Public Affairs Students: 214 full-time (115 women), 85 part-time (48 women); includes 263 Black or African American, non-Hispanic/Latino; 14 Asian, non-Hispanic/Latino; 12 Hispanic/Latino, 2 international. Average age 34. 159 applicants, 99% accepted, 133 enrolled. *Faculty:* 14 full-time (5 women), 7 part-time/adjunct (0 women). Expenses: Contact institution. *Financial support:* In 2010–11, 39 research assistantships (averaging $7,560 per year), 22 teaching assistantships (averaging $3,100 per year) were awarded; fellowships, career-related internships or fieldwork, scholarships/grants, and unspecified assistantships also available. Financial award application deadline: 5/1; financial award applicants required to submit FAFSA. In 2010, 41 master's, 3 doctorates awarded. *Degree program information:* Part-time programs available. Offers administration of justice (MS, PhD); public administration (MPA); public affairs (MPA, MS, PhD); urban planning and environmental policy (MS, PhD). *Application deadline:* For fall admission, 7/1 for domestic and international students; for spring admission, 11/1 for domestic and international students. Applications are processed on a rolling basis. *Application fee:* $50 ($75 for international students). Electronic applications accepted. *Application Contact:* Pinkie Cotton, Administrative Assistant, 713-313-7311, E-mail: cotton_pe@tsu.edu. *Interim Dean*, Dr. Helen Taylor-Greene, 713-313-7864, E-mail: greeneht@tsu.edu.

School of Science and Technology Students: 106 full-time (55 women), 81 part-time (53 women); includes 124 Black or African American, non-Hispanic/Latino; 41 Asian, non-Hispanic/Latino; 6 Hispanic/Latino, 5 international. Average age 32. 64 applicants, 97% accepted, 48 enrolled. *Faculty:* 33 full-time (10 women), 3 part-time/adjunct (1 woman). Expenses: Contact institution. *Financial support:* In 2010–11, 8 fellowships (averaging $28,000 per year), 37 research assistantships (averaging $5,448 per year), 44 teaching assistantships (averaging $4,622 per year) were awarded; career-related internships or fieldwork, scholarships/grants, tuition waivers (partial), and unspecified assistantships also available. Financial award application deadline: 5/1. In 2010, 12 master's, 1 doctorate awarded. *Degree program information:* Part-time and evening/weekend programs available. Offers biology (MS); chemistry (MS); computer science (MS); environmental toxicology (MS, PhD); industrial technology (MS); mathematics (MS); science and technology (MS, PhD); transportation, planning and management (MS). *Application deadline:* For fall admission, 7/1 for domestic and international students; for spring admission, 11/1 for domestic and international students. Applications are processed on a rolling basis. *Application fee:* $50 ($75 for international students). Electronic applications accepted. *Application Contact:* Charlotte Whaley, Administrative Secretary, 713-313-7009, E-mail: whaley@tsu.edu. *Dean*, Dr. Lei Yu, 713-313-7007, E-mail: yu_lx@tsu.edu.

Tavis Smiley School of Communication Students: 21 full-time (9 women), 45 part-time (36 women); includes 61 Black or African American, non-Hispanic/Latino; 1 Asian, non-Hispanic/Latino; 1 Hispanic/Latino, 2 international. Average age 30. 25 applicants, 100% accepted, 21 enrolled. *Faculty:* 4 full-time (3 women), 1 part-time/adjunct (0 women). Expenses: Contact institution. *Financial support:* In 2010–11, 5 teaching assistantships (averaging $3,500 per year) were awarded; unspecified assistantships also available. Financial award application deadline: 5/1. In 2010, 6 master's awarded. *Degree program information:* Part-time programs available. Offers communication (MA). *Application deadline:* For fall admission, 7/1 for domestic and international students; for spring admission, 11/1 for domestic and international students. Applications are processed on a rolling basis. *Application fee:* $50 ($75 for international students). Electronic applications accepted. *Application Contact:* Dr. Louis Browne, Graduate Advisor, 713-313-7024. *Dean*, Dr. James Ward, 713-313-7740, E-mail: ward_jw@tsu.edu.

Thurgood Marshall School of Law Students: 565 full-time (301 women), 6 part-time (3 women); includes 257 Black or African American, non-Hispanic/Latino; 3 American Indian or Alaska Native, non-Hispanic/Latino; 41 Asian, non-Hispanic/Latino; 161 Hispanic/Latino, 5 international. Average age 28. 241 applicants, 100% accepted, 210 enrolled. *Faculty:* 37 full-time (21 women), 22 part-time/adjunct (9 women). Expenses: Contact institution. *Financial support:* In 2010–11, 75 students received support, including 1 research assistantship (averaging $6,000 per year), 107 teaching assistantships (averaging $1,600 per year); career-related internships or fieldwork, scholarships/grants, tuition waivers (partial), and unspecified assistantships also available. Financial award application deadline: 4/1; financial award applicants required to submit FAFSA. In 2010, 133 JDs awarded. Offers law (JD). *Application deadline:* For fall admission, 4/1 for domestic and international students. Applications are processed on a rolling basis. *Application fee:* $55. Electronic applications accepted. *Application Contact:* Edward Rene, Director of Admissions, 713-313-7115 Ext. 1004, Fax: 713-313-1049, E-mail: erene@tsulaw.edu. *Dean*, Dr. Dannye Holley, 713-313-7388, Fax: 713-313-1049, E-mail: dholley@tsulaw.edu.

TEXAS STATE UNIVERSITY–SAN MARCOS, San Marcos, TX 78666

General Information State-supported, coed, university. CGS member. *Enrollment:* 32,572 graduate, professional, and undergraduate students; 1,999 full-time matriculated graduate/professional students (1,225 women), 2,405 part-time matriculated graduate/professional students (1,555 women). *Enrollment by degree level:* 120 first professional, 4,016 master's, 268 doctoral. *Graduate faculty:* 535 full-time (237 women), 82 part-time/adjunct (42 women). Tuition, state resident: full-time $6024; part-time $251 per credit hour. Tuition, nonresident: full-time $13,536; part-time $564 per credit hour. *Required fees:* $1776; $50 per credit hour. $306 per semester. *Graduate housing:* Rooms and/or apartments available on a first-come, first-served basis to single and married students. Housing application deadline: 7/1. *Student services:* Campus employment opportunities, campus safety program, career counseling, exercise/wellness program, free psychological counseling, international student services, low-cost health insurance, multicultural affairs office, services for students with disabilities, teacher training, writing training. *Library facilities:* Alkek Library plus 1 other. *Online resources:* library catalog, web page, access to other libraries' catalogs. *Collection:* 1.5 million titles, 14,764 serial subscriptions, 276,062 audiovisual materials. *Research affiliation:* Lower Colorado River Authority (environmental conservation), Edwards Aquifer Authority (conservation), ITT Corporation (engineering), Advanced Materials and Processes (environmental and industrial science), New Vectors (risk assessment), Nanohmics (nano technology).

Computer facilities: Computer purchase and lease plans are available. 1,792 computers available on campus for general student use. A campuswide network can be accessed from student residence rooms and from off campus. Online class registration is available. *Web address:* http://www.txstate.edu/.

General Application Contact: Dr. J. Michael Willoughby, Dean of Graduate School, 512-245-2581, Fax: 512-245-8365, E-mail: gradcollege@txstate.edu.

GRADUATE UNITS

Graduate School Students: 1,999 full-time (1,225 women), 2,405 part-time (1,555 women); includes 1,318 minority (228 Black or African American, non-Hispanic/Latino; 12 American Indian or Alaska Native, non-Hispanic/Latino; 125 Asian, non-Hispanic/Latino; 882 Hispanic/Latino; 3 Native Hawaiian or other Pacific Islander, non-Hispanic/Latino; 68 Two or more races, non-Hispanic/Latino), 141 international. Average age 31. 2,484 applicants, 67% accepted, 1151 enrolled. *Faculty:* 498 full-time (215 women), 73 part-time/adjunct (44 women). Expenses: Contact institution. *Financial support:* In 2010–11, 1,703 students received support, including 275 research assistantships (averaging $4,489 per year), 688 teaching assistantships (averaging $4,150 per year); fellowships, career-related internships or fieldwork, Federal Work-Study, institutionally sponsored loans, scholarships/grants, unspecified assistantships, and laboratory instructorships, stipends also available. Support available to part-time students. Financial award application deadline: 4/1; financial award applicants required to submit FAFSA. In 2010, 1,247 master's, 26 doctorates awarded. *Degree program information:* Part-time and evening/weekend programs available. Postbaccalaureate distance learning degree programs offered (minimal on-campus study). Offers biology (MSIS); educational

Texas State University–San Marcos (continued)

administration and psychological services (MAIS); elementary mathematics, science, and technology (MSIS); health, physical education, and recreation (MAIS); interdisciplinary studies in political science (MAIS); international studies (MA); modern languages (MAIS); occupational education (M Ed, MSIS); psychology (MAIS, MSIS). *Application deadline:* For fall admission, 6/15 for domestic students, 6/1 for international students; for spring admission, 10/15 for domestic students, 10/1 for international students. Applications are processed on a rolling basis. *Application fee:* $40 ($90 for international students). Electronic applications accepted. *Application Contact:* Dr. J. Michael Willoughby, Dean of Graduate School, 512-245-2581, Fax: 512-245-8365, E-mail: gradcollege@txstate.edu. *Dean,* Dr. J. Michael Willoughby, 512-245-2581, Fax: 512-245-8365, E-mail: gradcollege@txstate.edu.

College of Applied Arts Students: 171 full-time (129 women), 269 part-time (191 women); includes 34 Black or African American, non-Hispanic/Latino; 2 American Indian or Alaska Native, non-Hispanic/Latino; 6 Asian, non-Hispanic/Latino; 126 Hispanic/Latino; 8 Two or more races, non-Hispanic/Latino, 3 international. Average age 32. 410 applicants, 53% accepted, 142 enrolled. *Faculty:* 28 full-time (11 women), 3 part-time/adjunct (2 women). Expenses: Contact institution. *Financial support:* In 2010–11, 215 students received support, including 34 research assistantships (averaging $5,572 per year), 50 teaching assistantships (averaging $4,157 per year); career-related internships or fieldwork, Federal Work-Study, and institutionally sponsored loans also available. Support available to part-time students. Financial award application deadline: 4/1; financial award applicants required to submit FAFSA. In 2010, 178 master's awarded. *Degree program information:* Part-time and evening/weekend programs available. Offers agriculture (M Ed); applied arts (M Ed, MS, MSCJ, MSW, PhD); criminal justice (MSCJ, PhD); family and child studies (MS); human nutrition (MS); management of technical education (M Ed); social work (MSW). *Application deadline:* For fall admission, 6/15 priority date for domestic students, 6/1 for international students; for spring admission, 10/15 priority date for domestic students, 10/1 for international students. Applications are processed on a rolling basis. *Application fee:* $40 ($90 for international students). Electronic applications accepted. *Application Contact:* Dr. J. Michael Willoughby, Dean of Graduate School, 512-245-2581, Fax: 512-245-8365, E-mail: gradcollege@txstate.edu. *Dean,* Dr. Jaime Chahin, 512-245-3333, Fax: 512-245-3338, E-mail: tc03@txstate.edu.

College of Education Students: 531 full-time (411 women), 942 part-time (740 women); includes 454 minority (90 Black or African American, non-Hispanic/Latino; 3 American Indian or Alaska Native, non-Hispanic/Latino; 31 Asian, non-Hispanic/Latino; 309 Hispanic/Latino; 1 Native Hawaiian or other Pacific Islander, non-Hispanic/Latino; 20 Two or more races, non-Hispanic/Latino), 8 international. Average age 32. 652 applicants, 76% accepted, 329 enrolled. *Faculty:* 95 full-time (57 women), 39 part-time/adjunct (30 women). Expenses: Contact institution. *Financial support:* In 2010–11, 535 students received support, including 105 research assistantships (averaging $4,721 per year), 74 teaching assistantships (averaging $3,736 per year); fellowships, career-related internships or fieldwork, Federal Work-Study, and institutionally sponsored loans also available. Support available to part-time students. Financial award application deadline: 4/1; financial award applicants required to submit FAFSA. In 2010, 428 master's, 14 doctorates awarded. *Degree program information:* Part-time and evening/weekend programs available. Offers adult, professional, and community education (PhD); athletic training (MS); counseling and guidance (M Ed); developmental and adult education (MA, PhD); early childhood education (M Ed, MA); education (M Ed, MA, MSRLS, PhD, SSP); educational leadership (M Ed, MA); elementary education (M Ed, MA); elementary education-bilingual/bicultural (M Ed, MA); health education (M Ed); physical education (M Ed); professional counseling (MA); reading education (M Ed); recreation and leisure services (MSRLS); school psychology (SSP); secondary education (M Ed, MA); special education (M Ed). *Application deadline:* For fall admission, 6/15 priority date for domestic students, 6/1 for international students; for spring admission, 10/15 priority date for domestic students, 10/1 for international students. Applications are processed on a rolling basis. *Application fee:* $40 ($90 for international students). Electronic applications accepted. *Application Contact:* Dr. J. Michael Willoughby, Dean of Graduate School, 512-245-2581, Fax: 512-245-8365, E-mail: gradcollege@txstate.edu. *Dean,* Dr. Stan Carpenter, 512-245-2150, Fax: 512-245-3158, E-mail: sc33@txstate.edu.

College of Fine Arts and Communication Students: 140 full-time (76 women), 84 part-time (54 women); includes 6 Black or African American, non-Hispanic/Latino; 2 American Indian or Alaska Native, non-Hispanic/Latino; 5 Asian, non-Hispanic/Latino; 51 Hispanic/Latino; 3 Two or more races, non-Hispanic/Latino, 12 international. Average age 30. 134 applicants, 74% accepted, 73 enrolled. *Faculty:* 72 full-time (31 women), 6 part-time/adjunct (3 women). Expenses: Contact institution. *Financial support:* In 2010–11, 109 students received support, including 4 research assistantships (averaging $5,154 per year), 80 teaching assistantships (averaging $3,716 per year); career-related internships or fieldwork, Federal Work-Study, institutionally sponsored loans, scholarships/grants, and unspecified assistantships also available. Support available to part-time students. Financial award application deadline: 4/1; financial award applicants required to submit FAFSA. In 2010, 67 master's awarded. *Degree program information:* Part-time and evening/weekend programs available. Offers communication design (MFA); communication studies (MA); fine arts and communication (MA, MFA, MM); journalism and mass communication (MA); music education (MM); music performance (MM); theatre arts (MA). *Application deadline:* For fall admission, 6/15 priority date for domestic students, 6/1 for international students; for spring admission, 10/15 priority date for domestic students, 10/1 for international students. Applications are processed on a rolling basis. *Application fee:* $40 ($90 for international students). Electronic applications accepted. *Application Contact:* Dr. J. Michael Willoughby, Dean of Graduate School, 512-245-2581, Fax: 512-245-8365, E-mail: gradcollege@txstate.edu. *Dean,* Dr. Timothy Mottet, 512-245-2308, Fax: 512-245-8334, E-mail: tm15@txstate.edu.

College of Health Professions Students: 177 full-time (122 women), 92 part-time (64 women); includes 80 minority (9 Black or African American, non-Hispanic/Latino; 1 American Indian or Alaska Native, non-Hispanic/Latino; 5 Asian, non-Hispanic/Latino; 61 Hispanic/Latino; 4 Two or more races, non-Hispanic/Latino), 4 international. Average age 27. 255 applicants, 25% accepted, 59 enrolled. *Faculty:* 32 full-time (17 women), 4 part-time/adjunct (0 women). Expenses: Contact institution. *Financial support:* In 2010–11, 155 students received support, including 14 research assistantships (averaging $3,096 per year), 40 teaching assistantships (averaging $2,583 per year); fellowships, career-related internships or fieldwork, Federal Work-Study, institutionally sponsored loans, scholarships/grants, unspecified assistantships, and stipends also available. Support available to part-time students. Financial award application deadline: 4/1; financial award applicants required to submit FAFSA. In 2010, 51 master's awarded. *Degree program information:* Part-time and evening/weekend programs available. Offers communication disorders (MA, MSCD); health administration (MHA, MS); health professions (MA, MHA, MS, MSCD, DPT); health services research (MS); healthcare administration (MHA); healthcare human resources (MS); physical therapy (DPT). *Application deadline:* For fall admission, 6/15 for domestic students, 6/1 for international students; for spring admission, 10/15 priority date for domestic students, 10/1 for international students. Applications are processed on a rolling basis. *Application fee:* $40 ($90 for international students). Electronic applications accepted. *Application Contact:* Dr. J. Michael Willoughby, Dean of Graduate School, 512-245-2581, Fax: 512-245-8365, E-mail: gradcollege@txstate.edu. *Dean,* Dr. Ruth Welborn, 512-245-3300, Fax: 512-245-3791, E-mail: mw01@txstate.edu.

College of Liberal Arts Students: 518 full-time (287 women), 556 part-time (318 women); includes 317 minority (51 Black or African American, non-Hispanic/Latino; 3 American Indian or Alaska Native, non-Hispanic/Latino; 18 Asian, non-Hispanic/Latino; 222 Hispanic/Latino; 1 Native Hawaiian or other Pacific Islander, non-Hispanic/Latino; 22 Two or more races, non-Hispanic/Latino), 16 international. Average age 31. 626 applicants, 70% accepted, 314 enrolled. *Faculty:* 151 full-time (63 women), 13 part-time/adjunct (2 women). Expenses: Contact institution. *Financial support:* In 2010–11, 445 students received support, including 275 research assistantships (averaging $4,489 per year), 239 teaching assistantships (averaging $4,128 per year); fellowships, career-related internships or fieldwork, Federal Work-Study, institutionally sponsored loans, scholarships/grants, and unspecified assistantships also available. Support available to part-time students. Financial award application deadline: 4/1; financial award applicants required to submit FAFSA. In 2010, 232 master's, 7 doctorates awarded. *Degree program information:* Part-time and evening/weekend programs available. Offers anthropology (MA); applied geography (MAG); applied sociology (MS); creative writing (MFA); criminal justice (MSIS); environmental geography (PhD); environmental geography, geography education, and geography information science (PhD); geographic information science (MAG); geography (MAG, MS); geography education (PhD); health psychology (MA); history (M Ed, MA); information science (PhD); land/area studies (MAG); legal studies (MA); liberal arts (M Ed, MA, MAG, MAIS, MFA, MPA, MS, MSIS, PhD); literature (MA); political science (MA); public administration (MPA); resource and environmental studies (MAG); rhetoric and composition (MA); sociology (MA); Spanish (MA); technical communication (MA). *Application deadline:* For fall admission, 6/15 priority date for domestic students, 6/1 for international students; for spring admission, 10/15 priority date for domestic students, 10/1 for international students. Applications are processed on a rolling basis. *Application fee:* $40 ($90 for international students). Electronic applications accepted. *Application Contact:* Dr. J. Michael Willoughby, Dean of Graduate School, 512-245-2581, Fax: 512-245-8365, E-mail: gradcollege@txstate.edu. *Dean,* Dr. Michael Hennessy, 512-245-2317, Fax: 512-245-8291, E-mail: ae02@txstate.edu.

College of Science Students: 270 full-time (114 women), 178 part-time (75 women); includes 108 minority (16 Black or African American, non-Hispanic/Latino; 1 American Indian or Alaska Native, non-Hispanic/Latino; 28 Asian, non-Hispanic/Latino; 57 Hispanic/Latino; 6 Two or more races, non-Hispanic/Latino), 71 international. Average age 30. 212 applicants, 88% accepted, 107 enrolled. *Faculty:* 89 full-time (23 women), 6 part-time/adjunct (0 women). Expenses: Contact institution. *Financial support:* In 2010–11, 127 students received support, including 54 research assistantships (averaging $4,088 per year), 178 teaching assistantships (averaging $4,737 per year); career-related internships or fieldwork, Federal Work-Study, institutionally sponsored loans, scholarships/grants, health care benefits, unspecified assistantships, and laboratory instructorships also available. Support available to part-time students. Financial award application deadline: 4/1; financial award applicants required to submit FAFSA. In 2010, 123 master's, 5 doctorates awarded. *Degree program information:* Part-time and evening/weekend programs available. Offers aquatic resources (MS, PhD); biochemistry (MS); biology (M Ed, MA, MS, PhD); chemistry (MA, MS); computer science (MA, MS); industrial mathematics (MS); industrial technology (MST); material physics (PhD); mathematics (M Ed, MS, PhD); mathematics education (PhD); middle school mathematics teaching (M Ed); physics (MS); population and conservation biology (MS); science (M Ed, MA, MS, MST, PhD); software engineering (MS); wildlife ecology (MS). *Application deadline:* For fall admission, 6/15 priority date for domestic students, 6/1 priority date for international students; for spring admission, 10/15 priority date for domestic students, 10/1 priority date for international students. Applications are processed on a rolling basis. *Application fee:* $40 ($90 for international students). Electronic applications accepted. *Application Contact:* Dr. J. Michael Willoughby, Dean of Graduate School, 512-245-2581, Fax: 512-245-8365, E-mail: gradcollege@txstate.edu. *Dean,* Dr. Stephen Seidman, 512-245-2119, Fax: 512-245-8095, E-mail: ss76@txstate.edu.

Emmett and Miriam McCoy College of Business Administration Students: 191 full-time (85 women), 283 part-time (113 women); includes 116 minority (22 Black or African American, non-Hispanic/Latino; 32 Asian, non-Hispanic/Latino; 56 Hispanic/Latino; 1 Native Hawaiian or other Pacific Islander, non-Hispanic/Latino; 5 Two or more races, non-Hispanic/Latino), 27 international. Average age 29. 191 applicants, 85% accepted, 125 enrolled. *Faculty:* 42 full-time (16 women), 3 part-time/adjunct (0 women). Expenses: Contact institution. *Financial support:* In 2010–11, 115 students received support, including 9 research assistantships (averaging $5,080 per year), 27 teaching assistantships (averaging $5,108 per year); Federal Work-Study, institutionally sponsored loans, scholarships/grants, health care benefits, and unspecified assistantships also available. Support available to part-time students. Financial award application deadline: 4/1; financial award applicants required to submit FAFSA. In 2010, 168 master's awarded. *Degree program information:* Part-time programs available. Offers accounting (M Acy); accounting and information technology (MS); business administration (M Acy, MBA, MS). *Application deadline:* For fall admission, 6/1 for domestic and international students; for spring admission, 10/1 for domestic and international students. Applications are processed on a rolling basis. *Application fee:* $40 ($90 for international students). Electronic applications accepted. *Application Contact:* Dr. J. Michael Willoughby, Dean of Graduate School, 512-245-2581, Fax: 512-245-8365, E-mail: gradcollege@txstate.edu. *Dean,* Dr. Denise Smart, 512-245-2311, Fax: 512-245-8375, E-mail: ds37@txstate.edu.

TEXAS TECH UNIVERSITY, Lubbock, TX 79409

General Information State-supported, coed, university. CGS member. *Enrollment:* 31,637 graduate, professional, and undergraduate students; 4,009 full-time matriculated graduate/professional students (1,730 women), 2,166 part-time matriculated graduate/professional students (1,160 women). *Enrollment by degree level:* 670 first professional, 3,100 master's, 1,833 doctoral, 572 other advanced degrees. *Graduate faculty:* 797 full-time (247 women), 36 part-time/adjunct (8 women). Tuition, state resident: full-time $5496; part-time $228.99 per credit hour. Tuition, nonresident: full-time $12,936; part-time $538.99 per credit hour. *Required fees:* $2674; $36 per credit hour. $905 per semester. *Graduate housing:* Room and/or apartments available on a first-come, first-served basis to single students; on-campus housing not available to married students. Typical cost: $4100 per year ($7800 including board). Room and board charges vary according to board plan and housing facility selected. Housing application deadline: 4/1. *Student services:* Campus employment opportunities, campus safety program, career counseling, exercise/wellness program, free psychological counseling, international student services, low-cost health insurance, multicultural affairs office, services for students with disabilities, teacher training, writing training. *Library facilities:* Texas Tech Library plus 2 others. *Online resources:* library catalog, web page, access to other libraries' catalogs. *Collection:* 2.7 million titles, 60,297 serial subscriptions, 57,117 audiovisual materials. *Research affiliation:* U.S Dept of Agriculture (food safety; development and production in agriculture), U.S. Dept of Energy (research and development in wind energy), U.S. Dept of Defense / U.S. Army (pulsed power and nanotechnology for defense applications), Bayer Crop Science (cotton genetics and production), Howard Hughes Medical Institute (undergraduate research), National Cattlemen's Beef Association (development and production of beef).

Computer facilities: Computer purchase and lease plans are available. 3,000 computers available on campus for general student use. A campuswide network can be accessed from student residence rooms and from off campus. Online class registration, online degree plans, accounts, transcripts, schedules are available. *Web address:* http://www.ttu.edu/.

General Application Contact: Dr. Duane Crawford, Assistant Dean of Graduate Admissions and Recruitment, 806-742-2781 Ext. 231, Fax: 806-742-4038, E-mail: gradschool@ttu.edu.

GRADUATE UNITS

Center for Biotechnology and Genomics Students: 26 full-time (16 women), 3 part-time (2 women); includes 1 Asian, non-Hispanic/Latino, 25 international. Average age 22. 90 applicants, 23% accepted, 9 enrolled. *Faculty:* 1 full-time (0 women). Expenses: Contact institution. *Financial support:* In 2010–11, 11 students received support, including 1 research assistantship with partial tuition reimbursement available (averaging $9,602 per year), 1 teaching assistantship with partial tuition reimbursement available (averaging $9,724 per year). Financial award application deadline: 4/15; financial award applicants required to submit FAFSA. In 2010, 14 master's awarded. *Degree program information:* Part-time programs available. Offers biotechnology (MS). *Application deadline:* For fall admission, 6/1 priority date for domestic students, 1/15 priority date for international students; for spring admission, 9/1 priority date for domestic students, 6/15 priority date for international students. Applications are processed on a rolling basis. *Application fee:* $50 ($75 for international students). Electronic applications accepted. *Application Contact:* Jatindra Tripathy, Senior Research Associate, 806-742-3722 Ext. 229, Fax: 806-742-3788, E-mail: jatindra.tripathy@ttu.edu. *Advisor,* Dr. David B. Knaff, 806-742-0288, Fax: 806-742-1289, E-mail: david.knaff@ttu.edu.

Graduate School Students: 4,009 full-time (1,730 women), 2,166 part-time (1,160 women); includes 827 minority (159 Black or African American, non-Hispanic/Latino; 33 American Indian or Alaska Native, non-Hispanic/Latino; 81 Asian, non-Hispanic/Latino; 514 Hispanic/Latino; 2 Native Hawaiian or other Pacific Islander, non-Hispanic/Latino; 38 Two or more races, non-Hispanic/Latino), 1,431 international. Average age 28. 6,488 applicants, 45%

accepted, 1526 enrolled. *Faculty:* 760 full-time (234 women), 33 part-time/adjunct (8 women). Expenses: Contact institution. *Financial support:* In 2010–11, 2,192 students received support, including 485 research assistantships with partial tuition reimbursements available (averaging $4,649 per year), 571 teaching assistantships with partial tuition reimbursements available (averaging $5,768 per year); career-related internships or fieldwork, Federal Work-Study, institutionally sponsored loans, scholarships/grants, traineeships, health care benefits, and unspecified assistantships also available. Support available to part-time students. Financial award application deadline: 4/15; financial award applicants required to submit FAFSA. In 2010, 1,266 master's, 264 doctorates awarded. *Degree program information:* Part-time and evening/weekend programs available. Postbaccalaureate distance learning degree programs offered (minimal on-campus study). Offers heritage management (MS); interdisciplinary studies (MA, MS); museum science (MA). *Application deadline:* For fall admission, 6/1 priority date for domestic students, 1/15 for international students; for spring admission, 9/1 priority date for domestic students, 6/15 for international students. Applications are processed on a rolling basis. *Application fee:* $50 ($75 for international students). Electronic applications accepted. *Application Contact:* Shannon Samson, Coordinator of Graduate School Recruitment, 806-742-2781 Ext. 239, Fax: 806-742-4038, E-mail: gradschool@ttu.edu. *Dean,* Dr. Peggy Gordon Miller, 806-742-2781, Fax: 806-742-1746, E-mail: peggy.miller@ttu.edu.

College of Agricultural Sciences and Natural Resources Students: 245 full-time (110 women), 103 part-time (41 women); includes 5 Black or African American, non-Hispanic/Latino; 3 American Indian or Alaska Native, non-Hispanic/Latino; 1 Asian, non-Hispanic/Latino; 13 Hispanic/Latino; 3 Two or more races, non-Hispanic/Latino, 85 international. Average age 28. 257 applicants, 49% accepted, 87 enrolled. *Faculty:* 57 full-time (8 women), 7 part-time/adjunct (0 women). Expenses: Contact institution. *Financial support:* In 2010–11, 211 students received support, including 81 research assistantships with partial tuition reimbursements available (averaging $5,146 per year), 8 teaching assistantships with partial tuition reimbursements available (averaging $7,149 per year); career-related internships or fieldwork, Federal Work-Study, institutionally sponsored loans, scholarships/grants, traineeships, health care benefits, and unspecified assistantships also available. Support available to part-time students. Financial award application deadline: 4/15; financial award applicants required to submit FAFSA. In 2010, 63 master's, 31 doctorates awarded. *Degree program information:* Part-time programs available. Postbaccalaureate distance learning degree programs offered (minimal on-campus study). Offers agribusiness (MAB); agricultural and applied economics (MS, PhD); agricultural communication (MS); agricultural education (MS, Ed D); agricultural sciences and natural resources (M Agr, MAB, MLA, MS, Ed D, PhD); animal science (MS, PhD); crop science (MS); fisheries science (MS, PhD); food science (MS); horticulture (MS); landscape architecture (MLA); plant and soil science (PhD); plant protection (MS); range science (MS, PhD); soil science (MS); wildlife science (MS, PhD); wildlife, aquatic, and wildlands science and management (MS, PhD). *Application deadline:* For fall admission, 6/1 priority date for domestic students, 1/15 priority date for international students; for spring admission, 9/1 priority date for domestic students, 6/15 priority date for international students. Applications are processed on a rolling basis. *Application fee:* $50 ($75 for international students). Electronic applications accepted. *Application Contact:* Dr. Cindy Akers, Director, Student Services Center, 806-742-2808, Fax: 806-742-2836, E-mail: cindy.akers@ttu.edu. *Dean,* Dr. John M. Burns, 806-742-2810, E-mail: john.burns@ttu.edu.

College of Architecture Students: 104 full-time (24 women), 26 part-time (9 women); includes 35 minority (1 American Indian or Alaska Native, non-Hispanic/Latino; 4 Asian, non-Hispanic/Latino; 29 Hispanic/Latino; 1 Two or more races, non-Hispanic/Latino), 13 international. Average age 25. 104 applicants, 41% accepted, 32 enrolled. *Faculty:* 22 full-time (4 women), 1 part-time/adjunct (0 women). Expenses: Contact institution. *Financial support:* In 2010–11, 11 students received support, including 3 research assistantships with partial tuition reimbursements available (averaging $4,324 per year); career-related internships or fieldwork, Federal Work-Study, institutionally sponsored loans, scholarships/grants, traineeships, health care benefits, and unspecified assistantships also available. Support available to part-time students. Financial award application deadline: 4/15; financial award applicants required to submit FAFSA. In 2010, 60 master's awarded. *Degree program information:* Part-time programs available. Offers architecture (M Arch, MS, PhD); land-use planning, management, and design (PhD). *Application deadline:* For fall admission, 6/1 priority date for domestic students, 1/15 priority date for international students; for spring admission, 9/1 priority date for domestic students, 6/15 priority date for international students. Applications are processed on a rolling basis. *Application fee:* $50 ($75 for international students). Electronic applications accepted. *Application Contact:* Jess Schwintz, Coordinator of Academic Programs, 806-742-3169 Ext. 247, Fax: 806-742-1400, E-mail: jess.schwintz@ttu.edu. *Dean,* Dr. Andrew Vernooy, 806-742-3136, Fax: 806-742-1400, E-mail: andrew.vernoy@ttu.edu.

College of Arts and Sciences Students: 1,026 full-time (458 women), 271 part-time (146 women); includes 25 Black or African American, non-Hispanic/Latino; 5 American Indian or Alaska Native, non-Hispanic/Latino; 18 Asian, non-Hispanic/Latino; 95 Hispanic/Latino; 11 Two or more races, non-Hispanic/Latino, 407 international. Average age 28. 1,509 applicants, 37% accepted, 307 enrolled. *Faculty:* 309 full-time (86 women), 8 part-time/adjunct (2 women). Expenses: Contact institution. *Financial support:* In 2010–11, 953 students received support, including 113 research assistantships with partial tuition reimbursements available (averaging $6,072 per year), 359 teaching assistantships with partial tuition reimbursements available (averaging $6,386 per year); career-related internships or fieldwork, Federal Work-Study, institutionally sponsored loans, scholarships/grants, traineeships, health care benefits, and unspecified assistantships also available. Support available to part-time students. Financial award application deadline: 4/15; financial award applicants required to submit FAFSA. In 2010, 251 master's, 80 doctorates awarded. *Degree program information:* Part-time and evening/weekend programs available. Offers anthropology (MA); applied linguistics (MA); applied physics (MS); arts and sciences (MA, MPA, MS, PhD); atmospheric science (MS); biology (MS, PhD); chemistry (MS, PhD); classics (MA); clinical psychology (PhD); communication studies (MA); counseling psychology (MA, PhD); economics (MA, PhD); English (MA, PhD); environmental toxicology (MS, PhD); exercise and sport sciences (MS); experimental psychology (MA, PhD); geosciences (MS, PhD); German (MA); history (MA, PhD); mathematics (MA, MS, PhD); microbiology (MS); philosophy (MA); physics (MS, PhD); political science (MA, PhD); psychology (MA, PhD); Romance language (MA); Romance languages-French (MA); Romance languages-Spanish (MA); sociology (MA); Spanish (PhD); statistics (MS); technical communication (MA); technical communication and rhetoric (PhD); zoology (MS, PhD). *Application deadline:* For fall admission, 6/1 priority date for domestic students, 1/15 priority date for international students; for spring admission, 9/1 priority date for domestic students, 6/15 priority date for international students. Applications are processed on a rolling basis. *Application fee:* $50 ($75 for international students). Electronic applications accepted. *Application Contact:* Dr. Jorge Iber, Associate Dean, 806-742-3833, Fax: 806-742-3893, E-mail: jorge.iber@ttu.edu. *Dean,* Dr. Lawrence E. Schovanec, 806-742-3831, Fax: 806-742-3893, E-mail: lawrence.schovanec@ttu.edu.

College of Education Students: 328 full-time (243 women), 713 part-time (535 women); includes 228 minority (53 Black or African American, non-Hispanic/Latino; 4 American Indian or Alaska Native, non-Hispanic/Latino; 7 Asian, non-Hispanic/Latino; 157 Hispanic/Latino; 1 Native Hawaiian or other Pacific Islander, non-Hispanic/Latino; 6 Two or more races, non-Hispanic/Latino), 62 international. Average age 34. 643 applicants, 54% accepted, 274 enrolled. *Faculty:* 58 full-time (36 women), 4 part-time/adjunct (3 women). Expenses: Contact institution. *Financial support:* In 2010–11, 102 students received support, including 32 research assistantships with partial tuition reimbursements available (averaging $4,102 per year), 12 teaching assistantships with partial tuition reimbursements available (averaging $6,734 per year); career-related internships or fieldwork, Federal Work-Study, institutionally sponsored loans, scholarships/grants, traineeships, health care benefits, and unspecified assistantships also available. Support available to part-time students. Financial award application deadline: 4/15; financial award applicants required to submit FAFSA. In 2010, 163 master's, 42 doctorates awarded. *Degree program information:* Part-time programs available. Offers bilingual education (M Ed); counselor education (M Ed, PhD); curriculum and instruction (M Ed, PhD); education (M Ed, MS, Ed D, PhD); educational leadership (M Ed, Ed D); educational psychology (M Ed, PhD); elementary education (M Ed); higher

Texas Tech University (continued)

education (M Ed, Ed D); higher education: higher education research (PhD); instructional technology (M Ed, Ed D); instructional technology: distance education (M Ed); language and literacy education (M Ed); secondary education (M Ed); special education (M Ed, Ed D). *Application deadline:* For fall admission, 6/1 priority date for domestic students, 1/15 priority date for international students; for spring admission, 9/1 priority date for domestic students, 6/15 priority date for international students. Applications are processed on a rolling basis. *Application fee:* $50 ($75 for international students). Electronic applications accepted. *Application Contact:* Stephenie Allyn McDaniel, Administrative Assistant, 806-742-1988 Ext. 434, Fax: 806-742-2179, E-mail: stephenie.mcdaniel@ttu.edu. *Interim Dean,* Dr. Charles Ruch, 806-742-1998 Ext. 450, Fax: 806-742-2179, E-mail: charles.ruch@ttu.edu.

College of Human Sciences Students: 272 full-time (174 women), 97 part-time (47 women); includes 11 Black or African American, non-Hispanic/Latino; 4 American Indian or Alaska Native, non-Hispanic/Latino; 4 Asian, non-Hispanic/Latino; 33 Hispanic/Latino, 88 international. Average age 29. 321 applicants, 60% accepted, 111 enrolled. *Faculty:* 53 full-time (35 women), 3 part-time/adjunct (2 women). Expenses: Contact institution. *Financial support:* In 2010–11, 151 students received support, including 26 research assistantships with partial tuition reimbursements available (averaging $2,966 per year), 50 teaching assistantships with partial tuition reimbursements available (averaging $3,480 per year); career-related internships or fieldwork, Federal Work-Study, institutionally sponsored loans, scholarships/grants, traineeships, health care benefits, and unspecified assistantships also available. Support available to part-time students. Financial award application deadline: 4/15; financial award applicants required to submit FAFSA. In 2010, 88 master's, 28 doctorates awarded. *Degree program information:* Part-time and evening/weekend programs available. Postbaccalaureate distance learning degree programs offered (minimal on-campus study). Offers family and consumer sciences education (MS, PhD); gerontology (MS); hospitality administration (PhD); hospitality and retail management (MS); human development and family studies (MS, PhD); human sciences (MS, PhD); interior and environmental design (MS, PhD); marriage and family therapy (MS, PhD); nutritional sciences (MS, PhD); personal financial planning (MS, PhD). *Application deadline:* For fall admission, 6/1 priority date for domestic students, 1/15 priority date for international students; for spring admission, 9/1 priority date for domestic students, 6/15 priority date for international students. Applications are processed on a rolling basis. *Application fee:* $50 ($75 for international students). Electronic applications accepted. *Application Contact:* Dr. Lynn Huffman, Executive Associate Dean, 806-742-3031, Fax: 806-742-1849, E-mail: lynn.huffman@ttu.edu. *Dean,* Dr. Linda C. Hoover, 806-742-3031, Fax: 806-742-1849.

College of Mass Communications Students: 47 full-time (19 women), 19 part-time (11 women); includes 5 Hispanic/Latino, 17 international. Average age 29. 72 applicants, 49% accepted, 20 enrolled. *Faculty:* 11 full-time (3 women). Expenses: Contact institution. *Financial support:* In 2010–11, 36 students received support, including 6 research assistantships with partial tuition reimbursements available (averaging $5,949 per year), 12 teaching assistantships with partial tuition reimbursements available (averaging $5,482 per year); career-related internships or fieldwork, Federal Work-Study, institutionally sponsored loans, scholarships/grants, traineeships, health care benefits, and unspecified assistantships also available. Support available to part-time students. Financial award application deadline: 4/15; financial award applicants required to submit FAFSA. In 2010, 7 master's, 3 doctorates awarded. *Degree program information:* Part-time programs available. Offers mass communications (MA, PhD). *Application deadline:* For fall admission, 6/1 priority date for domestic students, 1/15 priority date for international students; for spring admission, 9/1 priority date for domestic students, 6/15 priority date for international students. Applications are processed on a rolling basis. *Application fee:* $50 ($75 for international students). Electronic applications accepted. *Application Contact:* Dr. Coy Callison, Associate Dean of Graduate Studies, 806-742-3385 Ext. 235, Fax: 806-742-1085, E-mail: coy.callison@ttu.edu. *Dean,* Dr. Jerry C. Hudson, 806-742-3385 Ext. 224, Fax: 806-742-1085, E-mail: jerry.hudson@ttu.edu.

College of Visual and Performing Arts Students: 196 full-time (93 women), 85 part-time (45 women); includes 9 Black or African American, non-Hispanic/Latino; 3 American Indian or Alaska Native, non-Hispanic/Latino; 3 Asian, non-Hispanic/Latino; 24 Hispanic/Latino; 4 Two or more races, non-Hispanic/Latino, 47 international. Average age 31. 245 applicants, 56% accepted, 74 enrolled. *Faculty:* 73 full-time (31 women), 2 part-time/adjunct (0 women). Expenses: Contact institution. *Financial support:* In 2010–11, 163 students received support, including 3 research assistantships with partial tuition reimbursements available (averaging $7,143 per year), 81 teaching assistantships with partial tuition reimbursements available (averaging $5,495 per year); career-related internships or fieldwork, Federal Work-Study, institutionally sponsored loans, scholarships/grants, traineeships, health care benefits, and unspecified assistantships also available. Support available to part-time students. Financial award application deadline: 4/15; financial award applicants required to submit FAFSA. In 2010, 47 master's, 22 doctorates awarded. *Degree program information:* Part-time programs available. Offers art (MFA); art education (MAE); art history (MA); arts (PhD); music (MM, DMA); music education (MM Ed); theatre arts (MA, MFA); visual and performing arts (MA, MAE, MFA, MM, MM Ed, DMA, PhD). *Application deadline:* For fall admission, 6/1 priority date for domestic students, 1/15 priority date for international students; for spring admission, 9/1 priority date for domestic students, 6/15 priority date for international students. Applications are processed on a rolling basis. *Application fee:* $50 ($75 for international students). Electronic applications accepted. *Application Contact:* Shannon Samson, Coordinator of Graduate School Recruitment, 806-742-2781 Ext. 239, Fax: 806-742-4038, E-mail: gradschool@ttu.edu. *Dean,* Dr. Carol Edwards, 806-742-0700, Fax: 806-742-0695.

Edward E. Whitacre Jr. College of Engineering Students: 585 full-time (111 women), 182 part-time (35 women); includes 8 Black or African American, non-Hispanic/Latino; 6 Asian, non-Hispanic/Latino; 25 Hispanic/Latino; 3 Two or more races, non-Hispanic/Latino, 510 international. Average age 26. 1,849 applicants, 35% accepted, 207 enrolled. *Faculty:* 107 full-time (18 women), 6 part-time/adjunct (1 woman). Expenses: Contact institution. *Financial support:* In 2010–11, 414 students received support, including 170 research assistantships with partial tuition reimbursements available (averaging $4,118 per year), 34 teaching assistantships with partial tuition reimbursements available (averaging $3,836 per year); career-related internships or fieldwork, Federal Work-Study, institutionally sponsored loans, scholarships/grants, traineeships, health care benefits, and unspecified assistantships also available. Support available to part-time students. Financial award application deadline: 4/15; financial award applicants required to submit FAFSA. In 2010, 213 master's, 51 doctorates awarded. *Degree program information:* Part-time programs available. Offers chemical engineering (MS Ch E, PhD); civil engineering (MSCE, PhD); computer science (MS, PhD); electrical engineering (MSEE, PhD); engineering (M Engr, MENVEGR, MS, MS Ch E, MSCE, MSEE, MSIE, MSME, MSMSE, MSPE, MSSEM, PhD); environmental engineering (MENVEGR); industrial engineering (MSIE, PhD); manufacturing systems engineering (MSMSE); mechanical engineering (MSME, PhD); petroleum engineering (MSPE, PhD); software engineering (MS); systems and engineering management (MSSEM, PhD). *Application deadline:* For fall admission, 6/1 priority date for domestic students, 1/15 priority date for international students; for spring admission, 9/1 priority date for domestic students, 6/15 priority date for international students. Applications are processed on a rolling basis. *Application fee:* $50 ($75 for international students). Electronic applications accepted. *Application Contact:* Dr. John E. Kobza, Senior Associate Dean, 806-742-3451, Fax: 806-742-3493, E-mail: john.kobza@ttu.edu. *Dean,* Dr. Albert Sacco, 806-742-3451, Fax: 806-742-3493, E-mail: al.sacco-jr@ttu.edu.

Jerry S. Rawls College of Business Administration Students: 317 full-time (122 women), 564 part-time (158 women); includes 146 minority (32 Black or African American, non-Hispanic/Latino; 6 American Indian or Alaska Native, non-Hispanic/Latino; 36 Asian, non-Hispanic/Latino; 65 Hispanic/Latino; 7 Two or more races, non-Hispanic/Latino), 147 international. Average age 28. 811 applicants, 72% accepted, 439 enrolled. *Faculty:* 71 full-time (10 women), 5 part-time/adjunct (0 women). Expenses: Contact institution. *Financial support:* In 2010–11, 130 students received support, including 54 research assistantships (averaging $8,800 per year), 24 teaching assistantships (averaging $18,000 per year); fellowships, career-related internships or fieldwork, Federal Work-Study, scholarships/grants, health care benefits, and unspecified assistantships also available. Financial award applicants required to submit FAFSA. In 2010, 310 master's, 7 doctorates awarded. *Degree program information:* Part-time and evening/weekend programs available. Offers accounting (PhD); agricultural business (MBA); audit/financial reporting (MSA); business administration (IMBA, MBA, MS, MSA, PhD, Certificate); business statistics (MBA, MS, PhD); entrepreneurship and innovation (MBA); finance (MS, PhD); general business (MBA); health organization management (MBA); healthcare management (MS); international business (MBA); management (PhD); management and leadership skills (MBA); management information systems (MBA, MS, PhD); marketing (PhD); production and operations management (MS, PhD); real estate (MBA); risk management (MS); taxation (MSA). *Application deadline:* For fall admission, 4/1 priority date for domestic students, 1/15 for international students; for spring admission, 9/1 priority date for domestic students, 6/15 for international students. Applications are processed on a rolling basis. *Application fee:* $50 ($75 for international students). Electronic applications accepted. *Application Contact:* Cynthia D. Barnes, Director, Graduate Services Center, 806-742-3184, Fax: 806-742-3958, E-mail: ba_grad@ttu.edu. *Dean,* Dr. Allen T. McInnes, 806-742-1300, Fax: 806-742-1092, E-mail: allen.mcinnes@ttu.edu.

School of Law Students: 663 full-time (273 women), 7 part-time (3 women); includes 154 minority (19 Black or African American, non-Hispanic/Latino; 6 American Indian or Alaska Native, non-Hispanic/Latino; 25 Asian, non-Hispanic/Latino; 102 Hispanic/Latino; 1 Native Hawaiian or other Pacific Islander, non-Hispanic/Latino; 1 Two or more races, non-Hispanic/Latino), 9 international. Average age 24. 1,186 applicants, 42% accepted, 244 enrolled. *Faculty:* 37 full-time (13 women), 3 part-time/adjunct (0 women). Expenses: Contact institution. *Financial support:* Federal Work-Study and scholarships/grants available. Financial award application deadline: 4/15; financial award applicants required to submit FAFSA. In 2010, 207 first professional degrees awarded. Offers law (JD). *Application deadline:* For fall admission, 2/1 priority date for domestic and international students. Applications are processed on a rolling basis. *Application fee:* $50. Electronic applications accepted. *Application Contact:* Terence Cook, Assistant Dean of Admissions and Recruitment, 806-742-3990 Ext. 273, Fax: 806-742-4617, E-mail: terence.cook@ttu.edu. *Dean,* Walter Burl Huffman, 806-742-3793, Fax: 806-742-4014, E-mail: walter.huffman@ttu.edu.

See Display on previous page and Close-Up on page 983.

TEXAS TECH UNIVERSITY HEALTH SCIENCES CENTER, Lubbock, TX 79430

General Information State-supported, coed, graduate-only institution. *Graduate housing:* On-campus housing not available.

GRADUATE UNITS

Graduate School of Biomedical Sciences Offers biochemistry and molecular genetics (MS, PhD); biomedical sciences (MS, PhD); biotechnology (MS); cell and molecular biology (MS, PhD); cell physiology and molecular biophysics (MS, PhD); medical microbiology (MS, PhD); pharmaceutical sciences (MS, PhD); pharmacology and neuroscience (MS, PhD). Electronic applications accepted.

School of Allied Health Sciences Students: 654 full-time (480 women), 304 part-time (179 women); includes 61 Black or African American, non-Hispanic/Latino; 6 American Indian or Alaska Native, non-Hispanic/Latino; 51 Asian, non-Hispanic/Latino; 131 Hispanic/Latino, 3 international. Average age 30. 2,042 applicants, 22% accepted, 458 enrolled. *Faculty:* 75 full-time (38 women). Expenses: Contact institution. *Financial support:* Fellowships, research assistantships, teaching assistantships, career-related internships or fieldwork, institutionally sponsored loans, scholarships/grants, and tuition waivers (full) available. Financial award application deadline: 9/1; financial award applicants required to submit FAFSA. In 2010, 202 master's, 67 doctorates awarded. Offers allied health sciences (MAT, MOT, MPAS, MRC, MS, Au D, DPT, PhD, Sc D); athletic training (MAT); clinical practice management (MS); molecular pathology (MS); occupational therapy (MOT); physical therapy (DPT, Sc D); physician assistant studies (MPAS); rehabilitation counseling (MRC); rehabilitation sciences (PhD); speech, language and hearing sciences (MS, Au D, PhD). *Application fee:* $35. Electronic applications accepted. *Application Contact:* Jeri Moravcik, Assistant Director of Admissions and Student Affairs, 806-743-3220, Fax: 806-743-2994, E-mail: jeri.moravcik@ttuhsc.edu. *Assistant Dean for Admissions and Student Affairs,* Lindsay R. Johnson, 806-743-3220, Fax: 806-743-2994, E-mail: lindsay.johnson@ttuhsc.edu.

School of Medicine Offers medicine (MD). Open only to residents of Texas, eastern New Mexico, and southwestern Oklahoma; MD/PhD offered jointly with Texas Tech University; JD/MD with School of Law. Electronic applications accepted.

School of Nursing *Degree program information:* Part-time programs available. Postbaccalaureate distance learning degree programs offered (minimal on-campus study). Offers acute care nurse practitioner (MSN, Certificate); administration (MSN); advanced practice (DNP); education (MSN); executive leadership (DNP); family nurse practitioner (MSN, Certificate); geriatric nurse practitioner (MSN, Certificate); pediatric nurse practitioner (MSN, Certificate).

TEXAS WESLEYAN UNIVERSITY, Fort Worth, TX 76105-1536

General Information Independent-religious, coed, comprehensive institution. *Enrollment:* 3,378 graduate, professional, and undergraduate students; 1,011 full-time matriculated graduate/professional students (577 women), 523 part-time matriculated graduate/professional students (318 women). *Enrollment by degree level:* 768 first professional, 673 master's, 93 doctoral. *Graduate faculty:* 83 full-time (38 women), 47 part-time/adjunct (16 women). Tuition and fees vary according to course level, degree level and program. *Graduate housing:* Room and/or apartments available on a first-come, first-served basis to single students; on-campus housing not available to married students. Typical cost: $4050 per year ($6910 including board). *Student services:* Campus employment opportunities, career counseling, exercise/wellness program, free psychological counseling, international student services, low-cost health insurance, multicultural affairs office, services for students with disabilities, teacher training, writing training. *Library facilities:* Eunice and James L. West Library plus 1 other. *Online resources:* library catalog, web page, access to other libraries' catalogs. *Collection:* 237,916 titles, 949 serial subscriptions, 5,700 audiovisual materials.

Computer facilities: 77 computers available on campus for general student use. A campuswide network can be accessed from student residence rooms and from off campus. Online class registration is available. *Web address:* http://www.txwes.edu/.

General Application Contact: Beth Hargrove, Coordinator of Graduate Admissions, 817-531-4930, Fax: 817-531-4261, E-mail: bhargrove@txwes.edu.

GRADUATE UNITS

Graduate Programs *Degree program information:* Part-time and evening/weekend programs available. Postbaccalaureate distance learning degree programs offered (no on-campus study). Offers business administration (MBA); education (M Ed, Ed D); health services administration (MS); management (MiM); marriage and family therapy (MSMFT); nurse anesthesia (MHS, MSNA, DNAP); professional counseling (MA); school counseling (MS). Electronic applications accepted.

School of Law *Degree program information:* Part-time and evening/weekend programs available. Offers law (JD). Electronic applications accepted.

TEXAS WOMAN'S UNIVERSITY, Denton, TX 76201

General Information State-supported, coed, primarily women, university. CGS member. *Enrollment:* 14,180 graduate, professional, and undergraduate students; 2,175 full-time matriculated graduate/professional students (1,883 women), 3,522 part-time matriculated graduate/professional students (3,117 women). *Enrollment by degree level:* 284 first professional, 4,640 master's, 773 doctoral. *Graduate faculty:* 415 full-time (309 women), 21 part-time/adjunct (17 women). Tuition, state resident: full-time $3834; part-time $213 per credit hour. Tuition, nonresident: full-time $9468; part-time $526 per credit hour. *Required fees:* $1247; $220 per credit hour. *Graduate housing:* Rooms and/or apartments available on a first-come, first-served basis to single and married students. Typical cost: $3410 per year ($6200 including board) for single students. Room and board charges vary according to board plan and housing facility selected. *Student services:* Campus employment opportunities, campus safety program, career counseling, exercise/wellness program, free psychological counseling, grant writing training, international student services, low-cost health insurance, multicultural affairs office, services for students with disabilities, teacher training, writing training. *Library facilities:* Blagg-Huey Library. *Online resources:* library catalog, web page, access to other libraries' catalogs. *Collection:* 686,056 titles, 46,164 serial subscriptions, 6,307 audiovisual materials.

Computer facilities: 1,000 computers available on campus for general student use. A campuswide network can be accessed from student residence rooms and from off campus. Online class registration is available. *Web address:* http://www.twu.edu/.

General Application Contact: Dr. Samuel Wheeler, Assistant Director of Admissions, 940-898-3188, Fax: 940-898-3081, E-mail: wheelersr@twu.edu.

GRADUATE UNITS

Graduate School Students: 2,175 full-time (1,883 women), 3,522 part-time (3,117 women); includes 1,098 Black or African American, non-Hispanic/Latino; 50 American Indian or Alaska Native, non-Hispanic/Latino; 468 Asian, non-Hispanic/Latino; 636 Hispanic/Latino, 235 international. Average age 35. 3,176 applicants, 63% accepted, 1310 enrolled. *Faculty:* 415 full-time (309 women), 21 part-time/adjunct (17 women). Expenses: Contact institution. *Financial support:* In 2010–11, 1,346 students received support, including 298 research assistantships (averaging $12,044 per year), 93 teaching assistantships (averaging $12,044 per year); career-related internships or fieldwork, Federal Work-Study, institutionally sponsored loans, scholarships/grants, traineeships, health care benefits, tuition waivers (partial), and unspecified assistantships also available. Support available to part-time students. Financial award application deadline: 3/1; financial award applicants required to submit FAFSA. In 2010, 1,508 master's, 209 doctorates awarded. *Degree program information:* Part-time and evening/weekend programs available. Postbaccalaureate distance learning degree programs offered. *Application deadline:* For fall admission, 7/1 priority date for domestic students, 3/1 for international students; for spring admission, 12/1 priority date for domestic students, 7/1 for international students. Applications are processed on a rolling basis. *Application fee:* $50 ($75 for international students). Electronic applications accepted. *Application Contact:* Dr. Samuel Wheeler, Assistant Director of Admissions, 940-898-3188, Fax: 940-898-3081, E-mail: wheelersr@twu.edu. *Vice Provost/Dean of the Graduate School,* Dr. Jennifer L. Martin, 940-898-3415, Fax: 940-898-3412, E-mail: gradschool@twu.edu.

College of Arts and Sciences Students: 858 full-time (709 women), 815 part-time (669 women); includes 464 Black or African American, non-Hispanic/Latino; 16 American Indian or Alaska Native, non-Hispanic/Latino; 142 Asian, non-Hispanic/Latino; 165 Hispanic/Latino, 103 international. Average age 35. 760 applicants, 70% accepted, 230 enrolled. *Faculty:* 138 full-time (83 women), 4 part-time/adjunct (2 women). Expenses: Contact institution. *Financial support:* In 2010–11, 365 students received support, including 162 research assistantships (averaging $12,208 per year), 69 teaching assistantships (averaging $12,208 per year); career-related internships or fieldwork, Federal Work-Study, institutionally sponsored loans, scholarships/grants, traineeships, health care benefits, and unspecified assistantships also available. Support available to part-time students. Financial award application deadline: 3/1; financial award applicants required to submit FAFSA. In 2010, 552 master's, 24 doctorates awarded. *Degree program information:* Part-time and evening/weekend programs available. Postbaccalaureate distance learning degree programs offered (minimal on-campus study). Offers art (MA, MFA); arts (MA, MFA, PhD); arts and sciences (MA, MBA, MFA, MHSM, MS, PhD, SSP); biology (MS); business administration (MBA); chemistry (MS); counseling psychology (MA, PhD); dance (MA, MFA, PhD); drama (MA); English (MA); government (MA); health systems management (MHSM); history (MA); mathematics (MA, MS); mathematics teaching (MS); molecular biology (PhD); music (MA); rhetoric (PhD); school psychology (PhD, SSP); sociology (MA, PhD); women's studies (MA, PhD). *Application deadline:* For fall admission, 7/1 priority date for domestic students, 3/1 for international students; for spring admission, 12/1 priority date for domestic students, 7/1 for international students. Applications are processed on a rolling basis. *Application fee:* $50 ($75 for international students). Electronic applications accepted. *Application Contact:* Dr. Samuel Wheeler, Assistant Director of Admissions, 940-898-3188, Fax: 940-898-3081, E-mail: wheelersr@twu.edu. *Dean,* Dr. Ann Staton, 940-898-3326, Fax: 940-898-3366, E-mail: cas@twu.edu.

College of Health Sciences Students: 953 full-time (841 women), 550 part-time (468 women); includes 150 Black or African American, non-Hispanic/Latino; 12 American Indian or Alaska Native, non-Hispanic/Latino; 12 Asian, non-Hispanic/Latino; 201 Hispanic/Latino, 82 international. Average age 30. 1,152 applicants, 44% accepted, 341 enrolled. *Faculty:* 113 full-time (82 women), 9 part-time/adjunct (7 women). Expenses: Contact institution. *Financial support:* In 2010–11, 468 students received support, including 85 research assistantships (averaging $11,499 per year), 15 teaching assistantships (averaging $11,499 per year); career-related internships or fieldwork, Federal Work-Study, institutionally sponsored loans, scholarships/grants, traineeships, health care benefits, and unspecified assistantships also available. Support available to part-time students. Financial award application deadline: 3/1; financial award applicants required to submit FAFSA. In 2010, 323 master's, 122 doctorates awarded. *Degree program information:* Part-time and evening/weekend programs available. Postbaccalaureate distance learning degree programs offered. Offers adapted physical education (MS, PhD); biomechanics (MS, PhD); coaching (MS); education of the deaf (MS); exercise and sports nutrition (MS); exercise physiology (MS, PhD); food science (MS); food systems administration (MS); health care administration (MHA); health sciences (MA, MHA, MOT, MS, DPT, Ed D, PhD); health studies (MS, Ed D, PhD); nutrition (MS, PhD); occupational therapy (MA, MOT, PhD); pedagogy (MS); physical therapy (DPT, PhD); speech/language pathology (MS); sport management (MS, PhD). *Application deadline:* For fall admission, 7/1 priority date for domestic students, 3/1 for international students; for spring admission, 12/1 priority date for domestic students, 7/1 for international students. Applications are processed on a rolling basis. *Application fee:* $50 ($75 for international students). Electronic applications accepted. *Application Contact:* Dr. Samuel Wheeler, Assistant Director of Admissions, 940-898-3188, Fax: 940-898-3081, E-mail: wheelersr@twu.edu. *Dean,* Dr. Jimmy Ishee, 940-898-2852, Fax: 940-898-2853, E-mail: jishee@twu.edu.

College of Nursing Students: 77 full-time (72 women), 799 part-time (746 women); includes 212 Black or African American, non-Hispanic/Latino; 5 American Indian or Alaska Native, non-Hispanic/Latino; 138 Asian, non-Hispanic/Latino; 70 Hispanic/Latino, 18 international. Average age 39. 379 applicants, 76% accepted, 219 enrolled. *Faculty:* 98 full-time (94 women), 7 part-time/adjunct (all women). Expenses: Contact institution. *Financial support:* In 2010–11, 134 students received support, including 7 research assistantships (averaging $12,942 per year), 5 teaching assistantships (averaging $12,942 per year); career-related internships or fieldwork, Federal Work-Study, institutionally sponsored loans, scholarships/grants, traineeships, health care benefits, and unspecified assistantships also available. Support available to part-time students. Financial award application deadline: 3/1; financial award applicants required to submit FAFSA. In 2010, 149 master's, 38 doctorates awarded. *Degree program information:* Part-time programs available. Postbaccalaureate distance learning degree programs offered. Offers acute care nurse practitioner (MS); adult health clinical nurse specialist (MS); adult health nurse practitioner (MS); child health clinical nurse specialist (MS); clinical nurse leader (MS); family nurse practitioner (MS); health systems management (MS); nursing education (MS); nursing practice (DNP); nursing science (PhD); pediatric nurse practitioner (MS); women's health clinical nurse specialist (MS); women's health nurse practitioner (MS). *Application deadline:* For fall admission, 5/1 priority date for domestic students, 3/1 for international students; for spring admission, 9/15 priority date for domestic students, 7/1 for international students. Applications are processed on a rolling basis. *Application fee:* $50 ($75 for international students). Electronic applications accepted. *Application Contact:* Dr. Samuel Wheeler, Assistant Director of Admissions, 940-898-3188, Fax: 940-898-3081, E-mail: wheelersr@twu.edu. *Interim Dean,* Dr. Patricia Holden-Huchton, 940-898-2401, Fax: 940-898-2437, E-mail: nursing@twu.edu.

College of Professional Education Students: 287 full-time (261 women), 1,358 part-time (1,234 women); includes 272 Black or African American, non-Hispanic/Latino; 17 American Indian or Alaska Native, non-Hispanic/Latino; 57 Asian, non-Hispanic/Latino; 200 Hispanic/Latino, 32 international. Average age 37. 565 applicants, 68% accepted, 307 enrolled. *Faculty:* 66 full-time (50 women), 1 (woman) part-time/adjunct. Expenses: Contact institution. *Financial support:* In 2010–11, 378 students received support, including 44 research assistantships (averaging $12,164 per year), 4 teaching assistantships (averaging $12,164 per year); career-related internships or fieldwork, Federal Work-Study, institutionally sponsored loans, scholarships/grants, traineeships, health care benefits, and unspecified assistantships also available. Support available to part-time students. Financial award application deadline: 3/1; financial award applicants required to submit FAFSA. In 2010, 484 master's, 25 doctorates awarded. *Degree program information:* Part-time and evening/weekend programs available. Offers administration (M Ed, MA); child development (MS); counseling and development (MS); early childhood development and education (PhD); early childhood education (M Ed, MA, MS); family studies (MS, PhD); family therapy (MS, PhD); library science (MA, MLS, PhD); professional education (M Ed, MA, MAT, MLS, MS, Ed D, PhD); reading education (M Ed, MA, MS, Ed D, PhD); special education (M Ed, MA, PhD); teaching (MAT); teaching, learning, and curriculum (M Ed). *Application deadline:* For fall admission, 7/1 priority date for domestic students, 3/1 for international students; for spring admission, 12/1 priority date for domestic students, 7/1 for international students. Applications are processed on a rolling basis. *Application fee:* $50 ($75 for international students). Electronic applications accepted. *Application Contact:* Dr. Samuel Wheeler, Assistant Director of Admissions, 940-898-3188, Fax: 940-898-3081, E-mail: wheelersr@twu.edu. *Dean,* Dr. Nan L. Restine, 940-898-2202, Fax: 940-898-2209, E-mail: cope@twu.edu.

THOMAS COLLEGE, Waterville, ME 04901-5097

General Information Independent, coed, comprehensive institution. *Graduate housing:* On-campus housing not available.

GRADUATE UNITS

Graduate School *Degree program information:* Part-time and evening/weekend programs available. Offers business (MBA); computer technology education (MS); education (MS); human resource management (MBA). Electronic applications accepted.

THOMAS EDISON STATE COLLEGE, Trenton, NJ 08608-1176

General Information State-supported, coed, comprehensive institution. CGS member. *Enrollment:* 18,736 graduate, professional, and undergraduate students; 1,014 part-time matriculated graduate/professional students (648 women). *Enrollment by degree level:* 829 master's, 185 other advanced degrees. *Graduate housing:* On-campus housing not available. *Student services:* Services for students with disabilities.

Computer facilities: A campuswide network can be accessed from off campus. Online class registration, undergraduate and Nursing students are able to schedule appointments online with their advisors are available. *Web address:* http://www.tesc.edu/.

General Application Contact: David Hoftiezer, Director of Admissions, 888-442-8372, Fax: 609-984-8447, E-mail: admissions@tesc.edu.

GRADUATE UNITS

Heavin School of Arts and Sciences Students: 281 part-time (172 women); includes 46 Black or African American, non-Hispanic/Latino; 1 American Indian or Alaska Native, non-Hispanic/Latino; 6 Asian, non-Hispanic/Latino; 18 Hispanic/Latino, 2 international. Average age 41. Expenses: Contact institution. *Financial support:* Applicants required to submit FAFSA. In 2010, 36 master's, 15 other advanced degrees awarded. *Degree program information:* Part-time programs available. Postbaccalaureate distance learning degree programs offered (no on-campus study). Offers arts and sciences (MAEL, MALS, Graduate Certificate); educational leadership (MAEL); homeland security (Graduate Certificate); liberal studies (MALS); online learning and teaching (Graduate Certificate). *Application deadline:* For fall admission, 8/15 priority date for domestic and international students; for winter admission, 11/15 priority date for domestic and international students; for spring admission, 2/15 priority date for domestic and international students. Applications are processed on a rolling basis. *Application fee:* $75. Electronic applications accepted. *Application Contact:* David Hoftiezer, Director of Admissions, 888-442-8372, Fax: 609-984-8447, E-mail: admissions@tesc.edu. *Dean, Heavin School of Arts and Sciences,* Dr. Susan Davenport, 609-984-1130, Fax: 609-984-0740, E-mail: info@tesc.edu.

School of Applied Science and Technology Students: 22 part-time (15 women); includes 3 Black or African American, non-Hispanic/Latino; 2 Asian, non-Hispanic/Latino; 3 Hispanic/Latino. Average age 42. Expenses: Contact institution. *Financial support:* Applicants required to submit FAFSA. In 2010, 3 Graduate Certificates awarded. *Degree program information:* Part-time programs available. Postbaccalaureate distance learning degree programs offered (no on-campus study). Offers applied science and technology (Graduate Certificate); clinical trials management (Graduate Certificate). *Application deadline:* For fall admission, 8/15 priority date for domestic and international students; for winter admission, 11/15 priority date for domestic and international students; for spring admission, 2/15 priority date for domestic students, 1/15 priority date for international students. Applications are processed on a rolling basis. *Application fee:* $75. Electronic applications accepted. *Application Contact:* David Hoftiezer, Director of Admissions, 888-442-8372, Fax: 609-984-8447, E-mail: admissions@tesc.edu. *Dean, School of Applied Science and Technology,* Dr. Marcus Tillery, 609-984-1130, Fax: 609-984-3898, E-mail: info@tesc.edu.

School of Business and Management Students: 445 part-time (205 women); includes 96 Black or African American, non-Hispanic/Latino; 2 American Indian or Alaska Native, non-Hispanic/Latino; 16 Asian, non-Hispanic/Latino; 28 Hispanic/Latino, 8 international. Average age 41. Expenses: Contact institution. *Financial support:* Applicants required to submit FAFSA. In 2010, 62 master's, 8 other advanced degrees awarded. *Degree program information:* Part-time programs available. Postbaccalaureate distance learning degree programs offered. Offers business and management (MSHRM, MSM, Graduate Certificate); human resources management (MSHRM, Graduate Certificate); management (MSM); organizational leadership (Graduate Certificate); public service leadership (Graduate Certificate). *Application deadline:* For fall admission, 8/15 priority date for domestic and international students; for winter admission, 11/15 priority date for domestic and international students; for spring admission, 2/15 priority date for domestic and international students. Applications are processed on a rolling basis. *Application fee:* $75. Electronic applications accepted. *Application Contact:* David Hoftiezer, Director of Admissions, 888-442-8372, Fax: 609-984-8447, E-mail: admissions@tesc.edu. *Dean, School of Business and Management,* Dr. Susan Gilbert, 609-984-1130, Fax: 609-984-3898, E-mail: infor@tesc.edu.

School of Nursing Students: 297 part-time (275 women); includes 49 Black or African American, non-Hispanic/Latino; 1 American Indian or Alaska Native, non-Hispanic/Latino; 12 Asian, non-Hispanic/Latino; 13 Hispanic/Latino; 2 Native Hawaiian or other Pacific Islander, non-Hispanic/Latino, 1 international. Average age 46. Expenses: Contact institution. *Financial support:* Applicants required to submit FAFSA. In 2010, 15 master's, 1 other advanced degree awarded. *Degree program information:* Part-time programs available. Postbaccalaureate distance learning degree programs offered (no on-campus study). Offers nurse educator (Post-Master's Certificate); nursing (MSN, Post-Master's Certificate). *Application deadline:* For fall admission, 8/15 for domestic and international students; for winter admission, 11/15 for domestic and international students; for spring admission, 2/15 for domestic and international students. *Application fee:* $75. Electronic applications accepted. *Application Contact:* David Hoftiezer, Director of Admissions, 888-442-8372, Fax: 609-984-8447, E-mail: admissions@tesc.edu. *Dean, School of Nursing,* Dr. Susan O'Brien, 609-633-6460, Fax: 609-292-8279, E-mail: nursing@tesc.edu.

THOMAS JEFFERSON SCHOOL OF LAW, San Diego, CA 92110-2905

General Information Independent, coed, graduate-only institution. *Graduate housing:* Rooms and/or apartments available to single and married students. Housing application deadline: 5/1.

GRADUATE UNITS

Graduate Programs

Professional Program *Degree program information:* Part-time and evening/weekend programs available. Offers law (JD). Electronic applications accepted.

THOMAS JEFFERSON UNIVERSITY, Philadelphia, PA 19107

General Information Independent, coed, university. CGS member. *Enrollment:* 1,173 full-time matriculated graduate/professional students (592 women), 115 part-time matriculated graduate/professional students (63 women). *Enrollment by degree level:* 1,035 first professional, 96 master's, 138 doctoral, 19 other advanced degrees. *Graduate housing:* Rooms and/or apartments available to single and married students. *Student services:* Campus employment opportunities, campus safety program, career counseling, child daycare facilities, exercise/wellness program, free psychological counseling, grant writing training, international student services, low-cost health insurance, multicultural affairs office, services for students with disabilities, writing training. *Library facilities:* Scott Memorial Library plus 1 other. *Online resources:* web page. *Research affiliation:* Christiana Care Health Services (biomedical research), Lankenau Institute for Medical Research (biomedical research), A. I. du Pont for Children Nemours (biomedical research), University of Delaware (biomedical research).

Computer facilities: A campuswide network can be accessed from off campus. *Web address:* http://www.jefferson.edu/.

General Application Contact: Marc E. Stearns, Director of Admissions, 215-503-0155, Fax: 215-503-9920, E-mail: jcgs-info@jefferson.edu.

GRADUATE UNITS

Jefferson College of Graduate Studies Students: 138 full-time (77 women), 115 part-time (63 women); includes 36 minority (16 Black or African American, non-Hispanic/Latino; 19 Asian, non-Hispanic/Latino; 1 Native Hawaiian or other Pacific Islander, non-Hispanic/Latino), 38 international. Average age 29. 508 applicants, 29% accepted, 101 enrolled. *Faculty:* 173 full-time (45 women), 23 part-time/adjunct (8 women). Expenses: Contact institution. *Financial support:* In 2010–11, 166 students received support, including 120 fellowships with full tuition reimbursements available (averaging $54,723 per year); Federal Work-Study, institutionally sponsored loans, scholarships/grants, and traineeships also available. Support available to part-time students. Financial award application deadline: 5/1; financial award applicants required to submit FAFSA. In 2010, 23 master's, 20 doctorates, 6 other advanced degrees awarded. *Degree program information:* Part-time and evening/weekend programs available. Postbaccalaureate distance learning degree programs offered (no on-campus study). Offers biochemistry and molecular biology (PhD); biomedical sciences (MS); cell and developmental biology (MS, PhD); clinical research, public health, and research management (Certificate); flexible-entry pathway (PhD); genetics (PhD); immunology and microbial pathogenesis (PhD); microbiology (MS); molecular pharmacology and structural biology (PhD); molecular physiology and biophysics (PhD); neuroscience (PhD); pharmacology (MS); tissue engineering and regenerative medicine (PhD). *Application deadline:* For fall admission, 1/15 priority date for domestic and international students; for winter admission, 6/1 priority date for international students; for spring admission, 9/1 priority date for international students. Applications are processed on a rolling basis. *Application fee:* $50. Electronic applications accepted. *Application Contact:* Marc E. Stearns, Director of Admissions, 215-503-0155, Fax: 215-503-9920, E-mail: jcgs-info@jefferson.edu. *Dean,* Dr. Gerald B. Grunwald, 215-503-4191, Fax: 215-503-6690, E-mail: gerald.grunwald@jefferson.edu.

Jefferson College of Health Professions Offers bioscience technologies (MS); family therapy (MS); health professions (Pharm D, MS, DPT); nursing (MS); occupational therapy (MS); physical therapy (MS, DPT).

School of Pharmacy Offers pharmacy (Pharm D).

Jefferson Medical College Students: 1,035 full-time (515 women); includes 325 minority (21 Black or African American, non-Hispanic/Latino; 2 American Indian or Alaska Native, non-Hispanic/Latino; 253 Asian, non-Hispanic/Latino; 49 Hispanic/Latino), 50 international. Average age 23. 9,761 applicants, 5% accepted, 260 enrolled. *Faculty:* 767 full-time (224 women), 46 part-time/adjunct (23 women). Expenses: Contact institution. *Financial support:* In 2010–11, 856 students received support. Federal Work-Study and institutionally sponsored loans available. Financial award application deadline: 3/1; financial award applicants required to submit FAFSA. In 2010, 256 first professional degrees awarded. Offers medicine (MD). *Application deadline:* For fall admission, 11/15 for domestic and international students. Applications are processed on a rolling basis. *Application fee:* $80. Electronic applications accepted. *Application Contact:* Dr. Clara Callahan, Dean for Admissions, 215-955-6983, Fax: 215-923-6939, E-mail: clara.callahan@jefferson.edu. *Interim Dean,* Dr. Mark Tykowcinski, 215-955-6980, Fax: 215-923-6939.

Jefferson School of Population Health 169 applicants, 71% accepted, 66 enrolled. *Faculty:* 9 full-time (5 women), 14 part-time/adjunct (6 women). Expenses: Contact institution. *Financial support:* In 2010–11, 3 students received support. Federal Work-Study and scholarships/grants available. *Degree program information:* Part-time and evening/weekend programs available. Postbaccalaureate distance learning degree programs offered (no on-campus study). Offers applied health economics and outcomes research (MS, PhD); behavioral health science (PhD); chronic care management (MS, PhD, Certificate); health policy (MS, Certificate); healthcare quality and safety (MS, PhD); public health (MPH, Certificate). *Application deadline:* For fall admission, 8/31 for domestic and international students; for spring admission, 12/31 for domestic and international students. Applications are processed on a rolling basis. *Application fee:* $25. Electronic applications accepted. *Application Contact:* April L. Smith, Admissions/Programs Coordinator, 215-503-5305, Fax: 215-923-6939, E-mail: april.smith@jefferson.edu. *Associate Dean, Academic and Student Affairs,* Dr. Caroline Golab, 215-503-8467, Fax: 215-923-6939, E-mail: caroline.golab@jefferson.edu.

THOMAS M. COOLEY LAW SCHOOL, Lansing, MI 48901-3038

General Information Independent, coed, graduate-only institution. *Enrollment by degree level:* 3,931 first professional, 70 other advanced degrees. *Graduate faculty:* 127 full-time (53 women), 196 part-time/adjunct (78 women). *Tuition:* Full-time $30,604; part-time $2186 per credit hour. *Required fees:* $40. *Graduate housing:* On-campus housing not available. *Student services:* Campus employment opportunities, career counseling, multicultural affairs office, services for students with disabilities, writing training. *Library facilities:* Thomas E. Brennan Law School Library plus 5 others. *Online resources:* library catalog, web page. *Collection:* 317,625 titles, 8,042 serial subscriptions, 3,233 audiovisual materials.

Computer facilities: 200 computers available on campus for general student use. A campuswide network can be accessed. Online class registration, Online financial aid information, online ledger are available. *Web address:* http://www.cooley.edu/.

General Application Contact: Stephanie Gregg, Dean of Admissions, 517-371-5140, Fax: 517-334-5718, E-mail: greggs@cooley.edu.

GRADUATE UNITS

Graduate Programs Students: 718 full-time (342 women), 3,283 part-time (1,607 women); includes 1,071 minority (532 Black or African American, non-Hispanic/Latino; 19 American Indian or Alaska Native, non-Hispanic/Latino; 207 Asian, non-Hispanic/Latino; 219 Hispanic/Latino; 10 Native Hawaiian or other Pacific Islander, non-Hispanic/Latino; 84 Two or more races, non-Hispanic/Latino), 215 international. Average age 26. 4,922 applicants, 83% accepted, 1583 enrolled. *Faculty:* 127 full-time (53 women), 196 part-time/adjunct (78 women). Expenses: Contact institution. *Financial support:* In 2010–11, 2,187 students received support. Federal Work-Study and scholarships/grants available. Support available to part-time students. Financial award applicants required to submit FAFSA. In 2010, 918 first professional degrees awarded. *Degree program information:* Part-time and evening/weekend programs available. Postbaccalaureate distance learning degree programs offered. Offers corporate law and finance (LL M); general, self-directed (LL M); insurance (LL M); intellectual property (LL M); law (JD); taxation (LL M); U. S. law for foreign attorneys (LL M). *Application deadline:* For fall admission, 9/1 for domestic and international students; for winter admission, 1/1 for domestic and international students; for spring admission, 5/1 for domestic and international students. Applications are processed on a rolling basis. *Application fee:* $0. Electronic applications accepted. *Application Contact:* Stephanie Gregg, Assistant Dean of Admissions, 517-371-5140, Fax: 517-334-5718, E-mail: greggs@cooley.edu. *President and Dean,* Don LeDuc, 517-371-5140.

THOMAS MORE COLLEGE, Crestview Hills, KY 41017-3495

General Information Independent-religious, coed, comprehensive institution. *Enrollment:* 1,886 graduate, professional, and undergraduate students; 124 full-time matriculated graduate/professional students (58 women), 30 part-time matriculated graduate/professional students (14 women). *Enrollment by degree level:* 154 master's. *Graduate faculty:* 11 full-time (5 women), 4 part-time/adjunct (2 women). *Tuition:* Full-time $11,691; part-time $570 per credit hour. Tuition and fees vary according to program. *Student services:* Career counseling, exercise/wellness program, free psychological counseling, international student services, multicultural affairs office, services for students with disabilities, teacher training. *Library facilities:* Thomas More Library. *Online resources:* library catalog, web page, access to other libraries' catalogs. *Collection:* 112,103 titles, 456 serial subscriptions, 2,435 audiovisual materials.

Computer facilities: 95 computers available on campus for general student use. A campuswide network can be accessed from student residence rooms and from off campus. Online class registration is available. *Web address:* http://www.thomasmore.edu/.

General Application Contact: Nathan Hartman, Director of Lifelong Learning, 859-344-3333, Fax: 859-344-3686, E-mail: nathan.hartman@thomasmore.edu.

GRADUATE UNITS

Program in Business Administration Students: 117 full-time (53 women); includes 12 minority (5 Black or African American, non-Hispanic/Latino; 3 Asian, non-Hispanic/Latino; 3 Hispanic/Latino; 1 Native Hawaiian or other Pacific Islander, non-Hispanic/Latino). Average age 33. 47 applicants, 91% accepted, 41 enrolled. *Faculty:* 6 full-time (1 woman), 2 part-time/adjunct (0 women). Expenses: Contact institution. *Financial support:* In 2010–11, 13 students received support. Federal Work-Study, institutionally sponsored loans, and scholarships/grants available. Financial award application deadline: 3/15; financial award applicants required to submit FAFSA. In 2010, 75 master's awarded. Offers business administration (MBA). *Application deadline:* Applications are processed on a rolling basis. *Application fee:* $25. Electronic applications accepted. *Application Contact:* Judy Bautista, Enrollment Manager, 859-341-4554, Fax: 859-578-3589, E-mail: judy.bautista@apollogrp.edu. *Director of Lifelong Learning,* Nathan Hartman, 859-344-3333, Fax: 859-344-3686, E-mail: nathan.hartman@thomasmore.edu.

Program in Teaching Students: 7 full-time (5 women), 30 part-time (14 women). Average age 32. 28 applicants, 96% accepted, 23 enrolled. *Faculty:* 5 full-time (4 women), 2 part-time/adjunct (both women). Expenses: Contact institution. *Financial support:* In 2010–11, 10 students received support. Federal Work-Study, institutionally sponsored loans, and scholarships/grants available. Financial award application deadline: 3/15; financial award applicants required to submit FAFSA. In 2010, 12 master's awarded. Offers teaching (MAT). *Application deadline:* For fall admission, 6/1 for domestic students. Applications are processed on a rolling basis. *Application fee:* $0. Electronic applications accepted. *Application Contact:* Joyce Hamberg, 859-344-3404, Fax: 859-344-3345, E-mail: joyce.hamberg@thomasmore.edu. *Director,* Joyce Hamberg, 859-344-3404, Fax: 859-344-3345, E-mail: joyce.hamberg@thomasmore.edu.

THOMAS UNIVERSITY, Thomasville, GA 31792-7499

General Information Independent, coed, comprehensive institution. *Graduate housing:* Room and/or apartments available on a first-come, first-served basis to single students; on-campus housing not available to married students. Housing application deadline: 8/1.

GRADUATE UNITS

Department of Business Administration *Degree program information:* Part-time programs available. Offers business administration (MBA). Electronic applications accepted.

Department of Education *Degree program information:* Part-time programs available. Offers education (M Ed). Electronic applications accepted.

Department of Human Services *Degree program information:* Part-time programs available. Offers community counseling (MSCC); rehabilitation counseling (MRC). Electronic applications accepted.

Department of Nursing *Degree program information:* Part-time programs available. Offers nursing (MSN). Electronic applications accepted.

THOMPSON RIVERS UNIVERSITY, Kamloops, BC V2C 5N3, Canada

General Information Province-supported, coed, comprehensive institution.

GRADUATE UNITS

Program in Business Administration *Degree program information:* Part-time programs available. Offers business administration (MBA).

Program in Education *Degree program information:* Part-time programs available. Offers education (M Ed).

Program in Environmental Science Offers environmental science (MS).

Program in Social Work Offers social work (MSW).

THUNDERBIRD SCHOOL OF GLOBAL MANAGEMENT, Glendale, AZ 85306-6000

General Information Independent, coed, graduate-only institution. *Enrollment by degree level:* 1,286 master's. *Graduate faculty:* 48 full-time (13 women). *Tuition:* Full-time $43,080; part-time $1436 per credit hour. *Required fees:* $300. Part-time tuition and fees vary according to program. *Graduate housing:* Room and/or apartments available on a first-come, first-served basis to single students; on-campus housing not available to married students. Typical cost: $4275 per year ($6360 including board). Room and board charges vary according to campus/location. Housing application deadline: 7/15. *Student services:* Campus employment opportunities, campus safety program, career counseling, exercise/wellness program, international student services, low-cost health insurance, multicultural affairs office, services for students with disabilities, writing training. *Library facilities:* The Merle A. Hinrichs International Business Information Centre plus 1 other. *Online resources:* library catalog, web page, access to other libraries' catalogs. *Collection:* 32,000 titles, 562 serial subscriptions, 2,464 audiovisual materials. *Research affiliation:* Wiley (publishing).

Computer facilities: 97 computers available on campus for general student use. A campuswide network can be accessed from student residence rooms and from off campus. Online class registration, My Thunderbird, campus intranet are available. *Web address:* http://www.thunderbird.edu/.

General Application Contact: Jay Bryant, Director of Admissions, 602-978-7294, Fax: 602-439-5432, E-mail: jay.bryant@thunderbird.edu.

GRADUATE UNITS

Executive MBA Program–Glendale Students: 89 part-time (20 women); includes 3 Black or African American, non-Hispanic/Latino; 1 American Indian or Alaska Native, non-Hispanic/Latino; 10 Asian, non-Hispanic/Latino; 5 Two or more races, non-Hispanic/Latino, 17 international. Average age 37. *Faculty:* 48 full-time (13 women). Expenses: Contact institution. *Financial support:* In 2010–11, 25 students received support. Application deadline: 6/7. In 2010, 48 master's awarded. *Degree program information:* Part-time and evening/weekend programs available. Offers global management (MBA). *Application deadline:* For fall admission, 6/10 priority date for domestic students, 4/30 priority date for international students. Applications are processed on a rolling basis. *Application fee:* $125. Electronic applications accepted. *Associate Vice President, EMBA Programs,* Barbara Carpenter, 602-978-7921, Fax: 602-978-7463, E-mail: barbara.carpenter@thunderbird.edu.

Full-Time MBA Programs Students: 538 full-time (153 women); includes 7 Black or African American, non-Hispanic/Latino; 1 American Indian or Alaska Native, non-Hispanic/Latino; 17 Asian, non-Hispanic/Latino; 14 Hispanic/Latino; 19 Two or more races, non-Hispanic/Latino, 237 international. 512 applicants, 80% accepted, 226 enrolled. *Faculty:* 48 full-time (13 women). Expenses: Contact institution. *Financial support:* In 2010–11, 501 students received support. Federal Work-Study and scholarships/grants available. Support available to part-time students. Financial award application deadline: 2/15; financial award applicants required to submit FAFSA. In 2010, 360 master's awarded. *Degree program information:* Part-time and evening/weekend programs available. Postbaccalaureate distance learning degree programs offered (minimal on-campus study). Offers business administration (GMBA, MBA). *Application deadline:* For spring admission, 6/10 for domestic students, 4/30 for international students. Applications are processed on a rolling basis. *Application fee:* $125. Electronic applications accepted. *Application Contact:* Jay Bryant, Director of Admissions, 602-978-7294, Fax: 602-439-5432, E-mail: jay.bryant@thunderbird.edu. *Vice President,* Dr. Kay Keck, 602-978-7077, Fax: 602-547-1356, E-mail: kay.keck@thunderbird.edu.

Global MBA—Latin American Managers Program Students: 286 part-time (77 women); includes 1 Asian, non-Hispanic/Latino; 3 Hispanic/Latino, 259 international. Average age 31. 217 applicants, 73% accepted, 159 enrolled. *Faculty:* 48 full-time (13 women). Expenses: Contact institution. *Financial support:* Scholarships/grants available. Financial award application deadline: 4/30. In 2010, 163 master's awarded. *Degree program information:* Part-time and evening/weekend programs available. Postbaccalaureate distance learning degree programs offered. Offers global business administration—Latin American management (GMBA). Offered jointly with Instituto Tecnológico y de Estudios Superiores de Monterrey. *Application deadline:* For spring admission, 4/25 priority date for domestic and international students. *Application fee:* $125. *Application Contact:* Dr. Bert Valencia, Vice President, 602-978-7534, Fax: 602-978-7729, E-mail: globalmba@thunderbird.edu. *Vice President,* Dr. Bert Valencia, 602-978-7534, Fax: 602-978-7729, E-mail: globalmba@thunderbird.edu.

GMBA—On Demand Program Students: 132 part-time (50 women); includes 3 Black or African American, non-Hispanic/Latino; 1 American Indian or Alaska Native, non-Hispanic/Latino; 6 Asian, non-Hispanic/Latino; 1 Hispanic/Latino; 5 Two or more races, non-Hispanic/Latino, 17 international. Average age 32. 81 applicants, 79% accepted, 46 enrolled. *Faculty:* 48 full-time (13 women). Expenses: Contact institution. *Financial support:* Scholarships/grants available. Financial award application deadline: 2/15. In 2010, 62 master's awarded. *Degree program information:* Part-time programs available. Postbaccalaureate distance learning degree programs offered (minimal on-campus study). Offers global business administration (GMBA). *Application deadline:* For fall admission, 6/10 for domestic students, 4/30 for international students. *Application fee:* $125. *Application Contact:* Jay Bryant, Director of Admissions, 602-978-7294, Fax: 602-439-5432, E-mail: jay.bryant@thunderbird.edu. *Vice President,* Dr. Bert Valencia, 602-978-7534, Fax: 602-978-7729, E-mail: globalmba@thunderbird.edu.

Master's Programs in Global Management Students: 139 full-time (74 women); includes 2 Black or African American, non-Hispanic/Latino; 1 American Indian or Alaska Native, non-Hispanic/Latino; 5 Asian, non-Hispanic/Latino; 2 Hispanic/Latino; 5 Two or more races, non-Hispanic/Latino, 68 international. 153 applicants, 45% accepted, 69 enrolled. *Faculty:* 48 full-time (13 women). Expenses: Contact institution. *Financial support:* Career-related internships or fieldwork, Federal Work-Study, scholarships/grants, and unspecified assistantships available. In 2010, 55 master's awarded. Offers global affairs and management (MA); global management (MS). *Application deadline:* For fall admission, 6/10 for domestic students, 4/30 for international students. *Application fee:* $125. *Application Contact:* Jay Bryant, Director of Admissions, 602-978-7294, Fax: 602-439-5432, E-mail: jay.bryant@thunderbird.edu. *Unit Head,* Dr. Glenn Fong, 602-978-7156.

TIFFIN UNIVERSITY, Tiffin, OH 44883-2161

General Information Independent, coed, comprehensive institution. *Enrollment:* 4,940 graduate, professional, and undergraduate students; 326 full-time matriculated graduate/professional students (190 women), 673 part-time matriculated graduate/professional students (416 women). *Enrollment by degree level:* 999 master's. *Graduate faculty:* 37 full-time (15 women), 48 part-time/adjunct (19 women). *Graduate housing:* Room and/or apartments available on a first-come, first-served basis to single students; on-campus housing not available to married students. Typical cost: $5550 per year. Housing application deadline: 8/1. *Student services:* Campus employment opportunities, campus safety program, career counseling, exercise/wellness program, free psychological counseling, international student services, low-cost health insurance, multicultural affairs office, services for students with disabilities. *Library facilities:* Pfeiffer Library. *Online resources:* library catalog, web page, access to other libraries' catalogs. *Collection:* 40,691 titles, 6,003 serial subscriptions, 579 audiovisual materials.

Computer facilities: Computer purchase and lease plans are available. 195 computers available on campus for general student use. A campuswide network can be accessed from student residence rooms and from off campus. Online class registration is available. *Web address:* http://www.tiffin.edu/.

General Application Contact: Kristi Krintzline, Director of Graduate Admissions and Student Services, 800-968-6446 Ext. 3445, Fax: 419-443-5002, E-mail: krintzlineka@tiffin.edu.

GRADUATE UNITS

Program in Business Administration Students: 186 full-time (93 women), 250 part-time (124 women). Average age 31. 532 applicants, 86% accepted, 229 enrolled. *Faculty:* 18 full-time (9 women), 22 part-time/adjunct (6 women). Expenses: Contact institution. *Financial support:* In 2010–11, 94 students received support. Available to part-time students. Application deadline: 7/31. In 2010, 340 master's awarded. *Degree program information:* Part-time and evening/weekend programs available. Postbaccalaureate distance learning degree programs offered (no on-campus study). Offers finance (MBA); general management (MBA); healthcare administration (MBA); human resources (MBA); international business (MBA); leadership (MBA); marketing (MBA); sports management (MBA). *Application deadline:* For fall admission, 8/15 for domestic students, 8/1 for international students; for spring admission, 1/9 for domestic students, 12/1 for international students. Applications are processed on a rolling basis. *Application fee:* $0. Electronic applications accepted. *Application Contact:* Kristi Krintzline, Director of Graduate Admissions and Student Services, 800-968-6446 Ext. 3445, Fax: 419-443-5002, E-mail: krintzlineka@tiffin.edu. *Dean of the School of Business,* Dr. Lillian Schumacher, 419-448-3053, Fax: 419-443-5002, E-mail: schumacherlb@tiffin.edu.

Program in Criminal Justice Students: 120 full-time (84 women), 312 part-time (205 women). Average age 31. 185 applicants, 58% accepted, 104 enrolled. *Faculty:* 13 full-time (3 women), 20 part-time/adjunct (9 women). Expenses: Contact institution. *Financial support:* In 2010–11, 64 students received support. Available to part-time students. Application deadline: 7/31. In 2010, 340 master's awarded. *Degree program information:* Part-time and evening/weekend programs available. Postbaccalaureate distance learning degree programs offered (no on-campus study). Offers crime analysis (MSCJ); criminal behavior (MSCJ); forensic psychology (MSCJ); homeland security administration (MSCJ); justice administration (MSCJ). *Application deadline:* For fall admission, 9/3 for domestic students, 8/1 for international students; for spring admission, 1/9 priority date for domestic students, 12/1 for international students. Applications are processed on a rolling basis. *Application fee:* $0. Electronic applications accepted. *Application Contact:* Kristi Krintzline, Director of Graduate Admissions, 800-968-6446 Ext. 3445, Fax: 419-443-5002, E-mail: krintzlineka@tiffin.edu. *Dean of Criminal Justice and Social Sciences,* Dr. Tim Shaw, 419-448-3305, Fax: 419-443-5002, E-mail: shawta@tiffin.edu.

Program in Humanities Students: 20 full-time (13 women), 111 part-time (87 women). 112 applicants, 79% accepted, 34 enrolled. *Faculty:* 6 full-time (3 women), 6 part-time/adjunct (4 women). Expenses: Contact institution. In 2010, 340 master's awarded. *Degree program information:* Part-time and evening/weekend programs available. Postbaccalaureate distance learning degree programs offered (no on-campus study). Offers humanities (MH). *Application deadline:* For fall admission, 9/1 for domestic students; for spring admission, 1/9 for domestic students. *Application fee:* $0. *Application Contact:* Kristi Krintzline, Director of Graduate Admissions, 800-968-6446 Ext. 3445, Fax: 419-443-5002, E-mail: krintzlineka@tiffin.edu. *Dean of Arts and Sciences,* Miriam Fankhauser, 419-448-3426, Fax: 419-443-5002, E-mail: mfankhau@tiffin.edu.

TORONTO SCHOOL OF THEOLOGY, Toronto, ON M5S 2C3, Canada

General Information Independent-religious, coed, graduate-only institution.

GRADUATE UNITS

Graduate Programs Postbaccalaureate distance learning degree programs offered (minimal on-campus study). Offers theology (M Div, M Mus, M Rel, MA, MAMS, MPS, MRE, MTS, Th M, D Min, PhD, Th D). Federation of seven Toronto-area theological colleges; basic degrees offered through the member colleges jointly with the University of Toronto. Electronic applications accepted.

TOURO COLLEGE, New York, NY 10010

General Information Independent, coed, comprehensive institution.

GRADUATE UNITS

Graduate School of Jewish Studies *Degree program information:* Part-time programs available. Offers Jewish studies (MA).

Jacob D. Fuchsberg Law Center *Degree program information:* Part-time and evening/weekend programs available. Offers law (JD); U.S. law for foreign lawyers (LL M).

School of Health Sciences Offers acupuncture (MS); occupational therapy (MS); oriental medicine (MSOM); physical therapy (DPT); public health (MPH); speech-language pathology (MS).

TOURO UNIVERSITY, Vallejo, CA 94592

General Information Independent, coed, graduate-only institution. *Enrollment by degree level:* 930 first professional, 399 master's. *Graduate faculty:* 93 full-time (52 women), 55 part-time/adjunct (28 women). *Graduate housing:* On-campus housing not available. *Student services:* Campus safety program, career counseling, exercise/wellness program, free psychological counseling, low-cost health insurance, multicultural affairs office, services for students with disabilities, teacher training. *Library facilities:* Touro Library plus 1 other. *Online resources:* library catalog, web page, access to other libraries' catalogs. *Research affiliation:* National Health Institute (cardiac arrest in teens), Genetech (cancer), Siemans/UCSF (cancer), NIH (diabetes).

Computer facilities: 65 computers available on campus for general student use. A campuswide network can be accessed from off campus. Online class registration is available. *Web address:* http://www.tu.edu/.

General Application Contact: Dr. Harold Borrero, Registrar, 707-638-5242, Fax: 707-638-5267, E-mail: harold.borrero@tu.edu.

GRADUATE UNITS

Graduate Programs Students: 1,329 full-time (805 women). 6,914 applicants, 12% accepted, 503 enrolled. *Faculty:* 93 full-time (52 women), 55 part-time/adjunct (28 women). Expenses: Contact institution. *Financial support:* In 2010–11, 1,236 students received support, including 119 fellowships (averaging $1,535 per year), 24 research assistantships (averaging $3,686 per year), 13 teaching assistantships (averaging $4,058 per year); Federal Work-Study and scholarships/grants also available. Support available to part-time students. Financial award applicants required to submit FAFSA. In 2010, 229 first professional degrees, 103 master's awarded. *Degree program information:* Part-time and evening/weekend programs available. Offers education (MA); health sciences (MPH); medical health sciences (MS); osteopathic medicine (DO); pharmacy (Pharm D); physician assistant studies (MS). *Application deadline:* For fall admission, 3/15 for domestic students; for winter admission, 12/1 for domestic students. Applications are processed on a rolling basis. *Application fee:* $100. Electronic applications accepted. *Application Contact:* Steve Davis, Associate Director of Admissions, 707-638-5270, Fax: 707-638-5250, E-mail: steven.davis@tu.edu.

TOWSON UNIVERSITY, Towson, MD 21252-0001

General Information State-supported, coed, university. CGS member. *Enrollment:* 21,840 graduate, professional, and undergraduate students; 1,265 full-time matriculated graduate/professional students (895 women), 2,338 part-time matriculated graduate/professional students (1,770 women). *Enrollment by degree level:* 3,286 master's, 154 doctoral, 163 other advanced degrees. *Graduate faculty:* 338 full-time (193 women), 143 part-time/adjunct (83 women). Tuition, state resident: part-time $324 per credit. Tuition, nonresident: part-time $681 per credit. *Required fees:* $95 per term. *Graduate housing:* Room and/or apartments available on a first-come, first-served basis to single students; on-campus housing not available to married students. Typical cost: $5520 per year ($9614 including board). Room and board charges vary according to board plan and campus/location. Housing application deadline: 5/2. *Student services:* Campus employment opportunities, campus safety program, career counseling, child daycare facilities, exercise/wellness program, free psychological counseling, international student services, low-cost health insurance, multicultural affairs office, services for students with disabilities, teacher training, writing training. *Library facilities:* Cook Library. *Online resources:* library catalog, web page, access to other libraries' catalogs. *Collection:* 639,983 titles, 7,108 serial subscriptions, 17,156 audiovisual materials.

Computer facilities: 1,200 computers available on campus for general student use. A campuswide network can be accessed from student residence rooms and from off campus. Online class registration is available. *Web address:* http://www.towson.edu/.

General Application Contact: Fran Musotto, Information Contact, 410-704-2501, Fax: 410-704-4675, E-mail: grads@towson.edu.

GRADUATE UNITS

Arts Integration Institute Students: 22 part-time (21 women); includes 2 minority (both Black or African American, non-Hispanic/Latino). Expenses: Contact institution. In 2010, 7 Certificates awarded. Offers arts integration (Certificate). Program offered jointly with The Johns Hopkins University and University of Maryland, College Park. *Application Contact:* Susan Rotkovitz, Program Director, 410-704-3658, E-mail: srotkovitz@towson.edu. *Program Director,* Susan Rotkovitz, 410-704-3658, E-mail: srotkovitz@towson.edu.

Baltimore Hebrew Institute Students: 19 full-time (10 women), 28 part-time (17 women); includes 4 minority (all Black or African American, non-Hispanic/Latino), 2 international. Expenses: Contact institution. In 2010, 9 master's, 1 doctorate, 1 other advanced degree awarded. Offers Jewish communal service (MAJCS); Jewish education (MAJE, Certificate); Jewish studies (MAJS). *Application Contact:* Erika Schon, Director, 410-704-7117, E-mail: eschon@towson.edu. *Director,* Erika Schon, 410-704-7117, E-mail: eschon@towson.edu.

Joint Program in Accounting and Business Advisory Services Students: 31 full-time (21 women), 33 part-time (26 women); includes 9 minority (7 Black or African American, non-Hispanic/Latino; 1 American Indian or Alaska Native, non-Hispanic/Latino; 1 Asian, non-Hispanic/Latino), 19 international. Average age 29. Expenses: Contact institution. In 2010, 16 master's awarded. *Degree program information:* Part-time and evening/weekend programs available. Offers accounting and business advisory services (MS). Program offered jointly with University of Baltimore. *Application deadline:* Applications are processed on a rolling basis. *Application fee:* $50. Electronic applications accepted. *Application Contact:* Carol Abraham, The Graduate School, 410-704-6163, Fax: 401-704-4675, E-mail: grads@towson.edu. *Graduate Program Director,* Martin Freedman, 410-704-4143, E-mail: mfreedman@towson.edu.

Master's Program in Applied Information Technology Students: 111 full-time (25 women), 232 part-time (62 women); includes 122 minority (75 Black or African American, non-Hispanic/Latino; 4 American Indian or Alaska Native, non-Hispanic/Latino; 31 Asian, non-Hispanic/Latino; 11 Hispanic/Latino; 1 Native Hawaiian or other Pacific Islander, non-Hispanic/Latino), 85 international. Expenses: Contact institution. In 2010, 75 master's, 9 doctorates, 74 other advanced degrees awarded. Offers applied information technology (MS, PhD); database management systems (Postbaccalaureate Certificate); information security and assurance (Postbaccalaureate Certificate); information systems management (Graduate Certificate); Internet applications development (Postbaccalaureate Certificate); networking technologies (Postbaccalaureate Certificate); software engineering (Postbaccalaureate Certificate). *Application Contact:* Mike O'Leary, Graduate Program Director, 410-704-4757, E-mail: moleary@towson.edu. *Graduate Program Director,* Mike O'Leary, 410-704-4757, E-mail: moleary@towson.edu.

Program in Applied and Industrial Mathematics Students: 12 full-time (4 women), 22 part-time (8 women); includes 2 minority (1 Asian, non-Hispanic/Latino; 1 Hispanic/Latino), 10

Towson University (continued)

international. Average age 30. Expenses: Contact institution. *Financial support:* Teaching assistantships with full tuition reimbursements, unspecified assistantships available. Financial award application deadline: 4/1; financial award applicants required to submit FAFSA. In 2010, 4 master's awarded. *Degree program information:* Part-time and evening/weekend programs available. Offers applied and industrial mathematics (MS). *Application deadline:* Applications are processed on a rolling basis. *Application fee:* $50. Electronic applications accepted. *Application Contact:* 410-704-2501, Fax: 410-704-4675, E-mail: grads@towson.edu. *Graduate Program Director,* Xuezhang Hou, 410-704-2578, Fax: 410-704-4149, E-mail: xhou@towson.edu.

Program in Applied Gerontology Students: 6 full-time (all women), 7 part-time (6 women); includes 4 minority (2 Black or African American, non-Hispanic/Latino; 2 Hispanic/Latino), 2 international. Average age 36. Expenses: Contact institution. *Financial support:* Application deadline: 4/1. In 2010, 6 master's awarded. Offers applied gerontology (MS, Certificate). *Application deadline:* Applications are processed on a rolling basis. *Application fee:* $50. Electronic applications accepted. *Application Contact:* 410-704-2501, Fax: 410-704-4675, E-mail: grads@towson.edu. *Graduate Program Director,* Mary McSweeney-Feld, 410-704-4219, E-mail: mmcsweeneyfeld@towson.edu.

Program in Applied Physics Students: 2 full-time (0 women), 3 part-time (2 women), 3 international. Expenses: Contact institution. Offers applied physics (MS). *Application Contact:* Dr. Raj Kolagani, Dean, 410-704-3134, E-mail: rkolagani@towson.edu. *Dean,* Dr. Raj Kolagani, 410-704-3134, E-mail: rkolagani@towson.edu.

Program in Art Education Students: 1 full-time (0 women), 31 part-time (29 women); includes 3 minority (2 Black or African American, non-Hispanic/Latino; 1 Asian, non-Hispanic/Latino). Average age 35. Expenses: Contact institution. *Financial support:* Federal Work-Study and unspecified assistantships available. Financial award application deadline: 4/1; financial award applicants required to submit FAFSA. In 2010, 13 master's awarded. *Degree program information:* Part-time and evening/weekend programs available. Offers art education (M Ed). *Application deadline:* Applications are processed on a rolling basis. *Application fee:* $50. Electronic applications accepted. *Application Contact:* 410-704-2501, Fax: 410-704-4675, E-mail: grads@towson.edu. *Graduate Program Director,* Kay Broadwater, 410-704-3689, Fax: 410-704-2810, E-mail: kbroadwater@towson.edu.

Program in Audiology Students: 31 full-time (30 women), 7 part-time (6 women); includes 6 minority (2 Black or African American, non-Hispanic/Latino; 1 Asian, non-Hispanic/Latino; 3 Hispanic/Latino). Average age 25. Expenses: Contact institution. *Financial support:* In 2010–11, 4 fellowships with tuition reimbursements, 1 research assistantship with tuition reimbursement were awarded; traineeships, tuition waivers (partial), and unspecified assistantships also available. Financial award application deadline: 4/1; financial award applicants required to submit FAFSA. In 2010, 11 doctorates awarded. Offers audiology (Au D). *Application deadline:* For fall admission, 2/1 for domestic students. *Application fee:* $50. Electronic applications accepted. *Application Contact:* 410-704-2501, Fax: 410-704-4675, E-mail: grads@towson.edu. *Graduate Program Director,* Dr. Diana Emanuel, 410-704-2417, Fax: 410-704-4131, E-mail: demanuel@towson.edu.

Program in Autism Studies Students: 1 (woman) full-time, 7 part-time (all women); includes 2 minority (1 Black or African American, non-Hispanic/Latino; 1 American Indian or Alaska Native, non-Hispanic/Latino). Expenses: Contact institution. In 2010, 2 Certificates awarded. Offers autism studies (Certificate). *Application Contact:* Janet DeLany, Dean, 410-704-2371, E-mail: jdelany@towson.edu. *Dean,* Janet DeLany, 410-704-2371, E-mail: jdelany@towson.edu.

Program in Biology Students: 32 full-time (13 women), 26 part-time (18 women); includes 16 minority (11 Black or African American, non-Hispanic/Latino; 4 Asian, non-Hispanic/Latino; 1 Two or more races, non-Hispanic/Latino), 5 international. Average age 27. Expenses: Contact institution. *Financial support:* In 2010–11, 4 research assistantships with full tuition reimbursements (averaging $11,000 per year), 12 teaching assistantships with full tuition reimbursements (averaging $11,000 per year) were awarded; career-related internships or fieldwork, Federal Work-Study, and unspecified assistantships also available. Support available to part-time students. Financial award application deadline: 4/1; financial award applicants required to submit FAFSA. In 2010, 28 master's awarded. *Degree program information:* Part-time and evening/weekend programs available. Offers biology (MS). *Application deadline:* Applications are processed on a rolling basis. *Application fee:* $50. Electronic applications accepted. *Application Contact:* 410-704-2501, Fax: 410-704-4675, E-mail: grads@towson.edu. *Graduate Program Co-Director,* Joel Snodgrass, 410-704-5033, Fax: 410-704-2405, E-mail: jsnodgrass@towson.edu.

Program in Child Life, Administration and Family Collaboration Students: 13 full-time (all women), 2 part-time (both women); includes 2 minority (1 Black or African American, non-Hispanic/Latino; 1 Hispanic/Latino), 1 international. Expenses: Contact institution. Offers child life, administration and family collaboration (MS). *Application Contact:* Lisa Martinelli Beasley, Dean, 410-704-3766, E-mail: lmartinelli@towson.edu. *Dean,* Lisa Martinelli Beasley, 410-704-3766, E-mail: lmartinelli@towson.edu.

Program in Clinical Psychology Students: 101 full-time (83 women), 29 part-time (18 women); includes 22 minority (13 Black or African American, non-Hispanic/Latino; 5 Asian, non-Hispanic/Latino; 3 Hispanic/Latino; 1 Two or more races, non-Hispanic/Latino), 1 international. Average age 26. Expenses: Contact institution. *Financial support:* Federal Work-Study and unspecified assistantships available. Financial award application deadline: 4/1; financial award applicants required to submit FAFSA. In 2010, 45 master's awarded. *Degree program information:* Part-time and evening/weekend programs available. Offers clinical psychology (MA). *Application deadline:* For fall admission, 2/1 for domestic and international students. *Application fee:* $50. Electronic applications accepted. *Application Contact:* The Graduate School, 410-704-2501, Fax: 410-704-4675, E-mail: grads@towson.edu. *Graduate Program Director,* Dr. Elizabeth Katz, 410-704-3201, Fax: 410-704-3800, E-mail: ekatz@towson.edu.

Program in Clinician-Administrator Transition Students: 15 full-time (all women), 10 part-time (all women); includes 6 minority (4 Black or African American, non-Hispanic/Latino; 1 Asian, non-Hispanic/Latino; 1 Hispanic/Latino), 2 international. Expenses: Contact institution. *Financial support:* Application deadline: 4/1. In 2010, 1 Certificate awarded. Offers clinician-administrator transition (Certificate). *Application deadline:* Applications are processed on a rolling basis. *Application fee:* $50. Electronic applications accepted. *Application Contact:* 410-704-2501, Fax: 410-704-4675, E-mail: grads@towson.edu. *Graduate Program Director,* Marcie Weinstein, 410-704-4049, E-mail: mweinstein@towson.edu.

Program in Communications Management Students: 10 full-time (5 women), 28 part-time (23 women); includes 9 minority (all Black or African American, non-Hispanic/Latino), 1 international. Average age 29. Expenses: Contact institution. *Financial support:* Application deadline: 4/1. In 2010, 8 master's awarded. Offers communications management (MS). *Application deadline:* For fall admission, 1/15 for domestic students. *Application fee:* $50. Electronic applications accepted. *Application Contact:* 410-704-2501, Fax: 410-704-4675, E-mail: grads@towson.edu. *Graduate Program Director,* Theodora Carabas, 410-704-4855, E-mail: tcarabas@towson.edu.

Program in Computer Science Students: 82 full-time (27 women), 51 part-time (9 women); includes 22 minority (15 Black or African American, non-Hispanic/Latino; 5 Asian, non-Hispanic/Latino; 1 Hispanic/Latino; 1 Two or more races, non-Hispanic/Latino), 63 international. Average age 28. Expenses: Contact institution. *Financial support:* Federal Work-Study and unspecified assistantships available. Support available to part-time students. Financial award application deadline: 4/1; financial award applicants required to submit FAFSA. In 2010, 36 master's awarded. *Degree program information:* Part-time and evening/weekend programs available. Offers computer science (MS). *Application deadline:* Applications are processed on a rolling basis. *Application fee:* $50. Electronic applications accepted. *Application Contact:* 410-704-2501, Fax: 410-704-4675, E-mail: grads@towson.edu. *Graduate Program Director,* Dr. Yanggon Kim, 410-704-3782, E-mail: ykim@towson.edu.

Program in Counseling Psychology Students: 1 (woman) full-time, 7 part-time (all women); includes 1 minority (Black or African American, non-Hispanic/Latino). Average age 43. Expenses: Contact institution. *Financial support:* Application deadline: 4/1. In 2010, 1 CAS awarded. *Degree program information:* Part-time and evening/weekend programs available. Offers counseling psychology (CAS). *Application fee:* $50. *Application Contact:* The Graduate School, 410-704-2501, Fax: 410-704-4675, E-mail: grads@towson.edu. *Graduate Program Director,* Christa Schmidt, 410-704-3063, E-mail: ckschmidt@towson.edu.

Program in Early Childhood Education Students: 15 full-time (all women), 187 part-time (180 women); includes 46 minority (37 Black or African American, non-Hispanic/Latino; 3 American Indian or Alaska Native, non-Hispanic/Latino; 3 Asian, non-Hispanic/Latino; 1 Hispanic/Latino; 1 Native Hawaiian or other Pacific Islander, non-Hispanic/Latino; 1 Two or more races, non-Hispanic/Latino), 4 international. Average age 36. Expenses: Contact institution. *Financial support:* Federal Work-Study and unspecified assistantships available. Financial award application deadline: 4/1; financial award applicants required to submit FAFSA. In 2010, 63 master's, 1 other advanced degree awarded. *Degree program information:* Part-time and evening/weekend programs available. Offers early childhood education (M Ed, CAS). *Application deadline:* Applications are processed on a rolling basis. *Application fee:* $50. Electronic applications accepted. *Application Contact:* 410-704-2460, Fax: 410-704-4675, E-mail: ecedgrads@towson.edu. *Graduate Program Director,* Dr. Edyth Wheeler, 410-704-2460, Fax: 410-704-2733, E-mail: ejwheeler@towson.edu.

Program in Elementary Education Students: 79 part-time (72 women); includes 13 minority (6 Black or African American, non-Hispanic/Latino; 1 Asian, non-Hispanic/Latino; 5 Hispanic/Latino; 1 Native Hawaiian or other Pacific Islander, non-Hispanic/Latino). Average age 28. Expenses: Contact institution. *Financial support:* Federal Work-Study and unspecified assistantships available. Financial award application deadline: 4/1; financial award applicants required to submit FAFSA. In 2010, 7 master's awarded. *Degree program information:* Part-time and evening/weekend programs available. Offers elementary education (M Ed). *Application deadline:* Applications are processed on a rolling basis. *Application fee:* $50. Electronic applications accepted. *Application Contact:* Rachel Carter, The Graduate School, 410-704-5388, Fax: 410-704-2733, E-mail: rcarter@towson.edu. *Graduate Program Director,* Linda Emerick, 410-704-4251, Fax: 410-704-2733, E-mail: eledmed@towson.edu.

Program in Environmental Science Students: 5 full-time (3 women), 29 part-time (16 women); includes 5 minority (1 Black or African American, non-Hispanic/Latino; 1 American Indian or Alaska Native, non-Hispanic/Latino; 2 Asian, non-Hispanic/Latino; 1 Hispanic/Latino), 2 international. Average age 31. Expenses: Contact institution. *Financial support:* Application deadline: 4/1. In 2010, 11 master's awarded. *Degree program information:* Part-time and evening/weekend programs available. Offers environmental science (MS, Certificate). *Application deadline:* Applications are processed on a rolling basis. *Application fee:* $50. Electronic applications accepted. *Application Contact:* 410-704-2501, Fax: 410-704-4675, E-mail: grads@towson.edu. *Graduate Program Director,* Dr. Steven Lev, 410-704-2744, Fax: 410-704-2604, E-mail: slev@towson.edu.

Program in Family-Professional Collaboration Students: 13 full-time (all women), 5 part-time (all women); includes 2 minority (1 Black or African American, non-Hispanic/Latino; 1 Hispanic/Latino), 2 international. Average age 25. Expenses: Contact institution. Offers family-professional collaboration (Certificate). *Application fee:* $50. *Application Contact:* The Graduate School, 410-704-2501, Fax: 410-704-4675, E-mail: grads@towson.edu. *Graduate Program Director,* Karen Eskow, 410-704-5851, E-mail: keskow@towson.edu.

Program in Forensic Science Students: 39 full-time (31 women), 9 part-time (7 women); includes 16 minority (12 Black or African American, non-Hispanic/Latino; 1 Asian, non-Hispanic/Latino; 2 Hispanic/Latino; 1 Two or more races, non-Hispanic/Latino), 2 international. Average age 26. Expenses: Contact institution. In 2010, 12 master's awarded. Offers forensic science (MS). *Application Contact:* Mark Profili, Graduate Program Director, 410-704-2668, E-mail: mprofili@towson.edu. *Graduate Program Director,* Mark Profili, 410-704-2668, E-mail: mprofili@towson.edu.

Program in Geography and Environmental Planning Students: 8 full-time (4 women), 26 part-time (17 women); includes 2 minority (both Black or African American, non-Hispanic/Latino), 1 international. Average age 30. Expenses: Contact institution. *Financial support:* In 2010–11, 1 teaching assistantship with full tuition reimbursement (averaging $4,000 per year) was awarded; Federal Work-Study and unspecified assistantships also available. Financial award application deadline: 4/1; financial award applicants required to submit FAFSA. In 2010, 3 master's awarded. *Degree program information:* Part-time and evening/weekend programs available. Offers geography and environmental planning (MA). *Application deadline:* Applications are processed on a rolling basis. *Application fee:* $50. Electronic applications accepted. *Application Contact:* 410-704-2501, Fax: 410-704-4675, E-mail: grads@towson.edu. *Graduate Program Director,* Martin Roberge, 410-704-5011, Fax: 410-704-3880, E-mail: mroberge@towson.edu.

Program in Health Science Students: 20 full-time (14 women), 94 part-time (86 women); includes 29 minority (25 Black or African American, non-Hispanic/Latino; 2 Asian, non-Hispanic/Latino; 1 Hispanic/Latino; 1 Two or more races, non-Hispanic/Latino), 6 international. Average age 31. Expenses: Contact institution. *Financial support:* Federal Work-Study and unspecified assistantships available. Financial award application deadline: 4/1; financial award applicants required to submit FAFSA. In 2010, 20 master's awarded. *Degree program information:* Part-time and evening/weekend programs available. Offers health science (MS). *Application deadline:* Applications are processed on a rolling basis. *Application fee:* $50. Electronic applications accepted. *Application Contact:* 410-704-2501, Fax: 410-704-4675, E-mail: grads@towson.edu. *Director,* Dr. Susan Radius, 410-704-4216, Fax: 410-704-4670, E-mail: sradius@towson.edu.

Program in Humanities Students: 3 full-time (2 women), 13 part-time (8 women); includes 5 minority (3 Black or African American, non-Hispanic/Latino; 1 American Indian or Alaska Native, non-Hispanic/Latino; 1 Two or more races, non-Hispanic/Latino). Average age 26. Expenses: Contact institution. *Financial support:* Application deadline: 4/1. In 2010, 4 master's awarded. *Degree program information:* Part-time and evening/weekend programs available. Offers humanities (MA). *Application deadline:* Applications are processed on a rolling basis. *Application fee:* $50. Electronic applications accepted. *Application Contact:* 410-704-2501, Fax: 410-704-4675, E-mail: grads@towson.edu. *Graduate Program Director,* Lana Portolano, 410-704-3770, E-mail: ghahn@towson.edu.

Program in Human Resource Development Students: 64 full-time (48 women), 186 part-time (145 women); includes 65 minority (47 Black or African American, non-Hispanic/Latino; 2 American Indian or Alaska Native, non-Hispanic/Latino; 9 Asian, non-Hispanic/Latino; 6 Hispanic/Latino; 1 Two or more races, non-Hispanic/Latino), 8 international. Average age 30. Expenses: Contact institution. *Financial support:* In 2010–11, 1 research assistantship with full and partial tuition reimbursement was awarded; career-related internships or fieldwork, Federal Work-Study, and unspecified assistantships also available. Financial award application deadline: 4/1; financial award applicants required to submit FAFSA. In 2010, 99 master's awarded. *Degree program information:* Part-time and evening/weekend programs available. Offers human resource development (MS). *Application deadline:* Applications are processed on a rolling basis. *Application fee:* $50. Electronic applications accepted. *Application Contact:* 410-704-2501, Fax: 410-704-4675, E-mail: grads@towson.edu. *Graduate Program Director,* Alan Clardy, 410-704-3069, E-mail: aclardy@towson.edu.

Program in Instructional Technology Students: 5 full-time (3 women), 248 part-time (214 women); includes 26 minority (17 Black or African American, non-Hispanic/Latino; 4 American Indian or Alaska Native, non-Hispanic/Latino; 4 Asian, non-Hispanic/Latino; 1 Hispanic/Latino), 2 international. Average age 39. Expenses: Contact institution. *Financial support:* In 2010–11, 1 fellowship with tuition reimbursement, 3 research assistantships with tuition reimbursements (averaging $4,000 per year) were awarded; career-related internships or fieldwork, Federal Work-Study, and unspecified assistantships also available. Financial award application deadline: 4/1; financial award applicants required to submit FAFSA. In 2010, 39 master's, 4 doctorates awarded. *Degree program information:* Part-time and evening/weekend programs available. Offers instructional design and training (MS); instructional technology (Ed D). *Application deadline:* For fall admission, 8/1 priority date for domestic students, 7/15 priority date for international students. Applications are processed on a rolling basis. *Application fee:* $50. Electronic applications accepted. *Application Contact:* 410-704-2501, Fax: 410-704-4675, E-mail: grads@towson.edu. *Ed D Program Director,* Bill Sadera, 410-704-2731.

Program in Integrated Homeland Security Management Students: 4 full-time (3 women), 41 part-time (19 women); includes 14 minority (10 Black or African American, non-Hispanic/Latino; 2 American Indian or Alaska Native, non-Hispanic/Latino; 2 Hispanic/Latino). Average age 32. Expenses: Contact institution. *Financial support:* Application deadline: 4/1. In 2010, 14 master's, 13 other advanced degrees awarded. *Degree program information:* Part-time and evening/weekend programs available. Offers integrated homeland security management (MS); security assessment and management (Certificate). *Application fee:* $50. *Application Contact:* The Graduate School, 410-704-2501, Fax: 410-704-4675, E-mail: grads@towson.edu. *Graduate Program Director*, Dr. Mike O'Leary, 410-704-4757, E-mail: moleary@towson.edu.

Program in Interactive Media Design Students: 1 (woman) full-time, 14 part-time (10 women); includes 5 minority (3 Black or African American, non-Hispanic/Latino; 1 American Indian or Alaska Native, non-Hispanic/Latino; 1 Asian, non-Hispanic/Latino), 1 international. Average age 43. Expenses: Contact institution. In 2010, 1 Certificate awarded. Postbaccalaureate distance learning degree programs offered (no on-campus study). Offers interactive media design (Certificate). *Application Contact:* Bridget Z. Sullivan, Director, 410-704-2802, E-mail: bsullivan@towson.edu. *Director*, Bridget Z. Sullivan, 410-704-2802, E-mail: bsullivan@towson.edu.

Program in Kinesiology Students: 10 part-time (5 women); includes 2 minority (both Black or African American, non-Hispanic/Latino), 1 international. Expenses: Contact institution. Offers kinesiology (MS). *Application Contact:* Heather Crowe, Graduate Program Director, 410-704-4399. *Graduate Program Director*, Heather Crowe, 410-704-4399.

Program in Management and Leadership Development Students: 8 full-time (6 women), 22 part-time (18 women); includes 13 minority (10 Black or African American, non-Hispanic/Latino; 1 American Indian or Alaska Native, non-Hispanic/Latino; 2 Asian, non-Hispanic/Latino). Average age 34. Expenses: Contact institution. In 2010, 4 Certificates awarded. *Degree program information:* Part-time and evening/weekend programs available. Offers management and leadership development (Certificate). *Application fee:* $50. *Application Contact:* The Graduate School, 410-704-2501, Fax: 410-704-2501, E-mail: grads@towson.edu. *Graduate Program Director*, Alan Clardy, 410-704-3069, E-mail: aclardy@towson.edu.

Program in Mathematics Education Students: 9 full-time (7 women), 78 part-time (59 women); includes 17 minority (13 Black or African American, non-Hispanic/Latino; 3 Asian, non-Hispanic/Latino; 1 Hispanic/Latino), 9 international. Average age 32. Expenses: Contact institution. *Financial support:* Application deadline: 4/1. In 2010, 62 master's awarded. Offers mathematics education (MS). *Application deadline:* Applications are processed on a rolling basis. *Application fee:* $50. Electronic applications accepted. *Application Contact:* 410-704-2501, Fax: 410-704-4675, E-mail: grads@towson.edu. *Graduate Program Director*, Dr. Maureen Yarnevich, 410-704-2988, Fax: 410-704-4143, E-mail: myarnevich@towson.edu.

Program in Music Education Students: 12 full-time (7 women), 31 part-time (19 women); includes 7 minority (5 Black or African American, non-Hispanic/Latino; 1 Asian, non-Hispanic/Latino; 1 Hispanic/Latino). Average age 30. Expenses: Contact institution. *Financial support:* Federal Work-Study and unspecified assistantships available. Financial award application deadline: 4/1; financial award applicants required to submit FAFSA. In 2010, 7 master's, 1 other advanced degree awarded. *Degree program information:* Part-time and evening/weekend programs available. Offers music education (MS, Certificate). *Application deadline:* Applications are processed on a rolling basis. *Application fee:* $50. Electronic applications accepted. *Application Contact:* 410-704-2501, Fax: 410-704-4675, E-mail: grads@towson.edu. *Graduate Program Director*, Dr. Dana Rothlisberger, 410-704-2765, Fax: 410-704-3434, E-mail: drothlisberger@towson.edu.

Program in Music Performance and Composition Students: 9 full-time (2 women), 8 part-time (2 women); includes 7 minority (2 Black or African American, non-Hispanic/Latino; 1 American Indian or Alaska Native, non-Hispanic/Latino; 2 Asian, non-Hispanic/Latino; 2 Hispanic/Latino), 3 international. Average age 30. Expenses: Contact institution. *Financial support:* Teaching assistantships, Federal Work-Study and unspecified assistantships available. Financial award application deadline: 4/1; financial award applicants required to submit FAFSA. In 2010, 5 master's awarded. *Degree program information:* Part-time and evening/weekend programs available. Offers music performance and composition (MM). *Application deadline:* Applications are processed on a rolling basis. *Application fee:* $50. Electronic applications accepted. *Application Contact:* 410-704-2501, Fax: 410-704-4675, E-mail: grads@towson.edu. *Graduate Program Director*, Dr. Luis Engelke, 410-704-4664, E-mail: lengelke@towson.edu.

Program in Nursing Students: 49 full-time (48 women), 78 part-time (74 women); includes 38 minority (29 Black or African American, non-Hispanic/Latino; 9 Asian, non-Hispanic/Latino), 1 international. Average age 50. Expenses: Contact institution. *Financial support:* Application deadline: 4/1. In 2010, 15 master's, 12 other advanced degrees awarded. *Degree program information:* Part-time programs available. Offers nursing (MS); nursing education (Certificate). *Application deadline:* Applications are processed on a rolling basis. *Application fee:* $50. Electronic applications accepted. *Application Contact:* 410-704-2501, Fax: 410-704-4675, E-mail: grads@towson.edu. *Graduate Program Director*, Kathleen Ogle, 410-704-4389, E-mail: kogle@towson.edu.

Program in Occupational Science Students: 1 (woman) full-time, 11 part-time (10 women); includes 1 minority (Black or African American, non-Hispanic/Latino), 1 international. Average age 45. Expenses: Contact institution. *Financial support:* In 2010–11, 2 fellowships with full tuition reimbursements (averaging $7,500 per year), teaching assistantships with partial tuition reimbursements (averaging $3,000 per year) were awarded; research assistantships with partial tuition reimbursements, career-related internships or fieldwork and unspecified assistantships also available. Financial award application deadline: 4/1; financial award applicants required to submit FAFSA. In 2010, 1 doctorate awarded. *Degree program information:* Part-time and evening/weekend programs available. Offers occupational science (Sc D). *Application deadline:* For fall admission, 8/15 priority date for domestic and international students; for winter admission, 11/15 priority date for domestic and international students; for spring admission, 1/15 priority date for domestic and international students. Applications are processed on a rolling basis. *Application fee:* $50. Electronic applications accepted. *Application Contact:* 410-704-2501, Fax: 410-704-4675, E-mail: grads@towson.edu. *Graduate Program Director*, Dr. Janet Delany, 410-704-2371, Fax: 410-704-2322, E-mail: jdelany@towson.edu.

Program in Occupational Therapy Students: 111 full-time (106 women), 3 part-time (2 women); includes 14 minority (10 Black or African American, non-Hispanic/Latino; 3 Asian, non-Hispanic/Latino; 1 Hispanic/Latino), 1 international. Average age 27. Expenses: Contact institution. *Financial support:* In 2010–11, teaching assistantships (averaging $2,000 per year); Federal Work-Study and unspecified assistantships also available. Financial award application deadline: 4/1; financial award applicants required to submit FAFSA. In 2010, 61 master's awarded. *Degree program information:* Part-time and evening/weekend programs available. Offers occupational therapy (MS). *Application deadline:* For spring admission, 8/1 for domestic students. Applications are processed on a rolling basis. *Application fee:* $50. *Application Contact:* Lynne Murphy, The Graduate School, 410-704-4439, Fax: 410-704-2322, E-mail: lmurphy@towson.edu. *Graduate Program Director*, Sonia Lawson, 410-704-2313, Fax: 410-704-2322, E-mail: slawson@towson.edu.

Program in Organizational Change Students: 17 full-time (12 women), 62 part-time (50 women); includes 20 minority (19 Black or African American, non-Hispanic/Latino; 1 American Indian or Alaska Native, non-Hispanic/Latino), 2 international. Average age 35. Expenses: Contact institution. In 2010, 1 CAS awarded. Offers organizational change (CAS). *Application deadline:* Applications are processed on a rolling basis. *Application fee:* $50. Electronic applications accepted. *Application Contact:* 410-704-2501, Fax: 410-704-4675, E-mail: grads@towson.edu. *Assistant Dean*, Jane Neapolitan, 410-704-4954, Fax: 410-704-2733, E-mail: jneapolitan@towson.edu.

Program in Physician Assistant Studies Students: 58 full-time (49 women); includes 5 minority (2 Black or African American, non-Hispanic/Latino; 1 Asian, non-Hispanic/Latino; 2 Hispanic/Latino), 2 international. Average age 29. Expenses: Contact institution. *Financial support:* Application deadline: 4/1. In 2010, 34 master's awarded. Offers physician assistant studies (MS). *Application fee:* $50. *Graduate Program Director*, Marcie Weinstein, 410-704-4049, E-mail: mweinstein@towson.edu.

Program in Professional Studies Students: 18 full-time (11 women), 32 part-time (22 women); includes 12 minority (11 Black or African American, non-Hispanic/Latino; 1 Hispanic/Latino), 1 international. Average age 32. Expenses: Contact institution. *Financial support:* Federal Work-Study and unspecified assistantships available. Financial award application deadline: 4/1; financial award applicants required to submit FAFSA. In 2010, 10 master's awarded. *Degree program information:* Part-time and evening/weekend programs available. Offers professional studies (MA). *Application deadline:* Applications are processed on a rolling basis. *Application fee:* $50. Electronic applications accepted. *Application Contact:* 410-704-2501, Fax: 410-704-4678, E-mail: grads@towson.edu. *Graduate Program Director*, Dr. James Smith, 410-704-4620, E-mail: jmsmith@towson.edu.

Program in Professional Writing Students: 21 full-time (9 women), 51 part-time (41 women); includes 13 minority (10 Black or African American, non-Hispanic/Latino; 1 American Indian or Alaska Native, non-Hispanic/Latino; 1 Asian, non-Hispanic/Latino; 1 Hispanic/Latino). Average age 32. Expenses: Contact institution. *Financial support:* Federal Work-Study and unspecified assistantships available. Financial award application deadline: 4/1; financial award applicants required to submit FAFSA. In 2010, 13 master's awarded. *Degree program information:* Part-time and evening/weekend programs available. Offers professional writing (MS). *Application deadline:* For fall admission, 3/1 for domestic students; for spring admission, 10/1 for domestic students. *Application fee:* $50. Electronic applications accepted. *Application Contact:* 410-704-2501, Fax: 410-704-4675, E-mail: grads@towson.edu. *Graduate Program Director*, Prof. Geoffrey Becker, 410-704-5196, Fax: 410-704-3434, E-mail: gbecker@towson.edu.

Program in Reading Students: 6 full-time (all women), 242 part-time (231 women); includes 30 minority (21 Black or African American, non-Hispanic/Latino; 2 American Indian or Alaska Native, non-Hispanic/Latino; 4 Asian, non-Hispanic/Latino; 2 Hispanic/Latino; 1 Two or more races, non-Hispanic/Latino). Average age 35. Expenses: Contact institution. *Financial support:* In 2010–11, 4 students received support. Federal Work-Study, scholarships/grants, and unspecified assistantships available. Financial award application deadline: 4/1; financial award applicants required to submit FAFSA. In 2010, 63 master's awarded. *Degree program information:* Part-time and evening/weekend programs available. Postbaccalaureate distance learning degree programs offered (minimal on-campus study). Offers reading (M Ed); reading education (CAS). *Application deadline:* Applications are processed on a rolling basis. *Application fee:* $50. Electronic applications accepted. *Application Contact:* Steve Mogge, The Graduate School, 410-704-5771, Fax: 410-704-3434, E-mail: reed@towson.edu. *Graduate Program Co-Director*, Dr. Barbara Laster, 410-704-2556, Fax: 410-704-3434, E-mail: reed@towson.edu.

Program in School Psychology Students: 11 full-time (all women), 2 part-time (both women); includes 3 minority (all Black or African American, non-Hispanic/Latino). Average age 26. Expenses: Contact institution. *Financial support:* In 2010–11, 5 students received support, including 5 fellowships with full tuition reimbursements available (averaging $4,000 per year); Federal Work-Study and unspecified assistantships also available. Financial award application deadline: 4/1; financial award applicants required to submit FAFSA. In 2010, 12 CASs awarded. *Degree program information:* Part-time and evening/weekend programs available. Offers school psychology (CAS). *Application deadline:* For fall admission, 1/15 for domestic students. *Application fee:* $50. Electronic applications accepted. *Application Contact:* 410-704-2501, Fax: 410-704-4675, E-mail: grads@towson.edu. *Graduate Program Director*, Dr. Susan Bartels, 410-704-3070, Fax: 410-704-3800, E-mail: sbartels@towson.edu.

Program in Science Education Students: 2 part-time (1 woman). Average age 28. Expenses: Contact institution. In 2010, 1 master's awarded. Offers science education (MS). *Application fee:* $50. *Application Contact:* 410-704-2501, Fax: 410-704-4675, E-mail: grads@towson.edu. *Graduate Program Director*, Sarah Haines, 410-704-2926, E-mail: shaines@towson.edu.

Program in Secondary Education Students: 1 (woman) full-time, 41 part-time (31 women); includes 5 minority (4 Black or African American, non-Hispanic/Latino; 1 Two or more races, non-Hispanic/Latino), 1 international. Average age 34. Expenses: Contact institution. *Financial support:* Federal Work-Study and unspecified assistantships available. Financial award application deadline: 4/1; financial award applicants required to submit FAFSA. In 2010, 35 master's awarded. *Degree program information:* Part-time and evening/weekend programs available. Offers secondary education (M Ed). *Application deadline:* Applications are processed on a rolling basis. *Application fee:* $50. Electronic applications accepted. *Application Contact:* 410-704-2501, Fax: 410-704-4675, E-mail: grads@towson.edu. *Graduate Program Director*, Todd Kenreich, 410-704-5897, E-mail: tkenreich@towson.edu.

Program in Social Science Students: 12 full-time (9 women), 19 part-time (11 women); includes 9 minority (6 Black or African American, non-Hispanic/Latino; 1 American Indian or Alaska Native, non-Hispanic/Latino; 1 Asian, non-Hispanic/Latino; 1 Hispanic/Latino), 2 international. Average age 31. Expenses: Contact institution. *Financial support:* Career-related internships or fieldwork, Federal Work-Study, and unspecified assistantships available. Support available to part-time students. Financial award application deadline: 4/1; financial award applicants required to submit FAFSA. In 2010, 9 master's awarded. *Degree program information:* Part-time and evening/weekend programs available. Offers social science (MS). *Application deadline:* For fall admission, 10/15 priority date for domestic and international students; for spring admission, 4/15 priority date for domestic and international students. Applications are processed on a rolling basis. *Application fee:* $50. Electronic applications accepted. *Application Contact:* 410-704-2501, Fax: 410-704-4675, E-mail: grads@towson.edu. *Graduate Program Director*, Michael Korzi, 410-704-5219, Fax: 410-704-5995, E-mail: mkorzi@towson.edu.

Program in Special Education Students: 6 full-time (all women), 113 part-time (103 women); includes 10 minority (1 Black or African American, non-Hispanic/Latino; 3 Asian, non-Hispanic/Latino; 4 Hispanic/Latino; 2 Two or more races, non-Hispanic/Latino). Average age 31. Expenses: Contact institution. *Financial support:* Career-related internships or fieldwork available. In 2010, 19 master's awarded. *Degree program information:* Part-time and evening/weekend programs available. Offers special education leadership (M Ed). *Application deadline:* For fall admission, 2/15 priority date for domestic and international students; for spring admission, 10/15 priority date for domestic and international students. Applications are processed on a rolling basis. *Application fee:* $50. Electronic applications accepted. *Application Contact:* 410-704-2501, Fax: 410-704-4675, E-mail: grads@towson.edu. *Graduate Program Director*, Lori Jackman, 410-704-3122, Fax: 410-704-2733, E-mail: ljackman@towson.edu.

Program in Speech-Language Pathology Students: 87 full-time (84 women); includes 4 minority (all Black or African American, non-Hispanic/Latino), 1 international. Average age 23. Expenses: Contact institution. *Financial support:* In 2010–11, 7 students received support. Federal Work-Study and unspecified assistantships available. Financial award application deadline: 4/1; financial award applicants required to submit FAFSA. In 2010, 45 master's awarded. Offers speech-language pathology (MS). *Application deadline:* For fall admission, 1/15 for domestic students. *Application fee:* $50. Electronic applications accepted. *Application Contact:* The Graduate School, 410-704-2449, Fax: 410-704-4675, E-mail: grads@towson.edu. *Graduate Program Director*, Dr. Celia Bassich, 410-704-2449, Fax: 410-704-4131, E-mail: cbassich@towson.edu.

Program in Strategic Public Relations and Integrated Communications Students: 3 part-time (all women); includes 1 minority (Black or African American, non-Hispanic/Latino). Expenses: Contact institution. *Financial support:* Fellowships, teaching assistantships, career-related internships or fieldwork, Federal Work-Study, and unspecified assistantships available. Support available to part-time students. Financial award application deadline: 4/1; financial award applicants required to submit FAFSA. In 2010, 6 Certificates awarded. *Degree program information:* Evening/weekend programs available. Postbaccalaureate distance learning degree programs offered (no on-campus study). Offers strategic public relations and integrated communications (Certificate). *Application deadline:* For fall admission, 1/15 for domestic students. *Application fee:* $50. Electronic applications accepted. *Application Contact:* 410-

Towson University (continued)

704-2501, Fax: 410-704-4675, E-mail: grads@towson.edu. *Graduate Program Director*, Theodora Carabas, 410-704-4855, E-mail: tcarabas@towson.edu.

Program in Studio Arts Students: 22 full-time (11 women), 5 part-time (3 women); includes 5 minority (2 Black or African American, non-Hispanic/Latino; 1 Asian, non-Hispanic/Latino; 2 Hispanic/Latino), 2 international. Average age 30. Expenses: Contact institution. *Financial support:* Federal Work-Study and unspecified assistantships available. Financial award application deadline: 4/1; financial award applicants required to submit FAFSA. In 2010, 5 master's awarded. Offers studio arts (MFA). *Application deadline:* For fall admission, 2/1 for domestic students; for spring admission, 11/1 for domestic students. *Application fee:* $50. Electronic applications accepted. *Application Contact:* 410-704-2501, Fax: 410-704-4675, E-mail: grads@towson.edu. *Graduate Program Director*, Tonia Matthews, 410-704-2803, E-mail: tmatthews@towson.edu.

Program in Teaching Students: 143 full-time (99 women), 98 part-time (77 women); includes 23 minority (15 Black or African American, non-Hispanic/Latino; 3 Asian, non-Hispanic/Latino; 3 Hispanic/Latino; 2 Two or more races, non-Hispanic/Latino), 8 international. Average age 30. Expenses: Contact institution. *Financial support:* Unspecified assistantships available. Financial award application deadline: 4/1; financial award applicants required to submit FAFSA. In 2010, 91 master's awarded. Offers teaching (MAT). *Application deadline:* For fall admission, 6/15 priority date for domestic and international students; for spring admission, 10/15 priority date for domestic and international students. Applications are processed on a rolling basis. *Application fee:* $50. Electronic applications accepted. *Application Contact:* 410-704-2501, Fax: 410-704-4675, E-mail: grads@towson.edu. *Graduate Program Director*, Judy Reber, 410-704-4935, Fax: 410-704-2733, E-mail: jreber@towson.edu.

Program in Theatre Students: 12 full-time (9 women), 5 part-time (4 women); includes 1 minority (Black or African American, non-Hispanic/Latino), 2 international. Average age 34. Expenses: Contact institution. *Financial support:* In 2010–11, 1 fellowship with tuition reimbursement (averaging $10,000 per year), 1 teaching assistantship with tuition reimbursement (averaging $6,000 per year) were awarded; unspecified assistantships also available. Financial award application deadline: 4/1; financial award applicants required to submit FAFSA. In 2010, 4 master's awarded. Offers theatre (MFA). *Application deadline:* For fall admission, 3/1 for domestic students. *Application fee:* $50. Electronic applications accepted. *Application Contact:* 410-704-2501, Fax: 410-704-4675, E-mail: grads@towson.edu. *Graduate Program Director*, Stephen Nunns, 410-704-4519, E-mail: snunns@towson.edu.

Program in Women's Studies Students: 24 full-time (23 women), 15 part-time (14 women); includes 11 minority (8 Black or African American, non-Hispanic/Latino; 1 Asian, non-Hispanic/Latino; 2 Two or more races, non-Hispanic/Latino), 3 international. Average age 33. Expenses: Contact institution. *Financial support:* Application deadline: 4/1. In 2010, 5 master's, 2 other advanced degrees awarded. Offers women's studies (MS, Certificate). *Application deadline:* Applications are processed on a rolling basis. *Application fee:* $50. Electronic applications accepted. *Application Contact:* 410-704-2501, Fax: 410-704-4675, E-mail: grads@towson.edu. *Graduate Program Director*, Celia Bardwell-Jones, 410-704-2860, Fax: 410-704-3469, E-mail: cbardwelljones@towson.edu.

TOYOTA TECHNOLOGICAL INSTITUTE OF CHICAGO, Chicago, IL 60637

General Information Proprietary, coed, graduate-only institution.

GRADUATE UNITS

Program in Computer Science Offers computer science (PhD).

TRADITIONAL CHINESE MEDICAL COLLEGE OF HAWAII, Kamuela, HI 96743-2288

General Information Proprietary, coed, graduate-only institution.

GRADUATE UNITS

Graduate Programs Offers Oriental medicine (MSOM).

TRENT UNIVERSITY, Peterborough, ON K9J 7B8, Canada

General Information Province-supported, coed, university. *Graduate housing:* Room and/or apartments available to single students; on-campus housing not available to married students. Housing application deadline: 7/10. *Research affiliation:* Watershed Science Centre (watershed studies), Ontario Power Generation, Inc. (acid rain deposition), Enbridge Consumers Gas (ozone depletion), Forensics Laboratory (DNA testing).

GRADUATE UNITS

Graduate Studies *Degree program information:* Part-time programs available. Offers anthropology (MA); applications of modeling in the natural and social sciences (MA); biology (M Sc, PhD); chemistry (M Sc); computer studies (M Sc); cultural studies (PhD); environmental and resource studies (M Sc, PhD); geography (M Sc, PhD); indigenous studies (PhD); materials science (M Sc); physics (M Sc).

The Frost Centre for Canadian Studies and Indigenous Studies *Degree program information:* Part-time programs available. Offers Canadian studies (PhD); Canadian studies and indigenous studies (MA).

TREVECCA NAZARENE UNIVERSITY, Nashville, TN 37210-2877

General Information Independent-religious, coed, comprehensive institution. *Enrollment:* 2,345 graduate, professional, and undergraduate students; 865 full-time matriculated graduate/professional students (612 women), 139 part-time matriculated graduate/professional students (96 women). *Enrollment by degree level:* 839 master's, 165 doctoral. *Graduate faculty:* 35 full-time (15 women), 42 part-time/adjunct (25 women). *Graduate housing:* Rooms and/or apartments available to single and married students. Housing application deadline: 6/15. *Student services:* Teacher training. *Library facilities:* Waggoner Library. *Online resources:* library catalog, web page, access to other libraries' catalogs. *Collection:* 151,985 titles, 34,471 serial subscriptions.

Computer facilities: 200 computers available on campus for general student use. A campuswide network can be accessed from student residence rooms and from off campus. Traditional undergraduate registration on-line by advisors available. *Web address:* http://www.trevecca.edu/.

General Application Contact: College of Lifelong Learning, 615-248-1200, E-mail: cll@trevecca.edu.

GRADUATE UNITS

Graduate Division Students: 865 full-time (612 women), 139 part-time (96 women); includes 194 minority (166 Black or African American, non-Hispanic/Latino; 2 American Indian or Alaska Native, non-Hispanic/Latino; 4 Asian, non-Hispanic/Latino; 11 Hispanic/Latino; 1 Native Hawaiian or other Pacific Islander, non-Hispanic/Latino; 10 Two or more races, non-Hispanic/Latino), 2 international. Average age 35. *Faculty:* 35 full-time (15 women), 42 part-time/adjunct (25 women). Expenses: Contact institution. *Financial support:* Applicants required to submit FAFSA. In 2010, 486 master's, 48 doctorates awarded. *Degree program information:* Part-time and evening/weekend programs available. Postbaccalaureate distance learning degree programs offered. Offers biblical studies (MA); business administration (MBA); clinical counseling (PhD); counseling (MA); counseling psychology (MA); information technology (MBA); management (MSM); marriage and family therapy (MMFT); organizational leadership (MOL); physician assistant (MS); preaching and practical theology (MA); systematic theology/historical theology (MA). *Application deadline:* Applications are processed on a rolling basis. *Application fee:* $25. *Application Contact:* College of Lifelong Learning, 615-248-1200. *Dean, College of Lifelong Learning*, Dr. David Phillips, 615-248-1200, E-mail: cll@trevecca.edu.

School of Education Students: 433 full-time (335 women), 44 part-time (35 women); includes 90 minority (79 Black or African American, non-Hispanic/Latino; 3 Asian, non-Hispanic/Latino; 6 Hispanic/Latino; 2 Two or more races, non-Hispanic/Latino), 2 international. Average age 36. *Faculty:* 13 full-time (9 women), 18 part-time/adjunct (11 women). Expenses: Contact institution. *Financial support:* Applicants required to submit FAFSA. In 2010, 319 master's, 48 doctorates awarded. *Degree program information:* Part-time and evening/weekend programs available. Offers curriculum, assessment, and instruction K-12 (M Ed); educational leadership (M Ed); English language learners (PreK-12) (M Ed); instructional technology (M Ed); leadership and professional practice (Ed D); leading instructional improvement for teachers PreK-12 (M Ed); library and information science (MLI Sc); reading PreK-12 (M Ed); teaching (MAT); teaching 7-12 (MAT); teaching K-6 (MAT). *Application deadline:* Applications are processed on a rolling basis. *Application fee:* $50. *Application Contact:* Admissions Office, 615-248-1201, Fax: 615-248-1597, E-mail: admissions_ged@trevecca.edu. *Dean/Director of Graduate Education Programs*, Dr. Esther Swink, 615-248-1201, Fax: 615-248-1597, E-mail: eswink@trevecca.edu.

TRINE UNIVERSITY, Angola, IN 46703-1764

General Information Independent, coed, comprehensive institution. *Graduate housing:* Room and/or apartments available on a first-come, first-served basis to single students; on-campus housing not available to married students. Housing application deadline: 8/1.

GRADUATE UNITS

Allen School of Engineering and Technology *Degree program information:* Part-time and evening/weekend programs available. Offers civil engineering (ME); mechanical engineering (ME).

Program in Criminal Justice Offers criminal justice (MS).

TRINITY BAPTIST COLLEGE, Jacksonville, FL 32221

General Information Independent-religious, coed, comprehensive institution. *Enrollment:* 7 part-time matriculated graduate/professional students (1 woman). *Enrollment by degree level:* 7 master's. *Graduate faculty:* 4 full-time (1 woman), 3 part-time/adjunct (0 women). *Graduate housing:* On-campus housing not available. *Library facilities:* Travis Hudson Library.

Computer facilities: A campuswide network can be accessed from student residence rooms and from off campus. Online class registration is available. *Web address:* http://www.tbc.edu/.

General Application Contact: Dr. Matthew Beemer, Senior Vice President, 904-596-2400, Fax: 904-596-2531, E-mail: mbeemer@tbc.edu.

GRADUATE UNITS

Graduate Programs Students: 7 part-time (1 woman). *Faculty:* 4 full-time (1 woman), 3 part-time/adjunct (0 women). Expenses: Contact institution. Postbaccalaureate distance learning degree programs offered. Offers educational leadership (M Ed); ministry (MA); special education (M Ed). *Application Contact:* Michael Nichols, Director of Graduate Studies, 904-596-2449, E-mail: graduatestudies@tbc.edu. *Senior Vice President*, Dr. Matthew Beemer, 904-596-2400, Fax: 904-596-2531, E-mail: mbeemer@tbc.edu.

TRINITY COLLEGE, Hartford, CT 06106-3100

General Information Independent, coed, comprehensive institution. *Graduate housing:* On-campus housing not available.

GRADUATE UNITS

Graduate Programs *Degree program information:* Part-time and evening/weekend programs available. Offers American studies (MA); economics (MA); English (MA); public policy studies (MA). Electronic applications accepted.

TRINITY INTERNATIONAL UNIVERSITY, Deerfield, IL 60015-1284

General Information Independent-religious, coed, university. *Graduate housing:* Rooms and/or apartments available on a first-come, first-served basis to single and married students.

GRADUATE UNITS

Trinity Evangelical Divinity School *Degree program information:* Part-time programs available. Postbaccalaureate distance learning degree programs offered (minimal on-campus study). Offers Biblical and Near Eastern archaeology and languages (MA); Christian studies (MA, Certificate); Christian thought (MA); church history (MA, Th M); congregational ministry: pastor-teacher (M Div); congregational ministry: team ministry (M Div); counseling ministries (MA); counseling psychology (MA); cross-cultural ministry (M Div); educational studies (PhD); evangelism (MA); history of Christianity in America (MA); intercultural studies (MA, PhD); leadership and ministry management (D Min); military chaplaincy (D Min); ministry (MA); mission and evangelism (Th M); missions and evangelism (D Min); New Testament (MA, Th M); Old Testament (Th M); Old Testament and Semitic languages (MA); pastoral care (M Div); pastoral care and counseling (D Min); pastoral counseling and psychology (Th M); pastoral theology (Th M); philosophy of religion (MA); preaching (D Min); religion (MA); research ministry (M Div); systematic theology (Th M); theological studies (PhD); urban ministry (MA). Electronic applications accepted.

Trinity Graduate School *Degree program information:* Part-time and evening/weekend programs available. Postbaccalaureate distance learning degree programs offered (minimal on-campus study). Offers bioethics (MA); communication and culture (MA); counseling psychology (MA); instructional leadership (M Ed); teaching (MA). Electronic applications accepted.

Trinity Law School *Degree program information:* Part-time and evening/weekend programs available. Offers law (JD).

TRINITY INTERNATIONAL UNIVERSITY, SOUTH FLORIDA CAMPUS, Miami, FL 33132-1996

General Information Independent-religious, coed, graduate-only institution. *Graduate housing:* On-campus housing not available.

GRADUATE UNITS

Divinity School Offers Christian studies (MA, Certificate).

Graduate School Offers counseling psychology (MA).

TRINITY LUTHERAN SEMINARY, Columbus, OH 43209-2334

General Information Independent-religious, coed, graduate-only institution. *Enrollment by degree level:* 120 first professional, 25 master's. *Graduate faculty:* 15 full-time (7 women), 7 part-time/adjunct (2 women). *Tuition:* Full-time $13,020; part-time $434 per semester hour. *Required fees:* $165 per semester. One-time fee: $150. *Graduate housing:* Rooms and/or apartments available on a first-come, first-served basis to single and married students. Typical cost: $3078 per year for single students. Housing application deadline: 5/15. *Student services:* Campus employment opportunities, international student services, low-cost health insurance, services for students with disabilities, writing training. *Library facilities:* Hamma Library. *Online resources:* library catalog, web page, access to other libraries' catalogs. *Collection:* 141,334 titles, 180 serial subscriptions, 6,862 audiovisual materials.

Computer facilities: 21 computers available on campus for general student use. A campuswide network can be accessed from student residence rooms and from off campus. *Web address:* http://www.trinitylutheranseminary.edu/.

General Application Contact: Rev. Sheri L. Ayers, Director of Admissions, 614-235-4136 Ext. 4614, Fax: 866-610-8572, E-mail: sayers@tls.edu.

GRADUATE UNITS

Graduate and Professional Programs Students: 110 full-time (42 women), 35 part-time (19 women); includes 21 minority (15 Black or African American, non-Hispanic/Latino; 4 Asian, non-Hispanic/Latino; 2 Hispanic/Latino), 4 international. Average age 35. 71 applicants, 77% accepted, 49 enrolled. *Faculty:* 15 full-time (7 women), 7 part-time/adjunct (2 women). Expenses: Contact institution. *Financial support:* In 2010–11, 102 students received support. Career-related internships or fieldwork, Federal Work-Study, institutionally sponsored loans, and scholarships/grants available. Support available to part-time students. Financial award application deadline: 5/1; financial award applicants required to submit FAFSA. In 2010, 29 first professional degrees, 9 master's awarded. *Degree program information:* Part-time programs available. Offers Christian education (MA); church music (MA); divinity (M Div); sacred theology (STM); theological studies (MTS); youth and family ministry (MA). *Application deadline:*

For fall admission, 7/15 priority date for domestic and international students. Applications are processed on a rolling basis. *Application fee:* $25. *Application Contact:* Rev. Sheri L. Ayers, Director of Admissions, 614-235-4136 Ext. 4614, Fax: 866-610-8572, E-mail: sayers@tls.edu. *Interim Academic Dean,* Dr. James Childs, 614-235-4136 Ext. 4670, Fax: 614-384-4635.

TRINITY SCHOOL FOR MINISTRY, Ambridge, PA 15003-2397

General Information Independent-religious, coed, graduate-only institution. *Graduate housing:* On-campus housing not available.

GRADUATE UNITS

Graduate Programs *Degree program information:* Part-time programs available. Offers Anglican studies (Diploma); basic Christian studies (Diploma); divinity (M Div); ministry (D Min); mission and evangelism (MAME, Diploma); religion (MAR); youth ministry (Diploma).

TRINITY UNIVERSITY, San Antonio, TX 78212-7200

General Information Independent-religious, coed, comprehensive institution. *Graduate housing:* On-campus housing not available.

GRADUATE UNITS

Department of Business Administration *Degree program information:* Part-time programs available. Offers accounting (MS).

Department of Education *Degree program information:* Part-time and evening/weekend programs available. Offers school administration (M Ed); school psychology (MA); teacher education (MAT).

Department of Health Care Administration *Degree program information:* Part-time programs available. Postbaccalaureate distance learning degree programs offered (minimal on-campus study). Offers health care administration (MS).

TRINITY (WASHINGTON) UNIVERSITY, Washington, DC 20017-1094

General Information Independent-religious, Undergraduate: women only; graduate: coed, comprehensive institution. *Graduate housing:* Room and/or apartments available on a first-come, first-served basis to single students; on-campus housing not available to married students.

GRADUATE UNITS

School of Education *Degree program information:* Part-time and evening/weekend programs available. Offers counseling (MA); early childhood education (MAT); educating for change (M Ed); educational administration (MSA); elementary education (MAT); school counseling (MA); secondary education (MAT); special education (MAT); teaching English as a second language (MAT); teaching English to speakers of other languages (M Ed); the teaching of reading (M Ed).

School of Professional Studies *Degree program information:* Part-time and evening/weekend programs available. Offers business administration (MBA); communication (MA); international security studies (MA); organizational management (MSA).

TRINITY WESTERN UNIVERSITY, Langley, BC V2Y 1Y1, Canada

General Information Independent-religious, coed, comprehensive institution. *Graduate housing:* On-campus housing not available.

GRADUATE UNITS

ACTS Seminaries *Degree program information:* Part-time programs available. Offers Christian studies (MA); cross cultural ministry (MA); theology (M Div, M Th, MAMFT, MLE, MTS, D Min).

School of Graduate Studies Offers biblical studies (MA); business (MA, Certificate); Christian ministry (MA); counseling psychology (MA); education (MA, Certificate); general humanities (MAIH); healthcare (MA, Certificate); international business (MBA); linguistics (MA); management of the growing enterprise (MBA); non-profit (MA, Certificate); non-profit and charitable organization management (MBA); specialized (MAIH); teaching English to speakers of other languages (TESOL) (MA).

School of Nursing Offers nursing (MSN).

TRI-STATE COLLEGE OF ACUPUNCTURE, New York, NY 10011

General Information Independent, coed, graduate-only institution. *Graduate housing:* On-campus housing not available.

GRADUATE UNITS

Program in Acupuncture *Degree program information:* Evening/weekend programs available. Offers acupuncture (MS); oriental medicine (MS); traditional Chinese herbology (Certificate).

TROY UNIVERSITY, Troy, AL 36082

General Information State-supported, coed, comprehensive institution. *Enrollment:* 29,322 graduate, professional, and undergraduate students; 1,773 full-time matriculated graduate/professional students (1,212 women), 4,304 part-time matriculated graduate/professional students (2,934 women). *Enrollment by degree level:* 5,956 master's, 26 doctoral, 95 other advanced degrees. *Graduate faculty:* 279 full-time (117 women), 180 part-time/adjunct (71 women). Tuition, state resident: full-time $4428; part-time $246 per credit hour. Tuition, nonresident: full-time $8856; part-time $492 per credit hour. *Required fees:* $432; $24 per credit hour. $50 per term. Tuition and fees vary according to program. *Graduate housing:* Rooms and/or apartments available to single and married students. Housing application deadline: 7/31. *Student services:* Campus employment opportunities, campus safety program, career counseling, child daycare facilities, exercise/wellness program, free psychological counseling, grant writing training, international student services, low-cost health insurance, services for students with disabilities, teacher training, writing training. *Library facilities:* Lurleen B. Wallace Library (Troy Campus) plus 2 others. *Online resources:* library catalog, web page. *Collection:* 578,549 titles, 3,313 serial subscriptions, 35,742 audiovisual materials. *Research affiliation:* Systemics Research Fund (protozoan symbionts), Birmingham Audubon Society (Alabama flora and fauna).

Computer facilities: 1,908 computers available on campus for general student use. A campuswide network can be accessed from student residence rooms and from off campus. Online class registration is available. *Web address:* http://www.troy.edu/.

General Application Contact: Brenda K. Campbell, Director of Graduate Admissions, 334-670-3178, Fax: 334-670-3733, E-mail: bcamp@troy.edu.

GRADUATE UNITS

Graduate School Students: 1,773 full-time (1,212 women), 4,304 part-time (2,934 women); includes 3,251 minority (2,810 Black or African American, non-Hispanic/Latino; 64 American Indian or Alaska Native, non-Hispanic/Latino; 50 Asian, non-Hispanic/Latino; 196 Hispanic/Latino; 1 Native Hawaiian or other Pacific Islander, non-Hispanic/Latino; 130 Two or more races, non-Hispanic/Latino), 221 international. Average age 33. 3,167 applicants, 76% accepted. *Faculty:* 279 full-time (117 women), 180 part-time/adjunct (71 women). Expenses: Contact institution. *Financial support:* Fellowships, career-related internships or fieldwork available. Support available to part-time students. Financial award application deadline: 5/1; financial award applicants required to submit FAFSA. In 2010, 2,248 master's, 55 other advanced degrees awarded. *Degree program information:* Part-time and evening/weekend programs available. Postbaccalaureate distance learning degree programs offered (no on-campus study). *Application deadline:* Applications are processed on a rolling basis. *Application fee:* $50. Electronic applications accepted. *Application Contact:* Brenda K. Campbell, Director of Graduate Admissions, 334-670-3178, Fax: 334-670-3733, E-mail: bcamp@troy.edu. *Associate Provost/Dean,* Dr. Dianne Barron, 334-670-3189, Fax: 334-370-3912, E-mail: dlbarron@troy.edu.

College of Arts and Sciences Students: 306 full-time (174 women), 1,099 part-time (623 women); includes 730 minority (595 Black or African American, non-Hispanic/Latino; 16 American Indian or Alaska Native, non-Hispanic/Latino; 42 Asian, non-Hispanic/Latino; 73 Hispanic/Latino; 2 Native Hawaiian or other Pacific Islander, non-Hispanic/Latino; 2 Two or more races, non-Hispanic/Latino). Average age 30. 1,003 applicants, 62% accepted. Expenses: Contact institution. *Financial support:* Available to part-time students. Applicants required to submit FAFSA. In 2010, 584 master's awarded. *Degree program information:* Part-time and evening/weekend programs available. Offers arts and sciences (MPA, MS); computer science (MS); criminal justice (MS); education (MPA); environmental analysis and management (MS); environmental management (MPA); government contracting (MPA); health care administration (MPA); justice administration (MPA); national security affairs (MPA, MS); nonprofit management (MPA); public human resources management (MPA); public management (MPA). *Application deadline:* Applications are processed on a rolling basis. *Application fee:* $50. Electronic applications accepted. *Application Contact:* Brenda K. Campbell, Director of Graduate Admissions, 334-670-3178, Fax: 334-670-3733, E-mail: bcamp@troy.edu. *Interim Dean,* Dr. Don Jeffrey, 334-670-3712, Fax: 334-670-3673, E-mail: djeffrey@troy.edu.

College of Business Students: 528 full-time (313 women), 1,545 part-time (1,032 women); includes 1,258 minority (1,045 Black or African American, non-Hispanic/Latino; 24 American Indian or Alaska Native, non-Hispanic/Latino; 140 Asian, non-Hispanic/Latino; 47 Hispanic/Latino; 2 Two or more races, non-Hispanic/Latino). Average age 35. 1,132 applicants, 75% accepted. Expenses: Contact institution. *Financial support:* In 2010–11, 5 research assistantships were awarded; career-related internships or fieldwork also available. Support available to part-time students. Financial award applicants required to submit FAFSA. In 2010, 836 master's awarded. *Degree program information:* Part-time and evening/weekend programs available. Postbaccalaureate distance learning degree programs offered. Offers accounting (EMBA, MBA); applied management (MSM); business (EMBA, MBA, MS, MSM, MTX, Certificate); criminal justice (EMBA); finance (MBA); general management (EMBA, MBA); healthcare management (EMBA, MSM); human resources management (MSM); information systems (EMBA, MBA, MSM); international economic development (MBA); international hospitality management (MSM); international management (MSM); leadership and organizational effectiveness (MSM); public management (MS, MSM); taxation (MTX, Certificate). *Application deadline:* Applications are processed on a rolling basis. *Application fee:* $50. Electronic applications accepted. *Application Contact:* Brenda K. Campbell, Director of Graduate Admissions, 334-670-3178, Fax: 334-670-3733, E-mail: bcamp@troy.edu. *Interim Dean,* Dr. Kay Sheridan, 334-670-3143, Fax: 334-670-3708, E-mail: ksheridan@troy.edu.

College of Education Students: 976 full-time (789 women), 1,243 part-time (1,029 women); includes 1,077 minority (1,003 Black or African American, non-Hispanic/Latino; 8 American Indian or Alaska Native, non-Hispanic/Latino; 9 Asian, non-Hispanic/Latino; 55 Hispanic/Latino; 2 Two or more races, non-Hispanic/Latino). Average age 34. 721 applicants, 86% accepted. Expenses: Contact institution. *Financial support:* Career-related internships or fieldwork available. Support available to part-time students. Financial award applicants required to submit FAFSA. In 2010, 756 master's, 55 other advanced degrees awarded. *Degree program information:* Part-time and evening/weekend programs available. Offers 5th year biology (MS); 5th year computer science (MS); 5th year early childhood (MS); 5th year history (MS); 5th year language arts (MS); 5th year mathematics (MS); 5th year social science (MS); adult education (MS); agency counseling (Ed S); alternative 5th year art education (MS); alternative 5th year instrumental (MS); alternative 5th year physical education (MS); alternative 5th year vocal/choral (MS); alternative K-6 elementary (MS); biology (M Ed); clinical mental health (MS); community counseling (MS, Ed S); corrections counseling (MS); criminal justice (M Ed); early childhood education (Ed S); education (M Ed, MS, Ed S); educational administration (MS, Ed S); elementary education (Ed S); English (M Ed); foundations of education (M Ed); general science (M Ed); higher education administration (M Ed); history (M Ed); instructional technology (M Ed); mathematics (M Ed); music industry (M Ed); physical fitness (M Ed); political science (M Ed); public administration (M Ed); rehabilitation counseling (MS); school counseling (MS, Ed S); school psychology (MS, Ed S); school psychometry (MS); social science (M Ed); social service counseling (MS); student affairs counseling (MS); substance abuse counseling (MS); teaching English (M Ed); traditional art education (MS); traditional biology (MS); traditional computer science (MS); traditional early childhood (MS); traditional gifted education (MS); traditional history (MS); traditional instrumental (MS); traditional K-6 elementary (MS); traditional language arts (MS); traditional mathematics (MS); traditional physical education (MS); traditional reading specialist (MS); traditional social science (MS); traditional vocal/choral (MS). *Application deadline:* For fall admission, 6/1 for international students; for spring admission, 10/15 for international students. Applications are processed on a rolling basis. *Application fee:* $50. Electronic applications accepted. *Application Contact:* Brenda K. Campbell, Director of Graduate Admissions, 334-670-3178, Fax: 334-670-3733, E-mail: bcamp@troy.edu. *Dean,* Dr. Lance Tatum, 334-670-3365, Fax: 334-670-3474, E-mail: ltatum@troy.edu.

College of Health and Human Services Students: 79 full-time (50 women), 182 part-time (132 women); includes 104 minority (96 Black or African American, non-Hispanic/Latino; 1 American Indian or Alaska Native, non-Hispanic/Latino; 6 Asian, non-Hispanic/Latino; 1 Hispanic/Latino). Average age 31. 171 applicants, 85% accepted. Expenses: Contact institution. *Financial support:* Tuition waivers and unspecified assistantships available. Support available to part-time students. Financial award application deadline: 4/5; financial award applicants required to submit FAFSA. In 2010, 66 master's awarded. *Degree program information:* Part-time and evening/weekend programs available. Offers adult health (MSN); clinical nurse specialist adult health (DNP); clinical nurse specialist maternal infant (DNP); family nurse fractioned (DNP); family nurse practitioner (MSN, PMC); health and human services (MS, MSN, DNP, PMC); informatics specialist (MSN); maternal infant (MSN); sport and fitness management (MS). *Application deadline:* Applications are processed on a rolling basis. *Application fee:* $50. Electronic applications accepted. *Application Contact:* Brenda K. Campbell, Director of Graduate Admissions, 334-670-3178, Fax: 334-670-3733, E-mail: bcamp@troy.edu. *Interim Dean,* Dr. Edith Smith, 334-670-3712, Fax: 334-670-3743, E-mail: esmith@troy.edu.

TRUMAN STATE UNIVERSITY, Kirksville, MO 63501-4221

General Information State-supported, coed, comprehensive institution. CGS member. *Graduate housing:* Rooms and/or apartments available on a first-come, first-served basis to single and married students. Housing application deadline: 5/1. *Research affiliation:* Gulf Coast Research Laboratory (marine science), Kirksville College of Osteopathic Medicine (biology).

GRADUATE UNITS

Graduate School Electronic applications accepted.

School of Arts and Letters Offers arts and letters (MA, MS); biology (MS); English (MA); music (MA). Electronic applications accepted.

School of Business Offers accounting (M Ac); business (M Ac). Electronic applications accepted.

School of Health Sciences and Education Offers communication disorders (MA); education (MAE); health sciences and education (MA, MAE). Electronic applications accepted.

School of Science and Mathematics Offers science and mathematics (MS).

TUFTS UNIVERSITY, Medford, MA 02155

General Information Independent, coed, university. CGS member. *Enrollment:* 10,480 graduate, professional, and undergraduate students; 4,529 full-time matriculated graduate/professional students (2,568 women), 467 part-time matriculated graduate/professional students (265 women). *Enrollment by degree level:* 1,828 first professional, 2,176 master's, 843 doctoral, 149 other advanced degrees. *Graduate faculty:* 816 full-time (321 women), 429 part-time/adjunct (194 women). *Tuition:* Full-time $39,624; part-time $3962 per course. *Required fees:* $40 per year. Full-time tuition and fees vary according to degree level, program and student level. Part-time tuition and fees vary according to course load. *Graduate housing:* Room and/or apartments available on a first-come, first-served basis to single students; on-campus housing not available to married students. Typical cost: $7204 per year ($8156 including board). Room and board charges vary according to board plan, campus/location and housing facility selected. Housing application deadline: 4/15. *Student services:* Campus employment opportunities, campus safety program, career counseling, child daycare facilities, exercise/wellness program, free psychological counseling, international student services, low-cost health insurance, multicultural affairs office, services for students with disabilities,

Tufts University (continued)

teacher training, writing training. *Library facilities:* Tisch Library plus 4 others. *Online resources:* library catalog, web page, access to other libraries' catalogs. *Collection:* 1.5 million titles, 38,829 serial subscriptions, 50,922 audiovisual materials. *Research affiliation:* Maine Medical Center (medicine), The Stockholm Environmental Institute (environmental science and policy), Caritas St. Elizabeth's Medical Center (medicine), Tufts-New England Medical Center (medicine), Lahey Clinic Medical Center (medicine), Baystate Medical Center (medicine).

Computer facilities: Computer purchase and lease plans are available. 300 computers available on campus for general student use. A campuswide network can be accessed from student residence rooms and from off campus. Online class registration is available. *Web address:* http://www.tufts.edu/.

General Application Contact: Information Contact, 617-628-5000.

GRADUATE UNITS

Cummings School of Veterinary Medicine Students: 344 full-time (291 women); includes 29 minority (3 Black or African American, non-Hispanic/Latino; 3 American Indian or Alaska Native, non-Hispanic/Latino; 10 Asian, non-Hispanic/Latino; 7 Hispanic/Latino; 1 Native Hawaiian or other Pacific Islander, non-Hispanic/Latino; 5 Two or more races, non-Hispanic/Latino), 3 international. Average age 25. 746 applicants, 35% accepted, 120 enrolled. *Faculty:* 90 full-time (39 women), 16 part-time/adjunct (7 women). Expenses: Contact institution. *Financial support:* In 2010–11, 62 students received support, including 6 research assistantships with full tuition reimbursements available (averaging $25,000 per year), 4 teaching assistantships (averaging $5,000 per year); career-related internships or fieldwork, Federal Work-Study, institutionally sponsored loans, scholarships/grants, and institutional aid awards also available. Financial award application deadline: 5/15; financial award applicants required to submit FAFSA. In 2010, 74 first professional degrees, 11 master's, 1 doctorate awarded. Offers animals and public policy (MS); conservation medicine (MS); infectious diseases/digestive diseases/neuroscience/reproductive biology (PhD); veterinary medicine (DVM). *Application deadline:* For fall admission, 11/1 for domestic and international students. *Application fee:* $70. Electronic applications accepted. *Application Contact:* Rebecca Russo, Director of Admissions, 508-839-7920, Fax: 508-887-4820, E-mail: vetadmissions@tufts.edu. *Dean,* Dr. Deborah T. Kochevar, 508-839-5302, Fax: 508-839-2953, E-mail: deborah.kochevar@tufts.edu.

Fletcher School of Law and Diplomacy Students: 541 full-time (278 women), 9 part-time (3 women); includes 73 minority (8 Black or African American, non-Hispanic/Latino; 30 Asian, non-Hispanic/Latino; 11 Hispanic/Latino; 24 Two or more races, non-Hispanic/Latino), 208 international. Average age 31. 1,875 applicants, 41% accepted, 296 enrolled. *Faculty:* 37 full-time (10 women), 48 part-time/adjunct (14 women). Expenses: Contact institution. *Financial support:* Federal Work-Study, institutionally sponsored loans, scholarships/grants, and tuition waivers (partial) available. Financial award application deadline: 1/15; financial award applicants required to submit FAFSA. In 2010, 297 master's, 14 doctorates awarded. Postbaccalaureate distance learning degree programs offered (minimal on-campus study). Offers law and diplomacy (LL M, MA, MAHA, MALD, MIB, PhD). *Application deadline:* For fall admission, 1/15 for domestic and international students; for spring admission, 10/15 for domestic and international students. *Application fee:* $70. Electronic applications accepted. *Application Contact:* Laurie A. Hurley, 617-627-3040, E-mail: fletcheradmissions@tufts.edu. *Dean,* Stephen W. Bosworth, 617-627-3050, Fax: 617-627-3712.

The Gerald J. and Dorothy R. Friedman School of Nutrition Science and Policy *Degree program information:* Part-time programs available. Offers humanitarian assistance (MAHA); nutrition (MS, PhD). Electronic applications accepted.

Graduate School of Arts and Sciences *Degree program information:* Part-time programs available. Offers analytical chemistry (MS, PhD); art history (MA); arts and sciences (MA, MAT, MFA, MPP, MS, OTD, PhD, CAGS, Certificate, Ed S); bioengineering (Certificate); biology (MS, PhD); bioorganic chemistry (MS, PhD); biotechnology (Certificate); biotechnology engineering (Certificate); child development (MA, PhD, CAGS); classical archaeology (MA); classics (MA); community development (MA); community environmental studies (Certificate); computer science (Certificate); computer science minor (Certificate); drama (MA); dramatic literature and criticism (PhD); early childhood education (MAT); economics (MS); education (MA, MAT, MS, PhD); English (MA, PhD); environmental chemistry (MS, PhD); environmental management (Certificate); environmental policy (MA); epidemiology (Certificate); ethnomusicology (MA); French (MA); German (MA); health and human welfare (MA); history (MA, PhD); housing policy (MA); human-computer interaction (Certificate); inorganic chemistry (MS, PhD); international environment/development policy (MA); management of community organizations (Certificate); manufacturing engineering (Certificate); mathematics (MA, MS, PhD); microwave and wireless engineering (Certificate); middle and secondary education (MA, MAT); museum studies (Certificate); music history and literature (MA); music theory and composition (MA); occupational therapy (Certificate); organic chemistry (MS, PhD); philosophy (MA); physical chemistry (MS, PhD); physics (MS, PhD); program evaluation (Certificate); psychology (MS, PhD); public policy (MPP); school psychology (MA, Ed S); secondary education (MA); studio art (MFA); theater history (PhD). Electronic applications accepted.

Sackler School of Graduate Biomedical Sciences Students: 194 full-time (122 women), 4 part-time (all women); includes 5 Black or African American, non-Hispanic/Latino; 19 Asian, non-Hispanic/Latino; 8 Hispanic/Latino, 33 international. Average age 29. 705 applicants, 10% accepted, 41 enrolled. *Faculty:* 173 full-time (55 women). Expenses: Contact institution. *Financial support:* In 2010–11, 174 students received support, including 24 fellowships, 174 research assistantships with full tuition reimbursements available (averaging $28,500 per year); scholarships/grants and health care benefits also available. Financial award application deadline: 12/15. In 2010, 18 master's, 38 doctorates awarded. Offers biochemistry (PhD); biomedical sciences (MS, PhD); cell, molecular and developmental biology (PhD); cellular and molecular physiology (PhD); genetics (PhD); immunology (PhD); integrated studies (PhD); molecular microbiology (PhD); neuroscience (PhD); pharmacology and experimental therapeutics (PhD). *Application deadline:* For fall admission, 12/15 priority date for domestic and international students. Applications are processed on a rolling basis. *Application fee:* $70. Electronic applications accepted. *Application Contact:* Kellie Johnston, Associate Director of Admissions, 617-636-6767, Fax: 617-636-0375, E-mail: sackler-school@tufts.edu. *Dean,* Dr. Naomi Rosenberg, 617-636-6767, Fax: 617-636-0375, E-mail: naomi.rosenberg@tufts.edu.

Division of Clinical Care Research Students: 23 full-time (15 women), 1 part-time (0 women); includes 1 Black or African American, non-Hispanic/Latino; 4 Asian, non-Hispanic/Latino, 10 international. Average age 33. 32 applicants, 41% accepted, 13 enrolled. *Faculty:* 37 full-time (11 women). Expenses: Contact institution. *Financial support:* In 2010–11, 27 fellowships with full tuition reimbursements were awarded. Financial award application deadline: 12/15. In 2010, 7 master's awarded. Offers clinical care research (MS, PhD). *Application deadline:* For fall admission, 12/15 for domestic and international students. Applications are processed on a rolling basis. *Application fee:* $70. Electronic applications accepted. *Application Contact:* Kellie Johnston, Associate Director of Admissions, 617-636-6767, Fax: 617-636-0375, E-mail: sackler-school@tufts.edu. *Program Director,* Dr. Harry P. Selker, 617-636-5009, Fax: 617-636-8023, E-mail: hselker@lifespan.org.

School of Dental Medicine Offers dental medicine (DMD, MS, Certificate); dentistry (Certificate).

School of Engineering *Degree program information:* Part-time programs available. Offers biomedical engineering (ME, MS, PhD); chemical and biological engineering (ME, MS, PhD); civil engineering (ME, MS, PhD); computer science (MS, PhD); electrical engineering (MS, PhD); engineering (ME, MS, MSEM, PhD); environmental engineering (ME, MS, PhD); human factors (MS); mechanical engineering (ME, MS, PhD). Electronic applications accepted.

The Gordon Institute *Degree program information:* Part-time programs available. Offers engineering management (MSEM). Electronic applications accepted.

School of Medicine Expenses: Contact institution. Offers biomedical sciences (MS); health communication (MS); medicine (MD, MPH, MS); pain research, education and policy (MS); public health (MPH). *Application Contact:* Information Contact, 617-636-7000. *Interim Dean,* Dr. Harris Berman, 617-636-6565.

TUI UNIVERSITY, Cypress, CA 90630

General Information Independent, coed, university. *Enrollment:* 7,311 graduate, professional, and undergraduate students; 1,333 full-time matriculated graduate/professional students (468 women), 2,893 part-time matriculated graduate/professional students (986 women). *Enrollment by degree level:* 3,774 master's, 452 doctoral. *Graduate faculty:* 68 full-time (30 women), 397 part-time/adjunct (156 women). *Tuition:* Full-time $11,040; part-time $345 per semester hour. *Student services:* Services for students with disabilities. *Library facilities:* Trident University International Library. *Online resources:* web page. *Collection:* 57,791 titles, 38,756 serial subscriptions.

Computer facilities: A campuswide network can be accessed from off campus. Online class registration is available. *Web address:* http://www.tuiu.edu/.

General Application Contact: Wei Ren, Registrar, 800-375-9878, Fax: 714-276-6589, E-mail: registration@tuiu.edu.

GRADUATE UNITS

College of Business Administration Students: 741 full-time (200 women), 1,585 part-time (410 women). 379 applicants, 81% accepted, 300 enrolled. Expenses: Contact institution. In 2010, 752 master's, 28 doctorates awarded. *Degree program information:* Part-time and evening/weekend programs available. Postbaccalaureate distance learning degree programs offered (no on-campus study). Offers business administration (MBA, PhD); conflict and negotiation management (MBA); criminal justice administration (MBA); entrepreneurship (MBA); finance (MBA); general management (MBA); government accounting (MBA); human resource management (MBA); information security and digital assurance management (MBA); information technology management (MBA); international business (MBA); logistics management (MBA); marketing (MBA); project management (MBA); public management (MBA); quality management (MBA); strategic leadership (MBA). *Application deadline:* For fall admission, 10/3 for domestic and international students; for winter admission, 12/22 for domestic and international students; for spring admission, 4/3 for domestic and international students. Applications are processed on a rolling basis. *Application fee:* $75. Electronic applications accepted. *Application Contact:* Wei Ren-Finaly, Registrar, 800-375-9878, Fax: 714-827-7407, E-mail: registration@tuiu.edu. *Dean,* Dr. Paul Watkins, 714-816-0366 Ext. 2054, Fax: 714-816-0367, E-mail: infocba@tuiu.edu.

College of Education Students: 173 full-time (86 women), 421 part-time (189 women). 112 applicants, 72% accepted, 81 enrolled. Expenses: Contact institution. In 2010, 227 master's, 16 doctorates awarded. *Degree program information:* Part-time and evening/weekend programs available. Postbaccalaureate distance learning degree programs offered (no on-campus study). Offers adult education (MA Ed); aviation education (MA Ed); children's literacy development (MA Ed); e-learning (MA Ed); e-learning leadership (MA Ed, PhD); early childhood education (MA Ed); education (MA Ed, PhD); educational leadership (MA Ed); enrollment management (MA Ed); higher education (MA Ed); higher education leadership (PhD); K-12 leadership (PhD); teaching and instruction (MA Ed); training and development (MA Ed). *Application deadline:* For fall admission, 10/3 for domestic and international students; for winter admission, 12/22 for domestic and international students; for spring admission, 4/3 for domestic and international students. Applications are processed on a rolling basis. *Application fee:* $75. Electronic applications accepted. *Application Contact:* Wei Ren-Finaly, Registrar, 800-375-9878, Fax: 714-827-7407, E-mail: registration@tuiu.edu. *Dean,* Dr. Michaela Tanasescu, 714-816-0366, Fax: 714-226-9844, E-mail: infocoe@tuiu.edu.

College of Health Sciences Students: 322 full-time (170 women), 709 part-time (357 women). 227 applicants, 80% accepted, 164 enrolled. Expenses: Contact institution. In 2010, 366 master's, 29 doctorates awarded. *Degree program information:* Part-time and evening/weekend programs available. Postbaccalaureate distance learning degree programs offered (no on-campus study). Offers clinical research administration (MS, Certificate); emergency and disaster management (MS, Certificate); environmental health science (Certificate); health care administration (PhD); health care management (MS); health education (MS, Certificate); health informatics (Certificate); health sciences (MS, PhD, Certificate); international health (MS); international health: educator or researcher option (PhD); international health: practitioner option (PhD); law and expert witness studies (MS, Certificate); public health (MS); quality assurance (Certificate). *Application deadline:* For fall admission, 10/3 for domestic and international students; for winter admission, 12/22 for domestic and international students; for spring admission, 4/3 for domestic and international students. Applications are processed on a rolling basis. *Application fee:* $75. Electronic applications accepted. *Application Contact:* Wei Ren-Finaly, Registrar, 800-375-9878, Fax: 714-827-7407, E-mail: registration@tuiu.edu. *Dean,* Dr. Michaela Tanasescu, 714-816-0366, Fax: 714-226-9844, E-mail: infocoe@tuiu.edu.

College of Information Systems Students: 83 full-time (12 women), 178 part-time (30 women). 67 applicants, 84% accepted, 50 enrolled. Expenses: Contact institution. In 2010, 116 master's awarded. *Degree program information:* Part-time and evening/weekend programs available. Postbaccalaureate distance learning degree programs offered (no on-campus study). Offers business intelligence (Certificate); information technology management (MS). *Application deadline:* For fall admission, 10/3 for domestic and international students; for winter admission, 12/22 for domestic and international students; for spring admission, 4/3 for domestic and international students. Applications are processed on a rolling basis. *Application fee:* $0. Electronic applications accepted. *Application Contact:* Wei Ren-Finaly, Registrar, 800-375-9878, Fax: 714-827-7407, E-mail: registration@tuiu.edu. *Dean,* Dr. Paul Watkins, 800-509-3901, E-mail: infocis@tuiu.edu.

TULANE UNIVERSITY, New Orleans, LA 70118-5669

General Information Independent, coed, university. CGS member. *Graduate housing:* Rooms and/or apartments available on a first-come, first-served basis to single and married students. Housing application deadline: 3/24.

GRADUATE UNITS

A. B. Freeman School of Business *Degree program information:* Part-time and evening/weekend programs available. Offers business (EMBA, M Acct, M Fin, MBA, PMBA, PhD). Electronic applications accepted.

Program in Liberal Arts *Degree program information:* Part-time programs available. Offers liberal arts (MLA).

School of Architecture *Degree program information:* Part-time programs available. Offers architecture (M Arch, MPS).

School of Law Offers admiralty (LL M); American business law (LL M); energy and environment (LL M); international and comparative law (LL M); law (JD, LL M, SJD). Electronic applications accepted.

School of Liberal Arts *Degree program information:* Part-time programs available. Offers anthropology (MA, PhD); art (MFA); art history (MA); classical studies (MA); design and technical production (MFA); economics (MA, PhD); English (MA, PhD); French (MA, PhD); history (MA, PhD); liberal arts (MA, MFA, MS, PhD); music (MA, MFA); philosophy (MA, PhD); political science (MA, PhD); Portuguese (MA); sociology (MA, PhD); Spanish (MA); Spanish and Portuguese (PhD). Electronic applications accepted.

The Payson Center for International Development and Technology Transfer *Degree program information:* Part-time programs available. Offers international development (MS, PhD). Electronic applications accepted.

Roger Thayer Stone Center for Latin American Studies Offers Latin American studies (MA, PhD). Electronic applications accepted.

School of Medicine Offers medicine (MD, MBS, MS, PhD).

Graduate Programs in Biomedical Sciences Offers biochemistry (MS, PhD); biomedical sciences (MBS, MS, PhD); human genetics (MBS, PhD); microbiology and immunology (MS, PhD); molecular and cellular biology (PhD); neuroscience (MS, PhD); pharmacology (MS, PhD); physiology (MS, PhD); structural and cellular biology (MS, PhD).

School of Public Health and Tropical Medicine *Degree program information:* Part-time and evening/weekend programs available. Postbaccalaureate distance learning degree programs offered (no on-campus study). Offers biostatistics (MS, MSPH, PhD, Sc D); clinical tropical medicine and travelers health (Diploma); environmental health sciences (MPH, MSPH, Dr PH, PhD); epidemiology (MPH, MS, Dr PH, PhD); health education and communication (MPH); health systems management (MHA, MMM, MPH, PhD, Sc D); international health and development (MPH, Dr PH, PhD); maternal and child health (MPH, Dr PH); nutrition (MPH); parasitology (MSPH, PhD); public health and tropical medicine (MHA, MMM, MPH, MPHTM, MS, MSPH, Dr PH, PhD, Sc D, Diploma); vector borne infectious diseases (MS, PhD). MS, PhD offered through the Graduate School. Electronic applications accepted.

School of Science and Engineering *Degree program information:* Part-time programs available. Offers applied mathematics (MS); biomedical engineering (MS, PhD); cell and molecular biology (MS, PhD); chemical and biomolecular engineering (PhD); chemistry (MS, PhD); ecology and evolutionary biology (MS, PhD); interdisciplinary studies (PhD); mathematics (MS, PhD); neuroscience (MS, PhD); physics (PhD); psychology (MS, PhD); science and engineering (M Eng, MS, PhD); statistics (MS). MS and PhD offered through the Graduate School. Electronic applications accepted.

School of Social Work *Degree program information:* Part-time programs available. Offers social work (MSW). Electronic applications accepted.

TUSCULUM COLLEGE, Greeneville, TN 37743-9997

General Information Independent-religious, coed, comprehensive institution. *Graduate housing:* On-campus housing not available.

GRADUATE UNITS

Graduate School *Degree program information:* Evening/weekend programs available. Offers adult education (MA Ed); K–12 (MA Ed); organizational management (MAOM).

TUSKEGEE UNIVERSITY, Tuskegee, AL 36088

General Information Independent, coed, comprehensive institution. *Enrollment:* 2,946 graduate, professional, and undergraduate students; 442 full-time matriculated graduate/professional students (307 women), 23 part-time matriculated graduate/professional students (11 women). *Enrollment by degree level:* 259 first professional, 175 master's, 31 doctoral. *Graduate faculty:* 112 full-time (17 women), 11 part-time/adjunct (5 women). *Tuition:* Full-time $16,100; part-time $665 per credit hour. *Required fees:* $650. *Graduate housing:* Rooms and/or apartments available to single and married students. Typical cost: $7570 (including board) for single students. Housing application deadline: 5/1. *Student services:* Campus employment opportunities, campus safety program, career counseling, child daycare facilities, exercise/wellness program, free psychological counseling, international student services, low-cost health insurance, services for students with disabilities, writing training. *Library facilities:* Hollis B. Frissell Library plus 3 others. *Online resources:* library catalog. *Collection:* 623,824 titles, 81,157 serial subscriptions.

Computer facilities: 1,000 computers available on campus for general student use. A campuswide network can be accessed from student residence rooms and from off campus. Online class registration is available. *Web address:* http://www.tuskegee.edu/.

General Application Contact: Dr. Cynthia D. Cellers, Vice President/Director of Admissions and Enrollment Management, 334-727-8580, Fax: 334-727-5750, E-mail: planey@tuskegee.edu.

GRADUATE UNITS

Graduate Programs Students: 442 full-time (307 women), 23 part-time (11 women); includes 287 Black or African American, non-Hispanic/Latino; 2 Asian, non-Hispanic/Latino; 22 Hispanic/Latino; 2 Native Hawaiian or other Pacific Islander, non-Hispanic/Latino, 57 international. Average age 28. 1,197 applicants, 62% accepted, 465 enrolled. *Faculty:* 112 full-time (17 women), 11 part-time/adjunct (5 women). Expenses: Contact institution. *Financial support:* Fellowships, research assistantships, teaching assistantships, career-related internships or fieldwork, Federal Work-Study, institutionally sponsored loans, and scholarships/grants available. Support available to part-time students. Financial award application deadline: 4/15; financial award applicants required to submit FAFSA. In 2010, 54 first professional degrees, 61 master's, 6 doctorates awarded. *Degree program information:* Part-time programs available. *Application deadline:* For fall admission, 7/15 for domestic students. Applications are processed on a rolling basis. *Application fee:* $25 ($35 for international students). *Application Contact:* Dr. Robert L. Laney, Vice President/Director of Admissions and Enrollment Management, 334-727-8580, Fax: 334-727-5750, E-mail: planey@tuskegee.edu. *Interim Provost and Vice President for Institutional Research and Planning,* Dr. John A. Williams, 334-727-8164.

College of Agricultural, Environmental and Natural Sciences Students: 77 full-time (52 women), 5 part-time (3 women); includes 54 Black or African American, non-Hispanic/Latino, 18 international. Average age 29. 46 applicants, 65% accepted, 17 enrolled. *Faculty:* 26 full-time (12 women), 1 part-time/adjunct (0 women). Expenses: Contact institution. *Financial support:* Fellowships, research assistantships, teaching assistantships, career-related internships or fieldwork, Federal Work-Study, and institutionally sponsored loans available. Support available to part-time students. Financial award application deadline: 4/15. In 2010, 22 master's awarded. Offers agricultural and resource economics (MS); agricultural, environmental and natural sciences (MS, PhD); animal and poultry sciences (MS); biology (MS); chemistry (MS); environmental sciences (MS); food and nutritional sciences (MS); integrative bio-science (PhD); integrative biosciences (PhD); plant and soil sciences (MS). *Application deadline:* For fall admission, 7/15 for domestic students. Applications are processed on a rolling basis. *Application fee:* $25 ($35 for international students). *Application Contact:* Dr. Robert L. Laney, Vice President/Director of Admissions and Enrollment Management, 334-727-8580, Fax: 334-727-5750, E-mail: planey@tuskegee.edu. *Dean,* Dr. Walter A. Hill, 334-727-8157.

College of Engineering, Architecture and Physical Sciences Students: 60 full-time (19 women), 13 part-time (4 women); includes 37 Black or African American, non-Hispanic/Latino, 31 international. Average age 28. 104 applicants, 59% accepted. *Faculty:* 19 full-time (0 women). Expenses: Contact institution. *Financial support:* Fellowships, research assistantships, teaching assistantships, career-related internships or fieldwork, Federal Work-Study, and institutionally sponsored loans available. Support available to part-time students. Financial award application deadline: 4/15. In 2010, 14 master's awarded. Offers electrical engineering (MSEE); engineering, architecture and physical sciences (MSEE, MSME, PhD); material science and engineering (PhD); mechanical engineering (MSME). *Application deadline:* For fall admission, 7/15 for domestic students. Applications are processed on a rolling basis. *Application fee:* $25 ($35 for international students). *Application Contact:* Dr. Robert L. Laney, Vice President/Director of Admissions and Enrollment Management, 334-727-8580, Fax: 334-727-5750, E-mail: planey@tuskegee.edu. *Acting Dean,* Dr. Legand L. Burge, 334-727-8356.

College of Veterinary Medicine, Nursing and Allied Health Students: 273 full-time (210 women), 5 part-time (4 women); includes 168 Black or African American, non-Hispanic/Latino; 2 American Indian or Alaska Native, non-Hispanic/Latino; 2 Asian, non-Hispanic/Latino; 22 Hispanic/Latino, 8 international. Average age 27. *Faculty:* 62 full-time (6 women). Expenses: Contact institution. *Financial support:* Fellowships, research assistantships, teaching assistantships, career-related internships or fieldwork, Federal Work-Study, institutionally sponsored loans, and scholarships/grants available. Support available to part-time students. Financial award application deadline: 4/15. In 2010, 57 first professional degrees, 6 master's awarded. Offers veterinary medicine (DVM, MS); veterinary medicine, nursing and allied health (DVM, MS). *Application deadline:* For fall admission, 7/15 for domestic students. Applications are processed on a rolling basis. *Application fee:* $25 ($35 for international students). *Application Contact:* Dr. Robert L. Laney, Vice President/Director of Admissions and Enrollment Management, 334-727-8580, Fax: 334-727-5750, E-mail: planey@tuskegee.edu. *Dean,* Dr. Tsegaye Habtemariam, 334-727-8174, Fax: 334-727-8177.

TYNDALE UNIVERSITY COLLEGE & SEMINARY, Toronto, ON M2M 4B3, Canada

General Information Independent-religious, coed, comprehensive institution. *Graduate housing:* Room and/or apartments available on a first-come, first-served basis to single students; on-campus housing not available to married students.

GRADUATE UNITS

Graduate Programs *Degree program information:* Part-time programs available. Postbaccalaureate distance learning degree programs offered (no on-campus study). Offers Biblical studies (M Div); Christian foundations (MTS); Christian studies (Diploma); counseling (M Div); educational ministry (M Div); missions (M Div, Diploma); pastoral and Chinese ministry (M Div); pastoral ministry (M Div); Pentecostal studies (MTS); spiritual formation (M Div, Diploma); theological studies (M Div); theology (Th M); worship and liturgy (M Div, MTS); youth and family ministry (M Div). Electronic applications accepted.

UNIFICATION THEOLOGICAL SEMINARY, Barrytown, NY 12507

General Information Independent-religious, coed, primarily men, graduate-only institution. *Enrollment by degree level:* 19 first professional, 56 master's, 29 doctoral. *Graduate faculty:* 4 full-time (1 woman), 11 part-time/adjunct (2 women). *Tuition:* Full-time $10,440; part-time $435 per credit. *Required fees:* $125 per semester. *Graduate housing:* Rooms and/or apartments available on a first-come, first-served basis to single and married students. Typical cost: $3600 per year ($6050 including board) for single students; $8760 per year ($11,210 including board) for married students. Room and board charges vary according to board plan, campus/location and housing facility selected. *Student services:* Campus employment opportunities, career counseling, international student services, low-cost health insurance. *Library facilities:* UTS Library plus 1 other. *Online resources:* library catalog, web page, access to other libraries' catalogs. *Collection:* 55,100 titles, 75 serial subscriptions, 2,000 audiovisual materials.

Computer facilities: 10 computers available on campus for general student use. A campuswide network can be accessed from student residence rooms. *Web address:* http://www.uts.edu/.

General Application Contact: Davetta Ogunlola, Director of Admissions, 212-563-6647 Ext. 105, Fax: 212-563-6431, E-mail: d.ogunlola@uts.edu.

GRADUATE UNITS

Graduate Program, Main Campus Students: 37 full-time (9 women), 1 part-time (0 women); includes 10 Black or African American, non-Hispanic/Latino; 1 American Indian or Alaska Native, non-Hispanic/Latino; 4 Asian, non-Hispanic/Latino; 1 Hispanic/Latino, 9 international. Average age 45. *Faculty:* 4 full-time (1 woman), 3 part-time/adjunct (0 women). Expenses: Contact institution. *Financial support:* Career-related internships or fieldwork, institutionally sponsored loans, scholarships/grants, and tuition waivers (partial) available. Support available to part-time students. Financial award applicants required to submit FAFSA. In 2010, 2 first professional degrees, 14 master's, 3 doctorates awarded. *Degree program information:* Part-time and evening/weekend programs available. Offers divinity (M Div); ministry (D Min); religious education (MRE); religious studies (MA). *Application deadline:* For fall admission, 8/15 priority date for domestic students; for spring admission, 1/15 priority date for domestic students. Applications are processed on a rolling basis. *Application fee:* $30. *Application Contact:* Davetta Ogunlola, Director of Admissions, 212-563-6647 Ext. 105, Fax: 212-563-6431, E-mail: d.ogunlola@uts.edu. *Academic Dean,* Dr. Kathy Winings, 845-752-3000 Ext. 228, Fax: 845-752-3014, E-mail: academics@uts.edu.

Graduate Program, New York Extension Students: 42 full-time (17 women), 21 part-time (12 women); includes 25 Black or African American, non-Hispanic/Latino; 2 Asian, non-Hispanic/Latino; 1 Hispanic/Latino, 30 international. Average age 40. *Faculty:* 3 full-time (0 women), 9 part-time/adjunct (2 women). Expenses: Contact institution. *Financial support:* Career-related internships or fieldwork, institutionally sponsored loans, scholarships/grants, and tuition waivers (partial) available. Support available to part-time students. Financial award applicants required to submit FAFSA. *Degree program information:* Part-time and evening/weekend programs available. Offers divinity (M Div); religious education (MRE); religious studies (MA). *Application deadline:* For fall admission, 8/15 priority date for domestic students; for spring admission, 1/15 priority date for domestic students. Applications are processed on a rolling basis. *Application fee:* $30. *Application Contact:* Davetta Ogunlola, Admissions Officer, 212-563-6647 Ext. 105, Fax: 212-563-6431, E-mail: d.ogunlola@uts.edu. *Academic Dean,* Dr. Kathy Winings, 212-563-6647 Ext. 101, Fax: 212-563-6431, E-mail: academics@uts.edu.

UNIFORMED SERVICES UNIVERSITY OF THE HEALTH SCIENCES, Bethesda, MD 20814-4799

General Information Federally supported, coed, graduate-only institution. *Enrollment by degree level:* 670 first professional, 44 master's, 110 doctoral. *Graduate faculty:* 372 full-time (119 women), 4,044 part-time/adjunct (908 women). *Graduate housing:* On-campus housing not available. *Student services:* Career counseling, exercise/wellness program, free psychological counseling, grant writing training, low-cost health insurance, multicultural affairs office. *Library facilities:* Learning Resource Center. *Online resources:* library catalog, web page, access to other libraries' catalogs. *Collection:* 522,672 titles, 3,200 serial subscriptions. *Research affiliation:* U. S. Armed Forces Radiobiology Research Institute, National Institutes of Health, National Library of Medicine, Walter Reed Army Institute of Research, Armed Forces Institute of Pathology.

Computer facilities: 80 computers available on campus for general student use. A campuswide network can be accessed. Online class registration is available. *Web address:* http://www.usuhs.mil/.

General Application Contact: Elena Marina Sherman, Graduate Program Coordinator, 301-295-3913, Fax: 301-295-6772, E-mail: elena.sherman@usuhs.mil.

GRADUATE UNITS

Graduate School of Nursing Students: 70 full-time (33 women); includes 24 minority (14 Black or African American, non-Hispanic/Latino; 7 Asian, non-Hispanic/Latino; 1 Hispanic/Latino; 2 Native Hawaiian or other Pacific Islander, non-Hispanic/Latino). Average age 36. 120 applicants, 58% accepted, 70 enrolled. *Faculty:* 25 full-time (20 women), 7 part-time/adjunct (5 women). Expenses: Contact institution. In 2010, 44 master's awarded. Offers family nurse practitioner (MSN); nurse anesthesia (MSN); perioperative clinical nurse specialty (MSN); psychiatric mental health nurse practitioner (MSN). Available to military officers only. *Application deadline:* For fall admission, 7/1 for domestic students; for winter admission, 2/15 for domestic students. *Application fee:* $0. Electronic applications accepted. *Application Contact:* Terry Lynn Malavakis, Recording Secretary for Admissions Committee, 301-295-1055, Fax: 301-295-1707, E-mail: tmalavakis@usuhs.mil. *Associate Dean for Academic Affairs,* Dr. Carol A. Romano, 301-295-1180, Fax: 301-295-1707, E-mail: carol.romano@usuhs.mil.

School of Medicine Offers medicine (MD, MPH, MSPH, MTMH, Dr PH, PhD).

Graduate Programs in the Biomedical Sciences and Public Health Students: 176 full-time (96 women); includes 6 Black or African American, non-Hispanic/Latino; 4 American Indian or Alaska Native, non-Hispanic/Latino; 14 Asian, non-Hispanic/Latino; 7 Hispanic/Latino, 11 international. Average age 28. 278 applicants, 20% accepted, 47 enrolled. *Faculty:* 372 full-time (119 women), 4,044 part-time/adjunct (908 women). Expenses: Contact institution. *Financial support:* In 2010–11, fellowships with full tuition reimbursements (averaging $26,000 per year), research assistantships with full tuition reimbursements (averaging $26,000 per year) were awarded; career-related internships or fieldwork, scholarships/grants, health care benefits, and tuition waivers (full) also available. In 2010, 36 master's, 17 doctorates awarded. Offers clinical psychology (PhD); emerging infectious diseases (PhD); environmental health science (PhD); medical and clinical psychology (PhD); medical and clinical psychology (clinical/dual track) (PhD); medical and clinical psychology (research track) (PhD); medical zoology (PhD); molecular and cell biology (PhD); neuroscience (PhD); preventive medicine and biometrics (MPH, MSPH, MTMH, Dr PH, PhD); public health (MPH, MSPH, Dr PH); tropical medicine and hygiene (MTMH). *Application deadline:* For fall admission, 1/1 priority date for domestic and international students. Applications are processed on a rolling basis. *Application fee:* $0. Electronic applications accepted. *Application Contact:* Elena Marina Sherman, Graduate Program Coordinator, 301-295-3913, Fax: 301-295-6772, E-mail: elena.sherman@usuhs.mil. *Associate Dean,* Dr. Eleanor S. Metcalf, 301-295-1104, E-mail: emetcalf@usuhs.mil.

UNION COLLEGE, Barbourville, KY 40906-1499

General Information Independent-religious, coed, comprehensive institution. *Graduate housing:* Rooms and/or apartments available to single and married students.

GRADUATE UNITS

Graduate Programs *Degree program information:* Part-time and evening/weekend programs available. Offers clinical psychology (MA); counseling psychology (MA); elementary education (MA); health (MA Ed); health and physical education (MA); middle grades (MA); music education (MA); principalship (MA); reading specialist (MA); school psychology (MA); secondary education (MA); special education (MA).

UNION COLLEGE, Lincoln, NE 68506-4300

General Information Independent-religious, coed, comprehensive institution. *Graduate housing:* Rooms and/or apartments available on a first-come, first-served basis to single and married students.

GRADUATE UNITS

Physician Assistant Program Offers physician assistant (MPAS). Electronic applications accepted.

UNION GRADUATE COLLEGE, Schenectady, NY 12308-3107

General Information Independent, coed, graduate-only institution. *Enrollment by degree level:* 428 master's, 23 other advanced degrees. *Graduate faculty:* 24 full-time (4 women), 41 part-time/adjunct (12 women). *Tuition:* Part-time $750 per credit. One-time fee: $350 part-time. Tuition and fees vary according to course load and program. *Graduate housing:* On-campus housing not available. *Student services:* Campus employment opportunities, campus safety program, career counseling, free psychological counseling, international student services, low-cost health insurance, services for students with disabilities, teacher training. *Library facilities:* Schaeffer Library. *Online resources:* library catalog, web page, access to other libraries' catalogs. *Collection:* 634,183 titles, 12,500 serial subscriptions, 13,501 audiovisual materials.

Computer facilities: 30 computers available on campus for general student use. A campuswide network can be accessed from off campus. Online class registration is available. *Web address:* http://www.uniongraduatecollege.edu/.

General Application Contact: Erin Wheeler, Director of Recruiting, 518-631-9850, Fax: 518-631-9901, E-mail: wheelere@uniongraduatecollege.edu.

GRADUATE UNITS

Center for Bioethics and Clinical Leadership Students: 9 full-time (5 women), 50 part-time (32 women); includes 2 Black or African American, non-Hispanic/Latino; 16 Asian, non-Hispanic/Latino; 3 Hispanic/Latino, 3 international. Average age 33. 45 applicants, 67% accepted, 20 enrolled. *Faculty:* 2 full-time (0 women), 22 part-time/adjunct (10 women). Expenses: Contact institution. *Financial support:* Federal Work-Study, scholarships/grants, health care benefits, and tuition waivers (partial) available. Support available to part-time students. Financial award applicants required to submit FAFSA. In 2010, 15 master's, 3 other advanced degrees awarded. *Degree program information:* Part-time and evening/weekend programs available. Postbaccalaureate distance learning degree programs offered (minimal on-campus study). Offers bioethics (MS); clinical ethics (AC); clinical leadership in health management (MS); health, policy and law (AC). *Application deadline:* Applications are processed on a rolling basis. *Application fee:* $60. Electronic applications accepted. *Application Contact:* Ann Nolte, Assistant Director, 518-631-9860, Fax: 518-631-9903, E-mail: noltea@uniongraduatecollege.edu. *Director,* Dr. Robert B. Baker, 518-631-9860, Fax: 518-631-9903, E-mail: bakerr@union.edu.

School of Education Students: 50 full-time (37 women), 23 part-time (19 women); includes 4 minority (3 Asian, non-Hispanic/Latino; 1 Hispanic/Latino), 1 international. Average age 32. 70 applicants, 86% accepted, 48 enrolled. *Faculty:* 3 full-time (1 woman), 23 part-time/adjunct (8 women). Expenses: Contact institution. *Financial support:* Career-related internships or fieldwork, Federal Work-Study, scholarships/grants, health care benefits, and tuition waivers (partial) available. Support available to part-time students. Financial award applicants required to submit FAFSA. In 2010, 47 master's, 18 other advanced degrees awarded. Offers biology (MAT, MS); chemistry (MAT); Chinese (MAT); earth science (MAT); English (MAT); French (MAT); general science (MAT); German (MAT); Greek (MAT); languages (MAT); Latin (MAT); mathematics (MAT); mathematics and technology (MS); mentoring and teacher leadership (AC); middle childhood extension (AC); national board certificate and teacher leadership (AC); physical science (MS); physics (MAT); social studies (MAT); Spanish (MAT). *Application deadline:* Applications are processed on a rolling basis. *Application fee:* $60. Electronic applications accepted. *Application Contact:* Christine Angley, Assistant, 518-631-9871, Fax: 518-631-9903, E-mail: angleyc@uniongraduatecollege.edu. *Dean,* Dr. Patrick Allen, 518-631-9870, Fax: 518-631-9901.

School of Engineering and Computer Science Students: 15 full-time (1 woman), 89 part-time (13 women); includes 1 Black or African American, non-Hispanic/Latino; 1 American Indian or Alaska Native, non-Hispanic/Latino; 7 Asian, non-Hispanic/Latino; 6 Hispanic/Latino, 2 international. Average age 27. 52 applicants, 79% accepted, 39 enrolled. *Faculty:* 3 full-time (0 women), 9 part-time/adjunct (0 women). Expenses: Contact institution. *Financial support:* Research assistantships, Federal Work-Study, scholarships/grants, health care benefits, and tuition waivers (full and partial) available. Support available to part-time students. Financial award applicants required to submit FAFSA. In 2010, 24 master's awarded. *Degree program information:* Part-time and evening/weekend programs available. Offers computer science (MS); electrical engineering (MS); engineering and management systems (MS); mechanical engineering (MS). *Application deadline:* Applications are processed on a rolling basis. *Application fee:* $60. Electronic applications accepted. *Application Contact:* Diane Trzaskos, Coordinator, Admissions, 518-631-9837, Fax: 518-631-9901, E-mail: trzaskod@uniongraduatecollege.edu. *Dean,* Robert Kozik, 515-631-9881, Fax: 518-631-9902, E-mail: kozikr@union.edu.

School of Management Students: 129 full-time (61 women), 86 part-time (42 women); includes 27 minority (4 Black or African American, non-Hispanic/Latino; 16 Asian, non-Hispanic/Latino; 4 Hispanic/Latino; 3 Two or more races, non-Hispanic/Latino), 17 international. Average age 27. 115 applicants, 77% accepted, 71 enrolled. *Faculty:* 16 full-time (3 women), 7 part-time/adjunct (2 women). Expenses: Contact institution. *Financial support:* Research assistantships, career-related internships or fieldwork, Federal Work-Study, scholarships/grants, health care benefits, and tuition waivers (partial) available. Support available to part-time students. Financial award applicants required to submit FAFSA. In 2010, 78 master's, 17 other advanced degrees awarded. *Degree program information:* Part-time and evening/weekend programs available. Offers business administration (MBA); financial management (Certificate); general management (Certificate); health systems administration (MBA, Certificate); human resources (Certificate). *Application deadline:* Applications are processed on a rolling basis. *Application fee:* $60. *Application Contact:* Diane Trzaskos, Admissions Coordinator, 518-631-9837, Fax: 518-631-9901, E-mail: trzaskod@uniongraduatecollege.edu. *Dean,* Dr. Eric Lewis, 518-631-9890, Fax: 518-631-9902, E-mail: lewise@uniongraduatecollege.edu.

UNION INSTITUTE & UNIVERSITY, Cincinnati, OH 45206-1925

General Information Independent, coed, university. *Enrollment:* 1,508 graduate, professional, and undergraduate students; 325 full-time matriculated graduate/professional students (236 women), 215 part-time matriculated graduate/professional students (167 women). *Enrollment by degree level:* 289 master's, 241 doctoral, 10 other advanced degrees. *Graduate faculty:* 24 full-time (8 women), 79 part-time/adjunct (49 women). *Tuition:* Full-time $16,430; part-time $685 per credit hour. *Required fees:* $174; $44 per term. Tuition and fees vary according to course load, degree level and program. *Graduate housing:* On-campus housing not available. *Student services:* Career counseling, services for students with disabilities, teacher training, writing training. *Library facilities:* Union Institute & University Virtual Library. *Online resources:* library catalog, web page, access to other libraries' catalogs. *Collection:* 60,000 titles, 75 serial subscriptions, 500 audiovisual materials.

Computer facilities: Computer purchase and lease plans are available. 65 computers available on campus for general student use. A campuswide network can be accessed from off campus. Online class registration, CampusWeb-online access to basic information and grades are available. *Web address:* http://www.myunion.edu/.

General Application Contact: Admissions Office, 513-861-6400, E-mail: admissions@myunion.edu.

GRADUATE UNITS

Education Programs Students: 60 full-time (50 women), 60 part-time (46 women); includes 46 minority (40 Black or African American, non-Hispanic/Latino; 2 American Indian or Alaska Native, non-Hispanic/Latino; 4 Hispanic/Latino). Average age 52. *Faculty:* 6 full-time (1 woman), 18 part-time/adjunct (14 women). Expenses: Contact institution. *Financial support:* Federal Work-Study and scholarships/grants available. In 2010, 19 master's awarded. Postbaccalaureate distance learning degree programs offered (minimal on-campus study). Offers adult and higher education (M Ed); curriculum and instruction (M Ed); educational leadership (M Ed, Ed D); guidance and counseling (Ed S); higher education (Ed D); issues in education (M Ed); reading (Ed S). M Ed offered online and in Vermont and Florida, concentrations vary by location; Ed S offered in Florida; Ed D program is a hybrid (online with limited residency) offered in Ohio. *Application deadline:* Applications are processed on a rolling basis. *Application fee:* $50. *Application Contact:* Josefina Rosario, Admissions Counselor, 800-294-8884, E-mail: josefina.rosario@myunion.edu. *Dean*, Dr. Arlene Sacks, 305-653-6713, E-mail: arlene.sacks@myunion.edu.

Master of Arts Program–Online Students: 27 full-time (26 women), 119 part-time (98 women); includes 34 minority (25 Black or African American, non-Hispanic/Latino; 3 American Indian or Alaska Native, non-Hispanic/Latino; 6 Hispanic/Latino). Average age 40. *Faculty:* 2 full-time (1 woman), 18 part-time/adjunct (11 women). Expenses: Contact institution. *Financial support:* Career-related internships or fieldwork and tuition waivers available. Financial award applicants required to submit FAFSA. In 2010, 26 master's awarded. *Degree program information:* Part-time programs available. Postbaccalaureate distance learning degree programs offered (no on-campus study). Offers creativity studies (MA); education (MA); health and wellness (MA); history and culture (MA); leadership, public policy, and social issues (MA); literature and writing (MA); psychology (MA). *Application deadline:* Applications are processed on a rolling basis. *Application fee:* $50. Electronic applications accepted. *Application Contact:* Diane Robinson, Director of Admissions, 888-828-8575, E-mail: diane.robinson@myunion.edu. *Program Director*, Dr. Brian Webb, 802-828-8777, E-mail: brian.webb@tui.edu.

PhD Program in Interdisciplinary Studies Students: 103 full-time (60 women), 3 part-time (1 woman); includes 42 minority (40 Black or African American, non-Hispanic/Latino; 1 American Indian or Alaska Native, non-Hispanic/Latino; 1 Hispanic/Latino). Average age 46. *Faculty:* 4 full-time (1 woman), 14 part-time/adjunct (9 women). Expenses: Contact institution. *Financial support:* Federal Work-Study, scholarships/grants, and tuition waivers (partial) available. Financial award application deadline: 5/1; financial award applicants required to submit FAFSA. In 2010, 2 doctorates awarded. Postbaccalaureate distance learning degree programs offered (minimal on-campus study). Offers ethical and creative leadership (PhD); humanities and culture (PhD); public policy and social change (PhD). Program requires participation in brief on-campus residencies twice each year (January and July). *Application deadline:* Applications are processed on a rolling basis. *Application fee:* $50. *Application Contact:* Michelle Flick, Admissions Counselor, 800-486-3116 Ext. 1225. *Dean*, Dr. Larry Preston, 513-861-6400 Ext. 1151, E-mail: larry.preston@myunion.edu.

Programs in Psychology and Counseling Students: 93 full-time (66 women), 11 part-time (10 women); includes 14 minority (6 Black or African American, non-Hispanic/Latino; 1 Asian, non-Hispanic/Latino; 7 Hispanic/Latino). Average age 44. *Faculty:* 6 full-time (4 women), 17 part-time/adjunct (6 women). Expenses: Contact institution. *Financial support:* Federal Work-Study available. Financial award applicants required to submit FAFSA. In 2010, 21 master's awarded. Postbaccalaureate distance learning degree programs offered (minimal on-campus study). Offers clinical mental health counseling (MA); clinical psychology (Psy D); counseling psychology (MA); counselor education and supervision (CAGS); developmental psychology (MA); educational psychology (MA); human development and wellness (CAGS); organizational psychology (MA); psychology education (CAGS). Psy D offered in Ohio and Vermont. *Application deadline:* Applications are processed on a rolling basis. *Application fee:* $50. Electronic applications accepted. *Application Contact:* Diane Robinson, Director of Admissions, 888-828-8575, E-mail: diane.robinson@myunion.edu. *Dean*, Dr. Bill Lax, 802-254-0152, E-mail: bill.lax@myunion.edu.

See Display on previous page and Close-Up on page 985.

UNION PRESBYTERIAN SEMINARY, Richmond, VA 23227-4597

General Information Independent-religious, coed, graduate-only institution. *Enrollment by degree level:* 232 master's, 41 doctoral. *Graduate faculty:* 32 full-time (9 women), 16 part-time/adjunct (10 women). *Tuition:* Full-time $12,320; part-time $1232 per credit. *Required fees:* $200; $12 per term. Part-time tuition and fees vary according to campus/location. *Graduate housing:* Rooms and/or apartments available on a first-come, first-served basis to single and married students. Typical cost: $2840 per year for single students; $8040 per year for married students. Room charges vary according to campus/location and housing facility selected. Housing application deadline: 6/30. *Student services:* Campus employment opportunities, campus safety program, career counseling, free psychological counseling, international student services, low-cost health insurance, writing training. *Library facilities:* William Smith Morton Library. *Online resources:* library catalog, web page. *Collection:* 331,000 titles, 1,276 serial subscriptions, 99,772 audiovisual materials.

Computer facilities: 10 computers available on campus for general student use. A campuswide network can be accessed. Online class registration is available. *Web address:* http://www.upsem.edu/.

General Application Contact: Katherine Fiedler Boswell, Director of Admissions, 804-355-0671 Ext. 222, Fax: 804-355-3919, E-mail: kboswell@upsem.edu.

GRADUATE UNITS

Graduate and Professional Programs Students: 172 full-time (88 women), 101 part-time (69 women). 181 applicants, 64% accepted, 94 enrolled. *Faculty:* 32 full-time (9 women), 16 part-time/adjunct (10 women). Expenses: Contact institution. *Financial support:* In 2010–11, 67 students received support; fellowships, teaching assistantships, career-related internships or fieldwork and institutionally sponsored loans available. Financial award application deadline: 5/15; financial award applicants required to submit FAFSA. *Degree program information:* Part-time and evening/weekend programs available. Postbaccalaureate distance learning degree programs offered (minimal on-campus study). *Application deadline:* For fall admission, 3/15 for domestic students; for winter admission, 9/1 for domestic students; for spring admission, 12/1 for domestic students. Applications are processed on a rolling basis. *Application fee:* $45. *Application Contact:* Katherine Fiedler Boswell, Director of Admissions, 804-355-0671 Ext. 222, Fax: 804-355-3919, E-mail: kboswell@upsem.edu. *Dean*, 804-254-8047, Fax: 804-355-3919.

UNION THEOLOGICAL SEMINARY IN THE CITY OF NEW YORK, New York, NY 10027-5710

General Information Independent-religious, coed, graduate-only institution. *Graduate housing:* Rooms and/or apartments available on a first-come, first-served basis to single and married students. Housing application deadline: 5/15.

GRADUATE UNITS

Graduate and Professional Programs *Degree program information:* Part-time programs available. Offers theology (M Div, MA, STM, Ed D, PhD). Ed D offered jointly with Teachers College, Columbia University; M Div/MSSW with Columbia University.

UNION UNIVERSITY, Jackson, TN 38305-3697

General Information Independent-religious, coed, comprehensive institution. *Graduate housing:* Rooms and/or apartments available on a first-come, first-served basis to single and married students.

GRADUATE UNITS

Institute for International and Intercultural Studies *Degree program information:* Part-time and evening/weekend programs available. Offers international and intercultural studies (MAIS). Electronic applications accepted.

McAfee School of Business Administration *Degree program information:* Evening/weekend programs available. Offers business administration (MBA). Also available at Germantown campus. Electronic applications accepted.

School of Christian Studies Offers Christian studies (MCS); expository preaching (D Min).

School of Education *Degree program information:* Part-time and evening/weekend programs available. Offers education (M Ed, MA Ed); education administration generalist (Ed S); educational leadership (Ed D); educational supervision (Ed S); higher education (Ed D). M Ed also available at Germantown campus.

School of Nursing Offers executive leadership (DNP); nurse anesthesia (DNP); nurse anesthetist (PMC); nurse practitioner (DNP); nursing education (MSN, PMC). Electronic applications accepted.

UNITED STATES ARMY COMMAND AND GENERAL STAFF COLLEGE, Fort Leavenworth, KS 66027-2301

General Information Federally supported, coed, primarily men, graduate-only institution. *Graduate housing:* Rooms and/or apartments available to single and married students.

GRADUATE UNITS

Graduate Program Offers military art and science (MMAS). Only career military officers are selected to attend United States Army Command and General Staff College; Graduate Program is voluntary for first-year students, but mandatory for second-year students.

UNITED STATES INTERNATIONAL UNIVERSITY, Nairobi 00800, Kenya

General Information Independent, coed, comprehensive institution. *Enrollment:* 4,692 graduate, professional, and undergraduate students; 517 full-time matriculated graduate/professional students (287 women), 151 part-time matriculated graduate/professional students (85 women). *Enrollment by degree level:* 668 master's. *Graduate faculty:* 85 full-time (22 women), 133 part-time/adjunct (42 women). *Graduate housing:* Room and/or apartments available on a first-come, first-served basis to single students; on-campus housing not available to married students. Housing application deadline: 7/31. *Student services:* Campus employment opportunities, campus safety program, career counseling, exercise/wellness program, free psychological counseling, international student services, low-cost health insurance, services for students with disabilities, teacher training, writing training. *Library facilities:* Lillian K. Beam Library. *Web address:* http://www.usiu.ac.ke/.

General Application Contact: George Lumbasi, Director of Admissions, 254-02-3606563, Fax: 254-02-3606100, E-mail: glumbasi@usiu.ac.ke.

GRADUATE UNITS

School of Arts and Sciences Students: 94 full-time (60 women), 22 part-time (all women). Average age 30. 93 applicants, 80% accepted, 64 enrolled. *Faculty:* 43 full-time (14 women), 69 part-time/adjunct (28 women). Expenses: Contact institution. *Financial support:* In 2010–11, 56 students received support, including 3 research assistantships (averaging $1,400 per year), 7 teaching assistantships (averaging $1,400 per year); career-related internships or fieldwork, scholarships/grants, and unspecified assistantships also available. Support available to part-time students. Financial award application deadline: 6/30; financial award applicants required to submit FAFSA. In 2010, 33 master's awarded. *Degree program information:* Part-time and evening/weekend programs available. Offers counseling psychology (MA); international relations (MA). *Application deadline:* For fall admission, 6/30 priority date for domestic and international students. *Application fee:* $50. *Application Contact:* George Lumbasi, Director of Admissions, 254-02-3606563, Fax: 254-02-3606100, E-mail: glumbasi@usiu.ac.ke. *Dean*, Prof. Mulinge Munyae, 254-02-3606-434, E-mail: mmulinge@usiu.ac.ke.

School of Business Administration Students: 423 full-time (227 women), 129 part-time (63 women). Average age 29. 110 applicants, 79% accepted, 78 enrolled. *Faculty:* 42 full-time (8 women), 64 part-time/adjunct (14 women). Expenses: Contact institution. *Financial support:* In 2010–11, 30 students received support, including 8 research assistantships (averaging $1,400 per year), 4 teaching assistantships (averaging $1,400 per year); career-related internships or fieldwork, scholarships/grants, and unspecified assistantships also available. Support available to part-time students. Financial award application deadline: 6/30; financial award applicants required to submit FAFSA. In 2010, 164 master's awarded. *Degree program information:* Part-time and evening/weekend programs available. Offers business administration (GEMBA); entrepreneurship (MBA); finance (MBA); human resource management (MBA); information technology management (MBA); integrated studies (MBA); international business administration (MBA); management and organizational development (MS); marketing (MBA); organizational development (EMS); strategic management (MBA). *Application deadline:* For fall admission, 6/30 priority date for domestic and international students; for spring admission, 9/30 for domestic and international students. Applications are processed on a rolling basis. *Application fee:* $50. *Application Contact:* George Lumbasi, Director of Admissions, 254-02-3606563, Fax: 254-02-3606100, E-mail: glumbasi@usiu.ac.ke. *Dean*, Dr. Damary Sikalieh, 254-02-3606-415, E-mail: dsikalieh@usiu.ac.ke.

UNITED STATES SPORTS ACADEMY, Daphne, AL 36526-7055

General Information Independent, coed, upper-level institution. *Graduate housing:* On-campus housing not available.

GRADUATE UNITS

Graduate Programs *Degree program information:* Part-time programs available. Postbaccalaureate distance learning degree programs offered (no on-campus study). Offers sport management (MSS, Ed D); sport studies (MSS); sports coaching (MSS); sports fitness and health (MSS); sports medicine (MSS). Electronic applications accepted.

UNITED STATES UNIVERSITY, National City, CA 91950

General Information Proprietary, coed, comprehensive institution.

GRADUATE UNITS

Family Nurse Practitioner Program Offers family nurse practitioner (MSN).

UNITED TALMUDICAL SEMINARY, Brooklyn, NY 11211

General Information Independent-religious, men only, comprehensive institution.

GRADUATE UNITS

Graduate Programs

UNITED THEOLOGICAL SEMINARY, Trotwood, OH 45426

General Information Independent-religious, coed, graduate-only institution. *Enrollment by degree level:* 136 first professional, 35 master's, 184 doctoral, 5 other advanced degrees. *Graduate faculty:* 14 full-time (5 women), 30 part-time/adjunct (9 women). *Tuition:* Full-time $10,836; part-time $477 per credit hour. *Required fees:* $105 per semester. Tuition and fees vary according to course load and program. *Student services:* Campus employment opportunities, exercise/wellness program, international student services, writing training. *Library facilities:* Memorial Library. *Collection:* 138,384 titles, 518 serial subscriptions, 8,038 audiovisual materials.

Computer facilities: 12 computers available on campus for general student use. A campuswide network can be accessed. *Web address:* http://www.united.edu/.

General Application Contact: Evan Abla, Admissions Officer, 937-529-2201, Fax: 866-359-9350, E-mail: utsadmis@united.edu.

GRADUATE UNITS

Graduate and Professional Programs Students: 311 full-time (123 women), 49 part-time (22 women); includes 183 minority (171 Black or African American, non-Hispanic/Latino; 9

United Theological Seminary (continued)

Asian, non-Hispanic/Latino; 3 Hispanic/Latino), 3 international. *Faculty:* 14 full-time (5 women), 30 part-time/adjunct (9 women). Expenses: Contact institution. *Financial support:* Career-related internships or fieldwork, Federal Work-Study, and scholarships/grants available. Financial award application deadline: 4/1; financial award applicants required to submit CSS PROFILE or FAFSA. *Degree program information:* Part-time and evening/weekend programs available. Postbaccalaureate distance learning degree programs offered (minimal on-campus study). Offers theology (M Div, MA, MATS, D Min). *Application deadline:* For fall admission, 8/1 for domestic students, 1/15 for international students; for spring admission, 1/1 for domestic students. Applications are processed on a rolling basis. *Application fee:* $40. Electronic applications accepted. *Application Contact:* Evan Abla, Admissions Officer, 937-529-2201, E-mail: utsadmis@united.edu. *Academic Dean*, Dr. Richard Eslinger, 937-529-2201, E-mail: reslinger@united.edu.

UNITED THEOLOGICAL SEMINARY OF THE TWIN CITIES, New Brighton, MN 55112-2598

General Information Independent-religious, coed, graduate-only institution. *Enrollment by degree level:* 91 first professional, 25 master's, 35 doctoral. *Graduate faculty:* 9 full-time (6 women), 28 part-time/adjunct (16 women). *Tuition:* Full-time $13,014; part-time $482 per credit hour. One-time fee: $170. Tuition and fees vary according to course load, degree level and program. *Graduate housing:* Rooms and/or apartments available on a first-come, first-served basis to single and married students. Typical cost: $664 per year for single students; $883 per year for married students. *Student services:* Campus employment opportunities, free psychological counseling, international student services, multicultural affairs office, services for students with disabilities, writing training. *Library facilities:* Spencer Library. *Online resources:* library catalog, web page. *Collection:* 94,315 titles, 171 serial subscriptions, 559 audiovisual materials.

Computer facilities: 13 computers available on campus for general student use. A campuswide network can be accessed from student residence rooms. Software discount program available. *Web address:* http://www.unitedseminary.edu/.

General Application Contact: Rev. Glen Herrington-Hall, Director of Admissions, 651-255-6107, Fax: 651-633-4315, E-mail: gherrington-hall@unitedseminary.edu.

GRADUATE UNITS

Graduate Programs Students: 57 full-time (41 women), 94 part-time (61 women); includes 6 minority (5 Black or African American, non-Hispanic/Latino; 1 Hispanic/Latino), 1 international. Average age 47. 49 applicants, 98% accepted, 41 enrolled. *Faculty:* 8 full-time (5 women), 28 part-time/adjunct (16 women). Expenses: Contact institution. *Financial support:* In 2010–11, 120 students received support. Career-related internships or fieldwork, institutionally sponsored loans, and scholarships/grants available. Support available to part-time students. Financial award application deadline: 5/1; financial award applicants required to submit FAFSA. In 2010, 10 first professional degrees, 6 master's, 4 doctorates, 2 other advanced degrees awarded. *Degree program information:* Part-time and evening/weekend programs available. Offers advanced theological studies (Diploma); justice and peace studies (M Div, MA); leadership toward racial justice (M Div, MA, Certificate); Methodist studies (M Div, MA, Certificate); ministry (D Min); ministry renewal and professional development (Certificate); pastoral care and counseling (M Div, MA, MARL); religion and theology (MA); theological and religious studies (Certificate); theology and the arts (M Div, MA); urban ministry (M Div, MA, MARL); women's studies: religion, theology and ministry (M Div, MA). *Application deadline:* For fall admission, 7/1 priority date for domestic students, 11/1 priority date for international students; for winter admission, 11/1 priority date for domestic students; for spring admission, 11/15 priority date for domestic students. Applications are processed on a rolling basis. *Application fee:* $50. *Application Contact:* Rev. Glen Herrington-Hall, Director of Admissions, 651-255-6107 Ext. 107, Fax: 651-633-4315, E-mail: gherrington-hall@unitedseminary.edu. *Dean of the Seminary*, Prof. Susan K. Ebbers, 651-255-6143 Ext. 108, Fax: 651-633-4315, E-mail: sebbers@unitedseminary.edu.

UNIVERSIDAD ADVENTISTA DE LAS ANTILLAS, Mayagüez, PR 00681-0118

General Information Independent-religious, coed, comprehensive institution. *Enrollment:* 25 full-time matriculated graduate/professional students (21 women), 17 part-time matriculated graduate/professional students (all women). *Enrollment by degree level:* 42 master's. *Graduate faculty:* 4 part-time/adjunct (3 women). *Tuition:* Full-time $1152; part-time $836 per year. *Required fees:* $260 per semester. *Graduate housing:* Rooms and/or apartments available on a first-come, first-served basis to single and married students. *Student services:* Campus employment opportunities, campus safety program, career counseling, international student services, low-cost health insurance. *Library facilities:* Dennis Soto Library plus 1 other. *Online resources:* library catalog, web page, access to other libraries' catalogs.

Computer facilities: 62 computers available on campus for general student use. A campuswide network can be accessed from student residence rooms and from off campus. Online class registration is available. *Web address:* http://www.uaa.edu/.

General Application Contact: Prof. Yolanda Ferrer, Director of Admission, 787-834-9595 Ext. 2261, Fax: 787-834-9597, E-mail: admissions@uaa.edu.

GRADUATE UNITS

EGECED Department Students: 25 full-time (21 women), 17 part-time (all women). *Faculty:* 4 part-time/adjunct (3 women). Expenses: Contact institution. *Financial support:* Fellowships, Federal Work-Study available. Offers curriculum and instruction (M Ed); health education (M Ed); medical surgical nursing (MN); pastoral theology (M Div); school administration and supervision (M Ed). *Application fee:* $175. Electronic applications accepted. *Application Contact:* Prof. Yolanda Ferrer, Director of Admission, 787-834-9595 Ext. 2261, Fax: 787-834-9597, E-mail: admissions@uaa.edu. *Director*, 787-834-9595 Ext. 2282, Fax: 787-834-9595.

UNIVERSIDAD CENTRAL DEL CARIBE, Bayamón, PR 00960-6032

General Information Independent, coed, comprehensive institution. *Graduate housing:* On-campus housing not available.

GRADUATE UNITS

Program in Substance Abuse Counseling Offers substance abuse counseling (MHS).

School of Medicine Offers anatomy and cell biology (MA, MS); biochemistry (MS); biomedical sciences (MA); cellular and molecular biology (PhD); medicine (MD, MA, MS, PhD); microbiology and immunology (MA, MS); pharmacology (MS); physiology (MS).

UNIVERSIDAD DE LAS AMERICAS, A.C., 06700 Mexico City, Mexico

General Information Independent, coed, comprehensive institution.

GRADUATE UNITS

Program in Business Administration Offers finance (MBA); marketing research (MBA); production and quality (MBA).

Program in Education Offers education (M Ed).

Program in International Organizations and Institutions Offers international organizations and institutions (MA).

Program in Psychology Offers family therapy (MA).

UNIVERSIDAD DE LAS AMÉRICAS–PUEBLA, 72820 Puebla, Mexico

General Information Independent, coed, university. *Graduate housing:* On-campus housing not available. *Research affiliation:* Empacadora San Marcos S. A. de C. U. (food service), Volkswagen de México S. A. de C. U. (mechanical engineering), Institute Mexicano del Tecnologá del agua (electronic engineering), Frugosa S. A. de C. U. (chemical engineering).

GRADUATE UNITS

Division of Graduate Studies *Degree program information:* Part-time and evening/weekend programs available.

School of Business and Economics *Degree program information:* Part-time and evening/weekend programs available. Offers business administration (MBA); finance (M Adm).

School of Engineering *Degree program information:* Part-time and evening/weekend programs available. Offers chemical engineering (MS); computer science (PhD); construction management (M Adm); electronic engineering (MS); engineering (M Adm, MS, PhD); food sciences (MS); food technology (MS); industrial engineering (MS); manufacturing administration (MS); production management (M Adm).

School of Humanities *Degree program information:* Part-time and evening/weekend programs available. Offers humanities (MA); information design (MA); linguistics (MA); literature (MA).

School of Sciences *Degree program information:* Part-time and evening/weekend programs available. Offers biotechnology (MS); clinical analysis (biomedicine) (MS); sciences (MS).

School of Social Sciences *Degree program information:* Part-time and evening/weekend programs available. Offers American studies (MA); anthropology (MA); archaeology (MA); economics (MA); education (MA); finance (M Adm); psychology (MA); social sciences (M Adm, MA).

UNIVERSIDAD DEL ESTE, Carolina, PR 00984

General Information Independent, coed, comprehensive institution.

GRADUATE UNITS

Graduate School

UNIVERSIDAD DEL TURABO, Gurabo, PR 00778-3030

General Information Independent, coed, university. CGS member. *Enrollment:* 1,392 full-time matriculated graduate/professional students (969 women), 1,469 part-time matriculated graduate/professional students (1,046 women). *Enrollment by degree level:* 2,499 master's, 362 doctoral. *Graduate faculty:* 154 full-time (76 women), 777 part-time/adjunct (406 women). *Graduate housing:* On-campus housing not available. *Student services:* Campus employment opportunities, career counseling, child daycare facilities, free psychological counseling, services for students with disabilities, teacher training.

Computer facilities: A campuswide network can be accessed from off campus. *Web address:* http://www.suagm.edu/ut/.

General Application Contact: Carmen Rivera, Director of Admissions and Financial Aid, 787-743-7979 Ext. 4352, E-mail: ut_crivera@suagm.edu.

GRADUATE UNITS

Graduate Programs *Degree program information:* Part-time and evening/weekend programs available. Postbaccalaureate distance learning degree programs offered. Offers administration of school libraries (Certificate); athletic training (MPHE); coaching (MPHE); curriculum and instruction and appropriate environment (D Ed); curriculum and teaching (M Ed); educational administration (M Ed); educational leadership (D Ed); environmental analysis (MSE); environmental management (MSE); environmental science (D Sc); guidance counseling (M Ed); library service and information technology (M Ed); special education (M Ed); teaching at primary level (M Ed); teaching English as a second language (M Ed); teaching of fine arts (M Ed); wellness (MPHE).

School in Business Administration *Degree program information:* Part-time and evening/weekend programs available. Offers accounting (MBA); business administration (MBA, DBA); human resources (MBA); logistics and materials management (MBA); management (MBA, DBA); management of information systems (MBA); marketing (MBA); office systems management (MBA, DBA); project management (MBA); quality management (MBA).

School of Engineering Offers engineering (MS); telecommunication and network administration (MS).

School of Health Sciences Offers clinical nurse leader (MSN); family nurse practitioner (MSN); family nurse practitioner—adult nursing (MSN); health sciences (MS, MSN, ND); naturopathy (ND); speech and language pathology (MS).

School of Social Sciences and Humanities Offers arts administration (MPA); conflict and mediation studies (MPA); counseling psychology (M Psych, Psy D, Certificate); criminal justice studies (MPA); forensic science (MPA); human services administration (MPA); social sciences and humanities (M Psych, MPA, Psy D, Certificate).

UNIVERSIDAD DE MONTERREY, 66238 San Pedro Garza GarcÝa, NL, Mexico

General Information Independent-religious, coed, comprehensive institution.

GRADUATE UNITS

Graduate Programs

UNIVERSIDAD FLET, Miami, FL 33186

General Information Independent-religious, coed, comprehensive institution.

GRADUATE UNITS

Department of Graduate Studies Offers education (M Ed); theological studies (MTS).

UNIVERSIDAD METROPOLITANA, San Juan, PR 00928-1150

General Information Independent, coed, comprehensive institution. *Graduate housing:* On-campus housing not available. *Research affiliation:* Berkeley National Laboratories (bioremediation), University Corporation for Atmospheric Research (computer science, atmospheric science), University of Colorado at Boulder (computer science, biology), University of Puerto Rico (physics, chemistry), University of Utah (computational chemistry), Howard University (computational chemistry).

GRADUATE UNITS

School of Business Administration *Degree program information:* Part-time and evening/weekend programs available. Offers accounting (MBA); finance (MBA); human resources management (MBA); international business (MBA); management (MBA); management information systems (MBA); marketing (MBA). Electronic applications accepted.

School of Education *Degree program information:* Part-time and evening/weekend programs available. Offers administration and supervision (M Ed); curriculum and teaching (M Ed); education (M Ed, Ed D); educational administration and supervision (M Ed); managing recreation and sports services (M Ed); pedagogy (PhD); pre-school centers administration (M Ed); special education (M Ed); teaching of adult physical education (M Ed); teaching of elementary physical education (M Ed); teaching of physical education (M Ed); teaching of secondary physical education (M Ed). Electronic applications accepted.

School of Environmental Affairs *Degree program information:* Part-time programs available. Offers environmental management (MSEM); environmental planning (MP); environmental studies (MAES). Electronic applications accepted.

School of Health Sciences Offers case management (Certificate); health sciences (MSN, Certificate); nursing (MSN); oncology nursing (Certificate).

School of Social Sciences, Humanities and Communications Offers counseling psychology (MA).

UNIVERSITÉ DE MONCTON, Moncton, NB E1A 3E9, Canada

General Information Province-supported, coed, comprehensive institution. *Graduate housing:* Rooms and/or apartments available on a first-come, first-served basis to single and married students.

GRADUATE UNITS

Faculty of Administration Students: 32 full-time (5 women), 17 international. Average age 28. 142 applicants, 60% accepted, 20 enrolled. *Faculty:* 22 full-time (7 women), 20 part-time/adjunct (1 woman). Expenses: Contact institution. *Financial support:* In 2010–11, 7 fellowships (averaging $2,500 per year) were awarded; teaching assistantships, institutionally sponsored loans also available. Support available to part-time students. Financial award application deadline: 5/30. In 2010, 15 master's awarded. *Degree program information:* Part-time and evening/weekend programs available. Postbaccalaureate distance learning degree programs offered (no on-campus study). Offers administration (MBA). *Application deadline:* For fall admission, 6/1 for domestic students, 2/1 for international students; for winter admission, 11/15 for domestic students, 9/1 for international students; for spring admission, 3/31 for domestic students, 1/1 for international students. Applications are processed on a rolling basis. *Application fee:* $39. Electronic applications accepted. *Application Contact:* Natalie Allain, Admission Counselor, 506-858-4273, Fax: 506-858-4093, E-mail: natalie.allain@umoncton.ca. *Director*, Dr. Nha Nguyen, 506-858-4231, Fax: 506-858-4093, E-mail: nha.nguyen@umoncton.ca.

Faculty of Arts and Social Sciences *Degree program information:* Part-time programs available. Offers arts and social sciences (MA, MPA, MSW, PhD); economics (MA); French studies (MA, PhD); history (MA); public administration (MPA). Electronic applications accepted.
School of Social Work Offers social work (MSW).

Faculty of Education *Degree program information:* Part-time programs available. Offers education (M Ed, MA Ed).
Graduate Studies in Education *Degree program information:* Part-time programs available. Offers educational psychology (M Ed, MA Ed); guidance (M Ed, MA Ed); school administration (M Ed, MA Ed); teaching (M Ed, MA Ed).

Faculty of Engineering Offers civil engineering (M Sc A); electrical engineering (M Sc A); industrial engineering (M Sc A); mechanical engineering (M Sc A).

Faculty of Science *Degree program information:* Part-time programs available. Offers biochemistry (M Sc); biology (M Sc); chemistry (M Sc); information technology (M Sc, Certificate, Diploma); mathematics (M Sc); physics and astronomy (M Sc); science (M Sc, Certificate, Diploma). Electronic applications accepted.

School of Food Science, Nutrition and Family Studies *Degree program information:* Part-time programs available. Offers foods/nutrition (M Sc). Electronic applications accepted.

UNIVERSITÉ DE MONTRÉAL, Montréal, QC H3C 3J7, Canada

General Information Independent, coed, university. CGS member. *Graduate housing:* Room and/or apartments available on a first-come, first-served basis to single students; on-campus housing not available to married students. Housing application deadline: 2/1. *Research affiliation:* Centre Hospitalier Universitaire Mère-Enfant de lHôpital Sainte-Justine, Centre de Recherche de L&a'Hôpital Sacré-Coeur, Institut de Recherches Cliniques de Montréal, Institut de Cardiologie de Montréal, Institut Universitaire de gériatric de Montréal.

GRADUATE UNITS

Department of Kinesiology Offers kinesiology (M Sc, DESS); physical activity (M Sc, PhD). Electronic applications accepted.

Faculty of Arts and Sciences *Degree program information:* Part-time programs available. Offers anthropology (M Sc, PhD); applied human sciences (PhD); art history (MA, PhD); arts and sciences (M Sc, MA, MIS, PhD, DESS); biological sciences (M Sc, PhD); chemistry (M Sc, PhD); classical studies (MA); communication (PhD); communication sciences (M Sc); comparative literature (MA); computer systems (M Sc, PhD); demography (M Sc, PhD); economics (M Sc, PhD); electronic commerce (M Sc); English studies (MA, PhD); environment and durable development (DESS); film studies (MA, PhD); French literature (MA, PhD); geography (M Sc, PhD, DESS); German literature (PhD); German studies (MA); Hispanic literature (PhD); Hispanic studies (MA); history (MA, PhD); international studies (M Sc, DESS); linguistics (MA, PhD); literature (PhD); mathematical and computational finance (M Sc, DESS); mathematics (M Sc, PhD); museology (MA); philosophy (MA, PhD); physics (M Sc, PhD); political science (M Sc, PhD); psychology (M Sc, PhD); societies, public policies and health (DESS); sociology (M Sc, PhD); statistics (M Sc, PhD); translation (MA, PhD, DESS). Electronic applications accepted.
School of Criminology Offers criminology (M Sc, PhD). Electronic applications accepted.
School of Industrial Relations *Degree program information:* Part-time programs available. Offers industrial relations (M Sc, PhD, DESS). Electronic applications accepted.
School of Library and Information Sciences Offers information sciences (MIS, PhD). Electronic applications accepted.
School of Psychoeducation *Degree program information:* Part-time programs available. Offers psychoeducation (M Sc, PhD). Electronic applications accepted.
School of Social Service *Degree program information:* Part-time programs available. Offers social administration (DESS); social work (M Sc, PhD). M Sc and PhD offered jointly with McGill University. Electronic applications accepted.

Faculty of Dental Medicine Offers dental medicine (M Sc, Certificate); multidisciplinary residency (Certificate); oral and dental sciences (M Sc); orthodontics (M Sc); pediatric dentistry (M Sc); prosthodontics rehabilitation (M Sc); stomatology residency (Certificate). Electronic applications accepted.

Faculty of Education *Degree program information:* Part-time and evening/weekend programs available. Offers administration and foundations of education (M Ed, MA, PhD, DESS); didactics (M Ed, MA, PhD, DESS); education (M Ed, MA, PhD, DESS); psychopedagogy and andragogy (M Ed, MA, PhD, DESS). Electronic applications accepted.

Faculty of Environmental Design and Planning Offers environmental design and planning (M Sc A, PhD); environmental planning and design projects (DESS); game design (DESS); urban management for developing countries (DESS); urban planning (M Urb). DESS programs offered jointly with HEC Montreal and École Polytechnique de Montréal. Electronic applications accepted.

Faculty of Law *Degree program information:* Part-time programs available. Offers business law (DESS); common law (North America) (JD); international law (DESS); law (LL B, LL M, LL D, DDN, DESS); tax law (LL M). Electronic applications accepted.

Faculty of Medicine Offers biochemistry (M Sc, PhD, DEPD); bioethics (MA, DESS); bioinformatics (M Sc, PhD); biomedical sciences (M Sc, PhD); clinical biochemistry (DEPD); community health (M Sc, DESS); echography transoephagian perioperatoryenvironment, health and disaster management (DESS); environmental and occupational health (M Sc); genetic counseling (DESS); health administration (M Sc, DESS); health sciencesinsurance medicine and expertise (English) (DESS); insurance medicine and expertise in health sciences (DESS); medical genetics (DESS); medicine (MD, M Sc, M Sc A, MA, PMS, DES, PhD, DEPD, DESS); microbiology and immunology (M Sc, PhD); mobility and posture (DESS); molecular biology (M Sc, PhD); neurological sciences (M Sc, PhD); nutrition (M Sc, PhD, DESS); occupational therapy (DESS); pathology and cellular biology (M Sc, PhD); pharmacology (M Sc, PhD); physiology (M Sc, PhD); public health (PhD); toxicology and risk analysis (DESS). Electronic applications accepted.
Institute of Biomedical Engineering Offers biomedical engineering (M Sc A, PhD, DESS). M Sc A and PhD programs offered jointly with École Polytechnique de Montréal. Electronic applications accepted.
School of Speech Therapy and Audiology Offers audiology (PMS); speech therapy (PMS, DESS). Electronic applications accepted.

Faculty of Music Offers composition (M Mus, D Mus); interpretation (M Mus, D Mus, DESS); music (MA, PhD); orchestral repertoire (DESS). Electronic applications accepted.

Faculty of Nursing *Degree program information:* Part-time programs available. Offers nursing (M Sc, PhD, Certificate, DESS). PhD offered jointly with McGill University. Electronic applications accepted.

Faculty of Pharmacy *Degree program information:* Part-time programs available. Offers drugs development (DESS); pharmaceutical care (DESS); pharmaceutical practice (M Sc); pharmaceutical sciences (M Sc, PhD); pharmacist-supervisor teacher (DESS). Electronic applications accepted.

Faculty of Theology and Sciences of Religions Offers health, spirituality and bioethics (DESS); practical theology (MA, PhD); religious sciences (MA, PhD); theology (MA, D Th, PhD, L Th); theology-Biblical studies (PhD). Electronic applications accepted.

Faculty of Veterinary Medicine Offers veterinary medicine (M Sc, DES, PhD); veterinary sciences (M Sc, PhD); virology and immunology (PhD). Electronic applications accepted.

School of Optometry *Degree program information:* Part-time programs available. Offers optometry (OD, M Sc, DESS); vision sciences (M Sc); visual impairment intervention-orientation and mobility (DESS); visual impairment intervention-readaptation (DESS). Electronic applications accepted.

UNIVERSITÉ DE SHERBROOKE, Sherbrooke, QC J1K 2R1, Canada

General Information Independent, coed, university. *Graduate housing:* Room and/or apartments available to single students; on-campus housing not available to married students. Housing application deadline: 6/1. *Research affiliation:* Société de Microélectronique Industrielle.

GRADUATE UNITS

Faculty of Administration Students: 833 full-time (360 women), 986 part-time (386 women). 2,127 applicants, 57% accepted, 692 enrolled. *Faculty:* 91 full-time (33 women). Expenses: Contact institution. *Financial support:* In 2010–11, 110 students received support, including 3 research assistantships (averaging $4,000 per year); career-related internships or fieldwork also available. In 2010, 502 master's, 7 doctorates, 212 other advanced degrees awarded. *Degree program information:* Part-time and evening/weekend programs available. Offers accounting (M Sc); administration (EMBA, M Adm, M Sc, M Tax, MBA, DBA, PhD, Diploma); business administration (EMBA, MBA, DBA); e-commerce (M Sc); economic development (PhD); economics (M Sc); executive business administration (EMBA); finance (M Sc); general management (MBA); governance, audit and security of information technology (M Adm); international business (M Sc); management and governance of cooperatives and mutuals (M Adm); management information systems (M Sc); marketing (M Sc); marketing communications (M Adm); organizational change and intervention (M Sc); public management (M Adm); taxation (M Tax, Diploma). *Application deadline:* For fall admission, 4/30 for domestic and international students. *Application fee:* $70. *Application Contact:* France Myette, Registrar, 819-821-7685, Fax: 819-821-7966, E-mail: france.myette@usherbrooke.ca. *Dean*, Prof. Francine Turmel, 819-821-7311, Fax: 819-821-7928, E-mail: francine.turmel@usherbrooke.ca.

Faculty of Education *Degree program information:* Part-time and evening/weekend programs available. Offers education (M Ed, MA, Diploma); elementary education (M Ed, Diploma); postsecondary education training (M Ed, Diploma); school administration (M Ed); sciences of education (MA); special education (M Ed, Diploma).

Faculty of Engineering *Degree program information:* Part-time programs available. Offers chemical engineering (M Sc A, PhD); civil engineering (M Sc A, PhD); electrical engineering (M Sc A, PhD); engineering (M Eng, M Env, M Sc A, PhD, Diploma); engineering management (M Eng, Diploma); environment (M Env); mechanical engineering (M Sc A, PhD). Electronic applications accepted.

Faculty of Law *Degree program information:* Part-time and evening/weekend programs available. Offers alternative dispute resolution (LL M, Diploma); biotechnology (LL B); business administration (LL B); business law (Diploma); health law (LL M, Diploma); law (LL B, LL D); legal management (Diploma); notarial law (DDN); transnational law (Diploma). Electronic applications accepted.

Faculty of Letters and Human Sciences *Degree program information:* Part-time programs available. Offers comparative Canadian literature (MA, PhD); economics (MA); French literature (MA, PhD); geography and remote sensing (M Sc, PhD); gerontology (MA); history (MA); letters and human sciences (M Psych, M Sc, MA, MSS, PhD, Diploma); linguistics (MA); philosophy (MA); social service (MSS); theatre (MA).
Institute of Management and Development of Cooperatives Offers management and development of cooperatives (MA, Diploma).

Faculty of Medicine and Health Sciences *Degree program information:* Part-time programs available. Offers medicine (MD); medicine and health sciences (MD, M Sc, PhD). Electronic applications accepted.
Graduate Programs in Medicine *Degree program information:* Part-time programs available. Offers biochemistry (M Sc, PhD); cell biology (M Sc, PhD); clinical sciences (M Sc, PhD); immunology (M Sc, PhD); medicine (M Sc, PhD); microbiology (M Sc, PhD); pharmacology (M Sc, PhD); physiology and biophysics (M Sc, PhD); radiobiology (M Sc, PhD). Electronic applications accepted.

Faculty of Physical Education and Sports *Degree program information:* Part-time programs available. Offers kinanthropology (M Sc); physical activity (Diploma); physical education (M Sc, Diploma).

Faculty of Sciences Offers biology (M Sc, PhD, Diploma); chemistry (M Sc, PhD, Diploma); informatics (M Sc, PhD); mathematics (M Sc, PhD); physics (M Sc, PhD); sciences (M Sc, PhD, Diploma).
Centre de Formation en Technologies de L'information Offers information technologies (M Sc, Diploma). Electronic applications accepted.
Centre Universitaire de Formation en Environnement Postbaccalaureate distance learning degree programs offered (no on-campus study). Offers environment (M Sc, Diploma). Electronic applications accepted.

Faculty of Theology, Ethics and Philosophy *Degree program information:* Part-time and evening/weekend programs available. Postbaccalaureate distance learning degree programs offered. Offers applied ethics (Diploma); human science of religions (MA); intercultural training (Diploma); philosophy (MA, PhD); spiritual anthropology (Diploma); theology (MA, PhD, Diploma).

UNIVERSITÉ DU QUÉBEC À CHICOUTIMI, Chicoutimi, QC G7H 2B1, Canada

General Information Province-supported, coed, university. CGS member. *Graduate housing:* Room and/or apartments available to single students; on-campus housing not available to married students.

GRADUATE UNITS

Graduate Programs *Degree program information:* Part-time programs available. Offers didactics of French-mother tongue (Diploma); earth sciences (M Sc A); education (M Ed, MA, PhD); engineering (M Sc A, PhD); ethics (Diploma); fine arts (MA); genetics (M Sc); linguistics (MA); literary studies (MA); mineral resources (PhD); project management (M Sc); regional studies (MA); renewable resources (M Sc); small and medium-sized organization management (M Sc); theology (pastoral studies) (MA, PhD).

UNIVERSITÉ DU QUÉBEC À MONTRÉAL, Montréal, QC H3C 3P8, Canada

General Information Province-supported, coed, university. CGS member. *Graduate housing:* Room and/or apartments available to single students; on-campus housing not available to married students. *Research affiliation:* Labopharm, Inc. (pharmacology), Hydro-Québec (environmental sciences), Bell (computer sciences), Microcréatif (computer sciences), University Corporation for Atmospheric Research.

GRADUATE UNITS

Graduate Programs *Degree program information:* Part-time programs available. Offers accounting (M Sc, MPA, Diploma); actuarial sciences (Diploma); art history (PhD); art studies (MA); atmospheric sciences (M Sc); biology (M Sc, PhD); business administration (PhD);

Université du Québec à Montréal (continued)

business administration (research) (MBA); chemistry (M Sc, PhD); communications (MA, PhD); dance (MA); death (Diploma); Earth and atmospheric sciences (PhD); Earth science (M Sc); earth sciences (M Sc); economics (M Sc, PhD); education (M Ed, MA, PhD); education of the environmental sciences (Diploma); environmental sciences (M Sc, PhD, Certificate); ergonomics in occupational health and safety (Diploma); finance (Diploma); fine arts (MA); geographical information systems (Diploma); geography (M Sc); history (MA, PhD); human movement studies (M Sc); linguistics (MA, PhD); literary studies (MA, PhD); management consultant (Diploma); management information systems (M Sc, M Sc A); mathematics (M Sc, PhD); meteorology (PhD, Diploma); mineral resources (PhD); museology (MA); non-renewable resources (DESS); philosophy (MA, PhD); political science (MA, PhD); project management (MGP, Diploma); psychology (D Ps, PhD); religious sciences (MA, PhD); semiology (PhD); sexology (MA); social and labor law (Certificate); social intervention (MA); sociology (MA, PhD); study and practices of the arts (PhD); urban analysis and management (MA); urban studies (MA, PhD).

UNIVERSITÉ DU QUÉBEC À RIMOUSKI, Rimouski, QC G5L 3A1, Canada

General Information Province-supported, coed, comprehensive institution. CGS member. *Graduate housing:* Rooms and/or apartments available on a first-come, first-served basis to single and married students. *Research affiliation:* Institut des Sciences de la Mer de Rimouski (ISMER) (marine sciences), CRDT (territory development), Centre d'Etudes Nordiques (nordicity), Quebec Ocean (oceans), Centre Recherche en Forestene (forest).

GRADUATE UNITS

Graduate Programs *Degree program information:* Part-time programs available. Offers biology (PhD); business administration (MBA); education (M Ed, MA, PhD, Diploma); engineering (M Sc A); ethics (MA, Diploma); literary studies (MA, PhD); management of marine resources (M Sc, Diploma); management of people in working situation (M Sc, Diploma); nursing studies (M Sc, Diploma); oceanography (M Sc, PhD); project management (M Sc, Diploma); psychosocial studies (MA); regional development (MA, PhD, Diploma); wildlife resources management (M Sc, Diploma).

UNIVERSITÉ DU QUÉBEC À TROIS-RIVIÈRES, Trois-Rivières, QC G9A 5H7, Canada

General Information Province-supported, coed, university. CGS member. *Graduate housing:* Room and/or apartments available to single students; on-campus housing not available to married students. Housing application deadline: 2/1.

GRADUATE UNITS

Graduate Programs *Degree program information:* Part-time programs available. Offers accounting science (MBA); biophysics and cellular biology (M Sc, PhD); business administration (MBA, DBA); chemistry (M Sc); chiropractic (DC); education (M Ed, PhD); educational administration (DESS); electrical engineering (M Sc A, PhD); environmental sciences (M Sc, PhD); finance (DESS); industrial engineering (M Sc, DESS); labor relations (DESS); leisure, culture and tourism sciences (MA, DESS); literary studies (MA); mathematics and computer science (M Sc); matter and energy (MS, PhD); nursing sciences (M Sc, DESS); philosophy (MA, PhD); physical education (M Sc); psychoeducation (M Ed, PhD); psychology (PhD, Certificate); social communication (MA, DESS).

UNIVERSITÉ DU QUÉBEC, ÉCOLE DE TECHNOLOGIE SUPÉRIEURE, Montréal, QC H3C 1K3, Canada

General Information Province-supported, coed, primarily men, comprehensive institution. CGS member. *Graduate housing:* Rooms and/or apartments available on a first-come, first-served basis to single and married students.

GRADUATE UNITS

Graduate Programs Postbaccalaureate distance learning degree programs offered (minimal on-campus study). Offers engineering (M Eng, PhD, Diploma).

UNIVERSITÉ DU QUÉBEC, ÉCOLE NATIONALE D'ADMINISTRATION PUBLIQUE, Quebec, QC G1K 9E5, Canada

General Information Province-supported, coed, graduate-only institution. CGS member. *Graduate housing:* On-campus housing not available.

GRADUATE UNITS

Graduate Program in Public Administration *Degree program information:* Part-time programs available. Offers international administration (MAP, Diploma); public administration (MAGU, MAP, PhD, Diploma); urban analysis and management (MAGU).

UNIVERSITÉ DU QUÉBEC EN ABITIBI-TÉMISCAMINGUE, Rouyn-Noranda, QC J9X 5E4, Canada

General Information Province-supported, coed, comprehensive institution. CGS member. *Graduate housing:* Room and/or apartments available on a first-come, first-served basis to single students; on-campus housing not available to married students. Housing application deadline: 3/1.

GRADUATE UNITS

Graduate Programs *Degree program information:* Part-time programs available. Offers biology (MS); business administration (MBA); education (M Ed, MA, PhD, DESS); engineering (ME); environmental sciences (PhD); mineral engineering (ME); mining engineering (DESS); organization management (M Sc); project management (M Sc, DESS); social work (MSW); sustainable forest ecosystem management (MS).

UNIVERSITÉ DU QUÉBEC EN OUTAOUAIS, Gatineau, QC J8X 3X7, Canada

General Information Province-supported, coed, university. CGS member. *Enrollment:* 6,003 graduate, professional, and undergraduate students; 588 full-time matriculated graduate/professional students, 692 part-time matriculated graduate/professional students. *Enrollment by degree level:* 1,158 master's, 122 doctoral. *Graduate faculty:* 65. *Graduate housing:* Rooms and/or apartments available on a first-come, first-served basis to single and married students. *Student services:* Campus employment opportunities, campus safety program, career counseling, child daycare facilities, free psychological counseling, international student services, low-cost health insurance, multicultural affairs office, services for students with disabilities, teacher training, writing training. *Library facilities:* Bibliotheque UQO plus 1 other. *Online resources:* library catalog, web page. *Collection:* 230,910 titles, 12,351 serial subscriptions.

Computer facilities: 500 computers available on campus for general student use. A campuswide network can be accessed from student residence rooms. Online class registration, pay tuition fees online are available. *Web address:* http://www.uqo.ca/.

General Application Contact: Registrar's Office, 819-773-1850, Fax: 819-773-1835, E-mail: registraire@uqo.ca.

GRADUATE UNITS

Graduate Programs Students: 1,280, 82 international. Expenses: Contact institution. *Financial support:* Fellowships, research assistantships, teaching assistantships available. *Degree program information:* Part-time and evening/weekend programs available. Offers accounting (MA, DESS, Diploma); andragogy (DESS); computer science (M Sc, PhD); education (M Ed, MA, PhD, Diploma); executive certified management accounting (MBA, DESS); financial services (MBA, DESS, Diploma); industrial relations (M Sc, MA, PhD, Diploma); localisation (DESS); nursing (M Sc, DESS, Diploma); project management (M Sc, MA, DESS, Diploma); psychoéducation (M Ed, MA); regional development (MA); second and foreign language teaching (Diploma); social work (MA). *Application deadline:* For fall admission, 6/1 for domestic students, 3/1 for international students; for winter admission, 11/1 for domestic students, 10/1 for international students. *Application fee:* $30 Canadian dollars. Electronic applications accepted. *Application Contact:* Registrar Office, 819-773-1850, Fax: 819-773-1835, E-mail: registraire@uqo.ca. *Dean*, Denis Hurtubise, 819-595-3985, Fax: 819-595-3985, E-mail: denis.hurtubise@uqo.ca.

UNIVERSITÉ DU QUÉBEC, INSTITUT NATIONAL DE LA RECHERCHE SCIENTIFIQUE, Québec, QC G1K 9A9, Canada

General Information Province-supported, coed, graduate-only institution. CGS member. *Enrollment by degree level:* 270 master's, 356 doctoral, 90 other advanced degrees. *Graduate faculty:* 154. *Graduate housing:* On-campus housing not available. *Student services:* Campus employment opportunities, international student services. *Library facilities:* Service de documentation et d'information spécialisées (SDIS) plus 3 others. *Online resources:* library catalog, web page, access to other libraries' catalogs. *Collection:* 54,010 titles, 7,986 serial subscriptions, 293 audiovisual materials.

Computer facilities: A campuswide network can be accessed from student residence rooms and from off campus. *Web address:* http://www.inrs.ca/.

General Application Contact: Yvonne Boisvert, Registrar, 418-654-3861, Fax: 418-654-3858, E-mail: registrariat@adm.inrs.ca.

GRADUATE UNITS

Graduate Programs Students: 674 full-time (303 women), 42 part-time (15 women), 252 international. Average age 31. *Faculty:* 154. Expenses: Contact institution. *Financial support:* Fellowships, research assistantships, teaching assistantships available. In 2010, 66 master's, 61 doctorates awarded. *Degree program information:* Part-time programs available. Offers demography (M Sc, PhD); research and public action (MA); urban studies (M Sc, PhD). *Application deadline:* For fall admission, 3/30 for domestic and international students; for winter admission, 11/1 for domestic and international students; for spring admission, 3/1 for domestic and international students. *Application fee:* $30. *Application Contact:* Yvonne Boisvert, Registrar, 418-654-3861, Fax: 418-654-3858, E-mail: registrariat@adm.inrs.ca. *Scientific Director*, Alain Fournier, 450-687-5010 Ext. 4123, E-mail: alain.fournier@adm.inrs.ca.

Research Center—Energy, Materials and Telecommunications Students: 171 full-time (44 women), 6 part-time (1 woman), 88 international. Average age 32. *Faculty:* 40. Expenses: Contact institution. *Financial support:* Fellowships, research assistantships, teaching assistantships available. In 2010, 15 master's, 23 doctorates awarded. *Degree program information:* Part-time programs available. Offers energy and materials science (M Sc, PhD); telecommunications (M Sc, PhD). Programs given in French; PhD programs offered jointly with Université du Québec à Trois-Rivières. *Application deadline:* For fall admission, 3/30 for domestic and international students; for winter admission, 11/1 for domestic and international students; for spring admission, 3/1 for domestic and international students. *Application fee:* $30. *Application Contact:* Yvonne Boisvert, Registrar, 418-654-3861, Fax: 418-654-3858, E-mail: registrariat@adm.inrs.ca. *Director*, Jean-Claude Kieffer, 450-929-8100, E-mail: kieffer@emt.inrs.ca.

Research Center—INRS—Institut Armand-Frappier—Human Health Students: 157 full-time (92 women), 6 part-time (4 women), 54 international. Average age 30. *Faculty:* 36. Expenses: Contact institution. *Financial support:* Fellowships, research assistantships, teaching assistantships available. In 2010, 20 master's, 13 doctorates awarded. *Degree program information:* Part-time programs available. Offers applied microbiology (M Sc); biology (PhD); experimental health sciences (M Sc); virology and immunology (M Sc, PhD). Programs given in French. *Application deadline:* For fall admission, 3/30 for domestic and international students; for winter admission, 11/1 for domestic and international students; for spring admission, 3/1 for domestic and international students. *Application fee:* $30 Canadian dollars. *Application Contact:* Yvonne Boisvert, Registrar, 418-654-3861, Fax: 418-654-3858, E-mail: registrariat@adm.inrs.ca. *Director*, Charles Dozois, 450-687-5010, Fax: 450-686-5501, E-mail: charles.dozois@iaf.inrs.ca.

Research Center—Water, Earth and Environment Students: 196 full-time (79 women), 17 part-time (5 women), 94 international. Average age 30. *Faculty:* 41. Expenses: Contact institution. *Financial support:* Fellowships, research assistantships, teaching assistantships available. In 2010, 19 master's, 17 doctorates awarded. *Degree program information:* Part-time programs available. Offers earth sciences (M Sc, PhD); earth sciences-environmental technologies (M Sc); water sciences (M Sc, PhD). *Application deadline:* For fall admission, 3/30 for domestic and international students; for winter admission, 11/1 for domestic and international students; for spring admission, 3/1 for domestic and international students. *Application fee:* $30. *Application Contact:* Yvonne Boisvert, Registrar, 418-654-3861, Fax: 418-654-3858, E-mail: registrariat@adm.inrs.ca. *Director*, Yves Begin, 418-654-2524, Fax: 418-654-2600, E-mail: info@ete.inrs.ca.

UNIVERSITÉ LAVAL, Québec, QC G1K 7P4, Canada

General Information Independent, coed, university. *Graduate housing:* Room and/or apartments available on a first-come, first-served basis to single students; on-campus housing not available to married students. *Research affiliation:* Centre Hospitalier Universitaire de Québec (biomedical research), Institut National d'optique (optics and photonics), Centre de Développement de la Geomatique (applied geomatics), Institut Maurice-Lamontagne (oceanography), Forintek Canada (forestry and wood processing), Société des pades de Sciences Naturelles du Québec (biology).

GRADUATE UNITS

Faculty of Administrative Sciences *Degree program information:* Part-time programs available. Postbaccalaureate distance learning degree programs offered (no on-campus study). Offers accounting (MBA); administrative sciences (M Sc, MBA, PhD, Diploma); administrative studies (M Sc, PhD); agri-food management (MBA); electronic business (MBA, Diploma); factory management and logistics (MBA); finance (MBA); financial engineering (M Sc); firm management (MBA); geomatic management (MBA); information technology management (MBA); international management (MBA); management (MBA); management accounting (MBA, Diploma); marketing (MBA); modeling and organizational decision (MBA); occupational health and safety management (MBA); organizations management and development (Diploma); pharmacy management (MBA); public accountancy (MBA, Diploma); social and environmental responsibility (MBA); technological entrepreneurship (Diploma). Electronic applications accepted.

Faculty of Agricultural and Food Sciences *Degree program information:* Part-time programs available. Offers agri-food engineering (M Sc); agricultural and food sciences (M Sc, PhD, Diploma); agricultural economics (M Sc); agricultural microbiology (M Sc); agro-food microbiology (PhD); animal sciences (M Sc, PhD); consumer sciences (Diploma); environmental technology (M Sc); food sciences and technology (M Sc, PhD); integrated rural development (Diploma); nutrition (M Sc, PhD); plant biology (M Sc, PhD); soils and environment science (M Sc, PhD). Electronic applications accepted.

Faculty of Architecture, Planning and Visual Arts Offers architecture, planning and visual arts (M Arch, M Sc, MA, MATDR, PhD); planning and regional development (MATDR, PhD). Electronic applications accepted.

School of Architecture *Degree program information:* Part-time programs available. Offers architecture (M Arch, M Sc). Electronic applications accepted.

School of Visual Arts Offers graphic design and multimedia (MA); visual arts (MA). Electronic applications accepted.

Faculty of Dentistry Offers buccal and maxillofacial surgery (DESS); dentistry (DMD, M Sc, DESS); gerodontology (DESS); multidisciplinary dentistry (DESS); periodontics (DESS). Electronic applications accepted.

Faculty of Education *Degree program information:* Part-time programs available. Offers didactics (MA, PhD); education (MA, PhD, Diploma); educational administration and evaluation (MA, PhD); educational pedagogy (Diploma); educational practice (Diploma); educational psychology (MA, PhD); orientation sciences (MA, PhD); pedagogy management and development (Diploma); school adaptation (Diploma); teaching technology (MA, PhD). Electronic applications accepted.

Faculty of Forestry and Geomatics Offers agroforestry (M Sc); forestry and geomatics (M Sc, M Sc Geogr, PhD); forestry sciences (M Sc, PhD); geographical sciences (M Sc Geogr, PhD); geography (M Sc Geogr, PhD); geomatics sciences (M Sc, PhD); wood sciences (M Sc, PhD). Electronic applications accepted.

Faculty of Law *Degree program information:* Part-time programs available. Offers environment, sustainable development and food safety (LL M); international and transnational law (LL M, Diploma); law (LL M, LL D, Diploma); law of business (LL M, Diploma); notarial law (Diploma). Electronic applications accepted.

Faculty of Letters *Degree program information:* Part-time programs available. Offers ancient civilization (MA, PhD); archaeology (MA, PhD); art history (MA, PhD); English literatures (MA, PhD); ethnology of French-speaking people in North America (MA, PhD); history (MA, PhD, Diploma); international journalism (Diploma); letters (MA, PhD, Diploma); linguistics (MA, PhD); literary studies (MA, PhD); literature and arts of the screen and stage (PhD); literature and arts of the screen and stage (MA); museology (Diploma); public communication (MA, PhD); public relations (Diploma); Spanish literature (MA, PhD); terminology and translation (MA, Diploma). Electronic applications accepted.

Faculty of Medicine *Degree program information:* Part-time programs available. Offers accident prevention and occupational health and safety management (Diploma); anatomy and physiology (M Sc, PhD); anatomy–pathology (DESS); anesthesiology (DESS); cardiology (DESS); care of older people (Diploma); cellular and molecular biology (M Sc, PhD); clinical research (DESS); community health (M Sc, PhD, DESS); dermatology (DESS); diagnostic radiology (DESS); emergency medicine (Diploma); epidemiology (M Sc, PhD); experimental medicine (M Sc, PhD); family medicine (DESS); general surgery (DESS); geriatrics (DESS); hematology (DESS); internal medicine (DESS); kinesiology (M Sc, PhD); maternal and fetal medicine (Diploma); medical biochemistry (DESS); medical microbiology and infectious diseases (DESS); medical oncology (DESS); medicine (MD, M Sc, PhD, DESS, Diploma); microbiology-immunology (M Sc, PhD); nephrology (DESS); neurobiology (M Sc, PhD); neurology (DESS); neurosurgery (DESS); obstetrics and gynecology (DESS); ophthalmology (DESS); orthopedic surgery (DESS); oto-rhino-laryngology (DESS); palliative medicine (Diploma); pediatrics (DESS); physiology-endocrinology (M Sc, PhD); plastic surgery (DESS); psychiatry (DESS); pulmonary medicine (DESS); radiology–oncology (DESS); speech therapy (M Sc); thoracic surgery (DESS); urology (DESS). Electronic applications accepted.

Faculty of Music Offers composition (M Mus); instrumental didactics (M Mus); interpretation (M Mus); music (M Mus, PhD); music education (M Mus, PhD); musicology (M Mus, PhD). Electronic applications accepted.

Faculty of Nursing Offers nursing (M Sc, PhD, DESS, Diploma). Electronic applications accepted.

Faculty of Pharmacy *Degree program information:* Part-time programs available. Offers community pharmacy (DESS); hospital pharmacy (M Sc); pharmacy (M Sc, PhD, DESS). Electronic applications accepted.

Faculty of Philosophy Offers philosophy (MA, PhD). Electronic applications accepted.

Faculty of Sciences and Engineering *Degree program information:* Part-time programs available. Offers aerospace engineering (M Sc); biochemistry (M Sc, PhD); biology (M Sc, PhD); chemical engineering (M Sc, PhD); chemistry (M Sc, PhD); civil engineering (M Sc, PhD); computer science (M Sc, PhD); earth sciences (M Sc, PhD); electrical engineering (M Sc, PhD); environmental technologies (M Sc); environmental technology (M Sc); geology (M Sc, PhD); industrial engineering (Diploma); mathematics (M Sc, PhD); mechanical engineering (M Sc, PhD); metallurgical engineering (M Sc, PhD); microbiology (M Sc, PhD); mining engineering (M Sc, PhD); oceanography (PhD); physics (M Sc, PhD); sciences and engineering (M Sc, PhD, Diploma); software engineering (Diploma); statistics (M Sc); urban infrastructure engineering (Diploma). Electronic applications accepted.

Faculty of Social Sciences *Degree program information:* Part-time programs available. Offers anthropology (MA, PhD); economics (MA, PhD); feminist studies (Diploma); industrial relations (MA, PhD); policy analysis (MA); political science (MA, PhD); social sciences (M Serv Soc, MA, PhD, Psy D, Diploma); sociology (MA, PhD). Electronic applications accepted.

School of Psychology Offers clinical psychology (PhD); community psychology (PhD); psychology (PhD, Psy D). Electronic applications accepted.

School of Social Work Offers social work (M Serv Soc, PhD). Electronic applications accepted.

Faculty of Theology and Religious Sciences Offers applied ethics (DESS); human sciences of religion (MA, PhD); practical theology (D Th P); theology (MA, PhD); theology and religious sciences (MA, D Th P, PhD, DESS). Electronic applications accepted.

Québec Institute for Advanced International Studies Offers advanced international studies (MA, PhD); international relations (MA, PhD). Electronic applications accepted.

UNIVERSITY AT ALBANY, STATE UNIVERSITY OF NEW YORK, Albany, NY 12222-0001

General Information State-supported, coed, university. CGS member. *Graduate housing:* Rooms and/or apartments available on a first-come, first-served basis to single and married students. Housing application deadline: 9/1. *Research affiliation:* Wadsworth Laboratories, New York State Department of Health (biomedical sciences, epidemiology, environmental health), Naval Research Laboratories (organizational structures (public administration)), General Electric Corporate Research and Development Center (nanoscale science and engineering), IBM–Watson Research Laboratories (artificial intelligence, computer science), Whiteface Mountain Observatory (earth and atmospheric sciences), Woods Hole Oceanographic Institution.

GRADUATE UNITS

College of Arts and Sciences *Degree program information:* Part-time and evening/weekend programs available. Offers African studies (MA); Afro-American studies (MA); anthropology (MA, PhD); art (MA, MFA); arts and sciences (MA, MFA, MRP, MS, DA, PhD, Certificate); atmospheric science (MS, PhD); autism (Certificate); biodiversity, conservation, and policy (MS); biopsychology (PhD); chemistry (MS, PhD); clinical psychology (PhD); communication (MA); demography (Certificate); ecology, evolution, and behavior (MS, PhD); economics (MA, PhD); English (MA, PhD); forensic molecular biology (MS); French (MA, PhD); general/experimental psychology (PhD); geographic information systems and spatial analysis (Certificate); geography (MA, Certificate); geology (MS, PhD); history (MA, PhD); industrial/organizational psychology (PhD); Italian (MA); Latin American, Caribbean, and US Latino studies (MA, Certificate); liberal studies (MA); mathematics (PhD); molecular, cellular, developmental, and neural biology (MS, PhD); philosophy (MA, PhD); physics (MS, PhD); psychology (MA); public history (Certificate); regional planning (MRP); regulatory economics (Certificate); Russian (MA, Certificate); Russian translation (Certificate); secondary teaching (MA); social/personality psychology (PhD); sociology (MA, PhD); sociology and communication (PhD); Spanish (MA, PhD); statistics (MA); theatre (MA); urban policy (Certificate); women's studies (MA, DA).

College of Computing and Information *Degree program information:* Part-time programs available. Offers computer science (MS, PhD); information science (MS, PhD, CAS); information studies (MS, CAS). Electronic applications accepted.

College of Nanoscale Science and Engineering Offers nanoscale science and engineering (MS, PhD).

Nelson A. Rockefeller College of Public Affairs and Policy *Degree program information:* Part-time programs available. Offers administrative behavior (PhD); comparative and development administration (MPA, PhD); human resources (MPA); legislative administration (MPA); nonprofit leadership and management (Certificate); planning and policy analysis (CAS); policy analysis (MPA); political science (MA, PhD); program analysis and evaluation (PhD); public affairs and policy (MA); public finance (MPA, PhD); public management (MPA, PhD); women and public policy (Certificate). Electronic applications accepted.

School of Business *Degree program information:* Part-time and evening/weekend programs available. Offers accounting (MS); business (MBA, MS); finance (MBA); human resource systems (MBA); information technology management (MBA); marketing (MBA); taxation (MS). Electronic applications accepted.

School of Criminal Justice *Degree program information:* Part-time programs available. Offers criminal justice (MA, PhD). Electronic applications accepted.

School of Education *Degree program information:* Part-time and evening/weekend programs available. Offers counseling psychology (MS, PhD, CAS); curriculum and instruction (MS, Ed D, CAS); curriculum planning and development (MA); education (MA, MS, Ed D, PhD, Psy D, CAS); educational administration and policy studies (MS, PhD, CAS); educational communications (MS, CAS); educational psychology (Ed D); educational psychology and statistics (MS); measurements and evaluation (Ed D); reading (MS, Ed D, CAS); rehabilitation counseling (MS); school counselor (CAS); school psychology (Psy D, CAS); special education (MS); statistics and research design (Ed D). Electronic applications accepted.

School of Public Health Offers biochemistry, molecular biology, and genetics (MS, PhD); cell and molecular structure (MS, PhD); environmental and analytical chemistry (MS, PhD); environmental and occupational health (MS, PhD); epidemiology and biostatistics (MS, PhD); health policy, management, and behavior (MS); immunobiology and immunochemistry (MS, PhD); molecular pathogenesis (MS, PhD); neuroscience (MS, PhD); public health (MPH, MS, Dr PH, PhD, Certificate); toxicology (MS, PhD). Electronic applications accepted.

School of Social Welfare *Degree program information:* Part-time and evening/weekend programs available. Offers social welfare (MSW, PhD). Electronic applications accepted.

UNIVERSITY AT BUFFALO, THE STATE UNIVERSITY OF NEW YORK, Buffalo, NY 14260

General Information State-supported, coed, university. CGS member. *Enrollment:* 29,048 graduate, professional, and undergraduate students; 7,521 full-time matriculated graduate/professional students (3,687 women), 1,786 part-time matriculated graduate/professional students (1,050 women). *Enrollment by degree level:* 1,975 first professional, 4,627 master's, 2,547 doctoral, 158 other advanced degrees. *Graduate faculty:* 1,576 full-time (562 women), 218 part-time/adjunct (88 women). *Graduate housing:* Rooms and/or apartments available on a first-come, first-served basis to single students and available to married students. Housing application deadline: 5/1. *Student services:* Campus employment opportunities, campus safety program, career counseling, child daycare facilities, exercise/wellness program, free psychological counseling, international student services, low-cost health insurance, multicultural affairs office, services for students with disabilities, teacher training, writing training. *Library facilities:* Lockwood Memorial Library plus 9 others. *Online resources:* library catalog, web page, access to other libraries' catalogs. *Collection:* 4.1 million titles, 81,643 serial subscriptions, 283,118 audiovisual materials. *Research affiliation:* Hauptman-Woodward Medical Research Institute, Roswell Park Cancer Institute, Veterans Administration Medical Center, Calspan–University of Buffalo Research Center, Roswell Park Cancer Institute.

Computer facilities: Computer purchase and lease plans are available. 2,300 computers available on campus for general student use. A campuswide network can be accessed from student residence rooms and from off campus. Online class registration is available. *Web address:* http://www.buffalo.edu/.

General Application Contact: Christopher S. Connor, Director of Graduate Enrollment Management Services, 716-645-3482, Fax: 716-645-6998, E-mail: cconnor@buffalo.edu.

GRADUATE UNITS

Graduate School Students: 7,521 full-time (3,687 women), 1,786 part-time (1,050 women); includes 304 Black or African American, non-Hispanic/Latino; 41 American Indian or Alaska Native, non-Hispanic/Latino; 541 Asian, non-Hispanic/Latino; 192 Hispanic/Latino, 2,438 international. 29,337 applicants, 23% accepted, 2888 enrolled. *Faculty:* 1,576 full-time (562 women), 218 part-time/adjunct (88 women). Expenses: Contact institution. *Financial support:* In 2010–11, 2,451 students received support; fellowships with full and partial tuition reimbursements available, research assistantships with full and partial tuition reimbursements available, teaching assistantships with full and partial tuition reimbursements available, career-related internships or fieldwork, Federal Work-Study, institutionally sponsored loans, scholarships/grants, traineeships, tuition waivers (full and partial), unspecified assistantships, and stipends available. Support available to part-time students. Financial award applicants required to submit FAFSA. In 2010, 610 first professional degrees, 2,031 master's, 323 doctorates, 182 other advanced degrees awarded. *Degree program information:* Part-time and evening/weekend programs available. Postbaccalaureate distance learning degree programs offered. *Application deadline:* Applications are processed on a rolling basis. *Application fee:* $50. Electronic applications accepted. *Application Contact:* Christopher S. Connor, Director of Graduate Enrollment Management Services, 716-645-3482, Fax: 716-645-6998, E-mail: gradrecruit@buffalo.edu. *Associate Provost/Executive Director,* Dr. Myron A. Thompson, 716-645-2939, Fax: 716-645-6142, E-mail: gradschl@buffalo.edu.

College of Arts and Sciences Students: 1,089 full-time (569 women), 865 part-time (407 women); includes 155 minority (38 Black or African American, non-Hispanic/Latino; 11 American Indian or Alaska Native, non-Hispanic/Latino; 58 Asian, non-Hispanic/Latino; 48 Hispanic/Latino), 610 international. Average age 29. 4,521 applicants, 29% accepted, 525 enrolled. *Faculty:* 489 full-time (140 women), 237 part-time/adjunct (93 women). Expenses: Contact institution. *Financial support:* In 2010–11, 125 students received support, including 125 fellowships with full and partial tuition reimbursements available (averaging $2,500 per year), 155 research assistantships with full tuition reimbursements available (averaging $15,100 per year), 670 teaching assistantships with full tuition reimbursements available (averaging $15,275 per year); career-related internships or fieldwork, Federal Work-Study, institutionally sponsored loans, scholarships/grants, health care benefits, tuition waivers (full and partial), and unspecified assistantships also available. Support available to part-time students. Financial award applicants required to submit FAFSA. In 2010, 445 master's, 145 doctorates awarded. *Degree program information:* Part-time programs available. Offers American studies (MA, PhD); anthropology (MA, PhD); art (MFA); art history (MA, Certificate); arts and sciences (MA, MAH, MFA, MM, MS, Au D, PhD, Certificate); audiology (Au D); behavioral neuroscience (PhD); biological sciences (MA, MS, PhD); Caribbean cultural studies (MAH); chemistry (MA, PhD); classics (MA, PhD); clinical psychology (PhD); cognitive psychology (PhD); communication (MA, PhD); communicative disorders and sciences (MA, PhD); comparative literature (MA, PhD); critical museum studies (Certificate); earth systems science (MA); economic geography and international business and world trade (MA); economics (MA, MS, PhD); English (MA, PhD); environmental and earth systems science (MS); environmental modeling and analysis (MA); evolution, ecology and behavior (MS, PhD, Certificate); film studies (MAH); financial economics (Certificate); fine arts (MFA); French (MA, PhD); general psychology (MA); geographic information science (MA, Certificate); geographic information systems and science (MS); geography (MA, PhD); geology (MA, MS, PhD); health services (Certificate); historical musicology and music theory (PhD); history (MA, PhD); information and Internet economics (Certificate); international economics (Certificate); law and regulation (Certificate); linguistics (MA, PhD); mathematics (MA, PhD); media arts production (MFA); media study (PhD); medicinal chemistry (MS, PhD); music composition (MA, PhD); music history (MA); music performance (MM); music theory (MA); new media design (Certificate); philosophy (MA, PhD); physics (MS, PhD); political science (MA, PhD); social-personality psychology (PhD); sociology (MA, PhD); Spanish (MA, PhD); urban and regional economics (Certificate); urban and regional geography (MA). *Application deadline:* Applications are processed on a rolling basis. *Application fee:* $75. Electronic applications accepted. *Application Contact:* Joseph C. Syracuse, Graduate Enrollment Manager, 716-645-2711, Fax: 716-645-3888, E-mail: jcs32@buffalo.edu. *Dean,* Dr. Bruce D. McCombe, 716-645-2711, Fax: 716-645-3888, E-mail: cas-dean@buffalo.edu.

Graduate Programs in Cancer Research and Biomedical Sciences at Roswell Park Cancer Institute Students: 151 full-time (88 women), 33 part-time (11 women); includes 8 Black or African American, non-Hispanic/Latino; 12 Asian, non-Hispanic/Latino; 6 Hispanic/Latino, 55 international. Average age 24. 249 applicants, 32% accepted, 50 enrolled. *Faculty:* 129 full-time (34 women). Expenses: Contact institution. *Financial support:* In 2010–11, 120 students received support, including fellowships with full tuition reimburse-

University at Buffalo, the State University of New York (continued)

ments available (averaging $24,000 per year), research assistantships with full tuition reimbursements available (averaging $24,000 per year), teaching assistantships with full tuition reimbursements available (averaging $8,500 per year); Federal Work-Study, institutionally sponsored loans, scholarships/grants, and unspecified assistantships also available. Financial award application deadline: 2/1; financial award applicants required to submit FAFSA. In 2010, 24 master's, 12 doctorates awarded. Offers biomedical sciences and cancer research (MS); cancer immunology (PhD); cancer pathology and prevention (PhD); cancer research and biomedical sciences (MS, PhD); cellular molecular biology/genetics (PhD); molecular and cellular biophysics and biochemistry (PhD); molecular pharmacology and cancer therapeutics (PhD). *Application deadline:* For fall admission, 2/1 priority date for domestic and international students. Applications are processed on a rolling basis. *Application fee:* $50. Electronic applications accepted. *Application Contact:* Craig R. Johnson, Director of Admissions, 716-845-2339, Fax: 716-845-8178, E-mail: craig.johnson@roswellpark.org. *Assistant Dean,* Dr. Adam Kisailus, 716-845-2339, Fax: 716-845-8178, E-mail: adam.kisailus@roswellpark.org.

Graduate School of Education Students: 743 full-time (527 women), 730 part-time (536 women); includes 78 Black or African American, non-Hispanic/Latino; 8 American Indian or Alaska Native, non-Hispanic/Latino; 28 Asian, non-Hispanic/Latino; 40 Hispanic/Latino, 121 international. Average age 31. 1,478 applicants, 60% accepted, 585 enrolled. *Faculty:* 75 full-time (48 women), 113 part-time/adjunct (89 women). Expenses: Contact institution. *Financial support:* Fellowships with full tuition reimbursements, research assistantships with full tuition reimbursements, teaching assistantships with full tuition reimbursements, career-related internships or fieldwork, Federal Work-Study, institutionally sponsored loans, tuition waivers (full and partial), and unspecified assistantships available. Financial award applicants required to submit FAFSA. In 2010, 423 master's, 41 doctorates, 106 other advanced degrees awarded. *Degree program information:* Part-time programs available. Postbaccalaureate distance learning degree programs offered (no on-campus study). Offers biology education (Ed M, Certificate); chemistry education (Ed M, Certificate); childhood education (Ed M); childhood education with bilingual extension (Ed M); counseling/school psychology (PhD); counselor education (PhD); early childhood education (Ed M); earth science education (Ed M, MA, MLS, MS, Ed D, PhD, Certificate, Certificate/Ed M); educational administration (Ed M, Ed D, PhD); educational psychology (MA, PhD); educational technology and new literacies (Certificate); elementary education (Ed D, PhD); English education (Ed M, PhD, Certificate); English for speakers of other languages (Ed M); foreign and second language education (PhD); French education (Ed M, Certificate); general education (Ed M); German education (Ed M, Certificate); gifted education (online) (Certificate); higher education administration (Ed M, Ed D, PhD); Latin education (Ed M, Certificate); library and information studies (MLS, Certificate); library and information studies (online) (MLS); literary specialist (Ed M); mathematics education (Ed M, PhD, Certificate); mental health counseling (MS); music education (Ed M, Certificate); physics education (Ed M, Certificate); reading education (PhD); rehabilitation counseling (MS); school building leadership (LIFTS) (Certificate); school business and human resource administration (Certificate); school counseling (Ed M, Certificate); school district business leadership (LIFTS) (Certificate); school district leadership (LIFTS) (Certificate); science and the public (online) (Ed M); science education (PhD); Singapore school counseling (Ed M); social foundations (PhD); social studies education (Ed M, Certificate); Spanish education (Ed M, Certificate); special education (PhD); teaching and leading for diversity (Certificate); teaching English to speakers of other languages (Ed M). *Application deadline:* Applications are processed on a rolling basis. *Application fee:* $50. Electronic applications accepted. *Application Contact:* Dr. Radhika Suresh, Director of Graduate Admissions and Student Services, 716-645-2110, Fax: 716-645-7937, E-mail: gse-info@buffalo.edu. *Dean,* Dr. Mary H. Gresham, 716-645-6640, Fax: 716-645-2479, E-mail: gse-info@buffalo.edu.

Law School Students: 706 full-time (330 women), 11 part-time (7 women); includes 104 minority (37 Black or African American, non-Hispanic/Latino; 6 American Indian or Alaska Native, non-Hispanic/Latino; 29 Asian, non-Hispanic/Latino; 25 Hispanic/Latino; 1 Native Hawaiian or other Pacific Islander, non-Hispanic/Latino; 6 Two or more races, non-Hispanic/Latino), 27 international. Average age 26. 1,896 applicants, 36% accepted, 219 enrolled. *Faculty:* 60 full-time (28 women), 123 part-time/adjunct (43 women). Expenses: Contact institution. *Financial support:* In 2010–11, 660 students received support, including 6 fellowships with full tuition reimbursements available (averaging $16,010 per year), 21 research assistantships (averaging $519 per year); career-related internships or fieldwork, Federal Work-Study, institutionally sponsored loans, scholarships/grants, tuition waivers (full and partial), and unspecified assistantships also available. Financial award application deadline: 3/1; financial award applicants required to submit FAFSA. In 2010, 265 first professional degrees awarded. Offers criminal law (LL M); general law (LL M); law (JD). *Application deadline:* For fall admission, 3/15 priority date for domestic and international students. Applications are processed on a rolling basis. *Application fee:* $75. Electronic applications accepted. *Application Contact:* Lillie V. Wiley-Upshaw, Vice Dean/Director of Admissions and Financial Aid, 716-645-2907, Fax: 716-645-6676, E-mail: law-admissions@buffalo.edu. *Dean,* Dr. Makau Mutua, 716-645-2311, Fax: 716-645-2064, E-mail: mutua@buffalo.edu.

School of Architecture and Planning Students: 199 full-time (83 women), 17 part-time (9 women); includes 10 Black or African American, non-Hispanic/Latino; 1 American Indian or Alaska Native, non-Hispanic/Latino; 7 Asian, non-Hispanic/Latino; 8 Hispanic/Latino, 43 international. Average age 27. 501 applicants, 37% accepted, 82 enrolled. *Faculty:* 38 full-time (10 women), 26 part-time/adjunct (7 women). Expenses: Contact institution. *Financial support:* In 2010–11, 9 fellowships with full tuition reimbursements (averaging $9,600 per year), 19 research assistantships with full and partial tuition reimbursements (averaging $5,365 per year), 42 teaching assistantships with partial tuition reimbursements (averaging $4,800 per year) were awarded; career-related internships or fieldwork, Federal Work-Study, institutionally sponsored loans, scholarships/grants, tuition waivers (partial), and unspecified assistantships also available. Support available to part-time students. Financial award application deadline: 3/1; financial award applicants required to submit FAFSA. In 2010, 79 master's awarded. *Degree program information:* Part-time programs available. Offers architecture (M Arch, MS); architecture and planning (M Arch, MS, MUP); urban and regional planning (MUP). *Application fee:* $75. Electronic applications accepted. *Application Contact:* Shannon Phillips, Director of Program Development, 716-829-3485 Ext. 128, Fax: 716-829-3256, E-mail: smp2@buffalo.edu. *Dean,* Robert Shibley, 716-829-3485 Ext. 121, Fax: 716-829-2297, E-mail: rshibley@buffalo.edu.

School of Dental Medicine Offers advanced education in general dentistry (Certificate); biomaterials (MS); combined prosthodontics (Certificate); dental medicine (DDS, MS, PhD, Certificate); endodontics (Certificate); general practice residency (Certificate); oral and maxillofacial pathology (Certificate); oral and maxillofacial surgery (Certificate); oral biology (PhD); oral diagnostic sciences (MS); oral sciences (MS); orthodontics (MS); pediatric dentistry (Certificate); periodontics (Certificate); temporomandibular disorders and oralfacial pain (Certificate). Electronic applications accepted.

School of Engineering and Applied Sciences Students: 1,132 full-time (224 women), 148 part-time (22 women); includes 13 Black or African American, non-Hispanic/Latino; 1 American Indian or Alaska Native, non-Hispanic/Latino; 30 Asian, non-Hispanic/Latino; 12 Hispanic/Latino, 936 international. Average age 26. 5,084 applicants, 29% accepted, 397 enrolled. *Faculty:* 147 full-time (18 women), 25 part-time/adjunct (2 women). Expenses: Contact institution. *Financial support:* In 2010–11, 42 fellowships with full tuition reimbursements (averaging $28,908 per year), 210 research assistantships with full and partial tuition reimbursements (averaging $21,300 per year), 168 teaching assistantships with full tuition reimbursements (averaging $20,900 per year) were awarded; career-related internships or fieldwork, Federal Work-Study, institutionally sponsored loans, scholarships/grants, tuition waivers (full and partial), and unspecified assistantships also available. Support available to part-time students. Financial award applicants required to submit FAFSA. In 2010, 298 master's, 42 doctorates awarded. *Degree program information:* Part-time and evening/weekend programs available. Postbaccalaureate distance learning degree programs offered (minimal on-campus study). Offers aerospace engineering (ME, MS, PhD); chemical and biological engineering (ME, MS, PhD); civil engineering (ME, MS, PhD); computer science and engineering (MS, PhD); electrical engineering (ME, MS, PhD); engineering and applied sciences (ME, MS, PhD); engineering science (MS); industrial and systems engineering (ME, MS, PhD); mechanical engineering (ME, MS, PhD). *Application deadline:* Applications are processed on a rolling basis. *Application fee:* $50. Electronic applications accepted. *Application Contact:* Dr. Rajan Batta, Associate Dean for Graduate Education, 716-645-2772, Fax: 716-645-2495, E-mail: batta@buffalo.edu. *Dean,* Dr. Harvey G. Stenger, 716-645-2771, Fax: 716-645-2495, E-mail: dean@.buffalo.edu.

School of Management Students: 626 full-time (229 women), 202 part-time (69 women); includes 43 minority (18 Black or African American, non-Hispanic/Latino; 2 American Indian or Alaska Native, non-Hispanic/Latino; 18 Asian, non-Hispanic/Latino; 5 Hispanic/Latino), 351 international. Average age 27. 1,553 applicants, 46% accepted, 400 enrolled. *Faculty:* 65 full-time (18 women), 32 part-time/adjunct (8 women). Expenses: Contact institution. *Financial support:* In 2010–11, 91 students received support, including 5 fellowships with full and partial tuition reimbursements available (averaging $4,000 per year), 41 research assistantships with full and partial tuition reimbursements available (averaging $16,000 per year), 28 teaching assistantships with full and partial tuition reimbursements available (averaging $15,000 per year); career-related internships or fieldwork, Federal Work-Study, institutionally sponsored loans, scholarships/grants, health care benefits, and unspecified assistantships also available. Financial award application deadline: 2/15; financial award applicants required to submit FAFSA. In 2010, 287 master's, 4 doctorates, 3 other advanced degrees awarded. *Degree program information:* Part-time and evening/weekend programs available. Offers accounting (MS); business administration (EMBA, MBA, PMBA); finance (MS); information assurance (Certificate); management (PhD); management information systems (MS); supply chains and operations management (MS). *Application deadline:* For fall admission, 5/2 priority date for domestic students, 3/1 priority date for international students. Applications are processed on a rolling basis. *Application fee:* $100. Electronic applications accepted. *Application Contact:* David W. Frasier, Assistant Dean, 716-645-3204, Fax: 716-645-2341, E-mail: davidf@buffalo.edu. *Assistant Dean,* David W. Frasier, 716-645-3204, Fax: 716-645-2341, E-mail: davidf@buffalo.edu.

School of Medicine and Biomedical Sciences Students: 716 full-time (380 women), 16 part-time (10 women); includes 15 Black or African American, non-Hispanic/Latino; 3 American Indian or Alaska Native, non-Hispanic/Latino; 138 Asian, non-Hispanic/Latino; 9 Hispanic/Latino, 60 international. Average age 26. 3,971 applicants, 12% accepted. *Faculty:* 154 full-time (32 women), 351 part-time/adjunct (100 women). Expenses: Contact institution. *Financial support:* In 2010–11, fellowships with full tuition reimbursements (averaging $24,000 per year), research assistantships with full tuition reimbursements (averaging $21,000 per year), teaching assistantships with full tuition reimbursements (averaging $21,000 per year) were awarded; career-related internships or fieldwork, Federal Work-Study, institutionally sponsored loans, scholarships/grants, traineeships, health care benefits, and unspecified assistantships also available. Financial award application deadline: 2/1; financial award applicants required to submit FAFSA. In 2010, 131 first professional degrees, 21 master's, 27 doctorates awarded. Offers anatomical sciences (MA, PhD); biochemical pharmacology (MS); biochemistry (MA, PhD); biomedical sciences (PhD); biophysics (MS, PhD); biotechnology (MS); medicine (MD); medicine and biomedical sciences (MD, MA, MS, PhD); microbiology and immunology (MA, PhD); neuroscience (MS, PhD); pathology (MA, PhD); pharmacology (MA, PhD); physiology (MA, PhD); structural biology (MS, PhD). *Application deadline:* For fall admission, 2/1 priority date for domestic and international students. Applications are processed on a rolling basis. *Application fee:* $50. Electronic applications accepted. *Application Contact:* Amy J. Kuzdale, Staff Associate, 716-829-3399, Fax: 716-829-2437, E-mail: akuzdale@buffalo.edu. *Dean,* Dr. Michael E. Cain, 716-829-3955, Fax: 716-829-3395, E-mail: mcain@buffalo.edu.

School of Nursing Students: 130 full-time (106 women), 69 part-time (59 women); includes 15 Black or African American, non-Hispanic/Latino; 1 American Indian or Alaska Native, non-Hispanic/Latino; 12 Asian, non-Hispanic/Latino; 7 Hispanic/Latino, 17 international. Average age 34. 361 applicants, 25% accepted, 65 enrolled. *Faculty:* 34 full-time (31 women), 17 part-time/adjunct (16 women). Expenses: Contact institution. *Financial support:* In 2010–11, 78 students received support, including 5 fellowships with full tuition reimbursements available (averaging $17,000 per year), 5 research assistantships with full tuition reimbursements available (averaging $10,600 per year), 8 teaching assistantships with full tuition reimbursements available (averaging $10,600 per year); scholarships/grants, traineeships, health care benefits, and unspecified assistantships also available. Financial award application deadline: 3/15; financial award applicants required to submit FAFSA. In 2010, 5 doctorates, 9 other advanced degrees awarded. *Degree program information:* Part-time programs available. Postbaccalaureate distance learning degree programs offered (minimal on-campus study). Offers adult clinical nurse practitioner (DNP); adult nurse practitioner (DNP); family nurse practitioner (DNP); nursing (PhD); nursing education (Certificate). *Application deadline:* For fall admission, 8/15 for domestic students, 4/1 for international students; for spring admission, 11/1 for domestic students, 10/1 for international students. *Application fee:* $75. Electronic applications accepted. *Application Contact:* Dr. David J. Lang, Director of Student Affairs, 716-829-2537, Fax: 716-829-2067, E-mail: langdj@buffalo.edu. *Dean and Professor,* Dr. Jean K. Brown, 716-829-2533, Fax: 716-829-2566, E-mail: ubnursingdean@buffalo.edu.

School of Pharmacy and Pharmaceutical Sciences Students: 373 full-time (227 women), 33 part-time (17 women); includes 15 Black or African American, non-Hispanic/Latino; 3 American Indian or Alaska Native, non-Hispanic/Latino; 87 Asian, non-Hispanic/Latino; 8 Hispanic/Latino, 54 international. Average age 24. 1,603 applicants, 9% accepted, 143 enrolled. *Faculty:* 38 full-time (11 women), 9 part-time/adjunct (3 women). Expenses: Contact institution. *Financial support:* In 2010–11, 291 students received support, including 4 fellowships (averaging $40,000 per year), 33 research assistantships with full tuition reimbursements available (averaging $23,500 per year); scholarships/grants, health care benefits, tuition waivers (full), and unspecified assistantships also available. Financial award application deadline: 3/1; financial award applicants required to submit FAFSA. In 2010, 114 first professional degrees, 4 master's, 1 doctorate awarded. Offers pharmaceutical sciences (MS, PhD); pharmacy (Pharm D); pharmacy and pharmaceutical sciences (Pharm D, MS, PhD). *Application deadline:* For fall admission, 2/1 priority date for domestic and international students. Applications are processed on a rolling basis. *Application fee:* $50. Electronic applications accepted. *Application Contact:* Dr. Jennifer M. Hess, Assistant Dean, 716-645-2825 Ext. 1, Fax: 716-645-3688, E-mail: pharm-admin@buffalo.edu. *Dean,* Dr. Wayne K. Anderson, 716-645-2823, Fax: 716-645-3688.

School of Public Health and Health Professions Students: 315 full-time (204 women), 85 part-time (54 women); includes 17 Black or African American, non-Hispanic/Latino; 30 Asian, non-Hispanic/Latino; 9 Hispanic/Latino, 62 international. Average age 30. 526 applicants, 50% accepted, 110 enrolled. *Faculty:* 65 full-time (30 women), 43 part-time/adjunct (26 women). Expenses: Contact institution. *Financial support:* In 2010–11, 21 students received support, including 12 fellowships with full tuition reimbursements available (averaging $2,500 per year), 2 research assistantships with full tuition reimbursements available (averaging $15,000 per year), 15 teaching assistantships with full tuition reimbursements available (averaging $8,500 per year); career-related internships or fieldwork, Federal Work-Study, institutionally sponsored loans, scholarships/grants, tuition waivers (full and partial), and unspecified assistantships also available. Financial award application deadline: 3/15; financial award applicants required to submit FAFSA. In 2010, 90 master's, 11 doctorates awarded. *Degree program information:* Part-time programs available. Offers assistive and rehabilitation technology (Certificate); biostatistics (MA, PhD); epidemiology (MS, PhD); exercise science (MS, PhD); nutrition (MS); occupational therapy (MS); physical therapy (DPT); public health (MPH); public health and health professions (MA, MPH, MS, DPT, PhD, Certificate). *Application deadline:* For fall admission, 2/1 priority date for domestic and international students. *Application fee:* $50. Electronic applications accepted. *Application Contact:* Allison Garvey, Project Director, Office of Academic and Student Affairs, 716-829-6766, Fax: 716-829-2034, E-mail: sphhp-mph@buffalo.edu. *Dean,* Dr. Lynn Kozlowski, 716-829-6951, Fax: 716-829-6040, E-mail: lk22@buffalo.edu.

School of Social Work Students: 293 full-time (241 women), 202 part-time (182 women); includes 53 Black or African American, non-Hispanic/Latino; 1 American Indian or Alaska Native, non-Hispanic/Latino; 8 Asian, non-Hispanic/Latino; 13 Hispanic/Latino, 17 international. Average age 30. 474 applicants, 65% accepted, 229 enrolled. *Faculty:* 23 full-time (16 women), 36 part-time/adjunct (28 women). Expenses: Contact institution. *Financial support:*

In 2010–11, 91 students received support, including 3 fellowships with full tuition reimbursements available (averaging $7,500 per year), 4 research assistantships with full tuition reimbursements available (averaging $15,000 per year), 6 teaching assistantships with full tuition reimbursements available (averaging $3,000 per year); Federal Work-Study, scholarships/grants, health care benefits, tuition waivers (partial), unspecified assistantships, and instructorships and research grants (PhD) also available. Financial award application deadline: 4/30; financial award applicants required to submit FAFSA. In 2010, 160 master's, 3 doctorates awarded. *Degree program information:* Part-time programs available. Offers social work (MSW, PhD). *Application deadline:* For fall admission, 3/1 priority date for domestic and international students. Applications are processed on a rolling basis. *Application fee:* $50. Electronic applications accepted. *Application Contact:* Maria Soos, Admissions Processor, 716-645-3381, Fax: 716-645-3456, E-mail: sw-info@buffalo.edu. *Dean*, Dr. Nancy J. Smyth, 716-645-3381, Fax: 716-645-3883, E-mail: sw-dean@buffalo.edu.

UNIVERSITY OF ADVANCING TECHNOLOGY, Tempe, AZ 85283-1042

General Information Proprietary, coed, primarily men, comprehensive institution. *Enrollment:* 1,073 graduate, professional, and undergraduate students; 55 full-time matriculated graduate/professional students (9 women), 4 part-time matriculated graduate/professional students (1 woman). *Enrollment by degree level:* 59 master's. *Graduate faculty:* 42 full-time (11 women), 35 part-time/adjunct (6 women). *Tuition:* Full-time $18,300. *Graduate housing:* Room and/or apartments available on a first-come, first-served basis to single students; on-campus housing not available to married students. *Student services:* Campus employment opportunities, career counseling. *Library facilities:* University of Advancing Computer Technology Library. *Online resources:* library catalog, web page. *Collection:* 27,500 titles, 92 serial subscriptions, 1,200 audiovisual materials.

Computer facilities: Computer purchase and lease plans are available. 400 computers available on campus for general student use. A campuswide network can be accessed from student residence rooms and from off campus. Online class registration is available. *Web address:* http://www.uat.edu/.

General Application Contact: Michelle Wilcox, Admissions Office, 800-658-5744, Fax: 602-383-8222, E-mail: mkable@uat.edu.

GRADUATE UNITS

Master of Science Program in Technology Students: 55 full-time (9 women), 4 part-time (1 woman). Average age 25. *Faculty:* 9 full-time (3 women), 3 part-time/adjunct (1 woman). Expenses: Contact institution. *Financial support:* Career-related internships or fieldwork, Federal Work-Study, and scholarships/grants available. Financial award applicants required to submit FAFSA. In 2010, 5 master's awarded. Offers advancing computer science (MS); emerging technologies (MS); game production and management (MS); information assurance (MS); technology leadership (MS). *Application deadline:* For fall admission, 8/15 priority date for domestic students, 7/15 priority date for international students; for winter admission, 12/15 priority date for domestic students, 11/15 priority date for international students; for spring admission, 4/1 priority date for domestic students, 3/1 priority date for international students. Applications are processed on a rolling basis. *Application fee:* $100 ($250 for international students). Electronic applications accepted. *Application Contact:* Information Contact, 800-658-5744, Fax: 602-383-8222. *Dean of Graduate Education*, Robert Marshall, 602-383-8283, Fax: 602-383-8222, E-mail: rmarshall@uat.edu.

THE UNIVERSITY OF AKRON, Akron, OH 44325

General Information State-supported, coed, university. CGS member. *Enrollment:* 27,076 graduate, professional, and undergraduate students; 2,371 full-time matriculated graduate/professional students (1,236 women), 2,276 part-time matriculated graduate/professional students (1,462 women). *Enrollment by degree level:* 510 first professional, 3,101 master's, 793 doctoral, 243 other advanced degrees. *Graduate faculty:* 806 full-time (342 women), 1,087 part-time/adjunct (589 women). Tuition, state resident: full-time $6800; part-time $378 per credit hour. Tuition, nonresident: full-time $11,644; part-time $647 per credit hour. *Required fees:* $1265. One-time fee: $30 full-time. *Graduate housing:* Room and/or apartments available on a first-come, first-served basis to single students; on-campus housing not available to married students. Housing application deadline: 3/1. *Student services:* Campus employment opportunities, campus safety program, career counseling, child daycare facilities, exercise/wellness program, free psychological counseling, grant writing training, international student services, low-cost health insurance, multicultural affairs office, services for students with disabilities, teacher training, writing training. *Library facilities:* Bierce Library plus 2 others. *Online resources:* library catalog, web page, access to other libraries' catalogs. *Collection:* 1.3 million titles, 46,053 audiovisual materials.

Computer facilities: Computer purchase and lease plans are available. 3,100 computers available on campus for general student use. A campuswide network can be accessed from student residence rooms and from off campus. Online class registration, library laptops for student checkout are available. *Web address:* http://www.uakron.edu/.

General Application Contact: Dr. Mark Tausig, Associate Dean, 330-972-6266, Fax: 330-972-6475, E-mail: mtausig@uakron.edu.

GRADUATE UNITS

Graduate School Students: 2,081 full-time (1,122 women), 2,059 part-time (1,352 women); includes 434 minority (287 Black or African American, non-Hispanic/Latino; 4 American Indian or Alaska Native, non-Hispanic/Latino; 61 Asian, non-Hispanic/Latino; 64 Hispanic/Latino; 2 Native Hawaiian or other Pacific Islander, non-Hispanic/Latino; 16 Two or more races, non-Hispanic/Latino), 675 international. Average age 31. 3,199 applicants, 56% accepted, 1067 enrolled. *Faculty:* 806 full-time (342 women), 1,087 part-time/adjunct (589 women). Expenses: Contact institution. *Financial support:* In 2010–11, 66 fellowships with full tuition reimbursements, 383 research assistantships with full and partial tuition reimbursements, 797 teaching assistantships with full and partial tuition reimbursements were awarded; Federal Work-Study, institutionally sponsored loans, scholarships/grants, and administrative assistantships also available. Support available to part-time students. In 2010, 1,091 master's, 86 doctorates awarded. *Degree program information:* Part-time and evening/weekend programs available. *Application deadline:* For fall admission, 1/15 priority date for domestic and international students; for spring admission, 10/1 priority date for domestic and international students. Applications are processed on a rolling basis. *Application fee:* $30 ($40 for international students). Electronic applications accepted. *Application Contact:* Dr. Mark Tausig, Associate Dean, 330-972-6266, Fax: 330-972-6475, E-mail: mtausig@uakron.edu. *Vice President for Research/Dean*, Dr. George R. Newkome, 330-972-6458, Fax: 330-972-2413, E-mail: newkome@uakron.edu.

Buchtel College of Arts and Sciences Students: 571 full-time (276 women), 241 part-time (137 women); includes 75 Black or African American, non-Hispanic/Latino; 2 American Indian or Alaska Native, non-Hispanic/Latino; 14 Asian, non-Hispanic/Latino; 17 Hispanic/Latino; 4 Two or more races, non-Hispanic/Latino, 160 international. Average age 30. 761 applicants, 54% accepted, 197 enrolled. *Faculty:* 260 full-time (85 women), 238 part-time/adjunct (132 women). Expenses: Contact institution. *Financial support:* In 2010–11, 60 research assistantships with full tuition reimbursements, 367 teaching assistantships with full tuition reimbursements were awarded; career-related internships or fieldwork, Federal Work-Study, institutionally sponsored loans, scholarships/grants, and unspecified assistantships also available. Support available to part-time students. In 2010, 163 master's, 28 doctorates awarded. *Degree program information:* Part-time and evening/weekend programs available. Offers applied mathematics (MS); applied politics (MA); arts and sciences (MA, MFA, MPA, MS, PhD); biology (MS); chemistry (MS, PhD); composition (MA); computer science (MS); counseling psychology (MA, PhD); creative writing (MFA); earth science (MS); economics (MA); environmental geology (MS); geographic information science (MS); geology (MS); geophysics (MS); history (MA, PhD); industrial/organizational psychology (MA, PhD); integrated bioscience (PhD); literature (MA); mathematics (MS); physics (MS); political science (MA); psychology (MA); public administration (MPA); sociology (MA, PhD); Spanish (MA); statistics (MS); urban planning (MA); urban studies (MA, PhD); urban studies and public affairs (PhD). *Application deadline:* For fall admission, 1/15 for domestic and international students. Applications are processed on a rolling basis. *Application fee:* $30 ($40 for international students). Electronic applications accepted. *Application Contact:* Dr. Chand Midha, Dean, 330-972-7882, E-mail: cmidha@uakron.edu. *Dean*, Dr. Chand Midha, 330-972-7882, E-mail: cmidha@uakron.edu.

College of Business Administration Students: 200 full-time (85 women), 238 part-time (90 women); includes 11 Black or African American, non-Hispanic/Latino; 9 Asian, non-Hispanic/Latino; 5 Hispanic/Latino; 1 Two or more races, non-Hispanic/Latino, 96 international. Average age 29. 321 applicants, 64% accepted, 128 enrolled. *Faculty:* 65 full-time (14 women), 35 part-time/adjunct (1 woman). Expenses: Contact institution. *Financial support:* In 2010–11, 18 research assistantships with full tuition reimbursements, 66 teaching assistantships with full tuition reimbursements were awarded. In 2010, 180 master's awarded. *Degree program information:* Part-time and evening/weekend programs available. Offers accountancy (MS); accounting-information systems (MS); business administration (MBA, MS, MSM, MT); electronic business (MBA); entrepreneurship (MBA); finance (MBA); international business (MBA); international business for international executive (MBA); management (MBA); management of technology (MBA); management-health services administration (MSM); management-human resources (MSM); management-information systems (MSM); management-supply chain management (MSM); strategic marketing (MBA); taxation (MT). *Application deadline:* For fall admission, 7/15 for domestic and international students; for spring admission, 11/15 for domestic and international students. *Application fee:* $30 ($40 for international students). Electronic applications accepted. *Application Contact:* Dr. Susan Hanlon, Director of Graduate Business Programs, 330-972-7043, Fax: 330-972-6588, E-mail: shanlon@uakron.edu. *Interim Dean*, Dr. Ravi Krovi, 330-972-7442, E-mail: cbadean@uakron.edu.

College of Creative and Professional Arts Students: 115 full-time (74 women), 55 part-time (32 women); includes 7 Black or African American, non-Hispanic/Latino; 1 Asian, non-Hispanic/Latino; 7 Hispanic/Latino, 13 international. Average age 32. 128 applicants, 75% accepted, 55 enrolled. *Faculty:* 82 full-time (33 women), 108 part-time/adjunct (60 women). Expenses: Contact institution. *Financial support:* In 2010–11, 1 research assistantship with full and partial tuition reimbursement, 76 teaching assistantships with full and partial tuition reimbursements were awarded; career-related internships or fieldwork, Federal Work-Study, institutionally sponsored loans, tuition waivers, and unspecified assistantships also available. Support available to part-time students. In 2010, 49 master's awarded. *Degree program information:* Part-time and evening/weekend programs available. Offers arts administration (MA); communication (MA); composition (MM); creative and professional arts (MA, MM); music education (MM); music history and literature (MM); music technology (MM); performance (MM); theatre arts (MA); theory (MM). *Application deadline:* For fall admission, 3/15 priority date for domestic students, 3/14 priority date for international students. Applications are processed on a rolling basis. Electronic applications accepted. *Application Contact:* Neil Sapienza, Interim Associate Dean, 330-972-7543, E-mail: nbs@uakron.edu. *Dean*, Dr. Chand Midha, 330-972-7543, E-mail: cmidha@uakron.edu.

College of Education Students: 493 full-time (340 women), 939 part-time (704 women); includes 169 minority (128 Black or African American, non-Hispanic/Latino; 12 Asian, non-Hispanic/Latino; 21 Hispanic/Latino; 1 Native Hawaiian or other Pacific Islander, non-Hispanic/Latino; 7 Two or more races, non-Hispanic/Latino), 15 international. Average age 33. 685 applicants, 74% accepted, 366 enrolled. *Faculty:* 71 full-time (52 women), 140 part-time/adjunct (84 women). Expenses: Contact institution. *Financial support:* In 2010–11, 38 research assistantships with full tuition reimbursements, 86 teaching assistantships with full tuition reimbursements were awarded. In 2010, 429 master's, 7 doctorates awarded. *Degree program information:* Part-time programs available. Offers classroom guidance for teachers (MA, MS); community counseling (MA, MS); counseling psychology (PhD); counselor education and supervision (PhD); education (MA, MS, Ed D, PhD); educational leadership (Ed D); elementary education (MA, MS, PhD); elementary education—literacy (MA); elementary education with licensure (MS); exercise physiology/adult fitness (MA, MS); higher education administration (MA, MS); marriage and family therapy (MA, MS); principalship (MA, MS); school counseling (MA, MS); school psychology (MS); secondary education (MA, MS, PhD); secondary education with licensure (MS); special education (MA, MS); sports science/coaching (MA, MS); technical education (MS). *Application deadline:* For fall admission, 3/1 for domestic and international students; for spring admission, 10/15 for domestic and international students. Applications are processed on a rolling basis. *Application fee:* $30 ($40 for international students). Electronic applications accepted. *Application Contact:* Dr. Mark Shermis, Dean, 330-972-7680, E-mail: shermis@uakron.edu. *Dean*, Dr. Mark Shermis, 330-972-7680, E-mail: shermis@uakron.edu.

College of Engineering Students: 270 full-time (62 women), 85 part-time (17 women); includes 16 minority (2 Black or African American, non-Hispanic/Latino; 11 Asian, non-Hispanic/Latino; 1 Hispanic/Latino; 1 Native Hawaiian or other Pacific Islander, non-Hispanic/Latino; 1 Two or more races, non-Hispanic/Latino), 207 international. Average age 27. 427 applicants, 58% accepted, 99 enrolled. *Faculty:* 84 full-time (13 women), 16 part-time/adjunct (1 woman). Expenses: Contact institution. *Financial support:* In 2010–11, 4 fellowships with full tuition reimbursements, 74 research assistantships with full tuition reimbursements, 156 teaching assistantships with full tuition reimbursements were awarded; career-related internships or fieldwork and Federal Work-Study also available. In 2010, 56 master's, 18 doctorates awarded. *Degree program information:* Part-time and evening/weekend programs available. Offers biomedical engineering (MS, PhD); chemical and biomolecular engineering (MS, PhD); civil engineering (MS, PhD); electrical and computer engineering (MS, PhD); engineering (MS, PhD); engineering (biomedical engineering specialization) (MS); engineering (management specialization) (MS); engineering (polymer specialization) (MS); engineering applied mathematics (PhD); interdisciplinary engineering (PhD); mechanical engineering (MS, PhD). *Application deadline:* Applications are processed on a rolling basis. *Application fee:* $30 ($40 for international students). Electronic applications accepted. *Application Contact:* Dr. Craig Menzemer, Associate Dean, 330-972-5536, E-mail: ccmenze@uakron.edu. *Dean*, Dr. George Haritos, 330-972-6978, E-mail: haritos@uakron.edu.

College of Health Sciences and Human Services Students: 220 full-time (202 women), 65 part-time (58 women); includes 23 Black or African American, non-Hispanic/Latino; 1 American Indian or Alaska Native, non-Hispanic/Latino; 1 Asian, non-Hispanic/Latino; 4 Hispanic/Latino, 6 international. Average age 29. 441 applicants, 28% accepted, 96 enrolled. *Faculty:* 41 full-time (33 women), 97 part-time/adjunct (66 women). Expenses: Contact institution. *Financial support:* In 2010–11, 49 fellowships with full tuition reimbursements, 40 research assistantships with full tuition reimbursements, 37 teaching assistantships with full tuition reimbursements were awarded. In 2010, 106 master's, 10 doctorates awarded. Offers audiology (Au D); child and family development (MA); child development (MA); child life (MA); clothing, textiles and interiors (MA); family development (MA); health sciences and human services (MA, MS, Au D); nutrition and dietetics (MS); social work (MS); speech-language pathology (MA). *Application deadline:* For fall admission, 1/1 for domestic and international students. Electronic applications accepted. *Application Contact:* Dr. James Lynn, Interim Dean, 330-972-6519, E-mail: jlynn@uakron.edu. *Interim Dean*, Dr. James Lynn, 330-972-6519, E-mail: jlynn@uakron.edu.

College of Nursing Students: 64 full-time (53 women), 237 part-time (215 women); includes 18 Black or African American, non-Hispanic/Latino; 6 Asian, non-Hispanic/Latino; 5 Hispanic/Latino; 1 Two or more races, non-Hispanic/Latino, 4 international. Average age 35. 175 applicants, 83% accepted, 76 enrolled. *Faculty:* 46 full-time (44 women), 34 part-time/adjunct (33 women). Expenses: Contact institution. *Financial support:* In 2010–11, 12 fellowships with full tuition reimbursements, 1 research assistantship with full tuition reimbursement, 9 teaching assistantships with full tuition reimbursements were awarded; career-related internships or fieldwork and Federal Work-Study also available. In 2010, 75 master's, 1 doctorate awarded. *Degree program information:* Part-time programs available. Offers nursing (MSN, PhD); public health (MPH). PhD offered jointly with Kent State University. *Application deadline:* For fall admission, 7/15 for domestic and international students. Applications are processed on a rolling basis. *Application fee:* $30 ($40 for international students). Electronic applications accepted. *Application Contact:* Dr. Marlene Huff, Graduate Director, 330-972-7555, E-mail: mhuff@uakron.edu. *Dean*, Dr. Margaret Wineman, 330-972-7551, E-mail: wineman@uakron.edu.

The University of Akron (continued)

College of Polymer Science and Polymer Engineering Students: 159 full-time (41 women), 28 part-time (10 women); includes 4 Black or African American, non-Hispanic/Latino; 3 Asian, non-Hispanic/Latino; 1 Hispanic/Latino, 137 international. Average age 28. 260 applicants, 25% accepted, 50 enrolled. *Faculty:* 29 full-time (2 women), 5 part-time/adjunct (0 women). Expenses: Contact institution. *Financial support:* In 2010–11, 1 fellowship with full tuition reimbursement, 151 research assistantships with full tuition reimbursements were awarded; teaching assistantships, scholarships/grants and tuition waivers also available. In 2010, 3 master's, 21 doctorates awarded. *Degree program information:* Part-time and evening/weekend programs available. Offers polymer engineering (MS, PhD); polymer science (MS, PhD). *Application deadline:* For fall admission, 12/1 priority date for domestic and international students. *Application fee:* $30 ($40 for international students). Electronic applications accepted. *Application Contact:* Dr. Stephen Cheng, Dean, 330-972-7500, E-mail: scheng@uakron.edu. *Dean,* Dr. Stephen Cheng, 330-972-7500, E-mail: scheng@uakron.edu.

School of Law Students: 290 full-time (114 women), 220 part-time (110 women); includes 31 Black or African American, non-Hispanic/Latino; 1 American Indian or Alaska Native, non-Hispanic/Latino; 14 Asian, non-Hispanic/Latino; 20 Hispanic/Latino; 2 Two or more races, non-Hispanic/Latino, 1 international. Average age 27. 1,876 applicants, 39% accepted, 202 enrolled. *Faculty:* 38 full-time (16 women), 16 part-time/adjunct (4 women). Expenses: Contact institution. *Financial support:* In 2010–11, 171 students received support. Career-related internships or fieldwork, scholarships/grants, and tuition waivers (full and partial) available. Support available to part-time students. Financial award applicants required to submit FAFSA. In 2010, 131 first professional degrees awarded. *Degree program information:* Part-time and evening/weekend programs available. Offers intellectual property (LL M); law (JD). *Application deadline:* For fall admission, 3/1 priority date for domestic and international students. Applications are processed on a rolling basis. *Application fee:* $0. Electronic applications accepted. *Application Contact:* Lauri S. File, Assistant Dean of Admission and Financial Aid, 330-972-7331, Fax: 330-258-2343, E-mail: lfile@uakron.edu. *Dean,* Martin H. Belsky, 330-972-6359, Fax: 330-258-2343, E-mail: belsky@uakron.edu.

THE UNIVERSITY OF ALABAMA, Tuscaloosa, AL 35487

General Information State-supported, coed, university. CGS member. *Enrollment:* 30,127 graduate, professional, and undergraduate students; 2,972 full-time matriculated graduate/professional students (1,582 women), 2,186 part-time matriculated graduate/professional students (1,351 women). *Enrollment by degree level:* 519 first professional, 2,953 master's, 1,578 doctoral, 108 other advanced degrees. *Graduate faculty:* 853 full-time (302 women), 69 part-time/adjunct (21 women). Tuition, state resident: full-time $7900. Tuition, nonresident: full-time $20,500. *Graduate housing:* Room and/or apartments available on a first-come, first-served basis to single students; on-campus housing not available to married students. Typical cost: $4700 per year ($8214 including board). Housing application deadline: 4/1. *Student services:* Campus employment opportunities, campus safety program, career counseling, child daycare facilities, exercise/wellness program, free psychological counseling, grant writing training, international student services, low-cost health insurance, multicultural affairs office, services for students with disabilities, teacher training, writing training. *Library facilities:* Amelia Gayle Gorgas Library plus 8 others. *Online resources:* library catalog, web page, access to other libraries' catalogs. *Collection:* 3.5 million titles, 88,083 serial subscriptions, 32,881 audiovisual materials. *Research affiliation:* Wyle Info Systems (information technology), QRxPharma (Pharma), Grandis, Inc. (materials science), Baxter Healthcare (Pharma), Gates Foundation (environmental chemistry), Abbott Laboratories (Pharma).

Computer facilities: 2,200 computers available on campus for general student use. A campuswide network can be accessed from student residence rooms and from off campus. Online class registration is available. *Web address:* http://www.ua.edu/.

General Application Contact: Patrick D. Fuller, Senior Graduate Admissions Counselor, 205-348-5923, Fax: 205-348-0400, E-mail: patrick.d.fuller@ua.edu.

GRADUATE UNITS

Graduate School Students: 2,493 full-time (1,373 women), 2,006 part-time (1,281 women); includes 817 minority (579 Black or African American, non-Hispanic/Latino; 22 American Indian or Alaska Native, non-Hispanic/Latino; 64 Asian, non-Hispanic/Latino; 105 Hispanic/Latino; 1 Native Hawaiian or other Pacific Islander, non-Hispanic/Latino; 46 Two or more races, non-Hispanic/Latino), 465 international. Average age 32. 4,686 applicants, 50% accepted, 1433 enrolled. *Faculty:* 783 full-time (274 women), 21 part-time/adjunct (14 women). Expenses: Contact institution. *Financial support:* In 2010–11, 844 students received support, including research assistantships with full and partial tuition reimbursements available (averaging $9,123 per year); fellowships with full and partial tuition reimbursements available, teaching assistantships with full and partial tuition reimbursements available, career-related internships or fieldwork, Federal Work-Study, institutionally sponsored loans, scholarships/grants, traineeships, health care benefits, tuition waivers (full and partial), and unspecified assistantships also available. Support available to part-time students. Financial award application deadline: 2/15. In 2010, 1,375 master's, 253 doctorates, 44 other advanced degrees awarded. *Degree program information:* Part-time and evening/weekend programs available. Postbaccalaureate distance learning degree programs offered. *Application deadline:* For fall admission, 7/1 priority date for domestic students, 3/15 for international students; for spring admission, 11/1 priority date for domestic students, 7/1 for international students. Applications are processed on a rolling basis. *Application fee:* $50 ($60 for international students). Electronic applications accepted. *Application Contact:* Patrick D. Fuller, Admissions Officer, 205-348-5923, Fax: 205-348-0400, E-mail: patrick.d.fuller@ua.edu. *Dean,* Dr. David A. Francko, 205-348-8280, Fax: 205-348-0400, E-mail: dfrancko@ua.edu.

Capstone College of Nursing Students: 51 full-time (48 women), 169 part-time (148 women); includes 67 minority (55 Black or African American, non-Hispanic/Latino; 2 American Indian or Alaska Native, non-Hispanic/Latino; 2 Asian, non-Hispanic/Latino; 7 Hispanic/Latino; 1 Two or more races, non-Hispanic/Latino). Average age 45. 141 applicants, 74% accepted, 78 enrolled. *Faculty:* 17 full-time (15 women). Expenses: Contact institution. *Financial support:* In 2010–11, 2 fellowships with full tuition reimbursements (averaging $14,000 per year) were awarded; scholarships/grants and traineeships also available. Financial award application deadline: 8/1; financial award applicants required to submit FAFSA. In 2010, 35 master's, 52 doctorates awarded. *Degree program information:* Part-time programs available. Postbaccalaureate distance learning degree programs offered (no on-campus study). Offers nursing (MSN, DNP, Ed D). *Application deadline:* For fall admission, 6/1 priority date for domestic students; for winter admission, 1/1 priority date for domestic students; for spring admission, 4/15 priority date for domestic students. Applications are processed on a rolling basis. *Application fee:* $50 ($60 for international students). Electronic applications accepted. *Application Contact:* Dr. Marietta Stanton, Assistant Dean, Graduate Programs, 205-348-1020, Fax: 205-348-5559, E-mail: mstanton@bama.ua.edu. *Dean,* Dr. Sara E. Barger, 205-348-1040, Fax: 205-348-5559, E-mail: sbarger@bama.ua.edu.

College of Arts and Sciences Students: 713 full-time (408 women), 428 part-time (211 women); includes 144 minority (71 Black or African American, non-Hispanic/Latino; 2 American Indian or Alaska Native, non-Hispanic/Latino; 22 Asian, non-Hispanic/Latino; 38 Hispanic/Latino; 1 Native Hawaiian or other Pacific Islander, non-Hispanic/Latino; 10 Two or more races, non-Hispanic/Latino), 165 international. Average age 28. 1,486 applicants, 35% accepted, 310 enrolled. *Faculty:* 374 full-time (120 women), 11 part-time/adjunct (7 women). Expenses: Contact institution. *Financial support:* In 2010–11, 555 students received support; fellowships with full tuition reimbursements available, research assistantships with full tuition reimbursements available, teaching assistantships with full and partial tuition reimbursements available, career-related internships or fieldwork, Federal Work-Study, institutionally sponsored loans, scholarships/grants, tuition waivers (full and partial), and unspecified assistantships also available. Support available to part-time students. Financial award applicants required to submit FAFSA. In 2010, 221 master's, 59 doctorates awarded. *Degree program information:* Part-time programs available. Postbaccalaureate distance learning degree programs offered. Offers acting (MFA); American studies (MA); anthropology (MA, PhD); applied mathematics (PhD); arranging (MM); art history (MA); arts and sciences (MA, MATESOL, MFA, MM, MPA, MS, DMA, PhD); biological sciences (MS, PhD); chemistry (MS, PhD); choral conducting (MM, DMA); clinical psychology (PhD); composition (MM, DMA); composition and rhetoric (PhD); costume design (MFA); creative writing (MFA); criminal justice (MS); directing (MFA); experimental psychology (PhD); French (MA, PhD); French and Spanish (PhD); geography (MS); geological sciences (MS, PhD); German (MA); history (MA, PhD); literature (MA, PhD); mathematics (MA, PhD); music education (MA, PhD); music history (MM); performance (MM, DMA); physics (MS, PhD); political science (MA, PhD); public administration (MPA); pure mathematics (PhD); rhetoric and composition (MA); Romance languages (MA, PhD); scene design/technical production (MFA); Spanish (MA, PhD); speech language pathology (MS); stage management (MFA); studio art (MA, MFA); teaching English as a second language (MATESOL); theatre (MFA); theatre management/administration (MFA); theory (MM); wind conducting (MM, DMA); women's studies (MA). *Application fee:* $50 ($60 for international students). Electronic applications accepted. *Application Contact:* Patrick D. Fuller, Senior Graduate Admissions Counselor, 205-348-5923, Fax: 205-348-0400, E-mail: patrick.d.fuller@ua.edu. *Dean,* Dr. Robert F. Olin, 205-348-7007, Fax: 205-348-0272, E-mail: olin@as.ua.edu.

College of Communication and Information Sciences Students: 204 full-time (137 women), 248 part-time (178 women); includes 49 minority (24 Black or African American, non-Hispanic/Latino; 3 American Indian or Alaska Native, non-Hispanic/Latino; 6 Asian, non-Hispanic/Latino; 12 Hispanic/Latino; 4 Two or more races, non-Hispanic/Latino), 18 international. Average age 33. 497 applicants, 47% accepted, 144 enrolled. *Faculty:* 55 full-time (26 women), 3 part-time/adjunct (all women). Expenses: Contact institution. *Financial support:* In 2010–11, 78 students received support, including 3 fellowships with tuition reimbursements available (averaging $15,000 per year), 34 research assistantships with tuition reimbursements available (averaging $13,045 per year), 38 teaching assistantships with tuition reimbursements available (averaging $13,045 per year); institutionally sponsored loans, health care benefits, and unspecified assistantships also available. Financial award application deadline: 2/15. In 2010, 169 master's, 12 doctorates awarded. Offers advertising and public relations (MA); book arts (MFA); communication and information sciences (MA, MFA, MLIS, PhD); communication studies (MA); journalism (MA); library and information studies (MLIS, PhD); telecommunication and film (MA). *Application deadline:* For fall admission, 2/15 priority date for domestic and international students; for winter admission, 11/1 priority date for international students; for spring admission, 11/1 priority date for domestic students. Applications are processed on a rolling basis. *Application fee:* $50 ($60 for international students). Electronic applications accepted. *Application Contact:* Diane Shaddix, Information Contact, 205-348-8593, Fax: 205-348-6774, E-mail: dshaddix@bama.ua.edu. *Associate Dean for Graduate Studies,* Dr. Jennings Bryant, 205-348-8593, Fax: 205-348-6774.

College of Education Students: 419 full-time (276 women), 635 part-time (447 women); includes 210 minority (162 Black or African American, non-Hispanic/Latino; 13 American Indian or Alaska Native, non-Hispanic/Latino; 7 Asian, non-Hispanic/Latino; 17 Hispanic/Latino; 11 Two or more races, non-Hispanic/Latino), 30 international. Average age 35. 492 applicants, 67% accepted, 216 enrolled. *Faculty:* 80 full-time (43 women), 3 part-time/adjunct (all women). Expenses: Contact institution. *Financial support:* In 2010–11, 42 research assistantships with full and partial tuition reimbursements were awarded; teaching assistantships with full and partial tuition reimbursements, career-related internships or fieldwork, Federal Work-Study, institutionally sponsored loans, scholarships/grants, and unspecified assistantships also available. Financial award applicants required to submit FAFSA. In 2010, 171 master's, 76 doctorates, 44 other advanced degrees awarded. *Degree program information:* Part-time programs available. Postbaccalaureate distance learning degree programs offered (minimal on-campus study). Offers alternative sport pedagogy (MA); choral music education (MA); collaborative teacher program (M Ed, Ed S); early intervention (M Ed, Ed S); education (M Ed, MA, Ed D, PhD, Ed S); educational administration (Ed D, PhD); educational leadership (MA, Ed S); educational studies in psychology, research methodology and counseling (MA, Ed D, PhD, Ed S); elementary education (MA, Ed D, PhD, Ed S); exercise science (MA, PhD); gifted education (M Ed, Ed S); higher education administration (MA, Ed D, PhD); human performance (MA); instructional leadership (Ed D, PhD); instrumental music education (MA); multiple abilities program (M Ed); music education (Ed D, PhD, Ed S); secondary education (MA, Ed D, PhD, Ed S); special education (Ed D, PhD); sport management (MA); sport pedagogy (MA, PhD). *Application deadline:* For fall admission, 7/1 for domestic and international students; for spring admission, 11/15 for domestic students, 11/17 for international students. Applications are processed on a rolling basis. *Application fee:* $50 ($60 for international students). *Application Contact:* Dr. Kathy S. Wetzel, Assistant Dean for Student Services, 205-348-1154, Fax: 205-348-0080, E-mail: kwetzel@bamaed.ua.edu. *Dean,* Dr. James E. McLean, 205-348-6052.

College of Engineering Students: 214 full-time (34 women), 105 part-time (18 women); includes 27 minority (17 Black or African American, non-Hispanic/Latino; 5 Asian, non-Hispanic/Latino; 3 Hispanic/Latino; 2 Two or more races, non-Hispanic/Latino), 139 international. Average age 28. 429 applicants, 49% accepted, 82 enrolled. *Faculty:* 104 full-time (15 women), 1 part-time/adjunct (0 women). Expenses: Contact institution. *Financial support:* In 2010–11, 188 students received support, including 23 fellowships with full tuition reimbursements available (averaging $16,022 per year), 85 research assistantships with full tuition reimbursements available (averaging $16,022 per year), 73 teaching assistantships with full tuition reimbursements available (averaging $16,022 per year); career-related internships or fieldwork, Federal Work-Study, and institutionally sponsored loans also available. Financial award application deadline: 2/15. In 2010, 79 master's, 28 doctorates awarded. *Degree program information:* Part-time programs available. Postbaccalaureate distance learning degree programs offered (no on-campus study). Offers aerospace engineering (MAE); chemical and biological engineering (MS Ch E, PhD); civil engineering (MSCE, PhD); computer science (MS, PhD); electrical engineering (MS, PhD); engineering (MAE, MES, MS, MS Ch E, MS Met E, MSCE, PhD); engineering science and mechanics (MES, PhD); environmental engineering (MS); materials science (PhD); mechanical engineering (MS, PhD); metallurgical and materials engineering (MS Met E, PhD). *Application deadline:* For fall admission, 7/1 for domestic students, 4/15 for international students; for spring admission, 11/15 for domestic students, 9/1 for international students. Applications are processed on a rolling basis. *Application fee:* $50 ($60 for international students). Electronic applications accepted. *Application Contact:* Dr. David A. Francko, Dean, 205-348-8280, Fax: 205-348-0400, E-mail: dfrancko@ua.edu. *Dean,* Dr. Charles Karr, 205-348-6405, Fax: 205-348-8573.

College of Human Environmental Sciences Students: 168 full-time (118 women), 281 part-time (197 women); includes 117 minority (95 Black or African American, non-Hispanic/Latino; 2 American Indian or Alaska Native, non-Hispanic/Latino; 3 Asian, non-Hispanic/Latino; 7 Hispanic/Latino; 10 Two or more races, non-Hispanic/Latino), 4 international. Average age 32. 333 applicants, 79% accepted, 172 enrolled. *Faculty:* 39 full-time (26 women), 2 part-time/adjunct (1 woman). Expenses: Contact institution. *Financial support:* In 2010–11, 2 research assistantships with full tuition reimbursements (averaging $9,000 per year) were awarded; fellowships with tuition reimbursements, teaching assistantships with full tuition reimbursements, career-related internships or fieldwork, Federal Work-Study, institutionally sponsored loans, and scholarships/grants also available. In 2010, 174 master's, 5 doctorates awarded. *Degree program information:* Part-time and evening/weekend programs available. Postbaccalaureate distance learning degree programs offered (no on-campus study). Offers clothing, textiles, and interior design (MSHES); consumer sciences (MS); family financial planning and counseling (MS); health education and promotion (PhD); health studies (MA); human development and family studies (MSHES); human environmental sciences (MA, MS, MSHES, PhD); human nutrition and hospitality management (MSHES); interactive technology (MS); quality management (MS); restaurant and meeting management (MS); rural community health (MS); sport management (MS). *Application deadline:* For fall admission, 7/6 for domestic students. Applications are processed on a rolling basis. *Application fee:* $50 ($60 for international students). Electronic applications accepted. *Application Contact:* Dr. Milla D. Boschung, Dean, 205-348-6250, Fax: 205-348-1786, E-mail: mboschun@ches.ua.edu. *Dean,* Dr. Milla D. Boschung, 205-348-6250, Fax: 205-348-1786, E-mail: mboschun@ches.ua.edu.

Manderson Graduate School of Business Students: 564 full-time (194 women), 80 part-time (25 women); includes 80 minority (41 Black or African American, non-Hispanic/Latino; 1 American Indian or Alaska Native, non-Hispanic/Latino; 16 Asian, non-Hispanic/Latino;

17 Hispanic/Latino; 5 Two or more races, non-Hispanic/Latino), 101 international. Average age 28. 962 applicants, 49% accepted, 299 enrolled. *Faculty:* 94 full-time (17 women), 1 part-time/adjunct (0 women). Expenses: Contact Institution. *Financial support:* In 2010–11, 60 research assistantships with full and partial tuition reimbursements (averaging $20,000 per year), 60 teaching assistantships with full and partial tuition reimbursements (averaging $20,000 per year) were awarded; fellowships with full and partial tuition reimbursements, career-related internships or fieldwork, Federal Work-Study, institutionally sponsored loans, and scholarships/grants also available. Support available to part-time students. In 2010, 362 master's, 15 doctorates awarded. *Degree program information:* Part-time and evening/weekend programs available. Postbaccalaureate distance learning degree programs offered (no on-campus study). Offers accounting (M Acc, PhD); applied statistics (MS, PhD); business (EMBA, M Acc, MA, MBA, MS, MTA, PhD); economics (MA, PhD); finance (MS, PhD); general commerce and business (EMBA, MBA); information systems, statistics, and management science—applied statistics (MS, PhD); information systems, statistics, and management science—operations management (MS, PhD); management (MA, MS, PhD); marketing (MS, PhD); operations management (MS, PhD); tax accounting (MTA). *Application deadline:* For winter admission, 1/2 priority date for domestic students, 1/1 priority date for international students; for spring admission, 4/15 for domestic and international students. Applications are processed on a rolling basis. *Application fee:* $50 ($60 for international students). Electronic applications accepted. *Application Contact:* Blake Bedsole, Coordinator of Graduate Recruiting/Admissions, 205-348-9122, Fax: 205-348-4504, E-mail: bbedsole@cba.ua.edu. *Dean,* Dr. J. Barry Mason, 205-348-8935, Fax: 205-348-5308, E-mail: jbmason@cba.ua.edu.

School of Social Work Students: 210 full-time (194 women), 76 part-time (66 women); includes 132 minority (121 Black or African American, non-Hispanic/Latino; 2 Asian, non-Hispanic/Latino; 5 Hispanic/Latino; 4 Two or more races, non-Hispanic/Latino), 5 international. Average age 31. 327 applicants, 67% accepted, 134 enrolled. *Faculty:* 18 full-time (12 women). Expenses: Contact institution. *Financial support:* In 2010–11, 113 students received support, including 4 fellowships (averaging $3,750 per year), 9 research assistantships with full tuition reimbursements available (averaging $9,394 per year), 3 teaching assistantships with full tuition reimbursements available (averaging $9,396 per year); career-related internships or fieldwork, scholarships/grants, health care benefits, tuition waivers (partial), and unspecified assistantships also available. Financial award application deadline: 2/1; financial award applicants required to submit FAFSA. In 2010, 164 master's, 6 doctorates awarded. Postbaccalaureate distance learning degree programs offered (no on-campus study). Offers social work (MSW, PhD). *Application deadline:* For fall admission, 2/1 priority date for domestic students; for spring admission, 9/1 priority date for domestic students. Applications are processed on a rolling basis. *Application fee:* $50 ($60 for international students). Electronic applications accepted. *Application Contact:* Casey Barnes, Admissions Coordinator, 205-348-8413, Fax: 205-348-9419, E-mail: credmill@sw.ua.edu. *Dean,* Dr. James A. Hall, 205-348-3924, Fax: 205-348-9419, E-mail: jhall1@sw.ua.edu.

Interdisciplinary Programs Students: 6 full-time (2 women), 6 part-time (4 women); includes 3 minority (all Black or African American, non-Hispanic/Latino). Average age 39. 4 applicants, 25% accepted, 0 enrolled. *Faculty:* 2 full-time (0 women). Expenses: Contact institution. Offers interdisciplinary studies (PhD). *Application Contact:* Patrick D. Fuller, Senior Graduate Admissions Counselor, 205-348-5923, Fax: 205-348-0400, E-mail: patrick.d.fuller@ua.edu.

School of Law Students: 538 full-time (230 women), 182 part-time (71 women); includes 107 minority (63 Black or African American, non-Hispanic/Latino; 5 American Indian or Alaska Native, non-Hispanic/Latino; 18 Asian, non-Hispanic/Latino; 16 Hispanic/Latino; 5 Two or more races, non-Hispanic/Latino), 3 international. Average age 28. 2,639 applicants, 28% accepted, 298 enrolled. *Faculty:* 35 full-time (12 women), 47 part-time/adjunct (7 women). Expenses: Contact institution. *Financial support:* In 2010–11, 383 students received support. Applicants required to submit FAFSA. In 2010, 179 first professional degrees, 76 master's awarded. Offers law (JD, LL M, LL M in Tax). *Application deadline:* Applications are processed on a rolling basis. *Application fee:* $50 ($60 for international students). Electronic applications accepted. *Application Contact:* Page Thead Pulliam, Assistant Director for Admissions, 205-348-7945, Fax: 205-348-3917, E-mail: ppulliam@law.ua.edu. *Dean,* Aaron V. Latham, 205-348-5195, Fax: 205-348-6397, E-mail: alatham@law.ua.edu.

THE UNIVERSITY OF ALABAMA AT BIRMINGHAM, Birmingham, AL 35294

General Information State-supported, coed, university. CGS member. *Enrollment:* 17,543 graduate, professional, and undergraduate students; 3,660 full-time matriculated graduate/professional students (2,125 women), 2,382 part-time matriculated graduate/professional students (1,674 women). *Enrollment by degree level:* 1,032 first professional, 3,454 master's, 1,397 doctoral, 159 other advanced degrees. *Graduate faculty:* 1,769 full-time (622 women), 120 part-time/adjunct (48 women). Tuition, state resident: full-time $5482. Tuition, nonresident: full-time $12,430. Tuition and fees vary according to program. *Graduate housing:* Rooms and/or apartments available on a first-come, first-served basis to single and married students. Housing application deadline: 5/1. *Student services:* Campus employment opportunities, campus safety program, career counseling, child daycare facilities, exercise/wellness program, free psychological counseling, grant writing training, international student services, low-cost health insurance, multicultural affairs office, services for students with disabilities, teacher training, writing training. *Library facilities:* Mervyn Sterne Library plus 1 other. *Online resources:* library catalog, web page, access to other libraries' catalogs. *Collection:* 1.4 million titles, 70,088 serial subscriptions. *Research affiliation:* Southern Research Institute (cancer therapeutics, biodefense).

Computer facilities: A campuswide network can be accessed from student residence rooms and from off campus. Online class registration, transcript requests are available. *Web address:* http://www.uab.edu/.

General Application Contact: Julie Bryant, Director of Graduate Admissions, 205-934-8227, Fax: 205-934-8413, E-mail: jbryant@uab.edu.

GRADUATE UNITS

College of Arts and Sciences Students: 365 full-time (200 women), 134 part-time (88 women); includes 95 minority (59 Black or African American, non-Hispanic/Latino; 2 American Indian or Alaska Native, non-Hispanic/Latino; 14 Asian, non-Hispanic/Latino; 15 Hispanic/Latino; 5 Two or more races, non-Hispanic/Latino), 91 international. Average age 29. 442 applicants, 45% accepted, 106 enrolled. Expenses: Contact institution. *Financial support:* Fellowships, research assistantships, teaching assistantships, career-related internships or fieldwork, Federal Work-Study, and institutionally sponsored loans available. Support available to part-time students. In 2010, 137 master's, 20 doctorates awarded. *Degree program information:* Part-time and evening/weekend programs available. Offers anthropology (MA); applied mathematics (PhD); art history (MA); arts and sciences (MA, MA Ed, MPA, MS, MSCJ, MSFS, Ed D, PhD, Ed S); biology (MS, PhD); chemistry (MS, PhD); communication management (MA); computer and information sciences (MS, PhD); computer forensics and security management (MS); criminal justice (MSCJ); English (MA); forensic science (MSFS); history (MA); mathematics (MS); medical sociology (PhD); physics (MS, PhD); psychology (MA, PhD); public administration (MPA); sociology (MA). *Application deadline:* Applications are processed on a rolling basis. Electronic applications accepted. *Application Contact:* Julie Bryant, Director of Graduate Admissions, 205-934-8227, Fax: 205-934-8413, E-mail: jbryant@uab.edu. *Dean,* Dr. Thomas DiLorenzo, 205-934-5643.

School of Education Students: 351 full-time (271 women), 541 part-time (422 women); includes 214 minority (195 Black or African American, non-Hispanic/Latino; 10 Asian, non-Hispanic/Latino; 7 Hispanic/Latino; 2 Two or more races, non-Hispanic/Latino), 9 international. Average age 33. 212 applicants, 93% accepted, 164 enrolled. Expenses: Contact institution. *Financial support:* Fellowships, career-related internships or fieldwork and Federal Work-Study available. Support available to part-time students. In 2010, 304 master's, 9 doctorates, 42 other advanced degrees awarded. *Degree program information:* Part-time and evening/weekend programs available. Offers arts education (MA Ed); counseling (MA); early childhood education (MA Ed, PhD); education (MA, MA Ed, Ed D, PhD, Ed S); educational leadership (MA Ed, Ed D, PhD, Ed S); elementary education (MA Ed); health education (MA Ed); health education and promotion (PhD); high school education (MA Ed); physical education (MA Ed); special education (MA Ed). *Application deadline:* Applications are processed on a rolling basis. Electronic applications accepted. *Application Contact:* Julie Bryant, Director of Graduate Admissions, 205-934-8227, Fax: 205-934-8413, E-mail: jbryant@uab.edu. *Dean,* Dr. Deborah Voltz, 205-934-8320, Fax: 205-975-7581.

Graduate Programs in Joint Health Sciences Students: 410 full-time (175 women), 12 part-time (2 women); includes 65 minority (34 Black or African American, non-Hispanic/Latino; 3 American Indian or Alaska Native, non-Hispanic/Latino; 19 Asian, non-Hispanic/Latino; 9 Hispanic/Latino), 95 international. Average age 27. 642 applicants, 18% accepted, 52 enrolled. Expenses: Contact institution. *Financial support:* Fellowships, career-related internships or fieldwork available. In 2010, 5 master's, 71 doctorates awarded. Offers basic medical sciences (MSBMS); biochemistry and molecular genetics (PhD); cell biology (PhD); cellular and molecular physiology (PhD); genetics (PhD); joint health sciences (MSBMS, PhD); microbiology (PhD); neurobiology (PhD); pathology (PhD); pharmacology and toxicology (PhD). *Application deadline:* Applications are processed on a rolling basis. Electronic applications accepted. *Application Contact:* Julie Bryant, Director of Graduate Admissions, 205-934-8227, Fax: 205-934-8413, E-mail: jbryant@uab.edu. *Vice President/Dean, School of Medicine,* Dr. Ray L. Watts, 205-934-1111, Fax: 205-934-0333.

School of Business Students: 123 full-time (38 women), 228 part-time (68 women); includes 56 minority (25 Black or African American, non-Hispanic/Latino; 23 Asian, non-Hispanic/Latino; 5 Hispanic/Latino; 3 Two or more races, non-Hispanic/Latino), 11 international. Average age 29. 143 applicants, 73% accepted, 68 enrolled. Expenses: Contact institution. *Financial support:* Fellowships, career-related internships or fieldwork available. In 2010, 129 master's awarded. Offers accounting (M Acct); business (M Acct, MBA); business administration (MBA). *Application deadline:* Applications are processed on a rolling basis. Electronic applications accepted. *Application Contact:* Director, 205-934-8817. *Dean,* Dr. David R. Klock, 205-934-8800, Fax: 205-934-8886, E-mail: dklock@uab.edu.

School of Dentistry Students: 239 full-time (106 women); includes 40 minority (8 Black or African American, non-Hispanic/Latino; 2 American Indian or Alaska Native, non-Hispanic/Latino; 20 Asian, non-Hispanic/Latino; 9 Hispanic/Latino; 1 Two or more races, non-Hispanic/Latino), 8 international. Average age 25. 4 applicants, 100% accepted, 0 enrolled. Expenses: Contact institution. *Financial support:* Fellowships, Federal Work-Study available. In 2010, 52 first professional degrees, 14 master's awarded. Offers dentistry (DMD, MS). *Application Contact:* Dr. Steven J. Filler, Director of Dentistry Admissions, 205-934-5424, Fax: 205-975-6519, E-mail: sfiller@uab.edu. *Dean,* Dr. Huw F. Thomas, 205-934-4720, Fax: 205-934-9283.

School of Engineering Students: 117 full-time (33 women), 238 part-time (53 women); includes 103 minority (67 Black or African American, non-Hispanic/Latino; 1 American Indian or Alaska Native, non-Hispanic/Latino; 21 Asian, non-Hispanic/Latino; 12 Hispanic/Latino; 2 Two or more races, non-Hispanic/Latino), 66 international. Average age 32. 274 applicants, 69% accepted, 128 enrolled. Expenses: Contact institution. *Financial support:* Fellowships with full tuition reimbursements, research assistantships with full tuition reimbursements, career-related internships or fieldwork, Federal Work-Study, institutionally sponsored loans, and tuition waivers (full and partial) available. Support available to part-time students. In 2010, 134 master's, 6 doctorates awarded. *Degree program information:* Evening/weekend programs available. Offers advanced safety engineering and management (M Eng); biomedical engineering (MSBME, PhD); civil engineering (MSCE, PhD); computer engineering (PhD); construction engineering management (M Eng); electrical engineering (MSEE); engineering (M Eng, MS Mt E, MSBME, MSCE, MSEE, MSME, PhD); information engineering and management (M Eng); interdisciplinary engineering (PhD); materials engineering (MS Mt E, PhD); materials science (PhD); mechanical engineering (MSME). *Application deadline:* Applications are processed on a rolling basis. Electronic applications accepted. *Application Contact:* Julie Bryant, Director of Graduate Admissions, 205-934-8227, Fax: 205-934-8413, E-mail: jbryant@uab.edu. *Dean,* Dr. Melinda Lalor, 205-934-8410, Fax: 205-934-8437.

School of Health Professions Students: 742 full-time (521 women), 197 part-time (142 women); includes 142 minority (98 Black or African American, non-Hispanic/Latino; 4 American Indian or Alaska Native, non-Hispanic/Latino; 19 Asian, non-Hispanic/Latino; 17 Hispanic/Latino; 4 Two or more races, non-Hispanic/Latino), 36 international. Average age 30. 422 applicants, 74% accepted, 257 enrolled. Expenses: Contact institution. *Financial support:* Fellowships, research assistantships, teaching assistantships, career-related internships or fieldwork, Federal Work-Study, institutionally sponsored loans, scholarships/grants, traineeships, and unspecified assistantships available. Support available to part-time students. In 2010, 206 master's, 35 doctorates awarded. *Degree program information:* Part-time programs available. Offers administration/health services (D Sc, PhD); clinical laboratory science (MS); clinical nutrition and dietetics (MS); genetic counseling (MS); health administration (MSHA); health informatics (MSHI); health professions (MNA, MS, MSHA, MSHI, MSPAS, D Sc, DPT, PhD); nurse anesthesia (MNA); nutrition sciences (PhD); occupational therapy (MS); physical therapy (DPT); physician assistant studies (MSPAS); rehabilitation science (PhD). Electronic applications accepted. *Application Contact:* Julie Bryant, Director of Graduate Admissions, 205-934-8227, Fax: 205-934-8413, E-mail: jbryant@uab.edu. *Dean,* Dr. Harold P. Jones, 205-934-5149, Fax: 205-934-2412, E-mail: jonesh@uab.edu.

School of Medicine Students: 617 full-time (260 women); includes 38 Black or African American, non-Hispanic/Latino; 2 American Indian or Alaska Native, non-Hispanic/Latino; 87 Asian, non-Hispanic/Latino; 2 Hispanic/Latino; 1 Two or more races, non-Hispanic/Latino. Average age 25. 2,224 applicants, 175 enrolled. Expenses: Contact institution. *Financial support:* Fellowships, career-related internships or fieldwork available. Financial award application deadline: 5/1; financial award applicants required to submit FAFSA. In 2010, 164 first professional degrees awarded. Offers medicine (MD). *Application Contact:* Dr. George S. Hand, Assistant Dean for Admissions, 205-934-2333, Fax: 205-934-8724, E-mail: ghand@uab.edu. *Vice President/Dean, School of Medicine,* Dr. Ray L. Watts, 205-934-1111, Fax: 205-934-0333.

School of Nursing Students: 257 full-time (233 women), 929 part-time (847 women); includes 251 minority (185 Black or African American, non-Hispanic/Latino; 5 American Indian or Alaska Native, non-Hispanic/Latino; 28 Asian, non-Hispanic/Latino; 21 Hispanic/Latino; 12 Two or more races, non-Hispanic/Latino), 15 international. Average age 35. 294 applicants, 99% accepted, 244 enrolled. Expenses: Contact institution. *Financial support:* In 2010–11, 3 fellowships (averaging $12,833 per year), 1 research assistantship, teaching assistantships (averaging $6,760 per year) were awarded; Federal Work-Study also available. Support available to part-time students. In 2010, 217 master's, 62 doctorates awarded. Offers nursing (MSN, DNP, PhD). *Application deadline:* Applications are processed on a rolling basis. Electronic applications accepted. *Application Contact:* Dr. Lynda L. Harrison, Associate for Graduate Studies, 205-934-6787. *Dean,* Dr. Doreen C. Harper, 205-934-5360, E-mail: dcharper@uab.edu.

School of Optometry Students: 197 full-time (128 women), 2 part-time (0 women); includes 44 minority (19 Black or African American, non-Hispanic/Latino; 2 American Indian or Alaska Native, non-Hispanic/Latino; 17 Asian, non-Hispanic/Latino; 4 Hispanic/Latino; 2 Two or more races, non-Hispanic/Latino), 5 international. Average age 25. 17 applicants, 59% accepted, 8 enrolled. Expenses: Contact institution. *Financial support:* In 2010–11, 137 students received support. Federal Work-Study available. Financial award application deadline: 5/1; financial award applicants required to submit FAFSA. In 2010, 42 first professional degrees, 1 master's, 6 doctorates awarded. Offers optometry (OD, MS, PhD); vision science (MS, PhD). *Application deadline:* Applications are processed on a rolling basis. *Application Contact:* Dr. Gerald Simon, Director, Optometry Student Affairs, 205-935-0739, Fax: 205-934-6758, E-mail: gsimonod@uab.edu. *Dean,* Dr. Rodney Nowakowski, 205-934-6724, Fax: 205-974-6758.

School of Public Health Students: 242 full-time (160 women), 101 part-time (52 women); includes 79 minority (47 Black or African American, non-Hispanic/Latino; 24 Asian, non-Hispanic/Latino; 7 Hispanic/Latino; 1 Two or more races, non-Hispanic/Latino), 64 international. Average age 31. 489 applicants, 57% accepted, 95 enrolled. Expenses: Contact institution. *Financial support:* In 2010–11, 115 students received support; fellowships, career-related internships or fieldwork, Federal Work-Study, scholarships/grants, and unspecified assistantships available. Support available to part-time students. Financial award application deadline: 2/15. In 2010, 150 master's, 20 doctorates awarded. *Degree program information:* Part-time programs available. Offers biostatistics (MS, PhD); environmental health sciences (PhD);

The University of Alabama at Birmingham (continued)

epidemiology (PhD); health education and promotion (PhD); public health (MPH, MS, MSPH, DPH, PhD). *Application deadline:* Applications are processed on a rolling basis. Electronic applications accepted. *Application Contact:* Nancy O. Pinson, Coordinator of Student Admissions, 205-934-4993, Fax: 205-975-5484. *Dean,* Dr. Max Michael, 205-975-7742, Fax: 205-975-5484, E-mail: maxm@uab.edu.

THE UNIVERSITY OF ALABAMA IN HUNTSVILLE, Huntsville, AL 35899

General Information State-supported, coed, university. CGS member. *Enrollment:* 7,614 graduate, professional, and undergraduate students; 470 full-time matriculated graduate/professional students (197 women), 1,010 part-time matriculated graduate/professional students (387 women). *Enrollment by degree level:* 1,132 master's, 327 doctoral, 21 other advanced degrees. *Graduate faculty:* 251 full-time (63 women), 40 part-time/adjunct (10 women). Tuition, state resident: full-time $7250; part-time $407.75 per credit hour. Tuition, nonresident: full-time $17,358; part-time $970.05 per credit hour. *Required fees:* $246.80 per semester. Tuition and fees vary according to course load and program. *Graduate housing:* Rooms and/or apartments available on a first-come, first-served basis to single and married students. Typical cost: $4540 per year ($6790 including board) for single students; $6900 per year ($9150 including board) for married students. Housing application deadline: 6/1. *Student services:* Campus employment opportunities, campus safety program, career counseling, child daycare facilities, exercise/wellness program, free psychological counseling, grant writing training, international student services, low-cost health insurance, multicultural affairs office, services for students with disabilities, teacher training, writing training. *Library facilities:* University of Alabama in Huntsville Library. *Online resources:* library catalog, web page. *Collection:* 322,645 titles, 633 serial subscriptions, 2,677 audiovisual materials. *Research affiliation:* Oak Ridge, Lawrence Livermore and Savannah River National Laboratories–National Security Complex (neutron science, energy, high-performance computing, systems biology, materials science at the nanoscale, and national security), Cummings Research Park/Boeing/ADTRAN/SAIC/Teledyne Brown Engineering/Lockheed Martin/Dynetics, Inc. (computer science, aerospace engineering, information systems, space systems, defense systems, informatics), National Oceanic and Atmospheric Administration (NOAA) (weather, climate, oceans, satellites), Hudson Alpha Institute for Biotechnology (medical, biotechnology, genetic research, molecular biology), Department of Defense/U. S. Army Aviation and Missile Command (missile research, development and engineering and manufacturing technology), NASA/Marshall Space Flight Center/Goddard Space Flight Center (space science, earth science, information technology, materials science, optical science).

Computer facilities: 1,213 computers available on campus for general student use. A campuswide network can be accessed from student residence rooms and from off campus. Online class registration is available. *Web address:* http://www.uah.edu/.

General Application Contact: Dr. Rhonda Kay Gaede, Dean of Graduate Studies, 256-824-6002, Fax: 256-824-6405, E-mail: deangrad@uah.edu.

GRADUATE UNITS

School of Graduate Studies Students: 470 full-time (197 women), 1,010 part-time (387 women); includes 105 Black or African American, non-Hispanic/Latino; 17 American Indian or Alaska Native, non-Hispanic/Latino; 43 Asian, non-Hispanic/Latino; 15 Hispanic/Latino; 5 Two or more races, non-Hispanic/Latino, 192 international. Average age 32. 1,332 applicants, 63% accepted, 533 enrolled. *Faculty:* 251 full-time (63 women), 40 part-time/adjunct (10 women). Expenses: Contact institution. *Financial support:* In 2010–11, 291 students received support, including 2 fellowships (averaging $17,250 per year), 105 research assistantships with full and partial tuition reimbursements available (averaging $12,921 per year), 155 teaching assistantships with full and partial tuition reimbursements available (averaging $10,334 per year); career-related internships or fieldwork, Federal Work-Study, institutionally sponsored loans, scholarships/grants, traineeships, health care benefits, tuition waivers (full and partial), and unspecified assistantships also available. Support available to part-time students. Financial award application deadline: 4/1; financial award applicants required to submit FAFSA. In 2010, 364 master's, 38 doctorates, 16 other advanced degrees awarded. *Degree program information:* Part-time and evening/weekend programs available. Postbaccalaureate distance learning degree programs offered (minimal on-campus study). *Application deadline:* For fall admission, 7/15 priority date for domestic students, 4/1 priority date for international students; for spring admission, 11/30 priority date for domestic students, 9/1 priority date for international students. Applications are processed on a rolling basis. *Application fee:* $40 ($50 for international students). Electronic applications accepted. *Application Contact:* Kathy Biggs, Graduate Studies Admissions Manager, 256-824-6199, Fax: 256-824-6405, E-mail: biggsk@email.uah.edu. *Dean of Graduate Studies,* Dr. Rhonda Kay Gaede, 256-824-6002, Fax: 256-824-6405, E-mail: deangrad@uah.edu.

College of Business Administration Students: 58 full-time (25 women), 206 part-time (90 women); includes 42 minority (23 Black or African American, non-Hispanic/Latino; 7 American Indian or Alaska Native, non-Hispanic/Latino; 8 Asian, non-Hispanic/Latino; 3 Hispanic/Latino; 1 Two or more races, non-Hispanic/Latino), 17 international. Average age 32. 193 applicants, 62% accepted, 100 enrolled. *Faculty:* 29 full-time (7 women), 10 part-time/adjunct (1 woman). Expenses: Contact institution. *Financial support:* In 2010–11, 5 students received support, including 2 research assistantships with full and partial tuition reimbursements available (averaging $11,475 per year), 3 teaching assistantships with full and partial tuition reimbursements available (averaging $9,157 per year); career-related internships or fieldwork, Federal Work-Study, institutionally sponsored loans, scholarships/grants, health care benefits, and unspecified assistantships also available. Support available to part-time students. Financial award application deadline: 4/1; financial award applicants required to submit FAFSA. In 2010, 85 master's awarded. *Degree program information:* Part-time and evening/weekend programs available. Offers accounting (M Acc); business administration (M Acc, MBA, MSIS); information systems (MSIS); management (MBA). *Application deadline:* For fall admission, 8/1 for domestic students, 4/1 for international students; for spring admission, 12/1 for domestic students, 9/1 for international students. Applications are processed on a rolling basis. *Application fee:* $40 ($50 for international students). Electronic applications accepted. *Application Contact:* Jennifer Pettitt, Director of Graduate Programs, 256-824-6681, Fax: 256-824-7571, E-mail: jennifer.pettitt@uah.edu. *Dean,* Dr. Caron St. John, 256-824-6736, Fax: 256-824-7571, E-mail: caron.stjohn@uah.edu.

College of Engineering Students: 138 full-time (32 women), 447 part-time (86 women); includes 66 minority (31 Black or African American, non-Hispanic/Latino; 5 American Indian or Alaska Native, non-Hispanic/Latino; 18 Asian, non-Hispanic/Latino; 9 Hispanic/Latino; 3 Two or more races, non-Hispanic/Latino), 69 international. Average age 32. 484 applicants, 62% accepted, 186 enrolled. *Faculty:* 63 full-time (7 women), 14 part-time/adjunct (2 women). Expenses: Contact institution. *Financial support:* In 2010–11, 97 students received support, including 44 research assistantships with full and partial tuition reimbursements available (averaging $11,769 per year), 54 teaching assistantships with full and partial tuition reimbursements available (averaging $10,694 per year); career-related internships or fieldwork, Federal Work-Study, institutionally sponsored loans, scholarships/grants, health care benefits, tuition waivers, and unspecified assistantships also available. Support available to part-time students. Financial award application deadline: 4/1; financial award applicants required to submit FAFSA. In 2010, 124 master's, 15 doctorates awarded. *Degree program information:* Part-time and evening/weekend programs available. Postbaccalaureate distance learning degree programs offered (minimal on-campus study). Offers aerospace engineering (MSE); aerospace systems engineering (MS, PhD); chemical engineering (MSE); civil and environmental engineering (PhD); civil engineering (MSE); computer engineering (MSE, PhD); electrical engineering (MSE, PhD); engineering (MS, MSE, MSOR, MSSE, PhD); industrial and systems engineering (PhD); industrial engineering (MSE); mechanical engineering (MSE, PhD); operations research (MSOR); optical science and engineering (PhD); optics and photonics (MSE); software engineering (MSSE). *Application deadline:* For fall admission, 7/15 for domestic students, 4/1 for international students; for spring admission, 11/30 for domestic students, 9/1 for international students. Applications are processed on a rolling basis. *Application fee:* $40 ($50 for international students). Electronic applications accepted. *Application Contact:* Kathy Biggs, Graduate Studies Admissions Manager, 256-824-6199, Fax: 256-824-6405, E-mail: deangrad@uah.edu. *Dean,* Dr. Shankar Mahalingam, 256-824-6474, Fax: 256-824-6843, E-mail: shankar.mahalingam@uah.edu.

College of Liberal Arts Students: 41 full-time (26 women), 74 part-time (48 women); includes 21 minority (16 Black or African American, non-Hispanic/Latino; 1 American Indian or Alaska Native, non-Hispanic/Latino; 1 Asian, non-Hispanic/Latino; 2 Hispanic/Latino; 1 Two or more races, non-Hispanic/Latino), 1 international. Average age 32. 73 applicants, 75% accepted, 34 enrolled. *Faculty:* 46 full-time (25 women), 1 part-time/adjunct (0 women). Expenses: Contact institution. *Financial support:* In 2010–11, 24 students received support, including 2 research assistantships with full and partial tuition reimbursements available (averaging $11,475 per year), 6 teaching assistantships with full and partial tuition reimbursements available (averaging $8,460 per year); career-related internships or fieldwork, Federal Work-Study, institutionally sponsored loans, scholarships/grants, health care benefits, tuition waivers (full and partial), and unspecified assistantships also available. Support available to part-time students. Financial award application deadline: 4/1; financial award applicants required to submit FAFSA. In 2010, 32 master's, 2 other advanced degrees awarded. *Degree program information:* Part-time and evening/weekend programs available. Offers English (MA); experimental psychology (MA); history (MA); industrial and organizational psychology (MA); liberal arts (MA, Certificate); public affairs (MA); teaching of English to speakers of other languages (Certificate); technical communications (Certificate). *Application deadline:* For fall admission, 7/15 for domestic students, 4/1 for international students; for spring admission, 11/30 for domestic students, 9/1 for international students. Applications are processed on a rolling basis. *Application fee:* $40 ($50 for international students). Electronic applications accepted. *Application Contact:* Kathy Biggs, Graduate Studies Admissions Manager, 256-824-6199, Fax: 256-824-6405, E-mail: deangrad@uah.edu. *Dean,* Glenn Dasher, 256-824-6200, Fax: 256-824-6949, E-mail: dasherg@uah.edu.

College of Nursing Students: 40 full-time (36 women), 124 part-time (111 women); includes 15 minority (11 Black or African American, non-Hispanic/Latino; 1 American Indian or Alaska Native, non-Hispanic/Latino; 2 Asian, non-Hispanic/Latino; 1 Hispanic/Latino), 3 international. Average age 38. 156 applicants, 76% accepted, 77 enrolled. *Faculty:* 19 full-time (18 women), 6 part-time/adjunct (4 women). Expenses: Contact institution. *Financial support:* In 2010–11, 9 students received support, including 9 teaching assistantships with full tuition reimbursements available (averaging $10,041 per year); career-related internships or fieldwork, Federal Work-Study, institutionally sponsored loans, scholarships/grants, traineeships, health care benefits, and unspecified assistantships also available. Support available to part-time students. Financial award application deadline: 4/1; financial award applicants required to submit FAFSA. In 2010, 51 master's, 10 doctorates, 5 other advanced degrees awarded. *Degree program information:* Part-time and evening/weekend programs available. Postbaccalaureate distance learning degree programs offered (minimal on-campus study). Offers family nurse practitioner (Certificate); nursing (MSN, DNP); nursing education (Certificate). DNP offered jointly with The University of Alabama at Birmingham. *Application deadline:* For fall admission, 7/15 for domestic students, 4/1 for international students; for spring admission, 11/30 for domestic students, 9/1 for international students. Applications are processed on a rolling basis. *Application fee:* $40 ($50 for international students). Electronic applications accepted. *Application Contact:* Charles Davis, Associate Director of Nursing Student Affairs Graduate Programs, 256-824-6669, Fax: 256-824-6026, E-mail: charles.davis@uah.edu. *Dean,* Dr. Fay Raines, 256-824-6345, Fax: 256-824-6026, E-mail: rainesc@uah.edu.

College of Science Students: 157 full-time (62 women), 128 part-time (45 women); includes 31 minority (17 Black or African American, non-Hispanic/Latino; 1 American Indian or Alaska Native, non-Hispanic/Latino; 13 Asian, non-Hispanic/Latino), 83 international. Average age 30. 348 applicants, 57% accepted, 104 enrolled. *Faculty:* 74 full-time (6 women), 8 part-time/adjunct (3 women). Expenses: Contact institution. *Financial support:* In 2010–11, 124 students received support, including 2 fellowships (averaging $17,250 per year), 55 research assistantships with full and partial tuition reimbursements available (averaging $13,191 per year), 68 teaching assistantships with full and partial tuition reimbursements available (averaging $10,322 per year); career-related internships or fieldwork, Federal Work-Study, institutionally sponsored loans, scholarships/grants, health care benefits, tuition waivers, and unspecified assistantships also available. Support available to part-time students. Financial award application deadline: 4/1; financial award applicants required to submit FAFSA. In 2010, 69 master's, 8 doctorates, 1 other advanced degree awarded. *Degree program information:* Part-time and evening/weekend programs available. Offers applied mathematics (PhD); atmospheric and environmental science (MS, PhD); biological sciences (MS); chemistry (MS); computer science (MS, PhD); mathematics (MA, MS); optics and photonics technology (MS); physics (MS, PhD); science (MA, MS, MSSE, PhD, Certificate); software engineering (MSSE, Certificate). *Application deadline:* For fall admission, 7/15 for domestic students, 4/1 for international students; for spring admission, 11/30 for domestic students, 9/1 for international students. Applications are processed on a rolling basis. *Application fee:* $40 ($50 for international students). Electronic applications accepted. *Application Contact:* Kathy Biggs, Graduate Studies Admissions Manager, 256-824-6199, Fax: 256-824-6405, E-mail: deangrad@uah.edu. *Dean,* Dr. Jack Fix, 256-824-6605, Fax: 256-824-6819, E-mail: fixj@uah.edu.

Interdisciplinary Studies Students: 36 full-time (16 women), 31 part-time (7 women); includes 10 minority (7 Black or African American, non-Hispanic/Latino; 2 American Indian or Alaska Native, non-Hispanic/Latino; 1 Asian, non-Hispanic/Latino), 19 international. Average age 34. 78 applicants, 54% accepted, 32 enrolled. *Faculty:* 66 full-time (8 women), 7 part-time/adjunct (0 women). Expenses: Contact institution. *Financial support:* In 2010–11, 32 students received support, including 14 research assistantships with full and partial tuition reimbursements available (averaging $13,049 per year), 18 teaching assistantships with full and partial tuition reimbursements available (averaging $11,208 per year); career-related internships or fieldwork, Federal Work-Study, institutionally sponsored loans, scholarships/grants, health care benefits, and unspecified assistantships also available. Support available to part-time students. Financial award application deadline: 4/1; financial award applicants required to submit FAFSA. In 2010, 3 master's, 5 doctorates, 8 other advanced degrees awarded. *Degree program information:* Part-time and evening/weekend programs available. Offers biotechnology science and engineering (PhD); information assurance and cybersecurity (MS, Certificate); interdisciplinary studies (MS, PhD, Certificate); materials science (MS, PhD); modeling and simulation (MS, PhD, Certificate); optical science and engineering (PhD). *Application deadline:* For fall admission, 7/15 for domestic students, 4/1 for international students; for spring admission, 11/30 for domestic students, 9/1 for international students. Applications are processed on a rolling basis. *Application fee:* $40 ($50 for international students). Electronic applications accepted. *Application Contact:* Kathy Biggs, Graduate Studies Admissions Manager, 256-824-6199, Fax: 256-824-6405, E-mail: deangrad@uah.edu. *Dean of Graduate Studies,* Dr. Rhonda Kay Gaede, 256-824-6002, Fax: 256-824-6405, E-mail: rhonda.gaede@uah.edu.

UNIVERSITY OF ALASKA ANCHORAGE, Anchorage, AK 99508

General Information State-supported, coed, comprehensive institution. CGS member. *Graduate housing:* Rooms and/or apartments available on a first-come, first-served basis to single and married students. Housing application deadline: 7/1. *Research affiliation:* Conoco Phillips (energy), Habitat for Humanity (project management), BP Alaska (energy), Municipality of Anchorage (government), Providence Hospital (health care).

GRADUATE UNITS

College of Arts and Sciences *Degree program information:* Part-time programs available. Offers anthropology (MA); arts and sciences (MA, MFA, MS, PhD); biological sciences (MS); clinical psychology (MS); clinical-community psychology with rural-indigenous emphasis (PhD); creative writing and literary arts (MFA); English (MA); interdisciplinary studies (MA, MS).

College of Business and Public Policy *Degree program information:* Part-time and evening/weekend programs available. Offers business administration (MBA); business and public policy (MBA, MPA, MS, Certificate); global supply chain management (MS); public administration (MPA); supply chain management (Certificate).

College of Education *Degree program information:* Part-time programs available. Offers adult education (M Ed); counseling and guidance (M Ed); early childhood special education

(M Ed); education (M Ed, MAT, Certificate); educational leadership (M Ed); master teacher (M Ed); principal licensure (Certificate); special education (M Ed, Certificate); superintendent (Certificate); teaching (MAT).

College of Health and Social Welfare *Degree program information:* Part-time and evening/weekend programs available. Offers health and social welfare (MPH, MS, MSW, Certificate).

Division of Health Sciences *Degree program information:* Part-time programs available. Offers public health practice (MPH).

School of Nursing *Degree program information:* Part-time and evening/weekend programs available. Offers family nurse practitioner (Certificate); nursing (MS); nursing education (Certificate); psychiatric nurse practitioner (Certificate).

School of Social Work *Degree program information:* Part-time and evening/weekend programs available. Postbaccalaureate distance learning degree programs offered (no on-campus study). Offers clinical social work practice (Certificate); social work (MSW); social work management (Certificate). Electronic applications accepted.

School of Engineering *Degree program information:* Part-time and evening/weekend programs available. Offers applied environmental science and technology (M AEST, MS); arctic engineering (MS); civil engineering (MCE, MS); engineering (M AEST, MCE, MS, Certificate); engineering management (MS); port and coastal engineering (Certificate); project management (MS); science management (MS).

UNIVERSITY OF ALASKA FAIRBANKS, Fairbanks, AK 99775-7520

General Information State-supported, coed, university. CGS member. *Enrollment:* 9,855 graduate, professional, and undergraduate students; 650 full-time matriculated graduate/professional students (328 women), 497 part-time matriculated graduate/professional students (313 women). *Enrollment by degree level:* 763 master's, 361 doctoral, 23 other advanced degrees. *Graduate faculty:* 300 full-time (96 women), 91 part-time/adjunct (43 women). Tuition, state resident: full-time $5688; part-time $316 per credit. Tuition, nonresident: full-time $11,628; part-time $646 per credit. *Required fees:* $289 per semester. Tuition and fees vary according to course load and reciprocity agreements. *Graduate housing:* Rooms and/or apartments available on a first-come, first-served basis to single and married students. Typical cost: $4060 per year ($7410 including board) for single students; $6750 per year ($10,100 including board) for married students. Room and board charges vary according to board plan and housing facility selected. Housing application deadline: 8/1. *Student services:* Campus employment opportunities, campus safety program, career counseling, exercise/wellness program, free psychological counseling, grant writing training, international student services, low-cost health insurance, multicultural affairs office, services for students with disabilities, teacher training, writing training. *Library facilities:* Rasmuson Library plus 2 others. *Online resources:* library catalog, web page, access to other libraries' catalogs. *Collection:* 966,394 titles, 58,000 serial subscriptions, 63,676 audiovisual materials. *Research affiliation:* Institute of Northern Forestry, Alaska Cooperative Fishery and Wildlife Research Unit.

Computer facilities: Computer purchase and lease plans are available. 125 computers available on campus for general student use. A campuswide network can be accessed from student residence rooms and from off campus. Online class registration, university portal, campus wireless access are available. *Web address:* http://www.uaf.edu/.

General Application Contact: Mike Earnest, Director of Admissions, 907-474-7500, Fax: 907-474-5379, E-mail: admissions@uaf.edu.

GRADUATE UNITS

College of Engineering and Mines Students: 103 full-time (27 women), 31 part-time (6 women); includes 10 minority (3 Black or African American, non-Hispanic/Latino; 1 American Indian or Alaska Native, non-Hispanic/Latino; 3 Asian, non-Hispanic/Latino; 3 Two or more races, non-Hispanic/Latino), 56 international. Average age 29. 152 applicants, 36% accepted, 39 enrolled. *Faculty:* 67 full-time (13 women), 1 part-time/adjunct (0 women). Expenses: Contact institution. *Financial support:* In 2010–11, 57 research assistantships with tuition reimbursements (averaging $12,602 per year), 34 teaching assistantships with tuition reimbursements (averaging $7,084 per year) were awarded; fellowships with tuition reimbursements, career-related internships or fieldwork, Federal Work-Study, scholarships/grants, health care benefits, and unspecified assistantships also available. Support available to part-time students. Financial award application deadline: 7/1; financial award applicants required to submit FAFSA. In 2010, 29 master's, 3 doctorates awarded. *Degree program information:* Part-time programs available. Offers arctic engineering (MS, PhD); civil engineering (MCE, MS, PhD); computer science (MS); electrical engineering (MEE, MS, PhD); engineering (PhD); engineering and mines (MCE, MEE, MS, MSE, PhD); engineering and science management (MS, PhD); engineering management (MS, PhD); environmental engineering (MS, PhD); environmental quality science (MS); geological engineering (MS, PhD); mechanical engineering (MS); mineral preparation engineering (MS); mining engineering (MS, PhD); petroleum engineering (MS, PhD); science management (MS); software engineering (MSE). *Application deadline:* For fall admission, 6/1 for domestic students, 3/1 for international students; for spring admission, 10/15 for domestic students, 9/1 for international students. Applications are processed on a rolling basis. *Application fee:* $60. Electronic applications accepted. *Application Contact:* Dr. Douglas J. Goering, Dean, 907-474-7730, Fax: 907-474-6994, E-mail: fycem@uaf.edu. *Dean,* Dr. Douglas J. Goering, 907-474-7730, Fax: 907-474-6994, E-mail: fycem@uaf.edu.

College of Liberal Arts Students: 119 full-time (72 women), 125 part-time (85 women); includes 41 minority (3 Black or African American, non-Hispanic/Latino; 15 American Indian or Alaska Native, non-Hispanic/Latino; 4 Asian, non-Hispanic/Latino; 6 Hispanic/Latino; 13 Two or more races, non-Hispanic/Latino), 15 international. Average age 35. 181 applicants, 51% accepted, 74 enrolled. *Faculty:* 121 full-time (54 women), 1 (woman) part-time/adjunct. Expenses: Contact institution. *Financial support:* In 2010–11, 17 research assistantships with tuition reimbursements (averaging $12,044 per year), 80 teaching assistantships with tuition reimbursements (averaging $10,861 per year) were awarded; fellowships with tuition reimbursements, career-related internships or fieldwork, Federal Work-Study, scholarships/grants, health care benefits, and unspecified assistantships also available. Support available to part-time students. Financial award application deadline: 7/1; financial award applicants required to submit FAFSA. In 2010, 67 master's, 6 doctorates awarded. *Degree program information:* Part-time programs available. Postbaccalaureate distance learning degree programs offered. Offers anthropology (MA, PhD); applied linguistics (MA); art (MFA); ceramics (MFA); clinical-community psychology (PhD); computer art (MFA); conducting (MA); creative writing (MFA); cross cultural studies (MA); drawing (MFA); environmental politics and policy (MA); justice (MA); liberal arts (MA, MFA, PhD); literature (MA); music education (MA); music history (MA); music theory/composition (MA); Native arts (MFA); Northern history (MA); painting (MFA); performance (MA); photography (MFA); printmaking (MFA); professional communications (MA); sculpture (MFA). *Application deadline:* For fall admission, 6/1 for domestic students, 3/1 for international students; for spring admission, 10/15 for domestic students, 9/1 for international students. Applications are processed on a rolling basis. *Application fee:* $60. Electronic applications accepted. *Application Contact:* Burns Cooper, Interim Dean, 907-474-7231, Fax: 907-474-5817, E-mail: fycla@uaf.edu. *Interim Dean,* Burns Cooper, 907-474-7231, Fax: 907-474-5817, E-mail: fycla@uaf.edu.

College of Natural Sciences and Mathematics Students: 223 full-time (106 women), 70 part-time (39 women); includes 33 minority (3 Black or African American, non-Hispanic/Latino; 5 American Indian or Alaska Native, non-Hispanic/Latino; 8 Asian, non-Hispanic/Latino; 3 Hispanic/Latino; 1 Native Hawaiian or other Pacific Islander, non-Hispanic/Latino; 13 Two or more races, non-Hispanic/Latino), 45 international. Average age 31. 220 applicants, 29% accepted, 58 enrolled. *Faculty:* 65 full-time (24 women). Expenses: Contact institution. *Financial support:* In 2010–11, 129 research assistantships with tuition reimbursements (averaging $12,149 per year), 58 teaching assistantships with tuition reimbursements (averaging $13,264 per year) were awarded; fellowships with tuition reimbursements, career-related internships or fieldwork, Federal Work-Study, scholarships/grants, health care benefits, and unspecified assistantships also available. Support available to part-time students. Financial award application deadline: 7/1; financial award applicants required to submit FAFSA. In 2010, 30 master's, 26 doctorates awarded. *Degree program information:* Part-time programs available. Offers atmospheric science (MS, PhD); biochemistry and molecular biology (MS, PhD); biological sciences (MS, PhD); biology (MAT, MS); chemistry (MA, MS); computational physics (MS); environmental chemistry (MS, PhD); geology (MS, PhD); geophysics (MS, PhD); mathematics (MAT, PhD); natural sciences and mathematics (MA, MAT, MS, PhD); physics (MAT, MS, PhD); space physics (MS, PhD); statistics (MS); wildlife biology (MS). *Application deadline:* For fall admission, 6/1 for domestic students, 3/1 for international students; for spring admission, 10/15 for domestic students, 9/1 for international students. Applications are processed on a rolling basis. *Application fee:* $60. Electronic applications accepted. *Application Contact:* Dr. Paul Layer, Interim Dean, 907-474-7608, Fax: 907-474-5101, E-mail: fycnsm@uaf.edu. *Interim Dean,* Dr. Paul Layer, 907-474-7608, Fax: 907-474-5101, E-mail: fycnsm@uaf.edu.

College of Rural and Community Development Students: 5 full-time (all women), 27 part-time (20 women); includes 21 minority (17 American Indian or Alaska Native, non-Hispanic/Latino; 4 Two or more races, non-Hispanic/Latino), 2 international. Average age 39. 14 applicants, 57% accepted, 7 enrolled. *Faculty:* 22 full-time (14 women). Expenses: Contact institution. *Financial support:* Fellowships with tuition reimbursements, Federal Work-Study, scholarships/grants, and health care benefits available. Support available to part-time students. Financial award application deadline: 2/15; financial award applicants required to submit FAFSA. In 2010, 10 master's awarded. *Degree program information:* Part-time programs available. Postbaccalaureate distance learning degree programs offered (no on-campus study). Offers rural and community development (MA); rural development (MA). *Application deadline:* For fall admission, 6/1 for domestic students, 3/1 for international students; for spring admission, 10/15 for domestic students, 9/1 for international students. Applications are processed on a rolling basis. *Application fee:* $60. Electronic applications accepted. *Application Contact:* Bernice Joseph, Vice Chancellor for Rural, Community and Native Education, 907-474-7143, Fax: 907-474-5824, E-mail: fyrural@uaf.edu. *Vice Chancellor for Rural, Community and Native Education,* Bernice Joseph, 907-474-7143, Fax: 907-474-5824, E-mail: fyrural@uaf.edu.

Graduate School for Interdisciplinary Studies Students: 2 full-time (both women), 18 part-time (14 women); includes 9 minority (7 American Indian or Alaska Native, non-Hispanic/Latino; 2 Two or more races, non-Hispanic/Latino). Average age 48. 25 applicants, 52% accepted, 13 enrolled. Expenses: Contact institution. *Financial support:* In 2010–11, 1 teaching assistantship with tuition reimbursement (averaging $7,300 per year) was awarded; fellowships with tuition reimbursements, research assistantships with tuition reimbursements, career-related internships or fieldwork, Federal Work-Study, scholarships/grants, health care benefits, and unspecified assistantships also available. Support available to part-time students. Financial award application deadline: 2/15; financial award applicants required to submit FAFSA. In 2010, 2 master's, 4 doctorates awarded. *Degree program information:* Part-time programs available. Offers indigenous studies (PhD); interdisciplinary studies (MA, MS, PhD). *Application deadline:* For fall admission, 6/1 for domestic students, 3/1 for international students; for spring admission, 10/15 for domestic students, 9/1 for international students. Applications are processed on a rolling basis. *Application fee:* $60. Electronic applications accepted. *Application Contact:* Lawrence Duffy, Interim Dean, 907-474-7716, Fax: 907-474-1984, E-mail: fyinds@uaf.edu. *Interim Dean,* Lawrence Duffy, 907-474-7716, Fax: 907-474-1984, E-mail: fyinds@uaf.edu.

School of Education Students: 44 full-time (32 women), 119 part-time (91 women); includes 27 minority (3 Black or African American, non-Hispanic/Latino; 10 American Indian or Alaska Native, non-Hispanic/Latino; 2 Asian, non-Hispanic/Latino; 2 Hispanic/Latino; 1 Native Hawaiian or other Pacific Islander, non-Hispanic/Latino; 9 Two or more races, non-Hispanic/Latino), 1 international. Average age 35. 106 applicants, 64% accepted, 51 enrolled. *Faculty:* 23 full-time (14 women), 1 (woman) part-time/adjunct. Expenses: Contact institution. *Financial support:* In 2010–11, 1 research assistantship with tuition reimbursement (averaging $11,823 per year), 3 teaching assistantships with tuition reimbursements (averaging $10,065 per year) were awarded; fellowships with tuition reimbursements, career-related internships or fieldwork, Federal Work-Study, scholarships/grants, health care benefits, and unspecified assistantships also available. Support available to part-time students. Financial award application deadline: 2/15; financial award applicants required to submit FAFSA. In 2010, 29 master's, 1 doctorate, 27 other advanced degrees awarded. Postbaccalaureate distance learning degree programs offered. Offers counseling (M Ed); curriculum and instruction (M Ed); education (M Ed, PhD, Graduate Certificate); elementary education (M Ed); guidance and counseling (M Ed); interdisciplinary (PhD); language and literacy (M Ed); reading (M Ed); secondary education (M Ed). *Application deadline:* For fall admission, 3/1 for domestic and international students; for spring admission, 10/15 for domestic students, 9/1 for international students. *Application fee:* $60. Electronic applications accepted. *Application Contact:* Dr. Eric C. Madsen, Dean, 907-474-7341, Fax: 907-474-5451, E-mail: fysoed@uaf.edu. *Dean,* Dr. Eric C. Madsen, 907-474-7341, Fax: 907-474-5451, E-mail: fysoed@uaf.edu.

School of Fisheries and Ocean Sciences Students: 93 full-time (52 women), 43 part-time (23 women); includes 9 minority (1 American Indian or Alaska Native, non-Hispanic/Latino; 3 Asian, non-Hispanic/Latino; 4 Hispanic/Latino; 1 Two or more races, non-Hispanic/Latino), 9 international. Average age 31. 103 applicants, 37% accepted, 35 enrolled. *Faculty:* 59 full-time (23 women), 5 part-time/adjunct (3 women). Expenses: Contact institution. *Financial support:* In 2010–11, 65 research assistantships with tuition reimbursements (averaging $13,094 per year), 19 teaching assistantships with tuition reimbursements (averaging $9,396 per year) were awarded; fellowships with tuition reimbursements, career-related internships or fieldwork, Federal Work-Study, scholarships/grants, health care benefits, and unspecified assistantships also available. Support available to part-time students. Financial award application deadline: 2/15; financial award applicants required to submit FAFSA. In 2010, 22 master's, 3 doctorates awarded. *Degree program information:* Part-time programs available. Offers fisheries (MS, PhD); marine biology (MS, PhD); marine sciences and limnology (MS, PhD); oceanography (PhD); seafood science and nutrition (MS, PhD). *Application deadline:* For fall admission, 6/1 for domestic students, 3/1 for international students; for spring admission, 10/15 for domestic students, 9/1 for international students. Applications are processed on a rolling basis. *Application fee:* $60. Electronic applications accepted. *Application Contact:* Christina Neumann, Academic Manager, 907-474-7289, Fax: 907-474-5863, E-mail: cneumann@alaska.edu. *Dean,* Michael Castellini, 907-474-7824, Fax: 907-474-7204, E-mail: academics@sfos.uaf.edu.

School of Management Students: 30 full-time (10 women), 40 part-time (25 women); includes 18 minority (5 Black or African American, non-Hispanic/Latino; 5 American Indian or Alaska Native, non-Hispanic/Latino; 4 Asian, non-Hispanic/Latino; 2 Hispanic/Latino; 1 Native Hawaiian or other Pacific Islander, non-Hispanic/Latino; 1 Two or more races, non-Hispanic/Latino), 5 international. Average age 31. 45 applicants, 69% accepted, 24 enrolled. *Faculty:* 23 full-time (6 women), 1 part-time/adjunct (0 women). Expenses: Contact institution. *Financial support:* In 2010–11, 3 research assistantships with tuition reimbursements (averaging $9,613 per year), 10 teaching assistantships with tuition reimbursements (averaging $11,267 per year) were awarded; fellowships with tuition reimbursements, career-related internships or fieldwork, Federal Work-Study, scholarships/grants, health care benefits, and unspecified assistantships also available. Support available to part-time students. Financial award application deadline: 7/1; financial award applicants required to submit FAFSA. In 2010, 27 master's awarded. *Degree program information:* Part-time programs available. Offers capital markets (MBA); general management (MBA); management (MBA, MS); resource and applied economics (MS). *Application deadline:* For fall admission, 6/1 priority date for domestic students, 2/15 for international students; for spring admission, 10/15 priority date for domestic students, 9/1 for international students. Applications are processed on a rolling basis. *Application fee:* $60. Electronic applications accepted. *Application Contact:* Dr. Mark Herrmann, Dean, 907-474-7461, Fax: 907-474-5219, E-mail: dean.som@uaf.edu. *Dean,* Dr. Mark Herrmann, 907-474-7461, Fax: 907-474-5219, E-mail: dean.som@uaf.edu.

School of Natural Resources and Agricultural Sciences Students: 31 full-time (22 women), 24 part-time (10 women); includes 5 minority (2 American Indian or Alaska Native, non-Hispanic/Latino; 1 Hispanic/Latino; 2 Two or more races, non-Hispanic/Latino), 6 international. Average age 33. 42 applicants, 26% accepted, 8 enrolled. *Faculty:* 37 full-time (12 women), 5 part-time/adjunct (4 women). Expenses: Contact institution. *Financial support:* In 2010–11, 17 research assistantships (averaging $11,187 per year), 4 teaching assistantships (averaging $8,943 per year) were awarded; fellowships, career-related internships or fieldwork, Federal Work-Study, scholarships/grants, health care benefits, and unspecified assistant-

University of Alaska Fairbanks (continued)

ships also available. Support available to part-time students. Financial award application deadline: 2/15; financial award applicants required to submit FAFSA. In 2010, 3 master's, 2 doctorates awarded. *Degree program information:* Part-time programs available. Offers natural resource and sustainability (PhD); natural resource management (MS); natural resource management and geography (MNRM, MS). *Application deadline:* For fall admission, 6/1 for domestic students, 3/1 for international students; for spring admission, 10/15 for domestic students, 9/1 for international students. Applications are processed on a rolling basis. *Application fee:* $60. Electronic applications accepted. *Application Contact:* Veazey David, Director of Enrollment Management, 907-474-5276, Fax: 907-474-6567, E-mail: dave.veazey@alaska.edu. *Dean*, Dr. Carol E. Lewis, 907-474-7083, Fax: 907-474-6567, E-mail: fysnras@uaf.edu.

UNIVERSITY OF ALASKA SOUTHEAST, Juneau, AK 99801

General Information State-supported, coed, comprehensive institution. *Graduate housing:* Rooms and/or apartments available on a first-come, first-served basis to single and married students. Housing application deadline: 5/1. *Research affiliation:* National Park Service (environmental resources, cultural studies), North Pacific Research Board (marine biology, oceanography), U. S. Department of Education (DOE) (teaching, early childhood education), National Science Foundation (marine biology, undergraduate research), U. S. Department of Agriculture (USDA) (forest service), Alaska Department of Education (teaching).

GRADUATE UNITS

Graduate Programs *Degree program information:* Part-time and evening/weekend programs available. Postbaccalaureate distance learning degree programs offered (minimal on-campus study). Offers business administration (MBA); early childhood education (M Ed, MAT); educational technology (M Ed); elementary education (MAT); public administration (MPA); reading (M Ed); secondary education (MAT). Electronic applications accepted.

UNIVERSITY OF ALBERTA, Edmonton, AB T6G 2E1, Canada

General Information Province-supported, coed, university. CGS member. *Graduate housing:* Rooms and/or apartments available on a first-come, first-served basis to single and married students.

GRADUATE UNITS

Faculty of Extension Offers communications and technology (MA).

Faculty of Graduate Studies and Research *Degree program information:* Part-time and evening/weekend programs available. Offers accounting (PhD); adult education (M Ed, Ed D, PhD); agricultural economics (M Ag, M Sc, PhD); agricultural, food and nutritional science (M Ag, M Eng, M Sc, PhD); agroforestry (M Ag, M Sc, MF); ancient history (PhD); anthropology (MA, PhD); applied linguistics (Germanic, Romance, Slavic) (MA); applied mathematics (M Sc, PhD); applied music (M Mus); astrophysics (M Sc, PhD); biostatistics (M Sc); business administration (Exec MBA); chemical engineering (M Eng, M Sc, PhD); chemistry (M Sc, PhD); Chinese literature (MA); choral conducting (M Mus); classical archaeology (MA, PhD); classical literature (PhD); classics (MA); communications (M Eng, M Sc, PhD); communications and technology (MACT); composition (M Mus); computer engineering (M Eng, M Sc, PhD); computing science (M Sc, PhD); condensed matter (M Sc, PhD); conservation biology (M Sc, PhD); construction engineering and management (M Eng, M Sc, PhD); counseling psychology (M Ed, PhD); criminal justice (MA); demography (MA, PhD); design (MFA); directing (MFA); drama (MA); drawing (MFA); earth and atmospheric sciences (M Sc, MA, PhD); East Asian interdisciplinary studies (MA); economics (MA, PhD); economics and finance (MA); educational administration and leadership (M Ed, Ed D, PhD, Postgraduate Diploma); educational psychology (M Ed, PhD); electromagnetics (M Eng, M Sc, PhD); elementary education (M Ed, Ed D, PhD); engineering management (M Eng); English (MA, PhD); environmental and natural resource economics (PhD); environmental biology and ecology (M Sc, PhD); environmental engineering (M Eng, M Sc, PhD); environmental science (M Sc, PhD); experimental linguistics (M Sc, PhD); family ecology and practice (M Sc, PhD); finance (PhD); First Nations education (M Ed, Ed D, PhD); forest biology and management (M Sc, PhD); forest economics (M Ag, M Sc, PhD); French language, literatures and linguistics (PhD); French language, literatures, and linguistics (MA); geoenvironmental engineering (M Eng, M Sc, PhD); geophysics (M Sc, PhD); geotechnical engineering (M Eng, M Sc, PhD); Germanic languages, literatures and linguistics (PhD); Germanic languages, literatures, and linguistics (MA); history (MA, PhD); history of art, design, and visual culture (MA); human resources/industrial relations (PhD); industrial design (M Des); instructional technology (M Ed); international business (MBA); Italian studies (MA); Japanese literature (MA); land reclamation and remediation (M Sc, PhD); leisure and sport management (MBA); management science (PhD); marketing (PhD); materials engineering (M Eng, M Sc, PhD); mathematical finance (M Sc, PhD); mathematical physics (M Sc, PhD); mathematics (M Sc, PhD); mechanical engineering (M Eng, M Sc, PhD); medical physics (M Sc, PhD); microbiology and biotechnology (M Sc, PhD); mining engineering (M Eng, M Sc, PhD); molecular biology and genetics (M Sc, PhD); music (PhD); nanotechnology and microdevices (M Eng, M Sc, PhD); natural resources and energy (MBA); occupational therapy (M Sc, PhD); organ and choral conductors (D Mus); organizational analysis (PhD); painting (MFA); petroleum engineering (M Eng, M Sc, PhD); pharmacology (M Sc, PhD); pharmacy and pharmaceutical sciences (M Sc, PhD); philosophy (MA, PhD); physical education (M Sc); physical therapy (M Sc, PhD); physiology and cell biology (M Sc, PhD); piano (D Mus); plant biology (M Sc, PhD); political science (MA, PhD); power/power electronics (M Eng, M Sc, PhD); printmaking (MFA); process control (M Eng, M Sc, PhD); protected areas and wildlands management (M Sc, PhD); psychology (M Sc, MA, PhD); recreation and physical education (MA, PhD); rural sociology (M Ag, M Sc); school counseling (M Ed); school psychology (M Ed, PhD); sculpture (MFA); secondary education (M Ed, Ed D, PhD); Slavic languages and literatures (Russian, Ukrainian) (MA, PhD); Slavic linguistics (Russian, Ukrainian) (MA, PhD); sociology (MA, PhD); soil science (M Ag, M Sc, PhD); Spanish and Latin American studies (MA, PhD); special education (M Ed, PhD); special education-deafness studies (M Ed); speech pathology and audiology (PhD); speech-language pathology (M Sc); statistics (M Sc, PhD, Postgraduate Diploma); structural engineering (M Eng, M Sc, PhD); subatomic physics (M Sc, PhD); systematics and evolution (M Sc, PhD); systems (M Eng, M Sc, PhD); teaching English as a second language (M Ed); technology commercialization (MBA); textiles and clothing (M Sc, MA, PhD); theoretical, cultural and international studies in education (M Ed, Ed D, PhD); Ukrainian folklore (MA, PhD); visual communication design (M Des); water and land resources (M Ag, M Sc, PhD); water resources (M Eng, M Sc, PhD); welding (M Eng); wildlife ecology and management (M Sc, PhD). Electronic applications accepted.

Faculté Saint Jean *Degree program information:* Part-time and evening/weekend programs available. Postbaccalaureate distance learning degree programs offered (minimal on-campus study). Offers education (M Ed).

Faculty of Nursing *Degree program information:* Part-time programs available. Offers nursing (MN, PhD).

Faculty of Rehabilitation Medicine Offers rehabilitation medicine (PhD). Electronic applications accepted.

School of Library and Information Studies Offers library and information studies (MLIS). Electronic applications accepted.

Faculty of Law *Degree program information:* Part-time programs available. Offers law (LL B, LL M). Electronic applications accepted.

Faculty of Medicine and Dentistry Offers dental hygiene (Diploma); dentistry (DDS); medicine and dentistry (DDS, MD, M Sc, PhD, Diploma); orthodontics (M Sc, PhD); TMD/orofacial pain (M Sc). Electronic applications accepted.

Graduate Programs in Medicine *Degree program information:* Part-time programs available. Offers biochemistry (M Sc, PhD); biomedical engineering (M Sc); cell and molecular biology (M Sc, PhD); medical genetics (M Sc, PhD); medical microbiology and immunology (M Sc, PhD); medical sciences (M Sc, PhD); medicine (MD, M Sc, PhD); neuroscience (M Sc, PhD); obstetrics and gynecology (MD); oncology (M Sc, PhD); ophthalmology (M Sc, PhD); pediatrics (M Sc, PhD); physiology (M Sc, PhD); psychiatry (M Sc, PhD); radiology and diagnostic imaging (M Sc); surgery (M Sc, PhD).

School of Public Health Offers clinical epidemiology (M Sc, MPH); environmental and occupational health (MPH); environmental health sciences (M Sc); epidemiology (M Sc); global health (M Sc, MPH); health policy and management (MPH); health policy research (M Sc); health technology assessment (MPH); occupational health (M Sc); population health (M Sc); public health (M Sc, MPH, PhD, Postgraduate Diploma); public health leadership (MPH); public health sciences (PhD); quantitative methods (MPH).

Centre for Health Promotion Studies *Degree program information:* Part-time programs available. Postbaccalaureate distance learning degree programs offered. Offers health promotion (M Sc, Postgraduate Diploma).

THE UNIVERSITY OF ARIZONA, Tucson, AZ 85721

General Information State-supported, coed, university. CGS member. *Enrollment:* 39,086 graduate, professional, and undergraduate students; 5,869 full-time matriculated graduate/professional students (2,983 women), 1,772 part-time matriculated graduate/professional students (983 women). *Enrollment by degree level:* 1,469 first professional, 2,881 master's, 3,176 doctoral, 115 other advanced degrees. *Graduate faculty:* 1,307 full-time (429 women), 159 part-time/adjunct (53 women). Tuition, state resident: full-time $7692. *Graduate housing:* Rooms and/or apartments available on a first-come, first-served basis to single students and available to married students. Housing application deadline: 5/1. *Student services:* Campus employment opportunities, campus safety program, career counseling, child daycare facilities, exercise/wellness program, free psychological counseling, grant writing training, international student services, low-cost health insurance, multicultural affairs office, services for students with disabilities, teacher training, writing training. *Library facilities:* University of Arizona Main Library. *Online resources:* library catalog, web page, access to other libraries' catalogs. *Research affiliation:* Research Corporation (astronomy), Smithsonian Astrophysical Observatory (astronomy), National Center for Atmospheric Research (atmospheric physics), Kitt Peak National Observatory (astronomy), Argonne National Laboratory (physics).

Computer facilities: A campuswide network can be accessed from student residence rooms and from off campus. Online class registration is available. *Web address:* http://www.arizona.edu/.

General Application Contact: Graduate College Admissions Information Desk, 520-621-3471, Fax: 520-621-4101, E-mail: gradadm@grad.arizona.edu.

GRADUATE UNITS

College of Agriculture and Life Sciences Students: 305 full-time (169 women), 91 part-time (52 women); includes 9 Black or African American, non-Hispanic/Latino; 1 American Indian or Alaska Native, non-Hispanic/Latino; 6 Asian, non-Hispanic/Latino; 39 Hispanic/Latino; 29 Two or more races, non-Hispanic/Latino, 97 international. Average age 31. 358 applicants, 37% accepted, 66 enrolled. *Faculty:* 120 full-time (36 women), 5 part-time/adjunct (1 woman). Expenses: Contact institution. *Financial support:* In 2010–11, 126 research assistantships with full and partial tuition reimbursements (averaging $16,919 per year), 47 teaching assistantships with full and partial tuition reimbursements (averaging $15,942 per year) were awarded; fellowships with full and partial tuition reimbursements, career-related internships or fieldwork, Federal Work-Study, institutionally sponsored loans, scholarships/grants, traineeships, health care benefits, tuition waivers (full and partial), and unspecified assistantships also available. In 2010, 73 master's, 32 doctorates awarded. *Degree program information:* Part-time programs available. Offers agricultural and biosystems engineering (MS, PhD); agricultural and resource economics (MS); agricultural education (M Ag Ed, MS); agriculture and life sciences (M Ag Ed, MHE Ed, MS, PhD); animal sciences (MS, PhD); arid lands resource sciences (PhD); microbiology (MS, PhD); microbiology and pathobiology (MS, PhD); nutritional sciences (MS, PhD); plant pathology (PhD); plant sciences (MS, PhD); soil, water and environmental science (MS, PhD). *Application deadline:* For fall admission, 1/1 for domestic students, 12/1 for international students. Applications are processed on a rolling basis. *Application fee:* $75. Electronic applications accepted. *Application Contact:* Dr. David E. Cox, Associate Dean, 520-621-3612, Fax: 520-621-8662. *Dean*, Dr. Eugene G. Sander, 520-621-7621, Fax: 520-621-7196.

School of Family and Consumer Sciences Students: 33 full-time (21 women), 3 part-time (2 women); includes 2 Black or African American, non-Hispanic/Latino; 4 Hispanic/Latino; 1 Two or more races, non-Hispanic/Latino, 10 international. Average age 33. 25 applicants, 44% accepted, 8 enrolled. *Faculty:* 16 full-time (12 women). Expenses: Contact institution. *Financial support:* In 2010–11, 19 research assistantships with full and partial tuition reimbursements (averaging $13,821 per year), 8 teaching assistantships with full and partial tuition reimbursements (averaging $13,778 per year) were awarded; fellowships, career-related internships or fieldwork, Federal Work-Study, institutionally sponsored loans, scholarships/grants, health care benefits, tuition waivers (full), and unspecified assistantships also available. Financial award application deadline: 3/1. In 2010, 1 master's, 3 doctorates awarded. *Degree program information:* Part-time programs available. Offers family and consumer sciences (MS, PhD). *Application deadline:* Applications are processed on a rolling basis. *Application fee:* $75. *Application Contact:* Mary Helen Scott, Program Coordinator, 520-621-5884, Fax: 520-621-9445, E-mail: mhscott@ag.arizona.edu. *Director*, Dr. Soyeon Shim, 520-621-1075, Fax: 520-621-9445, E-mail: shim@ag.arizona.edu.

School of Natural Resources Students: 73 full-time (38 women), 41 part-time (22 women); includes 1 Asian, non-Hispanic/Latino; 13 Hispanic/Latino; 7 Two or more races, non-Hispanic/Latino, 14 international. Average age 34. 50 applicants, 44% accepted, 15 enrolled. *Faculty:* 21 full-time (2 women), 2 part-time/adjunct (0 women). Expenses: Contact institution. *Financial support:* In 2010–11, 51 research assistantships with full and partial tuition reimbursements (averaging $18,483 per year), 2 teaching assistantships with full and partial tuition reimbursements (averaging $18,035 per year) were awarded; fellowships, career-related internships or fieldwork, scholarships/grants, health care benefits, tuition waivers (full and partial), and unspecified assistantships also available. In 2010, 15 master's, 10 doctorates awarded. Offers natural resources (MS, PhD); rangeland science and management (MS, PhD); watershed resources (MS, PhD); wildlife, fisheries conservation, and management (MS, PhD). *Application deadline:* For fall admission, 6/1 for domestic students, 12/1 for international students; for spring admission, 10/1 for domestic students, 6/1 for international students. *Application fee:* $75. *Application Contact:* Cheryl L. Craddock, Academic Coordinator, 520-621-7260, Fax: 520-621-8801, E-mail: ccraddoc@email.arizona.edu. *Director*, Dr. Lisa J. Graumlich, 520-621-7257, E-mail: lisag@cals.arizona.edu.

College of Architecture and Landscape Architecture Students: 97 full-time (44 women), 16 part-time (8 women); includes 4 Black or African American, non-Hispanic/Latino; 1 American Indian or Alaska Native, non-Hispanic/Latino; 3 Asian, non-Hispanic/Latino; 14 Hispanic/Latino; 9 Two or more races, non-Hispanic/Latino, 18 international. Average age 33. 147 applicants, 59% accepted, 42 enrolled. *Faculty:* 15 full-time (6 women), 1 part-time/adjunct (0 women). Expenses: Contact institution. *Financial support:* In 2010–11, 19 research assistantships with full tuition reimbursements (averaging $13,030 per year), 18 teaching assistantships with full tuition reimbursements (averaging $13,290 per year) were awarded; career-related internships or fieldwork, Federal Work-Study, scholarships/grants, health care benefits, tuition waivers (full), and unspecified assistantships also available. In 2010, 38 master's awarded. *Degree program information:* Part-time programs available. Offers architecture and landscape architecture (M Arch, ML Arch, MS); landscape architecture (ML Arch); planning (MS). *Application deadline:* For fall admission, 2/1 for domestic students, 1/1 for international students. Applications are processed on a rolling basis. *Application fee:* $75. *Application Contact:* Ronald Stoltz, Associate Dean, 520-626-7730, Fax: 520-621-8700, E-mail: rstoltz@u.arizona.edu. *Dean*, Janice A. Cervelli, 520-621-6754, Fax: 520-621-8700, E-mail: jcervell@email.arizona.edu.

School of Architecture Students: 29 full-time (8 women), 8 part-time (5 women); includes 2 Black or African American, non-Hispanic/Latino; 6 Hispanic/Latino; 4 Two or more races, non-Hispanic/Latino, 9 international. Average age 30. 64 applicants, 45% accepted, 16 enrolled. *Faculty:* 10 full-time (3 women). Expenses: Contact institution. *Financial support:* In 2010–11, 17 research assistantships with full tuition reimbursements (averaging $13,000 per year), 9 teaching assistantships with full tuition reimbursements (averaging $13,000 per year) were awarded; health care benefits and unspecified assistantships also available. In 2010, 12 master's awarded. Offers architecture (M Arch). *Application deadline:* For fall admission, 2/1 for domestic students, 12/1 for international students; for spring admission, 2/1 for domestic and international students. *Application fee:* $75. Electronic applications accepted. *Application Contact:* Linda Erasmus, 520-621-9819, Fax: 520-621-8700, E-mail: erasmus@email.arizona.edu. *Interim Director*, Mary Hardin, 520-621-6752, E-mail: mchardin@u.arizona.edu.

College of Education Students: 383 full-time (282 women), 296 part-time (220 women); includes 1 American Indian or Alaska Native, non-Hispanic/Latino; 8 Asian, non-Hispanic/Latino; 111 Hispanic/Latino; 54 Two or more races, non-Hispanic/Latino, 44 international. Average age 39. 399 applicants, 66% accepted, 177 enrolled. *Faculty:* 49 full-time (31 women), 1 (woman) part-time/adjunct. Expenses: Contact institution. *Financial support:* In 2010–11, 47 research assistantships with full tuition reimbursements (averaging $16,678 per year), 49 teaching assistantships with full tuition reimbursements (averaging $15,930 per year) were awarded; career-related internships or fieldwork, Federal Work-Study, institutionally sponsored loans, scholarships/grants, health care benefits, tuition waivers (full and partial), and unspecified assistantships also available. Support available to part-time students. Financial award application deadline: 3/1. In 2010, 220 master's, 49 doctorates awarded. *Degree program information:* Part-time programs available. Postbaccalaureate distance learning degree programs offered (no on-campus study). Offers bilingual education (M Ed); bilingual/multicultural education (MA); education (M Ed, MA, MS, Ed D, PhD, Ed S); educational leadership (M Ed, Ed D, Ed S); educational psychology (MA, PhD, Ed S); family studies and human development (M Ed); higher education (MA); language, reading and culture (MA, Ed D, PhD, Ed S); rehabilitation (MA, PhD); school counseling (M Ed); school counseling and guidance (M Ed); school psychology (PhD, Ed S); special education (Ed D). *Application deadline:* For fall admission, 2/1 priority date for domestic and international students; for spring admission, 10/1 priority date for domestic students, 9/1 priority date for international students. Applications are processed on a rolling basis. *Application fee:* $75. Electronic applications accepted. *Application Contact:* General Information, 520-621-3471, Fax: 520-621-4101, E-mail: gradadm@grad.arizona.edu. *Dean*, Dr. Ronald Marx, 520-621-1081, Fax: 520-621-9271, E-mail: ronmarx@email.arizona.edu.

College of Engineering Students: 408 full-time (93 women), 135 part-time (22 women); includes 14 Black or African American, non-Hispanic/Latino; 1 American Indian or Alaska Native, non-Hispanic/Latino; 14 Asian, non-Hispanic/Latino; 36 Hispanic/Latino; 27 Two or more races, non-Hispanic/Latino, 268 international. Average age 30. 1,110 applicants, 36% accepted, 109 enrolled. *Faculty:* 99 full-time (11 women), 12 part-time/adjunct (2 women). Expenses: Contact institution. *Financial support:* In 2010–11, 236 research assistantships with full tuition reimbursements (averaging $23,836 per year), 57 teaching assistantships with full tuition reimbursements (averaging $23,586 per year) were awarded; institutionally sponsored loans, scholarships/grants, health care benefits, and unspecified assistantships also available. In 2010, 121 master's, 38 doctorates awarded. *Degree program information:* Part-time programs available. Postbaccalaureate distance learning degree programs offered (no on-campus study). Offers aerospace engineering (MS, PhD); chemical engineering (MS, PhD); civil engineering (MS, PhD); electrical and computer engineering (M Eng, MS, PhD); engineering (M Eng, ME, MS, PhD, Certificate); engineering mechanics (MS, PhD); environmental engineering (MS, PhD); geological engineering (MS, PhD); industrial engineering (MS); materials science and engineering (MS, PhD); mechanical engineering (MS, PhD); mine health and safety (Certificate); mine information and production technology (Certificate); mining engineering (M Eng, Certificate); reliability and quality engineering (MS); rock mechanics (Certificate); systems and industrial engineering (MS, PhD); systems engineering (MS, PhD). *Application fee:* $75. *Application Contact:* General Information, 520-621-3471, Fax: 520-621-7112, E-mail: gradadm@grad.arizona.edu. *Dean*, Dr. Thomas W. Peterson, 520-621-6594, Fax: 520-621-2232, E-mail: twp@engr.arizona.edu.

College of Fine Arts Students: 207 full-time (106 women), 119 part-time (65 women); includes 3 Black or African American, non-Hispanic/Latino; 2 American Indian or Alaska Native, non-Hispanic/Latino; 11 Asian, non-Hispanic/Latino; 22 Hispanic/Latino; 20 Two or more races, non-Hispanic/Latino, 43 international. Average age 33. 411 applicants, 39% accepted, 88 enrolled. *Faculty:* 100 full-time (46 women), 4 part-time/adjunct (3 women). Expenses: Contact institution. *Financial support:* In 2010–11, 1 research assistantship with full tuition reimbursement (averaging $15,200 per year), 143 teaching assistantships with full tuition reimbursements (averaging $16,580 per year) were awarded; career-related internships or fieldwork, Federal Work-Study, institutionally sponsored loans, scholarships/grants, health care benefits, tuition waivers (full and partial), and unspecified assistantships also available. Support available to part-time students. In 2010, 82 master's, 23 doctorates awarded. *Degree program information:* Part-time programs available. Offers fine arts (MA, MFA, MM, A Mus D, PhD). *Application fee:* $75. *Application Contact:* General Information, 520-621-1301, Fax: 520-621-1307, E-mail: finearts@email.arizona.edu. *Dean*, Dr. Maurice Sevigny, 520-621-7886, Fax: 520-621-1307.

School of Art Students: 68 full-time (43 women), 30 part-time (24 women); includes 21 minority (2 American Indian or Alaska Native, non-Hispanic/Latino; 2 Asian, non-Hispanic/Latino; 5 Hispanic/Latino; 12 Two or more races, non-Hispanic/Latino), 3 international. Average age 31. 181 applicants, 36% accepted, 41 enrolled. *Faculty:* 32 full-time (16 women), 2 part-time/adjunct (both women). Expenses: Contact institution. *Financial support:* In 2010–11, 9 research assistantships with full tuition reimbursements (averaging $15,204 per year), 87 teaching assistantships with full tuition reimbursements (averaging $16,581 per year) were awarded; career-related internships or fieldwork, Federal Work-Study, institutionally sponsored loans, scholarships/grants, health care benefits, tuition waivers (full and partial), and unspecified assistantships also available. Support available to part-time students. Financial award application deadline: 4/1. In 2010, 27 master's awarded. *Degree program information:* Part-time programs available. Offers art education (MA); art history (MA, PhD); history and theory of art (PhD); studio art (MFA). *Application deadline:* Applications are processed on a rolling basis. *Application fee:* $75. Electronic applications accepted. *Application Contact:* Megan Bartel, Graduate Program Coordinator, 520-621-8518, Fax: 520-621-2955, E-mail: mbartel@email.arizona.edu. *Director*, Dennis L. Jones, 520-621-7000, Fax: 520-621-2955, E-mail: dennisj@email.arizona.edu.

School of Dance Students: 11 full-time (7 women), 1 part-time; includes 5 minority (2 Asian, non-Hispanic/Latino; 3 Two or more races, non-Hispanic/Latino), 1 international. Average age 33. 15 applicants, 40% accepted, 6 enrolled. *Faculty:* 7 full-time (5 women). Expenses: Contact institution. *Financial support:* In 2010–11, 10 teaching assistantships with full tuition reimbursements (averaging $16,581 per year) were awarded. In 2010, 5 master's awarded. Offers dance (MFA). *Application fee:* $75. *Application Contact:* General Information, 520-621-1301, Fax: 520-621-1307, E-mail: finearts@email.arizona.edu. *Interim Dean and Director*, Jory Hancock, 520-626-8030, E-mail: jory@email.arizona.edu.

School of Media Arts Students: 8 full-time (5 women), 2 part-time (0 women); includes 1 Hispanic/Latino, 1 international. Average age 29. 34 applicants, 47% accepted, 10 enrolled. *Faculty:* 8. Expenses: Contact institution. *Financial support:* In 2010–11, 9 teaching assistantships with full tuition reimbursements (averaging $16,581 per year) were awarded; career-related internships or fieldwork, scholarships/grants, health care benefits, tuition waivers (full and partial), and unspecified assistantships also available. Financial award applicants required to submit FAFSA. In 2010, 5 master's awarded. *Degree program information:* Part-time programs available. Offers media arts (MA). *Application deadline:* For fall admission, 2/15 for domestic students, 1/31 for international students. Applications are processed on a rolling basis. *Application fee:* $75. Electronic applications accepted. *Application Contact:* Sylvia Jo Miles, Administrative Secretary, 520-626-2847, Fax: 520-621-9662, E-mail: sjmiles@u.arizona.edu. *Interim Director*, Beverly Seckinger, 520-621-1239, Fax: 520-621-9662, E-mail: bsecking@email.arizona.edu.

School of Music Students: 107 full-time (41 women), 83 part-time (40 women); includes 3 Black or African American, non-Hispanic/Latino; 7 Asian, non-Hispanic/Latino; 14 Hispanic/Latino; 3 Two or more races, non-Hispanic/Latino, 38 international. Average age 34. 162 applicants, 48% accepted, 50 enrolled. *Faculty:* 41 full-time (12 women), 1 part-time/adjunct (0 women). Expenses: Contact institution. *Financial support:* In 2010–11, 64 teaching assistantships with full tuition reimbursements (averaging $16,132 per year) were awarded; career-related internships or fieldwork, institutionally sponsored loans, scholarships/grants, health care benefits, tuition waivers (full), and unspecified assistantships also available. Support available to part-time students. Financial award application deadline: 2/15; financial award applicants required to submit FAFSA. In 2010, 19 master's, 15 doctorates awarded. *Degree program information:* Part-time programs available. Offers composition (MM, A Mus D); conducting (MM, A Mus D); music education (MM, PhD); music theory (MM, PhD); musicology (MM); performance (MM, A Mus D). *Application deadline:* For fall admission, 6/1 for domestic students, 12/1 for international students; for spring admission, 10/1 for domestic students, 6/1 for international students. Applications are processed on a rolling basis. *Application fee:* $75. Electronic applications accepted. *Application Contact:* Lyneen Elmore, 520-621-5929, Fax: 520-621-8118, E-mail: lyneen@u.arizona.edu. *Director*, Dr. Peter A. McAllister, 520-621-7023, Fax: 520-621-1351, E-mail: pmcallis@email.arizona.edu.

School of Theatre Arts Students: 11 full-time (8 women), 2 part-time (0 women); includes 4 minority (2 Hispanic/Latino; 2 Two or more races, non-Hispanic/Latino). Average age 28. 12 applicants, 33% accepted, 2 enrolled. *Faculty:* 14. Expenses: Contact institution. *Financial support:* In 2010–11, 11 teaching assistantships with full tuition reimbursements (averaging $16,581 per year) were awarded; career-related internships or fieldwork, Federal Work-Study, institutionally sponsored loans, scholarships/grants, health care benefits, tuition waivers (full), and unspecified assistantships also available. Financial award application deadline: 3/1; financial award applicants required to submit FAFSA. In 2010, 6 master's awarded. Offers theatre arts (MA, MFA). *Application deadline:* For fall admission, 2/15 for domestic students, 12/1 for international students. Applications are processed on a rolling basis. *Application fee:* $75. Electronic applications accepted. *Application Contact:* Justine M. Collins, Assistant to Director of Administration, 520-621-7007, Fax: 520-621-2412, E-mail: jcollins@email.arizona.edu. *Interim Director*, Jerry Dickey, 520-621-8740, E-mail: jdickey@email.arizona.edu.

College of Humanities Students: 239 full-time (153 women), 106 part-time (63 women); includes 4 Black or African American, non-Hispanic/Latino; 1 American Indian or Alaska Native, non-Hispanic/Latino; 7 Asian, non-Hispanic/Latino; 58 Hispanic/Latino; 19 Two or more races, non-Hispanic/Latino, 49 international. Average age 31. 822 applicants, 24% accepted, 91 enrolled. *Faculty:* 106 full-time (45 women), 7 part-time/adjunct (2 women). Expenses: Contact institution. *Financial support:* In 2010–11, 7 research assistantships with full tuition reimbursements (averaging $19,680 per year), 317 teaching assistantships with full tuition reimbursements (averaging $19,813 per year) were awarded; career-related internships or fieldwork, Federal Work-Study, institutionally sponsored loans, scholarships/grants, health care benefits, tuition waivers (full and partial), and unspecified assistantships also available. Support available to part-time students. In 2010, 74 master's, 24 doctorates awarded. *Degree program information:* Part-time programs available. Offers classics (MA); creative writing (MFA); East Asian studies (MA, PhD); English (MA, PhD); English language/linguistics (MA); ESL (MA); French (MA); German (MA); humanities (MA, MFA, PhD); rhetoric, composition and the teaching of English (PhD); Russian (MA); Spanish (MA, PhD). *Application deadline:* Applications are processed on a rolling basis. *Application fee:* $75. Electronic applications accepted. *Application Contact:* General Information, 520-621-3471, Fax: 520-621-7112, E-mail: gradadm@grad.arizona.edu. *Interim Dean*, Dr. Mary Wildner-Bassett, 520-621-1044, Fax: 520-621-5594.

College of Medicine Students: 647 full-time (346 women), 11 part-time (8 women); includes 9 Black or African American, non-Hispanic/Latino; 44 Asian, non-Hispanic/Latino; 44 Hispanic/Latino; 56 Two or more races, non-Hispanic/Latino, 7 international. Average age 29. *Faculty:* 167 full-time (46 women), 44 part-time/adjunct (9 women). Expenses: Contact institution. *Financial support:* In 2010–11, 88 research assistantships (averaging $22,255 per year), 22 teaching assistantships (averaging $17,000 per year) were awarded; fellowships, career-related internships or fieldwork, Federal Work-Study, institutionally sponsored loans, scholarships/grants, traineeships, tuition waivers (full and partial), and unspecified assistantships also available. Support available to part-time students. In 2010, 107 first professional degrees, 2 master's, 7 doctorates awarded. *Degree program information:* Part-time programs available. Offers cell biology and anatomy (PhD); immunobiology (MS, PhD); medicine (MD, MS, PhD). MD program open only to state residents. *Application Contact:* Dr. Shirley Nickols Fahey, Associate Dean for Admissions, 520-621-2211. *Dean*, Dr. Steven RGoldschmid, 520-626-0998, E-mail: sgoldsch@email.arizona.edu.

College of Nursing Students: 119 full-time (107 women), 33 part-time (29 women); includes 44 minority (10 Black or African American, non-Hispanic/Latino; 4 American Indian or Alaska Native, non-Hispanic/Latino; 7 Asian, non-Hispanic/Latino; 16 Hispanic/Latino; 1 Native Hawaiian or other Pacific Islander, non-Hispanic/Latino; 6 Two or more races, non-Hispanic/Latino), 3 international. Average age 42. *Faculty:* 19 full-time (18 women). Expenses: Contact institution. *Financial support:* In 2010–11, 9 research assistantships with full tuition reimbursements (averaging $18,220 per year), 1 teaching assistantship (averaging $18,327 per year) were awarded; career-related internships or fieldwork, institutionally sponsored loans, scholarships/grants, traineeships, health care benefits, tuition waivers (full), and unspecified assistantships also available. Financial award application deadline: 6/1. In 2010, 28 master's, 20 doctorates awarded. *Degree program information:* Part-time programs available. Postbaccalaureate distance learning degree programs offered (minimal on-campus study). Offers health care informatics (Certificate); nurse practitioner (MS, Certificate); nursing (DNP, PhD); rural health (Certificate). *Application deadline:* For fall admission, 1/15 for domestic and international students. Applications are processed on a rolling basis. *Application fee:* $75. Electronic applications accepted. *Application Contact:* Sally J. Reel, Assistant Dean, Student Affairs, 520-626-6767, Fax: 520-626-6424, E-mail: sreel@nursing.arizona.edu. *Associate Dean*, Dr. Carolyn Murdaugh, 520-626-7124, Fax: 520-626-6424, E-mail: cmurdaugh@nursing.arizona.edu.

College of Optical Sciences Students: 141 full-time (30 women), 121 part-time (22 women); includes 43 minority (6 Black or African American, non-Hispanic/Latino; 1 American Indian or Alaska Native, non-Hispanic/Latino; 16 Asian, non-Hispanic/Latino; 11 Hispanic/Latino; 1 Native Hawaiian or other Pacific Islander, non-Hispanic/Latino; 8 Two or more races, non-Hispanic/Latino), 73 international. Average age 32. 261 applicants, 29% accepted, 53 enrolled. *Faculty:* 26 full-time (3 women), 2 part-time/adjunct (0 women). Expenses: Contact institution. *Financial support:* In 2010–11, 105 research assistantships with full tuition reimbursements (averaging $22,192 per year), 29 teaching assistantships with full tuition reimbursements (averaging $20,978 per year) were awarded; fellowships, scholarships/grants also available. Financial award application deadline: 1/1. In 2010, 44 master's, 23 doctorates awarded. *Degree program information:* Part-time programs available. Offers optical sciences (MS, PhD). *Application deadline:* For fall admission, 1/1 for domestic students, 12/1 for international students. Applications are processed on a rolling basis. *Application fee:* $75. Electronic applications accepted. *Application Contact:* Gail Varin, Coordinator, Graduate Academic Progress, 520-626-0888, E-mail: gail@optics.arizona.edu. *Dean*, Dr. James Wyant, 520-621-6997, Fax: 520-621-9613, E-mail: jcwyant@optics.arizona.edu.

College of Pharmacy Students: 483 full-time (287 women), 7 part-time (6 women); includes 8 Black or African American, non-Hispanic/Latino; 33 Asian, non-Hispanic/Latino; 51 Hispanic/Latino; 83 Two or more races, non-Hispanic/Latino, 45 international. Average age 30. 139 applicants, 118 enrolled. *Faculty:* 27 full-time (6 women), 2 part-time/adjunct (0 women). Expenses: Contact institution. *Financial support:* In 2010–11, 49 research assistantships with full tuition reimbursements (averaging $22,320 per year) were awarded; career-related internships or fieldwork, Federal Work-Study, institutionally sponsored loans, scholarships/grants, health care benefits, tuition waivers (full and partial), and unspecified assistantships also available. Support available to part-time students. In 2010, 84 first professional degrees, 7 master's, 12 doctorates awarded. Offers medical pharmacology (MS, PhD); medicinal and natural products chemistry (MS, PhD); perfusion science (MS); pharmaceutical economics (MS, PhD); pharmaceutics and pharmacokinetics (MS, PhD); pharmacy (Pharm D, MS, PhD). *Application deadline:* For fall admission, 1/1 for domestic and international students. *Application fee:* $65. *Application Contact:* Dr. J. Lyle Bootman, Dean, 520-626-1657. *Dean*, Dr. J. Lyle Bootman, 520-626-1657.

College of Science Students: 661 full-time (277 women), 202 part-time (104 women); includes 118 minority (8 Black or African American, non-Hispanic/Latino; 2 American Indian or Alaska Native, non-Hispanic/Latino; 8 Asian, non-Hispanic/Latino; 52 Hispanic/Latino; 2 Native Hawaiian or other Pacific Islander, non-Hispanic/Latino; 46 Two or more races, non-Hispanic/Latino), 225 international. Average age 31. 2,626 applicants, 13% accepted, 194 enrolled. *Faculty:* 280 full-time (58 women), 31 part-time/adjunct (6 women). Expenses: Contact institution. *Financial support:* In 2010–11, 348 research assistantships with full tuition reimbursements (averaging $22,263 per year), 381 teaching assistantships with full tuition reimburse-

The University of Arizona (continued)

ments (averaging $21,647 per year) were awarded; career-related internships or fieldwork, Federal Work-Study, institutionally sponsored loans, scholarships/grants, health care benefits, tuition waivers (full and partial), and unspecified assistantships also available. Support available to part-time students. In 2010, 101 master's, 84 doctorates awarded. *Degree program information:* Part-time programs available. Offers applied and industrial physics (PMS); applied biosciences (PSM); applied science and business (PMS); astronomy (MS, PhD); atmospheric sciences (MS, PhD); biochemistry (PhD); chemistry (PhD); computer science (MS, PhD); ecology and evolutionary biology (MS, PhD); geosciences (MS, PhD); hydrology and water resources (MS, PhD); mathematical sciences (PMS); mathematics (MA, MS, PhD); molecular and cellular biology (MS, PhD); physics (MS, PhD); planetary sciences (MS, PhD); psychology (MA, PhD); science (MA, MS, PMS, PSM, Au D, PhD); speech, language, and hearing sciences (MS, Au D, PhD). *Application fee:* $75. Electronic applications accepted. *Application Contact:* General Information, 520-621-4090, Fax: 520-621-8389, E-mail: uasci@email.arizona.edu. *Dean*, Dr. Joaquin Ruiz, 520-621-4090, Fax: 520-621-8389, E-mail: jruiz@email.arizona.edu.

College of Social and Behavioral Sciences Students: 615 full-time (347 women), 373 part-time (242 women); includes 8 Black or African American, non-Hispanic/Latino; 9 Asian, non-Hispanic/Latino; 98 Hispanic/Latino; 58 Two or more races, non-Hispanic/Latino, 103 international. Average age 34. 1,209 applicants, 19% accepted, 160 enrolled. *Faculty:* 166 full-time (73 women), 32 part-time/adjunct (20 women). Expenses: Contact institution. *Financial support:* In 2010–11, 70 research assistantships with full tuition reimbursements (averaging $19,321 per year), 337 teaching assistantships (averaging $19,240 per year) were awarded; career-related internships or fieldwork, Federal Work-Study, institutionally sponsored loans, scholarships/grants, health care benefits, tuition waivers (full and partial), and unspecified assistantships also available. Support available to part-time students. In 2010, 239 master's, 73 doctorates awarded. *Degree program information:* Part-time and evening/weekend programs available. Offers anthropology (MA, PhD); communication (MA, PhD); gender and women's studies (MA, PhD); geography (MA, PhD); history (MA, PhD); human language technology (MS); linguistics and anthropology (PhD); Native American linguistics (MA); Near Eastern studies (MA, PhD); philosophy (MA, PhD); political science (MA, PhD); social and behavioral sciences (MA, MS, PhD); sociology (PhD); theoretical linguistics (PhD). *Application fee:* $75. Electronic applications accepted. *Application Contact:* General Information, 520-621-3471, Fax: 520-621-7112, E-mail: gradadm@grad.arizona.edu. *Dean*, Dr. Edward Donnerstein, 520-621-1112, Fax: 520-621-9424, E-mail: edonners@u.arizona.edu.

Center for Latin American Studies Students: 17 full-time (7 women), 9 part-time (2 women); includes 7 Hispanic/Latino; 1 Two or more races, non-Hispanic/Latino. Average age 27. 69 applicants, 52% accepted, 15 enrolled. *Faculty:* 2 full-time (1 woman). Expenses: Contact institution. *Financial support:* In 2010–11, 4 research assistantships with full tuition reimbursements (averaging $18,237 per year), 5 teaching assistantships with full tuition reimbursements (averaging $17,542 per year) were awarded; career-related internships or fieldwork, Federal Work-Study, institutionally sponsored loans, scholarships/grants, health care benefits, tuition waivers (full and partial), and unspecified assistantships also available. In 2010, 10 master's awarded. *Degree program information:* Part-time programs available. Offers Latin American studies (MA). *Application deadline:* For fall admission, 2/1 for domestic students, 12/1 for international students. *Application fee:* $65. Electronic applications accepted. *Application Contact:* Brittany Kaza, Information Contact, 520-626-3317, Fax: 520-626-7248, E-mail: bkaza@email.arizona.edu. *Director*, Dr. Scott Whiteford, 520-626-7207, Fax: 520-626-7248, E-mail: eljete@email.arizona.edu.

School of Information Resources and Library Science Students: 85 full-time (59 women), 160 part-time (123 women); includes 3 Black or African American, non-Hispanic/Latino; 2 American Indian or Alaska Native, non-Hispanic/Latino; 1 Asian, non-Hispanic/Latino; 30 Hispanic/Latino; 20 Two or more races, non-Hispanic/Latino, 1 international. Average age 38. 22 applicants, 36% accepted, 7 enrolled. *Faculty:* 7 full-time (4 women), 1 (woman) part-time/adjunct. Expenses: Contact institution. *Financial support:* In 2010–11, 5 research assistantships with full tuition reimbursements (averaging $18,244 per year), 29 teaching assistantships with full tuition reimbursements (averaging $20,287 per year) were awarded; career-related internships or fieldwork, Federal Work-Study, institutionally sponsored loans, scholarships/grants, health care benefits, tuition waivers (full and partial), and unspecified assistantships also available. Financial award application deadline: 3/1. In 2010, 121 master's awarded. *Degree program information:* Part-time programs available. Offers information resources and library science (MA, PhD). *Application deadline:* For spring admission, 9/1 for domestic and international students. Applications are processed on a rolling basis. *Application fee:* $65. Electronic applications accepted. *Application Contact:* Geraldme Fragoso, Program Manager, 520-621-3565, Fax: 520-621-3279, E-mail: gfragoso@email.arizona.edu. *Director*, Dr. Jana Bradley, 520-621-3565, Fax: 520-621-3279, E-mail: janabrad@email.arizona.edu.

Eller College of Management Students: 633 full-time (249 women), 67 part-time (22 women); includes 16 Black or African American, non-Hispanic/Latino; 4 American Indian or Alaska Native, non-Hispanic/Latino; 28 Asian, non-Hispanic/Latino; 70 Hispanic/Latino; 32 Two or more races, non-Hispanic/Latino, 177 international. Average age 31. 1,656 applicants, 46% accepted, 294 enrolled. *Faculty:* 67 full-time (18 women), 7 part-time/adjunct (1 woman). Expenses: Contact institution. *Financial support:* In 2010–11, 48 research assistantships with full tuition reimbursements (averaging $21,909 per year), 64 teaching assistantships with full tuition reimbursements (averaging $21,830 per year) were awarded; career-related internships or fieldwork, Federal Work-Study, scholarships/grants, health care benefits, tuition waivers (partial), and unspecified assistantships also available. Financial award application deadline: 3/15. In 2010, 407 master's, 23 doctorates awarded. *Degree program information:* Evening/weekend programs available. Offers accounting (M Ac); business administration (MBA); economics (MA, PhD); finance (MS, PhD); management (M Ac, MA, MBA, MPA, MS, PhD); management information systems (MS); marketing (MS, PhD). *Application deadline:* Applications are processed on a rolling basis. *Application fee:* $75. Electronic applications accepted. *Application Contact:* Information Contact, 520-621-2165, Fax: 520-621-8105, E-mail: mbaadmissions@eller.arizona.edu. *Dean*, Dr. Paul R. Portney, 520-621-2125, Fax: 520-621-8105, E-mail: pportney@email.arizona.edu.

School of Public Administration and Policy Students: 64 full-time (38 women), 22 part-time (11 women); includes 2 Black or African American, non-Hispanic/Latino; 1 American Indian or Alaska Native, non-Hispanic/Latino; 2 Asian, non-Hispanic/Latino; 15 Hispanic/Latino; 8 Two or more races, non-Hispanic/Latino, 5 international. Average age 31. 76 applicants, 70% accepted, 27 enrolled. Expenses: Contact institution. *Financial support:* In 2010–11, 1 research assistantship with full tuition reimbursement (averaging $9,429 per year) was awarded; teaching assistantships with full tuition reimbursements, career-related internships or fieldwork, scholarships/grants, health care benefits, tuition waivers (full and partial), and unspecified assistantships also available. Financial award application deadline: 4/15. In 2010, 23 master's awarded. Offers public administration (MPA); public administration and policy (PhD). *Application deadline:* For fall admission, 2/15 priority date for domestic students, 2/15 for international students. Applications are processed on a rolling basis. *Application fee:* $75. Electronic applications accepted. *Application Contact:* Pamela Adams, Administrative Associate, 520-621-3128, Fax: 520-621-5549. *Director*, Dr. H. Brinton Milward, 520-621-7476, Fax: 520-626-5549, E-mail: bmilward@eller.arizona.edu.

Graduate Interdisciplinary Programs Students: 275 full-time (156 women), 61 part-time (27 women); includes 8 Black or African American, non-Hispanic/Latino; 9 American Indian or Alaska Native, non-Hispanic/Latino; 8 Asian, non-Hispanic/Latino; 27 Hispanic/Latino; 50 Two or more races, non-Hispanic/Latino, 59 international. Average age 36. 529 applicants, 31% accepted, 80 enrolled. *Faculty:* 8 full-time (6 women). Expenses: Contact institution. *Financial support:* In 2010–11, 115 research assistantships with full tuition reimbursements (averaging $22,536 per year), 38 teaching assistantships with full tuition reimbursements (averaging $21,205 per year) were awarded; career-related internships or fieldwork, Federal Work-Study, institutionally sponsored loans, scholarships/grants, health care benefits, tuition waivers (full and partial), and unspecified assistantships also available. Support available to part-time students. In 2010, 42 master's, 42 doctorates awarded. *Degree program information:* Part-time programs available. Offers American Indian studies (MA, PhD); applied mathematics (MS, PMS, PhD); biomedical engineering (MS, PhD); cancer biology (PhD); entomology (MA); entomology and insect science (MS, PhD); genetics (MS, PhD); mathematical sciences (PMS); neuroscience (PhD); physiological sciences (MS, PhD); second language acquisition and teaching (PhD); statistics (MS, PhD). *Application deadline:* For fall admission, 2/1 for domestic students, 1/15 for international students. *Application fee:* $65. *Application Contact:* Jolene M. Gruener, Associate Director, 520-621-8368, E-mail: gidp@email.arizona.edu. *Dean*, Dr. Andrew Comrie, 520-621-3512, Fax: 520-621-4101, E-mail: gradadm@grad.arizona.edu.

James E. Rogers College of Law Offers indigenous peoples law and policy (LL M); international trade and business law (LL M); law (JD). Electronic applications accepted.

Mel and Enid Zuckerman College of Public Health Students: 168 full-time (124 women), 79 part-time (59 women); includes 10 Black or African American, non-Hispanic/Latino; 7 American Indian or Alaska Native, non-Hispanic/Latino; 7 Asian, non-Hispanic/Latino; 40 Hispanic/Latino; 28 Two or more races, non-Hispanic/Latino, 16 international. Average age 35. 483 applicants, 41% accepted, 62 enrolled. *Faculty:* 19 full-time (10 women), 10 part-time/adjunct (7 women). Expenses: Contact institution. *Financial support:* In 2010–11, 46 research assistantships with full tuition reimbursements (averaging $18,151 per year), 30 teaching assistantships with full tuition reimbursements (averaging $18,151 per year) were awarded; health care benefits and unspecified assistantships also available. In 2010, 56 master's, 2 doctorates awarded. Offers biostatistics (PhD); epidemiology (MS, PhD); public health (MPH, MS, Dr PH, PhD). *Application deadline:* For fall admission, 1/1 for domestic and international students. Applications are processed on a rolling basis. *Application fee:* $75. Electronic applications accepted. *Application Contact:* Lorraine Varela, Special Assistant to the Dean, 520-626-3201, E-mail: varelal@coph.arizona.edu. *Interim Dean*, Dr. Iman Hakim, 520-626-7083, E-mail: ihakim@email.arizona.edu.

UNIVERSITY OF ARKANSAS, Fayetteville, AR 72701-1201

General Information State-supported, coed, university. CGS member. *Enrollment:* 21,405 graduate, professional, and undergraduate students; 1,006 full-time matriculated graduate/professional students (489 women), 1,795 part-time matriculated graduate/professional students (840 women). *Enrollment by degree level:* 1,849 master's, 912 doctoral, 40 other advanced degrees. *Graduate faculty:* 655 full-time (169 women), 13 part-time/adjunct (2 women). *Graduate housing:* Room and/or apartments available on a first-come, first-served basis to single students; on-campus housing not available to married students. *Student services:* Campus employment opportunities, campus safety program, career counseling, exercise/wellness program, free psychological counseling, international student services, low-cost health insurance, multicultural affairs office, services for students with disabilities, teacher training, writing training. *Library facilities:* David W. Mullins Library plus 5 others. *Online resources:* library catalog, web page, access to other libraries' catalogs. *Collection:* 1.9 million titles, 26,130 serial subscriptions, 31,704 audiovisual materials. *Research affiliation:* Southern Regional Education Board, Southeastern Universities Research Association, Southern Regional Education Board Uncommon Facilities Program, Oak Ridge Associated Universities, Science Coalition, National Minority Graduate Feeder Project.

Computer facilities: Computer purchase and lease plans are available. 3,014 computers available on campus for general student use. A campuswide network can be accessed from student residence rooms and from off campus. Online class registration is available. *Web address:* http://www.uark.edu/.

GRADUATE UNITS

Graduate School Students: 1,188 full-time (639 women), 2,094 part-time (949 women); includes 223 Black or African American, non-Hispanic/Latino; 44 American Indian or Alaska Native, non-Hispanic/Latino; 59 Asian, non-Hispanic/Latino; 68 Hispanic/Latino, 583 international. Expenses: Contact institution. *Financial support:* In 2010–11, 304 fellowships with tuition reimbursements, 772 research assistantships, 469 teaching assistantships with full tuition reimbursements were awarded; career-related internships or fieldwork, Federal Work-Study, institutionally sponsored loans, scholarships/grants, traineeships, and unspecified assistantships also available. Support available to part-time students. Financial award application deadline: 4/1; financial award applicants required to submit FAFSA. In 2010, 930 master's, 144 doctorates, 8 other advanced degrees awarded. *Degree program information:* Part-time programs available. Postbaccalaureate distance learning degree programs offered (no on-campus study). Offers cell and molecular biology (MS, PhD); comparative literature and cultural studies (MA, PhD); environmental dynamics (PhD); microelectronics and photonics (MS, PhD); public policy (PhD); space and planetary sciences (MS, PhD). *Application deadline:* Applications are processed on a rolling basis. *Application fee:* $40 ($50 for international students). Electronic applications accepted. *Application Contact:* Graduate Admissions, 479-575-6246, Fax: 479-575-5908, E-mail: gradinfo@uark.edu. *Associate Dean*, Dr. Patricia R. Koski, 479-575-4401, Fax: 479-575-5908, E-mail: gradinfo@uark.edu.

College of Education and Health Professions Students: 447 full-time (345 women), 584 part-time (419 women); includes 154 minority (101 Black or African American, non-Hispanic/Latino; 23 American Indian or Alaska Native, non-Hispanic/Latino; 10 Asian, non-Hispanic/Latino; 19 Hispanic/Latino; 1 Native Hawaiian or other Pacific Islander, non-Hispanic/Latino), 40 international. 314 applicants, 91% accepted. Expenses: Contact institution. *Financial support:* In 2010–11, 46 fellowships with tuition reimbursements, 101 research assistantships, 24 teaching assistantships were awarded; career-related internships or fieldwork and Federal Work-Study also available. Support available to part-time students. Financial award application deadline: 4/1; financial award applicants required to submit FAFSA. In 2010, 311 master's, 28 doctorates, 5 other advanced degrees awarded. Offers athletic training (MAT); childhood education (MAT); communication disorders (MS); counseling (MS, PhD, Ed S); curriculum and instruction (M Ed, MAT, MS, Ed D, PhD, Ed S); education and health professions (M Ed, MAT, MAT, MS, MSN, Ed D, PhD, Ed S); education policy (PhD); educational leadership (M Ed, Ed D, Ed S); educational statistics and research methods (MS, PhD); educational technology (M Ed); elementary education (M Ed, Ed S); health science (MS, PhD); higher education (M Ed, Ed D, Ed S); kinesiology (MS, PhD); middle-level education (MAT); nursing (MSN); physical education (M Ed, MAT); recreation (M Ed, Ed D); rehabilitation (MS, PhD); secondary education (M Ed, MAT, Ed S); special education (M Ed, MAT); vocational education (MAT); workforce development education (M Ed, Ed D). *Application deadline:* For fall admission, 4/1 for international students; for spring admission, 10/1 for international students. Applications are processed on a rolling basis. *Application fee:* $40 ($50 for international students). Electronic applications accepted. *Application Contact:* Graduate Admissions, 479-575-6246, Fax: 479-575-5908, E-mail: gradinfo@uark.edu. *Dean*, Dr. Thomas E. Smith, 479-575-3208, Fax: 479-575-3119, E-mail: tecsmith@uark.edu.

College of Engineering Students: 134 full-time (33 women), 630 part-time (144 women); includes 114 minority (70 Black or African American, non-Hispanic/Latino; 7 American Indian or Alaska Native, non-Hispanic/Latino; 24 Asian, non-Hispanic/Latino; 12 Hispanic/Latino; 1 Native Hawaiian or other Pacific Islander, non-Hispanic/Latino), 165 international. 421 applicants, 71% accepted. Expenses: Contact institution. *Financial support:* In 2010–11, 39 fellowships with tuition reimbursements, 189 research assistantships, 23 teaching assistantships were awarded; career-related internships or fieldwork and Federal Work-Study also available. Support available to part-time students. Financial award application deadline: 4/1; financial award applicants required to submit FAFSA. In 2010, 272 master's, 28 doctorates awarded. Offers biological and agricultural engineering (MSE, PhD); biological engineering (MSBE); biomedical engineering (MSBME); chemical engineering (MS Ch E, MSE, PhD); civil engineering (MS En E, MSCE, MSE, MSTE, PhD); computer engineering (MS Cmp E, MSE, PhD); computer science (MS, PhD); electrical engineering (MSEE, PhD); engineering (MS, MS Cmp E, MS Ch E, MS En E, MS Tc E, MSBE, MSBME, MSCE, MSE, MSEE, MSIE, MSME, MSOR, MSTE, PhD); environmental engineering (MS En E, MSE); industrial engineering (MSE, MSIE, PhD); mechanical engineering (MSE, MSME, PhD); operations management (MS); operations research (MSE, MSOR); telecommunications engineering (MS Tc E); transportation engineering (MSE, MSTE). *Application deadline:* For fall admission, 4/1 for international students; for spring admission, 10/1 for international students. Applications are processed on a rolling basis. *Application fee:* $40 ($50 for international students). Electronic applications accepted. *Application Contact:* Dr. Terry Martin, Associate Dean for Academic Affairs, 479-575-3052, E-mail: tmartin@uark.edu. *Dean*, Ashok Saxena, 479-575-4153, Fax: 479-575-4346, E-mail: asaxena@uark.edu.

Dale Bumpers College of Agricultural, Food and Life Sciences Students: 113 full-time (53 women), 196 part-time (103 women); includes 16 minority (8 Black or African American, non-Hispanic/Latino; 2 American Indian or Alaska Native, non-Hispanic/Latino; 2 Asian, non-Hispanic/Latino; 4 Hispanic/Latino), 88 international. 164 applicants, 59% accepted. Expenses: Contact institution. *Financial support:* In 2010–11, 14 fellowships with tuition reimbursements, 168 research assistantships, 8 teaching assistantships were awarded; career-related internships or fieldwork, Federal Work-Study, scholarships/grants, and unspecified assistantships also available. Support available to part-time students. Financial award application deadline: 4/1; financial award applicants required to submit FAFSA. In 2010, 81 master's, 18 doctorates awarded. Offers agricultural and extension education (MS); agricultural economics (MS); agricultural, food and life sciences (MS, PhD); agronomy (MS, PhD); animal science (MS, PhD); entomology (MS, PhD); food science (MS, PhD); horticulture (MS); human environmental sciences (MS); plant pathology (MS); plant science (PhD); poultry science (MS, PhD). *Application deadline:* For fall admission, 4/1 for international students; for spring admission, 10/1 for international students. Applications are processed on a rolling basis. *Application fee:* $40 ($50 for international students). Electronic applications accepted. *Application Contact:* Graduate Admissions, 479-575-6246, Fax: 479-575-5908, E-mail: gradinfo@uark.edu. *Dean,* Dr. Michael E. Vayda, 479-575-2034, Fax: 479-575-7273, E-mail: mvayda@uark.edu.

J. William Fulbright College of Arts and Sciences Students: 392 full-time (203 women), 449 part-time (206 women); includes 63 minority (18 Black or African American, non-Hispanic/Latino; 10 American Indian or Alaska Native, non-Hispanic/Latino; 11 Asian, non-Hispanic/Latino; 24 Hispanic/Latino), 147 international. 412 applicants, 75% accepted. Expenses: Contact institution. *Financial support:* In 2010–11, 140 fellowships, 149 research assistantships, 368 teaching assistantships with full tuition reimbursements were awarded; career-related internships or fieldwork, Federal Work-Study, institutionally sponsored loans, and traineeships also available. Support available to part-time students. Financial award application deadline: 4/1; financial award applicants required to submit FAFSA. In 2010, 185 master's, 41 doctorates awarded. Offers anthropology (MA, PhD); applied physics (MS); art (MFA); arts and sciences (MA, MFA, MM, MPA, MS, MSW, PhD); biological sciences (MA, MS, PhD); chemistry (MS, PhD); communication (MA); creative writing (MFA); drama (MA, MFA); English (MA, PhD); French (MA); geography (MA); geology (MS); German (MA); history (MA, PhD); journalism (MA); mathematics (MS, PhD); music (MM); philosophy (MA, PhD); physics (MS, PhD); physics education (MA); political science (MA); psychology (MA, PhD); public administration (MPA); secondary mathematics (MA); social work (MSW); sociology (MA); Spanish (MA); statistics (MS); translation (MFA). *Application deadline:* For fall admission, 4/1 for international students; for spring admission, 10/1 for international students. Applications are processed on a rolling basis. *Application fee:* $40 ($50 for international students). Electronic applications accepted. *Application Contact:* Dr. Charles Adams, Associate Dean for Academic Affairs and International Programs, 479-575-3711, E-mail: cadams@uark.edu. *Dean,* Dr. Bill Schwab, 479-575-4801, Fax: 479-575-2642.

Sam M. Walton College of Business Administration Students: 118 full-time (36 women), 145 part-time (38 women); includes 23 minority (7 Black or African American, non-Hispanic/Latino; 3 American Indian or Alaska Native, non-Hispanic/Latino; 10 Asian, non-Hispanic/Latino; 2 Hispanic/Latino; 1 Native Hawaiian or other Pacific Islander, non-Hispanic/Latino), 46 international. 193 applicants, 68% accepted. Expenses: Contact institution. *Financial support:* In 2010–11, 37 fellowships, 80 research assistantships, 20 teaching assistantships were awarded; career-related internships or fieldwork and Federal Work-Study also available. Support available to part-time students. Financial award application deadline: 4/1; financial award applicants required to submit FAFSA. In 2010, 158 master's, 3 doctorates awarded. Offers accounting (M Acc); business administration (M Acc, MA, MBA, MIS, PhD); economics (MA, PhD); information systems (MIS). *Application fee:* $40 ($50 for international students). *Application Contact:* Rebel Smith, Assistant Director of Marketing and Recruiting, 479-575-6123, E-mail: gsb@walton.uark.edu. *Dean,* Dr. Dan Worrell, 479-575-5949, E-mail: dworrell@walton.uark.edu.

School of Law Students: 405 full-time (179 women); includes 67 minority (32 Black or African American, non-Hispanic/Latino; 5 American Indian or Alaska Native, non-Hispanic/Latino; 11 Asian, non-Hispanic/Latino; 14 Hispanic/Latino; 5 Two or more races, non-Hispanic/Latino), 3 international. Expenses: Contact institution. *Financial support:* In 2010–11, fellowships with full tuition reimbursements (averaging $6,000 per year), 12 research assistantships (averaging $2,500 per year) were awarded; teaching assistantships, career-related internships or fieldwork, Federal Work-Study, and scholarships/grants also available. Support available to part-time students. Financial award application deadline: 4/1; financial award applicants required to submit FAFSA. In 2010, 139 first professional degrees, 14 master's awarded. Offers agricultural law (LL M); law (JD). *Application deadline:* For fall admission, 4/1 for domestic students. Applications are processed on a rolling basis. *Application fee:* $0. *Application Contact:* James K. Miller, Associate Dean for Students, 479-575-3102, E-mail: jkmiller@uark.edu. *Dean,* Cynthia Nance, 479-575-5601, Fax: 479-575-3320, E-mail: cnance@uark.edu.

UNIVERSITY OF ARKANSAS AT LITTLE ROCK, Little Rock, AR 72204-1099

General Information State-supported, coed, university. CGS member. *Graduate housing:* Room and/or apartments available on a first-come, first-served basis to single students; on-campus housing not available to married students.

GRADUATE UNITS

Graduate School *Degree program information:* Part-time and evening/weekend programs available. Postbaccalaureate distance learning degree programs offered. Electronic applications accepted.

Clinton School of Public Service Offers public service (MPS, Graduate Certificate).

College of Arts, Humanities, and Social Science *Degree program information:* Part-time and evening/weekend programs available. Offers applied psychology (MAP); art education (MA); art history (MA); arts, humanities, and social science (MA, MALS, MAP, Graduate Certificate); gerontology (Graduate Certificate); philosophy and liberal studies (MALS); professional and technical writing (MA); public history (MA); second languages (MA); studio art (MA).

College of Business Administration *Degree program information:* Part-time and evening/weekend programs available. Offers accountancy (M Acc, Graduate Certificate); business administration (MBA); construction management (Graduate Certificate); management (Graduate Certificate); management information system (MIS); management information systems (Graduate Certificate); management information systems leadership (Graduate Certificate); taxation (MS, Graduate Certificate).

College of Education *Degree program information:* Part-time and evening/weekend programs available. Offers adult education (M Ed); college student affairs (MA); counselor education (M Ed); early childhood education (M Ed); education (M Ed, MA, Ed D, Ed S, Graduate Certificate); educational administration (M Ed, Ed D, Ed S); educational administration and supervision (Ed D); higher education administration (Ed D); higher education: two-year college teaching (MA); learning systems technology (M Ed); literacy coach (Graduate Certificate); middle childhood education (M Ed); orientation and mobility of the blind (Graduate Certificate); reading (M Ed, Ed S); reading education (M Ed, Ed S, Graduate Certificate); rehabilitation counseling (MA, Graduate Certificate); rehabilitation of the blind (MA); school counseling (M Ed); secondary education (M Ed); special education (M Ed); teaching advanced placement (Graduate Certificate); teaching deaf and hard of hearing (M Ed); teaching the gifted and talented (M Ed); teaching the visually impaired (M Ed).

College of Professional Studies *Degree program information:* Part-time and evening/weekend programs available. Offers advanced direct practice (MSW); applied communication studies (MA); conflict mediation (Graduate Certificate); criminal justice (MA, MS, PhD); health sciences (MS); journalism (MA); management and community practice (MSW); marriage and family therapy (Graduate Certificate); nonprofit management (Graduate Certificate); professional studies (MA, MPA, MS, MSW, Graduate Certificate); public administration (MPA); social work (MSW, Graduate Certificate).

College of Science and Mathematics Offers applied statistics (Graduate Certificate); biology (MS); chemistry (MA, MS); geospatial technology (Graduate Certificate); integrated science and mathematics (MS); mathematical sciences (MS); science and mathematics (MA, MS, Graduate Certificate).

George W. Donaghey College of Engineering and Information Technology *Degree program information:* Part-time and evening/weekend programs available. Offers applied science (MS, PhD); bioinformatics (MS, PhD); computer and information science (MS); engineering and information technology (MS, PhD, Graduate Certificate); information quality (MS); systems engineering (Graduate Certificate).

William H. Bowen School of Law *Degree program information:* Part-time and evening/weekend programs available. Offers law (JD). Electronic applications accepted.

UNIVERSITY OF ARKANSAS AT MONTICELLO, Monticello, AR 71656

General Information State-supported, coed, comprehensive institution. *Graduate housing:* Rooms and/or apartments guaranteed to single students and available on a first-come, first-served basis to married students. Housing application deadline: 8/15.

GRADUATE UNITS

School of Education *Degree program information:* Part-time and evening/weekend programs available. Postbaccalaureate distance learning degree programs offered (minimal on-campus study). Offers education (M Ed, MAT); educational leadership (M Ed). Electronic applications accepted.

School of Forest Resources *Degree program information:* Part-time programs available. Offers forest resources (MS). Electronic applications accepted.

UNIVERSITY OF ARKANSAS AT PINE BLUFF, Pine Bluff, AR 71601-2799

General Information State-supported, coed, comprehensive institution. *Graduate housing:* Rooms and/or apartments available to single and married students. Housing application deadline: 8/1.

GRADUATE UNITS

Program in Education *Degree program information:* Part-time and evening/weekend programs available. Offers elementary education (M Ed); secondary education (M Ed).

School of Agriculture, Fisheries and Human Sciences Offers aquaculture and fisheries (MS).

School of Arts and Sciences Offers addiction studies (MS).

UNIVERSITY OF ARKANSAS FOR MEDICAL SCIENCES, Little Rock, AR 72205-7199

General Information State-supported, coed, university. *Graduate housing:* Rooms and/or apartments available on a first-come, first-served basis to single students and available to married students. *Research affiliation:* National Center for Toxicological Research, Veterans Administration Hospital, Oak Ridge Associated Universities, Arkansas Children's Hospital.

GRADUATE UNITS

College of Medicine Offers medicine (MD).

College of Pharmacy Offers pharmaceutical evaluation and policy (MS); pharmacy (Pharm D, MS).

Graduate School *Degree program information:* Part-time programs available. Offers clinical nutrition (MS); communicative disorders (MS, PhD); genetic counseling (MS); health promotion and prevention research (PhD); health systems research (PhD); occupational and environmental health (MS, Certificate).

College of Nursing *Degree program information:* Part-time programs available. Offers nursing (PhD).

Graduate Programs in Biomedical Sciences Offers biochemistry and molecular biology (MS, PhD); biomedical sciences (MS, PhD, Certificate); microbiology and immunology (MS, PhD); neurobiology and developmental sciences (MS, PhD); pathology (MS); pharmacology (MS, PhD); physiology and biophysics (MS, PhD); toxicology (MS, PhD). Electronic applications accepted.

UNIVERSITY OF ATLANTA, Atlanta, GA 30360

General Information Independent, coed, comprehensive institution.

GRADUATE UNITS

Graduate Programs Postbaccalaureate distance learning degree programs offered. Offers business (MS); business administration (Exec MBA, MBA); computer science (MS); educational leadership (MS, Ed D); healthcare administration (MS, D Sc, Graduate Certificate); information technology for management (Graduate Certificate); international project management (Graduate Certificate); law (JD); managerial science (DBA); project management (Graduate Certificate); social science (MS).

UNIVERSITY OF BALTIMORE, Baltimore, MD 21201-5779

General Information State-supported, coed, comprehensive institution. *Graduate housing:* On-campus housing not available.

GRADUATE UNITS

Graduate School *Degree program information:* Part-time and evening/weekend programs available. Postbaccalaureate distance learning degree programs offered (no on-campus study). Electronic applications accepted.

Merrick School of Business *Degree program information:* Part-time and evening/weekend programs available. Postbaccalaureate distance learning degree programs offered (no on-campus study). Offers accounting and business advisory services (MS); accounting fundamentals (Graduate Certificate); business (MBA, MS, Graduate Certificate); business/finance (MS); business/marketing and venturing (MS); forensic accounting (Graduate Certificate); taxation (MS). Electronic applications accepted.

The Yale Gordon College of Liberal Arts *Degree program information:* Part-time and evening/weekend programs available. Offers applied psychology (MS); communications design (DCD); creative writing and publishing arts (MFA); criminal justice (MS); health systems management (MS); human services administration (MS); human-computer interaction (MS); integrated design (MFA); interaction design and information technology (MS); legal and ethical studies (MA); liberal arts (MA, MFA, MPA, MS, DCD, DPA); negotiations and conflict management (MS); public administration (MPA, DPA); publications design (MA). Electronic applications accepted.

Joint University of Baltimore/Towson University (UB/Towson) MBA Program *Degree program information:* Part-time and evening/weekend programs available. Postbaccalaureate distance learning degree programs offered (no on-campus study). Offers business administration (MBA). MBA/MSN, MBA/PharmD offered jointly with University of Maryland, Baltimore.

School of Law Students: 718 full-time (367 women), 353 part-time (169 women); includes 79 Black or African American, non-Hispanic/Latino; 2 American Indian or Alaska Native, non-Hispanic/Latino; 55 Asian, non-Hispanic/Latino; 28 Hispanic/Latino, 4 international. Average age 27. 2,443 applicants, 43% accepted, 363 enrolled. *Faculty:* 62 full-time (28 women), 75 part-time/adjunct (26 women). Expenses: Contact institution. *Financial support:* In 2010–11, 162 students received support; research assistantships, teaching assistantships, career-related internships or fieldwork, Federal Work-Study, institutionally sponsored loans, and scholarships/grants available. Support available to part-time students. Financial award application deadline: 4/1; financial award applicants required to submit FAFSA. In 2010, 318 first professional degrees awarded. *Degree program information:* Part-time and evening/weekend programs available. Offers law (JD); law of the United States (LL M); taxation (LL M). JD/MS offered jointly with Division of Criminology, Criminal Justice, and Social Policy; JD/PhD with University of Maryland, Baltimore. *Application deadline:* For fall admission, 4/1 priority date

University of Baltimore (continued)

for domestic and international students. Applications are processed on a rolling basis. *Application fee:* $60. Electronic applications accepted. *Application Contact:* Jeffrey L. Zavrotny, Assistant Dean for Admissions, 410-837-4454, Fax: 410-837-4450, E-mail: jzavrotny@ubalt.edu. *Dean*, Phillip J. Closius, 410-837-4458.

UNIVERSITY OF BRIDGEPORT, Bridgeport, CT 06604

General Information Independent, coed, comprehensive institution. CGS member. *Enrollment:* 5,155 graduate, professional, and undergraduate students; 1,424 full-time matriculated graduate/professional students (680 women), 1,197 part-time matriculated graduate/professional students (677 women). *Enrollment by degree level:* 192 first professional, 2,122 master's, 181 doctoral, 126 other advanced degrees. *Graduate faculty:* 120 full-time (45 women), 364 part-time/adjunct (164 women). *Tuition:* Full-time $22,000; part-time $575 per credit hour. *Required fees:* $90 per semester. Tuition and fees vary according to course level, course load and program. *Graduate housing:* Room and/or apartments guaranteed to single students; on-campus housing not available to married students. Typical cost: $11,400 (including board). Housing application deadline: 8/15. *Student services:* Campus employment opportunities, campus safety program, career counseling, exercise/wellness program, free psychological counseling, international student services, low-cost health insurance, multicultural affairs office, services for students with disabilities, teacher training. *Library facilities:* Wahlstrom Library. *Online resources:* library catalog, web page, access to other libraries' catalogs. *Collection:* 293,440 titles, 57,006 serial subscriptions, 3,624 audiovisual materials. *Research affiliation:* Connecticut Medicine Research Consortia, Marine Biology Station (Hummingbird Cay, Bahamas), Burndy Library.

Computer facilities: 100 computers available on campus for general student use. A campuswide network can be accessed from student residence rooms. Online class registration is available. *Web address:* http://www.bridgeport.edu/.

General Application Contact: Bryan J. Gross, Associate Vice President for Admissions, 203-576-4552, Fax: 203-576-4941, E-mail: admit@bridgeport.edu.

GRADUATE UNITS

Acupuncture Institute Students: 17 full-time (13 women), 8 part-time (5 women); includes 8 minority (2 Black or African American, non-Hispanic/Latino; 1 American Indian or Alaska Native, non-Hispanic/Latino; 3 Asian, non-Hispanic/Latino; 2 Hispanic/Latino), 1 international. Average age 40. 25 applicants, 56% accepted, 6 enrolled. *Faculty:* 2 full-time (1 woman), 8 part-time/adjunct (2 women). Expenses: Contact institution. In 2010, 7 master's awarded. *Degree program information:* Part-time programs available. Offers acupuncture (MS). *Application deadline:* For fall admission, 8/1 priority date for domestic students, 8/1 for international students; for spring admission, 12/1 priority date for domestic students, 12/1 for international students. Applications are processed on a rolling basis. *Application fee:* $50. Electronic applications accepted. *Application Contact:* Michael B. Grandison, Director of Health Sciences Admission, 203-576-4348, Fax: 203-576-4941, E-mail: acup@bridgeport.edu. *Director*, Dr. Jennifer Brett, 203-576-4122, Fax: 203-576-4107, E-mail: acup@bridgeport.edu.

College of Chiropractic Offers chiropractic (DC). Electronic applications accepted.

College of Naturopathic Medicine Offers naturopathic medicine (ND). Electronic applications accepted.

Fones School of Dental Hygiene *Degree program information:* Part-time and evening/weekend programs available. Postbaccalaureate distance learning degree programs offered (no on-campus study). Offers dental hygiene (MS).

International College *Degree program information:* Part-time and evening/weekend programs available. Offers global development and peace (MA).

Nutrition Institute *Degree program information:* Part-time and evening/weekend programs available. Postbaccalaureate distance learning degree programs offered (no on-campus study). Offers human nutrition (MS). Electronic applications accepted.

School of Business *Degree program information:* Part-time and evening/weekend programs available. Offers business (MBA); business administration (MBA). Electronic applications accepted.

School of Education and Human Resources *Degree program information:* Part-time and evening/weekend programs available. Offers education and human resources (MS, Ed D, Diploma). Electronic applications accepted.

Division of Education *Degree program information:* Part-time and evening/weekend programs available. Offers computer specialist (Diploma); early childhood education (MS, Diploma); education (MS, Ed D, Diploma); educational management (Ed D, Diploma); elementary education (MS, Diploma); intermediate administrator or supervisor (Diploma); international education (Diploma); leadership (Ed D); reading specialist (MS, Diploma); secondary education (MS, Diploma). Electronic applications accepted.

Division of Human Resources *Degree program information:* Part-time and evening/weekend programs available. Offers college student personnel (MS); community counseling (MS); human resource development (MS); human service (MS). Electronic applications accepted.

School of Engineering *Degree program information:* Part-time and evening/weekend programs available. Postbaccalaureate distance learning degree programs offered (no on-campus study). Offers computer engineering (MS); computer science (MS); computer science and engineering (PhD); electrical engineering (MS); engineering (MS, PhD); mechanical engineering (MS); technology management (MS). Electronic applications accepted.

THE UNIVERSITY OF BRITISH COLUMBIA, Vancouver, BC V6T 1Z1, Canada

General Information Province-supported, coed, university. CGS member. *Enrollment:* 47,094 graduate, professional, and undergraduate students; 8,999 full-time matriculated graduate/professional students. *Enrollment by degree level:* 5,425 master's, 3,574 doctoral. *Graduate tuition:* Tuition charges are reported in Canadian dollars. *International tuition:* $7344 Canadian dollars full-time. *Tuition, area resident:* Full-time $4179 Canadian dollars. *Graduate housing:* Rooms and/or apartments available on a first-come, first-served basis to single and married students. Typical cost: $4500 Canadian dollars per year for single students; $5000 Canadian dollars per year for married students. Room charges vary according to board plan and housing facility selected. Housing application deadline: 3/1. *Student services:* Campus employment opportunities, campus safety program, career counseling, child daycare facilities, exercise/wellness program, free psychological counseling, grant writing training, international student services, low-cost health insurance, multicultural affairs office, services for students with disabilities, teacher training, writing training. *Library facilities:* UBC Library plus 9 others. *Online resources:* library catalog, web page, access to other libraries' catalogs. *Collection:* 6.4 million titles, 778,063 serial subscriptions, 840,987 audiovisual materials. *Research affiliation:* Pulp and Paper Research Institute of Canada (pulp and paper research), Pacific Environment Institute, Pacific Biological Station (fisheries and oceanography), British Columbia Research (chemical and biological science technology), Forintek Canada (forest technology), National Research Council of Canada Institute of Machinery Research (machinery research).

Computer facilities: 1,500 computers available on campus for general student use. A campuswide network can be accessed from student residence rooms and from off campus. Online class registration is available. *Web address:* http://www.ubc.ca/.

General Application Contact: Vincy Yung, Student Academic Services Application Clerk, 604-822-3907, Fax: 604-822-5802, E-mail: grad.admissions@ubc.ca.

GRADUATE UNITS

College for Interdisciplinary Studies Tuition charges are reported in Canadian dollars.

Faculty of Applied Science Tuition charges are reported in Canadian dollars. *Degree program information:* Part-time programs available. Offers applied science (M Arch, M Eng, M Sc, MA Sc, MASA, MASLA, MLA, MSN, MSS, PhD); chemical engineering (M Eng, M Sc, MA Sc, PhD); civil engineering (M Eng, MA Sc, PhD); electrical and computer engineering (M Eng, MA Sc, PhD); materials and metallurgy (M Sc, PhD); mechanical engineering (M Eng, MA Sc, PhD); metals and materials engineering (MA Sc, PhD); mining engineering (M Eng, MA Sc, PhD); nursing (MSN, PhD); software systems (MSS). Electronic applications accepted.

School of Architecture and Landscape Architecture Offers architecture (M Arch, MASA); landscape architecture (MASLA, MLA). Electronic applications accepted.

Faculty of Arts Tuition charges are reported in Canadian dollars. Offers ancient culture, religion, and ethnicity (MA); anthropology (MA, PhD); art history (MA, PhD, Diploma); arts (M Mus, M Sc, MA, MAS, MFA, MJ, MLIS, MSW, DMA, PhD, CAS, Diploma); Asian studies (MA, PhD); behavioral neuroscience (MA, PhD); classical and near eastern archaeology (MA); classics (MA, PhD); clinical psychology (MA, PhD); cognitive science (MA, PhD); creative writing (MFA); creative writing and film (MFA); creative writing and film production (MFA); creative writing and theatre (MFA); critical and curatorial studies (MA); developmental psychology (MA, PhD); economics (MA, PhD); English (MA, PhD); film (MA, MFA, Diploma); film production (MFA, Diploma); film studies (MA); French (MA, PhD); geography (M Sc, MA, PhD); Germanic studies (MA, PhD); health psychology (MA, PhD); Hispanic studies (MA, PhD); history (MA, PhD); linguistics (MA, PhD); philosophy (MA, PhD); political science (MA, PhD); quantitative methods (MA, PhD); religious studies (MA, PhD); social/personality psychology (MA, PhD); sociology (MA, PhD); theatre (MA, MFA, PhD); theatre design (MFA); theatre directing (MFA); visual art (MFA). Electronic applications accepted.

The School of Journalism Offers journalism (MJ). Electronic applications accepted.

School of Library, Archival and Information Studies Tuition charges are reported in Canadian dollars. *Degree program information:* Part-time programs available. Offers archival studies (MAS, CAS); children's literature (MA); library and information studies (MLIS, CAS); library, archival and information studies (PhD). Electronic applications accepted.

School of Music Tuition charges are reported in Canadian dollars. *Degree program information:* Part-time programs available. Offers music (M Mus, MA, DMA, PhD). Electronic applications accepted.

School of Social Work Tuition charges are reported in Canadian dollars. Offers social work (MSW, PhD). Electronic applications accepted.

Faculty of Dentistry *Degree program information:* Part-time programs available. Offers dental science (M Sc, PhD); dentistry (DMD, M Sc, PhD, Certificate, Diploma); periodontics (Diploma). Electronic applications accepted.

Faculty of Education *Degree program information:* Part-time and evening/weekend programs available. Postbaccalaureate distance learning degree programs offered (no on-campus study). Offers adult education (M Ed, MA); adult learning and global change (M Ed); art education (M Ed, MA); business education (MA); counseling psychology (M Ed, MA, PhD); curriculum studies (M Ed, MA, PhD); development, learning and culture (PhD); education (M Ed, M Sc, MA, MET, MHK, Ed D, PhD, Diploma); educational administration (M Ed, MA); educational leadership and policy (Ed D); educational studies (PhD); guidance studies (Diploma); higher education (M Ed, MA); home economics education (M Ed, MA); human development, learning and culture (M Ed, MA); library education (M Ed); literacy education (M Ed, MA, PhD); math education (M Ed, MA); measurement and evaluation and research methodology (M Ed); measurement, evaluation and research methodology (MA); measurement, evaluation, and research methodology (PhD); modern language education (M Ed, MA, PhD); music education (M Ed, MA); physical education (M Ed, MA); school psychology (M Ed, MA, PhD); science education (M Ed, MA); social studies education (M Ed, MA); society, culture and politics in education (M Ed, MA); special education (M Ed, MA, PhD, Diploma); teaching English as a second language (M Ed, MA, PhD); technology studies education (M Ed, MA). Electronic applications accepted.

Centre for Cross-Faculty Inquiry in Education Tuition charges are reported in Canadian dollars. *Degree program information:* Part-time and evening/weekend programs available. Offers curriculum and instruction (M Ed, MA, PhD); early childhood education (M Ed, MA). Electronic applications accepted.

School of Human Kinetics Tuition charges are reported in Canadian dollars. *Degree program information:* Part-time programs available. Offers human kinetics (M Sc, MA, MHK, PhD). Electronic applications accepted.

Faculty of Forestry Tuition charges are reported in Canadian dollars. *Degree program information:* Part-time programs available. Offers forestry (M Sc, MA Sc, MF, PhD). Electronic applications accepted.

Faculty of Land and Food Systems Tuition charges are reported in Canadian dollars. Offers agricultural economics (M Sc); animal science (M Sc, PhD); food science (M Sc, MFS, PhD); human nutrition (M Sc, PhD); land and food systems (M Sc, MFS, PhD); plant science (M Sc, PhD); soil science (M Sc, PhD). Electronic applications accepted.

Faculty of Law Tuition charges are reported in Canadian dollars. *Degree program information:* Part-time programs available. Offers law (LL M, LL M CL, PhD). Electronic applications accepted.

Faculty of Medicine *Degree program information:* Part-time programs available. Offers anatomy and cell biology (M Sc, PhD); anesthesiology, pharmacology and therapeutics (M Sc, PhD); biochemistry and molecular biology (M Sc, PhD); experimental medicine (M Sc, PhD); experimental pathology (M Sc, PhD); genetic counselling (M Sc); medical genetics (M Sc, PhD); medicine (MD, M Sc, MH Sc, MHA, MOT, MPH, MPT, MRSc, PhD); occupational science and occupational therapy (MOT); physiology (M Sc, PhD); reproductive and developmental sciences (M Sc, PhD); surgery (M Sc). Open only to Canadian residents.

School of Audiology and Speech Sciences Tuition charges are reported in Canadian dollars. Offers audiology and speech sciences (M Sc, PhD). Electronic applications accepted.

School of Population and Public Health Tuition charges are reported in Canadian dollars. Postbaccalaureate distance learning degree programs offered (minimal on-campus study). Offers health administration (MHA); health care and epidemiology (MH Sc, PhD); public health (MPH). Electronic applications accepted.

School of Rehabilitation Sciences Tuition charges are reported in Canadian dollars. Offers rehabilitation sciences (M Sc, MOT, MPT, MRSc, PhD). Electronic applications accepted.

Faculty of Pharmaceutical Sciences Students: 55 full-time (23 women). Average age 28. 84 applicants, 21% accepted, 14 enrolled. *Faculty:* 30 full-time (9 women), 26 part-time/adjunct (11 women). Expenses: Contact institution. *Financial support:* In 2010–11, 55 students received support, including 10 fellowships (averaging $19,000 per year), 45 research assistantships (averaging $13,127 per year), 27 teaching assistantships (averaging $7,503 per year); career-related internships or fieldwork, institutionally sponsored loans, scholarships/grants, traineeships, health care benefits, and unspecified assistantships also available. In 2010, 6 master's, 7 doctorates awarded. Offers pharmaceutical sciences (Pharm D, M Sc, PhD). *Application deadline:* For fall admission, 3/15 for domestic students, 2/15 for international students. Applications are processed on a rolling basis. *Application fee:* $90 Canadian dollars ($150 Canadian dollars for international students). Electronic applications accepted. *Application Contact:* Dr. Barb Conway, Research Grants Facilitator and Graduate Program Coordinator, 604-822-2390, Fax: 604-822-3035, E-mail: baconway@mail.ubc.ca. *Dean*, Dr. Robert D. Sindelar, 604-822-2343, Fax: 604-822-3035, E-mail: sindelar@mail.ubc.ca.

Faculty of Science Tuition charges are reported in Canadian dollars. *Degree program information:* Part-time programs available. Offers astronomy (M Sc, PhD); atmospheric science (M Sc, PhD); botany (M Sc, PhD); chemistry (M Sc, PhD); computer science (M Sc, PhD); geological engineering (M Eng, MA Sc, PhD); geological sciences (M Sc, PhD); geophysics (M Sc, MA Sc, PhD); mathematics (M Sc, MA, PhD); microbiology and immunology (M Sc, PhD); oceanography (M Sc, PhD); physics (M Sc, PhD); science (M Eng, M Sc, MA, MA Sc, PhD); statistics (M Sc, PhD); zoology (M Sc, PhD). Electronic applications accepted.

Genetics Graduate Program Tuition charges are reported in Canadian dollars. Offers genetics (M Sc, PhD).

Institute of Applied Mathematics Tuition charges are reported in Canadian dollars. Offers applied mathematics (M Sc, PhD).

Institute of Asian Research Tuition charges are reported in Canadian dollars. Offers Asian research (MAPPS). Electronic applications accepted.

Program in Resource Management and Environmental Studies Tuition charges are reported in Canadian dollars. Offers resource management and environmental studies (M Sc, MA, PhD). Electronic applications accepted.

Sauder School of Business *Degree program information:* Part-time and evening/weekend programs available. Offers accounting (PhD); business (IMBA, M Sc, MBA, MM, PhD); business administration (IMBA, MBA); finance (PhD); international business (PhD); management information systems (PhD); management science (PhD); marketing (PhD); operations research (MM); organizational behavior (PhD); strategy and business economics (PhD); transportation and logistics (PhD); urban land economics (PhD). Electronic applications accepted.

School of Community and Regional Planning Tuition charges are reported in Canadian dollars. Offers community and regional planning (M Sc P, MAP, PhD). Electronic applications accepted.

School of Environmental Health Tuition charges are reported in Canadian dollars. *Degree program information:* Part-time programs available. Offers environmental health (M Sc, PhD). Electronic applications accepted.

UNIVERSITY OF CALGARY, Calgary, AB T2N 1N4, Canada

General Information Province-supported, coed, university. CGS member. *Graduate housing:* Rooms and/or apartments available on a first-come, first-served basis to single and married students. Housing application deadline: 3/31. *Research affiliation:* Alta Telecommunications Research Centre, Alberta Sulphur Research, Calgary Society for Students with Learning Difficulties, Canadian Institute of Resources Law, Canadian Music Centre, Canadian Energy Research Institute.

GRADUATE UNITS

Faculty of Graduate Studies *Degree program information:* Part-time and evening/weekend programs available. Postbaccalaureate distance learning degree programs offered (minimal on-campus study). Offers interdisciplinary research (M Sc, MA, PhD); resources and the environment (M Sc, MA, PhD).

Centre for Military and Strategic Studies *Degree program information:* Part-time programs available. Offers military and strategic studies (MSS, PhD). PhD offered in special cases only.

Faculty of Arts *Degree program information:* Part-time and evening/weekend programs available. Offers arts (MA, PhD); English (MA, PhD); French (MA, PhD); German (MA); Greek and Roman studies (MA, PhD); philosophy (MA, PhD); religious studies (MA, PhD); Spanish (MA, PhD). Electronic applications accepted.

Faculty of Communication and Culture *Degree program information:* Part-time and evening/weekend programs available. Offers communication and culture (MA, MCS, PhD). Electronic applications accepted.

Faculty of Education *Degree program information:* Part-time and evening/weekend programs available. Postbaccalaureate distance learning degree programs offered (minimal on-campus study). Offers community rehabilitation and disability studies (M Ed, M Sc, Ed D, PhD, Graduate Certificate, Graduate Diploma); counseling psychology (M Ed, M Sc, PhD); curriculum, teaching and learning (M Ed, M Sc, MA, Ed D, PhD, Graduate Certificate, Graduate Diploma); education (M Ed, M Sc, MA, Ed D, PhD, Graduate Certificate, Graduate Diploma); educational contexts (M Ed, MA, Ed D, PhD, Graduate Certificate, Graduate Diploma); educational leadership (M Ed, MA, Ed D, PhD, Graduate Certificate, Graduate Diploma); educational technology (M Ed, M Sc, MA, Ed D, PhD, Graduate Certificate, Graduate Diploma); gifted education (M Sc, MA, Ed D, PhD, Graduate Certificate, Graduate Diploma); higher education administration (Ed D); human development and learning (M Ed, M Sc, PhD); interpretive studies in education (M Ed, M Sc, MA, Ed D, PhD, Graduate Certificate, Graduate Diploma); school psychology (M Ed, M Sc, PhD); second language teaching (M Ed, Ed D, PhD, Graduate Certificate, Graduate Diploma); special education (M Ed, M Sc, PhD); teaching English as a second language (M Ed, M Sc, MA, Ed D, PhD, Graduate Certificate, Graduate Diploma); workplace and adult learning (M Ed, MA, Ed D, PhD, Graduate Certificate, Graduate Diploma). Electronic applications accepted.

Faculty of Environmental Design Offers architecture (M Arch); environmental design (M Env Des, PhD).

Faculty of Fine Arts Offers art (MA, MFA); design and technical theatre (MFA); directing (MFA); fine arts (M Mus, MA, MFA, PhD); music (M Mus, MA, PhD); playwriting (MFA); theatre studies (MFA). Electronic applications accepted.

Faculty of Kinesiology Offers biomedical engineering (M Sc, PhD); kinesiology (M Kin, M Sc, PhD). Electronic applications accepted.

Faculty of Nursing Students: 86 full-time (76 women), 47 part-time (46 women). Average age 30. 58 applicants, 84% accepted, 36 enrolled. *Faculty:* 31 full-time (29 women). Expenses: Contact institution. *Financial support:* In 2010–11, 36 students received support, including 14 teaching assistantships (averaging $3,900 per year); institutionally sponsored loans, scholarships/grants, health care benefits, and unspecified assistantships also available. Support available to part-time students. Financial award application deadline: 2/1. In 2010, 22 master's, 2 doctorates, 8 other advanced degrees awarded. *Degree program information:* Part-time programs available. Offers nursing (MN, PhD, PMD). *Application deadline:* For fall admission, 2/1 for domestic and international students; for winter admission, 9/15 for domestic and international students. *Application fee:* $100 ($130 for international students). Electronic applications accepted. *Application Contact:* Laura Thomas, Graduate Programs Student Advisor, 403-220-6241, Fax: 403-284-4803, E-mail: lthomas@ucalgary.ca. *Associate Dean, Graduate Programs,* Dr. Shelley Raffin Bouchal, 403-220-6258, Fax: 403-284-4803, E-mail: raffin@ucalgary.ca.

Faculty of Science *Degree program information:* Part-time programs available. Offers analytical chemistry (M Sc, PhD); applied chemistry (M Sc, PhD); biological sciences (M Sc, PhD); computer science (M Sc, PhD); geology (M Sc, PhD); geophysics (M Sc, PhD); inorganic chemistry (M Sc, PhD); mathematics and statistics (M Sc, PhD); organic chemistry (M Sc, PhD); physical chemistry (M Sc, PhD); physics and astronomy (M Sc, PhD); polymer chemistry (M Sc, PhD); science (M Sc, PhD); software engineering (M Sc); theoretical chemistry (M Sc, PhD).

Faculty of Social Sciences *Degree program information:* Part-time and evening/weekend programs available. Offers anthropology (MA, PhD); archaeology (MA, PhD); clinical psychology (M Sc, PhD); economics (M Ec, MA, PhD); geography (M Sc, MA, MGIS, PhD); history (MA, PhD); linguistics (MA, PhD); political science (MA, PhD); psychology (M Sc, PhD); social sciences (M Ec, M Sc, MA, MGIS, PhD); sociology (MA, PhD).

Faculty of Social Work Offers social work (MSW, PhD, Postgraduate Diploma). Electronic applications accepted.

Haskayne School of Business *Degree program information:* Part-time and evening/weekend programs available. Offers business (EMBA, MBA, PhD); business administration (EMBA, MBA); management (MBA, PhD).

Schulich School of Engineering *Degree program information:* Part-time and evening/weekend programs available. Offers biomedical engineering (M Eng, M Sc, PhD); chemical and petroleum engineering (M Eng, M Sc, PhD); civil engineering (M Eng, M Sc, MPM, PhD); electrical and computer engineering (M Eng, M Sc, PhD); engineering (M Eng, M Sc, MPM, PhD); geomatics engineering (M Eng, M Sc, PhD); mechanical and manufacturing engineering (M Eng, M Sc, PhD).

Faculty of Law Students: 303 full-time (159 women), 4 part-time (3 women). Average age 26. 1,180 applicants, 9% accepted, 110 enrolled. Expenses: Contact institution. *Financial support:* In 2010–11, 2 research assistantships (averaging $4,100 per year) were awarded; scholarships/grants and study awards also available. Financial award application deadline: 2/1. In 2010, 91 first professional degrees awarded. Offers law (JD, LL B, LL M, Postbaccalaureate Certificate); natural resources, energy and environmental law (LL M, Postbaccalaureate Certificate). *Application deadline:* For fall admission, 11/1 for domestic and international students. *Application fee:* $100 ($130 for international students). *Application Contact:* Karen Argento, Admissions and Student Affairs Officer, 403-220-8154, Fax: 403-210-9662, E-mail: kargento@ucalgary.ca. *Dean,* Alastair Lucas, 403-220-5447, Fax: 403-282-8325, E-mail: lawdean@ucalgary.ca.

Faculty of Medicine *Degree program information:* Part-time programs available. Offers biochemistry and molecular biology (M Sc, PhD); biomedical technology (MBT); cancer biology (M Sc, PhD); cardiovascular and respiratory sciences (M Sc, PhD); community health sciences (M Sc, MCM, PhD); gastrointestinal sciences (M Sc, PhD); immunology (M Sc, PhD); joint injury and arthritis research (M Sc, PhD); medical education (M Sc, PhD); medical science (M Sc, PhD); medicine (MD, M Sc, MBT, MCM, PhD); microbiology and infectious diseases (M Sc, PhD); mountain medicine and high altitude physiology (M Sc); neuroscience (M Sc, PhD). Electronic applications accepted.

UNIVERSITY OF CALIFORNIA, BERKELEY, Berkeley, CA 94720-1500

General Information State-supported, coed, university. CGS member. *Graduate housing:* Rooms and/or apartments available to single and married students.

GRADUATE UNITS

Graduate Division *Degree program information:* Part-time and evening/weekend programs available. Offers Asian studies (PhD); bioengineering (PhD); comparative biochemistry (PhD); East Asian studies (MA); energy and resources (MA, MS, PhD); international and area studies (MA, PhD); Latin American studies (MA); neuroscience (PhD); Northeast Asian studies (MA); South Asian studies (MA); Southeast Asian studies (MA); vision science (MS, PhD).

College of Chemistry Offers chemical engineering (MS, PhD); chemistry (MS, PhD).

College of Engineering Offers applied science and technology (PhD); computer science (MS, PhD); electrical engineering (MS, PhD); engineering (M Eng, MS, D Eng, PhD); engineering and project management (M Eng, MS, D Eng, PhD); engineering science (M Eng, MS, PhD); environmental engineering (M Eng, MS, D Eng, PhD); geoengineering (M Eng, MS, D Eng, PhD); industrial engineering and operations research (M Eng, MS, D Eng, PhD); mechanical engineering (M Eng, MS, D Eng, PhD); nuclear engineering (M Eng, MS, D Eng, PhD); structural engineering, mechanics and materials (M Eng, MS, D Eng, PhD); transportation engineering (M Eng, MS, D Eng, PhD).

College of Environmental Design Offers architecture (M Arch); building science (MS, PhD); building structures, construction and materials (MS, PhD); city and regional planning (MCP, PhD); design (MA); design theories, methods, and practices (MS, PhD); environmental design (M Arch, MA, MCP, MLA, MS, MUD, PhD); environmental design in developing countries (MS, PhD); history of architecture and urbanism (MS, PhD); landscape architecture (MLA); landscape architecture and environmental planning (PhD); social and cultural processes in architecture and urbanism (MS, PhD); urban design (MUD).

College of Letters and Science Offers African American studies (PhD); ancient history and Mediterranean archaeology (MA, PhD); anthropology (MA, PhD); applied mathematics (PhD); art practice (MFA); astrophysics (PhD); biophysics (PhD); Buddhist studies (PhD); Chinese language (PhD); classical archaeology (MA, PhD); classics (MA, PhD); comparative literature (PhD); composition (PhD); Czech (PhD); demography (PhD); economics (PhD); endocrinology (MA, PhD); English (PhD); ethnic studies (PhD); ethnomusicology (PhD); folklore (MA); French (PhD); geography (PhD); geology (MA, MS, PhD); geophysics (MA, MS, PhD); German (PhD); Greek (MA); Hindi (MA, PhD); Hispanic languages and literature (PhD); history (PhD); history of art (PhD); Indonesian (MA, PhD); integrative biology (PhD); Italian (PhD); Italian studies (PhD); Japanese language (PhD); Jewish studies (PhD); Latin (MA); letters and science (MA, MFA, MS, PhD); linguistics (PhD); logic and the methodology of science (PhD); mathematics (MA, PhD); medical anthropology (PhD); molecular and cell biology (PhD); musicology (PhD); Near Eastern religions (PhD); Near Eastern studies (MA, PhD); performance studies (PhD); philosophy (PhD); physics (PhD); Polish (PhD); political science (PhD); psychology (PhD); rhetoric (PhD); Russian (PhD); Sanskrit (MA, PhD); Scandinavian languages and literatures (PhD); Serbo-Croatian (PhD); sociology (PhD); sociology and demography (MA, PhD); Spanish (PhD); statistics (MA, PhD); Tamil (MA, PhD). Electronic applications accepted.

College of Natural Resources Offers agricultural and resource economics (PhD); environmental science, policy, and management (MS, PhD); forestry (MF); microbiology (PhD); molecular and biochemical nutrition (PhD); molecular toxicology (PhD); natural resources (MF, MS, PhD); plant biology (PhD); range management (MS).

Graduate School of Journalism Offers journalism (MJ).

Graduate School of Public Policy Offers public policy (MPP, PhD).

Haas School of Business Students: 638 full-time (181 women), 929 part-time (242 women); includes 351 minority (13 Black or African American, non-Hispanic/Latino; 2 American Indian or Alaska Native, non-Hispanic/Latino; 279 Asian, non-Hispanic/Latino; 41 Hispanic/Latino; 1 Native Hawaiian or other Pacific Islander, non-Hispanic/Latino; 15 Two or more races, non-Hispanic/Latino), 611 international. *Faculty:* 90 full-time (21 women), 127 part-time/adjunct (20 women). Expenses: Contact institution. *Financial support:* Fellowships, research assistantships, teaching assistantships, career-related internships or fieldwork, Federal Work-Study, institutionally sponsored loans, scholarships/grants, tuition waivers (full), and unspecified assistantships available. Support available to part-time students. Financial award application deadline: 3/1; financial award applicants required to submit FAFSA. In 2010, 624 master's, 17 doctorates awarded. *Degree program information:* Part-time and evening/weekend programs available. Offers accounting (PhD); business (MBA, MFE, PhD); business administration (MBA, PhD); business and public policy (PhD); finance (PhD); financial engineering (MFE); management of organizations (PhD); marketing (PhD); operations management (PhD); real estate (PhD). *Application fee:* $200. *Application Contact:* MBA Admissions Office, 510-642-1405, Fax: 510-643-6659. *Dean,* Richard K. Lyons, 510-643-2027, Fax: 510-642-9128, E-mail: lyons@haas.berkeley.edu.

School of Education Offers development in mathematics and science (MA); education (MA, PhD); education in mathematics, science, and technology (MA, PhD); human development and education (MA, PhD); science and mathematics education (PhD); special education (PhD).

School of Information Management and Systems Offers information management and systems (MIMS, PhD).

School of Public Health Offers biostatistics (MA, PhD); environmental health sciences (MPH, MS, Dr PH, PhD); epidemiology (MS, PhD); health services and policy analysis (PhD); infectious diseases (MPH, PhD); infectious diseases and immunity (PhD); public health (MA, MPH, MS, Dr PH, PhD).

School of Social Welfare Offers social welfare (MSW, PhD).

School of Law Offers jurisprudence and social policy (PhD); law (JD, LL M, JSD).

School of Optometry Offers optometry (OD, Certificate). Electronic applications accepted.

UC Berkeley Extension *Degree program information:* Part-time and evening/weekend programs available. Postbaccalaureate distance learning degree programs offered. Offers accounting (Certificate); alcohol and drug abuse studies (Certificate); business administration (Certificate); clinical research conduct and management (Certificate); college admissions and career planning (Certificate); construction management (Certificate); finance (Certificate); global business management (Certificate); human resource management (Certificate); HVAC (Certificate); information systems and management (Postbaccalaureate Certificate); integrated circuit design and techniques (online) (Certificate); interior design and interior architecture (Certificate); landscape architecture (Certificate); leadership in sustainability and environmental management (Professional Certificate); management (Certificate); marketing (Certificate); project management (Certificate); solar energy and green building (Professional Certificate); sustainable design (Professional Certificate); teaching English as a second language (Certificate); UNIX/LINUX system administration (Certificate); visual arts (Postbaccalaureate Certificate); writing (Postbaccalaureate Certificate).

UNIVERSITY OF CALIFORNIA, DAVIS, Davis, CA 95616

General Information State-supported, coed, university. CGS member. *Graduate housing:* Rooms and/or apartments available to single and married students. Housing application deadline: 4/1.

University of California, Davis (continued)

GRADUATE UNITS

College of Engineering *Degree program information:* Part-time programs available. Offers aeronautical engineering (M Engr, MS, D Engr, PhD, Certificate); applied science (MS, PhD); biological systems engineering (M Engr, MS, D Engr, PhD); biomedical engineering (MS, PhD); chemical engineering (MS, PhD); civil and environmental engineering (M Engr, MS, D Engr, PhD, Certificate); computer science (MS, PhD); electrical and computer engineering (MS, PhD); engineering (M Engr, MS, D Engr, PhD, Certificate); materials science and engineering (MS, PhD); mechanical engineering (M Engr, MS, D Engr, PhD, Certificate); transportation, technology and policy (MS, PhD). Electronic applications accepted.

Graduate School of Management Students: 117 full-time (41 women), 432 part-time (124 women); includes 202 minority (9 Black or African American, non-Hispanic/Latino; 3 American Indian or Alaska Native, non-Hispanic/Latino; 147 Asian, non-Hispanic/Latino; 37 Hispanic/Latino; 2 Native Hawaiian or other Pacific Islander, non-Hispanic/Latino; 4 Two or more races, non-Hispanic/Latino), 63 international. Average age 31. 642 applicants, 41% accepted, 173 enrolled. *Faculty:* 31 full-time (13 women), 29 part-time/adjunct (1 woman). Expenses: Contact institution. *Financial support:* In 2010–11, 125 students received support; research assistantships with partial tuition reimbursements available, teaching assistantships with partial tuition reimbursements available, career-related internships or fieldwork, Federal Work-Study, institutionally sponsored loans, scholarships/grants, health care benefits, tuition waivers (partial), and unspecified assistantships available. Support available to part-time students. Financial award application deadline: 3/1; financial award applicants required to submit FAFSA. *Degree program information:* Part-time and evening/weekend programs available. Offers business administration (MBA); management (MBA). *Application deadline:* For fall admission, 11/1 priority date for domestic students, 11/3 priority date for international students; for winter admission, 1/5 priority date for domestic and international students; for spring admission, 3/1 for domestic students, 3/2 for international students. Applications are processed on a rolling basis. *Application fee:* $125. Electronic applications accepted. *Application Contact:* Heather O'Leary, Director, Admissions, 530-752-7658, Fax: 530-754-9355, E-mail: admissions@gsm.ucdavis.edu. *Dean,* Dr. Steven C. Currall, 530-752-7366, Fax: 530-752-2924, E-mail: scc@ucdavis.edu.

Graduate Studies Offers acting (MFA); agricultural and environmental chemistry (MS, PhD); agricultural and resource economics (MS, PhD); animal behavior (PhD); animal biology (MAM, MS, PhD); anthropology (MA, PhD); applied linguistics (MA, PhD); applied mathematics (MS, PhD); art (MFA); art history (MA); atmospheric sciences (MS, PhD); avian sciences (MS); biochemistry and molecular biology (MS, PhD); biophysics (MS, PhD); biostatistics (MS, PhD); cell and developmental biology (MS, PhD); chemistry (MS, PhD); child development (MS); clinical research (MAS); communication (MA); community development (MS); comparative literature (PhD); comparative pathology (MS, PhD); composition (MA, PhD); conducting (MA, PhD); creative writing (MA); cultural studies (MA, PhD); dramatic art (PhD); ecology (MS, PhD); economics (MA, PhD); education (MA, Ed D); English (MA, PhD); entomology (MS, PhD); epidemiology (MS, PhD); exercise science (MS); food science (MS, PhD); forensic science (MS); French (PhD); genetics (MS, PhD); geography (MA, PhD); geology (MS, PhD); German (MA, PhD); health informatics (MS); history (MA, PhD); horticulture and agronomy (MS); human development (PhD); hydrologic sciences (MS, PhD); immunology (MS, PhD); instructional studies (PhD); integrated pest management (MS); international agricultural development (MS); linguistics (MA); mathematics (MA, MAT, PhD); microbiology (MS, PhD); molecular, cellular and integrative physiology (MS, PhD); musicology (MA, PhD); Native American studies (MA, PhD); neuroscience (PhD); nutrition (MS, PhD); pharmacology/toxicology (MS, PhD); philosophy (MA, PhD); physics (MS, PhD); plant biology (MS, PhD); plant pathology (MS, PhD); political science (MA, PhD); population biology (PhD); psychological studies (PhD); psychology (PhD); sociocultural studies (PhD); sociology (MA, PhD); soils and biogeochemistry (MS, PhD); Spanish (MA, PhD); statistics (MS, PhD); textile arts and costume design (MFA); textiles (MS); viticulture and enology (MS, PhD). Electronic applications accepted.

School of Law Students: 589 full-time (290 women); includes 10 Black or African American, non-Hispanic/Latino; 6 American Indian or Alaska Native, non-Hispanic/Latino; 136 Asian, non-Hispanic/Latino; 47 Hispanic/Latino; 1 Native Hawaiian or other Pacific Islander, non-Hispanic/Latino, 15 international. Average age 24. 4,020 applicants, 23% accepted, 196 enrolled. *Faculty:* 52 full-time (28 women), 18 part-time/adjunct (5 women). Expenses: Contact institution. *Financial support:* In 2010–11, 495 students received support, including 6 research assistantships with partial tuition reimbursements available, 35 teaching assistantships with partial tuition reimbursements available; Federal Work-Study, institutionally sponsored loans, scholarships/grants, and health care benefits also available. Financial award application deadline: 3/2; financial award applicants required to submit FAFSA. In 2010, 195 first professional degrees, 16 master's awarded. Offers law (JD, LL M). *Application deadline:* For fall admission, 2/1 for domestic and international students. Applications are processed on a rolling basis. *Application fee:* $75. Electronic applications accepted. *Application Contact:* Sharon Pinkney, Director, Admissions, 530-752-6477, Fax: 530-754-8371, E-mail: lawadmissions@ucdavis.edu. *Dean,* Kevin R. Johnson, 530-752-0243, Fax: 530-752-7279, E-mail: krjohnson@ucdavis.edu.

School of Medicine Students: 434 full-time (249 women); includes 242 minority (23 Black or African American, non-Hispanic/Latino; 2 American Indian or Alaska Native, non-Hispanic/Latino; 136 Asian, non-Hispanic/Latino; 49 Hispanic/Latino; 4 Native Hawaiian or other Pacific Islander, non-Hispanic/Latino; 28 Two or more races, non-Hispanic/Latino). Average age 27. 4,596 applicants, 5% accepted, 96 enrolled. *Faculty:* 684 full-time (218 women), 130 part-time/adjunct (54 women). Expenses: Contact institution. *Financial support:* In 2010–11, 387 students received support, including 15 fellowships with full tuition reimbursements available (averaging $22,367 per year), 7 research assistantships with partial tuition reimbursements available (averaging $22,320 per year), 5 teaching assistantships with partial tuition reimbursements available (averaging $1,919 per year); institutionally sponsored loans and scholarships/grants also available. Support available to part-time students. Financial award application deadline: 3/1; financial award applicants required to submit FAFSA. In 2010, 91 first professional degrees awarded. Offers medicine (MD). *Application deadline:* For fall admission, 11/1 for domestic and international students. Applications are processed on a rolling basis. *Application fee:* $70. Electronic applications accepted. *Application Contact:* Edward D. Dagang, Director of Admissions and Outreach, 916-734-4800, Fax: 916-734-4050, E-mail: ed.dagang@ucdmc.ucdavis.edu. *Dean/Vice Chancellor, Human Health Sciences,* Dr. Claire Pomeroy, 916-734-7131, Fax: 916-734-7055, E-mail: claire.pomeroy@ucdmc.ucdavis.edu.

School of Veterinary Medicine Offers preventive veterinary medicine (MPVM); veterinary medicine (DVM, MPVM, Certificate).

UNIVERSITY OF CALIFORNIA, HASTINGS COLLEGE OF THE LAW, San Francisco, CA 94102-4978

General Information State-supported, coed, graduate-only institution. *Enrollment by degree level:* 1,247 first professional. *Graduate faculty:* 86 full-time (38 women), 102 part-time/adjunct (41 women). Tuition, state resident: full-time $36,000. Tuition, nonresident: full-time $47,225. One-time fee: $2906 full-time. *Graduate housing:* Rooms and/or apartments available on a first-come, first-served basis to single and married students. *Student services:* Campus employment opportunities, campus safety program, career counseling, free psychological counseling, international student services, low-cost health insurance, services for students with disabilities, writing training. *Library facilities:* Hastings Law Library. *Online resources:* library catalog, web page. *Collection:* 459,233 titles, 4,176 serial subscriptions, 1,310 audiovisual materials.

Computer facilities: 146 computers available on campus for general student use. A campuswide network can be accessed from student residence rooms and from off campus. Online class registration, Specialized research data bases; job/career website; campus-wide software licenses (MS Office, antivirus, exam software) are available. *Web address:* http://www.uchastings.edu/.

General Application Contact: Greg Canada, Director of Admissions, 415-565-4623, Fax: 415-565-4863, E-mail: canadag@uchastings.edu.

GRADUATE UNITS

Graduate Programs Students: 1,247 full-time (669 women), 1 (woman) part-time; includes 412 minority (39 Black or African American, non-Hispanic/Latino; 6 American Indian or Alaska Native, non-Hispanic/Latino; 288 Asian, non-Hispanic/Latino; 79 Hispanic/Latino), 18 international. Average age 26. 5,142 applicants, 27% accepted, 401 enrolled. *Faculty:* 86 full-time (38 women), 102 part-time/adjunct (41 women). Expenses: Contact institution. *Financial support:* In 2010–11, 1,138 students received support. Career-related internships or fieldwork, Federal Work-Study, institutionally sponsored loans, and scholarships/grants available. Support available to part-time students. Financial award application deadline: 3/2; financial award applicants required to submit FAFSA. In 2010, 417 first professional degrees, 16 master's awarded. Offers law (JD, LL M). *Application deadline:* For fall admission, 3/1 priority date for domestic and international students. Applications are processed on a rolling basis. *Application fee:* $75. Electronic applications accepted. *Application Contact:* Greg Canada, Director of Admissions, 415-565-4623, Fax: 415-565-4863, E-mail: canadag@uchastings.edu.

UNIVERSITY OF CALIFORNIA, IRVINE, Irvine, CA 92697

General Information State-supported, coed, university. CGS member. *Enrollment:* 26,994 graduate, professional, and undergraduate students; 4,275 full-time matriculated graduate/professional students (1,794 women), 593 part-time matriculated graduate/professional students (217 women). *Enrollment by degree level:* 453 first professional, 1,656 master's, 2,661 doctoral, 95 other advanced degrees. *Graduate housing:* Rooms and/or apartments available on a first-come, first-served basis to single and married students. *Student services:* Campus employment opportunities, campus safety program, career counseling, child daycare facilities, exercise/wellness program, free psychological counseling, grant writing training, international student services, low-cost health insurance, multicultural affairs office, services for students with disabilities, teacher training, writing training. *Library facilities:* Jack Langson Library plus 3 others. *Online resources:* library catalog, web page, access to other libraries' catalogs. *Collection:* 3.1 million titles, 53,981 serial subscriptions, 115,097 audiovisual materials.

Computer facilities: 1,500 computers available on campus for general student use. A campuswide network can be accessed from student residence rooms and from off campus. Online class registration is available. *Web address:* http://www.uci.edu/.

General Application Contact: Sheree McPeak, Graduate Division, 949-824-4611, Fax: 949-824-9096, E-mail: ogsfront@uci.edu.

GRADUATE UNITS

Claire Trevor School of the Arts Students: 144 full-time (82 women), 2 part-time (0 women); includes 8 Black or African American, non-Hispanic/Latino; 1 American Indian or Alaska Native, non-Hispanic/Latino; 9 Asian, non-Hispanic/Latino; 18 Hispanic/Latino; 7 Two or more races, non-Hispanic/Latino, 8 international. Average age 28. 446 applicants, 16% accepted, 55 enrolled. Expenses: Contact institution. *Financial support:* Fellowships, teaching assistantships, institutionally sponsored loans, traineeships, health care benefits, and unspecified assistantships available. Financial award application deadline: 3/1; financial award applicants required to submit FAFSA. In 2010, 48 master's, 1 doctorate awarded. Offers accompanying (MFA); acting (MFA); arts (MFA, PhD); choral conducting (MFA); composition and technology (MFA); dance (MFA); design and stage management (MFA); directing (MFA); drama (MFA); drama and theatre (PhD); guitar/lute performance (MFA); instrumental performance (MFA); jazz instrumental/composition (MFA); piano performance (MFA); studio art (MFA); vocal performance (MFA). *Application deadline:* For fall admission, 1/15 for domestic and international students. Applications are processed on a rolling basis. *Application fee:* $80 ($100 for international students). Electronic applications accepted. *Application Contact:* Prof. Antoinette Lafarge, Associate Dean, 949-824-4088, Fax: 949-824-5297, E-mail: alafarge@uci.edu. *Dean,* Dr. Joseph S. Lewis, 949-824-8792, Fax: 949-824-2450, E-mail: jslewis@uci.edu.

College of Health Sciences Students: 35 full-time (25 women), 27 part-time (22 women); includes 27 minority (1 Black or African American, non-Hispanic/Latino; 16 Asian, non-Hispanic/Latino; 8 Hispanic/Latino; 2 Two or more races, non-Hispanic/Latino), 3 international. Average age 28. 208 applicants, 42% accepted, 41 enrolled. Expenses: Contact institution. In 2010, 7 master's awarded. Offers health sciences (MPH, MSN, PhD); medicinal chemistry and pharmacology (PhD); nursing science (MSN); public health (MPH, PhD). *Application fee:* $80 ($100 for international students). *Application Contact:* Sheree McPeak, Graduate Division, 949-824-4611, Fax: 949-824-9096, E-mail: ogsfront@uci.edu.

Department of Education Students: 252 full-time (188 women), 10 part-time (7 women); includes 140 minority (5 Black or African American, non-Hispanic/Latino; 1 American Indian or Alaska Native, non-Hispanic/Latino; 77 Asian, non-Hispanic/Latino; 39 Hispanic/Latino; 1 Native Hawaiian or other Pacific Islander, non-Hispanic/Latino; 17 Two or more races, non-Hispanic/Latino), 7 international. Average age 28. 516 applicants, 76% accepted, 194 enrolled. Expenses: Contact institution. *Financial support:* Fellowships, research assistantships with full tuition reimbursements, institutionally sponsored loans, traineeships, health care benefits, and unspecified assistantships available. Financial award application deadline: 3/1; financial award applicants required to submit FAFSA. In 2010, 154 master's, 16 doctorates awarded. *Degree program information:* Part-time and evening/weekend programs available. Offers educational administration (Ed D); educational administration and leadership (Ed D); elementary and secondary education (MAT). *Application deadline:* For fall admission, 1/2 priority date for domestic students, 1/2 for international students. *Application fee:* $80 ($100 for international students). Electronic applications accepted. *Application Contact:* Sarah K. Singh, Credential Program Counselor, 949-824-6673, Fax: 949-824-9103, E-mail: sksingh@uci.edu. *Chair,* Deborah L. Vandell, 949-824-8026, Fax: 949-824-3968, E-mail: dvandell@uci.edu.

Donald Bren School of Information and Computer Sciences Students: 340 full-time (73 women), 28 part-time (5 women); includes 55 minority (2 Black or African American, non-Hispanic/Latino; 45 Asian, non-Hispanic/Latino; 6 Hispanic/Latino; 2 Two or more races, non-Hispanic/Latino), 218 international. Average age 28. 1,501 applicants, 24% accepted, 128 enrolled. Expenses: Contact institution. *Financial support:* Fellowships, research assistantships with full tuition reimbursements, teaching assistantships, institutionally sponsored loans, traineeships, health care benefits, and unspecified assistantships available. Financial award applicants required to submit FAFSA. In 2010, 67 master's, 29 doctorates awarded. Offers computer science (MS, PhD); informatics (MS, PhD); information and computer science (MS, PhD); networked systems (MS, PhD); statistics (MS, PhD). *Application deadline:* For fall admission, 1/15 for domestic and international students. *Application fee:* $80 ($100 for international students). Electronic applications accepted. *Application Contact:* Prof. Tony D. Givargis, Associate Dean, 949-824-9357, E-mail: givargis@uci.edu. *Dean,* Prof. Hal S. Stern, 949-824-7405, Fax: 949-824-3976, E-mail: sternh@uci.edu.

The Paul Merage School of Business Students: 424 full-time (134 women), 372 part-time (128 women); includes 255 minority (8 Black or African American, non-Hispanic/Latino; 5 American Indian or Alaska Native, non-Hispanic/Latino; 210 Asian, non-Hispanic/Latino; 29 Hispanic/Latino; 3 Native Hawaiian or other Pacific Islander, non-Hispanic/Latino), 121 international. Average age 28. 1,463 applicants, 34% accepted, 267 enrolled. Expenses: Contact institution. *Financial support:* Career-related internships or fieldwork, Federal Work-Study, institutionally sponsored loans, scholarships/grants, traineeships, health care benefits, and unspecified assistantships available. Support available to part-time students. Financial award application deadline: 3/1; financial award applicants required to submit FAFSA. In 2010, 331 master's, 5 doctorates awarded. *Degree program information:* Part-time and evening/weekend programs available. Offers business (EMBA, MBA, PhD); business administration (EMBA, MBA); health care (MBA); management (PhD). *Application deadline:* For fall admission, 1/2 priority date for domestic and international students. Applications are processed on a rolling basis. *Application fee:* $80 ($100 for international students). Electronic applications accepted. *Application Contact:* Prof. L. Robin Keller, Program Director, 949-824-6348, Fax: 949-824-2835, E-mail: lrkeller@uci.edu. *Dean,* Andrew John Policano, 949-824-8470, Fax: 949-824-8469, E-mail: policano@uci.edu.

School of Biological Sciences Students: 277 full-time (148 women), 1 (woman) part-time; includes 103 minority (3 Black or African American, non-Hispanic/Latino; 1 American Indian or Alaska Native, non-Hispanic/Latino; 54 Asian, non-Hispanic/Latino; 38 Hispanic/Latino; 7 Two or more races, non-Hispanic/Latino), 29 international. Average age 28. 749 applicants, 25% accepted, 77 enrolled. Expenses: Contact institution. *Financial support:* Fellowships with full tuition reimbursements, research assistantships with full tuition reimbursements, teaching assistantships with full tuition reimbursements, career-related internships or fieldwork, institutionally sponsored loans, scholarships/grants, traineeships, health care benefits, and unspecified assistantships available. Financial award application deadline: 3/1; financial award applicants required to submit FAFSA. In 2010, 21 master's, 44 doctorates awarded. Offers biological science (MS); biological sciences (MS, PhD); biotechnology (MS); cellular and molecular biosciences (PhD); mathematical, computational and systems biology (PhD); neuroscience (PhD). *Application deadline:* For fall admission, 12/15 for domestic and international students. Applications are processed on a rolling basis. *Application fee:* $80 ($100 for international students). Electronic applications accepted. *Application Contact:* Prof. R. Michael Mulligan, Associate Dean, 949-824-8433, Fax: 949-824-4709, E-mail: rmmullig@uci.edu. *Dean,* Prof. Albert F. Bennett, 949-824-5315, Fax: 949-824-3035, E-mail: abennett@uci.edu.

School of Engineering Students: 647 full-time (138 women), 70 part-time (19 women); includes 175 minority (2 Black or African American, non-Hispanic/Latino; 2 American Indian or Alaska Native, non-Hispanic/Latino; 137 Asian, non-Hispanic/Latino; 26 Hispanic/Latino; 1 Native Hawaiian or other Pacific Islander, non-Hispanic/Latino; 7 Two or more races, non-Hispanic/Latino), 357 international. Average age 27. 2,410 applicants, 25% accepted, 215 enrolled. Expenses: Contact institution. *Financial support:* Fellowships with tuition reimbursements, research assistantships with full tuition reimbursements, teaching assistantships with tuition reimbursements, institutionally sponsored loans, traineeships, health care benefits, and unspecified assistantships available. Financial award application deadline: 3/1; financial award applicants required to submit FAFSA. In 2010, 150 master's, 70 doctorates awarded. *Degree program information:* Part-time programs available. Offers biomedical engineering (MS, PhD); chemical and biochemical engineering (MS, PhD); civil and environmental engineering (MS, PhD); electrical engineering and computer science (MS, PhD); engineering (MS, PhD); materials science and engineering (MS, PhD); mechanical and aerospace engineering (MS, PhD); networked systems (MS, PhD). *Application deadline:* For fall admission, 1/15 priority date for domestic students, 1/15 for international students. Applications are processed on a rolling basis. *Application fee:* $80 ($100 for international students). Electronic applications accepted. *Application Contact:* Prof. John C. LaRue, Associate Dean, 949-824-6737, Fax: 949-824-8585, E-mail: jclarue@uci.edu. *Dean,* Dr. Gregory Washington, 949-824-6002, Fax: 949-824-8200, E-mail: engineeringdean@uci.edu.

School of Humanities Students: 397 full-time (207 women), 16 part-time (8 women); includes 94 minority (4 Black or African American, non-Hispanic/Latino; 1 American Indian or Alaska Native, non-Hispanic/Latino; 34 Asian, non-Hispanic/Latino; 49 Hispanic/Latino; 6 Two or more races, non-Hispanic/Latino), 29 international. Average age 28. 1,203 applicants, 12% accepted, 74 enrolled. Expenses: Contact institution. *Financial support:* Fellowships with full and partial tuition reimbursements, research assistantships with full tuition reimbursements, teaching assistantships with full and partial tuition reimbursements, institutionally sponsored loans, traineeships, health care benefits, and unspecified assistantships available. Financial award application deadline: 3/1; financial award applicants required to submit FAFSA. In 2010, 83 master's, 53 doctorates awarded. Offers Chinese (MA, PhD); classics (MA, PhD); comparative literature (MA, PhD); creative writing (MFA); culture and theory (PhD); East Asian languages and literatures (MA, PhD); English (MA, PhD); English and American literature (PhD); French (MA, PhD); German (MA, PhD); history (MA, PhD); humanities (MA, MAT, MFA, PhD); Japanese (MA, PhD); philosophy (MA, PhD); Spanish (MA, MAT, PhD); visual studies (PhD); writing (MFA). *Application deadline:* For fall admission, 1/15 for domestic and international students. Applications are processed on a rolling basis. *Application fee:* $80 ($100 for international students). Electronic applications accepted. *Application Contact:* Glen Masato Mimura, Associate Dean, 949-824-4724, Fax: 949-824-2464, E-mail: gmimura@uci.edu. *Dean,* Vicki Lynn Ruiz, 949-824-5131, Fax: 949-824-2379, E-mail: vruiz@uci.edu.

School of Law Offers law (JD).

School of Medicine Students: 576 full-time (295 women), 33 part-time (12 women); includes 240 minority (14 Black or African American, non-Hispanic/Latino; 2 American Indian or Alaska Native, non-Hispanic/Latino; 165 Asian, non-Hispanic/Latino; 54 Hispanic/Latino; 4 Native Hawaiian or other Pacific Islander, non-Hispanic/Latino; 1 Two or more races, non-Hispanic/Latino), 13 international. Average age 28. Expenses: Contact institution. *Financial support:* Fellowships, research assistantships with full tuition reimbursements, teaching assistantships, career-related internships or fieldwork, institutionally sponsored loans, traineeships, health care benefits, and unspecified assistantships available. Financial award application deadline: 3/1; financial award applicants required to submit FAFSA. In 2010, 13 master's, 19 doctorates awarded. Offers biological sciences (MS, PhD); epidemiology (MS, PhD); experimental pathology (PhD); genetic counseling (MS); medicine (MD, MS, PhD); pharmacology and toxicology (MS, PhD). *Application deadline:* For fall admission, 1/15 for domestic and international students. *Application fee:* $80 ($100 for international students). Electronic applications accepted. *Application Contact:* Prof. F. Allan Hubbell, Associate Dean, 949-824-3975, Fax: 949-824-2676, E-mail: fahubbel@uci.edu. *Dean,* Prof. Ralph Victor Clayman, 949-824-5926, Fax: 949-824-2676, E-mail: rclayman@uci.edu.

School of Physical Sciences Students: 516 full-time (164 women), 2 part-time (1 woman); includes 96 minority (7 Black or African American, non-Hispanic/Latino; 65 Asian, non-Hispanic/Latino; 16 Hispanic/Latino; 8 Two or more races, non-Hispanic/Latino), 129 international. Average age 28. 825 applicants, 37% accepted, 109 enrolled. Expenses: Contact institution. *Financial support:* Fellowships, research assistantships with full tuition reimbursements, teaching assistantships, career-related internships or fieldwork, institutionally sponsored loans, traineeships, health care benefits, and unspecified assistantships available. Financial award application deadline: 3/1; financial award applicants required to submit FAFSA. In 2010, 59 master's, 58 doctorates awarded. Offers chemical and material physics (PhD); chemical and materials physics (MS, PhD); chemistry (MS, PhD); earth system science (MS, PhD); mathematics (MS, PhD); physical sciences (MS, PhD); physics (MS, PhD). *Application deadline:* For fall admission, 1/15 priority date for domestic and international students. Applications are processed on a rolling basis. *Application fee:* $80 ($100 for international students). Electronic applications accepted. *Application Contact:* Prof. Robert Doedens, Associate Dean, 949-824-6605, Fax: 949-824-4759, E-mail: rjdoeden@uci.edu. *Dean,* Kenneth C. Janda, 949-824-6022, Fax: 949-824-2261, E-mail: kcjanda@uci.edu.

School of Social Ecology Students: 295 full-time (182 women), 26 part-time (12 women); includes 105 minority (11 Black or African American, non-Hispanic/Latino; 2 American Indian or Alaska Native, non-Hispanic/Latino; 43 Asian, non-Hispanic/Latino; 41 Hispanic/Latino; 8 Two or more races, non-Hispanic/Latino), 37 international. Average age 28. 626 applicants, 35% accepted, 114 enrolled. Expenses: Contact institution. *Financial support:* Fellowships, research assistantships with full tuition reimbursements, teaching assistantships, institutionally sponsored loans, traineeships, health care benefits, and unspecified assistantships available. Financial award application deadline: 3/1; financial award applicants required to submit FAFSA. In 2010, 64 master's, 22 doctorates awarded. Offers criminology, law and society (MAS, PhD); environmental analysis and design (PhD); epidemiology and public health (PhD); planning, policy and design (PhD); psychology and social behavior (PhD); social ecology (MA, MAS, MURP, PhD); urban and regional planning (MURP). *Application deadline:* For fall admission, 1/15 priority date for domestic students, 1/15 for international students. Applications are processed on a rolling basis. *Application fee:* $80 ($100 for international students). Electronic applications accepted. *Application Contact:* Prof. James W. Meeker, Associate Dean of Students, 949-824-1463, Fax: 949-824-1845, E-mail: jwmeeker@uci.edu. *Dean,* Prof. Valerie Jenness, 949-824-6094, Fax: 949-824-1845, E-mail: jenness@uci.edu.

School of Social Sciences Students: 372 full-time (158 women), 6 part-time (2 women); includes 101 minority (2 Black or African American, non-Hispanic/Latino; 1 American Indian or Alaska Native, non-Hispanic/Latino; 61 Asian, non-Hispanic/Latino; 31 Hispanic/Latino; 6 Two or more races, non-Hispanic/Latino), 43 international. Average age 28. 848 applicants, 23% accepted, 94 enrolled. Expenses: Contact institution. *Financial support:* Fellowships, research assistantships with full tuition reimbursements, teaching assistantships, institutionally sponsored loans, traineeships, health care benefits, and unspecified assistantships available. Financial award application deadline: 3/1; financial award applicants required to submit FAFSA. In 2010, 64 master's, 34 doctorates awarded. Offers anthropology (MA, PhD); demographic and social analysis (MA); economics (MA, PhD); philosophy (PhD); political psychology (PhD); political sciences (PhD); psychology (PhD); public choice (MA, PhD); social networks (PhD); social networks-social science (MA); social science (MA, PhD); social sciences (MA, PhD); sociology and social relations-social science (MA, PhD); transportation economics (MA, PhD); transportation science (MA, PhD). *Application deadline:* For fall admission, 1/15 priority date for domestic students, 1/15 for international students. Applications are processed on a rolling basis. *Application fee:* $80 ($100 for international students). Electronic applications accepted. *Application Contact:* Prof. Bill M. Maurer, Associate Dean, 949-824-6680, Fax: 949-824-0646, E-mail: wmmaurer@uci.edu. *Dean,* Prof. Barbara Anne Dosher, 949-824-6802, Fax: 949-824-3995, E-mail: bdosher@uci.edu.

UNIVERSITY OF CALIFORNIA, LOS ANGELES, Los Angeles, CA 90095

General Information State-supported, coed, university. CGS member. *Enrollment:* 39,593 graduate, professional, and undergraduate students; 11,898 full-time matriculated graduate/professional students (5,510 women). *Enrollment by degree level:* 2,058 first professional, 5,118 master's, 4,713 doctoral, 9 other advanced degrees. *Graduate faculty:* 1,883 full-time (526 women). *Graduate housing:* Rooms and/or apartments available on a first-come, first-served basis to single and married students. *Student services:* Campus employment opportunities, campus safety program, career counseling, child daycare facilities, exercise/wellness program, free psychological counseling, grant writing training, international student services, low-cost health insurance, multicultural affairs office, services for students with disabilities, teacher training, writing training. *Library facilities:* Charles E. Young Research Library plus 13 others. *Online resources:* library catalog, web page, access to other libraries' catalogs. *Collection:* 9 million titles, 38,975 serial subscriptions, 316,523 audiovisual materials.

Computer facilities: 3,930 computers available on campus for general student use. A campuswide network can be accessed from student residence rooms and from off campus. Online class registration is available. *Web address:* http://www.ucla.edu/.

General Application Contact: Graduate Admissions Office, 310-825-1711.

GRADUATE UNITS

David Geffen School of Medicine Students: 990 full-time (480 women); includes 214 minority (19 Black or African American, non-Hispanic/Latino; 1 American Indian or Alaska Native, non-Hispanic/Latino; 124 Asian, non-Hispanic/Latino; 66 Hispanic/Latino; 1 Native Hawaiian or other Pacific Islander, non-Hispanic/Latino; 3 Two or more races, non-Hispanic/Latino), 56 international. Average age 26. 7,085 applicants, 5% accepted, 196 enrolled. Expenses: Contact institution. *Financial support:* In 2010–11, 401 fellowships, 264 research assistantships, 75 teaching assistantships were awarded; career-related internships or fieldwork, Federal Work-Study, institutionally sponsored loans, scholarships/grants, and tuition waivers (full and partial) also available. In 2010, 166 first professional degrees, 22 master's, 61 doctorates awarded. Offers medicine (MD, MS, PhD). *Application fee:* $70. Electronic applications accepted. *Application Contact:* School of Medicine Admissions, 310-825-6081. *Vice Chancellor, Health Sciences/Dean,* Dr. A. Eugene Washington, 310-825-5687, E-mail: ewashington@mednet.ucla.edu.

Graduate Programs in Medicine Students: 339 full-time (164 women); includes 98 minority (5 Black or African American, non-Hispanic/Latino; 1 American Indian or Alaska Native, non-Hispanic/Latino; 58 Asian, non-Hispanic/Latino; 31 Hispanic/Latino; 1 Native Hawaiian or other Pacific Islander, non-Hispanic/Latino; 2 Two or more races, non-Hispanic/Latino), 53 international. Average age 28. 382 applicants, 19% accepted, 38 enrolled. Expenses: Contact institution. *Financial support:* In 2010–11, 324 fellowships, 263 research assistantships, 75 teaching assistantships were awarded; career-related internships or fieldwork, Federal Work-Study, institutionally sponsored loans, scholarships/grants, and tuition waivers (full and partial) also available. Financial award application deadline: 3/1. In 2010, 22 master's, 61 doctorates awarded. Offers anatomy and cell biology (PhD); biological chemistry (MS, PhD); biomathematics (MS, PhD); biomedical physics (MS, PhD); cellular and molecular pathology (MS, PhD); clinical research (MS); experimental pathology (MS, PhD); human genetics (MS, PhD); medicine (MS, PhD); microbiology, immunology and molecular genetics (MS, PhD); molecular and medical pharmacology (PhD); neuroscience (PhD); physiology (PhD). *Application fee:* $70 ($90 for international students). Electronic applications accepted. *Application Contact:* Office of Continuing Medical Education, 310-794-2620. *Senior Associate Dean for Student Affairs and Graduate Medical Education,* Dr. Neil H. Parker, 310-825-6774, E-mail: nhparker@mednet.ucla.edu.

Graduate Division Students: 9,830 full-time (4,513 women); includes 3,327 minority (338 Black or African American, non-Hispanic/Latino; 29 American Indian or Alaska Native, non-Hispanic/Latino; 1,949 Asian, non-Hispanic/Latino; 868 Hispanic/Latino; 18 Native Hawaiian or other Pacific Islander, non-Hispanic/Latino; 125 Two or more races, non-Hispanic/Latino), 1,955 international. 22,395 applicants, 28% accepted, 3130 enrolled. Expenses: Contact institution. *Financial support:* In 2010–11, 4,963 fellowships with full and partial tuition reimbursements, 2,745 research assistantships with full tuition reimbursements, 2,903 teaching assistantships with full tuition reimbursements were awarded; career-related internships or fieldwork, Federal Work-Study, institutionally sponsored loans, scholarships/grants, health care benefits, tuition waivers (full and partial), and unspecified assistantships also available. Support available to part-time students. Financial award application deadline: 3/1; financial award applicants required to submit FAFSA. In 2010, 2,639 master's, 747 doctorates awarded. *Application fee:* $70 ($90 for international students). Electronic applications accepted. *Application Contact:* Graduate Admissions, 310-825-1711. *Interim Dean/Vice Provost,* Dr. Michael Goldstein, 310-825-4383, E-mail: mgoldstein@gdnet.ucla.edu.

College of Letters and Science Students: 2,643 full-time (1,315 women); includes 842 minority (75 Black or African American, non-Hispanic/Latino; 13 American Indian or Alaska Native, non-Hispanic/Latino; 339 Asian, non-Hispanic/Latino; 191 Hispanic/Latino; 4 Native Hawaiian or other Pacific Islander, non-Hispanic/Latino; 20 Two or more races, non-Hispanic/Latino), 492 international. Average age 28. 5,992 applicants, 19% accepted, 512 enrolled. Expenses: Contact institution. *Financial support:* In 2010–11, 2,152 fellowships with full tuition reimbursements, 1,187 research assistantships with full tuition reimbursements, 1,573 teaching assistantships with full tuition reimbursements were awarded; Federal Work-Study, institutionally sponsored loans, scholarships/grants, traineeships, health care benefits, tuition waivers (full and partial), and unspecified assistantships also available. Financial award application deadline: 3/1; financial award applicants required to submit FAFSA. In 2010, 321 master's, 360 doctorates awarded. Offers Afro-American studies (MA); American Indian studies (MA); anthropology (MA, PhD); applied linguistics (PhD); applied linguistics and teaching English as a second language (MA); archaeology (MA, PhD); art history (MA, PhD); Asian languages and cultures (MA, PhD); Asian-American studies (MA); astronomy (MAT, MS, PhD); atmospheric sciences (MS, PhD); biochemistry and molecular biology (MS, PhD); bioinformatics (MS, PhD); biological chemistry (PhD); cellular and molecular pathology (PhD); chemistry (MS, PhD); classics (MA, PhD); comparative literature (MA, PhD); conservation of archaeological and ethnographic materials (MA); ecology and evolutionary biology (MA, PhD); economics (MA, PhD); English (MA, PhD); French and Francophone studies (MA, PhD); geochemistry (MS, PhD); geography (MA, PhD); geology (MS, PhD); geophysics and space physics (MS, PhD); Germanic languages (MA, PhD); Greek (MA); Hispanic languages and literature (PhD); history (MA, PhD); human genetics (PhD); Indo-European studies (PhD); Italian (MA, PhD); Latin (MA); letters and science (MA, MAT, MS, PhD, Certificate); linguistics (MA, PhD); mathematics (MA, MAT, PhD); microbiology, immunology, and molecular genetics (PhD); molecular biology (PhD); molecular toxicology (PhD); molecular, cell and developmental biology (PhD); molecular, cellular and integrative physiology (PhD); musicology (MA, PhD); Near Eastern languages and cultures (MA, PhD); neurobiology (PhD); oral biology (PhD); philosophy (MA, PhD); physics (MAT, MS, PhD); physics education (MAT); physiological science (MS); physiology (PhD); political science (MA, PhD); Portuguese (MA); psychology (MA, PhD); Scandinavian (MA); Slavic languages and literatures (MA, PhD); sociology (MA, PhD); Spanish (MA); statistics (MS, PhD); teaching English as a second language (Certificate); women's studies (MA, PhD). *Application fee:* $70 ($90 for international students). Electronic applications accepted. *Application Contact:* Dr. Judith L. Smith, Vice Provost/Dean, 310-206-3961, E-mail: judis@college.ucla.edu. *Vice Provost/Dean,* Dr. Judith L. Smith, 310-206-3961, E-mail: judis@college.ucla.edu.

Graduate School of Education and Information Studies *Degree program information:* Part-time and evening/weekend programs available. Offers archival studies (MLIS); educa-

University of California, Los Angeles (continued)

tion (M Ed, MA, Ed D, PhD); education and information studies (M Ed, MA, MLIS, Ed D, PhD, Certificate); educational leadership (Ed D); informatics (MLIS); information studies (PhD); library and information science (Certificate); library studies (MLIS); moving image archive studies (MA); special education (PhD). Electronic applications accepted.

Henry Samueli School of Engineering and Applied Science Students: 1,783 full-time (360 women); includes 26 Black or African American, non-Hispanic/Latino; 1 American Indian or Alaska Native, non-Hispanic/Latino; 432 Asian, non-Hispanic/Latino; 59 Hispanic/Latino; 7 Native Hawaiian or other Pacific Islander, non-Hispanic/Latino, 737 international. 3,914 applicants, 38% accepted, 601 enrolled. *Faculty:* 155 full-time (19 women), 21 part-time/adjunct (0 women). Expenses: Contact institution. *Financial support:* In 2010–11, 482 fellowships, 1,870 research assistantships, 448 teaching assistantships were awarded; career-related internships or fieldwork, Federal Work-Study, institutionally sponsored loans, and tuition waivers (full and partial) also available. Financial award application deadline: 3/2; financial award applicants required to submit FAFSA. In 2010, 438 master's, 164 doctorates awarded. *Degree program information:* Evening/weekend programs available. Postbaccalaureate distance learning degree programs offered (no on-campus study). Offers aerospace engineering (MS, PhD); biomedical engineering (MS, PhD); chemical and biomolecular engineering (MS, PhD); civil and environmental engineering (MS, PhD); computer science (MS, PhD); electrical engineering (MS, PhD); engineering (MS); engineering and applied science (MS, PhD); manufacturing engineering (MS); materials science and engineering (MS, PhD); mechanical engineering (MS, PhD). *Application deadline:* For fall admission, 12/15 for domestic and international students. *Application fee:* $70 ($90 for international students). Electronic applications accepted. *Application Contact:* Jan LaBuda, Director, Office of Academic and Student Affairs, 310-825-2514, Fax: 310-825-2473, E-mail: jan@ea.ucla.edu. *Associate Dean, Academic and Student Affairs,* Dr. Richard D. Wesel, 310-825-2942.

International Institute Students: 57 full-time (30 women); includes 29 minority (5 Black or African American, non-Hispanic/Latino; 8 Asian, non-Hispanic/Latino; 16 Hispanic/Latino), 6 international. Average age 30. 112 applicants, 55% accepted, 20 enrolled. Expenses: Contact institution. *Financial support:* In 2010–11, 40 fellowships, 8 research assistantships, 13 teaching assistantships were awarded; Federal Work-Study, scholarships/grants, and unspecified assistantships also available. In 2010, 35 master's awarded. Offers African studies (MA); East Asian studies (MA); Islamic studies (MA, PhD); Latin American studies (MA). *Application fee:* $70 ($90 for international students). Electronic applications accepted. *Application Contact:* Department Office, 310-825-4811, E-mail: info-intl@international.ucla.edu. *Interim Vice Provost, International Studies,* Dr. Randal Johnson, 310-825-4921, E-mail: rjohnson@international.ucla.edu.

School of Nursing Students: 346 full-time (306 women); includes 176 minority (30 Black or African American, non-Hispanic/Latino; 4 American Indian or Alaska Native, non-Hispanic/Latino; 82 Asian, non-Hispanic/Latino; 45 Hispanic/Latino; 2 Native Hawaiian or other Pacific Islander, non-Hispanic/Latino; 13 Two or more races, non-Hispanic/Latino), 7 international. Average age 32. 734 applicants, 27% accepted, 156 enrolled. *Faculty:* 31 full-time (all women). Expenses: Contact institution. *Financial support:* In 2010–11, 241 fellowships with full and partial tuition reimbursements, 9 research assistantships with full and partial tuition reimbursements, 35 teaching assistantships with full and partial tuition reimbursements were awarded; Federal Work-Study, institutionally sponsored loans, scholarships/grants, health care benefits, tuition waivers (full and partial), and unspecified assistantships also available. Financial award application deadline: 3/1; financial award applicants required to submit FAFSA. In 2010, 153 master's, 8 doctorates awarded. Offers nursing (MSN, PhD). *Application deadline:* For fall admission, 12/1 priority date for domestic and international students. *Application fee:* $70 ($90 for international students). Electronic applications accepted. *Application Contact:* Departmental Office, 310-794-7461, E-mail: sonsaff@sonnet.ucla.edu. *Dean,* Prof. Courtney H. Lyder, 310-206-7433, E-mail: clyder@sonnet.ucla.edu.

School of Public Affairs Offers public affairs (MA, MPP, MSW, PhD); public policy (MPP); social welfare (MSW, PhD); urban planning (MA, PhD). Electronic applications accepted.

School of Public Health Offers biostatistics (MPH, MS, Dr PH, PhD); environmental health sciences (MS, PhD); environmental science and engineering (D Env); epidemiology (MPH, MS, Dr PH, PhD); health services (MPH, MS, Dr PH, PhD); molecular toxicology (PhD); public health (MPH, MS, D Env, Dr PH, PhD). Electronic applications accepted.

School of the Arts and Architecture Students: 394 full-time (178 women); includes 108 minority (16 Black or African American, non-Hispanic/Latino; 52 Asian, non-Hispanic/Latino; 37 Hispanic/Latino; 1 Native Hawaiian or other Pacific Islander, non-Hispanic/Latino; 2 Two or more races, non-Hispanic/Latino), 62 international. Average age 28. 1,945 applicants, 14% accepted, 129 enrolled. Expenses: Contact institution. *Financial support:* In 2010–11, 365 students received support, including 225 fellowships, 25 research assistantships, 174 teaching assistantships; Federal Work-Study, institutionally sponsored loans, scholarships/grants, tuition waivers (full and partial), and unspecified assistantships also available. Financial award application deadline: 3/1. In 2010, 96 master's, 19 doctorates awarded. Offers architecture and urban design (M Arch, MA, PhD); art (MA, MFA); arts and architecture (M Arch, MA, MFA, MM, DMA, PhD); composition (MA, PhD); culture and performance (MA, PhD); dance (MFA); design/media arts (MFA); ethnomusicology (MA, PhD); performance (MM, DMA). *Application fee:* $70 ($90 for international students). Electronic applications accepted. *Application Contact:* Office of Enrollment Management and Outreach, 310-825-8981. *Dean,* Christopher Waterman, 310-206-6465, E-mail: cwater@arts.ucla.edu.

School of Theater, Film and Television Students: 387 full-time (190 women); includes 115 minority (32 Black or African American, non-Hispanic/Latino; 5 American Indian or Alaska Native, non-Hispanic/Latino; 34 Asian, non-Hispanic/Latino; 37 Hispanic/Latino; 1 Native Hawaiian or other Pacific Islander, non-Hispanic/Latino; 6 Two or more races, non-Hispanic/Latino), 39 international. Average age 29. 1,619 applicants, 12% accepted, 134 enrolled. Expenses: Contact institution. *Financial support:* In 2010–11, 286 fellowships with full and partial tuition reimbursements, 17 research assistantships with full and partial tuition reimbursements, 164 teaching assistantships with full and partial tuition reimbursements were awarded; career-related internships or fieldwork, Federal Work-Study, institutionally sponsored loans, scholarships/grants, traineeships, health care benefits, tuition waivers (full and partial), and unspecified assistantships also available. Financial award application deadline: 3/1; financial award applicants required to submit FAFSA. In 2010, 115 master's, 7 doctorates awarded. Offers film and television (MA, MFA, PhD); moving image archive studies (MA); theater (MA, MFA); theater and performance studies (PhD); theater, film and television (MA, MFA, PhD). *Application fee:* $70 ($90 for international students). Electronic applications accepted. *Application Contact:* Departmental Office, 310-825-8787, E-mail: info@tft.ucla.edu. *Executive Director,* Peter Heller, 310-206-3620, E-mail: pheller@tft.ucla.edu.

UCLA Anderson School of Management Students: 833 full-time (270 women), 1,052 part-time (271 women); includes 592 minority (25 Black or African American, non-Hispanic/Latino; 3 American Indian or Alaska Native, non-Hispanic/Latino; 482 Asian, non-Hispanic/Latino; 60 Hispanic/Latino; 6 Native Hawaiian or other Pacific Islander, non-Hispanic/Latino; 16 Two or more races, non-Hispanic/Latino), 445 international. *Faculty:* 102 full-time (17 women), 43 part-time/adjunct (6 women). Expenses: Contact institution. *Financial support:* Fellowships, research assistantships, teaching assistantships, career-related internships or fieldwork, institutionally sponsored loans, scholarships/grants, health care benefits, and tuition waivers (partial) available. Financial award application deadline: 3/2; financial award applicants required to submit FAFSA. In 2010, 735 master's, 10 doctorates awarded. *Degree program information:* Part-time programs available. Offers accounting (PhD); business administration (MBA); decisions, operations and technology management (PhD); finance (PhD); financial engineering (MFE); global economics and management (PhD); human resources and organizational behavior (PhD); marketing (PhD); strategy and policy (PhD). *Application deadline:* For fall admission, 10/20 for domestic and international students; for winter admission, 1/5 for domestic and international students; for spring admission, 4/13 for domestic and international students. *Application fee:* $200. Electronic applications accepted. *Application Contact:* Mae Jennifer Shores, Assistant Dean and Director of Full-time MBA Admissions and Financial Aid, 310-825-6944, Fax: 310-825-8582, E-mail: mba.admissions@anderson.ucla.edu. *Dean,* Judy D. Olian, 310-825-7982, Fax: 310-206-2073.

School of Dentistry Students: 410 full-time (193 women); includes 84 minority (9 Black or African American, non-Hispanic/Latino; 2 American Indian or Alaska Native, non-Hispanic/Latino; 58 Asian, non-Hispanic/Latino; 9 Hispanic/Latino; 6 Two or more races, non-Hispanic/Latino), 23 international. 1,877 applicants, 7% accepted, 102 enrolled. *Faculty:* 42 full-time (8 women). Expenses: Contact institution. *Financial support:* In 2010–11, 29 fellowships, 3 research assistantships, 3 teaching assistantships were awarded; Federal Work-Study, institutionally sponsored loans, scholarships/grants, traineeships, tuition waivers (full and partial), and unspecified assistantships also available. Financial award application deadline: 3/1. In 2010, 98 first professional degrees, 11 master's, 2 doctorates awarded. Offers dentistry (DDS, MS, PhD, Certificate); oral biology (MS, PhD). *Application deadline:* For fall admission, 1/15 for domestic students. *Application fee:* $70 ($90 for international students). Electronic applications accepted. *Application Contact:* Noemi Benitez, Coordinator, Admissions, 310-794-7971, E-mail: nbenitez@dentistry.ucla.edu. *Dean,* Dr. No-Hee Park, 310-206-6063, E-mail: nhpark@dentistry.ucla.edu.

School of Law Students: 1,079 full-time (523 women); includes 337 minority (44 Black or African American, non-Hispanic/Latino; 19 American Indian or Alaska Native, non-Hispanic/Latino; 161 Asian, non-Hispanic/Latino; 92 Hispanic/Latino; 1 Native Hawaiian or other Pacific Islander, non-Hispanic/Latino; 20 Two or more races, non-Hispanic/Latino), 75 international. Average age 25. 8,748 applicants, 16% accepted, 308 enrolled. *Faculty:* 110 full-time (43 women), 59 part-time/adjunct (17 women). Expenses: Contact institution. *Financial support:* In 2010–11, 682 students received support. Career-related internships or fieldwork, Federal Work-Study, institutionally sponsored loans, scholarships/grants, and tuition waivers (full and partial) available. Financial award application deadline: 3/2. In 2010, 346 first professional degrees, 72 master's, 1 doctorate awarded. Offers law (JD, LL M, SJD). *Application deadline:* For fall admission, 2/1 for domestic students. Applications are processed on a rolling basis. *Application fee:* $75. Electronic applications accepted. *Application Contact:* Admissions Office, 310-825-2080. *Dean,* Rachel F. Moran, 310-825-8202.

UNIVERSITY OF CALIFORNIA, MERCED, Merced, CA 95343

General Information State-supported, coed, university.

GRADUATE UNITS

Division of Graduate Studies *Degree program information:* Part-time programs available. Electronic applications accepted.

School of Engineering Offers electrical engineering and computer science (MS, PhD).

School of Natural Sciences Offers applied mathematics (MS, PhD); biological engineering and small-scale technologies (MS, PhD); environmental systems (MS, PhD); mechanical engineering and applied mechanics (MS, PhD); physics and chemistry (PhD); quantitative and systems biology (MS, PhD).

School of Social Sciences, Humanities and Arts Offers social and cognitive sciences (MA, PhD); world cultures (MA, PhD).

UNIVERSITY OF CALIFORNIA, RIVERSIDE, Riverside, CA 92521-0102

General Information State-supported, coed, university. CGS member. *Enrollment:* 2,368 full-time matriculated graduate/professional students (1,306 women), 30 part-time matriculated graduate/professional students (17 women). *Enrollment by degree level:* 557 master's, 1,841 doctoral. *Graduate faculty:* 664 full-time (210 women). *Graduate housing:* Rooms and/or apartments available on a first-come, first-served basis to single and married students. Housing application deadline: 6/1. *Student services:* Campus safety program, career counseling, child daycare facilities, exercise/wellness program, free psychological counseling, international student services, low-cost health insurance, multicultural affairs office, services for students with disabilities, teacher training, writing training. *Library facilities:* Tomas Rivera Library plus 6 others. *Online resources:* library catalog, web page, access to other libraries' catalogs. *Collection:* 3 million titles, 90,153 serial subscriptions, 45,372 audiovisual materials. *Research affiliation:* Fermi National Accelerator Laboratory (physics), Los Alamos National Laboratory (botany and plant sciences, chemistry, earth sciences, physics), Brookhaven National Laboratory (chemistry, physics), U. S. Salinity Laboratory (environmental sciences, biochemistry), J. Paul Getty Museum (art history), Lawrence Livermore National Laboratory (archaeology).

Computer facilities: Computer purchase and lease plans are available. 1,072 computers available on campus for general student use. A campuswide network can be accessed from student residence rooms and from off campus. Online class registration, online viewing of financial information are available. *Web address:* http://www.ucr.edu/.

General Application Contact: Graduate Admissions, 951-827-3313, Fax: 951-827-2238, E-mail: grdadmis@ucr.edu.

GRADUATE UNITS

Graduate Division Students: 2,368 full-time (1,306 women), 30 part-time (17 women); includes 71 Black or African American, non-Hispanic/Latino; 9 American Indian or Alaska Native, non-Hispanic/Latino; 252 Asian, non-Hispanic/Latino; 191 Hispanic/Latino; 8 Native Hawaiian or other Pacific Islander, non-Hispanic/Latino, 702 international. Average age 29. 4,833 applicants, 28% accepted, 656 enrolled. *Faculty:* 664 full-time (210 women). Expenses: Contact institution. *Financial support:* Fellowships with full and partial tuition reimbursements, research assistantships with full and partial tuition reimbursements, teaching assistantships with full and partial tuition reimbursements, career-related internships or fieldwork, Federal Work-Study, institutionally sponsored loans, scholarships/grants, and tuition waivers (full and partial) available. Financial award applicants required to submit FAFSA. In 2010, 457 master's, 215 doctorates awarded. *Degree program information:* Part-time and evening/weekend programs available. Offers anthropology (MA, MS, PhD); applied statistics (PhD); archival management (MA); art history (MA); biochemistry and molecular biology (MS, PhD); bioengineering (MS, PhD); biomedical sciences (PhD); cell, molecular, and developmental biology (MS, PhD); chemical and environmental engineering (MS, PhD); chemistry (MS, PhD); classics (PhD); comparative literature (MA, PhD); composition (PhD); computer science (MS, PhD); creative writing and writing for the performing arts (MFA); critical dance studies (PhD); economics (MA, PhD); electrical engineering (MS, PhD); English (MA, PhD); entomology (MS, PhD); environmental toxicology (MS, PhD); ethnic studies (PhD); ethnomusicology (MA, PhD); evolution and ecology (PhD); evolution, ecology and organismal biology (MS, PhD); experimental choreography (MFA); genomics and bioinformatics (PhD); geological sciences (MS, PhD); historic preservation (MA); history (MA, PhD); materials science and engineering (MS, PhD); mathematics (MA, MS, PhD); mechanical engineering (MS, PhD); microbiology (MS, PhD); molecular genetics (PhD); museum curatorship (MA); musicology (PhD); neuroscience (PhD); philosophy (MA, PhD); physics (MS, PhD); plant biology (MS, PhD); plant pathology (MS, PhD); political science (MA, PhD); population and evolutionary genetics (PhD); psychology (MA, PhD); sociology (MA, PhD); soil and water sciences (MS, PhD); Southeast Asian studies (MA); Spanish (MA, PhD); statistics (MS); visual arts (MFA). *Application deadline:* For fall admission, 5/1 for domestic students, 2/1 for international students; for winter admission, 2/1 for domestic students, 7/1 for international students; for spring admission, 12/1 for domestic students, 10/1 for international students. Applications are processed on a rolling basis. *Application fee:* $80 ($100 for international students). Electronic applications accepted. *Application Contact:* Graduate Admissions, 951-827-3313, Fax: 951-827-2238, E-mail: grdadmis@ucr.edu. *Dean,* Dr. Joseph W. Childers, 951-827-3313, Fax: 951-827-2238.

A. Gary Anderson Graduate School of Management Students: 170 full-time (78 women), 5 part-time (3 women); includes 8 Black or African American, non-Hispanic/Latino; 34 Asian, non-Hispanic/Latino; 9 Hispanic/Latino; 1 Native Hawaiian or other Pacific Islander, non-Hispanic/Latino, 88 international. Average age 33. 311 applicants, 47% accepted, 64 enrolled. *Faculty:* 29 full-time (3 women), 14 part-time/adjunct (2 women). Expenses: Contact institution. *Financial support:* In 2010–11, 44 students received support, including 44 fellowships with partial tuition reimbursements available (averaging $19,770 per year), 47 teaching assistantships with partial tuition reimbursements available (averaging $16,500 per year); research assistantships, career-related internships or fieldwork, institutionally sponsored loans, scholarships/grants, and tuition waivers (full) also available. Financial award application deadline: 5/1; financial award applicants required to submit FAFSA. In 2010, 73 master's awarded. *Degree program information:* Part-time and evening/weekend programs available. Offers management (MBA). *Application deadline:* For fall admission, 9/1 for domestic students, 5/1 for international students; for winter admission, 12/1 for domestic students, 9/1 for international students; for spring admission, 3/1 for domestic students, 10/1 for international students. Applications are processed on a rolling basis. *Application fee:* $100 ($125 for international students). *Application Contact:* Dr. Yunzeng Wang, Associate Dean/Adviser, 951-827-2932, Fax: 951-827-3970, E-mail: mba@ucr.edu. *Dean,* Dr. David W. Stewart, 951-827-6329, Fax: 951-827-3970, E-mail: mba@ucr.edu.

Graduate School of Education Students: 171 full-time (123 women); includes 9 Black or African American, non-Hispanic/Latino; 1 American Indian or Alaska Native, non-Hispanic/Latino; 18 Asian, non-Hispanic/Latino; 19 Hispanic/Latino, 5 international. Average age 31. 165 applicants, 66% accepted, 80 enrolled. *Faculty:* 23 full-time (12 women), 8 part-time/adjunct (5 women). Expenses: Contact institution. *Financial support:* In 2010–11, 53 students received support, including 30 fellowships with full and partial tuition reimbursements available (averaging $29,836 per year), 24 research assistantships with full and partial tuition reimbursements available (averaging $14,239 per year), 1 teaching assistantship with full and partial tuition reimbursement available (averaging $16,969 per year); career-related internships or fieldwork, Federal Work-Study, institutionally sponsored loans, scholarships/grants, and unspecified assistantships also available. Financial award application deadline: 1/5. In 2010, 67 master's, 14 doctorates awarded. Offers autism (M Ed); curriculum and instruction (MA, PhD); diversity and equity (M Ed); educational psychology (MA, PhD); general education (M Ed); higher education administration and policy (M Ed, PhD); reading (M Ed); school psychology (PhD); special education (M Ed, MA, PhD). *Application deadline:* For fall admission, 9/1 for domestic students, 4/1 for international students; for winter admission, 12/1 for domestic students, 7/1 for international students; for spring admission, 3/1 for domestic students, 10/1 for international students. Applications are processed on a rolling basis. *Application fee:* $80 ($100 for international students). Electronic applications accepted. *Application Contact:* Prof. John Wills, Graduate Advisor for Admission, 951-827-6362, Fax: 951-827-3291, E-mail: edgrad@ucr.edu. *Interim Dean,* Prof. John Levin, 951-827-5802, Fax: 951-827-3942, E-mail: john.levin@ucr.edu.

UNIVERSITY OF CALIFORNIA, SAN DIEGO, La Jolla, CA 92093

General Information State-supported, coed, university. CGS member. *Graduate housing:* Rooms and/or apartments available to single and married students. *Research affiliation:* Salk Institute, Veterans Administration Medical Center, Scripps Clinic and Research Foundation, La Jolla Institute.

GRADUATE UNITS

Office of Graduate Studies Offers acting (MFA); aerospace engineering (MS, PhD); anthropology (PhD); applied mathematics (MA); applied mechanics (MS, PhD); applied ocean science (MS, PhD); applied physics (MS, PhD); bilingual education (MA); bioengineering (M Eng, MS, PhD); bioinformatics (PhD); biophysics (MS, PhD); chemical engineering (MS, PhD); chemistry (MS, PhD); clinical psychology (PhD); cognitive science (PhD); cognitive science/anthropology (PhD); cognitive science/communication (PhD); cognitive science/computer science and engineering (PhD); cognitive science/linguistics (PhD); cognitive science/neuroscience (PhD); cognitive science/philosophy (PhD); cognitive science/psychology (PhD); cognitive science/sociology (PhD); communication (MA, PhD); communication theory and systems (MS, PhD); comparative literature (MA, PhD); computer engineering (MS, PhD); computer science (MS, PhD); curriculum design (MA); design (MFA); directing (MFA); drama and theatre (PhD); earth sciences (PhD); economics (PhD); economics and international affairs (PhD); electrical engineering (M Eng); electronic circuits and systems (MS, PhD); engineering physics (MS, PhD); ethnic studies (MA, PhD); French literature (MA); German literature (MA); health law (MAS); history (MA, PhD); intelligent systems, robotics and control (MS, PhD); Judaic studies (MA); language and communicative disorders (PhD); Latin American studies (MA); linguistics (PhD); literature (PhD); literatures in English (MA); marine biodiversity and conservation (MAS); marine biology (PhD); materials science and engineering (MS, PhD); mathematics (MA, PhD); mathematics and science education (PhD); mechanical engineering (MS, PhD); music (MA, DMA, PhD); oceanography (PhD); philosophy (PhD); photonics (MS, PhD); physics (MS, PhD); physics/materials physics (MS); playwriting (MFA); political science (PhD); political science and international affairs (PhD); psychology (PhD); public health and epidemiology (PhD); science studies (PhD); signal and image processing (MS, PhD); sociology (PhD); Spanish literature (MA); stage management (MFA); statistics (MS); structural engineering (MS, PhD); structural health monitoring, prognosis, and validated simulations (MS); teacher education (M Ed); teaching and learning (Ed D); theatre (PhD); visual arts (MFA, PhD). Electronic applications accepted.

Division of Biological Sciences Offers biochemistry (PhD); biology (MS); cell and developmental biology (PhD); ecology, behavior, and evolution (PhD); genetics and molecular biology (PhD); immunology, virology, and cancer biology (PhD); molecular and cellular biology (PhD); neurobiology (PhD); plant molecular biology (PhD); plant systems biology (PhD); signal transduction (PhD). Offered in association with the Salk Institute; fall admission only. Electronic applications accepted.

Graduate School of International Relations and Pacific Studies Offers economics and international affairs (PhD); Pacific international affairs (MPIA); political science and international affairs (PhD). Electronic applications accepted.

Rady School of Management Offers management (MBA).

School of Medicine Offers audiology (Au D); bioinformatics (PhD); cancer biology/oncology (PhD); cardiovascular sciences and disease (PhD); clinical research (MAS); leadership in healthcare organizations (MAS); medicine (MD, MAS, Au D, PhD); microbiology (PhD); molecular pathology (PhD); neurological disease (PhD); neurosciences (PhD); stem cell and developmental biology (PhD); structural biology/drug design (PhD).

Graduate Studies in Biomedical Sciences Offers molecular cell biology (PhD); pharmacology (PhD); physiology (PhD); regulatory biology (PhD). Electronic applications accepted.

School of Pharmacy and Pharmaceutical Sciences Offers pharmacy and pharmaceutical sciences (Pharm D).

UNIVERSITY OF CALIFORNIA, SAN FRANCISCO, San Francisco, CA 94143

General Information State-supported, coed, graduate-only institution. CGS member. *Graduate housing:* Rooms and/or apartments available to single and married students.

GRADUATE UNITS

Graduate Division *Degree program information:* Part-time programs available. Offers anatomy (PhD); biochemistry and molecular biology (PhD); bioengineering (PhD); cell biology (PhD); developmental biology (PhD); endocrinology (PhD); experimental pathology (PhD); genetics (PhD); history of health sciences (MA, PhD); medical anthropology (PhD); microbiology and immunology (PhD); neuroscience (PhD); oral and craniofacial sciences (MS, PhD); physical therapy (MS, DPT, DPTSc); physiology (PhD).

School of Nursing Offers nursing (MS, PhD); sociology (PhD).

School of Dentistry Offers dentistry (DDS).

School of Medicine Students: 618 full-time (321 women); includes 320 minority (43 Black or African American, non-Hispanic/Latino; 2 American Indian or Alaska Native, non-Hispanic/Latino; 122 Asian, non-Hispanic/Latino; 90 Hispanic/Latino; 20 Native Hawaiian or other Pacific Islander, non-Hispanic/Latino; 43 Two or more races, non-Hispanic/Latino). Average age 24. 6,413 applicants, 4% accepted, 149 enrolled. *Faculty:* 1,931 full-time (678 women), 58 part-time/adjunct (11 women). Expenses: Contact institution. *Financial support:* In 2010–11, 543 students received support. Federal Work-Study, institutionally sponsored loans, scholarships/grants, and tuition waivers (partial) available. Financial award application deadline: 2/1; financial award applicants required to submit FAFSA. In 2010, 163 first professional degrees awarded. Offers epidemiology and translational science (PhD); medicine (MD, PhD). *Application deadline:* For fall admission, 10/15 for domestic students. Applications are processed on a rolling basis. *Application fee:* $60 ($80 for international students). Electronic applications accepted. *Application Contact:* Hallen Chung, Director of Admissions, 415-476-8090, Fax: 415-476-5490, E-mail: chungh@medsch.ucsf.edu. *Dean,* Dr. Sam Hawgood, 415-476-2342, Fax: 415-476-0689, E-mail: sam.hawgood@ucsf.edu.

School of Pharmacy Students: 654 full-time (411 women); includes 14 Black or African American, non-Hispanic/Latino; 280 Asian, non-Hispanic/Latino; 52 Hispanic/Latino, 10 international. Average age 26. 1,904 applicants, 12% accepted, 152 enrolled. *Faculty:* 87 full-time (38 women), 15 part-time/adjunct (6 women). Expenses: Contact institution. *Financial support:* In 2010–11, 434 students received support, including 50 fellowships with full tuition reimbursements available (averaging $28,000 per year), 76 research assistantships with full tuition reimbursements available (averaging $28,000 per year), 10 teaching assistantships with partial tuition reimbursements available (averaging $28,000 per year); career-related internships or fieldwork, Federal Work-Study, institutionally sponsored loans, scholarships/grants, traineeships, and tuition waivers (full) also available. Financial award applicants required to submit FAFSA. In 2010, 122 first professional degrees, 4 master's, 22 doctorates awarded. Offers biological and medical informatics (PhD); biophysics (PhD); chemistry and chemical biology (PhD); pharmaceutical sciences and pharmacogenomics (PhD); pharmacy (Pharm D, MS, PhD). *Application fee:* $70 ($90 for international students). Electronic applications accepted. *Application Contact:* Cynthia Watchmaker, Assistant Dean/Director, Student Affairs, 415-476-2732, Fax: 415-476-6805, E-mail: osaca@pharmacy.ucsf.edu. *Dean,* Mary Anne Koda-Kimble, 415-476-8010.

UNIVERSITY OF CALIFORNIA, SANTA BARBARA, Santa Barbara, CA 93106-2014

General Information State-supported, coed, university. CGS member. *Enrollment:* 22,218 graduate, professional, and undergraduate students; 2,993 full-time matriculated graduate/professional students (1,383 women). *Enrollment by degree level:* 13 first professional, 659 master's, 2,321 doctoral. *Graduate faculty:* 838 full-time (260 women). *Graduate housing:* Rooms and/or apartments available on a first-come, first-served basis to single and married students. Housing application deadline: 5/15. *Student services:* Campus employment opportunities, campus safety program, career counseling, child daycare facilities, exercise/wellness program, free psychological counseling, grant writing training, international student services, low-cost health insurance, multicultural affairs office, services for students with disabilities, teacher training, writing training. *Library facilities:* Davidson Library plus 1 other. *Online resources:* library catalog, web page, access to other libraries' catalogs. *Collection:* 3.4 million titles, 36,990 serial subscriptions, 146,142 audiovisual materials. *Research affiliation:* Mitsubishi Chemical Center for Advanced Materials, Center for Stem Cell Biology and Engineering, California NanoSystems Institute, National Center for Ecological Analysis and Synthesis, Intercampus Research Program on Mexican Literary and Cultural Studies, Orfalea Center for Global and International Studies.

Computer facilities: 700 computers available on campus for general student use. A campuswide network can be accessed from student residence rooms and from off campus. Online class registration is available. *Web address:* http://www.ucsb.edu/.

General Application Contact: Sierra Gray, Assistant Director of Graduate Admissions, 805-893-8000, Fax: 805-893-8259, E-mail: gradadmissions@graddiv.ucsb.edu.

GRADUATE UNITS

Graduate Division Students: 2,993 full-time (1,383 women); includes 52 Black or African American, non-Hispanic/Latino; 13 American Indian or Alaska Native, non-Hispanic/Latino; 568 Asian, non-Hispanic/Latino; 264 Hispanic/Latino; 5 Native Hawaiian or other Pacific Islander, non-Hispanic/Latino. Average age 28. 7,609 applicants, 25% accepted, 748 enrolled. *Faculty:* 838 full-time (260 women). Expenses: Contact institution. *Financial support:* In 2010–11, 2,520 students received support, including 1,420 fellowships with full and partial tuition reimbursements available (averaging $8,402 per year), 997 research assistantships with full and partial tuition reimbursements available (averaging $12,597 per year), 1,359 teaching assistantships with full and partial tuition reimbursements available (averaging $10,723 per year); career-related internships or fieldwork, Federal Work-Study, institutionally sponsored loans, scholarships/grants, traineeships, health care benefits, tuition waivers (full and partial), and unspecified assistantships also available. Support available to part-time students. Financial award applicants required to submit FAFSA. In 2010, 527 master's, 321 doctorates awarded. *Application fee:* $70 ($90 for international students). Electronic applications accepted. *Application Contact:* Graduate Admissions Coordinator, 805-893-2278, Fax: 805-893-8259, E-mail: gradadmissions@graddiv.ucsb.edu. *Dean,* Dr. Gale M. Morrison, 805-893-2013, Fax: 805-893-8259, E-mail: graddeans@graddiv.ucsb.edu.

College of Engineering Students: 663 full-time (133 women); includes 4 Black or African American, non-Hispanic/Latino; 2 American Indian or Alaska Native, non-Hispanic/Latino; 244 Asian, non-Hispanic/Latino; 23 Hispanic/Latino; 2 Native Hawaiian or other Pacific Islander, non-Hispanic/Latino. Average age 26. 2,463 applicants, 22% accepted, 176 enrolled. *Faculty:* 145 full-time (16 women), 17 part-time/adjunct (3 women). Expenses: Contact institution. *Financial support:* In 2010–11, 563 students received support, including 213 fellowships with full and partial tuition reimbursements available (averaging $9,216 per year), 455 research assistantships with full and partial tuition reimbursements available (averaging $14,350 per year), 204 teaching assistantships with partial tuition reimbursements available (averaging $8,128 per year); career-related internships or fieldwork, Federal Work-Study, institutionally sponsored loans, scholarships/grants, traineeships, health care benefits, tuition waivers (full and partial), and unspecified assistantships also available. Financial award applicants required to submit FAFSA. In 2010, 92 master's, 77 doctorates awarded. Offers chemical engineering (PhD); cognitive science (PhD); communications, control and signal processing (PhD); computational science and engineering (MS, PhD); computer engineering (MS); computer science (MS, PhD); electronics and photonics (MS); engineering (MS, PhD); materials (MS, PhD); mechanical engineering (MS, PhD); technology and society (PhD). *Application fee:* $70 ($90 for international students). Electronic applications accepted. *Application Contact:* 805-893-3207, E-mail: engrdean@engineering.ucsb.edu. *Dean,* Dr. Matthew Tirrell, 805-893-3141.

College of Letters and Sciences Students: 1,700 full-time (797 women); includes 28 Black or African American, non-Hispanic/Latino; 7 American Indian or Alaska Native, non-Hispanic/Latino; 232 Asian, non-Hispanic/Latino; 163 Hispanic/Latino; 3 Native Hawaiian or other Pacific Islander, non-Hispanic/Latino. Average age 29. 3,942 applicants, 22% accepted, 336 enrolled. *Faculty:* 788 full-time (255 women), 198 part-time/adjunct (85 women). Expenses: Contact institution. *Financial support:* In 2010–11, 1,583 students received support, including 902 fellowships with full and partial tuition reimbursements available (averaging $9,032 per year), 440 research assistantships with full and partial tuition reimbursements available (averaging $12,054 per year), 1,058 teaching assistantships with partial tuition reimbursements available (averaging $11,527 per year); career-related internships or fieldwork, Federal Work-Study, institutionally sponsored loans, scholarships/grants, traineeships, health care benefits, tuition waivers (full and partial), and unspecified assistantships also available. Support available to part-time students. Financial award applicants required to submit FAFSA. In 2010, 237 master's, 189 doctorates awarded. Offers ancient history (MA, PhD); ancient Mediterranean studies (PhD); ancient Mediterranean studies (PhD); applied linguistics (PhD); applied mathematics (MA); archaeology (MA); art (MFA); art history (PhD); biochemistry and molecular biology (PhD); biosocial anthropology (MA, PhD); brass (MM); chemistry (MA, MS, PhD); classics (MA, PhD); cognitive science (PhD); communication (PhD); comparative literature (PhD); composition (MA, PhD); computational science and engineering (MA); computational sciences and engineering (PhD); conducting (MM, DMA); East Asian language and cultural studies (MA, PhD); East Asian literatures (PhD); ecology, evolution, and marine biology (MA, PhD); economics (MA, PhD); economics and environmental science (PhD); electronic music and sound design (MA); English (PhD); ethnomusicology (MA, PhD); European medieval studies (PhD); feminist studies (PhD); film and media studies (PhD); financial mathematics and statistics (PhD); French (PhD); geography (MA, PhD); geological sciences (PhD); geophysics (MS); global culture and religion (MA); global government and human rights (MA); global studies (PhD); Hispanic languages and literatures (PhD); Hispanic linguistics (MA); history (PhD); humanities and fine arts (MA, MFA, MM, MS, DMA, PhD); keyboard (MM, DMA); language, interaction and social organization (PhD); language, interaction, and

University of California, Santa Barbara (continued)

social organizations (PhD); Latin American and Iberian studies (MA); letters and sciences (MA, MFA, MM, MS, DMA, PhD); linguistics (PhD); literature and theory (PhD); literature and theory (MA, PhD); Luso-Brazilian literature (MA); marine science (MS, PhD); mathematics (MA, PhD); mathematics, life, and physical sciences (MA, MS, PhD); media arts and technology (PhD); molecular, cellular, and developmental biology (MA, PhD); multimedia engineering (MS); musicology (MA, PhD); philosophy (PhD); physics (PhD); piano accompanying (MM); political economy, sustainable development, and the environment (MA); political science (MA, PhD); psychology (PhD); public history (PhD); quantitative methods in the social sciences (PhD); religious studies (MA, PhD); social sciences (MA, PhD); society and technology (PhD); sociocultural anthropology (MA, PhD); sociology (PhD); Spanish or Spanish-American literature (MA); statistics (MA); statistics and applied probability (PhD); strings (MM, DMA); technology and society (PhD); theater studies (MA, PhD); theory (MA, PhD); translation studies (PhD); transportation (PhD); visual and spatial arts (MA); voice (MM, DMA); woodwinds (MM). *Application fee:* $70 ($90 for international students). Electronic applications accepted. *Application Contact:* Dr. David Marshall, Executive Dean, 805-893-4327, E-mail: dmarshall@ltsc.ucsb.edu. *Executive Dean,* Dr. David Marshall, 805-893-4327, E-mail: dmarshall@ltsc.ucsb.edu.

Donald Bren School of Environmental Science and Management Students: 219 full-time (128 women); includes 1 Black or African American, non-Hispanic/Latino; 1 American Indian or Alaska Native, non-Hispanic/Latino; 33 Asian, non-Hispanic/Latino; 11 Hispanic/Latino. Average age 28. 521 applicants, 40% accepted, 82 enrolled. *Faculty:* 17 full-time (3 women), 2 part-time/adjunct (0 women). Expenses: Contact institution. *Financial support:* In 2010–11, 105 students received support, including 83 fellowships with full and partial tuition reimbursements available (averaging $6,929 per year), 27 research assistantships with full and partial tuition reimbursements available (averaging $8,918 per year), 32 teaching assistantships with partial tuition reimbursements available (averaging $8,112 per year); career-related internships or fieldwork and tuition waivers (full and partial) also available. Financial award application deadline: 12/15; financial award applicants required to submit FAFSA. In 2010, 75 master's awarded. Offers economics and environmental science (PhD); environmental science and management (MESM, PhD); technology and society (PhD). *Application deadline:* For fall admission, 12/15 priority date for domestic and international students. *Application fee:* $70 ($90 for international students). Electronic applications accepted. *Application Contact:* Graduate Advisor, 805-893-7611, Fax: 805-893-7612, E-mail: admissions@bren.ucsb.edu. *Assistant Dean, Planning and Administration,* Bryant Wieneke, 805-893-2212, Fax: 805-893-7612, E-mail: bryant@bren.ucsb.edu.

Gevirtz Graduate School of Education Students: 411 full-time (325 women); includes 19 Black or African American, non-Hispanic/Latino; 3 American Indian or Alaska Native, non-Hispanic/Latino; 59 Asian, non-Hispanic/Latino; 67 Hispanic/Latino. Average age 29. 683 applicants, 38% accepted, 154 enrolled. *Faculty:* 40 full-time (22 women), 5 part-time/adjunct (1 woman). Expenses: Contact institution. *Financial support:* In 2010–11, 269 students received support, including 222 fellowships with partial tuition reimbursements available (averaging $5,615 per year), 75 research assistantships with full tuition reimbursements available (averaging $6,470 per year), 65 teaching assistantships with partial tuition reimbursements available (averaging $7,059 per year); career-related internships or fieldwork also available. Financial award applicants required to submit FAFSA. In 2010, 128 master's, 58 doctorates awarded. Postbaccalaureate distance learning degree programs offered (minimal on-campus study). Offers counseling, clinical and school psychology (PhD); education (M Ed, MA, PhD); educational leadership (Ed D); school psychology (M Ed). *Application fee:* $70 ($90 for international students). Electronic applications accepted. *Application Contact:* Kathryn Marie Tucciarone, Student Affairs Officer, 805-893-2137, Fax: 805-893-2588, E-mail: katiet@education.ucsb.edu. *Graduate Advisor,* Carol North Dixon, 805-893-2185, E-mail: dixon@education.ucsb.edu.

UNIVERSITY OF CALIFORNIA, SANTA CRUZ, Santa Cruz, CA 95064

General Information State-supported, coed, university. CGS member. *Enrollment:* 17,175 graduate, professional, and undergraduate students; 1,423 full-time matriculated graduate/professional students (663 women), 95 part-time matriculated graduate/professional students (32 women). *Enrollment by degree level:* 307 master's, 1,192 doctoral, 19 other advanced degrees. *Graduate faculty:* 495 full-time (175 women). *Graduate housing:* Rooms and/or apartments available on a first-come, first-served basis to single and married students. Typical cost: $11,652 per year for single students; $16,884 per year for married students. Room charges vary according to board plan, campus/location and housing facility selected. Housing application deadline: 5/20. *Student services:* Campus employment opportunities, campus safety program, career counseling, child daycare facilities, exercise/wellness program, free psychological counseling, grant writing training, international student services, low-cost health insurance, multicultural affairs office, services for students with disabilities, teacher training, writing training. *Library facilities:* UCSC Library. *Online resources:* library catalog, web page, access to other libraries' catalogs. *Collection:* 2.2 million titles, 36,882 serial subscriptions, 66,139 audiovisual materials. *Research affiliation:* Center for Biomimetic MicroElectronic Systems (science and engineering), Center for Information Technology Research in the Interest of Society (science and engineering), Institute for Regenerative Medicine (science and engineering), Center for Adaptive Optics (science and engineering), Center for Biomolecular Science and Engineering (science and engineering), Institute for Quantitative Biology (science and engineering).

Computer facilities: A campuswide network can be accessed from student residence rooms and from off campus. Online class registration is available. *Web address:* http://www.ucsc.edu/.

General Application Contact: Veronica Williams, Graduate Admissions Assistant, 831-459-5905, Fax: 831-459-4843, E-mail: gradadm@ucsc.edu.

GRADUATE UNITS

Division of Graduate Studies Students: 1,423 full-time (663 women), 95 part-time (32 women); includes 343 minority (25 Black or African American, non-Hispanic/Latino; 4 American Indian or Alaska Native, non-Hispanic/Latino; 127 Asian, non-Hispanic/Latino; 153 Hispanic/Latino; 5 Native Hawaiian or other Pacific Islander, non-Hispanic/Latino; 29 Two or more races, non-Hispanic/Latino), 218 international. Average age 30. 3,288 applicants, 29% accepted, 414 enrolled. *Faculty:* 495 full-time (175 women). Expenses: Contact institution. *Financial support:* Fellowships, research assistantships, teaching assistantships, institutionally sponsored loans, health care benefits, and tuition waivers (full and partial) available. Support available to part-time students. Financial award applicants required to submit FAFSA. In 2010, 270 master's, 152 doctorates, 17 other advanced degrees awarded. *Application fee:* $70 ($90 for international students). Electronic applications accepted. *Application Contact:* Veronica Williams, Graduate Admissions Assistant, 831-459-5905, Fax: 831-459-4843, E-mail: gradadm@ucsc.edu. *Dean of Graduate Studies,* Tyrus Miller, 831-459-5079, Fax: 831-459-4843.

Division of Humanities Students: 160 full-time (81 women), 8 part-time (3 women); includes 6 Black or African American, non-Hispanic/Latino; 12 Asian, non-Hispanic/Latino; 14 Hispanic/Latino, 8 international. Average age 31. 299 applicants, 77% accepted, 113 enrolled. Expenses: Contact institution. *Financial support:* Fellowships, research assistantships, teaching assistantships, institutionally sponsored loans and tuition waivers available. Financial award applicants required to submit FAFSA. In 2010, 30 master's, 23 doctorates awarded. Offers history (MA, PhD); history of consciousness (PhD); humanities (MA, PhD); linguistics (MA, PhD); literature (MA, PhD); philosophy (MA, PhD). *Application fee:* $70 ($90 for international students). Electronic applications accepted. *Application Contact:* Veronica Williams, Graduate Admissions Assistant, 831-459-5905, Fax: 831-459-4843, E-mail: gradadm@ucsc.edu. *Dean,* William Ladusaw, 831-459-2696, E-mail: humdean@ucsc.edu.

Division of Physical and Biological Sciences Students: 455 full-time (211 women), 6 part-time (3 women); includes 6 Black or African American, non-Hispanic/Latino; 1 American Indian or Alaska Native, non-Hispanic/Latino; 25 Asian, non-Hispanic/Latino; 43 Hispanic/Latino; 7 Two or more races, non-Hispanic/Latino, 52 international. Average age 28. 1,052 applicants, 22% accepted, 113 enrolled. Expenses: Contact institution. *Financial support:* Fellowships, research assistantships, teaching assistantships, institutionally sponsored loans and tuition waivers available. Financial award applicants required to submit FAFSA. In 2010, 26 master's, 57 doctorates, 9 other advanced degrees awarded. Offers astronomy and astrophysics (PhD); chemistry and biochemistry (MS, PhD); earth and planetary sciences (MS, PhD); ecology and evolutionary biology (MA, PhD); environmental toxicology (MS, PhD); mathematics (MA, PhD); molecular, cellular, and developmental biology (MA, PhD); ocean sciences (MS, PhD); physical and biological sciences (MA, MS, PhD, Certificate); physics (MS, PhD); science communication (Certificate). *Application fee:* $70 ($90 for international students). Electronic applications accepted. *Application Contact:* Veronica Williams, Graduate Admissions Assistant, 831-459-5905, Fax: 831-459-4843, E-mail: gradadm@ucsc.edu. *Dean,* Dr. Stephen E. Thorsett, 831-459-2931, E-mail: pbsdean@lists.pbsci.ucsc.edu.

Division of Social Sciences Students: 434 full-time (263 women), 26 part-time (22 women); includes 137 minority (9 Black or African American, non-Hispanic/Latino; 2 American Indian or Alaska Native, non-Hispanic/Latino; 38 Asian, non-Hispanic/Latino; 69 Hispanic/Latino; 1 Native Hawaiian or other Pacific Islander, non-Hispanic/Latino; 18 Two or more races, non-Hispanic/Latino), 56 international. Average age 30. 975 applicants, 40% accepted, 181 enrolled. Expenses: Contact institution. *Financial support:* Fellowships, research assistantships, teaching assistantships, institutionally sponsored loans and tuition waivers (partial) available. Financial award applicants required to submit FAFSA. In 2010, 144 master's, 37 doctorates awarded. Offers applied economics and finance (MS); cultural anthropology (PhD); education (MA, PhD); environmental studies (PhD); international economics (PhD); politics (PhD); psychology (PhD); social documentation (MA); social sciences (MA, MS, PhD); sociology (PhD). *Application fee:* $70 ($90 for international students). Electronic applications accepted. *Application Contact:* Sheldon Kamieniecki, Dean, 831-459-3212, E-mail: socialsciences@ucsc.edu. *Dean,* Sheldon Kamieniecki, 831-459-3212, E-mail: socialsciences@ucsc.edu.

Division of the Arts Students: 60 full-time (27 women), 5 part-time (2 women); includes 18 minority (1 Black or African American, non-Hispanic/Latino; 10 Asian, non-Hispanic/Latino; 4 Hispanic/Latino; 1 Native Hawaiian or other Pacific Islander, non-Hispanic/Latino; 2 Two or more races, non-Hispanic/Latino), 4 international. Average age 32. 244 applicants, 23% accepted, 35 enrolled. Expenses: Contact institution. *Financial support:* Fellowships, research assistantships, teaching assistantships, institutionally sponsored loans and tuition waivers available. Financial award application deadline: 2/1; financial award applicants required to submit FAFSA. In 2010, 25 master's, 1 doctorate, 8 other advanced degrees awarded. Offers arts (MA, MFA, DMA, PhD, Certificate); digital arts and new media (MFA); ethnomusicology (MA); film and digital media (PhD); music (PhD); music composition (MA, DMA); music composition (DMA); performance practice (MA); theater arts (Certificate); visual studies (PhD). *Application fee:* $70 ($90 for international students). Electronic applications accepted. *Application Contact:* David Yager, Dean, 831-459-4940, E-mail: artsdiv@ucsc.edu. *Dean,* David Yager, 831-459-4940, E-mail: artsdiv@ucsc.edu.

Jack Baskin School of Engineering Students: 314 full-time (81 women), 51 part-time (3 women); includes 71 minority (3 Black or African American, non-Hispanic/Latino; 1 American Indian or Alaska Native, non-Hispanic/Latino; 42 Asian, non-Hispanic/Latino; 23 Hispanic/Latino; 2 Two or more races, non-Hispanic/Latino), 98 international. Average age 31. 718 applicants, 30% accepted, 67 enrolled. Expenses: Contact institution. *Financial support:* Fellowships, research assistantships, teaching assistantships, institutionally sponsored loans and tuition waivers available. Financial award applicants required to submit FAFSA. In 2010, 45 master's, 34 doctorates awarded. Offers bioinformatics (MS, PhD); computer engineering (MS, PhD); computer science (MS, PhD); electrical engineering (MS, PhD); engineering (MS, PhD); network engineering (MS); statistics and applied mathematics (MS, PhD); technology and information management (MS, PhD). *Application fee:* $70 ($90 for international students). Electronic applications accepted. *Application Contact:* Veronica Williams, Graduate Admissions Assistant, 831-459-5905, Fax: 831-459-4843, E-mail: gradadm@ucsc.edu. *Dean,* Arthur Ramirez, 831-459-2158, Fax: 831-459-4046, E-mail: apr@soe.ucsc.edu.

UNIVERSITY OF CENTRAL ARKANSAS, Conway, AR 72035-0001

General Information State-supported, coed, university. CGS member. *Enrollment:* 754 full-time matriculated graduate/professional students (540 women), 828 part-time matriculated graduate/professional students (668 women). *Graduate housing:* Rooms and/or apartments available on a first-come, first-served basis to single and married students. Housing application deadline: 7/1. *Student services:* Campus employment opportunities, campus safety program, career counseling, exercise/wellness program, free psychological counseling, grant writing training, international student services, low-cost health insurance, multicultural affairs office, services for students with disabilities, teacher training, writing training. *Library facilities:* Torreyson Library. *Online resources:* library catalog. *Collection:* 600,084 titles, 804 serial subscriptions, 2,063 audiovisual materials. *Research affiliation:* 3M Corporation, State Farm Foundation (insurance), Arkansas Game and Fish Commission, Acxiom (math, computers), AETN.

Computer facilities: 608 computers available on campus for general student use. A campuswide network can be accessed from student residence rooms and from off campus. Online class registration is available. *Web address:* http://www.uca.edu/.

General Application Contact: Brenda Herring, Admissions Assistant, 501-450-3124, Fax: 501-450-5678, E-mail: bherring@uca.edu.

GRADUATE UNITS

Graduate School Students: 756 full-time (542 women), 865 part-time (700 women); includes 215 minority (139 Black or African American, non-Hispanic/Latino; 19 American Indian or Alaska Native, non-Hispanic/Latino; 19 Asian, non-Hispanic/Latino; 31 Hispanic/Latino; 7 Two or more races, non-Hispanic/Latino), 33 international. Average age 31. 728 applicants, 92% accepted. *Faculty:* 220 full-time (83 women), 7 part-time/adjunct (4 women). Expenses: Contact institution. *Financial support:* In 2010–11, 48 research assistantships with partial tuition reimbursements (averaging $6,000 per year), 34 teaching assistantships with partial tuition reimbursements (averaging $9,000 per year) were awarded; career-related internships or fieldwork, Federal Work-Study, scholarships/grants, traineeships, tuition waivers (partial), and unspecified assistantships also available. Support available to part-time students. Financial award application deadline: 2/15; financial award applicants required to submit FAFSA. In 2010, 547 master's, 54 doctorates awarded. *Degree program information:* Part-time programs available. *Application deadline:* For fall admission, 3/1 priority date for domestic and international students; for spring admission, 10/1 priority date for domestic and international students. Applications are processed on a rolling basis. *Application fee:* $25 ($50 for international students). *Application Contact:* Brenda Herring, Admissions Assistant, 501-450-5065, Fax: 501-450-5678, E-mail: bherring@uca.edu. *Dean,* Dr. Elaine M. McNiece, 501-450-3124, Fax: 501-450-5678, E-mail: elainem@uca.edu.

College of Business Administration Students: 45 full-time (17 women), 20 part-time (10 women); includes 7 minority (4 Black or African American, non-Hispanic/Latino; 1 American Indian or Alaska Native, non-Hispanic/Latino; 1 Asian, non-Hispanic/Latino; 1 Two or more races, non-Hispanic/Latino), 5 international. Average age 25. *Faculty:* 27 full-time (6 women). Expenses: Contact institution. *Financial support:* In 2010–11, 8 research assistantships with full tuition reimbursements (averaging $7,000 per year) were awarded; career-related internships or fieldwork, Federal Work-Study, scholarships/grants, and unspecified assistantships also available. Support available to part-time students. Financial award application deadline: 2/15; financial award applicants required to submit FAFSA. In 2010, 50 master's awarded. *Degree program information:* Part-time and evening/weekend programs available. Offers accounting (M Acc); business administration (M Acc, MBA). *Application deadline:* For fall admission, 3/1 priority date for domestic and international students; for spring admission, 10/1 priority date for domestic and international students. Applications are processed on a rolling basis. *Application fee:* $25 ($50 for international students). *Application Contact:* Dr. Pat Cantrell, Dean, 501-450-5323, E-mail: patc@uca.edu. *Dean,* Dr. Pat Cantrell, 501-450-5323, E-mail: patc@uca.edu.

College of Education Students: 103 full-time (78 women), 446 part-time (376 women); includes 86 minority (65 Black or African American, non-Hispanic/Latino; 5 American Indian or Alaska Native, non-Hispanic/Latino; 5 Asian, non-Hispanic/Latino; 7 Hispanic/Latino; 4

Two or more races, non-Hispanic/Latino), 2 international. Average age 32. Expenses: Contact institution. *Financial support:* Career-related internships or fieldwork, Federal Work-Study, scholarships/grants, tuition waivers (partial), and unspecified assistantships available. Financial award application deadline: 2/15; financial award applicants required to submit FAFSA. In 2010, 2,138 master's awarded. *Degree program information:* Part-time programs available. Offers collaborative instructional specialist (ages 0-8) (MSE); collaborative instructional specialist (grades 4-12) (MSE); college student personnel (MS); education (MAT, MS, MSE, Ed S); educational leadership—district level (Ed S); instructional technology (MS); library media and information technology (MS); reading education (MSE); school counseling (MS); school leadership (MS); special education (MSE); teaching (MAT); teaching and learning (MAT, MSE). *Application deadline:* For fall admission, 3/1 priority date for domestic and international students; for spring admission, 10/1 priority date for domestic and international students. Applications are processed on a rolling basis. *Application fee:* $25 ($50 for international students). *Application Contact:* Bridget Burroughs, Admissions Assistant, 501-450-3124, Fax: 501-450-5678, E-mail: bburroughs@uca.edu. *Interim Dean,* Dr. Diane Pounder, 501-450-5401, Fax: 501-450-5424, E-mail: dpounder@uca.edu.

College of Fine Arts and Communication Students: 31 full-time (11 women), 13 part-time (4 women); includes 5 minority (3 Black or African American, non-Hispanic/Latino; 1 American Indian or Alaska Native, non-Hispanic/Latino; 1 Asian, non-Hispanic/Latino), 3 international. Average age 29. Expenses: Contact institution. *Financial support:* Federal Work-Study, scholarships/grants, tuition waivers (partial), and unspecified assistantships available. Financial award application deadline: 2/15; financial award applicants required to submit FAFSA. In 2010, 10 master's awarded. *Degree program information:* Part-time programs available. Offers choral conducting (MM); digital filmmaking (MFA); fine arts and communication (MFA, MM); instrumental conducting (MM); music education (MM); music theory (MM); performance (MM). *Application deadline:* For fall admission, 3/1 priority date for domestic students; for spring admission, 10/1 priority date for domestic students. Applications are processed on a rolling basis. *Application fee:* $25 ($50 for international students). *Application Contact:* Susan Wood, Admissions Assistant, 501-450-5065, Fax: 501-450-5678, E-mail: swood@uca.edu. *Dean,* Dr. Rollin Potter, 501-450-3167, Fax: 501-450-3296, E-mail: rpotter@uca.edu.

College of Health and Behavioral Sciences Students: 491 full-time (395 women), 263 part-time (243 women); includes 85 minority (52 Black or African American, non-Hispanic/Latino; 9 American Indian or Alaska Native, non-Hispanic/Latino; 10 Asian, non-Hispanic/Latino; 14 Hispanic/Latino), 5 international. Average age 28. Expenses: Contact institution. *Financial support:* Career-related internships or fieldwork, Federal Work-Study, scholarships/grants, traineeships, tuition waivers (partial), and unspecified assistantships available. Support available to part-time students. Financial award application deadline: 2/15; financial award applicants required to submit FAFSA. In 2010, 228 master's, 54 doctorates awarded. Offers clinical nurse specialist (MSN); communication sciences and disorders (PhD); community counseling (MS); counseling psychology (MS); family and consumer sciences (MS); health and behavioral sciences (MS, MSN, DPT, PhD); health education (MS); health systems (MS); kinesiology (MS); nurse practitioner (MSN); occupational therapy (MS); physical therapy (DPT, PhD); school psychology (MS, PhD); speech-language pathology (MS). *Application deadline:* For fall admission, 3/1 priority date for domestic and international students; for spring admission, 10/1 for domestic and international students. Applications are processed on a rolling basis. *Application fee:* $25 ($50 for international students). *Application Contact:* Susan Wood, Administrative Assistant, 501-450-3124, Fax: 501-450-5678, E-mail: swood@uca.edu. *Dean,* Dr. Neil Hattlestad, 501-450-3122, Fax: 501-450-5503, E-mail: neilh@uca.edu.

College of Liberal Arts Students: 35 full-time (18 women), 61 part-time (23 women); includes 17 minority (9 Black or African American, non-Hispanic/Latino; 1 American Indian or Alaska Native, non-Hispanic/Latino; 5 Hispanic/Latino; 2 Two or more races, non-Hispanic/Latino), 2 international. Average age 31. 46 applicants, 98% accepted, 38 enrolled. *Faculty:* 39 full-time (8 women). Expenses: Contact institution. *Financial support:* In 2010–11, 2 teaching assistantships with partial tuition reimbursements (averaging $10,000 per year) were awarded; Federal Work-Study, scholarships/grants, and unspecified assistantships also available. Financial award application deadline: 2/15; financial award applicants required to submit FAFSA. In 2010, 24 master's awarded. *Degree program information:* Part-time programs available. Offers community and economic development (MS); English (MA); foreign languages (MA); geographic information systems (MGIS, Certificate); history (MA); liberal arts (MA, MGIS, MS, Certificate). *Application deadline:* For fall admission, 3/1 priority date for domestic students; for spring admission, 10/1 priority date for domestic students. Applications are processed on a rolling basis. *Application fee:* $25 ($50 for international students). *Application Contact:* Susan Wood, Admissions Assistant, 501-450-3124, Fax: 501-450-5678, E-mail: swood@uca.edu. *Dean,* Maurice Lee, 501-450-3167, Fax: 501-450-5185, E-mail: mauricel@uca.edu.

College of Natural Sciences and Math Students: 49 full-time (21 women), 25 part-time (12 women); includes 6 minority (2 Black or African American, non-Hispanic/Latino; 1 American Indian or Alaska Native, non-Hispanic/Latino; 2 Asian, non-Hispanic/Latino; 1 Hispanic/Latino), 15 international. Average age 28. 49 applicants, 94% accepted, 28 enrolled. *Faculty:* 40 full-time (10 women). Expenses: Contact institution. *Financial support:* In 2010–11, 4 research assistantships (averaging $8,000 per year) were awarded; career-related internships or fieldwork, Federal Work-Study, and unspecified assistantships also available. Financial award application deadline: 2/15; financial award applicants required to submit FAFSA. In 2010, 27 master's awarded. *Degree program information:* Part-time programs available. Offers applied computing (MS); applied mathematics (MS); biological science (MS); math education (MA); natural sciences and math (MA, MS). *Application deadline:* For fall admission, 3/1 priority date for domestic and international students; for spring admission, 10/1 priority date for domestic and international students. Applications are processed on a rolling basis. *Application fee:* $25 ($50 for international students). *Application Contact:* Susan Wood, Admissions Assistant, 501-450-3124, Fax: 501-450-5678, E-mail: swood@uca.edu. *Dean,* Dr. Steven Runge, 501-450-3199, Fax: 501-450-5084.

UNIVERSITY OF CENTRAL FLORIDA, Orlando, FL 32816

General Information State-supported, coed, university. CGS member. *Enrollment:* 56,235 graduate, professional, and undergraduate students; 3,974 full-time matriculated graduate/professional students (2,187 women), 3,943 part-time matriculated graduate/professional students (2,405 women). *Enrollment by degree level:* 5,457 master's, 1,716 doctoral, 374 other advanced degrees. *Graduate faculty:* 1,149 full-time (434 women), 529 part-time/adjunct (278 women). Tuition, state resident: part-time $256.56 per credit hour. Tuition, nonresident: part-time $1011.52 per credit hour. Part-time tuition and fees vary according to program. *Graduate housing:* Room and/or apartments available on a first-come, first-served basis to single students; on-campus housing not available to married students. Typical cost: $5700 per year ($8765 including board). Room and board charges vary according to board plan, campus/location and housing facility selected. Housing application deadline: 3/1. *Student services:* Campus employment opportunities, campus safety program, career counseling, child daycare facilities, exercise/wellness program, free psychological counseling, grant writing training, international student services, low-cost health insurance, multicultural affairs office, services for students with disabilities, teacher training, writing training. *Library facilities:* University Library. *Online resources:* library catalog, web page, access to other libraries' catalogs. *Collection:* 2.4 million titles, 29,659 serial subscriptions, 50,517 audiovisual materials.

Computer facilities: Computer purchase and lease plans are available. 3,200 computers available on campus for general student use. A campuswide network can be accessed from student residence rooms and from off campus. Online class registration is available. *Web address:* http://www.ucf.edu/.

General Application Contact: Barbara Rodriguez, Associate Director, Admissions and Registration, 407-823-2766, Fax: 407-823-6442, E-mail: gradadmissions@ucf.edu.

GRADUATE UNITS

College of Arts and Humanities Students: 268 full-time (120 women), 266 part-time (133 women); includes 18 Black or African American, non-Hispanic/Latino; 1 American Indian or Alaska Native, non-Hispanic/Latino; 24 Asian, non-Hispanic/Latino; 63 Hispanic/Latino; 3 Two or more races, non-Hispanic/Latino, 16 international. Average age 31. 502 applicants, 59% accepted, 207 enrolled. *Faculty:* 251 full-time (114 women), 108 part-time/adjunct (59 women). Expenses: Contact institution. *Financial support:* In 2010–11, 116 students received support, including 29 fellowships with partial tuition reimbursements available (averaging $7,500 per year), 22 research assistantships with partial tuition reimbursements available (averaging $6,600 per year), 82 teaching assistantships with partial tuition reimbursements available (averaging $7,200 per year); career-related internships or fieldwork, Federal Work-Study, institutionally sponsored loans, scholarships/grants, tuition waivers (partial), and unspecified assistantships also available. Financial award application deadline: 3/1; financial award applicants required to submit FAFSA. In 2010, 133 master's, 5 doctorates, 25 other advanced degrees awarded. *Degree program information:* Part-time and evening/weekend programs available. Offers arts and humanities (MA, MFA, MS, PhD, Certificate); creative writing (MFA); digital media (MA); emerging media (MFA); English (MA, MFA, Certificate); history (MA); music (MA); professional writing (Certificate); Spanish (MA); teaching English to speakers of other languages (MA, Certificate); texts and technology (PhD); theatre (MA, MFA). *Application fee:* $30. Electronic applications accepted. *Application Contact:* Dr. Jose Fernandez, Dean, 407-823-2573, E-mail: jfernandez@mail.ucf.edu. *Dean,* Dr. Jose Fernandez, 407-823-2573, E-mail: jfernandez@mail.ucf.edu.

Division of Film and Digital Media Students: 14 full-time (3 women), 4 part-time (0 women); includes 1 Black or African American, non-Hispanic/Latino; 2 Hispanic/Latino, 1 international. Average age 27. 21 applicants, 38% accepted, 7 enrolled. *Faculty:* 16 full-time (5 women), 3 part-time/adjunct (2 women). Expenses: Contact institution. *Financial support:* In 2010–11, 10 students received support, including 2 fellowships with partial tuition reimbursements available (averaging $5,300 per year), 9 teaching assistantships (averaging $5,500 per year). In 2010, 5 master's awarded. Offers film and digital media (MFA). *Application fee:* $30. *Application Contact:* Stephen Schlow, Interim Chair, 407-823-2845, Fax: 407-823-3659, E-mail: sschlow@mail.ucf.edu. *Interim Chair,* Stephen Schlow, 407-823-2845, Fax: 407-823-3659, E-mail: sschlow@mail.ucf.edu.

Florida Interactive Entertainment Academy Students: 60 full-time (11 women), 48 part-time (5 women); includes 2 Black or African American, non-Hispanic/Latino; 11 Asian, non-Hispanic/Latino; 17 Hispanic/Latino, 7 international. Average age 25. 133 applicants, 57% accepted, 59 enrolled. Expenses: Contact institution. Offers interactive entertainment (MS). *Application Contact:* Ben Noel, Executive Director, 407-235-3612, Fax: 407-317-7094, E-mail: bnoel@fiea.ucf.edu. *Executive Director,* Ben Noel, 407-235-3612, Fax: 407-317-7094, E-mail: bnoel@fiea.ucf.edu.

College of Business Administration Students: 444 full-time (181 women), 457 part-time (188 women); includes 203 minority (61 Black or African American, non-Hispanic/Latino; 4 American Indian or Alaska Native, non-Hispanic/Latino; 62 Asian, non-Hispanic/Latino; 71 Hispanic/Latino; 3 Native Hawaiian or other Pacific Islander, non-Hispanic/Latino; 2 Two or more races, non-Hispanic/Latino), 69 international. Average age 29. 861 applicants, 47% accepted, 301 enrolled. *Faculty:* 110 full-time (31 women), 19 part-time/adjunct (4 women). Expenses: Contact institution. *Financial support:* In 2010–11, 119 students received support, including 14 fellowships with partial tuition reimbursements available (averaging $8,000 per year), 47 research assistantships with partial tuition reimbursements available (averaging $4,900 per year), 82 teaching assistantships with partial tuition reimbursements available (averaging $11,400 per year); career-related internships or fieldwork, Federal Work-Study, institutionally sponsored loans, tuition waivers (partial), and unspecified assistantships also available. Financial award application deadline: 3/1; financial award applicants required to submit FAFSA. In 2010, 444 master's, 12 doctorates, 9 other advanced degrees awarded. *Degree program information:* Part-time and evening/weekend programs available. Offers business administration (MBA, MSA, MSBM, MSM, MSRE, MST, PhD, Graduate Certificate); entrepreneurship (Graduate Certificate); management (MSM); sport business management (MSBM); technology ventures (Graduate Certificate). *Application deadline:* For spring admission, 11/1 priority date for domestic students. *Application fee:* $30. Electronic applications accepted. *Application Contact:* Judy Ryder, Director, Graduate Admissions, 407-823-2364, Fax: 407-823-0219, E-mail: jryder@bus.ucf.edu. *Interim Dean,* Dr. Foard F. Jones, 407-823-0508, E-mail: thomas.keon@bus.ucf.edu.

Dr. P. Phillips School of Real Estate Expenses: Contact institution. *Degree program information:* Part-time programs available. Offers real estate (MSRE). *Application Contact:* Judy Ryder, Director, Graduate Admissions, 407-823-2364, Fax: 407-823-0219, E-mail: jryder@bus.ucf.edu. *Chair,* Dr. Randy I. Anderson, 407-823-3575, Fax: 407-823-6676, E-mail: randerson@bus.ucf.edu.

Kenneth G. Dixon School of Accounting Students: 108 full-time (47 women), 114 part-time (56 women); includes 10 Black or African American, non-Hispanic/Latino; 22 Asian, non-Hispanic/Latino; 16 Hispanic/Latino; 2 Native Hawaiian or other Pacific Islander, non-Hispanic/Latino, 10 international. Average age 28. 166 applicants, 58% accepted, 69 enrolled. *Faculty:* 21 full-time (9 women), 2 part-time/adjunct (1 woman). Expenses: Contact institution. *Financial support:* In 2010–11, 7 students received support, including 1 research assistantship (averaging $7,100 per year), 6 teaching assistantships with partial tuition reimbursements available (averaging $6,400 per year); career-related internships or fieldwork, Federal Work-Study, institutionally sponsored loans, tuition waivers (partial), and unspecified assistantships also available. Financial award application deadline: 3/1; financial award applicants required to submit FAFSA. In 2010, 89 master's awarded. *Degree program information:* Part-time and evening/weekend programs available. Offers accounting (MSA, MST); taxation (MST). *Application deadline:* For fall admission, 6/15 priority date for domestic students; for spring admission, 11/1 priority date for domestic students. Electronic applications accepted. *Application Contact:* Dr. Sean Robb, Director, 407-823-2871, Fax: 407-823-3881, E-mail: srobb@bus.ucf.edu. *Director,* Dr. Sean Robb, 407-823-2871, Fax: 407-823-3881, E-mail: srobb@bus.ucf.edu.

College of Education Students: 744 full-time (545 women), 1,073 part-time (854 women); includes 380 minority (185 Black or African American, non-Hispanic/Latino; 3 American Indian or Alaska Native, non-Hispanic/Latino; 38 Asian, non-Hispanic/Latino; 140 Hispanic/Latino; 1 Native Hawaiian or other Pacific Islander, non-Hispanic/Latino; 13 Two or more races, non-Hispanic/Latino), 44 international. Average age 32. 1,145 applicants, 66% accepted, 518 enrolled. *Faculty:* 129 full-time (83 women), 140 part-time/adjunct (96 women). Expenses: Contact institution. *Financial support:* In 2010–11, 152 students received support, including 63 fellowships with partial tuition reimbursements available (averaging $6,200 per year), 72 research assistantships with partial tuition reimbursements available (averaging $5,500 per year), 77 teaching assistantships with partial tuition reimbursements available (averaging $7,100 per year); career-related internships or fieldwork, Federal Work-Study, institutionally sponsored loans, tuition waivers (partial), and unspecified assistantships also available. Financial award application deadline: 3/1; financial award applicants required to submit FAFSA. In 2010, 414 master's, 63 doctorates, 224 other advanced degrees awarded. *Degree program information:* Part-time and evening/weekend programs available. Offers autism spectrum disorders (Certificate); career counseling (Certificate); communication sciences and disorders (PhD); community college education (Certificate); counselor education (M Ed, MA, PhD, Ed S); early childhood development and education (MS); early childhood education (MS); education (M Ed, MA, MAT, MS, Ed D, PhD, Certificate, Ed S); educational leadership (MA, Ed D); elementary education (PhD); exceptional education (PhD); exceptional student education (M Ed, MA, Certificate); exercise physiology (PhD); health and wellness (Certificate); higher education (PhD); hospitality education (PhD); instructional design for simulations (Certificate); instructional systems (MA, Certificate); instructional technology (PhD); marriage and family therapy (MA, Certificate); mathematics education (PhD); mental health counseling (MA); online educational media (Certificate); play therapy (Certificate); reading education (PhD); school counseling (M Ed, MA, Ed S); school psychology (Ed S); science education (PhD); severe or profound disabilities (Certificate); social science education (PhD); special education (Certificate); sport and exercise science (MS, Certificate); sports leadership (Certificate); TESOL (PhD). *Application fee:* $30. Electronic applications accepted. *Application Contact:* Dr. Sandra L. Robinson, Dean, 407-823-5529, E-mail: sandra.robinson@ucf.edu. *Dean,* Dr. Sandra L. Robinson, 407-823-5529, E-mail: sandra.robinson@ucf.edu.

School of Teaching, Learning, and Leadership Students: 210 full-time (170 women), 569 part-time (474 women); includes 158 minority (68 Black or African American, non-Hispanic/Latino; 2 American Indian or Alaska Native, non-Hispanic/Latino; 17 Asian, non-Hispanic/

University of Central Florida (continued)

Latino; 63 Hispanic/Latino; 1 Native Hawaiian or other Pacific Islander, non-Hispanic/Latino; 7 Two or more races, non-Hispanic/Latino), 13 international. Average age 32. 383 applicants, 71% accepted, 190 enrolled. *Faculty:* 73 full-time (49 women), 85 part-time/adjunct (64 women). Expenses: Contact institution. *Financial support:* In 2010–11, 12 students received support, including 1 fellowship with partial tuition reimbursement available (averaging $1,300 per year), 3 research assistantships with partial tuition reimbursements available (averaging $4,800 per year), 7 teaching assistantships with partial tuition reimbursements available (averaging $9,700 per year); career-related internships or fieldwork, Federal Work-Study, institutionally sponsored loans, tuition waivers (partial), and unspecified assistantships also available. Financial award application deadline: 3/1; financial award applicants required to submit FAFSA. In 2010, 163 master's, 69 other advanced degrees awarded. *Degree program information:* Part-time and evening/weekend programs available. Offers applied learning and instruction (MA); art education (M Ed, MAT); career and technical education (MA); community college education (Certificate); e-learning (MA, Certificate); education (Ed S); educational leadership (Ed S); educational studies (MA, Certificate, Ed S); educational technology (MA, Certificate); elementary education (M Ed, MA); English language arts education (M Ed, MAT); gifted education (Certificate); global and comparative education (Certificate); initial teacher professional preparation (Certificate); instructional technology/media (MA, Certificate); K-8 mathematics and science education (M Ed, Certificate); mathematics education (M Ed, MAT); reading education (M Ed, Certificate); science education (M Ed, MAT); social science education (M Ed, MAT); teacher education (MAT); teacher leadership (M Ed); teaching excellence (Certificate); urban education (Certificate). *Application deadline:* For fall admission, 7/15 for domestic students; for spring admission, 12/15 for domestic students. *Application fee:* $30. Electronic applications accepted. *Application Contact:* Dr. Michael C. Hynes, Chair, 407-823-6076, E-mail: hynes@mail.ucf.edu. *Chair*, Dr. Michael C. Hynes, 407-823-6076, E-mail: hynes@mail.ucf.edu.

College of Engineering and Computer Science Students: 644 full-time (139 women), 654 part-time (145 women); includes 279 minority (69 Black or African American, non-Hispanic/Latino; 2 American Indian or Alaska Native, non-Hispanic/Latino; 73 Asian, non-Hispanic/Latino; 120 Hispanic/Latino; 2 Native Hawaiian or other Pacific Islander, non-Hispanic/Latino; 13 Two or more races, non-Hispanic/Latino), 377 international. Average age 30. 1,233 applicants, 71% accepted, 367 enrolled. *Faculty:* 114 full-time (15 women), 40 part-time/adjunct (4 women). Expenses: Contact institution. *Financial support:* In 2010–11, 320 students received support, including 64 fellowships with partial tuition reimbursements available (averaging $6,000 per year), 289 research assistantships with partial tuition reimbursements available (averaging $8,300 per year), 140 teaching assistantships with partial tuition reimbursements available (averaging $7,700 per year); career-related internships or fieldwork, Federal Work-Study, institutionally sponsored loans, tuition waivers (partial), and unspecified assistantships also available. Financial award application deadline: 3/1; financial award applicants required to submit FAFSA. In 2010, 250 master's, 67 doctorates, 35 other advanced degrees awarded. *Degree program information:* Part-time and evening/weekend programs available. Offers aerospace engineering (MSAE); applied operations research (Certificate); CAD/CAM technology (Certificate); civil engineering (MS, MSCE, PhD, Certificate); computer engineering (MS Cp E, PhD); computer science (MS, PhD); construction engineering (Certificate); design for usability (Certificate); digital forensics (MS); electrical engineering (MSEE, PhD, Certificate); electronic circuits (Certificate); engineering and computer science (MS, MS Cp E, MS Env E, MSAE, MSCE, MSEE, MSIE, MSME, MSMSE, PhD, Certificate); environmental engineering (MS, MS Env E, PhD); HVAC engineering (Certificate); industrial engineering (MSIE, PhD); industrial engineering and management systems (MS); industrial ergonomics and safety (Certificate); materials science and engineering (MSMSE, PhD); mechanical engineering (MSME, PhD, Certificate); project engineering (Certificate); quality assurance (Certificate); structural engineering (Certificate); systems engineering (Certificate); systems simulation for engineers (Certificate); training simulation (Certificate); transportation engineering (Certificate). *Application deadline:* For fall admission, 7/15 for domestic students; for spring admission, 12/1 for domestic students. *Application fee:* $30. Electronic applications accepted. *Application Contact:* Dr. Marwan Simaan, Dean, 407-823-2156, E-mail: simaan@eecs.ucf.edu. *Dean*, Dr. Marwan Simaan, 407-823-2156, E-mail: simaan@eecs.ucf.edu.

College of Graduate Studies Students: 132 full-time (61 women), 72 part-time (22 women); includes 6 Black or African American, non-Hispanic/Latino; 1 American Indian or Alaska Native, non-Hispanic/Latino; 8 Asian, non-Hispanic/Latino; 20 Hispanic/Latino, 40 international. Average age 33. 143 applicants, 61% accepted, 58 enrolled. Expenses: Contact institution. *Financial support:* In 2010–11, 85 students received support, including 18 fellowships (averaging $8,000 per year), 82 research assistantships (averaging $9,700 per year), 36 teaching assistantships (averaging $9,400 per year). In 2010, 25 master's, 14 doctorates awarded. Offers biomedical sciences (MS, PhD); interdisciplinary studies (MA, MS); modeling and simulation (MS, PhD). *Application Contact:* Dr. Patricia Bishop, Vice Provost and Dean, 407-823-2766, Fax: 407-823-6442, E-mail: pbishop@mail.ucf.edu. *Vice Provost and Dean*, Dr. Patricia Bishop, 407-823-2766, Fax: 407-823-6442, E-mail: pbishop@mail.ucf.edu.

College of Health and Public Affairs Students: 871 full-time (679 women), 818 part-time (599 women); includes 520 minority (297 Black or African American, non-Hispanic/Latino; 8 American Indian or Alaska Native, non-Hispanic/Latino; 64 Asian, non-Hispanic/Latino; 140 Hispanic/Latino; 2 Native Hawaiian or other Pacific Islander, non-Hispanic/Latino; 9 Two or more races, non-Hispanic/Latino), 42 international. Average age 30. 1,277 applicants, 71% accepted, 625 enrolled. *Faculty:* 130 full-time (67 women), 108 part-time/adjunct (54 women). Expenses: Contact institution. *Financial support:* In 2010–11, 81 students received support, including 27 fellowships with partial tuition reimbursements available (averaging $8,400 per year), 30 research assistantships with partial tuition reimbursements available (averaging $5,700 per year), 43 teaching assistantships with partial tuition reimbursements available (averaging $5,300 per year); career-related internships or fieldwork, Federal Work-Study, institutionally sponsored loans, traineeships, tuition waivers (partial), and unspecified assistantships also available. Financial award application deadline: 3/1; financial award applicants required to submit FAFSA. In 2010, 358 master's, 38 doctorates, 47 other advanced degrees awarded. *Degree program information:* Part-time and evening/weekend programs available. Offers child language disorders (Certificate); communication sciences and disorders (MA); corrections leadership (Certificate); crime analysis (Certificate); criminal justice (MS); emergency management and homeland security (Certificate); health and public affairs (MA, MNM, MPA, MS, MSW, DPT, PhD, Certificate); health care informatics (MS, Certificate); health sciences (MS); juvenile justice leadership (Certificate); medical speech-language pathology (Certificate); non-profit management (MNM, Certificate); physical therapy (DPT); police leadership (Certificate); public administration (MPA, Certificate); public affairs (PhD); research administration (MS); urban and regional planning (Certificate). Electronic applications accepted. *Application Contact:* Dr. Michael Frumkin, Dean, 407-823-0171, E-mail: mfrumkin@mail.ucf.edu. *Dean*, Dr. Michael Frumkin, 407-823-0171, E-mail: mfrumkin@mail.ucf.edu.

School of Social Work Students: 190 full-time (176 women), 169 part-time (138 women); includes 78 Black or African American, non-Hispanic/Latino; 2 American Indian or Alaska Native, non-Hispanic/Latino; 6 Asian, non-Hispanic/Latino; 38 Hispanic/Latino; 4 Two or more races, non-Hispanic/Latino, 3 international. Average age 32. 337 applicants, 82% accepted, 207 enrolled. *Faculty:* 20 full-time (16 women), 23 part-time/adjunct (18 women). Expenses: Contact institution. *Financial support:* In 2010–11, 4 students received support, including 3 fellowships with partial tuition reimbursements available (averaging $10,000 per year), 1 research assistantship with partial tuition reimbursement available (averaging $7,100 per year); career-related internships or fieldwork, Federal Work-Study, institutionally sponsored loans, and unspecified assistantships also available. Financial award application deadline: 3/1; financial award applicants required to submit FAFSA. In 2010, 88 master's, 5 other advanced degrees awarded. *Degree program information:* Part-time and evening/weekend programs available. Offers aging studies (Certificate); children's services (Certificate); social work (MSW); social work administration (Certificate). *Application deadline:* For fall admission, 3/1 for domestic students. *Application fee:* $30. Electronic applications accepted. *Application Contact:* Dr. John Ronnau, Director, 407-823-2114, Fax: 407-823-5697, E-mail: jronnau@mail.ucf.edu. *Director*, Dr. John Ronnau, 407-823-2114, Fax: 407-823-5697, E-mail: jronnau@mail.ucf.edu.

College of Medicine *Faculty:* 50 full-time (18 women), 12 part-time/adjunct (4 women). Expenses: Contact institution. *Financial support:* Fellowships, research assistantships, teaching assistantships available. Offers medicine (MD, MS). *Application Contact:* Dr. Deborah C. German, Dean, 407-823-1829, E-mail: medical@mail.ucf.edu. *Dean*, Dr. Deborah C. German, 407-823-1829, E-mail: medical@mail.ucf.edu.

Burnett School of Biomedical Sciences Students: 37 full-time (25 women), 7 part-time (5 women); includes 4 Asian, non-Hispanic/Latino; 4 Hispanic/Latino, 20 international. Average age 26. 105 applicants, 41% accepted, 19 enrolled. *Faculty:* 27 full-time (7 women), 3 part-time/adjunct (1 woman). Expenses: Contact institution. *Financial support:* In 2010–11, 12 students received support, including 21 research assistantships (averaging $4,500 per year), 27 teaching assistantships (averaging $6,300 per year). In 2010, 14 master's awarded. Offers biomedical sciences (MS); biotechnology (MS). *Application Contact:* Dr. Pappachan E. Kolattukudy, Director, 407-823-1206, Fax: 407-823-0956, E-mail: pk@mail.ucf.edu. *Director*, Dr. Pappachan E. Kolattukudy, 407-823-1206, Fax: 407-823-0956, E-mail: pk@mail.ucf.edu.

College of Nursing Students: 127 full-time (121 women), 367 part-time (345 women); includes 137 minority (67 Black or African American, non-Hispanic/Latino; 1 American Indian or Alaska Native, non-Hispanic/Latino; 27 Asian, non-Hispanic/Latino; 37 Hispanic/Latino; 1 Native Hawaiian or other Pacific Islander, non-Hispanic/Latino; 4 Two or more races, non-Hispanic/Latino), 7 international. Average age 40. 206 applicants, 76% accepted, 120 enrolled. *Faculty:* 42 full-time (37 women), 56 part-time/adjunct (54 women). Expenses: Contact institution. *Financial support:* In 2010–11, 66 students received support, including 66 fellowships with partial tuition reimbursements available (averaging $1,300 per year), 2 teaching assistantships with partial tuition reimbursements available (averaging $4,500 per year); research assistantships with partial tuition reimbursements available, career-related internships or fieldwork, Federal Work-Study, institutionally sponsored loans, traineeships, and unspecified assistantships also available. Financial award application deadline: 3/1; financial award applicants required to submit FAFSA. In 2010, 93 master's, 5 doctorates, 20 other advanced degrees awarded. *Degree program information:* Part-time and evening/weekend programs available. Offers adult-gerontology clinical nurse specialist (Post-Master's Certificate); adult-gerontology nurse practitioner (Post-Master's Certificate); clinical nurse leader (Post-Master's Certificate); clinical nurse specialist (Post-Master's Certificate); family nurse practitioner (Post-Master's Certificate); nursing (MSN, PhD); nursing education (Post-Master's Certificate); nursing practice (DNP). *Application deadline:* For fall admission, 2/15 for domestic students; for spring admission, 9/15 for domestic students. *Application fee:* $30. Electronic applications accepted. *Application Contact:* Dr. Jean D. Leuner, Dean, 407-823-5496, Fax: 407-823-5675, E-mail: jleuner@mail.ucf.edu. *Dean*, Dr. Jean D. Leuner, 407-823-5496, Fax: 407-823-5675, E-mail: jleuner@mail.ucf.edu.

College of Optics and Photonics Students: 119 full-time (17 women), 19 part-time (1 woman); includes 2 Black or African American, non-Hispanic/Latino; 3 Asian, non-Hispanic/Latino; 5 Hispanic/Latino, 72 international. Average age 28. 232 applicants, 28% accepted, 33 enrolled. *Faculty:* 20 full-time (0 women). Expenses: Contact institution. *Financial support:* In 2010–11, 85 students received support, including 5 fellowships with partial tuition reimbursements available (averaging $8,700 per year), 116 research assistantships with partial tuition reimbursements available (averaging $11,700 per year); career-related internships or fieldwork, Federal Work-Study, institutionally sponsored loans, tuition waivers (partial), and unspecified assistantships also available. Financial award application deadline: 3/1; financial award applicants required to submit FAFSA. In 2010, 21 master's, 17 doctorates awarded. *Degree program information:* Part-time and evening/weekend programs available. Offers optics (MS, PhD). *Application deadline:* For fall admission, 2/1 priority date for domestic students; for spring admission, 12/1 for domestic students. *Application fee:* $30. Electronic applications accepted. *Application Contact:* Dr. Bahaa E. Saleh, Dean and Director, 407-882-3326, E-mail: besaleh@creol.ucf.edu. *Dean and Director*, Dr. Bahaa E. Saleh, 407-882-3326, E-mail: besaleh@creol.ucf.edu.

College of Sciences Students: 608 full-time (312 women), 193 part-time (108 women); includes 141 minority (43 Black or African American, non-Hispanic/Latino; 3 American Indian or Alaska Native, non-Hispanic/Latino; 25 Asian, non-Hispanic/Latino; 66 Hispanic/Latino; 1 Native Hawaiian or other Pacific Islander, non-Hispanic/Latino; 3 Two or more races, non-Hispanic/Latino), 145 international. Average age 29. 1,075 applicants, 41% accepted, 217 enrolled. *Faculty:* 285 full-time (88 women), 66 part-time/adjunct (21 women). Expenses: Contact institution. *Financial support:* In 2010–11, 441 students received support, including 67 fellowships (averaging $5,400 per year), 192 research assistantships (averaging $9,000 per year), 364 teaching assistantships (averaging $8,900 per year). In 2010, 162 master's, 36 doctorates, 19 other advanced degrees awarded. Offers anthropology (MA); applied experimental and human factors psychology (MA, PhD); applied mathematics (Certificate); applied sociology (MA); biology (MS); chemistry (MS, PhD); clinical psychology (MA, MS, PhD); computer forensics (Certificate); conservation biology (MS, PhD, Certificate); industrial/organizational psychology (MS, PhD); mathematical science (MS); mathematics (PhD); Maya studies (Certificate); physics (MS, PhD); political science (MA); SAS data mining (Certificate); sciences (MA, MS, PhD, Certificate); sociology (PhD); statistical computing (MS). *Application Contact:* Dr. Peter Panousis, Dean, 407-823-1911, E-mail: ppanousis@mail.ucf.edu. *Dean*, Dr. Peter Panousis, 407-823-1911, E-mail: ppanousis@mail.ucf.edu.

Nicholson School of Communication Students: 43 full-time (31 women), 33 part-time (26 women); includes 8 Black or African American, non-Hispanic/Latino; 2 American Indian or Alaska Native, non-Hispanic/Latino; 1 Asian, non-Hispanic/Latino; 5 Hispanic/Latino, 7 international. Average age 28. 64 applicants, 67% accepted, 19 enrolled. *Faculty:* 44 full-time (19 women), 23 part-time/adjunct (8 women). Expenses: Contact institution. *Financial support:* In 2010–11, 17 students received support, including 4 fellowships with partial tuition reimbursements available (averaging $5,300 per year), 2 research assistantships with partial tuition reimbursements available (averaging $8,100 per year), 16 teaching assistantships with partial tuition reimbursements available (averaging $6,400 per year); career-related internships or fieldwork, Federal Work-Study, institutionally sponsored loans, tuition waivers (partial), and unspecified assistantships also available. Financial award application deadline: 3/1; financial award applicants required to submit FAFSA. In 2010, 36 master's awarded. *Degree program information:* Part-time and evening/weekend programs available. Offers communication (MA). *Application deadline:* For fall admission, 7/15 for domestic students; for spring admission, 12/7 for domestic students. *Application fee:* $30. Electronic applications accepted. *Application Contact:* Dr. Robert Chandler, Director, 407-823-2683, Fax: 407-823-5216, E-mail: rcchandl@mail.ucf.edu. *Director*, Dr. Robert Chandler, 407-823-2683, Fax: 407-823-5216, E-mail: rcchandl@mail.ucf.edu.

Rosen College of Hospitality Management Students: 45 full-time (30 women), 40 part-time (28 women); includes 3 Black or African American, non-Hispanic/Latino; 4 Asian, non-Hispanic/Latino; 3 Hispanic/Latino; 1 Two or more races, non-Hispanic/Latino, 13 international. Average age 28. 69 applicants, 58% accepted, 28 enrolled. *Faculty:* 35 full-time (12 women), 29 part-time/adjunct (12 women). Expenses: Contact institution. *Financial support:* In 2010–11, 1 student received support, including 1 fellowship with partial tuition reimbursement available (averaging $10,000 per year). In 2010, 25 master's awarded. Offers hospitality and tourism management (MS). *Application deadline:* For fall admission, 2/1 for domestic students. *Application fee:* $30. Electronic applications accepted. *Application Contact:* Dr. Abraham C. Pizam, Dean, 407-903-8010, E-mail: apizam@mail.ucf.edu. *Dean*, Dr. Abraham C. Pizam, 407-903-8010, E-mail: apizam@mail.ucf.edu.

UNIVERSITY OF CENTRAL MISSOURI, Warrensburg, MO 64093

General Information State-supported, coed, comprehensive institution. CGS member. *Graduate housing:* Rooms and/or apartments available on a first-come, first-served basis to single and married students. Housing application deadline: 8/1.

GRADUATE UNITS

The Graduate School *Degree program information:* Part-time programs available. Electronic applications accepted.

College of Arts, Humanities and Social Sciences *Degree program information:* Part-time programs available. Offers English (MA); history (MA); mass communication (MA); music (MA); psychology (MS); speech communication (MA); teaching English as a second language (MA); theatre (MA). Electronic applications accepted.

College of Education *Degree program information:* Part-time programs available. Postbaccalaureate distance learning degree programs offered. Offers career and technical education administration (MS); career and technical education industry training (MS); career and technical education leadership/teaching (MS); college student personnel administration (MS); counseling (MS); curriculum and instruction (Ed S); educational leadership (Ed D); educational technology (MS); elementary education/educational foundations and literacy (MSE); elementary school administration (MSE); elementary school principalship (Ed S); human services/learning resources (Ed S); human services/professional counseling (Ed S); human services/special education (Ed S); human services/technology and occupational education (Ed S); K-12 education/educational foundations and literacy (MSE); K-12 special education (MSE); library science and information services (MS); literacy education (MSE); secondary education/educational foundations & literacy (MSE); secondary school administration (MSE); secondary school principalship (Ed S); superintendency (Ed S); teaching (MAT). Ed D offered jointly with University of Missouri. Electronic applications accepted.

College of Health and Human Services *Degree program information:* Part-time programs available. Postbaccalaureate distance learning degree programs offered. Offers criminal justice (MS); industrial hygiene (MS); occupational safety management (MS); physical education/exercise and sport science (MS); rural family nursing (MS); social gerontology (MS); sociology (MA); speech language pathology and audiology (MS). Electronic applications accepted.

College of Science and Technology *Degree program information:* Part-time programs available. Postbaccalaureate distance learning degree programs offered. Offers applied mathematics (MS); aviation safety (MS); biology (MS); computer science (MS); environmental studies (MA); industrial management (MS); mathematics (MS); technology (MS); technology management (PhD). PhD is offered jointly with Indiana State University. Electronic applications accepted.

Harmon College of Business Administration *Degree program information:* Part-time programs available. Postbaccalaureate distance learning degree programs offered. Offers accountancy (MA); accounting (MBA); ethical strategic leadership (MBA); finance (MBA); general business (MBA); information systems (MBA); information technology (MS); marketing (MBA). Electronic applications accepted.

UNIVERSITY OF CENTRAL OKLAHOMA, Edmond, OK 73034-5209

General Information State-supported, coed, comprehensive institution. CGS member. *Graduate housing:* Rooms and/or apartments available on a first-come, first-served basis to single and married students. Housing application deadline: 7/1. *Research affiliation:* U. S. Department of Agriculture (USDA)–Agricultural Research Service (grazing lands), National Geographic Society (global positioning system education).

GRADUATE UNITS

College of Graduate Studies and Research *Degree program information:* Part-time and evening/weekend programs available. Electronic applications accepted.

College of Business Administration *Degree program information:* Part-time programs available. Postbaccalaureate distance learning degree programs offered (minimal on-campus study). Offers business administration (MBA). Electronic applications accepted.

College of Education *Degree program information:* Part-time programs available. Offers adult education (M Ed); community services (M Ed); counseling psychology (MS); early childhood education (M Ed); education (M Ed, MA, MS); educational administration (M Ed); elementary education (M Ed); family and child studies (MS); family and consumer science education (MS); general education (M Ed); general psychology (MA); gerontology (M Ed); guidance and counseling (M Ed); instructional media (M Ed); interior design (MS); nutrition-food management (MS); professional health occupations (M Ed); reading (M Ed); secondary education (M Ed); special education (M Ed); speech-language pathology (M Ed). Electronic applications accepted.

College of Fine Arts and Design *Degree program information:* Part-time and evening/weekend programs available. Postbaccalaureate distance learning degree programs offered (minimal on-campus study). Offers design and interior design (MFA); fine arts and design (MFA, MM); music education (MM); performance (MM). Electronic applications accepted.

College of Liberal Arts *Degree program information:* Part-time programs available. Offers composition skills (MA); contemporary literature (MA); creative writing (MA); criminal justice management and administration (MA); history (MA); international affairs (MA); liberal arts (MA); museum studies (MA); political science (MA); social studies teaching (MA); Southwestern studies (MA); teaching English as a second language (MA); traditional studies (MA); urban affairs (MA). Electronic applications accepted.

College of Mathematics and Science *Degree program information:* Part-time programs available. Offers applied mathematical sciences (MS); biology (MS); chemistry (MS); mathematics and science (MS); physics and engineering (MS). Electronic applications accepted.

UNIVERSITY OF CHARLESTON, Charleston, WV 25304-1099

General Information Independent, coed, comprehensive institution. *Enrollment:* 1,518 graduate, professional, and undergraduate students; 381 full-time matriculated graduate/professional students (190 women), 2 part-time matriculated graduate/professional students (1 woman). *Enrollment by degree level:* 295 first professional, 88 master's. *Graduate faculty:* 28 full-time (14 women). Part-time tuition and fees vary according to course load and program. *Graduate housing:* Rooms and/or apartments available on a first-come, first-served basis to single and married students. *Student services:* Campus employment opportunities, campus safety program, career counseling, free psychological counseling, international student services, low-cost health insurance, services for students with disabilities. *Library facilities:* Schoenbaum Library. *Online resources:* library catalog, web page, access to other libraries' catalogs. *Collection:* 164,457 titles, 14,192 serial subscriptions, 3,759 audiovisual materials. *Research affiliation:* Walmart (pharmacy).

Computer facilities: 200 computers available on campus for general student use. A campuswide network can be accessed from student residence rooms and from off campus. Online class registration is available. *Web address:* http://www.ucwv.edu/.

General Application Contact: Amanda Pritt, Director of Admissions, 800-995-4682, Fax: 304-357-4750, E-mail: ucadmissions@ucwv.edu.

GRADUATE UNITS

Executive Master of Business Administration Program Students: 57 full-time (22 women); includes 1 minority (Native Hawaiian or other Pacific Islander, non-Hispanic/Latino). Average age 34. 37 applicants, 89% accepted, 33 enrolled. *Faculty:* 4 full-time (0 women), 1 (woman) part-time/adjunct. Expenses: Contact institution. *Financial support:* In 2010–11, 3 students received support. Scholarships/grants available. Support available to part-time students. Financial award application deadline: 3/1; financial award applicants required to submit FAFSA. In 2010, 38 master's awarded. *Degree program information:* Part-time and evening/weekend programs available. Offers business administration (EMBA). *Application deadline:* Applications are processed on a rolling basis. *Application fee:* $40. Electronic applications accepted. *Application Contact:* Dr. Robert B. Bliss, Associate Dean, 304-357-4865, Fax: 304-357-4872, E-mail: robertbliss@ucwv.edu. *Associate Dean,* Dr. Robert B. Bliss, 304-357-4865, Fax: 304-357-4872, E-mail: robertbliss@ucwv.edu.

Executive Master of Forensic Accounting Program Students: 7 full-time (4 women). Average age 35. 12 applicants, 83% accepted. *Faculty:* 6 part-time/adjunct (1 woman). Expenses: Contact institution. *Financial support:* In 2010–11, 1 student received support. Applicants required to submit FAFSA. In 2010, 9 master's awarded. *Degree program information:* Part-time and evening/weekend programs available. Offers forensic accounting (EMFA). *Application deadline:* Applications are processed on a rolling basis. *Application fee:* $50. Electronic applications accepted. *Application Contact:* Dr. Robert B. Bliss, Associate Dean, 304-357-4865, Fax: 304-357-4872, E-mail: robertbliss@ucwv.edu. *Associate Dean,* Dr. Robert B. Bliss, 304-357-4865, Fax: 304-357-4872, E-mail: robertbliss@ucwv.edu.

Master of Business Administration and Leadership Program Students: 24 full-time (12 women); includes 3 minority (all Black or African American, non-Hispanic/Latino), 7 international. Average age 23. 46 applicants, 57% accepted, 11 enrolled. *Faculty:* 3 full-time (1 woman). Expenses: Contact institution. *Financial support:* Career-related internships or fieldwork and scholarships/grants available. Financial award application deadline: 3/1; financial award applicants required to submit FAFSA. In 2010, 10 master's awarded. Offers business administration and leadership (MBA). *Application deadline:* Applications are processed on a rolling basis. *Application fee:* $0. Electronic applications accepted. *Application Contact:* Cheryl Fout, Administrative Assistant to the Dean, 304-357-4373, E-mail: cherylfout@ucwv.edu. *Dean,* Dr. J. Bart Morrison, 304-357-4373, E-mail: bartmorrison@ucwv.edu.

School of Pharmacy Students: 293 full-time (152 women), 2 part-time (1 woman); includes 48 minority (18 Black or African American, non-Hispanic/Latino; 22 Asian, non-Hispanic/Latino; 6 Hispanic/Latino; 2 Native Hawaiian or other Pacific Islander, non-Hispanic/Latino), 4 international. Average age 26. 450 applicants, 36% accepted, 70 enrolled. *Faculty:* 25 full-time (13 women). Expenses: Contact institution. *Financial support:* Application deadline: 3/1. In 2010, 70 Pharm Ds awarded. Offers pharmacy (Pharm D). *Application deadline:* For fall admission, 2/1 priority date for domestic and international students. Applications are processed on a rolling basis. *Application fee:* $50. Electronic applications accepted. *Application Contact:* Dr. Mary Euler, Associate Dean, Academic Affairs, 304-357-4860, Fax: 304-357-4868, E-mail: maryeuler@ucwv.edu. *Dean,* Dr. Michelle Easton, 304-357-4858, Fax: 304-357-4868, E-mail: michelleeaston@ucwv.edu.

UNIVERSITY OF CHICAGO, Chicago, IL 60637-1513

General Information Independent, coed, university. CGS member. *Enrollment:* 12,781 graduate, professional, and undergraduate students; 4,471 full-time matriculated graduate/professional students (1,923 women), 2,788 part-time matriculated graduate/professional students (784 women). *Enrollment by degree level:* 1,035 first professional, 5,113 master's, 1,111 doctoral. *Graduate faculty:* 2,173 full-time (707 women), 662 part-time/adjunct (270 women). *Graduate housing:* Rooms and/or apartments available on a first-come, first-served basis to single and married students. *Student services:* Campus employment opportunities, campus safety program, career counseling, exercise/wellness program, free psychological counseling, grant writing training, international student services, low-cost health insurance, multicultural affairs office, services for students with disabilities, teacher training, writing training. *Library facilities:* Joseph Regenstein Library plus 6 others. *Online resources:* library catalog, web page, access to other libraries' catalogs. *Collection:* 9 million titles, 50,000 serial subscriptions. *Research affiliation:* National Opinion Research Center (social science), Smithsonian Tropical Research Institute (biology), Field Museum of Natural History (archaeology, zoology), McDonald Observatory (astronomy), Fermilab (high-energy physics), Argonne National Laboratory (energy, materials).

Computer facilities: 1,000 computers available on campus for general student use. A campuswide network can be accessed from student residence rooms and from off campus. Online class registration is available. *Web address:* http://www.uchicago.edu/.

General Application Contact: Martha Jackson, Manager, Office of Graduate Affairs, 773-702-7813, Fax: 773-702-1194, E-mail: graduate-affairs-admissions@uchicago.edu.

GRADUATE UNITS

Booth School of Business Offers accounting (MBA); analytic finance (MBA); analytic management (MBA); business (IMBA, MBA, PhD); business administration (MBA); econometrics and statistics (MBA); economics (MBA); entrepreneurship (MBA); executive business administration (MBA); finance (MBA); general management (MBA); human resource management (MBA); international business (MBA); international business administration (IMBA); managerial and organizational behavior (MBA); marketing management (MBA); operations management (MBA); strategic management (MBA).

Divinity School *Degree program information:* Part-time programs available. Offers divinity (M Div, AM, AMRS, PhD). Electronic applications accepted.

Division of Biological Sciences Offers biochemistry and molecular biology (PhD); biological sciences (MD, MS, PhD); cancer biology (PhD); cell and molecular biology (PhD); cell physiology (PhD); cellular and molecular physiology (PhD); cellular differentiation (PhD); computational neuroscience (PhD); developmental biology (PhD); developmental endocrinology (PhD); developmental genetics (PhD); developmental neurobiology (PhD); ecology and evolution (PhD); evolutionary biology (PhD); functional and evolutionary biology (PhD); gene expression (PhD); genetics, genomics and systems biology (PhD); health studies (MS, PhD); human genetics (PhD); immunology (PhD); integrative neuroscience (PhD); interdisciplinary scientist training (PhD); medical physics (PhD); microbiology (PhD); molecular metabolism and nutrition (PhD); molecular pathogenesis and molecular medicine (PhD); neurobiology (PhD); ophthalmology and visual science (PhD); organismal biology and anatomy (PhD); pathology (PhD); pharmacological and physiological sciences (PhD). Electronic applications accepted.

Pritzker School of Medicine Students: 400 full-time (196 women); includes 45 Black or African American, non-Hispanic/Latino; 2 American Indian or Alaska Native, non-Hispanic/Latino; 87 Asian, non-Hispanic/Latino; 17 Hispanic/Latino, 6 international. Average age 25. 5,884 applicants, 4% accepted, 88 enrolled. *Faculty:* 905 full-time (315 women). Expenses: Contact institution. *Financial support:* In 2010–11, 354 students received support, including 8 fellowships with full tuition reimbursements available (averaging $27,000 per year), 75 teaching assistantships; career-related internships or fieldwork, Federal Work-Study, institutionally sponsored loans, and scholarships/grants also available. Financial award application deadline: 4/1; financial award applicants required to submit FAFSA. In 2010, 113 first professional degrees awarded. Offers medicine (MD). *Application deadline:* For fall admission, 10/15 for domestic and international students. Applications are processed on a rolling basis. *Application fee:* $75. Electronic applications accepted. *Application Contact:* Sylvia Robertson, Assistant Dean for Admissions and Financial Aid, 773-702-1937, Fax: 773-834-5412, E-mail: sroberts@bsd.uchicago.edu.

Division of Social Sciences Offers anthropology (PhD); comparative human development (PhD); conceptual and historical studies of science (PhD); economics (PhD); history (PhD); international relations (AM); Latin American and Caribbean studies (AM); Middle Eastern studies (AM); political science (PhD); psychology (PhD); social sciences (AM, PhD); social thought (PhD); sociology (PhD). Electronic applications accepted.

Division of the Humanities Offers ancient philosophy (AM, PhD); anthropology and linguistics (PhD); art history (AM, PhD); cinema and media studies (AM, PhD); classical archaeology (AM, PhD); classical languages and literatures (AM, PhD); comparative literature (AM, PhD); East Asian languages and civilizations (AM, PhD); English language and literature (AM, PhD); French (AM, PhD); Germanic languages and literatures (AM, PhD); humanities (AM, MA, MFA, PhD); Italian (AM, PhD); linguistics (AM, PhD); music (AM, PhD); Near Eastern languages and civilizations (AM, PhD); philosophy (AM, PhD); Slavic languages and literatures (AM, PhD); South Asian languages and civilizations (AM, PhD); Spanish (AM, PhD); visual arts (MFA).

Division of the Physical Sciences Offers applied mathematics (SM, PhD); astronomy and astrophysics (MS, PhD); atmospheric sciences (SM, PhD); biophysical science (PhD); chemistry (PhD); computer science (SM, PhD); earth sciences (SM, PhD); financial mathematics (MS); mathematics (SM, PhD); paleobiology (PhD); physical sciences (MS, SM, PhD); physics (PhD); planetary and space sciences (SM, PhD); statistics (SM, PhD). Electronic applications accepted.

Irving B. Harris Graduate School of Public Policy Studies *Degree program information:* Part-time programs available. Offers environmental science and policy (MS); public policy studies (AM, MPP, PhD). Electronic applications accepted.

The Law School Students: 634 full-time (281 women); includes 37 Black or African American, non-Hispanic/Latino; 1 American Indian or Alaska Native, non-Hispanic/Latino; 57 Asian, non-Hispanic/Latino; 63 Hispanic/Latino; 20 Two or more races, non-Hispanic/Latino, 13 international. Average age 24. 5,579 applicants, 15% accepted, 205 enrolled. *Faculty:* 74 full-time (24 women). Expenses: Contact institution. *Financial support:* In 2010–11, 294 students received support; fellowships, research assistantships, teaching assistantships, career-related internships or fieldwork, institutionally sponsored loans, and scholarships/

University of Chicago (continued)

grants available. Financial award application deadline: 3/1; financial award applicants required to submit FAFSA. In 2010, 199 first professional degrees, 65 master's, 4 doctorates awarded. Offers law (JD, LL M, MCL, DCL, JSD). *Application deadline:* For fall admission, 2/1 priority date for domestic students. Applications are processed on a rolling basis. *Application fee:* $75. Electronic applications accepted. *Application Contact:* Ann K. Perry, Dean of Admissions, 773-834-4425, Fax: 773-834-0942, E-mail: admissions@law.uchicago.edu. *Dean,* Michael Schill, 773-702-9494, Fax: 773-834-4409.

School of Social Service Administration *Degree program information:* Part-time and evening/weekend programs available. Offers social service administration (PhD); social work (AM). Electronic applications accepted.

UNIVERSITY OF CINCINNATI, Cincinnati, OH 45221

General Information State-supported, coed, university. CGS member. *Graduate housing:* Rooms and/or apartments available on a first-come, first-served basis to single and married students. Housing application deadline: 7/1.

GRADUATE UNITS

College of Law Students: 411 full-time (174 women); includes 62 minority (25 Black or African American, non-Hispanic/Latino; 18 Asian, non-Hispanic/Latino; 11 Hispanic/Latino; 1 Native Hawaiian or other Pacific Islander, non-Hispanic/Latino; 7 Two or more races, non-Hispanic/Latino), 3 international. Average age 25. 1,823 applicants, 43% accepted, 144 enrolled. *Faculty:* 28 full-time (15 women), 28 part-time/adjunct (9 women). Expenses: Contact institution. *Financial support:* In 2010–11, 275 students received support, including 257 fellowships (averaging $7,741 per year); research assistantships, career-related internships or fieldwork, Federal Work-Study, scholarships/grants, tuition waivers (full and partial), and unspecified assistantships also available. Financial award application deadline: 3/1; financial award applicants required to submit FAFSA. In 2010, 105 first professional degrees awarded. Offers law (JD). *Application deadline:* For fall admission, 3/1 priority date for domestic students. Applications are processed on a rolling basis. *Application fee:* $35. Electronic applications accepted. *Application Contact:* Al Watson, Assistant Dean and Director of Admissions, 513-556-0077, Fax: 513-556-2391, E-mail: alfred.watson@uc.edu. *Dean,* Louis D. Bilionis, 513-556-0121, Fax: 513-556-2391, E-mail: louis.bilionis@uc.edu.

College of Pharmacy *Degree program information:* Part-time programs available. Offers pharmacy (Pharm D, MS, PhD).

Division of Pharmaceutical Sciences Offers pharmaceutical sciences (MS, PhD).

Division of Pharmacy Practice Offers pharmacy practice (Pharm D).

Graduate School *Degree program information:* Part-time and evening/weekend programs available. Offers neuroscience (PhD). Electronic applications accepted.

College-Conservatory of Music Offers arts administration (MA); choral conducting (MM, DMA); composition (MM, DMA); directing (MFA); keyboard studies (MM, DMA, AD); music (MA, MFA, MM, DMA, PhD, AD); music education (MM); music history (MM); music theory (MM, PhD); musicology (PhD); orchestral conducting (MM, DMA); performance (MM, DMA, AD); theater design and production (MFA); voice and opera (MM, DMA); wind conducting (MM, DMA). Electronic applications accepted.

College of Allied Health Sciences *Degree program information:* Part-time programs available. Offers allied health sciences (MA, MS, Au D, DPT, PhD); blood transfusion medicine (MS); cellular therapies (MS); communication sciences and disorders (MA, Au D, PhD); medical genetics (MS); nutritional science (MS); rehabilitation science (DPT).

College of Business Students: 293 full-time (103 women), 213 part-time (79 women); includes 42 minority (11 Black or African American, non-Hispanic/Latino; 1 American Indian or Alaska Native, non-Hispanic/Latino; 19 Asian, non-Hispanic/Latino; 7 Hispanic/Latino; 1 Native Hawaiian or other Pacific Islander, non-Hispanic/Latino; 3 Two or more races, non-Hispanic/Latino), 160 international. Average age 28. 736 applicants, 55% accepted, 241 enrolled. *Faculty:* 79 full-time (22 women), 71 part-time/adjunct (24 women). Expenses: Contact institution. *Financial support:* In 2010–11, 110 students received support, including 29 research assistantships with full and partial tuition reimbursements available (averaging $14,640 per year), 10 teaching assistantships with full and partial tuition reimbursements available (averaging $5,400 per year); scholarships/grants, tuition waivers (full and partial), and unspecified assistantships also available. Financial award application deadline: 2/15; financial award applicants required to submit FAFSA. In 2010, 208 master's, 5 doctorates awarded. *Degree program information:* Part-time and evening/weekend programs available. Offers accounting (MS, PhD); business (MBA, MS, PhD); business administration (MBA); finance (PhD); information systems (MS, PhD); management (PhD); marketing (MS, PhD); quantitative analysis (MS); quantitative analysis and operations management (PhD). *Application deadline:* For fall admission, 1/15 priority date for domestic students, 4/1 for international students. Applications are processed on a rolling basis. *Application fee:* $45. Electronic applications accepted. *Application Contact:* Dona Clary, Director, Graduate Programs Office, 513-556-3546, Fax: 513-558-7006, E-mail: dona.clary@uc.edu. *Dean,* Dr. David Szymanski, 513-556-7001, Fax: 513-556-4891, E-mail: david.szymanski@uc.edu.

College of Design, Architecture, Art, and Planning *Degree program information:* Part-time programs available. Offers architecture (M Arch); art education (MA); art history (MA); community planning (MCP); design, architecture, art, and planning (M Arch, M Des, MA, MCP, MFA, PhD); fashion design (M Des); fine arts (MFA); graphic design (M Des); industrial design (M Des); interaction design (M Des); planning (MCP); product development (M Des); regional development planning (PhD). Electronic applications accepted.

College of Education, Criminal Justice, and Human Services *Degree program information:* Part-time programs available. Postbaccalaureate distance learning degree programs offered (no on-campus study). Offers community health (MS); counseling (Ed D); counselor education (CAGS); criminal justice (MS, PhD); curriculum and instruction (M Ed, Ed D); deaf studies (Certificate); early childhood education (M Ed); education, criminal justice, and human services (M Ed, MA, MS, Ed D, PhD, CAGS, Certificate, Ed S); educational leadership (M Ed, Ed S); educational studies (M Ed, Ed D, PhD, Ed S); health education (MS, PhD); health promotion and education (M Ed); human services (M Ed, MA, MS, Ed D, PhD, CAGS, Ed S); mental health (MA); middle childhood education (M Ed); postsecondary literacy instruction (Certificate); reading/literacy (M Ed, Ed D); school counseling (M Ed); school psychology (PhD, Ed S); secondary education (M Ed); special education (M Ed, Ed D); teaching English as a second language (M Ed, Ed D, Certificate); teaching science (MS); urban educational leadership (Ed D). Electronic applications accepted.

College of Engineering *Degree program information:* Part-time and evening/weekend programs available. Offers aerospace engineering and engineering mechanics (MS, PhD); bioinformatics (PhD); biomechanics (PhD); chemical engineering (MS, PhD); civil engineering (MS, PhD); computer engineering (MS); computer science (MS); computer science and engineering (PhD); electrical engineering (MS, PhD); engineering (MS, PhD); environmental engineering (MS, PhD); environmental sciences (MS, PhD); health physics (MS); industrial engineering (MS, PhD); materials engineering (MS, PhD); materials science and engineering (MS, PhD); mechanical engineering (MS, PhD); medical imaging (PhD); nuclear engineering (MS, PhD); tissue engineering (PhD).

College of Medicine Offers biomedical sciences (MS, PhD); cell and cancer biology (PhD); cell biophysics (PhD); environmental and industrial hygiene (MS, PhD); environmental and occupational medicine (MS); environmental genetics and molecular toxicology (MS, PhD); epidemiology and biostatistics (MS, PhD); immunobiology (MS, PhD); medical physics (MS); medicine (MD, MS, PhD); molecular and developmental biology (PhD); molecular genetics, biochemistry and microbiology (MS, PhD); occupational safety and ergonomics (MS, PhD); pathology (PhD); pharmacology (PhD); physiology (PhD). Electronic applications accepted.

College of Nursing *Degree program information:* Part-time programs available. Postbaccalaureate distance learning degree programs offered (no on-campus study). Offers clinical nurse specialist (MSN); nurse anesthesia (MSN); nurse midwifery (MSN); nurse practitioner (MSN); nursing (PhD). Electronic applications accepted.

McMicken College of Arts and Sciences *Degree program information:* Part-time and evening/weekend programs available. Offers analytical chemistry (MS, PhD); anthropology (MA); applied economics (MA); applied mathematics (MS, PhD); arts and sciences (MA, MALER, MAT, MS, PhD, Certificate); biochemistry (MS, PhD); biological sciences (MS, PhD); classics (MA, PhD); clinical psychology (PhD); communication (MA); English (MA, MAT, PhD); experimental psychology (PhD); French (MA, PhD); geography (MA, PhD); geology (MS, PhD); German studies (MA, PhD); history (MA, PhD); inorganic chemistry (MS, PhD); interdisciplinary studies (PhD); labor and employment relations (MALER); mathematics education (MAT); organic chemistry (MS, PhD); organizational leadership (MALER); philosophy (MA, PhD); physical chemistry (MS, PhD); physics (MS, PhD); political science (MA, PhD); polymer chemistry (MS, PhD); pure mathematics (MS, PhD); Romance languages and literatures (PhD); sensors (PhD); sociology (MA, PhD); Spanish (MA, PhD); statistics (MS, PhD); women's, gender, and sexuality studies (MA, Certificate).

School of Social Work *Degree program information:* Part-time programs available. Offers social work (MSW). Electronic applications accepted.

UNIVERSITY OF COLORADO AT COLORADO SPRINGS, Colorado Springs, CO 80933-7150

General Information State-supported, coed, university. *Enrollment:* 9,348 graduate, professional, and undergraduate students; 1,091 full-time matriculated graduate/professional students (574 women), 459 part-time matriculated graduate/professional students (262 women). *Enrollment by degree level:* 8 first professional, 1,350 master's, 125 doctoral, 67 other advanced degrees. *Graduate faculty:* 310 full-time (154 women), 50 part-time/adjunct (26 women). Tuition, state resident: full-time $7916. Tuition, nonresident: full-time $16,610. Tuition and fees vary according to course load, degree level, program, reciprocity agreements and student level. *Graduate housing:* Room and/or apartments available on a first-come, first-served basis to single students; on-campus housing not available to married students. Typical cost: $9118 per year ($9493 including board). Room and board charges vary according to board plan and housing facility selected. *Student services:* Campus employment opportunities, campus safety program, career counseling, child daycare facilities, exercise/wellness program, free psychological counseling, grant writing training, international student services, low-cost health insurance, multicultural affairs office, services for students with disabilities, teacher training, writing training. *Library facilities:* Kraemer Family Library. *Online resources:* library catalog, web page, access to other libraries' catalogs. *Collection:* 400,254 titles, 4,807 serial subscriptions, 9,459 audiovisual materials. *Research affiliation:* Omegatech (genetics), Colorado Vintage Companies (radon mitigation), Symetrix (ferroelectronics).

Computer facilities: Computer purchase and lease plans are available. 500 computers available on campus for general student use. A campuswide network can be accessed from student residence rooms and from off campus. Online class registration, student portal, learning management system (Blackboard) are available. *Web address:* http://www.uccs.edu/.

General Application Contact: Michael Sanderson, Graduate Recruitment Coordinator, 719-255-3072, Fax: 719-255-3045, E-mail: michael.sanderson@uccs.edu.

GRADUATE UNITS

Beth-El College of Nursing and Health Sciences Students: 121 full-time (103 women), 47 part-time (5 women); includes 5 Black or African American, non-Hispanic/Latino; 2 American Indian or Alaska Native, non-Hispanic/Latino; 6 Asian, non-Hispanic/Latino; 17 Hispanic/Latino, 5 international. Average age 34. 105 applicants, 84% accepted, 46 enrolled. *Faculty:* 26 full-time (21 women), 3 part-time/adjunct (2 women). Expenses: Contact institution. *Financial support:* Fellowships, career-related internships or fieldwork, Federal Work-Study, and scholarships/grants available. Support available to part-time students. Financial award application deadline: 3/1; financial award applicants required to submit FAFSA. In 2010, 57 master's awarded. *Degree program information:* Part-time programs available. Postbaccalaureate distance learning degree programs offered (minimal on-campus study). Offers adult health nurse practitioner and clinical specialist (MSN); family practitioner (MSN); neonatal nurse practitioner and clinical specialist (MSN); nursing administration (MSN); nursing practice (DNP); women nurse practitioner (MSN). *Application deadline:* For fall admission, 3/15 priority date for domestic students; for spring admission, 11/15 for domestic students. *Application fee:* $60 ($75 for international students). Electronic applications accepted. *Application Contact:* Jackie Crouch, Graduate Recruitment Coordinator, 719-255-4493, Fax: 719-255-4416, E-mail: jcrouch@uccs.edu. *Dean,* Dr. Nancy Smith, 719-255-4411, Fax: 719-255-4416, E-mail: nsmith2@uccs.edu.

College of Education Students: 302 full-time (214 women), 134 part-time (111 women); includes 20 Black or African American, non-Hispanic/Latino; 4 American Indian or Alaska Native, non-Hispanic/Latino; 12 Asian, non-Hispanic/Latino; 39 Hispanic/Latino; 1 Two or more races, non-Hispanic/Latino. Average age 37. 113 applicants, 81% accepted, 71 enrolled. *Faculty:* 24 full-time (16 women), 10 part-time/adjunct (5 women). Expenses: Contact institution. *Financial support:* Career-related internships or fieldwork, Federal Work-Study, and scholarships/grants available. Support available to part-time students. Financial award application deadline: 3/1; financial award applicants required to submit FAFSA. In 2010, 212 master's, 6 doctorates awarded. *Degree program information:* Part-time and evening/weekend programs available. Postbaccalaureate distance learning degree programs offered (minimal on-campus study). Offers counseling and human services (MA); curriculum and instruction (MA); educational administration (MA); educational leadership (MA, PhD); special education (MA). *Application deadline:* For fall admission, 2/28 priority date for domestic students; for spring admission, 10/15 for domestic students. Applications are processed on a rolling basis. *Application fee:* $60 ($75 for international students). *Application Contact:* Melissa Schecter, Student Services Manager, 719-255-4526, Fax: 719-255-4110, E-mail: mschedte@uccs.edu. *Dean,* Dr. David Fenell, 719-255-4133, Fax: 719-262-4133, E-mail: dfenell@uccs.edu.

College of Engineering and Applied Science Students: 166 full-time (27 women), 84 part-time (10 women); includes 5 Black or African American, non-Hispanic/Latino; 15 Asian, non-Hispanic/Latino; 11 Hispanic/Latino; 1 Two or more races, non-Hispanic/Latino, 25 international. Average age 33. 102 applicants, 79% accepted, 61 enrolled. *Faculty:* 30 full-time (5 women), 1 part-time/adjunct (0 women). Expenses: Contact institution. *Financial support:* Fellowships, research assistantships, teaching assistantships, career-related internships or fieldwork, Federal Work-Study, and scholarships/grants available. Support available to part-time students. Financial award application deadline: 3/1; financial award applicants required to submit FAFSA. In 2010, 59 master's, 3 doctorates awarded. *Degree program information:* Part-time and evening/weekend programs available. Offers computer science (MS); electrical engineering (ME, MS, PhD); engineering (PhD); engineering and applied science (ME, MS, PhD); engineering management (ME); information operations (ME); manufacturing (ME); mechanical engineering (MS); software engineering (ME); space operations (ME); space systems (MS). *Application deadline:* For fall admission, 5/1 for domestic students; for spring admission, 10/1 for domestic students. Applications are processed on a rolling basis. *Application fee:* $60 ($75 for international students). *Application Contact:* Tina Moore, Director, Office of Student Support, 719-255-3347, E-mail: tmoore@uccs.edu. *Dean,* Dr. Ramaswami Dandapani, 719-255-3543, Fax: 719-255-3542, E-mail: rdan@cas.uccs.edu.

College of Letters, Arts and Sciences Students: 184 full-time (103 women), 63 part-time (36 women); includes 7 Black or African American, non-Hispanic/Latino; 5 Asian, non-Hispanic/Latino; 16 Hispanic/Latino; 1 Two or more races, non-Hispanic/Latino, 4 international. Average age 32. 170 applicants, 74% accepted, 76 enrolled. *Faculty:* 189 full-time (97 women), 28 part-time/adjunct (16 women). Expenses: Contact institution. *Financial support:* Fellowships, research assistantships, teaching assistantships, career-related internships or fieldwork, Federal Work-Study, and scholarships/grants available. Support available to part-time students. Financial award application deadline: 3/1; financial award applicants required to submit FAFSA. In 2010, 68 master's, 3 doctorates awarded. *Degree program information:* Part-time and evening/weekend programs available. Offers applied mathematics (MS); applied science (PhD); applied science—bioscience (M Sc); applied science—physics (M Sc); biology (M Sc); chemistry (M Sc); communication (MA); geography and environmental studies (MA); health promotion (M Sc); history (MA); letters, arts and sciences (M Sc, MA, MS, PhD); mathematics (M Sc); physics (M Sc); psychology (MA, PhD); sociology (MA); sports medicine (M Sc); sports nutrition (M Sc). *Application deadline:* Applications are processed on a rolling basis. *Applica-*

tion fee: $60. *Application Contact:* Michael Sanderson, Information Contact, 719-255-3417, Fax: 719-255-3045, E-mail: gradschl@uccs.edu. *Dean,* Dr. Tom Christensen, 719-255-4550, Fax: 719-255-4200, E-mail: tchriste@uccs.edu.

Graduate School of Business Administration Students: 250 full-time (84 women), 94 part-time (39 women); includes 10 Black or African American, non-Hispanic/Latino; 1 American Indian or Alaska Native, non-Hispanic/Latino; 12 Asian, non-Hispanic/Latino; 16 Hispanic/Latino, 14 international. Average age 32. 169 applicants, 73% accepted, 68 enrolled. *Faculty:* 32 full-time (11 women), 8 part-time/adjunct (3 women). Expenses: Contact institution. *Financial support:* Career-related internships or fieldwork, Federal Work-Study, and scholarships/grants available. Support available to part-time students. Financial award application deadline: 3/1; financial award applicants required to submit FAFSA. In 2010, 117 master's awarded. *Degree program information:* Part-time and evening/weekend programs available. Offers business administration (MBA). *Application deadline:* For fall admission, 6/1 for domestic students; for spring admission, 11/1 for domestic students. *Application fee:* $60 ($75 for international students). *Application Contact:* Windy Haddad, MBA Program Director, 719-255-3401, Fax: 719-255-3100, E-mail: whaddad@uccs.edu. *Dean,* Dr. Venkateshwar Reddy, 719-255-3113, Fax: 719-255-3100, E-mail: vreddy@uccs.edu.

Graduate School of Public Affairs Students: 14 full-time (9 women), 3 part-time (1 woman); includes 1 Black or African American, non-Hispanic/Latino; 2 Asian, non-Hispanic/Latino; 4 Hispanic/Latino. Average age 34. 56 applicants, 88% accepted. *Faculty:* 7 full-time (2 women). Expenses: Contact institution. *Financial support:* Career-related internships or fieldwork, Federal Work-Study, and scholarships/grants available. Support available to part-time students. Financial award application deadline: 3/1; financial award applicants required to submit FAFSA. In 2010, 18 master's awarded. *Degree program information:* Part-time and evening/weekend programs available. Offers criminal justice (MCJ); public administration (MPA). *Application deadline:* For fall admission, 6/1 priority date for domestic students; for spring admission, 11/1 priority date for domestic students. Applications are processed on a rolling basis. *Application fee:* $60 ($75 for international students). *Application Contact:* Mary Lou Kartis, Program Assistant, 719-255-4182, Fax: 719-255-4183, E-mail: mkartis@uccs.edu. *Dean,* Dr. Terry Schwartz, 719-255-4047, Fax: 719-255-4183, E-mail: tschwart@uccs.edu.

UNIVERSITY OF COLORADO BOULDER, Boulder, CO 80309

General Information State-supported, coed, university. CGS member. *Enrollment:* 32,378 graduate, professional, and undergraduate students; 4,798 full-time matriculated graduate/professional students (1,950 women), 977 part-time matriculated graduate/professional students (450 women). *Graduate faculty:* 1,067 full-time (336 women). *Graduate housing:* Rooms and/or apartments available to single and married students. *Student services:* Campus employment opportunities, campus safety program, career counseling, child daycare facilities, free psychological counseling, international student services, low-cost health insurance. *Library facilities:* Norlin Library plus 6 others. *Online resources:* library catalog, web page, access to other libraries' catalogs. *Collection:* 4.3 million titles, 60,805 serial subscriptions, 1.1 million audiovisual materials. *Research affiliation:* National Center for Atmospheric Research, National Institute of Standards and Technology (NIST), National Oceanic and Atmospheric Administration (NOAA), U. S. West Advanced Technologies, National Aeronautics and Space Administration (NASA).

Computer facilities: Computer purchase and lease plans are available. 1,823 computers available on campus for general student use. A campuswide network can be accessed from student residence rooms and from off campus. Online class registration, standard and academic software, student government voting are available. *Web address:* http://www.colorado.edu/.

GRADUATE UNITS

Graduate School Students: 3,832 full-time (1,554 women), 958 part-time (439 women); includes 521 minority (50 Black or African American, non-Hispanic/Latino; 37 American Indian or Alaska Native, non-Hispanic/Latino; 178 Asian, non-Hispanic/Latino; 239 Hispanic/Latino; 17 Two or more races, non-Hispanic/Latino), 840 international. Average age 30. 9,320 applicants, 1182 enrolled. *Faculty:* 979 full-time (313 women). Expenses: Contact institution. *Financial support:* In 2010–11, 1,023 fellowships with full tuition reimbursements (averaging $9,106 per year), research assistantships with full tuition reimbursements (averaging $13,490 per year), 70 teaching assistantships with full tuition reimbursements (averaging $17,591 per year) were awarded; career-related internships or fieldwork, Federal Work-Study, institutionally sponsored loans, scholarships/grants, traineeships, tuition waivers (full and partial), and unspecified assistantships also available. Support available to part-time students. Financial award applicants required to submit FAFSA. In 2010, 1,125 master's, 409 doctorates awarded. *Degree program information:* Part-time programs available. Postbaccalaureate distance learning degree programs offered. Offers museum and field studies (MS). *Application fee:* $50 ($60 for international students). Electronic applications accepted.

ATLAS Institute (Alliance for Technology, Learning, and Society) Students: 17 full-time (12 women), 1 (woman) part-time; includes 3 minority (1 Black or African American, non-Hispanic/Latino; 1 American Indian or Alaska Native, non-Hispanic/Latino; 1 Asian, non-Hispanic/Latino), 1 international. Average age 33. 24 applicants, 10 enrolled. Expenses: Contact institution. *Financial support:* In 2010–11, 2 fellowships (averaging $33,692 per year), 5 research assistantships (averaging $13,970 per year) were awarded. Financial award application deadline: 1/15. Offers technology, media, and society (PhD). *Application deadline:* For fall admission, 1/28 for domestic students, 12/1 for international students.

College of Arts and Sciences Students: 2,076 full-time (984 women), 260 part-time (124 women); includes 25 Black or African American, non-Hispanic/Latino; 25 American Indian or Alaska Native, non-Hispanic/Latino; 68 Asian, non-Hispanic/Latino; 95 Hispanic/Latino; 7 Two or more races, non-Hispanic/Latino, 315 international. Average age 29. 5,761 applicants, 532 enrolled. *Faculty:* 691 full-time (234 women). Expenses: Contact institution. *Financial support:* In 2010–11, 589 fellowships with full tuition reimbursements (averaging $9,547 per year), 947 research assistantships with full tuition reimbursements (averaging $13,053 per year) were awarded; career-related internships or fieldwork, Federal Work-Study, institutionally sponsored loans, scholarships/grants, traineeships, tuition waivers (full), and unspecified assistantships also available. Support available to part-time students. In 2010, 408 master's, 246 doctorates awarded. *Degree program information:* Part-time programs available. Offers animal behavior (MA); anthropology (MA, PhD); applied mathematics (MS, PhD); art history (MA); arts and sciences (MA, MFA, MS, Au D, PhD); astrophysics (MS, PhD); atmospheric and oceanic sciences (MS, PhD); audiology (Au D, PhD); biochemistry (PhD); biology (MA, PhD); cellular structure and function (MA, PhD); ceramics (MFA); chemical physics (PhD); chemistry (MS); Chinese (MA, PhD); classics (MA, PhD); clinical research and practice in audiology (PhD); communication (MA, PhD); comparative literature and humanities (MA, PhD); dance (MFA); developmental biology (MA, PhD); drawing (MFA); economics (MA, PhD); environmental biology (MA, PhD); environmental studies (MS, PhD); evolutionary biology (MA, PhD); French (MA, PhD); geography (MA, PhD); geology (MS, PhD); geophysics (PhD); German (MA); Hispanic linguistics (MA); history (MA, PhD); integrative physiology (MS, PhD); international affairs (MA); Japanese (MA, PhD); linguistics (MA, PhD); liquid crystal science and technology (PhD); literature (MA, PhD); mathematical physics (PhD); mathematics (MA, MS, PhD); medical physics (PhD); medieval/early modern Hispanic literatures (PhD); molecular biology (MA, PhD); neurobiology (MA); optical sciences and engineering (PhD); painting (MFA); philosophy (MA, PhD); photography and media arts (MFA); physics (MS, PhD); planetary science (MS, PhD); political science (MA, PhD); population biology (MA); population genetics (PhD); printmaking (MFA); psychology and neuroscience (MA, PhD); public policy (MA); religious studies (MA); sculpture (MFA); sociology (PhD); Spanish and Spanish American literatures (MA, PhD); speech, language and hearing science (MA); speech-language pathology (MA, PhD); speech-language-hearing sciences (PhD); theatre (MA, PhD). *Application fee:* $50 ($60 for international students). Electronic applications accepted.

College of Engineering and Applied Science Students: 1,245 full-time (259 women), 398 part-time (89 women); includes 15 Black or African American, non-Hispanic/Latino; 8 American Indian or Alaska Native, non-Hispanic/Latino; 82 Asian, non-Hispanic/Latino; 52 Hispanic/Latino; 6 Two or more races, non-Hispanic/Latino, 478 international. Average age 28. 2,497 applicants, 403 enrolled. *Faculty:* 179 full-time (32 women). Expenses: Contact institution. *Financial support:* In 2010–11, 247 fellowships with full tuition reimbursements (averaging $12,287 per year), 413 research assistantships with full tuition reimbursements (averaging $15,375 per year), 70 teaching assistantships with full tuition reimbursements (averaging $17,591 per year) were awarded; career-related internships or fieldwork, scholarships/grants, traineeships, and tuition waivers (full) also available. In 2010, 445 master's, 109 doctorates awarded. *Degree program information:* Part-time programs available. Postbaccalaureate distance learning degree programs offered. Offers aerospace engineering sciences (MS, PhD); building systems (MS, PhD); chemical and biological engineering (ME, MS, PhD); computer science (ME, MS, PhD); construction engineering management (MS, PhD); electrical, computer and energy engineering (ME, MS, PhD); engineering and applied science (ME, MS, PhD); environmental engineering (MS, PhD); geotechnical engineering and geomechanics (MS, PhD); hydrology, water resources and environmental fluid mechanics (MS, PhD); mechanical engineering (ME, MS, PhD); operations and logistics (ME); quality and process (ME); research and development (ME); structural engineering and structural mechanics (MS, PhD); telecommunications (MS). *Application fee:* $50 ($60 for international students). Electronic applications accepted.

College of Music Students: 202 full-time (101 women), 56 part-time (29 women); includes 3 Black or African American, non-Hispanic/Latino; 11 Asian, non-Hispanic/Latino; 13 Hispanic/Latino; 3 Two or more races, non-Hispanic/Latino, 28 international. Average age 30. 493 applicants, 83 enrolled. *Faculty:* 56 full-time (20 women). Expenses: Contact institution. *Financial support:* In 2010–11, 88 fellowships (averaging $3,325 per year), 38 research assistantships (averaging $6,550 per year) were awarded; tuition waivers (full) also available. Financial award application deadline: 3/1. In 2010, 46 master's, 34 doctorates awarded. Offers composition (M Mus, D Mus A); conducting (M Mus); instrumental conducting and literature (D Mus A); literature and performance of choral music (D Mus A); music education (M Mus Ed, PhD); musicology (PhD); performance (M Mus, D Mus A); performance/pedagogy (M Mus, D Mus A); theory (M Mus). *Application deadline:* For fall admission, 3/1 priority date for domestic students, 12/1 for international students. Applications are processed on a rolling basis. *Application fee:* $50 ($60 for international students).

School of Education Students: 198 full-time (134 women), 231 part-time (189 women); includes 103 minority (7 Black or African American, non-Hispanic/Latino; 3 American Indian or Alaska Native, non-Hispanic/Latino; 16 Asian, non-Hispanic/Latino; 77 Hispanic/Latino), 7 international. Average age 33. 319 applicants, 110 enrolled. *Faculty:* 31 full-time (16 women). Expenses: Contact institution. *Financial support:* In 2010–11, 82 fellowships (averaging $3,279 per year), 50 research assistantships (averaging $12,516 per year) were awarded; career-related internships or fieldwork, Federal Work-Study, scholarships/grants, and tuition waivers (full and partial) also available. Support available to part-time students. In 2010, 180 master's, 14 doctorates awarded. *Degree program information:* Part-time programs available. Offers education (MA, PhD); educational and psychological studies (MA, PhD); educational foundations, policy, and practice (MA, PhD); instruction and curriculum (MA, PhD); research and evaluation methodologies (PhD); social multicultural and bilingual foundations (MA, PhD). *Application deadline:* For fall admission, 2/1 priority date for domestic students, 12/1 for international students; for spring admission, 9/1 for domestic students, 12/1 for international students. *Application fee:* $50 ($60 for international students).

School of Journalism and Mass Communication Students: 78 full-time (49 women), 10 part-time (6 women); includes 4 minority (1 Black or African American, non-Hispanic/Latino; 2 Hispanic/Latino; 1 Two or more races, non-Hispanic/Latino), 11 international. Average age 30. 154 applicants, 35 enrolled. *Faculty:* 22 full-time (11 women). Expenses: Contact institution. *Financial support:* In 2010–11, 14 fellowships (averaging $1,807 per year), 21 research assistantships with tuition reimbursements (averaging $11,554 per year) were awarded; institutionally sponsored loans and unspecified assistantships also available. Financial award application deadline: 3/1. In 2010, 35 master's, 6 doctorates awarded. *Degree program information:* Part-time programs available. Offers communication (PhD); mass communication research (MA); media studies (PhD); newsgathering (MA). *Application deadline:* For fall admission, 2/15 for domestic students, 12/1 for international students. Applications are processed on a rolling basis. *Application fee:* $50 ($60 for international students).

Leeds School of Business Students: 438 full-time (139 women), 6 part-time (4 women); includes 24 minority (1 Black or African American, non-Hispanic/Latino; 2 American Indian or Alaska Native, non-Hispanic/Latino; 17 Asian, non-Hispanic/Latino; 4 Hispanic/Latino), 46 international. Average age 29. 342 applicants, 125 enrolled. *Faculty:* 52 full-time (10 women). Expenses: Contact institution. *Financial support:* In 2010–11, 95 fellowships (averaging $5,033 per year), 27 research assistantships (averaging $16,982 per year), 11 teaching assistantships (averaging $12,576 per year) were awarded; career-related internships or fieldwork, Federal Work-Study, scholarships/grants, and unspecified assistantships also available. In 2010, 199 master's, 12 doctorates awarded. *Degree program information:* Part-time and evening/weekend programs available. Offers accounting (MS, PhD); business (MBA, MS, PhD); business administration (MBA, MS, PhD); finance (PhD); information systems (PhD); marketing (PhD); operations (PhD); strategic, organizational, and entrepreneurial studies (PhD). *Application deadline:* For fall admission, 3/1 priority date for domestic students, 3/1 for international students. Applications are processed on a rolling basis. *Application fee:* $50 ($60 for international students). Electronic applications accepted.

School of Law Students: 528 full-time (257 women), 13 part-time (7 women); includes 110 minority (16 Black or African American, non-Hispanic/Latino; 20 American Indian or Alaska Native, non-Hispanic/Latino; 33 Asian, non-Hispanic/Latino; 41 Hispanic/Latino), 1 international. Average age 27. *Faculty:* 36 full-time (13 women). Expenses: Contact institution. *Financial support:* In 2010–11, 218 fellowships (averaging $8,399 per year), 1 research assistantship (averaging $432 per year) were awarded; Federal Work-Study and institutionally sponsored loans also available. Financial award applicants required to submit FAFSA. In 2010, 188 first professional degrees awarded. Offers law (JD). *Application deadline:* For fall admission, 2/15 for domestic students. Applications are processed on a rolling basis. *Application fee:* $50 ($60 for international students).

UNIVERSITY OF COLORADO DENVER, Denver, CO 80217-3364

General Information State-supported, coed, university. CGS member. *Enrollment:* 24,108 graduate, professional, and undergraduate students; 6,740 full-time matriculated graduate/professional students (3,850 women), 1,864 part-time matriculated graduate/professional students (1,184 women). *Enrollment by degree level:* 2,018 first professional, 5,661 master's, 726 doctoral, 170 other advanced degrees. *Graduate faculty:* 2,782 full-time (1,404 women), 864 part-time/adjunct (483 women). Tuition, state resident: full-time $7332; part-time $355 per credit hour. Tuition, nonresident: full-time $18,990; part-time $1055 per credit hour. *Required fees:* $998. Tuition and fees vary according to course level, course load, degree level, campus/location, program, reciprocity agreements and student level. *Student services:* Campus employment opportunities, campus safety program, career counseling, child daycare facilities, exercise/wellness program, free psychological counseling, international student services, low-cost health insurance, services for students with disabilities, teacher training, writing training. *Library facilities:* Auraria Library (UCD) and Health Sciences Library (AMC). *Online resources:* library catalog, web page, access to other libraries' catalogs. *Research affiliation:* The Children's Hospital (pediatrics), National Jewish Health (pediatrics, immunology, respiratory disease), Denver Health (trauma, primary care, under-served populations).

Computer facilities: 750 computers available on campus for general student use. A campuswide network can be accessed from student residence rooms and from off campus. Online class registration is available. *Web address:* http://www.ucdenver.edu/.

General Application Contact: Graduate School Admissions, 303-556-2704, E-mail: admissions@ucdenver.edu.

GRADUATE UNITS

Business School Students: 1,266 full-time (491 women), 298 part-time (121 women); includes 29 Black or African American, non-Hispanic/Latino; 9 American Indian or Alaska Native, non-Hispanic/Latino; 100 Asian, non-Hispanic/Latino; 77 Hispanic/Latino; 1 Two or more races, non-Hispanic/Latino, 114 international. Average age 30. 853 applicants, 64% accepted, 393 enrolled. *Faculty:* 63 full-time (23 women), 29 part-time/adjunct (8 women). Expenses: Contact institution. *Financial support:* In 2010–11, 89 students received support. Federal Work-Study, scholarships/grants, and unspecified assistantships available. Support available

University of Colorado Denver (continued)

to part-time students. Financial award application deadline: 4/1; financial award applicants required to submit FAFSA. In 2010, 505 master's, 4 doctorates awarded. *Degree program information:* Part-time and evening/weekend programs available. Postbaccalaureate distance learning degree programs offered (no on-campus study). Offers accounting and information systems audit and control (MS); auditing and forensic accounting (MS); brand management and marketing communication (MS); business (MBA, MS, MSIB, PhD); business administration (MBA); business intelligence (MS); communications management (MS); computer science and information systems (PhD); decision sciences (MS); enterprise technology management (MS, PhD); entrepreneurship and innovation (MS); finance (MS); financial accounting (MS); financial management (MS); global energy management (MS); global management (MS); global marketing (MS); health administration (MBA); health information technology management (MS); high-tech/entrepreneurial marketing (MS); human resources management (MS); information systems audit control (MS); international business (MSIB); international health management and policy (MS); Internet marketing (MS); leadership (MS); market research (MS); marketing and business intelligence (MS); marketing for sustainability (MS); marketing in nonprofit organizations (MS); quantitative decision methods (MS); sports and entertainment management (MS); sports and entertainment marketing (MS); strategic management (MS); sustainability management (MS); taxation (MS); web and mobile computing (MS). *Application deadline:* For fall admission, 4/1 for domestic students, 3/15 for international students; for spring admission, 10/1 for domestic and international students. *Application fee:* $50 ($75 for international students). Electronic applications accepted. *Application Contact:* Shelly Townley, Admissions Director, Graduate Programs, 303-315-8202, E-mail: shelly.townley@ucdenver.edu. *Dean,* Dr. Sueann Ambron, 303-556-5802, Fax: 303-556-5914, E-mail: sueann.ambron@ucdenver.edu.

College of Architecture and Planning Students: 544 full-time (262 women), 28 part-time (17 women); includes 10 Black or African American, non-Hispanic/Latino; 3 American Indian or Alaska Native, non-Hispanic/Latino; 15 Asian, non-Hispanic/Latino; 31 Hispanic/Latino, 41 international. Average age 30. 712 applicants, 54% accepted, 178 enrolled. *Faculty:* 43 full-time (14 women), 33 part-time/adjunct (9 women). Expenses: Contact institution. *Financial support:* In 2010–11, 136 students received support; fellowships with partial tuition reimbursements available, research assistantships, teaching assistantships, Federal Work-Study, scholarships/grants, and unspecified assistantships available. Support available to part-time students. Financial award application deadline: 4/1; financial award applicants required to submit FAFSA. In 2010, 185 master's, 2 doctorates awarded. *Degree program information:* Part-time programs available. Offers architecture and planning (MLA, MS, MUD, MURP, PhD); economic and community development planning (MURP); historic preservation (MS); history of architecture, landscape and urbanism (PhD); land use and environmental planning (MURP); landscape architecture (MLA); sustainable and healthy environments (PhD); urban design (MUD); urban place making (MURP). *Application deadline:* For fall admission, 2/15 for domestic students; for spring admission, 10/1 for domestic students. *Application fee:* $50 ($75 for international students). Electronic applications accepted. *Application Contact:* Michael Harper, Administrative Coordinator, Graduate Admissions and PhD Program, 303-556-6042, E-mail: michael.t.harper@ucdenver.edu. *Dean,* Dr. Mark Gelernter, 303-556-5938, E-mail: mark.gelernter@ucdenver.edu.

College of Arts and Media Students: 13 full-time (0 women), 2 part-time (0 women); includes 1 Hispanic/Latino. Average age 30. 20 applicants, 45% accepted, 8 enrolled. *Faculty:* 34 full-time (11 women), 2 part-time/adjunct (0 women). Expenses: Contact institution. *Financial support:* In 2010–11, 2 students received support. Federal Work-Study and scholarships/grants available. Financial award application deadline: 4/1; financial award applicants required to submit FAFSA. In 2010, 4 master's awarded. *Degree program information:* Part-time and evening/weekend programs available. Offers recording arts (MS). *Application deadline:* For fall admission, 2/15 for domestic students, 1/1 for international students. *Application fee:* $50 ($75 for international students). Electronic applications accepted. *Application Contact:* Clark Strickland, Assistant Dean for Programs and Resources, 303-556-2279, Fax: 303-556-2335, E-mail: clark.strickland@ucdenver.edu. *Dean,* Dr. David Dynak, 303-556-2279, Fax: 303-556-2335, E-mail: david.dynak@ucdenver.edu.

College of Engineering and Applied Science Students: 268 full-time (70 women), 160 part-time (30 women); includes 18 Black or African American, non-Hispanic/Latino; 26 Asian, non-Hispanic/Latino; 19 Hispanic/Latino, 128 international. Average age 32. 335 applicants, 50% accepted, 105 enrolled. *Faculty:* 44 full-time (5 women), 13 part-time/adjunct (3 women). Expenses: Contact institution. *Financial support:* In 2010–11, 41 students received support; research assistantships, teaching assistantships, Federal Work-Study and scholarships/grants available. Financial award application deadline: 4/1; financial award applicants required to submit FAFSA. In 2010, 84 master's, 4 doctorates awarded. *Degree program information:* Part-time and evening/weekend programs available. Offers bioengineering (PhD); civil engineering (M Eng, PhD); clinical imaging (MS); computer science (MS); computer science and information systems (PhD); device design and entrepreneurship (MS); electrical engineering (M Eng); engineering and applied science (M Eng, MS, PhD); environmental and sustainability engineering (MS); geographic information systems (MS); geotechnical engineering (MS); hydrology and hydraulics (MS); mechanical engineering (M Eng, MS); research (MS); structural engineering (MS); transportation engineering (MS). *Application fee:* $50 ($75 for international students). Electronic applications accepted. *Application Contact:* Dr. Paul Rakowski, Assistant Dean of Student Services, 303-556-6771, Fax: 303-556-2511, E-mail: paul.rakowski@ucdenver.edu. *Assistant Dean of Student Services,* Dr. Paul Rakowski, 303-556-6771, Fax: 303-556-2511, E-mail: paul.rakowski@ucdenver.edu.

College of Liberal Arts and Sciences Students: 448 full-time (257 women), 220 part-time (131 women); includes 95 minority (17 Black or African American, non-Hispanic/Latino; 8 American Indian or Alaska Native, non-Hispanic/Latino; 23 Asian, non-Hispanic/Latino; 46 Hispanic/Latino; 1 Two or more races, non-Hispanic/Latino), 37 international. Average age 32. 585 applicants, 48% accepted, 179 enrolled. *Faculty:* 201 full-time (79 women), 24 part-time/adjunct (11 women). Expenses: Contact institution. *Financial support:* In 2010–11, 77 students received support; fellowships, research assistantships, teaching assistantships, Federal Work-Study, scholarships/grants, and unspecified assistantships available. Support available to part-time students. Financial award application deadline: 4/1; financial award applicants required to submit FAFSA. In 2010, 201 master's, 6 doctorates awarded. *Degree program information:* Part-time and evening/weekend programs available. Offers academic track (MA); applied linguistics (MA); applied mathematics (MS, PhD); applied science (MIS); archaeological studies (MA); biological anthropology (MA); biology (MS); chemistry (MS); clinical psychology (MA); community health science (MSS); computer science (MIS); economics (MA); environmental sciences (MS); European history (MA); global history (MA); health and behavioral sciences (PhD); humanities (MH); international studies (MSS); liberal arts and sciences (MA, MH, MIS, MS, MSS, PhD); literature (MA); mathematics (MIS); medical anthropology (MA); political science (MA); professional track/communication management (MA); public history (MA); rhetoric and teaching of writing (MA); social science (MSS); society and the environment (MSS); sociology (MA); Spanish (MA); sustainable development and political ecology (MA); technical communication (MS); U. S. history (MA); women's and gender studies (MSS). *Application fee:* $50 ($75 for international students). Electronic applications accepted. *Application Contact:* College of Liberal Arts and Sciences, 303-556-2557, E-mail: clas@ucdenver.edu. *Professor and Dean,* Dr. Daniel Howard, 303-556-2624, Fax: 303-556-4861, E-mail: dan.howard@ucdenver.edu.

College of Nursing Students: 269 full-time (248 women), 121 part-time (114 women); includes 9 Black or African American, non-Hispanic/Latino; 7 American Indian or Alaska Native, non-Hispanic/Latino; 8 Asian, non-Hispanic/Latino; 21 Hispanic/Latino; 1 Two or more races, non-Hispanic/Latino, 7 international. Average age 37. 242 applicants, 49% accepted, 108 enrolled. *Faculty:* 69 full-time (65 women), 68 part-time/adjunct (64 women). Expenses: Contact institution. *Financial support:* In 2010–11, 40 students received support; fellowships, research assistantships, teaching assistantships, Federal Work-Study, scholarships/grants, and unspecified assistantships available. Support available to part-time students. Financial award application deadline: 3/15; financial award applicants required to submit FAFSA. In 2010, 59 master's, 1 doctorate awarded. *Degree program information:* Part-time and evening/weekend programs available. Postbaccalaureate distance learning degree programs offered (minimal on-campus study). Offers adult clinical nurse specialist (MS); adult nurse practitioner (MS); family nurse practitioner (MS); family psychiatric mental health nurse practitioner (MS); health care informatics (MS); nurse-midwifery (MS); nursing (DNP, PhD); nursing leadership and health care systems (MS); pediatric nurse practitioner (MS); pediatric nursing leadership (MS); special studies (MS); women's health care (MS). *Application deadline:* For fall admission, 4/1 for domestic students; for spring admission, 9/1 for domestic students. *Application fee:* $65. Electronic applications accepted. *Application Contact:* Judy Campbell, Graduate Programs Coordinator, 303-724-8503, E-mail: judy.campbell@ucdenver.edu. *Dean,* Dr. Patricia Moritz, 303-724-1679, E-mail: pat.moritz@ucdenver.edu.

Colorado School of Public Health Students: 216 full-time (162 women), 46 part-time (35 women); includes 7 Black or African American, non-Hispanic/Latino; 5 American Indian or Alaska Native, non-Hispanic/Latino; 13 Asian, non-Hispanic/Latino; 14 Hispanic/Latino; 2 Two or more races, non-Hispanic/Latino, 10 international. Average age 30. 312 applicants, 72% accepted, 127 enrolled. *Faculty:* 79 full-time (58 women), 18 part-time/adjunct (6 women). Expenses: Contact institution. *Financial support:* In 2010–11, 51 students received support; fellowships, research assistantships, Federal Work-Study, scholarships/grants, and unspecified assistantships available. Support available to part-time students. Financial award application deadline: 4/1. In 2010, 64 master's, 12 doctorates awarded. *Degree program information:* Part-time programs available. Offers biostatistics and informatics (MS, PhD); community and behavioral health (MPH, Dr PH); environmental and occupational health (MPH); epidemiology (MS, PhD); health services research (PhD); health systems, management & policy (MPH); public health (MPH, MS, Dr PH, PhD). *Application fee:* $65. Electronic applications accepted. *Application Contact:* Office of Academic and Student Affairs, 303-724-4613, E-mail: colorado.sph@ucdenver.edu.

School of Dental Medicine Students: 265 full-time (117 women); includes 7 Black or African American, non-Hispanic/Latino; 2 American Indian or Alaska Native, non-Hispanic/Latino; 32 Asian, non-Hispanic/Latino; 26 Hispanic/Latino, 22 international. Average age 28. 1,267 applicants, 4% accepted, 32 enrolled. *Faculty:* 73 full-time (26 women), 40 part-time/adjunct (14 women). Expenses: Contact institution. *Financial support:* In 2010–11, 64 students received support. Application deadline: 4/1. In 2010, 71 DDSs awarded. Offers dental medicine (DDS). *Application deadline:* For fall admission, 12/31 for domestic students. *Application fee:* $50. Electronic applications accepted. *Application Contact:* Dr. Randy L. Kluender, Assistant Dean for Admissions and Student Affairs, 303-724-7120, E-mail: randy.kluender@ucdenver.edu. *Dean,* Dr. Denise K. Kassebaum, 303-724-7100, Fax: 303-724-7109, E-mail: denise.kassebaum@ucdenver.edu.

School of Education and Human Development Students: 1,125 full-time (901 women), 497 part-time (425 women); includes 34 Black or African American, non-Hispanic/Latino; 7 American Indian or Alaska Native, non-Hispanic/Latino; 45 Asian, non-Hispanic/Latino; 102 Hispanic/Latino; 1 Two or more races, non-Hispanic/Latino, 29 international. Average age 32. 605 applicants, 77% accepted, 367 enrolled. *Faculty:* 63 full-time (44 women), 97 part-time/adjunct (73 women). Expenses: Contact institution. *Financial support:* In 2010–11, 49 students received support; fellowships, research assistantships, teaching assistantships, Federal Work-Study, scholarships/grants, and unspecified assistantships available. Support available to part-time students. Financial award application deadline: 4/1; financial award applicants required to submit FAFSA. In 2010, 452 master's, 4 doctorates, 28 other advanced degrees awarded. *Degree program information:* Part-time and evening/weekend programs available. Postbaccalaureate distance learning degree programs offered (no on-campus study). Offers administrative leadership and policy studies (MA, Ed S); e-learning (MA); early childhood education (MA); education and human development (MA, Ed D, PhD, Ed S); educational psychology (MA); educational studies and research (PhD); elementary linguistically diverse education (MA); elementary math and science education (MA); elementary math education (MA); elementary reading and writing (MA); elementary science education (MA); instructional design and adult learning (MA); K-12 teaching (MA); leadership for educational equity (Ed D); school counseling (MA); school library and instructional leadership (MA); school psychology (Ed S); secondary English education (MA); secondary linguistically diverse education (MA); secondary math education (MA); secondary reading and writing (MA); secondary science education (MA); special education (MA). *Application fee:* $50 ($75 for international students). Electronic applications accepted. *Application Contact:* Student Services Center, 303-315-6300, Fax: 303-315-6311, E-mail: education@ucdenver.edu.

School of Medicine Students: 1,228 full-time (716 women), 65 part-time (44 women); includes 20 Black or African American, non-Hispanic/Latino; 15 American Indian or Alaska Native, non-Hispanic/Latino; 80 Asian, non-Hispanic/Latino; 56 Hispanic/Latino; 1 Two or more races, non-Hispanic/Latino, 29 international. Average age 28. 5,269 applicants, 9% accepted, 320 enrolled. *Faculty:* 1,984 full-time (1,021 women), 460 part-time/adjunct (249 women). Expenses: Contact institution. *Financial support:* Fellowships, research assistantships, teaching assistantships, career-related internships or fieldwork, Federal Work-Study, scholarships/grants, and unspecified assistantships available. Support available to part-time students. Financial award application deadline: 3/15; financial award applicants required to submit FAFSA. In 2010, 205 first professional degrees, 67 master's, 45 doctorates awarded. Offers biochemistry (PhD); bioinformatics (PhD); biomedical sciences (MS, PhD); biomolecular structure (PhD); cancer biology (PhD); cell biology, stem cells, and developmental biology (PhD); child health associate (MPAS); clinical investigation (PhD); clinical sciences (MS); computational bioscience (PhD); genetic counseling (MS); health information technology (PhD); health services research (PhD); human medical genetics (PhD); immunology (PhD); medicine (MD, MPAS, MS, DPT, PhD); microbiology (PhD); molecular biology (PhD); neuroscience (PhD); pharmacology (PhD); physical therapy (DPT); physiology (PhD). Electronic applications accepted. *Application Contact:* Office of Admissions, 303-724-8025, E-mail: somadmin@ucdenver.edu. *Dean,* Dr. Richard Krugman, 303-724-0882.

School of Pharmacy Students: 681 full-time (402 women), 216 part-time (131 women); includes 61 Black or African American, non-Hispanic/Latino; 8 American Indian or Alaska Native, non-Hispanic/Latino; 184 Asian, non-Hispanic/Latino; 43 Hispanic/Latino; 2 Two or more races, non-Hispanic/Latino, 24 international. Average age 31. 1,002 applicants, 24% accepted, 169 enrolled. *Faculty:* 103 full-time (45 women), 63 part-time/adjunct (39 women). Expenses: Contact institution. *Financial support:* Fellowships, research assistantships, teaching assistantships, Federal Work-Study and scholarships/grants available. Support available to part-time students. Financial award application deadline: 3/15; financial award applicants required to submit FAFSA. In 2010, 163 first professional degrees, 11 doctorates awarded. Postbaccalaureate distance learning degree programs offered (no on-campus study). Offers clinical pharmaceutical sciences (PhD); pharmaceutical biotechnology (PhD); pharmaceutical outcomes research (PhD); pharmacy (Pharm D, PhD); toxicology (PhD). *Application deadline:* For fall admission, 12/1 for domestic students. *Application fee:* $150. Electronic applications accepted. *Application Contact:* Julie Rodriguez, Admissions, 303-724-2634, E-mail: julie.rodriguez@ucdenver.edu. *Dean,* Ralpha Altiere, 303-724-2631, E-mail: ralph.altiere@ucdenver.edu.

School of Public Affairs Students: 352 full-time (204 women), 193 part-time (120 women); includes 18 Black or African American, non-Hispanic/Latino; 4 American Indian or Alaska Native, non-Hispanic/Latino; 21 Asian, non-Hispanic/Latino; 40 Hispanic/Latino; 1 Two or more races, non-Hispanic/Latino, 37 international. Average age 33. 315 applicants, 68% accepted, 133 enrolled. *Faculty:* 26 full-time (13 women), 17 part-time/adjunct (7 women). Expenses: Contact institution. *Financial support:* In 2010–11, 44 students received support, including 3 fellowships with full tuition reimbursements available (averaging $15,000 per year); research assistantships, teaching assistantships, Federal Work-Study, scholarships/grants, and unspecified assistantships also available. Support available to part-time students. Financial award application deadline: 4/1; financial award applicants required to submit FAFSA. In 2010, 147 master's, 4 doctorates awarded. *Degree program information:* Part-time and evening/weekend programs available. Postbaccalaureate distance learning degree programs offered (no on-campus study). Offers criminal justice (MCJ); public administration (MPA); public affairs (PhD). *Application deadline:* For fall admission, 3/15 priority date for domestic students; for spring admission, 10/15 priority date for domestic students. *Application fee:* $50 ($75 for international students). Electronic applications accepted. *Application Contact:* Antoinette Sandoval, Student Service Specialist, 303-315-2487, Fax: 303-315-2229, E-mail: antoinette.sandoval@ucdenver.edu. *Dean,* Paul Teske, 303-315-2805, Fax: 303-315-2229, E-mail: paul.teske@ucdenver.edu.

UNIVERSITY OF CONNECTICUT, Storrs, CT 06269

General Information State-supported, coed, university. CGS member. *Graduate housing:* Rooms and/or apartments available on a first-come, first-served basis to single and married students. Housing application deadline: 4/1. *Research affiliation:* U. S. Navy–Submarine Medical Research Laboratory, Haskins Laboratories.

GRADUATE UNITS

Graduate School Students: 3,792 full-time (2,013 women), 2,358 part-time (1,145 women); includes 901 minority (306 Black or African American, non-Hispanic/Latino; 16 American Indian or Alaska Native, non-Hispanic/Latino; 303 Asian, non-Hispanic/Latino; 276 Hispanic/Latino), 1,224 international. Average age 31. 8,167 applicants, 18% accepted, 977 enrolled. *Faculty:* 1,360 full-time (453 women). Expenses: Contact institution. *Financial support:* In 2010–11, 1,031 teaching assistantships with full tuition reimbursements were awarded; fellowships, research assistantships with full tuition reimbursements, career-related internships or fieldwork and Federal Work-Study also available. Financial award application deadline: 2/1; financial award applicants required to submit FAFSA. In 2010, 1,511 master's, 285 doctorates, 134 other advanced degrees awarded. *Degree program information:* Part-time and evening/weekend programs available. Postbaccalaureate distance learning degree programs offered (minimal on-campus study). *Application deadline:* For fall admission, 2/1 priority date for domestic and international students; for spring admission, 11/1 for domestic students, 10/1 for international students. Applications are processed on a rolling basis. *Application fee:* $55. Electronic applications accepted. *Application Contact:* Anne K. Lanzit, Associate Director of Graduate Admissions, 860-486-3617, Fax: 860-486-6739, E-mail: anne.lanzit@uconn.edu. *Interim Dean*, Dr. Lee Aggison, 860-486-3614, Fax: 860-486-6739, E-mail: lee.aggison@uconn.edu.

Center for Continuing Studies Postbaccalaureate distance learning degree programs offered. Offers continuing studies (MPS); homeland security leadership (MPS); humanitarian services administration (MPS); labor relations (MPS); occupational safety and health management (MPS); personnel (MPS).

College of Agriculture and Natural Resources Offers agricultural and resource economics (MS, PhD); agriculture and natural resources (MS, PhD); allied health sciences (MS); animal science (MS, PhD); natural resources management and engineering (MS, PhD); nutritional sciences (MS, PhD); pathobiology (MS, PhD); plant and soil sciences (MS, PhD). Electronic applications accepted.

College of Liberal Arts and Sciences Offers actuarial science (MS, PhD); African studies (MA); anthropology (MA, PhD); applied financial mathematics (MS); applied genomics (MS, PSM); audiology (Au D, PhD); behavioral neuroscience (PhD); biochemistry (MS, PhD); biophysics and structural biology (MS, PhD); biopsychology (PhD); botany (MS, PhD); cell and developmental biology (MS, PhD); chemistry (MS, PhD); clinical psychology (MA, PhD); cognition and instruction (PhD); communication processes (MA); communication processes and marketing communication (PhD); comparative literature and cultural studies (MA, PhD); comparative physiology (MS, PhD); culture, health and human development (Graduate Certificate); developmental psychology (MA, PhD); ecological psychology (PhD); ecology (MS, PhD); economics (MA, PhD); endocrinology (MS, PhD); English (MA, PhD); entomology (MS, PhD); European studies (MA); experimental psychology (PhD); French (MA, PhD); general psychology (MA, PhD); genetics, genomics, and bioinformatics (MS, PhD); geographic information systems (Certificate); geography (MS, PhD); geological sciences (MS, PhD); German (MA, PhD); health psychology (Graduate Certificate); history (MA, PhD); human development and family studies (MA, PhD); industrial/organizational psychology (PhD); international studies (MA, Graduate Certificate); Italian (MA, PhD); Italian history and culture (MA); Judaic studies (MA); language and cognition (PhD); Latin American studies (MA); liberal arts and sciences (MA, MPA, MS, PSM, Au D, PhD, Certificate, Graduate Certificate); linguistics (MA, PhD); marine sciences (MS, PhD); mathematics (MS, PhD); medieval studies (MA, PhD); microbial systems analysis (MS, PSM); microbiology (MS, PhD); neurobiology (MS, PhD); neuroscience (PhD); nonprofit management (Graduate Certificate); occupational health psychology (Graduate Certificate); philosophy (MA, PhD); physics (MS, PhD); plant cell and molecular biology (MS, PhD); political science (MA, PhD); public administration (MPA, Graduate Certificate); public financial management (Graduate Certificate); quantitative research methods (Graduate Certificate); social psychology (MA, PhD); sociology (MA, PhD); Spanish (MA, PhD); speech-language pathology (MA, PhD); statistics (MS, PhD); survey research (MA, Graduate Certificate); zoology (MS, PhD). Electronic applications accepted.

Neag School of Education Offers adult learning (MA, PhD); agriculture (MA); agriculture education (PhD, Post-Master's Certificate); bilingual and bicultural education (MA, PhD, Post-Master's Certificate); cognition and instruction (MA, PhD, Post-Master's Certificate); counseling psychology (MA, PhD, Post-Master's Certificate); education (MA, DPT, Ed D, PhD, Post-Master's Certificate); education policy analysis (PhD); educational administration (Ed D, PhD, Post-Master's Certificate); elementary education (MA, PhD, Post-Master's Certificate); English education (MA, PhD, Post-Master's Certificate); exercise science (MA, PhD); gifted and talented education (MA, PhD, Post-Master's Certificate); higher education and student affairs (MA); history and social sciences education (MA, PhD, Post-Master's Certificate); learning technology (MA, PhD, Post-Master's Certificate); mathematics education (MA, PhD, Post-Master's Certificate); measurement, evaluation, and assessment (MA, PhD, Post-Master's Certificate); physical therapy (DPT); reading education (MA, PhD, Post-Master's Certificate); school counseling (MA, Post-Master's Certificate); school psychology (MA, PhD, Post-Master's Certificate); science education (MA, PhD); secondary education (MA, PhD, Post-Master's Certificate); special education (MA, PhD, Post-Master's Certificate); sport management and sociology (MA, PhD); world languages education (MA, PhD, Post-Master's Certificate). Electronic applications accepted.

School of Business Offers accounting (MS, PhD); business administration (Exec MBA, MBA, PhD); finance (PhD); health care management and insurance studies (MBA); management (PhD); management consulting (MBA); marketing (PhD); marketing intelligence (MBA). Electronic applications accepted.

School of Engineering Offers biomedical engineering (MS, PhD); chemical engineering (MS, PhD); civil engineering (MS, PhD); computer science (MS, PhD); electrical engineering (MS, PhD); engineering (M Eng, MS, PhD); environmental engineering (MS, PhD); materials science and engineering (MS, PhD); mechanical engineering (MS, PhD); metallurgy and materials engineering (MS, PhD). Electronic applications accepted.

School of Fine Arts Offers acting (MFA); art history (MA); conducting (M Mus, DMA); costume design (MFA); fine arts (M Mus, MA, MFA, DMA, PhD, Performer's Certificate); historical musicology (MA); lighting design (MFA); music (Performer's Certificate); music education (M Mus, PhD); music theory (MA); music theory and history (PhD); performance (M Mus, DMA); puppetry (MA, MFA); scenic design (MFA); studio art (MFA). Electronic applications accepted.

School of Nursing Offers nursing (MS, PhD, Post-Master's Certificate). Electronic applications accepted.

School of Pharmacy Offers medicinal chemistry (MS, PhD); pharmaceutics (MS, PhD); pharmacology (MS, PhD); pharmacology and toxicology (MS, PhD); pharmacy (Pharm D, MS, PhD); toxicology (MS, PhD). Electronic applications accepted.

School of Social Work Offers social work (MSW, PhD). Electronic applications accepted.

University of Connecticut Health Center Offers biomedical science (PhD); clinical and translational research (MS); dental science (M Dent Sc); health (M Dent Sc, MPH, MS, PhD); public health (MPH). Electronic applications accepted.

Institute of Materials Science Offers materials science (MS, PhD); polymer science and engineering (MS, PhD).

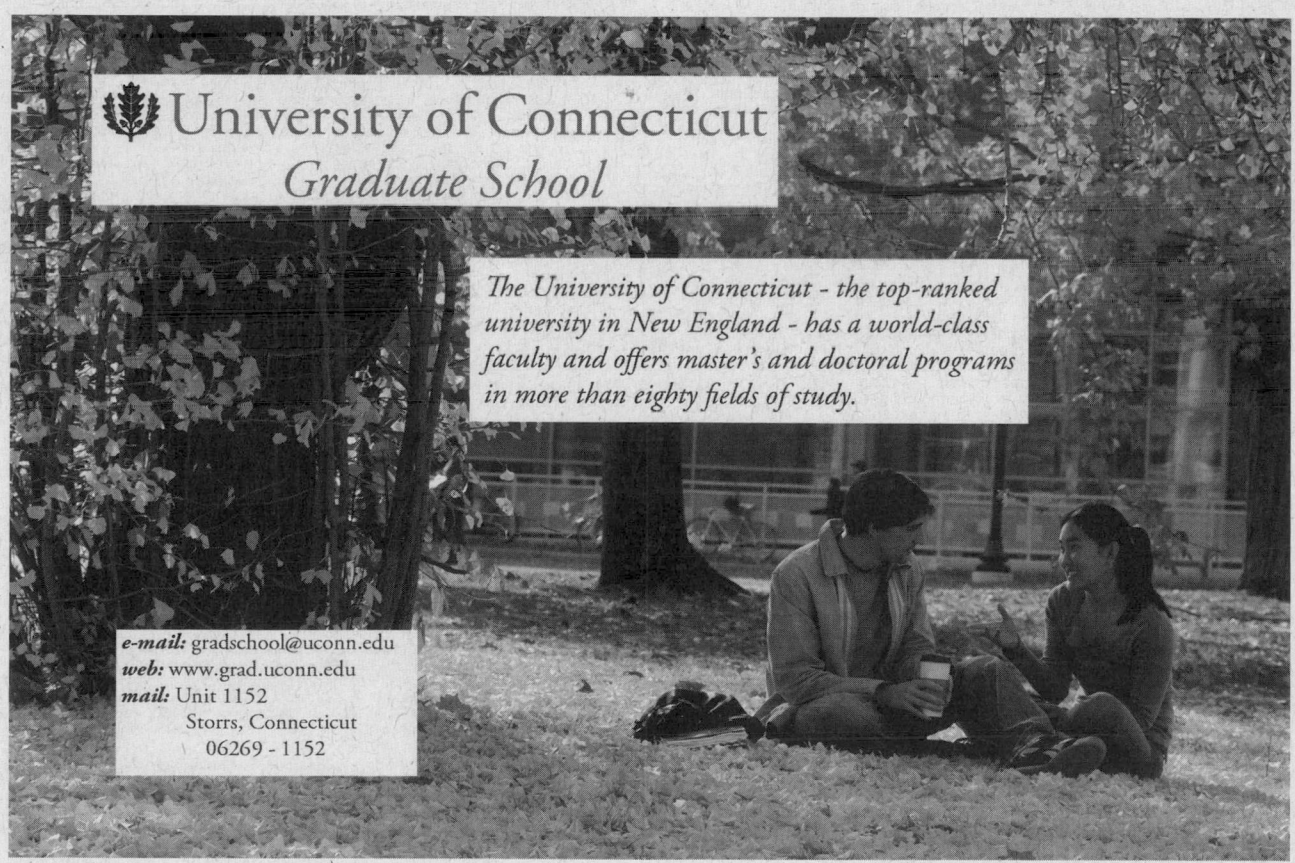

School of Law Students: 450 full-time (203 women), 242 part-time (106 women); includes 31 Black or African American, non-Hispanic/Latino; 3 American Indian or Alaska Native, non-Hispanic/Latino; 50 Asian, non-Hispanic/Latino; 54 Hispanic/Latino, 12 international. Average age 25. 2,376 applicants, 25% accepted, 186 enrolled. *Faculty:* 54 full-time (24 women), 54 part-time/adjunct (11 women). Expenses: Contact institution. *Financial support:* In 2010–11, 294 students received support. Federal Work-Study, scholarships/grants, and tuition waivers

University of Connecticut (continued)

(full and partial) available. Financial award application deadline: 3/15; financial award applicants required to submit FAFSA. In 2010, 212 first professional degrees awarded. *Degree program information:* Part-time programs available. Offers law (JD). *Application deadline:* For fall admission, 3/15 for domestic and international students. Applications are processed on a rolling basis. *Application fee:* $60. Electronic applications accepted. *Application Contact:* Karen Lynn DeMeola, Assistant Dean for Admissions and Student Finance, 860-570-5162, Fax: 860-570-5153, E-mail: karen.demeola@law.uconn.edu. *Dean,* Jeremy Paul, 860-570-5127, Fax: 860-570-5218.

See Display on previous page and Close-Up on page 987.

UNIVERSITY OF CONNECTICUT HEALTH CENTER, Farmington, CT 06030

General Information State-supported, coed, graduate-only institution. *Enrollment by degree level:* 516 first professional, 159 master's, 179 doctoral, 102 other advanced degrees. *Graduate faculty:* 393 full-time (124 women), 116 part-time/adjunct (65 women). *Graduate housing:* On-campus housing not available. *Student services:* Campus safety program, career counseling, child daycare facilities, free psychological counseling, grant writing training, international student services, low-cost health insurance, services for students with disabilities. *Library facilities:* Lyman Maynard Stowe Library. *Online resources:* library catalog, web page, access to other libraries' catalogs. *Collection:* 200,526 titles, 1,497 serial subscriptions, 1,620 audiovisual materials.

Computer facilities: 66 computers available on campus for general student use. A campuswide network can be accessed from off campus. Online class registration is available. *Web address:* http://www.uchc.edu/.

General Application Contact: Tricia Avolt, Graduate Admissions Coordinator, 860-679-2175, Fax: 860-679-1899, E-mail: robertson@nso2.uchc.edu.

GRADUATE UNITS

Graduate School Students: 197 full-time (113 women), 129 part-time (80 women); includes 58 minority (20 Black or African American, non-Hispanic/Latino; 1 American Indian or Alaska Native, non-Hispanic/Latino; 26 Asian, non-Hispanic/Latino; 11 Hispanic/Latino), 86 international. Expenses: Contact institution. *Financial support:* In 2010–11, 173 research assistantships with full and partial tuition reimbursements (averaging $27,000 per year) were awarded. Financial award applicants required to submit FAFSA. In 2010, 27 doctorates awarded. *Degree program information:* Part-time and evening/weekend programs available. Offers biomedical sciences (PhD); biomedical sciences—integrated (PhD); cell analysis and modeling (PhD); cell biology (PhD); clinical and translational research (MS); genetics and developmental biology (PhD); immunology (PhD); molecular biology and biochemistry (PhD); neuroscience (PhD); public health (MPH); skeletal, craniofacial and oral biology (PhD). *Application deadline:* Applications are processed on a rolling basis. *Application Contact:* Tricia Avolt, Graduate Admissions Coordinator, 860-679-2175, Fax: 860-679-1899, E-mail: robertson@nso2.uchc.edu. *Associate Dean,* Dr. Barbara Kream, 860-679-3849, Fax: 860-679-1258, E-mail: kream@nso1.uchc.edu.

School of Dental Medicine Students: 178 full-time (98 women); includes 49 minority (6 Black or African American, non-Hispanic/Latino; 1 American Indian or Alaska Native, non-Hispanic/Latino; 29 Asian, non-Hispanic/Latino; 12 Hispanic/Latino; 1 Two or more races, non-Hispanic/Latino), 6 international. Average age 25. 1,192 applicants, 4% accepted, 43 enrolled. Expenses: Contact institution. *Financial support:* In 2010–11, 114 students received support, including 2 research assistantships with full tuition reimbursements available (averaging $27,000 per year); fellowships, teaching assistantships, Federal Work-Study and institutionally sponsored loans also available. Financial award application deadline: 4/15; financial award applicants required to submit FAFSA. In 2010, 40 DMDs awarded. Offers dental medicine (DMD, MDS, Certificate); dental science (MDS). *Application deadline:* For fall admission, 2/1 for domestic students. *Application fee:* $75. Electronic applications accepted. *Application Contact:* Tricia Avolt, Graduate Admissions Coordinator, 860-679-2175, Fax: 860-679-1899, E-mail: robertson@nso2.uchc.edu. *Associate Dean for Dental Academic Affairs,* Dr. R. Lamont MacNeil, 860-679-2207, Fax: 860-679-1899, E-mail: macneil@nso.uchc.edu.

School of Medicine Students: 348 full-time (198 women), 4 part-time (2 women); includes 126 minority (35 Black or African American, non-Hispanic/Latino; 3 American Indian or Alaska Native, non-Hispanic/Latino; 65 Asian, non-Hispanic/Latino; 21 Hispanic/Latino; 2 Two or more races, non-Hispanic/Latino), 6 international. Average age 26. 3,141 applicants, 7% accepted, 89 enrolled. *Faculty:* 396 full-time (130 women), 104 part-time/adjunct (54 women). Expenses: Contact institution. *Financial support:* In 2010–11, 217 students received support, including 31 research assistantships (averaging $27,000 per year); institutionally sponsored loans also available. Financial award application deadline: 4/15; financial award applicants required to submit FAFSA. In 2010, 75 first professional degrees awarded. Offers medicine (MD). *Application deadline:* For fall admission, 12/15 for domestic and international students. *Application fee:* $85. Electronic applications accepted. *Application Contact:* Dr. Richard Zeff, Assistant Dean and Director, 860-679-2112, Fax: 860-679-1282, E-mail: zeff@neuron.uchc.edu. *Dean,* Dr. Cato Laurencin, 860-679-2413, Fax: 860-679-1282.

UNIVERSITY OF DALLAS, Irving, TX 75062-4736

General Information Independent-religious, coed, university. *Enrollment:* 2,843 graduate, professional, and undergraduate students; 371 full-time matriculated graduate/professional students (148 women), 1,094 part-time matriculated graduate/professional students (454 women). *Enrollment by degree level:* 1,359 master's, 76 doctoral, 30 other advanced degrees. *Graduate faculty:* 54 full-time (13 women), 36 part-time/adjunct (7 women). *Tuition:* Full-time $7500; part-time $720 per credit hour. *Required fees:* $500; $60 per credit hour. $300 per semester. One-time fee: $150. Tuition and fees vary according to program and student level. *Graduate housing:* Room and/or apartments available on a first-come, first-served basis to single students; on-campus housing not available to married students. Typical cost: $3150 per year ($5163 including board). Room and board charges vary according to board plan and housing facility selected. Housing application deadline: 6/1. *Student services:* Campus employment opportunities, career counseling, exercise/wellness program, international student services, services for students with disabilities, teacher training. *Library facilities:* William A. Blakley Library. *Online resources:* library catalog, web page, access to other libraries' catalogs. *Collection:* 245,228 titles, 1,310 serial subscriptions, 1,317 audiovisual materials.

Computer facilities: Computer purchase and lease plans are available. 125 computers available on campus for general student use. A campuswide network can be accessed from student residence rooms and from off campus. Online class registration is available. *Web address:* http://www.udallas.edu/.

General Application Contact: Dr. David Sweet, Dean, Braniff Graduate School, 972-721-5288, Fax: 972-721-5280, E-mail: dsweet@udallas.edu.

GRADUATE UNITS

Braniff Graduate School of Liberal Arts *Degree program information:* Part-time programs available. Offers American studies (MAS); art (MA, MFA); English literature (MA, MENG); humanities (M Hum, MA); liberal arts (M Hum, M Pol, M Psych, M Th, MA, MAS, MCSL, MEL, MENG, MFA, MPM, MRE, MTS, PhD); philosophy (MA); politics (M Pol, MA); psychology (M Psych, MA); theology (M Th, MA).

Institute of Philosophic Studies Offers literature (PhD); philosophy (PhD); politics (PhD).

Graduate School of Management *Degree program information:* Part-time and evening/weekend programs available. Postbaccalaureate distance learning degree programs offered (no on-campus study). Offers accounting (MBA, MM, MS); business management (MBA, MM); corporate finance (MBA, MM); financial services (MBA); global business (MBA, MM); health services management (MBA, MM); human resource management (MBA, MM); information assurance (MBA, MM, MS); information technology (MBA, MM, MS); information technology service management (MBA, MM, MS); marketing management (MBA, MM); organization development (MBA, MM); project management (MBA, MM); sports and entertainment management (MBA, MM); strategic leadership (MBA, MM); supply chain management (MBA); supply chain management and market logistics (MM). Electronic applications accepted.

Institute for Religious and Pastoral Studies *Degree program information:* Part-time and evening/weekend programs available. Postbaccalaureate distance learning degree programs offered (no on-campus study). Offers religious and pastoral studies (MCSL, MPM, MRE, MTS).

UNIVERSITY OF DAYTON, Dayton, OH 45469-1300

General Information Independent-religious, coed, university. CGS member. *Enrollment:* 11,214 graduate, professional, and undergraduate students; 1,930 full-time matriculated graduate/professional students (933 women), 886 part-time matriculated graduate/professional students (537 women). *Enrollment by degree level:* 625 first professional, 1,971 master's, 195 doctoral, 25 other advanced degrees. *Graduate faculty:* 308 full-time (100 women), 175 part-time/adjunct (71 women). *Tuition:* Full-time $7800; part-time $650 per credit hour. *Graduate housing:* Room and/or apartments available on a first-come, first-served basis to single students; on-campus housing not available to married students. Typical cost: $4640 per year. *Student services:* Campus employment opportunities, campus safety program, career counseling, child daycare facilities, exercise/wellness program, free psychological counseling, grant writing training, international student services, low-cost health insurance, multicultural affairs office, services for students with disabilities, teacher training, writing training. *Library facilities:* Roesch Library plus 2 others. *Online resources:* library catalog, web page, access to other libraries' catalogs. *Collection:* 1.3 million titles, 24,325 serial subscriptions, 7,641 audiovisual materials. *Research affiliation:* American Chemical Council (material testing), The IAMS Company (insulin studies), Knights Templar Eye Foundation (eye research), Miami Valley Hospital (water research), Research Corporation (DNA research), Ohio Space Grant Consortium (flight simulation).

Computer facilities: Computer purchase and lease plans are available. A campuswide network can be accessed from student residence rooms and from off campus. Online class registration, applications, admission/enrollment status, virtual orientation, online digital resources, online courses, assistive technology, learning management system, multimedia labs, payment, cyber cafes, centrally-licensed, downloadable software and training are available. *Web address:* http://www.udayton.edu/.

General Application Contact: Alexander Popovski, Associate Director of International and Graduate Admissions, 937-229-2357, Fax: 937-229-4729, E-mail: alex.popovski@notes.udayton.edu.

GRADUATE UNITS

Graduate School Students: 1,930 full-time (933 women), 886 part-time (537 women); includes 312 minority (204 Black or African American, non-Hispanic/Latino; 7 American Indian or Alaska Native, non-Hispanic/Latino; 48 Asian, non-Hispanic/Latino; 47 Hispanic/Latino; 6 Two or more races, non-Hispanic/Latino), 289 international. Average age 30. 1,997 applicants, 61% accepted, 685 enrolled. *Faculty:* 308 full-time (100 women), 175 part-time/adjunct (71 women). Expenses: Contact institution. *Financial support:* In 2010–11, 262 research assistantships with full and partial tuition reimbursements (averaging $11,000 per year), 115 teaching assistantships with full and partial tuition reimbursements (averaging $10,750 per year) were awarded; fellowships, career-related internships or fieldwork, institutionally sponsored loans, scholarships/grants, traineeships, health care benefits, and unspecified assistantships also available. Support available to part-time students. Financial award applicants required to submit FAFSA. In 2010, 758 master's, 28 doctorates, 10 other advanced degrees awarded. *Degree program information;* Part-time and evening/weekend programs available. Postbaccalaureate distance learning degree programs offered (no on-campus study). *Application deadline:* For fall admission, 3/1 priority date for domestic and international students; for winter admission, 7/1 priority date for international students; for spring admission, 1/1 priority date for international students. Applications are processed on a rolling basis. *Application fee:* $0 ($50 for international students). Electronic applications accepted. *Application Contact:* Alexander Popovski, Associate Director of International and Graduate Admissions, 937-229-4411, Fax: 937-229-4729, E-mail: gradadmission@udayton.edu. *Associate Provost/Dean,* Dr. Paul Vanderburgh, 937-229-2390, Fax: 937-229-2400, E-mail: udgradschool@udayton.edu.

College of Arts and Sciences Students: 202 full-time (116 women), 66 part-time (35 women); includes 26 minority (11 Black or African American, non-Hispanic/Latino; 2 American Indian or Alaska Native, non-Hispanic/Latino; 3 Asian, non-Hispanic/Latino; 9 Hispanic/Latino; 1 Two or more races, non-Hispanic/Latino), 44 international. Average age 30. 353 applicants, 49% accepted, 75 enrolled. *Faculty:* 117 full-time (37 women), 14 part-time/adjunct (4 women). Expenses: Contact institution. *Financial support:* In 2010–11, 4 fellowships with full tuition reimbursements (averaging $15,814 per year), 22 research assistantships with full and partial tuition reimbursements (averaging $10,500 per year), 67 teaching assistantships with full tuition reimbursements (averaging $12,538 per year) were awarded; career-related internships or fieldwork, Federal Work-Study, institutionally sponsored loans, scholarships/grants, traineeships, health care benefits, tuition waivers (full and partial), and unspecified assistantships also available. Support available to part-time students. Financial award application deadline: 3/1; financial award applicants required to submit FAFSA. In 2010, 90 master's, 1 doctorate awarded. *Degree program information:* Part-time and evening/weekend programs available. Postbaccalaureate distance learning degree programs offered (no on-campus study). Offers applied mathematics (MAS); arts and sciences (MA, MAS, MCS, MFM, MME, MPA, MS, PhD); biology (MS, PhD); chemistry (MS); clinical psychology (MA); communication (MA); computer science (MCS); English (MA); financial mathematics (MFM); general psychology (MA); mathematics education (MME); pastoral ministry (MA); public administration (MPA); theological studies (MA); theology (PhD). *Application deadline:* For fall admission, 3/1 priority date for domestic and international students; for winter admission, 7/1 priority date for international students; for spring admission, 1/1 priority date for international students. Applications are processed on a rolling basis. *Application fee:* $0 ($50 for international students). Electronic applications accepted. *Application Contact:* Alexander Popovski, Associate Director of International and Graduate Admissions, 937-229-2357, Fax: 937-229-4729, E-mail: gradadmission@udayton.edu. *Dean,* Dr. Paul Benson, 937-229-2601, Fax: 937-229-2615.

School of Business Administration Students: 184 full-time (72 women), 110 part-time (34 women); includes 23 minority (7 Black or African American, non-Hispanic/Latino; 7 Asian, non-Hispanic/Latino; 8 Hispanic/Latino; 1 Two or more races, non-Hispanic/Latino), 31 international. Average age 28. 220 applicants, 85% accepted, 103 enrolled. *Faculty:* 25 full-time (7 women), 14 part-time/adjunct (2 women). Expenses: Contact institution. *Financial support:* In 2010–11, 15 research assistantships with full and partial tuition reimbursements (averaging $7,020 per year) were awarded; career-related internships or fieldwork, institutionally sponsored loans, scholarships/grants, health care benefits, and unspecified assistantships also available. Support available to part-time students. Financial award application deadline: 3/15; financial award applicants required to submit FAFSA. In 2010, 113 master's awarded. *Degree program information:* Part-time and evening/weekend programs available. Offers accounting (MBA); business intelligence (MBA); cyber security (MBA); entrepreneurship (MBA); finance (MBA); international business (MBA); marketing (MBA); MIS (MBA); operations management (MBA); technology-enhanced business/e-commerce (MBA). *Application deadline:* For fall admission, 3/1 priority date for international students; for winter admission, 7/1 priority date for international students; for spring admission, 1/1 priority date for international students. Applications are processed on a rolling basis. *Application fee:* $0 ($50 for international students). Electronic applications accepted. *Application Contact:* Jeffrey Carter, Assistant Director, MBA Program, 937-229-3733, Fax: 937-229-3882, E-mail: jeff.carter@notes.udayton.edu. *Director, MBA Program,* Janice M. Glynn, 937-229-3733, Fax: 937-229-3882, E-mail: glynn@udayton.edu.

School of Education and Allied Professions Students: 628 full-time (449 women), 574 part-time (435 women); includes 152 minority (124 Black or African American, non-Hispanic/Latino; 3 American Indian or Alaska Native, non-Hispanic/Latino; 14 Asian, non-Hispanic/Latino; 9 Hispanic/Latino; 2 Two or more races, non-Hispanic/Latino), 14 international. Average age 33. 821 applicants, 63% accepted, 344 enrolled. *Faculty:* 57 full-time (30 women), 86 part-time/adjunct (55 women). Expenses: Contact institution. *Financial support:* In 2010–11, 32 research assistantships with full tuition reimbursements (averaging $9,378 per year), 2 teaching assistantships with full tuition reimbursements (averaging $9,378 per year) were awarded. Financial award applicants required to submit FAFSA. In 2010, 434 master's, 5 doctorates, 10 other advanced degrees awarded. *Degree program information:*

Part-time and evening/weekend programs available. Postbaccalaureate distance learning degree programs offered (no on-campus study). Offers adolescent/young adult (MS Ed); art education (MS Ed); college student personnel (MS Ed); community counseling (MS Ed); early childhood education (MS Ed); early childhood leadership advocacy (MS Ed); education administration (Ed S); education and allied professions (MS Ed, DPT, PhD, Ed S); educational leadership (MS Ed, PhD, Ed S); exercise science (MS Ed); higher education administration (MS Ed); human services (MS Ed); inclusive early childhood (MS Ed); interdisciplinary education (MS Ed); intervention specialist education, mild/moderate (MS Ed); literacy (MS Ed); middle childhood (MS Ed); multi-age education (MS Ed); music education (MS Ed); physical therapy (DPT); school counseling (MS Ed); school psychology (MS Ed, Ed S); teacher as leader (MS Ed); technology in education (MS Ed). *Application deadline:* For fall admission, 3/15 priority date for domestic students, 3/1 priority date for international students; for winter admission, 7/1 priority date for international students; for spring admission, 1/1 priority date for international students. Applications are processed on a rolling basis. *Application fee:* $0 ($50 for international students). Electronic applications accepted. *Application Contact:* Alexander Popovski, Associate Director of International and Graduate Admissions, 937-229-2357, Fax: 937-229-4729, E-mail: gradadmission@udayton.edu. *Dean,* Dr. Kevin Kelly, 937-229-3146, Fax: 937-229-3199, E-mail: kevin.kelly@notes.udayton.edu.

School of Engineering Students: 394 full-time (94 women), 128 part-time (30 women); includes 59 minority (31 Black or African American, non-Hispanic/Latino; 17 Asian, non-Hispanic/Latino; 10 Hispanic/Latino; 1 Two or more races, non-Hispanic/Latino), 194 international. Average age 28. 597 applicants, 59% accepted, 163 enrolled. *Faculty:* 50 full-time (4 women), 36 part-time/adjunct (3 women). Expenses: Contact institution. *Financial support:* In 2010–11, 105 students received support, including 7 fellowships with full tuition reimbursements available (averaging $28,000 per year), 84 research assistantships with full tuition reimbursements available (averaging $15,000 per year), 14 teaching assistantships with full tuition reimbursements available (averaging $9,000 per year); career-related internships or fieldwork, institutionally sponsored loans, health care benefits, tuition waivers (full and partial), and unspecified assistantships also available. Financial award applicants required to submit FAFSA. In 2010, 121 master's, 22 doctorates awarded. *Degree program information:* Part-time and evening/weekend programs available. Postbaccalaureate distance learning degree programs offered (no on-campus study). Offers aerospace engineering (MSAE, DE, PhD); bioengineering instrumentation (MS); bioprocess engineering (MS); biosystems engineering (MS); electrical and computer engineering (MSEE, DE, PhD); electro-optics (MSEO, PhD); engineering (MS, MS Ch E, MS Mat E, MSAE, MSCE, MSE, MSEE, MSEM, MSEM, MSEO, MSME, MSMS, DE, PhD); engineering management (MSEM); engineering mechanics (MSEM); environmental engineering (MSCE); geotechnical engineering (MSCE); management science (MSMS); materials engineering (MS Mat E, DE, PhD); mechanical engineering (MSME, DE, PhD); renewable and clean energy (MS); structural engineering (MSCE); transportation engineering (MSCE); water resources engineering (MSCE). *Application deadline:* For fall admission, 8/1 priority date for domestic students, 3/1 priority date for international students; for winter admission, 7/1 priority date for international students; for spring admission, 1/1 priority date for international students. Applications are processed on a rolling basis. *Application fee:* $0 ($50 for international students). Electronic applications accepted. *Application Contact:* Alexander Popovski, Associate Director of International and Graduate Admissions, 937-229-4411, Fax: 937-229-4729, E-mail: gradadmission@udayton.edu. *Associate Dean,* Dr. John Weber, 937-229-2736, Fax: 937-229-2756, E-mail: john.weber@notes.udayton.edu.

School of Law Students: 522 full-time (202 women), 8 part-time (3 women); includes 53 minority (31 Black or African American, non-Hispanic/Latino; 2 American Indian or Alaska Native, non-Hispanic/Latino; 8 Asian, non-Hispanic/Latino; 11 Hispanic/Latino; 1 Two or more races, non-Hispanic/Latino), 5 international. Average age 26. 2,171 applicants, 55% accepted, 216 enrolled. *Faculty:* 55 full-time (21 women), 24 part-time/adjunct (7 women). Expenses: Contact institution. *Financial support:* Career-related internships or fieldwork, institutionally sponsored loans, scholarships/grants, and tuition waivers (partial) available. Financial award application deadline: 3/1; financial award applicants required to submit FAFSA. In 2010, 146 first professional degrees, 1 master's awarded. Offers law (JD, LL M, MSL). *Application deadline:* For fall admission, 5/1 priority date for domestic and international students; for spring admission, 3/1 priority date for domestic and international students. Applications are processed on a rolling basis. *Application fee:* $0 ($50 for international students). Electronic applications accepted. *Application Contact:* Janet L. Hein, Assistant Dean/Director of Admissions and Financial Aid, 937-229-3555, Fax: 937-229-4194, E-mail: lawinfo@notes.udayton.edu. *Dean,* Lisa A. Kloppenberg, 937-229-3795, Fax: 937-229-2469.

UNIVERSITY OF DELAWARE, Newark, DE 19716

General Information State-related, coed, university. CGS member. *Graduate housing:* Rooms and/or apartments available to single and married students. Housing application deadline: 3/15. *Research affiliation:* Hagley Museum, Winterthur Museum, Longwood Gardens, Bartol Research Foundation.

GRADUATE UNITS

Alfred Lerner College of Business and Economics *Degree program information:* Part-time and evening/weekend programs available. Offers accounting (MS); business administration (MBA); business and economics (MA, MBA, MS, PhD); economic education (PhD); economics (MA, MS, PhD); economics for entrepreneurship and educators (MA); finance (MS); hospitality information management (MS); information systems and technology management (MS). Electronic applications accepted.

College of Agriculture and Natural Resources *Degree program information:* Part-time programs available. Offers agricultural economics (MS); agricultural education (MA); agriculture and natural resources (MA, MS, PhD); agriculture and technical education (MA); animal sciences (MS, PhD); bioresources engineering (MS); entomology and applied ecology (MS, PhD); food sciences (MS); operations research (MS, PhD); plant and soil sciences (MS, PhD); public horticulture (MS); statistics (MS). Electronic applications accepted.

College of Arts and Sciences *Degree program information:* Part-time and evening/weekend programs available. Offers acting (MFA); applied mathematics (MS, PhD); art (MA, MFA); art history (MA, PhD); arts and sciences (MA, MALS, MFA, MM, MS, DPT, PhD); behavioral neuroscience (PhD); biochemistry (MA, MS, PhD); biomechanics and movement science (MS, PhD); biotechnology (MS); cancer biology (MS, PhD); cell and extracellular matrix biology (MS, PhD); cell and systems physiology (MS, PhD); chemistry (MA, MS, PhD); clinical psychology (PhD); cognitive psychology (PhD); communication (MA); composition (MM); criminology (MA, PhD); developmental biology (MS, PhD); early American culture (MA); ecology and evolution (MS, PhD); English and American literature (MA, PhD); fashion and apparel studies (MS); foreign languages and literatures (MA); foreign languages pedagogy (MA); history (MA, PhD); history of technology and industrialization (MA, PhD); liberal studies (MALS); linguistics (MA, PhD); mathematics (MS, PhD); microbiology (MS, PhD); molecular biology and genetics (MS, PhD); music education (MM); performance (MM); physical therapy (DPT); physics and astronomy (MS, PhD); political science and international relations (MA, PhD); practicing art conservation (MS); social psychology (PhD); sociology (MA, PhD); stage management (MFA); technical Chinese translation (MA); technical production (MFA). Electronic applications accepted.

College of Earth, Ocean, and Environment Offers geography (MA, MS, PhD); geological sciences (MA, PhD); geology (MS, PhD); marine science and policy (MMP, MS, PhD); ocean engineering (MS, PhD). Electronic applications accepted.

School of Marine Science and Policy Offers marine policy (MMP); marine studies (MS, PhD); oceanography (PhD).

College of Engineering *Degree program information:* Part-time and evening/weekend programs available. Postbaccalaureate distance learning degree programs offered (minimal on-campus study). Offers chemical engineering (M Ch E, PhD); computer and information sciences (MS, PhD); electrical and computer engineering (MSECE, PhD); engineering (M Ch E, MAS, MCE, MEM, MMSE, MS, MSECE, MSME, PhD); environmental engineering (MAS, MCE, PhD); geotechnical engineering (MAS, MCE, PhD); materials science and engineering (MMSE, PhD); mechanical engineering (MEM, MSME, PhD); ocean engineering (MAS, MCE, PhD); structural engineering (MAS, MCE, PhD); transportation engineering (MAS, MCE, PhD); water resource engineering (MAS, MCE, PhD). Electronic applications accepted.

College of Health Sciences *Degree program information:* Part-time and evening/weekend programs available. Postbaccalaureate distance learning degree programs offered. Offers adult nurse practitioner (MSN, PMC); cardiopulmonary clinical nurse specialist (MSN, PMC); cardiopulmonary clinical nurse specialist/adult nurse practitioner (MSN, PMC); exercise science (MS); family nurse practitioner (MSN, PMC); gerontology clinical nurse specialist (MSN, PMC); gerontology clinical nurse specialist geriatric nurse practitioner (PMC); gerontology clinical nurse specialist/geriatric nurse practitioner (MSN); health promotion (MS); health sciences (MS, MSN, PMC); health services administration (MSN, PMC); human nutrition (MS); kinesiology and applied physiology (MS, PhD); nursing of children clinical nurse specialist (MSN, PMC); nursing of children clinical nurse specialist/pediatric nurse practitioner (MSN, PMC); oncology/immune deficiency clinical nurse specialist (MSN, PMC); oncology/immune deficiency clinical nurse specialist/adult nurse practitioner (MSN, PMC); perinatal/women's health clinical nurse specialist (MSN, PMC); perinatal/women's health clinical nurse specialist/women's health nurse practitioner (MSN, PMC); psychiatric nursing clinical nurse specialist (MSN, PMC). Electronic applications accepted.

College of Human Services, Education and Public Policy *Degree program information:* Part-time and evening/weekend programs available. Offers counseling in higher education (M Ed, MA); human development and family studies (MS, PhD); human services, education and public policy (M Ed, MA, MEEP, MI, MPA, MS, Ed D, PhD, Ed S). Electronic applications accepted.

Center for Energy and Environmental Policy Offers community development and nonprofit leadership (MA); energy and environmental policy (MA); environmental and energy policy (MEEP, PhD); governance, planning and management (PhD); historic preservation (MA); social and urban policy (PhD); technology, environment and society (PhD); urban affairs and public policy (MA, PhD). Electronic applications accepted.

School of Education *Degree program information:* Part-time and evening/weekend programs available. Offers education (PhD); educational leadership (Ed D); higher education (M Ed); instruction (MI); reading (M Ed); school leadership (M Ed); school psychology (MA, Ed S); teaching English as a second language (TESL) (MA). Electronic applications accepted.

School of Public Policy and Administration *Degree program information:* Part-time and evening/weekend programs available. Offers public administration (MPA); public policy and administration (MPA). Electronic applications accepted.

UNIVERSITY OF DENVER, Denver, CO 80208

General Information Independent, coed, university. CGS member. *Enrollment:* 11,842 graduate, professional, and undergraduate students; 3,437 full-time matriculated graduate/professional students (2,036 women), 2,765 part-time matriculated graduate/professional students (1,495 women). *Enrollment by degree level:* 965 first professional, 4,187 master's, 733 doctoral, 317 other advanced degrees. *Graduate faculty:* 640 full-time (273 women), 604 part-time/adjunct (311 women). *Tuition:* Full-time $35,604; part-time $29,670 per year. *Required fees:* $687 per year. Tuition and fees vary according to program. *Graduate housing:* Rooms and/or apartments available on a first-come, first-served basis to single and married students. Housing application deadline: 5/1. *Student services:* Campus employment opportunities, campus safety program, career counseling, exercise/wellness program, free psychological counseling, international student services, low-cost health insurance, multicultural affairs office, services for students with disabilities, teacher training, writing training. *Library facilities:* Penrose Library plus 1 other. *Online resources:* library catalog, web page, access to other libraries' catalogs. *Collection:* 1.5 million titles, 39,271 serial subscriptions, 20,015 audiovisual materials. *Research affiliation:* National Center for Atmospheric Research (infrared measurement).

Computer facilities: Computer purchase and lease plans are available. 200 computers available on campus for general student use. A campuswide network can be accessed from student residence rooms and from off campus. Online class registration is available. *Web address:* http://www.du.edu/.

General Application Contact: Office of Graduate Studies, 303-871-2706, E-mail: gstcomm@du.edu.

GRADUATE UNITS

Daniels College of Business Students: 540 full-time (193 women), 485 part-time (191 women); includes 103 minority (13 Black or African American, non-Hispanic/Latino; 4 American Indian or Alaska Native, non-Hispanic/Latino; 36 Asian, non-Hispanic/Latino; 44 Hispanic/Latino; 1 Native Hawaiian or other Pacific Islander, non-Hispanic/Latino; 5 Two or more races, non-Hispanic/Latino), 271 international. Average age 29. 1,870 applicants, 50% accepted, 381 enrolled. *Faculty:* 117 full-time (27 women), 59 part-time/adjunct (19 women). Expenses: Contact institution. *Financial support:* In 2010–11, 99 teaching assistantships with full and partial tuition reimbursements (averaging $1,669 per year) were awarded; career-related internships or fieldwork, Federal Work-Study, institutionally sponsored loans, scholarships/grants, and unspecified assistantships also available. Support available to part-time students. Financial award application deadline: 2/15; financial award applicants required to submit FAFSA. In 2010, 587 master's awarded. *Degree program information:* Part-time and evening/weekend programs available. Offers business (EMS, IMBA, M Acc, MBA, MS); business administration (MBA); business intelligence (MS); data mining (MS); general business administration (IMBA, MBA, MS); information technology (IMBA, MBA); international business/management (IMBA, MBA); management (MS); marketing (IMBA, MBA, MS). *Application deadline:* For fall admission, 1/15 priority date for domestic students. Applications are processed on a rolling basis. *Application fee:* $60. Electronic applications accepted. *Application Contact:* Admissions, 303-871-3416, Fax: 303-871-4466, E-mail: daniels@du.edu. *Dean,* Dr. Chris Riordan, 303-871-4324, E-mail: christine.riordan@du.edu.

Franklin L. Burns School of Real Estate and Construction Management Students: 40 full-time (8 women), 65 part-time (11 women); includes 11 minority (4 Black or African American, non-Hispanic/Latino; 3 Asian, non-Hispanic/Latino; 4 Hispanic/Latino), 14 international. Average age 32. 91 applicants, 77% accepted, 41 enrolled. *Faculty:* 8 full-time (1 woman), 8 part-time/adjunct (2 women). Expenses: Contact institution. *Financial support:* In 2010–11, 3 teaching assistantships with full and partial tuition reimbursements (averaging $1,966 per year) were awarded; career-related internships or fieldwork, Federal Work-Study, institutionally sponsored loans, scholarships/grants, and unspecified assistantships also available. Support available to part-time students. Financial award application deadline: 3/15; financial award applicants required to submit FAFSA. In 2010, 62 master's awarded. *Degree program information:* Part-time and evening/weekend programs available. Offers construction management (IMBA, MS); real estate (IMBA, MBA, MS); real estate and construction management (EMS). *Application deadline:* For fall admission, 11/15 priority date for domestic students; for spring admission, 10/15 priority date for domestic students. Applications are processed on a rolling basis. *Application fee:* $100. Electronic applications accepted. *Application Contact:* Victoria Chen, Graduate Admissions Manager, 303-871-3826, E-mail: victoria.chen@du.edu. *Director,* Dr. Mark Levine, 303-871-2142, E-mail: mark.levine@du.edu.

Reiman School of Finance Students: 47 full-time (13 women), 80 part-time (32 women); includes 7 minority (1 Black or African American, non-Hispanic/Latino; 5 Asian, non-Hispanic/Latino; 1 Hispanic/Latino), 82 international. Average age 26. 518 applicants, 32% accepted, 41 enrolled. *Faculty:* 15 full-time (3 women), 4 part-time/adjunct (2 women). Expenses: Contact institution. *Financial support:* In 2010–11, 17 teaching assistantships with partial tuition reimbursements (averaging $1,425 per year) were awarded; career-related internships or fieldwork, Federal Work-Study, institutionally sponsored loans, scholarships/grants, and unspecified assistantships also available. Support available to part-time students. Financial award application deadline: 3/15; financial award applicants required to submit FAFSA. In 2010, 92 master's awarded. *Degree program information:* Part-time and evening/weekend programs available. Offers finance (IMBA, MBA, MS). *Application deadline:* For fall admission, 11/15 priority date for domestic students; for spring admission, 10/15 priority date for domestic students. Applications are processed on a rolling basis. *Application fee:* $100. Electronic applications accepted. *Application Contact:* Tara Stenbakken, Graduate Admissions Manager, 303-871-4211, E-mail: tara.stenbakken@du.edu. *Co-Director,* Dr. Ron Rizzuto, 303-871-2010, E-mail: ronald.rizzuto@du.edu.

University of Denver (continued)

School of Accountancy Students: 26 full-time (17 women), 73 part-time (54 women); includes 9 minority (3 Asian, non-Hispanic/Latino; 6 Hispanic/Latino), 58 international. Average age 26. 291 applicants, 53% accepted, 57 enrolled. *Faculty:* 15 full-time (5 women), 5 part-time/adjunct (1 woman). Expenses: Contact institution. *Financial support:* In 2010–11, 11 teaching assistantships with full and partial tuition reimbursements (averaging $1,493 per year) were awarded; career-related internships or fieldwork, Federal Work-Study, institutionally sponsored loans, scholarships/grants, and unspecified assistantships also available. Support available to part-time students. Financial award application deadline: 3/15; financial award applicants required to submit FAFSA. In 2010, 51 master's awarded. *Degree program information:* Part-time and evening/weekend programs available. Offers accountancy (M Acc); accounting (MBA). *Application deadline:* For fall admission, 11/15 priority date for domestic students; for spring admission, 10/15 priority date for domestic students. Applications are processed on a rolling basis. *Application fee:* $100. Electronic applications accepted. *Application Contact:* Victoria Chen, Graduate Admissions Manager, 303-871-3826, E-mail: victoria.chen@du.edu. *Director,* Dr. Sharon Lassar, 303-871-2032, E-mail: slassar@du.edu.

Division of Arts, Humanities and Social Sciences Students: 195 full-time (138 women), 152 part-time (95 women); includes 49 minority (7 Black or African American, non-Hispanic/Latino; 3 American Indian or Alaska Native, non-Hispanic/Latino; 14 Asian, non-Hispanic/Latino; 18 Hispanic/Latino; 2 Native Hawaiian or other Pacific Islander, non-Hispanic/Latino; 5 Two or more races, non-Hispanic/Latino), 22 international. Average age 28. 1,171 applicants, 41% accepted, 258 enrolled. *Faculty:* 134 full-time (62 women), 66 part-time/adjunct (30 women). Expenses: Contact institution. *Financial support:* In 2010–11, 68 teaching assistantships with full and partial tuition reimbursements (averaging $11,415 per year) were awarded; career-related internships or fieldwork, Federal Work-Study, institutionally sponsored loans, scholarships/grants, and unspecified assistantships also available. Support available to part-time students. Financial award applicants required to submit FAFSA. In 2010, 127 master's, 16 doctorates, 3 other advanced degrees awarded. *Degree program information:* Part-time programs available. Offers advertising management (MS); affective science (PhD); affective/social psychology (PhD); archaeology (MA); arts, humanities and social sciences (MA, MFA, MM, MPP, MS, PhD, Certificate); clinical child psychology (PhD); communication studies (MA, PhD); creative writing (PhD); cultural anthropology (MA); developmental cognitive neuroscience (PhD); developmental psychology (PhD); digital media studies (MA); economics (MA); international and intercultural communication (MA); literary studies (MA, PhD); media, film, and journalism studies (MA); museum studies (MA); public policy (MPP); religious studies (MA); rhetoric and theory (PhD); strategic communication (MS). *Application deadline:* Applications are processed on a rolling basis. *Application fee:* $60. Electronic applications accepted. *Application Contact:* Information Contact, 360-871-4449, Fax: 303-871-4436, E-mail: ahss@du.edu. *Dean,* Dr. Anne McCall, 303-871-4449.

Lamont School of Music Students: 22 full-time (12 women), 43 part-time (22 women); includes 8 minority (1 Black or African American, non-Hispanic/Latino; 3 Asian, non-Hispanic/Latino; 2 Hispanic/Latino; 1 Native Hawaiian or other Pacific Islander, non-Hispanic/Latino; 1 Two or more races, non-Hispanic/Latino), 6 international. Average age 28. 97 applicants, 58% accepted, 34 enrolled. *Faculty:* 26 full-time (8 women), 41 part-time/adjunct (20 women). Expenses: Contact institution. *Financial support:* In 2010–11, 35 teaching assistantships with full and partial tuition reimbursements (averaging $6,600 per year) were awarded; career-related internships or fieldwork, Federal Work-Study, institutionally sponsored loans, scholarships/grants, and unspecified assistantships also available. Support available to part-time students. Financial award application deadline: 3/1; financial award applicants required to submit FAFSA. In 2010, 24 master's, 3 other advanced degrees awarded. *Degree program information:* Part-time programs available. Offers choral conducting (MA); composition (MA); jazz and commercial music (Certificate); jazz studies (MM); music theory (MA); musicology (MA); orchestral conducting (MM); performance (MM); piano pedagogy (MM); Suzuki pedagogy (MA, MM); Suzuki teaching (Certificate); wind conducting (MM). *Application deadline:* Applications are processed on a rolling basis. *Application fee:* $60. Electronic applications accepted. *Application Contact:* Jerrod Price, Director of Admission, 303-871-6950, Fax: 303-871-3118, E-mail: jerrod.price@du.edu. *Director,* Joseph Docksey, 303-871-6986, Fax: 303-871-3118, E-mail: jdocksey@du.edu.

School of Art and Art History Students: 14 full-time (12 women), 11 part-time (10 women); includes 2 minority (both Hispanic/Latino). Average age 29. 61 applicants, 46% accepted, 11 enrolled. *Faculty:* 13 full-time (7 women), 10 part-time/adjunct (3 women). Expenses: Contact institution. *Financial support:* In 2010–11, 2 teaching assistantships with full and partial tuition reimbursements (averaging $10,500 per year) were awarded; career-related internships or fieldwork, Federal Work-Study, institutionally sponsored loans, scholarships/grants, and unspecified assistantships also available. Support available to part-time students. Financial award application deadline: 3/1; financial award applicants required to submit FAFSA. In 2010, 19 master's awarded. *Degree program information:* Part-time programs available. Offers art history (MA); art history/museum studies (MA); electronic media arts and design (MFA). *Application deadline:* Applications are processed on a rolling basis. *Application fee:* $60. Electronic applications accepted. *Application Contact:* Dr. Annabeth Headrick, Graduate Admissions Coordinator, 303-871-3574, E-mail: saah-interest@du.edu. *Director,* Dr. M. E. Warlick, 303-871-2371, E-mail: mwarlick@du.edu.

DU-Iliff Joint PhD Program in Religious and Theological Studies Students: 42 full-time (20 women), 50 part-time (20 women); includes 13 minority (3 Black or African American, non-Hispanic/Latino; 2 American Indian or Alaska Native, non-Hispanic/Latino; 2 Asian, non-Hispanic/Latino; 5 Hispanic/Latino; 1 Two or more races, non-Hispanic/Latino), 3 international. Average age 39. 53 applicants, 49% accepted, 15 enrolled. *Faculty:* 20 full-time (10 women), 3 part-time/adjunct (0 women). Expenses: Contact institution. In 2010, 8 doctorates awarded. *Degree program information:* Part-time programs available. Offers religious and theological studies (PhD). Program jointly offered with Iliff School of Theology. *Application deadline:* For fall admission, 1/15 for domestic students. *Application fee:* $60. *Application Contact:* Meghan Laurvick, Coordinator, 303-765-3166, E-mail: jointphd@iliff.edu. *Director,* Dr. Ted Vial, 303-765-3166, E-mail: tvial@iliff.edu.

Faculty of Natural Sciences and Mathematics Students: 35 full-time (14 women), 110 part-time (54 women); includes 12 minority (1 Black or African American, non-Hispanic/Latino; 2 American Indian or Alaska Native, non-Hispanic/Latino; 3 Asian, non-Hispanic/Latino; 6 Hispanic/Latino), 22 international. Average age 29. 207 applicants, 56% accepted, 61 enrolled. *Faculty:* 76 full-time (20 women), 10 part-time/adjunct (6 women). Expenses: Contact institution. *Financial support:* In 2010–11, 23 research assistantships with full and partial tuition reimbursements (averaging $17,600 per year), 63 teaching assistantships with full and partial tuition reimbursements (averaging $17,500 per year) were awarded; career-related internships or fieldwork, Federal Work-Study, institutionally sponsored loans, and scholarships/grants also available. Support available to part-time students. Financial award application deadline: 3/1; financial award applicants required to submit FAFSA. In 2010, 25 master's, 10 doctorates awarded. *Degree program information:* Part-time and evening/weekend programs available. Offers biological sciences (MS, PhD); chemistry (MA, MS, PhD); geographic information science (MS); geography (MA, PhD); mathematics (MA, MS, PhD); natural sciences and mathematics (MA, MS, PhD); physics and astronomy (MS, PhD). *Application deadline:* Applications are processed on a rolling basis. *Application fee:* $60. Electronic applications accepted. *Application Contact:* Kirsten Norwood, Executive Assistant to the Dean, 303-871-2693, E-mail: knorwood@du.edu. *Dean,* Dr. Alayne Parson, 303-871-2693, E-mail: alayne.parson@du.edu.

Graduate School of Professional Psychology Students: 209 full-time (170 women), 36 part-time (25 women); includes 26 minority (7 Black or African American, non-Hispanic/Latino; 2 American Indian or Alaska Native, non-Hispanic/Latino; 5 Asian, non-Hispanic/Latino; 9 Hispanic/Latino; 3 Two or more races, non-Hispanic/Latino), 4 international. Average age 26. 612 applicants, 30% accepted, 124 enrolled. *Faculty:* 15 full-time (8 women), 24 part-time/adjunct (11 women). Expenses: Contact institution. *Financial support:* In 2010–11, 38 teaching assistantships with full and partial tuition reimbursements (averaging $2,952 per year) were awarded; career-related internships or fieldwork, Federal Work-Study, institutionally sponsored loans, scholarships/grants, unspecified assistantships, and clinical assistantships also available. Support available to part-time students. Financial award application deadline: 3/1; financial award applicants required to submit FAFSA. In 2010, 74 master's, 38 doctorates awarded. Offers clinical psychology (Psy D); forensic psychology (MA); international disaster psychology (MA); psychology (MA); sport and performance psychology (MA). *Application fee:* $60. Electronic applications accepted. *Application Contact:* Admissions Counselor, 303-871-3736, Fax: 303-871-7656, E-mail: gsppinfo@du.edu. *Dean,* Dr. Peter Buirski, 303-871-2382, E-mail: pbuirski@du.edu.

Graduate School of Social Work Students: 428 full-time (388 women), 19 part-time (15 women); includes 70 minority (12 Black or African American, non-Hispanic/Latino; 9 American Indian or Alaska Native, non-Hispanic/Latino; 12 Asian, non-Hispanic/Latino; 25 Hispanic/Latino; 2 Native Hawaiian or other Pacific Islander, non-Hispanic/Latino; 10 Two or more races, non-Hispanic/Latino), 4 international. Average age 29. 689 applicants, 75% accepted, 255 enrolled. *Faculty:* 21 full-time (14 women), 96 part-time/adjunct (80 women). Expenses: Contact institution. *Financial support:* In 2010–11, 1 research assistantship with full and partial tuition reimbursement (averaging $19,636 per year), 13 teaching assistantships with full and partial tuition reimbursements (averaging $14,462 per year) were awarded; unspecified assistantships also available. Financial award applicants required to submit FAFSA. In 2010, 228 master's, 11 doctorates, 77 other advanced degrees awarded. *Degree program information:* Part-time and evening/weekend programs available. Offers adoption competent practice (Certificate); animals and human health (Certificate); social work (MSW, PhD). *Application deadline:* For fall admission, 2/1 priority date for domestic students. Applications are processed on a rolling basis. *Application fee:* $60. Electronic applications accepted. *Application Contact:* Colin Schneider, Director of Admission and Financial Aid, 303-871-2841, Fax: 303-871-2845, E-mail: gssw-admission@du.edu. *Dean,* Dr. James Herbert Williams, 303-871-2203, E-mail: james.herbert@du.edu.

Josef Korbel School of International Studies Students: 461 full-time (279 women), 52 part-time (27 women); includes 71 minority (8 Black or African American, non-Hispanic/Latino; 3 American Indian or Alaska Native, non-Hispanic/Latino; 25 Asian, non-Hispanic/Latino; 25 Hispanic/Latino; 2 Native Hawaiian or other Pacific Islander, non-Hispanic/Latino; 8 Two or more races, non-Hispanic/Latino), 42 international. Average age 28. 1,056 applicants, 69% accepted, 259 enrolled. *Faculty:* 33 full-time (13 women), 38 part-time/adjunct (11 women). Expenses: Contact institution. *Financial support:* In 2010–11, 1 teaching assistantship with partial tuition reimbursement (averaging $9,999 per year) was awarded; career-related internships or fieldwork, Federal Work-Study, institutionally sponsored loans, scholarships/grants, and unspecified assistantships also available. Support available to part-time students. Financial award applicants required to submit FAFSA. In 2010, 230 master's, 5 doctorates, 42 other advanced degrees awarded. *Degree program information:* Part-time programs available. Offers conflict resolution (MA); development practice (MDP); global finance, trade and economic integration (MA); global health affairs (Certificate); homeland security (Certificate); humanitarian assistance (Certificate); international development (MA); international human rights (MA); international security (MA); international studies (MA, PhD). *Application deadline:* For fall admission, 1/15 priority date for domestic students, 12/15 priority date for international students; for winter admission, 10/15 priority date for domestic and international students. Applications are processed on a rolling basis. *Application fee:* $60. Electronic applications accepted. *Application Contact:* Brad Miller, Director of Graduate Admissions and Financial Aid, 303-871-2989, Fax: 303-871-2124, E-mail: korbeladm@du.edu. *Dean,* Ambassador Christopher R. Hill, 303-871-2539, Fax: 303-871-2124, E-mail: christopher.r.hill@du.edu.

Morgridge College of Education Students: 405 full-time (311 women), 423 part-time (326 women); includes 171 minority (53 Black or African American, non-Hispanic/Latino; 5 American Indian or Alaska Native, non-Hispanic/Latino; 17 Asian, non-Hispanic/Latino; 88 Hispanic/Latino; 8 Two or more races, non-Hispanic/Latino), 19 international. Average age 33. 934 applicants, 66% accepted, 381 enrolled. *Faculty:* 48 full-time (33 women), 68 part-time/adjunct (52 women). Expenses: Contact institution. *Financial support:* In 2010–11, 1 research assistantship with full and partial tuition reimbursement (averaging $18,297 per year), 26 teaching assistantships with full and partial tuition reimbursements (averaging $12,341 per year) were awarded; career-related internships or fieldwork, Federal Work-Study, institutionally sponsored loans, scholarships/grants, and unspecified assistantships also available. Support available to part-time students. Financial award application deadline: 3/1; financial award applicants required to submit FAFSA. In 2010, 203 master's, 59 doctorates, 108 other advanced degrees awarded. *Degree program information:* Part-time and evening/weekend programs available. Postbaccalaureate distance learning degree programs offered (no on-campus study). Offers counseling psychology (MA, PhD); curriculum and instruction (MA, PhD, Certificate); educational administration and policy studies (Certificate); educational psychology (MA, PhD, Ed S); higher education and adult studies (MA, PhD); library and information science (MLIS); library and information sciences (Certificate); school administration (PhD). *Application deadline:* Applications are processed on a rolling basis. *Application fee:* $60. Electronic applications accepted. *Application Contact:* Janet Erickson, Director of Graduate Admission, 303-871-2485, E-mail: edinfo@du.edu. *Dean,* Dr. Gregory M. Anderson, 303-871-3665, E-mail: gregory.m.anderson@du.edu.

School of Engineering and Computer Science Students: 10 full-time (2 women), 231 part-time (39 women); includes 25 minority (3 Black or African American, non-Hispanic/Latino; 9 Asian, non-Hispanic/Latino; 12 Hispanic/Latino; 1 Two or more races, non-Hispanic/Latino), 55 international. Average age 32. 259 applicants, 71% accepted, 61 enrolled. *Faculty:* 26 full-time (3 women), 7 part-time/adjunct (2 women). Expenses: Contact institution. *Financial support:* In 2010–11, 4 research assistantships with full and partial tuition reimbursements (averaging $10,772 per year), 2 teaching assistantships with full and partial tuition reimbursements (averaging $18,298 per year) were awarded; Federal Work-Study, scholarships/grants, and unspecified assistantships also available. Financial award applicants required to submit FAFSA. In 2010, 53 master's, 6 doctorates awarded. Offers bioengineering (MS); computer engineering (MS); computer science (MS, PhD); computer science and engineering (MS); computer science systems engineering (MS); electrical and computer engineering (PhD); electrical engineering (MS); engineering (MS, PhD); engineering and computer science (MS, PhD); interdisciplinary engineering (PhD); materials science (MS, PhD); mechanical engineering (MS, PhD); mechatronic systems engineering (MS); nanoscale science and engineering (PhD). *Application deadline:* Applications are processed on a rolling basis. *Application fee:* $60. Electronic applications accepted. *Application Contact:* Information Request, 303-871-2716, E-mail: secs@du.edu. *Dean,* Dr. Rahmat Shoureshi, 303-871-2621, E-mail: rshoures@du.edu.

Sturm College of Law Students: 992 full-time (483 women), 75 part-time (52 women); includes 178 minority (27 Black or African American, non-Hispanic/Latino; 14 American Indian or Alaska Native, non-Hispanic/Latino; 45 Asian, non-Hispanic/Latino; 77 Hispanic/Latino; 15 Two or more races, non-Hispanic/Latino), 20 international. Average age 28. 3,225 applicants, 36% accepted, 397 enrolled. *Faculty:* 62 full-time (15 women), 65 part-time/adjunct (30 women). Expenses: Contact institution. *Financial support:* Career-related internships or fieldwork, Federal Work-Study, institutionally sponsored loans, and tutorships available. Support available to part-time students. Financial award application deadline: 2/15; financial award applicants required to submit FAFSA. In 2010, 340 first professional degrees, 64 master's, 4 other advanced degrees awarded. *Degree program information:* Part-time and evening/weekend programs available. Offers American and comparative law (LL M); international natural resources law (LL M, MRLS); law (JD, LL M, MRLS, MSLA, MT, Certificate); legal administration (MSLA, Certificate); taxation (LL M, MT). *Application deadline:* For fall admission, 3/1 priority date for domestic students. Applications are processed on a rolling basis. *Application fee:* $60. Electronic applications accepted. *Application Contact:* Wende Best Conway, Assistant Director of Admissions, 303-871-6192, Fax: 303-871-6992, E-mail: admissions@law.du.edu. *Dean,* Martin Katz, 303-871-6103, Fax: 303-871-6992, E-mail: martin.katz@du.edu.

University College Students: 52 full-time (19 women), 1,044 part-time (625 women); includes 196 minority (81 Black or African American, non-Hispanic/Latino; 7 American Indian or Alaska Native, non-Hispanic/Latino; 30 Asian, non-Hispanic/Latino; 66 Hispanic/Latino; 3 Native Hawaiian or other Pacific Islander, non-Hispanic/Latino; 9 Two or more races, non-Hispanic/Latino), 76 international. Average age 36. 488 applicants, 91% accepted, 339 enrolled. *Faculty:* 7 full-time (2 women), 212 part-time/adjunct (83 women). Expenses: Contact institution. *Financial support:* Applicants required to submit FAFSA. In 2010, 286 master's, 130 other advanced degrees awarded. *Degree program information:* Part-time and evening/weekend programs available. Postbaccalaureate distance learning degree programs offered (no on-campus study). Offers arts and culture (MLS, Certificate); environmental policy and management (MAS, Certificate); geographic information systems (MAS, Certificate); global affairs (MLS, Certificate); healthcare leadership (MPH, Certificate); information and communications technology (MCIS, Certificate); leadership and organizations (MPS, Certificate); organizational and professional communication (MPS, Certificate); security management (MAS, Certificate); strategic human resource management (MPS, Certificate). *Application deadline:* For fall admission, 6/22 priority date for domestic students, 6/10 priority date for international students; for winter admission, 9/15 priority date for domestic students, 9/6 priority date for international students; for spring admission, 2/3 priority date for domestic students, 12/15 priority date for international students. Applications are processed on a rolling basis. *Application fee:* $75. Electronic applications accepted. *Application Contact:* Information Contact, 303-871-3155, Fax: 303-871-4047, E-mail: ucolinfo@du.edu. *Dean,* Dr. James Davis, 303-871-2291, Fax: 303-871-4047, E-mail: jdavis@du.edu.

UNIVERSITY OF DETROIT MERCY, Detroit, MI 48221

General Information Independent-religious, coed, university. *Graduate housing:* Rooms and/or apartments available to single and married students.

GRADUATE UNITS

College of Business Administration *Degree program information:* Part-time and evening/weekend programs available. Offers business administration (EMBA, MBA, MS, MSCIS, Certificate); business turnaround management (MS, Certificate); computer information systems (MSCIS); information assurance (MS).

College of Engineering and Science *Degree program information:* Part-time and evening/weekend programs available. Offers chemistry (MS); civil and environmental engineering (ME, DE); computer engineering (ME, DE); computer science (MSCS); computer science education (MATM); computer systems applications (MSCS); engineering and science (M Eng Mgt, MATM, ME, MS, MSCS, DE); engineering management (M Eng Mgt); mathematics education (MATM); mechanical engineering (ME, DE); mechatronics systems (ME, DE); signals and systems (ME, DE); software engineering (MSCS).

College of Health Professions Offers family nurse practitioner (MSN, Certificate); health professions (MHSA, MS, MSN, Certificate); health services administration (MHSA); health systems management (MSN); nurse anesthesiology (MS); physician assistant (MS).

College of Liberal Arts and Education *Degree program information:* Part-time and evening/weekend programs available. Offers addiction counseling (MA); addiction studies (Certificate); clinical psychology (MA, PhD); community counseling (MA); counseling (MA); criminal justice (MA); curriculum and instruction (MA); educational administration (MA); emotionally impaired (MA); industrial/organizational psychology (MA); intelligence analysis (MS); learning disabilities (MA); liberal arts and education (MA, MALS, MS, PhD, Certificate, Spec); liberal studies (MALS); religious studies (MA); school counseling (MA); school psychology (Spec); security administration (MS); special education (MA).

School of Architecture Offers architecture (M Arch).

School of Dentistry Offers dentistry (DDS, MS, Certificate); endodontics (MS, Certificate); orthodontics (MS, Certificate); periodontics (MS, Certificate).

School of Law *Degree program information:* Part-time programs available. Offers law (JD).

UNIVERSITY OF DUBUQUE, Dubuque, IA 52001-5099

General Information Independent-religious, coed, comprehensive institution. *Graduate housing:* Rooms and/or apartments available on a first-come, first-served basis to single students and available to married students.

GRADUATE UNITS

Program in Business Administration *Degree program information:* Part-time and evening/weekend programs available. Offers business administration (MBA). Electronic applications accepted.

Program in Communication *Degree program information:* Part-time and evening/weekend programs available. Offers information technologies communication (MAC); leadership and management (MAC); strategic and corporate communication (MAC). Electronic applications accepted.

Theological Seminary Students: 142 full-time (56 women), 16 part-time (9 women); includes 4 Black or African American, non-Hispanic/Latino; 1 American Indian or Alaska Native, non-Hispanic/Latino; 1 Asian, non-Hispanic/Latino; 3 Hispanic/Latino, 5 international. Average age 41. 72 applicants, 92% accepted, 56 enrolled. *Faculty:* 12 full-time (3 women), 8 part-time/adjunct (4 women). Expenses: Contact institution. *Financial support:* In 2010–11, 69 students received support. Career-related internships or fieldwork, Federal Work-Study, institutionally sponsored loans, scholarships/grants, and tuition waivers (full and partial) available. Support available to part-time students. Financial award application deadline: 6/1; financial award applicants required to submit FAFSA. In 2010, 28 master's, 3 doctorates awarded. Postbaccalaureate distance learning degree programs offered (minimal on-campus study). Offers theology (M Div, MAMC, D Min). *Application deadline:* For fall admission, 4/15 priority date for domestic students, 12/1 priority date for international students; for spring admission, 11/1 priority date for domestic students. Applications are processed on a rolling basis. *Application fee:* $30. *Application Contact:* Peggy Sell, Director, Seminary Admissions, 563-589-3287, E-mail: psell@dbq.edu. *Dean,* Dr. Bradley Longfield, 319-589-3122, Fax: 319-589-3110, E-mail: blongfie@dbq.edu.

UNIVERSITY OF EVANSVILLE, Evansville, IN 47722

General Information Independent-religious, coed, comprehensive institution. *Enrollment:* 2,898 graduate, professional, and undergraduate students; 153 full-time matriculated graduate/professional students (112 women), 28 part-time matriculated graduate/professional students (20 women). *Enrollment by degree level:* 110 master's, 71 doctoral. *Graduate faculty:* 17 full-time (8 women), 14 part-time/adjunct (8 women). *Tuition:* Full-time $7830. Tuition and fees vary according to course load and program. *Graduate housing:* On-campus housing not available. *Student services:* Career counseling, free psychological counseling, international student services, multicultural affairs office, services for students with disabilities. *Library facilities:* University of Evansville Libraries. *Online resources:* library catalog, web page, access to other libraries' catalogs. *Collection:* 280,833 titles, 575 serial subscriptions, 13,721 audiovisual materials. *Research affiliation:* Council of Independent Colleges (higher education administration), The New American Colleges and Universities (higher education administration), Independent Colleges of Indiana (higher education administration), Military Family Research Institute (higher education administration).

Computer facilities: 385 computers available on campus for general student use. A campuswide network can be accessed from student residence rooms and from off campus. Online class registration is available. *Web address:* http://www.evansville.edu/.

General Application Contact: Carla Doty, Director of Center for Adult Education, 812-488-2981, Fax: 812-488-2432, E-mail: cd39@evansville.edu.

GRADUATE UNITS

Center for Adult Education Students: 62 full-time (45 women), 2 part-time (0 women); includes 10 minority (all Black or African American, non-Hispanic/Latino), 1 international. Average age 36. 24 applicants, 96% accepted, 19 enrolled. *Faculty:* 4 full-time (2 women), 7 part-time/adjunct (3 women). Expenses: Contact institution. *Financial support:* In 2010–11, 10 students received support. Unspecified assistantships available. Financial award application deadline: 6/1; financial award applicants required to submit FAFSA. In 2010, 31 master's awarded. *Degree program information:* Part-time and evening/weekend programs available. Offers public service administration (MS). *Application deadline:* For fall admission, 7/15 priority date for domestic students; for spring admission, 11/30 priority date for domestic students. Applications are processed on a rolling basis. *Application fee:* $35. *Application Contact:* Carla Doty, Director, 812-488-2981, Fax: 812-488-2432, E-mail: cd39@evansville.edu. *Director,* Carla Doty, 812-488-2981, Fax: 812-488-2432, E-mail: cd39@evansville.edu.

College of Education and Health Sciences Students: 82 full-time (65 women), 25 part-time (19 women); includes 4 minority (1 Black or African American, non-Hispanic/Latino; 1 Asian, non-Hispanic/Latino; 2 Two or more races, non-Hispanic/Latino), 6 international. Average age 26. 133 applicants, 53% accepted, 60 enrolled. *Faculty:* 12 full-time (6 women), 6 part-time/adjunct (4 women). Expenses: Contact institution. *Financial support:* In 2010–11, 82 students received support. Scholarships/grants available. Financial award application deadline: 4/1; financial award applicants required to submit FAFSA. In 2010, 12 master's, 35 doctorates awarded. Offers education and health sciences (MS, MS Ed, DPT); health services administration (MS); physical therapy (DPT). *Application deadline:* Applications are processed on a rolling basis. *Application Contact:* Dr. Lynn Penland, Dean, 812-488-2360, Fax: 812-488-1146, E-mail: lp22@evansville.edu. *Dean,* Dr. Lynn Penland, 812-488-2360, Fax: 812-488-1146, E-mail: lp22@evansville.edu.

School of Education Students: 18 part-time (12 women). Average age 31. 19 applicants, 100% accepted, 17 enrolled. *Faculty:* 2 full-time (0 women). Expenses: Contact institution. *Financial support:* In 2010–11, 7 students received support. Teach Grants for teaching in Title I schools teaching 'high need field" available. Financial award application deadline: 6/1; financial award applicants required to submit FAFSA. Postbaccalaureate distance learning degree programs offered (minimal on-campus study). Offers education (MS Ed). *Application deadline:* Applications are processed on a rolling basis. *Application fee:* $35. *Application Contact:* Dr. Charles Watson, Chair, 812-488-2004, Fax: 812-488-6998, E-mail: cw73@evansville.edu. *Chair,* Dr. Charles Watson, 812-488-2004, Fax: 812-488-6998, E-mail: cw73@evansville.edu.

College of Engineering and Computer Science Students: 1 (woman) part-time. Average age 28. 1 applicant, 0% accepted, 0 enrolled. *Faculty:* 2 full-time (0 women). Expenses: Contact institution. *Financial support:* Scholarships/grants available. Financial award application deadline: 6/1; financial award applicants required to submit FAFSA. *Degree program information:* Part-time programs available. Offers electrical engineering and computer science (MS); engineering and computer science (MS). *Application deadline:* For fall admission, 5/1 priority date for domestic and international students. Applications are processed on a rolling basis. *Application fee:* $25 ($50 for international students). *Application Contact:* Dr. Dick Blandford, Department Chair, 812-488-2570, Fax: 812-488-2662, E-mail: blandford@evansville.edu. *Dean,* Dr. Philip Gerhart, 812-488-2651, Fax: 812-488-2780, E-mail: pg3@evansville.edu.

Schroeder Family School of Business Administration Students: 9 full-time (2 women); includes 1 minority (Hispanic/Latino). Average age 41. 16 applicants, 81% accepted, 8 enrolled. *Faculty:* 1 (woman) part-time/adjunct. Expenses: Contact institution. *Financial support:* In 2010–11, 3 students received support. Application deadline: 6/1. In 2010, 6 master's awarded. *Degree program information:* Part-time and evening/weekend programs available. Offers executive business administration (MBA). *Application deadline:* For fall admission, 6/1 for domestic students, 4/1 for international students. Applications are processed on a rolling basis. *Application fee:* $75. *Application Contact:* Dr. Peter Rosen, Chair, EMBA Admissions, 812-488-2851, Fax: 812-488-2872, E-mail: emba@evansville.edu. *Interim Dean,* Dr. Peter Sherman, 812-488-2851, Fax: 812-488-2872, E-mail: ps45@evansville.edu.

THE UNIVERSITY OF FINDLAY, Findlay, OH 45840-3653

General Information Independent-religious, coed, comprehensive institution. CGS member. *Enrollment:* 5,542 graduate, professional, and undergraduate students; 435 full-time matriculated graduate/professional students (297 women), 648 part-time matriculated graduate/professional students (342 women). *Enrollment by degree level:* 119 first professional, 835 master's, 129 doctoral. *Graduate faculty:* 120 full-time (65 women), 30 part-time/adjunct (14 women). *Tuition:* Full-time $17,000; part-time $700 per semester hour. *Required fees:* $680; $35 per semester hour. Tuition and fees vary according to course load and program. *Graduate housing:* Room and/or apartments available on a first-come, first-served basis to single students; on-campus housing not available to married students. *Student services:* Campus employment opportunities, campus safety program, career counseling, exercise/wellness program, free psychological counseling, grant writing training, international student services, low-cost health insurance, multicultural affairs office, services for students with disabilities, teacher training, writing training. *Library facilities:* Shafer Library plus 1 other. *Online resources:* library catalog, access to other libraries' catalogs. *Collection:* 145,948 titles, 7,479 serial subscriptions, 4,448 audiovisual materials. *Research affiliation:* Ohio State University Research Foundation (biology research), Rollin M. Gerstacker Foundation (environmental research), Department of Agriculture (wildlife research), Department of Education (bilingual teaching research), Department of Education (technology innovation), Department of Health and Human Services (terrorism preparedness).

Computer facilities: Computer purchase and lease plans are available. 274 computers available on campus for general student use. A campuswide network can be accessed from student residence rooms and from off campus. Online class registration is available. *Web address:* http://www.findlay.edu/.

General Application Contact: Heather Riffle, Assistant Director, Graduate and Professional Studies, 419-434-4640, Fax: 419-434-5517, E-mail: riffle@findlay.edu.

GRADUATE UNITS

Graduate and Professional Studies Students: 435 full-time (297 women), 648 part-time (342 women); includes 62 minority (22 Black or African American, non-Hispanic/Latino; 2 American Indian or Alaska Native, non-Hispanic/Latino; 29 Asian, non-Hispanic/Latino; 9 Hispanic/Latino), 159 international. Average age 35. 417 applicants, 82% accepted, 228 enrolled. *Faculty:* 120 full-time (65 women), 30 part-time/adjunct (14 women). Expenses: Contact institution. *Financial support:* In 2010–11, 13 research assistantships with full and partial tuition reimbursements (averaging $4,000 per year), 10 teaching assistantships with full and partial tuition reimbursements (averaging $6,000 per year) were awarded; career-related internships or fieldwork, Federal Work-Study, health care benefits, and unspecified assistantships also available. Financial award application deadline: 4/1; financial award applicants required to submit FAFSA. In 2010, 50 first professional degrees, 519 master's awarded. *Degree program information:* Part-time and evening/weekend programs available. Postbaccalaureate distance learning degree programs offered (no on-campus study). Offers administration (MA Ed); early childhood (MA Ed); elementary education (MA Ed); human resource development (MA Ed); leadership (MA Ed); special education (MA Ed); technology (MA Ed); web instruction (MA Ed). *Application deadline:* Applications are processed on a rolling basis. *Application fee:* $25. Electronic applications accepted. *Application Contact:* Heather Riffle, Assistant Director, Graduate and Professional Studies, 419-434-4640, Fax: 419-434-5517, E-mail: riffle@findlay.edu. *Dean,* Dr. Thomas Dillon, 419-434-4640, Fax: 419-434-5517, E-mail: dillon@findlay.edu.

College of Business Students: 25 full-time (11 women), 239 part-time (112 women); includes 15 minority (5 Black or African American, non-Hispanic/Latino; 9 Asian, non-Hispanic/Latino; 1 Hispanic/Latino), 98 international. Average age 25. 93 applicants, 86% accepted, 70 enrolled. *Faculty:* 20 full-time (5 women), 6 part-time/adjunct (0 women). Expenses: Contact institution. *Financial support:* In 2010–11, 8 research assistantships with full and partial tuition reimbursements (averaging $4,200 per year) were awarded; career-related internships or fieldwork, Federal Work-Study, health care benefits, and unspecified assistantships also available. Financial award application deadline: 4/1; financial award applicants required to submit FAFSA. In 2010, 283 master's awarded. *Degree program information:* Part-time and evening/weekend programs available. Postbaccalaureate distance learning degree programs offered (no on-campus study). Offers health care management (MBA); hospitality management (MBA); organizational leadership (MBA); public management (MBA). *Application deadline:* Applications are processed on a rolling basis. *Application fee:* $25. Electronic applications accepted. *Application Contact:* Heather Riffle, Assistant Director, Graduate and Professional Studies, 419-434-4640, Fax: 419-434-5517, E-mail: riffle@findlay.edu. *Dean,* Dr. Paul Sears, 419-434-4704, Fax: 419-434-4822.

College of Health Professions Students: 195 full-time (147 women), 47 part-time (35 women); includes 9 minority (3 Black or African American, non-Hispanic/Latino; 1 American Indian or Alaska Native, non-Hispanic/Latino; 3 Asian, non-Hispanic/Latino; 2 Hispanic/Latino), 1 international. Average age 35. 159 applicants, 78% accepted, 53 enrolled. *Faculty:* 36 full-time (26 women), 7 part-time/adjunct (4 women). Expenses: Contact institution. *Financial support:* In 2010–11, 2 research assistantships with full and partial

The University of Findlay (continued)

tuition reimbursements (averaging $3,600 per year), 3 teaching assistantships with full and partial tuition reimbursements (averaging $6,000 per year) were awarded; Federal Work-Study, health care benefits, and unspecified assistantships also available. Financial award applicants required to submit FAFSA. In 2010, 102 master's awarded. *Degree program information:* Evening/weekend programs available. Offers athletic training (MAT); health professions (MAT, MOT, MPA, DPT); occupational therapy (MOT); physical therapy (DPT); physician assistant (MPA). *Application deadline:* Applications are processed on a rolling basis. *Application fee:* $25. Electronic applications accepted. *Application Contact:* Heather Riffle, Assistant Director, Graduate and Professional Studies, 419-434-4640, Fax: 419-434-5517, E-mail: riffle@findlay.edu. *Dean,* Dr. Andrea Koepke, 419-434-4677, Fax: 419-434-4822, E-mail: koepke@findlay.edu.

College of Liberal Arts Students: 10 full-time (6 women), 26 part-time (21 women), 14 international. Average age 35. 13 applicants, 69% accepted, 6 enrolled. *Faculty:* 14 full-time (7 women). Expenses: Contact institution. *Financial support:* In 2010–11, 1 teaching assistantship with full tuition reimbursement (averaging $6,000 per year) was awarded; Federal Work-Study and health care benefits also available. Financial award application deadline: 4/1; financial award applicants required to submit FAFSA. In 2010, 15 master's awarded. *Degree program information:* Part-time and evening/weekend programs available. Offers bilingual education (MA); liberal arts (MA); teaching English to speakers of other languages (MA). *Application deadline:* Applications are processed on a rolling basis. *Application fee:* $25. Electronic applications accepted. *Application Contact:* Heather Riffle, Assistant Director, Graduate and Professional Studies, 419-434-4640, Fax: 419-434-5517, E-mail: riffle@findlay.edu. *Dean,* Dr. Gary Johnson, 419-434-4643, Fax: 419-434-4822, E-mail: gjohnson@findlay.edu.

College of Pharmacy Students: 119 full-time (80 women); includes 17 minority (4 Black or African American, non-Hispanic/Latino; 11 Asian, non-Hispanic/Latino; 2 Hispanic/Latino), 4 international. Average age 25. 197 applicants, 67% accepted, 77 enrolled. *Faculty:* 18 full-time (6 women). Expenses: Contact institution. *Financial support:* Federal Work-Study, health care benefits, and unspecified assistantships available. Financial award application deadline: 4/1; financial award applicants required to submit FAFSA. In 2010, 50 Pharm Ds awarded. Offers pharmacy (Pharm D). *Application deadline:* Applications are processed on a rolling basis. Electronic applications accepted. *Application Contact:* Heather Riffle, Assistant Director, Graduate and Professional Studies, 419-434-4640, Fax: 419-434-5517, E-mail: riffle@findlay.edu. *Dean,* Dr. Donald Stansloski, 419-434-5327, Fax: 419-434-4822, E-mail: stansloski@findlay.edu.

College of Sciences Students: 3 full-time (1 woman), 87 part-time (34 women); includes 10 minority (4 Black or African American, non-Hispanic/Latino; 1 American Indian or Alaska Native, non-Hispanic/Latino; 5 Asian, non-Hispanic/Latino), 28 international. Average age 25. 29 applicants, 83% accepted, 20 enrolled. *Faculty:* 11 full-time (3 women), 3 part-time/adjunct (2 women). Expenses: Contact institution. *Financial support:* In 2010–11, 1 research assistantship with full and partial tuition reimbursement (averaging $4,000 per year), 1 teaching assistantship with full and partial tuition reimbursement (averaging $6,000 per year) were awarded; career-related internships or fieldwork, Federal Work-Study, health care benefits, and unspecified assistantships also available. Financial award application deadline: 4/1; financial award applicants required to submit FAFSA. In 2010, 30 master's awarded. *Degree program information:* Part-time and evening/weekend programs available. Postbaccalaureate distance learning degree programs offered (no on-campus study). Offers environmental, safety and health management (MSEM); sciences (MSEM). *Application deadline:* Applications are processed on a rolling basis. *Application fee:* $25. Electronic applications accepted. *Application Contact:* Heather Riffle, Assistant Director, Graduate and Professional Studies, 419-434-4640, Fax: 419-434-5517, E-mail: riffle@findlay.edu. *Dean,* Dr. Terry Schwaner, 419-434-5377, E-mail: schwaner@findlay.edu.

UNIVERSITY OF FLORIDA, Gainesville, FL 32611

General Information State-supported, coed, university. CGS member. *Enrollment:* 49,827 graduate, professional, and undergraduate students; 9,437 full-time matriculated graduate/professional students (4,195 women), 3,280 part-time matriculated graduate/professional students (1,758 women). *Enrollment by degree level:* 7,540 master's, 4,969 doctoral, 205 other advanced degrees. *Graduate faculty:* 1,538 full-time (457 women), 127 part-time/adjunct (59 women). Tuition, state resident: full-time $10,916. Tuition, nonresident: full-time $28,309. *Graduate housing:* Rooms and/or apartments available on a first-come, first-served basis to single and married students. Typical cost: $6770 per year ($10,110 including board) for single students. *Student services:* Campus employment opportunities, campus safety program, career counseling, child daycare facilities, exercise/wellness program, free psychological counseling, grant writing training, international student services, low-cost health insurance, multicultural affairs office, services for students with disabilities, teacher training, writing training. *Library facilities:* George A. Smathers Libraries plus 8 others. *Online resources:* library catalog, web page, access to other libraries' catalogs. *Collection:* 6 million titles, 109,181 serial subscriptions, 76,492 audiovisual materials. *Research affiliation:* Los Alamos National Laboratory (high magnetic field research), National Center for Automated Information Research (law and business data), Oracle Corporation (database management), IBM (information infrastructure), Association of Universities for Research in Astronomy (Gemini multinational telescope).

Computer facilities: 2,200 computers available on campus for general student use. A campuswide network can be accessed from student residence rooms and from off campus. Online class registration, course management system are available. *Web address:* http://www.ufl.edu/.

General Application Contact: Graduate Admissions, 352-392-1365, E-mail: webrequests@admissions.ufl.edu.

GRADUATE UNITS

College of Dentistry Offers dentistry (DMD, MS, PhD, Certificate); endodontics (MS, Certificate); foreign trained dentistry (Certificate); oral biology (PhD); orthodontics (MS, Certificate); periodontology (MS, Certificate); prosthodontics (MS, Certificate).

College of Medicine Offers biochemistry and molecular biology (MS, PhD); biomedical sciences (PhD); clinical investigation (MS); epidemiology (MS); genetics (PhD); imaging science and technology (MS, PhD); immunology and microbiology (PhD); immunology and molecular pathology (PhD); medicine (MD, MPAS, MPH, MS, PhD); molecular cell biology (PhD); molecular genetics and microbiology (MS, PhD); neuroscience (MS, PhD); pharmacology and therapeutics (PhD); physician assistant (MPAS); physiology and functional genomics (PhD); physiology and pharmacology (PhD); public health (MPH). Electronic applications accepted.

College of Pharmacy Students: 147 full-time (84 women), 370 part-time (251 women); includes 55 Black or African American, non-Hispanic/Latino; 7 American Indian or Alaska Native, non-Hispanic/Latino; 39 Asian, non-Hispanic/Latino; 40 Hispanic/Latino, 66 international. Average age 33. 461 applicants, 38% accepted, 151 enrolled. *Faculty:* 32 full-time (13 women). Expenses: Contact institution. *Financial support:* In 2010–11, 68 students received support, including 16 fellowships, 6 research assistantships (averaging $16,365 per year), 46 teaching assistantships (averaging $18,469 per year); Federal Work-Study, institutionally sponsored loans, tuition waivers (full), and unspecified assistantships also available. Support available to part-time students. Financial award application deadline: 4/15; financial award applicants required to submit FAFSA. In 2010, 155 master's, 13 doctorates awarded. *Degree program information:* Part-time and evening/weekend programs available. Postbaccalaureate distance learning degree programs offered (minimal on-campus study). Offers clinical pharmaceutical sciences (PhD); clinical toxicology (Certificate); drug chemistry (Certificate); environmental forensics (Certificate); forensic death investigation (Certificate); forensic DNA and serology (MSP, Certificate); forensic drug chemistry (MSP); forensic science (MSP); forensic toxicology (Certificate); medicinal chemistry (MSP, PhD); pharmaceutical outcomes and policy (MSP, PhD); pharmaceutical sciences (MSP, PhD); pharmaceutics (MSP, PhD); pharmacodynamics (MSP, PhD); pharmacology (PhD); pharmacy (Pharm D, MSP, PhD, Certificate). *Application deadline:* For fall admission, 5/1 for domestic and international students; for winter admission, 8/1 for domestic and international students; for spring admission, 2/1 for domestic and international students. Applications are processed on a rolling basis. *Application fee:* $30. Electronic applications accepted. *Application Contact:* Dr. William J. Millard, Executive Associate Dean, 352-273-6311, Fax: 352-273-6306, E-mail: millard@cop.ufl.edu. *Dean,* Dr. William H. Riffee, 352-273-6309, Fax: 352-273-6306, E-mail: riffee@cop.ufl.edu.

College of Veterinary Medicine *Degree program information:* Part-time programs available. Offers forensic toxicology (Certificate); veterinary medical sciences (MS, PhD); veterinary medicine (DVM, MS, PhD, Certificate).

Graduate School Students: 9,437 full-time (4,195 women), 3,280 part-time (1,758 women); includes 568 Black or African American, non-Hispanic/Latino; 54 American Indian or Alaska Native, non-Hispanic/Latino; 600 Asian, non-Hispanic/Latino; 984 Hispanic/Latino, 3,630 international. Average age 30. 19,066 applicants, 33% accepted, 3238 enrolled. *Faculty:* 1,538 full-time (457 women), 127 part-time/adjunct (59 women). Expenses: Contact institution. *Financial support:* In 2010–11, 5,025 students received support, including 981 fellowships, 2,561 research assistantships (averaging $17,628 per year), 1,483 teaching assistantships (averaging $15,933 per year); career-related internships or fieldwork, Federal Work-Study, institutionally sponsored loans, and unspecified assistantships also available. Support available to part-time students. Financial award applicants required to submit FAFSA. In 2010, 68 first professional degrees, 3,672 master's, 874 doctorates awarded. *Degree program information:* Part-time and evening/weekend programs available. Postbaccalaureate distance learning degree programs offered. *Application deadline:* Applications are processed on a rolling basis. *Application fee:* $30. Electronic applications accepted. *Application Contact:* Office of Admissions, 352-392-1365, E-mail: gradinfo@ufl.edu. *Dean,* Dr. Henry T. Frierson, 352-392-6622, Fax: 352-392-8729, E-mail: hfrierson@ufl.edu.

College of Agricultural and Life Sciences Students: 904 full-time (447 women), 268 part-time (158 women); includes 25 Black or African American, non-Hispanic/Latino; 5 American Indian or Alaska Native, non-Hispanic/Latino; 40 Asian, non-Hispanic/Latino; 61 Hispanic/Latino, 387 international. Average age 30. 614 applicants, 43% accepted, 192 enrolled. *Faculty:* 346 full-time (93 women), 12 part-time/adjunct (4 women). Expenses: Contact institution. *Financial support:* In 2010–11, 744 students received support, including 155 fellowships with tuition reimbursements available, 515 research assistantships with tuition reimbursements available (averaging $17,173 per year), 74 teaching assistantships with tuition reimbursements available (averaging $17,409 per year); career-related internships or fieldwork, Federal Work-Study, institutionally sponsored loans, and unspecified assistantships also available. Support available to part-time students. Financial award application deadline: 2/1; financial award applicants required to submit FAFSA. In 2010, 217 master's, 129 doctorates awarded. *Degree program information:* Part-time programs available. Offers agricultural and life sciences (M Ag, MAB, MFAS, MFRC, MFYCS, MS, DPM, PhD); agricultural education and communication (M Ag, MS, PhD); agronomy (M Ag, MS, PhD); anatomy and development (MS, PhD); animal sciences (MS, PhD); biochemistry and molecular biology (MS, PhD); breeding and genetics (MS, PhD); ecology (MS, PhD); entomology and nematology (MS, PhD); family, youth, and community sciences (M Ag, MFYCS, MS); fisheries and aquatic sciences (MFAS, MS, PhD); food and resource economics (MAB, MS, PhD); food science (MS, PhD); forest resources and conservation (MFRC, MS, PhD); microbiology and cell science (MS, PhD); nutritional sciences (MS, PhD); plant biotechnology (MS, PhD); plant breeding and genetics (MS, PhD); plant medicine (DPM); plant molecular and cellular biology (MS, PhD); plant pathology (MS, PhD); plant production and nutrient management (MS, PhD); postharvest biology (MS, PhD); soil and water science (MS, PhD); stress physiology (MS, PhD); sustainable/organic practice (MS, PhD); taxonomy (MS, PhD); tissue culture (MS, PhD); weed science (MS, PhD); wildlife ecology and conservation (MS, PhD). *Application deadline:* Applications are processed on a rolling basis. *Application fee:* $30. Electronic applications accepted. *Application Contact:* Dr. Jane E. Luzar, Associate Dean for Academic Programs, 352-392-2251, Fax: 352-392-8988, E-mail: ejluzar@ufl.edu. *Interim Associate Dean,* Dr. Allen F. Wysocki, 352-392-1963, Fax: 352-392-8988, E-mail: wysocki@ufl.edu.

College of Design, Construction and Planning Students: 412 full-time (183 women), 80 part-time (34 women); includes 22 Black or African American, non-Hispanic/Latino; 3 American Indian or Alaska Native, non-Hispanic/Latino; 26 Asian, non-Hispanic/Latino; 44 Hispanic/Latino, 102 international. Average age 28. 518 applicants, 48% accepted, 85 enrolled. *Faculty:* 59 full-time (19 women), 2 part-time/adjunct (both women). Expenses: Contact institution. *Financial support:* In 2010–11, 129 students received support, including 18 fellowships, 61 research assistantships (averaging $8,664 per year), 50 teaching assistantships (averaging $8,585 per year); career-related internships or fieldwork, Federal Work-Study, and unspecified assistantships also available. Support available to part-time students. Financial award applicants required to submit FAFSA. In 2010, 134 master's, 6 doctorates awarded. *Degree program information:* Part-time programs available. Offers architecture (M Arch, MSAS); building construction (MBC, MICM, MSBC, PhD); design, construction and planning (M Arch, MAURP, MBC, MICM, MID, MLA, MSAS, MSBC, PhD); historic preservation (PhD); interior design (MID, PhD); landscape architecture (MLA); urban and regional planning (MAURP). *Application deadline:* Applications are processed on a rolling basis. *Application fee:* $30. Electronic applications accepted. *Application Contact:* Dr. Christopher Silver, Dean, 352-392-4836, Fax: 352-392-7266, E-mail: silver2@ufl.edu. *Dean,* Dr. Christopher Silver, 352-392-4836, Fax: 352-392-7266, E-mail: silver2@ufl.edu.

College of Education Students: 761 full-time (630 women), 673 part-time (543 women); includes 129 Black or African American, non-Hispanic/Latino; 5 American Indian or Alaska Native, non-Hispanic/Latino; 52 Asian, non-Hispanic/Latino; 186 Hispanic/Latino, 76 international. Average age 32. 741 applicants, 48% accepted, 226 enrolled. *Faculty:* 72 full-time (49 women). Expenses: Contact institution. *Financial support:* In 2010–11, 220 students received support, including 14 fellowships with tuition reimbursements available, 135 research assistantships with tuition reimbursements available (averaging $18,136 per year), 71 teaching assistantships with tuition reimbursements available (averaging $10,509 per year); career-related internships or fieldwork, Federal Work-Study, and unspecified assistantships also available. Support available to part-time students. Financial award applicants required to submit FAFSA. In 2010, 445 master's, 56 doctorates, 68 other advanced degrees awarded. *Degree program information:* Part-time and evening/weekend programs available. Postbaccalaureate distance learning degree programs offered (minimal on-campus study). Offers bilingual/ESOL education (M Ed, MAE, Ed D, PhD, Ed S); curriculum and instruction (M Ed, MAE, Ed D, PhD, Ed S); early childhood education (Ed D, PhD, Ed S); education (M Ed, MAE, Ed D, PhD, Ed S); educational leadership (M Ed, MAE, Ed D, PhD, Ed S); educational psychology (M Ed, MAE, Ed D, PhD, Ed S); elementary education (M Ed, MAE); English education (M Ed, MAE); higher education administration (Ed D, PhD, Ed S); marriage and family counseling (M Ed, MAE, Ed D, PhD, Ed S); mathematics education (M Ed, MAE); mental health counseling (M Ed, MAE, Ed D, PhD, Ed S); reading education (M Ed, MAE); research and evaluation methodology (M Ed, MAE, Ed D, PhD, Ed S); school counseling and guidance (M Ed, MAE, Ed D, PhD, Ed S); school psychology (M Ed, MAE, Ed D, PhD, Ed S); science education (M Ed, MAE); social foundations (M Ed, MAE, Ed D, PhD); social studies education (M Ed, MAE); special education (M Ed, MAE, Ed D, PhD, Ed S); student personnel in higher education (M Ed, MAE). *Application deadline:* For fall admission, 2/15 for domestic students, 12/1 for international students; for spring admission, 9/15 for domestic students, 3/1 for international students. Applications are processed on a rolling basis. *Application fee:* $30. Electronic applications accepted. *Application Contact:* Dr. Thomasenia L. Adams, Interim Associate Dean for Research and Faculty Development, 352-273-4194, Fax: 352-392-9193, E-mail: tla@coe.ufl.edu. *Dean,* Dr. Catherine A. Emihovich, 352-273-4135, Fax: 352-392-6930, E-mail: cemihovich@coe.ufl.edu.

College of Engineering Students: 2,461 full-time (525 women), 643 part-time (157 women); includes 68 Black or African American, non-Hispanic/Latino; 5 American Indian or Alaska Native, non-Hispanic/Latino; 125 Asian, non-Hispanic/Latino; 157 Hispanic/Latino, 1,772 international. Average age 27. 5,463 applicants, 43% accepted, 853 enrolled. *Faculty:* 235 full-time (25 women), 12 part-time/adjunct (3 women). Expenses: Contact institution. *Financial support:* In 2010–11, 1,181 students received support, including 78 fellowships with full tuition reimbursements available, 976 research assistantships with full tuition reimbursements available (averaging $19,823 per year), 127 teaching assistantships with full tuition reimbursements available (averaging $17,179 per year); career-related internships or fieldwork, Federal Work-Study, institutionally sponsored loans, and unspecified assistantships also available. Support available to part-time students. Financial award applicants required to submit FAFSA. In 2010, 893 master's, 224 doctorates awarded. *Degree program information:* Part-time programs available. Postbaccalaureate distance learning degree programs offered (no on-campus study). Offers aerospace engineering (ME, MS, PhD, Engr); agricultural and biological engineering (ME, MS, PhD, Engr); biomedical engineering (ME, MS, PhD, Certificate); chemical engineering (ME, MS, PhD); civil engineering (MCE, MS, PhD, Engr); coastal and oceanographic engineering (ME, MS, PhD, Engr); computer engineering (ME, MS, PhD); computer science (MS); digital arts and sciences (MS); electrical and computer engineering (ME, MS, PhD, Engr); engineering (MCE, ME, MS, PhD, Certificate, Engr); environmental engineering sciences (ME, MS, PhD, Engr); industrial and systems engineering (ME, MS, PhD, Engr); materials science and engineering (ME, MS, PhD, Engr); mechanical engineering (ME, MS, PhD, Engr); nuclear engineering sciences (ME, MS, PhD, Engr). *Application deadline:* Applications are processed on a rolling basis. *Application fee:* $30. Electronic applications accepted. *Application Contact:* Dr. David Norton, Associate Dean for Research and Graduate Programs, 352-392-0946, E-mail: dnort@eng.ufl.edu. *Dean,* Dr. Cammy R. Abernathy, 352-392-6000, E-mail: caber@ufl.edu.

College of Fine Arts Students: 230 full-time (132 women), 86 part-time (69 women); includes 18 Black or African American, non-Hispanic/Latino; 2 American Indian or Alaska Native, non-Hispanic/Latino; 9 Asian, non-Hispanic/Latino; 24 Hispanic/Latino, 38 international. Average age 31. 420 applicants, 38% accepted, 115 enrolled. *Faculty:* 80 full-time (30 women). Expenses: Contact institution. *Financial support:* In 2010–11, 94 students received support, including 16 fellowships, 15 research assistantships (averaging $15,385 per year), 63 teaching assistantships (averaging $12,436 per year); career-related internships or fieldwork, Federal Work-Study, institutionally sponsored loans, and unspecified assistantships also available. Support available to part-time students. Financial award applicants required to submit FAFSA. In 2010, 58 master's, 7 doctorates awarded. Postbaccalaureate distance learning degree programs offered. Offers art (MFA); art education (MA); art history (MA, PhD); choral conducting (MM, PhD); composition/theory (MM, PhD); digital arts and sciences (MA); ethnomusicology (PhD); fine arts (MA, MFA, MM, PhD); instrumental conducting (MM, PhD); museology (museum studies) (MA); music (MM, PhD); music education (MM, PhD); music history and literature (MM); musicology (PhD); performance (MM); sacred music (MM); theatre (MFA). *Application deadline:* For spring admission, 11/1 for domestic and international students. Applications are processed on a rolling basis. *Application fee:* $30. Electronic applications accepted. *Application Contact:* Edward Schaefer, Associate Dean for Academic and Student Affairs, 352-273-1482 Ext. 230, Fax: 352-392-3802, E-mail: eschaefer@arts.ufl.edu. *Interim Dean,* Lucinda Lavelli, 352-392-0207, Fax: 352-392-3802, E-mail: llavelli@arts.ufl.edu.

College of Health and Human Performance Students: 257 full-time (126 women), 46 part-time (20 women); includes 20 Black or African American, non-Hispanic/Latino; 1 American Indian or Alaska Native, non-Hispanic/Latino; 10 Asian, non-Hispanic/Latino; 25 Hispanic/Latino, 66 international. Average age 26. 694 applicants, 35% accepted, 158 enrolled. *Faculty:* 25 full-time (12 women), 1 (woman) part-time/adjunct. Expenses: Contact institution. *Financial support:* In 2010–11, 112 students received support, including 21 fellowships, 55 research assistantships (averaging $14,166 per year), 36 teaching assistantships (averaging $14,603 per year); career-related internships or fieldwork, Federal Work-Study, institutionally sponsored loans, and unspecified assistantships also available. Support available to part-time students. Financial award application deadline: 2/1; financial award applicants required to submit FAFSA. In 2010, 103 master's, 13 doctorates awarded. *Degree program information:* Part-time programs available. Offers athletic training/sport medicine (MS); biobehavioral science (MS, PhD); clinical exercise physiology (MS); exercise physiology (MS, PhD); health and human performance (PhD); health behavior (PhD); health communication (Graduate Certificate); health education and behavior (MS); human performance (MS); recreational studies (MS). *Application deadline:* For fall admission, 3/1 priority date for domestic students, 2/1 for international students; for spring admission, 9/15 for domestic students, 7/1 for international students. Applications are processed on a rolling basis. *Application fee:* $30. Electronic applications accepted. *Application Contact:* Dr. William Chen, Associate Dean, Research and Graduate Programs, 352-392-0583 Ext. 1284, Fax: 352-392-1909, E-mail: wchen@hhp.ufl.edu. *Dean,* Dr. Steve Dorman, 352-392-0578 Ext. 1225, Fax: 352-392-1909, E-mail: sdorman@hhp.ufl.edu.

College of Journalism and Communications Students: 164 full-time (123 women), 33 part-time (23 women); includes 15 Black or African American, non-Hispanic/Latino; 1 American Indian or Alaska Native, non-Hispanic/Latino; 14 Asian, non-Hispanic/Latino; 10 Hispanic/Latino, 82 international. Average age 29. 458 applicants, 35% accepted, 55 enrolled. *Faculty:* 36 full-time (17 women), 1 part-time/adjunct (0 women). Expenses: Contact institution. *Financial support:* In 2010–11, 69 students received support, including 11 fellowships with full and partial tuition reimbursements available, 11 research assistantships with full tuition reimbursements available (averaging $15,656 per year), 47 teaching assistantships with full tuition reimbursements available (averaging $15,518 per year); career-related internships or fieldwork, Federal Work-Study, institutionally sponsored loans, and unspecified assistantships also available. Support available to part-time students. Financial award application deadline: 3/15; financial award applicants required to submit FAFSA. In 2010, 63 master's, 12 doctorates awarded. *Degree program information:* Part-time programs available. Offers advertising (M Adv); journalism (MAMC); mass communication (MAMC, PhD); public relations (MAMC); telecommunication (MAMC). *Application deadline:* For fall admission, 1/15 for domestic and international students; for spring admission, 7/15 for domestic and international students. Applications are processed on a rolling basis. *Application fee:* $30. Electronic applications accepted. *Application Contact:* Dr. Debbie M. Treise, Associate Dean for Graduate Programs, 352-392-6557. *Dean,* Dr. John W. Wright, 352-392-0466, Fax: 352-392-1794, E-mail: dtreise@jou.ufl.edu.

College of Liberal Arts and Sciences Students: 1,791 full-time (811 women), 253 part-time (136 women); includes 66 Black or African American, non-Hispanic/Latino; 9 American Indian or Alaska Native, non-Hispanic/Latino; 70 Asian, non-Hispanic/Latino; 142 Hispanic/Latino, 592 international. Average age 29. 5,212 applicants, 16% accepted, 415 enrolled. *Faculty:* 486 full-time (135 women), 66 part-time/adjunct (30 women). Expenses: Contact institution. *Financial support:* In 2010–11, 1,789 students received support, including 488 fellowships, 368 research assistantships (averaging $18,017 per year), 933 teaching assistantships (averaging $17,248 per year); career-related internships or fieldwork, Federal Work-Study, institutionally sponsored loans, and unspecified assistantships also available. Support available to part-time students. Financial award applicants required to submit FAFSA. In 2010, 243 master's, 224 doctorates awarded. *Degree program information:* Part-time programs available. Offers African history (MA, PhD); African studies (Certificate); American history (MA, PhD); anthropology (MA, PhD); astronomy (MS, PhD); behavior analysis (PhD); behavioral neuroscience (MS, PhD); botany (M Ag, MS, MST, PhD); chemistry (MS, MST, PhD); classical studies (MA, PhD); cognitive and sensory processes (PhD); counseling psychology (PhD); creative writing (MFA); criminology, law and society (MA, PhD); developmental psychology (PhD); English (MA, PhD); European history (MA, PhD); gender and development (Graduate Certificate); geography (MA, MS, PhD); geology (MS, MST, PhD); German (MA, PhD); Germanic and Slavic studies (MA, PhD); international development policy and administration (MA, Certificate); international relations (MA, MAT); languages, literatures and culture (MA, PhD); Latin (MA, MAT, ML); Latin American history (MA, PhD); Latin American studies (MA, Certificate); liberal arts and sciences (M Ag, M Stat, MA, MAT, MFA, ML, MS, MS Stat, MST, MWS, PhD, Certificate, Graduate Certificate); linguistics (MA, PhD); mathematics (MA, MAT, MS, MST, PhD); philosophy (MA, PhD); physics (MS, MST, PhD); political campaigning (MA, Certificate); political science (MA, MAT, PhD); public affairs (MA, Certificate); religion and nature (MA); religion in the Americas (MA); religions of Asia (MA, PhD); social psychology (MS, PhD); sociology (MA, PhD); Spanish (MA, PhD); statistics (M Stat, MS Stat, PhD); teaching English as a second language (Certificate); women's studies (MA, Graduate Certificate); zoology (MS, MST, PhD). *Application deadline:* Applications are processed on a rolling basis. *Application fee:* $30. Electronic applications accepted. *Application Contact:* Dr. Albert R. Matheny, Associate Dean for Student Affairs, 352-392-1521, Fax: 351-392-3584, E-mail: matheny@polisci.ufl.edu. *Dean,* Dr. Paul D'Anieri, 352-392-0780, Fax: 352-392-3584, E-mail: danieri@clas.ufl.edu.

College of Nursing Students: 50 full-time (44 women), 71 part-time (70 women); includes 7 Black or African American, non-Hispanic/Latino; 1 Asian, non-Hispanic/Latino; 10 Hispanic/Latino, 3 international. Average age 36. 109 applicants, 39% accepted, 33 enrolled. *Faculty:* 20 full-time (19 women), 1 (woman) part-time/adjunct. Expenses: Contact institution. *Financial support:* In 2010–11, 9 students received support, including 8 fellowships with partial tuition reimbursements available, 1 teaching assistantship with partial tuition reimbursement available (averaging $30,900 per year); career-related internships or fieldwork and Federal Work-Study also available. Support available to part-time students. Financial award applicants required to submit FAFSA. In 2010, 38 master's, 7 doctorates awarded. *Degree program information:* Part-time programs available. Offers nursing (MSN); nursing sciences (PhD). *Application deadline:* For fall admission, 3/15 priority date for domestic students, 3/15 for international students. Applications are processed on a rolling basis. *Application fee:* $30. Electronic applications accepted. *Application Contact:* Sharon M. Bradley, Assistant Dean for Student Affairs, 352-273-6423, E-mail: sbradley@ufl.edu. *Dean,* Dr. Kathleen A. Long, 352-273-6324, Fax: 352-273-6505, E-mail: longka@ufl.edu.

College of Public Health and Health Professions Students: 591 full-time (442 women), 112 part-time (82 women); includes 62 Black or African American, non-Hispanic/Latino; 3 American Indian or Alaska Native, non-Hispanic/Latino; 48 Asian, non-Hispanic/Latino; 51 Hispanic/Latino, 70 international. Average age 29. 1,579 applicants, 18% accepted, 191 enrolled. *Faculty:* 76 full-time (36 women), 19 part-time/adjunct (10 women). Expenses: Contact institution. *Financial support:* In 2010–11, 167 students received support, including 33 fellowships, 117 research assistantships (averaging $16,126 per year), 17 teaching assistantships (averaging $11,478 per year); career-related internships or fieldwork, Federal Work-Study, institutionally sponsored loans, and unspecified assistantships also available. Support available to part-time students. Financial award applicants required to submit FAFSA. In 2010, 140 master's, 117 doctorates awarded. *Degree program information:* Part-time programs available. Offers audiology (Au D); biostatistics (MPH); clinical psychology (PhD); communication sciences and disorders (MA, Au D, PhD); environmental health (MPH); epidemiology (MPH); health administration (MHA); health services research (PhD); occupational therapy (MHS, MOT); physical therapy (DPT); public health and health professions (MA, MHA, MHS, MOT, MPH, Au D, DPT, PhD); public health management and policy (MPH); public health practice (MPH); rehabilitation science (PhD); social and behavioral sciences (MPH). *Application deadline:* Applications are processed on a rolling basis. *Application fee:* $30. Electronic applications accepted. *Application Contact:* Dr. Michael G. Perri, Dean, 352-273-6214, Fax: 352-273-6199, E-mail: mperri@phhp.ufl.edu. *Dean,* Dr. Michael G. Perri, 352-273-6214, Fax: 352-273-6199, E-mail: mperri@phhp.ufl.edu.

School of Natural Resources and Environment Students: 101 full-time (55 women), 29 part-time (15 women); includes 2 Black or African American, non-Hispanic/Latino; 1 American Indian or Alaska Native, non-Hispanic/Latino; 4 Asian, non-Hispanic/Latino; 7 Hispanic/Latino, 38 international. 65 applicants, 34% accepted, 18 enrolled. Expenses: Contact institution. *Financial support:* In 2010–11, 96 students received support, including 27 fellowships, 50 research assistantships (averaging $12,679 per year), 19 teaching assistantships (averaging $17,101 per year). Financial award applicants required to submit FAFSA. In 2010, 12 master's, 11 doctorates awarded. Offers interdisciplinary ecology (MS, PhD). *Application deadline:* For fall admission, 2/1 priority date for domestic students, 2/1 for international students. Applications are processed on a rolling basis. *Application fee:* $30. Electronic applications accepted. *Application Contact:* Dr. Stephen R. Humphrey, Director and Graduate Coordinator, 352-392-9230, Fax: 352-392-9748, E-mail: humphrey@ufl.edu. *Director and Graduate Coordinator,* Dr. Stephen R. Humphrey, 352-392-9230, Fax: 352-392-9748, E-mail: humphrey@ufl.edu.

Warrington College of Business Administration Students: 1,195 full-time (412 women), 570 part-time (173 women); includes 69 Black or African American, non-Hispanic/Latino; 7 American Indian or Alaska Native, non-Hispanic/Latino; 140 Asian, non-Hispanic/Latino; 199 Hispanic/Latino, 233 international. Average age 28. 1,545 applicants, 37% accepted, 343 enrolled. *Faculty:* 71 full-time (10 women). Expenses: Contact institution. *Financial support:* In 2010–11, 82 students received support, including 25 fellowships, 42 research assistantships (averaging $21,222 per year), 15 teaching assistantships (averaging $22,470 per year). Financial award applicants required to submit FAFSA. In 2010, 994 master's, 14 doctorates awarded. *Degree program information:* Part-time and evening/weekend programs available. Offers accounting (MBA); arts administration (MBA); business administration (MS); business strategy and public policy (MBA); competitive strategy (MBA); decision and information sciences (MBA, MS, PhD); economics (MA, PhD); electronic commerce (MBA); finance (MBA, PhD); financial services (Certificate); general business (MBA); global management (MBA); Graham-Buffett security analysis (MBA); health administration (MBA); human resources management (MBA); international business (MAIB); international studies (MBA); Latin American business (MBA); management (MBA, MSM, PhD); marketing (MS, PhD); real estate and urban analysis (PhD); sports administration (MBA); supply chain management (MS). *Application fee:* $30. *Application Contact:* Dr. Steve Slutsky, Graduate Coordinator, 352-392-8106, E-mail: steven.slutsky@warrington.ufl.edu. *Dean,* Dr. John Kraft, 352-392-2398, Fax: 352-392-8729, E-mail: john.kraft@warrington.ufl.edu.

Interdisciplinary Concentration in Animal Molecular and Cellular Biology Students: 2 full-time (both women), both international. Average age 27. 5 applicants, 80% accepted, 2 enrolled. Expenses: Contact institution. *Financial support:* In 2010–11, 2 students received support, including 1 fellowship, 1 research assistantship (averaging $25,749 per year). Financial award applicants required to submit FAFSA. Offers animal molecular and cellular biology (MS, PhD). Program offered jointly with College of Agricultural and Life Sciences, College of Liberal Arts and Sciences, College of Medicine, and College of Veterinary Medicine. *Application fee:* $30. Electronic applications accepted. *Application Contact:* Dr. Joel H. Brendemuhl, Assistant Chair, 352-392-8073, Fax: 352-392-5595, E-mail: brendj@ufl.edu. *Chair, Animal Sciences,* Dr. Geoffrey E. Dahl, 352-392-1981 Ext. 221, Fax: 352-392-5595, E-mail: gdahl@ufl.edu.

Levin College of Law Students: 1,175 full-time (518 women), 10 part-time (1 woman); includes 74 Black or African American, non-Hispanic/Latino; 16 American Indian or Alaska Native, non-Hispanic/Latino; 73 Asian, non-Hispanic/Latino; 112 Hispanic/Latino, 33 international. Average age 24. 3,357 applicants, 24% accepted, 310 enrolled. *Faculty:* 77 full-time (37 women), 36 part-time/adjunct (10 women). Expenses: Contact institution. *Financial support:* In 2010–11, 261 students received support, including 30 research assistantships (averaging $8,580 per year); Federal Work-Study, institutionally sponsored loans, scholarships/grants, health care benefits, and unspecified assistantships also available. Financial award application deadline: 4/7; financial award applicants required to submit FAFSA. In 2010, 382 first professional degrees awarded. Offers comparative law (LL M); environmental law (LL M); international taxation (LL M); law (JD); taxation (LL M, SJD). *Application deadline:* For fall admission, 1/15 for domestic and international students. Applications are processed on a rolling basis. *Application fee:* $30. Electronic applications accepted. *Application Contact:* Michelle Adorno, Assistant Dean for Admissions, 352-273-0890, Fax: 352-392-4087, E-mail: madorno@law.ufl.edu. *Dean,* Robert Jerry, 352-273-0600, Fax: 352-392-8727, E-mail: jerryr@law.ufl.edu.

UNIVERSITY OF GEORGIA, Athens, GA 30602

General Information State-supported, coed, comprehensive institution. CGS member. *Enrollment:* 34,677 graduate, professional, and undergraduate students; 5,062 full-time matriculated graduate/professional students (2,818 women), 2,015 part-time matriculated graduate/professional students (1,318 women). *Enrollment by degree level:* 3,711 master's, 2,836 doctoral, 530 other advanced degrees. *Graduate faculty:* 1,508 full-time (485 women), 66 part-time/adjunct (15 women). Tuition, state resident: full-time $7200; part-time $344 per credit hour. Tuition, nonresident: full-time $21,900; part-time $944 per credit hour. Tuition and fees vary according to course load and program. *Graduate housing:* Rooms and/or apartments available on a first-come, first-served basis to single and married students. Typical cost: $5360 per year for single students; $6000 per year for married students. *Student services:* Campus employment opportunities, campus safety program, career counseling, child daycare facilities, exercise/wellness program, free psychological counseling, grant writing training, international student services, low-cost health insurance, multicultural affairs office, services for students with disabilities, teacher training, writing training. *Library facilities:* Ilah Dunlap Little Memorial Library plus 3 others. *Online resources:* library catalog, web page,

University of Georgia (continued)

access to other libraries' catalogs. *Collection:* 4.7 million titles, 96,401 serial subscriptions. *Research affiliation:* Skidaway Institute of Oceanography, Southeast Water Laboratory, Russell Research Laboratory, Organization for Tropical Studies.

Computer facilities: 3,440 computers available on campus for general student use. A campuswide network can be accessed from student residence rooms and from off campus. Online class registration is available. *Web address:* http://www.uga.edu/.

General Application Contact: Dr. Melissa Barry, Assistant Dean of The Graduate School, 706-425-2934, Fax: 706-425-3093, E-mail: mjb14@uga.edu.

GRADUATE UNITS

Biomedical and Health Sciences Institute Students: 13 full-time (9 women), 1 (woman) part-time; includes 1 Black or African American, non-Hispanic/Latino; 1 Asian, non-Hispanic/Latino; 1 Hispanic/Latino, 4 international. 23 applicants, 13% accepted, 2 enrolled. Expenses: Contact institution. *Financial support:* Unspecified assistantships available. Financial award application deadline: 12/31. In 2010, 6 doctorates awarded. Offers neuroscience (PhD). *Application Contact:* Philip V. Holmes, Graduate Coordinator, 706-542-5922, Fax: 706-542-5285, E-mail: pvholmes@uga.edu. *Chair*, Dr. Gaylen Edwards, 706-542-5922, Fax: 706-542-5285, E-mail: gedwards@uga.edu.

College of Agricultural and Environmental Sciences Students: 343 full-time (170 women), 84 part-time (31 women); includes 21 Black or African American, non-Hispanic/Latino; 9 Asian, non-Hispanic/Latino; 8 Hispanic/Latino; 2 Two or more races, non-Hispanic/Latino, 155 international. 386 applicants, 44% accepted, 104 enrolled. *Faculty:* 207 full-time (37 women), 18 part-time/adjunct (4 women). Expenses: Contact institution. *Financial support:* Fellowships, research assistantships, teaching assistantships, career-related internships or fieldwork and unspecified assistantships available. In 2010, 96 master's, 29 doctorates awarded. Offers agricultural and environmental sciences (MA Ext, MADS, MAE, MAL, MCCS, MFT, MPPPM, MS, PhD); agricultural economics (MAE, MS, PhD); agricultural engineering (MS); agricultural leadership, education, and communication (MA Ext, MAL); animal and dairy science (PhD); animal and dairy sciences (MADS); animal nutrition (PhD); animal science (MS); biological and agricultural engineering (PhD); biological engineering (MS); crop and soil science (MS, PhD); crop and soil sciences (MCCS); dairy science (MS); entomology (MS, PhD); environmental economics (MS); food science (MS, PhD); food technology (MFT); horticulture (MS, PhD); plant pathology (MS, PhD); plant protection and pest management (MPPPM); poultry science (MS, PhD). *Application deadline:* For fall admission, 7/1 priority date for domestic students; for spring admission, 11/15 for domestic students. *Application fee:* $50. Electronic applications accepted. *Application Contact:* Krista Haynes, Director of Enrolled Student Services, 706-425-1789, Fax: 706-425-3094, E-mail: gradoff@uga.edu. *Dean*, Dr. J. Scott Angle, 706-542-3924, Fax: 706-542-0803, E-mail: caesdean@uga.edu.

Institute of Plant Breeding, Genetics and Genomics Students: 22 full-time (7 women), 5 part-time (1 woman), 12 international. 17 applicants, 24% accepted, 3 enrolled. Expenses: Contact institution. *Financial support:* Tuition waivers and unspecified assistantships available. In 2010, 3 master's awarded. Offers plant breeding, genetics and genomics (MS, PhD). *Application Contact:* Dr. Dayton Wilde, Graduate Coordinator, 706-542-5607, E-mail: pbgg@uga.edu. *Director*, Dr. E. Charles Brummer, 706-542-8847, Fax: 706-583-8120, E-mail: pbgg@uga.edu.

College of Arts and Sciences Students: 1,551 full-time (720 women), 237 part-time (116 women); includes 155 minority (66 Black or African American, non-Hispanic/Latino; 3 American Indian or Alaska Native, non-Hispanic/Latino; 37 Asian, non-Hispanic/Latino; 38 Hispanic/Latino; 3 Native Hawaiian or other Pacific Islander, non-Hispanic/Latino; 8 Two or more races, non-Hispanic/Latino), 443 international. 2,940 applicants, 29% accepted, 445 enrolled. *Faculty:* 591 full-time (172 women), 14 part-time/adjunct (3 women). Expenses: Contact institution. *Financial support:* Fellowships, research assistantships, teaching assistantships, Federal Work-Study, institutionally sponsored loans, and unspecified assistantships available. In 2010, 221 master's, 165 doctorates awarded. Offers analytical chemistry (MS, PhD); anthropology (MA, PhD); applied mathematical science (MAMS); archaeological resource management (MS); arts and sciences (MA, MAMS, MAT, MFA, MM, MS, DMA, PhD, Certificate); biochemistry and molecular biology (MS, PhD); cellular biology (MS, PhD); classical languages (MA); comparative literature (MA, PhD); computer science (MS, PhD); creative writing (MFA, PhD); English (MA, MAT, PhD); French (MA); genetics (MS, PhD); geography (MA, MS, PhD); geology (MS, PhD); German (MA); Greek (MA); history (MA, PhD); inorganic chemistry (MS, PhD); Latin (MA); linguistics (MA, PhD); marine sciences (MS, PhD); mathematics (MA, PhD); microbiology (MS, PhD); organic chemistry (MS, PhD); philosophy (MA, PhD); physical chemistry (MS, PhD); physics (MS, PhD); plant biology (MS, PhD); psychology (MS, PhD); religion (MA); Romance languages (MA, PhD); sociology (MA, PhD); Spanish (MA); speech communication (MA, PhD); statistics (MS, PhD); theatre (MFA, PhD). *Application deadline:* For fall admission, 7/1 priority date for domestic students; for spring admission, 11/15 for domestic students. *Application fee:* $50. Electronic applications accepted. *Application Contact:* Director of Enrolled Student Services. *Dean*, Dr. Garnett Stokes, 706-542-3400, Fax: 706-542-3422, E-mail: gstokes@franklin.uga.edu.

Artificial Intelligence Center Students: 20 full-time (4 women), 6 part-time (2 women); includes 2 Black or African American, non-Hispanic/Latino; 1 Hispanic/Latino, 10 international. 17 applicants, 59% accepted, 10 enrolled. *Faculty:* 1 full-time (0 women). Expenses: Contact institution. *Financial support:* Unspecified assistantships available. In 2010, 5 master's awarded. Offers artificial intelligence (MS). *Application deadline:* For fall admission, 7/1 priority date for domestic students; for spring admission, 11/15 for domestic students. *Application fee:* $50. Electronic applications accepted. *Application Contact:* Dr. Khaled M. Rasheed, Graduate Coordinator, 706-542-3444, Fax: 706-542-8864, E-mail: khaled@cs.uga.edu. *Director*, Dr. Walter Don Potter, 706-542-0361, E-mail: potter@uga.edu.

Hugh Hodgson School of Music Students: 102 full-time (48 women), 36 part-time (9 women); includes 4 Black or African American, non-Hispanic/Latino; 5 Asian, non-Hispanic/Latino; 1 Hispanic/Latino; 1 Native Hawaiian or other Pacific Islander, non-Hispanic/Latino, 11 international. 162 applicants, 49% accepted, 52 enrolled. *Faculty:* 38 full-time (10 women). Expenses: Contact institution. *Financial support:* Fellowships, research assistantships, teaching assistantships, unspecified assistantships available. In 2010, 18 master's, 16 doctorates awarded. Offers music (MA, MM, DMA, PhD). *Application deadline:* For fall admission, 7/1 priority date for domestic students; for spring admission, 11/15 for domestic students. *Application fee:* $50. Electronic applications accepted. *Application Contact:* Dr. Adrian Childs, Graduate Coordinator, 206-542-2765, E-mail: apchilds@uga.edu. *Director*, Dr. Dale Monson, 706-542-2776, Fax: 706-542-2773, E-mail: dmonson@uga.edu.

Institute for Women's Studies Students: 1 (woman) part-time; includes Black or African American, non-Hispanic/Latino. 1 applicant, 100% accepted, 1 enrolled. Expenses: Contact institution. Offers women's studies (Certificate). *Application Contact:* Dr. Susan R. Thomas, Assistant Director, 706-542-2763, Fax: 706-542-0049, E-mail: suthomas@uga.edu. *Director*, Dr. Juanita Johnson-Bailey, 706-542-2846, E-mail: jjb@uga.edu.

Lamar Dodd School of Art Students: 81 full-time (58 women), 12 part-time (9 women); includes 14 minority (1 Black or African American, non-Hispanic/Latino; 1 American Indian or Alaska Native, non-Hispanic/Latino; 5 Asian, non-Hispanic/Latino; 5 Hispanic/Latino; 1 Native Hawaiian or other Pacific Islander, non-Hispanic/Latino; 1 Two or more races, non-Hispanic/Latino), 3 international. 219 applicants, 23% accepted, 29 enrolled. *Faculty:* 34 full-time (13 women). Expenses: Contact institution. *Financial support:* Fellowships, research assistantships, teaching assistantships, unspecified assistantships available. In 2010, 15 master's, 3 doctorates awarded. Offers art (MA, MFA, PhD); art history (MA). *Application deadline:* For fall admission, 7/1 priority date for domestic students; for spring admission, 11/15 for domestic students. *Application fee:* $50. Electronic applications accepted. *Application Contact:* Dr. Carole Henry, Graduate Coordinator, 706-542-1624, Fax: 706-542-0226, E-mail: ckhenry@uga.edu. *Director*, Prof. Georgia Strange, 706-542-1600, Fax: 706-542-0226, E-mail: strange@uga.edu.

College of Education Students: 999 full-time (709 women), 1,102 part-time (807 women); includes 463 minority (333 Black or African American, non-Hispanic/Latino; 6 American Indian or Alaska Native, non-Hispanic/Latino; 57 Asian, non-Hispanic/Latino; 49 Hispanic/Latino; 4 Native Hawaiian or other Pacific Islander, non-Hispanic/Latino; 14 Two or more races, non-Hispanic/Latino), 149 international. 1,641 applicants, 46% accepted, 450 enrolled. *Faculty:* 177 full-time (90 women), 1 (woman) part-time/adjunct. Expenses: Contact institution. *Financial support:* Fellowships, research assistantships, teaching assistantships, unspecified assistantships available. In 2010, 465 master's, 127 doctorates, 76 other advanced degrees awarded. Offers adult education (M Ed, Ed D, PhD, Ed S); art education (MA Ed, Ed D, PhD, Ed S); college student affairs administration (M Ed, PhD); communication science and disorders (M Ed, MA, PhD, Ed S); counseling and student personnel (PhD); counseling psychology (PhD); early childhood education (M Ed, MAT, PhD, Ed S); education (M Ed, MA, MA Ed, MAT, MM Ed, MS, Ed D, PhD, Ed S); education of the gifted (Ed D); educational administration and policy (M Ed, PhD, Ed S); educational leadership (Ed D); educational psychology (M Ed, MA, Ed D, PhD, Ed S); elementary education (PhD); English education (M Ed, Ed S); higher education (PhD); human resource and organizational design (M Ed); human resources and organization design (M Ed); instructional technology (M Ed, PhD, Ed S); kinesiology (MS, PhD); language and literacy education (PhD); mathematics education (M Ed, Ed D, PhD, Ed S); middle school education (M Ed, PhD, Ed S); music education (MM Ed, Ed D, Ed S); occupational studies (MAT, Ed D, PhD, Ed S); professional counseling (M Ed); professional school counseling (Ed S); reading education (M Ed, Ed D, Ed S); recreation and leisure studies (M Ed, MA, PhD); science education (M Ed, Ed D, PhD, Ed S); social foundations of education (PhD); social studies education (M Ed, Ed D, PhD, Ed S); special education (M Ed, Ed D, PhD, Ed S); teaching additional languages (M Ed, Ed S). *Application deadline:* For fall admission, 7/1 priority date for domestic students; for spring admission, 11/15 for domestic students. *Application fee:* $50. Electronic applications accepted. *Application Contact:* Krista Haynes, Director of Enrolled Student Services, 706-425-1789, Fax: 706-425-3094, E-mail: gradoff@uga.edu. *Interim Dean*, Dr. Arthur M. Horne, 706-542-6446, Fax: 706-542-0360, E-mail: ahorne@uga.edu.

College of Environment and Design Students: 111 full-time (69 women), 25 part-time (15 women); includes 2 Black or African American, non-Hispanic/Latino; 1 Asian, non-Hispanic/Latino; 3 Two or more races, non-Hispanic/Latino, 9 international. 200 applicants, 56% accepted, 58 enrolled. *Faculty:* 29 full-time (8 women). Expenses: Contact institution. In 2010, 26 master's awarded. Offers environmental planning and design (MEPD); historic preservation (MHP); landscape architecture (MLA). *Application deadline:* For fall admission, 7/1 priority date for domestic students; for spring admission, 11/15 for domestic students. *Application fee:* $50. *Application Contact:* Prof. Brian J. LaHaie, Director of Enrolled Student Services, 706-542-4704, Fax: 706-542-4236, E-mail: blahaie@uga.edu. *Acting Dean*, Daniels J. Nadenicek, 706-542-1100, Fax: 706-542-4485, E-mail: dnadeni@uga.edu.

College of Family and Consumer Sciences Students: 113 full-time (92 women), 41 part-time (37 women); includes 19 Black or African American, non-Hispanic/Latino; 2 Asian, non-Hispanic/Latino; 3 Hispanic/Latino, 20 international. 184 applicants, 44% accepted, 37 enrolled. *Faculty:* 54 full-time (33 women). Expenses: Contact institution. *Financial support:* Fellowships, research assistantships, teaching assistantships, unspecified assistantships available. In 2010, 40 master's, 4 doctorates awarded. Offers child and family development (MS, PhD); early childhood education (MAT); family and consumer sciences (MAT, MFCS, MS, PhD); foods and nutrition (MFCS, MS, PhD); historic costume and textiles (MS); housing and consumer economics (MS, PhD); merchandising/international trade (MS); textile analysis (PhD); textile chemical processes (PhD); textile products and standards (PhD); textile science (MS). *Application deadline:* For fall admission, 7/1 priority date for domestic students; for spring admission, 11/15 for domestic students. *Application fee:* $50. Electronic applications accepted. *Application Contact:* Director of Enrolled Student Services. *Dean*, Dr. Laura Dunn Jolly, 706-542-4879, Fax: 706-542-4862, E-mail: dean@fcs.uga.edu.

College of Pharmacy Students: 50 full-time (28 women), 10 part-time (6 women); includes 6 Black or African American, non-Hispanic/Latino; 4 Asian, non-Hispanic/Latino; 1 Two or more races, non-Hispanic/Latino, 28 international. 205 applicants, 8% accepted, 12 enrolled. *Faculty:* 38 full-time (11 women), 4 part-time/adjunct (0 women). Expenses: Contact institution. *Financial support:* Fellowships, research assistantships, teaching assistantships, career-related internships or fieldwork, Federal Work-Study, institutionally sponsored loans, tuition waivers, and unspecified assistantships available. Support available to part-time students. Financial award application deadline: 2/15. In 2010, 123 first professional degrees, 1 master's, 12 doctorates awarded. Offers clinical trials design and management (Certificate); pharmacy (Pharm D, MS, PhD, Certificate); pharmacy and biomedical regulatory affairs (Certificate). *Application deadline:* For fall admission, 7/1 priority date for domestic students; for spring admission, 11/15 for domestic students. *Application fee:* $50. Electronic applications accepted. *Application Contact:* Dr. Svein Oie, Dean, 706-542-1914, Fax: 706-542-5269, E-mail: soie@rx.uga.edu. *Dean*, Dr. Svein Oie, 706-542-1914, Fax: 706-542-5269, E-mail: soie@rx.uga.edu.

College of Public Health Students: 164 full-time (115 women), 26 part-time (16 women); includes 28 Black or African American, non-Hispanic/Latino; 1 American Indian or Alaska Native, non-Hispanic/Latino; 17 Asian, non-Hispanic/Latino; 7 Hispanic/Latino; 4 Two or more races, non-Hispanic/Latino, 14 international. 311 applicants, 59% accepted, 88 enrolled. Expenses: Contact institution. In 2010, 44 master's, 2 doctorates awarded. Offers biostatistics (MPH); environmental health science (MPH, MSEH); epidemiology (MPH); health policy and management (MPH); health promotion and behavior (MPH, PhD); public health (MPH, MSEH, PhD, Certificate). *Application deadline:* For fall admission, 7/1 for domestic students; for spring admission, 11/15 for domestic students. *Application fee:* $50. *Application Contact:* Mitchela Salum, Graduate Coordinator, 706-583-0885, E-mail: msalum@uga.edu. *Dean*, Dr. Joel M. Lee, 706-542-3709, E-mail: joellee@uga.edu.

Institute of Gerontology Students: 3 part-time (all women). 3 applicants, 67% accepted. *Faculty:* 2 full-time (1 woman). Expenses: Contact institution. Offers gerontology (Certificate). *Application Contact:* Dr. Anne H. Glass, Graduate Coordinator, 706-425-3222, E-mail: aglass@geron.uga.edu. *Director*, Dr. Leonard W. Poon, 706-425-3222, E-mail: lpoon@geron.uga.edu.

College of Veterinary Medicine Students: 147 full-time (88 women), 4 part-time (2 women); includes 5 Black or African American, non-Hispanic/Latino; 5 Asian, non-Hispanic/Latino; 3 Hispanic/Latino, 44 international. 94 applicants, 35% accepted, 27 enrolled. *Faculty:* 25 full-time (8 women). Expenses: Contact institution. *Financial support:* Fellowships, research assistantships, teaching assistantships, Federal Work-Study, scholarships/grants, and unspecified assistantships available. Financial award applicants required to submit FAFSA. In 2010, 94 first professional degrees, 16 master's, 7 doctorates awarded. Offers food animal medicine (MFAM); infectious diseases (MS, PhD); pathology (MS, PhD); pharmacology (MS, PhD); physiology (MS, PhD); physiology and pharmacology (MS, PhD); population health (MAM, MFAM); toxicology (MS, PhD); veterinary anatomy (MS); veterinary anatomy and radiology (MS); veterinary medicine (DVM, MAM, MFAM, MS, PhD). *Application deadline:* For fall admission, 7/1 priority date for domestic students; for spring admission, 11/15 for domestic students. *Application fee:* $50. Electronic applications accepted. *Application Contact:* Malik McKinley, Director of Graduate Admissions, 706-542-5727, E-mail: dvmadmit@uga.edu. *Dean*, Dr. Sheila W. Allen, 706-542-3461, Fax: 706-542-8254, E-mail: sallen01@uga.edu.

Faculty of Engineering Students: 11 full-time (2 women), 3 part-time (2 women); includes 1 Hispanic/Latino; 1 Two or more races, non-Hispanic/Latino, 6 international. 17 applicants, 41% accepted, 4 enrolled. *Faculty:* 1 full-time (0 women). Expenses: Contact institution. In 2010, 3 master's awarded. Offers biochemical engineering (MS); engineering (MS); environmental engineering (MS). *Application Contact:* Dr. Melissa Barry, Assistant Dean of The Graduate School, 706-425-2934, Fax: 706-425-3093, E-mail: mjb14@uga.edu. Dr. E. Dale Threadgill.

Graduate Program in Law Students: 13 full-time (6 women), 3 part-time (all women); includes 3 Black or African American, non-Hispanic/Latino, 3 international. 49 applicants, 39% accepted, 12 enrolled. Expenses: Contact institution. *Financial support:* Fellowships, research assistantships, teaching assistantships, Federal Work-Study, institutionally sponsored loans, and unspecified assistantships available. Financial award application deadline: 4/15. In 2010, 13 master's awarded. Offers law (LL M). *Application deadline:* For fall admission, 4/15 for domestic and international students. *Application fee:* $50. *Application Contact:* Ambassador C. Donald Johnson, Director, 706-542-5135, Fax: 706-542-7822, E-mail: johnsocd@uga.edu. *Director*, Ambassador C. Donald Johnson, 706-542-5135, Fax: 706-542-7822, E-mail: johnsocd@uga.edu.

Grady School of Journalism and Mass Communication Students: 88 full-time (61 women), 24 part-time (16 women); includes 13 Black or African American, non-Hispanic/Latino; 4 Hispanic/Latino, 21 international. 297 applicants, 40% accepted, 48 enrolled. *Faculty:* 37 full-time (14 women). Expenses: Contact institution. *Financial support:* Research assistantships, teaching assistantships, tuition waivers (full) and unspecified assistantships available. In 2010, 31 master's, 5 doctorates awarded. Offers journalism and mass communication (MA); mass communication (PhD). *Application deadline:* For spring admission, 2/15 for domestic students. *Application fee:* $50. Electronic applications accepted. *Application Contact:* Dr. Jeffrey K. Springston, Graduate Coordinator, 706-542-5030, Fax: 706-542-2183, E-mail: jspring@grady.uga.edu. *Dean,* Dr. E. Culpepper Clark, 706-542-1704, Fax: 706-542-2183, E-mail: cully@uga.edu.

Institute of Bioinformatics Students: 46 full-time (21 women); includes 1 Black or African American, non-Hispanic/Latino; 3 Asian, non-Hispanic/Latino; 1 Hispanic/Latino, 35 international. 52 applicants, 23% accepted. Expenses: Contact institution. In 2010, 2 master's awarded. Offers bioinformatics (MS, PhD, Graduate Certificate). *Application Contact:* Dr. Jeff Dean, Graduate Coordinator, 706-542-1710, E-mail: jeffdean@uga.edu. *Director,* Dr. Ying Xu, 706-542-9779, E-mail: xyn@bmb.uga.edu.

School of Ecology Students: 62 full-time (35 women), 19 part-time (10 women); includes 1 Black or African American, non-Hispanic/Latino; 4 Hispanic/Latino; 1 Two or more races, non-Hispanic/Latino, 3 international. 93 applicants, 24% accepted, 14 enrolled. *Faculty:* 19 full-time (5 women), 4 part-time/adjunct (1 woman). Expenses: Contact institution. *Financial support:* Fellowships, research assistantships, teaching assistantships, unspecified assistantships available. In 2010, 4 master's, 9 doctorates awarded. Offers conservation ecology and sustainable development (MS); ecology (MS, PhD). *Application deadline:* For fall admission, 7/1 priority date for domestic students; for spring admission, 11/15 for domestic students. *Application fee:* $50. Electronic applications accepted. *Application Contact:* Dr. James Byers, Graduate Coordinator, 706-338-0012, Fax: 706-542-4819, E-mail: jebyers@uga.edu. *Dean,* Dr. John L. Gittleman, 706-542-2968, Fax: 706-542-4819, E-mail: ecohead@uga.edu.

School of Forestry and Natural Resources Students: 145 full-time (63 women), 28 part-time (6 women); includes 1 Black or African American, non-Hispanic/Latino; 1 Asian, non-Hispanic/Latino; 1 Two or more races, non-Hispanic/Latino, 18 international. 91 applicants, 66% accepted, 46 enrolled. *Faculty:* 41 full-time (6 women), 7 part-time/adjunct (1 woman). Expenses: Contact institution. *Financial support:* Fellowships, research assistantships, teaching assistantships, unspecified assistantships available. In 2010, 45 master's, 15 doctorates awarded. Offers forestry and natural resources (MFR, MS, PhD). *Application deadline:* For fall admission, 7/1 priority date for domestic students; for spring admission, 11/15 for domestic students. *Application fee:* $50. Electronic applications accepted. *Application Contact:* Dr. Laurence Schimleck, Graduate Coordinator, 706-542-0464, Fax: 706-542-8356, E-mail: lschimlect@warnell.uga.edu.

School of Law Students: 700 full-time (332 women), 5 part-time (2 women); includes 84 Black or African American, non-Hispanic/Latino; 1 American Indian or Alaska Native, non-Hispanic/Latino; 29 Asian, non-Hispanic/Latino; 12 Hispanic/Latino, 7 international. Expenses: Contact institution. *Financial support:* Fellowships, research assistantships, teaching assistantships, Federal Work-Study, institutionally sponsored loans, tuition waivers (partial), and unspecified assistantships available. Financial award application deadline: 1/31. In 2010, 217 first professional degrees awarded. Offers law (JD). *Application deadline:* For fall admission, 7/1 priority date for domestic students; for spring admission, 11/15 for domestic students. *Application fee:* $50. Electronic applications accepted. *Application Contact:* Paul M. Kurtz, Associate Dean for Academic and Student Affairs, 706-542-7140, E-mail: pmkurtz@uga.edu. *Dean,* Rebecca H. White, 706-542-7140, Fax: 706-542-5283, E-mail: rhwhite@uga.edu.

School of Public and International Affairs Students: 14 full-time (6 women); includes 2 Asian, non-Hispanic/Latino. 77 applicants, 30% accepted, 5 enrolled. *Faculty:* 13 full-time (2 women). Expenses: Contact institution. *Financial support:* Fellowships, research assistantships, teaching assistantships, unspecified assistantships available. In 2010, 1 master's awarded. Offers political science (MA, PhD); public administration (MPA, PhD); public and international affairs (MA, MPA, PhD). *Application deadline:* For fall admission, 7/1 priority date for domestic students; for spring admission, 11/15 for domestic students. *Application fee:* $50. Electronic applications accepted. *Application Contact:* Dr. Jeffrey K. Berejikian, Director of Graduate Admissions, 706-425-1789, E-mail: gradoff@uga.edu. *Dean,* Dr. Markus Crepaz, 706-542-2149, E-mail: mcrepaz@uga.edu.

School of Social Work Students: 282 full-time (243 women), 57 part-time (41 women); includes 65 Black or African American, non-Hispanic/Latino; 8 Asian, non-Hispanic/Latino; 6 Hispanic/Latino; 2 Two or more races, non-Hispanic/Latino, 6 international. Average age 34. 388 applicants, 58% accepted, 145 enrolled. *Faculty:* 22 full-time (13 women). Expenses: Contact institution. *Financial support:* In 2010–11, 39 students received support, including 4 fellowships (averaging $25,000 per year), 35 research assistantships with tuition reimbursements available (averaging $7,500 per year); teaching assistantships with tuition reimbursements available, career-related internships or fieldwork, Federal Work-Study, scholarships/grants, tuition waivers (full and partial), and unspecified assistantships also available. Support available to part-time students. Financial award application deadline: 2/10; financial award applicants required to submit FAFSA. In 2010, 159 master's, 4 doctorates awarded. *Degree program information:* Part-time and evening/weekend programs available. Offers social work (MA, MSW, PhD, Certificate). *Application deadline:* For fall admission, 7/1 priority date for domestic students, 7/1 for international students; for spring admission, 11/15 for domestic and international students. Applications are processed on a rolling basis. *Application fee:* $50. Electronic applications accepted. *Application Contact:* Dr. Jerome Schiele, Graduate Coordinator, 706-542-5429, Fax: 706-542-3282, E-mail: fschiele@uga.edu. *Dean,* Dr. Maurice C. Daniels, 706-542-5424, Fax: 706-542-3282, E-mail: daniels@uga.edu.

Institute for Non-Profit Organizations Students: 28 full-time (19 women), 4 part-time (2 women); includes 2 Black or African American, non-Hispanic/Latino, 1 international. 25 applicants, 80% accepted, 17 enrolled. Expenses: Contact institution. In 2010, 18 master's awarded. Offers non-profit organizations (MA, Certificate). *Application deadline:* For fall admission, 7/1 priority date for domestic students; for spring admission, 11/15 for domestic students. *Application fee:* $50. *Application Contact:* Dr. Michelle Mohr Carney, Director, 706-542-5429, Fax: 706-542-3282, E-mail: mmcarney@uga.edu. *Director,* Dr. Michelle Mohr Carney, 706-542-5429, Fax: 706-542-3282, E-mail: mmcarney@uga.edu.

Terry College of Business Students: 322 full-time (145 women), 20 part-time (7 women); includes 12 Black or African American, non-Hispanic/Latino; 14 Asian, non-Hispanic/Latino; 6 Hispanic/Latino; 3 Two or more races, non-Hispanic/Latino, 57 international. 707 applicants, 24% accepted, 110 enrolled. *Faculty:* 76 full-time (21 women). Expenses: Contact institution. *Financial support:* Fellowships, research assistantships, teaching assistantships, unspecified assistantships available. In 2010, 208 master's, 13 doctorates awarded. Offers business (M Acc, MA, MBA, MIT, MMR, PhD); business administration (MA, MBA, PhD); economics (MA, PhD); Internet technology (MIT); management information systems (PhD); marketing research (MMR). *Application deadline:* For fall admission, 7/1 priority date for domestic students; for spring admission, 11/15 for domestic students. *Application fee:* $50. Electronic applications accepted. *Application Contact:* Dr. Rich Daniels, Interim Associate Dean, 404-842-4862, E-mail: rdaniels@terry.uga.edu. *Dean,* Dr. Robert T. Sumichrast, 706-542-8100, Fax: 706-542-3835, E-mail: busdean@terry.uga.edu.

J. M. Tull School of Accounting Students: 138 full-time (80 women), 8 part-time (5 women); includes 6 Black or African American, non-Hispanic/Latino; 11 Asian, non-Hispanic/Latino; 2 Hispanic/Latino; 2 Two or more races, non-Hispanic/Latino, 7 international. 199 applicants, 32% accepted, 45 enrolled. *Faculty:* 17 full-time (7 women). Expenses: Contact institution. *Financial support:* Fellowships, research assistantships, teaching assistantships, unspecified assistantships available. In 2010, 104 master's awarded. Offers accounting (M Acc). *Application deadline:* For fall admission, 7/1 priority date for domestic students; for spring admission, 11/15 for domestic students. *Application fee:* $50. Electronic applications accepted. *Application Contact:* Dr. E. Michael Bamber, Graduate Coordinator, 706-542-3601, E-mail: mbamber@terry.uga.edu. *Director,* Dr. Benjamin C. Ayers, 706-542-1616, Fax: 706-542-3630, E-mail: bayers@terry.uga.edu.

UNIVERSITY OF GREAT FALLS, Great Falls, MT 59405

General Information Independent-religious, coed, comprehensive institution. *Graduate housing:* On-campus housing not available.

GRADUATE UNITS

Graduate Studies *Degree program information:* Part-time programs available. Postbaccalaureate distance learning degree programs offered (no on-campus study). Offers counseling (MSC); criminal justice (MSM); education (M Ed); human development (MSM); management (MSM); secondary teaching (MAT). Electronic applications accepted.

UNIVERSITY OF GUAM, Mangilao, GU 96923

General Information Territory-supported, coed, comprehensive institution. *Graduate housing:* Room and/or apartments available on a first-come, first-served basis to single students; on-campus housing not available to married students. Housing application deadline: 5/1. *Research affiliation:* Bernice Pauahi Bishop Museum (science, cultural preservation), Pilar Project, Inc. (salvage of artifacts, archaeology), Cancer Research Center of Hawaii (cancer research).

GRADUATE UNITS

Office of Graduate Studies *Degree program information:* Part-time programs available.

College of Liberal Arts and Social Sciences *Degree program information:* Part-time programs available. Offers ceramics (MA); English (MA); graphics (MA); liberal arts and social sciences (MA); Micronesian studies (MA); painting (MA).

College of Natural and Applied Sciences Offers environmental science (MS); natural and applied sciences (MS, MSW); social work (MSW); tropical marine biology (MS).

School of Business and Public Administration *Degree program information:* Part-time programs available. Offers business administration (PMBA); business and public administration (MPA, PMBA); public administration (MPA).

School of Education *Degree program information:* Part-time programs available. Offers administration and supervision (M Ed); counseling (MA); education (M Ed, MA); language and literacy (M Ed); secondary education (M Ed); special education (M Ed); teaching English to speakers of other languages (M Ed).

UNIVERSITY OF GUELPH, Guelph, ON N1G 2W1, Canada

General Information Province-supported, coed, university. *Graduate housing:* Rooms and/or apartments available to single and married students. Housing application deadline: 5/28.

GRADUATE UNITS

Graduate Studies *Degree program information:* Part-time and evening/weekend programs available. Postbaccalaureate distance learning degree programs offered (minimal on-campus study). Offers biophysics (M Sc, PhD). Electronic applications accepted.

Collaborative International Development Studies *Degree program information:* Part-time programs available. Offers international development studies (M Eng, M Sc, MA, MBA, PhD).

College of Arts *Degree program information:* Part-time programs available. Offers arts (MA, MFA, PhD); drama (MA); English (MA); European studies (MA); French studies (MA); history (MA, PhD); literary studies/theatre studies in English (PhD); philosophy (MA, PhD); studio art (MFA).

College of Biological Science *Degree program information:* Part-time programs available. Offers biochemistry (M Sc, PhD); biological science (M Sc, PhD); biophysics (M Sc, PhD); botany (M Sc, PhD); microbiology (M Sc, PhD); molecular biology and genetics (M Sc, PhD); nutritional sciences (M Sc, PhD); zoology (M Sc, PhD). Electronic applications accepted.

College of Management and Economics Offers economics (MA, PhD); food and agribusiness management (MBA); hospitality and tourism management (MBA); leadership (MA); management and economics (M Sc, MA, MBA, PhD); marketing and consumer studies (M Sc).

College of Physical and Engineering Science *Degree program information:* Part-time programs available. Offers applied computer science (M Sc); applied mathematics (PhD); applied statistics (PhD); biological engineering (M Eng, M Sc, MA Sc, PhD); chemistry and biochemistry (M Sc, PhD); computer science (PhD); engineering systems and computing (M Eng, M Sc, MA Sc, PhD); environmental engineering (M Eng, M Sc, MA Sc, PhD); mathematics and statistics (M Sc); physical and engineering science (M Eng, M Sc, MA Sc, PhD); physics (M Sc, PhD); water resources engineering (M Eng, M Sc, MA Sc, PhD).

College of Social and Applied Human Sciences *Degree program information:* Part-time programs available. Offers anthropology (MA); applied nutrition (MAN); applied social psychology (MA, PhD); clinical psychology applied development emphasis (PhD); clinical psychology applied developmental emphasis (MA); comparative politics (MA); crime and criminal justice policy (MA); criminology and criminal justice policy (MA); family relations and human development (M Sc, PhD); geography (M Sc, MA, PhD); industrial/organizational psychology (MA, PhD); international development (MA); neuroscience and applied cognitive science (MA, PhD); political science (MA); public policy and public administration (MA); social and applied human sciences (M Sc, MA, MAN, PhD); sociology (MA, PhD); the Americas (Canada emphasis) (MA).

Ontario Agricultural College *Degree program information:* Part-time programs available. Postbaccalaureate distance learning degree programs offered (minimal on-campus study). Offers agricultural economics (M Sc, PhD); agriculture (M Sc, MLA, PhD, Diploma); animal and poultry science (M Sc, PhD); aquaculture (M Sc); atmospheric science (M Sc, PhD); capacity development and extension (M Sc); collaborative international development studies (M Sc, PhD); entomology (M Sc, PhD); environmental and agricultural earth sciences (M Sc, PhD); environmental microbiology and biotechnology (M Sc, PhD); environmental toxicology (M Sc, PhD); food safety and quality assurance (M Sc); food science (M Sc, PhD); international rural planning and development (M Sc); land resources management (M Sc, PhD); landscape architecture (M Sc, MLA); plant agriculture (M Sc, PhD); plant and forest systems (M Sc, PhD); plant pathology (M Sc, PhD); rural planning and development (M Sc); rural planning and development in Canada (M Sc); rural studies (PhD); soil science (M Sc, PhD).

Ontario Veterinary College Offers toxicology (M Sc, PhD); veterinary medicine (M Sc, DV Sc, PhD, Diploma).

Graduate Programs in Veterinary Sciences Offers anatomic pathology (DV Sc, Diploma); anesthesiology (M Sc, DV Sc); cardiology (DV Sc, Diploma); clinical pathology (Diploma); clinical studies (Diploma); comparative pathology (M Sc, PhD); dermatology (M Sc); diagnostic imaging (M Sc, DV Sc); emergency/critical care (M Sc, DV Sc, Diploma); epidemiology (M Sc, DV Sc, PhD); health management (DV Sc); immunology (M Sc, PhD); laboratory animal science (DV Sc); medicine (M Sc, DV Sc); morphology (M Sc, DV Sc, PhD); neurology (M Sc, DV Sc); neuroscience (M Sc, DV Sc, PhD); ophthalmology (M Sc, DV Sc); pathology (M Sc, PhD, Diploma); pharmacology (M Sc, DV Sc, PhD); physiology (M Sc, DV Sc, PhD); population medicine and health management (M Sc); surgery (M Sc, DV Sc); swine health management (M Sc); theriogenology (M Sc, DV Sc); toxicology (M Sc, DV Sc, PhD); veterinary infectious diseases (M Sc, PhD); veterinary sciences (M Sc, DV Sc, PhD, Diploma); zoo animal/wildlife medicine (DV Sc).

UNIVERSITY OF HARTFORD, West Hartford, CT 06117-1599

General Information Independent, coed, comprehensive institution. CGS member. *Graduate housing:* On-campus housing not available.

GRADUATE UNITS

Barney School of Business *Degree program information:* Part-time and evening/weekend programs available. Offers business (MBA, MSAT, Certificate); business administration (MBA); professional accounting (Certificate); taxation (MSAT). Electronic applications accepted.

College of Arts and Sciences *Degree program information:* Part-time and evening/weekend programs available. Offers arts and sciences (MA, MS, Psy D); biology (MS); clinical practices

University of Hartford (continued)
(MA, Psy D); communication (MA); general experimental psychology (MA); neuroscience (MS); organizational behavior (MS); psychology (MA); school psychology (MS). Electronic applications accepted.

College of Education, Nursing, and Health Professions *Degree program information:* Part-time and evening/weekend programs available. Offers administration and supervision (CAGS); community/public health nursing (MSN); counseling (M Ed, MS, Sixth Year Certificate); early childhood education (M Ed); education, nursing, and health professions (M Ed, MS, MSN, MSPT, DPT, Ed D, CAGS, Sixth Year Certificate); educational leadership (Ed D, CAGS); educational technology (M Ed); elementary education (M Ed); nursing education (MSN); nursing management (MSN); physical therapy (MSPT, DPT). Electronic applications accepted.

College of Engineering, Technology and Architecture *Degree program information:* Part-time and evening/weekend programs available. Offers architecture (M Arch); engineering (M Eng); engineering, technology and architecture (M Arch, M Eng). Electronic applications accepted.

Hartford Art School *Degree program information:* Part-time programs available. Offers art (MFA). Electronic applications accepted.

The Hartt School *Degree program information:* Part-time programs available. Offers choral conducting (MM Ed); composition (MM, DMA, Artist Diploma, Diploma); conducting (MM, DMA, Artist Diploma, Diploma); early childhood education (MM Ed); instrumental conducting (MM Ed); Kodály (MM Ed); music (CAGS); music education (DMA, PhD); music history (MM); music theory (MM); pedagogy (MM Ed); performance (MM, MM Ed, DMA, Artist Diploma, Diploma); research (MM Ed); technology (MM Ed). Electronic applications accepted.

UNIVERSITY OF HAWAII AT HILO, Hilo, HI 96720-4091

General Information State-supported, coed, comprehensive institution.

GRADUATE UNITS

Program in China-US Relations Offers China-US relations (MA).

Program in Counseling Psychology Offers counseling psychology (MA).

Program in Education *Degree program information:* Part-time and evening/weekend programs available. Offers education (M Ed). Electronic applications accepted.

Program in Hawaiian and Indigenous Language and Cultural Revitalization Offers Hawaiian and indigenous language and cultural revitalization (PhD).

Program in Hawaiian Language and Literature Offers Hawaiian language and literature (MA).

Program in Indigenous Language and Culture Education Offers indigenous language and culture education (MA).

Program in Tropical Conservation Biology and Environmental Science Offers tropical conservation biology and environmental science (MS).

UNIVERSITY OF HAWAII AT MANOA, Honolulu, HI 96822

General Information State-supported, coed, university. CGS member. *Enrollment:* 20,337 graduate, professional, and undergraduate students; 4,158 full-time matriculated graduate/professional students (2,312 women), 2,223 part-time matriculated graduate/professional students (1,398 women). *Enrollment by degree level:* 698 first professional, 3,237 master's, 1,564 doctoral, 882 other advanced degrees. *Graduate faculty:* 1,343 full-time (479 women), 211 part-time/adjunct (58 women). *Graduate housing:* Rooms and/or apartments available to single and married students. Housing application deadline: 5/1. *Student services:* Campus employment opportunities, campus safety program, career counseling, child daycare facilities, exercise/wellness program, free psychological counseling, international student services, low-cost health insurance, multicultural affairs office, services for students with disabilities, teacher training, writing training. *Library facilities:* Hamilton Library plus 6 others. *Online resources:* library catalog, web page, access to other libraries' catalogs. *Collection:* 3.4 million titles, 58,434 serial subscriptions, 72,147 audiovisual materials. *Research affiliation:* Bernice Pauahi Bishop Museum (anthropology, zoology), Hawaiian Volcano Observatory (geology, geophysics), Honolulu Academy of Arts, East-West Center (communication, geography, economics), U. S. Geological Survey (USGS), Hawaii Agriculture Research Center.

Computer facilities: Computer purchase and lease plans are available. 400 computers available on campus for general student use. A campuswide network can be accessed from student residence rooms and from off campus. Online class registration is available. *Web address:* http://manoa.hawaii.edu/.

General Application Contact: Jarren Uyehara-Fujii, Director of Graduate Admissions, 808-956-8544, Fax: 808-956-4261, E-mail: admissions@grad.hawaii.edu.

GRADUATE UNITS

Graduate Division Students: 3,453 full-time (1,949 women), 1,615 part-time (1,043 women); includes 2,315 minority (63 Black or African American, non-Hispanic/Latino; 28 American Indian or Alaska Native, non-Hispanic/Latino; 873 Asian, non-Hispanic/Latino; 110 Hispanic/Latino; 755 Native Hawaiian or other Pacific Islander, non-Hispanic/Latino; 486 Two or more races, non-Hispanic/Latino), 979 international. Average age 32. 4,026 applicants, 54% accepted, 1426 enrolled. *Faculty:* 1,472 full-time (493 women), 180 part-time/adjunct (41 women). Expenses: Contact institution. *Financial support:* In 2010–11, 2,200 fellowships (averaging $3,800 per year), 741 research assistantships with full tuition reimbursements (averaging $18,800 per year), 524 teaching assistantships with full tuition reimbursements (averaging $14,850 per year) were awarded; career-related internships or fieldwork, Federal Work-Study, institutionally sponsored loans, scholarships/grants, and tuition waivers (full and partial) also available. Support available to part-time students. Financial award applicants required to submit FAFSA. In 2010, 1,107 master's, 187 doctorates, 38 other advanced degrees awarded. *Degree program information:* Part-time programs available. Offers communication and information sciences (PhD); ecology, evolution and conservation biology (MS, PhD); international cultural studies (Graduate Certificate). *Application fee:* $60. Electronic applications accepted. *Application Contact:* Graduate Division, 808-956-8544.

College of Arts and Humanities Students: 258 full-time (127 women), 108 part-time (50 women); includes 112 minority (1 Black or African American, non-Hispanic/Latino; 5 American Indian or Alaska Native, non-Hispanic/Latino; 45 Asian, non-Hispanic/Latino; 4 Hispanic/Latino; 14 Native Hawaiian or other Pacific Islander, non-Hispanic/Latino; 43 Two or more races, non-Hispanic/Latino), 40 international. Average age 33. 330 applicants, 52% accepted, 108 enrolled. Expenses: Contact institution. *Financial support:* In 2010–11, 67 students received support, including 97 fellowships, 8 research assistantships, 66 teaching assistantships; career-related internships or fieldwork, Federal Work-Study, institutionally sponsored loans, scholarships/grants, and tuition waivers (full and partial) also available. Support available to part-time students. Financial award applicants required to submit FAFSA. In 2010, 46 master's, 4 doctorates awarded. *Degree program information:* Part-time programs available. Offers American studies (MA, PhD); art history (MA); arts and humanities (M Mus, MA, MFA, PhD, Graduate Certificate); dance (MA, MFA); historic preservation (Graduate Certificate); history (MA, PhD); museum studies (Graduate Certificate); music (M Mus, MA, PhD); philosophy (MA, PhD); religion (MA); speech (MA); theatre (MA, MFA, PhD); visual arts (MFA). *Application Contact:* Thomas Bingham, Dean, 808-956-6460. *Dean,* Thomas Bingham, 808-956-6460.

College of Education Students: 508 full-time (348 women), 568 part-time (392 women); includes 673 minority (23 Black or African American, non-Hispanic/Latino; 7 American Indian or Alaska Native, non-Hispanic/Latino; 289 Asian, non-Hispanic/Latino; 23 Hispanic/Latino; 215 Native Hawaiian or other Pacific Islander, non-Hispanic/Latino; 116 Two or more races, non-Hispanic/Latino), 54 international. Average age 38. 971 applicants, 67% accepted, 509 enrolled. Expenses: Contact institution. *Financial support:* In 2010–11, 24 students received support, including 122 fellowships, 84 research assistantships, 9 teaching assistantships; career-related internships or fieldwork, Federal Work-Study, institutionally sponsored loans, and tuition waivers (full and partial) also available. Support available to part-time students. In 2010, 312 master's, 13 doctorates, 3 other advanced degrees awarded. *Degree program information:* Part-time and evening/weekend programs available. Offers curriculum and instruction (PhD); curriculum studies (M Ed); disability and diversity studies (Graduate Certificate); early childhood education (M Ed); education (M Ed, M Ed T, MS, Ed D, PhD, Graduate Certificate); educational administration (M Ed); educational foundations (PhD); educational policy studies (PhD); educational psychology (M Ed, PhD); educational technology (M Ed); exceptionalities (PhD); kinesiology (MS, PhD); professional practice (Ed D); special education (M Ed); teaching (M Ed T). *Application Contact:* Christine Sorensen, Dean, 808-956-7703. *Dean,* Christine Sorensen, 808-956-7703.

College of Engineering Students: 160 full-time (35 women), 45 part-time (11 women); includes 103 minority (1 Black or African American, non-Hispanic/Latino; 69 Asian, non-Hispanic/Latino; 3 Hispanic/Latino; 11 Native Hawaiian or other Pacific Islander, non-Hispanic/Latino; 19 Two or more races, non-Hispanic/Latino), 69 international. Average age 29. 208 applicants, 69% accepted, 84 enrolled. *Faculty:* 75 full-time (3 women). Expenses: Contact institution. *Financial support:* In 2010–11, 30 fellowships, 103 research assistantships, 21 teaching assistantships were awarded; career-related internships or fieldwork, Federal Work-Study, and tuition waivers (full and partial) also available. Financial award applicants required to submit FAFSA. In 2010, 35 master's, 10 doctorates awarded. *Degree program information:* Part-time programs available. Offers civil and environmental engineering (MS, PhD); electrical engineering (MS, PhD); engineering (MS, PhD); mechanical engineering (MS, PhD). *Application deadline:* Applications are processed on a rolling basis. *Application Contact:* Peter E. Crouch, Dean, 808-956-7727, Fax: 808-956-2291. *Dean,* Peter E. Crouch, 808-956-7727, Fax: 808-956-2291.

College of Languages, Linguistics and Literature Students: 307 full-time (204 women), 75 part-time (45 women); includes 133 minority (7 Black or African American, non-Hispanic/Latino; 2 American Indian or Alaska Native, non-Hispanic/Latino; 73 Asian, non-Hispanic/Latino; 11 Hispanic/Latino; 14 Native Hawaiian or other Pacific Islander, non-Hispanic/Latino; 26 Two or more races, non-Hispanic/Latino), 145 international. Average age 34. 462 applicants, 45% accepted, 128 enrolled. Expenses: Contact institution. *Financial support:* In 2010–11, 100 fellowships, 15 research assistantships, 135 teaching assistantships were awarded; career-related internships or fieldwork, Federal Work-Study, institutionally sponsored loans, and tuition waivers (full and partial) also available. Support available to part-time students. Financial award applicants required to submit FAFSA. In 2010, 100 master's, 22 doctorates, 1 other advanced degree awarded. *Degree program information:* Part-time programs available. Offers Chinese (MA, PhD); English (MA, PhD); English as a second language (MA, Graduate Certificate); French (MA); Japanese (MA, PhD); Korean (MA, PhD); languages, linguistics and literature (MA, PhD, Graduate Certificate); linguistics (MA, PhD); second language acquisition (PhD); Spanish (MA). *Application Contact:* Robert Bley-Vroman, Dean, 808-956-8516, Fax: 808-956-9879. *Dean,* Robert Bley-Vroman, 808-956-8516, Fax: 808-956-9879.

College of Natural Sciences Students: 309 full-time (116 women), 55 part-time (21 women); includes 105 minority (3 Black or African American, non-Hispanic/Latino; 3 American Indian or Alaska Native, non-Hispanic/Latino; 49 Asian, non-Hispanic/Latino; 12 Hispanic/Latino; 11 Native Hawaiian or other Pacific Islander, non-Hispanic/Latino; 27 Two or more races, non-Hispanic/Latino), 76 international. Average age 32. 409 applicants, 35% accepted, 83 enrolled. *Faculty:* 230 full-time (45 women), 17 part-time/adjunct (2 women). Expenses: Contact institution. *Financial support:* In 2010–11, 41 students received support, including 59 fellowships, 134 research assistantships, 108 teaching assistantships; institutionally sponsored loans and tuition waivers (full and partial) also available. Support available to part-time students. In 2010, 48 master's, 35 doctorates awarded. *Degree program information:* Part-time programs available. Offers advanced library and information science (Graduate Certificate); astronomy (MS, PhD); botany (MS, PhD); chemistry (MS, PhD); computer science (MS, PhD); library and information science (MLI Sc, Graduate Certificate); mathematics (MA, PhD); microbiology (MS, PhD); natural sciences (MA, MLI Sc, MS, PhD, Graduate Certificate); physics (MS, PhD); zoology (MS, PhD). *Application fee:* $60. *Application Contact:* William Ditto, Dean, 808-956-6451, E-mail: wditto@hawaii.edu. *Dean,* William Ditto, 808-956-6451, E-mail: wditto@hawaii.edu.

College of Social Sciences Students: 477 full-time (273 women), 174 part-time (109 women); includes 209 minority (3 Black or African American, non-Hispanic/Latino; 2 American Indian or Alaska Native, non-Hispanic/Latino; 81 Asian, non-Hispanic/Latino; 14 Hispanic/Latino; 54 Native Hawaiian or other Pacific Islander, non-Hispanic/Latino; 55 Two or more races, non-Hispanic/Latino), 205 international. Average age 33. 908 applicants, 40% accepted, 221 enrolled. *Faculty:* 239 full-time (82 women), 61 part-time/adjunct (19 women). Expenses: Contact institution. *Financial support:* In 2010–11, 2 students received support, including 142 fellowships, 117 research assistantships, 79 teaching assistantships; career-related internships or fieldwork, Federal Work-Study, institutionally sponsored loans, and tuition waivers (full and partial) also available. Support available to part-time students. Financial award applicants required to submit FAFSA. In 2010, 115 master's, 40 doctorates, 16 other advanced degrees awarded. *Degree program information:* Part-time and evening/weekend programs available. Offers advanced women's studies (Graduate Certificate); anthropology (MA, PhD); clinical psychology (PhD); communication (MA); community and cultural psychology (PhD); community and culture (MA); community planning and social policy (MURP); conflict resolution (Graduate Certificate); disaster preparedness and emergency management (Graduate Certificate); economics (MA, PhD); environmental planning and management (MURP); geography (MA, PhD); land use and infrastructure planning (MURP); ocean policy (Graduate Certificate); political science (MA, PhD); psychology (MA, PhD, Graduate Certificate); public administration (MPA, Graduate Certificate); public policy (Graduate Certificate); social sciences (MA, MPA, MURP, PhD, Graduate Certificate); sociology (MA, PhD); telecommunication and information resource management (Graduate Certificate); urban and regional planning (PhD, Graduate Certificate); urban and regional planning in Asia and Pacific (MURP). *Application fee:* $60. *Application Contact:* Richard Dubanoski, Dean, 808-956-6570, Fax: 808-956-2340, E-mail: dickd@hawaii.edu. *Dean,* Richard Dubanoski, 808-956-6570, Fax: 808-956-2340, E-mail: dickd@hawaii.edu.

College of Tropical Agriculture and Human Resources Students: 197 full-time (99 women), 54 part-time (26 women); includes 78 minority (1 Black or African American, non-Hispanic/Latino; 1 American Indian or Alaska Native, non-Hispanic/Latino; 44 Asian, non-Hispanic/Latino; 3 Hispanic/Latino; 13 Native Hawaiian or other Pacific Islander, non-Hispanic/Latino; 16 Two or more races, non-Hispanic/Latino), 90 international. Average age 34. 240 applicants, 57% accepted, 93 enrolled. Expenses: Contact institution. *Financial support:* In 2010–11, 12 students received support, including 37 fellowships, 129 research assistantships, 16 teaching assistantships; career-related internships or fieldwork, Federal Work-Study, institutionally sponsored loans, tuition waivers (full and partial), and unspecified assistantships also available. In 2010, 30 master's, 10 doctorates awarded. *Degree program information:* Part-time programs available. Offers animal sciences (MS); bioengineering (MS); entomology (MS, PhD); food science (MS); molecular bioscience and bioengineering (MS); molecular biosciences and bioengineering (PhD); natural resources and environmental management (MS, PhD); nutrition (PhD); nutritional sciences (MS, PhD); tropical agriculture and human resources (MS, PhD); tropical plant and soil sciences (MS, PhD); tropical plant pathology (MS, PhD). *Application Contact:* Sylvia Yuen, Interim Dean, 808-956-8234, Fax: 808-956-9105, E-mail: syuen@hawaii.edu. *Interim Dean,* Sylvia Yuen, 808-956-8234, Fax: 808-956-9105, E-mail: syuen@hawaii.edu.

Hawai'inuaka School of Hawaiian Knowledge Students: 35 full-time (25 women), 14 part-time (11 women); includes 47 minority (1 Asian, non-Hispanic/Latino; 40 Native Hawaiian or other Pacific Islander, non-Hispanic/Latino; 6 Two or more races, non-Hispanic/Latino), 1 international. Average age 34. 26 applicants, 62% accepted, 13 enrolled. *Faculty:* 20 full-time (11 women). Expenses: Contact institution. *Financial support:* In 2010–11, 19 fellowships, 9 research assistantships, 8 teaching assistantships were awarded. In 2010, 7 master's awarded. *Degree program information:* Part-time programs available. Offers Hawaiian (MA); Hawaiian studies (MA). *Application deadline:* For fall admission, 3/1 for domestic and international students. *Application fee:* $60. *Application Contact:* Maenette Ah Nee-Benham, Dean, 808-956-0980, Fax: 808-956-0411, E-mail: mbenham@hawaii.edu. *Dean,* Maenette Ah Nee-Benham, 808-956-0980, Fax: 808-956-0411, E-mail: mbenham@hawaii.edu.

School of Nursing and Dental Hygiene Students: 111 full-time (96 women), 136 part-time (120 women); includes 147 minority (6 Black or African American, non-Hispanic/Latino; 1 American Indian or Alaska Native, non-Hispanic/Latino; 71 Asian, non-Hispanic/Latino; 7

Hispanic/Latino; 38 Native Hawaiian or other Pacific Islander, non-Hispanic/Latino; 24 Two or more races, non-Hispanic/Latino), 1 international. Average age 41. 190 applicants, 52% accepted, 82 enrolled. *Faculty:* 32 full-time (27 women), 22 part-time/adjunct (11 women). Expenses: Contact institution. *Financial support:* In 2010–11, 78 fellowships (averaging $1,277 per year), 3 research assistantships (averaging $16,824 per year), 2 teaching assistantships (averaging $14,382 per year) were awarded. In 2010, 20 master's, 8 doctorates awarded. *Degree program information:* Part-time programs available. Postbaccalaureate distance learning degree programs offered (minimal on-campus study). Offers clinical nurse specialist (MS); nurse practitioner (MS); nursing (PhD, Graduate Certificate); nursing administration (MS). *Application deadline:* For fall admission, 2/1 for domestic and international students. *Application fee:* $60. *Application Contact:* Maureen Shannon, Graduate Chair, 808-956-5201, Fax: 808-956-3257, E-mail: maureens@hawaii.edu. *Dean,* Mary Boland, 808-956-8522, Fax: 808-956-3257, E-mail: mgboland@hawaii.edu.

School of Ocean and Earth Science and Technology Students: 169 full-time (75 women), 16 part-time (8 women); includes 36 minority (2 Black or African American, non-Hispanic/Latino; 15 Asian, non-Hispanic/Latino; 6 Hispanic/Latino; 4 Native Hawaiian or other Pacific Islander, non-Hispanic/Latino; 9 Two or more races, non-Hispanic/Latino), 51 international. Average age 31. 265 applicants, 32% accepted, 48 enrolled. *Faculty:* 170 full-time (30 women), 23 part-time/adjunct (3 women). Expenses: Contact institution. *Financial support:* In 2010–11, 25 students received support, including 18 fellowships, 140 research assistantships, 17 teaching assistantships; career-related internships or fieldwork, Federal Work-Study, institutionally sponsored loans, and tuition waivers (full and partial) also available. Financial award applicants required to submit FAFSA. In 2010, 25 master's, 19 doctorates awarded. *Degree program information:* Part-time programs available. Offers high-pressure geophysics and geochemistry (MS, PhD); hydrogeology and engineering geology (MS, PhD); marine biology (MS, PhD); marine geology and geophysics (MS, PhD); meteorology (MS, PhD); ocean and earth science and technology (MS, PhD); ocean and resources engineering (MS, PhD); oceanography (MS, PhD); planetary geosciences and remote sensing (MS, PhD); seismology and solid-earth geophysics (MS, PhD); volcanology, petrology, and geochemistry (MS, PhD). *Application fee:* $60. *Application Contact:* Brian Taylor, Dean, 808-956-6182, E-mail: taylorb@hawaii.edu. *Dean,* Brian Taylor, 808-956-6182, E-mail: taylorb@hawaii.edu.

School of Pacific and Asian Studies Students: 50 full-time (18 women), 18 part-time (11 women); includes 28 minority (2 Black or African American, non-Hispanic/Latino; 12 Asian, non-Hispanic/Latino; 3 Hispanic/Latino; 5 Native Hawaiian or other Pacific Islander, non-Hispanic/Latino; 6 Two or more races, non-Hispanic/Latino), 13 international. Average age 34. 111 applicants, 59% accepted, 38 enrolled. *Faculty:* 132 full-time (50 women), 1 part-time/adjunct (0 women). Expenses: Contact institution. *Financial support:* In 2010–11, 26 fellowships, 2 research assistantships, 12 teaching assistantships were awarded; career-related internships or fieldwork, Federal Work-Study, and tuition waivers (full) also available. In 2010, 28 master's awarded. *Degree program information:* Part-time programs available. Offers Asian studies (MA, Graduate Certificate); Chinese studies (Graduate Certificate); Japanese studies (Graduate Certificate); Korean studies (Graduate Certificate); Pacific and Asian studies (MA, Graduate Certificate); Pacific Island studies (MA, Graduate Certificate); Philippine studies (Graduate Certificate); Southeast Asian studies (Graduate Certificate). *Application fee:* $60. *Application Contact:* Edward J. Shultz, Dean, 808-956-8818, E-mail: shultz@hawaii.edu. *Dean,* Edward J. Shultz, 808-956-8818, E-mail: shultz@hawaii.edu.

School of Social Work Students: 190 full-time (156 women), 35 part-time (30 women); includes 138 minority (7 Black or African American, non-Hispanic/Latino; 1 American Indian or Alaska Native, non-Hispanic/Latino; 45 Asian, non-Hispanic/Latino; 10 Hispanic/Latino; 48 Native Hawaiian or other Pacific Islander, non-Hispanic/Latino; 27 Two or more races, non-Hispanic/Latino), 16 international. Average age 35. 194 applicants, 59% accepted, 70 enrolled. *Faculty:* 27 full-time (19 women). Expenses: Contact institution. *Financial support:* In 2010–11, 23 fellowships with full and partial tuition reimbursements (averaging $2,966 per year), 9 research assistantships with full and partial tuition reimbursements (averaging $16,793 per year), 1 teaching assistantship (averaging $14,382 per year) were awarded; career-related internships or fieldwork, Federal Work-Study, institutionally sponsored loans, and tuition waivers (full) also available. Support available to part-time students. Financial award application deadline: 2/1; financial award applicants required to submit FAFSA. In 2010, 108 master's awarded. *Degree program information:* Part-time programs available. Offers social welfare (PhD); social work (MSW). *Application deadline:* For fall admission, 1/15 for domestic and international students. Applications are processed on a rolling basis. *Application fee:* $60. *Application Contact:* Crystal Mills, Graduate Chair, 808-956-3832, Fax: 808-956-5964, E-mail: millsc@hawaii.edu. *Dean,* Jon Matsuoka, 808-956-6300, E-mail: jmatsuok@hawaii.edu.

School of Travel Industry Management Students: 10 full-time (7 women), 2 part-time (1 woman); includes 4 minority (3 Asian, non-Hispanic/Latino; 1 Two or more races, non-Hispanic/Latino), 2 international. Average age 31. 56 applicants, 32% accepted, 8 enrolled. *Faculty:* 8 full-time (3 women). Expenses: Contact institution. *Financial support:* In 2010–11, 1 fellowship with partial tuition reimbursement (averaging $6,000 per year) was awarded; career-related internships or fieldwork, scholarships/grants, tuition waivers (full and partial), and student assistantships also available. Financial award application deadline: 3/1. In 2010, 2 master's awarded. *Degree program information:* Part-time programs available. Offers travel industry management (MS). *Application deadline:* For fall admission, 3/1 for domestic and international students. Applications are processed on a rolling basis. *Application fee:* $60. Electronic applications accepted. *Application Contact:* Dexter J. L. Choy, Graduate Chair, 808-956-9840, Fax: 808-956-5378, E-mail: djlchoy@hawaii.edu.

Shidler College of Business Students: 262 full-time (101 women), 191 part-time (66 women); includes 228 minority (3 Black or African American, non-Hispanic/Latino; 137 Asian, non-Hispanic/Latino; 6 Hispanic/Latino; 38 Native Hawaiian or other Pacific Islander, non-Hispanic/Latino; 44 Two or more races, non-Hispanic/Latino), 96 international. Average age 33. Expenses: Contact institution. *Financial support:* In 2010–11, 32 students received support, including 113 fellowships, 36 research assistantships, 1 teaching assistantship; career-related internships or fieldwork, Federal Work-Study, and tuition waivers (full) also available. Support available to part-time students. In 2010, 260 master's, 4 doctorates awarded. *Degree program information:* Part-time and evening/weekend programs available. Offers accounting (M Acc); accounting law (M Acc); Asian business studies (MBA); Asian finance (PhD); business (EMBA, M Acc, MBA, MHRM, MS, PhD, Graduate Certificate); Chinese business studies (MBA); decision sciences (MBA); entrepreneurship (MBA, Graduate Certificate); executive business administration (EMBA); finance (MBA); finance and banking (MBA); financial engineering (MS); global information technology management (PhD); human resources management (MBA); information management (MBA); information systems (M Acc); information technology (MBA); international accounting (PhD); international business (MBA); international marketing (PhD); international organization and strategy (PhD); Japanese business studies (MBA); marketing (MBA); organizational behavior (MBA); organizational management (MBA); real estate (MBA); student-designed track (MBA); taxation (M Acc); Vietnam focused business administration (EMBA). *Application fee:* $60. *Application Contact:* V. Vance Roley, Dean, 808-956-8377. *Dean,* V. Vance Roley, 808-956-8377.

John A. Burns School of Medicine Students: 391 full-time (235 women), 41 part-time (28 women); includes 306 minority (2 Black or African American, non-Hispanic/Latino; 187 Asian, non-Hispanic/Latino; 2 Hispanic/Latino; 34 Native Hawaiian or other Pacific Islander, non-Hispanic/Latino; 81 Two or more races, non-Hispanic/Latino), 32 international. Expenses: Contact institution. *Financial support:* In 2010–11, 62 fellowships, 70 research assistantships, 2 teaching assistantships were awarded; career-related internships or fieldwork, Federal Work-Study, institutionally sponsored loans, and tuition waivers (full and partial) also available. Support available to part-time students. Financial award applicants required to submit FAFSA. In 2010, 23 master's, 10 doctorates, 1 other advanced degree awarded. *Degree program information:* Part-time programs available. Offers cell and molecular biology (MS, PhD); communication sciences and disorders (MS); developmental and reproductive biology (MS, PhD); epidemiology (PhD); gerontology (Graduate Certificate); global health and population studies (Graduate Certificate); medicine (MD, MPH, MS, Dr PH, PhD, Graduate Certificate); public health (MPH, MS, Dr PH). *Application Contact:* Dr. Jerris R. Hedges, Dean, 808-692-0881. *Dean,* Dr. Jerris R. Hedges, 808-692-0881.

Graduate Programs in Biomedical Sciences Students: 5 full-time (2 women), 6 part-time (4 women); includes 6 minority (5 Asian, non-Hispanic/Latino; 1 Two or more races, non-Hispanic/Latino), 2 international. Average age 42. 20 applicants, 55% accepted, 11 enrolled. *Faculty:* 17 full-time (10 women), 1 part-time/adjunct (0 women). Expenses: Contact institution. *Financial support:* In 2010–11, 1 fellowship (averaging $18,126 per year), 1 research assistantship (averaging $23,022 per year) were awarded; career-related internships or fieldwork, Federal Work-Study, institutionally sponsored loans, and tuition waivers (full and partial) also available. Support available to part-time students. In 2010, 1 master's, 3 doctorates awarded. *Degree program information:* Part-time programs available. Offers biomedical sciences (MS, PhD); tropical medicine (MS, PhD). *Application deadline:* For fall admission, 6/1 for domestic and international students. *Application fee:* $60. *Application Contact:* Rosanne Harrigan, Graduate Chairperson, 808-692-0904, Fax: 808-692-1247, E-mail: harrigan@hawaii.edu.

School of Architecture Students: 130 full-time (67 women), 21 part-time (6 women); includes 3 Black or African American, non-Hispanic/Latino; 62 Asian, non-Hispanic/Latino; 4 Hispanic/Latino; 12 Native Hawaiian or other Pacific Islander, non-Hispanic/Latino; 16 Two or more races, non-Hispanic/Latino, 16 international. Average age 33. *Faculty:* 10 full-time (3 women). Expenses: Contact institution. *Financial support:* In 2010–11, 31 students received support, including 11 fellowships (averaging $3,020 per year), 2 research assistantships with full tuition reimbursements available (averaging $17,496 per year); teaching assistantships with full tuition reimbursements available, institutionally sponsored loans, scholarships/grants, and unspecified assistantships also available. Financial award applicants required to submit FAFSA. *Degree program information:* Part-time programs available. Offers architecture (D Arch). *Application deadline:* For fall admission, 5/1 for domestic and international students; for spring admission, 9/1 for domestic students, 8/1 for international students. *Application fee:* $60. *Application Contact:* Spencer Leineweber, Graduate Field Chairperson, 808-956-7228, Fax: 808-956-7778, E-mail: aspencer@hawaii.edu.

William S. Richardson School of Law Students: 302 full-time (178 women), 56 part-time (29 women); includes 240 minority (3 Black or African American, non-Hispanic/Latino; 2 American Indian or Alaska Native, non-Hispanic/Latino; 97 Asian, non-Hispanic/Latino; 4 Hispanic/Latino; 67 Native Hawaiian or other Pacific Islander, non-Hispanic/Latino; 67 Two or more races, non-Hispanic/Latino), 15 international. *Faculty:* 32 full-time (15 women). Expenses: Contact institution. *Financial support:* In 2010–11, 73 fellowships (averaging $3,824 per year) were awarded; research assistantships, career-related internships or fieldwork, Federal Work-Study, institutionally sponsored loans, and tuition waivers (full and partial) also available. Financial award application deadline: 3/1; financial award applicants required to submit FAFSA. In 2010, 15 master's awarded. Offers law (JD, LL M, Graduate Certificate). *Application deadline:* For fall admission, 6/1 for domestic and international students. *Application Contact:* Elisabeth Steele Hutchinson, Assistant Dean, 808-956-5557, Fax: 808-956-6813, E-mail: lawadm@hawaii.edu.

UNIVERSITY OF HOUSTON, Houston, TX 77204

General Information State-supported, coed, university. CGS member. *Enrollment:* 38,752 graduate, professional, and undergraduate students; 5,605 full-time matriculated graduate/professional students (2,869 women), 2,459 part-time matriculated graduate/professional students (1,205 women). *Enrollment by degree level:* 1,740 first professional, 4,537 master's, 1,787 doctoral. *Graduate faculty:* 713 full-time (196 women), 426 part-time/adjunct (183 women). Tuition, state resident: full-time $8592; part-time $358 per credit hour. Tuition, nonresident: full-time $16,032; part-time $668 per credit hour. *Required fees:* $2889. Tuition and fees vary according to course load and program. *Graduate housing:* Rooms and/or apartments available on a first-come, first-served basis to single and married students. Typical cost: $4360 per year ($7300 including board) for single students. Room and board charges vary according to board plan and housing facility selected. *Student services:* Campus employment opportunities, campus safety program, career counseling, child daycare facilities, exercise/wellness program, free psychological counseling, international student services, low-cost health insurance, services for students with disabilities, teacher training, writing training. *Library facilities:* M.D. Anderson Library plus 5 others. *Online resources:* library catalog, web page, access to other libraries' catalogs. *Collection:* 2.7 million titles, 76,619 serial subscriptions, 29,128 audiovisual materials. *Research affiliation:* Keck Consortium.

Computer facilities: Computer purchase and lease plans are available. 1,476 computers available on campus for general student use. A campuswide network can be accessed from student residence rooms and from off campus. Online class registration is available. *Web address:* http://www.uh.edu/.

General Application Contact: Margaret D. Watson, Director, Graduate Studies Programs, 713-743-9118, Fax: 713-743-9089, E-mail: mwatson@uh.edu.

GRADUATE UNITS

Bauer College of Business Students: 774 full-time (311 women), 699 part-time (230 women); includes 533 minority (105 Black or African American, non-Hispanic/Latino; 4 American Indian or Alaska Native, non-Hispanic/Latino; 251 Asian, non-Hispanic/Latino; 159 Hispanic/Latino; 2 Native Hawaiian or other Pacific Islander, non-Hispanic/Latino; 12 Two or more races, non-Hispanic/Latino), 276 international. Average age 29. 1,173 applicants, 56% accepted, 481 enrolled. *Faculty:* 52 full-time (10 women), 44 part-time/adjunct (9 women). Expenses: Contact institution. *Financial support:* In 2010–11, 26 fellowships with partial tuition reimbursements (averaging $2,400 per year), 2 research assistantships with partial tuition reimbursements (averaging $8,800 per year), 54 teaching assistantships with partial tuition reimbursements (averaging $14,571 per year) were awarded; career-related internships or fieldwork, Federal Work-Study, institutionally sponsored loans, scholarships/grants, health care benefits, and unspecified assistantships also available. Support available to part-time students. Financial award application deadline: 2/1; financial award applicants required to submit FAFSA. In 2010, 601 master's, 14 doctorates awarded. *Degree program information:* Part-time and evening/weekend programs available. Offers accountancy (MS Accy); accountancy and taxation (PhD); business (MBA, MS, MS Accy, PhD); decision and information sciences (PhD); finance (MS); management (PhD); marketing (PhD). *Application deadline:* For fall admission, 6/1 for domestic students, 4/1 for international students; for spring admission, 11/1 for domestic students, 10/1 for international students. Applications are processed on a rolling basis. *Application fee:* $75 ($150 for international students). Electronic applications accepted. *Application Contact:* Dr. Latha Ramchand, Interim Dean, 713-743-4604, Fax: 713-743-4622, E-mail: ramchand@uh.edu. *Interim Dean,* Dr. Latha Ramchand, 713-743-4604, Fax: 713-743-4622, E-mail: ramchand@uh.edu.

College of Architecture Students: 92 full-time (40 women), 6 part-time (2 women); includes 1 Black or African American, non-Hispanic/Latino; 1 American Indian or Alaska Native, non-Hispanic/Latino; 9 Asian, non-Hispanic/Latino; 8 Hispanic/Latino; 3 Two or more races, non-Hispanic/Latino, 19 international. Average age 28. 192 applicants, 45% accepted, 47 enrolled. *Faculty:* 18 full-time (3 women), 13 part-time/adjunct (2 women). Expenses: Contact institution. *Financial support:* In 2010–11, 1 research assistantship with partial tuition reimbursement (averaging $7,720 per year), 11 teaching assistantships with partial tuition reimbursements (averaging $5,264 per year) were awarded; career-related internships or fieldwork, Federal Work-Study, institutionally sponsored loans, scholarships/grants, health care benefits, and unspecified assistantships also available. Support available to part-time students. Financial award application deadline: 2/1. In 2010, 21 master's awarded. Offers architecture (MS); architecture studies (MA); space architecture (MS). *Application deadline:* For fall admission, 2/1 priority date for domestic students, 2/1 for international students. Applications are processed on a rolling basis. *Application fee:* $50. Electronic applications accepted. *Application Contact:* Trang Phan, Assistant Dean, 713-743-2400, Fax: 713-743-2358, E-mail: tphan@uh.edu. *Dean,* Dr. Patricia Oliver, 713-743-2400, Fax: 713-743-2358, E-mail: poliver@central.uh.edu.

College of Education Students: 345 full-time (266 women), 435 part-time (343 women); includes 310 minority (121 Black or African American, non-Hispanic/Latino; 5 American Indian or Alaska Native, non-Hispanic/Latino; 58 Asian, non-Hispanic/Latino; 114 Hispanic/Latino; 2 Native Hawaiian or other Pacific Islander, non-Hispanic/Latino; 10 Two or more races, non-Hispanic/Latino), 39 international. Average age 33. 436 applicants, 68% accepted, 206 enrolled. *Faculty:* 63 full-time (30 women), 40 part-time/adjunct (27 women). Expenses: Contact institution. *Financial support:* In 2010–11, 2 fellowships with full tuition reimbursements (averaging $2,000 per year), 17 research assistantships with full tuition reimburse-

University of Houston (continued)

ments (averaging $8,634 per year), 82 teaching assistantships with full tuition reimbursements (averaging $8,697 per year) were awarded; career-related internships or fieldwork, Federal Work-Study, institutionally sponsored loans, scholarships/grants, health care benefits, and unspecified assistantships also available. Support available to part-time students. Financial award application deadline: 2/1; financial award applicants required to submit FAFSA. In 2010, 205 master's, 48 doctorates awarded. *Degree program information:* Part-time programs available. Offers administration and supervision (M Ed, Ed D); administration and supervision—higher education (M Ed); counseling (M Ed); counseling psychology (PhD); curriculum and instruction (M Ed, Ed D); education (M Ed, Ed D, PhD); educational psychology (M Ed); higher education (M Ed); historical, social, and cultural foundations of education (M Ed); professional leadership (Ed D); school psychology (PhD); school psychology and individual differences (PhD); special education (M Ed). *Application fee:* $45 ($75 for international students). Electronic applications accepted. *Application Contact:* Dr. Robert K. Wimpelberg, Dean, 713-743-5008, Fax: 713-743-5013, E-mail: rwimpelberg@uh.edu. *Dean,* Dr. Robert K. Wimpelberg, 713-743-5008, Fax: 713-743-5013, E-mail: rwimpelberg@uh.edu.

College of Liberal Arts and Social Sciences Students: 822 full-time (512 women), 354 part-time (223 women); includes 307 minority (74 Black or African American, non-Hispanic/Latino; 5 American Indian or Alaska Native, non-Hispanic/Latino; 56 Asian, non-Hispanic/Latino; 150 Hispanic/Latino; 1 Native Hawaiian or other Pacific Islander, non-Hispanic/Latino; 21 Two or more races, non-Hispanic/Latino), 162 international. Average age 30. 1,733 applicants, 29% accepted, 301 enrolled. *Faculty:* 207 full-time (79 women), 79 part-time/adjunct (41 women). Expenses: Contact institution. *Financial support:* In 2010–11, 64 fellowships with full tuition reimbursements (averaging $4,532 per year), 55 research assistantships with full tuition reimbursements (averaging $8,377 per year), 353 teaching assistantships with full tuition reimbursements (averaging $8,614 per year) were awarded; career-related internships or fieldwork, Federal Work-Study, institutionally sponsored loans, scholarships/grants, health care benefits, and unspecified assistantships also available. Support available to part-time students. Financial award application deadline: 2/1; financial award applicants required to submit FAFSA. In 2010, 237 master's, 56 doctorates awarded. *Degree program information:* Part-time programs available. Postbaccalaureate distance learning degree programs offered. Offers anthropology (MA); applied economics (MA); applied English linguistics (MA); art history (MA); clinical psychology (PhD); communication sciences and disorders (MA); creative writing (MFA); creative writing and literature (MA, PhD); developmental psychology (PhD); economics (MA, PhD); English (MA, PhD); exercise science (MS); history (MA, PhD); human nutrition (MS); human space exploration sciences (MS); industrial/organizational psychology (PhD); interdisciplinary practice and emerging forms (MFA); kinesiology (PhD); liberal arts and social sciences (M Ed, MA, MFA, MM, MS, DMA, PhD); painting (MFA); philosophy (MA); physical education (M Ed); political science (MA, PhD); psychology (MA); public administration (MA); social psychology (PhD); sociology (MA); Spanish (MA, PhD); studio art (MFA); world cultures and literatures (MA). *Application deadline:* For fall admission, 4/1 for international students; for spring admission, 10/1 for international students. *Application fee:* $75 for international students. Electronic applications accepted. *Application Contact:* Anna Marchese, Program Director, 713-743-4012, E-mail: amarches@uh.edu. *Dean,* Dr. John Roberts, 713-743-2992, Fax: 713-743-2990, E-mail: jwrobert@central.uh.edu.

Moores School of Music Students: 110 full-time (56 women), 42 part-time (21 women); includes 26 minority (6 Black or African American, non-Hispanic/Latino; 7 Asian, non-Hispanic/Latino; 6 Hispanic/Latino; 1 Native Hawaiian or other Pacific Islander, non-Hispanic/Latino; 6 Two or more races, non-Hispanic/Latino), 32 international. Average age 29. 128 applicants, 50% accepted, 42 enrolled. *Faculty:* 25 full-time (5 women), 21 part-time/adjunct (8 women). Expenses: Contact institution. *Financial support:* In 2010–11, 3 fellowships with full tuition reimbursements (averaging $8,767 per year), 56 teaching assistantships with full tuition reimbursements (averaging $5,112 per year) were awarded; career-related internships or fieldwork, Federal Work-Study, institutionally sponsored loans, scholarships/grants, health care benefits, and unspecified assistantships also available. Support available to part-time students. Financial award application deadline: 2/1. In 2010, 37 master's, 5 doctorates awarded. *Degree program information:* Part-time programs available. Offers accompanying and chamber music (MM); applied music (MM); composition (MM); music education (DMA); music theory (MM); performance (DMA). *Application deadline:* For fall admission, 3/1 for domestic and international students; for spring admission, 11/1 for domestic and international students. *Application fee:* $0 ($75 for international students). Electronic applications accepted. *Application Contact:* Douglas Goldberg, Graduate Advisor, 713-743-3314, Fax: 713-743-3166, E-mail: gradmusic@uh.edu. *Chairperson,* David Ashley White, 713-743-3009, Fax: 713-743-3166, E-mail: dwhite@uh.edu.

School of Communication Students: 47 full-time (39 women), 46 part-time (36 women); includes 15 Black or African American, non-Hispanic/Latino; 2 American Indian or Alaska Native, non-Hispanic/Latino; 3 Asian, non-Hispanic/Latino; 16 Hispanic/Latino, 19 international. Average age 28. 54 applicants, 70% accepted, 24 enrolled. *Faculty:* 11 full-time (6 women), 2 part-time/adjunct (0 women). Expenses: Contact institution. *Financial support:* In 2010–11, 28 teaching assistantships with full tuition reimbursements (averaging $8,111 per year) were awarded; career-related internships or fieldwork, Federal Work-Study, institutionally sponsored loans, scholarships/grants, health care benefits, and unspecified assistantships also available. Support available to part-time students. Financial award application deadline: 2/1. In 2010, 20 master's awarded. *Degree program information:* Part-time programs available. Offers health communication (MA); mass communication studies (MA); public relations studies (MA); speech communication (MA). *Application deadline:* For fall admission, 6/1 for domestic students, 4/1 for international students; for spring admission, 11/1 for domestic students, 10/1 for international students. Applications are processed on a rolling basis. *Application fee:* $50 ($100 for international students). Electronic applications accepted. *Application Contact:* Dr. Martha Haun, Director of Graduate Studies, 713-743-2886, E-mail: mhaun@uh.edu. *Chairperson,* Dr. Beth Olson, 713-743-2873, Fax: 713-743-2876, E-mail: bolson@uh.edu.

School of Theatre and Dance Students: 31 full-time (16 women); includes 2 Hispanic/Latino, 1 international. Average age 27. 12 applicants, 100% accepted, 12 enrolled. *Faculty:* 7 full-time (1 woman), 5 part-time/adjunct (2 women). Expenses: Contact institution. *Financial support:* Career-related internships or fieldwork, Federal Work-Study, institutionally sponsored loans, scholarships/grants, health care benefits, and unspecified assistantships available. Support available to part-time students. Financial award application deadline: 2/1. In 2010, 29 master's awarded. *Degree program information:* Part-time programs available. Offers theatre (MA, MFA). *Application deadline:* For fall admission, 4/1 for domestic and international students. *Application fee:* $25 ($75 for international students). Electronic applications accepted. *Application Contact:* Jack Young, Head of Graduate Acting and Directing, 713-743-0705, E-mail: jyoung2@mail.uh.edu. *Chairperson,* Steven Wallace, 713-743-3003, Fax: 713-743-2648, E-mail: swwallace@uh.edu.

College of Natural Sciences and Mathematics Students: 762 full-time (263 women), 190 part-time (68 women); includes 23 Black or African American, non-Hispanic/Latino; 54 Asian, non-Hispanic/Latino; 40 Hispanic/Latino; 4 Two or more races, non-Hispanic/Latino, 605 international. Average age 29. 1,010 applicants, 61% accepted, 226 enrolled. *Faculty:* 146 full-time (20 women), 22 part-time/adjunct (8 women). Expenses: Contact institution. *Financial support:* In 2010–11, 7 fellowships with partial tuition reimbursements (averaging $10,430 per year), 180 research assistantships with partial tuition reimbursements (averaging $12,043 per year), 176 teaching assistantships with partial tuition reimbursements (averaging $13,519 per year) were awarded; career-related internships or fieldwork, Federal Work-Study, institutionally sponsored loans, scholarships/grants, health care benefits, and unspecified assistantships also available. Support available to part-time students. Financial award application deadline: 2/1; financial award applicants required to submit FAFSA. In 2010, 163 master's, 62 doctorates awarded. *Degree program information:* Part-time programs available. Postbaccalaureate distance learning degree programs offered. Offers applied mathematics (MS); atmospheric science (PhD); biochemistry (MA, PhD); biology (MA); chemistry (MA, PhD); computer science (MA, PhD); geology (MA, PhD); geophysics (PhD); mathematics (MA, PhD); natural sciences and mathematics (MA, MS, PhD); physics (MA, PhD). *Application deadline:* Applications are processed on a rolling basis. *Application fee:* $75 for international students. Electronic applications accepted. *Application Contact:* Dr. Mark Smith, Dean, 713-743-2619, Fax: 713-743-8630, E-mail: markasmith@uh.edu. *Dean,* Dr. Mark Smith, 713-743-2619, Fax: 713-743-8630, E-mail: markasmith@uh.edu.

College of Optometry Students: 430 full-time (279 women), 11 part-time (7 women); includes 213 minority (11 Black or African American, non-Hispanic/Latino; 1 American Indian or Alaska Native, non-Hispanic/Latino; 154 Asian, non-Hispanic/Latino; 37 Hispanic/Latino; 2 Native Hawaiian or other Pacific Islander, non-Hispanic/Latino; 8 Two or more races, non-Hispanic/Latino), 31 international. Average age 25. 438 applicants, 27% accepted, 105 enrolled. *Faculty:* 25 full-time (6 women), 18 part-time/adjunct (12 women). Expenses: Contact institution. *Financial support:* In 2010–11, 2 fellowships with partial tuition reimbursements (averaging $6,500 per year), 7 research assistantships with partial tuition reimbursements (averaging $11,794 per year), 16 teaching assistantships with partial tuition reimbursements (averaging $15,378 per year) were awarded; career-related internships or fieldwork, Federal Work-Study, institutionally sponsored loans, scholarships/grants, health care benefits, and unspecified assistantships also available. Support available to part-time students. Financial award application deadline: 2/1. In 2010, 98 first professional degrees, 2 doctorates awarded. *Degree program information:* Part-time programs available. Offers optometry (OD, MS, PhD); physiological optics (MS, PhD). *Application deadline:* For winter admission, 2/15 for international students. Applications are processed on a rolling basis. *Application fee:* $50 for international students. Electronic applications accepted. *Application Contact:* Roger Boltz, Associate Dean, 713-743-1893, Fax: 713-743-0965, E-mail: boltz@uh.edu. *Dean,* Dr. Earl Smith, 713-743-1899, Fax: 713-743-0965, E-mail: esmith@uh.edu.

College of Pharmacy Students: 525 full-time (324 women), 43 part-time (24 women); includes 291 minority (25 Black or African American, non-Hispanic/Latino; 2 American Indian or Alaska Native, non-Hispanic/Latino; 219 Asian, non-Hispanic/Latino; 40 Hispanic/Latino; 1 Native Hawaiian or other Pacific Islander, non-Hispanic/Latino; 4 Two or more races, non-Hispanic/Latino), 78 international. Average age 25. 703 applicants, 28% accepted, 133 enrolled. *Faculty:* 26 full-time (7 women), 13 part-time/adjunct (9 women). Expenses: Contact institution. *Financial support:* In 2010–11, 3 fellowships with partial tuition reimbursements (averaging $2,000 per year), 9 research assistantships with partial tuition reimbursements (averaging $13,101 per year), 27 teaching assistantships with partial tuition reimbursements (averaging $13,123 per year) were awarded; career-related internships or fieldwork, Federal Work-Study, institutionally sponsored loans, scholarships/grants, health care benefits, and unspecified assistantships also available. Support available to part-time students. Financial award application deadline: 2/1. In 2010, 115 first professional degrees, 18 master's, 7 doctorates awarded. *Degree program information:* Part-time programs available. Offers pharmaceutics (MSPHR, PhD); pharmacology (MSPHR, PhD); pharmacy (Pharm D); pharmacy administration (MSPHR, PhD). *Application deadline:* For fall admission, 1/15 for domestic and international students. Applications are processed on a rolling basis. *Application fee:* $150. Electronic applications accepted. *Application Contact:* Barbara Lewis, Assistant Dean for Student and Professional Affairs, 713-743-1264, Fax: 713-743-1237, E-mail: pharmacyadmissions@uh.edu. *Dean,* Dr. Lamar Pritchard, 713-743-1253, Fax: 713-743-1259, E-mail: flpritchard@uh.edu.

College of Technology Students: 173 full-time (74 women), 167 part-time (73 women); includes 93 minority (37 Black or African American, non-Hispanic/Latino; 1 American Indian or Alaska Native, non-Hispanic/Latino; 24 Asian, non-Hispanic/Latino; 28 Hispanic/Latino; 1 Native Hawaiian or other Pacific Islander, non-Hispanic/Latino; 2 Two or more races, non-Hispanic/Latino), 132 international. Average age 30. 163 applicants, 90% accepted, 99 enrolled. *Faculty:* 24 full-time (11 women), 20 part-time/adjunct (8 women). Expenses: Contact institution. *Financial support:* In 2010–11, 17 research assistantships with partial tuition reimbursements (averaging $9,266 per year), 44 teaching assistantships with partial tuition reimbursements (averaging $7,791 per year) were awarded; career-related internships or fieldwork, Federal Work-Study, institutionally sponsored loans, scholarships/grants, health care benefits, and unspecified assistantships also available. Support available to part-time students. Financial award application deadline: 2/1. In 2010, 71 master's awarded. *Degree program information:* Part-time programs available. Offers construction management (MS); engineering technology (MS); future studies in commerce (MS); human resources development (MS); information security (MS); network communications (M Tech); supply chain and logistics technology (MS); technology (M Tech, MS); technology project management (MS). *Application deadline:* For fall admission, 7/1 for domestic students, 4/1 for international students; for spring admission, 12/1 for domestic students, 10/1 for international students. Applications are processed on a rolling basis. *Application fee:* $75 ($150 for international students). Electronic applications accepted. *Application Contact:* Tiffany Roosa, Graduate Advisor, 713-743-4100, Fax: 713-743-4151, E-mail: troosa@uh.edu. *Dean,* Dr. William Fitzgibbon, 713-743-3465, Fax: 713-743-4994, E-mail: fitz@uh.edu.

Conrad N. Hilton College of Hotel and Restaurant Management Students: 76 full-time (55 women), 25 part-time (20 women); includes 6 Black or African American, non-Hispanic/Latino; 9 Asian, non-Hispanic/Latino; 7 Hispanic/Latino; 2 Two or more races, non-Hispanic/Latino, 44 international. Average age 26. 79 applicants, 80% accepted, 43 enrolled. *Faculty:* 11 full-time (3 women), 10 part-time/adjunct (3 women). Expenses: Contact institution. *Financial support:* In 2010–11, 4 research assistantships with partial tuition reimbursements (averaging $5,600 per year), 24 teaching assistantships with partial tuition reimbursements (averaging $6,224 per year) were awarded; career-related internships or fieldwork, Federal Work-Study, institutionally sponsored loans, scholarships/grants, health care benefits, and unspecified assistantships also available. Support available to part-time students. Financial award application deadline: 2/1. In 2010, 21 master's awarded. *Degree program information:* Part-time programs available. Offers hospitality management (MS). *Application deadline:* For fall admission, 5/1 for domestic students, 4/1 for international students; for spring admission, 11/1 for domestic students, 10/1 for international students. Applications are processed on a rolling basis. *Application fee:* $50 ($75 for international students). Electronic applications accepted. *Application Contact:* Laura S. Gonzalez, Graduate Program Coordinator, 713-743-2457, Fax: 713-743-2218, E-mail: lgonzal3@central.uh.edu. *Dean,* Dr. John Bowen, 713-743-2607, Fax: 713-743-2482, E-mail: jbowen@uh.edu.

Cullen College of Engineering Students: 551 full-time (145 women), 242 part-time (57 women); includes 20 Black or African American, non-Hispanic/Latino; 66 Asian, non-Hispanic/Latino; 35 Hispanic/Latino; 2 Two or more races, non-Hispanic/Latino, 537 international. Average age 27. 1,215 applicants, 42% accepted, 182 enrolled. *Faculty:* 86 full-time (10 women), 24 part-time/adjunct (2 women). Expenses: Contact institution. *Financial support:* In 2010–11, 24 fellowships with partial tuition reimbursements (averaging $3,933 per year), 144 research assistantships with partial tuition reimbursements (averaging $11,985 per year), 73 teaching assistantships with partial tuition reimbursements (averaging $9,909 per year) were awarded; career-related internships or fieldwork, Federal Work-Study, institutionally sponsored loans, scholarships/grants, health care benefits, and unspecified assistantships also available. Support available to part-time students. Financial award application deadline: 2/1. In 2010, 189 master's, 37 doctorates awarded. *Degree program information:* Part-time programs available. Offers biomedical engineering (PhD); chemical engineering (MCHE, PhD); civil engineering (MCE, PhD); electrical engineering (MEE, MSEE, PhD); engineering (M Pet E, MCE, MCHE, MEE, MIE, MME, MSEE, MSME, PhD); industrial engineering (MIE, PhD); mechanical engineering (MME, MSME, PhD); petroleum engineering (M Pet E). *Application fee:* $25 ($75 for international students). *Application Contact:* Dr. Joseph Tedesco, Dean, 713-743-4242, Fax: 713-743-4214, E-mail: jtedesco@uh.edu. *Dean,* Dr. Joseph Tedesco, 713-743-4242, Fax: 713-743-4214, E-mail: jtedesco@uh.edu.

Graduate School of Social Work Students: 321 full-time (281 women), 46 part-time (42 women); includes 114 Black or African American, non-Hispanic/Latino; 1 American Indian or Alaska Native, non-Hispanic/Latino; 20 Asian, non-Hispanic/Latino; 66 Hispanic/Latino; 6 Two or more races, non-Hispanic/Latino, 4 international. Average age 32. 232 applicants, 85% accepted, 158 enrolled. *Faculty:* 13 full-time (6 women), 29 part-time/adjunct (23 women). Expenses: Contact institution. *Financial support:* In 2010–11, 5 research assistantships with partial tuition reimbursements (averaging $9,136 per year), 5 teaching assistantships with partial tuition reimbursements (averaging $9,136 per year) were awarded; career-related internships or fieldwork, Federal Work-Study, institutionally sponsored loans, scholarships/grants, health care benefits, and unspecified assistantships also available. Support available to part-time students. Financial award application deadline: 3/10; financial award applicants required to submit FAFSA. In 2010, 137 master's, 7 doctorates awarded. *Degree program* *information:* Part-time programs available. Offers social work (MSW, PhD). *Application deadline:* For fall admission, 2/1 priority date for domestic and international students; for spring admission, 11/1 for domestic and international students. Applications are processed on a rolling basis. *Application fee:* $40 ($115 for international students). *Application Contact:* Amber Mollhagen, Director of Recruitment and Admissions, 713-743-8082, Fax: 713-743-8149, E-mail: amollhagen@uh.edu. *Dean,* Dr. Ira C. Colby, 713-743-8085, Fax: 713-743-3267, E-mail: icolby@uh.edu.

Law Center Students: 734 full-time (319 women), 241 part-time (116 women); includes 285 minority (71 Black or African American, non-Hispanic/Latino; 5 American Indian or Alaska Native, non-Hispanic/Latino; 94 Asian, non-Hispanic/Latino; 100 Hispanic/Latino; 2 Native Hawaiian or other Pacific Islander, non-Hispanic/Latino; 13 Two or more races, non-Hispanic/Latino), 45 international. Average age 28. 1,059 applicants, 100% accepted, 361 enrolled. *Faculty:* 40 full-time (9 women), 85 part-time/adjunct (32 women). Expenses: Contact institution. *Financial support:* In 2010–11, 3 fellowships with partial tuition reimbursements (averaging $5,000 per year), 2 teaching assistantships with partial tuition reimbursements (averaging $7,720 per year) were awarded; career-related internships or fieldwork, Federal Work-Study, institutionally sponsored loans, scholarships/grants, health care benefits, and unspecified assistantships also available. Support available to part-time students. Financial award application deadline: 3/10; financial award applicants required to submit FAFSA. In 2010, 284 first professional degrees, 59 master's awarded. *Degree program information:* Part-time and evening/weekend programs available. Offers energy, environment, and natural resources (LL M); health law (LL M); intellectual property and information law (LL M); international law (LL M); law (JD, LL M); tax law (LL M). *Application deadline:* For fall admission, 11/15 priority date for domestic and international students. Applications are processed on a rolling basis. *Application fee:* $70. Electronic applications accepted. *Application Contact:* Jamie Dillon, Assistant Dean for Admissions, 713-743-2280, Fax: 713-743-2194, E-mail: jdillon@central.uh.edu. *Dean,* Raymond Nimmer, 713-743-2100, Fax: 713-743-2122, E-mail: rnimmer@uh.edu.

UNIVERSITY OF HOUSTON–CLEAR LAKE, Houston, TX 77058-1098

General Information State-supported, coed, upper-level institution. CGS member. *Graduate housing:* Rooms and/or apartments available on a first-come, first-served basis to single students and available to married students. *Research affiliation:* NASA–Johnson Space Center (computer science, computer engineering), Baylor College of Medicine (life sciences), Schlumberger (ergonomic software).

GRADUATE UNITS

School of Business *Degree program information:* Part-time and evening/weekend programs available. Offers accounting (MS); business (MA, MBA, MHA, MS); business administration (MBA); environmental management (MS); finance (MS); healthcare administration (MHA); human resource management (MA); management information systems (MS); professional accounting (MS). Electronic applications accepted.

School of Education *Degree program information:* Part-time and evening/weekend programs available. Offers counseling (MS); curriculum and instruction (MS); early childhood education (MS); education (MS, Ed D); educational leadership (Ed D); educational management (MS); instructional technology (MS); multicultural studies (MS); reading (MS); school library and information science (MS). Electronic applications accepted.

School of Human Sciences and Humanities *Degree program information:* Part-time and evening/weekend programs available. Offers behavioral sciences (MA); clinical psychology (MA); criminology (MA); cross cultural studies (MA); family therapy (MA); fitness and human performance (MA); history (MA); human sciences and humanities (MA); humanities (MA); literature (MA); school psychology (MA).

School of Science and Computer Engineering *Degree program information:* Part-time and evening/weekend programs available. Offers biological sciences (MS); biotechnology (MS); chemistry (MS); computer engineering (MS); computer information systems (MS); computer science (MS); environmental science (MS); mathematical sciences (MS); physics (MS); science and computer engineering (MS); software engineering (MS); statistics (MS); system engineering (MS).

UNIVERSITY OF HOUSTON–DOWNTOWN, Houston, TX 77002

General Information State-supported, coed, comprehensive institution. *Enrollment:* 12,900 graduate, professional, and undergraduate students; 15 full-time matriculated graduate/professional students (11 women), 139 part-time matriculated graduate/professional students (74 women). *Enrollment by degree level:* 154 master's. *Graduate faculty:* 30 full-time (17 women), 1 part-time/adjunct (0 women). Tuition, state resident: full-time $4280; part-time $183 per credit hour. Tuition, nonresident: full-time $9230; part-time $458 per credit hour. *Required fees:* $390 per term. *Graduate housing:* On-campus housing not available. *Student services:* Campus employment opportunities, campus safety program, career counseling, exercise/wellness program, free psychological counseling, international student services, low-cost health insurance, services for students with disabilities, teacher training. *Library facilities:* W. I. Dykes Library. *Online resources:* library catalog, web page, access to other libraries' catalogs. *Collection:* 301,428 titles, 8,543 serial subscriptions, 3,958 audiovisual materials.

Computer facilities: 1,860 computers available on campus for general student use. A campuswide network can be accessed from off campus. Online class registration is available. *Web address:* http://www.uhd.edu/.

General Application Contact: Traneshia Parker, Associate Director of International Student Services and Graduate Admissions, 713-221-8093, Fax: 713-221-8658, E-mail: parkert@uhd.edu.

GRADUATE UNITS

College of Humanities and Social Sciences Students: 4 full-time (all women), 17 part-time (12 women); includes 4 Black or African American, non-Hispanic/Latino; 1 Asian, non-Hispanic/Latino; 2 Hispanic/Latino, 1 international. Average age 35. 6 applicants, 83% accepted, 4 enrolled. *Faculty:* 9 full-time (4 women). Expenses: Contact institution. *Financial support:* Applicants required to submit FAFSA. In 2010, 7 master's awarded. *Degree program information:* Part-time and evening/weekend programs available. Offers humanities and social sciences (MS); professional writing and technical communication (MS). *Application deadline:* For fall admission, 3/15 for domestic and international students; for spring admission, 11/15 for domestic and international students. *Application fee:* $35 ($60 for international students). Electronic applications accepted. *Application Contact:* Dr. Michelle Moosally, Coordinator of MS in Professional Writing and Technical Communication and Professor, Department of English, 713-221-8013, Fax: 713-226-5205, E-mail: mspwtc@uhd.edu. *Dean,* Dr. Susan K. Ahern, 713-221-8009, Fax: 713-221-8106, E-mail: aherns@uhd.edu.

College of Public Service Students: 11 full-time (7 women), 122 part-time (62 women); includes 37 Black or African American, non-Hispanic/Latino; 8 Asian, non-Hispanic/Latino; 37 Hispanic/Latino; 1 Two or more races, non-Hispanic/Latino, 1 international. Average age 36. 47 applicants, 94% accepted, 41 enrolled. *Faculty:* 21 full-time (13 women), 1 part-time/adjunct (0 women). Expenses: Contact institution. *Financial support:* Federal Work-Study and scholarships/grants available. Financial award applicants required to submit FAFSA. In 2010, 41 master's awarded. *Degree program information:* Part-time and evening/weekend programs available. Offers bilingual education (MAT); criminal justice (MS); curriculum and instruction (MAT); elementary education (MAT); public service (MAT, MS, MSM); secondary education (MAT); security management for executives (MSM). *Application deadline:* For fall admission, 8/1 for domestic students, 5/1 for international students; for spring admission, 11/15 for domestic students, 10/1 for international students. Applications are processed on a rolling basis. *Application fee:* $35 ($60 for international students). Electronic applications accepted. *Application Contact:* Maryanne Denner, Senior Graduate Advisor, 713-221-8074, Fax: 713-226-5234, E-mail: dennerm@uhd.edu. *Dean,* Dr. Beth Pelz, 713-221-8194, Fax: 713-226-5274, E-mail: pelzb@uhd.edu.

UNIVERSITY OF HOUSTON–VICTORIA, Victoria, TX 77901-4450

General Information State-supported, coed, upper-level institution. *Enrollment:* 4,095 graduate, professional, and undergraduate students; 411 full-time matriculated graduate/professional students (243 women), 1,395 part-time matriculated graduate/professional students (862 women). *Enrollment by degree level:* 1,806 master's. *Graduate faculty:* 97 full-time (42 women). Tuition, state resident: full-time $4050; part-time $225 per credit hour. Tuition, nonresident: full-time $8730; part-time $485 per credit hour. *Required fees:* $810; $54 per credit hour. Tuition and fees vary according to course load. *Graduate housing:* On-campus housing not available. *Student services:* Campus employment opportunities, campus safety program, career counseling, exercise/wellness program, grant writing training, international student services, low-cost health insurance, services for students with disabilities, teacher training, writing training. *Library facilities:* VC/UHV Library plus 1 other. *Online resources:* library catalog, web page, access to other libraries' catalogs. *Collection:* 50,000 titles, 70,000 serial subscriptions, 12,773 audiovisual materials.

Computer facilities: 200 computers available on campus for general student use. A campuswide network can be accessed from student residence rooms and from off campus. Online class registration is available. *Web address:* http://www.uhv.edu/.

General Application Contact: Admissions and Records, 361-570-4359, Fax: 361-580-5500, E-mail: admissions@uhv.edu.

GRADUATE UNITS

School of Arts and Sciences Students: 95 full-time (61 women), 188 part-time (127 women); includes 63 Black or African American, non-Hispanic/Latino; 27 Asian, non-Hispanic/Latino; 52 Hispanic/Latino; 3 Two or more races, non-Hispanic/Latino, 21 international. Average age 34. 173 applicants, 72% accepted, 82 enrolled. *Faculty:* 39 full-time (12 women). Expenses: Contact institution. *Financial support:* In 2010–11, research assistantships with partial tuition reimbursements (averaging $2,000 per year), teaching assistantships with partial tuition reimbursements (averaging $2,000 per year) were awarded; Federal Work-Study, scholarships/grants, and unspecified assistantships also available. Support available to part-time students. Financial award application deadline: 4/15; financial award applicants required to submit FAFSA. In 2010, 38 master's awarded. *Degree program information:* Part-time and evening/weekend programs available. Postbaccalaureate distance learning degree programs offered (minimal on-campus study). Offers arts and sciences (MA, MAIS, MS); computer information systems (MS); counseling psychology (MA); interdisciplinary studies (MAIS); publishing (MS); school psychology (MA). *Application deadline:* For fall admission, 6/1 for international students; for spring admission, 10/1 for international students. Applications are processed on a rolling basis. *Application fee:* $0. Electronic applications accepted. *Application Contact:* Tracey Fox, Director of Services, 361-570-4233, Fax: 361-580-5507, E-mail: foxt@uhv.edu. *Dean,* Dr. Jeffrey Dileo, 361-570-4200, Fax: 361-580-5507, E-mail: dileoj@uhv.edu.

School of Business Administration Students: 234 full-time (108 women), 714 part-time (303 women); includes 542 minority (215 Black or African American, non-Hispanic/Latino; 1 American Indian or Alaska Native, non-Hispanic/Latino; 197 Asian, non-Hispanic/Latino; 124 Hispanic/Latino; 1 Native Hawaiian or other Pacific Islander, non-Hispanic/Latino; 4 Two or more races, non-Hispanic/Latino), 115 international. Average age 34. 362 applicants, 65% accepted, 147 enrolled. *Faculty:* 37 full-time (11 women). Expenses: Contact institution. *Financial support:* In 2010–11, research assistantships with partial tuition reimbursements (averaging $2,000 per year), teaching assistantships with partial tuition reimbursements (averaging $2,000 per year) were awarded; Federal Work-Study, scholarships/grants, and unspecified assistantships also available. Support available to part-time students. Financial award application deadline: 4/15; financial award applicants required to submit FAFSA. In 2010, 181 master's awarded. *Degree program information:* Part-time and evening/weekend programs available. Postbaccalaureate distance learning degree programs offered (minimal on-campus study). Offers accounting (MBA); economic development and entrepreneurship (MS); finance (GMBA, MBA); general business (MBA); international business (MBA); management (GMBA, MBA); marketing (MBA). *Application deadline:* For fall admission, 6/1 for international students; for spring admission, 10/1 for international students. Applications are processed on a rolling basis. *Application fee:* $0. Electronic applications accepted. *Application Contact:* Jane Mims, Assistant Dean, 361-570-4639, Fax: 361-580-5529, E-mail: mims@uhv.edu. *Dean,* Dr. Farhang Niroomand, 361-570-4230, Fax: 361-580-5599, E-mail: niroomandf@uhv.edu.

School of Education and Human Development Students: 71 full-time (65 women), 438 part-time (384 women); includes 220 minority (118 Black or African American, non-Hispanic/Latino; 2 American Indian or Alaska Native, non-Hispanic/Latino; 19 Asian, non-Hispanic/Latino; 76 Hispanic/Latino; 1 Native Hawaiian or other Pacific Islander, non-Hispanic/Latino; 4 Two or more races, non-Hispanic/Latino), 3 international. Average age 36. 193 applicants, 75% accepted, 107 enrolled. *Faculty:* 26 full-time (18 women). Expenses: Contact institution. *Financial support:* In 2010–11, research assistantships with partial tuition reimbursements (averaging $2,000 per year), teaching assistantships with partial tuition reimbursements (averaging $2,000 per year) were awarded; Federal Work-Study, scholarships/grants, and unspecified assistantships also available. Support available to part-time students. Financial award application deadline: 4/15; financial award applicants required to submit FAFSA. In 2010, 121 master's awarded. *Degree program information:* Part-time and evening/weekend programs available. Postbaccalaureate distance learning degree programs offered (minimal on-campus study). Offers administration and supervision (M Ed); counseling (M Ed); curriculum and instruction (M Ed); special education (M Ed). *Application deadline:* For fall admission, 6/1 for international students; for spring admission, 10/1 for international students. Applications are processed on a rolling basis. *Application fee:* $0. Electronic applications accepted. *Application Contact:* Sandy Hybner, Student Recruitment Coordinator, 361-570-4252, Fax: 361-580-5580, E-mail: hybners@uhv.edu. *Dean,* Dr. Lawrence Rossow, 361-570-4262, Fax: 361-580-5580, E-mail: rossowl@uhv.edu.

School of Nursing Students: 11 full-time (9 women), 52 part-time (47 women); includes 12 Black or African American, non-Hispanic/Latino; 11 Asian, non-Hispanic/Latino; 9 Hispanic/Latino, 5 international. Average age 40. 53 applicants, 26% accepted, 10 enrolled. *Faculty:* 13 full-time (all women). Expenses: Contact institution. *Financial support:* Federal Work-Study, scholarships/grants, and unspecified assistantships available. Support available to part-time students. Financial award application deadline: 4/15. In 2010, 13 master's awarded. Offers nursing (MSN). *Application deadline:* For fall admission, 6/1 for international students; for spring admission, 10/1 for international students. Applications are processed on a rolling basis. Electronic applications accepted. *Application Contact:* Tammy Whatley, Student Recruitment Coordinator, 361-570-4114, E-mail: whatleyt@uhv.edu. *Dean,* Dr. Kathryn Tart, 361-570-4295, E-mail: neilld@uhv.edu.

UNIVERSITY OF IDAHO, Moscow, ID 83844-2282

General Information State-supported, coed, university. CGS member. *Enrollment:* 12,302 graduate, professional, and undergraduate students; 1,431 full-time matriculated graduate/professional students (591 women), 1,052 part-time matriculated graduate/professional students (499 women). *Graduate faculty:* 443 full-time (124 women), 48 part-time/adjunct (20 women). Tuition, nonresident: part-time $580 per credit. *Required fees:* $306 per credit. *Graduate housing:* Rooms and/or apartments available on a first-come, first-served basis to single and married students. Typical cost: $9318 (including board) for single students. Room and board charges vary according to board plan and housing facility selected. *Student services:* Campus employment opportunities, campus safety program, career counseling, child daycare facilities, exercise/wellness program, free psychological counseling, grant writing training, international student services, low-cost health insurance, multicultural affairs office, services for students with disabilities, writing training. *Library facilities:* University of Idaho Library plus 1 other. *Online resources:* library catalog, web page, access to other libraries' catalogs. *Collection:* 1.2 million titles, 15,400 serial subscriptions, 15,113 audiovisual materials. *Research affiliation:* Idaho Mining and Materials Resources Research Institute, Idaho Research Foundation, Snake River Conservation Research Center, Battelle Pacific Northwest Laboratories, Idaho Nuclear Environmental Engineering Laboratory, Inland Northwest Research Alliance (INRA).

Computer facilities: Computer purchase and lease plans are available. 495 computers available on campus for general student use. A campuswide network can be accessed from student residence rooms and from off campus. Online class registration is available. *Web address:* http://www.uidaho.edu/.

University of Idaho (continued)

General Application Contact: Dr. Nilsa A. Bosque-Perez, Interim Dean of the College of Graduate Studies, 208-885-6243, Fax: 208-885-6198, E-mail: uigrad@uidaho.edu.

GRADUATE UNITS

College of Graduate Studies Students: 1,431 full-time (591 women), 1,052 part-time (499 women); includes 24 Black or African American, non-Hispanic/Latino; 21 American Indian or Alaska Native, non-Hispanic/Latino; 44 Asian, non-Hispanic/Latino; 105 Hispanic/Latino; 46 Two or more races, non-Hispanic/Latino, 280 international. Average age 34. 1,768 applicants, 87% accepted, 546 enrolled. *Faculty:* 443 full-time (124 women), 48 part-time/adjunct (20 women). Expenses: Contact institution. *Financial support:* Fellowships, research assistantships, teaching assistantships, career-related internships or fieldwork, Federal Work-Study, institutionally sponsored loans, scholarships/grants, and tuition waivers (full and partial) available. Support available to part-time students. Financial award applicants required to submit FAFSA. In 2010, 499 master's, 73 doctorates, 45 other advanced degrees awarded. Offers bioinformatics and computational biology (MS, PhD); bioregional planning and community design (MS); environmental science (MS, PhD); interdisciplinary studies (MA, MS); neuroscience (MS, PhD); water resources (MS, PhD). *Application deadline:* For fall admission, 8/1 for domestic students; for spring admission, 12/15 for domestic students. Applications are processed on a rolling basis. *Application fee:* $60. Electronic applications accepted. *Application Contact:* Erick Larson, Director of Graduate Admissions, 208-885-4723, E-mail: gadms@uidaho.edu. *Interim Dean of the College of Graduate Studies,* Dr. Nilsa A. Bosque-Perez, 208-885-6243, Fax: 208-885-6198, E-mail: uigrad@uidaho.edu.

College of Agricultural and Life Sciences Students: 94 full-time (54 women), 64 part-time (38 women). Average age 31. *Faculty:* 70 full-time, 1 part-time/adjunct. Expenses: Contact institution. *Financial support:* Research assistantships, teaching assistantships, career-related internships or fieldwork and Federal Work-Study available. Support available to part-time students. Financial award application deadline: 2/15; financial award applicants required to submit FAFSA. In 2010, 19 master's, 6 doctorates awarded. Offers agricultural and life sciences (MS, PhD); agricultural economics (MS); agricultural education (MS); animal physiology (PhD); animal science (MS); applied economics (MS); entomology (MS, PhD); family and consumer sciences (MS); food science (MS, PhD); microbiology, molecular biology and biochemistry (MS, PhD); plant science (MS, PhD); soil and land resources (MS, PhD). *Application deadline:* For fall admission, 8/1 for domestic students; for spring admission, 12/15 for domestic students. Applications are processed on a rolling basis. *Application fee:* $60. Electronic applications accepted. *Application Contact:* Dr. John Hammel, Dean, 208-885-6681, E-mail: ag@uidaho.edu. *Dean,* Dr. John Hammel, 208-885-6681, E-mail: ag@uidaho.edu.

College of Art and Architecture Students: 102 full-time, 15 part-time. Average age 27. *Faculty:* 19 full-time, 1 part-time/adjunct. Expenses: Contact institution. *Financial support:* Applicants required to submit FAFSA. In 2010, 31 master's awarded. Offers architecture (MS); architecture (professional degree) (M Arch); landscape architecture (MS); studio art (MFA); teaching art (MAT). *Application deadline:* For fall admission, 8/1 for domestic students; for spring admission, 12/15 for domestic students. Applications are processed on a rolling basis. *Application fee:* $60. Electronic applications accepted. *Application Contact:* Dr. Mark Elison Hoversten, Dean, 208-885-5423, E-mail: caa@uidaho.edu. *Dean,* Dr. Mark Elison Hoversten, 208-885-5423, E-mail: caa@uidaho.edu.

College of Business and Economics Students: 35 full-time, 11 part-time. Average age 33. *Faculty:* 13 full-time, 1 part-time/adjunct. Expenses: Contact institution. *Financial support:* Research assistantships, teaching assistantships, Federal Work-Study and scholarships/grants available. Support available to part-time students. Financial award applicants required to submit FAFSA. In 2010, 30 master's awarded. Offers accountancy (M Acct); business and economics (M Acct, MBA, MS); economics (MS); general management (MBA). *Application deadline:* For fall admission, 8/1 for domestic students; for spring admission, 12/15 for domestic students. Applications are processed on a rolling basis. *Application fee:* $60. Electronic applications accepted. *Application Contact:* Dr. John Morris, Dean, 208-885-6478, E-mail: cbe@uidaho.edu. *Dean,* Dr. John Morris, 208-885-6478, E-mail: cbe@uidaho.edu.

College of Education Students: 147 full-time (87 women), 435 part-time (282 women). Average age 39. *Faculty:* 53 full-time, 12 part-time/adjunct. Expenses: Contact institution. *Financial support:* Teaching assistantships, Federal Work-Study available. Support available to part-time students. Financial award applicants required to submit FAFSA. In 2010, 160 master's, 30 doctorates, 45 other advanced degrees awarded. Offers adult education (Ed S); adult/organizational learning and leadership (MS, Ed S); counseling and human services (M Ed, MS); curriculum and instruction (MS, Ed S); education (M Ed, MS, Ed D, PhD, Ed S); educational leadership (M Ed, MS, Ed S); movement and leisure sciences (MS); physical education (M Ed, MS); recreation (MS); school psychology (Ed S); special education (M Ed, MS). *Application deadline:* For fall admission, 8/1 for domestic students; for spring admission, 12/15 for domestic students. Applications are processed on a rolling basis. *Application fee:* $60. Electronic applications accepted. *Application Contact:* Dr. Corinne Mantle-Bromley, Dean, 208-885-6772, E-mail: coe@uidaho.edu. *Dean,* Dr. Corinne Mantle-Bromley, 208-885-6772, E-mail: coe@uidaho.edu.

College of Engineering Students: 188 full-time (24 women), 263 part-time (40 women). Average age 33. *Faculty:* 74 full-time, 6 part-time/adjunct. Expenses: Contact institution. *Financial support:* Fellowships, research assistantships, teaching assistantships, career-related internships or fieldwork and Federal Work-Study available. Support available to part-time students. Financial award applicants required to submit FAFSA. In 2010, 95 master's, 9 doctorates awarded. Offers biological and agricultural engineering (M Engr, MS, PhD); chemical engineering (MS); civil engineering (M Engr, MS, PhD); computer engineering (M Engr, MS); computer science (MS, PhD); electrical engineering (M Engr, MS, PhD); engineering (M Engr, MS, PhD); engineering management (M Engr); environmental engineering (M Engr, MS); geological engineering (MS); materials science and engineering (MS, PhD); mechanical engineering (M Engr, MS, PhD); metallurgical engineering (MS); mining engineering (PhD); nuclear engineering (M Engr, MS, PhD). *Application deadline:* For fall admission, 8/1 for domestic students; for spring admission, 12/15 for domestic students. Applications are processed on a rolling basis. *Application fee:* $60. Electronic applications accepted. *Application Contact:* Dr. Donald Blackletter, Dean, 208-885-6470, E-mail: deanengr@uidaho.edu. *Dean,* Dr. Donald Blackletter, 208-885-6470, E-mail: deanengr@uidaho.edu.

College of Letters, Arts and Social Sciences Students: 152 full-time (72 women), 70 part-time (35 women). Average age 32. *Faculty:* 107 full-time (25 women), 15 part-time/adjunct (8 women). Expenses: Contact institution. *Financial support:* Fellowships, research assistantships, teaching assistantships, Federal Work-Study available. Support available to part-time students. Financial award applicants required to submit FAFSA. In 2010, 60 master's, 1 doctorate awarded. Offers anthropology (MA); creative writing (MFA); English (MA, MAT, MFA); history (MA, PhD); letters, arts and social sciences (M Mus, MA, MAT, MFA, MPA, MS, PhD); music (M Mus, MA); political science (MA, PhD); psychology (MS); public administration (MPA); teaching English as a second language (MA); theatre arts (MFA). *Application deadline:* For fall admission, 8/1 for domestic students; for spring admission, 12/15 for domestic students. Applications are processed on a rolling basis. *Application fee:* $60. Electronic applications accepted. *Application Contact:* Dr. Katherine Aiken, Dean, 208-885-6426, E-mail: class@uidaho.edu. *Dean,* Dr. Katherine Aiken, 208-885-6426, E-mail: class@uidaho.edu.

College of Natural Resources Students: 119 full-time (62 women), 74 part-time (27 women). Average age 32. *Faculty:* 50 full-time, 2 part-time/adjunct. Expenses: Contact institution. *Financial support:* Fellowships, research assistantships, teaching assistantships, Federal Work-Study available. Support available to part-time students. Financial award applicants required to submit FAFSA. In 2010, 39 master's, 10 doctorates awarded. Offers natural resources (MNR, MS, PhD). *Application deadline:* For fall admission, 8/1 for domestic students; for spring admission, 12/15 for domestic students. Applications are processed on a rolling basis. *Application fee:* $60. Electronic applications accepted. *Application Contact:* Dr. Kurt Scott Pregitzer, Dean, 208-885-8981, Fax: 208-885-5534, E-mail: cnr@uidaho.edu. *Dean,* Dr. Kurt Scott Pregitzer, 208-885-8981, Fax: 208-885-5534, E-mail: cnr@uidaho.edu.

College of Science Students: 148 full-time (51 women), 36 part-time (16 women). Average age 31. *Faculty:* 56 full-time, 5 part-time/adjunct. Expenses: Contact institution. *Financial support:* Applicants required to submit FAFSA. In 2010, 39 master's, 10 doctorates awarded. Offers biology (MS, PhD); chemistry (MS, PhD); geography (MS, PhD); geology (MS, PhD); hydrology (MS); mathematics (MAT, MS, PhD); physics (MS, PhD); science (MAT, MS, PhD); statistics (MS). *Application deadline:* Applications are processed on a rolling basis. *Application fee:* $60. Electronic applications accepted. *Application Contact:* Dr. Scott Wood, Dean, 208-885-6195, E-mail: science@uidaho.edu. *Dean,* Dr. Scott Wood, 208-885-6195, E-mail: science@uidaho.edu.

College of Law Students: 342 full-time, 7 part-time. Average age 27. *Faculty:* 12 full-time, 1 part-time/adjunct. Expenses: Contact institution. *Financial support:* Career-related internships or fieldwork, Federal Work-Study, and institutionally sponsored loans available. Financial award applicants required to submit FAFSA. In 2010, 96 JDs awarded. Offers law (JD); Native American law (JD); natural resources and environmental law (JD). *Application deadline:* For fall admission, 2/15 for domestic students. Applications are processed on a rolling basis. *Application fee:* $50 ($60 for international students). Electronic applications accepted. *Application Contact:* Donald L. Burnett, Dean, 208-885-4977, E-mail: uilaw@uidaho.edu. *Dean,* Donald L. Burnett, 208-885-4977, E-mail: uilaw@uidaho.edu.

UNIVERSITY OF ILLINOIS AT CHICAGO, Chicago, IL 60607-7128

General Information State-supported, coed, university. CGS member. *Graduate housing:* Room and/or apartments available on a first-come, first-served basis to single students; on-campus housing not available to married students. Housing application deadline: 3/1. *Research affiliation:* U. S. Department of Energy National Laboratories (physics, environment, computational science), National Surgical Adjuvant Breast and Bowel Project (prevention of breast cancer), Chicago Manufacturing Technology Extension Center (manufacturing research and development, industrial research), Eastern Cooperative Oncology Group (clinical cancer research).

GRADUATE UNITS

College of Dentistry Offers dentistry (DDS, MS, PhD); oral sciences (MS, PhD). Electronic applications accepted.

College of Medicine *Degree program information:* Part-time programs available. Offers biochemistry and molecular genetics (PhD); cellular and systems neuroscience and cell biology (PhD); medical education (MHPE); medicine (MD, MHPE, MS, PhD); microbiology and immunology (PhD); neuroscience (PhD); pharmacology (PhD); physiology and biophysics (MS, PhD); surgery (MS).

College of Pharmacy Offers biopharmaceutical sciences (PhD); forensic science (MS); medicinal chemistry (MS, PhD); pharmacognosy (MS, PhD); pharmacy (Pharm D, MS, PhD); pharmacy administration (MS, PhD).

Center for Pharmaceutical Biotechnology Offers pharmaceutical biotechnology (PhD).

Graduate College *Degree program information:* Part-time and evening/weekend programs available. Postbaccalaureate distance learning degree programs offered. Offers neuroscience (PhD). Electronic applications accepted.

College of Applied Health Sciences *Degree program information:* Part-time programs available. Offers applied health sciences (MS, DPT, OTD, PhD); biomedical visualization (MS); disability and human development (MS); disability studies (PhD); health informatics (MS); kinesiology (MS, PhD); nutrition (MS, PhD); occupational therapy (MS, OTD); physical therapy (MS, DPT). Electronic applications accepted.

College of Architecture and Art *Degree program information:* Part-time and evening/weekend programs available. Offers architecture (M Arch, MS Arch); architecture and art (M Arch, MA, MFA, MS Arch, PhD); architecture in health design (MS Arch); art history (MA, PhD); electronic visualization (MFA); film animation (MFA); graphic design (MFA); industrial design (MFA); photography (MFA); studio arts (MFA). Electronic applications accepted.

College of Education *Degree program information:* Part-time and evening/weekend programs available. Offers curriculum studies (PhD); education (M Ed, Ed D, PhD); educational psychology (PhD); educational studies (M Ed); elementary education (M Ed); literacy, language and culture (M Ed, PhD); policy studies (M Ed); policy studies in urban education (PhD); secondary education (M Ed); special education (M Ed, PhD); urban education leadership (Ed D). Electronic applications accepted.

College of Engineering *Degree program information:* Part-time and evening/weekend programs available. Offers bioengineering (MS, PhD); chemical engineering (MS, PhD); civil engineering (MS, PhD); computer science (MS, PhD); electrical and computer engineering (MS, PhD); energy engineering (MEE); engineering (M Eng, MEE, MS, PhD); industrial engineering (MS); industrial engineering and operations research (PhD); materials engineering (MS, PhD); mechanical engineering (MS, PhD). Electronic applications accepted.

College of Liberal Arts and Sciences *Degree program information:* Part-time and evening/weekend programs available. Offers anthropology (MA, PhD); applied mathematics (MS, PhD); biological sciences (MS, PhD); chemistry (MS, PhD); communication (MA, PhD); computational finance (MS, PhD); computer science (MS, PhD); criminal justice (MA, PhD); earth and environmental sciences (MS, PhD); economics (MA, PhD); elementary (MST); English (MA, PhD); environmental and urban geography (MA); environmental studies (MA); French (MA); Germanic studies (MA, PhD); Hispanic linguistics (MA, PhD); Hispanic literary and cultural studies (MA, PhD); Hispanic studies (MA, PhD); history (MA, MAT, PhD); liberal arts and sciences (MA, MAT, MS, MST, DA, PhD); linguistics (MA); mathematics (DA); mathematics and information sciences for industry (MS); philosophy (MA, PhD); physics (MS, PhD); political science (MA, PhD); probability and statistics (PhD); psychology (PhD); pure mathematics (MS, PhD); secondary (MST); sociology (MA, PhD); statistics (MS); teaching English to speakers of other languages/applied linguistics (MA); teaching of mathematics (MST); urban geography (MA). Electronic applications accepted.

College of Nursing *Degree program information:* Part-time programs available. Offers acute care clinical nurse specialist (MS); acute care nurse practitioner (MS); administrative studies in nursing (MS); adult nurse practitioner (MS); adult/geriatric nurse practitioner (MS); advanced community health nurse specialist (MS); family nurse practitioner (MS); geriatric clinical nurse specialist (MS); geriatric nurse practitioner (MS); mental health clinical nurse specialist (MS); mental health nurse practitioner (MS); nurse midwifery (MS); nursing (MS, DNP, PhD); nursing practice (DNP); nursing science (PhD); occupational health/advanced community health nurse specialist (MS); occupational health/family nurse practitioner (MS); pediatric clinical nurse specialist (MS); pediatric nurse practitioner (MS); perinatal clinical nurse specialist (MS); school/advanced community health nurse specialist (MS); school/family nurse practitioner (MS); women's health nurse practitioner (MS). Electronic applications accepted.

College of Urban Planning and Public Affairs *Degree program information:* Part-time and evening/weekend programs available. Offers public administration (MPA, PhD); urban planning and policy (MUPP, PhD); urban planning and public affairs (MPA, MUPP, PhD). Electronic applications accepted.

Jane Addams College of Social Work *Degree program information:* Part-time programs available. Offers social work (MSW, PhD). Electronic applications accepted.

Liautaud Graduate School of Business *Degree program information:* Part-time and evening/weekend programs available. Offers accounting (MS); business (MA, MBA, MS, PhD); business administration (MBA, PhD); business statistics (PhD); management information systems (MS, PhD); real estate (MA). Electronic applications accepted.

School of Public Health *Degree program information:* Part-time programs available. Offers biostatistics (MS, PhD); cancer epidemiology (MS, PhD); clinical translational science (MS); community health sciences (MPH, MS, Dr PH, PhD); environmental and occupational health sciences (MPH, MS, Dr PH, PhD); epidemiology (MPH, MS, Dr PH, PhD); health policy (PhD); health policy and administration (Dr PH); health services research (PhD); healthcare (MHA); public health (MHA, MPH, MS, Dr PH, PhD); public health policy management (MPH); quantitative methods (MPH). Electronic applications accepted.

UNIVERSITY OF ILLINOIS AT SPRINGFIELD, Springfield, IL 62703-5407

General Information State-supported, coed, comprehensive institution. CGS member. *Enrollment:* 5,174 graduate, professional, and undergraduate students; 502 full-time matriculated graduate/professional students (256 women), 1,296 part-time matriculated graduate/professional students (719 women). *Enrollment by degree level:* 1,743 master's, 24 doctoral, 31 other advanced degrees. *Graduate faculty:* 165 full-time (63 women), 30 part-time/adjunct (12 women). Tuition, state resident: full-time $6774; part-time $282.25 per credit hour. Tuition, nonresident: full-time $15,078; part-time $628.25 per credit hour. *Required fees:* $15.25 per credit hour. $492 per term. *Graduate housing:* Rooms and/or apartments available on a first-come, first-served basis to single and married students. *Student services:* Campus employment opportunities, campus safety program, career counseling, child daycare facilities, exercise/wellness program, free psychological counseling, international student services, low-cost health insurance, multicultural affairs office, services for students with disabilities, teacher training, writing training. *Library facilities:* Norris L. Brookens Library. *Online resources:* library catalog, web page, access to other libraries' catalogs. *Collection:* 612,417 titles, 45,475 serial subscriptions, 15,404 audiovisual materials. *Research affiliation:* Council of Undergraduate Research, Interuniversity Consortium for Political and Social Research.

Computer facilities: 353 computers available on campus for general student use. A campuswide network can be accessed from student residence rooms and from off campus. Online class registration is available. *Web address:* http://www.uis.edu/.

General Application Contact: Dr. Cecelia Cornell, Faculty Associate, Office of Graduate Studies, 888-977-4847, Fax: 217-206-7623, E-mail: ccorn1@uis.edu.

GRADUATE UNITS

Graduate Programs *Degree program information:* Part-time and evening/weekend programs available. Postbaccalaureate distance learning degree programs offered (no on-campus study). Electronic applications accepted.

College of Business and Management *Degree program information:* Part-time and evening/weekend programs available. Postbaccalaureate distance learning degree programs offered (no on-campus study). Offers accountancy (MA); business administration (MBA); business and management (MA, MBA, MS); management information systems (MS). Electronic applications accepted.

College of Education and Human Services *Degree program information:* Part-time and evening/weekend programs available. Postbaccalaureate distance learning degree programs offered (no on-campus study). Offers alcoholism and substance abuse (MA); child and family services (MA); education and human services (MA); educational leadership (MA); gerontology (MA); human development counseling (MA); social services administration (MA); teacher leadership (MA). Electronic applications accepted.

College of Liberal Arts and Sciences *Degree program information:* Part-time and evening/weekend programs available. Postbaccalaureate distance learning degree programs offered (no on-campus study). Offers biology (MS); communication (MA); computer science (MS); English (MA); history (MA); liberal arts and sciences (MA, MS); liberal studies (MA). Electronic applications accepted.

College of Public Affairs and Administration *Degree program information:* Part-time and evening/weekend programs available. Postbaccalaureate distance learning degree programs offered (no on-campus study). Offers environmental science (MS); environmental studies (MA); legal studies (MA); political science (MA); public administration (MPA, DPA); public affairs and administration (MA, MPA, MPH, MS, DPA); public affairs reporting (MA); public health (MPH). Electronic applications accepted.

UNIVERSITY OF ILLINOIS AT URBANA–CHAMPAIGN, Champaign, IL 61820

General Information State-supported, coed, university. CGS member. *Enrollment:* 43,862 graduate, professional, and undergraduate students; 9,291 full-time matriculated graduate/professional students (4,293 women), 2,363 part-time matriculated graduate/professional students (1,271 women). *Graduate faculty:* 1,951 full-time (612 women), 141 part-time/adjunct (61 women). *Graduate housing:* Rooms and/or apartments available to single and married students. *Student services:* Campus employment opportunities, campus safety program, career counseling, exercise/wellness program, free psychological counseling, international student services, low-cost health insurance, multicultural affairs office, services for students with disabilities, teacher training, writing training. *Library facilities:* University Library plus 30 others. *Online resources:* library catalog, web page, access to other libraries' catalogs. *Collection:* 24 million titles. *Research affiliation:* Midwest Universities Research Association, Sandia National Laboratories, Fermi National Accelerator Laboratory, National Center for Atmospheric Research.

Computer facilities: Computer purchase and lease plans are available. A campuswide network can be accessed from student residence rooms and from off campus. Online class registration is available. *Web address:* http://www.illinois.edu/.

General Application Contact: Elizabeth Kibler, Director of Graduate and Professional Admissions, 217-244-4637, Fax: 217-333-8019, E-mail: bkibler@illinois.edu.

GRADUATE UNITS

College of Law Students: 730 full-time (329 women), 1 part-time (0 women); includes 163 minority (42 Black or African American, non-Hispanic/Latino; 4 American Indian or Alaska Native, non-Hispanic/Latino; 62 Asian, non-Hispanic/Latino; 41 Hispanic/Latino; 1 Native Hawaiian or other Pacific Islander, non-Hispanic/Latino; 13 Two or more races, non-Hispanic/Latino), 113 international. 676 applicants, 58% accepted, 319 enrolled. *Faculty:* 41 full-time (14 women), 32 part-time/adjunct (15 women). Expenses: Contact institution. *Financial support:* In 2010–11, 1 fellowship, 6 teaching assistantships were awarded; research assistantships, tuition waivers (full and partial) also available. In 2010, 197 first professional degrees, 83 master's, 3 doctorates awarded. Offers law (JD, LL M, MCL, JSD). *Application deadline:* Applications are processed on a rolling basis. *Application fee:* $75 ($90 for international students). Electronic applications accepted. *Application Contact:* Kelly J. Salefski, Director of Academic Administration and Student Records, 217-244-8663, Fax: 217-244-1478, E-mail: salefski@illinois.edu. *Dean,* Bruce Smith, 217-244-8446, Fax: 217-244-1478, E-mail: smithb@illinois.edu.

College of Veterinary Medicine Students: 527 full-time (412 women), 15 part-time (10 women); includes 4 Black or African American, non-Hispanic/Latino; 19 Asian, non-Hispanic/Latino; 29 Hispanic/Latino; 7 Two or more races, non-Hispanic/Latino, 24 international. 317 applicants, 67% accepted, 140 enrolled. *Faculty:* 58 full-time (26 women), 4 part-time/adjunct (3 women). Expenses: Contact institution. *Financial support:* In 2010–11, 12 fellowships, 26 research assistantships, 3 teaching assistantships were awarded; tuition waivers (full and partial) also available. In 2010, 106 first professional degrees, 7 master's, 8 doctorates awarded. Offers comparative biosciences (MS, PhD); pathobiology (MS, PhD); veterinary clinical medicine (MS, PhD); veterinary medical science (DVM); veterinary medicine (DVM, MS, PhD). *Application fee:* $75 ($90 for international students). Electronic applications accepted. *Application Contact:* Nikki Hausmann, Office Administrator, 217-333-4291, E-mail: nhausman@illinois.edu. *Dean,* Herbert E. Whiteley, 217-333-2760, Fax: 217-333-4628, E-mail: hwhitele@illinois.edu.

Graduate College Students: 8,176 full-time (3,648 women), 2,362 part-time (1,270 women); includes 1,547 minority (399 Black or African American, non-Hispanic/Latino; 10 American Indian or Alaska Native, non-Hispanic/Latino; 632 Asian, non-Hispanic/Latino; 386 Hispanic/Latino; 3 Native Hawaiian or other Pacific Islander, non-Hispanic/Latino; 117 Two or more races, non-Hispanic/Latino), 3,795 international. 21,144 applicants, 23% accepted, 3018 enrolled. *Faculty:* 1,951 full-time (612 women), 141 part-time/adjunct (61 women). Expenses: Contact institution. *Financial support:* In 2010–11, 1,338 fellowships, 3,598 research assistantships, 2,896 teaching assistantships were awarded; career-related internships or fieldwork and tuition waivers (full and partial) also available. In 2010, 3,023 master's, 763 doctorates, 14 other advanced degrees awarded. *Application deadline:* Applications are processed on a rolling basis. *Application fee:* $75 ($90 for international students). Electronic applications accepted. *Application Contact:* Gregory S. Harman, Admissions Support Staff, 217-244-4637. *Dean,* Debasish Dutta, 217-333-6715, Fax: 217-333-8019, E-mail: ddutta@illinois.edu.

College of Agricultural, Consumer and Environmental Sciences Students: 528 full-time (242 women), 168 part-time (69 women); includes 11 Black or African American, non-Hispanic/Latino; 26 Asian, non-Hispanic/Latino; 18 Hispanic/Latino; 6 Two or more races, non-Hispanic/Latino, 254 international. 747 applicants, 32% accepted, 181 enrolled. *Faculty:* 202 full-time (53 women), 5 part-time/adjunct (2 women). Expenses: Contact institution. *Financial support:* In 2010–11, 126 fellowships, 367 research assistantships, 121 teaching assistantships were awarded; tuition waivers (full and partial) also available. In 2010, 108 master's, 55 doctorates awarded. Offers agricultural and applied economics (MS, PhD); agricultural and biological engineering (MS, PhD); agricultural education (MS); agricultural production (MS); agricultural, consumer and environmental sciences (MS, PSM, PhD); animal sciences (MS, PhD); bioenergy (MS); bioinformatics: animal sciences (MS); bioinformatics: crop sciences (MS); crop sciences (MS, PhD); food science (MS); food science and human nutrition (MS, PhD); human and community development (MS, PhD); human nutrition (MS); natural resources and environmental science (MS, PhD); nutritional sciences (MS, PhD); technical systems management (MS, PSM). *Application deadline:* Applications are processed on a rolling basis. *Application fee:* $75 ($90 for international students). Electronic applications accepted. *Application Contact:* Robert Hauser, Interim Dean, 217-244-2807, Fax: 217-244-2911, E-mail: r-hauser@illinois.edu. *Interim Dean,* Robert Hauser, 217-244-2807, Fax: 217-244-2911, E-mail: r-hauser@illinois.edu.

College of Applied Health Sciences Students: 240 full-time (162 women), 90 part-time (46 women); includes 22 Black or African American, non-Hispanic/Latino; 1 American Indian or Alaska Native, non-Hispanic/Latino; 9 Asian, non-Hispanic/Latino; 10 Hispanic/Latino; 7 Two or more races, non-Hispanic/Latino, 52 international. 508 applicants, 24% accepted, 111 enrolled. *Faculty:* 61 full-time (34 women), 2 part-time/adjunct (0 women). Expenses: Contact institution. *Financial support:* In 2010–11, 20 fellowships, 88 research assistantships, 103 teaching assistantships were awarded; tuition waivers (full and partial) also available. In 2010, 63 master's, 15 doctorates awarded. Offers applied health sciences (MA, MPH, MS, MSPH, Au D, PhD); audiology (Au D); community health (MS, MSPH, PhD); kinesiology (MS, PhD); public health (MPH); recreation, sport and tourism (MS, PhD); rehabilitation (MS); speech and hearing science (MA, PhD). *Application deadline:* Applications are processed on a rolling basis. *Application fee:* $75 ($90 for international students). Electronic applications accepted. *Application Contact:* Tanya M. Gallagher, Dean, 217-333-2131, Fax: 217-333-0404, E-mail: tmgallag@illinois.edu. *Dean,* Tanya M. Gallagher, 217-333-2131, Fax: 217-333-0404, E-mail: tmgallag@illinois.edu.

College of Business Students: 958 full-time (423 women), 30 part-time (10 women); includes 30 Black or African American, non-Hispanic/Latino; 105 Asian, non-Hispanic/Latino; 8 Hispanic/Latino; 8 Two or more races, non-Hispanic/Latino, 466 international. 3,309 applicants, 28% accepted, 624 enrolled. *Faculty:* 93 full-time (18 women), 11 part-time/adjunct (2 women). Expenses: Contact institution. *Financial support:* In 2010–11, 49 fellowships, 75 research assistantships, 107 teaching assistantships were awarded; tuition waivers (full and partial) also available. In 2010, 781 master's, 12 doctorates awarded. Offers accountancy (MAS, MS, PhD); business (MAS, MBA, MS, PhD); business administration (MS, PhD); finance (MS, PhD); taxation (MS); technology management (MS). *Application deadline:* Applications are processed on a rolling basis. *Application fee:* $75 ($90 for international students). Electronic applications accepted. *Application Contact:* Lawrence M. DeBrock, Dean, 217-333-4553, Fax: 217-244-6678, E-mail: ldebrock@illinois.edu. *Dean,* Lawrence M. DeBrock, 217-333-4553, Fax: 217-244-6678, E-mail: ldebrock@illinois.edu.

College of Education Students: 384 full-time (265 women), 477 part-time (335 women); includes 119 Black or African American, non-Hispanic/Latino; 3 American Indian or Alaska Native, non-Hispanic/Latino; 43 Asian, non-Hispanic/Latino; 67 Hispanic/Latino; 11 Two or more races, non-Hispanic/Latino, 118 international. 640 applicants, 44% accepted, 153 enrolled. *Faculty:* 81 full-time (47 women), 2 part-time/adjunct (0 women). Expenses: Contact institution. *Financial support:* In 2010–11, 90 fellowships, 128 research assistantships, 146 teaching assistantships were awarded; tuition waivers (full and partial) also available. In 2010, 259 master's, 52 doctorates, 9 other advanced degrees awarded. Offers curriculum and instruction (Ed M, MA, MS, Ed D, PhD, CAS); early childhood education (Ed M); education (Ed M, MA, MS, Ed D, PhD, CAS); educational organization and leadership (Ed M, MS, Ed D, PhD, CAS); educational policy studies (Ed M, MA, PhD); educational psychology (Ed M, MA, MS, PhD, CAS); elementary education (Ed M); human resource education (Ed M, MS, Ed D, PhD, CAS); secondary education (Ed M); special education (Ed M, MS, Ed D, PhD, CAS). *Application deadline:* Applications are processed on a rolling basis. *Application fee:* $75 ($90 for international students). Electronic applications accepted. *Application Contact:* Mary A. Kalantzis, Dean, 217-333-0960, Fax: 217-333-5847, E-mail: kalantzi@illinois.edu. *Dean,* Mary A. Kalantzis, 217-333-0960, Fax: 217-333-5847, E-mail: kalantzi@illinois.edu.

College of Engineering Students: 2,097 full-time (365 women), 453 part-time (75 women); includes 17 Black or African American, non-Hispanic/Latino; 1 American Indian or Alaska Native, non-Hispanic/Latino; 180 Asian, non-Hispanic/Latino; 54 Hispanic/Latino; 19 Two or more races, non-Hispanic/Latino, 1,403 international. 6,259 applicants, 21% accepted, 586 enrolled. *Faculty:* 365 full-time (39 women), 14 part-time/adjunct (0 women). Expenses: Contact institution. *Financial support:* In 2010–11, 280 fellowships, 1,702 research assistantships, 690 teaching assistantships were awarded; tuition waivers (full and partial) also available. In 2010, 469 master's, 261 doctorates awarded. Offers aerospace engineering (MS, PhD); bioengineering (MS, PhD); bioinformatics (MS); civil engineering (MS); computer science (MCS, MS, PhD); electrical and computer engineering (MS, PhD); engineering (MCS, MS, PhD); environmental engineering in civil engineering (MS, PhD); environmental science in civil engineering (MS, PhD); financial engineering (MS); industrial engineering (MS, PhD); materials science and engineering (MS, PhD); mechanical engineering (MS, PhD); nuclear engineering (MS, PhD); physics (MS, PhD); systems and entrepreneurial engineering (MS, PhD); teaching of physics (MS); theoretical and applied mechanics (MS, PhD). *Application deadline:* Applications are processed on a rolling basis. *Application fee:* $75 ($90 for international students). Electronic applications accepted. *Application Contact:* Dr. Ilesanmi Adesida, Dean, 217-333-2150, Fax: 217-244-7705, E-mail: iadesida@illinois.edu. *Dean,* Dr. Ilesanmi Adesida, 217-333-2150, Fax: 217-244-7705, E-mail: iadesida@illinois.edu.

College of Fine and Applied Arts Students: 716 full-time (372 women), 120 part-time (65 women); includes 22 Black or African American, non-Hispanic/Latino; 32 Asian, non-Hispanic/Latino; 39 Hispanic/Latino; 15 Two or more races, non-Hispanic/Latino, 239 international. 1,781 applicants, 21% accepted, 265 enrolled. *Faculty:* 194 full-time (61 women), 23 part-time/adjunct (9 women). Expenses: Contact institution. *Financial support:* In 2010–11, 81 fellowships, 76 research assistantships, 270 teaching assistantships were awarded; tuition waivers (full and partial) also available. In 2010, 228 master's, 46 doctorates awarded. Offers architectural studies (MS); architecture (M Arch, PhD); art and design (Ed M, MA, MFA, PhD); art education (Ed M, MA, PhD); art history (MA, PhD); crafts (MFA); dance (MFA); fine and applied arts (Ed M, M Arch, M Mus, MA, MFA, MLA, MME, MS, MUP, DMA, Ed D, PhD, AD); graphic design (MFA); industrial design (MFA); landscape architecture (MLA, PhD); metals (MFA); music (M Mus, DMA, AD); music education (MME, Ed D, PhD); musicology (PhD); painting (MFA); photography (MFA); regional planning (PhD); sculpture (MFA); theatre (MA, MFA, PhD); urban planning (MUP). *Application deadline:* Applications are processed on a rolling basis. *Application fee:* $75 ($90 for international students). Electronic applications accepted. *Application Contact:* Robert B. Graves, Dean, 217-333-1660, Fax: 217-244-8381, E-mail: rbgraves@illinois.edu. *Dean,* Robert B. Graves, 217-333-1660, Fax: 217-244-8381, E-mail: rbgraves@illinois.edu.

College of Liberal Arts and Sciences Students: 2,236 full-time (1,069 women), 383 part-time (208 women); includes 368 minority (65 Black or African American, non-Hispanic/Latino; 4 American Indian or Alaska Native, non-Hispanic/Latino; 160 Asian, non-Hispanic/Latino; 106 Hispanic/Latino; 3 Native Hawaiian or other Pacific Islander, non-Hispanic/Latino; 30 Two or more races, non-Hispanic/Latino), 966 international. 5,713 applicants, 14% accepted, 508 enrolled. *Faculty:* 650 full-time (211 women), 22 part-time/adjunct (11 women). Expenses: Contact institution. *Financial support:* In 2010–11, 620 fellowships, 1,058 research assistantships, 1,346 teaching assistantships were awarded; tuition waivers (full and partial) also available. In 2010, 402 master's, 284 doctorates awarded. Offers

University of Illinois at Urbana–Champaign (continued)

African studies (MA); animal biology (ecology, ethology and evolution) (MS, PhD); anthropology (MA, PhD); applied mathematics (MS); applied mathematics: actuarial science (MS); applied statistics (MS); Asian studies (MA); astrochemistry (PhD); astronomy (PhD); atmospheric sciences (MS, PhD); biochemistry (MS, PhD); bioinformatics: chemical and biomolecular engineering (MS); biophysics and computational biology (MS, PhD); cell and developmental biology (PhD); chemical engineering (MS, PhD); chemical physics (PhD); chemical sciences (MA, MS, PhD); chemistry (MA, MS, PhD); classical philology (PhD); classics (MA); communication (MA); comparative literature (MA, PhD); creative writing (MFA); earth, society and environment (MA, MS, PhD); East Asian languages and cultures (PhD); ecology, evolution and conservation biology (MS, PhD); economics (MS, PhD); English (MA, PhD); entomology (MS, PhD); European Union studies (MA); French (MA, PhD); geography (MA, MS, PhD); geology (MS, PhD); German (MA, PhD); history (MA, PhD); integrative biology (MS, MST, PhD); Italian (MA, PhD); Latin American studies (MA); liberal arts and sciences (MA, MFA, MS, MST, PhD); linguistics (MA, PhD); literatures, cultures and linguistics (MA, MS, PhD); mathematics (MA, MS, PhD); microbiology (MS, PhD); molecular and cellular biology (MS, PhD); molecular and integrative physiology (MS, PhD); neuroscience (PhD); philosophy (MA, PhD); physiological and molecular plant biology (PhD); plant biology (MS, PhD); policy economics (MS); political science (MA, PhD); Portuguese (MA, PhD); psychology (MA, MS, PhD); Russian, East European and Eurasian studies (MA); Slavic languages and literatures (MA, PhD); sociology (MA, PhD); Spanish (MA, PhD); statistics (PhD); teaching of chemistry (MS); teaching of earth sciences (MS); teaching of English as a second language (MA); teaching of Latin (MA); teaching of mathematics (MS). *Application deadline:* Applications are processed on a rolling basis. *Application fee:* $75 ($90 for international students). Electronic applications accepted. *Application Contact:* Ruth V. Watkins, Dean, 217-333-1350, Fax: 217-333-9142, E-mail: rwatkins@illinois.edu. *Dean,* Ruth V. Watkins, 217-333-1350, Fax: 217-333-9142, E-mail: rwatkins@illinois.edu.

College of Media Students: 65 full-time (43 women), 26 part-time (16 women); includes 6 Black or African American, non-Hispanic/Latino; 3 Asian, non-Hispanic/Latino; 8 Hispanic/Latino; 3 Two or more races, non-Hispanic/Latino, 34 international. 301 applicants, 11% accepted, 32 enrolled. *Faculty:* 31 full-time (13 women), 1 (woman) part-time/adjunct. Expenses: Contact institution. *Financial support:* In 2010–11, 9 fellowships, 15 research assistantships, 53 teaching assistantships were awarded; tuition waivers (full and partial) also available. In 2010, 34 master's, 8 doctorates awarded. Offers advertising (MS); communications and media (PhD); journalism (MS); media (MS, PhD). *Application deadline:* Applications are processed on a rolling basis. *Application fee:* $75 ($90 for international students). Electronic applications accepted. *Application Contact:* Jan Slater, Interim Dean, 217-333-1602, Fax: 217-333-9882, E-mail: slaterj@illinois.edu. *Interim Dean,* Jan Slater, 217-333-1602, Fax: 217-333-9882, E-mail: slaterj@illinois.edu.

Graduate School of Library and Information Science Students: 352 full-time (258 women), 367 part-time (270 women); includes 124 minority (38 Black or African American, non-Hispanic/Latino; 1 American Indian or Alaska Native, non-Hispanic/Latino; 34 Asian, non-Hispanic/Latino; 40 Hispanic/Latino; 11 Two or more races, non-Hispanic/Latino), 27 international. 737 applicants, 58% accepted, 242 enrolled. *Faculty:* 23 full-time (11 women), 10 part-time/adjunct (7 women). Expenses: Contact institution. *Financial support:* In 2010–11, 37 fellowships, 37 research assistantships, 38 teaching assistantships were awarded; tuition waivers (full and partial) also available. In 2010, 272 master's, 5 doctorates, 2 other advanced degrees awarded. Postbaccalaureate distance learning degree programs offered. Offers bioinformatics (MS); digital libraries (CAS); library and information science (MS, PhD, CAS). *Application deadline:* Applications are processed on a rolling basis. *Application fee:* $75 ($90 for international students). Electronic applications accepted. *Application Contact:* Valerie Youngen, Admissions and Records Representative, 217-333-0734, Fax: 217-244-3302, E-mail: vyoungen@llinois.edu. *Dean,* John Unsworth, 217-333-3281, Fax: 217-244-3302, E-mail: unsworth@illinois.edu.

School of Labor and Employment Relations Students: 169 full-time (117 women), 24 part-time (11 women); includes 40 minority (15 Black or African American, non-Hispanic/Latino; 16 Asian, non-Hispanic/Latino; 7 Hispanic/Latino; 2 Two or more races, non-Hispanic/Latino), 66 international. 262 applicants, 43% accepted, 63 enrolled. *Faculty:* 15 full-time (4 women). Expenses: Contact institution. *Financial support:* In 2010–11, 8 fellowships, 10 research assistantships, 4 teaching assistantships were awarded; tuition waivers (full and partial) also available. In 2010, 99 master's, 1 doctorate awarded. *Degree program information:* Part-time programs available. Offers human resources and industrial relations (MHRIR, PhD). *Application fee:* $75 ($90 for international students). Electronic applications accepted. *Application Contact:* Elizabeth Barker, Director of Student Services, 217-333-2381, Fax: 217-244-9290, E-mail: ebarker@illinois.edu. *Dean,* Dr. Joel E. Cutcher-Gershenfeld, 217-333-1482, Fax: 217-244-9290, E-mail: joelcg@illinois.edu.

School of Social Work Students: 224 full-time (201 women), 94 part-time (82 women); includes 66 minority (31 Black or African American, non-Hispanic/Latino; 12 Asian, non-Hispanic/Latino; 19 Hispanic/Latino; 4 Two or more races, non-Hispanic/Latino), 16 international. 307 applicants, 47% accepted, 117 enrolled. *Faculty:* 18 full-time (12 women), 2 part-time/adjunct (both women). Expenses: Contact institution. *Financial support:* In 2010–11, 5 fellowships, 11 research assistantships, 6 teaching assistantships were awarded; tuition waivers (full and partial) also available. In 2010, 141 master's, 5 doctorates awarded. Offers advocacy, leadership, and social change (MSW); children, youth and family services (MSW); social work (PhD). *Application deadline:* Applications are processed on a rolling basis. *Application fee:* $75 ($90 for international students). Electronic applications accepted. *Application Contact:* Cheryl M. Street, Admissions and Records Officer, 217-333-2261, Fax: 217-244-5220, E-mail: street@illinois.edu. *Dean,* Wynne S. Korr, 217-333-2260, Fax: 217-244-5220, E-mail: wkorr@illinois.edu.

Informatics Institute Expenses: Contact institution. *Financial support:* Fellowships, research assistantships, teaching assistantships, tuition waivers (full and partial) available. *Degree program information:* Part-time programs available. Offers informatics (PhD). *Application fee:* $75 ($90 for international students). *Application Contact:* Judy Tolliver, Coordinator for Informatics Education Programs, 217-333-2322, E-mail: tolliver@illinois.edu. *Director,* John Unsworth, 217-333-3281, E-mail: unsworth@illinois.edu.

Institute of Aviation Students: 11 full-time (8 women), 6 international. 18 applicants, 28% accepted, 4 enrolled. Expenses: Contact institution. *Financial support:* In 2010–11, 5 research assistantships, 3 teaching assistantships were awarded; fellowships, tuition waivers (full and partial) also available. In 2010, 3 master's awarded. Offers human factors (MS). *Application deadline:* Applications are processed on a rolling basis. *Application fee:* $75 ($90 for international students). Electronic applications accepted. *Application Contact:* Peter Vlach, Information Systems Specialist, 217-265-9456, E-mail: pvlach@illinois.edu. *Acting Head,* Alex Kirlik, 217-244-8972, E-mail: kirlik@illinois.edu.

UNIVERSITY OF INDIANAPOLIS, Indianapolis, IN 46227-3697

General Information Independent-religious, coed, comprehensive institution. *Enrollment:* 5,290 graduate, professional, and undergraduate students; 469 full-time matriculated graduate/professional students (360 women), 716 part-time matriculated graduate/professional students (481 women). *Graduate faculty:* 59 full-time (29 women), 23 part-time/adjunct (16 women). Tuition and fees vary according to course load, degree level and program. *Graduate housing:* Rooms and/or apartments available on a first-come, first-served basis to single and married students. *Student services:* Campus employment opportunities, campus safety program, career counseling, exercise/wellness program, free psychological counseling, grant writing training, international student services, low-cost health insurance, services for students with disabilities, teacher training, writing training. *Library facilities:* Krannert Memorial Library. *Online resources:* library catalog, web page, access to other libraries' catalogs. *Collection:* 173,363 titles, 1,015 serial subscriptions.

Computer facilities: 222 computers available on campus for general student use. A campuswide network can be accessed from student residence rooms and from off campus. *Web address:* http://www.uindy.edu/.

General Application Contact: Dr. E. John McIlvried, Associate Provost and Dean of the Graduate School, 317-788-3477, E-mail: jmcilvried@uindy.edu.

GRADUATE UNITS

Graduate Programs Students: 469 full-time (360 women), 716 part-time (481 women); includes 46 Black or African American, non-Hispanic/Latino; 14 Asian, non-Hispanic/Latino; 19 Hispanic/Latino; 3 Two or more races, non-Hispanic/Latino, 100 international. Average age 30. *Faculty:* 59 full-time (29 women), 23 part-time/adjunct (16 women). Expenses: Contact institution. *Financial support:* Career-related internships or fieldwork, Federal Work-Study, scholarships/grants, tuition waivers (full and partial), and unspecified assistantships available. Support available to part-time students. Financial award application deadline: 5/1; financial award applicants required to submit FAFSA. In 2010, 301 master's, 85 doctorates, 1 other advanced degree awarded. *Degree program information:* Part-time and evening/weekend programs available. Postbaccalaureate distance learning degree programs offered. *Application deadline:* Applications are processed on a rolling basis. *Application Contact:* Dr. E. John McIlvried, Associate Provost and Dean of the Graduate School, 317-788-3477, E-mail: jmcilvried@uindy.edu. *Associate Provost and Dean of the Graduate School,* Dr. E. John McIlvried, 317-788-3477, E-mail: jmcilvried@uindy.edu.

Center for Aging and Community Students: 1 (woman) full-time, 24 part-time (22 women); includes 2 minority (both Black or African American, non-Hispanic/Latino). Average age 39. Expenses: Contact institution. *Financial support:* Career-related internships or fieldwork, Federal Work-Study, scholarships/grants, and tuition waivers (full and partial) available. Support available to part-time students. *Degree program information:* Part-time and evening/weekend programs available. Postbaccalaureate distance learning degree programs offered. Offers gerontology (MS, Certificate). *Application deadline:* Applications are processed on a rolling basis. *Application fee:* $50. *Application Contact:* Tamora Wolske, Academic Program Director, 317-791-5930, Fax: 317-791-5945, E-mail: wolsketl@uindy.edu. *Executive Director,* Dr. Ellen Miller, 317-791-5930, Fax: 317-791-5945, E-mail: emiller@uindy.edu.

College of Arts and Sciences Students: 43 full-time (28 women), 74 part-time (49 women); includes 14 minority (11 Black or African American, non-Hispanic/Latino; 2 Hispanic/Latino; 1 Two or more races, non-Hispanic/Latino), 18 international. Average age 30. *Faculty:* 26 full-time (10 women), 6 part-time/adjunct (4 women). Expenses: Contact institution. *Financial support:* Teaching assistantships, Federal Work-Study, scholarships/grants, and tuition waivers (full and partial) available. Support available to part-time students. Financial award application deadline: 5/1; financial award applicants required to submit FAFSA. *Degree program information:* Part-time and evening/weekend programs available. Offers anthropology (MS); applied sociology (MA); art (MA); arts and sciences (MA, MS); English (MA); history (MA); human biology (MS); international relations (MA). *Application deadline:* Applications are processed on a rolling basis. *Application fee:* $30. *Application Contact:* Linda Corn, 317-788-3395, E-mail: lcorn@uindy.edu. *Dean,* Dr. Daniel Briere, 317-788-3395, Fax: 317-788-3480, E-mail: dbriere@uindy.edu.

Krannert School of Physical Therapy Students: 124 full-time (90 women), 75 part-time (58 women); includes 4 minority (1 Black or African American, non-Hispanic/Latino; 2 Asian, non-Hispanic/Latino; 1 Hispanic/Latino), 46 international. Average age 26. *Faculty:* 11 full-time (6 women), 4 part-time/adjunct (all women). Expenses: Contact institution. *Financial support:* Teaching assistantships, career-related internships or fieldwork, Federal Work-Study, scholarships/grants, tuition waivers (full and partial), and unspecified assistantships available. Support available to part-time students. Financial award application deadline: 5/1; financial award applicants required to submit FAFSA. In 2010, 32 master's, 67 doctorates awarded. *Degree program information:* Part-time and evening/weekend programs available. Offers physical therapy (MHS, DHS, DPT, TDPT). *Application deadline:* For fall admission, 10/10 for domestic students. *Application fee:* $50. Electronic applications accepted. *Application Contact:* Kelly Wilson, Admissions Counselor, 317-788-4909, Fax: 317-788-3542, E-mail: kwilson@uindy.edu. *Dean, College of Health Sciences,* Dr. Stephanie Kelly, 317-788-3500, Fax: 317-788-3542, E-mail: huerm@uindy.edu.

School of Business Students: 28 full-time (9 women), 185 part-time (62 women); includes 15 minority (8 Black or African American, non-Hispanic/Latino; 2 Asian, non-Hispanic/Latino; 5 Hispanic/Latino), 13 international. Average age 30. *Faculty:* 4 full-time (2 women), 4 part-time/adjunct (1 woman). Expenses: Contact institution. *Financial support:* Tuition waivers (full and partial) and unspecified assistantships available. Support available to part-time students. Financial award application deadline: 5/1; financial award applicants required to submit FAFSA. In 2010, 77 master's awarded. *Degree program information:* Part-time and evening/weekend programs available. Offers business (EMBA, MBA, Graduate Certificate). *Application deadline:* Applications are processed on a rolling basis. *Application fee:* $50. *Application Contact:* Stephen A. Tokar, Director of Graduate Business Programs, 317-788-4905, E-mail: tokarsa@uindy.edu. *Dean,* Dr. Sheela Yadav, 317-788-3232, E-mail: syadav@uindy.edu.

School of Education Students: 40 full-time (26 women), 106 part-time (64 women); includes 9 minority (8 Black or African American, non-Hispanic/Latino; 1 Asian, non-Hispanic/Latino), 3 international. Average age 33. *Faculty:* 3 full-time (2 women), 2 part-time/adjunct (1 woman). Expenses: Contact institution. *Financial support:* Federal Work-Study available. Financial award application deadline: 5/1; financial award applicants required to submit FAFSA. In 2010, 44 master's awarded. *Degree program information:* Part-time and evening/weekend programs available. Offers art education (MAT); biology (MAT); chemistry (MAT); curriculum and instruction (MA); earth sciences (MAT); education (MA, MAT); educational leadership (MA); elementary education (MA); English (MAT); French (MAT); math (MAT); physical education (MAT); physics (MAT); secondary education (MA); social studies (MAT); Spanish (MAT). *Application deadline:* Applications are processed on a rolling basis. *Application fee:* $50. *Application Contact:* Chemain Slater, 317-788-2051, E-mail: slaterc@uindy.edu. *Dean,* Dr. Kathy Moran, 317-788-3285, Fax: 317-788-3300, E-mail: kmoran@uindy.edu.

School of Nursing Students: 25 full-time (23 women), 134 part-time (125 women); includes 13 minority (6 Black or African American, non-Hispanic/Latino; 1 American Indian or Alaska Native, non-Hispanic/Latino; 2 Asian, non-Hispanic/Latino; 3 Hispanic/Latino; 1 Two or more races, non-Hispanic/Latino), 5 international. Average age 38. *Faculty:* 4 full-time (3 women), 2 part-time/adjunct (both women). Expenses: Contact institution. *Financial support:* Federal Work-Study available. In 2010, 26 master's awarded. Offers family practice (post-RN) (MSN); gerontological nurse practitioner (MSN); nurse-midwifery (MSN); nursing (MSN); nursing administration (MSN); nursing education (MSN). *Application deadline:* For fall admission, 8/1 for domestic students; for winter admission, 12/15 for domestic students; for spring admission, 4/15 for domestic students. Applications are processed on a rolling basis. *Application fee:* $50. *Application Contact:* T. C. Crum, Information Contact, 317-788-2128, Fax: 317-788-3542, E-mail: tcrum@uindy.edu. *Dean,* Dr. Anne Thomas, 317-788-3206, E-mail: athomas@uindy.edu.

School of Occupational Therapy Students: 91 full-time (78 women), 74 part-time (65 women); includes 13 minority (4 Black or African American, non-Hispanic/Latino; 5 Asian, non-Hispanic/Latino; 4 Hispanic/Latino), 4 international. Average age 27. *Faculty:* 4 full-time (all women), 3 part-time/adjunct (2 women). Expenses: Contact institution. *Financial support:* Career-related internships or fieldwork, Federal Work-Study, tuition waivers (full and partial), and unspecified assistantships available. Financial award application deadline: 5/1; financial award applicants required to submit FAFSA. In 2010, 60 master's, 4 doctorates awarded. *Degree program information:* Part-time and evening/weekend programs available. Offers occupational therapy (MHS, MOT, DHS). *Application deadline:* For fall admission, 11/1 for domestic students, 2/1 for international students. *Application fee:* $55. *Application Contact:* Kelly Wilson, Director, Admissions, 317-788-3457, Fax: 317-788-3542, E-mail: kwilson@uindy.edu. *Dean, College of Health Sciences,* Dr. Stephanie Kelly, 317-788-3500, Fax: 317-788-3542, E-mail: spkelly@uindy.edu.

School of Psychological Sciences Students: 118 full-time (105 women), 44 part-time (37 women); includes 2 minority (1 Black or African American, non-Hispanic/Latino; 1 Hispanic/Latino), 11 international. Average age 26. *Faculty:* 6 full-time (1 woman), 1 (woman) part-time/adjunct. Expenses: Contact institution. *Financial support:* Federal Work-Study available. Offers clinical psychology (Psy D); clinical psychology/mental health counseling (MA). *Application deadline:* For fall admission, 2/25 for domestic students. *Application fee:* $50. *Application Contact:* Dr. Rick Holigrocki, Acting Dean, 317-788-6126, E-mail: rholigrocki@uindy.edu. *Acting Dean,* Dr. Rick Holigrocki, 317-788-6126, Fax: 317-788-3480, E-mail: rholigrocki@uindy.edu.

THE UNIVERSITY OF IOWA, Iowa City, IA 52242-1316

General Information State-supported, coed, university. CGS member. *Graduate housing:* Rooms and/or apartments available on a first-come, first-served basis to single and married students.

GRADUATE UNITS

College of Dentistry Offers dental public health (MS); dentistry (DDS, MS, PhD, Certificate); endodontics (MS, Certificate); operative dentistry (MS, Certificate); oral and maxillofacial pathology (Certificate); oral and maxillofacial radiology (Certificate); oral and maxillofacial surgery (MS, Certificate); oral pathology, radiology and medicine (MS, Certificate); oral science (MS, PhD); orthodontics (MS, Certificate); pediatric dentistry (Certificate); periodontics (MS, Certificate); preventive and community dentistry (MS); prosthodontics (MS, Certificate); stomatology (MS).

College of Law Offers law (JD, LL M). Electronic applications accepted.

College of Pharmacy Offers pharmacy (MS, PhD). Electronic applications accepted.

Graduate College *Degree program information:* Part-time and evening/weekend programs available. Postbaccalaureate distance learning degree programs offered (minimal on-campus study). Offers applied mathematical and computational sciences (PhD); bioinformatics and computational biology (Certificate); genetics (PhD); health informatics (MS, PhD, Certificate); human toxicology (MS, PhD); immunology (PhD); information science (MS, PhD, Certificate); molecular and cellular biology (PhD); neuroscience (PhD); second language acquisition (PhD); translational biomedicine (MS, PhD); urban and regional planning (MA, MS). Electronic applications accepted.

College of Education Offers administration and research (PhD); art education (PhD); community/rehabilitation counseling (MA); counseling psychology (PhD); counselor education and supervision (PhD); curriculum and supervision (MA, PhD); curriculum supervision (MA); developmental reading (MA); early childhood education and care (MA); education (MA, MAT, PhD, Ed S); educational administration (MA, PhD, Ed S); educational measurement and statistics (MA, PhD); educational psychology (MA, PhD); elementary education (MA, PhD); English education (MA, MAT); foreign language education (MA, MAT); foreign language/ESL education (PhD); higher education (MA, PhD, Ed S); language, literature and culture (PhD); math education (PhD); mathematics education (MA); rehabilitation counselor education (PhD); school counseling (MA); school psychology (PhD, Ed S); secondary education (MA, MAT, PhD); social foundations (MA, PhD); social studies (MA, PhD); special education (MA, PhD); student development (MA, PhD). Electronic applications accepted.

College of Engineering Students: 411 full-time (110 women); includes 28 minority (10 Black or African American, non-Hispanic/Latino; 13 Asian, non-Hispanic/Latino; 5 Hispanic/Latino), 196 international. Average age 26. 709 applicants, 30% accepted, 114 enrolled. *Faculty:* 83 full-time (10 women), 2 part-time/adjunct (1 woman). Expenses: Contact institution. *Financial support:* In 2010–11, 29 fellowships with partial tuition reimbursements (averaging $20,678 per year), 292 research assistantships with partial tuition reimbursements (averaging $20,739 per year), 84 teaching assistantships with partial tuition reimbursements (averaging $17,174 per year) were awarded; scholarships/grants, health care benefits, and unspecified assistantships also available. Financial award application deadline: 2/1; financial award applicants required to submit FAFSA. In 2010, 65 master's, 42 doctorates awarded. Offers biomedical engineering (MS, PhD); chemical and biochemical engineering (MS, PhD); civil and environmental engineering (MS, PhD); electrical and computer engineering (MS, PhD); engineering (MS, PhD); engineering design and manufacturing (MS, PhD); ergonomics (MS, PhD); information and engineering management (MS, PhD); mechanical engineering (MS, PhD); operations research (MS, PhD); quality engineering (MS, PhD). *Application deadline:* For fall admission, 7/15 for domestic students, 4/15 for international students; for spring admission, 12/1 for domestic students, 10/1 for international students. Applications are processed on a rolling basis. *Application fee:* $60 ($100 for international students). Electronic applications accepted. *Application Contact:* Michael Barron, Director of Admissions, 319-335-1525, Fax: 319-335-1535, E-mail: admissions@uiowa.edu. *Interim Dean,* Dr. Alec Scranton, 319-335-5766, Fax: 319-335-6086, E-mail: alec-scranton@uiowa.edu.

College of Liberal Arts and Sciences *Degree program information:* Part-time programs available. Postbaccalaureate distance learning degree programs offered (minimal on-campus study). Offers African American world studies (MA); American studies (MA, PhD); anthropology (MA, PhD); art (MA, MFA); art history (MA, PhD); Asian languages and literature (MA); astronomy (MS); biology (MS, PhD); cell and developmental biology (MS, PhD); chemistry (MS, PhD); classics (MA, PhD); communication research (MA, PhD); comparative literature (MA, PhD); comparative literature translation (MFA); computer science (MCS, MS, PhD); dance (MFA); English (PhD); evolution (MS, PhD); exercise science (MS); film and video production (MA, MFA); film studies (MA, PhD); French (MA, PhD); genetics (MS, PhD); geography (MA, PhD); geoscience (MS, PhD); German (MA, PhD); history (MA, PhD); integrative physiology (PhD); leisure and recreational sport management (MA); liberal arts and sciences (MA, MCS, MFA, MS, MSW, Au D, DMA, PhD); linguistics (MA, PhD); linguistics with TESL (MA); literary criticism (PhD); literary history (PhD); literary studies (MA); mass communication (PhD); mathematics (MS, PhD); media communication (MA); music (MA, MFA, DMA, PhD); neural and behavioral sciences (PhD); neurobiology (MS, PhD); nonfiction writing (MFA); philosophy (MA, PhD); physics (MS, PhD); political science (MA, PhD); professional journalism (MA); professional speech pathology and audiology (MA, Au D); psychology (MA, PhD); psychology of sport and physical activity (MA, PhD); religious studies (MA, PhD); rhetorical studies (MA, PhD); rhetorical theory and stylistics (PhD); science education (MS, PhD); social work (MSW, PhD); sociology (MA, PhD); Spanish (MA, PhD); speech and hearing science (PhD); sports studies (MA, PhD); statistics and actuarial science (MS, PhD); theatre arts (MFA); therapeutic recreation (MA); women's studies (PhD); writer's workshop (MFA). Electronic applications accepted.

College of Nursing Offers nursing (MSN, DNP, PhD). Electronic applications accepted.

College of Public Health Offers biostatistics (MS, PhD); clinical investigation (MS); community and behavioral health (MS, PhD); epidemiology (MS, PhD); health management and policy (MHA, PhD); occupational and environmental health (MS, PhD, Certificate); public health (MHA, MPH, MS, PhD, Certificate). Electronic applications accepted.

School of Library and Information Science Offers library and information science (MA). Electronic applications accepted.

Henry B. Tippie College of Business *Faculty:* 10 part-time/adjunct. Expenses: Contact institution. Offers accounting (M Ac, PhD); business (M Ac, MBA, PhD); business administration (PhD); economics (PhD); marketing (PhD). *Application Contact:* Jodi Schafer, Director, Admissions and Financial Aid, 319-335-0864, Fax: 319-335-3604, E-mail: jodi-schafer@uiowa.edu. *Dean,* Prof. William Curt Hunter, 319-335-0862, Fax: 319-335-1956, E-mail: william-hunter@uiowa.edu.

Henry B. Tippie School of Management Students: 242 full-time (46 women), 809 part-time (277 women); includes 95 minority (15 Black or African American, non-Hispanic/Latino; 3 American Indian or Alaska Native, non-Hispanic/Latino; 56 Asian, non-Hispanic/Latino; 21 Hispanic/Latino), 132 international. Average age 31. 652 applicants, 66% accepted, 380 enrolled. *Faculty:* 110 full-time (25 women), 19 part-time/adjunct (1 woman). Expenses: Contact institution. *Financial support:* In 2010–11, 111 students received support, including 121 fellowships (averaging $8,285 per year), 87 research assistantships with partial tuition reimbursements available (averaging $8,288 per year), 25 teaching assistantships with partial tuition reimbursements available (averaging $11,326 per year); career-related internships or fieldwork, scholarships/grants, health care benefits, and unspecified assistantships also available. Financial award application deadline: 4/15; financial award applicants required to submit FAFSA. In 2010, 333 master's awarded. *Degree program information:* Part-time and evening/weekend programs available. Offers corporate finance (MBA); investment management (MBA); marketing (MBA); process and operations excellence (MBA); strategic management and innovation (MBA). *Application deadline:* For fall admission, 7/30 for domestic students, 4/15 for international students; for spring admission, 12/15 for domestic and international students. Applications are processed on a rolling basis. *Application fee:* $60 ($100 for international students). Electronic applications accepted. *Application Contact:* Jodi Schafer, Director of Admissions and Financial Aid, 319-335-0864, Fax: 319-335-3604, E-mail: jodi-schafer@uiowa.edu. *Associate Dean, MBA Programs,* Prof. Jarjisu Sa-Aadu, 800-622-4692, Fax: 319-335-3604, E-mail: jsa-aadu@uiowa.edu.

Roy J. and Lucille A. Carver College of Medicine Students: 972 full-time (489 women), 4 part-time (1 woman); includes 170 minority (32 Black or African American, non-Hispanic/Latino; 8 American Indian or Alaska Native, non-Hispanic/Latino; 72 Asian, non-Hispanic/Latino; 38 Hispanic/Latino; 2 Native Hawaiian or other Pacific Islander, non-Hispanic/Latino; 18 Two or more races, non-Hispanic/Latino), 33 international. 5,091 applicants, 8% accepted, 254 enrolled. Expenses: Contact institution. *Financial support:* In 2010–11, 794 students received support; fellowships, research assistantships, teaching assistantships, career-related internships or fieldwork, Federal Work-Study, institutionally sponsored loans, scholarships/grants, health care benefits, and tuition waivers (full and partial) available. Support available to part-time students. Financial award applicants required to submit FAFSA. In 2010, 170 first professional degrees, 32 master's, 34 doctorates awarded. *Degree program information:* Part-time programs available. Offers anatomy and biology (PhD); biochemistry (PhD); biology (PhD); biomedical engineering (PhD); chemistry (PhD); free radical and radiation biology (PhD); genetics (PhD); human toxicology (PhD); immunology (PhD); medicine (MD, MA, MPAS, MS, DPT, PhD); microbiology (PhD); molecular and cellular biology (PhD); molecular physiology and biophysics (PhD); neuroscience (PhD); pharmacology (PhD); physical therapy and rehabilitation science (PhD); speech and hearing (PhD). Electronic applications accepted. *Application Contact:* Betty Wood, Associate Director of Admissions, 319-335-1525, Fax: 319-335-1535, E-mail: admissions@uiowa.edu. *Dean,* Dr. Paul B. Rothman, 319-384-4590, Fax: 319-335-8318, E-mail: paul-rothman@uiowa.edu.

Graduate Programs in Medicine Students: 309 full-time (176 women), 4 part-time (1 woman); includes 23 minority (4 Black or African American, non-Hispanic/Latino; 5 American Indian or Alaska Native, non-Hispanic/Latino; 9 Asian, non-Hispanic/Latino; 5 Hispanic/Latino), 30 international. 1,305 applicants, 9% accepted, 94 enrolled. *Faculty:* 133 full-time (30 women), 92 part-time/adjunct (42 women). Expenses: Contact institution. *Financial support:* In 2010–11, 160 students received support, including fellowships (averaging $25,000 per year), research assistantships (averaging $25,000 per year), teaching assistantships (averaging $25,000 per year); career-related internships or fieldwork, Federal Work-Study, institutionally sponsored loans, health care benefits, and tuition waivers (full and partial) also available. Support available to part-time students. Financial award applicants required to submit FAFSA. In 2010, 32 master's, 27 doctorates awarded. *Degree program information:* Part-time programs available. Offers anatomy and cell biology (PhD); biochemistry (MS, PhD); free radical and radiation biology (MS, PhD); general microbiology and microbial physiology (MS, PhD); immunology (MS, PhD); medicine (MA, MPAS, MS, DPT, PhD); microbial genetics (MS, PhD); molecular physiology and biophysics (MS, PhD); pathogenic bacteriology (MS, PhD); pathology (MS); pharmacology (MS, PhD); physical therapy (DPT); physician assistant (MPAS); rehabilitation science (PhD); virology (MS, PhD). Electronic applications accepted. *Application Contact:* Dr. Paul B. Rothman, Dean, 319-384-4590, Fax: 319-335-8318, E-mail: paul-rothman@uiowa.edu. *Dean,* Dr. Paul B. Rothman, 319-384-4590, Fax: 319-335-8318, E-mail: paul-rothman@uiowa.edu.

THE UNIVERSITY OF KANSAS, Lawrence, KS 66045

General Information State-supported, coed, university. CGS member. *Enrollment:* 28,696 graduate, professional, and undergraduate students; 8,157 matriculated graduate/professional students (4,477 women). *Enrollment by degree level:* 1,834 first professional, 3,979 master's, 2,320 doctoral, 24 other advanced degrees. *Graduate faculty:* 1,468. Tuition, state resident: full-time $7092; part-time $295.50 per credit hour. Tuition, nonresident: full-time $16,590; part-time $691.25 per credit hour. *Required fees:* $858; $71.49 per credit hour. Tuition and fees vary according to course load, campus/location and program. *Graduate housing:* Rooms and/or apartments available on a first-come, first-served basis to single and married students. Typical cost: $6982 (including board) for single students. Room and board charges vary according to board plan and housing facility selected. Housing application deadline: 3/1. *Student services:* Campus employment opportunities, campus safety program, career counseling, child daycare facilities, exercise/wellness program, free psychological counseling, grant writing training, international student services, low-cost health insurance, multicultural affairs office, services for students with disabilities, teacher training, writing training. *Library facilities:* Watson Library plus 11 others. *Online resources:* library catalog, web page, access to other libraries' catalogs. *Collection:* 5.1 million titles, 79,469 serial subscriptions, 70,271 audiovisual materials.

Computer facilities: 1,500 computers available on campus for general student use. A campuswide network can be accessed from student residence rooms and from off campus. Online class registration is available. *Web address:* http://www.ku.edu/.

General Application Contact: Graduate Studies, 785-864-8040, Fax: 785-864-7209, E-mail: graduate@ku.edu.

GRADUATE UNITS

Graduate Studies Students: 4,014 full-time (2,181 women), 1,494 part-time (739 women); includes 649 minority (155 Black or African American, non-Hispanic/Latino; 51 American Indian or Alaska Native, non-Hispanic/Latino; 165 Asian, non-Hispanic/Latino; 202 Hispanic/Latino; 2 Native Hawaiian or other Pacific Islander, non-Hispanic/Latino; 74 Two or more races, non-Hispanic/Latino), 909 international. Average age 30. 5,583 applicants, 48% accepted, 1610 enrolled. Expenses: Contact institution. *Financial support:* Fellowships with full and partial tuition reimbursements, research assistantships with full and partial tuition reimbursements, teaching assistantships with full and partial tuition reimbursements, career-related internships or fieldwork, Federal Work-Study, institutionally sponsored loans, scholarships/grants, traineeships, and unspecified assistantships available. Support available to part-time students. Financial award applicants required to submit FAFSA. In 2010, 1,484 master's, 298 doctorates, 6 other advanced degrees awarded. *Degree program information:* Part-time and evening/weekend programs available. Postbaccalaureate distance learning degree programs offered. *Application fee:* $55 ($65 for international students). Electronic applications accepted. *Application Contact:* Dr. John Augusto, Assistant Dean, 785-864-8040, Fax: 785-864-7209, E-mail: graduate@ku.edu.

College of Liberal Arts and Sciences Students: 1,703 full-time (885 women), 347 part-time (170 women); includes 216 minority (46 Black or African American, non-Hispanic/Latino; 27 American Indian or Alaska Native, non-Hispanic/Latino; 41 Asian, non-Hispanic/Latino; 73 Hispanic/Latino; 1 Native Hawaiian or other Pacific Islander, non-Hispanic/Latino; 28 Two or more races, non-Hispanic/Latino), 364 international. Average age 30. 2,471 applicants, 39% accepted, 526 enrolled. Expenses: Contact institution. *Financial support:* Fellowships, research assistantships with partial tuition reimbursements, teaching assistantships with full and partial tuition reimbursements, career-related internships or fieldwork, Federal Work-Study, institutionally sponsored loans, scholarships/grants, traineeships, and unspecified assistantships available. Support available to part-time students. Financial award applicants required to submit FAFSA. In 2010, 291 master's, 137 doctorates awarded. *Degree program information:* Part-time and evening/weekend programs available. Offers African and African-American studies (MA); African Studies (Graduate Certificate); American studies (MA, PhD); anthropology (MA, PhD); applied behavioral science (MA); atmospheric science (MS); audiology (PhD); behavioral psychology (PhD); biochemistry and biophysics (MA, PhD); botany (MA, PhD); Brazilian studies (Graduate Certificate); Central American and Mexican studies (Graduate Certificate); chemistry (MS, PhD); child language (MA, PhD); classics (MA); clinical child psychology (MA, PhD); clinical health and rehabilitation (PhD); cognitive psychology (PhD); communication studies (MA, PhD); computational physics and astronomy (MS); creative writing (MFA); developmental psychology (PhD); East Asian languages and cultures (MA); ecology and evolutionary biology (MA, PhD); economics (MA, PhD); English (MA, PhD); entomology (MA, PhD); film and media studies (MA, PhD); French (MA, PhD); geography (MA, PhD); geology (MS, PhD); German (MA, PhD); gerontology (MA, PhD, Graduate Certificate); global and international studies (MA); global indigenous nations studies (MA); history (MA, PhD); history of art (MA, PhD); Latin American studies (MA); liberal arts and sciences (MA, MFA, MPA, MS, PhD, Graduate Certificate); linguistics (MA, PhD); mathematics (MA, PhD); microbiology (MA, PhD); molecular, cellular, and developmental biology (MA, PhD); museum studies (MA); painting, printmaking (MFA); philosophy (MA, PhD); physics (MS, PhD); political science (MA, PhD);

The University of Kansas (continued)

public administration (MPA, PhD); quantitative psychology (PhD); religious studies (MA); Russian, East European and Eurasian studies (MA); Slavic languages and literatures (MA, PhD); social psychology (MA); sociology (MA, PhD); Spanish (MA, PhD); speech-language pathology (MA, PhD); theatre (MA, PhD); theatre design (MFA); visual art education (MA). *Application fee:* $55 ($65 for international students). Electronic applications accepted. *Application Contact:* Dr. Danny J. Anderson, Dean, 785-864-3661, Fax: 785-864-5331, E-mail: clasdean@ku.edu. *Dean*, Dr. Danny J. Anderson, 785-864-3661, Fax: 785-864-5331, E-mail: clasdean@ku.edu.

School of Architecture, Design, and Planning Students: 234 full-time (110 women), 49 part-time (25 women); includes 27 minority (6 Black or African American, non-Hispanic/Latino; 1 American Indian or Alaska Native, non-Hispanic/Latino; 3 Asian, non-Hispanic/Latino; 11 Hispanic/Latino; 6 Two or more races, non-Hispanic/Latino), 28 international. Average age 27. 203 applicants, 69% accepted, 77 enrolled. *Faculty:* 25 full-time (7 women), 6 part-time/adjunct (0 women). Expenses: Contact institution. *Financial support:* Fellowships, research assistantships with full and partial tuition reimbursements, teaching assistantships with full and partial tuition reimbursements, career-related internships or fieldwork, scholarships/grants, health care benefits, and unspecified assistantships available. Financial award application deadline: 2/1; financial award applicants required to submit FAFSA. In 2010, 85 master's awarded. *Degree program information:* Part-time programs available. Offers academic track (MA); architecture (PhD); architecture, design, and planning (M Arch, MA, MFA, MUP, PhD, Certificate); design (MA, MFA); design management (MA); facility management (Certificate); interaction design (MA); management track (MA); professional track (M Arch); urban planning (MUP). *Application deadline:* For fall admission, 3/1 priority date for domestic students, 2/1 priority date for international students; for spring admission, 11/1 priority date for domestic and international students. *Application fee:* $55 ($65 for international students). Electronic applications accepted. *Application Contact:* Gera Elliott, Admissions Coordinator, 785-864-3167, Fax: 785-864-5185, E-mail: archku@ku.edu. *Dean*, John C. Gaunt, 785-864-4281, E-mail: jgaunt@ku.edu.

School of Business Students: 406 full-time (137 women), 239 part-time (79 women); includes 89 minority (23 Black or African American, non-Hispanic/Latino; 3 American Indian or Alaska Native, non-Hispanic/Latino; 38 Asian, non-Hispanic/Latino; 20 Hispanic/Latino; 5 Two or more races, non-Hispanic/Latino), 80 international. Average age 29. 590 applicants, 53% accepted, 246 enrolled. Expenses: Contact institution. *Financial support:* Fellowships, research assistantships with full and partial tuition reimbursements, teaching assistantships with full and partial tuition reimbursements, career-related internships or fieldwork, Federal Work-Study, and unspecified assistantships available. Financial award application deadline: 6/1; financial award applicants required to submit FAFSA. In 2010, 254 master's, 2 doctorates awarded. *Degree program information:* Part-time and evening/weekend programs available. Offers accounting (M Acc); business (M Acc, MBA, PhD); finance (MBA); human resources management (MBA); information systems (MBA); international business (MBA); management (MBA); marketing (MBA); strategic management (MBA). *Application deadline:* Applications are processed on a rolling basis. *Application fee:* $60. Electronic applications accepted. *Application Contact:* Dee Steinle, Administrative Director of Master's Programs, 785-864-3795, Fax: 785-864-5328, E-mail: bschoolgrad@ku.edu. *Dean*, Dr. Neeli Bendapudi, 785-864-3795, E-mail: bschoolgrad@ku.edu.

School of Education Students: 762 full-time (552 women), 345 part-time (253 women); includes 137 minority (29 Black or African American, non-Hispanic/Latino; 10 American Indian or Alaska Native, non-Hispanic/Latino; 36 Asian, non-Hispanic/Latino; 43 Hispanic/Latino; 19 Two or more races, non-Hispanic/Latino), 122 international. Average age 32. 746 applicants, 66% accepted, 347 enrolled. Expenses: Contact institution. *Financial support:* Fellowships, research assistantships with partial tuition reimbursements, teaching assistantships with full and partial tuition reimbursements, career-related internships or fieldwork, scholarships/grants, and unspecified assistantships available. Financial award application deadline: 2/1. In 2010, 273 master's, 71 doctorates, 6 other advanced degrees awarded. *Degree program information:* Part-time programs available. Offers counseling psychology (MS, PhD); curriculum and instruction (MA, MS Ed, Ed D, PhD); education (MA, MS, MS Ed, Ed D, PhD, Ed S); educational administration (MS Ed); educational policy and leadership (Ed D, PhD); educational psychology and research (MS Ed, PhD); foundations (PhD); foundations of education (MS Ed); health and physical education (MS Ed, Ed D, PhD); higher education (MS Ed, Ed D, PhD); higher education administration (MS Ed); historical, philosophical, and social foundations of education (MS Ed); policy studies (PhD); school psychology (PhD, Ed S); special education (MS Ed, Ed D, PhD). *Application fee:* $55 ($65 for international students). Electronic applications accepted. *Application Contact:* Mary Ann Williams, Graduate Admissions Coordinator, 785-864-4510, E-mail: mwilliams@ku.edu. *Dean*, Dr. Rick Ginsberg, 785-864-4297.

School of Engineering Students: 342 full-time (100 women), 298 part-time (53 women); includes 67 minority (13 Black or African American, non-Hispanic/Latino; 5 American Indian or Alaska Native, non-Hispanic/Latino; 27 Asian, non-Hispanic/Latino; 17 Hispanic/Latino; 1 Native Hawaiian or other Pacific Islander, non-Hispanic/Latino; 4 Two or more races, non-Hispanic/Latino), 215 international. Average age 29. 705 applicants, 39% accepted, 112 enrolled. Expenses: Contact institution. *Financial support:* Fellowships, research assistantships with full and partial tuition reimbursements, teaching assistantships with full and partial tuition reimbursements, career-related internships or fieldwork, Federal Work-Study, scholarships/grants, and unspecified assistantships available. In 2010, 134 master's, 22 doctorates awarded. *Degree program information:* Part-time and evening/weekend programs available. Postbaccalaureate distance learning degree programs offered (no on-campus study). Offers aerospace engineering (ME, MS, DE, PhD); architectural engineering (MS); bioengineering (MS, PhD); chemical engineering (MS); chemical/petroleum engineering (PhD); civil engineering (MCE, MS, DE, PhD); computer engineering (MS); computer science (MS, PhD); construction management (MCM); electrical engineering (MS, DE, PhD); engineering (MCE, MCM, ME, MS, DE, PhD); engineering management (MS); environmental engineering (MS, PhD); environmental science (MS, PhD); information technology (MS); mechanical engineering (MS, DE, PhD); petroleum engineering (MS). *Application deadline:* Applications are processed on a rolling basis. *Application fee:* $55 ($65 for international students). Electronic applications accepted. *Application Contact:* Dr. Glen Marotz, Associate Dean, 785-864-2980, Fax: 785-864-5445, E-mail: gama@ku.edu. *Dean*, Dr. Stuart R. Bell, 785-864-3881, E-mail: kuengr@ku.edu.

School of Journalism and Mass Communications Students: 28 full-time (15 women), 56 part-time (35 women); includes 7 minority (3 Black or African American, non-Hispanic/Latino; 2 Asian, non-Hispanic/Latino; 1 Hispanic/Latino; 1 Two or more races, non-Hispanic/Latino), 7 international. Average age 30. 59 applicants, 69% accepted, 21 enrolled. *Faculty:* 25 full-time (9 women), 7 part-time/adjunct (4 women). Expenses: Contact institution. *Financial support:* Fellowships, research assistantships, teaching assistantships with full and partial tuition reimbursements, career-related internships or fieldwork, scholarships/grants, and unspecified assistantships available. Support available to part-time students. Financial award application deadline: 2/1; financial award applicants required to submit FAFSA. In 2010, 28 master's awarded. *Degree program information:* Part-time programs available. Offers journalism (MS). *Application deadline:* For fall admission, 2/1 priority date for domestic and international students; for spring admission, 11/1 priority date for domestic and international students. *Application fee:* $55 ($65 for international students). Electronic applications accepted. *Application Contact:* Cindy Nesvarba, Graduate Records Coordinator, 785-864-7649, Fax: 785-864-5318, E-mail: cnesvarb@ku.edu. *Dean*, Ann Brill, 785-864-4755, Fax: 785-864-4396, E-mail: abrill@ku.edu.

School of Music Students: 152 full-time (83 women), 55 part-time (36 women); includes 26 minority (4 Black or African American, non-Hispanic/Latino; 6 Asian, non-Hispanic/Latino; 11 Hispanic/Latino; 5 Two or more races, non-Hispanic/Latino), 36 international. Average age 30. 225 applicants, 56% accepted, 66 enrolled. Expenses: Contact institution. *Financial support:* Fellowships with full tuition reimbursements, research assistantships with full and partial tuition reimbursements, teaching assistantships with full and partial tuition reimbursements, scholarships/grants and unspecified assistantships available. In 2010, 37 master's, 22 doctorates awarded. Offers music (MM, MME, DMA, PhD); music education (MME, PhD); music therapy (MME). *Application fee:* $55 ($65 for international students). Electronic applications accepted. *Application Contact:* Dr. Robert Walzel, Dean, 785-864-3436, E-mail: music@ku.edu. *Dean*, Dr. Robert Walzel, 785-864-3436, E-mail: music@ku.edu.

School of Pharmacy Students: 95 full-time (52 women), 28 part-time (19 women); includes 11 minority (1 Black or African American, non-Hispanic/Latino; 7 Asian, non-Hispanic/Latino; 2 Hispanic/Latino; 1 Two or more races, non-Hispanic/Latino), 48 international. Average age 28. 239 applicants, 17% accepted, 24 enrolled. Expenses: Contact institution. *Financial support:* Fellowships with full tuition reimbursements, research assistantships with full and partial tuition reimbursements, teaching assistantships with full and partial tuition reimbursements, career-related internships or fieldwork, scholarships/grants, traineeships, and unspecified assistantships available. In 2010, 33 master's, 20 doctorates awarded. Offers medicinal chemistry (MS, PhD); neurosciences (MS, PhD); pharmaceutical chemistry (MS, PhD); pharmacology and toxicology (MS, PhD); pharmacy (MS, PhD); pharmacy practice (MS). *Application fee:* $55 ($65 for international students). Electronic applications accepted. *Application Contact:* Kenneth L. Audus, Dean, 785-864-3591, E-mail: pharmacy@ku.edu. *Dean*, Kenneth L. Audus, 785-864-3591, E-mail: pharmacy@ku.edu.

School of Social Welfare Students: 292 full-time (247 women), 77 part-time (69 women); includes 69 minority (30 Black or African American, non-Hispanic/Latino; 5 American Indian or Alaska Native, non-Hispanic/Latino; 5 Asian, non-Hispanic/Latino; 24 Hispanic/Latino; 5 Two or more races, non-Hispanic/Latino), 9 international. Average age 32. 345 applicants, 79% accepted, 191 enrolled. *Faculty:* 10 full-time (6 women), 28 part-time/adjunct (17 women). Expenses: Contact institution. *Financial support:* Fellowships, research assistantships with full and partial tuition reimbursements, teaching assistantships with full and partial tuition reimbursements, Federal Work-Study, scholarships/grants, and tuition waivers (partial) available. Support available to part-time students. Financial award applicants required to submit FAFSA. In 2010, 144 master's, 6 doctorates awarded. *Degree program information:* Part-time programs available. Postbaccalaureate distance learning degree programs offered (minimal on-campus study). Offers social welfare (MSW); social work (PhD). *Application deadline:* For fall admission, 2/1 for domestic and international students. *Application fee:* $45 ($55 for international students). Electronic applications accepted. *Application Contact:* Becky Hofer, Director of Admissions, 785-864-8956, Fax: 785-864-5277, E-mail: bhofer@ku.edu. *Dean*, Mary Ellen Kondrat, 785-864-4720, Fax: 785-864-5277.

School of Law Students: 497 full-time (195 women), 24 part-time (6 women); includes 92 minority (12 Black or African American, non-Hispanic/Latino; 12 American Indian or Alaska Native, non-Hispanic/Latino; 24 Asian, non-Hispanic/Latino; 27 Hispanic/Latino; 17 Two or more races, non-Hispanic/Latino), 20 international. Average age 25. 1,121 applicants, 37% accepted, 165 enrolled. *Faculty:* 41 full-time (17 women), 20 part-time/adjunct (7 women). Expenses: Contact institution. *Financial support:* In 2010–11, 252 students received support, including 7 fellowships (averaging $3,000 per year), 53 research assistantships, 18 teaching assistantships (averaging $3,600 per year); career-related internships or fieldwork, Federal Work-Study, institutionally sponsored loans, and scholarships/grants also available. Financial award application deadline: 3/1; financial award applicants required to submit FAFSA. In 2010, 173 first professional degrees awarded. Offers law (JD). *Application deadline:* For fall admission, 3/15 for domestic and international students. Applications are processed on a rolling basis. *Application fee:* $55. Electronic applications accepted. *Application Contact:* Wendy Rohleder-Sook, Associate Dean for Student Affairs, 866-220-3654, E-mail: admitlaw@ku.edu. *Dean*, Stephen W. Mazza, 785-864-4550, Fax: 785-864-5054.

University of Kansas Medical Center Students: 1,328 full-time (776 women), 482 part-time (410 women); includes 286 minority (79 Black or African American, non-Hispanic/Latino; 15 American Indian or Alaska Native, non-Hispanic/Latino; 107 Asian, non-Hispanic/Latino; 62 Hispanic/Latino; 23 Two or more races, non-Hispanic/Latino), 97 international. Average age 29. 3,476 applicants, 18% accepted, 503 enrolled. *Faculty:* 1,073. Expenses: Contact institution. In 2010, 227 first professional degrees, 205 master's, 17 doctorates, 33 other advanced degrees awarded. Offers health informatics (MS). *Application Contact:* Dr. Barbara Atkinson, Executive Vice Chancellor, 913-588-1440, E-mail: batkinson@kumc.edu. *Executive Vice Chancellor*, Dr. Barbara Atkinson, 913-588-1440, E-mail: batkinson@kumc.edu.

School of Allied Health Students: 321 full-time (249 women), 85 part-time (71 women); includes 10 Black or African American, non-Hispanic/Latino; 5 American Indian or Alaska Native, non-Hispanic/Latino; 14 Asian, non-Hispanic/Latino; 6 Hispanic/Latino; 4 Two or more races, non-Hispanic/Latino, 23 international. Average age 29. 475 applicants, 38% accepted, 147 enrolled. *Faculty:* 183. Expenses: Contact institution. In 2010, 76 master's, 1 doctorate, 16 other advanced degrees awarded. Offers allied health (MA, MOT, MS, Au D, DPT, OTD, PhD, Certificate); audiology (MA, Au D); dietetic internship (Certificate); dietetics and nutrition (MS); medical nutrition science (PhD); molecular biotechnology (MS); nurse anesthesia (MS); occupational therapy (MOT, MS, OTD); physical therapy (DPT); rehabilitation science (PhD); therapeutic science (PhD). *Application Contact:* Moffett Ferguson, Student Affairs Coordinator, 913-588-5275, Fax: 913-588-5254, E-mail: mfergus1@kumc.edu. *Dean*, Dr. Karen L. Miller, 913-588-5235, Fax: 913-588-5254, E-mail: kmiller@kumc.edu.

School of Medicine Students: 950 full-time (474 women), 85 part-time (54 women); includes 196 minority (46 Black or African American, non-Hispanic/Latino; 7 American Indian or Alaska Native, non-Hispanic/Latino; 83 Asian, non-Hispanic/Latino; 45 Hispanic/Latino; 15 Two or more races, non-Hispanic/Latino), 68 international. Average age 27. 2,851 applicants, 13% accepted, 289 enrolled. *Faculty:* 813. Expenses: Contact institution. In 2010, 169 first professional degrees, 51 master's, 9 doctorates awarded. Offers anatomy and cell biology (MA, PhD); biochemistry and molecular biology (MS, PhD); biomedical sciences (MA, MPH, MS, PhD); biostatistics (MS, PhD); clinical research (MS); epidemiology (MPH); generalist (MPH); health policy and management (PhD); health services administration (MHSA); medicine (MD, MA, MHSA, MPH, MS, PhD); microbiology (PhD); molecular and integrative physiology (MS, PhD); neuroscience (MS, PhD); pathology and laboratory medicine (MA, PhD); pharmacology (MS, PhD); social and behavioral health (MPH); toxicology (MS, PhD). *Application Contact:* Dr. Barbara Atkinson, Executive Dean, 913-588-1440, E-mail: batkinson@kumc.edu. *Executive Dean*, Dr. Barbara Atkinson, 913-588-1440, E-mail: batkinson@kumc.edu.

School of Nursing Students: 54 full-time (51 women), 307 part-time (283 women); includes 49 minority (22 Black or African American, non-Hispanic/Latino; 3 American Indian or Alaska Native, non-Hispanic/Latino; 9 Asian, non-Hispanic/Latino; 11 Hispanic/Latino; 4 Two or more races, non-Hispanic/Latino), 6 international. Average age 38. 142 applicants, 45% accepted, 62 enrolled. *Faculty:* 77. Expenses: Contact institution. *Financial support:* Research assistantships with full and partial tuition reimbursements, teaching assistantships with full and partial tuition reimbursements, traineeships available. Financial award application deadline: 2/14; financial award applicants required to submit FAFSA. In 2010, 78 master's, 7 doctorates, 17 other advanced degrees awarded. *Degree program information:* Part-time programs available. Postbaccalaureate distance learning degree programs offered (minimal on-campus study). Offers clinical research management (PMC); family nurse practitioner (PMC); health care informatics (PMC); health professions educator (PMC); nurse midwife (PMC); nursing (MS, DNP, PhD); organizational leadership (PMC); psychiatric/mental health nurse practitioner (PMC); public health nursing (PMC). *Application deadline:* For fall admission, 4/1 for domestic and international students; for spring admission, 9/1 for domestic and international students. *Application fee:* $60. Electronic applications accepted. *Application Contact:* Dr. Rita K. Clifford, Associate Dean, Student Affairs, 913-588-1619, Fax: 913-588-1615, E-mail: rcliffor@kumc.edu. *Dean*, Dr. Karen L. Miller, 913-588-1601, Fax: 913-588-1660, E-mail: kmiller@kumc.edu.

UNIVERSITY OF KENTUCKY, Lexington, KY 40506-0032

General Information State-supported, coed, university. CGS member. *Graduate housing:* Rooms and/or apartments available to single and married students. *Research affiliation:* Battelle Pacific Northwest Laboratories (environmental sciences), Continuous Electron Beam Accelerator Facility (high-energy physics), Oak Ridge National Laboratory (nuclear physics), National Institute of Occupational Health and Safety (environmental health), National Drug Addiction Center (drug abuse and prevention).

GRADUATE UNITS

College of Dentistry Students: 229 full-time (110 women); includes 20 Black or African American, non-Hispanic/Latino; 18 Asian, non-Hispanic/Latino; 5 Hispanic/Latino, 1 international.

Average age 28. 1,464 applicants, 6% accepted, 57 enrolled. Expenses: Contact institution. *Financial support:* In 2010–11, 65 students received support; fellowships, research assistantships, teaching assistantships, career-related internships or fieldwork, Federal Work-Study, institutionally sponsored loans, and scholarships/grants available. Support available to part-time students. Financial award application deadline: 4/15; financial award applicants required to submit FAFSA. In 2010, 51 DMDs awarded. Offers dentistry (DMD). *Application deadline:* For fall admission, 12/1 priority date for domestic students. Applications are processed on a rolling basis. *Application fee:* $65. Electronic applications accepted. *Application Contact:* Christine S. Harper, Director of Student Affairs, 859-323-6071, Fax: 859-257-5550, E-mail: christine.harper@uky.edu. *Dean,* Dr. Sharon P. Turner, 859-323-1884, Fax: 859-323-1042.

College of Law Offers law (JD). Electronic applications accepted.

College of Medicine Students: 452 full-time (185 women); includes 24 Black or African American, non-Hispanic/Latino; 29 Asian, non-Hispanic/Latino; 4 Hispanic/Latino, 12 international. Average age 23. 2,154 applicants, 113 enrolled. *Faculty:* 614 full-time (178 women), 283 part-time/adjunct (56 women). Expenses: Contact institution. *Financial support:* Institutionally sponsored loans available. Financial award applicants required to submit FAFSA. Offers medicine (MD). *Application deadline:* For fall admission, 11/1 for domestic students. Applications are processed on a rolling basis. *Application fee:* $50. Electronic applications accepted. *Application Contact:* Kimberly Scott, Assistant Director of Admissions, 859-323-6161, Fax: 859-323-2076, E-mail: kstahlma@email.uky.edu. *Associate Dean for Admissions,* Dr. Carol L. Elam, 859-323-6161.

College of Pharmacy Offers pharmacy (Pharm D).

Graduate School *Degree program information:* Part-time and evening/weekend programs available. Offers biomedical engineering (MSBE, PBME, PhD); dentistry (MS); health administration (MHA); nutritional sciences (MSNS, PhD); pharmaceutical sciences (MS, PhD); public administration (MPA, MPP, PhD). Electronic applications accepted.

College of Agriculture *Degree program information:* Part-time programs available. Offers agricultural economics (MS, PhD); agriculture (MS, MSFAM, MSFOR, PhD); animal sciences (MS, PhD); biosystems and agricultural engineering (MS, PhD); career, technology and leadership education (MS); crop science (MS, PhD); entomology (MS, PhD); family studies, human development, and resource management (MSFAM, PhD); forestry (MSFOR); hospitality and dietetic administration (MS); plant and soil science (MS); plant pathology (MS, PhD); plant physiology (PhD); soil science (PhD); veterinary science (MS, PhD). Electronic applications accepted.

College of Arts and Sciences *Degree program information:* Part-time programs available. Offers anthropology (MA, PhD); applied mathematics (MS); arts and sciences (MA, MS, PhD); biology (MS, PhD); chemistry (MS, PhD); classics (MA); clinical psychology (MA); English (MA, PhD); experimental psychology (MA); French (MA); geography (MA, PhD); geology (MS, PhD); German (MA); Hispanic studies (MA, PhD); history (MA, PhD); mathematics (MA, MS, PhD); philosophy (MA, PhD); physics (MS, PhD); political science (MA, PhD); sociology (MA, PhD); statistics (MS, PhD); teaching world languages (MA). Electronic applications accepted.

College of Communications and Information Studies *Degree program information:* Part-time programs available. Offers communication (MA, PhD); communications and information studies (MA, MSLS, PhD); library science (MA, MSLS). Electronic applications accepted.

College of Design Offers architecture (M Arch); design (M Arch, MAIDM, MHP, MSIDM); historic preservation (MHP); interior design, merchandising, and textiles (MAIDM, MSIDM). Electronic applications accepted.

College of Education *Degree program information:* Part-time and evening/weekend programs available. Offers administration and supervision (Ed S); counseling psychology (MS Ed, PhD, Ed S); curriculum and instruction (MA Ed, Ed D); early childhood special education (MS Ed); education (M Ed, MA Ed, MRC, MS, MS Ed, Ed D, PhD, Ed S); educational and counseling psychology (MS Ed); educational policy studies and evaluation (Ed D); educational psychology (Ed D, PhD, Ed S); exercise science (PhD); higher education (MS Ed, PhD); instruction and administration (Ed D); instruction system design (MS Ed); kinesiology (MS, Ed D); middle school education (MS Ed); rehabilitation counseling (MRC); school administration (M Ed); school psychometrist and school psychology (MA Ed); special education (MS Ed); special education leadership personnel preparation (Ed D). Electronic applications accepted.

College of Engineering *Degree program information:* Part-time programs available. Offers chemical engineering (MS, PhD); civil engineering (MCE, MSCE, PhD); computer science (MS, PhD); electrical engineering (MSEE, PhD); engineering (M Eng, MCE, MME, MS, MS Ch E, MS Min, MSCE, MSEE, MSEM, MSMAE, MSME, MSMSE, PhD); manufacturing systems engineering (MSMSE); materials science and engineering (MSMAE, PhD); mechanical engineering (MSME, PhD); mining engineering (MME, MS Min, PhD). Electronic applications accepted.

College of Fine Arts *Degree program information:* Part-time and evening/weekend programs available. Offers art education (MA); art history (MA); art studio (MFA); fine arts (MA, MFA, MM, DMA, PhD); music (PhD); music composition (MM); music education (MM); music performance (MM); music theory (MA); musical arts (DMA); musicology (MA); theatre (MA). Electronic applications accepted.

College of Health Sciences *Degree program information:* Part-time programs available. Offers clinical sciences (MS, DS); communication disorders (MSCD); health physics (MSHP); health sciences (MS, MSCD, MSHP, MSPAS, MSPT, MSRMP, DS, PhD); physical therapy (MSPT); physician assistant studies (MSPAS); radiological medical physics (MSRMP); rehabilitation sciences (PhD). Electronic applications accepted.

College of Public Health Offers gerontology (PhD); public health (MPH, PhD). Electronic applications accepted.

College of Social Work Offers social work (MSW, PhD). Electronic applications accepted.

Gatton College of Business and Economics *Degree program information:* Part-time and evening/weekend programs available. Offers accounting (MSACC); business administration (MBA, PhD); business and economics (MBA, MS, MSACC, PhD); economics (MS, PhD). Electronic applications accepted.

Graduate School Programs from the College of Medicine Offers anatomy (PhD); biochemistry (PhD); medical science (MS); medicine (MS, PhD); microbiology (PhD); pharmacology (PhD); physiology (MS, PhD); toxicology (MS, PhD). Electronic applications accepted.

Graduate School Programs in the College of Nursing Offers nursing (MSN, PhD). Electronic applications accepted.

Patterson School of Diplomacy and International Commerce Offers diplomacy and international commerce (MA). Electronic applications accepted.

UNIVERSITY OF LA VERNE, La Verne, CA 91750-4443

General Information Independent, coed, university. *Enrollment:* 4,468 graduate, professional, and undergraduate students; 1,862 full-time matriculated graduate/professional students (1,105 women), 1,895 part-time matriculated graduate/professional students (1,277 women). *Enrollment by degree level:* 425 first professional, 2,547 master's, 431 doctoral, 354 other advanced degrees. *Graduate faculty:* 119 full-time (65 women), 272 part-time/adjunct (142 women). *Tuition:* Part-time $620 per credit hour. Tuition and fees vary according to degree level and program. *Graduate housing:* Room and/or apartments available on a first-come, first-served basis to single students; on-campus housing not available to married students. Housing application deadline: 5/1. *Student services:* Campus employment opportunities, campus safety program, career counseling, exercise/wellness program, free psychological counseling, international student services, low-cost health insurance, multicultural affairs office, services for students with disabilities, teacher training, writing training. *Library facilities:* Wilson Library. *Online resources:* library catalog, web page, access to other libraries' catalogs. *Collection:* 196,842 titles, 28,178 serial subscriptions, 2,721 audiovisual materials. *Research affiliation:* Huntington Memorial Hospital (health services management), Southern California Healthcare Systems, Methodist Hospital of Southern California, San Antonio Community Hospital, Riverside Community Hospital, Presbyterian Intercommunity Hospital.

Computer facilities: 250 computers available on campus for general student use. A campuswide network can be accessed from student residence rooms and from off campus. Online class registration, MyULV (online) are available. *Web address:* http://www.laverne.edu/.

General Application Contact: Office of Admission, 909-593-3511 Ext. 4244, Fax: 909-392-2761, E-mail: gradadmission@laverne.edu.

GRADUATE UNITS

College of Arts and Sciences Students: 101 full-time (89 women), 78 part-time (63 women); includes 27 Black or African American, non-Hispanic/Latino; 14 Asian, non-Hispanic/Latino; 61 Hispanic/Latino. Average age 29. *Faculty:* 13 full-time (6 women), 25 part-time/adjunct (16 women). Expenses: Contact institution. *Financial support:* Career-related internships or fieldwork, institutionally sponsored loans, and scholarships/grants available. Financial award application deadline: 3/2; financial award applicants required to submit FAFSA. In 2010, 36 master's, 15 doctorates awarded. *Degree program information:* Part-time programs available. Offers arts and sciences (MS, Psy D); clinical-community psychology (Psy D); counseling (MS); marriage and family therapy (MS). *Application deadline:* Applications are processed on a rolling basis. *Application Contact:* Connie Hamlow, Admissions Information Specialist, 909-593-3511 Ext. 4244, Fax: 909-392-2761, E-mail: gradadmission@laverne.edu. *Interim Dean,* Dr. Jonathan Reed, 909-593-3511 Ext. 4366, E-mail: jreed@laverne.edu.

College of Business and Public Management Students: 684 full-time (364 women), 400 part-time (224 women); includes 686 minority (93 Black or African American, non-Hispanic/Latino; 5 American Indian or Alaska Native, non-Hispanic/Latino; 358 Asian, non-Hispanic/Latino; 230 Hispanic/Latino), 13 international. Average age 32. *Faculty:* 34 full-time (12 women), 36 part-time/adjunct (9 women). Expenses: Contact institution. *Financial support:* Career-related internships or fieldwork, institutionally sponsored loans, and scholarships/grants available. Financial award application deadline: 3/2; financial award applicants required to submit FAFSA. In 2010, 348 master's, 6 doctorates awarded. *Degree program information:* Part-time and evening/weekend programs available. Offers accounting (MBA); business and public management (MBA, MBA-EP, MHA, MPA, MS, DPA, Certificate); executive management (MBA-EP); finance (MBA, MBA-EP); financial management (MHA); gerontology (Certificate); gerontology administration (MS); health administration (MHA); health services management (MBA); human resources (MHA); information management (MHA); information technology (MBA, MBA-EP); international business (MBA, MBA-EP); leadership (MBA-EP); leadership and management (MHA); managed care (MBA, MHA); management (MBA, MBA-EP); marketing (MBA, MBA-EP); marketing and business development (MHA); nonprofit management (Certificate); organizational leadership (Certificate); organizational management and leadership (MS); public administration (MPA, DPA). *Application deadline:* Applications are processed on a rolling basis. *Application fee:* $50. *Application Contact:* Program and Admission Specialist, 909-593-3511 Ext. 4004, Fax: 909-392-2704, E-mail: cbpm@laverne.edu. *Dean,* Dr. Abe Helou, 909-539-3511 Ext. 4211, Fax: 909-392-2704, E-mail: ihelou@laverne.edu.

College of Education and Organizational Leadership Students: 281 full-time (208 women), 598 part-time (466 women); includes 71 Black or African American, non-Hispanic/Latino; 10 American Indian or Alaska Native, non-Hispanic/Latino; 37 Asian, non-Hispanic/Latino; 254 Hispanic/Latino, 1 international. Average age 35. *Faculty:* 31 full-time (22 women), 39 part-time/adjunct (30 women). Expenses: Contact institution. *Financial support:* Institutionally sponsored loans, scholarships/grants, and unspecified assistantships available. Financial award application deadline: 3/2; financial award applicants required to submit FAFSA. In 2010, 179 master's, 55 doctorates awarded. *Degree program information:* Part-time programs available. Offers advanced teaching skills (M Ed); child development (MS); child life (MS); education (special emphasis) (M Ed); education and organizational leadership (M Ed, MS, Ed D, Certificate, Credential); educational management (M Ed); multiple subject (Credential); organizational leadership (Ed D); preliminary administrative services (Credential); professional administrative services (Credential); pupil personnel services (Credential); reading (M Ed, Certificate); reading and language arts specialist (Credential); school counseling (MS); single subject (Credential). *Application deadline:* Applications are processed on a rolling basis. *Application fee:* $50. *Application Contact:* Christy Ranells, Admissions Information Specialist, 909-593-3511 Ext. 4644, Fax: 909-392-2761, E-mail: cranells@laverne.edu. *Dean,* Dr. Mark Goor, 909-593-3511 Ext. 4647, E-mail: mgoor@laverne.edu.

College of Law Students: 311 full-time (141 women), 114 part-time (51 women); includes 12 Black or African American, non-Hispanic/Latino; 6 American Indian or Alaska Native, non-Hispanic/Latino; 55 Asian, non-Hispanic/Latino; 69 Hispanic/Latino, 9 international. Average age 26. 1,462 applicants, 42% accepted, 150 enrolled. *Faculty:* 22 full-time (10 women), 25 part-time/adjunct (11 women). Expenses: Contact institution. *Financial support:* In 2010–11, 389 students received support. Federal Work-Study, scholarships/grants, and health care benefits available. Support available to part-time students. Financial award application deadline: 3/2; financial award applicants required to submit FAFSA. In 2010, 96 JDs awarded. *Degree program information:* Part-time and evening/weekend programs available. Offers law (JD). *Application deadline:* For fall admission, 7/1 priority date for domestic students; for spring admission, 11/1 priority date for domestic students. Applications are processed on a rolling basis. *Application fee:* $50. Electronic applications accepted. *Application Contact:* Alexis Thompson, Assistant Dean of Admissions and External Relations, 909-460-2001, Fax: 909-460-2082, E-mail: lawadm@laverne.edu. *Dean,* Allen K. Easley, 909-460-2000, Fax: 909-460-2081, E-mail: lawadm@laverne.edu.

Regional Campus Administration Students: 376 full-time (243 women), 656 part-time (422 women); includes 528 minority (123 Black or African American, non-Hispanic/Latino; 10 American Indian or Alaska Native, non-Hispanic/Latino; 105 Asian, non-Hispanic/Latino; 290 Hispanic/Latino). Average age 36. *Faculty:* 31 full-time (15 women), 191 part-time/adjunct (92 women). Expenses: Contact institution. *Financial support:* Institutionally sponsored loans available. Support available to part-time students. Financial award application deadline: 3/2; financial award applicants required to submit FAFSA. In 2010, 415 master's awarded. *Degree program information:* Part-time programs available. Offers business (MBA, MBA-EP); business administration (MBA); cross cultural language and academic development (Credential); educational management (M Ed); health administration (MHA); leadership and management (MS); multiple or single subject teaching credential (M Ed); multiple subject (Credential); school counseling (MS); single subject (Credential). *Application deadline:* Applications are processed on a rolling basis. *Application fee:* $50. *Application Contact:* Patti Noreen, 909-392-2718, Fax: 909-392-2761, E-mail: pnoreen@laverne.edu. *Dean,* Dr. Stephen E. Lesniak, 909-593-3511 Ext. 5300, E-mail: slesniak@laverne.edu.

UNIVERSITY OF LETHBRIDGE, Lethbridge, AB T1K 3M4, Canada

General Information Province-supported, coed, university. CGS member. *Graduate housing:* Rooms and/or apartments available on a first-come, first-served basis to single and married students. Housing application deadline: 4/1. *Research affiliation:* Monsanto Dow Agro-Sciences, Pacific Forestry Institution.

GRADUATE UNITS

School of Graduate Studies *Degree program information:* Part-time and evening/weekend programs available. Offers accounting (MScM); addictions counseling (M Sc); agricultural biotechnology (M Sc); agricultural studies (M Sc, MA); anthropology (MA); archaeology (MA); art (MA, MFA); biochemistry (M Sc); biological sciences (M Sc); biomolecular science (PhD); biosystems and biodiversity (PhD); Canadian studies (MA); chemistry (M Sc); computer science (M Sc); computer science and geographical information science (M Sc); counseling psychology (M Ed); dramatic arts (MA); earth, space, and physical science (PhD); economics (MA); educational leadership (M Ed); English (MA); environmental science (M Sc); evolution and behavior (PhD); exercise science (M Sc); finance (MScM); French (MA); French/German (MA); French/Spanish (MA); general education (M Ed); general management (MScM); geography (M Sc, MA); German (MA); health science (M Sc); history (MA); human resource management and labour relations (MScM); individualized multidisciplinary (M Sc, MA); information systems (MScM); international management (MScM); kinesiology (M Sc, MA); management (M Sc, MA); marketing (MScM); mathematics (M Sc); music (M Mus, MA); Native American studies (MA); neuroscience (M Sc, PhD); new media (MA); nursing (M Sc); philosophy

University of Lethbridge (continued)

(MA); physics (M Sc); policy and strategy (MScM); political science (MA); psychology (M Sc, MA); religious studies (MA); social sciences (MA); sociology (MA); theatre and dramatic arts (MFA); theoretical and computational science (PhD); urban and regional studies (MA); women's studies (MA).

UNIVERSITY OF LOUISIANA AT LAFAYETTE, Lafayette, LA 70504

General Information State-supported, coed, university. CGS member. *Graduate housing:* Rooms and/or apartments available on a first-come, first-served basis to single and married students. *Research affiliation:* National Wetlands Research Center (biology, wetlands restoration), Louisiana Universities Marine Consortium (marine biology), U. S. Fish and Wildlife Service (ecology), Army Corps of Engineers (wetlands), U. S. Geological Survey (USGS), U. S. Department of Agriculture (USDA).

GRADUATE UNITS

BI Moody III College of Business Administration MBA Program *Degree program information:* Part-time and evening/weekend programs available. Offers business administration (MBA).

College of Education *Degree program information:* Part-time programs available. Offers education (M Ed, Ed D). Electronic applications accepted.

Graduate Studies and Research in Education Offers administration and supervision (M Ed); curriculum and instruction (M Ed); education of the gifted (M Ed); educational leadership (M Ed, Ed D).

College of Engineering *Degree program information:* Part-time and evening/weekend programs available. Offers chemical engineering (MSE); civil engineering (MSE); computer engineering (MS, PhD); engineering (MS, MSE, MSET, MSTC, PhD); engineering and technology management (MSET); mechanical engineering (MSE); petroleum engineering (MSE); telecommunications (MSTC). Electronic applications accepted.

Center for Advanced Computer Studies *Degree program information:* Part-time programs available. Offers computer engineering (MS, PhD); computer science (MS, PhD). Electronic applications accepted.

College of Liberal Arts *Degree program information:* Part-time programs available. Offers British and American literature (MA); communicative disorders (MS, PhD); creative writing (PhD); Francophone studies (PhD); French (MA); history (MA); liberal arts (MA, MS, PhD); literature (PhD); mass communications (MS); psychology (MS); rehabilitation counseling (MS); rhetoric (PhD). Electronic applications accepted.

College of Nursing Offers nursing (MSN). Program offered jointly with Southern Louisiana University, McNeese State University, Southern University and Agricultural and Mechanical College. Electronic applications accepted.

College of Sciences *Degree program information:* Part-time programs available. Offers biology (MS); environmental and evolutionary biology (PhD); geology (MS); mathematics (MS, PhD); physics (MS); sciences (MS, PhD). Electronic applications accepted.

Institute of Cognitive Science Offers cognitive science (PhD). Electronic applications accepted.

College of the Arts Offers arts (M Arch, MM). Electronic applications accepted.

School of Architecture Offers architecture (M Arch). Electronic applications accepted.

School of Music Offers conducting (MM); pedagogy (MM); vocal and instrumental performance (MM). Electronic applications accepted.

Department of Counselor Education Offers counselor education (MS). Electronic applications accepted.

UNIVERSITY OF LOUISIANA AT MONROE, Monroe, LA 71209-0001

General Information State-supported, coed, university. *Enrollment:* 8,801 graduate, professional, and undergraduate students; 690 full-time matriculated graduate/professional students (438 women), 598 part-time matriculated graduate/professional students (420 women). *Enrollment by degree level:* 315 first professional, 614 master's, 93 doctoral, 266 other advanced degrees. *Graduate faculty:* 125 full-time (54 women), 34 part-time/adjunct (11 women). *International tuition:* $10,288 full-time. Tuition, state resident: full-time $2991; part-time $197 per credit hour. Tuition, nonresident: full-time $2991; part-time $197 per credit hour. *Graduate housing:* Room and/or apartments available on a first-come, first-served basis to single students; on-campus housing not available to married students. Typical cost: $3574 per year ($5984 including board). Housing application deadline: 7/1. *Student services:* Campus employment opportunities, career counseling, child daycare facilities, exercise/wellness program, free psychological counseling, international student services. *Library facilities:* University Library. *Online resources:* library catalog, access to other libraries' catalogs. *Collection:* 629,606 titles, 95 serial subscriptions, 61 audiovisual materials. *Research affiliation:* Juvenile Diabetes Research Foundation (pharmacology), Philip Morris, Inc. (medicinal chemistry), Harvard Hughes Medical Institute (biology), Xenoport, Inc. (pharmaceutics), U. S. Army Corps of Engineers (toxicology, environmental science), National Center for Toxicological Research (toxicology).

Computer facilities: Computer purchase and lease plans are available. A campuswide network can be accessed from student residence rooms and from off campus. Online class registration is available. *Web address:* http://www.ulm.edu/.

General Application Contact: Dr. William McCown, Interim Graduate Studies and Research Director, 318-342-1036, Fax: 318-342-1042, E-mail: mccown@ulm.edu.

GRADUATE UNITS

Graduate School Students: 11 full-time (6 women), 193 part-time (141 women); includes 29 Black or African American, non-Hispanic/Latino; 2 American Indian or Alaska Native, non-Hispanic/Latino; 3 Asian, non-Hispanic/Latino. Average age 39. Expenses: Contact institution. *Financial support:* Career-related internships or fieldwork, Federal Work-Study, institutionally sponsored loans, tuition waivers (full and partial), and unspecified assistantships available. Support available to part-time students. Financial award application deadline: 4/1; financial award applicants required to submit FAFSA. *Degree program information:* Part-time and evening/weekend programs available. *Application deadline:* For fall admission, 5/24 priority date for domestic students, 7/1 priority date for international students; for winter admission, 12/14 priority date for domestic students; for spring admission, 1/19 priority date for domestic students, 11/1 priority date for international students. Applications are processed on a rolling basis. *Application fee:* $20 ($30 for international students). Electronic applications accepted. *Application Contact:* Misty Wiggins, Coordinator of Enrollment Services, 318-342-1036, Fax: 318-342-1042, E-mail: mwiggins@ulm.edu. *Interim Graduate Studies and Research Director,* Dr. William McCown, 318-342-1036, Fax: 318-342-1042, E-mail: mccown@ulm.edu.

College of Arts and Sciences Students: 82 full-time (48 women), 58 part-time (41 women); includes 29 Black or African American, non-Hispanic/Latino; 2 American Indian or Alaska Native, non-Hispanic/Latino; 4 Asian, non-Hispanic/Latino, 4 international. Average age 30. *Faculty:* 49 full-time (25 women), 2 part-time/adjunct (1 woman). Expenses: Contact institution. *Financial support:* In 2010–11, 14 research assistantships with full tuition reimbursements (averaging $3,171 per year), 33 teaching assistantships with full tuition reimbursements (averaging $3,470 per year) were awarded; career-related internships or fieldwork, Federal Work-Study, institutionally sponsored loans, and unspecified assistantships also available. Support available to part-time students. Financial award application deadline: 4/1; financial award applicants required to submit FAFSA. In 2010, 38 master's awarded. *Degree program information:* Part-time and evening/weekend programs available. Offers arts and sciences (MA, MM, MS, CGS); biology (MS); communication (MA); criminal justice (MA); English (MA); gerontology (MA, CGS); history (MA); music (MM); visual and performing arts (MM). *Application deadline:* For fall admission, 8/24 priority date for domestic students, 7/1 for international students; for winter admission, 12/14 priority date for domestic students; for spring admission, 1/19 priority date for domestic students, 11/1 for international students. Applications are processed on a rolling basis. *Application fee:* $20 ($30 for international students). Electronic applications accepted. *Application Contact:* Paul Karlowitz, Assistant Dean, 318-342-1758, Fax: 318-342-1755, E-mail: karlowitz@ulm.edu. *Dean,* Dr. Jeffrey D. Cass, 318-342-1750, Fax: 318-342-1755, E-mail: jcass@ulm.edu.

College of Business Administration Students: 44 full-time (15 women), 36 part-time (17 women); includes 10 Black or African American, non-Hispanic/Latino; 5 Asian, non-Hispanic/Latino, 9 international. Average age 28. 90 applicants. *Faculty:* 18 full-time (6 women), 2 part-time/adjunct (both women). Expenses: Contact institution. *Financial support:* In 2010–11, 12 research assistantships with full tuition reimbursements (averaging $2,500 per year), 1 teaching assistantship with full tuition reimbursement (averaging $2,500 per year) were awarded; career-related internships or fieldwork, Federal Work-Study, and unspecified assistantships also available. Financial award application deadline: 4/1; financial award applicants required to submit FAFSA. In 2010, 30 master's awarded. *Degree program information:* Part-time and evening/weekend programs available. Offers business administration (MBA). *Application deadline:* For fall admission, 8/24 for domestic students, 7/1 for international students; for winter admission, 12/14 for domestic students; for spring admission, 1/19 for domestic students, 11/1 for international students. Applications are processed on a rolling basis. *Application fee:* $20 ($30 for international students). Electronic applications accepted. *Application Contact:* Dr. Donna Walton Luse, Program Chair, 318-342-1106, Fax: 318-342-1101, E-mail: luse@ulm.edu. *Dean,* Dr. Ronald Berry, 318-342-1100, Fax: 318-342-1101, E-mail: rberry@ulm.edu.

College of Education and Human Development Students: 190 full-time (136 women), 294 part-time (212 women); includes 106 Black or African American, non-Hispanic/Latino; 2 American Indian or Alaska Native, non-Hispanic/Latino; 10 Asian, non-Hispanic/Latino; 1 Hispanic/Latino, 15 international. Average age 33. *Faculty:* 36 full-time (15 women), 8 part-time/adjunct (3 women). Expenses: Contact institution. *Financial support:* In 2010–11, 44 research assistantships (averaging $2,614 per year), 8 teaching assistantships (averaging $4,688 per year) were awarded; career-related internships or fieldwork, Federal Work-Study, institutionally sponsored loans, and unspecified assistantships also available. Financial award application deadline: 4/1; financial award applicants required to submit FAFSA. In 2010, 152 master's, 11 doctorates, 3 other advanced degrees awarded. *Degree program information:* Part-time and evening/weekend programs available. Postbaccalaureate distance learning degree programs offered. Offers administration and supervision (M Ed); applied exercise physiology (MS); clinical exercise physiology (MS); counseling (M Ed); curriculum and instruction (M Ed, Ed D); education and human development (M Ed, MA, MAT, MS, Ed D, PhD, SSP); educational leadership (M Ed, Ed D); elementary education (M Ed, MAT); elementary education (1-5) (M Ed); general psychology (MS); grades 1-5 (M Ed); marriage and family therapy (MA, PhD); multiple levels grades K-12 (MAT); reading education (K-12) (M Ed); school psychology (MS, SSP); secondary education 6-12 (M Ed, MAT); SPED-academically gifted education (K-12) (M Ed); SPED-early intervention education (birth-3) (M Ed); SPED-educational diagnostics education (PreK-12) (M Ed); substance abuse counseling (MA). *Application deadline:* For fall admission, 8/24 priority date for domestic students, 7/1 for international students; for winter admission, 12/14 priority date for domestic students; for spring admission, 1/19 priority date for domestic students, 11/1 for international students. Applications are processed on a rolling basis. *Application fee:* $20 ($30 for international students). Electronic applications accepted. *Application Contact:* Dr. Jack Palmer, Director of Graduate Studies, 318-342-1250, Fax: 318-342-1240, E-mail: palmer@ulm.edu. *Dean,* Dr. Sandra M. Lemoine, 318-342-1235, Fax: 318-342-1240, E-mail: slemoine@ulm.edu.

College of Health Sciences Students: 28 full-time (all women), 5 part-time (all women); includes 1 Black or African American, non-Hispanic/Latino; 2 Asian, non-Hispanic/Latino, 1 international. Average age 26. *Faculty:* 4 full-time (all women), 2 part-time/adjunct (both women). Expenses: Contact institution. *Financial support:* In 2010–11, 8 research assistantships with full tuition reimbursements (averaging $2,500 per year) were awarded; career-related internships or fieldwork, Federal Work-Study, and unspecified assistantships also available. Financial award application deadline: 4/1; financial award applicants required to submit FAFSA. In 2010, 17 master's awarded. Offers health sciences (MS); speech-language pathology (MS). *Application deadline:* For fall admission, 8/24 priority date for domestic students, 7/1 for international students; for winter admission, 12/14 priority date for domestic students; for spring admission, 1/19 for domestic students, 11/1 for international students. Applications are processed on a rolling basis. *Application fee:* $20 ($30 for international students). Electronic applications accepted. *Application Contact:* Dr. Paxton E. Oliver, Associate Dean, 318-342-1622, Fax: 318-342-1606, E-mail: poliver@ulm.edu. *Dean,* Dr. Denny Ryman, 318-342-1622, Fax: 318-342-1606, E-mail: ryman@ulm.edu.

College of Pharmacy Students: 335 full-time (205 women), 12 part-time (4 women); includes 18 Black or African American, non-Hispanic/Latino; 2 American Indian or Alaska Native, non-Hispanic/Latino; 42 Asian, non-Hispanic/Latino, 22 international. Average age 25. *Faculty:* 18 full-time (4 women), 20 part-time/adjunct (3 women). Expenses: Contact institution. *Financial support:* In 2010–11, 12 research assistantships with full tuition reimbursements (averaging $6,032 per year), 14 teaching assistantships (averaging $6,032 per year) were awarded; Federal Work-Study and unspecified assistantships also available. Financial award application deadline: 4/1; financial award applicants required to submit FAFSA. In 2010, 83 doctorates awarded. Offers pharmaceutical sciences (MS); pharmacy (MS, PhD). *Application deadline:* For fall admission, 8/24 priority date for domestic students, 7/1 for international students; for winter admission, 12/14 priority date for domestic students; for spring admission, 1/19 priority date for domestic students, 11/1 for international students. Applications are processed on a rolling basis. *Application fee:* $20 ($30 for international students). Electronic applications accepted. *Application Contact:* Dr. Paul W. Sylvester, Director of Graduate Studies and Research, 318-342-1958, Fax: 318-342-1606, E-mail: sylvester@ulm.edu. *Dean,* Dr. Benny L. Blaylock, 318-342-1600, Fax: 318-342-1606, E-mail: blaylock@ulm.edu.

UNIVERSITY OF LOUISVILLE, Louisville, KY 40292-0001

General Information State-supported, coed, university. CGS member. *Enrollment:* 21,234 graduate, professional, and undergraduate students; 3,763 full-time matriculated graduate/professional students (1,950 women), 1,538 part-time matriculated graduate/professional students (928 women). *Enrollment by degree level:* 1,427 first professional, 2,763 master's, 1,058 doctoral, 53 other advanced degrees. *Graduate faculty:* 1,620 full-time (592 women), 568 part-time/adjunct (308 women). Tuition, state resident: full-time $9144; part-time $508 per credit hour. Tuition, nonresident: full-time $19,026; part-time $1057 per credit hour. Tuition and fees vary according to program and reciprocity agreements. *Graduate housing:* Rooms and/or apartments available to single and married students. Typical cost: $4272 per year ($6602 including board) for single students. Room and board charges vary according to housing facility selected. *Student services:* Campus employment opportunities, campus safety program, career counseling, child daycare facilities, exercise/wellness program, free psychological counseling, grant writing training, international student services, low-cost health insurance, multicultural affairs office, services for students with disabilities. *Library facilities:* William F. Ekstrom Library plus 6 others. *Online resources:* library catalog, web page. *Collection:* 2.3 million titles, 73,105 serial subscriptions, 49,226 audiovisual materials. *Research affiliation:* Argonne National Laboratory, Oak Ridge National Laboratory.

Computer facilities: Computer purchase and lease plans are available. 400 computers available on campus for general student use. A campuswide network can be accessed from student residence rooms and from off campus. Online class registration is available. *Web address:* http://www.louisville.edu/.

General Application Contact: Libby Leggett, Executive Director, Graduate Admissions and Recruitment, 502-852-3108, E-mail: gradadm@louisville.edu.

GRADUATE UNITS

Graduate School 8,266 applicants, 26% accepted, 1404 enrolled. Expenses: Contact institution. *Financial support:* Fellowships with full tuition reimbursements, research assistantships with full tuition reimbursements, teaching assistantships with full and partial tuition reimbursements, career-related internships or fieldwork, Federal Work-Study, institutionally sponsored loans, scholarships/grants, traineeships, tuition waivers (partial), and unspecified assistantships available. Financial award applicants required to submit FAFSA. *Degree program information:* Part-time and evening/weekend programs available. *Application deadline:* Applications are processed on a rolling basis. *Application fee:* $50. Electronic applications accepted. *Application Contact:* Libby Leggett, Director, Graduate Admissions, 502-852-3101, Fax: 502-852-6536, E-mail: gradadm@louisville.edu. *Interim Dean,* Dr. William M. Pierce, 502-852-6495, Fax: 502-852-6616, E-mail: wmpier01@louisville.edu.

College of Arts and Sciences Students: 591 full-time (319 women), 272 part-time (150 women); includes 118 minority (76 Black or African American, non-Hispanic/Latino; 2 American Indian or Alaska Native, non-Hispanic/Latino; 13 Asian, non-Hispanic/Latino; 17 Hispanic/Latino; 2 Native Hawaiian or other Pacific Islander, non-Hispanic/Latino; 8 Two or more races, non-Hispanic/Latino), 107 international. Average age 31. 810 applicants, 50% accepted, 260 enrolled. *Faculty:* 385 full-time (159 women), 177 part-time/adjunct (87 women). Expenses: Contact institution. *Financial support:* In 2010–11, 226 students received support; fellowships with full tuition reimbursements available, research assistantships with full tuition reimbursements available, teaching assistantships with full tuition reimbursements available, career-related internships or fieldwork, institutionally sponsored loans, scholarships/grants, tuition waivers (partial), and unspecified assistantships available. In 2010, 181 master's, 37 doctorates awarded. *Degree program information:* Part-time and evening/weekend programs available. Postbaccalaureate distance learning degree programs offered (no on-campus study). Offers African and Diaspora studies (MA); African-American studies (MA); analytical chemistry (MS, PhD); anthropology (MA); applied and industrial mathematics (PhD); applied geography (MS); art history (MA, PhD); arts and sciences (MA, MFA, MPA, MS, MUP, PhD, Certificate); biochemistry (MS, PhD); biology (MS); chemical physics (PhD); clinical psychology (PhD); communication (MA); creative art (MA); curatorial studies (MA); English (MA); English rhetoric and composition (PhD); environmental biology (PhD); experimental psychology (PhD); French (MA); history (MA); humanities (MA, PhD); inorganic chemistry (MS, PhD); justice administration (MS); mathematics (MA); organic chemistry (MS, PhD); performance (MFA); philosophy (MA); physical chemistry (MS, PhD); physics (MS, PhD); political science (MA); public administration (MPA); public history (Certificate); sociology (MA); Spanish (MA); urban and public affairs (PhD); urban planning (MUP); women's and gender studies (MA, Certificate). *Application deadline:* Applications are processed on a rolling basis. *Application fee:* $50. *Application Contact:* Libby Leggett, Director, Graduate Admissions, 502-852-3101, Fax: 502-852-6536, E-mail: gradadm@louisville.edu. *Dean,* Dr. J. Blaine Hudson, 502-852-2234, Fax: 502-852-6888, E-mail: jbhuds01@louisville.edu.

College of Business Students: 37 full-time (11 women), 218 part-time (71 women); includes 22 minority (8 Black or African American, non-Hispanic/Latino; 1 American Indian or Alaska Native, non-Hispanic/Latino; 8 Asian, non-Hispanic/Latino; 4 Hispanic/Latino; 1 Native Hawaiian or other Pacific Islander, non-Hispanic/Latino), 20 international. Average age 29. 395 applicants, 41% accepted, 135 enrolled. *Faculty:* 48 full-time (10 women), 4 part-time/adjunct (0 women). Expenses: Contact institution. *Financial support:* In 2010–11, 18 students received support, including 6 fellowships (averaging $21,000 per year), 10 research assistantships (averaging $12,000 per year), 2 teaching assistantships (averaging $18,000 per year); scholarships/grants, health care benefits, and unspecified assistantships also available. Financial award application deadline: 3/15; financial award applicants required to submit FAFSA. In 2010, 115 master's, 2 doctorates awarded. *Degree program information:* Part-time programs available. Offers accountancy (MAC); business (MAC, MBA, PMBA, PhD); entrepreneurship (PhD); global business (PMBA); global business (full time) (MBA). *Application deadline:* For fall admission, 7/15 for domestic students; for winter admission, 11/15 for domestic students; for spring admission, 4/15 for domestic students. Applications are processed on a rolling basis. *Application fee:* $50. Electronic applications accepted. *Application Contact:* Joshua M. Philpot, Graduate Programs Manager, 502-852-7257, Fax: 502-852-4901, E-mail: josh.philpot@louisville.edu. *Dean,* Dr. Charles Moyer, 502-852-6443, Fax: 502-852-7557, E-mail: charlie.moyer@louisville.edu.

College of Education and Human Development Students: 514 full-time (343 women), 676 part-time (499 women); includes 177 minority (110 Black or African American, non-Hispanic/Latino; 1 American Indian or Alaska Native, non-Hispanic/Latino; 22 Asian, non-Hispanic/Latino; 26 Hispanic/Latino; 2 Native Hawaiian or other Pacific Islander, non-Hispanic/Latino; 16 Two or more races, non-Hispanic/Latino), 24 international. Average age 33. 705 applicants, 59% accepted, 295 enrolled. *Faculty:* 90 full-time (54 women), 43 part-time/adjunct (35 women). Expenses: Contact institution. *Financial support:* In 2010–11, 295 students received support, including 6 fellowships with full tuition reimbursements available (averaging $18,000 per year), 29 research assistantships with full tuition reimbursements available (averaging $18,000 per year), 11 teaching assistantships with full tuition reimbursements available (averaging $18,000 per year); career-related internships or fieldwork, Federal Work-Study, scholarships/grants, and health care benefits also available. Financial award application deadline: 6/1. In 2010, 422 master's, 39 doctorates, 11 other advanced degrees awarded. *Degree program information:* Part-time and evening/weekend programs available. Postbaccalaureate distance learning degree programs offered. Offers art education (MAT); community health education (M Ed); counseling and personnel services (M Ed, PhD); curriculum and instruction (PhD); early elementary education (MAT); education and human development (M Ed, MA, MAT, MS, Ed D, PhD, Ed S); educational leadership and organizational development (Ed D, PhD); exercise physiology (MS); health and physical education (MAT); higher education (MA); human resource education (MS); instructional technology (M Ed); interdisciplinary early childhood education (MAT); middle school education (MAT); music education (MAT); P-12 educational administration (M Ed, Ed S); reading education (M Ed); secondary education (MAT); special education (M Ed, MAT); sport administration (MS); teacher leadership (M Ed). *Application fee:* $50. Electronic applications accepted. *Application Contact:* Libby Leggett, Director, Graduate Admissions, 502-852-3101, Fax: 502-852-6536, E-mail: gradadm@louisville.edu. *Interim Dean,* Dr. Blake Haselton, 502-852-6411, Fax: 502-852-1464, E-mail: blake.haselton@louisville.edu.

Raymond A. Kent School of Social Work Students: 259 full-time (209 women), 71 part-time (60 women); includes 84 minority (66 Black or African American, non-Hispanic/Latino; 1 American Indian or Alaska Native, non-Hispanic/Latino; 3 Asian, non-Hispanic/Latino; 6 Hispanic/Latino; 8 Two or more races, non-Hispanic/Latino), 7 international. Average age 32. 249 applicants, 78% accepted, 141 enrolled. *Faculty:* 23 full-time (15 women), 38 part-time/adjunct (21 women). Expenses: Contact institution. *Financial support:* In 2010–11, 70 students received support, including 9 research assistantships with full tuition reimbursements available (averaging $19,000 per year), 1 teaching assistantship (averaging $19,000 per year); Federal Work-Study, institutionally sponsored loans, scholarships/grants, health care benefits, and unspecified assistantships also available. Support available to part-time students. Financial award application deadline: 5/15; financial award applicants required to submit FAFSA. In 2010, 141 master's, 7 doctorates awarded. *Degree program information:* Part-time and evening/weekend programs available. Offers marriage and family therapy (PMC); social work (MSSW, PhD). *Application deadline:* For fall admission, 7/31 for domestic and international students. Applications are processed on a rolling basis. *Application fee:* $50. Electronic applications accepted. *Application Contact:* Libby Leggett, Director, Graduate Admissions, 502-852-3101, Fax: 502-852-6536, E-mail: gradadm@louisville.edu. *Dean,* Dr. Terry Singer, 502-852-6402, Fax: 502-852-0422, E-mail: terry.singer@louisville.edu.

School of Music Students: 57 full-time (22 women), 4 part-time (3 women); includes 1 Black or African American, non-Hispanic/Latino; 1 Asian, non-Hispanic/Latino; 2 Hispanic/Latino; 1 Two or more races, non-Hispanic/Latino, 13 international. Average age 27. 73 applicants, 70% accepted, 31 enrolled. *Faculty:* 33 full-time (10 women), 38 part-time/adjunct (10 women). Expenses: Contact institution. *Financial support:* In 2010–11, 50 students received support, including 3 fellowships with full tuition reimbursements available (averaging $12,000 per year), 24 teaching assistantships with full tuition reimbursements available (averaging $12,000 per year); scholarships/grants, health care benefits, tuition waivers (full and partial), and unspecified assistantships also available. Financial award application deadline: 3/1; financial award applicants required to submit FAFSA. In 2010, 28 master's awarded. *Degree program information:* Part-time and evening/weekend programs available. Offers music composition (MM); music education (MME); music history and literature (MM); music theory (MM); performance (MM). *Application deadline:* For fall admission, 3/15 priority date for domestic and international students; for spring admission, 11/15 priority date for domestic and international students. Applications are processed on a rolling basis. *Application fee:* $50. Electronic applications accepted. *Application Contact:* Toni Robinson, Admissions Counselor, 502-852-1623, Fax: 502-852-0520, E-mail: toni.robinson@louisville.edu. *Dean,* Dr. Christopher Doane, 502-852-6907, Fax: 502-852-1874, E-mail: doane@louisville.edu.

School of Nursing Students: 85 full-time (81 women), 68 part-time (63 women); includes 10 Black or African American, non-Hispanic/Latino; 1 American Indian or Alaska Native, non-Hispanic/Latino; 5 Asian, non-Hispanic/Latino; 2 Hispanic/Latino; 1 Two or more races, non-Hispanic/Latino, 8 international. Average age 34. 121 applicants, 14% accepted, 16 enrolled. *Faculty:* 28 full-time (25 women), 4 part-time/adjunct (3 women). Expenses: Contact institution. *Financial support:* In 2010–11, 45 students received support, including 2 fellowships with full tuition reimbursements available (averaging $20,000 per year), 5 research assistantships with full tuition reimbursements available (averaging $19,500 per year), 5 teaching assistantships with full tuition reimbursements available (averaging $19,500 per year); institutionally sponsored loans, scholarships/grants, traineeships, health care benefits, and unspecified assistantships also available. Support available to part-time students. Financial award application deadline: 4/15; financial award applicants required to submit FAFSA. In 2010, 32 master's, 1 doctorate awarded. *Degree program information:* Part-time programs available. Offers adult nurse practitioner (MSN); family nurse practitioner (MSN); health professions education (MSN); neonatal nurse practitioner (MSN); nursing research (PhD); psychiatric mental health nurse practitioner (MSN). *Application deadline:* For fall admission, 4/1 priority date for domestic students, 4/1 for international students. Applications are processed on a rolling basis. *Application fee:* $50. Electronic applications accepted. *Application Contact:* Dr. Rosalie O'Dell Mainous, Associate Dean for Graduate Academic Affairs and Research, 502-852-8387, Fax: 502-852-0704, E-mail: romain01@louisville.edu. *Dean,* Dr. Marcia J. Hern, 502-852-8300, Fax: 502-852-5044, E-mail: m.hern@gwise.louisville.edu.

School of Public Health and Information Sciences Students: 105 full-time (69 women), 61 part-time (39 women); includes 19 Black or African American, non-Hispanic/Latino; 14 Asian, non-Hispanic/Latino; 4 Hispanic/Latino; 2 Two or more races, non-Hispanic/Latino, 23 international. Average age 32. 218 applicants, 48% accepted, 66 enrolled. *Faculty:* 32 full-time (14 women), 6 part-time/adjunct (1 woman). Expenses: Contact institution. *Financial support:* In 2010–11, 30 students received support, including 11 research assistantships with full tuition reimbursements available (averaging $20,000 per year); scholarships/grants, health care benefits, and unspecified assistantships also available. Financial award application deadline: 5/1; financial award applicants required to submit FAFSA. In 2010, 48 master's, 4 doctorates awarded. *Degree program information:* Part-time and evening/weekend programs available. Offers bioinformatics and biostatistics (MS, PhD); biostatistics (MS, PhD); clinical investigation sciences (M Sc, Certificate); decision science (MS); environmental and occupational health sciences (MPH, PhD); epidemiology (MPH, MS, PhD); epidemiology and population health (MS); epidemiology and public health (MPH, PhD); health management and systems sciences (PhD); health promotion (PhD); health promotion and behavioral sciences (PhD); public health (PhD); public health sciences (PhD); public health sciences—health management (PhD). *Application deadline:* For fall admission, 2/1 for domestic and international students. Applications are processed on a rolling basis. *Application fee:* $50. Electronic applications accepted. *Application Contact:* Vicki Lewis, Administrative Assistant, 502-852-1798, Fax: 502-852-3294, E-mail: vicki.lewis@louisville.edu. *Associate Dean for Academic Affairs,* Dr. Pete Walton, 502-852-4493, Fax: 502-852-3291, E-mail: pete.walton@gwise.louisville.edu.

J. B. Speed School of Engineering Students: 375 full-time (74 women), 152 part-time (30 women); includes 61 Two or more races, non-Hispanic/Latino. Average age 27. 241 applicants, 48% accepted, 60 enrolled. *Faculty:* 74 full-time (9 women). Expenses: Contact institution. *Financial support:* In 2010–11, 87 students received support, including 17 fellowships with full tuition reimbursements available (averaging $20,000 per year), 29 research assistantships with full tuition reimbursements available (averaging $20,000 per year), 41 teaching assistantships with full tuition reimbursements available (averaging $20,000 per year); scholarships/grants also available. Financial award application deadline: 1/25; financial award applicants required to submit FAFSA. In 2010, 181 master's, 24 doctorates awarded. *Degree program information:* Part-time programs available. Postbaccalaureate distance learning degree programs offered (no on-campus study). Offers chemical engineering (M Eng, MS, PhD); civil engineering (M Eng, MS, PhD); computer engineering and computer science (M Eng); computer science (MS); computer science and engineering (PhD); data mining (Certificate); electrical and computer engineering (M Eng, MS, PhD); engineering (M Eng, MS, PhD, Certificate); engineering management (M Eng); industrial engineering (M Eng, MS, PhD); logistics and distribution (Certificate); mechanical engineering (M Eng, MS, PhD); network and information security (Certificate). *Application deadline:* For fall admission, 5/1 priority date for domestic and international students; for spring admission, 11/1 priority date for domestic and international students. Applications are processed on a rolling basis. *Application fee:* $50. Electronic applications accepted. *Application Contact:* Dr. Michael Day, Associate Dean, 502-852-6195, Fax: 502-852-7294, E-mail: day@louisville.edu. *Dean,* Dr. Mickey R. Wilhelm, 502-852-6281, Fax: 502-852-7033, E-mail: wilhelm@louisville.edu.

Louis D. Brandeis School of Law Students: 378 full-time (173 women), 47 part-time (16 women); includes 16 Black or African American, non-Hispanic/Latino; 4 Asian, non-Hispanic/Latino; 13 Hispanic/Latino, 3 international. Average age 25. 1,769 applicants, 30% accepted, 143 enrolled. *Faculty:* 31 full-time (8 women), 16 part-time/adjunct (6 women). Expenses: Contact institution. *Financial support:* In 2010–11, 173 students received support; fellowships, research assistantships, teaching assistantships, career-related internships or fieldwork, scholarships/grants, and tuition waivers (partial) available. Support available to part-time students. Financial award application deadline: 6/1; financial award applicants required to submit FAFSA. In 2010, 133 first professional degrees awarded. *Degree program information:* Part-time programs available. Offers law (JD). *Application deadline:* For fall admission, 3/15 for domestic and international students. Applications are processed on a rolling basis. *Application fee:* $50. Electronic applications accepted. *Application Contact:* Brandon L. Hamilton, Assistant Dean for Admission and Financial Aid, 502-852-6365, Fax: 502-852-8971, E-mail: lawadmissions@louisville.edu. *Dean,* James Ming Chen, 502-852-6879, Fax: 502-852-0862, E-mail: jim.chen@louisville.edu.

School of Dentistry Students: 389 full-time (165 women), 11 part-time (8 women); includes 28 Black or African American, non-Hispanic/Latino; 6 American Indian or Alaska Native, non-Hispanic/Latino; 27 Asian, non-Hispanic/Latino; 8 Hispanic/Latino; 4 Two or more races, non-Hispanic/Latino, 10 international. Average age 26. 174 applicants, 92% accepted, 132 enrolled. *Faculty:* 63 full-time (20 women), 84 part-time/adjunct (22 women). Expenses: Contact institution. *Financial support:* In 2010–11, 331 students received support, including 1 research assistantship with full tuition reimbursement available (averaging $20,000 per year). Financial award application deadline: 3/15; financial award applicants required to submit FAFSA. In 2010, 81 first professional degrees, 15 master's awarded. *Degree program information:* Part-time programs available. Offers oral biology (MS). *Application deadline:* For fall admission, 1/1 for domestic and international students. Applications are processed on a rolling basis. *Application fee:* $50. Electronic applications accepted. *Application Contact:* Robin Benningfield, Admissions Counselor, 502-852-5081, Fax: 502-852-1210, E-mail: dmdadms@louisville.edu. *Dean,* Dr. John J. Sauk, 502-852-1304, Fax: 502-852-3364, E-mail: jjsauk01@louisville.edu.

School of Interdisciplinary and Graduate Studies Students: 9 full-time (5 women), 8 part-time (4 women); includes 2 Black or African American, non-Hispanic/Latino; 1 Asian, non-Hispanic/Latino. Average age 33. 27 applicants, 70% accepted, 10 enrolled. Expenses: Contact institution. *Financial support:* In 2010–11, 61 fellowships with full tuition reimbursements (averaging $18,068 per year) were awarded; career-related internships or fieldwork, Federal Work-Study, institutionally sponsored loans, scholarships/grants, health care benefits, and tuition waivers (full and partial) also available. Financial award application deadline: 2/1; financial award applicants required to submit FAFSA. In 2010, 3 master's awarded. *Degree program information:* Part-time and evening/weekend programs available. Offers interdisciplinary studies (MA, MS, PhD). *Application deadline:* For fall admission, 5/1 for international students; for spring admission, 11/1 for international students. Applications are processed on a rolling basis. *Application fee:* $50. Electronic applications accepted. *Application Contact:* Libby Leggett, Executive Director of Graduate Admissions and Recruitment, 502-852-3108, Fax: 502-852-3111, E-mail: melegg02@louisville.edu. *Interim Dean/Associate Provost for Faculty Personnel/Professor of English,* Dr. Beth A. Boehm, 502-852-6590, Fax: 502-852-6616, E-mail: beth.boehm@louisville.edu.

University of Louisville (continued)

School of Medicine Students: 887 full-time (455 women), 28 part-time (10 women); includes 152 minority (60 Black or African American, non-Hispanic/Latino; 1 American Indian or Alaska Native, non-Hispanic/Latino; 70 Asian, non-Hispanic/Latino; 15 Hispanic/Latino; 2 Native Hawaiian or other Pacific Islander, non-Hispanic/Latino; 4 Two or more races, non-Hispanic/Latino), 60 international. Average age 26. 3,060 applicants, 14% accepted, 260 enrolled. *Faculty:* 689 full-time (206 women), 74 part-time/adjunct (24 women). Expenses: Contact institution. *Financial support:* Career-related internships or fieldwork, institutionally sponsored loans, scholarships/grants, traineeships, and unspecified assistantships available. Financial award applicants required to submit FAFSA. In 2010, 134 first professional degrees, 57 master's, 38 doctorates awarded. Offers anatomical sciences and neurobiology (MS, PhD); audiology (Au D); biochemistry and molecular biology (MS, PhD); communicative disorders (MS); medicine (MD, MS, Au D, PhD); microbiology and immunology (MS, PhD); pharmacology and toxicology (MS, PhD); physiology and biophysics (MS, PhD). *Application deadline:* For fall admission, 10/15 for domestic and international students. Applications are processed on a rolling basis. *Application fee:* $75. Electronic applications accepted. *Application Contact:* Pamela D. Osborne, Director of Admissions, 502-852-5193, Fax: 502-852-6849, E-mail: pdosbo01@gwise.louisville.edu. *Dean,* Dr. Edward C. Halperin, 502-852-1499, Fax: 502-852-1484, E-mail: edward.halperin@louisville.edu.

UNIVERSITY OF MAINE, Orono, ME 04469

General Information State-supported, coed, university. CGS member. *Enrollment:* 11,501 graduate, professional, and undergraduate students; 1,055 full-time matriculated graduate/professional students (619 women), 660 part-time matriculated graduate/professional students (402 women). *Enrollment by degree level:* 1,175 master's, 458 doctoral, 82 other advanced degrees. *Graduate faculty:* 535 full-time (186 women), 284 part-time/adjunct (172 women). Tuition, state resident: full-time $400. Tuition, nonresident: full-time $1050. *Graduate housing:* Rooms and/or apartments available on a first-come, first-served basis to single and married students. Typical cost: $6256 per year ($7256 including board) for single students; $7500 per year for married students. Housing application deadline: 8/1. *Student services:* Campus employment opportunities, campus safety program, career counseling, child daycare facilities, exercise/wellness program, free psychological counseling, grant writing training, international student services, low-cost health insurance, multicultural affairs office, services for students with disabilities, teacher training, writing training. *Library facilities:* Fogler Library. *Online resources:* library catalog, web page, access to other libraries' catalogs. *Collection:* 1.1 million titles, 16,988 serial subscriptions. *Research affiliation:* Jackson Laboratory (medical genetics), Bigelow Laboratories for Ocean Sciences (marine science), Mount Desert Island Biological Laboratory (marine molecular biology), Sensor Research Development Corporation (electrical sensors), Maine Medical Center Research Institute (clinical medicine), Maine Institute for Human Genetics (medical genetics).

Computer facilities: Computer purchase and lease plans are available. 500 computers available on campus for general student use. A campuswide network can be accessed from student residence rooms and from off campus. Online class registration, online housing and financial aid information are available. *Web address:* http://www.umaine.edu/.

General Application Contact: Scott G. Delcourt, Associate Dean of the Graduate School, 207-581-3291, Fax: 207-581-3232, E-mail: graduate@maine.edu.

GRADUATE UNITS

Graduate School Students: 1,055 full-time (619 women), 660 part-time (402 women); includes 7 Black or African American, non-Hispanic/Latino; 31 American Indian or Alaska Native, non-Hispanic/Latino; 19 Asian, non-Hispanic/Latino; 12 Hispanic/Latino, 160 international. Average age 33. 1,460 applicants, 38% accepted, 468 enrolled. *Faculty:* 535 full-time (186 women), 284 part-time/adjunct (172 women). Expenses: Contact institution. *Financial support:* In 2010–11, 30 fellowships with tuition reimbursements (averaging $20,400 per year), 250 research assistantships with tuition reimbursements (averaging $17,600 per year), 250 teaching assistantships with tuition reimbursements (averaging $13,120 per year) were awarded; career-related internships or fieldwork, Federal Work-Study, institutionally sponsored loans, scholarships/grants, tuition waivers (full and partial), and unspecified assistantships also available. Support available to part-time students. Financial award application deadline: 3/1; financial award applicants required to submit FAFSA. In 2010, 424 master's, 55 doctorates, 28 other advanced degrees awarded. *Degree program information:* Part-time and evening/weekend programs available. Offers biomedical engineering (PhD); cell and molecular biology (PhD); communication (PhD); functional genomics (PhD); information systems (MS); Maine studies (MA); mass communication (PhD); neuroscience (PhD); new media (MA); ocean engineering (PhD); peace studies (MA); toxicology (PhD). *Application deadline:* For fall admission, 1/15 priority date for domestic students; for spring admission, 11/15 priority date for domestic students. Applications are processed on a rolling basis. *Application fee:* $65. Electronic applications accepted. *Application Contact:* Scott G. Delcourt, Associate Dean of the Graduate School, 207-581-3291, Fax: 207-581-3232, E-mail: graduate@maine.edu. *Associate Dean of the Graduate School,* Scott G. Delcourt, 207-581-3291, Fax: 207-581-3232, E-mail: graduate@maine.edu.

Climate Change Institute Students: 9 full-time (5 women), 1 (woman) part-time, 1 international. Average age 27. 14 applicants, 29% accepted, 2 enrolled. Expenses: Contact institution. *Financial support:* In 2010–11, 8 research assistantships with tuition reimbursements (averaging $17,425 per year), 2 teaching assistantships (averaging $12,790 per year) were awarded. Financial award application deadline: 3/1. *Degree program information:* Part-time programs available. Offers climate change (MS). *Application deadline:* For fall admission, 2/1 priority date for domestic students. Applications are processed on a rolling basis. *Application fee:* $65. Electronic applications accepted. *Application Contact:* Scott G. Delcourt, Associate Dean of the Graduate School, 207-581-3291, Fax: 207-581-3232, E-mail: graduate@maine.edu. *Director,* Dr. Paul Mayewski, 207-581-3019, Fax: 207-581-1203.

College of Business, Public Policy and Health Students: 192 full-time (135 women), 38 part-time (20 women); includes 14 minority (9 American Indian or Alaska Native, non-Hispanic/Latino; 2 Asian, non-Hispanic/Latino; 1 Hispanic/Latino; 2 Two or more races, non-Hispanic/Latino), 9 international. Average age 35. 125 applicants, 60% accepted, 69 enrolled. *Faculty:* 34 full-time (13 women), 10 part-time/adjunct (8 women). Expenses: Contact institution. *Financial support:* In 2010–11, research assistantships with tuition reimbursements (averaging $12,790 per year), teaching assistantships with tuition reimbursements (averaging $12,790 per year) were awarded; career-related internships or fieldwork, Federal Work-Study, institutionally sponsored loans, scholarships/grants, tuition waivers (full and partial), and unspecified assistantships also available. Support available to part-time students. Financial award application deadline: 3/1. In 2010, 88 degrees awarded. *Degree program information:* Part-time and evening/weekend programs available. Offers accounting (MBA); business and sustainability (MBA); business, public policy and health (MBA, MPA, MSW, PhD); finance (MBA); management (MBA); public administration (MPA, PhD); social work (MSW). *Application deadline:* Applications are processed on a rolling basis. *Application fee:* $65. Electronic applications accepted. *Application Contact:* Scott G. Delcourt, Associate Dean of the Graduate School, 207-581-3291, Fax: 207-581-3232, E-mail: graduate@maine.edu. *Dean,* Dr. John Mahon, 207-581-1968, Fax: 207-581-1930.

College of Education and Human Development Students: 215 full-time (166 women), 320 part-time (253 women); includes 21 minority (5 Black or African American, non-Hispanic/Latino; 8 American Indian or Alaska Native, non-Hispanic/Latino; 2 Asian, non-Hispanic/Latino; 5 Hispanic/Latino; 1 Two or more races, non-Hispanic/Latino), 7 international. Average age 37. 226 applicants, 60% accepted, 120 enrolled. *Faculty:* 35 full-time (21 women), 47 part-time/adjunct (37 women). Expenses: Contact institution. *Financial support:* In 2010–11, 21 teaching assistantships with tuition reimbursements (averaging $12,790 per year) were awarded; career-related internships or fieldwork, Federal Work-Study, institutionally sponsored loans, and unspecified assistantships also available. Support available to part-time students. Financial award application deadline: 3/1. In 2010, 186 master's, 10 doctorates, 28 other advanced degrees awarded. *Degree program information:* Part-time and evening/weekend programs available. Offers counselor education (M Ed, MA, MS, Ed D, CAS); curriculum and instruction (M Ed); curriculum, assessment, and instruction (M Ed); earth sciences (MST); educational leadership (M Ed, Ed D, CAS); elementary and secondary education (M Ed); elementary education (M Ed, MAT, MS, CAS); exercise science (MS); generalist (MST); higher education (M Ed, MA, MS, Ed D, CAS); human development (MS); human development and family relations (MS); instructional technology (M Ed); kinesiology and physical education (M Ed, MS); literacy education (M Ed, MA, MS, Ed D, CAS); mathematics (MST); physics and astronomy (MST); science education (M Ed, MS, CAS); secondary education (M Ed, MA, MAT, MS, CAS); social studies education (M Ed, MA, MS, CAS); special education (M Ed, CAS); teaching (MST). *Application deadline:* For fall admission, 2/1 priority date for domestic students. Applications are processed on a rolling basis. *Application fee:* $65. Electronic applications accepted. *Application Contact:* Scott G. Delcourt, Associate Dean of the Graduate School, 207-581-3291, Fax: 207-581-3232, E-mail: graduate@maine.edu. *Dean,* Dr. Ann Pooler, 207-581-2441, Fax: 207-581-2423.

College of Engineering Students: 97 full-time (18 women), 53 part-time (8 women); includes 8 minority (1 Black or African American, non-Hispanic/Latino; 2 American Indian or Alaska Native, non-Hispanic/Latino; 4 Asian, non-Hispanic/Latino; 1 Two or more races, non-Hispanic/Latino), 50 international. Average age 30. 136 applicants, 33% accepted, 34 enrolled. *Faculty:* 65 full-time (6 women), 11 part-time/adjunct (5 women). Expenses: Contact institution. *Financial support:* In 2010–11, 1 research assistantship with tuition reimbursement (averaging $12,790 per year) was awarded; Federal Work-Study, institutionally sponsored loans, scholarships/grants, and tuition waivers (full and partial) also available. Financial award application deadline: 3/1. In 2010, 38 master's, 6 doctorates awarded. *Degree program information:* Part-time programs available. Offers biological engineering (MS); chemical engineering (MS, PhD); computer engineering (MS); electrical engineering (MS, PhD); engineering (MS, PhD); mechanical engineering (MS, PhD); spatial information science and engineering (MS, PhD); water resources (MS). *Application deadline:* For fall admission, 2/1 priority date for domestic students. Applications are processed on a rolling basis. *Application fee:* $65. Electronic applications accepted. *Application Contact:* Scott G. Delcourt, Associate Dean of the Graduate School, 207-581-3291, Fax: 207-581-3232, E-mail: graduate@maine.edu. *Interim Dean,* Dr. Dana Humphrey, 207-581-2216, Fax: 207-581-2220.

College of Liberal Arts and Sciences Students: 228 full-time (114 women), 95 part-time (33 women); includes 14 minority (7 American Indian or Alaska Native, non-Hispanic/Latino; 4 Asian, non-Hispanic/Latino; 3 Hispanic/Latino), 34 international. Average age 31. 378 applicants, 30% accepted, 93 enrolled. *Faculty:* 171 full-time (59 women), 81 part-time/adjunct (41 women). Expenses: Contact institution. *Financial support:* Career-related internships or fieldwork, Federal Work-Study, institutionally sponsored loans, scholarships/grants, and tuition waivers (full and partial) available. Support available to part-time students. Financial award application deadline: 3/1. In 2010, 70 master's, 17 doctorates awarded. *Degree program information:* Part-time and evening/weekend programs available. Offers American studies (MA, PhD); Canadian studies (MA, PhD); chemistry (MS, PhD); choral conducting (MM); clinical (PhD); collaborative piano (MM); communication (MA); communication sciences and disorders (MA); composition and pedagogy (MA); computer science (MS, PhD); creative (MA); developmental (MA, PhD); East Asian (MA); engineering physics (M Eng); environmental (MA); European (MA); experimental (MA); French (MA, MAT); gender and literature (MA); instrumental (MM); instrumental conducting (MM); liberal arts and sciences (M Eng, MA, MAT, MM, MS, PhD); mass communication (MA); mathematics (MA); North American French (MA); physics (MS, PhD); poetry and poetics (MA); psychological sciences (MA, PhD); technology (MA); vocal (MM). *Application deadline:* For fall admission, 2/1 priority date for domestic students. Applications are processed on a rolling basis. *Application fee:* $65. Electronic applications accepted. *Application Contact:* Scott G. Delcourt, Associate Dean of the Graduate School, 207-581-3291, Fax: 207-581-3232, E-mail: graduate@maine.edu. *Dean,* Dr. Jeffrey E. Hecker, 207-581-1954, Fax: 207-581-1947.

College of Natural Sciences, Forestry, and Agriculture Students: 259 full-time (145 women), 91 part-time (53 women); includes 10 minority (2 American Indian or Alaska Native, non-Hispanic/Latino; 6 Asian, non-Hispanic/Latino; 1 Hispanic/Latino; 1 Two or more races, non-Hispanic/Latino), 47 international. Average age 30. 456 applicants, 27% accepted, 98 enrolled. *Faculty:* 152 full-time (54 women), 43 part-time/adjunct (26 women). Expenses: Contact institution. *Financial support:* Career-related internships or fieldwork, Federal Work-Study, institutionally sponsored loans, scholarships/grants, tuition waivers (full and partial), and unspecified assistantships available. Support available to part-time students. Financial award application deadline: 3/1. In 2010, 77 master's, 17 doctorates, 1 other advanced degree awarded. *Degree program information:* Part-time and evening/weekend programs available. Offers animal sciences (MPS, MS); biochemistry (MPS, MS); biochemistry and molecular biology (PhD); biological sciences (MS, PhD); botany and plant pathology (MS); ecology and environmental science (MS, PhD); ecology and environmental sciences (MS, PhD); entomology (MS); food and nutritional sciences (PhD); food science and human nutrition (MS); forest resources (PhD); forestry (MF, MS); horticulture (MS); individualized track (MS, CAS); marine biology (MS, PhD); marine policy (MS); microbiology (MPS, MS, PhD); natural sciences, forestry, and agriculture (MF, MPS, MS, MWC, PhD, CAS); oceanography (MS, PhD); plant science (PhD); plant, soil, and environmental sciences (MS); resource economics and policy (MS); resource utilization (MS); rural health family nurse practitioner (MS, CAS); water resources (MS, PhD); wildlife conservation (MWC); wildlife ecology (MS, PhD); zoology (MS, PhD). *Application deadline:* For fall admission, 2/1 priority date for domestic students. Applications are processed on a rolling basis. *Application fee:* $65. Electronic applications accepted. *Application Contact:* Scott G. Delcourt, Associate Dean of the Graduate School, 207-581-3291, Fax: 207-581-3232, E-mail: graduate@maine.edu. *Dean,* Dr. Edward Ashworth, 207-581-3206, Fax: 207-581-3207.

UNIVERSITY OF MAINE AT FARMINGTON, Farmington, ME 04938-1990

General Information State-supported, coed, comprehensive institution. *Enrollment:* 2,392 graduate, professional, and undergraduate students; 55 full-time matriculated graduate/professional students (46 women). *Enrollment by degree level:* 55 master's. *Graduate faculty:* 10 full-time (9 women), 9 part-time/adjunct (7 women). Tuition, state resident: part-time $364 per credit. *Required fees:* $81 per semester. One-time fee: $160 part-time. Part-time tuition and fees vary according to course load. *Library facilities:* Mantor Library. *Online resources:* library catalog, web page, access to other libraries' catalogs. *Collection:* 98,935 titles, 498 serial subscriptions, 8,550 audiovisual materials.

Computer facilities: Computer purchase and lease plans are available. 180 computers available on campus for general student use. A campuswide network can be accessed from student residence rooms and from off campus. Online class registration, laptop initiative are available. *Web address:* http://www.umf.maine.edu/.

General Application Contact: Eileen Reading, Assistant Director of Admission, 207-778-7052, Fax: 207-778-8182, E-mail: eileen.reading@maine.edu.

GRADUATE UNITS

Program in Education Students: 55 full-time (46 women); includes 2 minority (1 American Indian or Alaska Native, non-Hispanic/Latino; 1 Hispanic/Latino). 11 applicants, 100% accepted, 10 enrolled. *Faculty:* 10 full-time (9 women), 9 part-time/adjunct (7 women). Expenses: Contact institution. *Degree program information:* Part-time and evening/weekend programs available. Postbaccalaureate distance learning degree programs offered (minimal on-campus study). Offers early childhood education (MS Ed); educational leadership (MS Ed). *Application deadline:* Applications are processed on a rolling basis. *Application fee:* $60.

UNIVERSITY OF MANAGEMENT AND TECHNOLOGY, Arlington, VA 22209

General Information Proprietary, coed, comprehensive institution. *Graduate housing:* On-campus housing not available.

GRADUATE UNITS

Program in Business Administration *Degree program information:* Part-time and evening/weekend programs available. Postbaccalaureate distance learning degree programs offered (no on-campus study). Offers acquisition management (DBA); general management (MBA, DBA); project management (MBA, DBA). Electronic applications accepted.

Program in Computer Science and Information Technology *Degree program information:* Part-time and evening/weekend programs available. Postbaccalaureate distance learning degree programs offered (no on-campus study). Offers computer science (MS); information technology (AC); information technology project management (MS); management information systems (MS); project management (AC); software engineering (MS). Electronic applications accepted.

Program in Criminal Justice Offers criminal justice (MS).

Program in Management *Degree program information:* Part-time and evening/weekend programs available. Postbaccalaureate distance learning degree programs offered (no on-campus study). Offers acquisition management (MS, AC); general management (MS); project management (MS, AC); public administration (MPA, MS, AC). Electronic applications accepted.

THE UNIVERSITY OF MANCHESTER, Manchester M13 9PL, United Kingdom

General Information Public, comprehensive institution.

GRADUATE UNITS

Faculty of Life Sciences Offers adaptive organismal biology (M Phil, PhD); animal biology (M Phil, PhD); biochemistry (M Phil, PhD); bioinformatics (M Phil, PhD); biomolecular sciences (M Phil, PhD); biotechnology (M Phil, PhD); cell biology (M Phil, PhD); cell matrix research (M Phil, PhD); channels and transporters (M Phil, PhD); developmental biology (M Phil, PhD); Egyptology (M Phil, PhD); environmental biology (M Phil, PhD); evolutionary biology (M Phil, PhD); gene expression (M Phil, PhD); genetics (M Phil, PhD); history of science, technology and medicine (M Phil, PhD); immunology (M Phil, PhD); integrative neurobiology and behavior (M Phil, PhD); membrane trafficking (M Phil, PhD); microbiology (M Phil, PhD); molecular and cellular neuroscience (M Phil, PhD); molecular biology (M Phil, PhD); molecular cancer studies (M Phil, PhD); neuroscience (M Phil, PhD); ophthalmology (M Phil, PhD); optometry (M Phil, PhD); organelle function (M Phil, PhD); pharmacology (M Phil, PhD); physiology (M Phil, PhD); plant sciences (M Phil, PhD); stem cell research (M Phil, PhD); structural biology (M Phil, PhD); systems neuroscience (M Phil, PhD); toxicology (M Phil, PhD).

Manchester Business School Offers accounting (M Phil, PhD); business (M Ent, D Ent); business and management (M Phil); business management (PhD).

School of Arts, Histories and Cultures Offers anthropology, media and performance (PhD); applied theatre professional (PhD); archaeology (PhD); art history and visual studies (PhD); arts management and cultural policy (PhD); classics and ancient history (PhD); composition (PhD); creative writing (PhD); drama (PhD); economic and social history (PhD); electroacoustic composition (PhD); English and American studies (PhD); history (PhD); humanitarianism and conflict response (PhD); museology (PhD); music (PhD); musicology (PhD); religions and theology (PhD).

School of Chemical Engineering and Analytical Science Offers biocatalysis (M Phil, PhD); chemical engineering (M Phil, PhD); chemical engineering and analytical science (M Phil, D Eng, PhD); colloids, crystals, interfaces and materials (M Phil, PhD); environment and sustainable technology (M Phil, PhD); instrumentation (M Phil, PhD); multi-scale modeling (M Phil, PhD); process integration (M Phil, PhD); systems biology (M Phil, PhD).

School of Chemistry Offers biological chemistry (PhD); chemistry (M Ent, M Phil, M Sc, D Ent, PhD); inorganic chemistry (PhD); materials chemistry (PhD); nanoscience (PhD); nuclear fission (PhD); organic chemistry (PhD); physical chemistry (PhD); theoretical chemistry (PhD).

School of Computer Science Offers computer science (M Phil, PhD).

School of Dentistry Offers basic dental sciences (cancer studies) (M Phil, PhD); basic dental sciences (molecular genetics) (M Phil, PhD); basic dental sciences (stem cell biology) (M Phil, PhD); biomaterials sciences and dental technology (M Phil, PhD); dental public health/community dentistry (M Phil, PhD); dental science (clinical) (PhD); endodontology (M Phil, PhD); fixed and removable prosthodontics (M Phil, PhD); operative dentistry (M Phil, PhD); oral and maxillofacial surgery (M Phil, PhD); oral radiology (M Phil, PhD); orthodontics (M Phil, PhD); restorative dentistry (M Phil, PhD).

School of Earth, Atmospheric and Environmental Sciences Offers atmospheric sciences (M Phil, M Sc, PhD); basin studies and petroleum geosciences (M Phil, M Sc, PhD); earth, atmospheric and environmental sciences (M Phil, M Sc, PhD); environmental geochemistry and cosmochemistry (M Phil, M Sc, PhD); isotope geochemistry and cosmochemistry (M Phil, M Sc, PhD); paleontology (M Phil, M Sc, PhD); physics and chemistry of minerals and fluids (M Phil, M Sc, PhD); structural and petrological geosciences (M Phil, M Sc, PhD).

School of Education Offers counseling (D Couns); counseling psychology (D Couns); education (M Phil, Ed D, PhD); educational and child psychology (Ed D); educational psychology (Ed D).

School of Electrical and Electronic Engineering Offers electrical and electronic engineering (M Phil, PhD).

School of Environment and Development Offers architecture (M Phil, PhD); development policy and management (M Phil, PhD); human geography (M Phil, PhD); physical geography (M Phil, PhD); planning and landscape (M Phil, PhD).

School of Languages, Linguistics and Cultures Offers Arab world studies (PhD); Chinese studies (M Phil, PhD); East Asian studies (M Phil, PhD); English language (PhD); French studies (M Phil, PhD); German studies (M Phil, PhD); interpreting studies (PhD); Italian studies (M Phil, PhD); Japanese studies (M Phil, PhD); Latin American cultural studies (M Phil, PhD); linguistics (M Phil, PhD); Middle Eastern studies (M Phil, PhD); Polish studies (M Phil, PhD); Portuguese studies (M Phil, PhD); Russian studies (M Phil, PhD); Spanish studies (M Phil, PhD); translation and intercultural studies (M Phil, PhD).

School of Law Offers bioethics and medical jurisprudence (PhD); criminology (M Phil, PhD); law (M Phil, PhD).

School of Materials Offers advanced aerospace materials engineering (M Sc); advanced metallic systems (PhD); biomedical materials (M Phil, M Sc, PhD); ceramics and glass (M Phil, M Sc, PhD); composite materials (M Sc, PhD); corrosion and protection (M Phil, M Sc, PhD); materials (M Phil, PhD); metallic materials (M Phil, M Sc, PhD); nanostructural materials (M Phil, M Sc, PhD); paper science (M Phil, M Sc, PhD); polymer science and engineering (M Phil, M Sc, PhD); technical textiles (M Sc); textile design, fashion and management (M Phil, M Sc, PhD); textile science and technology (M Phil, M Sc, PhD); textiles (M Phil, PhD); textiles and fashion (M Ent).

School of Mathematics Offers actuarial science (PhD); applied mathematics (M Phil, PhD); applied numerical computing (M Phil, PhD); financial mathematics (M Phil, PhD); mathematical logic (M Phil); probability (M Phil, PhD); pure mathematics (M Phil, PhD); statistics (M Phil, PhD).

School of Mechanical, Aerospace and Civil Engineering Offers advanced manufacturing technology (M Ent); aerospace engineering (M Phil, M Sc, PhD); civil engineering (M Phil, M Sc, PhD); environmental engineering (M Phil, PhD); management of projects (M Phil, M Sc, PhD); mechanical engineering (M Phil, M Sc, PhD); mechanical engineering design (M Ent); nuclear engineering (M Phil, D Eng, PhD).

School of Medicine Offers medicine (M Phil, PhD).

School of Nursing, Midwifery and Social Work Offers nursing (M Phil, PhD); social work (M Phil, PhD).

School of Pharmacy and Pharmaceutical Sciences Offers pharmacy and pharmaceutical sciences (M Phil, PhD).

School of Physics and Astronomy Offers astronomy and astrophysics (M Sc, PhD); biological physics (M Sc, PhD); condensed matter physics (M Sc, PhD); nonlinear and liquid crystals physics (M Sc, PhD); nuclear physics (M Sc, PhD); particle physics (M Sc, PhD); photon physics (M Sc, PhD); physics (M Sc, PhD); theoretical physics (M Sc, PhD).

School of Psychological Sciences Offers audiology (M Phil, PhD); clinical psychology (M Phil, PhD, Psy D); psychology (M Phil, PhD).

School of Social Sciences Offers ethnographic documentary (M Phil); interdisciplinary study of culture (PhD); philosophy (PhD); politics (PhD); social anthropology (PhD); social anthropology with visual media (PhD); social change (PhD); social statistics (PhD); sociology (PhD); visual anthropology (M Phil).

UNIVERSITY OF MANITOBA, Winnipeg, MB R3T 2N2, Canada

General Information Province-supported, coed, university. CGS member. *Graduate housing:* Rooms and/or apartments available to single and married students. *Research affiliation:* Canada Department of Agriculture Research Station, Freshwater Institute, Atomic Energy of Canada, Manitoba Department of Mines, Resources, and Environmental Management, Northern Scientific Training Program (Northern studies), Taiga Biological Research Trust.

GRADUATE UNITS

Faculty of Dentistry Offers dental diagnostic and surgical sciences (M Dent); dentistry (DMD, M Dent, M Sc, PhD); oral and maxillofacial surgery (M Dent); oral biology (M Sc, PhD); orthodontics (M Sc); periodontology (M Dent); preventive dental science (M Sc); restorative dentistry (M Dent).

Faculty of Graduate Studies *Degree program information:* Part-time programs available.

Asper School of Business Offers business (M Sc, MBA, PhD).

Clayton H. Riddell Faculty of Environment, Earth, and Resources Offers environment (M Env); environment and geography (M Sc); environment, earth, and resources (M Env, M Sc, MA, MNRM, PhD); geography (MA, PhD); geology (M Sc, PhD); geophysics (M Sc, PhD); natural resources and environmental management (PhD); natural resources management (MNRM).

College Universitaire de Saint Boniface Offers Canadian studies (MA); education (M Ed).

Faculty of Agricultural and Food Sciences Offers agribusiness (M Sc, PhD); agricultural and food sciences (M Sc, PhD); agronomy and plant protection (M Sc, PhD); animal science (M Sc, PhD); entomology (M Sc, PhD); food and nutritional sciences (PhD); food science (M Sc); foods and nutrition (M Sc); horticulture (M Sc, PhD); plant breeding and genetics (M Sc, PhD); plant physiology-biochemistry (M Sc, PhD); soil science (M Sc, PhD).

Faculty of Architecture Offers architecture (M Arch, M Land Arch, MCP, MID); city planning (MCP); interior design (MID); landscape architecture (M Land Arch).

Faculty of Arts Offers anthropology (MA, PhD); archival studies (MA); arts (MA, MPA, PhD); classics (MA); clinical psychology (PhD); economics (MA, PhD); English (MA, PhD); French (MA, PhD); German language and literature (MA); history (MA, PhD); Icelandic language and literature (MA); linguistics (MA, PhD); native studies (MA); philosophy (MA); political studies (MA); psychology (MA, PhD); public administration (MPA); religion (MA, PhD); school psychology (MA); Slavic languages and literatures (MA); sociology (MA, PhD).

Faculty of Education Offers adult and post-secondary education (M Ed); education (M Ed, PhD); educational administration (M Ed); guidance and counseling (M Ed); inclusive special education (M Ed); language and literacy (M Ed); second language education (M Ed); social foundations of education (M Ed); studies in curriculum, teaching and learning (M Ed).

Faculty of Engineering Offers biosystems engineering (M Eng, M Sc, PhD); civil engineering (M Eng, M Sc, PhD); electrical and computer engineering (M Eng, M Sc, PhD); engineering (M Eng, M Sc, PhD); mechanical and manufacturing engineering (M Eng, M Sc, PhD).

Faculty of Human Ecology Offers family social sciences (M Sc); human ecology (M Sc); human nutritional sciences (M Sc); textile sciences (M Sc).

Faculty of Kinesiology and Recreation Management Offers kinesiology and recreation management (M Sc); recreation studies (MA).

Faculty of Law Students: 7 full-time (2 women), 1 part-time (0 women); includes 3 Black or African American, non-Hispanic/Latino; 2 Asian, non-Hispanic/Latino; 1 Hispanic/Latino. *Faculty:* 24 full-time (8 women). Expenses: Contact institution. *Financial support:* In 2010–11, 7 students received support, including 7 fellowships with full tuition reimbursements available (averaging $6,000 per year); scholarships/grants also available. Financial award application deadline: 3/15. In 2010, 3 master's awarded. Offers law (LL M). *Application deadline:* For fall admission, 6/15 for domestic students, 3/15 for international students. Applications are processed on a rolling basis. Electronic applications accepted. *Application Contact:* Sonja De Gannes, Student Program Officer, 204-474-6129, Fax: 204-474-7580, E-mail: sonja_degannes@umanitoba.ca. *Associate Dean, Research and Graduate Studies*, Dr. Jennifer L. Schulz, 204-474-7958, Fax: 204-474-7580, E-mail: j_schulz@umanitoba.ca.

Faculty of Nursing Offers cancer nursing (MN); nursing (MN).

Faculty of Pharmacy Offers pharmacy (M Sc, PhD).

Faculty of Science Offers botany (M Sc, PhD); chemistry (M Sc, PhD); computer science (M Sc, PhD); ecology (M Sc, PhD); mathematical, computational and statistical sciences (MMCSS); mathematics (M Sc, PhD); microbiology (M Sc, PhD); physics and astronomy (M Sc, PhD); science (M Sc, MMCSS, PhD); statistics (M Sc, PhD); zoology (M Sc, PhD).

Faculty of Social Work Offers social work (MSW, PhD).

Interdisciplinary Programs Offers disability studies (M Sc, MA); individual interdisciplinary studies (M Sc, MA, PhD); interdisciplinary studies (M Sc, MA, PhD).

Marcel A. Desautels Faculty of Music Offers music (M Mus).

School of Medical Rehabilitation Offers applied health sciences (PhD); occupational therapy (MOT); physical therapy (MPT); rehabilitation (M Sc).

Faculty of Medicine *Degree program information:* Part-time programs available. Offers medicine (M Sc, PhD). Electronic applications accepted.

Graduate Programs in Medicine *Degree program information:* Part-time programs available. Offers biochemistry and medical genetics (M Sc, PhD); community health sciences (M Sc, MPH, PhD, G Dip); human anatomy and cell science (M Sc, PhD); immunology (M Sc, PhD); medical microbiology (M Sc, PhD); medicine (M Sc, MPH, PhD, G Dip); pathology (M Sc); pediatrics and child health (M Sc); pharmacology and therapeutics (M Sc, PhD); physiology (M Sc, PhD); psychiatry (M Sc); rehabilitation (M Sc); surgery (M Sc).

UNIVERSITY OF MARY, Bismarck, ND 58504-9652

General Information Independent-religious, coed, comprehensive institution. *Enrollment:* 596 full-time matriculated graduate/professional students (424 women), 472 part-time matriculated graduate/professional students (297 women). *Enrollment by degree level:* 1,009 master's, 59 doctoral. *Graduate faculty:* 20 full-time (14 women), 107 part-time/adjunct (53 women). *Tuition:* Full-time $10,800; part-time $450 per credit. Tuition and fees vary according to course load, degree level, program and student level. *Graduate housing:* Room and/or apartments available on a first-come, first-served basis to single students; on-campus housing not available to married students. Typical cost: $4600 per year ($7240 including board). Housing application deadline: 7/15. *Student services:* Campus employment opportunities, campus safety program, career counseling, exercise/wellness program, free psychological counseling, international student services, services for students with disabilities, teacher training. *Library facilities:* University of Mary Library. *Online resources:* library catalog, access to other libraries' catalogs. *Collection:* 64,524 titles, 210 serial subscriptions, 4,346 audiovisual materials.

Computer facilities: 100 computers available on campus for general student use. A campuswide network can be accessed from student residence rooms and from off campus. Online class registration is available. *Web address:* http://www.umary.edu/.

General Application Contact: Dr. Kathy Perrin, Director of Graduate Studies, 701-355-8119, Fax: 701-255-7687, E-mail: kperrin@umary.edu.

GRADUATE UNITS

Gary Tharaldson School of Business Students: 232 full-time (123 women), 226 part-time (115 women); includes 63 minority (30 Black or African American, non-Hispanic/Latino; 23

University of Mary (continued)

American Indian or Alaska Native, non-Hispanic/Latino; 5 Asian, non-Hispanic/Latino; 3 Hispanic/Latino; 1 Native Hawaiian or other Pacific Islander, non-Hispanic/Latino; 1 Two or more races, non-Hispanic/Latino), 20 international. Average age 36. 209 applicants, 98% accepted, 189 enrolled. *Faculty:* 2 full-time (0 women), 73 part-time/adjunct (27 women). Expenses: Contact institution. *Financial support:* Application deadline: 8/1. In 2010, 265 master's awarded. *Degree program information:* Part-time and evening/weekend programs available. Offers accountancy (MBA); business administration (MBA); health care (MBA); human resource management (MBA); management (MBA); project management (MPM); strategic leadership (MSSL). *Application deadline:* Applications are processed on a rolling basis. *Application fee:* $40. *Application Contact:* Wayne G. Maruska, Graduate Program Advisor, 701-355-8134, Fax: 701-255-7687, E-mail: wmaruska@umary.edu. *Director of the School of Accelerated and Distance Education,* Dr. Shanda Traiser, 701-355-8160, Fax: 701-255-7687, E-mail: straiser@umary.edu.

School of Education and Behavioral Sciences Expenses: Contact institution. Offers addiction counseling (MSC); college teaching (M Ed); community counseling (MSC); curriculum, instruction and assessment (M Ed); early childhood education (M Ed); early childhood special education (M Ed); education and behavioral sciences (M Ed, MSC); elementary administration (M Ed); emotional disorders (M Ed); learning disabilities (M Ed); reading (M Ed); school counseling (MSC); secondary administration (M Ed); special education strategist (M Ed); student affairs counseling (MSC). *Application Contact:* Dr. Kathy Perrin, Director of Graduate Studies, 701-355-8119, Fax: 701-255-7687, E-mail: kperrin@umary.edu. *Dean,* Dr. Rod Jonas, 701-355-8097, Fax: 701-255-7687, E-mail: rjonas@umary.edu.

School of Health Sciences Expenses: Contact institution. Offers health sciences (MS, MSN, MSOT, DPT); occupational therapy (MSOT); physical therapy (DPT); respiratory therapy (MS). *Application Contact:* Dr. Kathy Perrin, Director of Graduate Studies, 701-355-8119, Fax: 701-255-7687, E-mail: kperrin@umary.edu.

Division of Nursing Students: 195 full-time (182 women), 89 part-time (82 women); includes 23 minority (9 Black or African American, non-Hispanic/Latino; 3 American Indian or Alaska Native, non-Hispanic/Latino; 3 Asian, non-Hispanic/Latino; 6 Hispanic/Latino; 1 Native Hawaiian or other Pacific Islander, non-Hispanic/Latino; 1 Two or more races, non-Hispanic/Latino), 2 international. Average age 40. *Faculty:* 6 full-time (5 women), 15 part-time/adjunct (14 women). Expenses: Contact institution. *Financial support:* In 2010–11, 14 fellowships with partial tuition reimbursements, 3 teaching assistantships with partial tuition reimbursements were awarded. Financial award application deadline: 8/1; financial award applicants required to submit FAFSA. In 2010, 80 master's awarded. *Degree program information:* Part-time and evening/weekend programs available. Postbaccalaureate distance learning degree programs offered (minimal on-campus study). Offers family nurse practitioner (MSN); nurse administrator (MSN); nursing educator (MSN). *Application deadline:* Applications are processed on a rolling basis. *Application fee:* $40. Electronic applications accepted. *Application Contact:* Joanne Lassiter, Nurse Recruiter, 701-355-8379, Fax: 701-255-7687, E-mail: jllassiter@umary.edu. *Director,* Glenda Reemts, 701-255-7500 Ext. 8041, Fax: 701-255-7687, E-mail: greemts@umary.edu.

UNIVERSITY OF MARY HARDIN-BAYLOR, Belton, TX 76513

General Information Independent-religious, coed, comprehensive institution. *Enrollment:* 2,956 graduate, professional, and undergraduate students; 164 full-time matriculated graduate/professional students (88 women), 139 part-time matriculated graduate/professional students (84 women). *Enrollment by degree level:* 233 master's, 70 doctoral. *Graduate faculty:* 36 full-time (22 women), 6 part-time/adjunct (2 women). *Graduate housing:* On-campus housing not available. *Student services:* Campus employment opportunities, career counseling, exercise/wellness program, free psychological counseling, international student services, multicultural affairs office, services for students with disabilities, teacher training. *Library facilities:* Townsend Memorial Library. *Online resources:* library catalog.

Computer facilities: Computer purchase and lease plans are available. 275 computers available on campus for general student use. A campuswide network can be accessed from student residence rooms and from off campus. Online class registration is available. *Web address:* http://www.umhb.edu/.

General Application Contact: Rachel Haynes, Director of Graduate Admissions, 254-295-4020, Fax: 254-295-5301, E-mail: rhaynes@umhb.edu.

GRADUATE UNITS

Graduate Studies in Business Administration Students: 29 full-time (10 women), 26 part-time (13 women); includes 12 minority (3 Black or African American, non-Hispanic/Latino; 9 Hispanic/Latino), 23 international. Average age 29. 71 applicants, 72% accepted, 27 enrolled. *Faculty:* 6 full-time (3 women), 2 part-time/adjunct (0 women). Expenses: Contact institution. *Financial support:* Federal Work-Study and scholarships (for some active duty military personnel only) available. Financial award applicants required to submit FAFSA. In 2010, 7 master's awarded. *Degree program information:* Part-time and evening/weekend programs available. Offers accounting (MBA); information systems management (MBA); management (MBA). *Application deadline:* For fall admission, 6/1 priority date for domestic students; for spring admission, 11/1 for domestic students. Applications are processed on a rolling basis. *Application fee:* $35 ($135 for international students). Electronic applications accepted. *Application Contact:* Dr. Terry Fox, Program Director, 254-295-5406, E-mail: terry.fox@umhb.edu. *Program Director,* Dr. Terry Fox, 254-295-5406, E-mail: terry.fox@umhb.edu.

Graduate Studies in Counseling and Psychology Students: 33 full-time (23 women), 18 part-time (10 women); includes 11 minority (6 Black or African American, non-Hispanic/Latino; 4 Hispanic/Latino; 1 Two or more races, non-Hispanic/Latino), 1 international. Average age 29. 46 applicants, 50% accepted, 19 enrolled. *Faculty:* 7 full-time (4 women). Expenses: Contact institution. *Financial support:* Research assistantships with full tuition reimbursements, Federal Work-Study and scholarships (for some active duty military personnel only) available. Support available to part-time students. Financial award applicants required to submit FAFSA. In 2010, 44 master's awarded. *Degree program information:* Part-time and evening/weekend programs available. Offers clinical mental health counseling (MA); marriage and family Christian counseling (MA); psychology and counseling (MA); school counseling and psychology (MA). *Application deadline:* For fall admission, 6/1 priority date for domestic students; for spring admission, 11/1 for domestic students. Applications are processed on a rolling basis. *Application fee:* $35 ($135 for international students). Electronic applications accepted. *Application Contact:* Dr. Isaac Gusukuma, Interim Graduate Program Director, 254-295-5017, E-mail: isaac.gusukuma@umhb.edu. *Interim Graduate Program Director,* Dr. Isaac Gusukuma, 254-295-5017, E-mail: isaac.gusukuma@umhb.edu.

Graduate Studies in Education Students: 37 full-time (25 women), 88 part-time (57 women); includes 44 minority (25 Black or African American, non-Hispanic/Latino; 3 Asian, non-Hispanic/Latino; 16 Hispanic/Latino), 2 international. Average age 37. 41 applicants, 73% accepted, 18 enrolled. *Faculty:* 16 full-time (10 women), 2 part-time/adjunct (0 women). Expenses: Contact institution. *Financial support:* Federal Work-Study, scholarships/grants, and scholarships (for some active duty military personnel only) available. Support available to part-time students. Financial award application deadline: 6/1; financial award applicants required to submit FAFSA. In 2010, 25 master's awarded. *Degree program information:* Part-time and evening/weekend programs available. Offers curriculum and instruction (M Ed); educational administration (M Ed, Ed D); educational psychology (M Ed); exercise and sport science (M S Ed); general studies (M Ed); reading education (M Ed). *Application deadline:* For fall admission, 6/1 priority date for domestic students; for spring admission, 11/1 for domestic students. Applications are processed on a rolling basis. *Application fee:* $35 ($135 for international students). Electronic applications accepted. *Application Contact:* Dr. Austin Vasek, Program Director, 254-295-4185, Fax: 254-295-4480, E-mail: austin.vasek@umhb.edu. *Program Director,* Dr. Austin Vasek, 254-295-4185, Fax: 254-295-4480, E-mail: austin.vasek@umhb.edu.

Graduate Studies in Information Systems Students: 47 full-time (16 women), 8 part-time (3 women); includes 1 minority (Black or African American, non-Hispanic/Latino), 52 international. Average age 23. 148 applicants, 100% accepted, 32 enrolled. *Faculty:* 3 full-time (1 woman). Expenses: Contact institution. *Financial support:* Federal Work-Study and scholarships (for some active duty military personnel only) available. Support available to part-time students. Financial award applicants required to submit FAFSA. In 2010, 2 master's awarded. *Degree program information:* Part-time and evening/weekend programs available. Offers information systems (MS). *Application deadline:* For fall admission, 6/1 priority date for domestic students; for spring admission, 11/1 for domestic students. Applications are processed on a rolling basis. *Application fee:* $35 ($135 for international students). Electronic applications accepted. *Application Contact:* Dr. Nancy Bonner, Graduate Program Director, 254-295-5405, E-mail: nbonner@umhb.edu. *Graduate Program Director,* Dr. Nancy Bonner, 254-295-5405, E-mail: nbonner@umhb.edu.

Graduate Studies in Nursing Students: 8 full-time (7 women), 3 part-time (all women); includes 3 minority (all Black or African American, non-Hispanic/Latino), 4 international. Average age 39. *Faculty:* 4 full-time (all women), 2 part-time/adjunct (both women). Expenses: Contact institution. *Financial support:* Applicants required to submit FAFSA. *Degree program information:* Part-time and evening/weekend programs available. Offers nursing (MSN). *Application deadline:* For fall admission, 6/1 priority date for domestic students; for spring admission, 11/1 priority date for domestic students. Applications are processed on a rolling basis. *Application fee:* $35 ($135 for international students). Electronic applications accepted. *Application Contact:* Dr. Margaret Prydun, Program Director, 254-295-4674, E-mail: margaret.prydun@umhb.edu. *Program Director,* Dr. Margaret Prydun, 254-295-4674, E-mail: margaret.prydun@umhb.edu.

UNIVERSITY OF MARYLAND, BALTIMORE, Baltimore, MD 21201

General Information State-supported, coed, graduate-only institution. CGS member. *Enrollment by degree level:* 2,990 first professional, 1,931 master's, 448 doctoral, 76 other advanced degrees. *Graduate faculty:* 1,746 full-time (751 women), 769 part-time/adjunct (464 women). Part-time tuition and fees vary according to course load, degree level and program. *Graduate housing:* Rooms and/or apartments available on a first-come, first-served basis to single and married students. *Student services:* Campus employment opportunities, campus safety program, career counseling, exercise/wellness program, free psychological counseling, grant writing training, international student services, low-cost health insurance, services for students with disabilities, writing training. *Library facilities:* Health Sciences and Human Services Library plus 1 other. *Online resources:* web page. *Collection:* 403,222 titles, 31,001 serial subscriptions. *Research affiliation:* University of Maryland Medical System (medical), University of Maryland BioPark (biology), University of Maryland Biotechnology Institute (biology).

Computer facilities: A campuswide network can be accessed from student residence rooms and from off campus. Online class registration is available. *Web address:* http://www.umaryland.edu/.

General Application Contact: Keith T. Brooks, Director, Graduate Enrollment Affairs, 410-706-7131, Fax: 410-706-3473, E-mail: kbrooks@umaryland.edu.

GRADUATE UNITS

Graduate School *Degree program information:* Part-time and evening/weekend programs available. Offers biochemistry (MS, PhD); biochemistry and molecular biology (MS, PhD); biomedical sciences—dental (MS, PhD); cancer biology (PhD); cell and molecular physiology (PhD); dental hygiene (MS); epidemiology (MS, PhD); gerontology (PhD); human genetics and genomic medicine (PhD); marine-estuarine-environmental sciences (MS, PhD); medical and research technology (MS); molecular medicine (MS, PhD); molecular microbiology and immunology (PhD); molecular toxicology and pharmacology (PhD); neuroscience (PhD); oral biology (MS); oral pathology (MS, PhD); pharmaceutical health service research (MS, PhD); pharmaceutical sciences (PhD); pharmacy administration (PhD); physical rehabilitation science (PhD); toxicology (MS, PhD). Electronic applications accepted.

School of Nursing *Degree program information:* Part-time programs available. Offers community health nursing (MS); direct nursing (PhD); gerontological nursing (MS); indirect nursing (PhD); maternal-child nursing (MS); medical-surgical nursing (MS); nurse-midwifery education (MS); nursing (MS, PhD); nursing administration (MS); nursing education (MS); nursing health policy (MS); primary care nursing (MS); psychiatric nursing (MS). MS/MBA offered jointly with University of Baltimore. Electronic applications accepted.

School of Social Work Offers social work (MSW, PhD). MSW/MA offered jointly with Baltimore Hebrew University; MBA/MSW with University of Maryland, College Park; MSW/MPH with The Johns Hopkins University. Electronic applications accepted.

Professional and Advanced Education Programs in Dentistry Students: 588 full-time (297 women), 2 part-time (both women); includes 35 Black or African American, non-Hispanic/Latino; 1 American Indian or Alaska Native, non-Hispanic/Latino; 124 Asian, non-Hispanic/Latino; 27 Hispanic/Latino, 20 international. Average age 26. Expenses: Contact institution. *Financial support:* Career-related internships or fieldwork, Federal Work-Study, scholarships/grants, and traineeships available. Financial award application deadline: 3/1; financial award applicants required to submit FAFSA. In 2010, 117 first professional degrees, 38 other advanced degrees awarded. Offers advanced general dentistry (Certificate); dentistry (DDS); endodontics (Certificate); oral-maxillofacial surgery (Certificate); orthodontics (Certificate); pediatric dentistry (Certificate); periodontics (Certificate); prosthodontics (Certificate). *Application deadline:* Applications are processed on a rolling basis. *Application fee:* $85. Electronic applications accepted. *Application Contact:* Dr. Patricia Meehan, Assistant Dean for Admissions, 410-706-7472, Fax: 410-706-0945, E-mail: ddsadmissions@umaryland.edu. *Dean,* Dr. Christian S. Stohler, 410-706-7461.

Professional Program in Pharmacy Students: 631 full-time (412 women); includes 65 Black or African American, non-Hispanic/Latino; 2 American Indian or Alaska Native, non-Hispanic/Latino; 282 Asian, non-Hispanic/Latino; 10 Hispanic/Latino. Average age 25. 1,366 applicants, 12% accepted, 161 enrolled. *Faculty:* 72 full-time (37 women), 60 part-time/adjunct (11 women). Expenses: Contact institution. *Financial support:* In 2010–11, 350 students received support. Career-related internships or fieldwork, Federal Work-Study, institutionally sponsored loans, and scholarships/grants available. Support available to part-time students. Financial award application deadline: 3/1; financial award applicants required to submit FAFSA. In 2010, 114 first professional degrees awarded. Offers pharmacy (Pharm D). *Application deadline:* For fall admission, 1/5 for domestic and international students. *Application fee:* $45. Electronic applications accepted. *Application Contact:* Patrice Sharp, Admissions Officer, 410-706-7653, Fax: 410-706-2158, E-mail: pharmdhelp@umaryland.edu. *Associate Dean for Student Affairs,* Dr. Jill Morgan, 410-706-4332, Fax: 410-706-2158, E-mail: jmorgan@rx.umaryland.edu.

School of Law Students: 739 full-time (363 women), 233 part-time (104 women); includes 105 Black or African American, non-Hispanic/Latino; 3 American Indian or Alaska Native, non-Hispanic/Latino; 91 Asian, non-Hispanic/Latino; 82 Hispanic/Latino, 8 international. Average age 27. 3,853 applicants, 18% accepted, 296 enrolled. *Faculty:* 65 full-time (34 women), 50 part-time/adjunct (16 women). Expenses: Contact institution. *Financial support:* In 2010–11, 819 students received support, including 21 fellowships (averaging $4,000 per year); Federal Work-Study, institutionally sponsored loans, and scholarships/grants also available. Support available to part-time students. Financial award application deadline: 3/1; financial award applicants required to submit FAFSA. In 2010, 281 first professional degrees awarded. *Degree program information:* Part-time and evening/weekend programs available. Offers law (JD, LL M). *Application deadline:* For fall admission, 4/1 priority date for domestic and international students. Applications are processed on a rolling basis. *Application fee:* $70. Electronic applications accepted. *Application Contact:* Connie Beals, Executive Director of Admissions and Student Recruiting, 410-706-3492, Fax: 410-706-1793, E-mail: admissions@law.umaryland.edu. *Dean/Professor,* Phoebe A. Haddon, 410-706-7214, Fax: 410-706-4045, E-mail: phaddon@law.umaryland.edu.

School of Medicine Students: 1,048 full-time (627 women), 173 part-time (122 women); includes 109 Black or African American, non-Hispanic/Latino; 1 American Indian or Alaska Native, non-Hispanic/Latino; 193 Asian, non-Hispanic/Latino; 36 Hispanic/Latino, 55 international. Average age 27. Expenses: Contact institution. *Financial support:* In 2010–11, research assistantships with partial tuition reimbursements (averaging $25,000 per year); fellowships, Federal Work-Study, scholarships/grants, health care benefits, and unspecified assistantships also available. Financial award application deadline: 3/1; financial award applicants required to submit FAFSA. In 2010, 227 first professional degrees, 39 master's, 54 doctorates awarded. *Degree program information:* Part-time programs available. Offers biostatistics

(MS); clinical research (MS); epidemiology and preventative medicine (PhD); epidemiology and preventive medicine (MPH, MS); genetic counseling (MGC); gerontology (PhD); human genetics and genomic (PhD); human genetics and genomic medicine (MS); medicine (MD, MGC, MPH, MS, DPT, PhD); molecular epidemiology (MS, PhD); pathologists' assistant (MS); physical rehabilitation science (PhD); physical therapy and rehabilitation science (DPT); toxicology (MS, PhD). Electronic applications accepted. *Application Contact:* Dr. E. Albert Reece, Dean and Vice President for Medical Affairs, 410-706-7410, Fax: 410-706-0235, E-mail: deanmed@som.umaryland.edu. *Dean and Vice President for Medical Affairs*, Dr. E. Albert Reece, 410-706-7410, Fax: 410-706-0235, E-mail: deanmed@som.umaryland.edu.

UNIVERSITY OF MARYLAND, BALTIMORE COUNTY, Baltimore, MD 21250

General Information State-supported, coed, university. CGS member. *Enrollment:* 12,888 graduate, professional, and undergraduate students; 1,135 full-time matriculated graduate/professional students (602 women), 1,296 part-time matriculated graduate/professional students (688 women). *Enrollment by degree level:* 1,532 master's, 756 doctoral, 143 other advanced degrees. *Graduate faculty:* 338 full-time, 109 part-time/adjunct. *Graduate housing:* Room and/or apartments available on a first-come, first-served basis to single students; on-campus housing not available to married students. Housing application deadline: 6/1. *Student services:* Campus employment opportunities, campus safety program, career counseling, child daycare facilities, exercise/wellness program, free psychological counseling, grant writing training, international student services, low-cost health insurance, multicultural affairs office, services for students with disabilities, teacher training, writing training. *Library facilities:* Albin O. Kuhn Library and Gallery plus 1 other. *Online resources:* library catalog, web page, access to other libraries' catalogs. *Collection:* 1 million titles, 33,078 serial subscriptions, 2.2 million audiovisual materials. *Research affiliation:* Sciences Applications International Corporation (information systems and technology), Halliburton Energy Services (provider of products and services to oil and gas industries), IBM (computers and information technology), BouMatic (dairy industry), Pfizer, Inc. (pharmaceuticals), Fujitsu Laboratories of America (information technology and communications).

Computer facilities: 875 computers available on campus for general student use. A campuswide network can be accessed from student residence rooms and from off campus. Online class registration, student account information are available. *Web address:* http://www.umbc.edu/.

General Application Contact: Kathryn Nee, Coordinator of Domestic Admissions, 410-455-2944, E-mail: nee@umbc.edu.

GRADUATE UNITS

Graduate School Students: 1,135 full-time (602 women), 1,296 part-time (688 women); includes 252 Black or African American, non-Hispanic/Latino; 2 American Indian or Alaska Native, non-Hispanic/Latino; 159 Asian, non-Hispanic/Latino; 76 Hispanic/Latino; 17 Two or more races, non-Hispanic/Latino, 443 international. Average age 31. 2,468 applicants, 62% accepted, 813 enrolled. *Faculty:* 338 full-time, 109 part-time/adjunct. Expenses: Contact institution. *Financial support:* In 2010–11, 673 students received support, including 35 fellowships with tuition reimbursements available (averaging $16,231 per year), 292 research assistantships with tuition reimbursements available (averaging $16,231 per year), 327 teaching assistantships with tuition reimbursements available (averaging $16,231 per year); career-related internships or fieldwork, Federal Work-Study, scholarships/grants, traineeships, health care benefits, and unspecified assistantships also available. Financial award applicants required to submit FAFSA. In 2010, 505 master's, 84 doctorates, 126 other advanced degrees awarded. *Degree program information:* Part-time and evening/weekend programs available. Postbaccalaureate distance learning degree programs offered (no on-campus study). Offers aging policy for the elderly (PhD); epidemiology of aging (PhD); marine-estuarine-environmental sciences (MS, PhD); social, cultural, and behavioral sciences (PhD). *Application deadline:* For fall admission, 1/1 for international students; for spring admission, 5/1 for international students. Applications are processed on a rolling basis. *Application fee:* $50. Electronic applications accepted. *Application Contact:* Kathryn Nee, Coordinator of Domestic Admissions, 410-455-2944, E-mail: nee@umbc.edu. *Dean and Vice Provost for Graduate Education*, Dr. Janet C. Rutledge, 410-455-2199.

College of Arts, Humanities and Social Sciences Students: 470 full-time (335 women), 710 part-time (503 women); includes 122 Black or African American, non-Hispanic/Latino; 2 American Indian or Alaska Native, non-Hispanic/Latino; 58 Asian, non-Hispanic/Latino; 41 Hispanic/Latino; 10 Two or more races, non-Hispanic/Latino, 82 international. Average age 33. 924 applicants, 63% accepted, 337 enrolled. *Faculty:* 405 full-time, 148 part-time/adjunct. Expenses: Contact institution. *Financial support:* Fellowships, research assistantships, teaching assistantships, career-related internships or fieldwork, scholarships/grants, health care benefits, and unspecified assistantships available. Financial award applicants required to submit FAFSA. In 2010, 260 master's, 22 doctorates, 97 other advanced degrees awarded. Offers administration, planning, and policy (MS); American contemporary music (Postbaccalaureate Certificate); applied behavioral analysis (MA); applied developmental psychology (PhD); applied sociology (MA, Postbaccalaureate Certificate); arts, humanities and social science (MA, MAT, MFA, MPP, MPS, MS, PhD, Certificate, Graduate Certificate, Postbaccalaureate Certificate); computer/web-based instruction (Postbaccalaureate Certificate); distance education (Graduate Certificate, Postbaccalaureate Certificate); e-learning in instructional design (Graduate Certificate); early childhood education (MAT); economic policy analysis (MA); economics (PhD); education (MA, MPP, MS, PhD); elementary education (MAT); elementary/middle science education (Postbaccalaureate Certificate); emergency health services (MS); emergency management (Postbaccalaureate Certificate); evaluation (MPP); gender and women's studies (Postbaccalaureate Certificate); geographic information systems (MPS, Certificate); geography and environmental systems (MS, PhD); health (MPP, PhD); historical studies (MA); human services psychology (MA, PhD); human services psychology/clinical (PhD); imaging and digital arts (MFA); industrial organizational psychology (MPS); instructional systems development (MA, Graduate Certificate); instructional systems development: training systems (MA, Graduate Certificate); instructional technology (Graduate Certificate); intercultural communication (MA); language, literacy, and culture (PhD); language, literacy, culture (PhD); management (MPP, PhD); math education (Postbaccalaureate Certificate); mathematics education (MA); nonprofit sector (Postbaccalaureate Certificate); policy history (PhD); preventive medicine and epidemiology (MS); psychology (MPS); public policy (MPP, PhD); science education (MA); secondary education (MAT); secondary science (MAT); STEM education (MA, Postbaccalaureate Certificate); teaching (MAT); teaching English to speakers of other languages (MA, Postbaccalaureate Certificate); urban (MPP, PhD). *Application deadline:* For fall admission, 1/1 for international students; for spring admission, 5/1 for international students. Applications are processed on a rolling basis. *Application fee:* $50. Electronic applications accepted. *Application Contact:* Kathryn Nee, Coordinator of Domestic Admissions, 410-455-2944, E-mail: nee@umbc.edu. *Dean*, Dr. John Jeffries, 410-455-2312, Fax: 410-455-1045, E-mail: jeffries@umbc.edu.

College of Engineering and Information Technology Students: 391 full-time (117 women), 515 part-time (149 women); includes 202 minority (96 Black or African American, non-Hispanic/Latino; 72 Asian, non-Hispanic/Latino; 28 Hispanic/Latino; 6 Two or more races, non-Hispanic/Latino), 263 international. Average age 30. 883 applicants, 58% accepted, 230 enrolled. *Faculty:* 111 full-time (29 women), 39 part-time/adjunct (8 women). Expenses: Contact institution. *Financial support:* In 2010–11, 7 fellowships with full tuition reimbursements (averaging $25,000 per year), 113 research assistantships with full tuition reimbursements (averaging $22,000 per year), 82 teaching assistantships with full tuition reimbursements (averaging $17,000 per year) were awarded; career-related internships or fieldwork, Federal Work-Study, scholarships/grants, health care benefits, tuition waivers (partial), and unspecified assistantships also available. Support available to part-time students. Financial award application deadline: 6/30; financial award applicants required to submit FAFSA. In 2010, 172 master's, 30 doctorates, 25 other advanced degrees awarded. *Degree program information:* Part-time and evening/weekend programs available. Postbaccalaureate distance learning degree programs offered (no on-campus study). Offers biochemical regulatory engineering (Postbaccalaureate Certificate); chemical and biochemical engineering (MS, PhD, Postbaccalaureate Certificate); civil engineering (MS, PhD); computational thermal/fluid dynamics (Postbaccalaureate Certificate); computer engineering (MS, PhD); computer science (MS, PhD); electrical engineering (MS, PhD); engineering and information technology (MS, PhD, Postbaccalaureate Certificate); engineering management (MS, Postbaccalaureate Certificate); human-centered computing (MS, PhD); information systems (MS, PhD); mechanical engineering (MS, PhD); mechatronics (Postbaccalaureate Certificate); systems engineering (MS, Postbaccalaureate Certificate). *Application deadline:* For fall admission, 6/1 for domestic students, 1/1 for international students; for spring admission, 11/1 for domestic students, 6/1 for international students. Applications are processed on a rolling basis. *Application fee:* $50. Electronic applications accepted. *Application Contact:* Graduate School, 410-455-2537, E-mail: umbcgrad@umbc.edu. *Dean*, Dr. Warren R. DeVries, 410-455-3270, Fax: 410-455-3559, E-mail: wdevries@umbc.edu.

College of Natural and Mathematical Sciences Students: 244 full-time (132 women), 71 part-time (36 women); includes 66 minority (32 Black or African American, non-Hispanic/Latino; 27 Asian, non-Hispanic/Latino; 6 Hispanic/Latino; 1 Two or more races, non-Hispanic/Latino), 98 international. Average age 28. 373 applicants, 48% accepted, 86 enrolled. *Faculty:* 93 full-time (23 women). Expenses: Contact institution. *Financial support:* In 2010–11, 78 research assistantships with full and partial tuition reimbursements, 110 teaching assistantships with full tuition reimbursements were awarded. In 2010, 50 master's, 32 doctorates awarded. *Degree program information:* Part-time programs available. Offers applied mathematics (MS, PhD); applied molecular biology (MS); applied physics (MS, PhD); astrophysics (PhD); atmospheric physics (MS, PhD); biochemistry (MS, PhD); biological sciences (MS, PhD); biostatistics (PhD); chemistry (MS, PhD); environmental statistics (MS); molecular and cell biology (PhD); natural and mathematical sciences (MS, PhD, Postbaccalaureate Certificate); neurosciences and cognitive sciences (PhD); optics (MS, PhD); quantum optics (PhD); solid state physics (MS, PhD); statistics (MS, PhD). *Application deadline:* Applications are processed on a rolling basis. Electronic applications accepted. *Application Contact:* Kathryn Nee, Coordinator of Domestic Admissions, 410-455-2944, E-mail: nee@umbc.edu. *Dean*, Dr. Philip J. Rous, 410-455-5827, Fax: 410-455-5831, E-mail: rous@umbc.edu.

Continuing and Professional Studies Students: 8 full-time (7 women), 25 part-time (12 women); includes 2 Black or African American, non-Hispanic/Latino; 9 Asian, non-Hispanic/Latino; 1 Hispanic/Latino. 32 applicants, 50% accepted, 12 enrolled. *Faculty:* 10 part-time/adjunct (4 women). Expenses: Contact institution. Offers biotechnology management (Graduate Certificate). *Application deadline:* For fall admission, 8/15 for domestic students, 1/1 for international students; for spring admission, 12/15 for domestic students. Electronic applications accepted. *Application Contact:* Nancy Clements, Program Specialist, 410-455-5536, E-mail: nancyc@umbc.edu. *Interim Vice Provost for Graduate Education*, Dr. Chris Morris, 410-455-1570, E-mail: morrisc@umbc.edu.

Erickson School of Aging Studies Students: 30 full-time (18 women); includes 4 Black or African American, non-Hispanic/Latino; 1 Asian, non-Hispanic/Latino; 1 Hispanic/Latino. Average age 39. 50 applicants, 84% accepted, 30 enrolled. *Faculty:* 3 full-time (0 women), 5 part-time/adjunct (1 woman). Expenses: Contact institution. *Financial support:* In 2010–11, 8 students received support, including 1 teaching assistantship with tuition reimbursement available (averaging $21,600 per year). Financial award applicants required to submit FAFSA. In 2010, 30 master's awarded. Offers management of aging services (MA). *Application deadline:* Applications are processed on a rolling basis. *Application fee:* $50. Electronic applications accepted. *Application Contact:* Megan Risavi, Administrative Assistant, 443-543-5633, E-mail: meganr2@umbc.edu. *Graduate Program Director*, Dr. Joseph Gribbin, 443-543-5603, E-mail: gribbin@umbc.edu.

UNIVERSITY OF MARYLAND, COLLEGE PARK, College Park, MD 20742

General Information State-supported, coed, university. CGS member. *Enrollment:* 37,595 graduate, professional, and undergraduate students; 7,095 full-time matriculated graduate/professional students (3,387 women), 3,624 part-time matriculated graduate/professional students (1,671 women). *Enrollment by degree level:* 117 first professional, 5,177 master's, 4,599 doctoral, 826 other advanced degrees. *Graduate faculty:* 3,147 full-time (1,148 women), 976 part-time/adjunct (410 women). Tuition, state resident: part-time $471 per credit hour. Tuition, nonresident: part-time $1016 per credit hour. *Required fees:* $337 per term. *Graduate housing:* On-campus housing not available. *Student services:* Campus employment opportunities, campus safety program, career counseling, child daycare facilities, exercise/wellness program, free psychological counseling, international student services, low-cost health insurance, multicultural affairs office, services for students with disabilities. *Library facilities:* McKeldin Library plus 6 others. *Online resources:* library catalog, web page, access to other libraries' catalogs. *Collection:* 3.9 million titles, 68,514 serial subscriptions, 382,037 audiovisual materials. *Research affiliation:* Waters Technology Corporation (food safety training), Battelle–Pacific Northwest National Laboratory (high performance company), MacroSystems Research & Technology (travel modeling), Bill & Melinda Gates Foundation (international aid and outreach), American Cancer Society (prostate cancer research and community outreach), Lockheed martin Corporation (science and technology).

Computer facilities: Computer purchase and lease plans are available. 11,637 computers available on campus for general student use. A campuswide network can be accessed from student residence rooms and from off campus. Online class registration, student account information, financial aid summary are available. *Web address:* http://www.maryland.edu/.

General Application Contact: Dr. Charles Caramello, Dean of Graduate School, 301-405-0358, Fax: 301-314-9305.

GRADUATE UNITS

Academic Affairs Students: 7,095 full-time (3,387 women), 3,624 part-time (1,671 women); includes 2,232 minority (804 Black or African American, non-Hispanic/Latino; 12 American Indian or Alaska Native, non-Hispanic/Latino; 845 Asian, non-Hispanic/Latino; 383 Hispanic/Latino; 5 Native Hawaiian or other Pacific Islander, non-Hispanic/Latino; 183 Two or more races, non-Hispanic/Latino), 2,455 international. Average age 30. 22,649 applicants, 27% accepted, 3341 enrolled. *Faculty:* 3,147 full-time (1,148 women), 976 part-time/adjunct (410 women). Expenses: Contact institution. *Financial support:* In 2010–11, 464 fellowships with full and partial tuition reimbursements (averaging $15,808 per year), 1,416 research assistantships (averaging $20,129 per year), 2,658 teaching assistantships (averaging $17,120 per year) were awarded; career-related internships or fieldwork, Federal Work-Study, institutionally sponsored loans, and scholarships/grants also available. Support available to part-time students. Financial award applicants required to submit FAFSA. In 2010, 2,262 master's, 643 doctorates awarded. *Degree program information:* Part-time and evening/weekend programs available. Postbaccalaureate distance learning degree programs offered (no on-campus study). Offers history, library, and information services. *Application deadline:* For fall admission, 2/1 for domestic and international students; for spring admission, 6/1 for domestic and international students. Applications are processed on a rolling basis. *Application fee:* $75. Electronic applications accepted. *Application Contact:* Dean of Graduate School, 301-405-0358, Fax: 301-314-9305. *Dean of the Graduate School*, Dr. Charles Caramello, 301-405-0358, Fax: 301-314-9305, E-mail: ccaramel@umd.edu.

A. James Clark School of Engineering Students: 1,179 full-time (278 women), 700 part-time (157 women); includes 375 minority (111 Black or African American, non-Hispanic/Latino; 2 American Indian or Alaska Native, non-Hispanic/Latino; 182 Asian, non-Hispanic/Latino; 58 Hispanic/Latino; 22 Two or more races, non-Hispanic/Latino), 724 international. 4,073 applicants, 32% accepted, 707 enrolled. *Faculty:* 455 full-time (54 women), 115 part-time/adjunct (19 women). Expenses: Contact institution. *Financial support:* In 2010–11, 64 fellowships with full and partial tuition reimbursements (averaging $15,595 per year), 646 research assistantships (averaging $21,597 per year), 144 teaching assistantships (averaging $18,294 per year) were awarded; career-related internships or fieldwork, Federal Work-Study, institutionally sponsored loans, and scholarships/grants also available. Support available to part-time students. Financial award applicants required to submit FAFSA. In 2010, 341 master's, 109 doctorates awarded. *Degree program information:* Part-time and evening/weekend programs available. Postbaccalaureate distance learning degree programs offered. Offers aerospace engineering (M Eng, MS, PhD); bioengineering (MS, PhD); chemical engineering (M Eng, MS, PhD); civil and environmental engineering (M Eng, MS, PhD); electrical and computer engineering (M Eng, MS, PhD); electrical engineering (MS, PhD); electronic packaging and reliability (MS, PhD); engineering (M Eng, ME, MS,

University of Maryland, College Park (continued)

PhD, Certificate); engineering and public policy (MS); fire protection engineering (M Eng, MS); manufacturing and design (MS, PhD); materials science and engineering (MS, PhD); mechanics and materials (MS, PhD); nuclear engineering (ME, MS, PhD); reliability engineering (M Eng, MS, PhD); systems engineering (M Eng, MS); telecommunications (MS); thermal and fluid sciences (MS, PhD). *Application deadline:* For fall admission, 1/15 for domestic and international students; for spring admission, 10/15 for domestic students, 6/1 for international students. Applications are processed on a rolling basis. *Application fee:* $75. Electronic applications accepted. *Application Contact:* Dr. Charles A. Caramello, Dean of the Graduate School, 301-405-0358, Fax: 301-314-9305, E-mail: ccaramel@umd.edu. *Dean*, Dr. Darryll Pines, 301-405-3868, Fax: 301-314-5908, E-mail: pines@umd.edu.

College of Agriculture and Natural Resources Students: 338 full-time (211 women), 21 part-time (12 women); includes 9 Black or African American, non-Hispanic/Latino; 21 Asian, non-Hispanic/Latino; 13 Hispanic/Latino; 1 Native Hawaiian or other Pacific Islander, non-Hispanic/Latino; 3 Two or more races, non-Hispanic/Latino, 95 international. 546 applicants, 26% accepted, 82 enrolled. *Faculty:* 320 full-time (139 women), 40 part-time/adjunct (21 women). Expenses: Contact institution. *Financial support:* In 2010–11, 4 fellowships with full and partial tuition reimbursements (averaging $16,452 per year), 88 research assistantships with tuition reimbursements (averaging $17,447 per year), 84 teaching assistantships with tuition reimbursements (averaging $16,542 per year) were awarded; career-related internships or fieldwork, Federal Work-Study, and scholarships/grants also available. Support available to part-time students. Financial award applicants required to submit FAFSA. In 2010, 28 first professional degrees, 27 master's, 23 doctorates awarded. *Degree program information:* Part-time and evening/weekend programs available. Offers agriculture and natural resources (DVM, MS, PhD); agriculture economics (MS, PhD); animal sciences (MS, PhD); environmental science and technology (MS, PhD); food science (MS, PhD); horticulture (MS, PhD); landscape architecture (MLA); natural resource sciences (MS, PhD); nutrition (MS, PhD); resource economics (MS, PhD); veterinary medical sciences (MS, PhD); veterinary medicine (DVM, MS, PhD). *Application deadline:* For fall admission, 12/15 for domestic and international students; for spring admission, 6/1 for international students. Applications are processed on a rolling basis. *Application fee:* $75. Electronic applications accepted. *Application Contact:* Dr. Charles A. Caramello, Dean of Graduate School, 301-405-0358, Fax: 301-314-9305, E-mail: ccaramel@umd.edu. *Dean*, Dr. Cheng-i Wei, 301-405-2072, Fax: 301-314-9146, E-mail: wei@umd.edu.

College of Arts and Humanities Students: 841 full-time (487 women), 134 part-time (68 women); includes 161 minority (58 Black or African American, non-Hispanic/Latino; 2 American Indian or Alaska Native, non-Hispanic/Latino; 49 Asian, non-Hispanic/Latino; 39 Hispanic/Latino; 1 Native Hawaiian or other Pacific Islander, non-Hispanic/Latino; 12 Two or more races, non-Hispanic/Latino), 141 international. 2,558 applicants, 16% accepted, 200 enrolled. *Faculty:* 449 full-time (222 women), 236 part-time/adjunct (127 women). Expenses: Contact institution. *Financial support:* In 2010–11, 80 fellowships with full and partial tuition reimbursements (averaging $13,640 per year), 18 research assistantships (averaging $18,494 per year), 539 teaching assistantships (averaging $17,113 per year) were awarded; career-related internships or fieldwork, Federal Work-Study, and scholarships/grants also available. Support available to part-time students. Financial award applicants required to submit FAFSA. In 2010, 159 master's, 113 doctorates awarded. *Degree program information:* Part-time and evening/weekend programs available. Offers American studies (MA, PhD); Arabic (MPS, Graduate Certificate); art (MFA); art history (MA, PhD); arts and humanities (M Ed, MA, MFA, MM, MPS, DMA, Ed D, PhD, Graduate Certificate); classics (MA); communication (MA, PhD); comparative literature (MA, PhD); creative writing (MA, MFA, PhD); dance (MFA); English language and literature (MA, PhD); ethnomusicology (MA); French language and literature (MA); Germanic language and literature (MA, PhD); history (MA, PhD); Jewish studies (MA); languages, literature, and cultures (MA, PhD); linguistics (MA, PhD); modern French studies (PhD); music (M Ed, MA, MM, DMA, Ed D, PhD); performance (MFA); Persian (MPS, Graduate Certificate); philosophy (MA, PhD); second language instruction (PhD); second language learning (PhD); second language measurement and assessment (PhD); second language use (PhD); Spanish and Portuguese (MA, PhD); theatre and performance studies (MA, PhD); theatre design (MFA); women's studies (MA, PhD). *Application deadline:* For fall admission, 1/15 for domestic students, 2/1 for international students; for spring admission, 6/1 for international students. Applications are processed on a rolling basis. *Application fee:* $75. Electronic applications accepted. *Application Contact:* Charles A. Caramello, Dean of Graduate School, 301-405-0358, Fax: 301-314-9305. *Dean*, Elizabeth Loizeaux, 301-405-5646, Fax: 301-314-9148, E-mail: loizeau@umd.edu.

College of Behavioral and Social Sciences Students: 696 full-time (415 women), 178 part-time (84 women); includes 134 minority (45 Black or African American, non-Hispanic/Latino; 2 American Indian or Alaska Native, non-Hispanic/Latino; 38 Asian, non-Hispanic/Latino; 35 Hispanic/Latino; 1 Native Hawaiian or other Pacific Islander, non-Hispanic/Latino; 13 Two or more races, non-Hispanic/Latino), 213 international. 2,819 applicants, 14% accepted, 201 enrolled. *Faculty:* 409 full-time (175 women), 108 part-time/adjunct (49 women). Expenses: Contact institution. *Financial support:* In 2010–11, 59 fellowships with full and partial tuition reimbursements (averaging $16,924 per year), 62 research assistantships (averaging $16,638 per year), 425 teaching assistantships (averaging $16,683 per year) were awarded; career-related internships or fieldwork, Federal Work-Study, and scholarships/grants also available. Support available to part-time students. Financial award applicants required to submit FAFSA. In 2010, 174 master's, 90 doctorates awarded. *Degree program information:* Part-time and evening/weekend programs available. Offers American politics (PhD); applied anthropology (MAA); audiology (MA, PhD); behavioral and social sciences (MA, MAA, MS, Au D, PhD); clinical psychology (PhD); comparative politics (PhD); criminology and criminal justice (MA, PhD); developmental psychology (PhD); economics (MA, PhD); experimental psychology (PhD); geography (MA, PhD); hearing and speech sciences (Au D); industrial psychology (MA, MS, PhD); international relations (PhD); language pathology (MA, PhD); neuroscience (PhD); neurosciences and cognitive sciences (PhD); political economy (PhD); political theory (PhD); social psychology (PhD); sociology (MA, PhD); speech (MA, PhD); survey methodology (MS, PhD). *Application deadline:* For fall admission, 1/15 for domestic students, 2/1 for international students; for spring admission, 1/15 for domestic students, 6/1 for international students. Applications are processed on a rolling basis. *Application fee:* $75. Electronic applications accepted. *Application Contact:* Dr. Charles A. Caramello, Dean of Graduate School, 301-405-0358, Fax: 301-314-9305, E-mail: ccaramel@umd.edu. *Dean*, Dr. John Townshend, 301-405-1691, Fax: 301-314-9086, E-mail: jtownshe@umd.edu.

College of Computer, Mathematical and Natural Sciences Students: 1,289 full-time (465 women), 232 part-time (106 women); includes 185 minority (49 Black or African American, non-Hispanic/Latino; 1 American Indian or Alaska Native, non-Hispanic/Latino; 86 Asian, non-Hispanic/Latino; 34 Hispanic/Latino; 15 Two or more races, non-Hispanic/Latino), 529 international. 4,095 applicants, 17% accepted, 314 enrolled. *Faculty:* 956 full-time (235 women), 133 part-time/adjunct (29 women). Expenses: Contact institution. *Financial support:* In 2010–11, 80 fellowships with full and partial tuition reimbursements (averaging $17,921 per year), 541 research assistantships (averaging $19,627 per year), 542 teaching assistantships (averaging $18,566 per year) were awarded; career-related internships or fieldwork, Federal Work-Study, and scholarships/grants also available. Support available to part-time students. Financial award applicants required to submit FAFSA. In 2010, 163 master's, 163 doctorates awarded. *Degree program information:* Part-time and evening/weekend programs available. Postbaccalaureate distance learning degree programs offered. Offers analytical chemistry (MS, PhD); applied mathematics (MS, PhD); astronomy (MS, PhD); atmospheric and oceanic science (MS, PMS, PhD); behavior, ecology, and systematics (PhD); behavior, ecology, evolution, and systematics (MS, PhD); biochemistry (MS, PhD); biology (MS, PhD); biophysics (PhD); cell biology and molecular genetics (MS, PhD); chemical physics (MS, PhD); chemistry (MS, PhD); computer science (MS, PhD); computer, mathematical and natural sciences (MA, MLS, MS, PMS, PhD); entomology (MS, PhD); geology (MS, PhD); inorganic chemistry (MS, PhD); life sciences (MLS); marine-estuarine-environmental sciences (MS, PhD); mathematical statistics (MA, PhD); mathematics (MA, MS, PhD); molecular and cellular biology (PhD); organic chemistry (MS, PhD); physical chemistry (MS, PhD); physics (MS, PhD); plant biology (MS, PhD); sustainable development and conservation biology (MS). *Application deadline:* For fall admission, 12/1 for domestic students, 2/1 for international students; for spring admission, 10/1 for domestic students, 6/1 for international students. Applications are processed on a rolling basis. *Application fee:* $75. Electronic applications accepted. *Application Contact:* Dr. Charles A. Caramello, Dean of Graduate School, 301-405-0358, Fax: 301-314-9305, E-mail: ccaramel@umd.edu. *Dean*, Dr. Stephen Halperin, 301-405-4906, Fax: 301-405-9377, E-mail: shalper@umd.edu.

College of Education Students: 768 full-time (596 women), 377 part-time (295 women); includes 160 Black or African American, non-Hispanic/Latino; 2 American Indian or Alaska Native, non-Hispanic/Latino; 87 Asian, non-Hispanic/Latino; 76 Hispanic/Latino; 21 Two or more races, non-Hispanic/Latino, 112 international. 1,430 applicants, 29% accepted, 269 enrolled. *Faculty:* 202 full-time (142 women), 79 part-time/adjunct (59 women). Expenses: Contact institution. *Financial support:* In 2010–11, 69 fellowships with full and partial tuition reimbursements (averaging $14,628 per year), 36 research assistantships (averaging $16,994 per year), 298 teaching assistantships (averaging $16,640 per year) were awarded; career-related internships or fieldwork, Federal Work-Study, and scholarships/grants also available. Support available to part-time students. Financial award applicants required to submit FAFSA. In 2010, 333 master's, 77 doctorates awarded. *Degree program information:* Part-time and evening/weekend programs available. Postbaccalaureate distance learning degree programs offered. Offers college student personnel (M Ed, MA); college student personnel administration (PhD); community counseling (CAGS); community/career counseling (M Ed, MA); counseling and personnel services (M Ed, MA, PhD); counseling psychology (PhD); counselor education (PhD); curriculum and educational communications (M Ed, MA, Ed D, PhD); early childhood/elementary education (M Ed, MA, Ed D, PhD); education (M Ed, MA, Ed D, PhD, AGSC, CAGS); education leadership, higher education and international education (MA, Ed D, PhD); education policy studies (M Ed, MA, PhD); human development (M Ed, MA, Ed D, PhD); measurement (MA, PhD); program evaluation (MA, PhD); reading (M Ed, MA, PhD, CAGS); rehabilitation counseling (M Ed, MA, AGSC); school counseling (M Ed, MA); school psychology (M Ed, MA, PhD); secondary education (M Ed, MA, Ed D, PhD, CAGS); social foundations of education (M Ed, MA, Ed D, PhD, CAGS); special education (M Ed, MA, PhD, CAGS); statistics (MA, PhD); teaching English to speakers of other languages (M Ed). *Application deadline:* For fall admission, 12/15 for domestic students, 2/1 for international students; for spring admission, 6/1 for international students. Applications are processed on a rolling basis. *Application fee:* $75. Electronic applications accepted. *Application Contact:* Dean of Graduate School, 301-405-0376, Fax: 301-314-9305. *Dean*, Donna L. Wiseman, 301-405-2336, Fax: 301-314-9890, E-mail: dlwise@umd.edu.

College of Information Studies Students: 257 full-time (177 women), 228 part-time (164 women); includes 71 minority (30 Black or African American, non-Hispanic/Latino; 1 American Indian or Alaska Native, non-Hispanic/Latino; 20 Asian, non-Hispanic/Latino; 12 Hispanic/Latino; 8 Two or more races, non-Hispanic/Latino), 63 international. 833 applicants, 38% accepted, 147 enrolled. *Faculty:* 27 full-time (13 women), 19 part-time/adjunct (11 women). Expenses: Contact institution. *Financial support:* In 2010–11, 1 fellowship with partial tuition reimbursement (averaging $10,800 per year), 11 research assistantships (averaging $16,705 per year), 74 teaching assistantships (averaging $16,440 per year) were awarded; career-related internships or fieldwork, Federal Work-Study, scholarships/grants, and tuition waivers (full and partial) also available. Support available to part-time students. Financial award application deadline: 2/1; financial award applicants required to submit FAFSA. In 2010, 186 master's, 4 doctorates awarded. *Degree program information:* Part-time and evening/weekend programs available. Offers information studies (MIM, MLS, PhD). *Application deadline:* For fall admission, 12/1 for domestic students, 11/15 for international students; for spring admission, 10/1 for domestic students, 6/1 for international students. Applications are processed on a rolling basis. *Application fee:* $75. Electronic applications accepted. *Application Contact:* Dr. Charles A. Caramello, Dean of Graduate School, 301-405-0358, Fax: 301-314-9305, E-mail: ccaramel@umd.edu. *Dean*, Dr. Jennifer Preece, 301-405-2036, Fax: 301-314-9145, E-mail: preece@umd.edu.

Phillip Merrill College of Journalism Students: 76 full-time (46 women), 14 part-time (7 women); includes 20 minority (12 Black or African American, non-Hispanic/Latino; 5 Asian, non-Hispanic/Latino; 3 Hispanic/Latino), 11 international. 243 applicants, 37% accepted, 26 enrolled. *Faculty:* 18 full-time (10 women), 43 part-time/adjunct (18 women). Expenses: Contact institution. *Financial support:* In 2010–11, 3 fellowships with full and partial tuition reimbursements (averaging $11,667 per year), 22 teaching assistantships with tuition reimbursements (averaging $16,647 per year) were awarded; research assistantships with tuition reimbursements, career-related internships or fieldwork, Federal Work-Study, and scholarships/grants also available. Support available to part-time students. Financial award applicants required to submit FAFSA. In 2010, 26 master's, 5 doctorates awarded. *Degree program information:* Part-time and evening/weekend programs available. Offers broadcast journalism (MA); journalism (MA); journalism and media studies (PhD); online news (MA); public affairs reporting (MA). *Application deadline:* For fall admission, 1/15 for domestic and international students. Applications are processed on a rolling basis. *Application fee:* $75. Electronic applications accepted. *Application Contact:* Dr. Charles A. Caramello, Dean of Graduate School, 301-405-0358, Fax: 301-314-9305, E-mail: ccaramel@umd.edu. *Dean and Professor*, Kevin Klose, 301-405-2383, E-mail: kklose@jmail.umd.edu.

Robert H. Smith School of Business Students: 873 full-time (325 women), 781 part-time (263 women); includes 447 minority (151 Black or African American, non-Hispanic/Latino; 1 American Indian or Alaska Native, non-Hispanic/Latino; 243 Asian, non-Hispanic/Latino; 40 Hispanic/Latino; 1 Native Hawaiian or other Pacific Islander, non-Hispanic/Latino; 11 Two or more races, non-Hispanic/Latino), 368 international. 2,838 applicants, 37% accepted, 651 enrolled. *Faculty:* 146 full-time (37 women), 42 part-time/adjunct (10 women). Expenses: Contact institution. *Financial support:* In 2010–11, 50 fellowships with full and partial tuition reimbursements (averaging $18,808 per year), 1 research assistantship with tuition reimbursement (averaging $24,500 per year), 199 teaching assistantships with tuition reimbursements (averaging $17,426 per year) were awarded; Federal Work-Study and scholarships/grants also available. Support available to part-time students. Financial award applicants required to submit FAFSA. In 2010, 615 master's, 13 doctorates awarded. *Degree program information:* Part-time and evening/weekend programs available. Postbaccalaureate distance learning degree programs offered. Offers business (EMBA, MBA, MS, PhD); business administration (MBA); business and management (MS, PhD); executive business administration (EMBA). *Application deadline:* For fall admission, 12/15 for domestic students, 2/1 for international students; for spring admission, 11/30 for domestic students, 6/1 for international students. Applications are processed on a rolling basis. *Application fee:* $75. Electronic applications accepted. *Application Contact:* Dr. Charles A. Caramello, Dean of Graduate School, 301-405-0358, Fax: 301-314-9305, E-mail: ccaramel@umd.edu. *Dean*, Dr. Anand Anandalingam, 301-405-0582, E-mail: ganand@umd.edu.

School of Architecture, Planning and Preservation Students: 193 full-time (99 women), 81 part-time (29 women); includes 56 minority (27 Black or African American, non-Hispanic/Latino; 11 Asian, non-Hispanic/Latino; 11 Hispanic/Latino; 7 Two or more races, non-Hispanic/Latino), 22 international. 669 applicants, 33% accepted, 87 enrolled. *Faculty:* 34 full-time (9 women), 35 part-time/adjunct (4 women). Expenses: Contact institution. *Financial support:* In 2010–11, 8 fellowships with full and partial tuition reimbursements (averaging $11,133 per year), 104 teaching assistantships (averaging $15,311 per year) were awarded; research assistantships, career-related internships or fieldwork, Federal Work-Study, and scholarships/grants also available. Support available to part-time students. Financial award applicants required to submit FAFSA. In 2010, 70 master's awarded. *Degree program information:* Part-time and evening/weekend programs available. Offers architecture (M Arch); architecture, planning and preservation (M Arch, MCP, MHP, MRED, PhD, Certificate); historic preservation (MHP, Certificate); real estate development (MRED); urban and regional planning/design (PhD); urban studies and planning (MCP). *Application deadline:* For fall admission, 12/15 for domestic and international students. Applications are processed on a rolling basis. *Application fee:* $75. Electronic applications accepted. *Application Contact:* Dr. Charles A. Caramello, Dean of Graduate School, 301-405-0358, Fax: 301-314-9305. *Dean*, David Cronrath, 301-405-9421, E-mail: cronrath@umd.edu.

School of Public Health Students: 170 full-time (116 women), 51 part-time (46 women); includes 64 minority (36 Black or African American, non-Hispanic/Latino; 16 Asian, non-

Hispanic/Latino; 8 Hispanic/Latino; 4 Two or more races, non-Hispanic/Latino), 29 international. 646 applicants, 14% accepted, 59 enrolled. *Faculty:* 103 full-time (63 women), 44 part-time/adjunct (29 women). Expenses: Contact institution. *Financial support:* In 2010–11, 18 fellowships with full and partial tuition reimbursements (averaging $18,452 per year), 11 research assistantships (averaging $15,838 per year), 89 teaching assistantships (averaging $15,997 per year) were awarded; career-related internships or fieldwork, Federal Work-Study, and scholarships/grants also available. Support available to part-time students. Financial award applicants required to submit FAFSA. In 2010, 38 master's, 13 doctorates awarded. *Degree program information:* Part-time and evening/weekend programs available. Offers biostatistics (MPH); community health education (MPH); environmental health sciences (MPH); epidemiology (MPH, PhD); family studies (PhD); health services administration (MHA, PhD); kinesiology (MA, PhD); marriage and family therapy (MS); maternal and child health (PhD); public health (MA, MHA, MPH, MS, PhD); public/community health (PhD). *Application deadline:* For fall admission, 1/15 for domestic students, 2/1 for international students; for spring admission, 6/1 for international students. Applications are processed on a rolling basis. *Application fee:* $75. Electronic applications accepted. *Application Contact:* Dr. Charles A. Carmello, Dean of Graduate School, 301-405-0358. *Dean,* Dr. Robert Gold, 301-405-2437, Fax: 301-314-9167, E-mail: rsgold@umd.edu.

School of Public Policy Students: 315 full-time (135 women), 95 part-time (49 women); includes 65 minority (25 Black or African American, non-Hispanic/Latino; 20 Asian, non-Hispanic/Latino; 16 Hispanic/Latino; 4 Two or more races, non-Hispanic/Latino), 102 international. 963 applicants, 47% accepted, 166 enrolled. *Faculty:* 33 full-time (7 women), 29 part-time/adjunct (12 women). Expenses: Contact institution. *Financial support:* In 2010–11, 18 fellowships with full and partial tuition reimbursements (averaging $14,001 per year), 2 research assistantships with tuition reimbursements (averaging $19,347 per year), 131 teaching assistantships with tuition reimbursements (averaging $14,979 per year) were awarded; Federal Work-Study and scholarships/grants also available. Support available to part-time students. Financial award applicants required to submit FAFSA. In 2010, 114 master's, 5 doctorates awarded. *Degree program information:* Part-time and evening/weekend programs available. Postbaccalaureate distance learning degree programs offered. Offers policy studies (PhD); public management (MPM); public policy (MPM, MPP, PhD). *Application deadline:* For fall admission, 4/1 for domestic students, 2/1 for international students; for spring admission, 10/15 for domestic students, 6/1 for international students. Applications are processed on a rolling basis. *Application fee:* $75. Electronic applications accepted. *Application Contact:* Dr. Charles A. Carmello, Dean of Graduate School, 301-405-0358, Fax: 301-314-9305, E-mail: ccaramel@umd.edu. *Dean,* Dr. Donald Kettl, 301-405-6356, E-mail: kettl@umd.edu.

UNIVERSITY OF MARYLAND EASTERN SHORE, Princess Anne, MD 21853-1299

General Information State-supported, coed, university. CGS member. *Graduate housing:* On-campus housing not available.

GRADUATE UNITS

Graduate Programs *Degree program information:* Part-time and evening/weekend programs available. Offers applied computer science (MS); career and technology education (M Ed); criminology and criminal justice (MS); education leadership (Ed D); food and agricultural sciences (MS); food science and technology (PhD); guidance and counseling (M Ed); marine-estuarine-environmental sciences (MS, PhD); organizational leadership (PhD); physical therapy (DPT); rehabilitation counseling (MS); special education (M Ed); teaching (MAT); toxicology (MS, PhD). Electronic applications accepted.

UNIVERSITY OF MARYLAND UNIVERSITY COLLEGE, Adelphi, MD 20783

General Information State-supported, coed, comprehensive institution. CGS member. *Enrollment:* 39,577 graduate, professional, and undergraduate students; 263 full-time matriculated graduate/professional students (160 women), 13,184 part-time matriculated graduate/professional students (7,349 women). *Enrollment by degree level:* 12,418 master's, 322 doctoral, 707 other advanced degrees. *Graduate faculty:* 215 full-time (102 women), 1,978 part-time/adjunct (826 women). *Graduate housing:* On-campus housing not available. *Student services:* Campus employment opportunities, career counseling, international student services, services for students with disabilities, writing training. *Library facilities:* Information and Library Services. *Online resources:* library catalog, web page, access to other libraries' catalogs. *Collection:* 1,280 titles, 96,240 serial subscriptions, 33 audiovisual materials.

Computer facilities: Computer purchase and lease plans are available. 281 computers available on campus for general student use. A campuswide network can be accessed from off campus. Online class registration is available. *Web address:* http://www.umuc.edu/.

General Application Contact: Coordinator, Graduate Admissions, 800-888-UMUC, Fax: 240-684-2151, E-mail: newgrad@umuc.edu.

GRADUATE UNITS

Graduate School of Management and Technology Students: 263 full-time (160 women), 13,184 part-time (7,349 women); includes 6,971 minority (5,328 Black or African American, non-Hispanic/Latino; 50 American Indian or Alaska Native, non-Hispanic/Latino; 809 Asian, non-Hispanic/Latino; 645 Hispanic/Latino; 23 Native Hawaiian or other Pacific Islander, non-Hispanic/Latino; 116 Two or more races, non-Hispanic/Latino), 355 international. Average age 35. 5,269 applicants, 100% accepted, 3127 enrolled. *Faculty:* 215 full-time (102 women), 1,978 part-time/adjunct (826 women). Expenses: Contact institution. *Financial support:* Federal Work-Study and scholarships/grants available. Support available to part-time students. Financial award application deadline: 6/1; financial award applicants required to submit FAFSA. In 2010, 2,758 master's, 42 doctorates, 410 other advanced degrees awarded. *Degree program information:* Part-time and evening/weekend programs available. Postbaccalaureate distance learning degree programs offered (no on-campus study). Offers accounting and financial management (MS, Certificate); accounting and information technology (MS, Certificate); biotechnology studies (MS, Certificate); business administration (MBA, Certificate); cybersecurity (MS, Certificate); cybersecurity policy (MS); distance education (MDE, Certificate); education (M Ed); environmental management (MS, Certificate); financial management and information systems (MS, Certificate); health administration informatics (MS, Certificate); health care administration (MS, Certificate); information technology (MS, Certificate); international management (MIM, Certificate); management (MS, DM, Certificate); management and technology (M Ed, MAT, MBA, MDE, MIM, MS, DM, Certificate); teaching (MAT); technology management (MS, Certificate). *Application deadline:* Applications are processed on a rolling basis. *Application fee:* $50. Electronic applications accepted. *Application Contact:* Coordinator, Graduate Admissions, 800-888-8682, Fax: 240-684-2151, E-mail: newgrad@umuc.edu. *Vice Provost and Dean of Graduate Studies,* Dr. Michael S. Frank, 240-684-2400, Fax: 240-684-2401.

UNIVERSITY OF MARY WASHINGTON, Fredericksburg, VA 22401-5358

General Information State-supported, coed, comprehensive institution. *Enrollment:* 5,203 graduate, professional, and undergraduate students; 171 full-time matriculated graduate/professional students (115 women), 678 part-time matriculated graduate/professional students (483 women). *Graduate faculty:* 25 full-time (17 women), 20 part-time/adjunct (10 women). *Graduate housing:* On-campus housing not available. *Student services:* Campus employment opportunities, career counseling, free psychological counseling, international student services, multicultural affairs office, services for students with disabilities, teacher training, writing training. *Library facilities:* Simpson Library plus 2 others. *Online resources:* library catalog, web page, access to other libraries' catalogs. *Collection:* 467,101 titles, 62,931 serial subscriptions, 2,136 audiovisual materials.

Computer facilities: Computer purchase and lease plans are available. 306 computers available on campus for general student use. A campuswide network can be accessed from student residence rooms and from off campus. Online class registration, Library resources, foreign languages resources, course management system are available. *Web address:* http://www.umw.edu/.

General Application Contact: Matthew E. Mejia, Associate Dean of Admissions, 540-286-8017, Fax: 540-286-8085, E-mail: mmejia@umw.edu.

GRADUATE UNITS

College of Business Students: 107 full-time (57 women), 253 part-time (123 women); includes 78 Black or African American, non-Hispanic/Latino; 1 American Indian or Alaska Native, non-Hispanic/Latino; 8 Asian, non-Hispanic/Latino; 13 Hispanic/Latino, 5 international. Average age 36. 131 applicants, 56% accepted, 53 enrolled. *Faculty:* 11 full-time (4 women), 9 part-time/adjunct (1 woman). Expenses: Contact institution. *Financial support:* Available to part-time students. Application deadline: 3/15. In 2010, 85 master's awarded. *Degree program information:* Part-time and evening/weekend programs available. Offers business administration (MBA); management information systems (MSMIS). *Application deadline:* For fall admission, 6/1 priority date for domestic students, 6/1 for international students; for spring admission, 10/1 for domestic and international students. *Application fee:* $50. Electronic applications accepted. *Application Contact:* Matthew E. Mejia, Associate Dean of Admissions, 540-286-8088, Fax: 540-286-8085, E-mail: mmejia@umw.edu. *Acting Dean,* Dr. Larry W. Penwell, 540-654-1561, E-mail: lpenwell@umw.edu.

College of Education Students: 303 part-time (249 women); includes 54 minority (27 Black or African American, non-Hispanic/Latino; 2 American Indian or Alaska Native, non-Hispanic/Latino; 3 Asian, non-Hispanic/Latino; 16 Hispanic/Latino; 6 Two or more races, non-Hispanic/Latino). 126 applicants, 65% accepted, 65 enrolled. *Faculty:* 19 full-time (17 women), 1 part-time/adjunct (0 women). Expenses: Contact institution. *Financial support:* In 2010–11, 10 students received support. Application deadline: 3/15. In 2010, 173 master's awarded. *Degree program information:* Part-time and evening/weekend programs available. Offers education (M Ed, MS). *Application deadline:* For fall admission, 4/15 for domestic and international students; for spring admission, 9/15 for domestic and international students. *Application fee:* $50. Electronic applications accepted. *Application Contact:* Matthew E. Mejia, Associate Dean of Admissions, 540-286-8088, Fax: 540-286-8085, E-mail: mmejia@umw.edu. *Dean,* Dr. Mary L. Gendernalik-Cooper, 540-654-1290.

UNIVERSITY OF MASSACHUSETTS AMHERST, Amherst, MA 01003

General Information State-supported, coed, university. CGS member. *Enrollment:* 27,569 graduate, professional, and undergraduate students; 3,200 full-time matriculated graduate/professional students (1,649 women), 2,477 part-time matriculated graduate/professional students (1,184 women). *Enrollment by degree level:* 3,122 master's, 2,510 doctoral, 45 other advanced degrees. *Graduate faculty:* 1,269 full-time (423 women). Tuition, state resident: full-time $2640. *Required fees:* $8282. One-time fee: $357 full-time. *Graduate housing:* Rooms and/or apartments available on a first-come, first-served basis to single and married students. Typical cost: $6400 per year ($11,800 including board) for single students. Room and board charges vary according to board plan and housing facility selected. Housing application deadline: 8/15. *Student services:* Campus employment opportunities, campus safety program, career counseling, child daycare facilities, exercise/wellness program, free psychological counseling, grant writing training, international student services, low-cost health insurance, multicultural affairs office, services for students with disabilities, teacher training. *Library facilities:* W. E. B. Du Bois Library plus 2 others. *Online resources:* library catalog, web page, access to other libraries' catalogs. *Collection:* 3.7 million titles, 66,343 serial subscriptions, 29,028 audiovisual materials.

Computer facilities: 419 computers available on campus for general student use. A campuswide network can be accessed from student residence rooms and from off campus. Online class registration, online housing assignments, bill payment, Learning Management System, file storage, web hosting, blogs are available. *Web address:* http://www.umass.edu/.

General Application Contact: Jean M. Ames, Supervisor of Admissions, 413-545-0722, Fax: 413-577-0010, E-mail: gradadm@grad.umass.edu.

GRADUATE UNITS

Graduate School Students: 3,200 full-time (1,649 women), 2,477 part-time (1,184 women); includes 794 minority (202 Black or African American, non-Hispanic/Latino; 12 American Indian or Alaska Native, non-Hispanic/Latino; 241 Asian, non-Hispanic/Latino; 250 Hispanic/Latino; 7 Native Hawaiian or other Pacific Islander, non-Hispanic/Latino; 82 Two or more races, non-Hispanic/Latino), 1,292 international. Average age 32. 9,996 applicants, 33% accepted, 1556 enrolled. *Faculty:* 1,269 full-time (423 women). Expenses: Contact institution. *Financial support:* In 2010–11, 3,455 students received support, including 473 fellowships with full tuition reimbursements available (averaging $10,462 per year), 1,758 research assistantships with full tuition reimbursements available (averaging $12,436 per year), 1,835 teaching assistantships with full tuition reimbursements available (averaging $9,234 per year); career-related internships or fieldwork, Federal Work-Study, scholarships/grants, traineeships, health care benefits, tuition waivers (full), and unspecified assistantships also available. Support available to part-time students. Financial award application deadline: 2/1; financial award applicants required to submit FAFSA. In 2010, 1,207 master's, 294 doctorates awarded. *Degree program information:* Part-time and evening/weekend programs available. *Application deadline:* For fall admission, 2/1 for domestic and international students; for spring admission, 10/1 for domestic and international students. Applications are processed on a rolling basis. *Application fee:* $50 ($65 for international students). Electronic applications accepted. *Application Contact:* Jean M. Ames, Supervisor of Admissions, 413-545-0721, Fax: 413-577-0100, E-mail: gradadm@grad.umass.edu. *Dean,* Dr. John R. Mullin, 413-545-5271, Fax: 413-545-3754.

College of Engineering Students: 410 full-time (108 women), 67 part-time (14 women); includes 30 minority (3 Black or African American, non-Hispanic/Latino; 8 Asian, non-Hispanic/Latino; 13 Hispanic/Latino; 1 Native Hawaiian or other Pacific Islander, non-Hispanic/Latino; 5 Two or more races, non-Hispanic/Latino), 286 international. Average age 26. 1,644 applicants, 31% accepted, 151 enrolled. *Faculty:* 119 full-time (12 women). Expenses: Contact institution. *Financial support:* In 2010–11, 33 fellowships with full tuition reimbursements (averaging $12,641 per year), 350 research assistantships with full tuition reimbursements, 76 teaching assistantships with full tuition reimbursements (averaging $6,461 per year) were awarded; career-related internships or fieldwork, Federal Work-Study, scholarships/grants, traineeships, health care benefits, tuition waivers (full), and unspecified assistantships also available. Support available to part-time students. Financial award applicants required to submit FAFSA. In 2010, 72 master's, 30 doctorates awarded. *Degree program information:* Part-time programs available. Offers chemical engineering (MSChE, PhD); civil engineering (MSCE, PhD); electrical and computer engineering (MSECE, PhD); engineering (MS, MSCE, MSChE, MSECE, MSME, PhD); environmental engineering (MS); industrial engineering and operations research (MS, PhD); mechanical engineering (MSME, PhD). *Application deadline:* Applications are processed on a rolling basis. *Application fee:* $50 ($65 for international students). Electronic applications accepted. *Application Contact:* Jean M. Ames, Supervisor of Admissions, 413-545-0722, Fax: 413-577-0010, E-mail: gradadm@grad.umass.edu. *Dean,* Dr. Michael Malone, 413-545-6388, Fax: 413-545-6388.

College of Humanities and Fine Arts Students: 499 full-time (272 women), 252 part-time (152 women); includes 111 minority (33 Black or African American, non-Hispanic/Latino; 3 American Indian or Alaska Native, non-Hispanic/Latino; 18 Asian, non-Hispanic/Latino; 47 Hispanic/Latino; 1 Native Hawaiian or other Pacific Islander, non-Hispanic/Latino; 9 Two or more races, non-Hispanic/Latino), 105 international. Average age 31. 1,680 applicants, 28% accepted, 224 enrolled. *Faculty:* 256 full-time (111 women). Expenses: Contact institution. *Financial support:* In 2010–11, 37 fellowships with full tuition reimbursements (averaging $6,342 per year), 43 research assistantships with full tuition reimbursements (averaging $7,564 per year), 370 teaching assistantships with full tuition reimbursements (averaging $11,693 per year) were awarded; career-related internships or fieldwork, Federal Work-Study, scholarships/grants, traineeships, health care benefits, tuition waivers (full), and unspecified assistantships also available. Support available to part-time students. In 2010, 145 master's, 28 doctorates awarded. *Degree program information:* Part-time programs available. Offers Afro-American studies (MA, PhD); ancient history (MA); architecture and design (M Arch, MS); art (MA, MFA); art education (MA); art history (MA); Asian languages and literatures (MA); British Empire history (MA); Chinese (MA); comparative literature

University of Massachusetts Amherst (continued)

(MA, PhD); creative writing (MFA); design (MA); English and American literature (MA, PhD); European (medieval and modern) history (MA, PhD); French (MA, MAT); French and Francophone studies (MA, MAT); German and Scandinavian studies (MA, PhD); Hispanic literatures, cultures and linguistics (MA, MAT, PhD); historic preservation (MS); humanities and fine arts (M Arch, MA, MAT, MFA, MM, MS, PhD); interior design (MS); Islamic history (MA); Italian studies (MAT); Japanese (MA); Latin American history (MA, PhD); Latin and classical humanities (MAT); linguistics (MA, PhD); modern global history (MA); music (MM, PhD); philosophy (MA, PhD); public history (MA); science and technology history (MA); studio art (MFA); teaching Spanish (MAT); theater (MFA); U. S. history (MA, PhD). *Application deadline:* Applications are processed on a rolling basis. *Application fee:* $50 ($65 for international students). Electronic applications accepted. *Application Contact:* Jean M. Ames, Supervisor of Admissions, 413-545-0722, Fax: 413-577-0010, E-mail: gradadm@grad.umass.edu. *Dean,* Dr. Julie C. Hayes, 413-545-4169, Fax: 413-545-4171.

College of Natural Sciences Students: 797 full-time (329 women), 171 part-time (66 women); includes 82 minority (21 Black or African American, non-Hispanic/Latino; 1 American Indian or Alaska Native, non-Hispanic/Latino; 22 Asian, non-Hispanic/Latino; 24 Hispanic/Latino; 14 Two or more races, non-Hispanic/Latino), 417 international. Average age 29. 2,674 applicants, 18% accepted, 217 enrolled. *Faculty:* 461 full-time (106 women). Expenses: Contact institution. *Financial support:* In 2010–11, 76 fellowships with full tuition reimbursements (averaging $8,301 per year), 650 research assistantships with full tuition reimbursements (averaging $14,267 per year), 466 teaching assistantships with full tuition reimbursements (averaging $10,233 per year) were awarded; career-related internships or fieldwork, Federal Work-Study, scholarships/grants, traineeships, health care benefits, tuition waivers (full), and unspecified assistantships also available. Support available to part-time students. Financial award applicants required to submit FAFSA. In 2010, 124 master's, 93 doctorates awarded. *Degree program information:* Part-time programs available. Offers animal biotechnology and biomedical sciences (MS, PhD); applied mathematics (MS); astronomy (MS, PhD); biochemistry (MS); building systems (MS, PhD); chemistry (MS, PhD); clinical psychology (MS, PhD); cognitive psychology (MS, PhD); computer science (MS, PhD); developmental science (MS, PhD); entomology (MS, PhD); environmental policy and human dimensions (MS, PhD); food science (MS, PhD); forest resources (MS, PhD); geography (MS); geosciences (MS, PhD); mathematics and statistics (MS, PhD); microbiology (MS, PhD); natural sciences (MS, PhD); physics (MS, PhD); plant and soil sciences (MS, PhD); polymer science and engineering (MS, PhD); psychology of peace and violence (MS, PhD); social psychology (MS, PhD); soil science (MS); water, wetlands and watersheds (MS, PhD); wildlife and fisheries conservation (MS, PhD). *Application deadline:* Applications are processed on a rolling basis. *Application fee:* $50 ($65 for international students). Electronic applications accepted. *Application Contact:* Jean M. Ames, Supervisor of Admissions, 413-545-0722, Fax: 413-577-0010, E-mail: gradadm@grad.umass.edu. *Dean,* Dr. Steven D. Goodwin, 413-545-2766, Fax: 413-545-1242.

College of Social and Behavioral Sciences Students: 389 full-time (226 women), 175 part-time (97 women); includes 91 minority (22 Black or African American, non-Hispanic/Latino; 5 American Indian or Alaska Native, non-Hispanic/Latino; 16 Asian, non-Hispanic/Latino; 34 Hispanic/Latino; 14 Two or more races, non-Hispanic/Latino), 140 international. Average age 33. 1,009 applicants, 32% accepted, 115 enrolled. *Faculty:* 156 full-time (63 women). Expenses: Contact institution. *Financial support:* In 2010–11, 10 fellowships with full tuition reimbursements (averaging $6,092 per year), 127 research assistantships with full tuition reimbursements (averaging $7,150 per year), 273 teaching assistantships with full tuition reimbursements (averaging $10,107 per year) were awarded; career-related internships or fieldwork, Federal Work-Study, scholarships/grants, traineeships, health care benefits, tuition waivers (full), and unspecified assistantships also available. Support available to part-time students. Financial award applicants required to submit FAFSA. In 2010, 84 master's, 33 doctorates awarded. *Degree program information:* Part-time programs available. Postbaccalaureate distance learning degree programs offered (minimal on-campus study). Offers anthropology (MA, PhD); communication (MA, PhD); economics (MA, PhD); labor studies (MS); landscape architecture (MLA); landscape architecture and regional planning (MLA, MRP, PhD); political science (MA, PhD); public policy and administration (MPPA); regional planning (MRP, PhD); social and behavioral sciences (MA, MLA, MPPA, MRP, MS, PhD); sociology (MA, PhD); union leadership and administration (MS). *Application deadline:* Applications are processed on a rolling basis. *Application fee:* $50 ($65 for international students). Electronic applications accepted. *Application Contact:* Jean M. Ames, Supervisor of Admissions, 413-545-0722, Fax: 413-577-0010, E-mail: gradadm@grad.umass.edu. *Dean,* Dr. Robert S. Feldman, 413-545-4173, Fax: 413-577-0905.

Interdisciplinary Programs Students: 185 full-time (99 women), 6 part-time (5 women); includes 31 minority (3 Black or African American, non-Hispanic/Latino; 11 Asian, non-Hispanic/Latino; 12 Hispanic/Latino; 1 Native Hawaiian or other Pacific Islander, non-Hispanic/Latino; 4 Two or more races, non-Hispanic/Latino), 38 international. Average age 28. 427 applicants, 29% accepted, 58 enrolled. Expenses: Contact institution. *Financial support:* In 2010–11, 1 fellowship with full tuition reimbursement (averaging $11,144 per year), 14 research assistantships with full tuition reimbursements (averaging $7,297 per year) were awarded; teaching assistantships, career-related internships or fieldwork, Federal Work-Study, scholarships/grants, traineeships, health care benefits, tuition waivers (full), and unspecified assistantships also available. Support available to part-time students. In 2010, 19 master's, 21 doctorates awarded. *Degree program information:* Part-time programs available. Offers animal behavior (PhD); animal behavior and learning (PhD); biochemistry and metabolism (MS, PhD); biological chemistry and molecular biophysics (PhD); biomedicine (PhD); cell biology and physiology (MS, PhD); cellular and developmental biology (PhD); ecology (PhD); environmental, ecological and integrative (PhD); environmental, ecological and integrative biology (MS); evolutionary biology (PhD); genetics and evolution (MS, PhD); interdisciplinary studies (MS, PhD); marine science and technology (MS, PhD); molecular and cellular neuroscience (PhD); neural and behavioral development (PhD); neuroendocrinology (PhD); neuroscience and behavior (MS); organismal biology (PhD); organismic and evolutionary biology (MS); public policy and business administrationsensorimotor, cognitive, and computational neuroscience (PhD); sports management and business administration. *Application deadline:* Applications are processed on a rolling basis. *Application fee:* $50 ($65 for international students). Electronic applications accepted. *Application Contact:* Jean M. Ames, Supervisor of Admissions, 413-545-0722, Fax: 413-577-0010, E-mail: gradadm@grad.umass.edu. *Graduate Dean,* Dr. John R. Mullin, 413-545-0722, Fax: 413-577-0010, E-mail: gradadm@grad.umass.edu.

Isenberg School of Management Students: 232 full-time (89 women), 1,076 part-time (310 women); includes 219 minority (36 Black or African American, non-Hispanic/Latino; 2 American Indian or Alaska Native, non-Hispanic/Latino; 126 Asian, non-Hispanic/Latino; 37 Hispanic/Latino; 3 Native Hawaiian or other Pacific Islander, non-Hispanic/Latino; 15 Two or more races, non-Hispanic/Latino), 135 international. Average age 35. 910 applicants, 55% accepted, 336 enrolled. *Faculty:* 97 full-time (22 women). Expenses: Contact institution. *Financial support:* In 2010–11, 21 fellowships with full tuition reimbursements (averaging $5,396 per year), 97 research assistantships with full tuition reimbursements (averaging $8,163 per year), 94 teaching assistantships with full tuition reimbursements (averaging $8,875 per year) were awarded; career-related internships or fieldwork, Federal Work-Study, scholarships/grants, traineeships, health care benefits, tuition waivers (full), and unspecified assistantships also available. Support available to part-time students. Financial award application deadline: 2/1; financial award applicants required to submit FAFSA. In 2010, 412 master's, 12 doctorates awarded. *Degree program information:* Part-time and evening/weekend programs available. Postbaccalaureate distance learning degree programs offered (no on-campus study). Offers accounting (MSA); business administration (MBA); hospitality and tourism management (MS); management (MBA, MS, MSA, PhD); resource economics (MS, PhD); sport management (MS, PhD). *Application deadline:* For fall admission, 2/1 for domestic and international students. Applications are processed on a rolling basis. *Application fee:* $50 ($65 for international students). Electronic applications accepted. *Application Contact:* Jean M. Ames, Supervisor of Admissions, 413-545-0722, Fax: 413-577-0010, E-mail: gradadm@grad.umass.edu. *Dean,* Dr. Mark A. Fuller, 415-545-5583, Fax: 413-577-2234.

School of Education Students: 390 full-time (275 women), 338 part-time (229 women); includes 113 minority (42 Black or African American, non-Hispanic/Latino; 1 American Indian or Alaska Native, non-Hispanic/Latino; 16 Asian, non-Hispanic/Latino; 43 Hispanic/Latino; 11 Two or more races, non-Hispanic/Latino), 94 international. Average age 35. 821 applicants, 58% accepted, 253 enrolled. *Faculty:* 75 full-time (41 women). Expenses: Contact institution. *Financial support:* In 2010–11, 20 fellowships with full tuition reimbursements (averaging $7,887 per year), 77 research assistantships with full tuition reimbursements (averaging $8,564 per year), 57 teaching assistantships with full tuition reimbursements (averaging $4,936 per year) were awarded; career-related internships or fieldwork, Federal Work-Study, scholarships/grants, traineeships, health care benefits, tuition waivers (full), and unspecified assistantships also available. Support available to part-time students. Financial award application deadline: 1/15; financial award applicants required to submit FAFSA. In 2010, 217 master's, 46 doctorates awarded. *Degree program information:* Part-time programs available. Postbaccalaureate distance learning degree programs offered (minimal on-campus study). Offers bilingual, English as a second language, and multicultural education (M Ed, CAGS); child study and early education (M Ed); children, families and schools (Ed D, CAGS); early childhood and elementary teacher education (M Ed); education (M Ed, Ed D, PhD, CAGS); education policy and leadership (CAGS); educational administration (CAGS); educational leadership (M Ed); educational policy and leadership (Ed D); higher education (M Ed, CAGS); international education (M Ed); language, literacy and culture (Ed D); learning, media and technology (M Ed, CAGS); mathematics, science, and learning technologies (Ed D); policy studies (M Ed); policy studies in education (CAGS); reading and writing (M Ed); research and evaluation methods (Ed D); school counselor education (M Ed, CAGS); school psychology (M Ed, PhD, CAGS); science education (CAGS); secondary teacher education (M Ed); social justice education (M Ed, Ed D, CAGS); special education (M Ed, Ed D, CAGS). *Application deadline:* For fall admission, 1/15 for domestic and international students. Applications are processed on a rolling basis. *Application fee:* $50 ($65 for international students). Electronic applications accepted. *Application Contact:* Jean M. Ames, Supervisor of Admissions, 413-545-0722, Fax: 413-577-0010, E-mail: gradadm@grad.umass.edu. *Dean,* Dr. Christine B. McCormick, 413-545-6984, Fax: 413-545-4240.

School of Nursing Students: 59 full-time (52 women), 150 part-time (141 women); includes 175 minority (21 Black or African American, non-Hispanic/Latino; 135 American Indian or Alaska Native, non-Hispanic/Latino; 6 Asian, non-Hispanic/Latino; 10 Hispanic/Latino; 3 Two or more races, non-Hispanic/Latino). Average age 43. 111 applicants, 81% accepted, 65 enrolled. *Faculty:* 12 full-time (all women). Expenses: Contact institution. *Financial support:* In 2010–11, 2 fellowships with full tuition reimbursements (averaging $27,234 per year), 1 research assistantship with full tuition reimbursement (averaging $6,236 per year), 19 teaching assistantships with full tuition reimbursements (averaging $5,659 per year) were awarded; career-related internships or fieldwork, Federal Work-Study, scholarships/grants, traineeships, health care benefits, tuition waivers (full), and unspecified assistantships also available. Support available to part-time students. Financial award application deadline: 2/1; financial award applicants required to submit FAFSA. In 2010, 6 master's, 20 doctorates awarded. *Degree program information:* Part-time programs available. Postbaccalaureate distance learning degree programs offered (minimal on-campus study). Offers nursing (MS, DNP, PhD). *Application deadline:* For fall admission, 2/1 for domestic and international students. Applications are processed on a rolling basis. *Application fee:* $50 ($65 for international students). Electronic applications accepted. *Application Contact:* Jean M. Ames, Supervisor of Admissions, 413-545-0722, Fax: 413-577-0010, E-mail: gradadm@grad.umass.edu. *Graduate Program Director,* Dr. Donna Zucker, 413-577-2322, Fax: 413-577-2550.

School of Public Health and Health Sciences Students: 239 full-time (199 women), 242 part-time (170 women); includes 66 minority (21 Black or African American, non-Hispanic/Latino; 18 Asian, non-Hispanic/Latino; 19 Hispanic/Latino; 1 Native Hawaiian or other Pacific Islander, non-Hispanic/Latino; 7 Two or more races, non-Hispanic/Latino), 67 international. Average age 34. 719 applicants, 42% accepted, 136 enrolled. *Faculty:* 82 full-time (50 women). Expenses: Contact institution. *Financial support:* In 2010–11, 23 fellowships with full tuition reimbursements (averaging $11,688 per year), 82 research assistantships with full tuition reimbursements (averaging $8,373 per year), 70 teaching assistantships with full tuition reimbursements (averaging $6,600 per year) were awarded; career-related internships or fieldwork, Federal Work-Study, scholarships/grants, traineeships, health care benefits, tuition waivers (full), and unspecified assistantships also available. Support available to part-time students. Financial award application deadline: 2/1; financial award applicants required to submit FAFSA. In 2010, 128 master's, 11 doctorates awarded. *Degree program information:* Part-time and evening/weekend programs available. Postbaccalaureate distance learning degree programs offered (no on-campus study). Offers biostatistics (MPH, MS, PhD); communication disorders (MA, Au D, PhD); community health education (MPH, MS, PhD); environmental health sciences (MPH, MS, PhD); epidemiology (MPH, MS, PhD); health policy and management (MPH, MS, PhD); kinesiology (MS, PhD); nutrition (MPH, MS, PhD); public health (PhD); public health and health sciences (MA, MPH, MS, Au D, PhD); public health practice (MPH). *Application deadline:* For fall admission, 2/1 for domestic and international students. Applications are processed on a rolling basis. *Application fee:* $50 ($65 for international students). Electronic applications accepted. *Application Contact:* Jean M. Ames, Supervisor of Admissions, 413-545-0722, Fax: 413-577-0010, E-mail: gradadm@grad.umass.edu. *Dean,* Dr. C. Marjorie Aelion, 413-545-2526, Fax: 413-545-0501.

UNIVERSITY OF MASSACHUSETTS BOSTON, Boston, MA 02125-3393

General Information State-supported, coed, university. CGS member. *Graduate housing:* On-campus housing not available. *Research affiliation:* John F. Kennedy Presidential Library (twentieth century history and politics).

GRADUATE UNITS

Office of Graduate Studies *Degree program information:* Part-time and evening/weekend programs available. Postbaccalaureate distance learning degree programs offered.

College of Liberal Arts *Degree program information:* Part-time and evening/weekend programs available. Offers American studies (MA); applied sociology (MA); archival methods (MA); bilingual education (MA); clinical psychology (PhD); English (MA); English as a second language (MA); foreign language pedagogy (MA); historical archaeology (MA); history (MA); liberal arts (MA, PhD).

College of Management *Degree program information:* Part-time and evening/weekend programs available. Offers business administration (MBA); management (MBA).

College of Nursing and Health Sciences *Degree program information:* Part-time and evening/weekend programs available. Offers nursing (MS, PhD).

College of Public and Community Service *Degree program information:* Part-time and evening/weekend programs available. Offers dispute resolution (MA, Certificate); human services (MS); public and community service (MA, MS, Certificate).

College of Science and Mathematics *Degree program information:* Part-time and evening/weekend programs available. Offers applied physics (MS); biology (MS); biotechnology and biomedical science (MS); chemistry (MS); computer science (MS, PhD); environmental biology (PhD); environmental sciences (MS); environmental, earth and ocean sciences (PhD); molecular, cellular and organismal biology (PhD); science and mathematics (MS, PhD).

Division of Continuing Education *Degree program information:* Part-time and evening/weekend programs available. Offers continuing education (Certificate); women in politics and government (Certificate).

Graduate College of Education *Degree program information:* Part-time and evening/weekend programs available. Offers critical and creative thinking (MA, Certificate); education (M Ed, Ed D); educational administration (M Ed, CAGS); elementary and secondary education/certification (M Ed); family therapy (M Ed, CAGS); forensic counseling (M Ed, CAGS); higher education administration (Ed D); instructional design (M Ed); mental health counseling (M Ed, CAGS); rehabilitation counseling (M Ed, CAGS); school guidance counseling (M Ed, CAGS); school psychology (M Ed, CAGS); special education (M Ed); teacher certification (M Ed); urban school leadership (Ed D).

John W. McCormack Graduate School of Policy Studies *Degree program information:* Part-time and evening/weekend programs available. Offers gerontology (MA, MS, PhD, Certificate); gerontology research (MA); management in aging services (MA); public affairs (MS); public policy (PhD); women in politics and government (Certificate). Certificate program in women in politics and government offered jointly with Division of Continuing Education.

UNIVERSITY OF MASSACHUSETTS DARTMOUTH, North Dartmouth, MA 02747-2300

General Information State-supported, coed, university. *Enrollment:* 9,432 graduate, professional, and undergraduate students; 645 full-time matriculated graduate/professional students (304 women), 877 part-time matriculated graduate/professional students (509 women). *Enrollment by degree level:* 316 first professional, 922 master's, 130 doctoral, 154 other advanced degrees. *Graduate faculty:* 286 full-time (113 women), 178 part-time/adjunct (94 women). Tuition, state resident: full-time $2071; part-time $86 per credit. Tuition, nonresident: full-time $8099; part-time $337 per credit. *Required fees:* $9446; $394 per credit. One-time fee: $75. Part-time tuition and fees vary according to class time, course load, degree level and reciprocity agreements. *Graduate housing:* Room and/or apartments available on a first-come, first-served basis to single students; on-campus housing not available to married students. Typical cost: $6317 per year ($9134 including board). Room and board charges vary according to board plan, campus/location and housing facility selected. Housing application deadline: 3/14. *Student services:* Campus employment opportunities, campus safety program, career counseling, child daycare facilities, exercise/wellness program, free psychological counseling, grant writing training, international student services, low-cost health insurance, multicultural affairs office, services for students with disabilities, teacher training, writing training. *Library facilities:* University of Massachusetts Dartmouth Library plus 1 other. *Online resources:* library catalog, web page, access to other libraries' catalogs. *Collection:* 461,338 titles, 2,783 serial subscriptions, 8,115 audiovisual materials. *Research affiliation:* National Aeronautics and Space Administration (NASA) (marine science and technology), National Oceanic and Atmospheric Administration (NOAA) (marine sciences), Cape Cod Cranberry Growers Association (agriculture), Woods Hole Oceanographic Institution (marine sciences), Office of Naval Research (ONR) (engineering), Newton Photonics (chemistry).

Computer facilities: 368 computers available on campus for general student use. A campuswide network can be accessed from student residence rooms and from off campus. Online class registration is available. *Web address:* http://www.umassd.edu/.

General Application Contact: Elan Turcotte-Shamski, Graduate Admissions Officer, 508-999-8604, Fax: 508-999-8183, E-mail: graduate@umassd.edu.

GRADUATE UNITS

Graduate School Students: 645 full-time (304 women), 877 part-time (509 women); includes 70 Black or African American, non-Hispanic/Latino; 5 American Indian or Alaska Native, non-Hispanic/Latino; 28 Asian, non-Hispanic/Latino; 48 Hispanic/Latino; 15 Two or more races, non-Hispanic/Latino, 232 international. Average age 31. 1,661 applicants, 72% accepted, 631 enrolled. *Faculty:* 286 full-time (113 women), 178 part-time/adjunct (94 women). Expenses: Contact institution. *Financial support:* In 2010–11, 10 fellowships with full tuition reimbursements (averaging $11,015 per year), 103 research assistantships with full tuition reimbursements (averaging $10,685 per year), 121 teaching assistantships with full tuition reimbursements (averaging $8,021 per year) were awarded; career-related internships or fieldwork, Federal Work-Study, scholarships/grants, and unspecified assistantships also available. Support available to part-time students. Financial award application deadline: 3/1; financial award applicants required to submit FAFSA. In 2010, 288 master's, 3 doctorates, 25 other advanced degrees awarded. *Degree program information:* Part-time programs available. Postbaccalaureate distance learning degree programs offered. Offers biomedical engineering and biotechnology (PhD). *Application deadline:* Applications are processed on a rolling basis. *Application fee:* $40 ($60 for international students). Electronic applications accepted. *Application Contact:* Elan Turcotte-Shamski, Graduate Admissions Officer, 508-999-8604, Fax: 508-999-8183, E-mail: graduate@umassd.edu. *Director for Graduate Studies and Admissions,* Scott Webster, 508-999-8202, Fax: 508-999-8183, E-mail: swebster@umassd.edu.

Charlton College of Business Students: 99 full-time (38 women), 123 part-time (62 women); includes 4 Black or African American, non-Hispanic/Latino; 2 American Indian or Alaska Native, non-Hispanic/Latino; 3 Asian, non-Hispanic/Latino; 8 Hispanic/Latino; 1 Two or more races, non-Hispanic/Latino, 45 international. Average age 30. 185 applicants, 76% accepted, 79 enrolled. *Faculty:* 40 full-time (13 women), 28 part-time/adjunct (8 women). Expenses: Contact institution. *Financial support:* In 2010–11, 1 research assistantship with full tuition reimbursement (averaging $6,000 per year) was awarded; teaching assistantships, Federal Work-Study and unspecified assistantships also available. Support available to part-time students. Financial award application deadline: 3/1; financial award applicants required to submit FAFSA. In 2010, 79 master's, 12 other advanced degrees awarded. *Degree program information:* Part-time programs available. Offers accounting (Postbaccalaureate Certificate); business (MBA, PMC, Postbaccalaureate Certificate); business administration (MBA); e-commerce (PMC); finance (PMC); general management (PMC); leadership (PMC); management (Postbaccalaureate Certificate); marketing (PMC); supply chain management (PMC). *Application deadline:* For fall admission, 6/1 for domestic students, 5/1 for international students; for spring admission, 10/1 for domestic students, 8/1 for international students. Applications are processed on a rolling basis. *Application fee:* $40 ($60 for international students). Electronic applications accepted. *Application Contact:* Elan Turcotte-Shamski, Graduate Admissions Officer, 508-999-8604, Fax: 508-999-8183, E-mail: graduate@umassd.edu. Dr. Norm Barber, 508-999-8543, Fax: 508-999-8779, E-mail: nbarber@umassd.edu.

College of Arts and Sciences Students: 71 full-time (52 women), 110 part-time (77 women); includes 8 Black or African American, non-Hispanic/Latino; 2 Asian, non-Hispanic/Latino; 8 Hispanic/Latino; 1 Two or more races, non-Hispanic/Latino, 22 international. Average age 30. 207 applicants, 50% accepted, 73 enrolled. *Faculty:* 82 full-time (33 women), 52 part-time/adjunct (30 women). Expenses: Contact institution. *Financial support:* In 2010–11, 15 research assistantships with full tuition reimbursements (averaging $11,360 per year), 43 teaching assistantships with full tuition reimbursements (averaging $10,417 per year) were awarded; career-related internships or fieldwork, Federal Work-Study, and unspecified assistantships also available. Support available to part-time students. Financial award application deadline: 3/1; financial award applicants required to submit FAFSA. In 2010, 38 master's awarded. *Degree program information:* Part-time programs available. Offers arts and sciences (MA, MS, PhD, Postbaccalaureate Certificate); behavior analyst (Postbaccalaureate Certificate); biology (MS); chemistry (MS, PhD); clinical psychology (MA); general psychology (MA); Luso-Afro-Brazilian studies (PhD); marine biology (MS); Portuguese (MA); professional writing (MA, Postbaccalaureate Certificate). *Application fee:* $40 ($60 for international students). *Application Contact:* Elan Turcotte-Shamski, Graduate Admissions Officer, 508-999-8604, Fax: 508-999-8183, E-mail: graduate@umassd.edu. *Dean,* Dr. William Hogan, 508-999-8200, Fax: 508-999-8183, E-mail: whogan@umassd.edu.

College of Engineering Students: 100 full-time (23 women), 124 part-time (22 women); includes 2 Black or African American, non-Hispanic/Latino; 1 American Indian or Alaska Native, non-Hispanic/Latino; 4 Asian, non-Hispanic/Latino; 4 Hispanic/Latino, 120 international. Average age 26. 296 applicants, 81% accepted, 68 enrolled. *Faculty:* 60 full-time (9 women), 11 part-time/adjunct (0 women). Expenses: Contact institution. *Financial support:* In 2010–11, 5 fellowships with full tuition reimbursements (averaging $12,707 per year), 52 research assistantships with full tuition reimbursements (averaging $9,501 per year), 37 teaching assistantships with full tuition reimbursements (averaging $10,140 per year) were awarded; Federal Work-Study and unspecified assistantships also available. Support available to part-time students. Financial award application deadline: 3/1; financial award applicants required to submit FAFSA. In 2010, 28 master's, 1 doctorate, 1 other advanced degree awarded. *Degree program information:* Part-time programs available. Offers acoustics (Postbaccalaureate Certificate); civil and environmental engineering (MS); communications (Postbaccalaureate Certificate); computer engineering (MS, PhD); computer networks and distributed systems (Postbaccalaureate Certificate); computer science (MS); computer systems (Postbaccalaureate Certificate); computer systems engineering (Postbaccalaureate Certificate); digital signal processing (Postbaccalaureate Certificate); electrical engineering (MS, PhD); electrical engineering systems (Postbaccalaureate Certificate); engineering (MS, PhD, Postbaccalaureate Certificate); mechanical engineering (MS); physics (MS); software development and design (Postbaccalaureate Certificate); textile chemistry (MS); textile technology (MS). *Application deadline:* Applications are processed on a rolling basis. *Application fee:* $40 ($60 for international students). Electronic applications accepted. *Application Contact:* Elan Turcotte-Shamski, Graduate Admissions Officer, 508-999-8604, Fax: 508-999-8183, E-mail: graduate@umassd.edu. *Dean,* Dr. Robert Peck, 508-999-8539, Fax: 508-999-9137, E-mail: rpeck@umassd.edu.

College of Nursing Students: 7 full-time (6 women), 90 part-time (83 women); includes 3 Black or African American, non-Hispanic/Latino; 1 American Indian or Alaska Native, non-Hispanic/Latino; 2 Asian, non-Hispanic/Latino; 2 Hispanic/Latino, 1 international. Average age 39. 57 applicants, 84% accepted, 29 enrolled. *Faculty:* 27 full-time (all women), 33 part-time/adjunct (32 women). Expenses: Contact institution. *Financial support:* In 2010–11, 11 teaching assistantships with full tuition reimbursements (averaging $3,359 per year) were awarded; Federal Work-Study and scholarships/grants also available. Support available to part-time students. Financial award application deadline: 3/1; financial award applicants required to submit FAFSA. In 2010, 18 master's, 1 other advanced degree awarded. *Degree program information:* Part-time programs available. Offers adult health/adult nurse practitioner (MS); adult health/advanced practice (MS); adult nurse practitioner (PMC); community nursing/advanced practice (MS); individualized nursing (PMC); nursing (PhD). *Application deadline:* For fall admission, 4/20 for domestic students, 2/20 for international students; for spring admission, 10/15 for domestic students, 8/15 for international students. *Application fee:* $40 ($60 for international students). Electronic applications accepted. *Application Contact:* Elan Turcotte-Shamski, Graduate Admissions Officer, 508-999-8604, Fax: 508-999-8183, E-mail: graduate@umassd.edu. *Director,* Dr. Gail Russell, 508-999-8251, Fax: 508-999-9127, E-mail: grussell@umassd.edu.

College of Visual and Performing Arts Students: 52 full-time (38 women), 40 part-time (34 women); includes 1 Asian, non-Hispanic/Latino; 1 Hispanic/Latino; 2 Two or more races, non-Hispanic/Latino, 5 international. Average age 31. 146 applicants, 54% accepted, 39 enrolled. *Faculty:* 39 full-time (17 women), 9 part-time/adjunct (4 women). Expenses: Contact institution. *Financial support:* In 2010–11, 3 fellowships with full tuition reimbursements (averaging $5,333 per year), 1 research assistantship with full tuition reimbursement (averaging $7,400 per year), 28 teaching assistantships with full tuition reimbursements (averaging $3,088 per year) were awarded; Federal Work-Study and unspecified assistantships also available. Support available to part-time students. Financial award application deadline: 3/1; financial award applicants required to submit FAFSA. In 2010, 25 master's, 1 other advanced degree awarded. *Degree program information:* Part-time programs available. Offers art education (MAE); ceramics (MFA, Postbaccalaureate Certificate); digital media (MFA); drawing (MFA); fibers (MFA); fibers/textiles (Postbaccalaureate Certificate); graphic design (MFA); illustration (MFA); jewelry/metals (MFA, Postbaccalaureate Certificate); painting (MFA); photography (MFA); printmaking (MFA); sculpture (MFA); typography (MFA); visual and performing arts (MAE, MFA, Postbaccalaureate Certificate); wood/furniture design (MFA, Postbaccalaureate Certificate). *Application deadline:* Applications are processed on a rolling basis. *Application fee:* $40 ($60 for international students). Electronic applications accepted. *Application Contact:* Elan Turcotte-Shamski, Graduate Admissions Officer, 508-999-8604, Fax: 508-999-8183, E-mail: graduate@umassd.edu. *Dean,* Adrian Tio, 508-999-9295, Fax: 508-999-9126, E-mail: atio@umassd.edu.

School of Education, Public Policy, and Civic Engagement Students: 65 full-time (34 women), 234 part-time (151 women); includes 8 Black or African American, non-Hispanic/Latino; 6 Hispanic/Latino; 5 Two or more races, non-Hispanic/Latino. Average age 35. 283 applicants, 85% accepted, 167 enrolled. *Faculty:* 17 full-time (9 women), 12 part-time/adjunct (8 women). Expenses: Contact institution. *Financial support:* In 2010–11, 3 research assistantships with full tuition reimbursements (averaging $5,333 per year) were awarded; Federal Work-Study, scholarships/grants, and unspecified assistantships also available. Support available to part-time students. Financial award application deadline: 3/1; financial award applicants required to submit FAFSA. In 2010, 65 master's, 10 other advanced degrees awarded. *Degree program information:* Part-time programs available. Offers education, public policy, and civic engagement (MAT, MPP, PhD, Postbaccalaureate Certificate); elementary education (MAT, Postbaccalaureate Certificate); environmental policy (Postbaccalaureate Certificate); math education (PhD); middle school education (MAT); principal initial licensure (Postbaccalaureate Certificate); public policy (MPP); secondary school education (MAT). *Application deadline:* For fall admission, 4/20 for domestic students, 2/20 for international students; for spring admission, 11/15 for domestic students, 9/15 for international students. *Application fee:* $40 ($60 for international students). Electronic applications accepted. *Application Contact:* Elan Turcotte-Shamski, Graduate Admissions Officer, 508-999-8604, Fax: 508-999-8183, E-mail: graduate@umassd.edu. *Interim Dean,* Dr. Ismael Ramirez-Soto, 508-999-9050, E-mail: iramirezsoto@umassd.edu.

School of Marine Science and Technology Students: 42 full-time (16 women), 23 part-time (12 women), 19 international. Average age 31. 41 applicants, 34% accepted, 10 enrolled. *Faculty:* 14 full-time (1 woman), 1 part-time/adjunct (0 women). Expenses: Contact institution. *Financial support:* In 2010–11, 2 fellowships with full tuition reimbursements (averaging $15,307 per year), 31 research assistantships with full tuition reimbursements (averaging $13,121 per year), 2 teaching assistantships with full tuition reimbursements (averaging $12,000 per year) were awarded. Financial award application deadline: 3/1; financial award applicants required to submit FAFSA. In 2010, 5 master's, 2 doctorates awarded. Offers marine science and technology (MS, PhD). *Application deadline:* For fall admission, 4/20 priority date for domestic students, 2/20 for international students. Applications are processed on a rolling basis. *Application fee:* $40 ($60 for international students). Electronic applications accepted. *Application Contact:* Elan Turcotte-Shamski, Graduate Admissions Officer, 508-999-8604, Fax: 508-999-8183, E-mail: graduate@umassd.edu. *Associate Dean,* Dr. Avijit Gangopadhyay, 508-910-6330, Fax: 508-999-8197, E-mail: avijit@umassd.edu.

University of Massachusetts School of Law at Dartmouth Students: 191 full-time (85 women), 125 part-time (67 women); includes 45 Black or African American, non-Hispanic/Latino; 1 American Indian or Alaska Native, non-Hispanic/Latino; 16 Asian, non-Hispanic/Latino; 19 Hispanic/Latino, 3 international. Average age 30. 446 applicants, 74% accepted, 166 enrolled. *Faculty:* 8 full-time (5 women), 32 part-time/adjunct (12 women). Expenses: Contact institution. *Financial support:* Research assistantships, scholarships/grants, tuition waivers (full and partial), and summer stipends available. Support available to part-time students. Financial award application deadline: 6/30; financial award applicants required to submit FAFSA. *Degree program information:* Part-time and evening/weekend programs available. Offers law (JD). *Application deadline:* For fall admission, 6/30 for domestic students. Applications are processed on a rolling basis. *Application fee:* $50. *Application Contact:* Nancy Fitzsimmons Hebert, Director of Admission, 508-998-9400 Ext. 113, Fax: 508-998-9561, E-mail: nhebert@umassd.edu. *Dean,* Robert V. Ward, 508-998-9600 Ext. 170, Fax: 508-998-9561, E-mail: rward@umassd.edu.

UNIVERSITY OF MASSACHUSETTS LOWELL, Lowell, MA 01854-2881

General Information State-supported, coed, university. *Graduate housing:* Rooms and/or apartments available on a first-come, first-served basis to single students and available to married students. Housing application deadline: 4/1.

GRADUATE UNITS

College of Arts and Sciences *Degree program information:* Part-time and evening/weekend programs available. Offers analytical chemistry (PhD); applied mathematics (MS); applied mechanics (PhD); applied physics (MS, PhD); arts and sciences (MA, MM, MS, PhD, Sc D, Graduate Certificate); atmospheric science (MS, PhD); biochemistry (PhD); biological sciences (MS); biotechnology (MS); chemistry (MS, PhD); community social psychology (MA); computational mathematics (PhD); computer science (MS, PhD, Sc D); criminal justice and criminology (MA); environmental studies (PhD); green chemistry (PhD); inorganic chemistry (PhD); mathematics (MS); music education (MM); organic chemistry (PhD); physics (MS,

PhD); polymer science (MS); radiological science and protection (MS); regional economic and social development (MA, Graduate Certificate); sound recording technology (MM).

College of Management *Degree program information:* Part-time and evening/weekend programs available. Offers business administration (MBA); foundations of business (Graduate Certificate); new venture creation (Graduate Certificate).

Graduate School of Education *Degree program information:* Part-time and evening/weekend programs available. Postbaccalaureate distance learning degree programs offered (no on-campus study). Offers administration, planning, and policy (CAGS); curriculum and instruction (M Ed, CAGS); educational administration (M Ed); language arts and literacy (Ed D); leadership in schooling (Ed D); math and science education (Ed D); reading and language (M Ed, CAGS). Electronic applications accepted.

James B. Francis College of Engineering *Degree program information:* Part-time and evening/weekend programs available. Offers chemical engineering (MS Eng, D Eng, PhD); civil and environmental engineering (MS Eng, Certificate); computer engineering (MS Eng); elastomers (Graduate Certificate); electrical engineering (MS Eng, D Eng); energy engineering (MS Eng, D Eng, PhD); engineering (MS Eng, MSES, D Eng, PhD, Certificate, Graduate Certificate); environmental engineering (MSES, D Eng); environmental studies (MSES, PhD, Certificate); mechanical engineering (MS Eng, D Eng, PhD); medical plastics design and manufacturing (Graduate Certificate); plastics design (Graduate Certificate); plastics engineering (MS Eng, D Eng, PhD); plastics engineering fundamentals (Graduate Certificate); plastics materials (Graduate Certificate); plastics processing (Graduate Certificate); polymer science/plastics engineering (PhD); sustainable infrastructure for developing nations (Certificate).

School of Health and Environment *Degree program information:* Part-time programs available. Offers adult psychiatric and mental health nursing (MS, Graduate Certificate); cleaner production and pollution prevention (MS, Sc D); clinical laboratory sciences (MS); clinical pathology (Graduate Certificate); environmental risk assessment (Certificate); epidemiology (MS, Sc D); ergonomics and safety (MS, Sc D); family health nursing (MS); gerontological nursing (MS, Graduate Certificate); geropsychiatric nursing (Graduate Certificate); health and environment (MS, DPT, PhD, Sc D, Certificate, Graduate Certificate); health management and policy (MS, Graduate Certificate); identification and control of ergonomic hazards (Certificate); job stress and healthy job redesign (Certificate); nursing (PhD); nursing education (Graduate Certificate); nutritional sciences (Graduate Certificate); occupational and environmental hygiene (MS, Sc D); palliative and end-of-life nursing care (Graduate Certificate); physical therapy (DPT); public health laboratory sciences (Graduate Certificate); radiological health physics and general work environment protection (Certificate); work environment policy (MS, Sc D).

See Display on this page and Close-Up on page 989.

UNIVERSITY OF MASSACHUSETTS WORCESTER, Worcester, MA 01655-0115

General Information State-supported, coed, graduate-only institution. CGS member. *Enrollment by degree level:* 496 first professional, 139 master's, 465 doctoral. *Graduate faculty:* 1,059 full-time (357 women), 145 part-time/adjunct (100 women). Tuition, state resident: full-time $2640. Tuition, nonresident: full-time $9856. Full-time tuition and fees vary according to program. *Graduate housing:* On-campus housing not available. *Student services:* Campus employment opportunities, campus safety program, career counseling, child daycare facilities, exercise/wellness program, free psychological counseling, grant writing training, international student services, low-cost health insurance, multicultural affairs office, services for students with disabilities, teacher training, writing training. *Library facilities:* Lamar Soutter Library. *Online resources:* library catalog, web page, access to other libraries' catalogs. *Collection:* 202,000 titles, 5,302 serial subscriptions, 657 audiovisual materials. *Research affiliation:* Abbott Bioresearch Center (biomedical research and training), Charles River Laboratories (pre-clinical biomedical research).

Computer facilities: 115 computers available on campus for general student use. A campuswide network can be accessed from off campus. Online class registration, Student account (Bursar) and Blackboard Vista Web management are available. *Web address:* http://www.umass.edu/.

General Application Contact: Karen Lawton, Director of Admissions, 508-856-2323, Fax: 508-856-3629, E-mail: admissions@umassmed.edu.

GRADUATE UNITS

Graduate School of Biomedical Sciences Students: 438 full-time (239 women), 1 (woman) part-time; includes 44 minority (9 Black or African American, non-Hispanic/Latino; 31 Asian, non-Hispanic/Latino; 4 Hispanic/Latino), 148 international. Average age 29. 687 applicants, 28% accepted, 116 enrolled. *Faculty:* 1,059 full-time (357 women), 145 part-time/adjunct (100 women). Expenses: Contact institution. *Financial support:* In 2010–11, 439 students received support, including 439 research assistantships with full tuition reimbursements available (averaging $28,350 per year); scholarships/grants, health care benefits, tuition waivers (full), and unspecified assistantships also available. Financial award application deadline: 4/20. In 2010, 6 master's, 45 doctorates awarded. Offers biochemistry and molecular pharmacology (PhD); bioinformatics and computational biology (PhD); cancer biology (PhD); cell biology (PhD); clinical and population health research (PhD); clinical investigation (MS); immunology and virology (PhD); interdisciplinary graduate program (PhD); molecular genetics and microbiology (PhD); neuroscience (PhD). *Application deadline:* For fall admission, 12/15 for domestic and international students; for winter admission, 1/15 for domestic students; for spring admission, 5/15 for domestic students. *Application fee:* $35. Electronic applications accepted. *Application Contact:* Dr. Kendall Knight, Associate Dean and Interim Director of Admissions and Recruitment, 508-856-5628, Fax: 508-856-3659, E-mail: kendall.knight@umassmed.edu. *Dean,* Dr. Anthony Carruthers, 508-856-4135, E-mail: anthony.carruthers@umassmed.edu.

Graduate School of Nursing Students: 169 full-time (146 women), 5 part-time (all women); includes 19 minority (10 Black or African American, non-Hispanic/Latino; 6 Asian, non-Hispanic/Latino; 3 Hispanic/Latino), 1 international. Average age 36. 197 applicants, 44% accepted, 68 enrolled. *Faculty:* 15 full-time (13 women), 29 part-time/adjunct (25 women). Expenses: Contact institution. *Financial support:* In 2010–11, 60 students received support. Institutionally sponsored loans, scholarships/grants, and traineeships available. Support available to part-time students. Financial award application deadline: 5/18; financial award applicants required to submit FAFSA. In 2010, 37 master's, 2 doctorates awarded. Offers adult acute/critical care nurse practitioner (MS, Post Master's Certificate); adult acute/critical care nurse practitioner and gerontological nurse practitioner (MS, Post Master's Certificate); adult primary care nurse practitioner (MS, Post Master's Certificate); adult primary care nurse practitioner and gerontological nurse practitioner (MS, Post Master's Certificate); advanced practice nursing (DNP); family nurse practitioner (MS); gerontological nurse practitioner (Post Master's Certificate); leadership (DNP); nurse education (Post Master's Certificate); nurse educator (MS); nursing (PhD). *Application deadline:* For fall admission, 1/15 priority date for domestic students. Applications are processed on a rolling basis. *Application fee:* $40 ($60 for international students). *Application Contact:* Diane Brescia, Admissions Coordinator, 508-856-3488, Fax: 508-856-5851, E-mail: diane.brescia@umassmed.edu. *Dean,* Dr. Paulette Seymour-Route, 508-856-5801, Fax: 508-856-6552, E-mail: paulette.seymour-route@umassmed.edu.

School of Medicine Students: 487 full-time (263 women); includes 115 minority (20 Black or African American, non-Hispanic/Latino; 1 American Indian or Alaska Native, non-Hispanic/Latino; 78 Asian, non-Hispanic/Latino; 16 Hispanic/Latino). Average age 27. 944 applicants, 21% accepted, 125 enrolled. *Faculty:* 1,059 full-time (357 women), 145 part-time/adjunct (100 women). Expenses: Contact institution. *Financial support:* In 2010–11, 426 students received support. Institutionally sponsored loans, scholarships/grants, health care benefits, tuition waivers (partial), and unspecified assistantships available. Financial award application deadline: 4/20; financial award applicants required to submit FAFSA. In 2010, 101 first professional degrees awarded. Offers medicine (MD). *Application deadline:* For fall admission, 12/15 for domestic students. Applications are processed on a rolling basis. *Application fee:* $75. Electronic applications accepted. *Application Contact:* Karen Lawton, Director of Admissions, 508-856-2323, Fax: 508-856-3629, E-mail: admissions@umassmed.edu. *Dean/Provost/Executive Deputy Chancellor,* Dr. Terence R. Flotte, 508-856-8000.

UNIVERSITY OF MEDICINE AND DENTISTRY OF NEW JERSEY, Newark, NJ 07107-1709

General Information State-supported, coed, comprehensive institution. CGS member. *Graduate housing:* Room and/or apartments available on a first-come, first-served basis to single students; on-campus housing not available to married students. *Research affiliation:* Robert Wood Johnson University Hospital (adult care hospitalization), Public Health Research Institute (public health), Kessler Institute for Rehabilitation (physical rehabilitation), Coriell Institute for Medical Research (cancer and human development).

GRADUATE UNITS

Graduate School of Biomedical Sciences Students: 694 full-time (398 women), 122 part-time (78 women); includes 76 Black or African American, non-Hispanic/Latino; 2 American Indian or Alaska Native, non-Hispanic/Latino; 175 Asian, non-Hispanic/Latino; 49 Hispanic/Latino, 132 international. Average age 27. Expenses: Contact institution. *Financial support:* Fellowships, research assistantships, teaching assistantships, career-related internships or fieldwork, Federal Work-Study, institutionally sponsored loans, traineeships, and tuition waivers (full and partial) available. Financial award application deadline: 5/1. In 2010, 166 master's, 72 doctorates awarded. Offers biochemistry and molecular biology (MS, PhD); biodefense (Certificate); biomedical engineering (MS, PhD); biomedical science (MS); biomedical sciences (MBS, MS); biomedical sciences (interdisciplinary) (PhD); biomedical sciences (multidisciplinary) (PhD); cell and molecular biology (MS, PhD); cell biology and molecular medicine (PhD); cellular and molecular pharmacology (MS, PhD); cellular biology, neuroscience and physiology (PhD); clinical and translational science (MS); environmental sciences/exposure assessment (PhD); infection, immunity and inflammation (PhD); integrative neuroscience (PhD); microbiology and molecular genetics (PhD); molecular biology, genetics and cancer (PhD); molecular biosciences (PhD); molecular genetics, microbiology and immunology (MS, PhD); molecular pathology and immunology (PhD); neuroscience (MS, PhD); pharmacological sciences (Certificate); pharmacology and physiology (PhD); physiology and integrative biology (MS, PhD); stem cell (Certificate); toxicology (PhD). *Application deadline:* Applications are processed on a rolling basis. *Application fee:* $40. Electronic applications accepted. *Application Contact:* University Registrar, 973-972-5338. *Interim Dean,* Dr. Kathleen W. Scotto, 973-972-5332, Fax: 973-972-7068, E-mail: scottoka@umdnj.edu.

New Jersey Dental School Offers dental science (MS); dentistry (DMD); endodontics (Certificate); oral medicine (Certificate); orthodontics (Certificate); pediatric dentistry (Certificate); periodontics (Certificate); prosthodontics (Certificate). DMD/MPH offered jointly with New Jersey Institute of Technology, Rutgers, The State University of New Jersey, Camden. Electronic applications accepted.

New Jersey Medical School Offers medicine (MD). Electronic applications accepted.

Robert Wood Johnson Medical School Offers medicine (MD). Electronic applications accepted.

School of Health Related Professions Students: 435 full-time (303 women), 462 part-time (348 women); includes 79 Black or African American, non-Hispanic/Latino; 112 Asian, non-Hispanic/Latino; 59 Hispanic/Latino, 57 international. Average age 32. 869 applicants, 43% accepted, 277 enrolled. Expenses: Contact institution. *Financial support:* Fellowships, research assistantships, teaching assistantships, Federal Work-Study and institutionally sponsored loans available. Financial award application deadline: 5/1. In 2010, 106 master's, 60 doctorates, 24 other advanced degrees awarded. *Degree program information:* Part-time programs available. Offers biomedical informatics (MS, PhD); cardiopulmonary sciences (PhD); clinical laboratory sciences (PhD); clinical nutrition (MS, DCN); clinical trials (MS); dietetic internship (Certificate); health care informatics (Certificate); health related professions (MPT, MS, DCN, DPT, PhD, Certificate); health sciences (MS, PhD); health systems (MS); interdisciplinary studies (PhD); nurse midwifery (Certificate); nutrition (PhD); physical therapy (MPT, DPT); physical therapy/movement science (PhD); physician assistant (MS); professional counseling (Certificate); psychiatric rehabilitation (MS, PhD); radiologist assistant (MS); rehabilitation counseling (MS); vocational rehabilitation (MS). *Application deadline:* Applications are processed on a rolling basis. *Application fee:* $50. Electronic applications accepted. *Application Contact:* Douglas Lomonaco, Assistant Dean for Enrollment Services, 973-972-5454, Fax: 973-972-7463, E-mail: shrpadm@umdnj.edu. *Interim Dean,* Dr. Julie O'Sullivan Maillet, 973-972-4276, Fax: 973-972-7028, E-mail: maillet@umdnj.edu.

School of Nursing *Degree program information:* Part-time programs available. Offers adult health (MSN); adult occupational health (MSN); advanced practice nursing (MSN, Post Master's Certificate); family nurse practitioner (MSN); nurse anesthesia (MSN); nursing (MSN); nursing informatics (MSN); urban health (PhD); women's health practitioner (MSN). Electronic applications accepted.

School of Osteopathic Medicine Offers osteopathic medicine (DO). Electronic applications accepted.

UMDNJ–School of Public Health (UMDNJ, Rutgers, NJIT) Newark Campus Expenses: Contact institution. *Degree program information:* Part-time and evening/weekend programs available. Offers clinical epidemiology (Certificate); dental public health (MPH); general public health (Certificate); public policy and oral health services administration (Certificate); quantitative methods (MPH); urban health (MPH). *Application deadline:* For fall admission, 5/1 for domestic students; for spring admission, 10/1 for domestic students. *Application fee:* $115. Electronic applications accepted. *Application Contact:* Yvette J. Holding-Ford, Information Contact, 973-972-7212, Fax: 973-972-8032, E-mail: holdinys@umdnj.edu.

UMDNJ–School of Public Health (UMDNJ, Rutgers, NJIT) Piscataway/New Brunswick Campus Expenses: Contact institution. *Degree program information:* Part-time and evening/weekend programs available. Offers biostatistics (MPH, MS, Dr PH, PhD); clinical epidemiology (Certificate); environmental and occupational health (MPH, Dr PH, PhD, Certificate); epidemiology (MPH, Dr PH, PhD); general public health (Certificate); health education and behavioral science (MPH, Dr PH, PhD); health systems and policy (MPH, PhD); public health preparedness (Certificate). *Application deadline:* For fall admission, 5/1 for domestic students; for spring admission, 10/1 for domestic students. *Application fee:* $115. Electronic applications accepted. *Application Contact:* Janet Zamorski, Staff Assistant, 732-235-4646, E-mail: zamorsja@umdnj.edu. *Program Coordinator,* Tina Greco, 732-235-4646, Fax: 732-235-5476, E-mail: grecotm@umdnj.edu.

UMDNJ–School of Public Health (UMDNJ, Rutgers, NJIT) Stratford/Camden Campus Expenses: Contact institution. *Degree program information:* Part-time and evening/weekend programs available. Offers general public health (Certificate); health systems and policy (MPH). *Application deadline:* For fall admission, 5/1 for domestic students; for spring admission, 10/1 for domestic students. *Application fee:* $115. Electronic applications accepted. *Application Contact:* Tina Greco, Program Coordinator, 856-566-2790, Fax: 856-566-2882, E-mail: grecotm@umdnj.edu. *Program Coordinator,* Tina Greco, 856-566-2790, Fax: 856-566-2882, E-mail: grecotm@umdnj.edu.

UNIVERSITY OF MEMPHIS, Memphis, TN 38152

General Information State-supported, coed, university. CGS member. *Enrollment:* 22,421 graduate, professional, and undergraduate students; 1,873 full-time matriculated graduate/professional students (1,081 women), 2,605 part-time matriculated graduate/professional students (1,763 women). *Enrollment by degree level:* 411 first professional, 3,115 master's, 875 doctoral. *Graduate faculty:* 562 full-time (197 women), 117 part-time/adjunct (49 women). *Graduate housing:* Rooms and/or apartments available on a first-come, first-served basis to single students and available to married students. Housing application deadline: 7/1. *Student services:* Campus employment opportunities, campus safety program, career counseling, child daycare facilities, exercise/wellness program, free psychological counseling, grant writing training, international student services, low-cost health insurance, multicultural affairs office, services for students with disabilities, teacher training, writing training. *Library facilities:* McWherter Library plus 4 others. *Online resources:* library catalog, web page, access to other libraries' catalogs. *Collection:* 1.5 million titles, 6,771 serial subscriptions, 34,093 audiovisual materials. *Research affiliation:* Memphis Biotech Foundation, Campbell Clinic Orthopaedics, Federal Express, Oak Ridge National Laboratory, St. Jude Children's Research Hospital, Gulf Coast Research Laboratory.

Computer facilities: 1,600 computers available on campus for general student use. A campuswide network can be accessed from student residence rooms and from off campus. Online class registration is available. *Web address:* http://www.memphis.edu/.

General Application Contact: Dr. Karen Weddle-West, Information Contact, 901-678-2531, Fax: 901-678-5023, E-mail: gradsch@memphis.edu.

GRADUATE UNITS

Cecil C. Humphreys School of Law Students: 408 full-time (167 women), 24 part-time (10 women); includes 55 minority (35 Black or African American, non-Hispanic/Latino; 4 American Indian or Alaska Native, non-Hispanic/Latino; 8 Asian, non-Hispanic/Latino; 8 Hispanic/Latino). Average age 26. 965 applicants, 31% accepted, 158 enrolled. *Faculty:* 20 full-time (8 women), 28 part-time/adjunct (8 women). Expenses: Contact institution. *Financial support:* In 2010–11, 114 students received support, including 24 research assistantships with full and partial tuition reimbursements available (averaging $3,000 per year), 2 teaching assistantships (averaging $3,000 per year); career-related internships or fieldwork, Federal Work-Study, scholarships/grants, tuition waivers (partial), and unspecified assistantships also available. Support available to part-time students. Financial award application deadline: 4/1; financial award applicants required to submit FAFSA. In 2010, 124 first professional degrees awarded. *Degree program information:* Part-time programs available. Offers law (JD). *Application deadline:* For fall admission, 3/1 priority date for domestic and international students. Applications are processed on a rolling basis. *Application fee:* $25 ($40 for international students). Electronic applications accepted. *Application Contact:* Dr. Sue Ann McClellan, Assistant Dean for Law Admissions, Recruiting and Scholarships, 901-678-5403, Fax: 901-678-5210, E-mail: smcclell@memphis.edu. *Dean,* Dr. Kevin H. Smith, 901-678-2421, Fax: 901-678-5210, E-mail: ksmith@memphis.edu.

Graduate School Students: 1,873 full-time (1,081 women), 2,605 part-time (1,763 women); includes 1,404 minority (1,171 Black or African American, non-Hispanic/Latino; 7 American Indian or Alaska Native, non-Hispanic/Latino; 89 Asian, non-Hispanic/Latino; 71 Hispanic/Latino; 2 Native Hawaiian or other Pacific Islander, non-Hispanic/Latino; 64 Two or more races, non-Hispanic/Latino), 433 international. Average age 33. 2,666 applicants, 74% accepted, 604 enrolled. *Faculty:* 528 full-time (176 women), 102 part-time/adjunct (43 women). Expenses: Contact institution. *Financial support:* In 2010–11, 2,179 students received support; fellowships with full tuition reimbursements available, research assistantships with full tuition reimbursements available, teaching assistantships with full tuition reimbursements available, career-related internships or fieldwork, Federal Work-Study, institutionally sponsored loans, scholarships/grants, and unspecified assistantships available. Support available to part-time students. Financial award application deadline: 2/15; financial award applicants required to submit FAFSA. In 2010, 861 master's, 126 doctorates, 38 other advanced degrees awarded. *Degree program information:* Part-time and evening/weekend programs available. Postbaccalaureate distance learning degree programs offered. *Application deadline:* For fall admission, 7/1 for domestic students, 5/1 for international students; for spring admission, 12/1 for domestic students, 9/15 for international students. Applications are processed on a rolling basis. *Application fee:* $35 ($60 for international students). Electronic applications accepted. *Application Contact:* Dr. Karen D. Weddle-West, Vice Provost for Graduate Studies, 901-678-4653, Fax: 901-678-0378, E-mail: gradsch@memphis.edu. *Vice Provost for Graduate Studies,* Dr. Karen D. Weddle-West, 901-678-4653, Fax: 901-678-0378, E-mail: gradsch@memphis.edu.

College of Arts and Sciences Students: 647 full-time (343 women), 395 part-time (242 women); includes 169 Black or African American, non-Hispanic/Latino; 2 American Indian or Alaska Native, non-Hispanic/Latino; 15 Asian, non-Hispanic/Latino; 13 Hispanic/Latino, 184 international. Average age 32. 774 applicants, 60% accepted, 237 enrolled. *Faculty:* 222 full-time (70 women), 27 part-time/adjunct (6 women). Expenses: Contact institution. *Financial support:* In 2010–11, 467 students received support; fellowships with full tuition reimbursements available, research assistantships with full tuition reimbursements available, teaching assistantships with full tuition reimbursements available, career-related internships or fieldwork, Federal Work-Study, institutionally sponsored loans, scholarships/grants, tuition waivers (full and partial), and unspecified assistantships available. Financial award application deadline: 2/15; financial award applicants required to submit FAFSA. In 2010, 210 master's, 47 doctorates, 14 other advanced degrees awarded. *Degree program information:* Part-time and evening/weekend programs available. Offers African-American literature (Graduate Certificate); analytical chemistry (MS, PhD); ancient Egyptian history (MA, PhD); applied computer science (MS); applied linguistics (PhD); applied mathematics (MS); applied statistics (PhD); archaeology (MS); arts and sciences (MA, MCRP, MFA, MPA, MS, PhD, Ed S, Graduate Certificate); bioinformatics (MS); biology (MS, PhD); city and regional planning (MCRP); composition studies (PhD); computational chemistry (MS, PhD); computer science (MS, PhD); computer sciences (MS); creative writing (MFA); criminology and criminal justice (MA); earth sciences (PhD); English as a second language (MA); French (MA); geographic information systems (Graduate Certificate); geography (MA, MS); geology (MS); geophysics (MS); inorganic chemistry (MS, PhD); interdisciplinary (MS); interdisciplinary studies (MA, MS, Graduate Certificate); linguistics (MA); literary and cultural studies (PhD); literature (MA); mathematics (MS, PhD); medical anthropology (MA); nonprofit administration (MPA); organic chemistry (MS, PhD); philosophy (MA, PhD); physical chemistry (MS, PhD); physics (MS); political science (MA); professional writing (MA, PhD); psychology (MS, PhD); public management and policy (MPA); school psychology (MA, Ed S); sociology (MA); Spanish (MA); statistics (MS, PhD); teaching English as a second language (Graduate Certificate); urban anthropology (MA); urban management and planning (MPA). *Application deadline:* Applications are processed on a rolling basis. *Application fee:* $35 ($60 for international students). Electronic applications accepted. *Application Contact:* Dr. Linda Bennett, Associate Dean for Graduate Studies and Research, 901-678-2253, Fax: 901-678-4831, E-mail: lbennett@memphis.edu. *Dean,* Dr. Henry A. Kurtz, 901-678-3067, Fax: 901-678-4831, E-mail: hkurtz@memphis.edu.

College of Communication and Fine Arts Students: 201 full-time (111 women), 99 part-time (55 women); includes 37 Black or African American, non-Hispanic/Latino; 2 American Indian or Alaska Native, non-Hispanic/Latino; 6 Hispanic/Latino, 32 international. Average age 32. 220 applicants, 75% accepted, 100 enrolled. *Faculty:* 87 full-time (27 women), 16 part-time/adjunct (9 women). Expenses: Contact institution. *Financial support:* In 2010–11, 182 students received support; research assistantships with full tuition reimbursements available, teaching assistantships with full tuition reimbursements available, career-related internships or fieldwork, Federal Work-Study, institutionally sponsored loans, scholarships/grants, and unspecified assistantships available. Financial award application deadline: 2/15; financial award applicants required to submit FAFSA. In 2010, 49 master's, 14 doctorates, 5 other advanced degrees awarded. *Degree program information:* Part-time programs available. Postbaccalaureate distance learning degree programs offered (no on-campus study). Offers applied music (M Mu, DMA); architecture (M Arch); art (Graduate Certificate); art history (MA); ceramics (MFA); communication (MA); communication and fine arts (M Arch, M Mu, MA, MFA, DMA, PhD, Graduate Certificate); communication arts (PhD); composition (M Mu, DMA); conducting (M Mu, DMA); film and video production (MA); general journalism (MA); graphic design (MFA); historical musicology (PhD); interior design (MFA); jazz and studio performance (M Mu); journalism administration (MA); music education (M Mu, DMA); musicology (M Mu); painting (MFA); printmaking/photography (MFA); sculpture (MFA); theatre (MFA). *Application deadline:* For fall admission, 8/1 for domestic students; for spring admission, 12/1 for domestic students. Applications are processed on a rolling basis. *Application fee:* $35 ($60 for international students). Electronic applications accepted. *Application Contact:* Moira J. Logan, Associate Dean/Director of Research and Graduate Studies, 901-678-2350, Fax: 901-678-5118, E-mail: mlogan1@memphis.edu. *Dean,* Dr. Richard R. Ranta, 901-678-2350, Fax: 901-678-5118, E-mail: rranta@memphis.edu.

College of Education Students: 316 full-time (223 women), 906 part-time (693 women); includes 503 Black or African American, non-Hispanic/Latino; 5 American Indian or Alaska Native, non-Hispanic/Latino; 6 Asian, non-Hispanic/Latino; 16 Hispanic/Latino, 17 international. Average age 34. 489 applicants, 73% accepted, 121 enrolled. *Faculty:* 94 full-time (55 women), 41 part-time/adjunct (23 women). Expenses: Contact institution. *Financial support:* In 2010–11, 921 students received support; research assistantships with full tuition reimbursements available, teaching assistantships with full tuition reimbursements available, career-

University of Memphis (continued)

related internships or fieldwork, Federal Work-Study, scholarships/grants, tuition waivers (partial), and unspecified assistantships available. Financial award application deadline: 2/15; financial award applicants required to submit FAFSA. In 2010, 230 master's, 37 doctorates, 17 other advanced degrees awarded. *Degree program information:* Part-time and evening/weekend programs available. Offers adult education (Ed D); clinical nutrition (MS); counseling (MS, Ed D); counseling psychology (PhD); early childhood education (MAT, MS, Ed D); education (M Ed, MAT, MS, Ed D, PhD, Graduate Certificate); educational leadership (Ed D); educational psychology and research (MS, PhD); elementary education (MAT); exercise and sport science (MS); health promotion (MS); higher education (Ed D); instruction and curriculum (MS, Ed D); instruction design and technology (MS, Ed D); leadership (MS); middle grades education (MAT); physical education teacher education (MS); policy studies (Ed D); reading (MS, Ed D); school administration and supervision (MS); secondary education (MAT); special education (MAT, MS, Ed D); sport and leisure commerce (MS). *Application deadline:* Applications are processed on a rolling basis. *Application fee:* $35 ($60 for international students). *Application Contact:* Dr. Ernest A. Rakow, Associate Dean of Administration and Graduate Programs, 901-678-2363, Fax: 901-678-4778, E-mail: erakow@memphis.edu. *Dean,* Dr. Donald J. Wagner, 901-678-4265, Fax: 901-678-4778, E-mail: djwagner@memphis.edu.

Fogelman College of Business and Economics Students: 290 full-time (117 women), 205 part-time (80 women); includes 53 Black or African American, non-Hispanic/Latino; 3 American Indian or Alaska Native, non-Hispanic/Latino; 19 Asian, non-Hispanic/Latino; 6 Hispanic/Latino, 120 international. Average age 31. 413 applicants, 74% accepted, 128 enrolled. *Faculty:* 64 full-time (11 women), 5 part-time/adjunct (0 women). Expenses: Contact institution. *Financial support:* In 2010–11, 199 students received support; research assistantships with full tuition reimbursements available, teaching assistantships with full tuition reimbursements available, career-related internships or fieldwork, Federal Work-Study, scholarships/grants, and unspecified assistantships available. Financial award application deadline: 2/15; financial award applicants required to submit FAFSA. In 2010, 170 master's, 17 doctorates awarded. *Degree program information:* Part-time and evening/weekend programs available. Postbaccalaureate distance learning degree programs offered (minimal on-campus study). Offers accounting (MBA, MS, PhD); accounting systems (MS); business and economics (IMBA, MA, MBA, MS, PhD); economics (MA, PhD); executive business administration (MBA); finance (PhD); finance, insurance, and real estate (MBA, MS); international business administration (IMBA); management (MBA, MS, PhD); management information systems (MBA, MS, PhD); management science (MBA); marketing (MBA, MS); marketing and supply chain management (PhD); real estate development (MS); taxation (MS). *Application deadline:* For fall admission, 7/1 for domestic students, 5/1 for international students; for winter admission, 9/15 for international students; for spring admission, 12/1 for domestic students. *Application fee:* $35 ($60 for international students). *Application Contact:* Melodie V. Patterson, MBA Advisor, 901-678-5394, Fax: 901-678-4705, E-mail: mvpttrsn@memphis.edu. *MBA Program Manager,* Brenda Williams, 901-678-3405, Fax: 901-678-4705, E-mail: bmwllms3@memphis.edu.

Herff College of Engineering Students: 117 full-time (35 women), 57 part-time (13 women); includes 13 Black or African American, non-Hispanic/Latino; 3 Asian, non-Hispanic/Latino; 1 Hispanic/Latino, 80 international. Average age 29. 77 applicants, 84% accepted, 62 enrolled. *Faculty:* 40 full-time (3 women), 4 part-time/adjunct (1 woman). Expenses: Contact institution. *Financial support:* In 2010–11, 30 students received support; fellowships with full tuition reimbursements available, research assistantships with full tuition reimbursements available, teaching assistantships with full tuition reimbursements available, career-related internships or fieldwork, Federal Work-Study, scholarships/grants, tuition waivers (full and partial), and unspecified assistantships available. Financial award application deadline: 2/15; financial award applicants required to submit FAFSA. In 2010, 34 master's, 7 doctorates awarded. *Degree program information:* Part-time programs available. Offers automatic control systems (MS); biomedical engineering (MS, PhD); biomedical systems (MS); civil engineering (PhD); communications and propagation systems (MS); computer engineering (PhD); computer engineering technology (MS); design and mechanical engineering (MS); electrical engineering (PhD); electronics engineering technology (MS); energy systems (MS); engineering (MS, PhD); engineering computer systems (MS); environmental engineering (MS); foundation engineering (MS); industrial engineering (MS); manufacturing engineering technology (MS); mechanical engineering (PhD); mechanical systems (MS); power systems (MS); structural engineering (MS); transportation engineering (MS); water resources engineering (MS). *Application deadline:* For fall admission, 7/1 for domestic students, 5/1 for international students; for spring admission, 12/1 for domestic students, 9/15 for international students. *Application fee:* $35 ($60 for international students). Electronic applications accepted. *Application Contact:* Dr. Deborah Hochstein, Associate Dean, 901-678-3298, Fax: 901-678-5030, E-mail: dhochstn@memphis.edu. *Dean,* Dr. Richard C. Warder, 901-678-4306, Fax: 901-678-4180, E-mail: rcwarder@memphis.edu.

School of Audiology and Speech-Language Pathology Students: 76 full-time (71 women), 11 part-time (all women); includes 2 Black or African American, non-Hispanic/Latino; 3 Asian, non-Hispanic/Latino, 3 international. Average age 26. 203 applicants, 37% accepted, 37 enrolled. *Faculty:* 14 full-time (6 women), 1 (woman) part-time/adjunct. Expenses: Contact institution. *Financial support:* In 2010–11, 64 students received support; research assistantships with full tuition reimbursements available, Federal Work-Study, scholarships/grants, and unspecified assistantships available. Financial award application deadline: 2/15; financial award applicants required to submit FAFSA. In 2010, 22 master's, 2 doctorates awarded. *Degree program information:* Part-time programs available. Offers audiology and speech-language pathology (MA, Au D, PhD). *Application deadline:* For fall admission, 2/1 for domestic students. *Application fee:* $35 ($60 for international students). *Application Contact:* Dr. David J. Wark, Coordinator of Graduate Studies, 901-678-5891, E-mail: dwark@memphis.edu. *Dean,* Dr. Maurice Mendel, 901-678-5800, Fax: 901-525-1282, E-mail: dlluna@memphis.edu.

School of Public Health Students: 45 full-time (23 women), 29 part-time (14 women); includes 19 Black or African American, non-Hispanic/Latino; 6 Asian, non-Hispanic/Latino; 2 Hispanic/Latino, 7 international. Average age 32. 57 applicants, 70% accepted, 22 enrolled. *Faculty:* 5 full-time (2 women), 4 part-time/adjunct (2 women). Expenses: Contact institution. *Financial support:* In 2010–11, 46 students received support; research assistantships with full tuition reimbursements available, Federal Work-Study, scholarships/grants, and unspecified assistantships available. Financial award application deadline: 2/15; financial award applicants required to submit FAFSA. In 2010, 17 master's awarded. *Degree program information:* Part-time and evening/weekend programs available. Postbaccalaureate distance learning degree programs offered. Offers biostatistics (MPH); environmental health (MPH); epidemiology (MPH); health systems management (MPH); public health (MHA); social and behavioral sciences (MPH). *Application deadline:* For fall admission, 4/1 for domestic students; for spring admission, 11/1 for domestic students. *Application fee:* $35 ($60 for international students). Electronic applications accepted. *Application Contact:* Dr. Lisa M. Klesges, Director, 901-678-4637, E-mail: lmklsges@memphis.edu. *Director,* Dr. Lisa M. Klesges, 901-678-4637, E-mail: lmklsges@memphis.edu.

University College Students: 30 full-time (19 women), 122 part-time (93 women); includes 88 Black or African American, non-Hispanic/Latino; 1 American Indian or Alaska Native, non-Hispanic/Latino; 1 Asian, non-Hispanic/Latino; 1 Hispanic/Latino, 1 international. Average age 40. 89 applicants, 74% accepted, 8 enrolled. *Faculty:* 3 full-time (2 women), 3 part-time/adjunct (1 woman). Expenses: Contact institution. *Financial support:* In 2010–11, 123 students received support; research assistantships with full tuition reimbursements available, teaching assistantships with tuition reimbursements available, Federal Work-Study, scholarships/grants, and unspecified assistantships available. Financial award application deadline: 2/15; financial award applicants required to submit FAFSA. In 2010, 41 master's awarded. *Degree program information:* Part-time and evening/weekend programs available. Offers liberal studies (MALS); merchandising and consumer science (MS); strategic leadership (MPS). *Application deadline:* For fall admission, 7/1 for domestic students, 5/1 for international students; for spring admission, 11/1 for domestic students, 9/15 for international students. Applications are processed on a rolling basis. *Application fee:* $35 ($60 for international students). Electronic applications accepted. *Application Contact:* Dr. Herbert McCree, Coordinator of Graduate Studies, 901-678-4171, Fax: 901-678-3363, E-mail: hmccree@memphis.edu. *Dean,* Dr. Dan Lattimore, 901-678-2991.

Loewenberg School of Nursing Students: 20 full-time (all women), 226 part-time (217 women); includes 71 Black or African American, non-Hispanic/Latino; 6 Asian, non-Hispanic/Latino; 4 Hispanic/Latino, 2 international. Average age 35. 111 applicants, 80% accepted, 20 enrolled. *Faculty:* 15 full-time (all women), 3 part-time/adjunct (all women). Expenses: Contact institution. *Financial support:* In 2010–11, 147 students received support. Federal Work-Study and scholarships/grants available. Financial award application deadline: 2/15; financial award applicants required to submit FAFSA. In 2010, 47 master's, 2 other advanced degrees awarded. *Degree program information:* Part-time and evening/weekend programs available. Postbaccalaureate distance learning degree programs offered. Offers advance practice-family nurse practitioner (MSN); executive nursing leadership (MSN); nursing (Graduate Certificate); nursing administration (MSN); nursing education (MSN); nursing informatics (MSN). *Application deadline:* For fall admission, 2/15 for domestic and international students; for spring admission, 10/1 for domestic and international students. *Application fee:* $35 ($60 for international students). *Associate Dean,* Dr. Robert Koch, 901-678-3908, Fax: 901-678-4907, E-mail: rakoch@memphis.edu.

UNIVERSITY OF MIAMI, Coral Gables, FL 33124

General Information Independent, coed, university. CGS member. *Graduate housing:* On-campus housing not available. *Research affiliation:* Howard Hughes Medical Institute (biology), The Buoniconti Fund: Miami Project to Cure Paralysis (paralysis research), Organization for Tropical Studies, National Center for Atmospheric Research (atmospheric science).

GRADUATE UNITS

Graduate School *Degree program information:* Part-time and evening/weekend programs available. Postbaccalaureate distance learning degree programs offered. Offers international administration (MAIA). Electronic applications accepted.

College of Arts and Sciences *Degree program information:* Part-time and evening/weekend programs available. Offers adult clinical (PhD); art history (MA); arts and sciences (MA, MAIA, MALS, MFA, MPA, MS, PhD); behavioral neuroscience (PhD); biology (MS, PhD); ceramics/glass (MFA); chemistry (MS); child clinical (PhD); computer science (MS, PhD); creative writing (MFA); developmental psychology (PhD); English (MA, PhD); genetics and evolution (MS, PhD); geography (MA); graphic design/multimedia (MFA); health clinical (PhD); history (MA, PhD); inorganic chemistry (PhD); international studies (MA, PhD); Latin American studies (MA); liberal studies (MALS); mathematics (MA, MS, PhD); organic chemistry (PhD); painting (MFA); philosophy (MA, PhD); photography/digital imaging (MFA); physical chemistry (PhD); physics (MS, PhD); political science (MPA); printmaking (MFA); psychology (MS); romance studies (PhD); sculpture (MFA); sociology (MA, PhD). Electronic applications accepted.

College of Engineering *Degree program information:* Part-time and evening/weekend programs available. Offers architectural engineering (MSAE); biomedical engineering (MSBE, PhD); civil engineering (MSCE, PhD); electrical and computer engineering (MSECE, PhD); engineering (MS, MSAE, MSBE, MSCE, MSECE, MSEVH, MSIE, MSME, MSOES, PhD); environmental health and safety (MS); ergonomics (PhD); industrial engineering (MSIE, PhD); management of technology (MS); mechanical and aerospace engineering (MSME, PhD); occupational ergonomics and safety (MS, MSOES). Electronic applications accepted.

Frost School of Music Offers accompanying and chamber music (MM, DMA); choral conducting (MM, DMA); composition (MM, DMA); electronic music (MM); instrumental conducting (MM, DMA); instrumental performance (MM, DMA, AD); jazz composition (DMA); jazz pedagogy (MM); jazz performance (MM, DMA); keyboard performance and pedagogy (MM, DMA); media writing and production (MM); multiple woodwinds (MM, DMA); music (MM, MS, DMA, PhD, AD, Spec M); music business and entertainment industries (MM); music education (MM, PhD, Spec M); music engineering (MS); music theory (MM); music therapy (MM); musicology (MM); piano performance (MM, DMA, AD); studio jazz writing (MM); vocal pedagogy (DMA); vocal performance (MM, DMA, AD). Electronic applications accepted.

Miller School of Medicine Students: 237 full-time (121 women), 19 part-time (10 women); includes 15 Black or African American, non-Hispanic/Latino; 16 Asian, non-Hispanic/Latino; 32 Hispanic/Latino; 4 Two or more races, non-Hispanic/Latino, 80 international. Expenses: Contact institution. *Financial support:* In 2010–11, 480 students received support; fellowships with partial tuition reimbursements available, research assistantships with partial tuition reimbursements available, teaching assistantships, Federal Work-Study, institutionally sponsored loans, scholarships/grants, and health care benefits available. Financial award applicants required to submit FAFSA. In 2010, 131 first professional degrees awarded. Offers biochemistry and molecular biology (PhD); cancer biology (PhD); epidemiology (PhD); medicine (MD, MPH, MSPH, DPT, PhD); microbiology and immunology (PhD); molecular and cellular pharmacology (PhD); molecular cell and developmental biology (PhD); neuroscience (PhD); physical therapy (DPT, PhD); physiology and biophysics (PhD); public health (MPH, MSPH). *Application deadline:* Applications are processed on a rolling basis. Electronic applications accepted. *Application Contact:* Dr. John L. Bixby, Associate Dean, 305-243-1094, Fax: 305-243-3593, E-mail: biomedgrad@miami.edu. *Vice President for Medical Affairs/Dean,* Dr. Paschal Goldschmidt, 305-243-6545.

Rosenstiel School of Marine and Atmospheric Science *Degree program information:* Part-time programs available. Offers applied marine physics (MS, PhD); marine affairs and policy (MA, MS); marine and atmospheric chemistry (MS, PhD); marine and atmospheric science (MA, MS, PhD); marine biology and fisheries (MA, MS, PhD); marine geology and geophysics (MS, PhD); meteorology (MS, PhD); physical oceanography (MS, PhD). Electronic applications accepted.

School of Architecture Offers architecture (M Arch); suburb and town design (M Arch). Electronic applications accepted.

School of Business Administration *Degree program information:* Part-time and evening/weekend programs available. Offers accounting (MBA); business administration (MA, MBA, MP Acc, MS, MS Tax, MSPM, PhD); computer information systems (MBA); economic development (MA, PhD); environmental economics (PhD); executive and professional (MBA); finance (MBA); human resource economics (MA, PhD); international business (MBA); international economics (MA, PhD); macroeconomics (PhD); management (MBA); management science (MBA); marketing (MBA); professional accounting (MP Acc); professional management (MSPM); taxation (MS Tax). Electronic applications accepted.

School of Communication *Degree program information:* Part-time programs available. Offers communication (PhD); communication studies (MA); film studies (MA, PhD); motion pictures (MFA); print journalism (MA); public relations (MA); Spanish language journalism (MA); television broadcast journalism (MA). Electronic applications accepted.

School of Education Students: 184 full-time (125 women), 98 part-time (71 women); includes 114 minority (32 Black or African American, non-Hispanic/Latino; 4 Asian, non-Hispanic/Latino; 73 Hispanic/Latino; 5 Two or more races, non-Hispanic/Latino), 27 international. Average age 28. 538 applicants, 42% accepted, 117 enrolled. *Faculty:* 38 full-time (19 women). Expenses: Contact institution. *Financial support:* In 2010–11, 144 students received support, including 3 fellowships with full tuition reimbursements available (averaging $18,900 per year), 53 research assistantships with full and partial tuition reimbursements available (averaging $18,900 per year), 5 teaching assistantships with full and partial tuition reimbursements available (averaging $18,900 per year); career-related internships or fieldwork, institutionally sponsored loans, scholarships/grants, traineeships, health care benefits, tuition waivers (full and partial), and unspecified assistantships also available. Support available to part-time students. Financial award application deadline: 3/1; financial award applicants required to submit FAFSA. In 2010, 89 master's, 17 doctorates, 1 other advanced degree awarded. Offers advanced professional studies (MS Ed, Ed S); community and social change (MS Ed); counseling (MS Ed, Certificate); counseling and research (MS Ed); counseling psychology (PhD); early childhood special education (MS Ed, Ed S); education (MS Ed, Ed D, PhD, Certificate, Ed S); education and social change (MS Ed); enrollment management (MS Ed, Certificate); exercise physiology (MS Ed, PhD); exercise physiology strength and conditioning (MS Ed); higher education administration (MS Ed, Ed D, Certificate); higher education leadership (Ed D); language and literacy learning in multilingual settings

(PhD); Latino mental health (Certificate); marriage and family therapy (MS Ed); mental health counseling (MS Ed); research, measurement, and evaluation (MS Ed, PhD); science, technology, engineering and mathematics (PhD); special education (PhD); sport administration (MS Ed); sports medicine (MS Ed); student life and development (MS Ed, Certificate); teaching and learning (PhD); women's health (Certificate). *Application deadline:* For fall admission, 10/15 for international students. *Application fee:* $65. Electronic applications accepted. *Application Contact:* Lois Heffernan, Graduate Admissions Coordinator, 305-284-2167, Fax: 305-284-3003, E-mail: lheffernan@miami.edu. *Senior Associate Dean,* Dr. Walter Secada, 305-284-2102, Fax: 305-284-6998, E-mail: wsecada@miami.edu.

School of Law Students: 1,353 full-time (573 women); includes 368 minority (99 Black or African American, non-Hispanic/Latino; 7 American Indian or Alaska Native, non-Hispanic/Latino; 51 Asian, non-Hispanic/Latino; 206 Hispanic/Latino; 1 Native Hawaiian or other Pacific Islander, non-Hispanic/Latino; 4 Two or more races, non-Hispanic/Latino), 25 international. Average age 24. 4,972 applicants, 46% accepted, 489 enrolled. Expenses: Contact institution. *Financial support:* In 2010–11, 432 students received support; fellowships, research assistantships, career-related internships or fieldwork, Federal Work-Study, institutionally sponsored loans, scholarships/grants, and unspecified assistantships available. Financial award application deadline: 3/1; financial award applicants required to submit FAFSA. In 2010, 462 first professional degrees awarded. Offers comparative law (LL M); estate planning (LL M); international law, inter-American law, and transnational law for foreign lawyers (LL M); law (JD); ocean and coastal law (LL M); real property development (LL M); taxation (LL M). *Application deadline:* For fall admission, 1/1 priority date for domestic students, 1/2 priority date for international students. Applications are processed on a rolling basis. *Application fee:* $60. Electronic applications accepted. *Application Contact:* Therese Lambert, Director of Student Recruitment, 305-284-6746, Fax: 305-284-3084, E-mail: tlambert@law.miami.edu. *Assistant Dean of Admissions,* Michael Goodnight, 305-284-2527, Fax: 305-284-3084, E-mail: mgoodnig@law.miami.edu.

School of Nursing and Health Studies *Degree program information:* Part-time programs available. Offers acute care (MSN); nursing (PhD); primary care (MSN). Electronic applications accepted.

UNIVERSITY OF MICHIGAN, Ann Arbor, MI 48109

General Information State-supported, coed, university. CGS member. *Enrollment:* 41,924 graduate, professional, and undergraduate students; 13,128 full-time matriculated graduate/professional students (6,153 women), 1,522 part-time matriculated graduate/professional students (569 women). *Enrollment by degree level:* 2,598 first professional, 6,620 master's, 5,367 doctoral, 65 other advanced degrees. *Graduate faculty:* 4,000 full-time (1,449 women), 1,007 part-time/adjunct (540 women). *International tuition:* $35,994 full-time. Tuition, state resident: full-time $17,784; part-time $1116 per credit hour. Tuition, nonresident: full-time $35,944; part-time $2125 per credit hour. *Required fees:* $95 per semester. Tuition and fees vary according to course load, degree level and program. *Graduate housing:* Rooms and/or apartments available on a first-come, first-served basis to single and married students. *Student services:* Campus employment opportunities, campus safety program, career counseling, child daycare facilities, exercise/wellness program, free psychological counseling, grant writing training, international student services, low-cost health insurance, multicultural affairs office, services for students with disabilities, teacher training, writing training. *Library facilities:* Shapiro Undergraduate Library plus 27 others. *Online resources:* library catalog, web page, access to other libraries' catalogs. *Collection:* 10.3 million titles, 83,062 serial subscriptions, 126,011 audiovisual materials.

Computer facilities: Computer purchase and lease plans are available. 2,529 computers available on campus for general student use. A campuswide network can be accessed from student residence rooms and from off campus. Online class registration, file storage are available. *Web address:* http://www.umich.edu/.

General Application Contact: Admissions Office, 734-764-8129, Fax: 734-647-7740, E-mail: rackadmis@umich.edu.

GRADUATE UNITS

College of Pharmacy Offers medicinal chemistry (PhD); pharmaceutical sciences (PhD); pharmacy (Pharm D, PhD); social and administrative sciences (PhD).

Law School Students: 1,134 full-time (506 women); includes 46 Black or African American, non-Hispanic/Latino; 22 American Indian or Alaska Native, non-Hispanic/Latino; 133 Asian, non-Hispanic/Latino; 42 Hispanic/Latino; 1 Native Hawaiian or other Pacific Islander, non-Hispanic/Latino, 24 international. 6,312 applicants, 19% accepted, 379 enrolled. *Faculty:* 87 full-time (26 women), 40 part-time/adjunct (14 women). Expenses: Contact institution. *Financial support:* In 2010–11, 808 students received support. Career-related internships or fieldwork, Federal Work-Study, institutionally sponsored loans, and scholarships/grants available. Financial award applicants required to submit FAFSA. In 2010, 358 first professional degrees, 43 master's, 2 doctorates awarded. Offers comparative law (MCL); international tax (LL M); law (JD, LL M, SJD). *Application deadline:* For fall admission, 2/15 for domestic students. Applications are processed on a rolling basis. *Application fee:* $75. Electronic applications accepted. *Application Contact:* Sarah C. Zearfoss, Assistant Dean and Director of Admissions, 734-764-0537, Fax: 734-647-3218, E-mail: law.jd.admissions@umich.edu. *Dean,* Evan H. Caminker, 734-764-1358.

Medical School *Degree program information:* Part-time programs available. Offers medicine (MD, MS, PhD). Electronic applications accepted.

Rackham Graduate School Students: 7,159 full-time (3,185 women), 856 part-time (426 women); includes 1,351 minority (265 Black or African American, non-Hispanic/Latino; 15 American Indian or Alaska Native, non-Hispanic/Latino; 566 Asian, non-Hispanic/Latino; 349 Hispanic/Latino; 156 Two or more races, non-Hispanic/Latino), 2,693 international. Average age 28. 21,449 applicants, 28% accepted, 2287 enrolled. Expenses: Contact institution. *Financial support:* Fellowships with full and partial tuition reimbursements, research assistantships with full and partial tuition reimbursements, teaching assistantships with full and partial tuition reimbursements, career-related internships or fieldwork, Federal Work-Study, scholarships/grants, traineeships, health care benefits, and unspecified assistantships available. Support available to part-time students. Offers chemical biology (PhD); education and psychology (PhD); English and education (PhD); modern Middle Eastern and North African studies (AM); survey methodology (MS, PhD, Certificate). *Application deadline:* Applications are processed on a rolling basis. *Application fee:* $65 ($75 for international students). Electronic applications accepted. *Application Contact:* Admissions Office, 734-764-8129, E-mail: rackadmis@umich.edu. *Dean/Vice President for Academic Affairs,* Dr. Janet A. Weiss, 734-764-4400.

College of Engineering Students: 2,618 full-time (567 women), 337 part-time (45 women). 6,449 applicants, 34% accepted, 901 enrolled. *Faculty:* 353 full-time (56 women). Expenses: Contact institution. *Financial support:* Fellowships, research assistantships, teaching assistantships, career-related internships or fieldwork, Federal Work-Study, institutionally sponsored loans, scholarships/grants, traineeships, health care benefits, tuition waivers (full and partial), and unspecified assistantships available. Support available to part-time students. Financial award applicants required to submit FAFSA. In 2010, 810 master's, 231 doctorates awarded. *Degree program information:* Part-time programs available. Postbaccalaureate distance learning degree programs offered (no on-campus study). Offers aerospace engineering (M Eng, MS, MSE, PhD); atmospheric and space sciences (MS, PhD); biomedical engineering (MS, MSE, PhD); chemical engineering (MSE, PhD, Ch E); civil engineering (MSE, PhD, CE); computer science and engineering (MS, MSE, PhD); concurrent marine design (M Eng); construction engineering and management (M Eng, MSE); electrical engineering and computer science (MS, MSE, PhD); engineering (M Eng, MS, MSE, D Eng, PhD, CE, Certificate, Ch E, Mar Eng, Nav Arch, Nuc E); environmental engineering (MSE, PhD); geoscience and remote sensing (PhD); industrial and operations engineering (MS, MSE, PhD); macromolecular science and engineering (MS, MSE, PhD); materials science and engineering (MS, PhD); mechanical engineering (MSE, PhD); naval architecture and marine engineering (MS, MSE, PhD, Mar Eng, Nav Arch); nuclear engineering (Nuc E); nuclear engineering and radiological sciences (MSE, PhD); nuclear science (MS, PhD); space and planetary sciences (PhD); space engineering (M Eng); structural engineering (M Eng). *Application deadline:* Applications are processed on a rolling basis. *Application fee:* $65 ($75 for international students). Electronic applications accepted. *Application Contact:* Mike Nazareth, Recruiting Contact, 734-647-7030, Fax: 734-647-7045, E-mail: mikenaz@umich.edu. *Chair,* Prof. David C. Munson, 734-647-7010, Fax: 734-647-7009, E-mail: munson@umich.edu.

College of Literature, Science, and the Arts Students: 2,331 full-time (1,144 women). Expenses: Contact institution. *Financial support:* Fellowships with full and partial tuition reimbursements, research assistantships with full and partial tuition reimbursements, teaching assistantships with full and partial tuition reimbursements, Federal Work-Study, scholarships/grants, traineeships, health care benefits, tuition waivers (full and partial), and unspecified assistantships available. In 2010, 531 master's, 318 doctorates awarded. Offers American culture (AM, PhD); analytical chemistry (PhD); ancient Near Eastern studies (AM, PhD); anthropology (PhD); anthropology and history (PhD); applied and interdisciplinary mathematics (AM, MS, PhD); applied economics (AM); applied physics (PhD); applied statistics (AM); Arabic for professional purposes (AM); Arabic language and literature (AM, PhD); Armenian studies (AM, PhD); Asian languages and cultures (MA, PhD); Asian studies: China (AM, Graduate Certificate); astronomy and astrophysics (PhD); biophysics (PhD); biopsychology (PhD); chemical biology (PhD); Christianity in late antiquity (AM, PhD); classical art and archaeology (PhD); classical studies (PhD); clinical psychology (PhD); cognition and perception (PhD); communication studies (PhD); comparative literature (PhD); creative writing (MFA); developmental psychology (PhD); ecology and evolutionary biology (MS, PhD); ecology and evolutionary biology-Frontiers (MS); economics (AM, PhD); Egyptology (AM, PhD); English and education (PhD); English and women's studies (PhD); English language and literature (PhD); French (PhD); geology (MS, PhD); German (AM, PhD); Greek and Roman history (PhD, Certificate); Hebrew Bible and ancient Israel (AM, PhD); Hebrew literature (AM, PhD); history (PhD); history and women's studies (PhD); history of art (PhD); inorganic chemistry (PhD); Islamic studies (AM, PhD); Italian (PhD); Japanese studies (AM); Jewish cultural studies (AM, PhD); Jewish mysticism (AM, PhD); Judaic studies (MA, Graduate Certificate); lesbian, gay, bisexual, transgender, queer (LGBTQ) studies (Certificate); linguistics (PhD); linguistics and Romance languages and literatures (PhD); literature, science, and the arts (AM, MA, MAT, MFA, MS, PhD, Certificate, Graduate Certificate); material chemistry (PhD); mathematics (AM, MS, PhD); medieval and early modern studies (Certificate); molecular, cellular, and developmental biology (MS, PhD); organic chemistry (PhD); Persian and Iranian studies (AM, PhD); personality and social contexts (PhD); philosophy (AM, PhD); physical chemistry (PhD); physics (MS, PhD); political science (AM, PhD); psychology and women's studies (PhD); public policy and economics (PhD); public policy and sociology (PhD); Rabbinic literature (AM, PhD); Romance linguistics (PhD); Russian (AM); Russian and East European studies (AM, Certificate); screen arts and cultures (PhD, Certificate); Second Temple Judaism (AM, PhD); Slavic languages and literatures (PhD); social psychology (PhD); social work and economics (PhD); social work and political science (PhD); social work and sociology (PhD); sociology (PhD); sociology and women's studies (PhD); South Asian studies (MA, Certificate); Southeast Asian studies (MA, Graduate Certificate); Spanish (PhD); statistics (AM, PhD); teaching Latin (MAT); teaching of Arabic as a foreign language (AM); Turkish studies (AM, PhD); women's studies (Certificate); women's studies and sociology (PhD). *Application fee:* $65 ($75 for international students). Electronic applications accepted. *Application Contact:* Rackham Graduate School Admissions Office, 734-764-8129, E-mail: rackadmis@umich.edu. *Dean,* Dr. Terrence J. McDonald, 734-764-1817.

Gerald R. Ford School of Public Policy *Degree program information:* Part-time programs available. Offers public policy (MPA, MPP, PhD). Electronic applications accepted.

Program in Biomedical Sciences (PIBS) Students: 100 full-time (50 women); includes 19 minority (4 Black or African American, non-Hispanic/Latino; 6 Asian, non-Hispanic/Latino; 6 Hispanic/Latino; 3 Two or more races, non-Hispanic/Latino), 14 international. Average age 24. 617 applicants, 38% accepted, 100 enrolled. *Faculty:* 464 full-time. Expenses: Contact institution. *Financial support:* In 2010–11, 100 students received support, including 91 fellowships with full tuition reimbursements available (averaging $26,500 per year); scholarships/grants, health care benefits, tuition waivers (full), and unspecified assistantships also available. Financial award application deadline: 12/1. Offers bioinformatics (MS, PhD); biological chemistry (PhD); biomedical sciences (MS, PhD); cell and developmental biology (PhD); cellular and molecular biology (PhD); genetic counseling (MS); human genetics (MS, PhD); immunology (PhD); microbiology and immunology (PhD); molecular and cellular pathology (PhD); molecular and integrative physiology (PhD); neuroscience (PhD); pharmacology (MS, PhD). *Application deadline:* For fall admission, 12/1 for domestic and international students. *Application fee:* $60 ($75 for international students). Electronic applications accepted. *Application Contact:* Michelle S. Melis, Director of Student Life, 734-615-6538, Fax: 734-647-7022, E-mail: pibs@umich.edu. *Assistant Dean/Director/Professor of Molecular and Integrative Physiology and Pharmacology,* Dr. Lori L. Isom, 734-615-7005, Fax: 734-647-7022, E-mail: lisom@umich.edu.

School of Art and Design Offers art and design (MFA). Electronic applications accepted.

School of Education Students: 413 full-time (305 women), 34 part-time (27 women); includes 29 Black or African American, non-Hispanic/Latino; 1 American Indian or Alaska Native, non-Hispanic/Latino; 27 Asian, non-Hispanic/Latino; 48 Hispanic/Latino; 16 Two or more races, non-Hispanic/Latino, 43 international. 714 applicants, 60% accepted, 210 enrolled. *Faculty:* 52 full-time (30 women). Expenses: Contact institution. *Financial support:* In 2010–11, 371 students received support, including 740 fellowships (averaging $4,217 per year), 161 research assistantships with full tuition reimbursements available (averaging $17,270 per year), 74 teaching assistantships with full tuition reimbursements available (averaging $17,200 per year); career-related internships or fieldwork, Federal Work-Study, institutionally sponsored loans, scholarships/grants, health care benefits, tuition waivers, and unspecified assistantships also available. Support available to part-time students. Financial award application deadline: 12/1; financial award applicants required to submit FAFSA. In 2010, 146 master's, 39 doctorates awarded. Offers academic affairs and student development (PhD); cross specialization (PhD); curriculum development (MA); development (AM); early childhood education (MA, PhD); education (AM, MA, MS, PhD); educational administration and policy (MA, PhD); educational foundations and policy (MA, PhD); English education (MA); English language learning in school settings (MA); higher education (AM); individually designed concentration (PhD); learning technologies (MA, PhD); literacy, language, and culture (MA, PhD); mathematics education (MA, PhD); medical and professional education (AM); organizational behavior and management (PhD); postsecondary science education (MS); public policy (PhD); research methods (MA); research, evaluation, and assessment (PhD); science education (MA, PhD); social studies education (MA); teaching and teacher education (PhD). *Application deadline:* For fall admission, 12/1 priority date for domestic students, 12/1 for international students. *Application fee:* $65 ($75 for international students). Electronic applications accepted. *Application Contact:* Laura Mayers, Student Services Assistant, 734-764-7563, Fax: 734-763-1495, E-mail: ed.grad.admit@umich.edu. *Dean,* Dr. Deborah Loewenberg Ball, 734-615-4415, Fax: 734-764-3473, E-mail: dball@umich.edu.

School of Information Offers archives and records management (MSI); community informatics (MSI); health informatics (MS); human computer interaction (MSI); information (PhD); information analysis and retrieval (MSI); information economics for management (MSI); information policy (MSI); library and information science (MSI); preservation of information (MSI); school library media (MSI); social computing (MSI). Electronic applications accepted.

School of Kinesiology Students: 66 full-time (34 women); includes 5 minority (1 Black or African American, non-Hispanic/Latino; 2 Asian, non-Hispanic/Latino; 2 Hispanic/Latino), 20 international. 121 applicants, 45% accepted, 29 enrolled. *Faculty:* 28 full-time (10 women). Expenses: Contact institution. *Financial support:* In 2010–11, 11 fellowships, 14 research assistantships, 11 teaching assistantships were awarded; Federal Work-Study, scholarships/grants, health care benefits, and unspecified assistantships also available. Financial award application deadline: 1/15. In 2010, 23 master's, 2 doctorates awarded. Offers kinesiology (MS, PhD); sport management (AM). *Application deadline:* For fall admission, 1/15 priority date for domestic students, 1/15 for international students. Applications are processed on a rolling basis. *Application fee:* $60 ($75 for international students). Electronic applications accepted. *Application Contact:* Charlene F. Ruloff, Graduate Program Coordinator, 734-764-1343, Fax: 734-647-2808, E-mail: cruloff@umich.edu. *Associate Dean for Graduate Programs and Faculty Affairs,* Dr. Rodney D. Fort, 734-647-8989.

University of Michigan (continued)

School of Music, Theatre, and Dance Offers composition (MA, MM, A Mus D); composition and theory (PhD); conducting (MM, A Mus D); design (MFA); media arts (MA); modern dance performance and choreography (MFA); music education (MM, PhD, Spec M); music, theatre, and dance (MA, MFA, MM, A Mus D, PhD, Spec M); musicology (MA, PhD); performance (MM, A Mus D, Spec M); theatre (PhD); theory (MA, PhD). Electronic applications accepted.

School of Nursing *Degree program information:* Part-time programs available. Postbaccalaureate distance learning degree programs offered (minimal on-campus study). Offers adult acute care nurse practitioner (MS); adult nurse practitioner (Post Master's Certificate); adult primary care/adult nurse practitioner (MS); community care (Post Master's Certificate); community care/home care (MS); community health nursing (MS, Post Master's Certificate); family nurse practitioner (MS, Post Master's Certificate); gerontology nurse practitioner (MS); gerontology nursing (MS); gerontology-clinical nurse specialist (MS); infant, child, adolescent health nurse practitioner (MS); medical-surgical clinical nurse specialist (MS); nurse midwifery (MS, Post Master's Certificate); nursing (MS, PhD, Post Master's Certificate); nursing business and health systems (MS); occupational health nursing (MS); parent-child nursing (MS, Post Master's Certificate); psychiatric mental health nurse practitioner (MS); psychiatric mental health nursing (MS); psychiatric mental health nursing- clinical nurse specialist (MS). Electronic applications accepted.

Ross School of Business at the University of Michigan *Degree program information:* Part-time and evening/weekend programs available. Offers business (M Acc, MBA); business administration (PhD). Electronic applications accepted.

School of Dentistry *Degree program information:* Part-time programs available. Offers biomaterials (MS); dental hygiene (MS); dentistry (DDS, MS, PhD, Certificate); endodontics (MS); oral health sciences (PhD); orthodontics (MS); pediatric dentistry (MS); periodontics (MS); prosthodontics (MS); restorative dentistry (MS). Electronic applications accepted.

School of Natural Resources and Environment Students: 450 (254 women); includes 7 Black or African American, non-Hispanic/Latino; 2 American Indian or Alaska Native, non-Hispanic/Latino; 35 Asian, non-Hispanic/Latino; 13 Hispanic/Latino; 6 Two or more races, non-Hispanic/Latino, 50 international. Average age 28. 692 applicants. *Faculty:* 42 full-time, 23 part-time/adjunct. Expenses: Contact institution. *Financial support:* Fellowships with tuition reimbursements, research assistantships with tuition reimbursements, teaching assistantships with tuition reimbursements, career-related internships or fieldwork, Federal Work-Study, institutionally sponsored loans, scholarships/grants, health care benefits, unspecified assistantships, and Peace Corps Fellows available. Support available to part-time students. Financial award application deadline: 1/5; financial award applicants required to submit FAFSA. In 2010, 133 master's, 11 doctorates awarded. Offers aquatic sciences: research and management (MS); behavior, education and communication (MS); conservation biology (MS); conservation ecology (MS); environmental informatics (MS); environmental justice (MS, Certificate); environmental policy and planning (MS); industrial ecology (Certificate); landscape architecture (MLA, PhD); natural resources and environment (MS, PhD); spatial analysis (Certificate); sustainable systems (MS); terrestrial ecosystems (MS). *Application deadline:* For fall admission, 1/5 priority date for domestic and international students. Applications are processed on a rolling basis. *Application fee:* $65 ($75 for international students). Electronic applications accepted. *Application Contact:* Adam D. Ancira, Recruiting and Admissions Coordinator, 734-764-6453, Fax: 734-936-2195, E-mail: snre.admissions@umich.edu. *Dean,* Dr. Rosina Bierbaum, 734-764-2550, Fax: 734-763-8965, E-mail: rbierbau@umich.edu.

School of Public Health Students: 708 full-time (501 women), 178 part-time (114 women); includes 216 minority (60 Black or African American, non-Hispanic/Latino; 3 American Indian or Alaska Native, non-Hispanic/Latino; 109 Asian, non-Hispanic/Latino; 25 Hispanic/Latino; 19 Two or more races, non-Hispanic/Latino), 166 international. Average age 27. 2,083 applicants, 61% accepted, 386 enrolled. *Faculty:* 143 full-time (59 women), 82 part-time/adjunct (34 women). Expenses: Contact institution. *Financial support:* Fellowships, research assistantships with full and partial tuition reimbursements, teaching assistantships with full and partial tuition reimbursements, career-related internships or fieldwork, Federal Work-Study, institutionally sponsored loans, scholarships/grants, traineeships, health care benefits, and unspecified assistantships available. Support available to part-time students. In 2010, 326 master's, 46 doctorates awarded. *Degree program information:* Part-time and evening/weekend programs available. Offers biostatistics (MPH, MS, PhD); clinical research design and statistical analysis (MS); dental public health (MPH); environmental health sciences (MS, PhD); environmental quality and health (MPH); epidemiological science (PhD); epidemiology (MS); general epidemiology (MPH); health behavior and health education (MPH, PhD); health management and policy (MHSA, MPH, MS); health services organization and policy (PhD); hospital and molecular epidemiology (MPH); human nutrition (MPH); industrial hygiene (MPH, MS); international health (MPH); nutritional sciences (MS); occupational and environmental epidemiology (MPH); public health (MHSA, MPH, MS, PhD); toxicology (MPH, MS, PhD). MS and PhD offered through the Horace H. Rackham School of Graduate Studies. *Application deadline:* For fall admission, 12/1 priority date for domestic students, 1/15 priority date for international students. Applications are processed on a rolling basis. *Application fee:* $65 ($75 for international students). Electronic applications accepted. *Application Contact:* Kiran Dhiman, Admissions Coordinator, 734-764-5425, Fax: 734-763-5455, E-mail: sph.inquiries@umich.edu. *Dean,* Martin Philbert, 734-763-4523, Fax: 734-763-5455, E-mail: philbert@umich.edu.

School of Social Work Students: 576 full-time (502 women), 12 part-time (10 women); includes 161 minority (83 Black or African American, non-Hispanic/Latino; 12 American Indian or Alaska Native, non-Hispanic/Latino; 37 Asian, non-Hispanic/Latino; 29 Hispanic/Latino), 18 international. Average age 27. 1,029 applicants, 62% accepted, 341 enrolled. *Faculty:* 52 full-time (30 women), 59 part-time/adjunct (40 women). Expenses: Contact institution. *Financial support:* In 2010–11, 538 students received support. Career-related internships or fieldwork, Federal Work-Study, scholarships/grants, traineeships, and unspecified assistantships available. Financial award application deadline: 3/15; financial award applicants required to submit FAFSA. In 2010, 306 master's, 9 doctorates awarded. Offers social work (MSW, PhD); social work and social science (PhD). PhD offered through the Horace H. Rackham School of Graduate Studies. *Application deadline:* For fall admission, 3/1 priority date for domestic students, 2/1 priority date for international students. Applications are processed on a rolling basis. *Application fee:* $50. Electronic applications accepted. *Application Contact:* Timothy Colenback, Assistant Dean for Student Services, 734-936-0961, Fax: 734-936-1961, E-mail: timot@umich.edu. *Dean,* Laura Lein, 734-764-5347, Fax: 734-764-9954, E-mail: leinl@umich.edu.

Taubman College of Architecture and Urban Planning *Degree program information:* Part-time programs available. Offers architecture (M Arch, M Sc, PhD); architecture and urban planning (M Arch, M Sc, MUD, MUP, PhD, Certificate); real estate development (Certificate); urban and regional planning (MUP, PhD, Certificate); urban design (MUD); urban planning (MUP). Electronic applications accepted.

UNIVERSITY OF MICHIGAN–DEARBORN, Dearborn, MI 48128-1491

General Information State-supported, coed, comprehensive institution. *Enrollment:* 8,599 graduate, professional, and undergraduate students; 263 full-time matriculated graduate/professional students (115 women), 1,326 part-time matriculated graduate/professional students (599 women). *Enrollment by degree level:* 1,523 master's, 66 doctoral. *Graduate faculty:* 173 full-time (58 women), 42 part-time/adjunct (12 women). *Graduate housing:* On-campus housing not available. *Student services:* Campus employment opportunities, campus safety program, career counseling, child daycare facilities, exercise/wellness program, free psychological counseling, grant writing training, international student services, low-cost health insurance, multicultural affairs office, services for students with disabilities, teacher training, writing training. *Library facilities:* Mardigian Library. *Online resources:* library catalog, web page, access to other libraries' catalogs. *Collection:* 382,065 titles, 576 serial subscriptions, 6,070 audiovisual materials.

Computer facilities: Computer purchase and lease plans are available. 695 computers available on campus for general student use. A campuswide network can be accessed from off campus. Online class registration, tuition and application payments accepted online are available. *Web address:* http://www.umd.umich.edu/.

General Application Contact: Kimberly Lewandowski, Graduate Programs Coordinator, 313-593-1494, Fax: 313-436-9156, E-mail: umdgrad@umd.umich.edu.

GRADUATE UNITS

College of Arts, Sciences, and Letters Students: 73 full-time (49 women), 143 part-time (91 women); includes 30 Black or African American, non-Hispanic/Latino; 1 American Indian or Alaska Native, non-Hispanic/Latino; 9 Asian, non-Hispanic/Latino; 5 Hispanic/Latino. Average age 35. 120 applicants, 82% accepted, 86 enrolled. *Faculty:* 52 full-time (21 women), 12 part-time/adjunct (2 women). Expenses: Contact institution. *Financial support:* In 2010–11, 1 fellowship (averaging $2,500 per year), 2 research assistantships (averaging $2,500 per year) were awarded; Federal Work-Study and scholarships/grants also available. Support available to part-time students. Financial award application deadline: 4/1; financial award applicants required to submit FAFSA. In 2010, 50 master's awarded. *Degree program information:* Part-time and evening/weekend programs available. Offers applied and computational mathematics (MS); arts, sciences, and letters (MA, MPA, MPP, MS, Certificate); assessment and evaluation (Certificate); clinical health psychology (MS); environmental science (MS); health psychology (MS); liberal studies (MA); nonprofit leadership (Certificate); public administration (MPA); public policy (MPP). *Application deadline:* For fall admission, 8/1 priority date for domestic students, 4/1 for international students; for winter admission, 12/1 priority date for domestic students, 11/1 for international students; for spring admission, 4/1 for domestic students, 3/1 for international students. Applications are processed on a rolling basis. *Application fee:* $60 ($75 for international students). Electronic applications accepted. *Application Contact:* Carol Ligienza, Coordinator, CASL Graduate Programs, 313-593-1183, Fax: 313-583-6700, E-mail: caslgrad@umd.umich.edu. *Dean,* Dr. Jerold L. Hale, 313-593-5490, Fax: 313-593-5552, E-mail: jhale@umd.umich.edu.

College of Engineering and Computer Science Students: 63 full-time (9 women), 431 part-time (86 women); includes 23 Black or African American, non-Hispanic/Latino; 64 Asian, non-Hispanic/Latino; 19 Hispanic/Latino, 84 international. Average age 31. 230 applicants, 61% accepted, 105 enrolled. *Faculty:* 52 full-time (3 women), 12 part-time/adjunct (1 woman). Expenses: Contact institution. *Financial support:* In 2010–11, 12 students received support, including 7 fellowships (averaging $18,331 per year), 27 research assistantships with full tuition reimbursements available (averaging $56,894 per year), 12 teaching assistantships (averaging $3,400 per year); career-related internships or fieldwork and Federal Work-Study also available. Financial award application deadline: 4/1; financial award applicants required to submit FAFSA. In 2010, 121 master's awarded. *Degree program information:* Part-time and evening/weekend programs available. Offers automotive systems engineering (MSE, PhD); computer and information science (MS); computer engineering (MSE); electrical engineering (MSE); engineering and computer science (MS, MSE, PhD); engineering management (MS); industrial and systems engineering (MSE); information systems and technology (MS); information systems engineering (PhD); manufacturing systems engineering (MSE); mechanical engineering (MSE); program and project management (MS); software engineering (MS). *Application deadline:* For fall admission, 6/15 for domestic students, 4/1 for international students; for winter admission, 12/1 for domestic students, 10/15 for international students; for spring admission, 2/15 for domestic and international students. Applications are processed on a rolling basis. *Application fee:* $60 ($75 for international students). Electronic applications accepted. *Application Contact:* Dr. Keshav Varde, Associate Dean, 313-593-5117, Fax: 313-593-9967, E-mail: varde@engin.umd.umich.edu. *Dean,* Dr. Subrata Sengupta, 313-593-5290, Fax: 313-593-9967, E-mail: razal@engin.umd.umich.edu.

School of Education Students: 15 full-time (7 women), 376 part-time (318 women); includes 51 minority (23 Black or African American, non-Hispanic/Latino; 14 Asian, non-Hispanic/Latino; 8 Hispanic/Latino; 4 Native Hawaiian or other Pacific Islander, non-Hispanic/Latino; 2 Two or more races, non-Hispanic/Latino). Average age 35. 165 applicants, 74% accepted, 121 enrolled. *Faculty:* 29 full-time (17 women), 16 part-time/adjunct (8 women). Expenses: Contact institution. *Financial support:* Career-related internships or fieldwork and Federal Work-Study available. Support available to part-time students. Financial award application deadline: 4/1; financial award applicants required to submit FAFSA. In 2010, 191 master's awarded. *Degree program information:* Part-time and evening/weekend programs available. Postbaccalaureate distance learning degree programs offered. Offers curriculum and practice (Ed D); education (M Ed, MA, MAT, MS, Ed D, Certificate); educational leadership (Ed D); educational psychology/special education (Ed D); emotional impairments endorsement (M Ed); inclusion specialist (M Ed); learning disabilities endorsement (M Ed); metropolitan education (Ed D); science education (MS); secondary teaching certificate (MAT); teaching (MAT). *Application deadline:* For fall admission, 8/1 priority date for domestic students, 8/3 for international students; for winter admission, 12/1 for domestic students, 1/4 for international students; for spring admission, 4/1 for domestic students, 3/4 for international students. Applications are processed on a rolling basis. *Application fee:* $60 ($75 for international students). Electronic applications accepted. *Application Contact:* Graduate Secretary, 313-593-5091. *Interim Dean,* Dr. Paul Fossum, 313-593-5435, E-mail: pfossum@umd.umich.edu.

School of Management Students: 71 full-time (26 women), 403 part-time (134 women); includes 68 minority (19 Black or African American, non-Hispanic/Latino; 1 American Indian or Alaska Native, non-Hispanic/Latino; 39 Asian, non-Hispanic/Latino; 6 Hispanic/Latino; 1 Native Hawaiian or other Pacific Islander, non-Hispanic/Latino; 2 Two or more races, non-Hispanic/Latino), 89 international. Average age 30. 185 applicants, 51% accepted, 67 enrolled. *Faculty:* 40 full-time (17 women), 2 part-time/adjunct (1 woman). Expenses: Contact institution. *Financial support:* Career-related internships or fieldwork, Federal Work-Study, and scholarships/grants available. Support available to part-time students. Financial award application deadline: 9/1; financial award applicants required to submit FAFSA. In 2010, 150 master's awarded. *Degree program information:* Part-time and evening/weekend programs available. Postbaccalaureate distance learning degree programs offered (no on-campus study). Offers accounting (MBA, MS); finance (MBA, MS); information systems (MS); international business (MBA); management (MBA); management information systems (MBA); marketing (MBA); supply chain management (MBA). *Application deadline:* For fall admission, 8/1 priority date for domestic students, 6/1 for international students; for winter admission, 12/1 priority date for domestic students, 10/1 for international students; for spring admission, 4/1 priority date for domestic students, 2/1 for international students. Applications are processed on a rolling basis. *Application fee:* $60. Electronic applications accepted. *Application Contact:* Joan Doherty, Academic Advisor/Counselor, 313-593-5460, Fax: 313-271-9838, E-mail: gradbusiness@umd.umich.edu. *Dean,* Dr. Kim Schatzel, 313-593-5248, Fax: 313-271-9835, E-mail: schatzel@umd.umich.edu.

UNIVERSITY OF MICHIGAN–FLINT, Flint, MI 48502-1950

General Information State-supported, coed, comprehensive institution. CGS member. *Graduate housing:* Room and/or apartments available on a first-come, first-served basis to single students; on-campus housing not available to married students. Housing application deadline: 2/1.

GRADUATE UNITS

College of Arts and Sciences *Degree program information:* Part-time programs available. Offers arts and sciences (MA, MS); biology (MS); computer science and information systems (MS); English (MA); social sciences (MA). Electronic applications accepted.

Graduate Programs *Degree program information:* Part-time and evening/weekend programs available. Postbaccalaureate distance learning degree programs offered (minimal on-campus study). Offers American culture (MLS); public administration (MPA). Electronic applications accepted.

School of Education and Human Services *Degree program information:* Part-time programs available. Offers education (MA); education and human services (MA); elementary education with teaching certification (MA); literacy (K-12) (MA); special education (MA); technology in education (MA).

School of Health Professions and Studies *Degree program information:* Part-time programs available. Offers anesthesia (MSA); health education (MS); health professions and studies (MS, MSA, DNP, DPT); nursing (DNP); online transitional (DPT); traditional entry-level (DPT). Electronic applications accepted.

School of Management *Degree program information:* Part-time programs available. Postbaccalaureate distance learning degree programs offered (minimal on-campus study). Offers management (MBA). Electronic applications accepted.

UNIVERSITY OF MINNESOTA, DULUTH, Duluth, MN 55812-2496

General Information State-supported, coed, comprehensive institution. *Graduate housing:* Room and/or apartments available to single students; on-campus housing not available to married students. Housing application deadline: 3/1. *Research affiliation:* Environmental Protection Agency Environmental Research Laboratory (aquatic biology), Minnesota Geological Survey, Northeastern Minnesota National Historical Center (local history), U. S. Forest Service, Northcentral Forest Experiment Station.

GRADUATE UNITS

Graduate School *Degree program information:* Part-time and evening/weekend programs available. Postbaccalaureate distance learning degree programs offered (minimal on-campus study). Offers toxicology (MS, PhD).

College of Education and Human Service Professions *Degree program information:* Part-time and evening/weekend programs available. Postbaccalaureate distance learning degree programs offered (minimal on-campus study). Offers communication sciences and disorders (MA); education (Ed D); education and human service professions (MA, MSW, Ed D); social work (MSW).

College of Liberal Arts *Degree program information:* Part-time programs available. Offers criminology (MA); English (MA); liberal arts (MA, MLS); liberal studies (MLS).

Labovitz School of Business and Economics *Degree program information:* Part-time and evening/weekend programs available. Offers business administration (MBA); business and economics (MBA).

School of Fine Arts *Degree program information:* Part-time programs available. Offers fine arts (MFA, MM); graphic design (MFA); music education (MM); performance (MM).

Swenson College of Science and Engineering *Degree program information:* Part-time and evening/weekend programs available. Postbaccalaureate distance learning degree programs offered (minimal on-campus study). Offers applied and computational mathematics (MS); chemistry and biochemistry (MS); computer science (MS); electrical and computer engineering (MSECE); engineering management (MSEM); environmental health and safety (MEHS); geological sciences (MS, PhD); integrated biosciences (MS, PhD); physics (MS); science and engineering (MEHS, MS, MSECE, MSEM, PhD).

Medical School *Degree program information:* Part-time programs available. Offers biochemistry, molecular biology and biophysics (MS); biology and biophysics (PhD); medicine (MD, MS, PhD); microbiology, immunology and molecular pathobiology (MS, PhD); pharmacology (MS, PhD); physiology (MS, PhD); social, administrative, and clinical pharmacy (MS, PhD); toxicology (MS, PhD).

UNIVERSITY OF MINNESOTA, TWIN CITIES CAMPUS, Minneapolis, MN 55455-0213

General Information State-supported, coed, comprehensive institution. CGS member. *Graduate housing:* Rooms and/or apartments available on a first-come, first-served basis to single and married students. Housing application deadline: 5/1.

GRADUATE UNITS

Carlson School of Management Students: 531 full-time (282 women), 1,695 part-time (604 women); includes 32 Black or African American, non-Hispanic/Latino; 4 American Indian or Alaska Native, non-Hispanic/Latino; 134 Asian, non-Hispanic/Latino; 33 Hispanic/Latino, 294 international. Average age 28. *Faculty:* 144 full-time (43 women), 83 part-time/adjunct (34 women). Expenses: Contact institution. *Financial support:* Fellowships with full and partial tuition reimbursements, research assistantships with full tuition reimbursements, teaching assistantships with full and partial tuition reimbursements, career-related internships or fieldwork, Federal Work-Study, institutionally sponsored loans, scholarships/grants, health care benefits, tuition waivers (full and partial), and unspecified assistantships available. Support available to part-time students. Financial award application deadline: 4/1; financial award applicants required to submit FAFSA. In 2010, 676 master's, 13 doctorates awarded. *Degree program information:* Part-time and evening/weekend programs available. Offers accountancy (M Acc); accounting (PhD); business taxation (MBT); finance (MBA, PhD); human resources and industrial relations (MA, PhD); information and decision sciences (PhD); information technology (MBA); management (EMBA, M Acc, MA, MBA, MBT, PhD); marketing (MBA); marketing and logistics management (PhD); medical industry orientation (MBA); operations and management science (PhD); strategic management and organization (PhD); supply chain and operations (MBA). Electronic applications accepted. *Application Contact:* Dr. Alison Davis-Blake, Dean, 612-626-9636, Fax: 612-624-6374, E-mail: csdean@umn.edu. *Dean,* Dr. Alison Davis-Blake, 612-626-9636, Fax: 612-624-6374, E-mail: csdean@umn.edu.

College of Pharmacy *Degree program information:* Part-time programs available. Offers experimental and clinical pharmacology (MS, PhD); medicinal chemistry (MS, PhD); pharmaceutics (PhD); pharmacy (Pharm D, MS, PhD); social and administrative pharmacy (MS, PhD); social, administrative and clinical pharmacy (MS, PhD).

College of Veterinary Medicine *Degree program information:* Part-time programs available. Offers comparative and molecular bioscience (MS, PhD); veterinary medicine (MS, PhD). Electronic applications accepted.

Graduate School *Degree program information:* Part-time and evening/weekend programs available. Postbaccalaureate distance learning degree programs offered (minimal on-campus study). Offers biophysical sciences and medical physics (MS, PhD); genetic counseling (MS); health informatics (MHI, MS, PhD); history of science, technology and medicine (MA, PhD); integrative biology and physiology (PhD); microbial engineering (MS); microbiology, immunology and cancer biology (PhD); molecular, cellular, developmental biology and genetics (PhD); neuroscience (MS, PhD); scientific computation (MS, PhD); stem cell biology (MS). Electronic applications accepted.

College of Biological Sciences *Degree program information:* Part-time programs available. Offers biochemistry, molecular biology and biophysics (PhD); biological science (MBS); biological sciences (MBS, MS, PhD); ecology, evolution, and behavior (MS, PhD); plant biological sciences (MS, PhD). Electronic applications accepted.

College of Design Offers apparel (MA, MS, PhD); architecture (M Arch); design (M Arch, MA, MFA, MLA, MS, PhD, Postbaccalaureate Certificate); design communication (MA, MS, PhD); housing studies (MA, MS, PhD, Postbaccalaureate Certificate); interactive design (MFA); interior design (MA, MS, PhD); landscape architecture (MLA, MS); sustainable design (MS). Electronic applications accepted.

College of Education and Human Development Students: 1,672 full-time (1,237 women), 1,021 part-time (689 women); includes 155 Black or African American, non-Hispanic/Latino; 28 American Indian or Alaska Native, non-Hispanic/Latino; 118 Asian, non-Hispanic/Latino; 57 Hispanic/Latino, 239 international. Average age 33. 2,224 applicants, 56% accepted, 948 enrolled. *Faculty:* 178 full-time (92 women). Expenses: Contact institution. *Financial support:* In 2010–11, 70 fellowships (averaging $26,111 per year), 337 research assistantships with full tuition reimbursements (averaging $26,943 per year), 230 teaching assistantships with full tuition reimbursements (averaging $28,379 per year) were awarded; scholarships/grants and tuition waivers (partial) also available. Financial award applicants required to submit FAFSA. In 2010, 985 master's, 127 doctorates, 164 other advanced degrees awarded. *Degree program information:* Part-time programs available. Offers adapted physical education (MA, PhD); adult education (M Ed, MA, Ed D, PhD, Certificate); agricultural, food and environmental education (M Ed, MA, Ed D, PhD); art education (M Ed, MA, PhD); biomechanics (MA); biomechanics and neural control (PhD); business and industry education (M Ed, MA, Ed D, PhD); business education (M Ed); child psychology (MA, PhD); children's literature (M Ed, MA, PhD); Chinese (M Ed); coaching (Certificate); comparative and international development education (MA, PhD); counseling and student personnel psychology (MA, PhD, Ed S); curriculum and instruction (MA, PhD); developmental adapted physical education (M Ed); disability policy and services (Certificate); early childhood education (M Ed, MA, PhD); earth science (M Ed); education and human development (M Ed, MA, MSW, Ed D, PhD, Certificate, Ed S); educational administration (MA, Ed D, PhD); educational psychology (PhD); elementary education (M Ed, MA, PhD); elementary special education (M Ed); English (M Ed); English as a second language (M Ed); English education (MA, PhD); environmental education (M Ed); evaluation studies (MA, PhD); exercise physiology (MA, PhD); family education (M Ed, MA, Ed D, PhD); French (M Ed); German (M Ed); Hebrew (M Ed); higher education (MA, PhD); human factors/ergonomics (MA, PhD); human resource development (M Ed, MA, Ed D, PhD, Certificate); instructional systems and technology (M Ed, MA, PhD); international/comparative sport (MA, PhD); Japanese (M Ed); kinesiology (M Ed, MA, PhD, Certificate); language arts (MA, PhD); language immersion education (Certificate); leisure services/management (MA, PhD); life sciences (M Ed); literacy education (MA); marketing education (M Ed); marriage and family therapy (MA, PhD); mathematics (M Ed); mathematics education (MA, PhD); middle school science (M Ed); motor development (MA, PhD); motor learning/control (MA, PhD); outdoor education/recreation (MA, PhD); physical education (M Ed); postsecondary administration (Ed D); program evaluation (Certificate); psychological foundations of education (MA, PhD, Ed S); reading education (MA, PhD); recreation, park, and leisure studies (M Ed, MA, PhD); school psychology (MA, PhD, Ed S); school-to-work (Certificate); science (M Ed); science education (MA, PhD); second languages and cultures (M Ed); second languages and cultures education (MA, PhD); social studies (M Ed); social studies education (MA, PhD); social work (MSW, PhD); Spanish (M Ed); special education (M Ed, MA, PhD, Ed S); sport and exercise science (M Ed); sport management (M Ed, MA, PhD); sport psychology (MA, PhD); sport sociology (MA, PhD); staff development (Certificate); talent development and gifted education (Certificate); teacher leadership (M Ed); teaching (M Ed); technical education (Certificate); technology education (M Ed, MA); technology enhanced learning (Certificate); therapeutic recreation (MA, PhD); work and human resource education (M Ed, MA, Ed D, PhD); writing education (M Ed, MA, PhD); youth development leadership (M Ed). *Application fee:* $55. *Application Contact:* Dr. Jennifer Engler, Associate Dean, 612-626-2887, Fax: 612-626-7496, E-mail: engle009@umn.edu. *Dean,* Dr. Jean K. Quam, 612-626-9252, Fax: 612-626-7496, E-mail: jquam@umn.edu.

College of Food, Agricultural and Natural Resource Sciences Students: 480 full-time (253 women), 52 part-time (20 women); includes 48 minority (5 Black or African American, non-Hispanic/Latino; 1 American Indian or Alaska Native, non-Hispanic/Latino; 36 Asian, non-Hispanic/Latino; 6 Two or more races, non-Hispanic/Latino), 152 international. Average age 30. 850 applicants, 29% accepted, 170 enrolled. *Faculty:* 713 full-time (172 women). Expenses: Contact institution. *Financial support:* In 2010–11, fellowships with full tuition reimbursements (averaging $23,500 per year), research assistantships with full and partial tuition reimbursements (averaging $18,000 per year), teaching assistantships with full and partial tuition reimbursements (averaging $18,000 per year) were awarded; career-related internships or fieldwork, institutionally sponsored loans, scholarships/grants, health care benefits, tuition waivers (full), and unspecified assistantships also available. Support available to part-time students. Financial award application deadline: 12/15. In 2010, 71 master's, 43 doctorates awarded. *Degree program information:* Part-time programs available. Offers animal science (MS, PhD); applied economics (MS, PhD); applied plant sciences (MS, PhD); bioproducts and biosystems science, engineering and management (MS, PhD); conservation biology (MS, PhD); entomology (MS, PhD); food science (MS, PhD); food, agricultural and natural resource sciences (MS, PhD); land and atmospheric science (MS, PhD); natural resources science and management (MS, PhD); nutrition (MS, PhD); plant pathology (MS, PhD); water resources science (MS, PhD). *Application deadline:* For fall admission, 12/15 priority date for domestic and international students; for spring admission, 10/15 for domestic and international students. Applications are processed on a rolling basis. *Application fee:* $75 ($95 for international students). Electronic applications accepted. *Application Contact:* Lisa Wiley, Graduate Programs Coordinator, 612-624-2748, Fax: 612-625-1260, E-mail: lwiley@umn.edu. *Senior Associate Dean,* Dr. F. Abel Ponce de Leon, 612-625-4772, Fax: 612-625-1260, E-mail: apl@umn.edu.

College of Liberal Arts *Degree program information:* Part-time and evening/weekend programs available. Offers American studies (PhD); ancient and medieval art and archaeology (MA, PhD); anthropology (MA, PhD); art (MFA); art history (MA, PhD); Asian literatures, cultures, and media (PhD); audiology (Au D); biological psychopathology (PhD); classics (MA, PhD); clinical psychology (PhD); cognitive and biological psychology (PhD); communication studies (MA, PhD); comparative literature (PhD); comparative studies in discourse and society (PhD); counseling psychology (PhD); design technology (MFA); economics (PhD); English (MA, MFA, PhD); English as a second language (MA); feminist studies (PhD); French (MA, PhD); geographic information science (MGIS); geography (MA, PhD); Germanic studies: German and Scandinavian studies track (PhD); Germanic studies: German track (MA, PhD); Germanic studies: Germanic medieval studies track (MA, PhD); Germanic studies: Scandinavian studies track (MA); Germanic studies: teaching track (MA); Greek (MA, PhD); Hispanic and Lusophone literatures, cultures and linguistics (PhD); Hispanic linguistics (MA); Hispanic literature (MA); history (MA, PhD); industrial/organizational psychology (PhD); Latin (MA, PhD); liberal arts (MA, MFA, MGIS, MM, MS, Au D, DMA, PhD); linguistics (MA, PhD); Lusophone literature (MA); mass communication (MA, PhD); music (MA, MM, DMA, PhD); personality, individual differences, and behavior genetics (PhD); philosophy (MA, PhD); political science (PhD); quantitative/psychometric methods (PhD); religions in antiquity (MA); school psychology (PhD); social psychology (PhD); sociology (MA, PhD); speech-language pathology (MA); speech-language-hearing sciences (PhD); statistics (MS, PhD); strategic communication (professional program) (MA); theatre arts and dance (MA, PhD). Electronic applications accepted.

Hubert H. Humphrey School of Public Affairs Students: 328 full-time (185 women), 200 part-time (125 women); includes 91 minority (39 Black or African American, non-Hispanic/Latino; 4 American Indian or Alaska Native, non-Hispanic/Latino; 28 Asian, non-Hispanic/Latino; 14 Hispanic/Latino; 1 Native Hawaiian or other Pacific Islander, non-Hispanic/Latino; 5 Two or more races, non-Hispanic/Latino), 28 international. Average age 30. 588 applicants, 69% accepted, 208 enrolled. *Faculty:* 33 full-time (14 women), 29 part-time/adjunct (15 women). Expenses: Contact institution. *Financial support:* In 2010–11, 68 students received support, including fellowships with full tuition reimbursements available (averaging $8,500 per year), research assistantships with full and partial tuition reimbursements available (averaging $5,270 per year), teaching assistantships with full and partial tuition reimbursements available (averaging $5,270 per year); career-related internships or fieldwork, scholarships/grants, tuition waivers (full and partial), and unspecified assistantships also available. Financial award application deadline: 12/15. In 2010, 171 master's awarded. *Degree program information:* Part-time and evening/weekend programs available. Postbaccalaureate distance learning degree programs offered (minimal on-campus study). Offers advanced policy analysis methods (MPP); economic and community development (MPP); environmental planning (MURP); foreign policy (MPP); housing and community development (MURP); international development (MDP); land use and urban design (MURP); public affairs (MDP, MPA, MPP, MS, MURP); public and nonprofit leadership and management (MPP); regional, economic and workforce development (MURP); science technology and environmental policy (MPP); science, technology, and environmental policy (MS); social policy (MPP); transportation planning (MURP); women and public policy (MPP). *Application deadline:* For fall admission, 4/1 for domestic and international students. Applications are processed on a rolling basis. *Application fee:* $75 ($95 for international students). Electronic applications accepted. *Application Contact:* Julie Harrold, Director of Admissions, 612-624-3800, Fax: 612-626-0002, E-mail: hhhadmit@umn.edu. *Interim Dean,* Greg Lindey, 612-624-3800, Fax: 612-626-0002, E-mail: hhhadmit@umn.edu.

School of Nursing *Degree program information:* Part-time programs available. Postbaccalaureate distance learning degree programs offered (minimal on-campus study). Offers adolescent nursing (MS); adult health clinical nurse specialist (MS); advanced clinical specialist in gerontology (MS); children with special health care needs (MS); family nurse practitioner (MS); gerontological nurse practitioner (MS); nurse anesthetist (MS); nurse midwifery (MS); nursing (MN, MS, DNP, PhD); nursing and health care systems administration (MS); pediatric clinical nurse specialist (MS); pediatric nurse practitioner (MS); psychiatric mental health clinical nurse specialist (MS); public health nursing (MS); women's health nurse practitioner (MS).

Institute of Technology *Degree program information:* Part-time and evening/weekend programs available. Postbaccalaureate distance learning degree programs offered (minimal on-campus study). Offers aerospace engineering (M Aero E); aerospace engineering and

University of Minnesota, Twin Cities Campus (continued)
mechanics (MS, PhD); biomedical engineering (MS, PhD); chemical engineering (M Ch E, MS Ch E, PhD); chemistry (MS, PhD); civil engineering (MCE, MS, PhD); computer and information sciences (MCIS, MS, PhD); computer engineering (M Comp E, MS); electrical and computer engineering (MSEE, PhD); geological engineering (M Geo E, MS, PhD); geology (MS, PhD); geophysics (MS, PhD); history of science and technology (MA, PhD); industrial engineering (MSIE, PhD); materials science and engineering (M Mat SE, MS Mat SE, PhD); mechanical engineering (MSME, PhD); technology (M Aero E, M Ch E, M Comp E, M Geo E, M Mat SE, MA, MCE, MCIS, MCS, MEE, MS, MS Ch E, MS Mat SE, MSEE, MSIE, MSISE, MSME, MSMOT, MSST, PhD). Electronic applications accepted.

School of Mathematics *Degree program information:* Part-time programs available. Offers mathematics (MS, PhD).

School of Physics and Astronomy *Degree program information:* Part-time programs available. Offers astronomy (MS, PhD); astrophysics (MS, PhD); physics (MS, PhD).

Technological Leadership Institute *Degree program information:* Evening/weekend programs available. Offers infrastructure systems engineering (MSISE); management of technology (MSMOT); security technologies (MSST). Electronic applications accepted.

Law School Students: 752 full-time (315 women); includes 24 Black or African American, non-Hispanic/Latino; 7 American Indian or Alaska Native, non-Hispanic/Latino; 56 Asian, non-Hispanic/Latino; 29 Hispanic/Latino, 19 international. Average age 25. 3,866 applicants, 27% accepted, 260 enrolled. *Faculty:* 65 full-time (25 women), 184 part-time/adjunct (86 women). Expenses: Contact institution. *Financial support:* In 2010–11, 480 students received support; fellowships, research assistantships, teaching assistantships, career-related internships or fieldwork, Federal Work-Study, institutionally sponsored loans, scholarships/grants, and tuition waivers (partial) available. Financial award application deadline: 5/1; financial award applicants required to submit FAFSA. In 2010, 284 first professional degrees, 31 master's awarded. Offers law (JD, LL M). *Application deadline:* For fall admission, 4/1 for domestic students. Applications are processed on a rolling basis. *Application fee:* $75. Electronic applications accepted. *Application Contact:* Nick Wallace, Director of Admissions, 612-625-0718, Fax: 612-625-2011, E-mail: umnlsadm@umn.edu. *Dean,* David Wippman, 612-625-4841.

Medical School *Degree program information:* Part-time and evening/weekend programs available. Offers medicine (MD, MA, MS, DPT, PhD); pharmacology (MS, PhD); physical therapy (DPT).

Graduate Programs in Medicine *Degree program information:* Part-time and evening/weekend programs available. Offers medicine (MA).

School of Dentistry Offers dentistry (DDS, MS, PhD, Certificate); endodontics (MS, Certificate); oral biology (MS, PhD); oral health services for older adults (geriatrics) (MS, Certificate); orthodontics (MS); pediatric dentistry (MS); periodontology (MS); prosthodontics (MS); temporomandibular joint disorders (MS).

School of Public Health *Degree program information:* Part-time programs available. Postbaccalaureate distance learning degree programs offered (minimal on-campus study). Offers biostatistics (MPH, MS, PhD); clinical research (MS); community health education (MPH); core concepts (Certificate); environmental and occupational epidemiology (MPH, MS, PhD); environmental chemistry (MS, PhD); environmental health policy (MPH, MS, PhD); environmental infectious diseases (MPH, MS, PhD); environmental toxicology (MPH, MS, PhD); epidemiology (MPH, PhD); exposure sciences (MS); food safety and biosecurity (Certificate); general environmental health (MPH, MS); global environmental health (MPH, MS, PhD); health services research, policy, and administration (MS, PhD); healthcare administration (MHA); industrial hygiene (MPH, MS, PhD); maternal and child health (MPH); occupational health and safety (Certificate); occupational health nursing (MPH, MS, PhD); occupational medicine (MPH); preparedness, response and recovery (Certificate); public health (MHA, MPH, MS, PhD, Certificate); public health administration and policy (MPH); public health nutrition (MPH); public health practice (MPH). Electronic applications accepted.

UNIVERSITY OF MISSISSIPPI, Oxford, University, MS 38677

General Information State-supported, coed, university. CGS member. *Enrollment:* 17,085 graduate, professional, and undergraduate students; 2,115 full-time matriculated graduate/professional students (1,088 women), 713 part-time matriculated graduate/professional students (468 women). *Enrollment by degree level:* 812 first professional, 1,299 master's, 631 doctoral, 86 other advanced degrees. *Graduate housing:* Rooms and/or apartments available to single and married students. *Student services:* Campus employment opportunities, campus safety program, career counseling, free psychological counseling, international student services, low-cost health insurance, teacher training. *Library facilities:* J. D. Williams Library plus 3 others. *Online resources:* library catalog, web page, access to other libraries' catalogs. *Collection:* 1.4 million titles, 218,625 serial subscriptions, 105,789 audiovisual materials. *Research affiliation:* ElSohly Laboratories (national products research), Greenstone Industries (engineering), Combustion Research and Flow Technology, Inc. (fluid dynamics), Research Corporation (advancement of science), Cumberland Emerging Technologies (pharmaceutics).

Computer facilities: A campuswide network can be accessed from student residence rooms and from off campus. Online class registration, application for admission, registration for orientation are available. *Web address:* http://www.olemiss.edu/.

General Application Contact: Dr. Christy M. Wyandt, Associate Dean of Graduate School, 662-915-7474, Fax: 662-915-7577, E-mail: cwyandt@olemiss.edu.

GRADUATE UNITS

Graduate School Students: 2,115 full-time (1,088 women), 713 part-time (468 women); includes 503 minority (365 Black or African American, non-Hispanic/Latino; 11 American Indian or Alaska Native, non-Hispanic/Latino; 43 Asian, non-Hispanic/Latino; 46 Hispanic/Latino; 3 Native Hawaiian or other Pacific Islander, non-Hispanic/Latino; 35 Two or more races, non-Hispanic/Latino), 283 international. Expenses: Contact institution. *Financial support:* Fellowships, research assistantships, teaching assistantships, career-related internships or fieldwork, Federal Work-Study, institutionally sponsored loans, scholarships/grants, tuition waivers (full), and unspecified assistantships available. Financial award application deadline: 3/1; financial award applicants required to submit FAFSA. *Degree program information:* Part-time programs available. *Application deadline:* For fall admission, 4/1 for domestic students; for spring admission, 10/1 for domestic students. Applications are processed on a rolling basis. *Application fee:* $25. Electronic applications accepted. *Application Contact:* Dr. Christy M. Wyandt, Associate Dean, 662-915-7474, Fax: 662-915-7577, E-mail: cwyandt@olemiss.edu. *Dean,* Dr. Maurice Eftink, 662-915-7474, E-mail: eftink@olemiss.edu.

College of Liberal Arts Students: 513 full-time (251 women), 74 part-time (45 women); includes 101 minority (57 Black or African American, non-Hispanic/Latino; 2 American Indian or Alaska Native, non-Hispanic/Latino; 6 Asian, non-Hispanic/Latino; 23 Hispanic/Latino; 2 Native Hawaiian or other Pacific Islander, non-Hispanic/Latino; 11 Two or more races, non-Hispanic/Latino), 83 international. Expenses: Contact institution. *Financial support:* Fellowships, research assistantships, teaching assistantships, career-related internships or fieldwork, Federal Work-Study, institutionally sponsored loans, scholarships/grants, and unspecified assistantships available. Financial award application deadline: 3/1; financial award applicants required to submit FAFSA. In 2010, 97 master's, 38 doctorates awarded. *Degree program information:* Part-time programs available. Offers anthropology (MA); art education (MA); art history (MA); biology (MS, PhD); chemistry and biochemistry (MS, DA, PhD); clinical psychology (PhD); economics (MA, PhD); English (MA, MFA, PhD); experimental psychology (PhD); fine arts (MFA); French (MA); German (MA); history (MA, PhD); liberal arts (MA, MFA, MM, MS, MSS, DA, PhD); mathematics (MA, MS, PhD); music (MM, DA); philosophy (MA); physics (MA, MS, PhD); political science (MA, PhD); psychology (MA); sociology (MA, MSS); Southern studies (MA); Spanish (MA). *Application deadline:* For fall admission, 4/1 for domestic students; for spring admission, 10/1 for domestic students. Applications are processed on a rolling basis. *Application fee:* $25. Electronic applications accepted. *Application Contact:* Dr. Christy M. Wyandt, Associate Dean, 662-915-7474, Fax: 662-915-7577, E-mail: cwyandt@olemiss.edu. *Dean,* Dr. Glenn Hopkins, 662-915-7177, Fax: 662-915-5792, E-mail: ghopkins@olemiss.edu.

School of Accountancy Students: 112 full-time (43 women), 16 part-time (12 women); includes 12 minority (7 Black or African American, non-Hispanic/Latino; 1 American Indian or Alaska Native, non-Hispanic/Latino; 2 Asian, non-Hispanic/Latino; 2 Two or more races, non-Hispanic/Latino), 5 international. *Faculty:* 14 full-time (5 women), 3 part-time/adjunct (1 woman). Expenses: Contact institution. *Financial support:* Scholarships/grants available. Financial award application deadline: 3/1; financial award applicants required to submit FAFSA. In 2010, 70 master's awarded. Offers accountancy (M Acc, PhD); taxation accounting (M Tax). *Application deadline:* For fall admission, 4/1 for domestic students; for spring admission, 10/1 for domestic students. Applications are processed on a rolling basis. *Application fee:* $25. *Application Contact:* Dr. Christy M. Wyandt, Associate Dean, 662-915-7474, Fax: 662-915-7577, E-mail: cwyandt@olemiss.edu. *Interim Dean,* Dr. Mark Wilder, 662-915-7468, Fax: 662-915-7483, E-mail: umaccy@olemiss.edu.

School of Applied Sciences Students: 146 full-time (102 women), 75 part-time (53 women); includes 38 minority (32 Black or African American, non-Hispanic/Latino; 1 Hispanic/Latino; 1 Native Hawaiian or other Pacific Islander, non-Hispanic/Latino; 4 Two or more races, non-Hispanic/Latino), 10 international. Expenses: Contact institution. *Financial support:* Scholarships/grants available. Financial award application deadline: 3/1; financial award applicants required to submit FAFSA. In 2010, 34 master's, 1 doctorate awarded. Offers applied sciences (MA, MS, MSW, PhD); communicative disorders (MS); exercise science (MS); exercise science and leisure management (PhD); family and consumer sciences (MS); legal studies (MS); park and recreation management (MA); social work (MSW); wellness (MS). *Application deadline:* For fall admission, 4/1 for domestic students; for spring admission, 10/1 for domestic students. Applications are processed on a rolling basis. *Application fee:* $25. Electronic applications accepted. *Application Contact:* Dr. Christy M. Wyandt, Associate Dean, 662-915-7474, Fax: 662-915-7577, E-mail: cwyandt@olemiss.edu. *Dean,* Dr. Linda Chitwood, 662-915-7916, Fax: 662-915-5717, E-mail: lchitwoo@olemiss.edu.

School of Business Administration Students: 96 full-time (30 women), 49 part-time (8 women); includes 17 minority (8 Black or African American, non-Hispanic/Latino; 2 Asian, non-Hispanic/Latino; 2 Hispanic/Latino; 5 Two or more races, non-Hispanic/Latino), 16 international. Expenses: Contact institution. *Financial support:* Fellowships, career-related internships or fieldwork, scholarships/grants, tuition waivers (full), and unspecified assistantships available. Financial award application deadline: 3/1; financial award applicants required to submit FAFSA. In 2010, 46 master's, 9 doctorates awarded. Offers business administration (MBA, PhD); systems management (MS). *Application deadline:* For fall admission, 2/1 for domestic students; for spring admission, 10/1 for domestic students. Applications are processed on a rolling basis. *Application fee:* $25. Electronic applications accepted. *Application Contact:* Dr. Christy M. Wyandt, Associate Dean, 662-915-7474, Fax: 662-915-7577, E-mail: cwyandt@olemiss.edu. *Dean,* Dr. Ken Cyree, 662-915-5820, Fax: 662-915-5821, E-mail: info@bus.olemiss.edu.

School of Education Students: 210 full-time (166 women), 435 part-time (331 women); includes 187 minority (171 Black or African American, non-Hispanic/Latino; 1 American Indian or Alaska Native, non-Hispanic/Latino; 2 Asian, non-Hispanic/Latino; 5 Hispanic/Latino; 8 Two or more races, non-Hispanic/Latino), 15 international. Expenses: Contact institution. *Financial support:* Scholarships/grants available. Financial award application deadline: 3/1; financial award applicants required to submit FAFSA. In 2010, 227 master's, 24 doctorates awarded. Offers counselor education (M Ed, PhD, Specialist); curriculum and instruction (M Ed, Ed D, Ed S); education (PhD); educational leadership (PhD); educational leadership and counselor education (M Ed, MA, Ed D, Ed S); higher education/student personnel (MA). *Application deadline:* For fall admission, 4/1 for domestic students; for spring admission, 10/1 for domestic students. Applications are processed on a rolling basis. *Application fee:* $25. Electronic applications accepted. *Application Contact:* Dr. Christy M. Wyandt, Associate Dean, 662-915-7474, Fax: 662-915-7577, E-mail: cwyandt@olemiss.edu. *Interim Dean,* Dr. David Rock, 662-915-7063, Fax: 662-915-7249, E-mail: soe@olemiss.edu.

School of Engineering Students: 124 full-time (35 women), 37 part-time (9 women); includes 19 minority (11 Black or African American, non-Hispanic/Latino; 6 Asian, non-Hispanic/Latino; 2 Hispanic/Latino), 78 international. Expenses: Contact institution. *Financial support:* Scholarships/grants available. Financial award application deadline: 3/1; financial award applicants required to submit FAFSA. In 2010, 33 master's, 9 doctorates awarded. Offers engineering science (MS, PhD). *Application deadline:* For fall admission, 4/1 for domestic students; for spring admission, 10/1 for domestic students. Applications are processed on a rolling basis. *Application fee:* $25. Electronic applications accepted. *Application Contact:* Dr. Christy M. Wyandt, Associate Dean, 662-915-7474, Fax: 662-915-7577, E-mail: cwyandt@olemiss.edu. Dr. Alexander Cheng, 662-915-7407, Fax: 662-915-1287, E-mail: engineer@olemiss.edu.

School of Journalism and New Media Students: 14 full-time (8 women), 6 part-time (3 women); includes 2 Black or African American, non-Hispanic/Latino. *Faculty:* 19 full-time (9 women), 4 part-time/adjunct (2 women). Expenses: Contact institution. In 2010, 5 master's awarded. Offers journalism (MA). *Application Contact:* Dr. Christy M. Wyandt, Associate Dean, 662-915-7474, Fax: 662-915-7577, E-mail: cwyandt@olemiss.edu. *Dean,* Dr. Will Norton, 662-915-7146.

School of Pharmacy Students: 384 full-time (223 women), 19 part-time (7 women); includes 47 minority (18 Black or African American, non-Hispanic/Latino; 1 American Indian or Alaska Native, non-Hispanic/Latino; 21 Asian, non-Hispanic/Latino; 3 Hispanic/Latino; 4 Two or more races, non-Hispanic/Latino), 72 international. Expenses: Contact institution. *Financial support:* Scholarships/grants available. Financial award application deadline: 3/1; financial award applicants required to submit FAFSA. In 2010, 66 first professional degrees, 8 master's, 10 doctorates awarded. Offers medicinal chemistry (PhD); pharmaceutical sciences (MS); pharmaceutics (PhD); pharmacognosy (PhD); pharmacology (PhD); pharmacy (Pharm D, MS, PhD); pharmacy administration (PhD). *Application deadline:* For fall admission, 4/1 for domestic students. Applications are processed on a rolling basis. *Application fee:* $25. *Application Contact:* Dr. Christy M. Wyandt, Associate Dean, 662-915-7474, Fax: 662-915-7577, E-mail: cwyandt@olemiss.edu. *Dean,* Dr. Barbara G. Wells, 662-915-7265, Fax: 662-915-5704, E-mail: pharmacy@olemiss.edu.

School of Law Students: 516 full-time (230 women), 2 part-time (0 women); includes 80 minority (59 Black or African American, non-Hispanic/Latino; 6 American Indian or Alaska Native, non-Hispanic/Latino; 4 Asian, non-Hispanic/Latino; 10 Hispanic/Latino; 1 Two or more races, non-Hispanic/Latino), 4 international. Average age 24. 1,069 applicants, 42% accepted, 160 enrolled. Expenses: Contact institution. *Financial support:* Fellowships, research assistantships, teaching assistantships, career-related internships or fieldwork, Federal Work-Study, institutionally sponsored loans, and scholarships/grants available. Support available to part-time students. Financial award application deadline: 3/1; financial award applicants required to submit FAFSA. In 2010, 149 first professional degrees awarded. Offers law (JD). *Application deadline:* For fall admission, 4/1 for domestic students. *Application fee:* $40. *Application Contact:* Barbara Vinson, Director of Admissions and Recruiting, 662-915-7361, E-mail: bvinson@olemiss.edu. *Dean,* Dr. Ira Richard Gershon, 662-915-6900, Fax: 662-915-6895, E-mail: igershon@olemiss.edu.

UNIVERSITY OF MISSISSIPPI MEDICAL CENTER, Jackson, MS 39216-4505

General Information State-supported, coed, upper-level institution. *Graduate housing:* On-campus housing not available. *Research affiliation:* NASA–Stennis Space Center (imaging technology), Catfish Genetics Research Unit (immunology), Oak Ridge National Laboratory (physiology, biomedical engineering), Gulf Coast Research Laboratory (microbiology).

GRADUATE UNITS

School of Dentistry Offers craniofacial and dental research (MS, PhD); dentistry (DMD, MS, PhD).

School of Graduate Studies in the Health Sciences Offers anatomy (MS, PhD); biochemistry (MS, PhD); clinical health sciences (MS, PhD); health sciences (MS, MSN, PhD); maternal-fetal medicine (MS); microbiology (MS, PhD); nursing (MSN, PhD); pathology (MS, PhD); pharmacology (MS, PhD); physiology and biophysics (MS, PhD); toxicology (MS, PhD).

School of Health Related Professions *Degree program information:* Part-time programs available. Offers health related professions (MOT, MPT); occupational therapy (MOT); physical therapy (MPT).

School of Medicine Offers medicine (MD).

UNIVERSITY OF MISSOURI, Columbia, MO 65211

General Information State-supported, coed, university. CGS member. *Graduate housing:* Rooms and/or apartments available on a first-come, first-served basis to single and married students. Housing application deadline: 10/1.

GRADUATE UNITS

College of Veterinary Medicine Offers laboratory animal medicine (MS); pathobiology (MS, PhD); veterinary biomedical sciences (MS); veterinary medicine (DVM, MS, PhD); veterinary medicine and surgery (MS); veterinary pathobiology (MS, PhD).

Graduate School *Degree program information:* Part-time and evening/weekend programs available. Offers dispute resolution (LL M); genetics (PhD); health administration (MHA); health informatics (MHA); health services management (MHA); neuroscience (MS, PhD); public health (MPH).

College of Agriculture, Food and Natural Resources *Degree program information:* Part-time programs available. Offers agricultural economics (MS, PhD); agricultural education (MS, PhD); agriculture, food and natural resources (MS, PhD, Graduate Certificate); animal sciences (MS, PhD); biochemistry (MS, PhD); crop, soil and pest management (MS, PhD); entomology (MS, PhD); food science (MS, PhD); foods and food systems management (MS); horticulture (MS, PhD); human nutrition (MS); plant biology and genetics (MS, PhD); plant stress biology (MS, PhD); rural sociology (MS, PhD). Electronic applications accepted.

College of Arts and Sciences *Degree program information:* Part-time programs available. Offers analytical chemistry (MS, PhD); anthropology (MA, PhD); applied mathematics (MS); art (MFA); art history and archaeology (MA, PhD); arts and sciences (MA, MFA, MM, MS, MST, PhD); classical languages (MA, PhD); classical studies (MA, PhD); communication (MA, PhD); economics (MA, PhD); English (MA, PhD); evolutionary biology and ecology (MA, PhD); French (MA, PhD); genetic, cellular and developmental biology (MA, PhD); geography (MA); geological sciences (MS, PhD); German (MA); history (MA, PhD); inorganic chemistry (MS, PhD); literature (MA); mathematics (MA, MST, PhD); music (MA, MM); neurobiology and behavior (MA, PhD); organic chemistry (MS, PhD); philosophy (MA, PhD); physical chemistry (MS, PhD); physics and astronomy (MS, PhD); political science (MA, PhD); psychological sciences (MA, MS, PhD); religious studies (MA); sociology (MA, PhD); Spanish (MA, PhD); statistics (MA, PhD); teaching (MA); theatre (MA, PhD). Electronic applications accepted.

College of Education *Degree program information:* Part-time and evening/weekend programs available. Offers administration and supervision of special education (PhD); agricultural education (M Ed, PhD, Ed S); art education (M Ed, PhD, Ed S); behavior disorders (M Ed, PhD); business and office education (M Ed, PhD, Ed S); counseling psychology (M Ed, MA, PhD, Ed S); curriculum development of exceptional students (M Ed, PhD); early childhood education (M Ed, PhD, Ed S); early childhood special education (M Ed, PhD); education (M Ed, MA, Ed D, PhD, Ed S); education administration (M Ed, MA, Ed D, PhD, Ed S); educational psychology (M Ed, MA, PhD, Ed S); educational technology (M Ed, Ed S); elementary education (M Ed, PhD, Ed S); English education (M Ed, PhD, Ed S); foreign language education (M Ed, PhD, Ed S); general special education (M Ed, MA, PhD); health education and promotion (M Ed, PhD); higher and adult education (M Ed, MA, Ed D, PhD, Ed S); information science and learning technology (PhD); learning and instruction (M Ed); learning disabilities (M Ed, PhD); library science (MA); marketing education (M Ed, PhD, Ed S); mathematics education (M Ed, PhD, Ed S); mental retardation (M Ed, PhD); music education (M Ed, PhD, Ed S); reading education (M Ed, PhD, Ed S); school psychology (M Ed, MA, PhD, Ed S); science education (M Ed, PhD, Ed S); social studies education (M Ed, PhD, Ed S); vocational education (M Ed, PhD, Ed S).

College of Engineering *Degree program information:* Part-time programs available. Offers agricultural engineering (MS); biological engineering (MS, PhD); chemical engineering (MS, PhD); civil engineering (MS, PhD); computer science (MS, PhD); electrical and computer engineering (MS, PhD); engineering (ME, MS, PhD); environmental engineering (MS, PhD); geotechnical engineering (MS, PhD); industrial and manufacturing systems engineering (MS, PhD); mechanical and aerospace engineering (MS, PhD); structural engineering (MS, PhD); transportation and highway engineering (MS); water resources (MS, PhD).

College of Human Environmental Science *Degree program information:* Part-time programs available. Offers design with digital media (MA, MS); environmental design (MS); exercise physiology (MA, PhD); human development and family studies (MA, MS, PhD); human environmental science (MA, MS, PhD); nutritional sciences (MS, PhD); personal financial planning (MS); textile and apparel management (MA, MS).

Harry S Truman School of Public Affairs Offers public affairs (MPA).

Informatics Institute Offers informatics (PhD).

Nuclear Science and Engineering Institute Offers nuclear power engineering (MS, PhD).

Robert J. Trulaske, Sr. College of Business *Degree program information:* Part-time programs available. Offers accountancy (M Acc, PhD); business (M Acc, MBA, PhD); business administration (MBA, PhD).

School of Journalism *Degree program information:* Part-time programs available. Offers journalism (MA, PhD).

School of Natural Resources *Degree program information:* Part-time programs available. Offers atmospheric science (MS, PhD); fisheries and wildlife (MS, PhD); forestry (MS, PhD); natural resources (MNR, MS, PhD); parks, recreation and tourism (MS); soil science (MS, PhD).

School of Social Work *Degree program information:* Part-time programs available. Offers social work (MSW).

Sinclair School of Nursing *Degree program information:* Part-time programs available. Offers nursing (MS, PhD).

School of Health Professions Offers communication science and disorders (MHS); diagnostic medical ultrasound (MHS); health professions (MHS, MOT, MPT); occupational therapy (MOT); physical therapy (MPT).

School of Law Offers law (JD, LL M).

School of Medicine *Degree program information:* Part-time programs available. Offers medicine (MD, MS, PhD); public health (MS).

Graduate Programs in Medicine *Degree program information:* Part-time programs available. Offers medicine (MS, PhD); molecular microbiology and immunology (MS, PhD); pathology and anatomical sciences (MS); pharmacology (MS, PhD); physiology (MS, PhD).

UNIVERSITY OF MISSOURI–KANSAS CITY, Kansas City, MO 64110-2499

General Information State-supported, coed, university. CGS member. *Enrollment:* 2,845 full-time matriculated graduate/professional students (1,438 women), 2,346 part-time matriculated graduate/professional students (1,351 women). *Enrollment by degree level:* 1,632 first professional, 2,815 master's, 664 doctoral, 80 other advanced degrees. *Graduate faculty:* 741 full-time (327 women), 427 part-time/adjunct (207 women). Tuition, state resident: full-time $5522; part-time $306.80 per credit hour. Tuition, nonresident: full-time $7128; part-time $792 per credit hour. *Required fees:* $261.15 per term. *Graduate housing:* Room and/or apartments available on a first-come, first-served basis to single students; on-campus housing not available to married students. Typical cost: $6022 per year ($8754 including board). Room and board charges vary according to board plan and housing facility selected. *Student services:* Campus employment opportunities, campus safety program, career counseling, child daycare facilities, exercise/wellness program, free psychological counseling, international student services, multicultural affairs office, services for students with disabilities, teacher training, writing training. *Library facilities:* Miller-Nichols Library plus 3 others. *Online resources:* library catalog, web page, access to other libraries' catalogs. *Collection:* 1.8 million titles, 48,869 serial subscriptions, 456,219 audiovisual materials. *Research affiliation:* St. Luke's Hospital (health sciences), Children's Mercy Hospital (health sciences), Truman Medical Center (health sciences), Veterans Administration Hospital (health sciences), Midwest Research Institute (health sciences).

Computer facilities: Computer purchase and lease plans are available. 730 computers available on campus for general student use. A campuswide network can be accessed from student residence rooms and from off campus. Online class registration is available. *Web address:* http://www.umkc.edu/.

General Application Contact: W. C. Vance, Director of Admissions, 816-235-1111, Fax: 816-235-5544, E-mail: admit@umkc.edu.

GRADUATE UNITS

College of Arts and Sciences Students: 270 full-time (171 women), 420 part-time (257 women); includes 143 minority (82 Black or African American, non-Hispanic/Latino; 6 American Indian or Alaska Native, non-Hispanic/Latino; 14 Asian, non-Hispanic/Latino; 33 Hispanic/Latino; 1 Native Hawaiian or other Pacific Islander, non-Hispanic/Latino; 7 Two or more races, non-Hispanic/Latino), 37 international. Average age 33. 588 applicants, 46% accepted, 223 enrolled. *Faculty:* 230 full-time (96 women), 165 part-time/adjunct (79 women). Expenses: Contact institution. *Financial support:* In 2010–11, 49 research assistantships with full and partial tuition reimbursements (averaging $12,927 per year), 176 teaching assistantships with full and partial tuition reimbursements (averaging $12,460 per year) were awarded; career-related internships or fieldwork, Federal Work-Study, institutionally sponsored loans, scholarships/grants, and tuition waivers (full and partial) also available. Support available to part-time students. Financial award application deadline: 3/1; financial award applicants required to submit FAFSA. In 2010, 173 master's, 4 doctorates awarded. *Degree program information:* Part-time and evening/weekend programs available. Offers acting (MFA); analytical chemistry (MS, PhD); art history (MA, PhD); arts and sciences (MA, MFA, MS, MSW, PhD); clinical psychology (PhD); community psychology (PhD); creative writing and media arts (MFA); criminal justice and criminology (MS); design technology (MFA); economics (MA, PhD); English (MA, PhD); environmental and urban geosciences (MS); geosciences (PhD); health psychology (PhD); history (MA, PhD); inorganic chemistry (MS, PhD); mathematics and statistics (MA, MS, PhD); organic chemistry (MS, PhD); physical chemistry (MS, PhD); physics (MS, PhD); political science (MA, PhD); polymer chemistry (MS, PhD); psychology (MA); Romance languages and literatures (MA); sociology (MA, PhD); studio art (MA); theatre (MA). *Application deadline:* Applications are processed on a rolling basis. *Application fee:* $45 ($50 for international students). Electronic applications accepted. *Application Contact:* W. C. Vance, Director of Admissions, 816-235-1111, Fax: 816-235-5544, E-mail: admit@umkc.edu. *Dean*, Dr. Karen Vorst, 816-235-1307, Fax: 816-235-1308.

School of Social Work Students: 99 full-time (85 women), 91 part-time (77 women); includes 40 Black or African American, non-Hispanic/Latino; 2 American Indian or Alaska Native, non-Hispanic/Latino; 2 Asian, non-Hispanic/Latino; 8 Hispanic/Latino; 2 Two or more races, non-Hispanic/Latino, 1 international. Average age 34. 104 applicants, 63% accepted, 57 enrolled. *Faculty:* 10 full-time (8 women), 12 part-time/adjunct (7 women). Expenses: Contact institution. *Financial support:* In 2010–11, 4 research assistantships with partial tuition reimbursements (averaging $11,280 per year) were awarded; career-related internships or fieldwork and institutionally sponsored loans also available. Financial award application deadline: 3/1; financial award applicants required to submit FAFSA. In 2010, 56 master's awarded. *Degree program information:* Part-time and evening/weekend programs available. Offers social work (MSW). *Application deadline:* For fall admission, 4/30 for domestic and international students; for spring admission, 12/1 for domestic and international students. Applications are processed on a rolling basis. *Application fee:* $45 ($50 for international students). *Application Contact:* Dr. Monica Nandan, Program Director, 816-235-2203, E-mail: soc-wk@umkc.edu. *Program Director*, Dr. Monica Nandan, 816-235-2203, E-mail: soc-wk@umkc.edu.

Conservatory of Music Students: 135 full-time (59 women), 101 part-time (51 women); includes 16 minority (10 Black or African American, non-Hispanic/Latino; 3 Asian, non-Hispanic/Latino; 3 Hispanic/Latino), 56 international. Average age 29. 335 applicants, 25% accepted, 74 enrolled. *Faculty:* 58 full-time (25 women), 33 part-time/adjunct (13 women). Expenses: Contact institution. *Financial support:* In 2010–11, 56 teaching assistantships with partial tuition reimbursements (averaging $8,835 per year) were awarded; career-related internships or fieldwork, Federal Work-Study, institutionally sponsored loans, scholarships/grants, tuition waivers (partial), and unspecified assistantships also available. Support available to part-time students. Financial award application deadline: 3/1; financial award applicants required to submit FAFSA. In 2010, 56 master's, 20 doctorates awarded. *Degree program information:* Part-time programs available. Offers composition (MM, DMA); conducting (MM, DMA); music (MA); music education (MME, PhD); music history and literature (MM); music theory (MM); performance (MM, DMA). PhD (interdisciplinary) offered through the School of Graduate Studies. *Application deadline:* For fall admission, 1/15 priority date for domestic students, 1/15 for international students. *Application fee:* $45 ($50 for international students). *Application Contact:* William Everett, Associate Dean, 816-235-2857, Fax: 816-235-5264, E-mail: everettw@umkc.edu. *Dean*, Peter Witte, 816-235-2731, Fax: 816-235-5265, E-mail: wittep@umkc.edu.

Henry W. Bloch School of Management Students: 280 full-time (134 women), 435 part-time (193 women); includes 91 minority (44 Black or African American, non-Hispanic/Latino; 19 Asian, non-Hispanic/Latino; 23 Hispanic/Latino; 5 Two or more races, non-Hispanic/Latino), 50 international. Average age 30. 426 applicants, 255 enrolled. *Faculty:* 49 full-time (16 women), 21 part-time/adjunct (5 women). Expenses: Contact institution. *Financial support:* In 2010–11, 26 research assistantships with partial tuition reimbursements (averaging $7,767 per year), 5 teaching assistantships with partial tuition reimbursements (averaging $8,430 per year) were awarded; career-related internships or fieldwork, Federal Work-Study, institutionally sponsored loans, scholarships/grants, tuition waivers (full and partial), and unspecified assistantships also available. Support available to part-time students. Financial award application deadline: 3/1; financial award applicants required to submit FAFSA. In 2010, 254 master's awarded. *Degree program information:* Part-time and evening/weekend programs available. Offers accounting (MS); business administration (MBA); entrepreneurship and innovation (PhD); public affairs (MPA, PhD). PhD (interdisciplinary) offered through the School of Graduate Studies. *Application deadline:* For fall admission, 5/1 priority date for domestic and international students; for spring admission, 10/1 priority date for domestic and international students. Applications are processed on a rolling basis. *Application fee:* $45 ($50 for international students). Electronic applications accepted. *Application Contact:* 816-235-1111, E-mail: admit@umkc.edu. *Dean*, Dr. Teng-Kee Tan, 816-235-2215, Fax: 816-235-2206.

School of Biological Sciences Students: 23 full-time (14 women), 33 part-time (19 women); includes 12 minority (3 Black or African American, non-Hispanic/Latino; 6 Asian, non-Hispanic/Latino; 2 Hispanic/Latino; 1 Two or more races, non-Hispanic/Latino), 3 international. Average age 30. 56 applicants, 52% accepted, 25 enrolled. *Faculty:* 42 full-time (11 women). Expenses: Contact institution. *Financial support:* In 2010–11, 17 research assistantships with full tuition reimbursements (averaging $21,098 per year), 9 teaching assistantships with full tuition reimbursements (averaging $22,000 per year) were awarded; Federal Work-Study, institutionally sponsored loans, scholarships/grants, tuition waivers (full and partial), and unspecified assistantships also available. Support available to part-time students. Financial award application deadline: 3/1; financial award applicants required to submit FAFSA. In 2010, 23 master's awarded. *Degree program information:* Part-time and evening/weekend programs available. Offers biology (MA); cell biology and biophysics (PhD); cellular and molecular biology (MS); molecular biology and biochemistry (PhD). PhD (interdisciplinary) offered through the School of Graduate Studies. *Application deadline:* For fall admission, 2/15 priority date for domestic and international students. Applications are processed on a rolling basis. *Application fee:* $45 ($50 for international students). *Application Contact:* Laura Batenic, Information Contact, 816-235-2352, Fax: 816-235-5158, E-mail: batenicl@umkc.edu. *Dean*, Dr. Lawrence A. Dreyfus, 816-235-5246, Fax: 816-235-5158, E-mail: dreyfusl@umkc.edu.

School of Computing and Engineering Students: 160 full-time (32 women), 194 part-time (41 women); includes 21 minority (5 Black or African American, non-Hispanic/Latino; 9 Asian, non-Hispanic/Latino; 6 Hispanic/Latino; 1 Two or more races, non-Hispanic/Latino), 273

University of Missouri–Kansas City (continued)

international. Average age 25. 440 applicants, 55% accepted, 104 enrolled. *Faculty:* 36 full-time (5 women), 21 part-time/adjunct (0 women). Expenses: Contact institution. *Financial support:* In 2010–11, 35 research assistantships with partial tuition reimbursements (averaging $14,340 per year), 20 teaching assistantships with partial tuition reimbursements (averaging $13,351 per year) were awarded; career-related internships or fieldwork, Federal Work-Study, scholarships/grants, tuition waivers (partial), and unspecified assistantships also available. Support available to part-time students. Financial award application deadline: 3/1; financial award applicants required to submit FAFSA. In 2010, 135 master's awarded. *Degree program information:* Part-time programs available. Offers civil engineering (MS); computer and electrical engineering (PhD); computer science (MS); computer science and informatics (PhD); computing (PhD); electrical engineering (MS); engineering (PhD); mechanical engineering (MS); telecommunications (PhD). PhD (interdisciplinary) offered through the School of Graduate Studies. *Application deadline:* For fall admission, 1/15 priority date for domestic students, 1/15 for international students. Applications are processed on a rolling basis. *Application fee:* $45 ($50 for international students). *Application Contact:* Dr. Kevin Z. Truman, Dean, 816-235-2399, Fax: 816-235-5159. *Dean,* Dr. Kevin Z. Truman, 816-235-2399, Fax: 816-235-5159.

School of Dentistry Students: 405 full-time (172 women), 52 part-time (32 women); includes 59 minority (8 Black or African American, non-Hispanic/Latino; 2 American Indian or Alaska Native, non-Hispanic/Latino; 33 Asian, non-Hispanic/Latino; 15 Hispanic/Latino; 1 Two or more races, non-Hispanic/Latino), 1 international. Average age 27. 505 applicants, 26% accepted, 113 enrolled. *Faculty:* 98 full-time (41 women), 72 part-time/adjunct (23 women). Expenses: Contact institution. *Financial support:* In 2010–11, 5 fellowships (averaging $60,900 per year), 2 research assistantships (averaging $16,206 per year) were awarded; career-related internships or fieldwork, Federal Work-Study, institutionally sponsored loans, and tuition waivers (full and partial) also available. Support available to part-time students. Financial award application deadline: 3/1; financial award applicants required to submit FAFSA. In 2010, 96 first professional degrees, 7 master's awarded. Offers advanced education in dentistry (Graduate Dental Certificate); dental hygiene education (MS); dental specialties (Graduate Dental Certificate); dentistry (DDS); diagnostic sciences (Graduate Dental Certificate); oral and maxillofacial surgery (Graduate Dental Certificate); oral biology (MS, PhD); orthodontics and dentofacial orthopedics (Graduate Dental Certificate); pediatric dentistry (Graduate Dental Certificate); periodontics (Graduate Dental Certificate); prosthodontics (Graduate Dental Certificate). PhD (interdisciplinary) offered through the School of Graduate Studies. *Application deadline:* For fall admission, 2/1 for domestic and international students. *Application fee:* $45 ($50 for international students). *Application Contact:* 816-235-2080. *Dean,* Dr. Marsha Pyle, 816-235-2010.

School of Education Students: 213 full-time (154 women), 410 part-time (300 women); includes 127 minority (91 Black or African American, non-Hispanic/Latino; 1 American Indian or Alaska Native, non-Hispanic/Latino; 14 Asian, non-Hispanic/Latino; 20 Hispanic/Latino; 1 Two or more races, non-Hispanic/Latino), 19 international. Average age 33. 422 applicants, 243 enrolled. *Faculty:* 61 full-time (51 women), 38 part-time/adjunct (28 women). Expenses: Contact institution. *Financial support:* In 2010–11, 19 research assistantships with partial tuition reimbursements (averaging $10,920 per year) were awarded; career-related internships or fieldwork, Federal Work-Study, institutionally sponsored loans, and tuition waivers (full and partial) also available. Support available to part-time students. Financial award application deadline: 3/1; financial award applicants required to submit FAFSA. In 2010, 152 master's, 5 doctorates, 33 other advanced degrees awarded. *Degree program information:* Part-time and evening/weekend programs available. Offers administration (Ed D); counseling and guidance (MA, Ed S); counseling psychology (PhD); curriculum and instruction (MA, Ed S); education (PhD); educational administration (Ed S); reading education (MA, Ed S); special education (MA). PhD (education) offered through the School of Graduate Studies. *Application deadline:* For fall admission, 4/1 priority date for domestic and international students; for spring admission, 11/1 priority date for domestic and international students. Applications are processed on a rolling basis. *Application fee:* $45 ($50 for international students). *Application Contact:* Erica Hernandez-Scott, Student Recruiter, 816-235-1295, Fax: 816-235-5270, E-mail: hernandeze@umkc.edu. *Dean,* Dr. Wanda Blanchett, 816-235-2234, Fax: 816-235-5270, E-mail: education@umkc.edu.

School of Graduate Studies Students: 73 full-time (32 women), 316 part-time (127 women); includes 32 minority (16 Black or African American, non-Hispanic/Latino; 9 Asian, non-Hispanic/Latino; 6 Hispanic/Latino; 1 Two or more races, non-Hispanic/Latino), 169 international. Average age 35. 335 applicants, 26% accepted, 69 enrolled. Expenses: Contact institution. *Financial support:* Career-related internships or fieldwork, Federal Work-Study, tuition waivers (partial), and unspecified assistantships available. Support available to part-time students. Financial award application deadline: 3/1; financial award applicants required to submit FAFSA. In 2010, 32 doctorates awarded. Offers interdisciplinary studies (PhD). *Application deadline:* For fall admission, 1/15 priority date for domestic and international students. Applications are processed on a rolling basis. *Application fee:* $45 ($50 for international students). Electronic applications accepted. *Application Contact:* Qunicy Bennett Johnson, Administrative Assistant, 816-235-1559, Fax: 816-235-1310, E-mail: bennettq@umkc.edu. *Dean,* Dr. Ronald MacQuarrie, 816-235-1301, Fax: 816-235-1310, E-mail: macquarrier@umkc.edu.

School of Law Students: 476 full-time (186 women), 51 part-time (21 women); includes 67 minority (29 Black or African American, non-Hispanic/Latino; 3 American Indian or Alaska Native, non-Hispanic/Latino; 15 Asian, non-Hispanic/Latino; 20 Hispanic/Latino), 23 international. Average age 27. 967 applicants, 22% accepted, 201 enrolled. *Faculty:* 31 full-time (15 women), 5 part-time/adjunct (2 women). Expenses: Contact institution. *Financial support:* In 2010–11, 40 teaching assistantships with partial tuition reimbursements (averaging $2,133 per year) were awarded; career-related internships or fieldwork, Federal Work-Study, institutionally sponsored loans, scholarships/grants, and tuition waivers (full and partial) also available. Support available to part-time students. Financial award application deadline: 3/1; financial award applicants required to submit FAFSA. In 2010, 156 first professional degrees, 32 master's awarded. *Degree program information:* Part-time programs available. Offers law (JD, LL M). *Application deadline:* For fall admission, 3/1 priority date for domestic and international students. Applications are processed on a rolling basis. *Application fee:* $50. Electronic applications accepted. *Application Contact:* Debbie Brooks, Director of Admissions, 816-235-1672, Fax: 816-235-5276, E-mail: brooksdv@umkc.edu. *Dean,* Ellen Y. Suni, 816-235-1677, Fax: 816-235-5276, E-mail: sunie@umkc.edu.

School of Medicine Students: 406 full-time (213 women), 4 part-time (2 women); includes 213 minority (24 Black or African American, non-Hispanic/Latino; 172 Asian, non-Hispanic/Latino; 16 Hispanic/Latino; 1 Two or more races, non-Hispanic/Latino), 1 international. Average age 23. 779 applicants, 13% accepted, 95 enrolled. *Faculty:* 44 full-time (11 women), 15 part-time/adjunct (6 women). Expenses: Contact institution. *Financial support:* Career-related internships or fieldwork, Federal Work-Study, institutionally sponsored loans, scholarships/grants, and tuition waivers (partial) available. Financial award application deadline: 3/1; financial award applicants required to submit FAFSA. In 2010, 92 first professional degrees, 4 master's awarded. Offers anesthesia (MS); bioinformatics (MS); medicine (MD). *Application deadline:* For fall admission, 11/15 for domestic and international students. *Application fee:* $50. *Application Contact:* Kelly Kasper-Cushman, Selection Administrative Assistant, 816-235-1870, Fax: 816-235-6579, E-mail: kasperkm@umkc.edu. *Dean,* Dr. Betty Drees, 816-235-1808, E-mail: dreesb@umkc.edu.

School of Nursing Students: 52 full-time (46 women), 330 part-time (308 women); includes 39 minority (15 Black or African American, non-Hispanic/Latino; 1 American Indian or Alaska Native, non-Hispanic/Latino; 10 Asian, non-Hispanic/Latino; 11 Hispanic/Latino; 2 Two or more races, non-Hispanic/Latino). Average age 36. 227 applicants, 78% accepted, 123 enrolled. *Faculty:* 38 full-time (32 women), 49 part-time/adjunct (47 women). Expenses: Contact institution. *Financial support:* In 2010–11, 1 research assistantship (averaging $13,200 per year), 18 teaching assistantships with partial tuition reimbursements (averaging $5,468 per year) were awarded; fellowships, career-related internships or fieldwork, Federal Work-Study, institutionally sponsored loans, and tuition waivers (full and partial) also available. Support available to part-time students. Financial award application deadline: 3/1; financial award applicants required to submit FAFSA. In 2010, 74 master's, 22 doctorates awarded. *Degree program information:* Part-time programs available. Postbaccalaureate distance learning degree programs offered (minimal on-campus study). Offers adult clinical nurse specialist (MSN); family nurse practitioner (MSN); neonatal nurse practitioner (MSN); nurse educator (MSN); nurse executive (MSN); nursing (PhD); nursing practice (DNP); pediatric nurse practitioner (MSN). *Application deadline:* For fall admission, 2/1 priority date for domestic and international students; for spring admission, 9/1 priority date for domestic and international students. *Application fee:* $45 ($50 for international students). *Application Contact:* Leah Wilder, Coordinator for Admissions and Recruitment, 816-235-5768, Fax: 816-235-1701, E-mail: wilderl@umkc.edu. *Dean,* Dr. Lora Lacey-Haun, 816-235-1700, Fax: 816-235-1701, E-mail: lacey-haunc@umkc.edu.

School of Pharmacy Students: 352 full-time (225 women); includes 39 minority (13 Black or African American, non-Hispanic/Latino; 1 American Indian or Alaska Native, non-Hispanic/Latino; 21 Asian, non-Hispanic/Latino; 2 Hispanic/Latino; 2 Two or more races, non-Hispanic/Latino), 6 international. Average age 26. 461 applicants, 28% accepted, 127 enrolled. *Faculty:* 54 full-time (24 women), 7 part-time/adjunct (3 women). Expenses: Contact institution. *Financial support:* In 2010–11, 39 research assistantships with full and partial tuition reimbursements (averaging $8,992 per year), 20 teaching assistantships with full tuition reimbursements (averaging $11,511 per year) were awarded; career-related internships or fieldwork, Federal Work-Study, institutionally sponsored loans, tuition waivers (full and partial), and unspecified assistantships also available. Financial award application deadline: 3/1; financial award applicants required to submit FAFSA. In 2010, 111 first professional degrees awarded. Postbaccalaureate distance learning degree programs offered (minimal on-campus study). Offers pharmaceutical sciences (PhD); pharmacy (Pharm D). *Application deadline:* For fall admission, 12/5 for domestic students, 12/15 for international students; for spring admission, 10/1 for domestic students. Applications are processed on a rolling basis. *Application fee:* $45 ($50 for international students). Electronic applications accepted. *Application Contact:* Shelly M. Janasz, Director, Student Services, 816-235-2400, Fax: 816-235-5190, E-mail: janaszs@umkc.edu. *Dean,* Dr. Russell B. Melchert, 816-235-1609, Fax: 816-235-5190, E-mail: melchertr@umkc.edu.

UNIVERSITY OF MISSOURI–ST. LOUIS, St. Louis, MO 63121

General Information State-supported, coed, university. CGS member. *Enrollment:* 16,802 graduate, professional, and undergraduate students; 938 full-time matriculated graduate/professional students (563 women), 2,340 part-time matriculated graduate/professional students (1,622 women). *Enrollment by degree level:* 2,568 master's, 573 doctoral, 137 other advanced degrees. *Graduate faculty:* 411 full-time (161 women), 185 part-time/adjunct (102 women). Tuition, state resident: full-time $5522; part-time $306.80 per credit hour. Tuition, nonresident: full-time $14,253; part-time $792.10 per credit hour. *Required fees:* $658; $49 per credit hour. One-time fee: $12. Tuition and fees vary according to program. *Graduate housing:* Rooms and/or apartments available on a first-come, first-served basis to single and married students. *Student services:* Campus employment opportunities, campus safety program, career counseling, child daycare facilities, exercise/wellness program, free psychological counseling, grant writing training, international student services, low-cost health insurance, multicultural affairs office, services for students with disabilities. *Library facilities:* Thomas Jefferson Library plus 2 others. *Online resources:* library catalog, web page, access to other libraries' catalogs. *Collection:* 1.2 million titles, 3,000 serial subscriptions, 3,966 audiovisual materials. *Research affiliation:* Express Scripts (business), St. Louis Zoo (biology), Missouri Botanical Garden (biology), Donald Danforth Plant Science Center (biology).

Computer facilities: Computer purchase and lease plans are available. 1,326 computers available on campus for general student use. A campuswide network can be accessed from student residence rooms and from off campus. Online class registration is available. *Web address:* http://www.umsl.edu/.

General Application Contact: Graduate Admissions, 314-516-5458, Fax: 314-516-6996, E-mail: gradadm@umsl.edu.

GRADUATE UNITS

College of Arts and Sciences Students: 386 full-time (237 women), 522 part-time (300 women); includes 104 minority (59 Black or African American, non-Hispanic/Latino; 7 American Indian or Alaska Native, non-Hispanic/Latino; 27 Asian, non-Hispanic/Latino; 10 Hispanic/Latino; 1 Two or more races, non-Hispanic/Latino), 105 international. Average age 31. *Faculty:* 223 full-time (78 women), 176 part-time/adjunct (98 women). Expenses: Contact institution. *Financial support:* In 2010–11, 128 research assistantships with full and partial tuition reimbursements (averaging $11,330 per year), 146 teaching assistantships with full and partial tuition reimbursements (averaging $10,906 per year) were awarded; career-related internships or fieldwork, Federal Work-Study, health care benefits, and unspecified assistantships also available. Support available to part-time students. Financial award applicants required to submit FAFSA. In 2010, 254 master's, 35 doctorates, 9 other advanced degrees awarded. *Degree program information:* Part-time and evening/weekend programs available. Offers American literature (MA); American politics (MA); applied mathematics (PhD); arts and sciences (MA, MFA, MS, MSW, PhD, Certificate); behavioral neuroscience (PhD); biotechnology (Certificate); cell and molecular biology (MS, PhD); chemistry (MS, PhD); clinical community psychology (PhD); clinical psychology respecialization (Certificate); comparative politics (MA); computer science (MS); creative writing (MFA); criminology and criminal justice (MA, PhD); ecology, evolution and systematics (MS, PhD); English literature (MA); gender studies (Certificate); general economics (MA); general psychology (MA); gerontology (MS, Certificate); history (MA); industrial/organizational psychology (PhD); international politics (MA); international studies (Certificate); linguistics (MA); long term care administration (Certificate); mathematics (MA); museum studies (MA, Certificate); philosophy (MA); physics (MS, PhD); political process and behavior (MA); political science (PhD); public administration and public policy (MA); teaching of writing (Certificate); trauma studies (Certificate); tropical biology and conservation (Certificate); urban and regional politics (MA). *Application deadline:* For fall admission, 7/1 for domestic and international students; for spring admission, 12/1 for domestic and international students. *Application fee:* $35 ($40 for international students). Electronic applications accepted. *Application Contact:* Graduate Admissions, 314-516-5458, Fax: 314-516-6996, E-mail: gradadm@umsl.edu. *Dean,* Dr. Ronald Yasbin, 314-516-5501.

School of Social Work Students: 66 full-time (60 women), 69 part-time (62 women); includes 18 minority (16 Black or African American, non-Hispanic/Latino; 1 Asian, non-Hispanic/Latino; 1 Hispanic/Latino), 2 international. Average age 31. *Faculty:* 10 full-time (8 women), 5 part-time/adjunct (3 women). Expenses: Contact institution. *Financial support:* In 2010–11, 1 research assistantship with full and partial tuition reimbursement (averaging $9,900 per year), 7 teaching assistantships with full and partial tuition reimbursements (averaging $8,360 per year) were awarded. Financial award applicants required to submit FAFSA. In 2010, 50 master's, 3 other advanced degrees awarded. Offers gerontology (MS, Certificate); nonprofit organization management and leadership (Certificate); social work (MSW). *Application deadline:* For fall admission, 2/15 for domestic and international students. *Application fee:* $35 ($40 for international students). Electronic applications accepted. *Application Contact:* 314-516-5458, Fax: 314-516-6996, E-mail: gradadm@umsl.edu. *Graduate Program Director,* Dr. Lois Pierce, 314-516-6364, Fax: 314-516-5816, E-mail: socialwork@umsl.edu.

College of Business Administration Students: 188 full-time (88 women), 359 part-time (156 women); includes 68 minority (25 Black or African American, non-Hispanic/Latino; 1 American Indian or Alaska Native, non-Hispanic/Latino; 27 Asian, non-Hispanic/Latino; 12 Hispanic/Latino; 1 Native Hawaiian or other Pacific Islander, non-Hispanic/Latino; 2 Two or more races, non-Hispanic/Latino), 71 international. Average age 34. 320 applicants, 60% accepted, 121 enrolled. *Faculty:* 47 full-time (11 women), 10 part-time/adjunct (1 woman). Expenses: Contact institution. *Financial support:* In 2010–11, 22 research assistantships with full and partial tuition reimbursements (averaging $7,414 per year), 4 teaching assistantships with full and partial tuition reimbursements (averaging $13,950 per year) were awarded; career-related internships or fieldwork, Federal Work-Study, and institutionally sponsored loans also available. Support available to part-time students. Financial award application deadline: 4/1; financial award applicants required to submit FAFSA. In 2010, 158 master's, 2 doctorates, 9 other advanced degrees awarded. *Degree program information:* Part-time and evening/weekend programs available. Offers accounting (M Acc); business administration

(M Acc, MBA, MSIS, PhD, Certificate); finance (MBA); human resource management (Certificate); information systems (MBA, MSIS, PhD); local government (Certificate); logistics and supply chain management (MBA, PhD, Certificate); marketing (MBA); marketing management (Certificate); operations management (MBA). *Application deadline:* For fall admission, 7/1 priority date for domestic and international students; for spring admission, 12/1 priority date for domestic and international students. Applications are processed on a rolling basis. *Application fee:* $35 ($40 for international students). Electronic applications accepted. *Application Contact:* 314-516-5458, Fax: 314-516-6996, E-mail: gradadm@umsl.edu. *Assistant Director,* Karl Kottemann, 314-516-5885, Fax: 314-516-6420, E-mail: mba@umsl.edu.

College of Education Students: 231 full-time (156 women), 1,182 part-time (910 women); includes 343 minority (273 Black or African American, non-Hispanic/Latino; 5 American Indian or Alaska Native, non-Hispanic/Latino; 30 Asian, non-Hispanic/Latino; 31 Hispanic/Latino; 4 Two or more races, non-Hispanic/Latino), 31 international. Average age 31. *Faculty:* 70 full-time (33 women), 82 part-time/adjunct (53 women). Expenses: Contact institution. *Financial support:* In 2010–11, 32 research assistantships with full and partial tuition reimbursements (averaging $10,700 per year), 8 teaching assistantships with full and partial tuition reimbursements (averaging $12,400 per year) were awarded. Financial award application deadline: 4/1; financial award applicants required to submit FAFSA. In 2010, 34 master's, 49 doctorates, 10 other advanced degrees awarded. *Degree program information:* Part-time and evening/weekend programs available. Offers adult and higher education (Ed D); counseling (PhD); counselor education (Ed D); education (M Ed, Ed D, PhD, Certificate, Ed S); educational administration (Ed D); educational leadership and policy studies (PhD); educational psychology (PhD). *Application deadline:* For fall admission, 7/1 priority date for domestic and international students; for spring admission, 12/1 priority date for domestic and international students. Applications are processed on a rolling basis. *Application fee:* $35 ($40 for international students). Electronic applications accepted. *Application Contact:* 314-516-5458, Fax: 314-516-6996, E-mail: gradadm@umsl.edu. *Director of Graduate Studies,* Dr. Kathleen Haywood, 314-516-5483, Fax: 314-516-5227, E-mail: kathleen_haywood@umsl.edu.

Division of Counseling Students: 50 full-time (44 women), 165 part-time (135 women); includes 40 minority (33 Black or African American, non-Hispanic/Latino; 2 Asian, non-Hispanic/Latino; 5 Hispanic/Latino), 4 international. Average age 31. 97 applicants, 52% accepted, 32 enrolled. *Faculty:* 7 full-time (3 women), 11 part-time/adjunct (7 women). Expenses: Contact institution. *Financial support:* In 2010–11, 1 research assistantship with full and partial tuition reimbursement (averaging $12,240 per year), 1 teaching assistantship with full and partial tuition reimbursement (averaging $10,381 per year) were awarded. Financial award application deadline: 4/1; financial award applicants required to submit FAFSA. In 2010, 61 master's awarded. *Degree program information:* Part-time and evening/weekend programs available. Offers community counseling (M Ed); elementary school counseling (M Ed); secondary school counseling (M Ed). *Application deadline:* For fall admission, 6/1 for domestic and international students; for spring admission, 10/1 for domestic and international students. *Application fee:* $35 ($40 for international students). Electronic applications accepted. *Application Contact:* 314-516-5458, Fax: 314-516-6996, E-mail: gradadm@umsl.edu. *Chair,* Dr. Mark Pope, 314-516-5782.

Division of Educational Leadership and Policy Studies Students: 22 full-time (13 women), 171 part-time (125 women); includes 81 minority (75 Black or African American, non-Hispanic/Latino; 3 Asian, non-Hispanic/Latino; 3 Hispanic/Latino), 3 international. Average age 36. *Faculty:* 20 full-time (10 women), 7 part-time/adjunct (5 women). Expenses: Contact institution. *Financial support:* In 2010–11, 2 research assistantships (averaging $6,812 per year) were awarded. Financial award application deadline: 4/1; financial award applicants required to submit FAFSA. In 2010, 74 master's, 17 other advanced degrees awarded. *Degree program information:* Part-time and evening/weekend programs available. Offers adult and higher education (M Ed); educational administration (M Ed, Ed S); institutional research (Certificate). *Application deadline:* For fall admission, 7/1 priority date for domestic and international students; for spring admission, 12/1 priority date for domestic and international students. Applications are processed on a rolling basis. *Application fee:* $35 ($40 for international students). Electronic applications accepted. *Application Contact:* 314-516-5458, Fax: 314-516-6996, E-mail: gradadm@umsl.edu. *Chair,* Dr. E. Paulette Savage, 514-516-5944.

Division of Educational Psychology, Research, and Evaluation Students: 16 full-time (13 women), 8 part-time (1 woman); includes 3 minority (2 Black or African American, non-Hispanic/Latino; 1 Asian, non-Hispanic/Latino), 2 international. Average age 26. 29 applicants, 52% accepted, 8 enrolled. *Faculty:* 10 full-time (3 women), 9 part-time/adjunct (3 women). Expenses: Contact institution. *Financial support:* In 2010–11, 1 research assistantship (averaging $5,625 per year), 1 teaching assistantship (averaging $10,380 per year) were awarded. Financial award application deadline: 4/1; financial award applicants required to submit FAFSA. In 2010, 7 Ed Ss awarded. Offers program evaluation and assessment (Certificate); school psychology (Ed S). *Application deadline:* For fall admission, 3/1 for domestic and international students. *Application fee:* $35 ($40 for international students). Electronic applications accepted. *Application Contact:* 314-516-5458, Fax: 314-516-6996, E-mail: gradadm@umsl.edu. *Chairperson,* Dr. Matthew Keefer, 314-516-5783, Fax: 314-516-5784, E-mail: keefer@umsl.edu.

Division of Teaching and Learning Students: 117 full-time (68 women), 618 part-time (495 women); includes 150 minority (106 Black or African American, non-Hispanic/Latino; 2 American Indian or Alaska Native, non-Hispanic/Latino; 19 Asian, non-Hispanic/Latino; 19 Hispanic/Latino; 4 Two or more races, non-Hispanic/Latino), 17 international. Average age 30. 352 applicants, 83% accepted, 203 enrolled. *Faculty:* 33 full-time (17 women), 55 part-time/adjunct (38 women). Expenses: Contact institution. *Financial support:* In 2010–11, 5 research assistantships with full and partial tuition reimbursements (averaging $10,288 per year), 4 teaching assistantships with full and partial tuition reimbursements (averaging $6,800 per year) were awarded. Financial award application deadline: 4/1; financial award applicants required to submit FAFSA. In 2010, 212 master's, 4 other advanced degrees awarded. *Degree program information:* Part-time and evening/weekend programs available. Offers elementary education (M Ed); secondary education (M Ed); secondary school teaching (Certificate); special education (M Ed); teaching English to speakers of other languages (Certificate). *Application deadline:* For fall admission, 7/1 priority date for domestic and international students; for spring admission, 12/1 priority date for domestic and international students. *Application fee:* $35 ($40 for international students). Electronic applications accepted. *Application Contact:* 314-516-5458, Fax: 314-516-6996, E-mail: gadadm@umsl.edu. *Chair,* Dr. Joseph Polman, 314-516-5791.

College of Fine Arts and Communication Students: 9 full-time (all women), 38 part-time (24 women); includes 9 minority (8 Black or African American, non-Hispanic/Latino; 1 Hispanic/Latino), 1 international. Average age 30. *Faculty:* 22 full-time (10 women), 6 part-time/adjunct (3 women). Expenses: Contact institution. *Financial support:* In 2010–11, 6 teaching assistantships (averaging $11,571 per year) were awarded. In 2010, 23 master's awarded. Offers communication (MA); fine arts and communication (MA, MME); music education (MME). *Application deadline:* For fall admission, 7/1 priority date for domestic and international students; for spring admission, 12/1 priority date for domestic and international students. Applications are processed on a rolling basis. *Application fee:* $35 ($40 for international students). Electronic applications accepted. *Application Contact:* 314-516-5458, Fax: 314-516-6996, E-mail: gradadm@umsl.edu. *Dean,* Dr. Jim Richards, 314-516-5911, Fax: 314-516-5910.

College of Nursing Students: 4 full-time (3 women), 256 part-time (242 women); includes 32 minority (28 Black or African American, non-Hispanic/Latino; 1 Asian, non-Hispanic/Latino; 2 Hispanic/Latino; 1 Two or more races, non-Hispanic/Latino). Average age 37. *Faculty:* 14 full-time (13 women), 20 part-time/adjunct (19 women). Expenses: Contact institution. *Financial support:* In 2010–11, 3 research assistantships with full and partial tuition reimbursements (averaging $12,339 per year), 2 teaching assistantships with full and partial tuition reimbursements (averaging $12,339 per year) were awarded. Financial award application deadline: 4/1; financial award applicants required to submit FAFSA. In 2010, 66 master's, 4 doctorates, 4 other advanced degrees awarded. *Degree program information:* Part-time programs available. Offers adult nurse practitioner (DNP, Post Master's Certificate); clinical nurse specialist (DNP); family mental health nurse practitioner (DNP); family nurse practitioner (MSN, DNP, Post Master's Certificate); neonatal nurse practitioner (MSN); nurse educator (MSN); nurse leader (MSN); nurse practitioner (Post Master's Certificate); nursing (PhD); pediatric clinical nurse specialist (DNP); pediatric nurse practitioner (MSN, DNP, Post Master's Certificate); women's health nurse practitioner (MSN, Post Master's Certificate). *Application deadline:* For fall admission, 2/15 for domestic and international students. *Application fee:* $35 ($40 for international students). Electronic applications accepted. *Application Contact:* 314-516-5458, Fax: 314-516-6996, E-mail: gradadm@umsl.edu. *Dean,* Juliann Sebastian, 314-516-6066.

College of Optometry Students: 172 full-time (101 women), 4 part-time (1 woman); includes 7 Black or African American, non-Hispanic/Latino; 1 American Indian or Alaska Native, non-Hispanic/Latino; 19 Asian, non-Hispanic/Latino; 3 Hispanic/Latino, 3 international. Average age 23. 375 applicants, 30% accepted, 40 enrolled. *Faculty:* 23 full-time (6 women), 14 part-time/adjunct (4 women). Expenses: Contact institution. *Financial support:* In 2010–11, 140 students received support, including 6 research assistantships with full and partial tuition reimbursements available (averaging $500 per year), 4 teaching assistantships with full and partial tuition reimbursements available (averaging $23,000 per year); fellowships with full tuition reimbursements available, Federal Work-Study, institutionally sponsored loans, scholarships/grants, tuition waivers (partial), and unspecified assistantships also available. Financial award applicants required to submit FAFSA. In 2010, 43 first professional degrees awarded. Offers optometry (OD, MS, PhD); vision science (MS, PhD). *Application deadline:* For fall admission, 2/15 for domestic and international students. Applications are processed on a rolling basis. *Application fee:* $50. Electronic applications accepted. *Application Contact:* Dr. Edward S. Bennett, Director, Student Services, 314-516-6263, Fax: 314-516-6708, E-mail: optstuaff@umsl.edu. *Dean,* Dr. Larry J. Davis, 314-516-5606, Fax: 314-516-6708, E-mail: optometry@umsl.edu.

Graduate School Students: 36 full-time (21 women), 59 part-time (33 women); includes 17 minority (13 Black or African American, non-Hispanic/Latino; 2 American Indian or Alaska Native, non-Hispanic/Latino; 1 Asian, non-Hispanic/Latino; 1 Hispanic/Latino), 11 international. Average age 31. 60 applicants, 68% accepted, 24 enrolled. *Faculty:* 9 full-time (4 women), 8 part-time/adjunct (6 women). Expenses: Contact institution. *Financial support:* In 2010–11, 23 fellowships with full tuition reimbursements (averaging $4,564 per year), 3 research assistantships with full tuition reimbursements (averaging $11,000 per year) were awarded. Financial award application deadline: 4/1; financial award applicants required to submit FAFSA. In 2010, 23 master's, 17 Certificates awarded. *Degree program information:* Part-time and evening/weekend programs available. Offers health policy (MPPA); local government management (MPPA); managing human resources and organization (MPPA); nonprofit organization management (MPPA); nonprofit organization management and leadership (Certificate); policy research and analysis (MPPA). *Application deadline:* For fall admission, 7/1 priority date for domestic and international students; for spring admission, 12/1 priority date for domestic and international students. Applications are processed on a rolling basis. *Application fee:* $35 ($40 for international students). Electronic applications accepted. *Application Contact:* Graduate Admissions, 314-516-5458, Fax: 314-516-6996, E-mail: gradadm@umsl.edu. *Dean,* Dr. Judith Walker de Felix, 314-516-5900, Fax: 314-516-7015, E-mail: graduate@umsl.edu.

UNIVERSITY OF MOBILE, Mobile, AL 36613

General Information Independent-religious, coed, comprehensive institution. *Enrollment:* 1,673 graduate, professional, and undergraduate students; 50 full-time matriculated graduate/professional students (42 women), 143 part-time matriculated graduate/professional students (111 women). *Enrollment by degree level:* 193 master's. *Graduate faculty:* 17 full-time (7 women), 7 part-time/adjunct (5 women). *Tuition:* Full-time $3915; part-time $435 per credit hour. *Required fees:* $63 per semester. *Graduate housing:* Room and/or apartments available on a first-come, first-served basis to single students; on-campus housing not available to married students. Typical cost: $4590 per year ($7780 including board). Housing application deadline: 8/15. *Student services:* Campus employment opportunities, career counseling, free psychological counseling, international student services, low-cost health insurance. *Library facilities:* J. L. Bedsole Library. *Online resources:* library catalog, web page. *Collection:* 109,840 titles, 288 serial subscriptions, 1,908 audiovisual materials.

Computer facilities: 110 computers available on campus for general student use. A campuswide network can be accessed from student residence rooms and from off campus. Online class registration is available. *Web address:* http://www.umobile.edu/.

General Application Contact: Dr. Anne B. Lowery, Dean, Graduate Programs, 251-442-2332, Fax: 251-442-2523, E-mail: alowery@umobile.edu.

GRADUATE UNITS

Graduate Programs Students: 50 full-time (42 women), 143 part-time (111 women); includes 101 Black or African American, non-Hispanic/Latino; 4 American Indian or Alaska Native, non-Hispanic/Latino; 1 Asian, non-Hispanic/Latino; 1 Two or more races, non-Hispanic/Latino, 7 international. Average age 35. 67 applicants, 97% accepted, 54 enrolled. *Faculty:* 17 full-time (7 women), 7 part-time/adjunct (5 women). Expenses: Contact institution. In 2010, 56 master's awarded. *Degree program information:* Part-time and evening/weekend programs available. Offers biblical/theological studies (MA); business administration (MBA); education (MA); marriage and family counseling (MA); nursing (MSN); religious studies (MA). *Application deadline:* For fall admission, 8/3 priority date for domestic students. Applications are processed on a rolling basis. *Application fee:* $40 ($50 for international students). *Application Contact:* Tammy C. Eubanks, Administrative Assistant to the Dean of Graduate Programs, 251-442-2270, Fax: 251-442-2523, E-mail: teubanks@umobile.edu. *Dean,* Dr. Anne B. Lowery, 251-442-2332, Fax: 251-442-2523, E-mail: alowery@umobile.edu.

THE UNIVERSITY OF MONTANA, Missoula, MT 59812-0002

General Information State-supported, coed, university. CGS member. *Graduate housing:* Rooms and/or apartments available on a first-come, first-served basis to single and married students. *Research affiliation:* Arthur Carhart National Wilderness Training Center (environmental), Nature Center at Ft. Missoula Museum (environmental), World Trade Center (business), Rocky Mountain National Laboratories (medical), Community Hospital Medical Center (medical), Aldo Leopold Wilderness Institute (forestry).

GRADUATE UNITS

Graduate School *Degree program information:* Part-time programs available. Offers individual interdisciplinary programs (IIP) (PhD); interdisciplinary studies (MIS).

College of Arts and Sciences *Degree program information:* Part-time programs available. Offers anthropology (MA); applied geoscience (PhD); arts and sciences (MA, MFA, MPA, MS, PhD, Ed S); biochemistry (MS); biochemistry and microbiology (MS, PhD); chemistry (MS, PhD); clinical psychology (PhD); communication studies (MA); computer science (MS); creative writing (MFA); criminology (MA); cultural heritage (MA); cultural heritage studies (PhD); ecology of infectious disease (PhD); economics (MA); environmental studies (MS); experimental psychology (PhD); fiction (MFA); forensic anthropology (MA); French (MA); geography (MA); geology (MS, PhD); German (MA); historical anthropology (PhD); history (MA, PhD); integrative microbiology and biochemistry (PhD); linguistics (MA); literature (MA); mathematics (MA, PhD); mathematics education (MA); microbial ecology (MS, PhD); microbiology (MS); non-fiction (MFA); organismal biology and ecology (MS, PhD); philosophy (MA); poetry (MFA); political science (MA, MPA); public administration (MPA); rural and environmental change (MA); school psychology (MA, PhD, Ed S); sociology (MA); Spanish (MA); teaching (MA).

College of Forestry and Conservation Offers ecosystem management (MEM, MS); fish and wildlife biology (PhD); forestry (MS, PhD); recreation management (MS); resource conservation (MS); wildlife biology (MS).

College of Health Professions and Biomedical Sciences Offers biomedical and pharmaceutical sciences (MS, PhD); biomedical sciences (PhD); health professions and biomedical sciences (Pharm D, MPH, MS, MSW, DPT, PhD, CPH); neuroscience (MS, PhD); pharmaceutical sciences (MS); pharmacy (Pharm D); physical therapy (DPT); public health (MPH, CPH); social work (MSW); toxicology (MS, PhD).

School of Business Administration *Degree program information:* Part-time and evening/weekend programs available. Postbaccalaureate distance learning degree programs offered (minimal on-campus study). Offers accounting (M Acct); business administration (M Acct, MBA).

The University of Montana (continued)

School of Education *Degree program information:* Part-time programs available. Offers counselor education (MA, Ed D, Ed S); counselor education and supervision (Ed D); curriculum and instruction (M Ed, Ed D); education (M Ed, MA, MS, Ed D, Ed S); educational leadership (M Ed, Ed D, Ed S); exercise science (MS); health and human performance (MS); health promotion (MS); mental health counseling (MA); school counseling (MA).

School of Fine Arts Offers fine arts (MA, MFA); music (MM).

School of Journalism Offers journalism (MA). Electronic applications accepted.

School of Law Offers law (JD).

UNIVERSITY OF MONTEVALLO, Montevallo, AL 35115

General Information State-supported, coed, comprehensive institution. *Enrollment:* 3,050 graduate, professional, and undergraduate students; 234 full-time matriculated graduate/professional students (177 women), 268 part-time matriculated graduate/professional students (213 women). *Enrollment by degree level:* 398 master's, 104 other advanced degrees. Tuition, state resident: full-time $6264; part-time $261 per credit hour. Tuition, nonresident: full-time $12,528; part-time $502 per credit hour. *Required fees:* $251 per semester. *Graduate housing:* Room and/or apartments guaranteed to single students; on-campus housing not available to married students. Typical cost: $4924 (including board). *Student services:* Campus employment opportunities, campus safety program, career counseling, free psychological counseling, international student services, low-cost health insurance, writing training. *Library facilities:* Carmichael Library. *Online resources:* library catalog, web page, access to other libraries' catalogs. *Collection:* 266,236 titles, 27,962 serial subscriptions, 4,693 audiovisual materials.

Computer facilities: 340 computers available on campus for general student use. A campuswide network can be accessed from student residence rooms and from off campus. Online class registration is available. *Web address:* http://www.montevallo.edu/.

General Application Contact: Rebecca Hartley, Coordinator for Graduate Studies, 205-665-6350, Fax: 205-665-6353, E-mail: hartleyrs@montevallo.edu.

GRADUATE UNITS

College of Arts and Sciences Students: 41 full-time (39 women), 10 part-time (8 women); includes 5 minority (3 Black or African American, non-Hispanic/Latino; 2 Hispanic/Latino). Expenses: Contact institution. *Financial support:* Federal Work-Study, scholarships/grants, and unspecified assistantships available. In 2010, 25 master's awarded. *Degree program information:* Part-time and evening/weekend programs available. Offers arts and sciences (MA, MS); English literature (MA); speech-language pathology (MS). *Application deadline:* For fall admission, 7/15 for domestic students; for spring admission, 11/15 for domestic students. *Application fee:* $25. *Application Contact:* Rebecca Hartley, Coordinator for Graduate Studies, 205-665-6350, Fax: 205-665-6353, E-mail: hartleyrs@montevallo.edu. *Dean*, Dr. Mary Beth Armstrong, 205-665-6508.

College of Education Students: 187 full-time (135 women), 247 part-time (200 women); includes 89 minority (77 Black or African American, non-Hispanic/Latino; 3 American Indian or Alaska Native, non-Hispanic/Latino; 2 Hispanic/Latino; 7 Two or more races, non-Hispanic/Latino), 2 international. Expenses: Contact institution. *Financial support:* Federal Work-Study, scholarships/grants, and unspecified assistantships available. In 2010, 176 master's, 32 other advanced degrees awarded. *Degree program information:* Part-time and evening/weekend programs available. Offers community counseling (M Ed); education (M Ed, Ed S); elementary education (M Ed); instructional leadership (M Ed, Ed S); marriage and family (M Ed); school counseling (M Ed); secondary/high school education (M Ed). *Application deadline:* For fall admission, 7/15 for domestic students; for spring admission, 11/15 for domestic students. *Application fee:* $25. *Application Contact:* Rebecca Hartley, Assistant Director, 205-665-6350, E-mail: hartleyrs@montevallo.edu. *Dean*, Dr. Anna E. McEwan, 205-665-6360, E-mail: mcewanae@montevallo.edu.

Stephens College of Business Students: 6 full-time (3 women), 11 part-time (5 women); includes 4 minority (2 Black or African American, non-Hispanic/Latino; 1 Hispanic/Latino; 1 Two or more races, non-Hispanic/Latino). Expenses: Contact institution. *Degree program information:* Part-time and evening/weekend programs available. Offers business (MBA). *Application deadline:* For fall admission, 7/15 for domestic students; for spring admission, 11/15 for domestic students. *Application fee:* $25. *Application Contact:* Rebecca Hartley, Coordinator for Graduate Studies, 205-665-6350, Fax: 205-665-6353, E-mail: hartleyrs@montevallo.edu. *Dean*, Dr. Stephen H. Craft, 205-665-6540.

UNIVERSITY OF NEBRASKA AT KEARNEY, Kearney, NE 68849-0001

General Information State-supported, coed, comprehensive institution. CGS member. *Graduate housing:* Rooms and/or apartments available on a first-come, first-served basis to single and married students.

GRADUATE UNITS

College of Graduate Study *Degree program information:* Part-time and evening/weekend programs available.

College of Business and Technology *Degree program information:* Part-time and evening/weekend programs available. Offers business administration (MBA); business and technology (MBA). Electronic applications accepted.

College of Education *Degree program information:* Part-time and evening/weekend programs available. Offers adapted physical education (MA Ed); counseling (MS Ed, Ed S); curriculum and instruction (MS Ed); education (MA Ed, MS Ed, Ed S); educational administration (MA Ed, Ed S); exercise science (MA Ed); instructional technology (MS Ed); master teacher (MA Ed); reading education (MA Ed); school psychology (Ed S); special education (MA Ed); speech pathology (MS Ed); supervisor (MA Ed). Electronic applications accepted.

College of Fine Arts and Humanities *Degree program information:* Part-time and evening/weekend programs available. Offers art education (MA Ed); creative writing (MA); fine arts and humanities (MA, MA Ed); French (MA Ed); German (MA Ed); literature (MA); music education (MA Ed); Spanish (MA Ed). Electronic applications accepted.

College of Natural and Social Sciences *Degree program information:* Part-time and evening/weekend programs available. Offers biology (MS); history (MA); natural and social sciences (MA, MS, MS Ed); science education (MS Ed). Electronic applications accepted.

UNIVERSITY OF NEBRASKA AT OMAHA, Omaha, NE 68182

General Information State-supported, coed, university. CGS member. *Enrollment:* 14,665 graduate, professional, and undergraduate students; 656 full-time matriculated graduate/professional students (361 women), 1,635 part-time matriculated graduate/professional students (968 women). *Graduate faculty:* 319 full-time (132 women). *Graduate housing:* Room and/or apartments available on a first-come, first-served basis to single students; on-campus housing not available to married students. *Student services:* Campus employment opportunities, campus safety program, career counseling, child daycare facilities, exercise/wellness program, free psychological counseling, grant writing training, international student services, low-cost health insurance, multicultural affairs office, services for students with disabilities, teacher training, writing training. *Library facilities:* Criss Library. *Online resources:* library catalog, web page, access to other libraries' catalogs. *Collection:* 1.5 million titles, 71,187 serial subscriptions, 13,003 audiovisual materials.

Computer facilities: Computer purchase and lease plans are available. 2,000 computers available on campus for general student use. A campuswide network can be accessed from student residence rooms and from off campus. Online class registration is available. *Web address:* http://www.unomaha.edu/.

General Application Contact: Penny Harmoney, Director, Graduate Studies, 402-554-2341, Fax: 402-554-3143, E-mail: graduate@unomaha.edu.

GRADUATE UNITS

Graduate Studies Students: 671 full-time (371 women), 1,635 part-time (968 women); includes 199 minority (91 Black or African American, non-Hispanic/Latino; 6 American Indian or Alaska Native, non-Hispanic/Latino; 42 Asian, non-Hispanic/Latino; 56 Hispanic/Latino; 4 Two or more races, non-Hispanic/Latino), 197 international. Average age 33. 1,320 applicants, 51% accepted, 533 enrolled. *Faculty:* 323 full-time (134 women). Expenses: Contact institution. *Financial support:* In 2010–11, 1,193 students received support; fellowships, research assistantships with tuition reimbursements available, teaching assistantships with tuition reimbursements available, career-related internships or fieldwork, Federal Work-Study, institutionally sponsored loans, tuition waivers (partial), and unspecified assistantships available. Support available to part-time students. Financial award application deadline: 3/1; financial award applicants required to submit FAFSA. In 2010, 680 master's, 21 doctorates, 57 other advanced degrees awarded. *Degree program information:* Part-time and evening/weekend programs available. Postbaccalaureate distance learning degree programs offered (no on-campus study). Offers writing (MFA). *Application deadline:* Applications are processed on a rolling basis. *Application fee:* $45. Electronic applications accepted. *Application Contact:* Penny Harmoney, Director, Graduate Studies, 402-554-2341, Fax: 402-554-3143, E-mail: graduate@unomaha.edu. *Dean*, Dr. Deborah Smith-Howell, 402-554-4849.

College of Arts and Sciences Students: 118 full-time (62 women), 239 part-time (132 women); includes 30 minority (6 Black or African American, non-Hispanic/Latino; 4 American Indian or Alaska Native, non-Hispanic/Latino; 4 Asian, non-Hispanic/Latino; 14 Hispanic/Latino; 2 Two or more races, non-Hispanic/Latino), 14 international. Average age 33. 222 applicants, 53% accepted, 96 enrolled. *Faculty:* 110 full-time (41 women). Expenses: Contact institution. *Financial support:* In 2010–11, 219 students received support; fellowships, research assistantships with tuition reimbursements available, teaching assistantships with tuition reimbursements available, career-related internships or fieldwork, Federal Work-Study, institutionally sponsored loans, scholarships/grants, tuition waivers (partial), and unspecified assistantships available. Support available to part-time students. Financial award application deadline: 3/1; financial award applicants required to submit FAFSA. In 2010, 90 master's, 2 doctorates, 21 other advanced degrees awarded. *Degree program information:* Part-time and evening/weekend programs available. Offers advanced writing (Certificate); arts and sciences (MA, MAT, MS, PhD, Certificate, Ed S); biology (MS); developmental psychology (PhD); English (MA); geographic information science (Certificate); geography (MA); history (MA); industrial/organizational psychology (MS, PhD); language teaching (MA); mathematics (MA, MAT, MS); political science (MS); psychobiology (PhD); psychology (MA); school psychology (MS, Ed S); teaching English to speakers of other languages (Certificate); technical communication (Certificate). *Application deadline:* For fall admission, 3/1 priority date for domestic students; for spring admission, 10/1 priority date for domestic students. Applications are processed on a rolling basis. *Application fee:* $45. Electronic applications accepted. *Application Contact:* Penny Harmoney, Director, Graduate Studies, 402-554-2341, Fax: 402-554-3143, E-mail: graduate@unomaha.edu. *Dean*, Dr. David Boocker, 402-554-2338.

College of Business Administration Students: 128 full-time (47 women), 294 part-time (98 women); includes 46 minority (18 Black or African American, non-Hispanic/Latino; 1 American Indian or Alaska Native, non-Hispanic/Latino; 17 Asian, non-Hispanic/Latino; 10 Hispanic/Latino), 51 international. Average age 31. 254 applicants, 48% accepted, 104 enrolled. *Faculty:* 40 full-time (12 women). Expenses: Contact institution. *Financial support:* In 2010–11, 158 students received support; fellowships, research assistantships with tuition reimbursements available, career-related internships or fieldwork, Federal Work-Study, institutionally sponsored loans, scholarships/grants, tuition waivers (partial), and unspecified assistantships available. Support available to part-time students. Financial award application deadline: 3/1; financial award applicants required to submit FAFSA. In 2010, 144 master's awarded. *Degree program information:* Part-time and evening/weekend programs available. Offers accounting (M Acc); business administration (EMBA, M Acc, MA, MBA, MS); economics (MA, MS). *Application deadline:* For fall admission, 7/1 priority date for domestic students; for spring admission, 12/1 priority date for domestic students. Applications are processed on a rolling basis. *Application fee:* $45. Electronic applications accepted. *Application Contact:* Lex Kaczmarek, Director, 402-554-2303. *Associate*, Dr. Louis Pol, 402-554-2303.

College of Communication, Fine Arts and Media Students: 37 full-time (23 women), 88 part-time (58 women); includes 16 minority (10 Black or African American, non-Hispanic/Latino; 4 Asian, non-Hispanic/Latino; 2 Hispanic/Latino), 2 international. Average age 34. 64 applicants, 72% accepted, 36 enrolled. *Faculty:* 41 full-time (17 women). Expenses: Contact institution. *Financial support:* In 2010–11, 88 students received support; fellowships, research assistantships with tuition reimbursements available, career-related internships or fieldwork, Federal Work-Study, institutionally sponsored loans, traineeships, tuition waivers (full), and unspecified assistantships available. Support available to part-time students. Financial award application deadline: 3/1; financial award applicants required to submit FAFSA. In 2010, 27 master's awarded. *Degree program information:* Part-time and evening/weekend programs available. Offers communication (MA); communication, fine arts and media (MA, MM); music (MM); theatre (MA). *Application deadline:* For fall admission, 7/1 priority date for domestic students; for spring admission, 12/1 priority date for domestic students. Applications are processed on a rolling basis. *Application fee:* $45. Electronic applications accepted. *Application Contact:* Penny Harmoney, Director, Graduate Studies, 402-554-2341, Fax: 402-554-3143, E-mail: graduate@unomaha.edu. *Dean*, Dr. Gail Baker, 402-554-2231.

College of Education Students: 124 full-time (79 women), 621 part-time (484 women); includes 52 minority (34 Black or African American, non-Hispanic/Latino; 4 Asian, non-Hispanic/Latino; 14 Hispanic/Latino), 10 international. Average age 33. 194 applicants, 65% accepted, 97 enrolled. *Faculty:* 52 full-time (27 women). Expenses: Contact institution. *Financial support:* In 2010–11, 355 students received support; fellowships, research assistantships with tuition reimbursements available, teaching assistantships with tuition reimbursements available, career-related internships or fieldwork, Federal Work-Study, institutionally sponsored loans, scholarships/grants, tuition waivers (full), and unspecified assistantships available. Support available to part-time students. Financial award application deadline: 3/1; financial award applicants required to submit FAFSA. In 2010, 226 master's, 11 doctorates, 1 other advanced degree awarded. *Degree program information:* Part-time and evening/weekend programs available. Offers community counseling (MA, MS); counseling gerontology (MA, MS); education (MA, MS, Ed D, Certificate, Ed S); educational administration and supervision (MS, Ed D, Ed S); elementary education (MA, MS); health, physical education, and recreation (MA, MS); instruction in urban schools (Certificate); instructional technology (Certificate); reading education (MS); school counseling (MA, MS); secondary education (MA, MS); special education (MA, MS); speech-language pathology (MA, MS); student affairs practice in higher education (MA, MS). *Application deadline:* For fall admission, 3/1 priority date for domestic students; for spring admission, 10/1 priority date for domestic students. Applications are processed on a rolling basis. *Application fee:* $45. *Application Contact:* Penny Harmoney, Director, Graduate Studies, 402-554-2341, Fax: 402-554-3143, E-mail: graduate@unomaha.edu. *Chairperson*, Dr. Nancy Edick, 402-554-2212.

College of Information Science and Technology Students: 83 full-time (22 women), 138 part-time (38 women); includes 17 minority (7 Black or African American, non-Hispanic/Latino; 6 Asian, non-Hispanic/Latino; 3 Hispanic/Latino; 1 Two or more races, non-Hispanic/Latino), 103 international. Average age 40. 242 applicants, 40% accepted, 63 enrolled. *Faculty:* 27 full-time (8 women). Expenses: Contact institution. *Financial support:* In 2010–11, 111 students received support; fellowships, research assistantships with tuition reimbursements available, teaching assistantships with tuition reimbursements available, career-related internships or fieldwork, Federal Work-Study, institutionally sponsored loans, scholarships/grants, tuition waivers (full), and unspecified assistantships available. Financial award application deadline: 3/1; financial award applicants required to submit FAFSA. In 2010, 58 master's, 5 doctorates, 23 other advanced degrees awarded. *Degree program information:* Part-time and evening/weekend programs available. Offers computer science (MA, MS); information science and technology (MA, MS, PhD, Certificate); information systems and quantitative analysis (Certificate); information technology (PhD); management information systems (MS). *Application deadline:* For fall admission, 7/1 priority date for domestic students; for spring admission, 12/1 priority date for domestic students. Applications are processed on a rolling basis. *Application fee:* $45. Electronic applications accepted. *Application Contact:* Penny Harmoney, Director, Graduate Studies, 402-554-2341, Fax: 402-554-3143, E-mail: graduate@unomaha.edu. *Dean*, Dr. Hesham Ali, 402-554-2276.

College of Public Affairs and Community Service Students: 166 full-time (128 women), 255 part-time (158 women); includes 35 minority (15 Black or African American, non-Hispanic/Latino; 1 American Indian or Alaska Native, non-Hispanic/Latino; 7 Asian, non-Hispanic/Latino; 11 Hispanic/Latino; 1 Two or more races, non-Hispanic/Latino), 17 international. Average age 30. 322 applicants, 48% accepted, 128 enrolled. *Faculty:* 49 full-time (27 women). Expenses: Contact institution. *Financial support:* In 2010–11, 262 students received support, including 28 research assistantships with tuition reimbursements available; fellowships, teaching assistantships with tuition reimbursements available, career-related internships or fieldwork, Federal Work-Study, institutionally sponsored loans, scholarships/grants, tuition waivers (partial), and unspecified assistantships also available. Support available to part-time students. Financial award application deadline: 3/1; financial award applicants required to submit FAFSA. In 2010, 116 master's, 3 doctorates, 10 other advanced degrees awarded. *Degree program information:* Part-time and evening/weekend programs available. Postbaccalaureate distance learning degree programs offered (no on-campus study). Offers criminal justice (MA, MS, PhD); gerontology (Certificate); public administration (MPA, PhD); public affairs and community service (MA, MPA, MS, MSW, PhD, Certificate); public management (Certificate); social gerontology (MA); social work (MSW); urban studies (MS). *Application deadline:* Applications are processed on a rolling basis. *Application fee:* $45. Electronic applications accepted. *Application Contact:* Penny Harmoney, Director, Graduate Studies, 402-554-2341, Fax: 402-554-3143, E-mail: graduate@unomaha.edu. *Chairperson*, Dr. Burton J. Reed, 402-554-2276.

UNIVERSITY OF NEBRASKA–LINCOLN, Lincoln, NE 68588

General Information State-supported, coed, university. CGS member. *Graduate housing:* Rooms and/or apartments available on a first-come, first-served basis to single and married students. Housing application deadline: 7/1. *Research affiliation:* U. S. Meat Animal Research Center.

GRADUATE UNITS

College of Law Offers law (JD); legal studies (MLS); space and telecommunications law (LL M). Electronic applications accepted.

Graduate College *Degree program information:* Part-time and evening/weekend programs available. Postbaccalaureate distance learning degree programs offered. Offers environmental health, occupational health and toxicology (MS, PhD); survey research and methodology (MS, PhD). Electronic applications accepted.

College of Agricultural Sciences and Natural Resources Offers agribusiness (MBA); agricultural economics (MS, PhD); agricultural sciences and natural resources (M Ag, MA, MBA, MS, PhD); agronomy (MS, PhD); animal science (MS, PhD); biochemistry (MS, PhD); community development (M Ag); distance education specialization (MS); entomology (MS, PhD); food science and technology (MS, PhD); geography (PhD); horticulture (MS, PhD); leadership development (MS); leadership education (MS); mechanized systems management (MS); natural resources (MS, PhD); nutrition (MS, PhD); nutrition outreach education specialization (MS); statistics (MS, PhD); teaching and extension education specialization (MS); veterinary science (MS). Electronic applications accepted.

College of Architecture Offers architecture (M Arch, MCRP, MS, PhD); community and regional planning (MCRP); interior design (MS). Electronic applications accepted.

College of Arts and Sciences Offers analytical chemistry (PhD); anthropology (MA); arts and sciences (M Sc T, MA, MAT, MS, PhD, Graduate Certificate); astronomy (MS, PhD); biochemistry (PhD); bioinformatics (MS, PhD); biological sciences (MA, MS, PhD); biopsychology (PhD); chemistry (MS); classics and religious studies (MA); clinical psychology (PhD); cognitive psychology (PhD); composition and rhetoric (MA, PhD); computer engineering (MS, PhD); computer science (MS, PhD); creative writing (MA, PhD); developmental psychology (PhD); French (MA, PhD); geography (MA, PhD); geosciences (MS, PhD); German (MA, PhD); history (MA, PhD); information technology (PhD); inorganic chemistry (PhD); instructional communication (MA, PhD); interpersonal communication (MA, PhD); literature studies (MA, PhD); marketing, communication studies, and advertising (MA, PhD); materials chemistry (PhD); mathematics (MA, MAT, MS, PhD); mathematics and computer science (PhD); organic chemistry (PhD); organizational communication (MA, PhD); philosophy (MA, PhD); physical chemistry (PhD); physics (MS, PhD); political science (MA, PhD); professional archaeology (MA); psychology (MA); public policy analysis (Graduate Certificate); rhetoric and culture (MA, PhD); social/personality psychology (PhD); sociology (MA, PhD); Spanish (MA, PhD). Electronic applications accepted.

College of Business Administration *Degree program information:* Part-time and evening/weekend programs available. Offers accountancy (MPA, PhD); actuarial science (MS); business (MA, MBA, PhD); business administration (MA, MBA, MPA, MS, PhD); economics (MA, PhD); finance (MA, PhD); management (MA, PhD); marketing (MA, PhD). Electronic applications accepted.

College of Education and Human Sciences Offers administration, curriculum and instruction (Ed D, PhD); adult and continuing education (MA); audiology and hearing science (Au D); audiology research (PhD); child development/early childhood education (MS, PhD); child, youth and family studies (MS); clinical audiology (Au D); cognition, learning and development (MA); community nutrition and health promotion (MS); counseling psychology (MA); education and human sciences (M Ed, MA, MS, MST, Au D, Ed D, PhD, Certificate, Ed S); educational administration (M Ed, MA, Ed D, Certificate); educational psychology (MA, Ed S); educational studies (Ed D, PhD); family and consumer sciences education (MS, PhD); family financial planning (MS); family science (MS, PhD); gerontology (PhD); human sciences (PhD); marriage and family therapy (MS); medical family therapy (PhD); merchandising (MS); nutrition (MS, PhD); nutrition and exercise (MS); nutrition and health sciences (MS, PhD); psychological studies in education (PhD); quantitative, qualitative, and psychometric methods (MA); school psychology (MA, Ed S); special education (M Ed, MA, Ed S); speech-language pathology and audiology (MS, Au D); teaching, learning and teacher education (M Ed, MA, MST, Ed D, PhD); textile history/quilt studies (MA); textile science (MS); textile-apparel (MA); textiles, clothing and design (MA, MS); vocational and adult education (M Ed, MA); youth development (MS). Electronic applications accepted.

College of Engineering Offers agricultural and biological systems engineering (MS, PhD); architectural engineering (M Eng, MAE, MS, PhD); chemical and biomolecular engineering (MS, PhD); chemical and materials engineering (PhD); civil engineering (MS, PhD); electrical engineering (MS, PhD); engineering (M Eng, MAE, MEE, MS, PhD); engineering management (M Eng); engineering mechanics (MS, PhD); environmental engineering (MS, PhD); industrial and management systems engineering (MS, PhD); manufacturing systems engineering (MS); mechanical engineering (MS, PhD); mechanized systems management (MS). Electronic applications accepted.

College of Fine and Performing Arts Offers acting (MFA); art and art history (MA, MFA); art history (MA); composition (MM, DMA); conducting (MM, DMA); costume (MFA); directing (MFA); fine and performing arts (MA, MFA, MM, DMA, PhD); music education (MM, PhD); music history (MM); music theory (MM); performance (MM, DMA); piano pedagogy (MM); stage design (MFA); studio art (MFA); woodwind specialties (MM). Electronic applications accepted.

College of Journalism and Mass Communications Postbaccalaureate distance learning degree programs offered (no on-campus study). Offers marketing, communication and advertising (MA); professional journalism (MA). Electronic applications accepted.

UNIVERSITY OF NEBRASKA MEDICAL CENTER, Omaha, NE 68198

General Information State-supported, coed, upper-level institution. CGS member. *Enrollment:* 1,560 full-time matriculated graduate/professional students (864 women), 482 part-time matriculated graduate/professional students (409 women). *Enrollment by degree level:* 913 first professional, 625 master's, 443 doctoral, 61 other advanced degrees. *Graduate faculty:* 951 full-time (396 women), 205 part-time/adjunct (95 women). Tuition, state resident: part-time $198.25 per semester hour. *Required fees:* $63 per semester. *Graduate housing:* On-campus housing not available. *Student services:* Campus employment opportunities, campus safety program, child daycare facilities, exercise/wellness program, free psychological counseling, international student services, low-cost health insurance, multicultural affairs office, services for students with disabilities. *Library facilities:* McGoogan Medical Library. *Online resources:* library catalog, web page, access to other libraries' catalogs. *Collection:* 238,074 titles, 6,403 serial subscriptions. *Research affiliation:* UNeMed Corporation (biotechnology).

Computer facilities: 100 computers available on campus for general student use. A campuswide network can be accessed from off campus. Various software packages available. *Web address:* http://www.unmc.edu/.

General Application Contact: Tymaree Tonjes, Student Records Technician, 402-559-6468, Fax: 402-559-6796, E-mail: ttonjes@unmc.edu.

GRADUATE UNITS

College of Dentistry Students: 183 full-time (89 women), 11 part-time (7 women); includes 1 Black or African American, non-Hispanic/Latino; 16 Asian, non-Hispanic/Latino; 5 Hispanic/Latino. Average age 25. 845 applicants, 6% accepted, 47 enrolled. *Faculty:* 56 full-time (11 women), 57 part-time/adjunct (18 women). Expenses: Contact institution. *Financial support:* Federal Work-Study, scholarships/grants, and stipends available. Support available to part-time students. Financial award application deadline: 3/10; financial award applicants required to submit FAFSA. In 2010, 47 first professional degrees awarded. Offers dentistry (DDS, MS, PhD, Certificate). *Application deadline:* For fall admission, 12/1 priority date for domestic students; for spring admission, 2/1 for domestic students. *Application fee:* $50. *Application Contact:* Glenda Canfield, Admissions Secretary, 402-472-1363, Fax: 402-472-5290, E-mail: gmcanfie@unmc.edu. *Dean*, Dr. John W. Reinhardt, 402-472-1344.

College of Medicine Offers medicine (MD, Certificate). Electronic applications accepted.

College of Pharmacy Students: 235 full-time (147 women); includes 6 Black or African American, non-Hispanic/Latino; 17 Asian, non-Hispanic/Latino; 2 Hispanic/Latino. Average age 23. 170 applicants, 33% accepted, 43 enrolled. *Faculty:* 29 full-time (4 women), 18 part-time/adjunct (11 women). Expenses: Contact institution. *Financial support:* Career-related internships or fieldwork, Federal Work-Study, institutionally sponsored loans, and scholarships/grants available. Financial award application deadline: 4/1; financial award applicants required to submit FAFSA. In 2010, 69 Pharm Ds awarded. Offers pharmacy (Pharm D). *Application deadline:* For fall admission, 12/1 for domestic students. Applications are processed on a rolling basis. *Application fee:* $45. Electronic applications accepted. *Application Contact:* Dr. Charles H. Krobot, Associate Dean for Student Affairs, 402-559-4333, Fax: 402-559-5060, E-mail: ckrobot@unmc.edu. *Dean*, Dr. Courtney V. Fletcher, 402-559-4333, Fax: 402-559-5060, E-mail: cfletcher@unmc.edu.

Graduate Studies Students: 1,267 full-time (870 women), 430 part-time (372 women); includes 17 Black or African American, non-Hispanic/Latino; 1 American Indian or Alaska Native, non-Hispanic/Latino; 45 Asian, non-Hispanic/Latino; 19 Hispanic/Latino, 110 international. Average age 34. 3,926 applicants, 20% accepted, 667 enrolled. *Faculty:* 321 full-time (105 women), 203 part-time/adjunct (180 women). Expenses: Contact institution. *Financial support:* In 2010–11, 8 fellowships with tuition reimbursements (averaging $21,000 per year), 26 research assistantships with tuition reimbursements (averaging $21,000 per year), teaching assistantships with tuition reimbursements (averaging $16,500 per year) were awarded; career-related internships or fieldwork, institutionally sponsored loans, scholarships/grants, traineeships, tuition waivers (full), and unspecified assistantships also available. Support available to part-time students. Financial award applicants required to submit FAFSA. In 2010, 165 master's, 34 doctorates awarded. *Degree program information:* Part-time programs available. Postbaccalaureate distance learning degree programs offered. Offers biochemistry and molecular biology (MS, PhD); cancer research (PhD); environmental health, occupational health and toxicology (MS, PhD); genetics, cell biology and anatomy (MS, PhD); medical sciences (MS, PhD); neuroscience (MS, PhD); nursing (MSN, PhD); pathology and microbiology (MS, PhD); pharmaceutical sciences (MS, PhD); pharmacology (MS, PhD); physiology (MS, PhD); public health (MPH). *Application deadline:* For fall admission, 6/1 for domestic students, 4/1 for international students; for spring admission, 10/1 for domestic students, 8/1 for international students. Applications are processed on a rolling basis. *Application fee:* $45. Electronic applications accepted. *Application Contact:* Dan Teet, Graduate Studies Associate, 402-559-6531, Fax: 402-559-7845, E-mail: unmcgraduatestudies@unmc.edu. *Executive Associate Dean*, Dr. David A. Crouse, 402-559-6531, Fax: 402-559-7845, E-mail: dcrouse@unmc.edu.

School of Allied Health Professions 821 applicants, 22% accepted, 183 enrolled. Expenses: Contact institution. *Financial support:* Scholarships/grants available. Financial award applicants required to submit FAFSA. In 2010, 50 master's, 50 doctorates, 10 other advanced degrees awarded. Offers allied health professions (MPAS, MPS, DPT, Certificate); cytotechnology (Certificate); dietetic internship (Certificate); distance education perfusion education (MPS); perfusion science (MPS); physical therapy education (DPT); physician assistant education (MPAS). *Application fee:* $70. *Application Contact:* Anne Constantino, Director of Student Affairs, 402-559-6673, Fax: 402-559-8696, E-mail: sahpadmissions@unmc.edu. *Senior Associate Dean*, Kyle P. Meyer, 402-559-6680, E-mail: kpmeyer@unmc.edu.

UNIVERSITY OF NEVADA, LAS VEGAS, Las Vegas, NV 89154

General Information State-supported, coed, university. CGS member. *Enrollment:* 28,222 graduate, professional, and undergraduate students; 2,170 full-time matriculated graduate/professional students (1,230 women), 1,693 part-time matriculated graduate/professional students (1,053 women). *Enrollment by degree level:* 2,857 master's, 930 doctoral, 76 other advanced degrees. *Graduate faculty:* 692 full-time (228 women), 161 part-time/adjunct (74 women). Tuition, state resident: part-time $239.50 per credit. Tuition, nonresident: part-time $503 per credit. *Required fees:* $108 per semester. Tuition and fees vary according to course load, program and reciprocity agreements. *Graduate housing:* Room and/or apartments available on a first-come, first-served basis to single students; on-campus housing not available to married students. Typical cost: $3273 per year ($5078 including board). Room and board charges vary according to board plan. Housing application deadline: 5/1. *Student services:* Campus employment opportunities, campus safety program, career counseling, child daycare facilities, exercise/wellness program, free psychological counseling, grant writing training, international student services, low-cost health insurance, multicultural affairs office, services for students with disabilities, teacher training, writing training. *Library facilities:* Lied Library plus 4 others. *Online resources:* library catalog, web page, access to other libraries' catalogs.

Computer facilities: A campuswide network can be accessed from student residence rooms and from off campus. Online class registration is available. *Web address:* http://www.unlv.edu/.

General Application Contact: Dr. Frederick Krauss, Director of Graduate Outreach, 702-895-5773, Fax: 702-895-4180, E-mail: frederick.krauss@unlv.edu.

GRADUATE UNITS

Graduate College Students: 2,170 full-time (1,230 women), 1,693 part-time (1,053 women); includes 1,437 minority (184 Black or African American, non-Hispanic/Latino; 16 American Indian or Alaska Native, non-Hispanic/Latino; 152 Asian, non-Hispanic/Latino; 309 Hispanic/Latino; 30 Native Hawaiian or other Pacific Islander, non-Hispanic/Latino; 746 Two or more races, non-Hispanic/Latino), 414 international. Average age 31. 2,656 applicants, 57% accepted, 1042 enrolled. *Faculty:* 692 full-time (228 women), 161 part-time/adjunct (74 women). Expenses: Contact institution. *Financial support:* In 2010–11, 895 students received support, including 4 fellowships with full tuition reimbursements available (averaging $17,000 per year), 372 research assistantships with partial tuition reimbursements available (averaging $11,822 per year), 518 teaching assistantships with partial tuition reimbursements available (averaging $10,905 per year); institutionally sponsored loans, scholarships/grants, health care benefits, and unspecified assistantships also available. Financial award application deadline: 3/1. In 2010, 1,252 master's, 115 doctorates, 48 other advanced degrees awarded. *Degree program information:* Part-time and evening/weekend programs available. *Application deadline:* Applications are processed on a rolling basis. *Application fee:* $60 ($95 for international students). Electronic applications accepted. *Application Contact:* Graduate College Admissions Evaluator, 702-895-3320, Fax: 702-895-4180, E-mail: gradcollege@unlv.edu. *Vice President for Research/Dean*, Dr. Ronald Smith, 702-895-4070, Fax: 702-895-4180, E-mail: ron.smith@unlv.edu.

University of Nevada, Las Vegas (continued)

College of Business Students: 260 full-time (99 women), 158 part-time (70 women); includes 124 minority (7 Black or African American, non-Hispanic/Latino; 1 American Indian or Alaska Native, non-Hispanic/Latino; 41 Asian, non-Hispanic/Latino; 19 Hispanic/Latino; 56 Two or more races, non-Hispanic/Latino), 63 international. Average age 30. 272 applicants, 72% accepted, 120 enrolled. *Faculty:* 55 full-time (6 women), 6 part-time/adjunct (2 women). Expenses: Contact institution. *Financial support:* In 2010–11, 36 students received support, including 34 research assistantships with partial tuition reimbursements available (averaging $10,000 per year), 2 teaching assistantships with partial tuition reimbursements available (averaging $10,000 per year); institutionally sponsored loans, scholarships/grants, health care benefits, and unspecified assistantships also available. Financial award application deadline: 3/1. In 2010, 170 master's, 1 other advanced degree awarded. *Degree program information:* Part-time and evening/weekend programs available. Offers accounting (MS, Advanced Certificate, Certificate); business (Exec MBA, MA, MBA, MS, Advanced Certificate, Certificate); business administration (Exec MBA, MBA); economics (MA); finance (Certificate); management (Certificate); management information systems (MS, Certificate); new venture management (Certificate). *Application fee:* $60 ($95 for international students). *Application Contact:* Graduate College Admissions Evaluator, 702-895-3320, Fax: 702-895-4180, E-mail: gradcollege@unlv.edu. *Dean,* Dr. Paul Jarley, 702-895-3362, Fax: 702-895-4090, E-mail: paul.jarley@unlv.edu.

College of Education Students: 568 full-time (418 women), 686 part-time (484 women); includes 467 minority (83 Black or African American, non-Hispanic/Latino; 8 American Indian or Alaska Native, non-Hispanic/Latino; 33 Asian, non-Hispanic/Latino; 125 Hispanic/Latino; 13 Native Hawaiian or other Pacific Islander, non-Hispanic/Latino; 205 Two or more races, non-Hispanic/Latino), 36 international. Average age 34. 495 applicants, 77% accepted, 291 enrolled. *Faculty:* 108 full-time (58 women), 55 part-time/adjunct (40 women). Expenses: Contact institution. *Financial support:* In 2010–11, 115 students received support, including 1 fellowship with full tuition reimbursement available (averaging $14,000 per year), 49 research assistantships with partial tuition reimbursements available (averaging $10,781 per year), 65 teaching assistantships with partial tuition reimbursements available (averaging $9,396 per year); institutionally sponsored loans, scholarships/grants, health care benefits, and unspecified assistantships also available. Financial award application deadline: 3/1. In 2010, 534 master's, 32 doctorates, 14 other advanced degrees awarded. *Degree program information:* Part-time and evening/weekend programs available. Offers clinical mental health counseling (MS); community mental health counseling (Advanced Certificate); curriculum and instruction (M Ed, MS, Ed D, PhD); early childhood education (M Ed); education (M Ed, MS, Ed D, PhD, Advanced Certificate, Ed S); educational leadership (M Ed, MS, PhD); educational psychology (MS); learning and technology (PhD); physical education (M Ed, MS); rehabilitation counseling (Advanced Certificate); school counseling (M Ed); school psychology (PhD, Ed S); special education (MS, Ed D, PhD, Ed S); sports education leadership (PhD); teacher education (PhD). *Application fee:* $60 ($95 for international students). *Application Contact:* Graduate College Admissions Evaluator, 702-895-3320, Fax: 702-895-4180, E-mail: gradcollege@unlv.edu. *Interim Dean,* Dr. William Speer, 702-895-3375, Fax: 702-895-4068, E-mail: william.speer@unlv.edu.

College of Fine Arts Students: 163 full-time (73 women), 53 part-time (29 women); includes 70 minority (8 Black or African American, non-Hispanic/Latino; 5 Asian, non-Hispanic/Latino; 11 Hispanic/Latino; 46 Two or more races, non-Hispanic/Latino), 20 international. Average age 31. 222 applicants, 64% accepted, 87 enrolled. *Faculty:* 58 full-time (11 women), 33 part-time/adjunct (7 women). Expenses: Contact institution. *Financial support:* In 2010–11, 103 students received support, including 31 research assistantships with partial tuition reimbursements available (averaging $10,625 per year), 72 teaching assistantships with partial tuition reimbursements available (averaging $10,690 per year); institutionally sponsored loans, scholarships/grants, health care benefits, and unspecified assistantships also available. Financial award application deadline: 3/1. In 2010, 52 master's, 5 doctorates awarded. *Degree program information:* Part-time programs available. Offers architecture (M Arch); art (MFA); fine arts (M Arch, MA, MFA, MM, DMA); music (MM); musical arts (DMA); screenwriting (MFA); theatre arts (MA, MFA). *Application fee:* $60 ($95 for international students). *Application Contact:* Graduate College Admissions Evaluator, 702-895-3320, Fax: 702-895-4180, E-mail: gradcollege@unlv.edu. *Dean,* Dr. Jeffrey Koep, 702-895-4210, Fax: 702-895-4194, E-mail: jeffrey.koep@unlv.edu.

College of Liberal Arts Students: 224 full-time (135 women), 139 part-time (78 women); includes 157 minority (11 Black or African American, non-Hispanic/Latino; 8 Asian, non-Hispanic/Latino; 31 Hispanic/Latino; 3 Native Hawaiian or other Pacific Islander, non-Hispanic/Latino; 104 Two or more races, non-Hispanic/Latino), 19 international. Average age 33. 505 applicants, 22% accepted, 85 enrolled. *Faculty:* 130 full-time (51 women), 12 part-time/adjunct (5 women). Expenses: Contact institution. *Financial support:* In 2010–11, 204 students received support, including 2 fellowships with full tuition reimbursements available (averaging $20,000 per year), 46 research assistantships with partial tuition reimbursements available (averaging $11,926 per year), 156 teaching assistantships with partial tuition reimbursements available (averaging $11,278 per year); institutionally sponsored loans, scholarships/grants, health care benefits, and unspecified assistantships also available. Financial award application deadline: 3/1. In 2010, 52 master's, 18 doctorates, 2 other advanced degrees awarded. *Degree program information:* Part-time programs available. Offers anthropology and ethnic studies (MA, PhD); creative writing (MFA); English (MA, PhD); ethics and policy studies (MA); Hispanic studies (MA); history (MA, PhD); liberal arts (MA, MFA, PhD, Certificate); political science (MA, PhD); psychology (MA, PhD); sociology (MA, PhD); women's studies (Certificate). *Application fee:* $60 ($95 for international students). *Application Contact:* Graduate College Admissions Evaluator, 702-895-3320, Fax: 702-895-4180, E-mail: gradcollege@unlv.edu. *Dean,* Dr. Chris Hudgins, 702-895-3401, Fax: 702-895-4097, E-mail: chris.hudgins@unlv.edu.

College of Science Students: 185 full-time (78 women), 56 part-time (24 women); includes 79 minority (3 Black or African American, non-Hispanic/Latino; 1 American Indian or Alaska Native, non-Hispanic/Latino; 4 Asian, non-Hispanic/Latino; 10 Hispanic/Latino; 2 Native Hawaiian or other Pacific Islander, non-Hispanic/Latino; 59 Two or more races, non-Hispanic/Latino), 67 international. Average age 30. 184 applicants, 44% accepted, 45 enrolled. *Faculty:* 108 full-time (16 women), 11 part-time/adjunct (3 women). Expenses: Contact institution. *Financial support:* In 2010–11, 169 students received support, including 2 fellowships with full tuition reimbursements available (averaging $17,000 per year), 45 research assistantships with partial tuition reimbursements available (averaging $15,838 per year), 122 teaching assistantships with partial tuition reimbursements available (averaging $12,488 per year); institutionally sponsored loans, scholarships/grants, health care benefits, and unspecified assistantships also available. Financial award application deadline: 3/1. In 2010, 27 master's, 15 doctorates awarded. *Degree program information:* Part-time programs available. Offers astronomy (MS, PhD); biochemistry (MS); biological sciences (MS, PhD); chemistry (MS, PhD); geoscience (MS, PhD); mathematical sciences (MS, PhD); physics (MS, PhD); radiochemistry (PhD); science (MA, MS, PhD); water resources management (MS). *Application fee:* $60 ($95 for international students). *Application Contact:* Graduate College Admissions Evaluator, 702-895-3320, Fax: 702-895-4180, E-mail: gradcollege@unlv.edu. *Dean,* Dr. Timothy Porter, 702-895-2058, Fax: 702-895-4159, E-mail: tim.porter@unlv.edu.

Greenspun College of Urban Affairs Students: 264 full-time (187 women), 198 part-time (134 women); includes 207 minority (44 Black or African American, non-Hispanic/Latino; 2 American Indian or Alaska Native, non-Hispanic/Latino; 20 Asian, non-Hispanic/Latino; 66 Hispanic/Latino; 5 Native Hawaiian or other Pacific Islander, non-Hispanic/Latino; 70 Two or more races, non-Hispanic/Latino), 20 international. Average age 33. 369 applicants, 60% accepted, 156 enrolled. *Faculty:* 45 full-time (16 women), 11 part-time/adjunct (7 women). Expenses: Contact institution. *Financial support:* In 2010–11, 54 students received support, including 22 research assistantships with partial tuition reimbursements available (averaging $11,237 per year), 32 teaching assistantships with partial tuition reimbursements available (averaging $10,444 per year); institutionally sponsored loans, scholarships/grants, health care benefits, and unspecified assistantships also available. Financial award application deadline: 3/1. In 2010, 145 master's, 3 doctorates, 27 other advanced degrees awarded. *Degree program information:* Part-time and evening/weekend programs available. Offers communication studies (MA); criminal justice (MA); crisis and emergency management (MS); environmental science (MS, PhD); forensic social work (Advanced Certificate); journalism and media studies (MA); marriage and family therapy (MS); non-profit management (Certificate); public administration (MPA); public affairs (PhD); public management (Certificate); social work (MSW); urban affairs (MA, MPA, MS, MSW, PhD, Advanced Certificate, Certificate). *Application fee:* $60 ($95 for international students). *Application Contact:* Graduate College Admissions Evaluator, 702-895-3320, Fax: 702-895-4180, E-mail: gradcollege@unlv.edu. *Dean,* Dr. E. Lee Bernick, 702-895-3291, Fax: 702-895-4231, E-mail: lee.burnick@unlv.edu.

Howard R. Hughes College of Engineering Students: 149 full-time (29 women), 91 part-time (20 women); includes 67 minority (4 Black or African American, non-Hispanic/Latino; 2 American Indian or Alaska Native, non-Hispanic/Latino; 9 Asian, non-Hispanic/Latino; 12 Hispanic/Latino; 1 Native Hawaiian or other Pacific Islander, non-Hispanic/Latino; 39 Two or more races, non-Hispanic/Latino), 102 international. Average age 30. 148 applicants, 78% accepted, 67 enrolled. *Faculty:* 67 full-time (9 women), 18 part-time/adjunct (0 women). Expenses: Contact institution. *Financial support:* In 2010–11, 121 students received support, including 57 research assistantships with partial tuition reimbursements available (averaging $12,288 per year), 64 teaching assistantships with partial tuition reimbursements available (averaging $10,751 per year); institutionally sponsored loans, scholarships/grants, health care benefits, and unspecified assistantships also available. Financial award application deadline: 3/1. In 2010, 64 master's, 13 doctorates awarded. *Degree program information:* Part-time programs available. Offers aerospace engineering (MS); biomedical engineering (MS); civil and environmental engineering (PhD); computer science (MS, PhD); construction management (MS); electrical and computer engineering (MSE, PhD); engineering (MS, MSE, PhD); informatics (MS, PhD); materials and nuclear engineering (MS); mechanical engineering (MSE, PhD); transportation (MS). *Application fee:* $60 ($95 for international students). *Application Contact:* Graduate College Admissions Evaluator, 702-895-3320, Fax: 702-895-4180, E-mail: gradcollege@unlv.edu. *Interim Dean,* Dr. Rama Venkat, 702-895-1094, Fax: 702-895-4059, E-mail: venkat@ee.unlv.edu.

School of Allied Health Sciences Students: 130 full-time (61 women), 21 part-time (14 women); includes 40 minority (1 American Indian or Alaska Native, non-Hispanic/Latino; 6 Asian, non-Hispanic/Latino; 10 Hispanic/Latino; 23 Two or more races, non-Hispanic/Latino), 5 international. Average age 27. 64 applicants, 72% accepted, 25 enrolled. *Faculty:* 29 full-time (10 women), 3 part-time/adjunct (2 women). Expenses: Contact institution. *Financial support:* In 2010–11, 34 students received support, including 31 research assistantships with partial tuition reimbursements available (averaging $10,986 per year), 3 teaching assistantships with partial tuition reimbursements available (averaging $10,000 per year); institutionally sponsored loans, scholarships/grants, health care benefits, and unspecified assistantships also available. Financial award application deadline: 3/1. In 2010, 13 master's, 30 doctorates awarded. *Degree program information:* Part-time programs available. Offers allied health sciences (MS, DPT); exercise physiology (MS); health physics (MS); kinesiology (MS); physical therapy (DPT). *Application fee:* $60 ($95 for international students). *Application Contact:* Graduate College Admissions Evaluator, 702-895-3320, Fax: 702-895-4180, E-mail: gradcollege@unlv.edu. *Interim Dean,* Dr. Carolyn Yucha, 702-895-3906, Fax: 702-895-5050, E-mail: carolyn.yucha@unlv.edu.

School of Community Health Sciences Students: 81 full-time (55 women), 109 part-time (75 women); includes 85 minority (21 Black or African American, non-Hispanic/Latino; 17 Asian, non-Hispanic/Latino; 11 Hispanic/Latino; 2 Native Hawaiian or other Pacific Islander, non-Hispanic/Latino; 34 Two or more races, non-Hispanic/Latino), 14 international. Average age 33. 88 applicants, 74% accepted, 44 enrolled. *Faculty:* 15 full-time (5 women). Expenses: Contact institution. *Financial support:* In 2010–11, 18 students received support, including 18 research assistantships with partial tuition reimbursements available (averaging $11,109 per year); institutionally sponsored loans, scholarships/grants, health care benefits, and unspecified assistantships also available. Financial award application deadline: 3/1. In 2010, 47 master's awarded. Offers community health sciences (M Ed, MHA, MPH, PhD); health care administration (MHA); health care promotion (M Ed); public health (MPH, PhD). *Application fee:* $60 ($95 for international students). *Application Contact:* Dr. Mary Guinan, Dean, 702-895-5090, Fax: 702-895-5184, E-mail: mary.guinan@unlv.edu. *Dean,* Dr. Mary Guinan, 702-895-5090, Fax: 702-895-5184, E-mail: mary.guinan@unlv.edu.

School of Nursing Students: 46 full-time (41 women), 91 part-time (80 women); includes 76 minority (1 Black or African American, non-Hispanic/Latino; 6 Asian, non-Hispanic/Latino; 7 Hispanic/Latino; 2 Native Hawaiian or other Pacific Islander, non-Hispanic/Latino; 60 Two or more races, non-Hispanic/Latino), 6 international. Average age 37. 126 applicants, 50% accepted, 52 enrolled. *Faculty:* 35 full-time (30 women), 5 part-time/adjunct (all women). Expenses: Contact institution. *Financial support:* In 2010–11, 9 students received support, including 8 research assistantships with partial tuition reimbursements available (averaging $14,275 per year), 1 teaching assistantship (averaging $12,000 per year); institutionally sponsored loans, scholarships/grants, health care benefits, and unspecified assistantships also available. Financial award application deadline: 3/1. In 2010, 40 master's, 7 doctorates, 5 other advanced degrees awarded. *Degree program information:* Part-time programs available. Postbaccalaureate distance learning degree programs offered (minimal on-campus study). Offers family nurse practitioner (Advanced Certificate); nursing (MS, DNP, PhD); nursing education (Advanced Certificate); pediatric nurse practitioner (Post-Master's Certificate). *Application deadline:* For fall admission, 2/15 priority date for domestic and international students. Applications are processed on a rolling basis. *Application fee:* $60 ($95 for international students). Electronic applications accepted. *Application Contact:* Graduate College Admissions Evaluator, 702-895-3320, Fax: 702-895-4180, E-mail: gradcollege@unlv.edu. *Interim Dean,* Dr. Carolyn Yucha, 702-895-3906, Fax: 702-895-5050, E-mail: carolyn.yucha@unlv.edu.

William F. Harrah College of Hotel Administration Students: 100 full-time (54 women), 91 part-time (45 women); includes 65 minority (2 Black or African American, non-Hispanic/Latino; 1 American Indian or Alaska Native, non-Hispanic/Latino; 3 Asian, non-Hispanic/Latino; 7 Hispanic/Latino; 2 Native Hawaiian or other Pacific Islander, non-Hispanic/Latino; 50 Two or more races, non-Hispanic/Latino), 62 international. Average age 32. 183 applicants, 54% accepted, 70 enrolled. *Faculty:* 42 full-time (16 women), 7 part-time/adjunct (3 women). Expenses: Contact institution. *Financial support:* In 2010–11, 32 students received support, including 31 research assistantships with partial tuition reimbursements available (averaging $10,981 per year), 1 teaching assistantship with partial tuition reimbursement available (averaging $12,000 per year); institutionally sponsored loans, scholarships/grants, health care benefits, and unspecified assistantships also available. Financial award application deadline: 3/1. In 2010, 53 master's, 6 doctorates awarded. *Degree program information:* Part-time programs available. Offers hospitality administration (MHA, PhD); hotel administration (MHA, MS, PhD); sport and leisure services management (MS). *Application fee:* $60 ($95 for international students). *Application Contact:* Graduate College Admissions Evaluator, 702-895-3320, Fax: 702-895-4180, E-mail: gradcollege@unlv.edu. *Interim Dean,* Dr. Don Snyder, 702-895-3308, Fax: 702-895-4109, E-mail: donald.snyder@unlv.edu.

William S. Boyd School of Law *Faculty:* 42 full-time (20 women), 15 part-time/adjunct (4 women). Expenses: Contact institution. *Financial support:* Career-related internships or fieldwork and scholarships/grants available. Support available to part-time students. Financial award application deadline: 2/1; financial award applicants required to submit FAFSA. *Degree program information:* Part-time and evening/weekend programs available. Offers law (JD). *Application deadline:* For fall admission, 3/15 for domestic and international students. Applications are processed on a rolling basis. *Application fee:* $50. Electronic applications accepted. *Application Contact:* Elizabeth M. Karl, Admissions and Records Assistant III, 702-895-2424, Fax: 702-895-2414, E-mail: elizabeth.karl@unlv.edu. *Dean,* John V. White, 702-895-3671, Fax: 702-895-1095.

UNIVERSITY OF NEVADA, RENO, Reno, NV 89557

General Information State-supported, coed, university. CGS member. *Enrollment:* 17,679 graduate, professional, and undergraduate students; 1,273 full-time matriculated graduate/professional students (734 women), 1,231 part-time matriculated graduate/professional students (664 women). *Enrollment by degree level:* 1,680 master's, 797 doctoral, 27 other advanced degrees. *Graduate faculty:* 955 full-time (370 women). *International tuition:* $9009 full-time. Tuition, state resident: full-time $2219; part-time $246 per credit. Tuition, nonresident: part-time $510 per credit. *Required fees:* $59 per term. One-time fee: $101. Tuition and fees vary according to course load. *Graduate housing:* Rooms and/or apartments available on a first-come, first-served basis to single and married students. Housing application deadline: 5/16. *Student services:* Campus employment opportunities, campus safety program, child daycare facilities, exercise/wellness program, free psychological counseling, international student services, low-cost health insurance, multicultural affairs office, services for students with disabilities, teacher training, writing training. *Library facilities:* Mathewson-IGT Knowledge Center. *Online resources:* library catalog, web page, access to other libraries' catalogs. *Research affiliation:* NIH (nursing), Desert Research Institute (natural resource sciences, environmental sciences).

Computer facilities: Computer purchase and lease plans are available. A campuswide network can be accessed from student residence rooms and from off campus. Online class registration is available. *Web address:* http://www.unr.edu/.

General Application Contact: Lisa Oliveto, Recruitment Coordinator, 775-327-2361, Fax: 775-784-6064, E-mail: loliveto@unr.edu.

GRADUATE UNITS

Graduate School Students: 998 full-time (583 women), 1,618 part-time (906 women); includes 57 Black or African American, non-Hispanic/Latino; 23 American Indian or Alaska Native, non-Hispanic/Latino; 200 Asian, non-Hispanic/Latino; 167 Hispanic/Latino, 359 international. Average age 33. 1,986 applicants, 51% accepted, 709 enrolled. *Faculty:* 1,035 full-time (321 women). Expenses: Contact institution. *Financial support:* In 2010–11, 4 fellowships with partial tuition reimbursements (averaging $26,328 per year), 423 research assistantships with partial tuition reimbursements (averaging $14,000 per year), 485 teaching assistantships with partial tuition reimbursements (averaging $14,000 per year) were awarded; career-related internships or fieldwork, Federal Work-Study, institutionally sponsored loans, scholarships/grants, health care benefits, and unspecified assistantships also available. Support available to part-time students. Financial award application deadline: 3/1; financial award applicants required to submit FAFSA. In 2010, 626 master's, 112 doctorates, 4 other advanced degrees awarded. *Degree program information:* Part-time and evening/weekend programs available. Postbaccalaureate distance learning degree programs offered (no on-campus study). Offers atmospheric sciences (MS, PhD); Basque studies (PhD); biomedical engineering (MS, PhD); cell and molecular biology (MS, PhD); cellular and molecular pharmacology and physiology (PhD); chemical physics (PhD); ecology, evolution, and conservation biology (PhD); environmental sciences and health (MS, PhD); hydrogeology (MS, PhD); hydrology (MS, PhD); social psychology (PhD). *Application deadline:* Applications are processed on a rolling basis. *Application fee:* $60 ($95 for international students). Electronic applications accepted. *Application Contact:* Michele Sandberg, Application Contact, 775-784-7026, Fax: 775-784-6064, E-mail: gradschool@unr.edu. *Dean*, Dr. Marsha Read, 775-784-6869, Fax: 775-784-6064, E-mail: read@unr.edu.

College of Agriculture, Biotechnology and Natural Resources Offers agriculture, biotechnology and natural resources (MS, PhD); animal science (MS); biochemistry (MS, PhD); biotechnology (MS); natural resources and environmental sciences (MS); nutrition (MS); resource economics (MS, PhD). Electronic applications accepted.

College of Business Administration *Degree program information:* Part-time programs available. Postbaccalaureate distance learning degree programs offered. Offers accounting and information systems (M Acc); business administration (M Acc, MA, MBA, MS); economics (MA, MS); finance (MS); information systems (MS). Electronic applications accepted.

College of Education Offers counseling and educational psychology (M Ed, MA, MS, Ed D, PhD, Ed S); curriculum and instruction (PhD); curriculum, teaching and learning (Ed D, PhD); education (M Ed, MA, MS, Ed D, PhD, Ed S); educational leadership (M Ed, MA, MS, Ed D, PhD, Ed S); educational specialties (M Ed, MA, MS, Ed D, PhD); elementary education (M Ed, MA, MS); human development and family studies (MS); literacy studies (M Ed, MA, Ed D, PhD); secondary education (M Ed, MA, MS); special education (M Ed, MA, MS, Ed D, PhD); special education and disability studies (PhD); teaching English to speakers of other languages (MA). Electronic applications accepted.

College of Engineering Offers chemical engineering (MS, PhD); civil and environmental engineering (MS, PhD); computer engineering (MS); computer science (MS); computer science and engineering (MS, PhD); electrical engineering (MS, PhD); engineering (MS, PhD); materials science and engineering (MS, PhD); mechanical engineering (MS, PhD). Electronic applications accepted.

College of Liberal Arts *Degree program information:* Part-time and evening/weekend programs available. Postbaccalaureate distance learning degree programs offered (no on-campus study). Offers anthropology (MA, PhD); behavior analysis (MA, PhD); clinical psychology (MA, PhD); cognitive brain science (MA, PhD); criminal justice (MA); English (MA, MATE, PhD); fine arts (MFA); French (MA); German (MA); history (MA, PhD); judicial studies (MJS, PhD); justice management (MJM); liberal arts (MA, MATE, MFA, MJM, MJS, MM, MPA, PhD); music (MA, MM); philosophy (MA); political science (MA, PhD); public administration (MPA); public administration and policy (MPA); social research and justice studies (MA, MJM, MJS, PhD); sociology (MA); Spanish (MA); speech communications (MA). Electronic applications accepted.

College of Science Offers biology (MS); chemistry (MS, PhD); earth sciences and engineering (MS, PhD); geochemistry (MS, PhD); geography (MS, PhD); geological engineering (MS, PhD); geology (MS, PhD); geophysics (MS, PhD); land use planning (MS); mathematics (MS); mining engineering (MS); physics (MS, PhD); science (MATM, MS, PhD); teaching mathematics (MATM). Electronic applications accepted.

Division of Health Sciences Offers health sciences (MPH, MS, MSN, MSW, DNP, PhD); nursing (MSN, DNP); public health (MPH, PhD); social work (MSW); speech pathology (PhD); speech pathology and audiology (MS). Electronic applications accepted.

Donald W. Reynolds School of Journalism Offers journalism (MA). Electronic applications accepted.

School of Medicine Offers medicine (MD).

UNIVERSITY OF NEW BRUNSWICK FREDERICTON, Fredericton, NB E3B 5A3, Canada

General Information Province-supported, coed, university. *Enrollment:* 10,859 graduate, professional, and undergraduate students; 939 full-time matriculated graduate/professional students (398 women), 538 part-time matriculated graduate/professional students (355 women). *Graduate faculty:* 424 full-time (146 women), 103 part-time/adjunct (37 women). *International tuition:* $6300 full-time. *Tuition, area resident:* Full-time $3708; part-time $927 per term. *Required fees:* $50 per term. *Graduate housing:* Rooms and/or apartments available on a first-come, first-served basis to single and married students. Typical cost: $7000 per year ($8000 including board) for single students; $5760 per year for married students. Room and board charges vary according to board plan, campus/location and housing facility selected. Housing application deadline: 5/31. *Student services:* Campus employment opportunities, campus safety program, career counseling, child daycare facilities, exercise/wellness program, free psychological counseling, grant writing training, international student services, low-cost health insurance, multicultural affairs office, services for students with disabilities, teacher training, writing training. *Library facilities:* Harriet Irving Library plus 4 others. *Online resources:* library catalog, web page, access to other libraries' catalogs. *Collection:* 1.7 million titles, 37,550 serial subscriptions, 6,686 audiovisual materials. *Research affiliation:* Petroleum Research Atlantic Canada (petroleum), Huntsman Marine Science Centre (marine sciences), Atlantic Association for Research in the Mathematical Sciences (mathematical sciences), Atlantic Hydrogen, Inc. (hydrogen), Pulp and Paper Research Institute of Canada (pulp and paper), National Research Council Institute for Information Technology (information technology).

Computer facilities: 1,400 computers available on campus for general student use. A campuswide network can be accessed from student residence rooms and from off campus. Online class registration is available. *Web address:* http://www.unb.ca/.

General Application Contact: Dr. Edmund Biden, Dean of Graduate Studies, 506-458-7154, Fax: 506-453-4817, E-mail: biden@unb.ca.

GRADUATE UNITS

Faculty of Law Students: 230 full-time (108 women). *Faculty:* 16 full-time (5 women), 9 part-time/adjunct (6 women). Expenses: Contact institution. *Financial support:* Scholarships/grants available. Offers law (LL B). *Application deadline:* For fall admission, 3/1 for domestic students. Applications are processed on a rolling basis. *Application fee:* $50. Electronic applications accepted. *Application Contact:* Wanda Foster, Law Admissions Officer, 506-453-4703, Fax: 506-458-7722, E-mail: wfoster@unb.ca. *Interim Dean*, David A. Townsend, 506-453-4702, Fax: 506-453-4604, E-mail: townsend@unb.ca.

School of Graduate Studies Students: 939 full-time (398 women), 538 part-time (355 women). *Faculty:* 424 full-time (146 women), 103 part-time/adjunct (37 women). Expenses: Contact institution. *Financial support:* Fellowships, research assistantships, teaching assistantships, scholarships/grants and tuition waivers available. Support available to part-time students. In 2010, 253 master's, 48 doctorates awarded. *Degree program information:* Part-time and evening/weekend programs available. Postbaccalaureate distance learning degree programs offered (minimal on-campus study). Offers applied health services (MAHSR); interdisciplinary studies (M IDST, PhD); people, property and alternative dispute resolution (M Phil); philosophy politics and economics (M Phil); sustainable development (M Phil). *Application deadline:* 1/31 for domestic and international students. Applications are processed on a rolling basis. *Application fee:* $50 Canadian dollars. *Application Contact:* Dr. Edmund Biden, Acting Dean, 506-458-7150, Fax: 506-453-4817, E-mail: biden@unb.ca. *Acting Dean*, Dr. Edmund Biden, 506-458-7150, Fax: 506-453-4817, E-mail: biden@unb.ca.

Faculty of Arts Students: 184 full-time (97 women), 35 part-time (18 women). *Faculty:* 79 full-time (36 women), 27 part-time/adjunct (11 women). Expenses: Contact institution. *Financial support:* Research assistantships, teaching assistantships available. In 2010, 30 master's, 18 doctorates awarded. *Degree program information:* Part-time programs available. Offers anthropology (MA); applied economics and finance (M Sc); arts (M Sc, MA, PhD); classics (MA); economics (MA); English (MA, PhD); history (MA, PhD); political science (MA); psychology (MA, PhD); sociology (MA, PhD). *Application deadline:* For fall admission, 1/31 priority date for domestic students; for winter admission, 1/31 priority date for domestic students; for spring admission, 1/31 priority date for domestic students. Applications are processed on a rolling basis. *Application fee:* $50 Canadian dollars. *Application Contact:* Dr. Edmund Biden, Dean of Graduate Studies, 506-458-7154, Fax: 506-453-4817, E-mail: biden@unb.ca. *Dean*, Dr. James Murray, 506-458-7485, Fax: 506-453-5102, E-mail: jsm@unb.ca.

Faculty of Business Administration Students: 43 full-time (18 women), 35 part-time (20 women). *Faculty:* 23 full-time (3 women), 5 part-time/adjunct (2 women). Expenses: Contact institution. *Financial support:* In 2010–11, 4 research assistantships (averaging $4,500 per year), 13 teaching assistantships (averaging $2,250 per year) were awarded. In 2010, 29 master's awarded. *Degree program information:* Part-time programs available. Offers business administration (MBA); engineering management (MBA); entrepreneurship (MBA); sports and recreation management (MBA). *Application deadline:* For fall admission, 3/1 priority date for domestic students. Applications are processed on a rolling basis. *Application fee:* $50 Canadian dollars. *Application Contact:* Marilyn Davis, Acting Graduate Secretary, 506-453-4766, Fax: 506-453-3561, E-mail: mbacontact@unb.ca. *Director of Graduate Studies*, Judy Roy, 506-458-7307, Fax: 506-453-3561, E-mail: jroy@unb.ca.

Faculty of Computer Science Students: 72 full-time (16 women), 18 part-time (4 women). *Faculty:* 25 full-time (6 women), 10 part-time/adjunct (0 women). Expenses: Contact institution. *Financial support:* In 2010–11, 53 research assistantships, 27 teaching assistantships were awarded. In 2010, 13 master's, 3 doctorates awarded. *Degree program information:* Part-time programs available. Offers computer science (M Sc CS, PhD). *Application deadline:* For fall admission, 3/1 priority date for domestic students. *Application fee:* $50 Canadian dollars. Electronic applications accepted. *Application Contact:* Jodi O'Neill, Graduate Secretary, 506-458-7285, Fax: 506-453-3566, E-mail: jodio@unb.ca. *Director of Graduate Studies*, Dr. Eric Aubanel, 506-458-7268, Fax: 506-453-3566, E-mail: aubanel@unb.ca.

Faculty of Education Students: 67 full-time (49 women), 338 part-time (254 women). *Faculty:* 33 full-time (18 women), 21 part-time/adjunct (13 women). Expenses: Contact institution. *Financial support:* In 2010–11, research assistantships (averaging $2,600 per year), teaching assistantships (averaging $3,777 per year) were awarded; tuition waivers also available. In 2010, 148 master's, 3 doctorates awarded. *Degree program information:* Part-time programs available. Postbaccalaureate distance learning degree programs offered. Offers education (M Ed, PhD). *Application deadline:* 1/31 priority date for domestic and international students. *Application fee:* $50 Canadian dollars. Electronic applications accepted. *Application Contact:* Carolyn King, Graduate Secretary, 506-458-7147, Fax: 506-453-3569, E-mail: kingc@unb.ca. *Director of Graduate Studies*, Dr. Kirk Anderson, 506-447-3343, Fax: 506-453-3569, E-mail: andersk@unb.ca.

Faculty of Engineering Students: 234 full-time (47 women), 35 part-time (3 women). *Faculty:* 68 full-time (10 women), 17 part-time/adjunct (1 woman). Expenses: Contact institution. *Financial support:* In 2010–11, 284 research assistantships, 209 teaching assistantships were awarded; career-related internships or fieldwork also available. In 2010, 55 master's, 19 doctorates awarded. *Degree program information:* Part-time programs available. Offers applied mechanics (M Eng, M Sc E, PhD); chemical engineering (M Eng, M Sc E, PhD); construction engineering and management (M Eng, M Sc E, PhD); electrical and computer engineering (M Eng, M Sc E, PhD); engineering (M Eng, M Sc E, PhD, Certificate, Diploma); environmental engineering (M Eng, M Sc E, PhD); environmental studies (M Eng); geotechnical engineering (M Eng, M Sc E, PhD); groundwater/hydrology (M Eng, M Sc E, PhD); land information management (Diploma); mapping, charting and geodesy (Diploma); materials (M Eng, M Sc E, PhD); mechanical engineering (M Eng, M Sc E, PhD); pavements (M Eng, M Sc E, PhD); structures (M Eng, M Sc E, PhD); surveying engineering (M Eng, M Sc E, PhD); transportation (M Eng, M Sc E, PhD). *Application deadline:* For fall admission, 3/1 priority date for domestic students. Applications are processed on a rolling basis. *Application fee:* $50 Canadian dollars. *Application Contact:* Dr. David Coleman, Dean, 506-453-4570, Fax: 506-453-4569, E-mail: dcoleman@unb.ca. *Dean*, Dr. David Coleman, 506-453-4570, Fax: 506-453-4569, E-mail: dcoleman@unb.ca.

Faculty of Forestry and Environmental Management Students: 68 full-time (29 women), 7 part-time (2 women). *Faculty:* 22 full-time (3 women), 1 part-time/adjunct (0 women). Expenses: Contact institution. *Financial support:* In 2010–11, 54 research assistantships, 46 teaching assistantships were awarded. In 2010, 20 master's, 4 doctorates awarded. *Degree program information:* Part-time programs available. Offers ecological foundations of forest management (PhD); environmental management (MEM); forest engineering (M Sc FE, MFE); forest products marketing (MBA); forest resources (M Sc F, MF, PhD). *Application deadline:* For fall admission, 3/1 priority date for domestic students. *Application fee:* $50 Canadian dollars. Electronic applications accepted. *Application Contact:* Faith Sharpe, Graduate Secretary, 506-458-7520, Fax: 506-453-3538, E-mail: fsharpe@unb.ca. *Director of Graduate Studies*, Dr. John Kershaw, 506-453-4933, Fax: 506-453-3538, E-mail: kershaw@unb.ca.

Faculty of Kinesiology Students: 38 full-time (16 women), 3 part-time (all women). *Faculty:* 15 full-time (7 women). Expenses: Contact institution. *Financial support:* Fellowships with tuition reimbursements, research assistantships, teaching assistantships, career-related internships or fieldwork and scholarships/grants available. In 2010, 6 master's awarded. *Degree program information:* Part-time programs available. Offers exercise and sport science (M Sc); sport and recreation management (MBA); sport and recreation studies (MA). *Application deadline:* For winter admission, 1/31 for domestic students; for spring admission, 3/31 for domestic students. Applications are processed on a rolling basis. *Application fee:* $50 Canadian dollars. Electronic applications accepted. *Application Contact:* Leslie Harquail, Graduate Secretary, 506-453-4575, Fax: 506-453-3511, E-mail: harquail@unb.ca. *Acting Director of Graduate Studies*, Dr. Tim McGarry, 506-458-7109, Fax: 506-453-3511, E-mail: tmcgarry@unb.ca.

Faculty of Nursing Students: 11 full-time (10 women), 32 part-time (31 women). *Faculty:* 24 full-time (all women), 1 part-time/adjunct (0 women). Expenses: Contact institution. *Financial support:* In 2010–11, 4 research assistantships, 3 teaching assistantships were awarded. In 2010, 9 master's awarded. *Degree program information:* Part-time programs available. Postbaccalaureate distance learning degree programs offered. Offers nurse educator (MN);

University of New Brunswick Fredericton (continued)

nurse practitioner (MN); nursing (MN). *Application deadline:* For winter admission, 2/5 for domestic students. *Application fee:* $50 Canadian dollars. Electronic applications accepted. *Application Contact:* Francis Perry, Graduate Secretary, 506-451-6844, Fax: 506-447-3057, E-mail: fperry@unb.ca. *Director of Graduate Studies,* Gail Storr, 506-458-7643, Fax: 506-447-3057, E-mail: storr@unb.ca.

Faculty of Science Students: 172 full-time (75 women), 16 part-time (7 women). *Faculty:* 92 full-time (15 women), 15 part-time/adjunct (3 women). Expenses: Contact institution. *Financial support:* Research assistantships, teaching assistantships available. In 2010, 20 master's, 8 doctorates awarded. *Degree program information:* Part-time programs available. Offers biology (M Sc, PhD); chemistry (M Sc, PhD); geology (M Sc, PhD); mathematics and statistics (M Sc, PhD); physics (M Sc, PhD); science (M Sc, PhD). *Application deadline:* For fall admission, 3/1 priority date for domestic students. Applications are processed on a rolling basis. *Application fee:* $50 Canadian dollars. *Application Contact:* Dean of Graduate Studies. *Dean,* Dr. David MaGee, 506-470-5625, Fax: 506-453-3570, E-mail: dmagee@unb.ca.

UNIVERSITY OF NEW BRUNSWICK SAINT JOHN, Saint John, NB E2L 4L5, Canada

General Information Province-supported, coed, comprehensive institution. *Graduate faculty:* 42 full-time (9 women), 15 part-time/adjunct (8 women). *Graduate housing:* Rooms and/or apartments available on a first-come, first-served basis to single and married students. Housing application deadline: 3/31. *Student services:* Campus employment opportunities, campus safety program, career counseling, exercise/wellness program, free psychological counseling, grant writing training, international student services, low-cost health insurance, multicultural affairs office, services for students with disabilities, teacher training, writing training. *Library facilities:* Ward Chipman Library. *Online resources:* library catalog, web page, access to other libraries' catalogs. *Collection:* 155,500 titles, 700 serial subscriptions.

Computer facilities: 100 computers available on campus for general student use. A campuswide network can be accessed from student residence rooms and from off campus. Online class registration is available. *Web address:* http://www.unb.ca/.

General Application Contact: Dr. Bruce MacDonald, Associate Dean of Graduate Studies, 506-648-5620, Fax: 506-648-5528, E-mail: bmacdon@unb.ca.

GRADUATE UNITS

Department of Biology Students: 44 full-time (26 women), 6 part-time (3 women). *Faculty:* 14 full-time (1 woman). Expenses: Contact institution. *Financial support:* In 2010–11, 118 fellowships, 42 research assistantships (averaging $4,000 per year), 1 teaching assistantship (averaging $4,000 per year) were awarded; scholarships/grants and unspecified assistantships also available. In 2010, 5 master's, 1 doctorate awarded. *Degree program information:* Part-time programs available. Offers biology (M Sc, PhD). *Application deadline:* For fall admission, 2/15 for domestic and international students. Applications are processed on a rolling basis. *Application fee:* $50 Canadian dollars. *Application Contact:* Christine Robson, Secretary, 506-648-5605, Fax: 506-648-5811, E-mail: crobson@unb.ca. *Director of Graduate Studies,* Dr. Kate Frego, 506-648-5566, Fax: 506-648-5811, E-mail: frego@unbsj.ca.

Department of Psychology Students: 4 full-time (1 woman). *Faculty:* 9 full-time (4 women), 1 part-time/adjunct (0 women). Expenses: Contact institution. *Financial support:* In 2010–11, 2 research assistantships (averaging $9,000 per year), 7 teaching assistantships (averaging $4,500 per year) were awarded; fellowships, unspecified assistantships also available. Support available to part-time students. Financial award application deadline: 2/1. In 2010, 1 doctorate awarded. *Degree program information:* Part-time programs available. Offers applied and experimental psychology (PhD); clinical psychology (PhD); experimental psychology (MA). *Application deadline:* For fall admission, 2/1 for domestic students. *Application fee:* $50. *Application Contact:* Frances Stevens, Secretary, 506-648-5640, Fax: 506-648-5780, E-mail: fstevens@unb.ca. *Director of Graduate Studies,* Dr. Lily Both, 506-648-5769, Fax: 506-648-5780, E-mail: lboth@unbsj.ca.

Faculty of Business Students: 47 full-time (18 women), 55 part-time (21 women). 93 applicants, 78% accepted, 25 enrolled. *Faculty:* 19 full-time (4 women), 14 part-time/adjunct (8 women). Expenses: Contact institution. *Financial support:* In 2010–11, 4 students received support. Career-related internships or fieldwork and scholarships/grants available. In 2010, 36 master's awarded. *Degree program information:* Part-time programs available. Offers administration (MBA); electronic commerce (MBA); international business (MBA); natural resource management (MBA). *Application deadline:* For fall admission, 5/15 for domestic and international students. Applications are processed on a rolling basis. *Application fee:* $100. Electronic applications accepted. *Application Contact:* Tammy Morin, Secretary, 506-648-5746, Fax: 506-648-5574, E-mail: tmorin@unbsj.ca. *Director of Graduate Studies,* Henryk Sterniczuk, 506-648-5573, Fax: 506-648-5574, E-mail: sterniczl@unbsj.ca.

UNIVERSITY OF NEW ENGLAND, Biddeford, ME 04005-9526

General Information Independent, coed, comprehensive institution. *Enrollment:* 5,168 graduate, professional, and undergraduate students; 2,158 full-time matriculated graduate/professional students (1,524 women), 281 part-time matriculated graduate/professional students (235 women). *Enrollment by degree level:* 733 first professional, 1,268 master's. *Graduate housing:* On-campus housing not available. *Student services:* Campus employment opportunities, campus safety program, career counseling, exercise/wellness program, free psychological counseling, low-cost health insurance, multicultural affairs office, services for students with disabilities. *Library facilities:* Jack S. Ketchum Library plus 1 other. *Online resources:* library catalog, web page, access to other libraries' catalogs. *Collection:* 156,752 titles, 39,705 serial subscriptions, 10,656 audiovisual materials.

Computer facilities: Computer purchase and lease plans are available. 150 computers available on campus for general student use. A campuswide network can be accessed from student residence rooms and from off campus. Online class registration is available. *Web address:* http://www.une.edu/.

General Application Contact: Stacy Gato, Director of Graduate and Professional Admissions, 207-221-4225, Fax: 207-523-1925, E-mail: gradadmissions@une.edu.

GRADUATE UNITS

College of Arts and Sciences Students: 614 full-time (467 women), 195 part-time (160 women); includes 33 Black or African American, non-Hispanic/Latino; 6 American Indian or Alaska Native, non-Hispanic/Latino; 5 Asian, non-Hispanic/Latino; 16 Hispanic/Latino; 7 Two or more races, non-Hispanic/Latino. 484 applicants, 95% accepted, 435 enrolled. Expenses: Contact institution. *Financial support:* Available to part-time students. Application deadline: 5/1. In 2010, 354 master's, 66 other advanced degrees awarded. *Degree program information:* Part-time programs available. Postbaccalaureate distance learning degree programs offered (minimal on-campus study). Offers advanced educational leadership (CAGS); applied biosciences (MS); arts and sciences (MS, MS Ed, CAGS); curriculum and instruction strategies (CAGS); curriculum and instruction strategy (MS Ed); educational leadership (MS Ed, CAGS); general studies (MS Ed); inclusion education (MS Ed); leadership, ethics and change (CAGS); literacy K-12 (MS Ed, CAGS); marine sciences (MS); teaching methodologies (MS Ed). *Application deadline:* Applications are processed on a rolling basis. *Application fee:* $40. *Application Contact:* Stacy Gato, Assistant Director of Graduate Admissions, 207-221-4225, Fax: 207-221-4898, E-mail: gradadmissions@une.edu. *Dean,* Christine A. Brown, 207-283-0171, E-mail: sbrown@une.edu.

College of Graduate Studies Expenses: Contact institution. Offers public health (MPH, Certificate). *Application Contact:* Stacy Gato, Assistant Director of Graduate Admissions, 207-221-4225, Fax: 207-221-4898, E-mail: gradadmissions@une.edu. *Dean,* Timothy Ford, 207-602-2334, E-mail: tford@une.edu.

College of Osteopathic Medicine Students: 541 full-time (306 women), 4 part-time (1 woman); includes 57 minority (5 Black or African American, non-Hispanic/Latino; 29 Asian, non-Hispanic/Latino; 11 Hispanic/Latino; 5 Native Hawaiian or other Pacific Islander, non-Hispanic/Latino; 7 Two or more races, non-Hispanic/Latino), 2 international. 1,324 applicants, 18% accepted, 132 enrolled. Expenses: Contact institution. *Financial support:* Federal Work-Study, institutionally sponsored loans, and scholarships/grants available. Support available to part-time students. Financial award application deadline: 5/1; financial award applicants required to submit FAFSA. In 2010, 109 first professional degrees awarded. Offers medical education leadership (MS); osteopathic medicine (DO). *Application deadline:* For fall admission, 3/1 for domestic students. *Application fee:* $55. *Application Contact:* Stacy Gato, Director of Graduate and Professional Admissions, 207-283-0171, Fax: 207-602-5900, E-mail: gradadmissions@une.edu. *Dean,* Dr. Marc Hahn, 207-602-2340, Fax: 207-878-2434, E-mail: deanunecom@une.edu.

College of Pharmacy Students: 194 full-time (112 women); includes 67 minority (14 Black or African American, non-Hispanic/Latino; 1 American Indian or Alaska Native, non-Hispanic/Latino; 43 Asian, non-Hispanic/Latino; 4 Hispanic/Latino; 3 Native Hawaiian or other Pacific Islander, non-Hispanic/Latino; 2 Two or more races, non-Hispanic/Latino), 2 international. 675 applicants, 21% accepted, 93 enrolled. Expenses: Contact institution. Offers pharmacy (Pharm D). *Application Contact:* Stacy Gato, Assistant Director of Graduate Admissions, 207-221-4225, Fax: 207-221-4898, E-mail: gradadmissions@une.edu. *Dean,* Gayle A. Brazeau, 207-221-4500, Fax: 207-523-1927, E-mail: gbrazeau@une.edu.

Westbrook College of Health Professions Students: 769 full-time (605 women), 61 part-time (57 women); includes 108 minority (52 Black or African American, non-Hispanic/Latino; 4 American Indian or Alaska Native, non-Hispanic/Latino; 17 Asian, non-Hispanic/Latino; 20 Hispanic/Latino; 5 Native Hawaiian or other Pacific Islander, non-Hispanic/Latino; 10 Two or more races, non-Hispanic/Latino). 2,422 applicants, 34% accepted, 590 enrolled. Expenses: Contact institution. *Financial support:* Career-related internships or fieldwork and Federal Work-Study available. Support available to part-time students. Financial award application deadline: 5/1; financial award applicants required to submit FAFSA. In 2010, 162 master's awarded. *Degree program information:* Part-time programs available. Postbaccalaureate distance learning degree programs offered (minimal on-campus study). Offers health professions (MS, MSW, DPT, Certificate); nurse anesthesia (MS); occupational therapy (MS); physical therapy (DPT); physician assistant (MS); post professional occupational therapy (MS); post professional physical therapy (DPT). *Application deadline:* Applications are processed on a rolling basis. *Application fee:* $40. *Application Contact:* Stacy Gato, Director of Graduate and Professional Admissions, 207-221-4225, Fax: 207-523-1925, E-mail: gradadmissions@une.edu. *Dean,* Dr. David Ward, 207-221-4520 Ext. 4520, E-mail: dward1@une.edu.

School of Social Work Students: 361 full-time (323 women), 61 part-time (57 women); includes 83 minority (48 Black or African American, non-Hispanic/Latino; 3 American Indian or Alaska Native, non-Hispanic/Latino; 5 Asian, non-Hispanic/Latino; 16 Hispanic/Latino; 2 Native Hawaiian or other Pacific Islander, non-Hispanic/Latino; 9 Two or more races, non-Hispanic/Latino). 276 applicants, 75% accepted, 181 enrolled. Expenses: Contact institution. *Financial support:* In 2010–11, 40 students received support. Scholarships/grants and tuition waivers (partial) available. Financial award application deadline: 5/1; financial award applicants required to submit FAFSA. In 2010, 44 master's awarded. *Degree program information:* Part-time programs available. Offers addictions counseling (Certificate); gerontology (Certificate); social work (MSW). *Application deadline:* For fall admission, 1/15 priority date for domestic students; for spring admission, 3/31 priority date for domestic students, 3/31 for international students. Applications are processed on a rolling basis. *Application fee:* $40. Electronic applications accepted. *Application Contact:* Stacy Gato, Assistant Director of Graduate Admissions, 207-221-4225, Fax: 207-221-4898, E-mail: gradadmissions@une.edu. *Director,* Martha Wilson, 207-221-4513, E-mail: mwilson@une.edu.

UNIVERSITY OF NEW HAMPSHIRE, Durham, NH 03824

General Information State-supported, coed, university. CGS member. *Enrollment:* 15,155 graduate, professional, and undergraduate students; 1,282 full-time matriculated graduate/professional students (768 women), 1,004 part-time matriculated graduate/professional students (541 women). *Enrollment by degree level:* 1,720 master's, 510 doctoral, 56 other advanced degrees. *Graduate faculty:* 607 full-time (199 women). *Graduate housing:* Rooms and/or apartments available on a first-come, first-served basis to single and married students. Housing application deadline: 7/15. *Student services:* Campus employment opportunities, campus safety program, career counseling, child daycare facilities, exercise/wellness program, free psychological counseling, grant writing training, international student services, low-cost health insurance, multicultural affairs office, services for students with disabilities, teacher training, writing training. *Library facilities:* Dimond Library plus 4 others. *Online resources:* library catalog, web page, access to other libraries' catalogs. *Collection:* 2.1 million titles, 98,923 serial subscriptions, 18,072 audiovisual materials.

Computer facilities: Computer purchase and lease plans are available. 448 computers available on campus for general student use. A campuswide network can be accessed from student residence rooms and from off campus. Online class registration is available. *Web address:* http://www.unh.edu/.

General Application Contact: Dovev Levine, Graduate Admissions Officer, 603-862-3000, Fax: 603-862-0275, E-mail: grad.school@unh.edu.

GRADUATE UNITS

Center for Graduate and Professional Studies Students: 97 full-time (65 women), 159 part-time (85 women); includes 20 minority (11 Black or African American, non-Hispanic/Latino; 1 American Indian or Alaska Native, non-Hispanic/Latino; 6 Asian, non-Hispanic/Latino; 2 Hispanic/Latino), 2 international. 119 applicants, 71% accepted, 61 enrolled. Expenses: Contact institution. *Financial support:* In 2010–11, 21 students received support, including 1 fellowship, 1 teaching assistantship; research assistantships, Federal Work-Study, scholarships/grants, health care benefits, and unspecified assistantships also available. Support available to part-time students. Financial award application deadline: 3/1; financial award applicants required to submit FAFSA. In 2010, 79 master's, 1 other advanced degree awarded. *Degree program information:* Part-time and evening/weekend programs available. Offers business administration (MBA); counseling (M Ed); education (M Ed, MAT); educational administration and supervision (M Ed, Ed S); industrial statistics (Certificate); public administration (MPA); public health (MPH, Certificate); social work (MSW); software systems engineering (Certificate). *Application deadline:* For fall admission, 6/1 for domestic students, 4/1 for international students; for spring admission, 12/1 for domestic students. Applications are processed on a rolling basis. *Application fee:* $65. Electronic applications accepted. *Application Contact:* Graduate Admissions Office, 603-862-3000, Fax: 603-862-0275, E-mail: grad.school@unh.edu. *Director,* Kate Ferreira, 603-641-4313, E-mail: unhm.gradcenter@unh.edu.

Graduate School Students: 1,282 full-time (768 women), 1,004 part-time (541 women); includes 121 minority (22 Black or African American, non-Hispanic/Latino; 11 American Indian or Alaska Native, non-Hispanic/Latino; 41 Asian, non-Hispanic/Latino; 31 Hispanic/Latino; 1 Native Hawaiian or other Pacific Islander, non-Hispanic/Latino; 15 Two or more races, non-Hispanic/Latino), 222 international. Average age 33. 2,529 applicants, 50% accepted, 678 enrolled. *Faculty:* 607 full-time (199 women). Expenses: Contact institution. *Financial support:* In 2010–11, 859 students received support, including 34 fellowships, 186 research assistantships, 426 teaching assistantships; Federal Work-Study, scholarships/grants, health care benefits, tuition waivers, and unspecified assistantships also available. Support available to part-time students. Financial award application deadline: 3/1; financial award applicants required to submit FAFSA. In 2010, 743 master's, 73 doctorates, 20 other advanced degrees awarded. *Degree program information:* Part-time and evening/weekend programs available. Offers college teaching (MST); development policy and practice (MA); earth and environmental science (PhD); environmental education (MA); interdisciplinary studies (Post-baccalaureate Certificate); natural resources and earth system science (PhD); natural resources and environmental studies (PhD). *Application deadline:* For fall admission, 7/1 priority date for domestic students, 4/1 priority date for international students; for spring admission, 2/1 for domestic students. Applications are processed on a rolling basis. *Application fee:* $65. Electronic applications accepted. *Application Contact:* Dovev L. Levine, Admissions Officer, 603-862-3000, Fax: 603-862-0275, E-mail: grad.school@unh.edu. *Dean,* Dr. Harry J. Richards, 603-862-3005, Fax: 603-862-0275, E-mail: harry.richards@unh.edu.

College of Engineering and Physical Sciences Students: 240 full-time (81 women), 239 part-time (53 women); includes 25 minority (1 Black or African American, non-Hispanic/Latino; 3 American Indian or Alaska Native, non-Hispanic/Latino; 8 Asian, non-Hispanic/Latino; 5 Hispanic/Latino; 8 Two or more races, non-Hispanic/Latino), 145 international.

Average age 30. 620 applicants, 59% accepted, 159 enrolled. *Faculty:* 162 full-time (25 women). Expenses: Contact institution. *Financial support:* In 2010–11, 326 students received support, including 7 fellowships, 131 research assistantships, 153 teaching assistantships; career-related internships or fieldwork, Federal Work-Study, scholarships/grants, and tuition waivers also available. Support available to part-time students. Financial award application deadline: 3/15; financial award applicants required to submit FAFSA. In 2010, 89 master's, 28 doctorates, 9 other advanced degrees awarded. *Degree program information:* Part-time and evening/weekend programs available. Offers applied mathematics (MS); chemical engineering (MS, PhD); chemistry (MS, MST, PhD); chemistry education (PhD); civil engineering (MS, PhD); computer science (MS, PhD); earth sciences (MS); electrical engineering (MS, PhD); engineering and physical sciences (MS, MST, PhD, Postbaccalaureate Certificate); hydrology (MS); industrial statistics (Postbaccalaureate Certificate); materials science (MS, PhD); mathematics (MS, MST, PhD); mathematics education (PhD); mechanical engineering (MS, PhD); ocean engineering (MS, PhD); ocean mapping (MS, Postbaccalaureate Certificate); physics (MS, PhD); software systems engineering (Postbaccalaureate Certificate); statistics (MS); systems design (PhD). *Application deadline:* For fall admission, 7/1 priority date for domestic students, 4/1 for international students; for winter admission, 12/1 priority date for domestic students. Applications are processed on a rolling basis. *Application fee:* $65. Electronic applications accepted. *Application Contact:* Samuel Mukasa, Dean, 603-862-1781. *Dean,* Samuel Mukasa, 603-862-1781.

College of Liberal Arts Students: 404 full-time (263 women), 428 part-time (289 women); includes 37 minority (6 Black or African American, non-Hispanic/Latino; 3 American Indian or Alaska Native, non-Hispanic/Latino; 10 Asian, non-Hispanic/Latino; 13 Hispanic/Latino; 1 Native Hawaiian or other Pacific Islander, non-Hispanic/Latino; 4 Two or more races, non-Hispanic/Latino), 14 international. Average age 35. 821 applicants, 50% accepted, 205 enrolled. *Faculty:* 193 full-time (90 women). Expenses: Contact institution. *Financial support:* In 2010–11, 214 students received support, including 8 fellowships, 4 research assistantships, 133 teaching assistantships; career-related internships or fieldwork, Federal Work-Study, scholarships/grants, and tuition waivers (full and partial) also available. Support available to part-time students. In 2010, 281 master's, 27 doctorates, 4 other advanced degrees awarded. *Degree program information:* Part-time programs available. Offers counseling (M Ed, MA); early childhood education (M Ed); education (M Ed, MA, MAT, PhD, Ed S, Postbaccalaureate Certificate); educational administration (M Ed, Ed S); elementary education (M Ed, MAT); English (MFA, PhD); English education (MST); history (MA, PhD); justice studies (MA); language and linguistics (MA); liberal arts (M Ed, MA, MALS, MAT, MFA, MPA, MST, PhD, Ed S, Postbaccalaureate Certificate); liberal studies (MALS); literature (MA); museum studies (MA); music education (MA); music history (MA); painting (MFA); political science (MA); psychology (PhD); public administration (MPA); reading (M Ed); secondary education (M Ed, MAT); sociology (MA, PhD); Spanish (MA); special education (M Ed, Postbaccalaureate Certificate); special needs (M Ed); teacher leadership (M Ed, Postbaccalaureate Certificate); writing (MA). *Application deadline:* For fall admission, 3/1 for domestic students, 4/1 for international students; for spring admission, 12/1 for domestic students. Applications are processed on a rolling basis. *Application fee:* $65. Electronic applications accepted. *Application Contact:* Dr. Kenneth Fuld, Dean, 603-862-2062. *Dean,* Dr. Kenneth Fuld, 603-862-2062.

College of Life Sciences and Agriculture Students: 90 full-time (46 women), 88 part-time (50 women); includes 15 minority (1 Black or African American, non-Hispanic/Latino; 7 Asian, non-Hispanic/Latino; 4 Hispanic/Latino; 3 Two or more races, non-Hispanic/Latino), 21 international. Average age 31. 235 applicants, 29% accepted, 37 enrolled. *Faculty:* 125 full-time (31 women). Expenses: Contact institution. *Financial support:* In 2010–11, 118 students received support, including 8 fellowships, 26 research assistantships, 76 teaching assistantships; career-related internships or fieldwork, Federal Work-Study, scholarships/grants, and tuition waivers (full and partial) also available. Support available to part-time students. Financial award application deadline: 3/1. In 2010, 34 master's, 8 doctorates awarded. *Degree program information:* Part-time programs available. Offers animal and nutritional sciences (PhD); animal science (MS); biochemistry (MS, PhD); environmental conservation (MS); forestry (MS); genetics (MS, PhD); integrated coastal ecosystem science, policy, management (MS); life sciences and agriculture (MS, PhD); microbiology (MS, PhD); natural resources (MS); nutritional sciences (MS); plant biology (MS, PhD); resource administration (MS); resource economics (MS); water resources (MS); wildlife (MS); zoology (MS, PhD). *Application deadline:* For fall admission, 7/1 for domestic students, 4/1 for international students. Applications are processed on a rolling basis. *Application fee:* $65. Electronic applications accepted. *Application Contact:* Tom Brady, Dean, 603-862-1453. *Dean,* Tom Brady, 603-862-1453.

School of Health and Human Services Students: 324 full-time (284 women), 138 part-time (112 women); includes 27 minority (11 Black or African American, non-Hispanic/Latino; 3 American Indian or Alaska Native, non-Hispanic/Latino; 6 Asian, non-Hispanic/Latino; 7 Hispanic/Latino), 7 international. Average age 34. 524 applicants, 52% accepted, 157 enrolled. *Faculty:* 79 full-time (43 women). Expenses: Contact institution. *Financial support:* In 2010–11, 84 students received support, including 29 teaching assistantships; fellowships, research assistantships, career-related internships or fieldwork, Federal Work-Study, scholarships/grants, and tuition waivers (full and partial) also available. Support available to part-time students. Financial award application deadline: 3/1. In 2010, 206 master's, 6 other advanced degrees awarded. *Degree program information:* Part-time and evening/weekend programs available. Offers communication sciences and disorders (Postbaccalaureate Certificate); early childhood intervention (MS); family practitioner (Postbaccalaureate Certificate); family studies (MS); health and human services (MPH, MS, MSW, Postbaccalaureate Certificate); kinesiology (MS); language and literature disabilities (MS); marriage and family therapy (MS); nursing (MS); occupational therapy (MS, Postbaccalaureate Certificate); public health (MPH, Postbaccalaureate Certificate); recreation administration (MS); social work (MSW, Postbaccalaureate Certificate); therapeutic recreation (MS). *Application deadline:* For fall admission, 7/1 priority date for domestic students, 4/1 for international students; for winter admission, 12/1 priority date for domestic students. Applications are processed on a rolling basis. *Application fee:* $65. Electronic applications accepted. *Application Contact:* Dr. Barbara Arrington, Dean, 603-862-1178. *Dean,* Dr. Barbara Arrington, 603-862-1178.

Whittemore School of Business and Economics Students: 158 full-time (55 women), 87 part-time (22 women); includes 12 minority (3 Black or African American, non-Hispanic/Latino; 2 American Indian or Alaska Native, non-Hispanic/Latino; 5 Asian, non-Hispanic/Latino; 2 Hispanic/Latino), 23 international. Average age 34. 280 applicants, 49% accepted, 112 enrolled. *Faculty:* 47 full-time (10 women). Expenses: Contact institution. *Financial support:* In 2010–11, 70 students received support, including 1 fellowship, 1 research assistantship, 25 teaching assistantships; career-related internships or fieldwork, Federal Work-Study, scholarships/grants, and tuition waivers (full and partial) also available. Support available to part-time students. Financial award application deadline: 2/15. In 2010, 174 master's, 2 doctorates awarded. *Degree program information:* Part-time and evening/weekend programs available. Offers accounting (MS); business administration (MBA); business and economics (MA, MBA, MS, PhD, Postbaccalaureate Certificate); economics (MA, PhD); executive business administration (MBA); health management (MBA); management of technology (MS, Postbaccalaureate Certificate). *Application deadline:* For fall admission, 6/1 for domestic students, 4/1 for international students; for spring admission, 12/1 for domestic students. Applications are processed on a rolling basis. *Application fee:* $65. Electronic applications accepted. *Application Contact:* Dr. Daniel Innis, Dean, 603-862-1983. *Dean,* Dr. Daniel Innis, 603-862-1983.

UNIVERSITY OF NEW HAVEN, West Haven, CT 06516-1916

General Information Independent, coed, comprehensive institution. CGS member. *Enrollment:* 5,949 graduate, professional, and undergraduate students; 984 full-time matriculated graduate/professional students (547 women), 762 part-time matriculated graduate/professional students (398 women). *Enrollment by degree level:* 1,172 master's, 5 doctoral, 21 other advanced degrees. *Graduate housing:* On-campus housing not available. *Student services:* Campus employment opportunities, campus safety program, career counseling, free psychological counseling, international student services, low-cost health insurance, multicultural affairs office, services for students with disabilities, writing training. *Library facilities:*

University of New Haven (continued)

Marvin K. Peterson Library. *Online resources:* library catalog, web page. *Collection:* 408,619 titles, 21,038 serial subscriptions, 1,436 audiovisual materials.

Computer facilities: Computer purchase and lease plans are available. 300 computers available on campus for general student use. A campuswide network can be accessed from student residence rooms. Online class registration, computer repair services are available. *Web address:* http://www.newhaven.edu/.

General Application Contact: Eloise Gormley, Director of Graduate Admissions, 203-932-7449, Fax: 203-932-7137, E-mail: gradinfo@newhaven.edu.

GRADUATE UNITS

Graduate School Students: 984 full-time (547 women), 762 part-time (398 women); includes 291 minority (156 Black or African American, non-Hispanic/Latino; 6 American Indian or Alaska Native, non-Hispanic/Latino; 58 Asian, non-Hispanic/Latino; 71 Hispanic/Latino), 402 international. Average age 30. 1,712 applicants, 97% accepted, 722 enrolled. *Faculty:* 85 full-time (23 women), 117 part-time/adjunct (39 women). Expenses: Contact institution. *Financial support:* In 2010–11, 182 students received support, including 34 research assistantships with partial tuition reimbursements available (averaging $5,784 per year), 52 teaching assistantships with partial tuition reimbursements available (averaging $5,784 per year); career-related internships or fieldwork, Federal Work-Study, and unspecified assistantships also available. Support available to part-time students. Financial award applicants required to submit FAFSA. In 2010, 672 master's, 68 other advanced degrees awarded. *Degree program information:* Part-time and evening/weekend programs available. *Application deadline:* For fall admission, 5/31 for international students; for winter admission, 10/15 for international students; for spring admission, 1/15 for international students. Applications are processed on a rolling basis. *Application fee:* $50. Electronic applications accepted. *Application Contact:* Eloise Gormley, Director of Graduate Admissions, 203-932-7449, Fax: 203-932-7137, E-mail: gradinfo@newhaven.edu. *Associate Provost and Dean of Graduate Studies,* Dr. Ira Kleinfeld, 203-932-7063.

College of Arts and Sciences Students: 321 full-time (231 women), 220 part-time (153 women); includes 49 minority (22 Black or African American, non-Hispanic/Latino; 2 American Indian or Alaska Native, non-Hispanic/Latino; 9 Asian, non-Hispanic/Latino; 16 Hispanic/Latino), 52 international. Average age 28. 430 applicants, 91% accepted, 221 enrolled. Expenses: Contact institution. *Financial support:* Research assistantships with partial tuition reimbursements, teaching assistantships with partial tuition reimbursements, career-related internships or fieldwork, Federal Work-Study, scholarships/grants, tuition waivers, and unspecified assistantships available. Support available to part-time students. Financial award application deadline: 5/1; financial award applicants required to submit FAFSA. In 2010, 236 master's, 4 other advanced degrees awarded. *Degree program information:* Part-time and evening/weekend programs available. Offers applications of psychology (Certificate); arts and sciences (MA, MS, Certificate); cellular and molecular biology (MS); community clinical services (MA); conflict management (MA); environmental ecology (Certificate); environmental geoscience (MS); environmental health and management (MS); environmental science (MS); forensic psychology (Certificate); geographical information systems (Certificate); human nutrition (MS); human resource management (MA); industrial organizational psychology (MA); organizational development (MA); professional education (MS); psychology of conflict management (Certificate); teacher certification (MS). *Application deadline:* For fall admission, 5/31 for international students; for winter admission, 10/15 for international students; for spring admission, 1/15 for international students. Applications are processed on a rolling basis. *Application fee:* $50. Electronic applications accepted. *Application Contact:* Eloise Gormley, Director of Graduate Admissions, 203-932-7449, Fax: 203-932-7137, E-mail: gradinfo@newhaven.edu. *Dean,* Dr. Ronald Nowaczyk, 203-932-7257.

Henry C. Lee College of Criminal Justice and Forensic Sciences Students: 164 full-time (108 women), 108 part-time (53 women); includes 30 Black or African American, non-Hispanic/Latino; 2 American Indian or Alaska Native, non-Hispanic/Latino; 5 Asian, non-Hispanic/Latino; 20 Hispanic/Latino, 20 international. Average age 29. 219 applicants, 97% accepted, 121 enrolled. Expenses: Contact institution. *Financial support:* Research assistantships with partial tuition reimbursements, teaching assistantships with partial tuition reimbursements, career-related internships or fieldwork, Federal Work-Study, scholarships/grants, tuition waivers, and unspecified assistantships available. Support available to part-time students. Financial award applicants required to submit FAFSA. In 2010, 93 master's, 24 other advanced degrees awarded. *Degree program information:* Part-time and evening/weekend programs available. Offers advanced investigation (MS, Certificate); crime analysis (MS); criminal justice (PhD); criminal justice and forensic sciences (MS, PhD, Certificate); criminal justice management (MS); criminalistics (MS, Certificate); emergency management (Certificate); fire administration (MS); fire science (MS); fire science technology (Certificate); fire/arson investigation (MS, Certificate); forensic computer investigation (MS, Certificate); forensic psychology (MS); forensic science/fire science (Certificate); information protection and security (MS); national security (Certificate); national security administration (Certificate); public safety management (MS, Certificate); victim advocacy and services management (Certificate); victimology (MS). *Application deadline:* For fall admission, 5/31 for international students; for winter admission, 10/15 for international students; for spring admission, 1/15 for international students. Applications are processed on a rolling basis. *Application fee:* $50. Electronic applications accepted. *Application Contact:* Eloise Gormley, Director of Graduate Admissions, 203-932-7449, Fax: 203-932-7137, E-mail: gradinfo@newhaven.edu. *Dean,* Dr. Richard Ward, 203-932-7260.

School of Business Students: 338 full-time (174 women), 327 part-time (173 women); includes 93 Black or African American, non-Hispanic/Latino; 2 American Indian or Alaska Native, non-Hispanic/Latino; 35 Asian, non-Hispanic/Latino; 32 Hispanic/Latino, 176 international. Average age 32. 511 applicants, 99% accepted, 246 enrolled. Expenses: Contact institution. *Financial support:* Research assistantships with partial tuition reimbursements, teaching assistantships with partial tuition reimbursements, career-related internships or fieldwork, Federal Work-Study, scholarships/grants, tuition waivers, and unspecified assistantships available. Support available to part-time students. Financial award application deadline: 5/1; financial award applicants required to submit FAFSA. In 2010, 264 master's, 28 other advanced degrees awarded. *Degree program information:* Part-time and evening/weekend programs available. Offers accounting (MBA, Certificate); business (EMBA, MBA, MPA, MS, Certificate); business administration (EMBA, MBA, Certificate); business management (Certificate); business policy and strategy (MBA); facility management (MS); finance (MBA, Certificate); finance and financial services (MS); financial accounting (MS); global marketing (MBA); health care management (Certificate); health care marketing (MS); health policy and finance (MS); human resource management (Certificate); human resource management in health care (MS); human resources management (MBA); international business (Certificate); long-term care (MS); long-term health care (Certificate); managed care (MS); management of sports industries (Certificate); managerial accounting (MS); marketing (Certificate); medical group management (MS); personnel and labor relations (MPA); public administration (MPA, Certificate); sports management (MBA, MS); taxation (MS); telecommunications management (Certificate). *Application deadline:* For fall admission, 5/31 for international students; for winter admission, 10/15 for international students; for spring admission, 1/15 for international students. Applications are processed on a rolling basis. *Application fee:* $50. Electronic applications accepted. *Application Contact:* Eloise Gormley, Director of Graduate Admissions, 203-932-7449, Fax: 203-932-7137, E-mail: gradinfo@newhaven.edu. *Dean,* Dr. Richard Highfield, 203-932-7115.

Tagliatela College of Engineering Students: 161 full-time (34 women), 91 part-time (10 women); includes 11 Black or African American, non-Hispanic/Latino; 9 Asian, non-Hispanic/Latino; 3 Hispanic/Latino, 153 international. Average age 29. 529 applicants, 99% accepted, 118 enrolled. Expenses: Contact institution. *Financial support:* Research assistantships with partial tuition reimbursements, teaching assistantships with partial tuition reimbursements, career-related internships or fieldwork, Federal Work-Study, scholarships/grants, tuition waivers, and unspecified assistantships available. Support available to part-time students. Financial award applicants required to submit FAFSA. In 2010, 78 master's, 9 other advanced degrees awarded. *Degree program information:* Part-time and evening/weekend programs available. Offers communications/digital signal processing (MS); computer science (MS, Certificate); control system (MS); electrical and computer engineering (MS); electrical engineering (MS); engineering (EMS, MS, MSIE, Certificate); engineering and operations management (MS); environmental engineering (MS); industrial and hazardous wastes (MS); industrial engineering (MSIE); lean-Six Sigma (Certificate); mechanical engineering (MS); network systems (MS); quality engineering (Certificate); water and wastewater treatment (MS); water resources (Certificate). *Application deadline:* For fall admission, 5/30 for international students; for winter admission, 10/15 for international students; for spring admission, 1/15 for international students. Applications are processed on a rolling basis. *Application fee:* $50. Electronic applications accepted. *Application Contact:* Eloise Gormley, Director of Graduate Admissions, 203-932-7449, Fax: 203-932-7137, E-mail: gradinfo@newhaven.edu. *Dean,* Dr. Barry Farbrother, 203-932-7167.

See Display on previous page and Close-Up on page 991.

UNIVERSITY OF NEW MEXICO, Albuquerque, NM 87131-2039

General Information State-supported, coed, university. CGS member. *Enrollment:* 28,688 graduate, professional, and undergraduate students; 4,091 full-time matriculated graduate/professional students (2,239 women), 2,138 part-time matriculated graduate/professional students (1,317 women). *Enrollment by degree level:* 1,045 first professional, 3,234 master's, 1,914 doctoral, 36 other advanced degrees. *Graduate faculty:* 2,215 full-time (943 women), 1,129 part-time/adjunct (639 women). Tuition, state resident: full-time $5991; part-time $251 per credit hour. Tuition, nonresident: full-time $14,405; part-time $800.20 per credit hour. Tuition and fees vary according to course level, course load, program and reciprocity agreements. *Graduate housing:* Rooms and/or apartments available on a first-come, first-served basis to single and married students. Typical cost: $4822 per year ($7638 including board) for single students; $6552 per year for married students. Room and board charges vary according to board plan, campus/location and housing facility selected. Housing application deadline: 7/16. *Student services:* Campus employment opportunities, campus safety program, career counseling, child daycare facilities, exercise/wellness program, free psychological counseling, international student services, low-cost health insurance, services for students with disabilities, teacher training. *Library facilities:* The University of New Mexico University Libraries plus 7 others. *Online resources:* library catalog, web page, access to other libraries' catalogs. *Collection:* 3.4 million titles, 85,916 serial subscriptions, 1.2 million audiovisual materials. *Research affiliation:* Sandia National Laboratories, Los Alamos National Laboratory, Lovelace Respiratory Research Institute, Phillips Laboratory, Oak Ridge National Laboratories.

Computer facilities: 766 computers available on campus for general student use. A campuswide network can be accessed from student residence rooms and from off campus. Online class registration is available. *Web address:* http://www.unm.edu/.

General Application Contact: Deborah Kieltyka, Associate Director, Admissions, 505-277-3140, Fax: 505-277-6686, E-mail: deborahk@unm.edu.

GRADUATE UNITS

Graduate School Students: 2,825 full-time (1,510 women), 1,752 part-time (1,112 women); includes 1,514 minority (98 Black or African American, non-Hispanic/Latino; 195 American Indian or Alaska Native, non-Hispanic/Latino; 154 Asian, non-Hispanic/Latino; 1,011 Hispanic/Latino; 7 Native Hawaiian or other Pacific Islander, non-Hispanic/Latino; 49 Two or more races, non-Hispanic/Latino), 514 international. Average age 34. 3,945 applicants, 35% accepted, 900 enrolled. *Faculty:* 1,292 full-time (602 women), 866 part-time/adjunct (493 women). Expenses: Contact institution. *Financial support:* In 2010–11, 3,216 students received support, including 176 fellowships (averaging $5,966 per year), 735 research assistantships (averaging $13,651 per year), 763 teaching assistantships (averaging $10,171 per year); career-related internships or fieldwork, Federal Work-Study, institutionally sponsored loans, scholarships/grants, health care benefits, tuition waivers (full and partial), and project assistantships, residencies also available. Support available to part-time students. Financial award application deadline: 3/1; financial award applicants required to submit FAFSA. In 2010, 85 first professional degrees, 779 master's, 178 doctorates, 23 other advanced degrees awarded. *Degree program information:* Part-time and evening/weekend programs available. Postbaccalaureate distance learning degree programs offered. Offers computational science and engineering (Post-Doctoral Certificate); hydroscience (MWR); nanoscience and microsystems (MS, PhD); policy management (MWR). *Application fee:* $50. Electronic applications accepted. *Application Contact:* Deborah Kieltyka, Associate Director, Admissions, 505-277-3140, Fax: 505-277-6686, E-mail: deborahk@unm.edu. *Dean,* Dr. Amy Wohlert, 505-277-2711, Fax: 505-277-7405, E-mail: awohlert@unm.edu.

College of Arts and Sciences Students: 1,091 full-time (597 women), 300 part-time (157 women); includes 305 minority (12 Black or African American, non-Hispanic/Latino; 33 American Indian or Alaska Native, non-Hispanic/Latino; 31 Asian, non-Hispanic/Latino; 213 Hispanic/Latino; 2 Native Hawaiian or other Pacific Islander, non-Hispanic/Latino; 14 Two or more races, non-Hispanic/Latino), 190 international. Average age 33. 1,687 applicants, 30% accepted, 296 enrolled. *Faculty:* 699 full-time (300 women), 568 part-time/adjunct (324 women). Expenses: Contact institution. *Financial support:* In 2010–11, 1,159 students received support, including 110 fellowships (averaging $6,560 per year), 364 research assistantships with tuition reimbursements available (averaging $12,446 per year), 576 teaching assistantships with tuition reimbursements available (averaging $11,221 per year); scholarships/grants, health care benefits, tuition waivers (full and partial), and unspecified assistantships also available. Financial award application deadline: 3/1; financial award applicants required to submit FAFSA. In 2010, 158 master's, 86 doctorates, 1 other advanced degree awarded. *Degree program information:* Part-time programs available. Offers American studies (MA, PhD); anthropology (MA, MS, PhD); arts and sciences (MA, MFA, MS, PhD, Graduate Certificate); biology (MS, PhD); biomedical physics (MS, PhD); chemistry and chemical biology (MS, PhD); clinical psychology (MS, PhD); communication (MA, PhD); comparative literature and cultural studies (MA); creative writing (MFA); earth and planetary sciences (MS, PhD); English (MA, MFA, PhD); environmental/natural resources (MA, PhD); French (MA); French studies (PhD); geography (MS); German studies (MA); history (MA, PhD); international/development (MA, PhD); labor/human resources (MA, PhD); Latin American studies (MA, PhD); linguistics (MA, PhD); mathematics (MS, PhD); optical science and engineering (MS, PhD); philosophy (MA, PhD); physics (MS, PhD); political science (MA, PhD); Portuguese (MA); psychology (PhD); public finance (MA, PhD); sociology (MA, PhD); Spanish (MA); Spanish and Portuguese (PhD); speech-language pathology (MS); statistics (MS, PhD); women studies (Graduate Certificate). *Application fee:* $50. Electronic applications accepted. *Application Contact:* Vicki Hall, Academic Administrator III, 505-277-6131, Fax: 505-277-0351, E-mail: vhall@unm.edu. *Dean,* Dr. Brenda J. Claiborne, 505-277-6131, Fax: 505-277-0351, E-mail: brendac@unm.edu.

College of Education Students: 518 full-time (366 women), 807 part-time (612 women); includes 566 minority (54 Black or African American, non-Hispanic/Latino; 66 American Indian or Alaska Native, non-Hispanic/Latino; 34 Asian, non-Hispanic/Latino; 391 Hispanic/Latino; 2 Native Hawaiian or other Pacific Islander, non-Hispanic/Latino; 19 Two or more races, non-Hispanic/Latino), 68 international. Average age 37. 679 applicants, 52% accepted, 269 enrolled. *Faculty:* 203 full-time (141 women), 115 part-time/adjunct (87 women). Expenses: Contact institution. *Financial support:* In 2010–11, 761 students received support, including 25 fellowships with partial tuition reimbursements available (averaging $3,285 per year), 19 research assistantships with partial tuition reimbursements available (averaging $9,053 per year), 68 teaching assistantships with full tuition reimbursements available (averaging $8,189 per year); career-related internships or fieldwork, Federal Work-Study, scholarships/grants, health care benefits, and unspecified assistantships also available. Support available to part-time students. Financial award application deadline: 3/1; financial award applicants required to submit FAFSA. In 2010, 311 master's, 28 doctorates, 9 other advanced degrees awarded. *Degree program information:* Part-time and evening/weekend programs available. Postbaccalaureate distance learning degree programs offered (minimal on-campus study). Offers art education (MA); counselor education (MA, PhD); curriculum and instruction (Ed S); education (MA, MS, Ed D, PhD, EDSPC, Ed S, Graduate Certificate); educational leadership (MA, Ed D, EDSPC); educational linguistics (PhD); educational psychology (MA, PhD); elementary education (MA); family studies (MA, PhD); health education (MS); intensive social, language and behavioral needs

(Graduate Certificate); language, literacy and sociocultural studies (MA, PhD); multicultural teacher and childhood education (Ed D, PhD); nutrition (MS); organizational learning and instructional technologies (MA, PhD, EDSPC); physical education (MS); physical education, sports and exercise science (PhD); secondary education (MA); special education (MA, Ed D, PhD, EDSPC). *Application deadline:* For fall admission, 3/1 for domestic students; for spring admission, 8/1 for domestic students. *Application fee:* $50. Electronic applications accepted. *Application Contact:* Receptionist, 505-277-3190, Fax: 505-277-8427. *Dean,* Dr. Richard Howell, 505-277-7267, Fax: 505-277-8427, E-mail: rhowell@unm.edu.

College of Fine Arts Students: 144 full-time (90 women), 59 part-time (37 women); includes 46 minority (4 Black or African American, non-Hispanic/Latino; 4 American Indian or Alaska Native, non-Hispanic/Latino; 5 Asian, non-Hispanic/Latino; 33 Hispanic/Latino), 20 international. Average age 32. 358 applicants, 30% accepted, 71 enrolled. *Faculty:* 140 full-time (60 women), 112 part-time/adjunct (65 women). Expenses: Contact institution. *Financial support:* In 2010–11, 172 students received support, including 5 fellowships (averaging $6,620 per year), 21 research assistantships (averaging $4,322 per year), 58 teaching assistantships (averaging $5,427 per year); unspecified assistantships also available. Financial award application deadline: 3/1; financial award applicants required to submit FAFSA. In 2010, 28 master's, 15 doctorates awarded. *Degree program information:* Part-time programs available. Offers art history (MA, PhD); collaborative piano (M Mu); conducting (M Mu); dance (MFA); dance history (MA); dramatic writing (MFA); fine arts (M Mu, MA, MFA, PhD); music education (M Mu); music history and literature (M Mu); performance (M Mu); studio arts (MFA); theatre education and outreach (MA); theory and composition (M Mu). *Application fee:* $50. *Application Contact:* Deanna Sanchez-Mulcahy, Associate Director, Admissions, 505-277-4817, Fax: 505-277-0708, E-mail: dmulcahy@unm.edu. *Dean,* Dr. Jim Linnell, 505-277-2112, Fax: 505-277-0708, E-mail: jlinnell@unm.edu.

College of Nursing Students: 50 full-time (48 women), 140 part-time (126 women); includes 58 minority (4 Black or African American, non-Hispanic/Latino; 5 American Indian or Alaska Native, non-Hispanic/Latino; 6 Asian, non-Hispanic/Latino; 43 Hispanic/Latino). Average age 42. 35 applicants, 3% accepted, 1 enrolled. *Faculty:* 50 full-time (44 women), 1 (woman) part-time/adjunct. Expenses: Contact institution. *Financial support:* In 2010–11, 89 students received support, including 10 fellowships (averaging $3,557 per year), 2 research assistantships with partial tuition reimbursements available (averaging $6,323 per year), 7 teaching assistantships with partial tuition reimbursements available (averaging $3,890 per year); institutionally sponsored loans, scholarships/grants, traineeships, and unspecified assistantships also available. Support available to part-time students. Financial award application deadline: 3/1; financial award applicants required to submit FAFSA. In 2010, 59 master's, 5 doctorates awarded. *Degree program information:* Part-time programs available. Postbaccalaureate distance learning degree programs offered (minimal on-campus study). Offers nursing (MSN, PhD). *Application fee:* $50. Electronic applications accepted. *Application Contact:* Karen Wells, Student Academic Advisor, 505-272-4223, Fax: 505-272-3970, E-mail: kwells@salud.unm.edu. *Dean,* Dr. Nancy Ridenour, 505-272-6284, Fax: 505-272-4343, E-mail: nridenour@salud.unm.edu.

College of Pharmacy Students: 354 full-time (199 women), 10 part-time (5 women); includes 188 minority (10 Black or African American, non-Hispanic/Latino; 19 American Indian or Alaska Native, non-Hispanic/Latino; 50 Asian, non-Hispanic/Latino; 104 Hispanic/Latino; 1 Native Hawaiian or other Pacific Islander, non-Hispanic/Latino; 4 Two or more races, non-Hispanic/Latino), 10 international. Average age 27. 68 applicants, 10% accepted, 4 enrolled. *Faculty:* 41 full-time (23 women), 6 part-time/adjunct (4 women). Expenses: Contact institution. *Financial support:* In 2010–11, 331 students received support, including 6 research assistantships with full and partial tuition reimbursements available (averaging $9,569 per year); residencies also available. Financial award application deadline: 3/1; financial award applicants required to submit FAFSA. In 2010, 85 first professional degrees, 3 master's, 1 doctorate awarded. *Degree program information:* Part-time programs available. Offers pharmaceutical sciences (MS, PhD); pharmacy (Pharm D, MS, PhD). *Application deadline:* For fall admission, 1/1 for domestic and international students. *Application fee:* $50. Electronic applications accepted. *Application Contact:* Krystal McCutchen, Coordinator, Academic Advisement, 505-272-0583, Fax: 505-272-8324, E-mail: kmccutchen@salud.unm.edu. *Interim Dean,* Dr. Donald Godwin, 505-272-3241, E-mail: dgodwin@salud.unm.edu.

School of Architecture and Planning Students: 183 full-time (79 women), 50 part-time (29 women); includes 2 Black or African American, non-Hispanic/Latino; 24 American Indian or Alaska Native, non-Hispanic/Latino; 4 Asian, non-Hispanic/Latino; 51 Hispanic/Latino; 2 Two or more races, non-Hispanic/Latino, 8 international. Average age 32. 250 applicants, 37% accepted, 61 enrolled. *Faculty:* 25 full-time (11 women), 31 part-time/adjunct (8 women). Expenses: Contact institution. *Financial support:* In 2010–11, 185 students received support, including 8 fellowships (averaging $6,238 per year), 10 research assistantships with full and partial tuition reimbursements available (averaging $8,590 per year), 3 teaching assistantships with full and partial tuition reimbursements available (averaging $7,124 per year). Financial award application deadline: 3/1; financial award applicants required to submit FAFSA. In 2010, 55 master's, 10 other advanced degrees awarded. Offers architecture (M Arch); architecture and planning (M Arch, MCRP, MLA, Graduate Certificate); community and regional planning (MCRP); historic preservation and regionalism (Graduate Certificate); landscape architecture (MLA); town design (Graduate Certificate). *Application deadline:* For fall admission, 2/1 for domestic and international students. *Application fee:* $50. Electronic applications accepted. *Application Contact:* Elizabeth M. Rowe, Senior Academic Adviser, 505-277-1303, Fax: 505-277-0076, E-mail: erowe@unm.edu. *Dean,* Geraldine C. Forbes Isais.

School of Engineering Students: 373 full-time (78 women), 191 part-time (31 women); includes 113 minority (6 Black or African American, non-Hispanic/Latino; 5 American Indian or Alaska Native, non-Hispanic/Latino; 17 Asian, non-Hispanic/Latino; 80 Hispanic/Latino; 1 Native Hawaiian or other Pacific Islander, non-Hispanic/Latino; 4 Two or more races, non-Hispanic/Latino), 182 international. Average age 31. 624 applicants, 32% accepted, 116 enrolled. *Faculty:* 123 full-time (20 women), 30 part-time/adjunct (3 women). Expenses: Contact institution. *Financial support:* In 2010–11, 357 students received support, including 16 fellowships (averaging $7,301 per year), 277 research assistantships (averaging $16,471 per year), 38 teaching assistantships (averaging $7,468 per year). Financial award application deadline: 3/1; financial award applicants required to submit FAFSA. In 2010, 117 master's, 36 doctorates awarded. *Degree program information:* Part-time and evening/weekend programs available. Offers biomedical engineering (PhD); chemical engineering (MS, PhD); civil engineering (MSCE); computer engineering (MS, PhD); computer science (MS, PhD); construction management (MCM); electrical engineering (MS, PhD); engineering (MCM, MEME, MS, MSCE, PhD, Post-Doctoral Certificate); manufacturing engineering (MEME); mechanical engineering (MS, PhD); nuclear engineering (MS, PhD). *Application deadline:* Applications are processed on a rolling basis. *Application fee:* $50. Electronic applications accepted. *Application Contact:* Dr. Joseph L. Cecchi, Dean, 505-277-5522, Fax: 505-277-1422, E-mail: cecchi@unm.edu. *Dean,* Dr. Joseph L. Cecchi, 505-277-5522, Fax: 505-277-1422, E-mail: cecchi@unm.edu.

School of Public Administration Students: 60 full-time (35 women), 159 part-time (100 women); includes 138 minority (6 Black or African American, non-Hispanic/Latino; 32 American Indian or Alaska Native, non-Hispanic/Latino; 5 Asian, non-Hispanic/Latino; 88 Hispanic/Latino; 1 Native Hawaiian or other Pacific Islander, non-Hispanic/Latino; 6 Two or more races, non-Hispanic/Latino), 4 international. Average age 35. 145 applicants, 57% accepted, 64 enrolled. *Faculty:* 10 full-time (3 women), 3 part-time/adjunct (1 woman). Expenses: Contact institution. *Financial support:* In 2010–11, 104 students received support, including 2 fellowships with tuition reimbursements available (averaging $5,400 per year), 3 research assistantships with tuition reimbursements available (averaging $7,171 per year); career-related internships or fieldwork, scholarships/grants, health care benefits, and unspecified assistantships also available. Financial award application deadline: 3/31; financial award applicants required to submit FAFSA. In 2010, 31 master's awarded. *Degree program information:* Part-time and evening/weekend programs available. Postbaccalaureate distance learning degree programs offered (no on-campus study). Offers public administration (MPA). *Application deadline:* For fall admission, 6/1 for domestic students, 3/1 for international students; for spring admission, 11/1 for domestic students, 8/1 for international students. *Application fee:* $50. Electronic applications accepted. *Application Contact:* Kristen L. Cole, Department Administrator, 505-277-9196, Fax: 505-277-2529, E-mail: klcole@unm.edu. *Director,* Dr. Uday Desai, 505-277-1092, Fax: 505-277-2529, E-mail: ucdesai@unm.edu.

Robert O. Anderson Graduate School of Management *Degree program information:* Part-time and evening/weekend programs available. Offers accounting (MBA); advanced accounting (M Acct); finance (MBA); human resources management (MBA); information assurance (MBA); international management (MBA); international management in Latin America (MBA); management (EMBA, M Acct, MBA); management information systems (MBA); management of technology (MBA); marketing management (MBA); operations management (MBA); policy and planning (MBA); professional accounting (M Acct); tax accounting (M Acct). Electronic applications accepted.

School of Law Students: 351 full-time (186 women); includes 150 minority (15 Black or African American, non-Hispanic/Latino; 26 American Indian or Alaska Native, non-Hispanic/Latino; 3 Asian, non-Hispanic/Latino; 100 Hispanic/Latino; 5 Native Hawaiian or other Pacific Islander, non-Hispanic/Latino; 1 Two or more races, non-Hispanic/Latino), 1 international. 1,200 applicants, 21% accepted, 116 enrolled. *Faculty:* 34 full-time (20 women), 36 part-time/adjunct (18 women). Expenses: Contact institution. *Financial support:* Career-related internships or fieldwork, Federal Work-Study, and scholarships/grants available. Financial award application deadline: 3/1; financial award applicants required to submit FAFSA. In 2010, 107 first professional degrees awarded. Offers law (JD). *Application deadline:* For fall admission, 2/15 priority date for domestic and international students. Applications are processed on a rolling basis. *Application fee:* $50. Electronic applications accepted. *Application Contact:* Susan L. Mitchell, Assistant Dean for Admissions and Financial Aid, 505-277-0959, Fax: 505-277-9958, E-mail: mitchell@law.unm.edu. *Dean,* Kevin Washburn, 505-277-4700, Fax: 505-277-9558, E-mail: washburn@law.unm.edu.

School of Medicine Students: 609 full-time (386 women), 65 part-time (51 women); includes 247 minority (10 Black or African American, non-Hispanic/Latino; 24 American Indian or Alaska Native, non-Hispanic/Latino; 36 Asian, non-Hispanic/Latino; 174 Hispanic/Latino; 3 Two or more races, non-Hispanic/Latino), 23 international. Average age 29. 361 applicants, 29% accepted, 95 enrolled. *Faculty:* 687 full-time (230 women), 110 part-time/adjunct (71 women). Expenses: Contact institution. *Financial support:* In 2010–11, 267 students received support, including 6 fellowships (averaging $663 per year), 105 research assistantships with full tuition reimbursements available (averaging $16,442 per year), 2 teaching assistantships with full tuition reimbursements available (averaging $2,415 per year); scholarships/grants also available. Financial award application deadline: 5/1; financial award applicants required to submit FAFSA. In 2010, 75 first professional degrees, 70 master's, 55 doctorates awarded. Offers biochemistry and molecular biology (MS, PhD); cell biology and physiology (MS, PhD); clinical and translational science (Certificate); clinical laboratory science (MS); dental hygiene (MS); medicine (MD, MOT, MPH, MS, DPT, PhD, Certificate); molecular genetics and microbiology (MS, PhD); neuroscience (MS, PhD); occupational therapy (MOT); pathology (MS, PhD); physical therapy (DPT); physician assistant studies (MS); public health (MPH); toxicology (MS, PhD); university science teaching (Certificate). *Application fee:* $50. Electronic applications accepted. *Application Contact:* Dr. Roberto Gomez, Associate Dean of Students, 505-272-3414, Fax: 505-272-6857, E-mail: rgomez@unm.edu. *Dean,* Dr. Paul B. Roth, 505-272-8273, Fax: 505-272-6857.

UNIVERSITY OF NEW ORLEANS, New Orleans, LA 70148

General Information State-supported, coed, university. CGS member. *Graduate housing:* Room and/or apartments available on a first-come, first-served basis to single students; on-campus housing not available to married students. *Research affiliation:* John C. Stennis Space Center (acoustics, computer science), Northrop Grumman Corporation (engineering), TJ Watson Research Center–IBM (chemistry), Paratek Microwave, Inc. (nanotechnology), Applied Research Lab-Penn State University (engineering), Lockheed Martin Corporation (materials).

GRADUATE UNITS

Graduate School *Degree program information:* Part-time and evening/weekend programs available. Postbaccalaureate distance learning degree programs offered (minimal on-campus study). Electronic applications accepted.

College of Business Administration *Degree program information:* Part-time and evening/weekend programs available. Offers accounting (MS); business administration (MBA, MS, PhD); economics and finance (MS); financial economics (PhD); health care management (MS); hospitality and tourism management (MS); taxation (MS). Electronic applications accepted.

College of Education and Human Development *Degree program information:* Part-time programs available. Postbaccalaureate distance learning degree programs offered. Offers counselor education (M Ed, PhD, GCE); curriculum and instruction (M Ed, PhD, GCE); education and human development (M Ed, MAT, PhD, GCE); educational leadership (M Ed, PhD, GCE); special education (M Ed, PhD, GCE). Electronic applications accepted.

College of Engineering *Degree program information:* Part-time programs available. Offers engineering (MS, PhD, Certificate); engineering and applied sciences (PhD); engineering management (MS, Certificate); mechanical engineering (MS). Electronic applications accepted.

College of Liberal Arts *Degree program information:* Part-time and evening/weekend programs available. Offers arts administration (MA); English (MA); film production (MFA); fine arts (MFA); foreign languages (MA); geography (MA); history (MA); liberal arts (MA, MFA, MM, MPA, MS, MURP, PhD); music (MM); political science (MA, PhD); public administration (MPA); sociology (MA); theatre directing (MFA); theatre performance (MFA); urban and regional planning (MURP); urban planning and regional studies (MS, MURP, PhD); urban studies (MS, PhD). Electronic applications accepted.

College of Sciences *Degree program information:* Part-time and evening/weekend programs available. Offers biological sciences (MS, PhD); chemistry (MS, PhD); computer science (MS); earth and environmental sciences (MS); mathematics (MS); physics (MS, PhD); psychology (MS, PhD); sciences (MS, PhD). Electronic applications accepted.

UNIVERSITY OF NORTH ALABAMA, Florence, AL 35632-0001

General Information State-supported, coed, comprehensive institution. *Enrollment:* 7,209 graduate, professional, and undergraduate students; 408 full-time matriculated graduate/professional students (215 women), 640 part-time matriculated graduate/professional students (390 women). *Enrollment by degree level:* 1,028 master's, 20 other advanced degrees. *Graduate faculty:* 16 full-time (9 women), 62 part-time/adjunct (23 women). Tuition, state resident: full-time $5472; part-time $228 per credit hour. Tuition, nonresident: full-time $10,944; part-time $456 per credit hour. *Required fees:* $986. Tuition and fees vary according to course load. *Graduate housing:* Rooms and/or apartments available on a first-come, first-served basis to single and married students. *Student services:* Campus employment opportunities, career counseling, child daycare facilities, exercise/wellness program, grant writing training, international student services, multicultural affairs office, services for students with disabilities. *Library facilities:* Collier Library plus 3 others. *Online resources:* library catalog, web page, access to other libraries' catalogs. *Collection:* 405,406 titles, 3,711 serial subscriptions, 14,236 audiovisual materials.

Computer facilities: 1,000 computers available on campus for general student use. A campuswide network can be accessed from student residence rooms and from off campus. Online class registration is available. *Web address:* http://www.una.edu/.

General Application Contact: Kim Mauldin, Director of Admissions, 256-765-4608, Fax: 256-765-4960, E-mail: komauldin@una.edu.

GRADUATE UNITS

College of Arts and Sciences Students: 35 full-time (16 women), 51 part-time (33 women); includes 12 minority (11 Black or African American, non-Hispanic/Latino; 1 Two or more races, non-Hispanic/Latino), 5 international. Average age 31. *Faculty:* 4 full-time (0 women), 25 part-time/adjunct (8 women). Expenses: Contact institution. In 2010, 14 master's awarded. *Degree program information:* Part-time and evening/weekend programs available. Offers arts

University of North Alabama (continued)

and sciences (MA, MAEN, MSCJ); criminal justice (MSCJ); English (MAEN); history and political science (MA). *Application deadline:* For fall admission, 7/1 priority date for domestic students; for spring admission, 12/1 for domestic students. Applications are processed on a rolling basis. *Application fee:* $25. *Application Contact:* Kim Mauldin, Director of Admissions, 256-765-4608, Fax: 256-765-4960, E-mail: komauldin@una.edu. *Dean,* Dr. Vagn Hansen, 256-765-4288, Fax: 256-765-4778, E-mail: vhansen@una.edu.

College of Business Students: 248 full-time (113 women), 326 part-time (154 women); includes 288 minority (42 Black or African American, non-Hispanic/Latino; 5 American Indian or Alaska Native, non-Hispanic/Latino; 231 Asian, non-Hispanic/Latino; 3 Hispanic/Latino; 2 Native Hawaiian or other Pacific Islander, non-Hispanic/Latino; 5 Two or more races, non-Hispanic/Latino), 49 international. Average age 35. *Faculty:* 3 full-time (0 women), 17 part-time/adjunct (4 women). Expenses: Contact institution. *Financial support:* Federal Work-Study available. Support available to part-time students. Financial award application deadline: 4/1. In 2010, 268 master's awarded. *Degree program information:* Part-time and evening/weekend programs available. Offers business (MBA). *Application deadline:* For fall admission, 7/1 priority date for domestic students; for spring admission, 12/1 for domestic students. Applications are processed on a rolling basis. *Application fee:* $25. Electronic applications accepted. *Application Contact:* Kim Mauldin, Director of Admissions, 256-765-4608, Fax: 256-765-4960, E-mail: komauldin@una.edu. *Dean,* Dr. Kerry Gatlin, 256-765-4261, Fax: 256-765-4170, E-mail: kpgatlin@una.edu.

College of Education Students: 116 full-time (78 women), 213 part-time (154 women); includes 460 minority (23 Black or African American, non-Hispanic/Latino; 41 American Indian or Alaska Native, non-Hispanic/Latino; 1 Asian, non-Hispanic/Latino; 393 Hispanic/Latino; 2 Two or more races, non-Hispanic/Latino). Average age 32. *Faculty:* 7 full-time (all women), 19 part-time/adjunct (10 women). Expenses: Contact institution. *Financial support:* Federal Work-Study available. Support available to part-time students. Financial award application deadline: 4/1. In 2010, 90 master's, 8 other advanced degrees awarded. *Degree program information:* Part-time and evening/weekend programs available. Offers collaborative teacher special education (MA Ed); counseling (MA Ed); education (MA, MA Ed, Ed S); education leadership (Ed S); elementary education (MA Ed); learning disabilities (MA Ed); mentally retarded (MA Ed); mild learning handicapped (MA Ed); non-school-based counseling (MA); non-school-based teaching (MA); secondary education (MA Ed, Ed S). *Application deadline:* For fall admission, 7/1 priority date for domestic students; for spring admission, 12/1 for domestic students. Applications are processed on a rolling basis. *Application fee:* $25. Electronic applications accepted. *Application Contact:* Kim Mauldin, Director of Admissions, 256-765-4608, Fax: 256-765-4960, E-mail: komauldin@una.edu. *Dean,* Dr. Donna Jacobs, 256-765-4252, Fax: 256-765-4664, E-mail: dpjacobs@una.edu.

College of Nursing and Allied Health Students: 9 full-time (8 women), 50 part-time (49 women); includes 12 minority (11 Black or African American, non-Hispanic/Latino; 1 Two or more races, non-Hispanic/Latino). Average age 37. *Faculty:* 2 full-time (both women), 1 (woman) part-time/adjunct. Expenses: Contact institution. In 2010, 9 master's awarded. Offers nursing and allied health (MSN). *Application Contact:* Kim Mauldin, Director of Admissions, 256-465-4608, Fax: 256-765-4960, E-mail: komauldin@una.edu. *Dean,* Dr. Birdie Bailey, 256-765-4984, E-mail: bibailey@una.edu.

THE UNIVERSITY OF NORTH CAROLINA AT ASHEVILLE, Asheville, NC 28804-3299

General Information State-supported, coed, comprehensive institution. *Enrollment:* 3,967 graduate, professional, and undergraduate students; 45 part-time matriculated graduate/professional students (27 women). *Enrollment by degree level:* 23 master's. *Graduate faculty:* 8 full-time (5 women), 5 part-time/adjunct (2 women). Tuition, state resident: full-time $3110. Tuition, nonresident: full-time $15,706. *Required fees:* $2097. *Graduate housing:* On-campus housing not available. *Student services:* Campus employment opportunities, career counseling, exercise/wellness program, free psychological counseling, international student services, low-cost health insurance, multicultural affairs office, services for students with disabilities, teacher training, writing training. *Library facilities:* D. Hidden Ramsey Library. *Online resources:* library catalog, web page, access to other libraries' catalogs. *Collection:* 275,323 titles, 13,592 serial subscriptions, 9,185 audiovisual materials.

Computer facilities: Computer purchase and lease plans are available. 360 computers available on campus for general student use. A campuswide network can be accessed from student residence rooms and from off campus. Online class registration is available. *Web address:* http://www.unca.edu/.

General Application Contact: Director, 828-250-2399.

GRADUATE UNITS

Graduate Studies Students: 45 part-time (27 women); includes 1 Asian, non-Hispanic/Latino; 2 Two or more races, non-Hispanic/Latino. Average age 43. 29 applicants, 97% accepted, 15 enrolled. *Faculty:* 8 full-time (5 women), 5 part-time/adjunct (2 women). Expenses: Contact institution. *Financial support:* Federal Work-Study and institutionally sponsored loans available. Support available to part-time students. Financial award application deadline: 5/1; financial award applicants required to submit FAFSA. In 2010, 8 master's awarded. *Degree program information:* Part-time and evening/weekend programs available. *Application deadline:* For fall admission, 4/15 for domestic students; for spring admission, 11/15 for domestic students. Applications are processed on a rolling basis. *Application fee:* $50.

THE UNIVERSITY OF NORTH CAROLINA AT CHAPEL HILL, Chapel Hill, NC 27599

General Information State-supported, coed, university. CGS member. *Enrollment:* 29,390 graduate, professional, and undergraduate students; 8,685 full-time matriculated graduate/professional students (4,931 women), 875 part-time matriculated graduate/professional students (609 women). *Enrollment by degree level:* 2,469 first professional, 3,700 master's, 3,391 doctoral. *Graduate faculty:* 3,235 full-time (1,867 women), 284 part-time/adjunct (122 women). *Graduate housing:* Rooms and/or apartments available on a first-come, first-served basis to single and married students. *Student services:* Campus employment opportunities, campus safety program, career counseling, child daycare facilities, exercise/wellness program, free psychological counseling, grant writing training, international student services, low-cost health insurance, multicultural affairs office, services for students with disabilities, teacher training, writing training. *Library facilities:* Davis Library plus 19 others. *Online resources:* library catalog, web page, access to other libraries' catalogs. *Collection:* 7 million titles, 87,639 serial subscriptions, 430,892 audiovisual materials. *Research affiliation:* Centers for Disease Control, Research Triangle Institute, Triangle Universities Nuclear Laboratory.

Computer facilities: Computer purchase and lease plans are available. 740 computers available on campus for general student use. A campuswide network can be accessed from student residence rooms and from off campus. Online class registration is available. *Web address:* http://www.unc.edu/.

GRADUATE UNITS

Eshelman School of Pharmacy Students: 99 full-time (48 women); includes 7 Black or African American, non-Hispanic/Latino; 7 Asian, non-Hispanic/Latino, 29 international. Average age 26. 204 applicants, 7% accepted, 14 enrolled. *Faculty:* 88 full-time (34 women), 2 part-time/adjunct (1 woman). Expenses: Contact institution. *Financial support:* In 2010–11, 16 students received support, including 16 fellowships with full tuition reimbursements available (averaging $22,500 per year), 65 research assistantships with full tuition reimbursements available (averaging $22,500 per year), 18 teaching assistantships with full tuition reimbursements available (averaging $22,500 per year); career-related internships or fieldwork, Federal Work-Study, institutionally sponsored loans, scholarships/grants, traineeships, health care benefits, and unspecified assistantships also available. Financial award application deadline: 4/1. In 2010, 4 master's, 17 doctorates awarded. *Degree program information:* Part-time programs available. Postbaccalaureate distance learning degree programs offered (minimal on-campus study). Offers pharmacy (MS, PhD). *Application deadline:* For fall admission, 4/1 for domestic and international students. Applications are processed on a rolling basis. *Application fee:* $75. Electronic applications accepted. *Application Contact:* Amber M. Allen, Graduate Services Manager, 919-843-9759, Fax: 919-966-3525, E-mail: amber_allen@unc.edu. *Dean,* Dr. Robert A. Blouin, 919-966-1122, Fax: 919-966-6919, E-mail: bob_blouin@unc.edu.

Graduate School Students: 5,266 full-time (3,268 women), 693 part-time (453 women); includes 412 Black or African American, non-Hispanic/Latino; 31 American Indian or Alaska Native, non-Hispanic/Latino; 161 Asian, non-Hispanic/Latino; 229 Hispanic/Latino, 786 international. Average age 28. 13,958 applicants, 25% accepted, 1833 enrolled. *Faculty:* 1,113 full-time (463 women), 75 part-time/adjunct (35 women). Expenses: Contact institution. *Financial support:* In 2010–11, 225 fellowships with full and partial tuition reimbursements, 1,034 research assistantships with full and partial tuition reimbursements, 985 teaching assistantships with full and partial tuition reimbursements were awarded; career-related internships or fieldwork, Federal Work-Study, institutionally sponsored loans, scholarships/grants, traineeships, health care benefits, and unspecified assistantships also available. Support available to part-time students. Financial award applicants required to submit FAFSA. In 2010, 1,223 master's, 509 doctorates awarded. Postbaccalaureate distance learning degree programs offered (minimal on-campus study). *Application deadline:* For fall admission, 12/15 priority date for domestic and international students. Applications are processed on a rolling basis. Electronic applications accepted. *Application Contact:* Director of Admissions and Enrolled Students. *Dean.*

College of Arts and Sciences *Degree program information:* Part-time programs available. Offers acting (MFA); anthropology (MA, PhD); art history (MA, PhD); arts and sciences (MA, MCRP, MFA, MPA, MRP, MS, MSRA, PhD, Certificate); athletic training (MA); biological psychology (PhD); botany (MA, MS, PhD); cell biology, development, and physiology (MA, MS, PhD); cell motility and cytoskeleton (PhD); chemistry (MA, MS, PhD); city and regional planning (MCRP); classical archaeology (MA, PhD); classics (MA, PhD); clinical psychology (PhD); cognitive psychology (PhD); communication studies (PhD); computer science (MS, PhD); costume production (MFA); developmental psychology (PhD); ecology (MA, MS, PhD); ecology and behavior (MA, MS, PhD); economics (MS, PhD); English (MA, PhD); exercise physiology (MA); folklore (MA); French (MA, PhD); genetics and molecular biology (MA, MS, PhD); geography (MA, PhD); geological sciences (MS, PhD); history (MA, PhD); Italian (MA, PhD); Latin American studies (Certificate); linguistics (MA); literature and linguistics (MA, PhD); marine sciences (MS, PhD); materials science (MS, PhD); mathematics (MA, MS, PhD); morphology, systematics, and evolution (MA, MS, PhD); music (MA, PhD); operations research (MS, PhD); philosophy (MA, PhD); physics (MS, PhD); planning (PhD); Polish literature (PhD); political science (MA, PhD); Portuguese (MA, PhD); public policy (PhD); public policy analysis (PhD); quantitative psychology (PhD); religious studies (MA, PhD); Romance languages (MA, PhD); Romance philology (MA, PhD); Russian and east Euorpean studies (MA); Russian and east European studies (MA); Russian literature (MA, PhD); Serbo-Croatian literature (PhD); Slavic linguistics (MA, PhD); social psychology (PhD); sociology (MA, PhD); Spanish (MA, PhD); sport administration (MA); statistics (MS, PhD); studio art (MFA); technical production (MFA); trans-Atlantic studies (MA). Electronic applications accepted.

School of Education Students: 379 full-time (274 women), 187 part-time (160 women); includes 135 minority (100 Black or African American, non-Hispanic/Latino; 5 American Indian or Alaska Native, non-Hispanic/Latino; 7 Asian, non-Hispanic/Latino; 17 Hispanic/Latino; 4 Native Hawaiian or other Pacific Islander, non-Hispanic/Latino; 2 Two or more races, non-Hispanic/Latino), 18 international. Average age 33. 665 applicants, 57% accepted, 235 enrolled. *Faculty:* 50 full-time (33 women), 34 part-time/adjunct (17 women). Expenses: Contact institution. *Financial support:* Fellowships with full and partial tuition reimbursements, research assistantships with full and partial tuition reimbursements, teaching assistantships with full tuition reimbursements, Federal Work-Study, scholarships/grants, traineeships, health care benefits, and unspecified assistantships available. Financial award application deadline: 3/1; financial award applicants required to submit FAFSA. In 2010, 165 master's, 28 doctorates awarded. *Degree program information:* Part-time programs available. Offers culture, curriculum and change (MA, PhD); early childhood intervention and family support (M Ed); early childhood, intervention and literacy (MA, PhD); education (M Ed, MA, MAT, MSA, Ed D, PhD); education for experienced teachers (K-12) (M Ed); educational leadership (Ed D); educational psychology, measurement and evaluation (MA, PhD); English (Grades 9-12) (MAT); English as a second language (MAT); French (Grades K-12) (MAT); German (Grades K-12) (MAT); Japanese (Grades K-12) (MAT); Latin (Grades 9-12) (MAT); mathematics (Grades 9-12) (MAT); music (Grades K-12) (MAT); school administration (MSA); school counseling (M Ed); school psychology (M Ed, MA, PhD); science (Grades 9-12) (MAT); social studies (Grades 9-12) (MAT); Spanish (Grades K-12) (MAT). *Application deadline:* For fall admission, 12/15 priority date for domestic and international students; for spring admission, 11/1 priority date for domestic and international students. Applications are processed on a rolling basis. *Application fee:* $77. Electronic applications accepted. *Application Contact:* Amy Butler, Student Services Assistant, 919-966-1346, Fax: 919-962-1533, E-mail: abutler@email.unc.edu. *Dean,* Dr. Bill McDiarmid, 919-966-7000, Fax: 919-962-1533.

School of Government Students: 43 full-time (27 women); includes 9 minority (8 Black or African American, non-Hispanic/Latino; 1 Hispanic/Latino). Average age 25. 98 applicants, 34% accepted, 24 enrolled. *Faculty:* 15 full-time (3 women), 2 part-time/adjunct (both women). Expenses: Contact institution. *Financial support:* In 2010–11, 35 students received support, including fellowships with full tuition reimbursements available (averaging $7,000 per year), 25 research assistantships with full tuition reimbursements available (averaging $5,000 per year), 1 teaching assistantship with full tuition reimbursement available (averaging $7,000 per year); career-related internships or fieldwork, Federal Work-Study, and scholarships/grants also available. Financial award application deadline: 3/1; financial award applicants required to submit FAFSA. In 2010, 18 master's awarded. Offers government (MPA). *Application deadline:* For fall admission, 1/1 priority date for domestic students. Applications are processed on a rolling basis. *Application fee:* $60. Electronic applications accepted. *Application Contact:* Jessica C. Russell, Admissions Coordinator, 919-962-0425, Fax: 919-962-8271, E-mail: mpastaff@iogmail.iog.unc.edu. *Director,* Dr. David N. Ammons, 919-962-7696, Fax: 919-962-8271, E-mail: ammons@iogmail.iog.unc.edu.

School of Information and Library Science Students: 321 full-time (232 women), 34 part-time (19 women); includes 7 Black or African American, non-Hispanic/Latino; 1 American Indian or Alaska Native, non-Hispanic/Latino; 15 Hispanic/Latino, 14 international. Average age 28. 468 applicants, 57% accepted, 119 enrolled. *Faculty:* 25 full-time (10 women), 46 part-time/adjunct (23 women). Expenses: Contact institution. *Financial support:* In 2010–11, 58 fellowships with full tuition reimbursements (averaging $2,436 per year), 153 research assistantships with full tuition reimbursements (averaging $10,018 per year), 4 teaching assistantships with full tuition reimbursements (averaging $11,000 per year) were awarded; career-related internships or fieldwork, Federal Work-Study, institutionally sponsored loans, health care benefits, and unspecified assistantships also available. Financial award application deadline: 12/15. In 2010, 111 master's, 14 doctorates awarded. *Degree program information:* Part-time programs available. Offers information and library science (MSIS, MSLS, PhD, CAS). *Application deadline:* For fall admission, 12/15 priority date for domestic and international students; for spring admission, 10/15 for domestic and international students. Applications are processed on a rolling basis. *Application fee:* $77. Electronic applications accepted. *Application Contact:* Lara Bailey, Student Services Manager, 919-962-8366, Fax: 919-962-8071, E-mail: info@ils.unc.edu. *Dean,* Dr. Gary Marchionini, 919-962-8363, Fax: 919-962-8071, E-mail: gary@ils.unc.edu.

School of Journalism and Mass Communication Students: 82 full-time (59 women), 1 (woman) part-time; includes 7 Black or African American, non-Hispanic/Latino; 8 Asian, non-Hispanic/Latino; 3 Hispanic/Latino. Average age 30. 278 applicants, 18% accepted, 33 enrolled. *Faculty:* 48 full-time (21 women). Expenses: Contact institution. *Financial support:* In 2010–11, 14 research assistantships with full tuition reimbursements (averaging $14,000 per year) were awarded; institutionally sponsored loans and health care benefits also available. Financial award application deadline: 3/1; financial award applicants required to submit FAFSA. In 2010, 20 master's, 5 doctorates awarded. *Degree program information:* Part-time programs available. Offers mass communication (MA, PhD). *Application deadline:* For fall admission, 1/1 for domestic and international students. *Application fee:* $77. Electronic applications accepted. *Application Contact:* Graduate Program Administrator, 919-962-1204, E-mail: jomcgrad@unc.edu. *Dean,* Dr. Jean Folkerts, 919-962-1204, Fax: 919-962-0620.

School of Public Health Students: 655 full-time (465 women), 271 part-time (192 women); includes 65 Black or African American, non-Hispanic/Latino; 3 American Indian or Alaska Native, non-Hispanic/Latino; 55 Asian, non-Hispanic/Latino; 29 Hispanic/Latino, 106 international. Average age 27. 2,342 applicants, 41% accepted, 490 enrolled. *Faculty:* 217 full-time (114 women), 16 part-time/adjunct (9 women). Expenses: Contact institution. *Financial support:* Fellowships with tuition reimbursements, research assistantships with tuition reimbursements, teaching assistantships with tuition reimbursements, career-related internships or fieldwork, Federal Work-Study, institutionally sponsored loans, scholarships/grants, traineeships, and unspecified assistantships available. Support available to part-time students. Financial award application deadline: 11/15; financial award applicants required to submit FAFSA. In 2010, 351 master's, 91 doctorates awarded. *Degree program information:* Part-time programs available. Postbaccalaureate distance learning degree programs offered (minimal on-campus study). Offers air, radiation and industrial hygiene (MPH, MS, MSEE, MSPH, PhD); aquatic and atmospheric sciences (MPH, MS, MSPH, PhD); biostatistics (MPH, MS, Dr PH, PhD); environmental engineering (MPH, MS, MSEE, MSPH, PhD); environmental health sciences (MPH, MS, MSPH, PhD); environmental management and policy (MPH, MS, MSPH, PhD); epidemiology (MPH, MSCR, PhD); health behavior and health education (MPH, PhD); health care and prevention (MPH); health policy and management (MHA, MPH, MSPH, Dr PH, PhD); leadership (MPH); maternal and child health (MPH, MSPH, Dr PH, PhD); nutrition (MPH, Dr PH, PhD); nutritional biochemistry (MS); occupational health nursing (MPH); professional practice program (MPH); public health (MHA, MPH, MS, MSCR, MSEE, MSPH, Dr PH, PhD); public health nursing (MS). *Application deadline:* For fall admission, 12/15 priority date for domestic and international students. Applications are processed on a rolling basis. *Application fee:* $77. Electronic applications accepted. *Application Contact:* Sherry Rhodes, Director of Student Services, 919-966-0064, Fax: 919-966-6352, E-mail: srhodes@email.unc.edu. *Dean,* Dr. Barbara K. Rimer, 919-966-3245, Fax: 919-966-7678.

School of Social Work *Degree program information:* Part-time programs available. Offers social work (MSW, PhD). Electronic applications accepted.

Kenan-Flagler Business School *Degree program information:* Evening/weekend programs available. Postbaccalaureate distance learning degree programs offered (minimal on-campus study). Offers accounting (PhD); business (MAC, MBA, PhD); business administration (MBA, PhD); finance (PhD); marketing (PhD); operations management (PhD); organizational behavior (PhD); strategy (PhD). Electronic applications accepted.

School of Dentistry Offers dental hygiene (MS); dentistry (DDS, MS, PhD); endodontics (MS); epidemiology (PhD); operative dentistry (MS); oral and maxillofacial pathology (MS); oral and maxillofacial radiology (MS); oral biology (PhD); orthodontics (MS); pediatric dentistry (MS); periodontology (MS); prosthodontics (MS). Electronic applications accepted.

School of Law Offers law (JD). JD/MAPPS offered jointly with Duke University. Electronic applications accepted.

School of Medicine Offers allied health sciences (MPT, MS, Au D, DPT, PhD); audiology (Au D); biochemistry and biophysics (MS, PhD); bioinformatics and computational biology (PhD); biomedical engineering (MS, PhD); cell and developmental biology (PhD); cell and molecular physiology (PhD); experimental pathology (PhD); genetics and molecular biology (PhD); human movement science (PhD); immunology (MS, PhD); medicine (MD, MPT, MS, Au D, DPT, PhD); microbiology (MS, PhD); microbiology and immunology (MS, PhD); neurobiology (PhD); occupational science (MS, PhD); pathology and laboratory medicine (PhD); pharmacology (PhD); physical therapy (DPT); physical therapy—off campus (DPT); physical therapy—on campus (DPT); rehabilitation counseling and psychology (MS); speech and hearing sciences (MS, Au D, PhD); toxicology (MS, PhD). Electronic applications accepted.

School of Nursing *Degree program information:* Part-time programs available. Offers nursing (MSN, PhD, PMC).

THE UNIVERSITY OF NORTH CAROLINA AT CHARLOTTE, Charlotte, NC 28223-0001

General Information State-supported, coed, university. CGS member. *Enrollment:* 25,063 graduate, professional, and undergraduate students; 1,869 full-time matriculated graduate/professional students (980 women), 3,439 part-time matriculated graduate/professional students (2,238 women). *Enrollment by degree level:* 3,010 master's, 828 doctoral, 1,470 other advanced degrees. *Graduate faculty:* 750 full-time (278 women), 64 part-time/adjunct (39 women). Tuition, state resident: full-time $3464. Tuition, nonresident: full-time $14,297. *Required fees:* $2094. Tuition and fees vary according to course load. *Graduate housing:* Room and/or apartments available on a first-come, first-served basis to single students; on-campus housing not available to married students. Typical cost: $4850 per year ($8280 including board). Room and board charges vary according to housing facility selected. Housing application deadline: 5/1. *Student services:* Campus employment opportunities, campus safety program, career counseling, exercise/wellness program, free psychological counseling, grant writing training, international student services, low-cost health insurance, multicultural affairs office, services for students with disabilities, writing training. *Library facilities:* J. Murrey Atkins Library. *Online resources:* library catalog, web page, access to other libraries' catalogs. *Collection:* 1.1 million titles, 46,966 serial subscriptions, 18,468 audiovisual materials.

Computer facilities: 3,500 computers available on campus for general student use. A campuswide network can be accessed from student residence rooms and from off campus. Online class registration is available. *Web address:* http://www.uncc.edu/.

General Application Contact: Kathy B. Giddings, Director of Graduate Admissions, 704-687-5503, Fax: 704-687-3279, E-mail: gradcounselor@uncc.edu.

GRADUATE UNITS

Graduate School Students: 1,869 full-time (980 women), 3,439 part-time (2,238 women); includes 1,035 minority (693 Black or African American, non-Hispanic/Latino; 14 American Indian or Alaska Native, non-Hispanic/Latino; 142 Asian, non-Hispanic/Latino; 153 Hispanic/Latino; 2 Native Hawaiian or other Pacific Islander, non-Hispanic/Latino; 31 Two or more races, non-Hispanic/Latino), 777 international. Average age 31. 3,470 applicants, 68% accepted, 1269 enrolled. *Faculty:* 750 full-time (278 women), 64 part-time/adjunct (39 women). Expenses: Contact institution. *Financial support:* In 2010–11, 795 students received support, including 35 fellowships (averaging $34,686 per year), 229 research assistantships (averaging $9,864 per year), 510 teaching assistantships (averaging $10,302 per year); career-related internships or fieldwork, institutionally sponsored loans, scholarships/grants, traineeships, unspecified assistantships, and administrative assistantships also available. Support available to part-time students. Financial award application deadline: 4/1; financial award applicants required to submit FAFSA. In 2010, 1,142 master's, 95 doctorates awarded. *Degree program information:* Part-time and evening/weekend programs available. Postbaccalaureate distance learning degree programs offered (no on-campus study). *Application deadline:* For fall admission, 7/15 for domestic students, 5/1 for international students; for spring admission, 11/15 for domestic students, 10/1 for international students. Applications are processed on a rolling basis. *Application fee:* $55. Electronic applications accepted. *Application Contact:* Kathy B. Giddings, Director of Graduate Admissions, 704-687-5503, Fax: 704-687-3279, E-mail: gradadm@uncc.edu. *Dean and Associate Provost,* Dr. Thomas L. Reynolds, 704-687-5503, Fax: 687-687-3279, E-mail: gradadm@uncc.edu.

Belk College of Business Students: 260 full-time (103 women), 436 part-time (138 women); includes 114 minority (51 Black or African American, non-Hispanic/Latino; 41 Asian, non-Hispanic/Latino; 19 Hispanic/Latino; 3 Two or more races, non-Hispanic/Latino), 199 international. Average age 30. 579 applicants, 82% accepted, 238 enrolled. *Faculty:* 72 full-time (17 women), 2 part-time/adjunct (0 women). Expenses: Contact institution. *Financial support:* In 2010–11, 68 students received support, including 2 research assistantships (averaging $18,000 per year), 65 teaching assistantships (averaging $12,142 per year); career-related internships or fieldwork, institutionally sponsored loans, scholarships/grants, unspecified assistantships, and administrative assistantship also available. Support available to part-time students. Financial award application deadline: 4/1; financial award applicants required to submit FAFSA. In 2010, 345 master's, 1 doctorate awarded. *Degree program information:* Part-time and evening/weekend programs available. Offers accounting (M Acc); business (M Acc, MBA, MS, PhD, Certificate, Post-Master's Certificate); business administration (PhD); economics (MS); Hong Kong (MBA); mathematical finance (MS); MBA-plus (Post-Master's Certificate); Mexico (MBA); real estate finance and development (Certificate); sports marketing and management (MBA); Taiwan (MBA); U. S. (MBA). *Application deadline:* For fall admission, 7/15 for domestic students, 5/1 for international students; for spring admission, 11/15 for domestic students, 10/1 for international students. Applications are processed on a rolling basis. *Application fee:* $55. Electronic applications accepted. *Application Contact:* Kathy B. Giddings, Director of Graduate Admissions, 704-687-5503, Fax: 704-687-3279, E-mail: gradadm@uncc.edu. *Interim Dean,* Dr. Joe Mazzola, 704-687-7577, Fax: 704-687-4014, E-mail: jmazzola@uncc.edu.

College of Arts and Architecture Students: 76 full-time (36 women), 6 part-time (5 women); includes 8 minority (5 Black or African American, non-Hispanic/Latino; 2 Asian, non-Hispanic/Latino; 1 Hispanic/Latino), 1 international. Average age 27. 72 applicants, 67% accepted, 32 enrolled. *Faculty:* 34 full-time (12 women), 3 part-time/adjunct (0 women). Expenses: Contact institution. *Financial support:* In 2010–11, 12 students received support, including 5 research assistantships (averaging $9,032 per year), 7 teaching assistantships (averaging $8,451 per year); career-related internships or fieldwork, institutionally sponsored loans, scholarships/grants, and unspecified assistantships also available. Support available to part-time students. Financial award application deadline: 4/1; financial award applicants required to submit FAFSA. In 2010, 29 master's awarded. Offers architecture (M Arch); urban design (MUD). *Application deadline:* For fall admission, 2/15 for domestic students, 1/31 for international students. *Application fee:* $55. Electronic applications accepted. *Application Contact:* Kathy B. Giddings, Director of Graduate Admissions, 704-687-5503, Fax: 704-687-3279, E-mail: gradadm@uncc.edu. *Dean,* Kenneth A. Lambla, 704-687-4024, Fax: 704-687-3353, E-mail: kalambla@uncc.edu.

College of Arts and Sciences Students: 431 full-time (236 women), 472 part-time (283 women); includes 149 minority (97 Black or African American, non-Hispanic/Latino; 2 American Indian or Alaska Native, non-Hispanic/Latino; 18 Asian, non-Hispanic/Latino; 21 Hispanic/Latino; 2 Native Hawaiian or other Pacific Islander, non-Hispanic/Latino; 9 Two or more races, non-Hispanic/Latino), 124 international. Average age 29. 878 applicants, 47% accepted, 241 enrolled. *Faculty:* 326 full-time (121 women), 14 part-time/adjunct (7 women). Expenses: Contact institution. *Financial support:* In 2010–11, 350 students received support, including 21 fellowships (averaging $36,471 per year), 94 research assistantships (averaging $10,374 per year), 228 teaching assistantships (averaging $10,575 per year); career-related internships or fieldwork, institutionally sponsored loans, scholarships/grants, and administrative assistantships also available. Support available to part-time students. Financial award application deadline: 4/1; financial award applicants required to submit FAFSA. In 2010, 165 master's, 25 doctorates awarded. *Degree program information:* Part-time and evening/weekend programs available. Offers applied ethics (Certificate); applied mathematics (MS, PhD); applied physics (MS); arts and sciences (MA, MPA, MS, PhD, Certificate); biology (MA, MS, PhD); chemistry (MS); community/clinical psychology (MA); criminal justice (MS); earth sciences (MS); emergency management (Certificate); English (MA); English education (MA); ethics and applied philosophy (MA); geography (MA); geography and urban regional analysis (PhD); gerontology (MA, Certificate); health communication (MA); health psychology (PhD); health research (MA); history (MA); industrial/organizational psychology (MA); Latin American studies (MA); liberal studies (MA); mathematical sociology and quantitative methods (MA); mathematics (MS); mathematics education (MA); media/rhetorical critical studies (MA); nanoscale science (PhD); non-profit management (Certificate); optical science and engineering (MS, PhD); organizational communication (MA); organizational science (PhD); organizations, occupations, and work (MA); political sociology (MA); public administration (MPA, PhD); public finance (Certificate); public policy (PhD); public relations (MA); race and gender (MA); religious studies (MA); social psychology (MA); social theory (MA); sociology of education (MA); Spanish (MA); stratification (MA); technical/professional writing (Certificate); urban management and policy (Certificate); women's studies (Certificate). *Application deadline:* For fall admission, 7/15 for domestic students, 5/1 for international students; for spring admission, 11/15 for domestic students, 10/1 for international students. Applications are processed on a rolling basis. *Application fee:* $55. Electronic applications accepted. *Application Contact:* Kathy B. Giddings, Director of Graduate Admissions, 704-687-5503, Fax: 704-687-3279, E-mail: gradadm@uncc.edu. *Dean,* Dr. Nancy A. Gutierrez, 704-687-4303, Fax: 704-687-3228, E-mail: ngutierr@uncc.edu.

College of Computing and Informatics Students: 277 full-time (80 women), 111 part-time (37 women); includes 50 minority (27 Black or African American, non-Hispanic/Latino; 1 American Indian or Alaska Native, non-Hispanic/Latino; 12 Asian, non-Hispanic/Latino; 8 Hispanic/Latino; 2 Two or more races, non-Hispanic/Latino), 211 international. Average age 28. 466 applicants, 82% accepted, 115 enrolled. *Faculty:* 5 full-time (0 women), 52 part-time/adjunct (16 women). Expenses: Contact institution. *Financial support:* In 2010–11, 107 students received support, including 11 fellowships (averaging $32,060 per year), 37 research assistantships (averaging $11,279 per year), 59 teaching assistantships (averaging $11,190 per year); career-related internships or fieldwork, institutionally sponsored loans, scholarships/grants, and unspecified assistantships also available. Support available to part-time students. Financial award application deadline: 4/1; financial award applicants required to submit FAFSA. In 2010, 108 master's, 19 doctorates awarded. *Degree program information:* Part-time and evening/weekend programs available. Offers advance databases and knowledge discovery (Certificate); bioinformatics (MS); computer science (MS); computing and informatics (MS, PhD, Certificate); game design and development (Certificate); health care information (Certificate); information security/privacy (Certificate); information technology (MS, PhD, Certificate). *Application deadline:* For fall admission, 7/1 for domestic students, 5/1 for international students; for spring admission, 11/1 for domestic students, 10/1 for international students. Applications are processed on a rolling basis. *Application fee:* $55. Electronic applications accepted. *Application Contact:* Kathy B. Giddings, Director of Graduate Admissions, 704-687-5503, Fax: 704-687-3279, E-mail: gradadm@uncc.edu. *Dean,* Dr. Mirsad Hadzikadic, 704-687-3119, Fax: 704-687-6979, E-mail: mirsad@uncc.edu.

College of Education Students: 327 full-time (260 women), 1,659 part-time (1,324 women); includes 355 Black or African American, non-Hispanic/Latino; 68 Hispanic/Latino; 11 Two or more races, non-Hispanic/Latino, 15 international. Average age 33. 519 applicants, 87% accepted, 364 enrolled. *Faculty:* 104 full-time (60 women), 25 part-time/adjunct (20 women). Expenses: Contact institution. *Financial support:* In 2010–11, 40 students received support, including 11 research assistantships (averaging $14,648 per year), 23 teaching assistantships (averaging $9,961 per year); career-related internships or fieldwork, institutionally sponsored loans, scholarships/grants, and administrative assistantship also available. Support available to part-time students. Financial award application deadline: 4/1; financial award applicants required to submit FAFSA. In 2010, 258 master's, 30 doctorates awarded. *Degree program information:* Part-time and evening/weekend programs available. Postbaccalaureate distance learning degree programs offered (no on-campus study). Offers art education (MAT); child and family studies (M Ed); counseling (MA, PhD); curriculum and instruction (PhD); curriculum and supervision (M Ed); dance education (MAT); education (M Ed, MA, MAT, MSA, Ed D, PhD, Certificate, Post-Master's Certificate); educational leadership (Ed D); elementary education (M Ed, MAT); foreign language education (MAT); instructional systems technology (M Ed); middle grades and secondary education (M Ed); middle grades education (MAT); music education (MAT); play therapy (Certificate); reading, language and literacy (M Ed); school administration (MSA); school counseling (MA); secondary education (MAT); special education (M Ed, PhD); teaching English as a second language (M Ed); theatre education (MAT). *Application deadline:* For fall admission, 7/1 for domestic students, 5/1 for international students; for spring admission, 11/1 for domestic students, 10/1 for international students. Applications are processed on a rolling basis. *Application fee:* $55. Electronic applications accepted. *Application Contact:* Kathy B. Giddings, Director of Graduate Admissions, 704-687-5503, Fax: 704-687-3279, E-mail: gradadm@uncc.edu. *Dean,* Dr. Mary Lynne Calhoun, 704-687-8722, Fax: 704-687-4705, E-mail: mlcalhou@uncc.edu.

College of Health and Human Services Students: 255 full-time (206 women), 257 part-time (218 women); includes 117 minority (84 Black or African American, non-Hispanic/Latino; 1 American Indian or Alaska Native, non-Hispanic/Latino; 17 Asian, non-Hispanic/Latino; 13 Hispanic/Latino; 2 Two or more races, non-Hispanic/Latino), 15 international. Average age 32. 435 applicants, 63% accepted, 189 enrolled. *Faculty:* 57 full-time (41 women), 15

The University of North Carolina at Charlotte (continued)

part-time/adjunct (11 women). Expenses: Contact institution. *Financial support:* In 2010–11, 43 students received support, including 14 research assistantships (averaging $7,653 per year), 23 teaching assistantships (averaging $7,942 per year); career-related internships or fieldwork, institutionally sponsored loans, scholarships/grants, traineeships, and administrative assistantship also available. Support available to part-time students. Financial award application deadline: 4/1; financial award applicants required to submit FAFSA. In 2010, 160 master's, 4 doctorates awarded. *Degree program information:* Part-time and evening/weekend programs available. Postbaccalaureate distance learning degree programs offered (no on-campus study). Offers administration (Post-Master's Certificate); advanced clinical (MSN, Post-Master's Certificate); anesthesia (MSN, Post-Master's Certificate); clinical exercise physiology (MS); community health (MSN, Certificate); family nurse practitioner (MSN, Post-Master's Certificate); health administration (MHA, MSN); health and human services (MHA, MS, MSN, MSPH, MSW, PhD, Certificate, Post-Master's Certificate); health services research (PhD); mental health (MSN); nurse educator (MSN, Post-Master's Certificate); public health (MSPH); social work (MSW); systems population (MSN). *Application deadline:* For fall admission, 7/1 for domestic students, 5/1 for international students; for spring admission, 11/1 for domestic students, 10/1 for international students. Applications are processed on a rolling basis. Electronic applications accepted. *Application Contact:* Kathy B. Giddings, Director of Graduate Admissions, 704-687-5503, Fax: 704-687-3279, E-mail: gradadm@uncc.edu. *Dean,* Dr. Karen Schmaling, 704-687-4651, Fax: 704-687-3180, E-mail: kbschaml@uncc.edu.

The William States Lee College of Engineering Students: 213 full-time (44 women), 173 part-time (37 women); includes 38 minority (18 Black or African American, non-Hispanic/Latino; 2 American Indian or Alaska Native, non-Hispanic/Latino; 8 Asian, non-Hispanic/Latino; 9 Hispanic/Latino; 1 Two or more races, non-Hispanic/Latino), 201 international. Average age 27. 431 applicants, 61% accepted, 64 enrolled. *Faculty:* 82 full-time (8 women), 1 (woman) part-time/adjunct. Expenses: Contact institution. *Financial support:* In 2010–11, 169 students received support, including 3 fellowships (averaging $31,815 per year), 65 research assistantships (averaging $7,814 per year), 101 teaching assistantships (averaging $8,748 per year); career-related internships or fieldwork, institutionally sponsored loans, scholarships/grants, and administrative assistantship also available. Support available to part-time students. Financial award application deadline: 4/1; financial award applicants required to submit FAFSA. In 2010, 77 master's, 16 doctorates awarded. *Degree program information:* Part-time and evening/weekend programs available. Offers civil engineering (MSCE); electrical engineering (MSEE, PhD); engineering (MS, MSCE, MSE, MSEE, MSME, PhD); engineering management (MS); infrastructure and environmental systems (PhD); mechanical engineering (MSE, MSME, PhD). *Application deadline:* For fall admission, 7/1 for domestic students, 5/1 for international students; for spring admission, 11/1 for domestic students, 10/1 for international students. Applications are processed on a rolling basis. *Application fee:* $55. Electronic applications accepted. *Application Contact:* Kathy B. Giddings, Director of Graduate Admissions, 704-687-5503, Fax: 704-687-3279, E-mail: gradadm@uncc.edu. *Dean,* Dr. Robert E. Johnson, 704-687-2301, Fax: 704-687-2352, E-mail: robejohn@.uncc.edu.

THE UNIVERSITY OF NORTH CAROLINA AT GREENSBORO, Greensboro, NC 27412-5001

General Information State-supported, coed, university. CGS member. *Graduate housing:* Room and/or apartments available to single students; on-campus housing not available to married students. Housing application deadline: 5/15. *Research affiliation:* Moses Cone Memorial Hospital, North Carolina Zoological Park, North Carolina Baptist Hospital.

GRADUATE UNITS

Graduate School *Degree program information:* Part-time and evening/weekend programs available. Postbaccalaureate distance learning degree programs offered (minimal on-campus study). Offers conflict resolution (MA, Certificate); genetic counseling (MS); gerontology (MS, Certificate); liberal studies (MALS). Electronic applications accepted.

Bryan School of Business and Economics *Degree program information:* Part-time programs available. Offers accounting (MS); accounting systems (MS); applied economics (MA); business administration (MBA, PMC, Postbaccalaureate Certificate); business and economics (MA, MBA, MS, PhD, Certificate, PMC, Postbaccalaureate Certificate); economics (PhD); financial accounting and reporting (MS); financial analysis (PMC); financial economics (MA); information systems (PhD); information technology (Certificate); information technology and management (MS); supply chain management (Certificate); tax concentration (MS). Electronic applications accepted.

College of Arts and Sciences *Degree program information:* Part-time programs available. Offers acting (MFA); advanced Spanish language and Hispanic cultural studies (Certificate); American literature (PhD); applied geography (MA); arts and sciences (M Ed, MA, MFA, MPA, MS, PhD, Certificate); biochemistry (MS); biology (MS); chemistry (MS); clinical psychology (MA, PhD); cognitive psychology (MA, PhD); communication studies (MA); computer science (MS); creative writing (MFA); criminology (MA); design (MFA); developmental psychology (MA, PhD); directing (MFA); English (M Ed, MA, PhD, Certificate); English literature (PhD); film and video production (MFA); French (MA); geographic information science (Certificate); geography (PhD); historic preservation (Certificate); history (MA); Latin (M Ed); mathematics (MA, PhD); museum studies (Certificate); nonprofit management (Certificate); public affairs (MPA); rhetoric and composition (PhD); social psychology (MA, PhD); sociology (MA); Spanish (MA, Certificate); studio arts (MFA); theater education (M Ed); theater for youth (MFA); U.S. history (PhD); urban and economic development (Certificate); women's and gender studies (MA, Certificate). Electronic applications accepted.

School of Education *Degree program information:* Part-time and evening/weekend programs available. Offers advanced school counseling (PMC); college teaching and adult learning (Certificate); counseling and counselor education (PhD); counseling and educational development (MS); couple and family counseling (PMC); cross-categorical special education (M Ed); curriculum and instruction (M Ed); curriculum and teaching (PhD); education (M Ed, MLIS, MS, MSA, Ed D, PhD, Certificate, Ed S, PMC); educational leadership (Ed D, Ed S); educational research, measurement and evaluation (PhD); English as a second language (Certificate); higher education (M Ed, PhD); interdisciplinary studies in special education (M Ed); leadership early care and education (Certificate); library and information studies (MLIS); school administration (MSA); school counseling (PMC); special education (M Ed, PhD); supervision (M Ed); teacher education and development (PhD). Electronic applications accepted.

School of Health and Human Performance Offers community health education (MPH, Dr PH); dance (MA, MFA); exercise and sports science (M Ed, MS, Ed D, PhD); health and human performance (M Ed, MA, MFA, MPH, MS, Dr PH, Ed D, PhD); parks and recreation management (MS); speech language pathology (PhD); speech pathology and audiology (MA). Electronic applications accepted.

School of Human Environmental Sciences Offers consumer, apparel, and retail studies (MS, PhD); historic preservation (Certificate); human development and family studies (M Ed, MS, PhD); human environmental sciences (M Ed, MS, MSW, PhD, Certificate); interior architecture (MS); museum studies (Certificate); nutrition (MS, PhD); social work (MSW). Electronic applications accepted.

School of Music Offers composition (MM); education (MM); music education (PhD); performance (MM, DMA). Electronic applications accepted.

School of Nursing Offers adult clinical nurse specialist (MSN, PMC); adult/gerontological nurse practitioner (MSN, PMC); nurse anesthesia (MSN, PMC); nursing (PhD); nursing administration (MSN); nursing education (MSN). Electronic applications accepted.

THE UNIVERSITY OF NORTH CAROLINA AT PEMBROKE, Pembroke, NC 28372-1510

General Information State-supported, coed, comprehensive institution. CGS member. *Graduate housing:* Room and/or apartments available to single students; on-campus housing not available to married students. Housing application deadline: 4/15.

GRADUATE UNITS

Graduate Studies *Degree program information:* Part-time and evening/weekend programs available. Offers art education (MA, MAT); English education (MA, MAT); mathematics education (MA, MAT); music education (MA, MAT); physical education (MA, MAT); public administration (MPA); science education (MA); service agency counseling (MA); social studies education (MA, MAT).

School of Business *Degree program information:* Part-time and evening/weekend programs available. Offers business (MBA); business administration (MBA).

School of Education *Degree program information:* Part-time and evening/weekend programs available. Offers elementary education (MA Ed); middle grades education (MA Ed, MAT); reading education (MA Ed); school administration (MSA); school counseling (MA Ed).

UNIVERSITY OF NORTH CAROLINA SCHOOL OF THE ARTS, Winston-Salem, NC 27127-2188

General Information State-supported, coed, comprehensive institution. *Enrollment:* 872 graduate, professional, and undergraduate students; 126 full-time matriculated graduate/professional students (68 women). *Enrollment by degree level:* 126 master's. *Graduate faculty:* 76. Tuition, state resident: full-time $4946. Tuition, nonresident: full-time $17,253. *Required fees:* $2092. *Graduate housing:* Room and/or apartments available on a first-come, first-served basis to single students. Typical cost: $7256 (including board). Housing application deadline: 5/16. *Student services:* Campus employment opportunities, campus safety program, career counseling, exercise/wellness program, free psychological counseling, grant writing training, international student services, low-cost health insurance, services for students with disabilities, writing training. *Library facilities:* Semans Library plus 1 other. *Online resources:* library catalog, access to other libraries' catalogs. *Collection:* 87,917 titles, 490 serial subscriptions.

Computer facilities: 60 computers available on campus for general student use. A campuswide network can be accessed from student residence rooms and from off campus. *Web address:* http://www.uncsa.edu/.

General Application Contact: Sheeler Lawson, Director of Admissions, 336-770-3290, Fax: 336-770-3370, E-mail: admissions@uncsa.edu.

GRADUATE UNITS

School of Design and Production Students: 73 full-time (50 women); includes 3 Black or African American, non-Hispanic/Latino; 2 American Indian or Alaska Native, non-Hispanic/Latino; 3 Asian, non-Hispanic/Latino; 2 Hispanic/Latino, 3 international. Average age 25. 86 applicants, 77% accepted, 48 enrolled. *Faculty:* 19 full-time (4 women), 16 part-time/adjunct (6 women). Expenses: Contact institution. *Financial support:* In 2010–11, 2 teaching assistantships with partial tuition reimbursements (averaging $1,500 per year) were awarded; career-related internships or fieldwork, Federal Work-Study, unspecified assistantships, and Academic Common Market also available. Support available to part-time students. Financial award application deadline: 3/15; financial award applicants required to submit FAFSA. In 2010, 21 master's awarded. Offers costume design (MFA); costume technology (MFA); performance arts management (MFA); scene design (MFA); scene painting/properties (MFA); sound design (MFA); stage automation (MFA); technical direction (MFA); wig and make-up design (MFA). *Application deadline:* For fall admission, 4/1 priority date for domestic students. Applications are processed on a rolling basis. *Application fee:* $60 ($100 for international students). Electronic applications accepted. *Application Contact:* Sheeler Lawson, Director of Admissions, 336-770-3290, Fax: 336-770-3370, E-mail: admissions@uncsa.edu. *Dean,* Joseph A. Tilford, 336-770-3214 Ext. 103, Fax: 336-770-3213, E-mail: tilford@uncsa.edu.

School of Filmmaking Students: 6 full-time (1 woman); includes 1 Asian, non-Hispanic/Latino. Average age 25. 6 applicants, 33% accepted, 2 enrolled. *Faculty:* 1 full-time (0 women). Expenses: Contact institution. *Financial support:* In 2010–11, fellowships (averaging $2,000 per year); career-related internships or fieldwork, Federal Work-Study, and Academic Common Market also available. Support available to part-time students. Financial award application deadline: 3/15; financial award applicants required to submit FAFSA. In 2010, 3 master's awarded. Offers film music composition (MFA). *Application deadline:* For fall admission, 4/1 priority date for domestic students. Applications are processed on a rolling basis. *Application fee:* $60 ($100 for international students). *Application Contact:* Sheeler Lawson, Director of Admissions, 336-770-3290, Fax: 336-770-3370, E-mail: admissions@uncsa.edu. *Dean,* Jordan Kerner, 336-770-1330, Fax: 336-770-1339, E-mail: kernerj@uncsa.edu.

School of Music Students: 46 full-time (18 women); includes 6 Black or African American, non-Hispanic/Latino; 1 American Indian or Alaska Native, non-Hispanic/Latino; 1 Asian, non-Hispanic/Latino; 1 Hispanic/Latino, 3 international. Average age 25. *Faculty:* 30 full-time (9 women), 11 part-time/adjunct (3 women). Expenses: Contact institution. *Financial support:* In 2010–11, 8 fellowships with partial tuition reimbursements (averaging $2,000 per year), 3 teaching assistantships with partial tuition reimbursements (averaging $3,000 per year) were awarded; career-related internships or fieldwork and Federal Work-Study also available. Financial award application deadline: 3/15; financial award applicants required to submit FAFSA. In 2010, 20 master's awarded. Offers music performance (MM). *Application deadline:* For fall admission, 4/1 priority date for domestic students. Applications are processed on a rolling basis. *Application fee:* $60 ($100 for international students). *Application Contact:* Sheeler Lawson, Director of Admissions, 336-770-3290, Fax: 336-770-3370, E-mail: admissions@uncsa.edu. *Dean,* Dr. Wade Weast, 336-770-3251, Fax: 336-770-3248, E-mail: weastw@uncsa.edu.

THE UNIVERSITY OF NORTH CAROLINA WILMINGTON, Wilmington, NC 28403-3297

General Information State-supported, coed, comprehensive institution. CGS member. *Enrollment:* 13,071 graduate, professional, and undergraduate students; 449 full-time matriculated graduate/professional students (284 women), 852 part-time matriculated graduate/professional students (529 women). *Enrollment by degree level:* 1,257 master's, 44 doctoral. *Graduate faculty:* 285 full-time (107 women), 29 part-time/adjunct (12 women). *Graduate housing:* Room and/or apartments available on a first-come, first-served basis to single students; on-campus housing not available to married students. Housing application deadline: 3/31. *Student services:* Campus employment opportunities, campus safety program, career counseling, exercise/wellness program, free psychological counseling, international student services, low-cost health insurance, services for students with disabilities. *Library facilities:* William Madison Randall Library. *Online resources:* library catalog, web page, access to other libraries' catalogs. *Collection:* 1.1 million titles, 30,000 serial subscriptions, 114,113 audiovisual materials.

Computer facilities: Computer purchase and lease plans are available. 1,111 computers available on campus for general student use. A campuswide network can be accessed from student residence rooms and from off campus. Online class registration is available. *Web address:* http://www.uncw.edu/.

General Application Contact: Dr. Robert D. Roer, Dean, Graduate School and Research, 910-962-7303, Fax: 910-962-3787, E-mail: roer@uncw.edu.

GRADUATE UNITS

Center for Marine Science Students: 8 full-time (6 women), 20 part-time (11 women); includes 1 Hispanic/Latino; 1 Two or more races, non-Hispanic/Latino. Average age 27. 28 applicants, 46% accepted, 7 enrolled. *Faculty:* 66 full-time (16 women). Expenses: Contact institution. *Financial support:* In 2010–11, research assistantships with full and partial tuition reimbursements (averaging $10,000 per year), 11 teaching assistantships with full and partial tuition reimbursements (averaging $10,000 per year) were awarded; scholarships/grants and unspecified assistantships also available. Support available to part-time students. In 2010, 10 master's awarded. *Degree program information:* Part-time programs available. Offers marine science (MS). *Application deadline:* For fall admission, 3/15 for domestic students. *Application fee:* $60. *Application Contact:* Dr. Joan Willey, Graduate Coordinator, 910-962-3459, E-mail: willeyj@uncw.edu. *Director,* Dr. Daniel Baden, 910-962-2301, E-mail: badend@uncw.edu.

College of Arts and Sciences Students: 208 full-time (133 women), 370 part-time (219 women); includes 27 Black or African American, non-Hispanic/Latino; 2 American Indian or

Alaska Native, non-Hispanic/Latino; 15 Asian, non-Hispanic/Latino; 22 Hispanic/Latino, 24 international. Average age 30. 812 applicants, 44% accepted, 218 enrolled. *Faculty:* 207 full-time (63 women), 20 part-time/adjunct (9 women). Expenses: Contact institution. *Financial support:* In 2010–11, research assistantships with full and partial tuition reimbursements (averaging $10,000 per year), 207 teaching assistantships with full and partial tuition reimbursements (averaging $10,000 per year) were awarded; career-related internships or fieldwork and Federal Work-Study also available. Support available to part-time students. Financial award application deadline: 3/15. In 2010, 176 master's, 1 doctorate awarded. *Degree program information:* Part-time programs available. Offers applied gerontology (MS); arts and sciences (MA, MFA, MPA, MS, MSW, PhD, Graduate Certificate); biology (MS); chemistry and biochemistry (MS); coastal management (MA); computer science and information systems (MS); creative writing (MFA); criminology (MA); English (MA); environmental education and interpretation (MA); environmental management (MA); geology (MS); Hispanic studies (Graduate Certificate); history (MA); individualized study (MA); liberal studies (MA); marine biology (MS, PhD); marine science (MS); mathematical sciences (MS); psychology (MA); public and international affairs (MPA); public sociology (MA); social work (MSW); Spanish (MA). *Application deadline:* Applications are processed on a rolling basis. *Application fee:* $45. *Application Contact:* Dr. Robert D. Roer, Dean, Graduate School and Research, 910-962-4117, Fax: 910-962-3787, E-mail: roer@uncw.edu. *Dean,* Dr. David Cordle, 910-962-3111, Fax: 910-962-3114, E-mail: cordled@uncw.edu.

School of Business *Degree program information:* Part-time and evening/weekend programs available. Offers accountancy (MSA); business (MBA, MSA); business administration (MBA).

School of Nursing Students: 21 full-time (19 women), 27 part-time (all women); includes 5 Black or African American, non-Hispanic/Latino; 7 American Indian or Alaska Native, non-Hispanic/Latino; 1 Asian, non-Hispanic/Latino; 1 Two or more races, non-Hispanic/Latino. Average age 36. 30 applicants, 83% accepted, 23 enrolled. *Faculty:* 15 full-time (all women). Expenses: Contact institution. *Financial support:* In 2010–11, 2 teaching assistantships with full and partial tuition reimbursements (averaging $9,500 per year) were awarded. Financial award application deadline: 3/15. In 2010, 2 master's awarded. Offers family nurse practitioner (MSN); nurse educator (MSN). *Application deadline:* For fall admission, 3/1 for domestic students. Applications are processed on a rolling basis. *Application fee:* $60. Electronic applications accepted. *Application Contact:* Dr. Julie Taylor, Graduate Coordinator, 910-962-7927, E-mail: taylorjs@uncw.edu. *Graduate Program Coordinator,* Dr. Ruthanne Kuiper, 910-962-3343, E-mail: kuiperr@uncw.edu.

Watson School of Education *Degree program information:* Part-time and evening/weekend programs available. Offers curriculum, instruction and supervision (M Ed); education (M Ed, MAT, MS, MSA, Ed D); educational leadership (MSA, Ed D); educational leadership and administration (Ed D); elementary education (M Ed); instructional technology (MS); language and literacy education (M Ed); middle grades education (M Ed, MS); school administration (MSA); secondary education (M Ed); teaching (MAT).

UNIVERSITY OF NORTH DAKOTA, Grand Forks, ND 58202

General Information State-supported, coed, university. CGS member. *Enrollment:* 14,194 graduate, professional, and undergraduate students; 1,875 full-time matriculated graduate/professional students (1,088 women), 1,419 part-time matriculated graduate/professional students (926 women). *Enrollment by degree level:* 636 first professional, 1,050 master's, 619 doctoral, 989 other advanced degrees. *Graduate faculty:* 695 full-time (290 women), 87 part-time/adjunct (25 women). Tuition, state resident: full-time $5857; part-time $306.74 per credit. Tuition, nonresident: full-time $15,666; part-time $729.77 per credit. *Required fees:* $53.42 per credit. Tuition and fees vary according to course load, program and reciprocity agreements. *Graduate housing:* Rooms and/or apartments guaranteed to single students and available on a first-come, first-served basis to married students. *Student services:* Campus employment opportunities, campus safety program, career counseling, child daycare facilities, exercise/wellness program, free psychological counseling, grant writing training, international student services, low-cost health insurance, multicultural affairs office, services for students with disabilities, writing training. *Library facilities:* Chester Fritz Library plus 2 others. *Online resources:* library catalog, web page. *Collection:* 1.1 million titles, 43,394 serial subscriptions, 20,687 audiovisual materials. *Research affiliation:* North Dakota Geological Survey, U. S. Department of Agriculture (USDA)–Human Nutrition Research Center, Neuropsychiatric Research Institute (neurosciences), Environmental Energy Research Center.

Computer facilities: Computer purchase and lease plans are available. 1,500 computers available on campus for general student use. A campuswide network can be accessed from student residence rooms and from off campus. Online class registration is available. *Web address:* http://www.und.nodak.edu/.

General Application Contact: Evan A. Nelson, Director of Admissions, 701-777-2945, Fax: 701-777-3619, E-mail: gradschool@mail.und.nodak.edu.

GRADUATE UNITS

Graduate School Students: 1,117 full-time (679 women), 1,463 part-time (940 women); includes 223 minority (62 Black or African American, non-Hispanic/Latino; 61 American Indian or Alaska Native, non-Hispanic/Latino; 48 Asian, non-Hispanic/Latino; 45 Hispanic/Latino; 1 Native Hawaiian or other Pacific Islander, non-Hispanic/Latino; 6 Two or more races, non-Hispanic/Latino), 219 international. Average age 33. 1,787 applicants, 40% accepted, 612 enrolled. *Faculty:* 578 full-time (240 women), 89 part-time/adjunct (25 women). Expenses: Contact institution. *Financial support:* In 2010–11, 613 students received support, including 254 research assistantships with full and partial tuition reimbursements available (averaging $13,000 per year), 285 teaching assistantships with full and partial tuition reimbursements available (averaging $13,000 per year); fellowships with full and partial tuition reimbursements available, career-related internships or fieldwork, Federal Work-Study, institutionally sponsored loans, scholarships/grants, traineeships, health care benefits, tuition waivers (full and partial), and unspecified assistantships also available. Support available to part-time students. Financial award application deadline: 3/15; financial award applicants required to submit FAFSA. In 2010, 746 master's, 78 doctorates, 51 other advanced degrees awarded. *Degree program information:* Part-time and evening/weekend programs available. Postbaccalaureate distance learning degree programs offered (minimal on-campus study). Offers anatomy and cell biology (MS, PhD); biochemistry and molecular biology (MS, PhD); clinical laboratory science (MS); medicine (MOT, MPAS, MPT, MS, DPT, PhD); microbiology and immunology (MS, PhD); occupational therapy (MOT); pharmacology (MS, PhD); physical therapy (MPT, DPT); physician assistant (MPAS); physiology (MS, PhD). *Application deadline:* For fall admission, 8/1 priority date for domestic and international students; for spring admission, 12/1 priority date for domestic and international students. Applications are processed on a rolling basis. *Application fee:* $35. Electronic applications accepted. *Application Contact:* Evan Nelson, Director of Graduate Admissions and Recruitment, 701-777-2945, Fax: 701-777-3619, E-mail: evan.nelson@gradschool.und.edu. *Dean,* Dr. Joseph N. Benoit, 701-777-2786, Fax: 701-777-3619, E-mail: joseph.benoit@und.edu.

College of Arts and Sciences Students: 267 full-time (170 women), 218 part-time (136 women); includes 50 minority (6 Black or African American, non-Hispanic/Latino; 24 American Indian or Alaska Native, non-Hispanic/Latino; 9 Asian, non-Hispanic/Latino; 9 Hispanic/Latino; 2 Two or more races, non-Hispanic/Latino), 52 international. Average age 31. 372 applicants, 34% accepted, 107 enrolled. *Faculty:* 193 full-time (69 women), 25 part-time/adjunct (7 women). Expenses: Contact institution. *Financial support:* In 2010–11, 208 students received support, including 38 research assistantships with full tuition reimbursements available (averaging $8,763 per year), 158 teaching assistantships with full tuition reimbursements available (averaging $9,300 per year); fellowships with full and partial tuition reimbursements available, career-related internships or fieldwork, Federal Work-Study, institutionally sponsored loans, scholarships/grants, health care benefits, tuition waivers (full and partial), and unspecified assistantships also available. Support available to part-time students. Financial award application deadline: 3/15; financial award applicants required to submit FAFSA. In 2010, 70 master's, 26 doctorates awarded. *Degree program information:* Part-time programs available. Postbaccalaureate distance learning degree programs offered. Offers arts and sciences (M Ed, M Mus, MA, MFA, MS, DA, DMEd, PhD); botany (MS, PhD); chemistry (MS, PhD); clinical psychology (PhD); communication (MA); communication and public discourse (PhD); communication sciences and disorders (PhD); counseling psychology (PhD); criminal justice (PhD); ecology (MS, PhD); English (MA, PhD); entomology (MS, PhD); environmental biology (MS, PhD); experimental psychology (PhD); fisheries/wildlife (MS, PhD); forensic psychology (MA, MS); genetics (MS, PhD); geography (MA, MS); history (MA, DA, PhD); linguistics (MA); mathematics (M Ed, MS); music (M Mus); music education (M Mus, DMEd); physics (MS, PhD); psychology (MA); sociology (MA); speech-language pathology (MS); theatre arts (MA); visual arts (MFA); zoology (MS, PhD). *Application deadline:* For fall admission, 8/1 for domestic and international students; for spring admission, 12/15 for domestic and international students. *Application fee:* $35. Electronic applications accepted. *Application Contact:* Evan Nelson, Director of Admissions and Recruitment, 701-777-2945, Fax: 701-777-3619, E-mail: evan.nelson@gradschool.und.edu. *Dean,* Dr. Kathleen Tiemann, 701-777-2749, Fax: 701-777-4397, E-mail: kathleen.tiemann@as.und.edu.

College of Business and Public Administration Students: 74 full-time (25 women), 121 part-time (46 women); includes 16 minority (4 Black or African American, non-Hispanic/Latino; 3 American Indian or Alaska Native, non-Hispanic/Latino; 5 Asian, non-Hispanic/Latino; 3 Hispanic/Latino; 1 Two or more races, non-Hispanic/Latino), 17 international. Average age 30. 134 applicants, 62% accepted, 70 enrolled. *Faculty:* 57 full-time (12 women), 2 part-time/adjunct (0 women). Expenses: Contact institution. *Financial support:* In 2010–11, 44 students received support, including research assistantships with full tuition reimbursements available (averaging $5,625 per year), 4 teaching assistantships with full tuition reimbursements available (averaging $6,728 per year); fellowships with full and partial tuition reimbursements available, Federal Work-Study, institutionally sponsored loans, scholarships/grants, health care benefits, tuition waivers (full and partial), and unspecified assistantships also available. Support available to part-time students. Financial award application deadline: 3/15; financial award applicants required to submit FAFSA. In 2010, 64 master's awarded. *Degree program information:* Part-time and evening/weekend programs available. Postbaccalaureate distance learning degree programs offered. Offers accountancy (M Acc); applied economics (MSAE); business administration (MBA); business and public administration (M Acc, MBA, MPA, MSAE, MSIT); public administration (MPA); technology (MSIT). *Application deadline:* For fall admission, 8/1 priority date for domestic and international students; for spring admission, 12/1 priority date for domestic and international students. Applications are processed on a rolling basis. *Application fee:* $35. Electronic applications accepted. *Application Contact:* Evan Nelson, Director of Graduate Admissions and Recruitment, 701-777-2945, Fax: 701-777-3619, E-mail: evan.nelson@gradschool.und.edu. *Dean,* Dr. Dennis J. Elbert, 701-777-2135, Fax: 701-777-5099, E-mail: dennis.elbert@mail.und.nodak.edu.

College of Education and Human Development Students: 216 full-time (167 women), 607 part-time (464 women); includes 76 minority (26 Black or African American, non-Hispanic/Latino; 25 American Indian or Alaska Native, non-Hispanic/Latino; 5 Asian, non-Hispanic/Latino; 18 Hispanic/Latino; 2 Two or more races, non-Hispanic/Latino), 28 international. Average age 33. 387 applicants, 48% accepted, 164 enrolled. *Faculty:* 74 full-time (44 women), 18 part-time/adjunct (9 women). Expenses: Contact institution. *Financial support:* In 2010–11, 83 students received support, including 14 research assistantships with full and partial tuition reimbursements available (averaging $7,232 per year), 54 teaching assistantships with full and partial tuition reimbursements available (averaging $8,026 per year); fellowships with full and partial tuition reimbursements available, career-related internships or fieldwork, Federal Work-Study, institutionally sponsored loans, scholarships/grants, tuition waivers (full and partial), and unspecified assistantships also available. Support available to part-time students. Financial award application deadline: 3/15; financial award applicants required to submit FAFSA. In 2010, 148 master's, 41 doctorates, 27 other advanced degrees awarded. *Degree program information:* Part-time and evening/weekend programs available. Postbaccalaureate distance learning degree programs offered (minimal on-campus study). Offers counseling (MA); early childhood education (MS); education and human development (M Ed, MA, MS, MSW, Ed D, PhD, Specialist); education/general studies (MS); educational leadership (M Ed, MS, Ed D, PhD, Specialist); elementary education (M Ed, MS); instructional design and technology (M Ed, MS); kinesiology (MS); measurement and statistics (Ed D, PhD); reading education (M Ed, MS); secondary education (Ed D, PhD); social work (MSW); special education (Ed D, PhD). *Application deadline:* Applications are processed on a rolling basis. *Application fee:* $35. Electronic applications accepted. *Application Contact:* Evan Nelson, Director of Admissions and Recruitment, 701-777-2945, Fax: 701-777-3619, E-mail: evan.nelson@gradschool.und.edu. *Dean,* Dr. Dan R. Rice, 701-777-4255, Fax: 701-777-4393, E-mail: dan.rice@mail.und.nodak.edu.

College of Nursing Students: 99 full-time (85 women), 131 part-time (122 women); includes 15 minority (6 Black or African American, non-Hispanic/Latino; 4 American Indian or Alaska Native, non-Hispanic/Latino; 4 Asian, non-Hispanic/Latino; 1 Hispanic/Latino), 6 international. Average age 38. 261 applicants, 35% accepted, 84 enrolled. *Faculty:* 25 full-time (24 women), 6 part-time/adjunct (5 women). Expenses: Contact institution. *Financial support:* In 2010–11, 13 students received support, including 3 research assistantships with full and partial tuition reimbursements available (averaging $10,498 per year), 6 teaching assistantships with full and partial tuition reimbursements available (averaging $10,669 per year); fellowships with full and partial tuition reimbursements available, Federal Work-Study, institutionally sponsored loans, scholarships/grants, traineeships, health care benefits, and tuition waivers (full and partial) also available. Support available to part-time students. Financial award application deadline: 3/15; financial award applicants required to submit FAFSA. In 2010, 36 master's, 2 doctorates awarded. *Degree program information:* Part-time and evening/weekend programs available. Postbaccalaureate distance learning degree programs offered (minimal on-campus study). Offers advanced public health nursing (MS); family nurse practitioner (MS); gerontological nursing (MS); nurse anesthesia (MS); nursing (MS, PhD); nursing education (MS); psychiatric and mental health (MS). *Application deadline:* For fall admission, 1/15 for domestic and international students. *Application fee:* $35. Electronic applications accepted. *Application Contact:* Matt Anderson, Admissions Specialist, 701-777-2947, Fax: 701-777-3619, E-mail: matthew.anderson@gradschool.und.edu. *Associate Dean of Graduate Studies,* Dr. Darla Adams, 701-777-4509, Fax: 701-777-4096, E-mail: darla.adams@email.und.edu.

John D. Odegard School of Aerospace Sciences Students: 59 full-time (20 women), 108 part-time (25 women); includes 15 minority (4 Black or African American, non-Hispanic/Latino; 2 American Indian or Alaska Native, non-Hispanic/Latino; 4 Asian, non-Hispanic/Latino; 5 Hispanic/Latino), 32 international. Average age 31. 115 applicants, 70% accepted, 52 enrolled. *Faculty:* 48 full-time (8 women), 10 part-time/adjunct (3 women). Expenses: Contact institution. *Financial support:* In 2010–11, 49 students received support, including 30 research assistantships with full and partial tuition reimbursements available (averaging $8,146 per year), 16 teaching assistantships with full and partial tuition reimbursements available (averaging $8,460 per year); fellowships with full and partial tuition reimbursements available, career-related internships or fieldwork, Federal Work-Study, institutionally sponsored loans, scholarships/grants, health care benefits, tuition waivers (full and partial), and unspecified assistantships also available. Support available to part-time students. Financial award application deadline: 3/15; financial award applicants required to submit FAFSA. In 2010, 42 master's awarded. *Degree program information:* Part-time and evening/weekend programs available. Postbaccalaureate distance learning degree programs offered (minimal on-campus study). Offers aerospace sciences (MEM, MS, PhD); atmospheric sciences (MS, PhD); aviation (MS); computer science (MS, PhD); earth system science and policy (MEM, MS, PhD); space studies (MS). *Application deadline:* For fall and spring admission, 8/1 priority date for domestic and international students. Applications are processed on a rolling basis. *Application fee:* $35. Electronic applications accepted. *Application Contact:* Matt Anderson, Admissions Specialist, 701-777-2947, Fax: 701-777-3619, E-mail: matthew.anderson@gradschool.und.edu. *Dean,* Bruce A. Smith, 701-777-2791, Fax: 701-777-3016, E-mail: bsmith@aero.und.nodak.edu.

School of Engineering and Mines Students: 87 full-time (10 women), 53 part-time (5 women); includes 13 minority (4 Black or African American, non-Hispanic/Latino; 6 Asian, non-Hispanic/Latino; 3 Hispanic/Latino), 45 international. Average age 28. 129 applicants, 41% accepted, 38 enrolled. *Faculty:* 41 full-time (3 women), 13 part-time/adjunct (0 women). Expenses: Contact institution. *Financial support:* In 2010–11, 70 students received support, including 46 research assistantships with full and partial tuition reimbursements available (averaging $7,685 per year), 23 teaching assistantships with full and partial tuition reimbursements available (averaging $7,059 per year); fellowships with full and partial tuition reimburse-

University of North Dakota (continued)

ments available, career-related internships or fieldwork, Federal Work-Study, institutionally sponsored loans, scholarships/grants, health care benefits, tuition waivers (full and partial), and unspecified assistantships also available. Support available to part-time students. Financial award application deadline: 3/15; financial award applicants required to submit FAFSA. In 2010, 21 master's, 2 doctorates awarded. *Degree program information:* Part-time programs available. Offers chemical engineering (M Engr, MS); civil engineering (M Engr); electrical engineering (M Engr, MS); engineering (PhD); engineering and mines (M Engr, MA, MS, PhD); environmental engineering (M Engr, MS); geological engineering (M Engr, MS); geology (MA, MS, PhD); mechanical engineering (M Engr, MS); sanitary engineering (M Engr). *Application deadline:* For fall admission, 8/1 priority date for domestic and international students; for spring admission, 12/1 priority date for domestic and international students. Applications are processed on a rolling basis. *Application fee:* $35. Electronic applications accepted. *Application Contact:* Evan Nelson, Director of Graduate Admissions and Recruitment, 701-777-2945, Fax: 701-777-3619, E-mail: evan.nelson@gradschool.und.edu. *Dean,* Dr. Hesham El-Rewini, 701-777-3411, Fax: 701-777-4838, E-mail: rewini@mail.und.edu.

School of Law Students: 248 full-time (113 women), 6 part-time (3 women); includes 12 minority (2 Black or African American, non-Hispanic/Latino; 7 American Indian or Alaska Native, non-Hispanic/Latino; 1 Asian, non-Hispanic/Latino; 2 Hispanic/Latino), 9 international. Average age 27. 534 applicants, 38% accepted, 85 enrolled. *Faculty:* 18 full-time (8 women). Expenses: Contact institution. *Financial support:* In 2010–11, 4 teaching assistantships with full tuition reimbursements were awarded; career-related internships or fieldwork, Federal Work-Study, scholarships/grants, and tuition waivers (full and partial) also available. Financial award application deadline: 4/15; financial award applicants required to submit FAFSA. In 2010, 74 JDs awarded. Offers law (JD). *Application deadline:* For fall admission, 4/1 priority date for domestic students. Applications are processed on a rolling basis. *Application fee:* $35. *Application Contact:* Ben Hoffman, Admissions and Records Officer, 701-777-2260, Fax: 701-777-2217, E-mail: hoffman@law.und.edu. *Dean/Professor,* Kathryn R. L. Rand, 701-777-2104, E-mail: rand@law.und.edu.

School of Medicine and Health Sciences Students: 240 full-time (121 women), 1 part-time (0 women); includes 23 minority (16 American Indian or Alaska Native, non-Hispanic/Latino; 6 Asian, non-Hispanic/Latino; 1 Hispanic/Latino), 2 international. Average age 28. 317 applicants, 20% accepted, 62 enrolled. *Faculty:* 99 full-time (42 women). Expenses: Contact institution. *Financial support:* Fellowships, research assistantships, teaching assistantships, Federal Work-Study, institutionally sponsored loans, and tuition waivers (full and partial) available. Support available to part-time students. Financial award applicants required to submit FAFSA. In 2010, 56 first professional degrees awarded. Postbaccalaureate distance learning degree programs offered (minimal on-campus study). Offers medicine (MD); medicine and health sciences (MD). *Application Contact:* Judy L. DeMers, Associate Dean, Student Affairs and Admissions, 701-777-4221, Fax: 701-777-4942. *Dean,* Dr. Joshua Wynne, 701-777-2514, Fax: 701-777-3527, E-mail: dean@medicine.nodak.edu.

UNIVERSITY OF NORTHERN BRITISH COLUMBIA, Prince George, BC V2N 4Z9, Canada

General Information Province-supported, coed, university. *Graduate housing:* Room and/or apartments available on a first-come, first-served basis to single students; on-campus housing not available to married students. Housing application deadline: 2/15. *Research affiliation:* Houston Forest Products (forestry–wood debris management), TRC Cedar Ltd. (forestry–cyanolicen growth rate study), Remote Law Online Systems Corporation (computer science), Canadian Natural Oils Ltd. (chemistry–oil fractionation), Stella Jones, Inc. (forestry–Douglas fir cores), Insurance Corporation of British Columbia (moose involved in highway traffic accidents).

GRADUATE UNITS

Office of Graduate Studies *Degree program information:* Part-time and evening/weekend programs available. Postbaccalaureate distance learning degree programs offered (no on-campus study).

UNIVERSITY OF NORTHERN COLORADO, Greeley, CO 80639

General Information State-supported, coed, university. CGS member. *Enrollment:* 12,358 graduate, professional, and undergraduate students; 705 full-time matriculated graduate/professional students (445 women), 675 part-time matriculated graduate/professional students (480 women). *Enrollment by degree level:* 793 master's, 433 doctoral, 154 other advanced degrees. *Graduate faculty:* 330 full-time (152 women). Tuition, state resident: full-time $6199; part-time $344 per credit hour. Tuition, nonresident: full-time $14,834; part-time $824 per credit hour. *Required fees:* $1091; $60.60 per credit hour. Tuition and fees vary according to course load, degree level and program. *Graduate housing:* Rooms and/or apartments available on a first-come, first-served basis to single and married students. Typical cost: $4188 per year ($8920 including board) for single students; $4188 per year ($8920 including board) for married students. Room and board charges vary according to board plan and housing facility selected. Housing application deadline: 5/30. *Student services:* Campus employment opportunities, campus safety program, career counseling, exercise/wellness program, free psychological counseling, international student services, low-cost health insurance, multicultural affairs office, services for students with disabilities, teacher training. *Library facilities:* James A. Michener Library plus 1 other. *Online resources:* library catalog, web page, access to other libraries' catalogs. *Collection:* 1.1 million titles, 3,701 serial subscriptions, 33,778 audiovisual materials.

Computer facilities: Computer purchase and lease plans are available. 1,513 computers available on campus for general student use. A campuswide network can be accessed from student residence rooms and from off campus. Online class registration is available. *Web address:* http://www.unco.edu/.

General Application Contact: Linda Sisson, Graduate Student Admission Coordinator, 970-351-1807, Fax: 970-351-2371, E-mail: linda.sisson@unco.edu.

GRADUATE UNITS

Graduate School Students: 705 full-time (445 women), 675 part-time (480 women); includes 43 Black or African American, non-Hispanic/Latino; 12 American Indian or Alaska Native, non-Hispanic/Latino; 55 Asian, non-Hispanic/Latino; 73 Hispanic/Latino, 51 international. Average age 33. 1,442 applicants, 60% accepted, 418 enrolled. *Faculty:* 330 full-time (152 women). Expenses: Contact institution. *Financial support:* In 2010–11, 280 research assistantships (averaging $7,295 per year), 154 teaching assistantships (averaging $8,110 per year) were awarded; fellowships, career-related internships or fieldwork, Federal Work-Study, institutionally sponsored loans, scholarships/grants, traineeships, tuition waivers (partial), and unspecified assistantships also available. Support available to part-time students. Financial award application deadline: 3/1; financial award applicants required to submit FAFSA. In 2010, 501 master's, 74 doctorates, 40 other advanced degrees awarded. *Degree program information:* Part-time and evening/weekend programs available. Postbaccalaureate distance learning degree programs offered (minimal on-campus study). *Application deadline:* Applications are processed on a rolling basis. *Application fee:* $50 ($60 for international students). Electronic applications accepted. *Application Contact:* Linda Sisson, Graduate Student Admission Coordinator, 970-351-1807, Fax: 970-351-2371, E-mail: linda.sisson@unco.edu. *Assistant Vice President, Research and Extended Studies/Dean,* Dr. Robbyn Wacker, 970-351-2817, Fax: 970-351-2371.

College of Education and Behavioral Sciences Students: 302 full-time (221 women), 390 part-time (295 women); includes 18 Black or African American, non-Hispanic/Latino; 9 American Indian or Alaska Native, non-Hispanic/Latino; 23 Asian, non-Hispanic/Latino; 41 Hispanic/Latino, 21 international. Average age 34. 479 applicants, 66% accepted, 145 enrolled. *Faculty:* 101 full-time (52 women). Expenses: Contact institution. *Financial support:* In 2010–11, 92 research assistantships (averaging $7,328 per year), 25 teaching assistantships (averaging $5,209 per year) were awarded; fellowships, unspecified assistantships also available. Financial award application deadline: 3/1; financial award applicants required to submit FAFSA. In 2010, 275 master's, 44 doctorates, 40 other advanced degrees awarded. *Degree program information:* Part-time programs available. Postbaccalaureate distance learning degree programs offered. Offers applied statistics and research methods (MS, PhD); clinical counseling (MA); counselor education and supervision (MA, PhD, Ed S); early childhood education (MA); education and behavioral sciences (MA, MAT, MS, Ed D, PhD, Ed S); educational leadership (MA, Ed D, Ed S); educational leadership and policy studies (MA, Ed D, Ed S); educational psychology (MA, PhD); educational studies (MAT, Ed D); educational technology (MA, PhD); higher education and student affairs leadership (PhD); psychological sciences (MA, PhD); reading (MA); school counseling (MA); school library education (MA); school psychology (PhD, Ed S); special education (MA, Ed D); teacher education (MA, MAT, Ed D). *Application deadline:* Applications are processed on a rolling basis. *Application fee:* $50 ($60 for international students). *Application Contact:* Linda Sisson, Graduate Student Admission Coordinator, 970-351-1807, Fax: 970-351-2371, E-mail: linda.sisson@unco.edu. *Dean,* Dr. Eugene P. Sheehan, 970-351-2817, Fax: 970-351-2312, E-mail: coeinfo@unco.edu.

College of Humanities and Social Sciences Students: 53 full-time (27 women), 51 part-time (30 women); includes 8 Black or African American, non-Hispanic/Latino; 2 American Indian or Alaska Native, non-Hispanic/Latino; 4 Asian, non-Hispanic/Latino; 13 Hispanic/Latino, 6 international. Average age 30. 64 applicants, 72% accepted, 32 enrolled. *Faculty:* 59 full-time (28 women). Expenses: Contact institution. *Financial support:* In 2010–11, 7 research assistantships (averaging $7,081 per year), 35 teaching assistantships (averaging $9,644 per year) were awarded; fellowships, unspecified assistantships also available. Financial award application deadline: 3/1; financial award applicants required to submit FAFSA. In 2010, 29 master's awarded. *Degree program information:* Part-time programs available. Offers communication (MA); communication studies (MA); criminal justice (MA); English (MA); history (MA); humanities and social sciences (MA); modern languages and cultural studies (MA); sociology (MA); Spanish/teaching (MA). *Application deadline:* Applications are processed on a rolling basis. *Application fee:* $50 ($60 for international students). Electronic applications accepted. *Application Contact:* Linda Sisson, Graduate Student Admission Coordinator, 970-351-1807, Fax: 970-351-2371, E-mail: linda.sisson@unco.edu. *Dean,* Dr. David Caldwell, 970-351-2707, Fax: 970-351-1571.

College of Natural and Health Sciences Students: 25 full-time (13 women), 6 part-time (1 woman); includes 1 American Indian or Alaska Native, non-Hispanic/Latino; 1 Asian, non-Hispanic/Latino; 3 Hispanic/Latino, 1 international. Average age 30. 23 applicants, 52% accepted, 8 enrolled. *Faculty:* 16 full-time (3 women). Expenses: Contact institution. *Financial support:* In 2010–11, 81 research assistantships (averaging $6,619 per year), 61 teaching assistantships (averaging $10,582 per year) were awarded; fellowships, unspecified assistantships also available. Financial award application deadline: 3/1; financial award applicants required to submit FAFSA. In 2010, 9 master's, 27 doctorates awarded. Offers audiology (Au D); biological education (PhD); biological sciences (MS, PhD); chemical education (MS, PhD); chemistry (MS); clinical nurse specialist in chronic illness (MS); earth sciences (MA); earth sciences and physics (MA); exercise science (MS, PhD); family nurse practitioner (MS); gerontology (MA); human rehabilitation (PhD); human sciences (MA, MPH, Au D, PhD); mathematical teaching (MA); mathematics (MA, PhD); mathematics education (PhD); mathematics: liberal arts (MA); natural and health sciences (MA, MPH, MS, Au D, PhD); nursing education (MS, PhD); public health education (MPH); rehabilitation counseling (MA); speech language pathology (MA); sport administration (MS, PhD); sport pedagogy (MS, PhD). *Application deadline:* Applications are processed on a rolling basis. *Application fee:* $50 ($60 for international students). Electronic applications accepted. *Application Contact:* Linda Sisson, Graduate Student Admission Coordinator, 970-351-1807, Fax: 970-351-2371, E-mail: linda.sisson@unco.edu. *Dean,* Dr. Denise A. Battles, 970-351-2877, Fax: 970-351-2176.

College of Performing and Visual Arts Students: 91 full-time (38 women), 32 part-time (21 women); includes 14 minority (5 Black or African American, non-Hispanic/Latino; 7 Asian, non-Hispanic/Latino; 2 Hispanic/Latino), 9 international. Average age 30. 114 applicants, 68% accepted, 38 enrolled. *Faculty:* 39 full-time (12 women). Expenses: Contact institution. *Financial support:* In 2010–11, 50 research assistantships (averaging $4,609 per year), 24 teaching assistantships (averaging $4,158 per year) were awarded; fellowships, unspecified assistantships also available. Financial award application deadline: 3/1; financial award applicants required to submit FAFSA. In 2010, 37 master's, 3 doctorates awarded. *Degree program information:* Part-time programs available. Offers collaborative keyboard (MM); conducting (MM); instrumental performance (MM); jazz studies (MM); music conducting (DA); music education (MM, DA); music history and literature (MM, DA); music performance (DA); music theory and composition (MM, DA); performing and visual arts (MA, MM, DA); visual arts (MA); vocal performance (MM). *Application deadline:* Applications are processed on a rolling basis. *Application fee:* $50 ($60 for international students). Electronic applications accepted. *Application Contact:* Linda Sisson, Graduate Student Admission Coordinator, 970-351-1807, Fax: 970-351-2371, E-mail: linda.sisson@unco.edu. *Dean,* Dr. Andrew J. Svedlow, 970-351-2515, Fax: 970-351-2699.

Monfort College of Business Students: 8 full-time (4 women). Average age 27. 10 applicants, 80% accepted, 6 enrolled. *Faculty:* 9 full-time (3 women). Expenses: Contact institution. Offers accounting (MA). *Application Contact:* Linda Sisson, Graduate Student Admission Coordinator, 970-351-1807, Fax: 970-351-2371, E-mail: linda.sisson@unco.edu. *Dean,* Donald Gudmundson, 970-351-1217, E-mail: don.gudmundson@unco.edu.

UNIVERSITY OF NORTHERN IOWA, Cedar Falls, IA 50614

General Information State-supported, coed, comprehensive institution. CGS member. *Enrollment:* 13,201 graduate, professional, and undergraduate students; 671 full-time matriculated graduate/professional students (448 women), 681 part-time matriculated graduate/professional students (461 women). *Enrollment by degree level:* 1,215 master's, 120 doctoral, 17 other advanced degrees. *Graduate housing:* Rooms and/or apartments available on a first-come, first-served basis to single students and available to married students. *Student services:* Campus employment opportunities, campus safety program, career counseling, child daycare facilities, exercise/wellness program, free psychological counseling, grant writing training, international student services, low-cost health insurance, multicultural affairs office, services for students with disabilities. *Library facilities:* Rod Library. *Online resources:* library catalog, web page, access to other libraries' catalogs. *Collection:* 1.3 million titles, 46,396 serial subscriptions, 34,370 audiovisual materials.

Computer facilities: Computer purchase and lease plans are available. 1,900 computers available on campus for general student use. A campuswide network can be accessed from student residence rooms and from off campus. Online class registration, course registration, student account, degree audit, program of study are available. *Web address:* http://www.uni.edu/.

General Application Contact: Laurie S. Russell, Record Analyst, 319-273-2623, Fax: 319-273-2885, E-mail: laurie.russell@uni.edu.

GRADUATE UNITS

Graduate College Students: 671 full-time (448 women), 681 part-time (461 women); includes 67 Black or African American, non-Hispanic/Latino; 2 American Indian or Alaska Native, non-Hispanic/Latino; 15 Asian, non-Hispanic/Latino; 36 Hispanic/Latino; 6 Two or more races, non-Hispanic/Latino, 125 international. Average age 32. 1,091 applicants, 48% accepted, 341 enrolled. Expenses: Contact institution. *Financial support:* In 2010–11, 1,084 students received support; fellowships, research assistantships, teaching assistantships, career-related internships or fieldwork, Federal Work-Study, institutionally sponsored loans, scholarships/grants, tuition waivers (full and partial), and unspecified assistantships available. Support available to part-time students. Financial award application deadline: 2/1; financial award applicants required to submit FAFSA. In 2010, 561 master's, 20 doctorates, 6 other advanced degrees awarded. *Degree program information:* Part-time and evening/weekend programs available. Offers philanthropy and nonprofit development (MA); public policy (MPP); women's and gender studies (MA). *Application deadline:* For fall admission, 8/1 for domestic students, 2/1 for international students; for winter admission, 12/1 for domestic students. Applications are processed on a rolling basis. *Application fee:* $50 ($70 for international students). Electronic applications accepted. *Application Contact:* Laurie S. Russell, Record Analyst, 319-273-2623, Fax: 319-273-2885, E-mail: laurie.russell@uni.edu. *Dean,* Dr. Michael Licari, 319-273-2748, Fax: 319-273-2243, E-mail: michael.licari@uni.edu.

College of Business Administration Students: 37 full-time (16 women), 28 part-time (7 women); includes 1 Black or African American, non-Hispanic/Latino; 2 Hispanic/Latino, 22 international. 107 applicants, 43% accepted, 33 enrolled. Expenses: Contact institution. *Financial support:* Career-related internships or fieldwork, Federal Work-Study, scholarships/grants, and tuition waivers (full and partial) available. Support available to part-time students. Financial award application deadline: 2/1. In 2010, 69 master's awarded. *Degree program information:* Part-time and evening/weekend programs available. Offers accounting (M Acc); business administration (M Acc, MBA). *Application deadline:* For fall admission, 8/1 priority date for domestic students. Applications are processed on a rolling basis. *Application fee:* $50 ($70 for international students). *Application Contact:* Laurie S. Russell, Record Analyst, 319-273-2623, Fax: 319-273-2885, E-mail: laurie.russell@uni.edu. *Dean,* Dr. Farzad Moussavi, 319-273-6240, Fax: 319-273-2922, E-mail: farzad.moussavi@uni.edu.

College of Education Students: 163 full-time (114 women), 353 part-time (252 women); includes 60 minority (43 Black or African American, non-Hispanic/Latino; 4 Asian, non-Hispanic/Latino; 12 Hispanic/Latino; 1 Two or more races, non-Hispanic/Latino), 24 international. 280 applicants, 60% accepted, 109 enrolled. Expenses: Contact institution. *Financial support:* Career-related internships or fieldwork, Federal Work-Study, institutionally sponsored loans, scholarships/grants, and tuition waivers (full and partial) available. Support available to part-time students. Financial award application deadline: 2/1. In 2010, 209 master's, 18 doctorates, 6 other advanced degrees awarded. *Degree program information:* Part-time and evening/weekend programs available. Offers athletic training (MS, Ed D); community health education (Ed D); curriculum and instruction (MA, MAE, Ed D); curriculum and instruction: instructional technology school library endorsement (MA); curriculum and instruction: literacy education (MAE); early childhood education (MAE); education (MA, MAE, MS, Ed D, Ed S); education of the gifted (MAE); educational leadership (MAE, Ed D); educational psychology (MAE); elementary education (MAE); health education (MA); health promotion and education (MA, Ed D); instructional technology (MA); kinesiology (MA); leisure services (Ed D); leisure, youth, and human services (MA, Ed D); middle school/junior high education (MAE); performance and training technology (MA); physical education (MA); postsecondary education (MAE); principalship (MAE); professional development for teachers (MAE); reading (MAE); rehabilitation studies (Ed D); school library media studies (MA); school psychology (Ed S); special education (MAE, Ed D); student affairs (MAE); teacher of students with visual impairments (MAE); teaching/coaching (MA); youth and human services (MA). *Application deadline:* For fall admission, 8/1 priority date for domestic students. Applications are processed on a rolling basis. *Application fee:* $50 ($70 for international students). Electronic applications accepted. *Application Contact:* Laurie S. Russell, Record Analyst, 319-273-2623, Fax: 319-273-2885, E-mail: laurie.russell@uni.edu. *Dean,* Dr. Dwight Watson, 319-273-2717, Fax: 319-273-2607, E-mail: dwight.watson@uni.edu.

College of Humanities and Fine Arts Students: 194 full-time (156 women), 97 part-time (78 women); includes 29 minority (9 Black or African American, non-Hispanic/Latino; 5 Asian, non-Hispanic/Latino; 13 Hispanic/Latino; 2 Two or more races, non-Hispanic/Latino), 30 international. 245 applicants, 47% accepted, 88 enrolled. Expenses: Contact institution. *Financial support:* Career-related internships or fieldwork, Federal Work-Study, scholarships/grants, and tuition waivers (full and partial) available. Support available to part-time students. Financial award application deadline: 2/1. In 2010, 115 master's awarded. *Degree program information:* Part-time and evening/weekend programs available. Offers art education (MA); communication studies (MA); composition (MM); conducting (MM); creative writing (MA); English (MA); French (MA); German (MA); humanities and fine arts (MA, MM); jazz pedagogy (MM); literature (MA); music (MA, MM); music education (MM); music history (MM); performance (MM); piano performance and pedagogy (MM); Spanish (MA); speech-language pathology (MA); teaching English in secondary schools (TESS) (MA); teaching English to speakers of other languages (MA); teaching English to speakers of other languages/French (MA); teaching English to speakers of other languages/German (MA); teaching English to speakers of other languages/Spanish (MA). *Application deadline:* For fall admission, 8/1 priority date for domestic students. Applications are processed on a rolling basis. *Application fee:* $50 ($70 for international students). Electronic applications accepted. *Application Contact:* Laurie S. Russell, Record Analyst, 319-273-2623, Fax: 319-273-2885, E-mail: laurie.russell@uni.edu. *Interim Dean,* Dr. Joel Haack, 319-273-2585, Fax: 319-273-2731, E-mail: joel.haack@uni.edu.

College of Natural Sciences Students: 81 full-time (33 women), 97 part-time (47 women); includes 6 minority (1 Black or African American, non-Hispanic/Latino; 2 Asian, non-Hispanic/Latino; 1 Hispanic/Latino; 2 Two or more races, non-Hispanic/Latino), 37 international. 145 applicants, 46% accepted, 36 enrolled. Expenses: Contact institution. *Financial support:* Teaching assistantships, career-related internships or fieldwork, Federal Work-Study, scholarships/grants, and tuition waivers (full and partial) available. Support available to part-time students. Financial award application deadline: 2/1. In 2010, 59 master's, 2 doctorates awarded. *Degree program information:* Part-time and evening/weekend programs available. Offers applied chemistry and biochemistry (PSM); applied physics (PSM); biology (MA, MS); biotechnology (PSM); chemistry (MA, MS); computer science (MS); earth science education (MA); ecosystem management (PSM); environmental health (MS); environmental science (MS); industrial mathematics (PSM); industrial technology (MS, PSM, DIT); mathematics (MA); mathematics for middle grades 4-8 (MA); natural sciences (MA, MS, PSM, PSM, DIT); physics education (MA); science education (MA). *Application deadline:* For fall admission, 8/1 priority date for domestic students. Applications are processed on a rolling basis. *Application fee:* $50 ($70 for international students). Electronic applications accepted. *Application Contact:* Laurie S. Russell, Record Analyst, 319-273-2623, Fax: 319-273-2885, E-mail: laurie.russell@uni.edu. *Dean,* Dr. Joel Haack, 319-273-2585, Fax: 319-273-2893, E-mail: joel.haack@uni.edu.

College of Social and Behavioral Sciences Students: 165 full-time (114 women), 90 part-time (62 women); includes 22 minority (8 Black or African American, non-Hispanic/Latino; 2 American Indian or Alaska Native, non-Hispanic/Latino; 4 Asian, non-Hispanic/Latino; 7 Hispanic/Latino; 1 Two or more races, non-Hispanic/Latino), 9 international. 266 applicants, 36% accepted, 62 enrolled. Expenses: Contact institution. *Financial support:* Career-related internships or fieldwork, Federal Work-Study, scholarships/grants, and tuition waivers (full and partial) available. Support available to part-time students. Financial award application deadline: 2/1. In 2010, 99 master's awarded. *Degree program information:* Part-time and evening/weekend programs available. Offers counseling (MA, MAE); criminology (MA); geography (MA); history (MA); mental health counseling (MA); political science (MA); psychology (MA); public history (MA); school counseling (MAE); social and behavioral sciences (MA, MAE, MSW); social science (MA); social work (MSW); sociology (MA). *Application deadline:* For fall admission, 8/1 priority date for domestic students. Applications are processed on a rolling basis. *Application fee:* $50 ($70 for international students). Electronic applications accepted. *Application Contact:* Laurie S. Russell, Record Analyst, 319-273-2623, Fax: 319-273-2885, E-mail: laurie.russell@uni.edu. *Dean/Professor,* Dr. Philip Mauceri, 319-273-2221, Fax: 319-273-2222, E-mail: philip.mauceri@uni.edu.

UNIVERSITY OF NORTH FLORIDA, Jacksonville, FL 32224

General Information State-supported, coed, comprehensive institution. *Enrollment:* 16,153 graduate, professional, and undergraduate students; 766 full-time matriculated graduate/professional students (483 women), 1,039 part-time matriculated graduate/professional students (637 women). *Enrollment by degree level:* 1,600 master's, 205 doctoral. *Graduate faculty:* 387 full-time (171 women), 22 part-time/adjunct (10 women). Tuition, state resident: full-time $7646; part-time $318.60 per credit hour. Tuition, nonresident: full-time $23,502; part-time $979.24 per credit hour. *Required fees:* $1209; $50.37 per credit hour. Tuition and fees vary according to course load and program. *Graduate housing:* Room and/or apartments available on a first-come, first-served basis to single students; on-campus housing not available to married students. Typical cost: $8322 (including board). Room and board charges vary according to board plan and housing facility selected. Housing application deadline: 7/15. *Student services:* Campus employment opportunities, campus safety program, career counseling, child daycare facilities, exercise/wellness program, free psychological counseling, international student services, low-cost health insurance, multicultural affairs office, services for students with disabilities, teacher training, writing training. *Library facilities:* Thomas G. Carpenter Library. *Online resources:* library catalog, web page, access to other libraries' catalogs. *Collection:* 840,423 titles, 2,800 serial subscriptions, 30,274 audiovisual materials.

Computer facilities: Computer purchase and lease plans are available. 750 computers available on campus for general student use. A campuswide network can be accessed from student residence rooms and from off campus. Online class registration, applications software are available. *Web address:* http://www.unf.edu/.

General Application Contact: Lilith Richardson, Assistant Director, The Graduate School, 904-620-1360, Fax: 904-620-1362, E-mail: graduateschool@unf.edu.

GRADUATE UNITS

Brooks College of Health Students: 329 full-time (234 women), 161 part-time (124 women); includes 33 Black or African American, non-Hispanic/Latino; 3 American Indian or Alaska Native, non-Hispanic/Latino; 24 Asian, non-Hispanic/Latino; 28 Hispanic/Latino; 4 Two or more races, non-Hispanic/Latino, 10 international. Average age 32. 790 applicants, 25% accepted, 142 enrolled. *Faculty:* 64 full-time (43 women), 8 part-time/adjunct (4 women). Expenses: Contact institution. *Financial support:* In 2010–11, 138 students received support, including 1 research assistantship (averaging $80 per year); teaching assistantships, career-related internships or fieldwork, Federal Work-Study, scholarships/grants, and tuition waivers (partial) also available. Support available to part-time students. Financial award application deadline: 4/1; financial award applicants required to submit FAFSA. In 2010, 99 master's, 31 doctorates awarded. *Degree program information:* Part-time and evening/weekend programs available. Offers aging services (Certificate); athletic training and physical therapy (DPT); community health (MPH); geriatric management (MSH); health (MHA, MPH, MS, MSH, MSN, DNP, DPT, Certificate); health administration (MHA); nutrition and dietetics (MSH); rehabilitation counseling (MS). *Application deadline:* For fall admission, 7/1 priority date for domestic students, 5/1 for international students; for spring admission, 11/1 priority date for domestic students, 10/1 for international students. Applications are processed on a rolling basis. *Application fee:* $30. Electronic applications accepted. *Application Contact:* Heather Kenney, Director of Advising, 904-620-2810, Fax: 904-620-1030, E-mail: heather.kenney@unf.edu. *Dean,* Dr. Pamela Chally, 904-620-2810, Fax: 904-620-1030, E-mail: pchally@unf.edu.

School of Nursing Students: 106 full-time (73 women), 73 part-time (65 women); includes 15 Black or African American, non-Hispanic/Latino; 1 American Indian or Alaska Native, non-Hispanic/Latino; 13 Asian, non-Hispanic/Latino; 11 Hispanic/Latino; 2 Two or more races, non-Hispanic/Latino. Average age 35. 210 applicants, 21% accepted, 38 enrolled. *Faculty:* 26 full-time (19 women), 1 (woman) part-time/adjunct. Expenses: Contact institution. *Financial support:* In 2010–11, 62 students received support; research assistantships available. Financial award application deadline: 4/1; financial award applicants required to submit FAFSA. In 2010, 25 master's, 3 doctorates awarded. *Degree program information:* Part-time programs available. Offers clinical nurse leader (MSN); clinical nurse specialist (MSN); nurse anesthetist (MSN); nurse practitioner (MSN); nursing practice (DNP); primary care nurse practitioner (Certificate). *Application deadline:* For fall admission, 3/15 for domestic students, 4/1 for international students. Applications are processed on a rolling basis. *Application fee:* $30. Electronic applications accepted. *Application Contact:* Beth Dibble, 904-620-2684, Fax: 904-620-1832, E-mail: nursingadmissions@unf.edu. *Director,* Dr. Lillia Loriz, 904-620-2684, E-mail: lloriz@unf.edu.

Coggin College of Business Students: 157 full-time (63 women), 306 part-time (132 women); includes 17 Black or African American, non-Hispanic/Latino; 1 American Indian or Alaska Native, non-Hispanic/Latino; 24 Asian, non-Hispanic/Latino; 13 Hispanic/Latino; 4 Two or more races, non-Hispanic/Latino, 29 international. Average age 29. 282 applicants, 57% accepted, 106 enrolled. *Faculty:* 54 full-time (15 women), 3 part-time/adjunct (0 women). Expenses: Contact institution. *Financial support:* In 2010–11, 48 students received support; research assistantships, teaching assistantships, career-related internships or fieldwork, Federal Work-Study, scholarships/grants, and tuition waivers (partial) available. Financial award application deadline: 4/1; financial award applicants required to submit FAFSA. In 2010, 210 master's awarded. *Degree program information:* Part-time and evening/weekend programs available. Offers accountancy (M Acc); accounting (MBA); business (M Acc, MBA); construction management (MBA); e-commerce (MBA); economics (MBA); finance (MBA); human resource management (MBA); international business (MBA); logistics (MBA); management applications (MBA). *Application deadline:* For fall admission, 7/1 priority date for domestic students, 5/1 for international students; for spring admission, 11/1 priority date for domestic students, 10/1 for international students. Applications are processed on a rolling basis. *Application fee:* $30. Electronic applications accepted. *Application Contact:* Cheryl Campbell, Director of Student Services, 904-620-2575, Fax: 904-620-2832, E-mail: ccampbell@unf.edu. *Dean,* Dr. Ajay Samant, 904-620-2590, Fax: 904-620-2590, E-mail: ajay.samant@unf.edu.

College of Arts and Sciences Students: 146 full-time (78 women), 169 part-time (108 women); includes 54 minority (21 Black or African American, non-Hispanic/Latino; 2 American Indian or Alaska Native, non-Hispanic/Latino; 9 Asian, non-Hispanic/Latino; 16 Hispanic/Latino; 1 Native Hawaiian or other Pacific Islander, non-Hispanic/Latino; 5 Two or more races, non-Hispanic/Latino), 9 international. Average age 30. 231 applicants, 48% accepted, 68 enrolled. *Faculty:* 181 full-time (70 women), 4 part-time/adjunct (1 woman). Expenses: Contact institution. *Financial support:* In 2010–11, 96 students received support, including 5 research assistantships (averaging $2,539 per year), 41 teaching assistantships (averaging $5,713 per year); career-related internships or fieldwork, Federal Work-Study, scholarships/grants, and tuition waivers (partial) also available. Support available to part-time students. Financial award application deadline: 4/1; financial award applicants required to submit FAFSA. In 2010, 117 master's awarded. *Degree program information:* Part-time and evening/weekend programs available. Offers applied ethics (Graduate Certificate); arts and sciences (MA, MAC, MPA, MS, MSCJ, Graduate Certificate); biology (MA, MS); counseling psychology (MAC); criminal justice (MSCJ); English (MA); European history (MA); general psychology (MA); mathematical sciences (MS); nonprofit management (Graduate Certificate); practical philosophy and applied ethics (MA); public administration (MPA); statistics (MS); U. S. history (MA). *Application deadline:* For fall admission, 7/1 priority date for domestic students, 5/1 for international students; for spring admission, 11/1 priority date for domestic students, 10/1 for international students. Applications are processed on a rolling basis. *Application fee:* $30. Electronic applications accepted. *Application Contact:* Lilith Richardson, Assistant Director, The Graduate School, 904-620-1360, Fax: 904-620-1362, E-mail: graduateschool@unf.edu. *Dean,* Dr. Barbara Hetrick, 904-620-2560, Fax: 904-620-2929, E-mail: barbara.hetrick@unf.edu.

College of Computing, Engineering, and Construction Students: 17 full-time (6 women), 76 part-time (19 women); includes 7 Black or African American, non-Hispanic/Latino; 3 Asian, non-Hispanic/Latino; 6 Hispanic/Latino; 3 Two or more races, non-Hispanic/Latino, 20 international. Average age 31. 90 applicants, 49% accepted, 24 enrolled. *Faculty:* 37 full-time (8 women). Expenses: Contact institution. *Financial support:* In 2010–11, 25 students received support, including 12 research assistantships (averaging $2,864 per year), 5 teaching assistantships (averaging $761 per year); Federal Work-Study, scholarships/grants, tuition waivers (partial), and unspecified assistantships also available. Support available to part-time students. Financial award application deadline: 4/1; financial award applicants required to submit FAFSA. In 2010, 8 master's awarded. *Degree program information:* Part-time programs available. Offers computing, engineering, and construction (MS, MSCE, MSEE, MSME). *Application deadline:* For fall admission, 7/1 priority date for domestic students, 5/1 for international students; for spring admission, 11/1 priority date for domestic students, 10/1 for international students. Applications are processed on a rolling basis. *Application fee:* $30. Electronic applications accepted. *Application Contact:* Lillith Richardson, Assistant Director, The Graduate School, 904-620-1360, Fax: 904-620-1362, E-mail: graduateschool@unf.edu. *Dean,* Dr. Neal Coulter, 904-620-1350, E-mail: ncoulter@unf.edu.

School of Computing Students: 12 full-time (4 women), 35 part-time (14 women); includes 5 Black or African American, non-Hispanic/Latino; 2 Asian, non-Hispanic/Latino; 2 Hispanic/Latino; 2 Two or more races, non-Hispanic/Latino, 14 international. Average age 32. 45 applicants, 58% accepted, 11 enrolled. *Faculty:* 15 full-time (4 women). Expenses: Contact institution. *Financial support:* In 2010–11, 9 students received support, including 1 teaching assistantship (averaging $2,000 per year); Federal Work-Study, scholarships/grants, and unspecified assistantships also available. Financial award application deadline: 4/1; financial award applicants required to submit FAFSA. In 2010, 5 master's awarded. *Degree program information:* Part-time programs available. Offers computer science (MS); information systems (MS); software engineering (MS). *Application deadline:* For fall admission, 7/1 for domestic students, 5/1 for international students; for spring admission, 11/1 for domestic students,

University of North Florida (continued)

10/1 for international students. Applications are processed on a rolling basis. *Application fee:* $30. Electronic applications accepted. *Application Contact:* Lillith Richardson, Assistant Director, The Graduate School, 904-620-1360, Fax: 904-620-1362, E-mail: graduateschool@unf.edu. *Dean*, Dr. Neal Coulter, 904-620-1350, E-mail: ncoulter@unf.edu.

School of Engineering Students: 5 full-time (2 women), 41 part-time (5 women); includes 2 Black or African American, non-Hispanic/Latino; 1 Asian, non-Hispanic/Latino; 4 Hispanic/Latino; 1 Two or more races, non-Hispanic/Latino, 6 international. Average age 29. 45 applicants, 40% accepted, 13 enrolled. *Faculty:* 15 full-time (2 women). Expenses: Contact institution. *Financial support:* In 2010–11, 16 students received support, including research assistantships (averaging $2,669 per year), teaching assistantships (averaging $451 per year); Federal Work-Study, scholarships/grants, tuition waivers, and unspecified assistantships also available. Financial award application deadline: 4/1; financial award applicants required to submit FAFSA. In 2010, 3 master's awarded. *Degree program information:* Part-time programs available. Offers engineering (MSCE, MSEE, MSME). *Application deadline:* For fall admission, 7/1 for domestic students, 5/1 for international students; for spring admission, 11/1 for domestic students, 10/1 for international students. *Application fee:* $30. *Application Contact:* Lillith Richardson, Assistant Director, The Graduate School, 904-320-1360, Fax: 904-620-1362, E-mail: graduateschool@unf.edu. *Associate Dean*, Gerald Merckel, 904-620-1390, E-mail: gmerckel@unf.edu.

College of Education and Human Services Students: 102 full-time (84 women), 297 part-time (222 women); includes 53 Black or African American, non-Hispanic/Latino; 3 American Indian or Alaska Native, non-Hispanic/Latino; 9 Asian, non-Hispanic/Latino; 17 Hispanic/Latino, 1 international. Average age 35. 121 applicants, 45% accepted, 31 enrolled. *Faculty:* 53 full-time (34 women). Expenses: Contact institution. *Financial support:* In 2010–11, 110 students received support, including 4 research assistantships (averaging $2,870 per year), 1 teaching assistantship (averaging $5,700 per year); career-related internships or fieldwork, Federal Work-Study, scholarships/grants, and tuition waivers (partial) also available. Support available to part-time students. Financial award application deadline: 4/1; financial award applicants required to submit FAFSA. In 2010, 152 master's, 15 doctorates awarded. *Degree program information:* Part-time and evening/weekend programs available. Offers adult learning (M Ed); American sign language/English interpreting (M Ed); applied behavior analysis (M Ed); autism (M Ed); counselor education (M Ed); deaf education (M Ed); disability services (M Ed); education and human services (M Ed, Ed D); educational leadership (M Ed, Ed D); exceptional student education (M Ed); literacy K-12 (M Ed); professional education (M Ed); professional education—elementary education (M Ed); TESOL K-12 (M Ed). *Application deadline:* For fall admission, 7/1 priority date for domestic students, 5/1 for international students; for spring admission, 11/1 priority date for domestic students, 10/1 for international students. Applications are processed on a rolling basis. *Application fee:* $30. Electronic applications accepted. *Application Contact:* Dr. John Kemppainen, Director, Office of Student Services, 904-620-2530, Fax: 904-620-1135, E-mail: jkemppai@unf.edu. *Dean*, Dr. Larry Daniel, 904-620-2520, E-mail: ldaniel@unf.edu.

UNIVERSITY OF NORTH TEXAS, Denton, TX 76203

General Information State-supported, coed, university. CGS member. *Enrollment:* 36,067 graduate, professional, and undergraduate students; 3,227 full-time matriculated graduate/professional students (1,753 women), 4,557 part-time matriculated graduate/professional students (2,966 women). *Enrollment by degree level:* 36 first professional, 5,992 master's, 1,656 doctoral. *Graduate faculty:* 706 full-time (238 women), 146 part-time/adjunct (80 women). Tuition, state resident: full-time $4298; part-time $239 per credit hour. Tuition, nonresident: full-time $10,782; part-time $549 per credit hour. *Required fees:* $1292; $270 per credit hour. *Graduate housing:* Rooms and/or apartments available on a first-come, first-served basis to single and married students. Typical cost: $6716 (including board) for single students. Room and board charges vary according to board plan and housing facility selected. *Student services:* Campus employment opportunities, campus safety program, career counseling, exercise/wellness program, free psychological counseling, grant writing training, international student services, low-cost health insurance, multicultural affairs office, services for students with disabilities, teacher training. *Library facilities:* Willis Library plus 4 others. *Online resources:* library catalog, web page, access to other libraries' catalogs. *Collection:* 2.5 million titles, 95,597 serial subscriptions, 232,620 audiovisual materials. *Research affiliation:* Cotton, Incorporated (natural science), Semiconductor Research Corporation (materials science), Delta and Pine Land Company (natural science), Semiconductor Research Corporation (materials science), Sematech (physical science), Texas Utilities (physical science).

Computer facilities: 755 computers available on campus for general student use. A campuswide network can be accessed from student residence rooms and from off campus. Online class registration is available. *Web address:* http://www.unt.edu/.

General Application Contact: Toulouse School of Graduate Studies, 940-565-2383, Fax: 940-565-2141, E-mail: gradsch@unt.edu.

GRADUATE UNITS

College of Information Expenses: Contact institution. Offers applied technology, training and development (M Ed, MS, Ed D, PhD); computer education and cognitive systems (MS); educational computing (PhD); information (M Ed, MS, Ed D, PhD); information science (MS, PhD); learning technologies (M Ed, Ed D); library science (MS).

Toulouse Graduate School Expenses: Contact institution. *Financial support:* Fellowships with partial tuition reimbursements, research assistantships with partial tuition reimbursements, teaching assistantships, career-related internships or fieldwork, Federal Work-Study, institutionally sponsored loans, scholarships/grants, and library assistantships available. Support available to part-time students. Financial award applicants required to submit FAFSA. *Degree program information:* Part-time and evening/weekend programs available. Postbaccalaureate distance learning degree programs offered. *Application deadline:* For fall admission, 7/15 for domestic students; for spring admission, 11/15 for domestic students. Applications are processed on a rolling basis. Electronic applications accepted.

College of Arts and Sciences Expenses: Contact institution. *Financial support:* In 2010–11, teaching assistantships (averaging $1 per year); fellowships, research assistantships, career-related internships or fieldwork, Federal Work-Study, institutionally sponsored loans, tuition waivers (partial), and unspecified assistantships also available. Support available to part-time students. Financial award applicants required to submit FAFSA. *Degree program information:* Part-time and evening/weekend programs available. Offers arts and sciences (MA, MFA, MJ, MS, Au D, PhD, Graduate Certificate); audiology (Au D); biochemistry (MS, PhD); biology (MA, MS, PhD); chemistry (MS, PhD); clinical psychology (PhD); communication studies (MA, MS); counseling psychology (MA, MS, PhD); creative writing (MA); economic research (MS); economics (MA, MS); English (MA, PhD); environmental science (MS, PhD); experimental psychology (MA, MS, PhD); French (MA); geography (MS); health psychology and behavioral medicine (PhD); history (MA, MS, PhD); journalism (MA, MJ); labor and industrial relations (MS); mathematics (MA, MS, PhD); molecular biology (MA, MS, PhD); narrative journalism (Graduate Certificate); philosophy (MA, PhD); physics (MA, MS, PhD); political science (MA, MS, PhD); radio, television and film (MA, MFA, MS); Spanish (MA); speech-language pathology (MA, MS). *Application deadline:* For fall admission, 7/15 for international students; for spring admission, 11/15 for international students. *Application Contact:* Dr. Lawrence J. Schneider, Associate Dean, 940-565-2383, Fax: 940-565-2141. *Dean*, Dr. Warren Burggren, 940-565-2497, Fax: 940-565-4517, E-mail: burggren@unt.edu.

College of Business Administration Expenses: Contact institution. *Financial support:* Fellowships, research assistantships, teaching assistantships, career-related internships or fieldwork, Federal Work-Study, and institutionally sponsored loans available. Financial award applicants required to submit FAFSA. *Degree program information:* Part-time and evening/weekend programs available. Offers accounting (MS, PhD); business administration (MBA, MS, PhD); business computer information systems (PhD); decision technologies (MS); finance (PhD); finance, insurance, real estate, and law (MS); information technology (MS); managementmanagement science (PhD); marketing and logistics (PhD); real estate (MS); taxation (MS). *Application deadline:* Applications are processed on a rolling basis. Electronic applications accepted. *Application Contact:* Associate Dean for Graduate Programs, 940-565-8977, Fax: 940-369-8978, E-mail: mbacoba@unt.edu.

College of Education Expenses: Contact institution. *Financial support:* Fellowships, research assistantships, teaching assistantships, career-related internships or fieldwork, Federal Work-Study, institutionally sponsored loans, and tuition waivers (partial) available. Support available to part-time students. Financial award application deadline: 4/15; financial award applicants required to submit FAFSA. *Degree program information:* Part-time and evening/weekend programs available. Offers adolescent counseling (Certificate); adult counseling (Certificate); alternative initial certification (Certificate); autism intervention (M Ed); behavioral specialist (Certificate); child counseling/play therapy (Certificate); college/university counseling (Certificate); community college counseling (MS); community counseling (Certificate); counseling (M Ed, MS, PhD, Certificate); couple/family counseling (Certificate); curriculum and instruction (M Ed, Ed D, PhD); development and family studies (MS, Certificate); early childhood education (MS, Ed D); EC-12 generalist certification (M Ed); education (M Ed, MS, Ed D, PhD, Certificate); educational administration (M Ed, Ed D, PhD); educational psychology (MS); educational research (PhD); elementary school counseling (M Ed, MS); emotional/behavioral disorders (M Ed); gifted education (Certificate); group counseling (Certificate); higher education (M Ed, MS, Ed D, PhD); higher education (Certificate); kinesiology (MS); reading education (M Ed, MS, Ed D, PhD); recreation and leisure studies (MS, Certificate); recreation management (Certificate); school psychology (MS); secondary education (M Ed, Certificate); secondary school counseling (M Ed); special education (M Ed, PhD, Certificate); teaching students with traumatic brain injury (Certificate); transition (M Ed); transition specialist (Certificate); traumatic brain injury (M Ed); university counseling (M Ed). *Application Contact:* Associate Dean, 940-565-2383, Fax: 940-565-2141.

College of Engineering Expenses: Contact institution. *Financial support:* Fellowships with full tuition reimbursements, research assistantships with full tuition reimbursements, teaching assistantships with full tuition reimbursements available. Financial award applicants required to submit FAFSA. Offers computer science (MS); computer science and engineering (PhD); electrical engineering (MS); engineering (MS, PhD); engineering technology (MS); materials science and engineering (MS, PhD). *Application deadline:* Applications are processed on a rolling basis. Electronic applications accepted.

College of Music Expenses: Contact institution. *Financial support:* Fellowships with partial tuition reimbursements, research assistantships, teaching assistantships with partial tuition reimbursements, career-related internships or fieldwork, Federal Work-Study, institutionally sponsored loans, and scholarships/grants available. Financial award application deadline: 4/1. Offers composition (MM, DMA); jazz studies (MM); music (MA); music education (MM, MME, PhD); music theory (MM, PhD); musicology (MM, PhD); performance (MM, DMA). *Application deadline:* Applications are processed on a rolling basis. Electronic applications accepted. *Application Contact:* Admissions and Scholarship Services, 940-367-7771, Fax: 940-565-2002.

College of Public Affairs and Community Service Expenses: Contact institution. *Financial support:* Fellowships, research assistantships, teaching assistantships, career-related internships or fieldwork, Federal Work-Study, institutionally sponsored loans, scholarships/grants, and tuition waivers (full and partial) available. Support available to part-time students. Financial award applicants required to submit FAFSA. *Degree program information:* Part-time and evening/weekend programs available. Offers aging (Certificate); applied anthropology (MA, MS); applied economics (MS); applied gerontology (PhD); behavior analysis (MS); criminal justice (MS); general studies in aging (MA, MS); global and comparative (PhD); health and illness (PhD); long term care, senior housing, and aging services (MA, MS); public administration (MPA); public administration and management (PhD); public affairs and community service (MA, MPA, MS, PhD, Certificate); rehabilitation counseling (MS); social stratification and inequality (PhD); sociology (MA, MS). *Application deadline:* Applications are processed on a rolling basis. Electronic applications accepted.

College of Visual Arts and Design Expenses: Contact institution. *Financial support:* Fellowships, teaching assistantships, career-related internships or fieldwork, Federal Work-Study, institutionally sponsored loans, and unspecified assistantships available. Support available to part-time students. Financial award application deadline: 4/1. *Degree program information:* Part-time programs available. Offers art education (MA, PhD); art history (MA); art museum education (Certificate); arts leadership (Certificate); design (MFA); metalsmithing and jewelry (MFA); visual arts and design (MA, MFA, MS, PhD, Certificate). *Application deadline:* Applications are processed on a rolling basis.

Interdisciplinary Studies Expenses: Contact institution. *Financial support:* Fellowships, career-related internships or fieldwork, Federal Work-Study, and institutionally sponsored loans available. Financial award application deadline: 4/1; financial award applicants required to submit FAFSA. *Degree program information:* Part-time programs available. Offers interdisciplinary studies (MA, MS). *Application deadline:* Applications are processed on a rolling basis. Electronic applications accepted.

School of Merchandising and Hospitality Management Expenses: Contact institution. *Financial support:* Fellowships, research assistantships, teaching assistantships, career-related internships or fieldwork, Federal Work-Study, and institutionally sponsored loans available. Financial award application deadline: 4/1; financial award applicants required to submit FAFSA. *Degree program information:* Part-time programs available. Postbaccalaureate distance learning degree programs offered (no on-campus study). Offers hospitality management (MS); merchandising (MS). *Application deadline:* Applications are processed on a rolling basis. Electronic applications accepted. *Application Contact:* Coordinator, 940-565-4757, Fax: 940-565-4348, E-mail: kennon@smhm.unt.edu.

UNIVERSITY OF NORTH TEXAS HEALTH SCIENCE CENTER AT FORT WORTH, Fort Worth, TX 76107-2699

General Information State-supported, coed, graduate-only institution. CGS member. *Graduate housing:* On-campus housing not available. *Research affiliation:* Myogen, Inc. (cardiac research), My-tech, Inc. (cardiovascular research), Novopharm, Inc. (gene control), Ethnobotanical Product Investigation Consortium (natural plant products), Genelink (familial DNA depository), Botanical Research Institutions of Texas.

GRADUATE UNITS

Graduate School of Biomedical Sciences Offers anatomy and cell biology (MS, PhD); biochemistry and molecular biology (MS, PhD); biomedical sciences (MS, PhD); biotechnology (MS); forensic genetics (MS); integrative physiology (MS, PhD); medical science (MS); microbiology and immunology (MS, PhD); pharmacology (MS, PhD); science education (MS).

School of Public Health *Degree program information:* Part-time and evening/weekend programs available. Offers biostatistics (MPH); community health (MPH); disease control and prevention (Dr PH); environmental and occupational health sciences (MPH); epidemiology (MPH); health administration (MHA); health policy and management (MPH, Dr PH). MPH offered jointly with University of North Texas; DO/MPH with Texas College of Osteopathic Medicine. Electronic applications accepted.

Texas College of Osteopathic Medicine Offers osteopathic medicine (DO); physician assistant studies (MPAS). DO/MPH offered jointly with University of North Texas. Electronic applications accepted.

School of Health Professions Offers health professions (MPAS).

UNIVERSITY OF NOTRE DAME, Notre Dame, IN 46556

General Information Independent-religious, coed, university. CGS member. *Graduate housing:* Rooms and/or apartments available on a first-come, first-served basis to single and married students. Housing application deadline: 5/1. *Research affiliation:* Space Telescope Science Institute, Brookhaven National Laboratory, Fermi National Accelerator Laboratory, Argonne National Laboratory.

GRADUATE UNITS

Graduate School *Degree program information:* Part-time programs available. Electronic applications accepted.

College of Arts and Letters *Degree program information:* Part-time programs available. Offers art history (MA); arts and letters (M Div, M Ed, MA, MFA, MMS, MSM, MTS, PhD); cognitive psychology (PhD); counseling psychology (PhD); creative writing (MFA); design (MFA); developmental psychology (PhD); early Christian studies (MA); economics and econometrics (MA, PhD); educational initiatives (M Ed, MA); English (MA, PhD); French and Francophone studies (MA); history (MA, PhD); history and philosophy of science (MA, PhD); humanities (M Div, MA, MFA, MMS, MSM, MTS, PhD); Iberian and Latin American studies (MA); international peace studies (MA, PhD); Italian studies (MA); literature (PhD); medieval studies (MMS, PhD); philosophy (PhD); political science (PhD); quantitative psychology (PhD); Romance literatures (MA); social science (M Ed, MA, PhD); sociology (PhD); studio art (MFA); theology (M Div, MA, MSM, MTS, PhD); theology and science (PhD). Electronic applications accepted.

College of Engineering Offers aerospace and mechanical engineering (M Eng, PhD); aerospace engineering (MS Aero E); bioengineering (MS Bio E); chemical and biomolecular engineering (MS Ch E, PhD); civil engineering (MSCE); civil engineering and geological sciences (PhD); computer science and engineering (MSCSE, PhD); electrical engineering (MSEE, PhD); engineering (M Eng, MEME, MS, MS Aero E, MS Bio E, MS Ch E, MS Env E, MSCE, MSCSE, MSEE, MSME, PhD); environmental engineering (MS Env E); geological sciences (MS); mechanical engineering (MEME, MSME). Electronic applications accepted.

College of Science Offers algebra (PhD); algebraic geometry (PhD); applied mathematics (MSAM); aquatic ecology, evolution and environmental biology (MS, PhD); biochemistry (MS, PhD); cellular and molecular biology (MS, PhD); complex analysis (PhD); differential geometry (PhD); genetics (MS, PhD); inorganic chemistry (MS, PhD); logic (PhD); organic chemistry (MS, PhD); partial differential equations (PhD); physical chemistry (MS, PhD); physics (MS, PhD); physiology (MS, PhD); science (MS, MSAM, PhD); topology (PhD); vector biology and parasitology (MS, PhD). Electronic applications accepted.

School of Architecture Offers architectural design and urbanism (M ADU); architecture (M Arch). Electronic applications accepted.

Law School Students: 590 full-time (250 women); includes 161 minority (29 Black or African American, non-Hispanic/Latino; 7 American Indian or Alaska Native, non-Hispanic/Latino; 45 Asian, non-Hispanic/Latino; 64 Hispanic/Latino; 1 Native Hawaiian or other Pacific Islander, non-Hispanic/Latino; 15 Two or more races, non-Hispanic/Latino), 28 international. 4,022 applicants, 16% accepted, 172 enrolled. *Faculty:* 58 full-time (18 women), 40 part-time/adjunct (14 women). Expenses: Contact institution. *Financial support:* In 2010–11, 440 students received support, including 440 fellowships with tuition reimbursements available (averaging $15,337 per year); research assistantships, teaching assistantships, career-related internships or fieldwork, Federal Work-Study, institutionally sponsored loans, scholarships/grants, health care benefits, unspecified assistantships, and university dormitory rector assistants also available. Financial award application deadline: 2/28; financial award applicants required to submit FAFSA. In 2010, 172 first professional degrees, 19 master's, 1 doctorate awarded. Offers human rights (LL M, JSD); international and comparative law (LL M); law (JD). *Application deadline:* For fall admission, 11/1 priority date for domestic students; for winter admission, 2/15 for domestic students. Applications are processed on a rolling basis. *Application fee:* $65. Electronic applications accepted. *Application Contact:* Melissa Ann Fruscione, Director of Admissions and Financial Aid, 574-631-6626, Fax: 574-631-5474, E-mail: lawadmit@nd.edu. *Dean,* Nell Jessup Newton, 574-631-6789, Fax: 574-631-8400, E-mail: nell.newton@nd.edu.

Mendoza College of Business Students: 701 full-time (189 women), 55 part-time (34 women); includes 111 minority (26 Black or African American, non-Hispanic/Latino; 10 American Indian or Alaska Native, non-Hispanic/Latino; 44 Asian, non-Hispanic/Latino; 28 Hispanic/Latino; 3 Two or more races, non-Hispanic/Latino), 77 international. Average age 29. 1,548 applicants, 40% accepted, 392 enrolled. *Faculty:* 60 full-time (8 women), 18 part-time/adjunct (3 women). Expenses: Contact institution. *Financial support:* In 2010–11, 350 students received support, including 350 fellowships with full and partial tuition reimbursements available (averaging $12,041 per year); career-related internships or fieldwork, Federal Work-Study, institutionally sponsored loans, scholarships/grants, tuition waivers (full and partial), and unspecified assistantships also available. Financial award applicants required to submit FAFSA. In 2010, 422 master's awarded. Offers business (MBA, MNA, MS); business administration (MBA); executive business administration (MBA); financial reporting and assurance services (MS); nonprofit administration (MNA); tax services (MS). *Application deadline:* Applications are processed on a rolling basis. Electronic applications accepted. *Application Contact:* Dr. Carolyn Y. Woo, Dean, 574-631-7236, Fax: 574-631-4825, E-mail: woo.5@nd.edu. *Dean,* Dr. Carolyn Y. Woo, 574-631-7236, Fax: 574-631-4825, E-mail: woo.5@nd.edu.

UNIVERSITY OF OKLAHOMA, Norman, OK 73019-0390

General Information State-supported, coed, university. CGS member. *Enrollment:* 26,478 graduate, professional, and undergraduate students; 3,481 full-time matriculated graduate/professional students (1,676 women), 3,108 part-time matriculated graduate/professional students (1,588 women). *Enrollment by degree level:* 533 first professional, 4,457 master's, 1,520 doctoral, 79 other advanced degrees. *Graduate faculty:* 1,046 full-time (337 women), 93 part-time/adjunct (37 women). Tuition, state resident: full-time $3893; part-time $162.20 per credit hour. Tuition, nonresident: full-time $14,167; part-time $590.30 per credit hour. *Required fees:* $2523; $94.60 per credit hour. Tuition and fees vary according to course load and degree level. *Graduate housing:* Rooms and/or apartments available on a first-come, first-served basis to single and married students. *Student services:* Campus employment opportunities, campus safety program, career counseling, child daycare facilities, exercise/wellness program, free psychological counseling, grant writing training, international student services, low-cost health insurance, services for students with disabilities, writing training. *Library facilities:* Bizzell Memorial Library plus 7 others. *Online resources:* library catalog, web page, access to other libraries' catalogs. *Collection:* 5.3 million titles, 102,639 serial subscriptions, 5,983 audiovisual materials. *Research affiliation:* Federal Aviation Administration Aeronautical Center, Oklahoma Geological Survey, National Severe Storms Laboratory, Oklahoma Climatological Survey.

Computer facilities: Computer purchase and lease plans are available. 3,600 computers available on campus for general student use. A campuswide network can be accessed from student residence rooms and from off campus. Online class registration is available. *Web address:* http://www.ou.edu/.

General Application Contact: Mark McMasters, Director of Admissions, 405-325-2252, Fax: 405-325-7124, E-mail: mmcmasters@ou.edu.

GRADUATE UNITS

College of Architecture Students: 69 full-time (27 women), 32 part-time (12 women); includes 16 minority (2 Black or African American, non-Hispanic/Latino; 4 American Indian or Alaska Native, non-Hispanic/Latino; 3 Asian, non-Hispanic/Latino; 2 Hispanic/Latino; 1 Native Hawaiian or other Pacific Islander, non-Hispanic/Latino; 4 Two or more races, non-Hispanic/Latino), 17 international. Average age 30. 77 applicants, 79% accepted, 36 enrolled. *Faculty:* 32 full-time (9 women). Expenses: Contact institution. *Financial support:* In 2010–11, 78 students received support, including 11 research assistantships with partial tuition reimbursements available (averaging $10,465 per year), 9 teaching assistantships with partial tuition reimbursements available (averaging $9,938 per year); career-related internships or fieldwork, scholarships/grants, and unspecified assistantships also available. Financial award applicants required to submit FAFSA. In 2010, 41 master's awarded. Offers architecture (M Arch, MLA, MRCP, MS). *Application deadline:* For fall admission, 4/1 for domestic and international students; for spring admission, 11/1 for domestic students, 9/1 for international students. Applications are processed on a rolling basis. *Application fee:* $40 ($90 for international students). Electronic applications accepted. *Application Contact:* James Patterson, Associate Dean for Graduate and Research Programs, 405-325-2444, Fax: 405-325-7558, E-mail: jampatt@ou.edu. *Dean,* Charles W. Graham, 405-325-2444, Fax: 405-325-7558, E-mail: cwgraham@ou.edu.

Division of Architecture Students: 26 full-time (7 women), 10 part-time (5 women); includes 6 minority (1 American Indian or Alaska Native, non-Hispanic/Latino; 2 Asian, non-Hispanic/Latino; 1 Native Hawaiian or other Pacific Islander, non-Hispanic/Latino; 2 Two or more races, non-Hispanic/Latino), 8 international. Average age 31. 26 applicants, 69% accepted, 12 enrolled. *Faculty:* 26 full-time (7 women). Expenses: Contact institution. *Financial support:* In 2010–11, 23 students received support, including 4 teaching assistantships with partial tuition reimbursements available (averaging $9,586 per year); unspecified assistantships also available. Financial award applicants required to submit FAFSA. In 2010, 11 master's awarded. Offers architecture (M Arch, MS). *Application deadline:* For fall admission, 4/1 for domestic and international students; for spring admission, 11/1 for domestic students, 9/1 for international students. Applications are processed on a rolling basis. *Application fee:* $40 ($90 for international students). Electronic applications accepted. *Application Contact:* Lee Fithian, Associate Professor, 405-325-2444, Fax: 405-325-7558, E-mail: leefithian@ou.edu. *Interim Director,* Joel K. Dietrich, 405-325-6792, Fax: 405-325-7558, E-mail: dietrich@ou.edu.

Division of Construction Science Students: 13 full-time (4 women), 13 part-time (2 women); includes 6 minority (1 Black or African American, non-Hispanic/Latino; 1 American Indian or Alaska Native, non-Hispanic/Latino; 2 Hispanic/Latino; 2 Two or more races, non-Hispanic/Latino), 3 international. Average age 31. 19 applicants, 74% accepted, 12 enrolled. *Faculty:* 2 full-time (1 woman). Expenses: Contact institution. *Financial support:* In 2010–11, 19 students received support, including 42 research assistantships with partial tuition reimbursements available (averaging $11,025 per year), 3 teaching assistantships with partial tuition reimbursements available (averaging $10,641 per year); career-related internships or fieldwork, scholarships/grants, tuition waivers (partial), and unspecified assistantships also available. Support available to part-time students. Financial award applicants required to submit FAFSA. In 2010, 10 master's awarded. *Degree program information:* Part-time and evening/weekend programs available. Offers construction administration (MS). *Application deadline:* For fall admission, 4/1 for domestic and international students; for spring admission, 11/1 for domestic students, 9/1 for international students. Applications are processed on a rolling basis. *Application fee:* $40 ($90 for international students). Electronic applications accepted. *Application Contact:* Richard C. Ryan, Professor, 405-325-3976, Fax: 405-325-7558, E-mail: rryan@ou.edu. *Director,* Kenneth Robson, 405-325-6404, Fax: 405-325-7558, E-mail: krobson@ou.edu.

Division of Landscape Architecture Students: 11 full-time (6 women), 6 part-time (2 women); includes 2 minority (1 American Indian or Alaska Native, non-Hispanic/Latino; 1 Asian, non-Hispanic/Latino), 1 international. Average age 31. 20 applicants, 90% accepted, 5 enrolled. *Faculty:* 2 full-time (0 women). Expenses: Contact institution. *Financial support:* In 2010–11, 3 research assistantships with partial tuition reimbursements (averaging $9,586 per year) were awarded; career-related internships or fieldwork, Federal Work-Study, institutionally sponsored loans, scholarships/grants, and unspecified assistantships also available. Financial award applicants required to submit FAFSA. In 2010, 2 master's awarded. *Degree program information:* Part-time programs available. Offers landscape architecture (MLA). *Application deadline:* For fall admission, 4/1 for domestic and international students; for spring admission, 11/1 for domestic students, 9/1 for international students. Applications are processed on a rolling basis. *Application fee:* $40 ($90 for international students). Electronic applications accepted. *Application Contact:* Thomas Woodfin, Interim Director, 405-325-2299, Fax: 405-325-7558, E-mail: twoodfin@ou.edu. *Interim Director,* Thomas Woodfin, 405-325-2299, Fax: 405-325-7558, E-mail: twoodfin@ou.edu.

Division of Regional and City Planning Students: 18 full-time (9 women), 3 part-time (all women); includes 2 minority (1 Black or African American, non-Hispanic/Latino; 1 American Indian or Alaska Native, non-Hispanic/Latino), 5 international. Average age 28. 12 applicants, 92% accepted, 7 enrolled. *Faculty:* 2 full-time (1 woman). Expenses: Contact institution. *Financial support:* In 2010–11, 16 students received support, including 1 research assistantship with partial tuition reimbursement available (averaging $13,500 per year); career-related internships or fieldwork, institutionally sponsored loans, scholarships/grants, tuition waivers (partial), and unspecified assistantships also available. Support available to part-time students. Financial award applicants required to submit FAFSA. In 2010, 18 master's awarded. *Degree program information:* Part-time programs available. Offers regional and city planning (MRCP). *Application deadline:* For fall admission, 4/1 for domestic and international students; for spring admission, 11/1 for domestic students, 9/1 for international students. Applications are processed on a rolling basis. *Application fee:* $40 ($90 for international students). Electronic applications accepted. *Application Contact:* Charles Warnken, Interim Director, 405-325-3871, Fax: 405-325-7558, E-mail: cwarnken@ou.edu. *Interim Director,* Charles Warnken, 405-325-3871, Fax: 405-325-7558, E-mail: cwarnken@ou.edu.

College of Arts and Sciences Students: 1,393 full-time (801 women), 1,234 part-time (734 women); includes 590 minority (256 Black or African American, non-Hispanic/Latino; 138 American Indian or Alaska Native, non-Hispanic/Latino; 70 Asian, non-Hispanic/Latino; 72 Hispanic/Latino; 4 Native Hawaiian or other Pacific Islander, non-Hispanic/Latino; 50 Two or more races, non-Hispanic/Latino), 259 international. Average age 32. 1,235 applicants, 70% accepted, 570 enrolled. *Faculty:* 495 full-time (175 women), 57 part-time/adjunct (28 women). Expenses: Contact institution. *Financial support:* In 2010–11, 1,525 students received support, including 48 fellowships with full tuition reimbursements available (averaging $4,633 per year), 226 research assistantships with full and partial tuition reimbursements available (averaging $13,368 per year), 557 teaching assistantships with full and partial tuition reimbursements available (averaging $14,010 per year); career-related internships or fieldwork, Federal Work-Study, institutionally sponsored loans, scholarships/grants, traineeships, health care benefits, tuition waivers (full and partial), and unspecified assistantships also available. Support available to part-time students. Financial award applicants required to submit FAFSA. In 2010, 821 master's, 89 doctorates awarded. Offers anthropology (MA, PhD); applied economics (MA); applied linguistic anthropology (MA); arts and sciences (M Nat Sci, MA, MHR, MLIS, MPA, MS, MSW, PhD, Graduate Certificate); botany (MS, PhD); cellular and behavioral neurobiology (PhD); chemistry and biochemistry (MS, PhD); communication (MA, PhD); ecology and evolutionary biology (PhD); economics (PhD); English (MA, PhD); French (MA, PhD); German (MA); health and exercise science (MS, PhD); history (MA, PhD); history of science (MA, PhD); human relations (MHR); human relations licensure (Graduate Certificate); industrial and organizational psychology (MS, PhD); managerial economics (MA); mathematics (MA, MS, PhD); microbiology (MS, PhD); Native American studies (MA); natural science (M Nat Sci); organizational dynamics (MA); philosophy (MA, PhD); physics (MS, PhD); political science (MA, PhD); psychology (MS, PhD); public administration (MPA); sociology (MA, PhD); Spanish (MA, PhD); women's and gender studies (Graduate Certificate); zoology (M Nat Sci, MS, PhD). *Application deadline:* For fall admission, 4/1 for domestic and international students; for spring admission, 11/1 for domestic students, 9/1 for international students. Applications are processed on a rolling basis. *Application fee:* $40 ($90 for international students). Electronic applications accepted. *Application Contact:* Paul B. Bell, Dean and Vice Provost, 405-325-2077, Fax: 405-325-7709, E-mail: pbell@ou.edu. *Dean and Vice Provost,* Paul B. Bell, 405-325-2077, Fax: 405-325-7709, E-mail: pbell@ou.edu.

School of Library and Information Studies Students: 60 full-time (47 women), 123 part-time (98 women); includes 32 minority (8 Black or African American, non-Hispanic/Latino; 13 American Indian or Alaska Native, non-Hispanic/Latino; 4 Asian, non-Hispanic/Latino; 3 Hispanic/Latino; 4 Two or more races, non-Hispanic/Latino), 3 international. Average age 32. 79 applicants, 92% accepted, 47 enrolled. *Faculty:* 11 full-time (8 women). Expenses: Contact institution. *Financial support:* In 2010–11, 90 students received support, including 2 research assistantships (averaging $9,586 per year), 5 teaching assistantships with partial tuition reimbursements available (averaging $9,586 per year); Federal Work-Study, scholarships/grants, health care benefits, and unspecified assistantships also available. Support available to part-time students. Financial award applicants required to submit FAFSA. In 2010, 60 master's awarded. *Degree program information:* Part-time and evening/weekend programs available. Postbaccalaureate distance learning degree programs offered (minimal on-campus study). Offers library and information studies (MLIS, Graduate Certificate); library information studies (Graduate Certificate). *Application deadline:* For fall admission, 4/1 priority date for domestic students, 4/1 for international students; for spring admission, 11/1 for domestic students, 9/1 for international students. Applications are processed on a rolling basis. *Application fee:* $40 ($90 for international students). Electronic applications accepted. *Application Contact:* Maggie Ryan, Coordinator of Admissions, 405-325-3921, Fax: 405-325-7648, E-mail: mryan@ou.edu. *Director,* Cecelia Brown, 405-325-3921, Fax: 405-325-7648, E-mail: cbrown@ou.edu.

University of Oklahoma (continued)

School of Social Work Students: 204 full-time (172 women), 120 part-time (107 women); includes 91 minority (34 Black or African American, non-Hispanic/Latino; 26 American Indian or Alaska Native, non-Hispanic/Latino; 7 Asian, non-Hispanic/Latino; 17 Hispanic/Latino; 1 Native Hawaiian or other Pacific Islander, non-Hispanic/Latino; 6 Two or more races, non-Hispanic/Latino), 1 international. Average age 33. 170 applicants, 79% accepted, 92 enrolled. *Faculty:* 22 full-time (13 women), 11 part-time/adjunct (9 women). Expenses: Contact institution. *Financial support:* In 2010–11, 144 students received support, including 23 research assistantships with partial tuition reimbursements available (averaging $9,586 per year); Federal Work-Study, scholarships/grants, and unspecified assistantships also available. Financial award application deadline: 3/1; financial award applicants required to submit FAFSA. In 2010, 125 master's awarded. Offers social work (MSW). *Application deadline:* For fall admission, 3/1 priority date for domestic students, 4/1 for international students; for spring admission, 11/1 for domestic students, 9/1 for international students. *Application fee:* $40 ($90 for international students). Electronic applications accepted. *Application Contact:* Chrsitine Young, Administrative Assistant to Graduate Administration, 405-325-2821, Fax: 405-325-7072, E-mail: cdyoung@ou.edu. *Director*, Dr. Donald R. Baker, 405-325-2821, Fax: 405-325-7072, E-mail: drralph@ou.edu.

College of Atmospheric and Geographic Sciences Students: 113 full-time (37 women), 29 part-time (8 women); includes 7 minority (1 Black or African American, non-Hispanic/Latino; 3 American Indian or Alaska Native, non-Hispanic/Latino; 3 Asian, non-Hispanic/Latino), 25 international. Average age 28. 98 applicants, 24% accepted, 18 enrolled. *Faculty:* 52 full-time (8 women), 7 part-time/adjunct (2 women). Expenses: Contact institution. *Financial support:* In 2010–11, 13 fellowships with full tuition reimbursements (averaging $5,000 per year), 85 research assistantships with partial tuition reimbursements (averaging $17,152 per year), 30 teaching assistantships with partial tuition reimbursements (averaging $16,863 per year) were awarded; career-related internships or fieldwork, scholarships/grants, health care benefits, tuition waivers (partial), and unspecified assistantships also available. Financial award application deadline: 2/1; financial award applicants required to submit FAFSA. In 2010, 17 master's, 7 doctorates awarded. *Degree program information:* Part-time programs available. Offers atmospheric and geographic sciences (MA, MS, PhD); geography (MA, PhD). *Application deadline:* For fall admission, 2/1 priority date for domestic students, 4/1 for international students; for spring admission, 11/1 for domestic students, 9/1 for international students. Applications are processed on a rolling basis. *Application fee:* $40 ($90 for international students). Electronic applications accepted. *Application Contact:* Miranda Sowell, Coordinator of Graduate Admissions, 405-325-3811, Fax: 405-325-5346, E-mail: mgsowell@ou.edu. *Dean*, Dr. Berrien Moore, 405-325-3095, Fax: 405-325-3148, E-mail: berrien@ou.edu.

School of Meteorology Students: 85 full-time (23 women), 15 part-time (3 women); includes 5 minority (1 Black or African American, non-Hispanic/Latino; 1 American Indian or Alaska Native, non-Hispanic/Latino; 3 Asian, non-Hispanic/Latino), 15 international. Average age 27. 78 applicants, 14% accepted, 11 enrolled. *Faculty:* 37 full-time (4 women), 6 part-time/adjunct (1 woman). Expenses: Contact institution. *Financial support:* In 2010–11, 10 fellowships with full tuition reimbursements (averaging $5,000 per year), 75 research assistantships (averaging $17,281 per year), 17 teaching assistantships with partial tuition reimbursements (averaging $17,885 per year) were awarded; health care benefits and unspecified assistantships also available. Financial award application deadline: 2/1; financial award applicants required to submit FAFSA. In 2010, 14 master's, 3 doctorates awarded. Offers meteorology (MS, PhD); professional meteorology (MS). *Application deadline:* For fall admission, 2/1 priority date for domestic students, 4/1 for international students; for spring admission, 11/1 for domestic students, 9/1 for international students. Applications are processed on a rolling basis. *Application fee:* $40 ($90 for international students). Electronic applications accepted. *Application Contact:* Celia Jones, Coordinator, Academic Student Services, 405-325-6571, Fax: 405-325-7689, E-mail: cjones@ou.edu. *Director*, David Parsons, 405-325-8565, Fax: 405-325-7689, E-mail: dparsons@ou.edu.

College of Earth and Energy Students: 158 full-time (42 women), 71 part-time (17 women); includes 12 minority (4 Black or African American, non-Hispanic/Latino; 3 American Indian or Alaska Native, non-Hispanic/Latino; 2 Asian, non-Hispanic/Latino; 2 Hispanic/Latino; 1 Two or more races, non-Hispanic/Latino), 153 international. Average age 28. 245 applicants, 27% accepted, 47 enrolled. *Faculty:* 37 full-time (2 women), 1 part-time/adjunct (0 women). Expenses: Contact institution. *Financial support:* In 2010–11, 188 students received support, including 2 fellowships (averaging $5,000 per year), 108 research assistantships (averaging $14,670 per year), 39 teaching assistantships (averaging $16,269 per year); career-related internships or fieldwork, scholarships/grants, tuition waivers (partial), and unspecified assistantships also available. Financial award applicants required to submit FAFSA. In 2010, 28 master's, 10 doctorates awarded. Offers earth and energy (MS, PhD). *Application deadline:* For fall admission, 2/1 priority date for domestic students, 4/1 for international students; for spring admission, 9/1 for domestic and international students. Applications are processed on a rolling basis. *Application fee:* $40 ($90 for international students). Electronic applications accepted. *Application Contact:* Linda Goeringer, Academic Counselor, 405-325-3821, Fax: 405-325-3180, E-mail: lgoeringer@ou.edu. *Associate Provost/Director*, Doug Elmore, 405-325-3253, Fax: 405-325-3140, E-mail: delmore@ou.edu.

ConocoPhillips School of Geology and Geophysics Students: 73 full-time (24 women), 30 part-time (10 women); includes 7 minority (3 American Indian or Alaska Native, non-Hispanic/Latino; 2 Asian, non-Hispanic/Latino; 1 Hispanic/Latino; 1 Two or more races, non-Hispanic/Latino), 44 international. Average age 28. 101 applicants, 28% accepted, 21 enrolled. *Faculty:* 21 full-time (2 women). Expenses: Contact institution. *Financial support:* In 2010–11, 90 students received support, including 2 fellowships (averaging $5,000 per year), 36 research assistantships with partial tuition reimbursements available (averaging $18,446 per year), 26 teaching assistantships with partial tuition reimbursements available (averaging $18,346 per year); scholarships/grants, health care benefits, tuition waivers (partial), and unspecified assistantships also available. Financial award application deadline: 2/1; financial award applicants required to submit FAFSA. In 2010, 17 master's, 7 doctorates awarded. Offers geology (MS, PhD); geophysics (MS, PhD). *Application deadline:* For fall admission, 2/1 priority date for domestic students, 4/1 for international students; for spring admission, 9/1 for domestic and international students. Applications are processed on a rolling basis. *Application fee:* $40 ($90 for international students). Electronic applications accepted. *Application Contact:* Donna S. Mullins, Coordinator of Administrative Student Services, 405-325-3255, Fax: 405-325-3140, E-mail: dsmullins@ou.edu. *Director and Associate Provost*, Dr. Douglas Elmore, 405-325-3253, Fax: 405-325-3140, E-mail: delmore@ou.edu.

School of Petroleum and Geological Engineering Students: 85 full-time (18 women), 41 part-time (7 women); includes 7 minority (3 American Indian or Alaska Native, non-Hispanic/Latino; 2 Asian, non-Hispanic/Latino; 1 Hispanic/Latino; 1 Two or more races, non-Hispanic/Latino), 109 international. Average age 28. 144 applicants, 27% accepted, 26 enrolled. *Faculty:* 16 full-time (0 women), 1 part-time/adjunct (0 women). Expenses: Contact institution. *Financial support:* In 2010–11, 98 students received support, including 52 research assistantships with partial tuition reimbursements available (averaging $12,868 per year), 13 teaching assistantships with partial tuition reimbursements available (averaging $12,115 per year); traineeships also available. Financial award application deadline: 4/15; financial award applicants required to submit FAFSA. In 2010, 11 master's, 3 doctorates awarded. *Degree program information:* Part-time programs available. Offers geological engineering (MS, PhD); natural gas engineering and management (MS); petroleum engineering (MS, PhD). *Application deadline:* For fall admission, 6/1 priority date for domestic students, 4/1 for international students; for spring admission, 11/1 for domestic students, 9/1 for international students. Applications are processed on a rolling basis. *Application fee:* $40 ($90 for international students). Electronic applications accepted. *Application Contact:* Shalli Young, Executive Assistant to the Graduate Liaison, 405-325-2921, Fax: 405-325-7477, E-mail: syoung@ou.edu. *Director*, Dr. Chandra Rai, 405-325-2921, Fax: 405-325-7477, E-mail: crai@ou.edu.

College of Engineering Students: 386 full-time (92 women), 194 part-time (36 women); includes 46 minority (11 Black or African American, non-Hispanic/Latino; 12 American Indian or Alaska Native, non-Hispanic/Latino; 19 Asian, non-Hispanic/Latino; 3 Hispanic/Latino; 1 Two or more races, non-Hispanic/Latino), 322 international. Average age 28. 325 applicants, 62% accepted, 90 enrolled. *Faculty:* 131 full-time (19 women), 2 part-time/adjunct (0 women). Expenses: Contact institution. *Financial support:* In 2010–11, 532 students received support, including 5 fellowships with full tuition reimbursements available (averaging $9,500 per year), 232 research assistantships with partial tuition reimbursements available (averaging $14,093 per year), 76 teaching assistantships with partial tuition reimbursements available (averaging $12,126 per year); career-related internships or fieldwork, Federal Work-Study, institutionally sponsored loans, scholarships/grants, traineeships, tuition waivers (full and partial), and unspecified assistantships also available. Support available to part-time students. Financial award applicants required to submit FAFSA. In 2010, 114 master's, 40 doctorates awarded. Offers electrical and computer engineering (MS, PhD); engineering (M Env Sc, MS, PhD); engineering physics (MS, PhD); telecommunications engineering (MS). *Application deadline:* For fall admission, 6/1 for domestic students, 4/1 for international students; for spring admission, 11/1 for domestic students, 9/1 for international students. Applications are processed on a rolling basis. *Application fee:* $40 ($90 for international students). Electronic applications accepted. *Application Contact:* Miranda Sowell, Coordinator of Graduate Admissions, 405-325-3811, Fax: 405-325-5346, E-mail: mgsowell@ou.edu. *Dean*, Dr. Thomas Landers, 405-325-2621, Fax: 405-325-7508, E-mail: landers@ou.edu.

Center for Bioengineering Students: 19 full-time (4 women), 10 part-time (2 women); includes 3 minority (1 Black or African American, non-Hispanic/Latino; 2 Asian, non-Hispanic/Latino), 15 international. Average age 29. 7 applicants, 86% accepted, 6 enrolled. Expenses: Contact institution. *Financial support:* Tuition waivers and unspecified assistantships available. Financial award applicants required to submit FAFSA. In 2010, 8 master's, 2 doctorates awarded. Offers bioengineering (MS, PhD). *Application deadline:* For fall admission, 6/1 priority date for domestic students, 4/1 priority date for international students; for spring admission, 11/1 priority date for domestic students, 9/1 priority date for international students. *Application fee:* $40 ($90 for international students). Electronic applications accepted. *Application Contact:* Dr. Ulli Nollert, Graduate Program Coordinator and Associate Professor, 405-325-4366, Fax: 405-325-5813, E-mail: nollert@ou.edu. *Director*, Dr. David Schmidtke.

School of Aerospace and Mechanical Engineering Students: 47 full-time (1 woman), 31 part-time (2 women); includes 11 minority (2 Black or African American, non-Hispanic/Latino; 3 American Indian or Alaska Native, non-Hispanic/Latino; 5 Asian, non-Hispanic/Latino; 1 Hispanic/Latino), 32 international. Average age 28. 58 applicants, 43% accepted, 14 enrolled. *Faculty:* 20 full-time (3 women). Expenses: Contact institution. *Financial support:* In 2010–11, 66 students received support, including 25 research assistantships with partial tuition reimbursements available (averaging $11,852 per year), 25 teaching assistantships with partial tuition reimbursements available (averaging $11,655 per year); unspecified assistantships also available. Financial award application deadline: 3/1; financial award applicants required to submit FAFSA. In 2010, 26 master's, 9 doctorates awarded. *Degree program information:* Part-time programs available. Offers aerospace engineering (MS, PhD); mechanical engineering (MS, PhD). *Application deadline:* For fall admission, 1/15 priority date for domestic and international students; for spring admission, 10/1 priority date for domestic and international students. Applications are processed on a rolling basis. *Application fee:* $40 ($90 for international students). Electronic applications accepted. *Application Contact:* Dr. David Miller, Graduate Liaison, 405-325-1094, Fax: 405-325-1088, E-mail: dpmiller@ou.edu. *Director*, Farrokh Mistree, 405-325-5011, Fax: 405-325-1088, E-mail: farrokh.mistree@ou.edu.

School of Chemical, Biological and Materials Engineering Students: 55 full-time (20 women), 9 part-time (4 women), 52 international. Average age 25. 33 applicants, 55% accepted, 13 enrolled. *Faculty:* 18 full-time (1 woman), 1 part-time/adjunct (0 women). Expenses: Contact institution. *Financial support:* In 2010–11, 61 research assistantships with partial tuition reimbursements (averaging $16,485 per year) were awarded; tuition waivers and unspecified assistantships also available. Financial award application deadline: 3/1; financial award applicants required to submit FAFSA. In 2010, 5 master's, 7 doctorates awarded. Offers chemical engineering (MS, PhD). *Application deadline:* For fall admission, 6/1 priority date for domestic students, 4/1 for international students; for spring admission, 11/1 for domestic students, 9/1 for international students. Applications are processed on a rolling basis. *Application fee:* $40 ($90 for international students). Electronic applications accepted. *Application Contact:* Dr. Ulli Nollert, Graduate Program Coordinator and Associate Professor, 405-325-4366, Fax: 405-325-5813, E-mail: nollert@ou.edu. *Director*, Dr. Lance Lobban, 405-325-5811, Fax: 405-325-5813, E-mail: llobban@ou.edu.

School of Civil Engineering and Environmental Science Students: 54 full-time (18 women), 29 part-time (9 women); includes 9 minority (2 Black or African American, non-Hispanic/Latino; 5 American Indian or Alaska Native, non-Hispanic/Latino; 1 Asian, non-Hispanic/Latino; 1 Hispanic/Latino), 36 international. Average age 28. 42 applicants, 40% accepted, 11 enrolled. *Faculty:* 23 full-time (5 women). Expenses: Contact institution. *Financial support:* In 2010–11, 2 fellowships with full tuition reimbursements (averaging $5,000 per year), 44 research assistantships with partial tuition reimbursements (averaging $13,343 per year), 4 teaching assistantships with partial tuition reimbursements (averaging $11,522 per year) were awarded; scholarships/grants also available. Financial award application deadline: 3/1; financial award applicants required to submit FAFSA. In 2010, 21 master's, 5 doctorates awarded. *Degree program information:* Part-time programs available. Offers air (M Env Sc); civil engineering (MS, PhD); environmental engineering (MS, PhD); environmental science (M Env Sc, PhD). *Application deadline:* For fall admission, 4/1 priority date for domestic students, 4/1 for international students; for spring admission, 11/1 for domestic students, 9/1 for international students. Applications are processed on a rolling basis. *Application fee:* $40 ($90 for international students). Electronic applications accepted. *Application Contact:* Susan Williams, Graduate Programs Specialist, 405-325-2344, Fax: 405-325-4217, E-mail: srwilliams@ou.edu. *Director*, Robert C. Knox, 405-325-5911, Fax: 405-325-4217, E-mail: rknox@ou.edu.

School of Computer Science Students: 63 full-time (12 women), 43 part-time (4 women); includes 4 minority (1 American Indian or Alaska Native, non-Hispanic/Latino; 3 Asian, non-Hispanic/Latino), 61 international. Average age 28. 64 applicants, 81% accepted, 15 enrolled. *Faculty:* 17 full-time (3 women). Expenses: Contact institution. *Financial support:* In 2010–11, 85 students received support, including 3 fellowships (averaging $3,000 per year), 16 research assistantships with partial tuition reimbursements available (averaging $15,006 per year), 16 teaching assistantships with partial tuition reimbursements available (averaging $14,116 per year); unspecified assistantships also available. Financial award application deadline: 3/1; financial award applicants required to submit FAFSA. In 2010, 18 master's, 1 doctorate awarded. Offers computer science (MS, PhD). *Application deadline:* For fall admission, 1/15 priority date for domestic students, 4/1 for international students; for spring admission, 11/1 for domestic students, 9/1 for international students. Applications are processed on a rolling basis. *Application fee:* $40 ($90 for international students). Electronic applications accepted. *Application Contact:* Sridhar Radhakrishnan, Professor and Director, 405-325-4042, Fax: 405-325-4044, E-mail: sridhar@ou.edu. *Professor and Director*, Sridhar Radhakrishnan, 405-325-4042, Fax: 405-325-4044, E-mail: sridhar@ou.edu.

School of Industrial Engineering Students: 37 full-time (11 women), 23 part-time (7 women); includes 5 minority (3 Black or African American, non-Hispanic/Latino; 1 American Indian or Alaska Native, non-Hispanic/Latino; 1 Two or more races, non-Hispanic/Latino), 32 international. Average age 28. 58 applicants, 72% accepted, 12 enrolled. *Faculty:* 14 full-time (5 women). Expenses: Contact institution. *Financial support:* In 2010–11, 48 students received support, including 12 research assistantships with partial tuition reimbursements available (averaging $13,300 per year), 10 teaching assistantships with partial tuition reimbursements available (averaging $10,350 per year); scholarships/grants and unspecified assistantships also available. Financial award application deadline: 5/1; financial award applicants required to submit FAFSA. In 2010, 7 master's, 5 doctorates awarded. *Degree program information:* Part-time programs available. Offers industrial engineering (MS, PhD). *Application deadline:* For fall admission, 6/1 priority date for domestic students, 4/1 for international students; for spring admission, 11/1 for domestic students, 9/1 for international students. Applications are processed on a rolling basis. *Application fee:* $40 ($90 for international students). Electronic applications accepted. *Application Contact:*

Amy J. Piper, Student Services Coordinator, 405-325-3721, Fax: 405-325-7555, E-mail: ajpiper@ou.edu. *Director*, Dr. Randa Shehab, 405-325-3721, Fax: 405-325-7555, E-mail: rlshehab@ou.edu.

College of International Studies Students: 14 full-time (4 women), 5 part-time (4 women); includes 1 minority (Asian, non-Hispanic/Latino), 2 international. Average age 26. 17 applicants, 47% accepted, 4 enrolled. *Faculty:* 17 full-time (5 women). Expenses: Contact institution. *Financial support:* In 2010–11, 4 research assistantships (averaging $11,611 per year), 7 teaching assistantships with partial tuition reimbursements (averaging $13,616 per year) were awarded; career-related internships or fieldwork, scholarships/grants, health care benefits, tuition waivers (full), and unspecified assistantships also available. Financial award applicants required to submit FAFSA. In 2010, 6 master's awarded. *Degree program information:* Part-time programs available. Offers area studies (MAIS, Graduate Certificate); global studies (MAIS, Graduate Certificate). *Application deadline:* For fall admission, 2/15 for domestic students, 4/1 for international students; for spring admission, 10/15 for domestic students, 9/1 for international students. Applications are processed on a rolling basis. *Application fee:* $40 ($90 for international students). Electronic applications accepted. *Application Contact:* Eric Heinze, Director of Graduate Studies, 405-325-5802, Fax: 405-325-7738, E-mail: eheinze@ou.edu. *Director*, Mark Fraizer, 405-325-1584, Fax: 405-325-7738, E-mail: markfrazier@ou.edu.

College of Law Students: 535 full-time (242 women), 4 part-time (1 woman); includes 64 minority (15 Black or African American, non-Hispanic/Latino; 24 American Indian or Alaska Native, non-Hispanic/Latino; 17 Asian, non-Hispanic/Latino; 4 Hispanic/Latino; 4 Two or more races, non-Hispanic/Latino), 4 international. Average age 25. 901 applicants, 35% accepted, 152 enrolled. *Faculty:* 66 full-time (27 women), 29 part-time/adjunct (13 women). Expenses: Contact institution. *Financial support:* In 2010–11, 408 students received support. Career-related internships or fieldwork, Federal Work-Study, institutionally sponsored loans, scholarships/grants, and tuition waivers (full and partial) available. Financial award application deadline: 3/1; financial award applicants required to submit FAFSA. In 2010, 179 first professional degrees awarded. Offers law (JD, LL M). *Application deadline:* For fall admission, 3/15 for domestic students, 4/1 for international students. Applications are processed on a rolling basis. *Application fee:* $50 ($90 for international students). Electronic applications accepted. *Application Contact:* Vicki Ferguson, Admissions Coordinator, 405-325-4728, Fax: 405-325-0502, E-mail: admissions@law.ou.edu. *Dean*, Dr. Joseph Harroz, 405-325-4699, Fax: 405-325-7712, E-mail: jharroz@ou.edu.

College of Liberal Studies Students: 30 full-time (18 women), 432 part-time (221 women); includes 99 minority (31 Black or African American, non-Hispanic/Latino; 33 American Indian or Alaska Native, non-Hispanic/Latino; 4 Asian, non-Hispanic/Latino; 21 Hispanic/Latino; 10 Two or more races, non-Hispanic/Latino), 1 international. Average age 36. 159 applicants, 94% accepted, 113 enrolled. *Faculty:* 16 full-time (12 women), 13 part-time/adjunct (4 women). Expenses: Contact institution. *Financial support:* In 2010–11, 358 students received support. Career-related internships or fieldwork, institutionally sponsored loans, scholarships/grants, and tuition waivers (partial) available. Support available to part-time students. Financial award applicants required to submit FAFSA. In 2010, 114 master's awarded. *Degree program information:* Part-time programs available. Postbaccalaureate distance learning degree programs offered (no on-campus study). Offers human and health services administration (MA); integrated studies (MA); museum studies (MA); prevention science (MPS). *Application deadline:* For fall admission, 7/15 priority date for domestic students, 4/1 for international students; for spring admission, 12/1 for domestic students, 9/1 for international students. Applications are processed on a rolling basis. *Application fee:* $40 ($90 for international students). Electronic applications accepted. *Application Contact:* Kelly Collyar, Coordinator, Recruitment and Admissions, 800-522-4389, Fax: 405-325-7132, E-mail: clsinfo@ou.edu. *Dean and Vice President for University Outreach*, Dr. James Pappas, 405-325-6361, Fax: 405-325-7196, E-mail: jpappas@ou.edu.

Gaylord College of Journalism and Mass Communication Students: 43 full-time (28 women), 38 part-time (19 women); includes 12 minority (5 Black or African American, non-Hispanic/Latino; 5 American Indian or Alaska Native, non-Hispanic/Latino; 1 Asian, non-Hispanic/Latino; 1 Hispanic/Latino), 8 international. Average age 29. 44 applicants, 73% accepted, 17 enrolled. *Faculty:* 29 full-time (8 women), 3 part-time/adjunct (1 woman). Expenses: Contact institution. *Financial support:* In 2010–11, 58 students received support, including 4 fellowships (averaging $5,000 per year), 15 research assistantships (averaging $13,334 per year), 20 teaching assistantships (averaging $14,087 per year); Federal Work-Study, scholarships/grants, health care benefits, tuition waivers (full and partial), and unspecified assistantships also available. Support available to part-time students. Financial award application deadline: 2/1; financial award applicants required to submit FAFSA. In 2010, 25 master's awarded. *Degree program information:* Part-time programs available. Offers advertising and public relations (MA); broadcasting and electronic media (MA); journalism (MA); journalism and mass communication (MA); mass communication (PhD); mass communication management (MA); professional writing (MPW). *Application deadline:* For fall admission, 7/1 for domestic students, 4/1 for international students; for spring admission, 11/1 for domestic students, 9/1 for international students. *Application fee:* $40 ($90 for international students). Electronic applications accepted. *Application Contact:* David Craig, Director of Graduate Studies, 405-325-5206, Fax: 405-325-7565, E-mail: dcraig@ou.edu. *Dean*, Joe Foote, 405-325-2721, Fax: 405-325-7565, E-mail: jfoote@ou.edu.

Graduate College Students: 117 full-time (46 women), 463 part-time (172 women); includes 99 minority (42 Black or African American, non-Hispanic/Latino; 6 American Indian or Alaska Native, non-Hispanic/Latino; 15 Asian, non-Hispanic/Latino; 28 Hispanic/Latino; 3 Native Hawaiian or other Pacific Islander, non-Hispanic/Latino; 5 Two or more races, non-Hispanic/Latino), 5 international. Average age 34. 135 applicants, 93% accepted, 70 enrolled. *Faculty:* 25 full-time (15 women). Expenses: Contact institution. *Financial support:* Career-related internships or fieldwork, Federal Work-Study, institutionally sponsored loans, scholarships/grants, traineeships, health care benefits, tuition waivers (full and partial), and unspecified assistantships available. Support available to part-time students. Financial award applicants required to submit FAFSA. In 2010, 132 master's, 6 doctorates awarded. *Degree program information:* Part-time and evening/weekend programs available. Postbaccalaureate distance learning degree programs offered (no on-campus study). Offers interdisciplinary studies (MA, MS, PhD). *Application deadline:* For fall admission, 4/1 for domestic and international students; for spring admission, 11/1 for domestic students, 9/1 for international students. Applications are processed on a rolling basis. *Application fee:* $40 ($90 for international students). Electronic applications accepted. *Application Contact:* Miranda Sowell, Coordinator of Graduate Admissions, 405-325-3811, Fax: 405-325-5346, E-mail: mgsowell@ou.edu. *Dean*, Dr. Lee Williams, 405-325-3811, Fax: 405-325-5346, E-mail: lwilliams@ou.edu.

Jeannine Rainbolt College of Education Students: 350 full-time (226 women), 438 part-time (309 women); includes 163 minority (74 Black or African American, non-Hispanic/Latino; 48 American Indian or Alaska Native, non-Hispanic/Latino; 14 Asian, non-Hispanic/Latino; 15 Hispanic/Latino; 1 Native Hawaiian or other Pacific Islander, non-Hispanic/Latino; 11 Two or more races, non-Hispanic/Latino), 26 international. Average age 34. 335 applicants, 69% accepted, 178 enrolled. *Faculty:* 70 full-time (43 women), 3 part-time/adjunct (0 women). Expenses: Contact institution. *Financial support:* In 2010–11, 538 students received support, including 6 fellowships with full tuition reimbursements available (averaging $5,000 per year), 59 research assistantships with partial tuition reimbursements available (averaging $14,363 per year), 25 teaching assistantships with partial tuition reimbursements available (averaging $10,134 per year); career-related internships or fieldwork, Federal Work-Study, institutionally sponsored loans, scholarships/grants, tuition waivers (full and partial), and unspecified assistantships also available. Support available to part-time students. Financial award applicants required to submit FAFSA. In 2010, 127 master's, 35 doctorates awarded. *Degree program information:* Evening/weekend programs available. Postbaccalaureate distance learning degree programs offered (no on-campus study). Offers adult and higher education (M Ed, PhD); college teaching (Graduate Certificate); communication, culture and pedagogy for Hispanic populations in educational settings (Graduate Certificate); community counseling (M Ed); counseling psychology (PhD); curriculum and supervision (M Ed); education (M Ed, Ed D, PhD, Graduate Certificate); education administration (M Ed, Ed D, PhD); educational administration, curriculum and supervision (M Ed, Ed D, PhD); educational studies (M Ed, PhD); instructional leadership and academic curriculum (M Ed, PhD); instructional psychology and technology (M Ed, PhD); law and policy (M Ed); special education (M Ed, PhD); technology leadership (M Ed). *Application deadline:* For fall admission, 6/1 for domestic students, 4/1 for international students; for spring admission, 11/1 for domestic students, 9/1 for international students. Applications are processed on a rolling basis. *Application fee:* $40 ($90 for international students). Electronic applications accepted. *Application Contact:* Dr. Joan Karen Smith, Dean, 405-325-1081, Fax: 405-325-7390, E-mail: jksmith@ou.edu. *Dean*, Dr. Joan Karen Smith, 405-325-1081, Fax: 405-325-7390, E-mail: jksmith@ou.edu.

Michael F. Price College of Business Students: 188 full-time (60 women), 151 part-time (40 women); includes 40 minority (4 Black or African American, non-Hispanic/Latino; 10 American Indian or Alaska Native, non-Hispanic/Latino; 18 Asian, non-Hispanic/Latino; 4 Hispanic/Latino; 4 Two or more races, non-Hispanic/Latino), 55 international. Average age 28. 359 applicants, 45% accepted, 118 enrolled. *Faculty:* 52 full-time (12 women), 5 part-time/adjunct (1 woman). Expenses: Contact institution. *Financial support:* In 2010–11, 238 students received support, including 13 fellowships with full tuition reimbursements available (averaging $5,300 per year), 62 research assistantships with partial tuition reimbursements available (averaging $11,878 per year), 18 teaching assistantships with partial tuition reimbursements available (averaging $13,695 per year); career-related internships or fieldwork, Federal Work-Study, scholarships/grants, tuition waivers (full and partial), and unspecified assistantships also available. Support available to part-time students. Financial award applicants required to submit FAFSA. In 2010, 117 master's, 6 doctorates awarded. Offers business (M Acc, MBA, MS, PhD, Graduate Certificate); business administration (MBA, PhD). *Application deadline:* For fall admission, 4/1 for domestic and international students; for spring admission, 11/1 for domestic students, 9/1 for international students. Applications are processed on a rolling basis. *Application fee:* $40 ($90 for international students). Electronic applications accepted. *Application Contact:* Gina Amundson, Director of Graduate Programs, 405-325-4107, Fax: 405-325-7753, E-mail: gamundson@ou.edu. *Dean*, Dr. Kenneth Evans, 405-325-2070, Fax: 405-325-3421, E-mail: evansk@ou.edu.

Division of Management Information Systems Students: 17 full-time (3 women), 18 part-time (3 women); includes 4 minority (1 Black or African American, non-Hispanic/Latino; 3 Asian, non-Hispanic/Latino), 6 international. Average age 28. 14 applicants, 79% accepted, 10 enrolled. *Faculty:* 9 full-time (3 women). Expenses: Contact institution. *Financial support:* In 2010–11, 24 students received support, including 11 research assistantships with full tuition reimbursements available (averaging $11,603 per year), 4 teaching assistantships with full tuition reimbursements available (averaging $11,021 per year); scholarships/grants and unspecified assistantships also available. Financial award applicants required to submit FAFSA. In 2010, 6 master's awarded. *Degree program information:* Part-time and evening/weekend programs available. Offers management information systems (MS, PhD, Graduate Certificate). *Application deadline:* For fall admission, 3/15 for domestic students, 3/1 for international students; for spring admission, 11/1 for domestic students, 9/1 for international students. Applications are processed on a rolling basis. *Application fee:* $40 ($90 for international students). Electronic applications accepted. *Application Contact:* Amber Hasbrook, Academic Counselor, 405-325-4107, Fax: 405-325-7753, E-mail: amber.hasbrook@ou.edu. *Director*, Laku Chidambaram, 405-325-5721, Fax: 405-325-2096, E-mail: laku@ou.edu.

School of Accounting Students: 38 full-time (21 women), 11 part-time (5 women); includes 9 minority (1 Black or African American, non-Hispanic/Latino; 2 American Indian or Alaska Native, non-Hispanic/Latino; 5 Asian, non-Hispanic/Latino; 1 Two or more races, non-Hispanic/Latino), 5 international. Average age 26. 38 applicants, 39% accepted, 9 enrolled. *Faculty:* 12 full-time (4 women), 1 part-time/adjunct (0 women). Expenses: Contact institution. *Financial support:* In 2010–11, 44 students received support, including 7 research assistantships with partial tuition reimbursements available (averaging $14,887 per year), 5 teaching assistantships with partial tuition reimbursements available (averaging $14,683 per year); career-related internships or fieldwork, scholarships/grants, and unspecified assistantships also available. Financial award application deadline: 4/1; financial award applicants required to submit FAFSA. In 2010, 16 master's awarded. *Degree program information:* Part-time programs available. Offers accounting (M Acc). *Application deadline:* For fall admission, 6/15 for domestic students, 4/1 for international students; for spring admission, 11/15 for domestic students, 9/1 for international students. Applications are processed on a rolling basis. *Application fee:* $40 ($90 for international students). Electronic applications accepted. *Application Contact:* Amber Hasbrook, Academic Counselor, 405-325-4107, Fax: 405-325-7753, E-mail: amber.hasbrook@ou.edu. *Director*, Dr. Frances L. Ayres, 405-325-4221, Fax: 405-325-2096, E-mail: fayres@ou.edu.

Weitzenhoffer Family College of Fine Arts Students: 139 full-time (77 women), 71 part-time (42 women); includes 24 minority (4 Black or African American, non-Hispanic/Latino; 9 American Indian or Alaska Native, non-Hispanic/Latino; 4 Asian, non-Hispanic/Latino; 3 Hispanic/Latino; 2 Native Hawaiian or other Pacific Islander, non-Hispanic/Latino; 2 Two or more races, non-Hispanic/Latino), 21 international. Average age 31. 174 applicants, 54% accepted, 63 enrolled. *Faculty:* 90 full-time (29 women), 2 part-time/adjunct (1 woman). Expenses: Contact institution. *Financial support:* In 2010–11, 182 students received support, including 12 fellowships (averaging $4,900 per year), 28 research assistantships with partial tuition reimbursements available (averaging $10,733 per year), 92 teaching assistantships with partial tuition reimbursements available (averaging $10,290 per year); scholarships/grants, health care benefits, tuition waivers (partial), and unspecified assistantships also available. Financial award application deadline: 4/7; financial award applicants required to submit FAFSA. In 2010, 41 master's, 12 doctorates awarded. *Degree program information:* Part-time programs available. Offers fine arts (M Mus, M Mus Ed, MA, MFA, DMA, PhD). *Application deadline:* For fall admission, 6/1 for domestic students, 4/1 for international students; for spring admission, 11/1 for domestic students, 9/1 for international students. Applications are processed on a rolling basis. *Application fee:* $40 ($90 for international students). Electronic applications accepted. *Application Contact:* Jonathan Hils, Graduate Liaison, 405-325-2691, Fax: 405-325-1668, E-mail: hils@ou.edu. *Dean*, Dr. Rich Taylor, 405-325-7370, Fax: 405-325-1667, E-mail: rich.taylor@ou.edu.

School of Art and Art History Students: 26 full-time (17 women), 8 part-time (6 women); includes 8 minority (6 American Indian or Alaska Native, non-Hispanic/Latino; 2 Native Hawaiian or other Pacific Islander, non-Hispanic/Latino), 3 international. Average age 29. 38 applicants, 47% accepted, 13 enrolled. *Faculty:* 26 full-time (10 women). Expenses: Contact institution. *Financial support:* In 2010–11, 10 research assistantships with partial tuition reimbursements (averaging $9,592 per year), 7 teaching assistantships with partial tuition reimbursements (averaging $9,592 per year) were awarded; career-related internships or fieldwork, Federal Work-Study, institutionally sponsored loans, scholarships/grants, health care benefits, tuition waivers (full and partial), and unspecified assistantships also available. Financial award application deadline: 4/7; financial award applicants required to submit FAFSA. In 2010, 9 master's awarded. Offers art (MFA); art history (MA, PhD). *Application deadline:* For fall admission, 2/1 priority date for domestic students, 2/1 for international students; for spring admission, 10/1 for domestic and international students. Applications are processed on a rolling basis. *Application fee:* $40 ($90 for international students). Electronic applications accepted. *Application Contact:* Jonathan Hils, Graduate Liaison, 405-325-2691, Fax: 405-325-1668, E-mail: hils@ou.edu. *Director*, Mary Jo Watson, 405-325-2691, Fax: 405-325-1668, E-mail: mjwatson@ou.edu.

School of Dance Students: 6 full-time (all women), 1 (woman) part-time. Average age 36. 4 applicants, 50% accepted, 1 enrolled. *Faculty:* 7 full-time (3 women). Expenses: Contact institution. *Financial support:* In 2010–11, 5 students received support, including 5 fellowships with full tuition reimbursements available (averaging $4,800 per year), 6 teaching assistantships with partial tuition reimbursements available (averaging $14,034 per year); health care benefits and unspecified assistantships also available. Support available to part-time students. Financial award application deadline: 3/15; financial award applicants required to submit FAFSA. In 2010, 1 master's awarded. Offers dance (MFA). *Application deadline:* For fall admission, 6/1 for domestic students, 4/1 for international students; for spring admission, 11/1 for domestic students, 9/1 for international students. Applications are processed on a rolling basis. *Application fee:* $40 ($90 for international students). Electronic applications accepted. *Application Contact:* Jeremy Lindberg, Associate Professor, 405-325-0567, Fax: 405-325-7024, E-mail: jlindberg@ou.edu. *Director*, Mary Margaret Holt, 405-325-4051, Fax: 405-325-7024, E-mail: marymholt@ou.edu.

University of Oklahoma (continued)

School of Drama Students: 9 full-time (4 women); includes 1 minority (Two or more races, non-Hispanic/Latino). Average age 32. 6 applicants, 33% accepted, 2 enrolled. *Faculty:* 9 full-time (4 women). Expenses: Contact institution. *Financial support:* In 2010–11, 1 research assistantship with partial tuition reimbursement (averaging $9,586 per year), 6 teaching assistantships with partial tuition reimbursements (averaging $9,586 per year) were awarded; Federal Work-Study also available. Financial award application deadline: 4/7; financial award applicants required to submit FAFSA. In 2010, 5 master's awarded. *Degree program information:* Part-time programs available. Offers drama (MA, MFA). *Application deadline:* For fall admission, 3/1 for domestic and international students; for spring admission, 11/1 for domestic students, 9/1 for international students. Applications are processed on a rolling basis. *Application fee:* $40 ($90 for international students). Electronic applications accepted. *Application Contact:* Dr. Kae Koger, Graduate Liaison, 405-325-4021, Fax: 405-325-0400, E-mail: akoger@ou.edu. *Director,* Dr. Tom Orr, 405-325-4021, Fax: 405-325-0400, E-mail: thorr@ou.edu.

School of Music Students: 98 full-time (50 women), 62 part-time (35 women); includes 15 minority (4 Black or African American, non-Hispanic/Latino; 3 American Indian or Alaska Native, non-Hispanic/Latino; 4 Asian, non-Hispanic/Latino; 3 Hispanic/Latino; 1 Two or more races, non-Hispanic/Latino), 18 international. Average age 31. 126 applicants, 57% accepted, 47 enrolled. *Faculty:* 48 full-time (12 women), 2 part-time/adjunct (1 woman). Expenses: Contact institution. *Financial support:* In 2010–11, 131 students received support, including 7 fellowships with full tuition reimbursements available (averaging $5,000 per year), 17 research assistantships with partial tuition reimbursements available (averaging $11,472 per year), 73 teaching assistantships with partial tuition reimbursements available (averaging $10,107 per year); unspecified assistantships also available. Financial award application deadline: 4/7; financial award applicants required to submit FAFSA. In 2010, 25 master's, 12 doctorates awarded. Offers choral conducting (M Mus, M Mus Ed); conducting (DMA); instrumental conducting (M Mus, M Mus Ed); music composition (M Mus, DMA); music education (M Mus Ed, PhD); music theory (M Mus); musicology (M Mus); organ (M Mus, DMA); piano (M Mus, DMA); piano pedagogy (M Mus Ed); vocal/general (M Mus Ed); voice (M Mus, DMA); wind/percussion/string (M Mus, DMA). *Application deadline:* For fall admission, 6/1 priority date for domestic students, 4/1 for international students; for spring admission, 11/1 for domestic students, 9/1 for international students. Applications are processed on a rolling basis. *Application fee:* $40 ($90 for international students). Electronic applications accepted. *Application Contact:* Jan Russell, Office Assistant, 405-325-5393, Fax: 405-325-7574, E-mail: jrussell@ou.edu. *Director,* Dr. Steven Curtis, 405-325-2081, Fax: 405-325-7574, E-mail: scurtis@ou.edu.

See Close-Up on page 993.

UNIVERSITY OF OKLAHOMA HEALTH SCIENCES CENTER, Oklahoma City, OK 73190

General Information State-supported, coed, upper-level institution. CGS member. *Graduate housing:* Rooms and/or apartments available on a first-come, first-served basis to single and married students. *Research affiliation:* Oklahoma Children's Memorial Hospital (pediatrics), Veterans Administration Medical Center (clinical and applied medicine), University of Oklahoma Medical Center, Oklahoma Medical Research Foundation, Dean A. McGee Eye Institute (ophthalmology).

GRADUATE UNITS

College of Dentistry Offers dentistry (DDS, MS, Certificate); general dentistry (Certificate); orthodontics (MS); periodontics (MS). Electronic applications accepted.

College of Medicine Offers biochemistry (MS, PhD); biochemistry and molecular biology (MS, PhD); biological psychology (MS, PhD); cell biology (MS, PhD); genetic counseling (MS); immunology (MS, PhD); medical radiation physics (MS, PhD); medical sciences (MS); medicine (MD, MHS, MS, PhD); microbiology (MS, PhD); microbiology and immunology (MS, PhD); molecular biology (MS, PhD); neuroscience (MS, PhD); pathology (PhD); physician associate (MHS); physiology (MS, PhD); psychiatry and behavioral sciences (MS, PhD); radiological sciences (MS, PhD). Electronic applications accepted.

College of Pharmacy Offers pharmacy (Pharm D, MS, PhD).

Graduate College *Degree program information:* Part-time and evening/weekend programs available.

College of Allied Health *Degree program information:* Part-time programs available. Offers allied health (MOT, MPT, MS, Au D, PhD, Certificate); allied health sciences (PhD); audiology (MS, Au D, PhD); communication sciences and disorders (Certificate); education of the deaf (MS); nutritional sciences (MS); occupational therapy (MOT); physical therapy (MPT); rehabilitation sciences (MS); speech-language pathology (MS, PhD).

College of Nursing *Degree program information:* Part-time programs available. Offers nursing (MS). MS/MBA offered jointly with Oklahoma State University, University of Oklahoma.

College of Public Health *Degree program information:* Part-time programs available. Offers biostatistics (MPH, MS, Dr PH, PhD); epidemiology (MPH, MS, Dr PH, PhD); general public health (MPH, Dr PH); health administration and policy (MHA, MPH, MS, Dr PH, PhD); health promotion sciences (MPH, MS, Dr PH, PhD); occupational and environmental health (MPH, MS, Dr PH, PhD); preparedness and terrorism (MPH); public health (MHA, MPH, MS, Dr PH, PhD).

UNIVERSITY OF OREGON, Eugene, OR 97403

General Information State-supported, coed, university. CGS member. *Graduate housing:* Rooms and/or apartments available to single and married students. *Research affiliation:* Oregon Research Institute, Decision Research, Battelle Pacific Northwest Laboratories, National Renewable Energy Laboratory (NREL), Stanford Linear Accelerator Center, Naval Research Laboratories.

GRADUATE UNITS

Graduate School *Degree program information:* Part-time and evening/weekend programs available. Offers applied information management (MS).

Charles H. Lundquist College of Business *Degree program information:* Part-time and evening/weekend programs available. Offers accounting (M Actg, PhD); business (M Actg, MA, MBA, MS, PhD); decision sciences (MA, MS); finance (PhD); management (PhD); management: general business (MBA); marketing (PhD).

College of Arts and Sciences *Degree program information:* Part-time and evening/weekend programs available. Offers anthropology (MA, MS, PhD); arts and sciences (MA, MFA, MS, PhD); Asian studies (MA); biochemistry (MA, MS, PhD); chemistry (MA, MS, PhD); Chinese (MA, PhD); classical civilization (MA); classics (MA); clinical psychology (PhD); cognitive psychology (MA, MS, PhD); comparative literature (MA, PhD); computer and information science (MA, MS, PhD); creative writing (MFA); developmental psychology (MA, MS, PhD); ecology and evolution (MA, MS, PhD); economics (MA, MS, PhD); English (MA, PhD); environmental science, studies, and policy (PhD); environmental studies (MA, MS); French (MA); geography (MA, MS, PhD); geological sciences (MA, MS, PhD); Germanic languages and literatures (MA, PhD); Greek (MA); history (MA, PhD); human physiology (MS, PhD); independent study: folklore (MA, MS); international studies (MA); Italian (MA); Japanese (MA, PhD); Latin (MA); linguistics (MA, PhD); marine biology (MA, MS, PhD); mathematics (MA, MS, PhD); molecular, cellular and genetic biology (PhD); neuroscience and development (PhD); philosophy (MA, PhD); physics (MA, MS, PhD); physiological psychology (MA, MS, PhD); political science (MA, MS, PhD); psychology (MA, MS, PhD); Romance languages (MA, PhD); Russian and East European Studies (MA); social/personality psychology (MA, MS, PhD); sociology (MA, MS, PhD); Spanish (MA); theater arts (MA, MFA, MS, PhD).

College of Education *Degree program information:* Part-time programs available. Offers education (M Ed, MA, MS, D Ed, PhD).

School of Architecture and Allied Arts *Degree program information:* Part-time and evening/weekend programs available. Offers architecture (M Arch); architecture and allied arts (M Arch, MA, MCRP, MFA, MI Arch, MLA, MPA, MS, PhD); art (MFA); art history (MA, PhD); arts management (MA, MS); community and regional planning (MCRP); historic preservation (MS); interior architecture (MI Arch); landscape architecture (MLA); media management (MA, MS); public policy and management (MA, MPA, MS).

School of Journalism and Communication *Degree program information:* Part-time programs available. Offers journalism and communication (MA, MS, PhD).

School of Music *Degree program information:* Part-time programs available. Offers composition (M Mus, DMA, PhD); conducting (M Mus); dance (MA, MS); jazz studies (M Mus); music (M Mus, MA, MS, DMA, PhD); music education (M Mus, DMA, PhD); music history (PhD); music theory (PhD); performance (M Mus, DMA); piano pedagogy (M Mus).

School of Law Offers law (JD, MA, MS).

UNIVERSITY OF OTTAWA, Ottawa, ON K1N 6N5, Canada

General Information Province-supported, coed, university. CGS member. *Graduate housing:* Rooms and/or apartments available on a first-come, first-served basis to single and married students. *Research affiliation:* Bell Canada (telecommunications, data security), Virox Technologies (disinfectants), Shipley (advanced materials), EnPharma Pharmaceuticals (medical drug development), Communications and Information Technology Ontario (CITO) (telecommunications), Oncology, Inc. (cancer, neuromuscular diseases, genetics).

GRADUATE UNITS

Faculty of Graduate and Postdoctoral Studies *Degree program information:* Part-time and evening/weekend programs available. Offers biomedical engineering (MA Sc); e-business technologies (M Sc, MEBT); globalization and international development (MA); population health (PhD); systems science (M Sc, M Sys Sc, Certificate). MCL, MRE, MP Th offered jointly with Saint Paul University. Electronic applications accepted.

Faculty of Arts *Degree program information:* Part-time and evening/weekend programs available. Offers arts (M Geog, M Mus, M Sc, MA, PhD, Certificate); classical studies (MA); communication (MA); directing for theatre (MA); economics (PhD); English (PhD); geography (PhD); history (MA, PhD); interpreting (MA); lettres Françaises (MA, PhD); linguistics (MA, PhD); music (M Mus, MA); orchestral studies (Certificate); philosophy (MA, PhD); piano pedagogy research (Certificate); political science (PhD); psychology (PhD); religious studies (PhD); Spanish (MA, PhD); Spanish translation (MA); translation (MA); translation studies (PhD). Electronic applications accepted.

Faculty of Education Postbaccalaureate distance learning degree programs offered (minimal on-campus study). Offers education (M Ed, MA Ed, PhD, Certificate). Electronic applications accepted.

Faculty of Engineering Offers chemical engineering (M Eng, MA Sc, PhD); civil engineering (M Eng, MA Sc, PhD); computer science (MCS, PhD); electrical and computer engineering (M Eng, MA Sc, PhD); engineering (M Eng, MA Sc, MCS, PhD, Certificate); engineering management (M Eng); information technology (Certificate); mechanical and aerospace engineering (M Eng, MA Sc, PhD); project management (Certificate). Electronic applications accepted.

Faculty of Health Sciences *Degree program information:* Part-time and evening/weekend programs available. Offers audiology (M Sc); health sciences (M Sc, MA, PhD, Certificate); human kinetics (MA); nurse practitioner (Certificate); nursing (M Sc, PhD); nursing/primary health care (M Sc); orthophony (M Sc). Electronic applications accepted.

Faculty of Law *Degree program information:* Part-time and evening/weekend programs available. Offers law (LL M, LL D). Electronic applications accepted.

Faculty of Medicine Offers biochemistry (M Sc, PhD); cellular and molecular medicine (M Sc, PhD); epidemiology (M Sc); medicine (MD, M Sc, PhD); microbiology and immunology (M Sc, PhD). Electronic applications accepted.

Faculty of Science *Degree program information:* Part-time and evening/weekend programs available. Offers biology (M Sc, PhD); chemistry (M Sc, PhD); earth sciences (M Sc, PhD); mathematics and statistics (M Sc, PhD); physics (M Sc, PhD); science (M Sc, PhD). Electronic applications accepted.

Faculty of Social Sciences *Degree program information:* Part-time and evening/weekend programs available. Offers criminology (MA, MCA); economics (MA, PhD); education (MA); English (MA); history (MA); human kinetics (MA); law (LL M); lettres Françaises (MA); nursing (M Sc); pastoral studies (MA); political science (MA); political studies (MA, PhD); psychology (PhD); religious studies (MA); social sciences (LL M, M Sc, MA, MCA, MSS, PhD); social work (MSS); sociology (MA); sociology and anthropology (MA). Electronic applications accepted.

Telfer School of Management *Degree program information:* Part-time and evening/weekend programs available. Offers business administration (MBA); executive business administration (EMBA); health administration (MHA); management (EMBA, MBA, MHA). Electronic applications accepted.

UNIVERSITY OF PENNSYLVANIA, Philadelphia, PA 19104

General Information Independent, coed, university. CGS member. *Enrollment:* 19,842 graduate, professional, and undergraduate students; 10,729 full-time matriculated graduate/professional students (5,502 women), 1,694 part-time matriculated graduate/professional students (1,010 women). *Enrollment by degree level:* 2,415 first professional, 6,345 master's, 3,467 doctoral, 196 other advanced degrees. *Graduate faculty:* 2,528 full-time (761 women), 1,859 part-time/adjunct (654 women). *Tuition:* Full-time $25,660; part-time $4758 per course. *Required fees:* $2152; $270 per course. Tuition and fees vary according to course load, degree level and program. *Graduate housing:* Rooms and/or apartments available on a first-come, first-served basis to single and married students. Housing application deadline: 4/1. *Student services:* Campus employment opportunities, campus safety program, career counseling, child daycare facilities, exercise/wellness program, free psychological counseling, international student services, low-cost health insurance, multicultural affairs office, services for students with disabilities, writing training. *Library facilities:* Van Pelt Library plus 21 others. *Online resources:* library catalog, web page, access to other libraries' catalogs. *Collection:* 5.9 million titles, 98,145 serial subscriptions, 121,233 audiovisual materials. *Research affiliation:* Children's Hospital of Philadelphia, Wistar Institute of Anatomy and Biology, BioAdvance, Regional Nanotechnology Center.

Computer facilities: Computer purchase and lease plans are available. A campuswide network can be accessed from student residence rooms and from off campus. Online class registration, billing information, financial aid application, status, academic records, student services are available. *Web address:* http://www.upenn.edu/.

General Application Contact: Karen Lawrence, Associate Director for Graduate Education, 215-898-1842, Fax: 215-898-6567, E-mail: graded@pobox.upenn.edu.

GRADUATE UNITS

Annenberg School for Communication Students: 78 full-time (52 women), 3 part-time (0 women); includes 8 Black or African American, non-Hispanic/Latino; 2 Asian, non-Hispanic/Latino; 1 Hispanic/Latino, 25 international. 537 applicants, 4% accepted, 13 enrolled. *Faculty:* 19 full-time (8 women), 3 part-time/adjunct (0 women). Expenses: Contact institution. *Financial support:* In 2010–11, 86 students received support; fellowships, research assistantships, teaching assistantships, institutionally sponsored loans, scholarships/grants, traineeships, health care benefits, and unspecified assistantships available. Financial award application deadline: 12/15. In 2010, 13 doctorates awarded. Offers communication (PhD). *Application deadline:* For fall admission, 1/2 for domestic students. *Application fee:* $70. Electronic applications accepted. *Application Contact:* Beverly Henry, Graduate Studies Coordinator, 215-573-1091, Fax: 215-898-2024, E-mail: bhenry@asc.upenn.edu. *Dean,* Dr. Michael X. Delli Carpini.

Graduate School of Education Students: 1,252 full-time (889 women), 198 part-time (153 women); includes 167 Black or African American, non-Hispanic/Latino; 4 American Indian or Alaska Native, non-Hispanic/Latino; 79 Asian, non-Hispanic/Latino; 54 Hispanic/Latino, 221 international. 2,135 applicants, 57% accepted, 750 enrolled. *Faculty:* 62 full-time (26 women), 38 part-time/adjunct (17 women). Expenses: Contact institution. *Financial support:* In 2010–11, 101 students received support; fellowships, research assistantships, teaching assistantships, institutionally sponsored loans, scholarships/grants, traineeships, health care benefits, and unspecified assistantships available. Financial award application deadline: 12/15. In 2010, 410 master's, 74 doctorates awarded. Offers applied psychology and human development (M Phil, MS Ed, PhD); counseling and mental health services (MS Ed); counseling and psychological services (PhD); education (M Phil, MS Ed, Ed D, PhD); education policy (MS Ed, PhD); education, culture and society (MS Ed, PhD); educational leadership (MS Ed, Ed D, PhD); educational linguistics (PhD); elementary and secondary education (MS Ed); foundations and practices in education (MS Ed, Ed D, PhD); human development (MS Ed, PhD); intercultural communication (MS Ed, Ed D, PhD); learning science and technologies (MS Ed); policy research, evaluation, and measurement (M Phil, PhD); professional counseling (M Phil); reading, writing, and literacy (MS Ed, Ed D, PhD); school counseling (MS Ed); teaching English to speakers of other languages (MS Ed); teaching English to speakers of other languages and intercultural communication (MS Ed, PhD). *Application deadline:* For fall admission, 12/15 priority date for domestic students. Applications are processed on a rolling basis. *Application fee:* $70. Electronic applications accepted. *Application Contact:* Alyssa D'Alconzo, Associate Director, Admissions, 215-898-6415, Fax: 215-746-6884, E-mail: admissions@gse.upenn.edu. *Dean,* Dr. Andrew Porter, 215-898-7014.

Law School Students: 802 full-time (382 women), 1 part-time (0 women); includes 60 Black or African American, non-Hispanic/Latino; 113 Asian, non-Hispanic/Latino; 37 Hispanic/Latino, 25 international. Average age 24. 6,003 applicants, 14% accepted, 250 enrolled. *Faculty:* 67 full-time (16 women), 40 part-time/adjunct (11 women). Expenses: Contact institution. *Financial support:* In 2010–11, 599 students received support, including 1 fellowship (averaging $10,000 per year), 1 research assistantship with tuition reimbursement available (averaging $22,280 per year), 22 teaching assistantships (averaging $2,500 per year); career-related internships or fieldwork, Federal Work-Study, institutionally sponsored loans, and scholarships/grants also available. Financial award application deadline: 3/1; financial award applicants required to submit FAFSA. In 2010, 276 first professional degrees, 89 master's, 4 doctorates awarded. Offers law (JD, LL CM, LL M, SJD). *Application deadline:* For fall admission, 2/15 for domestic students. Applications are processed on a rolling basis. *Application fee:* $75. Electronic applications accepted. *Application Contact:* Renee Post, Associate Dean of Admissions and Financial Aid, 215-898-7400, Fax: 215-898-9606, E-mail: admissions@law.upenn.edu. *Dean,* Michael A. Fitts, 215-898-7463, Fax: 215-573-2025.

Perelman School of Medicine Students: 1,618 full-time (805 women), 150 part-time (92 women); includes 101 Black or African American, non-Hispanic/Latino; 6 American Indian or Alaska Native, non-Hispanic/Latino; 302 Asian, non-Hispanic/Latino; 110 Hispanic/Latino, 89 international. Average age 26. 7,810 applicants, 8% accepted, 370 enrolled. *Faculty:* 2,420 full-time (856 women), 1,241 part-time/adjunct (537 women). Expenses: Contact institution. *Financial support:* In 2010–11, 1,421 students received support; fellowships, research assistantships, teaching assistantships, career-related internships or fieldwork, Federal Work-Study, institutionally sponsored loans, scholarships/grants, and unspecified assistantships available. Financial award application deadline: 5/1; financial award applicants required to submit FAFSA. In 2010, 156 first professional degrees, 91 master's, 115 doctorates awarded. *Degree program information:* Part-time programs available. Offers bioethics (MBE, MD/MBE); environmental health (MPH); generalist (MPH); global health (MPH); health policy research (MS); medicine (MD, MBE, MPH, MS, MSCE, MTR, PhD, MD/MBE, MD/MSCE); translational therapeutics (MTR). *Application deadline:* For fall admission, 10/15 for domestic students. Applications are processed on a rolling basis. *Application fee:* $80. Electronic applications accepted. *Application Contact:* Gaye Sheffler, Director, Admissions, 215-898-8001, Fax: 215-898-0833, E-mail: sheffler@mail.med.upenn.edu. *Dean,* Dr. Arthur M. Rubenstein, 215-898-6796, Fax: 215-573-2030, E-mail: amrdean@mail.med.upenn.edu.

Biomedical Graduate Studies Students: 761 full-time (392 women), 128 part-time (78 women); includes 38 Black or African American, non-Hispanic/Latino; 6 American Indian or Alaska Native, non-Hispanic/Latino; 137 Asian, non-Hispanic/Latino; 45 Hispanic/Latino, 76 international. 1,341 applicants, 25% accepted, 172 enrolled. *Faculty:* 783. Expenses: Contact institution. *Financial support:* In 2010–11, 693 students received support; fellowships, research assistantships, scholarships/grants, traineeships, and unspecified assistantships available. Financial award application deadline: 12/8. In 2010, 52 master's, 109 doctorates awarded. Offers biochemistry and molecular biophysics (PhD); biomedical studies (MS, PhD); biostatistics (MS, PhD); cancer biology (PhD); cell biology and physiology (PhD); developmental stem cell regenerative biology (PhD); gene therapy and vaccines (PhD); genetics and gene regulation (PhD); genomics and computational biology (PhD); immunology (PhD); microbiology, virology, and parasitology (PhD); neuroscience (PhD); pharmacology (PhD). *Application deadline:* For fall admission, 12/8 priority date for domestic and international students. Applications are processed on a rolling basis. *Application fee:* $70. Electronic applications accepted. *Application Contact:* Sarah Gormley, Admissions Coordinator, 215-898-1030, Fax: 215-898-2671, E-mail: gormley@mail.med.upenn.edu. *Director,* Dr. Susan R. Ross, 215-898-1030.

Center for Clinical Epidemiology and Biostatistics Students: 91 full-time (52 women), 4 part-time (2 women); includes 6 Black or African American, non-Hispanic/Latino; 22 Asian, non-Hispanic/Latino; 5 Hispanic/Latino. Average age 30. 41 applicants, 95% accepted, 34 enrolled. *Faculty:* 72 full-time (27 women), 119 part-time/adjunct (40 women). Expenses: Contact institution. *Financial support:* In 2010–11, 65 students received support, including 60 fellowships with full and partial tuition reimbursements available (averaging $42,000 per year); career-related internships or fieldwork, scholarships/grants, health care benefits, and unspecified assistantships also available. Financial award application deadline: 11/15. In 2010, 28 master's awarded. *Degree program information:* Part-time programs available. Offers clinical epidemiology (MSCE); epidemiology (PhD). PhD offered through the School of Arts and Sciences. *Application deadline:* For fall admission, 12/1 priority date for domestic and international students. Applications are processed on a rolling basis. *Application fee:* $80. Electronic applications accepted. *Application Contact:* Jennifer E. Kuklinski, Associate Director for Graduate Training in Epidemiology, 215-573-2382, Fax: 215-573-5315, E-mail: jkuklins@mail.med.upenn.edu. *Director,* Dr. Harold I. Feldman, 215-573-0901, Fax: 215-573-2265, E-mail: hfeldman@mail.med.upenn.edu.

School of Arts and Sciences Students: 1,651 full-time (833 women), 562 part-time (340 women); includes 77 Black or African American, non-Hispanic/Latino; 4 American Indian or Alaska Native, non-Hispanic/Latino; 101 Asian, non-Hispanic/Latino; 59 Hispanic/Latino, 540 international. 7,088 applicants, 14% accepted, 530 enrolled. *Faculty:* 467 full-time (141 women), 22 part-time/adjunct (8 women). Expenses: Contact institution. *Financial support:* In 2010–11, 1,830 students received support; fellowships, research assistantships, teaching assistantships, institutionally sponsored loans, scholarships/grants, traineeships, health care benefits, and unspecified assistantships available. Financial award application deadline: 12/15. In 2010, 494 master's, 201 doctorates awarded. *Degree program information:* Part-time and evening/weekend programs available. Offers Africana studies (MA, PhD); ancient history (AM, PhD); anthropology (AM, MS, PhD); applied mathematics and computational science (PhD); art and archaeology of the Mediterranean world (AM, PhD); arts and sciences (AM, MA, MBA, MES, MGA, MLA, MS, PhD); biology (PhD); chemistry (MS, PhD); classical studies (AM, PhD); comparative literature (AM, PhD); criminology (MA, MS, PhD); demography (AM, PhD); earth and environmental science (MS, PhD); East Asian languages and civilization (AM, PhD); economics (AM, PhD); English (AM, PhD); French (AM, PhD); Germanic languages (AM, PhD); history (AM, PhD); history and sociology of science (AM, PhD); history of art (AM, PhD); international studies (AM); Italian (AM, PhD); linguistics (AM, PhD); literary theory (AM, PhD); mathematics (AM, PhD); medical physics (MS); music (AM, PhD); near eastern languages and civilization (AM, PhD); organizational dynamics (MS); philosophy (AM, PhD); physics (PhD); political science (AM, PhD); psychology (PhD); religious studies (PhD); sociology (AM, PhD); South Asian regional studies (AM, PhD); Spanish (AM, PhD). *Application deadline:* For fall admission, 12/15 priority date for domestic students. Applications are processed on a rolling basis. *Application fee:* $70. Electronic applications accepted. *Application Contact:* Patricia Rea, Associate Director for Admissions, 215-573-5816, Fax: 215-573-8068, E-mail: gdasadmis@sas.upenn.edu. *Associate Dean for Graduate Studies,* Dr. Ralph M. Rosen, 215-898-7156, Fax: 215-573-8068, E-mail: gdasdmis@sas.upenn.edu.

College of Liberal and Professional Studies Students: 97 full-time (63 women), 256 part-time (165 women); includes 15 Black or African American, non-Hispanic/Latino; 1 American Indian or Alaska Native, non-Hispanic/Latino; 16 Asian, non-Hispanic/Latino; 15 Hispanic/Latino, 33 international. 600 applicants, 46% accepted, 213 enrolled. Expenses: Contact institution. In 2010, 151 master's awarded. Offers environmental studies (MES); individualized study (MLA). *Application deadline:* For fall admission, 12/1 priority date for domestic students. *Application fee:* $70. Electronic applications accepted. *Application Contact:* Patricia Rea, Coordinator for Admissions, 215-573-5816, Fax: 215-573-8068, E-mail: gdasadmis@sas.upenn.edu. *Associate Dean/Director,* Dr. Kristine Billmyer, 215-898-8681, E-mail: gdasdmis@sas.upenn.edu.

Fels Institute of Government Students: 57 full-time (23 women), 69 part-time (39 women); includes 12 Black or African American, non-Hispanic/Latino; 3 Asian, non-Hispanic/Latino; 4 Hispanic/Latino, 13 international. 476 applicants, 44% accepted, 99 enrolled. Expenses: Contact institution. *Financial support:* Fellowships, institutionally sponsored loans and scholarships/grants available. Financial award application deadline: 1/15; financial award applicants required to submit FAFSA. In 2010, 48 master's awarded. *Degree program information:* Part-time and evening/weekend programs available. Offers government (MGA). *Application deadline:* For fall admission, 1/15 for domestic students. Applications are processed on a rolling basis. *Application fee:* $70. *Application Contact:* Ilene Ford, Administrative Coordinator, 215-898-2600, Fax: 215-898-6238, E-mail: felsinstitute@sas.upenn.edu. *Director,* David B. Thornburgh, 215-898-2600.

Joseph H. Lauder Institute of Management and International Studies Students: 125 full-time (53 women). Average age 27. Expenses: Contact institution. *Financial support:* Fellowships with full and partial tuition reimbursements, career-related internships or fieldwork and scholarships/grants available. In 2010, 68 master's awarded. Offers international studies (MA); management and international studies (MBA). Applications must be made concurrently and separately to the Wharton MBA program. *Application deadline:* For fall admission, 10/1 for domestic and international students; for winter admission, 1/3 for domestic and international students. Electronic applications accepted. *Application Contact:* Marcy R. Bevan, Director of Admissions, 215-898-1215, Fax: 215-898-2067, E-mail: lauderinfo@wharton.upenn.edu. *Director,* Dr. Mauro Guillen, 215-898-1215.

School of Dental Medicine Offers dental medicine (DMD).

School of Design Students: 615 full-time (335 women), 22 part-time (10 women); includes 24 Black or African American, non-Hispanic/Latino; 58 Asian, non-Hispanic/Latino; 26 Hispanic/Latino, 146 international. 2,064 applicants, 36% accepted, 281 enrolled. *Faculty:* 35 full-time (14 women), 18 part-time/adjunct (5 women). Expenses: Contact institution. *Financial support:* In 2010–11, 29 students received support; fellowships, research assistantships, teaching assistantships, institutionally sponsored loans, scholarships/grants, traineeships, health care benefits, and unspecified assistantships available. Financial award application deadline: 12/15. In 2010, 288 master's, 9 doctorates, 57 other advanced degrees awarded. *Degree program information:* Part-time programs available. Offers architecture (M Arch, PhD); city and regional planning (MCP, PhD, Certificate); conservation and heritage management (Certificate); design (M Arch, MCP, MFA, MLA, MS, PhD, Certificate); fine arts (MFA); historic conservation (Certificate); historic preservation (MS); landscape architecture and regional planning (MLA); landscape studies (Certificate); real estate design and development (PhD, Certificate); urban design (PhD, Certificate). *Application deadline:* For fall admission, 1/2 priority date for domestic students. *Application fee:* $70. *Application Contact:* Joan Weston, Director of Admissions and Financial Aid, 215-898-6520, Fax: 215-573-6809, E-mail: admissions@design.upenn.edu. *Associate Dean,* Patricia Woldar, 215-898-3425, Fax: 215-573-6654, E-mail: admissions@design.upenn.edu.

School of Engineering and Applied Science Students: 990 full-time (274 women), 315 part-time (67 women); includes 23 Black or African American, non-Hispanic/Latino; 1 American Indian or Alaska Native, non-Hispanic/Latino; 153 Asian, non-Hispanic/Latino; 24 Hispanic/Latino, 617 international. 3,875 applicants, 32% accepted, 621 enrolled. *Faculty:* 105 full-time (14 women), 24 part-time/adjunct (1 woman). Expenses: Contact institution. *Financial support:* In 2010–11, 393 students received support; fellowships, research assistantships, teaching assistantships, institutionally sponsored loans, scholarships/grants, traineeships, health care benefits, and unspecified assistantships available. Financial award application deadline: 12/15. In 2010, 396 master's, 60 doctorates awarded. *Degree program information:* Part-time and evening/weekend programs available. Offers applied mechanics (MSE, PhD); bioengineering (MSE, PhD); biotechnology (MS); chemical engineering (MSE, PhD); computer and information science (MCIT, MSE, PhD); computer graphics and game technology (MSE); electrical and systems engineering (MSE, PhD); engineering and applied science (EMBA, MCIT, MS, MSE, PhD, AC); materials science and engineering (MSE, PhD); mechanical engineering (MSE, PhD); technology management (EMBA); telecommunications and networking (MSE). *Application deadline:* For fall admission, 6/1 priority date for domestic students, 5/1 priority date for international students; for spring admission, 11/1 priority date for domestic students, 10/1 priority date for international students. Applications are processed on a rolling basis. *Application fee:* $70. Electronic applications accepted. *Application Contact:* Academic Programs Office, 215-898-4542, Fax: 215-573-5577, E-mail: engstats@seas.upenn.edu. *Dean,* Eduardo D. Glandt, 215-898-7244, Fax: 215-573-2018, E-mail: seasdean@seas.upenn.edu.

School of Nursing Students: 247 full-time (219 women), 238 part-time (219 women); includes 25 Black or African American, non-Hispanic/Latino; 3 American Indian or Alaska Native, non-Hispanic/Latino; 36 Asian, non-Hispanic/Latino; 14 Hispanic/Latino, 13 international. 727 applicants, 46% accepted, 311 enrolled. *Faculty:* 55 full-time (50 women), 46 part-time/adjunct (41 women). Expenses: Contact institution. *Financial support:* In 2010–11, 71 students received support; fellowships, research assistantships, teaching assistantships, institutionally sponsored loans, scholarships/grants, traineeships, health care benefits, and unspecified assistantships available. Financial award application deadline: 12/15. In 2010, 169 master's, 8 doctorates, 12 other advanced degrees awarded. *Degree program information:* Part-time programs available. Postbaccalaureate distance learning degree programs offered. Offers acute care nurse practitioner (MSN); administration/consulting (MSN); adult and special populations (MSN); adult health nurse practitioner (MSN); adult oncology nurse practitioner (MSN); child and family (MSN); family health nurse practitioner (MSN, Certificate); geropsychiatrics (MSN); health leadership (MSN); neonatal nurse practitioner (MSN); nurse anesthetist (MSN); nurse midwifery (MSN); nursing (MSN, PhD, Certificate); nursing and health care administration (MSN, PhD); pediatric acute/chronic care nurse practitioner (MSN); pediatric critical care nurse practitioner (MSN); pediatric nurse practitioner (MSN); pediatric oncology nurse practitioner (MSN); perinatal advanced practice nurse specialist (MSN); primary care (MSN); women's healthcare nurse practitioner (MSN). *Application deadline:* For fall admission, 2/15 priority date for domestic students. Applications are processed on a rolling basis. *Application fee:* $70. *Application Contact:* Sylvia V. J. English, Enrollment Management Coordinator, 866-867-6877, Fax: 215-573-8439, E-mail: admissions@nursing.upenn.edu. *Assistant Dean of Admissions and Financial Aid,* 866-867-6877, Fax: 215-573-8439, E-mail: admissions@nursing.upenn.edu.

School of Social Policy and Practice Students: 379 full-time (341 women), 94 part-time (76 women); includes 62 Black or African American, non-Hispanic/Latino; 4 American Indian or Alaska Native, non-Hispanic/Latino; 42 Asian, non-Hispanic/Latino; 15 Hispanic/Latino. Average age 28. 750 applicants, 62% accepted, 251 enrolled. *Faculty:* 19 full-time (10 women), 48 part-time/adjunct (30 women). Expenses: Contact institution. *Financial support:* In 2010–11, 320 students received support, including fellowships (averaging $20,200 per year); career-related internships or fieldwork, Federal Work-Study, institutionally sponsored loans, scholarships/grants, tuition waivers (partial), and unspecified assistantships also available. Support available to part-time students. Financial award applicants required to submit FAFSA. In 2010, 150 master's, 13 doctorates awarded. Offers social policy and practice (MNPL, MSSP, MSW, DSW, PhD, MSSP/MGA, MSSP/MPH, MSW/MSSP); social welfare (PhD); social work (MSW, DSW). *Application deadline:* For fall admission, 4/15 for domestic and international students. Applications are processed on a rolling basis. *Application fee:* $65. Electronic applications accepted. *Application Contact:* Mary C. Mazzola, Associate Dean, Enrollment Management, 215-898-5550, Fax: 215-573-2099, E-mail: mmazzola@sp2.upenn.edu. *Dean,* Richard Gelles, 215-898-5541, Fax: 215-573-2099, E-mail: gelles@sp2.upenn.edu.

School of Veterinary Medicine Students: 464 full-time (355 women), 16 part-time (11 women); includes 9 Black or African American, non-Hispanic/Latino; 20 Asian, non-Hispanic/Latino; 17 Hispanic/Latino, 3 international. Average age 24. 1,226 applicants, 11% accepted, 114 enrolled. *Faculty:* 126 full-time (57 women), 26 part-time/adjunct (11 women). Expenses: Contact institution. *Financial support:* Career-related internships or fieldwork, Federal Work-Study, and institutionally sponsored loans available. In 2010, 112 VMDs awarded. Offers veterinary medicine (VMD). *Application deadline:* For fall admission, 10/1 for domestic students.

University of Pennsylvania (continued)

Application fee: $0. *Application Contact:* Malcolm Keiter, Assistant Dean for Admissions, 215-898-5434, Fax: 215-573-8819, E-mail: admissions@vet.upenn.edu. *Dean,* Dr. Joan C. Hendricks, 215-898-8841, Fax: 215-573-8837, E-mail: vetdean@vet.upenn.edu.

Wharton School *Degree program information:* Evening/weekend programs available. Offers accounting (PhD); applied economics (PhD); business (MBA, PhD); business administration (MBA); business and public policy (MBA, PhD); ethics and legal studies (PhD); finance (MBA, PhD); health care management (MBA, PhD); health care management and economics (PhD); insurance and risk management (MBA, PhD); legal studies and business ethics (MBA, PhD); management (MBA, PhD); marketing (PhD); operations and information management (PhD); real estate (MBA, PhD); statistics (MBA, PhD). Electronic applications accepted.

The Wharton MBA Program for Executives *Degree program information:* Evening/weekend programs available. Offers executive business administration (MBA).

UNIVERSITY OF PHILOSOPHICAL RESEARCH, Los Angeles, CA 90027

General Information Proprietary, coed, graduate-only institution.

GRADUATE UNITS

Program in Consciousness Studies Offers consciousness studies (MA).

Program in Transformational Psychology Offers transformational psychology (MA).

UNIVERSITY OF PHOENIX, Phoenix, AZ 85034-7209

General Information Proprietary, coed, comprehensive institution. *Enrollment:* 54,371 full-time matriculated graduate/professional students (38,647 women). *Enrollment by degree level:* 46,664 master's, 6,882 doctoral, 825 other advanced degrees. *Tuition:* Full-time $16,440. One-time fee: $45 full-time. Full-time tuition and fees vary according to course load, degree level, campus/location and program. *Graduate housing:* On-campus housing not available. *Student services:* Career counseling, exercise/wellness program, free psychological counseling, services for students with disabilities, writing training. *Library facilities:* University Library. *Online resources:* library catalog, web page. *Collection:* 16,781 serial subscriptions.

Computer facilities: Computer purchase and lease plans are available. A campuswide network can be accessed from off campus. Online class registration is available. *Web address:* http://www.uopxonline.com/.

General Application Contact: Student Contact Center, 866-766-0766.

GRADUATE UNITS

College of Criminal Justice and Security Students: 1,855 full-time (1,247 women); includes 734 minority (562 Black or African American, non-Hispanic/Latino; 24 American Indian or Alaska Native, non-Hispanic/Latino; 15 Asian, non-Hispanic/Latino; 122 Hispanic/Latino; 6 Native Hawaiian or other Pacific Islander, non-Hispanic/Latino; 5 Two or more races, non-Hispanic/Latino), 24 international. Average age 38. Expenses: Contact institution. *Financial support:* Scholarships/grants available. Financial award applicants required to submit FAFSA. *Degree program information:* Evening/weekend programs available. Postbaccalaureate distance learning degree programs offered. Offers administration of justice and security (MS). Programs are offered at the online campus. *Application deadline:* Applications are processed on a rolling basis. *Application fee:* $45. Electronic applications accepted. *Application Contact:* James Ness, Dean, 602-557-7430, E-mail: james.ness@phoenix.edu. *Dean,* James Ness, 602-557-7430, E-mail: james.ness@phoenix.edu.

College of Education Students: 11,467 full-time (8,895 women); includes 3,367 minority (2,450 Black or African American, non-Hispanic/Latino; 59 American Indian or Alaska Native, non-Hispanic/Latino; 143 Asian, non-Hispanic/Latino; 610 Hispanic/Latino; 46 Native Hawaiian or other Pacific Islander, non-Hispanic/Latino; 59 Two or more races, non-Hispanic/Latino), 210 international. Average age 39. Expenses: Contact institution. *Financial support:* Scholarships/grants available. Financial award applicants required to submit FAFSA. *Degree program information:* Evening/weekend programs available. Postbaccalaureate distance learning degree programs offered. Offers administration and supervision (MAEd); adult education and training (MAEd); curriculum and instruction (MAEd); early childhood (MAEd); elementary teacher education (MAEd); secondary teacher education (MAEd); special education (MAEd); teacher leadership (MAEd). Programs are offered at the online campus. *Application deadline:* Applications are processed on a rolling basis. *Application fee:* $45. Electronic applications accepted. *Application Contact:* Dr. Meredith Curley, Dean/Executive Director, 480-557-1217, Fax: 480-557-1588, E-mail: meredith.curley@phoenix.edu. *Dean/Executive Director,* Dr. Meredith Curley, 480-557-1217, Fax: 480-557-1588, E-mail: meredith.curley@phoenix.edu.

College of Information Systems and Technology Students: 1,816 full-time (630 women); includes 580 minority (364 Black or African American, non-Hispanic/Latino; 15 American Indian or Alaska Native, non-Hispanic/Latino; 60 Asian, non-Hispanic/Latino; 112 Hispanic/Latino; 20 Native Hawaiian or other Pacific Islander, non-Hispanic/Latino; 9 Two or more races, non-Hispanic/Latino), 124 international. Average age 40. Expenses: Contact institution. *Financial support:* Scholarships/grants available. Financial award applicants required to submit FAFSA. *Degree program information:* Evening/weekend programs available. Postbaccalaureate distance learning degree programs offered. Offers information systems (MIS). Programs are offered at the online campus. *Application deadline:* Applications are processed on a rolling basis. *Application fee:* $45. Electronic applications accepted. *Application Contact:* Dr. Blair Sith, Dean/Executive Director, 480-557-1241, E-mail: blair.smitha@phoenix.edu. *Dean/Executive Director,* Dr. Blair Sith, 480-557-1241, E-mail: blair.smitha@phoenix.edu.

College of Natural Sciences Students: 2,644 full-time (2,223 women); includes 947 minority (728 Black or African American, non-Hispanic/Latino; 20 American Indian or Alaska Native, non-Hispanic/Latino; 61 Asian, non-Hispanic/Latino; 119 Hispanic/Latino; 11 Native Hawaiian or other Pacific Islander, non-Hispanic/Latino; 8 Two or more races, non-Hispanic/Latino), 81 international. Average age 39. Expenses: Contact institution. *Financial support:* Scholarships/grants available. Financial award applicants required to submit FAFSA. *Degree program information:* Evening/weekend programs available. Postbaccalaureate distance learning degree programs offered. Offers gerontology (MHA); health administration (MHA); health administration education (MHA); informatics (MHA). Programs are offered at the online campus. *Application deadline:* Applications are processed on a rolling basis. *Application fee:* $45. Electronic applications accepted. *Application Contact:* Dr. Hinrich Eylers, Dean/Executive Director, 602-557-7428, Fax: 602-794-8454, E-mail: hinrich.eylers@phoenix.edu. *Dean/Executive Director,* Dr. Hinrich Eylers, 602-557-7428, Fax: 602-794-8454, E-mail: hinrich.eylers@phoenix.edu.

College of Nursing Students: 5,255 full-time (4,828 women); includes 1,283 minority (774 Black or African American, non-Hispanic/Latino; 36 American Indian or Alaska Native, non-Hispanic/Latino; 242 Asian, non-Hispanic/Latino; 170 Hispanic/Latino; 48 Native Hawaiian or other Pacific Islander, non-Hispanic/Latino; 13 Two or more races, non-Hispanic/Latino), 274 international. Average age 42. Expenses: Contact institution. *Financial support:* Scholarships/grants available. Financial award applicants required to submit FAFSA. *Degree program information:* Evening/weekend programs available. Postbaccalaureate distance learning degree programs offered. Offers health care education (MSN); informatics (MSN); nursing (MSN). Programs are offered at the online campus. *Application deadline:* Applications are processed on a rolling basis. *Application fee:* $45. Electronic applications accepted. *Application Contact:* Dr. Pam Fuller, Dean/Executive Director, 480-557-1140, Fax: 480-929-7164, E-mail: pam.fuller@phoenix.edu. *Dean/Executive Director,* Dr. Pam Fuller, 480-557-1140, Fax: 480-929-7164, E-mail: pam.fuller@phoenix.edu.

College of Social Science Students: 4,215 full-time (3,585 women); includes 1,544 minority (1,161 Black or African American, non-Hispanic/Latino; 34 American Indian or Alaska Native, non-Hispanic/Latino; 32 Asian, non-Hispanic/Latino; 280 Hispanic/Latino; 22 Native Hawaiian or other Pacific Islander, non-Hispanic/Latino; 15 Two or more races, non-Hispanic/Latino), 85 international. Average age 38. Expenses: Contact institution. *Financial support:* Scholarships/grants available. Financial award applicants required to submit FAFSA. *Degree program information:* Evening/weekend programs available. Postbaccalaureate distance learning degree programs offered. Offers clinical mental health counseling (MSC); community counseling (MSC); psychology (MS). Programs are offered at the online campus. *Application deadline:* Applications are processed on a rolling basis. *Application fee:* $45. Electronic applications accepted. *Application Contact:* Rob Olding, Associate Dean, Human Service/Psychology, 602-551-3073, E-mail: rob.olding@phoenix.edu. *Associate Dean, Human Service/Psychology,* Rob Olding, 602-551-3073, E-mail: rob.olding@phoenix.edu.

School of Advanced Studies Students: 6,882 full-time (4,598 women); includes 2,871 minority (2,251 Black or African American, non-Hispanic/Latino; 50 American Indian or Alaska Native, non-Hispanic/Latino; 133 Asian, non-Hispanic/Latino; 378 Hispanic/Latino; 46 Native Hawaiian or other Pacific Islander, non-Hispanic/Latino; 13 Two or more races, non-Hispanic/Latino), 375 international. Average age 46. Expenses: Contact institution. *Financial support:* Scholarships/grants available. Financial award applicants required to submit FAFSA. *Degree program information:* Evening/weekend programs available. Postbaccalaureate distance learning degree programs offered. Offers business administration (DBA); education (Ed D); educational leadership (Ed D); health administration (DHA); higher education administration (PhD); industrial organizational psychology (PhD); nursing (PhD); organizational leadership and technology (DM). *Application deadline:* Applications are processed on a rolling basis. *Application fee:* $45. Electronic applications accepted. *Application Contact:* Dr. Jeremy Moreland, Dean/Executive Director, 480-557-3231, E-mail: jeremy.moreland@phoenix.edu. *Dean/Executive Director,* Dr. Jeremy Moreland, 480-557-3231, E-mail: jeremy.moreland@phoenix.edu.

School of Business Students: 20,237 full-time (12,641 women); includes 6,424 minority (4,376 Black or African American, non-Hispanic/Latino; 150 American Indian or Alaska Native, non-Hispanic/Latino; 546 Asian, non-Hispanic/Latino; 1,137 Hispanic/Latino; 155 Native Hawaiian or other Pacific Islander, non-Hispanic/Latino; 60 Two or more races, non-Hispanic/Latino), 1,149 international. Average age 39. Expenses: Contact institution. *Financial support:* Scholarships/grants available. Financial award applicants required to submit FAFSA. *Degree program information:* Evening/weekend programs available. Postbaccalaureate distance learning degree programs offered. Offers accounting (MBA, MSA); business administration (MBA); energy management (MBA); global management (MBA); health care management (MBA); human resources management (MM); international management (MM); management (MM); marketing (MBA); project management (MBA); public administration (MPA); technology management (MBA). Programs are offered at the online campus. *Application deadline:* Applications are processed on a rolling basis. *Application fee:* $45. Electronic applications accepted. *Application Contact:* Dr. Bill Berry, Director, 480-557-1824, E-mail: bill.berry@phoenix.edu. *Director,* Dr. Bill Berry, 480-557-1824, E-mail: bill.berry@phoenix.edu.

UNIVERSITY OF PHOENIX–ATLANTA CAMPUS, Sandy Springs, GA 30350-4153

General Information Proprietary, coed, comprehensive institution. *Graduate housing:* On-campus housing not available.

GRADUATE UNITS

College of Information Systems and Technology *Degree program information:* Evening/weekend programs available. Offers information systems (MIS); technology management (MBA). Electronic applications accepted.

College of Nursing *Degree program information:* Evening/weekend programs available. Postbaccalaureate distance learning degree programs offered. Offers health administration (MHA); nursing (MSN); nursing/health care education (MSN). Electronic applications accepted.

School of Business *Degree program information:* Evening/weekend programs available. Postbaccalaureate distance learning degree programs offered. Offers accounting (MBA); business administration (MBA); global management (MBA); human resources management (MBA, MM); management (MM); marketing (MBA); public administration (MM).

UNIVERSITY OF PHOENIX–AUGUSTA CAMPUS, Augusta, GA 30909-4583

General Information Proprietary, coed, comprehensive institution.

GRADUATE UNITS

College of Criminal Justice and Security Offers administration of justice and security (MS).

College of Information Systems and Technology Offers information systems (MIS); technology management (MBA).

College of Nursing Postbaccalaureate distance learning degree programs offered. Offers health administration (MHA); nursing (MSN); nursing/health care education (MSN).

School of Business Postbaccalaureate distance learning degree programs offered. Offers accounting (MBA); business administration (MBA); business and management (MBA, MM); global management (MBA); human resources management (MBA, MM); management (MM); marketing (MBA); public administration (MBA, MM).

UNIVERSITY OF PHOENIX–AUSTIN CAMPUS, Austin, TX 78759

General Information Proprietary, coed, comprehensive institution.

GRADUATE UNITS

College of Criminal Justice and Security Postbaccalaureate distance learning degree programs offered. Offers administration of justice and security (MS).

College of Education Offers curriculum and instruction (MA Ed).

College of Information Systems and Technology Offers information systems (MIS); technology management (MBA).

College of Nursing Postbaccalaureate distance learning degree programs offered. Offers health administration (MHA).

School of Business Postbaccalaureate distance learning degree programs offered. Offers accounting (MBA); business administration (MBA); business and management (MBA); e-business (MBA); global management (MBA); human resources management (MBA, MM); management (MM); marketing (MBA); public administration (MBA).

UNIVERSITY OF PHOENIX–BIRMINGHAM CAMPUS, Birmingham, AL 35244

General Information Proprietary, coed, comprehensive institution.

GRADUATE UNITS

College of Graduate Business and Management Offers accounting (MBA); business administration (MBA); global management (MBA); human resources management (MBA, MM); management (MM); marketing (MBA); public administration (MM).

College of Health and Human Services Offers education (MHA); gerontology (MHA); health administration (MHA); health care management (MBA); informatics (MHA); nursing (MSN); nursing/health care education (MSN).

College of Information Systems and Technology Offers information systems (MIS); technology management (MBA).

College of Social and Behavioral Science Offers administration of justice and security (MS); psychology (MS).

UNIVERSITY OF PHOENIX–BOSTON CAMPUS, Braintree, MA 02184-4949

General Information Proprietary, coed, comprehensive institution. *Graduate housing:* On-campus housing not available.

GRADUATE UNITS

College of Information Systems and Technology *Degree program information:* Evening/weekend programs available. Offers technology management (MBA). Electronic applications accepted.

School of Business *Degree program information:* Evening/weekend programs available. Offers administration (MBA); global management (MBA).

UNIVERSITY OF PHOENIX–CENTRAL FLORIDA CAMPUS, Maitland, FL 32751-7057

General Information Proprietary, coed, comprehensive institution. *Graduate housing:* On-campus housing not available.

GRADUATE UNITS

College of Education *Degree program information:* Evening/weekend programs available. Offers administration and supervision (MA Ed); curriculum and instruction (MA Ed); curriculum and instruction-computer education (MA Ed); curriculum and instruction-mathematics education (MA Ed); early childhood education (MA Ed); elementary teacher education (MA Ed); secondary teacher education (MA Ed). Electronic applications accepted.

College of Information Systems and Technology *Degree program information:* Evening/weekend programs available. Offers management (MIS); technology management (MBA). Electronic applications accepted.

College of Nursing *Degree program information:* Evening/weekend programs available. Offers health administration (MHA); health and human services (MSN); nursing (MSN); nursing/health care education (MSN). Electronic applications accepted.

School of Business *Degree program information:* Evening/weekend programs available. Offers accounting (MBA); business administration (MBA); business and management (MM); global management (MBA); human resources management (MBA, MM); management (MM); marketing (MBA); public administration (MBA, MM). Electronic applications accepted.

UNIVERSITY OF PHOENIX–CENTRAL MASSACHUSETTS CAMPUS, Westborough, MA 01581-3906

General Information Proprietary, coed, comprehensive institution. *Graduate housing:* On-campus housing not available.

GRADUATE UNITS

College of Education *Degree program information:* Evening/weekend programs available. Offers education (MA Ed). Electronic applications accepted.

College of Information Systems and Technology *Degree program information:* Evening/weekend programs available. Offers technology management (MBA). Electronic applications accepted.

School of Business *Degree program information:* Evening/weekend programs available. Offers business administration (MBA); global management (MBA). Electronic applications accepted.

UNIVERSITY OF PHOENIX–CENTRAL VALLEY CAMPUS, Fresno, CA 93720-1562

General Information Proprietary, coed, comprehensive institution.

GRADUATE UNITS

College of Education Offers curriculum and instruction (MA Ed); curriculum and instruction-computer education (MA Ed); elementary teacher education (MA Ed); secondary teacher education (MA Ed).

College of Human Services Offers marriage, family and child therapy (MSC).

College of Information Systems and Technology Offers information systems (MIS); technology management (MBA).

College of Nursing Offers education (MHA); gerontology (MHA); health administration (MHA); nursing (MSN).

School of Business Offers accounting (MBA); business administration (MBA); global management (MBA); human resources management (MBA, MM); management (MM); marketing (MBA); public administration (MBA, MM).

UNIVERSITY OF PHOENIX–CHARLOTTE CAMPUS, Charlotte, NC 28273-3409

General Information Proprietary, coed, comprehensive institution. *Graduate housing:* On-campus housing not available.

GRADUATE UNITS

College of Information Systems and Technology *Degree program information:* Evening/weekend programs available. Offers information systems (MIS); information systems management (MISM); technology management (MBA). Electronic applications accepted.

College of Nursing *Degree program information:* Evening/weekend programs available. Offers education (MHA); gerontology (MHA); health administration (MHA); informatics (MHA, MSN); nursing (MSN); nursing/health care education (MSN). Electronic applications accepted.

School of Business *Degree program information:* Evening/weekend programs available. Offers accounting (MBA); business administration (MBA); global management (MBA). Electronic applications accepted.

UNIVERSITY OF PHOENIX–CHATTANOOGA CAMPUS, Chattanooga, TN 37421-3707

General Information Proprietary, coed, comprehensive institution.

GRADUATE UNITS

College of Education Offers administration and supervision (MA Ed); curriculum and instruction (MA Ed); elementary teacher education (MA Ed); secondary teacher education (MA Ed).

College of Information Systems and Technology Postbaccalaureate distance learning degree programs offered. Offers information systems (MIS); technology management (MBA).

College of Nursing Offers education (MHA); gerontology (MHA); health administration (MHA).

College of Social Services Postbaccalaureate distance learning degree programs offered. Offers industrial/organizational psychology (PhD); psychology (MSP).

School of Business Postbaccalaureate distance learning degree programs offered. Offers accounting (MBA); business administration (MBA); business and management (MBA); global management (MBA); human resources management (MBA, MM); management (MM); marketing (MBA); public administration (MBA, MM).

UNIVERSITY OF PHOENIX–CHEYENNE CAMPUS, Cheyenne, WY 82009

General Information Proprietary, coed, comprehensive institution.

GRADUATE UNITS

College of Criminal Justice and Security Postbaccalaureate distance learning degree programs offered. Offers administration of justice and security (MS).

College of Information Systems and Technology Offers information systems (MIS); technology management (MBA).

College of Nursing Postbaccalaureate distance learning degree programs offered. Offers health administration (MHA); nursing (MSN); nursing/health care education (MSN).

School of Business Postbaccalaureate distance learning degree programs offered. Offers global management (MBA); human resources management (MBA, MM); management (MM); marketing (MBA); public administration (MBA, MM).

UNIVERSITY OF PHOENIX–CHICAGO CAMPUS, Schaumburg, IL 60173-4399

General Information Proprietary, coed, comprehensive institution. *Graduate housing:* On-campus housing not available.

GRADUATE UNITS

College of Information Systems and Technology *Degree program information:* Evening/weekend programs available. Offers e-business (MBA); information systems (MIS); management (MM); technology management (MBA). Electronic applications accepted.

School of Business *Degree program information:* Evening/weekend programs available. Offers business administration (MBA); global management (MBA); human resources management (MBA); information systems (MIS); management (MM). Electronic applications accepted.

UNIVERSITY OF PHOENIX–CINCINNATI CAMPUS, West Chester, OH 45069-4875

General Information Proprietary, coed, comprehensive institution. *Graduate housing:* On-campus housing not available.

GRADUATE UNITS

College of Information Systems and Technology *Degree program information:* Evening/weekend programs available. Postbaccalaureate distance learning degree programs offered. Offers electronic business (MBA); information systems (MIS); technology management (MBA). Electronic applications accepted.

College of Social Services *Degree program information:* Evening/weekend programs available. Postbaccalaureate distance learning degree programs offered. Offers psychology (MS). Electronic applications accepted.

School of Business *Degree program information:* Evening/weekend programs available. Offers accounting (MBA); business administration (MBA); global management (MBA); human resources management (MBA, MM); management (MM); marketing (MBA); public administration (MM). Electronic applications accepted.

UNIVERSITY OF PHOENIX–CLEVELAND CAMPUS, Independence, OH 44131-2194

General Information Proprietary, coed, comprehensive institution. *Graduate housing:* On-campus housing not available.

GRADUATE UNITS

College of Information Systems and Technology *Degree program information:* Evening/weekend programs available. Postbaccalaureate distance learning degree programs offered (no on-campus study). Offers information management (MIS); technology management (MBA). Electronic applications accepted.

College of Nursing *Degree program information:* Evening/weekend programs available. Postbaccalaureate distance learning degree programs offered. Offers nursing (MSN, PhD). Electronic applications accepted.

School of Business *Degree program information:* Evening/weekend programs available. Postbaccalaureate distance learning degree programs offered (no on-campus study). Offers accounting (MBA); business administration (MBA); global management (MBA); human resources management (MBA, MM); management (MM); marketing (MBA); public administration (MBA, MM). Electronic applications accepted.

UNIVERSITY OF PHOENIX–COLUMBIA CAMPUS, Columbia, SC 29223

General Information Proprietary, coed, comprehensive institution.

GRADUATE UNITS

College of Information Systems and Technology Offers technology management (MBA).

School of Business Postbaccalaureate distance learning degree programs offered. Offers business (MBA).

UNIVERSITY OF PHOENIX–COLUMBUS GEORGIA CAMPUS, Columbus, GA 31904-6321

General Information Proprietary, coed, comprehensive institution. *Graduate housing:* On-campus housing not available.

GRADUATE UNITS

College of Information Systems and Technology *Degree program information:* Evening/weekend programs available. Postbaccalaureate distance learning degree programs offered. Offers e-business (MBA); information systems (MIS); technology management (MBA). Electronic applications accepted.

College of Nursing Postbaccalaureate distance learning degree programs offered. Offers health administration (MHA); nursing (MSN). Electronic applications accepted.

School of Business *Degree program information:* Evening/weekend programs available. Offers accounting (MBA); business administration (MBA); global management (MBA); human resources management (MBA, MM); management (MM); marketing (MBA); public administration (MBA). Electronic applications accepted.

UNIVERSITY OF PHOENIX–COLUMBUS OHIO CAMPUS, Columbus, OH 43240-4032

General Information Proprietary, coed, comprehensive institution. *Graduate housing:* On-campus housing not available.

GRADUATE UNITS

College of Information Systems and Technology Postbaccalaureate distance learning degree programs offered. Offers information systems (MIS); technology management (MBA).

College of Nursing *Degree program information:* Evening/weekend programs available. Postbaccalaureate distance learning degree programs offered. Offers nursing (MSN, PhD). Electronic applications accepted.

School of Business *Degree program information:* Evening/weekend programs available. Postbaccalaureate distance learning degree programs offered. Offers accounting (MBA); business administration (MBA); global management (MBA); human resources management (MBA, MM); management (MM); marketing (MBA); public administration (MM). Electronic applications accepted.

UNIVERSITY OF PHOENIX–DALLAS CAMPUS, Dallas, TX 75251-2009

General Information Proprietary, coed, comprehensive institution. *Graduate housing:* On-campus housing not available.

GRADUATE UNITS

College of Criminal Justice and Security Postbaccalaureate distance learning degree programs offered. Offers administration of justice and security (MS). Electronic applications accepted.

College of Education Offers curriculum and instruction (MA Ed).

College of Information Systems and Technology *Degree program information:* Evening/weekend programs available. Offers e-business (MBA); information systems (MIS); technology management (MBA). Electronic applications accepted.

School of Business *Degree program information:* Evening/weekend programs available. Postbaccalaureate distance learning degree programs offered. Offers accounting (MBA); business administration (MBA); global management (MBA); human resources management (MBA, MM); management (MM); marketing (MBA); public administration (MBA, MM). Electronic applications accepted.

UNIVERSITY OF PHOENIX–DENVER CAMPUS, Lone Tree, CO 80124-5453

General Information Proprietary, coed, comprehensive institution. *Graduate housing:* On-campus housing not available.

GRADUATE UNITS

College of Education *Degree program information:* Evening/weekend programs available. Offers administration and supervision (MAEd); curriculum instruction (MAEd); elementary teacher education (MAEd); school counseling (MSC); secondary teacher education (MAEd). Electronic applications accepted.

College of Information Systems and Technology *Degree program information:* Evening/weekend programs available. Postbaccalaureate distance learning degree programs offered. Offers e-business (MBA); management (MIS); technology management (MBA). Electronic applications accepted.

College of Nursing *Degree program information:* Evening/weekend programs available. Postbaccalaureate distance learning degree programs offered. Offers health administration (MHA); nursing (MSN). Electronic applications accepted.

School of Business *Degree program information:* Evening/weekend programs available. Postbaccalaureate distance learning degree programs offered. Offers accountancy (MSA); accounting (MBA); business administration (MBA); e-business (MBA); global management (MBA); human resources management (MBA, MM); management (MM); marketing (MBA); public administration (MBA, MM). Electronic applications accepted.

UNIVERSITY OF PHOENIX–DES MOINES CAMPUS, Des Moines, IA 50266

General Information Proprietary, coed, comprehensive institution.

GRADUATE UNITS

College of Criminal Justice and Security Postbaccalaureate distance learning degree programs offered. Offers administration of justice and security (MS).

College of Information Systems and Technology Postbaccalaureate distance learning degree programs offered. Offers information systems (MIS); technology management (MBA).

College of Nursing Offers education (MHA); gerontology (MHA); health administration (MHA, DHA); informatics (MHA, MSN); nursing (MSN, PhD); nursing/health care education (MSN).

School of Business Postbaccalaureate distance learning degree programs offered. Offers accounting (MBA); business administration (MBA); global management (MBA); human resources management (MBA, MM); management (MM); marketing (MBA); public administration (MBA, MM).

UNIVERSITY OF PHOENIX–EASTERN WASHINGTON CAMPUS, Spokane Valley, WA 99212-2531

General Information Proprietary, coed, comprehensive institution. *Graduate housing:* On-campus housing not available.

GRADUATE UNITS

College of Information Systems and Technology Offers technology management (MBA).

School of Business *Degree program information:* Evening/weekend programs available. Offers accounting (MBA); business administration (MBA); human resources management (MBA); marketing (MBA); public administration (MBA). Electronic applications accepted.

UNIVERSITY OF PHOENIX–FAIRFIELD COUNTY CAMPUS, Norwalk, CT 06854-1799

General Information Proprietary, coed, comprehensive institution.

GRADUATE UNITS

School of Business Offers business (MBA).

UNIVERSITY OF PHOENIX–HARRISBURG CAMPUS, Harrisburg, PA 17112

General Information Proprietary, coed, comprehensive institution.

GRADUATE UNITS

College of Criminal Justice and Security Postbaccalaureate distance learning degree programs offered. Offers administration of justice and security (MS).

College of Information Systems and Technology Postbaccalaureate distance learning degree programs offered. Offers information systems (MIS); technology management (MBA).

College of Nursing Postbaccalaureate distance learning degree programs offered. Offers health administration (MHA); nursing (MSN); nursing/health care education (MSN).

School of Business Postbaccalaureate distance learning degree programs offered. Offers accounting (MBA); business administration (MBA); business and management (MBA); global management (MBA); human resources management (MBA, MM); management (MM); marketing (MBA); public administration (MBA, MM).

UNIVERSITY OF PHOENIX–HAWAII CAMPUS, Honolulu, HI 96813-4317

General Information Proprietary, coed, comprehensive institution. *Graduate housing:* On-campus housing not available.

GRADUATE UNITS

College of Education *Degree program information:* Evening/weekend programs available. Offers administration and supervision (MA Ed); curriculum and instruction (MA Ed); elementary education (MA Ed); secondary education (MA Ed); special education (MA Ed); teacher education for elementary licensure (MA Ed). Electronic applications accepted.

College of Information Systems and Technology *Degree program information:* Evening/weekend programs available. Offers information systems (MIS); technology management (MBA). Electronic applications accepted.

College of Nursing *Degree program information:* Evening/weekend programs available. Offers education (MHA); family nurse practitioner (MSN); gerontology (MHA); health administration (MHA); nursing (MSN); nursing/health care education (MSN). Electronic applications accepted.

School of Business *Degree program information:* Evening/weekend programs available. Offers accounting (MBA); business administration (MBA); global management (MBA); human resources management (MBA, MM); management (MM); marketing (MBA); public administration (MBA, MM). Electronic applications accepted.

UNIVERSITY OF PHOENIX–HOUSTON CAMPUS, Houston, TX 77079-2004

General Information Proprietary, coed, comprehensive institution. *Graduate housing:* On-campus housing not available.

GRADUATE UNITS

College of Education Offers curriculum and instruction (MA Ed).

College of Information Systems and Technology *Degree program information:* Evening/weekend programs available. Postbaccalaureate distance learning degree programs offered. Offers e-business (MBA); information systems (MIS); technology management (MBA). Electronic applications accepted.

College of Nursing Postbaccalaureate distance learning degree programs offered. Offers health administration (MHA). Electronic applications accepted.

School of Business *Degree program information:* Evening/weekend programs available. Postbaccalaureate distance learning degree programs offered. Offers accounting (MBA); business administration (MBA); global management (MBA); human resources management (MBA, MM); management (MM); marketing (MBA); public administration (MBA, MM). Electronic applications accepted.

UNIVERSITY OF PHOENIX–IDAHO CAMPUS, Meridian, ID 83642-3014

General Information Proprietary, coed, comprehensive institution. *Graduate housing:* On-campus housing not available.

GRADUATE UNITS

College of Education *Degree program information:* Evening/weekend programs available. Offers administration and supervision (MA Ed); curriculum and instruction (MA Ed); elementary teacher education (MA Ed); secondary teacher education (MA Ed). Electronic applications accepted.

College of Information Systems and Technology *Degree program information:* Evening/weekend programs available. Offers information systems (MIS); technology management (MBA). Electronic applications accepted.

College of Nursing *Degree program information:* Evening/weekend programs available. Postbaccalaureate distance learning degree programs offered. Offers health administration (MHA); nursing (MSN); nursing/health care education (MSN). Electronic applications accepted.

School of Business *Degree program information:* Evening/weekend programs available. Postbaccalaureate distance learning degree programs offered. Offers accounting (MBA); administration (MBA); global management (MBA); human resources management (MBA, MM); management (MM); marketing (MBA); public administration (MM). Electronic applications accepted.

UNIVERSITY OF PHOENIX–INDIANAPOLIS CAMPUS, Indianapolis, IN 46250-932

General Information Proprietary, coed, comprehensive institution. *Graduate housing:* On-campus housing not available.

GRADUATE UNITS

College of Education Offers elementary teacher education (MA Ed); secondary teacher education (MA Ed).

College of Information Systems and Technology *Degree program information:* Evening/weekend programs available. Offers information systems (MIS); technology management (MBA). Electronic applications accepted.

College of Nursing *Degree program information:* Evening/weekend programs available. Postbaccalaureate distance learning degree programs offered. Offers health administration (MHA); nursing (MSN); nursing/health care education (MSN). Electronic applications accepted.

School of Business *Degree program information:* Evening/weekend programs available. Offers accounting (MBA); business administration (MBA); global management (MBA); human resources management (MBA, MM); management (MM); marketing (MBA); public administration (MM). Electronic applications accepted.

UNIVERSITY OF PHOENIX–JERSEY CITY CAMPUS, Jersey City, NJ 07310

General Information Proprietary, coed, comprehensive institution.

GRADUATE UNITS

College of Criminal Justice and Security Postbaccalaureate distance learning degree programs offered. Offers administration of justice and security (MS).

College of Information Systems and Technology Postbaccalaureate distance learning degree programs offered. Offers information systems (MIS); technology management (MBA).

College of Social Services Postbaccalaureate distance learning degree programs offered. Offers psychology (MS).

School of Business Offers accounting (MBA); business administration (MBA); global management (MBA); human resources management (MBA, MM); management (MM); marketing (MBA); public administration (MBA, MM).

UNIVERSITY OF PHOENIX–KANSAS CITY CAMPUS, Kansas City, MO 64131-4517

General Information Proprietary, coed, comprehensive institution. *Graduate housing:* On-campus housing not available.

GRADUATE UNITS

College of Criminal Justice and Security *Degree program information:* Evening/weekend programs available. Postbaccalaureate distance learning degree programs offered. Offers administration of justice and security (MS).

College of Education Postbaccalaureate distance learning degree programs offered. Offers administration and supervision (MA Ed).

College of Information Systems and Technology *Degree program information:* Evening/weekend programs available. Offers management (MIS); technology management (MBA). Electronic applications accepted.

School of Business *Degree program information:* Evening/weekend programs available. Offers accounting (MBA); business administration (MBA); global management (MBA); human resources management (MBA, MM); management (MM); marketing (MBA); public administration (MBA). Electronic applications accepted.

UNIVERSITY OF PHOENIX–LAS VEGAS CAMPUS, Las Vegas, NV 89128

General Information Proprietary, coed, comprehensive institution. *Graduate housing:* On-campus housing not available.

GRADUATE UNITS

College of Education *Degree program information:* Evening/weekend programs available. Offers administration and supervision (MA Ed); curriculum and instruction (MA Ed); school counseling (MSC); teacher education-elementary licensure (MA Ed). Electronic applications accepted.

College of Human Services Postbaccalaureate distance learning degree programs offered. Offers marriage, family, and child therapy (MSC); mental health counseling (MSC); school counseling (MSC). Electronic applications accepted.

College of Information Systems and Technology *Degree program information:* Evening/weekend programs available. Offers information systems (MIS); technology management (MBA). Electronic applications accepted.

School of Business *Degree program information:* Evening/weekend programs available. Postbaccalaureate distance learning degree programs offered (no on-campus study). Offers accounting (MBA); business administration (MBA); global management (MBA); human resources management (MBA, MM); management (MM); marketing (MBA); public administration (MM). Electronic applications accepted.

UNIVERSITY OF PHOENIX–LITTLE ROCK CAMPUS, Little Rock, AR 72211-3500

General Information Proprietary, coed, comprehensive institution. *Graduate housing:* On-campus housing not available.

GRADUATE UNITS

School of Business *Degree program information:* Evening/weekend programs available. Offers business (MBA, MM). Electronic applications accepted.

UNIVERSITY OF PHOENIX–LOUISIANA CAMPUS, Metairie, LA 70001-2082

General Information Proprietary, coed, comprehensive institution. *Graduate housing:* On-campus housing not available.

GRADUATE UNITS

College of Education Postbaccalaureate distance learning degree programs offered. Offers curriculum and instruction (MA Ed); early childhood education (MA Ed).

College of Information Systems and Technology *Degree program information:* Evening/weekend programs available. Offers information systems/management (MIS); technology management (MBA). Electronic applications accepted.

College of Nursing *Degree program information:* Evening/weekend programs available. Postbaccalaureate distance learning degree programs offered (no on-campus study). Offers health administration (MHA); nursing (MSN). Electronic applications accepted.

School of Business *Degree program information:* Evening/weekend programs available. Offers accounting (MBA); business administration (MBA); global management (MBA); human resources management (MBA, MM); management (MM); marketing (MBA); public administration (MBA). Electronic applications accepted.

UNIVERSITY OF PHOENIX–LOUISVILLE CAMPUS, Louisville, KY 40223-3839

General Information Proprietary, coed, comprehensive institution.

GRADUATE UNITS

College of Information Systems and Technology Postbaccalaureate distance learning degree programs offered. Offers technology management (MBA).

College of Nursing Postbaccalaureate distance learning degree programs offered. Offers education (MHA); gerontology (MHA); health administration (MHA); informatics (MHA, MSN); nursing (MSN); nursing/health care education (MSN).

School of Business Postbaccalaureate distance learning degree programs offered. Offers business administration (MBA); e-business (MBA); management (MM).

UNIVERSITY OF PHOENIX–MADISON CAMPUS, Madison, WI 53718-2416

General Information Proprietary, coed, comprehensive institution.

GRADUATE UNITS

College of Education Offers education (Ed S); educational leadership (Ed D); educational leadership: curriculum and instruction (Ed D); higher education administration (PhD).

College of Information Systems and Technology Offers information systems (MIS); management (MIS); technology management (MBA).

School of Business Offers accounting (MBA); business and management (MBA); e-business (MBA); global management (MBA); human resources management (MBA, MM); management (MM); marketing (MBA); public administration (MBA).

UNIVERSITY OF PHOENIX–MARYLAND CAMPUS, Columbia, MD 21045-5424

General Information Proprietary, coed, comprehensive institution. *Graduate housing:* On-campus housing not available.

GRADUATE UNITS

College of Information Systems and Technology *Degree program information:* Evening/weekend programs available. Offers information systems (MIS); technology management (MBA). Electronic applications accepted.

College of Nursing *Degree program information:* Evening/weekend programs available. Offers health administration (MHA); health care education (MSN); nursing (MSN). Electronic applications accepted.

School of Business *Degree program information:* Evening/weekend programs available. Offers accounting (MBA); business administration (MBA); e-business (MBA); global management (MBA); human resources management (MBA, MM); management (MM); marketing (MBA); public administration (MBA, MM). Electronic applications accepted.

UNIVERSITY OF PHOENIX–MEMPHIS CAMPUS, Cordova, TN 38018

General Information Proprietary, coed, comprehensive institution.

GRADUATE UNITS

College of Criminal Justice and Security Offers administration of justice and security (MS).

College of Education Offers administration and supervision (MA Ed); curriculum and instruction (MA Ed); elementary teacher education (MA Ed); secondary teacher education (MA Ed).

College of Information Systems and Technology Offers information systems (MIS); technology management (MBA).

College of Nursing Offers health administration (MHA, DHA).

School of Business Offers accounting (MBA); business and management (MBA); e-business (MBA); global management (MBA); human resources management (MBA, MM); management (MM); marketing (MBA); public administration (MBA, MM).

UNIVERSITY OF PHOENIX–METRO DETROIT CAMPUS, Troy, MI 48098-2623

General Information Proprietary, coed, comprehensive institution. *Graduate housing:* On-campus housing not available.

GRADUATE UNITS

College of Education *Degree program information:* Evening/weekend programs available. Offers administration and supervision (MA Ed); elementary teacher education (MA Ed); secondary teacher education (MA Ed); special education (MA Ed). Electronic applications accepted.

College of Information Systems and Technology *Degree program information:* Evening/weekend programs available. Offers information systems and technology (MIS). Electronic applications accepted.

College of Nursing *Degree program information:* Evening/weekend programs available. Offers health care education (MSN); nursing (MSN). Electronic applications accepted.

School of Business *Degree program information:* Evening/weekend programs available. Offers business (MBA, MIS, MM, MS). Electronic applications accepted.

UNIVERSITY OF PHOENIX–MILWAUKEE CAMPUS, Milwaukee, WI 53045

General Information Proprietary, coed, comprehensive institution.

GRADUATE UNITS

College of Criminal Justice and Security Offers administration of justice and security (MS).

College of Education Offers curriculum and instruction (MA Ed, Ed D); education (Ed S); educational leadership (Ed D); English as a second language (MA Ed); higher education administration (PhD).

College of Information Systems and Technology Offers information systems (MIS); organziational leadership/information systems and technology (DM).

College of Nursing Offers education (MHA); gerontology (MHA); health administration (MHA, DHA); informatics (MHA, MSN); nursing (MSN, PhD); nursing/health care education (MSN).

College of Social Sciences Offers industrial/organizational psychology (PhD); psychology (MS).

School of Business Offers accounting (MS); business administration (MBA, DBA); human resources management (MM); management (MM); organizational leadership (DM); public administration (MPA).

UNIVERSITY OF PHOENIX–MINNEAPOLIS/ST. LOUIS PARK CAMPUS, St. Louis Park, MN 55426

General Information Proprietary, coed, comprehensive institution.

GRADUATE UNITS

College of Human Services Offers community counseling (MSC).

College of Information Systems and Technology Offers technology management (MBA).

School of Business Offers accounting (MBA); business administration (MBA); global management (MBA); human resources management (MBA); management (MM); marketing (MBA); public administration (MBA).

UNIVERSITY OF PHOENIX–NASHVILLE CAMPUS, Nashville, TN 37214-5048

General Information Proprietary, coed, comprehensive institution. *Graduate housing:* On-campus housing not available.

GRADUATE UNITS

College of Education *Degree program information:* Evening/weekend programs available. Offers administration and supervision (MA Ed); curriculum and instruction (MA Ed); elementary teacher education (MA Ed); secondary teacher education (MA Ed). Electronic applications accepted.

College of Information Systems and Technology *Degree program information:* Evening/weekend programs available. Offers technology management (MBA). Electronic applications accepted.

College of Nursing *Degree program information:* Evening/weekend programs available. Offers health administration (MHA). Electronic applications accepted.

School of Business *Degree program information:* Evening/weekend programs available. Offers business administration (MBA); human resources management (MBA); management (MM). Electronic applications accepted.

UNIVERSITY OF PHOENIX–NEW MEXICO CAMPUS, Albuquerque, NM 87113-1570

General Information Proprietary, coed, comprehensive institution. *Graduate housing:* On-campus housing not available.

GRADUATE UNITS

College of Education *Degree program information:* Evening/weekend programs available. Offers administration and supervision (MAEd); curriculum and instruction (MAEd); elementary teacher education (MAEd); school counseling (MSC); secondary teacher education (MAEd). Electronic applications accepted.

College of Information Systems and Technology *Degree program information:* Evening/weekend programs available. Offers e-business (MBA); information systems (MS); technology management (MBA). Electronic applications accepted.

College of Nursing *Degree program information:* Evening/weekend programs available. Offers health administration (MHA); health care education (MSN); nursing (MSN). Electronic applications accepted.

School of Business *Degree program information:* Evening/weekend programs available. Offers accounting (MBA); business administration (MBA); global management (MBA); human resource management (MBA); human resources management (MM); management (MM); marketing (MBA). Electronic applications accepted.

UNIVERSITY OF PHOENIX–NORTHERN NEVADA CAMPUS, Reno, NV 89521-5862

General Information Proprietary, coed, comprehensive institution.

GRADUATE UNITS

College of Criminal Justice and Security Offers administration of justice and security (MS).

College of Education Offers administration and supervision (MA Ed); curriculum and instruction (MA Ed); elementary teacher education (MA Ed); secondary teacher education (MA Ed).

College of Information Systems and Technology Offers information systems (MIS); technology management (MBA).

College of Nursing Offers health administration (MHA); health care education (MSN); nursing (MSN).

School of Business Offers accounting (MBA); business administration (MBA); global management (MBA); human resources management (MBA, MM); management (MM); marketing (MBA); public administration (MBA, MM).

UNIVERSITY OF PHOENIX–NORTHERN VIRGINIA CAMPUS, Reston, VA 20190

General Information Proprietary, coed, comprehensive institution. *Enrollment:* 143 full-time matriculated graduate/professional students (50 women). *Enrollment by degree level:* 143 master's. *Tuition:* Full-time $16,440. One-time fee: $45 full-time. Full-time tuition and fees vary according to course load, degree level, campus/location and program. *Graduate housing:* On-campus housing not available. *Student services:* Career counseling, exercise/wellness program, free psychological counseling, services for students with disabilities, writing training. *Library facilities:* University Library. *Online resources:* library catalog. *Collection:* 16,781 serial subscriptions.

Computer facilities: A campuswide network can be accessed from off campus. *Web address:* http://www.phoenix.edu/.

GRADUATE UNITS

College of Criminal Justice and Security Offers administration of justice and security (MS).

College of Education Offers administration and supervision (MA Ed).

College of Information Systems and Technology Students: 8 full-time (0 women); includes 3 Black or African American, non-Hispanic/Latino. Average age 38. Expenses: Contact institution. *Financial support:* Scholarships/grants available. Financial award applicants required to submit FAFSA. *Degree program information:* Evening/weekend programs available. Postbaccalaureate distance learning degree programs offered. Offers information systems and technology (MIS). *Application deadline:* Applications are processed on a rolling basis. *Application fee:* $45. Electronic applications accepted. *Application Contact:* Dr. Blair Smith, Dean/Executive Director, 480-557-1241, E-mail: blair.smith@phoenix.edu. *Dean/Executive Director,* Dr. Blair Smith, 480-557-1241, E-mail: blair.smith@phoenix.edu.

College of Nursing Offers health administration (MHA); nursing (MSN).

School of Business Students: 135 full-time (50 women); includes 43 Black or African American, non-Hispanic/Latino; 3 Asian, non-Hispanic/Latino; 3 Hispanic/Latino, 6 international. Average age 40. Expenses: Contact institution. *Financial support:* Scholarships/grants available. Financial award applicants required to submit FAFSA. *Degree program information:* Evening/weekend programs available. Postbaccalaureate distance learning degree programs offered. Offers business administration (MBA); public accounting (MPA). *Application deadline:* Applications are processed on a rolling basis. *Application fee:* $45. Electronic applications accepted.

University of Phoenix–Northern Virginia Campus (continued)

Application Contact: Erik Greenberg, Campus Director, 703-376-6150, E-mail: erik.greenberg@phoenix.edu. *Campus Director,* Erik Greenberg, 703-376-6150, E-mail: erik.greenberg@phoenix.edu.

UNIVERSITY OF PHOENIX–NORTH FLORIDA CAMPUS, Jacksonville, FL 32216-0959

General Information Proprietary, coed, comprehensive institution. *Graduate housing:* On-campus housing not available.

GRADUATE UNITS

College of Education *Degree program information:* Evening/weekend programs available. Offers administration and supervision (MA Ed); curriculum and instruction (MA Ed); early childhood education (MA Ed); elementary teacher education (MA Ed); secondary teacher education (MA Ed). Electronic applications accepted.

College of Information Systems and Technology *Degree program information:* Evening/weekend programs available. Offers information systems (MIS); management (MIS). Electronic applications accepted.

College of Nursing *Degree program information:* Evening/weekend programs available. Offers health administration (MHA); health care education (MSN); nursing (MSN). Electronic applications accepted.

School of Business *Degree program information:* Evening/weekend programs available. Offers accounting (MBA); business administration (MBA); global management (MBA); human resources management (MBA, MM); management (MM); marketing (MBA); public administration (MBA, MM). Electronic applications accepted.

UNIVERSITY OF PHOENIX–NORTHWEST ARKANSAS CAMPUS, Rogers, AR 72756-9615

General Information Proprietary, coed, comprehensive institution.

GRADUATE UNITS

College of Criminal Justice and Security Offers administration of justice and security (MS).

College of Information Systems and Technology Offers information systems (MIS); technology management (MBA).

College of Nursing Offers health administration (MHA); health care education (MSN); nursing (MSN).

School of Business Offers accounting (MBA); business and management (MBA); global management (MBA); human resources management (MBA, MM); management (MM); marketing (MBA); public administration (MBA, MM).

UNIVERSITY OF PHOENIX–OKLAHOMA CITY CAMPUS, Oklahoma City, OK 73116-8244

General Information Proprietary, coed, comprehensive institution. *Graduate housing:* On-campus housing not available.

GRADUATE UNITS

College of Information Systems and Technology *Degree program information:* Evening/weekend programs available. Offers e-business (MBA); technology management (MBA). Electronic applications accepted.

College of Nursing Offers nursing (MSN).

School of Business *Degree program information:* Evening/weekend programs available. Offers accounting (MBA); business administration (MBA); global management (MBA); human resource management (MBA); management (MM); marketing (MBA). Electronic applications accepted.

UNIVERSITY OF PHOENIX–OMAHA CAMPUS, Omaha, NE 68154-5240

General Information Proprietary, coed, comprehensive institution.

GRADUATE UNITS

College of Criminal Justice and Security Offers administration of justice and security (MS).

College of Education Offers administration and supervision (MA Ed); curriculum and instruction (MA Ed); elementary teacher education (MA Ed); secondary teacher education (MA Ed); special education (MA Ed).

College of Information Systems and Technology Offers information systems (MIS); technology management (MBA).

College of Nursing Offers health administration (MHA).

School of Business Offers accounting (MBA); business and management (MBA); global management (MBA); human resources management (MBA, MM); management (MM); marketing (MBA); public administration (MBA, MM).

UNIVERSITY OF PHOENIX–OREGON CAMPUS, Tigard, OR 97223

General Information Proprietary, coed, comprehensive institution. *Graduate housing:* On-campus housing not available.

GRADUATE UNITS

College of Education *Degree program information:* Evening/weekend programs available. Offers curriculum and instruction (MA Ed); early childhood education (MA Ed); elementary education (MA Ed); secondary education (MA Ed). Electronic applications accepted.

College of Information Systems and Technology *Degree program information:* Evening/weekend programs available. Offers information systems (MIS); technology management (MBA). Electronic applications accepted.

College of Nursing *Degree program information:* Evening/weekend programs available. Offers health administration (MHA); nursing (MSN). Electronic applications accepted.

School of Business *Degree program information:* Evening/weekend programs available. Offers accounting (MBA); business administration (MBA); global management (MBA); human resource management (MM); human resources management (MBA); management (MM); marketing (MBA); public administration (MM). Electronic applications accepted.

UNIVERSITY OF PHOENIX–PHILADELPHIA CAMPUS, Wayne, PA 19087-2121

General Information Proprietary, coed, comprehensive institution. *Graduate housing:* On-campus housing not available.

GRADUATE UNITS

College of Information Systems and Technology *Degree program information:* Evening/weekend programs available. Offers information systems (MIS); technology management (MBA). Electronic applications accepted.

College of Social Services *Degree program information:* Evening/weekend programs available. Offers psychology (MS). Electronic applications accepted.

School of Business *Degree program information:* Evening/weekend programs available. Offers accounting (MBA); business administration (MBA); global management (MBA); human resources management (MBA, MM); management (MM); marketing (MBA); public administration (MM). Electronic applications accepted.

UNIVERSITY OF PHOENIX–PHOENIX CAMPUS, Phoenix, AZ 85040-1958

General Information Proprietary, coed, comprehensive institution. *Enrollment:* 1,596 full-time matriculated graduate/professional students (950 women). *Enrollment by degree level:* 1,585 master's, 11 other advanced degrees. *Tuition:* Full-time $13,560. One-time fee: $45 full-time. Full-time tuition and fees vary according to course load, degree level, campus/location and program. *Graduate housing:* On-campus housing not available. *Student services:* Career counseling, exercise/wellness program, free psychological counseling, services for students with disabilities, writing training. *Library facilities:* University Library. *Online resources:* library catalog, web page. *Collection:* 16,781 serial subscriptions, 3,000 audiovisual materials.

Computer facilities: Computer purchase and lease plans are available. A campuswide network can be accessed from off campus. *Web address:* http://www.phoenix.edu/.

General Application Contact: 866-766-0766.

GRADUATE UNITS

College of Education Students: 301 full-time (202 women); includes 52 minority (23 Black or African American, non-Hispanic/Latino; 3 American Indian or Alaska Native, non-Hispanic/Latino; 24 Hispanic/Latino; 1 Native Hawaiian or other Pacific Islander, non-Hispanic/Latino; 1 Two or more races, non-Hispanic/Latino), 3 international. Average age 35. Expenses: Contact institution. *Financial support:* Scholarships/grants available. Financial award applicants required to submit FAFSA. *Degree program information:* Evening/weekend programs available. Postbaccalaureate distance learning degree programs offered. Offers administration and supervision (MA Ed); curriculum instruction (MA Ed); education and training (MA Ed); elementary teacher education (MA Ed); secondary teacher education (MA Ed); special education (MA Ed); teacher leadership (MA Ed). *Application deadline:* Applications are processed on a rolling basis. *Application fee:* $45. Electronic applications accepted. *Application Contact:* 866-766-0766. *Dean/Executive Director,* Dr. Meredith Curley, 480-557-1217, Fax: 480-557-1588, E-mail: meredith.curley@phoenix.edu.

College of Natural Sciences Students: 14 full-time (8 women); includes 7 minority (4 Black or African American, non-Hispanic/Latino; 1 American Indian or Alaska Native, non-Hispanic/Latino; 2 Hispanic/Latino). Average age 37. Expenses: Contact institution. *Financial support:* Scholarships/grants available. Financial award applicants required to submit FAFSA. *Degree program information:* Evening/weekend programs available. Postbaccalaureate distance learning degree programs offered. Offers health administration (MHA). *Application deadline:* Applications are processed on a rolling basis. *Application fee:* $45. Electronic applications accepted. *Application Contact:* Campus Information Center, 480-804-7600, Fax: 480-537-2320. *Dean/Executive Director,* Dr. Hinrich Eylers, 602-557-7428, E-mail: hinrich.eylers@phoenix.edu.

College of Nursing Students: 150 full-time (132 women); includes 20 minority (5 Black or African American, non-Hispanic/Latino; 6 Asian, non-Hispanic/Latino; 8 Hispanic/Latino; 1 Native Hawaiian or other Pacific Islander, non-Hispanic/Latino), 8 international. Average age 40. Expenses: Contact institution. *Financial support:* Scholarships/grants available. Financial award applicants required to submit FAFSA. *Degree program information:* Evening/weekend programs available. Postbaccalaureate distance learning degree programs offered. Offers family nurse practitioner (MSN); health care education (MSN); informatics (MSN); nursing (MSN). *Application deadline:* Applications are processed on a rolling basis. *Application fee:* $45. Electronic applications accepted. *Application Contact:* 866-766-0766. *Dean/Executive Director,* Dr. Pam Fuller, 480-557-1140, E-mail: pam.fuller@phoenix.edu.

College of Social Sciences Students: 181 full-time (140 women); includes 23 minority (7 Black or African American, non-Hispanic/Latino; 2 Asian, non-Hispanic/Latino; 14 Hispanic/Latino), 7 international. Average age 34. Expenses: Contact institution. *Financial support:* Scholarships/grants available. Financial award applicants required to submit FAFSA. *Degree program information:* Evening/weekend programs available. Postbaccalaureate distance learning degree programs offered. Offers community counseling (MC); counseling (MSC); psychology (MSP). *Application deadline:* Applications are processed on a rolling basis. *Application fee:* $45. Electronic applications accepted. *Application Contact:* Campus Information Center, 866-766-0766. *Dean/Executive Director,* Dr. Lynn Hall, 520-247-4364, E-mail: lynn.hall@phoenix.edu.

School of Business Students: 950 full-time (468 women); includes 194 minority (59 Black or African American, non-Hispanic/Latino; 11 American Indian or Alaska Native, non-Hispanic/Latino; 27 Asian, non-Hispanic/Latino; 84 Hispanic/Latino; 10 Native Hawaiian or other Pacific Islander, non-Hispanic/Latino; 3 Two or more races, non-Hispanic/Latino), 47 international. Average age 34. Expenses: Contact institution. *Financial support:* Scholarships/grants available. Financial award applicants required to submit FAFSA. *Degree program information:* Evening/weekend programs available. Postbaccalaureate distance learning degree programs offered. Offers accounting (MSA); business administration (MBA); management (MM). *Application deadline:* Applications are processed on a rolling basis. *Application fee:* $45. Electronic applications accepted. *Application Contact:* Campus Information Center, 800-766-0766. *Director,* Bill Berry, 480-557-1824, Fax: 480-557-1854, E-mail: bill.berry@phoenix.edu.

UNIVERSITY OF PHOENIX–PITTSBURGH CAMPUS, Pittsburgh, PA 15276

General Information Proprietary, coed, comprehensive institution. *Graduate housing:* On-campus housing not available.

GRADUATE UNITS

College of Information Systems and Technology *Degree program information:* Evening/weekend programs available. Offers e-business (MBA); information systems (MIS); technology management (MBA). Electronic applications accepted.

College of Nursing *Degree program information:* Evening/weekend programs available. Offers health administration (MHA); health care education (MSN); nursing (MSN). Electronic applications accepted.

School of Business *Degree program information:* Evening/weekend programs available. Offers accounting (MBA); business administration (MBA); global management (MBA); human resources management (MBA, MM); management (MM); marketing (MBA); public administration (MBA, MM). Electronic applications accepted.

UNIVERSITY OF PHOENIX–PUERTO RICO CAMPUS, Guaynabo, PR 00968

General Information Proprietary, coed, comprehensive institution. *Graduate housing:* On-campus housing not available.

GRADUATE UNITS

College of Education *Degree program information:* Evening/weekend programs available. Offers administration and supervision (MA Ed); early childhood education (MA Ed); school counselor (MSC). Electronic applications accepted.

College of Human Services *Degree program information:* Evening/weekend programs available. Offers marriage and family counseling (MSC); mental health counseling (MSC). Electronic applications accepted.

College of Information Systems and Technology *Degree program information:* Evening/weekend programs available. Offers technology management (MBA). Electronic applications accepted.

School of Business *Degree program information:* Evening/weekend programs available. Offers accounting (MBA); energy management (MBA); global management (MBA); human resource management (MBA); marketing (MBA); project management (MBA); small business administration (MBA). Electronic applications accepted.

UNIVERSITY OF PHOENIX–RALEIGH CAMPUS, Raleigh, NC 27606

General Information Proprietary, coed, comprehensive institution.

GRADUATE UNITS

College of Information Systems and Technology Offers information systems and technology (MIS); management (MIS); technology management (MBA).

College of Nursing Offers education (MHA); gerontology (MHA); health administration (MHA, DHA); informatics (MHA, MSN); nursing (MSN, PhD); nursing/health care education (MSN).

School of Business Offers accounting (MBA); business administration (MBA); e-business (MBA); global management (MBA); human resources management (MBA); marketing (MBA).

UNIVERSITY OF PHOENIX–RICHMOND CAMPUS, Richmond, VA 23230

General Information Proprietary, coed, comprehensive institution. *Graduate housing:* On-campus housing not available.

GRADUATE UNITS

College of Education Offers administration and supervision (MA Ed); curriculum and instruction (MA Ed).

College of Information Systems and Technology *Degree program information:* Evening/weekend programs available. Offers information systems (MIS); technology management (MBA). Electronic applications accepted.

College of Nursing *Degree program information:* Evening/weekend programs available. Offers health administration (MHA); health care education (MSN); nursing (MSN). Electronic applications accepted.

School of Business *Degree program information:* Evening/weekend programs available. Offers accounting (MBA); business administration (MBA); global management (MBA); human resources management (MBA, MM); management (MM); marketing (MBA); public administration (MBA, MM). Electronic applications accepted.

UNIVERSITY OF PHOENIX–SACRAMENTO VALLEY CAMPUS, Sacramento, CA 95833-3632

General Information Proprietary, coed, comprehensive institution. *Graduate housing:* On-campus housing not available.

GRADUATE UNITS

College of Education *Degree program information:* Evening/weekend programs available. Offers adult education (MA Ed); curriculum instruction (MA Ed); elementary teacher education (MA Ed); secondary teacher education (MA Ed); teacher education (Certificate). Electronic applications accepted.

College of Information Systems and Technology *Degree program information:* Evening/weekend programs available. Offers management (MIS); technology management (MBA). Electronic applications accepted.

College of Nursing *Degree program information:* Evening/weekend programs available. Offers family nurse practitioner (MSN); health administration (MHA); health care education (MSN); nursing (MSN). Electronic applications accepted.

School of Business *Degree program information:* Evening/weekend programs available. Offers accounting (MBA); business administration (MBA); global management (MBA); human resources management (MBA, MM); management (MM); marketing (MBA); public administration (MBA, MM). Electronic applications accepted.

UNIVERSITY OF PHOENIX–ST. LOUIS CAMPUS, St. Louis, MO 63043-4828

General Information Proprietary, coed, comprehensive institution. *Graduate housing:* On-campus housing not available.

GRADUATE UNITS

College of Criminal Justice and Security *Degree program information:* Evening/weekend programs available. Offers administration of justice and security (MS). Electronic applications accepted.

College of Information Systems and Technology *Degree program information:* Evening/weekend programs available. Offers information systems (MIS); technology management (MBA). Electronic applications accepted.

School of Business *Degree program information:* Evening/weekend programs available. Offers accounting (MBA); business administration (MBA); global management (MBA); human resources management (MBA, MM); management (MM); marketing (MBA); public administration (MM). Electronic applications accepted.

UNIVERSITY OF PHOENIX–SAN ANTONIO CAMPUS, San Antonio, TX 78230

General Information Proprietary, coed, comprehensive institution.

GRADUATE UNITS

College of Criminal Justice and Security Offers administration of justice and security (MS).

College of Education Offers curriculum and instruction (MA Ed).

College of Information Systems and Technology Offers information systems (MIS); technology management (MBA).

College of Nursing Offers health administration (MHA).

School of Business Offers accounting (MBA); business administration (MBA); e-business (MBA); global management (MBA); human resources management (MBA, MM); management (MM); marketing (MBA); public administration (MBA, MM).

UNIVERSITY OF PHOENIX–SAN DIEGO CAMPUS, San Diego, CA 92123

General Information Proprietary, coed, comprehensive institution. *Graduate housing:* On-campus housing not available.

GRADUATE UNITS

College of Education *Degree program information:* Evening/weekend programs available. Offers curriculum and instruction (MA Ed); elementary teacher education (MA Ed); secondary teacher education (MA Ed). Electronic applications accepted.

College of Information Systems and Technology *Degree program information:* Evening/weekend programs available. Offers management (MIS); technology management (MBA). Electronic applications accepted.

College of Nursing *Degree program information:* Evening/weekend programs available. Offers health care education (MSN); nursing (MSN). Electronic applications accepted.

School of Business *Degree program information:* Evening/weekend programs available. Offers accounting (MBA); business administration (MBA); global management (MBA); human resources management (MBA, MM); management (MM); marketing (MBA); public administration (MBA, MM). Electronic applications accepted.

UNIVERSITY OF PHOENIX–SAVANNAH CAMPUS, Savannah, GA 31405-7400

General Information Proprietary, coed, comprehensive institution.

GRADUATE UNITS

College of Criminal Justice and Security Offers administration of justice and security (MS).

College of Information Systems and Technology Offers information systems and technology (MIS); technology management (MBA).

College of Nursing Offers health administration (MHA); nursing (MSN); nursing/health care education (MSN).

School of Business Offers accounting (MBA); business administration (MBA); global management (MBA); human resources management (MBA, MM); management (MM); marketing (MBA); public administration (MBA, MM).

UNIVERSITY OF PHOENIX–SOUTHERN ARIZONA CAMPUS, Tucson, AZ 85711

General Information Proprietary, coed, comprehensive institution. *Graduate housing:* On-campus housing not available.

GRADUATE UNITS

College of Education *Degree program information:* Evening/weekend programs available. Offers administration and supervision (MA Ed); adult education and training (MA Ed); curriculum instruction (MA Ed); educational counseling (MA Ed); elementary teacher education (MA Ed); school counseling (MSC); secondary teacher education (MA Ed); special education (MA Ed, Certificate). Electronic applications accepted.

College of Information Systems and Technology *Degree program information:* Evening/weekend programs available. Offers information systems (MIS); technology management (MBA). Electronic applications accepted.

College of Social Sciences *Degree program information:* Evening/weekend programs available. Offers psychology (MS). Electronic applications accepted.

School of Business *Degree program information:* Evening/weekend programs available. Offers accountancy (MS); accounting (MBA); business administration (MBA); global management (MBA); human resources management (MBA); management (MM); marketing (MBA). Electronic applications accepted.

UNIVERSITY OF PHOENIX–SOUTHERN CALIFORNIA CAMPUS, Costa Mesa, CA 92626

General Information Proprietary, coed, comprehensive institution. *Graduate housing:* On-campus housing not available.

GRADUATE UNITS

College of Education *Degree program information:* Evening/weekend programs available. Offers administration and supervision (MA Ed); adult education and training (MA Ed); curriculum and instruction (MA Ed); early childhood education (MA Ed); special education (MA Ed); teacher leadership (MA Ed). Electronic applications accepted.

College of Nursing *Degree program information:* Evening/weekend programs available. Offers family nurse practitioner (MSN); health care education (MSN); nursing (MSN). Electronic applications accepted.

College of Social Sciences *Degree program information:* Evening/weekend programs available. Offers administration of justice and security (MS); community counseling (MSC); marriage, family and child therapy (MSC); mental health counseling (MSC); psychology (MS); school counseling (MSC). Electronic applications accepted.

School of Business *Degree program information:* Evening/weekend programs available. Offers business (MBA, MIS, MM). Electronic applications accepted.

UNIVERSITY OF PHOENIX–SOUTHERN COLORADO CAMPUS, Colorado Springs, CO 80919-2335

General Information Proprietary, coed, comprehensive institution. *Graduate housing:* On-campus housing not available.

GRADUATE UNITS

College of Education *Degree program information:* Evening/weekend programs available. Offers administration and supervision (MA Ed); curriculum and instruction (MA Ed); elementary teacher education (MA Ed); principal licensure certification (Certificate); school counseling (MSC); secondary teacher education (MA Ed). Electronic applications accepted.

College of Information Systems and Technology *Degree program information:* Evening/weekend programs available. Offers technology management (MBA). Electronic applications accepted.

College of Nursing *Degree program information:* Evening/weekend programs available. Offers education (MHA); gerontology (MHA); health administration (MHA); nursing (MSN). Electronic applications accepted.

School of Business *Degree program information:* Evening/weekend programs available. Offers accounting (MBA); business administration (MBA); global management (MBA); human resources management (MBA, MM); management (MM); marketing (MBA); public administration (MM). Electronic applications accepted.

UNIVERSITY OF PHOENIX–SOUTH FLORIDA CAMPUS, Fort Lauderdale, FL 33309

General Information Proprietary, coed, comprehensive institution. *Graduate housing:* On-campus housing not available.

GRADUATE UNITS

College of Education *Degree program information:* Evening/weekend programs available. Offers administration and supervision (MA Ed); curriculum and instruction (MA Ed); early childhood education (MA Ed); elementary teacher education (MA Ed); secondary teacher education (MA Ed). Electronic applications accepted.

College of Information Systems and Technology *Degree program information:* Evening/weekend programs available. Offers management (MIS); technology management (MBA). Electronic applications accepted.

College of Nursing *Degree program information:* Evening/weekend programs available. Offers health administration (MHA); health care education (MSN); nursing (MSN). Electronic applications accepted.

School of Business *Degree program information:* Evening/weekend programs available. Offers accounting (MBA); business administration (MBA); global management (MBA); human resource management (MBA); human resources management (MM); management (MM); marketing (MBA); public administration (MBA, MM). Electronic applications accepted.

UNIVERSITY OF PHOENIX–SPRINGFIELD CAMPUS, Springfield, MO 65804-7211

General Information Proprietary, coed, comprehensive institution.

GRADUATE UNITS

College of Criminal Justice and Security Offers administration of justice and security (MS).

College of Education Offers administration and supervision (MA Ed); curriculum and instruction (MA Ed); English and language arts education (MA Ed).

College of Information Systems and Technology Offers information systems (MIS); technology management (MBA).

College of Nursing Offers health administration (MHA); nursing (MSN).

School of Business Offers accounting (MBA); business administration (MBA); global management (MBA); human resources management (MBA, MM); management (MM); marketing (MBA); public administration (MBA, MM).

UNIVERSITY OF PHOENIX–TULSA CAMPUS, Tulsa, OK 74134-1412

General Information Proprietary, coed, comprehensive institution. *Graduate housing:* On-campus housing not available.

GRADUATE UNITS

College of Information Systems and Technology Offers information systems and technology (MIS); technology management (MBA).

University of Phoenix–Tulsa Campus (continued)

College of Nursing Offers nursing (MSN).

School of Business *Degree program information:* Evening/weekend programs available. Offers accounting (MBA); business (MM); business administration (MBA); global management (MBA); human resources management (MBA); marketing (MBA).

UNIVERSITY OF PHOENIX–UTAH CAMPUS, Salt Lake City, UT 84123-4617

General Information Proprietary, coed, comprehensive institution. *Graduate housing:* On-campus housing not available.

GRADUATE UNITS

College of Education *Degree program information:* Evening/weekend programs available. Offers administration and supervision (MA Ed); curriculum and instruction (MA Ed); elementary teacher education (MA Ed); school counseling (MSC); secondary teacher education (MA Ed); special education (MA Ed). Electronic applications accepted.

College of Information Systems and Technology *Degree program information:* Evening/weekend programs available. Offers information systems and technology (MIS). Electronic applications accepted.

College of Nursing *Degree program information:* Evening/weekend programs available. Offers health care education (MSN); nursing (MSN). Electronic applications accepted.

School of Business *Degree program information:* Evening/weekend programs available. Offers accounting (MBA); business administration (MBA); global management (MBA); human resource management (MBA, MM); management (MM); marketing (MBA); technology management (MBA). Electronic applications accepted.

UNIVERSITY OF PHOENIX–VANCOUVER CAMPUS, Burnaby, BC V5C 6G9, Canada

General Information Proprietary, coed, comprehensive institution. *Graduate housing:* On-campus housing not available.

GRADUATE UNITS

The Artemis School *Degree program information:* Evening/weekend programs available. Electronic applications accepted.

College of Education *Degree program information:* Evening/weekend programs available. Offers administration and supervision (MA Ed); curriculum and instruction (MA Ed). Electronic applications accepted.

College of Health and Human Services *Degree program information:* Evening/weekend programs available. Offers health care management (MBA). Electronic applications accepted.

John Sperling School of Business *Degree program information:* Evening/weekend programs available. Offers business (MBA, MM). Electronic applications accepted.

College of Graduate Business and Management *Degree program information:* Evening/weekend programs available. Offers accounting (MBA); business administration (MBA); global management (MBA); human resources management (MBA, MM); marketing (MBA). Electronic applications accepted.

College of Information Systems and Technology *Degree program information:* Evening/weekend programs available. Offers technology management (MBA). Electronic applications accepted.

UNIVERSITY OF PHOENIX–WASHINGTON CAMPUS, Seattle, WA 98188-7500

General Information Proprietary, coed, comprehensive institution. *Graduate housing:* On-campus housing not available.

GRADUATE UNITS

College of Criminal Justice and Security *Degree program information:* Evening/weekend programs available. Offers administration of justice and security (MS). Electronic applications accepted.

School of Business *Degree program information:* Evening/weekend programs available. Offers business (MBA). Electronic applications accepted.

UNIVERSITY OF PHOENIX–WASHINGTON D.C. CAMPUS, Washington, DC 20001

General Information Proprietary, coed, comprehensive institution.

GRADUATE UNITS

College of Criminal Justice and Security Offers administration of justice and security (MS).

College of Education Offers administration and supervision (MA Ed); adult education and training (MA Ed); computer ed (MA Ed); curriculum and instruction (MA Ed, Ed D); early childhood education (MA Ed); education (Ed S); educational leadership (Ed D); educational technology (Ed D); elementary teacher education (MA Ed); English and language arts education (MA Ed); English as a second language (MA Ed); higher education administration (PhD); mathematics education (MA Ed); secondary teacher education (MA Ed); special education (MA Ed); teacher leadership (MA Ed).

College of Information Systems and Technology Offers information systems (MIS); organizational leadership/information systems and technology (DM).

College of Nursing Offers education (MHA); gerontology (MHA); health administration (MHA, DHA); informatics (MHA, MSN); nursing (MSN, PhD); nursing/health care education (MSN).

College of Social Sciences Offers industrial/organizational psychology (PhD); psychology (MS).

School of Business Offers accountancy (MS); business administration (MBA, DBA); human resources management (MM); management (MM); organizational leadership (DM); public administration (MPA).

UNIVERSITY OF PHOENIX–WEST FLORIDA CAMPUS, Temple Terrace, FL 33637

General Information Proprietary, coed, comprehensive institution. *Graduate housing:* On-campus housing not available.

GRADUATE UNITS

College of Education *Degree program information:* Evening/weekend programs available. Offers administration and supervision (MA Ed); curriculum and instruction (MA Ed); curriculum and technology (MA Ed); early childhood education (MA Ed); elementary teacher education (MA Ed); secondary teacher education (MA Ed).

College of Information Systems and Technology *Degree program information:* Evening/weekend programs available. Offers information systems (MIS); technology management (MBA). Electronic applications accepted.

College of Nursing *Degree program information:* Evening/weekend programs available. Postbaccalaureate distance learning degree programs offered. Offers health administration (MHA); health care education (MSN); nursing (MSN). Electronic applications accepted.

School of Business *Degree program information:* Evening/weekend programs available. Offers accounting (MBA); business administration (MBA); global management (MBA); human resources management (MBA, MM); management (MM); marketing (MBA); public administration (MBA, MM). Electronic applications accepted.

UNIVERSITY OF PHOENIX–WEST MICHIGAN CAMPUS, Walker, MI 49544

General Information Proprietary, coed, comprehensive institution. *Graduate housing:* On-campus housing not available.

GRADUATE UNITS

School of Business *Degree program information:* Evening/weekend programs available. Offers business (MBA, MSA). Electronic applications accepted.

UNIVERSITY OF PHOENIX–WICHITA CAMPUS, Wichita, KS 67226-4011

General Information Proprietary, coed, comprehensive institution. *Graduate housing:* On-campus housing not available.

GRADUATE UNITS

School of Business *Degree program information:* Evening/weekend programs available. Offers business (MBA). Electronic applications accepted.

UNIVERSITY OF PITTSBURGH, Pittsburgh, PA 15260

General Information State-related, coed, university. CGS member. *Enrollment:* 28,823 graduate, professional, and undergraduate students; 7,574 full-time matriculated graduate/professional students (4,041 women), 2,878 part-time matriculated graduate/professional students (1,678 women). *Enrollment by degree level:* 1,900 first professional, 4,678 master's, 3,236 doctoral, 638 other advanced degrees. *Graduate faculty:* 3,945 full-time (1,512 women), 852 part-time/adjunct (434 women). Tuition, state resident: full-time $17,304; part-time $701 per credit. Tuition, nonresident: full-time $29,554; part-time $1210 per credit. *Required fees:* $740; $214 per term. Tuition and fees vary according to program. *Student services:* Campus employment opportunities, campus safety program, career counseling, exercise/wellness program, free psychological counseling, international student services, low-cost health insurance, services for students with disabilities, writing training. *Library facilities:* Hillman Library plus 16 others. *Online resources:* library catalog, web page, access to other libraries' catalogs. *Collection:* 6.1 million titles, 87,417 serial subscriptions, 1.2 million audiovisual materials. *Research affiliation:* Technology Collaboration (formerly Pittsburgh Digital Greenhouse), Innovation Works (formerly Ben Franklin Technology Center of Western Pennsylvania), Pittsburgh Life Sciences Greenhouse.

Computer facilities: Computer purchase and lease plans are available. 2,000 computers available on campus for general student use. A campuswide network can be accessed from student residence rooms and from off campus. Online class registration, online class listings, online tuition payment are available. *Web address:* http://www.pitt.edu/.

General Application Contact: Information Contact, 412-624-4141, E-mail: graduate@pitt.edu.

GRADUATE UNITS

Graduate School of Public and International Affairs Students: 371 full-time (187 women), 92 part-time (47 women); includes 32 minority (16 Black or African American, non-Hispanic/Latino; 1 American Indian or Alaska Native, non-Hispanic/Latino; 8 Asian, non-Hispanic/Latino; 7 Hispanic/Latino), 63 international. Average age 25. 708 applicants, 70% accepted, 198 enrolled. *Faculty:* 30 full-time (12 women), 67 part-time/adjunct (25 women). Expenses: Contact institution. *Financial support:* In 2010–11, 132 students received support, including 18 fellowships (averaging $41,325 per year), 5 research assistantships (averaging $41,325 per year); scholarships/grants, tuition waivers (full and partial), unspecified assistantships, and Student employment also available. Support available to part-time students. Financial award application deadline: 2/1. In 2010, 188 master's, 11 doctorates awarded. *Degree program information:* Part-time and evening/weekend programs available. Offers development planning (MPPM); development policy (PhD); foreign and security policy (PhD); international development (MPPM); international political economy (MPPM, PhD); international security studies (MPPM); management of non profit organizations (MPPM); metropolitan management and regional development (MPPM); policy analysis and evaluation (MPPM); public administration (PhD); public and international affairs (MID, MPA, MPIA, MPPM, PhD, MPA/MID); public policy (PhD). *Application deadline:* For fall admission, 2/1 for domestic students, 1/15 for international students; for spring admission, 11/1 for domestic students, 8/1 for international students. *Application fee:* $50. Electronic applications accepted. *Application Contact:* Michael T. Rizzi, Associate Director of Student Services, 412-648-7640, Fax: 412-648-7641, E-mail: rizzim@pitt.edu. *Dean and Professor*, Dr. John T. S. Keeler, 412-648-7636, Fax: 412-648-2605, E-mail: keeler@pitt.edu.

Division of International Development Students: 66 full-time (46 women), 7 part-time (5 women); includes 7 minority (1 Black or African American, non-Hispanic/Latino; 3 Asian, non-Hispanic/Latino; 3 Hispanic/Latino), 11 international. Average age 25. 125 applicants, 82% accepted, 39 enrolled. *Faculty:* 30 full-time (12 women), 67 part-time/adjunct (25 women). Expenses: Contact institution. *Financial support:* In 2010–11, 28 students received support. Scholarships/grants, tuition waivers (full and partial), unspecified assistantships, and student employment available. Financial award application deadline: 2/1. In 2010, 35 master's awarded. *Degree program information:* Part-time programs available. Offers development planning and environmental sustainability (MID); human security (MID); nongovernmental organizations and civil society (MID). *Application deadline:* For fall admission, 2/1 for domestic students, 1/5 for international students; for spring admission, 11/1 for domestic students, 8/1 for international students. *Application fee:* $50. Electronic applications accepted. *Application Contact:* Elizabeth Hruby, Graduate Enrollment Counselor, 412-648-7640, Fax: 412-648-7641, E-mail: eah44@pitt.edu. *Director*, Dr. Paul J. Nelson, 412-648-7645, Fax: 412-648-2605, E-mail: pjnelson@pitt.edu.

Division of Public and Urban Affairs Students: 61 full-time (29 women), 22 part-time (16 women); includes 4 Black or African American, non-Hispanic/Latino; 1 Asian, non-Hispanic/Latino; 1 Hispanic/Latino, 8 international. Average age 25. 119 applicants, 76% accepted, 38 enrolled. *Faculty:* 30 full-time (12 women), 67 part-time/adjunct (25 women). Expenses: Contact institution. *Financial support:* In 2010–11, 18 students received support. Scholarships/grants, tuition waivers (full and partial), unspecified assistantships, and student employment available. Financial award application deadline: 2/1. In 2010, 24 master's awarded. *Degree program information:* Part-time and evening/weekend programs available. Offers policy research and analysis (MPA); public and nonprofit management (MPA); urban and regional affairs (MPA). *Application deadline:* For fall admission, 2/1 for domestic students, 1/15 for international students; for spring admission, 11/1 for domestic students, 8/1 for international students. *Application fee:* $50. Electronic applications accepted. *Application Contact:* Elizabeth A. Hruby, Graduate Enrollment Counselor, 412-648-7640, Fax: 412-648-7641, E-mail: eah44@pitt.edu. *Director*, Dr. David Y. Miller, 412-648-7606, Fax: 412-648-2605, E-mail: dymiller@pitt.edu.

International Affairs Division Students: 187 full-time (93 women), 26 part-time (7 women); includes 17 minority (9 Black or African American, non-Hispanic/Latino; 1 American Indian or Alaska Native, non-Hispanic/Latino; 4 Asian, non-Hispanic/Latino; 3 Hispanic/Latino), 17 international. Average age 25. 325 applicants, 73% accepted, 100 enrolled. *Faculty:* 30 full-time (12 women), 67 part-time/adjunct (25 women). Expenses: Contact institution. *Financial support:* In 2010–11, 44 students received support. Scholarships/grants, tuition waivers (full and partial), unspecified assistantships, and student employment available. Financial award application deadline: 2/1. In 2010, 92 master's awarded. *Degree program information:* Part-time and evening/weekend programs available. Offers global political economy (MPIA); human security (MPIA); security and intelligence studies (MPIA). *Application deadline:* For fall admission, 3/1 for domestic students, 1/15 for international students; for spring admission, 11/1 for domestic students, 8/1 for international students. *Application fee:* $50. Electronic applications accepted. *Application Contact:* Kelly C. McDevitt, Graduate Enrollment Counselor, 412-648-7640, Fax: 412-648-7641, E-mail: mcdevitt@pitt.edu. *Director, International Affairs and International Development Divisions*, Dr. Martin Staniland, 412-648-7656, Fax: 412-648-2605, E-mail: mstan@pitt.edu.

Graduate School of Public Health Students: 404 full-time (290 women), 228 part-time (148 women); includes 47 Black or African American, non-Hispanic/Latino; 1 American Indian or Alaska Native, non-Hispanic/Latino; 39 Asian, non-Hispanic/Latino; 11 Hispanic/Latino; 4 Two or more races, non-Hispanic/Latino, 150 international. Average age 28. 1,555 applicants, 59% accepted, 201 enrolled. *Faculty:* 158 full-time (73 women), 205 part-time/adjunct (88 women). Expenses: Contact institution. *Financial support:* In 2010–11, 184 students received support, including 10 fellowships with full and partial tuition reimbursements available (averaging $4,200 per year), 153 research assistantships with full and partial tuition reimbursements available (averaging $21,698 per year), 21 teaching assistantships with full and partial tuition reimbursements available (averaging $19,964 per year); career-related internships or fieldwork, scholarships/grants, traineeships, health care benefits, tuition waivers (full and partial), and unspecified assistantships also available. Support available to part-time students. In 2010, 153 master's, 45 doctorates awarded. *Degree program information:* Part-time programs available. Offers behavioral and community health sciences (MPH, Dr PH); bioscience of infectious diseases (MPH); biostatistics (MPH, MS, Dr PH, PhD); community and behavioral intervention of infectious diseases (MPH); community-based participatory research and practice (Certificate); environmental and occupational health (MPH, MS, PhD); environmental health risk assessment (Certificate); epidemiology (MPH, MS, Dr PH, PhD); genetic counseling (MS); health policy and management (MHA, MPH); human genetics (MS, PhD); infectious diseases and microbiology (MS, Dr PH, PhD); lesbian, gay, bisexual and transgender health and wellness (Certificate); LGBT health and wellness (Certificate); minority health and health disparities (Certificate); program evaluation (Certificate); public health (MHA, MPH, MS, Dr PH, PhD, Certificate); public health and aging (Certificate); public health genetics (MPH, Certificate); public health preparedness (Certificate). *Application deadline:* For fall admission, 1/4 priority date for domestic and international students; for winter admission, 11/1 priority date for domestic students, 8/1 priority date for international students; for spring admission, 3/1 priority date for domestic students, 2/1 priority date for international students. Applications are processed on a rolling basis. *Application fee:* $115. Electronic applications accepted. *Application Contact:* Karrie Presutti, Admissions Manager, 412-624-3003, Fax: 412-624-3755, E-mail: stuaff@pitt.edu. *Dean,* Dr. Donald S. Burke, 412-624-3001, Fax: 412-624-3013, E-mail: donburke@pitt.edu.

Joint CMU-Pitt PhD Program in Computational and Systems Biology Students: 46 full-time (9 women); includes 22 Asian, non-Hispanic/Latino; 2 Hispanic/Latino; 1 Native Hawaiian or other Pacific Islander, non-Hispanic/Latino, 18 international. Average age 25. 133 applicants, 16% accepted, 7 enrolled. *Faculty:* 78 full-time (17 women). Expenses: Contact institution. *Financial support:* In 2010–11, 46 students received support, including 10 fellowships with full tuition reimbursements available, 36 research assistantships with full tuition reimbursements available (averaging $25,500 per year). Offers computational and systems biology (PhD). *Application deadline:* For fall admission, 1/15 priority date for domestic and international students. *Application fee:* $50. Electronic applications accepted. *Application Contact:* Kelly Gentille, Assistant Programs Coordinator, 412-648-8107, Fax: 412-648-3163, E-mail: kmg120@pitt.edu. *Director,* Dr. Takis Benos, 412-648-3315, Fax: 412-648-3163, E-mail: benos@pitt.edu.

Katz Graduate School of Business Students: 448 full-time (147 women), 506 part-time (173 women); includes 45 Black or African American, non-Hispanic/Latino; 1 American Indian or Alaska Native, non-Hispanic/Latino; 36 Asian, non-Hispanic/Latino; 17 Hispanic/Latino, 204 international. Average age 30. 1,626 applicants, 35% accepted, 306 enrolled. *Faculty:* 82 full-time (25 women), 22 part-time/adjunct (5 women). Expenses: Contact institution. *Financial support:* In 2010–11, 149 students received support, including 11 fellowships (averaging $19,000 per year), 19 research assistantships with full tuition reimbursements available (averaging $19,000 per year), 10 teaching assistantships with full tuition reimbursements available (averaging $23,745 per year); career-related internships or fieldwork, Federal Work-Study, scholarships/grants, health care benefits, and unspecified assistantships also available. Financial award application deadline: 3/1; financial award applicants required to submit FAFSA. In 2010, 365 master's, 4 doctorates awarded. *Degree program information:* Part-time and evening/weekend programs available. Offers accounting (PhD); business (EMBA, MBA, MS, MSIS, PhD, Certificate); business administration (EMBA, MBA, PhD, Certificate); finance (MBA, PhD); information systems (MBA, PhD); international business administration (MBA); marketing (MBA, PhD); operations management (MBA); operations/decision sciences/ artificial intelligence (PhD); organizational behavior and human resource management (MBA, PhD); organizational leadership (Certificate); six sigma (Certificate); strategic planning (PhD); strategy, environment and organizations (MBA); technology, innovation and entrepreneurship (Certificate). *Application deadline:* For fall admission, 4/1 priority date for domestic students, 2/1 priority date for international students. *Application fee:* $50. Electronic applications accepted. *Application Contact:* Cliff McCormick, Director of MBA Admissions, 412-648-1700, Fax: 412-648-1659, E-mail: mba@katz.pitt.edu. *Dean,* Dr. John T. Delaney, 412-648-1556, Fax: 412-648-1552, E-mail: jtdelaney@katz.pitt.edu.

Program in Cultural Studies Expenses: Contact institution. *Financial support:* In 2010–11, 2 fellowships were awarded. Offers cultural studies (Certificate). *Application Contact:* Information Contact, 412-624-4141, E-mail: graduate@pitt.edu.

School of Arts and Sciences Students: 1,577 full-time (728 women), 85 part-time (56 women); includes 186 minority (39 Black or African American, non-Hispanic/Latino; 3 American Indian or Alaska Native, non-Hispanic/Latino; 80 Asian, non-Hispanic/Latino; 57 Hispanic/ Latino; 1 Native Hawaiian or other Pacific Islander, non-Hispanic/Latino; 6 Two or more races, non-Hispanic/Latino), 462 international. 4,450 applicants, 18% accepted, 403 enrolled. *Faculty:* 737 full-time (243 women), 101 part-time/adjunct (35 women). Expenses: Contact institution. *Financial support:* In 2010–11, 1,041 students received support, including 361 fellowships with full tuition reimbursements available (averaging $19,949 per year), 595 research assistantships with full tuition reimbursements available (averaging $17,475 per year), 609 teaching assistantships with full and partial tuition reimbursements available (averaging $16,897 per year); career-related internships or fieldwork, Federal Work-Study, institutionally sponsored loans, scholarships/grants, traineeships, health care benefits, tuition waivers (full and partial), and unspecified assistantships also available. Support available to part-time students. Financial award applicants required to submit FAFSA. In 2010, 143 master's, 150 doctorates, 12 other advanced degrees awarded. *Degree program information:* Part-time programs available. Offers anthropology (MA, PhD); applied linguistics (PhD); applied mathematics (MA, MS); applied statistics (MA, MS); arts and sciences (MA, MFA, MS, PM Sc, PhD, Certificate, Doctoral Certificate, Master's Certificate); chemistry (MS, PhD); classics (MA, PhD); communication (MA, PhD); composition and theory (MA, PhD); computer science (MS, PhD); cultural and critical studies (PhD); East Asian studies (MA); ecology and evolution (PhD); economics (PhD); English (MA); ethnomusicology (MA, PhD); film studies (Certificate); French (MA, PhD); geographical information systems (PM Sc); geology and planetary science (MS, PhD); German (MA, PhD); Hispanic languages and literatures (MA, PhD); Hispanic linguistics (MA, PhD); historical musicology (MA, PhD); history (MA, PhD); history and philosophy of science (MA, PhD); history of art and architecture (MA, PhD); intelligent systems (MS, PhD); Italian (MA); jazz studies (MA, PhD); linguistics (MA); mathematics (MA, MS, PhD); medieval and Renaissance studies (Certificate); molecular, cellular, and developmental biology (PhD); performance pedagogy (MFA); philosophy (MA, PhD); physics (MS, PhD); political science (MA, PhD); psychology (MS, PhD); religion (PhD); religious studies (MA); Slavic languages and literatures (MA, PhD); sociolinguistics (PhD); sociology (MA, PhD); statistics (MA, MS, PhD); TESOL—teaching English to speakers of other languages (Certificate); theatre and performance studies (MA, PhD); women's studies (Doctoral Certificate, Master's Certificate); writing (MFA). *Application deadline:* Applications are processed on a rolling basis. *Application fee:* $50. Electronic applications accepted. *Application Contact:* Dave R. Carmen, Administrative Secretary, 412-624-6094, Fax: 412-624-6855, E-mail: drc41@pitt.edu. *Associate Dean, Graduate Studies and Research,* Dr. Nicole Constable, 412-624-6094, Fax: 412-624-6855, E-mail: constable@fcas.pitt.edu.

Center for Bioethics and Health Law Students: 11 full-time (5 women), 8 part-time (7 women). Average age 35. 11 applicants, 45% accepted, 2 enrolled. *Faculty:* 4 full-time (1 woman), 3 part-time/adjunct (1 woman). Expenses: Contact institution. *Financial support:* Tuition waivers (partial) available. In 2010, 1 master's awarded. *Degree program information:* Part-time programs available. Offers bioethics (MA). *Application deadline:* For fall admission, 2/1 priority date for domestic students, 6/30 for international students. Applications are processed on a rolling basis. *Application fee:* $50. Electronic applications accepted. *Application Contact:* Janet E. Malis, Administrative Assistant, 412-647-5785, Fax: 412-647-5877, E-mail: bioethic@pitt.edu. *Director of Graduate Education,* Dr. Lisa S. Parker, 412-647-5780, Fax: 412-647-5877, E-mail: lisap@pitt.edu.

Center for Neuroscience Students: 77 full-time (37 women); includes 2 Black or African American, non-Hispanic/Latino; 8 Asian, non-Hispanic/Latino; 1 Hispanic/Latino, 14 international. Average age 25. 138 applicants, 22% accepted, 14 enrolled. *Faculty:* 95 full-time (25 women). Expenses: Contact institution. *Financial support:* In 2010–11, 77 students received support, including 35 fellowships with full tuition reimbursements available (averaging $25,550 per year), 40 research assistantships with full tuition reimbursements available (averaging $25,550 per year), 2 teaching assistantships with full tuition reimbursements available (averaging $25,550 per year). Financial award application deadline: 12/1. In 2010, 9 doctorates awarded. Offers neurobiology (PhD); neuroscience (PhD). *Application deadline:* For fall admission, 12/1 priority date for domestic and international students. *Application fee:* $50. Electronic applications accepted. *Application Contact:* Joan M. Blaney, Administrator, 412-624-5043, Fax: 412-624-9198, E-mail: jblaney@pitt.edu. *Co-Director,* Dr. Alan Sved, 412-624-6996, Fax: 412-624-9188.

School of Dental Medicine Students: 376 full-time (135 women); includes 108 minority (11 Black or African American, non-Hispanic/Latino; 1 American Indian or Alaska Native, non-Hispanic/Latino; 72 Asian, non-Hispanic/Latino; 23 Hispanic/Latino; 1 Two or more races, non-Hispanic/Latino), 7 international. Average age 27. 2,660 applicants, 8% accepted, 105 enrolled. *Faculty:* 90 full-time (39 women), 186 part-time/adjunct (50 women). Expenses: Contact institution. *Financial support:* In 2010–11, 258 students received support. Scholarships/ grants and stipends available. Financial award application deadline: 4/30; financial award applicants required to submit FAFSA. In 2010, 73 DMDs, 18 other advanced degrees awarded. Offers craniofacial and maxillofacial surgery (Certificate); dental anesthesia (Certificate); dental medicine (DMD, MDS, Certificate); endodontics (MDS, Certificate); general dentistry (Certificate); general practice residency (Certificate); oral and maxillofacial pathology (Certificate); oral and maxillofacial surgery (Certificate); orthodontics and dentofacial orthopedics (MDS, Certificate); pediatric dentistry (MDS, Certificate); periodontics (MDS, Certificate); prosthodontics (MDS, Certificate). *Application deadline:* For fall admission, 12/1 for domestic and international students. Applications are processed on a rolling basis. *Application fee:* $35 ($50 for international students). Electronic applications accepted. *Application Contact:* Rosemary Mangold, Recruitment/Financial Aid Officer, 412-648-8437, Fax: 412-648-9571, E-mail: mangold@pitt.edu. *Dean,* Dr. Thomas W. Braun, 412-648-8900, Fax: 412-648-8219, E-mail: twb3@pitt.edu.

School of Education Students: 557 full-time (389 women), 579 part-time (410 women); includes 124 minority (76 Black or African American, non-Hispanic/Latino; 17 Asian, non-Hispanic/Latino; 18 Hispanic/Latino; 13 Two or more races, non-Hispanic/Latino), 77 international. Average age 31. 726 applicants, 69% accepted, 326 enrolled. *Faculty:* 98 full-time (55 women), 115 part-time/adjunct (74 women). Expenses: Contact institution. *Financial support:* In 2010–11, 18 fellowships with full and partial tuition reimbursements (averaging $16,462 per year), 86 research assistantships with full and partial tuition reimbursements (averaging $16,000 per year), 50 teaching assistantships with full and partial tuition reimbursements (averaging $14,862 per year) were awarded; career-related internships or fieldwork, Federal Work-Study, institutionally sponsored loans, scholarships/grants, traineeships, tuition waivers (partial), and unspecified assistantships also available. Support available to part-time students. Financial award applicants required to submit FAFSA. In 2010, 363 master's, 33 doctorates awarded. *Degree program information:* Part-time and evening/weekend programs available. Postbaccalaureate distance learning degree programs offered (minimal on-campus study). Offers applied developmental psychology (M Ed, MS, PhD); cognitive studies (PhD); developmental movement (MS); early childhood education (M Ed); early education of disabled students (M Ed); education (M Ed, MA, MAT, MS, Ed D, PhD); education of students with mental and physical disabilities (M Ed); elementary education (M Ed, MAT); English/ communications education (M Ed, MAT); exercise physiology (MS, PhD); foreign languages education (M Ed, MAT); general special education (M Ed); higher education (M Ed, Ed D); higher education management (M Ed, Ed D); learning sciences and policy (PhD); mathematics education (M Ed, MAT, Ed D); reading education (M Ed, Ed D, PhD); research methodology (M Ed, MA, PhD); school leadership (M Ed, Ed D); science education (M Ed, MAT, MS, Ed D); secondary education (M Ed, MAT, MS, Ed D, PhD); social and comparative analysis in education (M Ed, MA, Ed D, PhD); social studies education (M Ed, MAT); special education (M Ed, Ed D, PhD); vision studies (M Ed). *Application deadline:* For fall admission, 2/1 priority date for domestic students, 2/1 for international students; for spring admission, 11/15 priority date for domestic students, 7/1 for international students. Applications are processed on a rolling basis. *Application fee:* $50. Electronic applications accepted. *Application Contact:* Marianne L. Budziszewski, Director of Admissions and Enrollment Services, 412-648-7056, Fax: 412-648-1899, E-mail: soeinfo@pitt.edu. *Dean,* Dr. Alan Lesgold, 412-648-1773, Fax: 412-648-1825, E-mail: al@pitt.edu.

School of Engineering Students: 508 full-time (137 women), 307 part-time (51 women); includes 53 minority (17 Black or African American, non-Hispanic/Latino; 21 Asian, non-Hispanic/Latino; 15 Hispanic/Latino), 293 international. 2,154 applicants, 34% accepted, 237 enrolled. *Faculty:* 112 full-time (16 women), 192 part-time/adjunct (22 women). Expenses: Contact institution. *Financial support:* In 2010–11, 397 students received support, including 72 fellowships with full tuition reimbursements available (averaging $20,772 per year), 247 research assistantships with full tuition reimbursements available (averaging $22,000 per year), 78 teaching assistantships with full tuition reimbursements available (averaging $21,000 per year); scholarships/grants, traineeships, and tuition waivers (full and partial) also available. Financial award application deadline: 4/15. In 2010, 132 master's, 52 doctorates awarded. *Degree program information:* Part-time programs available. Offers bioengineering (MSBENG, PhD); chemical engineering (MS Ch E, PhD); civil and environmental engineering (MSCEE, PhD); computer engineering (MS, PhD); electrical engineering (MSEE, PhD); engineering (MS, MS Ch E, MSBENG, MSCEE, MSEE, MSIE, MSME, MSPE, PhD); industrial engineering (MSIE, PhD); mechanical engineering and materials science (MSME, PhD); petroleum engineering (MSPE). *Application deadline:* For fall admission, 3/1 priority date for domestic students; for spring admission, 7/1 priority date for domestic students. Applications are processed on a rolling basis. *Application fee:* $50. Electronic applications accepted. *Application Contact:* 412-624-9800, Fax: 412-624-9808, E-mail: admin@engrng.pitt.edu. *Dean,* Dr. Gerald D. Holder, 412-624-9811, Fax: 412-624-0412, E-mail: holder@engrng.pitt.edu.

School of Health and Rehabilitation Sciences Students: 625 full-time (463 women), 117 part-time (85 women); includes 53 minority (19 Black or African American, non-Hispanic/ Latino; 19 Asian, non-Hispanic/Latino; 9 Hispanic/Latino; 1 Native Hawaiian or other Pacific Islander, non-Hispanic/Latino; 5 Two or more races, non-Hispanic/Latino), 128 international. Average age 28. 1,687 applicants, 36% accepted, 319 enrolled. *Faculty:* 86 full-time (49 women), 28 part-time/adjunct (12 women). Expenses: Contact institution. *Financial support:* In 2010–11, 44 research assistantships with full and partial tuition reimbursements (averaging $32,720 per year), 6 teaching assistantships with full tuition reimbursements (averaging $34,603 per year) were awarded; fellowships with full tuition reimbursements, career-related internships or fieldwork, Federal Work-Study, scholarships/grants, traineeships, and unspecified assistantships also available. Financial award applicants required to submit FAFSA. In 2010, 220 master's, 71 doctorates awarded. *Degree program information:* Part-time programs available. Offers communication science and disorders (MA, MS, Au D, CScD, PhD); dietetics (MS); health and rehabilitation sciences (MA, MOT, MS, Au D, CScD, DPT, PhD); occupational therapy (MOT); physical therapy (DPT); physician assistant studies (MS); prosthetics and orthotics (MS); rehabilitation science (PhD). *Application deadline:* For fall admission, 1/31 for international students. Applications are processed on a rolling basis. *Application fee:* $50. Electronic applications accepted. *Application Contact:* Shameem Gangjee, Director of Admissions, 412-383-6558, Fax: 412-383-6535, E-mail: admissions@shrs.pitt.edu. *Dean,* Dr. Clifford E. Brubaker, 412-383-6560, Fax: 412-383-6535, E-mail: cliffb@pitt.edu.

School of Information Sciences Students: 376 full-time (217 women), 284 part-time (182 women); includes 23 Black or African American, non-Hispanic/Latino; 3 American Indian or Alaska Native, non-Hispanic/Latino; 15 Asian, non-Hispanic/Latino; 16 Hispanic/Latino, 175 international. 705 applicants, 85% accepted, 238 enrolled. *Faculty:* 28 full-time (6 women), 10 part-time/adjunct (6 women). Expenses: Contact institution. *Financial support:* Fellowships with partial tuition reimbursements, research assistantships with full and partial tuition reimbursements, teaching assistantships with full and partial tuition reimbursements, career-related internships or fieldwork, scholarships/grants, health care benefits, tuition waivers (full and partial), and unspecified assistantships available. Financial award application deadline: 1/15; financial award applicants required to submit FAFSA. In 2010, 315 master's, 15 doctorates, 1 other advanced degree awarded. *Degree program information:* Part-time and evening/ weekend programs available. Postbaccalaureate distance learning degree programs offered (minimal on-campus study). Offers health sciences librarianship (Certificate); information

University of Pittsburgh (continued)

science and technology (MSIS, PhD, Certificate); information sciences (MLIS, MSIS, MST, PhD, Certificate); library and information science (MLIS, PhD); telecommunications and networking (MST, PhD, Certificate). *Application deadline:* For fall admission, 1/15 priority date for domestic and international students; for winter admission, 9/15 priority date for domestic students, 6/15 for international students; for spring admission, 1/15 priority date for domestic students, 12/15 priority date for international students. Applications are processed on a rolling basis. *Application fee:* $50. Electronic applications accepted. *Application Contact:* Shabana Reza, Student Recruiting Coordinator, 412-624-3988, Fax: 412-624-5231, E-mail: sisinq@sis.pitt.edu. *Dean and Professor,* Dr. Ronald L. Larsen, 412-624-5139, Fax: 412-624-5231, E-mail: rlarsen@sis.pitt.edu.

School of Law 2,177 applicants, 37% accepted, 235 enrolled. *Faculty:* 43 full-time (16 women), 104 part-time/adjunct (30 women). Expenses: Contact institution. *Financial support:* In 2010–11, 370 students received support, including 3 fellowships (averaging $6,667 per year), 36 research assistantships (averaging $5,440 per year); teaching assistantships, career-related internships or fieldwork, Federal Work-Study, scholarships/grants, and unspecified assistantships also available. Financial award application deadline: 3/1; financial award applicants required to submit FAFSA. In 2010, 7 first professional degrees, 9 master's awarded. Offers business law (MSL); civil litigation (Certificate); constitutional law (MSL); criminal law and justice (MSL); disabilities law (MSL); dispute resolution (MSL); education law (MSL); elder and estate planning law (MSL); employment and labor law (MSL); environment and real estate law (MSL); environmental law, science and policy (Certificate); family law (MSL); general law and jurisprudence (MSL); health law (Certificate); intellectual property and technology (MSL); intellectual property and technology law (Certificate); international and comparative law (LL M, MSL); international law (Certificate); law (JD, LL M, MSL, Certificate); personal injury and civil litigation (MSL); regulatory law (MSL); self-designed (MSL); sports and entertainment law (MSL). *Application deadline:* For fall admission, 3/1 for domestic students. Applications are processed on a rolling basis. *Application fee:* $55. Electronic applications accepted. *Application Contact:* Charmaine McCall, Assistant Dean of Admissions and Financial Aid, 412-648-1413, Fax: 412-648-1318, E-mail: cmccall@pitt.edu. *Dean,* Mary Crossley, 412-648-1401, Fax: 412-648-2647, E-mail: crossley@pitt.edu.

School of Medicine Students: 975 full-time (463 women), 85 part-time (36 women); includes 358 minority (60 Black or African American, non-Hispanic/Latino; 230 Asian, non-Hispanic/Latino; 48 Hispanic/Latino; 4 Native Hawaiian or other Pacific Islander, non-Hispanic/Latino; 16 Two or more races, non-Hispanic/Latino), 102 international. 6,239 applicants, 9% accepted, 255 enrolled. *Faculty:* 2,116 full-time (687 women), 68 part-time/adjunct (43 women). Expenses: Contact institution. *Financial support:* In 2010–11, 390 students received support, including fellowships with full tuition reimbursements available (averaging $24,650 per year), research assistantships with full tuition reimbursements available (averaging $24,650 per year); teaching assistantships, institutionally sponsored loans, scholarships/grants, traineeships, health care benefits, and unspecified assistantships also available. Financial award application deadline: 4/15; financial award applicants required to submit FAFSA. In 2010, 145 first professional degrees, 32 master's, 51 doctorates, 16 other advanced degrees awarded. Offers biomedical informatics (MS, PhD, Certificate); cell biology and molecular physiology (MS, PhD); cellular and molecular pathology (MS, PhD); clinical and translational science (PhD); clinical research (MS, Certificate); immunology (MS, PhD); integrative molecular biology (PhD); interdisciplinary biomedical sciences (PhD); medical education (MS, Certificate); medicine (MD, MS, PhD, Certificate); molecular biophysics and structural biology (PhD); molecular genetics and developmental biology (MS, PhD); molecular pharmacology (MS, PhD); molecular virology and microbiology (MS, PhD). *Application deadline:* For fall admission, 11/15 for domestic students; for winter admission, 1/15 priority date for domestic students. Applications are processed on a rolling basis. *Application fee:* $85. Electronic applications accepted. *Application Contact:* Dr. Arthur S. Levine, Dean and Senior Vice Chancellor, Health Sciences, 412-648-8975, Fax: 412-648-1236, E-mail: alevine@hs.pitt.edu. *Dean and Senior Vice Chancellor, Health Sciences,* Dr. Arthur S. Levine, 412-648-8975, Fax: 412-648-1236, E-mail: alevine@hs.pitt.edu.

School of Nursing Students: 177 full-time (142 women), 271 part-time (249 women); includes 16 Black or African American, non-Hispanic/Latino; 1 American Indian or Alaska Native, non-Hispanic/Latino; 20 Asian, non-Hispanic/Latino; 1 Hispanic/Latino. Average age 34. 273 applicants, 52% accepted, 122 enrolled. *Faculty:* 55 full-time (48 women). Expenses: Contact institution. *Financial support:* In 2010–11, 35 students received support, including 12 fellowships (averaging $12,700 per year), 13 research assistantships (averaging $10,400 per year), 10 teaching assistantships (averaging $13,100 per year); scholarships/grants, traineeships, health care benefits, and unspecified assistantships also available. Support available to part-time students. Financial award application deadline: 7/1; financial award applicants required to submit FAFSA. In 2010, 95 master's, 5 doctorates awarded. *Degree program information:* Part-time programs available. Offers acute care nurse practitioner (MSN, DNP); adult nurse practitioner (MSN, DNP); clinical nurse leader (MSN); family nurse practitioner (MSN, DNP); medical/surgical clinical nurse specialist (MSN, DNP); neonatal (MSN, DNP); nurse anesthesia (MSN, DNP); nursing (MSN, DNP, PhD); nursing administration (MSN, DNP); nursing informatics (MSN); nursing practice (DNP); pediatric nurse practitioner (MSN, DNP); psychiatric and mental health clinical nurse specialist (MSN, DNP); psychiatric primary care nurse practitioner (MSN, DNP). *Application deadline:* Applications are processed on a rolling basis. *Application fee:* $50. Electronic applications accepted. *Application Contact:* Laurie Lapsley, Administrator of Graduate Student Services, 412-624-9670, Fax: 412-624-2409, E-mail: lapsleyl@pitt.edu. *Dean,* Dr. Jacqueline Dunbar-Jacob, 412-624-7838, Fax: 412-624-2401, E-mail: dunbar@pitt.edu.

School of Pharmacy Students: 479 full-time (271 women), 1 part-time (0 women); includes 60 minority (15 Black or African American, non-Hispanic/Latino; 2 American Indian or Alaska Native, non-Hispanic/Latino; 38 Asian, non-Hispanic/Latino; 5 Hispanic/Latino), 27 international. Average age 23. 1,003 applicants, 15% accepted, 123 enrolled. *Faculty:* 75 full-time (35 women), 61 part-time/adjunct (29 women). Expenses: Contact institution. *Financial support:* In 2010–11, 210 students received support, including 2 fellowships with full tuition reimbursements available (averaging $24,000 per year), 7 research assistantships with full tuition reimbursements available (averaging $24,500 per year), 16 teaching assistantships with full tuition reimbursements available (averaging $23,000 per year); career-related internships or fieldwork, Federal Work-Study, institutionally sponsored loans, scholarships/grants, and health care benefits also available. Financial award application deadline: 10/1. In 2010, 107 first professional degrees, 6 master's, 3 doctorates awarded. Offers pharmaceutical sciences (MS, PhD); pharmacy (Pharm D); pharmacy administration (MS). Electronic applications accepted. *Application Contact:* Marcia L. Borrelli, Director of Student Services, 412-383-9000, Fax: 412-383-9996, E-mail: borrelli@pitt.edu. *Dean,* Dr. Patricia Dowley Kroboth, 412-624-2400, Fax: 412-648-1086.

School of Social Work Students: 406 full-time (346 women), 218 part-time (178 women); includes 121 minority (74 Black or African American, non-Hispanic/Latino; 1 American Indian or Alaska Native, non-Hispanic/Latino; 19 Asian, non-Hispanic/Latino; 13 Hispanic/Latino; 1 Native Hawaiian or other Pacific Islander, non-Hispanic/Latino; 13 Two or more races, non-Hispanic/Latino). Average age 28. 603 applicants, 83% accepted, 293 enrolled. *Faculty:* 20 full-time (12 women), 39 part-time/adjunct (29 women). Expenses: Contact institution. *Financial support:* In 2010–11, 234 students received support, including 1 research assistantship with full tuition reimbursement available (averaging $12,670 per year), 3 teaching assistantships with full tuition reimbursements available (averaging $15,520 per year); fellowships, career-related internships or fieldwork, institutionally sponsored loans, scholarships/grants, traineeships, tuition waivers (full), and unspecified assistantships also available. Financial award application deadline: 3/31; financial award applicants required to submit FAFSA. In 2010, 227 master's, 8 doctorates awarded. *Degree program information:* Part-time programs available. Offers gerontology (Certificate); social work (MSW, PhD). *Application deadline:* For fall admission, 5/1 for domestic and international students. Applications are processed on a rolling basis. *Application fee:* $40. Electronic applications accepted. *Application Contact:* Philip Mack, Director of Admissions, 412-624-6346, Fax: 412-624-6323, E-mail: psm8@pitt.edu. *Dean,* Dr. Larry E. Davis, 412-624-6304, Fax: 412-624-6323, E-mail: ledavis@pitt.edu.

University Center for International Studies Students: 322 full-time (192 women), 19 part-time (14 women); includes 22 minority (8 Black or African American, non-Hispanic/Latino; 3 Asian, non-Hispanic/Latino; 6 Hispanic/Latino; 5 Two or more races, non-Hispanic/Latino), 134 international. Expenses: Contact institution. In 2010, 61 Certificates awarded. Offers African studies (Certificate); Asian studies (Certificate); European Union studies (Certificate); global studies (Certificate); Latin American studies (Certificate); Russian and East European studies (Certificate); West European studies (Certificate). *Application deadline:* Applications are processed on a rolling basis. *Application Contact:* Information Contact, 412-624-4141, E-mail: graduate@pitt.edu. *Director,* Dr. Lawrence F. Feick, 412-648-7374, Fax: 412-624-4672, E-mail: feick@pitt.edu.

UNIVERSITY OF PORTLAND, Portland, OR 97203-5798

General Information Independent-religious, coed, comprehensive institution. *Enrollment:* 3,936 graduate, professional, and undergraduate students; 194 full-time matriculated graduate/professional students (126 women), 357 part-time matriculated graduate/professional students (230 women). *Enrollment by degree level:* 457 master's, 28 doctoral, 66 other advanced degrees. *Graduate faculty:* 57 full-time (29 women), 20 part-time/adjunct (9 women). *Tuition:* Part-time $940 per credit hour. Tuition and fees vary according to program. *Graduate housing:* On-campus housing not available. *Student services:* Campus employment opportunities, campus safety program, career counseling, exercise/wellness program, free psychological counseling, international student services, low-cost health insurance, multicultural affairs office, services for students with disabilities, teacher training, writing training. *Library facilities:* Wilson M. Clark Library plus 1 other. *Online resources:* library catalog, web page, access to other libraries' catalogs. *Collection:* 251,547 titles, 1,103 serial subscriptions, 14,484 audiovisual materials. *Research affiliation:* Portland Area Nursing Consortium, Kaiser Center Health Resources, Oregon Graduate Institute of Science and Technology (applied engineering, applied physics).

Computer facilities: 575 computers available on campus for general student use. A campuswide network can be accessed from student residence rooms and from off campus. Online class registration is available. *Web address:* http://www.up.edu/.

General Application Contact: Dr. Thomas G. Greene, Assistant to the Provost and Dean of the Graduate School, 503-943-7107, Fax: 503-943-7315, E-mail: greene@up.edu.

GRADUATE UNITS

College of Arts and Sciences Expenses: Contact institution. *Financial support:* Teaching assistantships, career-related internships or fieldwork, Federal Work-Study, scholarships/grants, and tuition waivers (partial) available. Support available to part-time students. Financial award application deadline: 3/1; financial award applicants required to submit FAFSA. *Degree program information:* Part-time and evening/weekend programs available. Offers arts and sciences (MA, MFA, MS); communication (MA); directing (MFA); management communication (MS); pastoral ministry (MA). *Application deadline:* For fall admission, 7/15 priority date for domestic and international students; for spring admission, 12/15 priority date for domestic and international students. Applications are processed on a rolling basis. *Application fee:* $50. *Application Contact:* Chris James Olinger, Administrative Assistant, 503-943-7107, Fax: 503-943-7315, E-mail: olingerc@up.edu. *Dean,* Rev. Stephen Rowan, 503-943-7221, E-mail: rowan@up.edu.

Dr. Robert B. Pamplin, Jr. School of Business Students: 55 full-time (24 women), 81 part-time (29 women); includes 18 minority (2 Black or African American, non-Hispanic/Latino; 8 Asian, non-Hispanic/Latino; 5 Hispanic/Latino; 3 Two or more races, non-Hispanic/Latino), 23 international. Average age 30. *Faculty:* 12 full-time (2 women), 7 part-time/adjunct (2 women). Expenses: Contact institution. *Financial support:* Federal Work-Study, scholarships/grants, and tuition waivers (partial) available. Support available to part-time students. Financial award application deadline: 3/1; financial award applicants required to submit FAFSA. In 2010, 55 master's awarded. *Degree program information:* Part-time and evening/weekend programs available. Offers business administration (MBA); entrepreneurship (MBA); finance (MBA, MS); health care management (MBA); marketing (MBA); nonprofit management (EMBA); operations and technology management (MBA); sustainability (MBA). *Application deadline:* For fall admission, 7/15 priority date for domestic and international students; for spring admission, 12/15 priority date for domestic and international students. Applications are processed on a rolling basis. *Application fee:* $50. *Application Contact:* Melissa McCarthy, Academic Specialist, 503-943-7225, E-mail: mccarthy@up.edu. *Associate Dean,* Dr. Howard Feldman, 503-943-7224, E-mail: feldman@up.edu.

School of Education Students: 57 full-time (40 women), 193 part-time (137 women); includes 27 minority (1 Black or African American, non-Hispanic/Latino; 4 Asian, non-Hispanic/Latino; 7 Hispanic/Latino; 12 Native Hawaiian or other Pacific Islander, non-Hispanic/Latino; 3 Two or more races, non-Hispanic/Latino), 55 international. Average age 34. *Faculty:* 14 full-time (8 women), 9 part-time/adjunct (5 women). Expenses: Contact institution. *Financial support:* Federal Work-Study and scholarships/grants available. Support available to part-time students. Financial award application deadline: 3/1; financial award applicants required to submit FAFSA. In 2010, 140 master's awarded. *Degree program information:* Part-time and evening/weekend programs available. Offers education (M Ed, MA, MAT). M Ed also available through the Graduate Outreach Program for teachers residing in the Oregon and Washington state areas. *Application deadline:* For fall admission, 7/15 priority date for domestic and international students; for spring admission, 12/15 priority date for domestic and international students. Applications are processed on a rolling basis. *Application fee:* $50. *Application Contact:* Dr. Bruce Weitzel, Associate Dean, 503-943-7135, E-mail: weitzel@up.edu. *Dean,* Dr. Thomas Greene, 503-943-7135, Fax: 503-943-8042, E-mail: ciriello@up.edu.

School of Engineering Students: 1 full-time (0 women), all international. Average age 22. *Faculty:* 2 full-time (0 women). Expenses: Contact institution. *Financial support:* Teaching assistantships, career-related internships or fieldwork, Federal Work-Study, and scholarships/grants available. Support available to part-time students. Financial award application deadline: 3/1; financial award applicants required to submit FAFSA. In 2010, 1 master's awarded. *Degree program information:* Part-time and evening/weekend programs available. Offers engineering (ME). *Application deadline:* For fall admission, 7/15 priority date for domestic and international students; for spring admission, 12/15 priority date for domestic and international students. Applications are processed on a rolling basis. *Application fee:* $50. *Application Contact:* Dr. Khalid Khan, Director, 503-943-7276, E-mail: khan@up.edu. *Dean,* Dr. Zia Yamayee, 503-943-7314.

School of Nursing Students: 72 full-time (58 women), 47 part-time (41 women); includes 11 minority (2 Black or African American, non-Hispanic/Latino; 3 Asian, non-Hispanic/Latino; 3 Hispanic/Latino; 3 Two or more races, non-Hispanic/Latino), 2 international. Average age 33. *Faculty:* 8 full-time (7 women), 12 part-time/adjunct (10 women). Expenses: Contact institution. *Financial support:* Fellowships, research assistantships, Federal Work-Study and scholarships/grants available. Support available to part-time students. Financial award application deadline: 3/1; financial award applicants required to submit FAFSA. In 2010, 16 master's awarded. *Degree program information:* Part-time and evening/weekend programs available. Post-baccalaureate distance learning degree programs offered (minimal on-campus study). Offers clinical nurse leader (MS); nursing (DNP). *Application deadline:* For fall admission, 11/2 priority date for domestic and international students; for spring admission, 1/7 priority date for domestic and international students. Applications are processed on a rolling basis. *Application fee:* $50. *Application Contact:* Dr. Susan Mascato, Associate Dean, 503-943-7211, E-mail: mascato@up.edu. Dr. Joanne Warner, 503-943-7509, Fax: 503-943-7729, E-mail: warner@up.edu.

UNIVERSITY OF PRINCE EDWARD ISLAND, Charlottetown, PE C1A 4P3, Canada

General Information Province-supported, coed, comprehensive institution. *Graduate housing:* Room and/or apartments available on a first-come, first-served basis to single students; on-campus housing not available to married students. *Research affiliation:* Agriculture Canada Research Station, Diagnostic Chemicals, Ltd., National Research Council Canada Institute for Nutrisciences and Health, PEI Food Technology Centre, Canadian Food Inspection Agency, AquaHealth.

GRADUATE UNITS

Atlantic Veterinary College *Degree program information:* Part-time programs available. Offers anatomy (M Sc, PhD); bacteriology (M Sc, PhD); clinical pharmacology (M Sc, PhD);

clinical sciences (M Sc, PhD); epidemiology (M Sc, PhD); fish health (M Sc, PhD); food animal nutrition (M Sc, PhD); immunology (M Sc, PhD); microanatomy (M Sc, PhD); parasitology (M Sc, PhD); pathology (M Sc, PhD); pharmacology (M Sc, PhD); physiology (M Sc, PhD); toxicology (M Sc, PhD); veterinary medicine (DVM, M Sc, M Vet Sc, PhD); veterinary science (M Vet Sc); virology (M Sc, PhD).

Faculty of Arts *Degree program information:* Part-time programs available. Offers island studies (MA).

Faculty of Education *Degree program information:* Part-time programs available. Offers leadership and learning (M Ed).

Faculty of Science Offers biology (M Sc); chemistry (M Sc).

UNIVERSITY OF PUERTO RICO, MAYAGÜEZ CAMPUS, Mayagüez, PR 00681-9000

General Information Commonwealth-supported, coed, university. *Enrollment:* 924 full-time matriculated graduate/professional students (431 women), 128 part-time matriculated graduate/professional students (48 women). *Enrollment by degree level:* 883 master's, 169 doctoral. *Graduate faculty:* 694 full-time (243 women), 3 part-time/adjunct (all women). *International tuition:* $6126 full-time. Tuition, commonwealth resident: full-time $1188. Tuition, nonresident: full-time $1188. Tuition and fees vary according to course level and course load. *Graduate housing:* On-campus housing not available. *Student services:* Career counseling, child daycare facilities, free psychological counseling, international student services, low-cost health insurance, services for students with disabilities, teacher training. *Library facilities:* General Library plus 1 other. *Online resources:* library catalog, access to other libraries' catalogs. *Research affiliation:* Tropical Agriculture Research Station, Corporation for the Development and Administration of Marine Resources of Puerto Rico.

Computer facilities: A campuswide network can be accessed from off campus. Online class registration is available. *Web address:* http://www.uprm.edu/.

General Application Contact: Carmen Figueroa, Student Affairs Official, 787-265-3809, Fax: 787-265-5489, E-mail: carmen.figueroa11@upr.edu.

GRADUATE UNITS

Graduate Studies Students: 924 full-time (431 women), 128 part-time (48 women); includes 959 Hispanic/Latino, 75 international. Average age 25. 259 applicants, 58% accepted, 80 enrolled. Expenses: Contact institution. *Financial support:* In 2010–11, 426 research assistantships with tuition reimbursements (averaging $15,000 per year), 522 teaching assistantships with tuition reimbursements (averaging $8,500 per year) were awarded; career-related internships or fieldwork, Federal Work-Study, and institutionally sponsored loans also available. In 2010, 224 master's, 26 doctorates awarded. *Degree program information:* Part-time and evening/weekend programs available. *Application deadline:* For fall admission, 2/15 for domestic and international students; for spring admission, 9/15 for domestic and international students. Applications are processed on a rolling basis. *Application fee:* $25. Electronic applications accepted. *Application Contact:* Carmen Figueroa, Student Affairs Official, 787-265-3809, Fax: 787-265-5489, E-mail: carmen.figueroa11@upr.edu. *Director,* Dr. Anand D. Sharma, 787-265-3809.

College of Agricultural Sciences Students: 144 full-time (74 women), 14 part-time (3 women); includes 72 Hispanic/Latino, 8 international. 33 applicants, 76% accepted, 12 enrolled. Expenses: Contact institution. *Financial support:* In 2010–11, 60 research assistantships with tuition reimbursements (averaging $15,000 per year), 44 teaching assistantships with tuition reimbursements (averaging $8,500 per year) were awarded; career-related internships or fieldwork, Federal Work-Study, and institutionally sponsored loans also available. In 2010, 14 master's awarded. *Degree program information:* Part-time programs available. Offers agricultural economics (MS); agricultural education (MS); agricultural extension (MS); agricultural sciences (MS); agronomy (MS); animal industries (MS); crop protection (MS); food science and technology (MS); horticulture (MS); soils (MS). *Application deadline:* For fall admission, 2/15 for domestic and international students; for spring admission, 9/15 for domestic and international students. Applications are processed on a rolling basis. *Application fee:* $25. *Application Contact:* Carmen Figueroa, Student Affairs Official, 787-265-3809, Fax: 787-265-5489, E-mail: carmen.figueroa11@upr.edu. *Associate Dean,* Prof. Aristides Armstrong, 787-832-4040 Ext. 2181, E-mail: aristides.armstrong@upr.edu.

College of Arts and Sciences Students: 369 full-time (201 women), 24 part-time (16 women); includes 279 Hispanic/Latino, 103 international. 95 applicants, 47% accepted, 32 enrolled. Expenses: Contact institution. *Financial support:* In 2010–11, 379 students received support, including 98 research assistantships with tuition reimbursements available (averaging $15,000 per year), 258 teaching assistantships with tuition reimbursements available (averaging $8,500 per year); Federal Work-Study and institutionally sponsored loans also available. In 2010, 46 master's awarded. *Degree program information:* Part-time programs available. Offers applied mathematics (MS); arts and sciences (MA, MS, PhD); biology (MS); chemistry (MS, PhD); English education (MA); geology (MS); Hispanic studies (MA); marine sciences (MS, PhD); physical education (MA); physics (MS); pure mathematics (MS); scientific computation (MS); statistics (MS). *Application deadline:* For fall admission, 2/15 for domestic and international students; for spring admission, 9/15 for domestic and international students. Applications are processed on a rolling basis. *Application fee:* $25. *Application Contact:* Nancy Damiani, Secretary, 787-832-4040 Ext. 3828, Fax: 787-265-1225, E-mail: nancyi.damiani@upr.edu. *Dean,* Dr. Juan Lopez-Garriga, 787-832-4040 Ext. 3828, Fax: 787-265-1225, E-mail: juan.lopez16@upr.edu.

College of Business Administration Students: 47 full-time (28 women), 36 part-time (16 women); includes 79 Hispanic/Latino, 4 international. 19 applicants, 47% accepted, 4 enrolled. Expenses: Contact institution. *Financial support:* In 2010–11, fellowships (averaging $12,000 per year), 2 research assistantships (averaging $15,000 per year), teaching assistantships (averaging $8,500 per year) were awarded; Federal Work-Study and institutionally sponsored loans also available. In 2010, 15 master's awarded. *Degree program information:* Part-time and evening/weekend programs available. Offers business administration (MBA); finance (MBA); human resources (MBA); industrial management (MBA). *Application deadline:* For fall admission, 2/15 for domestic and international students; for spring admission, 9/15 for domestic and international students. Applications are processed on a rolling basis. *Application fee:* $25. *Application Contact:* Milagros Soto, Student Administrator, 787-265-3887, Fax: 787-832-5320, E-mail: milagros.soto1@upr.edu. *Graduate Student Coordinator,* Dr. Rosario Ortiz, 787-265-3800, Fax: 787-832-5320, E-mail: rosario.ortiz@upr.edu.

College of Engineering Students: 365 full-time (129 women), 53 part-time (12 women); includes 293 Hispanic/Latino, 124 international. 112 applicants, 64% accepted, 32 enrolled. Expenses: Contact institution. *Financial support:* In 2010–11, 294 students received support, including 1 fellowship (averaging $12,000 per year), 185 research assistantships (averaging $15,000 per year), 108 teaching assistantships (averaging $8,500 per year); Federal Work-Study and institutionally sponsored loans also available. In 2010, 51 master's, 3 doctorates awarded. *Degree program information:* Part-time programs available. Offers chemical engineering (ME, MS, PhD); civil engineering (ME, MS, PhD); computer and information sciences and engineering (PhD); computer engineering (ME, MS); computing and information sciences and engineering (PhD); electrical engineering (ME, MS); engineering (ME, MS, PhD); industrial engineering (ME, MS); management systems engineering (ME); mechanical engineering (ME, MS). *Application deadline:* For fall admission, 2/15 for domestic and international students; for spring admission, 9/15 for domestic and international students. Applications are processed on a rolling basis. *Application fee:* $25. *Application Contact:* Dr. Agustin Rullan, Graduate Affairs Officer, 787-265-3823, Fax: 787-833-6965, E-mail: agustin.rullan@upr.edu. *Dean,* Dr. Jaime Seguel, 787-265-3823, Fax: 787-833-1190, E-mail: jaime.seguel@upr.edu.

UNIVERSITY OF PUERTO RICO, MEDICAL SCIENCES CAMPUS, San Juan, PR 00936-5067

General Information Commonwealth-supported, coed, primarily women, university. *Graduate housing:* On-campus housing not available.

GRADUATE UNITS

Graduate School of Public Health *Degree program information:* Part-time programs available. Offers biostatistics (MPH); demography (MS); developmental disabilities-early intervention (Certificate); environmental health (MS, Dr PH); epidemiology (MPH, MS); evaluative research of health systems (MS); gerontology (MPH, Certificate); health services administration (MHSA, MS); industrial hygiene (MS); maternal and child health (MPH); nurse midwifery (MPH, Certificate); nutrition (MS); public health (MHSA, MPH, MPHE, MS, Dr PH, Certificate); public health education (MPHE); school health promotion (Certificate).

School of Dental Medicine Offers dental medicine (DMD, Certificate); dentistry (DMD, Certificate); general dentistry (Certificate); oral and maxillofacial surgery (Certificate); orthodontics (Certificate); pediatric dentistry (Certificate); prosthodontics (Certificate). Electronic applications accepted.

School of Health Professions Offers audiology (Au D); clinical laboratory science (MS); clinical research (MS, Graduate Certificate); cytotechnology (Certificate); dietetics (Certificate); health information administration (MS); health professions (MS, Au D, Certificate); medical technology (Certificate); occupational therapy (MS); physical therapy (MS); speech-language pathology (MS). Electronic applications accepted.

School of Medicine Offers medicine (MD, MS, PhD). Electronic applications accepted.

Division of Graduate Studies Offers anatomy (MS, PhD); biochemistry (MS, PhD); biomedical sciences (MS, PhD); microbiology and medical zoology (MS, PhD); pharmacology and toxicology (MS, PhD); physiology (MS, PhD). Electronic applications accepted.

School of Nursing Offers adult and elderly nursing (MSN); child and adolescent nursing (MSN); critical care nursing (MSN); family and community nursing (MSN); family nurse practitioner (MSN); maternity nursing (MSN); mental health and psychiatric nursing (MSN). Electronic applications accepted.

School of Pharmacy *Degree program information:* Part-time and evening/weekend programs available. Offers industrial pharmacy (MS); pharmaceutical sciences (MS); pharmacy (Pharm D). The MS in Pharmacy program is not admitting students in the academic year 2010-2011. Electronic applications accepted.

UNIVERSITY OF PUERTO RICO, RÍO PIEDRAS, San Juan, PR 00931-3300

General Information Commonwealth-supported, coed, university. CGS member. *Graduate housing:* Room and/or apartments available to single students; on-campus housing not available to married students. Housing application deadline: 6/15. *Research affiliation:* U. S. Department of Education (DOE) (social sciences, general studies), U. S. Department of Health and Human Services (social sciences, biology), National Science Foundation (ecology, biology), Ocean Conservancy (ecology, biology), Ford International (ecology), U. S. Department of Education (DOE) (physics, biology).

GRADUATE UNITS

College of Business Administration *Degree program information:* Part-time programs available. Offers accounting (MBA); finance (MBA, PhD); general business (MBA); human resources management (MBA); international trade and business (MBA, PhD); marketing (MBA); operations management (MBA); quantitative methods (MBA).

College of Education *Degree program information:* Part-time programs available. Offers biology education (M Ed); chemistry education (M Ed); curriculum and teaching (Ed D); early child education (M Ed); education (M Ed, MS, Ed D); educational research and evaluation (M Ed); exercise sciences (MS); family ecology and nutrition (M Ed); guidance and counseling (M Ed, Ed D); history education (M Ed); mathematics education (M Ed); physics education (M Ed); school administration and supervision (M Ed, Ed D); Spanish education (M Ed); special and differentiated education (M Ed); teaching English as a second language (M Ed).

College of Humanities *Degree program information:* Part-time programs available. Offers Caribbean history (PhD); Caribbean linguistics (PhD); Caribbean literature (PhD); comparative literature (MA); English (MA); Hispanic linguistics (PhD); Hispanic studies (MA); history (MA); humanities (MA, PhD, Certificate); Latin American literature (PhD); linguistics (MA); philosophy (MA); Puerto Rican history (PhD); Puerto Rican literature (PhD); Spanish literature (PhD); translation (MA, Certificate).

College of Natural Sciences *Degree program information:* Part-time programs available. Offers chemical physics (PhD); chemistry (MS, PhD); ecology/systematics (MS, PhD); environmental sciences (MS, PhD); evolution/genetics (MS, PhD); mathematics (MS, PhD); molecular/cellular biology (MS, PhD); natural sciences (MS, PhD); neuroscience (MS, PhD); physics (MS).

College of Social Sciences *Degree program information:* Part-time programs available. Offers clinical psychology (MA); economics (MA); industrial organizational psychology (MA); investigative academic psychology (MA); psychology (PhD); social sciences (MA, MPA, MRC, MSW, PhD); social-community psychology (MA); sociology (MA).

Graduate School of Rehabilitation Counseling *Degree program information:* Part-time programs available. Offers rehabilitation counseling (MRC).

Graduate School of Social Work *Degree program information:* Part-time programs available. Offers social work (MSW, PhD).

School of Public Administration *Degree program information:* Part-time programs available. Offers public administration (MPA).

Graduate School of Information Sciences and Technologies *Degree program information:* Part-time programs available. Offers administration of academic libraries (PMC); administration of public libraries (PMC); administration of special libraries (PMC); consultant in information services (PMC); documents and files administration (Post-Graduate Certificate); electronic information resources analyst (Post-Graduate Certificate); information science (MIS); librarianship and information services (MLS); school librarian (Post-Graduate Certificate); school librarian distance education mode (Post-Graduate Certificate); specialist in legal information (PMC).

Graduate School of Planning *Degree program information:* Part-time programs available. Offers economic planning systems (MP); environmental planning (MP); social policy and planning (MP); urban and territorial planning (MP).

School of Architecture *Degree program information:* Part-time programs available. Offers architecture (M Arch).

School of Communication *Degree program information:* Part-time programs available. Offers communication (MA); communication theory and research (MA); journalism (MA).

School of Law *Degree program information:* Part-time and evening/weekend programs available. Offers law (JD, LL M).

UNIVERSITY OF PUGET SOUND, Tacoma, WA 98416

General Information Independent, coed, comprehensive institution. *Graduate housing:* On-campus housing not available.

GRADUATE UNITS

Graduate Studies Electronic applications accepted.

School of Education Offers education (M Ed, MAT); elementary education (MAT); mental health counseling (M Ed); pastoral counseling (M Ed); school counseling (M Ed); secondary education (MAT). Electronic applications accepted.

School of Occupational Therapy and Physical Therapy Offers occupational therapy (MOT, MSOT); occupational therapy and physical therapy (MOT, MSOT, DPT); physical therapy (DPT). Electronic applications accepted.

UNIVERSITY OF REDLANDS, Redlands, CA 92373-0999

General Information Independent, coed, comprehensive institution. *Graduate housing:* Rooms and/or apartments available on a first-come, first-served basis to single students and available to married students. Housing application deadline: 8/19. *Research affiliation:* Environmental Systems Research Institute (geographic information systems).

University of Redlands (continued)

GRADUATE UNITS

College of Arts and Sciences Offers arts and sciences (MM, MS); communicative disorders (MS); geographic information systems (MS). Electronic applications accepted.

School of Music *Degree program information:* Part-time programs available. Offers music (MM).

School of Business *Degree program information:* Evening/weekend programs available. Offers business (MBA); information technology (MS); management (MA).

School of Education *Degree program information:* Part-time and evening/weekend programs available. Offers education (MA, Ed D, Certificate).

UNIVERSITY OF REGINA, Regina, SK S4S 0A2, Canada

General Information Province-supported, coed, university. *Enrollment:* 11,913 graduate, professional, and undergraduate students; 724 full-time matriculated graduate/professional students (338 women), 528 part-time matriculated graduate/professional students (338 women). *Enrollment by degree level:* 1,023 master's, 224 doctoral. *Graduate faculty:* 514 full-time (187 women), 287 part-time/adjunct (119 women). *Graduate tuition:* Tuition and fees charges are reported in Canadian dollars. *International tuition:* $4745 Canadian dollars full-time. *Tuition, area resident:* Full-time $3245 Canadian dollars; part-time $180.25 Canadian dollars per credit hour. *Required fees:* $494 Canadian dollars; $115.25 Canadian dollars per credit hour. $115.25 Canadian dollars per semester. Tuition and fees vary according to program. *Graduate housing:* Room and/or apartments available on a first-come, first-served basis to single students; on-campus housing not available to married students. Typical cost: $6000 Canadian dollars per year ($12,000 Canadian dollars including board). Room and board charges vary according to board plan, campus/location and housing facility selected. *Student services:* Campus employment opportunities, campus safety program, career counseling, child daycare facilities, exercise/wellness program, free psychological counseling, grant writing training, international student services, low-cost health insurance, multicultural affairs office, services for students with disabilities, teacher training, writing training. *Library facilities:* Dr. John Archer Library plus 3 others. *Online resources:* library catalog, web page, access to other libraries' catalogs. *Collection:* 1.1 million titles, 29,253 serial subscriptions, 13,612 audiovisual materials. *Research affiliation:* TR Labs (telecommunications), Regional Centre of Expertise on Education for Sustainable Development in Saskatchewan (sustainable development), Saskatchewan Population Health and Evaluation Research Unit (health research), Petroleum Technology Research Center (green energy technologies), Canadian Plains Research Centre (CPRC) (climate change adaptation), Prairie Adaptation Research Collaborative (PARC-UR) (climate change and adaptation options).

Computer facilities: 193 computers available on campus for general student use. A campuswide network can be accessed from student residence rooms. Online class registration is available. *Web address:* http://www.uregina.ca/.

General Application Contact: Dr. Dongyan Blachford, Associate Dean, 306-585-5186, Fax: 306-337-2444, E-mail: grad.studies@uregina.ca.

GRADUATE UNITS

Faculty of Graduate Studies and Research Students: 724 full-time (338 women), 528 part-time (338 women). 1,315 applicants, 37% accepted. *Faculty:* 514 full-time (187 women), 287 part-time/adjunct (119 women). Expenses: Contact institution. *Financial support:* In 2010–11, 115 fellowships (averaging $19,115 per year), 42 research assistantships (averaging $11,138 per year), 160 teaching assistantships (averaging $6,925 per year) were awarded; career-related internships or fieldwork, institutionally sponsored loans, and scholarships/grants also available. Financial award application deadline: 6/15. In 2010, 307 master's, 31 doctorates awarded. *Degree program information:* Part-time and evening/weekend programs available. *Application deadline:* For fall admission, 3/15 priority date for domestic students, 3/15 for international students; for winter admission, 8/15 priority date for domestic students, 8/15 for international students; for spring admission, 9/15 priority date for domestic students, 9/15 for international students. Applications are processed on a rolling basis. *Application fee:* $100. Electronic applications accepted. *Application Contact:* Dr. Dongyan Blachford, Associate Dean, 306-585-5186, Fax: 306-337-2444, E-mail: dongyan.blachford@uregina.ca. *Dean,* Dr. Rod Kelln, 306-585-5185, Fax: 306-337-2444, E-mail: rod.kelln@uregina.ca.

Faculty of Arts Students: 118 full-time (78 women), 47 part-time (31 women). 106 applicants, 48% accepted. *Faculty:* 108 full-time (47 women), 12 part-time/adjunct (5 women). Expenses: Contact institution. *Financial support:* In 2010–11, 19 fellowships (averaging $19,263 per year), 8 research assistantships (averaging $16,500 per year), 22 teaching assistantships (averaging $6,819 per year) were awarded; career-related internships or fieldwork and scholarships/grants also available. Financial award application deadline: 6/15. In 2010, 35 master's awarded. *Degree program information:* Part-time programs available. Offers anthropology (MA); applied economics and public policy (MA); arts (M Sc, MA, PhD); Canadian plains studies (MA, PhD); clinical psychology (MA, PhD); English (MA); experimental and applied psychology (MA, PhD); French (MA); geography (M Sc, MA); gerontology (M Sc, MA); history (MA); human justice (MA); justice studies (MA); linguistics (MA); philosophy (MA); police studies (MA); political science (MA); religious studies (MA); social and political thought (MA); social studies (MA); sociology (MA); women's studies (MA). *Application deadline:* For fall admission, 2/15 for domestic and international students; for winter admission, 9/15 for domestic and international students. Applications are processed on a rolling basis. *Application fee:* $100. Electronic applications accepted. *Application Contact:* Dr. Thomas Bredohl, Associate Dean, Research and Graduate Studies, 306-585-5324, Fax: 306-585-5368, E-mail: thomas.bredohl@uregina.ca. *Dean,* Dr. Richard Kleer, 306-585-4895, Fax: 306-585-5368, E-mail: richard.kleer@uregina.ca.

Faculty of Education Students: 89 full-time (67 women), 227 part-time (174 women). 218 applicants, 75% accepted. *Faculty:* 40 full-time (22 women), 2 part-time/adjunct (0 women). Expenses: Contact institution. *Financial support:* In 2010–11, 17 fellowships (averaging $19,412 per year), 1 research assistantship (averaging $16,500 per year), 7 teaching assistantships (averaging $6,853 per year) were awarded; career-related internships or fieldwork and scholarships/grants also available. Financial award application deadline: 6/15. In 2010, 78 master's, 3 doctorates awarded. *Degree program information:* Part-time programs available. Offers adult education (MA Ed); curriculum and instruction (M Ed); education (M Ed, MA Ed, MHRD, PhD, Master's Certificate); educational administration (M Ed); educational psychology (M Ed); human resources development (MHRD). *Application deadline:* 2/15 for domestic and international students. *Application fee:* $100. Electronic applications accepted. *Application Contact:* Tania Gates, Graduate Program Coordinator, 306-585-4506, Fax: 306-585-5387, E-mail: edgrad@uregina.ca. *Associate Dean, Research and Graduate Programs,* Dr. Rod Dolmage, 306-585-4816, Fax: 306-585-5387, E-mail: rod.dolmage@uregina.ca.

Faculty of Engineering and Applied Science Students: 180 full-time (38 women), 27 part-time (6 women). 323 applicants, 46% accepted. *Faculty:* 45 full-time (7 women), 2 part-time/adjunct (0 women). Expenses: Contact institution. *Financial support:* In 2010–11, 22 fellowships (averaging $18,955 per year), 12 research assistantships (averaging $17,125 per year), 32 teaching assistantships (averaging $6,893 per year) were awarded; career-related internships or fieldwork and scholarships/grants also available. Financial award application deadline: 6/15. In 2010, 35 master's, 11 doctorates awarded. *Degree program information:* Part-time programs available. Offers electronic systems engineering (M Eng, MA Sc, PhD); engineering and applied science (M Eng, MA Sc, PhD); environmental systems engineering (M Eng, MA Sc, PhD); industrial systems engineering (M Eng, MA Sc, PhD); petroleum systems engineering (M Eng, MA Sc, PhD); process systems engineering (M Eng, MA Sc, PhD); software systems engineering (M Eng, MA Sc, PhD). *Application deadline:* For fall admission, 3/31 for domestic and international students; for winter admission, 7/31 for domestic and international students; for spring admission, 11/30 for domestic and international students. *Application fee:* $100. Electronic applications accepted. *Application Contact:* Melissa Dyck, Administrative Contact, 306-337-2603, Fax: 306-585-4855, E-mail: melissa.dyck@uregina.ca. *Dean,* Dr. Paitoon Tontiwachwuthikul, 306-585-4160, Fax: 306-585-4855, E-mail: paitoon.tontiwachwuthikul@uregina.ca.

Faculty of Fine Arts Students: 18 full-time (9 women), 1 (woman) part-time. 13 applicants, 69% accepted. *Faculty:* 32 full-time (18 women). Expenses: Contact institution. *Financial support:* In 2010–11, 9 students received support, including 3 fellowships (averaging $18,000 per year), 2 research assistantships (averaging $18,000 per year), 4 teaching assistantships (averaging $6,759 per year); scholarships/grants also available. Financial award application deadline: 6/15. In 2010, 1 master's awarded. *Degree program information:* Part-time programs available. Offers ceramics (MFA); conducting (MMus); drawing (MFA); fine arts (MA, MFA, MMus); intermedia (MFA); media production (MFA); media studies (MA); music theory (MA); musicology (MA); painting (MFA); sculpture (MFA). *Application deadline:* For fall admission, 2/15 for domestic and international students. *Application fee:* $100. *Application Contact:* Dr. Carmen Robertson, Graduate Program Coordinator, 306-337-2227, Fax: 306-585-5526, E-mail: carmen.robertson@uregina.ca. *Dean,* Dr. Sheila Petty, 306-585-5510, Fax: 306-585-5544, E-mail: sheila.petty@uregina.ca.

Faculty of Kinesiology and Health Studies Students: 18 full-time (8 women), 14 part-time (9 women). 14 applicants, 86% accepted. *Faculty:* 17 full-time (9 women), 1 (woman) part-time/adjunct. Expenses: Contact institution. *Financial support:* In 2010–11, 5 fellowships (averaging $18,000 per year), 2 research assistantships (averaging $16,500 per year), 6 teaching assistantships (averaging $6,759 per year) were awarded; scholarships/grants also available. Financial award application deadline: 6/15. In 2010, 5 master's, 2 doctorates awarded. Offers kinesiology and health studies (M Sc, PhD). *Application deadline:* Applications are processed on a rolling basis. *Application fee:* $100. Electronic applications accepted. *Application Contact:* Dr. Shanthi Johnson, Graduate Program Coordinator, 306-585-3180, Fax: 306-585-5693, E-mail: shanthi.johnson@uregina.ca. *Dean,* Dr. Craig Chamberlin, 306-585-4535, Fax: 306-585-5441, E-mail: shanthi.johnson@uregina.ca.

Faculty of Science Students: 123 full-time (52 women), 26 part-time (6 women). 149 applicants, 42% accepted. *Faculty:* 69 full-time (12 women). Expenses: Contact institution. *Financial support:* In 2010–11, 25 fellowships (averaging $20,040 per year), 9 research assistantships (averaging $17,667 per year), 32 teaching assistantships (averaging $7,567 per year) were awarded; career-related internships or fieldwork and scholarships/grants also available. Financial award application deadline: 6/15. In 2010, 33 master's, 11 doctorates awarded. *Degree program information:* Part-time programs available. Offers analytical/environmental chemistry (M Sc, PhD); biology (M Sc, PhD); biophysics of biological interfaces (M Sc, PhD); computer science (M Sc, PhD); enzymology/chemical biology (M Sc, PhD); geology (M Sc, PhD); inorganic/organometallic chemistry (M Sc, PhD); mathematics (M Sc, MA, PhD); physics (M Sc, PhD); science (M Sc, MA, PhD); signal transduction and mechanisms of cancer cell regulation (M Sc, PhD); statistics (M Sc, MA, PhD); supramolecular organic photochemistry and photophysics (M Sc, PhD); synthetic organic chemistry (M Sc, PhD); theoretical/computational chemistry (M Sc, PhD). *Application deadline:* Applications are processed on a rolling basis. *Application fee:* $100. Electronic applications accepted. *Application Contact:* Information Contact. *Dean,* Dr. Brien Maguire, 306-585-4143, Fax: 306-585-4291, E-mail: brien.maguire@uregina.ca.

Faculty of Social Work Students: 26 full-time (25 women), 37 part-time (29 women). 43 applicants, 72% accepted. *Faculty:* 17 full-time (10 women), 1 (woman) part-time/adjunct. Expenses: Contact institution. *Financial support:* In 2010–11, 3 fellowships (averaging $18,000 per year), 2 teaching assistantships (averaging $6,759 per year) were awarded; research assistantships, career-related internships or fieldwork and scholarships/grants also available. Financial award application deadline: 6/15. In 2010, 22 master's awarded. *Degree program information:* Part-time programs available. Offers social work (MASW, MSW). *Application deadline:* For fall admission, 1/31 for domestic and international students. *Application fee:* $100. Electronic applications accepted. *Application Contact:* Dr. Judy White, Graduate Program Coordinator, 306-664-7375, E-mail: judy.white@uregina.ca. *Dean,* Dr. David Schantz, 306-585-4037, E-mail: david.schantz@uregina.ca.

Johnson-Shoyama Graduate School of Public Policy Students: 60 full-time (28 women), 71 part-time (36 women). 101 applicants, 72% accepted. *Faculty:* 7 full-time (3 women). Expenses: Contact institution. *Financial support:* In 2010–11, 11 fellowships (averaging $18,000 per year), 2 research assistantships (averaging $16,500 per year), 15 teaching assistantships (averaging $6,759 per year) were awarded; scholarships/grants also available. Financial award application deadline: 6/15. In 2010, 48 master's awarded. *Degree program information:* Part-time programs available. Offers economic analysis for public policy (Master's Certificate); health systems management (Master's Certificate); health systems research (MPP); non-profit management (Master's Certificate); public management (MPA, Master's Certificate); public policy (MPA, MPP, PhD); public policy analysis (Master's Certificate). *Application deadline:* For fall admission, 2/1 for domestic and international students. *Application fee:* $100. Electronic applications accepted. *Application Contact:* Elaine Groenendyk, Program Advisor, 306-585-5462, Fax: 306-585-5461, E-mail: elaine.groenendyk@uregina.ca. *Director,* Dr. Michael Atkinson, 306-996-1984, Fax: 306-585-5461, E-mail: michael.atkinson@usask.ca.

Kenneth Levene Graduate School of Business Students: 85 full-time (28 women), 73 part-time (43 women). 191 applicants, 75% accepted. *Faculty:* 51 full-time (14 women), 10 part-time/adjunct (0 women). Expenses: Contact institution. *Financial support:* In 2010–11, 9 fellowships (averaging $18,000 per year), 2 research assistantships (averaging $16,500 per year), 8 teaching assistantships (averaging $6,759 per year) were awarded; scholarships/grants also available. Financial award application deadline: 6/15. In 2010, 46 master's awarded. *Degree program information:* Part-time and evening/weekend programs available. Offers business (Master's Certificate); business administration (MBA); executive business administration (MBA); human resources management (MHRM, Master's Certificate); international business (MBA); leadership (M Admin); organizational leadership (Master's Certificate); project management (Master's Certificate). *Application deadline:* Applications are processed on a rolling basis. *Application fee:* $100. Electronic applications accepted. *Application Contact:* Steve Wield, Manager, 306-337-8463, Fax: 306-585-5361, E-mail: steve.wield@uregina.ca. *Dean,* Dr. Anne Lavack, 306-585-4162, Fax: 306-585-4805, E-mail: anne.lavack@uregina.ca.

UNIVERSITY OF RHODE ISLAND, Kingston, RI 02881

General Information State-supported, coed, university. CGS member. *Enrollment:* 16,294 graduate, professional, and undergraduate students; 1,819 full-time matriculated graduate/professional students (1,062 women), 1,012 part-time matriculated graduate/professional students (589 women). *Enrollment by degree level:* 629 first professional, 1,378 master's, 654 doctoral, 170 other advanced degrees. *Graduate faculty:* 556 full-time (240 women), 56 part-time/adjunct (23 women). Tuition, state resident: full-time $9588; part-time $533 per credit hour. Tuition, nonresident: full-time $22,968; part-time $1276 per credit hour. *Required fees:* $1282; $68 per semester. Tuition and fees vary according to program. *Graduate housing:* Rooms and/or apartments available on a first-come, first-served basis to single and married students. Typical cost: $6878 per year for single students; $7812 per year for married students. Housing application deadline: 5/1. *Student services:* Campus employment opportunities, campus safety program, career counseling, free psychological counseling, international student services, low-cost health insurance, multicultural affairs office, services for students with disabilities. *Library facilities:* Robert L. Carothers Library & Learning Commons. *Online resources:* library catalog, web page. *Research affiliation:* U. S. Department of Agriculture (USDA)/University of Rhode Island (food stamp nutrition education project), Sustainable Coastal Communities and Ecosystems (SUCCESS)–Leader with Associates, Rhode Island Network for Molecular Toxicology, Rhode Island Sea Grant Omnibus 2008-2010, Rhode Island Teacher Education Renewal (RITER), Toward the 'First Census of Marine Life"-Education and Outreach Strategies.

Computer facilities: Computer purchase and lease plans are available. 488 computers available on campus for general student use. A campuswide network can be accessed from student residence rooms and from off campus. Online class registration is available. *Web address:* http://www.uri.edu/.

General Application Contact: Nasser H. Zawia, Dean of the Graduate School, 401-874-5909, Fax: 401-874-5787, E-mail: nzawia@uri.edu.

GRADUATE UNITS

Graduate School Students: 1,819 full-time (1,062 women), 1,012 part-time (589 women); includes 330 minority (81 Black or African American, non-Hispanic/Latino; 11 American Indian or Alaska Native, non-Hispanic/Latino; 123 Asian, non-Hispanic/Latino; 84 Hispanic/Latino; 24 Native Hawaiian or other Pacific Islander, non-Hispanic/Latino; 7 Two or more races, non-Hispanic/Latino), 223 international. *Faculty:* 556 full-time (240 women), 46 part-time/adjunct (23 women). Expenses: Contact institution. *Financial support:* In 2010–11, 144 research assistantships with full and partial tuition reimbursements (averaging $10,444 per year), 299 teaching assistantships with full and partial tuition reimbursements (averaging $11,406 per year) were awarded. Financial award applicants required to submit FAFSA. In 2010, 91 first professional degrees, 508 master's, 114 doctorates awarded. *Degree program information:* Part-time and evening/weekend programs available. *Application fee:* $65. Electronic applications accepted. *Application Contact:* Dr. Nasser H. Zawia, Dean of the Graduate School, 401-874-5909, Fax: 401-874-5787, E-mail: nzawia@uri.edu. *Dean of the Graduate School,* Dr. Nasser H. Zawia, 401-874-5909, Fax: 401-874-5787, E-mail: nzawia@uri.edu.

College of Arts and Sciences Students: 324 full-time (196 women), 281 part-time (191 women); includes 66 minority (22 Black or African American, non-Hispanic/Latino; 1 American Indian or Alaska Native, non-Hispanic/Latino; 17 Asian, non-Hispanic/Latino; 24 Hispanic/Latino; 2 Two or more races, non-Hispanic/Latino), 48 international. *Faculty:* 193 full-time (81 women), 15 part-time/adjunct (6 women). Expenses: Contact institution. *Financial support:* In 2010–11, 16 research assistantships with full and partial tuition reimbursements (averaging $9,243 per year), 142 teaching assistantships with full and partial tuition reimbursements (averaging $12,566 per year) were awarded. Financial award applicants required to submit FAFSA. In 2010, 152 master's, 33 doctorates awarded. *Degree program information:* Part-time and evening/weekend programs available. Offers applied mathematical sciences (MS, PhD); applied mathematics (PhD); arts and sciences (MA, MLIS, MM, MPA, MS, PhD, Graduate Certificate); behavioral science (PhD); chemistry (MS, PhD); clinical psychology (MA, PhD); communication studies (MA); computer science (MS, PhD); digital forensics (Graduate Certificate); English (MA, PhD); history (MA); library and information studies (MLIS); mathematics (MS, PhD); music education (MM); music performance (MM); physics (MS, PhD); political science (MA); public policy and administration (MPA); school psychology (MS, PhD); Spanish (MA); statistics (MS). *Application fee:* $65. Electronic applications accepted. *Application Contact:* Dr. Winifed E. Brownell, Dean, 401-874-4101, Fax: 401-874-2892, E-mail: winnie@uri.edu. *Dean,* Dr. Winifed E. Brownell, 401-874-4101, Fax: 401-874-2892, E-mail: winnie@uri.edu.

College of Business Administration Students: 82 full-time (31 women), 218 part-time (77 women); includes 31 minority (6 Black or African American, non-Hispanic/Latino; 1 American Indian or Alaska Native, non-Hispanic/Latino; 13 Asian, non-Hispanic/Latino; 11 Hispanic/Latino), 29 international. *Faculty:* 54 full-time (15 women), 3 part-time/adjunct (2 women). Expenses: Contact institution. *Financial support:* In 2010–11, 13 teaching assistantships with full and partial tuition reimbursements (averaging $12,432 per year) were awarded. Financial award applicants required to submit FAFSA. In 2010, 78 master's, 3 doctorates awarded. *Degree program information:* Part-time and evening/weekend programs available. Offers accounting (MS); business administration (MBA, PhD); finance (MBA); general business (MBA); management (MBA); marketing (MBA); supply chain management (MBA). *Application fee:* $65. Electronic applications accepted. *Application Contact:* Lisa Lancellotta, Coordinator, MBA Programs, 401-874-4241, Fax: 401-874-4312, E-mail: mba@uri.edu. *Dean,* Dr. Mark Higgins, 401-874-4244, Fax: 401-874-4312, E-mail: markhiggins@uri.edu.

College of Engineering Students: 127 full-time (24 women), 93 part-time (15 women); includes 25 minority (5 Black or African American, non-Hispanic/Latino; 1 American Indian or Alaska Native, non-Hispanic/Latino; 11 Asian, non-Hispanic/Latino; 6 Hispanic/Latino; 2 Two or more races, non-Hispanic/Latino), 54 international. *Faculty:* 61 full-time (10 women), 8 part-time/adjunct (1 woman). Expenses: Contact institution. *Financial support:* In 2010–11, 37 research assistantships with full and partial tuition reimbursements (averaging $9,791 per year), 19 teaching assistantships with full and partial tuition reimbursements (averaging $9,033 per year) were awarded. Financial award applicants required to submit FAFSA. In 2010, 53 master's, 8 doctorates awarded. *Degree program information:* Part-time programs available. Offers chemical engineering (MS, PhD); civil and environmental engineering (MS, PhD); electrical, computer and biomedical engineering (MS, PhD, Graduate Certificate); engineering (MS, PhD, Graduate Certificate); mechanical, industrial and systems engineering (MS, PhD); ocean engineering (MS, PhD). *Application fee:* $65. Electronic applications accepted. *Application Contact:* Dr. Raymond Wright, Dean, 401-874-2186, Fax: 401-782-1066, E-mail: dean@egr.uri.edu. *Dean,* Dr. Raymond Wright, 401-874-2186, Fax: 401-782-1066, E-mail: dean@egr.uri.edu.

College of Human Science and Services Students: 276 full-time (222 women), 166 part-time (129 women); includes 54 minority (16 Black or African American, non-Hispanic/Latino; 6 American Indian or Alaska Native, non-Hispanic/Latino; 7 Asian, non-Hispanic/Latino; 17 Hispanic/Latino; 8 Native Hawaiian or other Pacific Islander, non-Hispanic/Latino), 7 international. *Faculty:* 70 full-time (46 women), 6 part-time/adjunct (5 women). Expenses: Contact institution. *Financial support:* In 2010–11, 4 research assistantships with full and partial tuition reimbursements (averaging $12,271 per year), 19 teaching assistantships with full and partial tuition reimbursements (averaging $7,443 per year) were awarded. Financial award applicants required to submit FAFSA. In 2010, 84 master's, 33 doctorates awarded. *Degree program information:* Part-time and evening/weekend programs available. Offers adult education (MA); college student personnel (MS); cultural studies of sport and physical culture (MS); education (PhD); elementary education (MA); exercise science (MS); human development and family studies (MS); human science and services (MA, MM, MS, DPT, PhD); marriage and family therapy (MS); music education (MM); physical education pedagogy (MS); physical therapy (DPT); psychosocial/behavioral aspects of physical activity (MS); reading education (MA); secondary education (MA); special education (MA); speech-language pathology (MS); textiles, fashion merchandising and design (MS). *Application fee:* $65. Electronic applications accepted. *Application Contact:* Dr. W. Lynn McKinney, Dean, 401-874-4014, Fax: 401-874-2581, E-mail: lynnm@uri.edu. *Dean,* Dr. W. Lynn McKinney, 401-874-4014, Fax: 401-874-2581, E-mail: lynnm@uri.edu.

College of Nursing Students: 25 full-time (all women), 76 part-time (71 women); includes 2 minority (both Black or African American, non-Hispanic/Latino), 5 international. *Faculty:* 27 full-time (26 women), 2 part-time/adjunct (1 woman). Expenses: Contact institution. *Financial support:* In 2010–11, 4 teaching assistantships with full and partial tuition reimbursements (averaging $9,817 per year) were awarded. Financial award application deadline: 4/15; financial award applicants required to submit FAFSA. In 2010, 26 master's, 1 doctorate awarded. *Degree program information:* Part-time programs available. Offers administration (MS); clinical nurse leader (MS); clinical specialist in gerontology (MS); clinical specialist in psychiatric/mental health (MS); family nurse practitioner (MS); gerontological nurse practitioner (MS); nursing (DNP, PhD); nursing education (MS). *Application deadline:* For fall admission, 4/15 for domestic students, 2/1 for international students; for spring admission, 11/15 for domestic students, 7/15 for international students. *Application fee:* $65. Electronic applications accepted. *Application Contact:* Dr. Mary C. Sullivan, Director of Graduate Studies, 401-874-5339, Fax: 401-874-2061, E-mail: mcsullivan@uri.edu. *Dean,* Dr. Dayle Joseph, 401-874-2766, Fax: 401-874-2061, E-mail: dayle@uri.edu.

College of Pharmacy Students: 670 full-time (391 women), 17 part-time (6 women); includes 95 minority (16 Black or African American, non-Hispanic/Latino; 61 Asian, non-Hispanic/Latino; 15 Hispanic/Latino; 3 Two or more races, non-Hispanic/Latino), 43 international. *Faculty:* 47 full-time (26 women), 4 part-time/adjunct (1 woman). Expenses: Contact institution. *Financial support:* In 2010–11, 8 research assistantships with partial tuition reimbursements (averaging $8,572 per year), 15 teaching assistantships with full and partial tuition reimbursements (averaging $11,446 per year) were awarded. Financial award applicants required to submit FAFSA. In 2010, 7 master's, 8 doctorates awarded. *Degree program information:* Part-time programs available. Offers medicinal chemistry and pharmacognosy (MS, PhD); pharmaceutical sciences (MS, PhD); pharmaceutics and pharmacokinetics (MS, PhD); pharmacology and toxicology (MS, PhD); pharmacy (MS, PhD). *Application fee:* $65. Electronic applications accepted. *Application Contact:* Dr. Ronald Jordan, Dean, 401-874-5003, Fax: 401-874-2181, E-mail: ronjordan@uri.edu. *Dean,* Dr. Ronald Jordan, 401-874-5003, Fax: 401-874-2181, E-mail: ronjordan@uri.edu.

College of the Environment and Life Sciences Students: 205 full-time (114 women), 91 part-time (61 women); includes 28 minority (7 Black or African American, non-Hispanic/Latino; 11 Asian, non-Hispanic/Latino; 10 Hispanic/Latino), 27 international. *Faculty:* 78 full-time (29 women), 10 part-time/adjunct (4 women). Expenses: Contact institution. *Financial support:* In 2010–11, 52 research assistantships with full and partial tuition reimbursements (averaging $12,411 per year), 60 teaching assistantships with full and partial tuition reimbursements (averaging $11,282 per year) were awarded. Financial award applicants required to submit FAFSA. In 2010, 68 master's, 17 doctorates awarded. *Degree program information:* Part-time programs available. Offers animal health and disease (MS); animal science (MS); aquaculture (MS); aquatic pathology (MS); biochemistry (MS, PhD); biological sciences (MS, PhD); clinical laboratory sciences (MS); entomology (MS, PhD); environment and life sciences (MA, MESM, MMA, MS, PhD); environmental and natural resource economics (MESM, MS, PhD); environmental science and management (MESM); environmental sciences (MS, PhD); fisheries (MS); food science (MS, PhD); marine affairs (MA, MESM, MMA, PhD); microbiology (MS, PhD); molecular genetics (MS, PhD); natural resources science (MESM, MS, PhD); nutrition (MS, PhD); plant sciences (MS, PhD). *Application fee:* $65. Electronic applications accepted. *Application Contact:* Dr. John Kirby, Dean, 401-874-2957, Fax: 401-874-4017, E-mail: jdkirby@uri.edu. *Dean,* Dr. John Kirby, 401-874-2957, Fax: 401-874-4017, E-mail: jdkirby@uri.edu.

Graduate School of Oceanography Students: 64 full-time (35 women), 18 part-time (12 women); includes 3 minority (all Asian, non-Hispanic/Latino), 7 international. *Faculty:* 25 full-time (7 women), 5 part-time/adjunct (1 woman). Expenses: Contact institution. *Financial support:* In 2010–11, 29 research assistantships with full and partial tuition reimbursements (averaging $9,617 per year), 9 teaching assistantships with full and partial tuition reimbursements (averaging $9,724 per year) were awarded. Financial award application deadline: 1/15; financial award applicants required to submit FAFSA. In 2010, 10 master's, 10 doctorates awarded. *Degree program information:* Part-time programs available. Offers oceanography (MO, MS, PhD, MBA/MO, PhD/MMA). *Application deadline:* For fall admission, 1/15 for domestic and international students; for spring admission, 11/15 for domestic students, 7/15 for international students. *Application fee:* $65. Electronic applications accepted. *Application Contact:* Dr. David M. Farmer, Dean, 401-874-6222, Fax: 401-874-6889, E-mail: thedean@gso.uri.edu. *Dean,* Dr. David M. Farmer, 401-874-6222, Fax: 401-874-6889, E-mail: thedean@gso.uri.edu.

Labor Research Center Students: 24 full-time (20 women), 31 part-time (23 women); includes 14 minority (5 Black or African American, non-Hispanic/Latino; 1 Hispanic/Latino; 8 Native Hawaiian or other Pacific Islander, non-Hispanic/Latino), 3 international. *Faculty:* 1 full-time (0 women), 3 part-time/adjunct (2 women). Expenses: Contact institution. *Financial support:* In 2010–11, 2 teaching assistantships with full tuition reimbursements (averaging $13,894 per year) were awarded; institutionally sponsored loans also available. Financial award application deadline: 2/1; financial award applicants required to submit FAFSA. In 2010, 8 master's awarded. *Degree program information:* Part-time and evening/weekend programs available. Offers labor relations and human resources (MS). *Application deadline:* For fall admission, 7/15 for domestic students, 2/1 for international students; for spring admission, 11/15 for domestic students, 7/15 for international students. *Application fee:* $65. Electronic applications accepted. *Application Contact:* Dr. Richard W. Scholl, Director, 401-874-4347, Fax: 401-874-2954, E-mail: rscholl@uri.edu. *Director,* Dr. Richard W. Scholl, 401-874-4347, Fax: 401-874-2954, E-mail: rscholl@uri.edu.

UNIVERSITY OF RICHMOND, Richmond, University of Richmond, VA 23173

General Information Independent, coed, comprehensive institution. *Graduate housing:* On-campus housing not available.

GRADUATE UNITS

Robins School of Business *Degree program information:* Part-time and evening/weekend programs available. Offers business (MBA). Electronic applications accepted.

School of Law Offers law (JD). JD/MSW, JD/MHA, JD/MPA offered jointly with Virginia Commonwealth University; JD/MURP with Virginia Commonwealth University; JD/MA with Department of History; JD/MS with Department of Biology. Electronic applications accepted.

UNIVERSITY OF RIO GRANDE, Rio Grande, OH 45674

General Information Independent, coed, comprehensive institution. *Graduate housing:* Room and/or apartments guaranteed to single students; on-campus housing not available to married students.

GRADUATE UNITS

Graduate School *Degree program information:* Part-time and evening/weekend programs available. Offers classroom teaching (M Ed).

UNIVERSITY OF ROCHESTER, Rochester, NY 14627

General Information Independent, coed, university. CGS member. *Graduate housing:* Rooms and/or apartments available on a first-come, first-served basis to single and married students. Housing application deadline: 5/15. *Research affiliation:* Brookhaven National Laboratory, Fermi National Accelerator Laboratory, Argonne National Laboratory, Lawrence Livermore National Laboratory, Los Alamos National Laboratory.

GRADUATE UNITS

Eastman School of Music *Degree program information:* Part-time programs available. Offers composition (MA, MM, DMA, PhD); conducting (MM, DMA); education (MA, PhD); ethnomusicologyjazz studies/contemporary media (MM); music compositionmusic education (MM, DMA); music theorymusic theory pedagogymusicologypedagogy of music theory (MA); performance and literature (MM, DMA); piano accompanying and chamber music (MM, DMA); theory (MA, PhD).

Hajim School of Engineering and Applied Sciences *Degree program information:* Part-time programs available. Offers alternative energybiomedical engineering (MS, PhD); chemical engineering (MS, PhD); computer science (MS, PhD); electrical and computer engineering (MS, PhD); electrical engineeringengineering and applied sciences (MS, PhD); materials science (MS, PhD); mechanical engineering (MS, PhD).

Center for Entrepreneurship Offers technical entrepreneurship and management (TEAM) (MS).

Institute of Optics Offers optics (MS, PhD).

Margaret Warner Graduate School of Education and Human Development *Degree program information:* Part-time and evening/weekend programs available. Offers counselingeducationeducation and human development (MAT, MS, Ed D, PhD); educational policyhigher educationhuman developmentschool leadershipteaching and curriculum.

School of Arts and Sciences *Degree program information:* Part-time programs available. Offers applied mathematicsarts and sciences (MA, MS, PhD); biology (MS, PhD); brain and cognitive sciences (MS, PhD); chemistry (MS, PhD); clinical psychology (PhD); comparative literaturedevelopmental psychologyeconomics (MA, PhD); englishEnglish (MA, PhD); frenchgeological sciences (MS, PhD); germanhistory (MA, PhD); linguisticsliterary translation studiesmathematical methodsmathematics (MA, MS, PhD); modern languages and culturesphilosophy (MA, PhD); physics (MA, MS, PhD); physics and astronomy (PhD); political science (MA, PhD); psychology (MA); social personality psychologysocial-personality psychology (PhD); spanishstatisticsvisual and cultural studies (MA, PhD). Electronic applications accepted.

School of Medicine and Dentistry *Degree program information:* Part-time programs available. Offers medicine (MD); medicine and dentistry (MD, MA, MPH, MS, PhD, Certificate). Electronic applications accepted.

Graduate Programs in Medicine and Dentistry *Degree program information:* Part-time programs available. Offers biochemistry (MS, PhD); biomedical genetics (MS, PhD); biophysics (MS, PhD); clinical translational researchepidemiology (MS, PhD); health services research and policy (PhD); marriage and family therapy (MS); medical microbiologymedical statistics (MS); medicine and dentistry (MA, MPH, MS, PhD); microbiology (MS, PhD); microbiology and immunology (MS, PhD); neurobiology and anatomy (MS, PhD); neuroscience (MS, PhD); oral biology (MS); pathology (MS, PhD); pharmacology (MS, PhD); physiology (MS, PhD); public health (MPH); public health and clinical investigation (MPH); statistics (MA, PhD); toxicology (MS, PhD); translational biomedical science. Electronic applications accepted.

University of Rochester (continued)

School of Nursing *Degree program information:* Part-time programs available. Postbaccalaureate distance learning degree programs offered (minimal on-campus study). Offers acute care nurse practitioner (MS); adult nurse practitioner (MS); adult psychiatric mental health nurse practitioner (MS); adult/geriatric nurse practitioner (MS); care of children and families/pediatric nurse practitioner (MS); care of children and families/pediatric nurse practitioner with pediatric behavioral health (MS); care of children and families/pediatric nurse practitioner/neonatal nurse practitioner (MS); child and adolescent psychiatric mental health nurse practitioner (MS); clinical nurse leader (MS); disaster response and emergency preparedness (MS); family nurse practitioner (MS); health care organization management and leadership (MS); health practice research (PhD); health promotion, education and technology (MS); nursing (Certificate).

William E. Simon Graduate School of Business Administration *Degree program information:* Part-time and evening/weekend programs available. Offers accountancybusiness administration (MBA, MS, PhD).

UNIVERSITY OF ST. AUGUSTINE FOR HEALTH SCIENCES, St. Augustine, FL 32086

General Information Proprietary, coed, graduate-only institution. *Graduate housing:* On-campus housing not available.

GRADUATE UNITS

Graduate Programs *Degree program information:* Part-time programs available. Postbaccalaureate distance learning degree programs offered (minimal on-campus study).

Division of Advanced Studies *Degree program information:* Part-time programs available. Postbaccalaureate distance learning degree programs offered (minimal on-campus study). Offers advanced studies (MH Sc, DH Sc, TDPT).

Division of Entry-Level Physical Therapy Offers entry-level physical therapy (DPT).

Division of Occupational Therapy Offers occupational therapy (MOT, OTD).

Division of Physical Therapy Offers physical therapy (DPT, Certificate).

UNIVERSITY OF ST. FRANCIS, Joliet, IL 60435-6169

General Information Independent-religious, coed, comprehensive institution. *Enrollment:* 2,171 graduate, professional, and undergraduate students; 280 full-time matriculated graduate/professional students (204 women), 990 part-time matriculated graduate/professional students (811 women). *Enrollment by degree level:* 1,228 master's, 25 doctoral, 17 other advanced degrees. *Graduate faculty:* 39 full-time (27 women), 76 part-time/adjunct (36 women). *Tuition:* Part-time $628 per credit. Part-time tuition and fees vary according to degree level, campus/location and program. *Student services:* Campus employment opportunities, campus safety program, career counseling, exercise/wellness program, free psychological counseling, multicultural affairs office, services for students with disabilities, teacher training, writing training. *Library facilities:* University of St. Francis Library. *Online resources:* library catalog, web page, access to other libraries' catalogs. *Collection:* 138,882 titles, 18,231 serial subscriptions, 4,701 audiovisual materials.

Computer facilities: 382 computers available on campus for general student use. A campuswide network can be accessed from student residence rooms and from off campus. Online class registration, billing/payment are available. *Web address:* http://www.stfrancis.edu/.

General Application Contact: Sandra Sloka, Director of Admissions for Graduate and Degree Completion Programs, 800-735-7500, Fax: 815-740-5032, E-mail: ssloka@stfrancis.edu.

GRADUATE UNITS

College of Arts and Sciences Students: 88 full-time (62 women), 15 part-time (13 women); includes 30 minority (14 Black or African American, non-Hispanic/Latino; 1 American Indian or Alaska Native, non-Hispanic/Latino; 3 Asian, non-Hispanic/Latino; 12 Hispanic/Latino). Average age 32. 36 applicants, 53% accepted, 16 enrolled. *Faculty:* 6 full-time (4 women). Expenses: Contact institution. *Financial support:* In 2010–11, 20 students received support. Federal Work-Study, scholarships/grants, and tuition waivers (partial) available. Support available to part-time students. Financial award applicants required to submit FAFSA. In 2010, 39 master's awarded. Offers physician assistant practice (MS); social work (MSW). *Application deadline:* Applications are processed on a rolling basis. *Application fee:* $30. Electronic applications accepted. *Application Contact:* Sandra Sloka, Director of Admissions for Graduate and Degree Completion Programs, 800-735-7500, Fax: 815-740-5032, E-mail: ssloka@stfrancis.edu. *Dean,* Dr. Robert Kase, 815-740-3367, Fax: 815-740-6366.

College of Business and Health Administration Expenses: Contact institution. *Financial support:* In 2010–11, 67 students received support. Tuition waivers (partial) available. Support available to part-time students. Financial award applicants required to submit FAFSA. *Degree program information:* Part-time and evening/weekend programs available. Postbaccalaureate distance learning degree programs offered (no on-campus study). Offers business and health administration (MBA, MS, MSM). *Application deadline:* Applications are processed on a rolling basis. *Application fee:* $30. Electronic applications accepted. *Application Contact:* Sandra Sloka, Director of Admissions for Graduate and Degree Completion Programs, 800-735-7500, Fax: 815-740-5032, E-mail: ssloka@stfrancis.edu. *Dean,* Dr. Michael LaRocco, 815-740-3395, Fax: 815-774-2920, E-mail: mlarocco@stfrancis.edu.

School of Business Students: 38 full-time (23 women), 115 part-time (64 women); includes 31 minority (22 Black or African American, non-Hispanic/Latino; 8 Hispanic/Latino; 1 Two or more races, non-Hispanic/Latino). Average age 37. 88 applicants, 59% accepted, 31 enrolled. *Faculty:* 6 full-time (2 women), 7 part-time/adjunct (2 women). Expenses: Contact institution. *Financial support:* In 2010–11, 35 students received support. Federal Work-Study, scholarships/grants, and tuition waivers (partial) available. Support available to part-time students. Financial award applicants required to submit FAFSA. In 2010, 58 master's awarded. *Degree program information:* Part-time and evening/weekend programs available. Postbaccalaureate distance learning degree programs offered (no on-campus study). Offers business (MBA, MSM). *Application deadline:* Applications are processed on a rolling basis. *Application fee:* $30. Electronic applications accepted. *Application Contact:* Sandra Sloka, Director of Admissions for Graduate and Degree Completion Programs, 800-735-7500, Fax: 815-740-5032, E-mail: ssloka@stfrancis.edu. *Dean,* Dr. Michael LaRocco, 815-740-5025, Fax: 815-774-2920, E-mail: mlarocco@stfrancis.edu.

School of Health Administration Students: 95 full-time (74 women), 348 part-time (288 women); includes 85 minority (43 Black or African American, non-Hispanic/Latino; 1 American Indian or Alaska Native, non-Hispanic/Latino; 10 Asian, non-Hispanic/Latino; 26 Hispanic/Latino; 5 Two or more races, non-Hispanic/Latino), 2 international. Average age 43. 181 applicants, 70% accepted, 89 enrolled. *Faculty:* 5 full-time (1 woman), 28 part-time/adjunct (9 women). Expenses: Contact institution. *Financial support:* In 2010–11, 78 students received support. Tuition waivers (partial) available. Support available to part-time students. Financial award applicants required to submit FAFSA. In 2010, 209 master's awarded. *Degree program information:* Part-time and evening/weekend programs available. Postbaccalaureate distance learning degree programs offered (no on-campus study). Offers health administration (MS). *Application deadline:* Applications are processed on a rolling basis. *Application fee:* $30. Electronic applications accepted. *Application Contact:* Sandra Sloka, Director of Admissions for Graduate and Degree Completion Programs, 800-735-7500, Fax: 815-740-5032, E-mail: ssloka@stfrancis.edu. *Dean,* Dr. Michael LaRocco, 815-740-5025, Fax: 815-774-2920, E-mail: mlarocco@stfrancis.edu.

School of Professional Studies Students: 6 full-time (5 women), 25 part-time (23 women); includes 10 minority (6 Black or African American, non-Hispanic/Latino; 1 Asian, non-Hispanic/Latino; 2 Hispanic/Latino; 1 Native Hawaiian or other Pacific Islander, non-Hispanic/Latino). Average age 41. 23 applicants, 48% accepted, 9 enrolled. *Faculty:* 1 (woman) full-time, 5 part-time/adjunct (0 women). Expenses: Contact institution. *Financial support:* In 2010–11, 14 students received support. Tuition waivers (partial) available. Support available to part-time students. Financial award applicants required to submit FAFSA. In 2010, 17 master's awarded. *Degree program information:* Part-time and evening/weekend programs available. Postbaccalaureate distance learning degree programs offered (no on-campus study). Offers training and development (MS). *Application deadline:* Applications are processed on a rolling basis. *Application fee:* $30. Electronic applications accepted. *Application Contact:* Sandra Sloka, Director of Admissions for Graduate and Degree Completion Programs, 800-735-7500, Fax: 815-740-5032, E-mail: ssloka@stfrancis.edu. *Dean,* Dr. Michael LaRocco, 815-740-5025, Fax: 815-774-2920, E-mail: mlarocco@stfrancis.edu.

College of Education Students: 35 full-time (25 women), 297 part-time (244 women); includes 35 minority (13 Black or African American, non-Hispanic/Latino; 4 Asian, non-Hispanic/Latino; 16 Hispanic/Latino; 1 Native Hawaiian or other Pacific Islander, non-Hispanic/Latino; 1 Two or more races, non-Hispanic/Latino), 1 international. Average age 32. 218 applicants, 61% accepted, 104 enrolled. *Faculty:* 9 full-time (7 women), 22 part-time/adjunct (13 women). Expenses: Contact institution. *Financial support:* In 2010–11, 28 students received support. Federal Work-Study, scholarships/grants, tuition waivers (partial), and unspecified assistantships available. Support available to part-time students. Financial award applicants required to submit FAFSA. In 2010, 197 master's awarded. *Degree program information:* Part-time and evening/weekend programs available. Postbaccalaureate distance learning degree programs offered (no on-campus study). Offers educational leadership (MS); elementary education certification (M Ed); reading (MS); secondary education certification (M Ed); special education (M Ed); teaching and learning (MS). *Application deadline:* Applications are processed on a rolling basis. *Application fee:* $30. Electronic applications accepted. *Application Contact:* Sandra Sloka, Director of Admissions for Graduate and Degree Completion Programs, 800-735-7500, Fax: 815-740-5032, E-mail: ssloka@stfrancis.edu. *Dean,* Dr. John Gambro, 815-740-3332, Fax: 815-740-2264, E-mail: jgambro@stfrancis.edu.

College of Nursing and Allied Health Students: 12 full-time (11 women), 183 part-time (169 women); includes 53 minority (26 Black or African American, non-Hispanic/Latino; 9 Asian, non-Hispanic/Latino; 14 Hispanic/Latino; 4 Two or more races, non-Hispanic/Latino). Average age 40. 231 applicants, 39% accepted, 71 enrolled. *Faculty:* 12 full-time (all women), 14 part-time/adjunct (12 women). Expenses: Contact institution. *Financial support:* In 2010–11, 62 students received support. Scholarships/grants, traineeships, and tuition waivers (partial) available. Support available to part-time students. Financial award applicants required to submit FAFSA. In 2010, 27 master's awarded. *Degree program information:* Part-time and evening/weekend programs available. Postbaccalaureate distance learning degree programs offered (no on-campus study). Offers nursing (MSN); nursing practice (DNP). *Application deadline:* Applications are processed on a rolling basis. *Application fee:* $30. Electronic applications accepted. *Application Contact:* Sandra Sloka, Director of Admissions for Graduate and Degree Completion Programs, 800-735-7500, Fax: 815-740-5032, E-mail: ssloka@stfrancis.edu. *Dean,* Dr. Carol Wilson, 815-740-3859, Fax: 815-740-4243, E-mail: cwilson@stfrancis.edu.

UNIVERSITY OF SAINT FRANCIS, Fort Wayne, IN 46808-3994

General Information Independent-religious, coed, comprehensive institution. *Enrollment:* 340 matriculated graduate/professional students (265 women). *Enrollment by degree level:* 340 master's. *Graduate faculty:* 36 full-time (24 women), 17 part-time/adjunct (10 women). *Tuition:* Part-time $770 per semester hour. Part-time tuition and fees vary according to program. *Graduate housing:* Room and/or apartments available on a first-come, first-served basis to single students; on-campus housing not available to married students. *Student services:* Campus employment opportunities, career counseling, free psychological counseling, international student services, low-cost health insurance, services for students with disabilities. *Library facilities:* Lee and Jim Vann Library. *Online resources:* library catalog, web page, access to other libraries' catalogs. *Collection:* 95,991 titles, 567 serial subscriptions.

Computer facilities: Computer purchase and lease plans are available. 297 computers available on campus for general student use. A campuswide network can be accessed from student residence rooms. Online class registration is available. *Web address:* http://www.sf.edu/.

General Application Contact: James Cashdollar, Admissions Counselor, 260-434-3279, E-mail: jcashdollar@sf.edu.

GRADUATE UNITS

Graduate School *Degree program information:* Part-time and evening/weekend programs available. Offers business administration (MBA); fine art (MA); general psychology (MS); mental health counseling (MS); nursing (MSN); pastoral counseling (MS); physician assistant studies (MS); school counseling (MS Ed); special education (MS Ed).

UNIVERSITY OF SAINT MARY, Leavenworth, KS 66048-5082

General Information Independent-religious, coed, comprehensive institution. *Graduate housing:* On-campus housing not available.

GRADUATE UNITS

Graduate Programs *Degree program information:* Part-time and evening/weekend programs available. Postbaccalaureate distance learning degree programs offered (no on-campus study). Offers business administration (MBA); curriculum and instruction (MAT); education (MA, MAT); management (MS); psychology (MA); special education (MA); teaching (MA). Electronic applications accepted.

UNIVERSITY OF SAINT MARY OF THE LAKE–MUNDELEIN SEMINARY, Mundelein, IL 60060

General Information Independent-religious, men only, graduate-only institution. *Enrollment by degree level:* 166 first professional, 9 master's, 17 doctoral, 20 other advanced degrees. *Graduate faculty:* 42 full-time (6 women), 15 part-time/adjunct (3 women). *Tuition:* Full-time $20,622. *Required fees:* $250. *Graduate housing:* Room and/or apartments guaranteed to single students; on-campus housing not available to married students. Housing application deadline: 8/1. *Student services:* Campus employment opportunities, campus safety program, free psychological counseling, international student services, low-cost health insurance, multicultural affairs office. *Library facilities:* Feehan Memorial Library. *Online resources:* library catalog, web page. *Collection:* 20,152 titles, 435 serial subscriptions, 700 audiovisual materials.

Computer facilities: 20 computers available on campus for general student use. A campuswide network can be accessed from student residence rooms. *Web address:* http://www.usml.edu/.

General Application Contact: Very Rev. Dennis J. Lyle, Rector-President, 847-566-6401, Fax: 847-566-7330.

GRADUATE UNITS

Graduate School of Theology Students: 212 full-time (13 women); includes 10 minority (2 Black or African American, non-Hispanic/Latino; 3 Asian, non-Hispanic/Latino; 5 Hispanic/Latino), 78 international. 95 applicants, 75% accepted, 71 enrolled. *Faculty:* 42 full-time (6 women), 15 part-time/adjunct (3 women). Expenses: Contact institution. *Financial support:* Career-related internships or fieldwork available. Offers theology (M Div, MA, D Min). *Application deadline:* Applications are processed on a rolling basis. *Application fee:* $0. Electronic applications accepted. *Application Contact:* Rev. Raymond J. Webb, Academic Dean, 847-566-6401. *Academic Dean,* Rev. Raymond J. Webb, 847-566-6401.

UNIVERSITY OF ST. MICHAEL'S COLLEGE, Toronto, ON M5S 1J4, Canada

General Information Independent-religious, coed, graduate-only institution. *Graduate housing:* Rooms and/or apartments available on a first-come, first-served basis to single and married students. Housing application deadline: 8/15.

GRADUATE UNITS

Faculty of Theology *Degree program information:* Part-time programs available. Offers Catholic leadership (MA); eastern Christian studies (Diploma); religious education (Diploma); theological studies (Diploma); theology (M Div, MA, MRE, MTS, D Min, PhD, Th D); theology and Jewish studies (MA). Th D offered jointly with University of Toronto. Electronic applications accepted.

UNIVERSITY OF ST. THOMAS, St. Paul, MN 55105-1096

General Information Independent-religious, coed, university. *Enrollment:* 10,832 graduate, professional, and undergraduate students; 1,252 full-time matriculated graduate/professional students (680 women), 3,127 part-time matriculated graduate/professional students (1,659 women). *Enrollment by degree level:* 561 first professional, 3,360 master's, 221 doctoral, 237 other advanced degrees. *Graduate housing:* On-campus housing not available. *Student services:* Campus employment opportunities, campus safety program, career counseling, child daycare facilities, exercise/wellness program, free psychological counseling, international student services, low-cost health insurance, multicultural affairs office, services for students with disabilities. *Library facilities:* O'Shaughnessy-Frey Library. *Online resources:* library catalog, web page, access to other libraries' catalogs.

Computer facilities: A campuswide network can be accessed from student residence rooms and from off campus. Online class registration is available. *Web address:* http://www.stthomas.edu/.

General Application Contact: Dr. Michael Cogan, Associate Vice President of Records and Institutional Effectiveness, 651-962-6657, Fax: 651-962-6702, E-mail: mfcogan@stthomas.edu.

GRADUATE UNITS

Graduate Studies Students: 1,252 full-time (680 women), 3,127 part-time (1,659 women); includes 538 minority (175 Black or African American, non-Hispanic/Latino; 13 American Indian or Alaska Native, non-Hispanic/Latino; 201 Asian, non-Hispanic/Latino; 89 Hispanic/Latino; 6 Native Hawaiian or other Pacific Islander, non-Hispanic/Latino; 54 Two or more races, non-Hispanic/Latino), 171 international. Average age 31. Expenses: Contact institution. *Financial support:* Fellowships, research assistantships, teaching assistantships, career-related internships or fieldwork, institutionally sponsored loans, and scholarships/grants available. Support available to part-time students. In 2010, 154 first professional degrees, 1,209 master's, 32 doctorates, 31 other advanced degrees awarded. *Degree program information:* Part-time and evening/weekend programs available. Postbaccalaureate distance learning degree programs offered (no on-campus study). Offers advanced studies in software engineering (Certificate); business analysis (Certificate); computer security (Certificate); information systems (Certificate); software design and development (Certificate); software engineering (MS); software management (MS); software systems (MSS). *Application Contact:* Dr. Michael Cogan, Associate Vice President of Records and Institutional Effectiveness, 651-962-6657, Fax: 651-962-6702, E-mail: mfcogan@stthomas.edu. *Executive Vice President for Academic Affairs,* Dr. Susan J. Huber, 651-962-6720, Fax: 651-962-6702, E-mail: sjhuber@stthomas.edu.

College of Arts and Sciences Students: 16 full-time (10 women), 115 part-time (74 women); includes 3 American Indian or Alaska Native, non-Hispanic/Latino; 1 Asian, non-Hispanic/Latino; 1 Hispanic/Latino, 2 international. Average age 31. 68 applicants, 88% accepted, 31 enrolled. *Faculty:* 35 full-time (19 women), 45 part-time/adjunct (24 women). Expenses: Contact institution. *Financial support:* In 2010–11, 79 students received support, including 5 fellowships (averaging $4,000 per year); research assistantships, teaching assistantships, career-related internships or fieldwork, institutionally sponsored loans, and scholarships/grants also available. Support available to part-time students. Financial award application deadline: 4/1; financial award applicants required to submit FAFSA. In 2010, 41 master's awarded. *Degree program information:* Part-time and evening/weekend programs available. Offers art history (MA); arts and sciences (MA); Catholic studies (MA); choral (MA); Dalcroze (MA); English (MA); instrumental (MA); Kodaly (MA); Orff (MA); piano pedagogy (MA). *Application deadline:* For fall admission, 4/1 for domestic students, 5/1 priority date for international students; for spring admission, 11/1 for domestic students, 10/1 priority date for international students. *Application fee:* $50. *Application Contact:* Dr. Angeline Barretta-Herman, Associate Vice President for Academic Affairs, 651-962-6033, Fax: 651-962-6702, E-mail: a9barrettahe@stthomas.edu. *Dean,* Dr. Marisa Kelly, 651-962-6000, Fax: 651-962-6004, E-mail: mjkelly1@stthomas.edu.

Graduate School of Professional Psychology Students: 68 full-time (54 women), 141 part-time (113 women); includes 5 Black or African American, non-Hispanic/Latino; 13 Asian, non-Hispanic/Latino; 3 Hispanic/Latino, 4 international. Average age 29. 578 applicants, 42% accepted. *Faculty:* 11 full-time (5 women), 13 part-time/adjunct (6 women). Expenses: Contact institution. *Financial support:* In 2010–11, 2 fellowships (averaging $5,000 per year) were awarded; research assistantships, institutionally sponsored loans and scholarships/grants also available. Support available to part-time students. Financial award application deadline: 8/1; financial award applicants required to submit FAFSA. In 2010, 22 master's, 11 doctorates awarded. *Degree program information:* Part-time and evening/weekend programs available. Offers counseling psychology (MA, Psy D); marriage and family psychology (MA, Certificate). *Application deadline:* For fall admission, 3/1 priority date for domestic students; for winter admission, 2/1 priority date for domestic students; for spring admission, 9/15 priority date for domestic students, 3/1 for international students. *Application fee:* $50. *Application Contact:* Laurie Dupont, Administrative Assistant, 651-962-4669, Fax: 651-962-4651, E-mail: ldupont@stthomas.edu. *Associate Dean,* Dr. Christopher S. Vye, 651-962-4666, Fax: 651-962-4666, E-mail: bnolan@stthomas.edu.

Opus College of Business Students: 144 full-time (57 women), 1,265 part-time (549 women); includes 150 minority (34 Black or African American, non-Hispanic/Latino; 6 American Indian or Alaska Native, non-Hispanic/Latino; 72 Asian, non-Hispanic/Latino; 28 Hispanic/Latino; 1 Native Hawaiian or other Pacific Islander, non-Hispanic/Latino; 9 Two or more races, non-Hispanic/Latino), 52 international. *Faculty:* 106 full-time (33 women), 35 part-time/adjunct (7 women). Expenses: Contact institution. In 2010, 519 master's awarded. Offers accountancy (MS); business (MBA, MBC, MS); business administration (MBA); business communication (MBC); executive business administration (MBA); health care business administration (MBA); real estate (MS). *Application Contact:* William Woodson, Assistant Dean, 651-962-4200, Fax: 651-962-4129, E-mail: ustmba@stthomas.edu. *Dean,* Dr. Christopher Puto, 651-962-4200, Fax: 651-962-4129, E-mail: cob@stthomas.edu.

The Saint Paul Seminary School of Divinity Students: 97 full-time (5 women), 20 part-time (10 women); includes 2 minority (both Hispanic/Latino), 10 international. Average age 30. 32 applicants, 100% accepted, 30 enrolled. *Faculty:* 13 full-time (5 women), 5 part-time/adjunct (2 women). Expenses: Contact institution. *Financial support:* In 2010–11, 52 students received support; fellowships, research assistantships, institutionally sponsored loans and scholarships/grants available. Support available to part-time students. Financial award application deadline: 4/1; financial award applicants required to submit FAFSA. In 2010, 9 first professional degrees, 23 master's awarded. *Degree program information:* Part-time and evening/weekend programs available. Offers divinity (M Div, MA, MARE). *Application deadline:* For fall admission, 6/1 priority date for domestic students. Applications are processed on a rolling basis. *Application fee:* $40. Electronic applications accepted. *Application Contact:* Rev. Peter A. Laird, Vice Rector and Admissions Chair, 651-962-5070, Fax: 651-962-5790, E-mail: palaird@stthomas.edu. *Rector,* Rev. Msgr. Aloysius R. Callaghan, 651-962-5052, Fax: 651-962-5790, E-mail: arcallaghan@stthomas.edu.

School of Education Students: 115 full-time (92 women), 929 part-time (630 women); includes 132 minority (60 Black or African American, non-Hispanic/Latino; 3 American Indian or Alaska Native, non-Hispanic/Latino; 30 Asian, non-Hispanic/Latino; 25 Hispanic/Latino; 4 Native Hawaiian or other Pacific Islander, non-Hispanic/Latino; 10 Two or more races, non-Hispanic/Latino), 22 international. Average age 35. 428 applicants, 75% accepted, 258 enrolled. *Faculty:* 33 full-time (21 women), 74 part-time/adjunct (43 women). Expenses: Contact institution. *Financial support:* Fellowships, research assistantships, career-related internships or fieldwork, institutionally sponsored loans, and scholarships/grants available. Support available to part-time students. Financial award applicants required to submit FAFSA. In 2010, 264 master's, 19 doctorates, 148 other advanced degrees awarded. *Degree program information:* Part-time and evening/weekend programs available. Offers athletics and activities administration (MA); autism spectrum disorders (MA, Certificate); career development (Certificate); community education administration (MA); critical pedagogy (Ed D); curriculum and instruction (MA); developmental disabilities (MA); director of special education (Ed S); e-learning (Certificate); early childhood special education (MA); education (MA, MAT, Ed D, Certificate, Ed S); educational leadership (Ed S); educational leadership and administration (MA); elementary (MAT); emotional behavioral disorders (MA); engineering education (Certificate); English as a second language (MA); gifted, creative, and talented education (MA); human resource development (Certificate); human resource management (Certificate); human resources and change leadership (MA); international leadership (MA, Certificate); leadership (Ed D); leadership in student affairs (MA, Certificate); learning disabilities (MA); learning technology (Certificate); learning technology for learning development and change (MA); math education (Certificate); multicultural education (Certificate); organization development (Ed D, Certificate); Orton-Gillingham reading (Certificate); police leadership (MA); public policy and leadership (MA, Certificate); reading (MA, Certificate); special education (MA). *Application deadline:* For fall admission, 6/1 priority date for domestic students; for spring admission, 11/1 priority date for domestic students. Applications are processed on a rolling basis. *Application fee:* $50. *Application Contact:* Vicky L. Rasmusson, Admissions Coordinator, 651-962-4430, Fax: 651-962-4169, E-mail: vlrasmusson@stthomas.edu. *Dean,* Dr. Bruce H. Kramer, 651-962-4435, Fax: 651-962-4169, E-mail: bhkramer@stthomas.edu.

School of Engineering Expenses: Contact institution. *Financial support:* Fellowships, research assistantships, institutionally sponsored loans and scholarships/grants available. Support available to part-time students. Financial award application deadline: 4/1; financial award applicants required to submit FAFSA. Offers manufacturing engineering and operations (MS); mechanical engineering (MS); medical device development (Certificate); regulatory science (MS); software engineering (MS); software management (MS); software systems (MSS); systems engineering (MS); technology management (MS). *Application deadline:* For fall admission, 8/1 priority date for domestic students; for spring admission, 1/1 priority date for domestic students. Applications are processed on a rolling basis. *Application fee:* $30. Electronic applications accepted. *Application Contact:* Joyce A. Taylor, Graduate Programs Coordinator, 651-962-5756, Fax: 651-962-6419, E-mail: jataylor1@stthomas.edu. *Dean,* Don Weinkauf, 651-962-5760, Fax: 651-962-6419, E-mail: dhweinkauf@stthomas.edu.

School of Law Students: 473 full-time (205 women), 2 part-time (1 woman); includes 14 Black or African American, non-Hispanic/Latino; 2 American Indian or Alaska Native, non-Hispanic/Latino; 25 Asian, non-Hispanic/Latino; 9 Hispanic/Latino; 5 Two or more races, non-Hispanic/Latino, 2 international. Average age 25. 1,801 applicants, 51% accepted, 168 enrolled. *Faculty:* 39 full-time (16 women), 56 part-time/adjunct (18 women). Expenses: Contact institution. *Financial support:* In 2010–11, 278 students received support. Scholarships/grants available. Financial award application deadline: 7/1; financial award applicants required to submit FAFSA. In 2010, 145 first professional degrees awarded. Offers law (JD). *Application deadline:* For fall admission, 7/1 priority date for domestic and international students. Applications are processed on a rolling basis. *Application fee:* $0. Electronic applications accepted. *Application Contact:* Cari Haaland, Assistant Dean for Admissions and International Programs, 651-962-4895, Fax: 651-962-4876, E-mail: lawschool@stthomas.edu. *Dean,* Thomas M. Mengler, 651-962-4880, Fax: 651-962-4881, E-mail: tmmengler@stthomas.edu.

School of Social Work Students: 228 full-time (202 women), 153 part-time (143 women); includes 9 Black or African American, non-Hispanic/Latino; 1 American Indian or Alaska Native, non-Hispanic/Latino; 6 Asian, non-Hispanic/Latino; 5 Hispanic/Latino; 8 Two or more races, non-Hispanic/Latino, 1 international. Average age 31. 321 applicants, 76% accepted, 141 enrolled. *Faculty:* 17 full-time (13 women), 21 part-time/adjunct (15 women). Expenses: Contact institution. *Financial support:* In 2010–11, 350 students received support, including 8 fellowships, 15 research assistantships; career-related internships or fieldwork, Federal Work-Study, institutionally sponsored loans, scholarships/grants, and unspecified assistantships also available. Support available to part-time students. Financial award application deadline: 7/1; financial award applicants required to submit FAFSA. In 2010, 133 master's awarded. *Degree program information:* Part-time and evening/weekend programs available. Postbaccalaureate distance learning degree programs offered (minimal on-campus study). Offers social work (MSW). *Application deadline:* For fall admission, 1/10 for domestic students. *Application fee:* $35. Electronic applications accepted. *Application Contact:* Lisa Dalsin, Program Manager, 651-962-5810, Fax: 651-962-5819, E-mail: msw@stthomas.edu. *Dean and Professor,* Dr. Barbara W. Shank, 651-962-5801, Fax: 651-962-5819, E-mail: bwshank@stthomas.edu.

UNIVERSITY OF ST. THOMAS, Houston, TX 77006-4696

General Information Independent-religious, coed, comprehensive institution. *Enrollment:* 3,520 graduate, professional, and undergraduate students; 300 full-time matriculated graduate/professional students (122 women), 1,203 part-time matriculated graduate/professional students (863 women). *Enrollment by degree level:* 96 first professional, 1,369 master's, 21 doctoral, 17 other advanced degrees. *Graduate faculty:* 89 full-time (33 women), 57 part-time/adjunct (30 women). *Tuition:* Full-time $15,696; part-time $872 per credit hour. *Required fees:* $236; $83 per term. One-time fee: $100. Tuition and fees vary according to course load, campus/location and program. *Graduate housing:* Room and/or apartments available on a first-come, first-served basis to single students; on-campus housing not available to married students. Typical cost: $4800 per year ($7900 including board). *Student services:* Campus employment opportunities, campus safety program, career counseling, free psychological counseling, international student services, services for students with disabilities. *Library facilities:* Doherty Library. *Online resources:* library catalog, web page. *Collection:* 306,793 titles, 48,323 serial subscriptions, 1,865 audiovisual materials.

Computer facilities: Computer purchase and lease plans are available. 287 computers available on campus for general student use. A campuswide network can be accessed from student residence rooms. Online class registration is available. *Web address:* http://www.stthom.edu/.

General Application Contact: Fr. Joseph Pilsner, Dean, School of Arts and Sciences, 713-942-5081, Fax: 713-525-3849, E-mail: pilsnerj@stthom.edu.

GRADUATE UNITS

Cameron School of Business Students: 137 full-time (74 women), 235 part-time (123 women); includes 156 minority (44 Black or African American, non-Hispanic/Latino; 29 Asian, non-Hispanic/Latino; 81 Hispanic/Latino; 2 Two or more races, non-Hispanic/Latino), 80 international. Average age 30. 134 applicants, 95% accepted, 87 enrolled. *Faculty:* 24 full-time (7 women), 3 part-time/adjunct (0 women). Expenses: Contact institution. *Financial support:* In 2010–11, 21 students received support. Federal Work-Study, scholarships/grants, unspecified assistantships, and state work-study, institutional employment available. Support available to part-time students. Financial award application deadline: 4/15; financial award applicants required to submit FAFSA. In 2010, 179 master's awarded. *Degree program information:* Part-time and evening/weekend programs available. Offers business (MBA, MSA). *Application deadline:* Applications are processed on a rolling basis. *Application fee:* $35. Electronic applications accepted. *Application Contact:* Sandra Flanagan, Assistant Director, 713-525-2100, Fax: 713-525-2110, E-mail: cameron@stthom.edu. *Dean,* Dr. Bahman Mirshab, 713-525-2100, Fax: 713-525-2110, E-mail: cameron@stthom.edu.

Center for Faith and Culture Students: 6 full-time (3 women), 6 part-time (2 women); includes 5 minority (1 Black or African American, non-Hispanic/Latino; 1 Asian, non-Hispanic/Latino; 2 Hispanic/Latino; 1 Two or more races, non-Hispanic/Latino), 1 international. Average age 38. 13 applicants, 100% accepted, 12 enrolled. *Faculty:* 1 full-time (0 women), 2 part-time/adjunct (0 women). Expenses: Contact institution. *Financial support:* In 2010–11, 12 students received support. Federal Work-Study, scholarships/grants, and state work-study, institutional employment available. Support available to part-time students. Financial award application deadline: 4/15; financial award applicants required to submit FAFSA. *Degree program information:* Part-time programs available. Offers faith and culture (MA). *Application deadline:* Applications are processed on a rolling basis. *Application fee:* $35. Electronic applications accepted. *Application Contact:* Dr. Adam Martinez, Program Director, 713-942-5066, E-mail: cfc@stthom.edu. *Director,* Fr. Donald S. Nesti, 713-942-5066, E-mail: cfc@stthom.edu.

Center for Thomistic Studies Students: 9 full-time (2 women), 22 part-time (2 women); includes 7 minority (2 Asian, non-Hispanic/Latino; 5 Hispanic/Latino), 3 international. Average age 33. 16 applicants, 75% accepted, 8 enrolled. *Faculty:* 7 full-time (1 woman). Expenses: Contact institution. *Financial support:* In 2010–11, 9 students received support. Federal Work-Study, scholarships/grants, unspecified assistantships, and state work-study, institutional employment available. Support available to part-time students. Financial award application

University of St. Thomas (continued)

deadline: 4/15; financial award applicants required to submit FAFSA. In 2010, 3 master's awarded. *Degree program information:* Part-time programs available. Offers philosophy (MA, PhD). *Application deadline:* Applications are processed on a rolling basis. *Application fee:* $35. Electronic applications accepted. *Application Contact:* Valerie Hall, Administrative Assistant II, 713-525-3591, Fax: 713-942-3464, E-mail: hallvl@stthom.edu. *Director,* Dr. Mary Catherine Sommers, 713-525-3591, Fax: 713-942-3464, E-mail: sommers@stthom.edu.

Program in Liberal Arts Students: 47 full-time (30 women), 122 part-time (84 women); includes 61 minority (22 Black or African American, non-Hispanic/Latino; 1 American Indian or Alaska Native, non-Hispanic/Latino; 8 Asian, non-Hispanic/Latino; 26 Hispanic/Latino; 1 Native Hawaiian or other Pacific Islander, non-Hispanic/Latino; 3 Two or more races, non-Hispanic/Latino), 16 international. Average age 34. 63 applicants, 94% accepted, 49 enrolled. *Faculty:* 34 full-time (14 women), 15 part-time/adjunct (7 women). Expenses: Contact institution. *Financial support:* In 2010–11, 19 students received support. Federal Work-Study, scholarships/grants, and state work-study, institutional employment available. Support available to part-time students. Financial award application deadline: 4/15; financial award applicants required to submit FAFSA. In 2010, 30 master's awarded. *Degree program information:* Part-time and evening/weekend programs available. Offers liberal arts (MLA). *Application deadline:* Applications are processed on a rolling basis. *Application fee:* $35. Electronic applications accepted. *Application Contact:* Kate Henderson, Program Assistant, 713-525-6951, Fax: 713-525-6924, E-mail: mla@stthom.edu. *Dean,* Dr. Ravi Srinivas, 713-525-6951, Fax: 713-525-6924, E-mail: mla@stthom.edu.

School of Education Students: 10 full-time (8 women), 705 part-time (613 women); includes 436 minority (145 Black or African American, non-Hispanic/Latino; 5 American Indian or Alaska Native, non-Hispanic/Latino; 18 Asian, non-Hispanic/Latino; 262 Hispanic/Latino; 6 Two or more races, non-Hispanic/Latino), 22 international. Average age 36. 490 applicants, 96% accepted, 355 enrolled. *Faculty:* 17 full-time (9 women), 34 part-time/adjunct (23 women). Expenses: Contact institution. *Financial support:* In 2010–11, 22 students received support. Federal Work-Study, scholarships/grants, and state work-study, institutional employment available. Support available to part-time students. Financial award application deadline: 4/15; financial award applicants required to submit FAFSA. In 2010, 87 master's awarded. *Degree program information:* Part-time and evening/weekend programs available. Postbaccalaureate distance learning degree programs offered (no on-campus study). Offers education (M Ed). *Application deadline:* Applications are processed on a rolling basis. *Application fee:* $35. Electronic applications accepted. *Application Contact:* Paula C. Hollis, Administrative Assistant, 713-525-3540, Fax: 713-525-3871, E-mail: education@stthom.edu. *Dean,* Dr. Robert M. LeBlanc, 713-525-3540, Fax: 713-525-3871, E-mail: education@stthom.edu.

School of Theology Students: 91 full-time (5 women), 113 part-time (39 women); includes 71 minority (9 Black or African American, non-Hispanic/Latino; 21 Asian, non-Hispanic/Latino; 38 Hispanic/Latino; 3 Two or more races, non-Hispanic/Latino), 21 international. Average age 41. 43 applicants, 100% accepted, 35 enrolled. *Faculty:* 8 full-time (2 women), 5 part-time/adjunct (0 women). Expenses: Contact institution. *Financial support:* In 2010–11, 10 students received support. Federal Work-Study, scholarships/grants, and state work-study, institutional employment available. Support available to part-time students. Financial award application deadline: 4/15; financial award applicants required to submit FAFSA. In 2010, 13 first professional degrees, 23 master's awarded. *Degree program information:* Part-time programs available. Offers theology (M Div, MAPS, MAT). *Application deadline:* Applications are processed on a rolling basis. *Application fee:* $35. Electronic applications accepted. *Application Contact:* Connie Henry, Office Manager, 713-686-4345, Fax: 713-683-8673, E-mail: sms@stthom.edu. *Dean,* Dr. Sandra C. Magie, 713-686-4345, Fax: 713-683-8673, E-mail: sms@stthom.edu.

UNIVERSITY OF SAN DIEGO, San Diego, CA 92110-2492

General Information Independent-religious, coed, university. CGS member. *Enrollment:* 8,201 graduate, professional, and undergraduate students; 1,603 full-time matriculated graduate/professional students (916 women), 974 part-time matriculated graduate/professional students (575 women). *Enrollment by degree level:* 1,007 first professional, 1,301 master's, 210 doctoral, 59 other advanced degrees. *Graduate faculty:* 150 full-time (71 women), 213 part-time/adjunct (124 women). *Tuition:* Full-time $21,744; part-time $1208 per unit. *Required fees:* $224. Full-time tuition and fees vary according to course load and degree level. *Graduate housing:* Room and/or apartments available on a first-come, first-served basis to single students; on-campus housing not available to married students. Typical cost: $11,602 (including board). Housing application deadline: 6/15. *Student services:* Campus employment opportunities, career counseling, child daycare facilities, free psychological counseling, international student services, low-cost health insurance, multicultural affairs office, services for students with disabilities, teacher training. *Library facilities:* Helen K. and James S. Copley Library plus 1 other. *Online resources:* library catalog, access to other libraries' catalogs. *Collection:* 852,714 titles, 38,940 serial subscriptions, 16,781 audiovisual materials. *Research affiliation:* Leon R. Hubbard Hatchery (marine science), Southwest Fisheries Science Center (marine science), Hubbs Seaworld Research Institute (marine science), old Globe Theater (dramatic arts), Old Globe Theater (dramatic arts).

Computer facilities: Computer purchase and lease plans are available. 1,283 computers available on campus for general student use. A campuswide network can be accessed from student residence rooms and from off campus. Online class registration is available. *Web address:* http://www.sandiego.edu/.

General Application Contact: Dr. John Mosby, Associate Director of Graduate Admissions, 619-260-4524, Fax: 619-260-4158, E-mail: grads@sandiego.edu.

GRADUATE UNITS

College of Arts and Sciences Students: 49 full-time (28 women), 39 part-time (20 women); includes 3 Black or African American, non-Hispanic/Latino; 1 American Indian or Alaska Native, non-Hispanic/Latino; 1 Asian, non-Hispanic/Latino; 11 Hispanic/Latino; 3 Two or more races, non-Hispanic/Latino, 2 international. Average age 28. 469 applicants, 14% accepted, 35 enrolled. *Faculty:* 10 full-time (4 women), 5 part-time/adjunct (1 woman). Expenses: Contact institution. *Financial support:* In 2010–11, 54 students received support, including 14 fellowships; career-related internships or fieldwork, Federal Work-Study, institutionally sponsored loans, scholarships/grants, and unspecified assistantships also available. Support available to part-time students. Financial award application deadline: 4/1; financial award applicants required to submit FAFSA. In 2010, 34 master's awarded. *Degree program information:* Part-time and evening/weekend programs available. Offers arts and sciences (MA, MFA, MS); dramatic arts (MFA); history (MA); international relations (MA); marine science (MS). *Application deadline:* Applications are processed on a rolling basis. *Application fee:* $45. Electronic applications accepted. *Application Contact:* Stephen Pultz, Director of Admissions and Enrollment, 619-260-4506, Fax: 619-260-6836, E-mail: admissions@sandiego.edu. *Dean,* Dr. Mary K. Boyd, 619-260-4545, E-mail: deanboyd@sandiego.edu.

Hahn School of Nursing and Health Science Students: 146 full-time (124 women), 173 part-time (151 women); includes 108 minority (14 Black or African American, non-Hispanic/Latino; 7 American Indian or Alaska Native, non-Hispanic/Latino; 37 Asian, non-Hispanic/Latino; 37 Hispanic/Latino; 1 Native Hawaiian or other Pacific Islander, non-Hispanic/Latino; 12 Two or more races, non-Hispanic/Latino), 7 international. Average age 38. 483 applicants, 45% accepted, 123 enrolled. *Faculty:* 21 full-time (19 women), 38 part-time/adjunct (34 women). Expenses: Contact institution. *Financial support:* In 2010–11, 270 students received support. Scholarships/grants and traineeships available. Support available to part-time students. Financial award application deadline: 4/1; financial award applicants required to submit FAFSA. In 2010, 116 master's, 10 doctorates awarded. *Degree program information:* Part-time and evening/weekend programs available. Offers adult nurse practitioner/family nurse practitioner (MSN); adult-gerontology clinical nurse specialist (MSN); clinical nursing (MSN); entry-level nursing (for non-RNs) (MSN); executive nurse leader (MSN); family nurse practitioner (MSN); healthcare informatics (MS, MSN); nursing (PhD); nursing practice (DNP); pediatric nurse practitioner/family nurse practitioner (MSN); psychiatric-mental health nurse practitioner (MSN). *Application deadline:* For fall admission, 3/1 priority date for domestic students, 3/1 for international students; for spring admission, 11/1 priority date for domestic students, 11/1 for international students. Applications are processed on a rolling basis. *Application fee:* $45. Electronic applications accepted. *Application Contact:* Stephen Pultz, Director of Admissions and Enrollment, 619-260-4506, Fax: 619-260-6836, E-mail: admissions@sandiego.edu. *Dean,* Dr. Sally Hardin, 619-260-4550, Fax: 619-260-6814.

Joan B. Kroc School of Peace Studies Students: 33 full-time (21 women), 1 (woman) part-time; includes 1 Black or African American, non-Hispanic/Latino; 3 Hispanic/Latino, 9 international. Average age 31. 100 applicants, 64% accepted, 26 enrolled. *Faculty:* 4 full-time (2 women), 1 part-time/adjunct (0 women). Expenses: Contact institution. *Financial support:* In 2010–11, 20 students received support, including 9 fellowships; career-related internships or fieldwork, Federal Work-Study, institutionally sponsored loans, scholarships/grants, and unspecified assistantships also available. Support available to part-time students. Financial award application deadline: 4/1; financial award applicants required to submit FAFSA. In 2010, 15 master's awarded. Offers peace and justice studies (MA). *Application deadline:* For fall admission, 2/15 for domestic and international students. *Application fee:* $45. Electronic applications accepted. *Application Contact:* Stephen Pultz, Director of Admissions and Enrollment, 619-260-4506, Fax: 619-260-6836, E-mail: admissions@sandiego.edu. *Dean,* Fr. William Headley, 619-260-7919, E-mail: wheadley@sandiego.edu.

School of Business Administration Students: 207 full-time (85 women), 269 part-time (93 women); includes 98 minority (10 Black or African American, non-Hispanic/Latino; 2 American Indian or Alaska Native, non-Hispanic/Latino; 30 Asian, non-Hispanic/Latino; 46 Hispanic/Latino; 2 Native Hawaiian or other Pacific Islander, non-Hispanic/Latino; 8 Two or more races, non-Hispanic/Latino), 41 international. Average age 31. 591 applicants, 54% accepted, 216 enrolled. *Faculty:* 33 full-time (7 women), 14 part-time/adjunct (6 women). Expenses: Contact institution. *Financial support:* In 2010–11, 247 students received support. Career-related internships or fieldwork, Federal Work-Study, institutionally sponsored loans, scholarships/grants, and unspecified assistantships available. Support available to part-time students. Financial award application deadline: 4/1; financial award applicants required to submit FAFSA. In 2010, 239 master's awarded. *Degree program information:* Part-time and evening/weekend programs available. Offers accountancy (MS); accountancy and taxation (MS); business administration (IMBA, MBA, MS, Certificate); executive leadership (MS); global leadership (MS); international business administration (IMBA); real estate (MS); supply chain management (MS, Certificate); taxation (MS). *Application fee:* $80. Electronic applications accepted. *Application Contact:* Stephen Pultz, Director of Admissions and Enrollment, 619-260-4506, Fax: 619-260-6836, E-mail: admissions@sandiego.edu. *Dean,* Dr. David Pyke, 619-260-4886, E-mail: sbadean@sandiego.edu.

School of Law Students: 881 full-time (435 women), 226 part-time (96 women); includes 336 minority (13 Black or African American, non-Hispanic/Latino; 3 American Indian or Alaska Native, non-Hispanic/Latino; 161 Asian, non-Hispanic/Latino; 113 Hispanic/Latino; 2 Native Hawaiian or other Pacific Islander, non-Hispanic/Latino; 44 Two or more races, non-Hispanic/Latino), 30 international. Average age 26. 4,808 applicants, 32% accepted, 295 enrolled. *Faculty:* 50 full-time (21 women), 66 part-time/adjunct (18 women). Expenses: Contact institution. *Financial support:* In 2010–11, 973 students received support. Career-related internships or fieldwork, Federal Work-Study, institutionally sponsored loans, and scholarships/grants available. Support available to part-time students. Financial award application deadline: 3/1; financial award applicants required to submit FAFSA. In 2010, 318 first professional degrees, 72 master's awarded. *Degree program information:* Part-time and evening/weekend programs available. Offers business and corporate law (LL M); comparative law (LL M); general studies (LL M); international law (LL M); law (JD); taxation (LL M, Diploma). *Application deadline:* For fall admission, 2/1 priority date for domestic students. Applications are processed on a rolling basis. *Application fee:* $50. Electronic applications accepted. *Application Contact:* Carl J. Eging, Director of Admissions and Financial Aid, 619-260-4528, Fax: 619-260-2218, E-mail: eging@sandiego.edu. *Dean,* Kevin Cole, 619-260-2330, Fax: 619-260-2218.

School of Leadership and Education Sciences Students: 252 full-time (214 women), 301 part-time (223 women); includes 199 minority (29 Black or African American, non-Hispanic/Latino; 2 American Indian or Alaska Native, non-Hispanic/Latino; 31 Asian, non-Hispanic/Latino; 111 Hispanic/Latino; 5 Native Hawaiian or other Pacific Islander, non-Hispanic/Latino; 21 Two or more races, non-Hispanic/Latino), 17 international. Average age 31. 803 applicants, 56% accepted, 185 enrolled. *Faculty:* 32 full-time (18 women), 89 part-time/adjunct (65 women). Expenses: Contact institution. *Financial support:* In 2010–11, 446 students received support. Career-related internships or fieldwork, Federal Work-Study, institutionally sponsored loans, unspecified assistantships, and stipends available. Support available to part-time students. Financial award application deadline: 4/1; financial award applicants required to submit FAFSA. In 2010, 208 master's, 15 doctorates awarded. *Degree program information:* Part-time and evening/weekend programs available. Offers clinical mental health counseling (MA); curriculum and instruction (M Ed); higher education leadership (MA); leadership and education sciences (M Ed, MA, MAT, PhD, Certificate); leadership studies (MA, PhD); marital and family therapy (MA); nonprofit leadership and management (MA, Certificate); school counseling (MA); special education (M Ed); special education with deaf and hard of hearing (M Ed); teaching (MAT); TESOL, literacy and culture (M Ed). *Application fee:* $45. *Application Contact:* Stephen Pultz, Director of Admissions and Enrollment, 619-260-4506, Fax: 619-260-6836, E-mail: admissions@sandiego.edu. *Dean,* Dr. Paula A. Cordeiro, 619-260-4540, Fax: 619-260-6835, E-mail: cordeiro@sandiego.edu.

UNIVERSITY OF SAN FRANCISCO, San Francisco, CA 94117-1080

General Information Independent-religious, coed, university. *Enrollment:* 9,494 graduate, professional, and undergraduate students; 3,105 full-time matriculated graduate/professional students (1,922 women), 619 part-time matriculated graduate/professional students (378 women). *Enrollment by degree level:* 764 first professional, 2,663 master's, 297 doctoral. *Graduate faculty:* 118 full-time (52 women), 277 part-time/adjunct (138 women). *Tuition:* Full-time $20,070; part-time $1115 per credit hour. Tuition and fees vary according to course load, degree level and program. *Graduate housing:* Room and/or apartments available on a first-come, first-served basis to single students; on-campus housing not available to married students. Typical cost: $8240 per year ($12,250 including board). Room and board charges vary according to campus/location and housing facility selected. *Student services:* Campus employment opportunities, career counseling, free psychological counseling, international student services, low-cost health insurance, multicultural affairs office, services for students with disabilities, teacher training. *Library facilities:* Gleeson Library plus 2 others. *Online resources:* library catalog, web page, access to other libraries' catalogs. *Collection:* 1.1 million titles, 5,560 serial subscriptions. *Research affiliation:* NASA–Ames Research Center.

Computer facilities: Computer purchase and lease plans are available. 350 computers available on campus for general student use. A campuswide network can be accessed from student residence rooms and from off campus. Online class registration is available. *Web address:* http://www.usfca.edu/.

General Application Contact: Information Contact, 415-422-4723, Fax: 415-422-2217, E-mail: graduate@usfca.edu.

GRADUATE UNITS

College of Arts and Sciences Students: 680 full-time (343 women), 150 part-time (62 women); includes 220 minority (25 Black or African American, non-Hispanic/Latino; 2 American Indian or Alaska Native, non-Hispanic/Latino; 100 Asian, non-Hispanic/Latino; 62 Hispanic/Latino; 1 Native Hawaiian or other Pacific Islander, non-Hispanic/Latino; 30 Two or more races, non-Hispanic/Latino), 222 international. Average age 29. 1,841 applicants, 45% accepted, 375 enrolled. *Faculty:* 37 full-time (13 women), 41 part-time/adjunct (13 women). Expenses: Contact institution. *Financial support:* In 2010–11, 468 students received support; fellowships, research assistantships, teaching assistantships, career-related internships or fieldwork, Federal Work-Study, institutionally sponsored loans, and tuition waivers (partial) available. Support available to part-time students. Financial award application deadline: 3/2; financial award applicants required to submit FAFSA. In 2010, 325 master's awarded. *Degree program information:* Part-time and evening/weekend programs available. Offers arts and sciences (MA, MFA, MPA, MS); Asia Pacific studies (MA); biology (MS); chemistry (MS); computer science (MS); economics (MA); environmental management (MS); financial analysis (MS); international and development economics (MA); international studies (MA); investor relations (MA); public affairs and practical politics (MPA); risk management (MS); sport management

(MA); Web science (MS); writing (MFA). *Application deadline:* Applications are processed on a rolling basis. *Application fee:* $55 ($65 for international students). *Application Contact:* Information Contact, 415-422-5135, Fax: 415-422-2217, E-mail: asgraduate@usfca.edu. *Dean,* Dr. Jennifer Turpin, 415-422-6373.

School of Business and Professional Studies Students: 439 full-time (288 women), 18 part-time (14 women); includes 223 minority (47 Black or African American, non-Hispanic/Latino; 4 American Indian or Alaska Native, non-Hispanic/Latino; 84 Asian, non-Hispanic/Latino; 61 Hispanic/Latino; 4 Native Hawaiian or other Pacific Islander, non-Hispanic/Latino; 23 Two or more races, non-Hispanic/Latino), 23 international. Average age 33. 315 applicants, 77% accepted, 164 enrolled. *Faculty:* 11 full-time (4 women), 40 part-time/adjunct (19 women). Expenses: Contact institution. *Financial support:* In 2010–11, 265 students received support. Available to part-time students. Application deadline: 3/2. In 2010, 177 master's awarded. *Degree program information:* Part-time and evening/weekend programs available. Offers business and professional studies (MBA, MGEM, MNA, MPA, MS); health services administration (MPA); information systems (MS); nonprofit administration (MNA); organization development (MS); project management (MS); public administration (MPA). *Application fee:* $55 ($65 for international students). *Application Contact:* 415-422-6000, E-mail: graduate@usfca.edu. *Dean,* Dr. Michael Duffy, 415-422-2592.

Masagung Graduate School of Management Students: 350 full-time (170 women), 11 part-time (6 women); includes 133 minority (8 Black or African American, non-Hispanic/Latino; 76 Asian, non-Hispanic/Latino; 31 Hispanic/Latino; 3 Native Hawaiian or other Pacific Islander, non-Hispanic/Latino; 15 Two or more races, non-Hispanic/Latino), 57 international. Average age 30. 592 applicants, 62% accepted, 132 enrolled. *Faculty:* 19 full-time (4 women), 18 part-time/adjunct (8 women). Expenses: Contact institution. *Financial support:* In 2010–11, 211 students received support; fellowships, research assistantships, teaching assistantships, career-related internships or fieldwork, Federal Work-Study, and institutionally sponsored loans available. Support available to part-time students. Financial award application deadline: 3/2; financial award applicants required to submit FAFSA. In 2010, 184 master's awarded. *Degree program information:* Part-time and evening/weekend programs available. Offers business administration (MBA); business economics (MBA); e-business (MBA); entrepreneurship (MBA); finance (MBA); global entrepreneurship and management (MGEM); international business (MBA); management (MBA, MGEM); marketing (MBA); telecommunications management and policy (MBA). *Application deadline:* For fall admission, 7/1 priority date for domestic students; for spring admission, 11/30 for domestic students. Applications are processed on a rolling basis. *Application Contact:* Kelly Brookes, Director, MBA Program, 415-422-2221, Fax: 415-422-6315, E-mail: mba@usfca.edu. *Dean,* Dr. Michael Duffy, 415-422-6771, Fax: 415-422-2502.

School of Education Students: 770 full-time (575 women), 225 part-time (157 women); includes 363 minority (55 Black or African American, non-Hispanic/Latino; 3 American Indian or Alaska Native, non-Hispanic/Latino; 118 Asian, non-Hispanic/Latino; 139 Hispanic/Latino; 2 Native Hawaiian or other Pacific Islander, non-Hispanic/Latino; 46 Two or more races, non-Hispanic/Latino), 50 international. Average age 34. 1,055 applicants, 65% accepted, 386 enrolled. *Faculty:* 22 full-time (15 women), 97 part-time/adjunct (62 women). Expenses: Contact institution. *Financial support:* In 2010–11, 624 students received support; fellowships, research assistantships, teaching assistantships available. Financial award application deadline: 3/2; financial award applicants required to submit FAFSA. In 2010, 301 master's, 47 doctorates awarded. *Degree program information:* Part-time and evening/weekend programs available. Offers Catholic school leadership (MA, Ed D); Catholic school teaching (MA); counseling (MA); counseling psychology (Ed D); digital media and learning (MA); education (MA, Ed D); international and multicultural education (MA, Ed D); learning and instruction (MA, Ed D); multicultural literature for children and young adults (MA); organization and leadership (MA, Ed D); teaching (MA); teaching English as a second language (MA); teaching reading (MA). *Application fee:* $55 ($65 for international students). *Application Contact:* Beth Teabue, Associate Director of Graduate Outreach, 415-422-5467, E-mail: schoolofeducation@usfca.edu. *Dean,* Dr. Walter Gmelch, 415-422-6525.

School of Law Students: 613 full-time (340 women), 151 part-time (78 women); includes 271 minority (50 Black or African American, non-Hispanic/Latino; 4 American Indian or Alaska Native, non-Hispanic/Latino; 96 Asian, non-Hispanic/Latino; 82 Hispanic/Latino; 2 Native Hawaiian or other Pacific Islander, non-Hispanic/Latino; 37 Two or more races, non-Hispanic/Latino), 31 international. Average age 27. 4,949 applicants, 32% accepted, 271 enrolled. *Faculty:* 27 full-time (13 women), 49 part-time/adjunct (18 women). Expenses: Contact institution. *Financial support:* In 2010–11, 667 students received support. Career-related internships or fieldwork, Federal Work-Study, and institutionally sponsored loans available. Support available to part-time students. Financial award application deadline: 3/2; financial award applicants required to submit FAFSA. In 2010, 191 first professional degrees awarded. *Degree program information:* Part-time and evening/weekend programs available. Offers intellectual property and technology law (LL M); international transactions and comparative law (LL M); law (JD, LL M). *Application deadline:* For fall admission, 4/1 for domestic students. Applications are processed on a rolling basis. *Application Contact:* Alan P. Guerrero, Director of Admissions, 415-422-2975, E-mail: lawadmissions@usfca.edu. *Dean,* Jeffrey Brand, 415-422-6304.

School of Nursing Students: 253 full-time (206 women), 64 part-time (61 women); includes 147 minority (18 Black or African American, non-Hispanic/Latino; 1 American Indian or Alaska Native, non-Hispanic/Latino; 72 Asian, non-Hispanic/Latino; 42 Hispanic/Latino; 1 Native Hawaiian or other Pacific Islander, non-Hispanic/Latino; 13 Two or more races, non-Hispanic/Latino), 4 international. Average age 38. 422 applicants, 37% accepted, 89 enrolled. *Faculty:* 7 full-time (all women), 31 part-time/adjunct (30 women). Expenses: Contact institution. *Financial support:* In 2010–11, 220 students received support. Institutionally sponsored loans available. Financial award application deadline: 3/2. In 2010, 103 master's, 7 doctorates awarded. *Degree program information:* Part-time programs available. Offers clinical nurse leader (MSN); family nurse practitioner (DNP); healthcare systems leadership (MSN, DNP); nursing practice (DNP). *Application deadline:* Applications are processed on a rolling basis. *Application fee:* $40. *Application Contact:* Information Contact, 415-422-4723, Fax: 415-422-2217. *Dean,* Dr. Judith Karshmer, 415-422-6681, Fax: 415-422-6877, E-mail: nursing@usfca.edu.

UNIVERSITY OF SASKATCHEWAN, Saskatoon, SK S7N 5A2, Canada

General Information Province-supported, coed, university. *Graduate housing:* Rooms and/or apartments available on a first-come, first-served basis to single and married students. *Research affiliation:* Canada Agriculture, Saskatchewan Research Council, University Hospital, Innovation Place, Vaccine and Infectious Disease Organization/InterVac Libratory (vaccinology and immunothereaputics), Canadian Light Source.

GRADUATE UNITS

College of Dentistry Offers dentistry (DMD). Electronic applications accepted.

College of Graduate Studies and Research *Degree program information:* Part-time programs available. Electronic applications accepted.

College of Agriculture *Degree program information:* Part-time programs available. Offers agricultural economics (M Ag, M Sc, MA, PhD, PGD); agriculture (M Ag, M Sc, MA, PhD, Diploma, PGD); animal and poultry science (M Ag, M Sc, PhD); applied microbiology and food science (M Ag, M Sc, PhD); plant sciences (M Sc, PhD); soil science (M Ag, M Sc, PhD, Diploma).

College of Arts and Sciences *Degree program information:* Part-time programs available. Offers archaeology (MA, PhD); art and art history (MFA); arts and sciences (M Math, M Mus, M Sc, MA, MFA, PhD, Diploma); biology (M Sc, PhD); chemistry (M Sc, PhD); computer science (M Sc, PhD); drama (MA); economics (MA, Diploma); English (MA, PhD); geography (M Sc, MA, PhD); geological sciences (M Sc, PhD, Diploma); history (MA, PhD); languages and linguistics (MA); mathematics and statistics (M Math, MA, PhD); music (M Mus, MA); native studies (MA, PhD); philosophy (MA); physics and engineering physics (M Sc, PhD); political studies (MA); psychology (MA, PhD); religious studies and anthropology (MA); sociology (MA, PhD); women's and gender studies (MA, PhD). Electronic applications accepted.

College of Education *Degree program information:* Part-time programs available. Offers curriculum studies (M Ed, PhD, Diploma); education (M Ed, MC Ed, PhD, Diploma); educational administration (M Ed, PhD, Diploma); educational foundations (M Ed, MC Ed, PhD, Diploma); educational psychology and special education (M Ed, PhD, Diploma). Electronic applications accepted.

College of Engineering Offers agricultural and bioresource engineering (M Eng, M Sc, PhD); biomedical engineering (M Eng, M Sc, PhD); chemical engineering (M Eng, M Sc, PhD); civil and geological engineering (M Eng, M Sc, PhD); electrical engineering (M Eng, M Sc, PhD); engineering (M Eng, M Sc, PhD, Diploma); environmental engineering (M Eng, M Sc, PhD, Diploma); mechanical engineering (M Sc, PhD).

College of Kinesiology Offers kinesiology (M Sc, PhD, Diploma).

College of Law *Degree program information:* Part-time programs available. Offers law (LL B, LL M).

College of Nursing *Degree program information:* Part-time programs available. Offers nursing (MN).

College of Pharmacy and Nutrition Offers pharmacy and nutrition (M Sc, PhD).

Edwards School of Business *Degree program information:* Part-time programs available. Offers accounting (M Sc, MP Acc); agribusiness management (MBA); biotechnology management (MBA); business (M Sc, MBA, MP Acc); finance (M Sc); health services management (MBA); indigenous management (MBA); industrial relations and organizational behavior (M Sc); international business management (MBA); marketing (M Sc).

School of Environment and Sustainability Offers environment and sustainability (MES).

School of Public Policy Offers public policy (MIT, MPA, MPP, PhD).

Toxicology Centre Offers toxicology (M Sc, PhD, Diploma).

College of Medicine Offers anatomy and cell biology (M Sc, PhD); biochemistry (M Sc, PhD); community health and epidemiology (M Sc, PhD); medicine (MD, M Sc, DPT, PhD); microbiology and immunology (M Sc, PhD); obstetrics, gynecology and reproductive services (M Sc, PhD); pathology (M Sc, PhD); pharmacology (M Sc, PhD); physiology (M Sc, PhD); psychiatry (M Sc, PhD); surgery (M Sc).

Western College of Veterinary Medicine Students: 127 full-time (76 women); includes 9 Black or African American, non-Hispanic/Latino. *Faculty:* 43 full-time (15 women), 15 part-time/adjunct (3 women). Expenses: Contact institution. *Financial support:* Fellowships, teaching assistantships available. Financial award application deadline: 1/31. In 2010, 16 master's, 10 doctorates awarded. Offers large animal clinical sciences (M Sc, M Vet Sc, PhD); small animal clinical sciences (M Sc, M Vet Sc, PhD); veterinary anatomy (M Sc); veterinary anesthesiology, radiology and surgery (M Vet Sc); veterinary biomedical sciences (M Sc, M Vet Sc, PhD); veterinary internal medicine (M Vet Sc); veterinary medicine (DVM, M Sc, M Vet Sc, PhD); veterinary microbiology (M Sc, M Vet Sc, PhD); veterinary pathology (M Sc, M Vet Sc, PhD); veterinary physiological sciences (M Sc, PhD). *Application deadline:* For fall admission, 7/1 priority date for domestic students. *Application Contact:* Dr. Norman C. Rawlings, Associate Dean, Research, 306-966-7068, Fax: 306-966-8747, E-mail: norman.rawlings@usask.ca. *Dean,* Dr. C. S. Rhodes, 306-966-7447, Fax: 306-966-8747, E-mail: charles.rhodes@usask.ca.

THE UNIVERSITY OF SCRANTON, Scranton, PA 18510

General Information Independent-religious, coed, comprehensive institution. CGS member. *Enrollment:* 6,070 graduate, professional, and undergraduate students; 1,224 full-time matriculated graduate/professional students (754 women), 639 part-time matriculated graduate/professional students (392 women). *Enrollment by degree level:* 1,727 master's, 136 doctoral. *Graduate faculty:* 135 full-time (57 women), 68 part-time/adjunct (29 women). *Graduate housing:* Room and/or apartments available to single students; on-campus housing not available to married students. *Student services:* Campus employment opportunities, campus safety program, career counseling, exercise/wellness program, free psychological counseling, international student services, multicultural affairs office, services for students with disabilities, writing training. *Library facilities:* Harry and Jeanette Weinberg Memorial Library plus 1 other. *Online resources:* library catalog, web page, access to other libraries' catalogs. *Collection:* 393,189 titles, 48,201 serial subscriptions. *Research affiliation:* Lackawanna River Corridor Association (environment), Universidad Iberoamericana (counseling and human services), Wyoming Valley Health Care System (nursing), Community Medical Center (health services), National Health Management Center (health care management), Allied Services (rehabilitation).

Computer facilities: Computer purchase and lease plans are available. 945 computers available on campus for general student use. A campuswide network can be accessed from student residence rooms and from off campus. Online class registration is available. *Web address:* http://www.scranton.edu/.

General Application Contact: Joseph M. Roback, Director of Admissions, 570-941-4385, Fax: 570-941-5995, E-mail: robackj2@scranton.edu.

GRADUATE UNITS

College of Graduate and Continuing Education Students: 1,224 full-time (754 women), 639 part-time (392 women); includes 107 Black or African American, non-Hispanic/Latino; 37 Asian, non-Hispanic/Latino; 42 Hispanic/Latino, 88 International. Average age 32. 1,182 applicants, 71% accepted. *Faculty:* 135 full-time (57 women), 68 part-time/adjunct (29 women). Expenses: Contact institution. *Financial support:* In 2010–11, 128 students received support, including 128 teaching assistantships with full and partial tuition reimbursements available (averaging $5,870 per year); fellowships, career-related internships or fieldwork, Federal Work-Study, and unspecified assistantships also available. Support available to part-time students. Financial award application deadline: 3/1. In 2010, 635 master's, 37 doctorates awarded. *Degree program information:* Part-time and evening/weekend programs available. Postbaccalaureate distance learning degree programs offered (no on-campus study). Offers accounting (MBA); adult health nursing (MSN); biochemistry (MA, MS); chemistry (MA, MS); clinical chemistry (MA, MS); community counseling (MS); curriculum and instruction (MA, MS); early childhood education (MA, MS); educational administration (MS); elementary education (MS); English as a second language (MS); family nurse practitioner (MSN, PMC); finance (MBA); general business administration (MBA); health administration (MHA); health care management (MBA); history (MA); human resources (MS); human resources administration (MS); human resources development (MS); international business (MBA); management information systems (MBA); marketing (MBA); nurse anesthesia (MSN, PMC); occupational therapy (MS); operations management (MBA); organizational leadership (MS); physical therapy (MPT, DPT); professional counseling (CAGS); reading education (MS); rehabilitation counseling (MS); school counseling (MS); secondary education (MS); software engineering (MS); special education (MS); theology (MA). *Application deadline:* Applications are processed on a rolling basis. *Application fee:* $0. Electronic applications accepted. *Application Contact:* Joseph M. Roback, Director of Admissions, 570-941-4385, Fax: 570-941-5928, E-mail: robackj2@scranton.edu. *Dean,* Dr. W. Jeffrey Welsh, 570-941-6300, Fax: 570-941-7621, E-mail: welshw2@scranton.edu.

UNIVERSITY OF SIOUX FALLS, Sioux Falls, SD 57105-1699

General Information Independent-religious, coed, comprehensive institution. *Graduate housing:* Rooms and/or apartments available on a first-come, first-served basis to single and married students.

GRADUATE UNITS

Fredrikson School of Education *Degree program information:* Part-time and evening/weekend programs available. Offers leadership (M Ed); reading (M Ed); superintendent (Ed S); teaching (M Ed); technology (M Ed). Summer admission only.

John T. Vucurevich School of Business *Degree program information:* Part-time and evening/weekend programs available. Offers business (MBA).

UNIVERSITY OF SOUTH AFRICA, Pretoria 0003, South Africa

General Information Private, coed, university.

University of South Africa (continued)

GRADUATE UNITS

College of Agriculture and Environmental Sciences Offers agriculture (MS); consumer science (MCS); environmental management (MA, MS, PhD); environmental science (MA, MS, PhD); geography (MA, MS, PhD); horticulture (M Tech); human ecology (MHE); life sciences (MS); nature conservation (M Tech).

College of Economic and Management Sciences Offers accounting (D Admin, D Com); accounting science (DA); auditing (D Admin, D Com); business administration (M Tech); business economics (D Admin); business leadership (DBL); business management (D Admin, D Com); economic management analysis (M Tech); economics (D Admin, D Com, PhD); human resource development (M Tech); industrial psychology (D Admin, D Com, PhD); logistics (D Com); marketing (M Tech); public administration (D Admin, D Com, DPA, PhD); public management (M Tech); quantitative management (D Admin, D Com); real estate (M Tech); statistics (D Admin, PhD); tourism management (D Admin, D Com); transport economics (D Admin, D Com).

College of Human Sciences Offers adult education (M Ed); African languages (MA, PhD); African politics (MA, PhD); Afrikaans (MA, PhD); ancient history (MA, PhD); ancient Near Eastern studies (MA, PhD); anthropology (MA, PhD); applied linguistics (MA); Arabic (MA, PhD); archaeology (MA); art history (MA); Biblical archaeology (MA); Biblical studies (M Th, D Th, PhD); Christian spirituality (M Th, D Th); church history (M Th, D Th); classical studies (MA, PhD); clinical psychology (MA); communication (MA, PhD); comparative education (M Ed, Ed D); consulting psychology (D Admin, D Com, PhD); curriculum studies (M Ed, Ed D); development studies (M Admin, MA, D Admin, PhD); didactics (M Ed, Ed D); education (M Tech); education management (M Ed, Ed D); educational psychology (M Ed); English (MA); environmental education (M Ed); French (MA, PhD); German (MA, PhD); Greek (MA); guidance and counseling (M Ed); health studies (MA, PhD); history (MA, PhD); history of education (Ed D); inclusive education (M Ed, Ed D); information and communications technology policy and regulation (MA); information science (MA, MIS, PhD); international politics (MA, PhD); Islamic studies (MA, PhD); Italian (MA, PhD); Judaica (MA, PhD); linguistics (MA, PhD); mathematical education (M Ed); mathematics education (MA); missiology (M Th, D Th); modern Hebrew (MA, PhD); musicology (MA, MMus, D Mus, PhD); natural science education (M Ed); New Testament (M Th, D Th); Old Testament (D Th); pastoral therapy (M Th, D Th); philosophy (MA); philosophy of education (M Ed, Ed D); politics (MA, PhD); Portuguese (MA, PhD); practical theology (M Th, D Th); psychology (MA, MS, PhD); psychology of education (M Ed, Ed D); public health (MA); religious studies (MA, D Th, PhD); Romance languages (MA); Russian (MA, PhD); Semitic languages (MA, PhD); social behavior studies in HIV/AIDS (MA); social science (mental health) (MA); social science in development studies (MA); social science in psychology (MA); social science in social work (MA); social science in sociology (MA); social work (MSW, DSW, PhD); socio-education (M Ed, Ed D); sociolinguistics (MA); sociology (MA, PhD); Spanish (MA, PhD); systematic theology (M Th, D Th); TESOL (teaching English to speakers of other languages) (MA); theological ethics (M Th, D Th); theory of literature (MA, PhD); urban ministries (D Th); urban ministry (M Th).

College of Law Offers correctional services management (M Tech); criminology (MA, PhD); law (LL M, LL D); penology (MA, PhD); police science (MA, PhD); policing (M Tech); security risk management (M Tech); social science in criminology (MA).

College of Science, Engineering and Technology Offers chemical engineering (M Tech); information technology (M Tech).

Graduate School of Business Leadership Offers business leadership (MBA, MBL, DBL).

Institute for Science and Technology Education Offers mathematics, science and technology education (M Sc, PhD).

UNIVERSITY OF SOUTH ALABAMA, Mobile, AL 36688-0002

General Information State-supported, coed, university. CGS member. *Enrollment:* 14,776 graduate, professional, and undergraduate students; 2,519 full-time matriculated graduate/professional students (1,838 women), 599 part-time matriculated graduate/professional students (452 women). *Enrollment by degree level:* 299 first professional, 2,274 master's, 420 doctoral, 49 other advanced degrees. *Graduate faculty:* 349 full-time (120 women), 1 (woman) part-time/adjunct. Tuition, state resident: part-time $300 per credit hour. Tuition, nonresident: part-time $600 per credit hour. *Required fees:* $150 per semester. *Graduate housing:* Rooms and/or apartments available to single and married students. Typical cost: $2708 per year ($5608 including board) for single students; $2708 per year ($5608 including board) for married students. Room and board charges vary according to board plan. Housing application deadline: 5/21. *Student services:* Campus employment opportunities, campus safety program, career counseling, exercise/wellness program, free psychological counseling, grant writing training, international student services, low-cost health insurance, multicultural affairs office, services for students with disabilities, writing training. *Library facilities:* University Library plus 1 other. *Online resources:* library catalog, web page, access to other libraries' catalogs. *Collection:* 7.6 million titles, 1,137 serial subscriptions, 7,424 audiovisual materials. *Research affiliation:* Gulf Coast Universities Consortium, Alabama EPSCoR Programs, Von Braun Center for Science and Innovation, Oak Ridge Associated Universities, Rand Gulf State Policy Institute, Dauphin Island Marine Laboratory.

Computer facilities: 500 computers available on campus for general student use. A campuswide network can be accessed from student residence rooms and from off campus. Online class registration is available. *Web address:* http://www.southalabama.edu/.

General Application Contact: Dr. B. Keith Harrison, Dean, Graduate School, 251-460-6310, Fax: 251-461-1513, E-mail: kharriso@usouthal.edu.

GRADUATE UNITS

College of Medicine Students: 353 full-time (165 women), 4 part-time (3 women); includes 61 minority (24 Black or African American, non-Hispanic/Latino; 4 American Indian or Alaska Native, non-Hispanic/Latino; 27 Asian, non-Hispanic/Latino; 3 Hispanic/Latino; 2 Native Hawaiian or other Pacific Islander, non-Hispanic/Latino; 1 Two or more races, non-Hispanic/Latino), 12 international. Average age 25. *Faculty:* 50 full-time (9 women), 1 part-time/adjunct (0 women). Expenses: Contact institution. *Financial support:* Fellowships, research assistantships, institutionally sponsored loans and unspecified assistantships available. Financial award applicants required to submit FAFSA. In 2010, 63 first professional degrees awarded. Offers basic medical sciences (PhD); medicine (MD, PhD). *Application deadline:* For fall admission, 6/1 for domestic and international students. *Application fee:* $35. Electronic applications accepted. *Application Contact:* Dean of the Graduate School. *Director of Graduate Studies*, Dr. Keith Harrison, 251-460-6310, E-mail: kharriso@usouthal.edu.

Graduate School Students: 2,819 full-time (2,159 women), 599 part-time (452 women); includes 576 minority (430 Black or African American, non-Hispanic/Latino; 29 American Indian or Alaska Native, non-Hispanic/Latino; 47 Asian, non-Hispanic/Latino; 61 Hispanic/Latino; 4 Native Hawaiian or other Pacific Islander, non-Hispanic/Latino; 5 Two or more races, non-Hispanic/Latino), 300 international. 2,063 applicants, 50% accepted, 701 enrolled. *Faculty:* 333 full-time (114 women), 4 part-time/adjunct (2 women). Expenses: Contact institution. *Financial support:* Fellowships, research assistantships, teaching assistantships, career-related internships or fieldwork, institutionally sponsored loans, and traineeships available. Support available to part-time students. Financial award application deadline: 4/1. In 2010, 66 first professional degrees, 707 master's, 112 doctorates awarded. *Degree program information:* Part-time and evening/weekend programs available. Offers clinical and counseling psychology (PhD); environmental toxicology (MS). *Application deadline:* For fall admission, 7/15 priority date for domestic students, 6/15 for international students; for spring admission, 12/1 for domestic students, 11/1 for international students. Applications are processed on a rolling basis. *Application fee:* $35. *Application Contact:* Dr. B. Keith Harrison, Dean of the Graduate School, 251-460-6310, Fax: 251-461-1513, E-mail: kharriso@usouthal.edu. *Dean of the Graduate School*, Dr. B. Keith Harrison, 251-460-6310, Fax: 251-461-1513, E-mail: kharriso@usouthal.edu.

College of Allied Health Professions Students: 338 full-time (278 women), 22 part-time (17 women); includes 23 minority (13 Black or African American, non-Hispanic/Latino; 5 Asian, non-Hispanic/Latino; 3 Hispanic/Latino; 1 Native Hawaiian or other Pacific Islander, non-Hispanic/Latino; 1 Two or more races, non-Hispanic/Latino), 2 international. 119 applicants, 98% accepted, 72 enrolled. *Faculty:* 28 full-time (14 women), 1 part-time/adjunct (0 women). Expenses: Contact institution. *Financial support:* Fellowships, research assistantships, career-related internships or fieldwork available. Support available to part-time students. Financial award application deadline: 4/1. In 2010, 73 master's, 66 doctorates awarded. Offers allied health professions (MHS, MS, Au D, DPT, PhD); audiology (Au D); communication sciences and disorders (PhD); occupational therapy (MS); physical therapy (DPT); physician assistant studies (MHS); speech and hearing sciences (MS). *Application deadline:* For fall admission, 7/15 priority date for domestic students, 6/15 for international students; for spring admission, 12/1 for domestic students, 11/1 for international students. Applications are processed on a rolling basis. *Application fee:* $35. *Application Contact:* Dr. Julio Turrens, Director of Graduate Studies, 251-445-9250. *Dean*, Dr. Richard Talbott, 251-445-9250.

College of Arts and Sciences Students: 171 full-time (115 women), 83 part-time (53 women); includes 37 minority (27 Black or African American, non-Hispanic/Latino; 3 American Indian or Alaska Native, non-Hispanic/Latino; 2 Asian, non-Hispanic/Latino; 4 Hispanic/Latino; 1 Native Hawaiian or other Pacific Islander, non-Hispanic/Latino), 17 international. 119 applicants, 98% accepted, 72 enrolled. *Faculty:* 126 full-time (37 women), 2 part-time/adjunct (1 woman). Expenses: Contact institution. *Financial support:* Fellowships, research assistantships, teaching assistantships, career-related internships or fieldwork available. Support available to part-time students. Financial award application deadline: 4/1. In 2010, 56 master's, 4 doctorates awarded. *Degree program information:* Part-time and evening/weekend programs available. Offers arts and sciences (MA, MPA, MS, PhD, Certificate); biological sciences (MS); clinical and counseling psychology (PhD); communication (MA); English (MA); gerontology (Certificate); history (MA); marine sciences (MS, PhD); mathematics (MS); psychology (MS); public administration (MPA); sociology (MA). *Application deadline:* For fall admission, 7/15 priority date for domestic students, 6/15 for international students; for spring admission, 12/1 for domestic students, 11/1 for international students. Applications are processed on a rolling basis. *Application fee:* $35. *Application Contact:* Dr. S. L. Varghese, Director of Graduate Studies, 251-460-6280, Fax: 251-460-7928. *Dean*, Dr. Andrzej Wierzbicki, 251-460-6280, Fax: 251-460-7928.

College of Education Students: 315 full-time (250 women), 217 part-time (182 women); includes 128 minority (112 Black or African American, non-Hispanic/Latino; 5 American Indian or Alaska Native, non-Hispanic/Latino; 3 Asian, non-Hispanic/Latino; 7 Hispanic/Latino; 1 Native Hawaiian or other Pacific Islander, non-Hispanic/Latino), 11 international. 208 applicants, 48% accepted, 86 enrolled. *Faculty:* 46 full-time (23 women), 1 (woman) part-time/adjunct. Expenses: Contact institution. *Financial support:* In 2010–11, 23 research assistantships, 10 teaching assistantships were awarded; career-related internships or fieldwork also available. Support available to part-time students. Financial award application deadline: 4/1. In 2010, 187 master's, 10 doctorates awarded. *Degree program information:* Part-time programs available. Offers community counseling (MS); early childhood education (M Ed); education (M Ed, MS, PhD, Ed S); educational administration (Ed S); educational leadership (M Ed); educational media (M Ed, MS); elementary education (M Ed); exercise science (MS); health education (M Ed); instructional design and development (MS, PhD); physical education (M Ed); reading education (M Ed); rehabilitation counseling (MS); school counseling (M Ed); school psychometry (M Ed); science education (M Ed); secondary education (M Ed); special education (M Ed, Ed S); therapeutic recreation (MS). *Application deadline:* For fall admission, 7/15 priority date for domestic students, 6/15 priority date for international students; for spring admission, 12/1 priority date for domestic students, 11/1 priority date for international students. Applications are processed on a rolling basis. *Application fee:* $35. *Application Contact:* Dr. Abigail Baxter, Director of Graduate Studies, 251-460-6310, Fax: 251-461-1513, E-mail: kharriso@usouthal.edu. *Dean*, Dr. Richard Hayes, 251-380-2738.

College of Engineering Students: 114 full-time (16 women), 51 part-time (11 women); includes 9 minority (2 Black or African American, non-Hispanic/Latino; 4 Asian, non-Hispanic/Latino; 3 Hispanic/Latino), 121 international. 174 applicants, 50% accepted, 39 enrolled. *Faculty:* 28 full-time (2 women). Expenses: Contact institution. *Financial support:* Research assistantships, career-related internships or fieldwork and institutionally sponsored loans available. Support available to part-time students. Financial award application deadline: 4/1. In 2010, 63 master's awarded. *Degree program information:* Part-time programs available. Offers chemical engineering (MS Ch E); civil engineering (MSCE); electrical engineering (MSEE); engineering (MS Ch E, MSCE, MSEE, MSME); mechanical engineering (MSME). *Application deadline:* For fall admission, 7/15 priority date for domestic students, 6/15 for international students; for spring admission, 12/1 for domestic students, 11/1 for international students. Applications are processed on a rolling basis. *Application fee:* $35. *Application Contact:* Dr. B. Keith Harrison, Director of Graduate Studies, 251-460-6160. *Director of Graduate Studies*, Dr. Thomas G. Thomas, 251-460-6140.

College of Nursing Students: 1,057 full-time (958 women), 189 part-time (173 women); includes 227 minority (161 Black or African American, non-Hispanic/Latino; 13 American Indian or Alaska Native, non-Hispanic/Latino; 20 Asian, non-Hispanic/Latino; 28 Hispanic/Latino; 1 Native Hawaiian or other Pacific Islander, non-Hispanic/Latino; 4 Two or more races, non-Hispanic/Latino), 8 international. 887 applicants, 45% accepted, 324 enrolled. *Faculty:* 21 full-time (20 women). Expenses: Contact institution. In 2010, 268 master's, 28 doctorates awarded. Offers adult health nursing (MSN); community/mental health nursing (MSN); maternal/child nursing (MSN); nursing (DNP). *Application deadline:* For fall admission, 7/15 for domestic students; for spring admission, 12/1 for domestic students. *Application fee:* $35. *Application Contact:* Dr. B. Keith Harrison, Dean of the Graduate School, 251-460-6310, Fax: 251-461-1513, E-mail: kharriso@usouthal.edu. *Director of Graduate Education*, Dr. Rosemary Rhodes, 251-445-9409, Fax: 251-445-9416.

Mitchell College of Business Students: 91 full-time (36 women), 10 part-time (7 women); includes 13 minority (8 Black or African American, non-Hispanic/Latino; 1 American Indian or Alaska Native, non-Hispanic/Latino; 2 Asian, non-Hispanic/Latino; 2 Hispanic/Latino), 11 international. 175 applicants, 26% accepted, 30 enrolled. *Faculty:* 22 full-time (7 women). Expenses: Contact institution. *Financial support:* Research assistantships available. Support available to part-time students. Financial award application deadline: 4/1. In 2010, 39 master's awarded. *Degree program information:* Part-time and evening/weekend programs available. Offers accounting (M Acc); business (M Acc, MBA); general management (MBA). *Application deadline:* For fall admission, 7/1 priority date for domestic students, 6/15 priority date for international students; for spring admission, 12/1 priority date for domestic students, 11/1 priority date for international students. Applications are processed on a rolling basis. *Application fee:* $35. *Application Contact:* Dr. B. Keith Harrison, Dean of the Graduate School, 251-460-6310, Fax: 251-461-1513, E-mail: kharriso@usouthal.edu. *Director of Graduate Studies*, Dr. John Gamble, 251-460-6418, Fax: 251-460-6529.

School of Computer and Information Sciences Students: 81 full-time (23 women), 20 part-time (4 women); includes 7 minority (4 Black or African American, non-Hispanic/Latino; 2 Asian, non-Hispanic/Latino; 1 Hispanic/Latino), 68 international. 164 applicants, 71% accepted, 31 enrolled. *Faculty:* 9 full-time (0 women). Expenses: Contact institution. *Financial support:* Research assistantships, career-related internships or fieldwork and institutionally sponsored loans available. Support available to part-time students. Financial award application deadline: 4/1. In 2010, 20 master's awarded. *Degree program information:* Part-time and evening/weekend programs available. Offers computer science (MS); information systems (MS). *Application deadline:* For fall admission, 7/15 priority date for domestic students, 6/15 priority date for international students; for spring admission, 12/1 for domestic students, 11/1 priority date for international students. Applications are processed on a rolling basis. *Application fee:* $35. *Application Contact:* Dr. B. Keith Harrison, Dean of the Graduate School, 251-460-6310, Fax: 251-461-1513, E-mail: kharriso@usouthal.edu. *Director of Graduate Studies*, Dr. Roy Daigle, 251-460-6390.

UNIVERSITY OF SOUTH CAROLINA, Columbia, SC 29208

General Information State-supported, coed, university. CGS member. *Graduate housing:* Rooms and/or apartments available to single and married students. *Research affiliation:* E. I. du Pont de Nemours and Company (engineering, chemical engineering), Westinghouse/Savannah River Corporation (environmental restoration, hazardous waste remediation), Motorola Corporation–Energy Production Division (electrochemical engineering), Glaxo-Wellcome (pharmaceuticals), NCR Corporation (electrical and computer engineering).

GRADUATE UNITS

The Graduate School *Degree program information:* Part-time and evening/weekend programs available. Postbaccalaureate distance learning degree programs offered. Offers gerontology (Certificate). Electronic applications accepted.

Arnold School of Public Health *Degree program information:* Part-time programs available. Postbaccalaureate distance learning degree programs offered (minimal on-campus study). Offers biostatistics (MPH, MSPH, Dr PH, PhD); communication sciences and disorders (MCD, MSP, PhD); environmental health science (MS); environmental quality (MPH, MS, MSPH, PhD); epidemiology (MPH, MSPH, Dr PH, PhD); exercise science (MS, DPT, PhD); general public health (MPH); hazardous materials management (MPH, MSPH, PhD); health education (MAT); health promotion, education, and behavior (MPH, MS, MSPH, Dr PH, PhD); health services policy and management (MHA, MPH, Dr PH, PhD); industrial hygiene (MPH, MSPH, PhD); physical activity and public health (MPH); public health (MAT, MCD, MHA, MPH, MS, MSP, MSPH, DPT, Dr PH, PhD, Certificate); school health education (Certificate). Electronic applications accepted.

College of Arts and Sciences *Degree program information:* Part-time and evening/weekend programs available. Offers anthropology (MA, PhD); applied statistics (CAS); archives (MA); art education (IMA, MA, MAT); art history (MA); art studio (MA); arts and sciences (IMA, M Math, MA, MAT, MFA, MIS, MMA, MPA, MS, PSM, PhD, CAS, Certificate); biology (MS, PhD); biology education (IMA, MAT); chemistry and biochemistry (IMA, MAT, MS, PhD); clinical/community psychology (MA, PhD); comparative literature (MA, PhD); creative writing (MFA); criminology and criminal justice (MA, PhD); ecology, evolution and organismal biology (MS, PhD); English (MA, PhD); English education (MAT); experimental psychology (MA, PhD); foreign languages (MAT); French (MA); general psychology (MA); geography (MA, MS, PhD); geography education (IMA); geological sciences (MS, PhD); German (MA); historic preservation (MA); history (MA, PhD); industrial statistics (MIS); international studies (MA, PhD); linguistics (MA, PhD); marine science (MS, PhD); mathematics (MA, MS, PhD); mathematics education (M Math, MAT); media arts (MMA); molecular, cellular, and developmental biology (MS, PhD); museum (MA); museum management (Certificate); philosophy (MA, PhD); physics and astronomy (IMA, MAT, MS, PSM, PhD); political science (MA, PhD); public administration (MPA); public history (MA, Certificate); religious studies (MA); school psychology (PhD); sociology (MA, PhD); Spanish (MA); statistics (MS, PhD); studio art (MFA); teaching English to speakers of other languages (Certificate); theatre (MA, MAT, MFA); women's studies (Certificate). Electronic applications accepted.

College of Education *Degree program information:* Part-time and evening/weekend programs available. Postbaccalaureate distance learning degree programs offered (minimal on-campus study). Offers art education (IMA, MAT); business education (IMA, MAT); counseling education (PhD, Ed S); curriculum and instruction (Ed D); early childhood education (M Ed, Ed D, PhD); education (IMA, M Ed, MAT, MS, MT, Ed D, PhD, Certificate, Ed S); educational administration (M Ed, PhD, Ed S); educational psychology, research (M Ed, PhD); educational technology (M Ed); elementary education (MAT, Ed D, PhD); English (MAT); foreign language (MAT); foundations in education (PhD); health education (MAT); higher education and student affairs (M Ed); higher education leadership (Certificate); language and literacy (M Ed, PhD); mathematics (MAT); physical education (IMA, MAT, MS, PhD); science (IMA, MAT); secondary (Ed D); secondary education (IMA, MAT, MT, Ed D, PhD); social studies (MAT); special education (M Ed, MAT, PhD); teaching (M Ed, Ed S); theatre and speech (MAT). Electronic applications accepted.

College of Engineering and Computing *Degree program information:* Part-time and evening/weekend programs available. Postbaccalaureate distance learning degree programs offered (minimal on-campus study). Offers chemical engineering (ME, MS, PhD); civil engineering (ME, MS, PhD); computer science and engineering (ME, MS, PhD); electrical engineering (ME, MS, PhD); engineering and computing (ME, MS, PhD); mechanical engineering (ME, MS, PhD); nuclear engineering (ME, MS, PhD); software engineering (MS). Electronic applications accepted.

College of Hospitality, Retail, and Sport Management *Degree program information:* Part-time programs available. Postbaccalaureate distance learning degree programs offered (minimal on-campus study). Offers hospitality, retail, and sport management (MIHTM, MR, MS); hotel, restaurant and tourism management (MIHTM); live sport and entertainment events (MS); public assembly facilities management (MS); retailing (MR). Electronic applications accepted.

College of Mass Communications and Information Studies Offers journalism and mass communications (MA, MMC, PhD); library and information science (MLIS, PhD, Certificate, Specialist); mass communications and information studies (MA, MLIS, MMC, PhD, Certificate, Specialist).

College of Nursing *Degree program information:* Part-time programs available. Postbaccalaureate distance learning degree programs offered (minimal on-campus study). Offers acute care clinical specialist (MSN); acute care nurse practitioner (MSN, Certificate); adult nurse practitioner (MSN); advanced practice clinical nursing (MSN, Certificate); advanced practice nursing in primary care (MSN, Certificate); advanced practice nursing in psychiatric mental health (MSN, Certificate); clinical nursing (MSN); community mental health and psychiatric health nursing (MSN); community/public health clinical nurse specialist (MSN); family nurse practitioner (MSN); health nursing (MSN); nursing administration (MSN); nursing practice (DNP); nursing science (PhD); pediatric nurse practitioner (MSN); psychiatric/mental health nurse practitioner (MSN); psychiatric/mental health specialist (MSN); women's health nurse practitioner (MSN). Electronic applications accepted.

College of Social Work *Degree program information:* Part-time programs available. Offers social work (MSW, PhD). Electronic applications accepted.

Darla Moore School of Business Students: 438 full-time (196 women), 356 part-time (83 women); includes 90 minority (33 Black or African American, non-Hispanic/Latino; 3 American Indian or Alaska Native, non-Hispanic/Latino; 34 Asian, non-Hispanic/Latino; 20 Hispanic/Latino), 101 international. Average age 26. 1,109 applicants, 59% accepted, 389 enrolled. *Faculty:* 99 full-time (23 women), 33 part-time/adjunct (5 women). Expenses: Contact institution. *Financial support:* Fellowships with partial tuition reimbursements, research assistantships with partial tuition reimbursements, teaching assistantships with partial tuition reimbursements, career-related internships or fieldwork, Federal Work-Study, institutionally sponsored loans, and tuition waivers (partial) available. Financial award application deadline: 12/1; financial award applicants required to submit FAFSA. In 2010, 323 master's, 9 doctorates awarded. *Degree program information:* Part-time and evening/weekend programs available. Postbaccalaureate distance learning degree programs offered (minimal on-campus study). Offers accountancy (M Acc); business administration (MBA, PhD); business measurement and assurance (M Acc); economics (MA, PhD); human resources (MHR); international business administration (IMBA). *Application deadline:* For fall admission, 2/1 priority date for international students. Applications are processed on a rolling basis. Electronic applications accepted. *Application Contact:* Dr. Hildy J. Teegen, Dean, 803-777-3176, Fax: 803-777-9123, E-mail: teegen@moore.sc.edu. *Dean,* Dr. Hildy J. Teegen, 803-777-3176, Fax: 803-777-9123, E-mail: teegen@moore.sc.edu.

School of Music *Degree program information:* Part-time programs available. Offers composition (MM, DMA); conducting (MM, DMA); jazz studies (MM); music education (MM Ed, PhD); music history (MM); music performance (Certificate); music theory (MM); opera theater (MM); performance (MM, DMA); piano pedagogy (MM, DMA). Electronic applications accepted.

School of the Environment *Degree program information:* Part-time programs available. Postbaccalaureate distance learning degree programs offered (no on-campus study). Offers earth and environmental resources management (MEERM); environment (MEERM). Electronic applications accepted.

School of Law Offers law (JD).

School of Medicine Offers biomedical science (MBS, PhD); genetic counseling (MS); medicine (MD, MBS, MNA, MRC, MS, PhD, Certificate); nurse anesthesia (MNA); psychiatric rehabilitation (Certificate); rehabilitation counseling (MRC, Certificate). Electronic applications accepted.

University of South Carolina (continued)

South Carolina College of Pharmacy *Degree program information:* Part-time programs available. Offers pharmaceutical sciences (MS, PhD); pharmacy (Pharm D, MS, PhD). Electronic applications accepted.

See Display on previous page and Close-Up on page 995.

UNIVERSITY OF SOUTH CAROLINA AIKEN, Aiken, SC 29801-6309

General Information State-supported, coed, comprehensive institution. *Enrollment:* 3,254 graduate, professional, and undergraduate students; 24 full-time matriculated graduate/professional students (19 women), 46 part-time matriculated graduate/professional students (42 women). *Enrollment by degree level:* 70 master's. *Graduate faculty:* 10 full-time (6 women). Tuition, state resident: full-time $10,490; part-time $440 per credit hour. Tuition, nonresident: full-time $22,550; part-time $945 per credit hour. *Required fees:* $290; $9 per credit hour. $25 per semester. *Graduate housing:* Room and/or apartments available on a first-come, first-served basis to single students; on-campus housing not available to married students. Typical cost: $4250 per year ($6450 including board). *Student services:* Campus employment opportunities, campus safety program, career counseling, child daycare facilities, exercise/wellness program, free psychological counseling, grant writing training, international student services, multicultural affairs office, services for students with disabilities, teacher training, writing training. *Library facilities:* Gregg-Graniteville Library. *Online resources:* library catalog, web page, access to other libraries' catalogs.

Computer facilities: 546 computers available on campus for general student use. A campuswide network can be accessed from student residence rooms and from off campus. Online class registration is available. *Web address:* http://www.usca.edu/.

General Application Contact: Karen Morris, Graduate Studies Coordinator, 803-641-3489, E-mail: karenm@usca.edu.

GRADUATE UNITS

Program in Applied Clinical Psychology Students: 23 full-time (19 women), 7 part-time (all women); includes 7 minority (2 Black or African American, non-Hispanic/Latino; 1 Asian, non-Hispanic/Latino; 2 Hispanic/Latino; 2 Two or more races, non-Hispanic/Latino). Average age 26. 50 applicants, 54% accepted, 15 enrolled. *Faculty:* 7 full-time (5 women). Expenses: Contact institution. *Financial support:* In 2010–11, 21 students received support, including 21 research assistantships with partial tuition reimbursements available (averaging $3,805 per year); career-related internships or fieldwork, Federal Work-Study, scholarships/grants, tuition waivers (partial), and unspecified assistantships also available. Financial award application deadline: 3/15; financial award applicants required to submit FAFSA. In 2010, 8 master's awarded. *Degree program information:* Part-time programs available. Offers applied clinical psychology (MS). *Application deadline:* For fall admission, 5/1 priority date for domestic and international students. Applications are processed on a rolling basis. *Application fee:* $45. Electronic applications accepted. *Application Contact:* Karen Morris, Graduate Studies Coordinator, 803-641-3489, Fax: 803-641-3720, E-mail: karenm@usca.edu. *Director,* Dr. Jane Stafford, 803-641-3358, Fax: 803-641-3720, E-mail: jstafford@usca.edu.

Program in Educational Technology Students: 1 full-time (0 women), 16 part-time (13 women); includes 3 minority (1 Black or African American, non-Hispanic/Latino; 1 American Indian or Alaska Native, non-Hispanic/Latino; 1 Hispanic/Latino). Average age 38. 13 applicants, 54% accepted, 7 enrolled. *Faculty:* 3 full-time (1 woman). Expenses: Contact institution. *Financial support:* In 2010–11, 5 students received support. Career-related internships or fieldwork, Federal Work-Study, scholarships/grants, tuition waivers (partial), and unspecified assistantships available. Support available to part-time students. Financial award application deadline: 3/15; financial award applicants required to submit FAFSA. In 2010, 7 master's awarded. *Degree program information:* Part-time and evening/weekend programs available. Postbaccalaureate distance learning degree programs offered (no on-campus study). Offers educational technology (M Ed). *Application deadline:* Applications are processed on a rolling basis. *Application fee:* $45. Electronic applications accepted. *Application Contact:* Karen Morris, Graduate Studies Coordinator, 803-641-3489, E-mail: karenm@usca.edu. *Coordinator,* Dr. Tom Smyth, 803-641-3527.

UNIVERSITY OF SOUTH CAROLINA UPSTATE, Spartanburg, SC 29303-4999

General Information State-supported, coed, comprehensive institution. *Enrollment:* 5,494 graduate, professional, and undergraduate students; 8 full-time matriculated graduate/professional students (all women), 49 part-time matriculated graduate/professional students (46 women). *Enrollment by degree level:* 3 master's. *Graduate faculty:* 8 full-time (6 women), 5 part-time/adjunct (3 women). Tuition, state resident: full-time $9788; part-time $484 per credit hour. Tuition, nonresident: full-time $21,080; part-time $1028 per credit hour. *Graduate housing:* On-campus housing not available. *Student services:* Campus employment opportunities, campus safety program, career counseling, child daycare facilities, exercise/wellness program, free psychological counseling, grant writing training, international student services, low-cost health insurance, multicultural affairs office, services for students with disabilities, teacher training. *Library facilities:* University of South Carolina Upstate Library. *Online resources:* library catalog, web page, access to other libraries' catalogs. *Collection:* 235,570 titles, 31,063 serial subscriptions, 6,776 audiovisual materials.

Computer facilities: 400 computers available on campus for general student use. A campuswide network can be accessed from student residence rooms. Online class registration is available. *Web address:* http://www.uscupstate.edu/.

General Application Contact: Dr. Rebecca L. Stevens, Director of Graduate Programs, 864-503-5521, Fax: 864-503-5574, E-mail: rstevens@uscupstate.edu.

GRADUATE UNITS

Graduate Programs Students: 8 full-time (all women), 49 part-time (46 women); includes 6 Black or African American, non-Hispanic/Latino; 2 American Indian or Alaska Native, non-Hispanic/Latino; 2 Two or more races, non-Hispanic/Latino, 1 international. Average age 34. *Faculty:* 8 full-time (6 women), 5 part-time/adjunct (3 women). Expenses: Contact institution. *Financial support:* Institutionally sponsored loans and institutional work-study available. Financial award application deadline: 7/15; financial award applicants required to submit FAFSA. In 2010, 6 master's awarded. *Degree program information:* Part-time and evening/weekend programs available. Offers early childhood education (M Ed); elementary education (M Ed); special education: visual impairment (M Ed). *Application deadline:* Applications are processed on a rolling basis. *Application fee:* $40. *Application Contact:* Donette Stewart, Associate Vice Chancellor for Enrollment Services, 864-503-5280, E-mail: dstewart@uscupstate.edu. *Director of Graduate Programs,* Dr. Rebecca L. Stevens, 864-503-5521, Fax: 864-503-5574, E-mail: rstevens@uscupstate.edu.

THE UNIVERSITY OF SOUTH DAKOTA, Vermillion, SD 57069-2390

General Information State-supported, coed, university. CGS member. *Graduate housing:* Rooms and/or apartments available to single students and available on a first-come, first-served basis to married students.

GRADUATE UNITS

Graduate School *Degree program information:* Part-time and evening/weekend programs available. Postbaccalaureate distance learning degree programs offered (no on-campus study). Offers administrative studies (MS); interdisciplinary studies (MA). Electronic applications accepted.

College of Arts and Sciences *Degree program information:* Part-time programs available. Postbaccalaureate distance learning degree programs offered. Offers American political institutions (PhD); arts and sciences (MA, MNS, MPA, MS, Au D, PhD); audiology (Au D); biology (MA, MNS, MS, PhD); chemistry (MNS, MS, PhD); clinical psychology (MA, PhD); communication studies (MA); communications disorders (MA); computational sciences and statistics (PhD); computer science (MS); English (MA, PhD); history (MA); human factors (MA, PhD); mathematics (MA, MNS, MS); physics (MS, PhD); political science (MA); public administration (MPA, PhD); public policy (PhD); speech-language pathology (MA). Electronic applications accepted.

College of Fine Arts Offers art (MFA); fine arts (MA, MFA, MM); music (MM); theatre (MA, MFA). Electronic applications accepted.

School of Business *Degree program information:* Part-time and evening/weekend programs available. Postbaccalaureate distance learning degree programs offered (no on-campus study). Offers business (MBA, MP Acc); business administration (MBA); professional accountancy (MP Acc). Electronic applications accepted.

School of Education *Degree program information:* Part-time and evening/weekend programs available. Postbaccalaureate distance learning degree programs offered (no on-campus study). Offers counseling and psychology in education (MA, PhD, Ed S); curriculum and instruction (Ed D, Ed S); education (MA, MS, Ed D, PhD, Ed S); educational administration (MA, Ed D, Ed S); elementary education (MA); health, physical education and recreation (MA); secondary education (MA); special education (MA); technology for education and training (MS, Ed S). Electronic applications accepted.

School of Law *Degree program information:* Part-time programs available. Offers law (JD). Electronic applications accepted.

School of Medicine and Health Sciences *Degree program information:* Part-time programs available. Offers cardiovascular research (MS, PhD); cellular and molecular biology (MS, PhD); medicine (MD); medicine and health science (MD, MS, DPT, PhD); molecular microbiology and immunology (MS, PhD); neuroscience (MS, PhD); occupational therapy (MS); physical therapy (DPT); physician assistant studies (MS); physiology and pharmacology (MS, PhD).

UNIVERSITY OF SOUTHERN CALIFORNIA, Los Angeles, CA 90089

General Information Independent, coed, university. CGS member. *Enrollment:* 36,896 graduate, professional, and undergraduate students; 15,677 full-time matriculated graduate/professional students (7,941 women), 3,839 part-time matriculated graduate/professional students (1,461 women). *Enrollment by degree level:* 3,012 first professional, 10,300 master's, 3,888 doctoral, 208 other advanced degrees. *Graduate faculty:* 1,661 full-time (573 women), 1,303 part-time/adjunct (526 women). *Tuition:* Full-time $31,240; part-time $1420 per unit. *Required fees:* $600. One-time fee: $35 full-time. Full-time tuition and fees vary according to degree level and program. *Graduate housing:* Rooms and/or apartments available on a first-come, first-served basis to single and married students. Typical cost: $10,800 per year ($15,800 including board) for single students; $12,500 per year for married students. Room and board charges vary according to board plan, campus/location and housing facility selected. *Student services:* Campus employment opportunities, campus safety program, career counseling, child daycare facilities, exercise/wellness program, free psychological counseling, grant writing training, international student services, low-cost health insurance, multicultural affairs office, services for students with disabilities, teacher training, writing training. *Library facilities:* Doheny Memorial Library plus 18 others. *Online resources:* library catalog, web page, access to other libraries' catalogs. *Collection:* 4.5 million titles, 109,352 serial subscriptions, 75,012 audiovisual materials. *Research affiliation:* SETI Institute (astronomy/astrobiology), Rancho Los Amigos Medical Center (medicine), Children's Hospital Los Angeles (medicine), Doheny Eye Institute (medicine), House Ear Institute (medicine), Jet Propulsion Laboratory (engineering and technology).

Computer facilities: Computer purchase and lease plans are available. 2,500 computers available on campus for general student use. A campuswide network can be accessed from student residence rooms and from off campus. Online class registration, online degree progress, financial aid applications, document sharing, calendars, personal Web space, customizable Web portal, course management systems (including data and video) are available. *Web address:* http://www.usc.edu/.

General Application Contact: Joseph Sanosa, Associate Director of Graduate Admission, 213-740-1111, Fax: 213-821-0200, E-mail: gradadm@usc.edu.

GRADUATE UNITS

Graduate School Students: 15,677 full-time (7,941 women), 3,839 part-time (1,461 women); includes 6,567 minority (875 Black or African American, non-Hispanic/Latino; 34 American Indian or Alaska Native, non-Hispanic/Latino; 3,388 Asian, non-Hispanic/Latino; 1,882 Hispanic/Latino; 39 Native Hawaiian or other Pacific Islander, non-Hispanic/Latino; 349 Two or more races, non-Hispanic/Latino), 4,989 international. Expenses: Contact institution. *Financial support:* Fellowships, research assistantships, teaching assistantships available. In 2010, 661 first professional degrees, 3,748 master's, 552 doctorates, 281 other advanced degrees awarded. *Application fee:* $85. Electronic applications accepted. *Application Contact:* Dr. Sarah Pratt, Vice Provost for Graduate Programs, 213-740-9033. *Vice Provost for Graduate Programs,* Dr. Sarah Pratt, 213-740-9033.

Annenberg School for Communication and Journalism Students: 605 full-time, 104 part-time; includes 219 minority (45 Black or African American, non-Hispanic/Latino; 3 American Indian or Alaska Native, non-Hispanic/Latino; 75 Asian, non-Hispanic/Latino; 77 Hispanic/Latino; 1 Native Hawaiian or other Pacific Islander, non-Hispanic/Latino; 18 Two or more races, non-Hispanic/Latino), 183 international. Average age 27. 1,325 applicants, 38% accepted, 255 enrolled. *Faculty:* 74 full-time (24 women), 62 part-time/adjunct (18 women). Expenses: Contact institution. *Financial support:* In 2010–11, 22 fellowships with full tuition reimbursements (averaging $24,845 per year), 33 research assistantships with full tuition reimbursements (averaging $23,939 per year), 41 teaching assistantships with full tuition reimbursements (averaging $21,253 per year) were awarded; career-related internships or fieldwork, Federal Work-Study, institutionally sponsored loans, scholarships/grants, health care benefits, tuition waivers (partial), and unspecified assistantships also available. Support available to part-time students. Financial award application deadline: 2/1; financial award applicants required to submit FAFSA. In 2010, 471 master's, 14 doctorates awarded. *Degree program information:* Part-time and evening/weekend programs available. Offers communication (MA, PhD); communication and journalism (MA, MCM, MPD, PhD); communication management (MCM); global communicationjournalism (MA); online journalism (MA); print journalism (MA); public diplomacy (MPD); specialized journalism (MA); specialized journalism (the arts) (MA); strategic public relations (MA). *Application deadline:* For spring admission, 12/1 priority date for domestic students, 8/1 for international students. Applications are processed on a rolling basis. *Application fee:* $85. Electronic applications accepted. *Application Contact:* Allyson Hill, Assistant Dean, Admissions, 213-821-0770, Fax: 213-740-1933, E-mail: ascadm@usc.edu. *Dean,* Dr. Ernest Wilson, 213-740-6180, Fax: 213-740-3772, E-mail: ascdean@usc.edu.

Dana and David Dornsife College of Letters, Arts and Sciences Students: 1,488 full-time (728 women), 134 part-time (69 women); includes 333 minority (37 Black or African American, non-Hispanic/Latino; 5 American Indian or Alaska Native, non-Hispanic/Latino; 145 Asian, non-Hispanic/Latino; 121 Hispanic/Latino; 25 Two or more races, non-Hispanic/Latino), 601 international. Expenses: Contact institution. In 2010, 223 master's, 188 doctorates, 35 other advanced degrees awarded. Offers American studies and ethnicity (PhD); applied mathematics (MA, MS, PhD); art history (MA, PhD); biology (MS); brain and cognitive science (PhD); chemistry (PhD); classical Chinese literature (MA, PhD); classical Japanese literature (MA, PhD); classics (MA, PhD); clinical science (PhD); comparative literature (PhD); comparative media and culture (PhD); computational biology and bioinformatics (PhD); computational molecular biology (MS); developmental psychology (PhD); East Asian linguistics (PhD); East Asian studies (MA); economic development programming (MA, PhD); English (MA, PhD); geographic information science and technology (MS, Graduate Certificate); geological sciences (MS, PhD); Hispanic linguistics (PhD); history (PhD); human behavior (MHB); integrative and evolutionary biology (PhD); letters, arts and sciences (MA, MHB, MMM, MPW, MS, PhD, Graduate Certificate); linguistics (MA, PhD); literature and creative writing (PhD); marine and environmental biology (MS); marine biology and biological oceanography (MS, PhD); mathematical finance (MS); mathematics (MA, PhD); modern Chinese literature (MA, PhD); modern Japanese literature (MA, PhD); modern Korean literature (MA, PhD); molecular and computational biology (PhD); molecular biology (PhD); neurobiology (PhD); neuroscience (MS, PhD); ocean sciences (MS, PhD);

philosophy (MA, PhD); physical chemistry (PhD); physics (MA, MS, PhD); political science and international relations (PhD); professional writing (MPW); quantitative methods (PhD); Slavic languages and literatures (MA, PhD); Slavic linguistics (PhD); social psychology (PhD); sociology (PhD); Spanish and Latin American studies (PhD); statistics (MS); visual studies (Graduate Certificate). *Application fee:* $85. Electronic applications accepted. *Application Contact:* Howard Gillman, Dean. *Dean,* Howard Gillman.

Davis School of Gerontology Students: 102 full-time (83 women), 30 part-time (23 women); includes 40 minority (4 Black or African American, non-Hispanic/Latino; 17 Asian, non-Hispanic/Latino; 15 Hispanic/Latino; 4 Two or more races, non-Hispanic/Latino), 7 international. 83 applicants, 80% accepted, 57 enrolled. *Faculty:* 18 full-time (7 women), 7 part-time/adjunct (3 women). Expenses: Contact institution. *Financial support:* In 2010–11, 90 students received support, including 4 fellowships with full tuition reimbursements available (averaging $30,000 per year), 14 research assistantships with full tuition reimbursements available (averaging $19,000 per year), 2 teaching assistantships (averaging $19,000 per year); Federal Work-Study and scholarships/grants also available. Financial award application deadline: 3/15. In 2010, 24 master's, 4 doctorates, 7 other advanced degrees awarded. *Degree program information:* Part-time programs available. Postbaccalaureate distance learning degree programs offered (no on-campus study). Offers gerontology/social work (MA, MASM, MLTCA, MS, PhD, Graduate Certificate). *Application deadline:* For fall admission, 2/1 priority date for domestic and international students; for spring admission, 10/1 priority date for domestic and international students. Applications are processed on a rolling basis. *Application fee:* $85. Electronic applications accepted. *Application Contact:* Whitney Fountas, Admission Counselor, 213-740-5156, E-mail: ldsgero@usc.edu. *Assistant Dean,* Maria Henke, 213-740-5156, Fax: 213-740-7069, E-mail: ldsgero@usc.edu.

Gould School of Law Students: 783 full-time (380 women); includes 212 minority (48 Black or African American, non-Hispanic/Latino; 2 American Indian or Alaska Native, non-Hispanic/Latino; 88 Asian, non-Hispanic/Latino; 58 Hispanic/Latino; 16 Two or more races, non-Hispanic/Latino), 134 international. 6,587 applicants, 22% accepted, 220 enrolled. *Faculty:* 41 full-time (16 women), 50 part-time/adjunct (20 women). Expenses: Contact institution. *Financial support:* In 2010–11, 338 students received support. Application deadline: 3/2. In 2010, 203 first professional degrees, 96 master's awarded. Offers comparative law for foreign attorneys (MCL); law (JD); law for foreign-educated attorneys (LL M). *Application deadline:* For fall admission, 2/1 for domestic and international students. *Application fee:* $75. *Application Contact:* Chloe Reid, Associate Dean and Dean of Admissions, 213-740-2523, E-mail: creid@law.usc.edu. *Dean/Chair,* Robert K. Rasmussen, 213-740-2523, E-mail: dean@law.usc.edu.

Herman Ostrow School of Dentistry Students: 1,350 full-time (786 women), 8 part-time (6 women); includes 39 Black or African American, non-Hispanic/Latino; 5 American Indian or Alaska Native, non-Hispanic/Latino; 438 Asian, non-Hispanic/Latino; 94 Hispanic/Latino, 110 international. Expenses: Contact institution. In 2010, 289 first professional degrees, 135 master's, 8 doctorates awarded. Offers biokinesiology (MS, PhD); craniofacial biology (MS, PhD, Graduate Certificate); dentistry (DDS, MA, MS, DPT, OTD, PhD, Graduate Certificate); occupational science (PhD); occupational therapy (MA, OTD); physical therapy (DPT). Electronic applications accepted. *Application Contact:* Dr. Avishai Sadan, Dean, 213-740-2800. *Dean,* Dr. Avishai Sadan, 213-740-2800.

Marshall School of Business Students: 1,422 full-time (407 women), 586 part-time (173 women); includes 802 minority (45 Black or African American, non-Hispanic/Latino; 4 American Indian or Alaska Native, non-Hispanic/Latino; 623 Asian, non-Hispanic/Latino; 100 Hispanic/Latino; 3 Native Hawaiian or other Pacific Islander, non-Hispanic/Latino; 27 Two or more races, non-Hispanic/Latino), 332 international. Expenses: Contact institution. *Financial support:* Fellowships, research assistantships, teaching assistantships, institutionally sponsored loans and scholarships/grants available. In 2010, 911 master's, 11 doctorates awarded. Offers accounting (M Acc); business (M Acc, MBA, MBT, MMM, MS, PhD); business administration (MBA, MMM, MS, PhD); business taxation (MBT). Electronic applications accepted. *Application Contact:* James Ellis, Dean, 213-740-6422, E-mail: dean@marshall.usc.edu. *Dean,* James Ellis, 213-740-6422, E-mail: dean@marshall.usc.edu.

Roski School of Fine Arts Students: 39 full-time (26 women); includes 8 minority (1 Black or African American, non-Hispanic/Latino; 2 Asian, non-Hispanic/Latino; 5 Hispanic/Latino), 3 international. 301 applicants, 14% accepted. *Faculty:* 8 full-time (5 women), 9 part-time/adjunct (5 women). Expenses: Contact institution. *Financial support:* Fellowships, research assistantships, teaching assistantships, health care benefits and unspecified assistantships available. In 2010, 20 master's awarded. Offers art and curatorial practices in the public sphere (MA); fine arts (MA, MFA); new genres (MFA); painting/drawing (MFA); photography (MFA); sculpture (MFA). *Application fee:* $85. Electronic applications accepted. *Application Contact:* Penelope Jones, Director of Admissions, 213-740-9153, Fax: 213-740-8938, E-mail: penelope@usc.edu. *Dean,* Ruth Weisberg, 213-740-2787, Fax: 213-740-8938, E-mail: finearts@usc.edu.

Rossier School of Education Students: 1,708 full-time (1,221 women), 347 part-time (253 women); includes 1,066 minority (274 Black or African American, non-Hispanic/Latino; 9 American Indian or Alaska Native, non-Hispanic/Latino; 311 Asian, non-Hispanic/Latino; 392 Hispanic/Latino; 15 Native Hawaiian or other Pacific Islander, non-Hispanic/Latino; 65 Two or more races, non-Hispanic/Latino), 45 international. Expenses: Contact institution. *Financial support:* In 2010–11, 385 students received support; research assistantships with full and partial tuition reimbursements available, teaching assistantships with tuition reimbursements available, career-related internships or fieldwork, Federal Work-Study, scholarships/grants, health care benefits, and unspecified assistantships available. Support available to part-time students. Financial award applicants required to submit FAFSA. In 2010, 226 master's, 157 doctorates awarded. Offers education (MAT, ME, MMFT, Ed D, PhD); educational counseling (ME); educational psychology (Ed D, PhD); higher education administration (Ed D); higher education administration and policy (PhD); K-12 leadership in urban school settings (Ed D); K-12 policy and practice (PhD); marriage, family and child counseling (MMFT); postsecondary administration and student affairs ERROR!!!PASAERROR!!! (ME); school counseling (ME); teacher education in multicultural societies (Ed D); teaching (online) (MAT); teaching and teaching credential (MAT); teaching English to speakers of other languages (MAT). *Application fee:* $85. Electronic applications accepted. *Application Contact:* Karen Gallagher. Karen Gallagher.

School of Architecture Students: 203 full-time (119 women), 20 part-time (6 women); includes 45 minority (5 Black or African American, non-Hispanic/Latino; 1 American Indian or Alaska Native, non-Hispanic/Latino; 22 Asian, non-Hispanic/Latino; 15 Hispanic/Latino; 1 Native Hawaiian or other Pacific Islander, non-Hispanic/Latino; 1 Two or more races, non-Hispanic/Latino), 105 international. 424 applicants, 56% accepted, 88 enrolled. *Faculty:* 12 full-time (2 women), 31 part-time/adjunct (9 women). Expenses: Contact institution. *Financial support:* In 2010–11, 95 students received support. Federal Work-Study and scholarships/grants available. Financial award application deadline: 5/1; financial award applicants required to submit CSS PROFILE or FAFSA. In 2010, 40 master's awarded. Offers architecture (M Arch, MBS, MHP, MLA, PhD). *Application deadline:* For fall admission, 1/15 priority date for domestic and international students. *Application fee:* $85. Electronic applications accepted. *Application Contact:* Laarni Cutidioc, Graduate Admissions Coordinator, 213-821-2168, Fax: 213-740-8884, E-mail: archgrad@usc.edu. *Dean,* Qingyun Ma, 213-740-2420, Fax: 213-740-8884, E-mail: archdean@usc.edu.

School of Cinematic Arts Students: 674 full-time (269 women), 44 part-time (16 women); includes 187 minority (50 Black or African American, non-Hispanic/Latino; 2 American Indian or Alaska Native, non-Hispanic/Latino; 54 Asian, non-Hispanic/Latino; 60 Hispanic/Latino; 21 Two or more races, non-Hispanic/Latino), 114 international. Expenses: Contact institution. *Financial support:* Fellowships with tuition reimbursements, research assistantships with tuition reimbursements, teaching assistantships with tuition reimbursements, career-related internships or fieldwork, Federal Work-Study, institutionally sponsored loans, scholarships/grants, health care benefits, and unspecified assistantships available. Support available to part-time students. Financial award applicants required to submit FAFSA. In 2010, 155 master's, 9 doctorates awarded. Offers animation and digital arts (MFA); cinema-television (MA); cinema-television (critical studies) (PhD); cinematic arts (MA, MFA, PhD); film and television production (MFA); interactive media (MFA); media arts and practice (PhD); motion picture producing (MFA); writing for screen and television (MFA). *Application fee:* $85. Electronic applications accepted. *Application Contact:* L. Katherine Harrington, Associate Dean and Executive Director of Admissions. *Dean,* Elizabeth Daley.

School of Pharmacy Students: 844 full-time (553 women), 77 part-time (42 women); includes 571 minority (29 Black or African American, non-Hispanic/Latino; 484 Asian, non-Hispanic/Latino; 43 Hispanic/Latino; 2 Native Hawaiian or other Pacific Islander, non-Hispanic/Latino; 13 Two or more races, non-Hispanic/Latino), 69 international. Expenses: Contact institution. In 2010, 169 first professional degrees, 37 master's, 11 doctorates, 28 other advanced degrees awarded. Offers clinical and experimental therapeutics (PhD); clinical research design and management (Graduate Certificate); food safety (Graduate Certificate); patient and product safety (Graduate Certificate); pharmaceutical economics and policy (MS, PhD); pharmacology and pharmaceutical sciences (MS, PhD); pharmacy (Pharm D, MS, DRSc, PhD, Graduate Certificate); preclinical drug development (Graduate Certificate); regulatory and clinical affairs (Graduate Certificate); regulatory science (MS, DRSc). *Application fee:* $85. *Application Contact:* Pete Vanderveen, Dean. *Dean,* Pete Vanderveen.

School of Policy, Planning, and Development Students: 780 full-time (433 women), 240 part-time (120 women); includes 402 minority (52 Black or African American, non-Hispanic/Latino; 1 American Indian or Alaska Native, non-Hispanic/Latino; 184 Asian, non-Hispanic/Latino; 138 Hispanic/Latino; 6 Native Hawaiian or other Pacific Islander, non-Hispanic/Latino; 21 Two or more races, non-Hispanic/Latino), 184 international. Expenses: Contact institution. *Financial support:* In 2010–11, 251 students received support. Scholarships/grants, traineeships, and tuition waivers (full and partial) available. Financial award applicants required to submit FAFSA. In 2010, 321 master's, 17 doctorates, 34 other advanced degrees awarded. Offers ambulatory care (Graduate Certificate); health administration (EMHA, MHA, Graduate Certificate); homeland security and public policy (Graduate Certificate); international public policy and management (MPPM); leadership (EML); long-term care (Graduate Certificate); nonprofit management and policy (Graduate Certificate); policy, planning, and development (EMHA, EML, M Pl, MHA, MPA, MPP, MPPM, MRED, DPPD, PhD, Graduate Certificate, M Pl/MPP, M Pl/MRED); political management (Graduate Certificate); public administration (MPA); public management (Graduate Certificate); public policy (MPP, Graduate Certificate); public policy and management (PhD); real estate development (MRED, M Pl/MRED); sustainable cities (Graduate Certificate); transportation systems (Graduate Certificate); urban planning (M Pl); urban planning and development (PhD). *Application fee:* $85. Electronic applications accepted. *Application Contact:* Marisol R. Gonzalez, Director of Recruitment and Admission, 213-740-0550, Fax: 213-740-7573, E-mail: marisolr@usc.edu. *Head,* Dr. Jack H. Knott, 213-740-0350, Fax: 213-740-5379, E-mail: jhknott@usc.edu.

School of Social Work Students: 924 full-time (786 women), 162 part-time (128 women); includes 730 minority (137 Black or African American, non-Hispanic/Latino; 2 American Indian or Alaska Native, non-Hispanic/Latino; 120 Asian, non-Hispanic/Latino; 445 Hispanic/Latino; 4 Native Hawaiian or other Pacific Islander, non-Hispanic/Latino; 22 Two or more races, non-Hispanic/Latino), 34 international. 1,627 applicants, 50% accepted, 477 enrolled. *Faculty:* 68 full-time (43 women), 67 part-time/adjunct (49 women). Expenses: Contact institution. *Financial support:* In 2010–11, 32 students received support, including 29 fellowships with full tuition reimbursements available (averaging $35,000 per year), 1 research assistantship with full tuition reimbursement available (averaging $30,000 per year), 2 teaching assistantships with full tuition reimbursements available (averaging $35,000 per year); scholarships/grants, traineeships, health care benefits, and unspecified assistantships also available. Financial award applicants required to submit FAFSA. In 2010, 288 master's, 7 doctorates awarded. Offers community organization, planning and administration (MSW); families and children (MSW); health (MSW); mental health (MSW); military social work and veterans services (MSW); older adults (MSW); public child welfare (MSW); school settings (MSW); social work (MSW, PhD); systems of mental illness recovery (MSW); work and life (MSW). *Application deadline:* For fall admission, 12/1 for domestic and international students. Electronic applications accepted. *Application Contact:* Necole Yaacoub, Admissions and Operations Manager, 213-740-3595, Fax: 213-821-1235, E-mail: naanouh@usc.edu. *Director of Admissions and Financial Aid,* Janine Luzano, 213-740-2017, Fax: 213-821-1235, E-mail: janinelu@usc.edu.

School of Theatre Students: 48 full-time (26 women); includes 21 minority (7 Black or African American, non-Hispanic/Latino; 4 Asian, non-Hispanic/Latino; 5 Hispanic/Latino; 5 Two or more races, non-Hispanic/Latino), 2 international. *Faculty:* 10 full-time (3 women), 9 part-time/adjunct (6 women). Expenses: Contact institution. *Financial support:* In 2010–11, 6 teaching assistantships with partial tuition reimbursements (averaging $34,000 per year) were awarded; scholarships/grants and tuition waivers also available. Financial award application deadline: 1/12; financial award applicants required to submit FAFSA. In 2010, 13 master's awarded. Offers acting (MFA); applied theatre arts (MA); dramatic writing (MFA). *Application deadline:* For fall admission, 1/12 for domestic and international students. *Application fee:* $85. Electronic applications accepted. *Application Contact:* Sergio Ramirez, Director of Academic and Student Services, 213-821-4163, Fax: 213-821-1193, E-mail: sergio.ramirez@usc.edu. *Director of Academic and Student Services,* Sergio Ramirez, 213-821-4163, Fax: 213-821-1193, E-mail: sergio.ramirez@usc.edu.

Thornton School of Music Students: 399 full-time (172 women), 47 part-time (31 women); includes 106 minority (9 Black or African American, non-Hispanic/Latino; 2 American Indian or Alaska Native, non-Hispanic/Latino; 53 Asian, non-Hispanic/Latino; 20 Hispanic/Latino; 1 Native Hawaiian or other Pacific Islander, non-Hispanic/Latino; 12 Two or more races, non-Hispanic/Latino), 103 international. 934 applicants, 35% accepted, 192 enrolled. *Faculty:* 75 full-time (14 women), 120 part-time/adjunct (24 women). Expenses: Contact institution. *Financial support:* In 2010–11, 60 teaching assistantships with full tuition reimbursements (averaging $9,600 per year) were awarded; scholarships/grants and tuition waivers also available. Financial award application deadline: 12/1; financial award applicants required to submit FAFSA. In 2010, 54 master's, 2 doctorates, 96 other advanced degrees awarded. *Degree program information:* Part-time and evening/weekend programs available. Offers brass performance (MM, DMA, Graduate Certificate); choral and sacred music (MM, DMA); classical guitar (MM, DMA, Graduate Certificate); composition (MM, DMA); early music (MA, DMA); harp performance (MM, DMA, Graduate Certificate); historical musicology (PhD); jazz studies (MM, DMA, Graduate Certificate); keyboard collaborative arts (MM, DMA, Graduate Certificate); music education (MM, DMA); organ performance (MM, DMA, Graduate Certificate); percussion performance (MM, DMA, Graduate Certificate); piano performance (MM, DMA, Graduate Certificate); scoring for motion pictures and television (Graduate Certificate); strings performance (MM, DMA, Graduate Certificate); studio jazz guitar (MM, DMA, Graduate Certificate); teaching music (MA); vocal arts (classical voice/opera) (MM, DMA, Graduate Certificate); woodwind performance (MM, DMA, Graduate Certificate). *Application deadline:* For fall admission, 12/1 for domestic and international students; for spring admission, 10/1 for domestic and international students. *Application fee:* $85. Electronic applications accepted. *Application Contact:* Ligaya J. Jones, Admission Coordinator, 213-740-8986, E-mail: ljones@thornton.usc.edu. *Director of Admission,* P. J. Woolston, 213-740-8986, E-mail: woolston@usc.edu.

Viterbi School of Engineering Students: 2,688 full-time (585 women), 1,571 part-time (306 women); includes 648 minority (56 Black or African American, non-Hispanic/Latino; 422 Asian, non-Hispanic/Latino; 138 Hispanic/Latino; 32 Two or more races, non-Hispanic/Latino), 2,718 international. Expenses: Contact institution. *Financial support:* Institutionally sponsored loans and scholarships/grants available. Financial award application deadline: 12/1. In 2010, 1,205 master's, 139 doctorates, 16 other advanced degrees awarded. *Degree program information:* Part-time programs available. Postbaccalaureate distance learning degree programs offered (no on-campus study). Offers aerospace and mechanical engineering: computational fluid and solid mechanics (MS); aerospace and mechanical engineering: dynamics and control (MS); aerospace engineering (MS, PhD, Engr); applied mechanics (MS); astronautical engineering (MS, PhD, Engr, Graduate Certificate); biomedical engineering (MS, PhD, Engr); chemical engineering (MS, PhD, Engr); civil engineering (MS, PhD); computer engineering (MS, PhD); computer networks (MS); computer science (MS, PhD); computer security (MS); computer-aided engineering (ME, Graduate Certificate); construction management (MCM); digital supply chain management (MS); electric power (MS); electrical engineering (MS, PhD, Engr); engineering (MCM, ME, MS, PhD, Engr, Graduate Certificate); engineering management (MS); engineering technology commercialization

University of Southern California (continued)

(Graduate Certificate); engineering technology communication (Graduate Certificate); environmental engineering (MS, PhD); environmental quality management (ME); game development (MS); green technologies (MS); health systems operations (Graduate Certificate); high performance computing and simulations (MS); human language technology (MS); industrial and systems engineering (MS, PhD, Engr); intelligent robotics (MS); manufacturing engineering (MS); materials engineering (MS); materials science (MS, PhD, Engr); mechanical engineering (MS, PhD, Engr); medical device and diagnostic engineering (MS); medical imaging and imaging informatics (MS); multimedia and creative technologies (MS); operations research engineering (MS); optimization and supply chain management (Graduate Certificate); petroleum engineering (MS, PhD, Engr); product development engineering (MS); safety systems and security (MS); smart oilfield technologies (MS, Graduate Certificate); software engineering (MS); structural design (ME); sustainable cities (Graduate Certificate); systems architecting and engineering (MS, Graduate Certificate); systems safety and security (Graduate Certificate); telecommunications (MS); transportation systems (MS, Graduate Certificate); VLSI design (MS); water and waste management (MS); wireless health technology (MS). *Application deadline:* Applications are processed on a rolling basis. *Application fee:* $85. Electronic applications accepted. *Application Contact:* Margery Berti, Associate Dean, 213-740-6241, Fax: 213-740-2367, E-mail: berti@usc.edu. *Dean*, Dr. Yannis C. Yortsos, 213-740-0617, Fax: 213-740-8493, E-mail: engrdean@usc.edu.

Keck School of Medicine Students: 1,408 full-time (813 women), 3 part-time (2 women); includes 601 minority (58 Black or African American, non-Hispanic/Latino; 4 American Indian or Alaska Native, non-Hispanic/Latino; 334 Asian, non-Hispanic/Latino; 154 Hispanic/Latino; 4 Native Hawaiian or other Pacific Islander, non-Hispanic/Latino; 47 Two or more races, non-Hispanic/Latino), 235 international. Average age 26. 8,335 applicants, 9% accepted, 418 enrolled. *Faculty:* 1,325 full-time (498 women), 160 part-time/adjunct (82 women). Expenses: Contact institution. *Financial support:* In 2010–11, 742 students received support, including 29 fellowships with full and partial tuition reimbursements available, 250 research assistantships with full and partial tuition reimbursements available (averaging $27,600 per year), 34 teaching assistantships with full and partial tuition reimbursements available (averaging $27,600 per year); career-related internships or fieldwork, Federal Work-Study, institutionally sponsored loans, scholarships/grants, traineeships, health care benefits, and unspecified assistantships also available. Support available to part-time students. Financial award application deadline: 5/3; financial award applicants required to submit CSS PROFILE or FAFSA. In 2010, 174 first professional degrees, 153 master's, 60 doctorates awarded. Offers genetic, molecular and cellular biology (PhD); medicine (MD, MPAP, MPH, MS, PhD); systems biology and disease (PhD). *Application deadline:* Applications are processed on a rolling basis. *Application fee:* $85. Electronic applications accepted. *Application Contact:* Marisela Zuniga, Administrative Coordinator, Graduate Affairs, 323-442-1607, Fax: 323-442-1199, E-mail: mzuniga@usc.edu. *Dean*, Dr. Carmen A. Puliafito, 323-442-1900.

Graduate Programs in Medicine Students: 727 full-time (489 women), 3 part-time (2 women); includes 276 minority (28 Black or African American, non-Hispanic/Latino; 3 American Indian or Alaska Native, non-Hispanic/Latino; 167 Asian, non-Hispanic/Latino; 70 Hispanic/Latino; 1 Native Hawaiian or other Pacific Islander, non-Hispanic/Latino; 7 Two or more races, non-Hispanic/Latino), 225 international. Average age 27. 1,598 applicants, 26% accepted, 238 enrolled. *Faculty:* 263 full-time (80 women), 16 part-time/adjunct (6 women). Expenses: Contact institution. *Financial support:* In 2010–11, 396 students received support, including 29 fellowships with tuition reimbursements available, 243 research assistantships with tuition reimbursements available (averaging $27,060 per year), 34 teaching assistantships with tuition reimbursements available (averaging $27,060 per year); career-related internships or fieldwork, Federal Work-Study, institutionally sponsored loans, scholarships/grants, traineeships, health care benefits, and unspecified assistantships also available. Support available to part-time students. Financial award application deadline: 5/5; financial award applicants required to submit CSS PROFILE or FAFSA. In 2010, 153 master's, 60 doctorates awarded. Offers applied biostatistics/epidemiology (MS); biochemistry and molecular biology (MS, PhD); biostatistics (MS, PhD); biostatistics/epidemiology (MPH); cell and neurobiology (MS, PhD); child and family health (MPH); epidemiology (PhD); experimental and molecular pathology (MS); genetic epidemiology and statistical genetics (PhD); global health leadership (MPH); health behavior research (PhD); health communication (MPH); health promotion (MPH); medicine (MPAP, MPH, MS, PhD); molecular epidemiology (MS, PhD); molecular microbiology and immunology (MS, PhD); pathobiology (PhD); physiology and biophysics (MS, PhD); primary care physician assistant (MPAP); public health (MPH). *Application fee:* $85. Electronic applications accepted. *Application Contact:* Marisela Zuniga, Administrative Coordinator, 323-442-1607, Fax: 323-442-1199, E-mail: mzuniga@usc.edu. *Associate Dean for Graduate Affairs*, Dr. Debbie Johnson, 323-442-1446, Fax: 323-442-1199, E-mail: johnsond@usc.edu.

UNIVERSITY OF SOUTHERN INDIANA, Evansville, IN 47712-3590

General Information State-supported, coed, comprehensive institution. CGS member. *Enrollment:* 10,702 graduate, professional, and undergraduate students; 130 full-time matriculated graduate/professional students (94 women), 648 part-time matriculated graduate/professional students (509 women). *Enrollment by degree level:* 730 master's, 48 doctoral. *Graduate faculty:* 38 full-time (13 women), 2 part-time/adjunct (1 woman). Tuition, state resident: full-time $4823; part-time $267.95 per credit hour. Tuition, nonresident: full-time $9515; part-time $528.62 per credit hour. *Required fees:* $220; $22.75 per term. Tuition and fees vary according to course load and reciprocity agreements. *Graduate housing:* Rooms and/or apartments available on a first-come, first-served basis to single and married students. Typical cost: $3560 per year ($6920 including board) for single students; $3560 per year ($6920 including board) for married students. Housing application deadline: 3/1. *Student services:* Campus employment opportunities, campus safety program, career counseling, child daycare facilities, exercise/wellness program, free psychological counseling, international student services, low-cost health insurance, multicultural affairs office, services for students with disabilities. *Library facilities:* David L. Rice Library. *Online resources:* library catalog, web page, access to other libraries' catalogs. *Collection:* 352,349 titles, 34,424 serial subscriptions, 6,241 audiovisual materials.

Computer facilities: 497 computers available on campus for general student use. A campuswide network can be accessed from student residence rooms and from off campus. Online class registration is available. *Web address:* http://www.usi.edu/.

General Application Contact: Dr. Peggy F. Harrel, Director, Graduate Studies, 812-465-7015, Fax: 812-464-1956, E-mail: pharrel@usi.edu.

GRADUATE UNITS

Graduate Studies Students: 130 full-time (94 women), 648 part-time (509 women); includes 24 Black or African American, non-Hispanic/Latino; 1 American Indian or Alaska Native, non-Hispanic/Latino; 11 Asian, non-Hispanic/Latino; 5 Hispanic/Latino; 2 Native Hawaiian or other Pacific Islander, non-Hispanic/Latino, 21 international. Average age 34. 337 applicants, 94% accepted, 233 enrolled. *Faculty:* 38 full-time (13 women), 2 part-time/adjunct (1 woman). Expenses: Contact institution. *Financial support:* In 2010–11, 73 students received support. Federal Work-Study, scholarships/grants, tuition waivers (full and partial), and unspecified assistantships available. Financial award application deadline: 3/1; financial award applicants required to submit FAFSA. In 2010, 271 master's awarded. *Degree program information:* Part-time and evening/weekend programs available. *Application deadline:* Applications are processed on a rolling basis. *Application fee:* $25. Electronic applications accepted. *Application Contact:* Dr. Peggy F. Harrel, Director, Graduate Studies, 812-465-7015, Fax: 812-464-1956, E-mail: pharrel@usi.edu. *Director*, Dr. Peggy F. Harrel, 812-465-7015, Fax: 812-464-1956, E-mail: pharrel@usi.edu.

College of Business Students: 17 full-time (2 women), 77 part-time (23 women), 10 international. Average age 30. 13 applicants, 92% accepted, 10 enrolled. *Faculty:* 11 full-time (2 women). Expenses: Contact institution. *Financial support:* In 2010–11, 4 students received support. Federal Work-Study, scholarships/grants, tuition waivers (full and partial), and unspecified assistantships available. Financial award application deadline: 3/1; financial award applicants required to submit FAFSA. In 2010, 28 master's awarded. *Degree program information:* Part-time and evening/weekend programs available. Offers business (MBA); business administration (MBA). *Application deadline:* For fall admission, 8/15 for domestic students, 3/1 priority date for international students. Applications are processed on a rolling basis. *Application fee:* $25. Electronic applications accepted. *Application Contact:* Information Contact, 812-464-1803. *Dean*, Dr. Mohammed F. Khayum, 812-465-1926, E-mail: mkhayum@usi.edu.

College of Education and Human Services Students: 60 full-time (54 women), 119 part-time (90 women); includes 7 Black or African American, non-Hispanic/Latino; 1 Asian, non-Hispanic/Latino; 2 Hispanic/Latino; 1 Native Hawaiian or other Pacific Islander, non-Hispanic/Latino, 3 international. Average age 32. 88 applicants, 94% accepted, 65 enrolled. *Faculty:* 13 full-time (7 women), 1 part-time/adjunct (0 women). Expenses: Contact institution. *Financial support:* In 2010–11, 22 students received support. Federal Work-Study, scholarships/grants, tuition waivers (full and partial), and unspecified assistantships available. Financial award application deadline: 3/1; financial award applicants required to submit FAFSA. In 2010, 111 master's awarded. *Degree program information:* Part-time and evening/weekend programs available. Offers education and human services (MS, MSW); elementary education (MS); secondary education (MS); social work (MSW). *Application deadline:* Applications are processed on a rolling basis. *Application fee:* $25. Electronic applications accepted. *Application Contact:* Dr. Julie Edmister, Dean, 812-464-1811, E-mail: jhedmister@usi.edu. *Dean*, Dr. Julie Edmister, 812-464-1811, E-mail: jhedmister@usi.edu.

College of Liberal Arts Students: 11 full-time (4 women), 55 part-time (40 women); includes 2 Black or African American, non-Hispanic/Latino; 1 American Indian or Alaska Native, non-Hispanic/Latino; 2 Asian, non-Hispanic/Latino, 2 international. Average age 33. 23 applicants, 96% accepted, 21 enrolled. *Faculty:* 7 full-time (1 woman). Expenses: Contact institution. *Financial support:* In 2010–11, 12 students received support. Federal Work-Study, scholarships/grants, tuition waivers (full and partial), and unspecified assistantships available. Financial award application deadline: 3/1; financial award applicants required to submit FAFSA. In 2010, 22 master's awarded. *Degree program information:* Part-time and evening/weekend programs available. Offers communication (MA); liberal arts (MA, MPA); liberal studies (MA); public administration (MPA). *Application deadline:* For fall admission, 8/15 priority date for domestic students, 3/1 priority date for international students. Applications are processed on a rolling basis. *Application fee:* $25. Electronic applications accepted. *Application Contact:* Dr. Thomas M. Rivers, Director, 812-464-1753, E-mail: trivers@usi.edu. *Dean*, Dr. Michael L. Aakhus, 812-464-1853.

College of Nursing and Health Professions Students: 12 full-time (10 women), 377 part-time (351 women); includes 14 Black or African American, non-Hispanic/Latino; 7 Asian, non-Hispanic/Latino; 3 Hispanic/Latino; 1 Native Hawaiian or other Pacific Islander, non-Hispanic/Latino, 6 international. Average age 37. 200 applicants, 94% accepted, 135 enrolled. *Faculty:* 3 full-time (2 women). Expenses: Contact institution. *Financial support:* In 2010–11, 35 students received support. Federal Work-Study, scholarships/grants, tuition waivers (full and partial), and unspecified assistantships available. Financial award application deadline: 3/1; financial award applicants required to submit FAFSA. In 2010, 109 master's awarded. *Degree program information:* Part-time programs available. Postbaccalaureate distance learning degree programs offered (minimal on-campus study). Offers health administration (MHA); nursing (MSN, DNP); nursing and health professions (MHA, MSN, MSOT, DNP); occupational therapy (MSOT). *Application deadline:* Applications are processed on a rolling basis. *Application fee:* $25. Electronic applications accepted. *Application Contact:* Dr. Peggy F. Harrel, Director, Graduate Studies, 812-465-7015, Fax: 812-464-1956, E-mail: pharrel@usi.edu. *Dean*, Dr. Nadine Coudret, 812-465-1151, E-mail: ncoudret@usi.edu.

College of Science and Engineering Students: 12 part-time (4 women). Average age 33. 2 applicants, 100% accepted, 1 enrolled. *Faculty:* 5 full-time (2 women), 1 (woman) part-time/adjunct. Expenses: Contact institution. *Financial support:* Federal Work-Study, scholarships/grants, tuition waivers (full and partial), and unspecified assistantships available. Financial award application deadline: 3/1; financial award applicants required to submit FAFSA. In 2010, 1 master's awarded. *Degree program information:* Part-time and evening/weekend programs available. Offers industrial management (MS); science and engineering (MS). *Application deadline:* For fall admission, 8/15 priority date for domestic students, 3/1 priority date for international students. Applications are processed on a rolling basis. *Application fee:* $25. Electronic applications accepted. *Application Contact:* Dr. Peggy F. Harrel, Director, Graduate Studies, 812-465-7015, Fax: 812-464-1956, E-mail: pharrel@usi.edu. *Dean*, Dr. Scott A. Gordon, 812-465-7137, E-mail: sgordon@usi.edu.

UNIVERSITY OF SOUTHERN MAINE, Portland, ME 04104-9300

General Information State-supported, coed, comprehensive institution. CGS member. *Graduate housing:* Rooms and/or apartments available on a first-come, first-served basis to single and married students.

GRADUATE UNITS

College of Arts and Sciences *Degree program information:* Part-time and evening/weekend programs available. Postbaccalaureate distance learning degree programs offered (minimal on-campus study). Offers American and New England studies (MA); arts and sciences (MA, MFA, MM, MS, MSW); biology (MS); creative writing (MFA); music (MM); social work (MSW); statistics (MS). Electronic applications accepted.

College of Nursing and Health Professions Students: 57 full-time (48 women), 44 part-time (41 women); includes 3 minority (2 Asian, non-Hispanic/Latino; 1 Hispanic/Latino). Average age 36. 143 applicants, 44% accepted, 43 enrolled. *Faculty:* 15 full-time (13 women), 4 part-time/adjunct (2 women). Expenses: Contact institution. *Financial support:* In 2010–11, 10 students received support, including 5 research assistantships with tuition reimbursements available (averaging $3,375 per year), 3 teaching assistantships with tuition reimbursements available (averaging $3,375 per year); career-related internships or fieldwork, Federal Work-Study, scholarships/grants, traineeships, tuition waivers (full and partial), and unspecified assistantships also available. Support available to part-time students. Financial award application deadline: 2/15; financial award applicants required to submit FAFSA. In 2010, 37 master's awarded. *Degree program information:* Part-time programs available. Offers adult health nursing (PMC); adult psychiatric/mental health nurse practitioner (MS); clinical nurse leader (MS); clinical nurse specialist psychiatric-mental health nursing (MS); education (MS); family nursing (PMC); family psychiatric/mental health nurse practitioner (MS); management (MS); medical/surgical nursing (MS); nurse practitioner adult health nursing (MS); nurse practitioner family nursing (MS); psychiatric-mental health nursing (PMC). *Application deadline:* For fall admission, 4/1 for domestic and international students; for spring admission, 10/1 for domestic and international students. *Application fee:* $50. Electronic applications accepted. *Application Contact:* Mary Sloan, Office of Graduate Studies Assistant Director, 207-780-4386, Fax: 207-780-4969, E-mail: gradstudies@usm.maine.edu. *Director of Nursing Program*, Krista M. Meinersmann, 207-780-4505, Fax: 207-228-8177, E-mail: kmeinersmann@usm.maine.edu.

Edmund S. Muskie School of Public Service *Degree program information:* Part-time and evening/weekend programs available. Postbaccalaureate distance learning degree programs offered (minimal on-campus study). Offers child and family policy (Certificate); community planning and development (MCPD, Certificate); health policy and management (MS, Certificate); non-profit management (Certificate); public policy (PhD); public policy and management (MPPM); public service (MCPD, MPPM, MS, PhD, Certificate). Electronic applications accepted.

Lewiston-Auburn College Offers leadership studies (MLS).

Program in Occupational Therapy Offers occupational therapy (MOT). Electronic applications accepted.

School of Applied Science, Engineering, and Technology *Degree program information:* Part-time and evening/weekend programs available. Offers applied medical sciences (MS); applied science, engineering, and technology (MS); computer science (MS); manufacturing systems (MS). Electronic applications accepted.

School of Business *Degree program information:* Part-time and evening/weekend programs available. Offers business administration (MBA); finance (MBA); taxation (MBA). Electronic applications accepted.

School of Education and Human Development Students: 211 full-time (151 women), 423 part-time (322 women); includes 20 minority (4 Black or African American, non-Hispanic/Latino; 4 American Indian or Alaska Native, non-Hispanic/Latino; 4 Asian, non-Hispanic/Latino; 8 Hispanic/Latino), 2 international. 416 applicants, 70% accepted, 223 enrolled. *Faculty:* 38 full-time (23 women), 22 part-time/adjunct (14 women). Expenses: Contact institution. *Financial support:* In 2010–11, 81 students received support, including 15 research assistantships (averaging $4,500 per year); career-related internships or fieldwork, Federal Work-Study, institutionally sponsored loans, scholarships/grants, and unspecified assistantships also available. Support available to part-time students. Financial award application deadline: 3/1; financial award applicants required to submit FAFSA. In 2010, 175 master's, 7 doctorates, 21 other advanced degrees awarded. *Degree program information:* Part-time and evening/weekend programs available. Postbaccalaureate distance learning degree programs offered (minimal on-campus study). Offers adult and higher education (MS); adult learning (CAS); applied behavior analysis (MS, Certificate); applied literacy (MS Ed); assistant principal (Certificate); athletic administration (Certificate); clinical mental health (MS); counseling (CAS); early language and literacy (Certificate); education and human development (MS, MS Ed, Psy D, CAS, Certificate); educational leadership (MS Ed, CAS); English as a second language (MS Ed, CAS); gifted and talented (MS); literacy education (MS Ed, CAS, Certificate); mental health rehabilitation technician/community (Certificate); middle-level education (Certificate); professional educator (MS Ed); rehabilitation counseling (MS); school counseling (MS); school psychology (MS, Psy D); self-design in special education (MS); teaching all students (MS); teaching all students (Certificate); teaching and learning (MS Ed). *Application fee:* $65. Electronic applications accepted. *Application Contact:* Mary Sloan, Director of Graduate Admissions, 207-780-4386, Fax: 207-780-4969, E-mail: msloan@usm.maine.edu. *Director,* Catherine Fallona, 207-780-5371, Fax: 207-780-5315, E-mail: cfallona@usm.maine.edu.

University of Maine School of Law Students: 266 full-time (124 women), 6 part-time (3 women); includes 28 minority (6 Black or African American, non-Hispanic/Latino; 4 American Indian or Alaska Native, non-Hispanic/Latino; 2 Asian, non-Hispanic/Latino; 10 Hispanic/Latino; 6 Native Hawaiian or other Pacific Islander, non-Hispanic/Latino), 3 international. Average age 28. 1,171 applicants, 38% accepted, 95 enrolled. *Faculty:* 14 full-time (5 women), 12 part-time/adjunct (2 women). Expenses: Contact institution. *Financial support:* In 2010–11, 86 students received support, including 15 fellowships (averaging $3,000 per year), 11 research assistantships (averaging $1,800 per year), 6 teaching assistantships (averaging $2,400 per year); career-related internships or fieldwork, Federal Work-Study, scholarships/grants, and tuition waivers (full and partial) also available. Support available to part-time students. Financial award application deadline: 2/15; financial award applicants required to submit FAFSA. In 2010, 82 first professional degrees awarded. *Degree program information:* Part-time programs available. Offers law (JD). *Application deadline:* For fall admission, 3/1 for domestic and international students. Applications are processed on a rolling basis. *Application fee:* $50. Electronic applications accepted. *Application Contact:* David Pallozzi, Assistant Dean for Admissions, 207-780-4341, Fax: 207-780-4239, E-mail: mainelaw@usm.maine.edu. *Dean,* Peter R. Pitegoff, 207-780-4344, Fax: 207-780-4239.

UNIVERSITY OF SOUTHERN MISSISSIPPI, Hattiesburg, MS 39406-0001

General Information State-supported, coed, university. CGS member. *Enrollment:* 15,778 graduate, professional, and undergraduate students; 1,461 full-time matriculated graduate/professional students (880 women), 1,491 part-time matriculated graduate/professional students (1,035 women). *Enrollment by degree level:* 1,669 master's, 1,092 doctoral, 191 other advanced degrees. *Graduate faculty:* 511 full-time (201 women), 32 part-time/adjunct (8 women). *Graduate housing:* Room and/or apartments available on a first-come, first-served basis to single students; on-campus housing not available to married students. Housing application deadline: 3/1. *Student services:* Campus employment opportunities, career counseling, child daycare facilities, exercise/wellness program, free psychological counseling, grant writing training, international student services, low-cost health insurance, services for students with disabilities, teacher training. *Library facilities:* Cook Memorial Library plus 4 others. *Online resources:* library catalog, web page. *Collection:* 1.3 million titles, 152,186 serial subscriptions, 41,339 audiovisual materials. *Research affiliation:* Oak Ridge Associated Universities, Geological Sciences, Coastal Sciences (physics).

Computer facilities: Computer purchase and lease plans are available. 600 computers available on campus for general student use. A campuswide network can be accessed from student residence rooms and from off campus. Online class registration is available. *Web address:* http://www.usm.edu/.

General Application Contact: Dr. Susan Siltanen, Dean, Graduate School, 601-266-4369, Fax: 601-266-5138, E-mail: susan.siltanen@usm.edu.

GRADUATE UNITS

Graduate School Students: 1,461 full-time (880 women), 1,491 part-time (1,035 women); includes 504 Black or African American, non-Hispanic/Latino; 4 American Indian or Alaska Native, non-Hispanic/Latino; 25 Asian, non-Hispanic/Latino; 63 Hispanic/Latino; 40 Two or more races, non-Hispanic/Latino, 207 international. Average age 34. 1,907 applicants, 49% accepted, 671 enrolled. *Faculty:* 511 full-time (201 women), 32 part-time/adjunct (8 women). Expenses: Contact institution. *Financial support:* In 2010–11, 13 fellowships with full and partial tuition reimbursements (averaging $15,000 per year), 364 research assistantships with full and partial tuition reimbursements (averaging $9,970 per year), 374 teaching assistantships with full and partial tuition reimbursements (averaging $9,970 per year) were awarded; career-related internships or fieldwork, Federal Work-Study, institutionally sponsored loans, scholarships/grants, traineeships, and unspecified assistantships also available. Support available to part-time students. Financial award application deadline: 3/15; financial award applicants required to submit FAFSA. In 2010, 762 master's, 139 doctorates, 42 other advanced degrees awarded. *Degree program information:* Part-time and evening/weekend programs available. *Application deadline:* For fall admission, 2/1 priority date for domestic and international students. Applications are processed on a rolling basis. *Application fee:* $50. Electronic applications accepted. *Application Contact:* Shonna Breland, Manager of Graduate Admissions, 601-266-4369, Fax: 601-266-5138, E-mail: shonna.breland@usm.edu. *Dean,* Dr. Susan Siltanen, 601-266-4369, Fax: 601-266-5138, E-mail: susan.siltanen@usm.edu.

College of Arts and Letters Students: 287 full-time (131 women), 267 part-time (150 women); includes 52 Black or African American, non-Hispanic/Latino; 1 American Indian or Alaska Native, non-Hispanic/Latino; 4 Asian, non-Hispanic/Latino; 23 Hispanic/Latino; 10 Two or more races, non-Hispanic/Latino, 42 international. Average age 34. 358 applicants, 57% accepted, 138 enrolled. *Faculty:* 155 full-time (60 women), 5 part-time/adjunct (1 woman). Expenses: Contact institution. *Financial support:* In 2010–11, 14 fellowships with full tuition reimbursements (averaging $12,500 per year), 16 research assistantships with full tuition reimbursements (averaging $9,300 per year), 186 teaching assistantships with full tuition reimbursements (averaging $8,252 per year) were awarded; Federal Work-Study, institutionally sponsored loans, scholarships/grants, health care benefits, and unspecified assistantships also available. Financial award application deadline: 3/15; financial award applicants required to submit FAFSA. In 2010, 122 master's, 22 doctorates awarded. *Degree program information:* Part-time and evening/weekend programs available. Postbaccalaureate distance learning degree programs offered. Offers anthropology (MA); arts and letters (MA, MATL, MFA, MM, MME, MS, DMA, PhD); conducting (MM); creative writing (MA, PhD); directing (MFA); English literature (MA, PhD); French (MATL); history (MA, MS, PhD); history and literature (MM); international development (PhD); mass communication (MA, MS, PhD); music education (MME, PhD); performance (MFA, MM); performance and pedagogy (DMA); political science (MA, MS); public relations (MS); Spanish (MATL); speech communication (MA, MS, PhD); teaching English to speakers of other languages (TESOL) (MATL); technical (MFA); theory and composition (MM); woodwind performance (MM). *Application deadline:* For fall admission, 5/1 for domestic students, 3/1 for international students. Applications are processed on a rolling basis. *Application fee:* $50. Electronic applications accepted. *Application Contact:* Shonna Breland, Manager of Graduate Admissions, 601-266-4369, Fax: 601-266-5138, E-mail: shonna.breland@usm.edu. *Interim Dean,* Dr. Steven Moser, 601-266-4315, Fax: 601-266-6541, E-mail: steven.moser@usm.edu.

College of Business Students: 45 full-time (24 women), 34 part-time (18 women); includes 5 Black or African American, non-Hispanic/Latino; 1 Asian, non-Hispanic/Latino; 2 Hispanic/Latino; 1 Two or more races, non-Hispanic/Latino, 5 international. Average age 28. 76 applicants, 63% accepted, 39 enrolled. *Faculty:* 26 full-time (10 women), 3 part-time/adjunct (2 women). Expenses: Contact institution. *Financial support:* In 2010–11, 21 research assistantships with full tuition reimbursements (averaging $6,000 per year), 1 teaching assistantship with full tuition reimbursement (averaging $6,000 per year) were awarded; Federal Work-Study, institutionally sponsored loans, scholarships/grants, and health care benefits also available. Support available to part-time students. Financial award application deadline: 3/15; financial award applicants required to submit FAFSA. In 2010, 74 master's awarded. *Degree program information:* Part-time and evening/weekend programs available. Offers accountancy (MPA); business (MBA, MPA); business administration (MBA). *Application deadline:* For fall admission, 7/15 priority date for domestic students, 3/1 for international students; for spring admission, 11/15 priority date for domestic students, 11/5 for international students. Applications are processed on a rolling basis. *Application fee:* $59. Electronic applications accepted. *Application Contact:* Dr. Joseph Peyrefitte, Assistant Dean, 601-266-4664, Fax: 601-266-5814. *Dean,* Dr. Lance Nail, 601-266-4659, Fax: 601-266-5814.

College of Education and Psychology Students: 271 full-time (213 women), 699 part-time (541 women); includes 205 Black or African American, non-Hispanic/Latino; 1 American Indian or Alaska Native, non-Hispanic/Latino; 5 Asian, non-Hispanic/Latino; 17 Hispanic/Latino; 10 Two or more races, non-Hispanic/Latino, 14 international. Average age 36. 560 applicants, 36% accepted, 173 enrolled. *Faculty:* 98 full-time (51 women), 13 part-time/adjunct (4 women). Expenses: Contact institution. *Financial support:* In 2010–11, 80 research assistantships with full tuition reimbursements (averaging $9,586 per year), 53 teaching assistantships with full tuition reimbursements (averaging $7,775 per year) were awarded; career-related internships or fieldwork, Federal Work-Study, institutionally sponsored loans, scholarships/grants, health care benefits, and unspecified assistantships also available. Financial award application deadline: 3/15; financial award applicants required to submit FAFSA. In 2010, 252 master's, 62 doctorates, 40 other advanced degrees awarded. *Degree program information:* Part-time programs available. Offers adult education (Graduate Certificate); alternative secondary teacher education (MAT); business technology education (MS); child and family studies (MS); clinical psychology (MA, PhD); community college leadership (Graduate Certificate); counseling and personnel services (college) (M Ed); counseling psychology (MA, PhD); early childhood education (M Ed, Ed S); education (Ed D, PhD, Ed S); education (Ed D); education and psychology (M Ed, MA, MAT, MLIS, MS, Ed D, PhD, Ed S, Graduate Certificate); education of the gifted (M Ed, PhD, Ed S); education: educational leadership and research (Ed S); educational administration (M Ed); educational administration and supervision (M Ed); elementary education (M Ed, PhD, Ed S); experimental psychology (MA, PhD); higher education administration (Ed D, PhD); institutional research (Graduate Certificate); instructional technology (MS); library and information science (MLIS); marriage and family therapy (MS); reading (M Ed, MS); school psychology (MA, PhD); secondary education (M Ed, MS, PhD); special education (M Ed, PhD, Ed S); technical occupational education (MS). *Application deadline:* For fall admission, 3/1 priority date for domestic students, 3/1 for international students; for spring admission, 11/1 priority date for domestic students, 11/1 for international students. Applications are processed on a rolling basis. *Application fee:* $50. Electronic applications accepted. *Application Contact:* Shonna Breland, Manager of Graduate Admissions, 601-266-6563, Fax: 601-266-5138. *Dean,* Dr. Ann P. Blackwell, 601-266-4568, Fax: 601-266-4175.

College of Health Students: 401 full-time (318 women), 207 part-time (162 women); includes 165 Black or African American, non-Hispanic/Latino; 8 Asian, non-Hispanic/Latino; 10 Hispanic/Latino; 10 Two or more races, non-Hispanic/Latino, 13 international. Average age 33. 506 applicants, 51% accepted, 183 enrolled. *Faculty:* 72 full-time (46 women), 2 part-time/adjunct (0 women). Expenses: Contact institution. *Financial support:* In 2010–11, 1 fellowship with full tuition reimbursement (averaging $16,000 per year), 45 research assistantships with full tuition reimbursements (averaging $8,397 per year), 12 teaching assistantships with full tuition reimbursements (averaging $7,756 per year) were awarded; career-related internships or fieldwork, Federal Work-Study, institutionally sponsored loans, scholarships/grants, health care benefits, and unspecified assistantships also available. Financial award application deadline: 3/15; financial award applicants required to submit FAFSA. In 2010, 216 master's, 11 doctorates awarded. *Degree program information:* Part-time and evening/weekend programs available. Offers audiology (Au D); epidemiology and biostatistics (MPH); family nurse practitioner (MSN); health (MA, MPH, MS, MSN, MSW, Au D, DNP, PhD); health education (MPH); health policy/administration (MPH); human performance (MS, PhD); interscholastic athletic administration (MS); medical technology (MS); nursing (DNP, PhD); nursing executive (MSN); nutrition (MS, PhD); occupational/environmental health (MPH); psychiatric nurse practitioner (MSN); public health nutrition (MPH); recreation and leisure management (MS); social work (MSW); speech language pathology (MA, MS); sport administration (MS); sport and coaching education (MS); sport management (MS). *Application deadline:* For fall admission, 3/1 for domestic and international students; for spring admission, 1/10 priority date for domestic and international students. Applications are processed on a rolling basis. *Application fee:* $50. Electronic applications accepted. *Application Contact:* Shonna Breland, Manager of Graduate Admissions, 601-266-6563, Fax: 601-266-5138. *Dean,* Dr. Michael Forster, 601-266-4866.

College of Science and Technology Students: 414 full-time (159 women), 160 part-time (84 women); includes 51 Black or African American, non-Hispanic/Latino; 1 American Indian or Alaska Native, non-Hispanic/Latino; 6 Asian, non-Hispanic/Latino; 8 Hispanic/Latino; 5 Two or more races, non-Hispanic/Latino, 130 international. Average age 32. 407 applicants, 52% accepted, 138 enrolled. *Faculty:* 160 full-time (34 women), 9 part-time/adjunct (1 woman). Expenses: Contact institution. *Financial support:* In 2010–11, 4 fellowships with full tuition reimbursements (averaging $16,250 per year), 189 research assistantships with full tuition reimbursements (averaging $14,464 per year), 137 teaching assistantships with full tuition reimbursements (averaging $10,259 per year) were awarded; career-related internships or fieldwork, Federal Work-Study, institutionally sponsored loans, scholarships/grants, health care benefits, and unspecified assistantships also available. Financial award application deadline: 3/15; financial award applicants required to submit FAFSA. In 2010, 98 master's, 44 doctorates awarded. *Degree program information:* Part-time and evening/weekend programs available. Offers administration of justice (PhD); analytical chemistry (MS, PhD); biochemistry (MS, PhD); coastal sciences (MS, PhD); computational science (MS, PhD); computer science (MS); corrections (MA, MS); economic development (MS); environmental biology (MS, PhD); forensics (MS); geography (MS, PhD); geology (MS); human capital development (PhD); hydrographic science (MS); inorganic chemistry (MS, PhD); juvenile justice (MA, MS); law enforcement (MA, MS); logistics management and technology (MS); marine biology (MS, PhD); marine science (MS, PhD); mathematics (MS); microbiology (MS, PhD); molecular biology (MS, PhD); organic chemistry (MS, PhD); physical chemistry (MS, PhD); physics (MS); polymer science (MS); polymer science and engineering (MS, PhD); science and mathematics education (MS, PhD); science and technology (MA, MS, PhD); workforce training and development (MS). *Application deadline:* For fall admission, 3/1 priority date for domestic students, 3/1 for international students; for spring admission, 1/10 priority date for domestic and international students. Applications are processed on a rolling basis. *Application fee:* $50. *Application Contact:* Shonna Breland, Manager of Graduate School Admissions, 601-266-6567, Fax: 601-266-5138. *Dean,* Dr. Joe B. Whitehead, 601-266-4883, Fax: 601-266-5829.

UNIVERSITY OF SOUTH FLORIDA, Tampa, FL 33620-9951

General Information State-supported, coed, university. CGS member. *Enrollment:* 40,431 graduate, professional, and undergraduate students; 4,353 full-time matriculated graduate/professional students (2,544 women), 4,313 part-time matriculated graduate/professional students (2,796 women). *Enrollment by degree level:* 604 first professional, 5,773 master's, 2,289 doctoral. *Graduate faculty:* 551 full-time (206 women), 39 part-time/adjunct (20 women). *Graduate housing:* Rooms and/or apartments available on a first-come, first-served basis to single students and available to married students. Typical cost: $5380 per year for single students. Housing application deadline: 7/1. *Student services:* Campus employment opportunities, campus safety program, career counseling, child daycare facilities, exercise/wellness program, free psychological counseling, grant writing training, international student

University of South Florida (continued)

services, low-cost health insurance, multicultural affairs office, services for students with disabilities, writing training. *Library facilities:* Tampa Campus Library plus 5 others. *Online resources:* library catalog, web page. *Collection:* 2.4 million titles, 81,572 serial subscriptions. *Research affiliation:* Veterans Administration Medical Center, All Children's Hospital, Harris Corporation (electronics), Tampa General Hospital, Shriners Hospitals, H. L. Moffitt Cancer Center.

Computer facilities: Computer purchase and lease plans are available. 500 computers available on campus for general student use. A campuswide network can be accessed from student residence rooms and from off campus. Online class registration is available. *Web address:* http://www.usf.edu/.

General Application Contact: Dr. Karen Liller, Interim Dean, Graduate School/Associate Vice President for Research and Innovation, 813-974-2846, Fax: 813-974-5762, E-mail: kliller@grad.usf.edu.

GRADUATE UNITS

Graduate School Students: 4,353 full-time (2,544 women), 4,312 part-time (2,796 women); includes 2,190 minority (771 Black or African American, non-Hispanic/Latino; 39 American Indian or Alaska Native, non-Hispanic/Latino; 506 Asian, non-Hispanic/Latino; 809 Hispanic/Latino; 6 Native Hawaiian or other Pacific Islander, non-Hispanic/Latino; 59 Two or more races, non-Hispanic/Latino), 822 international. 8,883 applicants, 44% accepted, 2318 enrolled. Expenses: Contact institution. *Financial support:* Fellowships with full tuition reimbursements, research assistantships with full tuition reimbursements, teaching assistantships with full tuition reimbursements available. Financial award application deadline: 2/1; financial award applicants required to submit FAFSA. In 2010, 156 first professional degrees, 2,241 master's, 243 doctorates, 17 other advanced degrees awarded. *Degree program information:* Part-time and evening/weekend programs available. Postbaccalaureate distance learning degree programs offered. *Application deadline:* For fall admission, 5/1 for international students; for spring admission, 9/15 for international students. *Application fee:* $30. Electronic applications accepted. *Application Contact:* Francisco Vera, Assistant Director for Admissions, 813-974-8800, E-mail: fvera@usf.edu. *Dean,* Dr. Karen D. Liller, 813-974-7359, Fax: 813-974-5762, E-mail: kliller@grad.usf.edu.

College of Arts and Sciences Students: 1,160 full-time (618 women), 691 part-time (451 women); includes 100 Black or African American, non-Hispanic/Latino; 9 American Indian or Alaska Native, non-Hispanic/Latino; 55 Asian, non-Hispanic/Latino; 157 Hispanic/Latino; 15 Two or more races, non-Hispanic/Latino, 205 international. Average age 31. 2,058 applicants, 37% accepted, 467 enrolled. *Faculty:* 193 full-time (65 women), 10 part-time/adjunct (2 women). Expenses: Contact institution. *Financial support:* Career-related internships or fieldwork, Federal Work-Study, institutionally sponsored loans, scholarships/grants, tuition waivers (full and partial), and unspecified assistantships available. Support available to part-time students. Financial award applicants required to submit FAFSA. In 2010, 408 master's, 80 doctorates awarded. *Degree program information:* Part-time and evening/weekend programs available. Postbaccalaureate distance learning degree programs offered (minimal on-campus study). Offers Africana studies (MLA); American studies (MA); analytical chemistry (MS, PhD); applied anthropology (MA, PhD); applied physics (PhD); arts and sciences (MA, MFA, MLA, MPA, MS, Au D, PhD); biochemistry (MS, PhD); cancer biology (PhD); cell biology and molecular biology (MS); classics: Latin/Greek (MA); clinical psychology (PhD); coastal marine biology (MS); coastal marine biology and ecology (PhD); cognitive and neural sciences (PhD); communication (MA, PhD); computational chemistry (MS, PhD); conservation biology (MS, PhD); economics (MA, PhD); English (MA, MFA, PhD); environmental chemistry (MS, PhD); environmental science and policy (MS); film studies (MLA); French (MA); geography (MA, PhD); geology (MS, PhD); government (PhD); history (MA, PhD); humanities (MLA); industrial-organizational psychology (PhD); inorganic chemistry (MS, PhD); Latin American Caribbean and Latino Studies (MA); library and information science (MA); linguistics (MA); linguistics: ESL (MA); mass communications (MA); mathematics (MA, PhD); molecular and cell biology (PhD); organic chemistry (MS); philosophy (MA, PhD); physical chemistry (MS, PhD); physics (MS); political science (MA); polymer chemistry (PhD); public administration (MPA); religious studies (MA); sociology (MA, PhD); Spanish (MA); statistics (MA); women's studies (MA). *Application deadline:* For fall admission, 2/15 priority date for domestic students, 1/2 priority date for international students; for spring admission, 10/15 priority date for domestic students, 6/1 priority date for international students. *Application fee:* $30. *Application Contact:* Sylvia Gardner, Administrative Assistant, 813-974-0853, Fax: 813-974-5911, E-mail: gardner@cas.usf.edu. *Dean,* Dr. Eric Eisenberg, 813-974-2503, Fax: 813-974-5911, E-mail: eisenber@cas.usf.edu.

College of Behavioral and Community Sciences Students: 450 full-time (393 women), 248 part-time (193 women); includes 53 Black or African American, non-Hispanic/Latino; 24 Asian, non-Hispanic/Latino; 82 Hispanic/Latino; 3 Two or more races, non-Hispanic/Latino, 13 international. Average age 30. 974 applicants, 35% accepted, 215 enrolled. *Faculty:* 67 full-time (39 women), 10 part-time/adjunct (8 women). Expenses: Contact institution. In 2010, 276 master's, 21 doctorates awarded. Offers aging studies (PhD); applied behavior analysis (MA); audiology (Au D); behavioral and community sciences (MA, MS, MSW, Au D, PhD); criminal justice administration (MA); criminology (MA, PhD); gerontology (MA); hearing science (PhD); language and speech science (PhD); neurocommunicative science (PhD); rehabilitation and mental health counseling (MA); social work (MSW, PhD); speech-language pathology (MS). *Application Contact:* Dr. Junius J. Gonzales, Dean, 813-974-2365, Fax: 813-974-2365, E-mail: deansoffice@fmhi.usf.edu. *Dean,* Dr. Junius J. Gonzales, 813-974-2365, Fax: 813-974-2365, E-mail: deansoffice@fmhi.usf.edu.

College of Business Students: 416 full-time (167 women), 373 part-time (143 women); includes 38 Black or African American, non-Hispanic/Latino; 4 American Indian or Alaska Native, non-Hispanic/Latino; 58 Asian, non-Hispanic/Latino; 77 Hispanic/Latino; 5 Two or more races, non-Hispanic/Latino, 127 international. Average age 30. 1,051 applicants, 42% accepted, 257 enrolled. *Faculty:* 22 full-time (6 women). Expenses: Contact institution. *Financial support:* Career-related internships or fieldwork, scholarships/grants, health care benefits, and unspecified assistantships available. Financial award applicants required to submit FAFSA. In 2010, 327 master's, 10 doctorates awarded. *Degree program information:* Part-time and evening/weekend programs available. Offers accounting (M Acc, PhD); business (PhD); business administration (MBA, MSM, PhD); entrepreneurship (MS, Graduate Certificate); finance (MS, PhD); information systems (PhD); leadership and organizational effectiveness (MSM); management (MS); management and organization (MBA); management information systems (MS); marketing (MSM, PhD); real estate (MS). *Application deadline:* For fall admission, 6/1 for domestic students, 1/2 for international students; for spring admission, 10/15 for domestic students, 6/1 for international students. *Application fee:* $30. *Application Contact:* Wendy Baker, Assistant Director, Graduate Studies, 813-974-3335, Fax: 813-974-4518, E-mail: wbaker@usf.edu. *Dean,* Dr. Robert Forsythe, 813-974-4281, Fax: 813-974-3030, E-mail: forsythe@usf.edu.

College of Education Students: 619 full-time (450 women), 1,101 part-time (819 women); includes 197 Black or African American, non-Hispanic/Latino; 9 American Indian or Alaska Native, non-Hispanic/Latino; 41 Asian, non-Hispanic/Latino; 150 Hispanic/Latino; 14 Two or more races, non-Hispanic/Latino, 63 international. Average age 35. 815 applicants, 64% accepted, 388 enrolled. *Faculty:* 134 full-time (82 women), 36 part-time/adjunct (21 women). Expenses: Contact institution. *Financial support:* In 2010–11, 9 fellowships with full tuition reimbursements (averaging $15,000 per year), 2 research assistantships with full tuition reimbursements (averaging $15,000 per year) were awarded; career-related internships or fieldwork, Federal Work-Study, institutionally sponsored loans, scholarships/grants, health care benefits, and unspecified assistantships also available. Support available to part-time students. Financial award applicants required to submit FAFSA. In 2010, 503 master's, 55 doctorates, 51 other advanced degrees awarded. *Degree program information:* Part-time and evening/weekend programs available. Postbaccalaureate distance learning degree programs offered (no on-campus study). Offers adult education (MA, Ed D, PhD, Ed S); autism spectrum disorders and severe intellectual disabilities (MA); behavior disorders (MA); career and technical education (MA); career and workforce education (PhD); college student affairs (M Ed); counselor education (MA, PhD, Ed S); early childhood education (M Ed, MA, PhD); education (M Ed, MA, MAT, Ed D, PhD, Ed S); educational leadership (M Ed, Ed D, Ed S); elementary education (MA, MAT, PhD); English education (M Ed, MA, MAT, PhD); exceptional student education (MA, MAT); exercise science (MA); foreign language education/ESOL (M Ed, MA, MAT); gifted education (MA); higher education/community college teaching (MA, Ed D, PhD); instructional technology (M Ed, PhD, Ed S); interdisciplinary (PhD, Ed S); mathematics education (M Ed, MA, MAT, PhD, Ed S); measurement and evaluation (M Ed, PhD, Ed S); mental retardation (MA); physical education teacher preparation (MA); reading/language arts (MA, PhD, Ed S); school psychology (PhD, Ed S); science education (M Ed, MA, MAT, PhD); second language acquisition/instructional technology (PhD); secondary education (M Ed, PhD); secondary education/TESOL (M Ed); social science education (M Ed, MA, MAT); special education (PhD); specific learning disabilities (MA); teaching and learning in the content area (PhD); vocational education (Ed S). *Application deadline:* For fall admission, 2/15 for domestic students, 1/2 for international students; for spring admission, 10/15 for domestic students, 6/1 for international students. *Application fee:* $30. Electronic applications accepted. *Application Contact:* Dr. Diane Briscoe, Coordinator of Graduate Studies, 813-974-1804, Fax: 813-974-3391, E-mail: briscoe@usf.edu. *Dean,* Dr. Colleen S. Kennedy, 813-974-3400, Fax: 813-974-3826.

College of Engineering Students: 527 full-time (148 women), 293 part-time (62 women); includes 184 minority (57 Black or African American, non-Hispanic/Latino; 46 Asian, non-Hispanic/Latino; 75 Hispanic/Latino; 2 Native Hawaiian or other Pacific Islander, non-Hispanic/Latino; 4 Two or more races, non-Hispanic/Latino), 314 international. Average age 30. 933 applicants, 53% accepted, 249 enrolled. *Faculty:* 84 full-time (11 women), 2 part-time/adjunct (0 women). Expenses: Contact institution. *Financial support:* Career-related internships or fieldwork, Federal Work-Study, scholarships/grants, health care benefits, and unspecified assistantships available. Financial award application deadline: 3/1; financial award applicants required to submit FAFSA. In 2010, 181 master's, 51 doctorates awarded. *Degree program information:* Part-time and evening/weekend programs available. Offers biomedical engineering (MSBE, PhD); chemical and biomedical engineering (MCH, ME, MSES, PhD); chemical engineering (PhD); civil and environmental engineering (MSES); civil engineering (MCE, MSCE, PhD); computer engineering (MSCP); computer science (MSCS); computer science and engineering (PhD); electrical engineering (ME, MSEE, MSES, PhD); engineering (MCE, MCH, ME, MIE, MME, MSBE, MSBE, MSCE, MSCP, MSCS, MSEE, MSEM, MSES, MSIE, MSME, PhD); engineering management (MSEM, MSIE); engineering science (PhD); industrial engineering (MIE, MSIE, PhD); mechanical engineering (ME, MME, MSES, MSME, PhD). *Application deadline:* For fall admission, 2/15 for domestic students, 1/2 priority date for international students; for spring admission, 10/15 for domestic students, 6/1 priority date for international students. Applications are processed on a rolling basis. *Application fee:* $30. Electronic applications accepted. *Application Contact:* Marsha L. Brett, Administrative Assistant, 813-974-3782, Fax: 813-974-5094, E-mail: brett@eng.usf.edu. *Dean,* Dr. John Wieneck, 813-974-2530, Fax: 813-974-5094, E-mail: wieneck@eng.usf.edu.

College of Marine Science Students: 69 full-time (41 women), 35 part-time (20 women); includes 6 Black or African American, non-Hispanic/Latino; 11 Hispanic/Latino; 1 Two or more races, non-Hispanic/Latino, 11 international. Average age 31. 98 applicants, 29% accepted, 15 enrolled. *Faculty:* 24 full-time (6 women). Expenses: Contact institution. *Financial support:* In 2010–11, 73 students received support. Health care benefits and unspecified assistantships available. Financial award application deadline: 1/15. In 2010, 7 master's, 7 doctorates awarded. *Degree program information:* Part-time programs available. Offers biological oceanography (MS, PhD); chemical oceanography (MS, PhD); geological oceanography (MS, PhD); interdisciplinary (PhD); marine resource assessment (MS, PhD); physical oceanography (MS, PhD). *Application deadline:* For fall admission, 1/15 for domestic students, 1/2 for international students; for spring admission, 10/1 for domestic students, 7/1 for international students. Applications are processed on a rolling basis. *Application fee:* $30. *Application Contact:* Dawna L. Ishler, Academic Services Administrator, 727-553-3944, Fax: 727-553-1189, E-mail: dishler@usf.edu. *Professor and Director of Academic Programs and Student Affairs,* Dr. Edward S. Van Vleet, 727-553-1165, Fax: 727-553-1189, E-mail: vanvleet@marine.usf.edu.

College of Medicine Students: 412 full-time (252 women), 564 part-time (287 women); includes 395 minority (98 Black or African American, non-Hispanic/Latino; 7 American Indian or Alaska Native, non-Hispanic/Latino; 180 Asian, non-Hispanic/Latino; 103 Hispanic/Latino; 1 Native Hawaiian or other Pacific Islander, non-Hispanic/Latino; 6 Two or more races, non-Hispanic/Latino), 17 international. Average age 27. 778 applicants, 55% accepted, 353 enrolled. *Faculty:* 21 full-time (6 women). Expenses: Contact institution. In 2010, 146 first professional degrees, 191 master's, 17 doctorates awarded. *Degree program information:* Part-time programs available. Offers medical sciences (MS, MSMS, PhD); medicine (MD, MS, MSMS, DPT, PhD); physical therapy (MS, DPT). *Application deadline:* For fall admission, 2/15 for domestic students, 1/2 for international students. *Application fee:* $30. Electronic applications accepted. *Application Contact:* Michael Barber, Director, 813-974-9702, Fax: 813-974-3886, E-mail: mbarber@health.usf.edu. *Director,* Michael Barber, 813-974-9702, Fax: 813-974-3886, E-mail: mbarber@health.usf.edu.

College of Nursing Students: 117 full-time (101 women), 593 part-time (530 women); includes 182 minority (86 Black or African American, non-Hispanic/Latino; 5 American Indian or Alaska Native, non-Hispanic/Latino; 28 Asian, non-Hispanic/Latino; 60 Hispanic/Latino; 1 Native Hawaiian or other Pacific Islander, non-Hispanic/Latino; 2 Two or more races, non-Hispanic/Latino), 10 international. Average age 37. 474 applicants, 25% accepted, 95 enrolled. *Faculty:* 26 full-time (22 women), 6 part-time/adjunct (4 women). Expenses: Contact institution. *Financial support:* In 2010–11, 3 teaching assistantships (averaging $12,397 per year) were awarded; tuition waivers (partial) and unspecified assistantships also available. Financial award application deadline: 2/1; financial award applicants required to submit FAFSA. In 2010, 152 master's, 4 doctorates awarded. *Degree program information:* Part-time programs available. Offers nursing (MS, DNP, PhD). *Application deadline:* For fall admission, 2/15 for domestic students, 1/2 for international students; for spring admission, 10/15 for domestic students, 6/1 for international students. *Application fee:* $30. Electronic applications accepted. *Application Contact:* Mary Webb, Director, 813-974-3442, Fax: 813-974-3118, E-mail: mwebb@health.usf.edu.

College of Public Health *Degree program information:* Part-time and evening/weekend programs available. Postbaccalaureate distance learning degree programs offered (minimal on-campus study). Offers community and family health (MPH, MSPH, Dr PH, PhD); environmental and occupational health (MPH, MSPH, PhD); epidemiology and biostatistics (MPH, MSPH, PhD); global health (MPH, MSPH, Dr PH, PhD); health policy and management (MHA, MPH, MSPH, PhD); public health (MHA, MPH, MSPH, Dr PH, PhD); public health practice (MPH). Electronic applications accepted.

College of The Arts Students: 195 full-time (87 women), 77 part-time (33 women); includes 12 Black or African American, non-Hispanic/Latino; 4 American Indian or Alaska Native, non-Hispanic/Latino; 12 Asian, non-Hispanic/Latino; 42 Hispanic/Latino; 1 Two or more races, non-Hispanic/Latino, 16 international. Average age 30. 287 applicants, 41% accepted, 81 enrolled. *Faculty:* 38 full-time (12 women), 4 part-time/adjunct (1 woman). Expenses: Contact institution. *Financial support:* Unspecified assistantships available. Financial award applicants required to submit FAFSA. In 2010, 85 master's, 3 doctorates awarded. *Degree program information:* Part-time and evening/weekend programs available. Offers architecture and community design (M Arch); art history (MA); chamber music (MM); composition (MM); conducting (MM); electro-acoustic music (MM); jazz studies (MM); music education (MA, PhD); piano pedagogy (MM); studio art (MFA); the arts (M Arch, MA, MFA, MM, PhD); theory (MM). *Application deadline:* For fall admission, 1/15 for domestic students, 1/2 for international students. *Application fee:* $30. *Application Contact:* Prof. Barton Lee, Associate Dean, 813-974-2301, Fax: 813-974-2091, E-mail: blee@usf.edu. *Dean,* Dr. Ron Jones, 813-974-7380, Fax: 813-974-2091, E-mail: ronjones@usf.edu.

THE UNIVERSITY OF TAMPA, Tampa, FL 33606-1490

General Information Independent, coed, comprehensive institution. *Enrollment:* 6,427 graduate, professional, and undergraduate students; 305 full-time matriculated graduate/professional students (139 women), 431 part-time matriculated graduate/professional students (255 women). *Enrollment by degree level:* 736 master's. *Graduate faculty:* 91 full-time (44 women), 14 part-time/adjunct (9 women). *Tuition:* Part-time $504 per credit hour. *Required fees:* $40 per term. *Graduate housing:* Room and/or apartments available on a first-come, first-served basis to single students; on-campus housing not available to married students. Typical cost: $8590 (including board). Housing application deadline: 5/1. *Student services:* Campus employment opportunities, campus safety program, career counseling, exercise/wellness program, international student services, services for students with disabilities, writing training. *Library facilities:* Macdonald Kelce Library. *Online resources:* library catalog, web page. *Collection:* 275,297 titles, 46,306 serial subscriptions, 733 audiovisual materials. *Research affiliation:* Tampa General Hospital (nursing).

Computer facilities: Computer purchase and lease plans are available. 800 computers available on campus for general student use. A campuswide network can be accessed from student residence rooms and from off campus. Online class registration is available. *Web address:* http://www.ut.edu/.

General Application Contact: Brent Benner, Director of Enrollment Management/Admission, 813-257-3002, E-mail: bbenner@ut.edu.

GRADUATE UNITS

John H. Sykes College of Business Students: 235 full-time (89 women), 288 part-time (122 women); includes 74 minority (16 Black or African American, non-Hispanic/Latino; 2 American Indian or Alaska Native, non-Hispanic/Latino; 14 Asian, non-Hispanic/Latino; 34 Hispanic/Latino; 2 Native Hawaiian or other Pacific Islander, non-Hispanic/Latino; 6 Two or more races, non-Hispanic/Latino), 95 international. Average age 29. 457 applicants, 45% accepted, 175 enrolled. *Faculty:* 67 full-time (24 women), 11 part-time/adjunct (4 women). Expenses: Contact institution. *Financial support:* In 2010–11, 74 students received support. Career-related internships or fieldwork, scholarships/grants, unspecified assistantships, and grants available. Financial award applicants required to submit FAFSA. In 2010, 230 master's awarded. *Degree program information:* Part-time and evening/weekend programs available. Offers accounting (MS); entrepreneurship (MBA); finance (MBA, MS); information systems management (MBA); innovation management (MBA); international business (MBA); marketing (MBA, MS); nonprofit management (MBA). *Application deadline:* Applications are processed on a rolling basis. *Application fee:* $40. Electronic applications accepted. *Application Contact:* Charlene Tobie, Associate Director of Admissions, 813-257-3566, E-mail: ctobie@ut.edu. *Vice President, Enrollment/Admissions,* Dennis Nostrand, 813-257-1808, E-mail: dnostrand@ut.edu.

Nursing Programs Students: 3 full-time (all women), 134 part-time (125 women); includes 28 minority (13 Black or African American, non-Hispanic/Latino; 1 Asian, non-Hispanic/Latino; 13 Hispanic/Latino; 1 Two or more races, non-Hispanic/Latino), 1 international. Average age 36. 70 applicants, 64% accepted, 36 enrolled. *Faculty:* 13 full-time (all women), 12 part-time/adjunct (all women). Expenses: Contact institution. *Financial support:* In 2010–11, 2 students received support. Unspecified assistantships available. Financial award applicants required to submit FAFSA. In 2010, 24 master's awarded. *Degree program information:* Part-time programs available. Offers adult nurse practitioner (MSN); family nurse practitioner (MSN). *Application deadline:* Applications are processed on a rolling basis. *Application fee:* $40. Electronic applications accepted. *Application Contact:* Wendy Plant, Admissions Counselor, 813-257-3696, Fax: 813-259-5403, E-mail: wplant@ut.edu. *Director/Chair,* Dr. Maria Warda, 813-257-3302, Fax: 813-258-7214, E-mail: mwarda@ut.edu.

Program in Teaching Students: 67 full-time (47 women), 9 part-time (8 women); includes 1 Black or African American, non-Hispanic/Latino; 2 American Indian or Alaska Native, non-Hispanic/Latino; 2 Asian, non-Hispanic/Latino; 5 Hispanic/Latino; 1 Two or more races, non-Hispanic/Latino. Average age 34. 149 applicants, 50% accepted, 51 enrolled. *Faculty:* 14 full-time (10 women), 16 part-time/adjunct (11 women). Expenses: Contact institution. *Financial support:* In 2010–11, 50 students received support. Grants available. Financial award applicants required to submit FAFSA. In 2010, 38 master's awarded. *Degree program information:* Part-time and evening/weekend programs available. Offers curricula and instructional leadership (M Ed); teaching (M Ed). *Application deadline:* For fall admission, 5/1 for domestic students. Applications are processed on a rolling basis. *Application fee:* $40. Electronic applications accepted. *Application Contact:* Charlene Tobie, Associate Director, Graduate and Continuing Studies, 813-258-7409, Fax: 813-258-7451, E-mail: ctobie@ut.edu. *Dean, College of Social Sciences, Mathematics and Education,* Dr. Anne Gormly, 813-253-3333 Ext. 6262, E-mail: agormly@ut.edu.

THE UNIVERSITY OF TENNESSEE, Knoxville, TN 37996

General Information State-supported, coed, university. CGS member. *Enrollment:* 30,312 graduate, professional, and undergraduate students; 4,167 full-time matriculated graduate/professional students (2,206 women), 2,048 part-time matriculated graduate/professional students (1,079 women). *Enrollment by degree level:* 820 first professional, 3,439 master's, 1,956 doctoral. *Graduate faculty:* 1,287 full-time (430 women), 97 part-time/adjunct (19 women). Tuition, state resident: full-time $7440; part-time $414 per credit hour. Tuition, nonresident: full-time $22,478; part-time $1250 per credit hour. *Required fees:* $922; $43 per credit hour. Tuition and fees vary according to program. *Graduate housing:* Room and/or apartments available on a first-come, first-served basis to single students; on-campus housing not available to married students. Typical cost: $8228 (including board). Room and board charges vary according to board plan. Housing application deadline: 2/1. *Student services:* Campus employment opportunities, campus safety program, career counseling, exercise/wellness program, free psychological counseling, grant writing training, international student services, low-cost health insurance, multicultural affairs office, services for students with disabilities, teacher training, writing training. *Library facilities:* John C. Hodges Library plus 5 others. *Online resources:* library catalog, web page, access to other libraries' catalogs. *Collection:* 3.1 million titles, 61,039 serial subscriptions, 44,900 audiovisual materials. *Research affiliation:* 3M (chemical engineering), Siemens (medicalimaging), East Chemical Company (chemical engineering), Electric Power Research Institute (energy systems), SAIC (engineering and technology applications), Exxon Corporation (material sciences).

Computer facilities: Computer purchase and lease plans are available. 600 computers available on campus for general student use. A campuswide network can be accessed from student residence rooms and from off campus. Online class registration, Blackboard Course Management System are available. *Web address:* http://www.utk.edu.

General Application Contact: Yvonne Kilpatrick, Interim Director, Graduate and International Admissions, 865-974-3251, Fax: 865-974-6541, E-mail: graduateadmissions@utk.edu.

GRADUATE UNITS

College of Law Students: 482 full-time (209 women); includes 122 minority (56 Black or African American, non-Hispanic/Latino; 2 American Indian or Alaska Native, non-Hispanic/Latino; 25 Asian, non-Hispanic/Latino; 26 Hispanic/Latino; 13 Two or more races, non-Hispanic/Latino), 3 international. Average age 24. 1,508 applicants, 27% accepted, 169 enrolled. *Faculty:* 44 full-time (19 women), 61 part-time/adjunct (22 women). Expenses: Contact institution. *Financial support:* In 2010–11, 292 students received support, including 8 research assistantships with full tuition reimbursements available (averaging $4,400 per year); career-related internships or fieldwork, Federal Work-Study, institutionally sponsored loans, scholarships/grants, and unspecified assistantships also available. Support available to part-time students. Financial award application deadline: 3/1; financial award applicants required to submit FAFSA. In 2010, 168 first professional degrees awarded. Offers business transactions (JD); law (JD); trial advocacy and dispute resolution (JD). *Application deadline:* For fall admission, 3/1 priority date for domestic and international students. Applications are processed on a rolling basis. *Application fee:* $15. Electronic applications accepted. *Application Contact:* Janet S. Hatcher, Admissions and Financial Aid Advisor, 865-974-4131, Fax: 865-974-1572, E-mail: hatcher@utk.edu. *Director of Admissions, Financial Aid and Career Services,* Dr. Karen R. Britton, 865-974-4131, Fax: 865-974-1572, E-mail: lawadmit@utk.edu.

Graduate School *Degree program information:* Part-time and evening/weekend programs available. Postbaccalaureate distance learning degree programs offered (minimal on-campus study). Offers aviation systems (MS); comparative and experimental medicine (MS, PhD). Electronic applications accepted.

College of Agricultural Sciences and Natural Resources *Degree program information:* Part-time programs available. Postbaccalaureate distance learning degree programs offered (minimal on-campus study). Offers agricultural education (MS); agricultural extension education (MS); agricultural sciences and natural resources (MS, PhD); animal anatomy (PhD); biosystems engineering (MS, PhD); biosystems engineering technology (MS); breeding (MS, PhD); entomology (MS, PhD); floriculture (MS); food science and technology (MS, PhD); forestry (MS); integrated pest management and bioactive natural products (PhD); landscape design (MS); management (MS, PhD); nutrition (MS, PhD); physiology (MS, PhD); plant pathology (MS, PhD); public horticulture (MS); turfgrass (MS); wildlife and fisheries science (MS); woody ornamentals (MS). Electronic applications accepted.

College of Architecture and Design Offers architecture (professional) (M Arch); architecture (research) (M Arch); architecture and design (M Arch, MA, MLA, MS); landscape architecture (MLA); landscape architecture (research) (MA, MS). Electronic applications accepted.

College of Arts and Sciences *Degree program information:* Part-time and evening/weekend programs available. Offers accompanying (MM); American history (PhD); analytical chemistry (MS, PhD); applied linguistics (PhD); applied mathematics (MS); archaeology (MA, PhD); arts and sciences (M Math, MA, MFA, MM, MPA, MS, PhD); audiology (MA); behavior (MS, PhD); biochemistry, cellular and molecular biology (MS, PhD); biological anthropology (MA, PhD); ceramics (MFA); chemical physics (PhD); choral conducting (MM); clinical psychology (PhD); composition (MM); computer science (MS, PhD); costume design (MFA); criminology (MA, PhD); cultural anthropology (MA, PhD); drawing (MFA); ecology (MS, PhD); energy, environment, and resource policy (MA, PhD); English (MA, PhD); environmental chemistry (MS, PhD); European history (PhD); evolutionary biology (MS, PhD); experimental psychology (MA, PhD); French (MA, PhD); genome science and technology (MS, PhD); geography (MS, PhD); geology (MS, PhD); German (MA, PhD); graphic design (MFA); hearing science (PhD); history (MA); inorganic chemistry (MS, PhD); instrumental conducting (MM); inter-area studies (MFA); Italian (PhD); jazz (MM); lighting design (MFA); mathematical ecology (PhD); mathematics (M Math, MS, PhD); media arts (MFA); medical ethics (MA, PhD); microbiology (MS, PhD); modern foreign languages (PhD); music education (MM); music theory (MM); musicology (MM); organic chemistry (MS, PhD); painting (MFA); performance (MFA, MM); philosophy (MA, PhD); physical chemistry (MS, PhD); physics (MS, PhD); piano pedagogy and literature (MM); plant physiology and genetics (MS, PhD); political economy (MA, PhD); political science (MA, MPA, PhD); polymer chemistry (MS, PhD); Portuguese (PhD); printmaking (MFA); psychology (MA); public administration (MPA); religious studies (MA); Russian (PhD); scene design (MFA); sculpture (MFA); Spanish (MA); speech and hearing science (PhD); speech and language pathology (PhD); speech and language science (PhD); speech pathology (MA); theatre technology (MFA); theoretical chemistry (PhD); watercolor (MFA); zoo-archaeology (MA, PhD). Electronic applications accepted.

College of Business Administration *Degree program information:* Part-time programs available. Postbaccalaureate distance learning degree programs offered (minimal on-campus study). Offers accounting (M Acc, PhD); business administration (M Acc, MA, MBA, MS, PhD); economics (MA, PhD); finance (MBA, PhD); industrial and organizational psychology (PhD); industrial statistics (MS); logistics and transportation (MBA, PhD); management (PhD); management science (MS, PhD); marketing (MBA, PhD); operations management (MBA); professional business administration (MBA); statistics (MS, PhD); systems (M Acc); taxation (M Acc); teacher licensure (MS); training and development (MS). Electronic applications accepted.

College of Communication and Information *Degree program information:* Part-time and evening/weekend programs available. Postbaccalaureate distance learning degree programs offered (no on-campus study). Offers advertising (MS, PhD); broadcasting (MS, PhD); communications (MS, PhD); information sciences (MS, PhD); journalism (MS, PhD); public relations (MS, PhD); speech communication (MS, PhD). Electronic applications accepted.

College of Education, Health and Human Sciences *Degree program information:* Part-time and evening/weekend programs available. Postbaccalaureate distance learning degree programs offered (no on-campus study). Offers adult education (MS); applied educational psychology (MS); art education (MS); biomechanics/sports medicine (MS, PhD); child and family studies (MS, PhD); collaborative learning (Ed D); college student personnel (MS); community health (PhD); community health education (MPH); consumer services management (MS); counseling education (PhD); cultural studies in education (PhD); curriculum (MS, Ed S); curriculum, educational research and evaluation (Ed D, PhD); early childhood education (MS, PhD); early childhood special education (MS); education of deaf and hard of hearing (MS); education, health and human sciences (MPH, MS, Ed D, PhD, Ed S); educational administration and policy studies (Ed D, PhD); educational administration and supervision (MS, Ed S); educational psychology (Ed D, PhD); elementary education (MS, Ed S); elementary teaching (MS); English education (MS, Ed S); exercise physiology (MS, PhD); exercise science (MS, PhD); foreign language/ESL education (MS, Ed S); gerontology (MPH); health planning/administration (MPH); health promotion and health education (MS); hospitality management (MS); hotel, restaurant, and tourism management (MS); instructional technology (MS, Ed D, PhD, Ed S); literacy, language and ESL education (PhD); literacy, language education, and ESL education (Ed D); mathematics education (MS, Ed S); mental health counseling (MS); modified and comprehensive special education (MS); nutrition (MS); nutrition science (PhD); reading education (MS, Ed S); recreation and leisure studies (MS); rehabilitation counseling (MS); retail and consumer sciences (MS); retailing and consumer sciences (PhD); safety (MS); school counseling (MS, Ed S); school psychology (PhD, Ed S); science education (MS, Ed S); secondary teaching (MS); social foundations (MS); social science education (MS, Ed S); socio-cultural foundations of sports and education (PhD); special education (Ed S); sport management (MS); sport studies (MS, PhD); teacher education (Ed D, PhD); textile science (MS, PhD); therapeutic recreation (MS); tourism (MS). Electronic applications accepted.

College of Engineering Students: 599 full-time (113 women), 256 part-time (35 women); includes 28 Black or African American, non-Hispanic/Latino; 3 American Indian or Alaska Native, non-Hispanic/Latino; 23 Asian, non-Hispanic/Latino; 11 Hispanic/Latino, 314 international. Average age 26. 1,405 applicants, 29% accepted, 199 enrolled. *Faculty:* 148 full-time (15 women), 117 part-time/adjunct (5 women). Expenses: Contact institution. *Financial support:* In 2010–11, 484 students received support, including 53 fellowships with full tuition reimbursements available (averaging $17,140 per year), 390 research assistantships with full tuition reimbursements available (averaging $17,759 per year), 204 teaching assistantships with full tuition reimbursements available (averaging $13,560 per year); career-related internships or fieldwork, Federal Work-Study, institutionally sponsored loans, health care benefits, and unspecified assistantships also available. Financial award application deadline: 2/1; financial award applicants required to submit FAFSA. In 2010, 154 master's, 63 doctorates awarded. *Degree program information:* Part-time programs available. Postbaccalaureate distance learning degree programs offered (minimal on-campus study). Offers aerospace engineering (MS, PhD); biomedical engineering (MS, PhD); chemical engineering (MS, PhD); civil engineering (MS, PhD); computer engineering (MS, PhD); computer science (MS, PhD); electrical engineering (MS, PhD); engineering (MS, PhD); engineering management (MS); engineering science (MS, PhD); environmental engineering (MS); industrial engineering (MS, PhD); materials science and engineering (MS, PhD); mechanical engineering (MS, PhD); nuclear engineering (MS, PhD); polymer engineering (MS, PhD); reliability and maintainability engineering (MS). *Application deadline:* For fall admission, 2/1 priority date for domestic and international students; for spring admission, 6/15 for domestic and international students. Applications are processed on a rolling basis. *Application fee:* $35. Electronic applications accepted. *Application Contact:* Dr. Masood Parang, Associate Dean of Student Affairs, 865-974-2454, Fax: 865-974-9871, E-mail: mparang@utk.edu. *Dean,* Dr. Wayne T. Davis, 865-974-5321, Fax: 865-974-8890, E-mail: way@utk.edu.

College of Nursing *Degree program information:* Part-time programs available. Offers nursing (MSN, PhD). Electronic applications accepted.

College of Social Work *Degree program information:* Part-time programs available. Offers clinical social work practice (MSSW); social welfare management and community practice (MSSW); social work (PhD). Electronic applications accepted.

College of Veterinary Medicine Offers veterinary medicine (DVM).

THE UNIVERSITY OF TENNESSEE AT CHATTANOOGA, Chattanooga, TN 37403-2598

General Information State-supported, coed, comprehensive institution. CGS member. *Enrollment:* 10,781 graduate, professional, and undergraduate students; 636 full-time matriculated graduate/professional students (358 women), 916 part-time matriculated graduate/professional students (518 women). *Enrollment by degree level:* 75 first professional, 1,299 master's, 116 doctoral, 62 other advanced degrees. *Graduate faculty:* 111 full-time (37 women), 18 part-time/adjunct (10 women). *Graduate housing:* Rooms and/or apartments available on a first-come, first-served basis to single and married students. Housing application deadline: 8/1. *Student services:* Campus employment opportunities, campus safety program, career counseling, child daycare facilities, exercise/wellness program, free psychological counseling, international student services, low-cost health insurance, services for students with disabilities, teacher training, writing training. *Library facilities:* Lupton Library. *Online resources:* library catalog, web page, access to other libraries' catalogs. *Collection:* 541,364 titles, 20,327 audiovisual materials. *Research affiliation:* Tennessee Coalition against Domestic & Sexual Violence (criminal justice), Law Enforcement Innovation Center (criminal justice), Highland Biological Field Station (biology and environmental science), Tennessee Valley Authority, Gulf Coast Research Laboratory (biology and environmental science).

Computer facilities: 965 computers available on campus for general student use. A campuswide network can be accessed from student residence rooms and from off campus. Online class registration, pay fees are available. *Web address:* http://www.utc.edu/.

General Application Contact: Dr. Jerald Ainsworth, Dean of Graduate Studies, 423-425-4478, Fax: 423-425-5223, E-mail: jerald-ainsworth@utc.edu.

GRADUATE UNITS

Graduate School Students: 636 full-time (358 women), 916 part-time (518 women); includes 140 minority (93 Black or African American, non-Hispanic/Latino; 1 American Indian or Alaska Native, non-Hispanic/Latino; 15 Asian, non-Hispanic/Latino; 15 Hispanic/Latino; 16 Two or more races, non-Hispanic/Latino), 54 international. Average age 31. 913 applicants, 79% accepted, 584 enrolled. *Faculty:* 111 full-time (37 women), 18 part-time/adjunct (10 women). Expenses: Contact institution. *Financial support:* In 2010–11, 134 research assistantships with full and partial tuition reimbursements (averaging $5,500 per year), 9 teaching assistantships with full and partial tuition reimbursements (averaging $5,500 per year) were awarded; career-related internships or fieldwork, scholarships/grants, and unspecified assistantships also available. Support available to part-time students. In 2010, 407 master's, 52 doctorates, 53 other advanced degrees awarded. *Degree program information:* Part-time and evening/weekend programs available. Postbaccalaureate distance learning degree programs offered (no on-campus study). *Application deadline:* For fall admission, 8/1 priority date for domestic students, 6/1 for international students; for spring admission, 12/1 priority date for domestic students, 10/1 for international students. Applications are processed on a rolling basis. *Application fee:* $35. Electronic applications accepted. *Application Contact:* Dr. Jerald Ainsworth, Dean of Graduate Studies, 423-425-4478, Fax: 423-425-5223, E-mail: jerald-ainsworth@utc.edu. *Dean of Graduate Studies,* Dr. Jerald Ainsworth, 423-425-4478, Fax: 423-425-5223, E-mail: jerald-ainsworth@utc.edu.

College of Arts and Sciences Students: 119 full-time (77 women), 85 part-time (48 women); includes 14 minority (9 Black or African American, non-Hispanic/Latino; 1 Asian, non-Hispanic/Latino; 2 Hispanic/Latino; 2 Two or more races, non-Hispanic/Latino), 4 international. Average age 28. 175 applicants, 78% accepted, 104 enrolled. *Faculty:* 42 full-time (13 women), 1 part-time/adjunct (0 women). Expenses: Contact institution. *Financial support:* In 2010–11, 45 research assistantships with full and partial tuition reimbursements (averaging $5,500 per year), 8 teaching assistantships with full and partial tuition reimbursements (averaging $5,500 per year) were awarded; career-related internships or fieldwork, scholarships/grants, and unspecified assistantships also available. Support available to part-time students. In 2010, 79 master's, 1 other advanced degree awarded. *Degree program information:* Part-time and evening/weekend programs available. Offers arts and sciences (MA, MM, MPA, MS, MSCJ, Postbaccalaureate Certificate); creative writing (MA); criminal justice (MSCJ); environmental sciences (MS); industrial/organizational psychology (MS); literary study (MA); local government management (MPA); music education (MM); non profit management (MPA); performance (MM); public administration (MPA); public administration and non-profit management (Postbaccalaureate Certificate); research psychology (MS); rhetoric and writing (MA, Graduate Certificate). *Application deadline:* For fall admission, 8/1 priority date for domestic students, 6/1 for international students; for spring admission, 12/1 priority date for domestic students, 10/1 for international students. Applications are processed on a rolling basis. *Application fee:* $35. Electronic applications accepted. *Application Contact:* Dr. Jerald Ainsworth, Dean of Graduate Studies, 423-425-4478, Fax: 423-425-5223, E-mail: jerald-ainsworth@utc.edu. *Dean,* Dr. Herb Burhenn, 423-425-4635, Fax: 423-425-4279, E-mail: herbert-burhenn@utc.edu.

College of Business Students: 127 full-time (45 women), 178 part-time (78 women); includes 29 minority (16 Black or African American, non-Hispanic/Latino; 6 Asian, non-Hispanic/Latino; 3 Hispanic/Latino; 4 Two or more races, non-Hispanic/Latino), 11 international. Average age 28. 179 applicants, 77% accepted, 114 enrolled. *Faculty:* 14 full-time (4 women). Expenses: Contact institution. *Financial support:* In 2010–11, 9 research assistantships (averaging $5,500 per year) were awarded; career-related internships or fieldwork, scholarships/grants, and unspecified assistantships also available. Support available to part-time students. In 2010, 107 master's awarded. *Degree program information:* Part-time and evening/weekend programs available. Offers accountancy (M Acc); business (EMBA, M Acc, MBA); business administration (EMBA, MBA). *Application deadline:* For fall admission, 8/1 priority date for domestic students, 6/1 for international students; for spring admission, 12/1 priority date for domestic students, 10/1 for international students. Applications are processed on a rolling basis. *Application fee:* $35. Electronic applications accepted. *Application Contact:* Dr. Jerald Ainsworth, Dean of Graduate Studies, 423-425-4478, Fax: 423-425-5223, E-mail: jerald-ainsworth@utc.edu. *Interim Dean,* Dr. John Fulmer, 423-425-4313, Fax: 423-425-5255, E-mail: richard-casavant@utc.edu.

College of Engineering and Computer Science Students: 61 full-time (11 women), 129 part-time (22 women); includes 24 minority (15 Black or African American, non-Hispanic/Latino; 4 Asian, non-Hispanic/Latino; 5 Hispanic/Latino), 32 international. Average age 30. 114 applicants, 75% accepted, 56 enrolled. *Faculty:* 22 full-time (3 women), 2 part-time/adjunct (1 woman). Expenses: Contact institution. *Financial support:* In 2010–11, 39 research assistantships with full and partial tuition reimbursements (averaging $5,500 per year) were awarded; career-related internships or fieldwork, scholarships/grants, and unspecified assistantships also available. Support available to part-time students. In 2010, 46 master's, 1 doctorate, 22 other advanced degrees awarded. *Degree program information:* Part-time and evening/weekend programs available. Postbaccalaureate distance learning degree programs offered (no on-campus study). Offers chemical engineering (MS Engr); civil engineering (MS Engr); computational engineering (MS Engr); computer science (MS, Graduate Certificate); electrical engineering (MS Engr); engineering and computer science (MS, MS Engr, PhD, Graduate Certificate); engineering management (MS); fundamentals of engineering management (Graduate Certificate); industrial engineering (MS Engr); mechanical engineering (MS Engr); power systems management (Graduate Certificate); project and value management (Graduate Certificate); quality management (Graduate Certificate). *Application deadline:* For fall admission, 8/1 priority date for domestic students, 6/1 for international students; for spring admission, 12/1 priority date for domestic students, 10/1 for international students. Applications are processed on a rolling basis. *Application fee:* $35. Electronic applications accepted. *Application Contact:* Dr. Jerald Ainsworth, Dean of Graduate Studies, 423-425-4478, Fax: 423-425-5223, E-mail: jerald-ainsworth@utc.edu. *Dean,* Dr. William Sutton, 423-425-2256, Fax: 423-425-5229, E-mail: will-sutton@utc.edu.

College of Health, Education and Professional Studies Students: 312 full-time (218 women), 400 part-time (306 women); includes 42 Black or African American, non-Hispanic/Latino; 1 American Indian or Alaska Native, non-Hispanic/Latino; 2 Asian, non-Hispanic/Latino; 4 Hispanic/Latino; 8 Two or more races, non-Hispanic/Latino, 5 international. Average age 33. 338 applicants, 84% accepted, 223 enrolled. *Faculty:* 33 full-time (17 women), 15 part-time/adjunct (9 women). Expenses: Contact institution. *Financial support:* In 2010–11, 41 research assistantships with full and partial tuition reimbursements (averaging $5,500 per year) were awarded; career-related internships or fieldwork, scholarships/grants, and unspecified assistantships also available. Support available to part-time students. In 2010, 175 master's, 51 doctorates, 21 other advanced degrees awarded. *Degree program information:* Part-time and evening/weekend programs available. Postbaccalaureate distance learning degree programs offered (no on-campus study). Offers administration (MSN); athletic training (MSAT); certified nurse anesthetist (Post-Master's Certificate); community counseling (M Ed); counseling (M Ed); education (M Ed, MSN, Post-Master's Certificate); educational leadership (Ed D); educational specialist (Ed S); educational technology (Ed S); elementary education (M Ed); family nurse practitioner (MSN, Post-Master's Certificate); health and human performance (MS); health care informatics (Post-Master's Certificate); health, education and professional studies (M Ed, MS, MSAT, MSN, DNP, DPT, Ed D, Ed S, Post-Master's Certificate); learning and leadership (Ed D); nurse anesthesia (MSN); nurse education (Post-Master's Certificate); nursing (DNP); physical therapy (DPT); post professional (DPT); school counseling (M Ed); school leadership (M Ed, Post-Master's Certificate); school psychology (Ed S); secondary education (M Ed); special education (M Ed). *Application deadline:* For fall admission, 8/1 priority date for domestic students, 6/1 for international students; for spring admission, 12/1 priority date for domestic students, 10/1 for international students. Applications are processed on a rolling basis. *Application fee:* $35. Electronic applications accepted. *Application Contact:* Dr. Jerald Ainsworth, Dean of Graduate Studies, 423-425-4478, Fax: 423-425-5223, E-mail: jerald-ainsworth@utc.edu. *Dean,* Dr. Mary Tanner, 423-425-4249, Fax: 423-425-4044, E-mail: mary-tanner@utc.edu.

THE UNIVERSITY OF TENNESSEE AT MARTIN, Martin, TN 38238-1000

General Information State-supported, coed, comprehensive institution. *Enrollment:* 8,469 graduate, professional, and undergraduate students; 94 full-time matriculated graduate/professional students (63 women), 341 part-time matriculated graduate/professional students (229 women). *Enrollment by degree level:* 435 master's. *Graduate faculty:* 162. Tuition, state resident: full-time $7164; part-time $400 per credit hour. Tuition, nonresident: full-time $19,574; part-time $1090 per credit hour. *Required fees:* $1044; $60 per credit hour. *Graduate housing:* Rooms and/or apartments guaranteed to single students and available to married students. Typical cost: $4480 per year ($5973 including board) for single students. Housing application deadline: 3/1. *Student services:* Campus employment opportunities, campus safety program, career counseling, child daycare facilities, exercise/wellness program, free psychological counseling, international student services, low-cost health insurance, multicultural affairs office, services for students with disabilities, teacher training, writing training. *Library facilities:* Paul Meek Library. *Online resources:* library catalog, web page, access to other libraries' catalogs. *Collection:* 516,595 titles, 1,125 serial subscriptions, 15,861 audiovisual materials. *Research affiliation:* Oak Ridge National Laboratories (Science, Technology, Engineering, and Math (STEM)), U. S. Department of Justice (criminal justice), Health and Human Services (infant health), Department of Education (academic extensions), National Writing Project (humanities), University of Tennessee Research Foundation (science and technology).

Computer facilities: 786 computers available on campus for general student use. A campuswide network can be accessed from student residence rooms and from off campus. Online class registration, online fee payments, degree progress, financial aid data, housing applications, transcripts are available. *Web address:* http://www.utm.edu/.

General Application Contact: Linda S. Arant, Student Services Specialist, 731-881-7012, Fax: 731-881-7499, E-mail: larant@utm.edu.

GRADUATE UNITS

Graduate Programs Students: 435 (292 women); includes 36 Black or African American, non-Hispanic/Latino; 1 American Indian or Alaska Native, non-Hispanic/Latino; 5 Hispanic/Latino; 2 Two or more races, non-Hispanic/Latino, 15 international. 270 applicants, 66% accepted, 127 enrolled. *Faculty:* 162. Expenses: Contact institution. *Financial support:* In 2010–11, 36 students received support, including 31 research assistantships with full tuition reimbursements available (averaging $7,080 per year), 5 teaching assistantships with full tuition reimbursements available (averaging $6,535 per year); scholarships/grants and unspecified assistantships also available. Support available to part-time students. Financial award application deadline: 2/15; financial award applicants required to submit FAFSA. In 2010, 126 master's awarded. *Degree program information:* Part-time programs available. Postbaccalaureate distance learning degree programs offered (minimal on-campus study). *Application deadline:* For fall admission, 8/1 priority date for domestic students, 7/5 priority date for international students; for spring admission, 2/5 priority date for domestic students, 2/10 priority date for international students. Applications are processed on a rolling basis. *Application fee:* $30 ($130 for international students). Electronic applications accepted. *Application Contact:* Linda S. Arant, Student Services Specialist, 731-881-7012, Fax: 731-881-7499, E-mail: larant@utm.edu. *Assistant Vice Chancellor and Dean of Graduate Studies,* Dr. Victoria S. Seng, 731-881-7012, Fax: 731-881-7499, E-mail: vseng@utm.edu.

College of Agriculture and Applied Sciences Students: 77 (51 women); includes 9 Black or African American, non-Hispanic/Latino; 2 Hispanic/Latino; 1 Two or more races, non-Hispanic/Latino, 2 international. 63 applicants, 76% accepted, 24 enrolled. *Faculty:* 35. Expenses: Contact institution. *Financial support:* In 2010–11, 3 students received support, including 3 research assistantships with full tuition reimbursements available (averaging $7,902 per year); scholarships/grants and unspecified assistantships also available. Support available to part-time students. Financial award application deadline: 2/15; financial award applicants required to submit FAFSA. In 2010, 20 master's awarded. *Degree program information:* Part-time programs available. Postbaccalaureate distance learning degree programs offered (no on-campus study). Offers agricultural and natural resources management (MSANR); agriculture and applied sciences (MSANR, MSFCS); dietetics (MSFCS); general family and consumer sciences (MSFCS). *Application deadline:* For fall admission, 8/1 priority date for domestic students, 7/15 priority date for international students; for spring admission, 2/15 priority date for domestic students, 12/1 priority date for international students. Applications are processed on a rolling basis. *Application fee:* $30 ($130 for international students). Electronic applications accepted. *Application Contact:* Linda S. Arant, Student Services Specialist, 731-881-7012, Fax: 731-881-7499, E-mail: larant@utm.edu. *Interim Dean,* Dr. Jerry Gresham, 731-881-7250, E-mail: jgresham@utm.edu.

College of Business and Global Affairs Students: 70 (22 women); includes 3 Black or African American, non-Hispanic/Latino; 1 Hispanic/Latino, 12 international. 46 applicants, 61% accepted, 21 enrolled. *Faculty:* 29. Expenses: Contact institution. *Financial support:* In 2010–11, 13 students received support, including 12 research assistantships with full tuition reimbursements available (averaging $6,866 per year), 1 teaching assistantship (averaging $6,284 per year); unspecified assistantships also available. Support available to part-time students. Financial award application deadline: 2/15; financial award applicants required to submit FAFSA. In 2010, 31 master's awarded. *Degree program information:* Part-time programs available. Postbaccalaureate distance learning degree programs offered (no on-campus study). Offers business (MBA); business and global affairs (MBA). *Application deadline:* For fall admission, 8/1 priority date for domestic students, 7/15 priority date for international students; for spring admission, 12/15 priority date for domestic students, 12/1 priority date for international students. Applications are processed on a rolling basis. *Application fee:* $30 ($130 for international students). Electronic applications accepted. *Application Contact:* Linda S. Arant, Student Services Specialist, 731-881-7012, Fax: 731-881-7499, E-mail: larant@utm.edu. *Dean,* Dr. Ernest Moser, 731-881-7227, Fax: 731-881-7241, E-mail: emoser@utm.edu.

College of Education and Behavioral Sciences Students: 288 (219 women); includes 24 Black or African American, non-Hispanic/Latino; 1 American Indian or Alaska Native, non-Hispanic/Latino; 2 Hispanic/Latino, 1 international. 144 applicants, 67% accepted, 75 enrolled. *Faculty:* 57. Expenses: Contact institution. *Financial support:* In 2010–11, 20 students received support, including 16 research assistantships with full tuition reimbursements available (averaging $7,088 per year), 4 teaching assistantships with full tuition reimbursements available (averaging $6,598 per year); scholarships/grants and unspecified assistantships also available. Support available to part-time students. Financial award application deadline: 1/15; financial award applicants required to submit FAFSA. In 2010, 80 master's awarded. *Degree program information:* Part-time programs available. Postbaccalaureate distance learning degree programs offered (minimal on-campus study). Offers advanced (MS Ed); community counseling (MS Ed); education and behavioral sciences (MS Ed); educational leadership (MS Ed); initial licensure (MS Ed); initial licensure comprehensive (MS Ed); school counseling (MS Ed). *Application deadline:* For fall admission, 8/1 priority date for domestic students, 7/15 priority date for international students; for spring admission, 12/15 priority date for domestic students, 12/1 priority date for international students. Applications are processed on a rolling basis. *Application fee:* $30 ($130 for international students). Electronic applications accepted. *Application Contact:* Linda S. Arant, Student Services Specialist, 731-881-7012, Fax: 731-881-7499, E-mail: larant@utm.edu. *Dean*, Dr. Mary Lee Hall, 731-881-7127, Fax: 731-881-7975, E-mail: mlhall@utm.edu.

THE UNIVERSITY OF TENNESSEE HEALTH SCIENCE CENTER, Memphis, TN 38163-0002

General Information State-supported, coed, upper-level institution. CGS member. *Enrollment by degree level:* 1,513 first professional, 150 master's, 312 doctoral. *Graduate faculty:* 745 full-time, 169 part-time/adjunct. *Graduate housing:* Room and/or apartments available on a first-come, first-served basis to single students; on-campus housing not available to married students. Housing application deadline: 2/28. *Student services:* Campus employment opportunities, campus safety program, career counseling, child daycare facilities, free psychological counseling, low-cost health insurance, services for students with disabilities. *Library facilities:* Health Science Library plus 2 others. *Collection:* 165,200 titles, 1,784 serial subscriptions. *Research affiliation:* Saint Jude's Children's Research Hospital, Veterans Administration Medical Center, LePasses Rehabilitation Center, LeBonheur Children's Medical Center.

Computer facilities: 100 computers available on campus for general student use. A campuswide network can be accessed from student residence rooms and from off campus. *Web address:* http://www.uthsc.edu/.

General Application Contact: Ron K. Patterson, Director for Admission, 901-448-2747, Fax: 901-448-7772, E-mail: rpatte10@uthsc.edu.

GRADUATE UNITS

College of Allied Health Sciences Students: 463 full-time (371 women), 102 part-time (86 women); includes 97 minority (52 Black or African American, non-Hispanic/Latino; 1 American Indian or Alaska Native, non-Hispanic/Latino; 18 Asian, non-Hispanic/Latino; 9 Hispanic/Latino; 17 Native Hawaiian or other Pacific Islander, non-Hispanic/Latino), 10 international. Average age 26. 225 applicants, 57% accepted, 120 enrolled. *Faculty:* 23 full-time (18 women), 23 part-time/adjunct (17 women). Expenses: Contact institution. *Financial support:* In 2010–11, 2 teaching assistantships were awarded; Federal Work-Study, institutionally sponsored loans, and scholarships/grants also available. Support available to part-time students. Financial award application deadline: 2/15; financial award applicants required to submit FAFSA. In 2010, 2 master's, 2 doctorates awarded. *Degree program information:* Part-time and evening/weekend programs available. Postbaccalaureate distance learning degree programs offered (minimal on-campus study). Offers allied health sciences (MCP, MDH, MHIIM, MOT, MSCLS, MSPT, DPT, ScDPT, TDPT). *Application deadline:* For fall admission, 1/30 priority date for domestic students; for winter admission, 10/1 priority date for domestic students. *Application fee:* $50. Electronic applications accepted. *Application Contact:* Ron K. Patterson, Director for Admissions, 901-448-5560, Fax: 901-448-7772, E-mail: rpatte10@uthsc.edu. *Dean*, Dr. Noma Anderson, 901-528-5581, Fax: 901-528-7545, E-mail: nander13@uthsc.edu.

College of Dentistry Students: 323 full-time (121 women); includes 20 minority (5 Black or African American, non-Hispanic/Latino; 7 Asian, non-Hispanic/Latino; 1 Hispanic/Latino; 7 Native Hawaiian or other Pacific Islander, non-Hispanic/Latino), 18 international. Average age 23. 255 applicants, 37% accepted, 95 enrolled. *Faculty:* 57 full-time (8 women), 66 part-time/adjunct (6 women). Expenses: Contact institution. *Financial support:* In 2010–11, 276 students received support. Federal Work-Study and minority scholarships available. Support available to part-time students. Financial award application deadline: 2/15; financial award applicants required to submit FAFSA. In 2010, 72 first professional degrees, 6 master's awarded. Offers dentistry (DDS); oral and maxillofacial surgery (Certificate); orthodontics (MS); pediatric dentistry (MS, Certificate); periodontics (MS); prosthodontics (Certificate). *Application deadline:* For fall admission, 12/31 for domestic and international students. Applications are processed on a rolling basis. *Application fee:* $50. Electronic applications accepted. *Application Contact:* Ron K. Patterson, Director for Admissions, 901-448-5560, Fax: 901-448-7772, E-mail: rpatte10@uthsc.edu. *Dean*, Dr. Timothy L. Hottel, 901-448-6200, Fax: 901-448-1625, E-mail: thottel@uthsc.edu.

College of Graduate Health Sciences Students: 255 full-time (145 women), 44 part-time (27 women); includes 214 minority (33 Black or African American, non-Hispanic/Latino; 1 American Indian or Alaska Native, non-Hispanic/Latino; 88 Asian, non-Hispanic/Latino; 4 Hispanic/Latino; 87 Native Hawaiian or other Pacific Islander, non-Hispanic/Latino; 1 Two or more races, non-Hispanic/Latino), 106 international. Average age 25. 673 applicants, 10% accepted, 67 enrolled. *Faculty:* 318 full-time (92 women), 59 part-time/adjunct (16 women). Expenses: Contact institution. *Financial support:* In 2010–11, 2 fellowships, 85 research assistantships, 40 teaching assistantships were awarded; career-related internships or fieldwork, Federal Work-Study, institutionally sponsored loans, and tuition waivers (full and partial) also available. Support available to part-time students. Financial award application deadline: 2/25; financial award applicants required to submit FAFSA. In 2010, 16 master's, 29 doctorates awarded. *Degree program information:* Part-time programs available. Offers health sciences (MS, PhD). *Application deadline:* For fall admission, 5/15 priority date for domestic students. *Application fee:* $0. Electronic applications accepted. *Application Contact:* Ron K. Patterson, Director for Admissions, 901-448-5560, Fax: 901-448-7772, E-mail: rpatte10@uthsc.edu. *Dean*, Dr. Cheryl R. Scheid, 901-448-5506, E-mail: cscheid@uthsc.edu.

College of Medicine Students: 634 full-time (245 women), 2 part-time (0 women); includes 237 minority (64 Black or African American, non-Hispanic/Latino; 1 American Indian or Alaska Native, non-Hispanic/Latino; 78 Asian, non-Hispanic/Latino; 16 Hispanic/Latino; 78 Native Hawaiian or other Pacific Islander, non-Hispanic/Latino), 22 international. Average age 25. 1,355 applicants, 11% accepted. *Faculty:* 1,041 full-time (208 women), 990 part-time/adjunct (198 women). Expenses: Contact institution. *Financial support:* In 2010–11, 519 students received support. Career-related internships or fieldwork, Federal Work-Study, and institutionally sponsored loans available. Support available to part-time students. Financial award application deadline: 2/28. In 2010, 144 first professional degrees awarded. Offers medicine (MD, MS, PhD). *Application deadline:* For fall admission, 11/15 for domestic students. Applications are processed on a rolling basis. *Application fee:* $50. Electronic applications accepted. *Application Contact:* Ron K. Patterson, Director for Admissions, 901-448-2747, Fax: 901-448-7772, E-mail: rpatte10@uthsc.edu. *Dean*, Dr. David M. Stern, 901-448-5529, Fax: 901-448-7683, E-mail: dstern@uthsc.edu.

College of Nursing Students: 280 full-time (231 women), 19 part-time (18 women); includes 97 minority (80 Black or African American, non-Hispanic/Latino; 1 American Indian or Alaska Native, non-Hispanic/Latino; 13 Asian, non-Hispanic/Latino; 3 Hispanic/Latino), 10 international. Average age 29. 225 applicants, 43% accepted, 79 enrolled. *Faculty:* 19 full-time (17 women), 8 part-time/adjunct (5 women). Expenses: Contact institution. *Financial support:* In 2010–11, 44 students received support; fellowships with partial tuition reimbursements available, teaching assistantships, Federal Work-Study, institutionally sponsored loans, scholarships/grants, and traineeships available. Support available to part-time students. Financial award application deadline: 2/28; financial award applicants required to submit FAFSA. In 2010, 31 master's, 5 doctorates awarded. Postbaccalaureate distance learning degree programs offered (minimal on-campus study). Offers nursing (MSN, DNP, PhD). *Application deadline:* For fall admission, 2/1 for domestic students; for winter admission, 9/1 for domestic students. *Application fee:* $50. Electronic applications accepted. *Application Contact:* Ron K. Patterson, Director for Admissions, 901-448-2747, Fax: 901-448-7772, E-mail: rpatte10@uthsc.edu. *Dean*, Dr. Donna Hathaway, 901-448-6135, Fax: 901-448-4121, E-mail: dhathaway@uthsc.edu.

College of Pharmacy Students: 675 full-time (423 women), 1 (woman) part-time; includes 105 minority (58 Black or African American, non-Hispanic/Latino; 43 Asian, non-Hispanic/Latino; 4 Hispanic/Latino), 27 international. Average age 24. 850 applicants, 25% accepted, 215 enrolled. Expenses: Contact institution. *Financial support:* In 2010–11, 215 students received support; fellowships, research assistantships, teaching assistantships, career-related internships or fieldwork, Federal Work-Study, institutionally sponsored loans, and tuition waivers (full) available. Support available to part-time students. Financial award application deadline: 2/15. In 2010, 121 first professional degrees awarded. Offers pharmacy (Pharm D, MS, PhD). *Application deadline:* For fall admission, 2/1 for domestic students. Applications are processed on a rolling basis. *Application fee:* $50. Electronic applications accepted. *Application Contact:* Ron K. Patterson, Director for Admission, 901-448-2747, Fax: 901-448-7772, E-mail: rpatte10@uthsc.edu. *Dean*, Dr. Dick R. Gourley, 901-528-6036, Fax: 901-528-7053, E-mail: rgourley@uthsc.edu.

THE UNIVERSITY OF TENNESSEE–OAK RIDGE NATIONAL LABORATORY GRADUATE SCHOOL OF GENOME SCIENCE AND TECHNOLOGY, Oak Ridge, TN 37830-8026

General Information State-supported, coed, graduate-only institution. *Graduate housing:* Rooms and/or apartments available on a first-come, first-served basis to single and married students. *Research affiliation:* Oak Ridge National Laboratory.

GRADUATE UNITS

Graduate Program Offers life sciences (MS, PhD). Electronic applications accepted.

THE UNIVERSITY OF TENNESSEE SPACE INSTITUTE, Tullahoma, TN 37388-9700

General Information State-supported, coed, primarily men, graduate-only institution. *Enrollment by degree level:* 103 master's, 45 doctoral. *Graduate faculty:* 20 full-time (2 women), 25 part-time/adjunct (1 woman). *Graduate housing:* Room and/or apartments available on a first-come, first-served basis to single students; on-campus housing not available to married students. *Student services:* Campus employment opportunities, career counseling, free psychological counseling, international student services, low-cost health insurance, writing training. *Library facilities:* Helen and Arthur Mason Library. *Online resources:* web page. *Collection:* 25,000 titles, 125 serial subscriptions, 80 audiovisual materials. *Research affiliation:* Air Force Institute of Technology (aerospace engineering), International Space University (space engineering), RWTH Technical University (aerospace engineering), U. S. Air Force–Arnold Engineering Development Center (aerospace engineering).

Computer facilities: 100 computers available on campus for general student use. A campuswide network can be accessed from student residence rooms and from off campus. Online class registration is available. *Web address:* http://www.utsi.edu/.

General Application Contact: Dee Merriman, Coordinator III, 931-393-7213, Fax: 931-393-7211, E-mail: dmerrima@utsi.edu.

GRADUATE UNITS

Graduate Programs Students: 54 full-time (8 women), 94 part-time (15 women); includes 12 minority (6 Black or African American, non-Hispanic/Latino; 5 Asian, non-Hispanic/Latino; 1 Native Hawaiian or other Pacific Islander, non-Hispanic/Latino), 23 international. 25 applicants, 88% accepted, 19 enrolled. *Faculty:* 20 full-time (2 women), 25 part-time/adjunct (1 woman). Expenses: Contact institution. *Financial support:* In 2010–11, 4 fellowships with full and partial tuition reimbursements (averaging $1,425 per year), 41 research assistantships with full tuition reimbursements (averaging $17,791 per year) were awarded; career-related internships or fieldwork, Federal Work-Study, institutionally sponsored loans, health care benefits, tuition waivers (full and partial), and unspecified assistantships also available. In 2010, 59 master's, 3 doctorates awarded. *Degree program information:* Part-time programs available. Postbaccalaureate distance learning degree programs offered. Offers aerospace engineering (MS, PhD); applied mathematics (MS); aviation systems (MS); electrical engineering and computer science (MS, PhD); engineering and applied science (MS, PhD); engineering management (MS, PhD); engineering sciences (MS, PhD); materials science and engineering (MS); mechanical engineering (MS, PhD); mechanics (MS, PhD); physics (MS, PhD). *Application deadline:* For fall admission, 2/1 for international students; for spring admission, 6/15 for international students. Applications are processed on a rolling basis. *Application fee:* $35. Electronic applications accepted. *Application Contact:* Dee Merriman, Coordinator III, 931-393-7213, Fax: 931-393-7211, E-mail: dmerrima@utsi.edu. *Associate Executive Director*, Dr. Charles Johnson, 931-393-7318, Fax: 931-393-7211, E-mail: cjohnson@utsi.edu.

THE UNIVERSITY OF TEXAS AT ARLINGTON, Arlington, TX 76019

General Information State-supported, coed, university. CGS member. *Enrollment:* 32,975 graduate, professional, and undergraduate students; 3,337 full-time matriculated graduate/professional students (1,485 women), 4,507 part-time matriculated graduate/professional students (2,851 women). *Enrollment by degree level:* 6,808 master's, 1,036 doctoral. *Graduate faculty:* 614 full-time (178 women), 49 part-time/adjunct (19 women). *International tuition:* $13,250 full-time. Tuition, state resident: full-time $7500. Tuition, nonresident: full-time $13,080. *Graduate housing:* Rooms and/or apartments available on a first-come, first-served basis to single and married students. Typical cost: $3872 per year ($7472 including board) for single students; $3872 per year ($7472 including board) for married students. *Student services:* Campus employment opportunities, campus safety program, career counseling, child daycare facilities, exercise/wellness program, free psychological counseling, international student services, multicultural affairs office, services for students with disabilities, teacher training, writing training. *Library facilities:* Central Library plus 2 others. *Online resources:* library catalog, web page. *Collection:* 1.5 million titles, 52,951 serial subscriptions, 12,174 audiovisual materials. *Research affiliation:* Texas Instruments (medical technologies), Texas Health Resources (medical technologies), Center for Innovation, Arlington, TX (technology development and commercialization), Ethicon (non-invasive surgical tools), Department of Energy (bioengineering), National Science Foundation (materials science and engineering).

Computer facilities: 600 computers available on campus for general student use. A campuswide network can be accessed from student residence rooms and from off campus. Online class registration is available. *Web address:* http://www.uta.edu/.

General Application Contact: Dr. Phil Cohen, Dean of Graduate Studies, 817-272-3186, Fax: 817-272-2625, E-mail: graduate.school@uta.edu.

GRADUATE UNITS

Graduate School Students: 3,337 full-time (1,485 women), 4,507 part-time (2,851 women); includes 658 Black or African American, non-Hispanic/Latino; 23 American Indian or Alaska Native, non-Hispanic/Latino; 348 Asian, non-Hispanic/Latino; 578 Hispanic/Latino, 1,963 international. Average age 31. 4,802 applicants, 78% accepted, 2017 enrolled. *Faculty:* 614 full-time (178 women), 49 part-time/adjunct (19 women). Expenses: Contact institution. *Financial support:* Fellowships, research assistantships, teaching assistantships, career-related internships or fieldwork, Federal Work-Study, institutionally sponsored loans, scholarships/grants, traineeships, and tuition waivers (partial) available. Financial award application deadline: 6/1; financial award applicants required to submit FAFSA. In 2010, 1,888 master's, 131 doctorates awarded. *Degree program information:* Part-time and evening/weekend programs available. Postbaccalaureate distance learning degree programs offered (no on-campus study). Offers curriculum and instruction (M Ed); teaching (with certification) (M Ed T). *Application deadline:* For fall admission, 6/15 for domestic students. Applications are processed on a rolling basis. *Application fee:* $35 ($50 for international students). *Application Contact:* Dr. Phil Cohen, Dean of Graduate Studies, 817-272-3186, Fax: 817-272-2625, E-mail: graduate.school@uta.edu. *Dean of Graduate Studies*, Dr. Phil Cohen, 817-272-3186, Fax: 817-272-2625, E-mail: graduate.school@uta.edu.

College of Business Students: 826 full-time (322 women), 765 part-time (330 women); includes 367 minority (116 Black or African American, non-Hispanic/Latino; 4 American Indian or Alaska Native, non-Hispanic/Latino; 127 Asian, non-Hispanic/Latino; 101 Hispanic/Latino; 1 Native Hawaiian or other Pacific Islander, non-Hispanic/Latino; 18 Two or more races, non-Hispanic/Latino), 550 international. Average age 32. 746 applicants, 75% accepted, 355 enrolled. *Faculty:* 72 full-time (15 women), 2 part-time/adjunct (0 women). Expenses: Contact institution. *Financial support:* In 2010–11, 100 students received support, including 5 fellowships (averaging $1,000 per year), 30 research assistantships (averaging $6,000 per year), 45 teaching assistantships (averaging $13,000 per year);

The University of Texas at Arlington (continued)

career-related internships or fieldwork, Federal Work-Study, institutionally sponsored loans, and scholarships/grants also available. Financial award application deadline: 6/1; financial award applicants required to submit FAFSA. In 2010, 655 master's, 10 doctorates awarded. *Degree program information:* Part-time and evening/weekend programs available. Postbaccalaureate distance learning degree programs offered (no on-campus study). Offers accounting (MP Acc, MS, PhD); business (MA, MBA, MP Acc, MS, MSHRM, PhD); business statistics (PhD); economics (MA); finance (MBA, PhD); health care administration (MS); human resources (MSHRM); information systems (MBA, MS, PhD); management (MBA, PhD); marketing (MBA, PhD); marketing research (MS); operations management (MBA, PhD); quantitative finance (MS); real estate (MBA, MS); taxation (MS). *Application deadline:* For fall admission, 6/1 for domestic students, 4/1 for international students; for spring admission, 10/15 for domestic students, 9/15 for international students. Applications are processed on a rolling basis. *Application fee:* $35 ($50 for international students). Electronic applications accepted. *Application Contact:* Rebecca Neilson, Director of Graduate Business Services, 817-272-3649, Fax: 817-272-5799, E-mail: rneilson@uta.edu. *Dean*, Dr. Daniel Himarios, 817-272-2881, Fax: 817-272-2073, E-mail: himarios@uta.edu.

College of Engineering Students: 995 full-time (235 women), 597 part-time (119 women); includes 165 minority (44 Black or African American, non-Hispanic/Latino; 77 Asian, non-Hispanic/Latino; 40 Hispanic/Latino; 1 Native Hawaiian or other Pacific Islander, non-Hispanic/Latino; 3 Two or more races, non-Hispanic/Latino), 1,127 international. Average age 27. 1,499 applicants, 72% accepted, 425 enrolled. *Faculty:* 128 full-time (12 women), 8 part-time/adjunct (1 woman). Expenses: Contact institution. *Financial support:* Fellowships, research assistantships, teaching assistantships, career-related internships or fieldwork, Federal Work-Study, institutionally sponsored loans, scholarships/grants, and tuition waivers (partial) available. Financial award application deadline: 6/1; financial award applicants required to submit FAFSA. In 2010, 481 master's, 56 doctorates awarded. *Degree program information:* Part-time and evening/weekend programs available. Postbaccalaureate distance learning degree programs offered (minimal on-campus study). Offers aerospace engineering (M Engr, MS, PhD); bioengineering (MS, PhD); civil engineering (M Engr, MS, PhD); computer engineering (MS, PhD); computer science (MS, PhD); computer science and engineering (M Engr); electrical engineering (M Engr, MS, PhD); engineering (M Engr, MS, PhD); engineering management (MS); industrial engineering (MS, PhD); logistics (MS); materials science and engineering (M Engr, MS, PhD); mechanical engineering (M Engr, MS, PhD); software engineering (MS, PhD); systems engineering (MS). *Application deadline:* For fall admission, 6/6 for domestic students, 4/4 for international students; for spring admission, 10/15 for domestic students, 9/5 for international students. Applications are processed on a rolling basis. *Application fee:* $35 ($50 for international students). *Application Contact:* Dr. Lynn L. Peterson, Associate Dean for Academic Affairs, 817-272-2571, Fax: 817-272-2548, E-mail: peterson@uta.edu. *Dean*, Dr. Bill D. Carroll, 817-272-2571, Fax: 817-272-5110, E-mail: carroll@uta.edu.

College of Liberal Arts Students: 203 full-time (103 women), 420 part-time (240 women); includes 183 minority (65 Black or African American, non-Hispanic/Latino; 4 American Indian or Alaska Native, non-Hispanic/Latino; 19 Asian, non-Hispanic/Latino; 86 Hispanic/Latino; 1 Native Hawaiian or other Pacific Islander, non-Hispanic/Latino; 8 Two or more races, non-Hispanic/Latino), 37 international. Average age 35. 301 applicants, 73% accepted, 173 enrolled. *Faculty:* 174 full-time (66 women), 13 part-time/adjunct (5 women). Expenses: Contact institution. *Financial support:* Fellowships, research assistantships, teaching assistantships, career-related internships or fieldwork, Federal Work-Study, institutionally sponsored loans, and scholarships/grants available. Financial award application deadline: 3/1; financial award applicants required to submit FAFSA. In 2010, 109 master's, 14 doctorates awarded. Offers anthropology (MA); communication (MA); criminology and criminal justice (MA); education (MM); English (MA); film and video (MFA); French (MA); glass (MFA); history (MA); intermedia (MFA); liberal arts (MA, MFA, MM, PhD); linguistics (MA, PhD); literature (PhD); performance (MM); political science (MA); sociology (MA); Spanish (MA); teaching English to speakers of other languages (MA); transatlantic history (PhD); visual communication (MFA). *Application deadline:* For fall admission, 6/15 for domestic students. Applications are processed on a rolling basis. *Application fee:* $35 ($50 for international students). *Application Contact:* Dr. Kimberly Van Noort, Associate Dean, 817-272-3291, E-mail: vannoort@uta.edu. *Dean*, Dr. Beth S. Wright, 817-272-3291, Fax: 817-272-3255, E-mail: bwright@uta.edu.

College of Nursing Students: 58 full-time (50 women), 610 part-time (549 women); includes 205 minority (93 Black or African American, non-Hispanic/Latino; 5 American Indian or Alaska Native, non-Hispanic/Latino; 57 Asian, non-Hispanic/Latino; 45 Hispanic/Latino; 1 Native Hawaiian or other Pacific Islander, non-Hispanic/Latino; 4 Two or more races, non-Hispanic/Latino), 15 international. Average age 37. 356 applicants, 78% accepted, 138 enrolled. *Faculty:* 12 full-time (all women), 6 part-time/adjunct (all women). Expenses: Contact institution. *Financial support:* In 2010–11, 41 students received support, including 41 fellowships with partial tuition reimbursements available (averaging $5,500 per year), 6 research assistantships (averaging $7,992 per year), 7 teaching assistantships (averaging $10,080 per year); career-related internships or fieldwork and traineeships also available. Financial award application deadline: 6/1; financial award applicants required to submit FAFSA. In 2010, 142 master's, 4 doctorates awarded. *Degree program information:* Part-time and evening/weekend programs available. Postbaccalaureate distance learning degree programs offered (no on-campus study). Offers nurse practitioner (MSN); nursing administration (MSN); nursing education (MSN); nursing practice (DNP); nursing science (PhD). *Application deadline:* For fall admission, 6/1 for domestic students, 4/1 for international students; for spring admission, 10/7 for domestic students, 9/5 for international students. Applications are processed on a rolling basis. *Application fee:* $40 ($70 for international students). *Application Contact:* Dr. Mary Schira, Graduate Advisor/Associate Dean, 817-272-2329, Fax: 817-272-2065, E-mail: schira@uta.edu. *Dean*, Dr. Elizabeth C. Poster, 817-272-2776, Fax: 817-272-5006, E-mail: poster@uta.edu.

College of Science Students: 358 full-time (163 women), 211 part-time (113 women); includes 132 minority (42 Black or African American, non-Hispanic/Latino; 2 American Indian or Alaska Native, non-Hispanic/Latino; 31 Asian, non-Hispanic/Latino; 48 Hispanic/Latino; 1 Native Hawaiian or other Pacific Islander, non-Hispanic/Latino; 8 Two or more races, non-Hispanic/Latino), 162 international. Average age 31. 308 applicants, 55% accepted, 122 enrolled. *Faculty:* 121 full-time (23 women), 8 part-time/adjunct (0 women). Expenses: Contact institution. *Financial support:* In 2010–11, 21 fellowships (averaging $1,000 per year), 44 research assistantships (averaging $18,000 per year), 123 teaching assistantships (averaging $16,500 per year) were awarded; career-related internships or fieldwork, Federal Work-Study, institutionally sponsored loans, scholarships/grants, tuition waivers (partial), and unspecified assistantships also available. Financial award application deadline: 6/1; financial award applicants required to submit FAFSA. In 2010, 69 master's, 38 doctorates awarded. *Degree program information:* Part-time and evening/weekend programs available. Offers applied math (MS); biology (MS); chemistry (MS, PhD); environmental and earth sciences (MS, PhD); environmental science (MS, PhD); experimental psychology (PhD); geology (MS, PhD); health psychology (PhD); industrial organizational psychology (MS); mathematics (PhD); mathematics education (MA); physics (MS); physics and applied physics (PhD); psychology (MS); quantitative biology (PhD); science (MA, MS, PhD). *Application deadline:* For fall admission, 6/15 for domestic students. Applications are processed on a rolling basis. *Application fee:* $35 ($50 for international students). *Application Contact:* Dr. Edward T. Morton, Assistant Dean, 817-272-3491, Fax: 817-272-3511, E-mail: morton@uta.edu. *Dean*, Dr. Pamela E. Jansma, 817-272-3491, Fax: 817-272-3511, E-mail: pjansma@uta.edu.

School of Architecture Students: 175 full-time (72 women), 42 part-time (23 women); includes 55 minority (5 Black or African American, non-Hispanic/Latino; 19 Asian, non-Hispanic/Latino; 31 Hispanic/Latino), 36 international. Average age 30. 146 applicants, 98% accepted, 60 enrolled. *Faculty:* 23 full-time (5 women), 1 part-time/adjunct (0 women). Expenses: Contact institution. *Financial support:* In 2010–11, 5 fellowships with partial tuition reimbursements (averaging $1,000 per year), 2 research assistantships with partial tuition reimbursements (averaging $5,700 per year), 8 teaching assistantships with partial tuition reimbursements (averaging $5,700 per year) were awarded; career-related internships or fieldwork, Federal Work-Study, scholarships/grants, health care benefits, tuition waivers (partial), and unspecified assistantships also available. Support available to part-time students. Financial award application deadline: 1/15; financial award applicants required to submit FAFSA. In 2010, 45 master's awarded. *Degree program information:* Part-time programs available. Offers architecture (M Arch, MLA); landscape architecture (MLA). *Application deadline:* For fall admission, 6/15 for domestic students, 1/15 for international students. Applications are processed on a rolling basis. *Application fee:* $35 ($50 for international students). Electronic applications accepted. *Application Contact:* David Jones, Associate Dean, 817-272-2801, Fax: 817-272-5098, E-mail: djonesarch@uta.edu. *Dean*, Donald Gatzke, 817-272-2801, Fax: 817-272-5098, E-mail: gatzke@uta.edu.

School of Social Work Students: 321 full-time (293 women), 241 part-time (218 women); includes 124 Black or African American, non-Hispanic/Latino; 2 American Indian or Alaska Native, non-Hispanic/Latino; 21 Asian, non-Hispanic/Latino; 78 Hispanic/Latino, 16 international. Average age 32. 274 applicants, 98% accepted, 174 enrolled. *Faculty:* 27 full-time (13 women), 2 part-time/adjunct (1 woman). Expenses: Contact institution. *Financial support:* In 2010–11, 355 students received support, including 40 fellowships (averaging $2,000 per year), 10 research assistantships (averaging $6,000 per year), 10 teaching assistantships (averaging $6,000 per year); career-related internships or fieldwork, Federal Work-Study, institutionally sponsored loans, scholarships/grants, and unspecified assistantships also available. Support available to part-time students. Financial award application deadline: 6/1; financial award applicants required to submit FAFSA. In 2010, 217 master's, 10 doctorates awarded. *Degree program information:* Part-time and evening/weekend programs available. Postbaccalaureate distance learning degree programs offered (no on-campus study). Offers social work (MSSW, PhD). *Application deadline:* For fall admission, 6/5 for domestic students; for winter admission, 10/15 for domestic students. Applications are processed on a rolling basis. *Application fee:* $35 ($50 for international students). Electronic applications accepted. *Application Contact:* Darlene Santee, Director of Admissions, 817-272-3613, Fax: 817-272-5229. *Dean*, Dr. Scott D. Ryan, 817-272-1491, Fax: 817-272-5229, E-mail: sdryan@uta.edu.

School of Urban and Public Affairs Students: 186 full-time (87 women), 211 part-time (118 women); includes 155 minority (89 Black or African American, non-Hispanic/Latino; 2 American Indian or Alaska Native, non-Hispanic/Latino; 9 Asian, non-Hispanic/Latino; 48 Hispanic/Latino; 1 Native Hawaiian or other Pacific Islander, non-Hispanic/Latino; 6 Two or more races, non-Hispanic/Latino), 19 international. Average age 35. 176 applicants, 81% accepted, 112 enrolled. *Faculty:* 18 full-time (8 women), 1 (woman) part-time/adjunct. Expenses: Contact institution. *Financial support:* In 2010–11, 19 students received support, including 2 fellowships with full tuition reimbursements available (averaging $18,000 per year), 5 research assistantships (averaging $4,000 per year), 2 teaching assistantships with full tuition reimbursements available (averaging $18,000 per year); career-related internships or fieldwork and Federal Work-Study also available. Financial award application deadline: 6/1; financial award applicants required to submit FAFSA. In 2010, 65 master's, 3 doctorates awarded. *Degree program information:* Part-time and evening/weekend programs available. Postbaccalaureate distance learning degree programs offered. Offers city and regional planning (MCRP); interdisciplinary science (MA); public administration (MPA); urban and public affairs (MA, MCRP, MPA, PhD). *Application deadline:* For fall admission, 6/1 for domestic students, 4/1 for international students; for spring admission, 10/15 for domestic students, 9/15 for international students. Applications are processed on a rolling basis. *Application fee:* $35 ($50 for international students). Electronic applications accepted. *Application Contact:* Tangie Fields, Academic Advisor, 817-272-3340, Fax: 817-272-5008, E-mail: nfields@uta.edu. *Dean*, Dr. Barbara Becker, 817-272-3071, Fax: 817-272-3255, E-mail: bbecker@uta.edu.

THE UNIVERSITY OF TEXAS AT AUSTIN, Austin, TX 78712-1111

General Information State-supported, coed, university. CGS member. *Graduate housing:* Rooms and/or apartments available to single students and available on a first-come, first-served basis to married students.

GRADUATE UNITS

Graduate School *Degree program information:* Part-time and evening/weekend programs available. Offers computational and applied mathematics (MA, PhD); technology commercialization (MS); writing (MFA). Electronic applications accepted.

Cockrell School of Engineering *Degree program information:* Part-time and evening/weekend programs available. Offers aerospace engineering (MSE, PhD); architectural engineering (MSE); biomedical engineering (MS, PhD); chemical engineering (MSE, PhD); civil engineering (MS, PhD); electrical and computer engineering (MSE, PhD); energy and earth resources (MA); engineering (MA, MS, MSE, PhD); engineering mechanics (MS, PhD); environmental and water resources engineering (MS, PhD); materials science and engineering (MS, PhD); mechanical engineering (MS, PhD); operations research and industrial engineering (MS, PhD); petroleum engineering (MS, PhD). Electronic applications accepted.

College of Communication *Degree program information:* Part-time programs available. Offers advertising (MA, PhD); audiology (Au D, PhD); communication (MA, MFA, Au D, PhD); communication studies (MA, PhD); film and video production (MFA); journalism (MA, PhD); radio-television-film (MA, PhD); screenwriting (MFA); speech language pathology (MA, PhD). Electronic applications accepted.

College of Education *Degree program information:* Part-time programs available. Offers academic educational psychology (M Ed, MA); behavioral health (PhD); counseling psychology (PhD); counselor education (M Ed); curriculum and instruction (M Ed, MA, Ed D, PhD); education (M Ed, MA, Ed D, PhD); educational administration (M Ed, Ed D, PhD); exercise and sport psychology (M Ed, MA); foreign language education (MA, PhD); health education (M Ed, MA, Ed D, PhD); human development and culture (PhD); kinesiology (M Ed, MA); learning, cognition and instruction (PhD); quantitative methods (PhD); school psychology (PhD); science and mathematics education (M Ed, MA, PhD); special education (M Ed, MA, Ed D, PhD). Electronic applications accepted.

College of Fine Arts *Degree program information:* Part-time programs available. Offers acting (MFA); art education (MA); art history (MA, PhD); dance (MFA); design (MFA); directing (MFA); drama and theatre for youth (MFA); fine arts (M Music, MA, MFA, DMA, PhD); music (M Music, DMA, PhD); performance as public practice (MA, MFA, PhD); playwriting (MFA); studio art (MFA); theatre technology (MFA); theatrical design (MFA). Electronic applications accepted.

College of Liberal Arts *Degree program information:* Part-time programs available. Offers African Diaspora studies (MA, PhD); American studies (MA, PhD); Arabic (MA, PhD); archaeology (MA, PhD); Asian cultures and languages (MA, PhD); Asian studies (MA); classics (MA, PhD); comparative literature (MA, PhD); creative writing (MA); economics (MA, MS Econ, PhD); English (MA, PhD); folklore and public culture (MA, PhD); French (MA, PhD); French linguistics (MA, PhD); geography and the environment (MA, PhD); Germanic studies (MA, PhD); government (PhD); Hebrew (MA); Hispanic linguistics (MA, PhD); Hispanic literature (MA, PhD); history (MA, PhD); Italian studies (MA, PhD); Latin American studies (MA, PhD); liberal arts (MA, MS Econ, PhD); linguistic anthropology (MA, PhD); linguistics (MA, PhD); Luso-Brazilian literature (MA, PhD); Mexican American studies (MA); Middle Eastern studies (MA, PhD); philosophy (PhD); physical anthropology (MA, PhD); psychology (PhD); Romance linguistics (MA, PhD); Russian, East European, and Eurasian studies (MA); Slavic languages (MA, PhD); social anthropology (MA, PhD); sociology (MA, PhD). Electronic applications accepted.

College of Natural Sciences *Degree program information:* Part-time programs available. Offers analytical chemistry (MA, PhD); astronomy (MA, PhD); biochemistry (MA, PhD); biological sciences (MA, PhD); computer sciences (MA, MSCS, PhD); ecology, evolution and behavior (MA, PhD); human development and family sciences (MA, PhD); inorganic chemistry (MA, PhD); marine science (MS, PhD); mathematics (MA, PhD); microbiology (PhD); natural sciences (MA, MS, MS Stat, MSCS, PhD); nutrition (MA); nutritional sciences (MA, PhD); organic chemistry (MA, PhD); physical chemistry (MA, PhD); physics (MA, MS, PhD); plant biology (MA, PhD); statistics (MS Stat); textile and apparel technology (MS). Electronic applications accepted.

College of Pharmacy Offers pharmacy (Pharm D, MS, PhD). Electronic applications accepted.

Institute for Cellular and Molecular Biology Offers cellular and molecular biology (PhD).

The Institute for Neuroscience Offers neuroscience (PhD). Electronic applications accepted.

Jackson School of Geosciences *Degree program information:* Part-time programs available. Offers geosciences (MA, MS, PhD). Electronic applications accepted.

Lyndon B. Johnson School of Public Affairs *Degree program information:* Part-time programs available. Offers global policy studies (MGPS); public affairs (MP Aff); public policy (PhD). Electronic applications accepted.

McCombs School of Business Offers accounting (MPA, PhD); business (MBA, MPA, PhD); business administration (MBA); finance (PhD); information systems (PhD); management (PhD); marketing (PhD); risk analysis and decision making (PhD); supply chain and operations management (PhD). Electronic applications accepted.

School of Architecture Offers architecture (M Arch); community and regional planning (MSCRP, PhD); historic preservation (MS); history of architecture (MA, PhD); landscape architecture (MLA); urban design (MSUD). Electronic applications accepted.

School of Information *Degree program information:* Part-time programs available. Offers information (MS, PhD). Electronic applications accepted.

School of Nursing *Degree program information:* Part-time programs available. Offers nursing (MSN, PhD). Electronic applications accepted.

School of Social Work *Degree program information:* Part-time programs available. Offers social work (MSSW, PhD).

School of Law Students: 1,229 full-time (578 women); includes 56 Black or African American, non-Hispanic/Latino; 5 American Indian or Alaska Native, non-Hispanic/Latino; 62 Asian, non-Hispanic/Latino; 183 Hispanic/Latino, 13 international. Average age 24. 5,818 applicants, 23% accepted, 389 enrolled. *Faculty:* 111 full-time (41 women), 94 part-time/adjunct (34 women). Expenses: Contact institution. *Financial support:* In 2010–11, 737 students received support, including 100 research assistantships, 32 teaching assistantships (averaging $3,900 per year); career-related internships or fieldwork, scholarships/grants, and tuition waivers (full) also available. Financial award application deadline: 3/15; financial award applicants required to submit FAFSA. In 2010, 392 first professional degrees, 39 master's awarded. Offers law (JD, LL M, JD/MGPS). *Application deadline:* For fall admission, 2/1 for domestic students. *Application fee:* $70. Electronic applications accepted. *Application Contact:* 512-232-1200, Fax: 512-471-2765, E-mail: admissions@law.utexas.edu. *Dean,* Lawrence Sager, 512-232-1120, Fax: 512-471-6987, E-mail: lsager@law.utexas.edu.

THE UNIVERSITY OF TEXAS AT BROWNSVILLE, Brownsville, TX 78520-4991

General Information State-supported, coed, comprehensive institution. CGS member. *Graduate housing:* Room and/or apartments available to single students; on-campus housing not available to married students.

GRADUATE UNITS

Graduate Studies *Degree program information:* Part-time and evening/weekend programs available. Postbaccalaureate distance learning degree programs offered (no on-campus study).

College of Liberal Arts *Degree program information:* Part-time and evening/weekend programs available. Offers behavioral sciences (MAIS); English (MA); government (MAIS); history (MAIS); interdisciplinary studies (MAIS); liberal arts (MA, MAIS, MPPM); public policy and management (MPPM); Spanish (MA).

College of Science, Mathematics and Technology *Degree program information:* Part-time and evening/weekend programs available. Offers biological sciences (MS, MSIS); mathematics (MS); physics (MS).

School of Business *Degree program information:* Part-time and evening/weekend programs available. Postbaccalaureate distance learning degree programs offered (minimal on-campus study). Offers business (MBA).

School of Education *Degree program information:* Part-time and evening/weekend programs available. Postbaccalaureate distance learning degree programs offered (minimal on-campus study). Offers bilingual education (M Ed); counseling and guidance (M Ed); curriculum and instruction (M Ed); early childhood education (M Ed); educational administration (M Ed); educational technology (M Ed); English as a second language (M Ed); reading specialist (M Ed); special education/educational diagnostician (M Ed).

School of Health Sciences Offers health sciences (MSN).

THE UNIVERSITY OF TEXAS AT DALLAS, Richardson, TX 75080

General Information State-supported, coed, university. CGS member. *Enrollment:* 17,128 graduate, professional, and undergraduate students; 3,573 full-time matriculated graduate/professional students (1,600 women), 2,434 part-time matriculated graduate/professional students (947 women). *Enrollment by degree level:* 36 first professional, 4,864 master's, 1,107 doctoral. *Graduate faculty:* 453 full-time (101 women), 26 part-time/adjunct (6 women). Tuition, state resident: full-time $10,248; part-time $569 per credit hour. Tuition, nonresident: full-time $18,544; part-time $1030 per credit hour. Tuition and fees vary according to course load. *Graduate housing:* Rooms and/or apartments available on a first-come, first-served basis to single and married students. Typical cost: $8210 (including board) for single students; $8210 (including board) for married students. Housing application deadline: 5/31. *Student services:* Campus employment opportunities, campus safety program, career counseling, child daycare facilities, exercise/wellness program, free psychological counseling, grant writing training, international student services, low-cost health insurance, multicultural affairs office, services for students with disabilities, teacher training, writing training. *Library facilities:* Eugene McDermott Library plus 1 other. *Online resources:* library catalog, web page, access to other libraries' catalogs. *Collection:* 2.4 million titles, 46,826 serial subscriptions, 13,557 audiovisual materials.

Computer facilities: Computer purchase and lease plans are available. 630 computers available on campus for general student use. A campuswide network can be accessed from student residence rooms and from off campus. Online class registration is available. *Web address:* http://www.utdallas.edu/.

General Application Contact: Dr. Austin Cunningham, Dean of Graduate Studies, 972-883-2234, E-mail: cunning@utdallas.edu.

GRADUATE UNITS

Erik Jonsson School of Engineering and Computer Science Students: 865 full-time (195 women), 409 part-time (87 women); includes 135 minority (15 Black or African American, non-Hispanic/Latino; 1 American Indian or Alaska Native, non-Hispanic/Latino; 84 Asian, non-Hispanic/Latino; 32 Hispanic/Latino; 3 Two or more races, non-Hispanic/Latino), 908 international. Average age 27. 2,928 applicants, 49% accepted, 386 enrolled. *Faculty:* 99 full-time (12 women), 3 part-time/adjunct (1 woman). Expenses: Contact institution. *Financial support:* In 2010–11, 428 students received support, including 6 fellowships with partial tuition reimbursements available (averaging $15,960 per year), 251 research assistantships with partial tuition reimbursements available (averaging $16,306 per year), 84 teaching assistantships with partial tuition reimbursements available (averaging $15,416 per year); career-related internships or fieldwork, Federal Work-Study, institutionally sponsored loans, scholarships/grants, and unspecified assistantships also available. Support available to part-time students. Financial award application deadline: 4/30; financial award applicants required to submit FAFSA. In 2010, 377 master's, 56 doctorates awarded. *Degree program information:* Part-time and evening/weekend programs available. Offers biomedical engineering (MS, PhD); computer engineering (MS, PhD); computer science (MS, PhD); electrical engineering (MSEE, PhD); engineering and computer science (MS, MSEE, MSME, MSTE, PhD); materials science and engineering (MS, PhD); mechanical systems engineering (MSME); microelectromechanical systems (MSME); microelectronics (MSEE, PhD); software engineering (MS, PhD); telecommunications (MSEE, MSTE, PhD). *Application deadline:* For fall admission, 7/15 for domestic students, 5/1 priority date for international students; for spring admission, 11/15 for domestic students, 9/1 priority date for international students. Applications are processed on a rolling basis. *Application fee:* $50 ($100 for international students). Electronic applications accepted. *Application Contact:* Dr. Cy Cantrell, Senior Associate Dean, 972-883-6234, Fax: 972-883-2813, E-mail: gradecs@utdallas.edu. *Dean,* Dr. Mark W. Spong, 972-883-2974, Fax: 972-883-2813, E-mail: ecsdean@utdallas.edu.

School of Arts and Humanities Students: 259 full-time (129 women), 243 part-time (134 women); includes 112 minority (33 Black or African American, non-Hispanic/Latino; 5 American Indian or Alaska Native, non-Hispanic/Latino; 28 Asian, non-Hispanic/Latino; 39 Hispanic/Latino; 7 Two or more races, non-Hispanic/Latino), 37 international. Average age 36. 249 applicants, 64% accepted, 120 enrolled. *Faculty:* 60 full-time (22 women). Expenses: Contact institution. *Financial support:* In 2010–11, 245 students received support, including 36 research assistantships with partial tuition reimbursements available (averaging $10,915 per year), 96 teaching assistantships with partial tuition reimbursements available (averaging $10,153 per year); Federal Work-Study, institutionally sponsored loans, scholarships/grants, and unspecified assistantships also available. Support available to part-time students. Financial award application deadline: 4/30; financial award applicants required to submit FAFSA. In 2010, 85 master's, 20 doctorates awarded. *Degree program information:* Part-time and evening/weekend programs available. Offers aesthetic studies (MA, MAT, PhD); arts and humanities (MA, MAT, MFA, PhD); arts and technology (MA, MFA, PhD); emerging media and communication (MA); history (MA); history of ideas (MA, MAT, PhD); humanities (MA, PhD); Latin American studies (MA); studies in literature (MA, MAT, PhD). *Application deadline:* For fall admission, 7/15 for domestic students, 5/1 priority date for international students; for spring admission, 11/15 for domestic students, 9/1 priority date for international students. Applications are processed on a rolling basis. *Application fee:* $50 ($100 for international students). Electronic applications accepted. *Application Contact:* Dr. Michael Wilson, Associate Dean of Graduate Studies, 972-883-2756, Fax: 972-883-2989, E-mail: mwilson@utdallas.edu. *Dean,* Dr. Dennis M. Kratz, 972-883-2984, Fax: 972-883-2989, E-mail: dkratz@utdallas.edu.

School of Behavioral and Brain Sciences Students: 396 full-time (337 women), 73 part-time (52 women); includes 90 minority (15 Black or African American, non-Hispanic/Latino; 35 Asian, non-Hispanic/Latino; 37 Hispanic/Latino; 3 Two or more races, non-Hispanic/Latino), 35 international. Average age 27. 587 applicants, 30% accepted, 103 enrolled. *Faculty:* 45 full-time (19 women). Expenses: Contact institution. *Financial support:* In 2010–11, 297 students received support, including 24 research assistantships with partial tuition reimbursements available (averaging $13,856 per year), 49 teaching assistantships with partial tuition reimbursements available (averaging $12,635 per year); career-related internships or fieldwork, Federal Work-Study, institutionally sponsored loans, scholarships/grants, and unspecified assistantships also available. Support available to part-time students. Financial award application deadline: 4/30; financial award applicants required to submit FAFSA. In 2010, 152 master's, 10 doctorates awarded. *Degree program information:* Part-time and evening/weekend programs available. Offers applied cognition and neuroscience (MS); audiology (Au D); behavioral and brain sciences (MS, Au D, PhD); cognition and neuroscience (PhD); communication disorders (MS); communication sciences (PhD); early childhood disorders (MS); psychological sciences (MS, PhD). *Application deadline:* For fall admission, 7/15 for domestic students, 5/1 priority date for international students; for spring admission, 11/15 for domestic students, 9/1 priority date for international students. Applications are processed on a rolling basis. *Application fee:* $50 ($100 for international students). Electronic applications accepted. *Application Contact:* Dr. Robert D. Stillman, Associate Dean of Graduate Programs, 214-905-3106, E-mail: stillman@utdallas.edu. *Dean,* Dr. Bert Moore, 972-883-2355, Fax: 972-883-2491, E-mail: bmoore@utdallas.edu.

School of Economic, Political and Policy Sciences Students: 261 full-time (124 women), 220 part-time (94 women); includes 148 minority (67 Black or African American, non-Hispanic/Latino; 2 American Indian or Alaska Native, non-Hispanic/Latino; 28 Asian, non-Hispanic/Latino; 48 Hispanic/Latino; 3 Two or more races, non-Hispanic/Latino), 78 international. Average age 34. 434 applicants, 56% accepted, 132 enrolled. *Faculty:* 59 full-time (14 women), 9 part-time/adjunct (4 women). Expenses: Contact institution. *Financial support:* In 2010–11, 219 students received support, including 27 research assistantships with partial tuition reimbursements available (averaging $13,001 per year), 79 teaching assistantships with partial tuition reimbursements available (averaging $11,422 per year); career-related internships or fieldwork, Federal Work-Study, institutionally sponsored loans, scholarships/grants, and unspecified assistantships also available. Support available to part-time students. Financial award application deadline: 4/30; financial award applicants required to submit FAFSA. In 2010, 115 master's, 58 doctorates awarded. *Degree program information:* Part-time and evening/weekend programs available. Offers applied sociology (MS); constitutional law (MA); criminology (MS, PhD); economic, political and policy sciences (MA, MPA, MPP, MS, PhD); economics (MS, PhD); geospatial sciences (MS, PhD); international political economy (MS); justice administration and leadership (MS); legislative studies (MA); political science (MA, PhD); public affairs (MPA, PhD); public policy (MPP); public policy and political economy (PhD). *Application deadline:* For fall admission, 7/15 for domestic students, 5/1 priority date for international students; for spring admission, 11/15 for domestic students, 9/1 priority date for international students. Applications are processed on a rolling basis. *Application fee:* $50 ($100 for international students). Electronic applications accepted. *Application Contact:* Dr. Thomas L. Brunell, Associate Dean for Graduate Education, 972-883-4963, Fax: 972-883-6297, E-mail: tbrunell@utdallas.edu. *Dean,* Dr. James W. Marquart, 972-883-2935, Fax: 972-883-6297, E-mail: marquart@utdallas.edu.

School of Interdisciplinary Studies Students: 13 full-time (10 women), 26 part-time (15 women); includes 16 minority (7 Black or African American, non-Hispanic/Latino; 4 Asian, non-Hispanic/Latino; 5 Hispanic/Latino), 1 international. Average age 39. 17 applicants, 82% accepted, 11 enrolled. *Faculty:* 3 full-time (2 women). Expenses: Contact institution. *Financial support:* In 2010–11, 14 students received support; research assistantships with partial tuition reimbursements available, teaching assistantships with partial tuition reimbursements available, career-related internships or fieldwork, Federal Work-Study, institutionally sponsored loans, and scholarships/grants available. Support available to part-time students. Financial award application deadline: 4/30; financial award applicants required to submit FAFSA. In 2010, 13 master's awarded. *Degree program information:* Part-time and evening/weekend programs available. Offers interdisciplinary studies (MA). *Application deadline:* For fall admission, 7/15 for domestic students, 5/1 priority date for international students; for spring admission, 11/15 for domestic students, 9/1 priority date for international students. Applications are processed on a rolling basis. *Application fee:* $50 ($100 for international students). Electronic applications accepted. *Application Contact:* Dr. Elizabeth Salter, Associate Dean, 972-883-2323, Fax: 972-883-2440, E-mail: emsalter@utdallas.edu. *Dean,* Dr. George Fair, 972-883-2350, Fax: 972-883-2440, E-mail: gwfair@utdallas.edu.

School of Management Students: 1,471 full-time (676 women), 1,314 part-time (489 women); includes 643 minority (82 Black or African American, non-Hispanic/Latino; 6 American Indian or Alaska Native, non-Hispanic/Latino; 399 Asian, non-Hispanic/Latino; 147 Hispanic/Latino; 9 Two or more races, non-Hispanic/Latino), 1,065 international. Average age 30. 2,827 applicants, 57% accepted, 919 enrolled. *Faculty:* 78 full-time (14 women), 28 part-time/adjunct (6 women). Expenses: Contact institution. *Financial support:* In 2010–11, 837 students received support, including 6 research assistantships with partial tuition reimbursements available (averaging $11,239 per year), 170 teaching assistantships with partial tuition reimbursements available (averaging $12,706 per year); career-related internships or fieldwork, Federal Work-Study, institutionally sponsored loans, scholarships/grants, and unspecified assistantships also available. Support available to part-time students. Financial award application deadline: 4/30; financial award applicants required to submit FAFSA. In 2010, 964 master's, 17 doctorates awarded. *Degree program information:* Part-time and evening/weekend programs available. Postbaccalaureate distance learning degree programs offered. Offers accounting (PhD); audit and professional (MS); cohort (MBA); electronic commerce (MS); executive business administration (EMBA); finance (MS, PhD); financial analysis (MS); financial engineering and risk management (MS); global leadership (EMBA); global online (MBA); healthcare administration (MS); healthcare management (EMBA); information management (MS); information systems (MS, PhD); information technology management (MS); innovation and entrepreneurship (MS); international audit (MS); international management (MS); international services (MS); investment management (MS); leadership in organizations (MS); management (EMBA, MBA, MS, PhD); managerial (MS); marketing (MS, PhD); operations (MS); operations management (PhD); organizations (MS); professional business administration (MBA); project management (EMBA); real estate (MS); strategy (MS); supply chain management (MS); taxation (MS). *Application deadline:* For fall admission, 7/15 for

The University of Texas at Dallas (continued)

domestic students, 5/1 priority date for international students; for spring admission, 11/15 for domestic students, 9/1 priority date for international students. Applications are processed on a rolling basis. *Application fee:* $50 ($100 for international students). Electronic applications accepted. *Application Contact:* David B. Ritchey, Director of Advising, 972-883-2750, Fax: 972-883-6425, E-mail: davidr@utdallas.edu. *Dean,* Dr. Hasan Pirkul, 972-883-2705, Fax: 972-883-2799, E-mail: hpirkul@utdallas.edu.

School of Natural Sciences and Mathematics Students: 308 full-time (129 women), 149 part-time (76 women); includes 88 minority (24 Black or African American, non-Hispanic/Latino; 39 Asian, non-Hispanic/Latino; 23 Hispanic/Latino; 1 Native Hawaiian or other Pacific Islander, non-Hispanic/Latino; 1 Two or more races, non-Hispanic/Latino), 191 international. Average age 30. 717 applicants, 37% accepted, 89 enrolled. *Faculty:* 88 full-time (11 women), 6 part-time/adjunct (1 woman). Expenses: Contact institution. *Financial support:* In 2010–11, 260 students received support, including 86 research assistantships with partial tuition reimbursements available (averaging $14,135 per year), 123 teaching assistantships with partial tuition reimbursements available (averaging $14,259 per year); career-related internships or fieldwork, Federal Work-Study, institutionally sponsored loans, scholarships/grants, and unspecified assistantships also available. Support available to part-time students. Financial award application deadline: 4/30. In 2010, 96 master's, 26 doctorates awarded. *Degree program information:* Part-time and evening/weekend programs available. Offers applied mathematics (MS, PhD); applied physics (MS); bioinformatics and computational biology (MS); biotechnology (MS); chemistry (MS, PhD); engineering mathematics (MS); geochemistry (MS, PhD); geophysics (MS, PhD); geospatial information sciences (MS, PhD); hydrogeology (MS, PhD); mathematical science (MS); mathematics education (MAT); molecular and cell biology (MS, PhD); natural sciences and mathematics (MAT, MS, PhD); physics (MS, PhD); science education (MAT); sedimentary, stratigraphy, paleontology (PhD); statistics (MS, PhD); stratigraphy, paleontology (MS); structural geology and tectonics (MS, PhD). *Application deadline:* For fall admission, 7/15 for domestic students, 5/1 priority date for international students; for spring admission, 11/15 for domestic students, 9/1 priority date for international students. Applications are processed on a rolling basis. *Application fee:* $50 ($100 for international students). Electronic applications accepted. *Application Contact:* Dr. Juan E. Gonzalez, Associate Dean for Graduate Studies, 972-883-2526, Fax: 972-883-6371, E-mail: jgonzal@utdallas.edu. *Dean,* Dr. Myron B. Salamon, 972-883-2416, Fax: 972-883-6371, E-mail: salamon@utdallas.edu.

THE UNIVERSITY OF TEXAS AT EL PASO, El Paso, TX 79968-0001

General Information State-supported, coed, university. CGS member. *Enrollment:* 3,570 matriculated graduate/professional students. *Enrollment by degree level:* 3,097 master's, 473 doctoral. *Graduate housing:* Room and/or apartments available on a first-come, first-served basis to single students; on-campus housing not available to married students. *Student services:* Campus employment opportunities, career counseling, child daycare facilities, exercise/wellness program, free psychological counseling, grant writing training, international student services, low-cost health insurance, services for students with disabilities, teacher training, writing training. *Library facilities:* University Library. *Collection:* 1.3 million titles, 3,065 serial subscriptions, 194,088 audiovisual materials.

Computer facilities: A campuswide network can be accessed from student residence rooms and from off campus. Online class registration is available. *Web address:* http://www.utep.edu/.

General Application Contact: Dr. Patricia D. Witherspoon, Dean of the Graduate School, 915-747-5491, Fax: 915-747-5788, E-mail: withersp@utep.edu.

GRADUATE UNITS

Graduate School Students: 3,570 (1,983 women); includes 106 Black or African American, non-Hispanic/Latino; 5 American Indian or Alaska Native, non-Hispanic/Latino; 60 Asian, non-Hispanic/Latino; 2,134 Hispanic/Latino, 616 international. Average age 35. 2,237 applicants, 60% accepted. Expenses: Contact institution. *Financial support:* In 2010–11, 697 students received support; fellowships with partial tuition reimbursements available, research assistantships with partial tuition reimbursements available, teaching assistantships with partial tuition reimbursements available, institutionally sponsored loans, scholarships/grants, health care benefits, tuition waivers (full and partial), and unspecified assistantships available. Support available to part-time students. Financial award application deadline: 3/15; financial award applicants required to submit FAFSA. In 2010, 796 master's, 52 doctorates awarded. *Degree program information:* Part-time and evening/weekend programs available. Postbaccalaureate distance learning degree programs offered (no on-campus study). Offers environmental science and engineering (PhD); materials science and engineering (PhD). *Application deadline:* For fall admission, 8/1 priority date for domestic students, 3/1 for international students; for spring admission, 11/1 priority date for domestic students, 9/1 for international students. Applications are processed on a rolling basis. *Application fee:* $45 ($80 for international students). Electronic applications accepted. *Application Contact:* Yvonne Lopez, Assistant Dean, 915-747-5491, Fax: 915-747-5788, E-mail: selopez@utep.edu. *Dean of the Graduate School,* Dr. Patricia D. Witherspoon, 915-747-5491, Fax: 915-747-5788, E-mail: withersp@utep.edu.

College of Business Administration Students: 431 (186 women); includes 10 Black or African American, non-Hispanic/Latino; 10 Asian, non-Hispanic/Latino; 239 Hispanic/Latino, 101 international. Average age 30. 302 applicants, 65% accepted. Expenses: Contact institution. *Financial support:* In 2010–11, research assistantships with partial tuition reimbursements (averaging $18,750 per year), teaching assistantships with partial tuition reimbursements (averaging $15,000 per year) were awarded; fellowships with partial tuition reimbursements, institutionally sponsored loans, scholarships/grants, health care benefits, tuition waivers (partial), and unspecified assistantships also available. Support available to part-time students. Financial award application deadline: 3/15; financial award applicants required to submit FAFSA. In 2010, 126 master's, 3 doctorates awarded. *Degree program information:* Part-time and evening/weekend programs available. Postbaccalaureate distance learning degree programs offered. Offers accounting (M Acc); business administration (M Acc, MBA, MS, PhD, Certificate); economics (MS); international business (PhD). *Application deadline:* For fall admission, 8/1 for domestic students, 3/1 for international students; for spring admission, 11/1 priority date for domestic students, 9/1 for international students. Applications are processed on a rolling basis. *Application fee:* $45 ($80 for international students). Electronic applications accepted. *Application Contact:* Dr. Patricia D. Witherspoon, Dean of the Graduate School, 915-747-5491, Fax: 915-747-5788, E-mail: withersp@utep.edu. *Dean,* Dr. Robert Nachtmann, 915-747-5241, Fax: 915-747-5147, E-mail: nachtmann@utep.edu.

College of Education Students: 1,399 (1,012 women); includes 37 Black or African American, non-Hispanic/Latino; 15 Asian, non-Hispanic/Latino; 1,066 Hispanic/Latino, 51 international. Average age 34. 589 applicants, 79% accepted. Expenses: Contact institution. *Financial support:* In 2010–11, research assistantships with partial tuition reimbursements (averaging $16,642 per year), teaching assistantships with partial tuition reimbursements (averaging $13,314 per year) were awarded; fellowships with partial tuition reimbursements, institutionally sponsored loans, scholarships/grants, health care benefits, tuition waivers (partial), and unspecified assistantships also available. Support available to part-time students. Financial award application deadline: 3/15; financial award applicants required to submit FAFSA. In 2010, 263 master's, 9 doctorates awarded. *Degree program information:* Part-time and evening/weekend programs available. Postbaccalaureate distance learning degree programs offered. Offers education (M Ed, MA, Ed D, PhD); educational administration (M Ed); educational diagnostics (M Ed); educational leadership and administration (Ed D); guidance and counseling (M Ed); instruction (M Ed); reading education (M Ed); special education (M Ed); teaching, learning, and culture (PhD). *Application deadline:* For fall admission, 8/1 for domestic students, 3/1 for international students; for spring admission, 11/1 priority date for domestic students, 9/1 for international students. Applications are processed on a rolling basis. *Application fee:* $45 ($80 for international students). Electronic applications accepted. *Application Contact:* Dr. Patricia D. Witherspoon, Dean of the Graduate School, 915-747-5491, Fax: 915-747-5788, E-mail: withersp@utep.edu. *Dean,* Dr. Josie V. Tinajero, 915-747-5572, Fax: 915-747-5755, E-mail: tinajero@utep.edu.

College of Engineering Students: 431 (97 women); includes 3 Black or African American, non-Hispanic/Latino; 8 Asian, non-Hispanic/Latino; 150 Hispanic/Latino, 250 international. Average age 28. 338 applicants, 49% accepted. Expenses: Contact institution. *Financial support:* In 2010–11, research assistantships with partial tuition reimbursements (averaging $21,125 per year), teaching assistantships with partial tuition reimbursements (averaging $16,900 per year) were awarded; fellowships with partial tuition reimbursements, institutionally sponsored loans, scholarships/grants, health care benefits, tuition waivers (partial), and unspecified assistantships also available. Support available to part-time students. Financial award application deadline: 3/15; financial award applicants required to submit FAFSA. In 2010, 116 master's, 8 doctorates awarded. *Degree program information:* Part-time and evening/weekend programs available. Offers civil engineering (MS, PhD); computer engineering (MS); computer science (MS, PhD); construction management (MS, Certificate); electrical and computer engineering (PhD); electrical engineering (MS); engineering (MEENE, MS, MSENE, MSIT, PhD, Certificate); environmental engineering (MEENE, MSENE); industrial engineering (MS); information technology (MSIT); manufacturing engineering (MS); materials science and engineering (PhD); mechanical engineering (MS); metallurgical and materials engineering (MS); systems engineering (MS, Certificate). *Application deadline:* For fall admission, 8/1 priority date for domestic students, 3/1 for international students; for spring admission, 11/1 priority date for domestic students, 9/1 for international students. Applications are processed on a rolling basis. *Application fee:* $45 ($80 for international students). Electronic applications accepted. *Application Contact:* Dr. Patricia D. Witherspoon, Dean of the Graduate School, 915-747-5491, Fax: 915-747-5788, E-mail: withersp@utep.edu. *Dean,* Dr. Richard Schoephoerster, 915-747-6444, Fax: 915-747-5437, E-mail: schoephoerster@utep.edu.

College of Health Sciences Students: 280 (205 women); includes 6 Black or African American, non-Hispanic/Latino; 1 American Indian or Alaska Native, non-Hispanic/Latino; 12 Asian, non-Hispanic/Latino; 202 Hispanic/Latino, 3 international. Average age 34. Expenses: Contact institution. *Financial support:* In 2010–11, research assistantships with partial tuition reimbursements (averaging $18,825 per year), teaching assistantships with partial tuition reimbursements (averaging $18,000 per year) were awarded; career-related internships or fieldwork, Federal Work-Study, institutionally sponsored loans, scholarships/grants, and tuition waivers (partial) also available. Support available to part-time students. Financial award application deadline: 3/15; financial award applicants required to submit FAFSA. In 2010, 45 master's awarded. *Degree program information:* Part-time and evening/weekend programs available. Postbaccalaureate distance learning degree programs offered. Offers health sciences (MOT, MPH, MPT, MRC, MS, MSN, MSW, PhD); interdisciplinary health sciences (PhD); kinesiology (MS); kinesiology on-line (MS); occupational therapy (MOT); physical therapy (MPT); public health (MPH); rehabilitation counseling (MRC); social work (MSW); speech-language pathology (MS). *Application deadline:* For fall admission, 7/1 for domestic students, 3/1 for international students; for spring admission, 11/1 priority date for domestic students, 9/1 for international students. Applications are processed on a rolling basis. *Application fee:* $15 ($65 for international students). Electronic applications accepted. *Application Contact:* Dr. Charles H. Ambler, Dean of the Graduate School, 915-747-5491 Ext. 7886, Fax: 915-747-5788, E-mail: cambler@utep.edu. *Dean,* Dr. Kathleen A. Curtis, 915-747-7201, E-mail: kacurtis@utep.edu.

College of Liberal Arts Students: 412 (221 women); includes 10 Black or African American, non-Hispanic/Latino; 1 American Indian or Alaska Native, non-Hispanic/Latino; 2 Asian, non-Hispanic/Latino; 220 Hispanic/Latino, 58 international. Average age 34. 355 applicants, 47% accepted. Expenses: Contact institution. *Financial support:* In 2010–11, research assistantships with partial tuition reimbursements (averaging $18,625 per year), teaching assistantships with partial tuition reimbursements (averaging $14,900 per year) were awarded; fellowships with partial tuition reimbursements, institutionally sponsored loans, scholarships/grants, health care benefits, tuition waivers (partial), and unspecified assistantships also available. Support available to part-time students. Financial award application deadline: 3/15; financial award applicants required to submit FAFSA. In 2010, 75 master's, 10 doctorates awarded. *Degree program information:* Part-time and evening/weekend programs available. Postbaccalaureate distance learning degree programs offered. Offers art education (MA); bilingual professional writing (Certificate); border history (MA); borderlands history (PhD); clinical psychology (MA); communication (MA); creative writing (on-line) (MFA); creative writing in English (MFA); creative writing in Spanish (MFA); English and American literature (MA); experimental psychology (MA); history (MA); Latin American and border studies (MA, Certificate); liberal arts (MA, MAIS, MAT, MFA, MM, PhD, Certificate); linguistics (MA); music education (MM); music performance (MM); philosophy (MA); political science (MA); psychology (PhD); rhetoric and composition (PhD); rhetoric and writing studies (MA); sociology (MA); Spanish (MA); studio art (MA); teaching English (MAT); teaching English to speakers of other languages (Certificate); women's and gender studies (Certificate). *Application deadline:* For fall admission, 8/1 for domestic students, 3/1 for international students; for spring admission, 11/1 priority date for domestic students, 9/1 for international students. Applications are processed on a rolling basis. *Application fee:* $45 ($80 for international students). Electronic applications accepted. *Application Contact:* Dr. Patricia D. Witherspoon, Dean of the Graduate School, 915-747-5491, Fax: 915-747-5788, E-mail: withersp@utep.edu. *Dean,* Dr. Howard C. Daudistel, 915-747-5666, Fax: 915-747-5905, E-mail: hdaudistel@utep.edu.

College of Science Students: 242 (90 women); includes 1 Black or African American, non-Hispanic/Latino; 7 Asian, non-Hispanic/Latino; 113 Hispanic/Latino, 60 international. Average age 34. Expenses: Contact institution. *Financial support:* In 2010–11, research assistantships with partial tuition reimbursements (averaging $21,812 per year), teaching assistantships with partial tuition reimbursements (averaging $17,450 per year) were awarded; fellowships with partial tuition reimbursements, career-related internships or fieldwork, Federal Work-Study, institutionally sponsored loans, scholarships/grants, and tuition waivers (partial) also available. Support available to part-time students. Financial award application deadline: 3/15; financial award applicants required to submit FAFSA. In 2010, 49 master's awarded. *Degree program information:* Part-time and evening/weekend programs available. Offers bioinformatics (MS); biological sciences (MS, PhD); chemistry (MS, PhD); computational science (MS, PhD); environmental science (MS); geological sciences (MS, PhD); geophysics (MS); interdisciplinary studies (MSIS); mathematical sciences (MS); mathematics (teaching) (MAT); physics (MS); science (MAT, MS, MSIS, PhD); statistics (MS); teaching science (MAT). *Application deadline:* For fall admission, 7/1 for domestic students, 3/1 for international students; for spring admission, 11/1 for domestic students, 9/1 for international students. Applications are processed on a rolling basis. *Application fee:* $15 ($65 for international students). Electronic applications accepted. *Application Contact:* Dr. Charles H. Ambler, Dean of the Graduate School, 915-747-5491 Ext. 7886, Fax: 915-747-5788, E-mail: cambler@utep.edu. *Dean,* Dr. Anny Morrobel-Sosa, 915-747-5536, E-mail: amorrobel@utep.edu.

Institute for Policy and Economic Development Students: 187 (57 women); includes 19 Black or African American, non-Hispanic/Latino; 1 American Indian or Alaska Native, non-Hispanic/Latino; 5 Asian, non-Hispanic/Latino; 99 Hispanic/Latino, 5 international. 142 applicants, 77% accepted. Expenses: Contact institution. *Financial support:* Fellowships with partial tuition reimbursements, research assistantships with partial tuition reimbursements, teaching assistantships with partial tuition reimbursements, institutionally sponsored loans, scholarships/grants, health care benefits, tuition waivers (partial), and unspecified assistantships available. Support available to part-time students. Financial award application deadline: 3/15; financial award applicants required to submit FAFSA. In 2010, 76 master's awarded. *Degree program information:* Part-time and evening/weekend programs available. Offers border administration (Certificate); homeland security (Certificate); intelligence and national security (MS, Certificate); leadership studies (MA); public administration (MPA). *Application deadline:* For fall admission, 8/1 for domestic students, 3/1 for international students; for spring admission, 10/1 for domestic students, 9/1 for international students. Applications are processed on a rolling basis. *Application fee:* $45 ($80 for international students). Electronic applications accepted. *Application Contact:* Dr. Patricia

D. Witherspoon, Dean of the Graduate School, 915-747-5491, Fax: 915-747-5788, E-mail: withersp@utep.edu. *Director*, Dr. Dennis Soden, 915-747-7974, Fax: 915-747-7948, E-mail: desoden@utep.edu.

School of Nursing Students: 153 (124 women); includes 11 Black or African American, non-Hispanic/Latino; 1 American Indian or Alaska Native, non-Hispanic/Latino; 6 Asian, non-Hispanic/Latino; 82 Hispanic/Latino, 5 international. Average age 34. 91 applicants, 49% accepted. Expenses: Contact institution. *Financial support:* In 2010–11, research assistantships with partial tuition reimbursements (averaging $18,825 per year), teaching assistantships with partial tuition reimbursements (averaging $18,000 per year) were awarded; fellowships with partial tuition reimbursements, institutionally sponsored loans, scholarships/grants, health care benefits, tuition waivers (partial), and unspecified assistantships also available. Support available to part-time students. Financial award application deadline: 3/15; financial award applicants required to submit FAFSA. In 2010, 33 master's awarded. Offers evidence-based practice (Certificate); family nurse practitioner (MSN); health care leadership and management (Certificate); interdisciplinary health sciences (PhD); nurse clinical specialist (MSN); nursing (Post-Master's Certificate); nursing systems management (MSN). *Application deadline:* For fall admission, 8/1 for domestic students, 3/1 for international students; for spring admission, 11/1 for domestic students, 9/1 for international students. Applications are processed on a rolling basis. *Application fee:* $45 ($80 for international students). Electronic applications accepted. *Application Contact:* Dr. Patricia D. Witherspoon, Dean of the Graduate School, 915-747-5491, Fax: 915-747-5788, E-mail: withersp@utep.edu. *Dean*, Dr. Elias Provencio-Vasquez, 915-747-7273, Fax: 915-747-8266, E-mail: eprovenciovasquez@utep.edu.

THE UNIVERSITY OF TEXAS AT SAN ANTONIO, San Antonio, TX 78249-0617

General Information State-supported, coed, university. CGS member. *Enrollment:* 30,258 graduate, professional, and undergraduate students; 1,800 full-time matriculated graduate/professional students (906 women), 2,392 part-time matriculated graduate/professional students (1,447 women). *Enrollment by degree level:* 3,533 master's, 659 doctoral. *Graduate faculty:* 490 full-time (169 women), 71 part-time/adjunct (23 women). Tuition, state resident: full-time $4172; part-time $231.75 per credit hour. Tuition, nonresident: full-time $15,332; part-time $851.75 per credit hour. *Graduate housing:* Room and/or apartments available on a first-come, first-served basis to single students; on-campus housing not available to married students. Typical cost: $5796 per year ($8696 including board). Housing application deadline: 5/31. *Student services:* Campus employment opportunities, campus safety program, career counseling, child daycare facilities, exercise/wellness program, free psychological counseling, grant writing training, international student services, low-cost health insurance, multicultural affairs office, services for students with disabilities, teacher training, writing training. *Library facilities:* University of Texas at San Antonio Libraries plus 3 others. *Online resources:* library catalog, web page, access to other libraries' catalogs. *Research affiliation:* Korea Association of Small Business Innovation (biomedical engineering), Provid Pharmaceuticals, Inc. (infectious diseases), Hispanic Association of Colleges and Universities (psychology), Southwest Research Institute (biomedical engineering, physics), Booz Allen Hamilton (economic development), Northrop Grumman Corporation (information systems).

Computer facilities: A campuswide network can be accessed. Online class registration is available. *Web address:* http://www.utsa.edu/.

General Application Contact: Veronica Ramirez, Assistant Dean of the Graduate School, 210-458-4330, Fax: 210-458-4332, E-mail: graduatestudies@utsa.edu.

GRADUATE UNITS

College of Business Students: 319 full-time (114 women), 318 part-time (99 women); includes 188 minority (19 Black or African American, non-Hispanic/Latino; 2 American Indian or Alaska Native, non-Hispanic/Latino; 38 Asian, non-Hispanic/Latino; 119 Hispanic/Latino; 3 Native Hawaiian or other Pacific Islander, non-Hispanic/Latino; 7 Two or more races, non-Hispanic/Latino), 92 international. Average age 31. 608 applicants, 50% accepted, 215 enrolled. *Faculty:* 75 full-time (21 women), 18 part-time/adjunct (1 woman). Expenses: Contact institution. *Financial support:* In 2010–11, 99 students received support, including 1 fellowship (averaging $45,000 per year), 446 research assistantships (averaging $13,905 per year), 210 teaching assistantships (averaging $8,955 per year); career-related internships or fieldwork, scholarships/grants, tuition waivers, and unspecified assistantships also available. Support available to part-time students. Financial award application deadline: 3/31. In 2010, 229 master's, 10 doctorates awarded. *Degree program information:* Part-time and evening/weekend programs available. Offers accounting (PhD); applied statistics (MS, PhD); business (MBA); business economics (MBA); business finance (MBA); construction science and management (MS); economics (MA); finance (MS, PhD); information systems (MBA); information technology (MSIT, PhD); international business (MBA); management accounting (MBA); management and organization studies (PhD); management of technology (MBA); management science (MBA); management technology (MSMOT); marketing (PhD); marketing management (MBA); real estate finance (MBA); taxation (MBA). *Application deadline:* For fall admission, 7/1 for domestic students, 4/1 for international students; for spring admission, 11/1 for domestic students, 9/1 for international students. Applications are processed on a rolling basis. *Application fee:* $45 ($80 for international students). Electronic applications accepted. *Application Contact:* Veronica Ramirez, Assistant Dean of the Graduate School, 210-458-4330, Fax: 210-458-4332, E-mail: graduatestudies@utsa.edu. *Dean*, Dr. Lynda Y. de la Vina, 210-458-4317, Fax: 210-458-4308, E-mail: lynda.delavina@utsa.edu.

College of Education and Human Development Students: 461 full-time (345 women), 1,083 part-time (847 women); includes 894 minority (103 Black or African American, non-Hispanic/Latino; 5 American Indian or Alaska Native, non-Hispanic/Latino; 30 Asian, non-Hispanic/Latino; 730 Hispanic/Latino; 2 Native Hawaiian or other Pacific Islander, non-Hispanic/Latino; 24 Two or more races, non-Hispanic/Latino), 52 international. Average age 34. 571 applicants, 89% accepted, 363 enrolled. *Faculty:* 95 full-time (55 women), 13 part-time/adjunct (6 women). Expenses: Contact institution. *Financial support:* In 2010–11, 134 students received support, including 141 research assistantships (averaging $11,569 per year), 14 teaching assistantships (averaging $8,268 per year); career-related internships or fieldwork, scholarships/grants, and unspecified assistantships also available. Support available to part-time students. In 2010, 313 master's, 12 doctorates awarded. *Degree program information:* Part-time and evening/weekend programs available. Offers adult learning and teaching (MA); bicultural-bilingual studies (MA); counseling (MA); counselor education and supervision (PhD); culture, literacy, and language (PhD); education (MA); education and human development (M Ed, MA, MS, Ed D, PhD, Graduate Certificate); educational leadership (Ed D); educational leadership and policy studies (M Ed); health and kinesiology (MS); interdisciplinary learning and teaching (PhD); school psychology (MA); teaching English as a second language (MA). *Application deadline:* For fall admission, 7/1 for domestic students, 4/1 for international students; for spring admission, 11/1 for domestic students, 9/1 for international students. Applications are processed on a rolling basis. *Application fee:* $45 ($80 for international students). Electronic applications accepted. *Application Contact:* Veronica Ramirez, Assistant Dean of the Graduate School, 210-458-4330, Fax: 210-458-4332, E-mail: graduatestudies@utsa.edu. *Dean*, Dr. Betty M. Merchant, 210-458-4370, Fax: 210-458-4487, E-mail: betty.merchant@utsa.edu.

College of Engineering Students: 206 full-time (53 women), 183 part-time (39 women); includes 88 minority (10 Black or African American, non-Hispanic/Latino; 16 Asian, non-Hispanic/Latino; 58 Hispanic/Latino; 4 Two or more races, non-Hispanic/Latino), 181 international. Average age 29. 325 applicants, 72% accepted, 115 enrolled. *Faculty:* 53 full-time (7 women), 7 part-time/adjunct (1 woman). Expenses: Contact institution. *Financial support:* In 2010–11, 144 students received support, including 22 fellowships (averaging $31,817 per year), 176 research assistantships (averaging $14,156 per year), 56 teaching assistantships (averaging $10,880 per year); career-related internships or fieldwork, institutionally sponsored loans, scholarships/grants, tuition waivers, and unspecified assistantships also available. Support available to part-time students. Financial award application deadline: 3/31. In 2010, 102 master's, 14 doctorates awarded. *Degree program information:* Part-time and evening/weekend programs available. Offers advanced manufacturing and enterprise engineering (MS); biomedical engineering (MS, PhD); civil engineering (MS, MSCE); computer engineering (MS); electrical engineering (MS, PhD); engineering (MS, MSCE, PhD); environmental science and engineering (PhD); mechanical engineering (MS). *Application deadline:* For fall admission, 7/1 for domestic students, 4/1 for international students; for spring admission, 11/1 for domestic students, 9/1 for international students. Applications are processed on a rolling basis. *Application fee:* $45 ($80 for international students). Electronic applications accepted. *Application Contact:* Veronica Ramirez, Assistant Dean, 210-458-4330, Fax: 210-458-4332, E-mail: graduatestudies@utsa.edu. *Dean*, Dr. C. Mauli Agarwal, 210-458-4490, Fax: 210-458-5556, E-mail: mauli.agarwal@utsa.edu.

College of Liberal and Fine Arts Students: 222 full-time (139 women), 304 part-time (178 women); includes 237 minority (19 Black or African American, non-Hispanic/Latino; 3 American Indian or Alaska Native, non-Hispanic/Latino; 11 Asian, non-Hispanic/Latino; 194 Hispanic/Latino; 1 Native Hawaiian or other Pacific Islander, non-Hispanic/Latino; 9 Two or more races, non-Hispanic/Latino), 22 international. Average age 31. 335 applicants, 70% accepted, 166 enrolled. *Faculty:* 119 full-time (52 women), 6 part-time/adjunct (5 women). Expenses: Contact institution. *Financial support:* In 2010–11, 146 students received support, including 108 research assistantships (averaging $10,463 per year), 55 teaching assistantships (averaging $5,828 per year); career-related internships or fieldwork, scholarships/grants, tuition waivers (partial), and unspecified assistantships also available. Support available to part-time students. In 2010, 88 master's, 4 doctorates awarded. *Degree program information:* Part-time and evening/weekend programs available. Offers anthropology (MA, PhD); art (MFA); art history (MA); communication (MA); English (MA, PhD); history (MA); keyboard pedagogy (Graduate Certificate); keyboard performance (Graduate Certificate); liberal and fine arts (MA, MFA, MM, MS, PhD, Graduate Certificate); music (MM); political science (MA); psychology (MS); sociology (MS); Spanish (MA). *Application deadline:* For fall admission, 7/1 for domestic students, 4/1 for international students; for spring admission, 11/1 for domestic students, 9/1 for international students. Applications are processed on a rolling basis. *Application fee:* $45 ($80 for international students). Electronic applications accepted. *Application Contact:* Veronica Ramirez, Assistant Dean of the Graduate School, 210-458-4330, Fax: 210-458-4332, E-mail: graduatestudies@utsa.edu. *Dean*, Dr. Daniel J. Gelo, 210-458-4350, Fax: 210-458-4347, E-mail: colfa@utsa.edu.

College of Public Policy Students: 154 full-time (98 women), 283 part-time (197 women); includes 271 minority (46 Black or African American, non-Hispanic/Latino; 4 American Indian or Alaska Native, non-Hispanic/Latino; 13 Asian, non-Hispanic/Latino; 192 Hispanic/Latino; 1 Native Hawaiian or other Pacific Islander, non-Hispanic/Latino; 15 Two or more races, non-Hispanic/Latino), 12 international. Average age 33. 225 applicants, 75% accepted, 142 enrolled. *Faculty:* 35 full-time (15 women), 5 part-time/adjunct (3 women). Expenses: Contact institution. *Financial support:* In 2010–11, 31 students received support, including 89 research assistantships (averaging $12,017 per year); career-related internships or fieldwork, scholarships/grants, tuition waivers, and unspecified assistantships also available. Support available to part-time students. In 2010, 98 master's, 7 doctorates awarded. *Degree program information:* Part-time and evening/weekend programs available. Offers applied demography (PhD); justice policy (MS); public administration (MPA); public policy (MPA, MS, MSW, PhD); social work (MSW). *Application deadline:* For fall admission, 7/1 for domestic students, 4/1 for international students; for spring admission, 11/1 for domestic students, 9/1 for international students. Applications are processed on a rolling basis. *Application fee:* $45 ($80 for international students). Electronic applications accepted. *Application Contact:* Veronica Ramirez, Assistant Dean of the Graduate School, 210-458-4330, Fax: 210-458-4332, E-mail: graduatestudies@utsa.edu. *Interim Dean*, Dr. Dennis T. Haynes, 210-458-2606, Fax: 210-458-2919, E-mail: dennis.haynes@utsa.edu.

College of Sciences Students: 349 full-time (129 women), 200 part-time (78 women); includes 150 minority (17 Black or African American, non-Hispanic/Latino; 20 Asian, non-Hispanic/Latino; 100 Hispanic/Latino; 13 Two or more races, non-Hispanic/Latino), 204 international. Average age 28. 600 applicants, 57% accepted, 175 enrolled. *Faculty:* 96 full-time (12 women), 18 part-time/adjunct (3 women). Expenses: Contact institution. *Financial support:* In 2010–11, 210 students received support, including 83 fellowships (averaging $29,110 per year), 156 research assistantships (averaging $16,768 per year), 179 teaching assistantships (averaging $11,403 per year); career-related internships or fieldwork, scholarships/grants, tuition waivers, and unspecified assistantships also available. Support available to part-time students. In 2010, 75 master's, 26 doctorates awarded. *Degree program information:* Part-time and evening/weekend programs available. Offers applied mathematics-industrial mathematics (MS); biology (MS, PhD); biotechnology (MS); chemistry (MS, PhD); computer and information security (MS); computer science (MS, PhD); geological sciences (MS); mathematics (MS); mathematics education (MS); neurobiology (PhD); physics (MS, PhD); sciences (MS, PhD); software engineering (MS). *Application deadline:* For fall admission, 7/1 for domestic students, 4/1 for international students; for spring admission, 11/1 for domestic students, 9/1 for international students. Applications are processed on a rolling basis. *Application fee:* $45 ($80 for international students). Electronic applications accepted. *Application Contact:* Veronica Ramirez, Assistant Dean of the Graduate School, 210-458-4330, Fax: 210-458-4332, E-mail: graduatestudies@utsa.edu. *Dean*, Dr. George Perry, 210-458-4450, Fax: 210-458-4445, E-mail: george.perry@utsa.edu.

THE UNIVERSITY OF TEXAS AT TYLER, Tyler, TX 75799-0001

General Information State-supported, coed, comprehensive institution. CGS member. *Graduate housing:* Rooms and/or apartments available on a first-come, first-served basis to single and married students. *Research affiliation:* Embassy of Arab Republic of Egypt Cultural and Education Bureau (electrical engineering), TransAtlantic Lines, Inc. (civil engineering), American Society of Civil Engineers (civil engineering), McGraw-Hill Company (civil engineering), Renaissance Society of America (art history), American Lung Association of the Central States (biology).

GRADUATE UNITS

College of Arts and Sciences *Degree program information:* Part-time and evening/weekend programs available. Postbaccalaureate distance learning degree programs offered. Offers art history (MA); arts and sciences (MA, MAIS, MAT, MFA, MPA, MS, MSIS); biology (MS); communication (MA); criminal justice (MS); English (MA); history (MA); interdisciplinary (MAIS); interdisciplinary studies (MAIS, MSIS); mathematics (MS, MSIS); political science (MA); public administration (MPA); sociology (MS); studio art (MFA). Electronic applications accepted.

College of Business and Technology *Degree program information:* Part-time and evening/weekend programs available. Postbaccalaureate distance learning degree programs offered (no on-campus study). Offers business and technology (MBA, MS, PhD). Electronic applications accepted.

School of Business Administration *Degree program information:* Part-time programs available. Postbaccalaureate distance learning degree programs offered (no on-campus study). Offers business administration (MBA); general management (MBA); health care (MBA).

School of Human Resource Development and Technology *Degree program information:* Part-time and evening/weekend programs available. Postbaccalaureate distance learning degree programs offered (no on-campus study). Offers human resource development (MS, PhD); industrial management (MS). Electronic applications accepted.

College of Education and Psychology *Degree program information:* Part-time and evening/weekend programs available. Offers clinical psychology (MS); counseling psychology (MA); education and psychology (M Ed, MA, MS, MSIS); educational leadership (M Ed); interdisciplinary studies (MSIS); school counseling (MA).

School of Education *Degree program information:* Part-time and evening/weekend programs available. Offers early childhood education (M Ed, MA); reading (M Ed, MA); special education (M Ed, MA). Electronic applications accepted.

College of Engineering and Computer Science *Degree program information:* Part-time programs available. Offers computer science (MS); electrical engineering (MS); engineering and computer science (MS, MSIS); environmental engineering (MS); industrial safety (MS); interdisciplinary studies (MSIS); mechanical engineering (MS); structural engineering (MS); transportation engineering (MS); water resources engineering (MS). Electronic applications accepted.

The University of Texas at Tyler (continued)

College of Nursing and Health Sciences *Degree program information:* Part-time and evening/weekend programs available. Postbaccalaureate distance learning degree programs offered. Offers health and kinesiology (M Ed, MA); health sciences (MS); kinesiology (MS); nurse practitioner (MSN); nursing (PhD); nursing administration (MSN); nursing and health sciences (M Ed, MA, MS, MSN, PhD); nursing education (MSN). Electronic applications accepted.

THE UNIVERSITY OF TEXAS HEALTH SCIENCE CENTER AT HOUSTON, Houston, TX 77225-0036

General Information State-supported, coed, upper-level institution. *Graduate housing:* On-campus housing not available.

GRADUATE UNITS

Graduate School of Biomedical Sciences Offers biochemistry and molecular biology (MS, PhD); biomathematics and biostatistics (MS, PhD); biomedical sciences (MS, PhD); cancer biology (MS, PhD); cell and regulatory biology (MS, PhD); genes and development (MS, PhD); genetic counseling (MS); human and molecular genetics (MS, PhD); immunology (MS, PhD); medical physics (MS, PhD); microbiology and molecular genetics (MS, PhD); molecular carcinogenesis (MS, PhD); molecular pathology (MS, PhD); neuroscience (MS, PhD); virology and gene therapy (MS, PhD). Electronic applications accepted.

School of Health Information Sciences *Degree program information:* Part-time programs available. Postbaccalaureate distance learning degree programs offered (no on-campus study). Offers health informatics (MS, PhD, Certificate). Electronic applications accepted.

School of Nursing Students: 141 full-time (117 women), 209 part-time (186 women); includes 39 Black or African American, non-Hispanic/Latino; 1 American Indian or Alaska Native, non-Hispanic/Latino; 36 Asian, non-Hispanic/Latino; 37 Hispanic/Latino, 8 international. Average age 37. 343 applicants, 40% accepted, 109 enrolled. *Faculty:* 46 full-time (40 women), 15 part-time/adjunct (12 women). Expenses: Contact institution. *Financial support:* In 2010–11, 144 students received support; research assistantships with tuition reimbursements available, teaching assistantships with tuition reimbursements available, institutionally sponsored loans, scholarships/grants, traineeships, and tuition waivers available. Support available to part-time students. Financial award applicants required to submit FAFSA. In 2010, 71 master's, 13 doctorates awarded. *Degree program information:* Part-time programs available. Offers nursing (MSN, DNP, PhD). *Application deadline:* For fall admission, 4/1 priority date for domestic students, 3/1 for international students. Applications are processed on a rolling basis. *Application fee:* $30. Electronic applications accepted. *Application Contact:* Laurie G. Rutherford, Student Affairs, 713-500-2101, Fax: 713-500-2107, E-mail: soninfo@uth.tmc.edu. *Dean,* Dr. Patricia L. Starck, 713-500-2100, Fax: 713-500-2107.

University of Texas Medical School at Houston Students: 953 full-time (406 women); includes 50 Black or African American, non-Hispanic/Latino; 2 American Indian or Alaska Native, non-Hispanic/Latino; 148 Asian, non-Hispanic/Latino; 115 Hispanic/Latino, 5 international. Average age 23. 3,613 applicants, 11% accepted, 230 enrolled. *Faculty:* 966 full-time (379 women), 94 part-time/adjunct (40 women). Expenses: Contact institution. *Financial support:* In 2010–11, 323 students received support. Scholarships/grants available. Financial award application deadline: 3/1; financial award applicants required to submit FAFSA. In 2010, 222 first professional degrees awarded. Offers medicine (MD). *Application deadline:* For fall admission, 10/1 for domestic and international students. Applications are processed on a rolling basis. *Application fee:* $55 ($100 for international students). Electronic applications accepted. *Application Contact:* Dr. Margaret McNeese, Associate Dean of Admissions and Student Affairs, 713-500-5160, E-mail: margaret.c.mcneese@uth.tmc.edu. *Dean,* Dr. Giuseppe N. Colasurdo, 713-500-5012, E-mail: giuseppe.n.colasurdo@uth.tmc.edu.

The University of Texas School of Dentistry at Houston Students: 333 full-time (174 women); includes 5 Black or African American, non-Hispanic/Latino; 1 American Indian or Alaska Native, non-Hispanic/Latino; 90 Asian, non-Hispanic/Latino; 57 Hispanic/Latino. Average age 25. 1,161 applicants, 13% accepted, 84 enrolled. *Faculty:* 93 full-time (36 women), 83 part-time/adjunct (30 women). Expenses: Contact institution. *Financial support:* In 2010–11, 290 students received support. Institutionally sponsored loans and scholarships/grants available. Financial award application deadline: 3/1; financial award applicants required to submit FAFSA. In 2010, 72 first professional degrees awarded. Offers dentistry (DDS, MS). *Application deadline:* For fall admission, 10/1 for domestic students. Applications are processed on a rolling basis. *Application fee:* $80. Electronic applications accepted. *Application Contact:* Dr. H. Philip Pierpont, Associate Dean for Student and Alumni Affairs, 713-500-4151, Fax: 713-500-4425, E-mail: dbstudentaffairs@uthouston.edu. *Dean,* Dr. John A. Valenza, 713-500-4021, Fax: 713-500-4089.

The University of Texas School of Public Health *Degree program information:* Part-time programs available. Offers public health (MPH, MS, Dr PH, PhD, Certificate). JD/MPH and MSW/MPH offered jointly with University of Houston. Electronic applications accepted.

THE UNIVERSITY OF TEXAS HEALTH SCIENCE CENTER AT SAN ANTONIO, San Antonio, TX 78229-3900

General Information State-supported, coed, upper-level institution. CGS member. *Enrollment:* 2,023 full-time matriculated graduate/professional students (1,120 women), 284 part-time matriculated graduate/professional students (214 women). *Enrollment by degree level:* 1,306 first professional, 528 master's, 428 doctoral, 45 other advanced degrees. *Graduate faculty:* 1,138 full-time (434 women), 487 part-time/adjunct (162 women). Tuition, state resident: full-time $3072; part-time $128 per credit hour. Tuition, nonresident: full-time $11,928; part-time $497 per credit hour. *Required fees:* $1078; $1078 per year. One-time fee: $60. *Graduate housing:* On-campus housing not available. *Student services:* Campus safety program, exercise/wellness program, free psychological counseling, international student services, low-cost health insurance. *Library facilities:* Dolph Briso Library. *Research affiliation:* University Hospital, Southwest Research Institute, Southwest Foundation for Biomedical Research, Veterans Administration Hospital. *Web address:* http://www.uthscsa.edu/.

GRADUATE UNITS

Dental School Offers dentistry (DDS, MS, Certificate). Electronic applications accepted.

Graduate School of Biomedical Sciences Students: 368 full-time (197 women), 243 part-time (180 women); includes 27 Black or African American, non-Hispanic/Latino; 4 American Indian or Alaska Native, non-Hispanic/Latino; 41 Asian, non-Hispanic/Latino; 120 Hispanic/Latino, 144 international. Average age 33. 661 applicants, 30% accepted, 148 enrolled. *Faculty:* 203 full-time (77 women), 44 part-time/adjunct (13 women). Expenses: Contact institution. *Financial support:* In 2010–11, 24 fellowships (averaging $26,000 per year), 240 teaching assistantships (averaging $26,000 per year) were awarded; career-related internships or fieldwork, institutionally sponsored loans, scholarships/grants, and health care benefits also available. Financial award application deadline: 6/30; financial award applicants required to submit FAFSA. In 2010, 39 master's, 39 doctorates awarded. Offers biochemistry (MS, PhD); biomedical sciences (MS, MSN, PhD); cellular and structural biology (MS, PhD); clinical investigation (MS); microbiology and immunology (PhD); molecular medicine (MS, PhD); neuroscience (PhD); physiology (MS, PhD); radiological sciences (MS, PhD). *Application deadline:* For fall admission, 1/15 priority date for domestic and international students; for spring admission, 10/1 for domestic and international students. Applications are processed on a rolling basis. *Application fee:* $0. Electronic applications accepted. *Application Contact:* Dr. Nicquet Blake, Assistant Dean for Graduate Student Recruitment, 210-567-3709, Fax: 210-567-3719, E-mail: blaken@uthscsa.edu. *Interim Dean,* Dr. David S. Weiss, 210-567-3709, Fax: 210-567-3719, E-mail: weissd@uthscsa.edu.

School of Nursing Students: 48 full-time (40 women), 177 part-time (156 women); includes 14 Black or African American, non-Hispanic/Latino; 2 American Indian or Alaska Native, non-Hispanic/Latino; 24 Asian, non-Hispanic/Latino; 72 Hispanic/Latino. Average age 39. 112 applicants, 56% accepted, 52 enrolled. *Faculty:* 30 full-time (29 women), 8 part-time/adjunct (7 women). Expenses: Contact institution. *Financial support:* In 2010–11, 100 students received support, including 3 fellowships with full tuition reimbursements available (averaging $30,000 per year); research assistantships, teaching assistantships, institutionally sponsored loans and scholarships/grants also available. Financial award application deadline: 6/30; financial award applicants required to submit FAFSA. In 2010, 68 master's, 4 doctorates awarded. *Degree program information:* Part-time programs available. Offers nursing (MSN, PhD). *Application deadline:* For fall admission, 1/10 for domestic students; for spring admission, 7/1 for domestic students. *Application fee:* $45. Electronic applications accepted. *Application Contact:* Dr. Eileen T. Breslin, Dean, 210-567-5800, Fax: 210-567-5929, E-mail: breslin@uthscsa.edu. *Dean,* Dr. Eileen T. Breslin, 210-567-5800, Fax: 210-567-5929, E-mail: breslin@uthscsa.edu.

School of Allied Health Sciences Expenses: Contact institution. *Financial support:* Scholarships/grants and health care benefits available. Financial award application deadline: 6/30; financial award applicants required to submit FAFSA. Offers clinical laboratory sciences (MS); deaf education and hearing science (MED); dental hygiene (MS); occupational therapy (MOT); physical therapy (MPT); physician assistant studies (MS). *Application deadline:* For fall admission, 6/1 for domestic and international students; for spring admission, 10/1 for domestic and international students. Applications are processed on a rolling basis. Electronic applications accepted. *Application Contact:* Dr. Marilyn S. Harrington, Dean, 210-567-8800. *Dean,* Dr. Marilyn S. Harrington, 210-567-8800.

School of Medicine Offers medicine (MD, MPH).

THE UNIVERSITY OF TEXAS MEDICAL BRANCH, Galveston, TX 77555

General Information State-supported, coed, comprehensive institution. CGS member. *Graduate housing:* Rooms and/or apartments available on a first-come, first-served basis to single and married students. *Research affiliation:* Shriners Hospitals (burns and wound healing).

GRADUATE UNITS

Graduate School of Biomedical Sciences Offers biochemistry (PhD); bioinformatics (PhD); biomedical sciences (MA, MMS, MPH, MS, PhD); biophysics (PhD); cell biology (PhD); cellular physiology and molecular biophysics (MS, PhD); clinical science (MS, PhD); computational biology (PhD); emerging and tropical infectious diseases (PhD); experimental pathology (PhD); medical humanities (MA, PhD); medical science (MMS); microbiology and immunology (MS, PhD); neuroscience (PhD); nursing (PhD); pharmacology (MS); pharmacology and toxicology (PhD); preventive medicine and community health (MPH, MS, PhD); public health (MPH); structural biology (PhD). Electronic applications accepted.

Center for Biodefense and Emerging Infectious Diseases Offers biodefense training (PhD).

School of Health Professions Offers health professions (MOT, MPAS, MPT, DPT); occupational therapy (MOT); physical therapy (MPT, DPT); physician assistant studies (MPAS). Electronic applications accepted.

School of Medicine Offers medicine (MD).

School of Nursing *Degree program information:* Part-time programs available. Postbaccalaureate distance learning degree programs offered (minimal on-campus study). Offers nursing (MSN, PhD). Electronic applications accepted.

THE UNIVERSITY OF TEXAS OF THE PERMIAN BASIN, Odessa, TX 79762-0001

General Information State-supported, coed, comprehensive institution. *Graduate housing:* Rooms and/or apartments available on a first-come, first-served basis to single and married students. Housing application deadline: 6/15.

GRADUATE UNITS

Office of Graduate Studies *Degree program information:* Part-time and evening/weekend programs available.

College of Arts and Sciences *Degree program information:* Part-time and evening/weekend programs available. Offers applied research psychology (MA); arts and sciences (MA, MS); biology (MS); clinical psychology (MA); computer science (MS); criminal justice administration (MS); English (MA); geology (MS); history (MA); kinesiology (MS); political science (MPA); Spanish (MA).

School of Business *Degree program information:* Part-time and evening/weekend programs available. Offers accountancy (MPA); business (MBA, MPA); management (MBA).

School of Education Offers bilingual/English as a second language education (MA); counseling (MA); early childhood education (MA); education (MA); educational leadership (MA); professional education (MA); reading (MA); special education (MA).

THE UNIVERSITY OF TEXAS–PAN AMERICAN, Edinburg, TX 78539

General Information State-supported, coed, comprehensive institution. CGS member. *Graduate housing:* Room and/or apartments available on a first-come, first-served basis to single students; on-campus housing not available to married students. *Research affiliation:* Lockheed Martin Corporation (manufacturing engineering), Texas Instruments (curriculum and instruction), Pfizer, Inc. (health disparities), Howard Hughes Medical Institute (medical science), The Boeing Company (engineering), Robert Wood Johnson (health science).

GRADUATE UNITS

College of Arts and Humanities *Degree program information:* Part-time and evening/weekend programs available. Offers art (MFA); arts and humanities (M Mus, MA, MAIS, MFA, MSIS); communication (MA); English (MA, MAIS); English as a second language (MA); ethnomusicology (M Mus); history (MA, MAIS); interdisciplinary studies (MAIS); music education (M Mus); performance (M Mus); Spanish (MA); theatre (MA).

College of Business Administration *Degree program information:* Part-time and evening/weekend programs available. Offers accounting (M Acc, MS); business administration (M Acc, MBA, MS, PhD); computer information systems (PhD); economics (PhD); finance (PhD); management (PhD); marketing (PhD).

College of Education *Degree program information:* Part-time and evening/weekend programs available. Offers bilingual education (M Ed); counseling (M Ed); early childhood education (M Ed); education (M Ed, MA, MS, Ed D); educational diagnostician (M Ed); educational leadership (M Ed, Ed D); elementary education (M Ed); gifted education (M Ed); kinesiology (MS); reading (M Ed); school psychology (MA); secondary education (M Ed); special education (M Ed). Ed D offered jointly with The University of Texas at Austin.

College of Health Sciences and Human Services *Degree program information:* Part-time and evening/weekend programs available. Offers adult health nursing (MSN); communication sciences and disorders (MS); family nurse practitioner (MSN); health sciences and human services (MS, MSN, MSSW, PhD); occupational therapy (MS); pediatric nurse practitioner (MSN); rehabilitation counseling (MS, PhD); social work (MSSW).

College of Science and Engineering *Degree program information:* Part-time and evening/weekend programs available. Offers biology (MS); chemistry (MS); computer science (MS); electrical engineering (MS); manufacturing engineering (MS); mathematical science (MS); mathematics teaching (MS); mechanical engineering (MS); science and engineering (MS).

College of Social and Behavioral Sciences *Degree program information:* Part-time and evening/weekend programs available. Postbaccalaureate distance learning degree programs offered (minimal on-campus study). Offers criminal justice (MS); psychology (MA); public administration (MPA); social and behavioral sciences (MA, MPA, MS); sociology (MS).

THE UNIVERSITY OF TEXAS SOUTHWESTERN MEDICAL CENTER AT DALLAS, Dallas, TX 75390

General Information State-supported, coed, upper-level institution. *Enrollment:* 2,499 graduate, professional, and undergraduate students; 1,765 full-time matriculated graduate/professional students (926 women), 669 part-time matriculated graduate/professional students (283 women). *Enrollment by degree level:* 1,041 first professional, 235 master's, 574 doctoral, 584 other advanced degrees. *Graduate faculty:* 1,539 full-time, 425 part-time/adjunct. *Graduate housing:* Rooms and/or apartments available on a first-come, first-served basis to single and married students. *Student services:* Campus employment opportunities, campus safety program, exercise/wellness program, free psychological counseling, grant writing training, international student services, low-cost health insurance, multicultural affairs office, services for students with disabilities, writing training. *Library facilities:* University of Texas Southwestern Library plus 1 other. *Online resources:* library catalog, web page, access to other libraries' catalogs. *Collection:* 257,782 titles, 2,865 serial subscriptions.

Computer facilities: 150 computers available on campus for general student use. A campuswide network can be accessed from off campus. *Web address:* http://www.utsouthwestern.edu/.

General Application Contact: Anne Mclane, Associate Director of Admissions, 214-648-5617, Fax: 214-648-3289, E-mail: admissions@utsouthwestern.edu.

GRADUATE UNITS

Southwestern Graduate School of Biomedical Sciences Students: 566 full-time (272 women), 669 part-time (283 women); includes 215 minority (25 Black or African American, non-Hispanic/Latino; 12 American Indian or Alaska Native, non-Hispanic/Latino; 99 Asian, non-Hispanic/Latino; 78 Hispanic/Latino; 1 Two or more races, non-Hispanic/Latino), 584 international. Average age 26. 1,482 applicants, 10% accepted, 111 enrolled. *Faculty:* 345 full-time (80 women), 89 part-time/adjunct (18 women). Expenses: Contact institution. *Financial support:* Fellowships, research assistantships, teaching assistantships, career-related internships or fieldwork, Federal Work-Study, institutionally sponsored loans, scholarships/grants, traineeships, and tuition waivers (full and partial) available. Financial award application deadline: 3/1; financial award applicants required to submit FAFSA. In 2010, 32 master's, 85 doctorates awarded. Offers biological chemistry (PhD); biomedical engineering (MS, PhD); biomedical sciences (MCS, MS, MSCS, PhD); cancer biology (PhD); cell regulation (PhD); genetics and development (PhD); immunology (PhD); integrative biology (PhD); medical scientist training (PhD); molecular biophysics (PhD); molecular microbiology (PhD); neuroscience (PhD). *Application deadline:* For fall admission, 12/15 priority date for domestic students. Applications are processed on a rolling basis. *Application fee:* $0. Electronic applications accepted. *Application Contact:* 214-648-5617, Fax: 214-648-3289, E-mail: admissions@utsouthwestern.edu. *Interim Dean,* Dr. Michael Roth, 214-645-6122, Fax: 214-648-2102.

Division of Clinical Science Students: 40 full-time (31 women), 65 part-time (37 women); includes 34 minority (4 Black or African American, non-Hispanic/Latino; 1 American Indian or Alaska Native, non-Hispanic/Latino; 18 Asian, non-Hispanic/Latino; 10 Hispanic/Latino; 1 Two or more races, non-Hispanic/Latino), 6 international. Average age 26. 230 applicants, 16% accepted, 23 enrolled. Expenses: Contact institution. *Financial support:* Applicants required to submit FAFSA. In 2010, 10 master's, 12 doctorates awarded. Offers clinical psychology (PhD); clinical science (MCS, MSCS, PhD). *Application Contact:* Dr. Melanie H. Cobb, Dean, 214-645-6122, Fax: 214-648-2102, E-mail: melanie.cobb@utsouthwestern.edu. *Dean,* Dr. Melanie H. Cobb, 214-645-6122, Fax: 214-648-2102, E-mail: melanie.cobb@utsouthwestern.edu.

Southwestern Medical School Students: 926 full-time (438 women); includes 485 minority (51 Black or African American, non-Hispanic/Latino; 1 American Indian or Alaska Native, non-Hispanic/Latino; 318 Asian, non-Hispanic/Latino; 115 Hispanic/Latino), 27 international. Average age 26. 3,483 applicants, 12% accepted, 228 enrolled. *Faculty:* 1,464 full-time, 402 part-time/adjunct. Expenses: Contact institution. *Financial support:* In 2010–11, 700 students received support. Federal Work-Study and institutionally sponsored loans available. Financial award application deadline: 3/15; financial award applicants required to submit FAFSA. In 2010, 207 first professional degrees awarded. Offers medicine (MD). *Application deadline:* For fall admission, 10/15 for domestic students. Applications are processed on a rolling basis. *Application fee:* $65. Electronic applications accepted. *Application Contact:* Anne Mclane, Associate Director of Admissions, 214-648-5617, Fax: 214-648-3289, E-mail: admissions@utsouthwestern.edu. *Dean,* Dr. Greg Fitz, 214-648-2509.

Southwestern School of Health Professions Students: 238 full-time (183 women), 70 part-time (57 women); includes 61 minority (13 Black or African American, non-Hispanic/Latino; 1 American Indian or Alaska Native, non-Hispanic/Latino; 21 Asian, non-Hispanic/Latino; 25 Hispanic/Latino; 1 Two or more races, non-Hispanic/Latino), 3 international. Average age 26. 1,376 applicants, 10% accepted, 96 enrolled. *Faculty:* 85 full-time (58 women). Expenses: Contact institution. *Financial support:* Application deadline: 3/1. In 2010, 47 master's awarded. Offers biomedical communications (MA); clinical nutrition (MCN); health professions (MA, MCN, MPAS, MPO, MRC, DPT); physical therapy (DPT); physician assistant studies (MPAS); prosthetics—orthotics (MPO); rehabilitation counseling psychology (MRC). *Application Contact:* Anne Mclane, Associate Director of Admissions, 214-648-6708, Fax: 214-648-2102, E-mail: admissions@utsouthwestern.edu. *Dean,* Dr. Raul Caetano, 214-648-1500.

THE UNIVERSITY OF THE ARTS, Philadelphia, PA 19102-4944

General Information Independent, coed, comprehensive institution. *Graduate housing:* Room and/or apartments available to single students; on-campus housing not available to married students. Housing application deadline: 6/1. *Research affiliation:* Ben Franklin Technology Partners (high tech department and creative/cultural production in Philadelphia), The Franklin Institute (general science education), Philadelphia Museum of Art (arts and culture), School District of Philadelphia (education).

GRADUATE UNITS

College of Art, Media and Design *Degree program information:* Part-time programs available. Offers art education (MA); art, media and design (MA, MAT, MFA, MID); book arts/printmaking (MFA); industrial design (MID); museum communication (MA); museum education (MA); museum exhibition planning and design (MFA); studio art (MFA); visual arts (MAT). Electronic applications accepted.

College of Performing Arts *Degree program information:* Part-time programs available. Offers performing arts (MAT, MM).

School of Music *Degree program information:* Part-time programs available. Offers jazz studies (MM); music education (MAT, MM). Electronic applications accepted.

UNIVERSITY OF THE CUMBERLANDS, Williamsburg, KY 40769-1372

General Information Independent-religious, coed, comprehensive institution. *Enrollment:* 3,300 graduate, professional, and undergraduate students; 1,293 full-time matriculated graduate/professional students (864 women), 277 part-time matriculated graduate/professional students (176 women). *Enrollment by degree level:* 1,379 master's, 67 doctoral, 124 other advanced degrees. *Graduate faculty:* 38 full-time (17 women), 46 part-time/adjunct (21 women). *Tuition:* Full-time $6984; part-time $291 per credit hour. *Required fees:* $50 per term. Tuition and fees vary according to course level, course load and program. *Graduate housing:* Room and/or apartments available on a first-come, first-served basis to single students; on-campus housing not available to married students. *Student services:* Campus employment opportunities, campus safety program, career counseling, low-cost health insurance, multicultural affairs office. *Library facilities:* Norma Perkins Hagan Memorial Library. *Online resources:* library catalog, web page, access to other libraries' catalogs. *Collection:* 206,136 titles, 25,857 serial subscriptions, 3,248 audiovisual materials.

Computer facilities: 225 computers available on campus for general student use. A campuswide network can be accessed from student residence rooms and from off campus. Online class registration is available. *Web address:* http://www.ucumberlands.edu/.

General Application Contact: Donna Stanfill, Director of Graduate Admissions, 606-539-2200 Ext. 4390, Fax: 606-539-4534, E-mail: donna.stanfill@ucumberlands.edu.

GRADUATE UNITS

Graduate Programs in Education Students: 1,198 full-time (818 women), 260 part-time (168 women); includes 44 Black or African American, non-Hispanic/Latino; 4 American Indian or Alaska Native, non-Hispanic/Latino; 7 Asian, non-Hispanic/Latino; 10 Hispanic/Latino, 2 international. Average age 33. *Faculty:* 33 full-time (15 women), 26 part-time/adjunct (12 women). Expenses: Contact institution. *Financial support:* Unspecified assistantships available. In 2010, 291 master's, 97 other advanced degrees awarded. *Degree program information:* Part-time and evening/weekend programs available. Postbaccalaureate distance learning degree programs offered. Offers all grades (P-12) (M Ed); business and marketing (MA Ed, MAT); director of pupil personnel (Certificate); director of special education (Certificate); educational administration and supervision (Ed S); educational leadership (Ed D); elementary education (MA Ed, MAT); instructional leadership—principalship (MA Ed); instructional leadership—school principal (Certificate); middle school education (MA Ed, MAT); reading and writing (MA Ed); school counseling (MA Ed); school superintendent (Certificate); secondary education (MA Ed, MAT); special education (MAT); supervisor of instruction (Certificate); teacher leader (MA Ed). *Application deadline:* Applications are processed on a rolling basis. *Application fee:* $30. Electronic applications accepted. *Application Contact:* Donna Stanfill, Director of Graduate Admissions, 606-539-4390. *Department Chair,* Dr. Robert Heffern, 800-549-2200 Ext. 4588, Fax: 606-539-4588, E-mail: robert.heffern@ucumberlands.edu.

Hutton School of Business Students: 46 full-time (16 women), 12 part-time (5 women); includes 1 Asian, non-Hispanic/Latino; 1 Hispanic/Latino, 1 international. Average age 37. *Faculty:* 1 (woman) full-time, 9 part-time/adjunct (3 women). Expenses: Contact institution. In 2010, 16 master's awarded. *Degree program information:* Part-time programs available. Postbaccalaureate distance learning degree programs offered (no on-campus study). Offers business (MBA). *Application deadline:* Applications are processed on a rolling basis. *Application fee:* $30. Electronic applications accepted. *Application Contact:* Donna Stanfil, Director, Graduate Admissions, 606-549-2200 Ext. 4496, Fax: 606-539-4534, E-mail: donna.stanfill@cumberlandcollege.edu. *Director, MBA and Business Online Programs,* Dr. Vonda Moore, 606-539-4293, E-mail: vonda.moore@ucumberlands.edu.

Program in Christian Studies Students: 9 full-time (2 women), 2 part-time (1 woman); includes 1 Black or African American, non-Hispanic/Latino. Average age 28. *Faculty:* 4 full-time (0 women), 4 part-time/adjunct (0 women). Expenses: Contact institution. *Degree program information:* Part-time and evening/weekend programs available. Postbaccalaureate distance learning degree programs offered (no on-campus study). Offers Christian studies (MA). *Application deadline:* Applications are processed on a rolling basis. *Application fee:* $30. Electronic applications accepted. *Application Contact:* Donna Stanfill, Director, Graduate Admissions, 606-549-2200 Ext. 4496, Fax: 606-539-4534, E-mail: donna.stanfill@cumberlandcollege.edu. *Director,* Dr. Keith Goforth, 606-539-4222, E-mail: macs@ucumberlands.edu.

Program in Clinical Psychology Expenses: Contact institution. *Degree program information:* Part-time and evening/weekend programs available. Postbaccalaureate distance learning degree programs offered (minimal on-campus study). Offers clinical psychology (PhD). *Application Contact:* Donna Stanfill, Director, Graduate Admissions, 606-549-2200 Ext. 4496, Fax: 606-539-4534, E-mail: donna.stanfill@cumberlandcollege.edu. *Professor,* Dr. Peter Geissler, 800-323-4574, E-mail: peter.geissler@ucumberlands.edu.

Program in Physician Assistant Studies Students: 28 full-time (18 women); includes 1 Hispanic/Latino, 1 international. Average age 27. *Faculty:* 2 full-time (1 woman), 7 part-time/adjunct (5 women). Expenses: Contact institution. Offers physician assistant studies (MPAS). *Application deadline:* Applications are processed on a rolling basis. *Application fee:* $30. Electronic applications accepted. *Application Contact:* Donna Stanfill, Director, Graduate Admissions, 606-549-2200 Ext. 4496, Fax: 606-539-4534, E-mail: donna.stanfill@cumberlandcollege.edu. *Program Director,* Dr. Eddie Perkins, 606-539-4384, E-mail: eddie.perkins@ucumberlands.edu.

Program in Professional Counseling Students: 12 full-time (10 women), 3 part-time (2 women); includes 1 Black or African American, non-Hispanic/Latino. Average age 33. *Faculty:* 2 full-time (1 woman), 2 part-time/adjunct (1 woman). Expenses: Contact institution. *Degree program information:* Part-time and evening/weekend programs available. Postbaccalaureate distance learning degree programs offered (minimal on-campus study). Offers professional counseling (MA). Program also offered in San Francisco. *Application deadline:* Applications are processed on a rolling basis. *Application fee:* $30. Electronic applications accepted. *Application Contact:* Donna Stanfill, Director, Graduate Admissions, 606-549-2200 Ext. 4496, Fax: 606-539-4534, E-mail: donna.stanfill@cumberlandcollege.edu. *Department Chair,* Dr. Dennis Trickett, 606-539-4153, E-mail: dennis.trickett@ucumberlands.edu.

UNIVERSITY OF THE DISTRICT OF COLUMBIA, Washington, DC 20008-1175

General Information District-supported, coed, comprehensive institution. CGS member. *Enrollment:* 5,518 graduate, professional, and undergraduate students; 126 full-time matriculated graduate/professional students (89 women), 81 part-time matriculated graduate/professional students (40 women). *Enrollment by degree level:* 207 master's. *Graduate faculty:* 30. Tuition, district resident: full-time $7580; part-time $421 per credit. Tuition, nonresident: full-time $14,580; part-time $810 per credit. *Required fees:* $620; $30 per credit. One-time fee: $100 part-time. *Graduate housing:* On-campus housing not available. *Student services:* Campus employment opportunities, campus safety program, career counseling, child daycare facilities, free psychological counseling, international student services, low-cost health insurance, multicultural affairs office, services for students with disabilities. *Library facilities:* Learning Resources Division Library plus 1 other. *Online resources:* library catalog, web page, access to other libraries' catalogs. *Collection:* 554,412 titles, 647 serial subscriptions.

Computer facilities: 1,586 computers available on campus for general student use. A campuswide network can be accessed. Online class registration is available. *Web address:* http://www.udc.edu/.

General Application Contact: Ann Marie Waterman, Associate Vice President for Admission, Recruitment and Financial Aid, 202-274-6110.

GRADUATE UNITS

College of Arts and Sciences *Degree program information:* Part-time and evening/weekend programs available. Offers applied statistics (MS); arts and sciences (MA, MS, MST); cancer biology, prevention and control (MS); clinical psychology (MS); counseling (MS); early childhood education (MA); English composition and rhetoric (MA); nutrition and dietetics (MS); special education (MA); speech and language pathology (MS); teaching mathematics (MST).

David A. Clarke School of Law Students: 256 full-time (151 women), 65 part-time (36 women); includes 97 Black or African American, non-Hispanic/Latino; 1 American Indian or Alaska Native, non-Hispanic/Latino; 24 Asian, non-Hispanic/Latino; 31 Hispanic/Latino. Average age 28. 1,742 applicants, 24% accepted, 131 enrolled. *Faculty:* 21 full-time (9 women), 22 part-time/adjunct (12 women). Expenses: Contact institution. *Financial support:* In 2010–11, 156 students received support, including teaching assistantships (averaging $3,500 per year); career-related internships or fieldwork, Federal Work-Study, scholarships/grants, and tuition waivers (full and partial) also available. Financial award application deadline: 5/1; financial award applicants required to submit FAFSA. In 2010, 81 first professional degrees awarded. *Degree program information:* Part-time and evening/weekend programs available. Offers clinical teaching and social justice (LL M); law (JD). *Application deadline:* For fall admission, 3/15 for domestic and international students. Applications are processed on a rolling basis. *Application fee:* $35. Electronic applications accepted. *Application Contact:* Vivian W. Canty, Assistant Dean of Admission, 202-274-7336, Fax: 202-274-5583, E-mail: vcanty@udc.edu. *Dean,* Katherine S. Broderick, 202-274-7400, Fax: 202-274-5583, E-mail: sbroderick@udc.edu.

School of Business and Public Administration *Degree program information:* Part-time and evening/weekend programs available. Offers business administration (MBA); business and public administration (MBA, MPA); public administration (MPA).

School of Engineering and Applied Science Offers computer science (MS); electrical engineering (MS); engineering and applied science (MS).

UNIVERSITY OF THE FRASER VALLEY, Abbotsford, BC V2S 7M8, Canada

General Information Province-supported, coed, comprehensive institution. *Graduate housing:* Room and/or apartments available on a first-come, first-served basis to single students. Housing application deadline: 5/15.

University of the Fraser Valley (continued)

GRADUATE UNITS

Graduate Studies *Degree program information:* Evening/weekend programs available. Offers criminal justice (MA). Electronic applications accepted.

UNIVERSITY OF THE INCARNATE WORD, San Antonio, TX 78209-6397

General Information Independent-religious, coed, comprehensive institution. *Enrollment:* 7,214 graduate, professional, and undergraduate students; 766 full-time matriculated graduate/professional students (477 women), 984 part-time matriculated graduate/professional students (613 women). *Enrollment by degree level:* 509 first professional, 1,054 master's, 187 doctoral. *Graduate faculty:* 76 full-time (40 women), 49 part-time/adjunct (26 women). *Tuition:* Part-time $725 per contact hour. *Required fees:* $890 per semester. *Graduate housing:* Room and/or apartments available on a first-come, first-served basis to single students; on-campus housing not available to married students. Typical cost: $5760 per year ($9658 including board). Room and board charges vary according to board plan. Housing application deadline: 5/1. *Student services:* Campus employment opportunities, campus safety program, career counseling, exercise/wellness program, free psychological counseling, grant writing training, international student services, low-cost health insurance, services for students with disabilities, teacher training, writing training. *Library facilities:* J.E. and M.E. Mabee Library plus 1 other. *Online resources:* library catalog, web page. *Collection:* 271,657 titles, 46,637 serial subscriptions, 14,988 audiovisual materials.

Computer facilities: Computer purchase and lease plans are available. 180 computers available on campus for general student use. A campuswide network can be accessed from student residence rooms. Online class registration is available. *Web address:* http://www.uiw.edu/.

General Application Contact: Elizabeth Levy, Graduate Admissions Counselor, 210-805-3554, Fax: 210-829-3921, E-mail: admis@uiwtx.edu.

GRADUATE UNITS

Extended Academic Programs Students: 19 full-time (9 women), 339 part-time (191 women); includes 33 Black or African American, non-Hispanic/Latino; 1 American Indian or Alaska Native, non-Hispanic/Latino; 7 Asian, non-Hispanic/Latino; 166 Hispanic/Latino, 2 international. Expenses: Contact institution. *Financial support:* Applicants required to submit FAFSA. In 2010, 119 degrees awarded. *Degree program information:* Part-time and evening/weekend programs available. Offers administration (MAA); business administration (MBA); education (M Ed, MA). *Application Contact:* Julie Weber, Director of Marketing and Recruitment, 210-832-2100, Fax: 210-829-2756, E-mail: eapadmission@uiwtx.edu. *Vice President*, Dr. Cyndi Porter, 877-603-1130, E-mail: porter@uiwtx.edu.

Feik School of Pharmacy Students: 384 full-time (264 women), 3 part-time (2 women); includes 34 Black or African American, non-Hispanic/Latino; 2 American Indian or Alaska Native, non-Hispanic/Latino; 105 Asian, non-Hispanic/Latino; 114 Hispanic/Latino, 12 international. Average age 27. *Faculty:* 34 full-time (21 women). Expenses: Contact institution. *Financial support:* Federal Work-Study and scholarships/grants available. Financial award applicants required to submit FAFSA. In 2010, 68 Pharm Ds awarded. Offers pharmacy (Pharm D). *Application deadline:* For fall admission, 1/5 for domestic students. *Application fee:* $100. *Application Contact:* Dr. Kevin Lord, Assistant Dean, Office of Student Affairs, 210-883-1060, Fax: 210-822-1521, E-mail: lord@uiwtx.edu. *Founding Dean*, Dr. Arcelia Johnson-Fannin, 210-883-1015, Fax: 210-822-1516, E-mail: johnsonf@uiwtx.edu.

School of Graduate Studies and Research Students: 241 full-time (137 women), 652 part-time (430 women); includes 64 Black or African American, non-Hispanic/Latino; 3 American Indian or Alaska Native, non-Hispanic/Latino; 19 Asian, non-Hispanic/Latino; 379 Hispanic/Latino; 2 Two or more races, non-Hispanic/Latino, 124 international. Average age 35. *Faculty:* 55 full-time (29 women), 49 part-time/adjunct (26 women). Expenses: Contact institution. *Financial support:* In 2010–11, 20 research assistantships (averaging $3,600 per year) were awarded; Federal Work-Study, scholarships/grants, and tuition waivers (partial) also available. Financial award applicants required to submit FAFSA. In 2010, 220 master's, 13 doctorates awarded. *Degree program information:* Part-time and evening/weekend programs available. Postbaccalaureate distance learning degree programs offered (no on-campus study). *Application deadline:* Applications are processed on a rolling basis. *Application fee:* $20. Electronic applications accepted. *Application Contact:* Andrea Cyterski-Acosta, Dean of Enrollment, 210-829-6005, Fax: 210-829-3921, E-mail: admis@uiwtx.edu. *Dean*, Dr. Kevin Vichcales, 210-829-3157, Fax: 210-805-3559, E-mail: vichcale@uiwtx.edu.

College of Humanities, Arts, and Social Sciences Students: 1 (woman) full-time, 23 part-time (15 women); includes 14 minority (1 Black or African American, non-Hispanic/Latino; 13 Hispanic/Latino). Average age 42. *Faculty:* 1 (woman) full-time, 1 part-time/adjunct (0 women). Expenses: Contact institution. *Financial support:* In 2010–11, 2 research assistantships were awarded; Federal Work-Study, scholarships/grants, and tuition waivers (partial) also available. Financial award applicants required to submit FAFSA. In 2010, 6 master's awarded. *Degree program information:* Part-time and evening/weekend programs available. Offers humanities, arts, and social sciences (MA); multidisciplinary studies (MA); religious studies (MA). *Application deadline:* Applications are processed on a rolling basis. *Application fee:* $20. Electronic applications accepted. *Application Contact:* Andrea Cyterski-Acosta, Dean of Enrollment, 210-829-6005, Fax: 210-829-3921, E-mail: admis@uiwtx.edu. *Dean*, Dr. Bob Connelly, 210-829-6022, Fax: 210-829-3880, E-mail: bobc@uiwtx.edu.

Dreeben School of Education Students: 16 full-time (7 women), 261 part-time (181 women); includes 28 Black or African American, non-Hispanic/Latino; 2 American Indian or Alaska Native, non-Hispanic/Latino; 2 Asian, non-Hispanic/Latino; 114 Hispanic/Latino; 1 Two or more races, non-Hispanic/Latino, 31 international. Average age 39. *Faculty:* 14 full-time (5 women), 12 part-time/adjunct (9 women). Expenses: Contact institution. *Financial support:* In 2010–11, 4 research assistantships were awarded; Federal Work-Study, scholarships/grants, and tuition waivers (partial) also available. Financial award applicants required to submit FAFSA. In 2010, 40 master's, 13 doctorates awarded. *Degree program information:* Part-time and evening/weekend programs available. Postbaccalaureate distance learning degree programs offered. Offers adult education (M Ed, MA); all-level teaching (MAT); cross-cultural education (M Ed, MA); early childhood literacy (M Ed, MA); education (M Ed, MA, MAT, PhD); elementary teaching (MAT); general education (M Ed, MA); higher education (PhD); instructional technology (M Ed, MA); international education and entrepreneurship (PhD); kinesiology (M Ed, MA); literacy (M Ed, MA); organizational leadership (PhD); organizational learning and learning (M Ed, MA); reading (M Ed, MA); secondary teaching (MAT); special education (M Ed, MA); teacher leadership (M Ed, MA). *Application deadline:* Applications are processed on a rolling basis. *Application fee:* $20. Electronic applications accepted. *Application Contact:* Andrea Cyterski-Acosta, Dean of Enrollment, 210-829-6005, Fax: 210-829-3921, E-mail: admis@uiwtx.edu. *Dean*, Dr. Denise Staudt, 210-829-2761, Fax: 210-829-2765, E-mail: staudt@uiwtx.edu.

H-E-B School of Business and Administration Students: 175 full-time (97 women), 216 part-time (123 women); includes 22 Black or African American, non-Hispanic/Latino; 1 American Indian or Alaska Native, non-Hispanic/Latino; 11 Asian, non-Hispanic/Latino; 170 Hispanic/Latino, 55 international. Average age 33. *Faculty:* 17 full-time (8 women), 27 part-time/adjunct (12 women). Expenses: Contact institution. *Financial support:* In 2010–11, 2 research assistantships were awarded; Federal Work-Study, scholarships/grants, and tuition waivers (partial) also available. Financial award applicants required to submit FAFSA. In 2010, 204 master's awarded. *Degree program information:* Part-time and evening/weekend programs available. Postbaccalaureate distance learning degree programs offered (no on-campus study). Offers accounting (MS); adult education (MAA); applied administration (MAA); business and administration (MAA, MBA, MHA, MS, Certificate); communication arts (MAA); general business (MBA); health administration (MHA); healthcare administration (MAA); instructional technology (MAA); international business (MBA, Certificate); international business strategy (MBA); nutrition (MAA); organizational development (MAA, Certificate); project management (Certificate); sports management (MAA, MBA). *Application deadline:* Applications are processed on a rolling basis. *Application fee:* $20. Electronic applications accepted. *Application Contact:* Andrea Cyterski-Acosta, Dean of Enrollment, 210-829-6005, Fax: 210-829-3921, E-mail: admis@uiwtx.edu. *Dean*, Dr. Shawn Daly, 210-829-3924, Fax: 210-805-3564, E-mail: sdaly@uiwtx.edu.

School of Interactive Media and Design Students: 9 full-time (4 women), 39 part-time (21 women); includes 3 Black or African American, non-Hispanic/Latino; 30 Hispanic/Latino; 1 Two or more races, non-Hispanic/Latino, 2 international. Average age 30. *Faculty:* 5 full-time (1 woman), 6 part-time/adjunct (all women). Expenses: Contact institution. *Financial support:* Federal Work-Study, scholarships/grants, and tuition waivers (partial) available. Financial award applicants required to submit FAFSA. In 2010, 8 master's awarded. *Degree program information:* Part-time and evening/weekend programs available. Offers communication arts (MA); interactive media and design (MA). *Application deadline:* Applications are processed on a rolling basis. *Application fee:* $20. Electronic applications accepted. *Application Contact:* Andrea Cyterski-Acosta, Dean of Enrollment, 210-829-6005, Fax: 210-829-3921, E-mail: admis@uiwtx.edu. *Dean*, Dr. Sharon Welkey, 210-829-6091, Fax: 210-829-3196, E-mail: welkey@uiwtx.edu.

School of Mathematics, Science, and Engineering Students: 16 full-time (13 women), 51 part-time (38 women); includes 2 Black or African American, non-Hispanic/Latino; 3 Asian, non-Hispanic/Latino; 30 Hispanic/Latino, 2 international. Average age 31. *Faculty:* 23 full-time (12 women), 3 part-time/adjunct (2 women). Expenses: Contact institution. *Financial support:* In 2010–11, 2 research assistantships were awarded; Federal Work-Study and scholarships/grants also available. Financial award applicants required to submit FAFSA. In 2010, 17 master's awarded. *Degree program information:* Part-time and evening/weekend programs available. Offers administration (MS); biology (MA, MS); mathematics teaching (MA); mathematics, science, and engineering (MA, MS); medical nutrition therapy (MS); multidisciplinary sciences (MA); nutrition education and health promotion (MS); nutrition services administration (MS); research statistics (MS). *Application deadline:* Applications are processed on a rolling basis. *Application fee:* $20. Electronic applications accepted. *Application Contact:* Andrea Cyterski-Acosta, Dean of Enrollment, 210-829-6005, Fax: 210-829-3921, E-mail: admis@uiwtx.edu. *Dean*, Dr. Glenn Edward James, 210-829-3152, Fax: 210-829-3153, E-mail: gjames@uiwtx.edu.

School of Nursing and Health Professions Students: 24 full-time (15 women), 61 part-time (52 women); includes 10 Black or African American, non-Hispanic/Latino; 3 Asian, non-Hispanic/Latino; 22 Hispanic/Latino, 34 international. Average age 36. *Faculty:* 12 full-time (9 women), 6 part-time/adjunct (4 women). Expenses: Contact institution. *Financial support:* Research assistantships, Federal Work-Study, scholarships/grants, and tuition waivers (partial) available. Financial award applicants required to submit FAFSA. In 2010, 10 master's awarded. *Degree program information:* Part-time and evening/weekend programs available. Offers kinesiology (MS); nursing (MSN); nursing and health professions (MS, MSN, Certificate); sport management (MS, Certificate); sport pedagogy (Certificate). *Application deadline:* Applications are processed on a rolling basis. *Application fee:* $20. Electronic applications accepted. *Application Contact:* Andrea Cyterski-Acosta, Dean of Enrollment, 210-829-6005, Fax: 210-829-3921, E-mail: admis@uiwtx.edu. *Dean*, Dr. Kathleen Light, 210-829-3982, Fax: 210-829-3174, E-mail: light@uiwtx.edu.

School of Optometry Students: 122 full-time (67 women); includes 1 Black or African American, non-Hispanic/Latino; 44 Asian, non-Hispanic/Latino; 7 Hispanic/Latino, 13 international. Average age 25. Expenses: Contact institution. *Financial support:* Federal Work-Study and scholarships/grants available. Financial award applicants required to submit FAFSA. Offers optometry (OD). *Application deadline:* For fall admission, 7/15 for domestic students. Applications are processed on a rolling basis. *Application fee:* $50. Electronic applications accepted. *Application Contact:* Kristine Benne, Director of Admissions and Student Services, School of Optometry, 210-883-1199, Fax: 210-883-1191, E-mail: optometry@uiwtx.edu. *Founding Dean*, Dr. Hani Ghazi-Birry, 210-883-1190, Fax: 210-883-1191, E-mail: optometry@uiwtx.edu.

UNIVERSITY OF THE PACIFIC, Stockton, CA 95211-0197

General Information Independent, coed, university. CGS member. *Enrollment:* 6,717 graduate, professional, and undergraduate students; 2,234 full-time matriculated graduate/professional students (1,256 women), 680 part-time matriculated graduate/professional students (396 women). *Enrollment by degree level:* 2,161 first professional, 495 master's, 254 doctoral, 4 other advanced degrees. *Graduate faculty:* 280 full-time (114 women), 269 part-time/adjunct (109 women). *Graduate housing:* Rooms and/or apartments available on a first-come, first-served basis to single and married students. Housing application deadline: 7/1. *Student services:* Campus employment opportunities, campus safety program, career counseling, free psychological counseling, international student services, low-cost health insurance, multicultural affairs office, services for students with disabilities, teacher training. *Library facilities:* University of the Pacific Library plus 1 other. *Online resources:* library catalog, web page. *Research affiliation:* Lawrence Hall of Science.

Computer facilities: A campuswide network can be accessed from student residence rooms and from off campus. Online class registration is available. *Web address:* http://www.pacific.edu/.

General Application Contact: Office of Graduate Admissions, 209-946-2344.

GRADUATE UNITS

Arthur A. Dugoni School of Dentistry Students: 513 full-time (268 women); includes 6 Black or African American, non-Hispanic/Latino; 1 American Indian or Alaska Native, non-Hispanic/Latino; 195 Asian, non-Hispanic/Latino; 29 Hispanic/Latino, 41 international. Average age 26. 3,063 applicants, 7% accepted, 139 enrolled. *Faculty:* 75 full-time (22 women), 177 part-time/adjunct (60 women). Expenses: Contact institution. *Financial support:* Institutionally sponsored loans, scholarships/grants, and stipends available. Support available to part-time students. Financial award application deadline: 3/2; financial award applicants required to submit FAFSA. In 2010, 141 DDSs, 5 master's awarded. Offers dentistry (DDS, MSD, Certificate). *Application deadline:* For fall admission, 9/15 priority date for international students. Applications are processed on a rolling basis. Electronic applications accepted. *Application Contact:* Dr. Craig S. Yarborough, Associate Dean for Institutional Advancement and Student Services, 415-929-6491. *Dean*, Dr. Arthur A. Dugoni, 415-929-6424.

College of the Pacific Students: 5 full-time (3 women), 78 part-time (44 women); includes 5 Black or African American, non-Hispanic/Latino; 14 Asian, non-Hispanic/Latino; 3 Hispanic/Latino, 8 international. Average age 25. 103 applicants, 43% accepted, 31 enrolled. *Faculty:* 40 full-time (15 women), 9 part-time/adjunct (4 women). Expenses: Contact institution. *Financial support:* Teaching assistantships, institutionally sponsored loans available. Support available to part-time students. Financial award application deadline: 3/1; financial award applicants required to submit FAFSA. In 2010, 16 master's awarded. Offers biological sciences (MS); communication (MA); psychology (MA); sport sciences (MA). *Application fee:* $75. *Application Contact:* Information Contact, 209-946-2261. *Dean*, Dr. Tom Krise, 209-946-2023.

Conservatory of Music Students: 17 full-time (13 women), 10 part-time (8 women); includes 3 Asian, non-Hispanic/Latino; 1 Hispanic/Latino, 4 international. Average age 28. 42 applicants, 48% accepted, 9 enrolled. *Faculty:* 4 full-time (3 women), 3 part-time/adjunct (2 women). Expenses: Contact institution. *Financial support:* Teaching assistantships, institutionally sponsored loans available. Support available to part-time students. Financial award application deadline: 3/1; financial award applicants required to submit FAFSA. In 2010, 3 master's awarded. Offers music (MA, MM); music education (MM); music therapy (MA). *Application deadline:* For fall admission, 3/1 priority date for domestic students; for spring admission, 10/1 priority date for domestic students. Applications are processed on a rolling basis. *Application fee:* $75. *Application Contact:* Dr. Therese West, Chairperson, 209-946-3194. *Dean*, Dr. Giulio Ongaro, 209-946-2417.

Eberhardt School of Business Students: 49 full-time (20 women), 1 (woman) part-time; includes 1 American Indian or Alaska Native, non-Hispanic/Latino; 19 Asian, non-Hispanic/Latino; 1 Hispanic/Latino, 14 international. Average age 25. 81 applicants, 60% accepted, 28 enrolled. *Faculty:* 24 full-time (7 women), 1 (woman) part-time/adjunct. Expenses: Contact institution. *Financial support:* Fellowships, research assistantships, Federal Work-Study and institutionally sponsored loans available. Support available to part-time students. Financial award application deadline: 3/1; financial award applicants required to submit FAFSA. In 2010, 28 master's awarded. *Degree program information:* Part-time programs available. Offers business (MBA). *Application deadline:* For fall admission, 7/31 priority date for domestic students; for spring admission, 11/30 for domestic students. Applications are processed on a rolling basis. *Application fee:* $75. *Application Contact:* Dr. Chris Lozano, MBA Recruiting Director, 209-946-2597, Fax: 209-946-2586, E-mail: clozano@pacific.edu. *Dean,* Dr. Richard Flaherty, 209-946-2466, Fax: 209-946-2586.

McGeorge School of Law Students: 756 full-time (362 women), 303 part-time (148 women); includes 27 Black or African American, non-Hispanic/Latino; 19 American Indian or Alaska Native, non-Hispanic/Latino; 150 Asian, non-Hispanic/Latino; 60 Hispanic/Latino, 27 international. Average age 27. 3,209 applicants, 42% accepted, 344 enrolled. *Faculty:* 49 full-time (22 women), 45 part-time/adjunct (15 women). Expenses: Contact institution. *Financial support:* Fellowships, research assistantships, teaching assistantships, career-related internships or fieldwork, Federal Work-Study, institutionally sponsored loans, and scholarships/grants available. Support available to part-time students. Financial award applicants required to submit FAFSA. In 2010, 307 first professional degrees, 36 master's awarded. *Degree program information:* Part-time and evening/weekend programs available. Offers advocacy (JD); criminal justice (JD); experiential law teaching (LL M); intellectual property (JD); international legal studies (JD); international water resources law (LL M, JSD); law (JD); public law and policy (JD); public policy and law (LL M); tax (JD); transnational business practice (LL M). *Application deadline:* For fall admission, 3/15 priority date for domestic students. Applications are processed on a rolling basis. *Application fee:* $50. Electronic applications accepted. *Application Contact:* 916-739-7105, Fax: 916-739-7301, E-mail: mcgeorge@pacific.edu. *Dean,* Elizabeth Rindskopf Parker, 916-739-7151, E-mail: elizabeth@pacific.edu.

School of Education Students: 98 full-time (68 women), 207 part-time (160 women); includes 21 Black or African American, non-Hispanic/Latino; 1 American Indian or Alaska Native, non-Hispanic/Latino; 85 Asian, non-Hispanic/Latino; 39 Hispanic/Latino, 6 international. Average age 33. 213 applicants, 78% accepted, 128 enrolled. *Faculty:* 20 full-time (11 women), 2 part-time/adjunct (1 woman). Expenses: Contact institution. *Financial support:* In 2010–11, 13 teaching assistantships were awarded; institutionally sponsored loans also available. Support available to part-time students. Financial award application deadline: 3/1; financial award applicants required to submit FAFSA. In 2010, 109 master's, 26 doctorates awarded. Offers curriculum and instruction (M Ed, MA, Ed D); education (M Ed); educational administration (MA, Ed D); educational psychology (MA, Ed D); school psychology (Ed S); special education (MA). *Application deadline:* For fall admission, 3/1 priority date for domestic students; for spring admission, 10/15 for domestic students. Applications are processed on a rolling basis. *Application fee:* $75. *Application Contact:* Office of Graduate Admissions, 209-946-2344. *Dean,* Dr. Lynn Beck, 209-946-2683, E-mail: lbeck@pacific.edu.

School of International Studies *Faculty:* 8 full-time (4 women), 1 part-time/adjunct (0 women). Expenses: Contact institution. *Financial support:* Application deadline: 3/1. In 2010, 6 master's awarded. Offers intercultural relations (MA); international studies (MA). *Application fee:* $75. *Application Contact:* Office of Graduate Admissions, 209-946-2344. *Dean,* Dr. Cynthia Weick, 209-946-2650, E-mail: mensign@pacific.edu.

School of Pharmacy and Health Sciences Students: 769 full-time (517 women), 73 part-time (32 women); includes 14 Black or African American, non-Hispanic/Latino; 4 American Indian or Alaska Native, non-Hispanic/Latino; 451 Asian, non-Hispanic/Latino; 31 Hispanic/Latino, 53 international. Average age 24. 537 applicants, 24% accepted, 74 enrolled. *Faculty:* 60 full-time (30 women), 31 part-time/adjunct (26 women). Expenses: Contact institution. *Financial support:* In 2010–11, 33 teaching assistantships were awarded; career-related internships or fieldwork, Federal Work-Study, and institutionally sponsored loans also available. Support available to part-time students. Financial award application deadline: 3/1; financial award applicants required to submit FAFSA. In 2010, 202 first professional degrees, 28 master's, 38 doctorates awarded. Offers pharmaceutical and chemical sciences (MS, PhD); pharmacy (Pharm D); pharmacy and health sciences (Pharm D, MS, DPT, PhD); physical therapy (MS, DPT); speech-language pathology (MS). *Application fee:* $75. *Application Contact:* Cyndi Porter, Outreach Officer, 209-946-3957, Fax: 209-946-2410, E-mail: cporter@pacific.edu. *Dean,* Dr. Philip Oppenheimer, 209-946-2561, Fax: 209-946-2410.

UNIVERSITY OF THE ROCKIES, Colorado Springs, CO 80903

General Information Independent, coed, graduate-only institution.

GRADUATE UNITS

Graduate Programs Offers psychology (MA, Psy D).

UNIVERSITY OF THE SACRED HEART, San Juan, PR 00914-0383

General Information Independent-religious, coed, comprehensive institution. *Graduate housing:* Room and/or apartments available on a first-come, first-served basis to single students; on-campus housing not available to married students. Housing application deadline: 5/31.

GRADUATE UNITS

Graduate Programs *Degree program information:* Part-time and evening/weekend programs available. Offers contemporary culture and media (MA); creative writing (MFA, Certificate); digital journalism (MA, Certificate); early childhood education (M Ed); editing for media (MA, Certificate); human resource management (MBA); human rights and anti-discriminatory processes (MASJ); information systems auditing (MS); information systems management (MBA); information technology (Certificate); information technology and multimedia (Certificate); instruction systems and education technology (M Ed); international marketing (MBA); management information systems (MBA); mediation and transformation of conflicts (MASJ); nonprofit organization administration (MBA); occupational health and safety (MS); occupational nursing (MSN); production and marketing of special events (Certificate); public relations (MA, Certificate); publicity (MA, Certificate); scriptwriting (MA, Certificate); taxation (MBA).

UNIVERSITY OF THE SCIENCES IN PHILADELPHIA, Philadelphia, PA 19104-4495

General Information Independent, coed, university. CGS member. *Graduate housing:* On-campus housing not available. *Research affiliation:* Progenra (molecular biology), Biotech Pharma & Device (drug delivery), Encapsulation Systems (analytical chemistry), Johnson & Johnson (cell biology), Ortho-McNeil Pharmaceuticals, Inc. (pharmacy), Polymedix (computational chemistry).

GRADUATE UNITS

College of Graduate Studies *Degree program information:* Part-time and evening/weekend programs available. Offers biochemistry (MS, PhD); bioinformatics (MS); biomedical writing (MS); cell and molecular biology (PhD); cell biology (MS); chemistry (MS, PhD); health policy (MPH, MS); health psychology (MS); medical marketing writing (Certificate); pharmaceutical business (MBA); pharmaceutics (MS, PhD); pharmacognosy (MS, PhD); pharmacology (MS, PhD); pharmacy administration (MS); public health (MPH); regulatory affairs writing (Certificate); toxicology (MS, PhD). Electronic applications accepted.

Mayes College of Healthcare Business and Policy Offers healthcare business and policy (MBA, MPH, MS, PhD, Certificate); public health (MPH).

Misher College of Arts and Sciences Offers arts and sciences (MS, PhD); cell and molecular biology (PhD).

Philadelphia College of Pharmacy Offers pharmacy (Pharm D, MS, PhD).

UNIVERSITY OF THE SOUTHWEST, Hobbs, NM 88240-9129

General Information Independent-religious, coed, comprehensive institution. *Enrollment:* 538 graduate, professional, and undergraduate students; 169 full-time matriculated graduate/professional students (125 women), 59 part-time matriculated graduate/professional students (42 women). *Enrollment by degree level:* 228 master's. *Graduate faculty:* 13 full-time (6 women), 28 part-time/adjunct (17 women). *Tuition:* Part-time $512 per credit hour. *Graduate housing:* On-campus housing not available. *Student services:* Campus employment opportunities, teacher training. *Library facilities:* Scarborough Memorial Library. *Online resources:* library catalog. *Collection:* 76,869 titles, 217 serial subscriptions, 538 audiovisual materials.

Computer facilities: 35 computers available on campus for general student use. A campuswide network can be accessed from student residence rooms. Online class registration is available. *Web address:* http://www.usw.edu/.

General Application Contact: Dr. Brad Moser, Vice President of Enrollment Services, 575-492-2116 Ext. 2116, E-mail: bmoser@usw.edu.

GRADUATE UNITS

Graduate Programs Students: 169 full-time (125 women), 59 part-time (42 women); includes 87 minority (16 Black or African American, non-Hispanic/Latino; 68 Hispanic/Latino; 3 Two or more races, non-Hispanic/Latino), 1 international. Average age 36. 94 applicants, 65% accepted, 36 enrolled. *Faculty:* 13 full-time (6 women), 28 part-time/adjunct (17 women). Expenses: Contact institution. *Financial support:* In 2010–11, 188 students received support; research assistantships with partial tuition reimbursements available, Federal Work-Study, scholarships/grants, and tuition waivers (partial) available. Support available to part-time students. Financial award application deadline: 4/1; financial award applicants required to submit FAFSA. In 2010, 41 master's awarded. *Degree program information:* Part-time and evening/weekend programs available. Postbaccalaureate distance learning degree programs offered (no on-campus study). Offers business administration (MBA); curriculum and instruction (MSE); curriculum and instruction: reading (MSE); early childhood education (MSE); educational administration (MSE); educational diagnostician (MSE); mental health counseling (MSE); school counseling (MSE); special education (MSE); sports management (MBA). *Application deadline:* For fall admission, 3/1 priority date for domestic students; for spring admission, 10/1 for domestic students. Applications are processed on a rolling basis. *Application fee:* $50. Electronic applications accepted. *Application Contact:* Melissa Mitchell, Graduate Program Advisor, 575-492-2142 Ext. 2142, Fax: 575-392-6006, E-mail: mmitchell@usw.edu. *Dean of Education,* Dr. Mary Harris, 575-492-2162 Ext. 2162, Fax: 575-392-6006, E-mail: mharris@usw.edu.

UNIVERSITY OF THE VIRGIN ISLANDS, Saint Thomas, VI 00802-9990

General Information Territory-supported, coed, comprehensive institution. *Graduate housing:* On-campus housing not available.

GRADUATE UNITS

Graduate Programs *Degree program information:* Part-time and evening/weekend programs available.

Division of Business Administration *Degree program information:* Part-time and evening/weekend programs available. Offers business administration (MBA).

Division of Education *Degree program information:* Part-time and evening/weekend programs available. Offers education (MAE).

Division of Humanities and Social Sciences *Degree program information:* Part-time and evening/weekend programs available. Offers humanities and social sciences (MPA).

Division of Science and Mathematics *Degree program information:* Part-time programs available. Postbaccalaureate distance learning degree programs offered. Offers environmental and marine science (MS); mathematics for secondary teachers (MA); science and mathematics (MA, MS).

UNIVERSITY OF THE WEST, Rosemead, CA 91770

General Information Independent, coed, comprehensive institution. *Graduate housing:* Room and/or apartments guaranteed to single students; on-campus housing not available to married students.

GRADUATE UNITS

Department of Business Administration *Degree program information:* Part-time and evening/weekend programs available. Offers business administration (EMBA); finance (MBA); information technology and management (MBA); international business (MBA); nonprofit organization management (MBA).

Department of Psychology Offers psychology (MA).

Department of Religious Studies *Degree program information:* Part-time and evening/weekend programs available. Offers Buddhist studies (MA, DBS); comparative religions (MA); religious studies (PhD).

THE UNIVERSITY OF TOLEDO, Toledo, OH 43606-3390

General Information State-supported, coed, university. CGS member. *Enrollment:* 23,085 graduate, professional, and undergraduate students; 3,340 full-time matriculated graduate/professional students (1,717 women), 1,457 part-time matriculated graduate/professional students (934 women). *Enrollment by degree level:* 687 first professional, 2,381 master's, 1,617 doctoral, 112 other advanced degrees. *Graduate faculty:* 750. Tuition, state resident: full-time $11,426; part-time $476 per credit hour. Tuition, nonresident: full-time $21,660; part-time $903 per credit hour. One-time fee: $62. *Graduate housing:* Room and/or apartments available to single students; on-campus housing not available to married students. Typical cost: $6142 per year ($9472 including board). Room and board charges vary according to board plan and housing facility selected. *Student services:* Campus employment opportunities, campus safety program, career counseling, child daycare facilities, exercise/wellness program, free psychological counseling, grant writing training, international student services, low-cost health insurance, multicultural affairs office, services for students with disabilities, teacher training, writing training. *Library facilities:* Carlson Library plus 3 others. *Online resources:* library catalog, web page, access to other libraries' catalogs. *Collection:* 2.1 million titles, 1,841 serial subscriptions, 42,941 audiovisual materials. *Research affiliation:* NASA–Glen Research Center at Lewis Field (aerospace engineering), Merck & Company, Inc. (pharmaceutical research), Midwest Astronomical Data Reduction and Analysis Facility (astronomy), Edison Industrial Systems Center (systems integration, quality control, mathematical modeling), Ohio Aerospace Institute (aerospace research), National Renewable Energy Laboratory (NREL) (thin films, photovoltaics).

Computer facilities: Computer purchase and lease plans are available. 5,000 computers available on campus for general student use. A campuswide network can be accessed from student residence rooms and from off campus. Online class registration, online transcripts, student account are available. *Web address:* http://www.utoledo.edu/.

General Application Contact: Graduate School Office, 419-530-4723, Fax: 419-530-4724, E-mail: gradsch@utnet.utoledo.edu.

GRADUATE UNITS

College of Graduate Studies Students: 2,234 full-time (1,245 women), 1,413 part-time (912 women); includes 412 minority (253 Black or African American, non-Hispanic/Latino; 4 American Indian or Alaska Native, non-Hispanic/Latino; 75 Asian, non-Hispanic/Latino; 68 Hispanic/Latino; 12 Two or more races, non-Hispanic/Latino), 721 international. Average age 30. 3,459 applicants, 43% accepted, 980 enrolled. *Faculty:* 750. Expenses: Contact institution. *Financial support:* In 2010–11, 1,425 students received support, including 729 research assistantships with full and partial tuition reimbursements available (averaging $11,089 per year), 562 teaching assistantships with full and partial tuition reimbursements available (averaging $10,432 per year); fellowships with tuition reimbursements available, career-related internships or fieldwork, Federal Work-Study, institutionally sponsored loans, scholarships/grants, traineeships, tuition waivers (full and partial), unspecified assistantships, and administrative assistantships also available. Support available to part-time students. In 2010, 975 master's, 137 doctorates, 75 other advanced degrees awarded. *Degree program information:* Part-time and evening/weekend programs available. Postbaccalaureate distance learning degree programs offered. *Application deadline:* For fall admission, 1/15 priority date for domestic and international students. Applications are processed on a rolling basis. *Application fee:* $45 ($75 for international students). Electronic applications accepted. *Application Contact:* Graduate School Office, 419-530-4723, Fax: 419-530-4724, E-mail: grdsch@utnet.utoledo.edu. *Dean,* Dr. Patricia Komuniecki, 419-530-4968, E-mail: patricia.komuniecki@utoledo.edu.

College of Business and Innovation Students: 248 full-time (99 women), 194 part-time (76 women); includes 19 Black or African American, non-Hispanic/Latino; 4 Asian, non-Hispanic/Latino; 8 Hispanic/Latino; 2 Two or more races, non-Hispanic/Latino, 169 international.

The University of Toledo (continued)

Average age 27. 254 applicants, 67% accepted, 124 enrolled. *Faculty:* 37. Expenses: Contact institution. *Financial support:* In 2010–11, 47 research assistantships with full and partial tuition reimbursements (averaging $6,967 per year) were awarded; career-related internships or fieldwork, Federal Work-Study, institutionally sponsored loans, scholarships/grants, tuition waivers (full and partial), unspecified assistantships, and administrative assistantships also available. Support available to part-time students. In 2010, 238 master's, 4 doctorates, 1 other advanced degree awarded. *Degree program information:* Part-time and evening/weekend programs available. Offers accounting (MSA); administration (MBA); business and innovation (EMBA, MBA, MSA, DME, Certificate); entrepreneurship (MBA); executive management (MBA); finance (MBA); human resource management (MBA); information systems (MBA); international business (MBA); leadership (MBA); management (MBA); manufacturing management (DME); marketing (MBA); operations management (MBA); supply chain management (Certificate). *Application deadline:* For fall admission, 1/15 priority date for domestic and international students. Applications are processed on a rolling basis. *Application fee:* $45 ($75 for international students). Electronic applications accepted. *Application Contact:* Graduate School Office, 419-530-4723, Fax: 419-530-4724, E-mail: grdsch@utnet.utoledo.edu. *Dean*, Dr. Thomas G. Gutteridge, 419-530-4060, Fax: 419-530-7260, E-mail: mba@uoft01.utoledo.edu.

College of Engineering *Degree program information:* Part-time and evening/weekend programs available. Postbaccalaureate distance learning degree programs offered (minimal on-campus study). Offers bioengineering (MS, PhD); biomedical engineering (PhD); chemical engineering (MS, PhD); civil engineering (MS, PhD); computer science (MS, PhD); electrical engineering (MS, PhD); engineering (MS, PhD); general engineering (MS); industrial engineering (MS, PhD); mechanical engineering (MS, PhD). Electronic applications accepted.

College of Language, Literature and Social Sciences Students: 171 full-time (100 women), 117 part-time (78 women); includes 45 minority (36 Black or African American, non-Hispanic/Latino; 1 American Indian or Alaska Native, non-Hispanic/Latino; 2 Asian, non-Hispanic/Latino; 5 Hispanic/Latino; 1 Two or more races, non-Hispanic/Latino), 32 international. Average age 31. 427 applicants, 40% accepted, 126 enrolled. *Faculty:* 116. Expenses: Contact institution. *Financial support:* In 2010–11, 65 research assistantships with tuition reimbursements (averaging $6,625 per year), 123 teaching assistantships with tuition reimbursements (averaging $9,923 per year) were awarded; career-related internships or fieldwork, Federal Work-Study, institutionally sponsored loans, scholarships/grants, tuition waivers (full and partial), and unspecified assistantships also available. Support available to part-time students. In 2010, 81 master's, 10 doctorates, 15 other advanced degrees awarded. *Degree program information:* Part-time programs available. Offers clinical psychology (MA, PhD); communication studies (Certificate); economics (MA); English as a second language (MA); experimental psychology (MA, PhD); French (MA); geographic information systems and applied geographics (Certificate); geography (MA); German (MA); health care administration (Certificate); history (MA, PhD); language, literature and social sciences (MA, MLS, MPA, PhD, Certificate); liberal studies (MLS); literature (MA); management of non-profit organizations (Certificate); philosophy (MA); planning (MA); political science (MA); public administration (MPA); sociology (MA); Spanish (MA); spatially-integrated social sciences (PhD); teaching of writing (Certificate). *Application deadline:* For fall admission, 1/15 priority date for domestic and international students. Applications are processed on a rolling basis. *Application fee:* $45 ($75 for international students). Electronic applications accepted. *Application Contact:* Graduate School Office, 419-530-4723, Fax: 419-530-4724, E-mail: grdsch@utnet.utoledo.edu. *Dean*, Dr. Alice Skeens, 419-530-2413, E-mail: alice.skeens@utoledo.edu.

College of Medicine and Life Sciences Students: 338 full-time (202 women), 62 part-time (40 women); includes 35 Black or African American, non-Hispanic/Latino; 24 Asian, non-Hispanic/Latino; 7 Hispanic/Latino, 51 international. Average age 27. 540 applicants, 57% accepted, 202 enrolled. *Faculty:* 129. Expenses: Contact institution. *Financial support:* In 2010–11, 144 students received support, including 117 research assistantships with full tuition reimbursements available (averaging $21,180 per year); fellowships with full tuition reimbursements available, career-related internships or fieldwork, Federal Work-Study, institutionally sponsored loans, scholarships/grants, tuition waivers (full and partial), and unspecified assistantships also available. Support available to part-time students. In 2010, 128 master's, 22 doctorates, 38 other advanced degrees awarded. *Degree program information:* Part-time and evening/weekend programs available. Offers biochemistry and cancer biology (MSBS, PhD); bioinformatics/proteomics/genomics (MSBS, Certificate); biostatistics and epidemiology (Certificate); cardiovascular and metabolic diseases (MSBS, PhD); contemporary gerontological practice (Certificate); environmental and occupational health and safety (MPH); epidemiology (MPH, Certificate); health administration (MPH); health promotion (MPH); human donation sciences (MSBS); infection, immunity, and transplantation (MSBS, PhD); medical physics (MSBS); medicine (MPH, MS, MSBS, MSOH, PhD, Certificate, PhD/MSBS); neurosciences (MSBS, PhD); nutrition (MPH); occupational health (MSOH, Certificate); oral biology (MSBS); orthopedic surgery (MSBS); pathology (Certificate); physician assistant studies (MSBS). *Application deadline:* For fall admission, 5/1 priority date for domestic and international students. Applications are processed on a rolling basis. *Application fee:* $45 ($75 for international students). Electronic applications accepted. *Application Contact:* Christine Wile, Admissions Analyst, 419-383-4116, Fax: 419-383-6140, E-mail: christine.wile@utoledo.edu. *Dean*, Dr. Jeffrey P. Gold.

College of Natural Sciences and Mathematics Students: 236 full-time (79 women), 45 part-time (30 women); includes 8 minority (3 Black or African American, non-Hispanic/Latino; 3 Asian, non-Hispanic/Latino; 2 Hispanic/Latino), 144 international. Average age 28. 408 applicants, 23% accepted, 79 enrolled. *Faculty:* 128. Expenses: Contact institution. *Financial support:* In 2010–11, 171 research assistantships with tuition reimbursements (averaging $13,285 per year), 199 teaching assistantships with tuition reimbursements (averaging $13,670 per year) were awarded; Federal Work-Study, institutionally sponsored loans, scholarships/grants, tuition waivers (full and partial), and unspecified assistantships also available. Support available to part-time students. In 2010, 32 master's, 21 doctorates awarded. *Degree program information:* Part-time programs available. Offers analytical chemistry (MS, PhD); applied mathematics (MS, PhD); biological chemistry (MS, PhD); cell biology (MS, PhD); ecology (MS, PhD); geology (MS); inorganic chemistry (MS, PhD); mathematics (MA, PhD); natural sciences and mathematics (MA, MS, PhD); organic chemistry (MS, PhD); physical chemistry (MS, PhD); physics (MS, PhD); statistics (MS, PhD). *Application deadline:* For fall admission, 1/15 priority date for domestic and international students. Applications are processed on a rolling basis. *Application fee:* $45 ($75 for international students). Electronic applications accepted. *Application Contact:* Graduate School Office, 419-530-4723, Fax: 419-530-4724, E-mail: grdsch@utnet.utoledo.edu. *Dean*, Dr. Karen Bjorkman, 419-530-7835, E-mail: karen.bjorkman@utoledo.edu.

College of Nursing Students: 99 full-time (84 women), 165 part-time (148 women); includes 10 Black or African American, non-Hispanic/Latino; 6 Asian, non-Hispanic/Latino; 5 Hispanic/Latino; 2 Two or more races, non-Hispanic/Latino, 2 international. Average age 38. 184 applicants, 55% accepted, 90 enrolled. *Faculty:* 45. Expenses: Contact institution. *Financial support:* In 2010–11, 6 students received support. Federal Work-Study, institutionally sponsored loans, scholarships/grants, traineeships, and tuition waivers (full and partial) available. In 2010, 60 master's, 7 other advanced degrees awarded. *Degree program information:* Part-time programs available. Postbaccalaureate distance learning degree programs offered (no on-campus study). Offers adult nurse practitioner (Certificate); adult nurse practitioner/clinical nurse specialist (MSN); clinical nurse leader (MSN); family nurse practitioner (MSN, Certificate); health promotions, outcomes, systems, and policy (DNP); nurse educator (MSN, Certificate); nursing (MSN, DNP, Certificate); pediatric nurse practitioner (MSN, Certificate); psychiatric-mental health clinical nurse specialist (MSN, Certificate). *Application deadline:* For fall admission, 2/1 for domestic and international students; for spring admission, 10/1 for domestic and international students. *Application fee:* $45 ($75 for international students). Electronic applications accepted. *Application Contact:* Kathleen Mitchell, Nursing Advisor, 419-383-5841, E-mail: kathleen.mitchell@utoledo.edu. *Dean*, Dr. Timothy Gaspar, 419-383-5858, E-mail: admitnurse@utoledo.edu.

College of Pharmacy Offers administrative pharmacy (MSPS); industrial pharmacy (MSPS); medicinal and biological chemistry (MS, PhD); pharmacology toxicology (MSPS); pharmacy (MS, MSPS, PhD). Electronic applications accepted.

College of Visual and Performing Arts Students: 8 full-time (2 women), 1 (woman) part-time; includes 1 minority (Hispanic/Latino), 2 international. Average age 31. 10 applicants, 40% accepted, 3 enrolled. *Faculty:* 13. Expenses: Contact institution. In 2010, 4 master's awarded. Offers music performance (MMP); visual and performing arts (MMP). *Application deadline:* For fall admission, 1/15 priority date for domestic and international students. Applications are processed on a rolling basis. *Application fee:* $45 ($75 for international students). Electronic applications accepted. *Application Contact:* Graduate School Office, 419-530-4723, Fax: 419-530-4724, E-mail: grdsch@utnet.utoledo.edu. *Dean*, Dr. Debra Davis, 419-530-2448.

Judith Herb College of Education, Health Science and Human Service Students: 656 full-time (467 women), 679 part-time (507 women); includes 137 Black or African American, non-Hispanic/Latino; 3 American Indian or Alaska Native, non-Hispanic/Latino; 18 Asian, non-Hispanic/Latino; 37 Hispanic/Latino; 7 Two or more races, non-Hispanic/Latino, 38 international. Average age 33. 1,022 applicants, 42% accepted, 332 enrolled. *Faculty:* 149. Expenses: Contact institution. *Financial support:* In 2010–11, 219 research assistantships with full and partial tuition reimbursements (averaging $9,747 per year), 206 teaching assistantships with full and partial tuition reimbursements (averaging $9,045 per year) were awarded; career-related internships or fieldwork, Federal Work-Study, institutionally sponsored loans, scholarships/grants, tuition waivers (full and partial), unspecified assistantships, and administrative assistantships also available. Support available to part-time students. In 2010, 339 master's, 64 doctorates, 13 other advanced degrees awarded. *Degree program information:* Part-time and evening/weekend programs available. Offers art education (ME); career and technical education (ME, Ed S); counselor education (MA, PhD, Ed S); criminal justice (MA); curriculum and instruction (ME, DE, PhD, Ed S); early childhood education (ME, Ed S); education and biology (MES); education and chemistry (MES); education and economics (MAE); education and English (MAE); education and French (MAE); education and geography (MAE); education and geology (MES); education and German (MAE); education and history (MAE); education and mathematics (MAE, MES); education and physics (MES); education and political science (MAE); education and sociology (MAE); education and Spanish (MAE); education, health science and human service (MA, MAE, ME, MES, MME, MSW, MSX, DE, DPT, OTD, PhD, Certificate, Ed S); educational administration and supervision (ME, DE, Ed S); educational media (DE, PhD, Ed S); educational psychology (ME, DE, PhD); educational research and measurement (ME, PhD); educational sociology (DE, PhD); educational technology (ME); educational theory and social foundations (ME); elder law (Certificate); elementary education (DE, PhD); English as a second language (MAE); exercise science (MSX, PhD); foundations of education (DE, PhD); gifted and talented (DE, PhD); health education (ME, PhD); higher education (ME, PhD); history of education (DE, PhD); middle childhood education (ME); music education (MME); occupational therapy (OTD); patient advocacy (Certificate); philosophy of education (DE, PhD); physical education (ME); physical therapy (DPT); school psychology (MA, Ed S); secondary education (ME, DE, PhD, Ed S); social work (MSW); special education (ME, DE, PhD, Ed S); speech-language pathology (MA). *Application deadline:* For fall admission, 1/15 priority date for domestic and international students. Applications are processed on a rolling basis. *Application fee:* $45 ($75 for international students). Electronic applications accepted. *Application Contact:* Graduate School Office, 419-530-4723, Fax: 419-530-4724, E-mail: grdsch@utnet.utoledo.edu. *Dean*, Dr. Beverly Schmoll, 419-530-2495, E-mail: beverly.schmoll@utoledo.edu.

College of Law *Degree program information:* Part-time and evening/weekend programs available. Offers law (JD). Electronic applications accepted.

UNIVERSITY OF TORONTO, Toronto, ON M5S 1A1, Canada

General Information Province-supported, coed, university. CGS member. *Graduate housing:* Rooms and/or apartments available on a first-come, first-served basis to single students and available to married students. *Research affiliation:* Fields Institute for Research in Mathematical Sciences, Canadian Institute for Theoretical Astrophysics, Royal Ontario Museum, Pontifical Institute of Medieval Studies, Hospital for Sick Children, Center for Addiction and Mental Health.

GRADUATE UNITS

Faculty of Dentistry Offers dental anesthesia (M Sc); dental public health (M Sc); dentistry (DDS, M Sc, PhD); endodontics (M Sc); oral and maxillofacial surgery and anesthesia (M Sc); oral pathology (M Sc); oral radiology (M Sc); orthodontics (M Sc); pediatric dentistry (M Sc); periodontology (M Sc); prosthodontics (M Sc).

Faculty of Law *Degree program information:* Part-time programs available. Offers law (JD, LL M, MSL, SJD).

Faculty of Medicine Offers medicine (MD, M Sc, M Sc BMC, M Sc OT, M Sc PT, MH Sc, PhD).

School of Graduate Studies *Degree program information:* Part-time and evening/weekend programs available. Electronic applications accepted.

Humanities Division *Degree program information:* Part-time programs available. Offers art history (MA, PhD); cinema studies (MA); classics (MA, PhD); comparative literature (MA, PhD); composition (M Mus, DMA); drama (MA, PhD); East Asian studies (MA, PhD); English (MA, PhD); French language and literature (MA, PhD); Germanic languages and literatures (MA, PhD); history (MA, PhD); history and philosophy of science and technology (MA, PhD); humanities (M Mus, MA, MM St, MVS, DMA, PhD); Italian studies (MA, PhD); linguistics (MA, PhD); medieval studies (MA, PhD); museum studies (MM St); music education (MA, PhD); musicology/theory (MA, PhD); Near and Middle Eastern civilizations (MA, PhD); performance (M Mus, DMA); philosophy (MA, PhD); religion (MA, PhD); Slavic languages and literatures (MA, PhD); South Asian studies (MA, PhD); Spanish and Portuguese (MA, PhD); visual studies (MVS); women and gender studies (MA).

Life Sciences Division *Degree program information:* Part-time programs available. Offers biochemistry (M Sc, PhD); bioethics (MH Sc); biomedical communications (M Sc BMC); biotechnology (MBiotech); cell and systems biology (M Sc, PhD); ecology and evolutionary biology (M Sc, PhD); forestry (M Sc F, MFC, PhD); genetic counseling (M Sc); health administration (MHS); health informatics (MHI); health policy, management and evaluation (M Sc, PhD); immunology (M Sc, PhD); laboratory medicine and pathobiology (M Sc, PhD); life sciences (M Sc, M Sc BMC, M Sc F, MA, MFC, MH Sc, MN, PhD); management of innovation (MMI); medical biophysics (M Sc, PhD); medical science (M Sc, PhD); molecular and medical genetics (M Sc, PhD); nursing science (MN, PhD); nutritional sciences (M Sc, PhD); occupational therapy (M Sc OT); pharmaceutical sciences (M Sc, PhD); pharmacology and toxicology (M Sc, PhD); physical education and health (M Sc, PhD); physical therapy (M Sc PT); physiology (M Sc, PhD); psychology (MA, PhD); public health sciences (M Sc, MH Sc, PhD); rehabilitation science (M Sc, PhD); speech-language pathology (M Sc, MH Sc, PhD).

Physical Sciences Division *Degree program information:* Part-time programs available. Offers aerospace science and engineering (M Eng, MA Sc, PhD); applied science and engineering (M Eng, MA Sc, MH Sc, PhD); astronomy and astrophysics (M Sc, PhD); biomedical engineering (MA Sc, PhD); chemical engineering and applied chemistry (M Eng, MA Sc, PhD); chemistry (M Sc, PhD); civil engineering (M Eng, MA Sc, PhD); clinical biomedical engineering (MH Sc); computer science (M Sc, PhD); design and manufacturing (M Eng); electrical and computer engineering (M Eng, MA Sc, PhD); environmental science (M Env Sc, PhD); geology (M Sc, MA Sc, PhD); materials science and engineering (M Eng, MA Sc, PhD); mathematical finance (MMF); mathematics (M Sc, MMF, PhD); mechanical and industrial engineering (M Eng, MA Sc, PhD); physical sciences (M Eng, M Sc, MA Sc, MH Sc, MMF, PhD); physics (M Sc, PhD); statistics (M Sc, PhD).

Social Sciences Division *Degree program information:* Part-time and evening/weekend programs available. Offers anthropology (M Sc, MA, PhD); architecture, landscape and design (M Arch, MLA, MUD); criminology (MA, PhD); economics (MA, MFE, PhD); education (M Ed, MA, MT, Ed D, PhD); European, Russian and Eurasian studies (MA); financial economics (MFE); geography (M Sc, MA, PhD); global affairs (MGA); industrial relations and human resources (MHRIR, PhD); information studies (MI St, PhD, G Dip); management (MBA, MMPA, PhD); planning (M Sc Pl); political science (MA, PhD); social sciences

(M Arch, M Ed, M Sc, M Sc Pl, MA, MBA, MFE, MHRIR, MI St, MLA, MMPA, MSW, MT, MUD, Ed D, PhD, G Dip); social work (MSW, PhD); sociology (M Ed, MA, Ed D, PhD); urban design studies (MUD).

UNIVERSITY OF TRINITY COLLEGE, Toronto, ON M5S 1H8, Canada

General Information Independent-religious, coed, graduate-only institution. *Enrollment by degree level:* 40 first professional, 37 master's, 27 doctoral. *Graduate faculty:* 3 full-time (1 woman), 31 part-time/adjunct (4 women). *Graduate housing:* Room and/or apartments available on a first-come, first-served basis to single students; on-campus housing not available to married students. Typical cost: $11,800 Canadian dollars (including board). Housing application deadline: 7/15. *Student services:* Campus employment opportunities, campus safety program, career counseling, child daycare facilities, exercise/wellness program, free psychological counseling, international student services, low-cost health insurance, multicultural affairs office, services for students with disabilities. *Library facilities:* The John W. Graham Library. *Online resources:* library catalog, web page, access to other libraries' catalogs. *Collection:* 200,000 titles, 400 serial subscriptions, 1,500 audiovisual materials.

Computer facilities: 5 computers available on campus for general student use. A campuswide network can be accessed from student residence rooms. Online class registration is available. *Web address:* http://www.trinity.utoronto.ca/.

General Application Contact: Rachel Richards, Administrative Assistant to the Dean, Faculty of Divinity, 416-978-2133, Fax: 416-978-4949, E-mail: divinity@trinity.utoronto.ca.

GRADUATE UNITS

Faculty of Divinity Students: 50 full-time (15 women), 84 part-time (39 women). Average age 45. *Faculty:* 3 full-time (1 woman), 31 part-time/adjunct (4 women). Expenses: Contact institution. *Financial support:* Fellowships, teaching assistantships, career-related internships or fieldwork, institutionally sponsored loans, and bursaries available. Support available to part-time students. Financial award application deadline: 5/15. *Degree program information:* Part-time programs available. Offers ministry (Diploma); ministry for church musicians (Diploma); theology (M Div, MA, MTS, Th M, D Min, PhD, Th D, Diploma, L Th). *Application deadline:* For fall admission, 3/31 priority date for domestic and international students; for winter admission, 12/31 for domestic and international students; for spring admission, 4/30 priority date for domestic and international students. Applications are processed on a rolling basis. *Application fee:* $0. *Application Contact:* Rachel Richards, Administrative Assistant to the Dean, 416-978-2133, Fax: 416-978-4949, E-mail: divinity@trinity.utoronto.ca. *Dean,* Dr. David Neelands, 416-978-7750, Fax: 416-978-4949, E-mail: divdean@trinity.utoronto.ca.

UNIVERSITY OF TULSA, Tulsa, OK 74104-3189

General Information Independent, coed, university. CGS member. *Enrollment:* 4,185 graduate, professional, and undergraduate students; 463 full-time matriculated graduate/professional students (205 women), 217 part-time matriculated graduate/professional students (96 women). *Enrollment by degree level:* 513 master's, 151 doctoral. *Graduate faculty:* 184 full-time (49 women), 21 part-time/adjunct (8 women). *Tuition:* Full-time $16,902; part-time $939 per credit hour. *Required fees:* $1020; $4 per credit hour. Tuition and fees vary according to course load. *Graduate housing:* Rooms and/or apartments available on a first-come, first-served basis to single and married students. Typical cost: $5060 per year ($9068 including board) for single students; $8060 per year ($12,068 including board) for married students. Room and board charges vary according to board plan, campus/location and housing facility selected. Housing application deadline: 2/1. *Student services:* Campus employment opportunities, campus safety program, career counseling, child daycare facilities, exercise/wellness program, free psychological counseling, international student services, low-cost health insurance, multicultural affairs office, services for students with disabilities, teacher training, writing training. *Library facilities:* McFarlin Library plus 1 other. *Online resources:* library catalog, web page, access to other libraries' catalogs. *Collection:* 1.1 million titles, 27,905 serial subscriptions, 20,362 audiovisual materials. *Research affiliation:* Network of Excellence in Training (NEXT) (petrophysics), Chevron Texaco (petroleum engineering).

Computer facilities: Computer purchase and lease plans are available. 900 computers available on campus for general student use. A campuswide network can be accessed from student residence rooms and from off campus. Online class registration is available. *Web address:* http://www.utulsa.edu/.

General Application Contact: Dr. Janet A. Haggerty, Associate Vice President of Research and Dean of the Graduate School, 918-631-2336, Fax: 918-631-2156, E-mail: grad@utulsa.edu.

GRADUATE UNITS

College of Law Students: 368 full-time (140 women), 38 part-time (18 women); includes 10 Black or African American, non-Hispanic/Latino; 36 American Indian or Alaska Native, non-Hispanic/Latino; 8 Asian, non-Hispanic/Latino; 14 Hispanic/Latino; 12 Two or more races, non-Hispanic/Latino, 1 international. Average age 27. 1,373 applicants, 43% accepted, 146 enrolled. *Faculty:* 28 full-time (12 women), 20 part-time/adjunct (5 women). Expenses: Contact institution. *Financial support:* In 2010–11, 176 students received support. Career-related internships or fieldwork, Federal Work-Study, and scholarships/grants available. Support available to part-time students. Financial award applicants required to submit FAFSA. In 2010, 130 first professional degrees, 6 master's awarded. *Degree program information:* Part-time programs available. Offers American Indian and indigenous law (LL M); American law for foreign lawyers (LL M); comparative and international law (Certificate); entrepreneurial law (Certificate); health law (Certificate); law (JD); Native American law (Certificate); public policy (Certificate); resources, energy, and environmental law (Certificate). *Application deadline:* For fall admission, 2/1 priority date for domestic and international students. Applications are processed on a rolling basis. *Application fee:* $30. Electronic applications accepted. *Application Contact:* April M. Fox, Assistant Dean of Admissions and Financial Aid, 918-631-2406, Fax: 918-631-3630, E-mail: april-fox@utulsa.edu. *Dean,* Janet Levit, 918-631-2400, Fax: 918-631-3126, E-mail: janet-levit@utulsa.edu.

Graduate School Students: 372 full-time (201 women), 197 part-time (84 women); includes 43 minority (9 Black or African American, non-Hispanic/Latino; 17 American Indian or Alaska Native, non-Hispanic/Latino; 7 Asian, non-Hispanic/Latino; 10 Hispanic/Latino), 202 international. Average age 28. 1,006 applicants, 42% accepted, 171 enrolled. *Faculty:* 210 full-time (64 women), 13 part-time/adjunct (5 women). Expenses: Contact institution. *Financial support:* In 2010–11, 442 students received support, including 97 fellowships with full and partial tuition reimbursements available (averaging $6,031 per year), 173 research assistantships with full and partial tuition reimbursements available (averaging $8,874 per year), 247 teaching assistantships with full and partial tuition reimbursements available (averaging $11,054 per year); career-related internships or fieldwork, Federal Work-Study, institutionally sponsored loans, scholarships/grants, traineeships, health care benefits, tuition waivers (partial), and unspecified assistantships also available. Support available to part-time students. Financial award application deadline: 2/1; financial award applicants required to submit FAFSA. In 2010, 209 master's, 28 doctorates awarded. *Degree program information:* Part-time and evening/weekend programs available. Offers anthropology (MA); general (MA); history (MA); Native American (MA). *Application deadline:* Applications are processed on a rolling basis. *Application fee:* $40. Electronic applications accepted. *Application Contact:* Graduate School, 918-631-2336, Fax: 918-631-2156, E-mail: grad@utulsa.edu. *Associate Vice President of Research and Dean of the Graduate School,* Dr. Janet A. Haggerty, 918-631-2336, Fax: 918-631-2156, E-mail: grad@utulsa.edu.

College of Arts and Sciences Students: 139 full-time (105 women), 44 part-time (32 women); includes 18 minority (4 Black or African American, non-Hispanic/Latino; 8 American Indian or Alaska Native, non-Hispanic/Latino; 2 Asian, non-Hispanic/Latino; 4 Hispanic/Latino), 12 international. Average age 30. 261 applicants, 44% accepted, 52 enrolled. *Faculty:* 59 full-time (26 women), 9 part-time/adjunct (4 women). Expenses: Contact institution. *Financial support:* In 2010–11, 134 students received support, including 30 fellowships with full and partial tuition reimbursements available (averaging $8,387 per year), 16 research assistantships with full and partial tuition reimbursements available (averaging $9,611 per year), 101 teaching assistantships with full and partial tuition reimbursements available (averaging $10,956 per year); career-related internships or fieldwork, Federal Work-Study, scholarships/grants, traineeships, health care benefits, tuition waivers (full and partial), and unspecified assistantships also available. Support available to part-time students. Financial award application deadline: 2/1; financial award applicants required to submit FAFSA. In 2010, 35 master's, 19 doctorates awarded. *Degree program information:* Part-time and evening/weekend programs available. Offers anthropology (MA); art (MTA); arts and sciences (M Ed, MA, MFA, MS, MSMSE, MTA, PhD); biology (MTA); clinical psychology (MA, PhD); education (M Ed, MA); elementary certification (M Ed); English (MTA); English language and literature (MA, MTA, PhD); history (MA, MTA); industrial/organizational psychology (MA, PhD); mathematics (MTA); mathematics and science education (MSMSE); secondary certification (M Ed); speech-language pathology (MS); teaching arts (MTA); theatre (MTA). *Application deadline:* Applications are processed on a rolling basis. *Application fee:* $40. Electronic applications accepted. *Application Contact:* Graduate School, 918-631-2336, Fax: 918-631-2156, E-mail: grad@utulsa.edu. *Dean,* Dr. Dale Thomas Benediktson, 918-631-2222, Fax: 918-631-3721, E-mail: dale-benediktson@utulsa.edu.

College of Engineering and Natural Sciences Students: 232 full-time (61 women), 75 part-time (19 women); includes 17 minority (3 Black or African American, non-Hispanic/Latino; 9 American Indian or Alaska Native, non-Hispanic/Latino; 3 Asian, non-Hispanic/Latino; 2 Hispanic/Latino), 167 international. Average age 26. 542 applicants, 35% accepted, 76 enrolled. *Faculty:* 100 full-time (10 women), 2 part-time/adjunct (1 woman). Expenses: Contact institution. *Financial support:* In 2010–11, 231 students received support, including 36 fellowships with full and partial tuition reimbursements available (averaging $4,439 per year), 151 research assistantships with full and partial tuition reimbursements available (averaging $10,677 per year), 99 teaching assistantships with full and partial tuition reimbursements available (averaging $10,018 per year); career-related internships or fieldwork, Federal Work-Study, scholarships/grants, health care benefits, tuition waivers (full and partial), and unspecified assistantships also available. Support available to part-time students. Financial award application deadline: 2/1; financial award applicants required to submit FAFSA. In 2010, 89 master's, 9 doctorates awarded. *Degree program information:* Part-time programs available. Offers biochemistry (MS); biological sciences (MS, MTA, PhD); chemical engineering (ME, MSE, PhD); chemistry (MS, PhD); computer science (MS, PhD); electrical engineering (ME, MSE); engineering and natural sciences (ME, MS, MSE, MTA, PhD); engineering physics (MS); geosciences (MS, PhD); mathematical sciences (MS, MTA); mechanical engineering (ME, MSE, PhD); petroleum engineering (ME, MSE, PhD); physics (MS). *Application deadline:* Applications are processed on a rolling basis. *Application fee:* $40. Electronic applications accepted. *Application Contact:* Graduate School, 918-631-2336, Fax: 918-631-2156, E-mail: grad@utulsa.edu. *Dean,* Dr. Steve J. Bellovich, 918-631-2288, E-mail: steven-bellovich@utulsa.edu.

Collins College of Business Students: 67 full-time (29 women), 78 part-time (33 women); includes 7 minority (1 Black or African American, non-Hispanic/Latino; 2 Asian, non-Hispanic/Latino; 4 Hispanic/Latino), 23 international. Average age 28. 189 applicants, 53% accepted, 37 enrolled. *Faculty:* 42 full-time (27 women), 2 part-time/adjunct (0 women). Expenses: Contact institution. *Financial support:* In 2010–11, 73 students received support, including 31 fellowships with full and partial tuition reimbursements available (averaging $5,267 per year), 6 research assistantships with full and partial tuition reimbursements available (averaging $9,304 per year), 38 teaching assistantships with full and partial tuition reimbursements available (averaging $10,202 per year); career-related internships or fieldwork, Federal Work-Study, institutionally sponsored loans, scholarships/grants, health care benefits, tuition waivers (full and partial), and unspecified assistantships also available. Support available to part-time students. Financial award application deadline: 2/1; financial award applicants required to submit FAFSA. In 2010, 85 master's awarded. *Degree program information:* Part-time and evening/weekend programs available. Postbaccalaureate distance learning degree programs offered (minimal on-campus study). Offers accounting (MBA); business (M Tax, MBA, MS); business administration (MBA); corporate finance (MS); energy management (MBA); finance (MBA); international business (MBA); investments and portfolio management (MS); management information systems (MBA); risk management (MS); taxation (M Tax). *Application deadline:* Applications are processed on a rolling basis. *Application fee:* $40. Electronic applications accepted. *Application Contact:* Information Contact, 918-631-2242, E-mail: graduate-business@utulsa.edu. *Dean,* Dr. W. Gale Sullenburger, 918-631-2213, E-mail: gale-sullenberger@utulsa.edu.

UNIVERSITY OF UTAH, Salt Lake City, UT 84112-1107

General Information State-supported, coed, university. CGS member. *Enrollment:* 30,819 graduate, professional, and undergraduate students; 5,666 full-time matriculated graduate/professional students (2,439 women), 1,782 part-time matriculated graduate/professional students (813 women). *Enrollment by degree level:* 1,330 first professional, 3,864 master's, 2,247 doctoral, 7 other advanced degrees. *Graduate faculty:* 1,594 full-time (508 women), 271 part-time/adjunct (176 women). *Tuition, area resident:* Part-time $179.19 per credit hour. Tuition, state resident: full-time $4384. Tuition, nonresident: full-time $16,684; part-time $630.67 per credit hour. *Required fees:* $350 per semester. Tuition and fees vary according to course load, degree level and program. *Graduate housing:* Rooms and/or apartments available on a first-come, first-served basis to single and married students. Typical cost: $3495 per year ($6734 including board) for single students; $6300 per year for married students. Room and board charges vary according to board plan and housing facility selected. Housing application deadline: 4/1. *Student services:* Campus employment opportunities, campus safety program, career counseling, child daycare facilities, exercise/wellness program, free psychological counseling, grant writing training, international student services, low-cost health insurance, multicultural affairs office, services for students with disabilities, teacher training, writing training. *Library facilities:* J. Willard Marriott Library plus 3 others. *Online resources:* library catalog, web page, access to other libraries' catalogs. *Collection:* 4.2 million titles, 68,225 serial subscriptions, 91,667 audiovisual materials. *Research affiliation:* Watson Laboratory (pharmaceutical research), Myriad Genetics (pharmaceutical research/manufacturing), Neuropsychiatric Institute (brain research, mental health and substance abuse treatment), ARUP (medical laboratory and medical research), John A. Moran Eye Center (vision treatment and research institute).

Computer facilities: 3,000 computers available on campus for general student use. A campuswide network can be accessed from student residence rooms and from off campus. Online class registration, online classes are available. *Web address:* http://www.utah.edu/.

General Application Contact: Office of Admissions, 801-581-7281, Fax: 801-585-3034, E-mail: admissionweb_grad@saff.utah.edu.

GRADUATE UNITS

Graduate School Students: 5,666 full-time (2,439 women), 1,782 part-time (813 women); includes 725 minority (56 Black or African American, non-Hispanic/Latino; 34 American Indian or Alaska Native, non-Hispanic/Latino; 256 Asian, non-Hispanic/Latino; 287 Hispanic/Latino; 31 Native Hawaiian or other Pacific Islander, non-Hispanic/Latino; 61 Two or more races, non-Hispanic/Latino), 1,081 international. Average age 31. 6,769 applicants, 44% accepted, 2055 enrolled. *Faculty:* 1,618 full-time (525 women), 258 part-time/adjunct (78 women). Expenses: Contact institution. *Financial support:* Fellowships with full and partial tuition reimbursements, research assistantships with full and partial tuition reimbursements, teaching assistantships with full and partial tuition reimbursements, career-related internships or fieldwork, Federal Work-Study, institutionally sponsored loans, scholarships/grants, traineeships, health care benefits, tuition waivers (full), and unspecified assistantships available. Support available to part-time students. Financial award application deadline: 2/1; financial award applicants required to submit FAFSA. In 2010, 353 first professional degrees, 1,571 master's, 279 doctorates awarded. *Degree program information:* Part-time and evening/weekend programs available. Offers biological chemistry (PhD); biostatistics (M Stat); biotechnology (PSM); computational science (PSM); econometrics (M Stat); educational psychology (M Stat); environmental science (PSM); mathematics (M Stat); science instrumentation (PSM); sociology (M Stat); statistics (M Stat). *Application deadline:* For fall admission, 4/1 priority date for domestic students, 4/1 for international students; for spring admission, 11/1 priority date for domestic students, 11/1 for international students. Applications are processed on a rolling basis. *Application fee:* $55 ($65 for international students). Electronic applications

University of Utah (continued)

accepted. *Application Contact:* Admissions Office, 801-581-7283, Fax: 801-585-7864, E-mail: graduate@sa.utah.edu. *Dean,* Dr. Charles A. Wight, 801-581-8796, Fax: 801-585-6749, E-mail: chuck.wight@gradschool.utah.edu.

College of Architecture and Planning Students: 153 full-time (53 women), 27 part-time (4 women); includes 14 minority (4 Asian, non-Hispanic/Latino; 6 Hispanic/Latino; 1 Native Hawaiian or other Pacific Islander, non-Hispanic/Latino; 3 Two or more races, non-Hispanic/Latino), 7 international. Average age 30. 144 applicants, 39% accepted, 52 enrolled. *Faculty:* 21 full-time (7 women), 15 part-time/adjunct (2 women). Expenses: Contact institution. *Financial support:* In 2010–11, 49 students received support, including 15 fellowships with partial tuition reimbursements available (averaging $2,875 per year), 5 research assistantships with partial tuition reimbursements available (averaging $2,875 per year), 36 teaching assistantships with partial tuition reimbursements available (averaging $2,875 per year); career-related internships or fieldwork, Federal Work-Study, and scholarships/grants also available. Financial award application deadline: 2/1; financial award applicants required to submit FAFSA. In 2010, 63 master's awarded. *Degree program information:* Part-time programs available. Offers architectural studies (MS); architecture (M Arch); architecture and planning (M Arch, MCMP, MS, PhD); city and metropolitan planning (MCMP); metropolitan planning, policy and design (PhD). *Application fee:* $55 ($65 for international students). Electronic applications accepted. *Application Contact:* Kassy Keen, Admissions and Academic Advisor, 801-581-7175, E-mail: advisor@arch.utah.edu. *Director,* Prof. Brenda Scheer, 801-581-8254, Fax: 801-581-8217, E-mail: scheer@arch.utah.edu.

College of Education Students: 278 full-time (204 women), 276 part-time (189 women); includes 101 minority (8 Black or African American, non-Hispanic/Latino; 9 American Indian or Alaska Native, non-Hispanic/Latino; 15 Asian, non-Hispanic/Latino; 52 Hispanic/Latino; 7 Native Hawaiian or other Pacific Islander, non-Hispanic/Latino; 10 Two or more races, non-Hispanic/Latino), 13 international. Average age 34. 417 applicants, 38% accepted, 116 enrolled. *Faculty:* 67 full-time (40 women), 9 part-time/adjunct (7 women). Expenses: Contact institution. *Financial support:* Fellowships with full tuition reimbursements, research assistantships with full tuition reimbursements, teaching assistantships with full and partial tuition reimbursements, career-related internships or fieldwork, Federal Work-Study, institutionally sponsored loans, scholarships/grants, tuition waivers (full and partial), and unspecified assistantships available. Support available to part-time students. Financial award application deadline: 2/1; financial award applicants required to submit FAFSA. In 2010, 148 master's, 32 doctorates awarded. *Degree program information:* Part-time and evening/weekend programs available. Offers counseling psychology (PhD); early childhood hearing impairments (M Ed, MS); early childhood special education (M Ed, PhD); early childhood vision impairments (M Ed, MS); education (M Ed, M Phil, M Stat, MA, MAT, MS, Ed D, PhD); education, culture, and society (M Ed, MA, MS, PhD); educational leadership and policy (M Ed, M Phil, Ed D, PhD); educational psychology (MA); elementary education (MAT); hearing impairments (M Ed, MS); instructional design and educational technology (M Ed); learning and cognition (MS, PhD); mild/moderate disabilities (M Ed, MS, PhD); professional counseling (MS); professional practice (M Ed); professional psychology (M Ed); reading and literacy (M Ed, PhD); research in special education (MS); school counseling (M Ed, MS); school psychology (MS, PhD); secondary education (MAT); severe disabilities (M Ed, MS, PhD); statistics (M Stat); teaching and learning (M Ed, M Phil, MA, MS, PhD); vision impairments (M Ed). *Application deadline:* For fall admission, 2/15 priority date for domestic and international students; for spring admission, 11/1 for domestic and international students. Applications are processed on a rolling basis. *Application fee:* $55 ($65 for international students). Electronic applications accepted. *Application Contact:* Mindy Jones, Executive Secretary, College Dean's Office, 801-581-8222, Fax: 801-581-5223, E-mail: mindy.jones@utah.edu. *Dean,* Michael Hardman, 801-581-8121, Fax: 801-585-6476, E-mail: michael.hardman@utah.edu.

College of Engineering Students: 688 full-time (90 women), 260 part-time (29 women); includes 47 minority (3 Black or African American, non-Hispanic/Latino; 1 American Indian or Alaska Native, non-Hispanic/Latino; 27 Asian, non-Hispanic/Latino; 15 Hispanic/Latino; 1 Two or more races, non-Hispanic/Latino), 360 international. Average age 28. 758 applicants, 55% accepted, 273 enrolled. *Faculty:* 153 full-time (19 women), 15 part-time/adjunct (0 women). Expenses: Contact institution. *Financial support:* Applicants required to submit FAFSA. In 2010, 210 master's, 60 doctorates awarded. Offers bioengineering (MS, PhD); chemical engineering (ME, MS, PhD); civil engineering (MS, PhD); computational engineering and science (MS); computer science (M Phil, MS, PhD); computing (MS, PhD); electrical engineering (ME, MS, PhD); engineering (M Phil, ME, MS, PhD); environmental engineering (MS, PhD); materials science and engineering (MS, PhD); mechanical engineering (M Phil, MS, PhD); nuclear engineering (ME, MS, PhD). *Application deadline:* Applications are processed on a rolling basis. *Application fee:* $55 ($65 for international students). *Application Contact:* Dianne Leonard, Coordinator, Administrative Program, 801-585-7769, Fax: 801-581-8692, E-mail: dleonard@coe.utah.edu. *Dean,* Dr. Richard B. Brown, 801-581-6912, E-mail: brown@coe.utah.edu.

College of Fine Arts Students: 153 full-time (97 women), 41 part-time (21 women); includes 19 minority (2 American Indian or Alaska Native, non-Hispanic/Latino; 6 Asian, non-Hispanic/Latino; 9 Hispanic/Latino; 1 Native Hawaiian or other Pacific Islander, non-Hispanic/Latino; 1 Two or more races, non-Hispanic/Latino), 28 international. Average age 30. 241 applicants, 43% accepted, 77 enrolled. *Faculty:* 85 full-time (38 women), 30 part-time/adjunct (7 women). Expenses: Contact institution. *Financial support:* Applicants required to submit FAFSA. In 2010, 52 master's, 3 doctorates awarded. Offers art history (MA); ballet (MFA); ceramics (MFA); community-based art education (MFA); drawing (MFA); film studies (MFA); fine arts (M Mus, MA, MFA, DMA, PhD); graphic design (MFA); modern dance (MFA); music (M Mus, MA, DMA, PhD); painting (MFA); photography/digital imaging (MFA); printmaking (MFA); sculpture/intermedia (MFA). *Application fee:* $55 ($65 for international students). *Application Contact:* Brent Lee Schneider, Associate Dean, 801-587-9811, Fax: 801-585-3066, E-mail: brent.schneider@utah.edu. *Dean and Associate Vice-President for the Arts,* Dr. Raymond Tymas Jones, 801-581-6764, Fax: 801-581-3066, E-mail: r.tymasjones@utah.edu.

College of Health Students: 482 full-time (302 women), 86 part-time (49 women); includes 42 minority (1 Black or African American, non-Hispanic/Latino; 2 American Indian or Alaska Native, non-Hispanic/Latino; 13 Asian, non-Hispanic/Latino; 19 Hispanic/Latino; 1 Native Hawaiian or other Pacific Islander, non-Hispanic/Latino; 6 Two or more races, non-Hispanic/Latino), 34 international. Average age 30. 871 applicants, 35% accepted, 201 enrolled. *Faculty:* 68 full-time (38 women), 5 part-time/adjunct (3 women). Expenses: Contact institution. *Financial support:* Applicants required to submit FAFSA. In 2010, 137 master's, 16 doctorates awarded. Offers audiology (Au D, PhD); exercise and sport science (MS, PhD); health (M Phil, MA, MOT, MS, Au D, DPT, Ed D, OTD, PhD, PPDPT); health promotion and education (M Phil, MS, Ed D, PhD); nutrition (MS); occupational therapy (MOT, OTD); parks, recreation, and tourism (M Phil, MS, Ed D, PhD); physical therapy (DPT, PPDPT); rehabilitation sciences (PhD); speech-language pathology (MA, MS, PhD). *Application deadline:* Applications are processed on a rolling basis. *Application fee:* $55 ($65 for international students). *Application Contact:* Shari A. Lindsey, Academic Advising Coordinator, 801-585-5764, Fax: 801-581-5580, E-mail: shari.lindsey@health.utah.edu. *Dean,* Dr. James E. Graves, 801-581-8537, Fax: 801-581-5580, E-mail: james.graves@health.utah.edu.

College of Humanities Students: 248 full-time (146 women), 163 part-time (81 women); includes 35 minority (2 Black or African American, non-Hispanic/Latino; 2 American Indian or Alaska Native, non-Hispanic/Latino; 13 Asian, non-Hispanic/Latino; 14 Hispanic/Latino; 1 Native Hawaiian or other Pacific Islander, non-Hispanic/Latino; 3 Two or more races, non-Hispanic/Latino), 34 international. Average age 33. 657 applicants, 30% accepted, 124 enrolled. *Faculty:* 152 full-time (71 women), 4 part-time/adjunct (0 women). Expenses: Contact institution. *Financial support:* In 2010–11, 133 students received support, including 40 fellowships with full and partial tuition reimbursements available (averaging $13,000 per year), 3 research assistantships with full and partial tuition reimbursements available (averaging $11,500 per year), 148 teaching assistantships with full and partial tuition reimbursements available (averaging $11,500 per year); career-related internships or fieldwork, Federal Work-Study, institutionally sponsored loans, scholarships/grants, and health care benefits also available. Financial award application deadline: 2/1; financial award applicants required to submit FAFSA. In 2010, 61 master's, 18 doctorates awarded. *Degree program information:* Part-time programs available. Offers American studies (PhD); anthropology (MA); applied linguistics (MA, PhD); Arabic (MA, PhD); Arabic and linguistics (MA, PhD); Asian studies (MA); British American literature (MA, PhD); communication (MA, MS, PhD); comparative literary and cultural studies (MA, PhD); creative writing (MA, MFA, PhD); French (MA, MALP); German (MA, MALP, PhD); Hebrew (MA); history (MA, PhD); humanities (MA, MALP, MAT, MFA, MS, PhD); linguistics (MA, PhD); literature (PhD); Persian (MA, PhD); philosophy (MA, MS, PhD); political science (MA, PhD); rhetoric and composition (PhD); rhetoric/composition (MA, PhD); Spanish (MA, MALP, PhD); Turkish (MA); world languages with secondary teaching licensure (MA). *Application deadline:* For fall admission, 4/1 for domestic and international students; for spring admission, 11/1 for domestic and international students. Applications are processed on a rolling basis. *Application fee:* $55 ($65 for international students). Electronic applications accepted. *Application Contact:* Dr. Mark Bergstrom, Associate Dean, 801-581-6214, Fax: 801-585-5190, E-mail: mark.bergstrom@utah.edu. *Dean and Associate Vice President of Interdisciplinary Studies,* Dr. Robert D. Newman, 801-581-6214, Fax: 801-585-5190, E-mail: robert.newman@utah.edu.

College of Mines and Earth Sciences Students: 129 full-time (35 women), 46 part-time (12 women); includes 8 minority (3 Asian, non-Hispanic/Latino; 5 Hispanic/Latino), 69 international. Average age 29. 227 applicants, 33% accepted, 40 enrolled. *Faculty:* 43 full-time (5 women), 8 part-time/adjunct (1 woman). Expenses: Contact institution. *Financial support:* In 2010–11, 8 fellowships (averaging $15,000 per year) were awarded; research assistantships, teaching assistantships, career-related internships or fieldwork and institutionally sponsored loans also available. Support available to part-time students. Financial award application deadline: 2/15; financial award applicants required to submit FAFSA. In 2010, 28 master's, 12 doctorates awarded. *Degree program information:* Part-time programs available. Offers atmospheric sciences (MS, PhD); environmental engineering (ME, MS, PhD); geological engineering (ME, MS, PhD); geology (MS, PhD); geophysics (MS, PhD); metallurgical engineering (ME, MS, PhD); mines and earth sciences (ME, MS, PhD); mining engineering (ME, MS, PhD). *Application deadline:* For fall admission, 4/1 for domestic and international students; for spring admission, 11/1 for domestic and international students. *Application fee:* $55 ($65 for international students). Electronic applications accepted. *Application Contact:* Sharon P. Christenson, Executive Assistant to the Dean, 801-585-9344, Fax: 801-581-5560, E-mail: sharon.christenson@utah.edu. *Dean,* Dr. Francis H. Brown, 801-581-8767, Fax: 801-581-5560, E-mail: frank.brown@utah.edu.

College of Nursing Students: 218 full-time (179 women), 101 part-time (89 women); includes 36 minority (4 Black or African American, non-Hispanic/Latino; 2 American Indian or Alaska Native, non-Hispanic/Latino; 11 Asian, non-Hispanic/Latino; 17 Hispanic/Latino; 2 Two or more races, non-Hispanic/Latino), 11 international. Average age 40. 239 applicants, 50% accepted, 95 enrolled. *Faculty:* 48 full-time (41 women), 20 part-time/adjunct (18 women). Expenses: Contact institution. *Financial support:* In 2010–11, 124 students received support, including 105 fellowships with full and partial tuition reimbursements available (averaging $6,060 per year), 6 research assistantships with full tuition reimbursements available (averaging $6,500 per year), 13 teaching assistantships with partial tuition reimbursements available (averaging $4,025 per year); scholarships/grants, traineeships, health care benefits, and unspecified assistantships also available. Support available to part-time students. Financial award application deadline: 3/15; financial award applicants required to submit FAFSA. In 2010, 38 master's, 6 doctorates awarded. *Degree program information:* Part-time programs available. Postbaccalaureate distance learning degree programs offered (minimal on-campus study). Offers gerontology (MS, Certificate); nursing (MS, DNP, PhD, Certificate). *Application deadline:* For fall admission, 1/15 priority date for domestic and international students; for spring admission, 11/1 for domestic and international students. *Application fee:* $55 ($65 for international students). Electronic applications accepted. *Application Contact:* Dr. Liz Leckie, Graduate Adviser, 801-585-6658, Fax: 801-585-9705, E-mail: liz.leckie@nurs.utah.edu. *Dean,* Dr. Maureen Keefe, 801-581-8262, Fax: 801-581-4642, E-mail: maureen.keefe@nurs.utah.edu.

College of Pharmacy Students: 268 full-time (129 women), 21 part-time (9 women); includes 32 minority (2 Black or African American, non-Hispanic/Latino; 1 American Indian or Alaska Native, non-Hispanic/Latino; 20 Asian, non-Hispanic/Latino; 7 Hispanic/Latino; 1 Native Hawaiian or other Pacific Islander, non-Hispanic/Latino; 1 Two or more races, non-Hispanic/Latino), 32 international. Average age 28. 319 applicants, 26% accepted, 73 enrolled. *Faculty:* 55 full-time (18 women), 44 part-time/adjunct (22 women). Expenses: Contact institution. *Financial support:* Federal Work-Study, institutionally sponsored loans, and scholarships/grants available. In 2010, 44 first professional degrees, 1 master's, 11 doctorates awarded. Offers medicinal chemistry (MS, PhD); pharmaceutics and pharmaceutical chemistry (MS, PhD); pharmacology and toxicology (PhD); pharmacotherapy (MS); pharmacy (Pharm D, MS, PhD). *Application deadline:* For fall admission, 12/1 for domestic and international students. *Application fee:* $55 ($65 for international students). Electronic applications accepted. *Application Contact:* Dr. Mark A. Munger, Associate Dean for Academic Affairs, 801-581-6731, Fax: 801-581-3716, E-mail: pharmd.admissions@pharm.utah.edu. *Interim Dean,* Dr. Chris M. Ireland, 801-581-6731.

College of Science Students: 360 full-time (107 women), 99 part-time (43 women); includes 27 minority (3 Black or African American, non-Hispanic/Latino; 9 Asian, non-Hispanic/Latino; 10 Hispanic/Latino; 1 Native Hawaiian or other Pacific Islander, non-Hispanic/Latino; 4 Two or more races, non-Hispanic/Latino), 146 international. Average age 29. 316 applicants, 41% accepted, 99 enrolled. *Faculty:* 155 full-time (21 women), 7 part-time/adjunct (0 women). Expenses: Contact institution. *Financial support:* Fellowships with full tuition reimbursements, research assistantships with full and partial tuition reimbursements, teaching assistantships with full and partial tuition reimbursements, career-related internships or fieldwork, Federal Work-Study, institutionally sponsored loans, scholarships/grants, traineeships, and health care benefits available. Financial award application deadline: 2/15; financial award applicants required to submit FAFSA. In 2010, 32 master's, 46 doctorates awarded. *Degree program information:* Part-time programs available. Offers biology (MS, PhD); chemical physics (PhD); chemistry (M Phil, MA, MS, PhD); mathematics (M Stat, MA, MS, PhD); medical physics (MS, PhD); physics (MA, MS, PhD); physics teaching (PhD); science (M Phil, M Stat, MA, MS, PhD); science teacher education (MS). *Application deadline:* For fall admission, 4/1 for domestic and international students; for spring admission, 11/1 for domestic and international students. Applications are processed on a rolling basis. *Application fee:* $55 ($65 for international students). *Application Contact:* Lisa Batchelder, Administrative Program Coordinator, 801-581-6958, E-mail: office@science.utah.edu. *Dean,* Pierre V. Sokolsky, 801-581-6958, Fax: 801-585-3169, E-mail: sokolsky@science.utah.edu.

College of Social and Behavioral Science Students: 356 full-time (172 women), 259 part-time (108 women); includes 55 minority (4 Black or African American, non-Hispanic/Latino; 1 American Indian or Alaska Native, non-Hispanic/Latino; 17 Asian, non-Hispanic/Latino; 25 Hispanic/Latino; 3 Native Hawaiian or other Pacific Islander, non-Hispanic/Latino; 5 Two or more races, non-Hispanic/Latino), 104 international. Average age 33. 842 applicants, 40% accepted, 234 enrolled. *Faculty:* 137 full-time (49 women), 13 part-time/adjunct (6 women). Expenses: Contact institution. *Financial support:* Fellowships, research assistantships, teaching assistantships, career-related internships or fieldwork, Federal Work-Study, and institutionally sponsored loans available. Support available to part-time students. Financial award application deadline: 2/1; financial award applicants required to submit FAFSA. In 2010, 133 master's, 24 doctorates awarded. *Degree program information:* Part-time programs available. Offers anthropology (M Phil, MA, MS, PhD); clinical psychology (PhD); early childhood education (M Ed); econometrics (M Stat); economics (M Phil, MA, MS, PhD); geography (MA, MS, PhD); human development and social policy (MS); international affairs and global enterprise (MS); political science (MA, MS, PhD); psychology (PhD); public administration (Exec MPA, MPA); public policy (MPP); social and behavioral science (Exec MPA, M Ed, M Phil, M Stat, MA, MPA, MPP, MS, PhD, Certificate); sociology (M Stat, MA, MS, PhD). *Application deadline:* Applications are processed on a rolling basis. *Application fee:* $55 ($65 for international students). *Application Contact:* Stephen E.

Reynolds, Associate Dean, 801-581-8620, Fax: 801-585-5081, E-mail: stephen.reynolds@csbs.utah.edu. *Dean,* Dr. M. David Rudd, 801-581-8620, Fax: 801-585-5081, E-mail: david.rudd@csbs.utah.edu.

College of Social Work Students: 307 full-time (230 women), 77 part-time (56 women); includes 50 minority (5 Black or African American, non-Hispanic/Latino; 6 American Indian or Alaska Native, non-Hispanic/Latino; 2 Asian, non-Hispanic/Latino; 27 Hispanic/Latino; 3 Native Hawaiian or other Pacific Islander, non-Hispanic/Latino; 7 Two or more races, non-Hispanic/Latino), 8 international. Average age 34. 380 applicants, 44% accepted, 106 enrolled. *Faculty:* 30 full-time (17 women), 5 part-time/adjunct (3 women). Expenses: Contact institution. *Financial support:* In 2010–11, 158 fellowships with full and partial tuition reimbursements (averaging $3,500 per year), 34 research assistantships with full and partial tuition reimbursements (averaging $7,000 per year), 6 teaching assistantships with full and partial tuition reimbursements (averaging $5,000 per year) were awarded; Federal Work-Study and institutionally sponsored loans also available. Support available to part-time students. Financial award application deadline: 3/15; financial award applicants required to submit FAFSA. In 2010, 147 master's, 6 doctorates awarded. *Degree program information:* Part-time programs available. Postbaccalaureate distance learning degree programs offered (minimal on-campus study). Offers social work (MSW, PhD). *Application deadline:* For fall admission, 4/1 for domestic and international students; for spring admission, 11/1 for domestic and international students. Applications are processed on a rolling basis. *Application fee:* $55 ($65 for international students). *Application Contact:* Dr. Mary Jane Taylor, Associate Dean, 801-581-8828, Fax: 801-585-3219, E-mail: maryjane.taylor@socwk.utah.edu. *Dean,* Dr. Jannah H. Mather, 801-581-6194, Fax: 801-585-3219, E-mail: jannah.mather@socwk.utah.edu.

David Eccles School of Business Students: 796 full-time (174 women), 99 part-time (31 women); includes 75 minority (5 Black or African American, non-Hispanic/Latino; 3 American Indian or Alaska Native, non-Hispanic/Latino; 37 Asian, non-Hispanic/Latino; 23 Hispanic/Latino; 7 Two or more races, non-Hispanic/Latino), 90 international. Average age 31. 1,340 applicants, 49% accepted, 464 enrolled. *Faculty:* 69 full-time (21 women), 1 part-time/adjunct (0 women). Expenses: Contact institution. *Financial support:* In 2010–11, 50 students received support, including 8 fellowships with partial tuition reimbursements available, 13 teaching assistantships with partial tuition reimbursements available; career-related internships or fieldwork and health care benefits also available. Financial award applicants required to submit FAFSA. In 2010, 383 master's, 8 doctorates awarded. *Degree program information:* Part-time and evening/weekend programs available. Offers accounting (M Acc, PhD); business (EMBA, M Acc, M Stat, MBA, MHA, MRED, MS, PMBA, PhD); business administration (EMBA, MBA, PMBA); finance (MS, PhD); healthcare administration (MHA, MS); information systems (MS); real estate development (MRED); statistics (M Stat). *Application fee:* $55 ($65 for international students). Electronic applications accepted. *Application Contact:* Andrea Chmelik, Program Coordinator, 801-581-7785, Fax: 801-581-3666, E-mail: andrea.chmelik@business.utah.edu. *Dean,* Dr. Taylor Randall, 801-587-3860, Fax: 801-581-3074, E-mail: dean@business.utah.edu.

School of Medicine Offers biochemistry (MS, PhD); biostatistics (M Stat); experimental pathology (PhD); human genetics (MS, PhD); laboratory medicine and biomedical science (MS); medical informatics (MS, PhD, Certificate); medicine (MD, M Phil, M Stat, MPAS, MPH, MS, MSPH, PhD, Certificate); molecular biology (PhD); neurobiology and anatomy (PhD); neuroscience (PhD); oncological sciences (M Phil, MS, PhD); physician assistant (MPAS); physiology (PhD); public health (MPH, MSPH, PhD).

S. J. Quinney College of Law Students: 400 full-time (172 women), 5 part-time (1 woman); includes 43 minority (3 Black or African American, non-Hispanic/Latino; 2 American Indian or Alaska Native, non-Hispanic/Latino; 11 Asian, non-Hispanic/Latino; 21 Hispanic/Latino; 2 Native Hawaiian or other Pacific Islander, non-Hispanic/Latino; 4 Two or more races, non-Hispanic/Latino), 3 international. Average age 29. 1,130 applicants, 32% accepted, 122 enrolled. *Faculty:* 38 full-time (11 women), 13 part-time/adjunct (4 women). Expenses: Contact institution. *Financial support:* In 2010–11, 167 students received support, including 45 fellowships with full and partial tuition reimbursements available (averaging $1,332 per year), 2 research assistantships with partial tuition reimbursements available (averaging $5,000 per year); career-related internships or fieldwork, Federal Work-Study, institutionally sponsored loans, and scholarships/grants also available. Financial award application deadline: 3/15; financial award applicants required to submit FAFSA. In 2010, 120 first professional degrees awarded. Offers law (JD, LL M). *Application deadline:* For fall admission, 2/1 for domestic and international students. Applications are processed on a rolling basis. *Application fee:* $60. *Application Contact:* Reyes Aguilar, Associate Dean for Admission and Financial Aid, 801-581-7479, Fax: 801-581-6897, E-mail: aguilarr@law.utah.edu. *Dean,* Hiram E. Chodosh, 801-581-6833, Fax: 801-581-6897.

UNIVERSITY OF VERMONT, Burlington, VT 05405

General Information State-supported, coed, university. CGS member. *Enrollment:* 13,554 graduate, professional, and undergraduate students; 1,932 matriculated graduate/professional students (1,134 women). *Enrollment by degree level:* 446 first professional, 943 master's, 543 doctoral. *Graduate faculty:* 702 full-time, 604 part-time/adjunct. Tuition, state resident: part-time $537 per credit hour. Tuition, nonresident: part-time $1355 per credit hour. *Graduate housing:* Rooms and/or apartments available on a first-come, first-served basis to single and married students. *Student services:* Career counseling, free psychological counseling, low-cost health insurance. *Library facilities:* Bailey-Howe Library plus 2 others. *Online resources:* library catalog, web page. *Collection:* 2.6 million titles, 20,093 serial subscriptions, 55,310 audiovisual materials. *Research affiliation:* Miner Institute (animal sciences).

Computer facilities: Computer purchase and lease plans are available. 850 computers available on campus for general student use. A campuswide network can be accessed from student residence rooms and from off campus. Online class registration, Web pages, online course support are available. *Web address:* http://www.uvm.edu/.

General Application Contact: Ralph Swenson, Director of Graduate Admissions, 802-656-2699, Fax: 802-656-0519, E-mail: graduate.admissions@uvm.edu.

GRADUATE UNITS

College of Medicine Students: 539 (280 women); includes 6 Black or African American, non-Hispanic/Latino; 51 Asian, non-Hispanic/Latino; 41 Hispanic/Latino, 25 international. 5,675 applicants, 5% accepted, 135 enrolled. *Faculty:* 284 full-time (59 women). Expenses: Contact institution. *Financial support:* Fellowships, research assistantships, teaching assistantships, Federal Work-Study available. In 2010, 108 first professional degrees, 3 master's, 4 doctorates awarded. Offers biochemistry (MS, PhD); clinical and translational science (MS, PhD); medicine (MD, MS, PhD); microbiology and molecular genetics (MS, PhD); molecular physiology and biophysics (MS, PhD); neuroscience (PhD); pathology (MS); pharmacology (MS, PhD). *Application deadline:* Applications are processed on a rolling basis. *Application Contact:* Dr. Frederick Morin, Dean, 802-656-2156. *Dean,* Dr. Frederick Morin, 802-656-2156.

Graduate College Students: 1,490 (908 women); includes 23 Black or African American, non-Hispanic/Latino; 8 American Indian or Alaska Native, non-Hispanic/Latino; 50 Asian, non-Hispanic/Latino; 50 Hispanic/Latino, 138 international. 2,573 applicants, 40% accepted, 345 enrolled. *Faculty:* 361. Expenses: Contact institution. *Financial support:* Fellowships, research assistantships, teaching assistantships, career-related internships or fieldwork, Federal Work-Study, traineeships, tuition waivers (full and partial), and analytical assistantships available. Support available to part-time students. In 2010, 372 master's, 112 doctorates awarded. *Degree program information:* Part-time programs available. Offers cell and molecular biology (MS, PhD). *Application deadline:* For fall admission, 4/1 priority date for domestic and international students; for spring admission, 11/15 priority date for domestic and international students. Applications are processed on a rolling basis. *Application fee:* $40. Electronic applications accepted. *Application Contact:* Dr. Domenico Grasso, Dean, 802-656-3160, Fax: 802-656-0519, E-mail: graduate.admissions@uvm.edu. *Dean,* Dr. Domenico Grasso, 802-656-3160, Fax: 802-656-0519, E-mail: graduate.admissions@uvm.edu.

College of Agriculture and Life Sciences Students: 146 (81 women); includes 1 Black or African American, non-Hispanic/Latino; 6 Asian, non-Hispanic/Latino; 1 Hispanic/Latino, 19 international. 206 applicants, 43% accepted, 32 enrolled. Expenses: Contact institution. *Financial support:* Fellowships, research assistantships, teaching assistantships, career-related internships or fieldwork, Federal Work-Study, and tuition waivers (full and partial) available. Financial award application deadline: 3/1. In 2010, 42 master's, 4 doctorates awarded. *Degree program information:* Part-time programs available. Offers agriculture and life sciences (MPA, MS, MSD, PhD); animal sciences (MS, PhD); animal, nutrition and food sciences (PhD); community development and applied economics (MS); dietetics (MSD); field naturalist (MS); microbiology and molecular genetics (MS, PhD); nutritional sciences (MS); plant and soil science (MS, PhD); plant biology (MS, PhD); public administration (MPA). *Application fee:* $40. Electronic applications accepted. *Application Contact:* Dr. Thomas C. Vogelmann, Dean, 802-656-2980. *Dean,* Dr. Thomas C. Vogelmann, 802-656-2980.

College of Arts and Sciences Students: 276 (163 women); includes 3 Black or African American, non-Hispanic/Latino; 4 American Indian or Alaska Native, non-Hispanic/Latino; 4 Asian, non-Hispanic/Latino; 12 Hispanic/Latino, 27 international. 683 applicants, 30% accepted, 81 enrolled. Expenses: Contact institution. *Financial support:* Fellowships, research assistantships, teaching assistantships, career-related internships or fieldwork and Federal Work-Study available. In 2010, 52 master's, 26 doctorates awarded. *Degree program information:* Part-time programs available. Offers arts and sciences (MA, MAT, MS, MST, PhD); biology (MS, PhD); biology education (MST); chemistry (MS, PhD); clinical psychology (PhD); communication sciences (MS); English (MA); French (MA); geology (MS); German (MA); Greek (MA); Greek and Latin (MAT); historic preservation (MS); history (MA); Latin (MA); physics (MS); psychology (PhD). *Application fee:* $40. Electronic applications accepted. *Application Contact:* . Dr. Eleanor Miller, Dean, 802-656-3166. *Dean,* Dr. Eleanor Miller, 802-656-3166.

College of Education and Social Services Students: 414 (322 women); includes 12 Black or African American, non-Hispanic/Latino; 1 American Indian or Alaska Native, non-Hispanic/Latino; 12 Asian, non-Hispanic/Latino; 13 Hispanic/Latino, 7 international. 547 applicants, 54% accepted, 116 enrolled. Expenses: Contact institution. *Financial support:* Fellowships, research assistantships, teaching assistantships, career-related internships or fieldwork and Federal Work-Study available. In 2010, 169 master's, 19 doctorates awarded. *Degree program information:* Part-time programs available. Offers counseling (MS); curriculum and instruction (M Ed, MAT); education and social services (M Ed, MAT, MS, MSW, Ed D); educational leadership (M Ed); educational leadership and policy studies (Ed D); educational studies (M Ed); higher education and student affairs administration (M Ed); interdisciplinary studies (M Ed); reading and language arts (M Ed); social work (MSW); special education (M Ed). *Application fee:* $40. Electronic applications accepted. *Application Contact:* Dr. Fayneese Miller, Dean, 802-656-3424. *Dean,* Dr. Fayneese Miller, 802-656-3424.

College of Engineering and Mathematics Students: 168 (46 women); includes 1 Black or African American, non-Hispanic/Latino; 5 Asian, non-Hispanic/Latino; 1 Hispanic/Latino, 50 international. 297 applicants, 44% accepted, 36 enrolled. Expenses: Contact institution. *Financial support:* Fellowships, research assistantships, teaching assistantships, Federal Work-Study available. Financial award application deadline: 3/1. In 2010, 40 master's, 11 doctorates awarded. *Degree program information:* Part-time programs available. Offers biomedical engineering (MS); biostatistics (MS); civil and environmental engineering (MS, PhD); computer science (MS, PhD); electrical engineering (MS, PhD); engineering and mathematics (MS, MST, PhD); materials science (MS, PhD); mathematics (MS, MST, PhD); mathematics education (MST); mechanical engineering (MS, PhD); statistics (MS). *Application deadline:* For fall admission, 4/1 priority date for domestic students. Applications are processed on a rolling basis. *Application fee:* $40. Electronic applications accepted. *Application Contact:* Prof. Jason Bates, Interim Director, 802-656-3333. *Interim Director,* Prof. Jason Bates, 802-656-3333.

College of Nursing and Health Sciences Students: 177 (143 women); includes 1 Black or African American, non-Hispanic/Latino; 1 American Indian or Alaska Native, non-Hispanic/Latino; 6 Asian, non-Hispanic/Latino; 5 Hispanic/Latino. 363 applicants, 39% accepted, 9 enrolled. Expenses: Contact institution. *Financial support:* Fellowships, research assistantships, teaching assistantships, Federal Work-Study available. Financial award application deadline: 3/1. In 2010, 23 master's, 28 doctorates awarded. *Degree program information:* Part-time programs available. Offers nursing (MS); nursing and health sciences (MS, DPT); physical therapy (DPT). *Application deadline:* For fall admission, 4/1 priority date for domestic students. Applications are processed on a rolling basis. *Application fee:* $40. Electronic applications accepted. *Application Contact:* Dr. Patricia Prelock, Dean, 802-656-3830. *Dean,* Dr. Patricia Prelock, 802-656-3830.

The Rubenstein School of Environment and Natural Resources Students: 102 (54 women); includes 2 Black or African American, non-Hispanic/Latino; 2 American Indian or Alaska Native, non-Hispanic/Latino; 7 Asian, non-Hispanic/Latino; 4 Hispanic/Latino, 5 international. 140 applicants, 32% accepted, 22 enrolled. Expenses: Contact institution. *Financial support:* Fellowships, research assistantships, teaching assistantships, Federal Work-Study available. Financial award application deadline: 3/1. In 2010, 22 master's, 8 doctorates awarded. *Degree program information:* Part-time programs available. Offers environment and natural resources (MS, PhD); natural resources (MS, PhD). *Application deadline:* For fall admission, 3/1 priority date for domestic students. Applications are processed on a rolling basis. *Application fee:* $40. Electronic applications accepted. *Application Contact:* Mary Watzin, Director/Coordinator, 802-656-2620. *Director/Coordinator,* Mary Watzin, 802-656-2620.

School of Business Administration Students: 58 (21 women); includes 2 Black or African American, non-Hispanic/Latino; 2 Asian, non-Hispanic/Latino; 2 Hispanic/Latino, 4 international. 70 applicants, 66% accepted, 14 enrolled. *Faculty:* 25. Expenses: Contact institution. *Financial support:* Fellowships, teaching assistantships, Federal Work-Study available. Financial award application deadline: 3/1. In 2010, 16 master's awarded. *Degree program information:* Part-time programs available. Offers accounting (M Acc); business administration (M Acc, MBA). *Application deadline:* For fall admission, 4/1 priority date for domestic students. Applications are processed on a rolling basis. *Application fee:* $40. Electronic applications accepted. *Application Contact:* Dr. Michael Gurdon, Coordinator, 802-656-4015. *Dean,* Dr. R. DeWitt, 802-656-0513.

UNIVERSITY OF VICTORIA, Victoria, BC V8W 2Y2, Canada

General Information Province-supported, coed, university. *Graduate housing:* Rooms and/or apartments available on a first-come, first-served basis to single and married students. Housing application deadline: 2/1. *Research affiliation:* Dominion Astrophysical Observatory, Bamfield Marine Research Station (marine biology), Tri-University Meson Facility, Canada/France/Hawaii Telescope Observatory, Institute of Ocean Sciences (geography, oceanography).

GRADUATE UNITS

Faculty of Graduate Studies *Degree program information:* Part-time programs available. Postbaccalaureate distance learning degree programs offered (no on-campus study). Electronic applications accepted.

Faculty of Business *Degree program information:* Part-time programs available. Offers business (MBA). Electronic applications accepted.

Faculty of Education Offers aboriginal communities counseling (M Ed); art education (M Ed, PhD); coaching studies (co-operative education) (M Ed); counseling (M Ed, MA); curriculum studies (M Ed, MA, PhD); early childhood education (M Ed, PhD); education (M Ed, M Sc, MA, PhD); educational psychology (M Ed, MA, PhD); educational studies (PhD); kinesiology (M Sc, MA); language and literacy (M Ed, MA, PhD); leadership studies (M Ed, MA); leisure service administration (MA); mathematics (M Ed, MA, PhD); music education (M Ed, MA, PhD); physical education (MA); science (M Ed, MA, PhD); social studies (M Ed, MA); social, cultural and foundational studies (MA, PhD); technology and environmental education (PhD).

Faculty of Engineering Offers computer science (M Sc, PhD); electrical and computer engineering (M Eng, MA Sc, PhD); engineering (M Eng, M Sc, MA Sc, PhD); mechanical engineering (M Eng, MA Sc, PhD).

Faculty of Fine Arts Offers composition (M Mus); design (MFA); digital multimedia (MFA); directing (MFA); drawing (MFA); fine arts (M Mus, MA, MFA, PhD); history in art (MA, PhD); musicology (MA, PhD); musicology with performance (MA); painting (MFA); performance (M Mus); photography (MFA); sculpture (MFA); theatre history (MA); video (MFA); writing (MFA).

University of Victoria (continued)

Faculty of Human and Social Development Offers advanced nursing practice (advanced practice leadership option) (MN); advanced nursing practice (nurse educator option) (MN); advanced nursing practice (nurse practitioner option) (MN); child and youth care (MA, PhD); dispute resolution (MADR); health information science (M Sc); human and social development (M Sc, MA, MADR, MN, MPA, MSW, PhD); indigenous governance (MA); nursing (PhD); public administration (MPA, PhD); social work (MSW); studies in policy and practice (MA).

Faculty of Humanities Offers applied linguistics (MA); English (MA, PhD); German studies (MA); Greek and Roman studies (MA, PhD); Hispanic and Italian studies (MA); Hispanic studies (MA); history (MA, PhD); humanities (MA, PhD); linguistics (MA, PhD); literature (MA); Pacific and Asian studies (MA); philosophy (MA); teaching emphasis (MA).

Faculty of Science Offers astronomy and astrophysics (M Sc, PhD); biochemistry (M Sc, PhD); biology (M Sc, PhD); chemistry (M Sc, PhD); condensed matter physics (M Sc, PhD); earth and ocean sciences (M Sc, PhD); experimental particle physics (M Sc, PhD); mathematics and statistics (M Sc, MA, PhD); medical physics (M Sc, PhD); microbiology (M Sc, PhD); ocean physics (M Sc, PhD); science (M Sc, MA, PhD); theoretical physics (M Sc, PhD). Electronic applications accepted.

Faculty of Social Sciences Offers anthropology (MA); clinical psychology (PhD); clinical psychology (neuropsychology) (M Sc); cognition and brain science (M Sc, PhD); economics (MA, PhD); experimental neuropsychology (M Sc); geography (M Sc, MA, PhD); individualized study (M Sc, PhD); life span development psychology (PhD); life span developmental psychology (M Sc); political science (MA, PhD); social psychology (M Sc, PhD); social sciences (M Sc, MA, PhD); sociology (MA, PhD).

Faculty of Law *Degree program information:* Part-time programs available. Offers law (JD, LL M, PhD). Electronic applications accepted.

UNIVERSITY OF VIRGINIA, Charlottesville, VA 22903

General Information State-supported, coed, university. CGS member. *Enrollment:* 24,391 graduate, professional, and undergraduate students; 5,906 full-time matriculated graduate/professional students (2,715 women), 424 part-time matriculated graduate/professional students (276 women). *Enrollment by degree level:* 1,683 first professional, 2,364 master's, 2,274 doctoral, 9 other advanced degrees. *Graduate faculty:* 2,069 full-time (651 women), 147 part-time/adjunct (86 women). *Graduate housing:* Rooms and/or apartments available on a first-come, first-served basis to single and married students. Housing application deadline: 6/1. *Student services:* Campus employment opportunities, campus safety program, career counseling, child daycare facilities, exercise/wellness program, free psychological counseling, grant writing training, international student services, low-cost health insurance, multicultural affairs office, services for students with disabilities, teacher training, writing training. *Library facilities:* Alderman Library plus 14 others. *Online resources:* library catalog, web page. *Collection:* 5.6 million titles, 184,340 serial subscriptions, 134,746 audiovisual materials. *Research affiliation:* The Judge Advocate General's School, U. S. Army, Federal Executive Institute, National Radio Astronomy Observatory.

Computer facilities: Computer purchase and lease plans are available. 691 computers available on campus for general student use. A campuswide network can be accessed from student residence rooms and from off campus. Online class registration, online course management tool are available. *Web address:* http://www.virginia.edu/.

General Application Contact: Dean, 434-924-0311.

GRADUATE UNITS

College and Graduate School of Arts and Sciences Students: 1,480 full-time (720 women), 23 part-time (13 women); includes 113 minority (25 Black or African American, non-Hispanic/Latino; 7 American Indian or Alaska Native, non-Hispanic/Latino; 40 Asian, non-Hispanic/Latino; 30 Hispanic/Latino; 2 Native Hawaiian or other Pacific Islander, non-Hispanic/Latino; 9 Two or more races, non-Hispanic/Latino), 317 international. Average age 28. 4,687 applicants, 15% accepted, 350 enrolled. *Faculty:* 572 full-time (169 women), 35 part-time/adjunct (16 women). Expenses: Contact institution. *Financial support:* Fellowships with partial tuition reimbursements, research assistantships, teaching assistantships with tuition reimbursements, career-related internships or fieldwork, Federal Work-Study, institutionally sponsored loans, traineeships, tuition waivers (full and partial), and unspecified assistantships available. Financial award applicants required to submit FAFSA. In 2010, 241 master's, 135 doctorates awarded. *Degree program information:* Part-time programs available. Offers anthropology (MA, PhD); art and architectural history (MA, PhD); arts and sciences (MA, MFA, MS, PhD); astronomy (MS, PhD); biology (MA, MS, PhD); chemistry (MA, MS, PhD); classics (MA, PhD); creative writing (MFA); drama (MFA); East Asian studies (MA); economics (MA, PhD); English (MA, PhD); environmental sciences (MA, MS, PhD); foreign affairs (MA, PhD); French (MA, PhD); German (MA, PhD); government (MA, PhD); history (MA, PhD); Italian (MA); linguistics (MA); math education (MA); mathematics (MA, MS, PhD); Middle Eastern and South Asian studies (MA); music (MA, PhD); philosophy (MA, PhD); physics (MA, MS, PhD); physics education (MA); psychology (MA, PhD); religious studies (MA, PhD); Slavic languages and literatures (MA, PhD); sociology (MA, PhD); Spanish (MA, PhD); statistics (MS, PhD). *Application deadline:* Applications are processed on a rolling basis. *Application fee:* $60. Electronic applications accepted. *Application Contact:* Robert Fatton, Associate Dean of Graduate Programs, 434-924-6739, Fax: 434-924-6737, E-mail: grad-a-s@virginia.edu. *Dean,* Meredith Jung-En Woo, 434-924-4611, Fax: 434-924-1317.

Center for Biomedical Ethics 5 applicants, 20% accepted, 0 enrolled. Expenses: Contact institution. *Financial support:* Applicants required to submit FAFSA. Offers bioethics (MA). *Application deadline:* Applications are processed on a rolling basis. *Application fee:* $60. Electronic applications accepted. *Application Contact:* Daniel Becker, Director, 434-924-5974, E-mail: dmb2y@virginia.edu. *Director,* Daniel Becker, 434-924-5974, E-mail: dmb2y@virginia.edu.

Curry School of Education Students: 696 full-time (539 women), 167 part-time (103 women); includes 111 minority (49 Black or African American, non-Hispanic/Latino; 2 American Indian or Alaska Native, non-Hispanic/Latino; 28 Asian, non-Hispanic/Latino; 25 Hispanic/Latino; 2 Native Hawaiian or other Pacific Islander, non-Hispanic/Latino; 5 Two or more races, non-Hispanic/Latino), 29 international. Average age 28. 870 applicants, 44% accepted, 201 enrolled. *Faculty:* 85 full-time (48 women), 5 part-time/adjunct (4 women). Expenses: Contact institution. *Financial support:* Fellowships, research assistantships, teaching assistantships, Federal Work-Study available. Financial award application deadline: 1/5; financial award applicants required to submit FAFSA. In 2010, 479 master's, 87 doctorates, 60 other advanced degrees awarded. Offers administration and supervision (M Ed, Ed D, Ed S); applied developmental science (M Ed, PhD); clinical and school psychology (PhD); communication disorders (M Ed); counselor education (M Ed, Ed S); curriculum and instruction (M Ed, Ed D, PhD, Ed S); early childhood-developmental risk (MT); education (M Ed, MT, Ed D, PhD, Ed S); education evaluation (PhD); educational evaluation (M Ed); educational policy studies (M Ed, Ed D); educational psychology (M Ed, Ed D, PhD, Ed S); educational research (Ed D, PhD); elementary (M Ed, MT, Ed D, PhD); English (M Ed, Ed D); English education (MT, PhD); foreign language (M Ed); foreign language education (MT); gifted education (M Ed); health and physical education (M Ed, Ed D); higher education (M Ed, Ed D, PhD, Ed S); instructional technology (M Ed, PhD, Ed S); kinesiology (M Ed, MT, Ed D, PhD); math education (PhD); mathematics (M Ed, Ed D); reading (M Ed, Ed D, Ed S); reading education (PhD); research statistics and evaluation (Ed D, PhD); school psychology (Ed D, PhD); science (Ed D); science education (PhD); social studies (M Ed); social studies education (MT, PhD); special education (M Ed, Ed D, PhD, Ed S); student affairs practice (M Ed); world languages education (MT). *Application deadline:* Applications are processed on a rolling basis. *Application fee:* $60. Electronic applications accepted. *Application Contact:* Joanne McNergney, Assistant Dean for Admissions and Student Services, 434-924-3334, E-mail: curry-admissions@virginia.edu. *Dean,* Robert C. Pianta, 434-924-3334.

Darden Graduate School of Business Administration Students: 774 full-time (214 women), 2 part-time (0 women); includes 37 Black or African American, non-Hispanic/Latino; 2 American Indian or Alaska Native, non-Hispanic/Latino; 52 Asian, non-Hispanic/Latino; 33 Hispanic/Latino; 5 Two or more races, non-Hispanic/Latino, 174 international. Average age 29. 2,411 applicants, 27% accepted, 339 enrolled. *Faculty:* 63 full-time (14 women), 5 part-time/adjunct (2 women). Expenses: Contact institution. *Financial support:* Career-related internships or fieldwork available. Financial award applicants required to submit FAFSA. In 2010, 387 master's, 3 doctorates awarded. Offers business administration (MBA, PhD). *Application deadline:* For fall admission, 3/1 for domestic students, 3/2 for international students. Applications are processed on a rolling basis. *Application fee:* $200. Electronic applications accepted. *Application Contact:* Sara Neher, Assistant Dean of MBA Admissions, 434-924-3900, E-mail: darden@virginia.edu. *Dean,* Robert F. Bruner, 434-924-3900, E-mail: darden@virginia.edu.

Frank Batten Sr. School of Leadership and Public Policy Students: 27 full-time (19 women); includes 4 Black or African American, non-Hispanic/Latino; 2 Asian, non-Hispanic/Latino; 2 Hispanic/Latino. Average age 22. *Faculty:* 4 full-time (2 women), 2 part-time/adjunct (1 woman). Expenses: Contact institution. In 2010, 29 master's awarded. Offers leadership and public policy (MPP); public policy (MPP). *Application deadline:* For fall admission, 2/20 for domestic and international students. Applications are processed on a rolling basis. Electronic applications accepted. *Application Contact:* Howard H. Hoege, Director of Graduate Admissions, 434-243-4383, Fax: 434-243-2318, E-mail: hhh@virginia.edu. *Dean,* Dr. Harry Harding, 434-924-0812, Fax: 434-243-2318.

McIntire School of Commerce Students: 223 full-time (89 women), 35 part-time (9 women); includes 11 Black or African American, non-Hispanic/Latino; 26 Asian, non-Hispanic/Latino; 15 Hispanic/Latino; 8 Two or more races, non-Hispanic/Latino, 27 international. Average age 26. 376 applicants, 64% accepted, 154 enrolled. *Faculty:* 61 full-time (19 women), 2 part-time/adjunct (1 woman). Expenses: Contact institution. *Financial support:* Fellowships, research assistantships, teaching assistantships, career-related internships or fieldwork and Federal Work-Study available. Financial award applicants required to submit FAFSA. In 2010, 228 master's awarded. Offers accounting (MS); commerce (MSC); financial services (MSC); management of information technology (MS); marketing and management (MSC). *Application deadline:* Applications are processed on a rolling basis. *Application fee:* $75. Electronic applications accepted. *Application Contact:* Carl Zeithaml, Dean, 434-924-3110, Fax: 434-924-7074, E-mail: mcs@virginia.edu. *Dean,* Carl Zeithaml, 434-924-3110, Fax: 434-924-7074, E-mail: mcs@virginia.edu.

School of Architecture Students: 200 full-time (120 women), 3 part-time (1 woman); includes 8 Black or African American, non-Hispanic/Latino; 8 Asian, non-Hispanic/Latino; 11 Hispanic/Latino, 17 international. Average age 26. 824 applicants, 21% accepted, 57 enrolled. *Faculty:* 35 full-time (14 women), 1 (woman) part-time/adjunct. Expenses: Contact institution. *Financial support:* Fellowships, career-related internships or fieldwork, Federal Work-Study, and institutionally sponsored loans available. Financial award applicants required to submit FAFSA. In 2010, 68 master's, 2 doctorates awarded. Offers architectural history (M Arch H, PhD); architecture (M Arch, M Arch H, M Land Arch, MUEP, PhD, JD/MUEP); landscape architecture (M Land Arch); urban and environmental planning (MUEP, JD/MUEP). *Application deadline:* Applications are processed on a rolling basis. *Application fee:* $60. Electronic applications accepted. *Application Contact:* Graduate Admissions Officer, 434-924-6442, Fax: 434-982-2678, E-mail: arch-admissions@virginia.edu. *Dean,* Kim M. Tanzer, 434-924-3715, Fax: 434-982-2678, E-mail: arch-web@virginia.edu.

School of Engineering and Applied Science Students: 600 full-time (144 women), 25 part-time (3 women); includes 72 minority (17 Black or African American, non-Hispanic/Latino; 40 Asian, non-Hispanic/Latino; 10 Hispanic/Latino; 5 Two or more races, non-Hispanic/Latino), 241 international. Average age 27. 1,570 applicants, 19% accepted, 114 enrolled. *Faculty:* 142 full-time (16 women), 4 part-time/adjunct (0 women). Expenses: Contact institution. *Financial support:* Fellowships with full tuition reimbursements, research assistantships with full tuition reimbursements, teaching assistantships with full tuition reimbursements, career-related internships or fieldwork available. Financial award application deadline: 1/15; financial award applicants required to submit FAFSA. In 2010, 170 master's, 55 doctorates awarded. *Degree program information:* Part-time programs available. Postbaccalaureate distance learning degree programs offered (no on-campus study). Offers biomedical engineering (ME, MS, PhD); chemical engineering (ME, MS, PhD); civil engineering (ME, MS, PhD); computer engineering (ME, MS, PhD); computer science (MCS, MS, PhD); electrical engineering (ME, MS, PhD); engineering and applied science (MCS, ME, MEP, MMSE, MS, PhD); engineering physics (MEP, MS, PhD); materials science (MMSE, MS, PhD); mechanical and aerospace engineering (ME, MS, PhD); systems and information engineering (ME, MS, PhD). *Application deadline:* For fall admission, 8/1 for domestic students, 4/1 for international students; for winter admission, 12/1 for domestic students, 8/1 for international students; for spring admission, 5/1 for domestic students, 1/1 for international students. Applications are processed on a rolling basis. *Application fee:* $60. Electronic applications accepted. *Application Contact:* Kathryn C. Thornton, Associate Dean for Graduate Programs, 434-924-3897, Fax: 434-982-3044, E-mail: seas-grad-admission@virginia.edu. *Dean,* James H. Aylor, 434-924-3072, Fax: 434-243-2083.

School of Law Students: 1,133 full-time (506 women), 1 (woman) part-time; includes 68 Black or African American, non-Hispanic/Latino; 9 American Indian or Alaska Native, non-Hispanic/Latino; 105 Asian, non-Hispanic/Latino; 58 Hispanic/Latino; 17 Two or more races, non-Hispanic/Latino, 35 international. Average age 25. 9,083 applicants, 22% accepted, 400 enrolled. *Faculty:* 83 full-time (21 women), 5 part-time/adjunct (2 women). Expenses: Contact institution. *Financial support:* Fellowships, career-related internships or fieldwork, Federal Work-Study, and institutionally sponsored loans available. Financial award application deadline: 3/1; financial award applicants required to submit FAFSA. In 2010, 373 first professional degrees, 38 master's, 1 doctorate awarded. Offers law (JD, LL M, SJD, JD/MUEP). *Application deadline:* For fall admission, 3/1 priority date for domestic students, 3/2 for international students. Applications are processed on a rolling basis. *Application fee:* $75. Electronic applications accepted. *Application Contact:* Jason Wu Trujillo, Senior Assistant Dean for Admissions, 434-924-7351, Fax: 434-982-2128, E-mail: lawadmit@virginia.edu. *Dean,* Paul G. Mahoney, 434-924-7351, Fax: 434-982-2128, E-mail: lawadmit@virginia.edu.

School of Medicine Students: 953 full-time (455 women), 24 part-time (9 women); includes 282 minority (69 Black or African American, non-Hispanic/Latino; 2 American Indian or Alaska Native, non-Hispanic/Latino; 129 Asian, non-Hispanic/Latino; 72 Hispanic/Latino; 10 Two or more races, non-Hispanic/Latino), 66 international. Average age 26. 4,760 applicants, 11% accepted, 230 enrolled. *Faculty:* 930 full-time (279 women), 76 part-time/adjunct (51 women). Expenses: Contact institution. *Financial support:* Institutionally sponsored loans and scholarships/grants available. Financial award applicants required to submit FAFSA. In 2010, 141 first professional degrees, 42 master's, 45 doctorates awarded. Offers biochemistry (PhD); biological and physical sciences (MS); biophysics (PhD); cell biology (PhD); clinical investigation and patient-oriented research (MS); clinical research (MS); experimental pathology (PhD); informatics in medicine (MS); medicine (MD, MPH, MS, PhD); microbiology (PhD); neuroscience (PhD); pharmacology (PhD); physiology (PhD); public health (MPH). *Application deadline:* Applications are processed on a rolling basis. *Application fee:* $80. Electronic applications accepted. *Application Contact:* Lesley L. Thomas, Director, Admissions Office, 434-924-5571, Fax: 434-982-2586, E-mail: medsch-adm@virginia.edu. *Vice President and Dean,* Steven T. DeKosky, 434-924-5118, E-mail: slh2m@virginia.edu.

School of Nursing Students: 153 full-time (128 women), 146 part-time (138 women); includes 25 Black or African American, non-Hispanic/Latino; 1 American Indian or Alaska Native, non-Hispanic/Latino; 11 Asian, non-Hispanic/Latino; 7 Hispanic/Latino; 2 Two or more races, non-Hispanic/Latino, 6 international. Average age 37. 172 applicants, 56% accepted, 75 enrolled. *Faculty:* 47 full-time (44 women), 5 part-time/adjunct (4 women). Expenses: Contact institution. *Financial support:* Fellowships, research assistantships, teaching assistantships, Federal Work-Study and scholarships/grants available. Financial award applicants required to submit FAFSA. In 2010, 77 master's, 18 doctorates awarded. *Degree program information:* Part-time programs available. Offers acute and specialty care (MSN); acute care nurse practitioner (MSN); clinical nurse leadership (MSN); community-public health leadership (MSN); nursing (DNP, PhD); psychiatric mental health counseling (MSN). *Application deadline:* Applications are processed on a rolling basis. *Application fee:* $60. Electronic applications accepted. *Application Contact:* Clay Hysell, Assistant Dean for Admissions and Financial Services, 434-924-0141, Fax: 434-982-1809, E-mail: nur-osa@virginia.edu. *Dean,* Dorrie K. Fontaine, 434-924-0141, Fax: 434-982-1809.

UNIVERSITY OF WASHINGTON, Seattle, WA 98195

General Information State-supported, coed, university. CGS member. *Graduate housing:* Rooms and/or apartments available on a first-come, first-served basis to single and married students. Housing application deadline: 5/1. *Research affiliation:* Fred Hutchinson Cancer Research Center, Children's Hospital and Regional Medical Center (pediatric research).

GRADUATE UNITS

Graduate School *Degree program information:* Part-time and evening/weekend programs available. Postbaccalaureate distance learning degree programs offered (minimal on-campus study). Offers biology for teachers (MS); education (M Ed, Professional Certificate); global trade, transportation and logistics studies (Certificate); museology (MA); Near and Middle Eastern studies (PhD); quantitative ecology and resource management (MS, PhD). Electronic applications accepted.

College of Arts and Sciences *Degree program information:* Part-time and evening/weekend programs available. Offers acting (MFA); animal behavior (PhD); anthropology (MA, PhD); applied mathematics (MS, PhD); art (MFA); art history (MA, PhD); arts and sciences (MA, MAIS, MAT, MC, MFA, MM, MS, Au D, DMA, PhD); astronomy (MS, PhD); atmospheric sciences (MS, PhD); audiology (Au D); biology (PhD); Buddhist studies (MA, PhD); Central Asian studies (MAIS); chemistry (MS, PhD); child psychology (PhD); China studies (MAIS); Chinese language and literature (MA, PhD); choral conducting (MM, DMA); classics (MA, PhD); classics and philosophy (PhD); clinical psychology (PhD); cognition and perception (PhD); communication (MA, MC, PhD); comparative literature (MA, PhD); comparative religion (MAIS); computational linguistics (MA); costume design (MFA); creative writing (MFA); dance (MFA); design (MFA); developmental psychology (PhD); directing (MFA); dramatic theory (PhD); East European studies (MAIS); economics (PhD); English as a second language (MAT); English literature and language (MA, MAT, PhD); ethnomusicology (MA); French (MA, PhD); French and Italian studies (MA, PhD); geography (MA, PhD); geology (MS, PhD); geophysics (MS, PhD); Germanics (MA, PhD); Hispanic literary and cultural studies (MA); history (MA, PhD); industrial design (MFA); international studies (MAIS); Italian (MA); Japan studies (MAIS); Japanese language and literature (MA, PhD); Korea studies (MAIS); Korean language and literature (MA, PhD); lighting design (MFA); linguistics (MA, PhD); mathematics (MA, MS, PhD); Middle East studies (MAIS); music (MA, MM, DMA, PhD); music education (MA, PhD); music history (MA, PhD); Near Eastern languages and civilization (MA); numerical analysis (MS); optimization (MS); painting and drawing (MFA); philosophy (MA, PhD); photography (MFA); physics (MS, PhD); political science (MA, PhD); quantitative psychology (PhD); Romance linguistics (MA, PhD); Russian literature (MA, PhD); Russian studies (MAIS); Russian, East European and Central Asian studies (MAIS); Scandinavian studies (MA, PhD); scenic design (MFA); Slavic linguistics (MA, PhD); social psychology and personality (PhD); sociology (MA, PhD); South Asian language and literature (MA, PhD); South Asian studies (MAIS); Southeast Asian studies (MAIS); Spanish and Portuguese (MA); speech and hearing sciences (PhD); speech-language pathology (MS); statistics (MS, PhD); theatre and performance history (PhD); visual communication design (MFA); women studies (PhD). Electronic applications accepted.

College of Built Environments *Degree program information:* Part-time and evening/weekend programs available. Offers architecture (M Arch, MS); built environment (PhD); built environments (M Arch, MLA, MS, MSCM, MSCPI, MUP, PhD, Certificate); construction management (MSCM); design computing (Certificate); design firm leadership and management (Certificate); historic preservation (Certificate); landscape architecture (MLA); lighting (Certificate); strategic planning for critical infrastructures (MSCPI); urban design (Certificate); urban design and planning (PhD); urban planning (MUP). Electronic applications accepted.

College of Education *Degree program information:* Part-time and evening/weekend programs available. Offers curriculum and instruction (M Ed, Ed D, PhD); early childhood special education (M Ed); educational leadership and policy studies (M Ed, Ed D, PhD); educational psychology (M Ed, PhD); emotional and behavioral disabilities (M Ed); human development and cognition (M Ed); instructional leadership (M Ed); intercollegiate athletic leadership (M Ed); learning disabilities (M Ed); learning sciences (M Ed, PhD); low-incidence disabilities (M Ed); measurement, statistics and research design (M Ed); school psychology (M Ed); severe disabilities (M Ed); special education (M Ed, Ed D, PhD); teacher education (MIT). Electronic applications accepted.

College of Engineering Students: 1,102 full-time (316 women), 697 part-time (146 women); includes 41 Black or African American, non-Hispanic/Latino; 4 American Indian or Alaska Native, non-Hispanic/Latino; 228 Asian, non-Hispanic/Latino; 58 Hispanic/Latino, 460 international. Average age 28. 4,490 applicants, 27% accepted, 517 enrolled. *Faculty:* 328 full-time (63 women), 80 part-time/adjunct (17 women). Expenses: Contact institution. *Financial support:* In 2010–11, 30 students received support, including 152 fellowships with full tuition reimbursements available (averaging $18,477 per year), 613 research assistantships with full tuition reimbursements available (averaging $17,217 per year), 153 teaching assistantships with full tuition reimbursements available (averaging $16,167 per year); career-related internships or fieldwork, Federal Work-Study, institutionally sponsored loans, scholarships/grants, traineeships, health care benefits, tuition waivers (full), unspecified assistantships, and stipend supplements also available. Financial award application deadline: 2/28; financial award applicants required to submit FAFSA. In 2010, 399 master's, 106 doctorates awarded. *Degree program information:* Part-time programs available. Postbaccalaureate distance learning degree programs offered (no on-campus study). Offers aeronautics and astronautics (MS, PhD); bioengineering (MS, PhD); bioengineering and nanotechnology (PhD); ceramic engineering (PhD); chemical engineering (MS, MSE, PhD); chemical engineering and nanotechnology (PhD); composite materials and structures (MAE); computer science (MS); computer science and engineering (PMS, PhD); construction engineering (MSCE); electrical engineering (MS, PhD); electrical engineering and nanotechnology (PhD); engineering (MAE, MME, MS, MSCE, MSE, MSME, PMS, PhD); environmental engineering (MS, MSCE, MSE, PhD); global technology and communication (MS, PhD); human centered design and engineering (MS, PhD); hydrology, water resources, and environmental fluid mechanics (MS, MSCE, MSE, PhD); industrial and systems engineering (MS, PhD); inter-engineering technical Japanese (MSE); materials science and engineering (MS, MSE, PhD); materials science and engineering and nanotechnology (PhD); mechanical engineering (MS, MSE, MSME, PhD); medical engineering (MME); pharmaceutical bioengineering (MS); structural and geotechnical engineering and mechanics (MS, MSCE, MSE, PhD); technical communication (MS, PhD); transportation and construction engineering (MS, MSE, PhD); transportation engineering (MSCE); user centered design (MS, PhD). *Application deadline:* For fall admission, 12/15 for domestic students, 11/15 priority date for international students. *Application fee:* $75. Electronic applications accepted. *Application Contact:* Dr. Eve Riskin, Associate Dean, Academic Affairs, 206-685-2313, Fax: 206-685-0666, E-mail: riskin@u.washington.edu. *Dean,* Dr. Matthew O'Donnell, 206-543-0340, Fax: 206-685-0666, E-mail: odonnel@uw.edu.

College of Forest Resources Offers bioresource science and engineering (MS, PhD); environmental horticulture (MEH); environmental horticulture and urban forestry (MS, PhD); forest ecology (MS, PhD); forest management (MFR); forest soils (MS, PhD); forest systems and bioenergy (MS, PhD); restoration ecology (MS, PhD); social sciences (MS, PhD); sustainable resource management (MS, PhD); wildlife science (MS, PhD). Electronic applications accepted.

College of Ocean and Fishery Sciences Offers aquatic and fishery sciences (MS, PhD); biological oceanography (MS, PhD); chemical oceanography (MS, PhD); marine affairs (MMA, Graduate Certificate); marine geology and geophysics (MS, PhD); ocean and fishery sciences (MMA, MS, PhD, Graduate Certificate); physical oceanography (MS, PhD). Electronic applications accepted.

Daniel J. Evans School of Public Affairs *Degree program information:* Part-time and evening/weekend programs available. Offers public administration (MPA); public policy and management (PhD). Electronic applications accepted.

The Information School Students: 275 full-time (178 women), 260 part-time (191 women); includes 12 Black or African American, non-Hispanic/Latino; 6 American Indian or Alaska Native, non-Hispanic/Latino; 51 Asian, non-Hispanic/Latino; 15 Hispanic/Latino, 67 international. Average age 32. 834 applicants, 47% accepted, 219 enrolled. *Faculty:* 36 full-time (15 women), 18 part-time/adjunct (11 women). Expenses: Contact institution. *Financial support:* In 2010–11, 71 students received support, including 4 fellowships with full tuition reimbursements available (averaging $18,450 per year), 21 research assistantships with full and partial tuition reimbursements available (averaging $17,994 per year), 19 teaching assistantships with full and partial tuition reimbursements available (averaging $18,143 per year); career-related internships or fieldwork, Federal Work-Study, institutionally sponsored loans, scholarships/grants, health care benefits, tuition waivers (full and partial), and unspecified assistantships also available. Support available to part-time students. Financial award application deadline: 2/28; financial award applicants required to submit FAFSA. In 2010, 200 master's, 1 doctorate awarded. *Degree program information:* Part-time and evening/weekend programs available. Postbaccalaureate distance learning degree programs offered (minimal on-campus study). Offers information management (MSIM); information science (PhD); library and information science (MLIS). MSIS degree available within PhD program. *Application deadline:* For fall admission, 12/1 for domestic and international students. *Application fee:* $75. Electronic applications accepted. *Application Contact:* Kari Brothers, Admissions Counselor, 206-616-5541, Fax: 206-616-3152, E-mail: kari683@uw.edu. *Dean,* Dr. Harry Bruce.

Michael G. Foster School of Business *Degree program information:* Part-time and evening/weekend programs available. Offers auditing and assurance (MP Acc); business (PhD); business administration (evening) (MBA); business administration (full-time) (MBA); executive business administration (MBA); global business administration (MBA); global executive business administration (MBA); taxation (MP Acc); technology management (MBA). Electronic applications accepted.

School of Dentistry Offers dental surgery (DDS); dentistry (DDS, MS, MSD, PhD, Certificate); endodontics (MSD, Certificate); oral biology (MS, MSD, PhD); oral medicine (MSD); orthodontics (MSD, Certificate); pediatric dentistry (MSD, Certificate); periodontics (MSD, PhD, Certificate); prosthodontics (MSD, Certificate).

School of Law Offers Asian law (LL M, PhD); intellectual property law and policy (LL M); law (JD); law of sustainable international development (LL M); taxation (LL M).

School of Medicine *Degree program information:* Part-time programs available. Offers biochemistry (PhD); bioethics (MA); biological structure (PhD); biomedical and health informatics (MS, PhD); comparative medicine (MS); experimental and molecular pathology (PhD); genome sciences (PhD); immunology (PhD); laboratory medicine (MS); medicine (MD, MA, MOT, MS, DPT, PhD); microbiology (PhD); molecular and cellular biology (PhD); neurobiology and behavior (PhD); occupational therapy (MOT); pharmacology (PhD); physical therapy (DPT); physiology and biophysics (PhD); rehabilitation science (PhD). Electronic applications accepted.

School of Nursing *Degree program information:* Part-time programs available. Offers nursing (MN, MS, DNP, PhD, Graduate Certificate).

School of Public Health Students: 595 full-time (400 women), 241 part-time (165 women); includes 19 Black or African American, non-Hispanic/Latino; 8 American Indian or Alaska Native, non-Hispanic/Latino; 105 Asian, non-Hispanic/Latino; 42 Hispanic/Latino, 79 international. Average age 32. 1,718 applicants, 34% accepted, 355 enrolled. *Faculty:* 229 full-time (105 women), 176 part-time/adjunct (73 women). Expenses: Contact institution. *Financial support:* In 2010–11, 414 students received support, including 110 fellowships with full and partial tuition reimbursements available (averaging $25,935 per year), 217 research assistantships with full and partial tuition reimbursements available (averaging $22,183 per year), 47 teaching assistantships with full and partial tuition reimbursements available (averaging $17,550 per year); career-related internships or fieldwork, Federal Work-Study, institutionally sponsored loans, scholarships/grants, traineeships, health care benefits, tuition waivers (full and partial), and unspecified assistantships also available. Support available to part-time students. In 2010, 241 master's, 51 doctorates awarded. *Degree program information:* Part-time and evening/weekend programs available. Postbaccalaureate distance learning degree programs offered (minimal on-campus study). Offers bioinformatics (PhD); biostatistics (MPH, MS, PhD); cancer prevention and control (PhD); clinical research (MS); community oriented public health practice (MPH); economics or finance (PhD); environmental and occupational health (MPH); environmental and occupational hygiene (PhD); environmental health (MS); epidemiology (MPH, MS, PhD); evaluation sciences (PhD); genetic epidemiology (MS); global health (MPH); global health—peace corps international (MPH); health behavior and health promotion (PhD); health care and population health research (MPH); health metrics and evaluation (MPH); health policy analysis and process (PhD); health policy and analysis and process (MPH); health services (MS, PhD); health services administration (EMHA, MHA); leadership, policy and management (MPH); maternal and child health (MPH, PhD); maternal/child health (MPH); nutritional sciences (MPH, MS, PhD); occupational and environmental exposure sciences (MS); occupational and environmental medicine (MPH); occupational health (PhD); pathobiology (PhD); population health and social determinants (PhD); public health (EMHA, MHA, MPH, MS, PhD); public health genetics (MPH, MS, PhD); social and behavioral sciences (MPH); sociology and demography (PhD); statistical genetics (PhD); toxicology (MS, PhD). *Application fee:* $75. Electronic applications accepted. *Application Contact:* Marcia Syverson, Manager, Student Services, 206-543-1144, Fax: 206-543-3813, E-mail: sphoss@u.washington.edu. *Dean,* Dr. Howard Frumkin, 206-543-1144.

School of Social Work *Degree program information:* Evening/weekend programs available. Postbaccalaureate distance learning degree programs offered (minimal on-campus study). Offers social work (MSW, PhD).

School of Social Work, Tacoma Campus *Degree program information:* Part-time and evening/weekend programs available. Offers social work (MSW). Electronic applications accepted.

School of Pharmacy *Degree program information:* Part-time and evening/weekend programs available. Postbaccalaureate distance learning degree programs offered. Offers medicinal chemistry (PhD); pharmaceutics (MS, PhD); pharmacy (Pharm D, MS, PhD).

UNIVERSITY OF WASHINGTON, BOTHELL, Bothell, WA 98011-8246

General Information State-supported, coed, comprehensive institution. *Enrollment:* 3,272 graduate, professional, and undergraduate students; 256 full-time matriculated graduate/professional students (122 women), 236 part-time matriculated graduate/professional students (170 women). *Enrollment by degree level:* 492 master's. Tuition, state resident: full-time $10,870; part-time $518 per quarter hour. Tuition, nonresident: full-time $24,210; part-time $1153 per quarter hour. *Required fees:* $495; $24 per quarter hour. Part-time tuition and fees vary according to course load, program and student level. *Graduate housing:* Room and/or apartments available on a first-come, first-served basis to single students; on-campus housing not available to married students. Typical cost: $9540 per year. Room charges vary according to housing facility selected. Housing application deadline: 5/1. *Student services:* Campus employment opportunities, campus safety program, career counseling, exercise/wellness program, international student services, low-cost health insurance, services for students with disabilities, writing training. *Library facilities:* Campus Library. *Online resources:* library catalog, web page, access to other libraries' catalogs. *Collection:* 98,503 titles, 429 serial subscriptions, 7,780 audiovisual materials. *Research affiliation:* Bill & Melinda Gates Foundation (improving health and reducing poverty in developing countries, providing opportunities to succeed in school and life in the U. S.), Carnegie Corporation of New York (doing 'real and permanent good in this world" by creating 'ladders on which the aspiring can rise"), Mathematica Policy Research, Inc. (health research, human services research, and surveys and information services), The Joyce Foundation (protecting the environment, reducing poverty and violence, and improving schools, jobs and culture in the Great Lakes region), Electric Power Research Institute (specific technology challenges of providing reliable, affordable, and environmentally responsible electricity), The Urban Institute (social and economic issues to foster sound public policy and effective government).

Computer facilities: 350 computers available on campus for general student use. A campuswide network can be accessed from student residence rooms. Online class registration, online course management system are available. *Web address:* http://www.uwb.edu/.

General Application Contact: Office of Graduate Admissions, 206-543-5929, Fax: 206-543-8798, E-mail: uwgrad@u.washington.edu.

GRADUATE UNITS

Business Program Students: 125 full-time (32 women), 1 part-time (0 women); includes 4 Black or African American, non-Hispanic/Latino; 20 Asian, non-Hispanic/Latino; 7 Hispanic/

University of Washington, Bothell (continued)

Latino, 3 international. Average age 33. 131 applicants, 53% accepted, 60 enrolled. *Faculty:* 18 full-time (2 women), 4 part-time/adjunct (2 women). Expenses: Contact institution. *Financial support:* In 2010–11, 67 students received support. Federal Work-Study and scholarships/grants available. Financial award application deadline: 2/28; financial award applicants required to submit FAFSA. In 2010, 36 master's awarded. *Degree program information:* Part-time and evening/weekend programs available. Offers leadership (MBA); technology (MBA). *Application deadline:* For fall admission, 4/16 priority date for domestic and international students. *Application fee:* $75. Electronic applications accepted. *Application Contact:* Kathryn Chester, MBA Admissions Coordinator, 425-352-3275, Fax: 425-352-5277, E-mail: kchester@uwb.edu. *Director*, Prof. Sandeep Krishnamurthy, 425-352-5229, Fax: 425-352-5277, E-mail: sandeep@uw.edu.

Program in Computing and Software Systems Students: 6 full-time (3 women), 45 part-time (6 women); includes 2 Black or African American, non-Hispanic/Latino; 11 Asian, non-Hispanic/Latino; 1 Hispanic/Latino, 4 international. Average age 33. 31 applicants, 74% accepted, 19 enrolled. *Faculty:* 8 full-time (1 woman). Expenses: Contact institution. *Financial support:* Applicants required to submit FAFSA. *Degree program information:* Part-time and evening/weekend programs available. Offers computing and software systems (MS). *Application deadline:* For fall admission, 7/1 for domestic students, 4/1 for international students; for winter admission, 11/1 for domestic students; for spring admission, 2/1 for domestic students. *Application fee:* $65. Electronic applications accepted. *Application Contact:* Megan Jewell, Graduate Advisor, 425-352-5279, E-mail: mjewell@uwb.edu. *Professor and Director*, Dr. Michael Stiber, 425-352-5279, E-mail: cssinfo@uwb.edu.

Program in Cultural Studies Students: 30 full-time (22 women), 1 (woman) part-time; includes 2 Black or African American, non-Hispanic/Latino; 1 American Indian or Alaska Native, non-Hispanic/Latino; 4 Asian, non-Hispanic/Latino; 2 Hispanic/Latino, 2 international. Average age 33. 39 applicants, 62% accepted, 18 enrolled. *Faculty:* 9 full-time (5 women), 5 part-time/adjunct (1 woman). Expenses: Contact institution. *Financial support:* In 2010–11, 9 students received support, including 5 fellowships (averaging $1,000 per year), 1 research assistantship (averaging $1,000 per year); Federal Work-Study and unspecified assistantships also available. In 2010, 14 master's awarded. *Degree program information:* Evening/weekend programs available. Offers cultural studies (MA). *Application deadline:* For fall admission, 2/1 for domestic and international students. *Application fee:* $65. Electronic applications accepted. *Application Contact:* Andrew Brusletten, Program Manager, 425-352-5427, Fax: 425-352-3462, E-mail: abrusletten@uwb.edu. *Director*, Prof. Bruce Burgett, 425-352-5452, Fax: 425-352-3462, E-mail: bburgett@uwb.edu.

Program in Education Students: 59 full-time (42 women), 108 part-time (87 women); includes 2 Black or African American, non-Hispanic/Latino; 8 Asian, non-Hispanic/Latino; 5 Hispanic/Latino. Average age 34. 91 applicants, 78% accepted, 61 enrolled. *Faculty:* 14 full-time (10 women), 1 (woman) part-time/adjunct. Expenses: Contact institution. *Financial support:* In 2010–11, 2 students received support. Federal Work-Study and unspecified assistantships available. Financial award application deadline: 5/2. In 2010, 61 master's awarded. *Degree program information:* Part-time and evening/weekend programs available. Offers education (M Ed); leadership development for educators (M Ed); secondary/middle level endorsement (M Ed). *Application deadline:* For fall admission, 8/14 priority date for domestic and international students; for spring admission, 4/7 priority date for domestic students, 11/1 priority date for international students. Applications are processed on a rolling basis. *Application fee:* $65. Electronic applications accepted. *Application Contact:* Amelia Bowers, Advisor, 425-352-5274, Fax: 425-352-5434, E-mail: abowers@uwb.edu. *Director/Professor*, Dr. Bradley S. Portin, 425-352-3482, Fax: 425-352-5234, E-mail: bportin@uwb.edu.

Program in Nursing Students: 11 full-time (all women), 80 part-time (72 women); includes 11 Black or African American, non-Hispanic/Latino; 8 Asian, non-Hispanic/Latino; 3 Hispanic/Latino, 1 international. Average age 43. 65 applicants, 68% accepted, 39 enrolled. *Faculty:* 8 full-time (all women). Expenses: Contact institution. *Financial support:* Federal Work-Study and unspecified assistantships available. In 2010, 23 master's awarded. *Degree program information:* Part-time programs available. Offers nursing (MN). *Application deadline:* For fall admission, 3/1 priority date for domestic and international students. Applications are processed on a rolling basis. *Application fee:* $65. Electronic applications accepted. *Application Contact:* Judy Lynn, Administrative Coordinator, 425-352-5376, Fax: 425-352-3237, E-mail: jlynn@uwb.edu. *Director*, Prof. Mary Baroni, 425-352-3543, Fax: 425-352-3237, E-mail: mbaroni@uwb.edu.

Program in Policy Studies Students: 27 full-time (13 women), 6 part-time (5 women); includes 8 minority (4 Black or African American, non-Hispanic/Latino; 3 Asian, non-Hispanic/Latino; 1 Hispanic/Latino), 2 international. Average age 32. 43 applicants, 63% accepted, 17 enrolled. *Faculty:* 9 full-time (4 women), 2 part-time/adjunct (both women). Expenses: Contact institution. *Financial support:* In 2010–11, 9 students received support, including 5 fellowships (averaging $1,000 per year), 1 research assistantship (averaging $1,000 per year); Federal Work-Study and unspecified assistantships also available. Financial award applicants required to submit FAFSA. In 2010, 22 master's awarded. *Degree program information:* Evening/weekend programs available. Offers policy studies (MA). *Application deadline:* For fall admission, 3/1 for domestic and international students. *Application fee:* $65. Electronic applications accepted. *Application Contact:* Andrew Brusletten, Program Manager, 425-352-5427, Fax: 425-352-3462, E-mail: abrusletten@uwb.edu. *Director*, Prof. Bruce Burgett, 425-352-5452, Fax: 425-352-3462, E-mail: bburgett@uwb.edu.

UNIVERSITY OF WASHINGTON, TACOMA, Tacoma, WA 98402-3100

General Information State-supported, coed, comprehensive institution. *Enrollment:* 3,331 graduate, professional, and undergraduate students; 251 full-time matriculated graduate/professional students (173 women), 324 part-time matriculated graduate/professional students (253 women). *Enrollment by degree level:* 575 master's. *Graduate faculty:* 139 full-time (73 women), 55 part-time/adjunct (32 women). *Graduate housing:* Room and/or apartments available on a first-come, first-served basis to single students; on-campus housing not available to married students. Typical cost: $13,578 (including board). Housing application deadline: 5/14. *Student services:* Campus employment opportunities, campus safety program, career counseling, exercise/wellness program, grant writing training, services for students with disabilities, teacher training, writing training. *Library facilities:* University of Washington Tacoma Library. *Online resources:* library catalog, web page, access to other libraries' catalogs. *Collection:* 7.5 million titles, 63,575 serial subscriptions, 136,325 audiovisual materials. *Research affiliation:* City of Tacoma/Port of Tacoma (water quality and sustainability studies), South Sound Public and Private Schools (internships and educational research).

Computer facilities: 178 computers available on campus for general student use. A campuswide network can be accessed from student residence rooms and from off campus. Online class registration, online courseware-Blackboard, Catalyst proprietary CMS are available. *Web address:* http://www.tacoma.washington.edu/.

General Application Contact: Director of Admissions, 206-543-5929, E-mail: uwgrad@u.washington.edu.

GRADUATE UNITS

Graduate Programs Students: 251 full-time (173 women), 324 part-time (253 women); includes 34 Black or African American, non-Hispanic/Latino; 3 American Indian or Alaska Native, non-Hispanic/Latino; 45 Asian, non-Hispanic/Latino; 32 Hispanic/Latino; 3 Native Hawaiian or other Pacific Islander, non-Hispanic/Latino. Average age 35. 339 applicants, 53% accepted, 141 enrolled. *Faculty:* 139 full-time (73 women), 55 part-time/adjunct (32 women). Expenses: Contact institution. *Financial support:* Federal Work-Study, institutionally sponsored loans, and scholarships/grants available. Support available to part-time students. In 2010, 154 master's awarded. *Degree program information:* Part-time and evening/weekend programs available. Offers accounting (MBA); advanced integrative practice (MSW); business administration (MBA); certified financial analyst (MBA); communities, populations and health (MN); computing and software systems (MS); education (M Ed); educational administration (principal or program administrator certification) (M Ed); elementary education teacher certification (M Ed); elementary education/special education teacher certification (M Ed); interdisciplinary studies (MA); leadership in healthcare (MN); nurse educator (MN); secondary science or math teacher certification (M Ed); social work (MSW). *Application deadline:* For fall admission, 4/15 priority date for domestic and international students; for winter admission, 10/15 priority date for domestic and international students; for spring admission, 1/15 priority date for domestic and international students. Applications are processed on a rolling basis. *Application fee:* $65 ($75 for international students). Electronic applications accepted. *Application Contact:* Dr. Debra Friedman, Chancellor, 253-692-5646. *Chancellor*, Dr. Debra Friedman, 253-692-5646.

UNIVERSITY OF WATERLOO, Waterloo, ON N2L 3G1, Canada

General Information Province-supported, coed, university. CGS member. *Graduate housing:* Rooms and/or apartments available on a first-come, first-served basis to single and married students. *Research affiliation:* Waterloo Maple, Inc. (symbolic computation research), Bell Canada, GM Canada (basic research), IBM (basic research), Com Dev International (telecommunications), Nortel (telecommunications).

GRADUATE UNITS

Graduate Studies *Degree program information:* Part-time and evening/weekend programs available. Postbaccalaureate distance learning degree programs offered (no on-campus study). Electronic applications accepted.

Centre for Business, Entrepreneurship and Technology Offers business, entrepreneurship and technology (MBET). Electronic applications accepted.

Faculty of Applied Health Sciences *Degree program information:* Part-time programs available. Offers applied health sciences (M Sc, MA, MPH, PhD); health studies and gerontology (M Sc, PhD); kinesiology (M Sc, PhD); public health (MPH); recreation and leisure studies (MA, PhD). Electronic applications accepted.

Faculty of Arts *Degree program information:* Part-time and evening/weekend programs available. Offers accounting (M Acc, PhD); ancient Mediterranean cultures (MA); anthropology (MA); arts (M Acc, M Tax, MA, MA Sc, MFA, PhD); economics (MA, PhD); English language and literature (PhD); finance (M Acc); French (MA, PhD); German (MA, PhD); global governance (MA, PhD); history (MA, PhD); literary studies (MA); philosophy (MA, PhD); psychology (MA, MA Sc, PhD); public issues (MA); religious diversity in North America (PhD); rhetoric and communication design (MA); Russian (MA); sociology (MA, PhD); studio art (MFA); taxation (M Tax). Electronic applications accepted.

Faculty of Engineering *Degree program information:* Part-time and evening/weekend programs available. Postbaccalaureate distance learning degree programs offered (no on-campus study). Offers applied operations research (MA Sc, MMS, PhD); architecture (M Arch); chemical engineering (M Eng, MA Sc, PhD); civil and environmental engineering (M Eng, MA Sc, PhD); electrical and computer engineering (M Eng, MA Sc, PhD); electrical and computer engineering (software engineering) (MA Sc); engineering (M Arch, M Eng, MA Sc, MBET, MMS, PhD); information systems (MA Sc, MMS, PhD); management of technology (MA Sc, MMS, PhD); mechanical engineering (M Eng, MA Sc, PhD); mechanical engineering design and manufacturing (M Eng); systems design engineering (M Eng, MA Sc, PhD). Electronic applications accepted.

Faculty of Environmental Studies *Degree program information:* Part-time programs available. Offers environment and resource studies (MES); environmental studies (MA, MAES, MES, PhD); geography (MA, PhD); local economic development (MAES); planning (MA, MAES, MES, PhD); tourism policy and planning (MAES). Electronic applications accepted.

Faculty of Mathematics Offers actuarial science (M Math, PhD); applied mathematics (M Math, PhD); biostatistics (PhD); combinatorics and optimization (M Math, PhD); computer science (M Math, PhD); mathematics (M Math, PhD); pure mathematics (M Math, PhD); software engineering (M Math); statistics (M Math, PhD); statistics and computing (M Math); statistics-biostatistics (M Math); statistics-computing (M Math); statistics-finance (M Math). Electronic applications accepted.

Faculty of Science *Degree program information:* Part-time programs available. Offers biology (M Sc, PhD); chemistry and biochemistry (M Sc, PhD); earth sciences (M Sc, PhD); physics (M Sc, PhD); science (M Sc, PhD); vision science (M Sc, PhD). Electronic applications accepted.

THE UNIVERSITY OF WEST ALABAMA, Livingston, AL 35470

General Information State-supported, coed, comprehensive institution. *Graduate housing:* Rooms and/or apartments available on a first-come, first-served basis to single students and available to married students.

GRADUATE UNITS

School of Graduate Studies *Degree program information:* Part-time and evening/weekend programs available.

College of Education *Degree program information:* Part-time and evening/weekend programs available. Offers continuing education (MSCE); early childhood education (M Ed); education (M Ed, MAT, MSCE); elementary education (M Ed); guidance and counseling (M Ed, MSCE); library media (M Ed); physical education (M Ed, MAT); school administration (M Ed); secondary education (MAT); special education (M Ed).

College of Liberal Arts Offers history (MAT); language arts (MAT); liberal arts (MAT); social science (MAT).

College of Natural Sciences and Mathematics Offers biological sciences (MAT); mathematics (MAT); natural sciences and mathematics (MAT).

THE UNIVERSITY OF WESTERN ONTARIO, London, ON N6A 5B8, Canada

General Information Province-supported, coed, university. *Graduate housing:* Rooms and/or apartments available on a first-come, first-served basis to single and married students.

GRADUATE UNITS

Faculty of Graduate Studies *Degree program information:* Part-time and evening/weekend programs available. Postbaccalaureate distance learning degree programs offered. Electronic applications accepted.

Biosciences Division *Degree program information:* Part-time programs available. Postbaccalaureate distance learning degree programs offered. Offers biochemistry (M Sc, PhD); biology (M Sc, PhD); biosciences (M Cl Sc, M Sc, MA, MPT, PhD, CAS); clinical neurological sciences (M Sc, PhD); epidemiology and biostatistics (M Sc, PhD); family medicine (M Cl Sc); manipulative therapy (CAS); medical biophysics (M Sc, PhD); microbiology and immunology (M Sc, PhD); pathology (M Sc, PhD); physical therapy (MPT); physiology (M Sc, PhD); plant and environmental sciences (M Sc); plant sciences (M Sc, PhD); plant sciences and environmental sciences (PhD); plant sciences and molecular biology (M Sc, PhD); psychology (MA, PhD); wound healing (CAS); zoology (M Sc, PhD).

Center for the Study of Theory and Criticism Offers theory and criticism (MA, PhD).

Faculty of Arts and Humanities *Degree program information:* Part-time programs available. Offers arts and humanities (M Mus, MA, PhD); Canadian literature (MA); classical studies (MA); comparative literature (MA, PhD); English (PhD); English literature (MA); French (MA, PhD); music (M Mus, PhD); philosophy (MA, PhD); popular music and culture (MA); Spanish (MA).

Faculty of Information and Media Studies Offers journalism (MA); library and information science (MLIS, PhD); media studies (MA, PhD).

Health Sciences Division Offers audiology (M Cl Sc, M Sc); health sciences (M Cl Sc, M Sc, M Sc N, MA, MCTS, MN NP, PhD); kinesiology (M Sc, MA, PhD); nurse practitioner (MN NP); nursing (M Sc N, MN NP, PhD); occupational therapy (M Sc); speech-language pathology (M Cl Sc, M Sc).

Physical Sciences Division *Degree program information:* Part-time programs available. Offers applied mathematics (M Sc, PhD); astronomy (M Sc, PhD); chemical and biochemical engineering (ME Sc, PhD); chemistry (M Sc, PhD); civil and environmental engineering (M Eng, ME Sc, PhD); computer science (M Sc, PhD); electrical and computer engineering (M Eng, ME Sc, PhD); environment and sustainability (MES); geology (M Sc, PhD); geology and environmental science (M Sc, PhD); geophysics (M Sc, PhD); geophysics and environmental science (M Sc, PhD); mathematics (M Sc, PhD); mechanical and materials engineering (M Eng, ME Sc, PhD); physical sciences (M Eng, M Sc, ME Sc, MES, PhD); physics (M Sc, PhD); statistical and actuarial sciences (M Sc, PhD); theoretical physics (PhD). Electronic applications accepted.

Social Sciences Division *Degree program information:* Part-time and evening/weekend programs available. Offers anthropology (MA, PhD); counseling psychology (M Ed); curriculum studies (M Ed); economics (MA, PhD); education (M Ed); educational policy studies (M Ed); educational psychology/special education (M Ed); geography (M Sc, MA, PhD); history (MA, PhD); political science (MA, MPA, PhD); social sciences (M Ed, M Sc, MA, MPA, PhD); sociology (MA, PhD).

Faculty of Law Offers law (LL B, LL M, Diploma).

Richard Ivey School of Business Offers business (EMBA, PhD); corporate strategy and leadership elective (MBA); entrepreneurship elective (MBA); finance elective (MBA); health sector stream (MBA); international management elective (MBA); marketing elective (MBA). Electronic applications accepted.

Schulich School of Medicine and Dentistry Offers medicine (MD); medicine and dentistry (DDS, MD, M Cl D, M Cl Sc, M Sc, MA, PhD).

School of Dentistry Offers dentistry (DDS, M Cl D); orthodontics (M Cl D).

UNIVERSITY OF WESTERN STATES, Portland, OR 97230-3099

General Information Independent, coed, graduate-only institution. *Graduate housing:* On-campus housing not available. *Research affiliation:* Consortial Center for Chiropractic Research (Palmer Chiropractic College) (chiropractic), Oregon Center for Complimentary and Alternative Medicine in Craniofacial Disorders (complimentary and alternative medicine).

GRADUATE UNITS

Professional Program Offers chiropractic (DC).

UNIVERSITY OF WEST FLORIDA, Pensacola, FL 32514-5750

General Information State-supported, coed, comprehensive institution. CGS member. *Enrollment:* 11,599 graduate, professional, and undergraduate students; 541 full-time matriculated graduate/professional students (356 women), 1,214 part-time matriculated graduate/professional students (740 women). *Enrollment by degree level:* 1,494 master's, 189 doctoral, 72 other advanced degrees. *Graduate faculty:* 143 full-time (48 women), 47 part-time/adjunct (28 women). Tuition, state resident: full-time $4982; part-time $208 per credit hour. Tuition, nonresident: full-time $20,059; part-time $836 per credit hour. *Required fees:* $1365; $57 per credit hour. *Graduate housing:* Room and/or apartments available on a first-come, first-served basis to single students; on-campus housing not available to married students. Typical cost: $4772 per year. *Student services:* Campus employment opportunities, campus safety program, career counseling, child daycare facilities, exercise/wellness program, free psychological counseling, international student services, low-cost health insurance, multicultural affairs office, services for students with disabilities, teacher training. *Library facilities:* John C. Pace Library plus 2 others. *Online resources:* library catalog, web page, access to other libraries' catalogs. *Collection:* 1 million titles, 4,588 serial subscriptions, 5,562 audiovisual materials. *Research affiliation:* Pensacola Bay Area Convention and Visitors Bureau (Pensacola tourism study), Software Engineering Research Consortium (Motorola, Northrup Grumman through Ball State University) (software engineering), University of Southern Mississippi Consortium on Coastal Estaurine Research (microbial biofilms and coastal estaurine research).

Computer facilities: Computer purchase and lease plans are available. 1,064 computers available on campus for general student use. A campuswide network can be accessed from student residence rooms and from off campus. Online class registration is available. *Web address:* http://www.uwf.edu/.

General Application Contact: Terry McCray, Assistant Director of Graduate Admissions, 850-473-7718, Fax: 850-473-7714, E-mail: gradadmissions@uwf.edu.

GRADUATE UNITS

College of Arts and Sciences: Arts Students: 150 full-time (98 women), 162 part-time (111 women); includes 39 minority (11 Black or African American, non-Hispanic/Latino; 2 American Indian or Alaska Native, non-Hispanic/Latino; 5 Asian, non-Hispanic/Latino; 13 Hispanic/Latino; 2 Native Hawaiian or other Pacific Islander, non-Hispanic/Latino; 6 Two or more races, non-Hispanic/Latino), 6 international. Average age 29. 283 applicants, 57% accepted, 77 enrolled. *Faculty:* 40 full-time (14 women), 3 part-time/adjunct (1 woman). Expenses: Contact institution. *Financial support:* In 2010–11, 66 fellowships with partial tuition reimbursements (averaging $721 per year), 117 research assistantships with partial tuition reimbursements (averaging $3,410 per year), 37 teaching assistantships with partial tuition reimbursements (averaging $4,882 per year) were awarded; unspecified assistantships also available. Financial award application deadline: 4/15; financial award applicants required to submit FAFSA. In 2010, 66 master's awarded. *Degree program information:* Part-time and evening/weekend programs available. Offers arts and sciences: arts (MA); communication arts (MA); counseling (MA); counseling-licensed mental health counselor (MA); creative writing (MA); general (MA); history (MA); industrial-organizational (MA); literature (MA); military history (MA); political science (MA); public history (MA). *Application deadline:* For fall admission, 6/1 for domestic students, 5/15 for international students; for spring admission, 10/1 for domestic and international students. Applications are processed on a rolling basis. *Application fee:* $30. *Application Contact:* Terry McCray, Assistant Director of Graduate Admissions, 850-473-7718, Fax: 850-473-7714, E-mail: gradadmissions@uwf.edu. *Dean,* Dr. Jane Halonen, 850-474-2688.

Division of Anthropology and Archaeology Students: 37 full-time (22 women), 31 part-time (22 women); includes 1 Black or African American, non-Hispanic/Latino; 2 Asian, non-Hispanic/Latino; 3 Hispanic/Latino; 2 Two or more races, non-Hispanic/Latino. Average age 29. 59 applicants, 53% accepted, 13 enrolled. *Faculty:* 6 full-time (2 women). Expenses: Contact institution. *Financial support:* In 2010–11, 2 fellowships with partial tuition reimbursements (averaging $3,702 per year), 39 research assistantships with partial tuition reimbursements (averaging $3,500 per year), 7 teaching assistantships with partial tuition reimbursements (averaging $3,760 per year) were awarded; unspecified assistantships also available. Financial award application deadline: 4/15; financial award applicants required to submit FAFSA. In 2010, 2 master's awarded. Offers anthropology (MA); historical archaeology (MA). *Application deadline:* For fall admission, 6/1 for domestic students, 5/15 for international students; for spring admission, 10/1 for domestic and international students. *Application fee:* $30. *Application Contact:* Terry McCray, Assistant Director of Graduate Admissions, 850-473-7718, Fax: 850-473-7714, E-mail: gradadmissions@uwf.edu. *Interim Chair,* Dr. John Bratten, 850-857-6278, E-mail: anthropology@uwf.edu.

College of Arts and Sciences: Sciences Students: 84 full-time (42 women), 248 part-time (103 women); includes 77 minority (28 Black or African American, non-Hispanic/Latino; 3 American Indian or Alaska Native, non-Hispanic/Latino; 20 Asian, non-Hispanic/Latino; 13 Hispanic/Latino; 1 Native Hawaiian or other Pacific Islander, non-Hispanic/Latino; 12 Two or more races, non-Hispanic/Latino), 8 international. Average age 34. 179 applicants, 76% accepted, 105 enrolled. *Faculty:* 36 full-time (7 women), 12 part-time/adjunct (6 women). Expenses: Contact institution. *Financial support:* In 2010–11, 64 fellowships with partial tuition reimbursements (averaging $488 per year), 41 research assistantships with partial tuition reimbursements (averaging $4,562 per year), 26 teaching assistantships with partial tuition reimbursements (averaging $6,608 per year) were awarded; unspecified assistantships also available. Financial award application deadline: 4/15; financial award applicants required to submit FAFSA. In 2010, 77 master's awarded. *Degree program information:* Part-time and evening/weekend programs available. Offers applied statistics (MS); arts and sciences: sciences (MPH, MS, MST); computer science (MS); database systems (MS); environmental science (MS); mathematical sciences (MS); software engineering (MS). *Application deadline:* For fall admission, 6/1 for domestic students, 5/15 for international students; for spring admission, 10/1 for domestic and international students. Applications are processed on a rolling basis. *Application fee:* $30. *Application Contact:* Terry McCray, Assistant Director of Graduate Admissions, 850-473-7715, Fax: 850-473-7714, E-mail: gradadmissions@uwf.edu. *Dean,* Dr. Jane Halonen, 850-474-2688.

School of Allied Health and Life Sciences Students: 35 full-time (26 women), 63 part-time (39 women); includes 16 Black or African American, non-Hispanic/Latino; 6 Asian, non-Hispanic/Latino; 1 Hispanic/Latino; 2 Two or more races, non-Hispanic/Latino, 2 international. Average age 31. 64 applicants, 63% accepted, 30 enrolled. *Faculty:* 11 full-time (2 women), 7 part-time/adjunct (4 women). Expenses: Contact institution. *Financial support:* In 2010–11, 20 fellowships with partial tuition reimbursements (averaging $523 per year), 18 research assistantships with partial tuition reimbursements (averaging $5,700 per year), 12 teaching assistantships with partial tuition reimbursements (averaging $8,042 per year) were awarded; unspecified assistantships also available. Financial award application deadline: 4/15; financial award applicants required to submit FAFSA. In 2010, 9 master's awarded. *Degree program information:* Part-time programs available. Offers allied health and life sciences (MPH, MS, MST); biological chemistry (MS); biology (MS); biology education (MST); biotechnology (MS); coastal zone studies (MS); environmental biology (MS); public health (MPH). *Application deadline:* For fall admission, 6/1 for domestic students, 5/15 for international students; for spring admission, 10/1 for domestic and international students. Applications are processed on a rolling basis. *Application fee:* $30. *Application Contact:* Terry McCray, Assistant Director of Graduate Admissions, 850-473-7718, Fax: 850-473-7714, E-mail: gradadmissions@uwf.edu. *Chairperson,* Dr. George L. Stewart, 850-474-2748.

College of Business Students: 42 full-time (19 women), 122 part-time (60 women); includes 12 Black or African American, non-Hispanic/Latino; 2 American Indian or Alaska Native, non-Hispanic/Latino; 7 Asian, non-Hispanic/Latino; 7 Hispanic/Latino, 19 international. Average age 30. 101 applicants, 72% accepted, 52 enrolled. *Faculty:* 17 full-time (2 women), 5 part-time/adjunct (2 women). Expenses: Contact institution. *Financial support:* In 2010–11, 58 fellowships (averaging $505 per year), 49 research assistantships with partial tuition reimbursements (averaging $3,354 per year) were awarded; unspecified assistantships also available. Financial award application deadline: 4/15; financial award applicants required to submit FAFSA. In 2010, 79 master's awarded. *Degree program information:* Part-time and evening/weekend programs available. Offers accounting (M Acc, MA); business (M Acc, MA, MBA); business administration (MBA). *Application deadline:* For fall admission, 6/30 for domestic students, 5/15 for international students; for spring admission, 10/1 for domestic and international students. Applications are processed on a rolling basis. *Application fee:* $30. *Application Contact:* Dr. W. Timothy O'Keefe, Associate Dean/Director, 850-474-2348. *Dean,* Dr. F. Edward Ranelli, 850-474-2348.

College of Professional Studies Students: 265 full-time (197 women), 682 part-time (466 women); includes 223 minority (141 Black or African American, non-Hispanic/Latino; 3 American Indian or Alaska Native, non-Hispanic/Latino; 20 Asian, non-Hispanic/Latino; 45 Hispanic/Latino; 6 Native Hawaiian or other Pacific Islander, non-Hispanic/Latino; 8 Two or more races, non-Hispanic/Latino), 10 international. Average age 37. 478 applicants, 66% accepted, 250 enrolled. *Faculty:* 50 full-time (25 women), 27 part-time/adjunct (19 women). Expenses: Contact institution. *Financial support:* In 2010–11, 85 fellowships (averaging $728 per year), 50 research assistantships (averaging $3,280 per year), 18 teaching assistantships (averaging $3,750 per year) were awarded; unspecified assistantships also available. Financial award application deadline: 4/15; financial award applicants required to submit FAFSA. In 2010, 227 master's, 21 doctorates, 27 other advanced degrees awarded. *Degree program information:* Part-time and evening/weekend programs available. Offers acquisition and contract administration (MSA); administration (MSA); aging studies (MS); biomedical/pharmaceutical (MSA); career and technical education (M Ed); clinical teaching (MA); college student personnel administration (M Ed); community health education (MS); criminal justice administration (MSA); curriculum and instruction (M Ed, Ed D, Ed S); curriculum and instruction: instructional technology (Ed D); curriculum and instruction: special education (M Ed); database administration (MSA); education (M Ed, MA, Ed D); education leadership (MSA); educational leadership (M Ed, Ed S); educational leadership—education specialist (Ed S); elementary education (M Ed); exercise science (MS); habilitative science (MA); health promotion and worksite wellness (MS); health, leisure, and exercise science (MS); healthcare administration (MSA); human performance technology (MSA); instructional technology (M Ed); leadership (MSA); middle and secondary level education and ESOL (M Ed); nursing administration (MSA); physical education (MS); primary education (M Ed); psychosocial (MS); public administration (MSA); reading education (M Ed); software engineering administration (MSA). *Application deadline:* For fall admission, 6/1 for domestic students, 5/15 for international students; for spring admission, 10/1 for domestic and international students. Applications are processed on a rolling basis. *Application fee:* $30. *Application Contact:* Terry McCray, Assistant Director of Graduate Admissions, 850-473-7718, Fax: 850-473-7714, E-mail: gradadmissions@uwf.edu. *Interim Dean,* Dr. Pam Northrup, 850-474-2769, Fax: 850-474-3205.

School of Justice Studies and Social Work Students: 93 full-time (75 women), 21 part-time (8 women); includes 36 minority (23 Black or African American, non-Hispanic/Latino; 1 American Indian or Alaska Native, non-Hispanic/Latino; 1 Asian, non-Hispanic/Latino; 8 Hispanic/Latino; 1 Native Hawaiian or other Pacific Islander, non-Hispanic/Latino; 2 Two or more races, non-Hispanic/Latino). Average age 36. 65 applicants, 69% accepted, 38 enrolled. *Faculty:* 10 full-time (2 women), 11 part-time/adjunct (9 women). Expenses: Contact institution. *Financial support:* In 2010–11, 24 fellowships (averaging $345 per year), 14 research assistantships (averaging $3,280 per year), 2 teaching assistantships (averaging $3,760 per year) were awarded. In 2010, 2 master's awarded. *Degree program information:* Part-time and evening/weekend programs available. Offers criminal justice (MS); justice studies and social work (MS, MSW); social work (MSW). *Application deadline:* For fall admission, 6/1 for domestic students, 5/1 for international students; for spring admission, 10/1 for domestic and international students. Applications are processed on a rolling basis. Electronic applications accepted. *Application Contact:* Terry McCray, Assistant Director of Graduate Admissions, 850-473-7718, Fax: 850-473-7714, E-mail: gradadmissions@uwf.edu. *Chair,* Dr. Glenn Rohrer, 850-474-2154, E-mail: grohrer@uwf.edu.

UNIVERSITY OF WEST GEORGIA, Carrollton, GA 30118

General Information State-supported, coed, comprehensive institution. CGS member. *Enrollment:* 11,283 graduate, professional, and undergraduate students; 529 full-time matriculated graduate/professional students (368 women), 1,047 part-time matriculated graduate/professional students (774 women). *Enrollment by degree level:* 1,024 master's, 108 doctoral, 444 other advanced degrees. *Graduate faculty:* 241 full-time (110 women), 30 part-time/adjunct (23 women). Tuition, state resident: full-time $4130; part-time $173 per semester hour. Tuition, nonresident: full-time $16,524; part-time $689 per semester hour. *Required fees:* $1586; $44.01 per semester hour. $397 per semester. Tuition and fees vary according to program. *Graduate housing:* Room and/or apartments available on a first-come, first-served basis to single students; on-campus housing not available to married students. Typical cost: $3700 per year ($7006 including board). Housing application deadline: 6/1. *Student services:* Campus employment opportunities, campus safety program, career counseling, child daycare facilities, exercise/wellness program, free psychological counseling, international student services, multicultural affairs office, services for students with disabilities, teacher training, writing training. *Library facilities:* Irvine Sullivan Ingram Library. *Online resources:* library catalog, web page, access to other libraries' catalogs. *Collection:* 853,832 titles, 65,054 serial subscriptions, 11,634 audiovisual materials.

Computer facilities: 1,200 computers available on campus for general student use. A campuswide network can be accessed from student residence rooms and from off campus. Online class registration is available. *Web address:* http://www.westga.edu/.

GRADUATE UNITS

College of Arts and Sciences Students: 146 full-time (70 women), 131 part-time (65 women); includes 52 minority (37 Black or African American, non-Hispanic/Latino; 3 American Indian or Alaska Native, non-Hispanic/Latino; 3 Asian, non-Hispanic/Latino; 6 Hispanic/Latino; 1 Native Hawaiian or other Pacific Islander, non-Hispanic/Latino; 2 Two or more races, non-Hispanic/Latino), 6 international. Average age 31. 162 applicants, 61% accepted, 36 enrolled. *Faculty:* 138 full-time (49 women), 4 part-time/adjunct (2 women). Expenses: Contact institution. *Financial support:* In 2010–11, 40 research assistantships with full tuition reimbursements (averaging $6,000 per year) were awarded; career-related internships or fieldwork and unspecified assistantships also available. Support available to part-time students. Financial award applicants required to submit FAFSA. In 2010, 63 master's, 14 other advanced degrees awarded. *Degree program information:* Part-time programs available. Offers applied

University of West Georgia (continued)

computer science (MS); arts and sciences (M Mus, MA, MPA, MS, MSM, Psy D, Certificate); biology (MS); criminology (MA); English (MA); geosciences (Certificate); history (MA); human centered computing (Certificate); individual, organizational, and community transformation: consciousness and society (Psy D); mathematics (MSM); museum studies (Certificate); music education (M Mus); performance (M Mus); political science (Certificate); psychology (MA); public administration (MPA); public history (Certificate); public management (Certificate); rural and small town planning (MS); sociology (MA); software development (Certificate); system and network administration (Certificate); teaching and applied mathematics (MS); Web technologies (Certificate). *Application deadline:* For fall admission, 7/17 for domestic students; for spring admission, 11/20 for domestic students. Applications are processed on a rolling basis. *Application fee:* $30. Electronic applications accepted. *Application Contact:* Dr. N. Jane McCandless, Interim Dean, 678-839-6405, Fax: 678-839-4898, E-mail: jmccandl@westga.edu. *Interim Dean,* Dr. N. Jane McCandless, 678-839-6405, Fax: 678-839-4898, E-mail: jmccandl@westga.edu.

College of Education Students: 317 full-time (258 women), 797 part-time (639 women); includes 225 Black or African American, non-Hispanic/Latino; 1 American Indian or Alaska Native, non-Hispanic/Latino; 6 Asian, non-Hispanic/Latino; 15 Hispanic/Latino; 12 Two or more races, non-Hispanic/Latino, 3 international. Average age 35. 323 applicants, 50% accepted, 87 enrolled. *Faculty:* 48 full-time (29 women), 16 part-time/adjunct (13 women). Expenses: Contact institution. *Financial support:* In 2010–11, 46 research assistantships with partial tuition reimbursements (averaging $6,000 per year) were awarded; career-related internships or fieldwork and unspecified assistantships also available. Support available to part-time students. Financial award applicants required to submit FAFSA. In 2010, 297 master's, 7 doctorates, 206 other advanced degrees awarded. *Degree program information:* Part-time and evening/weekend programs available. Offers art education (M Ed); art teacher education (Ed S); biology—secondary education (M Ed); biology/secondary education (Ed S); business education (M Ed, Ed S); chemistry/secondary education (Ed S); early childhood education (M Ed, Ed S); economics/secondary teacher education (Ed S); education (M Ed, Ed D, Ed S); education administration and supervision (M Ed); educational leadership (M Ed, Ed S); English teacher education (M Ed, Ed S); French language teacher education (M Ed, Ed S); guidance and counseling (M Ed, Ed S); history teacher education (Ed S); mathematics teacher education (M Ed, Ed S); media (M Ed, Ed S); middle grades education (M Ed, Ed S); physical education teaching and coaching (M Ed); physics/secondary education (Ed S); professional counseling (M Ed); professional counseling and supervision (Ed D); reading education (M Ed); school improvement (Ed S); science teacher education (M Ed, Ed S); secondary education (M Ed); social science—secondary education (M Ed); social science teacher education (M Ed); Spanish language teacher education (M Ed, Ed S); Spanish MAT (M Ed); special education-general (M Ed, Ed S); speech language pathology (M Ed); sports management (M Ed). *Application deadline:* For fall admission, 7/17 for domestic students; for spring admission, 11/20 for domestic students. Applications are processed on a rolling basis. *Application fee:* $30. Electronic applications accepted. *Application Contact:* Dr. Kim Metcalf, Dean, 678-839-6570, Fax: 678-839-6098, E-mail: kmetcalf@westga.edu. *Dean,* Dr. Kim Metcalf, 678-839-6570, Fax: 678-839-6098, E-mail: kmetcalf@westga.edu.

Richards College of Business Students: 52 full-time (26 women), 89 part-time (43 women); includes 21 Black or African American, non-Hispanic/Latino; 1 Asian, non-Hispanic/Latino; 4 Hispanic/Latino, 10 international. Average age 31. 93 applicants, 59% accepted, 15 enrolled. *Faculty:* 32 full-time (9 women), 2 part-time/adjunct (0 women). Expenses: Contact institution. *Financial support:* In 2010–11, 10 students received support; research assistantships with full tuition reimbursements available, career-related internships or fieldwork, tuition waivers (partial), and unspecified assistantships available. Financial award application deadline: 7/1; financial award applicants required to submit FAFSA. In 2010, 100 master's awarded. *Degree program information:* Part-time and evening/weekend programs available. Offers accounting and finance (MP Acc); business (MBA, MP Acc); business administration (MBA). *Application deadline:* For fall admission, 7/17 for domestic students; for spring admission, 11/20 for domestic students. Applications are processed on a rolling basis. *Application fee:* $30. Electronic applications accepted. *Application Contact:* Dr. Faye S. McIntyre, Dean, 678-839-6467, E-mail: fmclntyr@westga.edu. *Dean,* Dr. Faye S. McIntyre, 678-839-6467, E-mail: fmcintyr@westga.edu.

School of Nursing Students: 13 full-time (all women), 4 part-time (all women); includes 1 Black or African American, non-Hispanic/Latino. Average age 43. 21 applicants, 48% accepted, 1 enrolled. *Faculty:* 23 full-time (all women), 8 part-time/adjunct (all women). Expenses: Contact institution. *Financial support:* In 2010–11, 1 research assistantship with full tuition reimbursement (averaging $6,000 per year) was awarded. Financial award application deadline: 7/1; financial award applicants required to submit FAFSA. In 2010, 9 master's awarded. *Degree program information:* Part-time programs available. Offers health systems leadership (Post-Master's Certificate); nursing (MSN); nursing education (Post-Master's Certificate). *Application deadline:* For fall admission, 7/17 for domestic students; for spring admission, 11/20 for domestic students. Applications are processed on a rolling basis. *Application fee:* $30. Electronic applications accepted. *Application Contact:* Dr. Charles W. Clark, Dean, 678-839-6508, E-mail: cclark@westga.edu. *Dean,* Dr. Kathryn Mary Grams, 678-839-6552, Fax: 678-839-6553, E-mail: kgrams@westga.edu.

UNIVERSITY OF WINDSOR, Windsor, ON N9B 3P4, Canada

General Information Province-supported, coed, university. *Graduate housing:* Rooms and/or apartments available on a first-come, first-served basis to single and married students. Housing application deadline: 6/7. *Research affiliation:* Daimler/Chrysler Automotive Research and Development Centre.

GRADUATE UNITS

Faculty of Graduate Studies *Degree program information:* Part-time and evening/weekend programs available. Electronic applications accepted.

Faculty of Arts and Social Sciences *Degree program information:* Part-time programs available. Offers adult clinical (MA, PhD); applied social psychology (MA, PhD); arts and social sciences (MA, MFA, MSW, PhD); child clinical (MA, PhD); clinical neuropsychology (MA, PhD); communication and social justice (MA); criminology (MA); English: creative writing and language and literature (MA); English: language and literature (MA); history (MA); philosophy (MA); political science (MA); social work (MSW); sociology (MA); sociology-social justice (PhD); visual arts (MFA). Electronic applications accepted.

Faculty of Education *Degree program information:* Part-time and evening/weekend programs available. Offers education (M Ed); educational studies (PhD). Electronic applications accepted.

Faculty of Engineering *Degree program information:* Part-time programs available. Offers civil engineering (M Eng, MA Sc, PhD); electrical engineering (M Eng, MA Sc, PhD); engineering (M Eng, MA Sc, PhD); engineering materials (M Eng, MA Sc, PhD); environmental engineering (M Eng, MA Sc, PhD); industrial engineering (M Eng, MA Sc); manufacturing systems engineering (PhD); mechanical engineering (M Eng, MA Sc, PhD). Electronic applications accepted.

Faculty of Human Kinetics *Degree program information:* Part-time programs available. Offers human kinetics (MHK). Electronic applications accepted.

Faculty of Nursing Offers nursing (M Sc, MN). Electronic applications accepted.

Faculty of Science *Degree program information:* Part-time programs available. Offers biological sciences (M Sc, PhD); chemistry and biochemistry (M Sc, PhD); computer science (M Sc, PhD); earth sciences (M Sc, PhD); economics (MA); mathematics (M Sc); physics (M Sc, PhD); science (M Sc, MA, PhD); statistics (M Sc, PhD). Electronic applications accepted.

GLIER-Great Lakes Institute for Environmental Research Offers environmental science (M Sc, PhD). Electronic applications accepted.

Odette School of Business *Degree program information:* Evening/weekend programs available. Offers business (MBA, MM). Electronic applications accepted.

THE UNIVERSITY OF WINNIPEG, Winnipeg, MB R3B 2E9, Canada

General Information Province-supported, coed, comprehensive institution. *Graduate housing:* On-campus housing not available.

GRADUATE UNITS

Faculty of Theology *Degree program information:* Part-time programs available. Offers marriage and family therapy (MMFT, Certificate); sacred theology (STM); theology (M Div).

Graduate Studies *Degree program information:* Part-time and evening/weekend programs available. Offers history (MA); public administration (MPA); religious studies (MA).

UNIVERSITY OF WISCONSIN–EAU CLAIRE, Eau Claire, WI 54702-4004

General Information State-supported, coed, comprehensive institution. CGS member. *Enrollment:* 11,409 graduate, professional, and undergraduate students; 123 full-time matriculated graduate/professional students (91 women), 374 part-time matriculated graduate/professional students (223 women). *Enrollment by degree level:* 468 master's, 14 doctoral, 15 other advanced degrees. *Graduate faculty:* 349 full-time (152 women), 3 part-time/adjunct (all women). Tuition, state resident: full-time $7001; part-time $389 per credit. Tuition, nonresident: full-time $16,771; part-time $932 per credit. *Required fees:* $1057; $58.49 per credit. *Graduate housing:* Room and/or apartments guaranteed to single students; on-campus housing not available to married students. Typical cost: $2920 per year ($5830 including board). Room and board charges vary according to board plan and housing facility selected. Housing application deadline: 5/1. *Student services:* Campus employment opportunities, campus safety program, career counseling, child daycare facilities, exercise/wellness program, free psychological counseling, grant writing training, international student services, low-cost health insurance, multicultural affairs office, services for students with disabilities, teacher training, writing training. *Library facilities:* William D. McIntyre Library plus 1 other. *Online resources:* library catalog, web page, access to other libraries' catalogs. *Collection:* 1.9 million titles, 32,824 serial subscriptions, 12,152 audiovisual materials. *Research affiliation:* Research Corporation (chemistry), Camille and Henry Dreyfus Foundation, Inc. (chemistry), Chevron Phillips Chemical Company (chemistry), Resonant Microsystems (materials science), American Chemical Society Petroleum Research Fund (chemistry, geology), Magma Energy (U.S) Corp (geology).

Computer facilities: 900 computers available on campus for general student use. A campuswide network can be accessed from student residence rooms and from off campus. Online class registration, course management system, library reference staff online chat, ability to check where there are open seats in the general access computer labs, laptop check out pool are available. *Web address:* http://www.uwec.edu/.

General Application Contact: Kristina Anderson, Director of Admissions, 715-836-5415, Fax: 715-836-2409, E-mail: admissions@uwec.edu.

GRADUATE UNITS

College of Arts and Sciences Students: 36 full-time (20 women), 37 part-time (17 women); includes 5 minority (1 American Indian or Alaska Native, non-Hispanic/Latino; 3 Hispanic/Latino; 1 Two or more races, non-Hispanic/Latino), 1 international. Average age 31. 57 applicants, 63% accepted, 23 enrolled. *Faculty:* 258 full-time (101 women), 2 part-time/adjunct (both women). Expenses: Contact institution. *Financial support:* In 2010–11, 42 students received support. Application deadline: 3/1. In 2010, 22 master's, 6 other advanced degrees awarded. Offers arts and sciences (MA, MSE, Ed S); literature and textual interpretation (MA); public history (MA); school psychology (MSE, Ed S); writing (MA). *Application deadline:* For fall admission, 7/1 priority date for domestic students, 6/1 priority date for international students; for spring admission, 12/1 priority date for domestic students, 11/1 priority date for international students. Applications are processed on a rolling basis. *Application fee:* $56. Electronic applications accepted. *Application Contact:* Nancy Amdahl, Graduate Dean Assistant, 715-836-2721, Fax: 715-836-2902, E-mail: graduate@uwec.edu. *Dean,* Dr. Marty Wood, 715-836-2542, Fax: 715-836-3292, E-mail: mwood@uwec.edu.

College of Business Students: 11 full-time (1 woman), 229 part-time (106 women); includes 30 minority (8 Black or African American, non-Hispanic/Latino; 2 American Indian or Alaska Native, non-Hispanic/Latino; 16 Asian, non-Hispanic/Latino; 3 Hispanic/Latino; 1 Two or more races, non-Hispanic/Latino). Average age 32. 135 applicants, 81% accepted, 51 enrolled. *Faculty:* 31 full-time (11 women). Expenses: Contact institution. *Financial support:* In 2010–11, 34 students received support. Application deadline: 3/1. In 2010, 60 master's awarded. Offers business (MBA); business administration (MBA). *Application deadline:* For fall admission, 7/1 priority date for domestic students, 6/1 priority date for international students; for spring admission, 12/1 priority date for domestic students, 11/1 priority date for international students. Applications are processed on a rolling basis. *Application fee:* $56. Electronic applications accepted. *Application Contact:* Nancy Amdahl, Graduate Dean Assistant, 715-836-2721, Fax: 715-836-2902, E-mail: graduate@uwec.edu. *Dean,* Dr. Diane Hoadley, 715-836-5509, Fax: 715-836-4014, E-mail: cob@uwec.edu.

College of Education and Human Sciences Students: 40 full-time (37 women), 43 part-time (36 women); includes 7 minority (1 Black or African American, non-Hispanic/Latino; 2 American Indian or Alaska Native, non-Hispanic/Latino; 4 Asian, non-Hispanic/Latino), 1 international. Average age 29. 136 applicants, 31% accepted, 36 enrolled. *Faculty:* 36 full-time (23 women). Expenses: Contact institution. *Financial support:* In 2010–11, 37 students received support. Application deadline: 3/1. In 2010, 58 master's awarded. Offers communication sciences and disorders (MS); education and human sciences (MEPD, MS, MSE, MST); elementary education (MST); professional development (MEPD); reading (MST); special education (MSE). *Application deadline:* For fall admission, 7/1 priority date for domestic students, 6/1 priority date for international students; for spring admission, 12/1 priority date for domestic students, 11/1 priority date for international students. Applications are processed on a rolling basis. *Application fee:* $56. Electronic applications accepted. *Application Contact:* Nancy Amdahl, Graduate Dean Assistant, 715-836-2721, Fax: 715-836-2902, E-mail: graduate@uwec.edu. *Dean,* Dr. Gail Scukanec, 715-836-3264, Fax: 715-836-3245, E-mail: scukangp@uwec.edu.

College of Nursing and Health Sciences Students: 36 full-time (33 women), 65 part-time (64 women); includes 1 minority (Asian, non-Hispanic/Latino). Average age 36. 61 applicants, 79% accepted, 30 enrolled. *Faculty:* 15 full-time (14 women), 1 (woman) part-time/adjunct. Expenses: Contact institution. *Financial support:* In 2010–11, 48 students received support. Federal Work-Study and unspecified assistantships available. Financial award application deadline: 3/1; financial award applicants required to submit FAFSA. In 2010, 31 master's awarded. Offers adult-gerontologic-administration (MSN); adult-gerontologic-clinical nurse specialist (MSN); adult-gerontologic-education (MSN); adult-gerontologic-nurse practitioner (MSN); family health administration (MSN); family health in education (MSN); family health nurse practitioner (MSN); nursing and health sciences (MSN, DNP); nursing practice (DNP). *Application deadline:* For fall admission, 1/15 priority date for domestic and international students. Applications are processed on a rolling basis. *Application fee:* $86. Electronic applications accepted. *Application Contact:* Dr. Susan Peck, MSN Graduate Program Coordinator, 715-836-5375, E-mail: pecks@uwec.edu. *Interim Dean,* Dr. Mary Zwygart-Stauffacher, 715-836-4977, Fax: 715-836-5925, E-mail: zwygarmc@uwec.edu.

UNIVERSITY OF WISCONSIN–GREEN BAY, Green Bay, WI 54311-7001

General Information State-supported, coed, comprehensive institution. *Enrollment:* 6,636 graduate, professional, and undergraduate students; 38 full-time matriculated graduate/professional students (32 women), 108 part-time matriculated graduate/professional students (80 women). *Enrollment by degree level:* 146 master's. *Graduate faculty:* 20 full-time (8 women), 13 part-time/adjunct (9 women). Tuition, state resident: full-time $7001; part-time $389 per credit. Tuition, nonresident: full-time $16,771; part-time $932 per credit. *Required fees:* $1314; $110 per credit. Tuition and fees vary according to reciprocity agreements. *Graduate housing:* Room and/or apartments available on a first-come, first-served basis to single students; on-campus housing not available to married students. Housing application deadline: 5/1. *Student services:* Campus employment opportunities, campus safety program, career counseling, free psychological counseling, international student services, low-cost health insurance, multicultural affairs office, services for students with disabilities, teacher training. *Library facilities:* Cofrin Library. *Online resources:* library catalog, web page, access to other libraries' catalogs. *Collection:* 360,795 titles, 4,452 serial subscriptions, 48,563 audiovisual materials. *Research affiliation:* UW System Applied Research Program (biogas generation), UW Extension Solid and Hazardous Waste Education Center (sustainable use of natural resources), Abbott Laboratories (anaerobic digestion systems), Wisconsin Space Grant Consortium (space and aerospace science), UW Sea Grant Institute (Great Lakes and ocean sustainability and stewardship).

Computer facilities: Computer purchase and lease plans are available. 550 computers available on campus for general student use. A campuswide network can be accessed from student residence rooms and from off campus. Online class registration, online degree progress, online financial records and bill paying are available. *Web address:* http://www.uwgb.edu/.

General Application Contact: Pam Harvey-Jacobs, Director of Admissions, 920-465-2111, Fax: 920-465-5754, E-mail: uwgb@uwgb.edu.

GRADUATE UNITS

Graduate Studies Students: 38 full-time (32 women), 108 part-time (80 women); includes 23 minority (2 Black or African American, non-Hispanic/Latino; 11 American Indian or Alaska Native, non-Hispanic/Latino; 5 Asian, non-Hispanic/Latino; 5 Hispanic/Latino). Average age 31. 66 applicants, 91% accepted, 48 enrolled. *Faculty:* 20 full-time (8 women), 13 part-time/adjunct (9 women). Expenses: Contact institution. *Financial support:* In 2010–11, 80 students received support, including 4 teaching assistantships; research assistantships, career-related internships or fieldwork, Federal Work-Study, institutionally sponsored loans, and aid for veterans and their family members also available. Financial award application deadline: 7/15; financial award applicants required to submit FAFSA. In 2010, 48 master's awarded. *Degree program information:* Part-time and evening/weekend programs available. Offers applied leadership for teaching and learning (MS Ed); environmental science and policy (MS); management (MS); social work (MSW). *Application deadline:* For fall admission, 8/1 for domestic students; for spring admission, 11/1 for domestic students. Applications are processed on a rolling basis. *Application fee:* $56. Electronic applications accepted. *Application Contact:* Pam Harvey-Jacobs, Director of Admissions, 920-465-2111, Fax: 920-465-5754, E-mail: uwgb@uwgb.edu. *Interim Dean of Professional Studies and Outreach*, Dr. Derryl Block, 920-465-2123, Fax: 920-465-2728, E-mail: blockd@uwgb.edu.

UNIVERSITY OF WISCONSIN–LA CROSSE, La Crosse, WI 54601-3742

General Information State-supported, coed, comprehensive institution. CGS member. *Enrollment:* 9,948 graduate, professional, and undergraduate students; 504 full-time matriculated graduate/professional students (336 women), 468 part-time matriculated graduate/professional students (338 women). *Enrollment by degree level:* 845 master's, 127 doctoral. Tuition, state resident: full-time $7121; part-time $395.61 per credit. Tuition, nonresident: full-time $16,891; part-time $938.41 per credit. Part-time tuition and fees vary according to course load, program and reciprocity agreements. *Graduate housing:* Room and/or apartments available on a first-come, first-served basis to single students; on-campus housing not available to married students. Housing application deadline: 5/1. *Student services:* Campus employment opportunities, campus safety program, career counseling, child daycare facilities, exercise/wellness program, free psychological counseling, grant writing training, international student services, low-cost health insurance, multicultural affairs office, services for students with disabilities, teacher training, writing training. *Library facilities:* Murphy Library. *Online resources:* library catalog, web page, access to other libraries' catalogs. *Collection:* 546,766 titles, 8,120 serial subscriptions, 6,748 audiovisual materials.

Computer facilities: 575 computers available on campus for general student use. A campuswide network can be accessed from student residence rooms and from off campus. Online class registration is available. *Web address:* http://www.uwlax.edu/.

General Application Contact: Kathryn Kiefer, Director of Admissions, 608-785-8939, E-mail: admissions@uwlax.edu.

GRADUATE UNITS

Office of University Graduate Studies Students: 504 full-time (336 women), 468 part-time (338 women); includes 52 minority (8 Black or African American, non-Hispanic/Latino; 5 American Indian or Alaska Native, non-Hispanic/Latino; 17 Asian, non-Hispanic/Latino; 14 Hispanic/Latino; 2 Native Hawaiian or other Pacific Islander, non-Hispanic/Latino; 6 Two or more races, non-Hispanic/Latino), 75 international. Average age 29. 1,347 applicants, 36% accepted, 354 enrolled. Expenses: Contact institution. *Financial support:* Research assistantships with partial tuition reimbursements, Federal Work-Study, scholarships/grants, health care benefits, and tuition waivers (full and partial) available. Support available to part-time students. Financial award application deadline: 3/15; financial award applicants required to submit FAFSA. In 2010, 461 master's, 43 doctorates awarded. *Application fee:* $56. Electronic applications accepted. *Application Contact:* Kathryn Kiefer, Director of Admissions, 608-785-8939, E-mail: admissions@uwlax.edu. *Director*, Dr. Vijendra Agarwal, 608-785-8124, E-mail: gradstudies@uwlax.edu.

College of Business Administration Students: 26 full-time (11 women), 34 part-time (12 women); includes 2 minority (1 Asian, non-Hispanic/Latino; 1 Hispanic/Latino), 25 international. Average age 29. 95 applicants, 38% accepted, 26 enrolled. *Faculty:* 24 full-time (5 women). Expenses: Contact institution. *Financial support:* In 2010–11, 8 research assistantships with partial tuition reimbursements (averaging $5,011 per year) were awarded; Federal Work-Study, scholarships/grants, health care benefits, and tuition waivers (partial) also available. Support available to part-time students. Financial award application deadline: 3/15; financial award applicants required to submit FAFSA. In 2010, 32 master's awarded. *Degree program information:* Part-time and evening/weekend programs available. Offers business administration (MBA). *Application deadline:* For fall admission, 6/15 priority date for domestic and international students; for spring admission, 11/15 priority date for domestic and international students. Applications are processed on a rolling basis. *Application fee:* $56. Electronic applications accepted. *Application Contact:* Amelia Dittman, Assistant to the Dean, 608-785-8092, Fax: 608-785-6700, E-mail: dittman.amel@uwlax.edu. *Associate Dean*, Dr. Bruce May, 608-785-8095, Fax: 608-785-6700, E-mail: may.bruce@uwlax.edu.

College of Liberal Studies Students: 144 full-time (104 women), 278 part-time (227 women); includes 25 minority (5 Black or African American, non-Hispanic/Latino; 3 American Indian or Alaska Native, non-Hispanic/Latino; 7 Asian, non-Hispanic/Latino; 6 Hispanic/Latino; 1 Native Hawaiian or other Pacific Islander, non-Hispanic/Latino; 3 Two or more races, non-Hispanic/Latino), 1 international. 266 applicants, 59% accepted, 122 enrolled. Expenses: Contact institution. *Financial support:* Research assistantships with partial tuition reimbursements, Federal Work-Study, scholarships/grants, health care benefits, and tuition waivers (partial) available. Support available to part-time students. Financial award applicants required to submit FAFSA. In 2010, 247 master's awarded. Offers elementary education (MEPD); emotional disturbance (MS Ed); K-12 (MEPD); learning disabilities (MS Ed); liberal studies (MEPD, MS Ed, Ed S); professional development (MEPD); professional development-learning communities (MEPD); school psychology (MS Ed, Ed S); secondary education (MEPD); special education (MS Ed); student affairs administration (MS Ed). *Application fee:* $56. Electronic applications accepted. *Application Contact:* Kathryn Kiefer, Director of Admissions, 608-785-8939, E-mail: admissions@uwlax.edu. *Dean*, Dr. Ruthann Benson, 608-785-8113, Fax: 608-785-8119, E-mail: benson.ruth@uwlax.edu.

College of Science and Health Students: 334 full-time (221 women), 156 part-time (99 women); includes 25 minority (3 Black or African American, non-Hispanic/Latino; 2 American Indian or Alaska Native, non-Hispanic/Latino; 9 Asian, non-Hispanic/Latino; 7 Hispanic/Latino; 1 Native Hawaiian or other Pacific Islander, non-Hispanic/Latino; 3 Two or more races, non-Hispanic/Latino), 49 international. 986 applicants, 30% accepted, 206 enrolled. Expenses: Contact institution. *Financial support:* Research assistantships with partial tuition reimbursements, Federal Work-Study, scholarships/grants, health care benefits, and tuition waivers (partial) available. Support available to part-time students. Financial award applicants required to submit FAFSA. In 2010, 182 master's, 43 doctorates awarded. Offers applied sport science (MS); aquatic sciences (MS); biology (MS); cellular and molecular biology (MS); clinical exercise physiology (MS); clinical microbiology (MS); community health education (MPH, MS); human performance (MS); medical dosimetry (MS); microbiology (MS); nurse anesthesia (MS); occupational therapy (MS); physical education teaching (MS); physical therapy (MSPT, DPT); physician assistant studies (MS); physiology (MS); recreation management (MS); school health education (MS); science and health (MPH, MS, MSE, MSPT, DPT); software engineering (MSE); special/adapted physical education (MS); strength and conditioning (MS); therapeutic recreation (MS). *Application fee:* $56. Electronic applications accepted. *Application Contact:* Kathryn Kiefer, Director of Admissions, 608-785-8939, E-mail: admissions@uwlax.edu. *Interim Dean*, Dr. Bruce Riley, 608-785-8218, Fax: 608-785-8221, E-mail: riley.bruc@uwlax.edu.

UNIVERSITY OF WISCONSIN–MADISON, Madison, WI 53706-1380

General Information State-supported, coed, university. CGS member. *Enrollment:* 42,595 graduate, professional, and undergraduate students; 7,402 full-time matriculated graduate/professional students (3,555 women), 2,004 part-time matriculated graduate/professional students (1,064 women). *Enrollment by degree level:* 3,731 master's, 5,673 doctoral. *Graduate faculty:* 2,012 full-time (630 women), 228 part-time/adjunct (56 women). Tuition, state resident: full-time $9887; part-time $617.96 per credit. Tuition, nonresident: full-time $24,054; part-time $1503.40 per credit. *Required fees:* $67.63 per credit. Tuition and fees vary according to reciprocity agreements. *Graduate housing:* Rooms and/or apartments available on a first-come, first-served basis to single and married students. *Student services:* Campus employment opportunities, campus safety program, career counseling, child daycare facilities, exercise/wellness program, free psychological counseling, grant writing training, international student services, low-cost health insurance, multicultural affairs office, services for students with disabilities, teacher training, writing training. *Library facilities:* Memorial Library plus 40 others. *Online resources:* library catalog, web page, access to other libraries' catalogs. *Research affiliation:* Morgridge Institute for Research (life sciences: biological sciences), WiCell Research Institute (life sciences: biological sciences), University of Wisconsin Hospitals and Clinics (life sciences: health and medical sciences), William S. Middleton Memorial Veterans Hospital (life sciences: health and medical sciences), Universities Research Association, Inc. (physical and earth sciences: physics and astronomy), U.S. Department of Agriculture, Dairy Forage Center (life sciences: agriculture).

Computer facilities: 1,000 computers available on campus for general student use. A campuswide network can be accessed from student residence rooms and from off campus. Online class registration is available. *Web address:* http://www.wisc.edu/.

General Application Contact: Information Contact, 608-262-2433, Fax: 608-262-5134, E-mail: gsacserv@grad.wisc.edu.

GRADUATE UNITS

Development Studies Program Students: 15 full-time (7 women), 3 part-time (all women); includes 3 Black or African American, non-Hispanic/Latino; 1 Hispanic/Latino, 8 international. 15 applicants, 27% accepted, 2 enrolled. *Faculty:* 41 part-time/adjunct (15 women). Expenses: Contact institution. *Financial support:* In 2010–11, 1 fellowship, 1 research assistantship, 5 teaching assistantships were awarded. In 2010, 1 doctorate awarded. *Degree program information:* Part-time programs available. Offers development studies (PhD). *Application deadline:* For fall admission, 12/31 for domestic and international students; for spring admission, 9/30 for domestic and international students. *Application fee:* $56. Electronic applications accepted. *Application Contact:* Christine Elholm, Graduate Coordinator, 608-262-3412, E-mail: caelholm@wisc.edu. *Professor*, Dr. Gay Seidman, 608-262-3412, E-mail: seidman@ssc.wisc.edu.

Graduate School Students: 7,402 full-time (3,555 women), 2,004 part-time (1,064 women); includes 248 Black or African American, non-Hispanic/Latino; 93 American Indian or Alaska Native, non-Hispanic/Latino; 381 Asian, non-Hispanic/Latino; 327 Hispanic/Latino, 2,238 international. Average age 29. 19,477 applicants, 23% accepted, 2581 enrolled. *Faculty:* 2,012 full-time (630 women), 228 part-time/adjunct (56 women). Expenses: Contact institution. *Financial support:* In 2010–11, 6,735 students received support, including 894 fellowships with full and partial tuition reimbursements available (averaging $14,702 per year), 2,810 research assistantships with full and partial tuition reimbursements available (averaging $18,106 per year), 1,924 teaching assistantships with full and partial tuition reimbursements available (averaging $10,013 per year); career-related internships or fieldwork, Federal Work-Study, institutionally sponsored loans, scholarships/grants, traineeships, health care benefits, tuition waivers (full and partial), and unspecified assistantships also available. Support available to part-time students. Financial award applicants required to submit FAFSA. In 2010, 1,872 master's, 726 doctorates awarded. *Degree program information:* Part-time and evening/weekend programs available. Postbaccalaureate distance learning degree programs offered (minimal on-campus study). Offers biophysics (PhD); cellular and molecular biology (PhD); engine systems (ME); neuroscience (PhD); professional practice (ME). *Application deadline:* Applications are processed on a rolling basis. *Application fee:* $56. Electronic applications accepted. *Application Contact:* 608-262-2433, Fax: 608-262-5134, E-mail: gradadmiss@mail.bascom.wisc.edu. *Dean*, Martin Cadwallader, 608-262-1044.

College of Agricultural and Life Sciences *Degree program information:* Part-time programs available. Offers agricultural and applied economics (MA, MS, PhD); agricultural and life sciences (MA, MPS, MS, PhD); agroecology (MS); agronomy (MS, PhD); animal sciences (MS, PhD); bacteriology (MS); biochemistry (PhD); biological systems engineering (MS, PhD); dairy science (MS, PhD); entomology (MS, PhD); food science (MS, PhD); forestry (MS, PhD); genetic counseling (MS); genetics (MS, PhD); horticulture (MS, PhD); landscape architecture (MA, MS); life sciences communication (MPS, MS); mass communications (PhD); nutritional sciences (MS, PhD); plant breeding and plant genetics (MS, PhD); plant pathology (MS, PhD); soil science (MS, PhD); wildlife ecology (MS, PhD). Electronic applications accepted.

College of Engineering Students: 1,189 full-time (240 women), 83 part-time (15 women); includes 19 Black or African American, non-Hispanic/Latino; 3 American Indian or Alaska Native, non-Hispanic/Latino; 48 Asian, non-Hispanic/Latino; 34 Hispanic/Latino, 198 international. 3,671 applicants, 23% accepted, 282 enrolled. *Faculty:* 224 full-time (34 women), 93 part-time/adjunct (20 women). Expenses: Contact institution. *Financial support:* Fellowships with full and partial tuition reimbursements, research assistantships with full tuition reimbursements, teaching assistantships with full tuition reimbursements, career-related internships or fieldwork, Federal Work-Study, institutionally sponsored loans, scholarships/grants, and unspecified assistantships available. Support available to part-time students. In 2010, 285 master's, 87 doctorates awarded. *Degree program information:* Part-time programs available. Postbaccalaureate distance learning degree programs offered (minimal on-campus study). Offers biomedical engineering (MS, PhD); chemical engineering (MS, PhD); civil and environmental engineering (MS, PhD); electrical engineering (MS, PhD); energy systems (ME); engine systems (ME); engineering (ME, MS, PhD); engineering mechanics (MS, PhD); environmental chemistry and technology (MS, PhD); geological engineering (MS, PhD); industrial and systems engineering (MS, PhD); limnology and marine science (MS, PhD); manufacturing systems engineering (MS); materials engineering (MS, PhD); materials science (MS, PhD); mechanical engineering (MS, PhD); nuclear engineering and engineering physics (MS, PhD); polymers (ME). *Application deadline:* Applications are processed on a rolling basis. *Application fee:* $56. Electronic applications accepted. *Dean*, Paul S. Peercy, 608-262-3482, Fax: 608-262-6400, E-mail: peercy@engr.wisc.edu.

College of Letters and Science *Degree program information:* Part-time and evening/weekend programs available. Postbaccalaureate distance learning degree programs offered (minimal on-campus study). Offers African history (MA, PhD); African languages and literature (MA, PhD); Afro-American studies (MA); applied English linguistics (MA); archaeology (PhD); area studies (MA); art history (MA, PhD); astronomy (PhD); atmospheric and oceanic sciences (MS, PhD); biological anthropology (PhD); biology of brain and behavior (PhD); biometry (MS); botany (MS, PhD); cartography and geographic information systems (MS); Central Asian history (MA, PhD); chemistry (MS, PhD); Chinese literature (MA, PhD); Chinese thought (MA, PhD); choral (MM, DMA); civilizations and cultures (PhD); classics (MA, PhD); clinical psychology (PhD); cognitive neurosciences (PhD); communication

University of Wisconsin–Madison (continued)

science (MA, PhD); comparative literature (MA, PhD); comparative world history (MA, PhD); composition (MM, DMA); composition and rhetoric (PhD); computer sciences (MS, PhD); creative writing (MFA); cultural anthropology (PhD); curriculum and instruction (MS, PhD); developmental psychology (PhD); East Asian history (MA, PhD); economics (PhD); English language and linguistics (PhD); ethnomusicology (MA, PhD); European history (MA, PhD); family and consumer journalism (PhD); film (MA, PhD); folklore (PhD); French (MA, PhD); French studies (MFS, Certificate); gender and women's history (MA, PhD); geographic information systems (Certificate); geography (MS, PhD); geology (MS, PhD); geophysics (MS, PhD); German (MA, PhD); Greek (MA); Hebrew and Semitic studies (MA, PhD); historical musicology (PhD); history of medicine (MA); history of science (MA, PhD); instrumental (MM, DMA); international public affairs (MPIA); Italian (MA, PhD); Japanese linguistics (MA, PhD); Japanese literature (MA, PhD); journalism and mass communication (MA); languages and cultures of Asia (MA); languages and literatures (PhD); Latin (MA); Latin American and Caribbean history (MA, PhD); Latin American, Caribbean and Iberian studies (MA); letters and science (MA, MFA, MFS, MM, MPA, MPIA, MS, MSW, DMA, PhD, Certificate); library and information studies (MA, PhD); linguistics (MA, PhD); literary studies (MA, PhD); literature (MA, PhD); mass communication (PhD); mathematics (PhD); media and cultural studies (MA, PhD); Middle Eastern history (MA, PhD); music (MA, MM, DMA, PhD); music education (MM); music history (MA); music performance (MM, DMA); music theory (MA, PhD); normal aspects of speech, language and hearing (MS, PhD); orchestral (MM, DMA); perception (PhD); philology (PhD); philosophy (MA, PhD); physics (MA, MS, PhD); political science (PhD); Portuguese (MA, PhD); psychology (PhD); public affairs (MPA); religions of Asia (PhD); rhetoric (MA, PhD); rural sociology (MS); Slavic languages and literature (MA, PhD); social and personality psychology (PhD); social welfare (PhD); social work (MSW); sociology (MS, PhD); South Asian history (MA, PhD); Southeast Asian history (MA, PhD); Southeast Asian studies (MA); Spanish (MA, PhD); speech-language pathology (MS, PhD); statistics (MS, PhD); theatre and drama (MA, MFA, PhD); United States history (MA, PhD); urban and regional planning (MS, PhD); zoology (MA, MS, PhD). Electronic applications accepted.

Gaylord Nelson Institute for Environmental Studies Students: 175 (113 women); includes 3 Black or African American, non-Hispanic/Latino; 3 American Indian or Alaska Native, non-Hispanic/Latino; 7 Asian, non-Hispanic/Latino; 4 Hispanic/Latino, 17 international. Average age 30. 318 applicants, 39% accepted, 55 enrolled. *Faculty:* 16 full-time (3 women), 66 part-time/adjunct (19 women). Expenses: Contact institution. *Financial support:* In 2010–11, 103 students received support, including 21 fellowships with full tuition reimbursements available (averaging $18,756 per year), 34 research assistantships with full tuition reimbursements available (averaging $14,960 per year), 27 teaching assistantships with full tuition reimbursements available (averaging $9,392 per year); career-related internships or fieldwork, Federal Work-Study, scholarships/grants, traineeships, health care benefits, unspecified assistantships, and project assistantships also available. Financial award application deadline: 1/2. In 2010, 40 master's, 8 doctorates awarded. *Degree program information:* Part-time programs available. Offers conservation biology and sustainable development (MS); environment and resources (MS, PhD); environmental monitoring (MS, PhD); environmental studies (MS, PhD); water resources management (MS). *Application deadline:* For fall admission, 1/15 for domestic and international students; for spring admission, 10/15 for domestic and international students. *Application fee:* $56. Electronic applications accepted. *Application Contact:* Jim Miller, Student Services Coordinator, 608-263-4373, Fax: 608-262-2273, E-mail: jemiller@wisc.edu. *Associate Director*, Lewis E. Gilbert, 608-262-4510, Fax: 608-262-2273.

School of Education Students: 732 full-time (497 women), 406 part-time (263 women). *Faculty:* 145 full-time (65 women). Expenses: Contact institution. *Financial support:* In 2010–11, 46 fellowships with full tuition reimbursements, 20 research assistantships with full tuition reimbursements, 199 teaching assistantships with full tuition reimbursements were awarded; traineeships and project assistantships also available. In 2010, 211 master's, 78 doctorates awarded. Offers administration (Certificate); art (MA, MFA); art education (MA); counseling (MS); counseling psychology (MS, PhD); curriculum and instruction (MS, PhD); education (MA, MFA, MS, PhD, Certificate); education and mathematics (MA); educational policy (MS, PhD); educational policy studies (MA, PhD); educational psychology (MS, PhD); French education (MA); German education (MA); kinesiology (MS, PhD); music education (MS); occupational therapy (MS, PhD); rehabilitation psychology (MA, MS, PhD); science education (MS); Spanish education (MA); special education (MA, MS, PhD); therapeutic science (MS). *Application fee:* $56. *Application Contact:* Dr. Julie K. Underwood, Dean, 608-262-1763. *Dean*, Dr. Julie K. Underwood, 608-262-1763.

School of Human Ecology Students: 55 full-time (46 women), 9 part-time (8 women); includes 1 Black or African American, non-Hispanic/Latino; 4 Asian, non-Hispanic/Latino; 4 Hispanic/Latino. Average age 32. 118 applicants, 17% accepted, 16 enrolled. *Faculty:* 31 full-time (21 women). Expenses: Contact institution. *Financial support:* Fellowships with full tuition reimbursements, research assistantships with full tuition reimbursements, teaching assistantships with full tuition reimbursements, institutionally sponsored loans, scholarships/grants, health care benefits, and unspecified assistantships available. In 2010, 7 master's, 7 doctorates awarded. Offers consumer behavior and family economics (MS, PhD); design studies (MFA, MS, PhD); human development and family studies (MS, PhD). *Application deadline:* For fall admission, 1/3 for domestic and international students. *Application fee:* $56. Electronic applications accepted. *Application Contact:* Allison Murray, Student Academic Affairs, 608-262-1138, Fax: 608-265-3616, E-mail: armurray@wisc.edu. *Dean*, Robin A. Douthitt, 608-262-4847.

Wisconsin School of Business Students: 402 full-time (172 women), 174 part-time (52 women); includes 22 Black or African American, non-Hispanic/Latino; 4 American Indian or Alaska Native, non-Hispanic/Latino; 47 Asian, non-Hispanic/Latino; 17 Hispanic/Latino, 89 international. Average age 30. 1,235 applicants, 33% accepted, 350 enrolled. *Faculty:* 74 full-time (13 women), 24 part-time/adjunct (5 women). Expenses: Contact institution. *Financial support:* In 2010–11, 307 students received support, including 18 fellowships with partial tuition reimbursements available (averaging $18,567 per year), 6 research assistantships with full tuition reimbursements available (averaging $11,333 per year), 119 teaching assistantships with full tuition reimbursements available (averaging $17,218 per year); career-related internships or fieldwork, Federal Work-Study, institutionally sponsored loans, scholarships/grants, health care benefits, and unspecified assistantships also available. Support available to part-time students. Financial award applicants required to submit FAFSA. In 2010, 291 master's, 4 doctorates awarded. *Degree program information:* Part-time and evening/weekend programs available. Offers accounting and information systems (PhD); actuarial science (MS); actuarial science, risk management and insurance (PhD); applied security analysis (MBA); arts administration (MBA); audit (IM Acc); brand and product management (MBA); business (GM Acc, IM Acc, MBA, MS, PhD); business administration (MBA); corporate finance and investment banking (MBA); entrepreneurial management (MBA); finance, investment and banking (PhD); information systems (PhD); management and human resources (PhD); marketing (PhD); marketing research (MBA); operations and technology management (MBA); operations management (PhD); quantitative finance (MS); real estate (MBA); real estate and urban land economics (PhD); risk management and insurance (MBA); strategic human resource management (MBA); strategic management in the life and engineering sciences (MBA); supply chain management (MBA); tax (GM Acc). *Application deadline:* Applications are processed on a rolling basis. *Application fee:* $56. Electronic applications accepted. *Application Contact:* Erin L. C. Nickelsburg, Assistant Director of MBA Marketing and Recruiting, 608-262-4000, Fax: 608-265-4192, E-mail: enickelsburg@bus.wisc.edu. *Associate Dean for Master's Programs/Associate Professor of Finance*, Dr. Kenneth A. Kavajecz, 608-890-2496, Fax: 608-265-4192, E-mail: kkavajecz@bus.wisc.edu.

Law School Students: 821 full-time (376 women), 49 part-time (27 women); includes 59 Black or African American, non-Hispanic/Latino; 18 American Indian or Alaska Native, non-Hispanic/Latino; 46 Asian, non-Hispanic/Latino; 56 Hispanic/Latino, 82 international. Average age 24. 2,829 applicants, 21% accepted, 246 enrolled. *Faculty:* 70 full-time (32 women), 48 part-time/adjunct (16 women). Expenses: Contact institution. *Financial support:* In 2010–11, 695 students received support, including 79 fellowships with partial tuition reimbursements available (averaging $12,565 per year), 6 research assistantships with full tuition reimbursements available (averaging $10,685 per year), 1 teaching assistantship with full tuition reimbursement available (averaging $9,390 per year); career-related internships or fieldwork, Federal Work-Study, institutionally sponsored loans, scholarships/grants, tuition waivers (partial), and unspecified assistantships also available. Support available to part-time students. Financial award application deadline: 3/1; financial award applicants required to submit FAFSA. In 2010, 257 first professional degrees, 45 master's, 1 doctorate awarded. *Degree program information:* Part-time programs available. Offers law (JD, LL M, SJD). *Application deadline:* For fall admission, 3/1 for domestic and international students. Applications are processed on a rolling basis. *Application fee:* $56. Electronic applications accepted. *Application Contact:* Rebecca L. Scheller, Department of Admissions, 608-262-5914, Fax: 608-263-3190, E-mail: admissions@law.wisc.edu. *Dean*, Kenneth B. Davis, 608-262-0618, Fax: 608-262-5485.

School of Medicine and Public Health Expenses: Contact institution. *Financial support:* Fellowships with full tuition reimbursements, research assistantships with full tuition reimbursements, teaching assistantships with full tuition reimbursements, scholarships/grants, traineeships, and tuition waivers (full) available. *Degree program information:* Part-time programs available. Postbaccalaureate distance learning degree programs offered (minimal on-campus study). Offers biomolecular chemistry (MS, PhD); cancer biology (PhD); clinical research (MS, PhD); endocrinology-reproductive physiology (MS, PhD); epidemiology (MS, PhD); genetics and medical genetics (MS, PhD); health physics (MS); health services research (MS, PhD); medical physics (MS, PhD); medicine (MD, MPH, MS, PhD); medicine and public health (MD, MPH, MS, PhD); microbiology (PhD); molecular and cellular pharmacology (PhD); pathology and laboratory medicine (PhD); physiology (PhD); population health sciences (MPH, MS, PhD); social and behavioral health sciences (MS, PhD). Electronic applications accepted. *Application Contact:* Information Contact, 608-262-2433, Fax: 608-262-5134, E-mail: gradadmiss@mail.bascom.wisc.edu. *Dean*, Dr. Robert N. Golden, 608-263-4910, Fax: 608-265-3286, E-mail: rngolden@wisc.edu.

Molecular and Environmental Toxicology Center Students: 34 full-time (20 women); includes 1 American Indian or Alaska Native, non-Hispanic/Latino; 1 Asian, non-Hispanic/Latino; 3 Hispanic/Latino; 2 Native Hawaiian or other Pacific Islander, non-Hispanic/Latino, 8 international. Average age 28. 51 applicants, 31% accepted, 5 enrolled. *Faculty:* 77 full-time (25 women), 1 part-time/adjunct (0 women). Expenses: Contact institution. *Financial support:* In 2010–11, 5 research assistantships with tuition reimbursements (averaging $23,500 per year) were awarded; fellowships with tuition reimbursements, traineeships, health care benefits, and unspecified assistantships also available. In 2010, 1 master's, 10 doctorates awarded. Offers molecular and environmental toxicology (MS, PhD). *Application deadline:* For fall admission, 12/15 priority date for domestic and international students. *Application fee:* $56. Electronic applications accepted. *Application Contact:* Eileen M. Stevens, Program Administrator, 608-263-4580, Fax: 608-262-5245, E-mail: emstevens@wisc.edu. *Director*, Dr. Christopher Bradfield, 608-262-2024, E-mail: bradfield@oncology.wisc.edu.

School of Nursing Students: 43 full-time (41 women), 121 part-time (111 women); includes 2 Black or African American, non-Hispanic/Latino; 1 American Indian or Alaska Native, non-Hispanic/Latino; 3 Asian, non-Hispanic/Latino; 1 Hispanic/Latino, 13 international. Average age 34. 41 applicants, 63% accepted, 23 enrolled. *Faculty:* 22 full-time (all women), 11 part-time/adjunct (all women). Expenses: Contact institution. *Financial support:* In 2010–11, 8 fellowships with full tuition reimbursements (averaging $26,900 per year), 8 research assistantships with full tuition reimbursements (averaging $18,000 per year), 5 teaching assistantships with full tuition reimbursements (averaging $11,000 per year) were awarded; career-related internships or fieldwork, Federal Work-Study, institutionally sponsored loans, scholarships/grants, traineeships, health care benefits, and unspecified assistantships also available. Support available to part-time students. Financial award application deadline: 3/1; financial award applicants required to submit FAFSA. In 2010, 5 doctorates awarded. *Degree program information:* Part-time programs available. Offers adult/gerontology (DNP); nursing (PhD); pediatrics (DNP); psychiatric mental health (DNP). *Application deadline:* For fall admission, 2/1 priority date for domestic and international students. *Application fee:* $45. Electronic applications accepted. *Application Contact:* Marcia L. Voss, Program Coordinator, 608-263-5258, Fax: 608-263-5332, E-mail: mlvoss@wisc.edu. *Dean*, Dr. Katharyn A. May, 608-263-5155, Fax: 608-263-5323, E-mail: kamay@wisc.edu.

School of Pharmacy Offers pharmaceutical sciences (PhD); pharmacy (Pharm D, MS, PhD); social and administrative sciences in pharmacy (MS, PhD). Electronic applications accepted.

School of Veterinary Medicine Offers comparative biomedical sciences (MS, PhD); veterinary medicine (DVM, MS, PhD).

UNIVERSITY OF WISCONSIN–MILWAUKEE, Milwaukee, WI 53201-0413

General Information State-supported, coed, university. CGS member. *Enrollment:* 2,620 full-time matriculated graduate/professional students (1,470 women), 2,187 part-time matriculated graduate/professional students (1,413 women). *Enrollment by degree level:* 3,489 master's, 1,237 doctoral, 81 other advanced degrees. *Graduate faculty:* 877 full-time (342 women). *Graduate housing:* Room and/or apartments available on a first-come, first-served basis to single students; on-campus housing not available to married students. Housing application deadline: 4/7. *Student services:* Campus employment opportunities, campus safety program, career counseling, child daycare facilities, exercise/wellness program, free psychological counseling, grant writing training, international student services, low-cost health insurance, multicultural affairs office, services for students with disabilities, writing training. *Library facilities:* Golda Meir Library. *Online resources:* library catalog, web page, access to other libraries' catalogs. *Collection:* 1.4 million titles, 8,240 serial subscriptions. *Research affiliation:* We Energies (environment, wind turbine technology), Veolia Water S. A. (water research), Rockwell Automation (informatics, sensors and devices, materials), Johnson Controls (environment, advanced automation), GE Healthcare (informatics, biomedical/imaging).

Computer facilities: 1,000 computers available on campus for general student use. A campuswide network can be accessed from student residence rooms and from off campus. Online class registration is available. *Web address:* http://www.uwm.edu/.

General Application Contact: General Information Contact, 414-229-4982, Fax: 414-229-6967, E-mail: gradschool@uwm.edu.

GRADUATE UNITS

Graduate School Students: 2,620 full-time (1,470 women), 2,187 part-time (1,413 women); includes 215 Black or African American, non-Hispanic/Latino; 26 American Indian or Alaska Native, non-Hispanic/Latino; 148 Asian, non-Hispanic/Latino; 122 Hispanic/Latino, 515 international. Average age 30. 4,446 applicants, 52% accepted, 1195 enrolled. *Faculty:* 877 full-time (342 women). Expenses: Contact institution. *Financial support:* In 2010–11, 130 fellowships with partial tuition reimbursements (averaging $15,000 per year), 168 research assistantships with partial tuition reimbursements (averaging $17,200 per year), 865 teaching assistantships with full tuition reimbursements (averaging $18,100 per year) were awarded; career-related internships or fieldwork, Federal Work-Study, tuition waivers (partial), and unspecified assistantships also available. Support available to part-time students. Financial award application deadline: 4/15; financial award applicants required to submit FAFSA. In 2010, 1,349 master's, 126 doctorates awarded. *Degree program information:* Part-time and evening/weekend programs available. Offers multidisciplinary studies (PhD). *Application deadline:* For fall admission, 1/1 priority date for domestic students; for spring admission, 9/1 for domestic students. Applications are processed on a rolling basis. *Application fee:* $56 ($96 for international students). *Application Contact:* General Information Contact, 414-229-4982, Fax: 414-229-6967, E-mail: gradschool@uwm.edu. *Dean/Vice Chancellor for Research and Economic Development*, Colin Scanes, 414-229-2591, Fax: 414-229-2348, E-mail: scanes@uwm.edu.

College of Engineering and Applied Science Students: 186 full-time (37 women), 146 part-time (26 women); includes 15 Black or African American, non-Hispanic/Latino; 3 American Indian or Alaska Native, non-Hispanic/Latino; 8 Asian, non-Hispanic/Latino; 11 Hispanic/Latino, 33 international. Average age 31. 309 applicants, 65% accepted, 78 enrolled. *Faculty:* 80 full-time (9 women). Expenses: Contact institution. *Financial support:* In 2010–11, 31 research assistantships, 82 teaching assistantships were awarded; fellowships, career-related internships or fieldwork, Federal Work-Study, and unspecified assistantships also available. Support available to part-time students. Financial award application deadline: 4/15. In 2010, 55 master's, 19 doctorates awarded. *Degree program information:* Part-time programs available. Offers civil engineering (MS); computer science (MS, PhD); electrical and computer engineering (MS); energy engineering (Certificate); engineering (PhD); engineering and applied science (MS, PhD, Certificate); engineering management (MS); engineering mechanics (MS); ergonomics (Certificate); industrial and management engineering (MS); manufacturing engineering (MS); materials engineering (MS); mechanical engineering (MS); medical informatics (PhD). *Application deadline:* For fall admission, 1/1 priority date for domestic students; for spring admission, 9/1 for domestic students. Applications are processed on a rolling basis. *Application fee:* $56 ($96 for international students). *Application Contact:* Betty Warras, General Information Contact, 414-229-6169, Fax: 414-229-6958, E-mail: ceas-graduate@uwm.edu. *Interim Dean,* Dr. Tien-Chen Jen, 414-229-4126, E-mail: jent@uwm.edu.

College of Health Sciences Students: 183 full-time (141 women), 34 part-time (21 women); includes 30 minority (20 Black or African American, non-Hispanic/Latino; 7 Asian, non-Hispanic/Latino; 3 Hispanic/Latino), 28 international. Average age 30. 278 applicants, 22% accepted, 36 enrolled. *Faculty:* 46 full-time (25 women). Expenses: Contact institution. *Financial support:* In 2010–11, 6 research assistantships, 12 teaching assistantships were awarded; career-related internships or fieldwork, Federal Work-Study, and unspecified assistantships also available. Support available to part-time students. Financial award application deadline: 4/15. In 2010, 73 master's awarded. *Degree program information:* Part-time programs available. Offers biomedical sciences (MS); communication sciences and disorders (MS); ergonomics (Certificate); health sciences (MS, DPT, PhD, Certificate); healthcare informatics (MS, Certificate); kinesiology/human movement sciences (MS); occupational therapy (MS); physical therapy (DPT); therapeutic recreation (Certificate). *Application deadline:* For fall admission, 1/1 priority date for domestic students; for spring admission, 9/1 for domestic students. Applications are processed on a rolling basis. *Application fee:* $56 ($96 for international students). *Application Contact:* Roger O. Smith, General Information Contact, 414-229-6697, Fax: 414-229-6697, E-mail: smithro@uwm.edu. *Dean,* Chukuka S. Enwemeka, 414-229-4712, E-mail: enwemeka@uwm.edu.

College of Letters and Sciences Students: 744 full-time (361 women), 479 part-time (286 women); includes 44 Black or African American, non-Hispanic/Latino; 9 American Indian or Alaska Native, non-Hispanic/Latino; 35 Asian, non-Hispanic/Latino; 22 Hispanic/Latino, 205 international. Average age 32. 1,726 applicants, 50% accepted, 289 enrolled. *Faculty:* 423 full-time (145 women). Expenses: Contact institution. *Financial support:* In 2010–11, 14 fellowships, 67 research assistantships, 291 teaching assistantships were awarded; career-related internships or fieldwork, Federal Work-Study, unspecified assistantships, and project assistantships also available. Support available to part-time students. Financial award application deadline: 4/15. In 2010, 325 master's, 66 doctorates awarded. *Degree program information:* Part-time programs available. Offers Africology (PhD); anthropology (PhD); art history (MA); art museum studies (Certificate); biogeochemistry (PhD); biological sciences (MS, PhD); chemistry (MS, PhD); classics and Hebrew studies (MAFLL); clinical psychology (MS, PhD); communication (MA, PhD); comparative literature (MAFLL); creative writing (PhD); economics (MA, PhD); English (MA); French and Italian (MAFLL); geography (MA, MS, PhD); geological sciences (MS, PhD); German (MAFLL); global history (PhD); history (MA); human resources and labor relations (MHRLR); international human resources and labor relations (Certificate); international technical communication (Certificate); letters and sciences (MA, MAFLL, MHRLR, MLS, MPA, MS, PhD, Certificate); liberal studies (MLS); linguistics (PhD); mathematics (MS, PhD); media studies (MA); mediation and negotiation (Certificate); modern studies (PhD); museum studies (Certificate); philosophy (MA); physics (MS, PhD); political science (MA, PhD); professional writing (PhD); professional writing and communication (Certificate); psychology (MS, PhD); public administration (MPA); rhetoric and composition (PhD); rhetorical leadership (Certificate); Slavic studies (MAFLL); sociology (MA); Spanish (MA); translation (Certificate); urban history (PhD); urban studies (MS, PhD); women's studies (MA). *Application deadline:* For fall admission, 1/1 priority date for domestic students; for spring admission, 9/1 for domestic students. Applications are processed on a rolling basis. *Application fee:* $56 ($96 for international students). *Application Contact:* General Information Contact, 414-229-4982, Fax: 414-229-6967, E-mail: gradschool@uwm.edu. *Dean,* G. Richard Meadows, 414-229-5895, E-mail: meadows@uwm.edu.

College of Nursing Students: 104 full-time (93 women), 156 part-time (140 women); includes 1 Black or African American, non-Hispanic/Latino; 1 American Indian or Alaska Native, non-Hispanic/Latino; 9 Asian, non-Hispanic/Latino; 2 Hispanic/Latino, 4 international. Average age 40. 153 applicants, 57% accepted, 39 enrolled. *Faculty:* 31 full-time (30 women). Expenses: Contact institution. *Financial support:* In 2010–11, 3 fellowships, 1 research assistantship, 9 teaching assistantships were awarded; career-related internships or fieldwork, Federal Work-Study, health care benefits, unspecified assistantships, and project assistantships also available. Support available to part-time students. Financial award application deadline: 4/15; financial award applicants required to submit FAFSA. In 2010, 52 master's, 17 doctorates awarded. *Degree program information:* Part-time programs available. Offers family nursing practitioner (Post Master's Certificate); health professional education (Certificate); nursing (MS, PhD); public health (Certificate). *Application deadline:* For fall admission, 1/1 priority date for domestic students; for spring admission, 9/1 for domestic students. Applications are processed on a rolling basis. *Application fee:* $56 ($96 for international students). Electronic applications accepted. *Application Contact:* Kim Litwack, Representative, 414-229-5098. *Dean,* Dr. Sally Lundeen, 414-229-4189, E-mail: slundeen@uwm.edu.

Peck School of the Arts Students: 84 full-time (48 women), 27 part-time (12 women); includes 1 Black or African American, non-Hispanic/Latino; 7 Asian, non-Hispanic/Latino; 3 Hispanic/Latino, 11 international. Average age 30. 154 applicants, 37% accepted, 42 enrolled. *Faculty:* 76 full-time (40 women). Expenses: Contact institution. *Financial support:* In 2010–11, 24 teaching assistantships were awarded; career-related internships or fieldwork, Federal Work-Study, health care benefits, unspecified assistantships, and project assistantships also available. Support available to part-time students. Financial award application deadline: 4/15; financial award applicants required to submit FAFSA. In 2010, 42 master's awarded. *Degree program information:* Part-time programs available. Offers art (MA, MFA); art education (MA, MFA, MS); arts (MA, MFA, MM, MS, Certificate); chamber music performance (Certificate); dance (MFA); film (MFA); music composition (MM); music education (MM); music history and literature (MM); opera and vocal arts (Certificate); string pedagogy (MM); theatre (MFA). *Application deadline:* For fall admission, 1/1 priority date for domestic students; for spring admission, 9/1 for domestic students. Applications are processed on a rolling basis. *Application fee:* $56 ($96 for international students). Electronic applications accepted. *Application Contact:* General Information Contact, 414-229-4982, Fax: 414-229-6967, E-mail: gradschool@uwm.edu. *Dean,* Wade Hobgood, 414-229-4762, E-mail: whobgood@uwm.edu.

School of Architecture and Urban Planning Students: 234 full-time (78 women), 41 part-time (16 women); includes 6 Black or African American, non-Hispanic/Latino; 1 American Indian or Alaska Native, non-Hispanic/Latino; 8 Asian, non-Hispanic/Latino; 6 Hispanic/Latino, 19 international. Average age 29. 283 applicants, 70% accepted, 78 enrolled. *Faculty:* 31 full-time (6 women). Expenses: Contact institution. *Financial support:* In 2010–11, 5 fellowships, 24 teaching assistantships were awarded; research assistantships, career-related internships or fieldwork, Federal Work-Study, health care benefits, unspecified assistantships, and project assistantships also available. Support available to part-time students. Financial award application deadline: 4/15; financial award applicants required to submit FAFSA. In 2010, 36 master's awarded. *Degree program information:* Part-time programs available. Offers architecture (PhD); architecture and urban planning (M Arch, MUP, PhD, Certificate); geographic information systems (Certificate); preservation studies (Certificate); real estate development (Certificate); urban planning (MUP). *Application deadline:* For fall admission, 1/1 priority date for domestic students; for spring admission, 9/1 for domestic students. Applications are processed on a rolling basis. *Application fee:* $56 ($96 for international students). Electronic applications accepted. *Application Contact:* Joan Simuncak, Senior Admininistrative Program Specialist, 414-229-4015, Fax: 414-229-6967, E-mail: joanarch@uwm.edu. *Dean,* Robert Greenstreet, 414-229-4016, E-mail: bobg@uwm.edu.

School of Education Students: 312 full-time (243 women), 347 part-time (269 women); includes 80 Black or African American, non-Hispanic/Latino; 1 American Indian or Alaska Native, non-Hispanic/Latino; 25 Asian, non-Hispanic/Latino; 19 Hispanic/Latino, 20 international. Average age 34. 614 applicants, 57% accepted, 108 enrolled. *Faculty:* 74 full-time (50 women). Expenses: Contact institution. *Financial support:* In 2010–11, 7 teaching assistantships were awarded; fellowships, career-related internships or fieldwork, Federal Work-Study, health care benefits, unspecified assistantships, and project assistantships also available. Support available to part-time students. Financial award application deadline: 4/15; financial award applicants required to submit FAFSA. In 2010, 195 master's, 15 doctorates awarded. *Degree program information:* Part-time programs available. Offers administrative leadership and supervision in education (MS); adult and continuing education (PhD); assistive technology and accessible design (Certificate); counseling (school, community) (MS); counseling psychology (PhD); cultural foundations of education (MS); curriculum and instruction (PhD); curriculum planning and instruction improvement (MS); early childhood education (MS); education (MS, PhD, Certificate, Ed S); educational administration (PhD); educational and media technology (PhD); educational psychology (PhD); elementary education (MS); exceptional education (MS); junior high/middle school education (MS); learning and development (MS); multicultural studies (PhD); reading education (MS); research methodology (MS, PhD); school psychology (PhD, Ed S); secondary education (MS); social foundations of education (PhD); specialist in administrative leadership (Certificate); teaching and learning in higher education (Certificate); teaching in an urban setting (MS). *Application deadline:* For fall admission, 1/1 priority date for domestic students; for spring admission, 9/1 for domestic students. Applications are processed on a rolling basis. *Application fee:* $56 ($96 for international students). Electronic applications accepted. *Application Contact:* General Information Contact, 414-229-4982, Fax: 414-229-6967, E-mail: gradschool@uwm.edu. *Dean,* Alfonzo Thurman, 414-229-4181, E-mail: athurman@uwm.edu.

School of Freshwater Sciences Students: 11 full-time (4 women); includes 1 Two or more races, non-Hispanic/Latino, 1 international. Average age 33. 13 applicants, 62% accepted, 7 enrolled. *Faculty:* 3 full-time (0 women). Expenses: Contact institution. *Financial support:* Fellowships, research assistantships, teaching assistantships, unspecified assistantships available. Financial award applicants required to submit FAFSA. Offers freshwater sciences (PhD); freshwater sciences and technology (MS). *Application fee:* $56 ($96 for international students). *Application Contact:* General Information Contact, 414-229-4982, Fax: 414-229-6967, E-mail: gradschool@uwm.edu. *Acting Dean,* Dr. Mark Harris, 414-382-1700, E-mail: mtharris@uwm.edu.

School of Information Studies Students: 148 full-time (112 women), 458 part-time (367 women); includes 15 Black or African American, non-Hispanic/Latino; 1 American Indian or Alaska Native, non-Hispanic/Latino; 12 Asian, non-Hispanic/Latino; 4 Hispanic/Latino, 20 international. Average age 34. 337 applicants, 67% accepted, 126 enrolled. *Faculty:* 22 full-time (10 women). Expenses: Contact institution. *Financial support:* In 2010–11, 4 teaching assistantships were awarded; fellowships, research assistantships, career-related internships or fieldwork, Federal Work-Study, health care benefits, unspecified assistantships, and project assistantships also available. Support available to part-time students. Financial award application deadline: 4/15; financial award applicants required to submit FAFSA. In 2010, 198 master's awarded. *Degree program information:* Part-time programs available. Offers advanced studies in library and information science (CAS); archives and records administration (CAS); digital libraries (Certificate); information studies (MLIS, PhD). *Application deadline:* For fall admission, 1/1 priority date for domestic students; for spring admission, 9/1 for domestic students. Applications are processed on a rolling basis. *Application fee:* $56 ($96 for international students). Electronic applications accepted. *Application Contact:* Hur-Li Lee, Representative, 414-229-6838, E-mail: hurli@uwm.edu. *Dean,* Johannes Britz, 414-229-4709, Fax: 414-229-4848.

School of Social Welfare Students: 234 full-time (208 women), 123 part-time (109 women); includes 36 Black or African American, non-Hispanic/Latino; 1 American Indian or Alaska Native, non-Hispanic/Latino; 7 Asian, non-Hispanic/Latino; 5 Hispanic/Latino. Average age 30. 386 applicants, 54% accepted, 116 enrolled. *Faculty:* 26 full-time (12 women). Expenses: Contact institution. *Financial support:* In 2010–11, 1 fellowship with full tuition reimbursement, 5 research assistantships with full tuition reimbursements, 5 teaching assistantships with full tuition reimbursements were awarded; career-related internships or fieldwork, Federal Work-Study, health care benefits, unspecified assistantships, and project assistantships also available. Support available to part-time students. Financial award application deadline: 4/15; financial award applicants required to submit FAFSA. In 2010, 111 master's awarded. *Degree program information:* Part-time programs available. Offers administration (MS); applied gerontology (Certificate); corrections (MS); law enforcement (MS); marriage and family therapy (Certificate); non-profit management (Certificate); social welfare (MS, MSW, PhD, Certificate); social work (MSW, PhD). *Application deadline:* For fall admission, 1/1 priority date for domestic students; for spring admission, 9/1 for domestic students. Applications are processed on a rolling basis. *Application fee:* $56 ($96 for international students). Electronic applications accepted. *Application Contact:* Deborah Padgett, General Information Contact, 414-229-4851, Fax: 414-229-6967, E-mail: dpadgett@uwm.edu. *Dean,* Stan Stojkovic, 414-229-4400, E-mail: stojkovi@uwm.edu.

Sheldon B. Lubar School of Business Students: 343 full-time (125 women), 345 part-time (146 women); includes 18 Black or African American, non-Hispanic/Latino; 2 American Indian or Alaska Native, non-Hispanic/Latino; 37 Asian, non-Hispanic/Latino; 4 Hispanic/Latino, 66 international. Average age 32. 560 applicants, 57% accepted, 155 enrolled. *Faculty:* 59 full-time (13 women). Expenses: Contact institution. *Financial support:* In 2010–11, 5 fellowships with full tuition reimbursements, 2 research assistantships with full tuition reimbursements, 41 teaching assistantships with full tuition reimbursements were awarded; career-related internships or fieldwork, Federal Work-Study, health care benefits, unspecified assistantships, and project assistantships also available. Support available to part-time students. Financial award application deadline: 4/15; financial award applicants required to submit FAFSA. In 2010, 295 master's, 4 doctorates awarded. *Degree program information:* Part-time and evening/weekend programs available. Offers business administration (MBA); enterprise resource planning (Certificate); executive business administration (Exec MBA); investment management (Certificate); management science (MS, PhD); nonprofit management and leadership (MS, Certificate); state and local taxation (Certificate). *Application deadline:* For fall admission, 1/1 priority date for domestic students; for spring admission, 9/1 for domestic students. Applications are processed on a rolling basis. *Application fee:* $56 ($96 for international students). Electronic applications accepted. *Application Contact:* Matthew Jensen, 414-229-5403, E-mail: mba-ms@uwm.edu. *Dean,* Timothy L. Smunt, 414-229-6256, Fax: 414-229-2372, E-mail: tsmunt@uwm.edu.

UNIVERSITY OF WISCONSIN–OSHKOSH, Oshkosh, WI 54901

General Information State-supported, coed, comprehensive institution. *Graduate housing:* Room and/or apartments available on a first-come, first-served basis to single students; on-campus housing not available to married students.

GRADUATE UNITS

The Office of Graduate Studies *Degree program information:* Part-time and evening/weekend programs available. Offers social work (MSW). Electronic applications accepted.

College of Business *Degree program information:* Part-time programs available. Offers business (GMBA, MBA); business administration (MBA); global business administration (GMBA). Electronic applications accepted.

College of Education and Human Services *Degree program information:* Part-time and evening/weekend programs available. Offers counseling (MSE); cross-categorical (MSE); curriculum and instruction (MSE); early childhood: exceptional education needs (MSE); education and human services (MS, MSE); educational leadership (MS); non-licensure (MSE); reading education (MSE). Electronic applications accepted.

College of Letters and Science *Degree program information:* Part-time and evening/weekend programs available. Offers biology (MS); English (MA); experimental psychology

University of Wisconsin–Oshkosh (continued)
(MS); general agency (MPA); health care (MPA); industrial/organizational psychology (MS); letters and science (MA, MPA, MS, MSW); mathematics education (MS). Electronic applications accepted.

College of Nursing *Degree program information:* Part-time programs available. Offers adult health and illness (MSN); family nurse practitioner (MSN). Electronic applications accepted.

UNIVERSITY OF WISCONSIN–PARKSIDE, Kenosha, WI 53141-2000

General Information State-supported, coed, comprehensive institution. *Graduate housing:* Room and/or apartments available on a first-come, first-served basis to single students; on-campus housing not available to married students.

GRADUATE UNITS

College of Arts and Sciences Students: 10 full-time (5 women), 4 part-time (1 woman); includes 2 Asian, non-Hispanic/Latino, 2 international. Average age 27. 22 applicants, 64% accepted, 8 enrolled. *Faculty:* 9 full-time (3 women). Expenses: Contact institution. *Financial support:* Research assistantships, career-related internships or fieldwork and Federal Work-Study available. In 2010, 3 master's awarded. *Degree program information:* Part-time programs available. Offers applied molecular biology (MAMB); arts and sciences (MAMB). *Application deadline:* For fall admission, 7/1 priority date for domestic students. Applications are processed on a rolling basis. *Application fee:* $65 ($110 for international students). Electronic applications accepted. *Application Contact:* Dr. Daphne Pham, Chair of Molecular Biology Programs, 262-595-2172, Fax: 262-595-2056, E-mail: daphne.pham@uwp.edu. *Dean,* Dr. Dean Yohnk, 262-595-2188, Fax: 262-595-2056, E-mail: dean.yohnk@uwp.edu.

School of Business and Technology *Degree program information:* Part-time and evening/weekend programs available. Offers business administration (MBA); business and technology (MBA, MSCIS); computer and information systems (MSCIS). Electronic applications accepted.

UNIVERSITY OF WISCONSIN–PLATTEVILLE, Platteville, WI 53818-3099

General Information State-supported, coed, comprehensive institution. *Enrollment:* 7,874 graduate, professional, and undergraduate students; 65 full-time matriculated graduate/professional students (41 women), 565 part-time matriculated graduate/professional students (258 women). *Enrollment by degree level:* 630 master's. *Graduate faculty:* 5 full-time (2 women), 90 part-time/adjunct (16 women). Tuition, state resident: full-time $7000. Tuition, nonresident: full-time $16,800. *Required fees:* $756. *Graduate housing:* On-campus housing not available. *Student services:* Campus employment opportunities, campus safety program, career counseling, child daycare facilities, exercise/wellness program, free psychological counseling, grant writing training, international student services, low-cost health insurance, multicultural affairs office, services for students with disabilities, teacher training, writing training. *Library facilities:* Karrmann Library plus 1 other. *Online resources:* library catalog, web page, access to other libraries' catalogs. *Collection:* 535,989 titles, 981 serial subscriptions, 8,055 audiovisual materials.

Computer facilities: 1,200 computers available on campus for general student use. A campuswide network can be accessed from student residence rooms and from off campus. Online class registration is available. *Web address:* http://www.uwplatt.edu/.

General Application Contact: Lisa Popp, School of Graduate Studies, 608-342-1322, Fax: 608-342-1389, E-mail: poppl@uwplatt.edu.

GRADUATE UNITS

School of Graduate Studies Students: 65 full-time (41 women), 565 part-time (258 women); includes 85 minority (58 Black or African American, non-Hispanic/Latino; 6 American Indian or Alaska Native, non-Hispanic/Latino; 8 Asian, non-Hispanic/Latino; 10 Hispanic/Latino; 3 Native Hawaiian or other Pacific Islander, non-Hispanic/Latino), 91 international. 190 applicants, 59% accepted. *Faculty:* 5 full-time (2 women), 90 part-time/adjunct (16 women). Expenses: Contact institution. *Financial support:* Research assistantships with partial tuition reimbursements, career-related internships or fieldwork, Federal Work-Study, institutionally sponsored loans, scholarships/grants, and unspecified assistantships available. Support available to part-time students. Financial award applicants required to submit FAFSA. In 2010, 160 master's awarded. *Degree program information:* Part-time and evening/weekend programs available. Postbaccalaureate distance learning degree programs offered (no on-campus study). *Application deadline:* For fall admission, 7/1 priority date for domestic students; for spring admission, 11/1 for domestic students. Applications are processed on a rolling basis. *Application fee:* $56. Electronic applications accepted. *Application Contact:* Lisa Popp, School of Graduate Studies, 608-342-1322, Fax: 608-342-1389, E-mail: poppl@uwplatt.edu. *Dean,* Dr. David P. Van Buren, 608-342-1262, Fax: 608-342-1270, E-mail: vanburen@uwplatt.edu.

College of Engineering, Mathematics and Science Students: 6 full-time (0 women), 3 part-time (0 women), 4 international. 6 applicants, 67% accepted. Expenses: Contact institution. *Financial support:* Research assistantships with partial tuition reimbursements available. In 2010, 1 master's awarded. *Degree program information:* Part-time programs available. Offers computer science (MS); engineering, mathematics and science (MS). *Application deadline:* For fall admission, 7/1 priority date for domestic students; for spring admission, 11/1 for domestic students. *Application fee:* $56. *Application Contact:* Lisa Popp, School of Graduate Studies, 608-342-1322, Fax: 608-342-1389, E-mail: poppl@uwplatt.edu. *Dean,* Dr. Rich Shultz, 608-342-1561, Fax: 608-342-1566, E-mail: masoom@uwplatt.edu.

College of Liberal Arts and Education Students: 52 full-time (40 women), 185 part-time (135 women); includes 40 minority (32 Black or African American, non-Hispanic/Latino; 1 American Indian or Alaska Native, non-Hispanic/Latino; 6 Hispanic/Latino; 1 Native Hawaiian or other Pacific Islander, non-Hispanic/Latino), 53 international. 28 applicants, 64% accepted. *Faculty:* 4 full-time (1 woman), 54 part-time/adjunct (14 women). Expenses: Contact institution. *Financial support:* Research assistantships with partial tuition reimbursements, career-related internships or fieldwork, Federal Work-Study, institutionally sponsored loans, scholarships/grants, and unspecified assistantships available. Support available to part-time students. Financial award applicants required to submit FAFSA. In 2010, 108 master's awarded. *Degree program information:* Part-time programs available. Offers adult education (MSE); counselor education (MSE); elementary education (MSE); English education (MSE); liberal arts and education (MSE); middle school education (MSE); secondary education (MSE). *Application deadline:* For fall admission, 7/1 priority date for domestic students; for spring admission, 11/1 for domestic students. Applications are processed on a rolling basis. *Application fee:* $56. Electronic applications accepted. *Application Contact:* Lisa Popp, School of Graduate Studies, 608-342-1322, Fax: 608-342-1389, E-mail: poppl@uwplatt.edu. *Dean,* Dr. Laura Anderson, 608-342-1151, Fax: 608-342-1409.

Distance Learning Center Students: 7 full-time (1 woman), 377 part-time (123 women); includes 47 minority (26 Black or African American, non-Hispanic/Latino; 5 American Indian or Alaska Native, non-Hispanic/Latino; 8 Asian, non-Hispanic/Latino; 6 Hispanic/Latino; 2 Native Hawaiian or other Pacific Islander, non-Hispanic/Latino), 34 international. 174 applicants, 67% accepted, 76 enrolled. Expenses: Contact institution. *Financial support:* Scholarships/grants available. Support available to part-time students. In 2010, 101 master's awarded. *Degree program information:* Part-time and evening/weekend programs available. Postbaccalaureate distance learning degree programs offered (no on-campus study). Offers criminal justice (MS); engineering (MS); project management (MS). *Application deadline:* For fall admission, 7/1 priority date for domestic students; for spring admission, 11/1 priority date for domestic students. Applications are processed on a rolling basis. *Application fee:* $56. Electronic applications accepted. *Application Contact:* Chris Jentz, 800-362-5460, Fax: 608-342-1071, E-mail: disted@uwplatt.edu. *Executive Director,* Dawn Drake, 800-362-5460, Fax: 608-342-1071, E-mail: disted@uwplatt.edu.

UNIVERSITY OF WISCONSIN–RIVER FALLS, River Falls, WI 54022

General Information State-supported, coed, comprehensive institution. *Graduate housing:* Room and/or apartments available on a first-come, first-served basis to single students; on-campus housing not available to married students.

GRADUATE UNITS

Outreach and Graduate Studies *Degree program information:* Part-time programs available. Electronic applications accepted.

College of Agriculture, Food, and Environmental Sciences *Degree program information:* Part-time programs available. Offers agricultural education (MS); agriculture, food, and environmental sciences (MS). Electronic applications accepted.

College of Arts and Science *Degree program information:* Part-time programs available. Offers arts and science (MA, MSE); fine arts (MSE); mathematics education (MSE); science education (MSE); social science education (MSE); teaching English to speakers of other languages (MA). Electronic applications accepted.

College of Business and Economics Offers business and economics (MBA, MM). Electronic applications accepted.

College of Education and Professional Studies *Degree program information:* Part-time programs available. Offers communicative disorders (MS); counseling (MSE); education and professional studies (MS, MSE, Ed S); elementary education (MSE); professional development shared inquiry communities (MSE); reading (MSE); school psychology (MSE, Ed S); secondary education-communicative disorders (MSE).

UNIVERSITY OF WISCONSIN–STEVENS POINT, Stevens Point, WI 54481-3897

General Information State-supported, coed, comprehensive institution. *Graduate housing:* Room and/or apartments available on a first-come, first-served basis to single students; on-campus housing not available to married students.

GRADUATE UNITS

College of Fine Arts and Communication *Degree program information:* Part-time programs available. Offers fine arts and communication (MA, MM Ed); interpersonal communication (MA); mass communication (MA); music (MM Ed); organizational communication (MA); public relations (MA).

College of Letters and Science Offers biology (MST); business and economics (MBA); English (MST); history (MST); letters and science (MBA, MST).

College of Natural Resources *Degree program information:* Part-time programs available. Offers natural resources (MS).

College of Professional Studies *Degree program information:* Part-time programs available.

School of Communicative Disorders Offers audiology (Au D); speech-language pathology (MS).

School of Education *Degree program information:* Part-time programs available. Offers education—general/reading (MSE); education—general/special (MSE); educational administration (MSE); elementary education (MSE); guidance and counseling (MSE).

School of Health Promotion and Human Development *Degree program information:* Part-time programs available. Offers human and community resources (MS); nutritional sciences (MS).

UNIVERSITY OF WISCONSIN–STOUT, Menomonie, WI 54751

General Information State-supported, coed, comprehensive institution. *Graduate housing:* Room and/or apartments available on a first-come, first-served basis to single students; on-campus housing not available to married students.

GRADUATE UNITS

Graduate School *Degree program information:* Part-time programs available. Postbaccalaureate distance learning degree programs offered (minimal on-campus study). Electronic applications accepted.

College of Human Development *Degree program information:* Part-time programs available. Postbaccalaureate distance learning degree programs offered (no on-campus study). Offers applied psychology (MS); family studies and human development (MS); food and nutritional sciences (MS); human development (MS); marriage and family therapy (MS); mental health counseling (MS); vocational rehabilitation (MS). Electronic applications accepted.

College of Technology, Engineering, and Management *Degree program information:* Part-time programs available. Postbaccalaureate distance learning degree programs offered (minimal on-campus study). Offers information and communication technologies (MS); manufacturing engineering (MS); risk control (MS); technology management (MS); technology, engineering, and management (MS); training and development (MS). Electronic applications accepted.

School of Education *Degree program information:* Part-time programs available. Postbaccalaureate distance learning degree programs offered (no on-campus study). Offers career and technical education (MS, Ed S); education (MS, MS Ed, Ed S); industrial/technology education (MS); school counseling (MS); school psychology (MS Ed, Ed S). Electronic applications accepted.

UNIVERSITY OF WISCONSIN–SUPERIOR, Superior, WI 54880-4500

General Information State-supported, coed, comprehensive institution. *Enrollment:* 2,856 graduate, professional, and undergraduate students; 83 full-time matriculated graduate/professional students (53 women), 291 part-time matriculated graduate/professional students (179 women). *Enrollment by degree level:* 374 master's. *Graduate faculty:* 30 full-time (12 women), 6 part-time/adjunct (all women). *Graduate housing:* Rooms and/or apartments available on a first-come, first-served basis to single students and available to married students. Housing application deadline: 7/1. *Student services:* Campus employment opportunities, campus safety program, career counseling, child daycare facilities, exercise/wellness program, free psychological counseling, international student services, low-cost health insurance, multicultural affairs office, services for students with disabilities, teacher training, writing training. *Library facilities:* Jim Dan Hill Library. *Online resources:* library catalog, web page, access to other libraries' catalogs. *Collection:* 206,027 titles, 787 serial subscriptions, 4,482 audiovisual materials. *Research affiliation:* Great Lakes Indian Fish and Wildlife Commission, Wisconsin Department of Natural Resources (biology), Environmental Protection Agency (biology), The Mexican National Institute for Ecology (biology), The Mexican Marine National Park Service (biology), Coastal Zone Management Institute and Authority of Belize (biology), Fisheries Department, Government of Belize (biology).

Computer facilities: Computer purchase and lease plans are available. 343 computers available on campus for general student use. A campuswide network can be accessed from student residence rooms and from off campus. Online class registration is available. *Web address:* http://www.uwsuper.edu/.

General Application Contact: Sandra Wallgren, Student Status Examiner, 715-394-8295, Fax: 715-394-8146, E-mail: swallgr1@uwsuper.edu.

GRADUATE UNITS

Graduate Division *Degree program information:* Part-time and evening/weekend programs available. Postbaccalaureate distance learning degree programs offered (minimal on-campus study). Offers art education (MA); art history (MA); art therapy (MA); community counseling (MSE); educational administration (MSE, Ed S); emotional/behavior disabilities (MSE); human relations (MSE); instruction (MSE); learning disabilities (MSE); mass communication (MA); school counseling (MSE); special education (MSE); speech communication (MA); studio arts (MA); teaching reading (MSE); theater (MA). Electronic applications accepted.

UNIVERSITY OF WISCONSIN–WHITEWATER, Whitewater, WI 53190-1790

General Information State-supported, coed, comprehensive institution. *Graduate housing:* Rooms and/or apartments available on a first-come, first-served basis to single students and available to married students. Housing application deadline: 9/1. *Research affiliation:* Generac Power Systems (manufacturing), American Ag-Tec International (international marketing), American Family Insurance (insurance), R. A. Smith and Associates (civil engineering), Sho-Deen (property management and development), WEBCO (lightning radioactive transfer).

GRADUATE UNITS

School of Graduate Studies *Degree program information:* Part-time and evening/weekend programs available. Postbaccalaureate distance learning degree programs offered (no on-campus study). Electronic applications accepted.

College of Arts and Communications *Degree program information:* Part-time and evening/weekend programs available. Postbaccalaureate distance learning degree programs offered (no on-campus study). Offers arts and communications (MS); corporate communication (MS); mass communication (MS). Electronic applications accepted.

College of Business and Economics *Degree program information:* Part-time and evening/weekend programs available. Postbaccalaureate distance learning degree programs offered (no on-campus study). Offers accounting (MPA); business and economics (MBA, MPA, MS, MS Ed); finance (MBA); general business education (MS); human resource management (MBA); information technology management (MBA); international business (MBA); management (MBA); marketing (MBA); operations and supply chain management (MBA); post-secondary business education (MS); school business management (MS Ed); secondary business education (MS). Electronic applications accepted.

College of Education *Degree program information:* Part-time and evening/weekend programs available. Postbaccalaureate distance learning degree programs offered (no on-campus study). Offers communicative disorders (MS); community counseling (MS Ed); curriculum and instruction (MS); education (MS, MS Ed); higher education (MS Ed); reading (MS Ed); safety (MS); school counseling (MS Ed); special education (MS Ed). Electronic applications accepted.

College of Letters and Sciences *Degree program information:* Part-time and evening/weekend programs available. Offers letters and sciences (MS Ed, Ed S); school psychology (Ed S). Electronic applications accepted.

UNIVERSITY OF WYOMING, Laramie, WY 82070

General Information State-supported, coed, university. CGS member. *Graduate housing:* Rooms and/or apartments available on a first-come, first-served basis to single and married students.

GRADUATE UNITS

College of Agriculture and Natural Resources *Degree program information:* Part-time programs available. Offers agricultural and applied economics (MS); agriculture and natural resources (MA, MS, PhD); agroecology (MS, PhD); agronomy (MS, PhD); animal sciences (MS, PhD); early childhood development (MS); entomology (MS, PhD); entomology/water resources (MS, PhD); family and consumer sciences (MS); food science and human nutrition (MS); molecular biology (MA, MS, PhD); pathobiology (MS); rangeland ecology and watershed management (MS, PhD); rangeland ecology and watershed management/water resources (MS, PhD); reproductive biology (MS, PhD); soil science (MS); soil science/water resources (PhD). Electronic applications accepted.

College of Arts and Sciences *Degree program information:* Part-time programs available. Offers American studies (MA); anthropology (MA, PhD); arts and sciences (MA, MAT, MFA, MM, MME, MP, MPA, MS, MST, PhD); botany (MS, PhD); botany/water resources (MS); chemistry (MS, PhD); communication (MA); community and regional planning and natural resources (MP); creative writing (MFA); English (MA); French (MA); geography (MA, MP, MST); geography/water resources (MA); geology (MS, PhD); geophysics (MS, PhD); German (MA); history (MA, MAT); international peace corps (MA); international studies (MA); mathematics (MA, MAT, MS, MST, PhD); mathematics/computer science (PhD); music education (MME); performance (MM); philosophy (MA); political science (MA); psychology (MA, MS, PhD); public administration (MPA); rural planning and natural resources (MP); sociology (MA); Spanish (MA); statistics (MS, PhD); zoology and physiology (MS, PhD). Electronic applications accepted.

College of Business *Degree program information:* Part-time and evening/weekend programs available. Postbaccalaureate distance learning degree programs offered (minimal on-campus study). Offers accounting (MS); business (MBA, MS, PhD); business administration (MBA); economics (MS, PhD); economics and finance (MS, PhD); finance (MS).

College of Education Postbaccalaureate distance learning degree programs offered. Offers adult and postsecondary education (MA, Ed D, PhD, Ed S); community mental health (MS); counselor education and supervision (PhD); curriculum and instruction (MA, Ed D, PhD); distance education (Ed D, PhD); education (MA, MS, MST, Ed D, PhD, Certificate, Ed S); educational leadership (MA, Ed D, Certificate); instructional technology (MS, Ed D, PhD); school counseling (MS); special education (MA, PhD, Ed S); student affairs (MS). Electronic applications accepted.

Science and Mathematics Teaching Center Offers science and mathematics teaching (MS, MST). Electronic applications accepted.

College of Engineering and Applied Sciences *Degree program information:* Part-time programs available. Offers atmospheric science (MS, PhD); chemical engineering (MS, PhD); civil engineering (MS, PhD); computer science (MS, PhD); electrical engineering (MS, PhD); engineering and applied sciences (MS, PhD); environmental engineering (MS); mechanical engineering (MS, PhD); petroleum engineering (MS, PhD). Electronic applications accepted.

College of Health Sciences *Degree program information:* Part-time programs available. Postbaccalaureate distance learning degree programs offered (minimal on-campus study). Offers health sciences (Pharm D, MS, MSW). Electronic applications accepted.

Division of Communication Disorders *Degree program information:* Part-time programs available. Postbaccalaureate distance learning degree programs offered (minimal on-campus study). Offers speech-language pathology (MS). Electronic applications accepted.

Division of Kinesiology and Health *Degree program information:* Part-time programs available. Postbaccalaureate distance learning degree programs offered (no on-campus study). Offers kinesiology and health (MS). Electronic applications accepted.

Division of Social Work Offers social work (MSW).

Fay W. Whitney School of Nursing *Degree program information:* Part-time programs available. Postbaccalaureate distance learning degree programs offered (no on-campus study). Offers nursing (MS).

School of Pharmacy Offers pharmacy (Pharm D).

College of Law Offers law (JD). Electronic applications accepted.

Graduate Program in Molecular and Cellular Life Sciences Offers molecular and cellular life sciences (PhD).

Program in Ecology Offers ecology (MS, PhD).

UPPER IOWA UNIVERSITY, Fayette, IA 52142-1857

General Information Independent, coed, comprehensive institution.

GRADUATE UNITS

Master of Education Program Offers education (M Ed).

Online Master's Programs *Degree program information:* Part-time programs available. Postbaccalaureate distance learning degree programs offered (no on-campus study). Offers accounting (MBA); corporate financial management (MBA); global business (MBA); health and human services (MPA); higher education administration (MHEA); homeland security (MPA); human resources management (MBA); justice administration (MPA); organizational development (MBA); public personnel management (MPA); quality management (MBA). MBA also available at Madison, WI campus. Electronic applications accepted.

URBANA UNIVERSITY, Urbana, OH 43078-2091

General Information Independent, coed, comprehensive institution. *Graduate housing:* Room and/or apartments available on a first-come, first-served basis to single students; on-campus housing not available to married students.

GRADUATE UNITS

College of Education and Sports Studies *Degree program information:* Part-time and evening/weekend programs available. Offers classroom education (M Ed).

College of Nursing and Allied Health Offers nursing (MSN).

College of Social and Behavioral Sciences Offers criminal justice administration (MA).

Division of Business Administration *Degree program information:* Part-time and evening/weekend programs available. Offers business administration (MBA).

URSULINE COLLEGE, Pepper Pike, OH 44124-4398

General Information Independent-religious, coed, primarily women, comprehensive institution. *Enrollment:* 1,485 graduate, professional, and undergraduate students; 121 full-time matriculated graduate/professional students (101 women), 335 part-time matriculated graduate/professional students (295 women). *Enrollment by degree level:* 14 first professional, 418 master's, 24 other advanced degrees. *Graduate faculty:* 12 full-time (11 women), 42 part-time/adjunct (29 women). *Tuition:* Full-time $15,138; part-time $841 per credit. *Required fees:* $240; $120 per semester. *Graduate housing:* Room and/or apartments available on a first-come, first-served basis to single students; on-campus housing not available to married students. Typical cost: $10,464 (including board). Housing application deadline: 8/20. *Student services:* Career counseling, exercise/wellness program, free psychological counseling, multicultural affairs office, services for students with disabilities, teacher training. *Library facilities:* Ralph M. Besse Library. *Online resources:* library catalog, web page, access to other libraries' catalogs. *Collection:* 186,555 titles, 42,513 serial subscriptions, 8,929 audiovisual materials.

Computer facilities: 72 computers available on campus for general student use. A campuswide network can be accessed from student residence rooms. Online class registration is available. *Web address:* http://www.ursuline.edu/.

General Application Contact: Melissa Waclawik, Director, Graduate Admission, 440-646-8146, Fax: 440-684-6138, E-mail: graduateadmissions@ursuline.edu.

GRADUATE UNITS

School of Graduate Studies Students: 121 full-time (101 women), 335 part-time (295 women); includes 100 minority (84 Black or African American, non-Hispanic/Latino; 1 American Indian or Alaska Native, non-Hispanic/Latino; 7 Asian, non-Hispanic/Latino; 2 Hispanic/Latino; 1 Native Hawaiian or other Pacific Islander, non-Hispanic/Latino; 5 Two or more races, non-Hispanic/Latino), 1 international. Average age 37. 161 applicants, 88% accepted, 132 enrolled. *Faculty:* 12 full-time (11 women), 42 part-time/adjunct (29 women). Expenses: Contact institution. *Financial support:* In 2010–11, 45 students received support. Federal Work-Study available. Financial award application deadline: 3/1; financial award applicants required to submit FAFSA. In 2010, 116 master's awarded. *Degree program information:* Part-time programs available. Offers art education (MA); art therapy counseling (MA); business administration (MBA); care management (MSN); early childhood education (MA); education (MA); educational administration (MA); historic preservation (MA); language arts education (MA); liberal studies (MALS); life science education (MA); management (MMT); math education (MA); middle school education (MA); ministry (MA); nurse practitioner (MSN); nursing (DNP); nursing education (MSN); palliative care (MSN); social studies education (MA); special education (MA). *Application deadline:* For fall admission, 8/1 priority date for domestic students. Applications are processed on a rolling basis. *Application fee:* $25. Electronic applications accepted. *Application Contact:* Melanie Steele, Admission Assistant, 440-646-8119, Fax: 440-684-6088, E-mail: graduateadmissions@ursuline.edu. *Dean,* Dr. Debra Flrming, 440-646-8119, Fax: 440-684-6088, E-mail: graduateadmissions@ursuline.edu.

UTAH STATE UNIVERSITY, Logan, UT 84322

General Information State-supported, coed, university. CGS member. *Graduate housing:* Rooms and/or apartments available on a first-come, first-served basis to single and married students. *Research affiliation:* Boeing Aerospace and Engineering (science and engineering), Duke Energy Corporation (engineering), Kennecott Copper Corporation (natural resources), Kraft Foods, Inc. (agriculture), National Endowment for Financial Education (education).

GRADUATE UNITS

School of Graduate Studies *Degree program information:* Part-time and evening/weekend programs available. Postbaccalaureate distance learning degree programs offered (minimal on-campus study).

College of Agriculture *Degree program information:* Part-time programs available. Postbaccalaureate distance learning degree programs offered (minimal on-campus study). Offers agricultural systems technology (MS); agriculture (MDA, MFMS, MS, PhD); animal science (MS, PhD); biometeorology (MS, PhD); bioveterinary science (MS, PhD); dairy science (MS); dietetic administration (MDA); ecology (MS, PhD); family and consumer sciences education (MS); food microbiology and safety (MFMS); nutrition and food sciences (MS, PhD); nutrition science (MS, PhD); plant science (MS, PhD); soil science (MS, PhD); toxicology (MS, PhD).

College of Business *Degree program information:* Part-time and evening/weekend programs available. Postbaccalaureate distance learning degree programs offered (no on-campus study). Offers accountancy (M Acc); applied economics (MS); business (M Acc, MA, MBA, MS, Ed D, PhD); business administration (MBA); business education (MS); business information systems (MS); business information systems and education (Ed D); economics (MA, MS, PhD); education (PhD); human resource management (MS).

College of Education and Human Services *Degree program information:* Part-time and evening/weekend programs available. Postbaccalaureate distance learning degree programs offered (no on-campus study). Offers audiology (Au D, Ed S); business information systems (Ed D, PhD); clinical/counseling/school psychology (PhD); communication disorders and deaf education (M Ed); communicative disorders and deaf education (MA, MS); curriculum and instruction (Ed D, PhD); disability disciplines (PhD); education and human services (M Ed, MA, MFHD, MRC, MS, Au D, Ed D, PhD, Ed S); elementary education (M Ed, MA, MS); family and human development (MFHD); family, consumer, and human development (MS, PhD); health, physical education and recreation (M Ed, MS); instructional technology (M Ed, MS, PhD, Ed S); rehabilitation counselor education (MRC); research and evaluation (PhD); research and evaluation methodology (PhD); school counseling (MS); school psychology (MS); secondary education (M Ed, MA, MS); special education (M Ed, MS, Ed S).

College of Engineering *Degree program information:* Part-time and evening/weekend programs available. Offers aerospace engineering (MS, PhD); biological and agricultural engineering (MS, PhD); civil and environmental engineering (ME, MS, PhD, CE); electrical engineering (ME, MS, PhD); engineering (ME, MS, PhD, CE); industrial technology (MS); irrigation engineering (MS, PhD); mechanical engineering (ME, MS, PhD). Electronic applications accepted.

College of Humanities, Arts and Social Sciences *Degree program information:* Part-time and evening/weekend programs available. Postbaccalaureate distance learning degree programs offered (minimal on-campus study). Offers advanced technical practice (MFA); American studies (MA, MS); art (MA, MFA); bioregional planning (MS); design (MFA); English (MA, MS); folklore (MA, MS); history (MA, MS); humanities, arts and social sciences (MA, MFA, MLA, MS, MSLT, MSS, PhD); interior design (MS); journalism and communication (MA, MS); landscape architecture (MLA); political science (MA, MS); second language teaching (MSLT); sociology (MA, MS, MSS, PhD); theatre arts (MA, MFA); western American literature and culture (MA, MS).

College of Natural Resources *Degree program information:* Part-time programs available. Offers bioregional planning (MS); ecology (MS, PhD); fisheries biology (MS, PhD); forestry (MS, PhD); geography (MA, MS); human dimensions of ecosystem science and manage-

Utah State University (continued)

ment (MS, PhD); natural resources (MA, MNR, MS, PhD); range science (MS, PhD); recreation resource management (MS, PhD); watershed science (MS, PhD); wildlife biology (MS, PhD).

College of Science *Degree program information:* Part-time and evening/weekend programs available. Offers biochemistry (MS, PhD); biology (MS, PhD); chemistry (MS, PhD); computer science (MCS, MS, PhD); ecology (MS, PhD); geology (MS); industrial mathematics (MS); mathematical sciences (PhD); mathematics (M Math, MS); physics (MS, PhD); science (M Math, MCS, MS, PhD); statistics (MS).

UTAH VALLEY UNIVERSITY, Orem, UT 84058-5999

General Information State-supported, coed, comprehensive institution. *Enrollment:* 32,670 graduate, professional, and undergraduate students; 8 full-time matriculated graduate/professional students (6 women), 89 part-time matriculated graduate/professional students (38 women). *Enrollment by degree level:* 97 master's. *Graduate faculty:* 9 full-time (5 women). Tuition, state resident: full-time $5376; part-time $298 per credit. *Required fees:* $1232; $616 per semester. Tuition and fees vary according to course load and program. *Student services:* Campus employment opportunities, campus safety program, career counseling, child daycare facilities, exercise/wellness program, grant writing training, international student services, low-cost health insurance, multicultural affairs office, services for students with disabilities, teacher training. *Library facilities:* Utah Valley University Library plus 1 other. *Online resources:* library catalog, web page, access to other libraries' catalogs. *Collection:* 228,000 titles, 568 serial subscriptions, 20,788 audiovisual materials.

Computer facilities: 1,000 computers available on campus for general student use. A campuswide network can be accessed from off campus. Online class registration is available. *Web address:* http://www.uvu.edu/.

General Application Contact: Eric Wilding, Intermediate Research Analyst, 801-863-7923, E-mail: eric.wilding@uvu.edu.

GRADUATE UNITS

Program in Education Students: 2 full-time (both women), 47 part-time (30 women); includes 2 minority (1 Asian, non-Hispanic/Latino; 1 Hispanic/Latino). Average age 33. *Faculty:* 3 full-time (1 woman). Expenses: Contact institution. *Financial support:* Application deadline: 5/1. In 2010, 13 master's awarded. *Degree program information:* Part-time programs available. Offers education (M Ed). *Application deadline:* For fall admission, 3/15 for domestic and international students. *Application fee:* $45 ($100 for international students). Electronic applications accepted. *Application Contact:* Maggie Hewlett, Administrative Assistant, 801-863-8270, E-mail: mhewlett@uvu.edu. *Associate Vice President for Academic Affairs*, Kathie Debenham, 801-863-6815, E-mail: kathie.debenham@uvu.edu.

Program in Nursing Students: 5 full-time (3 women), 1 (woman) part-time. Average age 44. *Faculty:* 4 full-time (3 women). Expenses: Contact institution. *Financial support:* Application deadline: 5/1. *Degree program information:* Part-time programs available. Offers nursing (MSN). *Application deadline:* For fall admission, 4/1 for domestic and international students. *Application fee:* $45 ($100 for international students). Electronic applications accepted. *Application Contact:* Sam Rushforth, Dean of the College of Science and Health, 801-863-6441. *Dean of the College of Science and Health*, Sam Rushforth, 801-863-6441.

UTICA COLLEGE, Utica, NY 13502-4892

General Information Independent, coed, comprehensive institution. *Enrollment:* 206 full-time matriculated graduate/professional students (161 women), 711 part-time matriculated graduate/professional students (432 women). *Enrollment by degree level:* 261 first professional, 623 master's. *Graduate faculty:* 65 full-time (28 women). *Tuition:* Full-time $26,100; part-time $700 per credit hour. *Required fees:* $400; $60 per course. Tuition and fees vary according to course load, degree level and program. *Graduate housing:* Room and/or apartments available on a first-come, first-served basis to single students; on-campus housing not available to married students. Housing application deadline: 3/1. *Student services:* Campus employment opportunities, campus safety program, career counseling, international student services, low-cost health insurance, services for students with disabilities. *Library facilities:* Frank E. Gannett Memorial Library. *Online resources:* library catalog, web page. *Collection:* 17,884 titles, 1,480 serial subscriptions, 10,162 audiovisual materials.

Computer facilities: 179 computers available on campus for general student use. A campuswide network can be accessed from student residence rooms. Online class registration is available. *Web address:* http://www.utica.edu/.

General Application Contact: John D. Rowe, Director of Graduate Admissions, 315-792-3824, Fax: 315-792-3003, E-mail: jrowe@utica.edu.

GRADUATE UNITS

Department of Physical Therapy Students: 78 full-time (50 women), 188 part-time (106 women); includes 7 Black or African American, non-Hispanic/Latino; 57 Asian, non-Hispanic/Latino; 4 Hispanic/Latino, 69 international. Average age 33. *Faculty:* 8 full-time (4 women). Expenses: Contact institution. *Financial support:* Career-related internships or fieldwork, scholarships/grants, tuition waivers (partial), and unspecified assistantships available. Support available to part-time students. Financial award application deadline: 3/15; financial award applicants required to submit FAFSA. In 2010, 70 degrees awarded. *Degree program information:* Part-time and evening/weekend programs available. Postbaccalaureate distance learning degree programs offered (minimal on-campus study). Offers physical therapy (DPT, TDPT). *Application deadline:* Applications are processed on a rolling basis. *Application fee:* $50. Electronic applications accepted. *Application Contact:* John D. Rowe, Director of Graduate Admissions, 315-792-3824, Fax: 315-792-3003, E-mail: jrowe@utica.edu. *Director*, Dr. Shauna Malta, 315-792-3313, E-mail: smalta@utica.edu.

Liberal Studies Program Students: 18 part-time (14 women); includes 1 Black or African American, non-Hispanic/Latino; 1 Asian, non-Hispanic/Latino. Average age 28. *Faculty:* 19 full-time (8 women). Expenses: Contact institution. *Financial support:* Career-related internships or fieldwork, scholarships/grants, tuition waivers (partial), and unspecified assistantships available. Support available to part-time students. Financial award application deadline: 3/15; financial award applicants required to submit FAFSA. In 2010, 5 master's awarded. *Degree program information:* Part-time and evening/weekend programs available. Offers liberal studies (MS). *Application deadline:* Applications are processed on a rolling basis. *Application fee:* $50. Electronic applications accepted. *Application Contact:* John D. Rowe, Director of Graduate Admissions, 315-792-3824, Fax: 315-792-3003, E-mail: jrowe@utica.edu. *Coordinator*, Prof. Polly Smith, 315-792-3124, E-mail: laaronson@utica.edu.

Program in Accountancy Students: 18 part-time (15 women); includes 1 Black or African American, non-Hispanic/Latino; 2 Hispanic/Latino. Average age 31. *Faculty:* 7 full-time (0 women). Expenses: Contact institution. *Financial support:* Career-related internships or fieldwork, scholarships/grants, tuition waivers (partial), and unspecified assistantships available. Support available to part-time students. Financial award application deadline: 3/15; financial award applicants required to submit FAFSA. In 2010, 10 master's awarded. *Degree program information:* Part-time and evening/weekend programs available. Postbaccalaureate distance learning degree programs offered. Offers accountancy (MBA). *Application deadline:* Applications are processed on a rolling basis. *Application fee:* $50. Electronic applications accepted. *Application Contact:* John D. Rowe, Director of Graduate Admissions, 315-792-3824, Fax: 315-792-3003, E-mail: jrowe@utica.edu. *MBA Director*, Dr. Hartwell Herring, 315-792-3335, E-mail: hherring@utica.edu.

Program in Cybersecurity Students: 58 part-time (19 women); includes 9 minority (4 Black or African American, non-Hispanic/Latino; 1 Asian, non-Hispanic/Latino; 4 Hispanic/Latino), 1 international. Average age 33. Expenses: Contact institution. *Financial support:* Applicants required to submit FAFSA. *Degree program information:* Part-time and evening/weekend programs available. Postbaccalaureate distance learning degree programs offered. Offers cybersecurity (MS). *Application deadline:* Applications are processed on a rolling basis. Electronic applications accepted. *Application Contact:* John D. Rowe, Director of Graduate Admissions, 315-792-3824, Fax: 315-792-3003, E-mail: jrowe@utica.edu. *Chair*, Joseph Giordano, 315-792-2521.

Program in Economic Crime and Fraud Management Students: 3 full-time (2 women), 95 part-time (65 women); includes 11 Black or African American, non-Hispanic/Latino; 3 Asian, non-Hispanic/Latino; 3 Hispanic/Latino, 1 international. Average age 33. *Faculty:* 7 full-time (0 women). Expenses: Contact institution. *Financial support:* Career-related internships or fieldwork, scholarships/grants, tuition waivers (partial), and unspecified assistantships available. Support available to part-time students. Financial award application deadline: 3/15; financial award applicants required to submit FAFSA. In 2010, 41 master's awarded. *Degree program information:* Part-time and evening/weekend programs available. Postbaccalaureate distance learning degree programs offered (minimal on-campus study). Offers economic crime and fraud management (MBA). *Application deadline:* Applications are processed on a rolling basis. *Application fee:* $50. Electronic applications accepted. *Application Contact:* John D. Rowe, Director of Graduate Admissions, 315-792-3824, Fax: 315-792-3003, E-mail: jrowe@utica.edu. *Director of Economic Crime Graduate Programs*, Dr. R. Bruce McBride, 315-792-3808, E-mail: rmcbride@utica.edu.

Program in Economic Crime Management Students: 1 (woman) full-time, 103 part-time (51 women); includes 7 Black or African American, non-Hispanic/Latino; 1 American Indian or Alaska Native, non-Hispanic/Latino; 2 Asian, non-Hispanic/Latino; 6 Hispanic/Latino, 1 international. Average age 36. *Faculty:* 4 full-time (0 women). Expenses: Contact institution. *Financial support:* Career-related internships or fieldwork, scholarships/grants, tuition waivers (partial), and unspecified assistantships available. Support available to part-time students. Financial award application deadline: 3/15; financial award applicants required to submit FAFSA. In 2010, 35 master's awarded. *Degree program information:* Part-time programs available. Postbaccalaureate distance learning degree programs offered (minimal on-campus study). Offers economic crime management (MS). *Application deadline:* Applications are processed on a rolling basis. *Application fee:* $50. Electronic applications accepted. *Application Contact:* John D. Rowe, Director of Graduate Admissions, 315-792-3824, Fax: 315-792-3003, E-mail: jrowe@utica.edu. *Director of Economic Crime Graduate Programs*, Dr. R. Bruce McBride, 315-792-3808, E-mail: rmcbride@utica.edu.

Program in Health Care Administration Students: 7 full-time (4 women), 68 part-time (56 women); includes 8 Black or African American, non-Hispanic/Latino; 1 American Indian or Alaska Native, non-Hispanic/Latino; 1 Asian, non-Hispanic/Latino; 3 Hispanic/Latino, 1 international. Average age 33. Expenses: Contact institution. *Degree program information:* Part-time and evening/weekend programs available. Offers health care administration (MS). *Application deadline:* Applications are processed on a rolling basis. Electronic applications accepted. *Application Contact:* John D. Rowe, Director of Graduate Admissions, 315-792-3824, Fax: 315-792-3003, E-mail: jrowe@utica.edu. *Head*, Dr. Dana Hart, 315-792-3375, E-mail: dhart@utica.edu.

Program in Occupational Therapy Students: 79 full-time (75 women), 16 part-time (all women); includes 2 Black or African American, non-Hispanic/Latino; 1 Asian, non-Hispanic/Latino; 1 Hispanic/Latino, 5 international. Average age 29. *Faculty:* 7 full-time (all women). Expenses: Contact institution. *Financial support:* Career-related internships or fieldwork, scholarships/grants, tuition waivers (partial), and unspecified assistantships available. Support available to part-time students. Financial award application deadline: 3/15; financial award applicants required to submit FAFSA. In 2010, 27 master's awarded. *Degree program information:* Part-time and evening/weekend programs available. Offers occupational therapy (MS). *Application deadline:* Applications are processed on a rolling basis. *Application fee:* $50. Electronic applications accepted. *Application Contact:* John D. Rowe, Director of Graduate Admissions, 315-792-3824, Fax: 315-792-3003, E-mail: jrowe@utica.edu. *Director*, Sally Townsend, 315-792-3239, E-mail: stownsend@utica.edu.

Teacher Education Programs Students: 38 full-time (29 women), 88 part-time (56 women); includes 3 Black or African American, non-Hispanic/Latino; 2 Asian, non-Hispanic/Latino; 2 Hispanic/Latino. Average age 28. *Faculty:* 10 full-time (7 women). Expenses: Contact institution. *Financial support:* Career-related internships or fieldwork, scholarships/grants, tuition waivers (partial), and unspecified assistantships available. Support available to part-time students. Financial award application deadline: 3/15; financial award applicants required to submit FAFSA. In 2010, 64 master's awarded. Offers teacher education (MS, MS Ed, CAS). *Application deadline:* Applications are processed on a rolling basis. *Application fee:* $50. Electronic applications accepted. *Application Contact:* John D. Rowe, Director of Graduate Admissions, 315-792-3824, Fax: 315-792-3003, E-mail: jrowe@utica.edu. *Director, Institute for Excellence in Education*, Dr. Lois Fisch, 315-792-3815, E-mail: lfisch@utica.edu.

VALDOSTA STATE UNIVERSITY, Valdosta, GA 31698

General Information State-supported, coed, university. CGS member. *Enrollment:* 12,898 graduate, professional, and undergraduate students; 293 full-time matriculated graduate/professional students (225 women), 783 part-time matriculated graduate/professional students (601 women). *Enrollment by degree level:* 962 master's, 114 doctoral. *Graduate faculty:* 247 full-time (99 women). Tuition, state resident: full-time $5256; part-time $197 per credit hour. Tuition, nonresident: full-time $14,490; part-time $710 per credit hour. *Required fees:* $855 per semester. Tuition and fees vary according to course load and campus/location. *Graduate housing:* Rooms and/or apartments available on a first-come, first-served basis to single and married students. Typical cost: $1730 (including board) for single students; $1730 (including board) for married students. Housing application deadline: 7/1. *Student services:* Campus employment opportunities, campus safety program, career counseling, exercise/wellness program, free psychological counseling, grant writing training, international student services, low-cost health insurance, multicultural affairs office, services for students with disabilities, teacher training, writing training. *Library facilities:* Odum Library. *Online resources:* library catalog, web page, access to other libraries' catalogs. *Collection:* 637,522 titles, 2,594 serial subscriptions, 28,120 audiovisual materials.

Computer facilities: Computer purchase and lease plans are available. 1,225 computers available on campus for general student use. A campuswide network can be accessed from student residence rooms and from off campus. Online class registration is available. *Web address:* http://www.valdosta.edu/.

General Application Contact: Rebecca Waters, Graduate Admissions Coordinator, 229-333-5694, Fax: 229-245-3853, E-mail: rlwaters@valdosta.edu.

GRADUATE UNITS

Department of Early Childhood and Special Education Students: 67 full-time (56 women), 145 part-time (114 women); includes 38 Black or African American, non-Hispanic/Latino; 3 American Indian or Alaska Native, non-Hispanic/Latino; 2 Asian, non-Hispanic/Latino; 2 Hispanic/Latino; 1 Two or more races, non-Hispanic/Latino. Average age 26. 71 applicants, 69% accepted, 30 enrolled. *Faculty:* 17 full-time (13 women). Expenses: Contact institution. *Financial support:* In 2010–11, 5 students received support, including 5 research assistantships with full tuition reimbursements available (averaging $3,252 per year); institutionally sponsored loans, scholarships/grants, and unspecified assistantships also available. Support available to part-time students. Financial award application deadline: 7/1; financial award applicants required to submit FAFSA. In 2010, 48 master's awarded. *Degree program information:* Part-time and evening/weekend programs available. Postbaccalaureate distance learning degree programs offered (no on-campus study). Offers special education (M Ed, Ed S). *Application deadline:* For fall and spring admission, 7/1 for domestic and international students. Applications are processed on a rolling basis. *Application fee:* $35. Electronic applications accepted. *Application Contact:* Jessica DeVane, Admissions Specialist, 229-333-5694, Fax: 229-245-3853, E-mail: jldevane@valdosta.edu. *Acting Head*, Dr. Lynn C. Minor, 229-333-5929, E-mail: lcminor@valdosta.edu.

Department of English Students: 6 full-time (all women), 21 part-time (18 women); includes 1 Black or African American, non-Hispanic/Latino; 1 Asian, non-Hispanic/Latino; 3 Two or more races, non-Hispanic/Latino. Average age 25. 8 applicants, 88% accepted, 7 enrolled. *Faculty:* 19 full-time (9 women). Expenses: Contact institution. *Financial support:* In 2010–11, 13 students received support, including 6 research assistantships with full tuition reimbursements available (averaging $4,000 per year), 7 teaching assistantships with full tuition reimbursements available (averaging $8,000 per year); institutionally sponsored loans, scholarships/grants, and unspecified assistantships also available. Support available to part-time students. Financial award application deadline: 7/1; financial award applicants required to submit FAFSA. In 2010, 4 master's awarded. *Degree program information:* Part-time programs available. Offers English (MA). *Application deadline:* For fall admission, 7/1 for domestic and international students; for spring admission, 11/1 for domestic and international students. Applications are processed on a rolling basis. *Application fee:* $35. Electronic applications accepted. *Application Contact:* Misty Lamb, Admissions Specialist, 229-333-5694, Fax: 229-245-3853, E-mail: mllamb@valdosta.edu. *Head*, Dr. Mark Smith, 229-333-5946, E-mail: marksmit@valdosta.edu.

Department of History Students: 7 full-time (2 women), 10 part-time (4 women). Average age 22. 11 applicants, 73% accepted, 8 enrolled. *Faculty:* 11 full-time (3 women). Expenses: Contact institution. *Financial support:* In 2010–11, 5 students received support, including 5 research assistantships with full tuition reimbursements available (averaging $3,652 per year); scholarships/grants and unspecified assistantships also available. Support available to part-time students. Financial award application deadline: 7/1; financial award applicants required to submit FAFSA. In 2010, 1 master's awarded. *Degree program information:* Part-time programs available. Offers history (MA). *Application deadline:* For fall admission, 5/15 for domestic and international students; for spring admission, 11/15 for domestic and international students. Applications are processed on a rolling basis. *Application fee:* $35. Electronic applications accepted. *Application Contact:* Misty Lamb, Admissions Specialist, 229-333-5694, Fax: 229-245-3853, E-mail: mllamb@valdosta.edu. *Head*, Dr. Paul Riggs, 229-333-5947, Fax: 229-249-4865.

Department of Middle, Secondary, Reading and Deaf Education Students: 7 full-time (3 women), 22 part-time (17 women); includes 1 minority (Black or African American, non-Hispanic/Latino). Average age 25. 6 applicants, 67% accepted, 3 enrolled. *Faculty:* 9 full-time (7 women). Expenses: Contact institution. *Financial support:* In 2010–11, 4 students received support, including 4 research assistantships with full tuition reimbursements available (averaging $3,652 per year); institutionally sponsored loans, scholarships/grants, and unspecified assistantships also available. Support available to part-time students. Financial award application deadline: 7/1; financial award applicants required to submit FAFSA. In 2010, 24 master's, 5 other advanced degrees awarded. *Degree program information:* Part-time and evening/weekend programs available. Offers middle grades education (M Ed, Ed S); secondary education (M Ed, Ed S). *Application deadline:* For fall admission, 7/1 for domestic and international students; for spring admission, 11/15 for domestic and international students. Applications are processed on a rolling basis. *Application fee:* $35. Electronic applications accepted. *Application Contact:* Meg Moore, Director of GOML Programs, 229-333-5694, Fax: 229-245-3853, E-mail: mhgiddin@valdosta.edu. *Head*, Dr. Barbara Stanley, 229-333-5611, Fax: 229-333-7167.

Department of Psychology and Counseling Students: 65 full-time (47 women), 41 part-time (35 women); includes 38 minority (29 Black or African American, non-Hispanic/Latino; 3 Asian, non-Hispanic/Latino; 4 Hispanic/Latino; 2 Two or more races, non-Hispanic/Latino). Average age 27. 61 applicants, 51% accepted, 27 enrolled. *Faculty:* 19 full-time (6 women). Expenses: Contact institution. *Financial support:* In 2010–11, 6 students received support, including 2 research assistantships with full tuition reimbursements available (averaging $3,652 per year); institutionally sponsored loans and unspecified assistantships also available. Support available to part-time students. Financial award application deadline: 7/1; financial award applicants required to submit FAFSA. In 2010, 43 master's awarded. *Degree program information:* Part-time and evening/weekend programs available. Offers clinical/counseling psychology (MS); industrial/organizational psychology (MS); school counseling (M Ed, Ed S); school psychology (Ed S). *Application deadline:* For fall admission, 7/1 for domestic and international students; for spring admission, 11/15 for domestic and international students. Applications are processed on a rolling basis. *Application fee:* $35. Electronic applications accepted. *Application Contact:* Rebecca Waters, Coordinator of Graduate Admissions, 229-333-5694, Fax: 229-245-3853, E-mail: rlwaters@valdosta.edu. *Chair*, Dr. Robert Bauer, 229-333-5930, Fax: 229-259-5576, E-mail: bbauer@valdosta.edu.

Department of Sociology, Anthropology, and Criminal Justice Students: 3 full-time (2 women), 11 part-time (8 women); includes 6 minority (4 Black or African American, non-Hispanic/Latino; 1 American Indian or Alaska Native, non-Hispanic/Latino; 1 Asian, non-Hispanic/Latino). Average age 25. 6 applicants, 83% accepted, 5 enrolled. *Faculty:* 18 full-time (9 women). Expenses: Contact institution. *Financial support:* In 2010–11, 5 students received support, including 5 research assistantships with full tuition reimbursements available (averaging $3,652 per year); career-related internships or fieldwork, institutionally sponsored loans, scholarships/grants, and unspecified assistantships also available. Support available to part-time students. Financial award application deadline: 7/1; financial award applicants required to submit FAFSA. In 2010, 8 master's awarded. *Degree program information:* Part-time and evening/weekend programs available. Offers criminal justice (MS); marriage and family therapy (MS); sociology (MS). *Application deadline:* For fall admission, 7/1 for domestic and international students; for spring admission, 11/15 for domestic and international students. Applications are processed on a rolling basis. *Application fee:* $35. Electronic applications accepted. *Application Contact:* Misty Lamb, Admissions Specialist, 229-333-5694, Fax: 229-245-3853, E-mail: mllamb@valdosta.edu. *Acting Head*, Dr. Mike Capece, 229-333-5943, Fax: 229-333-5492.

Division of Social Work Students: 47 full-time (44 women), 64 part-time (58 women); includes 41 minority (38 Black or African American, non-Hispanic/Latino; 2 Asian, non-Hispanic/Latino; 1 Hispanic/Latino). Average age 26. 103 applicants, 46% accepted, 43 enrolled. *Faculty:* 7 full-time (4 women). Expenses: Contact institution. *Financial support:* In 2010–11, 4 students received support, including 2 research assistantships with full tuition reimbursements available (averaging $2,452 per year); career-related internships or fieldwork, institutionally sponsored loans, scholarships/grants, and unspecified assistantships also available. Financial award application deadline: 7/1; financial award applicants required to submit FAFSA. In 2010, 43 master's awarded. *Degree program information:* Part-time and evening/weekend programs available. Postbaccalaureate distance learning degree programs offered (minimal on-campus study). Offers social work (MSW). *Application deadline:* For fall admission, 3/15 for domestic and international students. Applications are processed on a rolling basis. *Application fee:* $35. *Application Contact:* Rebecca Waters, Coordinator of Graduate Admissions, 229-333-5694, Fax: 229-245-3853, E-mail: rlwaters@valdosta.edu. *Director*, Dr. Martha Giddings, 229-249-4864, Fax: 229-245-4341, E-mail: mgidding@valdosta.edu.

Program in Business Administration Students: 4 full-time (0 women), 61 part-time (30 women); includes 6 Black or African American, non-Hispanic/Latino; 1 Asian, non-Hispanic/Latino; 2 Two or more races, non-Hispanic/Latino, 1 international. Average age 26. 52 applicants, 46% accepted, 21 enrolled. *Faculty:* 6 full-time (1 woman). Expenses: Contact institution. *Financial support:* In 2010–11, 5 students received support, including 5 research assistantships with full tuition reimbursements available (averaging $3,652 per year); institutionally sponsored loans and scholarships/grants also available. Support available to part-time students. Financial award application deadline: 7/1; financial award applicants required to submit FAFSA. In 2010, 11 master's awarded. *Degree program information:* Part-time and evening/weekend programs available. Postbaccalaureate distance learning degree programs offered (no on-campus study). Offers business administration (MBA). *Application deadline:* For fall admission, 7/1 for domestic and international students; for spring admission, 11/1 for domestic students. Applications are processed on a rolling basis. *Application fee:* $35. Electronic applications accepted. *Application Contact:* Jessica DeVane, Coordinator of Graduate Admissions, 229-333-5694, Fax: 229-245-3853, E-mail: rlwaters@valdosta.edu. *Director*, Dr. Mel Schnake, 229-245-2233, Fax: 229-245-2795, E-mail: mschnake@valdosta.edu.

Program in Educational Leadership Students: 53 full-time (35 women), 146 part-time (93 women); includes 41 Black or African American, non-Hispanic/Latino; 2 American Indian or Alaska Native, non-Hispanic/Latino; 1 Asian, non-Hispanic/Latino; 5 Two or more races, non-Hispanic/Latino. Average age 24. 55 applicants, 47% accepted, 26 enrolled. *Faculty:* 16 full-time (7 women). Expenses: Contact institution. *Financial support:* In 2010–11, 4 students received support, including 4 research assistantships with full tuition reimbursements available (averaging $3,652 per year); institutionally sponsored loans, scholarships/grants, and unspecified assistantships also available. Support available to part-time students. Financial award application deadline: 7/1; financial award applicants required to submit FAFSA. In 2010, 100 master's, 7 doctorates awarded. Offers educational leadership (M Ed, Ed D, Ed S). *Application deadline:* For fall admission, 7/1 for domestic and international students; for spring admission, 11/15 for domestic and international students. Applications are processed on a rolling basis. *Application fee:* $35. Electronic applications accepted. *Application Contact:* Rebecca Waters, Coordinator of Graduate Programs, 229-333-5694, Fax: 229-245-3853, E-mail: rlwaters@valdosta.edu. Dr. Don Leech, 229-333-5633, E-mail: dwleech@valdosta.edu.

Program in Library and Information Science Students: 34 full-time (30 women), 262 part-time (224 women); includes 35 Black or African American, non-Hispanic/Latino; 1 American Indian or Alaska Native, non-Hispanic/Latino; 4 Asian, non-Hispanic/Latino; 1 Hispanic/Latino; 21 Two or more races, non-Hispanic/Latino, 6 international. Average age 30. 119 applicants, 64% accepted, 69 enrolled. *Faculty:* 4 full-time (2 women). Expenses: Contact institution. *Financial support:* In 2010–11, 4 students received support, including 4 research assistantships with full tuition reimbursements available (averaging $3,652 per year); institutionally sponsored loans, scholarships/grants, and unspecified assistantships also available. Support available to part-time students. Financial award application deadline: 7/1; financial award applicants required to submit FAFSA. In 2010, 69 master's awarded. Postbaccalaureate distance learning degree programs offered (minimal on-campus study). Offers library and information science (MLIS). *Application deadline:* For fall admission, 4/14 for domestic students, 4/15 for international students. *Application fee:* $35. *Application Contact:* Jessica DeVane, Admissions Specialist, 229-333-5694, Fax: 229-245-3853, E-mail: mllamb@valdosta.edu. *Director*, Dr. Wallace Koehler, 229-245-3732, Fax: 229-333-5862, E-mail: wkoehler@valdosta.edu.

VALLEY CITY STATE UNIVERSITY, Valley City, ND 58072

General Information State-supported, coed, comprehensive institution. *Enrollment:* 1,277 graduate, professional, and undergraduate students; 6 full-time matriculated graduate/professional students (5 women), 135 part-time matriculated graduate/professional students (77 women). *Enrollment by degree level:* 141 master's. *Graduate faculty:* 22 full-time (16 women), 3 part-time/adjunct (1 woman). Tuition, state resident: full-time $5655; part-time $314.15 per credit hour. Tuition, nonresident: full-time $5655; part-time $314.15 per credit hour. One-time fee: $35. *Library facilities:* Allen Memorial Library. *Online resources:* library catalog, web page, access to other libraries' catalogs. *Collection:* 150,000 titles, 35,000 serial subscriptions, 6,800 audiovisual materials.

Computer facilities: Computer purchase and lease plans are available. 995 computers available on campus for general student use. A campuswide network can be accessed from student residence rooms and from off campus. Online class registration is available. *Web address:* http://www.vcsu.edu/.

General Application Contact: Misty Lindgren, Administrative Assistant for Office of Graduate Studies and Research, 701-845-7303, Fax: 701-845-7305, E-mail: misty.lindgren@vcsu.edu.

GRADUATE UNITS

Online Master of Education Program Students: 6 full-time (5 women), 135 part-time (77 women); includes 1 Black or African American, non-Hispanic/Latino; 1 Asian, non-Hispanic/Latino, 1 international. Average age 36. 30 applicants, 80% accepted, 21 enrolled. *Faculty:* 22 full-time (16 women), 3 part-time/adjunct (1 woman). Expenses: Contact institution. *Financial support:* In 2010–11, 30 students received support. Scholarships/grants and tuition waivers (full and partial) available. Financial award application deadline: 5/30; financial award applicants required to submit FAFSA. In 2010, 30 master's awarded. *Degree program information:* Part-time and evening/weekend programs available. Postbaccalaureate distance learning degree programs offered (no on-campus study). Offers English language learners (ELL) (M Ed); library and information technologies (M Ed); teaching and technology (M Ed); technology education (M Ed). *Application deadline:* For fall admission, 5/23 priority date for domestic and international students; for winter admission, 12/10 priority date for domestic and international students; for spring admission, 4/20 priority date for domestic students, 4/23 priority date for international students. Applications are processed on a rolling basis. *Application fee:* $35. Electronic applications accepted. *Application Contact:* Misty Lindgren, 701-845-7303, Fax: 701-845-7305, E-mail: misty.lindgren@vcsu.edu. *Dean*, Dr. Gary Thompson, 701-845-7197, E-mail: gary.thompson@vcsu.edu.

VALLEY FORGE CHRISTIAN COLLEGE, Phoenixville, PA 19460

General Information Independent-religious, coed, comprehensive institution.

GRADUATE UNITS

Program in Christian Leadership Offers Christian leadership (MA).

Program in Music Technology Postbaccalaureate distance learning degree programs offered (minimal on-campus study). Offers music technology (MM).

Program in Theology Offers theology (MA).

Program in Worship Studies Offers worship studies (MA).

VALPARAISO UNIVERSITY, Valparaiso, IN 46383

General Information Independent-religious, coed, university. *Enrollment:* 4,056 graduate, professional, and undergraduate students; 884 full-time matriculated graduate/professional students (440 women), 272 part-time matriculated graduate/professional students (153 women). *Enrollment by degree level:* 567 first professional, 507 master's, 49 doctoral, 33 other advanced degrees. *Graduate faculty:* 31 full-time (8 women), 156 part-time/adjunct (75 women). *Tuition:* Full-time $9540; part-time $530 per credit hour. *Required fees:* $292; $95 per semester. Tuition and fees vary according to program. *Graduate housing:* Room and/or apartments available on a first-come, first-served basis to single students; on-campus housing not available to married students. Typical cost: $5150 per year. Room charges vary according to board plan and housing facility selected. *Student services:* Campus employment opportunities, campus safety program, career counseling, exercise/wellness program, free psychological counseling, international student services, low-cost health insurance, multicultural affairs office, services for students with disabilities, teacher training, writing training. *Library facilities:* Christopher Center for Library and Information Resources plus 1 other. *Online resources:* library catalog, web page. *Collection:* 528,494 titles, 37,673 serial subscriptions, 10,766 audiovisual materials.

Computer facilities: 900 computers available on campus for general student use. A campuswide network can be accessed from student residence rooms and from off campus. Online class registration, Web academic information, degree audit are available. *Web address:* http://www.valpo.edu/.

General Application Contact: Dr. David L. Rowland, Dean, Graduate School and Continuing Education/Associate Provost, 219-464-5313, Fax: 219-464-5381, E-mail: david.rowland@valpo.edu.

GRADUATE UNITS

Graduate School Students: 348 full-time (207 women), 235 part-time (137 women); includes 57 minority (22 Black or African American, non-Hispanic/Latino; 2 American Indian or Alaska Native, non-Hispanic/Latino; 7 Asian, non-Hispanic/Latino; 20 Hispanic/Latino; 6 Two or more races, non-Hispanic/Latino), 172 international. Average age 30. *Faculty:* 119 part-time/adjunct (57 women). Expenses: Contact institution. *Financial support:* Career-related internships or fieldwork, scholarships/grants, traineeships, and unspecified assistantships available. Support available to part-time students. Financial award applicants required to submit FAFSA. In 2010, 227 master's, 51 other advanced degrees awarded. *Degree program information:* Part-time and evening/weekend programs available. Postbaccalaureate distance learning degree programs offered (minimal on-campus study). Offers arts and entertainment administration (MA); business management (for counseling students) (Certificate); Chinese studies (MA); clinical mental health counseling (MA); community counseling (MA); digital media (MS); English (MALS, Post-Master's Certificate); English studies and communication (MA); ethics and values (MALS, Post-Master's Certificate); gerontology (MALS, Post-Master's Certificate); history (MALS, Post-Master's Certificate); human behavior and society (MALS, Post-Master's Certificate); individualized liberal studies (MALS); information technology (MS); initial licensure (M Ed); instructional leadership (M Ed); international commerce and policy (MS); international economics and finance (MS); legal studies and principles (Certificate); liberal studies (MALS, Post-Master's Certificate); sports administration (MS); sports media (MS, Certificate); teaching and learning (M Ed); teaching of English to speakers of other languages (TESOL) (Certificate); theology (MALS, Post-Master's Certificate); theology and ministry (MALS, Post-

Valparaiso University (continued)

Master's Certificate). *Application deadline:* Applications are processed on a rolling basis. *Application fee:* $30 ($50 for international students). Electronic applications accepted. *Application Contact:* Laura Groth, Coordinator of Student Services and Support, 219-464-5313, Fax: 219-464-5381, E-mail: laura.groth@valpo.edu. *Dean, Graduate School and Continuing Education/Associate Provost,* Dr. David L. Rowland, 219-464-5313, Fax: 219-464-5381, E-mail: david.rowland@valpo.edu.

College of Business Administration Students: 25 full-time (11 women), 48 part-time (18 women); includes 10 minority (4 Black or African American, non-Hispanic/Latino; 1 Asian, non-Hispanic/Latino; 4 Hispanic/Latino; 1 Two or more races, non-Hispanic/Latino), 4 international. Average age 31. *Faculty:* 15 part-time/adjunct (4 women). Expenses: Contact institution. *Financial support:* Available to part-time students. Applicants required to submit FAFSA. In 2010, 29 master's, 4 other advanced degrees awarded. *Degree program information:* Part-time and evening/weekend programs available. Postbaccalaureate distance learning degree programs offered (minimal on-campus study). Offers business administration (MBA); engineering management (MEM); management (Certificate). *Application deadline:* Applications are processed on a rolling basis. *Application fee:* $30 ($50 for international students). Electronic applications accepted. *Application Contact:* Cindy Scanlan, Assistant Director of Graduate Programs in Management, 219-465-7952, Fax: 219-464-5789, E-mail: cindy.scanlan@valpo.edu. *Director of Graduate Programs in Management,* Bruce MacLean, 219-465-7952, Fax: 219-464-5789, E-mail: bruce.maclean@valpo.edu.

College of Nursing Students: 34 full-time (29 women), 46 part-time (45 women); includes 6 minority (3 Black or African American, non-Hispanic/Latino; 1 Asian, non-Hispanic/Latino; 2 Hispanic/Latino), 10 international. Average age 39. *Faculty:* 10 part-time/adjunct (all women). Expenses: Contact institution. *Financial support:* Available to part-time students. Applicants required to submit FAFSA. In 2010, 10 master's, 9 other advanced degrees awarded. *Degree program information:* Part-time and evening/weekend programs available. Postbaccalaureate distance learning degree programs offered (minimal on-campus study). Offers management (Certificate); nursing education (MSN, Certificate). *Application deadline:* Applications are processed on a rolling basis. *Application fee:* $30 ($50 for international students). Electronic applications accepted. *Application Contact:* Laura Groth, Coordinator of Student Services and Support, 219-464-5313, Fax: 219-464-5381, E-mail: laura.groth@valpo.edu. *Dean,* Dr. Janet Brown, 219-464-5289, Fax: 219-464-5425, E-mail: janet.brown@valpo.edu.

School of Law *Faculty:* 41 full-time (13 women), 47 part-time/adjunct (20 women). Expenses: Contact institution. *Financial support:* Research assistantships, teaching assistantships, career-related internships or fieldwork, Federal Work-Study, institutionally sponsored loans, scholarships/grants, and tuition waivers (partial) available. Support available to part-time students. Financial award application deadline: 3/1; financial award applicants required to submit FAFSA. *Degree program information:* Part-time programs available. Offers law (JD, LL M). *Application deadline:* For fall admission, 3/1 priority date for domestic students. Applications are processed on a rolling basis. *Application fee:* $60. Electronic applications accepted. *Application Contact:* Diann Lapin, Executive Director of Admissions, 219-465-7891, Fax: 219-465-7975, E-mail: law.admissions@valpo.edu. *Dean,* Jay Conison, 219-465-7834, Fax: 219-465-7872, E-mail: jay.conison@valpo.edu.

VANCOUVER ISLAND UNIVERSITY, Nanaimo, BC V9R 5S5, Canada

General Information Province-supported, coed, comprehensive institution. *Graduate housing:* Room and/or apartments available on a first-come, first-served basis to single students; on-campus housing not available to married students. Housing application deadline: 3/5.

GRADUATE UNITS

Program in Business Administration *Degree program information:* Part-time and evening/weekend programs available. Offers business administration (EMBA, IMBA, MBA). Program offered jointly with University of Hertfordshire. Electronic applications accepted.

VANCOUVER SCHOOL OF THEOLOGY, Vancouver, BC V6T 1L4, Canada

General Information Independent-religious, coed, graduate-only institution. *Graduate housing:* Rooms and/or apartments guaranteed to single students and available to married students. Housing application deadline: 4/7.

GRADUATE UNITS

Graduate and Professional Programs *Degree program information:* Part-time programs available. Offers spiritual direction (Graduate Diploma); theological studies (MATS); theology (M Div, Th M, Dip CS). Electronic applications accepted.

VANDERBILT UNIVERSITY, Nashville, TN 37240-1001

General Information Independent, coed, university. CGS member. *Enrollment:* 12,714 graduate, professional, and undergraduate students; 5,017 full-time matriculated graduate/professional students (2,705 women), 761 part-time matriculated graduate/professional students (561 women). *Enrollment by degree level:* 1,328 first professional, 2,308 master's, 1,998 doctoral. *Graduate faculty:* 982 full-time (270 women), 4 part-time/adjunct (3 women). *Graduate housing:* On-campus housing not available. *Student services:* Campus employment opportunities, campus safety program, career counseling, child daycare facilities, exercise/wellness program, free psychological counseling, grant writing training, international student services, low-cost health insurance, multicultural affairs office, services for students with disabilities, teacher training, writing training. *Library facilities:* Jean and Alexander Heard Library plus 9 others. *Online resources:* library catalog, web page. *Collection:* 2.6 million titles, 67,249 serial subscriptions, 66,905 audiovisual materials. *Research affiliation:* Amgen (medicine), SAIC Frederick (engineering and computer science), Chevron Phillips Chemical Company (chemical engineering), Boeing Aerospace Corporation (engineering and computer science), BAE Systems (engineering and computer science), AstraZeneca (medicine).

Computer facilities: 400 computers available on campus for general student use. A campuswide network can be accessed from student residence rooms and from off campus. Online class registration, productivity and educational software are available. *Web address:* http://www.vanderbilt.edu/.

General Application Contact: Walter B. Bieschke, Program Coordinator for Graduate Admissions, 615-343-6321, Fax: 615-343-6687, E-mail: vandygrad@vanderbilt.edu.

GRADUATE UNITS

Divinity School Students: 246 full-time (131 women), 4 part-time (all women); includes 62 minority (48 Black or African American, non-Hispanic/Latino; 1 American Indian or Alaska Native, non-Hispanic/Latino; 9 Asian, non-Hispanic/Latino; 4 Hispanic/Latino). Average age 29. 201 applicants, 83% accepted, 86 enrolled. *Faculty:* 38 full-time (13 women), 3 part-time/adjunct (1 woman). Expenses: Contact institution. *Financial support:* In 2010–11, 246 students received support. Career-related internships or fieldwork, Federal Work-Study, institutionally sponsored loans, scholarships/grants, and tuition waivers (full and partial) available. Financial award application deadline: 5/1; financial award applicants required to submit CSS PROFILE or FAFSA. In 2010, 40 first professional degrees, 42 master's awarded. *Degree program information:* Part-time programs available. Offers divinity (M Div, MTS). *Application deadline:* For winter admission, 1/15 priority date for domestic and international students; for spring admission, 4/1 for domestic and international students. Applications are processed on a rolling basis. *Application fee:* $50. Electronic applications accepted. *Application Contact:* Rev. Katherine H. Smith, Director of Admissions and Student Services, 615-343-3963, Fax: 615-322-0691, E-mail: katherine.smith@vanderbilt.edu. *Dean,* Dr. James Hudnut-Beumler, 615-322-2776, Fax: 615-343-9957, E-mail: james.d.hudnut-beumler@vanderbilt.edu.

Graduate School Students: 2,063 full-time (1,003 women), 138 part-time (81 women); includes 125 Black or African American, non-Hispanic/Latino; 4 American Indian or Alaska Native, non-Hispanic/Latino; 84 Asian, non-Hispanic/Latino; 78 Hispanic/Latino; 40 Two or more races, non-Hispanic/Latino. Average age 29. 7,140 applicants, 13% accepted, 515 enrolled. *Faculty:* 1,065 full-time (301 women), 32 part-time/adjunct (10 women). Expenses: Contact institution. *Financial support:* Fellowships with full and partial tuition reimbursements, research assistantships with full tuition reimbursements, teaching assistantships with full tuition reimbursements, career-related internships or fieldwork, Federal Work-Study, institutionally sponsored loans, scholarships/grants, traineeships, health care benefits, tuition waivers (full and partial), and unspecified assistantships available. Support available to part-time students. Financial award application deadline: 1/15; financial award applicants required to submit CSS PROFILE or FAFSA. In 2010, 236 master's, 277 doctorates awarded. *Degree program information:* Part-time programs available. Offers analytical chemistry (MAT, MS, PhD); anthropology (MA, PhD); astronomy (MS); biochemistry (MS, PhD); biological sciences (MS, PhD); biomedical informatics (MS, PhD); cancer biology (MS, PhD); cell and developmental biology (MS, PhD); classics (MA); community research and action (MS, PhD); creative writing (MFA); earth and environmental sciences (MAT, MS); economic development (MA); economics (MA, MAT, PhD); English (MA, MAT, PhD); French (MA, MAT, PhD); German (MA, MAT, PhD); history (MA, MAT, PhD); human genetics (PhD); inorganic chemistry (MAT, MS, PhD); Latin (MAT); Latin American studies (MA); leadership and policy studies (PhD); learning, teaching and diversity (MS, PhD); liberal arts and science (MLAS); mathematics (MA, MAT, MS, PhD); microbiology and immunology (MS, PhD); molecular physiology and biophysics (MS, PhD); nursing science (PhD); organic chemistry (MAT, MS, PhD); pathology (PhD); pharmacology (PhD); philosophy (MA, PhD); physical chemistry (MAT, MS, PhD); physics (MA, MAT, MS, PhD); political science (MA, MAT, PhD); Portuguese (MA); psychological sciences (MA, MS, PhD); religion (MA, PhD); sociology (MA, PhD); Spanish (MA, MAT, PhD); Spanish and Portuguese (PhD); theoretical chemistry (MAT, MS, PhD). *Application deadline:* For fall admission, 1/15 for domestic and international students. *Application fee:* $0. Electronic applications accepted. *Application Contact:* Walter B. Bieschke, Program Coordinator for Graduate Admissions, 615-343-6321, Fax: 615-343-6687, E-mail: vandygrad@vanderbilt.edu. *Vice Provost for Research/Dean,* Dr. Dennis G. Hall, 615-322-2809, Fax: 615-343-9936, E-mail: dennis.g.hall@vanderbilt.edu.

Center for Medicine, Health, and Society Students: 3 full-time (all women); includes 1 Two or more races, non-Hispanic/Latino. Average age 23. 9 applicants, 44% accepted, 3 enrolled. Expenses: Contact institution. *Financial support:* Federal Work-Study, scholarships/grants, and health care benefits available. Financial award application deadline: 1/15; financial award applicants required to submit CSS PROFILE or FAFSA. In 2010, 1 master's awarded. Offers medicine, health, and society (MA). *Application deadline:* For fall admission, 1/15 for domestic and international students. *Application fee:* $0. Electronic applications accepted. *Application Contact:* Walter B. Bieschke, Program Coordinator for Graduate Admissions, 615-343-6321, Fax: 615-343-6687, E-mail: vandygrad@vanderbilt.edu. *Director,* Dr. Jonathan Metzl.

Owen Graduate School of Management Students: 531 full-time (134 women); includes 75 minority (19 Black or African American, non-Hispanic/Latino; 48 Asian, non-Hispanic/Latino; 5 Hispanic/Latino; 2 Native Hawaiian or other Pacific Islander, non-Hispanic/Latino; 1 Two or more races, non-Hispanic/Latino), 100 international. Average age 28. 1,713 applicants, 29% accepted, 301 enrolled. *Faculty:* 42 full-time (5 women), 23 part-time/adjunct (0 women). Expenses: Contact institution. *Financial support:* In 2010–11, 200 students received support. Scholarships/grants and tuition waivers (full and partial) available. Financial award application deadline: 5/1; financial award applicants required to submit FAFSA. In 2010, 361 master's awarded. *Degree program information:* Evening/weekend programs available. Offers accountancy (M Acc); business administration (MBA); executive business administration (EMBA); finance (MSF); management (EMBA, M Acc, MBA, MSF). Students in the 5-year MBA program enter as undergraduate freshmen. *Application deadline:* For fall admission, 11/15 priority date for domestic students, 11/15 for international students; for winter admission, 1/15 priority date for domestic students, 1/15 for international students; for spring admission, 3/1 for domestic and international students. Applications are processed on a rolling basis. *Application fee:* $0. Electronic applications accepted. *Application Contact:* Assistant Dean of Admissions and Career Management Services, 615-322-6469, Fax: 615-343-1175, E-mail: admissions@owen.vanderbilt.edu. *Dean,* Dr. James W. Bradford, 615-322-2316, Fax: 615-343-7110.

Peabody College Students: 461 full-time (366 women), 154 part-time (97 women); includes 92 minority (36 Black or African American, non-Hispanic/Latino; 1 American Indian or Alaska Native, non-Hispanic/Latino; 17 Asian, non-Hispanic/Latino; 24 Hispanic/Latino; 14 Two or more races, non-Hispanic/Latino), 36 international. Average age 28. 985 applicants, 56% accepted, 324 enrolled. *Faculty:* 166 full-time (83 women), 57 part-time/adjunct (32 women). Expenses: Contact institution. *Financial support:* In 2010–11, 473 students received support, including 5 fellowships with full and partial tuition reimbursements available, 152 research assistantships with full and partial tuition reimbursements available, 33 teaching assistantships with full and partial tuition reimbursements available; career-related internships or fieldwork, Federal Work-Study, institutionally sponsored loans, scholarships/grants, traineeships, tuition waivers (partial), and unspecified assistantships also available. Support available to part-time students. Financial award application deadline: 2/1; financial award applicants required to submit FAFSA. In 2010, 229 master's, 22 doctorates awarded. *Degree program information:* Part-time programs available. Offers child studies (M Ed); community development and action (M Ed); education and human development (M Ed, MPP, Ed D, PhD); education policy (MPP); educational leadership and policy (Ed D); elementary education (M Ed); English language learners (M Ed); higher education (M Ed); higher education, leadership and policy (Ed D); human development counseling (M Ed); international education policy and management (M Ed); leadership and organizational performance (M Ed); learning and instruction (M Ed); learning, diversity, and urban studies (M Ed); reading education (M Ed); secondary education (M Ed); special education (M Ed). *Application deadline:* For fall admission, 12/31 priority date for domestic and international students; for spring admission, 11/1 priority date for domestic and international students. Applications are processed on a rolling basis. *Application fee:* $0. Electronic applications accepted. *Application Contact:* Kimberly Brazil-Tanner, Recruitment Coordinator, 615-332-8410, Fax: 615-343-3474, E-mail: kim.brazil@vanderbilt.edu. *Dean,* Dr. Camilla P. Benbow, 615-322-8407, Fax: 615-322-8501, E-mail: camilla.benbow@vanderbilt.edu.

School of Engineering Students: 352 full-time (99 women); includes 15 Black or African American, non-Hispanic/Latino; 2 American Indian or Alaska Native, non-Hispanic/Latino; 12 Asian, non-Hispanic/Latino; 9 Hispanic/Latino, 146 international. Average age 26. 1,314 applicants, 15% accepted, 106 enrolled. *Faculty:* 121 full-time (22 women), 25 part-time/adjunct (2 women). Expenses: Contact institution. *Financial support:* Fellowships with full tuition reimbursements, research assistantships with full tuition reimbursements, teaching assistantships with full tuition reimbursements, career-related internships or fieldwork, Federal Work-Study, institutionally sponsored loans, scholarships/grants, traineeships, health care benefits, and tuition waivers (full and partial) available. Support available to part-time students. Financial award application deadline: 1/15; financial award applicants required to submit CSS PROFILE or FAFSA. In 2010, 70 master's, 45 doctorates awarded. *Degree program information:* Part-time programs available. Offers biomedical engineering (M Eng, MS, PhD); chemical and biomolecular engineering (M Eng, MS, PhD); civil engineering (M Eng, MS, PhD); computer science (M Eng, MS, PhD); electrical engineering (M Eng, MS, PhD); engineering (M Eng, MS, PhD); environmental engineering (M Eng, MS, PhD); environmental management (MS, PhD); materials science (M Eng, MS, PhD); mechanical engineering (M Eng, MS, PhD). MS and PhD offered through the Graduate School. *Application deadline:* For fall admission, 1/15 for domestic and international students; for spring admission, 11/1 for domestic and international students. *Application fee:* $0. Electronic applications accepted. *Application Contact:* Dolores A. Black, Coordinator, Graduate Student Recruiting, 615-343-3308, Fax: 615-343-8006, E-mail: dolores.black@vanderbilt.edu. *Dean,* Kenneth F. Galloway, 615-322-0720, Fax: 615-343-8006, E-mail: kenneth.f.galloway@vanderbilt.edu.

School of Medicine Students: 603 full-time (331 women); includes 169 minority (49 Black or African American, non-Hispanic/Latino; 5 American Indian or Alaska Native, non-Hispanic/Latino; 99 Asian, non-Hispanic/Latino; 16 Hispanic/Latino), 44 international. Average age 24. 4,892 applicants, 6% accepted, 111 enrolled. *Faculty:* 2,052 full-time (736 women), 987 part-time/adjunct (352 women). Expenses: Contact institution. *Financial support:* In 2010–11, 490 students received support. Institutionally sponsored loans and scholarships/grants available. Financial award application deadline: 3/1; financial award applicants required to submit FAFSA. In 2010, 118 first professional degrees, 70 master's, 11 doctorates awarded. Offers audiology (Au D, PhD); chemical and physical biology (PhD); clinical investigation (MS); deaf education (MED); medical physics (MS); medicine (MD, MDE, MMP, MPH, MS, MSCI, Au D, DMP, PhD); public health (MPH); speech-language pathology (MS). *Application deadline:* For fall admission, 11/15 for domestic and international students. Applications are processed on a rolling basis. *Application fee:* $50. Electronic applications accepted. *Application Contact:* Dr. John A. Zic, Associate Dean for Admissions, 615-322-2145, Fax: 615-343-8397. *Interim Dean*, Dr. Jeffrey R. Balser, 615-322-5191, E-mail: steven.gabbe@vanderbilt.edu.

School of Nursing *Degree program information:* Part-time programs available. Postbaccalaureate distance learning degree programs offered (minimal on-campus study). Offers adult acute care nurse practitioner (MSN); adult nurse practitioner/cardiovascular disease management and prevention (MSN); adult nurse practitioner/palliative care (MSN); clinical management (clinical nurse leader/specialist) (MSN); emergency nurse practitioner (MSN); family nurse practitioner (MSN); gerontology nurse practitioner (MSN); health systems management (MSN); neonatal nurse practitioner (MSN); nurse midwifery (MSN); nurse midwifery/family nurse practitioner (MSN); nursing informatics (MSN); nursing practice (DNP); nursing science (PhD); nutrition (MS); pediatric acute care nurse practitioner (MSN); pediatric primary care nurse practitioner (MSN); psychiatric-mental health nurse practitioner (MSN); women's health nurse practitioner (MSN); women's health nurse practitioner/adult nurse practitioner (MSN).

Vanderbilt University Law School Students: 612 full-time (289 women); includes 54 Black or African American, non-Hispanic/Latino; 3 American Indian or Alaska Native, non-Hispanic/Latino; 24 Asian, non-Hispanic/Latino; 28 Hispanic/Latino, 46 international. Average age 23. 4,885 applicants, 22% accepted, 193 enrolled. *Faculty:* 47 full-time (20 women), 71 part-time/adjunct (22 women). Expenses: Contact institution. *Financial support:* In 2010–11, 433 students received support. Career-related internships or fieldwork, Federal Work-Study, institutionally sponsored loans, scholarships/grants, and health care benefits available. Financial award application deadline: 2/15; financial award applicants required to submit FAFSA. In 2010, 204 first professional degrees, 28 master's awarded. Offers law (JD, LL M); law and economics (PhD). *Application deadline:* For fall admission, 3/15 for domestic and international students. Applications are processed on a rolling basis. *Application fee:* $50. Electronic applications accepted. *Application Contact:* Admissions Office, 615-322-6452, Fax: 615-322-1531, E-mail: admissions@law.vanderbilt.edu. *Assistant Dean of Admissions*, G. Todd Morton, 615-322-6452, Fax: 615-322-1531, E-mail: admissions@law.vanderbilt.edu.

VANDERCOOK COLLEGE OF MUSIC, Chicago, IL 60616-3731

General Information Independent, coed, comprehensive institution. *Enrollment:* 380 graduate, professional, and undergraduate students; 156 full-time matriculated graduate/professional students (89 women), 53 part-time matriculated graduate/professional students (26 women). *Enrollment by degree level:* 209 master's. *Graduate faculty:* 14 full-time (8 women), 53 part-time/adjunct (17 women). *Tuition:* Full-time $5520; part-time $460 per semester hour. *Required fees:* $500 per term. *Graduate housing:* Rooms and/or apartments available on a first-come, first-served basis to single and married students. Typical cost: $1878 per year ($2568 including board) for single students; $1578 per year ($2268 including board) for married students. Room and board charges vary according to board plan and campus/location. Housing application deadline: 6/1. *Student services:* Career counseling. *Library facilities:* Harry Ruppel Memorial Library. *Online resources:* library catalog, web page. *Collection:* 14,109 titles, 356 serial subscriptions, 4,628 audiovisual materials.

Computer facilities: 21 computers available on campus for general student use. A campuswide network can be accessed from student residence rooms and from off campus. *Web address:* http://www.vandercook.edu/.

General Application Contact: Amy Lenting, Director of Admissions, 312-225-6288 Ext. 230, Fax: 312-225-5211, E-mail: admissions@vandercook.edu.

GRADUATE UNITS

Master of Music Education Program Students: 156 full-time (89 women), 53 part-time (26 women); includes 12 Black or African American, non-Hispanic/Latino; 1 Asian, non-Hispanic/Latino; 5 Hispanic/Latino; 1 Two or more races, non-Hispanic/Latino, 6 international. Average age 31. 72 applicants, 92% accepted, 66 enrolled. *Faculty:* 13 full-time (8 women), 49 part-time/adjunct (14 women). Expenses: Contact institution. *Financial support:* In 2010–11, 12 students received support. Unspecified assistantships available. Financial award application deadline: 5/1; financial award applicants required to submit FAFSA. In 2010, 73 master's awarded. *Degree program information:* Part-time programs available. Offers music education (MM Ed). Offered during summer only. *Application deadline:* For fall admission, 4/1 for domestic and international students; for spring admission, 11/1 for domestic and international students. Applications are processed on a rolling basis. *Application fee:* $50. *Application Contact:* Amy Lenting, Director of Admissions, 312-225-6288 Ext. 230, Fax: 312-225-5211, E-mail: admissions@vandercook.edu. *Dean of Graduate Studies*, Ruth Rhodes, 312-225-6288 Ext. 231, Fax: 312-225-5211, E-mail: rrhodes@vandercook.edu.

VANGUARD UNIVERSITY OF SOUTHERN CALIFORNIA, Costa Mesa, CA 92626-9601

General Information Independent-religious, coed, comprehensive institution.

GRADUATE UNITS

Graduate Program in Business *Degree program information:* Part-time and evening/weekend programs available. Offers business (MBA). Electronic applications accepted.

Graduate Program in Clinical Psychology *Degree program information:* Part-time and evening/weekend programs available. Offers clinical psychology (MS). Electronic applications accepted.

Graduate Programs in Education *Degree program information:* Evening/weekend programs available. Offers education (MA). Electronic applications accepted.

Graduate Programs in Religion *Degree program information:* Part-time and evening/weekend programs available. Offers leadership studies (MA); theological studies (MTS). Electronic applications accepted.

VAUGHN COLLEGE OF AERONAUTICS AND TECHNOLOGY, Flushing, NY 11369

General Information Independent, coed, primarily men, comprehensive institution.

GRADUATE UNITS

Graduate Programs Offers airport management (MS).

VERMONT COLLEGE OF FINE ARTS, Montpelier, VT 05602

General Information Independent, coed, graduate-only institution. *Enrollment by degree level:* 273 master's. *Graduate faculty:* 71 full-time, 33 part-time/adjunct. *Tuition:* Full-time $17,820. *Required fees:* $270. *Student services:* Services for students with disabilities. *Library facilities:* Gary Library. *Online resources:* library catalog, web page. *Collection:* 52,500 titles, 26 serial subscriptions, 405 audiovisual materials.

Computer facilities: 26 computers available on campus for general student use. A campuswide network can be accessed from student residence rooms. Online student billing available. *Web address:* http://www.vermontcollege.edu/.

General Application Contact: Denise MacMartin, Director of Admissions, 802-828-8535.

GRADUATE UNITS

Program in Graphic Design Expenses: Contact institution. Postbaccalaureate distance learning degree programs offered (minimal on-campus study). Offers graphic design (MFA). *Application deadline:* For fall admission, 8/15 for domestic students. *Application Contact:* Debbie New, Assistant Director of Admissions, 802-828-8636, E-mail: debbie.new@vermontcollege.edu. *Program Director*, Jennifer Renko, 866-934-8232 Ext. 8896, E-mail: jennifer.renko@vermontcollege.edu.

Program in Music Composition Expenses: Contact institution. Postbaccalaureate distance learning degree programs offered (minimal on-campus study). Offers music composition (MFA). *Application Contact:* Debbie New, Assistant Director of Admissions, 802-828-8636, E-mail: debbie.new@vermontcollege.edu. *Program Director*, Carol Beatty, 866-934-8232 Ext. 8610, E-mail: carol.beatty@vermontcollege.edu.

Program in Visual Art Students: 47 full-time (33 women), 1 part-time; includes 1 Black or African American, non-Hispanic/Latino. Average age 42. 50 applicants, 68% accepted, 19 enrolled. *Faculty:* 10 full-time, 8 part-time/adjunct. Expenses: Contact institution. *Financial support:* Scholarships/grants available. Financial award applicants required to submit FAFSA. Postbaccalaureate distance learning degree programs offered (minimal on-campus study). Offers visual art (MFA). *Application deadline:* For fall admission, 2/15 priority date for domestic students, 2/15 for international students; for spring admission, 9/1 priority date for domestic students, 9/1 for international students. Applications are processed on a rolling basis. *Application fee:* $75. Electronic applications accepted. *Application Contact:* Denise MacMartin, Director of Admissions, 802-828-8535, E-mail: denise.macmartin@vermontcollege.edu. *Program Director*, Danielle Dahline, 802-828-8703, E-mail: danielle.dahline@vermontcollege.edu.

Program in Writing Students: 137 full-time (98 women); includes 1 Black or African American, non-Hispanic/Latino; 2 Asian, non-Hispanic/Latino; 2 Hispanic/Latino. Average age 38. 161 applicants, 61% accepted, 47 enrolled. *Faculty:* 31 full-time, 15 part-time/adjunct. Expenses: Contact institution. *Financial support:* Scholarships/grants available. Postbaccalaureate distance learning degree programs offered (minimal on-campus study). Offers writing (MFA). *Application deadline:* For fall admission, 2/1 for domestic and international students; for spring admission, 8/1 for domestic and international students. *Application fee:* $75. *Application Contact:* Jason Lamb, Assistant Director of Admissions, 802-828-8829, E-mail: jason.lamb@vermontcollege.edu. *Program Director*, Louise Crowley, 802-828-8840, E-mail: louise.crowley@vermontcollege.edu.

Program in Writing for Children and Young Adults Students: 88 full-time (78 women); includes 2 Black or African American, non-Hispanic/Latino; 1 Asian, non-Hispanic/Latino. Average age 38. 61 applicants, 74% accepted, 33 enrolled. *Faculty:* 20 full-time, 10 part-time/adjunct. Expenses: Contact institution. *Financial support:* Traineeships available. Financial award applicants required to submit FAFSA. Postbaccalaureate distance learning degree programs offered (minimal on-campus study). Offers writing for children and young adults (MFA). *Application deadline:* For fall admission, 3/1 for domestic and international students; for spring admission, 10/1 for domestic and international students. *Application fee:* $75. *Application Contact:* Jason Lamb, Assistant Director of Admissions, 802-828-8829, E-mail: jason.lamb@vermontcollege.edu. *Program Director*, Melissa Fisher, 802-828-8696, E-mail: melissa.fisher@vermontcollege.edu.

VERMONT LAW SCHOOL, South Royalton, VT 05068-0096

General Information Independent, coed, graduate-only institution. *Enrollment by degree level:* 607 first professional. *Graduate faculty:* 42 full-time (21 women), 26 part-time/adjunct (16 women). *Graduate housing:* On-campus housing not available. *Student services:* Campus employment opportunities, campus safety program, career counseling, child daycare facilities, exercise/wellness program, free psychological counseling, low-cost health insurance, multicultural affairs office, writing training. *Library facilities:* Cornell Library. *Online resources:* library catalog, access to other libraries' catalogs. *Collection:* 251,389 titles, 1,837 serial subscriptions, 3,905 audiovisual materials.

Computer facilities: 54 computers available on campus for general student use. A campuswide network can be accessed from off campus. *Web address:* http://www.vermontlaw.edu/.

General Application Contact: Kathy Hartman, Associate Dean for Enrollment Management, 802-831-1239, Fax: 802-831-1174, E-mail: admiss@vermontlaw.edu.

GRADUATE UNITS

Law School Students: 607 full-time (317 women); includes 14 Black or African American, non-Hispanic/Latino; 2 American Indian or Alaska Native, non-Hispanic/Latino; 18 Asian, non-Hispanic/Latino; 14 Hispanic/Latino; 10 Two or more races, non-Hispanic/Latino, 5 international. Average age 26. 1,056 applicants, 59% accepted, 212 enrolled. *Faculty:* 42 full-time (21 women), 26 part-time/adjunct (16 women). Expenses: Contact institution. *Financial support:* In 2010–11, 385 students received support, including 2 fellowships with full tuition reimbursements available (averaging $3,000 per year); career-related internships or fieldwork, Federal Work-Study, institutionally sponsored loans, scholarships/grants, and tuition waivers (partial) also available. Support available to part-time students. Financial award application deadline: 3/1; financial award applicants required to submit FAFSA. In 2010, 165 first professional degrees, 64 master's awarded. *Degree program information:* Part-time programs available. Offers law (JD, LL M, MELP, JD/MELP). *Application deadline:* For fall admission, 3/1 priority date for domestic students. Applications are processed on a rolling basis. *Application fee:* $60. Electronic applications accepted. *Application Contact:* Kathy Hartman, Associate Dean for Enrollment Management, 802-831-1239, Fax: 802-831-1174, E-mail: admiss@vermontlaw.edu. *President and Dean*, Geoffrey B. Shields, 802-831-1237, Fax: 802-763-2663, E-mail: hmccarthy@vermontlaw.edu.

Environmental Law Center Students: 64 full-time (35 women); includes 2 Black or African American, non-Hispanic/Latino; 1 American Indian or Alaska Native, non-Hispanic/Latino; 1 Two or more races, non-Hispanic/Latino. Average age 30. 92 applicants, 91% accepted, 48 enrolled. *Faculty:* 11 full-time (3 women), 13 part-time/adjunct (7 women). Expenses: Contact institution. *Financial support:* In 2010–11, 2 fellowships with full tuition reimbursements (averaging $5,000 per year) were awarded; career-related internships or fieldwork, Federal Work-Study, institutionally sponsored loans, scholarships/grants, and tuition waivers (partial) also available. Support available to part-time students. Financial award application deadline: 3/1; financial award applicants required to submit FAFSA. In 2010, 65 degrees awarded. *Degree program information:* Part-time programs available. Offers environmental law (LL M, MELP, JD/MELP). *Application deadline:* For fall admission, 3/1 priority date for domestic students. Applications are processed on a rolling basis. *Application fee:* $60. *Application Contact:* Anne Mansfield, Associate Director, 802-831-1338, Fax: 802-763-2940, E-mail: admiss@vermontlaw.edu. *Associate Dean*, Marc Mihaly, 802-831-1342, Fax: 802-763-2490, E-mail: admiss@vermontlaw.edu.

VICTORIA UNIVERSITY, Toronto, ON M5S 1K7, Canada

General Information Independent-religious, coed, graduate-only institution. *Graduate housing:* Rooms and/or apartments available on a first-come, first-served basis to single and married students. Housing application deadline: 6/30.

GRADUATE UNITS

Emmanuel College Offers theology (M Div, MA, MPS, MRE, MSMus, MTS, Th M, D Min, PhD, Th D, Certificate, Diploma, L Th). M Div, MRE, Th M, Th D, M Div/MA, M Div/MRE, M Div/MPS offered jointly with University of Toronto; MA, PhD with University of St. Michael's College. Electronic applications accepted.

VILLANOVA UNIVERSITY, Villanova, PA 19085-1699

General Information Independent-religious, coed, comprehensive institution. CGS member. *Enrollment:* 10,635 graduate, professional, and undergraduate students; 2,228 full-time matriculated graduate/professional students (1,029 women), 1,266 part-time matriculated graduate/professional students (635 women). *Enrollment by degree level:* 766 first professional, 2,515 master's, 133 doctoral, 80 other advanced degrees. *Graduate faculty:* 230 full-time (77 women), 150 part-time/adjunct (48 women). *Tuition:* Part-time $700 per credit. Part-time tuition and fees vary according to degree level and program. *Graduate housing:* On-campus housing not available. *Student services:* Campus employment opportunities, career counseling, exercise/wellness program, free psychological counseling, international student services, low-cost health insurance, multicultural affairs office, services for students with disabilities. *Library facilities:* Falvey Memorial Library plus 2 others. *Online resources:* library catalog, web page, access to other libraries' catalogs. *Collection:* 750,000 titles, 12,000 serial subscriptions, 9,000 audiovisual materials.

Computer facilities: Computer purchase and lease plans are available. 6,609 computers available on campus for general student use. A campuswide network can be accessed from student residence rooms and from off campus. Online class registration, learning management system with anti-plagiarism software, testing software, online faculty hours, video-

Villanova University (continued)

conferencing; electronic portfolios; data vaulting/backup service; emergency notification system; Citrix-based library of advanced software are available. *Web address:* http://www.villanova.edu/.

GRADUATE UNITS

College of Engineering Students: 75 full-time (13 women), 290 part-time (70 women); includes 13 Black or African American, non-Hispanic/Latino; 1 American Indian or Alaska Native, non-Hispanic/Latino; 18 Asian, non-Hispanic/Latino; 7 Hispanic/Latino, 49 international. *Faculty:* 72 full-time (11 women), 18 part-time/adjunct (2 women). Expenses: Contact institution. *Financial support:* In 2010–11, research assistantships with full and partial tuition reimbursements (averaging $13,500 per year); Federal Work-Study, scholarships/grants, tuition waivers (full and partial), and unspecified assistantships also available. Support available to part-time students. Financial award application deadline: 1/15. *Degree program information:* Part-time and evening/weekend programs available. Postbaccalaureate distance learning degree programs offered (minimal on-campus study). Offers biochemical engineering (Certificate); chemical engineering (MSChE); civil engineering (MSCE); computer architectures (Certificate); computer engineering (MSCPE, Certificate); electric power systems (Certificate); electrical engineering (MSEE, Certificate); electro mechanical systems (Certificate); electro-mechanical systems (Certificate); engineering (MSCPE, MSChE, MSEE, MSME, MSWREE, PhD, Certificate); environmental protection in the chemical process industries (Certificate); high frequency systems (Certificate); intelligent control systems (Certificate); machinery dynamics (Certificate); mechanical engineering (MSME); nonlinear dynamics and control (Certificate); thermofluid systems (Certificate); urban water resources design (Certificate); water resources and environmental engineering (MSWREE, Certificate); wireless and digital communications (Certificate). *Application deadline:* For fall admission, 8/1 priority date for domestic students, 4/1 priority date for international students; for spring admission, 12/1 for domestic students, 10/1 for international students. Applications are processed on a rolling basis. *Application fee:* $50. Electronic applications accepted. *Application Contact:* College of Engineering Graduate Programs Office, 610-519-5840, Fax: 610-519-5859, E-mail: engineering.grad@villanova.edu. *Dean,* Dr. Gary A. Gabriele, 610-519-4960, Fax: 610-519-5859, E-mail: gary.gabriele@villanova.edu.

College of Nursing Students: 37 full-time (30 women), 240 part-time (218 women); includes 18 Black or African American, non-Hispanic/Latino; 4 American Indian or Alaska Native, non-Hispanic/Latino; 12 Asian, non-Hispanic/Latino; 4 Hispanic/Latino; 1 Native Hawaiian or other Pacific Islander, non-Hispanic/Latino, 13 international. Average age 33. 169 applicants, 70% accepted, 86 enrolled. *Faculty:* 12 full-time (all women), 2 part-time/adjunct (both women). Expenses: Contact institution. *Financial support:* In 2010–11, 43 students received support, including 5 teaching assistantships with full tuition reimbursements available (averaging $13,100 per year); institutionally sponsored loans, scholarships/grants, traineeships, tuition waivers (full), and unspecified assistantships also available. Financial award application deadline: 7/1; financial award applicants required to submit FAFSA. In 2010, 43 master's, 4 doctorates, 10 other advanced degrees awarded. *Degree program information:* Part-time programs available. Postbaccalaureate distance learning degree programs offered (minimal on-campus study). Offers adult nurse practitioner (MSN, Post Master's Certificate); family nurse practitioner (MSN, Post Master's Certificate); health care administration (MSN); nurse anesthetist (MSN, Post Master's Certificate); nursing (PhD); nursing education (MSN, Post Master's Certificate); pediatric nurse practitioner (MSN, Post Master's Certificate). *Application deadline:* For fall admission, 7/1 priority date for domestic students, 7/1 for international students; for spring admission, 11/1 priority date for domestic students, 11/1 for international students. Applications are processed on a rolling basis. *Application fee:* $50. *Assistant Dean/Director, Graduate Programs,* Dr. Marguerite K. Schlag, 610-519-4907, Fax: 610-519-7650, E-mail: marguerite.schlag@villanova.edu.

Graduate School of Liberal Arts and Sciences Students: 793 full-time (450 women), 421 part-time (254 women); includes 192 minority (76 Black or African American, non-Hispanic/Latino; 2 American Indian or Alaska Native, non-Hispanic/Latino; 44 Asian, non-Hispanic/Latino; 51 Hispanic/Latino; 2 Native Hawaiian or other Pacific Islander, non-Hispanic/Latino; 17 Two or more races, non-Hispanic/Latino), 101 international. Average age 30. 946 applicants, 69% accepted, 397 enrolled. *Faculty:* 122 full-time (42 women), 51 part-time/adjunct (23 women). Expenses: Contact institution. *Financial support:* Research assistantships, teaching assistantships, career-related internships or fieldwork, Federal Work-Study, scholarships/grants, and unspecified assistantships available. Support available to part-time students. Financial award applicants required to submit FAFSA. In 2010, 419 master's, 1 doctorate awarded. *Degree program information:* Part-time and evening/weekend programs available. Postbaccalaureate distance learning degree programs offered (no on-campus study). Offers American studies (Certificate); ancient worlds (Certificate); applied statistics (MS); biology (MA, MS); chemistry (MS); clinical mental health counseling (MS); communication (MA); computer science (MS); counseling and human relations (MS); educational leadership (MA); elementary school counseling (MS); elementary teacher education (MA); English (MA); great books (Certificate); higher education (MA); Hispanic studies (MA); history (MA); human resource development (MS); humanities and Augustinian tradition (MA); interdisciplinary studies (Post-Master's Certificate); liberal arts and sciences (MA, MPA, MS, PhD, Certificate, Post-Master's Certificate); liberal studies (MA); mathematical sciences (MA, MS); peace and justice studies (Certificate); philosophy (PhD); political science (MA); psychology (MS); public administration (MPA); secondary school counseling (MS); secondary teacher education (MA); software engineering (MS); theatre (MA); theology (MA). *Application deadline:* For fall admission, 3/1 priority date for domestic and international students; for spring admission, 11/15 priority date for domestic and international students. Applications are processed on a rolling basis. *Application fee:* $50. Electronic applications accepted. *Application Contact:* Dean, Graduate School of Liberal Arts and Sciences. *Dean,* Dr. Adele Lindenmeyr, 610-519-7090, Fax: 610-519-7096.

School of Law Offers law (JD, LL M); tax (LL M). Electronic applications accepted.

Villanova School of Business Students: 45 full-time (10 women), 653 part-time (213 women); includes 16 Black or African American, non-Hispanic/Latino; 1 American Indian or Alaska Native, non-Hispanic/Latino; 50 Asian, non-Hispanic/Latino; 10 Hispanic/Latino; 1 Two or more races, non-Hispanic/Latino. Average age 31. *Faculty:* 81 full-time, 27 part-time/adjunct. Expenses: Contact institution. *Financial support:* In 2010–11, 19 research assistantships with full and partial tuition reimbursements (averaging $13,100 per year) were awarded; scholarships/grants and unspecified assistantships also available. Support available to part-time students. Financial award application deadline: 6/30; financial award applicants required to submit FAFSA. In 2010, 286 master's awarded. *Degree program information:* Part-time and evening/weekend programs available. Offers accountancy (MAC); business (EMBA, MAC, MBA, MSCM, MSF); church management (MSCM); executive business administration (EMBA); finance (MSF); health care management (MBA); international business (MBA); management information systems (MBA); marketing (MBA); real estate (MBA); strategic management (MBA). *Application deadline:* For fall admission, 6/30 for domestic students; for winter admission, 11/15 for domestic students; for spring admission, 3/31 for domestic students. *Application fee:* $50. Electronic applications accepted. *Application Contact:* Meredith L. Kwiatek, Assistant Director, 610-519-7016, Fax: 610-519-6273, E-mail: meredith.kwiatek@villanova.edu. *Associate Dean of Graduate Business Programs,* Robert F. Bonner, 610-519-4336, Fax: 610-519-6273, E-mail: robert.bonner@villanova.edu.

VIRGINIA COLLEGE AT BIRMINGHAM, Birmingham, AL 35209

General Information Proprietary, coed, comprehensive institution.

GRADUATE UNITS

Program in Business Administration *Degree program information:* Part-time and evening/weekend programs available. Postbaccalaureate distance learning degree programs offered (no on-campus study). Offers business administration (MBA).

Virginia College Online *Degree program information:* Part-time and evening/weekend programs available. Postbaccalaureate distance learning degree programs offered (no on-campus study). Offers business administration (MBA); criminal justice (MCJ); cybersecurity (MC).

VIRGINIA COMMONWEALTH UNIVERSITY, Richmond, VA 23284-9005

General Information State-supported, coed, university. CGS member. *Enrollment:* 32,303 graduate, professional, and undergraduate students; 5,163 full-time matriculated graduate/professional students (3,146 women), 3,391 part-time matriculated graduate/professional students (2,257 women). *Enrollment by degree level:* 1,640 first professional, 3,959 master's, 1,478 doctoral, 1,477 other advanced degrees. Tuition, state resident: full-time $4308; part-time $479 per credit hour. Tuition, nonresident: full-time $8942; part-time $994 per credit hour. *Required fees:* $2000; $85 per credit hour. Tuition and fees vary according to course level, course load, degree level, campus/location and program. *Graduate housing:* Room and/or apartments available on a first-come, first-served basis to single students; on-campus housing not available to married students. *Student services:* Campus employment opportunities, campus safety program, career counseling, child daycare facilities, exercise/wellness program, free psychological counseling, grant writing training, international student services, low-cost health insurance, multicultural affairs office, services for students with disabilities, teacher training, writing training. *Library facilities:* Cabell Library and Thompkins McCaw Library plus 6 others. *Online resources:* library catalog, web page, access to other libraries' catalogs. *Collection:* 2.1 million titles, 51,000 serial subscriptions. *Research affiliation:* Virginia Biotechnology Research Park (biotechnology), Virginia Biotechnology Research Park.

Computer facilities: Computer purchase and lease plans are available. 1,450 computers available on campus for general student use. A campuswide network can be accessed from student residence rooms and from off campus. Online class registration is available. *Web address:* http://www.vcu.edu/.

General Application Contact: Whitney A. Carswell, Recruitment Coordinator, Graduate School, 804-828-6916, Fax: 804-828-6949, E-mail: wcarswell@vcu.edu.

GRADUATE UNITS

Graduate School Students: 5,168 full-time (3,149 women), 3,473 part-time (2,325 women); includes 2,097 minority (961 Black or African American, non-Hispanic/Latino; 26 American Indian or Alaska Native, non-Hispanic/Latino; 746 Asian, non-Hispanic/Latino; 241 Hispanic/Latino; 13 Native Hawaiian or other Pacific Islander, non-Hispanic/Latino; 110 Two or more races, non-Hispanic/Latino), 529 international. 7,026 applicants, 49% accepted, 2269 enrolled. Expenses: Contact institution. *Financial support:* Fellowships, research assistantships, teaching assistantships, career-related internships or fieldwork, Federal Work-Study, institutionally sponsored loans, scholarships/grants, and tuition waivers (full and partial) available. Support available to part-time students. Financial award applicants required to submit FAFSA. In 2010, 1,726 master's, 298 doctorates, 321 other advanced degrees awarded. *Degree program information:* Part-time and evening/weekend programs available. Offers interdisciplinary studies (MIS). *Application fee:* $50. Electronic applications accepted. *Application Contact:* Dr. Sherry T. Sandkam, Associate Dean, 804-828-6916, Fax: 804-827-4546, E-mail: ssandkam@vcu.edu. *Dean, Graduate School,* Dr. F. Douglas Boudinot, 804-828-2233, Fax: 804-827-0724, E-mail: fdboudinot@vcu.edu.

College of Humanities and Sciences Students: 775 full-time (449 women), 1,057 part-time (654 women); includes 445 minority (249 Black or African American, non-Hispanic/Latino; 6 American Indian or Alaska Native, non-Hispanic/Latino; 88 Asian, non-Hispanic/Latino; 53 Hispanic/Latino; 3 Native Hawaiian or other Pacific Islander, non-Hispanic/Latino; 46 Two or more races, non-Hispanic/Latino), 117 international. 1,486 applicants, 40% accepted, 214 enrolled. Expenses: Contact institution. *Financial support:* Fellowships, research assistantships, teaching assistantships, career-related internships or fieldwork, Federal Work-Study, institutionally sponsored loans, scholarships/grants, and tuition waivers (full and partial) available. Support available to part-time students. Financial award applicants required to submit FAFSA. In 2010, 352 master's, 39 doctorates, 84 other advanced degrees awarded. *Degree program information:* Part-time and evening/weekend programs available. Offers analytical chemistry (MS, PhD); applied mathematics (MS); applied social research (CASR); art direction (MS); behavioral medicine (PhD); biology (MS); biopsychology (PhD); chemical physics (PhD); clinical child psychology (PhD); clinical psychology (PhD); communication strategy (MS); copywriting (MS); counseling psychology (PhD); creative brand management (MS); creative media planning (MS); creative writing (MFA); criminal justice (MS, CCJA); developmental psychology (PhD); English (MA); fiction (MFA); fictional poetry (MFA); forensic biology (MS); forensic chemistry/drugs and toxicology (MS); forensic chemistry/trace (MS); forensic physical evidence (MS); general psychology (PhD); geographic information systems (Certificate); government and public affairs (MA, MPA, MS, MURP, PhD, CASR, CCJA, CPM, CURP, Certificate, Graduate Certificate); health psychology (PhD); historic preservation planning (Certificate); history (MA); homeland security and emergency preparedness (MA, Graduate Certificate); humanities and sciences (MA, MFA, MPA, MS, MURP, PhD, CASR, CCJA, CPM, CURP, Certificate, Graduate Certificate); inorganic chemistry (MS, PhD); literature (MA); mass communications (MS, PhD); mathematics (MS); media, art, and text (PhD); medical physics (MS, PhD); multimedia journalism (MS); nanoscience and nanotechnology (PhD); nanosciences (PhD); nonprofit management (Graduate Certificate); operations research (MS); organic chemistry (MS, PhD); physical chemistry (MS, PhD); physics and applied physics (MS); poetry (MFA); public administration (MPA); public management (CPM); public policy and administration (PhD); social psychology (PhD); sociology (MS); statistical sciences and operations research (MS); strategic public relations (MS); urban and regional planning (MURP); urban revitalization (CURP); writing and rhetoric (MA). *Application fee:* $50. Electronic applications accepted. *Application Contact:* Dr. Fred M. Hawkridge, Interim Dean, 804-828-1674, E-mail: fmhawkri@vcu.edu. *Interim Dean,* Dr. Fred M. Hawkridge, 804-828-1674, E-mail: fmhawkri@vcu.edu.

School of Allied Health Professions Students: 774 full-time (556 women), 316 part-time (227 women). 608 applicants, 50% accepted, 210 enrolled. Expenses: Contact institution. *Financial support:* Fellowships, research assistantships, teaching assistantships, career-related internships or fieldwork and tuition waivers (full and partial) available. In 2010, 175 master's, 136 doctorates, 12 other advanced degrees awarded. *Degree program information:* Part-time programs available. Offers advanced physical therapy (MS); aging studies (CAS); allied health professions (MHA, MS, MSHA, MSNA, MSOT, DNAP, OTD, PhD, CAS, CPC); clinical laboratory sciences (MS); entry-level physical therapy (MS); gerontology (MS, PhD); health administration (MHA, MSHA, PhD); health related sciences (PhD); health services organization and research (PhD); nurse anesthesia (MSNA, DNAP); occupational therapy (MS, MSOT, OTD); patient counseling (MS, CPC); physical therapy (PhD); radiation sciences (PhD); rehabilitation counseling (MS, CPC); rehabilitation leadership (PhD). *Application fee:* $50. Electronic applications accepted. *Application Contact:* Monica L. White, Director of Student Services, 804-828-7247, Fax: 804-828-8656, E-mail: mlwhite1@vcu.edu. *Dean,* Dr. Cecil B. Drain, 804-828-7247.

School of Business Students: 246 full-time (104 women), 339 part-time (108 women); includes 139 minority (72 Black or African American, non-Hispanic/Latino; 4 American Indian or Alaska Native, non-Hispanic/Latino; 41 Asian, non-Hispanic/Latino; 14 Hispanic/Latino; 8 Two or more races, non-Hispanic/Latino), 67 international. 426 applicants, 59% accepted, 170 enrolled. Expenses: Contact institution. *Financial support:* Fellowships, research assistantships, teaching assistantships, Federal Work-Study, institutionally sponsored loans, and tuition waivers (full and partial) available. Support available to part-time students. Financial award application deadline: 3/15; financial award applicants required to submit FAFSA. In 2010, 240 master's, 2 doctorates, 61 other advanced degrees awarded. *Degree program information:* Part-time and evening/weekend programs available. Offers accounting (M Acc, MBA, PhD); business (M Acc, M Tax, MA, MBA, MS, PhD, Certificate, Postbaccalaureate Certificate); business administration (MBA, Postbaccalaureate Certificate); decision sciences (MBA, MS); economics (MA); finance, insurance, and real estate (MS); information systems (MS, PhD); management (Certificate); marketing and business law (MS); real estate and urban land development (Certificate); taxation (M Tax). *Application deadline:* Applications are processed on a rolling basis. *Application fee:* $50. *Application Contact:* Jana P. McQuaid, Assistant Dean of Master's Programs, 804-828-4622, Fax: 804-828-7174, E-mail: jpmcquaid@vcu.edu. *Dean,* Ed Grier, 804-828-1595, Fax: 804-828-8884.

School of Education Students: 389 full-time (311 women), 1,115 part-time (886 women). 625 applicants, 57% accepted, 249 enrolled. Expenses: Contact institution. *Financial support:*

Fellowships, research assistantships, teaching assistantships, career-related internships or fieldwork, Federal Work-Study, institutionally sponsored loans, and tuition waivers (full and partial) available. Support available to part-time students. Financial award application deadline: 3/1; financial award applicants required to submit FAFSA. In 2010, 398 master's, 34 doctorates, 83 other advanced degrees awarded. *Degree program information:* Part-time programs available. Offers adult literacy (M Ed); athletic training (MSAT); autism spectrum disorders (Certificate); college student development and counseling (M Ed); disability leadership (Certificate); early and elementary education (MT); early childhood (M Ed); education (M Ed, MS, MSAT, MT, Ed D, PhD, Certificate); educational leadership (PhD); educational psychology (PhD); general education (M Ed); health and movement sciences (MS); health and physical education (MT); human resource development (M Ed); instructional leadership (PhD); leadership (Ed D); reading (M Ed); reading specialist (Certificate); rehabilitation and movement science (PhD); research and evaluation (PhD); school counseling (M Ed); secondary 6-12 education (MT); secondary education (Certificate); severe disabilities (M Ed); special education and disability leadership (PhD); sport leadership (MS); teaching and learning with technology (M Ed); urban services leadership (PhD). *Application fee:* $50. Electronic applications accepted. *Application Contact:* Dr. Diane Simon, Associate Dean for Student Affairs, 804-828-3382, Fax: 804-828-1323, E-mail: dsimon@vcu.edu. *Interim Dean,* Dr. Michael D. Davis, 804-828-3382, E-mail: mddavis@vcu.edu.

School of Engineering Students: 157 full-time (50 women), 89 part-time (18 women); includes 49 minority (14 Black or African American, non-Hispanic/Latino; 24 Asian, non-Hispanic/Latino; 10 Hispanic/Latino; 1 Two or more races, non-Hispanic/Latino), 88 international. 245 applicants, 68% accepted, 108 enrolled. *Faculty:* 50 full-time (8 women). Expenses: Contact institution. *Financial support:* Applicants required to submit FAFSA. In 2010, 60 master's, 20 doctorates awarded. Offers biomedical engineering (MS, PhD); chemical and life science engineering (MS, PhD); computer science (MS, PhD); electrical engineering (MS, PhD); engineering (PhD); mechanical engineering (MS, PhD). *Application deadline:* For fall admission, 2/1 priority date for domestic students; for spring admission, 11/15 for domestic students. *Application fee:* $50. Electronic applications accepted. *Application Contact:* Mark D. Meadows, Director of Student Recruitment, 804-827-4005, E-mail: mdmeadows@vcu.edu. *Associate Dean for Graduate Affairs,* Dr. Rosalyn S. Hobson, 804-828-3925, E-mail: rhobson@vcu.edu.

School of Life Sciences Students: 61 full-time (32 women), 43 part-time (19 women); includes 15 minority (9 Black or African American, non-Hispanic/Latino; 1 American Indian or Alaska Native, non-Hispanic/Latino; 3 Asian, non-Hispanic/Latino; 1 Hispanic/Latino; 1 Two or more races, non-Hispanic/Latino), 14 international. 91 applicants, 55% accepted, 28 enrolled. Expenses: Contact institution. *Financial support:* Applicants required to submit FAFSA. In 2010, 18 master's, 3 doctorates awarded. Offers bioinformatics (MS); environmental studies (M Env Sc, MS); integrative life sciences (PhD); life sciences (M Env Sc, MB, MS, PhD). *Application fee:* $50. Electronic applications accepted. *Application Contact:* Dr. Greg Garman, Director, Center for Environmental Studies, 804-828-1574, E-mail: ggarman@vcu.edu. *Vice Provost,* Dr. Thomas F. Huff, 804-827-5600.

School of Nursing Students: 144 full-time (133 women), 156 part-time (145 women); includes 55 minority (26 Black or African American, non-Hispanic/Latino; 18 Asian, non-Hispanic/Latino; 5 Hispanic/Latino; 6 Two or more races, non-Hispanic/Latino), 1 international. 165 applicants, 58% accepted, 73 enrolled. Expenses: Contact institution. *Financial support:* Fellowships, research assistantships, teaching assistantships, career-related internships or fieldwork and institutionally sponsored loans available. Financial award applicants required to submit FAFSA. In 2010, 85 master's, 6 doctorates, 5 other advanced degrees awarded. *Degree program information:* Part-time and evening/weekend programs available. Offers adult health acute nursing (MS); adult health primary nursing (MS); biobehavioral clinical (PhD); child health nursing (MS); clinical nurse leader (MS); family health nursing (MS); nurse educator (MS); nurse practitioner (MS); nursing (Certificate); nursing administration (MS); psychiatric-mental health nursing (MS); women's health nursing (MS). *Application deadline:* For fall admission, 2/1 priority date for domestic students; for spring admission, 11/1 for domestic students. *Application fee:* $50. Electronic applications accepted. *Application Contact:* Susan Lipp, Assistant Dean, Enrollment and Student Services, 804-828-5171, Fax: 804-828-7743, E-mail: vcu_nurse@vcu.edu. *Dean,* Dr. Nancy F. Langston, 804-828-5174, Fax: 804-828-7743.

School of Social Work Students: 398 full-time (358 women), 147 part-time (129 women); includes 164 minority (99 Black or African American, non-Hispanic/Latino; 21 Asian, non-Hispanic/Latino; 35 Hispanic/Latino; 1 Native Hawaiian or other Pacific Islander, non-Hispanic/Latino; 8 Two or more races, non-Hispanic/Latino), 4 international. 632 applicants, 58% accepted, 211 enrolled. Expenses: Contact institution. *Financial support:* Fellowships, research assistantships, teaching assistantships, career-related internships or fieldwork, Federal Work-Study, institutionally sponsored loans, and tuition waivers (full and partial) available. Support available to part-time students. Financial award applicants required to submit FAFSA. In 2010, 217 master's, 5 doctorates awarded. Offers social work (MSW, PhD). *Application deadline:* For fall admission, 2/1 priority date for domestic students. *Application fee:* $50. Electronic applications accepted. *Application Contact:* Dr. Marcia P. Harrigan, Senior Associate Dean, Student and Academic Affairs, 804-828-0703, Fax: 804-828-0716, E-mail: mpharrig@vcu.edu. *Dean,* Dr. James E. Hinterlong, 804-828-1030, Fax: 804-828-0716, E-mail: jehinterlong@vcu.edu.

School of the Arts Students: 158 full-time (103 women), 116 part-time (96 women); includes 31 minority (10 Black or African American, non-Hispanic/Latino; 7 Asian, non-Hispanic/Latino; 11 Hispanic/Latino; 3 Two or more races, non-Hispanic/Latino), 9 international. 907 applicants, 18% accepted, 92 enrolled. Expenses: Contact institution. *Financial support:* Fellowships, teaching assistantships, career-related internships or fieldwork, Federal Work-Study, institutionally sponsored loans, and tuition waivers (full and partial) available. Support available to part-time students. Financial award applicants required to submit FAFSA. In 2010, 87 master's, 5 doctorates awarded. *Degree program information:* Part-time programs available. Offers architectural history (MA); art education (MAE); art history (MA, PhD); ceramics (MFA); costume design (MFA); design/visual communications (MFA); education (MM); fibers (MFA); furniture design (MFA); glassworking (MFA); graphic design (MFA); historical studies (MA); interior environment (MFA); jewelry/metalworking (MFA); kinetic imaging (MFA); museum studies (MA); music (MM); painting (MFA); pedagogy (MFA); printmaking (MFA); scene design/technical theater (MFA); sculpture (MFA); theatre (MFA). *Application deadline:* For fall admission, 1/15 priority date for domestic students. *Application fee:* $50. Electronic applications accepted. *Application Contact:* Jack H. Risley, Associate Dean for Academic Affairs, 804-828-2787, Fax: 804-828-6469, E-mail: jhrisley@vcu.edu. *Dean,* Joseph H. Seipel, 804-828-2787, Fax: 804-828-6469, E-mail: arts@vcu.edu.

Medical College of Virginia-Professional Programs Students: 2,213 full-time (1,164 women), 105 part-time (51 women); includes 711 minority (132 Black or African American, non-Hispanic/Latino; 9 American Indian or Alaska Native, non-Hispanic/Latino; 474 Asian, non-Hispanic/Latino; 60 Hispanic/Latino; 4 Native Hawaiian or other Pacific Islander, non-Hispanic/Latino; 32 Two or more races, non-Hispanic/Latino), 187 international. Expenses: Contact institution. *Financial support:* Fellowships, research assistantships, teaching assistantships, career-related internships or fieldwork, Federal Work-Study, institutionally sponsored loans, and tuition waivers (full and partial) available. In 2010, 406 first professional degrees, 94 master's, 54 doctorates awarded. *Degree program information:* Part-time programs available. Offers medicine (DDS, MD, Pharm D, MPH, MS, PhD). *Application deadline:* Applications are processed on a rolling basis. *Application fee:* $50. Electronic applications accepted. *Application Contact:* Whitney A. Carswell, Recruitment Coordinator, Graduate School, 804-828-6916, Fax: 804-828-6949, E-mail: wcarswell@vcu.edu. *Vice President for Health Sciences,* Dr. Sheldin M. Retchin, 804-828-7235, Fax: 804-828-8002, E-mail: vphsweb@vcu.edu.

School of Dentistry Students: 420 full-time (167 women), 11 part-time (5 women); includes 94 minority (14 Black or African American, non-Hispanic/Latino; 58 Asian, non-Hispanic/Latino; 17 Hispanic/Latino; 1 Native Hawaiian or other Pacific Islander, non-Hispanic/Latino; 4 Two or more races, non-Hispanic/Latino), 17 international. 141 applicants, 85% accepted, 117 enrolled. *Faculty:* 46 full-time (7 women). Expenses: Contact institution. *Financial support:* Fellowships available. In 2010, 90 first professional degrees, 13 master's awarded. Offers dentistry (DDS, MS). *Application deadline:* For fall admission, 9/1 for domestic students. Electronic applications accepted. *Application Contact:* Dr. Michael Healy, Assistant Dean of Student Affairs and Admissions, 804-828-9196, E-mail: mhealy@vcu.edu. *Dean/Associate Vice President for Health Sciences,* Dr. David C. Sarrett, 804-828-7235, E-mail: bmarcus@vcu.edu.

School of Medicine Students: 1,224 full-time (613 women), 67 part-time (35 women); includes 430 minority (81 Black or African American, non-Hispanic/Latino; 7 American Indian or Alaska Native, non-Hispanic/Latino; 287 Asian, non-Hispanic/Latino; 36 Hispanic/Latino; 19 Two or more races, non-Hispanic/Latino), 104 international. 1,300 applicants, 60% accepted, 329 enrolled. *Faculty:* 211 full-time (56 women). Expenses: Contact institution. *Financial support:* Fellowships, research assistantships, teaching assistantships, career-related internships or fieldwork, Federal Work-Study, institutionally sponsored loans, and tuition waivers (full and partial) available. In 2010, 186 first professional degrees, 77 master's, 46 doctorates, 74 other advanced degrees awarded. Offers anatomy (MS); anatomy and neurobiology (PhD); biochemistry (MS, PhD); biostatistics (MS, PhD); epidemiology (MPH, PhD); genetic counseling (MS); human genetics (PhD); medicine (MD, MPH, MS, PhD, Certificate); microbiology and immunology (MS, PhD); molecular biology (MS, PhD); molecular biology and genetics (MS, PhD); neurobiology (MS); neuroscience (PhD); pathology (PhD); pharmacology (Certificate); pharmacology and toxicology (MS, PhD); physical therapy (PhD); physiology (MS, PhD); public health practice (MPH); social and behavioral science (MPH). *Application deadline:* Applications are processed on a rolling basis. Electronic applications accepted. *Application Contact:* Dr. Jan Chlebowski, Associate Dean for Graduate Education, 804-828-1023, E-mail: jfchlebo@vcu.edu. *Dean,* Dr. Jerome F. Strauss, 804-828-9788, Fax: 804-828-7628.

School of Pharmacy Students: 569 full-time (384 women), 27 part-time (11 women); includes 187 minority (37 Black or African American, non-Hispanic/Latino; 2 American Indian or Alaska Native, non-Hispanic/Latino; 129 Asian, non-Hispanic/Latino; 7 Hispanic/Latino; 3 Native Hawaiian or other Pacific Islander, non-Hispanic/Latino; 9 Two or more races, non-Hispanic/Latino), 66 international. 398 applicants, 44% accepted, 165 enrolled. *Faculty:* 18 full-time (5 women). Expenses: Contact institution. *Financial support:* Fellowships, research assistantships, teaching assistantships, institutionally sponsored loans available. Financial award application deadline: 3/1. In 2010, 130 first professional degrees, 4 master's, 8 doctorates awarded. *Degree program information:* Part-time programs available. Offers medicinal chemistry (MS); pharmaceutical sciences (PhD); pharmaceutics (MS); pharmacotherapy and pharmacy administration (MS); pharmacy (Pharm D, MS, PhD). *Application deadline:* For fall admission, 12/1 priority date for domestic students. Applications are processed on a rolling basis. *Application fee:* $50. Electronic applications accepted. *Application Contact:* Dr. Thomas P. Reinders, Associate Dean for Admissions and Student Services, 804-828-3000, Fax: 804-827-0002, E-mail: reinders@vcu.edu. *Dean,* Dr. Victor A. Yanchick, 804-828-3000, Fax: 804-828-1815, E-mail: pharmacy@vcu.edu.

Program in Pre-Medical Basic Health Sciences Students: 86 full-time (43 women), 2 part-time (1 woman); includes 42 minority (5 Black or African American, non-Hispanic/Latino; 29 Asian, non-Hispanic/Latino; 5 Hispanic/Latino; 3 Two or more races, non-Hispanic/Latino). 314 applicants, 64% accepted. Expenses: Contact institution. In 2010, 70 CBHSs awarded. Offers anatomy (CBHS); biochemistry (CBHS); human genetics (CBHS); microbiology (CBHS); pharmacology (CBHS); physiology (CBHS). *Application deadline:* For fall admission, 6/1 for domestic students. *Application fee:* $50. Electronic applications accepted. *Application Contact:* Zack McDowell, Administrator, 804-828-9501, E-mail: premedcert@vcu.edu. *Director,* Dr. Louis J. De Felice, 804-828-9501, E-mail: premedcert@vcu.edu.

VIRGINIA INTERNATIONAL UNIVERSITY, Fairfax, VA 22030

General Information Proprietary, coed, comprehensive institution. *Graduate housing:* Rooms and/or apartments available on a first-come, first-served basis to single and married students. *Research affiliation:* Apple Federal Credit Union (financial management).

GRADUATE UNITS

School of Business *Degree program information:* Part-time programs available. Offers accounting (MBA); executive management (Graduate Certificate); global logistics (MBA); health care management (MBA); human resources management (MBA); international business management (MBA); international finance (MBA); marketing management (MBA). Electronic applications accepted.

School of Computer Information Systems *Degree program information:* Part-time programs available. Offers computer science (MS); information systems (MS). Electronic applications accepted.

School of English Language Studies *Degree program information:* Part-time programs available. Offers teaching English to speakers of other languages (MA, Graduate Certificate). Electronic applications accepted.

VIRGINIA POLYTECHNIC INSTITUTE AND STATE UNIVERSITY, Blacksburg, VA 24061

General Information State-supported, coed, university. CGS member. *Enrollment:* 31,006 graduate, professional, and undergraduate students; 4,874 full-time matriculated graduate/professional students (2,116 women), 2,442 part-time matriculated graduate/professional students (1,087 women). *Enrollment by degree level:* 372 first professional, 4,041 master's, 2,903 doctoral. *Graduate faculty:* 1,519 full-time (482 women), 14 part-time/adjunct (9 women). Tuition, state resident: full-time $9399; part-time $488 per credit hour. Tuition, nonresident: full-time $17,854; part-time $957.75 per credit hour. *Required fees:* $1534. Full-time tuition and fees vary according to program. *Graduate housing:* Room and/or apartments available on a first-come, first-served basis to single students; on-campus housing not available to married students. Typical cost: $4670 per year ($7388 including board). Room and board charges vary according to board plan, campus/location and housing facility selected. *Student services:* Campus employment opportunities, career counseling, exercise/wellness program, free psychological counseling, grant writing training, international student services, low-cost health insurance, multicultural affairs office, services for students with disabilities, teacher training, writing training. *Library facilities:* Newman Library plus 2 others. *Online resources:* library catalog, web page. *Collection:* 2.4 million titles, 27,150 serial subscriptions, 18,185 audiovisual materials. *Research affiliation:* The National Academies (transportation research), Southern States Energy Board (energy research), National Federation of the Blind (mechanical engineering/vehicle research), Oak Ridge National Laboratory (biological systems engineering/enzyme research), Virginia Uranium (uranium mining), Water Environment Research Foundation (water and wastewater pipe research).

Computer facilities: 8,000 computers available on campus for general student use. A campuswide network can be accessed from student residence rooms and from off campus. Online class registration is available. *Web address:* http://www.vt.edu/.

General Application Contact: Graduate School Applications, General Assistance, 540-231-8636, Fax: 540-231-2039, E-mail: gradappl@vt.edu.

GRADUATE UNITS

Graduate School Students: 4,874 full-time (2,116 women), 2,442 part-time (1,087 women); includes 392 Black or African American, non-Hispanic/Latino; 10 American Indian or Alaska Native, non-Hispanic/Latino; 299 Asian, non-Hispanic/Latino; 164 Hispanic/Latino, 1,824 international. Average age 31. 9,190 applicants, 33% accepted, 1870 enrolled. *Faculty:* 1,519 full-time (482 women), 14 part-time/adjunct (9 women). Expenses: Contact institution. *Financial support:* In 2010–11, 265 fellowships with full tuition reimbursements (averaging $8,235 per year), 1,458 research assistantships with full tuition reimbursements (averaging $20,091 per year), 980 teaching assistantships with full tuition reimbursements (averaging $15,706 per year) were awarded; career-related internships or fieldwork, Federal Work-Study, scholarships/grants, health care benefits, and unspecified assistantships also available. In 2010, 1,548 master's, 403 doctorates, 158 other advanced degrees awarded. *Degree program information:* Part-time and evening/weekend programs available. Postbaccalaureate distance learning degree programs offered (no on-campus study). *Application deadline:* For fall admission, 7/1 for domestic and international students; for spring admission, 12/1 for domestic and international students. Applications are processed on a rolling basis. *Application fee:* $65. Electronic applications accepted. *Application Contact:* Jacqueline Nottingham, Director of Graduate Admissions and Academic Progress, 540-231-3092, Fax: 540-231-3750, E-mail: ntnghm@

Virginia Polytechnic Institute and State University (continued)

vt.edu. *Vice President and Dean for Graduate Education*, Dr. Karen P. DePauw, 540-231-7581, Fax: 540-231-1670, E-mail: kpdepauw@vt.edu.

College of Agriculture and Life Sciences Students: 333 full-time (194 women), 85 part-time (47 women); includes 25 Black or African American, non-Hispanic/Latino; 2 American Indian or Alaska Native, non-Hispanic/Latino; 12 Asian, non-Hispanic/Latino; 11 Hispanic/Latino, 97 international. Average age 29. 352 applicants, 41% accepted, 84 enrolled. *Faculty:* 201 full-time (57 women), 1 (woman) part-time/adjunct. Expenses: Contact institution. *Financial support:* In 2010–11, 25 fellowships with full tuition reimbursements (averaging $6,007 per year), 216 research assistantships with full tuition reimbursements (averaging $19,621 per year), 87 teaching assistantships with full tuition reimbursements (averaging $14,846 per year) were awarded; career-related internships or fieldwork, Federal Work-Study, scholarships/grants, health care benefits, and unspecified assistantships also available. Financial award application deadline: 1/15. In 2010, 60 master's, 40 doctorates awarded. Offers agricultural and applied economics (MS, PhD); agricultural and life sciences (MS, MSLFS); agricultural extension education (MS, PhD); agriculture and life sciences (MS, MSLFS, PhD, Certificate); animal and poultry science (MS, PhD); biochemistry (MSLFS, PhD); crop and soil environmental sciences (MS, PhD); dairy science (MS, PhD); entomology (MSLFS, PhD); food science and technology (PhD); health product risk management (Certificate); horticulture (MS, PhD); human nutrition, foods and exercise (MS, PhD); plant pathology, physiology and weed science (MS, PhD); produce food safety (Certificate). *Application deadline:* For fall admission, 7/1 for domestic and international students; for spring admission, 12/1 for domestic and international students. Applications are processed on a rolling basis. *Application fee:* $65. Electronic applications accepted. *Application Contact:* Sheila Norman, Contact, 540-231-4152, Fax: 540-231-4163, E-mail: snorman@vt.edu. *Dean*, Dr. Alan L. Grant, 540-231-4152, Fax: 540-231-4163, E-mail: algrant@vt.edu.

College of Architecture and Urban Studies Students: 419 full-time (204 women), 268 part-time (123 women); includes 51 Black or African American, non-Hispanic/Latino; 1 American Indian or Alaska Native, non-Hispanic/Latino; 29 Asian, non-Hispanic/Latino; 22 Hispanic/Latino, 96 international. Average age 31. 815 applicants, 45% accepted, 176 enrolled. *Faculty:* 118 full-time (43 women), 2 part-time/adjunct (1 woman). Expenses: Contact institution. *Financial support:* In 2010–11, 14 fellowships with full tuition reimbursements (averaging $861 per year), 13 research assistantships with full tuition reimbursements (averaging $22,434 per year), 23 teaching assistantships with full tuition reimbursements (averaging $16,166 per year) were awarded; career-related internships or fieldwork, Federal Work-Study, scholarships/grants, health care benefits, and unspecified assistantships also available. Financial award application deadline: 1/15. In 2010, 142 master's, 17 doctorates awarded. Offers architecture (M Arch, MS); architecture and design research (PhD); architecture and urban studies (M Arch, MFA, MLA, MPA, MPIA, MS, MURPL, PhD, Certificate); building construction (MS); creative technologies (MFA); economic development (Certificate); environmental design and planning (PhD); government and international affairs (MPIA, PhD); homeland security policy (Certificate); landscape architecture (MLA, PhD); local government management (Certificate); nonprofit and nongovernmental organization management (Certificate); planning, governance and globalization (PhD); public administration and policy (Certificate); public administration and public affairs (MPA, PhD); urban and regional planning (MURPL). *Application deadline:* For fall admission, 7/1 for domestic and international students; for spring admission, 12/1 for domestic and international students. Applications are processed on a rolling basis. *Application fee:* $65. Electronic applications accepted. *Application Contact:* Liz Roberson, Contact, 540-231-6416, Fax: 540-231-6332, E-mail: eroberso@vt.edu. *Dean*, Dr. A. J. Davis, 540-231-6416, Fax: 540-231-6332, E-mail: davisa@vt.edu.

College of Engineering Students: 1,682 full-time (378 women), 402 part-time (79 women); includes 45 Black or African American, non-Hispanic/Latino; 92 Asian, non-Hispanic/Latino; 38 Hispanic/Latino, 955 international. Average age 28. 4,561 applicants, 20% accepted, 489 enrolled. *Faculty:* 331 full-time (49 women), 1 part-time/adjunct (0 women). Expenses: Contact institution. *Financial support:* In 2010–11, 185 fellowships with full tuition reimbursements (averaging $6,315 per year), 841 research assistantships with full tuition reimbursements (averaging $20,820 per year), 197 teaching assistantships with full tuition reimbursements (averaging $16,737 per year) were awarded; career-related internships or fieldwork, Federal Work-Study, scholarships/grants, health care benefits, and unspecified assistantships also available. Financial award application deadline: 1/15. In 2010, 452 master's, 154 doctorates awarded. Offers aerospace engineering (M Eng, MS, PhD); air transportation systems (Certificate); biological systems engineering (M Eng, MS, PhD); biomedical engineering and sciences (MS, PhD); chemical engineering (M Eng, MS, PhD); civil engineering (M Eng, MS, PhD); civil infrastructure systems (Certificate); computational engineering science and mechanics (Certificate); computer engineering (M Eng, MS, PhD); computer science and applications (MS, PhD); electrical engineering (M Eng, MS, PhD); emerging devices technologies (Certificate); engineering (M Eng, MEA, MS, PhD, Certificate); engineering education (PhD, Certificate); engineering mechanics (MS, PhD); environmental engineering (MS); environmental sciences and engineering (MS); human-computer interactions (Certificate); human-system integration (Certificate); industrial and systems engineering (MEA, PhD); information assurance engineering (Certificate); materials science and engineering (M Eng, MS, PhD); mechanical engineering (M Eng, MS, PhD); mining and minerals engineering (M Eng, MS, PhD); systems engineering (MS); traffic control and operations (Certificate); transportation systems engineering (Certificate); treatment process engineering (Certificate); urban hydrology and stormwater management (Certificate); water quality management (Certificate). *Application deadline:* For fall admission, 7/1 for domestic and international students; for spring admission, 12/1 for domestic and international students. Applications are processed on a rolling basis. *Application fee:* $65. Electronic applications accepted. *Application Contact:* Linda Perkins, Contact, 540-231-9752, Fax: 540-231-3362, E-mail: lperkins@vt.edu. *Dean*, Dr. Richard C. Benson, 540-231-9752, Fax: 540-231-3362, E-mail: deaneng@vt.edu.

College of Liberal Arts and Human Sciences Students: 711 full-time (460 women), 675 part-time (457 women); includes 153 Black or African American, non-Hispanic/Latino; 3 American Indian or Alaska Native, non-Hispanic/Latino; 22 Asian, non-Hispanic/Latino; 27 Hispanic/Latino, 85 international. Average age 35. 956 applicants, 46% accepted, 317 enrolled. *Faculty:* 762 full-time (388 women), 12 part-time/adjunct (8 women). Expenses: Contact institution. *Financial support:* In 2010–11, 2 fellowships with full tuition reimbursements (averaging $10,912 per year), 12 research assistantships with full tuition reimbursements (averaging $17,822 per year), 182 teaching assistantships with full tuition reimbursements (averaging $12,784 per year) were awarded; career-related internships or fieldwork, Federal Work-Study, scholarships/grants, health care benefits, and unspecified assistantships also available. Financial award application deadline: 1/15. In 2010, 422 master's, 88 doctorates, 23 other advanced degrees awarded. Offers apparel business and economics (MS, PhD); apparel product design and analysis (MS, PhD); apparel quality analysis (MS, PhD); career and technical education (MS Ed, Ed D, PhD, Ed S); cognition and education (Certificate); communication (MA); consumer studies (MS, PhD); counselor education (MA, PhD); creative writing (MFA); curriculum and instruction (MA Ed, Ed D, PhD, Ed S); directing and public dialogue (MFA); education (MA, MA Ed, MS Ed, Ed D, PhD, Certificate, Ed S); educational leadership and policy studies (MA, Ed D, PhD, Ed S); educational research, evaluation (PhD); English (MA); environmental politics and policy (Certificate); family financial management (MS, PhD); foreign languages and literatures (MA); foundations of political analysis (Certificate); gerontology (Certificate); higher education administration (Certificate); history (MA); history of science and technology (Certificate); household equipment (MS, PhD); housing (MS, PhD); human development (MS, PhD); information policy and society (Certificate); integrative STEM education (Certificate); interior design (MS, PhD); liberal arts (Certificate); liberal arts and human sciences (MA, MA Ed, MFA, MS, MS Ed, Ed D, PhD, Certificate, Ed S); marriage and family therapy (Certificate); philosophy (MA); philosophy of science and technology (Certificate); political science (MA); politics and policy studies of science and technology (Certificate); race and social policy (Certificate); religious studies (Certificate); resource management (MS, PhD); rhetoric and writing (PhD); science and technology studies (MS, PhD, Certificate); security studies (Certificate); social and cultural studies of science and technology (Certificate); social, political, ethical, and cultural thought (PhD, Certificate); sociology (MS, PhD); stage management (MFA); theatre design and technology (MFA); women's and gender studies (Certificate). *Application deadline:* For fall admission, 7/1 for domestic and international students; for spring admission, 12/1 for domestic and international students. Applications are processed on a rolling basis. *Application fee:* $65. Electronic applications accepted. *Application Contact:* Emily Oliver, Contact, 540-231-6779, Fax: 540-231-7157, E-mail: emilyo@vt.edu. *Dean*, Sue Ott Rowlands, 540-231-6779, Fax: 540-231-7157, E-mail: sottrowlands@vt.edu.

College of Natural Resources and Environment Students: 140 full-time (68 women), 92 part-time (47 women); includes 1 Black or African American, non-Hispanic/Latino; 1 American Indian or Alaska Native, non-Hispanic/Latino; 4 Asian, non-Hispanic/Latino; 4 Hispanic/Latino, 45 international. Average age 31. 44 applicants, 23% accepted, 10 enrolled. *Faculty:* 60 full-time (16 women). Expenses: Contact institution. *Financial support:* In 2010–11, 82 research assistantships with full tuition reimbursements (averaging $17,965 per year), 21 teaching assistantships with full tuition reimbursements (averaging $14,423 per year) were awarded; career-related internships or fieldwork, Federal Work-Study, scholarships/grants, health care benefits, and unspecified assistantships also available. Financial award application deadline: 1/15. In 2010, 35 master's, 11 doctorates awarded. Offers fisheries and wildlife sciences (MS, PhD); forestry (MS, PhD); geography (MS, PhD); geospatial and environmental analysis (PhD); natural resources (MNR, Certificate); natural resources and environment (MF, MNR, MS, PhD, Certificate); watershed management (Certificate); wood science and forest products (MF, MS, PhD). *Application deadline:* For fall admission, 7/1 for domestic and international students; for spring admission, 12/1 for domestic and international students. Applications are processed on a rolling basis. *Application fee:* $65. Electronic applications accepted. *Application Contact:* Peggy Quarterman, Contact, 540-231-3479, E-mail: pquarter@vt.edu. *Dean*, Dr. Paul M. Winistorfer, 540-231-8853, E-mail: pwinisto@vt.edu.

College of Science Students: 570 full-time (245 women), 25 part-time (10 women); includes 12 Black or African American, non-Hispanic/Latino; 1 American Indian or Alaska Native, non-Hispanic/Latino; 16 Asian, non-Hispanic/Latino; 14 Hispanic/Latino, 262 international. Average age 28. 931 applicants, 25% accepted, 127 enrolled. Expenses: Contact institution. *Financial support:* In 2010–11, 12 fellowships with full tuition reimbursements (averaging $12,444 per year), 147 research assistantships with full tuition reimbursements (averaging $17,826 per year), 312 teaching assistantships with full tuition reimbursements (averaging $16,378 per year) were awarded; career-related internships or fieldwork, Federal Work-Study, scholarships/grants, health care benefits, and unspecified assistantships also available. Financial award application deadline: 1/15. In 2010, 79 master's, 64 doctorates awarded. Offers biological sciences (MS, PhD); biomedical technology development and management (MS); chemistry (MS, PhD); economics (PhD); geosciences (MS, PhD); mathematics (MS, PhD); physics (MS, PhD); psychology (MS, PhD); science (MS, PhD); statistics (MS, PhD). *Application deadline:* For fall admission, 7/1 for domestic and international students; for spring admission, 12/1 for domestic and international students. Applications are processed on a rolling basis. *Application fee:* $65. Electronic applications accepted. *Application Contact:* Diane Stearns, Contact, 540-231-7515, Fax: 540-231-3380, E-mail: dstearns@vt.edu. *Dean*, Dr. Lay Nam Chang, 540-231-5422, Fax: 540-231-3380, E-mail: laynam@vt.edu.

Intercollege Students: 743 full-time (250 women), 148 part-time (64 women); includes 80 Black or African American, non-Hispanic/Latino; 2 American Indian or Alaska Native, non-Hispanic/Latino; 74 Asian, non-Hispanic/Latino; 29 Hispanic/Latino, 124 international. Average age 33. 756 applicants, 77% accepted, 390 enrolled. Expenses: Contact institution. *Financial support:* In 2010–11, 19 fellowships with full tuition reimbursements (averaging $23,872 per year), 134 research assistantships with full tuition reimbursements (averaging $20,375 per year), 59 teaching assistantships with full tuition reimbursements (averaging $15,212 per year) were awarded; career-related internships or fieldwork, Federal Work-Study, scholarships/grants, health care benefits, and unspecified assistantships also available. Financial award application deadline: 1/15. In 2010, 79 master's, 11 doctorates, 135 other advanced degrees awarded. Offers collaborative community leadership (Certificate); future professoriate (Certificate); genetics, bioinformatics and computational biology (PhD); geospatial information technology (Certificate); information technology (MIT); interdisciplinary studies (MIT, MS, PhD, Certificate); international research and development (Certificate); macromolecular interfaces with life sciences (Certificate); macromolecular science and engineering (MS, PhD); microbiology (PhD); molecular plant sciences (PhD); qualitative resource assessment (Certificate). *Application deadline:* For fall admission, 7/1 for domestic and international students; for spring admission, 12/1 for domestic and international students. Applications are processed on a rolling basis. *Application fee:* $65. Electronic applications accepted.

Pamplin College of Business Students: 417 full-time (164 women), 111 part-time (39 women); includes 16 Black or African American, non-Hispanic/Latino; 36 Asian, non-Hispanic/Latino; 11 Hispanic/Latino, 131 international. Average age 30. 603 applicants, 44% accepted, 199 enrolled. *Faculty:* 116 full-time (33 women), 2 part-time/adjunct (1 woman). Expenses: Contact institution. *Financial support:* In 2010–11, 3 fellowships with full tuition reimbursements (averaging $22,103 per year), 2 research assistantships with full tuition reimbursements (averaging $13,864 per year), 46 teaching assistantships with full tuition reimbursements (averaging $13,957 per year) were awarded; career-related internships or fieldwork, Federal Work-Study, scholarships/grants, health care benefits, and unspecified assistantships also available. Financial award application deadline: 1/15. In 2010, 264 master's, 15 doctorates awarded. Offers accounting and information systems (MACIS, PhD); business (MACIS, MBA, MS, PhD); business administration (MBA); business information technology (PhD); finance (MS, PhD); hospitality and tourism management (MS, PhD); management (PhD); marketing (MS, PhD). *Application deadline:* For fall admission, 7/1 for domestic and international students; for spring admission, 12/1 for domestic and international students. Applications are processed on a rolling basis. *Application fee:* $65. Electronic applications accepted. *Application Contact:* Denise Jones, Contact, 540-231-9647, Fax: 540-231-4487, E-mail: cdjones@vt.edu. *Dean*, Dr. Richard E. Sorensen, 540-231-6601, Fax: 540-231-4487, E-mail: sorensen@vt.edu.

Virginia-Maryland Regional College of Veterinary Medicine Students: 454 full-time (339 women), 41 part-time (35 women); includes 9 Black or African American, non-Hispanic/Latino; 14 Asian, non-Hispanic/Latino; 8 Hispanic/Latino, 29 international. Average age 27. 62 applicants, 63% accepted, 39 enrolled. *Faculty:* 83 full-time (32 women). Expenses: Contact institution. *Financial support:* In 2010–11, 5 fellowships with full tuition reimbursements (averaging $32,153 per year), 11 research assistantships with full tuition reimbursements (averaging $17,053 per year), 53 teaching assistantships with full tuition reimbursements (averaging $21,735 per year) were awarded; career-related internships or fieldwork, Federal Work-Study, scholarships/grants, health care benefits, and unspecified assistantships also available. Financial award application deadline: 1/15. In 2010, 87 first professional degrees, 15 master's, 3 doctorates awarded. Offers biomedical and veterinary sciences (MS, PhD); public health (MPH); veterinary medicine (DVM, MPH, MS, PhD). *Application deadline:* For fall admission, 7/1 for domestic and international students; for spring admission, 12/1 for domestic and international students. Applications are processed on a rolling basis. *Application fee:* $65. Electronic applications accepted. *Application Contact:* Shelia Steele, Contact, 540-231-7910, Fax: 540-231-9290, E-mail: ssteele@vt.edu. *Dean*, Dr. Gerhardt G. Schurig, 540-231-7666, Fax: 540-231-9290, E-mail: gschurig@vt.edu.

VT Online

VIRGINIA STATE UNIVERSITY, Petersburg, VA 23806-0001

General Information State-supported, coed, comprehensive institution. *Enrollment:* 5,634 graduate, professional, and undergraduate students; 274 full-time matriculated graduate/professional students (184 women), 285 part-time matriculated graduate/professional students (199 women). *Enrollment by degree level:* 459 master's, 36 doctoral, 13 other advanced degrees. *Graduate faculty:* 72 full-time (28 women). Tuition, state resident: full-time $5576; part-time $335 per credit hour. Tuition, nonresident: full-time $13,402; part-time $670 per credit hour. *Graduate housing:* Room and/or apartments available on a first-come, first-served basis to single students; on-campus housing not available to married students. Typical cost: $4640 per year ($8152 including board). Room and board charges vary according to housing facility selected. Housing application deadline: 5/1. *Student services:* Career counseling, international student services, services for students with disabilities. *Library facilities:* Johnston Memorial Library. *Online resources:* library catalog, web page, access to other libraries' catalogs. *Collection:* 331,289 titles, 27,676 audiovisual materials. *Research affiliation:* MCV/VCU (Medical College of Virginia/Virginia Commonwealth University) (biology), The College of William and Mary (biology), University of Massachusetts (biology), Rolls Royce USA (engineering), C-CAM (engineering).

Computer facilities: 1,461 computers available on campus for general student use. A campuswide network can be accessed from student residence rooms and from off campus. Online class registration is available. *Web address:* http://www.vsu.edu/.

General Application Contact: Patrice Randall, Graduate Programs Coordinator, 804-524-5385, Fax: 804-524-5104, E-mail: prandall@vsu.edu.

GRADUATE UNITS

School of Graduate Studies, Research, and Outreach *Degree program information:* Part-time and evening/weekend programs available. Offers interdisciplinary studies (MIS).

School of Agriculture Offers agriculture (MS); plant science (MS).

School of Engineering, Science and Technology Offers behavioral and community health sciences (PhD); biology (MS); clinical health psychology (PhD); clinical psychology (MS); computer science (MS); engineering, science and technology (M Ed, MS); general psychology (MS); mathematics (MS); mathematics education (M Ed); physics (MS).

School of Liberal Arts and Education *Degree program information:* Part-time and evening/weekend programs available. Offers career and technical studies (M Ed, MS, CAGS); economics (MA); education (M Ed, MS); educational administration and supervision (M Ed, MS); English (MA); history (MA); liberal arts and education (M Ed, MA, MS, CAGS).

VIRGINIA THEOLOGICAL SEMINARY, Alexandria, VA 22304

General Information Independent-religious, coed, graduate-only institution. *Graduate housing:* Room and/or apartments available on a first-come, first-served basis to single students; on-campus housing not available to married students. Housing application deadline: 5/1.

GRADUATE UNITS

Graduate and Professional Programs *Degree program information:* Part-time programs available. Offers theology (M Div, MACE, MTS, D Min).

VIRGINIA UNION UNIVERSITY, Richmond, VA 23220-1170

General Information Independent-religious, coed, comprehensive institution. *Graduate housing:* Room and/or apartments available on a first-come, first-served basis to single students; on-campus housing not available to married students.

GRADUATE UNITS

School of Theology *Degree program information:* Part-time and evening/weekend programs available. Offers theology (M Div, D Min).

VIRGINIA UNIVERSITY OF LYNCHBURG, Lynchburg, VA 24501-6417

General Information Independent-religious, coed, comprehensive institution.

GRADUATE UNITS

Graduate Programs

VITERBO UNIVERSITY, La Crosse, WI 54601-4797

General Information Independent-religious, coed, comprehensive institution. *Graduate housing:* Rooms and/or apartments available to single and married students. Housing application deadline: 4/2.

GRADUATE UNITS

Graduate Program in Business Offers business (MBA).

Graduate Program in Education *Degree program information:* Part-time and evening/weekend programs available. Offers education (MA). Courses held on weekends and during summer.

Graduate Program in Nursing *Degree program information:* Part-time programs available. Postbaccalaureate distance learning degree programs offered (minimal on-campus study). Offers nursing (MSN).

WAGNER COLLEGE, Staten Island, NY 10301-4495

General Information Independent, coed, comprehensive institution. *Enrollment:* 2,271 graduate, professional, and undergraduate students; 231 full-time matriculated graduate/professional students (136 women), 185 part-time matriculated graduate/professional students (137 women). *Enrollment by degree level:* 414 master's, 2 other advanced degrees. *Graduate faculty:* 26 full-time (18 women), 74 part-time/adjunct (44 women). *Tuition:* Full-time $15,570; part-time $865 per credit. *Graduate housing:* Room and/or apartments available on a first-come, first-served basis to single students; on-campus housing not available to married students. Typical cost: $10,170 (including board). Housing application deadline: 4/1. *Student services:* Campus employment opportunities, campus safety program, career counseling, child daycare facilities, exercise/wellness program, free psychological counseling, international student services, multicultural affairs office, services for students with disabilities, teacher training, writing training. *Library facilities:* August Horrmann Library. *Online resources:* library catalog, web page, access to other libraries' catalogs. *Collection:* 179,200 titles, 21,150 serial subscriptions, 3,815 audiovisual materials. *Research affiliation:* Staten Island University Hospital.

Computer facilities: 230 computers available on campus for general student use. A campuswide network can be accessed from student residence rooms and from off campus. Online class registration is available. *Web address:* http://www.wagner.edu/.

General Application Contact: Leigh-Ann Nowicki, Dean of Admissions, 718-420-4020, Fax: 718-390-3105, E-mail: leigh-ann.nowicki@wagner.edu.

GRADUATE UNITS

Division of Graduate Studies Students: 231 full-time (136 women), 187 part-time (139 women); includes 94 minority (31 Black or African American, non-Hispanic/Latino; 1 American Indian or Alaska Native, non-Hispanic/Latino; 23 Asian, non-Hispanic/Latino; 31 Hispanic/Latino; 8 Two or more races, non-Hispanic/Latino), 3 international. Average age 27. 245 applicants, 97% accepted, 187 enrolled. *Faculty:* 30 full-time (19 women), 80 part-time/adjunct (47 women). Expenses: Contact institution. *Financial support:* In 2010–11, 144 students received support. Career-related internships or fieldwork, Federal Work-Study, unspecified assistantships, and alumni fellowship grant available. Financial award application deadline: 4/1; financial award applicants required to submit FAFSA. In 2010, 170 master's, 1 other advanced degree awarded. *Degree program information:* Part-time and evening/weekend programs available. Offers accelerated business administration (MBA); accounting (MS); adolescent education (MS Ed); advanced physician assistant studies (MS); childhood education (MS Ed); early childhood education (birth-grade 2) (MS Ed); educational leadership (MS Ed); family nurse practitioner (Certificate); finance (MBA); health care administration (MBA); international business (MBA); literacy (B-6) (MS Ed); management (Exec MBA, MBA); marketing (MBA); microbiology (MS); middle level education (5-9) (MS Ed); nursing (MS, Certificate); school building leader (MS Ed). *Application deadline:* For fall admission, 5/1 priority date for domestic students, 3/1 priority date for international students; for spring admission, 11/1 priority date for domestic students, 10/1 priority date for international students. Applications are processed on a rolling basis. *Application fee:* $50 ($85 for international students). *Application Contact:* Patricia Clancy, Assistant Coordinator of Graduate Studies, 718-420-4464, Fax: 718-390-3105, E-mail: patricia.clancy@wagner.edu. *Coordinator,* Dr. Jeffrey Kraus, 718-390-3254, Fax: 718-390-3456, E-mail: jkraus@wagner.edu.

WAKE FOREST UNIVERSITY, Winston-Salem, NC 27109

General Information Independent, coed, university. CGS member. *Graduate housing:* On-campus housing not available.

GRADUATE UNITS

Graduate School of Arts and Sciences *Degree program information:* Part-time programs available. Offers accountancy (MSA); analytical chemistry (MS, PhD); arts and sciences (MA, MA Ed, MALS, MS, MSA, PhD); biology (MS, PhD); computer science (MS); counseling (MA); English (MA); health and exercise science (MS); inorganic chemistry (MS, PhD); liberal studies (MALS); mathematics (MA); organic chemistry (MS, PhD); physical chemistry (MS, PhD); physics (MS, PhD); psychology (MA); religion (MA); secondary education (MA Ed); speech communication (MA). Electronic applications accepted.

School of Law Offers law (JD, LL M, SJD). LL M for foreign law graduates in American law. Electronic applications accepted.

School of Medicine Offers medicine (MD, MS, PhD). Electronic applications accepted.

Graduate Programs in Medicine Offers biochemistry (PhD); cancer biology (PhD); comparative medicine (MS); health sciences research (MS); medicine (MS, PhD); microbiology and immunology (PhD); molecular and cellular pathobiology (MS, PhD); molecular genetics and genomics (PhD); molecular medicine (MS, PhD); neurobiology and anatomy (PhD); neuroscience (PhD); pharmacology (PhD); physiology (PhD). Electronic applications accepted.

Schools of Business Students: 584 full-time (186 women); includes 145 minority (94 Black or African American, non-Hispanic/Latino; 2 American Indian or Alaska Native, non-Hispanic/Latino; 23 Asian, non-Hispanic/Latino; 20 Hispanic/Latino; 6 Two or more races, non-Hispanic/Latino), 54 international. *Faculty:* 63 full-time (17 women), 30 part-time/adjunct (9 women). Expenses: Contact institution. *Financial support:* In 2010–11, 292 students received support. Scholarships/grants available. Financial award applicants required to submit FAFSA. In 2010, 376 master's awarded. *Degree program information:* Evening/weekend programs available. Offers assurance services (MSA); business (MA, MBA, MSA); business administration (MBA); consulting/general management (MBA); entrepreneurship (MBA); finance (MBA); health (MBA); management (MA); marketing (MBA); operations management (MBA); tax consulting (MSA); transaction services (MSA). *Application deadline:* Applications are processed on a rolling basis. *Application fee:* $100. Electronic applications accepted. *Application Contact:* Tamara Paquee, Administrative Assistant, 336-758-5422, Fax: 336-758-5830, E-mail: admissions@mba.wfu.edu. *Dean,* Steve Reinemund, 336-758-5422, Fax: 336-758-5830, E-mail: admissions@mba.wfu.edu.

Virginia Tech-Wake Forest University School of Biomedical Engineering and Sciences Offers biomedical engineering (MS, PhD). Electronic applications accepted.

WALDEN UNIVERSITY, Minneapolis, MN 55401

General Information Proprietary, coed, upper-level institution. CGS member. *Enrollment:* 47,456 graduate, professional, and undergraduate students; 30,418 full-time matriculated graduate/professional students (23,726 women), 7,486 part-time matriculated graduate/professional students (5,890 women). *Enrollment by degree level:* 21,954 master's, 15,127 doctoral, 823 other advanced degrees. *Graduate faculty:* 171 full-time (107 women), 1,884 part-time/adjunct (1,090 women). *Tuition:* Full-time $10,274; part-time $445 per credit. Tuition and fees vary according to course load, degree level and program. *Graduate housing:* On-campus housing not available. *Student services:* Career counseling, free psychological counseling, services for students with disabilities, writing training. *Library facilities:* Walden University Library. *Online resources:* library catalog, web page. *Collection:* 112,169 titles.

Computer facilities: Online class registration is available. *Web address:* http://www.waldenu.edu/.

General Application Contact: Jennifer Hall, Vice President of Enrollment Management, 866-4-WALDEN, E-mail: info@walden.edu.

GRADUATE UNITS

Graduate Programs Students: 30,418 full-time (23,726 women), 7,486 part-time (5,890 women); includes 15,346 minority (12,397 Black or African American, non-Hispanic/Latino; 279 American Indian or Alaska Native, non-Hispanic/Latino; 747 Asian, non-Hispanic/Latino; 1,515 Hispanic/Latino; 30 Native Hawaiian or other Pacific Islander, non-Hispanic/Latino; 378 Two or more races, non-Hispanic/Latino), 1,148 international. Average age 40. *Faculty:* 171 full-time (107 women), 1,884 part-time/adjunct (1,090 women). Expenses: Contact institution. *Financial support:* In 2010–11, 2 fellowships were awarded; Federal Work-Study, scholarships/grants, unspecified assistantships, and family tuition reduction, active duty/veteran tuition reduction, group tuition reduction, interest-free payment plans also available. Support available to part-time students. Financial award applicants required to submit FAFSA. In 2010, 7,782 master's, 584 doctorates, 67 other advanced degrees awarded. *Degree program information:* Part-time and evening/weekend programs available. Postbaccalaureate distance learning degree programs offered (minimal on-campus study). *Application deadline:* Applications are processed on a rolling basis. *Application fee:* $50. Electronic applications accepted. *Application Contact:* Jennifer Hall, Vice President of Enrollment Management, 866-4-WALDEN, E-mail: info@walden.edu. *President,* Jonathan A. Kaplan, 800-925-3368.

Richard W. Riley College of Education and Leadership Students: 13,130 full-time (10,679 women), 1,719 part-time (1,437 women); includes 5,153 minority (4,233 Black or African American, non-Hispanic/Latino; 89 American Indian or Alaska Native, non-Hispanic/Latino; 161 Asian, non-Hispanic/Latino; 542 Hispanic/Latino; 12 Native Hawaiian or other Pacific Islander, non-Hispanic/Latino; 116 Two or more races, non-Hispanic/Latino), 325 international. Average age 38. *Faculty:* 61 full-time (44 women), 822 part-time/adjunct (539 women). Expenses: Contact institution. *Financial support:* In 2010–11, 1 fellowship was awarded; Federal Work-Study, scholarships/grants, unspecified assistantships, and family tuition reduction, active duty/veteran tuition reduction, group tuition reduction, interest-free payment plans also available. Support available to part-time students. Financial award applicants required to submit FAFSA. In 2010, 4,656 master's, 306 doctorates, 65 other advanced degrees awarded. *Degree program information:* Part-time and evening/weekend programs available. Postbaccalaureate distance learning degree programs offered (minimal on-campus study). Offers administrator leadership for teaching and learning (Ed D, Ed S); adult learning (MS); college teaching and learning (Postbaccalaureate Certificate); curriculum, instruction and assessment (Ed D, Postbaccalaureate Certificate); curriculum, instruction, and professional development (Ed S); early childhood education (birth-grade 3) (MAT); early childhood studies (MS); education (MS, PhD); educational leadership and administration (principal preparation) (Ed S); educational technology (Ed S); engaging culturally diverse learners (Postbaccalaureate Certificate); enrollment management and institutional marketing (Postbaccalaureate Certificate); higher education (MS); higher education and adult learning (Ed D); higher education leadership (Ed D); instructional design (Postbaccalaureate Certificate); instructional design and technology (MS); integrating technology in the classroom (Postbaccalaureate Certificate); online learning (Postbaccalaureate Certificate); professional development (Postbaccalaureate Certificate); special education (Ed D, Ed S); special education: emotional/behavioral disorders (K-12) (MAT); special education: learning disabilities (K-12) (MAT); teacher leadership (Ed D, Ed S, Postbaccalaureate Certificate); training and performance management (Postbaccalaureate Certificate). *Application deadline:* Applications are processed on a rolling basis. *Application fee:* $50. Electronic applications accepted. *Application Contact:* Jennifer Hall, Vice President of Enrollment Management, 866-4-WALDEN, E-mail: info@waldenu.edu. *Dean,* Dr. Kate Steffens, 800-925-3368.

School of Counseling and Social Service Students: 2,687 full-time (2,269 women), 536 part-time (473 women); includes 1,582 minority (1,319 Black or African American, non-Hispanic/Latino; 34 American Indian or Alaska Native, non-Hispanic/Latino; 29 Asian, non-Hispanic/Latino; 142 Hispanic/Latino; 58 Two or more races, non-Hispanic/Latino), 47 international. Average age 38. *Faculty:* 25 full-time (17 women), 241 part-time/adjunct (162 women). Expenses: Contact institution. *Financial support:* Fellowships, Federal Work-Study, scholarships/grants, unspecified assistantships, and family tuition reduction, active duty/veteran tuition reduction, group tuition reduction, interest-free payment plans available. Support available to part-time students. Financial award applicants required to submit FAFSA. In 2010, 182 master's, 8 doctorates awarded. *Degree program information:* Part-time and evening/weekend programs available. Postbaccalaureate distance learning degree programs offered (minimal on-campus study). Offers career counseling (MS); counselor education and supervision (PhD); human services (PhD); marriage, couple, and family counseling (MS); mental health counseling (MS). *Application deadline:* Applications are processed on a rolling basis. *Application fee:* $50. Electronic applications accepted. *Application Contact:* Jennifer Hall, Vice President of Enrollment Management, 866-4-WALDEN, E-mail: info@waldenu.edu. *Associate Dean,* Dr. Savitri Dixon-Saxon, 800-925-3368.

Walden University (continued)

School of Health Sciences Students: 2,651 full-time (2,079 women), 932 part-time (731 women); includes 1,624 Black or African American, non-Hispanic/Latino; 24 American Indian or Alaska Native, non-Hispanic/Latino; 132 Asian, non-Hispanic/Latino; 145 Hispanic/Latino; 28 Two or more races, non-Hispanic/Latino, 177 international. Average age 39. *Faculty:* 15 full-time (11 women), 202 part-time/adjunct (94 women). Expenses: Contact institution. *Financial support:* Fellowships, Federal Work-Study, scholarships/grants, unspecified assistantships, and family tuition reduction, active duty/veteran tuition reduction, group tuition reduction, interest-free payment plans available. Support available to part-time students. Financial award applicants required to submit FAFSA. In 2010, 370 master's, 61 doctorates awarded. *Degree program information:* Part-time and evening/weekend programs available. Postbaccalaureate distance learning degree programs offered (minimal on-campus study). Offers clinical research administration (MS, Postbaccalaureate Certificate); health informatics (MS); health services (PhD); healthcare administration (MHA); public health (MPH, PhD). *Application deadline:* Applications are processed on a rolling basis. *Application fee:* $50. Electronic applications accepted. *Application Contact:* Jennifer Hall, Vice President of Enrollment Management, 866-4-WALDEN, E-mail: info@waldenu.edu. *Associate Dean,* Dr. Jorg Westermann, 800-925-3368.

School of Management Students: 3,705 full-time (1,956 women), 976 part-time (549 women); includes 2,432 minority (2,021 Black or African American, non-Hispanic/Latino; 32 American Indian or Alaska Native, non-Hispanic/Latino; 137 Asian, non-Hispanic/Latino; 193 Hispanic/Latino; 5 Native Hawaiian or other Pacific Islander, non-Hispanic/Latino; 44 Two or more races, non-Hispanic/Latino), 302 international. Average age 40. *Faculty:* 22 full-time (8 women), 291 part-time/adjunct (100 women). Expenses: Contact institution. *Financial support:* Fellowships, Federal Work-Study, scholarships/grants, unspecified assistantships, and family tuition reduction, active duty/veteran tuition reduction, group tuition reduction, interest-free payment plans available. Support available to part-time students. Financial award applicants required to submit FAFSA. In 2010, 658 master's, 86 doctorates awarded. *Degree program information:* Part-time and evening/weekend programs available. Postbaccalaureate distance learning degree programs offered (minimal on-campus study). Offers accounting (MS); accounting and management (MS); applied management and decision sciences (PhD); business information management (MISM); enterprise information security (MISM); entrepreneurship (MBA, DBA); finance (MBA, DBA); global management (MS); global supply chain management (DBA); health informatics (MISM); healthcare management (MBA, MS); healthcare system improvement (MBA); human resource management (MBA, MS); information systems (MS); information systems management (DBA); information technology (MS); international business (MBA, DBA); IT strategy and governance (MISM); leadership (MBA, MS, DBA); managers as leaders (MS); managing global software and service supply chains (MISM); marketing (MBA, DBA); project management (MBA, MS); research strategies (MS); risk management (MBA); self-designed (MBA, DBA); social impact management (DBA); strategy and operations (MS); sustainable futures (MBA); sustainable management (MS); technology (MBA); technology entrepreneurship (DBA); technology management (MS). *Application deadline:* Applications are processed on a rolling basis. *Application fee:* $50. Electronic applications accepted. *Application Contact:* Jennifer Hall, Vice President of Enrollment Management, 866-4-WALDEN, E-mail: info@waldenu.edu. *Associate Dean,* Dr. William Schulz, 800-925-3368.

School of Nursing Students: 3,360 full-time (3,115 women), 241 part-time (148 women); includes 1,036 minority (670 Black or African American, non-Hispanic/Latino; 30 American Indian or Alaska Native, non-Hispanic/Latino; 159 Asian, non-Hispanic/Latino; 142 Hispanic/Latino; 6 Native Hawaiian or other Pacific Islander, non-Hispanic/Latino; 29 Two or more races, non-Hispanic/Latino), 120 international. Average age 43. *Faculty:* 10 full-time (7 women), 121 part-time/adjunct (104 women). Expenses: Contact institution. *Financial support:* Fellowships, Federal Work-Study, scholarships/grants, unspecified assistantships, and family tuition reduction, active duty/veteran tuition reduction, group tuition reduction, interest-free payment plans available. Support available to part-time students. Financial award applicants required to submit FAFSA. In 2010, 988 master's awarded. *Degree program information:* Part-time and evening/weekend programs available. Postbaccalaureate distance learning degree programs offered (no on-campus study). Offers education (MSN); informatics (MSN); leadership and management (MSN); nursing (Post-Master's Certificate). *Application deadline:* Applications are processed on a rolling basis. *Application fee:* $50. Electronic applications accepted. *Application Contact:* Jennifer Hall, Vice President of Enrollment Management, 866-4-WALDEN, E-mail: info@walden.edu. *Associate Dean,* Dr. Sara Torres, 800-925-3368.

School of Psychology Students: 3,463 full-time (2,737 women), 1,400 part-time (1,130 women); includes 1,491 Black or African American, non-Hispanic/Latino; 59 American Indian or Alaska Native, non-Hispanic/Latino; 89 Asian, non-Hispanic/Latino; 283 Hispanic/Latino; 76 Two or more races, non-Hispanic/Latino, 126 international. Average age 40. *Faculty:* 41 full-time (25 women), 254 part-time/adjunct (131 women). Expenses: Contact institution. *Financial support:* In 2010–11, 1 fellowship was awarded; Federal Work-Study, scholarships/grants, unspecified assistantships, and family tuition reduction, active duty/veteran tuition reduction, group tuition reduction, interest-free payment plans also available. Support available to part-time students. Financial award applicants required to submit FAFSA. In 2010, 559 master's, 100 doctorates awarded. *Degree program information:* Part-time and evening/weekend programs available. Postbaccalaureate distance learning degree programs offered (minimal on-campus study). Offers clinical child psychology (Post-Doctoral Certificate); clinical psychology (MS, Post-Doctoral Certificate); counseling psychology (Post-Doctoral Certificate); forensic psychology (MS); general psychology (Post-Doctoral Certificate); health psychology (Post-Doctoral Certificate); organizational psychology (Post-Doctoral Certificate); organizational psychology and development (Postbaccalaureate Certificate); psychology (MS, PhD); teaching online (Post-Master's Certificate). *Application deadline:* Applications are processed on a rolling basis. *Application fee:* $50. Electronic applications accepted. *Application Contact:* Jennifer Hall, Vice President of Enrollment Management, 866-4-WALDEN, E-mail: info@waldenu.edu. *Associate Dean,* Dr. Melanie Storms, 800-925-3368.

School of Public Policy and Administration Students: 1,408 full-time (901 women), 599 part-time (392 women); includes 1,022 Black or African American, non-Hispanic/Latino; 11 American Indian or Alaska Native, non-Hispanic/Latino; 37 Asian, non-Hispanic/Latino; 64 Hispanic/Latino; 26 Two or more races, non-Hispanic/Latino, 47 international. Average age 40. *Faculty:* 10 full-time (5 women), 117 part-time/adjunct (49 women). Expenses: Contact institution. *Financial support:* Fellowships with tuition reimbursements, Federal Work-Study, scholarships/grants, unspecified assistantships, and family tuition reduction, active duty/veteran tuition reduction, group tuition reduction, interest-free payment plans available. Support available to part-time students. Financial award applicants required to submit FAFSA. In 2010, 311 master's, 23 doctorates awarded. *Degree program information:* Part-time and evening/weekend programs available. Postbaccalaureate distance learning degree programs offered (minimal on-campus study). Offers criminal justice (MPA); emergency management (MPA); government management (Postbaccalaureate Certificate); health policy (MPA); homeland security policy (MPA); homeland security policy and coordination (MPA); interdisciplinary policy studies (MPA); international nongovernmental organizations (ngos) (MPA); law and public policy (MPA); local government management for sustainable communities (MPA); nonprofit management (Postbaccalaureate Certificate); nonprofit management and leadership (MPA, MS); policy analysis (MPA); public management and leadership (MPA); public policy and administration (MPA, PhD); terrorism, mediation, and peace (MPA). *Application deadline:* Applications are processed on a rolling basis. *Application fee:* $50. Electronic applications accepted. *Application Contact:* Jennifer Hall, Vice President of Enrollment Management, 866-4-WALDEN, E-mail: info@waldenu.edu. *Associate Dean,* Dr. Mark Gordon, 800-925-3368.

WALLA WALLA UNIVERSITY, College Place, WA 99324-1198

General Information Independent-religious, coed, comprehensive institution. *Enrollment:* 1,791 graduate, professional, and undergraduate students; 217 full-time matriculated graduate/professional students (158 women), 25 part-time matriculated graduate/professional students (20 women). *Enrollment by degree level:* 238 master's. *Graduate faculty:* 25 full-time (13 women), 19 part-time/adjunct (13 women). *Graduate housing:* Rooms and/or apartments available on a first-come, first-served basis to single and married students. *Student services:* Campus employment opportunities, career counseling, free psychological counseling, international student services, low-cost health insurance, multicultural affairs office, services for students with disabilities. *Library facilities:* Peterson Memorial Library plus 3 others. *Online resources:* library catalog, web page, access to other libraries' catalogs.

Computer facilities: Computer purchase and lease plans are available. A campuswide network can be accessed from student residence rooms and from off campus. Online class registration, online forum, online classifieds, online student directory are available. *Web address:* http://www.wallawalla.edu/.

General Application Contact: Dr. Joe G. Galusha, Dean of Graduate Studies, 509-527-2421, Fax: 509-527-2237, E-mail: joe.galusha@wallawalla.edu.

GRADUATE UNITS

Graduate School Students: 214 full-time (148 women), 24 part-time (18 women); includes 4 Black or African American, non-Hispanic/Latino; 23 American Indian or Alaska Native, non-Hispanic/Latino; 7 Asian, non-Hispanic/Latino; 7 Hispanic/Latino, 1 international. Average age 36. 228 applicants, 75% accepted, 122 enrolled. *Faculty:* 25 full-time (13 women), 19 part-time/adjunct (13 women). Expenses: Contact institution. *Financial support:* In 2010–11, 200 students received support, including 10 teaching assistantships (averaging $11,109 per year); research assistantships, career-related internships or fieldwork, Federal Work-Study, scholarships/grants, tuition waivers (partial), and unspecified assistantships also available. Support available to part-time students. Financial award application deadline: 4/1; financial award applicants required to submit FAFSA. In 2010, 150 master's awarded. *Degree program information:* Part-time and evening/weekend programs available. Offers biology (MS). *Application deadline:* Applications are processed on a rolling basis. *Application fee:* $50. Electronic applications accepted. *Application Contact:* Christy Ann Bandy, Administrative Assistant to Graduate Dean, 509-527-2421, Fax: 509-527-2237, E-mail: christy.bandy@wallawalla.edu. *Dean of Graduate Studies,* Dr. Joe G. Galusha, 509-527-2421, Fax: 509-527-2237, E-mail: joe.galusha@wallawalla.edu.

School of Education and Psychology Students: 32 full-time (14 women), 9 part-time (7 women); includes 1 Black or African American, non-Hispanic/Latino; 1 American Indian or Alaska Native, non-Hispanic/Latino; 2 Asian, non-Hispanic/Latino; 1 Hispanic/Latino. Average age 30. 41 applicants, 80% accepted, 21 enrolled. *Faculty:* 7 full-time (3 women), 1 part-time/adjunct (0 women). Expenses: Contact institution. *Financial support:* In 2010–11, 29 students received support; research assistantships, teaching assistantships, Federal Work-Study and tuition waivers (partial) available. Support available to part-time students. Financial award application deadline: 4/1; financial award applicants required to submit FAFSA. In 2010, 29 master's awarded. *Degree program information:* Part-time programs available. Offers counseling psychology (MA); curriculum and instruction (M Ed, MA, MAT); educational leadership (M Ed, MA, MAT); literacy instruction (M Ed, MA, MAT); students at risk (M Ed, MA, MAT); teaching (MAT). *Application deadline:* For fall admission, 4/1 priority date for domestic students. Applications are processed on a rolling basis. *Application fee:* $50. Electronic applications accepted. *Application Contact:* Dr. Joe G. Galusha, Dean of Graduate Studies, 509-527-2421, Fax: 509-527-2237, E-mail: joe.galusha@wallawalla.edu. *Dean,* Dr. Julian Melgosa, 509-527-2272, Fax: 509-527-2248, E-mail: julian.melgosa@wallawalla.edu.

Wilma Hepker School of Social Work and Sociology Students: 173 full-time (129 women), 14 part-time (11 women); includes 4 Black or African American, non-Hispanic/Latino; 22 American Indian or Alaska Native, non-Hispanic/Latino; 4 Asian, non-Hispanic/Latino; 5 Hispanic/Latino. Average age 37. 178 applicants, 74% accepted, 95 enrolled. *Faculty:* 13 full-time (9 women), 17 part-time/adjunct (13 women). Expenses: Contact institution. *Financial support:* In 2010–11, 150 students received support. Career-related internships or fieldwork, Federal Work-Study, and scholarships/grants available. Support available to part-time students. Financial award application deadline: 4/1; financial award applicants required to submit FAFSA. In 2010, 115 master's awarded. *Degree program information:* Part-time programs available. Offers social work (MSW). *Application deadline:* For fall admission, 7/15 priority date for domestic students. Applications are processed on a rolling basis. *Application fee:* $50. Electronic applications accepted. *Application Contact:* Dr. Joe G. Galusha, Dean of Graduate Studies, 509-527-2421, Fax: 509-527-2237, E-mail: joe.galusha@wallawalla.edu. *Dean,* Dr. Pamela Cress, 509-527-2273, Fax: 509-527-2270, E-mail: pam.cress@wallawalla.edu.

WALSH COLLEGE OF ACCOUNTANCY AND BUSINESS ADMINISTRATION, Troy, MI 48007-7006

General Information Independent, coed, upper-level institution. *Graduate housing:* On-campus housing not available.

GRADUATE UNITS

Graduate Programs *Degree program information:* Part-time and evening/weekend programs available. Offers accountancy (MSPA); business administration (MBA); business information technology (MSBIT); finance (MSF); management (MSIB, MSSL); taxation (MST). Electronic applications accepted.

WALSH UNIVERSITY, North Canton, OH 44720-3396

General Information Independent-religious, coed, comprehensive institution. CGS member. *Enrollment:* 2,812 graduate, professional, and undergraduate students; 170 full-time matriculated graduate/professional students (121 women), 352 part-time matriculated graduate/professional students (233 women). *Enrollment by degree level:* 447 master's, 75 doctoral. *Graduate faculty:* 32 full-time (19 women), 40 part-time/adjunct (15 women). *Tuition:* Full-time $13,080; part-time $545 per credit hour. *Graduate housing:* Room and/or apartments available on a first-come, first-served basis to single students; on-campus housing not available to married students. Typical cost: $4420 per year ($8360 including board). Housing application deadline: 7/15. *Student services:* Campus employment opportunities, campus safety program, career counseling, exercise/wellness program, free psychological counseling, international student services, low-cost health insurance, multicultural affairs office, services for students with disabilities, teacher training, writing training. *Library facilities:* Brother Edmond Drouin Library. *Online resources:* library catalog, web page, access to other libraries' catalogs. *Collection:* 234,900 titles, 28,398 serial subscriptions, 3,810 audiovisual materials. *Research affiliation:* McKinley Freshman Academy, Battelle for Kids.

Computer facilities: 335 computers available on campus for general student use. A campuswide network can be accessed from student residence rooms and from off campus. Online class registration is available. *Web address:* http://www.walsh.edu/.

General Application Contact: Brett Freshour, Vice President of Enrollment Management, 330-490-7172, Fax: 330-490-7165, E-mail: bfreshour@walsh.edu.

GRADUATE UNITS

Graduate Studies Students: 170 full-time (121 women), 352 part-time (233 women); includes 48 minority (35 Black or African American, non-Hispanic/Latino; 1 American Indian or Alaska Native, non-Hispanic/Latino; 2 Asian, non-Hispanic/Latino; 5 Hispanic/Latino; 1 Native Hawaiian or other Pacific Islander, non-Hispanic/Latino; 4 Two or more races, non-Hispanic/Latino), 2 international. Average age 33. 228 applicants, 67% accepted, 106 enrolled. *Faculty:* 32 full-time (19 women), 40 part-time/adjunct (15 women). Expenses: Contact institution. *Financial support:* In 2010–11, 345 students received support, including 44 research assistantships with partial tuition reimbursements available (averaging $5,290 per year); unspecified assistantships also available. Support available to part-time students. Financial award application deadline: 12/31. In 2010, 128 master's, 19 doctorates awarded. *Degree program information:* Part-time and evening/weekend programs available. Offers education (MA); health care management (MBA); integrated marketing communications (MBA); management (MBA); mental health counseling (MA); physical therapy (DPT); school counseling (MA); theology (MA). *Application deadline:* Applications are processed on a rolling basis. *Application fee:* $25. Electronic applications accepted. *Application Contact:* Christine Haver, Assistant Director for Graduate and Transfer Admissions, 330-490-7177, Fax: 330-244-4925, E-mail: chaver@walsh.edu. *Director of Graduate Studies,* Dr. Chris Petrosino, 330-490-7370, Fax: 330-490-7371, E-mail: cpetrosino@walsh.edu.

WARNER PACIFIC COLLEGE, Portland, OR 97215-4099

General Information Independent-religious, coed, comprehensive institution. *Graduate housing:* Rooms and/or apartments available on a first-come, first-served basis to single and married students. Housing application deadline: 7/1.

GRADUATE UNITS

Graduate Programs *Degree program information:* Part-time programs available. Offers biblical and theological studies (MA); biblical studies (M Rel); education (M Ed); management/organizational leadership (MS); pastoral ministries (M Rel); religion and ethics (M Rel); teaching (MA); theology (M Rel).

WARNER UNIVERSITY, Lake Wales, FL 33859

General Information Independent-religious, coed, comprehensive institution. *Graduate housing:* Room and/or apartments available on a first-come, first-served basis to single students; on-campus housing not available to married students.

GRADUATE UNITS

School of Business *Degree program information:* Part-time and evening/weekend programs available. Offers business (MBA). Electronic applications accepted.

School of Professional Studies *Degree program information:* Part-time and evening/weekend programs available. Postbaccalaureate distance learning degree programs offered. Offers management (MSM). Electronic applications accepted.

Teacher Education Department *Degree program information:* Part-time and evening/weekend programs available. Offers teacher education (MAEd). Electronic applications accepted.

WARREN WILSON COLLEGE, Swannanoa, Asheville, NC 28815-9000

General Information Independent-religious, coed, comprehensive institution. *Graduate housing:* Room and/or apartments guaranteed to single students; on-campus housing not available to married students.

GRADUATE UNITS

MFA Program for Writers Postbaccalaureate distance learning degree programs offered (minimal on-campus study). Offers creative writing (MFA).

WARTBURG THEOLOGICAL SEMINARY, Dubuque, IA 52004-5004

General Information Independent-religious, coed, graduate-only institution. *Enrollment by degree level:* 134 first professional, 19 master's. *Graduate faculty:* 19 full-time (6 women), 9 part-time/adjunct (3 women). *Tuition:* Full-time $13,000; part-time $625 per semester hour. *Required fees:* $505; $50 per term. *Graduate housing:* Rooms and/or apartments available on a first-come, first-served basis to single and married students. Typical cost: $3333 per year for single students; $7150 per year for married students. Room charges vary according to campus/location and housing facility selected. Housing application deadline: 4/30. *Student services:* Campus employment opportunities, international student services, writing training. *Library facilities:* Reu Memorial Library. *Online resources:* library catalog, web page, access to other libraries' catalogs. *Collection:* 93,001 titles, 203 serial subscriptions, 625 audiovisual materials. *Research affiliation:* Menighetsfakultet, Augustana Theologische Hochschule.

Computer facilities: 19 computers available on campus for general student use. A campuswide network can be accessed from student residence rooms and from off campus. *Web address:* http://www.wartburgseminary.edu/.

General Application Contact: Rev. Karla Wildberger, Director of Admissions, 563-589-0203, Fax: 563-589-0333, E-mail: admissions@wartburgseminary.edu.

GRADUATE UNITS

Graduate and Professional Programs Students: 141 full-time (72 women), 12 part-time (8 women); includes 4 Black or African American, non-Hispanic/Latino; 2 American Indian or Alaska Native, non-Hispanic/Latino; 2 Asian, non-Hispanic/Latino; 2 Hispanic/Latino, 1 international. Average age 34. 58 applicants, 88% accepted, 50 enrolled. *Faculty:* 19 full-time (6 women), 9 part-time/adjunct (3 women). Expenses: Contact institution. *Financial support:* In 2010–11, 100 students received support, including 13 research assistantships with partial tuition reimbursements available (averaging $1,125 per year); career-related internships or fieldwork, Federal Work-Study, institutionally sponsored loans, and scholarships/grants also available. Support available to part-time students. Financial award application deadline: 6/15; financial award applicants required to submit FAFSA. In 2010, 39 first professional degrees, 14 master's awarded. Offers diaconal ministry (MA); ministry (M Div); theology (MA, MATDE, STM). *Application deadline:* For fall admission, 5/15 priority date for domestic students, 10/1 priority date for international students; for winter admission, 10/1 for international students; for spring admission, 12/15 priority date for domestic students, 10/1 for international students. Applications are processed on a rolling basis. *Application fee:* $0. Electronic applications accepted. *Application Contact:* Rev. Karla Wildberger, Director of Admissions, 563-589-0203, Fax: 563-589-0333, E-mail: admissions@wartburgseminary.edu. *Academic Dean,* Rev. Dr. Craig L. Nessan, 563-589-0207, Fax: 563-589-0333.

WASHBURN UNIVERSITY, Topeka, KS 66621

General Information City-supported, coed, comprehensive institution. CGS member. *Enrollment:* 7,230 graduate, professional, and undergraduate students; 604 full-time matriculated graduate/professional students (289 women), 305 part-time matriculated graduate/professional students (227 women). *Enrollment by degree level:* 455 first professional, 454 master's. Tuition, state resident: full-time $5130; part-time $285 per credit hour. Tuition, nonresident: full-time $10,476; part-time $582 per credit hour. *Required fees:* $86; $43 per semester. Tuition and fees vary according to program. *Graduate housing:* Room and/or apartments available on a first-come, first-served basis to single students; on-campus housing not available to married students. Typical cost: $3332 per year ($5982 including board). Room and board charges vary according to board plan and housing facility selected. *Student services:* Campus employment opportunities, campus safety program, career counseling, exercise/wellness program, free psychological counseling, international student services, low-cost health insurance, multicultural affairs office, services for students with disabilities, teacher training, writing training. *Library facilities:* Mabee Library plus 1 other. *Online resources:* library catalog, web page. *Collection:* 403,174 titles, 36,410 serial subscriptions, 13,600 audiovisual materials.

Computer facilities: 400 computers available on campus for general student use. A campuswide network can be accessed from student residence rooms and from off campus. Online class registration is available. *Web address:* http://www.washburn.edu/.

General Application Contact: Morgan Boyack, Director of Admissions, 785-670-1030, Fax: 785-670-1113, E-mail: admissions@washburn.edu.

GRADUATE UNITS

College of Arts and Sciences Students: 26 full-time (17 women), 64 part-time (48 women). Average age 35. Expenses: Contact institution. *Financial support:* Research assistantships, career-related internships or fieldwork, Federal Work-Study, institutionally sponsored loans, and scholarships/grants available. Support available to part-time students. Financial award applicants required to submit FAFSA. In 2010, 26 master's awarded. *Degree program information:* Part-time and evening/weekend programs available. Offers arts and sciences (M Ed, MA, MLS); clinical psychology (MA); curriculum and instruction (M Ed); educational leadership (M Ed); liberal studies (MLS); reading (M Ed); special education (M Ed). *Application Contact:* Dr. Gordon McQuere, Dean, 785-670-1561, Fax: 785-670-1297, E-mail: gordon.mcquere@washburn.edu. *Dean,* Dr. Gordon McQuere, 785-670-1561, Fax: 785-670-1297, E-mail: gordon.mcquere@washburn.edu.

School of Applied Studies Students: 73 full-time (60 women), 70 part-time (56 women). Average age 32. *Faculty:* 15 full-time (6 women), 27 part-time/adjunct (8 women). Expenses: Contact institution. *Financial support:* Career-related internships or fieldwork, Federal Work-Study, institutionally sponsored loans, and scholarships/grants available. Support available to part-time students. Financial award applicants required to submit FAFSA. In 2010, 55 master's awarded. *Degree program information:* Part-time and evening/weekend programs available. Postbaccalaureate distance learning degree programs offered. Offers applied studies (MCJ, MSW); clinical social work (MSW); criminal justice (MCJ). *Application deadline:* Applications are processed on a rolling basis. Electronic applications accepted. *Application Contact:* Dean. *Dean,* Dr. William Dunlap, 785-670-2111, Fax: 785-670-1027, E-mail: willie.dunlap@washburn.edu.

School of Business *Degree program information:* Part-time and evening/weekend programs available. Offers business (MBA). Electronic applications accepted.

School of Law Offers law (JD). Electronic applications accepted.

School of Nursing Students: 23 full-time (all women), 78 part-time (73 women). 52 applicants, 77% accepted, 40 enrolled. *Faculty:* 13 full-time (all women), 1 (woman) part-time/adjunct. Expenses: Contact institution. *Financial support:* Application deadline: 2/15. In 2010, 23 master's awarded. *Degree program information:* Part-time programs available. Offers adult nurse practitioner (MSN); clinical nurse leader (MSN); family nurse practitioner (MSN). *Application deadline:* For fall admission, 3/15 priority date for international students. *Application fee:* $35. *Application Contact:* Mary V. Allen, Director of Student Academic Support Services, 785-670-1533, E-mail: mary.allen@washburn.edu. *Dean,* Dr. Monica S. Scheibmeir, 785-670-1526, E-mail: monica.scheibmeir@washburn.edu.

WASHINGTON ADVENTIST UNIVERSITY, Takoma Park, MD 20912

General Information Independent-religious, coed, comprehensive institution. *Graduate housing:* Rooms and/or apartments available to single and married students.

GRADUATE UNITS

MBA Program *Degree program information:* Part-time programs available. Offers business administration (MBA).

Program in Counseling Psychology *Degree program information:* Part-time programs available. Offers counseling psychology (MA).

Program in Nursing—Business Leadership *Degree program information:* Part-time programs available. Offers nursing—business leadership (MSN).

Program in Professional Counseling Psychology *Degree program information:* Part-time programs available. Offers professional counseling psychology (MA).

Program in Public Administration *Degree program information:* Part-time programs available. Offers public administration (MPA).

Program in Religion *Degree program information:* Part-time programs available. Offers religion (MAR).

WASHINGTON AND LEE UNIVERSITY, Lexington, VA 24450-0303

General Information Independent, coed, comprehensive institution. *Enrollment:* 2,173 graduate, professional, and undergraduate students; 414 full-time matriculated graduate/professional students (172 women). *Enrollment by degree level:* 408 first professional, 6 other advanced degrees. *Graduate faculty:* 35 full-time (8 women), 25 part-time/adjunct (3 women). *Tuition:* Full-time $39,937. *Required fees:* $1062. *Graduate housing:* Room and/or apartments available on a first-come, first-served basis to single students. Typical cost: $5250 per year ($11,730 including board). Housing application deadline: 4/15. *Student services:* Campus employment opportunities, campus safety program, career counseling, exercise/wellness program, free psychological counseling, international student services, low-cost health insurance, multicultural affairs office, services for students with disabilities, writing training. *Library facilities:* James G. Leyburn Library plus 2 others. *Online resources:* library catalog, web page, access to other libraries' catalogs. *Collection:* 964,573 titles, 10,677 serial subscriptions, 17,393 audiovisual materials.

Computer facilities: 320 computers available on campus for general student use. A campuswide network can be accessed from student residence rooms and from off campus. Online class registration is available. *Web address:* http://www.wlu.edu/.

General Application Contact: Stephen Brett Twitty, Director of Admissions, 540-458-8503, Fax: 540-458-8586, E-mail: twittys@wlu.edu.

GRADUATE UNITS

School of Law Students: 414 full-time (172 women); includes 67 minority (26 Black or African American, non-Hispanic/Latino; 1 American Indian or Alaska Native, non-Hispanic/Latino; 17 Asian, non-Hispanic/Latino; 13 Hispanic/Latino; 1 Native Hawaiian or other Pacific Islander, non-Hispanic/Latino; 9 Two or more races, non-Hispanic/Latino), 8 international. Average age 25. 4,582 applicants, 22% accepted, 144 enrolled. *Faculty:* 35 full-time (8 women), 25 part-time/adjunct (3 women). Expenses: Contact institution. *Financial support:* In 2010–11, 244 students received support; fellowships, research assistantships, career-related internships or fieldwork, Federal Work-Study, institutionally sponsored loans, and scholarships/grants available. Financial award application deadline: 2/15; financial award applicants required to submit FAFSA. In 2010, 123 first professional degrees awarded. Offers law (JD); U. S. law (LL M). *Application deadline:* For fall admission, 3/1 priority date for domestic students. Applications are processed on a rolling basis. *Application fee:* $0. Electronic applications accepted. *Application Contact:* Stephen Brett Twitty, Director of Admissions, 540-458-8503, Fax: 540-458-8586, E-mail: twittys@wlu.edu. *Dean,* Mark H. Grunewald, 540-458-8502, Fax: 540-458-8488, E-mail: grunewaldm@wlu.edu.

WASHINGTON COLLEGE, Chestertown, MD 21620-1197

General Information Independent, coed, comprehensive institution. *Enrollment:* 1,473 graduate, professional, and undergraduate students; 3 full-time matriculated graduate/professional students (2 women), 76 part-time matriculated graduate/professional students (42 women). *Enrollment by degree level:* 79 master's. *Graduate faculty:* 28 full-time (10 women), 7 part-time/adjunct (2 women). *Tuition:* Part-time $1125 per course. *Required fees:* $100 per course. *Graduate housing:* On-campus housing not available. *Student services:* Campus employment opportunities, career counseling, exercise/wellness program, low-cost health insurance, multicultural affairs office, writing training. *Library facilities:* Clifton M. Miller Library. *Online resources:* library catalog, web page, access to other libraries' catalogs. *Collection:* 241,165 titles, 27,953 serial subscriptions, 8,736 audiovisual materials.

Computer facilities: Computer purchase and lease plans are available. 100 computers available on campus for general student use. A campuswide network can be accessed from student residence rooms and from off campus. Online class registration, thousands of wireless addresses available for students are available. *Web address:* http://www.washcoll.edu/.

General Application Contact: Dr. Kathryn W. Sack, Director of the Graduate Program and Assistant Dean, 800-422-1782 Ext. 7202, Fax: 410-778-7213, E-mail: ksack2@washcoll.edu.

GRADUATE UNITS

Graduate Programs Students: 3 full-time (2 women), 76 part-time (42 women); includes 1 Black or African American, non-Hispanic/Latino, 1 international. 19 applicants, 58% accepted, 6 enrolled. *Faculty:* 28 full-time (10 women), 7 part-time/adjunct (2 women). Expenses: Contact institution. In 2010, 11 master's awarded. *Degree program information:* Part-time and evening/weekend programs available. Offers English (MA); history (MA); psychology (MA). *Application deadline:* For fall admission, 8/1 priority date for domestic students; for winter admission, 12/1 priority date for domestic students; for spring admission, 4/15 priority date for domestic students. Applications are processed on a rolling basis. *Application fee:* $50. *Application Contact:* Dr. Kathryn W. Sack, Assistant Dean for Academic Affairs, 410-778-7213, Fax: 410-778-7850, E-mail: ksack2@washcoll.edu. *Provost/Dean,* Dr. Christopher Ames, 800-422-1782 Ext. 7202, Fax: 410-778-7850, E-mail: cames2@washcoll.edu.

WASHINGTON STATE UNIVERSITY, Pullman, WA 99164

General Information State-supported, coed, university. CGS member. *Enrollment:* 26,308 graduate, professional, and undergraduate students; 2,346 full-time matriculated graduate/professional students (1,148 women), 1,349 part-time matriculated graduate/professional

Washington State University (continued)

students (744 women). *Enrollment by degree level:* 1,832 master's, 1,575 doctoral, 288 other advanced degrees. *Graduate faculty:* 991. Tuition, state resident: full-time $8552; part-time $443 per credit. Tuition, nonresident: full-time $21,650; part-time $1083 per credit. *Required fees:* $846. *Graduate housing:* Rooms and/or apartments available on a first-come, first-served basis to single and married students. Housing application deadline: 3/1. *Student services:* Campus employment opportunities, campus safety program, career counseling, child daycare facilities, exercise/wellness program, free psychological counseling, grant writing training, international student services, low-cost health insurance, multicultural affairs office, services for students with disabilities, teacher training, writing training. *Library facilities:* Holland and Terrell Libraries plus 7 others. *Online resources:* library catalog, web page, access to other libraries' catalogs. *Collection:* 2.3 million titles, 42,987 serial subscriptions, 52,286 audiovisual materials. *Research affiliation:* Battelle Pacific Northwest Laboratories (biochemistry, engineering).

Computer facilities: 2,500 computers available on campus for general student use. A campuswide network can be accessed from student residence rooms and from off campus. Online class registration is available. *Web address:* http://www.wsu.edu/.

General Application Contact: Graduate School Admissions, 800-GRADWSU, Fax: 509-335-1949, E-mail: gradsch@wsu.edu.

GRADUATE UNITS

College of Veterinary Medicine Students: 496 full-time (370 women), 1 part-time (0 women); includes 1 Black or African American, non-Hispanic/Latino; 8 American Indian or Alaska Native, non-Hispanic/Latino; 20 Asian, non-Hispanic/Latino; 15 Hispanic/Latino; 3 Two or more races, non-Hispanic/Latino, 41 international. Average age 33. 1,157 applicants, 15% accepted, 138 enrolled. *Faculty:* 39 full-time (6 women), 21 part-time/adjunct (6 women). Expenses: Contact institution. *Financial support:* In 2010–11, 294 students received support, including 4 fellowships, 49 research assistantships, 9 teaching assistantships; career-related internships or fieldwork, Federal Work-Study, institutionally sponsored loans, scholarships/grants, traineeships, and health care benefits also available. Support available to part-time students. Financial award application deadline: 2/15; financial award applicants required to submit FAFSA. In 2010, 96 first professional degrees, 15 master's, 10 doctorates awarded. Offers neuroscience (MS, PhD); veterinary and comparative anatomy, pharmacology, and physiology (MS, PhD); veterinary clinical sciences (MS); veterinary medicine (DVM, MS, PhD); veterinary microbiology and pathology (MS, PhD); veterinary science (MS, PhD). *Application deadline:* For fall admission, 10/1 for domestic and international students. Applications are processed on a rolling basis. *Application fee:* $60. Electronic applications accepted. *Application Contact:* Julie K. Smith, Principal Assistant, 509-335-3164, E-mail: jksmith@vetmed.wsu.edu. *Dean,* Dr. Bryan K. Slinker, 509-335-9515, Fax: 509-335-0160, E-mail: vetmed-dean@vetmed.wsu.edu.

Graduate School Students: 2,346 full-time (1,148 women), 1,349 part-time (744 women); includes 363 minority (58 Black or African American, non-Hispanic/Latino; 27 American Indian or Alaska Native, non-Hispanic/Latino; 145 Asian, non-Hispanic/Latino; 115 Hispanic/Latino; 12 Native Hawaiian or other Pacific Islander, non-Hispanic/Latino; 6 Two or more races, non-Hispanic/Latino), 802 international. Average age 31. 6,587 applicants, 25% accepted, 1289 enrolled. *Faculty:* 723 full-time (160 women), 51 part-time/adjunct (15 women). Expenses: Contact institution. *Financial support:* In 2010–11, 266 fellowships with full tuition reimbursements (averaging $3,939 per year), 532 research assistantships with full tuition reimbursements (averaging $18,204 per year), 770 teaching assistantships with full tuition reimbursements (averaging $18,204 per year) were awarded; career-related internships or fieldwork, Federal Work-Study, institutionally sponsored loans, scholarships/grants, traineeships, tuition waivers (partial), unspecified assistantships, and staff assistantships, teaching associateships also available. Support available to part-time students. Financial award applicants required to submit FAFSA. In 2010, 748 master's, 185 doctorates awarded. *Degree program information:* Part-time programs available. Offers interdisciplinary studies (PhD). Campuses also located at Spokane, Tri-Cities, and Vancouver. *Application deadline:* For fall admission, 2/1 priority date for domestic students, 3/1 for international students; for spring admission, 9/1 priority date for domestic students, 7/1 for international students. Applications are processed on a rolling basis. *Application fee:* $50. Electronic applications accepted. *Application Contact:* Graduate School Admissions, 800-GRADWSU, Fax: 509-335-1949, E-mail: gradsch@wsu.edu. *Dean,* Dr. Howard Grimes, 509-335-6424, Fax: 509-335-1949, E-mail: grimes@wsu.edu.

College of Agricultural, Human, and Natural Resource Sciences Students: 372 full-time (186 women), 43 part-time (22 women); includes 27 minority (5 Black or African American, non-Hispanic/Latino; 4 American Indian or Alaska Native, non-Hispanic/Latino; 12 Asian, non-Hispanic/Latino; 4 Hispanic/Latino; 1 Native Hawaiian or other Pacific Islander, non-Hispanic/Latino; 1 Two or more races, non-Hispanic/Latino), 172 international. Average age 29. 689 applicants, 26% accepted, 146 enrolled. *Faculty:* 159. Expenses: Contact institution. *Financial support:* In 2010–11, 32 fellowships (averaging $18,204 per year), 87 research assistantships with full and partial tuition reimbursements (averaging $18,204 per year), 24 teaching assistantships with full and partial tuition reimbursements (averaging $18,204 per year) were awarded; career-related internships or fieldwork, Federal Work-Study, institutionally sponsored loans, tuition waivers (partial), unspecified assistantships, and staff assistantships, teaching associateships also available. Financial award application deadline: 4/1; financial award applicants required to submit FAFSA. In 2010, 64 master's, 21 doctorates awarded. *Degree program information:* Part-time programs available. Offers agribusiness (MA, Certificate); agricultural economics (MA, PhD); agricultural, human, and natural resource sciences (MA, MS, MSLA, PhD, Certificate); agriculture (MS); animal sciences (MS, PhD); apparel, merchandising, design and textiles (MA); applied economics (MA); applied statistics (MS); crop sciences (MS, PhD); economics (MA, PhD, Certificate); entomology (MS, PhD); food science (MS, PhD); horticulture (MS, PhD); human development (MA); interdisciplinary (PhD); interior design (MA); international business economics (Certificate); landscape architecture (MSLA); molecular plant sciences (MS, PhD); plant pathology (MS, PhD); soil sciences (MS, PhD); theoretical statistics (MS). *Application deadline:* For fall admission, 3/1 for international students; for spring admission, 7/1 for international students. Applications are processed on a rolling basis. *Application fee:* $50. Electronic applications accepted. *Application Contact:* Graduate School Admissions, 800-GRADWSU, Fax: 509-335-1949, E-mail: gradsch@wsu.edu. *Dean,* Dr. Daniel J. Bernardo, 509-335-4561.

College of Business Students: 164 full-time (67 women), 130 part-time (35 women); includes 24 minority (1 Black or African American, non-Hispanic/Latino; 17 Asian, non-Hispanic/Latino; 5 Hispanic/Latino; 1 Two or more races, non-Hispanic/Latino), 48 international. Average age 32. 470 applicants, 23% accepted, 110 enrolled. *Faculty:* 47. Expenses: Contact institution. *Financial support:* In 2010–11, 36 teaching assistantships with full and partial tuition reimbursements (averaging $18,204 per year) were awarded; career-related internships or fieldwork, Federal Work-Study, institutionally sponsored loans, tuition waivers (partial), and teaching associateships also available. Financial award application deadline: 4/1; financial award applicants required to submit FAFSA. In 2010, 86 master's, 5 doctorates awarded. Offers accounting and information systems (M Acc); accounting and taxation (M Acc); business (M Acc, MBA, PhD); business administration (MBA, PhD). *Application deadline:* For fall admission, 1/10 priority date for domestic students, 1/10 for international students. Applications are processed on a rolling basis. *Application fee:* $50. *Application Contact:* Graduate School Admissions, 800-GRADWSU, Fax: 509-335-1949, E-mail: gradsch@wsu.edu. *Chair,* Dr. Eric Spangenberg, 509-335-8150, Fax: 509-335-4275, E-mail: ers@wsu.edu.

College of Education Students: 163 full-time (110 women), 94 part-time (65 women); includes 55 minority (9 Black or African American, non-Hispanic/Latino; 1 American Indian or Alaska Native, non-Hispanic/Latino; 13 Asian, non-Hispanic/Latino; 28 Hispanic/Latino; 3 Native Hawaiian or other Pacific Islander, non-Hispanic/Latino; 1 Two or more races, non-Hispanic/Latino), 43 international. Average age 32. 652 applicants, 36% accepted, 97 enrolled. *Faculty:* 39. Expenses: Contact institution. *Financial support:* In 2010–11, 51 research assistantships with partial tuition reimbursements (averaging $18,204 per year), 32 teaching assistantships with partial tuition reimbursements (averaging $18,204 per year) were awarded; career-related internships or fieldwork, Federal Work-Study, institutionally sponsored loans, scholarships/grants, tuition waivers (partial), and staff assistantships, teaching associateships also available. Financial award application deadline: 2/15; financial award applicants required to submit FAFSA. In 2010, 69 master's, 23 doctorates awarded. Offers counseling psychology (Ed M, MA, PhD, Certificate); curriculum and instruction (Ed D, PhD); diverse languages (M Ed, MA); education (Ed M, M Ed, MA, MIT, MS, Ed D, PhD, Certificate); educational leadership (M Ed, MA, Ed D, PhD); educational psychology (Ed M, MA, PhD); elementary education (M Ed, MA, MIT); exercise science (MS); higher education (Ed M, MA, Ed D, PhD); higher education with sport management (Ed M); literacy education (M Ed, MA, PhD); math education (PhD); school psychologist (Certificate); secondary education (M Ed, MA). *Application deadline:* For fall admission, 1/10 for domestic and international students. *Application fee:* $50. Electronic applications accepted. *Application Contact:* Graduate School Admissions, 800-GRADWSU, Fax: 509-335-1949, E-mail: gradsch@wsu.edu. *Dean,* Dr. A. G. Rud, 509-335-4853, Fax: 509-335-2097, E-mail: ag.rud@wsu.edu.

College of Engineering and Architecture Students: 386 full-time (107 women), 57 part-time (12 women); includes 25 minority (2 Black or African American, non-Hispanic/Latino; 1 American Indian or Alaska Native, non-Hispanic/Latino; 17 Asian, non-Hispanic/Latino; 4 Hispanic/Latino; 1 Two or more races, non-Hispanic/Latino), 235 international. Average age 27. 1,013 applicants, 17% accepted, 92 enrolled. *Faculty:* 106. Expenses: Contact institution. *Financial support:* In 2010–11, 141 research assistantships with full and partial tuition reimbursements (averaging $18,204 per year), 92 teaching assistantships with full and partial tuition reimbursements (averaging $18,204 per year) were awarded; career-related internships or fieldwork, Federal Work-Study, institutionally sponsored loans, tuition waivers (partial), and teaching associateships also available. Financial award application deadline: 4/1; financial award applicants required to submit FAFSA. In 2010, 132 master's, 25 doctorates awarded. Offers architecture (M Arch); architecture design theory (MS); biological and agricultural engineering (MS, PhD); chemical engineering (MS, PhD); chemical engineering and bioengineering (MS, PhD); civil engineering (MS, PhD); computer engineering (MS, PhD); computer science (MS, PhD); electrical engineering (MS, PhD); electrical engineering and computer science (MS, PhD); engineering and architecture (M Arch, MS, PhD); environmental engineering (MS); material science engineering (MS); mechanical and materials engineering (MS, PhD); mechanical engineering (MS, PhD). *Application deadline:* For fall admission, 3/1 priority date for domestic students, 3/1 for international students; for spring admission, 7/1 priority date for domestic students, 7/1 for international students. Applications are processed on a rolling basis. *Application fee:* $50. *Application Contact:* Graduate School Admissions, 800-GRADWSU, Fax: 509-335-1949, E-mail: gradsch@wsu.edu. *Dean,* Dr. Candis Claiborn, 509-335-5593, Fax: 509-335-7632, E-mail: claiborn@wsu.edu.

College of Liberal Arts Students: 452 full-time (249 women), 80 part-time (36 women); includes 14 Black or African American, non-Hispanic/Latino; 13 American Indian or Alaska Native, non-Hispanic/Latino; 10 Asian, non-Hispanic/Latino; 33 Hispanic/Latino, 61 international. Average age 31. 1,020 applicants, 21% accepted, 147 enrolled. *Faculty:* 247. Expenses: Contact institution. *Financial support:* In 2010–11, 458 students received support, including 26 fellowships with tuition reimbursements available (averaging $4,109 per year), 39 research assistantships with full and partial tuition reimbursements available (averaging $13,917 per year), 301 teaching assistantships with full and partial tuition reimbursements available (averaging $13,056 per year); career-related internships or fieldwork, Federal Work-Study, institutionally sponsored loans, scholarships/grants, tuition waivers (partial), and unspecified assistantships also available. Support available to part-time students. Financial award applicants required to submit FAFSA. In 2010, 93 master's, 34 doctorates awarded. Offers archaeology (MA, PhD); ceramics (MFA); clinical psychology (PhD); composition (MA); crime and deviance (MA, PhD); criminal justice (MA, PhD); cultural anthropology (MA, PhD); digital media (MFA); drawing (MFA); early and modern European history (MA, PhD); English (MA, PhD); environmental history (MA, PhD); environments, community and demographics (MA, PhD); ethnic studies (MA, PhD); evolutionary anthropology (MA, PhD); experimental psychology (PhD); feminist studies (MA, PhD); foreign languages with emphasis in Spanish (MA); history (MA, PhD); institutions and social organizations (MA, PhD); jazz (MA); Latin American history (MA, PhD); liberal arts (MA, MFA, MS, PhD); literature (MA, PhD); modern East Asia history (MA, PhD); music (MA); music education (MA); painting (MFA); performance (MA); philosophy (MA); photography (MFA); political science (MA, PhD); political sociology (MA, PhD); print making (MFA); psychology (MS); public history (MA, PhD); sculpture (MFA); social inequality (MA, PhD); social psychology and life course (MA, PhD); teaching of English (MA); U. S. history (MA, PhD); women's history (MA, PhD); world history (MA, PhD). *Application deadline:* For fall admission, 3/1 for international students; for spring admission, 7/1 for international students. *Application fee:* $50. Electronic applications accepted. *Application Contact:* Graduate School Admissions, 800-GRADWSU, Fax: 509-335-1949, E-mail: gradsch@wsu.edu. *Dean,* Dr. Erich Lear, 509-335-4581, E-mail: learej@wsu.edu.

College of Pharmacy Students: 415 full-time (246 women), 14 part-time (9 women); includes 6 Black or African American, non-Hispanic/Latino; 6 American Indian or Alaska Native, non-Hispanic/Latino; 66 Asian, non-Hispanic/Latino; 13 Hispanic/Latino, 8 international. Average age 26. 919 applicants, 10% accepted, 94 enrolled. *Faculty:* 30. Expenses: Contact institution. *Financial support:* In 2010–11, 206 students received support, including 32 fellowships (averaging $4,982 per year), 10 research assistantships with full and partial tuition reimbursements available (averaging $13,917 per year), 4 teaching assistantships with full and partial tuition reimbursements available (averaging $13,056 per year); Federal Work-Study, institutionally sponsored loans, tuition waivers (partial), and staff assistantships, teaching associateships also available. Financial award application deadline: 4/1; financial award applicants required to submit FAFSA. In 2010, 76 first professional degrees, 11 master's, 4 doctorates awarded. Offers health policy and administration (MHPA); human nutrition (MS); nutrition (PhD); pharmaceutical sciences (Pharm D, PhD); pharmacy (Pharm D, MHPA, MS, PhD). *Application deadline:* For fall admission, 2/1 for domestic students. Applications are processed on a rolling basis. *Application fee:* $35. *Application Contact:* Graduate School Admissions, 800-GRADWSU, Fax: 509-335-1949, E-mail: gradsch@wsu.edu. *Dean,* Dr. James P. Kehrer, 509-335-4750, E-mail: kehrer@wsu.edu.

College of Sciences Students: 371 full-time (160 women), 31 part-time (11 women); includes 1 Black or African American, non-Hispanic/Latino; 2 American Indian or Alaska Native, non-Hispanic/Latino; 7 Asian, non-Hispanic/Latino; 10 Hispanic/Latino, 108 international. Average age 29. 788 applicants, 20% accepted, 96 enrolled. *Faculty:* 158. Expenses: Contact institution. *Financial support:* In 2010–11, 305 students received support, including 29 fellowships (averaging $4,199 per year), 105 research assistantships (averaging $13,917 per year), 166 teaching assistantships (averaging $13,056 per year); career-related internships or fieldwork, Federal Work-Study, institutionally sponsored loans, traineeships, tuition waivers (partial), and teaching associateships also available. Financial award applicants required to submit FAFSA. In 2010, 52 master's, 34 doctorates awarded. Offers applied mathematics (MS, PhD); biochemistry and biophysics (MS, PhD); biological sciences (MS, PhD); biology (MS); botany (MS, PhD); chemistry (MS, PhD); earth and environmental sciences (MS, PhD); environmental and natural resource sciences (PhD); environmental science (MS, PhD); genetics and cell biology (MS, PhD); geology (MS, PhD); materials science (PhD); mathematics teaching (MS, PhD); microbiology (MS, PhD); molecular biosciences (MS, PhD); natural resource sciences (MS); physics (MS, PhD); sciences (MS, PhD); zoology (MS, PhD). *Application deadline:* Applications are processed on a rolling basis. *Application fee:* $50. *Application Contact:* Graduate School Admissions, 800-GRADWSU, Fax: 509-335-1949, E-mail: gradsch@wsu.edu. *Dean,* Dr. Michael Griswold, 509-335-5548, E-mail: mgriswold@wsu.edu.

The Edward R. Murrow College of Communication Students: 43 full-time (26 women), 6 part-time (4 women); includes 1 Asian, non-Hispanic/Latino; 1 Hispanic/Latino, 19 international. Average age 30. 120 applicants, 22% accepted, 19 enrolled. *Faculty:* 30. Expenses: Contact institution. *Financial support:* In 2010–11, 46 students received support, including 2 fellowships (averaging $4,477 per year), 7 research assistantships with full and partial tuition reimbursements available (averaging $13,917 per year), 34 teaching assistantships with full and partial tuition reimbursements available (averaging $13,056 per year); career-related internships or fieldwork, Federal Work-Study, institutionally sponsored loans, tuition waivers (partial), and teaching associateships also available. Financial award application deadline: 4/1; financial award applicants required to submit FAFSA. In 2010, 22 master's, 1 doctorate awarded. Offers health communications (MA, PhD); intercultural and international communications (MA, PhD); media and society (MA, PhD); media process and effects (MA, PhD); organizational communications (MA, PhD). *Application deadline:* For fall admission, 1/15 priority date for domestic students, 3/1 for international students. Applications are processed on a rolling basis. *Application fee:* $50. Electronic applications accepted. *Application Contact:* Graduate School Admissions, 800-GRADWSU, Fax: 509-335-1949, E-mail: gradsch@wsu.edu. *Interim Director*, Dr. Erica Austin, 509-335-1556, E-mail: eaustin@wsu.edu.

WASHINGTON STATE UNIVERSITY SPOKANE, Spokane, WA 99210-1495

General Information State-supported, coed, graduate-only institution. *Enrollment by degree level:* 247 master's, 57 doctoral, 68 other advanced degrees. *Graduate faculty:* 257. *Student services:* Campus employment opportunities, campus safety program, career counseling, exercise/wellness program, free psychological counseling, grant writing training, international student services, low-cost health insurance, services for students with disabilities. *Library facilities:* Cooperative Academic Library Service. *Online resources:* library catalog, web page, access to other libraries' catalogs. *Collection:* 2.3 million titles, 30,122 serial subscriptions, 426,737 audiovisual materials.

Computer facilities: 48 computers available on campus for general student use. A campuswide network can be accessed from off campus. Online class registration is available. *Web address:* http://www.spokane.wsu.edu/.

General Application Contact: Graduate School Admissions, 509-358-7978, Fax: 509-350-7538, E-mail: enroll@wsu.edu.

GRADUATE UNITS

Graduate Programs Students: 201 full-time (139 women), 171 part-time (114 women); includes 2 Black or African American, non-Hispanic/Latino; 6 American Indian or Alaska Native, non-Hispanic/Latino; 6 Asian, non-Hispanic/Latino; 6 Hispanic/Latino, 24 international. *Faculty:* 257. Expenses: Contact institution. *Financial support:* In 2010–11, research assistantships with tuition reimbursements (averaging $14,634 per year), teaching assistantships with tuition reimbursements (averaging $13,383 per year) were awarded. Financial award application deadline: 2/15. Offers criminal justice (MA, PhD); educational leadership (Ed M, MA); engineering management (METM); exercise science (MS); health policy and administration (MHPA); principal (Certificate); professional certification for teachers (Certificate); program administrator (Certificate); school psychologist (Certificate); speech and hearing sciences (MA); superintendent (Certificate); teaching (MIT). *Application deadline:* For fall admission, 1/10 priority date for domestic students, 1/10 for international students; for spring admission, 7/1 priority date for domestic students, 7/1 for international students. *Application fee:* $50. *Application Contact:* Graduate School Admissions, 800-GRADWSU, Fax: 509-335-1949, E-mail: gradsch@wsu.edu. *Chancellor*, Dr. Brian L. Pitcher, 509-358-7551, Fax: 509-358-7538, E-mail: bpitcher@wsu.edu.

Intercollegiate College of Nursing Students: 39 full-time (33 women), 51 part-time (46 women); includes 2 American Indian or Alaska Native, non-Hispanic/Latino; 2 Asian, non-Hispanic/Latino; 3 Hispanic/Latino, 1 international. *Faculty:* 30. Expenses: Contact institution. *Financial support:* Teaching assistantships with tuition reimbursements available. Financial award application deadline: 4/1. In 2010, 26 master's awarded. Offers nursing (MN). *Application deadline:* For fall admission, 1/10 priority date for domestic students, 1/10 for international students; for spring admission, 7/1 priority date for domestic students, 7/1 for international students. *Application fee:* $50. *Application Contact:* Graduate School Admissions, 800-GRADWSU, Fax: 509-335-1949, E-mail: gradsch@wsu.edu. *Dean*, Dr. Patricia Butterfield, 509-324-7292, Fax: 509-858-7336.

Interdisciplinary Design Institute Students: 9 full-time (6 women), 2 part-time (both women); includes 1 Asian, non-Hispanic/Latino, 5 international. Average age 35. *Faculty:* 7. Expenses: Contact institution. *Financial support:* In 2010–11, research assistantships with full and partial tuition reimbursements (averaging $14,634 per year), teaching assistantships with full and partial tuition reimbursements (averaging $13,383 per year) were awarded. Financial award application deadline: 2/15. In 2010, 18 master's awarded. *Degree program information:* Part-time programs available. Offers architecture (M Arch, MS); design (Dr DES); interior design (MA); landscape architecture (MS). *Application deadline:* For fall admission, 1/10 priority date for domestic students, 1/10 for international students; for spring admission, 7/1 priority date for domestic students, 7/1 for international students. *Application fee:* $50. *Application Contact:* Graduate School Admissions, 800-GRADWSU, Fax: 509-335-1949, E-mail: gradsch@wsu.edu. *Director*, Dr. Nancy H. Blossom, 509-358-7513, E-mail: blossom@wsu.edu.

Program in Pharmacy Students: 408. *Faculty:* 39. Expenses: Contact institution. *Financial support:* Career-related internships or fieldwork, Federal Work-Study, and scholarships/grants available. Financial award application deadline: 2/15. Offers pharmacy (Pharm D). *Application deadline:* For fall admission, 1/10 priority date for domestic students, 1/10 for international students; for spring admission, 7/1 priority date for domestic students, 7/1 for international students. Applications are processed on a rolling basis. *Application fee:* $50. *Application Contact:* Teresa Woolverton, Academic Coordinator, 509-335-2356, E-mail: twool@wsu.edu. *Interim Dean*, Dr. William Campbell, 509-335-4750, E-mail: vburnham@wsu.edu.

WASHINGTON STATE UNIVERSITY TRI-CITIES, Richland, WA 99352-1671

General Information State-supported, coed, graduate-only institution. *Enrollment by degree level:* 154 master's, 15 doctoral. *Graduate faculty:* 87. *Graduate housing:* On-campus housing not available. *Student services:* Campus employment opportunities, campus safety program, career counseling, child daycare facilities, exercise/wellness program, free psychological counseling, grant writing training, international student services, low-cost health insurance, multicultural affairs office, services for students with disabilities, teacher training, writing training. *Library facilities:* Max E. Benitz Library plus 3 others. *Online resources:* library catalog, web page, access to other libraries' catalogs. *Collection:* 2.3 million titles, 30,122 serial subscriptions, 426,737 audiovisual materials.

Computer facilities: 50 computers available on campus for general student use. A campuswide network can be accessed from off campus. Online class registration is available. *Web address:* http://www.tricity.wsu.edu/.

General Application Contact: Admissions, 509-372-7250, E-mail: admiss@tricity.wsu.edu.

GRADUATE UNITS

Graduate Programs Students: 42 full-time (25 women), 127 part-time (107 women). Expenses: Contact institution. *Financial support:* In 2010–11, research assistantships (averaging $14,634 per year), teaching assistantships (averaging $13,383 per year) were awarded; Federal Work-Study, health care benefits, and unspecified assistantships also available. *Degree program information:* Part-time programs available. Offers applied environmental science (MS); biology (MS); chemistry (MS, PhD); counseling (Ed M); educational leadership (Ed M, Ed D); environmental science (PhD); literacy (Ed M); secondary certification (Ed M); teaching (MIT). *Application deadline:* For fall admission, 1/10 priority date for domestic students, 1/10 for international students; for spring admission, 7/1 priority date for domestic students, 7/1 for international students. Applications are processed on a rolling basis. *Application fee:* $50. Electronic applications accepted. *Application Contact:* Graduate School Admissions, 800-GRADWSU, Fax: 509-335-1949, E-mail: gradsch@wsu.edu. *Chancellor*, Dr. Vicky Carwein, 509-372-7258, Fax: 509-372-7354, E-mail: kshelton@tricity.wsu.edu.

College of Business Students: 11 full-time (5 women), 37 part-time (5 women); includes 1 American Indian or Alaska Native, non-Hispanic/Latino; 3 Asian, non-Hispanic/Latino; 2 Hispanic/Latino, 1 international. Average age 35. *Faculty:* 56. Expenses: Contact institution. *Financial support:* In 2010–11, 17 students received support. In 2010, 16 master's awarded. *Degree program information:* Part-time and evening/weekend programs available. Offers business management (MBA). *Application deadline:* For fall admission, 1/10 priority date for domestic students, 1/10 for international students; for spring admission, 7/1 priority date for domestic students, 7/1 for international students. *Application fee:* $50. *Application Contact:* Graduate School Admissions, 800-GRADWSU, Fax: 509-335-1949, E-mail: gradsch@wsu.edu. *Director*, Dr. John Thornton, 509-372-7246, Fax: 509-372-7354, E-mail: jthornt@tricity.wsu.edu.

College of Engineering and Computer Science Students: 4 full-time (0 women), 25 part-time (8 women); includes 2 Black or African American, non-Hispanic/Latino, 1 international. *Faculty:* 28. Expenses: Contact institution. *Financial support:* Application deadline: 3/1. *Degree program information:* Part-time programs available. Offers computer science (MS, PhD); electrical and computer engineering (PhD); electrical engineering (MS); mechanical engineering (MS, PhD). *Application deadline:* For fall admission, 1/10 priority date for domestic students, 1/10 for international students; for spring admission, 7/1 priority date for domestic students, 7/1 for international students. *Application fee:* $50. *Application Contact:* Dr. Scott Hudson, Associate Director, 509-372-7254, Fax: 509-335-1949, E-mail: hudson@tricity.wsu.edu. *Chair*, Dr. Ali Saberi, 509-372-7178, E-mail: sidra@eecs.wsu.edu.

Intercollegiate College of Nursing Students: 10 full-time (9 women), 19 part-time (18 women); includes 1 American Indian or Alaska Native, non-Hispanic/Latino. *Faculty:* 30. Expenses: Contact institution. *Financial support:* In 2010–11, 24 students received support, including fellowships (averaging $4,050 per year), teaching assistantships with tuition reimbursements available (averaging $13,056 per year). Financial award application deadline: 4/1; financial award applicants required to submit FAFSA. *Degree program information:* Part-time programs available. Postbaccalaureate distance learning degree programs offered (minimal on-campus study). Offers nursing (MN). *Application deadline:* For fall admission, 1/10 priority date for domestic students, 1/10 for international students; for spring admission, 7/1 priority date for domestic students, 7/1 for international students. *Application fee:* $50. *Application Contact:* Graduate School Admissions, 800-GRADWSU, Fax: 509-335-1949, E-mail: gradsch@wsu.edu. *Interim Director*, Phyllis Morris, 509-372-7196, Fax: 509-372-7116, E-mail: pmorris@tricity.wsu.edu.

WASHINGTON STATE UNIVERSITY VANCOUVER, Vancouver, WA 98686

General Information State-supported, coed, comprehensive institution. *Enrollment by degree level:* 384 master's, 61 doctoral, 100 other advanced degrees. *Graduate faculty:* 87. *Graduate housing:* On-campus housing not available. *Student services:* Campus employment opportunities, campus safety program, career counseling, free psychological counseling, grant writing training, low-cost health insurance, multicultural affairs office, services for students with disabilities, teacher training, writing training. *Web address:* http://www.vancouver.wsu.edu/.

General Application Contact: Office of Admissions, 800-GRADWSU, Fax: 360-546-9779, E-mail: admissions@vancouver.wsu.edu.

GRADUATE UNITS

Graduate Programs Students: 144 full-time (72 women), 401 part-time (276 women); includes 5 Black or African American, non-Hispanic/Latino; 5 American Indian or Alaska Native, non-Hispanic/Latino; 25 Asian, non-Hispanic/Latino; 9 Hispanic/Latino, 14 international. *Faculty:* 87. Expenses: Contact institution. *Financial support:* In 2010–11, research assistantships with partial tuition reimbursements (averaging $14,634 per year), teaching assistantships with partial tuition reimbursements (averaging $13,383 per year) were awarded; Federal Work-Study, scholarships/grants, and unspecified assistantships also available. Financial award application deadline: 2/15. *Degree program information:* Part-time programs available. Offers business administration (MBA); education (Ed M, MIT, Ed D); environmental science (MS); history (MA); public affairs (MPA). *Application deadline:* For fall admission, 1/10 priority date for domestic students, 1/10 for international students; for spring admission, 7/1 priority date for domestic students, 7/1 for international students. *Application fee:* $50. *Application Contact:* Graduate School Admissions, 800-GRADWSU, Fax: 509-335-1949, E-mail: gradsch@wsu.edu. *Chancellor*, Dr. Hal Dengerink, 360-546-9581, Fax: 360-546-9043, E-mail: dengerin@vancouver.wsu.edu.

Intercollegiate College of Nursing Students: 11 full-time (all women), 92 part-time (82 women); includes 6 Asian, non-Hispanic/Latino; 1 Hispanic/Latino. *Faculty:* 30. Expenses: Contact institution. *Financial support:* In 2010–11, research assistantships (averaging $14,634 per year), teaching assistantships with tuition reimbursements (averaging $13,383 per year) were awarded. Financial award application deadline: 2/15. In 2010, 34 master's awarded. Offers nursing (MN). *Application deadline:* For fall admission, 1/10 priority date for domestic students, 1/10 for international students; for spring admission, 7/1 priority date for domestic students, 7/1 for international students. Applications are processed on a rolling basis. *Application fee:* $50. Electronic applications accepted. *Application Contact:* Tami Kelly, Principal Assistant, 509-324-7334, E-mail: kelleyt@wsu.edu. *Regional Director*, Dr. Ginny Guido, 360-546-9244, Fax: 360-546-9038, E-mail: ginny_guido@vancouver.wsu.edu.

School of Engineering and Computer Science Students: 14 full-time (1 woman), 5 part-time (1 woman); includes 1 Asian, non-Hispanic/Latino, 5 international. *Faculty:* 9. Expenses: Contact institution. *Financial support:* In 2010–11, research assistantships with full tuition reimbursements (averaging $14,634 per year), teaching assistantships with full tuition reimbursements (averaging $13,383 per year) were awarded; health care benefits and unspecified assistantships also available. Financial award application deadline: 2/15. In 2010, 4 master's awarded. *Degree program information:* Part-time programs available. Offers computer science (MS); mechanical engineering (MS). *Application deadline:* For fall admission, 1/10 priority date for domestic students, 1/10 for international students; for spring admission, 7/1 priority date for domestic students, 7/1 for international students. Applications are processed on a rolling basis. *Application fee:* $50. *Application Contact:* Peggy Moore, Academic Coordinator, 360-546-9638, Fax: 360-546-9438, E-mail: moorep@vancouver.wsu.edu. *Director*, Dr. Hakan Gurocak, 360-546-9637, Fax: 360-546-9438, E-mail: hgurocak@vancouver.wsu.edu.

WASHINGTON THEOLOGICAL UNION, Washington, DC 20012

General Information Independent-religious, coed, graduate-only institution. *Enrollment by degree level:* 41 first professional, 128 master's, 35 doctoral. *Graduate faculty:* 18 full-time (3 women), 9 part-time/adjunct (2 women). *Tuition:* Part-time $660 per credit hour. *Required fees:* $90 per semester. *Graduate housing:* Rooms and/or apartments available on a first-come, first-served basis to single and married students. Typical cost: $5200 (including board) for single students; $8260 (including board) for married students. *Student services:* Campus employment opportunities, exercise/wellness program, international student services, low-cost health insurance. *Library facilities:* O'Toole Library. *Online resources:* library catalog, web page, access to other libraries' catalogs. *Collection:* 120,000 titles, 425 serial subscriptions.

Computer facilities: 10 computers available on campus for general student use. A campuswide network can be accessed from student residence rooms and from off campus. *Web address:* http://www.wtu.edu/.

General Application Contact: Cynthia Cameron, Director of Recruitment and Enrollment Services, 202-541-5210, Fax: 202-726-1716, E-mail: admissions@wtu.edu.

GRADUATE UNITS

Graduate and Professional Programs Students: 43 full-time (6 women), 197 part-time (75 women). Average age 32. 149 applicants, 95% accepted. *Faculty:* 18 full-time (3 women), 9 part-time/adjunct (2 women). Expenses: Contact institution. *Financial support:* In 2010–11, 40 students received support. Career-related internships or fieldwork and scholarships/grants available. Support available to part-time students. Financial award application deadline: 3/15; financial award applicants required to submit FAFSA. In 2010, 19 first professional degrees, 22 master's awarded. *Degree program information:* Part-time programs available. Postbaccalaureate distance learning degree programs offered. Offers theology (M Div, MA, MAPS, MTS, D Min). *Application deadline:* For fall admission, 4/1 priority date for domestic students; for spring admission, 11/15 priority date for domestic students. Applications are processed on a rolling basis. *Application fee:* $50. *Application Contact:* Cynthia Cameron, Director of Recruitment and Enrollment Services, 202-541-5210, Fax: 202-726-1716, E-mail: admissions@wtu.edu. *President*, Very Rev. Frederick J. Tillotson, OCARM, 202-541-5228, Fax: 202-726-1716.

WASHINGTON UNIVERSITY IN ST. LOUIS, St. Louis, MO 63130-4899

General Information Independent, coed, university. CGS member. *Graduate housing:* Rooms and/or apartments available on a first-come, first-served basis to single and married students.

GRADUATE UNITS

George Warren Brown School of Social Work Offers public health (MPH); social work (MSW, PhD). MSW/M Div, MSW/MAPS offered jointly with Eden Theological Seminary. Electronic applications accepted.

Graduate School of Arts and Sciences Offers American history (MA, PhD); anthropology (PhD); art history (MA, PhD); arts and sciences (MA, MA Ed, MAT, MFAW, MM, PhD); Asian history (MA, PhD); British history (MA, PhD); chemistry (PhD); Chinese (MA); Chinese and comparative literature (PhD); classical archaeology (MA, PhD); classics (MA); clinical psychology (PhD); comparative literature (MA, PhD); earth and planetary sciences (MA); East Asian studies (MA); economics (PhD); educational research (PhD); elementary education (MA Ed); English and American literature (MA, PhD); European history (MA, PhD); French (MA, PhD); general experimental psychology (PhD); Germanic languages and literature (MA, PhD); Japanese (MA); Japanese and comparative literature (PhD); Latin American history (MA, PhD); mathematics (MA, PhD); Middle Eastern history (MA, PhD); movement science (PhD); music (MM, PhD); philosophy (MA, PhD); philosophy/neuroscience/psychology (PhD); physics (PhD); planetary sciences (PhD); political economy and public policy (MA); political science (PhD); secondary education (MA Ed, MAT); social psychology (PhD); social work (PhD); Spanish (MA, PhD); statistics (MA); writing (MFAW). Electronic applications accepted.

Division of Biology and Biomedical Sciences Offers biochemistry (PhD); chemical biology (PhD); computational biology (PhD); developmental biology (PhD); ecology (PhD); environmental biology (PhD); evolution, ecology and population biology (PhD); evolutionary biology (PhD); genetics (PhD); immunology (PhD); molecular biophysics (PhD); molecular cell biology (PhD); molecular genetics (PhD); molecular microbiology and microbial pathogenesis (PhD); neurosciences (PhD); plant biology (PhD). Electronic applications accepted.

Olin Business School Students: 487 full-time (170 women), 503 part-time (127 women); includes 168 minority (34 Black or African American, non-Hispanic/Latino; 2 American Indian or Alaska Native, non-Hispanic/Latino; 93 Asian, non-Hispanic/Latino; 10 Hispanic/Latino; 29 Two or more races, non-Hispanic/Latino), 320 international. *Faculty:* 79 full-time (17 women), 42 part-time/adjunct (7 women). Expenses: Contact institution. Offers accounting (MS); business (EMBA, M Acc, MBA, MS, PhD); business administration (EMBA, MBA); finance (MS); supply chain management (MS). Electronic applications accepted. *Application Contact:* Dr. Mahendra Gupta, Dean, 314-935-6344. *Dean,* Dr. Mahendra Gupta, 314-935-6344.

Sam Fox School of Design and Visual Arts Offers architecture (M Arch, MLA); design and visual arts (M Arch, MFA, MLA, MUD); urban design (MUD).

Graduate School of Art Offers visual art (MFA). Electronic applications accepted.

School of Engineering and Applied Science Students: 423 full-time (107 women), 297 part-time (61 women); includes 25 Black or African American, non-Hispanic/Latino; 2 American Indian or Alaska Native, non-Hispanic/Latino; 47 Asian, non-Hispanic/Latino; 18 Hispanic/Latino; 7 Two or more races, non-Hispanic/Latino, 209 international. 1,304 applicants, 34% accepted, 248 enrolled. *Faculty:* 77 full-time, 74 part-time/adjunct. Expenses: Contact institution. *Financial support:* In 2010–11, 281 students received support, including 31 fellowships with full tuition reimbursements available, 241 research assistantships with full tuition reimbursements available, 5 teaching assistantships with full tuition reimbursements available; career-related internships or fieldwork, Federal Work-Study, institutionally sponsored loans, scholarships/grants, health care benefits, tuition waivers (full and partial), and unspecified assistantships also available. Financial award applicants required to submit FAFSA. In 2010, 187 master's, 50 doctorates awarded. *Degree program information:* Part-time and evening/weekend programs available. Offers biomedical engineering (MS, D Sc, PhD); chemical engineering (MS, D Sc); computer engineering (MS, PhD); computer science (MS, PhD); computer science and engineering (M Eng); electrical engineering (MS, D Sc, PhD); engineering and applied science (M Eng, MCE, MCM, MEM, MIM, MPM, MS, MSEE, MSEE, D Sc, PhD); environmental engineering (MS, D Sc); mechanical, aerospace and structural engineering (MS, D Sc, PhD); systems science and mathematics (MS, D Sc, PhD). *Application deadline:* For fall admission, 1/15 for domestic and international students. Applications are processed on a rolling basis. *Application fee:* $60. Electronic applications accepted. *Application Contact:* Beth Schnettler, Director of Graduate Admissions, 314-935-7974, Fax: 314-719-4703, E-mail: bethschnettler@seas.wustl.edu. *Dean,* Ralph S. Quatrano, 314-935-6350, E-mail: rsq@wustl.edu.

School of Law Offers law (JD, LL M, MJS, JSD). Electronic applications accepted.

School of Medicine Offers audiology (Au D); clinical investigation (MS); computational (MS); deaf education (MS); genetic epidemiology (Certificate); medicine (MD, MS, MSOT, Au D, DPT, OTD, PhD, Certificate, PPDPT); movement science (PhD); occupational therapy (MSOT, OTD); physical therapy (DPT, PhD, PPDPT); speech and hearing sciences (PhD).

See Close-Up on page 997.

WAYLAND BAPTIST UNIVERSITY, Plainview, TX 79072-6998

General Information Independent-religious, coed, comprehensive institution. *Graduate housing:* Rooms and/or apartments available on a first-come, first-served basis to single and married students.

GRADUATE UNITS

Graduate Programs *Degree program information:* Part-time and evening/weekend programs available. Postbaccalaureate distance learning degree programs offered (no on-campus study). Offers Christian ministry (MCM); counseling (MA); education administration (M Ed); general business (MBA); government administration (MPA); health care administration (MBA); higher education administration (M Ed); homeland security (MPA); human resource management (MBA); instructional leadership (M Ed); instructional technology (M Ed); international management (MBA); justice administration (MPA); management (MA, MBA); management information systems (MBA); multidisciplinary science (MS); religion (MA); special education (M Ed). Electronic applications accepted.

WAYNESBURG UNIVERSITY, Waynesburg, PA 15370-1222

General Information Independent-religious, coed, comprehensive institution. *Graduate housing:* Room and/or apartments available on a first-come, first-served basis to single students; on-campus housing not available to married students. Housing application deadline: 8/1.

GRADUATE UNITS

Graduate and Professional Studies *Degree program information:* Part-time and evening/weekend programs available. Offers business (MBA); counseling (MA); education (MAT); nursing (MSN); nursing practice (DNP); special education (M Ed); technology (M Ed). Electronic applications accepted.

WAYNE STATE COLLEGE, Wayne, NE 68787

General Information State-supported, coed, comprehensive institution. CGS member. *Graduate housing:* Room and/or apartments available on a first-come, first-served basis to single students; on-campus housing not available to married students. *Research affiliation:* Nebraska Business Development Center, Social Sciences Research Center.

GRADUATE UNITS

Department of Health, Human Performance and Sport *Degree program information:* Part-time and evening/weekend programs available. Offers exercise science (MSE); organizational management (MS). Electronic applications accepted.

School of Business and Technology *Degree program information:* Part-time and evening/weekend programs available. Postbaccalaureate distance learning degree programs offered (minimal on-campus study). Offers business and technology (MBA).

School of Education and Counseling *Degree program information:* Part-time and evening/weekend programs available. Offers alternative education (MSE); business and information technology education (MSE); communication arts education (MSE); counseling (MSE); counselor education (MSE); curriculum and instruction (MSE); early childhood education (MSE); education and counseling (MSE, Ed S); educational administration (MSE, Ed S); elementary administration (MSE); elementary and secondary administration (MSE); elementary education (MSE); English as a second language (MSE); English education (MSE); family and consumer sciences education (MSE); guidance and counseling (MSE); industrial technology and vocational education (MSE); learning communities (MSE); mathematics education (MSE); music education (MSE); school counseling (MSE); science education (MSE); secondary administration (MSE); social science education (MSE); special education (MSE).

WAYNE STATE UNIVERSITY, Detroit, MI 48202

General Information State-supported, coed, university. CGS member. *Enrollment:* 31,505 graduate, professional, and undergraduate students; 5,908 full-time matriculated graduate/professional students (3,298 women), 4,475 part-time matriculated graduate/professional students (2,823 women). *Enrollment by degree level:* 2,222 first professional, 5,971 master's, 1,820 doctoral, 370 other advanced degrees. *Graduate faculty:* 706 full-time (277 women), 290 part-time/adjunct (147 women). Tuition, state resident: full-time $7662; part-time $478.85 per credit hour. Tuition, nonresident: full-time $16,920; part-time $1057.55 per credit hour. *Required fees:* $571; $35.70 per credit hour. $188.05 per semester. Tuition and fees vary according to course load and program. *Graduate housing:* Rooms and/or apartments available on a first-come, first-served basis to single and married students. Typical cost: $8253 (including board) for single students. Room and board charges vary according to board plan and housing facility selected. *Student services:* Campus employment opportunities, career counseling, child daycare facilities, exercise/wellness program, free psychological counseling, grant writing training, international student services, low-cost health insurance, services for students with disabilities, writing training. *Library facilities:* David Adamany Undergraduate Library plus 6 others. *Online resources:* library catalog, web page, access to other libraries' catalogs. *Collection:* 3.7 million titles, 16,583 serial subscriptions, 80,713 audiovisual materials. *Research affiliation:* University of Michigan, Michigan State University, State of Michigan Department of Community Health, Henry Ford Health System, Novartis Pharmaceuticals, Research to Prevent Blindness, Inc.

Computer facilities: 2,877 computers available on campus for general student use. A campuswide network can be accessed from student residence rooms and from off campus. Online class registration is available. *Web address:* http://www.wayne.edu/.

General Application Contact: Kathy Lueckeman, Director, Graduate Enrollment Services, 313-577-8098, E-mail: klueckeman@wayne.edu.

GRADUATE UNITS

College of Education Students: 572 full-time (430 women), 1,179 part-time (867 women); includes 693 minority (598 Black or African American, non-Hispanic/Latino; 12 American Indian or Alaska Native, non-Hispanic/Latino; 39 Asian, non-Hispanic/Latino; 36 Hispanic/Latino; 1 Native Hawaiian or other Pacific Islander, non-Hispanic/Latino; 7 Two or more races, non-Hispanic/Latino), 44 international. Average age 37. 361 applicants, 63% accepted, 171 enrolled. *Faculty:* 78 full-time (43 women), 77 part-time/adjunct (52 women). Expenses: Contact institution. *Financial support:* In 2010–11, 3 fellowships with tuition reimbursements (averaging $15,154 per year), 11 research assistantships (averaging $16,054 per year), 5 teaching assistantships with tuition reimbursements (averaging $15,409 per year) were awarded; career-related internships or fieldwork, Federal Work-Study, and institutionally sponsored loans also available. Support available to part-time students. In 2010, 449 master's, 23 doctorates, 110 other advanced degrees awarded. *Degree program information:* Evening/weekend programs available. Offers education (M Ed, MA, MAT, Ed D, PhD, Certificate, Ed S). *Application deadline:* For fall admission, 7/1 for domestic students, 6/1 for international students; for winter admission, 10/1 for international students; for spring admission, 2/1 for international students. Applications are processed on a rolling basis. *Application fee:* $30 ($50 for international students). Electronic applications accepted. *Application Contact:* Janice Green, Assistant Dean, 313-577-1605, E-mail: jwgreen@wayne.edu. *Dean,* Dr. Carolyn Shields, 313-577-1620, Fax: 313-577-3606.

Division of Administrative and Organizational Studies Students: 80 full-time (52 women), 176 part-time (120 women); includes 115 minority (98 Black or African American, non-Hispanic/Latino; 3 American Indian or Alaska Native, non-Hispanic/Latino; 6 Asian, non-Hispanic/Latino; 8 Hispanic/Latino), 8 international. Average age 39. 48 applicants, 71% accepted, 24 enrolled. *Faculty:* 52 full-time (20 women), 40 part-time/adjunct (16 women). Expenses: Contact institution. *Financial support:* In 2010–11, 1 fellowship (averaging $11,711 per year), 4 research assistantships with tuition reimbursements (averaging $15,181 per year) were awarded; career-related internships or fieldwork, Federal Work-Study, and institutionally sponsored loans also available. Support available to part-time students. In 2010, 67 master's, 11 doctorates, 8 other advanced degrees awarded. Offers administration and supervision-secondary (Ed S); college and university teaching (Certificate); curriculum and instruction (PhD); educational leadership (M Ed, Ed S); educational leadership and policy studies (Ed D, PhD); elementary education curriculum and instruction (MA, Ed S); general administration and supervision (Ed D, PhD, Ed S); higher education (Ed D, PhD); instructional technology (M Ed, Ed D, PhD, Ed S); secondary curriculum and instruction (M Ed, Ed S). *Application deadline:* For fall admission, 7/1 for domestic students, 6/1 for international students; for winter admission, 10/1 for international students; for spring admission, 2/1 for international students. *Application fee:* $30 ($50 for international students). Electronic applications accepted. *Application Contact:* Janice Green, Assistant Dean, 313-577-1605, E-mail: jwgreen@wayne.edu. *Assistant Dean,* Dr. JoAnne Holbert, 313-577-1721, E-mail: jholbert@wayne.edu.

Division of Kinesiology, Health and Sports Studies Students: 43 full-time (25 women), 81 part-time (31 women); includes 42 minority (38 Black or African American, non-Hispanic/Latino; 1 American Indian or Alaska Native, non-Hispanic/Latino; 1 Asian, non-Hispanic/Latino; 1 Native Hawaiian or other Pacific Islander, non-Hispanic/Latino; 1 Two or more races, non-Hispanic/Latino), 4 international. Average age 31. 31 applicants, 84% accepted, 19 enrolled. *Faculty:* 36 full-time (12 women), 14 part-time/adjunct (5 women). Expenses: Contact institution. *Financial support:* In 2010–11, 2 research assistantships with tuition reimbursements (averaging $15,500 per year), 3 teaching assistantships with tuition reimbursements (averaging $15,466 per year) were awarded; career-related internships or fieldwork also available. In 2010, 55 master's awarded. Offers health education (M Ed); kinesiology (M Ed); physical education (M Ed); recreation and park services (MA); sports administration (MA). *Application deadline:* For fall admission, 7/1 for domestic students, 6/1 for international students; for winter admission, 10/1 for international students; for spring admission, 2/1 for international students. *Application fee:* $30 ($50 for international students). Electronic applications accepted. *Application Contact:* John Wirth, Assistant Professor, 313-993-7972, Fax: 313-577-5999, E-mail: johnwirth@wayne.edu. *Assistant Dean,* Dr. Sally Erbaugh, 313-577-6210, Fax: 313-577-5999, E-mail: serbaugh@coe.wayne.edu.

Division of Teacher Education Students: 256 full-time (197 women), 720 part-time (552 women); includes 368 minority (312 Black or African American, non-Hispanic/Latino; 5 American Indian or Alaska Native, non-Hispanic/Latino; 24 Asian, non-Hispanic/Latino; 23 Hispanic/Latino; 4 Two or more races, non-Hispanic/Latino), 15 international. Average age 35. 185 applicants, 63% accepted, 93 enrolled. *Faculty:* 532 full-time (362 women), 764 part-time/adjunct (599 women). Expenses: Contact institution. *Financial support:* In 2010–11, 2 research assistantships with tuition reimbursements (averaging $17,060 per year), 1 teaching assistantship (averaging $15,181 per year) were awarded. In 2010, 297 master's, 3 doctorates, 57 other advanced degrees awarded. Offers adult and continuing education (M Ed); art education (M Ed); bilingual/bicultural education (M Ed, MAT); business education (M Ed, MAT); career and technical education (M Ed, Ed D, PhD, Ed S); curriculum and instruction (Ed D, PhD, Ed S); distributive education (M Ed, MAT); early childhood education (M Ed); elementary education (M Ed, MAT, Ed D, PhD, Ed S); elementary education curriculum and instruction (M Ed); English education (M Ed); English education-secondary (M Ed, Ed S); foreign language education (M Ed); general education (Ed D, Ed S); health occupations education (M Ed); industrial education (M Ed); mathematics education (M Ed, Ed S); pre-school and parent education (M Ed); reading (M Ed, Ed D, Ed S); reading, languages and literature (Ed D); school music-vocal (M Ed); science education (M Ed, MAT, Ed S); secondary education (MAT); secondary school reading (M Ed); social studies education (M Ed, Ed S); special education (M Ed, Ed D, PhD, Ed S); teacher education (MAT, Ed D, PhD). *Application deadline:* For fall admission, 7/1 for domestic students, 6/1 for international students; for winter admission, 10/1 for international students; for spring admission, 2/1 for international students. *Application fee:* $30 ($50 for international students). Electronic applications accepted. *Application Contact:* Sharon Elliott, Assistant Dean, 313-577-0902, E-mail: sharon.elliott@wayne.edu. *Assistant Dean*, Dr. Sharon Elliot, 313-577-0902, E-mail: aa190@wayne.edu.

Division of Theoretical and Behavioral Foundations Students: 193 full-time (156 women), 202 part-time (164 women); includes 168 minority (150 Black or African American, non-Hispanic/Latino; 3 American Indian or Alaska Native, non-Hispanic/Latino; 8 Asian, non-Hispanic/Latino; 5 Hispanic/Latino; 2 Two or more races, non-Hispanic/Latino), 17 international. Average age 36. 97 applicants, 55% accepted, 35 enrolled. *Faculty:* 100 full-time (50 women), 60 part-time/adjunct (35 women). Expenses: Contact institution. *Financial support:* In 2010–11, 2 fellowships with tuition reimbursements (averaging $16,875 per year), 3 research assistantships with tuition reimbursements (averaging $17,785 per year), 1 teaching assistantship (averaging $15,181 per year) were awarded; career-related internships or fieldwork, Federal Work-Study, and institutionally sponsored loans also available. In 2010, 42 master's, 9 doctorates, 2 other advanced degrees awarded. *Degree program information:* Evening/weekend programs available. Offers counseling (M Ed, MA, Ed D, PhD, Ed S); education evaluation and research (M Ed, Ed D, PhD); educational psychology (M Ed, Ed D, PhD, Ed S); educational sociology (M Ed, Ed D, PhD, Ed S); history and philosophy of education (M Ed, Ed D, PhD); rehabilitation counseling and community inclusion (MA, Ed S); school and community psychology (MA, Ed S); school clinical psychology (Ed S). *Application deadline:* For fall admission, 7/1 for domestic students, 6/1 for international students; for winter admission, 10/1 for international students; for spring admission, 2/1 for international students. *Application fee:* $20 ($30 for international students). Electronic applications accepted. *Application Contact:* Janice Green, Assistant Dean, 313-577-1605, E-mail: jwgreen@wayne.edu. *Assistant Dean*, Dr. JoAnne Holbert, 313-577-1721, E-mail: jholbert@wayne.edu.

College of Engineering Students: 497 full-time (106 women), 309 part-time (84 women); includes 125 minority (46 Black or African American, non-Hispanic/Latino; 69 Asian, non-Hispanic/Latino; 7 Hispanic/Latino; 3 Two or more races, non-Hispanic/Latino), 336 international. Average age 30. 669 applicants, 56% accepted, 150 enrolled. *Faculty:* 65 full-time (8 women), 17 part-time/adjunct (2 women). Expenses: Contact institution. *Financial support:* In 2010–11, 17 fellowships (averaging $16,990 per year), 80 research assistantships with tuition reimbursements (averaging $17,053 per year), 54 teaching assistantships with tuition reimbursements (averaging $17,067 per year) were awarded; career-related internships or fieldwork, Federal Work-Study, institutionally sponsored loans, scholarships/grants, and tuition waivers (full and partial) also available. Support available to part-time students. In 2010, 190 master's, 29 doctorates, 2 other advanced degrees awarded. *Degree program information:* Part-time programs available. Offers biomedical engineering (MS, PhD); chemical engineering (MS, PhD); civil and environmental engineering (MS, PhD); computer engineering (MS, PhD); electric-drive vehicle engineering (MS, Graduate Certificate); electrical engineering (MS, PhD); electronics and computer control systems (MS); engineering (MS, PhD, Certificate, Graduate Certificate); engineering management (MS); industrial engineering (MS, PhD); manufacturing engineering (MS); materials science and engineering (MS, PhD, Certificate); mechanical engineering (MS, PhD); metallurgical engineering (MS, PhD); polymer engineering (Certificate); sustainable engineering (Certificate). *Application deadline:* For fall admission, 7/1 priority date for domestic students, 6/1 for international students; for winter admission, 10/1 for international students; for spring admission, 3/15 for domestic students, 2/1 for international students. Applications are processed on a rolling basis. *Application fee:* $30 ($50 for international students). *Application Contact:* Dr. Gerald O. Thompkins, Associate Dean, 313-577-3780. *Dean*, Dr. Ralph Kummler, 313-577-3861, Fax: 313-577-5300, E-mail: rkummler@eng.wayne.edu.

Division of Engineering Technology Students: 9 full-time (1 woman), 12 part-time (2 women); includes 9 minority (6 Black or African American, non-Hispanic/Latino; 3 Asian, non-Hispanic/Latino), 4 international. Average age 36. 9 applicants, 100% accepted, 6 enrolled. *Faculty:* 4 full-time (1 woman), 1 part-time/adjunct (0 women). Expenses: Contact institution. *Financial support:* In 2010–11, 2 students received support. Career-related internships or fieldwork, Federal Work-Study, and institutionally sponsored loans available. In 2010, 4 master's awarded. Offers engineering technology (MS). *Application deadline:* For fall admission, 7/1 priority date for domestic students, 6/1 for international students; for winter admission, 10/1 for international students; for spring admission, 3/15 for domestic students, 2/1 for international students. Applications are processed on a rolling basis. *Application fee:* $30 ($50 for international students). Electronic applications accepted. *Application Contact:* Dr. Gerald O. Thompkins, Associate Dean, 313-577-3780. *Department Chair*, Dr. Chih-Ping Yeh, 313-577-8076, Fax: 313-577-1781, E-mail: aa4771@wayne.edu.

College of Fine, Performing and Communication Arts Students: 145 full-time (76 women), 168 part-time (114 women); includes 71 minority (59 Black or African American, non-Hispanic/Latino; 2 American Indian or Alaska Native, non-Hispanic/Latino; 1 Asian, non-Hispanic/Latino; 5 Hispanic/Latino; 4 Two or more races, non-Hispanic/Latino), 15 international. Average age 33. 164 applicants, 59% accepted, 70 enrolled. *Faculty:* 74 full-time (32 women), 15 part-time/adjunct (4 women). Expenses: Contact institution. *Financial support:* In 2010–11, 10 fellowships with tuition reimbursements (averaging $15,340 per year), 37 research assistantships with tuition reimbursements (averaging $14,846 per year), 26 teaching assistantships with tuition reimbursements (averaging $14,682 per year) were awarded; career-related internships or fieldwork, Federal Work-Study, and institutionally sponsored loans also available. Support available to part-time students. In 2010, 87 master's, 10 doctorates, 3 other advanced degrees awarded. Offers art (MA, MFA); art history (MA); choral conducting (MM); communication studies (MA, PhD); composition (MM); design and merchandising (MA); dispute resolution (MADR, Certificate); fine, performing and communication arts (MA, MADR, MFA, MM, PhD, Certificate); music (MA, MM); music education (MM); orchestral studies (Certificate); performance (MM); public relations and organizational communication (MA); radio-TV-film (MA, PhD); speech communication (MA, PhD); theatre (MA, MFA, PhD); theory (MM). *Application deadline:* For fall admission, 4/1 for domestic students, 6/1 for international students; for winter admission, 10/1 for international students; for spring admission, 2/1 for international students. Applications are processed on a rolling basis. *Application fee:* $30 ($50 for international students). Electronic applications accepted. *Application Contact:* John Vander Weg, Associate Dean, 313-577-5342. *Interim Dean*, Dr. Matthew Seeger, 313-577-5342, Fax: 313-577-5355, E-mail: aa4331@wayne.edu.

College of Liberal Arts and Sciences Students: 1,089 full-time (612 women), 585 part-time (344 women); includes 318 minority (193 Black or African American, non-Hispanic/Latino; 10 American Indian or Alaska Native, non-Hispanic/Latino; 69 Asian, non-Hispanic/Latino; 41 Hispanic/Latino; 1 Native Hawaiian or other Pacific Islander, non-Hispanic/Latino; 4 Two or more races, non-Hispanic/Latino), 413 international. Average age 32. 1,858 applicants, 31% accepted, 353 enrolled. *Faculty:* 253 full-time (84 women), 26 part-time/adjunct (10 women). Expenses: Contact institution. *Financial support:* In 2010–11, 63 fellowships (averaging $16,840 per year), 152 research assistantships (averaging $18,285 per year), 374 teaching assistantships (averaging $16,855 per year) were awarded; career-related internships or fieldwork, Federal Work-Study, institutionally sponsored loans, scholarships/grants, and tuition waivers (full and partial) also available. Support available to part-time students. In 2010, 378 master's, 101 doctorates, 12 other advanced degrees awarded. *Degree program information:* Evening/weekend programs available. Offers anthropology (MA, PhD); applied mathematics (MA, PhD); Arabic (MA); audiology (MA, MS, Au D, PhD); biological sciences (MA, MS, PhD); chemistry (MA, MS, PhD); classics, Greek, and Latin (MA); communication disorders and science (MA, PhD); comparative literature (MA); computer science (MA, MS, PhD); criminal justice (MS); economics (MA, PhD); English (MA, PhD); French (MA, PhD); geography (MA); geology (MA, MS); German (MA, PhD); German and Slavic studies (MA, PhD); history (MA, PhD); industrial and organizational psychology (PhD); Italian (MA); language learning (MA); Latin (MA); liberal arts and sciences (MA, MPA, MS, MUP, Au D, PhD, Certificate); linguistics (MA); mathematical statistics (MA, PhD); mathematics (MA, MS, PhD); modern languages (PhD); molecular biotechnology (MS); multidisciplinary science (MA); Near Eastern and Asian studies (MA); Near Eastern studies (MA); nutrition and food science (MA, MS, PhD); philosophy (MA, PhD); physics (MA, MS, PhD); political science (MA, PhD); public administration (MPA); Russian (MA); scientific computing (Certificate); sociology (MA, PhD); Spanish (MA, PhD); speech-language pathology (MA, PhD); urban studies and planning (MUP). *Application deadline:* For fall admission, 6/1 for international students; for winter admission, 10/1 for international students; for spring admission, 2/1 for international students. *Application fee:* $30 ($50 for international students). *Application Contact:* Janet Hankin, Professor, 313-577-0841, E-mail: janet.hankin@wayne.edu. *Dean*, Robert Thomas, 313-577-2519, Fax: 313-577-8971, E-mail: aa0817@wayne.edu.

College of Nursing Students: 113 full-time (105 women), 316 part-time (294 women); includes 100 minority (73 Black or African American, non-Hispanic/Latino; 19 Asian, non-Hispanic/Latino; 8 Hispanic/Latino), 13 international. Average age 37. 161 applicants, 66% accepted, 93 enrolled. *Faculty:* 33 full-time (31 women), 2 part-time/adjunct (both women). Expenses: Contact institution. *Financial support:* In 2010–11, 3 fellowships with tuition reimbursements (averaging $14,404 per year), 5 teaching assistantships (averaging $26,400 per year) were awarded; research assistantships with tuition reimbursements, Federal Work-Study, institutionally sponsored loans, scholarships/grants, and traineeships also available. Support available to part-time students. Financial award application deadline: 7/1; financial award applicants required to submit FAFSA. In 2010, 86 master's, 6 doctorates, 10 other advanced degrees awarded. *Degree program information:* Part-time programs available. Offers adult acute care nursing (MSN); adult primary care nursing (MSN); advanced practice nursing with women, neonates and children (MSN); community health nursing (MSN); neonatal nurse practitioner (Certificate); nursing (MSN, PhD, Certificate); nursing education (Certificate); psychiatric mental health nurse practitioner (MSN, Certificate); transcultural nursing (MSN, Certificate). *Application deadline:* For fall admission, 6/1 for international students; for winter admission, 10/1 for international students; for spring admission, 2/1 for international students. Applications are processed on a rolling basis. *Application fee:* $30 ($50 for international students). Electronic applications accepted. *Application Contact:* Nancy Artinian, Professor, 313-577-4143, E-mail: n.artinian@wayne.edu. *Dean*, Dr. Barbara Redman, 313-577-4070, Fax: 313-577-4571, E-mail: ae9080@wayne.edu.

Eugene Applebaum College of Pharmacy and Health Sciences Students: 591 full-time (393 women), 91 part-time (53 women); includes 115 minority (24 Black or African American, non-Hispanic/Latino; 87 Asian, non-Hispanic/Latino; 4 Hispanic/Latino), 68 international. Average age 26. 289 applicants, 45% accepted, 112 enrolled. *Faculty:* 53 full-time (29 women), 15 part-time/adjunct (6 women). Expenses: Contact institution. *Financial support:* In 2010–11, 1 fellowship (averaging $1,800 per year), 11 research assistantships (averaging $23,682 per year) were awarded; teaching assistantships, career-related internships or fieldwork and scholarships/grants also available. Support available to part-time students. In 2010, 104 master's, 113 doctorates, 7 other advanced degrees awarded. *Degree program information:* Part-time and evening/weekend programs available. Offers experimental technology in pharmaceutical sciences (Certificate); health systems pharmacy management (MS); hospital pharmacy (MS); medicinal chemistry (MS, PhD); nurse anesthesia (MS); nursing anesthesia (MS, Certificate); occupational and environmental health sciences (MPH, MS, Certificate, Post-Master's Certificate); occupational therapy (MOT, MS); pediatric nurse anesthesia (Certificate); pharmaceutical administration (MS, PhD); pharmaceutical sciences (MS, PhD); pharmaceutics (MS, PhD); pharmacology (MS, PhD); pharmacy (Pharm D); pharmacy and health sciences (Pharm D, MOT, MPT, MS, DPT, PhD, Certificate, Post-Master's Certificate); physical therapy (DPT); physician assistant studies (MS); radiologist assistant studies (MS). *Application deadline:* For fall admission, 6/1 for international students; for winter admission, 10/1 for international students; for spring admission, 2/1 for international students. Applications are processed on a rolling basis. *Application fee:* $30 ($50 for international students). Electronic applications accepted. *Application Contact:* William Lindblad, Associate Professor, 313-577-0513, E-mail: wlindbl@wayne.edu. *Dean*, Beverly J. Schmoll, 313-577-1574, Fax: 313-577-5589, E-mail: aj4682@wayne.edu.

Graduate School Students: 28 full-time (13 women); includes 2 minority (both Asian, non-Hispanic/Latino), 10 international. Average age 27. 35 applicants, 20% accepted, 7 enrolled. *Faculty:* 2 full-time (0 women). Expenses: Contact institution. *Financial support:* In 2010–11, 5 fellowships with partial tuition reimbursements (averaging $18,795 per year), 22 research assistantships with tuition reimbursements (averaging $22,148 per year) were awarded; teaching assistantships with tuition reimbursements, career-related internships or fieldwork, Federal Work-Study, institutionally sponsored loans, scholarships/grants, and tuition waivers (full and partial) also available. Support available to part-time students. In 2010, 1 master's, 4 other advanced degrees awarded. *Degree program information:* Part-time and evening/weekend programs available. Offers molecular and cellular toxicology (MS, PhD); molecular biology and genetics (MS, PhD). *Application deadline:* For fall admission, 8/1 priority date for domestic students, 6/1 for international students; for winter admission, 10/1 for international students; for spring admission, 2/1 for international students. Applications are processed on a rolling basis. *Application fee:* $30 ($50 for international students). Electronic applications accepted. *Application Contact:* Gary Schickler, Director, 313-577-9753, Fax: 313-577-3536. *Dean*, Dr. Steve Salley, 313-577-2170, Fax: 313-577-2903.

Law School Students: 533 full-time (236 women), 123 part-time (58 women); includes 101 minority (47 Black or African American, non-Hispanic/Latino; 5 American Indian or Alaska Native, non-Hispanic/Latino; 34 Asian, non-Hispanic/Latino; 15 Hispanic/Latino), 18 international. Average age 28. 629 applicants, 98% accepted, 206 enrolled. *Faculty:* 36 full-time (13 women), 25 part-time/adjunct (5 women). Expenses: Contact institution. *Financial support:* Federal Work-Study available. Support available to part-time students. Financial award application deadline: 4/30; financial award applicants required to submit FAFSA. In 2010, 149 first professional degrees, 6 master's awarded. *Degree program information:* Part-time and evening/weekend programs available. Offers law (JD, LL M, PhD). *Application deadline:* For fall admission, 4/15 for domestic students, 6/1 for international students; for winter admission, 10/1 for international students; for spring admission, 2/1 for international students. *Application fee:* $30 ($50 for international students). Electronic applications accepted. *Application Contact:* Linda Fowler Sims, Assistant Dean for Recruitment and Admissions, 313-577-3937, Fax: 313-577-9049, E-mail: ab2594@wayne.edu. *Dean*, Frank Wu, 313-577-3933, Fax: 313-577-2620, E-mail: aw7545@wayne.edu.

School of Business Administration Students: 240 full-time (99 women), 800 part-time (419 women); includes 325 minority (180 Black or African American, non-Hispanic/Latino; 1 American Indian or Alaska Native, non-Hispanic/Latino; 118 Asian, non-Hispanic/Latino; 22 Hispanic/Latino; 4 Two or more races, non-Hispanic/Latino), 152 international. Average age 28. 529 applicants, 71% accepted, 287 enrolled. *Faculty:* 40 full-time (10 women), 8 part-time/adjunct (0 women). Expenses: Contact institution. *Financial support:* In 2010–11, 17 research assistantships (averaging $15,000 per year) were awarded; career-related internships or fieldwork, Federal Work-Study, and scholarships/grants also available. Support available to part-time students. Financial award applicants required to submit FAFSA. In 2010, 345 degrees awarded. *Degree program information:* Part-time and evening/weekend programs available. Postbaccalaureate distance learning degree programs offered. Offers accounting (MSA); business administration (MBA, PhD); taxation (MST). *Application deadline:* For fall admission, 6/1 for domestic students, 3/1 for international students; for winter admission, 10/1 for domestic students, 6/1 for international students; for spring admission, 2/1 for domestic students, 10/1 for international students. Applications are processed on a rolling basis. *Application fee:* $50. Electronic applications accepted. *Application Contact:* Linda Zaddach, Assistant Dean, 313-577-4510, E-mail: l.s.zaddach@wayne.edu. *Interim Dean*, Dr. Margaret Williams, 313-577-4501, Fax: 313-577-4557.

School of Library and Information Science Students: 149 full-time (109 women), 463 part-time (352 women); includes 64 minority (42 Black or African American, non-Hispanic/Latino; 2 American Indian or Alaska Native, non-Hispanic/Latino; 12 Asian, non-Hispanic/Latino; 4 Hispanic/Latino; 1 Native Hawaiian or other Pacific Islander, non-Hispanic/Latino; 3 Two or more races, non-Hispanic/Latino), 4 international. Average age 33. 230 applicants, 86% accepted, 133 enrolled. *Faculty:* 13 full-time (9 women), 22 part-time/adjunct (16 women). Expenses: Contact institution. *Financial support:* Research assistantships, career-related internships or fieldwork, Federal Work-Study, institutionally sponsored loans, and scholarships/grants available. Support available to part-time students. Financial award application deadline:

Wayne State University (continued)

5/15. In 2010, 193 master's, 38 other advanced degrees awarded. *Degree program information:* Part-time and evening/weekend programs available. Offers archival administration (Certificate); library and information science (MLIS, Spec); school library media (Spec). *Application deadline:* For fall admission, 7/1 for domestic students, 6/1 for international students; for winter admission, 10/1 for international students; for spring admission, 2/1 for international students. Applications are processed on a rolling basis. *Application fee:* $30 ($50 for international students). Electronic applications accepted. *Application Contact:* Matt Fredericks, Academic Services Officer, 313-577-2446, E-mail: aj8416@wayne.edu. *Dean*, Sandra Yee, 313-577-4020, Fax: 313-577-7563, E-mail: aj0533@wayne.edu.

School of Medicine Students: 1,485 full-time (690 women), 131 part-time (62 women); includes 443 minority (102 Black or African American, non-Hispanic/Latino; 5 American Indian or Alaska Native, non-Hispanic/Latino; 289 Asian, non-Hispanic/Latino; 23 Hispanic/Latino; 1 Native Hawaiian or other Pacific Islander, non-Hispanic/Latino; 23 Two or more races, non-Hispanic/Latino), 119 international. Average age 26. 4,310 applicants, 17% accepted, 463 enrolled. *Faculty:* 49 full-time (9 women), 1 part-time/adjunct (0 women). Expenses: Contact institution. *Financial support:* In 2010–11, 31 fellowships (averaging $25,064 per year), 102 research assistantships with tuition reimbursements (averaging $22,148 per year) were awarded; teaching assistantships with tuition reimbursements, career-related internships or fieldwork, Federal Work-Study, institutionally sponsored loans, scholarships/grants, and tuition waivers (full and partial) also available. Support available to part-time students. In 2010, 270 first professional degrees, 62 master's, 18 doctorates, 10 other advanced degrees awarded. *Degree program information:* Part-time and evening/weekend programs available. Offers anatomy (MS, PhD); basic medical science (MS); biochemistry and molecular biology (MS, PhD); cancer biology (MS, PhD); community health (MS); community health services (Certificate); immunology and microbiology (MS, PhD); medical physics (PhD); medical research (MS); medicine (MD, MPH, MS, PhD, Certificate); pharmacology (MS, PhD); physiology (MS, PhD); psychiatry (MS); public health (MPH); public health practice (Certificate); radiological physics (MS); translational neuroscience (PhD). *Application deadline:* For fall admission, 6/1 for international students; for winter admission, 10/1 for international students; for spring admission, 2/1 for international students. Applications are processed on a rolling basis. *Application fee:* $30 ($50 for international students). Electronic applications accepted. *Application Contact:* Dr. Kenneth C. Palmer, Assistant Dean, 313-577-1455, E-mail: kpalmer@med.wayne.edu. *Dean*, Dr. Robert M. Mentzer, 313-577-1450, Fax: 313-577-8777, E-mail: rmentzer@wayne.edu.

Graduate Programs in Medicine Students: 98 full-time (48 women), 34 part-time (12 women); includes 1 Black or African American, non-Hispanic/Latino; 1 American Indian or Alaska Native, non-Hispanic/Latino; 26 Asian, non-Hispanic/Latino; 3 Hispanic/Latino, 7 international. Average age 24. 149 applicants, 70% accepted, 77 enrolled. Expenses: Contact institution. *Financial support:* Fellowships, research assistantships, teaching assistantships, career-related internships or fieldwork, Federal Work-Study, institutionally sponsored loans, scholarships/grants, and tuition waivers (full and partial) available. Support available to part-time students. In 2010, 42 master's awarded. *Degree program information:* Part-time and evening/weekend programs available. Offers genetic counseling (MS); medical physics (PhD); medicine (MS, PhD); pathology (MS, PhD); radiological physics (MS). *Application deadline:* For fall admission, 6/1 for international students; for winter admission, 10/1 for international students; for spring admission, 2/1 for international students. Applications are processed on a rolling basis. *Application fee:* $30 ($50 for international students). Electronic applications accepted. *Application Contact:* Dr. Kenneth C. Palmer, Assistant Dean, 313-577-1455, E-mail: kpalmer@med.wayne.edu. *Assistant Dean*, Dr. Kenneth C. Palmer, 313-577-1455, E-mail: kpalmer@med.wayne.edu.

School of Social Work Students: 451 full-time (406 women), 159 part-time (141 women); includes 198 minority (172 Black or African American, non-Hispanic/Latino; 1 American Indian or Alaska Native, non-Hispanic/Latino; 8 Asian, non-Hispanic/Latino; 9 Hispanic/Latino; 8 Two or more races, non-Hispanic/Latino), 18 international. Average age 32. 330 applicants, 63% accepted, 146 enrolled. *Faculty:* 19 full-time (11 women), 36 part-time/adjunct (26 women). Expenses: Contact institution. *Financial support:* In 2010–11, 2 fellowships (averaging $19,500 per year), 4 research assistantships with tuition reimbursements (averaging $17,123 per year) were awarded; teaching assistantships, career-related internships or fieldwork, institutionally sponsored loans, scholarships/grants, and tuition waivers (partial) also available. Support available to part-time students. Financial award application deadline: 5/1; financial award applicants required to submit FAFSA. In 2010, 231 master's, 17 other advanced degrees awarded. *Degree program information:* Part-time and evening/weekend programs available. Offers interdisciplinary studies (PhD); social work (MSW); social work practice with families and couples (Certificate). *Application deadline:* For fall admission, 3/31 for domestic students, 6/1 for international students; for winter admission, 10/1 for international students; for spring admission, 2/28 for domestic students, 2/1 for international students. Applications are processed on a rolling basis. *Application fee:* $20 ($30 for international students). Electronic applications accepted. *Application Contact:* Janet Joiner, Assistant Dean, 313-577-4409, Fax: 313-577-4266, E-mail: ac2027@wayne.edu. *Dean*, Phyllis Vroom, 313-577-4400, Fax: 313-577-8770, E-mail: aa8773@wayne.edu.

WEBBER INTERNATIONAL UNIVERSITY, Babson Park, FL 33827-0096

General Information Independent, coed, comprehensive institution.

GRADUATE UNITS

Graduate School of Business *Degree program information:* Part-time and evening/weekend programs available. Offers accounting (MBA); management (MBA); security management (MBA); sports management (MBA).

WEBER STATE UNIVERSITY, Ogden, UT 84408-1001

General Information State-supported, coed, comprehensive institution. *Graduate housing:* Rooms and/or apartments available on a first-come, first-served basis to single and married students. *Research affiliation:* Raytheon Training Corporation (education).

GRADUATE UNITS

College of Arts and Humanities *Degree program information:* Part-time and evening/weekend programs available. Offers arts and humanities (MENG); English (MENG).

College of Health Professions *Degree program information:* Part-time and evening/weekend programs available. Offers health administration (MHA); health professions (MHA).

College of Social and Behavioral Sciences *Degree program information:* Part-time and evening/weekend programs available. Offers criminal justice (MCJ); social and behavioral sciences (MCJ).

Jerry and Vickie Moyes College of Education *Degree program information:* Part-time and evening/weekend programs available. Offers athletic training (MSAT); curriculum and instruction (M Ed); education (M Ed, MSAT).

John B. Goddard School of Business and Economics *Degree program information:* Part-time and evening/weekend programs available. Postbaccalaureate distance learning degree programs offered. Offers accounting (M Acc); business administration (MBA); business and economics (M Acc, M Tax, MBA); taxation (M Tax). Electronic applications accepted.

WEBSTER UNIVERSITY, St. Louis, MO 63119-3194

General Information Independent, coed, comprehensive institution. *Enrollment:* 4,189 full-time matriculated graduate/professional students (2,214 women), 11,942 part-time matriculated graduate/professional students (7,158 women). *Enrollment by degree level:* 15,830 master's, 61 doctoral, 240 other advanced degrees. *Graduate faculty:* 145 full-time, 1,485 part-time/adjunct. *Tuition:* Part-time $585 per credit hour. Tuition and fees vary according to degree level, campus/location and program. *Graduate housing:* Room and/or apartments available on a first-come, first-served basis to single students; on-campus housing not available to married students. Typical cost: $4970 per year ($9290 including board). Room and board charges vary according to board plan and housing facility selected. Housing application deadline: 7/1. *Student services:* Campus employment opportunities, campus safety program, career counseling, exercise/wellness program, free psychological counseling, international student services, multicultural affairs office, services for students with disabilities, teacher training, writing training. *Library facilities:* Emerson Library. *Online resources:* library catalog, web page, access to other libraries' catalogs. *Collection:* 279,928 titles, 1,536 serial subscriptions, 23,331 audiovisual materials. *Research affiliation:* Literacy Investment for Tomorrow.

Computer facilities: Computer purchase and lease plans are available. 450 computers available on campus for general student use. A campuswide network can be accessed from student residence rooms. Online class registration is available. *Web address:* http://www.webster.edu/.

General Application Contact: Associate Vice President for Enrollment Management/Dean of Admissions, 314-968-7089, Fax: 314-968-7462, E-mail: gadmit@webster.edu.

GRADUATE UNITS

College of Arts and Sciences *Degree program information:* Part-time and evening/weekend programs available. Postbaccalaureate distance learning degree programs offered. Offers arts and sciences (MA, MS, MSN, Certificate); counseling (MA); environmental management (MS); gerontology (MA); healthcare leadership (Certificate); intellectual property paralegal studies (Certificate); international nongovernmental organizations (MA); international relations (MA); legal analysis (MA); legal studies (MA); nurse anesthesia (MS); nursing (MSN); paralegal studies (Certificate); patent agency (MA); professional science management and leadership (MA).

George Herbert Walker School of Business and Technology *Degree program information:* Part-time and evening/weekend programs available. Postbaccalaureate distance learning degree programs offered (no on-campus study). Offers business (MA); business and organizational security management (MA, MBA); business and technology (MA, MBA, MHA, MPA, MS, DM, Certificate); computer resources and information management (MA, MBA); computer science/distributed systems (MS, Certificate); decision support systems (Certificate); environmental management (MBA, MS); finance (MA, MBA); government contracting (Certificate); health care management (MA); health services management (MA, MBA); human resources development (MA, MBA); human resources management (MA, MBA); international business (MA, MBA); management (DM); management and leadership (MA, MBA); marketing (MA, MBA); nonprofit management (Certificate); procurement and acquisitions management (MA, MBA); public administration (MA); quality management (MA, MBA); space systems operations management (MS); telecommunications management (MA, MBA); web services (Certificate).

Leigh Gerdine College of Fine Arts *Degree program information:* Part-time and evening/weekend programs available. Offers art (MA); arts management and leadership (MFA); church music (MM); composition (MM); conducting (MM); fine arts (MA, MFA, MM); jazz studies (MM); music (MA); music education (MM); performance (MM); piano (MM).

School of Communications *Degree program information:* Part-time and evening/weekend programs available. Postbaccalaureate distance learning degree programs offered. Offers advertising and marketing communications (MA); communications (MA); communications management (MA); media communications (MA); media literacy (MA); public relations (MA).

School of Education *Degree program information:* Part-time programs available. Postbaccalaureate distance learning degree programs offered (no on-campus study). Offers administrative leadership (Ed S); communications (MAT); early childhood education (MAT); education (MAT, Ed S); education leadership (Ed S); educational technology (MAT); mathematics (MAT); multidisciplinary studies (MAT); school systems, superintendency and leadership (Ed S); social science (MAT); special education (MAT).

WENTWORTH INSTITUTE OF TECHNOLOGY, Boston, MA 02115-5998

General Information Independent, coed, comprehensive institution. *Enrollment:* 3,845 graduate, professional, and undergraduate students; 78 full-time matriculated graduate/professional students (26 women), 28 part-time matriculated graduate/professional students (3 women). *Enrollment by degree level:* 106 master's. *Graduate faculty:* 22 full-time (5 women), 26 part-time/adjunct (7 women). *Tuition:* Full-time $31,200; part-time $1130 per credit hour. *Required fees:* $1000. *Graduate housing:* Room and/or apartments available on a first-come, first-served basis to single students; on-campus housing not available to married students. Typical cost: $11,300 (including board). Housing application deadline: 5/1. *Student services:* Campus employment opportunities, career counseling, exercise/wellness program, international student services, low-cost health insurance, multicultural affairs office, services for students with disabilities. *Library facilities:* Wentworth Alumni Library. *Online resources:* library catalog, web page, access to other libraries' catalogs. *Collection:* 124,694 titles, 37,974 serial subscriptions, 2,924 audiovisual materials.

Computer facilities: Computer purchase and lease plans are available. 120 computers available on campus for general student use. A campuswide network can be accessed from student residence rooms and from off campus. Online class registration is available. *Web address:* http://www.wit.edu/.

General Application Contact: Maureen Dischino, Executive Director of Admissions, 617-989-4009, Fax: 617-989-4010, E-mail: dischinom@wit.edu.

GRADUATE UNITS

Construction Management Program Students: 28 part-time (3 women); includes 3 Black or African American, non-Hispanic/Latino; 1 Asian, non-Hispanic/Latino; 1 Hispanic/Latino. Average age 36. 32 applicants, 97% accepted, 28 enrolled. *Faculty:* 5 full-time (1 woman), 4 part-time/adjunct (2 women). Expenses: Contact institution. *Financial support:* Application deadline: 5/1. *Degree program information:* Part-time and evening/weekend programs available. Offers construction management (MS). *Application deadline:* For fall admission, 5/1 for domestic students. *Application fee:* $50. *Application Contact:* Jacklyn Haas, Associate Director of Admissions for Continuing Education, 617-989-4258, Fax: 617-989-4399, E-mail: haasj@wit.edu. *Director*, Carl Sciple, 617-989-4817, Fax: 617-989-4399, E-mail: sciplec@wit.edu.

Department of Architecture Students: 78 full-time (26 women); includes 3 Asian, non-Hispanic/Latino; 2 Hispanic/Latino; 1 Two or more races, non-Hispanic/Latino, 6 international. Average age 23. 108 applicants, 78% accepted, 78 enrolled. *Faculty:* 17 full-time (4 women), 22 part-time/adjunct (5 women). Expenses: Contact institution. *Financial support:* In 2010–11, 78 students received support, including 78 fellowships (averaging $4,475 per year); Federal Work-Study and scholarships/grants also available. Financial award applicants required to submit FAFSA. Offers architecture (M Arch). *Application deadline:* For fall admission, 1/15 priority date for domestic and international students. Applications are processed on a rolling basis. *Application fee:* $50. Electronic applications accepted. *Application Contact:* Maureen Dischino, Executive Director of Admissions, 617-989-4009, Fax: 617-989-4010, E-mail: dischinom@wit.edu. *Dean of the College of Architecture, Design and Construction Management*, Dr. Glenn Wiggins, 617-989-4470, E-mail: wigginsg@wit.edu.

WESLEYAN COLLEGE, Macon, GA 31210-4462

General Information Independent-religious, Undergraduate: women only; graduate: coed, comprehensive institution. *Enrollment:* 671 graduate, professional, and undergraduate students; 57 full-time matriculated graduate/professional students (48 women), 6 part-time matriculated graduate/professional students (all women). *Enrollment by degree level:* 63 master's. *Graduate faculty:* 9 full-time (7 women), 9 part-time/adjunct (6 women). *Graduate housing:* Room and/or apartments available on a first-come, first-served basis to single students; on-campus housing not available to married students. Typical cost: $8100 (including board). Housing application deadline: 5/1. *Student services:* Campus safety program, career counseling, exercise/wellness program, low-cost health insurance, teacher training, writing training. *Library facilities:* Willet Memorial Library. *Online resources:* library catalog, web page, access to other libraries' catalogs. *Collection:* 145,571 titles, 431 serial subscriptions, 4,420 audiovisual materials.

Computer facilities: 22 computers available on campus for general student use. A campuswide network can be accessed from student residence rooms and from off campus. Online class registration, online payment are available. *Web address:* http://www.wesleyancollege.edu/.

General Application Contact: Danielle Lodge, Director, Recruiting and Non-Traditional Programs, 478-757-5263, Fax: 478-757-5148, E-mail: dlodge@wesleyancollege.edu.

GRADUATE UNITS

Department of Business and Economics Offers business administration (EMBA); business and economics (EMBA).

Department of Education *Degree program information:* Part-time programs available. Offers early childhood education (MA).

WESLEYAN UNIVERSITY, Middletown, CT 06459

General Information Independent, coed, university. CGS member. *Enrollment:* 3,215 graduate, professional, and undergraduate students; 162 full-time matriculated graduate/professional students (79 women). *Enrollment by degree level:* 54 master's, 88 doctoral. *Graduate faculty:* 76 full-time (21 women), 2 part-time/adjunct (both women). *Tuition:* Full-time $43,404. *Required fees:* $830. *Graduate housing:* Rooms and/or apartments available on a first-come, first-served basis to single and married students. Typical cost: $9084 per year for single students; $10,494 per year for married students. Room charges vary according to housing facility selected. Housing application deadline: 7/15. *Student services:* Campus employment opportunities, campus safety program, career counseling, child daycare facilities, exercise/wellness program, free psychological counseling, international student services, low-cost health insurance, multicultural affairs office, writing training. *Library facilities:* Olin Memorial Library. *Online resources:* library catalog, web page, access to other libraries' catalogs. *Research affiliation:* Woods Hole Oceanographic Institution, Cold Spring Harbor Laboratory.

Computer facilities: Computer purchase and lease plans are available. 1,600 computers available on campus for general student use. A campuswide network can be accessed from student residence rooms and from off campus. Online class registration, electronic portfolio, online course drop/add, Blackboard course management system are available. *Web address:* http://www.wesleyan.edu/.

General Application Contact: Jennifer Kriksciun, Interim Director, Graduate Program Student Services, 860-685-2390, Fax: 860-685-2439, E-mail: jkriksciun@wesleyan.edu.

GRADUATE UNITS

Graduate Liberal Studies Program Expenses: Contact institution. *Financial support:* Scholarships/grants available. Support available to part-time students. *Degree program information:* Part-time and evening/weekend programs available. Offers liberal studies (MALS, CAS). *Application deadline:* For fall admission, 6/20 for domestic students; for spring admission, 11/7 for domestic students. Applications are processed on a rolling basis. *Application fee:* $100. *Application Contact:* Jennifer M. Curran, Assistant Director, Admissions and Outreach, 860-685-3338, Fax: 860-685-2901, E-mail: jcurran@wesleyan.edu. *Director*, Sheryl Culotta, 860-685-3008, Fax: 860-685-2901, E-mail: sculotta@wesleyan.edu.

Graduate Programs Students: 137 full-time (63 women); includes 6 Black or African American, non-Hispanic/Latino; 2 American Indian or Alaska Native, non-Hispanic/Latino; 33 Asian, non-Hispanic/Latino; 11 Hispanic/Latino. Average age 27. 302 applicants, 19% accepted, 28 enrolled. *Faculty:* 76 full-time (21 women), 2 part-time/adjunct (both women). Expenses: Contact institution. *Financial support:* In 2010–11, 29 research assistantships with tuition reimbursements, 101 teaching assistantships with tuition reimbursements were awarded; fellowships with tuition reimbursements, institutionally sponsored loans and tuition waivers (full and partial) also available. Financial award application deadline: 4/15; financial award applicants required to submit FAFSA. In 2010, 36 master's, 10 doctorates awarded. Offers animal behavior (PhD); astronomy (MA); biochemistry (MA, PhD); bioformatics/genomics (PhD); cell biology (PhD); chemical physics (MA, PhD); composition (MA); developmental biology (PhD); earth and environmental sciences (MA); ethnomusicology (MA, PhD); evolution/ecology (PhD); genetics (PhD); inorganic chemistry (MA, PhD); mathematics and computer science (MA, PhD); molecular biology (PhD); neurobiology (PhD); organic chemistry (MA, PhD); physical chemistry (MA, PhD); physics (MA, PhD); population biology (PhD); theoretical chemistry (MA, PhD). *Application deadline:* Applications are processed on a rolling basis. Electronic applications accepted. *Application Contact:* Dr. Ishita Mukerji, Director of Graduate Studies, 860-685-2422, E-mail: imukerji@wesleyan.edu. *Director of Graduate Studies*, Dr. Ishita Mukerji, 860-685-2422, E-mail: imukerji@wesleyan.edu.

WESLEY BIBLICAL SEMINARY, Jackson, MS 39206

General Information Independent-religious, coed, graduate-only institution. *Graduate housing:* Room and/or apartments available on a first-come, first-served basis to single students; on-campus housing not available to married students. Housing application deadline: 7/30.

GRADUATE UNITS

Graduate Programs *Degree program information:* Part-time programs available. Offers apologetics (MA); Biblical studies (MA); Christian studies (MA); evangelism (M Div); family life ministry (M Div); honors research (M Div); missions (M Div); pastoral ministry (M Div); teaching (M Div); theological studies (MA). Electronic applications accepted.

WESLEY COLLEGE, Dover, DE 19901-3875

General Information Independent-religious, coed, comprehensive institution. *Graduate housing:* On-campus housing not available.

GRADUATE UNITS

Business Program *Degree program information:* Part-time and evening/weekend programs available. Offers environmental management (MBA); executive leadership (MBA); management (MBA). Executive leadership concentration also offered at New Castle, DE location.

Education Program *Degree program information:* Part-time and evening/weekend programs available. Offers education (M Ed, MA Ed, MAT).

Environmental Studies Program *Degree program information:* Part-time and evening/weekend programs available. Offers environmental studies (MS).

Nursing Program *Degree program information:* Part-time and evening/weekend programs available. Offers nursing (MSN). Electronic applications accepted.

WESLEY THEOLOGICAL SEMINARY, Washington, DC 20016-5690

General Information Independent-religious, coed, graduate-only institution. *Graduate housing:* Rooms and/or apartments available to single and married students. Housing application deadline: 7/1.

GRADUATE UNITS

Graduate and Professional Programs *Degree program information:* Part-time programs available. Offers theology (M Div, MA, MTS, D Min).

WEST CHESTER UNIVERSITY OF PENNSYLVANIA, West Chester, PA 19383

General Information State-supported, coed, comprehensive institution. CGS member. *Enrollment:* 14,490 graduate, professional, and undergraduate students; 667 full-time matriculated graduate/professional students (478 women), 1,102 part-time matriculated graduate/professional students (790 women). *Enrollment by degree level:* 1,720 master's, 49 other advanced degrees. Tuition, state resident: full-time $6966; part-time $387 per credit. Tuition, nonresident: full-time $11,146; part-time $619 per credit. *Required fees:* $1614; $133.24 per credit. Part-time tuition and fees vary according to campus/location. *Graduate housing:* Room and/or apartments available on a first-come, first-served basis to single students; on-campus housing not available to married students. Housing application deadline: 5/1. *Student services:* Campus employment opportunities, campus safety program, career counseling, child daycare facilities, exercise/wellness program, free psychological counseling, grant writing training, international student services, low-cost health insurance, multicultural affairs office, services for students with disabilities, teacher training, writing training. *Library facilities:* Francis Harvey Green Library plus 1 other. *Online resources:* library catalog, web page, access to other libraries' catalogs. *Collection:* 1.3 million titles, 21,125 serial

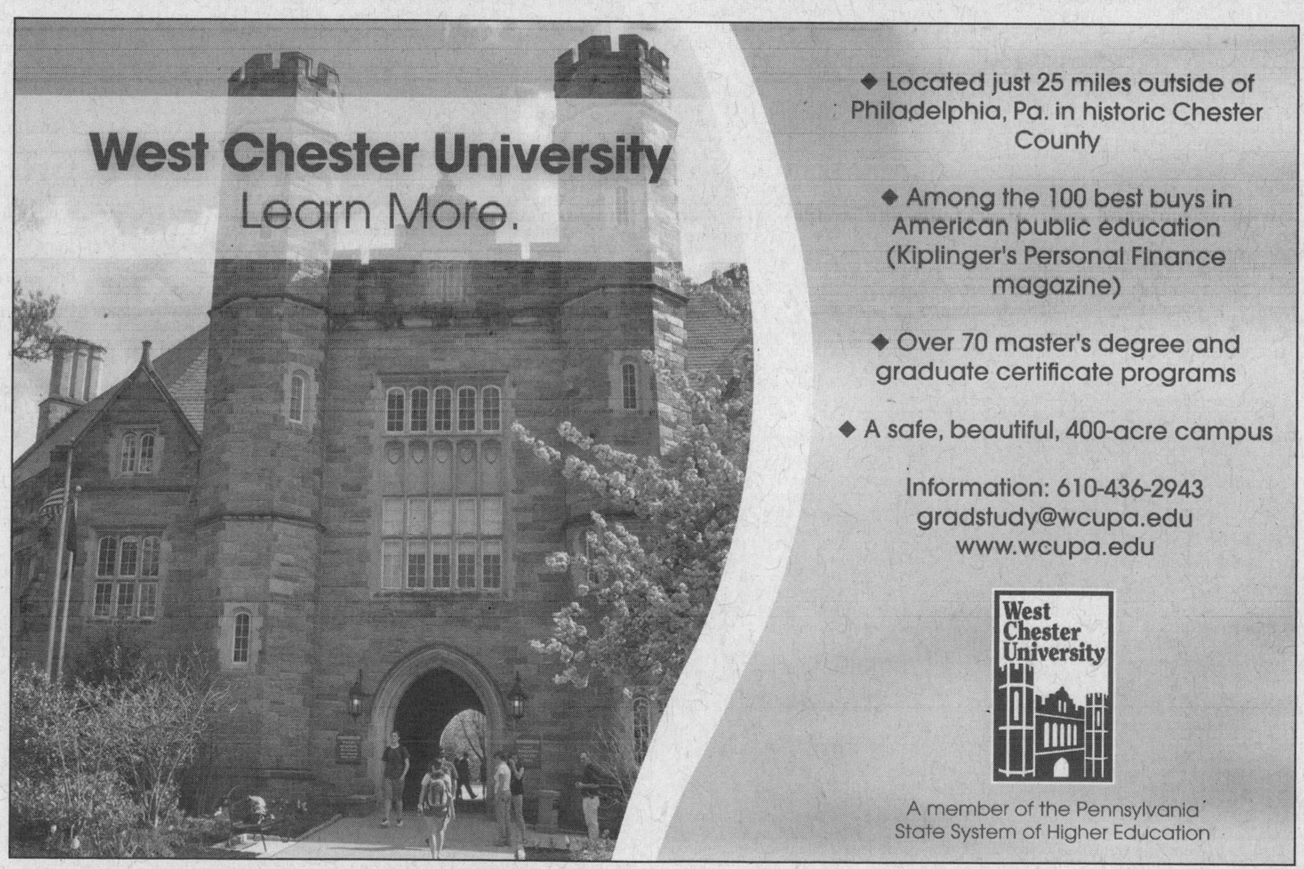

West Chester University of Pennsylvania (continued)

subscriptions, 140,044 audiovisual materials. *Research affiliation:* Agilent Technologies (chemistry), Hewlett-Packard (computer science), BASF (biology), HEAT Institute (health sciences), ENDO Pharmaceuticals (biology), Adidas (kinesiology).

Computer facilities: Computer purchase and lease plans are available. 1,700 computers available on campus for general student use. A campuswide network can be accessed from student residence rooms and from off campus. Online class registration is available. *Web address:* http://www.wcupa.edu/.

General Application Contact: Office of Graduate Studies, 610-436-2943, Fax: 610-436-2763, E-mail: gradstudy@wcupa.edu.

GRADUATE UNITS

Office of Graduate Studies Students: 667 full-time (478 women), 1,102 part-time (790 women); includes 265 minority (176 Black or African American, non-Hispanic/Latino; 6 American Indian or Alaska Native, non-Hispanic/Latino; 42 Asian, non-Hispanic/Latino; 40 Hispanic/Latino; 1 Two or more races, non-Hispanic/Latino), 58 international. Average age 30. 1,682 applicants, 64% accepted, 426 enrolled. Expenses: Contact institution. *Financial support:* Unspecified assistantships available. Support available to part-time students. Financial award application deadline: 2/15; financial award applicants required to submit FAFSA. In 2010, 626 master's, 56 other advanced degrees awarded. *Degree program information:* Part-time and evening/weekend programs available. *Application deadline:* For fall admission, 4/15 priority date for domestic students, 3/15 for international students; for spring admission, 10/15 for domestic students, 9/1 for international students. Applications are processed on a rolling basis. *Application fee:* $35. Electronic applications accepted. *Application Contact:* Office of Graduate Studies, 610-436-2943, Fax: 610-436-2763, E-mail: gradstudy@wcupa.edu. *Interim Dean*, Dr. Janet Susan Hickman, 610-436-2943, Fax: 610-436-2763, E-mail: jhickman@wcupa.edu.

College of Arts and Sciences Students: 199 full-time (121 women), 296 part-time (171 women); includes 73 minority (31 Black or African American, non-Hispanic/Latino; 1 American Indian or Alaska Native, non-Hispanic/Latino; 23 Asian, non-Hispanic/Latino; 18 Hispanic/Latino), 21 international. Average age 30. 497 applicants, 68% accepted, 145 enrolled. Expenses: Contact institution. *Financial support:* Unspecified assistantships available. Support available to part-time students. Financial award application deadline: 2/15; financial award applicants required to submit FAFSA. In 2010, 165 master's, 7 other advanced degrees awarded. *Degree program information:* Part-time and evening/weekend programs available. Offers applied statistics (MS, Certificate); arts and sciences (M Ed, MA, MPA, MS, MSA, Certificate, Teaching Certificate); biology (MS, Teaching Certificate); biology—thesis (MS); business ethics (Certificate); chemistry (Teaching Certificate); clinical mental health (Certificate); clinical psychology (MA); communication studies (MA); computer science (MS); computer security (Certificate); earth-space science (Teaching Certificate); English (MA, Teaching Certificate); French (M Ed, MA, Teaching Certificate); general psychology (MA); general science (Teaching Certificate); geoscience (MA); gerontology (Certificate); healthcare ethics (Certificate); history (M Ed, MA); holocaust and genocide studies (MA, Certificate); industrial psychology (MA); information systems (Certificate); long term health care (MPA, MSA); mathematics (MA, Teaching Certificate); philosophy: applied ethics (MA); philosophy: general (MA); physics (Teaching Certificate); Spanish (M Ed, MA, Teaching Certificate); TESL (MA, Certificate); Web technology (Certificate). *Application deadline:* For fall admission, 4/15 priority date for domestic students, 3/15 for international students; for spring admission, 10/15 for domestic students, 9/1 for international students. Applications are processed on a rolling basis. *Application fee:* $35. Electronic applications accepted. *Application Contact:* Office of Graduate Studies, 610-436-2943, Fax: 610-436-2763, E-mail: gradstudy@wcupa.edu. *Dean*, Dr. Lori Vermeulen, 610-436-3521, Fax: 610-436-3150, E-mail: lvermeulen@wcupa.edu.

College of Business and Public Affairs Students: 134 full-time (97 women), 186 part-time (106 women); includes 57 minority (42 Black or African American, non-Hispanic/Latino; 1 American Indian or Alaska Native, non-Hispanic/Latino; 4 Asian, non-Hispanic/Latino; 10 Hispanic/Latino), 6 international. Average age 30. 237 applicants, 92% accepted, 98 enrolled. Expenses: Contact institution. *Financial support:* Career-related internships or fieldwork and unspecified assistantships available. Support available to part-time students. Financial award application deadline: 2/15; financial award applicants required to submit FAFSA. In 2010, 113 master's, 19 other advanced degrees awarded. *Degree program information:* Part-time and evening/weekend programs available. Offers business (Certificate); business and public affairs (MA, MBA, MPA, MS, MSA, MSW, Certificate); criminal justice (MS); general business (MBA); general public administration (MPA); geographic technology (Certificate); geography (MA); human resource management (MPA, Certificate); marketing (MBA); non profit administration (Certificate); nonprofit administration (MPA); public administration (Certificate); regional planning (MPA, MSA); social work (MSW); urban regional planning (Certificate). *Application deadline:* For fall admission, 4/15 priority date for domestic students, 3/15 for international students; for spring admission, 10/15 for domestic students, 9/1 for international students. Applications are processed on a rolling basis. *Application fee:* $35. Electronic applications accepted. *Application Contact:* Office of Graduate Studies, 610-436-2943, Fax: 610-436-2763, E-mail: gradstudy@wcupa.edu. *Dean*, Dr. Christopher Fiorentino, 610-436-2824, E-mail: cfiorentino@wcupa.edu.

College of Education Students: 135 full-time (114 women), 165 part-time (122 women); includes 50 minority (35 Black or African American, non-Hispanic/Latino; 2 American Indian or Alaska Native, non-Hispanic/Latino; 4 Asian, non-Hispanic/Latino; 9 Hispanic/Latino). Average age 29. 389 applicants, 71% accepted, 64 enrolled. Expenses: Contact institution. *Financial support:* Unspecified assistantships available. Support available to part-time students. Financial award application deadline: 2/15; financial award applicants required to submit FAFSA. In 2010, 211 master's, 16 other advanced degrees awarded. *Degree program information:* Part-time and evening/weekend programs available. Offers applied studies in teaching and learning (M Ed); autism (Certificate); counseling (Teaching Certificate); early childhood education (M Ed, Teaching Certificate); education (M Ed, MS, Certificate, Teaching Certificate); education for sustainability (Certificate); elementary education (Teaching Certificate); elementary school counseling (M Ed); entrepreneurial education (Certificate); higher education counseling (MS); literacy (Certificate); literacy coaching (Certificate); professional counselor license preparation (Certificate); reading (M Ed, Teaching Certificate); secondary education (M Ed, Teaching Certificate); secondary school counseling (M Ed); special education (M Ed, Certificate, Teaching Certificate); special education: distance education (M Ed); teaching and learning with technology (Certificate); universal design for learning and assistive technology (Certificate); universal design for learning and assistive technology: distance education (Certificate). *Application deadline:* For fall admission, 4/15 priority date for domestic students, 3/15 for international students; for spring admission, 10/15 for domestic students, 9/1 for international students. Applications are processed on a rolling basis. *Application fee:* $35. Electronic applications accepted. *Application Contact:* Office of Graduate Studies, 610-436-2943, Fax: 610-436-2763, E-mail: gradstudy@wcupa.edu. *Interim Dean*, Dr. George P. Drake, 610-436-2321, E-mail: gdrake@wcupa.edu.

College of Health Sciences Students: 180 full-time (137 women), 165 part-time (122 women); includes 80 minority (65 Black or African American, non-Hispanic/Latino; 2 American Indian or Alaska Native, non-Hispanic/Latino; 9 Asian, non-Hispanic/Latino; 3 Hispanic/Latino; 1 Two or more races, non-Hispanic/Latino), 25 international. Average age 31. 406 applicants, 52% accepted, 106 enrolled. Expenses: Contact institution. *Financial support:* Unspecified assistantships available. Support available to part-time students. Financial award application deadline: 2/15; financial award applicants required to submit FAFSA. In 2010, 109 master's, 9 other advanced degrees awarded. *Degree program information:* Part-time and evening/weekend programs available. Offers adapted physical education (Certificate); communicative disorders (MA); emergency preparedness (Certificate); exercise/sport physiology (MS); health and physical education (MS, Teaching Certificate); health care management (MPH, Certificate); health sciences (M Ed, MA, MPA, MPH, MS, MSA, MSN, Certificate, Teaching Certificate); integrative health (Certificate); nursing education (Certificate); physical education (MS); public health nursing (MSN); school health (M Ed); school nursing (Teaching Certificate); speech correction (Teaching Certificate); sport management and athletics (MPA, MSA, Certificate). *Application deadline:* For fall admission, 4/15 priority date for domestic students, 3/15 for international students; for spring admission, 10/15 for domestic students, 9/1 for international students. Applications are processed on a rolling basis. *Application fee:* $35. Electronic applications accepted. *Application Contact:* Office of Graduate Studies, 610-436-2943, Fax: 610-436-2763, E-mail: gradstudy@wcupa.edu. *Dean*, Dr. Donald E. Barr, 610-436-2938, Fax: 610-436-2860, E-mail: dbarr@wcupa.edu.

College of Visual and Performing Arts Students: 19 full-time (9 women), 49 part-time (30 women); includes 5 minority (3 Black or African American, non-Hispanic/Latino; 2 Asian, non-Hispanic/Latino), 6 international. Average age 28. 53 applicants, 72% accepted, 13 enrolled. Expenses: Contact institution. *Financial support:* Unspecified assistantships available. Support available to part-time students. Financial award application deadline: 2/15; financial award applicants required to submit FAFSA. In 2010, 28 master's, 5 other advanced degrees awarded. *Degree program information:* Part-time and evening/weekend programs available. Offers accompanying (MM); Kodaly methodology (Certificate); music education (Teaching Certificate); music history (MA); music technology (Certificate); music: composition (MM); music: history and literature (MM); music: theory and composition (MM); Orff-Schulwerk (Certificate); performance (MM); piano pedagogy (MM, Certificate); research (MM); technology (MM); twenty-first century music education (Certificate); visual and performing arts (MA, MM, Certificate, Teaching Certificate). *Application deadline:* For fall admission, 4/15 priority date for domestic students, 3/15 for international students; for spring admission, 10/15 for domestic students, 9/1 for international students. Applications are processed on a rolling basis. *Application fee:* $35. Electronic applications accepted. *Application Contact:* Dr. J. Bryan Burton, Graduate Coordinator, 610-436-2222, E-mail: jburton@wcupa.edu. *Dean*, Dr. Timothy Blair, 610-436-2489, Fax: 610-436-2873, E-mail: tblair@wcupa.edu.

See Display on previous page and Close-Up on page 999.

WESTERN CAROLINA UNIVERSITY, Cullowhee, NC 28723

General Information State-supported, coed, comprehensive institution. CGS member. *Graduate housing:* Rooms and/or apartments available to single students and guaranteed to married students. *Research affiliation:* North Carolina Center for the Advancement of Teaching.

GRADUATE UNITS

Graduate School *Degree program information:* Part-time and evening/weekend programs available. Postbaccalaureate distance learning degree programs offered.

College of Arts and Sciences *Degree program information:* Part-time and evening/weekend programs available. Offers applied mathematics (MS); arts and sciences (MA, MPA, MS); biology (MS); chemistry (MS); English (MA); history (MA); political science and public affairs (MPA); teaching English as a second language or foreign language (MA).

College of Business *Degree program information:* Part-time and evening/weekend programs available. Postbaccalaureate distance learning degree programs offered. Offers accountancy (M Ac); business administration (MBA); entrepreneurship (ME); project management (MPM).

College of Education and Allied Professions *Degree program information:* Part-time and evening/weekend programs available. Postbaccalaureate distance learning degree programs offered. Offers community college administration (MA Ed); community college and higher education (MA Ed); community college teaching (MA Ed); community counseling (M Ed, MS); comprehensive education (MA Ed, MAT); counseling (M Ed, MA Ed, MS); education and allied professions (M Ed, MA, MA Ed, MAT, MS, MSA, Ed D, Ed S, PMC); educational leadership (MA Ed, MSA, Ed D, Ed S); educational supervision (MA Ed); general psychology (MA); human resources (MS); physical education (MA Ed); school counseling (MA Ed); school psychology (MA); teaching (MA Ed, MAT).

College of Fine and Performing Arts *Degree program information:* Part-time programs available. Offers art and design (MFA); comprehensive education: music (MA Ed, MAT); fine and performing arts (MA Ed, MAT, MFA, MM); music (MM).

College of Health and Human Sciences *Degree program information:* Part-time and evening/weekend programs available. Offers communication sciences and disorders (MS); health and human sciences (MHS, MPT, MS, MSN, MSW, PMC); health sciences (MHS); nurse educator (PMC); nursing (MSN); physical therapy (MPT); social work (MSW).

Kimmel School of Construction Management and Technology *Degree program information:* Part-time and evening/weekend programs available. Postbaccalaureate distance learning degree programs offered. Offers construction management (MCM); construction management and technology (MCM, MS); engineering and technology (MS).

WESTERN CONNECTICUT STATE UNIVERSITY, Danbury, CT 06810-6885

General Information State-supported, coed, comprehensive institution. CGS member. *Enrollment:* 6,582 graduate, professional, and undergraduate students; 90 full-time matriculated graduate/professional students (55 women), 466 part-time matriculated graduate/professional students (327 women). *Enrollment by degree level:* 497 master's, 49 doctoral, 10 other advanced degrees. *Graduate faculty:* 55 full-time (24 women), 49 part-time/adjunct (17 women). Tuition, state resident: full-time $5012; part-time $417 per credit hour. Tuition, nonresident: full-time $13,962; part-time $423 per credit hour. *Required fees:* $3886. Full-time tuition and fees vary according to course load, degree level and program. *Graduate housing:* Rooms and/or apartments available on a first-come, first-served basis to single and married students. Typical cost: $5698 per year ($9970 including board) for single students; $11,396 per year ($19,940 including board) for married students. Room and board charges vary according to board plan and housing facility selected. Housing application deadline: 4/1. *Student services:* Campus employment opportunities, career counseling, child daycare facilities, free psychological counseling, international student services, low-cost health insurance, multicultural affairs office, services for students with disabilities. *Library facilities:* Ruth Haas Library. *Online resources:* library catalog, web page, access to other libraries' catalogs. *Research affiliation:* The Jane Goodall Institute, Center for Financial Forensics and Informational Security, New England Educational Assessment Network, American Society for Microbiology, National Undergraduate Research Center, Smithsonian Institution Affiliations Program.

Computer facilities: A campuswide network can be accessed from student residence rooms and from off campus. Online class registration is available. *Web address:* http://www.wcsu.edu/.

General Application Contact: Chris Shankle, Associate Director of Graduate Studies, 203-837-9005, Fax: 203-837-8326, E-mail: shanklec@wcsu.edu.

GRADUATE UNITS

Division of Graduate Studies and External Programs Students: 90 full-time (55 women), 466 part-time (327 women); includes 40 minority (9 Black or African American, non-Hispanic/Latino; 7 Asian, non-Hispanic/Latino; 21 Hispanic/Latino; 3 Two or more races, non-Hispanic/Latino). Average age 35. 329 applicants, 50% accepted, 105 enrolled. *Faculty:* 55 full-time (24 women), 49 part-time/adjunct (17 women). Expenses: Contact institution. *Financial support:* In 2010–11, 17 students received support. Scholarships/grants available. Financial award application deadline: 5/1; financial award applicants required to submit FAFSA. In 2010, 175 master's, 11 doctorates awarded. *Degree program information:* Part-time programs available. *Application deadline:* For fall admission, 8/5 priority date for domestic students, 3/1 priority date for international students; for spring admission, 1/5 priority date for domestic students, 10/1 for international students. Applications are processed on a rolling basis. *Application fee:* $50. *Application Contact:* Chris Shankle, Associate Director of Graduate Studies, 203-837-9005, Fax: 203-837-8326, E-mail: shanklec@wcsu.edu. *Interim Dean*, Dr. Burton Peretti, 203-837-8386, Fax: 203-837-8326, E-mail: perettib@wcsu.edu.

Ancell School of Business Students: 8 full-time (3 women), 78 part-time (43 women); includes 9 minority (1 Black or African American, non-Hispanic/Latino; 4 Asian, non-Hispanic/Latino; 4 Hispanic/Latino). Average age 36. Expenses: Contact institution. *Financial support:* In 2010–11, 1 student received support. Scholarships/grants available. Financial award application deadline: 5/1; financial award applicants required to submit FAFSA. In 2010, 27 master's awarded. *Degree program information:* Part-time programs available. Offers accounting (MBA); business (MBA, MHA, MS); business administration (MBA); health administration (MHA); justice administration (MS). *Application deadline:* For fall admission, 8/5 priority date for domestic students; for spring admission, 1/5 priority date for domestic students. Applications are processed on a rolling basis. *Application fee:* $50. *Application Contact:* Chris Shankle, Associate Director of Graduate Studies, 203-837-9005, Fax: 203-837-8326, E-mail: shanklec@wcsu.edu. *Dean,* Dr. Allen Morton, 203-837-9600, Fax: 203-837-8527, E-mail: mortona@wcsu.edu.

School of Arts and Sciences Students: 43 full-time (22 women), 79 part-time (42 women); includes 11 minority (4 Black or African American, non-Hispanic/Latino; 6 Hispanic/Latino; 1 Two or more races, non-Hispanic/Latino). Average age 35. Expenses: Contact institution. *Financial support:* In 2010–11, 1 student received support. Scholarships/grants available. Financial award application deadline: 5/1; financial award applicants required to submit FAFSA. In 2010, 33 master's awarded. *Degree program information:* Part-time programs available. Offers arts and sciences (MA, MFA); biological and environmental sciences (MA); earth and planetary sciences (MA); English (MA); history (MA); literature option (MA); mathematics (MA); professional writing (MFA); TESOL option (MA); theoretical mathematics (MA); writing option (MA). *Application deadline:* For fall admission, 8/5 priority date for domestic students; for spring admission, 1/5 priority date for domestic students. Applications are processed on a rolling basis. *Application fee:* $50. *Application Contact:* Chris Shankle, Associate Director of Graduate Studies, 203-837-9005, Fax: 203-837-8326, E-mail: shanklec@wcsu.edu. *Interim Dean,* Dr. Abbey Zink, 203-837-8839, Fax: 203-837-8525, E-mail: zinka@wcsu.edu.

School of Professional Studies Students: 22 full-time (18 women), 288 part-time (228 women); includes 18 minority (3 Black or African American, non-Hispanic/Latino; 2 Asian, non-Hispanic/Latino; 11 Hispanic/Latino; 2 Two or more races, non-Hispanic/Latino). Average age 35. Expenses: Contact institution. *Financial support:* In 2010–11, 7 students received support. Scholarships/grants available. Financial award application deadline: 5/1; financial award applicants required to submit FAFSA. In 2010, 93 master's, 11 doctorates awarded. *Degree program information:* Part-time programs available. Offers adult nurse practitioner (MSN); biology option (MAT); clinical nurse specialist (MSN); community counseling (MS); counselor education (MS); curriculum (MS); English education (MS); instructional leadership (Ed D); instructional technology (MS); mathematics education (MS); mathematics option (MAT); reading (MS); school counseling (MS); secondary education (MAT); special education (MS). *Application deadline:* For fall admission, 8/5 priority date for domestic students; for spring admission, 1/5 priority date for domestic students. Applications are processed on a rolling basis. *Application fee:* $50. *Application Contact:* Chris Shankle, Associate Director of Graduate Admissions, 203-837-9005, Fax: 203-837-8326, E-mail: shanklec@wcsu.edu. *Interim Dean,* Dr. Maryann Rossi, 203-837-8950, Fax: 203-837-8526, E-mail: rossim@wcsu.edu.

School of Visual and Performing Arts Students: 17 full-time (12 women), 21 part-time (14 women); includes 2 minority (1 Black or African American, non-Hispanic/Latino; 1 Asian, non-Hispanic/Latino). Average age 31. Expenses: Contact institution. *Financial support:* In 2010–11, 8 students received support. Scholarships/grants available. Financial award applicants required to submit FAFSA. In 2010, 22 master's awarded. *Degree program information:* Part-time programs available. Offers illustration (MFA); music education (MS); painting (MFA); visual and performing arts (MFA, MS). *Application deadline:* For fall admission, 8/5 priority date for domestic students; for spring admission, 1/5 priority date for domestic students. *Application fee:* $50. *Application Contact:* Chris Shankle, Associate Director of Graduate Studies, 203-837-9005, Fax: 203-837-8326, E-mail: shanklec@wcsu.edu. *Dean,* Dr. Carol Hawkes, 203-837-8851, Fax: 203-837-3223, E-mail: hawkesc@wcsu.edu.

WESTERN GOVERNORS UNIVERSITY, Salt Lake City, UT 84107

General Information Independent, coed, comprehensive institution. *Graduate housing:* On-campus housing not available.

GRADUATE UNITS

Program in Information Security and Assurance Postbaccalaureate distance learning degree programs offered. Offers information security and assurance (MS).

Programs in Business Postbaccalaureate distance learning degree programs offered. Offers information technology management (MBA); management and strategy (MBA); strategic leadership (MBA). Electronic applications accepted.

Teachers College *Degree program information:* Part-time and evening/weekend programs available. Postbaccalaureate distance learning degree programs offered (no on-campus study). Offers English language learning (K-12) (MA); learning and technology (M Ed, MA); management and innovation (M Ed); mathematics education (5-12) (MA); mathematics education (5-9) (MA); mathematics education (K-6) (MA); measurement and evaluation (M Ed); science (5-12) (MA); science education (5-9) (MA); teaching (MAT); technology for principals (Post-Graduate Certificate). Electronic applications accepted.

WESTERN ILLINOIS UNIVERSITY, Macomb, IL 61455-1390

General Information State-supported, coed, comprehensive institution. CGS member. *Enrollment:* 12,585 graduate, professional, and undergraduate students; 858 full-time matriculated graduate/professional students (445 women), 980 part-time matriculated graduate/professional students (657 women). *Enrollment by degree level:* 1,695 master's, 46 doctoral, 97 other advanced degrees. Tuition, state resident: full-time $6370; part-time $265.40 per credit hour. Tuition, nonresident: full-time $12,740; part-time $530.80 per credit hour. *Required fees:* $75.67 per credit hour. *Graduate housing:* Rooms and/or apartments available on a first-come, first-served basis to single and married students. Typical cost: $4958 per year ($8138 including board) for single students; $5280 per year ($5280 including board) for married students. *Student services:* Campus employment opportunities, campus safety program, career counseling, exercise/wellness program, free psychological counseling, international student services, low-cost health insurance, multicultural affairs office, services for students with disabilities, teacher training, writing training. *Library facilities:* Leslie Malpass Library plus 4 others. *Online resources:* library catalog, web page. *Collection:* 998,041 titles, 3,200 serial subscriptions. *Research affiliation:* Innovative Design and Research Corporation (engineering technology), Petroleum Research Fund (chemistry), Center for the Study of the College Fraternity (sociology), McDonalds Corporation (education), The Ceres Trust (agriculture), Quad Cities Manufacturing Lab (engineering).

Computer facilities: 1,000 computers available on campus for general student use. A campuswide network can be accessed from student residence rooms and from off campus. Online class registration is available. *Web address:* http://www.wiu.edu/.

General Application Contact: Evelyn Hoing, Assistant Director of Graduate Studies, 309-298-1806, Fax: 309-298-2345, E-mail: grad-office@wiu.edu.

GRADUATE UNITS

School of Graduate Studies Students: 858 full-time (445 women), 980 part-time (657 women); includes 159 minority (77 Black or African American, non-Hispanic/Latino; 6 American Indian or Alaska Native, non-Hispanic/Latino; 17 Asian, non-Hispanic/Latino; 48 Hispanic/Latino; 11 Two or more races, non-Hispanic/Latino), 204 international. Average age 29. 1,272 applicants, 52% accepted. Expenses: Contact institution. *Financial support:* In 2010–11, 464 students received support, including 385 research assistantships with full tuition reimbursements available (averaging $7,280 per year), 79 teaching assistantships with full tuition reimbursements available (averaging $8,400 per year). Financial award applicants required to submit FAFSA. In 2010, 682 master's, 4 doctorates, 50 other advanced degrees awarded. *Degree program information:* Part-time programs available. Postbaccalaureate distance learning degree programs offered (no on-campus study). *Application fee:* $30. Electronic applications accepted. *Application Contact:* Evelyn Hoing, Assistant Director of Graduate Studies, 309-298-1806, Fax: 309-298-2345, E-mail: ea-hoing@wiu.edu. *Director/Associate Provost,* Dr. Judith Dallinger, 309-298-1806, Fax: 309-298-2345, E-mail: grad-office@wiu.edu.

College of Arts and Sciences Students: 277 full-time (144 women), 122 part-time (82 women); includes 51 minority (22 Black or African American, non-Hispanic/Latino; 2 American Indian or Alaska Native, non-Hispanic/Latino; 9 Asian, non-Hispanic/Latino; 15 Hispanic/Latino; 3 Two or more races, non-Hispanic/Latino), 64 international. Average age 28. 371 applicants, 51% accepted. Expenses: Contact institution. *Financial support:* In 2010–11, 171 students received support, including 128 research assistantships with full tuition reimbursements available (averaging $7,280 per year), 43 teaching assistantships with full tuition reimbursements available (averaging $8,400 per year). Financial award applicants required to submit FAFSA. In 2010, 125 master's, 36 other advanced degrees awarded. *Degree program information:* Part-time programs available. Offers applied math (Certificate); arts and sciences (MA, MLAS, MS, Certificate, SSP); biological sciences (MS); chemistry (MS); clinical/community mental health (MS); community development (Certificate); English (MA); environmental geographic information systems (Certificate); environmental GIS (Certificate); general psychology (MS); geography (MA); history (MA); liberal arts and sciences (MLAS); literary studies (Certificate); mathematics (MS); physics (MS); political science (MA); professional writing (Certificate); psychology (MS, SSP); school psychology (SSP); sociology (MA); teaching writing (Certificate); zoo and aquarium studies (Certificate). *Application deadline:* Applications are processed on a rolling basis. *Application fee:* $30. Electronic applications accepted. *Application Contact:* Evelyn Hoing, Assistant Director of Graduate Studies, 309-298-1806, Fax: 309-298-2345, E-mail: grad-office@wiu.edu. *Dean,* Dr. Susan Martinelli-Fernandez, 309-298-1828.

College of Business and Technology Students: 185 full-time (52 women), 80 part-time (25 women); includes 14 minority (11 Black or African American, non-Hispanic/Latino; 1 American Indian or Alaska Native, non-Hispanic/Latino; 1 Asian, non-Hispanic/Latino; 1 Hispanic/Latino), 97 international. Average age 27. 258 applicants, 69% accepted. Expenses: Contact institution. *Financial support:* In 2010–11, 63 students received support, including 54 research assistantships with full tuition reimbursements available (averaging $7,280 per year), 9 teaching assistantships with full tuition reimbursements available (averaging $8,400 per year). Financial award applicants required to submit FAFSA. In 2010, 125 master's awarded. *Degree program information:* Part-time programs available. Offers accountancy (M Acct); business administration (MBA); business and technology (M Acct, MA, MBA, MS, Certificate); community development (Certificate); computer science (MS); economics (MA); manufacturing engineering systems (MS). *Application deadline:* Applications are processed on a rolling basis. *Application fee:* $30. Electronic applications accepted. *Application Contact:* Evelyn Hoing, Assistant Director of Graduate Studies, 309-298-1806, Fax: 309-298-2345, E-mail: grad-office@wiu.edu. *Dean,* Dr. Tom Erekson, 309-298-2442.

College of Education and Human Services Students: 278 full-time (160 women), 748 part-time (527 women); includes 82 minority (40 Black or African American, non-Hispanic/Latino; 3 American Indian or Alaska Native, non-Hispanic/Latino; 4 Asian, non-Hispanic/Latino; 28 Hispanic/Latino; 7 Two or more races, non-Hispanic/Latino), 32 international. Average age 32. 415 applicants, 57% accepted. Expenses: Contact institution. *Financial support:* In 2010–11, 153 students received support, including 138 research assistantships with full tuition reimbursements available (averaging $7,280 per year), 15 teaching assistantships with full tuition reimbursements available (averaging $8,400 per year). Financial award applicants required to submit FAFSA. In 2010, 373 master's, 4 doctorates, 14 other advanced degrees awarded. *Degree program information:* Part-time and evening/weekend programs available. Postbaccalaureate distance learning degree programs offered (no on-campus study). Offers college student personnel (MS); counseling (MS Ed); distance learning (Certificate); education and human services (MA, MS, MS Ed, Ed D, Certificate, Ed S); educational and interdisciplinary studies (MS Ed, Certificate); educational leadership (MS Ed, Ed D, Ed S); educational technology specialist (Certificate); elementary education (MS Ed); graphic applications (Certificate); health education (MS); health services administration (Certificate); instructional design and technology (MS); kinesiology (MS); law enforcement and justice administration (MA); multimedia (Certificate); police executive administration (Certificate); reading (MS Ed); recreation, park, and tourism administration (MS); special education (MS Ed); sport management (MS); teaching English to speakers of other languages (Certificate); technology integration in education (Certificate); training development (Certificate). *Application deadline:* Applications are processed on a rolling basis. *Application fee:* $30. Electronic applications accepted. *Application Contact:* Evelyn Hoing, Assistant Director of Graduate Studies, 309-298-1806, Fax: 309-298-2345, E-mail: grad-office@wiu.edu. *Dean,* Dr. Sterling Saddler, 309-298-1690.

College of Fine Arts and Communication Students: 118 full-time (89 women), 30 part-time (23 women); includes 12 minority (4 Black or African American, non-Hispanic/Latino; 3 Asian, non-Hispanic/Latino; 4 Hispanic/Latino; 1 Two or more races, non-Hispanic/Latino), 11 international. Average age 28. 228 applicants, 28% accepted. Expenses: Contact institution. *Financial support:* In 2010–11, 77 students received support, including 65 research assistantships with full tuition reimbursements available (averaging $7,280 per year), 12 teaching assistantships with full tuition reimbursements available (averaging $8,400 per year). Financial award applicants required to submit FAFSA. In 2010, 59 master's awarded. *Degree program information:* Part-time programs available. Offers acting (MFA); communication (MA); communication sciences and disorders (MS); design (MFA); directing (MFA); fine arts and communication (MA, MFA, MM, MS, Certificate); museum studies (MA, Certificate); music (MM). *Application deadline:* Applications are processed on a rolling basis. *Application fee:* $30. Electronic applications accepted. *Application Contact:* Evelyn Hoing, Assistant Director of Graduate Studies, 309-298-1806, Fax: 309-298-2345, E-mail: grad-office@wiu.edu. *Interim Dean,* Dr. Sharon Evans, 309-298-1552.

WESTERN INTERNATIONAL UNIVERSITY, Phoenix, AZ 85021-2718

General Information Proprietary, coed, comprehensive institution. *Graduate housing:* On-campus housing not available.

GRADUATE UNITS

Graduate Programs in Business *Degree program information:* Evening/weekend programs available. Postbaccalaureate distance learning degree programs offered (no on-campus study). Offers business (MA, MBA, MPA, MS); business administration (MBA); finance (MBA); human dynamics (MA); information system engineering (MS); information technology (MBA); innovative leadership (MA); international business (MBA); management (MBA); marketing (MBA); organization development (MBA); public administration (MPA).

WESTERN KENTUCKY UNIVERSITY, Bowling Green, KY 42101

General Information State-supported, coed, comprehensive institution. CGS member. *Graduate housing:* Room and/or apartments guaranteed to single students; on-campus housing not available to married students. Housing application deadline: 4/1. *Research affiliation:* Bowling Green Field Station for Animal Studies (U. S. Fish and Wildlife Service), Roybal Center (gerontology).

GRADUATE UNITS

Graduate Studies *Degree program information:* Part-time and evening/weekend programs available. Postbaccalaureate distance learning degree programs offered (minimal on-campus study).

College of Education and Behavioral Sciences *Degree program information:* Part-time and evening/weekend programs available. Postbaccalaureate distance learning degree programs offered (no on-campus study). Offers adult education (MAE); clinical psychology (MA); counseling (MA Ed); education and behavioral sciences (MA, MAE, MS, Ed D, Ed S); educational leadership (Ed D); elementary education (MAE, Ed S); exceptional education: learning and behavioral disorders (MAE); exceptional education: moderate and severe disabilities (MAE); experimental psychology (MA); general psychology (MA); industrial/organizational psychology (MA); instructional design (MS); interdisciplinary early childhood education (MAE); library media education (MS); literacy education (MAE); middle grades education (MAE); school administration (Ed S); school counseling (P-12) (MA Ed); school principal (MAE); school psychology (Ed S); secondary education (MAE, Ed S); student affairs in higher education (MA Ed).

College of Health and Human Services *Degree program information:* Part-time and evening/weekend programs available. Offers athletic administration and coaching (MS); communication disorders (MS); health and human services (MHA, MPH, MS, MSN, MSW); healthcare administration (MHA); nursing (MSN); physical education (MS); public health (MPH); recreation and sport administration (MS); social work (MSW).

Gordon Ford College of Business *Degree program information:* Part-time and evening/weekend programs available. Offers applied economics (MA); business (MA, MBA); business administration (MBA).

Western Kentucky University (continued)

Ogden College of Science and Engineering *Degree program information:* Part-time and evening/weekend programs available. Offers agriculture (MA Ed, MS); biology (MS); chemistry (MA Ed, MS); computational mathematics (MS); computer science (MS); geoscience (MS); homeland security sciences (MS); mathematics (MA, MS); physics (MA Ed); science and engineering (MA Ed, MS); technology management (MS).

Potter College of Arts and Letters *Degree program information:* Part-time and evening/weekend programs available. Postbaccalaureate distance learning degree programs offered. Offers art education (MA Ed); arts and letters (MA, MA Ed, MPA); communication (MA); criminology (MA); education (MA); English (MA Ed); folk studies (MA); French (MA Ed); German (MA Ed); history (MA, MA Ed); literature (MA); music (MA Ed); organizational communication (Graduate Certificate); political science (MPA); sociology (MA); Spanish (MA Ed); teaching English as a second language (MA); writing (MA).

WESTERN MICHIGAN UNIVERSITY, Kalamazoo, MI 49008

General Information State-supported, coed, university. CGS member. *Graduate housing:* Rooms and/or apartments available on a first-come, first-served basis to single and married students. Housing application deadline: 7/1. *Research affiliation:* Argonne National Laboratory (particle physics), Central States Universities, Inc., Ames Research Center (manufacturing education), Copper Development Association, Inc. (plastics extrusion), Pharmacia and Upjohn Company (electron microscopy), Flowserve Corporation (mechanical pumps and seals).

GRADUATE UNITS

Graduate College *Degree program information:* Part-time and evening/weekend programs available.

College of Arts and Sciences *Degree program information:* Part-time programs available. Offers anthropology (MA); applied and computational mathematics (MS); applied economics (MA, PhD); arts and sciences (MA, MDA, MFA, MPA, MS, PhD, Graduate Certificate); behavior analysis (MA, PhD); biological sciences (MS, PhD); chemistry (MS, PhD); clinical psychology (PhD); communication (MA); comparative religion (MA); creative writing (MFA, PhD); earth science (MA); English (MA, PhD); English education (MA, PhD); geographic information science (Graduate Certificate); geography (MA); geosciences (MA, MS, PhD); health care administration (Graduate Certificate); history (MA, PhD); industrial/organizational psychology (MA); international development administration (MDA); mathematics (MA, PhD); mathematics education (MA, PhD); medieval studies (MA); nonprofit leadership and administration (Graduate Certificate); philosophy (MA); physics (MA, PhD); political science (MA, MDA, PhD); public administration (MPA, PhD); science education (MA, PhD); sociology (MA, PhD); Spanish (MA, PhD); statistics (MS, PhD).

College of Education and Human Development *Degree program information:* Part-time programs available. Offers career and technical education (MA); counseling psychology (MA, PhD); counselor education (MA, PhD); education and human development (MA, MS, Ed D, PhD, Ed S, Graduate Certificate); educational leadership (MA, PhD, Ed S); educational technology (MA, Graduate Certificate); evaluation, measurement and research (MA, PhD); exercise and sports medicine (MS); family and consumer sciences (MA); human resources development (MA); literacy studies (MA); physical education (MA); practice of teaching (MA); socio-cultural studies of education (MA); special education (MA, Ed D); teaching children with visual impairments (MA).

College of Engineering and Applied Sciences *Degree program information:* Part-time programs available. Offers civil engineering (MS); computer engineering (MSE); computer science (MS, PhD); electrical and computer engineering (PhD); electrical engineering (MSE); engineering and applied sciences (MS, MSE, PhD); engineering management (MS); industrial engineering (MSE, PhD); manufacturing engineering (MS); mechanical engineering (MSE, PhD); paper and imaging science and engineering (MS, PhD).

College of Fine Arts *Degree program information:* Part-time programs available. Offers art education (MA); composition (MM); conducting (MM); fine arts (MA, MFA, MM); music (MA); music education (MM); music therapy (MM); performance (MM); studio art (MFA).

College of Health and Human Services *Degree program information:* Part-time programs available. Offers audiology (Au D); health and human services (MA, MS, MSN, MSW, Au D, PhD); interdisciplinary health sciences (PhD); nursing (MSN); occupational therapy (MS); orientation and mobility (MA); orientation and mobility of children (MA); physician assistant (MS); social work (MSW); speech-language pathology (MA); vision rehabilitation teaching (MA).

The Evaluation Center Offers evaluation (PhD).

Haworth College of Business *Degree program information:* Part-time programs available. Offers accountancy (MSA); business (MBA, MSA); finance (MBA).

WESTERN NEW ENGLAND UNIVERSITY, Springfield, MA 01119

General Information Independent, coed, comprehensive institution. *Enrollment:* 3,710 graduate, professional, and undergraduate students; 386 full-time matriculated graduate/professional students (202 women), 577 part-time matriculated graduate/professional students (344 women). *Enrollment by degree level:* 602 first professional, 333 master's, 28 doctoral. *Tuition:* Full-time $35,582. *Graduate housing:* Room and/or apartments available to single students; on-campus housing not available to married students. *Student services:* Campus safety program, career counseling, exercise/wellness program, free psychological counseling, services for students with disabilities, writing training. *Library facilities:* D'Amour Library plus 1 other. *Online resources:* library catalog, web page, access to other libraries' catalogs. *Collection:* 130,900 titles, 208 serial subscriptions, 5,200 audiovisual materials.

Computer facilities: Computer purchase and lease plans are available. 400 computers available on campus for general student use. A campuswide network can be accessed from student residence rooms and from off campus. Online class registration is available. *Web address:* http://www.wne.edu/.

General Application Contact: Matt Fox, Director of Recruiting and Marketing for Adult Learners, 413-782-1517, Fax: 413-782-1777, E-mail: study@wnec.edu.

GRADUATE UNITS

School of Arts and Sciences Students: 156 part-time (125 women); includes 1 Asian, non-Hispanic/Latino; 6 Hispanic/Latino; 1 Two or more races, non-Hispanic/Latino, 4 international. Expenses: Contact institution. *Financial support:* Available to part-time students. Applicants required to submit FAFSA. *Degree program information:* Part-time and evening/weekend programs available. Postbaccalaureate distance learning degree programs offered. Offers applied behavior analysis (Postbaccalaureate Certificate); arts and sciences (M Ed, MAET, MAMT, PhD, Postbaccalaureate Certificate); behavior analysis (PhD); elementary education (M Ed); English for teachers (MAET); mathematics for teachers (MAMT). *Application deadline:* Applications are processed on a rolling basis. *Application fee:* $30. *Application Contact:* Matt Fox, Director of Recruiting and Marketing for Adult Learners, 413-782-1517, Fax: 413-782-1777, E-mail: study@wnec.edu. *Dean,* Dr. Saeed Ghahramani, 413-782-1218, Fax: 413-796-2118, E-mail: sghahram@wnec.edu.

School of Business Students: 158 part-time (75 women); includes 8 Black or African American, non-Hispanic/Latino; 2 Asian, non-Hispanic/Latino; 3 Hispanic/Latino; 1 Two or more races, non-Hispanic/Latino, 1 international. Expenses: Contact institution. *Financial support:* Available to part-time students. Applicants required to submit FAFSA. In 2010, 64 master's awarded. *Degree program information:* Part-time and evening/weekend programs available. Offers accounting (MSA); business (MBA, MSA); general business (MBA); sport management (MBA). *Application deadline:* Applications are processed on a rolling basis. *Application fee:* $30. *Application Contact:* Matt Fox, Director of Recruiting and Marketing for Adult Learners, 413-782-1517, Fax: 413-782-1777, E-mail: study@wnec.edu. *Dean,* Dr. Julie Siciliano, 413-782-1231.

School of Engineering Students: 48 part-time (14 women); includes 1 Black or African American, non-Hispanic/Latino; 3 Asian, non-Hispanic/Latino; 2 Hispanic/Latino; 1 Two or more races, non-Hispanic/Latino, 2 international. Expenses: Contact institution. *Financial support:* Available to part-time students. Applicants required to submit FAFSA. In 2010, 15 master's awarded. *Degree program information:* Part-time and evening/weekend programs available. Offers business and engineering information systems (MSEM); electrical engineering (MSEE); engineering (MSE, MSEE, MSEM, PhD); engineering management (MSEM, PhD); general engineering management (MSEM); mechanical engineering (MSE); production and manufacturing systems (MSEM); production management (MSEM); quality engineering (MSEM). *Application deadline:* Applications are processed on a rolling basis. *Application fee:* $30. *Application Contact:* Matt Fox, Director of Recruiting and Marketing for Adult Learners, 413-782-1517, Fax: 413-782-1777, E-mail: study@wnec.edu. *Dean,* Dr. S. Hossein Cheraghi, 413-782-1272, E-mail: cheraghi@wnec.edu.

School of Law Students: 386 full-time (202 women), 218 part-time (131 women); includes 18 Black or African American, non-Hispanic/Latino; 1 American Indian or Alaska Native, non-Hispanic/Latino; 26 Asian, non-Hispanic/Latino; 20 Hispanic/Latino, 1 international. 1,561 applicants, 57% accepted, 169 enrolled. *Faculty:* 34 full-time (16 women), 27 part-time/adjunct (5 women). Expenses: Contact institution. *Financial support:* Career-related internships or fieldwork, Federal Work-Study, institutionally sponsored loans, and scholarships/grants available. Support available to part-time students. Financial award application deadline: 4/1; financial award applicants required to submit FAFSA. In 2010, 193 first professional degrees awarded. *Degree program information:* Part-time and evening/weekend programs available. Offers estate planning/elder law (LL M); law (JD). *Application deadline:* For fall admission, 3/15 priority date for domestic students. Applications are processed on a rolling basis. *Application fee:* $50. Electronic applications accepted. *Application Contact:* Michael A. Johnson, Director of Admissions, 413-782-1406, E-mail: admissions@law.wnec.edu. *Dean,* Arthur R. Gaudio, 413-782-2201, E-mail: agaudio@wnec.edu.

WESTERN NEW MEXICO UNIVERSITY, Silver City, NM 88062-0680

General Information State-supported, coed, comprehensive institution. *Graduate housing:* Rooms and/or apartments available on a first-come, first-served basis to single and married students. Housing application deadline: 6/30.

GRADUATE UNITS

Graduate Division *Degree program information:* Part-time programs available. Postbaccalaureate distance learning degree programs offered (minimal on-campus study). Offers business administration (MBA); interdisciplinary studies (MA); occupational therapy (MOT); social work (MSW). Electronic applications accepted.

School of Education Offers bilingual education (MAT); counseling (MA); educational leadership (MA); elementary education (MAT); reading (MAT); school psychology (MA); secondary education (MAT); special education (MAT); TESOL (teaching English to speakers of other languages) (MAT). Electronic applications accepted.

WESTERN OREGON UNIVERSITY, Monmouth, OR 97361-1394

General Information State-supported, coed, comprehensive institution. *Graduate housing:* Room and/or apartments available on a first-come, first-served basis to single students; on-campus housing not available to married students. *Research affiliation:* Teaching Research Institute (education).

GRADUATE UNITS

Graduate Programs *Degree program information:* Part-time and evening/weekend programs available. Postbaccalaureate distance learning degree programs offered (minimal on-campus study).

College of Education *Degree program information:* Part-time and evening/weekend programs available. Postbaccalaureate distance learning degree programs offered (minimal on-campus study). Offers bilingual education (MS Ed); deaf education (MS Ed); early childhood special education (MS Ed); education (MAT, MS, MS Ed); health (MS Ed); humanities (MAT, MS Ed); information technology (MS Ed); initial licensure (MAT); mathematics (MAT, MS Ed); rehabilitation counseling (MS); science (MAT, MS Ed); secondary education (MAT, MS Ed); social science (MAT, MS Ed); special education (MS Ed).

College of Liberal Arts and Sciences *Degree program information:* Part-time and evening/weekend programs available. Offers contemporary music (MM); criminal justice (MA, MS); liberal arts and sciences (MA, MM, MS).

WESTERN SEMINARY, Portland, OR 97215-3367

General Information Independent-religious, coed, graduate-only institution. *Enrollment by degree level:* 544 master's, 62 doctoral, 46 other advanced degrees. *Graduate faculty:* 24 full-time (3 women), 40 part-time/adjunct (10 women). *Tuition:* Part-time $425 per credit. *Graduate housing:* On-campus housing not available. *Student services:* Campus employment opportunities, campus safety program, career counseling, international student services, low-cost health insurance, writing training. *Library facilities:* Cline-Tunnell Library. *Online resources:* library catalog, access to other libraries' catalogs. *Collection:* 55,895 titles, 673 serial subscriptions, 10,225 audiovisual materials.

Computer facilities: 14 computers available on campus for general student use. A campuswide network can be accessed from off campus. Online class registration is available. *Web address:* http://www.westernseminary.edu/.

General Application Contact: Brian LePort, Registrar/Dean of Student Development, 503-517-1820 Ext. 1807, Fax: 503-517-1801, E-mail: bleport@westernseminary.edu.

GRADUATE UNITS

Graduate Programs Students: 109 full-time (45 women), 543 part-time (185 women); includes 5 Black or African American, non-Hispanic/Latino; 1 American Indian or Alaska Native, non-Hispanic/Latino; 11 Asian, non-Hispanic/Latino; 3 Hispanic/Latino. Average age 29. 265 applicants, 77% accepted, 155 enrolled. *Faculty:* 29 full-time (4 women), 35 part-time/adjunct (9 women). Expenses: Contact institution. *Financial support:* Fellowships, career-related internships or fieldwork, institutionally sponsored loans, and scholarships/grants available. Support available to part-time students. Financial award applicants required to submit FAFSA. In 2010, 93 master's, 19 doctorates, 6 other advanced degrees awarded. *Degree program information:* Part-time and evening/weekend programs available. Postbaccalaureate distance learning degree programs offered. Offers biblical and theological studies (MA, G Dip); biblical studies (Certificate); chaplaincy (MA); coaching (MA); counseling (MA, Certificate); divinity (M Div); intercultural studies (MA, D Miss, Certificate, G Dip); Jewish ministry (MA); pastoral care to women (MA); pastoral counseling (M Div); theology (Th M); youth ministry (MA). *Application deadline:* For fall admission, 7/18 priority date for domestic students; for winter admission, 11/7 for domestic students; for spring admission, 11/1 priority date for domestic students. Applications are processed on a rolling basis. *Application fee:* $50. *Application Contact:* Dr. Robert W. Wiggins, Registrar/Dean of Student Development, 503-517-1820, Fax: 503-517-1801, E-mail: rwiggins@westernseminary.edu. *Academic Dean,* Dr. Randal R. Roberts, 503-517-1860, Fax: 503-517-1859, E-mail: rroberts@westernseminary.edu.

WESTERN SEMINARY–SACRAMENTO CAMPUS, Sacramento, CA 95821

General Information Independent-religious, coed, graduate-only institution.

GRADUATE UNITS

Graduate Certificate Programs Postbaccalaureate distance learning degree programs offered. Offers Bible (Graduate Certificate); coaching (Graduate Certificate); pastoral care to women (Graduate Certificate); theology (Graduate Certificate); youth and family (Graduate Certificate).

Graduate Diploma Programs Offers Bible and theology (Graduate Diploma); ministry (Graduate Diploma); pastoral care to women (Graduate Diploma).

Master of Divinity Program Offers divinity (M Div).

Program in Biblical and Theological Studies Offers biblical and theological studies (MA).

Program in Marital and Family Therapy Offers marital and family therapy (MA).

Program in Ministry and Leadership Offers ministry and leadership (MA).

WESTERN SEMINARY–SAN JOSE CAMPUS, Los Gatos, CA 95032-4520

General Information Independent-religious, coed, graduate-only institution. *Graduate faculty:* 4 full-time (1 woman), 20 part-time/adjunct (10 women). *Tuition:* Part-time $445 per unit. *Graduate housing:* On-campus housing not available. *Library facilities:* Main library plus 1 other.

Computer facilities: 2 computers available on campus for general student use. Online class registration is available. *Web address:* http://www.westernseminary.edu/SanJose/index.htm.

General Application Contact: Tony Cruz, Enrollment Team Lead, 408-356-6889 Ext. 416, E-mail: tcruz@westernseminary.edu.

GRADUATE UNITS

Graduate Programs Expenses: Contact institution. Postbaccalaureate distance learning degree programs offered. Offers Biblical and theological studies (MA); exposition ministry (M Div); marital and family therapy (MA); ministry and leadership (MA); open track (M Div); pastoral ministry (M Div); theology (Graduate Diploma).

WESTERN STATE COLLEGE OF COLORADO, Gunnison, CO 81231

General Information State-supported, coed, comprehensive institution.

GRADUATE UNITS

Graduate Programs in Education Postbaccalaureate distance learning degree programs offered (minimal on-campus study). Offers education administrator leadership (MA); reading leadership (MA); teacher leadership (MA).

Program in Creative Writing Postbaccalaureate distance learning degree programs offered (minimal on-campus study). Offers mainstream genre fiction (MFA); poetry (MFA); screenwriting (MFA).

WESTERN STATE UNIVERSITY COLLEGE OF LAW, Fullerton, CA 92831-3000

General Information Proprietary, coed, graduate-only institution. *Enrollment by degree level:* 468 first professional. *Graduate faculty:* 28 full-time (12 women), 19 part-time/adjunct (6 women). *Tuition:* Full-time $34,900; part-time $11,670 per term. *Required fees:* $145 per term. *Graduate housing:* On-campus housing not available. *Student services:* Campus employment opportunities, campus safety program, career counseling, free psychological counseling, international student services, low-cost health insurance, services for students with disabilities. *Library facilities:* Law Library. *Online resources:* library catalog, web page, access to other libraries' catalogs. *Collection:* 206,298 titles, 3,145 serial subscriptions, 91 audiovisual materials.

Computer facilities: 45 computers available on campus for general student use. A campuswide network can be accessed. Lexis, Westlaw, Dialog, Nexis, Cali, Authority, Hein Online, BNA, Intelliconnect, Legaltrac, ILP, Foreign Law Guide and LLMC available. *Web address:* http://www.wsulaw.edu/.

General Application Contact: Gloria Switzer, Assistant Dean of Admission, 714-459-1101, Fax: 714-441-1748, E-mail: adm@wsulaw.edu.

GRADUATE UNITS

Professional Program Students: 318 full-time (143 women), 150 part-time (79 women); includes 177 minority (25 Black or African American, non-Hispanic/Latino; 4 American Indian or Alaska Native, non-Hispanic/Latino; 70 Asian, non-Hispanic/Latino; 70 Hispanic/Latino; 2 Native Hawaiian or other Pacific Islander, non-Hispanic/Latino; 6 Two or more races, non-Hispanic/Latino), 2 international. Average age 27. 1,895 applicants, 56% accepted, 215 enrolled. *Faculty:* 28 full-time (12 women), 19 part-time/adjunct (6 women). Expenses: Contact institution. *Financial support:* In 2010–11, 8 fellowships (averaging $4,668 per year) were awarded; career-related internships or fieldwork, Federal Work-Study, and scholarships/grants also available. Support available to part-time students. Financial award application deadline: 9/15; financial award applicants required to submit FAFSA. In 2010, 79 JDs awarded. *Degree program information:* Part-time and evening/weekend programs available. Offers law (JD). *Application deadline:* For fall admission, 6/1 for domestic and international students; for spring admission, 12/1 for domestic and international students. Applications are processed on a rolling basis. *Application fee:* $50. Electronic applications accepted. *Application Contact:* Gloria Switzer, Assistant Dean of Admission, 714-459-1101, Fax: 714-441-1748, E-mail: adm@wsulaw.edu.

WESTERN THEOLOGICAL SEMINARY, Holland, MI 49423-3622

General Information Independent-religious, coed, graduate-only institution. *Enrollment by degree level:* 201 first professional, 17 master's, 21 doctoral. *Graduate faculty:* 18 full-time (4 women), 9 part-time/adjunct (5 women). *Tuition:* Full-time $11,680; part-time $365 per credit hour. *Required fees:* $90. *Graduate housing:* Rooms and/or apartments available on a first-come, first-served basis to single and married students. *Student services:* Campus employment opportunities, free psychological counseling, services for students with disabilities, writing training. *Library facilities:* Beardslee Library plus 1 other. *Online resources:* library catalog, web page, access to other libraries' catalogs. *Collection:* 109,662 titles, 442 serial subscriptions.

Computer facilities: 16 computers available on campus for general student use. A campuswide network can be accessed from student residence rooms and from off campus. *Web address:* http://www.westernsem.edu/.

General Application Contact: Rev. Mark Poppen, Director of Admissions, 616-392-8555, Fax: 616-392-7717, E-mail: mark@westernsem.edu.

GRADUATE UNITS

Graduate and Professional Programs Students: 170 full-time (67 women), 69 part-time (23 women); includes 24 minority (19 Black or African American, non-Hispanic/Latino; 1 Asian, non-Hispanic/Latino; 4 Hispanic/Latino), 1 international. 82 applicants, 98% accepted, 64 enrolled. *Faculty:* 18 full-time (4 women), 9 part-time/adjunct (5 women). Expenses: Contact institution. *Financial support:* Career-related internships or fieldwork, institutionally sponsored loans, and scholarships/grants available. Support available to part-time students. Financial award applicants required to submit FAFSA. In 2010, 35 first professional degrees, 5 master's, 1 doctorate awarded. *Degree program information:* Part-time programs available. Postbaccalaureate distance learning degree programs offered (minimal on-campus study). Offers theology (M Div, M Th, D Min). *Application deadline:* For fall admission, 5/1 priority date for domestic students. Applications are processed on a rolling basis. *Application fee:* $50. *Application Contact:* Rev. Mark Poppen, Director of Admissions, 616-392-8555, Fax: 616-392-7717, E-mail: mark@westernsem.edu. *President*, Dr. Timothy Brown, 616-392-8555, Fax: 616-392-7717, E-mail: tim.brown@westernsem.edu.

WESTERN UNIVERSITY OF HEALTH SCIENCES, Pomona, CA 91766-1854

General Information Independent, coed, graduate-only institution. *Enrollment by degree level:* 2,389 first professional, 528 master's. *Graduate faculty:* 223 full-time (107 women), 23 part-time/adjunct (11 women). *Tuition:* Full-time $41,530. *Graduate housing:* On-campus housing not available. *Student services:* Campus safety program, career counseling, exercise/wellness program, free psychological counseling, international student services, low-cost health insurance, services for students with disabilities, teacher training. *Library facilities:* Pumerantz Library plus 1 other. *Online resources:* library catalog, web page. *Collection:* 37,646 titles, 466 serial subscriptions, 3,604 audiovisual materials. *Research affiliation:* SafePath Laboratories (veterinary medicine), Amgen-UCSF-Partners in D-Medicare Outreach Program (MedOP) (pharmacy), Comprehensive Drup Enterprises Limited (pharmacy), DNA Genotek (veterinary medicine), Pall Corporation (veterinary medicine), Johnson and Johnson (pharmacy).

Computer facilities: A campuswide network can be accessed from off campus. Online class registration is available. *Web address:* http://www.westernu.edu/.

General Application Contact: Admissions Office, 909-469-5335, Fax: 909-469-5570, E-mail: admissions@westernu.edu.

GRADUATE UNITS

College of Allied Health Professions Students: 355 full-time (243 women), 43 part-time (33 women); includes 163 minority (9 Black or African American, non-Hispanic/Latino; 1 American Indian or Alaska Native, non-Hispanic/Latino; 121 Asian, non-Hispanic/Latino; 31 Hispanic/Latino; 1 Native Hawaiian or other Pacific Islander, non-Hispanic/Latino), 5 international. Average age 29. 1,393 applicants, 19% accepted, 191 enrolled. *Faculty:* 20 full-time (14 women), 1 (woman) part-time/adjunct. Expenses: Contact institution. *Financial support:* Institutionally sponsored loans and scholarships/grants available. Financial award application deadline: 3/2; financial award applicants required to submit FAFSA. In 2010, 114 master's awarded. Offers allied health professions (MS, DPT); health sciences (MS); physical therapy (DPT); physician assistant studies (MS). *Application deadline:* For fall admission, 12/1 for domestic students. Electronic applications accepted. *Application Contact:* Karen Hutton-Lopez, Director of Admissions, 909-469-5650, Fax: 909-469-5570, E-mail: admissions@westernu.edu. *Dean*, Dr. Stephanie Bowlin, 909-469-5383.

College of Dental Medicine Students: 144 full-time (58 women); includes 76 minority (3 Black or African American, non-Hispanic/Latino; 3 American Indian or Alaska Native, non-Hispanic/Latino; 62 Asian, non-Hispanic/Latino; 8 Hispanic/Latino), 4 international. Average age 27. 2,024 applicants, 8% accepted, 73 enrolled. *Faculty:* 15 full-time (7 women), 2 part-time/adjunct (0 women). Expenses: Contact institution. Offers dental medicine (DMD). *Application deadline:* For fall admission, 12/1 for domestic students. Applications are processed on a rolling basis. *Application fee:* $60. Electronic applications accepted. *Application Contact:* Marie Anderson, Director of Admissions, 909-469-5485, Fax: 909-469-5570, E-mail: admissions@westernu.edu. *Dean*, Dr. James J. Koelbl, 909-706-3504, E-mail: jkoelbl@westernu.edu.

College of Graduate Nursing Students: 286 full-time (251 women), 12 part-time (10 women); includes 154 minority (30 Black or African American, non-Hispanic/Latino; 1 American Indian or Alaska Native, non-Hispanic/Latino; 83 Asian, non-Hispanic/Latino; 40 Hispanic/Latino), 6 international. Average age 34. 547 applicants, 38% accepted, 131 enrolled. *Faculty:* 15 full-time (all women), 7 part-time/adjunct (all women). Expenses: Contact institution. *Financial support:* Institutionally sponsored loans, scholarships/grants, and veterans educational benefits available. Financial award application deadline: 3/2; financial award applicants required to submit FAFSA. In 2010, 56 master's awarded. *Degree program information:* Part-time and evening/weekend programs available. Postbaccalaureate distance learning degree programs offered (minimal on-campus study). Offers degree completion (MSN); entry-level (MSN); family nurse practitioner (MSN); nursing (DNP). *Application deadline:* For fall admission, 3/1 priority date for domestic students. Applications are processed on a rolling basis. *Application fee:* $60. *Application Contact:* Kathryn Ford, Director of Admissions/International Student Advisor, 909-469-5541, Fax: 909-469-5570, E-mail: admissions@westernu.edu. *Dean*, Karen J. Hanford, 909-469-5243, Fax: 909-469-5521, E-mail: khanford@westernu.edu.

College of Optometry Students: 163 full-time (117 women); includes 102 minority (96 Asian, non-Hispanic/Latino; 6 Hispanic/Latino), 12 international. Average age 26. 433 applicants, 36% accepted, 83 enrolled. *Faculty:* 20 full-time (9 women). Expenses: Contact institution. Offers optometry (OD). *Application deadline:* For fall admission, 5/1 for domestic and international students. *Application fee:* $65. Electronic applications accepted. *Application Contact:* Marie Anderson, Director of Admissions, 909-469-5485, Fax: 909-469-5570, E-mail: admissions@westernu.edu. *Dean*, Dr. Elizabeth Hoppe, 909-706-3497, E-mail: ehoppe@westernu.edu.

College of Osteopathic Medicine of the Pacific Students: 875 full-time (409 women); includes 379 minority (2 Black or African American, non-Hispanic/Latino; 1 American Indian or Alaska Native, non-Hispanic/Latino; 347 Asian, non-Hispanic/Latino; 27 Hispanic/Latino; 2 Native Hawaiian or other Pacific Islander, non-Hispanic/Latino), 15 international. Average age 27. 1,536 applicants, 14% accepted, 144 enrolled. *Faculty:* 53 full-time (17 women), 8 part-time/adjunct (2 women). Expenses: Contact institution. *Financial support:* Fellowships, research assistantships, teaching assistantships, institutionally sponsored loans, scholarships/grants, tuition waivers (full), unspecified assistantships, and veterans educational benefits available. Financial award application deadline: 3/2; financial award applicants required to submit FAFSA. In 2010, 206 DOs awarded. Offers osteopathic medicine (DO). *Application deadline:* For fall admission, 4/15 for domestic students. Applications are processed on a rolling basis. *Application fee:* $65. *Application Contact:* Susan Hanson, Director of Admissions, 909-469-5329, Fax: 909-469-5570, E-mail: admissions@westernu.edu. *Dean*, Dr. Clinton Adams, 909-469-5423, Fax: 909-469-5535, E-mail: aclinton@westernu.edu.

College of Pharmacy Students: 551 full-time (397 women); includes 350 minority (12 Black or African American, non-Hispanic/Latino; 1 American Indian or Alaska Native, non-Hispanic/Latino; 317 Asian, non-Hispanic/Latino; 20 Hispanic/Latino), 39 international. Average age 27. 1,620 applicants, 13% accepted, 144 enrolled. *Faculty:* 32 full-time (14 women), 1 part-time/adjunct (0 women). Expenses: Contact institution. *Financial support:* Institutionally sponsored loans, scholarships/grants, and veterans educational benefits available. Financial award application deadline: 3/2; financial award applicants required to submit FAFSA. In 2010, 136 first professional degrees, 5 master's awarded. Offers pharmaceutical sciences (MS); pharmacy (Pharm D, MS). *Application deadline:* For fall admission, 11/1 for domestic and international students. *Application fee:* $65. Electronic applications accepted. *Application Contact:* Kathryn Ford, Director of Admissions, 909-469-5542, Fax: 909-469-5570, E-mail: admissions@westernu.edu. *Dean*, Dr. Daniel Robinson, 909-469-5581, Fax: 909-469-5539.

College of Podiatric Medicine Students: 69 full-time (21 women); includes 31 minority (5 Black or African American, non-Hispanic/Latino; 22 Asian, non-Hispanic/Latino; 4 Hispanic/Latino), 1 international. Average age 26. 276 applicants, 27% accepted, 36 enrolled. *Faculty:* 9 full-time (4 women), 2 part-time/adjunct (0 women). Expenses: Contact institution. Offers podiatric medicine (DPM). *Application deadline:* For fall admission, 6/30 for domestic and international students. *Application fee:* $0. Electronic applications accepted. *Application Contact:* Marie Anderson, Director of Admissions, 909-469-5485, Fax: 909-469-5570, E-mail: admissions@westernu.edu. *Dean*, Dr. Lawrence B. Harkless, 909-706-3498, E-mail: lharkless@westernu.edu.

College of Veterinary Medicine Students: 391 full-time (305 women); includes 106 minority (5 Black or African American, non-Hispanic/Latino; 6 American Indian or Alaska Native, non-Hispanic/Latino; 63 Asian, non-Hispanic/Latino; 30 Hispanic/Latino; 2 Native Hawaiian or other Pacific Islander, non-Hispanic/Latino), 6 international. Average age 27. 669 applicants, 27% accepted, 100 enrolled. *Faculty:* 55 full-time (26 women), 2 part-time/adjunct (1 woman). Expenses: Contact institution. *Financial support:* Institutionally sponsored loans, scholarships/grants, and veterans educational benefits available. Financial award application deadline: 3/2; financial award applicants required to submit FAFSA. In 2010, 100 DVMs awarded. Offers veterinary medicine (DVM). *Application deadline:* For fall admission, 10/1 for domestic students. *Application fee:* $50. Electronic applications accepted. *Application Contact:* Karen Hutton-Lopez, Director of Admissions, 909-469-5650, Fax: 909-469-5570, E-mail: admissions@westernu.edu. *Dean*, Dr. Phil Nelson, 909-469-5637, Fax: 909-469-5635.

Graduate College of Biomedical Sciences Students: 28 full-time (16 women); includes 17 minority (4 Black or African American, non-Hispanic/Latino; 8 Asian, non-Hispanic/Latino; 3 Hispanic/Latino; 1 Native Hawaiian or other Pacific Islander, non-Hispanic/Latino; 1 Two or more races, non-Hispanic/Latino). Average age 26. 156 applicants, 19% accepted, 25 enrolled. *Faculty:* 4 full-time (1 woman). Expenses: Contact institution. Offers biomedical sciences (MS); medical sciences (MS). *Application deadline:* For fall admission, 5/15 for domestic students. *Application fee:* $50. Electronic applications accepted. *Application Contact:* Kathryn Ford, Director of Admissions/International Student Advisor, 909-469-5542, Fax: 909-469-5570, E-mail: kford@westernu.edu. *Founding Dean*, Dr. Steven J. Henriksen, 909-469-5299, E-mail: shenriksen@westernu.edu.

WESTERN WASHINGTON UNIVERSITY, Bellingham, WA 98225-5996

General Information State-supported, coed, comprehensive institution. CGS member. *Graduate housing:* Rooms and/or apartments available on a first-come, first-served basis to single

Western Washington University (continued)

and married students. Housing application deadline: 5/1. *Research affiliation:* Teck Cominco Ltd., Research Corporation, Dreyfus Foundation, Golden Associates, American Metals Technology, NARSAD (mental health).

GRADUATE UNITS

Graduate School *Degree program information:* Part-time programs available. Electronic applications accepted.

College of Business and Economics *Degree program information:* Part-time and evening/weekend programs available. Offers business and economics (MBA, MP Acc). Electronic applications accepted.

College of Fine and Performing Arts *Degree program information:* Part-time programs available. Offers fine and performing arts (M Mus, MA); music (M Mus). Electronic applications accepted.

College of Humanities and Social Sciences *Degree program information:* Part-time programs available. Offers anthropology (MA); communication sciences and disorders (MA); English (MA); exercise science (MS); experimental psychology (MS); history (MA); humanities and social sciences (M Ed, MA, MS); mental health counseling (MS); political science (MA); school counseling (M Ed); sport psychology (MS). Electronic applications accepted.

College of Sciences and Technology Offers biology (MS); chemistry (MS); computer science (MS); geology (MS); mathematics (MS); natural science/science education (M Ed); sciences and technology (M Ed, MS). Electronic applications accepted.

Huxley College of the Environment *Degree program information:* Part-time programs available. Offers environment (M Ed, MS); environmental education (M Ed); environmental science (MS); geography (MS); marine and estuarine science (MS). Electronic applications accepted.

Woodring College of Education *Degree program information:* Part-time programs available. Postbaccalaureate distance learning degree programs offered (minimal on-campus study). Offers continuing and college education (M Ed); education (M Ed, MA, MIT); educational administration (M Ed); elementary education (M Ed); rehabilitation counseling (MA); secondary education (MIT); special education (M Ed); student affairs administration (M Ed). Electronic applications accepted.

WESTFIELD STATE UNIVERSITY, Westfield, MA 01086

General Information State-supported, coed, comprehensive institution. *Graduate housing:* On-campus housing not available.

GRADUATE UNITS

Division of Graduate and Continuing Education *Degree program information:* Part-time and evening/weekend programs available. Offers applied behavior analysis (MA); criminal justice (MS); early childhood education (M Ed); elementary education (M Ed); English (MA); history (M Ed); mental health counseling (MA); occupational education (M Ed, CAGS); physical education (M Ed); reading (M Ed); school administration (M Ed, CAGS); school guidance (MA); secondary education (M Ed); special education (M Ed); technology for educators (M Ed).

WEST LIBERTY UNIVERSITY, West Liberty, WV 26074

General Information State-supported, coed, comprehensive institution.

GRADUATE UNITS

School of Education Offers education (MA Ed). Electronic applications accepted.

WESTMINSTER COLLEGE, New Wilmington, PA 16172-0001

General Information Independent-religious, coed, comprehensive institution. *Graduate housing:* On-campus housing not available.

GRADUATE UNITS

Programs in Education *Degree program information:* Part-time and evening/weekend programs available. Offers administration (M Ed, Certificate); general education (M Ed); guidance and counseling (M Ed, Certificate); reading (M Ed, Certificate).

WESTMINSTER COLLEGE, Salt Lake City, UT 84105-3697

General Information Independent, coed, comprehensive institution. *Enrollment:* 3,163 graduate, professional, and undergraduate students; 421 full-time matriculated graduate/professional students (215 women), 399 part-time matriculated graduate/professional students (182 women). *Enrollment by degree level:* 818 master's, 2 other advanced degrees. *Graduate faculty:* 75 full-time (37 women), 46 part-time/adjunct (23 women). *Tuition:* Part-time $880 per credit hour. Part-time tuition and fees vary according to program. *Graduate housing:* Room and/or apartments available on a first-come, first-served basis to single students; on-campus housing not available to married students. Typical cost: $4124 per year ($7274 including board). Room and board charges vary according to board plan and housing facility selected. *Student services:* Campus employment opportunities, campus safety program, career counseling, exercise/wellness program, free psychological counseling, grant writing training, international student services, low-cost health insurance, multicultural affairs office, services for students with disabilities, teacher training, writing training. *Library facilities:* Giovale Library plus 1 other. *Online resources:* library catalog, web page, access to other libraries' catalogs. *Collection:* 179,037 titles, 14,123 serial subscriptions, 4,896 audiovisual materials. *Research affiliation:* Key Bank (entrepreneurship), Zions Bank (entrepreneurship), International Psychotherapy (clinical training).

Computer facilities: 403 computers available on campus for general student use. A campuswide network can be accessed from student residence rooms and from off campus. Online class registration is available. *Web address:* http://www.westminstercollege.edu/.

General Application Contact: Joel Bauman, Vice President of Enrollment Services, 801-832-2200, Fax: 801-832-3101, E-mail: admission@westminstercollege.edu.

GRADUATE UNITS

The Bill and Vieve Gore School of Business Students: 175 full-time (44 women), 242 part-time (61 women); includes 2 Black or African American, non-Hispanic/Latino; 2 American Indian or Alaska Native, non-Hispanic/Latino; 8 Asian, non-Hispanic/Latino; 6 Hispanic/Latino; 2 Two or more races, non-Hispanic/Latino, 6 international. Average age 32. 342 applicants, 46% accepted, 113 enrolled. *Faculty:* 35 full-time (9 women), 22 part-time/adjunct (4 women). Expenses: Contact institution. *Financial support:* In 2010–11, 222 students received support. Career-related internships or fieldwork and tuition reimbursement, tuition remission available. Support available to part-time students. Financial award applicants required to submit FAFSA. In 2010, 196 master's, 75 other advanced degrees awarded. *Degree program information:* Part-time and evening/weekend programs available. Postbaccalaureate distance learning degree programs offered (minimal on-campus study). Offers accountancy (M Acc); business administration (MBA, Certificate); technology management (MBATM). *Application deadline:* Applications are processed on a rolling basis. *Application fee:* $50. Electronic applications accepted. *Application Contact:* Joel Bauman, Vice President of Enrollment Services, 801-832-2200, Fax: 801-832-3101, E-mail: admission@westminstercollege.edu. *Dean,* Gary Daynes, 801-832-2600, Fax: 801-832-3106, E-mail: gdaynes@westminstercollege.edu.

Program in Counseling Psychology Students: 27 full-time (18 women), 9 part-time (8 women); includes 1 Asian, non-Hispanic/Latino; 2 Hispanic/Latino; 1 Two or more races, non-Hispanic/Latino. Average age 28. 41 applicants, 46% accepted, 13 enrolled. *Faculty:* 8 full-time (all women), 3 part-time/adjunct (all women). Expenses: Contact institution. *Financial support:* In 2010–11, 26 students received support. Career-related internships or fieldwork and tuition reimbursement, tuition remission available. Support available to part-time students. Financial award applicants required to submit FAFSA. In 2010, 10 master's awarded. *Degree program information:* Part-time and evening/weekend programs available. Offers counseling psychology (MSPC). *Application deadline:* For fall admission, 4/15 for domestic students, 4/16 for international students. Applications are processed on a rolling basis. *Application fee:* $50. Electronic applications accepted. *Application Contact:* Joel Bauman, Vice President of Enrollment Services, 801-832-2200, Fax: 801-832-3101, E-mail: admission@westminstercollege.edu. *Director,* Janine Wanlass, 801-832-2428, E-mail: jwanlass@westminstercollege.edu.

Program in Professional Communication Students: 14 full-time (8 women), 50 part-time (37 women); includes 1 Native Hawaiian or other Pacific Islander, non-Hispanic/Latino; 1 Two or more races, non-Hispanic/Latino, 2 international. Average age 32. 35 applicants, 66% accepted, 17 enrolled. *Faculty:* 7 full-time (3 women), 5 part-time/adjunct (3 women). Expenses: Contact institution. *Financial support:* In 2010–11, 38 students received support. Career-related internships or fieldwork and tuition reimbursement, tuition remission available. Support available to part-time students. Financial award applicants required to submit FAFSA. In 2010, 15 master's awarded. *Degree program information:* Part-time and evening/weekend programs available. Offers professional communication (MPC). *Application deadline:* For fall admission, 7/9 for domestic and international students. Applications are processed on a rolling basis. *Application fee:* $50. Electronic applications accepted. *Application Contact:* Joel Bauman, Vice President of Enrollment Services, 801-832-2200, Fax: 801-832-3101, E-mail: admission@westminstercollege.edu. *Director,* Dr. Helen Hodgson, 801-832-2821, Fax: 801-832-3102, E-mail: hhodgson@westminstercollege.edu.

School of Education Students: 108 full-time (84 women), 73 part-time (59 women); includes 1 Black or African American, non-Hispanic/Latino; 2 American Indian or Alaska Native, non-Hispanic/Latino; 3 Asian, non-Hispanic/Latino; 5 Hispanic/Latino; 1 Two or more races, non-Hispanic/Latino, 3 international. Average age 33. 168 applicants, 77% accepted, 92 enrolled. *Faculty:* 12 full-time (10 women), 16 part-time/adjunct (13 women). Expenses: Contact institution. *Financial support:* In 2010–11, 105 students received support. Career-related internships or fieldwork and tuition reimbursement, tuition remission available. Support available to part-time students. Financial award applicants required to submit FAFSA. In 2010, 64 master's awarded. *Degree program information:* Part-time and evening/weekend programs available. Offers community leadership (MA); education (M Ed); teaching (MAT). *Application deadline:* Applications are processed on a rolling basis. *Application fee:* $50. Electronic applications accepted. *Application Contact:* Joel Bauman, Vice President of Enrollment Services, 801-832-2200, Fax: 801-832-3101, E-mail: admission@westminstercollege.edu. *Interim Dean,* Robert Shaw, 801-832-2470, Fax: 801-832-3105.

School of Nursing and Health Sciences Students: 97 full-time (61 women), 25 part-time (17 women); includes 1 Black or African American, non-Hispanic/Latino; 2 American Indian or Alaska Native, non-Hispanic/Latino; 3 Asian, non-Hispanic/Latino; 2 Hispanic/Latino, 1 international. Average age 35. 165 applicants, 37% accepted, 34 enrolled. *Faculty:* 13 full-time (7 women). Expenses: Contact institution. *Financial support:* In 2010–11, 79 students received support. Career-related internships or fieldwork and tuition reimbursement, tuition remission available. Support available to part-time students. Financial award applicants required to submit FAFSA. In 2010, 49 master's awarded. Offers family nurse practitioner (MSN); nurse anesthesia (MSNA); nurse education (MSNED); nursing (MSN); public health (MPH). *Application deadline:* Applications are processed on a rolling basis. *Application fee:* $50. Electronic applications accepted. *Application Contact:* Joel Bauman, Vice President of Enrollment Services, 801-832-2200, Fax: 801-832-3101, E-mail: admission@westminstercollege.edu. *Dean,* Dr. Sheryl Steadman, 801-832-2164, Fax: 801-832-3110, E-mail: ssteadman@westminstercollege.edu.

WESTMINSTER SEMINARY CALIFORNIA, Escondido, CA 92027-4128

General Information Independent-religious, coed, primarily men, graduate-only institution. *Graduate housing:* On-campus housing not available.

GRADUATE UNITS

Programs in Theology *Degree program information:* Part-time and evening/weekend programs available. Offers Biblical studies (MA); historical theology (MA); theological studies (M Div, MA).

WESTMINSTER THEOLOGICAL SEMINARY, Philadelphia, PA 19118

General Information Independent-religious, coed, primarily men, graduate-only institution. *Graduate housing:* Room and/or apartments available on a first-come, first-served basis to single students; on-campus housing not available to married students.

GRADUATE UNITS

Graduate and Professional Programs *Degree program information:* Part-time programs available. Offers apologetics (Th M); Biblical and urban studies (Certificate); Biblical counseling (MA); biblical studies (MAR); Christian studies (Certificate); church history (Th M); counseling (M Div); general studies (M Div, MAR); hermeneutics and Bible interpretations (PhD); historical and theological studies (PhD); historical theology (Th M); New Testament (Th M); Old Testament (Th M); pastoral counseling (D Min); pastoral ministry (M Div, D Min); systematic theology (Th M); theological studies (MAR); urban missions (M Div, MA, MAR, D Min).

WEST TEXAS A&M UNIVERSITY, Canyon, TX 79016-0001

General Information State-supported, coed, comprehensive institution. *Graduate housing:* Room and/or apartments available on a first-come, first-served basis to single students; on-campus housing not available to married students. *Research affiliation:* Agricultural Research (agriculture), Owens Corning (sports exercise), Agriculture Experiment Station (agriculture), Engineering Experiment Station (math, science), Pantex (chemistry).

GRADUATE UNITS

College of Agriculture, Nursing, and Natural Sciences *Degree program information:* Part-time and evening/weekend programs available. Offers agricultural business and economics (MS); agriculture (PhD); agriculture, nursing, and natural sciences (MS, MSN, PhD); animal science (MS); biology (MS); chemistry (MS); engineering technology (MS); environmental science (MS); mathematics (MS); nursing (MSN); plant science (MS). Electronic applications accepted.

College of Business *Degree program information:* Part-time and evening/weekend programs available. Postbaccalaureate distance learning degree programs offered (minimal on-campus study). Offers accounting (MP Acc); accounting/business administration (MPA); business (MBA, MP Acc, MPA, MS); business administration (MBA); finance and economics (MS); professional accounting (MPA). Electronic applications accepted.

College of Education and Social Sciences *Degree program information:* Part-time and evening/weekend programs available. Postbaccalaureate distance learning degree programs offered (minimal on-campus study). Offers administration (M Ed); counseling education (M Ed); criminal justice (MA); curriculum and instruction (M Ed); education and social sciences (M Ed, MA, MS); educational diagnostician (M Ed); educational technology (M Ed); history (MA); political science (MA); professional counseling (MA); psychology (MA); reading (M Ed); special education (M Ed); sports and exercise science (MS). Electronic applications accepted.

College of Fine Arts and Humanities *Degree program information:* Part-time and evening/weekend programs available. Offers art (MA); communication (MA); communication disorders (MS); English (MA); fine arts and humanities (MA, MFA, MM, MS); music (MA); performance (MM); studio art (MFA). Electronic applications accepted.

Program in Interdisciplinary Studies *Degree program information:* Part-time and evening/weekend programs available. Postbaccalaureate distance learning degree programs offered (minimal on-campus study). Offers interdisciplinary studies (MA, MS). Electronic applications accepted.

WEST VIRGINIA SCHOOL OF OSTEOPATHIC MEDICINE, Lewisburg, WV 24901-1196

General Information State-supported, coed, graduate-only institution. *Enrollment by degree level:* 790 first professional. *Graduate faculty:* 53 full-time (20 women), 1 part-time/adjunct (0 women). Tuition, state resident: full-time $19,950. Tuition, nonresident: full-time $49,950. *Graduate housing:* On-campus housing not available. *Student services:* Campus employment opportunities, campus safety program, career counseling, exercise/wellness program, multicultural affairs office, services for students with disabilities. *Library facilities:* WVSOM Library. *Online resources:* library catalog, web page. *Collection:* 33,000 titles, 150 serial subscriptions, 1,000 audiovisual materials.

Computer facilities: 19 computers available on campus for general student use. A campuswide network can be accessed from off campus. *Web address:* http://www.wvsom.edu/.

General Application Contact: Donna S. Varney, Director of Admissions, 304-647-6373, Fax: 304-647-6384, E-mail: dvarney@wvsom.edu.

GRADUATE UNITS

Professional Program Students: 790 full-time (367 women); includes 11 Black or African American, non-Hispanic/Latino; 3 American Indian or Alaska Native, non-Hispanic/Latino; 108 Asian, non-Hispanic/Latino; 24 Hispanic/Latino. Average age 26. 3,452 applicants, 14% accepted, 201 enrolled. *Faculty:* 46 full-time (16 women), 11 part-time/adjunct (4 women). Expenses: Contact institution. *Financial support:* In 2010–11, 2 students received support, including 10 teaching assistantships with full tuition reimbursements available; Federal Work-Study, scholarships/grants, tuition waivers (full), and unspecified assistantships also available. Financial award application deadline: 4/1; financial award applicants required to submit FAFSA. In 2010, 174 DOs awarded. Offers osteopathic medicine (DO). *Application deadline:* For fall admission, 2/15 for domestic students. Applications are processed on a rolling basis. *Application fee:* $80. Electronic applications accepted. *Application Contact:* Donna S. Varney, Director of Admissions, 304-647-6373, Fax: 304-647-6384, E-mail: dvarney@wvsom.edu. *President,* Dr. Michael D. Adelman, 304-645-6295, Fax: 304-645-4859, E-mail: madelman@osteo.wvsom.edu.

WEST VIRGINIA STATE UNIVERSITY, Institute, WV 25112-1000

General Information State-supported, coed, comprehensive institution. *Graduate housing:* Rooms and/or apartments available on a first-come, first-served basis to single and married students.

GRADUATE UNITS

Graduate Programs Offers biotechnology (MA, MS); media studies (MA).

WEST VIRGINIA UNIVERSITY, Morgantown, WV 26506

General Information State-supported, coed, university. CGS member. *Graduate housing:* Rooms and/or apartments available on a first-come, first-served basis to single and married students. Housing application deadline: 1/22. *Research affiliation:* Federal Bureau of Investigation (FBI) (biometrics research), NASA IV and V Center (GOCO addressing software verification/validation), Research Partnership for an Energy Secure America (energy research), Florida A&M (plasma physics), University of Pittsburgh and Carnegie Mellon University (energy research), National Energy Technology Laboratory (fossil energy and environmental research).

GRADUATE UNITS

College of Business and Economics *Degree program information:* Part-time programs available. Postbaccalaureate distance learning degree programs offered. Offers business administration (MBA); business and economics (MA, MBA, MPA, MSIR, PhD); industrial relations (MSIR). Electronic applications accepted.

Division of Accounting *Degree program information:* Part-time and evening/weekend programs available. Offers accounting (MPA). Electronic applications accepted.

Division of Economics and Finance Offers business analysis (MA); developmental financial economics (PhD); environmental and resource economics (PhD); international economics (PhD); mathematical economics (MA); monetary economics (PhD); public finance (PhD); public policy (MA); regional and urban economics (PhD); statistics and economics (MA). Electronic applications accepted.

College of Creative Arts *Degree program information:* Part-time programs available. Offers acting (MFA); art education (MA); art history (MA); ceramics (MFA); creative arts (MA, MFA, MM, DMA, PhD); graphic design (MFA); music composition (MM, DMA); music education (MM, PhD); music history (MM); music performance (MM, DMA); music theory (MM); painting (MFA); printmaking (MFA); sculpture (MFA); studio art (MA); theatre design/technology (MFA).

College of Engineering and Mineral Resources *Degree program information:* Part-time programs available. Offers aerospace engineering (MSAE, PhD); chemical engineering (MS Ch E, PhD); civil engineering (MSCE, MSE, PhD); computer engineering (PhD); computer science (MSCS, PhD); electrical engineering (MSEE, PhD); engineering (MSE); engineering and mineral resources (MS, MS Ch E, MS Min E, MSAE, MSCE, MSCS, MSE, MSEE, MSIE, MSME, MSPNGE, MSSE, PhD); industrial engineering (MSE, MSIE, PhD); industrial hygiene (MS); mechanical engineering (MSME, PhD); mining engineering (MS Min E, PhD); occupational safety and health (PhD); petroleum and natural gas engineering (MSPNGE, PhD); safety management (MS); software engineering (MSSE).

College of Human Resources and Education *Degree program information:* Part-time and evening/weekend programs available. Postbaccalaureate distance learning degree programs offered (no on-campus study). Offers audiology (Au D); autism spectrum disorder (5-adult) (MA); autism spectrum disorder (K-6) (MA); child development and family studies (MA); counseling (MA); counseling psychology (PhD); curriculum and instruction (Ed D); early intervention/early childhood special education (MA); educational leadership (Ed D); educational psychology (MA); elementary education (MA); gifted education (1-12) (MA); higher education administration (MA); higher education curriculum and teaching (MA); human resources and education (MA, MS, Au D, Ed D, PhD); instructional design and technology (MA, Ed D); low vision (PreK-adult) (MA); multicategorical special education (5-adult) (MA); multicategorical special education (K-6) (MA); public school administration (MA); reading (MA); rehabilitation counseling (MS); secondary education (MA); severe/multiple disabilities (K-adult) (MA); special education (MA, Ed D); speech-language pathology (MS); vision impairments (PreK-adult) (MA). Electronic applications accepted.

College of Law *Degree program information:* Part-time programs available. Offers law (JD). Electronic applications accepted.

Davis College of Agriculture, Forestry and Consumer Sciences *Degree program information:* Part-time programs available. Offers agricultural and extension education (MS, PhD); agricultural and resource economics (MS); agricultural sciences (PhD); agriculture, forestry and consumer sciences (M Agr, MS, MSF, PhD); agronomy (MS); animal and food sciences (PhD); animal and nutritional sciences (MS); animal breeding (MS, PhD); biochemical and molecular genetics (MS, PhD); breeding (MS); cytogenetics (MS, PhD); descriptive embryology (MS, PhD); developmental genetics (MS); entomology (MS); environmental microbiology (MS); experimental morphogenesis/teratology (MS); food sciences (MS); forest resource science (PhD); forestry (MSF); horticulture (MS); human and community development (PhD); human genetics (MS, PhD); immunogenetics (MS, PhD); life cycles of animals and plants (MS, PhD); molecular aspects of development (MS, PhD); mutagenesis (MS, PhD); natural resource economics (PhD); nutrition (MS); oncology (MS, PhD); physiology (MS); plant and soil sciences (PhD); plant genetics (MS, PhD); plant pathology (MS); population and quantitative genetics (MS, PhD); production management (MS); recreation, parks and tourism resources (MS); regeneration (MS, PhD); reproduction (MS); reproductive physiology (MS, PhD); resource management (PhD); resource management and sustainable development (PhD); teaching vocational-agriculture (MS); teratology (PhD); toxicology (MS, PhD); wildlife and fisheries resources (MS). Electronic applications accepted.

Eberly College of Arts and Sciences *Degree program information:* Part-time and evening/weekend programs available. Postbaccalaureate distance learning degree programs offered (minimal on-campus study). Offers African history (MA, PhD); African-American history (MA, PhD); American history (MA, PhD); American public policy and politics (MA); analytical chemistry (MS, PhD); Appalachian/regional history (MA, PhD); applied mathematics (MS, PhD); applied physics (MS, PhD); arts and sciences (MA, MALS, MFA, MLS, MPA, MS, MSW, PhD); astrophysics (MS, PhD); behavior analysis (PhD); cell and molecular biology (MS, PhD); chemical physics (MS, PhD); clinical psychology (MA, PhD); communication in instruction (MA); communication studies (PhD); communication theory and research (MA); condensed matter physics (MS, PhD); corporate and organizational communication (MA); creative writing (MFA); development psychology (PhD); discrete mathematics (PhD); East Asian history (MA, PhD); elementary particle physics (MS, PhD); energy and environmental resources (MA); English (MA, PhD); environmental and evolutionary biology (MS, PhD); European history (MA, PhD); forensic biology (MS, PhD); French (MA); genomic biology (MS, PhD); geographic information systems (PhD); geography (MA, PhD); geography-regional development (PhD); geology (MS, PhD); geomorphology (MS, PhD); geophysics (MS, PhD); GIS/cartographic analysis (MA); history of science and technology (MA, PhD); hydrogeology (MS, PhD); inorganic chemistry (MS, PhD); interdisciplinary mathematics (MS); international and comparative public policy and politics (MA); Latin American history (MA); liberal studies (MALS); linguistics (MA); literary/cultural studies (MA, PhD); materials physics (MS, PhD); mathematics for secondary education (MS); neurobiology (MS, PhD); organic chemistry (MS, PhD); paleontology (MS, PhD); petroleum geology (PhD); petrology (MS, PhD); physical chemistry (MS, PhD); plasma physics (MS, PhD); political science (PhD); psychology (MS); public policy analysis (PhD); pure mathematics (MS); regional development (MA); solid state physics (MS, PhD); Spanish (MA); statistical physics (MS, PhD); statistics (MS); stratigraphy (MS, PhD); structure (MS, PhD); teaching English to speakers of other languages (MA); theoretical chemistry (MS, PhD); theoretical physics (MS, PhD); writing (MA). Electronic applications accepted.

School of Applied Social Sciences *Degree program information:* Part-time programs available. Offers aging and health care (MSW); applied social research (MA); applied social sciences (MA, MLS, MPA, MSW); children and families (MSW); community mental health (MSW); community organization and social administration (MSW); direct (clinical) social work practice (MSW); legal studies (MLS); public administration (MPA).

Perley Isaac Reed School of Journalism *Degree program information:* Part-time programs available. Postbaccalaureate distance learning degree programs offered (no on-campus study). Offers digital marketing communications (Graduate Certificate); integrated marketing communications (MS); journalism (MSJ). MS program taught exclusively online. Electronic applications accepted.

School of Dentistry Offers dentistry (DDS, MS); endodontics (MS); orthodontics (MS); prosthodontics (MS).

Division of Dental Hygiene *Degree program information:* Part-time programs available. Offers dental hygiene (MS).

School of Medicine *Degree program information:* Part-time and evening/weekend programs available. Offers community health/preventative medicine (MPH); medicine (MD, MOT, MPH, MS, DPT, PhD); occupational therapy (MOT); physical therapy (DPT); public health (MPH); public health sciences (PhD).

Graduate Programs at the Health Sciences Center *Degree program information:* Part-time and evening/weekend programs available. Postbaccalaureate distance learning degree programs offered (minimal on-campus study). Offers biochemistry and molecular biology (MS, PhD); cancer cell biology (PhD); cellular and integrative physiology (MS, PhD); exercise physiology (MS, PhD); health sciences (MS, PhD); immunology and microbial pathogenesis (MS, PhD); neuroscience (PhD); pharmaceutical and pharmacological sciences (MS, PhD).

School of Nursing *Degree program information:* Part-time programs available. Postbaccalaureate distance learning degree programs offered (minimal on-campus study). Offers nurse practitioner (Certificate); nursing (MSN, DNP, PhD). Electronic applications accepted.

School of Pharmacy Offers administrative pharmacy (PhD); behavioral pharmacy (MS, PhD); biopharmaceutics/pharmacokinetics (MS, PhD); clinical pharmacy (Pharm D); industrial pharmacy (MS); medicinal chemistry (MS, PhD); pharmaceutical chemistry (MS, PhD); pharmaceutics (MS, PhD); pharmacology and toxicology (MS); pharmacy (MS); pharmacy administration (MS).

School of Physical Education Offers athletic coaching education (MS); athletic training (MS); physical education/teacher education (MS, PhD); sport and exercise psychology (PhD); sport management (MS). Electronic applications accepted.

WEST VIRGINIA UNIVERSITY INSTITUTE OF TECHNOLOGY, Montgomery, WV 25136

General Information State-supported, coed, comprehensive institution. *Graduate housing:* Room and/or apartments available to single students; on-campus housing not available to married students.

GRADUATE UNITS

College of Engineering *Degree program information:* Part-time programs available. Offers control systems engineering (MS); engineering (MS).

WEST VIRGINIA WESLEYAN COLLEGE, Buckhannon, WV 26201

General Information Independent-religious, coed, comprehensive institution. CGS member. *Graduate housing:* Room and/or apartments available to single students; on-campus housing not available to married students.

GRADUATE UNITS

Department of Business and Economics *Degree program information:* Part-time and evening/weekend programs available. Offers business and economics (MBA).

Department of Education Offers education (M Ed).

Department of Exercise Science Offers athletic training (MS).

Department of Nursing Offers nursing (MS).

WHEATON COLLEGE, Wheaton, IL 60187-5593

General Information Independent-religious, coed, comprehensive institution. CGS member. *Graduate housing:* Rooms and/or apartments available on a first-come, first-served basis to single and married students. Housing application deadline: 4/1.

GRADUATE UNITS

Graduate School Offers biblical and theological studies (MA, PhD); biblical archaeology (MA); biblical exegesis (MA); biblical studies (MA); Christian formation and ministry (MA); clinical psychology (MA, Psy D); counseling ministries (MA); elementary level (MAT); evangelism (MA); general history of Christianity (MA); historical and systematic theology (MA); intercultural studies (MA); intercultural studies/teaching English as a second language (MA); missions (MA); religion in American life (MA); secondary level (MAT); teaching English as a second language (Certificate).

WHEELING JESUIT UNIVERSITY, Wheeling, WV 26003-6295

General Information Independent-religious, coed, comprehensive institution. CGS member. *Graduate housing:* Room and/or apartments available on a first-come, first-served basis to married students; on-campus housing not available to single students.

GRADUATE UNITS

Center for Professional and Graduate Studies *Degree program information:* Part-time and evening/weekend programs available. Offers organizational leadership (MSOL). Electronic applications accepted.

Department of Business *Degree program information:* Part-time and evening/weekend programs available. Offers accounting (MS); business administration (MBA). Electronic applications accepted.

Department of Nursing *Degree program information:* Part-time and evening/weekend programs available. Postbaccalaureate distance learning degree programs offered (minimal on-campus study). Offers nursing (MSN). Electronic applications accepted.

Department of Physical Therapy Offers physical therapy (DPT). Electronic applications accepted.

WHEELOCK COLLEGE, Boston, MA 02215-4176

General Information Independent, coed, primarily women, comprehensive institution. *Graduate housing:* Room and/or apartments available on a first-come, first-served basis to single students; on-campus housing not available to married students. Housing application deadline: 5/1.

GRADUATE UNITS

Graduate Programs *Degree program information:* Part-time and evening/weekend programs available. Postbaccalaureate distance learning degree programs offered (minimal on-campus study). Offers education (MS, MSW).

Division of Arts and Sciences Offers human development (MS). Electronic applications accepted.

Division of Child and Family Studies *Degree program information:* Part-time programs available. Postbaccalaureate distance learning degree programs offered (minimal on-campus study). Offers family studies (MS); family support and parent education (MS); family, culture, and society (MS). Electronic applications accepted.

Division of Education Postbaccalaureate distance learning degree programs offered (minimal on-campus study). Offers early childhood education (MS); education leadership (MS); elementary education (MS); language, literacy, and reading (MS); teaching students with moderate disabilities (MS). Electronic applications accepted.

Division of Social Work Offers social work (MSW). Electronic applications accepted.

WHITTIER COLLEGE, Whittier, CA 90608-0634

General Information Independent, coed, comprehensive institution. *Graduate housing:* On-campus housing not available.

GRADUATE UNITS

Graduate Programs *Degree program information:* Part-time and evening/weekend programs available. Offers educational administration (MA Ed); elementary education (MA Ed); secondary education (MA Ed).

Whittier Law School *Degree program information:* Part-time and evening/weekend programs available. Offers foreign legal studies (LL M); law (JD). Electronic applications accepted.

WHITWORTH UNIVERSITY, Spokane, WA 99251-0001

General Information Independent-religious, coed, comprehensive institution. *Enrollment:* 62 full-time matriculated graduate/professional students (40 women), 227 part-time matriculated graduate/professional students (156 women). *Enrollment by degree level:* 273 master's, 16 other advanced degrees. *Graduate faculty:* 60 full-time (36 women), 219 part-time/adjunct (162 women). Tuition and fees vary according to course load and program. *Graduate housing:* Room and/or apartments available on a first-come, first-served basis to single students; on-campus housing not available to married students. Housing application deadline: 5/1. *Student services:* Campus employment opportunities, career counseling, exercise/wellness program, free psychological counseling, international student services, low-cost health insurance, multicultural affairs office, services for students with disabilities, teacher training, writing training. *Library facilities:* Harriet Cheney Cowles Library plus 2 others. *Online resources:* library catalog, web page. *Collection:* 17,982 titles, 773 serial subscriptions.

Computer facilities: 300 computers available on campus for general student use. A campuswide network can be accessed from student residence rooms and from off campus. Online class registration is available. *Web address:* http://www.whitworth.edu/.

General Application Contact: Office of Admissions, 509-777-1000.

GRADUATE UNITS

Master of Arts in Theology Program *Degree program information:* Part-time and evening/weekend programs available. Offers theology (MA).

School of Education *Degree program information:* Part-time and evening/weekend programs available. Postbaccalaureate distance learning degree programs offered (minimal on-campus study). Offers administration (M Ed); counseling (M Ed); education (M Ed, MAT, MIT); elementary education (M Ed); gifted and talented (MAT); school counselors (M Ed); secondary education (M Ed); social agency/church setting (M Ed); special education (MAT); teaching (MIT).

School of Global Commerce and Management Students: 7 full-time (1 woman), 38 part-time (26 women), 6 international. Average age 31. 27 applicants, 81% accepted, 21 enrolled. *Faculty:* 5 full-time (1 woman), 11 part-time/adjunct (2 women). Expenses: Contact institution. *Financial support:* In 2010–11, 9 students received support; fellowships with tuition reimbursements available, career-related internships or fieldwork, Federal Work-Study, institutionally sponsored loans, and scholarships/grants available. Support available to part-time students. Financial award application deadline: 3/1; financial award applicants required to submit FAFSA. In 2010, 18 master's awarded. *Degree program information:* Part-time and evening/weekend programs available. Offers international management (MBA, MIM). *Application deadline:* For fall admission, 8/1 priority date for domestic and international students; for spring admission, 1/8 priority date for domestic students. Applications are processed on a rolling basis. *Application fee:* $35. Electronic applications accepted. *Application Contact:* Bonnie Wakefield, Assistant Director, Graduate Studies in Business, 509-777-4606, Fax: 509-777-3723, E-mail: bwakefield@whitworth.edu. *Director, Graduate Studies in Business,* John Hengesh, 509-777-4455, Fax: 509-777-3723, E-mail: jhengesh@whitworth.edu.

WICHITA STATE UNIVERSITY, Wichita, KS 67260

General Information State-supported, coed, university. CGS member. *Enrollment:* 14,806 graduate, professional, and undergraduate students; 1,221 full-time matriculated graduate/professional students (688 women), 1,530 part-time matriculated graduate/professional students (827 women). *Enrollment by degree level:* 2,348 master's, 394 doctoral, 9 other advanced degrees. *Graduate faculty:* 412 full-time (147 women), 230 part-time/adjunct (120 women). *Graduate housing:* Rooms and/or apartments available on a first-come, first-served basis to single and married students. *Student services:* Campus employment opportunities, campus safety program, career counseling, child daycare facilities, exercise/wellness program, free psychological counseling, grant writing training, international student services, low-cost health insurance, multicultural affairs office, services for students with disabilities, teacher training, writing training. *Library facilities:* Ablah Library plus 2 others. *Online resources:* library catalog, web page, access to other libraries' catalogs. *Collection:* 1.8 million titles, 1.2 million serial subscriptions, 195,116 audiovisual materials. *Research affiliation:* Cisco Systems (computer engineering), LSI (computer engineering), Boeing Aircraft Company (aerospace engineering), General Atomics (aerospace engineering), Wesley Medical Center (industrial and manufacturing engineering), NASA Ames Research Center (aerospace engineering).

Computer facilities: 1,500 computers available on campus for general student use. A campuswide network can be accessed from student residence rooms and from off campus. Online class registration, online Blackboard are available. *Web address:* http://www.wichita.edu/.

General Application Contact: Carrie C. Henderson, Admissions Coordinator, 316-978-3095, Fax: 316-978-3253, E-mail: carrie.henderson@wichita.edu.

GRADUATE UNITS

Graduate School Students: 1,221 full-time (688 women), 1,530 part-time (827 women). *Faculty:* 412 full-time (147 women), 230 part-time/adjunct (120 women). Expenses: Contact institution. *Financial support:* Fellowships with partial tuition reimbursements, research assistantships with partial tuition reimbursements, teaching assistantships with partial tuition reimbursements, career-related internships or fieldwork, Federal Work-Study, institutionally sponsored loans, scholarships/grants, traineeships, health care benefits, and unspecified assistantships available. Support available to part-time students. Financial award application deadline: 4/1; financial award applicants required to submit FAFSA. In 2010, 777 master's, 66 doctorates, 5 other advanced degrees awarded. *Degree program information:* Part-time and evening/weekend programs available. *Application deadline:* For fall admission, 7/15 priority date for domestic students, 4/1 for international students; for spring admission, 12/1 priority date for domestic students, 8/1 for international students. Applications are processed on a rolling basis. *Application fee:* $50 ($65 for international students). Electronic applications accepted. *Application Contact:* Carrie C. Henderson, Admissions Coordinator, 316-978-3095, Fax: 316-978-3253, E-mail: carrie.henderson@wichita.edu. *Associate Provost for Research/Dean,* Dr. J. David McDonald, 316-978-3095, Fax: 316-978-3253, E-mail: david.mcdonald@wichita.edu.

College of Education Expenses: Contact institution. *Degree program information:* Part-time and evening/weekend programs available. Offers counseling (M Ed); curriculum and instruction (M Ed); education (M Ed, MAT, Ed D, Ed S); educational leadership (M Ed, Ed D); educational psychology (M Ed); exercise science (M Ed); school psychology (Ed S); special education (M Ed); sport management (M Ed); teaching (MAT). *Application Contact:* Dr. Pearl Sharon Iorio, Dean, 316-978-3301, Fax: 316-978-3302, E-mail: sharon.iorio@wichita.edu. *Dean,* Dr. Pearl Sharon Iorio, 316-978-3301, Fax: 316-978-3302, E-mail: sharon.iorio@wichita.edu.

College of Engineering Expenses: Contact institution. *Degree program information:* Part-time and evening/weekend programs available. Offers aerospace engineering (MS, PhD); computer networking (MS); computer science (MS); electrical engineering (MS, PhD); engineering (MEM, MS, PhD); industrial and manufacturing engineering (MEM, MS, PhD); mechanical engineering (MS, PhD). *Application Contact:* Dr. Zulma Toro-Ramos, Dean, 316-978-3400, Fax: 316-978-3853, E-mail: zulma.toro-ramos@wichita.edu. *Dean,* Dr. Zulma Toro-Ramos, 316-978-3400, Fax: 316-978-3853, E-mail: zulma.toro-ramos@wichita.edu.

College of Fine Arts Expenses: Contact institution. *Degree program information:* Part-time programs available. Offers fine arts (MFA, MM, MME); music (MM); music education (MME); studio arts (MFA). *Application Contact:* Dr. Rodney E. Miller, Dean, 316-978-3389, Fax: 316-978-3951, E-mail: rodney.miller@wichita.edu. *Dean,* Dr. Rodney E. Miller, 316-978-3389, Fax: 316-978-3951, E-mail: rodney.miller@wichita.edu.

College of Health Professions Expenses: Contact institution. *Degree program information:* Part-time programs available. Offers clinical nurse specialist (MSN); communication sciences and disorders (MA, Au D, PhD); gerontology (MA); health professions (MA, MPA, MSN, Au D, DNP, DPT, PhD); nurse midwifery (MSN); nurse practitioner (MSN); nursing and healthcare systems administration (MSN); nursing practice (DNP); physical therapy (DPT); physician assistant (MPA). *Application Contact:* Dr. Peter A. Cohen, Dean, 316-978-3600, Fax: 316-978-3025, E-mail: peter.cohen@wichita.edu. *Dean,* Dr. Peter A. Cohen, 316-978-3600, Fax: 316-978-3025, E-mail: peter.cohen@wichita.edu.

Fairmount College of Liberal Arts and Sciences Expenses: Contact institution. *Degree program information:* Part-time and evening/weekend programs available. Offers anthropology (MA); applied mathematics (PhD); biological sciences (MS); chemistry (MS, PhD); clinical (PhD); communication (MA); community (PhD); creative writing (MFA); criminal justice (MA); earth, environmental, and physical sciences (MS); English (MA); history (MA); human factors (PhD); liberal arts and sciences (MA, MFA, MPA, MS, MSW, PhD); liberal studies (MA); mathematics (MS); public administration (MPA); social work (MSW); sociology (MA); Spanish (MA). *Application Contact:* Dr. William Bischoff, Dean, 316-978-3100, Fax: 316-978-3234, E-mail: bill.bischoff@wichita.edu. *Dean,* Dr. William Bischoff, 316-978-3100, Fax: 316-978-3234, E-mail: bill.bischoff@wichita.edu.

W. Frank Barton School of Business Expenses: Contact institution. *Degree program information:* Part-time and evening/weekend programs available. Offers accountancy (M Acc); business (EMBA, M Acc, MA, MBA); business economics (MA); economic analysis (MA); economics (MA). *Application Contact:* Dr. Douglas Hensler, Dean, 316-978-3200, Fax: 316-978-3845, E-mail: douglas.hensler@wichita.edu. *Dean,* Dr. Douglas Hensler, 316-978-3200, Fax: 316-978-3845, E-mail: douglas.hensler@wichita.edu.

WIDENER UNIVERSITY, Chester, PA 19013-5792

General Information Independent, coed, comprehensive institution. CGS member. *Enrollment:* 6,630 graduate, professional, and undergraduate students; 2,135 full-time matriculated graduate/professional students (1,122 women), 1,130 part-time matriculated graduate/professional students (812 women). *Enrollment by degree level:* 1,452 first professional, 879 master's, 723 doctoral, 105 other advanced degrees. *Graduate faculty:* 194 full-time (97 women), 152 part-time/adjunct (61 women). *Graduate housing:* Rooms and/or apartments available on a first-come, first-served basis to single students and available to married students. Housing application deadline: 5/30. *Student services:* Campus employment opportunities, career counseling, child daycare facilities, exercise/wellness program, free psychological counseling, international student services, multicultural affairs office, services for students with disabilities, teacher training, writing training. *Library facilities:* Wolfgram Memorial Library. *Online resources:* library catalog, web page, access to other libraries' catalogs. *Collection:* 218,284 titles, 2,335 serial subscriptions. *Research affiliation:* Small Business Administration, Riverfront Development Corporation (engineering, management), Advanced Technology Center (engineering).

Computer facilities: 345 computers available on campus for general student use. A campuswide network can be accessed from student residence rooms and from off campus. Online class registration is available. *Web address:* http://www.widener.edu/.

General Application Contact: Dr. Roberta Nolan, Assistant to Associate Provost for Graduate Studies, 610-499-4125, Fax: 610-499-4676, E-mail: gradmc@mail.widener.edu.

GRADUATE UNITS

College of Arts and Sciences Students: 1 (woman) full-time, 56 part-time (37 women); includes 17 Black or African American, non-Hispanic/Latino; 1 American Indian or Alaska Native, non-Hispanic/Latino; 1 Asian, non-Hispanic/Latino; 1 Hispanic/Latino. Average age 31. 45 applicants, 89% accepted. *Faculty:* 9 full-time (2 women), 8 part-time/adjunct (1 woman). Expenses: Contact institution. *Financial support:* Career-related internships or fieldwork and institutionally sponsored loans available. Support available to part-time students. Financial award application deadline: 4/1. In 2010, 12 master's awarded. *Degree program information:* Part-time and evening/weekend programs available. Offers arts and sciences (MA, MPA); criminal justice (MA); liberal studies (MA); public administration (MPA). *Application deadline:* Applications are processed on a rolling basis. *Application fee:* $25 ($300 for international students). *Application Contact:* Dr. Roberta Nolan, Assistant to Associate Provost for Graduate Studies, 610-499-4125, Fax: 610-499-4676, E-mail: gradmc@mail.widener.edu. *Dean,* Dr. Matthew Poslusny, 610-499-4007, E-mail: mposlusny@widener.edu.

Graduate Programs in Engineering Students: 10 full-time (0 women), 29 part-time (2 women); includes 7 Black or African American, non-Hispanic/Latino, 9 international. Average age 29. 439 applicants, 46% accepted, 23 enrolled. *Faculty:* 10 full-time (1 woman), 4 part-time/adjunct (0 women). Expenses: Contact institution. *Financial support:* In 2010–11, 5 teaching assistantships with partial tuition reimbursements (averaging $8,000 per year) were awarded; research assistantships, unspecified assistantships also available. Financial award application deadline: 3/15. In 2010, 22 master's awarded. *Degree program information:* Part-time and evening/weekend programs available. Offers chemical engineering (M Eng); civil engineering (M Eng); computer and software engineering (M Eng); engineering management (M Eng); management and technology (MSMT); mechanical engineering (M Eng); telecommunications engineering (M Eng). *Application deadline:* For fall admission, 8/1 priority date for domestic students, 4/1 priority date for international students; for winter admission, 2/1 priority date for international students; for spring admission, 12/1 priority date for domestic students, 9/1 priority date for international students. Applications are processed on a rolling basis. *Application fee:* $25 ($300 for international students). *Application Contact:* Christine M. Weist, Assistant to Associate Provost for Graduate Studies, 610-499-4351, Fax: 610-499-4277, E-mail: christine.m.weist@widener.edu. *Assistant Dean,* Nora J. Kogut, 610-499-4037, Fax: 610-499-4059, E-mail: njkogut@widener.edu.

School of Business Administration Students: 25 full-time (12 women), 122 part-time (55 women); includes 34 minority (16 Black or African American, non-Hispanic/Latino; 2 American Indian or Alaska Native, non-Hispanic/Latino; 11 Asian, non-Hispanic/Latino; 3 Hispanic/Latino; 1 Native Hawaiian or other Pacific Islander, non-Hispanic/Latino; 1 Two or more races, non-Hispanic/Latino), 15 international. Average age 34. 254 applicants, 91% accepted. *Faculty:* 14 full-time (6 women), 6 part-time/adjunct (2 women). Expenses: Contact institution. *Financial support:* In 2010–11, 11 research assistantships with full tuition reimbursements were awarded; career-related internships or fieldwork, Federal Work-Study, and traineeships also available. Support available to part-time students. Financial award application deadline:

5/1. In 2010, 85 master's awarded. *Degree program information:* Part-time and evening/weekend programs available. Offers accounting information systems (MS); business administration (MBA, MHA, MHR, MS); health and medical services administration (MBA, MHA); human resource management (MHR, MS); taxation (MS). *Application deadline:* For fall admission, 8/1 priority date for domestic students; for spring admission, 12/1 for domestic students. Applications are processed on a rolling basis. *Application fee:* $25 ($300 for international students). Electronic applications accepted. *Application Contact:* Ann Seltzer, Graduate Enrollment Administrator, 610-499-4305, E-mail: apseltzer@widener.edu. *Dean*, Dr. Savas Ozatalay, 610-499-4300, Fax: 610-499-4615.

School of Human Service Professions Students: 581 full-time (435 women), 496 part-time (403 women); includes 280 minority (193 Black or African American, non-Hispanic/Latino; 2 American Indian or Alaska Native, non-Hispanic/Latino; 22 Asian, non-Hispanic/Latino; 43 Hispanic/Latino; 20 Two or more races, non-Hispanic/Latino), 8 international. Average age 34. 592 applicants, 71% accepted. *Faculty:* 64 full-time (39 women), 70 part-time/adjunct (34 women). Expenses: Contact institution. *Financial support:* Fellowships, research assistantships, teaching assistantships, career-related internships or fieldwork, Federal Work-Study, institutionally sponsored loans, tuition waivers (partial), unspecified assistantships, and stipends available. Support available to part-time students. Financial award applicants required to submit FAFSA. In 2010, 285 master's, 110 doctorates awarded. *Degree program information:* Part-time and evening/weekend programs available. Offers human service professions (M Ed, MS, MSW, DPT, Ed D, PhD, Psy D). *Application Contact:* Dr. Stephen C. Wilhite, Dean, 610-499-4351, Fax: 610-499-4277, E-mail: stephen.c.wilhite@widener.edu. *Dean*, Dr. Stephen C. Wilhite, 610-499-4351, Fax: 610-499-4277, E-mail: stephen.c.wilhite@widener.edu.

Center for Education Students: 203 full-time (154 women), 415 part-time (298 women); includes 34 Black or African American, non-Hispanic/Latino; 1 American Indian or Alaska Native, non-Hispanic/Latino; 5 Asian, non-Hispanic/Latino; 10 Hispanic/Latino, 3 international. Average age 39. 139 applicants, 88% accepted. *Faculty:* 34 full-time (22 women), 37 part-time/adjunct (14 women). Expenses: Contact institution. *Financial support:* Career-related internships or fieldwork, tuition waivers (full and partial), and unspecified assistantships available. Support available to part-time students. Financial award application deadline: 5/1. In 2010, 168 master's, 31 doctorates awarded. *Degree program information:* Part-time and evening/weekend programs available. Offers adult education (M Ed); counseling in higher education (M Ed); counselor education (M Ed); early childhood education (M Ed); educational foundations (M Ed); educational leadership (M Ed); educational psychology (M Ed); elementary education (M Ed); English and language arts (M Ed); health education (M Ed); higher education leadership (Ed D); home and school visitor (M Ed); human sexuality (M Ed); mathematics education (M Ed); middle school education (M Ed); principalship (M Ed); reading and language arts (Ed D); reading education (M Ed); school administration (Ed D); science education (M Ed); social studies education (M Ed); special education (M Ed); technology education (M Ed). *Application deadline:* Applications are processed on a rolling basis. *Application fee:* $25 ($300 for international students). Electronic applications accepted. *Application Contact:* Dr. Roberta D. Nolan, Director of Graduate Admissions, 610-499-4125, E-mail: rdnolan@widener.edu. *Associate Dean*, Dr. Michael W. LeDoux, 610-499-4294, Fax: 610-499-4623, E-mail: mwledoux@widener.edu.

Center for Social Work Education Students: 61 full-time (51 women), 218 part-time (196 women); includes 140 minority (123 Black or African American, non-Hispanic/Latino; 6 Asian, non-Hispanic/Latino; 6 Hispanic/Latino; 5 Two or more races, non-Hispanic/Latino), 2 international. Average age 33. 184 applicants, 95% accepted. *Faculty:* 15 full-time (9 women), 16 part-time/adjunct (9 women). Expenses: Contact institution. *Financial support:* In 2010–11, 11 students received support, including 6 fellowships; career-related internships or fieldwork, Federal Work-Study, institutionally sponsored loans, and unspecified assistantships also available. Support available to part-time students. Financial award applicants required to submit FAFSA. In 2010, 117 master's awarded. *Degree program information:* Part-time programs available. Offers social work education (MSW, PhD). *Application deadline:* For fall admission, 3/1 for domestic students. Applications are processed on a rolling basis. *Application fee:* $25 ($300 for international students). Electronic applications accepted. *Application Contact:* Jill L. Brinker, Secretary, 610-499-1513, Fax: 610-499-4617, E-mail: socialwork@widener.edu. *Associate Dean and Director*, Dr. Paula T. Silver, 610-499-1150, Fax: 610-499-4617, E-mail: socialwork@widener.edu.

Institute for Graduate Clinical Psychology Students: 176 full-time (129 women), 4 part-time (3 women); includes 32 minority (7 Black or African American, non-Hispanic/Latino; 10 Asian, non-Hispanic/Latino; 11 Hispanic/Latino; 4 Two or more races, non-Hispanic/Latino), 3 international. Average age 25. 208 applicants, 31% accepted. *Faculty:* 15 full-time (6 women), 18 part-time/adjunct (10 women). Expenses: Contact institution. *Financial support:* Research assistantships, teaching assistantships, career-related internships or fieldwork, Federal Work-Study, institutionally sponsored loans, scholarships/grants, and stipends available. In 2010, 26 doctorates awarded. Offers clinical psychology (Psy D). *Application deadline:* For fall admission, 12/31 for domestic students. *Application fee:* $75. Electronic applications accepted. *Application Contact:* Ellen Madison, Admissions Coordinator, 611-499-1206, Fax: 610-499-4625, E-mail: ellen.t.madison@widener.edu. *Associate Dean/Director*, Dr. Virginia Brabender, 610-499-1208, Fax: 610-499-4625, E-mail: graduate.psychology@widener.edu.

Institute for Physical Therapy Education Students: 101 full-time (62 women), 2 part-time (1 woman); includes 5 minority (1 Asian, non-Hispanic/Latino; 3 Hispanic/Latino; 1 Two or more races, non-Hispanic/Latino). 82 applicants, 93% accepted. *Faculty:* 8 full-time (5 women), 1 (woman) part-time/adjunct. Expenses: Contact institution. *Financial support:* Teaching assistantships, Federal Work-Study, institutionally sponsored loans, and scholarships/grants available. Financial award application deadline: 5/1; financial award applicants required to submit FAFSA. In 2010, 53 doctorates awarded. Offers physical therapy education (MS, DPT). *Application deadline:* For fall admission, 1/30 for domestic students. Applications are processed on a rolling basis. *Application fee:* $40. *Application Contact:* Dr. Robin L. Dole, Associate Dean and Director, 610-499-1159, Fax: 610-499-1231, E-mail: robin.l.dole@widener.edu. *Associate Dean and Director*, Dr. Robin L. Dole, 610-499-1159, Fax: 610-499-1231, E-mail: robin.l.dole@widener.edu.

School of Law at Harrisburg Students: 442 full-time (199 women), 11 part-time (7 women); includes 56 minority (12 Black or African American, non-Hispanic/Latino; 1 American Indian or Alaska Native, non-Hispanic/Latino; 19 Asian, non-Hispanic/Latino; 17 Hispanic/Latino; 7 Two or more races, non-Hispanic/Latino), 1 international. Average age 25. *Faculty:* 26 full-time (12 women), 18 part-time/adjunct (6 women). Expenses: Contact institution. *Financial support:* Fellowships, research assistantships, career-related internships or fieldwork, Federal Work-Study, institutionally sponsored loans, and scholarships/grants available. Support available to part-time students. Financial award application deadline: 2/15; financial award applicants required to submit FAFSA. In 2010, 120 JDs awarded. *Degree program information:* Part-time programs available. Offers law (JD). *Application deadline:* For fall admission, 5/15 for domestic students. Applications are processed on a rolling basis. *Application fee:* $60. Electronic applications accepted. *Application Contact:* Barbara L. Ayars, Assistant Dean of Admissions, 302-477-2210, Fax: 302-477-2224, E-mail: barbara.l.ayars@law.widener.edu. *Dean*, Linda L. Ammons, 302-477-2100, Fax: 302-477-2282, E-mail: llammons@widener.edu.

School of Law at Wilmington Students: 961 full-time (414 women), 37 part-time (25 women); includes 59 Black or African American, non-Hispanic/Latino; 5 American Indian or Alaska Native, non-Hispanic/Latino; 52 Asian, non-Hispanic/Latino; 12 Hispanic/Latino, 13 international. Average age 26. 2,376 applicants, 39% accepted, 351 enrolled. *Faculty:* 58 full-time (23 women), 42 part-time/adjunct (15 women). Expenses: Contact institution. *Financial support:* Career-related internships or fieldwork, Federal Work-Study, institutionally sponsored loans, and scholarships/grants available. Support available to part-time students. Financial award application deadline: 2/15; financial award applicants required to submit FAFSA. In 2010, 266 first professional degrees, 28 master's, 3 doctorates awarded. *Degree program information:* Part-time programs available. Offers corporate law and finance (LL M); health law (LL M, MJ, D Law); juridical science (SJD); law (JD). *Application deadline:* For fall admission, 5/15 for domestic students; for spring admission, 12/1 for domestic students. Applications are processed on a rolling basis. *Application fee:* $60. *Application Contact:* Barbara L. Ayars, Assistant Dean of Admissions, 302-477-2210, Fax: 302-477-2224, E-mail: barbara.l.ayars@law.widener.edu. *Dean*, Linda L. Ammons, 302-477-2100, Fax: 302-477-2282, E-mail: llammons@widener.edu.

School of Nursing Students: 25 full-time (23 women), 147 part-time (130 women); includes 34 minority (21 Black or African American, non-Hispanic/Latino; 1 American Indian or Alaska Native, non-Hispanic/Latino; 3 Asian, non-Hispanic/Latino; 3 Hispanic/Latino; 6 Two or more races, non-Hispanic/Latino), 1 international. Average age 33. 77 applicants, 79% accepted. *Faculty:* 12 full-time (all women), 4 part-time/adjunct (3 women). Expenses: Contact institution. *Financial support:* Career-related internships or fieldwork, Federal Work-Study, and traineeships available. Support available to part-time students. Financial award application deadline: 4/1. In 2010, 34 master's, 11 doctorates awarded. *Degree program information:* Part-time and evening/weekend programs available. Offers nursing (MSN, DN Sc, PhD, PMC). *Application deadline:* For fall admission, 7/1 for domestic students; for winter admission, 3/1 for domestic students; for spring admission, 11/1 for domestic students. Applications are processed on a rolling basis. *Application fee:* $25 ($300 for international students). Electronic applications accepted. *Application Contact:* Betty A. Boyles, Information Contact, 610-499-4207, Fax: 610-499-4216, E-mail: betty.a.boyles@widener.edu. *Assistant Dean for Graduate Studies*, Dr. Mary B. Walker, 610-499-4208, Fax: 610-499-4216, E-mail: mary.b.walker@widener.edu.

WILBERFORCE UNIVERSITY, Wilberforce, OH 45384

General Information Independent-religious, coed, comprehensive institution.

GRADUATE UNITS

Program in Rehabilitation Counseling Offers rehabilitation counseling (MS).

WILFRID LAURIER UNIVERSITY, Waterloo, ON N2L 3C5, Canada

General Information Province-supported, coed, comprehensive institution. *Enrollment:* 17,382 graduate, professional, and undergraduate students; 831 full-time matriculated graduate/professional students (519 women), 563 part-time matriculated graduate/professional students (253 women). *Graduate faculty:* 372 full-time (147 women), 127 part-time/adjunct (84 women). *Graduate tuition:* Tuition and fees charges are reported in Canadian dollars. *International tuition:* $21,300 Canadian dollars full-time. *Tuition, area resident:* Full-time $15,300 Canadian dollars; part-time $1200 Canadian dollars per credit. *Required fees:* $650 Canadian dollars; $100 Canadian dollars per credit. Tuition and fees vary according to course load, degree level, campus/location and program. *Student services:* Campus employment opportunities, campus safety program, career counseling, child daycare facilities, exercise/wellness program, free psychological counseling, grant writing training, international student services, low-cost health insurance, multicultural affairs office, services for students with disabilities, teacher training, writing training. *Library facilities:* Wilfrid Laurier University Library plus 1 other. *Online resources:* library catalog, web page, access to other libraries' catalogs. *Collection:* 14,671 serial subscriptions, 24,246 audiovisual materials.

Computer facilities: 383 computers available on campus for general student use. A campuswide network can be accessed from student residence rooms and from off campus. Online class registration is available. *Web address:* http://www.wlu.ca/.

General Application Contact: Sheila Verwey, Graduate Admissions and Records Assistant, 519-884-0710 Ext. 2617, Fax: 519-884-1020, E-mail: gradstudies@wlu.ca.

GRADUATE UNITS

Faculty of Graduate and Postdoctoral Studies Students: 831 full-time (519 women), 563 part-time (253 women). 1,857 applicants, 45% accepted, 419 enrolled. *Faculty:* 372 full-time (147 women), 127 part-time/adjunct (84 women). Expenses: Contact institution. *Financial support:* In 2010–11, 575 fellowships, 39 research assistantships, 575 teaching assistantships were awarded; career-related internships or fieldwork, scholarships/grants, health care benefits, and unspecified assistantships also available. In 2010, 576 master's, 24 doctorates awarded. *Degree program information:* Part-time and evening/weekend programs available. *Application deadline:* For fall admission, 1/2 priority date for domestic and international students. *Application fee:* $125. Electronic applications accepted. *Application Contact:* Jennifer Williams, Graduate Admissions and Records Officer, 519-884-0710 Ext. 3536, Fax: 519-884-1020, E-mail: gradstudies@wlu.ca. *Dean*, Dr. Joan Norris, 519-884-1970 Ext. 3324, Fax: 519-884-1020, E-mail: jnorris@wlu.ca.

Faculty of Arts Students: 198 full-time (110 women), 26 part-time (13 women). 533 applicants, 39% accepted, 107 enrolled. *Faculty:* 176 full-time (75 women), 6 part-time/adjunct (3 women). Expenses: Contact institution. *Financial support:* In 2010–11, 252 fellowships, 13 research assistantships, 252 teaching assistantships were awarded; career-related internships or fieldwork, scholarships/grants, health care benefits, and unspecified assistantships also available. In 2010, 90 master's, 13 doctorates awarded. *Degree program information:* Part-time programs available. Offers agency (MA); archaeology and classical studies (MA); arts (M Sc, MA, MES, MIPP, PhD); body politics (MA); Canadian political studies (MA); community (MA); comparative politics/international relations (MA); conflict and security (PhD); cultural representation and social theory (MA); environmental and resource management (MA, MES, PhD); environmental science (M Sc, MES, PhD); gender and genre (MA, PhD); gender, sexuality and embodiment (MA); geomatics (M Sc, MES, PhD); global environment (PhD); global governance (MIPP); global justice and human rights (PhD); global political economy (PhD); global social governance (PhD); globalization, identity and social movements (MA); health, family and well-being (MA); history (MA, PhD); human geography (MES, PhD); human security (MIPP); international economic relations (MIPP); international environmental policy (MIPP); internationalization, migration and human rights (MA); media, technology and culture (MA); multilateral institutions and diplomacy (PhD); nation, diaspora, culture (PhD); religion and culture (MA); religious diversity of North America (PhD); self (MA); textuality, media and print studies (PhD); visual communication and culture (MA). *Application deadline:* For fall admission, 2/1 priority date for domestic and international students. *Application fee:* $100. Electronic applications accepted. *Application Contact:* Jennifer Williams, Graduate Admissions and Records Officer, 519-884-0710 Ext. 3536, Fax: 519-884-1020, E-mail: gradstudies@wlu.ca. *Dean*, Dr. Michael Carroll, 519-884-0710 Ext. 3891, Fax: 519-884-8854, E-mail: mcarroll@wlu.ca.

Faculty of Music Students: 13 full-time (11 women). 13 applicants, 54% accepted, 5 enrolled. *Faculty:* 2 full-time (1 woman). Expenses: Contact institution. *Financial support:* In 2010–11, 9 fellowships, 9 teaching assistantships were awarded; career-related internships or fieldwork, scholarships/grants, health care benefits, and unspecified assistantships also available. In 2010, 9 master's awarded. Offers music (MMT). *Application deadline:* For fall admission, 4/15 priority date for domestic and international students. *Application fee:* $125. Electronic applications accepted. *Application Contact:* Jennifer Willaims, Graduate Admissions and Records Officer, 519-884-0710 Ext. 3536, Fax: 519-884-1020, E-mail: gradstudies@wlu.ca. *Graduate Coordinator*, Dr. Colin Lee, 519-884-1970 Ext. 2892, Fax: 519-747-9129, E-mail: clee@wlu.ca.

Faculty of Science Students: 145 full-time (86 women), 8 part-time (5 women). 159 applicants, 60% accepted, 55 enrolled. *Faculty:* 88 full-time (31 women), 20 part-time/adjunct (4 women). Expenses: Contact institution. *Financial support:* In 2010–11, 253 fellowships, 11 research assistantships, 253 teaching assistantships were awarded; career-related internships or fieldwork, scholarships/grants, health care benefits, and unspecified assistantships also available. In 2010, 47 master's, 5 doctorates awarded. Offers behavioral neuroscience (M Sc, PhD); chemistry (M Sc); cognitive neuroscience (M Sc, PhD); community psychology (MA, PhD); integrative biology (M Sc); mathematics for science and finance (M Sc); physical activity and health (M Sc); science (M Sc, MA, PhD); social and developmental psychology (MA, PhD). *Application deadline:* For fall admission, 2/1 priority date for domestic and international students. *Application fee:* $100. Electronic applications accepted. *Application Contact:* Rosemary Springett, Graduate Admission and Records Officer, 519-884-0710 Ext. 3078, Fax: 519-884-1020, E-mail: gradstudies@wlu.ca. *Dean*, Dr. Paul Jessop, 519-884-1970 Ext. 2401, Fax: 519-884-0464, E-mail: pjessop@wlu.ca.

Faculty of Social Work Students: 271 full-time (227 women), 111 part-time (100 women), 1 international. 621 applicants, 40% accepted, 132 enrolled. *Faculty:* 20 full-time (13 women), 50 part-time/adjunct (36 women). Expenses: Contact institution. *Financial support:* Career-related internships or fieldwork, scholarships/grants, health care benefits, and unspecified assistantships available. In 2010, 164 master's, 5 doctorates awarded. *Degree program information:* Part-time programs available. Offers Aboriginal studies (MSW); community, policy, planning and organizations (MSW); critical social policy and organizational studies

Wilfrid Laurier University (continued)

(PhD); individuals, families and groups (MSW); social work practice (individuals, families, groups and communities) (PhD); social work practice: individuals, families, groups and communities (PhD). *Application deadline:* For fall admission, 1/15 priority date for domestic and international students. *Application fee:* $125. Electronic applications accepted. *Application Contact:* Rosemary Springett, Graduate Admission and Records Officer, 519-884-0710 Ext. 3078, E-mail: gradstudies@wlu.ca. *Associate Dean*, Dr. Cheryl-Anne Cait, 519-884-1970 Ext. 5224, E-mail: ccait@wlu.ca.

School of Business and Economics Students: 204 full-time (85 women), 418 part-time (135 women). 531 applicants, 54% accepted, 120 enrolled. *Faculty:* 86 full-time (27 women), 14 part-time/adjunct (4 women). Expenses: Contact institution. *Financial support:* In 2010–11, 61 fellowships, 15 research assistantships, 61 teaching assistantships were awarded; career-related internships or fieldwork, scholarships/grants, health care benefits, and unspecified assistantships also available. In 2010, 266 master's, 1 doctorate awarded. *Degree program information:* Part-time and evening/weekend programs available. Offers accounting (PhD); business and economics (EMTM, M Fin, M Sc, MA, MBA, PhD); co-op (MBA); economics (MA); finance (M Fin); financial economics (PhD); full-time (MBA); marketing (PhD); operations and supply chain management (PhD); organizational behavior and human resource management (M Sc); organizational behaviour and human resource management (PhD); part-time (MBA); supply chain management (M Sc); technology management (EMTM). *Application deadline:* For fall admission, 2/1 priority date for domestic and international students. *Application fee:* $125. Electronic applications accepted. *Application Contact:* Jennifer Williams, Graduate Admissions and Records Officer, 519-884-0710 Ext. 3536, Fax: 519-884-1020, E-mail: gradstudies@wlu.ca. *Dean*, Dr. William Banks, 519-884-1970 Ext. 2671, Fax: 519-746-5733, E-mail: wbanks@wlu.ca.

Laurier Brantford *Faculty:* 13 full-time (6 women). Expenses: Contact institution. *Financial support:* Career-related internships or fieldwork, scholarships/grants, health care benefits, and unspecified assistantships available. Offers criminology (MA). *Application deadline:* For fall admission, 6/1 priority date for domestic students, 5/1 priority date for international students. *Application fee:* $100. Electronic applications accepted. *Application Contact:* Jennifer Williams, Graduate Admissions and Records Officer, 519-884-0710 Ext. 3536, Fax: 519-884-1020, E-mail: gradstudies@wlu.ca. *Graduate Coordinator*, Dr. Thomas Fleming, 519-756-8228 Ext. 5740, Fax: 519-759-2127, E-mail: tfleming@wlu.ca.

Waterloo Lutheran Seminary Expenses: Contact institution. *Financial support:* Career-related internships or fieldwork, institutionally sponsored loans, and scholarships/grants available. Financial award application deadline: 10/1. *Degree program information:* Part-time programs available. Offers divinity (M Div); multifaith spiritual care and counseling (Diploma); pastoral leadership (D Min); spiritual care and counseling (D Min); theology (M Th, MTS). *Application deadline:* For fall admission, 5/1 for domestic and international students; for winter admission, 9/1 for domestic and international students; for spring admission, 1/1 for domestic and international students. Applications are processed on a rolling basis. *Application fee:* $50. Electronic applications accepted. *Application Contact:* Sarina Wheeler, Student Advisor and Admissions Coordinator, 519-884-0710 Ext. 3498, Fax: 519-725-2434, E-mail: swheeler@wlu.ca. *Principal-Dean/Registrar*, Dr. David Pfrimmer, 519-884-0710 Ext. 3229, E-mail: dpfrimmer@wlu.ca.

WILKES UNIVERSITY, Wilkes-Barre, PA 18766-0002

General Information Independent, coed, comprehensive institution. CGS member. *Enrollment:* 5,926 graduate, professional, and undergraduate students; 509 full-time matriculated graduate/professional students (308 women), 3,233 part-time matriculated graduate/professional students (2,306 women). *Enrollment by degree level:* 279 first professional, 3,346 master's, 117 doctoral. Tuition and fees vary according to degree level and program. *Graduate housing:* On-campus housing not available. *Student services:* Campus employment opportunities, career counseling, free psychological counseling, international student services, low-cost health insurance, multicultural affairs office, services for students with disabilities. *Library facilities:* Eugene S. Farley Library. *Online resources:* library catalog, access to other libraries' catalogs.

Computer facilities: Computer purchase and lease plans are available. 739 computers available on campus for general student use. A campuswide network can be accessed from student residence rooms and from off campus. Online class registration is available. *Web address:* http://www.wilkes.edu/.

General Application Contact: Kathleen Houlihan, Director of Graduate Studies, 570-408-3235, Fax: 570-408-7846, E-mail: kathleen.houlihan@wilkes.edu.

GRADUATE UNITS

College of Graduate and Professional Studies Students: 509 full-time (308 women), 3,233 part-time (2,306 women); includes 136 minority (36 Black or African American, non-Hispanic/Latino; 28 Asian, non-Hispanic/Latino; 40 Hispanic/Latino; 2 Native Hawaiian or other Pacific Islander, non-Hispanic/Latino; 30 Two or more races, non-Hispanic/Latino), 35 international. Average age 33. Expenses: Contact institution. *Financial support:* Federal Work-Study and unspecified assistantships available. Financial award application deadline: 3/1; financial award applicants required to submit FAFSA. In 2010, 69 first professional degrees, 1,245 master's awarded. *Degree program information:* Part-time and evening/weekend programs available. Postbaccalaureate distance learning degree programs offered (minimal on-campus study). *Application deadline:* Applications are processed on a rolling basis. *Application fee:* $45 ($65 for international students). Electronic applications accepted. *Application Contact:* Kathleen Houlihan, Director of Graduate Studies, 570-408-3235, Fax: 570-408-7846, E-mail: kathleen.houlihan@wilkes.edu. *Dean*, Dr. Michael Speziale, 570-408-4679, Fax: 570-408-7846, E-mail: michael.speziale@wilkes.edu.

College of Arts, Humanities and Social Sciences Students: 81 full-time (48 women), 18 part-time (10 women); includes 17 minority (7 Black or African American, non-Hispanic/Latino; 1 Asian, non-Hispanic/Latino; 7 Hispanic/Latino; 1 Native Hawaiian or other Pacific Islander, non-Hispanic/Latino; 1 Two or more races, non-Hispanic/Latino). Average age 37. Expenses: Contact institution. *Financial support:* Federal Work-Study and unspecified assistantships available. Financial award application deadline: 3/1; financial award applicants required to submit FAFSA. In 2010, 45 master's awarded. *Degree program information:* Part-time and evening/weekend programs available. Postbaccalaureate distance learning degree programs offered (minimal on-campus study). Offers arts, humanities and social sciences (MA, MFA); creative writing (MA, MFA). *Application deadline:* Applications are processed on a rolling basis. *Application fee:* $35. Electronic applications accepted. *Application Contact:* Kathleen Houlihan, Director of Graduate Studies, 570-408-3235, Fax: 570-408-7846, E-mail: kathleen.houlihan@wilkes.edu. *Dean*, Dr. Linda Winkler, 570-408-4605, Fax: 570-408-7860, E-mail: linda.winkler@wilkes.edu.

College of Science and Engineering Students: 14 full-time (1 woman), 18 part-time (2 women); includes 1 Asian, non-Hispanic/Latino; 1 Two or more races, non-Hispanic/Latino, 8 international. Average age 29. Expenses: Contact institution. *Financial support:* Federal Work-Study and unspecified assistantships available. Financial award application deadline: 3/1; financial award applicants required to submit FAFSA. In 2010, 26 master's awarded. *Degree program information:* Part-time programs available. Offers electrical engineering (MSEE); engineering management (MS); mathematics (MS, MS Ed); mechanical engineering (MS); science and engineering (MS, MS Ed, MSEE). *Application deadline:* Applications are processed on a rolling basis. *Application fee:* $45 ($65 for international students). Electronic applications accepted. *Application Contact:* Kathleen Houlihan, Director of Graduate Studies, 570-408-3235, Fax: 570-408-7846, E-mail: kathleen.houlihan@wilkes.edu. *Dean*, Dr. Dale Bruns, 570-408-4600, Fax: 570-408-7860, E-mail: dale.bruns@wilkes.edu.

Jay S. Sidhu School of Business and Leadership Students: 39 full-time (16 women), 146 part-time (71 women); includes 5 Black or African American, non-Hispanic/Latino; 2 Asian, non-Hispanic/Latino; 1 Hispanic/Latino; 1 Two or more races, non-Hispanic/Latino, 16 international. Average age 30. Expenses: Contact institution. *Financial support:* Federal Work-Study and unspecified assistantships available. Financial award application deadline: 3/1; financial award applicants required to submit FAFSA. In 2010, 85 master's awarded. *Degree program information:* Part-time and evening/weekend programs available. Offers accounting (MBA); entrepreneurship (MBA); finance (MBA); health care administration (MBA); human resource management (MBA); international business (MBA); marketing (MBA); operations management (MBA); organizational leadership and development (MBA). *Application deadline:* Applications are processed on a rolling basis. *Application fee:* $45 ($65 for international students). Electronic applications accepted. *Application Contact:* Kathleen Houlihan, Director of Graduate Studies, 570-408-3235, Fax: 570-408-7846, E-mail: kathleen.houlihan@wilkes.edu. *Dean*, Dr. Paul Browne, 570-408-4701, Fax: 570-408-7846, E-mail: paul.browne@wilkes.edu.

Nesbitt College of Pharmacy and Nursing Students: 298 full-time (184 women), 44 part-time (41 women); includes 3 Black or African American, non-Hispanic/Latino; 4 Asian, non-Hispanic/Latino; 2 Hispanic/Latino; 3 Two or more races, non-Hispanic/Latino, 2 international. Average age 26. Expenses: Contact institution. *Financial support:* Federal Work-Study and unspecified assistantships available. Financial award application deadline: 3/1; financial award applicants required to submit FAFSA. In 2010, 69 first professional degrees, 16 master's awarded. *Degree program information:* Part-time and evening/weekend programs available. Offers nursing (MSN, DNP); pharmacy (Pharm D); pharmacy and nursing (Pharm D, MSN, DNP). *Application deadline:* Applications are processed on a rolling basis. *Application Contact:* Kathleen Houlihan, Director of Graduate Studies, 570-408-3235, Fax: 570-408-7846, E-mail: kathleen.houlihan@wilkes.edu. *Dean*, Dr. Bernard Graham, 570-408-4280, Fax: 570-408-7828, E-mail: bernard.graham@wilkes.edu.

School of Education Students: 73 full-time (55 women), 2,741 part-time (1,975 women); includes 88 minority (20 Black or African American, non-Hispanic/Latino; 18 Asian, non-Hispanic/Latino; 27 Hispanic/Latino; 1 Native Hawaiian or other Pacific Islander, non-Hispanic/Latino; 22 Two or more races, non-Hispanic/Latino), 8 international. Average age 33. Expenses: Contact institution. *Financial support:* Federal Work-Study and unspecified assistantships available. Financial award application deadline: 3/1; financial award applicants required to submit FAFSA. In 2010, 1,073 master's awarded. *Degree program information:* Part-time and evening/weekend programs available. Postbaccalaureate distance learning degree programs offered (minimal on-campus study). Offers art and science of teaching (MS Ed); classroom technology (MS Ed); early childhood literacy (MS Ed); educational computing (MS Ed); educational development and strategies (MS Ed); educational leadership (MS Ed); educational technology (Ed D); higher education administration (Ed D); instructional media (MS Ed); instructional technology (MS Ed); K-12 administration (Ed D); online teaching (MS Ed); school business leadership (MS Ed); secondary education (MS Ed); special education (MS Ed); teaching English as a second language (MS Ed); twenty-first century teaching and learning (MS Ed). *Application deadline:* Applications are processed on a rolling basis. *Application fee:* $45. Electronic applications accepted. *Application Contact:* Kathleen Houlihan, Director of Graduate Studies, 570-408-3235, Fax: 570-408-7846, E-mail: kathleen.houlihan@wilkes.edu. *Dean*, Dr. Michael Speziale, 570-408-4679, Fax: 570-408-4905, E-mail: michael.speziale@wilkes.edu.

WILLAMETTE UNIVERSITY, Salem, OR 97301-3931

General Information Independent-religious, coed, comprehensive institution. *Enrollment:* 2,851 graduate, professional, and undergraduate students; 778 full-time matriculated graduate/professional students (354 women), 92 part-time matriculated graduate/professional students (55 women). *Enrollment by degree level:* 420 first professional, 439 master's. *Graduate faculty:* 47 full-time (14 women), 52 part-time/adjunct (20 women). *Graduate housing:* Room and/or apartments available on a first-come, first-served basis to single students; on-campus housing not available to married students. Housing application deadline: 6/1. *Student services:* Campus employment opportunities, campus safety program, career counseling, free psychological counseling, international student services, low-cost health insurance, multicultural affairs office, services for students with disabilities, teacher training. *Library facilities:* Mark O. Hatfield Library plus 1 other. *Online resources:* library catalog, web page, access to other libraries' catalogs.

Computer facilities: A campuswide network can be accessed from student residence rooms and from off campus. Online class registration is available. *Web address:* http://www.willamette.edu/.

General Application Contact: Office of Graduate Admissions, 503-370-6300.

GRADUATE UNITS

College of Law Students: 426 full-time (185 women), 5 part-time (3 women); includes 77 minority (8 Black or African American, non-Hispanic/Latino; 7 American Indian or Alaska Native, non-Hispanic/Latino; 34 Asian, non-Hispanic/Latino; 27 Hispanic/Latino; 1 Native Hawaiian or other Pacific Islander, non-Hispanic/Latino), 4 international. Average age 27. 1,432 applicants, 37% accepted, 158 enrolled. *Faculty:* 34 full-time (12 women), 23 part-time/adjunct (5 women). Expenses: Contact institution. *Financial support:* In 2010–11, 404 students received support; fellowships with partial tuition reimbursements available, research assistantships with partial tuition reimbursements available, Federal Work-Study, scholarships/grants, and tuition waivers (full and partial) available. Financial award application deadline: 3/1; financial award applicants required to submit FAFSA. In 2010, 135 first professional degrees, 4 master's awarded. Offers law (JD, LL M). *Application deadline:* For fall admission, 3/1 priority date for domestic students, 3/1 for international students. Applications are processed on a rolling basis. *Application fee:* $50. Electronic applications accepted. *Application Contact:* Carolyn Dennis, Director of Admission, 503-370-6282, Fax: 503-370-6087, E-mail: law-admission@willamette.edu. *Dean*, Peter V. Letsou, 503-370-6402, Fax: 503-370-6828, E-mail: pletsou@willamette.edu.

George H. Atkinson Graduate School of Management Students: 203 full-time (85 women), 104 part-time (49 women); includes 43 minority (9 Black or African American, non-Hispanic/Latino; 1 American Indian or Alaska Native, non-Hispanic/Latino; 16 Asian, non-Hispanic/Latino; 13 Hispanic/Latino; 4 Two or more races, non-Hispanic/Latino), 73 international. Average age 28. 299 applicants, 86% accepted, 132 enrolled. *Faculty:* 17 full-time (4 women), 26 part-time/adjunct (8 women). Expenses: Contact institution. *Financial support:* In 2010–11, 177 students received support, including 12 research assistantships with tuition reimbursements available (averaging $1,500 per year); career-related internships or fieldwork, Federal Work-Study, scholarships/grants, unspecified assistantships, and scholarships are merit-based also available. Financial award application deadline: 5/1; financial award applicants required to submit FAFSA. In 2010, 100 master's awarded. *Degree program information:* Part-time and evening/weekend programs available. Offers management (MBA). *Application deadline:* For fall admission, 1/10 priority date for domestic and international students; for winter admission, 3/1 priority date for domestic and international students; for spring admission, 5/1 priority date for domestic and international students. Applications are processed on a rolling basis. *Application fee:* $0. Electronic applications accepted. *Application Contact:* Aimee Akimoff, Director of Recruitment, 503-370-6167, Fax: 503-370-3011, E-mail: aakimoff@willamette.edu. *Dean/Professor of Free Enterprise*, Dr. Debra J. Ringold, 503-370-6440, Fax: 503-370-3011, E-mail: dringold@willamette.edu.

Graduate School of Education Students: 139 full-time (79 women), 2 part-time (both women). Expenses: Contact institution. *Financial support:* Fellowships, career-related internships or fieldwork, institutionally sponsored loans, scholarships/grants, and tuition waivers (partial) available. Financial award application deadline: 2/1; financial award applicants required to submit FAFSA. *Degree program information:* Evening/weekend programs available. Offers environmental literacy (M Ed); reading (M Ed); special education (M Ed); teaching (MAT). *Application deadline:* Applications are processed on a rolling basis. *Application fee:* $50. Electronic applications accepted. *Application Contact:* Heather Daniels, Director of Admission, 503-375-5453, Fax: 503-375-5478, E-mail: hdaniels@willamette.edu. *Dean*, Julie Gess-Newsome, 503-370-6798, Fax: 503-375-5478, E-mail: jgessnew@willamette.edu.

WILLIAM CAREY UNIVERSITY, Hattiesburg, MS 39401-5499

General Information Independent-religious, coed, comprehensive institution. *Graduate housing:* Room and/or apartments available on a first-come, first-served basis to single students; on-campus housing not available to married students. Housing application deadline: 8/15.

GRADUATE UNITS

School of Business *Degree program information:* Part-time programs available. Offers business (MBA).

School of Education *Degree program information:* Part-time programs available. Offers art education (M Ed); art of teaching (M Ed); elementary education (M Ed, Ed S); English education (M Ed); gifted education (M Ed); history and social science (M Ed); mild/moderate disabilities (M Ed); secondary education (M Ed).

School of Nursing *Degree program information:* Part-time programs available. Offers nursing (MSN).

School of Psychology and Counseling *Degree program information:* Part-time programs available. Offers counseling psychology (MS).

WILLIAM HOWARD TAFT UNIVERSITY, Santa Ana, CA 92704

General Information Proprietary, coed, graduate-only institution.

GRADUATE UNITS

Graduate Programs

The Boyer Graduate School of Education Offers education (M Ed).

W. Edwards Deming School of Business Offers taxation (MS).

WILLIAM MITCHELL COLLEGE OF LAW, St. Paul, MN 55105-3076

General Information Independent, coed, graduate-only institution. *Enrollment by degree level:* 1,013 first professional. *Graduate faculty:* 37 full-time (17 women), 279 part-time/adjunct (141 women). *Tuition:* Full-time $35,660; part-time $25,790 per year. *Graduate housing:* On-campus housing not available. *Student services:* Campus employment opportunities, campus safety program, career counseling, free psychological counseling, international student services, multicultural affairs office, services for students with disabilities, writing training. *Library facilities:* Warren E. Burger Library. *Online resources:* library catalog, web page, access to other libraries' catalogs. *Collection:* 206,667 titles, 2,188 serial subscriptions, 844 audiovisual materials. *Research affiliation:* Haifa University (law), Suffolk University (law), University of Minnesota, Minneapolis (law), University of Nevada, Las Vegas (law), Haifa University (law).

Computer facilities: 50 computers available on campus for general student use. A campuswide network can be accessed from off campus. Online class registration, wireless network for all simultaneous users are available. *Web address:* http://www.wmitchell.edu/.

General Application Contact: Kendra Dane, Assistant Dean and Director of Admissions, 651-290-6343, Fax: 651-290-7535, E-mail: admissions@wmitchell.edu.

GRADUATE UNITS

Professional Program Students: 667 full-time (321 women), 346 part-time (184 women); includes 113 minority (24 Black or African American, non-Hispanic/Latino; 12 American Indian or Alaska Native, non-Hispanic/Latino; 47 Asian, non-Hispanic/Latino; 22 Hispanic/Latino; 1 Native Hawaiian or other Pacific Islander, non-Hispanic/Latino; 7 Two or more races, non-Hispanic/Latino), 8 international. Average age 29. 1,448 applicants, 55% accepted, 357 enrolled. *Faculty:* 37 full-time (17 women), 279 part-time/adjunct (141 women). Expenses: Contact institution. *Financial support:* In 2010–11, 720 students received support, including 111 research assistantships (averaging $2,000 per year); Federal Work-Study and scholarships/grants also available. Support available to part-time students. Financial award application deadline: 3/15; financial award applicants required to submit FAFSA. In 2010, 300 first professional degrees awarded. *Degree program information:* Part-time and evening/weekend programs available. Offers law (JD, LL M). *Application deadline:* For spring admission, 5/1 for domestic and international students. Applications are processed on a rolling basis. *Application fee:* $50. Electronic applications accepted. *Application Contact:* Kendra Dane, Assistant Dean and Director of Admissions, 651-290-6343, Fax: 651-290-7535, E-mail: admissions@wmitchell.edu. *President/Dean,* Eric S. Janus, 651-290-6310, Fax: 651-290-6426.

WILLIAM PATERSON UNIVERSITY OF NEW JERSEY, Wayne, NJ 07470-8420

General Information State-supported, coed, comprehensive institution. CGS member. *Graduate housing:* Room and/or apartments available on a first-come, first-served basis to single students; on-campus housing not available to married students.

GRADUATE UNITS

Christos M. Cotsakos College of Business *Degree program information:* Part-time and evening/weekend programs available. Offers business (MBA). Electronic applications accepted.

College of Education *Degree program information:* Part-time and evening/weekend programs available. Offers counseling services (M Ed); curriculum and learning (M Ed); educational leadership (M Ed); reading (M Ed); special education (M Ed); special education and counseling services (M Ed); teaching (MAT). Electronic applications accepted.

College of Humanities and Social Sciences *Degree program information:* Part-time and evening/weekend programs available. Offers clinical and counseling psychology (MA); English (MA); history (MA); public policy and international affairs (MA); sociology (MA). Electronic applications accepted.

College of Science and Health *Degree program information:* Part-time and evening/weekend programs available. Offers biotechnology (MS); communication disorders (MS); general biology (MS); nursing (MSN). Electronic applications accepted.

College of the Arts and Communication *Degree program information:* Part-time and evening/weekend programs available. Offers art (MFA); music (MM); professional communication (MA). Electronic applications accepted.

See Close-Up on page 1001.

WILLIAMS COLLEGE, Williamstown, MA 01267

General Information Independent, coed, comprehensive institution. *Graduate housing:* Room and/or apartments available on a first-come, first-served basis to single students; on-campus housing not available to married students. *Research affiliation:* Clark Art Institute.

GRADUATE UNITS

Program in the History of Art *Degree program information:* Part-time programs available. Offers history of art (MA). Offered jointly with Sterling and Francine Clark Art Institute. Electronic applications accepted.

WILLIAM WOODS UNIVERSITY, Fulton, MO 65251-1098

General Information Independent-religious, coed, comprehensive institution. *Graduate housing:* On-campus housing not available.

GRADUATE UNITS

Graduate and Adult Studies *Degree program information:* Evening/weekend programs available. Offers administration (Ed S); agriculture (MBA); athletic/activities administration (M Ed); curriculum and instruction (M Ed); curriculum leadership (Ed S); elementary administration (M Ed); health management (MBA); human resources (MBA); principalship (Ed S); secondary administration (M Ed); special education director (M Ed). Electronic applications accepted.

WILMINGTON COLLEGE, Wilmington, OH 45177

General Information Independent-religious, coed, comprehensive institution. *Graduate housing:* On-campus housing not available.

GRADUATE UNITS

Department of Education *Degree program information:* Part-time programs available. Offers reading (M Ed); special education (M Ed).

WILMINGTON UNIVERSITY, New Castle, DE 19720-6491

General Information Independent, coed, comprehensive institution. *Enrollment:* 10,605 graduate, professional, and undergraduate students; 1,079 full-time matriculated graduate/professional students (738 women), 2,457 part-time matriculated graduate/professional students (1,555 women). *Enrollment by degree level:* 2,457 master's, 263 doctoral. *Graduate faculty:* 70 full-time (25 women), 507 part-time/adjunct (316 women). *Tuition:* Full-time $7110; part-time $395 per credit hour. Tuition and fees vary according to campus/location. *Graduate housing:* On-campus housing not available. *Student services:* Career counseling, free psychological counseling, international student services, services for students with disabilities, teacher training. *Library facilities:* Robert C. and Dorothy M. Peoples Library plus 1 other. *Online resources:* library catalog, access to other libraries' catalogs. *Collection:* 98,713 titles, 425 serial subscriptions.

Computer facilities: 600 computers available on campus for general student use. A campuswide network can be accessed. Online class registration is available. *Web address:* http://www.wilmu.edu/.

General Application Contact: Laura Morris, Director of Admissions, 302-295-1179, Fax: 302-328-5164, E-mail: inquire@wilmcoll.edu.

GRADUATE UNITS

College of Business *Degree program information:* Part-time and evening/weekend programs available. Offers business administration (MBA); finance (MBA); health care administration (MBA, MS); homeland security (MBA, MS); human resource management (MS); management (MS); management information systems (MBA); organizational leadership (MS); public administration (MS); transportation and logistics (MBA, MS). Electronic applications accepted.

College of Education *Degree program information:* Part-time and evening/weekend programs available. Offers applied education technology (M Ed); career and technical education (M Ed); elementary and secondary school counseling (M Ed); elementary special education (M Ed); elementary studies (M Ed); instruction: gifted and talented (M Ed); instruction: teaching and learning (M Ed); literacy (M Ed); reading (M Ed); school leadership (M Ed); secondary teaching (MAT). Electronic applications accepted.

College of Health Professions *Degree program information:* Part-time programs available. Offers adult nurse practitioner (MSN); family nurse practitioner (MSN); gerontology (MSN); leadership (MSN); nursing (MSN); women's nurse practitioner (MSN). Electronic applications accepted.

College of Social and Behavioral Sciences *Degree program information:* Part-time and evening/weekend programs available. Offers administration of human services (MS); administration of justice (MS); community counseling (MS). Electronic applications accepted.

College of Technology *Degree program information:* Part-time and evening/weekend programs available. Offers corporate training (MS); information assurance (MS); information systems technologies (MS); Internet web design (MS); management information systems (MS). Electronic applications accepted.

Program in Innovation and Leadership *Degree program information:* Part-time programs available. Offers education innovation (Ed D); organizational leadership (Ed D). Electronic applications accepted.

WILSON COLLEGE, Chambersburg, PA 17201-1285

General Information Independent-religious, coed, primarily women, comprehensive institution.

GRADUATE UNITS

Program in Education *Degree program information:* Evening/weekend programs available. Offers education (M Ed). Electronic applications accepted.

WINEBRENNER THEOLOGICAL SEMINARY, Findlay, OH 45840

General Information Independent-religious, coed, graduate-only institution. *Enrollment by degree level:* 38 first professional, 31 master's, 13 doctoral. *Graduate faculty:* 7 full-time (1 woman), 2 part-time/adjunct (1 woman). *Tuition:* Full-time $10,920; part-time $426 per credit hour. *Required fees:* $115 per term. Tuition and fees vary according to degree level and program. *Graduate housing:* On-campus housing not available. *Student services:* Campus employment opportunities, career counseling, free psychological counseling, international student services. *Library facilities:* Winebrenner Seminary Library. *Online resources:* library catalog, access to other libraries' catalogs. *Collection:* 43,431 titles, 105 serial subscriptions, 748 audiovisual materials.

Computer facilities: A campuswide network can be accessed from off campus. *Web address:* http://www.winebrenner.edu/.

General Application Contact: Jim Wilder, Regional Coordinator, 419-434-4220, Fax: 419-434-4267, E-mail: admissions@winebrenner.edu.

GRADUATE UNITS

Graduate Programs Students: 38 full-time (7 women), 44 part-time (17 women); includes 11 Black or African American, non-Hispanic/Latino; 1 Two or more races, non-Hispanic/Latino, 2 international. Average age 40. 23 applicants, 100% accepted, 19 enrolled. *Faculty:* 7 full-time (1 woman), 2 part-time/adjunct (1 woman). Expenses: Contact institution. *Financial support:* In 2010–11, 26 students received support, including 1 research assistantship with partial tuition reimbursement available, 2 teaching assistantships with partial tuition reimbursements available; institutionally sponsored loans, scholarships/grants, and tuition waivers (partial) also available. Support available to part-time students. Financial award applicants required to submit FAFSA. In 2010, 12 first professional degrees, 17 master's, 3 doctorates awarded. *Degree program information:* Part-time and evening/weekend programs available. Offers church development (MA); family ministry (MA); theological study (MA); theological/ministerial studies (D Min); theology/ministerial studies (M Div). *Application deadline:* For fall admission, 8/15 priority date for domestic students, 7/15 priority date for international students; for winter admission, 12/15 priority date for domestic students, 11/15 priority date for international students; for spring admission, 4/15 priority date for domestic students, 3/15 priority date for international students. Applications are processed on a rolling basis. *Application fee:* $30. Electronic applications accepted. *Application Contact:* Jim Wilder, Regional Coordinator, 419-434-4220, Fax: 419-434-4267, E-mail: admissions@winebrenner.edu. *Interim Academic Dean,* Prof. Joel W. Cocklin, 419-434-4250, Fax: 419-434-4267, E-mail: jcocklin@winebrenner.edu.

WINGATE UNIVERSITY, Wingate, NC 28174-0159

General Information Independent-religious, coed, comprehensive institution. *Graduate housing:* Rooms and/or apartments available on a first-come, first-served basis to single and married students. Housing application deadline: 8/15.

GRADUATE UNITS

Program in Business Administration *Degree program information:* Part-time and evening/weekend programs available. Offers business administration (MBA). Electronic applications accepted.

Program in Education *Degree program information:* Part-time and evening/weekend programs available. Offers educational leadership (MA Ed); elementary education (MA Ed, MAT); physical education (MA Ed); sport administration (MA Ed).

School of Pharmacy Offers pharmacy (Pharm D). Electronic applications accepted.

WINONA STATE UNIVERSITY, Winona, MN 55987

General Information State-supported, coed, comprehensive institution. *Enrollment:* 8,539 graduate, professional, and undergraduate students; 261 full-time matriculated graduate/professional students (186 women), 130 part-time matriculated graduate/professional students (96 women). *Enrollment by degree level:* 387 master's, 4 doctoral. *Graduate housing:* Room and/or apartments available to single students; on-campus housing not available to married students. Housing application deadline: 3/2. *Student services:* Campus employment opportunities, campus safety program, career counseling, child daycare facilities, exercise/wellness program, free psychological counseling, international student services, low-cost health insurance, services for students with disabilities. *Library facilities:* Darrel W. Krueger. *Online resources:* library catalog, web page, access to other libraries' catalogs. *Collection:* 462,560 titles, 1,869 serial subscriptions, 8,191 audiovisual materials.

Winona State University (continued)

Computer facilities: Computer purchase and lease plans are available. 1,400 computers available on campus for general student use. A campuswide network can be accessed from student residence rooms and from off campus. Online class registration. *Web address:* http://www.winona.edu/.

General Application Contact: Dr. Nancy Jannik, Director of Graduate Studies, 507-457-5010, E-mail: njannik@winona.edu.

GRADUATE UNITS

College of Education Students: 186 full-time (127 women), 95 part-time (56 women); includes 16 minority (9 Black or African American, non-Hispanic/Latino; 1 American Indian or Alaska Native, non-Hispanic/Latino; 1 Asian, non-Hispanic/Latino; 2 Hispanic/Latino; 3 Two or more races, non-Hispanic/Latino), 5 international. Average age 31. Expenses: Contact institution. *Financial support:* Fellowships, career-related internships or fieldwork, Federal Work-Study, and unspecified assistantships available. Support available to part-time students. In 2010, 80 master's awarded. *Degree program information:* Part-time and evening/weekend programs available. Offers community counseling (MS); education (MS, Ed S); educational leadership (Ed S); general school leadership (MS); K-12 principalship (MS); outdoor education/adventure-based leadership (MS); professional development (MS); school counseling (MS); special education (MS); sports management (MS); teacher leadership (MS). *Application deadline:* For fall admission, 8/8 priority date for domestic students; for spring admission, 2/15 for domestic students. Applications are processed on a rolling basis. *Application fee:* $20. *Application Contact:* Patricia Cichosz, Office Manager, Graduate Studies, 507-457-5038, E-mail: pcichosz@winona.edu. *Dean*, Dr. Hank Rubin, 507-457-2570, E-mail: hrubin@winona.edu.

College of Liberal Arts Students: 20 full-time (11 women), 8 part-time (5 women); includes 1 minority (Asian, non-Hispanic/Latino), 9 international. Average age 30. Expenses: Contact institution. *Financial support:* Career-related internships or fieldwork, Federal Work-Study, and unspecified assistantships available. Support available to part-time students. Financial award applicants required to submit FAFSA. In 2010, 7 master's awarded. *Degree program information:* Part-time programs available. Offers English (MA, MS); liberal arts (MA, MS). *Application deadline:* For fall admission, 7/26 priority date for domestic students; for spring admission, 12/8 for domestic students. Applications are processed on a rolling basis. *Application fee:* $20. *Application Contact:* Patricia Cichosz, Office Manager, Graduate Studies, 507-457-5038, E-mail: pcichosz@winona.edu. *Dean*, Dr. Ralph Townsend, 507-457-5017, E-mail: rtownsend@winona.edu.

College of Nursing and Health Sciences Students: 55 full-time (48 women), 37 part-time (35 women); includes 5 minority (2 Black or African American, non-Hispanic/Latino; 2 Asian, non-Hispanic/Latino; 1 Two or more races, non-Hispanic/Latino), 4 international. Average age 34. Expenses: Contact institution. *Financial support:* Research assistantships with partial tuition reimbursements, Federal Work-Study, traineeships, and unspecified assistantships available. Support available to part-time students. Financial award application deadline: 8/15; financial award applicants required to submit FAFSA. In 2010, 35 master's, 4 doctorates awarded. *Degree program information:* Part-time programs available. Postbaccalaureate distance learning degree programs offered (no on-campus study). Offers adult nurse practitioner (MS, Post Master's Certificate); clinical nurse specialist (MS, Post Master's Certificate); family nurse practitioner (MS, Post Master's Certificate); nurse administrator (MS); nurse educator (MS, Post Master's Certificate); nursing (DNP). *Application deadline:* For fall admission, 12/1 for domestic and international students. *Application fee:* $20. *Application Contact:* Patricia Cichosz, Office Manager, Graduate Studies, 507-457-5038, E-mail: pcichosz@winona.edu. *Dean*, Dr. William J. McBreen, 507-457-5122, E-mail: wmcbreen@winona.edu.

WINSTON-SALEM STATE UNIVERSITY, Winston-Salem, NC 27110-0003

General Information State-supported, coed, comprehensive institution. CGS member. *Graduate housing:* On-campus housing not available.

GRADUATE UNITS

Department of Occupational Therapy Offers occupational therapy (MS). Electronic applications accepted.

Department of Physical Therapy Offers physical therapy (MPT). Electronic applications accepted.

Program in Business Administration *Degree program information:* Part-time and evening/weekend programs available. Postbaccalaureate distance learning degree programs offered (minimal on-campus study). Offers business administration (MBA). Electronic applications accepted.

Program in Computer Science and Information Technology *Degree program information:* Part-time programs available. Offers computer science and information technology (MS). Electronic applications accepted.

Program in Elementary Education *Degree program information:* Part-time and evening/weekend programs available. Postbaccalaureate distance learning degree programs offered (minimal on-campus study). Offers elementary education (M Ed). Electronic applications accepted.

Program in Nursing *Degree program information:* Part-time and evening/weekend programs available. Postbaccalaureate distance learning degree programs offered. Offers nursing (MSN). Electronic applications accepted.

Program in Rehabilitation Counseling *Degree program information:* Part-time programs available. Postbaccalaureate distance learning degree programs offered (minimal on-campus study). Offers rehabilitation counseling (MRC). Electronic applications accepted.

WINTHROP UNIVERSITY, Rock Hill, SC 29733

General Information State-supported, coed, comprehensive institution. CGS member. *Graduate housing:* Rooms and/or apartments available to single and married students. Housing application deadline: 3/1.

GRADUATE UNITS

College of Arts and Sciences *Degree program information:* Part-time programs available. Offers arts and sciences (MA, MLA, MS, SSP); biology (MS); English (MA); history (MA); human nutrition (MS); liberal arts (MLA); psychology (MS, SSP); social work (MA); Spanish (MA). Electronic applications accepted.

College of Business Administration *Degree program information:* Part-time and evening/weekend programs available. Postbaccalaureate distance learning degree programs offered (no on-campus study). Offers business administration (MBA, MS, Certificate); software development (MS); software project management (Certificate). Electronic applications accepted.

College of Education *Degree program information:* Part-time programs available. Offers agency counseling (M Ed); education (M Ed, MAT, MS); educational leadership (M Ed); middle level education (M Ed); physical education (MS); reading education (M Ed); school counseling (M Ed); secondary education (M Ed, MAT); special education (M Ed). Electronic applications accepted.

College of Visual and Performing Arts *Degree program information:* Part-time programs available. Offers art (MFA); art administration (MA); art education (MA); conducting (MM); music education (MME); performance (MM); visual and performing arts (MA, MFA, MM, MME). Electronic applications accepted.

WISCONSIN SCHOOL OF PROFESSIONAL PSYCHOLOGY, Milwaukee, WI 53225-4960

General Information Independent, coed, graduate-only institution. *Graduate housing:* On-campus housing not available.

GRADUATE UNITS

Program in Clinical Psychology *Degree program information:* Part-time and evening/weekend programs available. Offers clinical psychology (MA, Psy D).

WITTENBERG UNIVERSITY, Springfield, OH 45501-0720

General Information Independent-religious, coed, comprehensive institution.

GRADUATE UNITS

Graduate Program

WON INSTITUTE OF GRADUATE STUDIES, Glenside, PA 19038

General Information Proprietary, coed, graduate-only institution. *Enrollment by degree level:* 48 master's, 5 other advanced degrees. *Graduate faculty:* 7 full-time (4 women), 17 part-time/adjunct (11 women). *Tuition:* Full-time $16,900; part-time $400 per credit. *Required fees:* $150 per trimester. *Student services:* Career counseling, writing training. *Web address:* http://www.woninstitute.edu/.

General Application Contact: Zach Bremmer, Recruitment Manager, 215-884-8942 Ext. 219, Fax: 215-884-9002, E-mail: zach.bremmer@woninstitute.edu.

GRADUATE UNITS

Acupuncture Studies Program Students: 36 full-time (29 women); includes 2 Black or African American, non-Hispanic/Latino; 3 Asian, non-Hispanic/Latino; 1 Hispanic/Latino. 24 applicants, 83% accepted, 18 enrolled. *Faculty:* 4 full-time (2 women), 17 part-time/adjunct (11 women). Expenses: Contact institution. In 2010, 12 master's awarded. Offers acupuncture studies (M Ac). *Application deadline:* For fall admission, 7/15 for domestic students. *Application fee:* $75. Electronic applications accepted. *Application Contact:* Zach Bremmer, Recruitment Manager, 215-884-8942, E-mail: zach.bremmer@woninstitute.edu. *Chair*, Mary Ellen Scheckenbach, 215-884-8942, Fax: 215-884-8942, E-mail: maryellen.scheckenbach@woninstitute.edu.

Applied Meditation Studies Program Students: 5 part-time (4 women), 1 international. 3 applicants, 100% accepted, 3 enrolled. *Faculty:* 2 full-time (1 woman). Expenses: Contact institution. In 2010, 1 master's awarded. *Degree program information:* Part-time and evening/weekend programs available. Offers applied meditation studies (MA). *Application deadline:* For fall admission, 7/15 for domestic students. Applications are processed on a rolling basis. *Application fee:* $75. *Application Contact:* Dr. Glenn Wallis, Chair, 215-884-8942, Fax: 215-884-9002, E-mail: glenn.wallis@woninstitute.edu. *Chair*, Dr. Glenn Wallis, 215-884-8942, Fax: 215-884-9002, E-mail: glenn.wallis@woninstitute.edu.

Won Buddhist Studies Program Students: 5 full-time (4 women), 2 part-time (1 woman); includes 1 Black or African American, non-Hispanic/Latino, 5 international. Average age 27. 5 applicants, 100% accepted, 5 enrolled. *Faculty:* 2 full-time (both women). Expenses: Contact institution. *Financial support:* In 2010–11, 7 students received support. Application deadline: 8/1. In 2010, 2 master's awarded. *Degree program information:* Part-time programs available. Offers Won Buddhist studies (MA). *Application deadline:* For fall admission, 7/15 for domestic students, 2/15 for international students. Applications are processed on a rolling basis. *Application fee:* $75. *Application Contact:* Dr. Chungnam HA, Chair, 215-884-8942, E-mail: wbschair@woninstitute.edu. *Chair*, Dr. Chungnam HA, 215-884-8942, E-mail: wbschair@woninstitute.edu.

WOODBURY UNIVERSITY, Burbank, CA 91504-1099

General Information Independent, coed, comprehensive institution. *Enrollment:* 1,628 graduate, professional, and undergraduate students; 283 full-time matriculated graduate/professional students (153 women), 60 part-time matriculated graduate/professional students (35 women). *Enrollment by degree level:* 343 master's. *Graduate faculty:* 17 full-time (8 women), 37 part-time/adjunct (13 women). *Tuition:* Full-time $10,548; part-time $879 per credit. *Required fees:* $8 per credit. $50 per semester. One-time fee: $110. *Graduate housing:* Room and/or apartments available on a first-come, first-served basis to single students; on-campus housing not available to married students. Typical cost: $5816 per year ($9632 including board). Room and board charges vary according to board plan. *Student services:* Campus employment opportunities, campus safety program, career counseling, free psychological counseling, international student services, low-cost health insurance, writing training. *Library facilities:* Los Angeles Times Library. *Online resources:* library catalog, web page, access to other libraries' catalogs. *Collection:* 72,156 titles, 250 serial subscriptions, 12,751 audiovisual materials.

Computer facilities: 169 computers available on campus for general student use. A campuswide network can be accessed from off campus. Online class registration is available. *Web address:* http://www.woodbury.edu/.

General Application Contact: Ruth Lorenzana, Director of Admissions, 800-784-9663, Fax: 818-767-7520, E-mail: admissions@woodbury.edu.

GRADUATE UNITS

School of Architecture Students: 54 full-time (16 women); includes 21 minority (2 Black or African American, non-Hispanic/Latino; 8 Asian, non-Hispanic/Latino; 11 Hispanic/Latino), 9 international. Average age 28. 72 applicants, 60% accepted, 36 enrolled. *Faculty:* 6 full-time (4 women), 19 part-time/adjunct (6 women). Expenses: Contact institution. *Financial support:* In 2010–11, 52 students received support, including 36 fellowships (averaging $6,000 per year), 10 research assistantships (averaging $2,000 per year), 23 teaching assistantships (averaging $2,000 per year); scholarships/grants also available. In 2010, 13 degrees awarded. Offers architecture (M Arch); landscape and urbanism (M Arch); post-professional (M Arch). *Application deadline:* For fall admission, 3/1 priority date for domestic and international students. *Application fee:* $60. *Application Contact:* Glisery Colon, Director, Graduate Admissions, 818-252-5234, Fax: 818-252-5221, E-mail: glisery.colon@woodbury.edu. *Dean*, Norman Millar, 318-767-0888 Ext. 130, Fax: 318-504-9320, E-mail: norman.millar@woodbury.edu.

School of Business and Management Students: 178 full-time (109 women), 41 part-time (22 women); includes 66 minority (17 Black or African American, non-Hispanic/Latino; 12 Asian, non-Hispanic/Latino; 37 Hispanic/Latino), 45 international. Average age 30. 92 applicants, 54% accepted, 32 enrolled. *Faculty:* 10 full-time (3 women), 8 part-time/adjunct (1 woman). Expenses: Contact institution. *Financial support:* In 2010–11, 13 students received support. Scholarships/grants available. In 2010, 84 master's awarded. *Degree program information:* Part-time and evening/weekend programs available. Offers business administration (MBA); organizational leadership (MA). *Application deadline:* For fall admission, 8/1 priority date for domestic students; for spring admission, 12/1 for domestic and international students. Applications are processed on a rolling basis. *Application fee:* $35 ($50 for international students). *Application Contact:* Ani Khukoyan, Assistant Director, Graduate Admissions, 818-767-0888 Ext. 224, Fax: 818-767-7520, E-mail: ani.khukoyan@woodbury.edu. *Dean*, Dr. Andre Van Niekerk, 818-767-0888 Ext. 264, Fax: 818-767-0032.

WOODS HOLE OCEANOGRAPHIC INSTITUTION, Woods Hole, MA 02543-1541

General Information Independent, coed, graduate-only institution. CGS member. *Graduate housing:* Rooms and/or apartments guaranteed to single students and available on a first-come, first-served basis to married students.

GRADUATE UNITS

MIT/WHOI Joint Program in Oceanography/Applied Ocean Science and Engineering Offers applied ocean science and engineering (PhD); biological oceanography (PhD); chemical oceanography (PhD); marine geology and geophysics (PhD); physical oceanography (PhD). Program offered jointly with Massachusetts Institute of Technology. Electronic applications accepted.

WORCESTER POLYTECHNIC INSTITUTE, Worcester, MA 01609-2280

General Information Independent, coed, university. CGS member. *Enrollment:* 5,360 graduate, professional, and undergraduate students; 710 full-time matriculated graduate/professional students (218 women), 644 part-time matriculated graduate/professional students (134 women).

Enrollment by degree level: 1,079 master's, 212 doctoral, 63 other advanced degrees. *Graduate faculty:* 144 full-time (28 women), 33 part-time/adjunct (6 women). *Tuition:* Full-time $20,862; part-time $1159 per term. One-time fee: $15. *Graduate housing:* On-campus housing not available. *Student services:* Campus employment opportunities, campus safety program, career counseling, exercise/wellness program, free psychological counseling, grant writing training, international student services, low-cost health insurance, multicultural affairs office, services for students with disabilities, teacher training, writing training. *Library facilities:* George C. Gordon Library. *Online resources:* library catalog, web page, access to other libraries' catalogs. *Collection:* 563,590 titles, 84,460 serial subscriptions, 2,772 audiovisual materials. *Research affiliation:* Hewlett Packard (data and software development), Massachusetts Biomedical Initiatives (biotechnology, medical devices), University of Massachusetts Medical School at Worcester (basic transitional and clinical medical research), The MathWorks, Inc. (educational software), Raytheon BBN Technologies Corporation (electronic synchronization and pointing techniques), Huasheng Tianlong (HSTL) Photoelectric Co., Ltd (materials, casting technology).

Computer facilities: Computer purchase and lease plans are available. 500 computers available on campus for general student use. A campuswide network can be accessed from student residence rooms and from off campus. Online class registration, online course content are available. *Web address:* http://www.wpi.edu/.

General Application Contact: Lynne Dougherty, Administrative Assistant, 508-831-5301, Fax: 508-831-5717, E-mail: grad@wpi.edu.

GRADUATE UNITS

Graduate Studies Students: 710 full-time (218 women), 644 part-time (134 women); includes 28 Black or African American, non-Hispanic/Latino; 1 American Indian or Alaska Native, non-Hispanic/Latino; 87 Asian, non-Hispanic/Latino; 31 Hispanic/Latino, 415 international. 2,612 applicants, 58% accepted, 566 enrolled. *Faculty:* 144 full-time (28 women), 33 part-time/adjunct (6 women). Expenses: Contact institution. *Financial support:* Institutionally sponsored loans, scholarships/grants, tuition waivers, and unspecified assistantships available. Financial award application deadline: 1/1; financial award applicants required to submit FAFSA. In 2010, 384 master's, 34 doctorates awarded. *Degree program information:* Part-time and evening/weekend programs available. Postbaccalaureate distance learning degree programs offered (no on-campus study). Offers applied mathematics (MS); applied statistics (MS); biochemistry (MS, PhD); biology and biotechnology (MS); biomedical engineering (M Eng, MS, PhD, Graduate Certificate); bioscience administration (MS); biotechnology (PhD); chemical engineering (MS, PhD); chemistry (MS, PhD); civil and environmental engineering (Advanced Certificate, Graduate Certificate); civil engineering (ME, MS, PhD); computer and communications networks (MS); computer science (MS, PhD, Advanced Certificate, Graduate Certificate); construction project management (MS); electrical and computer engineering (Advanced Certificate, Graduate Certificate); electrical engineering (M Eng, MS, PhD); environmental engineering (MS); financial mathematics (MS); fire protection engineering (MS, PhD, Advanced Certificate, Graduate Certificate); impact engineering (MS); industrial mathematics (MS); interdisciplinary social science (PhD); manufacturing engineering (MS, PhD); manufacturing engineering management (MS); master builder environmental engineering (M Eng); materials process engineering (MS); materials science and engineering (MS, PhD); mathematical sciences (PhD, Graduate Certificate); mathematics (MME); mechanical engineering (MS, PhD, Graduate Certificate); physics (MS, PhD); power systems management (MS); robotics engineering (MS, PhD); social science (PhD); system dynamics (MS, Graduate Certificate); systems modeling (MS). *Application deadline:* For fall admission, 1/1 priority date for domestic and international students; for spring admission, 10/1 priority date for domestic and international students. Applications are processed on a rolling basis. *Application fee:* $70. Electronic applications accepted. *Application Contact:* Lynne Dougherty, Administrative Assistant, 508-831-5301, Fax: 508-831-5717, E-mail: grad@wpi.edu. *Dean,* Richard Sisson, 508-831-5633, Fax: 508-831-5178, E-mail: grad@wpi.edu.

School of Business Students: 112 full-time (53 women), 135 part-time (33 women); includes 5 Black or African American, non-Hispanic/Latino; 1 Hispanic/Latino; 15 Native Hawaiian or other Pacific Islander, non-Hispanic/Latino, 105 international. 396 applicants, 67% accepted, 79 enrolled. *Faculty:* 13 full-time (7 women), 9 part-time/adjunct (2 women). Expenses: Contact institution. *Financial support:* Career-related internships or fieldwork, institutionally sponsored loans, scholarships/grants, and unspecified assistantships available. Financial award application deadline: 6/1; financial award applicants required to submit FAFSA. In 2010, 69 degrees awarded. *Degree program information:* Part-time and evening/weekend programs available. Postbaccalaureate distance learning degree programs offered (minimal on-campus study). Offers information technology (MS); management (Graduate Certificate); marketing and technological innovation (MS); operations design and leadership (MS); technology (MBA). *Application deadline:* For fall admission, 6/1 priority date for domestic and international students; for spring admission, 11/1 priority date for domestic students, 10/1 priority date for international students. Applications are processed on a rolling basis. *Application fee:* $70. Electronic applications accepted. *Application Contact:* Alyssa Bates, Director, Graduate Management Programs, 508-831-4665, Fax: 508-831-5720, E-mail: ajbates@wpi.edu. *Dean,* Dr. Mark Rice, 508-831-4665, Fax: 508-831-5218, E-mail: rice@wpi.edu.

WORCESTER STATE UNIVERSITY, Worcester, MA 01602-2597

General Information State-supported, coed, comprehensive institution. *Enrollment:* 5,708 graduate, professional, and undergraduate students; 167 full-time matriculated graduate/professional students (146 women), 346 part-time matriculated graduate/professional students (257 women). *Enrollment by degree level:* 393 master's, 120 other advanced degrees. *Graduate faculty:* 39 full-time (27 women), 35 part-time/adjunct (15 women). Tuition, state resident: full-time $2700; part-time $150 per credit. Tuition, nonresident: full-time $2700; part-time $150 per credit. *Required fees:* $2016; $112 per credit. *Graduate housing:* On-campus housing not available. *Student services:* Campus safety program, career counseling, free psychological counseling, international student services, low-cost health insurance, multicultural affairs office, services for students with disabilities, teacher training, writing training. *Library facilities:* Worcester State University Library. *Online resources:* library catalog, web page, access to other libraries' catalogs. *Collection:* 204,259 titles, 419 serial subscriptions, 13,143 audiovisual materials.

Computer facilities: Computer purchase and lease plans are available. 500 computers available on campus for general student use. A campuswide network can be accessed from student residence rooms and from off campus. Online class registration is available. *Web address:* http://www.worcester.edu/.

General Application Contact: Sara Grady, Assistant Dean of Graduate and Continuing Education, 508-929-8787, Fax: 508-929-8100, E-mail: sara.grady@worcester.edu.

GRADUATE UNITS

Graduate Studies Students: 167 full-time (146 women), 346 part-time (257 women); includes 38 minority (7 Black or African American, non-Hispanic/Latino; 2 American Indian or Alaska Native, non-Hispanic/Latino; 7 Asian, non-Hispanic/Latino; 14 Hispanic/Latino; 8 Two or more races, non-Hispanic/Latino), 11 international. Average age 32. 677 applicants, 56% accepted, 159 enrolled. *Faculty:* 39 full-time (27 women), 35 part-time/adjunct (15 women). Expenses: Contact institution. *Financial support:* In 2010–11, 28 research assistantships with full tuition reimbursements (averaging $4,800 per year) were awarded; career-related internships or fieldwork, scholarships/grants, and unspecified assistantships also available. Financial award application deadline: 3/1; financial award applicants required to submit FAFSA. In 2010, 186 master's, 154 other advanced degrees awarded. *Degree program information:* Part-time and evening/weekend programs available. Offers accounting (MS); biotechnology (MS); community and public health nursing (MS); early childhood education (M Ed); elementary education (M Ed); English (MA); health care administration (MS); health education (M Ed); history (MA); leadership and administration (M Ed, CAGS); managerial leadership (MS); middle school education (M Ed); moderate special needs (M Ed); non-profit management (MS); nurse educator (MS); occupational therapy (MOT); reading (M Ed, CAGS); school psychology (M Ed, CAGS); secondary education (M Ed); Spanish (MA); speech-language pathology (MS). *Application deadline:* Applications are processed on a rolling basis. *Application fee:* $40. Electronic applications accepted. *Application Contact:* Sara Grady, Assistant Dean of Continuing Education, 508-929-8787, Fax: 508-929-8100, E-mail: sara.grady@worcester.edu. *Associate Vice President for Continuing Education and Outreach/Dean of the Graduate School,* Dr. William H. White, 508-929-8111, Fax: 508-929-8100, E-mail: william.white@worcester.edu.

WORLD MEDICINE INSTITUTE OF ACUPUNCTURE AND HERBAL MEDICINE, Honolulu, HI 96828

General Information Independent, coed, graduate-only institution. *Graduate housing:* On-campus housing not available.

GRADUATE UNITS

Program in Acupuncture and Oriental Medicine *Degree program information:* Part-time and evening/weekend programs available. Offers acupuncture and Oriental medicine (M Ac OM).

WRIGHT INSTITUTE, Berkeley, CA 94704-1796

General Information Independent, coed, graduate-only institution. *Enrollment by degree level:* 85 master's, 355 doctoral. *Graduate faculty:* 33 full-time (22 women), 110 part-time/adjunct (66 women). *Tuition:* Full-time $26,600. *Graduate housing:* On-campus housing not available. *Student services:* Campus employment opportunities, career counseling, low-cost health insurance. *Library facilities:* The Wright Institute Library plus 1 other. *Online resources:* library catalog, web page, access to other libraries' catalogs. *Collection:* 10,000 titles, 500 serial subscriptions, 600 audiovisual materials.

Computer facilities: 26 computers available on campus for general student use. A campuswide network can be accessed from off campus. Online class registration is available. *Web address:* http://www.wrightinst.edu/.

General Application Contact: Melissa Delaney, Director of Admissions, 510-841-9230 Ext. 170, Fax: 510-841-0167, E-mail: mdelaney@wi.edu.

GRADUATE UNITS

Doctoral Program in Clinical Psychology Students: 355 full-time (254 women); includes 95 minority (14 Black or African American, non-Hispanic/Latino; 2 American Indian or Alaska Native, non-Hispanic/Latino; 33 Asian, non-Hispanic/Latino; 29 Hispanic/Latino; 17 Two or more races, non-Hispanic/Latino). Average age 34. 323 applicants, 40% accepted, 59 enrolled. *Faculty:* 28 full-time (19 women), 93 part-time/adjunct (53 women). Expenses: Contact institution. *Financial support:* In 2010–11, 150 students received support, including 4 research assistantships (averaging $1,600 per year), 25 teaching assistantships (averaging $1,600 per year); career-related internships or fieldwork, Federal Work-Study, and scholarships/grants also available. Financial award application deadline: 11/30; financial award applicants required to submit FAFSA. In 2010, 45 degrees awarded. Offers clinical psychology (Psy D). *Application deadline:* For fall admission, 1/15 priority date for domestic students, 1/15 for international students. *Application fee:* $50. Electronic applications accepted. *Application Contact:* Melissa Delaney, Director of Admissions, 510-841-9230 Ext. 170, Fax: 510-841-0167, E-mail: mdelaney@wi.edu. *Dean,* Dr. Charles Alexander, 510-841-9230 Ext. 101, E-mail: calexander@wi.edu.

Program in Counseling Psychology Students: 85 full-time (69 women); includes 4 Black or African American, non-Hispanic/Latino; 3 Asian, non-Hispanic/Latino; 7 Hispanic/Latino; 7 Two or more races, non-Hispanic/Latino. Average age 38. 90 applicants, 54% accepted, 40 enrolled. *Faculty:* 5 full-time (3 women), 17 part-time/adjunct (13 women). Expenses: Contact institution. *Financial support:* In 2010–11, 22 students received support. Career-related internships or fieldwork, Federal Work-Study, and scholarships/grants available. Financial award application deadline: 11/30; financial award applicants required to submit FAFSA. In 2010, 30 degrees awarded. *Degree program information:* Part-time and evening/weekend programs available. Offers counseling psychology (MA). *Application deadline:* Applications are processed on a rolling basis. *Application fee:* $50. Electronic applications accepted. *Application Contact:* Melissa Delaney, Director of Admissions, 510-841-9230 Ext. 170, Fax: 510-841-0167, E-mail: mdelaney@wi.edu. *Program Director,* Dr. Milena Esherick, 510-841-9230.

WRIGHT STATE UNIVERSITY, Dayton, OH 45435

General Information State-supported, coed, university. CGS member. *Graduate housing:* Rooms and/or apartments available on a first-come, first-served basis to single students and available to married students. *Research affiliation:* Wright-Patterson Air Force Base (research and development, systems and logistics), Wright-Patterson Air Force Base Medical Center, Veterans Administration Medical Center, Scott-Kettering Magnetic Resonance Research Laboratory (medical science), Edison Biotechnology Center, Edison Materials Technology Center (processing).

GRADUATE UNITS

School of Graduate Studies *Degree program information:* Part-time and evening/weekend programs available. Offers interdisciplinary studies (MA, MS). Electronic applications accepted.

College of Education and Human Services *Degree program information:* Part-time and evening/weekend programs available. Offers adolescent young adult (M Ed, MA); advanced curriculum and instruction (Ed S); advanced educational leadership (Ed S); career, technology and vocational education (M Ed, MA); chemical dependency (MRC); classroom teacher education (M Ed, MA); computer/technology education (M Ed, MA); counseling (M Ed, MA, MS); curriculum and instruction: teacher leader (MA); early childhood education (M Ed, MA); education and human services (M Ed, MA, MRC, MS, MST, Ed S); educational administrative specialist: teacher leader (M Ed); educational administrative specialist: vocational education administration (M Ed, MA); educational leadership (M Ed, MA); gifted educational needs (M Ed, MA); health, physical education, and recreation (M Ed, MA); higher education-adult education (Ed S); intervention specialist (M Ed, MA); library/media (M Ed, MA); middle childhood education (M Ed, MA); mild to moderate educational needs (M Ed, MA); moderate to intensive educational needs (M Ed, MA); multi-age (M Ed, MA); pupil personnel services (M Ed, MA); rehabilitation counseling (MRC); severe disabilities (MRC); student affairs in higher education-administration (M Ed, MA); superintendent (Ed S); vocational education (M Ed, MA); workforce education (M Ed, MA).

College of Engineering and Computer Science *Degree program information:* Part-time and evening/weekend programs available. Offers biomedical and human factors engineering (MSE); biomedical engineering (MSE); computer engineering (MSCE); computer science (MS); computer science and engineering (MS, MSCE, PhD); electrical engineering (MSE); engineering (PhD); engineering and computer science (MS, MSCE, MSE, PhD); human factors engineering (MSE); materials science and engineering (MSE); mechanical and materials engineering (MSE); mechanical engineering (MSE).

College of Liberal Arts *Degree program information:* Part-time programs available. Offers composition and rhetoric (MA); criminal justice and social problems (MA); English (MA); history (MA); humanities (M Hum); international and comparative politics (MA); liberal arts (M Hum, M Mus, MA, MPA); literature (MA); music education (M Mus); performance (M Mus); public administration (MPA); teaching English to speakers of other languages (MA).

College of Nursing and Health *Degree program information:* Part-time and evening/weekend programs available. Offers acute care nurse practitioner (MS); administration of nursing and health care systems (MS); adult health (MS); child and adolescent health (MS); community health (MS); family nurse practitioner (MS); nurse practitioner (MS); nursing and health (MS); school nurse (MS).

College of Science and Mathematics *Degree program information:* Part-time and evening/weekend programs available. Offers anatomy (MS); applied mathematics (MS); applied statistics (MS); biochemistry and molecular biology (MS); biological sciences (MS); biomedical sciences (PhD); chemistry (MS); earth science education (MST); environmental sciences (PhD); geological sciences (MS); geophysics (MS); human factors and industrial/organizational psychology (MS, PhD); mathematics (MS); medical physics (MS); microbiology and immunology (MS); physics (MS); physics education (MST); physiology and biophysics (MS); science and mathematics (MS, MST, PhD).

Raj Soin College of Business *Degree program information:* Part-time and evening/weekend programs available. Offers accountancy (M Acc, MBA); accounting (MBA); business (M Acc, MBA, MIS, MS); business administration (MBA); business economics (MBA); finance (MBA); flexible business (MBA); health care management (MBA); information systems

Wright State University (continued)

(MIS); international business (MBA); logistics and supply chain management (MS); management information technology (MBA); management, innovation and change (MBA); marketing (MBA); project management (MBA); social and applied economics (MS); supply chain management (MBA).

School of Medicine Offers aerospace medicine (MS); health promotion and education (MPH); medicine (MD, MPH, MS, PhD); pharmacology and toxicology (MS); public health management (MPH); public health nursing (MPH).

School of Professional Psychology Offers clinical psychology (Psy D).

WYCLIFFE COLLEGE, Toronto, ON M5S 1H7, Canada

General Information Independent-religious, coed, graduate-only institution. *Graduate housing:* Rooms and/or apartments guaranteed to single students and available on a first-come, first-served basis to married students. Housing application deadline: 5/1.

GRADUATE UNITS

Division of Advanced Degree Studies *Degree program information:* Part-time programs available. Offers theology (MA, Th M, D Min, PhD, Th D). PhD, D Min, MA offered jointly with Toronto School of Theology; Th D, Th M with University of Toronto.

Division of Basic Degree Studies *Degree program information:* Part-time programs available. Offers Christian Studies (Diploma); theology (M Div, M Rel, MTS). M Div, M Rel, MTS offered jointly with University of Toronto.

XAVIER UNIVERSITY, Cincinnati, OH 45207

General Information Independent-religious, coed, comprehensive institution. *Enrollment:* 7,019 graduate, professional, and undergraduate students; 848 full-time matriculated graduate/professional students (517 women), 1,610 part-time matriculated graduate/professional students (900 women). *Enrollment by degree level:* 2,368 master's, 90 doctoral. *Graduate faculty:* 72 full-time (44 women), 96 part-time/adjunct (56 women). *Tuition:* Part-time $718 per credit hour. Tuition and fees vary according to degree level, campus/location and program. *Graduate housing:* On-campus housing not available. *Student services:* Campus employment opportunities, campus safety program, career counseling, exercise/wellness program, international student services, low-cost health insurance, multicultural affairs office, services for students with disabilities, teacher training, writing training. *Library facilities:* McDonald Memorial Library. *Online resources:* library catalog, web page, access to other libraries' catalogs. *Collection:* 373,952 titles, 86,539 serial subscriptions, 7,564 audiovisual materials.

Computer facilities: Computer purchase and lease plans are available. 320 computers available on campus for general student use. A campuswide network can be accessed from student residence rooms and from off campus. Online class registration is available. *Web address:* http://www.xu.edu/.

General Application Contact: Roger Bosse, Graduate Services Director, 513-745-3357, Fax: 513-745-1048, E-mail: bosse@xavier.edu.

GRADUATE UNITS

College of Arts and Sciences Students: 11 full-time (7 women), 30 part-time (15 women); includes 1 minority (Hispanic/Latino), 1 international. Average age 33. 28 applicants, 75% accepted, 11 enrolled. *Faculty:* 8 full-time (5 women). Expenses: Contact institution. *Financial support:* In 2010–11, 41 students received support. Scholarships/grants and unspecified assistantships available. Support available to part-time students. Financial award applicants required to submit FAFSA. In 2010, 16 master's awarded. *Degree program information:* Part-time programs available. Offers arts and sciences (MA); English (MA); health care mission integration (MA); theology (MA). *Application deadline:* Applications are processed on a rolling basis. *Application fee:* $35. Electronic applications accepted. *Application Contact:* Dr. Janice B. Walker, Dean, 513-745-3101, Fax: 513-745-1099, E-mail: walker@xavier.edu. *Dean*, Dr. Janice B. Walker, 513-745-3101, Fax: 513-745-1099, E-mail: walker@xavier.edu.

College of Social Sciences, Health and Education Students: 637 full-time (450 women), 845 part-time (646 women); includes 181 minority (133 Black or African American, non-Hispanic/Latino; 2 American Indian or Alaska Native, non-Hispanic/Latino; 22 Asian, non-Hispanic/Latino; 20 Hispanic/Latino; 4 Two or more races, non-Hispanic/Latino), 9 international. Average age 32. 1,066 applicants, 54% accepted, 379 enrolled. *Faculty:* 72 full-time (44 women), 96 part-time/adjunct (56 women). Expenses: Contact institution. *Financial support:* In 2010–11, 694 students received support. Career-related internships or fieldwork, scholarships/grants, traineeships, unspecified assistantships, and residency stipends available. Support available to part-time students. Financial award applicants required to submit FAFSA. In 2010, 537 master's, 16 doctorates awarded. Offers clinical psychology (Psy D); criminal justice (MS); health services administration (MHSA); occupational therapy (MOT); psychology (MA); social sciences, health and education (M Ed, MA, MHSA, MOT, MS, MSN, Psy D); sport administration (M Ed). *Application fee:* $35. *Application Contact:* Roger Bosse, Graduate Services Director, 513-745-3357, Fax: 513-745-1048, E-mail: bosse@xavier.edu. *Dean*, Dr. Mark Meyers, 513-745-3119, Fax: 513-745-1058, E-mail: meyersd3@xavier.edu.

School of Education Students: 352 full-time (266 women), 521 part-time (389 women); includes 120 minority (93 Black or African American, non-Hispanic/Latino; 11 Asian, non-Hispanic/Latino; 13 Hispanic/Latino; 3 Two or more races, non-Hispanic/Latino), 4 international. Average age 32. 306 applicants, 75% accepted, 177 enrolled. *Faculty:* 23 full-time (13 women), 58 part-time/adjunct (32 women). Expenses: Contact institution. *Financial support:* In 2010–11, 454 students received support. Applicants required to submit FAFSA. In 2010, 367 master's awarded. Offers community counseling (MA); education (M Ed, MA, MS); educational administration (M Ed); elementary education (M Ed); human resource development (MS); Montessori education (M Ed); multicultural literature for children (M Ed); reading (M Ed); school counseling (MA); secondary education (M Ed); special education (M Ed). *Application deadline:* Applications are processed on a rolling basis. *Application fee:* $35. Electronic applications accepted. *Application Contact:* Dr. Jennifer Fager, Associate Dean, 513-745-3495, Fax: 513-745-1052, E-mail: fagerj@xavier.edu. *Associate Dean*, Dr. Jennifer Fager, 513-745-3495, Fax: 513-745-1052, E-mail: fagerj@xavier.edu.

School of Nursing Students: 65 full-time (60 women), 167 part-time (164 women); includes 20 minority (17 Black or African American, non-Hispanic/Latino; 1 Asian, non-Hispanic/Latino; 1 Hispanic/Latino; 1 Two or more races, non-Hispanic/Latino). Average age 39. 261 applicants, 50% accepted, 86 enrolled. *Faculty:* 14 full-time (13 women), 13 part-time/adjunct (11 women). Expenses: Contact institution. *Financial support:* In 2010–11, 88 students received support. Applicants required to submit FAFSA. In 2010, 54 master's awarded. *Degree program information:* Part-time and evening/weekend programs available. Offers clinical nurse leader (MSN); education (MSN); forensic nursing (MSN); healthcare law (MSN); informatics (MSN); nursing administration (MSN); school nursing (MSN). *Application deadline:* Applications are processed on a rolling basis. *Application fee:* $35. Electronic applications accepted. *Application Contact:* Marilyn Volk Gomez, Director of Nursing Student Services, 513-745-4392, Fax: 513-745-1087, E-mail: gomez@xavier.edu. *Director*, Dr. Susan M. Schmidt, 513-745-3815, Fax: 513-745-1087, E-mail: schmidt@xavier.edu.

Williams College of Business Students: 200 full-time (60 women), 735 part-time (239 women); includes 128 minority (48 Black or African American, non-Hispanic/Latino; 3 American Indian or Alaska Native, non-Hispanic/Latino; 54 Asian, non-Hispanic/Latino; 22 Hispanic/Latino; 1 Native Hawaiian or other Pacific Islander, non-Hispanic/Latino), 32 international. Average age 30. 223 applicants, 85% accepted, 139 enrolled. *Faculty:* 37 full-time (13 women), 9 part-time/adjunct (2 women). Expenses: Contact institution. *Financial support:* In 2010–11, 176 students received support. Scholarships/grants, tuition waivers (partial), and unspecified assistantships available. Financial award application deadline: 3/1; financial award applicants required to submit FAFSA. In 2010, 323 master's awarded. *Degree program information:* Part-time and evening/weekend programs available. Offers business (Exec MBA, MBA); business administration (Exec MBA, MBA); business intelligence (MBA); finance (MBA); international business (MBA); management information systems (MBA); marketing (MBA). *Application deadline:* For fall admission, 8/1 priority date for domestic students, 5/1 for international students; for spring admission, 12/1 priority date for domestic students, 9/1 for international students. Applications are processed on a rolling basis. *Application fee:* $35. Electronic applications accepted. *Application Contact:* Jennifer Bush, Executive Director, MBA Programs, 513-745-3527, Fax: 513-745-2929, E-mail: bush@xavier.edu. *Dean*, Dr. Ali Malekzadeh, 513-745-3528, Fax: 513-745-3455, E-mail: malekzadeh@xavier.edu.

XAVIER UNIVERSITY OF LOUISIANA, New Orleans, LA 70125-1098

General Information Independent-religious, coed, comprehensive institution. CGS member. *Graduate housing:* On-campus housing not available.

GRADUATE UNITS

College of Pharmacy Offers pharmacy (Pharm D). Electronic applications accepted.

Graduate School *Degree program information:* Part-time and evening/weekend programs available. Offers curriculum and instruction (MA); education administration and supervision (MA); guidance and counseling (MA).

Institute for Black Catholic Studies *Degree program information:* Part-time programs available. Offers pastoral theology (Th M).

YALE UNIVERSITY, New Haven, CT 06520

General Information Independent, coed, university. CGS member. *Graduate housing:* Rooms and/or apartments available on a first-come, first-served basis to single and married students. Housing application deadline: 6/1. *Research affiliation:* Howard Hughes Medical Institute, J. B. Pierce Foundation (environmental physiology), Haskins Laboratories (speech, hearing, reading).

GRADUATE UNITS

Divinity School *Degree program information:* Part-time programs available. Offers divinity (M Div, MAR, STM). Electronic applications accepted.

Graduate School of Arts and Sciences *Degree program information:* Part-time programs available. Offers African studies (MA); African-American studies (PhD); American studies (PhD); anthropology (M Phil, MA, PhD); applied mathematics (M Phil, MS, PhD); Arabic and Islamic studies (MA, PhD); archaeological studies (MA); archaeology of the ancient Near East (MA, PhD); arts and sciences (M Phil, MA, MS, PhD); Assyriology (MA, PhD); astronomy (PhD); behavioral neuroscience (PhD); biochemistry, molecular biology and chemical biology (PhD); biogeochemistry (PhD); biophysical chemistry (PhD); cell biology (PhD); cellular and developmental biology (PhD); cellular and molecular physiology (PhD); classics (M Phil, MA, PhD); climate dynamics (PhD); clinical psychology (PhD); cognitive psychology (PhD); comparative and historical sociology (PhD); comparative literature (PhD); computer science (MS, PhD); cultural sociology and social theory (PhD); developmental psychology (PhD); East Asian languages and literatures (PhD); East Asian languages and literatures and film studies (PhD); East Asian studies (MA); ecology and evolutionary biology (PhD); economics (PhD); Egyptology (MA, PhD); English language and literature (MA, PhD); environmental sciences (PhD); experimental pathology (MS, PhD); film studies (PhD); forestry (PhD); French (M Phil, MA, PhD); genetics (PhD); geochemistry (PhD); geophysics (PhD); German (PhD); Graeco-Arabic studies (MA, PhD); history (M Phil, MA, PhD); history of art (PhD); history of science and medicine (MS, PhD); immunobiology (PhD); inorganic chemistry (PhD); international and development economics (MA); international relations (MA); Italian language and literature (PhD); Latin American literature (PhD); linguistics (PhD); Luso-Brazilian and Spanish/Spanish American literatures (PhD); mathematics (M Phil, MS, PhD); medieval Slavic literature and philology (PhD); medieval studies (M Phil, PhD); meteorology (PhD); molecular biophysics and biochemistry (PhD); music history (MA); music theory (MA); neurobiology (PhD); neuroscience (PhD); Northwest Semitic, Bible, comparative Semitics (MA, PhD); oceanography (PhD); organic chemistry (PhD); paleontology (PhD); paleooceanography (PhD); petrology (PhD); philosophy (PhD); physical and theoretical chemistry (PhD); physics (PhD); plant sciences (PhD); Polish literature (PhD); political science (PhD); religious studies (PhD); Renaissance studies (PhD); Russian and East European studies (MA); Russian literature (PhD); Slavic languages and literatures and film studies (PhD); social stratification and the life course (PhD); social/personality psychology (PhD); solar and terrestrial physics (PhD); Spanish peninsular literature (PhD); statistics (MA, PhD); tectonics (PhD).

School of Engineering and Applied Science *Degree program information:* Part-time programs available. Offers applied physics (MS, PhD); biomedical engineering (MS, PhD); chemical engineering (MS, PhD); electrical engineering (MS, PhD); engineering and applied science (MS, PhD); environmental engineering (MS, PhD); mechanical engineering (MS, PhD).

School of Architecture Offers architecture (M Arch, M Env Des, MEM, PhD).

School of Art Students: 121 full-time (64 women); includes 32 minority (7 Black or African American, non-Hispanic/Latino; 10 Asian, non-Hispanic/Latino; 15 Hispanic/Latino), 32 international. Average age 28. 1,222 applicants, 5% accepted, 57 enrolled. *Faculty:* 9 full-time (4 women), 35 part-time/adjunct (12 women). Expenses: Contact institution. *Financial support:* In 2010–11, 90 students received support, including 54 teaching assistantships (averaging $1,900 per year); Federal Work-Study, scholarships/grants, and unspecified assistantships also available. Financial award application deadline: 3/1; financial award applicants required to submit FAFSA. In 2010, 57 degrees awarded. Offers graphic design (MFA); painting/printmaking (MFA); photography (MFA); sculpture (MFA). *Application deadline:* For fall admission, 1/4 for domestic and international students. *Application fee:* $100. Electronic applications accepted. *Application Contact:* Patricia Ann DeChiara, Director of Academic Affairs, 203-432-2600, E-mail: artschool.info@yale.edu. *Dean*, Robert Storr, 203-432-2606.

School of Drama Students: 208 full-time (106 women); includes 42 minority (13 Black or African American, non-Hispanic/Latino; 2 American Indian or Alaska Native, non-Hispanic/Latino; 12 Asian, non-Hispanic/Latino; 14 Hispanic/Latino; 1 Two or more races, non-Hispanic/Latino), 27 international. Average age 27. 1,520 applicants, 4% accepted, 64 enrolled. *Faculty:* 66 full-time (43 women), 43 part-time/adjunct (23 women). Expenses: Contact institution. *Financial support:* In 2010–11, 193 students received support. Career-related internships or fieldwork, Federal Work-Study, institutionally sponsored loans, scholarships/grants, and health care benefits available. Financial award application deadline: 2/15; financial award applicants required to submit FAFSA. In 2010, 69 master's, 1 doctorate awarded. Offers drama (MFA, DFA, Certificate). *Application deadline:* For fall admission, 1/3 for domestic and international students. *Application fee:* $110. Electronic applications accepted. *Application Contact:* Maria Leveton, Registrar/Admissions Administrator, 203-432-1507, Fax: 203-432-9668. *Dean/Artistic Director of Yale Repertory Theatre*, James Bundy, 203-432-1505.

School of Forestry and Environmental Studies *Degree program information:* Part-time programs available. Offers forestry and environmental studies (MEM, MES, MF, MFS, PhD). Electronic applications accepted.

School of Medicine *Degree program information:* Part-time programs available. Offers biological and biomedical sciences (PhD); computational biology and bioinformatics (PhD); immunology (PhD); medicine (MD, APMPH, MM Sc, MPH, MS, PhD, MM Sc/MPH); microbiology (PhD); molecular biophysics and biochemistry (PhD); molecular cell biology, genetics, and development (PhD); neurobiology (PhD); neuroscience (PhD); pharmacological sciences and molecular medicine (PhD); pharmacology (PhD); physician associate (MM Sc, MM Sc/MPH); physiology and integrative medical biology (PhD). Electronic applications accepted.

Yale School of Public Health Students: 209 full-time (169 women), 8 part-time (4 women); includes 24 Black or African American, non-Hispanic/Latino; 44 Asian, non-Hispanic/Latino; 9 Hispanic/Latino, 21 international. Average age 26. 1,100 applicants, 117 enrolled. *Faculty:* 67 full-time (37 women), 53 part-time/adjunct (18 women). Expenses: Contact institution. *Financial support:* In 2010–11, 21 fellowships with full tuition reimbursements (averaging $12,560 per year), 4 research assistantships with full tuition reimbursements (averaging $24,910 per year) were awarded; teaching assistantships with full tuition reimbursements, career-related internships or fieldwork, Federal Work-Study, institutionally sponsored loans, scholarships/grants, and tuition waivers (full and partial) also available. Support available to part-time students. Financial award application deadline: 3/1; financial award applicants required to submit FAFSA. In 2010, 124 master's, 8 doctorates awarded. *Degree program information:* Part-time programs available. Offers applied biostatistics and epidemiology (APMPH); biostatistics (MPH, MS, PhD); chronic disease epidemiology (MPH, PhD); environmental health sciences (MPH, PhD); epidemiology of microbial diseases (MPH, PhD);

global health (APMPH); health management (MPH); health policy (MPH); health policy and administration (APMPH, PhD); occupational and environmental medicine (APMPH); preventive medicine (APMPH); social and behavioral sciences (APMPH, MPH). MS and PhD offered through the Graduate School. *Application deadline:* For fall admission, 1/15 priority date for domestic and international students. Applications are processed on a rolling basis. *Application fee:* $115. Electronic applications accepted. *Application Contact:* Jacqui R. Comshaw, Director of Admissions, 203-785-2844, Fax: 203-785-4845, E-mail: ysph.admissions@yale.edu. *Dean and Chairman,* Dr. Paul D. Cleary, 203-785-2867, Fax: 203-785-6103, E-mail: paul.cleary@yale.edu.

School of Music Students: 217 full-time (86 women); includes 5 Black or African American, non-Hispanic/Latino; 14 Asian, non-Hispanic/Latino; 2 Hispanic/Latino, 80 international. Average age 24. 1,463 applicants, 7% accepted, 98 enrolled. *Faculty:* 30 full-time (9 women), 29 part-time/adjunct (3 women). Expenses: Contact institution. *Financial support:* In 2010–11, 217 students received support, including 217 fellowships (averaging $31,000 per year); Federal Work-Study and scholarships/grants also available. Financial award application deadline: 5/30; financial award applicants required to submit FAFSA. In 2010, 79 master's, 6 doctorates, 31 other advanced degrees awarded. Offers music (MM, MMA, DMA, AD, Certificate). *Application deadline:* For fall admission, 12/1 for domestic and international students. *Application fee:* $100. Electronic applications accepted. *Application Contact:* Suzanne M. Stringer, Registrar and Financial Aid Administrator, 203-432-1962, Fax: 203-432-7448, E-mail: suzanne.stringer@yale.edu. *Dean,* Robert Blocker, 203-432-4160, Fax: 203-432-7542.

School of Nursing Students: 278 full-time (260 women), 43 part-time (41 women); includes 62 minority (15 Black or African American, non-Hispanic/Latino; 22 Asian, non-Hispanic/Latino; 14 Hispanic/Latino; 1 Native Hawaiian or other Pacific Islander, non-Hispanic/Latino; 10 Two or more races, non-Hispanic/Latino), 14 international. Average age 29. 445 applicants, 44% accepted, 105 enrolled. *Faculty:* 54 full-time (51 women), 95 part-time/adjunct (90 women). Expenses: Contact institution. *Financial support:* In 2010–11, 265 students received support, including 239 fellowships (averaging $5,905 per year), 13 research assistantships with tuition reimbursements available (averaging $28,450 per year); Federal Work-Study, scholarships/grants, traineeships, and health care benefits also available. Support available to part-time students. Financial award application deadline: 2/1; financial award applicants required to submit FAFSA. In 2010, 108 master's, 7 doctorates, 2 other advanced degrees awarded. *Degree program information:* Part-time programs available. Postbaccalaureate distance learning degree programs offered (minimal on-campus study). Offers nursing (MSN, PhD, Post Master's Certificate). *Application deadline:* For fall admission, 11/1 priority date for domestic students, 11/1 for international students. *Application fee:* $65. Electronic applications accepted. *Application Contact:* Office of Admissions, 203-737-1793, Fax: 203-737-5409, E-mail: yale.nurse@yale.edu. *Dean,* Dr. Margaret Grey, 203-785-2393, Fax: 203-785-6455, E-mail: margaret.grey@yale.edu.

Yale Law School Students: 629 full-time (310 women). Average age 26. 3,797 applicants, 7% accepted, 205 enrolled. *Faculty:* 65 full-time, 23 part-time/adjunct. Expenses: Contact institution. *Financial support:* Application deadline: 3/15. In 2010, 203 first professional degrees, 23 master's, 3 doctorates awarded. Offers law (JD, LL M, MSL, JSD). *Application deadline:* For fall admission, 2/15 for domestic students. Applications are processed on a rolling basis. *Application fee:* $75. Electronic applications accepted. *Application Contact:* Asha Rangappa, Associate Dean, 203-432-4995, E-mail: admissions.law@yale.edu. *Dean,* Robert Post, 203-432-1660.

Yale School of Management Students: 497 full-time (174 women). Average age 28. 2,963 applicants, 17% accepted, 231 enrolled. *Faculty:* 68 full-time (13 women), 27 part-time/adjunct (6 women). Expenses: Contact institution. *Financial support:* Career-related internships or fieldwork, Federal Work-Study, institutionally sponsored loans, scholarships/grants, and health care benefits available. Financial award application deadline: 3/1; financial award applicants required to submit FAFSA. In 2010, 187 master's, 9 doctorates awarded. Offers accounting (PhD); business administration (MBA, PhD); financial economics (PhD); management (MBA, PhD); marketing (PhD); organizations and management (PhD). *Application deadline:* For fall admission, 10/7 for domestic and international students; for winter admission, 1/6 for domestic and international students; for spring admission, 3/7 for domestic and international students. *Application fee:* $220. Electronic applications accepted. *Application Contact:* Bruce DelMonico, Director of Admissions, 203-432-5635, Fax: 203-432-7004, E-mail: mba.admissions@yale.edu. *Dean,* Sharon M. Oster, 203-432-6035, Fax: 203-432-5092.

YESHIVA BETH MOSHE, Scranton, PA 18505-2124

General Information Independent-religious, men only, comprehensive institution.

GRADUATE UNITS

Graduate Programs

YESHIVA DERECH CHAIM, Brooklyn, NY 11218

General Information Independent-religious, men only, comprehensive institution.

GRADUATE UNITS

Graduate Program Offers Talmudic studies (PhD).

YESHIVA KARLIN STOLIN RABBINICAL INSTITUTE, Brooklyn, NY 11204

General Information Independent-religious, men only, comprehensive institution. *Graduate housing:* On-campus housing not available.

GRADUATE UNITS

Graduate Programs

YESHIVA OF NITRA RABBINICAL COLLEGE, Mount Kisco, NY 10549

General Information Independent-religious, men only, comprehensive institution.

GRADUATE UNITS

Graduate Programs

YESHIVA SHAAR HATORAH TALMUDIC RESEARCH INSTITUTE, Kew Gardens, NY 11418-1469

General Information Independent-religious, men only, comprehensive institution.

GRADUATE UNITS

Graduate Programs

YESHIVATH VIZNITZ, Monsey, NY 10952

General Information Independent-religious, men only, comprehensive institution.

GRADUATE UNITS

Graduate Programs

YESHIVATH ZICHRON MOSHE, South Fallsburg, NY 12779

General Information Independent-religious, men only, comprehensive institution.

GRADUATE UNITS

Graduate Programs *Degree program information:* Part-time programs available.

YESHIVA TORAS CHAIM TALMUDICAL SEMINARY, Denver, CO 80204-1415

General Information Independent-religious, men only, comprehensive institution.

GRADUATE UNITS

Graduate Programs

YESHIVA UNIVERSITY, New York, NY 10033-3201

General Information Independent, coed, university. CGS member. *Graduate housing:* On-campus housing not available.

GRADUATE UNITS

Azrieli Graduate School of Jewish Education and Administration *Degree program information:* Part-time and evening/weekend programs available. Offers Jewish education and administration (MS, Ed D, Specialist).

Benjamin N. Cardozo School of Law Students: 1,122 full-time (585 women), 106 part-time (54 women); includes 54 Black or African American, non-Hispanic/Latino; 1 American Indian or Alaska Native, non-Hispanic/Latino; 101 Asian, non-Hispanic/Latino; 84 Hispanic/Latino, 75 international. Average age 24. 5,261 applicants, 26% accepted, 317 enrolled. *Faculty:* 59 full-time (19 women), 92 part-time/adjunct (31 women). Expenses: Contact institution. *Financial support:* In 2010–11, 919 students received support, including 111 research assistantships; career-related internships or fieldwork, Federal Work-Study, institutionally sponsored loans, scholarships/grants, health care benefits, and tuition waivers (full and partial) also available. Support available to part-time students. Financial award application deadline: 3/1; financial award applicants required to submit FAFSA. In 2010, 354 first professional degrees, 68 master's awarded. *Degree program information:* Part-time programs available. Offers comparative legal thought (LL M); dispute resolution and advocacy (LL M); general studies (LL M); intellectual property law (LL M); law (JD). *Application deadline:* For fall admission, 3/1 priority date for domestic students; for spring admission, 12/1 priority date for domestic students. Applications are processed on a rolling basis. *Application fee:* $75. Electronic applications accepted. *Application Contact:* David G. Martinidez, Dean of Admissions, 212-790-0274, Fax: 212-790-0482, E-mail: lawinfo@yu.edu. *Dean of Admissions,* David G. Martinidez, 212-790-0274, Fax: 212-790-0482, E-mail: lawinfo@yu.edu.

Bernard Revel Graduate School of Jewish Studies *Degree program information:* Part-time programs available. Offers Jewish studies (MA, PhD).

Ferkauf Graduate School of Psychology *Degree program information:* Part-time programs available. Offers clinical psychology (Psy D); health psychology (PhD); mental health counseling psychology (MA); psychology (MA, PhD, Psy D); school/clinical-child psychology (Psy D).

Sy Syms School of Business *Degree program information:* Part-time programs available. Offers accounting (MS).

Wurzweiler School of Social Work Students: 243 full-time (186 women), 95 part-time (65 women); includes 67 Black or African American, non-Hispanic/Latino; 2 Asian, non-Hispanic/Latino; 54 Hispanic/Latino. Average age 40. 376 applicants, 73% accepted, 218 enrolled. *Faculty:* 26 full-time (14 women), 40 part-time/adjunct (31 women). Expenses: Contact institution. *Financial support:* In 2010–11, 194 students received support, including 2 teaching assistantships (averaging $5,000 per year); career-related internships or fieldwork, Federal Work-Study, institutionally sponsored loans, and scholarships/grants also available. Financial award application deadline: 4/15; financial award applicants required to submit FAFSA. In 2010, 146 master's, 4 doctorates awarded. *Degree program information:* Part-time and evening/weekend programs available. Offers social work (MSW, PhD). *Application deadline:* For fall admission, 5/1 priority date for domestic students; for spring admission, 10/31 for domestic students. Applications are processed on a rolling basis. *Application fee:* $50. *Application Contact:* Ruth Bigman, Director of Admissions, 212-960-0811, Fax: 212-960-0822, E-mail: rbigman@yu.edu. *Dean,* Dr. Jade C. Docherty, 212-960-0829 Ext. 829, Fax: 212-960-0822, E-mail: docherty@yu.edu.

YORK COLLEGE OF PENNSYLVANIA, York, PA 17405-7199

General Information Independent, coed, comprehensive institution. *Enrollment:* 5,606 graduate, professional, and undergraduate students; 46 full-time matriculated graduate/professional students (23 women), 214 part-time matriculated graduate/professional students (129 women). *Enrollment by degree level:* 260 master's. *Graduate faculty:* 22 full-time (12 women), 20 part-time/adjunct (12 women). *Tuition:* Full-time $11,520; part-time $640 per credit hour. *Required fees:* $1500; $660 per year. *Graduate housing:* On-campus housing not available. *Student services:* Campus employment opportunities, campus safety program, career counseling, free psychological counseling, international student services, low-cost health insurance, multicultural affairs office, services for students with disabilities. *Library facilities:* Schmidt Library. *Online resources:* library catalog, web page, access to other libraries' catalogs. *Collection:* 331,226 titles, 43,044 serial subscriptions.

Computer facilities: 893 computers available on campus for general student use. A campuswide network can be accessed from student residence rooms and from off campus. Online class registration is available. *Web address:* http://www.ycp.edu/.

General Application Contact: Nancy Spataro, Director of Admissions, 717-815-1600, Fax: 717-849-1607, E-mail: admissions@ycp.edu.

GRADUATE UNITS

Department of Business Administration Students: 20 full-time (6 women), 111 part-time (44 women); includes 4 Black or African American, non-Hispanic/Latino; 1 Asian, non-Hispanic/Latino; 4 Hispanic/Latino, 2 international. Average age 30. 53 applicants, 91% accepted, 40 enrolled. *Faculty:* 11 full-time (2 women), 5 part-time/adjunct (1 woman). Expenses: Contact institution. *Financial support:* Scholarships/grants available. Financial award application deadline: 4/15; financial award applicants required to submit FAFSA. In 2010, 45 master's awarded. *Degree program information:* Part-time and evening/weekend programs available. Offers accounting (MBA); continuous improvement (MBA); finance (MBA); management (MBA); marketing (MBA). *Application deadline:* For fall admission, 7/15 priority date for domestic students; for spring admission, 12/15 priority date for domestic students. Applications are processed on a rolling basis. *Application fee:* $60. Electronic applications accepted. *Application Contact:* Brenda Adams, Assistant Director, MBA Program, 717-815-1749, Fax: 717-600-3999, E-mail: badams@ycp.edu. *MBA Director,* Dr. David Greisler, 717-815-6410, Fax: 717-600-3999, E-mail: dgreisle@ycp.edu.

Department of Education Students: 82 part-time (65 women). 5 applicants, 60% accepted, 2 enrolled. *Faculty:* 3 full-time (2 women), 8 part-time/adjunct (5 women). Expenses: Contact institution. In 2010, 29 master's awarded. *Degree program information:* Part-time and evening/weekend programs available. Offers educational leadership (M Ed); reading specialist (M Ed). *Application deadline:* For fall admission, 7/15 priority date for domestic students; for spring admission, 11/15 priority date for domestic students. Applications are processed on a rolling basis. *Application fee:* $60. Electronic applications accepted. *Application Contact:* Irene Z. Altland, Administrative Assistant, 717-815-6406, Fax: 717-849-1629, E-mail: med@ycp.edu. *Director,* Dr. Philip Monteith, 717-815-6406, E-mail: med@ycp.edu.

Department of Nursing Students: 26 full-time (17 women), 41 part-time (38 women); includes 1 Black or African American, non-Hispanic/Latino; 3 Asian, non-Hispanic/Latino, 1 international. Average age 37. 41 applicants, 68% accepted, 18 enrolled. *Faculty:* 8 full-time (all women), 9 part-time/adjunct (6 women). Expenses: Contact institution. *Financial support:* Federal Work-Study available. In 2010, 10 master's awarded. *Degree program information:* Part-time and evening/weekend programs available. Offers nursing (MS). *Application deadline:* For fall admission, 7/15 priority date for domestic students; for spring admission, 11/15 priority date for domestic students. Applications are processed on a rolling basis. *Application fee:* $60. Electronic applications accepted. *Application Contact:* Nancy Spataro, Director of Admissions, 717-815-1600, Fax: 717-849-1607, E-mail: admissions@ycp.edu. *Coordinator,* Lynn Warner, 717-815-1212, E-mail: lwarner@ycp.edu.

YORKTOWN UNIVERSITY, Denver, CO 80246

General Information Proprietary, coed, comprehensive institution.

GRADUATE UNITS

School of Business Offers entrepreneurship (MBA); sport management (MBA).

School of Government Offers American culture and the life of the citizen (MA); foundations of democracy in America and Western Europe (MA); political economy (MA); political theory (MA).

YORK UNIVERSITY, Toronto, ON M3J 1P3, Canada

General Information Province-supported, coed, university. CGS member. *Graduate housing:* Rooms and/or apartments available on a first-come, first-served basis to single and married students. *Research affiliation:* Imperial Oil Limited, National Palace Museum, Unicorn Children's Foundation (developmental and learning disorders), Smithsonian Institution (astronomy, physics, space), Beijing Municipality (management training), German Academic Exchange (German studies).

GRADUATE UNITS

Faculty of Graduate Studies *Degree program information:* Part-time and evening/weekend programs available. Offers communication and culture (MA, PhD); environmental studies (MES, PhD); interdisciplinary studies (MA); law (LL B, LL M, PhD). Electronic applications accepted.

Atkinson Faculty of Liberal and Professional Studies Offers disaster and emergency management (MA); human resources management (MHRM, PhD); liberal and professional studies (MA, MHRM, MPPAL, MSW, PhD); public policy, administration and law (MPPAL); social work (MSW, PhD).

Faculty of Arts *Degree program information:* Part-time programs available. Offers arts (M Sc, MA, PhD); economics (MA, PhD); English (MA, PhD); geography (M Sc, MA, PhD); history (MA, PhD); humanities (MA, PhD); international development studies (MA); philosophy (MA, PhD); political science (MA, PhD); social and political thought (MA, PhD); social anthropology (MA, PhD); sociology (MA, PhD); theoretical and applied linguistics (MA, PhD); women's studies (MA, PhD). Electronic applications accepted.

Faculty of Education *Degree program information:* Part-time programs available. Offers education (M Ed, PhD). Electronic applications accepted.

Faculty of Fine Arts *Degree program information:* Part-time programs available. Offers art history (MA, PhD); composition (MA); dance (MA, MFA); design (M Des); film (MA, MFA, PhD); fine arts (M Des, MA, MFA, PhD); musicology and ethnomusicology (MA, PhD); theatre (MFA); theatre studies (MA, PhD); visual arts (MFA, PhD). Electronic applications accepted.

Faculty of Health Offers critical disability studies (MA, PhD); health (M Sc, M Sc N, MA, PhD); kinesiology and health science (M Sc, MA, PhD); nursing (M Sc N); psychology (MA, PhD).

Faculty of Science and Engineering *Degree program information:* Part-time and evening/weekend programs available. Offers biology (M Sc, PhD); chemistry (M Sc, PhD); computer science (M Sc, PhD); earth and space science (M Sc, PhD); industrial and applied mathematics (M Sc); mathematics and statistics (MA, PhD); physics and astronomy (M Sc, PhD); science and engineering (M Sc, MA, PhD).

Glendon College Offers French studies (MA); public and international affairs (MA); translation (MA).

Schulich School of Business *Degree program information:* Part-time and evening/weekend programs available. Offers administration (PhD); business (MBA); finance (MF); international business (IMBA); public administration (MPA). Electronic applications accepted.

YO SAN UNIVERSITY OF TRADITIONAL CHINESE MEDICINE, Los Angeles, CA 90066

General Information Private, coed, graduate-only institution. *Graduate housing:* On-campus housing not available.

GRADUATE UNITS

Program in Acupuncture and Traditional Chinese Medicine *Degree program information:* Part-time programs available. Postbaccalaureate distance learning degree programs offered (no on-campus study). Offers acupuncture and traditional Chinese medicine (MATCM).

YOUNGSTOWN STATE UNIVERSITY, Youngstown, OH 44555-0001

General Information State-supported, coed, comprehensive institution. CGS member. *Graduate housing:* Room and/or apartments available on a first-come, first-served basis to single students; on-campus housing not available to married students. *Research affiliation:* BioRemedial Technologies Inc. (environmental bioremediation), Ohio Supercomputer Center (computational chemistry and physics), Northeast Ohio Universities College of Medicine (medicine), Parker-Hannifin Corporation (engineering technology), Ohio Mass Spectrometry Consortium (chemistry and biology).

GRADUATE UNITS

Graduate School *Degree program information:* Part-time and evening/weekend programs available.

Beeghly College of Education *Degree program information:* Part-time and evening/weekend programs available. Offers adolescent/young adult education (MS Ed); community counseling (MS Ed); content area concentration (MS Ed); early childhood education (MS Ed); education (MS Ed, Ed D); educational administration (MS Ed); educational leadership (Ed D); educational technology (MS Ed); gifted and talented education (MS Ed); literacy (MS Ed); middle childhood education (MS Ed); school counseling (MS Ed); special education (MS Ed).

Bitonte College of Health and Human Services *Degree program information:* Part-time and evening/weekend programs available. Offers criminal justice (MS); health and human services (MHHS, MPH, MS, MSN, DPT); nursing (MSN); physical therapy (DPT); public health (MPH).

College of Fine and Performing Arts *Degree program information:* Part-time and evening/weekend programs available. Offers fine and performing arts (MM); jazz studies (MM); music education (MM); music history and literature (MM); music theory and composition (MM); performance (MM).

College of Liberal Arts and Social Sciences *Degree program information:* Part-time programs available. Offers applied behavior analysis (MS); economics (MA); English (MA); environmental studies (MS); financial economics (MA); history (MA); industrial/institutional management (Certificate); liberal arts and social sciences (MA, MS, Certificate); risk management (Certificate).

College of Science, Technology, Engineering and Mathematics *Degree program information:* Part-time and evening/weekend programs available. Offers analytical chemistry (MS); applied mathematics (MS); biochemistry (MS); chemistry education (MS); civil and environmental engineering (MSE); computer engineering (MSE); computer science (MS); computing and information systems (MCIS); electrical engineering (MSE); environmental biology (MS); industrial and systems engineering (MSE); inorganic chemistry (MS); mechanical engineering (MSE); molecular biology, microbiology, and genetic (MS); organic chemistry (MS); physical chemistry (MS); physiology and anatomy (MS); science, technology, engineering and mathematics (MCIS, MSE); secondary mathematics (MS); statistics (MS).

Williamson College of Business Administration *Degree program information:* Part-time and evening/weekend programs available. Offers accounting (MBA); business administration (MBA, Certificate); enterprise resource planning (Certificate); marketing (MBA).

CLOSE-UPS OF INSTITUTIONS OFFERING GRADUATE AND PROFESSIONAL WORK

BARRY UNIVERSITY

Graduate Programs

Programs of Study

Barry University offers more than fifty high-quality graduate degree programs that prepare students for career change and advancement. Classes are offered on evenings or Saturdays for many programs to meet the needs of the working professional. The faculty provides personal attention and is well attuned to the learning styles of adult students. The experience at Barry is academically rewarding and challenging, with interaction with dedicated professors and diverse peers who bring real-world experience to the classroom.

The School of Adult and Continuing Education offers the M.A. in administration and Master of Public Administration (M.P.A.) at sites across the state of Florida.

The College of Arts and Sciences offers the M.A. in broadcast communication, liberal studies, pastoral ministry for Hispanics, practical theology, and public relations/corporate communications; the M.A. and M.F.A. in photography; and the M.S. in clinical psychology. The M.A. in pastoral theology is offered in Arcadia, Florida. The Doctor of Ministry (D.Min.) is offered at the main campus in Miami Shores.

The Andreas School of Business offers the Master of Business Administration (M.B.A.), with concentrations in accounting, finance, health-services administration, international business, management, and marketing. The School of Business also offers the M.S. in accounting and management.

The Adrian Dominican School of Education offers programs in Miami Shores and Orlando. Counseling programs (M.S. and Ed.S.) are available, with specializations in marital, couple, family counseling & therapy; mental health counseling; rehabilitation counseling; school counseling; and dual specializations in marital, couple, family counseling & therapy and mental health counseling; and mental health counseling and rehabilitation counseling. The Ph.D. in counseling is also offered. The M.S. is available in curriculum and instruction, educational leadership, exceptional student education (with endorsements in autism and gifted), Montessori education, and reading. The M.S. is also offered in organizational learning and leadership, with a specialization in higher education administration. The Ed.S. is available in educational leadership, Montessori education, and reading. Barry also offers a Specialist in School Psychology (S.S.P.) degree. The Ph.D. program in leadership and education has specializations in exceptional student education, higher education administration, human resource development, and leadership. The Ph.D. is available in curriculum and instruction, with specializations in culture, language, and literacy (TESOL); curriculum evaluation and research; early childhood education; elementary education; and reading.

The College of Health Sciences offers the M.S. in anesthesiology, biomedical science, clinical biology, health services administration, medical biotechnology, and occupational therapy. Students can also earn a dual degree in health services administration and a Master of Public Health (M.P.H.). Also available are a Master of Science in Nursing (M.S.N.), with specializations in nursing administration, nursing education, and nurse practitioner (family and acute care); an M.S.N./M.B.A. dual degree; a nursing Ph.D.; and Doctor of Nursing Practice (D.N.P.). There are also transitional and accelerated programs for qualified RNs to move seamlessly to the M.S.N.

The School of Human Performance and Leisure Sciences offers the Master of Science in sport management and an M.S./M.B.A. dual-degree program. The M.S. in movement science is also available, with a general M.S. option or specializations in exercise physiology, injury and sport biomechanics, and sport and exercise psychology.

The Dwayne O. Andreas School of Law offers the Juris Doctor (J.D.) degree.

The School of Podiatric Medicine offers programs leading to the Doctor of Podiatric Medicine and Surgery (D.P.M.) and D.P.M./M.B.A. and D.P.M./M.P.H. dual degrees. Also available are the M.S. in anatomy and a physician assistant program leading to certification and the Master of Clinical Medical Science (M.C.M.Sc.).

The School of Social Work offers the M.S.W. The Advanced Standing M.S.W. program is available to students with a recent B.S.W. from a school whose program is accredited by the Council on Social Work Education.

None of the graduate programs requires a foreign language for admission or graduation.

Research Facilities

Campus facilities include the Monsignor William Barry Memorial Library, photography and digital imaging labs, a human performance lab, an athletics training room, a biomechanics lab, a complete digital television production studio, an academic computing center, an education lab, multimedia business classrooms, art studios, a performing arts center, family counseling clinic, a nursing lab, and several other well-equipped science labs.

Financial Aid

Financial aid is available. Professional scholarships are available for full-time social work students, educators, nurses, and members of a religious community. Some schools offer scholarships and other forms of financial assistance. Barry University also participates in the full array of federal and state financial aid programs. Prospective students should contact their intended program for details. Additional information is also available from the Office of Financial Aid (phone: 305-899-3673; e-mail: finaid@mail.barry.edu).

Cost of Study

Tuition for 2011–12 is $905 per credit for master's programs and $1030 per credit for doctoral programs. Tuition for adult and continuing education, law, public health, physician assistant, and podiatric medicine programs vary.

Living and Housing Costs

Campus housing is available for full-time graduate students, space permitting. Barry University provides assistance in locating off-campus housing.

Student Group

The total University enrollment for 2010–11 was 8,995, with 4,055 students registered in graduate and professional programs. The majority of graduate students are studying part-time in evening and weekend classes.

Location

The University's 122-acre campus is located in Miami Shores, which is between the cities of Miami and Fort Lauderdale. This ideal location provides students with access to one of the nation's most dynamic multicultural environments and all of its business, cultural, and recreational opportunities.

The University

Barry University is an independent, coeducational university, with a history of distinguished graduate programs. Founded in 1940, the University has grown steadily in size and diversity, while maintaining a low student-faculty ratio, thus providing for the individual needs of its academic community. The University's various partnerships with local businesses, schools, hospitals, and community organizations ensure that students gain professional experience and hone their skills before graduation.

Applying

Applicants are expected to have earned a 3.0 cumulative GPA or above in undergraduate work and 3.25 or higher in graduate work for Ph.D. applicants. They are usually required to submit scores on standardized tests (such as the GRE, MAT, MCAT, or GMAT); the specific test requirement depends on the program. Applicants who do not give evidence of being native English speakers are required to submit a TOEFL score of at least 550 (paper-based), 213 (computer-based), or 79 (Internet-based); the minimum acceptable score is 600 for the School of Podiatric Medicine. The student's application and credentials (transcripts, recommendations, and test scores) should be sent to the university and should be received at least thirty days prior to the beginning of the term for which admission is desired. Students applying to the podiatric medicine and the physician assistant programs are required to apply via the national application process. Application deadlines, admission requirements, and start terms vary among programs. Prospective students should contact their intended program for details.

Correspondence and Information

Office of Admission
Barry University
11300 Northeast Second Avenue
Miami Shores, Florida 33161-6695

Phone: 305-899-3100
800-695-2279 (toll-free)
Fax: 305-899-2971
E-mail: gradadmissions@mail.barry.edu
Web site: http://www.barry.edu

FACULTY HEADS

School of Adult and Continuing Education
Carol-Rae Sodano, Ed.D., Widener; Dean.
Administration: Marilyn Jenkins, Ph.D., Barry; Academic Coordinator.
Public Administration: John Carroll, Ph.D., Florida Atlantic; Academic Coordinator.

College of Arts and Sciences
Karen A. Callaghan, Ph.D., Ohio State; Dean.
Clinical Psychology: Frank Muscarella, Ph.D., Louisville; Program Director.
Communication: Denis E. Vogel, Ph.D., Florida State; Chair.
Liberal Studies: Aphrodite Alexandrakis, Ph.D., Miami (Florida); Program Director.
Pastoral Ministry for Hispanics: Rev. Mario B. Vizcaino, Ph.D., Gregorian (Rome).
Photography: Silvia Lizama, M.F.A., RIT; Chair.
Theology: Mark Wedig, O.P., Ph.D., Catholic University; Chair.

School of Business
Tomislav Mandakovic, Ph.D., Pittsburgh; Dean.
Orlando R. Barreto, Ph.D., Barry; Assistant Dean.
Paola Moreno, M.B.A., Florida International; Assistant Dean.

Adrian Dominican School of Education
Terry Piper, Ph.D., Alberta; Dean.
John Dezek, Ed.D., Western Michigan; Associate Dean.
Catheryn Weitman, Ph.D., Texas A&M; Associate Dean.
Counseling: M. Sylvia Fernandez, Ph.D., Southern Illinois Carbondale; Chair.
Curriculum and Instruction: Jill Farrell, Ed.D., Florida International; Chair.
Educational Leadership: Joanne Calabro, Ed.D., Nova; Chair.
Exceptional Student Education: Judith Harris-Looby, Ph.D., Miami (Florida); Chair.
Leadership and Education: Carmen L. McCrink, Ph.D., Miami (Florida); Director.
Montessori Education: Heidy Lilchin, M.S., Barry; Program Director.
Organizational Learning and Leadership: David Kopp, Ph.D., Barry; Chair.
Reading: Joyce Warner, Ph.D., Pennsylvania; Program Director.
School Psychology: M. Sylvia Fernandez, Ph.D., Southern Illinois Carbondale; Program Coordinator.
Teaching English to Speakers of Other Languages (TESOL): Ruth Ban, Ph.D., South Florida; Program Coordinator.

College of Health Sciences
Pegge Bell, Ph.D., Virginia; Dean.
Anesthesiology: Anthony Umadhay, CRNA, M.S.N., Florida International; Program Director.
Biomedical Sciences: Ahmed Abdellatif, M.D., Ph.D.; Program Director.
Clinical Biology: Gerhild Packert, Ph.D., South Florida; Associate Dean and Program Director.
Health Services Administration and Public Health: Evelio Velis, M.D., M.S.; Program Director.
Medical Biotechnology: Graham Shaw, Ph.D., Aston; Program Director.
Nursing: Claudette Spalding, Ph.D., Barry; Associate Dean and Chair.
Occupational Therapy: Belkis Landa-Gonzalez, Ed.D., Florida International; Program Director.

School of Human Performance and Leisure Sciences
Darlene Kluka, Ph.D., D.Phil., Pretoria; Interim Dean.
Maritza Ryder, M.S., Barry; Assistant Dean.
Rev. Carl R. Cramer, Ed.D., Kansas State; Director of Graduate Programs.
Athletic Training: Rev. Carl R. Cramer, Ed.D., Kansas State; Program Director.
Exercise Science: Connie Mier, Ph.D., Texas; Program Coordinator.
Injury and Sport Biomechanics: Clare Egret, Ph.D., Rouen; Program Coordinator.
Sport and Exercise Psychology: Gualberto Cremades, Ph.D., Houston; Program Coordinator.
Sport Management: Darlene Kluka, Ph.D., D.Phil., Pretoria; Program Coordinator.

School of Law
Leticia M. Diaz, J.D., Ph.D., Rutgers; Dean.
Frank L. Schiavo, J.D., Villanova; Interim Assistant Dean for Academic Affairs.

School of Podiatric Medicine and Surgery
Jeffrey L. Jensen, D.P.M., California College of Podiatric Medicine; Dean.
Albert Armstrong, D.P.M., Barry; Associate Academic Dean.
Physician Assistant Program: Doreen Parkhurst, M.D., Boston University; Associate Dean and Program Director.

School of Social Work
Phyllis Scott, Ph.D., Barry; Interim Dean.
Social Work: Maria Teahan, A.C.S.W., L.C.S.W., C.T.S., M.S.W., Barry; Program Director.

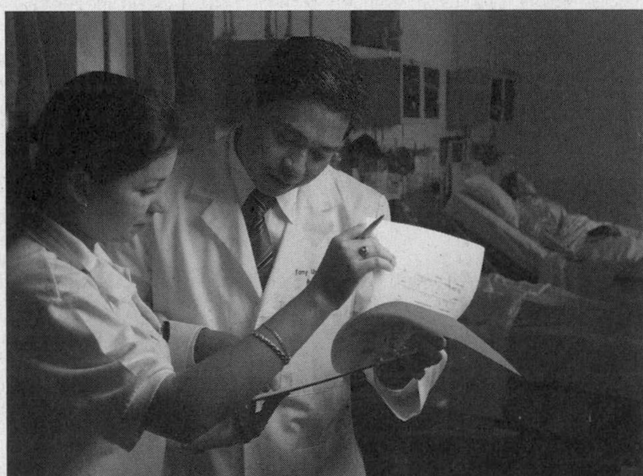

Barry University's faculty is well attuned to the learning styles of adult students, bringing personal attention and real-world experience to the classroom.

Barry's south Florida location gives students access to one of the nation's most dynamic multicultural environments.

BOWLING GREEN STATE UNIVERSITY

Graduate College

Programs of Study

Bowling Green State University (BGSU) offers Doctor of Philosophy (Ph.D.) programs in American culture studies applied philosophy, biological sciences, communication disorders, communication studies, English (rhetoric and composition), higher education administration, interdisciplinary studies, mathematics and statistics, photochemical sciences, psychology (clinical, developmental, industrial-organizational, and the neural and cognitive sciences), sociology, and theater and film. A Doctor of Education (Ed.D.) degree is offered in leadership studies, along with a Doctoral of Musical Arts (D.M.A.). A Ph.D. in technology management (consortium degree) is also offered. Specialist programs include education specialist in administration and supervision, and education specialist in reading.

Graduate certificates are offered in autism spectrum disorders, bioinformatics, ethnic studies, food and nutrition, geospatial technology, international scientific and technical communication, organizational change, performance studies, P–6 math endorsement, P–9 science endorsement, proteomics/genomics, public history, reading endorsement, quality systems, and women's studies.

BGSU offers the Master of Accountancy (M.Acc.) degree. The Master of Arts (M.A.) degree is offered in American culture studies, applied philosophy, architecture, art, art education, college student personnel, communication studies, cross-cultural and international education, economics, English (literacy and textual studies), French, German, history, mathematics, mental health and counseling, philosophy, political science (dual degree with German only), popular culture, psychology, sociology, Spanish, and theater and film. The Master of Arts in Teaching (M.A.T.) degree is offered in American culture studies, biological sciences, chemistry, French, geology, German, history, mathematics, physics, Spanish, and theater and film. The Master of Arts/Science is offered in interdisciplinary studies. The Master of Business Administration (M.B.A.) degree is offered in finance, management information systems, marketing, and supply chain management. The Master of Education (M.Ed.) degree is offered in business education; classroom technology; curriculum and teaching; educational administration and supervision; educational teaching and learning; human movement, sport, and leisure studies (developmental kinesiology, recreation and leisure, and sport administration); interdisciplinary studies; learning design; reading; and special education. BGSU also offers the Master of Family and Consumer Sciences (M.F.C.S.) degree. The Master of Fine Arts (M.F.A.) degree is offered in creative writing. The Master of Technology Management (M.T.M.) is offered in construction management and technology and engineering technology. BGSU also offers the Master of Music (M.M.) in composition, education, ethnomusicology, history, performance, and theory; Master of Organization Development (M.O.D.); Master of Public Administration (M.P.A.); and Master of Public Health (M.P.H.) degrees. The Master of Science (M.S.) degree is offered in applied statistics and operations research, biological sciences, chemistry, communication disorders, computer science, criminal justice, geology, and physics.

Ph.D. requirements include a minimum of 90 semester hours of graduate work beyond the baccalaureate. A minimum of 30 semester hours of graduate work beyond the baccalaureate is required for the master's degree; the choice of Plan I (thesis option) or Plan II (comprehensive examination option) is available in most programs. The Graduate College at BGSU is committed to helping students identify personal and professional goals. Through a comprehensive set of facilities and programs, opportunities are provided to pursue high-quality graduate education in an environment conducive to advanced study and research.

Research Facilities

The University libraries have approximately 2 million volumes and approximately 1.6 million microforms, including subscriptions to 6,000 periodicals and 600,000 government documents. In addition to providing a range of regular and specialized research facilities, the University supports a number of research centers and institutes. These include the Center for Archival Collections; the Center for Biomolecular Sciences; the Center for Family and Demographic Research; the Center for Neuroscience, Mind and Behavior; the Center for Photochemical Sciences; the Center for Regional Development; the Institute for the Study of Culture and Society; the Center for Microscopy and Microanalysis; the Institute for Great Lakes Research; the Institute for Psychological Research and Application; the Reading Center; the Social Philosophy and Policy Center; the National Institute for the Study of Digital Media; and the Statistical Consulting Center.

Financial Aid

Graduate assistantship assignments are available and may include instructional, research, or administrative service. Graduate assistants receive a stipend and a scholarship that can be applied to instructional and non-resident tuition fees. Assistantship appointments are generally made for the academic year. Stipend and scholarship amounts are set by each department. Graduate assistantships are available to students enrolled in at least 8 graduate credit hours in master's, specialist, or doctoral degree programs during fall and spring semesters. Student employment and loans are available as sources of graduate student support.

Cost of Study

Tuition for 2011–12 is $483 per credit hour for Ohio residents and $788 per credit hour for nonresidents.

Living and Housing Costs

On-campus housing is not available for graduate students. Numerous apartments and other housing are available near the campus. For more information, those interested should contact Off-Campus Housing at 419-372-2458 or visit the Web site at http://www.bgsu.edu/offices/sa/offcampus.

Student Group

The University maintains an enrollment of about 15,000 undergraduates and approximately 3,000 graduate students on the main campus. Students represent all fifty states and seventy countries. The opportunities to meet people and exchange ideas at Bowling Green are greatly enhanced by the residential nature of the campus.

Location

Bowling Green is a northwestern Ohio community, located 23 miles south of Toledo and within a 100-mile radius of Ann Arbor, Detroit, Cleveland, and Columbus. The community offers numerous recreational and cultural programs that supplement the activities offered by the University.

The University

Bowling Green, a state-assisted university, was founded in 1910. The University has a 1,250-acre campus. Graduate programs are offered in six academic colleges—Arts and Sciences, Business Administration, Education and Human Development, Health and Human Services, Musical Arts, and Technology—within the Graduate College. Each year, the University invites visiting scholars, guest artists, and celebrities to lecture, perform, and meet informally with students to exchange ideas and information.

Applying

Applicants must have graduated with a baccalaureate degree from a regionally accredited college or university. Assistantships are awarded for the academic year beginning in the fall semester. Applicants for financial aid are encouraged to complete the admission process by January 15. The application for admission to the Graduate College should be submitted with a $30 nonrefundable application fee. Students should apply six months in advance for admission to a Ph.D. program and three months in advance for a master's program. International students should allow more time for the application process. Two official transcripts from all colleges attended are required. GRE General Test or GMAT scores must be submitted. TOEFL scores must be submitted by all applicants whose first language is not English. Three letters of recommendation must be forwarded to the department to which admission is requested.

Correspondence and Information

Office of Admissions
110 McFall Center
Bowling Green State University
Bowling Green, Ohio 43403-0180
Phone: 1-866-CHOOSE-BGSU
Fax: 419-372-6955
E-mail: choosebgsu@bgsu.edu
Web site: http://www.bgsu.edu/gradcoll

FACULTY HEADS

GRADUATE COLLEGE

Timothy Messer-Kruse, Ph.D., Interim Vice Provost for Academic Programs and Graduate Dean, 419-372-5387.
Lisa Chavers, Ph.D., Assistant Dean for Graduate Studies and Director of Project Search, 419-372-0343.

ACADEMIC DEANS

Simon Morgan-Russell, Ph.D., Dean, College of Arts and Sciences, 419-372-2340.
Rodney Rogers, Ph.D., Dean, College of Business Administration, 419-372-2747.
Brad Colwell, Ph.D., Dean, College of Education and Human Development, 419-372-7403.
Linda Petrosino, Ph.D., Dean, College of Health and Human Services, 419-372-8243.
Jeffrey Showell, Ph.D., Dean, College of Musical Arts, 372-2188.
Faris Malhas, Ph.D., Dean, College of Technology, 419-372-7202.
Kay Flowers, Dean, College of University Libraries, 419-372-2856.
Marcia Salazar-Valentine, Ph.D., Executive Director, Continuing and Extended Education, 419-372-8185.

DEGREE PROGRAM GRADUATE COORDINATORS

College of Arts and Sciences

American Culture Studies: Radhika Gajjala, Ph.D., 419-372-0586 (radhik@bgsu.edu).
Art (School of): Dennis Wojtkiewicz, M.F.A., 419-372-2609 (dwojtki@bgsu.edu).
Biology: Ray Larsen, Ph.D., 419-372-9559 (larsera@bgsu.edu).
Chemistry: Tom Kinstle, Ph.D., 419-372-2658 (tkinstl@bgsu.edu).
Communication Studies: Joshua Atkinson, Ph.D., 419-372-3403 (jatkins@bgsu.edu).
Computer Science: Joseph Chao, Ph.D., 419-372-2364 (jchao@bgsu.edu).
English/Creative Writing: Lawrence Coates, Ph.D., 419-372-2111 (coatesl@bgsu.edu).
Ethnic Studies: Angela Nelson, Ph.D., Interim Chair, 419-372-6056 (anelson@bgsu.edu).
Geology: Jeff Snyder, Ph.D., 419-372-0533 (jasnyd@bgsu.edu).
German, Russian, and East Asian Languages: Edgar Landgraf, Ph.D., 419-372-9517 (elandgr@bgsu.edu).
History: Andrew Schocket, Ph.D., 419-372-8197 (aschock@bgsu.edu).
Mathematics and Statistics: Hanfeng Chen, Ph.D., 419-372-7463 (hchen@bgsu.edu).
Philosophy: Sara Worley, Ph.D., 419-372-2899 (sworley@bgsu.edu).
Photochemical Sciences: Felix N. Castellano, Ph.D., 419-372-7513 (castell@bgsu.edu).
Physics and Astronomy: Lewis Fulcher, Ph.D., 419-372-2635 (fulcher@bgsu.edu).
Political Science/Public Administration: Shannon Orr, Ph.D., 419-372-7593 (skorr@bgsu.edu).
Popular Culture: Jeffrey Brown, Ph.D., 419-372-2982 (jabrown@bgsu.edu).
Psychology: Rob Carels, Ph.D., 419-372-9405 (rcarels@bgsu.edu).
Romance & Classical Studies/French: Beatrice Guenther, Ph.D., 419-372-8069 (bguenth@bgsu.edu).
Romance & Classical Studies/Spanish: Amy Robinson, Ph.D., 419-372-2168 (arobins@bgsu.edu).
Sociology: Steve Demuth, Ph.D., 419-372-7260 (demuth@bgsu.edu).
Technical Writing: Gary Heba, Ph.D., 419-372-6835 (gheba@bgsu.edu).
Theater and Film: Lesa Lockford, Ph.D., 419-372-9381 (lockflo@bgsu.edu).
Women's Studies: Susana Pena, Ph.D., 419-372-7133 (susanap@bgsu.edu).

College of Business Administration

Accounting/MIS: David Stott, Ph.D., 419-372-2709 (dstott@bgsu.edu).
Applied Statistics/Operations Research: Richard McGrath, Ph.D., 419-372-8451 (rnmcgra@bgsu.edu).
Economics: Peter VanderHart, Ph.D., 419-372-8070 (pvander@bgsu.edu).
Graduate Studies in Business (M.B.A.): David Chatfield, Ph.D., 419-372-2488 (dchatfi@bgsu.edu).
Organization Development: Brian Childs, Ph.D., 419-372-8823 (bchilds@bgsu.edu).

College of Education and Human Development

DIS/School and Mental Health Counseling: Gregory Garske, Ph.D., 419-372-7319 (ggarske@bgsu.edu).
DIS/Special Education: Lessie Cochran, Ph.D., 419-372-7298 (llcochr@bgsu.edu).
DTL/Business Education: Bob Berns, Ph.D., 419-372-2904 (rberns@bgsu.edu).
DTL/Classroom Technology: Allison Goedde, Ph.D., 419-372-7394 (agoedde@bgnet.bgsu.edu).
DTL/Curriculum and Teaching: Tracy Huziak-Clark, Ph.D., 419-372-7363 (thuziak@bgsu.edu).
DTL/Reading: Cindy Hendricks, Ph.D., 419-372-7341 (cindyg@bgsu.edu).
Family and Consumer Sciences: Dawn Anderson, Ph.D., 419-372-8090 (dawna@bgsu.edu).
Human Movement/Sport/Leisure Studies: Dawn Anderson, Ph.D., 419-372-8090 (dawna@bgsu.edu).
LPS/College Student Personnel: Maureen Wilson, Ph.D., 419-372-7321 (mewilso@bgsu.edu).
LPS/Ed Foundations and Inquiry Program: Rachel Vannatta, Ph.D., 419-372-0451 (rvanna@bgsu.edu).
LPS/Ed Administration and Leadership Studies: Patrick Pauken, Ph.D., 419-372-2550 (paukenp@bgsu.edu).
LPS/Higher Education Administration: Maureen Wilson, Ph.D., 419-372-7321 (mewilso@bgsu.edu).
LPS/MACIE: Peggy Booth, Ph.D., 419-372-9950 (boothmz@bgsu.edu).

College of Health and Human Services

Communication Disorders: Tim Brackenbury, Ph.D., 419-372-2515 (tbracke@bgsu.edu).
Criminal Justice: Melissa Burek, Ph.D., 419-372-2326 (mwburek@bgsu.edu).
Gerontology: Nancy Orel, Ph.D., 419-372-7768 (norel@bgsu.edu).
Public Health: Hans Schmalzried, Ph.D., 419-372-9930 (hschmal@bgsu.edu).

College of Musical Arts

Robert Satterlee, Ph.D., 419-372-2360 (rsatter@bgsu.edu).

College of Technology

Architecture: Alan Atalah, Ph.D., 419-372-8354 (aatalah@bgsu.edu).
Learning Design: Terry Herman, Ph.D., 419-372-7265 (hermant@bgsu.edu).
Construction Management: Will Roudebush, Ph.D., 419-372-8275 (wroudeb@bgsu.edu).
Manufacturing Technology: Alan Atalah, Ph.D., 419-372-8354 (aatalah@bgsu.edu).

"Electric Falcon," the electric automobile developed by the College of Technology.

A professor with students and a telescope in the Physics and Astronomy Observatory.

Theater production of "The Good Times Are Killing Me."

CHAPMAN UNIVERSITY

Graduate Studies

Programs of Study

Chapman offers the Juris Doctor (law); the Ph.D. in education; the Doctor of Physical Therapy (D.P.T.); the Master of Arts (M.A.) in education, educational psychology, English, film studies, marriage and family therapy, international studies, school counseling, special education, teaching (elementary), or teaching (secondary); the Master of Fine Arts (M.F.A.) in creative writing, film production, film and television producing, production design, or screenwriting; and the Master of Science (M.S.) in food science, economic systems design, communication sciences and disorders, or health communication. Also offered are the Master of Business Administration; the Executive M.B.A.; the J.D./M.B.A.; the M.B.A./M.F.A. in film and television producing; and the M.B.A./M.S. in food science. Many of the degree programs offer specializations.

Public school credential programs include multiple subjects with bilingual emphasis, single subject, pupil personnel school counseling (PPS), special education credentials mild moderate and moderate severe Preliminary, special education credentials mild moderate and moderate severe Level II. Credential programs can be combined with one of the degree programs in education.

Required units vary with each degree; however, each program comprises courses that best prepare students to continue a career or enter a new profession. Program requirements include advancement to degree candidacy after the completion of 12 units. Some programs require a comprehensive examination, taken at the end of or during the final semester of course work. Some programs offer a thesis project option in place of the comprehensive examination. One or two internship courses that provide practical experience in the student's field are required for some programs. Course work from other accredited institutions may be transferred; a maximum of 6 credits may be applied to a program. At least 24 credits must be taken in residence.

Research projects are essential to many degree programs and are undertaken in research courses or through cooperative education. Because class sizes are kept small, students can readily communicate with faculty members about research projects and general academic work.

Research Facilities

Academic and research centers and institutes include the nationally recognized A. Gary Anderson Center for Economic Research, the Economic Science Institute, the Science of Teaching and Research Institute, Albert Schweitzer Institute, Ludie and David C. Henley Social Science Research Laboratory, Walter Schmid Center for International Business, Center for Global Trade and Development, Ralph W. Leatherby Center for Entrepreneurship Business Ethics, Roger C. Hobbs Institute for Real Estate, Law, and Environmental Studies, Institute for the Study of Media and the Public Interest, John Fowles Center for Creative Writing, Center for Educational and Social Equity, Barry and Phyllis Rodgers Center for Holocaust Education, a state-of-the-art human performance laboratory and research vivarium, food science and nutrition food-tasting and research laboratories, and a community clinic for psychological counseling and research. The computer lab has DEC MicroVAX and NCR Tower facilities, and there are also IBM PC and Apple Macintosh laboratories. The Chapman University Leatherby Libraries contain more than 220,000 volumes, more than 30,000 full text electronic journals, more than 8,000 electronic books, and 2,500 journal titles as well as DVDs, videos, CDs, and other media. Chapman has the largest collection of Albert Schweitzer memorabilia in the western United States; a permanent exhibit is on display in the Argyros Forum.

Financial Aid

Many financial aid opportunities are available for qualified students, including Chapman University Fellowships and loans, which are based on need and academic achievement; graduate assistantships; residence life positions; employment; California State Graduate Fellowships; Federal Direct Student Loans; Benefits for Veterans and Dependents; and an employer-paid tuition plan. Students interested in any of these opportunities should contact the Financial Aid Office (714-997-6741).

Cost of Study

Tuition for 2011–12 varies by program. Part-time and full-time students, as well as California and non-California residents, were charged the same tuition rate. Tuition for a full-time student (9 credits per semester) is approximately $12,000 to $50,000 per academic year, depending on the student's program. Books and personal expenses add to annual costs.

Living and Housing Costs

Chapman offers limited housing for graduate students. Off-campus housing is available.

Student Group

Graduate study programs enroll more than 1,600 students each year. Courses are scheduled so that both full- and part-time students can attend. Many students have been working in their field and bring practical experience to the classroom; they come from many states and countries, and about 50 percent of them are women. Students who choose to enroll at Chapman want a small-campus atmosphere, personalized attention, a superior faculty, and the education that will enable them to succeed in a highly competitive professional world. Opportunities for graduates are plentiful due to the concentration of business and industry in Orange County and throughout southern California. People for whom graduates may eventually work sit on many College advisory boards.

Location

The beautiful tree-lined campus in Orange, California, is 35 miles southeast of Los Angeles. Ocean breezes are less than 10 miles away; mountains and deserts are within an hour's drive. Just minutes from the University are major recreation and entertainment venues, including Orange County Performing Arts Center, Disneyland, Disney's California Adventure, Knott's Berry Farm, Angel Stadium, and Honda Center.

The University

Chapman is an independent, private institution and has provided liberal and professional education of distinction since it was founded in 1861 by the Christian Church (Disciples of Christ). It has continued to meet the needs of its students with fine academic programs and individualized attention. Undergraduate and graduate degree programs are offered. The graduate curricula are designed to offer advanced study in specific disciplines to broaden and deepen a student's knowledge. Faculty members include distinguished academicians and noted professional practitioners.

Chapman is accredited by and is a member of the Western Association of Schools and Colleges. It is also a member of the Independent Colleges of Southern California, the College Entrance Examination Board, the Western College Association, the Association of Independent California Colleges and Universities, the American Council on Education, the American Association of Colleges for Teacher Education, the Division of Higher Education of the Christian Church (Disciples of Christ), and the American Assembly of Collegiate Schools of Business. Its teacher training and credential programs are accredited by the California Commission on Teacher Credentialing. The College of Educational Studies is accredited by the Teacher Education Accreditation Council. The school psychology program is approved by the National Association of School Psychologists. The physical therapy program is accredited by the Commission on Accreditation in the Physical Therapy Education of the American Physical Therapy Association and by the Physical Therapy Examining Committee of the Board of Medical Quality Assurance of the State of California. The M.B.A. program is fully accredited by AACSB International—The Association to Advance Collegiate Schools of Business. The School of Law is fully approved by the American Bar Association. The marriage and family therapy program is accredited by COAMFTE, the Commission on Accreditation for Marriage and Family Therapy Education of AAMFT, the American Association for Marriage and Family Therapy. The communication sciences and disorders program is accredited by the Council of Academic Accreditation of ASHA, the American Speech-Language-Hearing Association. The program is in candidacy status.

Applying

Students are admitted in the fall, spring, and summer for most programs. Applicants should submit $60 and a completed Application for Graduate Studies; official transcripts of all postsecondary work, showing the completion of a bachelor's degree; scores on the GMAT, GRE (General or Subject test), MAT, or CSET; TOEFL, or IELTS scores, for international students; two letters of recommendation; and a statement of intent. Departments, however, should be consulted for specific program requirements.

Correspondence and Information

Office of Graduate Admission
Argyros Forum, Room 304
Chapman University
Orange, California 92866

Phone: 714-997-6786
888-CU-APPLY (toll-free)
Fax: 714-997-6713
E-mail: gradadmit@chapman.edu
Web site: http://www.chapman.edu

PROGRAM DIRECTORS

Business Administration: Jon Kaplan, Assistant Dean for Graduate and Executive Programs, Argyros School of Business and Economics; M.B.A., UCLA.
Creative Writing: Patrick Fuery, Chair, Department of English; Ph.D., Murdock University, Australia.
Communication Sciences and Disorders: Judy K. Montgomery, Professor of Education; Ph.D., Claremont.
Economic Systems Design: Stephen Rassenti, Professor of Economics and Mathematics and Director, Economic Science Institute; Ph.D., Arizona.
Education: Ky Kugler, Associate Dean of Education; Ed.D., New Mexico State.
Educational Psychology: Michael Hass, Associate Professor and Coordinator of Educational Psychology Programs; Ph.D., California, Irvine.
English: Patrick Fuery, Chair, Department of English; Ph.D., Murdock University, Australia.
Film Production, Film and Television Producing, Screenwriting, Production Design, M.B.A./M.F.A. Film and Television Producing, Film Studies, and J.D./M.F.A. Film and Television Producing: Alexandra Rose, Professor of Film and Television and Chair, Graduate Conservatory; B.A., Wisconsin–Madison.
Food Science: Anuradha Prakash, Associate Professor of Food Science and Program Director, Department of Physical Sciences; Ph.D., Ohio State.
Health Communication: Lisa Sparks, Professor of Communication Studies and Director, Health Communication Program, Ph.D., Oklahoma.
International Studies: Victoria Carty, Associate Professor of Sociology and Director, International Studies Program, Ph.D., New Mexico.
Law: Tom Campbell, Dean, School of Law; Ph.D., Chicago, J.D., Harvard.
Physical Therapy: Jaclyn Brechter, Chair, Department of Physical Therapy; Ph.D., USC.
Psychology: Georg Eifert, Professor of Psychology and Chair, Department of Psychology; Ph.D., Frankfurt (Germany).
School Counseling: John Brady, Associate Professor and Coordinator of Counselor Education Programs; Ph.D., US International.
Special Education: Dawn Hunter, Associate Professor of Education; Ph.D., Maryland, College Park.

Argyros Forum.

CHESTNUT HILL COLLEGE

Graduate Programs

Programs of Study

The School of Graduate Studies of Chestnut Hill College (CHC) offers master's degree and certificate programs in the following areas: Clinical and Counseling Psychology, Education, Educational Leadership, Instructional Technology, Holistic Spirituality, and Administration of Human Services. The School also offers an APA-accredited Doctor of Psychology (Psy.D.) degree in clinical psychology, state certification programs, LPC and LMFT licensure preparation, and a variety of post-master's programs. The College has also introduced a new post-bachelor's program for those who work and/or live with adults with autism spectrum disorder, the professional certificate in autism spectrum disorders.

The Clinical and Counseling Psychology program (M.A. and M.S. degrees) includes concentrations in child and adolescent therapy, marriage and family therapy, trauma studies, addictions treatment, and a new concentration in autism spectrum disorders. Students may also opt for a generalist curriculum. A post-master's certificate for licensure preparation prepares students for the licensure exam to become a LPC or LMFT in Pennsylvania and other states. Post-master's certificates are available in all areas of specialization. The APA-accredited Doctor of Psychology program is open to applicants who have a master's degree in counseling psychology or a closely related field. For applicants who have a bachelor's degree in psychology or the required four prerequisite courses, the combined M.S./Psy.D. track is available. All programs offered by the Department of Professional Psychology are practitioner based, and classes are taught by faculty members who are actively working in the field. Master's-level degrees/courses are also offered on the DeSales University campus in Center Valley, Pennsylvania.

The Education Department offers the M.Ed. in early childhood education, elementary education, secondary education, and educational leadership (accelerated/intensive format) with optional principal certification. Students may also opt for the following state certification programs: Early Education (pre-K to grade 4), Middle Level (grades 4 to 8), Instructional I and II, Special Education, Reading Specialist, and various secondary education areas. A Montessori certificate (AMS), with or without the M.Ed., is also offered.

The Instructional Technology program offers M.S. degrees and certificates in education and technology, instructional design and technology, and instructional technology specialist. CHC also offers Pennsylvania Department of Education (P.D.E.) Instructional Technology Specialist Certification. The instructional design program was created for students involved in technology who are challenged by cultural and technological changes. The courses present cutting-edge technology as the next wave in professional training, education, and design. The goal of the specializations is the preparation of professionals to assume leadership roles in the transformation of their work environments. The course work for these programs is offered through a combination distance/on-site format.

The M.A. in holistic spirituality and M.A. in holistic spirituality and spiritual direction programs offer students a way to turn a calling into a career. There is also a concentration in health care which is designed for those in the health-care employees, such as hospice workers, nurses, nurse practitioners, and hospital chaplains, who want to provide more holistic treatment for their patients and loved ones. Several certificate programs are also available, including new certificates in bereavement care and spirituality and sustainability. Each of the programs combine academic rigor with experiential learning in ways that promote the integration of theory and practice. The Holistic Spirituality programs presents an annual summer Festival of Spirituality featuring nationally known theologians in public lectures, extended conversations, and intensive course formats. Each summer's festival is designed to advance the relationships between spirituality and the Bible, justice issues, and/or ecological concerns.

The Administration of Human Services program (M.S. degree) combines courses in management, public policy, and social issues to prepare students for supervisory and leadership positions in health and human-service organizations. With an emphasis on social change and diversity, this degree provides a comprehensive knowledge base about organizations, their philosophy and structure, and the specialized services that are provided. This program is offered in an accelerated format. Post-bachelor's certificates of professional development in leadership development as well as adults and aging are also available.

The new professional certificate in autism spectrum disorders (ASD) for those who work and/or live with adults with ASD addresses the societal needs and challenges of this population. While resources and education for children with ASD have increased, adults, both young and old, have been largely overlooked. The certificate is a four-course sequence held on designated Saturdays over four eight-week terms. The total cost for the certificate is $5000, and company discounts are available.

Research Facilities

Chestnut Hill College provides access to state-of-the-art hardware and software in five computer labs and a new building offering computer access from every workstation. The Logue Library offers an electronic research center, an online catalog, and nearly 150,000 volumes on three floors of open stacks. Among the electronic resources are ERIC, PsychINFO, LexisNexis, ProQuestReligion, JSTOR, EBSCOhost Elite, and Wilson OmniFile Mega, MLA. Specialized psychology demonstration rooms are available for live observation and taping of clinical sessions. Studio TV labs are used by the applied technology program; video editing and specialized multimedia development labs are used by other graduate programs.

Financial Aid

Chestnut Hill College offers a number of graduate assistantships for students at the master's and doctoral levels. The majority of students finance their education through Stafford loans. The Financial Aid Office is available to assist students with the loan application process. Some graduate programs (Education and Holistic Spirituality) offer tuition discounts to full-time teachers, child care workers, and those in church-affiliated ministry.

Cost of Study

Tuition for 2011–12 is $550 per credit for the Administration of Human Services program, $525 per credit for Holistic Spirituality programs, $585 per credit for the Clinical and Counseling Psychology master's-level programs, $555 per credit for the Education programs, and $855 per credit for doctoral credits.

Living and Housing Costs

A variety of urban and suburban housing options are available within an easy commute to the campus. There are also a limited number of on-campus rooms for graduate students.

Student Group

With classes primarily in the evening and on weekends, the School of Graduate Studies at Chestnut Hill College caters to the needs of the working professional. Degree programs should be completed within six years of matriculation. Within that time frame, students can choose their own pace for most programs; some opt to study full-time, while others take one or two courses per semester. Small classes and a welcoming atmosphere make Chestnut Hill College an excellent choice for traditional students as well as working professionals and those who wish to change careers.

Location

Chestnut Hill College is located in the northwestern corner of Philadelphia, easily accessible to all of the Philadelphia neighborhoods, outlying areas, and adjoining states. It is also near numerous cultural, athletic, and recreational activities in the region. The campus has a suburban feel, while remaining accessible via public transportation and major routes.

The College

Chestnut Hill College, founded by the Sisters of St. Joseph in 1924, is an independent Catholic institution that fosters equality through education and welcomes women and men of all backgrounds. The School of Graduate Studies provides a quality education that takes into equal account the academic, professional, and personal needs of both women and men. The aim of the graduate programs is to graduate professionals who are skilled, ethical, knowledgeable, and confident practitioners in their respective fields.

Applying

Applications for all master's-level programs are considered on a rolling admissions basis. Master's degree students may begin in any semester: fall, spring, or summer. In order for files to be reviewed in time for registration, requirements should be received by the following dates: for fall, July 1; for spring; November 1, and for summer, March 1. Extensions may be granted by contacting the Director of Admissions. The Psy.D. program has a separate application process. The deadline for Psy.D. applications is January 15; cohorts begin each fall. Details are available on the Web site. Master's-level applicants are evaluated on the basis of the entire application packet, which includes the application, transcripts of all previous college study, three letters of recommendation, MAT or GRE General Test scores (PPST scores only for education), and a 400- to 600-word statement of professional goals. Applicants with previous graduate degrees may be exempt from one or more requirements. Special admission requirements apply to the Holistic Spirituality and Psy.D. programs. Interviews with department chairs are required for qualified applicants. Tours and/or interviews with a member of the admissions staff are available.

Correspondence and Information

For master's program information and all applications:
Jayne Mashett
Director of Graduate Admissions
Chestnut Hill College
9601 Germantown Avenue
Philadelphia, Pennsylvania 19118-2693
Phone: 215-248-7020
Fax: 215-248-7161
E-mail: gradadmissions@chc.edu
Web site: http://www.chc.edu/graduate

For Psy.D. program information:
Eileen Webb
Director of Psy.D. Admissions
Chestnut Hill College
9601 Germantown Avenue
Philadelphia, Pennsylvania 19118-2693
Phone: 215-248-7077
Fax: 215-248-7155
E-mail: profpsyc@chc.edu
Web site: http://www.chc.edu/graduate

THE FACULTY

Note: Research interests of the Psy.D. faculty members are available on the Web at http://www.chc.edu/graduate/psydfac.htm. Information on the entire faculty can be found at http://www.chc.edu/faculty/.

Stephen Berk, Assistant Professor of Education; Ph.D., Temple.
Richard W. Black, Assistant Professor of Education; Ed.D., Temple.
David Borsos, Assistant Professor of Psychology; Ph.D., Temple.
Scott W. Browning, Professor of Psychology; Ph.D., Berkeley.
Melanie Cohen-Goodman, Assistant Professor of Education; Ph.D., Temple.
Ana M. Caro, Assistant Professor of Psychology; Psy.D., Chestnut Hill.
Dominic Cotugno, Associate Professor of Education; Ed.D., Temple.
Joseph A. Diorio Jr., Assistant Professor of Psychology; Ph.D., Case Western Reserve.
Jeanne DiVincenzo Collins, Assistant Professor of Psychology; Psy.D., Chestnut Hill.
William J. Ernst, Assistant Professor of Psychology; Psy.D., James Madison.
Carolynne Ervin, Coordinator of Spiritual Direction Program; M.A., Creighton.
Mary Kay Flannery, S.S.J., Associate Professor of Religious Studies; D.Min., Catholic Theological Union.
Claudia Garcia-Leeds, Assistant Professor of Psychology; Ph.D., CUNY Graduate Center.
Elaine R. Green, Associate Professor of Sociology; Dean, School of Continuing Studies; and Chair, Administration of Human Services; Ed.D., Temple.
Barbara Hogan, Associate Professor of Human Services; Ph.D., Temple.
Jessica Kahn, Associate Professor of Education; Ph.D., Pennsylvania.
Yefim Kats, Assistant Professor and Coordinator of Instructional Technology; Ph.D., CUNY Graduate Center.
Thomas E. Klee, Associate Professor of Psychology; Ph.D., Temple.
Mary M. Lindsay, S.S.J., Assistant Professor of Psychology; Ph.D., Temple.
Susan Rosemarie Manfredi, Assistant Professor of Psychology; Psy.D., Widener.
Kevin McCarthy, Assistant Professor of Psychology; Ph.D., Pennsylvania.
Susan McGroarty, Assistant Professor of Psychology; Ph.D., Pennsylvania.
Joseph A. Micucci, Professor and Chair of Psychology; Ph.D., Minnesota.
Catherine Nerney, S.S.J., Associate Professor of Religious Studies; Ph.D., Catholic University.
Carol M. Pate, Assistant Professor and Chair, Education Department; Ed.D., Indiana.
Cheryll Rothery-Jackson, Associate Professor and Director of Clinical Training; Psy.D., Rutgers.
Leslie Parkes Shralow, Assistant Professor of Psychology; Ph.D., Temple.

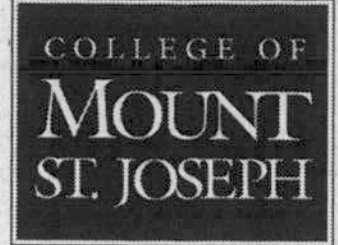

COLLEGE OF MOUNT ST. JOSEPH

Graduate Studies

Programs of Study

The advanced degree programs offered by the College of Mount St. Joseph (the Mount) specialize in the cultivation of ethical leadership skills in business, depth in ministry, and expertise in the teaching and health professions. Graduate degree programs include: a Master of Arts (M.A.) in education, a Master of Arts (M.A.) in religious studies, a Master of Science in Organizational Leadership (M.S.O.L.), a Master of Nursing (M.N.), and a Doctor of Physical Therapy (D.P.T.).

The M.A. degree programs in education meet the needs of college graduates who are prospective or experienced teachers. The major in teaching is offered to students who hold a bachelor's degree and are interested in seeking initial teacher licensure and a Master of Arts degree. The professional advancement programs are ideal for practicing teachers who wish to enhance their skills in the classroom or advance to positions of leadership while obtaining a Master of Arts degree. An intensive course of study integrates theory and field work in diverse educational settings. Classes meet during late afternoon and evening hours, in the summer months, and occasionally on weekends.

The TEAM (Teacher Education Accelerated Master's) programs prepare adults to enter the teaching profession through an intense learning and apprentice format. Three programs are offered: TEAM–IEC (Inclusive Early Childhood), TEAM–AYA (Adolescent/Young Adult), and TEAM–MSE (Multicultural/Special Education). The Mount's TEAM programs lead to a Master of Arts in education with a major in teaching, and can be completed in seventeen months. The programs are open to qualified students who have a bachelor's degree.

The Master of Arts in religious studies program, which concentrates on spiritual and pastoral care, is designed to enhance and integrate the interpersonal skills and theological knowledge of health-care professionals, educators, and ministers who serve in diverse populations and social contexts. Small classes, academic advising, and personal attention provide an environment conducive to the development of pastoral competence. Core courses are offered on weekends, enabling adult students to continue working while completing degree requirements in two years.

The Master of Science in Organizational Leadership program takes a multidisciplinary approach and emphasizes values, spirituality, and ethics while focusing on the development of effective leadership skills that can be used in any type of organization. Areas of study include leadership, people and organizations, organizational decision making, and technology. The M.S.O.L. degree can be completed in fewer than two years. All courses are offered on Saturdays.

The Master of Nursing program is a full-time, accelerated graduate-level program for individuals who have earned an undergraduate degree in a discipline other than nursing and would like to pursue a nursing career. The program includes advanced course work and can be completed with clinical experience in as little as fifteen months. The M.N. is accredited by the Commission on Collegiate Nursing Education and is supported by the Ohio Board of Nursing.

The Doctor of Physical Therapy program is designed to prepare clinicians who can think critically and solve problems; apply scientifically validated therapeutic skills and techniques effectively; respect the dignity of individuals; and understand the responsibilities of the health-care provider in the twenty-first century. This program is fully accredited by the Commission on Accreditation in Physical Therapy Education. Upon completion, a graduate must apply for and successfully pass the National Physical Therapy Examination conducted by each state's licensing board.

Research Facilities

The Mount's Archbishop Alter Library owns more than 96,000 volumes and provides access to more than 140 databases, online reference sources, and research assistance. Document delivery and interlibrary loan facilitate the prompt acquisition of materials available anywhere in the country. With FOCUS, the library's online public access catalog, patrons may search for materials available at the College library and other area libraries. OHIOLINK, a statewide network of public universities and private colleges, provides quick access to materials and full access to the Internet.

Financial Aid

Financial aid is available to all students enrolled at the Mount, with priority given to those in need of financial assistance. Students must complete a financial aid application. Five scholarships, each in the amount of $1000, are awarded annually to women who are graduate students in education and/or religious studies. To qualify, applicants must take at least 12 credit hours during the academic year.

A special grant is available to any individual enrolled in the religious studies graduate program who is a paid or volunteer minister serving in a congregation, hospital, health-care facility, social service agency, diocese, or educational institution. This grant reduces tuition during all semesters. Verification of employment/volunteer service and submission of a FAFSA form are required.

Cost of Study

Tuition for graduate programs is as follows: education (M.A.), $525 per hour; religious studies (M.A.), $525 per hour; organizational leadership (M.S.O.L.), $555 per hour; nursing (M.N.), $38,800 for the program; and physical therapy (D.P.T.), $81,000 for the program or $9000 per semester. The tuition rates for TEAM programs in education are: Inclusive Early Childhood (TEAM-IEC), $525 per hour; Adolescent/Young Adult (TEAM-AYA), $525 per hour; and Multicultural/Special Education (TEAM-MSE), $525 per hour.

Living and Housing Costs

Apartments are for rent at reasonable rates in the immediate area.

Student Group

Total enrollment at the Mount exceeds 2,400. There are more than 400 graduate students, with 53 percent attending full time.

Location

Located 15 minutes from downtown Cincinnati, the College of Mount St. Joseph is situated on a 92-acre suburban campus overlooking the Ohio River. The College is easily accessible from the airport, bus terminal, railway station, and interstate. Well known for its scenic and rolling hills, greater Cincinnati offers numerous parks, cultural and arts events, museums, theaters, professional athletics, shopping areas, and a wide assortment of fine restaurants.

The College

The College of Mount St. Joseph is a private, Catholic, coeducational college of 2,400 students that provides a professional and liberal arts education. Founded in 1920 by the Sisters of Charity, the Mount is dedicated to preparing the ethical leaders of tomorrow and equipping them with values, integrity, and social responsibility.

Small class sizes encourage individualized learning, and students have opportunities for career experience, leadership development, service learning, and participation in a wide variety of activities. In addition to its graduate programs, the Mount offers more than thirty-five undergraduate academic programs and nine associate degrees.

The Mount is fully accredited by the Higher Learning Commission of the North Central Association of Colleges and Schools and is consistently ranked among the top Midwest regional universities for quality and value by *U.S. News & World Report* in its guide to America's Best Colleges.

Applying

Students interested in applying should contact the Office of Graduate Admission to obtain application forms and other program materials.

Correspondence and Information

Office of Graduate Admission
College of Mount St. Joseph
5701 Delhi Road
Cincinnati, Ohio 45233

Phone: 513-244-GRAD
800-654-9314 (toll-free)
E-mail: admission@mail.msj.edu
Web site: http://www.msj.edu

THE FACULTY

Education: Mary West, Associate Professor and Chair; Ph.D., Ohio State; phone: 513-244-4935; fax: 513-244-4867; e-mail: mary_west@mail.msj.edu:.
Tsila Evers, Assistant Professor; Ph.D., Michigan.
James Green, Assistant Professor; Ph.D., Ohio State.
Kathleen Hulgin, Assistant Professor; Ph.D., Syracuse.
Steve McCafferty, Assistant Professor; Ed.D., Cincinnati.
Amy Murdoch, Assistant Professor; Ph.D., Cincinnati.
Jay Parks, Assistant Professor; M.Ed., Cincinnati.
Peggy Riegel, Instructor; M.Ed., Miami.
Clarissa Rosas, Associate Professor; Ph.D., New Mexico.
Rosemary Rotuno-Johnson, Assistant Professor; Ph.D., Miami.
Nursing: Mary Kishman, Associate Professor and Graduate Nursing Chair; Ph.D., Cincinnati; RN; phone: 513-244-4726; fax: 513-451-2547; e-mail: mary_kishman@mail.msj.edu.
Donna Glankler, Assistant Professor; M.S.N., Cincinnati; RN.
Susan Johnson, Professor and Division Dean; Ph.D., Cincinnati; RN.
Kelly Simmons, Assistant Professor; M.S.N., Northern Kentucky.
Organizational Leadership: Daryl Smith, Assistant Professor and Chair; Ph.D., Washington (Seattle); phone: 513-244-4920; fax: 513-244-4270; e-mail: daryl_smith@mail.msj.edu.
John Ballard, Associate Professor; Ph.D., Purdue.
Elizabeth Bartley, Professor; Ph.D., Cincinnati.
Mark Bell, Instructor; M.B.A., Maryland; CPA.
Mary Ann Edwards, Associate Professor; D.B.A., Argosy University.
Missy Houlette, Assistant Professor; Ph.D., Delaware.
David Kroger, Instructor; M.S., Dayton.
Charles Kroncke, Associate Professor; Ph.D., Auburn.
Judy Singleton, Assistant Professor; Ph.D., Cincinnati.
Georgana Taggart, Associate Professor; J.D., Northern Kentucky.
Ron White, Professor; Ph.D., Kentucky.
Physical Therapy: Karen Holtgrefe, Assistant Professor and Chair; D.H.S., Indianapolis; PT, OCS; phone: 513-244-3299; fax: 513-451-2547; e-mail: karen_holtgrefe@mail.msj.edu.
Adrick Caesar, Assistant Professor; M.P.T., Medical University of South Carolina; CSCS.
Lisa Dehner, Associate Professor; Ph.D., Virginia; PT.
Marsha Eifert Mangine, Assistant Professor; Ed.D., Cincinnati; PT, ATC.
Kevin Lawrence, Assistant Professor; D.H.S., Indianapolis; PT, OCS.
Renee Loftspring, Assistant Professor; Ed.D., Cincinnati; PT.
Peter Mosher, Assistant Professor; D.P.T., St. Louis; PT, ACCE.
Religious Studies: John Trokan, Associate Professor and Chair; D.Min., Saint Mary of the Lake–Muldelein Seminary; phone: 513-244-4496; fax: 513-244-4788; e-mail: john_trokan@mail.msj.edu.
Alan deCourcy, Associate Professor; D.Min., United Theological Seminary (Ohio).
Marge Kloos, S.C., Associate Professor; D.Min., United Theological Seminary (Ohio).
Harriet Luckman, Associate Professor; Ph.D., Marquette.
Jozef D. Zalot, Assistant Professor; Ph.D., Marquette.

The College of New Jersey

THE COLLEGE OF NEW JERSEY

Graduate Programs

Programs of Study

The College of New Jersey (TCNJ) offers the following advanced degrees: Master of Arts (M.A.) in counselor education or English; Master of Arts in Teaching (M.A.T.) in deaf and hard of hearing/elementary education (five-year program for TCNJ undergraduate students only), early childhood education, elementary education, health and physical education, secondary education, special education, or technology education; Master of Education (M.Ed.) in educational leadership–principal certification, educational leadership–instruction (a collaborative program in conjunction with the Regional Training Center), elementary and secondary education (Global Program only), health or physical education, reading K–12, special education, special education/teacher of students who are blind or visually impaired, or teaching English as a second language; Master of Science in Nursing (M.S.N.) in adult nurse practitioner studies, clinical nurse leader studies, family nurse practitioner studies, neonatal nurse practitioner studies, or school nurse certification (instructional and noninstructional options); and Educational Specialist (Ed.S.) in marriage and family therapy.

Graduate certificate programs and/or post-master's programs are offered in adult nurse practitioner studies; bilingual education (main campus and Global Program); educational leadership–principal certification; family nurse practitioner studies; adult nurse practitioner studies, school nurse certification (instructional and noninstructional options); instructional licensure-teacher of preschool–grade 3; learning disabilities teacher/consultant studies, reading specialist studies; substance awareness coordinator studies; teacher certification for international schools (Global Program only); teacher of students with disabilities; teaching English as a second language; or gender studies.

Global opportunities in education are also available for graduate students. Graduate global programs at TCNJ have been in existence for over thirty years and provide course work leading toward a master's degree in education and state of New Jersey certification in teaching and administration. Courses are taught by TCNJ faculty members and other internationally recognized professors. Courses are offered June through July at TCNJ sites in Mallorca, Spain; Bangkok, Thailand; and Johannesburg, South Africa. During the academic year, courses are available in Dubai, United Arab Emirates; Cairo, Egypt; and Hsinchu, Taiwan.

For the convenience of the majority of graduate students who pursue degrees while being employed full-time, graduate courses held on the Ewing campus are offered during the day and in the evening.

Research Facilities

TCNJ offers a state-of-the-art library that serves as an exciting intellectual, cultural, and social center for the College community. The five-story, 135,000-square-foot facility will provide cutting-edge services to the TCNJ community well into the twenty-first century. In addition to housing traditional library collections and services in an atmosphere that is both friendly and elegant, a key feature of the recently built library is its wide array of carefully considered and thoughtful amenities, which make using the facility both a pleasure and a convenience. The library provides twenty-four group-study rooms (one reserved for graduate students), ample and comfortable seating, tables and carrels, and both WiFi and LAN Internet access throughout, with power connections at every carrel and study table. Special design features include a café, a secure, late night/24-hour study area, and a 105-seat multipurpose auditorium. The library also houses the Instructional Technology Services facility, creating ideal one-stop shopping for students working on projects.

Library collections include more than 560,000 volumes and 200,000 microforms as well as subscriptions to more than 1,400 periodicals. The library also subscribes to more than seventy-five electronic indexes covering more than 14,000 scholarly journals, including full-text resources. A media facility offers viewing and listening equipment as well as sound recordings, videos, and interactive computer software. PCs are available for public access to electronic resources. Collections are constantly augmented by new acquisitions, and interlibrary loan and document delivery services are available as well. The library is also an active participant in a number of library networks and maintains cooperative arrangements with many regional academic libraries, from which students may borrow directly. TCNJ librarians are an important resource in and of themselves. In addition to advanced studies in library and information science, each subject-librarian has additional graduate degrees in one of the major academic areas, and students are encouraged to consult them in person and online.

In addition to providing new library facilities for the College community, TCNJ has met the challenge of the computer field's phenomenal growth with installations of computer facilities in each of its seven schools.

Financial Aid

The College of New Jersey offers financial aid to qualified matriculated students through a combination of loans, grants, and/or employment. To be considered for all financial aid programs, students must submit the Free Application for Federal Student Aid (FAFSA) to the College Financial Assistance Office. Graduate assistantships are available to qualified full-time students on a competitive basis.

Cost of Study

Tuition for graduate courses for 2011–12 is $623.50 per semester hour of credit for New Jersey residents and $983.40 per semester hour of credit for out-of-state residents. Additional fees include ID, student center, computer access and service fees, and health insurance (for full-time students). Tuition and fees are subject to change by action of the New Jersey State Legislature.

Living and Housing Costs

As the majority of TCNJ's graduate students attend classes part-time in the evenings, the College does not offer on-campus housing for graduate students. Graduate students who seek housing in the area can get assistance from the Office of Residence Life.

Student Group

The College of New Jersey had an enrollment of approximately 6,200 undergraduate students and 1,000 graduate students in 2010–11.

Student Outcomes

The College of New Jersey's excellent reputation has afforded graduates outstanding opportunities when entering their professional fields. Many TCNJ graduates receive job placements through various on-campus recruitment programs sponsored by the Office of Career Services.

Location

The College of New Jersey is located on 289 tree-lined acres in suburban Ewing, New Jersey, 7 miles from the state capital in Trenton. Woodlands and two lakes surround the academic and residential buildings. More than thirty-five buildings make up the physical plant, most of which are built in the classic Georgian Colonial architecture. The campus is 30 miles from Philadelphia and 60 miles from New York's theaters, museums, and other attractions. The nearby towns of Princeton and New Hope offer additional cultural activities.

The College

Founded in 1855, the College has grown from its early years as a teachers' college to a multipurpose institution comprising seven schools: Arts and Communication; Business; Education; Engineering; Humanities and Social Sciences; Nursing, Health, and Exercise Science; and Science. Graduate study is available in the Schools of Education, Humanities and Social Sciences, and Nursing, Health, and Exercise Science.

TCNJ introduced its first advanced degree program, a Master of Science in elementary education, in 1947. Over the years, the number of graduate programs has steadily increased. At present there are more than fifty specialized graduate degree and certificate programs.

TCNJ's academic programs are accredited by the Middle States Association of Colleges and Schools, the National Council for Accreditation of Teacher Education (NCATE), the Council for the Accreditation of Counseling and Related Educational Programs (CACREP), and other appropriate professional associations.

Applying

Students of proven ability with undergraduate degrees in appropriate fields are eligible to apply for graduate study. Applications should be submitted online (http://graduate.pages.tcnj.edu/apply) along with the $75 nonrefundable application fee. Transcripts of all previous college or university work and other supporting documentation as noted on the Web should be forwarded to the Office of Graduate Studies. Acceptable scores on the appropriate national standardized tests are required for most degree programs.

Application deadlines for matriculation and non-matriculation for the various graduate programs are located on the Graduate Studies Web site (http://graduate.pages.tcnj.edu/apply).

Correspondence and Information

Office of Graduate Studies
Paul Loser Hall, Room 109
The College of New Jersey
2000 Pennington Road
P.O. Box 7718
Ewing, New Jersey 08628

Phone: 609-771-2300
Fax: 609-637-5105
E-mail: graduate@tcnj.edu
Web site: http://graduate.pages.tcnj.edu

DEANS AND PROGRAM COORDINATORS

SCHOOL OF HUMANITIES AND SOCIAL SCIENCES
Benjamin Rifkin, Dean; Ph.D., Michigan.

Graduate Program Coordinator
English: Michele Tarter, Associate Professor; Ph.D., Colorado.

SCHOOL OF EDUCATION
Mark Kiselica, Interim Dean; Ph.D., Penn State.

Graduate Program Coordinators
Counselor Education: Mark Woodford, Assistant Professor and Chair; Ph.D., Virginia. Marion Cavallaro, Associate Professor; Ph.D., Ohio State. Mary Lou Ramsey, Professor; Ed.D., Fairleigh Dickinson. Atsuko Seto, Assistant Professor; Ph.D., Wyoming.
Deaf and Hard of Hearing/Elementary Education Five-Year Program: Barbara Strassman, Professor; Ed.D., Columbia Teachers College.
Early Childhood Education (P–3 Certificate): Jody Eberly, Assistant Professor; Ph.D.; Rutgers.
Educational Leadership–Instruction: Alan Amtzis, Director; Ph.D., Boston College.
Educational Leadership–Principal: Donald Leake, Associate Professor and Chair; Ph.D., Ohio State. Jacqueline Norris, Assistant Professor; Ed.D., Rutgers.
Elementary and Early Childhood Education (M.A.T.): Brenda Leake, Associate Professor; Ph.D., Ohio State.
Health and Physical Education: Anne Farrell, Assistant Professor and Chair; Ph.D., New Mexico.
Instructional Licensure–Teacher of Preschool–Grade 3: Jody Eberly, Assistant Professor; Ph.D., Rutgers.
Reading K–12: Kathryne Speaker, Assistant Professor; Ed.D., Temple.
School Personnel Licensure: Jody Eberly, Assistant Professor; Ph.D., Rutgers.
Secondary Education: Colette Gosselin, Assistant Professor; Ed.D., Rutgers. John Karsnitz, Professor; Ph.D., Ohio State.
Special Education: Shridevi Rao, Assistant Professor; Ph.D., Syracuse.
TESOL/Bilingual Education: Yiqiang Wu, Associate Professor; Ph.D., Texas A&M.

SCHOOL OF NURSING, HEALTH, AND EXERCISE SCIENCE
Marcia Blicharz, Interim Dean; M.S.N., Pennsylvania; Ed.D. Rutgers.

Graduate Program Coordinators
Nursing: Leslie Rice, Assistant Professor; M.S.N., Pennsylvania; Ph.D., New York.
Health and Exercise Science: Anne Farrell, Assistant Professor and Chair; Ph.D., New Mexico.

MAJOR RESEARCH PROJECTS

Grant Awards
Adaptive technology center; Dr. Amy G. Dell, School of Education.
Advanced education nursing traineeship program; Dr. Claire Lindberg, School of Nursing.
Infant functional status and discharge management; Dr. Susan Bakewell-Sachs, School of Nursing.
Preparing special and elementary educators to use inquiry and design-based learning; Dr. Amy Dell, School of Education.
Provisional teacher program; Dr. Anthony Evangelisto, School of Education.
TECH-NJ (Technology, Educators, and Children with Disabilities–New Jersey); Dr. Amy G. Dell, School of Education.
The New Jersey Teacher Quality Enhancement Recruitment Project; Dr. Sharon Sherman, School of Education and Dr. Cathy Liebars, School of Science.
Deaf/Blind Family and Community Educational Support; Dr. Jerry Petroff, School of Education.
Institute of Educational Design, Evaluation, and Assessment; Dr. Debra Frank, School of Education.

Support of Scholarly Activity Awards (SOSA)
Conversation analysis of native/nonnative speakers; Dr. Jean Wong, School of Education.
Facilitating transition from school to employment for individuals with challenging behavior; Dr. Shridevi Rao, School of Education.
HIV symptom distress project; Dr. Claire Lindberg, School of Nursing.
Issues of literacy and teaching elementary students of color; Dr. Deborah Thompson, School of Education.
The reception of Dante and Chaucer within the work of their literary successors; Dr. Glenn Steinberg, School of Culture and Society.
When boys become parents: understanding and helping teen fathers; Dr. Mark Kiselica, School of Education.
Writing the republic; Dr. David Blake, School of Culture and Society.

The clock tower above Green Hall, the main administrative building on campus, is a well-known symbol of TCNJ tradition.

The College is made up of more than thirty-eight Georgian-style buildings all situated on a 289-acre suburban campus.

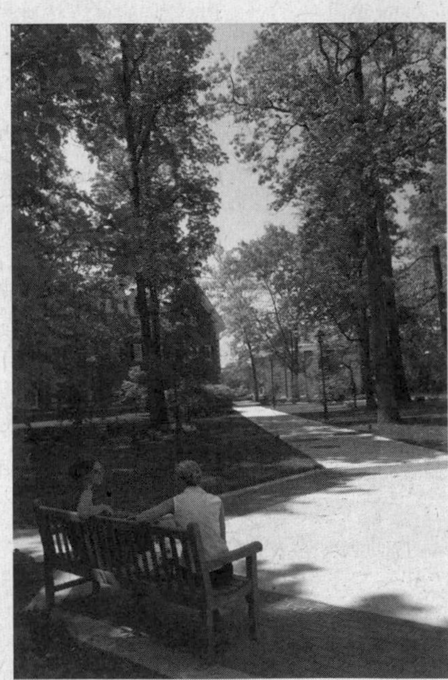
The College of New Jersey's tree-lined campus, which provides spectacular foliage, offers a beautiful setting for students all year long.

COLLEGE OF STATEN ISLAND OF THE CITY UNIVERSITY OF NEW YORK

Graduate Degree Programs

Programs of Study

The College of Staten Island (CSI) offers master's degrees in biology (M.S.); business management (M.S.); cinema and media studies (M.A.); computer science (M.S.); education: childhood (elementary) education (M.S.Ed.), adolescence (secondary) education (M.S.Ed.), special education (grades 1–6) (M.S.Ed.), special education (grades 7–12) (M.S.Ed.); English (M.A.); environmental science (M.S.); history (M.A.); liberal studies (M.A.); mental health counseling (M.A.); neuroscience, mental retardation, and developmental disabilities (M.S.); and nursing: adult health nursing (M.S.) and gerontological nursing (M.S.). Post-master's and advanced certificates are awarded in leadership in education, adult health nursing, gerontological nursing, cultural competence, and nursing education.

The doctoral programs in nursing (D.N.S.) and physical therapy (D.P.T.) are offered jointly with the Graduate Center of the City University of New York (CUNY). The College also participates in the Graduate Center's doctoral programs in biochemistry (Ph.D.), biology: specialty in neuroscience (Ph.D.), computer science (Ph.D.), physics (Ph.D.), and polymer chemistry (Ph.D.).

Research Facilities

The Center for Developmental Neuroscience and Developmental Disabilities is supported jointly with the New York State Institute for Basic Research (IBR). The center conducts, promotes, and sponsors research, education, and training in the developmental neurosciences, with special emphasis on research and educational programs in the specific field of developmental disabilities. The center provides for collaborative efforts between the College and IBR in offering the master's degree in neuroscience, developmental disabilities, and mental retardation, as well as with the University's doctoral programs in biology (subprogram in neuroscience), and in psychology (subprogram in learning processes). The center provides advanced research training for graduate students.

The Center for Environmental Science provides support for research and policy recommendations concerning environmental problems. One of the major purposes of the center is to define and solve environmental problems on Staten Island and its environs through research that includes studies of respiratory diseases, toxic and carcinogenic chemicals in the air, and the population at risk for lung cancer.

The Center for the Study of Staten Island: Staten Island Project (SIP) is designed to integrate the work of the College with the public affairs concerns of the people of Staten Island. To that end, it mediates and facilitates the collaboration of the College's faculty, students, and staff with government, civic organizations, and businesses in order to identify and assist in finding solutions to the borough's pressing public issues. The center serves as an information and consultation resource to prepare citizens and leaders to make better-informed decisions about public life; it fosters the development of faculty research and graduate education through engagement with the community; and it builds bridges to other public affairs institutes and local communities as a spur to innovations in public life on Staten Island.

The Center for Interdisciplinary Applied Mathematics and Computational Sciences brings together a diverse group of research faculty members and students with interests in interdisciplinary applications of mathematics and computational science. The center's activities include the use of the campus supercomputer, faculty collaboration, grant writing, student mentoring and research, and sponsored lectures.

The CUNY High-Performance Computing Center (HPCC) is located on the CSI campus. Goals of the HPCC are to: support the scientific computing needs of university faculty, student, staff, and their public and private sector partners; create opportunities for the CUNY research community to develop new partnerships with the government and private sectors; and leverage the center's capabilities to acquire additional research resources for its faculty and graduate students in existing and major new programs.

The Discovery Institute develops and manages educational programs using an interdisciplinary theme to engage intermediate, high school, and college students in learning more actively and effectively using the institute's discovery-based learning system. In addition, the institute works collaboratively with local public schools on professional development of teachers to develop new teaching strategies. The institute's Teaching Scholars program trains and places CSI students at public schools and partnering public/private institutions to serve as mentors and role models. These multiple programs are supported by the resources of the College and by grants from a variety of state, federal, and private institutions.

The Center for Engineered Polymeric Materials (CePM) is an initiative funded by the New York State Office of Science, Technology, and Academic Research (NYSTAR). The center's mission is to conduct cutting-edge research in polymeric and nanoscale materials and to provide a conduit for the transfer of technology involving synergistic interaction among New York State industries, academic institutions, and government laboratories. The University's doctoral program in polymer chemistry serves as the center's intellectual base.

Financial Aid

The Office of Student Financial Aid administers federal and state grant, loan, and work-study programs to assist students with financial need to attend the College of Staten Island. Students should contact the Office of Student Financial Aid early in the admission process to discuss eligibility requirements and responsibilities. In some departments, graduate assistant positions are available for full-time graduate students, and information about these positions may be obtained from the individual program departments.

Cost of Study

For the 2011–12 academic year, tuition for New York State residents is $345 per credit, or $4105 per semester for 12 or more credits. Tuition for nonresidents is $640 per credit.

Living and Housing Costs

For the 2011–12 academic year, dependent students budgeted a minimum of $1179 for books and supplies, $986 for local transportation, $2838 for meals and personal expenses, and $1655 for housing. Independent students budgeted the same amounts for books, supplies, and transportation, plus $14,737 for food, housing, and personal expenses for a nine-month academic year.

Student Group

Nearly 1,000 graduate students enrolled at the College of Staten Island in the 2011 fall semester. The graduate population reflects a wide range of ethnicity, social and economic backgrounds, educational and professional experiences, and aspirations.

Location

The College of Staten Island is located in New York City in the Borough of Staten Island. Completed in 1994, the 204-acre campus of the College of Staten Island is the largest one for a college in New York City. Set in a parklike landscape, the campus is centrally located on Staten Island and is accessible by automobile and public transportation.

The College

The College of Staten Island is a four-year senior college of the City University of New York that offers exceptional opportunities to all its students. Programs in the liberal arts and sciences and professional studies lead to bachelor's and associate degrees, in addition to the graduate programs listed above.

Applying

Requirements for admission and application deadlines vary by program and department. Students should contact the Graduate Admissions' Office for additional information or to arrange an admissions interview or campus tour.

Correspondence and Information

Sasha Spence, Assistant Director for Graduate Admissions
Office of Recruitment and Admissions
North Administration Building (2A), Room 103
College of Staten Island
2800 Victory Boulevard
Staten Island, New York 10314

Phone: 718-982-2019
Fax: 718-982-2500
E-mail: masterit@csi.cuny.edu
Web site: http://www.csi.cuny.edu/graduatestudies

GRADUATE PROGRAM FACULTY HEADS

A full listing of graduate program directors, contact information, and office hours is available at the College Web site. Please visit http://www.csi.cuny.edu/graduatestudies and click on "Graduate Program Coordinators."

The College of Staten Island is located in New York City in the Borough of Staten Island. The 204-acre campus is the largest one for a college in New York City.

Designed with inviting reading rooms, open shelves, and study carrels, the library's research and study facilities are enhanced by computer data-based operations available to all students.

DREW UNIVERSITY

The Caspersen School of Graduate Studies

Programs of Study

The Caspersen School of Graduate Studies offers students an opportunity to pursue graduate studies in a setting that emphasizes small class size, individual attention from faculty members, and the ability to explore a wide range of scholarly interests.

The M.A./Ph.D. program in History and Culture concentrates on the intellectual and cultural history of modern Europe and America. It trains students both for careers in academia and for related nonacademic work in publishing, cultural journalism, museums, and philanthropy.

The globally focused Master of Arts in Teaching (M.A.T.) program offers a one-year full-time track and a two-year part-time track. M.A.T. students learn leading-edge pedagogies while studying deeply in one of ten content areas (biology, chemistry, English, French, Italian, math, physics, social studies, Spanish, or theater arts).

The low-residency Master of Fine Arts in Poetry and Poetry in Translation program offers some of America's most talented poets as faculty mentors who work one-on-one with students. The program is divided into two 10-day on-campus residencies and two mentorship semesters each year.

Drew also offers an interdisciplinary Arts and Letters program (M.Litt., D.Litt.), emphasizing broad competence in the liberal arts, and an innovative Medical Humanities program (M.M.H., D.M.H.), conducted jointly by Drew, Overlook Hospital, and Saint Barnabas Medical Center. Medical Humanities addresses topics such as biomedical ethics, medical narrative, and the history of medicine. Full- or part-time study is available in both the Arts and Letters and Medical Humanities programs.

Research Facilities

The Rose Memorial Library houses 499,417 volumes plus a large collection of manuscripts, journals, and other primary source material. It also has an unusually large collection of periodicals with special strengths in the basic areas of graduate study offered at Drew. The library is a depository for the publications of the federal government and the state of New Jersey. It also collects the official documents of the United Nations. The Center for Holocaust Studies is located on campus, and the United Methodist Archive and History Center, adjacent to the library, houses one of the most extensive collections of American religious history and Methodistica in the world.

Financial Aid

Financial aid may take the form of scholarships, loans, employment, or any combination of these. Both need and achievement are taken into account in determining the amount of assistance to be made available. Merit-based awards range from 20 percent of tuition to 100 percent of tuition, plus stipend. Applicants must file financial aid forms.

Cost of Study

In 2011–12, tuition for the M.A./Ph.D. program is $2040 per credit. The Master of Arts in Teaching program is $855 per credit. Tuition for the M.F.A. in Poetry program is $443 per credit, plus a $900 residency fee. Arts and Letters and Medical Humanities tuition is $909 per credit, with reduced rates for senior citizens and full-time educators.

Living and Housing Costs

Drew offers a variety of housing options in dormitories or apartments for both single and married students. For 2011–12, the cost is approximately $7578 to $14,990 for the academic year, depending on size requirements. Meal plans can be provided for an additional charge. Commuter rooms are also available.

Student Group

The total University enrollment is 2,716 students; of this number, 394 are in the Graduate School. Of the total number of graduate students, 64 percent are women and 10 percent are self-identified members of minority groups.

Location

Drew is located on a beautiful, 186-acre campus in Madison, New Jersey (population 18,000), 25 miles west of Manhattan. Commuter rail and bus lines provide easy access to New York City and all its educational, cultural, and entertainment opportunities.

The University

One of the major characteristics of the Graduate School is the emphasis on interdisciplinary studies. Its size allows for graduate education on a personal level with many small seminars, one-to-one tutorials, and classes that encourage discussion and lively interaction. Faculty members excel in teaching as well as in scholarship and research.

Applying

Evaluation of an applicant's qualifications for admission is based on previous course work and grade point average, letters of recommendation, personal statement, and writing sample. GRE General Test scores are required of U.S. and Canadian citizens who apply for the M.A./Ph.D. program. International students who are not native English speakers are required to submit recent TOEFL and TWE scores. Arts and Letters and Medical Humanities candidates may be admitted for the fall, spring, or summer semester. M.F.A. in Poetry candidates may begin the program in January or June. Master of Arts in Teaching candidates are admitted for the June start term only. The deadline for receipt of admissions and financial aid forms varies by program; students should contact the Office of Graduate Admissions for more information.

Prospective students are encouraged to attend the Graduate Open House held each fall and spring.

Correspondence and Information

Director of Graduate Admissions
Drew University
Madison, New Jersey 07940
Phone: 973-408-3110
Fax: 973-408-3040
E-mail: gradm@drew.edu
Web site: http://www.drew.edu/grad

THE FACULTY

Fran Bernstein, Assistant Professor of History; Ph.D., Columbia.
William Campbell, Adjunct Professor of Parasitology and Fellow, Charles A. Dana Research Institute; Ph.D., Wisconsin.
Luis Campos, Assistant Professor of History; Ph.D., Harvard.
Robert Carnevale, Adjunct Assistant Professor of English; M.F.A., Columbia.
James Carter, Assistant Professor of History; Ph.D., Houston.
Philip E. Chase, Adjunct Assistant Professor of English; Ph.D., Drew.
Gabriel M. Coless, Affiliate Professor of Church History; S.Th.D., Pontificio Instituto Liturgico (Rome).
David A. Cowell, Professor of Political Science; Ph.D., Georgetown.
Paolo Cucchi, Professor of French and Italian and Dean; Ph.D., Princeton.
Phyllis D. DeJesse, Adjunct Assistant Professor of Medical Humanities; D.M.H., Drew.
Sloane Drason-Knigge, Adjunct Assistant Professor of Holocaust Studies; Ph.D., Drew.
Lillie Edwards, Associate Professor of History and African American Studies; Ph.D., Chicago.
C. Wyatt Evans, Assistant Professor of History; Ph.D., Drew.
Roxanne Friedenfels, Professor of Sociology; Ph.D., Michigan.
Jonathan Golden, Assistant Professor of Religious Studies, Associate Director of Caspersen Centers; Ph.D., Pennsylvania.
David Graybeal, Professor of Church and Society; Ph.D., Yale.
Richard Greenwald, Dean, Caspersen School of Graduate Studies, Associate Professor of History; Ph.D., NYU.
Yasuko Grosjean, Associate Professor of Japanese Literature and Culture; Ph.D., Drew.
James Paul Hala, Professor of English; Ph.D., Michigan.
Herbert Huffmon, Professor of Old Testament; Ph.D., Michigan.
Sandra Jamieson, Associate Professor of English; Ph.D., SUNY at Binghamton.
Donald F. Kent, Adjunct Associate Professor of Medical History; M.D., Pennsylvania, Ph.D., Drew.
Christine A. Kinealy, Professor of Irish History; Ph.D. Trinity College (Dublin).
Wendy Kolmar, Professor of English; Ph.D., Indiana.
Cassandra Laity, Associate Professor of English; Ph.D., Michigan.
Edwina Lawler, Associate Professor of German and Russian; Ph.D., Drew.
Perry Leavell Jr., Professor of History; Ph.D., Tulane.
John Lenz, Associate Professor of Classics; Ph.D., Columbia.
Neal Levi, Assistant Professor of English; Ph.D. Columbia.
Thomas Magnell, Professor of Philosophy; D.Phil., Oxford.
Richard A. Marfuggi, Adjunct Assistant Professor of Medical Humanities; D.M.H., Drew.
Rosemary McLaughlin, Associate Professor of Theater Arts; M.F.A., Rutgers.
Karen H. McNamara, Adjunct Assistant Professor of Children's Literature; D.Litt., Drew.
Margaret Micchelli, Adjunct Professor; Ph.D., Rutgers.
Jo Ann Middleton, Director of Medical Humanities; Ph.D., Drew.
John R. Middleton, Affiliate Associate Professor of Clinical Ethics; M.D., University of Medicine and Dentistry of New Jersey.
A. Johan Noordsij, Affiliate Professor of Psychiatry; M.D., Leiden (Netherlands).
Frank Occhiogrosso, Professor of English; Ph.D., Johns Hopkins.
Nadine Ollman, Professor of English; Ph.D., Pennsylvania.
Glen A. Olsen, Adjunct Assistant Professor of Music History; D.Litt., Drew.
Roberto Osti, Adjunct Assistant Professor of Medical Illustration; M.F.A., New York Academy of Art.
James H. Pain, Henry and Annie M. Pfeiffer Professor of Religion and Dean; D.Phil., Oxford.
Dale Patterson, Adjunct Assistant Professor of Religious History; Ph.D., Drew.
Philip Peek, Professor of Anthropology; Ph.D., Indiana.
Virginia Phelan, Affiliate Associate Professor of Comparative Literature; Ph.D., Rutgers.
Jonathan W. Reader, Associate Professor of Sociology; Ph.D., Cornell.
Robert Ready, Professor of English; Ph.D., Columbia.
William B. Rogers, Affiliate Professor of History and Associate Dean; Ph.D., Drew.
Joseph Romance, Associate Professor of Political Science; Ph.D., Rutgers.
Jonathan Rose, Assistant Professor of History; Ph.D., Pennsylvania.
Ann Saltzman, Associate Professor of Psychology; Ph.D., CUNY Graduate Center.
Peggy Samuels, Associate Professor of English; Ph.D., CUNY Graduate Center.
Philip C. Scibilia, Adjunct Assistant Professor of Medical Humanities; D.M.H., Drew.
Merrill M. Skaggs, Professor of English; Ph.D., Duke.
Geraldine Smith-Wright, Professor of English; Ph.D., Rutgers.
Sharon Sundue, Assistant Professor of History; Ph.D., Harvard.
Linda Swerdlow, Assistant Professor of Education, Director of M.A.T. Program; Ph.D., NYU.
Jerome A. Travers, Adjunct Assistant Professor of Family Studies; Ph.D., Fordham.
Linda Van Blerkom, Associate Professor of Anthropology; Ph.D., Colorado.
Jeremy Varon, Associate Professor of History; Ph.D., Cornell.
Jennifer Holly Wells, Adjunct Lecturer of English; M.Phil., Drew.
Laura Winters, Adjunct Associate Professor of English; Ph.D., Drew.
Carol A. Wipf, Adjunct Associate Professor of English; Ph.D., Illinois at Champaign–Urbana.
Eugene Zins, Adjunct Associate Professor of Medical Humanities; M.D., Pennsylvania.

Drew is located on a beautiful, 186-acre campus in Madison, New Jersey, just 25 miles from Manhattan.

The Caspersen School of Graduate Studies, Drew University.

D'YOUVILLE COLLEGE

Graduate Studies

Programs of Study

D'Youville College offers the Doctor of Education (Ed.D.) degree in educational leadership and health policy and health education. Doctor of Chiropractic (D.C.), Doctor of Pharmacy (Pharm.D.), and Doctor of Physical Therapy (D.P.T.) programs are also offered. Master of Science (M.S.) degrees are offered in business administration, clinical nurse specialist studies in community health nursing, education (childhood, adolescence, special education, and TESOL), health services administration, international business, nurse practitioner studies (master's degree and post-master's certificate), nursing (with choice of clinical focus), occupational therapy, and physical therapy. Advanced certificate programs in clinical research associate studies, health services administration, long-term-care administration, and nursing and health-related professions education are also available. Five-year B.S./M.S. degrees are offered in dietetics, international business, nursing, and occupational therapy.

Research Facilities

D'Youville's Library Resources Center contains 130,000 volumes, including microtext and software, and subscribes to 700 periodicals and newspapers. The library provides state-of-the-art computer reference facilities for both in-house and off-site users, including access to over 70 online databases. The multimillion-dollar Health Science Building houses laboratories, including those for anatomy, organic chemistry, quantitative analysis, and computer science.

Financial Aid

In order to apply for federal aid, the Free Application for Federal Student Aid (FAFSA) must be completed. Graduate students must be matriculated for 6 or more credit hours in a degree program. Sources of federal aid include Federal Perkins Loans, the Federal Work-Study Program, Veterans' Benefits, Federal Stafford Student Loans, and Graduate Nursing Loans. D'Youville College offers three forms of scholarships for graduate students matriculated in a master's degree program, including the Program Merit Scholarship, the Disadvantaged Student Scholarship, and the Retention Award. Nurse traineeship assistance is available to students enrolled for a minimum of 9 credit hours per semester in the Graduate Nursing Program. Canadian students (citizens and landed immigrants) are offered a 20 percent tuition reduction and may also apply for the Ontario Student Assistance Program (OSAP). Private education loans are also available to both U.S. and Canadian citizens.

Cost of Study

Graduate tuition for 2011–12 is $790 (M.S.) and $850 (Ed.D. and D.P.T.) per credit hour. The Doctor of Chiropractic is $10,725 per semester and the pharmacy program is $14,150 per semester. A general fee of between $50 and $155 is required, based on credit hours taken. A Student Association fee of $3 per credit hour is applied toward concerts, yearbooks, activities, and guest lectures.

Living and Housing Costs

Marquerite Hall, the residence facility, houses men and women students on separate floors, with the exception of the designated coed floors. For 2011–12, room and board cost $5000 per semester. Overnight accommodation is available, space permitting. A residence-apartment complex houses 175 junior, senior, and graduate students in one- and four-bedroom apartments. Rates for 2011–12 for this complex are around $4100 per semester, based on the type of apartment reserved.

Student Group

Graduate degree programs are enhanced by a 13:1 student-faculty ratio. The graduate enrollment is more than 783 full-time and 333 part-time students. Sixty-eight percent of the student population are women, 18 percent are from minority groups, and 44 percent are international students. D'Youville's proximity to the Canadian border accounts for the majority of the international student population.

Location

D'Youville's location is ideally set in a residential community of Buffalo, New York. D'Youville College is minutes from the Peace Bridge to Canada and is approximately 90 minutes from Toronto and 25 minutes from Niagara Falls, making it a gateway to recreation areas in western New York and Ontario.

The College

D'Youville College is a private, coeducational liberal arts and professional college located in residential Buffalo, New York, approximately 1 mile from the Peace Bridge. The Grey Nuns founded D'Youville College in 1908. With a student population of just over 3,200, D'Youville offers its students the diversity and resources of a much larger college and the attention and accessibility that are usually attributed to a small college. The College's 7-acre campus offers students comprehensive facilities, modern computer labs, state-of-the-art medical labs, and modern classrooms.

Applying

Completed application files are reviewed on a rolling admissions basis for most programs. The Doctor of Physical Therapy program has a November 30 application deadline for entry the following fall. The Doctor of Chiropractic program requires a minimum of 90 credit hours of undergraduate course work for application to the professional phase of the program. All other program candidates must have earned a baccalaureate degree from an accredited college or university. Candidates for the Ed.D. programs must have earned a master's degree from an accredited college or university. A baccalaureate degree in nursing from an approved or accredited college or university and RN licensure are required for admission to the graduate nursing programs. Licensure as a registered nurse in New York State and a minimum of one year of experience as a registered nurse are required of candidates applying to the nurse practitioner studies programs. Admission to graduate programs is based on an overall evaluation of credentials, including the applicant's undergraduate record, which should show approximately a B average or better in the major field. Applicants who do not fulfill admission requirements may be admitted provisionally. Applicants to the Ed.D. programs should show a 3.25 GPA or better in their master's course work. Admission to Ed.D. programs is competitive. Applicants whose native language is not English must submit a minimum TOEFL score of 500. The College does not require Graduate Record Examinations (GRE) or Miller Analogies Test (MAT) scores. Applicants for the M.B.A. program are required to take the GMAT. Applicants to the pharmacy program should refer to the School of Pharmacy for admissions requirements and deadlines.

Correspondence and Information

Linda E. Fisher
Director of Graduate Admissions
D'Youville College
One D'Youville Square
320 Porter Avenue
Buffalo, New York 14201-9985
Phone: 716-829-8400
800-777-3921 (toll-free)
Fax: 716-829-8408
E-mail: fisherl@dyc.edu
Web site: http://www.dyc.edu

THE FACULTY

Chiropractic
Kathleen Linaker, Executive Director of Chiropractic Program; D.C., Northwestern Health Sciences University; DACBR.
Steven Zajac, Coordinator of Clinical Services; D.C., National University of Health Sciences; DACBO.

Education
Jamie DeWaters, Professor; Ph.D., SUNY at Buffalo.
Robert J. Gamble, Associate Professor; Ph.D., SUNY at Buffalo.
Nancy M. Kaczmarek, GNSH, Associate Professor; Ph.D., SUNY at Buffalo.
James Lalley, Assistant Professor; Ph.D., SUNY at Buffalo.
Cathleen March, Assistant Professor; Ph.D., SUNY at Buffalo.
Thomas Traverse, Assistant Professor; M.A., SUNY at Buffalo.
Stephen E. Williams, Assistant Professor; Ed.D., Clark.

Educational Leadership
Mark Garrison, Associate Professor and Director of Doctoral Programs; Ph.D., SUNY at Buffalo.

Health Policy and Health Education
Mark Garrison, Associate Professor and Director of Doctoral Programs; Ph.D., SUNY at Buffalo.

Health Services Administration
Walter Iwanenko, Assistant Professor and Department Chair; Ph.D., SUNY at Buffalo.
Elizabeth Miranda, Assistant Professor; J.D., SUNY at Buffalo.
James Notaro, Assistant Professor; Ph.D., North Carolina at Chapel Hill.
Judith H. Schiffert, Assistant Professor; Ed.D., SUNY at Buffalo.

International Business
Peter Eimer, Assistant Professor; M.B.A., Pittsburgh.
Joseph Fennell, Associate Professor; M.B.A., Columbia.
Bonnie Fox-Garrity, Assistant Professor; Ed.D., D'Youville.

Nursing
Denise Dunford, Assistant Professor; Director of Nurse Practitioner; D.N.S., SUNY at Buffalo.
Carol A. Gutt, Associate Professor; Ed.D., SUNY at Buffalo.
Kathleen Mariano, Assistant Professor; D.N.S., SUNY at Buffalo.
Judith H. Lewis; Dean, School of Nursing; Ed.D., Cincinnati.
Abigail Mitchell; Assistant Professor, Nursing D.H.Ed., A. T. Still.
Eileen Nahigian; Assistant Professor; D.N.S., SUNY at Buffalo.

Occupational Therapy
Merlene Gingher, Associate Professor; Ed.D., SUNY at Buffalo.
Amy Nwora, Assistant Professor and Department Chair, Ph.D., SUNY at Buffalo.
Elizabeth Stanton, Associate Professor; Ph.D., SUNY at Buffalo.

Physical Therapy
James Karnes, Associate Professor; Ph.D., SUNY at Buffalo.
Lynn Rivers, Associate Professor and Department Chair; Ph.D., SUNY at Buffalo.
John Rouselle, Associate Professor; Ed.D., SUNY at Buffalo.
Brian Wrotniak, Assistant Professor; Ph.D., SUNY at Buffalo.

EMORY
LANEY GRADUATE SCHOOL

EMORY UNIVERSITY

James T. Laney School of Graduate Studies

Programs of Study

The Laney Graduate School at Emory University offers the Master of Arts (M.A.) in bioethics, educational studies, film studies, music, and sacred music; the Master of Science (M.S.) in biostatistics, computer science, and mathematics; and the Master of Science in Clinical Research (MSCR) program for physicians or Ph.D.'s in health-related sciences. Professional degrees awarded are the Master of Education (M.Ed.), Master of Arts in Teaching (M.A.T.), and the master's in development practice program. A diploma for advanced study in teaching is also available.

The Doctor of Philosophy (Ph.D.) is offered in anthropology, art history, behavioral sciences and health education, nine programs in the biological and biomedical sciences, biomedical engineering, biostatistics, business, chemistry, comparative literature, computer science and informatics, economics, educational studies, English, environmental health sciences, epidemiology, French, health sciences research and health policy, history, liberal arts, mathematics, nursing, philosophy, physics, political science, three programs in psychology, ten courses of study in religion, sociology, Spanish, and women's studies.

Programs within the Graduate Division of Biological and Biomedical Sciences include biochemistry, cell and developmental biology, cancer biology, genetics and molecular biology, immunology and molecular pathogenesis, microbiology and molecular genetics, molecular and systems pharmacology, neuroscience, nutrition and health sciences, and population biology, ecology, and evolution. A six-year Medical Scientist Program leads to a combined M.D./Ph.D. Programs in psychology include clinical psychology, cognitive and developmental psychology, and neuroscience and animal behavior. Courses of study within the Graduate Division of Religion include ethics and society; Hebrew Bible; historical studies in theology and religion; New Testament; person, community, and religious practices; theological studies; West and South Asian religion; and the J.D./Ph.D. program. The program in biomedical engineering is offered jointly with the Georgia Institute of Technology.

M.A. and M.S. degrees require a minimum of two semesters of residence; M.Ed. and M.A.T. degrees and the diploma require at least three semesters of residence; and the Ph.D. degree requires a minimum of four semesters of residence.

Research Facilities

Holdings of the five Emory libraries (Health Sciences Library, Law Library, Oxford College Library, Theology Library, and the General Libraries, made up of the Woodruff, Candler, Chemistry, and Math and Science Libraries) total approximately 2.7 million volumes. The libraries also offer access to thousands of electronic information resources. The Center for Library and Information Resources provides an integrated service environment that brings together technology and media specialists with librarians in a facility that includes an information commons, electronic classrooms, a distance learning classroom, the Center for Interactive Teaching, a state-of-the-art language lab and classrooms, the new high-tech Heilbrun Music and Media Library, the Electronic Services Data Center, group study rooms, and comfortable study spaces with data connections as well as wireless access throughout the building. The Special Collections and Archives Division of Woodruff Library contains modern literary manuscript archives, notable African American collections, and other major archival and manuscript holdings.

Facilities in the biomedical sciences include a large number of specialized laboratories as well as the opportunities associated with a number of affiliated or adjacent research institutions: the Robert W. Woodruff Health Sciences Center, the Winship Cancer Institute, the Yerkes National Primate Research Center, the Emory Vaccine Center, the U.S. Centers for Disease Control and Prevention, and the American Cancer Society.

Additional facilities include the Information Technology Division and the Michael C. Carlos Museum. The Carter Center of Emory University provides resources for the study of national and international policy issues.

Financial Aid

All Emory University graduate fellowships are based on academic merit. They provide stipend and tuition scholarships for five years. All applications are due by January 3. Some programs have earlier deadlines; prospective students should check with the program. Tuition assistance grants are awarded to some teachers who are admitted to master's programs in the Division of Educational Studies. Information regarding extra-University financial aid (loans, work-study, or veterans' benefits) may be obtained from the Financial Aid Office.

Cost of Study

In 2011–12, full-time tuition is $17,400 (12 semester hours or more); the computing fee is $50 per semester; and the student activity and recreation fee is $199 per semester. Students must either join the Emory student health insurance plan, which costs $2360 per year, or demonstrate equivalent coverage under another policy. Many scholarships include a health insurance subsidy.

Living and Housing Costs

A variety of on- and off-campus housing is available. On-campus housing includes the Campus Crossings apartments, a five-story complex with one-, two-, and three-bedroom furnished and unfurnished (except three-bedroom) apartments. The apartments have central heat and air-conditioning and are equipped with a full kitchen, washer and dryer units, and full bathrooms (one per bedroom).

Student Group

Total University enrollment is more than 13,000. In fall 2010, total enrollment in degree programs in the Laney Graduate School was 1,917; 796 men and 1,121 women.

Location

Emory University's wooded campus is located in an attractive residential section of Atlanta. Easily accessible by bus and metro from Emory, downtown Atlanta provides an exciting, progressive atmosphere with many recreational and cultural activities, often with reduced rates for students. Increased attention is being paid to the city's past and its historical development and the revitalization of the downtown area. With a population of 3 million, Atlanta is relatively close to the Appalachian Mountains, the Atlantic coast, and the Gulf coast.

The University

Founded by the Methodist Church in 1836, Emory received its university charter in 1915 and moved from Oxford, Georgia, to the northeast Atlanta campus. The University comprises the Laney Graduate School, Emory College, Oxford College, and the schools of business, law, medicine, nursing, public health, and theology. The Graduate School was organized as a division of the University in 1919, and named after Emory's seventeenth president in 2009. Extracurricular activities are plentiful.

Applying

Minimum requirements for admission include a baccalaureate degree from an accredited four-year college, an undergraduate academic average of C, an academic average of B for the last two undergraduate years, and satisfactory scores on the General Test of the GRE. Applicants are considered without regard to race, color, national origin, religion, sex, sexual orientation, age, handicap, or veteran status. Applicants may apply online. Applications are due by January 3. Some programs have earlier deadlines; students should check with the program.

Correspondence and Information

Emory University Laney Graduate School
209 Administration Building
201 Dowman Drive
Atlanta, Georgia 30322
Phone: 404-727-6028
E-mail: gradschool-l@listserv.cc.emory.edu
Web site: http://www.graduateschool.emory.edu

DIRECTORS OF GRADUATE STUDY AND THEIR RESEARCH

Anthropology: Bradd Shore, Director of Graduate Studies; Ph.D., Chicago, 1977. Cultural anthropology, symbolic and psychological anthropology; Oceania, Polynesia.
Art History: Bonna Daix Wescoat, Director of Graduate Studies; Ph.D., Oxford, 1983. Ancient Greek art and architecture with emphasis on Archaic and Hellenistic architectural trends and architectural sculpture.
Behavioral Sciences and Health Education: Kimberly Jacob Arriola, Director of Graduate Studies; Ph.D., Northeastern, 1998. Behavior and health, community-based research, HIV/AIDS.
Biochemistry, Cell and Developmental Biology: Richard A. Kahn, Director; Ph.D., Yale, 1980. Signal transduction and cell regulation by GTP-binding proteins, regulation of membrane traffic, Alzheimer's disease.
Bioethics: Toby Schonfeld, Director of the Master of Arts in Bioethics; Ph.D., Tennessee, Knoxville, 2001. Women's health, ethics education, religion and ethics, and research ethics.
Biological/Biomedical Sciences: Keith D. Wilkinson, Director; Ph.D., Michigan, 1977. Mechanism and regulation of protein synthesis and degradation.
Biomedical Engineering: Gilda Barabino, Associate Chair and Director of Graduate Studies; Ph.D., Rice, 1986. Sickle cell adhesion, cellular engineering, tissue engineering and bioreactors.
Biostatistics: John J. Hanfelt, Director of Graduate Studies; Ph.D., Johns Hopkins, 1994. Proteomics, Alzheimer's disease, the statistical analysis of sparse dependent data, estimating functions and artificial likelihood theory.
Business: Anand Swaminathan, Director of Doctoral Studies; Ph.D., Berkeley, 1993. Organizational theory and strategy, industry evolution, strategies for niche/specialist firms, market entry, applications of social network theory.
Cancer Biology: Erwin Van Meir, Director; Ph.D., Lausanne (Switzerland), 1989. Brain tumor biology and genetics, angiogenesis, cancer cell signaling, tumor suppressor, p53, hypoxia, HIF, oncolytic virus therapy, drug discovery.
Chemistry: Vincent Conticello, Director of Graduate Studies; Ph.D., Northwestern, 1990. Biomolecular chemistry.
Clinical Research: Henry Blumberg, Principal Investigator and Director; M.D., Vanderbilt, 1983. Hospital and molecular epidemiology, nosocomial and community control of tuberculosis, clinical research training.
Comparative Literature: Maximilian Aue, Director of Graduate Studies; Ph.D., Stanford, 1973. German studies, German modernism, fin de siècle, the experimental novel, Romanticism.
Development Practice: Carla Roncoli, Associate Director of Graduate Studies; Ph.D., SUNY Binghamton, 1994. Environmental anthropology, human dimensions of climate change, vulnerability and adaptation, agricultural livelihoods, participatory processes, gender, Africa.
Economics: Maria Arbatskaya, Director of Graduate Studies; Ph.D., Indiana, 1999. Industrial organization, applied game theory.
Educational Studies: George Engelhard, Director of Graduate Studies; Ph.D., Chicago, 1985. Educational measurement and evaluation, measurement history and theory.
English: Laura Otis, Director of Graduate Studies; Ph.D., Cornell, 1991. English, Spanish, German, French, North and South American literature especially nineteenth-century novels; memory identity formation, communication technologies.
Environmental Health Sciences: Gary W. Miller, Director of Graduate Studies; Ph.D., Georgia, 1995. Toxicology.
Epidemiology: Julie Gazmararian, Director of Graduate Studies; Ph.D., Michigan, 1992.
Film Studies: Karla Oeler, Director of Graduate Studies; Ph.D., Yale, 2000. Classical and contemporary film theory and aesthetics, masculinity and violence, Soviet cinema.
French: Valerie Loichot, Director of Graduate Studies; Ph.D., LSU, 1996. Francophone studies, Caribbean literature and culture, literature of the Americas, postcolonial theory.
Genetics and Molecular Biology: Andreas Fritz, Director; Ph.D., Basel (Switzerland), 1988. Molecular and genetic mechanisms of the early patterning of the nervous system and segmentation of the mesoderm.
Graduate Institute of the Liberal Arts: Kimberly Wallace-Sanders, Director of Graduate Studies; Ph.D., Boston University, 1996. Race, gender, and representation; nineteenth-century popular culture; African-American material culture; body theory and feminism; black mammy iconography.
Health Services Research and Health Policy: Walter M. Burnett, Director of Graduate Studies; Ph.D., Iowa, 1965.
History: James Melton, Director of Graduate Studies; Ph.D., Chicago, 1982. Enlightenment Europe, early modern German and Austrian history, the Atlantic World.
Immunology and Molecular Pathogenesis: Brian D. Evavold, Director; Ph.D., Chicago, 1989. T-cell activation, antigen recognition, EAE autoimmunity model, role of SHP-1 phosphatase in T-cell responses.
Mathematics and Computer Science: James Lu, Director of Graduate Studies; Ph.D., Northwestern, 1992. Logic programming and theorem proving, particularly inference techniques for certain non-standard logics. Data models, query processing, data integration, constraint databases, heuristic search and propositional satisfiability.
M.D./Ph.D. Program: Mary E. K. Horton, Director of Graduate Studies; M.P.H., M.A., Columbia, 1989. History of medicine, history of medical education in America, humanities in medical education.
Microbiology and Molecular Genetics: Philip Rather, Director; Ph.D., Emory, 1989. Mechanisms of cell-to-cell signaling and quorum sensing in bacteria.
Molecular and Systems Pharmacology: Eddie Morgan, Director; Ph.D., Glasgow, 1979. Regulation of drug metabolizing enzymes, cytochrome P-450, inflammation, biological effects of nitric oxide.
Music: Eric Nelson, Director of Graduate Studies; Ph.D., Indiana, 1990. Choral conducting and literature.
Neuroscience: Yoland Smith, Director; Ph.D., Laval, 1987. The pathophysiology of Parkinson's disease, changes in the synaptic plasticity of the basal ganglia in normal and pathological conditions.
Nursing: Ann Rogers, Director of Graduate Studies; Ph.D., Northwestern, 1986. Sleep, sleep medicine, sleep disorders, chronic disease management.
Nutrition and Health Sciences: Usha Ramakrishnan, Director; Ph.D., Cornell, 1993. Maternal and child nutrition, micronutrient malnutrition, nutrition assessment.
Philosophy: John Lysaker, Director of Graduate Studies; Ph.D., Vanderbilt, 1995. Philosophical psychology, aesthetics, social and political philosophy, nineteenth- and twentieth-century Continental and American philosophy.
Physics: Stefan Boettcher, Director of Graduate Studies; Ph.D., Washington (St. Louis), 1993. Theoretical soft condensed matter physics.
Political Science: Jennifer Gandhi, Director of Graduate Studies; Ph.D., NYU, 2004. Dictatorships, including their institutional design, modes of leadership succession, the role of ideology, and variations in economic performance.
Population Biology, Ecology, and Evolution: Michael Zwick, Director; Ph.D., California, Davis, 1998. Genetics of phenotypic evolution, population and comparative genomics.
Psychology: Hillary Rodman, Director of Graduate Studies; Ph.D., Princeton, 1986. Development, plasticity, and evolution of brain systems that govern high-level visual abilities such as object recognition and the awareness of stimuli.
Religion: Carl Holladay, Co-Director of Graduate Studies; Ph.D., Cambridge, 1975. Luke-Acts, Hellenistic Judaism, Christology. Gary Laderman, Co-Director of Graduate Studies; Ph.D., California, Santa Barbara, 1994. American religious history, religion, health and healing.
Sociology: Frank Lechner, Director of Graduate Studies; Ph.D., Pittsburgh, 1985. Global change, culture, religion, theory, national identity in globalization.
Spanish: Ricardo Gutiérrez-Mouat, Director of Graduate Studies; Ph.D., Princeton, 1978. Literary representations of violence, issues of globalization, the cultural discourses of post-dictatorship in the Southern Cone.
Women's Studies: Deboleena Roy, Director of Graduate Studies; Ph.D., Toronto, 2001. Feminist theory in science.

EMPORIA STATE UNIVERSITY

Graduate School

Programs of Study

Emporia State University (ESU) offers courses leading to the Master of Arts (M.A.) in biology, English, history, and teaching of English as a second language (TESOL).

The Master of Science (M.S.) is offered in art therapy; counseling; biology; business education (available totally online); clinical psychology; curriculum and instruction (pre-K–12 curriculum leadership, pre-K–12 effective practitioner, pre-K–12 national board certification); early childhood education; educational administration; health, physical education, and recreation; instructional design and technology; instructional leadership; master teacher studies (elementary subject matter, reading specialist); mathematics; mental health counseling; physical sciences (chemistry, earth science, physical sciences, physics); psychology; rehabilitation counseling; school counseling; school psychology; and special education.

The Master of Arts in Teaching (M.A.T.) is offered in social sciences. The University also offers Master of Business Administration (M.B.A.) with concentrations in accounting, enterprise resource planning, and information systems; Master of Library Science (M.L.S.); Master of Music (M.M.); and Master of Education in Teaching (M.Ed.) degree programs.

The Specialist in Education (Ed.S.) degree is offered in school psychology, and the Ph.D. is offered in library and information management.

Courses for the M.A. in TESOL are offered both online and in traditional face-to-face formats.

The University conducts an academic year of two semesters plus a nine-week summer session in which graduate courses are offered in every field.

The University is accredited by the North Central Association of Colleges and Schools and is a member of the Council of Graduate Schools in the United States. Its programs are recognized by the American Chemical Society, National Association of Schools of Music, AACSB International–The Association to Advance Collegiate Schools of Business, National Council for Accreditation of Teacher Education, American Library Association, American Art Therapy Association, Council on Rehabilitative Education, Kansas State Department of Education, and Council for Accreditation of Counseling and Related Educational Programs (CACREP).

Research Facilities

The William Allen White Library contains more than 1 million books, government documents, periodicals, theses, and nonprint materials. The library provides online access to a large number of bibliographic, full-text, and full-image databases. Other resources are available via the Internet at public access computers located in the library, via Web access through the home page, or through a proxy service for distance education students. Materials not available at ESU can be requested from other libraries throughout the world by utilizing the interlibrary loans service. Other key library resources are the Special Collections Department and the University Archives, both located in White Library.

The Departments of Biological Sciences and Physical Sciences utilize the Science of Mathematics Education Center, Johnston Geology Museum, Peterson Planetarium, Jones Biotechnology Laboratories, and the Jones Environmental Chemistry Laboratories, with state-of-the-art equipment. The University operates eight natural areas for biological research in tall grass prairie, upland and deciduous forest, and marshland. The Department of Psychology, Art Therapy, Rehabilitation, and Mental Health Counseling has a state-of-the-art research laboratory for students and faculty members. The Department of Special Education and School Counseling supports a state-of-the-art counseling clinic for training students and providing service to the community.

Financial Aid

Most departments offering graduate work, as well as numerous other units within the University, award graduate assistantships. During the academic year, the University employs at least 185 graduate assistants. To qualify for an assistantship, an applicant must have a minimum overall grade point average of 2.5 for four years or 2.75 for the last two years of undergraduate study, based on a 4.0 scale. Students may be eligible for tuition reductions during each term in which they hold an assistantship appointment. Nonresident full-time graduate assistants are assessed fees at the same rate as residents of Kansas.

Cost of Study

For the 2011–12 academic year, tuition and fees for a full graduate course load were $2886 per semester for state residents and $7798 per semester for nonresidents. For the summer session, resident tuition and fees were $261 per credit hour, and nonresident tuition and fees were $671 per credit hour. Fees are subject to change by action of the Board of Regents.

Living and Housing Costs

The Department of Residential Life offers graduate students a number of cost-effective living arrangements. Residence Hall rates range from $1573 to $2215 per semester. Emporia State Apartments rent for $254 to $341 per month (utilities not included). Students can contact the department by phone at 620-341-5264 or by e-mail (reslife@emporia.edu) for more information.

Student Group

The total on-campus enrollment is 6,314, with 299 full-time and 1,450 part-time graduate students. About 45 percent of the full-time graduate students receive financial assistance of some kind; 8.2 percent are international students.

Student Outcomes

Approximately 60 percent of the graduates find employment in their major fields of study within the state of Kansas, 29 percent of the graduates are employed in their major field of study outside the state of Kansas, 2 percent find employment outside their major field of study, 5 percent continue their education, and 4 percent are unemployed.

Location

Emporia, with a population of more than 26,000, is an educational, industrial, trade, and medical center serving 60,000 people in east-central Kansas. It is situated on the eastern edge of the famous Bluestem region of the Flint Hills and is surrounded by numerous lakes and recreational facilities. The city is located on the Kansas Turnpike, Interstate Highway 35. Three major metropolitan areas of the state—Topeka, Kansas City, and Wichita—are within 100 miles.

The University

The University, founded in 1863, has a long, diverse, and exciting history, which is reflected in its twenty-three different graduate programs in education, library science and information management, business, and liberal arts and sciences. Although all programs are of high quality, the University is particularly well known for its teacher education and library and information management programs. At ESU, small class sizes are the norm.

Applying

Applications for admission to the Graduate School should be made thirty days before the first day of an enrollment period. Some academic departments have earlier deadlines. For admission as a master's degree student, an applicant must have a minimum grade point average of 2.5 in the last 60 hours of undergraduate study. Applicants for the M.A. in English and the M.S. in special education must have at least a 2.75 grade point average or at least a 3.0 in the major. Applicants for the Specialist in Education degree must hold a master's degree from an accredited college or university with grades of B or better in three fourths of the credit hours taken for the degree. Applicants for the M.S. in psychology, school psychology, or art therapy must have a cumulative grade point average of at least 3.0 or at least 3.25 for the last 60 hours of an undergraduate program. Applicants for the M.A. in history must have a 3.0 GPA in 12 hours of history.

Correspondence and Information

Graduate School
Campus Box 4003
Emporia State University
Emporia, Kansas 66801-5087

Phone: 620-341-5403
800-950-GRAD (toll-free)
Fax: 620-341-5909
E-mail: gradinfo@emporia.edu
Web site: http://www.emporia.edu/grad

FACULTY HEADS

The following list shows specializations, research, and/or exhibits of the faculty within each graduate program and the chair or graduate adviser of each department.

Biological Sciences (M.S., M.A.): Scott Crupper, Ph.D., Coordinator of Graduate Studies. Animal and plant ecology, animal behavior, botany, cancer biology, cellular and molecular biology, endocrinology, entomology, environmental biochemistry and physiology, evolutionary biology, fisheries and wildlife management, herpetology, ichthyology, immunology, invertebrate and vertebrate zoology, mammalogy, microbiology, ornithology, population and molecular genetics, plant and animal anatomy/physiology, plant and animal taxonomy/systematics, biology education, soil science, and toxicology.

Business (M.B.A., M.S. in business education): Joseph Wen, Ph.D., Dean. Master in Business Administration with concentrations in accounting, enterprise resource planning (ERP), and information systems, and master in business education.

Special Education and School Counseling (M.S.): Jean Morrow, Ed.D., Interim Chair. Special education (adaptive concentration and gifted, talented, and creative concentration) and school counseling. Faculty specializations include assessment, inclusion, collaboration with teachers and parents, curriculum integration, special education attrition, mental retardation and autism, and implementation and management of school counseling program. The Department of Special Education and School Counseling supports a state-of-the-art counseling clinic for training students and providing service to the community.

Early Childhood/Elementary Teacher Education (M.S.): Jean Morrow, Ed.D., Chair. Master teacher (elementary subject matter, reading specialist), early childhood education, postbaccalaureate teacher certification. Faculty specializations include authentic assessment, cooperative learning, curriculum integration, literacy, inclusion, and multicultural education. Distance learning is available for all courses in these master's degree programs.

English (M.A.): Mel Storm, Ph.D., Director of Graduate Studies. Rhetoric and composition, creative writing, and English and American literatures. Courses for in-service teachers and for those who wish to pursue careers in community college teaching are also available. Dual master's degrees are offered with the School of Library and Information Management. Faculty specializations include medieval literature and language, Renaissance literature, eighteenth- and nineteenth-century British literature, nineteenth-century American literature, twentieth-century American literature, contemporary literature, world literature, women's studies, American studies, young adult fiction, English education, creative writing, folklore, popular culture, gender and ethnic studies, critical theory, rhetoric and composition, linguistics, and journalism.

Health, Physical Education, and Recreation (M.S.): Joan Brewer, Ed.D., Interim Chair. Pedagogy, exercise physiology, technology in health and physical education, sports ethics, administration, psychology of sport and physical education, motor behavior, health promotion and health education. The entire Master of Science in physical education may be completed through the online delivery.

History (M.A.): Deborah Gerish, Ph.D., Director of Graduate Studies. Faculty specialties include Colonial U.S., nineteenth-century U.S., political history of the South, women's history, twentieth-century political history in U.S. and Europe, Kansas history, Native American cultures, and public history. A dual master's degree is offered with the School of Library and Information Management.

Instructional Design and Technology (M.S.): Marcus Childress, Ph.D., Chair. Instructional design and technology. Faculty specializations include distance and online learning, online games/virtual reality, multimedia, instructional and curricular design, cooperative learning, integrating technology into teaching and learning, study skills, digital learning strategies (high-tech study skills), learning styles, digital storytelling, vocabulary acquisition methodologies, universal design, assistive technology, and heutagogy in distance learning. All courses in the M.S. program are offered via the Internet (http://idt.emporia.edu).

Library and Information Management (M.L.S., Ph.D.): Gwen Alexander, Ph.D., Dean. Analysis of information services and delivery systems, community analysis, economics of information, information brokering, information management, information transfer, library and information science education, management of library and information systems, organization and retrieval of information, psychology of information use, sociology of information, technology applications to information storage and retrieval. Dual master's degrees are offered with the Departments of Music, History, Social Sciences, and English and the School of Business. School library media and information management certification is also available. Regional programs are offered in various locations in the western half of the country.

Mathematics (M.S.): Joe Yanik, Ph.D., Chair. Algebra, analysis, applied mathematics, computer science, mathematics education, statistics, and topology. In addition to the on-campus option, the program can also be completed through online delivery.

Modern Languages and Literatures (M.A. in TESOL): Abdelilah Sehlaoui, Ed.D., and Manjula Shinge, Ph.D., Program Coordinators. Applied linguistics, sociolinguistics, second language acquisition, cross-/intercultural communication, CALL.

Music (M.M.): Allan Comstock, D.M.A., Interim Chair. Concentrations in music education and performance. Areas of study and research include elementary and secondary music education; choral and instrumental conducting; vocal and instrumental methods and performance; jazz performance and instruction; applied studies in voice, keyboard, woodwinds, brass, strings, and percussion; music computer applications; digital audio recordings. The music education concentration is delivered primarily through online course work.

Physical Sciences (M.S.): DeWayne Backhus, Ph.D., Chair. Concentrations in chemistry, earth science (with an online option), physical science, and physics. All programs are designed to prepare students for additional degree work at the doctoral level, industrial or government employment, or teaching. Research opportunities are available in a number of areas within each discipline; NASA-funded research exists in each discipline concentration.

Psychology, Art Therapy, Rehabilitation, and Mental Health Counseling (M.S., Ed.S.): Brian Schrader, Ph.D., Chair. Clinical psychology, general and industrial/organizational psychology, mental health counseling, rehabilitation counseling, art therapy counseling, and school psychology. Faculty specializations include teaching psychology at the secondary level, psychometrics, neuropsychology, cognition, behavioral toxicology, clinical applications of art, child and adolescent development, statistics, learning, performance appraisal, adolescent art therapy, human resources practices in organizations, autism, social skills training, at-risk youth, evaluation of intervention programs, bullying, study-abroad programs, refugee and immigrant populations, job/career satisfaction, school safety, and assessment and interventions in schools.

School Leadership/Middle and Secondary Teacher Education (M.S.): Jerry Will, Ph.D., Chair. Degree and certification programs in pre-K through 12 building and district levels, curriculum and instruction (effective practitioner studies, national board certification, curriculum leadership), master's program in teaching, instructional leadership master's program, postbaccalaureate teacher certification, and driver education. Varied courses are offered online and at the Metro Learning Center and ESU.

Social Sciences (M.A.T., M.A.): Darla Mallein, Ph.D., Coordinator. The multidisciplinary M.A.T. degree in social sciences, designed specifically for licensed secondary social studies teachers, allows candidates to concentrate their focus in the areas of American history, world history, geography, and political science. It emphasizes mastery of the methods of teaching the social sciences within the professional educational context, with the aim of developing each candidate's skills as critical thinkers, creative planners, and effective practitioners.

Relaxing campus environment.

Interactive classes.

Technology in the classroom.

FORDHAM UNIVERSITY

Graduate School of Arts and Sciences

Programs of Study

The Graduate School of Arts and Sciences is committed to the education of talented men and women in the liberal arts and sciences and offers programs of advanced study in a number of academic disciplines. Areas of study include both the traditional humanistic and scientific disciplines and interdisciplinary programs that may be oriented academically, toward the achievement of career goals, or for personal enrichment.

Master's and doctoral degrees are offered in biological sciences, classics, economics, English, history, philosophy, psychology, sociology, and theology. Master's degrees are also offered in computer science, elections and campaign management, political science, and public communications. Interdisciplinary programs include master's degrees in humanities and sciences and international political economy and a master's degree and a doctoral-level certificate in medieval studies. Advanced certificate programs in emerging markets and risk analysis, financial econometrics and data analysis, health-care ethics, and Latin American and Latino studies are also offered.

Research Facilities

The combined libraries of the University contain more than 2 million bound volumes, over 15,500 periodicals, and more than 18,000 electronic journals. The main collection is in the William D. Walsh Family University Library, an open-stack library that seats 1,600 readers. The Law School library and the Gerald Quinn Library Lincoln Center may also be used by Fordham students. In addition to the University libraries, graduate students may use the New York Public Library system, and they also have access to the libraries of the City University of New York, Columbia University, New School University, and New York University through the New York City Doctoral Consortium. The library subscribes to several computerized online services and data search networks.

The Computing Center houses up-to-date equipment that is available for use by students, faculty members, and administrators at all times of the day and night. It also maintains an extensive array of software packages. Terminals located at various sites on all three campuses provide convenient access for users.

Separate laboratory facilities are maintained by a number of departments, including biology, communications, computer science, and psychology. The Louis Calder Center–Biological Field Station is a 113-acre forested preserve, supporting education and research by students and faculty members in a diverse range of ecological topics. State-of-the-art laboratories in proximity to forest, old field, wetland, and aquatic habitats provide opportunities to conduct experiments in natural ecological systems 40 miles north of the most populous urban region in North America, New York City. In addition, the University is affiliated with a number of outside agencies, including the New York Botanical Garden and the New York Zoological Society.

Financial Aid

The Graduate School awards a number of graduate assistantships and fellowships, both teaching and research, and some that require no service. All assistantships and fellowships include stipends, and recipients usually receive a separate tuition scholarship. They are assigned on a competitive basis to full-time students with outstanding academic records, and reappointments are extended on the basis of proven competence and good academic standing. Scholarships for members of underrepresented groups are also available.

Cost of Study

Tuition for the 2011–12 academic year is $1270 per credit. Normally, a master's degree requires 30–36 credits and a doctoral degree 60–72 credits beyond the baccalaureate. Additional annual fees apply.

Living and Housing Costs

Rental costs for single students living in University apartments range from $7000 to $8000 a year. Shared rental units range from $600 to $750 per month in the immediate off-campus neighborhood.

Student Group

Of the approximately 15,000 students attending Fordham University, about 800 are enrolled in the various departments and programs of the Graduate School. Students come from all areas of the United States and many other countries. Many enroll either full-time or part-time in pursuit of a degree; some take individual courses for professional advancement or personal enrichment.

Location

New York City exposes students to the best the world has to offer in art, culture, and business and has the highly diversified atmosphere of a truly international city. Fordham encourages students to make the best possible use of the opportunities the city offers in class, at work, and during their leisure time. Professors draw upon the resources of the city to enrich their courses. Lectures, literary readings, Lincoln Center for the Performing Arts, museum exhibitions, art galleries, theaters, international film festivals, orchestras, and performances of every genre all combine to forge the intellects of Fordham students. Students can experience the city in their own personal and individual ways. The University is ideally located in a neighborhood bordered by the New York Bronx Zoo, the New York Botanical Garden, and "Arthur Ave," famous for Italian cuisine.

The University

Fordham is a university in the Jesuit tradition. Founded in 1841, it is governed as an institution under a charter granted by the State of New York. The Graduate School of Arts and Sciences is one of eleven colleges and schools at Fordham University. Founded in 1916, it carries on Fordham's oldest academic tradition, the education of talented men and women in the liberal arts and sciences, at the postgraduate level.

Applying

Online applications are available at the Fordham University Graduate School of Arts and Science Web site (http://www.fordham.edu/gsas). All applicants must submit a completed application form, official transcripts, Graduate Record Examinations (GRE) scores, three letters of recommendation, a resume, and a statement of intent. Some departments have additional requirements for which students should consult the individual department Web sites (http://www.fordham.edu/gsas). Students from abroad must have superior scholastic records and proficiency in written and spoken English. All international students are required to submit TOEFL scores. Transcripts should be comparable to the GPA grading system of 4.0.

Applications are accepted throughout the year for most programs. Specific deadline details for the various programs and terms are available via a link at http://www.fordham.edu/gsas.

Requests for program brochures and additional information should be directed to the Office of Admissions at the address provided.

Correspondence and Information

Office of Admissions
Graduate School of Arts and Sciences
216 Keating Hall
Fordham University
441 East Fordham Road
Bronx, New York 10458

Phone: 718-817-4416
Fax: 718-817-3566
E-mail: fuga@fordham.edu
Web site: http://www.fordham.edu/gsas/

FACULTY HEADS

Nancy Busch, Ph.D., Dean of GSAS and Associate Vice President for Academic Affairs/Chief Research Officer.
Department of Biological Sciences: William Thornhill, Ph.D., Chair.
Department of Classical Languages and Literature: Robert Penella, Ph.D., Chair.
Department of Communication and Media Studies: Paul Levinson, Ph.D., Chair.
Department of Computer and Information Science: Damian Lyons, Ph.D., Chair.
Department of Economics: Henry M. Schwalbenberg, Ph.D., Interim Chair.
Elections and Campaign Management: Costas Panagopoulos, Ph.D., Director.
Department of English Language and Literature: Nicola Pitchford, Ph.D., Chair.
Center for Ethics Education: Celia Fisher, Ph.D., Director.
Department of History: Doron Ben-Atar, Ph.D., Chair.
Humanities and Sciences Program: Hugo Benavides, Ph.D., Chair.
International Political Economy and Development: Henry M. Schwalbenberg, Ph.D., Director.
Latin American and Latino Studies: S. Elizabeth Penry, Ph.D., Director.
Medieval Studies Program: Maryanne Kowaleski, Ph.D., Director.
Philosophical Resources Program: Christopher Cullen, S.J., Ph.D., Director.
Department of Philosophy: John Drummond, Ph.D., Chair.
Department of Political Science: Bruce Berg, Ph.D., Chair.
Department of Psychology: Frederick J. Wertz, Ph.D., Chair.
Department of Sociology: Greta Gilbertson, Ph.D., Chair.
Department of Theology: Terrence Tilley, Ph.D., Chair.

RESEARCH

Biological Sciences. Two main areas of research are available: cell and molecular biology and ecology. Cell and molecular biology research programs include molecular and cellular analysis of immune response to cancer; immunomodulators and their molecular mechanisms of action; eukaryotic gene expression and RNA processing; genetic basis of aging; genetic toxicology; cytogenetic and molecular analysis of chromosomes; spermatogenesis and early development; cellular differentiation; regeneration in invertebrates; neuronal differentiation, structure, function, and analysis; role of growth factors. The ecology program spans behavioral, population, community, and ecosystem levels. Areas of emphasis include conservation biology, forest-microbial dynamics and function, ecology of phytoplankton and bacteria, insect-parasitoid interactions, medical entomology, paleoecology, plant-insect interactions, primate behavior and ecology, systematics and evolution of fishes, and vertebrate physiological ecology.

Classical Languages and Literature. Current research interests range widely over the following areas: Greek poetry, historiography, religion, archaeology, and philosophy; Latin lyric, elegiac, and epic poetry and historiography; Roman topography; textual criticism; the intellectual life of late antiquity; medieval and Renaissance Latin; and Latin paleography.

Communication and Media Studies. Support facilities provide a lab area for graduate study in interactive media, digital video, hypertext, computer graphics, Web page design, digital audio and video editing, news and magazine production, and public communications on the Internet as well as opportunities to work at the University's public radio station.

Computer and Information Science. Current research and concentrations are available in the following areas: information systems and applications, artificial intelligence, communications and networks, and computation and algorithms. Courses available include software system design, computer architecture, parallel computation, computer security and ethics, data communications and networks, graph theory and network design, internet computing and Java programming, data base systems, and artificial intelligence.

Economics. Research interests are broad, with perhaps slightly more emphasis given to areas of applied rather than theoretical economics. Topics include development economics, financial economics, international economics, monetary economics, and industrial organization.

Elections and Campaign Management. Current research interests focus on the theoretical and practical tools necessary to excel at managing political campaigns. Rigorous multidisciplinary instruction in voting behavior, candidate strategy, analysis of survey data, and media management is provided by leading academics and top industry professionals.

English Language and Literatures. The research interests of the faculty members are represented in virtually every field of English and American literature, from Old English literature to twentieth-century British and American literature as well as literary criticism and critical theory. The English department has particular strength in eighteenth-century literature and culture.

History. Current research interests range over diverse areas of medieval history, including England, France, Germany, Italy, and Spain, and include concentrations on the medieval Church, particularly liturgy, monasticism and canon law, medieval society and economy, notably women and family, towns, and trade; cultural history; and legal history. In European history the concentrations are Tudor-Stuart England; early modern and modern Britain, Ireland, France, and Germany; Protestant and Catholic reformations; European intellectual history; gender history; and Imperial and Soviet Russia. In American history research areas include women in colonial and modern America, Thomas Jefferson and the Republican era, the Civil War, the American South, the New Deal, foreign relations, African-American history, urban studies, immigration, and Latin America.

Humanities and Sciences. A unique course of study providing interdisciplinary approaches to individualized topics in areas that often cannot be addressed by more discipline-based graduate programs. Recent examples of study have explored the relationship between at least two fields or approaches to a particular topic. Such areas of study have included: the politics of culture, Native American approaches to science, and the historical economy of literature.

International Political Economy and Development. Current research efforts focus primarily on the interaction of political and economic institutions in the functioning of the global economy and their respective roles in facilitating political modernization and economic development. Ongoing research projects include the politics of economic stabilization programs, trade policies and economic growth, foreign assistance and economic reform efforts, and the political foundations of poverty. Participating faculty members have traditionally specialized in the following areas: corporative and international politics, development studies (project management, finance and development, economic and political development, community and social development), emerging markets and country risk analysis, international business and finance, and international and development economics.

Latin American and Latino Studies. The certificate program consists of three courses: an interdisciplinary course integrating the art, culture, and history of Latin Americans and Latinos in the United States; a course on the history of Latin America or Latinos in the U.S.; and an elective course on Latin American or Latino arts and humanities or social sciences.

Medieval Studies. The Center for Medieval Studies offers an interdisciplinary M.A. and a doctoral certificate in medieval studies, giving students the opportunity to broaden their knowledge of the Middle Ages and to integrate in a coherent whole the various facets of medieval civilization. Disciplines participating in the program include art, classics, English, history, modern languages and literature (French, German, Italian, and Spanish), music, philosophy, political science, and theology.

Philosophy. The department seeks to maintain a wide diversity of research interests and competencies. While strong in the history of philosophy, it has special capabilities in continental philosophy, analytic philosophy, classical American philosophy, medieval philosophy, and philosophy of religion. With respect to both historical and contemporary perspectives, it has strengths in epistemology and metaphysics as well as moral and political philosophy.

Political Science. Faculty members teach courses leading to the M.A. in the history of political philosophy, from classical to contemporary. Areas in American politics include institutions, political behavior, public policy, and urban politics. The department also offers M.A. and minor fields in political economy and comparative/international politics.

Psychology. Research is being undertaken in three areas: clinical, applied developmental, and psychometrics. Current clinical research interests are behavior therapy, family therapy, health psychology, neuropsychology, child therapy, social supports, and treatment planning and evaluation. Developmental research employs a life-span orientation in research on developmental processes and in the application of developmental principles to the design, implementation, and evaluation of prevention and intervention programs and to the assessment of children and families. Psychometrics research focuses on the quantitative aspects of psychology, especially test constructing, personnel selection, program evaluation, and advanced statistical procedures.

Sociology and Anthropology. Research centers on three specialization areas. Demography research includes family planning program efforts and fertility behavior; career histories and contraceptive behavior; gender, ethnic, and racial inequalities in the labor force; U.S. metropolitan migration; and residential segregation. Ethnic/minority research includes household structure among Dominican and Colombian immigrants, comorbidity of mental illness and problem behavior among Hispanic adolescents, and migration and adaptation of Hispanic groups. Sociology of religion research includes fundamentalist Catholic organizations, religion and social movements, and the abortion controversy and Catholic social thought. Other faculty research includes the sociology of emotions and the society of knowledge. The department also offers M.A. specialization in justice and criminology studies.

Theology. Faculty research represents the three areas of specialization in the department. In the biblical section, faculty research includes exegetical, theological, narrative, and historical interpretations. The historical theology faculty does research in Greek and Latin patristics, medieval theology, nineteenth- and twentieth-century European and American religious thought, and U.S. religious history. The systematic theology faculty, focusing on contemporary Catholic theology, is engaged in research in fundamental theology, Karl Rahner, liberation and feminist theologies, Christian social ethics, and moral theology.

GENEVA COLLEGE

Graduate Programs

Programs of Study

Geneva College offers seven master's degree programs intended to equip professionals for principled and wise Christian service in a variety of settings. The programs are available in a variety of formats and locations.

The Master of Business Administration (M.B.A.) degree program provides a rigorous and challenging education in excellent business practice. The required courses cover all of the major functional areas of business (e.g., accounting, finance, marketing), each of them taught from a managerial perspective.

The Master of Science (M.S.) in cardiovascular sciences program is geared to align with training in the two major areas of invasive cardiology: cardiac catheterization and electrophysiology. Both the didactic and clinical coursework is delivered at the Inova Heart and Vascular Institute (IHVI) in Falls Church, Virginia. This program is for students who have a B.S. degree in biology or nursing (B.S.N. or B.S./RN) from either Geneva College or other accredited four-year institutions.

The Master of Arts (M.A.) in counseling programs are specially designed for those who wish to integrate an understanding of Christian faith with professional counseling of diverse clients in a variety of religious and secular settings. A multidimensional holistic view of persons examines the interplay of physical, psychological, social, and spiritual aspects of life.

The Master of Arts (M.A.) in higher education program seeks to cultivate a vision for higher education that is rooted in a Christian view of life, characterized by a consideration of foundational issues, and committed to the preparation of perceptive and principled leaders for colleges and universities. The program provides solid theoretical and professional foundations for work in higher education.

The Master of Science in Organizational Leadership (M.S.O.L.) degree provides a practical blend of theory and field-based application. The curriculum for the program was developed by conducting field-based research among various area for-profit and nonprofit organizations and through input received from several noted leadership studies scholars.

The Master of Education (M.Ed.) in reading program prepares reading specialists to work in K–12 classrooms, Title One programs, reading centers, and adult literacy programs in order to foster learning in and through literacy.

The Master of Education (M.Ed.) in special education program seeks to provide in-service teachers and prospective in-service teachers with the methods, skills, and techniques needed to ensure K–12 students with special needs receive an appropriate education.

Research Facilities

Graduate students enrolled in Geneva College's traditional programs have access to the McCartney Library on the campus. Its resources and collections consist of over 400,000 items, including a growing database of resources available online. Students pursuing the M.S. in cardiovascular sciences will have the resources of Inova Heart and Vascular Institute in Falls Church, Virginia available for their use.

Financial Aid

Federal student loans are available. Several of the programs offer assistantships and grants. Students need to complete the Free Application for Federal Student Aid (FAFSA).

Cost of Study

Tuition for the counseling, higher education, special education, and reading programs is currently $625 per credit. Tuition for the M.B.A. program is $650 per credit. Cost for the M.S.O.L. program is $6480 per term. Cost for the full cardiovascular science program is $23,330.

Living and Housing

Geneva College does not provide graduate student housing; however, there are numerous housing options available in the nearby community.

Student Group

In the 2010–11 academic year there were 137 full-time and 104 part-time students enrolled in Geneva College's graduate programs.

Location

Located in the City of Beaver Falls, Pennsylvania, Geneva College offers the comfort of small-town living with the convenience of big-city attractions nearby. There are plenty of shops, restaurants, and parks within walking distance of campus and the professional sports and cultural venues of Pittsburgh are less than an hour away.

The cardiovascular sciences affiliate master's program is based in Falls Church, Virginia, which is a short drive from Washington, D.C.

The College

Geneva College provides rigorous academics built on a foundation of strong Christian values. Geneva offers distinctive and innovative programs in a variety of formats and locations to help students reach their professional and personal goals. Top-quality faculty members help graduate students to excel and achieve success. Geneva challenges students daily so that they can meet the challenges of the future. Geneva College is affiliated with the Reformed Presbyterian Church of North America.

Applying

Geneva College's graduate programs have a rolling application deadline. More information regarding specific program application requirements is available on the College's Web site at http://www.geneva.edu/graduate_programs.

Applications and inquiries about specific programs can be sent to the following locations: M.B.A.: mba@geneva.edu, Cardiovascular Science: dessig@geneva.edu, Counseling: counseling@geneva.edu, Higher Education: hed@geneva.edu, M.S.O.L.: msol@geneva.edu, Reading: lahartge@geneva.edu, and Special Education: lahartge@geneva.edu

Correspondence and Information

Geneva College
3200 College Avenue
Beaver Falls, Pennsylvania 15010
Phone: 724-846-5100
800-847-8255 (toll-free)
E-mail: admissions@geneva.edu
Web site: http://www.geneva.edu/graduate_programs

THE FACULTY

Business Administration

Ralph Ancil, Associate Professor; Ph.D, Michigan State. Economics. Phone: 724-847-6612, e-mail: reancil@geneva.edu.

Denise C. Murphy-Gerber, Associate Professor; Ph.D. candidate, Duquesne. International business, marketing. Phone: 724-847-5557, e-mail: dcmurphy@geneva.edu.

William Pearce, Associate Professor; Ph.D., Florida Tech. Business, marketing. Phone: 724-847-6881, e-mail: bpearce@geneva.edu.

Daniel Raver, Associate Professor; M.B.A., Pittsburgh. Business. Phone: 724-847-6618, e-mail: dhraver@geneva.edu.

Robert J. Reith, Associate Professor; J.D., Duquesne. Business, management, law. Phone: 724-847-6613, e-mail: rjreith@geneva.edu.

Gordon Richards, Professor; D.Sc. candidate, Robert Morris. Quantitative analysis, management of information systems. Phone: 724-847-6718, e-mail: gordan.richards@geneva.edu.

Amy C. Russin, Assistant Professor; M.B.A., Geneva. Accounting. Phone: 724-847-6616, e-mail: acrussin@geneva.edu.

Gary P. Vander Plaats, Associate Professor; D.B.A., Anderson. Finance. Phone: 724-847-6619, e-mail: gpvander@geneva.edu.

Cardiovascular Sciences

David Essig, Associate Professor/CVS Program Coordinator; Ph. D., Chicago. Biology. Phone: 724-847-6900, e-mail: dessig@geneva.edu.

Counseling

Carol Luce, Professor, Director of M.A. in Counseling Program; Ph.D., Pittsburgh. Psychology, counseling. Phone: 724-847-6622, e-mail: cbluce@geneva.edu.

Ronald Moslener, Professor; D.Min., Fuller Theological Seminary. Psychology, counseling, human services. Phone: 724-847-6629, e-mail: rwmoslen@geneva.edu.

Joseph Peters; Professor; Ph. D. Penn State. Psychology, counseling, human services. Phone: 724-847-6491, e-mail: jepeters@geneva.edu.

Diana Rice, Associate Professor; Ph.D., Syracuse. Social Psychology. Phone: 724-847-6773, e-mail: drrice@geneva.edu.

Higher Education

Bradshaw Frey, Professor; Ph.D., Pittsburgh. Sociology. Phone: 724-847-6558.

David Guthrie, Dean of Faculty Development and Professor of Higher Education; Ph.D. Penn State. Higher education, sociology. Phone: 724-847-5565, e-mail: dguthrie@geneva.edu.

Don Opitz, Professor, Director of M.A. in Higher Education Program; Ph.D., Boston University. Sociology. Phone: 724-847-6683, e-mail: ddopitz@geneva.edu.

Terry Thomas, Professor; Ph.D., Pittsburgh. Biblical studies, higher education. Phone: 724-847-6656, e-mail: tthomas@geneva.edu.

Organizational Leadership

Bonnie Budzowski, Professor; M.A., Trinity Episcopal School for the Ministry. Phone: 412-828-1629, e-mail: bonnie@inCredibleMessages.com.

Lutitia A. Clipper, Professor; Ph.D., Pittsburgh. Leadership, communication, research methods. Phone: 412-244-2583, e-mail: Dr.Lutitia.A.Clipper@alumni.pitt.edu.

Jim Dittmar, Professor; Ph.D., Pittsburgh. Leadership/organizational studies, education. Phone: 724-847-6853, e-mail: jkd@geneva.edu.

Ralph Fink, Professor; M.A., Rhode Island. Leadership. Phone: 724-847-2715, e-mail: ralphfink3@aol.com.

Diane Galbraith, Professor; D.Ed., Indiana of Pennsylvania. Leadership, management, human resource management, organizational development. Phone: 724-847-6756, e-mail: dianedgalbraith@aol.com.

Deborah A. Jeannette, Professor; M.Ed., Ed.D., Pittsburgh. Leadership studies. Phone: 724-847-6882, e-mail: djeannet@geneva.edu.

Mitchel Nickols, Professor; Ph.D., Pittsburgh. Leadership. Phone: 724-847-2715, e-mail: mitch.nickols@gmail.com.

Leo Salgado, Professor; M.B.A., Phoenix. Organizational leadership. Phone: 412-528-6130, e-mail: leo.j.salgado@gmail.com.

John Stahl-Wert, Professor; M.A., Mennonite Biblical Seminary. Transformational leadership, character and integrity. Phone: 412-281-3752, ext. 248, e-mail: stahlwert@servingleaders.com.

John Stanko, Professor; Ph.D., Liberty. Leadership, purpose, missions, theology, administration, pastoral ministry, personal productivity, time management. Phone: 412-321-4333 ext. 144, e-mail: johnstanko@gmail.com.

Daniel Straub, Professor; Ph.D., Pittsburgh. Leadership, management, public administration, judicial administration. Phone: 412-429-1322, e-mail: danielstraub@comcast.net.

Maureen Vanterpool, Professor; Ph.D., Ohio State. Leadership studies. Phone: 724-846-4247, e-mail: movanter@geneva.edu.

Donald Williams, Professor; M.B.A., Robert Morris. Business management, marketing, finance. Phone: 724-650-0863, e-mail: don@compoundingpros.com.

Reading

Adel Aiken, Professor, Reading Specialist; Ed.D., Pittsburgh. Phone: 724-847-5002, e-mail: aaiken@geneva.edu.

Natalie Heisey, Professor; Ed.D., Pittsburgh. Reading education. Phone: 724-847-6579, e-mail: ndheisey@geneva.edu.

Romaine Jesky-Smith, Professor; Ph.D. Pittsburgh. Education, elementary education, classroom management, children's literature, math for the elementary teacher, educational research, elementary education, reading specialist K–12. Phone: 724-847-6536, e-mail: rjs@geneva.edu.

Nancy Johnson, Professor; Ph.D., Penn State. Educational psychology, methods in the elementary school. Phone: 724-847-5798, e-mail: nhjohnso@geneva.edu.

Karen Schmalz, Professor; Ph.D., Regent University (Virginia). Special education. Phone: 724-847-6125, e-mail: kschmalz@geneva.edu.

Yvonne Devon Trotter, Professor; Ph.D., Kent State. Special education, elementary education, educational administration. Phone: 724-847-6534, e-mail: ydtrotte@geneva.edu.

Special Education

Adel Aiken, Professor, Reading Specialist; Ed.D., Pittsburgh.Phone: 724-847-5002, e-mail: aaiken@geneva.edu.

Beth Belcastro, Professor; Ed.D., Pittsburgh. Special education. Phone: 724-847-6132, e-mail: egbelcas@geneva.edu.

Natalie Heisey, Professor; Ed.D., Pittsburgh. Reading education. Phone: 724-847-6579, e-mail: ndheisey@geneva.edu.

Romaine Jesky-Smith, Professor; Ph.D. Pittsburgh. Education, elementary education, classroom management, children's literature, math for the elementary teacher, educational research, elementary education, reading specialist K–12. Phone: 724-847-6536, e-mail: rjs@geneva.edu.

Nancy Johnson, Professor; Ph.D., Penn State. Educational psychology, methods in the elementary school. Phone: 724-847-5798, e-mail: nhjohnso@geneva.edu.

Karen Schmalz, Professor; Ph.D., Regent University (Virginia). Special education. Phone: 724-847-6125, e-mail: kschmalz@geneva.edu.

Yvonne Devon Trotter, Professor; Ph.D., Kent State. Special education, elementary education, educational administration. Phone: 724-847-6534, e-mail: ydtrotte@geneva.edu.

Old Main.

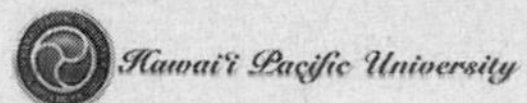

HAWAI'I PACIFIC UNIVERSITY

Graduate Studies

Programs of Study

Hawai'i Pacific University (HPU) offers leading master's degree programs in fourteen areas: business administration, clinical mental health counseling, communication, diplomacy and military studies, elementary education, global leadership and sustainable development, human resource management, information systems, nursing, marine science, organizational change, teaching English to speakers of other languages, social work, and secondary education. Some prerequisite courses may be required for all programs listed below.

The Master of Business Administration (M.B.A.) program offers concentrations in accounting, e-business, economics, finance, health-care management, human resource management, information systems, international business, management, marketing, organizational change, and travel industry management. It requires 42 semester hours of graduate work. The M.B.A. program is also available online with the same high-quality curriculum as the on-campus format. There is a complete set of online courses for five of the M.B.A. concentrations. Visit http://online.hpu.edu for more information.

The Master of Science in Information Systems (M.S.I.S.) program is designed to create decision makers and experts in information technology, systems design, and problem solving with automated resources. The program can be individualized with elective courses or concentrations in knowledge management, decision science, telecommunications security, and software engineering. Students lacking a background in the technical, scientific, and analytical realms must complete selected prerequisites to prepare fully for the program, which requires 36 semester hours of graduate work.

The Master of Arts in Human Resource Management (M.A./HRM) program requires 36 semester hours of graduate work and emphasizes the study and practices of human relations and managing personnel. These include human resource planning, recruitment, and selection; compensation management and benefits; human resource development; labor-management relations; employment law; safety and health; and global perspective on human resources.

The Master of Arts in Global Leadership and Sustainable Development (M.A./GLSD) program is designed to prepare students to become leaders in all types of organizations, including multinational, governmental, and not-for-profit. The program requires 42 semester hours of graduate work. Courses include comparative management systems, global markets in transition, international business management, and systems management.

The Master of Arts in Organizational Change (M.A./OC) program requires 42 semester hours of graduate work and emphasizes the management, design, implementation, and application of organizational change. Courses include organizational change and development, national and community change and development, culture and human organization, and organizational behavior.

The Master of Science in Nursing (M.S.N.) program offers concentrations for those interested in becoming family nurse practitioners or community-based health clinical nurse specialists. Students who have an RN but lack a Bachelor of Science in Nursing may enter the RN to M.S.N. Pathway. To complete the M.S.N. with a clinical nurse specialist concentration, 46 semester hours are required; 50 semester hours are required to complete the M.S.N. with a family nurse practitioner concentration.

The Master of Science in Marine Science (M.S.M.S.) program requires 34 hours of graduate work and is designed to provide students with the knowledge and skills necessary for marine-related technical positions in industry, government, and education or for entry into a doctoral marine science program. Courses include cell and molecular biology, aquatic chemistry, marine ecology, and toxicology.

The Master of Arts in Communication (M.A./COM) program, which requires 39 semester hours of graduate work, prepares students for careers in business communication, marketing, advertising, mass media, public relations, entertainment, broadcast or print journalism, sales, the Internet, writing, or education.

The Master of Arts in Teaching English to Speakers of Other Languages (M.A.T.E.S.O.L.) program requires 37 semester hours of graduate work. Courses include English phonology and teaching of pronunciation, English syntax and teaching of grammar, and methods of teaching oral/aural English.

The Master of Arts in Diplomacy and Military Studies (M.A./DMS) program requires 42 hours of graduate work and explores the complex relationships of politics, society, and the military. This degree is useful for professional military officers or those in government positions.

The Master of Arts in Social Work (M.S.W.) program is built on a foundation of liberal arts and is committed to the preparation of professional social work practitioners to help them become effective cross-cultural practitioners. The program requires 61 semester hours of graduate work and focuses on direct planning, administration, and community practice.

The Master of Education in Secondary Education (M.Ed./SE) program develops professional educators who are reflective practitioners dedicated to the scholarship of teaching and school renewal. The program, which requires 42 semester hours of graduate work, is based on an innovative, standards-driven, field-based curriculum that employs cutting-edge educational technology to integrate content and pedagogy.

The Master of Education in Elementary Education (M.Ed./EE) program requires 42 semester hours of graduate work and provides students with the most up-to-date knowledge available to meet the challenges of a changing world. Students are introduced to a variety of contemporary issues facing educators and are encouraged to use creative methodologies in the classroom.

The Master of Arts in Clinical Mental Health Counseling (M.A./CMHC) program prepares students to work as mental health counselors within a variety of community, medical, educational, and private practice settings. Through rigorous course work and clinical internship training, students learn to apply empirically supported methods of practice, assessment, and treatment. The program requires 60 semester hours of graduate work.

Research Facilities

To support graduate studies, HPU's Meader and Atherton libraries offer over 110,000 bound volumes, 350,000 microfiche items, and periodical subscriptions to 1,500 print titles and 30,000 electronic journals. Databases of public and state university libraries, legislative information, and business-oriented statistical data are also available in the libraries or online. HPU also provides free Wi-Fi enabling students to access HPU's library databases, course information, their academic information, and e-mail account through Pipeline, the University's internal Web site. HPU's accessible on-campus computer center houses more than 100 computers with specialized software to support graduate academic programs. A significant number of online courses are also available.

Financial Aid

The University participates in all federal financial aid programs designated for graduate students. These programs provide aid in the form of subsidized (need-based) and unsubsidized (non-need-based) Federal Stafford Student Loans. Through these loans, funds may be available to cover a student's entire cost of education. To apply for aid, students must submit the Free Application for Federal Student Aid (FAFSA) beginning January 1.

The University also offers several types of institutional graduate scholarships to new full-time, degree-seeking students. U.S. citizens, permanent residents, and international students who have a demonstrated financial need may apply. HPU's graduate scholarships include the Graduate Trustee Scholarship ($6000 for two semesters), the Graduate Dean Scholarship ($4000 for two semesters), and the Graduate Kokua Scholarship ($2000 for two semesters). Factors that may be considered when evaluating requests are previous academic record, community involvement and service, and professional work experience and achievement.

To be eligible for the best award package, students should apply by HPU's priority deadline of March 1. Applications received after March 1 are awarded on a funds-available basis. Mailing of student award letters usually begins by the end of March. Applicants are notified by mail as decisions are made.

Cost of Study

Tuition for graduate students enrolled in fall and spring semesters is determined on a per-credit basis; full-time status is 9 credits. Tuition for the optional winter and summer sessions is also determined on a per-credit basis. The estimated minimum funds needed for a nine-month academic year (September to May), based on 2011–12 school-year expenses, is $28,650. For the 2011–12 academic year, full-time tuition is $13,230 for most graduate degree programs. Other expenses, including books, personal expenses, fees, and a student bus pass, are estimated at $3190.

Living and Housing Costs

Most graduate students live in off-campus housing. The cost to live in off-campus apartments is approximately $12,230 for a double occupancy room.

Student Group

University enrollment currently stands at more than 8,200. HPU is one of the most culturally diverse universities in America with students from all fifty U.S. states and more than 100 countries. HPU strives to maintain a student profile that is one-third Hawai'i, one-third mainland USA, and one-third global.

Location

HPU combines the excitement of an urban, downtown campus with the serenity of a residential campus. Ideally located in downtown Honolulu—the business and financial center of the Pacific—the campus comprises six buildings and is home to the College of Business Administration and the College of Humanities and Social Sciences. The campus is within walking distance of shopping and dining. Just a few blocks away are Iolani Palace (the only U.S. palace), the State Capitol, City Hall, and the Blaisdell Concert Hall. The Honolulu Academy of Arts, Museum of Contemporary Art, and many other cultural attractions are located nearby.

Situated on 135 acres in Kaneohe 8 miles away, the windward Hawai'i Loa campus is the site of the College of Nursing and Health Sciences and the College of Natural and Computational Sciences. There are residence halls, a dining commons, the Educational Technology Center, a student center, and outdoor recreational facilities, including a soccer field, softball field, tennis courts, and more.

HPU is affiliated with the Oceanic Institute, an applied aquaculture research facility located on a 56-acre site at Makapu'u Point on the windward coast of Oahu, Hawaii. All three sites are linked by the HPU shuttle and are easily accessed by public transportation.

The University

Hawai'i Pacific University is a private, nonprofit university with approximately 8,200 students. Founded in 1965, HPU prides itself on maintaining strong academic programs, small class sizes, individual attention to students, and a diverse faculty and student population. HPU is recognized as a "Best Western" college by the *Princeton Review* and a "Best Buy in College Education" by *Barron's* business magazine. HPU offers more than fifty acclaimed undergraduate programs and fourteen distinguished graduate programs. The University has a faculty of more than 500, a student-faculty ratio of 15:1, and an average class size of fewer than 25 students. A wide range of counseling and other student support services are available. There are more than fifty student organizations on campus, including the Graduate Student Organization.

Applying

Students must have a baccalaureate degree from an accredited college or university in the United States or an equivalent degree from another country. Applicants should complete and forward a graduate admissions application, send in the $50 nonrefundable application fee, have official transcripts sent from all colleges or universities previously attended, and forward two letters of recommendation. A personal statement about the applicant's academic and career goals is required; submitting a resume is optional. Applicants who have taken the Graduate Management Admission Test (GMAT) should have their scores sent directly to the Graduate Admissions Office. International students should submit scores of a recognized English proficiency test, such as TOEFL. Admissions decisions are made on a rolling basis; applicants are notified one to two weeks after all documents have been submitted. Applicants are encouraged to submit applications online.

Correspondence and Information

Graduate Admissions
Hawai'i Pacific University
1164 Bishop Street, Suite 911
Honolulu, Hawaii 96813

Phone: 808-543-8034
866-GRAD-HPU (toll-free)
Fax: 808-544-0280
E-mail: graduate@hpu.edu
Web site: http://www.hpu.edu/grad

THE FACULTY

Valentina M. Abordonado, Professor of English, Education; Ph.D., Arizona.
Leina'ala Ahu Isa, Assistant Professor of Management; Ed.D., Hawaii at Manoa.
Michelle Alarcon-Catt, Assistant Professor of Management; M.B.A., Pepperdine.
Dale Allison, Professor of Nursing; Ph.D., Pennsylvania.
Margaret Anderson, Associate Professor of Nursing; Ed.D., San Francisco.
Pierre Asselin, Associate Professor of History; Ph.D., Hawaii at Manoa.
Margo Bare, Instructor in Social Work; M.S.W., Pennsylvania.
John Barnum, Associate Professor of Communication; Ph.D., Texas at Austin.
Patrick Bratton, Assistant Professor of Political Science; Ph.D., Catholic University.
Peter Britos, Associate Professor of Communication; Ph.D., USC.
Dale Burke, Instructor of Communication; D.Min., Ancilla Domini College, Graduate Theological Foundation.
Patricia Burrell, Professor of Nursing; Ph.D., Utah.
Randy Caine, Professor of Nursing; Ed.D, Pepperdine.
Brian Cannon, Assistant Professor of Communication; Ph.D., Regent University (Virginia).
Kathleen Cassity, Assistant Professor of English; Ph.D., Hawaii at Manoa.
Randall Chang, Assistant Professor of Economics; Ph.D., Claremont.
Grace Cheng, Associate Professor of Political Science; Ph.D., Hawaii at Manoa.
Richard Chepkevich, Instructor in Computer Science/Information Systems; M.S.S.M., USC.
Justin Gukhyun Cho, Associate Professor of Management; Ph.D., MIT.
Bee-Leng Chua, Associate Professor of Management; Ph.D., Ohio.
Katherine Clarke, Instructor of Communication; M.A., Denver.
Steven Combs, Professor of Communication; Ph.D., USC.
Kenneth Cook, Professor of Linguistics; Ph.D., California, San Diego.
Catherine Critz, Associate Professor of Nursing; Ph.D, Syracuse.
Cheryl Crozier-Garcia, Associate Professor of Human Resource Management; Ph.D., Walden.
ReNel Davis, Professor of Nursing; Ph.D., Colorado.
Thomas Dowd, Instructor of Communication; M.A., California State, Northridge.
Erik Drabkin, Affiliate Associate Professor of Economics; Ph.D., UCLA.
Jiason Fang, Associate Professor of Chemistry; Ph.D., Texas A&M.
Hobie Feagai, Associate Professor of Nursing; Ed.D., Argosy/okina: Hawai'i.
Mark Fox, Instructor of Social Work; M.S.W., Arizona State.
Susan Fox-Wolfgramm, Professor of Management; Ph.D., Texas Tech.
Matthew George, Assistant Professor of Communication; Ph.D., Berkeley.
Gerald Glover, Professor of Organizational Change; Ph.D., Florida.
Allison Gough, Associate Professor of Political Science, Ph.D., Hawaii.
John Gutrich, Associate Professor of Environmental Sciences; Ph.D., Ohio State.
Joseph Ha, Associate Professor of Marketing; Ph.D., Rutgers.
Barbara Hannum, Assistant Professor of English (ESL); M.A., Hawai'i at Manoa.
John P.Hart, Professor of Communication; Ph.D., Kansas.
Russell Hart, Associate Professor of History; Ph.D., Ohio State.
David Horgen, Associate Professor of Chemistry; Ph.D., Illinois at Chicago.
William Hummel, Instructor of Social Work; M.S.W., CUNY, Hunter.
Karl Hyrenbach, Assistant Professor of Oceanography; Ph.D., California, San Diego (Scripps).
Lowell Ing, Assistant Professor of Communication; M.F.A., CUNY, City College.
Brenda Jensen, Assistant Professor of Biology; Ph.D., California, San Diego (Scripps).
Gordon Jones, Professor of Computer Science and Information Systems; Ph.D., New Mexico.
Carlos Juarez, Professor of Political Science; Ph.D., UCLA.
Samuel Kahng, Assistant Professor of Oceanography; Ph.D., Hawaii at Manoa.
Anne Kennedy, Assistant Professor of Communication; Ph.D., Bowling Green State.
Jean Kirschenmann, Assistant Professor of English (ESL); M.A., Hawaii at Manoa.
Margo Kitts, Associate Professor of Humanities/Rel. Studies; Ph.D., Berkeley.
Edward Klein, Professor of Applied Linguistics; Ph.D., Hawall at Manoa.
Mark Lane, Associate Professor of Finance; Ph.D., Missouri.
Leroy Laney, Professor of Finance and Economics; Ph.D., Colorado.
Patricia Lange-Otsuka, Professor of Nursing; Ed.D., Nova Southeastern.
Laurence LeDoux, Assistant Professor of Communication; D.A., Oregon.
Candis Lee, Assistant Professor of English (ESL); Ed.D., USC.
Cathrine Linnes, Assistant Professor of Information Systems; Ph.D., Nova Southeastern.
Ernesto Lucas, Associate Professor of Economics; Ph.D., Hawaii at Manoa.
Marianne Luken, Instructor of Communication; M.I.A., School for International Training.
Lorraine Marais, Associate Professor of Social Work; Ed.D., Western Michigan.
Howard Markowitz, Assistant Professor of Psychology; Ph.D., Union (Ohio).
Sandra McKay, Professor of Linguistics; Ph.D., Minnesota.
Daniel Morgan, Instructor of Sociology; M.A., Miami (Florida).
Hanh Nguyen, Assistant Professor of Applied Linguistics; Ph.D., Wisconsin–Madison.
Patricia Nishimoto, Assistant Professor of Social Work; Ph.D., University of Hawaii, Manoa.
Scott Okamoto, Associate Professor of Social Work; Ph.D., Hawaii at Manoa.
Regina Ostergaard-Klem, Adjunct Professor of Mathematics; Ph.D., Johns Hopkins.
Aytun Ozturk, Associate Professor of Quantitative Methods; Ph.D., Pittsburgh.
Edgar Palafox, Instructor of Human Resource Management; M.S., Hawai'i Pacific.
Joseph Patoskie, Associate Professor of Travel Industry Management; Ph.D., Texas Tech.
Penny Pence Smith, Assistant Professor of Communication; Ph.D., North Carolina at Chapel Hill.
James Primm, Associate Professor of Political Science; Ph.D., Hawaii at Manoa.
Kenneth Rossi, Assistant Professor of Information Systems; Ed.D., USC.
Lawrence Rowland, Assistant Professor of Information Systems; Ed.D., USC.
Catherine Sajna, Assistant Professor of English; M.A., Hawaii at Manoa.
George Satterfield, Associate Professor of History, Ph.D., Illinois at Urbana-Champaign.
Mary Sheridan, Professor of Social Work; Ph.D., Hawaii at Manoa.
Malia Smith, Instructor of Communication; M.A., Hawai'i Pacific.
William Soderman, Associate Professor of Information Systems; Ph.D., Georgia.
Edward Souza, Instructor of Information Systems; M.S., Hawai'i Pacific.
Lisa Steinmueller, Assistant Professor of Nursing; MSN/MBA, Hawai'i Pacific.
Min Min Thaw, Assistant Professor of Economics; M.A., Hawaii at Manoa.
Paul Tran, Instructor of Social Work; M.S.W., San Francisco State.
Lewis Trusty, Instructor of Communication; M.A., USC.
Catherine Unabia, Assistant Professor of Biology; Ph.D., Hawaii at Manoa.
Edwin Van Gorder, Associate Professor of Mathematics; Ph.D., Stanford.
Eric Vetter, Associate Professor of Biology; Ph.D., California, San Diego (Scripps).
Niti Villinger, Associate Professor of Management; Ph.D., Cambridge.
Richard Ward, Associate Professor of Organizational Change; Ed.D., USC.
Warren Wee, Associate Professor of Accounting; Ph.D., Hawaii at Manoa.
Kristi West, Assistant Professor of Biology; Ph.D., L'Universite de la Polynesie Francaise, Hawaii at Manoa.
Arthur Whatley, Professor of Management; Ph.D., North Texas State.
Linda Wheeler, Assistant Professor of Education; Ed.D., Hawaii at Manoa.
James D. Whitfield, Professor of Communication; Ph.D., Texas Tech.
John Windrow, Instructor of Journalism; M.A., Missouri–Columbia.
Christopher Winn, Associate Professor of Oceanography; Ph.D., Hawaii at Manoa.
Yanjun Zhao; Ph.D., Southern Illinois Carbondale.
Larry Zimmerman, Assistant Professor of Organizational Change; Ph.D., Nebraska–Lincoln.

INDIANA STATE UNIVERSITY

College of Graduate and Professional Studies

Programs of Study

Indiana State University (ISU) offers more than 100 graduate courses of study leading to a graduate certificate or a master's, education specialist, or doctoral degree in the Colleges of Arts and Sciences; Business; Education; Nursing, Health, and Human Services; and Technology. The College of Arts and Sciences offers the Psy.D. in clinical psychology and the Ph.D. in biology and spatial and earth sciences. The Department of Art offers the M.F.A. The Department of Music offers the M.M. degree. The Department of Political Science offers the M.P.A. Both the M.A. and the M.S. are available in criminology and criminal justice, history, mathematics, political science, and psychology. The M.A. degree is offered in art, communication, English, geography, and linguistics/TESL/cross linguistics. The M.S. degree is offered in biology, computer science, earth and quaternary sciences, and science education. The College of Business offers the M.B.A. degree. The College of Education offers the Ph.D. in guidance and psychological services, educational administration, and curriculum and instruction. The Ed.S. degree is offered in school administration and school psychology. The M.Ed. is offered in curriculum and instruction, elementary education, school administration and supervision, school counseling, and school psychology. The M.A. and M.S. are offered in communication disorders and special education. The M.S. is offered in educational technology, clinical mental health counseling, and student affairs and higher education. The College of Nursing, Health, and Human Services offers the M.A. and M.S. in health and safety, as well as physical education. The M.S. is offered in athletic training, family and consumer sciences, nursing, physician assistant studies, and recreation and sport management. The College of Technology offers the Ph.D. in technology management. The M.S. is offered in career and technical education, electronics and computer technology, human resource development for higher education and industry, industrial technology, and technology education. Beginning in fall 2011, the College of Nursing, Health, and Human Services will begin offering courses of study leading to the Doctor of Nursing Practice and the Doctor of Physical Therapy degrees.

Research Facilities

Indiana State University Cunningham Memorial Library houses more than 2.5 million items, subscribes to more than 5,000 periodicals, and provides access to more than 20,000 full-text electronic periodicals. These can be accessed through an online system that also connects with other college libraries in Terre Haute and Indiana. The ISU library provides collaborative workstations to facilitate group and collaborative research. All students enrolled at ISU have access to a wireless network that allows them to access the Internet from most locations on the campus. Several departments offer specialized research facilities. The Instructional and Research Technology Services offers services (at no cost to students) that include statistical design consultation, research design consultation, design and analysis of sample research surveys, and presentation of statistical graphs and tables. The Psychology Clinic serves as a training facility for clinical psychology doctoral students. The Porter School Psychology Center provides research opportunities for students in counseling and school psychology. The ISU Remote Sensing Laboratory specializes in earth resources analysis using computer-aided processing of satellite data. The Technology Services Center engages in cooperative research with industry using CAD/CAM and other related technologies. A radiation laboratory provides students experience with the latest technology. The Center for Research and Management Services utilizes students to provide research for local area and statewide businesses in fields of economic development and targeted industry studies.

Financial Aid

Eligible graduate students may apply for institutional graduate assistantships through the respective academic departments. ISU graduate assistantships include a stipend and a tuition fee waiver. The tuition fee waivers are exclusive of building and student services fees, for up to 18 hours per academic year. For policies regarding graduate assistantships and fee waivers, students should visit the College of Graduate and Professional Studies Web site.

There are also opportunities for graduates to apply for scholarships and fellowships at ISU, some of which include the Paul A. Witty Fellowships, which are available for eligible students specializing in educating gifted and creative children and the Gertrude and Theodore Debs Memorial Fellowships, available for eligible students specializing in American labor and reform movements. There are also the Kweku Bentil Awards, which recognize full-time students who have shown exceptional scholarship and leadership skills. The Noyce Scholarship Program provides an assistantship and fee waiver for students in the College of Arts and Sciences. Detailed information regarding the application process for these fellowships can be found online at the College of Graduate and Professional Studies Web site. Applications received prior to March 1 are given preference.

The Office of Student Financial Aid assists ISU graduate students in obtaining further educational funding opportunities through the Federal Perkins Loan (National Direct Student Loans) and Federal Stafford Student Loan programs, PLUS loans, or the College Work-Study Program. The office can be contacted at 812-237-2215 or at http://www.indstate.edu/finaid/.

Cost of Study

Tuition and fees for the 2011–12 academic year are $353 per semester hour for in-state students and $694 per semester hour for out-of-state students. The maximum load for fall and spring semesters is 12 semester hours. Summer Session I runs eight weeks, with three-, five-, and eight-week class options. A maximum of 9 credit hours may be earned during Session I. Summer Session II runs five weeks, and a maximum of 6 credit hours may be earned.

Living and Housing Costs

In addition to traditional residence halls, Indiana State University offers furnished and unfurnished apartment-style housing for graduate students at its University Apartments at reasonable and competitive rental rates. Each apartment is self-contained with its own bedroom(s), bathroom, living/dining area, and kitchen with an electric range, refrigerator, and garbage disposal. Utilities and free local telephone service are also included. Furnished apartments have one- or two-bedroom options and range from $635 to $711 per month. Unfurnished apartments have one-, two-, or three-bedroom options and range from $675 to $794 per month. Low-cost housing is also available in the surrounding community.

Student Group

Since 1927, ISU's graduate programs have prepared students for careers in a wide range of teaching, research, and service professions. The campus has the highest diversity of students among four-year institutions in Indiana. Both the areas of study and the student population are diverse. Graduate programs attract applicants from all over the United States and from forty-three countries around the world. Approximately 15 percent of the graduate students are international, 33 percent are out-of-state students, 13 percent are members of minority groups, and 58 percent are women. The average graduate student age is 33.

Location

The campus is located adjacent to the central business district of Terre Haute, Indiana, which is an industrial and commercial city of approximately 61,000 located in west-central Indiana. Cultural activities include amateur and professional theatrical productions, symphonies, and art exhibits. Excellent county and state parks are within easy driving distance. The city is convenient to the four major metropolitan areas of Indianapolis, St. Louis, Chicago, and Cincinnati.

The University and The School

Indiana State University is listed as one of the nation's best-value colleges by the Princeton Review in its 2008 edition of *America's Best Value Colleges*. Indiana State University has grown during its 140-year history from Indiana State Normal School to Indiana State Teachers College and Indiana State College to full university status. With a graduate student population of approximately 2,000, students can be assured of a close mentoring experience and significant research opportunities within their academic program.

Applying

Applications to the College of Graduate and Professional Studies can be submitted online, by mail, or in person.

Prospective applicants should visit the College of Graduate and Professional Studies Web site at http://graduate.indstate.edu and check with their respective departments for specific deadlines and additional required admissions materials, such as test scores, letters of recommendation, and other documents. Students generally receive a response acknowledging receipt of the application and other communication from the College of Graduate and Professional Studies within one to two weeks. Once admitted, students receive instructions regarding academic advisement and registration.

International students must submit a TOEFL score of 550 or better and an Affidavit of Financial Support. For additional requirements and documentation, students should visit the Graduate School Web site or the International Programs and Services at http://www.indstate.edu/IPS.

Correspondence and Information

Dr. Jay D. Gatrell, Dean
College of Graduate and Professional Studies
Indiana State University
Terre Haute, Indiana 47809-1904
Phone: 812-237-3005
800-444-GRAD (4723) (toll-free)
Fax: 812-237-8060
E-mail: ISU-GradStudy@mail.indstate.edu
Web site: http://graduate.indstate.edu

For U.S. applicants, mail to:
Graduate Admissions
Indiana State University
Erickson Hall 218 North Sixth Street
Terre Haute, Indiana 47809-1904
Phone: 812-237-3005
800-444-GRAD (4723) (toll-free)
Fax: 812-237-8060
E-mail: ISU-GradStudy@mail.indstate.edu

For international applicants, mail to:
Graduate Admissions
Indiana State University
Erickson Hall 218 North Sixth Street
Terre Haute, Indiana 47809-1904
Phone: 812-237-3005
800-444-GRAD (4723) toll-free)
Fax: 812-237-8060
E-mail: ISU-GradStudy@mail.indstate.edu
Web site: http://graduate.indstate.edu

THE FACULTY

Deans
Jay D. Gatrell, Ph.D.; Dean, College of Graduate and Professional Studies.
John D. Murray, Ph.D.; Dean, College of Arts and Sciences.
Nancy J. Merritt, Ph.D.; Dean, Scott College of Business.
Bradley V. Balch, Ph.D.; Dean, Bayh College of Education.
Richard B. Williams, Ph.D.; Dean, College of Nursing, Health, and Human Services.
Bradford Sims, Ph.D.; Dean, College of Technology.

Directors of Graduate Degree Programs
Art: Nancy Nichols-Pethick, M.F.A., Assistant Professor.
Athletic Training: Susan Yeargin, Ph.D., Assistant Professor.
Biology: Elaina Tuttle, Ph.D., Associate Professor.
Business Administration: Dale L. Varble, Ph.D., Associate Dean and Professor.
Center for Science Education: James H. Speer, Ph.D., Assistant Professor.
Clinical Psychology: Liz O'Laughlin, Ph.D., Associate Professor.
Communication: Jay Clarkson, Ph.D., Assistant Professor.
Communication Disorders and School Counseling, School, and Educational Psychology: Vicki Hammen, Ph.D., Associate Professor.
Counseling Psychology: Tonya Balch, Ph.D., Assistant Professor.
Criminology and Criminal Justice: DeVere Woods, Ph.D., Associate Professor and Chairperson.
Curriculum, Instruction, and Media Technology: Susan Kiger, Ph.D., Associate Professor and Chairperson.
Educational and School Psychology: Damon Krug, Ph.D., Assistant Professor.
Educational Leadership, Administration, and Foundations: Steve Gruenert, Ph.D., Professor and Chairperson.
Electronics, Computer, and Mechanical Engineering Technology: Joe Ashby, Ph.D., Assistant Professor.
Elementary, Early, and Special Education: Karen Liu, Ph.D., Professor.
English: Matthew C. Brennan, Ph.D., Professor.
Earth and Environmental Systems: C. Russell Stafford, Ph.D., Professor and Chairperson.
Health, Safety, and Environmental Health Sciences: Yasenka Peterson, Ph.D., Associate Professor and Chairperson.
History: Richard Schneirov, Ph.D., Professor.
Human Resource Development: Dorothy Yaw, Ph.D., Associate Professor.
Industrial Technology: Michael Hayden, Ph.D., Professor.
Languages, Literatures, and Linguistics: Ronald Dunbar, Ph.D., Professor and Chairperson.
Mathematics and Computer Science: Steven Pontius, Ph.D., Professor.
Mental Health Counseling: Debra Leggett, Ph.D., Assistant Professor.
Music: Doug Keiser, Ph.D., Professor.
Nursing: Lea Hall, Ph.D., Assistant Professor and Chairperson.
Physical Education: Jolynn Kuhlman, Ph.D., Associate Professor.
Political Science: Michael Chambers, Ph.D., Professor and Chairperson.
Psychology: Veanne Anderson, Ph.D., Associate Professor.
Public Administration: Stan Buchanan, Ph.D., Associate Professor.
Recreation and Sport Management: Thomas H. Sawyer, Ed.D., Professor and Acting Chairperson.
School Administration and Supervision: Steve Gruenert, Ph.D., Professor and Chairperson.
School Counseling, M.Ed., and Licensure Programs: Tonya Balch, Ph.D., Assistant Professor.
School Psychology: Damon Krug, Ph.D., Assistant Professor.
Student Affairs and Higher Education: William, Barratt, Ph.D., Associate Professor.
Technology Education: Kara Harris, Ed.D., Assistant Professor.
Technology Management: George Maughan, Ph.D., Professor.

Tirey Hall on the campus of Indiana State University.

INDIANA UNIVERSITY OF PENNSYLVANIA

School of Graduate Studies and Research

Programs of Study

The School of Graduate Studies and Research at Indiana University of Pennsylvania (IUP) offers programs of study leading to the Doctor of Education, Doctor of Psychology, and Doctor of Philosophy degrees in the areas of administration and leadership studies (educational administration track or human services track), clinical psychology, communications media, criminology, curriculum and instruction, English, nursing, and school psychology.

IUP awards Master of Arts, Master of Science, Master of Business Administration, Master of Education, and Master of Fine Arts degrees. Programs are available in adult and community education, adult education and communications technology, applied archaeology, applied mathematics, art, biology, business administration, business and workforce development, chemistry, community counseling, criminology, education, educational psychology, education of exceptional persons, elementary and middle school mathematics education, secondary school mathematics education, elementary or secondary school counseling, employment and labor relations, English (teaching English, English generalist, literature, or teaching English to speakers of other languages), food and nutrition, geography, health and physical education, history, literacy, music, nursing, physics, public affairs, safety sciences, sociology, speech-language pathology, sport science, and student affairs in higher education. IUP also offers graduate programs in the Pittsburgh area.

IUP offers specialization or certification programs in elementary/secondary principal, geographic information science and geospatial techniques, reading specialist, safety sciences, school counseling, school psychology, elementary/secondary principal, special education, and supervisor of pupil services.

Residency requirements are established at the program level; thus, doctoral and M.F.A. students will find that residency requirements may vary from program to program. Students should check with their departments, the graduate coordinator, or the program handbook to determine the residency requirement for a particular program.

The University operates on an academic year of two semesters, plus summer and winter sessions.

Research Facilities

The University library contains more than 731,914 book volumes, 143,974 periodical volumes, 21,914 electronic serial subscriptions, and 2.4 million units of microform materials and other documents. The library is also a select federal depository. The computer center is available to members of the University community at all times. Specialized laboratories and research equipment are available for advanced master's, post-master's, and doctoral students. There are numerous research centers on campus.

Financial Aid

IUP offers a limited number of assistantships to degree-seeking graduate students. Full 20-hour assistantships currently pay a stipend plus a waiver of tuition for graduate course work during the terms of the assistantship. Various loan opportunities are available. Funds exist to support student research and attendance at professional meetings to present papers.

Cost of Study

In 2011–12, full-time graduate tuition was $416 per credit for in-state students and $624 per credit for out-of-state students. There are additional mandatory fees. Students enrolled in the high-demand differential programs are assessed an additional 5 percent tuition increase. Visit http://www.iup.edu/bursar/tuitionfees/ for the most current tuition and fee information.

Living and Housing Costs

University residence halls and off-campus rooms and apartments are available. Costs vary depending upon room size, proximity, and whether or not meals are included in the arrangement. Visit http://www.iup.edu/housing for specific information.

Student Group

Approximately 2,350 students are enrolled in programs leading to the various graduate degrees. The total University enrollment is approximately 14,640. Students represent American minority groups, most states, and a number of countries.

Location

Indiana, Pennsylvania, a community of 28,000, is 59 miles northeast of Pittsburgh. A wide variety of cultural and recreational activities in urban, suburban, and rural settings are available in and near the town of Indiana and in Pittsburgh.

The University

Founded as a higher education institution in 1875 and designated a university in 1965, IUP is classified as a Doctoral/Research University. It has three campuses and more than 700 faculty members.

Applying

An admissions packet is available by request from the School of Graduate Studies and Research or online at the School's Web site (http://www.iup.edu/admissions/graduate/howto). Information describing individual programs is available directly from departmental graduate coordinators, or online at http://www.iup.edu/graduatestudies/programs/.

Correspondence and Information

School of Graduate Studies and Research
Stright Hall, Room 101
210 South Tenth Street
Indiana University of Pennsylvania
Indiana, Pennsylvania 15705-1048
Phone: 724-357-2222
Fax: 724-357-4862
E-mail: graduate-admissions@iup.edu
Web site: http://www.iup.edu/graduatestudies

THE FACULTY

Listed below are IUP's graduate degree program areas. Each is followed by the name of the corresponding graduate coordinator and campus e-mail address.

PROGRAM AREAS

Administration and Leadership Studies, Education Track: Dr. Robert Millward (millward@iup.edu).
Administration and Leadership Studies, Human Services Track: Dr. John Anderson (jaa@iup.edu).
Adult and Community Education: Dr. Gary Dean (gjdean@iup.edu).
Adult Education and Communications Technology: Dr. Jeffrey Ritchey (jeffrey.ritchey@iup.edu).
Applied Archaeology: Dr. Phillip Neusius (phillip.neusius@iup.edu).
Art: Dr. Susan Palmisano (palmisan@iup.edu).
Biology: Dr. Robert Gendron (rgendron@iup.edu).
Business Administration: Dr. Krish Krishnan (krishnan@iup.edu).
Business and Workforce Development: Dr. Dawn Woodland (woodland@iup.edu).
Chemistry: Dr. Keith Kyler (keith.kyler@iup.edu).
Clinical Psychology: Dr. Beverly Goodwin (goodwin@iup.edu).
Communications Media: Dr. Mark Piwinsky (mark.piwinsky@iup.edu).
Community Counseling: Dr. Claire Dandeneau (cdanden@iup.edu).
Counselor Education: Dr. Claire Dandeneau (cdanden@iup.edu).
Criminology, M.A.: Dr. Shannon Phaneuf (s.phaneuf1@iup.edu).
Criminology, Ph.D.: Dr. Jennifer Roberts (jroberts@iup.edu).
Curriculum and Instruction: Dr. Mary Jalongo (mjalongo@iup.edu).
Education of Exceptional Persons: Dr. Becky Knickelbein (becky.knickelbein@iup.edu).
Educational Psychology: Dr. Mark McGowan (mmcgowan@iup.edu).
Employment and Labor Relations: Dr. Jennie Bullard (jbullard@iup.edu).
English, Generalist, Literature, and Literature and Criticism: Dr. David Downing (david.downing@iup.edu).
English, M.A., Teaching English: Dr. sj Miller (s.j.miller3@iup.edu).
English, M.A., TESOL: Dr. Lilia Savova (lilia.savova@iup.edu).
English, Ph.D., Composition and TESOL: Dr. Gian Pagnucci (gian.pagnucci@iup.edu).
Food and Nutrition: Dr. Stephanie Taylor-Davis (stdavis@iup.edu).
Geography: Dr. Richard Hoch (richard.hoch@iup.edu).
Health and Physical Education: Dr. Linda Klingaman (lrklinga@iup.edu).
History: Dr. Jeanine Mazak-Kahne (j.mkahne@iup.edu).
Literacy: Dr. Anne Creany (acreany@iup.edu).
Math, Applied: Dr. Yu-Ju Kuo (yjkuo@iup.edu).
Math Education, Elementary and Middle School: Dr. Larry Feldman (lmfeldmn@iup.edu).
Math Education, Secondary: Dr. Margaret Stempien (mmstemp@iup.edu).
Music, Performance, Education, Theory/Composition, History: Dr. Stephanie Caulder (scaulder@iup.edu).
Nursing, Education, Administration: Dr. Kristy Chunta (k.s.chunta@iup.edu).
Nursing, Ph.D.: Dr. Teresa Shellenbarger (tshell@iup.edu).
Physics: Dr. Gregory Kenning (ccpm@iup.edu).
Principal Certification: Dr. Cathy Kaufman (ckaufman@iup.edu).
Professional Studies, Master of Education: Dr. Crystal Machado (crystal.machado@iup.edu).
Public Affairs: Dr. Sarah Wheeler (SarahM.Wheeler@iup.edu).
Safety Sciences, Technical Track and Certificate of Recognition: Dr. Christopher Janicak (cjanicak@iup.edu).
School Psychology: Dr. Joseph Kovaleski (jkov@iup.edu).
Sociology: Dr. Valerie Gunter (val.gunter@iup.edu).
Speech-Language Pathology: Dr. David Stein (david.stein@iup.edu).
Sport Science: Dr. Mark Sloniger (mark.sloniger@iup.edu) and Dr. Robert Kostelnik (bkostel@iup.edu).
Student Affairs in Higher Education: Dr. Linda Hall (linda.hall@iup.edu).

IONA COLLEGE

School of Arts and Science and Hagan Business School Graduate Programs

Programs of Study

Iona College offers graduate programs leading to the degree of Master of Arts, Master of Science, Master of Science in Education, Master of Science in Teaching, or Master of Business Administration. Fields of study in the School of Arts & Science include computer science, criminal justice, education/teaching, educational leadership, English, history, Italian, marriage and family therapy, mental health counseling, psychology (experimental, industrial/organizational, school), public relations, and Spanish. Certificate programs are available in forensic criminology and criminal justice, and nonprofit public relations. Offered through the Hagan School of Business, the M.B.A. degree is available with specializations in accounting, financial management, health-care management, human resource management, information systems, management, and marketing. Certificates are available in business continuity and risk management, e-commerce, general accounting, health-care management, infrastructure management, international business, sports and entertainment studies, and more.

Graduate programs at Iona College are offered at the main campus in New Rochelle and at the Rockland Graduate Center (the College's branch campus in Pearl River, New York). These programs are specially designed to meet the needs of part-time students, although many programs serve the student who would like to attend full-time. Classes are conveniently scheduled in the late afternoon and early evening to accommodate students' workdays. Depending on the number of credits required of a graduate program, a dedicated part-time student can expect to complete his or her degree in as little as two years. Each program is designed with a core requirement and elective courses. Internships and practicum experiences are built into many programs so students may gain hands-on experience.

Research Facilities

The newly expanded and renovated main campus library opened in fall 2009. This transformed facility provides traditional library space, a multimedia seminar room, group study rooms, and a digital archive room. The library is also equipped with fifty-two dual-boot iMacs that can run both Microsoft Windows and the latest Mac OS; Iona is one of only a few colleges to invest in this cutting-edge technology. Iona College offers fully wireless facilities offering students high-speed access to the Internet and possesses more than 700 networked computers and two fully networked computer labs located at Iona's Graduate Center in Rockland County. Computer lab assistants are available to help students with their questions, and one lab stays open 24 hours a day, seven days a week.

Financial Aid

Iona College serves graduate students through a variety of state, federal, and institutional programs that include loans, scholarships, and assistantships. Scholarships are available based on undergraduate GPA or GRE or GMAT scores. To be eligible for federal loans, students must complete the FAFSA and the Iona College loan application.

Cost of Study

The cost of graduate tuition for the 2011–12 academic year is $872 per credit hour.

Living and Housing Costs

While Iona does not offer on-campus graduate housing, the Office of Off-Campus Housing provides information on living off campus, estimated apartment costs, and contact information for student-friendly real estate agents.

Student Group

There are approximately 900 students enrolled in graduate programs at Iona College. Most of these students are employed full-time and attend classes on a part-time basis in the evenings.

Student Outcomes

Some organizations that employ Iona graduates include American Express, Avon, Bristol-Meyers, Gannett Co., IBM, Lenox Hill and Sound Shore Hospitals, MasterCard, NBC, Sports Illustrated, top school districts, Verizon, Wyeth Pharmaceuticals, and Xerox.

Location

Iona's main campus is located on 35 acres in New Rochelle, New York, 20 minutes north of Manhattan. New Rochelle is a beautiful suburb of 70,000 located on Long Island Sound and is well served by mass transportation and highways. Iona's Rockland Graduate Center is 3 miles from the Palisades Parkway in Pearl River. Both campuses offer plentiful parking for evening students. The location of both campuses in the NYC metropolitan area allows students to take advantage of the many cultural, internship, and employment opportunities available.

The College

Iona College is a comprehensive, coed Catholic college, founded in 1940 by the Congregation of Christian Brothers. The overall enrollment is about 4,200 students, of whom 900 study at the graduate level.

Iona offers study in more than twenty graduate areas and is accredited by the Middle States Association of Colleges and Schools. In the School of Arts & Science, specialized recognitions are held by the following programs: education programs are accredited by NCATE: National Council for Accreditation of Teacher Education, public relations and journalism are accredited by ACEJMC: Accrediting Council of Education in Journalism and Mass Communication, and marriage and family therapy is accredited by COAMFTE: Commission on Accreditation for Marriage and Family Therapy Education. Graduates of mental health counseling and school psychology are licensure eligible. The Hagan School is accredited by AACSB International–The Association to Advance Collegiate Schools of Business.

Applying

Applications for Iona's School of Arts & Science graduate programs are available by mail or can be completed online at http://www.iona.edu/admissions/applyToIona.cfm. To be considered, an applicant must submit the application and required application fee, official transcripts from all colleges attended, a resume, and two letters of recommendation. Interviews (in person or by phone) and other application materials may be required by some programs. Applications should be submitted at least a month before the intended start term.

Candidates for the Hagan School of Business may enter the graduate program in the fall (September), winter (November), or spring (March) trimester or in the summer session. The completed application, with fee, must be accompanied by two letters of recommendation, official transcripts from all postsecondary schools, and GMAT scores. All documents must be received no later than two weeks prior to the start of the session for which the candidate is applying.

Correspondence and Information

Office of Graduate Admissions
School of Arts & Science
Iona College
715 North Avenue
New Rochelle, New York 10801
Phone: 914-633-2502
800-231-IONA (toll-free)
Fax: 914-633-2277
E-mail: admissions@iona.edu
Web site: http://www.iona.edu

Director of M.B.A. Admissions
Hagan School of Business
Iona College
715 North Avenue
New Rochelle, New York 10801
Phone: 914-633-2288
Fax: 914-633-2012
E-mail: hagan@iona.edu
Web site: http://www.iona.edu/hagan

Graduate Admissions Office
Rockland Graduate Center
Concourse Level
Two Blue Hill Plaza
P.O. Box 1522
Pearl River, New York 10965
Phone: 845-620-1350
Fax: 845-620-1260
E-mail: rockland@iona.edu
Web site: http://www.iona.edu/rockland

DEPARTMENT AND PROGRAM HEADS

Computer Science: Robert Schiaffino, Associate Professor and Chair; Ph.D., Polytechnic Institute of NYU.
Criminal Justice: Cathryn Lavery, Associate Professor and Chair; Ph.D., CUNY Graduate Center.
Education: Paul Beaudin, Professor and Assistant Department Chair; M.S.Ed., Iona.
English: Laura Shea, Professor and Chair; Ph.D., Boston University.
History: Br. James Carroll, Associate Professor and Chair; Ph.D., Notre Dame.
Italian and Spanish: Thomas Mussio, Associate Professor and Chair; Ph.D., Michigan.
Marriage and Family Therapy: Jerome M. Rubino, Associate Professor and Chair; M.A., St. John's (New York).
Psychology: Paul Greene, Professor and Chair; Ph.D., LIU, Brooklyn
Public Relations: Jim Eggensperger, Associate Professor; Ph.D., Capella.

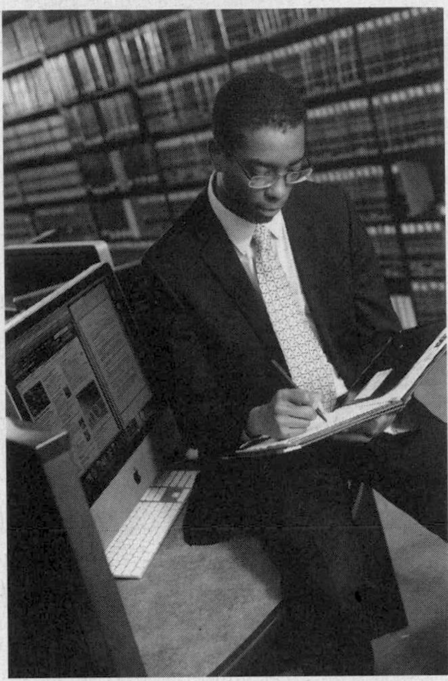
Iona College graduate student studying in the newly renovated Ryan Library.

Hagan School of Business, Iona College.

Ryan Library, Iona College.

KANSAS STATE UNIVERSITY

The Graduate School

Programs of Study

Kansas State University's (KSU) Graduate School offers advanced study in eighty-seven master's degree programs, fifty-one doctoral programs, five educational doctoral programs, and thirty-four certificate programs, with more than 4,000 graduate students enrolled. There is an increasing emphasis on innovative interdisciplinary programs.

Opportunities exist for research and scholarly activities in the areas of agriculture, architecture and design, biochemistry, business administration, education, engineering, food science, genetics, human ecology, humanities and fine arts, natural sciences, social sciences, and veterinary medicine. Examples of areas for graduate study and research include atomic physics, automated manufacturing, software engineering, space biology, infectious disease research, prairie ecology, rural sociology, wheat genetics, molecular biology, nutrition and public health, theater, cancer biology, materials science, industrial and organizational psychology, military history, high-energy physics, milling science, functional foods, food service, and human development.

The Graduate School requires 30 semester hours beyond the bachelor's degree to obtain the master's degree, although some programs require more than 30 semester hours. Many programs require a substantial research project, although a nonthesis option is available in some programs. In the professional programs, that option predominates.

Doctoral programs require 90 semester hours beyond the bachelor's degree to obtain a Ph.D. and 94 semester hours beyond to obtain an Ed.D. Both programs include original research and a dissertation. Admission to candidacy requires the successful completion of the preliminary examinations.

The Division of Continuing Education offers many courses and degree programs through distance education, using a variety of delivery methods, including the World Wide Web, DVDs, videotapes, audiotapes, Telenet 2, and other technologies. KSU offers the following through distance learning: the adult and continuing education master's program (Kansas City, Fort Leavenworth, or Wichita), an agribusiness master's degree, the classroom technology specialty, the educational administration and leadership master's program, engineering degree programs, English as a second language specialty in elementary/secondary education program, food science, gerontology, industrial/organization psychology, personal financial planning, and youth development. Several graduate certificate programs are also offered through the Division of Continuing Education.

Postbaccalaureate certificates provide a means to recognize mastery in a specialized area or to supplement a graduate degree. KSU currently offers thirty-four certificate programs in a variety of areas.

Research Facilities

KSU ranks among the nation's top seventy public research universities, with a growing foundation of research infrastructure to support rigorous training in scholarly research. Most recently, in 2008, KSU was selected as the location for the National Bio and Agro Defense Facility. The campus contains numerous specialized centers of interdisciplinary focused research, and these provide graduate students with dynamic training in their disciplines. Students should consult the KSU Research Facilities and Centers Web page at http://www.ksu.edu/Directories/research-facilities.html for a partial listing of these centers.

Financial Aid

Nearly half of KSU graduate students receive some type of financial assistance, including University graduate fellowships, teaching and research assistantships, or other forms of University employment and loans. Tuition waivers are given to graduate teaching assistants who receive at least a half-time appointment, and tuition reductions are available for graduate research assistants.

The KSU Office of Student Financial Assistance administers the federal assistance programs, work-study programs, and loans for which graduate students are eligible.

Cost of Study

For 2011–12, tuition for Kansas residents ranged from $310.10 for 1 graduate credit hour per semester to $3721.20 for 12 credit hours. Nonresident tuition ranged from $699.90 for 1 graduate credit hour per semester to $8398.80 for 12 credit hours. Fees in addition to tuition include campus privilege fees that range from $84.50 to $360.60. Some colleges have additional tuition surcharges and equipment fees.

Overall annual expenses, including living expenses, for a full-time student who completes 24 hours and is paying nonresident tuition are about $32,550.

Living and Housing Costs

KSU has over 700 apartment units for graduate students. Married couples with children and single parents have priority. One-bedroom apartments on a semester basis range from $378 to $546 per month for traditional and newly constructed units, respectively, and two-bedroom apartments range from $446 to $968 per month for traditional and newly constructed units. On a yearly basis in Manhattan, a typical unfurnished one-bedroom apartment ranges from $378 to $546 per month, and unfurnished two-bedroom apartments range from $446 to $968 per month.

Student Group

The KSU graduate student population of more than 4,000 is made up of approximately 50 percent men and 50 percent women. Approximately one fourth of the population is made up of international students from more than 100 countries. About two thirds of all graduate students are nontraditional (age 25 or older or married).

Student Outcomes

KSU graduates are highly sought after. They often receive multiple job offers, and many find employment well before graduation. They are leaders in public and private sectors, at government agencies, and at all levels of business and the private sector.

A sample of employers includes the National Institutes of Health, Argonne and Sandia National Labs, Nintendo, Merck, Pfizer, Cargill, Kellogg's, Hershey Foods, Anheuser-Busch, Motorola, AT&T Bell Labs, Texas Instruments, Rockwell International, and Sprint.

Location

KSU's picturesque 668-acre campus features many buildings of native limestone. KSU is centrally located in Manhattan (population 50,000), about 125 miles west of Kansas City. Manhattan has a new municipal airport, excellent schools, a daily newspaper, and numerous recreational facilities and cultural offerings. International festivals, Cinco de Mayo, Juneteenth, and Native American observances are held annually.

The University

Founded in 1863 as the first land-grant college, KSU is an internationally recognized, comprehensive research university with excellent academic programs carried out in a lively intellectual and cultural atmosphere.

In 1996, the University received the National Science Foundation's Recognition Award for the Integration of Research and Education. KSU was one of only ten universities selected.

Since 1974, KSU has ranked in the top 1 percent of all U.S. universities in the number of its graduates selected as Rhodes scholars.

Applying

Students should request admission applications and supplementary program information directly from the department or program coordinator. The Graduate School forwards correspondence to the appropriate program.

U.S. citizens should have all application materials on file by February 1 to receive priority consideration for full admission and for consideration for fellowships or graduate assistantships for the following fall semester. International students should apply no later than nine months prior to the term in which they wish to enroll.

Correspondence and Information

The Graduate School
103 Fairchild Hall
Kansas State University
Manhattan, Kansas 66506-1103

Phone: 785-532-6191
800-651-1816 (toll-free in the U.S.)
Fax: 785-532-2983
E-mail: grad@ksu.edu
Web site: http://www.k-state.edu/grad

PROGRAMS AND COORDINATORS

Students should contact the program coordinators listed below for more information.

COLLEGE OF AGRICULTURE

Agricultural Economics (M.S., Ph.D.): John Crespi.
Agricultural Economics–Agribusiness (M.A.B.): Allen Featherstone.
Agronomy (M.S., Ph.D.): Scott Staggenborg.
Animal Sciences and Industry (M.S., Ph.D.): Evan Titgmeyer.
Entomology (M.S., Ph.D.): David Margolies.
Grain Science and Industry (M.S., Ph.D.): Jon Faubion.
Horticulture (M.S., Ph.D.): Stuart Warren.
Plant Pathology (M.S., Ph.D.): Bill Bockus.

COLLEGE OF ARCHITECTURE PLANNING AND DESIGN

Postprofessional Master's Program in Architecture (M.S.Arch.): Todd Gabbard.
Professional Master's Programs. Architecture (M.Arch.): Peter Magyar.
Landscape Architecture (M.L.A.): Stephanie Rolley.
Regional and Community Planning (M.R.C.P.): Stephanie Rolley.
Community Development (M.S.): Stephanie Rolley.
Interior Architecture and Product Design (M.I.A.P.D.): Neal Hubbell.

COLLEGE OF ARTS AND SCIENCES

Sciences and Mathematics

Biology (M.S., Ph.D.): S. Keith Chapes.
Chemistry (M.S., Ph.D.): Christer Aakeroy.
Geology (M.S., cooperative Ph.D. with the University of Kansas): Adelmoneam Raef (international) and Matthew Brueseke (domestic).
Mathematics (M.S., Ph.D.): David Yetter.
Microbiology (Ph.D.): S. Keith Chapes.
Physics (M.S., Ph.D.): Michael O'Shea.
Statistics (M.S., Ph.D.): Weixing Song.

Humanities and Fine Arts

English (M.A.): Timothy Dayton.
Fine Arts (M.F.A.): Nancy Morrow.
History (M.A., Ph.D.): Louise Breen.
Modern Languages (M.A.): Claire Dehon.
Music (M.M.): Frederick Burrack.
Communication Studies, Theater, and Dance (M.A.). Speech: Bill Schenk-Hamlin. Theater: Sally Bailey.

Social Sciences

Economics (M.A., Ph.D.): Dong Li.
Geography (M.A., Ph.D.): Melinda Daniels.
Kinesiology (M.S.): Tom Barstow.
Journalism and Mass Communication (M.S.): Steven Smethers.
Political Science (M.A.): James Franke.
Psychology (M.S., Ph.D.): Clive Fullagar.
Public Administration (M.P.A.): Krishna Tummala.
Sociology (M.A., Ph.D.): Gerad Middendorf.

COLLEGE OF BUSINESS ADMINISTRATION

Accountancy (M.Acc.): Jeffrey Katz.
Business Administration (M.B.A.): Jeffrey Katz.

COLLEGE OF EDUCATION

Academic Advising (M.S.): Ken Hughey.
Adult and Continuing Education (M.S., Ed.D., Ph.D.): David Thompson.
Counseling and Student Development (M.S., Ed.D., Ph.D.): Ken Hughey.
Curriculum and Instruction (M.S., Ed.D., Ph.D.): Gail Shroyer.
Educational Administration and Leadership (M.S., Ed.D.): David Thompson.
Special Education (M.S., Ed.D.): Paul Burden.

COLLEGE OF ENGINEERING

Architectural Engineering (M.S.): Kimberly Kramer.
Biological and Agricultural Engineering (M.S., Ph.D.): Naiqian Zhang.
Chemical Engineering (M.S., Ph.D.): James Edgar.
Civil Engineering (M.S., Ph.D.): Hayder Rasheed.
Computer Science (M.S., Ph.D.): Dave Gustafson.
Electrical Engineering (M.S., Ph.D.): Andrew Rys.
Engineering Management (M.E.M.): E. Stanley Lee.
Industrial Engineering (M.S., Ph.D.): E. Stanley Lee.
Mechanical Engineering (M.S., Ph.D.): Steve Eckels.
Nuclear Engineering (M.S., Ph.D.): Steve Eckels.
Operations Research (M.S.): E. Stanley Lee.
Software Engineering (M.S.E.): Dave Gustafson.

COLLEGE OF HUMAN ECOLOGY

Apparel and Textiles (M.S.): Jana Hawley.
Dietetics (M.S.): Deborah Canter.
Family Studies and Human Services (M.S.): Connie Fechter.
Gerontology (M.S.): Gayle Doyle.
Food Service Hospitality Management and Dietetics Administration (M.S.): Deborah Canter.
Human Ecology (Ph.D.): Connie Fechter.
Apparel and Textiles: Sherry Haar.
Family Life Education and Consultation: Connie Fechter.
Food Service and Hospitality Management: Deborah Canter.
Life Span Human Development: Connie Fechter.
Marriage and Family Therapy: Connie Fechter.
Personal Financial Planning: Kim Misenhelter.
Human Nutrition (M.S., Ph.D.). Food Science: Edgar Chambers IV. Nutrition: Mark Haub.

COLLEGE OF VETERINARY MEDICINE

Biomedical Sciences (M.S.): Michael Kenney.
Pathobiology (Ph.D.): T. G. Nagaraja.
Anatomy and Physiology (Ph.D.): Bruce Schultz.

GRADUATE CERTIFICATE PROGRAMS

Academic Advising: Ken Hughey.
Agricultural Resources and Environmental Management: Kyle Douglas-Mankin.
Air Quality: Larry Erickson and Mo Hosni.
Applied Statistics: James Neill.
Biobased Products and Bioenergy: John Schlup.
Business Administration: Jeffrey Katz.
Community Planning and Development: Stephanie Rolley.
Complex Fluid Flows: Steve Eckels.
Conflict Resolution: Terrie McCants.
Digital Teaching and Learning: Rosemary Talab.
Entomology: Tom Phillips.
Food Safety and Defense: J. Scott Smith.
Food Science: J. Scott Smith.
Geoenvironmental: David Steward.
Geographic Information Science: J. M. Shawn Hutchinson.
Gerontology: Galye Doll.
Horticultural Therapy: Candice Shoemaker.
International Service: Jim Franke.
Management of Animal Health Related Organizations: Jeffrey Katz.
Occupational Health Psychology: Ron Downey.
Organizational Leadership: Jeffrey Katz.
Personal Financial Planning: John Grable.
Public Administration: Krishna Tummala.
Public Health Core Concepts: Michael Cates.
Real-Time Embedded System Design: Mitchell Neilsen.
Stem Cell Biotechnology: Duane Davis.
Teaching and Learning: Amanda Morales.
Teaching Students with Autism Spectrum Disorders: Marilyn Kaff.
Technical Writing and Professional Communications: Tim Dayton.
Transportation Engineering: Robert Stokes.
Women's Studies: Michelle Janette.
Youth Development Administration: Elaine Johannes.
Youth Development Professional: Elaine Johannes.

INTERDISCIPLINARY PROGRAMS

Biochemistry: (M.S., Ph.D.): Michal Zolkiewski.
Environmental Design and Planning (Ph.D.): Wendy Ornelas.
Food Science (M.S., Ph.D.): J. Scott Smith.
Genetics (M.S., Ph.D.): Barbara Valent.
Public Health (M.P.H.): Michael Cates.
Security Studies (M.A., Ph.D.): Craig Stapley.

LEE UNIVERSITY

Graduate Programs

Programs of Study

Lee University is a private, comprehensive Christian university that offers liberal arts and professional education at both the baccalaureate and master's levels. Lee's graduate programs serve adult students with various professional interests and diverse personal histories. Flexible scheduling for part-time and full-time students and personal attention from experts and practitioners in wide-ranging professional fields enable students to accommodate their personal goals and their intellectual progress in their chosen field of study.

Eighteen master's-level degree programs are offered at Lee through the following colleges or schools: College of Arts and Sciences (counseling), Helen DeVos College of Education, School of Music, and School of Religion. The Specialist in Education (Ed.S.) degree is offered through the Helen DeVos College of Education.

Research Facilities

The William G. Squires Library is a place of activity, collaboration, and study, staffed by a trained team of professionals who are experts at locating the most significant sources and are eager to teach students how to conduct research.

The library offers seating for about 250 with a mixture of casual seating, individual study carrels and group study tables, as well as quiet study areas, group study rooms, and a chapel. There are about sixty-five computers, including the LINK, a computer lab with thirty-two public computers). Students may use these computers to conduct research, write papers, browse the Internet, and send e-mail. Students may check out headphones and laptop computers for use in the library as well.

The library contains about 150,000 print volumes and subscribes to over 400 periodicals in print. In addition, the library provides access to 32,000 online journals and almost 110,000 electronic books available through subscriptions to numerous academic databases and e-book collections. Subscriptions to some casual reading magazines and current newspapers are provided also. The building also houses the Dixon Pentecostal Research Center, which serves as the official archives of the Church of God, with a large special collection of materials pertaining to the many aspects of the global Pentecostal/Charismatic movement.

More information is available at the library's Web site: http://library.leeuniversity.edu or follow the quick link from the Lee University home page.

Financial Aid

Eligibility for financial aid for graduate students is determined by filing the Free Application for Federal Student Aid (FAFSA) through the Federal processor. The FAFSA can be completed online at (www.fafsa.ed.gov.). In order to receive financial aid, a student must be fully accepted into a graduate program. Graduate students are eligible to apply for Stafford loans. Assistantships and scholarships are available for full-time and part-time graduate students. Information can be obtained from the Director of the Graduate Program in each area of study.

Cost of Study

In 2011–12, the estimated cost of tuition is $506 per credit, plus a registration fee of $25 per semester. Additional details regarding tuition and fees are available online at www.leegraduate.com.

Living and Housing

Lee University offers a residential life and housing program to meet the housing needs of graduate students who desire this service. Housing for married and nontraditional students is available but limited. Residence hall applications can be obtained by contacting the Office of Residential Life and Housing or visiting http:/www.leeuniversity.edu/residential-life.

Student Group

Lee's graduate students are highly qualified academically to pursue graduate studies in counseling, education, music, and religion. Fifty-six per cent of Lee's graduate students study part-time and the other 44 percent study full-time. Sixty-five percent are women, 35 percent are men.

Location

Lee University is a private, comprehensive university located in Cleveland, Tennessee, in the foothills of the Appalachian Mountains. Lee's 120-acre campus is located in a residential neighborhood at the center of the historic Ocoee street area near downtown Cleveland. The campus is 28 miles from Chattanooga, 124 miles from Atlanta, 172 miles from Birmingham, and 181 miles from Nashville.

The University

Lee University is emerging as a leader in higher education in the southeastern region and in 2010 was ranked in the Top Tier in the South for comprehensive–medium size universities by *U.S. News & World Report*. Lee is also listed by Princeton Review's Best Colleges as one of the 141 colleges named Best in the Southeast.

Applying

Graduate programs at Lee University are open to prospective students who hold a bachelor's degree from an accredited college or university and whose undergraduate or graduate work has been of sufficient quality and scope to enable them to profitably pursue graduate study.

Graduate applicants are required to meet specific admission criteria established by each of the graduate programs. All applications must be accompanied by a $25 nonrefundable application fee. Each Lee University graduate program has different requirements for admission. Applicants are advised to refer to appropriate sections in the University catalog for specific graduate program admission requirements or visit www.leegraduate.com.

Correspondence and Information

Office of Graduate Enrollment
Lee University
1120 North Ocoee Street
Cleveland, Tennessee 37320-3450
Phone: 423-614-8691
800-LEE-9930 (toll-free)
E-mail: gradstudies@leeuniversity.edu
Web site: http://www.leeuniversity.edu/admissions/graduate

THE ADMINISTRATION

College of Arts and Sciences
Matthew Melton, Dean, College of Arts and Sciences; Ph.D., Regent University (Virginia).
Trevor Milliron, Director of Graduate Studies in Counseling; Ph.D., Fuller Theological Seminary.

College of Education
Deborah Murray, Dean, Helen DeVos College of Education; Ed.D., Tennesse, Knoxville.
Gary Riggins Director of Graduate Studies in Education; Ed.D., Tennessee, Knoxville.

School of Music
William Green, Dean, School of Music; D.M.A., Kentucky.
Brad Moffett, Director of Graduate Studies in Music; D.W.S., Webber Institute for Worship Studies.

School of Religion
Terry Cross, Dean, School of Religion; Ph.D., Princeton Theological Seminary.
Lisa Long, Director of Graduate Studies in Christian Ministries; Ph.D., Biola.
Skip Jenkins, Director of Graduate Studies in Bible and Theology; Ph.D., Marquette.

Ignite Your Intellect.

Preparation with Purpose.

LOYOLA UNIVERSITY CHICAGO

The Graduate School

Programs of Study

The Graduate School oversees a variety of academic programs leading to doctoral (Ph.D.) and master's (M.A., M.S.) degrees. The School fosters graduate education and advanced research across traditionally defined disciplines as well as interdisciplinary environments. The students and faculty together strive to fulfill the University's mission of pursuing knowledge in the service of humanity.

Research Facilities

The combined libraries of the University contain more than 1 million volumes, with standing orders for more than 7,800 serials, 650,000 microforms, and 21,000 pieces of audiovisual material. The library subscribes to several computerized online services, data search networks, and interlibrary access and loan programs.

Loyola's campuses are interconnected by a high-speed fiber-optics network. Each campus has computing centers equipped with extensive software options and standard programming environments. Loyola's Wi-Fi wireless network allows students to access the University's network and the Internet from several locations on both campuses.

The Department of Computer Science provides a Linux-based laboratory with thirty-two new computing systems running the latest open source software. Students have access to experimental systems, including computational clusters and embedded systems, through its Emerging Technologies Laboratory.

Specialized laboratory facilities are maintained in the basic medical science, science, and social science departments.

Financial Aid

To learn about graduate financial aid at Loyola, students should visit http://LUC.edu/finaid, e-mail gradfinaid@luc.edu, or call 773-508-2984. Awards are offered on a competitive basis to Loyola's most talented Graduate School students and normally range from $14,000 to $25,000. Most awards are announced in the spring preceding enrollment, and most are renewable, based on academic performance, and can be held for up to four or five years.

Cost of Study

Students should visit http://LUC.edu/bursar to learn the latest tuition rates for nursing, social work, medical sciences, pastoral studies, and all other graduate programs. Tuition for courses offered by the Graduate School for the 2010–11 academic year was approximately $830 per credit hour.

Living and Housing Costs

Housing costs in the Chicago area vary considerably. Information is available through the Graduate School.

Student Group

Of the approximately 15,000 students attending Loyola University Chicago, more than 1,500 are enrolled in the various departments and programs of the Graduate School. Students come from all areas of the United States and many other countries.

Student Outcomes

More than 100,000 Loyola alumni are spread throughout every state of the nation and in at least 121 countries throughout the world. Among their ranks are hundreds of CEOs of major corporations and health-care institutions, dozens of state and national legislators, scores of circuit court and federal judges, and a number of presidents of nationally recognized universities.

Location

Graduate-level classes are held at Loyola's two Chicago campuses and at the Loyola University Medical Center in suburban Maywood. The Lake Shore Campus is located on Chicago's North Side, right along Lake Michigan, in a diverse and dynamic residential area. The Water Tower Campus in downtown Chicago is situated in the midst of the city's cultural and commercial center on the Magnificent Mile. The Loyola University Medical Center is one of the leading medical research and teaching institutions in the nation. Graduate programs also offer study-abroad options at Loyola's John Felice Rome Center in Italy and at other locations around the globe.

Loyola students have access to the world-renowned Newberry Center for Renaissance Studies, as well as such leading institutions as the Art Institute of Chicago, the Chicago Historical Society, and the Library of International Relations. In the social sciences, Loyola participates in the Inter-University Consortium for Political and Social Research.

The University

Founded in 1870, Loyola is a Jesuit, Catholic university dedicated to excellence in teaching, research, health care, and community service. Programs in the University's nine schools and colleges focus not only on intellectual growth but also on the social, cultural, and spiritual development of the students they serve.

Applying

All applicants must submit a completed application form and official transcripts. Most departments and programs also require the results of the Graduate Record Examinations. Additional material is required by some departments. Students should consult the *Graduate School Bulletin* for details. Applicants may apply online at http://LUC.edu/gpem.

Applications are accepted throughout the year by most departments. Students who wish to be considered for need-based financial aid and merit awards must have their completed applications on file by February 1. Because there are some exceptions to this deadline, students should consult the *Graduate School Bulletin* for details.

Students from abroad must have proficiency in written and spoken English. Students for whom English is not the native language are required to submit scores from the TOEFL. Students from other countries are tested for competence in the English language and may have to take ESL courses.

Detailed descriptions of programs and procedures are found in the *Graduate School Bulletin.*

Correspondence and Information

Requests for additional information and applications should be directed to:
Loyola University Chicago
820 North Michigan Avenue, Suite 800
Chicago, Illinois 60611
Phone: 312-915-8900
Web site: http://LUC.edu/gpem

GRADUATE PROGRAMS

Arts and Sciences
Applied Statistics (M.S.)
Biology (M.S.)
Chemistry (Ph.D., M.S.)
Child Development (Ph.D.)
Computer Science (M.S.)
Computer Science: Information Technology (M.S.)
Computer Science: Software Technology (M.S.)
Criminal Justice (M.A.)
Criminal Justice: Chicago Police Department Cohort (M.A.)
English (Ph.D., M.A.)
History (Ph.D., M.A.)
History: Public History (M.A.)
Mathematics and Statistics (M.S.)
Medical Sciences (M.A.)
Philosophy (Ph.D., M.A.)
Philosophy: Applied (M.A.)
Political Science (Ph.D., M.A.)
Public Policy (M.P.P.)
Psychology: Applied Social (Ph.D., M.A.)
Psychology: Clinical (Ph.D.)
Psychology: Developmental (Ph.D.)
Sociology (Ph.D., M.A.)
Sociology: Applied (M.A.)
Spanish (M.A.)
Theology (Ph.D., M.A.)
Urban Affairs (M.A.)
Women's Studies and Gender Studies (M.A., certificate)

Biomedical Sciences
Biochemistry, Molecular and Cellular (Ph.D., M.S.)
Bioethics (D.Be.)
Bioethics and Health Policy (online M.A., online certificate)
Cell and Molecular Physiology (Ph.D., M.S.)
Cellular Biology, Neurobiology, and Anatomy (Ph.D., M.S.)
Clinical Research Methods (M.S.)
Infectious Disease and Immunology (M.S.)
Integrated Program in the Biomedical Sciences (Ph.D.)
M.D./Ph.D. Program with Stritch School of Medicine
Microbiology and Immunology (Ph.D., M.S.)
Molecular Biology (Ph.D., M.S.)
Neuroscience (Ph.D., M.S.)
Pharmacology and Experimental Therapeutics (Ph.D., M.S.)
Public Health (M.P.H.)

Business
Accountancy (M.S.)
Business Administration (M.B.A.)
Business Administration for Executives (E.M.B.A.)
Business Administration: Health Care Management (M.B.A.)
Business Ethics (certificate)
Data Warehousing (certificate)
Finance (M.S.)
Human Resources (M.S.)
Information Systems Management (M.S.)
Integrated Marketing Communications (M.S.)

Education
Administration and Supervision (Ed.D.)
Behavior Intervention Specialist (M.Ed., certificate)
Community Counseling (M.A., M.Ed.)
Counseling Psychology (Ph.D.)
Cultural and Educational Policy Studies (Ph.D., M.A., M.Ed.)
Curriculum and Instruction (Ed.D., M.Ed.)
Educational Psychology (M.Ed.)
Elementary Education (M.Ed.)
Higher Education (Ph.D., M.Ed.)
Middle School Mathematics (M.Ed.)
Reading (M.Ed.)
Reading Teacher Endorsement (certificate)
Research Methodology (Ph.D., M.A., M.Ed.)
School Counseling (M.Ed., Type 73 certificate)
School Psychology (Ph.D., Ed.S., M.Ed.)
School Technology (M.Ed.)
Science Education (M.Ed.), with tracks in chemistry, earth and space science, and middle school mathematics.
Secondary Education (M.Ed.)
Special Education (M.Ed.)
Type 75 Superintendent (certificate)

Law: Master of Jurisprudence
Business Law (M.J.)
Child and Family Law (M.J.)
Health Law (online M.J.)

Law: Master of Laws
Trial Advocacy (L.L.M.)
Business and Corporate Governance Law (L.L.M.)
Child and Family Law (L.L.M.)
Health Law (L.L.M., online L.L.M.)
Tax Law (L.L.M.)

Nursing
Doctor of Nursing Practice (D.N.P.)
Nursing (Ph.D.)
Acute Care CNS or NP (M.S.N.)
Acute Care NP/Emergency NP (M.S.N.)
Adult CNS or NP (M.S.N.)
Adult with Cardio Subspecialty CNS or NP (M.S.N.)
Cardiovascular (online certificate)
Dietetics (M.S.)
Family NP (M.S.N.)
Family NP/Cardiovascular Subspecialty (M.S.N.)
Family NP/Oncology CNS (M.S.N.)
Family NP/Emergency NP (M.S.N.)
Health Care Informatics (online certificate)
Health Systems Management (M.S.N.)
Oncology CNS (M.S.N., online certificate)
Outcomes Performance Management (online certificate)
PICES: Population-based Infection Control and Environmental Safety (M.S.N., online certificate)
Post-Master's Nurse Practitioner (certificate)
Women's Health NP (M.S.N.).

Pastoral Studies
Divinity (M.Div.)
Congregational-based Community Development (certificate)
Fundamentals of Community Development (certificate)
Pastoral Counseling (M.A., certificate)
Pastoral Studies (M.A.)
Religious Education (M.A., certificate)
Social Justice (certificate)
Social Justice and Community Development (M.A.)
Spiritual Direction (certificate)
Spirituality (M.A.)

Social Work
Alcohol and Drug Abuse Counseling (CADC) (certificate)
Social Work (Ph.D., M.S.W.)
Family and School Partnerships–Advanced Practice in Schools (certificate)
Non-Profit Management and Philanthropy (certificate)
Type 73 (certificate)

MANHATTANVILLE COLLEGE

School of Graduate and Professional Studies

Programs of Study

Manhattanville's School of Graduate and Professional Studies offers career-oriented individuals the opportunity to acquire the skills they need to become effective leaders and advance their careers. The School offers undergraduate accelerated programs and part-time programs at both the undergraduate and graduate levels.

Manhattanville offers six Master of Science (M.S.) programs of study—Finance, Integrated Marketing Communications, International Management, Leadership and Strategic Management, Organizational Management and Human Resource Development, and Sport Business Management—in convenient one-weekend-per-month, weekday, and evening class schedules. A Certificate in Nonprofit Leadership program is also offered. The curriculum is designed and taught by executives presently employed in their field of expertise. Two Master of Arts (M.A.) programs are also offered: Liberal Studies and Writing. All master's programs have been developed to be completed within two years.

The Master of Science degree in Finance is a 36-credit program designed for working professionals who seek a career in finance or for experienced finance professionals who seek to enhance their knowledge of the field. Graduates of the program will be equipped for a variety of career opportunities including positions in multinational industrial corporations and financial institutions. The curriculum combines four elective courses with eight core courses to provide a broad management view of the world of finance and to address trends in the globally competitive financial marketplace. The program provides students a strong foundation in the principles and analytical techniques of finance upon which they will explore practical business applications.

The Master of Science in Integrated Marketing Communications is a 36-credit program. It provides advanced training in developing a communications strategy that is integrated with an organization's marketing and financial objectives. Students learn the principles of effective communications in global settings and the communication issues involved in marketing brand management and public relations. Degree requirements include eleven courses and a final integrative project.

The Master of Science in International Management program is a 36-credit program designed to prepare business leaders to meet the evolving challenges of international management and to seize opportunities for business success in both mature and expanding markets. Courses are designed to emphasize the development of practical management skills against a strong background of theory and values-based leadership principles. The learning environment promotes a high level of interaction between faculty members and students, and among students themselves. Degree requirements include eleven courses and a final integrative project.

The Master of Science in Leadership and Strategic Management is a 39-credit program providing advanced training in strategic management and planning and fostering the development of effective leadership skills. The learning is current, streamlined, and designed to allow managers and executives to excel in a rapidly changing and increasingly global work environment. Degree requirements include twelve courses and a final integrative project.

The Master of Science in Organizational Management and Human Resource Development is a 36-credit program that provides training in human resources skills and organizational management for professionals who want to enter or already work in the human resources field. Emphasis is on a strong theoretical background as well as development of practical, administrative, and management skills for individuals in corporations, small businesses, government, education, and the not-for-profit sector. Degree requirements include eleven courses and a thesis or final project option.

The Master of Science in Sport Business Management is a 36-credit program which provides individuals with the necessary knowledge and business skills to assume a leadership role in sports management. The course work provides an interdisciplinary approach to the study of sport management intended to provide a thorough foundation in sport and business while allowing flexibility for students to explore a wide variety of opportunities within the field. The program includes an internship to assist students in preparing for middle and upper level positions within a variety of markets including, but not limited to, professional sports, intercollegiate athletics, and amateur and youth athletic organizations.

The Master of Arts in Liberal Studies (M.A.L.S.), a 30-credit program, has been aptly described as a "time for your mind." This unique master's degree program cuts across many disciplines—art, literature, music, psychology, religion, sociology, philosophy, history, and politics. The M.A.L.S., designed for adult and part-time students, is self-paced and flexibly scheduled.

The Master of Arts in Writing is a 32-credit program designed for writers and aspiring writers. The program enables students to develop skills in writing while deepening their knowledge of the humanities. All required courses are scheduled in the evening, with the exception of the intensive Summer Writers' Week and Writers' Weekend. A final project of an original piece of writing is required.

The Certificate in Nonprofit Leadership requires 18 credits and may be completed in nine months. Under the guidance of executives and consultants currently working in the nonprofit and private sectors, the program targets key topics of concern to the leaders of nonprofit organizations with a focus on its application to day-to-day decisions. The curriculum is also well suited to accelerate the understanding of the challenges facing leaders in the nonprofit sector for those aspiring to leadership positions.

For those yet to complete their undergraduate degrees, Manhattanville offers three accelerated, part-time degree-completion programs: the Bachelor of Science (B.S.) in Behavioral Studies, the B.S. in Communications Management, and the B.S. in Organizational Management. Under a dual-degree arrangement, eligible students may take up to three graduate-level courses which can be applied to both their undergraduate and the related M.S. program.

Students may pursue a dual degree in Creative Writing. Those eligible may take up to 8 credits in graduate-level courses, which can be applied toward both the undergraduate degree and the Master of Arts in Writing. This program is designed for students with a grade point average of 3.4 or better. A dual-degree program may also be pursued with the School of Education. Eligible students may take up to five graduate-level education courses which can be applied toward both the undergraduate degree and the Master of Arts in Teaching.

These accelerated programs are designed for students who have earned an Associate of Arts degree or those who have accumulated undergraduate credits with a grade point average of 2.5 or better and now want the personal and professional benefits of earning a degree. To enroll, students must have at least two years of work experience. Most of these programs may be completed within eighteen months.

Research Facilities

Manhattanville has been named one of the Top 100 Wired Colleges in the U.S. The Manhattanville Library capitalizes on the power of the Internet to connect students with information and analysis found in powerful subscription databases, electronic journals, and electronic books. Manhattanville is one of the first colleges in the U.S. to outsource a service that enables students to interact online with experienced reference librarians at any time of the day or night from anywhere in the world. The virtual research service, Ask a Librarian 24/7, uses co-browsing to connect students with professional librarians who can answer questions about research and help students navigate the College's extensive array of subscription databases and other library resources. Manhattanville's teaching library, which supports the School of Education, ranks among the foremost undergraduate teaching libraries in the country. The Menendez Language Laboratory includes tapes and record libraries that provide materials for class instruction and individual practice in French, Spanish, Russian, Italian, German, Chinese, Japanese, Hindi, Marathi, modern Hebrew, and English as a second language. The College provides a writing clinic, a reading clinic, audiovisual facilities, and a bibliographic instruction program. The library building is open 24 hours a day, seven days a week through most of the fall and spring semesters, and it has computer labs, quiet study areas, group-study rooms, and a café, where students and faculty members can meet informally.

Financial Aid

Federal Stafford Student Loans, as well as a deferred payment plan, are available for graduate students. For further information, prospective students can contact the Office of Financial Aid, Reid Hall, Purchase, New York 10577 (phone: 914-323-5357).

Cost of Study

For 2011–12, tuition is $785 per credit for Master of Science degrees, $755 per credit for Master of Arts degrees, and $655 for the adult accelerated undergraduate degree completion programs. There is a semester registration fee of $60.

Living and Housing Costs

The programs offered by the School of Graduate and Professional Studies are nonresidential. Students live off campus and work in communities throughout Westchester and the surrounding counties.

Location

Manhattanville's 100-acre suburban campus is located in New York's Westchester County, just minutes from White Plains to the west and Greenwich, Connecticut, to the east. It is 30 miles from Manhattan. Many prominent corporate offices—IBM, MasterCard, Morgan Stanley, and PepsiCo—are headquartered nearby. The campus is accessible by public transportation.

The College

Manhattanville College is a coeducational, independent liberal arts college whose mission is to educate ethically and socially responsible leaders for the global community. Founded in 1841, the College has 1,650 undergraduate students and 1,100 graduate students. Manhattanville offers bachelor's, master's, and doctoral degrees in more than fifty academic concentrations in the arts and sciences. Its curriculum nurtures intellectual curiosity and independent thinking.

Applying

Applications to the School of Graduate and Professional Studies are reviewed on a continuing basis. Application requirements for the B.S. and M.S. programs include a completed application form, a resume, an autobiographical essay, an admissions interview, two recommendations, and official transcripts of all previous undergraduate and graduate college work.

For the Master of Arts in Writing program, submission of a 10- to 12-page creative writing sample, including at least five pages of prose, is substituted for the resume and letters of recommendation.

Correspondence and Information

Admissions Office
Graduate and Professional Studies
Manhattanville College
2900 Purchase Street
Purchase, New York 10277

Phone: 914-694-3425
Fax: 914-323-1988
E-mail: gps@mville.edu
Web site: http://www.mville.edu

THE FACULTY

School of Graduate and Professional Studies Administration

Anthony Davidson, Dean, School of Graudate and Professional Studies; Ph.D., London; M.B.A., CUNY, Baruch.
Efraim Berkovich, Director, M.S. in Finance and Assistant Professor of Finance; Ph.D., Pennsylvania.
Daniel Gerger, Director, Continuing Education; M.P.A, NYU.
Mark Nowak, Director, M.A. in Writing Program; M.F.A., Bowling Green State.
Ruth Mack, Interim Director, M.S. in Leadership and Strategic Manageement, Integrated Marketing Communications, Organizational Management and Human Resource Development, and International Management programs; M.B.A., North Carolina at Chapel Hill.
Dave Torromeo, Director of M.S. in Sport Business Management; M.S., Iona.
Nikhil Kumar, Director of Admissions; M.S.,Manhattanville.

MISSOURI STATE UNIVERSITY

Graduate College

Programs of Study

Missouri State University (MSU) offers forty-eight graduate programs leading to the Master of Accountancy (M.Acc.), Master of Arts (M.A.), Master of Arts in Teaching (M.A.T.), Master of Business Administration (M.B.A.), Master of Health Administration (M.H.A.), Master of Global Studies (M.G.S.), Master of Music (M.M.), Master of Natural and Applied Science (M.N.A.S.), Master of Public Administration (M.P.A.), Master of Public Health (M.P.H.), Master of Science (M.S.), Master of Science in Education (M.S.Ed.), Master of Science in Nursing (M.S.N.), Master of Social Work (M.S.W.), Specialist in Education (Ed.S.), and Doctorate in Educational Leadership (Ed.D.), Doctor of Audiology (Au.D.), and Doctor of Physical Therapy (D.P.T.) degrees. Programs of study are available in accounting, administrative studies, applied anthropology, audiology, biology, business administration, cell and molecular biology, chemistry, communication, communication sciences and disorders, computer information systems, counseling, criminology, defense and strategic studies, early childhood and family development, educational administration, educational leadership, educational technology, elementary education, English, geospatial sciences, global studies, health administration, health promotion and wellness management, history, literacy, materials science, mathematics, music, natural and applied science, nurse anesthesia, nursing, physical therapy, physician assistant studies, plant science, project management, psychology, public administration, public health, religious studies, secondary education, social work, special education, student affairs, teaching, theater, and writing. All programs are accredited by the North Central Association of Colleges and Schools, and many programs are professionally accredited.

Graduate certificate programs are offered in autism spectrum disorders, conflict and dispute resolution, defense and strategic studies, forensic accounting, forensic child psychology, geospatial information sciences, history for teachers, homeland security and defense, instructional technology specialist, orientation and mobility, Ozarks studies, post-master's nurse educator, post-master's family nurse practitioner, project management, public management, religious studies for the professions, screenwriting for television and film, sports management, tax accounting, and teaching English to speakers of other languages.

Research Facilities

Missouri State University libraries have comprehensive electronic resources, including an online catalog, electronic indexes and full-text resources, and Internet accessibility. The University is a member of the Center for Research Libraries and is both a U.S. and United Nations document depository. Other facilities include a K–12 laboratory school and numerous research centers, including the Bull Shoals Field Station, the Center for Archaeological Research, the Jordan Valley Innovation Center, the Center for Applied Science and Engineering, the Missouri State Fruit Experiment Station, and the Ozarks Environmental and Water Resources Institute.

Financial Aid

Financial assistance is available through a variety of scholarships, graduate assistantships, grants, loans, and work-study programs. Graduate assistantship stipends range from $8000 to $9730 for the nine-month academic year (2011–12) and include a tuition scholarship (resident or nonresident) for up to 15 hours a semester. Students on academic-year assistantships also receive a 6-hour tuition scholarship for the summer term. To be eligible for an assistantship, a student must be admitted to a graduate program and have a minimum GPA of 3.0 (cumulative or in the last 60 hours of undergraduate course work). The Missouri Outreach Graduate Opportunity (MOGO) Scholarship provides a partial remission of out-of-state fees for full-time students in eligible graduate programs who are not Missouri residents. The MOGO Scholarship has a value of three-fourths of the nonresident graduate student fees for 9 credit hours (5 credits hours in the summer).

Cost of Study

For the 2011–12 academic year, graduate-level course fees are $227–$410 per credit hour for Missouri residents and $235–$486 per credit hour for nonresidents (per credit hour rates vary by program and method of instruction). A student services fee is assessed per semester based on enrolled credit hours (courses taught via Internet excluded). This fee is $389 for full-time students (9 credit hours). Additional differential fees are assessed for some programs and courses.

Living and Housing Costs

The average cost per year for room and board in residence halls is $6598 in 2011–12. Exact rates depend on room style and meal plan. Furnished apartments are available for graduate, married, and nontraditional students for $6604 to $8774 per year (twelve-month lease). University and privately owned apartments are within a reasonable distance of the campus.

Student Group

The total student population is approximately 20,000, of which 15 percent are graduate students. Students come from across the United States and from approximately eighty countries.

Location

Missouri State University is located in Springfield, the third-largest city in Missouri with a metropolitan service region of more than 400,000. Located in the heart of the Ozarks recreational area, the University is within easy driving distance of numerous recreational lakes, streams, and parks. The community of Springfield is supported by an industrial/manufacturing base and an expanding service industry in tourism, with people drawn by the natural beauty and recreation of the Ozarks and the musical attractions in nearby Branson. Springfield has an extensive health and medical economy serving southwest Missouri, northwest Arkansas, southeast Kansas, and northeast Oklahoma.

The University

Missouri State University founded in 1905 is a multicampus metropolitan university system with a statewide mission in public affairs. The University offers more than 150 undergraduate majors and forty-eight graduate programs, many of which are the strongest of their kind in the state. The students experience college life at its best, with NCAA Division I athletics and more than 250 student organizations.

Applying

Missouri State University invites applications from students with strong records of undergraduate performance. To apply to a program, prospective students must complete the Graduate College application as well as submit a $35 application fee. To complete the application, the Graduate College also requires students to submit an official copy of their transcript, showing all prior academic work. Students should also contact the department or program to which they are applying to determine what additional materials (i.e., GRE, GMAT, letters of recommendation, resume, and/or other materials) are needed to complete their application. The application deadline to avoid a late fee is approximately three weeks prior to the beginning of the desired semester of entrance; however, students are strongly encouraged to submit required paperwork before this date to allow for appropriate processing time. Many programs admit students only once a year and have specific deadlines. Prospective students should refer to program admission requirements. The graduate catalog and admission application can be accessed via the Web site listed in this description.

Correspondence and Information

Pawan Kahol, Interim Dean
Graduate College
Missouri State University
901 South National Avenue
Springfield, Missouri 65897

Phone: 417-836-5335
417-836-4770 (MO Relay TDD)
866-767-4723 (toll-free)
Fax: 417-836-6888
E-mail: graduatecollege@missouristate.edu
Web site: http://graduate.missouristate.edu

FIELDS OF STUDY AND FACULTY ADVISERS

E-mail addresses of faculty members are in parentheses. All phone numbers are in area code 417.

Graduate College: Pawan Kahol, Interim Dean (pawankahol@missouristate.edu); Thomas Tomasi, Associate Dean (tomtomasi@missouristate.edu); 836-5335.
Administrative Studies (M.S.): Thomas Tomasi, Program Director (tomtomasi@missouristate.edu). This program is offered via the Internet. Options in applied communication, criminal justice, environmental management, homeland security and defense, project management, and sports management.
College of Arts and Letters: Carey Adams, Dean (careyadams@missouristate.edu); 836-5247.
Communication (M.A.): Dr. Heather Carmack, Program Director (heathercarmack@missouristate.edu); 836-4321. Graduate certificate program in conflict and dispute resolution.
English (M.A.): Dr. Matthew Calihman, Program Director (matthewcalihman@missouristate.edu); 836-4266. Tracks in literature, creative writing, and TESOL, and graduate certificate programs in TESOL and Ozarks Studies.
Media, Journalism, and Film (certificate): Diana Botsford, Program Director (dbotsford@missouristate.edu); 836-5029. Graduate certificate in screenwriting for television and film.
Music (M.M.): Robert Quebbeman, Program Director (robertquebbeman@missouristate.edu); 836-5648. Program accredited by the National Association of Schools of Music (NASM). Options in conducting, theory and composition, pedagogy, performance, and education.
Theater (M.A.): Dr. Christopher Herr, Program Director (jherr@missouristate.edu); 836-4400. Program accredited by the National Association of Schools of Theater.
Writing (M.A.): Dr. Linda Moser, Program Director (lmoser@missouristate.edu); 836-6606. Tracks in rhetoric and composition and technical and professional writing.
College of Business Administration: Stephanie Bryant, Dean (stephaniebryant@missouristate.edu); 836-5646. Programs accredited by AACSB International–The Association to Advance Collegiate Schools of Business.
Accounting (M.Acc.): School of Accountancy; Dr. David Byrd, Program Director (davidbyrd@missouristate.edu); 836-4183. Graduate certificate programs in forensic accounting and tax accounting.
Business Administration (M.B.A.): Dr. Elizabeth Rozell, Program Director (ERozell@missouristate.edu); 836-5616. Concentrations in accounting, computer information systems, finance, international management, management, and marketing.
Computer Information Systems (M.S.): Shannon McMurtrey, Program Director (shannonmcmurtrey@missouristate.edu); 836-4177.
Health Administration (M.H.A.): Michael Leibert, Program Director (mleibert@missouristate.edu); 836-4444.
Project Management (M.S.): Dr. Neal Callahan, Program Director (nelacallahan@missouristate.edu); 836-5160. Graduate certificate program in project management.
College of Education: Dennis J. Kear, Dean (denniskear@missouristate.edu); 836-5254. Programs accredited by the Department of Elementary and Secondary Education (DESE) and the National Council for Accreditation of Teacher Education (NCATE).
Counseling (M.S.): Dr. Joe Hulgus, Program Coordinator (josephhulgus@missouristate.edu); 836-6522.
Early Childhood and Family Development (M.S.): Joanna Cemore, Program Coordinator (joannacemore@missouristate.edu); 836-8403.
Educational Administration (Ed.S. and M.S.Ed.): Kim Finch, M.S.Ed. Program Coordinator (kimfinch@missouristate.edu), 836-5192; Robert Watson, Ed.S. Program Coordinator (robertwatson@missouristate.edu); 836-6951. Options in elementary principal, secondary principal, and superintendent.
Educational Leadership (Ed.D.): Cynthia MacGregor, Program Coordinator (cmacgregor@missouristate.edu); 836-6046. Cooperative program with the University of Missouri–Columbia (UMC). Degree conferred by UMC.
Elementary Education (M.S.Ed.): Cindy Wilson Hail, Program Coordinator (cindywilson@missouristate.edu); 836-6065.
Educational Technology (M.S.Ed.): School of Teacher Education, Fred H. Groves, Program Coordinator (fredgroves@missouristate.edu); 836-6769. Instructional Technology Specialist graduate certificate program.
Literacy (M.S.Ed.): Deanne Camp, Program Director (deannecamp@missouristate.edu); 836-6983. Program accredited by the International Reading Association (IRA).
Secondary Education (M.S.Ed.): For information, students should contact the area of emphasis department or Denise Frederick (dfrederick@missouristate.edu); 836-6204. Areas of emphasis include agriculture, art, biology, business, chemistry, earth science, English, family and consumer sciences, geography, history, mathematics, music, natural science, physical education, physics, social science, and speech and theater.
Special Education (M.S.Ed.): Dr. Tamara Arthaud, Department Head (TamaraArthaud@missouristate.edu); 836-6951. Emphasis areas in developmental disabilities, mild/moderate disabilities, orientation/mobility, and visual impairment. Graduate certificate programs in autism spectrum disorders and orientation/mobility.
Teaching (M.A.T.): Steven Hinch, Program Coordinator (shinch@missouristate.edu); 836-3170.
College of Health and Human Services: Helen Reid, Dean (helenreid@missouristate.edu); 836-4176.
Cell and Molecular Biology (M.S.): Scott Zimmerman, Program Director (scottzimmerman@missouristate.edu); 836-5478.
Communication Sciences and Disorders (M.S. and Au.D.): Neil DiSarno, Department Head, Program Director (neildisarno@missouristate.edu); 836-5368. Program options in audiology, education of the deaf/hard of hearing, and speech-language pathology. Audiology and speech-language pathology programs accredited by the American Speech-Language-Hearing Association. Education-of-the-deaf/hard-of-hearing program accredited by the Council of Education of the Deaf.
Health Promotion and Wellness Management (M.S.): Sarah McCallister, Department Head, Program Director (sarahmccallister@missouristate.edu); 836-5370. Graduate certificate program in sports management.
Nurse Anesthesia (M.S.): Ben Timson, Program Director (bentimson@missouristate.edu; 836-4145. Program accredited by the Council on Accreditation of Nurse Anesthesia Education Programs.
Nursing (M.S.N.): Kathryn Hope, Department Head, Program Director (kathrynhope@missouristate.edu); 836-5310. Post-master's graduate certificate programs for nurse educator and family nurse practitioner.
Physical Therapy (D.P.T.): Scott Wallentine, Program Admissions Coordinator (swallentine@missouristate.edu); 836-4514. Program accredited by the Commission on Accreditation in Physical Therapy Education (CAPTE).
Physician Assistant Studies (M.S.): Roberto Canales, Program Director (robertocanales@missouristate.edu); 836-615. Program accredited by the Accreditation Review Commission on Education for the Physician Assistant (ARC-PA).
Psychology (M.S.): Dr. David Lutz, Clinical Program Director (davidlutz@missouristate.edu); 836-5830. Dr. D. Wayne Mitchell, Experimental Program Director (waynemitchell@missouristate.edu); 836-6941. Dr. Carol Shoptaugh, Industrial Organizational Program Director (carolshoptaugh@missouristate.edu); 836-5788. Options in industrial/organizational, clinical, and experimental psychology. Graduate certificate program in forensic child psychology.
Public Health (M.P.H.): Vickie Sanchez, Program Director (vickiesanche@missouristate.edu); 836-5310.
Social Work (M.S.W.): Dr. Darry R. Haslam, Program Director (dhaslam@missouristate.edu); 836-4259. Program accredited by the Council on Social Work Education.
College of Humanities and Public Affairs: Victor H. Matthews, Dean (victormatthews@missouristate.edu); 836-5529. Graduate certificate program in homeland security and defense.
Applied Anthropology (M.S.): William Wedenoja, Program Director (billwedenoja@missouristate.edu); 836-5641.
Criminology (M.S.): Craig Hemmons, Department Head and Program Director (craighemmons@missouristate.edu); 836-3799.
Defense and Strategic Studies (M.S.): Keith B. Payne, Department Head, Program Director (kbpayne@missouristate.edu); 703-218-3565. Graduate certificate program in defense and strategic studies. Located in Fairfax, Virginia.
History (M.A.): F. Thornton Miller, Program Director (ftmiller@missouristate.edu); 836-5511. Tracks available in U.S. and world, American studies, and global area studies. Graduate certificate program in history for teachers.
Global Studies (M.G.S.); Dennis Hickey, Program Director (dennishickey@missouristate.edu), 836-5850.
Public Administration (M.P.A.): Mark Rushefsky, Program Director (markrushefsky@missouristate.edu); 836-5922. Graduate certificate program in public management.
Religious Studies (M.A.): Mark Given, Program Director (markgiven@missouristate.edu); 836-6681. Graduate certificate program in religious studies for the professions.
College of Natural and Applied Sciences: Tamera Jahnke, Dean (tamerajahnke@missouristate.edu); 836-5249.
Biology (M.S.): Dr. Alexander Wait, Program Director (alexanderwait@missouristate.edu); 836-5802.
Chemistry (M.S.): Dr. Erich D. Steinle, Program Director (esteinle@missouristate.edu); 836-5319.
Geospatial Sciences in Geography and Geology (M.S.): Bob Pavlowsky, Program Director (bobpavlowsky@missouristate.edu); 836-8473. Research concentration areas available in physical geography, geology, and human geography/planning. Graduate certificate program in geospatial information sciences.
Materials Science (M.S.): Kartik Ghosh, Program Director (kartikghosh@missouristate.edu); 836-6025.
Mathematics (M.S.): Yungchen Cheng, Department Head and Program Director (yungchencheng@missouristate.edu); 836-5112.
Natural and Applied Science (M.N.A.S.): Dr. Xingping Sun, Program Director (xsun@missouristate.edu). An interdisciplinary program in which students select from of the following primary emphasis areas: agriculture, biology, chemistry, computer science, geography/geology, mathematics, and physics/astronomy.
William H. Darr School of Agriculture: W. Anson Elliott, Director (ansonelliott@missouristate.edu); 836-5638.
Plant Science (M.S.): Dr. Arbindra Rimal, Program Director (arbindrarimal@missouristate.edu); 836-5094.

Carrington Hall, the main administration building, at Missouri State University.

Fountain near Missouri State University's Meyer Library.

MONMOUTH UNIVERSITY

Graduate School

Programs of Study

The Graduate School at Monmouth supports the University's goal to provide an exceptional educational experience at the postgraduate level. Graduate students have the chance to advance their knowledge and skills in their chosen fields and engage in challenging course work, scholarly research, clinical experience programs, and student teaching. The programs are offered through the School of Humanities and Social Sciences; the School of Nursing and Health Studies; the Leon Hess Business School; the School of Science; the School of Education; and the School of Social Work.

The School of Humanities and Social Sciences awards the Master of Arts (M.A.) in criminal justice, corporate and public communication, English, history, public policy, and psychological counseling, and a Master of Science (M.S) in mental health counseling. A Master of Arts in anthropology program is new in fall 2011. This school also offers graduate certificates in criminal justice administration, homeland security, public relations specialist, public service communication specialist, and human resource communication.

The School of Nursing and Health Studies introduced the Doctor of Nursing Practice (D.N.P.) in fall 2011—the first doctoral program to be offered at the University. The School also offers a Master of Science in Nursing (M.S.N.) as well as advanced practice nursing post-master's certificates in adult nurse practitioner, adult psychiatric and mental health practitioner, and family nurse practitioner; post-master's certificates in nursing education and nursing administration; and graduate certificates in forensic nursing, school nursing, and school nursing–noninstructional. An RN to M.S.N. direct program is offered that allows nurses to more quickly attain an M.S.N. degree.

The School of Science awards Master of Science (M.S.) degrees in computer science, financial mathematics, and software engineering. Certificates are available in computer science, software design and development, software development, and software engineering.

The School of Education offers three programs leading to master's degrees: the Master of Arts in Teaching (M.A.T.), the Master of Education (M.Ed.), and the Master of Science in Education (M.S.Ed.). The M.S.Ed. program offers concentrations in principal, principal–school administrator, special education, reading specialist, and school counseling. Graduate certificate programs are offered in autism, educational technology, and teaching English to speakers of other languages (TESOL). Education endorsement certification programs are available in bilingual/bicultural, Chinese, early childhood, ESL, substance awareness coordinator, and teacher of students with disabilities. Post-master's certificate programs are available in curriculum studies and education. Post-master's certification endorsement programs are offered in learning disabilities teacher-consultant, reading specialist, principal, supervisor, and director of school counseling services. An accelerated twelve-month M.A.T. program is offered, as are accelerated ESL endorsement programs.

The Leon Hess Business School offers the Master of Business Administration (M.B.A.) program with optional tracks in accounting, finance, and real estate and the M.B.A. with a concentration in health-care management. The school also offers post-master's certificate programs in accounting and health-care management. In addition, there is a full-time accelerated M.B.A. program that can be completed in one year.

The School of Social Work awards a Master of Social Work (M.S.W.) degree and a post-master's certificate in play therapy.

Research Facilities

The Monmouth University Library holds approximately 333,000 print and online monographs, 159 databases (including journals, videos, and e-books) and over 43,000 electronic journal subscriptions. Academic programs are amply supported by state-of-the-art computer hardware and software and classroom/laboratory facilities. Computer workstations that are specifically dedicated to student use are distributed among forty-five instructional and open-use laboratories and include both PC and Macintosh workstations. Wireless connectivity is available throughout most of the campus. All students receive a computer account that provides them with e-mail, World Wide Web browsing and authoring tools, and electronic access to the Monmouth University Library catalog.

Financial Aid

Financial aid is available in the form of fellowships, assistantships, and loans. Fellowships are awarded to qualified students on the basis of outstanding undergraduate cumulative grade point average. A limited number of assistantships are available to continuing students, with preference given to those maintaining a high grade point average. To determine eligibility for all other forms of aid, applicants must file the FAFSA form, which is available online at http://www.fafsa.ed.gov or at the Financial Aid Office. Monmouth University participates in the Federal Direct Student Loan Program, which makes both need- and non-need-based loans available to students who file the FAFSA. Alternative loan funding sources are available to those students who might not otherwise qualify for federal funding.

Cost of Study

Tuition for study in 2011–12 is $868 per credit. A University fee is assessed each semester.

Living and Housing Costs

Due to Monmouth's proximity to the beach, there are ample off-campus housing opportunities that are conveniently located near the University. These accommodations are relatively inexpensive since the academic year is also the off-season for tourism. A rental listing Web site is maintained by the Office of Off-Campus and Commuter Services and can be found at http://www.monmouth.edu/commuter.

Student Group

Monmouth University enrolls approximately 6,000 students, approximately 1,700 of whom are enrolled in the Graduate School. The diverse student body includes international students representing twenty-eight different countries.

Location

Monmouth University is located less than a mile from the Atlantic Ocean on a 156-acre campus in the quiet, suburban town of West Long Branch, New Jersey. The campus is only 1 hour from both New York City and Philadelphia. Both can be easily accessed by train. Commuter bus service is also available. The surrounding area has numerous activities, restaurants, and cultural events. The University's proximity to high-technology firms, financial institutions, and a thriving business-industrial sector provides Monmouth students and graduates with a wide variety of employment possibilities.

The University

Monmouth University is a private, moderate-sized coeducational teaching university committed to providing a learning environment that enables men and women to pursue their educational goals and realize their full potential for making significant contributions to their community and society. Small classes that allow for individual attention and student-faculty dialogue, together with careful academic advising and career counseling, are hallmarks of a Monmouth education. The Rebecca Stafford Student Center houses the Office of Student Services, the Center for Student Success, placement services, computer laboratories, study lounges, a full-service cafeteria, and student activities meeting rooms and offices. The University's NCAA Division I intercollegiate athletics program includes nine men's and eleven women's teams.

Applying

An application for admission to the Graduate School includes a completed application form with application fee, official transcript of the undergraduate record, score reports from the appropriate entrance examination, transcripts of any graduate work done elsewhere, and two letters of recommendation covering the candidate's personal and professional qualifications to pursue graduate work. Additional requirements may apply, based on the program. Students should contact the Office of Graduate Admission for details. International students must also provide evidence of English proficiency.

The application deadlines are July 15 for the fall term, November 15 for the spring term, and May 1 for the summer sessions. The deadline for applications to the M.S.W. program is March 15. An initial review of the complete application for admission is conducted by the Office of Graduate Admission. The file is then forwarded to the faculty director of the program for an admission decision. All correspondence should be conducted with the Office of Graduate Admission.

Correspondence and Information

Kevin L. Roane
Director of Graduate Admission
Monmouth University
400 Cedar Avenue
West Long Branch, New Jersey 07764-1898
Phone: 732-571-3452
800-320-7754 (toll-free)
Fax: 732-263-5123
E-mail: gradadm@monmouth.edu
Web site: http://www.monmouth.edu/admission

FACULTY HEADS AND PROGRAMS

Master of Arts in History (M.A.): Maryanne Rhett, Program Director and Assistant Professor of History and Anthropology; Ph.D., Washington State.

The program accommodates students who wish to specialize in European, United States, or world history. The program is designed not only for recent college graduates but also for secondary school teachers of history and social studies and professionals in government, the military, and business. Thesis and nonthesis options are available.

Master of Arts in Psychological Counseling (M.A.): George Kapalka, Program Director, Associate Professor of Psychology, and Chair of the Department of Psychological Counseling; Ph.D., Fairleigh Dickinson.

The program offers practical and theoretical courses in quantitative methods, intervention skills, and assessment methods. The program equips students with proficiencies in the traditional counseling field as well as in emerging areas. Upon completion of the program, students may pursue an advanced degree.

Master of Science in Mental Health Counseling (M.S.): George Kapalka, Program Director, Associate Professor of Psychology, and Chair of the Department of Psychological Counseling; Ph.D., Fairleigh Dickinson.

The program, which is accredited by the Council for Accreditation of Counseling and Related Educational Programs (CACREP), prepares students for the Professional Counselor Licensure Examination. Courses satisfy criteria prescribed by the New Jersey State Board of Professional Counselor Examiners. The curriculum concentrates on developing the basic course areas, specialty areas, research and evaluation skills, and practical experiences.

Master of Science in Software Engineering (M.S.): Daniela Rosca, Program Director and Associate Professor of Software Engineering; Ph.D., Old Dominion.

The software engineering program is accredited by the Engineering Accreditation Commission of ABET. Students learn to develop, validate, implement, and maintain high-quality software products. Specialization tracks are offered in embedded software, information management, organizational management, software technology, and telecommunications.

Master of Science in Computer Science (M.S.): Cui Yu, Program Director and Assistant Professor of Computer Science; Ph.D., National University of Singapore.

The program includes concentrations in computer networks, intelligent information systems, and security of information systems and networks. The computer networks concentration includes study in analysis/modeling and simulation. The program is open to students with undergraduate degrees other than computer science (some preparatory work may be required).

Master of Science in Nursing (M.S.N.): Laura Jannone, Program Director, and Associate Professor of Nursing; Ed.D., Columbia Teachers College.

The nursing program is designed to prepare the professional nurse for advanced practice nursing. Tracks are offered in adult or family nurse practitioner, nursing administration, adult psychiatric and mental health, school nursing, nursing education, and forensic nursing.

Master of Education (M.Ed.): Laurel Chehayl, M.Ed. Program Representative and Assistant Professor of Education; Ph.D., Kent State.

The Master of Education program is designed for fully certified teachers and other experienced education professionals to increase their knowledge and skills in specific content areas and earn additional credentials in the field of education. Graduates of the program master educational research and curriculum design as well as progressive theory and approaches to teaching.

Master of Science in Education (M.S.Ed.): Jason Barr, Chair, Program Director, and Assistant Professor of Educational Leadership, School Counseling, and Special Education; Ph.D., Fordham.

The Department of Educational Leadership, School Counseling, and Special Education provides research-based master's and endorsement programs that are linked to national, state, and local standards and effectively prepare individuals to serve as support specialists, leaders, literacy coaches, and master teachers in educational settings. Toward this end, faculty and staff members and students within the department value diversity; pursue reflective inquiry; apply problem-solving strategies; promote innovative, interdisciplinary educational practice; effectively integrate technology; and collaboratively support and assist colleagues within the professional areas of special education, reading, educational counseling, supervision, and educational administration. The School of Education is accredited by the Council for Accreditation of Counseling and Related Educational Programs (CACREP).

Master of Arts in Teaching (M.A.T.): William Stanley, Program Director and Professor of Education; Ed.D., Rutgers. Sarah Moore, Program Coordinator; M.A.Ed., Georgian Court.

The Master of Arts in Teaching (M.A.T.) provides initial certification in five program areas: early childhood (P–3), elementary education (K–5), elementary education and middle school specialization (K–8), secondary content certification (9–12), and elementary and secondary education (K–12). Programs have been designed to emphasize state and national curriculum standards and research-based best practices. The M.A.T. program ensures that its candidates are well prepared with appropriate knowledge, skills, and understanding in order to improve learning in educational systems through a commitment to lifelong learning and responsiveness to communities that represent diverse viewpoints, cultures, and learning styles. The M.A.T. program is offered in part-time, full-time, and accelerated formats. The School of Education is accredited by the National Council for Accreditation of Teacher Education (NCATE).

Master of Business Administration (M.B.A.): Douglas Stives, Program Director of the M.B.A. Program and Specialist Professor; M.B.A., CPA, Lehigh.

The comprehensive M.B.A. program provides a balance of theory and practice. Students learn the business disciplines as well as specific organizational functions. Current issues and realistic applications of skill and knowledge are discussed with prominent business executives who serve as visiting lecturers and adjunct professors. The program requires between 30 and 48 credit hours of study, depending on the student's background. The M.B.A. program is offered in part-time, full-time, and accelerated formats.

Master of Arts in Criminal Justice (M.A.): Gregory J. Coram, Program Director and Associate Professor; Psy.D., Indiana State.

The program offers a broad perspective on the criminal justice system and its various institutions and processes. The curriculum offers tracks in administration and in homeland security. The administration track prepares criminal justice professionals or precareer students for supervisory and administrative roles. The track in homeland security prepares individuals to assist in preventing, anticipating, and preparing for natural and man-made catastrophic events. This track will also provide opportunities for criminal justice professionals to work with federal, state, and local governmental agencies. In addition, trained professionals are finding many new opportunities in the private sector, protecting large multi-national companies and organizations.

Master of Arts in Corporate and Public Communication (M.A.): Sheila McAllister-Spooner, Program Director and Assistant Professor of Communication; Ph.D., Rutgers.

The program prepares students to become effective communication specialists in a number of fields, from interpersonal communication to mass media. Specialist certificates are available in human resources communication, public relations, and public service communication.

Master of Social Work (M.S.W.): Rosemary Barbera, Program Director, Associate Professor, and Associate Director of the Institute for Global Understanding; M.S.W., Ph.D., Bryn Mawr.

The program prepares students for professional practice aimed at improving the quality of life for vulnerable individuals, families, and communities, both locally and internationally. Social workers with master's degrees gain access to a new world of career opportunities, including licensing (either the License of Social Work or the License of Clinical Social Work) and specialized practice. The program offers two concentrations—one in services to families and children and one in international and community development.

Master of Arts in English (M.A.): Heide Estes, Program Director and Associate Professor of English; Ph.D., NYU.

The courses at Monmouth provide a broad education in English literature and a sound foundation for further graduate study. Secondary school teachers can fulfill their continuing education requirements and accrue credits toward salary increases by taking courses in the program. Those interested in personal enrichment or career advancement find that the course work improves critical-thinking abilities along with reading, speaking, and writing skills. To broaden the options for students in the program, four concentrations are offered: literature, creative writing, rhetoric and writing, and New Jersey studies.

Master of Arts in Public Policy (M.A.): Katherine Kloby, Program Director and Assistant Professor of Political Science; Ph.D., Rutgers.

The Master of Arts in public policy is a 30-credit program that appeals to those who wish to work in the public interest. The program focuses on the role of ethics in public policy and provides opportunities for experiential learning internships. Students can learn about the public policy process and policy analysis, improve critical thinking, increase oral and written communication skills, and develop research skills.

Master of Science in Financial Mathematics (M.S.F.M.): Joseph Coyle, Program Director and Associate Professor of Mathematics; Ph.D., Dayton.

The Master of Science in Financial Mathematics (M.S.F.M.) is for those seeking careers in major banking, insurance, and financial services companies. This 36-credit program integrates mathematics with financial analysis to produce graduates who are ready to enter a sophisticated workforce and employ an interdisciplinary experience that brings together the fields of mathematics, finance, and computational modeling or simulation. The curriculum is designed for those who wish to find employment as economists or statisticians, or those seeking careers in related fields.

NEW MEXICO INSTITUTE OF MINING AND TECHNOLOGY

Graduate Studies

Programs of Study

New Mexico Institute of Mining and Technology offers graduate courses and research opportunities leading to the M.S. degree in biology, chemistry, computer science, electrical engineering, mechanical engineering, civil and environmental engineering, geochemistry, geology, geophysics, hydrology, materials engineering, mathematics, mineral engineering, petroleum engineering, and physics. A Master of Engineering Management is also offered, as is a Master of Science for teachers (licensed K–12 teachers with at least one year of teaching experience).

The Institute offers programs of study and research leading to the Ph.D. degree in chemistry, computer science, geochemistry, geology, geophysics, hydrology, materials engineering, mathematics, petroleum engineering, and physics.

The Master of Engineering Management program is designed for engineers and applied scientists with work experience; offered both on campus and via Internet streaming.

The Master of Science for Teachers degree program is designed to provide classroom and laboratory instruction for teachers of science, mathematics, engineering, and/or technology. The emphasis is on content rather than pedagogy in the areas of geology, biology, chemistry, physics, mathematics, computer science, and technical communication. Courses are offered throughout the year via distance education and as live courses at the NMT campus and around the state. The teacher must select either a thesis (6 credits) or an independent study (3 credits) program under the guidance of an adviser and advisory committee.

The Institute is strongly research-oriented in fields of study dealing with natural physical resources, such as the atmosphere and water. Some research topics are hydrology and geofluids, geochemistry, volcanology (the Southwest and Antarctic), continental tectonics, fault mechanics, stratigraphy and sedimentation, economic geology, mineral exploration and recovery (including the biology and chemistry of leaching), fuel and energy research (petroleum exploration and production, geothermal, and environmental considerations, including carbon sequestration), climate change, nuclear and hazardous-waste hydrology, enhanced oil recovery, explosives (including the effect of high energized and strain rates on materials), mine ventilation and fire control, cave studies, seismological crustal studies, geotechnical and soil mechanics, environmental engineering, thunderstorm electrification and cloud physics, stellar and extragalactic processes, radio astronomy, atmospheric chemistry, and supporting information technology and computer security.

Research Facilities

Graduate research opportunities are supported by a number of on-campus research groups, such as the Bureau of Geology, the Petroleum Recovery Research Center, and the Research and Development Office, including the Geophysical Research Center (geophysics, hydrology, and climatology) and a Center for Explosives Technology Research. Special facilities include the Langmuir Laboratory for Atmospheric Research (for studies of lightning, atmospheric physics, chemistry, and air quality), the Magdalena Ridge Observatory, Waldo Experimental Mines, and the EMRTC Field Laboratory for explosives research. There are also materials characterization laboratories for structure/property correlation (TEM, SEM, EPMA, FIM, AFM, and mechanical testing). The Very Large Array Radio Telescope and the Very Large Baseline Array, both facilities of the National Radio Astronomy Observatory, are headquartered on the campus. Cooperative research opportunities are available with the Sandia National Laboratories and Kirtland Air Force Base in Albuquerque and with Los Alamos National Laboratory, as well as numerous government agencies. Modern computer and library facilities and a wide range of analytical equipment are available, including a liquid scintillation spectrometer, a stable isotope mass spectrometer, automated XRF and XRD spectrometers, a microprobe, a geochronology Ar/Ar laboratory, NMR spectrometers, a quadruple mass spectrometer, FT-IR UV/vis, fluorescence and GC/M spectrometers, GCs, HPLCs, DSC, seismological equipment, a thunderstorm-penetrating airplane, instrumented balloons and rockets, cloud physics radar, a fluid inclusion laboratory, and a quantitative mineralogy laboratory.

Financial Aid

In 2011, minimum stipends varied from $18,356 for nine months for beginning M.S. assistants to $40,900 for doctoral students who were on twelve-month appointments and had completed candidacy requirements.

Cost of Study

Tuition (based on a 12-credit-hour load) per semester for 2011–12 is $2424 for residents and $8020 for nonresidents. Those with teaching/research appointments qualify for resident tuition.

Living and Housing Costs

The cost of room and board for single students living in residence halls in 2011–12 is approximately $3500 per semester. Housing for married students started at approximately $600 per month for unfurnished one- or two-bedroom efficiency apartments. Housing in Socorro is also available.

Student Group

Tech has approximately 2,500 students, of whom about 600 are graduate students. About 51 percent of graduate students are women. International students from thirty-five countries constitute 10 percent of the student body.

Location

Socorro (population 9,000) is located in the Rio Grande Valley, in central New Mexico, 75 miles south of Albuquerque on Interstate 25. The campus is at an elevation of 1,400 meters. Nearby mountains reach 3,280 meters in elevation. The principal sources of income in New Mexico are scientific research, agriculture, minerals (including petroleum, copper, potash, and coal), lumbering, and tourism. New Mexico's cultural diversity provides an unusual political and social environment. Historic sites, ghost towns, and ancient Indian ruins are all within a short driving distance of the campus.

The Institute

New Mexico Tech, which started as the New Mexico School of Mines in 1889, has achieved international recognition in petroleum engineering, materials engineering, atmospheric physics, geosciences, mineral-resource engineering, and explosives technology. Its faculty is outstanding in such diverse areas as astrophysics, atmospheric physics, biomedical research, seismology, geochemistry, economic geology, mineral exploration, groundwater hydrology, bacteria leaching of ores, laser and ion surface modification, intermetallics, ceramic and metal matrix composites, solid oxide fuel cells, capacitor dielectrics and high-temperature superconductors, and all areas of chemistry and petroleum recovery.

Applying

Tech encourages interested people who have a bachelor's or master's degree from an accredited college and a record indicating potential for advanced study and research in science or engineering to apply for admission. Transcripts of previous college work, references from 3 professors and/or professionals, and GRE General Test and Subject Test scores are required. International students must also submit TOEFL scores.

Correspondence and Information

Lorie M. Liebrock
Dean of Graduate Studies
New Mexico Institute of Mining and Technology
801 Leroy Place
Socorro, New Mexico 87801
Phone: 505-835-5513
800-428-TECH (8324; toll-free)
E-mail: graduate@nmt.edu
Web site: http://www.nmt.edu

THE FACULTY AND THEIR RESEARCH

Biology. S. Rogelj, Chair: cell, cell adhesion, molecular biology, biosensors, nanoparticles, biofilms, antimicrobial materials, pathogen detection. T. Kieft: environmental biology, microbiology. K. Kirk: evolutionary ecology. J. Naik: vascular physiology, blood-flow control. R. Reiss: molecular biology and evolution. S. Shors: viral immunology.

Chemistry. A Kornienko, Chairman: organic chemistry, medicinal chemistry. J. Altig: physical chemistry, computational chemistry, chemical education. M. Heagy: organic chemistry, fluorescence, physical organic chemistry. I. Janser: organic chemistry, chemistry in aqueous media. M. Pullin: environmental chemistry, geochemistry. O. Wingenter: atmospheric chemistry.

Civil and Environmental Engineering. M. P. Cal, Chairman: air pollution engineering, fate and transport of pollutants, water resources engineering. P. V. Brady: aquatic chemistry, global change, groundwater remediation. Y. Dong: structural engineering. F. Y. C. Huang: hazardous waste management, biological and chemical waste treatment, environmental systems modeling, risk assessment. C. P. Richardson:water resources engineering, biological wastewater treatment, groundwater contamination, site remediation. C. Wilson: structural control, structural dynamics, earthquake engineering.

Computer Science (www.cs.nmt.edu). L. M. Liebrock, Chair: computer forensics, parallel processing, high-performance computing, well-posedness analysis, software security testing, visualization, information security. H. Clausen: operating systems and systems programming, broadband Internet, secure software construction. S. Mazumdar: databases, information systems, software integrity. D. Shin: access control, identity management, security engineering, software engineering. H. Soliman: computer networks, programming languages, sensor networks, fiber optics routing. A. Sung: computational intelligence, information security, bioinformatics. J. Zheng: wireless networking, computer architecture, image processing.

Earth and Environmental Science (www.ees.nmt.edu). G. Axen, Chairman: continental tectonics and fault mechanics; extensional, convergent, and wrench settings. J. Assad (visiting professor): petroleum exploration, geophysics. R. C. Aster: earthquake and volcanic seismology and seismic structure. S. Bilek: earthquake rupture processes, tsunami generation, fault-zone material properties. P. Boston: cave and karst studies, geomicrobiology, extraterrestrial life. A. R. Campbell: metallic ore deposits, stable isotope geochemistry, carbon sequestration. K. Condie: trace element and isotope geochemistry, Precambrian studies. B. Harrison: soil properties, recurrence intervals of earthquakes, soil salinization in arid environments, soil stability. J. Hendrickx: soil water physics, vadose zone hydrology, soil contamination. D. B. Johnson: biostratigraphy, pleozoic depositional environments. J. B. Johnson: volcano geophysics, infrasound, volcanic monitoring. P. R. Kyle: igneous geochemistry, antarctic geology, volcanology. W. C. McIntosh: argon geochronology, Cenozoic volcanism in southwestern U.S. and Antarctica. P. S. Mozley: environmental and petroleum geology, sedimentary petrology, low-temperature geochemistry, carbon sequestration. M. Murray (research faculty): geodesy (GPS) and active tectonics, volcano deformation. M. Person: paleohydrology, basin-scale numerical modeling, geothermal systems, role of groundwater in geologic processes. F. M. Phillips: groundwater chemistry, isotope hydrology, groundwater dating, quaternary studies. D. Reusch (research faculty): paleoclimatology, climate change and modeling, artificial neural network applications in geoscience. G. Spinelli: hydrogeology of oceanic lithosphere, groundwater–surface water interactions, sediment physical properties, sedimentology. D. Ulmer-Scholle (research faculty): carbonate diagenesis, fluid and thermal histories of carbonate basins, diagenesis. J. L. Wilson: groundwater hydrology, numerical and analytic modeling, stochastic hydrology, colloid and bacterial transport.

Electrical Engineering. K. Wedeward, Chairman: control and power systems. R. Arechiga: speech recognition. A. Jorgensen: optical interferometry techniques and astronomical instrumentation. R. Bond: design for test/manufacturability, teaching effectiveness. E. Calloni (adjunct): gravitational wave interferometry. A. El-Osery: wireless communications, control systems, soft computing. H. Erives: integration and calibration of hyperspectral and multispectral space sensors, airborne and space-borne image analysis. P. Krehbiel (adjunct): lightning, thunderstorms, radar. G. Mansfield (adjunct): radar systems. J. Meason (adjunct): nuclear, electromagnetic, and space radiation effects and directed energy. D. Reicher (adjunct): physics and simulation of thin films. S. R. Restaino (adjunct): adaptive optics, novel optical systems. W. Rison: atmospheric electricity, instrumentation, lightning protection. S. W. Teare: experimental adaptive optics, radiation effects on semiconductors, directed energy. R. Thomas (research): lightning, thunderstorms, and instrumentation. D. Wick (adjunct): experimental adaptive and active optics. H. Xiao (adjunct): photonic/fiber sensors, intelligent sensor networks, optical communications, computer vision.

Mechanical Engineering. W. Ostergren, Chairman: mechanics of materials, structural anlaysis, machine design, propulsion and power systems. S. Bakhtiyarov: non-Newtonian fluid mechanics, heat and mass transfer, rheology. J. Ford: technical communication, writing within engineering, organizational communication. P. Gerity: robotics, system integration, technology turnkey and licensing. A. Ghosh: macrobehavior of composites, biomechanics, finite element analysis. D. Grow: haptic technologies, robotics, dynamic modeling. A. R. Miller: finite element analysis, explosive synthesis of materials, high-temperature system and simulation, actuators and actuator controls. A. K. Miller: system dynamics, system modeling and simulation, nonlinear reduced order models, distributed turbulent pressure loads. K. Salehpoor: biomedical engineering (artificial organs, design of biomedical devices and implants, blood flow, prevention of hemolysis and blood coagulation in biomedical devices). N. Yilmaz: computational fluid dynamics, reactive flow, combustion and chemical kinetics, fire modeling, internal combustion engines. A. Zagrai: intelligent systems, structures and mechanisms, structural monitoring and infrastructure security.

Materials Engineering. B. Majumdar, Chairman: mechanisms and mechanics of deformation and fracture, thin films and interfaces, composites, advanced alloys. T. D. Burleigh: corrosion mechanisms and mechanisms of corrosion protection. P. Fuierer: electronic ceramics, magnetic ceramics, sol-gel thin films. D. Hirschfeld: engineering ceramics and advanced composites, processing, protective coatings, thermal spray, solid free-form fabrication. N. Kalugin: optoelectronics and nonlinear optics, nanostructures and nanotechnology, TeraHz lasers and photodetectors, solid-state physics of nanostructures, semiconductor materials and devices. C. Leclerc: biofuel conversion and production, thermo-catalysis, catalyst characterization, hydrogen production, aqueous phase reforming, millisecond contact time reactors.J. McCoy: polymer blends, phase transitions, interfaces. M. Tartis: lipid particle characterization, biomedical imaging, prodrugs, liposomes, microbubbles, ultrasound, fluorescence microscopy. Adjunct faculty: Browning, Curro, Hockensmith, Jacobson, Lowe, Ravi, Romig, Sickafus, Smith.

Mathematics. A. Hossain, Chairman: theory and applications of statistics, estimation, reliability and regression diagnostics. R. Altbayev: numerical partial differential equations, numerical analysis. I. Avramidi: geometric analysis, mathematical physics, quantum field theory, differential geometry. B. Borchers: optimization, inverse problems. G. Kerr: thermoelasticity, integral equations. O. Makhnin: stochastic processes, spatial statistics, computational statistics, time series. S. Schaffer: applied mathematics, numerical analysis, control theory. J. Starrett: dynamical systems, physics models, knot theory. W. D. Stone: differential equations, mathematical biology, industrial mathematics. B. Wang: partial differential equations, dynamical systems, applied mathematics.

Mineral Engineering. N. Mojtabai, Chairman: drilling and blasting, ground vibration analysis, mine planning and equipment selection, site investigation, rock slope stability, tunneling, computer applications. R. Abernathy: numerical modeling, computer application in explosive engineering. C. Aimone-Martin: drilling and blasting, vibration analysis. W. X. Chavez: mineral economics, ore mineralogy and petrology, applied mineral exploration and field mapping, mine waste characterization, ore deposits, natural resource utilization. A. Fahkimi: numerical modeling, code development, computer applications, geomechanics. C. Hockensmith: explosive engineering. V. McLemore: economic geology, industrial minerals. M. Razavi: soil mechanics, geotechnical engineering, computer applications, image possessing and photogrametry, X-ray computer tomography, soil-structure interaction, ground improvement, computer applications. C. Wimberly: natural resources law.

Petroleum and Chemical Engineering. T. Engler, Chairman, Petroleum Engineering: formation evaluation, petrophysics, unconventionial gas recovery. R. Balch: geophysics, artificial intelligence, reservoir characterization. J. Buckley: petrophysics and surface chemistry, reservoir wettability. H. Y. Chen: well testing, reservoir mechanics. R. Grigg: gas flooding processes, phase behavior. M. Kelly: well testing, production, and pressure transients; tight gas reservoirs; small production company operations. R. Lee: natural gas storage, applied numerical methods, phase behavior. T. Nguyen: drilling, advanced fluid mechanics, artificial lift. R. Seright: profile control, polymer, water and chemical flooding.

Physics. K. Eack, Chairman: production of energetic particles and gamma rays in thunderstorms. I. Avramidi: mathematical physics, analysis on manifolds, quantum field theory. K. Balasubramanian: spectroscopy and polarized radiative transfer dynamics for solar active regions, vector magnetometry. D. Buscher: optical/IR interferometry, atmospheric seeing measurement, adaptive optics, early and late stages of stellar evolution. S. Colgate: astrophysics, plasma physics, atmospheric physics. M. Creech-Eakman: stellar astrophysics, mass loss, optical/IR interferometry, IR instrumentation. J. Eilek: plasma astrophysics, quasars, radio galaxies, pulsars. M. Goss: radio astronomy, interstellar medium. C. Haniff: spatial interferometry at optical and near-infrared wavelengths, atmospheric turbulence, imaging theory, evolved stars. T. Hankins: radio astronomy of pulsars, instrumentation, signal processing. P. Hofner: star formation, interstellar medium, X-ray astronomy. R. M. Juberias: outer planets observations and atmospheric dynamics. D. Klinglesmith: asteroids, robotic telescope operations. P. Krehbiel: lightning studies, radar meteorology, thunderstorm electrification, remote sensing. G. Manney: atmospheric science, stratospheric dynamics/transport, stratospheric polar processes and ozone loss. J. Meason: nuclear physics, nuclear and space radiation effects, electromagnetic radiation effects and directed energy. D. Meier: astrochemistry in galaxies and star formation in dwarf/starburst galaxies. K. Minschwaner: radiative transfer and climate, physics of the middle and upper atmosphere. S. Myers: cosmology, extragalactic radio astronomy, interferometric imaging algorithms. D. Raymond: geophysical fluid dynamics, cloud physics, clouds and climate. W. Rison: atmospheric electricity, radar meteorology, instrumentation. V. Romereo: energetic materials, shock phenomena, high-energy physics. M. Rupen: gas and dust in galaxies, radio transients. E. Ryan: asteroid collisional physics, observational and theoretical studies. W. Ryan: asteroid astronomy, high-energy physics. S. Sessions: field theoretic approaches to atmospheric physics. R. Sonnenfeld: charge transport by lightning, embedded systems and instrumentation, tribocharging of ice. G. Taylor: very long baseline radio astronomy, active galactic nuclei. S. Teare: adaptive optics, instrumentation, astrophysics. R. Thomas: atmospheric physics, instrumentation. J. Ulvestad: compact radio sources, Seyfert galaxies, AGNs, space, VLBI techniques and future missions. D. Westpfahl: dynamics of spiral and dwarf galaxies. W. Winn: thunderstorm electrification, electric discharges in gases, instrumentation. L. Young: star formation and the interstellar medium, dwarf and elliptical galaxies.

Macey Conference Center and Turtle Bay.

NORTH DAKOTA STATE UNIVERSITY

Graduate School

Programs of Study

North Dakota State University (NDSU) offers the Doctor of Philosophy (Ph.D.), Doctor of Nursing Practice (D.N.P.), Doctor of Education (Ed.D.), Doctor of Musical Arts (D.M.A.), Master of Architecture (M. Arch.), Master of Arts (M.A.), Master of Business Administration (M.B.A.), Master of Education (M.Ed.), Master of Engineering (M.Eng.), Master of Music (M.M.), Master of Natural Resource Science (M.N.R.M.), Master of Science (M.S.), Master of Software Engineering (M.S.E.), Master of Transportation and Urban Systems (M.T.U.S.), Master of Athletic Training (M.A.Trg.), Master of Accountancy (M. Acct.) and Educational Specialist (Ed.S.) degrees.

The College of Agriculture, Food Systems, and Natural Resources offers the M.S. in agricultural and biosystems engineering, agricultural economics, animal and range sciences, cereal science, entomology, horticulture, international agribusiness, microbiology, plant pathology, plant sciences, range science, and soil science; the Ph.D. is offered in agricultural and biosystems engineering, animal sciences, cereal science, entomology, molecular pathogenesis, plant pathology, plant sciences, range science, and soil science.

The College of Arts, Humanities, and Social Sciences offers the master's degree in community development, criminal justice, emergency management, English, history, mass communication, music, anthropology, sociology, and speech communication; the Ph.D. is offered in communication, criminal justice, emergency management, history, rhetoric, writing, and culture; and the D.M.A. is offered in music.

The College of Business Administration offers the Master of Business Administration (M.B.A.) and the Master of Accountancy (M. Acct.) degrees.

The College of Engineering and Architecture offers the M.S. in agricultural and biosystems engineering, civil engineering, construction management and engineering, electrical engineering, environmental engineering, industrial engineering and management, manufacturing engineering, and mechanical engineering and the Ph.D. in agricultural and biosystems engineering, civil engineering, electrical and computer engineering, industrial and manufacturing engineering, and mechanical engineering. The Master of Engineering (M.Eng.) and the Master of Architecture (M.Arch.) are also offered.

The College of Human Development and Education offers the master's degree in agricultural education, human development and family science, counseling education, educational leadership, family and consumer sciences education, merchandising, health, nutrition and exercise sciences, and secondary education; the Master of Athletic Training (M.A.Trg.); the Ph.D. in human development and in education; and the Ed.D. in education. Certificates may be earned in family financial planning, gerontology, and merchandising. The Educational Specialist degree may be earned in education leadership.

The College of Pharmacy offers both the M.S. and Ph.D. in pharmaceutical sciences, the M.S. in nursing, and the D.N.P. in nursing practice.

The College of Science and Mathematics offers the M.S. in biochemistry, biology, botany, coatings and polymeric materials, chemistry, computer science, mathematics, physics, psychology, software engineering, statistics, and zoology and the Ph.D. in biochemistry, botany, chemistry, coatings and polymeric materials, computer science, mathematics, physics, psychology, psychological clinical science, software engineering, statistics, and zoology. The Master of Software Engineering (M.S.E.) degree is also offered. Certificate programs are available in software engineering, statistics, and digital enterprise.

The following programs are offered as interdisciplinary degrees: M.S. in environmental and conservation sciences, food safety, genomics and bioinformatics, natural resources management, and transportation and urban systems. The Master of Managerial Logistics (M.M.L.), Master of Natural Resources Management (M.N.R.M.), and Master of Transportation and Urban Systems (M.T.U.S.) are also offered. The Ph.D. is available in cellular and molecular biology; environmental and conservation sciences; food safety; genomics and bioinformatics; materials and nanotechnology; natural resources management; science, technology, engineering, mathematics (STEM); and transportation and logistics. Certificates are available in college teaching, food protection, transportation and leadership, and transportation and urban systems.

In addition, some graduate degrees (listed below) are available by distance coursework. Students enrolled in an on-campus degree program may choose to take a few distance and continuing education graduate-level online courses to minimize the number of classes they need to take on campus. Students need to check with their adviser to ensure the class will apply to their degree program.

The Great Plains Interactive Distance Education Alliance (Great Plains IDEA) is a consortium of human sciences colleges at eleven universities that can help students reach their goals. Each university brings a unique strength to the multi-institution academic programs. In a multi-institution degree program, students apply and are admitted at one university, enroll in all courses at that university, and graduate or receive a certificate from that university.

All graduate degrees offered through NDSU distance and continuing education or Great Plains IDEA degrees taken through NDSU are awarded an NDSU degree upon successful completion of coursework.

The following degree programs are available online: Master of Software Engineering (M.S.E.); M.S. or M.A. in mass communication; M.S. or M.A. in speech communication; M.S. in construction management; M.S. or M.A. in community development (Great Plains IDEA); M.S. in family and consumer sciences education (Great Plains IDEA); M.S. in health, nutrition, and exercise science: dietetics option (Great Plains IDEA); M.S. in human development and family science: family financial planning option (Great Plains IDEA); M.S. in human development and family science: gerontology option (Great Plains IDEA); M.S. in human development and family science: youth development option (Great Plains IDEA); and M.S. in merchandising (Great Plains IDEA).

The following graduate certificates are available through NDSU online: family financial planning certificate (Great Plains IDEA), food protection certificate, gerontology certificate (Great Plains IDEA), merchandising certificate (Great Plains IDEA), software engineering certificate, and transportation leadership graduate certificate.

Research Facilities

NDSU possesses state-of-the-art facilities in magnetic resonance imaging, high-performance computing, electron microscopy, and computer chip assembly. Located on campus, a Research and Technology Park houses both academic research units and industrial partners, strengthening links between the University and technology-based companies. Research specializations in a wide variety of disciplines have resulted in the establishment of centers, some of which are the Center of Nanoscale Science and Engineering, NSF Coatings Cooperative Research Center, the Bio-imaging and Sensing Center, the Center for Protease Research, the Quentin Burdick Center for Cooperatives, the Center for Agricultural Policy and Trade Studies, the Great Plains Institute of Food Safety, the Upper Great Plains Transportation Institute, and the Institute for Regional Studies. As the state's land-grant institution, NDSU houses the North Dakota Agricultural Experiment Station and Extension Service, with eight research and extension centers located across the state. An Internet2 institution, NDSU provides high-speed network access to classrooms and desktops, an Access Grid facility for global virtual conferencing, and high-speed connections to other universities and federal agencies for research and distance education. Library resources include current electronic and print subscriptions, and an extensive array of specialized, full-text electronic databases, as well as an online catalog that interfaces with other regional, national, and international library catalogs.

Financial Aid

Graduate teaching and research assistantships are awarded to qualified students upon recommendations from individual departments and include tuition waivers for all graduate credits. Approximately half of the graduate students are awarded graduate assistantships. Student activity fees are not waived. Stipend amounts vary widely by discipline. North Dakota's very successful National Science Foundation EPSCoR program is centered at NDSU; it provides generous funding for graduate education through dissertation fellowships and stipends. For more information, students should contact the Financial Aid Office (phone: 701-231-7533).

Cost of Study

In 2010–11, tuition per credit, through 12 credits, was $251.98 for North Dakota residents; $308.96 for Minnesota residents; $365.16 for residents of Saskatchewan, Manitoba, Indiana, Kansas, Michigan, Missouri, Nebraska, Wisconsin, South Dakota, and Montana; and $672.18 for other students. Student fees per credit, through 12 credits, were $42.57 in 2010–11.

Living and Housing Costs

Apartments for families, as well as single-occupancy units, are located near the University campus in University Village. For residence hall life, the combined room and meal plan cost approximately $6530 per academic year. Housing, utility, and food expenses for 2 people are estimated at $9300 on campus and $9400 off campus.

Student Group

Current enrollment at NDSU is more than 12,000 students on the central campus in Fargo. NDSU also serves several thousand people throughout the state in continuing education and extension programs. Graduate student enrollment is over 2,200 students. International students make up approximately 25 percent of the graduate student population, providing a wealth of diversity within both the academic and local communities.

Student Outcomes

North Dakota State University graduates more than 350 master's students and 70 Ph.D. students each year.

Location

With more than 200,000 people, Fargo-Moorhead is the largest metropolitan center between Minneapolis and Seattle and is nestled in the Red River Valley, which is rich in fertile farmlands. In Fargo-Moorhead, three universities and the technical colleges provide a wide variety of educational opportunities, while the community offers access to part-time jobs, internships, parks and other recreational facilities, entertainment, and cultural amenities.

The University

NDSU, the state's land-grant institution, was established in 1890. It is one of the two research institutions within North Dakota's university system of five 2-year schools, three 4-year schools, and four graduate institutions. NDSU is a comprehensive university that offers nationally recognized programs of study within a student-friendly community. Sixty-four master's programs, forty-four doctoral programs, nine certificate programs, and an Educational Administration (Ed.S.) Specialist program are offered. Over 100 undergraduate majors are offered.

Applying

All application materials are due one month before registration for U.S. students; some departments have earlier deadlines. For international students, the completed application packet (application form, application fee, official transcripts, three letters of reference, and statement of purpose) and required test scores should be received by the Graduate School by May 1 for the fall semester and August 1 for the spring semester. Please note that some departments require earlier application deadlines for graduate assistantships.

Correspondence and Information

The Graduate School
North Dakota State University
Dept. 2820
P.O. Box 6050
Fargo, North Dakota 58108

Phone: 701-231-7033
Fax: 701-231-6524
E-mail: ndsu.grad.school@ndsu.edu
Web site: http://www.ndsu.edu/gradschool
http://www.ndsu.edu

THE FACULTY

Listed below are North Dakota State University's deans, graduate degree programs, and corresponding phone numbers and e-mail addresses.

College of Agriculture, Food Systems, and Natural Resources: Ken Grafton, Ph.D.
Agribusiness and Applied Economics: 701-231-7466. (E-mail: robert.hearne@ndsu.edu)
Agricultural and Biosystems Engineering: 701-231-7274. (E-mail: lori.sholts@ndsu.edu)
Animal and Range Sciences: 701-231-8386. (E-mail: gregory.lardy@ndsu.nodak.edu)
Cereal and Food Sciences: 701-231-7712. (E-mail: deland.myers@ndsu.edu)
Entomology: 701-231-7902. (E-mail: marion.harris@ndsu.edu)
Horticulture: 701-231-7971. (E-mail: rhicard.horsley@ndsu.edu)
International Agribusiness: 701-231-7466. (E-mail: robert.hearne@ndsuext.nodak.edu)
Microbiology: 701-231-7511. (E-mail: eugene.berry@nsdu.edu)
Molecular Pathogenesis: 701-231-7511. (E-mail: eugene.berry@ndsu.edu)
Plant Pathology: 701-231-8362. (E-mail: jack.rasmussen@ndsu.edu)
Plant Sciences: 701-231-7971. (E-mail: richard.horsley@ndsu.edu)
Range Science: 701-231-8901. (E-mail: Kevin.sedivec@ndsu.edu)
Soil Science: 701-231-8903. (E-mail: frank.casey@ndsu.edu)

College of Arts, Humanities, and Social Sciences: Thomas Riley, Ph.D.
Anthropology: 701-231-7637. (E-mail: gary.goreham@ndsu.edu)
Communication: 701-231-7705. (E-mail for Ph.D.: judy.pearson@ndsu.edu; e-mail for master's: ross.collins@ndsu.edu)
Community Development: 701-231-7637. (E-mail: gary.goreham@ndsu.edu)
Criminal Justice: 701-231-8938. (E-mail: kevin.thompson@ndsu.edu)
Emergency Management: 701-231-8925. (E-mail: daniel.klenow@ndsu.edu)
English: 701-231-7147. (E-mail: kevin.brooks@ndsu.edu)
History: 701-231-8654. (E-mail: john.cox.1@ndsu.edu)
Mass Communication: 701-231-7705. (E-mail: ross.collins@ndsu.edu)
Musical Arts: 701-231-7932. (E-mail: ej.miller@ndsu.edu)
Rhetoric, Writing, and Culture: 701-231-7147. (E-mail: kevin.brooks@ndsu.edu)
Sociology: 701-231-8925. (E-mail: gary.goreham@ndsu.edu)
Speech Communication: 701-231-7705. (E-mail: ross.collins@ndsu.edu)

College of Business Administration: Ronald D. Johnson, Ph.D.
Business Administration: 701-231-8805. (E-mail: barb.geeslin@ndsu.edu)

College of Engineering and Architecture: Gary Smith, Ph.D.
Architecture: 701-231-5788. (E-mail: ganapathy.mahalingam@ndsu.edu)
Agricultural and Biosystems Engineering: 701-231-7261. (E-mail: lori.sholts@ndsu.edu)
Civil Engineering and Construction: 701-231-7245. (E-mail: kalpana.katti@ndsu.edu)
Construction Management and Engineering: 701-231-7879. (E-mail: charles.mcintyre@ndsu.edu)
Electrical and Computer Engineering: 701-231-7019. (E-mail: rajesh.kavasseri@ndsu.edu)
Engineering: 701-231-7494. (E-mail: gary.smith@ndsu.edu)
Environmental Engineering: 701-231-7245. (E-mail: kalpana.katti@ndsu.edu)
Industrial and Manufacturing Engineering: 701-231-7287. (E-mail: susan.l.peterson.2@ndsu.edu)
Manufacturing Engineering: 701-231-7287. (E-mail: susan.l.peterson.2@ndsu.edu)
Mechanical Engineering: 701-231-5859. (E-mail: g.karami@ndsu.edu)

College of Graduate and Interdisciplinary Programs: David Wittrock, Ph.D.
Cellular and Molecular Biology: 701-231-8110. (E-mail: mark.sheridan@ndsu.edu)
College Teaching: 701-231-7496. (E-mail for certificate: donald.schwert@ndsu.edu)
Environmental and Conservation Sciences: 701-231-8449. (E-mail: craig.stockwell@ndsu.edu)
Food Protection: 701-231-6359. (E-mail for certificate: charlene.hall@ndsu.edu)
Food Safety: 701-231-6359. (E-mail for certificate: charlene.kuss@ndsu.edu)
Genomics & Bioinformatics: 701-231-8443. (E-mail: phillip.mcclean@ndsu.edu)
Materials and Nontechnology: 701-231-7033. (E-mail: erik.hobbie@ndsu.edu)
Natural Resources Management: 701-231-8180. (E-mail: carolyn.grygiel@ndsu.edu)
STEM Education: 701-231-8221. (E-mail: donald.schwert@ndsu.edu)
Transportation and Logistics: 701-231-7190. (E-mail: jody.bohn@ndsu.edu)
Transportation and Urban Systems: 701-231-7190. (E-mail: jody.bohn@ndsu.edu)

College of Human Development and Education: Virginia Clark Johnson, Ph.D.
Human Development and Family Science: 701-231-8268. (E-mail: jim.deal@ndsu.edu)
Advanced Athletic Training: 701-231-8268. (E-mail: jim.deal@ndsu.edu)
Education Ph.D.: 701-231-7291. (E-mail: myron.eighmy@ndsu.edu)
Family Financial Planning: 701-231-8268. (E-mail for certificate: jim.deal@ndsu.edu)
Gerontology: 701-231-8268. (E-mail for certificate: jim.deal@ndsu.edu)
Health, Nutrition, and Exercise Sciences: 701-231-7474. (E-mail: gary.liguori@ndsu.edu or jim.deal@ndsu.edu)
Human Development: 701-231-8211. (E-mail: greg.sanders@ndsu.edu)
Merchandising: 701-231-8223. (E-mail for master's and certificate: holly.bastow-shoop@ndsu.edu)
School of Education: 701-231-7202. (E-mail: william.martin@ndsu.edu)
- Agricultural Education: 701-231-7439. (E-mail: brent.young@ndsu.edu)
- Counseling and Guidance (Counseling Education): 701-231-7676. (E-mail: jill.r.nelson@ndsu.edu)
- Educational Leadership: 701-231-9732. (E-mail: vicki.ihry@ndsu.edu)
- Family and Consumer Sciences Education: 701-231-7968. (E-mail: mari.borr@ndsu.edu)
- Secondary Education: 701-231-7108. (E-mail: justin.wageman@ndsu.edu)

College of Pharmacy: Charles Peterson, Ph.D.
Nursing: 701-231-7772. (E-mail: loretta.heuer@ndsu.edu)
Pharmaceutical Sciences: 701-231-7943. (E-mail: jagdish.singh@ndsu.edu)

College of Science and Mathematics: Kevin McCaul, Ph.D.
Biochemistry: 701-231-7413. (E-mail: gregory.cook@ndsu.edu)
Botany/Biology: 701-231-7087. (E-mail: william.bleier@ndsu.edu)
Chemistry: 701-231-7413. (E-mail: gregory.cook@ndsu.edu)
Coatings and Polymeric Materials: 701-231-7633. (E-mail: stuart.croll@ndsu.edu)
Computer Science: 701-231-8562. (E-mail: kendall.nygard@ndsu.edu)
Digital Enterprise: 701-231-8562. (E-mail for certificate: kendall.nygard@ndsu.edu)
Mathematics: 701-231-8561. (E-mail: ndsu.math@ndsu.edu)
Physics: 701-231-7049. (E-mail: dan.kroll@ndsu.edu)
Psychology: 701-231-8622. (E-mail: paul.rokke@ndsu.edu)
Psychological Clinical Science: 701-231-8622. (E-mail: paul.rokke@ndsu.edu)
Software Engineering: 701-231-8562. (E-mail for Ph.D., master's, and certificate: kenneth.magel@ndsu.edu)
Statistics: 701-231-7532. (E-mail for Ph.D., master's, and certificate: rhonda.magel@ndsu.edu)
Zoology: 701-231-7087. (E-mail: william.bleier@ndsu.edu)

QUEENS COLLEGE OF THE CITY UNIVERSITY OF NEW YORK

Graduate Programs in the Arts and Sciences

Programs of Study

Queens College (QC) offers programs of study leading to the Master of Arts in applied linguistics, art history, biology, chemistry, computer science, English literature, French, geology, history, Italian, mathematics, music, physics, psychology, psychology–behavioral neuroscience, sociology, Spanish, speech-language pathology, and urban affairs. Master of Science degrees are offered in accounting, applied environmental geoscience, nutrition and exercise science, and risk management. The interdisciplinary degrees of Master of Arts in Liberal Studies and Master of Arts in Social Sciences are also offered. The Master of Fine Arts degree is offered in English–creative writing and studio art. Master of Science in Education programs are available in bilingual elementary education, counselor education, early childhood education, elementary education, family and consumer sciences, literacy education (B–6 and 5–12), school psychology, secondary school education (art; English; French; general science–biology, chemistry, earth science, and physics; Italian; mathematics; music; physical education; social studies; and Spanish), special education (B–2, 1–6, and 7–12), and teaching English to speakers of other languages. Professional diplomas in applied behavior analysis, education, English language teaching, and school building leader are also offered.

For applicants who seek New York State provisional teacher certification but whose undergraduate programs did not include a background in education, the College offers postbaccalaureate advanced certificate programs in early childhood education, elementary education, and secondary education (art–visual arts, biology, chemistry, earth science, English, family and consumer science, French, Italian, mathematics, music, physical education, physics, social studies, and Spanish). Bilingual certification programs are available in counselor education, school psychology, and special education.

The Master of Library Science degree is available for public librarianship and school media specialist. Also offered are advanced certificates in archives and records management preservation and childhood/youth public library, and a post-master's advanced certificate in librarianship. All programs are accredited by the American Library Association. Concentrations in various areas also exist in a number of departments. Applicants should contact the Office of Graduate Admissions for more information.

Queens College is a major participant in the doctoral programs of the City University of New York (CUNY). Students interested in these programs should contact the CUNY Graduate Center, 365 Fifth Avenue, New York, New York 10016.

Research Facilities

QC's extensive laboratory facilities house state-of-the-art scientific instruments for research in biology, chemistry, computer science, geology, physics, psychology, and health and physical education. There is also a low-temperature physics laboratory. Computing equipment ranges from cutting-edge, high-technology personal computers to highly specialized minicomputers. There are diverse computer laboratories, including a well-equipped social science research laboratory. The Graduate School of Library and Information Studies maintains a fully integrated computer-intensive facility.

Gertz Speech and Hearing Center provides a facility for research and clinical practice experience in communicative disorders. The College is home to an electronic music studio and to one of the best music libraries on the East Coast. It also shares facilities with the American Museum of Natural History, Brookhaven National Laboratory, the Lamont-Doherty Geological Observatory, and leading hospitals. The Benjamin S. Rosenthal Library holds a print collection of approximately 900,000 volumes. The library subscribes to over 5,800 print and electronic periodicals and has online access to over 25,000 journal and periodical titles. The library also has a large (916,000 units) microform collection.

Financial Aid

A limited number of graduate fellowships, some requiring teaching and/or research, may be available from individual departments through the Office of the Assistant to the Provost for Graduate Admissions. Other kinds of financial aid include Board of Trustees partial tuition waivers, Federal Perkins Loans, the Federal Direct Student Loan Program, and Federal Work-Study Program awards. Applicants should contact the Financial Aid Office for information. The Cooperative Education Program helps students gain both academic credit and work experience in paid positions.

Cost of Study

In 2011–12, tuition per semester is $345 per credit (maximum $4105) for New York State residents and $640 per credit for nonresidents. Activity fees were additional.

Living and Housing Costs

The Summit, Queens College's first residence hall, opened in August 2009. The three-wing, 506-bed building, located in the heart of the campus, has rooms for study and music practice and a well-equipped exercise facility. The price per semester ranges from $4250 for accommodations in a shared bedroom to $7000 for a single bedroom. Each bedroom is in a multi-occupancy suite that includes a kitchenette, common living area, and a bath.

Student Group

Approximately 4,500 students are registered for master's and advanced certificate programs, and many CUNY doctoral students work under the direct supervision of Queens College faculty members. Students come from throughout the United States and from a number of other countries. The Graduate Student Association at Queens College, an elective body representing the interests of all graduate students, offers free help with income tax return preparation and legal counseling.

Location

Queens College is located close to the attractions of Manhattan. Opera, concerts, theater, and gallery and museum exhibits are accessible by public transportation; students can get tickets to many events at reduced prices. Parks and ocean beaches are nearby in Queens and on Long Island.

The College

Established in 1937, Queens College is a coeducational, publicly supported college with an emphasis on the liberal arts and sciences and education. It boasts an attractive, tree-lined, 77-acre campus that has some of the finest athletic facilities in the metropolitan area, including an Olympic-size pool and fully equipped fitness center. The College is home to the Kupferberg Center for the Arts, which schedules an extensive calendar of performances by internationally renowned artists. The beautiful LeFrak Concert Hall features a tracker organ and is the venue for the renowned Evening Readings series that brings to campus authors such as Toni Morrison, Salman Rushdie, Orhan Pamuk, and Margaret Atwood. Queens College administers the historic Louis Armstrong House Museum in Corona with its vast personal collection of Armstrong photographs, papers, recordings, and memorabilia that draws scholars and jazz fans from around the world. The Benjamin Rosenthal Library, with its soaring, light-filled atrium and art center, has more than 1 million print and electronic volumes.

Queens College is registered by the New York State Department of Education and accredited by the Middle States Association of Colleges and Schools. The American Association of Colleges for Teacher Education includes the College in its list of member colleges.

Applying

The admission decision is based on the baccalaureate record and evidence of the ability to pursue graduate work. Scores from the General Test and Subject Test of the Graduate Record Examinations are required for admission to certain programs. For fall semester admission, applications should be filed by April 1. For spring semester admission, applications should be filed by November 1 (not all programs admit students in the spring). Applications for school psychology must be filed by March 1 for fall admission (spring applications are not accepted). Applications for art studio must be filed by March 15 for fall admission and by October 15 for spring admission. Speech-language pathology applications must be filed by February 1 for fall admission (spring applications are not accepted). Counselor education applications must be submitted by March 1. Applications for English–creative writing must be filed by February 15 for fall admission (spring applications are not accepted). Applications for the postbaccalaureate advance certificate program in physical education (K–12) must be filed by March 1 for fall admission and by October 1 for spring admission. Financial aid applications should be filed as early as possible. This information is subject to change.

Correspondence and Information

For information about a particular program:
Chair (listed overleaf)
Department of (specify)
Queens College
Flushing, New York 11367

For admission and registration information:
Graduate Admissions Office
Queens College
Flushing, New York 11367
Phone: 718-997-5200
Fax: 718-997-5193
E-mail: graduate_admissions@qc.edu

For other information:
Office of Graduate Studies
Queens College
Flushing, New York 11367
Phone: 718-997-5190
Fax: 718-997-5198
E-mail: richard.bodnar@qc.cuny.edu

THE FACULTY

From its beginnings in 1937, Queens College has made every effort to build a faculty of dedicated teachers and scholars. The list of institutions that have conferred degrees on members of the faculty includes every major university in the United States and several major European universities. Faculty members have received numerous national and international awards and fellowships, as well as many sponsored research and training grants through the College's Office of Research and Sponsored Programs.

OFFICE OF GRADUATE STUDIES AND RESEARCH
Richard Bodnar, Ph.D., Acting Dean of Research and Graduate Studies.

OFFICE OF GRADUATE ADMISSIONS
Mario Caruso, M.A., Director of Graduate Admissions.

The following is a list of the heads of departments that offer graduate programs at the College. An asterisk (*) indicates that there is no master's or advanced certificate program in this area, but faculty members participate in the Ph.D. program at the CUNY Graduate Center. A dagger (†) indicates that the program is not currently accepting students.

DIVISION OF THE ARTS AND HUMANITIES
William McClure, Ph.D., Dean of the Faculty for the Arts and Humanities.

Art: Barbara Lane, Ph.D., Chair.
*__Classical, Middle Eastern, and Asian Languages and Cultures:__ Ammiel Alcalay (fall) and Joel Lidov (spring), Ph.D., Acting Chairs.
*__Comparative Literature:__ Ammiel Alcalay, Ph.D., Chair.
*__Drama, Dance, and Theatre:__ Charles Repole, Ph.D., Chair.
English: Glenn D. Burger, Ph.D., Chair.
European Languages and Literatures: David Andrew Jones, Ph.D., Chair.
Hispanic Languages and Literatures: Jose Martinez-Torrejon, Ph.D., Chair.
Linguistics and Communication Disorders: Robert Vago, Ph.D., Chair.
† **Media Studies:** Richard Maxwell, Ph.D., Chair.
Music: Edward Smaldone, Ph.D., Chair and Director, Aaron Copland School of Music.

DIVISION OF EDUCATION
Francine Peterman, Ph.D., Dean of the Faculty for Education.

Educational and Community Programs: Craig Michaels, Ph.D., Chair.
Elementary and Early Childhood Education and Services: Mary Bushnell Greiner, Ph.D., Chair.
Secondary Education and Youth Services: Eleanor Armour-Thomas, Ph.D., Chair.

DIVISION OF MATHEMATICS AND THE NATURAL SCIENCES
Larry Liebovitch, Ph.D., Dean of the Faculty for Mathematics and the Natural Sciences.

Biology: Pokay Ma, Ph.D., Chair.
Chemistry: Wilma Saffran, Ph.D., Chair.
Computer Science: Zhigang Xiang, Ph.D., Chair.
Earth and Environmental Sciences: Allan Ludman, Ph.D., Chair and Director, School of Earth and Environmental Sciences.
Family, Nutrition, and Exercise Sciences: Elizabeth Lowe, Ph.D., Chair.
Mathematics: Wallace Goldberg, Ph.D., Chair.
Physics: Alexander Lisyansky, Ph.D., Chair.
Psychology: Robert Lanson, Ph.D., Chair.

DIVISION OF THE SOCIAL SCIENCES
Elizabeth Hendrey, Ph.D., Dean of the Faculty for the Social Sciences.

Accounting and Information Systems: Israel Blumenfrucht, Ph.D., Chair.
*__Anthropology:__ Thomas Plummer, Ph.D., Chair.
† **Economics:** David Gabel, Ph.D., Chair.
History: Frank Warren, Ph.D., Chair.
Library Science: Thomas T. Surprenant, Ph.D., Chair and Director, Graduate School of Library and Information Studies.
† **Philosophy:** Stephen Grover, Ph.D., Chair.
† **Political Science:** Patricia Rachal, Ph.D., Chair.
Risk Management: Diane Coogan-Pushner, Ph.D., Coordinator.
Sociology: Andrew Beveridge, Ph.D., Chair.
Urban Studies: Leonard Rodberg, Ph.D., Chair.

INTERDISCIPLINARY STUDIES
Liberal Studies: James Jordon, Ph.D., Graduate Adviser.
Social Sciences: Martin Hanlon, Ph.D., Graduate Adviser.

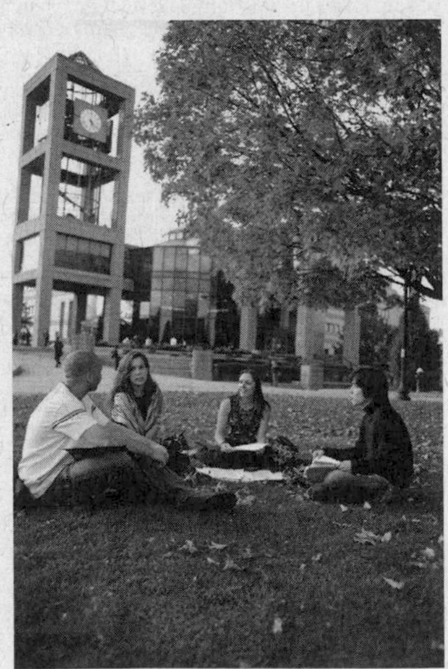

Queens College student learn inside and outside the classroom—taking full advantage of every learning opportunity.

Queens College is located just miles from Manhattan, and its 77-acre campus overlooks the New York City skyline—a unique suburban campus located within an exciting city.

ROBERT MORRIS UNIVERSITY

Programs of Study

Robert Morris University (RMU) offers more than twenty graduate degree programs, including ten master's programs available online. Doctoral programs include the Doctor of Science (D.Sc.) in information systems and communications, the Doctor of Philosophy (Ph.D.) in instructional management and leadership, and the Doctor of Nursing Practice (D.N.P.) offered as an adult nurse practitioner, family nurse practitioner, or adult psychiatric and mental health nurse practitioner, or as a completion of an existing master's degree. Master's programs available either online or on campus include the Master of Business Administration (M.B.A.) as well as Master of Science (M.S.) degrees in business education, competitive intelligence systems, engineering management, instructional leadership, Internet information systems, and organizational leadership. On-campus programs include a Master of Education (M.Ed.) in special education and M.S. programs in communications and information systems, information security and assurance, information systems management, IT project management, and taxation; M.S. degrees in human resource management and nonprofit management as well as the M.S.N. in nursing are solely online. Postbaccalaureate certification programs are also available for secondary and elementary teachers as well as instructional technology specialists.

The University is accredited by the Middle States Association of Colleges and Schools. RMU schools and programs are also accredited by the Association to Advance Collegiate Schools of Business International, the Teacher Education Accreditation Council, ABET Inc., and the Commission on Collegiate Nursing Education.

Research Facilities

Facilities supporting the graduate programs at Robert Morris University include nine open-access computer laboratories, two physical libraries, and an electronic library offering an array of research databases. Classrooms have been equipped with advanced computer and presentation technology equipment to facilitate teaching and learning.

To support a large number of holdings, the library has a state-of-the-art searchable catalog system. The RMU Electronic Library offers continual off-campus access to more than 100 major research databases. The library is a member of numerous resource-sharing consortia that greatly extend the amount of materials available to support graduate education.

Financial Aid

Graduate loans are available for those who qualify. Students are encouraged to file the Free Application for Federal Student Aid (FAFSA). Robert Morris University participates in the Federal Family Education Loan (FFEL) Program and also offers various interest-free payment plans.

Cost of Study

Tuition for the 2011–12 academic year for the M.B.A. program is $795 per credit. Tuition for the various M.S. programs is as follows: business, $775 per credit; taxation, $795 per credit; communications and information systems, $765 per credit; instructional leadership, education, business education, and the postbaccalaureate teacher certification programs, $735 per credit; nursing, $805 per credit; engineering management, $815 per credit; and organizational leadership, $690 per credit. Tuition for the D.Sc. in information systems and communications is $13,500 per semester. Tuition for the D.N.P. is $7983 per semester for full-time students, $815 per credit for part-time students, and $1080 per credit for students in the completion option. Tuition for the Ph.D. in instructional management and leadership is $6347 per semester.

Living and Housing Costs

Students find an abundance of residential living opportunities both on and off campus. The D.Sc. program fee includes the cost of the required residencies.

Student Group

RMU enrolls more than 1,100 students in its graduate degree programs. Women make up 56 percent of the graduate student population. Students come from diverse professional and academic backgrounds.

Location

Robert Morris University is located on a 230-acre campus in suburban Moon Township, 17 miles west of downtown Pittsburgh and 15 minutes from Pittsburgh International Airport. Many graduate programs and classes are also offered online.

The University

Robert Morris University, founded in 1921, is a four-year, private, coeducational, independent institution. It has developed a national reputation for its strong business programs and offers sixty undergraduate degrees and more than twenty master's and doctoral degree programs.

Applying

The graduate programs admit students on a rolling admission basis. However, students are encouraged to submit all required materials at least two months prior to the start of their desired term of entry. Applications can be filed for free through the University's Web site. Students should note that the M.S. in nonprofit management, the M.S. in nursing, the D.Sc. in information systems and communications, the D.N.P., and the Ph.D. in instructional management and leadership programs require an interview as part of the final selection process.

Correspondence and Information

Office of Graduate Admissions
Robert Morris University
6001 University Boulevard
Moon Township, Pennsylvania 15108-1189
Phone: 800-762-0097 (toll-free)
Web site: http://www.rmu.edu/graduate

THE FACULTY

SCHOOL OF BUSINESS
Derya A. Jacobs, Dean; Ph.D., Missouri–Rolla.
Kurt E. Shimmel, Associate Dean; D.B.A., Cleveland State.

Accounting and Taxation Faculty
Gerald J. Berenbaum, M.B.A., Massachusetts; CPA.
William G. Brucker, M.B.A., J.D., Duquesne; CPA.
Lois D. Bryan, D.Sc., Robert Morris; CPA.
Victoria A. Fratto, M.S., Robert Morris.
Fei Han, M.S., Connecticut.
Jerry Hanwell, M.B.A., South Carolina; J.D., Duquesne.
David Hess, M.B.A., Ohio State; CPA.
Katie Hetherington, J.D., Washington (Seattle); LL.M., Florida.
Timothy Hurley, J.D., Washburn; LL.M., NYU.
Louise Miller, Ph.D., Texas at Dallas.
Marc Ortegren, Ph.D., Texas Tech.
Tanya M. Lee, Ph.D., Arizona State.
James E. Rebele, Ph.D., Indiana.
Ronald R. Rubenfield, M.B.A., Shippensburg; CPA, CMA.
Zhaoyun Shangguan, Ph.D., Connecticut.

Finance Faculty
Robert G. Beaves, Ph.D., Iowa.
Zane Dennick-Ream, M.B.A., Iowa.
Riza Emekter, Ph.D., Nebraska.
Frank Flanegin, Ph.D., Central Florida.
Denise C. Letterman, M.B.A., Shippensburg.
Jianyu Ma, Ph.D., Texas–Pan American.
Stanko Racic, Ph.D., Pittsburgh.

Economics and Legal Studies Faculty
Mark J. Eschenfelder, Ph.D., Missouri.
Adora D. Holstein, Ph.D., Penn State.
Patrick J. Litzinger, Ph.D., Pittsburgh.
Min Lu, Ph.D., British Columbia–Vancouver.
J. Brian O'Roark, Ph.D., George Mason.
Ralph R. Reiland, M.B.A., Duquesne.
Louis B. Swartz, J.D., Duquesne.
Joel A. Waldman, J.D., Miami (Florida).

Management Faculty
Michele T. Cole, J.D., Ph.D., Pittsburgh.
Daria C. Crawley, Ph.D., Michigan.
Jeffery K. Guiler, Ph.D., Pittsburgh.
Nell T. Hartley, Ph.D., Vanderbilt.
Chia-Jung Lin, Ph.D., Southern Illinois Carbondale.
Marcel C. Minutolo, Ph.D., Pittsburgh.
Darlene Y. Motley, Ph.D., Pittsburgh.
Edward A. Nicholson, Ph.D., Ohio State.
Jodi A. Potter, Ph.D., Pittsburgh.
Yasmin S. Purohit, Ph.D., Drexel.
William F. Repack, M.S., Loyola.
David P. Synowka, Ph.D., Pittsburgh.
Michael A. Yahr, M.B.A., Pittsburgh.
Qin Yang, Ph.D., Temple.

Marketing Faculty
Artemisia Apostolopoulou, Ph.D., Massachusetts.
Scott Branvold, Ed.D., Utah.
Yun Chu, Ph.D., Texas–Pan American.
John S. Clark, Ph.D., Massachusetts Amherst.
Steven R. Clinton, Ph.D., Michigan State.
Cathleen S. Jones, D.Sc., Robert Morris.
Ersem Karadag, Ph.D., Oklahoma State.
Jill K. Maher, Ph.D., Kent State.
Dean R. Manna, Ph.D., Pittsburgh.
Gayle J. Marco, Ph.D., Pittsburgh.
Richard Mills, Ph.D., Duquesne
Denis P. Rudd, Ed.D., Nevada, Las Vegas; CHA, FMP.
Norman V. Schnurr, M.B.A., Pittsburgh.
Alan D. Smith, Ph.D., Akron; CPGS.
Yanbin Tu, Ph.D., Connecticut.

SCHOOL OF COMMUNICATIONS AND INFORMATION SYSTEMS
Barbara J. Levine, Dean; Ph.D., Wisconsin–Madison.
David F. Wood, Associate Dean; Ph.D., Pittsburgh.
Rex L. Crawley, Assistant Dean; Ph.D., Ohio

Communication Faculty
Barbara Burgess-Lefebvre, M.F.A., Illinois State.
Michele Reese Edwards, Ph.D., Ohio State.
Andrea Frantz, Ph.D., Iowa State.
Kenneth V. Gargaro, Ph.D., Pittsburgh.
Ann D. Jabro, Ph.D., Penn State.
Heather Pinson, Ph.D., Ohio.
Weiming Yao, Ph.D., Pittsburgh.

Computer and Information Systems Faculty
Jeanne M. Baugh, Ed.D., West Virginia.
Donald J. Caputo, Ph.D., Pittsburgh.
Gary A. Davis, D.Sc., Robert Morris.
Linda Kavanaugh, Ph.D., Pittsburgh.
Fred G. Kohun, Associate Provost for Research, Accreditation, and Program Support; Ph.D., Carnegie Mellon.
Paul J. Kovacs, Ph.D., Pittsburgh.
Joseph Laverty, Ph.D., Pittsburgh.
G. James Leone, Ph.D., Pittsburgh.
Sushma Mishra, Ph.D., Virginia Commonwealth.
Walter Pilof, M.B.A., Xavier (Cincinnati).
Valerie J. Powell, Ph.D., Texas at Austin.
Robert J. Skovira, Ph.D., Pittsburgh.
John Turchek, M.Ed., Duquesne.
Charles R. Woratschek, Ph.D., Pittsburgh.
Peter Wu, Ph.D., Rensselaer.
John Zeanchock, M.Ed., Indiana of Pennsylvania.

English Studies and Communications Skills Faculty
Diane Todd Bucci, Ph.D., Indiana of Pennsylvania.
Jay S. Carson, D.A., Carnegie Mellon.
Roger Gillan, M.A., Bucknell.
Arthur J. Grant, Ph.D., Wheaton (Illinois).
Edward Karshner, Ph.D., Bowling Green State.
John Lawson, Ph.D., Northern Illinois.
John D. O'Banion, Ph.D., Northern Illinois.
Sylvia A. Pamboukian, Ph.D., Indiana Bloomington.
Constance M. Ruzich, Ph.D., Pennsylvania.
H. James Vincent, M.A., Indiana.

Media Arts Faculty
Andrew Ames, M.F.A., Rhode Island School of Design.
Lutz Bacher, Ph.D., Wayne State.
Ferris Crane, M.F.A., Academy of Arts.
Timothy J. Hadfield, M.F.A., Chelsea College of Art and Design (London).
Christine Holtz, M.F.A., RIT.
Carolina Loyola-Garcia, M.F.A., Carnegie Mellon.
Jon A. Radermacher, M.F.A., Indiana.
Helena Vanhala, Ph.D., Oregon.
Hyla J. Willis, M.F.A., Carnegie Mellon.

Organizational Studies Faculty
Peter J. Draus, Ed.D., Pittsburgh.
Beatrice Kunka, Ed.D., University of the Pacific.
Anthony Petroy, D.M., Phoenix.
Elizabeth M. Stork, Ph.D., Pittsburgh.
Glenn Thiel, Ph.D., Pittsburgh.

SCHOOL OF EDUCATION AND SOCIAL SCIENCES
John E. Graham, Dean; Ed.D., Pittsburgh.
Donna Cellante, Associate Dean; Ed.D., Pittsburgh.

Elementary Education Faculty
Carianne Bernadowski, Ph.D., Pittsburgh.
Michele N. Hipsky, Ed.D., Duquesne.
Daniel J. Shelley, Ph.D., Pittsburgh.
Robert DelGreco, Ed.D., Pittsburgh.
Susan Parker, Ph.D., Pittsburgh.
Ronald Perry, Ph.D., Pittsburgh.

Secondary Education and Graduate Studies Faculty
James Bernauer, Ed.D., Pittsburgh.
Vicki Donne, Ed.D., Pittsburgh.
Bruce Golmic, Ed.D., Indiana of Pennsylvania.
Richard G. Fuller, D.Ed., Penn State.
Mary A. Hansen, Ph.D., Pittsburgh.
E. Gregory Holdan, Ph.D., Penn State.
Fan-Yu Lin, Ph.D., Penn State.
George W. Semich, Ed.D., Pittsburgh.
Darcy Tannehill, Ed.D., Pittsburgh.
Lawrence A. Tomei, Ed.D., USC.
John A. Zeanchock, Ed.D., Indiana of Pennsylvania.

Social Sciences Faculty
Daniel P. Barr, Ph.D., Kent State.
William R. Beaver, Ph.D., Carnegie Mellon.
Kathryn Dennick-Brecht, Ed.D., Duquesne.
Soren Fanning, Ph.D., Bowling Green State.
Philip J. Harold, Ph.D., Catholic University.
William E. Kelly, Ph.D., Louisiana Tech.
John M. McCarthy, Ph.D., Marquette.
Stephen T. Paul, Ph.D., Kansas.
David Wheeler, Ph.D., Washington (Seattle).

SCHOOL OF ENGINEERING, MATHEMATICS, AND SCIENCE
Maria V. Kalevitch, Dean; Ph.D., Academy of Sciences (Lithuania).
Jeffrey J. Mitchell, Associate Dean; Ph.D., Cornell.

Engineering Faculty
Sushil Acharya, D.Eng., Asian Institute of Technology (Thailand).
John Hayward, Ph.D., Penn State.
Giuseppe Iannelli, Ph.D., Tennessee, Knoxville.
Tony Kerzmann, M.S., Pittsburgh.
Priyadarshan A. Manohar, Ph.D., Wollongong (Australia).
Yildirim Omurtag, Ph.D., Iowa State.
Arif Sirinterlikci, Ph.D., Ohio State.

Mathematics Faculty
Len Asimow, Ph.D., Washington (Seattle).
Mark A. Ciancutti, Ph.D., Carnegie Mellon.
Renato Clavijo, Ph.D., Arkansas.
David G. Hudak, Ph.D., Carnegie Mellon.
Allen R. Lias, Ph.D., Pittsburgh.
Andris Niedra, Ph.D., Pittsburgh.
Jonathan Preisser, Ph.D., Iowa.
Qiang Sun, PhD., Pittsburgh.
Monica M. VanDieren, Ph.D., Carnegie Mellon.
Charles W. Zimmerman, Ph.D., Ohio State.

Science Faculty
Paul D. Badger, Ph.D., Pittsburgh.
Gavin Buxton, PhD., Sheffield Hallam (England).
William J. Dress, Ph.D., Ohio State.
Catherine Hanna, PhD., Louisville.
Kenneth A. Lasota, Ph.D., Pittsburgh.
Matthew Maurer, Ph.D., Ohio State.
Daniel Short, Ph.D., Liverpool (England).

SCHOOL OF NURSING AND HEALTH SCIENCES
Lynda J. Davidson, Dean; Ph.D., Pittsburgh; RN.
Lynn George, Associate Dean; Ph.D., Duquesne; RN.

Nuclear Medicine Faculty
Angela M. Bires, Ed.D., Duquesne.
Donna L. Mason, M.S., Carlow.
William Wentling, M.S., Buffalo State, SUNY.

Nursing Faculty
Mary Cothran, Ph.D., Pittsburgh.
Nadine C. Englert, Ph.D., Pittsburgh; RN.
Stephen Foreman, Ph.D., Berkeley.
Susan Hellier, Ph.D., Waynesburg.
Valerie M. Howard, Ed.D., Pittsburgh; RN.
Pamela Jackson, M.S., Robert Morris.
Judith A. Kaufmann, Dr.PH, Pittsburgh.
Kirstyn K. Kameg, D.N.P., Case Western Reserve; CRNP, RN.
Lisa W. Locasto, D.N.P., Robert Morris; RN.
Catherine Pyo, M.S., Indiana of Pennsylvania.
Denise Ramponi, D.N.P., Waynesburg.
Katherine Perozzi, M.S.N., Pittsburgh; RN.
Carl A. Ross, Ph.D., Duquesne; RN.
Janene Szpak, B.S.N., Carlow.
Susan Van Cleve, D.N.P., Robert Morris; CRNP, RN.

SARAH LAWRENCE COLLEGE

Graduate Programs

Programs of Study

Sarah Lawrence College has been a pioneer in several graduate fields, founding three outstanding programs in human genetics (genetic counseling), health advocacy, and women's history that have served as models nationwide. The College also offers master's degrees in areas where it has particular strength: the art of teaching, child development, creative writing, dance, and theatre. The College believes in the importance of close and extensive collaboration with the faculty. Many of the graduate programs combine small seminar classes with individual student-faculty conferences. In all programs, opportunity for fieldwork is extensive and varied. Most graduate programs are for two years of full-time study and require 36 course credits. Part-time study may be arranged in all programs, with the exception of dance and theatre.

The Art of Teaching Program leads to a Master of Science degree and recommendation for New York State certification in early childhood (birth–grade 2), childhood (grades 1–6), or dual certification (birth–grade 6). Special features of the program include study of child development, observation, and documentation; empirical courses in curriculum planning, with emphasis on language arts, mathematics, science, and social studies; and integration of theory with fieldwork from the first semester. Field placements and student teaching under master teachers are offered at the Sarah Lawrence Early Childhood Center and public schools in Westchester County and New York City.

The Child Development Program leads to an M.A. and is for students who seek in-depth understanding of childhood functioning in the context of contemporary society. Study of theoretical perspectives and research in developmental psychology is integrated with fieldwork experience. The program is unique in its ongoing combination of theory and fieldwork. Graduates of the program are prepared for direct work with young children in a variety of settings, for teaching child development at an intermediate level, or for pursuing more advanced study in psychology and related fields. In fall 2003, Sarah Lawrence College began offering a dual degree (M.A./M.S.W.) with the New York University School of Social Work and its Child Development Master's Program.

The Dance Program leads to an M.F.A. and is based on the premise that dance is a distinctive art form, calling for the integration of body, mind, and spirit. Daily modern and ballet technique classes are required of all graduate students. Basic physical skills, strength, and control are required for the central focus of the program, the creative use of the dance medium. The student is exposed to vital aspects of the art as a performer, creator, and observer, with music as an integral part. The curriculum centers on choreography, dance improvisation, music improvisation, composition, and the teaching of dance. The dance program offers dancers the opportunity to grow under the guidance of an excellent faculty made up of dancers and dance scholars with professional experience in the New York area and abroad.

The Human Genetics (Genetic Counseling) Program and the Health Advocacy Program, each leading to a master's degree, train health professionals devoted to the health concerns of patients. The interdisciplinary curriculum in each program consists of 40 academic course credits and 600 hours of clinical work or other fieldwork. The location of Sarah Lawrence College in the metropolitan New York area offers a rich network of settings—hospitals, clinics, and community agencies—in which on-site supervised training enables students to integrate theoretical knowledge with practice. The faculty includes professionals and academicians drawn from health and medical disciplines. Small classes and close faculty-student interaction offer a productive and stimulating environment for professional growth. Both programs make use of invited speakers, professional workshops, and community involvement to enrich the learning experience and expose students to new developments in the field. A joint degree in human genetics and health advocacy (M.S./M.A.) is also offered.

The Theatre Program leads to the M.F.A. and is based on the principle that learning comes through practical application, personal experience, and intensive workshops. Working with a faculty of New York City theater professionals, students explore playwriting, acting, directing, design, and technical work in small seminars, tutorials, and collaborative projects.

The Women's History Program leads to the M.A. It was the first in the nation to offer graduate study in the field and emphasizes the combination of scholarship and activism. A joint degree program in women's history and law is offered in cooperation with Pace University Law School.

The Writing Program leads to an M.F.A. This program offers an uncommon opportunity for students to develop as poets or creative nonfiction or fiction writers under the close attention of a nationally renowned faculty. At the center of the course of study are four successive seminars that students take during their two years in the program. In addition to the intensive student-faculty discussions in these seminars, students participate in individual conferences with faculty members every two weeks. This unique aspect of the Sarah Lawrence program provides further intensive scrutiny of students' writing and helps them create the substantial body of work needed to fulfill the program's requirements.

Research Facilities

The College's facilities include classrooms, laboratories, a computer center, and a state-of-the-art sports center; a modern library with 202,265 books and 880 periodicals, which is linked by computer to more than 6,000 other libraries; the Performing Arts Center, which consists of two theaters, a dance studio, and a concert hall; a music building, including a music library; a Science Center; the Early Childhood Center; the Center for Graduate Studies; and the Center for Continuing Education.

Financial Aid

Graduate students are welcome to apply for financial aid. There are two required forms for U.S. citizens (and other federally eligible students) and one form for international students. U.S. citizens should complete the Free Application for Federal Student Aid (FAFSA) and the Financial Aid PROFILE. International students may apply for Sarah Lawrence gift aid by filing the CSS profile. There are links to the forms at http://www.sarahlawrence.edu/finaid. March 1 is the College's preferential filing date. It is important that all applicants for financial aid complete either the PROFILE or the international application for aid at the same time as their application for admission. All financial aid is awarded on the basis of need. Students who complete the appropriate forms in a timely manner are automatically considered for all aid resources administered by Sarah Lawrence College. Grants (gift aid) and student loans comprise the two elements of a Sarah Lawrence financial aid package. Every federally eligible aid recipient is offered a student loan. Students are not required to accept the loan in order to receive Sarah Lawrence College gift aid. International students are advised to investigate financing opportunities offered by their government or private institutions. Detailed descriptions and a thorough explanation of financial aid procedures are available in *Financing Your Graduate Education at Sarah Lawrence College*, published and updated by the Office of Graduate Studies. A copy of the booklet is mailed to all students who apply to a graduate studies program.

Cost of Study

Tuition varies according to program. For more information, prospective students should visit http://www.slc.edu/student-accounts/Graduate_Tuition_and_Costs.php.

Living and Housing Costs

Estimated expenses for off-campus housing and food are $18,060 per year.

Student Group

Sarah Lawrence attracts students who seek a creative education and are eager to take responsibility for it. The College draws its approximately 350 graduate students from forty-nine states and thirty-one countries.

Location

The College is situated in the Bronxville/Yonkers community of Bronxville in southern Westchester County, just 15 miles north of midtown Manhattan in New York City. Highways and a commuter railroad make it possible to reach the city in about 30 minutes, enabling students to take advantage of its social, cultural, and intellectual riches and its internship possibilities.

The College

Founded in 1926, Sarah Lawrence is a small liberal arts college for men and women. It is a lively community of students, scholars, and artists, nationally renowned for its unique academic structure, which combines small classes with individual student-faculty conferences.

Applying

Applicants for graduate studies must have received a B.A. or an equivalent degree from an accredited college or university and have at least a 3.0 grade point average. They should request information on the program that interests them at the College address or by calling the College's telephone number. Applicants are asked to complete an application form and to furnish transcripts of all undergraduate work and two letters of recommendation, preferably from former teachers. Personal interviews may be arranged with the program directors and with the Director of Graduate Studies. The creative writing and the performing arts programs require demonstration of the candidate's ability. GRE scores are not required. Application deadlines vary according to program. Prospective students can apply online at https://data.slc.edu/graduate/index.php. Students should visit the Web site at http://www.slc.edu/graduate/index.php.

Correspondence and Information

Susan Guma, Dean of Graduate Studies
Sarah Lawrence College
1 Mead Way
Bronxville, New York 10708

Phone: 914-395-2371
Fax: 914-395-2664
E-mail: grad@sarahlawrence.edu
Web site: http://www.sarahlawrence.edu/graduate

THE FACULTY AND GRADUATE PROGRAM DIRECTORS

Art of Teaching
Sara Wilford, Director; M.S.Ed., M.Ed., Bank Street College of Education.
Mary Hebron, Associate Director; M.A., NYU.
Maggie Martinez DeLuca, M.S.Ed., Bank Street College of Education.
Jan Drucker, Ph.D., NYU.
David J. Eger, Ph.D., Michigan.
Linwood Lewis, Ph.D., CUNY.
Kathleen Ruen, Ph.D., NYU.

Child Development
Barbara Schecter, Director; Ph.D., Columbia Teachers College.
Carl Barenboim, Ph.D., Rochester.
Charlotte Doyle, Ph.D., Michigan.
Jan Drucker, Ph.D., NYU.
Kim Ferguson, Ph.D., Cornell.
Elizabeth Johnston, D.Phil., Oxford.
Linwood Lewis, Ph.D., CUNY.
Sara Wilford, M.S.Ed., M.Ed., Bank Street College of Education.

Dance
Sara Rudner, Director; M.F.A., Bennington.
Emily Devine, B.A., Connecticut College.
Dan Hurlin, B.A., Sarah Lawrence.
Rose Anne Thom, B.A., McGill.
John Yannelli, M.F.A., Sarah Lawrence.

Health Advocacy
Laura Weil, Director; M.A., Sarah Lawrence.
Bruce Berg, Ph.D., American. Department of Political Science at Fordham University.
Sayantani DasGupta, M.D./M.P.H., Johns Hopkins.
Catherine M. Handy, Ph.D., NYU.
Alice Herb, J.D., LL.M., NYU.
Rebecca O. Johnson, M.S., Southern New Hampshire; M.F.A., Sarah Lawrence.
Terry Mizrahi, M.S.W., Columbia; Ph.D., Virginia.
Constance Peterson, M.A., Sarah Lawrence.
Karen Porter, M.S., NYU; J.D., Yale.

Human Genetics
Caroline Lieber, Director; M.S., Sarah Lawrence.
James W. Speer, Associate Director; M.S., Sarah Lawrence.
Jessica Davis, Director of Clinical Training; M.D., Columbia.
Jacob Canick, Ph.D., Brandeis.
Susanne Carter, M.S., Sarah Lawrence.
Peggy Cottrell, M.S., Sarah Lawrence.
Siobhan Dolan, M.D., Harvard.
Judith Durcan, M.S., Sarah Lawrence.
Marvin Frankel, Ph.D., Chicago.
Eva Bostein Griepp, M.D., NYU.
Susan Gross, M.D., Toronto.
Alice Herb, J.D., LL.M., NYU.
Laura Hercher, M.S., Sarah Lawrence.
Judith Hull, M.S., Sarah Lawrence.
Daniel Iacoboni, M.S., Sarah Lawrence.
David Kronn, M.D., Trinity College, Dublin.
Sharon LaVigne, M.S., Sarah Lawrence.
Laura Long, M.S., Sarah Lawrence.
Robert Marion, M.D., Yeshiva (Einstein).
Diana Punales Morejon, M.S., Sarah Lawrence.
Sally Nolin, Ph.D., SUNY Health Science Center at Brooklyn.
Elsa Reich, M.S., Sarah Lawrence.
Michael J. Smith, D.S.W., Columbia.
Jennifer Scalia Wilbur, M.S., Sarah Lawrence.

Theatre
Christine Farrell, Director; M.F.A., Columbia.
Dan Hurlin, Graduate Director; B.A., Sarah Lawrence.
Robert Lyons, Creative Director; M.F.A., Brooklyn.
William D. McRee, Administrator; M.F.A., Sarah Lawrence.
Ernest Abuba, Member, Ensemble Studio Theatre; Rockefeller Foundation Fellowship.
Kevin Confoy, B.A., Rutgers.
Jill BC Du Boff, B.A., The New School.
Michael Early, M.F.A., Yale.
June Ekman, B.A., Goddard; ACAT, Alexander Technique.
Will Frears, M.F.A., Yale.
Paul Griffin, Founder, City at Peace, Inc., in Washington, D.C.
Shirley Kaplan, A.A., Briarcliff, Academie de la Grande Chaumiere (Paris).
Allen Lang, M.F.A., Sarah Lawrence.
Tom Lee, B.F.A., Carnegie Mellon.
Doug MacHugh, M.F.A., Sarah Lawrence.
Greg MacPherson, B.A., Vermont.
Thomas Mandel, B.A., Bowdoin.
Ella McGhee, B.A., Massachusetts.
Cassandra Medley, Michigan.
Greta Minsky, B.A., Kansas.
David Neumann, Artistic Director.
Dael Orlandersmith, OBIE Award winner.
Carol Ann Pelletier, B.A., Brandeis.
Fanchon Miller Scheier, M.F.A., Sarah Lawrence.
Edwin Sherin, Brown.
Stuart Spencer, B.A., Sarah Lawrence.
Sterling Swann, B.A., Vassar.
Lucy Thurber, Author.

Writing/Creative Nonfiction
Vijay Seshadri, Director; M.F.A., Columbia.
Alexandra Soiseth, Associate Director; M.F.A., Sarah Lawrence.
Gerald Albarelli, M.A., Brown.
Jo Ann Beard, M.A., Iowa.
Rachel Cohen, A.B., Harvard.
Ann Heppermann, Independent documentary writer/producer.
Stephen O'Connor, M.A., Berkeley.
Alice Truax, M.A., Middlebury.

Writing/Fiction
Brian Morton, Director; B.A., Sarah Lawrence.
Alexandra Soiseth, Associate Director; M.F.A., Sarah Lawrence.
Melvin Jules Bukiet, M.F.A., Columbia.
Carolyn Ferrell, M.A., CUNY, City College.
Myla Goldberg, B.A., Oberlin
Myra Goldberg, M.A., CUNY Graduate Center.
Kathleen Hill, Ph.D., Wisconsin.
Mary La Chapelle, M.F.A., Vermont.
Mary Morris, Director; M.Phil., Columbia.
Victoria Redel, M.F.A., Iowa.
Nelly Reifler, M.F.A., Sarah Lawrence.
Lucy Rosenthal, M.F.A., Yale.
Joan Silber, M.A., NYU.

Writing/Poetry
Kate Knapp Johnson, Director; M.F.A., Sarah Lawrence.
Alexandra Soiseth, Associate Director; M.F.A., Sarah Lawrence.
Tina Chang, M.F.A., Columbia.
Cynthia Cruz, MFA, Sarah Lawrence.
Thomas Sayers Ellis, M.F.A., Brown.
Suzanne Gardinier, M.F.A., Columbia.
Matthea Harvey, M.F.A., Iowa.
Cathy Park Hong, M.F.A., Columbia.
Suzanne Hoover, Ph.D., Columbia.
Marie Howe, M.F.A., Columbia.
Thomas Lux, B.A., Emerson; University of Iowa Writers Workshop.
Jeffrey McDaniel, M.F.A., George Mason.
Dennis Nurkse, B.A., Harvard.
Kevin Pilkington, M.A., Georgetown.
Victoria Redel, M.F.A., Iowa.
Martha Rhodes, poet and publisher.Name deleted after this line — Pat Rosal, M.F.A., Sarah Lawrence.
Vijay Seshadri, M.F.A., Columbia.

Women's History
Priscilla Murolo, Co-Director; Ph.D., Yale. U.S. labor history.
Rona Holub, Co-Director, Ph.D., Columbia.
Tara James, Associate Director; M.A., Sarah Lawrence.
David Bernstein, Ph.D., Harvard.
Persis Charles, Ph.D., Tufts.
Una Chung, Ph.D., CUNY Graduate Center.
Mary Dillard, Ph.D., UCLA.Name deleted after this line— Rona Holub, Ph.D., Columbia
Lyde Cullen Sizer, Ph.D., Brown. Women's literary cultures, American popular culture, the American Civil War.
Sarah Wilcox, Ph.D., Pennsylvania.
K. Komozi Woodard, Ph.D., Pennsylvania. African American history and culture, with emphasis on the black freedom movement, American urban history, and ghetto formation.

Affiliate Faculty in Women's History
Julie Abraham, Ph.D., Columbia. Lesbian and Gay Studies.
Eileen Ka-may Cheng, Ph.D., Yale. American history.
Alwin A. D. Jones, Ph.D., Virginia. Literature.
Patrisia Maciás, Ph.D., Berkeley. Sociology.
Gina Philogene, Ph.D., École des Hautes Études en Sciences Sociales (France). Social Psychology.
Sandra Robinson, Ph.D., Chicago. Asian Studies.
Shahnaz Rouse, Ph.D., Wisconsin–Madison. Sociology.
Matilde Zimmermann, Ph.D., Pittsburgh. History.

The College is set on a 40-acre campus reminiscent of a rural English village.

SOUTHERN CONNECTICUT STATE UNIVERSITY

School of Graduate Studies

Programs of Study

Southern Connecticut State University (SCSU) offers graduate programs leading to the degrees of Master of Arts, Master of Science, Master of Science in Education, Master of Science in Nursing, Master of Library Science, Master of Public Health, Master of Social Work, Master of Fine Arts, and Master of Business Administration, as well as Doctor of Education in educational leadership. Graduate programs leading to the Sixth-Year Professional Diploma in special areas of education and library science are also offered.

The Master of Arts degree is awarded in English, history, psychology, and women's studies. The Master of Science degree is offered in art education; bilingual education/TESOL; biology; chemistry; communications disorders; computer science; counseling; recreation and leisure studies; research, statistics, and measurement; sociology; and urban studies. The Master of Science in Education degree is awarded in art, bilingual/multicultural education/TESOL, biology, chemistry, counseling, elementary education, English, environmental education, exercise science, history, mathematics, reading, school health education, school psychology, science education, and special education. The Master of Fine Arts is offered in creative writing.

The Sixth-Year Professional Diploma is offered in counseling and school psychology, educational leadership, education–classroom teacher specialist studies, Information/library science, reading, school psychology, special education, and science education.

Most graduate programs are offered in the evening for the convenience of students, and some are offered online. Students follow a planned program that includes completing course requirements and taking a comprehensive examination, preparing a thesis, or completing a special project, as appropriate.

Research Facilities

The Hilton C. Buley Library, Southern Connecticut State University's center of education and research, plays an indispensable part in the academic experience of every student. Buley Library provides more than 400,000 monograph volumes, over 60,000 bound periodical volumes, 12,500 nonprint media items, 1,000 electronic books, and 100,000 volume equivalents in micro-format. Current periodical subscriptions include 2,060 individual journal titles; in addition, the library provides access to more than 43,000 full-text electronic journals, 130 Web-based indexes and databases, and over 1,000 e-book titles.

Financial Aid

There are a limited number of teaching and research assistantships available. The chief source of aid is the Federal Stafford Student Loan. Application forms for this loan are available from the Office of Financial Aid. The School of Graduate Studies also offers competitive research fellowships of approximately $8000.

Cost of Study

Tuition for full-time study for the 2011–12 academic year was $9145 for state residents and $19,721 for out-of-state residents. Part-time study cost $521 per credit hour plus a $55 registration fee and an $8-per-credit-hour information technology fee each semester. Students in some programs are charged differential tuition. Full-time, in-state students in the M.B.A. program and the M.L.S. program were charged $5029 per semester, and out-of-state students in these programs were charged $9861 per semester. Part-time students in these programs were charged $588 per credit. Students enrolled in the doctoral program were charged $731 per credit.

Living and Housing Costs

On-campus housing is available for graduate students. Off-campus accommodation is readily available close to the campus at a range of prices. Students may choose from a wide range of housing styles and options.

Student Group

Approximately 3,800 graduate students (including approximately 900 full-time) are enrolled in graduate programs in four schools of the University. SCSU has consistently ranked as one of the largest graduate schools in New England.

Location

New Haven, Connecticut's third largest city, is home to three universities, three colleges, and several private schools. New Haven serves as the gateway to New England, where I-95 and I-91 intersect and provide access to New York and Boston.

The University

Southern Connecticut State University is one of four institutions of the Connecticut State University System, which is authorized by the state of Connecticut. It receives its principal financial support from legislative appropriations. It is the policy of Southern Connecticut State University to accept students without regard to race, color, creed, sex, age, national origin, physical disability, or sexual orientation.

Applying

Application forms for the School of Graduate Studies are available in the Graduate Office, which is located in Engleman Hall Room B110, or may be obtained by mail or telephone request. An online application is also available at http://www.gradstudies.SouthernCT.edu. Students are advised to send the completed, signed application and official transcripts from every college and graduate school attended, along with a $50 application fee, to the School of Graduate Studies. International students must also send TOEFL scores to the graduate studies office. All other documents, such as requested letters of recommendation or any departmental forms, should be sent directly to the academic department to which application is being made. A personal interview with the appropriate department chairperson or a designated faculty member in the major area of study is a requirement for admission. Requests for appointments must be made to the department. The application and credentials should be submitted well in advance of the semester for which the student seeks admission.

Correspondence and Information

School of Graduate Studies
Southern Connecticut State University
501 Crescent Street
New Haven, Connecticut 06515-1355
Phone: 203-392-5240
800-448-0661 (toll-free)
Web site: http://www.gradstudies.southernct.edu

FACULTY HEADS

Listed below is the chairperson or graduate coordinator of each department.

Art Education: Jesse Whitehead, Coordinator.
Biology: Sean Grace, Coordinator.
Business Administration: Wafeek Abdelsayed, Director.
Chemistry: M.J. Gerald Lesley, Director.
Communication Disorders: Deborah Weiss, Director.
Computer Science: Lisa Lancor, Coordinator.
Counselor Education: Patricia DeBarbieri, Chair.
Creative Writing: Robin Troy, Coordinator.
Education: Maria Diamantis, Chair.
Educational Leadership: Peter Madonia, Chair.
English: Nicole Fluhr, Coordinator.
Exercise Science: Robert Axtell, Coordinator.
Foreign Languages: Elena Schmitt, Chair.
History: Christine Petto, Coordinator.
Information and Library Science: Chang Suk Kim, Chair.
Mathematics: Alain D'Amour, Coordinator.
Nursing: Leslie Neal-Boylan, Coordinator.
Political Science: John Critzer, Coordinator.
Psychology: W. Jerome Hauselt, Coordinator.
Public Health: Deborah Flynn, Coordinator.
Recreation and Leisure Studies: Jan Jones, Coordinator.
Research, Measurement, and Evaluation: William Diffley, Coordinator.
School Counseling: Margaret Generali, Coordinator.
School Health: Susan Calahan, Coordinator.
School Psychology: Joy Fopiano, Coordinator.
Science and Environmental Education: Susan Cusato, Chair.
Social Work: Todd Rofuth, Chair.
Sociology: Shirley Jackson, Coordinator.
Special Education: Deborah Newton, Chair.
Special Education and Reading: Ruth Eren, Coordinator.
Urban Studies: Eric West, Interim Chair.
Women's Studies: Tricia Lin, Coordinator.

There are many opportunities for graduate students at SCSU to enroll in small classes and work closely with faculty members.

Michael J. Adanti Student Center.

TEXAS TECH UNIVERSITY

Graduate School

Programs of Study

Texas Tech University prides itself on being a major comprehensive research university that retains the atmosphere of a smaller liberal arts institution. Although enrollment is over 31,000, Texas Tech students boast of one-on-one interaction with top faculty and an environment that stresses student accomplishment above all else. The University strives to be large enough to provide the best in facilities and academics, but small enough to focus on individual students. Through its Graduate School, School of Law, School of Allied Health, School of Nursing, School of Pharmacy, and School of Medicine, Texas Tech offers a diverse range of graduate studies.

The Graduate School offers degrees from ten academic colleges. The College of Agriculture offers the Doctor of Philosophy (Ph.D.), Master of Science (M.S.), Doctor of Education (Ed.D.), and Master of Agriculture (M.Ag.) in a variety of disciplines. In addition, the college offers the Master of Landscape Architecture (M.L.A.). The College of Architecture offers the Master of Architecture (M.Arch.), Master of Science in architecture, and Ph.D. degrees. The College of Arts and Sciences offers many degrees in a vast range of disciplines, including the Ph.D. in eighteen academic disciplines, the Master of Arts (M.A.) in eighteen fields, and the Master of Science in twelve fields. Texas Tech's College of Business Administration offers the Ph.D. in business administration, M.S. in business administration, Master of Science in Accounting (M.S.A.), and Master of Business Administration (M.B.A.) degree programs. Each degree offers concentrations in various areas. An M.B.A. is available as a joint degree with foreign languages, law, nursing, and medicine and also with architecture. The College of Education offers the Master of Education (M.Ed.) in twelve fields, the Doctor of Education, and the Ph.D. The College of Engineering offers the Ph.D. in seven engineering fields, the M.S. in ten fields, the Master of Engineering (M.Eng.), the Master of Science in Environmental Engineering (M.S.Env.E.), and the Master of Science in Environmental Technology Management (M.S.E.T.M.). The College of Human Sciences offers the M.S. as well as the Ph.D. in various fields. The College of Visual and Performing Arts offers Ph.D., M.A., Master of Fine Arts (M.F.A.), Master of Music (M.M.), and Master of Music Education (M.M.Ed.) degrees. In addition, the college offers the Doctor of Musical Arts (D.M.A.). The College of Mass Communication offers the Ph.D. in mass communication and M.S. in mass communication, both designed to prepare students for careers in communications research and academia. The College of Outreach and Distance Education offers a variety of online master's degrees and four online doctoral degrees: Doctor of Education in Agricultural Education (a joint program with Texas A&M University), Doctor of Philosophy in Systems and Engineering Management, Doctor of Education in Higher Education Administration, and Doctor of Philosophy in Technical Communication and Rhetoric (TRC). In addition to the online programs several distance degrees are offered through the University's teaching sites in Abilene, Amarillo, Fredericksburg, Marble Falls, and Junction, Texas.

Interdisciplinary degrees housed in the Graduate School include predesigned programs or self-designed programs that are coordinated to meet individual needs. Predesigned programs include applied linguistics, forensic science, heritage management, international affairs, museum science, public administration, sports health, and multidisciplinary science. Self-designed programs may be generated from any of the courses listed in the graduate catalog. Some of the more common minors or areas of interest include comparative literature, environmental evaluation, ethnic studies, fine arts management, land-use planning management and design, Latin American studies, legal studies, neural and behavioral science, risk-taking behavior, and women's studies. The School of Law offers the Doctor of Jurisprudence degree and joint-degree programs with the M.P.A., M.S. in agricultural economics; M.S. in accounting; and M.B.A. The School of Allied Health offers an M.S. in three disciplines: communication disorders (speech-language pathology or audiology), occupational therapy, and physical therapy. The School of Nursing offers a Ph.D. in Nursing, a Master of Science in Nursing, and a joint-degree program with the M.B.A. The School of Pharmacy offers the Doctor of Pharmacy (Pharm.D.). The School of Medicine offers the Doctor of Medicine, medical education in thirty residency programs, Ph.D. and M.S. degrees in six disciplines, and a joint M.B.A./M.D. degree.

Research Facilities

Graduate study is strongly supported by the University and its departments. The library houses more than 4 million volumes and more than 27,000 serials. The high-performance computer center provides students with up-to-date computing facilities. The Advanced Technology Learning Center gives students comprehensive access to the latest computer technology and software. Many departments feature their own library and computer facilities. Consistent dedication to quality and research has earned national and international respect for numerous departments. Every department has its own strengths, and each college possesses its special resources, centers for investigation, and research opportunities. A small sample of the numerous centers and institutes includes the Institute for Ergonomics Research, Institute for Banking and Financial Studies, Child Development Center, Center for Petroleum Mathematics, Southwest Center for German Studies, Institute for Disaster Research, International Center for Arid and Semi-Arid Land Studies, Center for the Study of Addiction, Center for Professional Development, and Institute of Environmental and Human Health. In the new Carnegie classification, Texas Tech was rated as an RU/H: Research University (high research activity), the highest category for graduate degree–granting institutions.

Financial Aid

Graduate students are eligible for an array of scholarships, fellowships, and research or teaching assistantships in many academic disciplines. Part-time employment is readily available both on and off campus. The University participates in most federal and state grant, loan, and work-study programs. Texas Tech University's Gelin Emergency Loan Fund is a special benefit for students in need. Non-Texas residents receiving approved scholarships, fellowships, or assistantships may be eligible to pay Texas resident tuition, which is among the lowest in the nation.

Cost of Study

Graduate School tuition and fees for the 2011–12 academic year for Texas residents is approximately $3500 for full-time students enrolled in 9 hours. Students employed at least half-time as teaching or research assistants pay the same tuition as Texas residents. Fees may vary but generally include the Texas Tech University identification fee, laboratory fee, informational technology fee, library fee, and general fees. Most fees are waived for half-time teaching and research assistants. Tuition and fees for law and nursing vary and may be confirmed in the course catalog or by contacting the school directly. Texas has no state income tax. Tuition and fees are subject to change.

Living and Housing Costs

Characteristics of Lubbock are low unemployment, low housing costs, and a low cost of living. Abundant privately owned housing in the city meets most price and amenity demands; more information is available at www.LubbockApartments.com.

Student Group

More than 50 percent of Texas Tech's 28,000 students have permanent homes more than 300 miles away, making Tech a residential campus. Students come from all parts of Texas, the nation, and more than 100 other countries. Tech's growing graduate and professional student population is about 6,000, most of whom are full-time students.

Location

With a population of approximately 240,000, Lubbock enjoys all the services of a major city. The city has more than sixty parks, numerous cultural and civic events, and a modern and convenient international airport that hosts several major airlines. Lubbock is the principal trade, medical, and financial center in a rich agricultural and petroleum area. Situated on the high plains of west Texas, Lubbock is about an hour's flight from Dallas, Houston, Albuquerque, and Denver. Lubbock enjoys 265 days of sunshine each year, a warm and dry climate, and pleasant weather year-round.

The University

Founded in 1923, Texas Tech is a state-assisted major research university. Texas Tech's campus features expansive lawns and impressive landscaping with unique Spanish Renaissance architecture. The beautiful, spacious campus—one of the largest in the nation—is well-equipped not only for research and study but also for cultural and recreational activities. A fulfilling after-study-hours life can be achieved by participating in the wide array of campus and community activities.

Applying

Application forms for admission can be provided upon request or accessed electronically through the Graduate School Web site. Applications are accepted throughout the year for the fall, spring, and two summer terms. The Graduate School requires a $50 application fee for U.S. citizens and permanent residents and $75 for international applicants.

Correspondence and Information

Shannon Samson
Coordinator for Graduate School Recruitment
Graduate Admissions
Texas Tech University
P.O. Box 41030
Lubbock, Texas 79409-1030
Phone: 806-742-2787 Ext. 239
E-mail: shannon.samson@ttu.edu
Web site: http://www.gradschool.ttu.edu

DEANS AND FACULTY HEADS

Graduate School: Peggy Gordon Miller, Dean; Ph.D., Indiana Northwest (phone: 806-742-2781).

Agricultural Sciences: Michael Galyean, Interim Dean; Ed.D., Oklahoma State (phone: 806-742-2810).
Associate Dean (Research): Sukant Misra, Ph.D., Mississippi State.
Assistant Dean (Academic and Student Programs): Cindy Akers, Ed.D, Texas Tech.
Agricultural and Applied Economics: Eduardo Segarra, Department Chair; Ph.D., Virginia Tech.
Agricultural Education and Communication: Steve Fraze, Department Chair; Ph.D., Texas A&M.
Animal and Food Science: Leslie D. Thompson, Department Chair; Ph.D., Florida.
Landscape Architecture: Alon Kvashny, Ed.D., Department Chair; West Virginia.
Plant and Soil Science: Richard Zartman, Department Chair; Ph.D., Kentucky.
Natural Resources Management: Mark Wallace, Interim Chairman; Ph.D., Arizona.

Architecture: Andrew Vernooy, Dean; M.D.S., Texas at Austin (phone: 806-742-3169).
Associate Dean (Academics): Clifton Ellis, Ph.D., Virginia.
Associate Dean (Research): Sair Haq, Ph.D., Georgia Tech.
Chair of Instruction: Maria Perbellini, M.Arch., Pratt.

Arts and Sciences: Lawrence Schovanec, Dean; Ph.D., Indiana (phone: 806-742-3833).
Associate Dean (Faculty and Graduate Affairs): Melanie Hart, Ph.D., Auburn.
Associate Dean (Academic Programs): David Roach, Ph.D., Ohio State.
Associate Dean (Research): John Zak, Ph.D., Calgary.
Associate Dean (Finance): Jeff Williams, Ph.D., Tennessee.
Assistant Dean: Philip Marshall, Ph.D., Illinois.
Biological Sciences: Lou Densmore, Department Chair; Ph.D., LSU Medical Center.
Chemistry and Biochemistry: Carol L. Korzeniewski, Department Chair; Ph.D., Utah.
Classical and Modern Languages and Literatures: Laura J. Beard, Interim Department Chair; Ph.D., Johns Hopkins.
Classical and Modern Languages and Literatures: Erin Collopy, Associate Department Chair; Ph.D., Washington (Seattle).
Communication Studies: Catherine Langford, Interim Department Chair; Ph.D., Penn State.
Economics: Klaus G. Becker, Department Chair; Ph.D., Kansas.
English: Sam Dragga, Department Chair; Ph.D., Ohio.
English: James Whitlark, Associate Chair; Ph.D., Chicago.
Environmental Toxicology: Ronald J. Kendall, Department Chair; Ph.D., Virginia Tech.
Geosciences: Cal Barnes, Department Chair; Ph.D., Oregon.
Health, Exercise, and Sports Sciences: Noreen Goggin, Department Chair; Ph.D., Texas Tech.
History: Randy McBee, Department Chair; Ph.D., Missouri–Columbia.
History: Aliza S. Wong, Associate Chair; Ph.D., Colorado at Boulder.
Mathematics and Statistics: Kent Pearce, Department Chair; Ph.D., SUNY at Albany.
Philosophy: Mark Webb, Department Chair; Ph.D., Syracuse.
Physics: Roger L. Lichti, Department Chair; Ph.D., Illinois.
Political Science: Dennis Patterson, Department Chair; Ph.D., UCLA.
Psychology: Lee Cohen, Department Chair; Ph.D., Oklahoma State.
Sociology, Anthropology, and Social Work: Yung-mei Tsai, Interim Department Chair; Ph.D., Colorado.

Business Administration: Allen McInnes, Dean; Ph.D., Texas at Austin (phone: 806-742-3188).
Senior Associate Dean: Debra Laverie, Ph.D., Arizona State.
Accounting: Robert Ricketts, Department Chair; Ph.D., North Texas.
Finance: Jeffrey M. Mercer, Department Chair (Wylie and Elizabeth Briscoe); Ph.D., Texas Tech.
Finance: Drew B. Winters, Department Chair (Lucille and Raymond Pickering); Ph.D., Georgia.
Information and Quantitative Sciences (MIS): Bradley T. Ewing, Area Coordinator; Ph.D., Purdue.
Management: William Gardner, Area Coordinator; Ph.D., Florida State.
Marketing: Bob McDonald, Area Coordinator; Ph.D., Connecticut.

Education: Scott Ridley, Dean; Ph.D., Texas at Austin (phone: 806-742-1837).
Autism Research: David Richman, Department Chair, postdoctoral fellow, Johns Hopkins University; Ph.D., Iowa.
Curriculum and Instruction: Doug Simpson, Department Chair; Ph.D., Oklahoma.
Curriculum and Instruction: Walter Smith, Department Chair; Ph.D., Indiana.
Educational Psychology and Leadership: William Lan, Department Chair; Ph.D., Iowa.

Engineering: Al Sacco, Dean; Ph.D., MIT (phone: 806-742-3451).
Chemical Engineering: M. Nazmul Karim, Department Chair; Ph.D., Manchester.
Civil and Environmental Engineering: H. Scott Norville, Department Chair; Ph.D., Purdue; PE.
Computer Science: William M. Marcy, Interim Chair; Ph.D., Texas Tech.
Construction Engineering and Engineering Technology: William R. Burkett, Department Chair; Ph.D., Texas at Austin.
Electrical and Computer Engineering: Michael Giesselmann, Department Chair; Ph.D., Darmstadt Tech (Germany).
Industrial Engineering: Patrick Patterson, Department Chair; Ph.D., Texas A&M.
Mechanical Engineering: Jharna Chaudhuri, Department Chair; Ph.D., Rutgers.
Petroleum Engineering: M. Y. Soliman, Ph.D., Stanford; PE.

Honors College: Stephen E. Fritz, Dean; Ph.D., Kentucky (phone: 806-742-1828).
Associate Dean: Marjean Puriton, Ph.D., Texas A&M.

Human Sciences: Linda Hoover, Dean; Ph.D., Texas Woman's (phone: 806-742-3031).
Assistant Dean (Research): Michael W. O'Boyle, Ph.D., USC.
Applies and Professional Studies: Vickie Hampton, Interim Chair; Ph.D., Illinois at Urbana-Champaign.
Applies and Professional Studies: Dottie Durband, Associate Chair; Ph.D., Virginia Tech.
Design: Cherif Amor, Department Chair; Ph.D., Missouri–Columbia.
Design: Don Collier, Associate Chair; M.F.A., Texas Tech.
Human Development and Family Studies: Jean Scott, Department Chair; Ph.D., North Carolina.
Nutrition, Hospitality, and Retailing: Shane Blum, Ph.D., Nevada.

School of Law: Darby Dickerson, Dean; J.D., Vanderbilt (phone: 806-742-3793).
Interim Dean: Susan Saab Fortney, J.D., Antioch Law.

Mass Communications: Jerry Hudson, Ph.D., North Texas (phone: 806-742-6500).
Associate Dean (Graduate Studies): Coy Callison, Ph.D., Alabama.
Associate Dean (Faculty Affairs): Kevin Stoker, Ph.D., Alabama.
Assistant Dean (Student Affairs): Marijane Wernsman, Ph.D., Tennessee–Knoxville.
Advertising: Samuel D. Bradley, Department Chair, Ph.D., Indiana.
Electronic Media and Communications: Leslie Todd Chambers, Department Chair; Ph.D., Tennessee.
Journalism: Randy Reddick, Department Chair; Ph.D., Ohio.
Public Relations: Trent Seltzer, Department Chair; Ph.D., Florida.

Visual and Performing Arts: Carol Edwards, Dean; Ph.D., Florida State (phone: 806-742-0700).
Associate Dean (Undergraduate and Curricular Issues): Robert Henry, Ph.D., North Texas.
Associate Dean (Graduate and Faculty Issues): Brian D. Steele, Ph.D., Iowa.
Art: Tina Fuentes, Director; M.F.A., North Texas.
Art: Andrew Martin, Associate Director; M.F.A., UCLA.
Music: William Ballenger, Director; M.A., Northeast Missouri State.
Music: Richard Bjella, Director of Choral Studies; M.M., Iowa.
Theater: Fred Christoffel, Department Chair; M.F.A., Illinois at Urbana-Champaign.

Interdisciplinary Studies: Clifford Fedler, Ph.D., Illinois; Ralph Ferguson, Coordinator; Ph.D., Texas Tech (phone: 806-742-2787).
Arid Land Studies: Aderbal C. Correa, Director; Ph.D., Stanford.
Biotechnology: David B. Knaff, Co-Director; Ph.D., Yale.
Biotechnology: Daniel M. Hardy, Co-Director; Ph.D., New Mexico.
Forensic Science: Kathy Sperry, Senior Director; Ph.D., Texas Tech (phone: 806-743-7901).
Forensic Science: James M. Childers, Director; M.S., Texas Tech.
Advanced Study of Museum Science and Heritage Management: Eileen Johnson, Executive Director; Ph.D., Texas Tech (phone: 806-742-2442).
Multidisciplinary Science: Jeff Lee, Ph.D., Arizona State.
Public Administration: Thomas Longoria, Ph.D., Texas A&M.
Wind Science and Engineering: John Schroeder, Director; Ph.D., Texas Tech.

Allied Health: Paul Brooke, Dean; Ph.D., Iowa; FACHE (phone: 806-743-3223).
Associate Dean and Chair: Hal S. Larsen, NIH (postdoctoral research fellowship) University of Tennessee; Ph.D., Nebraska Medical Center.
Athletic Training: LesLee Taylor, Program Director; Ph.D., Texas Tech.
Audiology: Candace Hicks, Program Director; Ph.D., Vanderbilt.
Clinical and Laboratory Science: Hal S. Larsen, Department Chair, NIH (postdoctoral research fellowship), University of Tennessee; Ph.D., Nebraska Medical Center.
Clinical and Laboratory Science: Lori Rice-Spearman, Program Director; Ph.D., Texas Tech University.
Clinical Practice Management: M. Nicholas Coppola, Program Director; Virginia Commonwealth.
Clinical Services Management: Michael J. Keller, Program Director; M.B.A.
Communication Sciences and Disorders: Rajinder Koul, Department Chair (Speech, Language, and Hearing Sciences); Ph.D., Purdue.
Molecular Pathology: Lori Rice-Spearman, Program Director; Ph.D., Texas Tech.
Occupational Therapy: Dawnra Meers Sechrist, Program Director; Ph.D., Texas Tech.
Physical Therapy: Kerry Gilbert, Program Director; Sc.D, Texas Tech.
Physical Therapy Doctor of Science: Phillip S. Sizer, Program Director; Ph.D., Texas Tech.
Physician Assistant: Elvin E. Maxwell Jr., Program Director and Regional Dean at Odessa; MPAS.
Rehabilitation Counseling: Evans H. Spears, Program Director; Ph.D., Arizona.
Rehabilitation Services: Steven Sawyer, Department Chair; Ph.D., San Diego.
Speech-Language Pathology: Sherry Sancibrian, Program Director; M.S., Texas Tech.

Graduate School of Biomedical Sciences: Douglas M. Stocco, Dean; Ph.D. (phone: 806-743-3000).
Interim Dean: Thomas A. Pressley, Ph.D., M.D., Medical University of South Carolina.
Cell Biology and Biochemistry: Harry Weitlauf, Department Chair; M.D., Washington (Seattle).
Microbiology and Immunology: Ronald Kennedy, Ph.D., Baylor College of Medicine.
Pharmacology: Reid L. Norman, Ph.D., Kansas.

Nursing: Alexia Green, Dean; Ph.D., Texas Woman's; RN (phone: 806-743-2737).
Interim Dean: Yondell Masten, Ph.D., RNC, WHNP.
Associate Dean (Practice and Research): Chris Esperat, Ph.D., RN.
Regional Dean: Josefina Lujan, Ph.D., Texas Health Science Center at Houston, RN.
Regional Dean: Pearl Merritt, Ed.D.
Regional Director, Sharon Cannon, Ed.D., RN.
Department Chair: Melinda Mitchell Jones, M.S.N., JD, RN.
Department Chair (Traditional Undergraduate Program): Cynthia O'Neal, Ph.D., Vanderbilt, RN.
Department Chair (Leadership Studies): Barbara Cherry, D.N.Sc., Texas Tech, RN.
Florence Thelma Hall Endowed Chair for Nursing Excellence in Women's Health: Chandice Covington, Ph.D., RN .

Medicine: Steven Lee Berk, Dean; M.D., Boston University (phone: 806-743-3000).
Luis Reuss, Department Chair; M.D., Chile.

Pharmacy: Arthur A. Nelson Jr., Dean; R.Ph., Ph.D., Iowa (phone: 806-356-4011).
Pharmacy Practice Management: Roland Patry, Department Chair; Dr.P.H., Texas Health Science Center at Houston.
Clinical Research and Science: Cynthia Raehl, Department Chair; Pharm.D., Kentucky.

UNION
INSTITUTE & UNIVERSITY

UNION INSTITUTE & UNIVERSITY

Programs of Study

With a legacy of over forty-five years of leadership and innovation in adult higher education, Union Institute & University (UI&U) offers graduate-level degree programs grounded in real-life application and designed exclusively for self-motivated adults. Program offerings include the Master of Arts, Master of Arts with a concentration in counseling psychology, Master of Education, Doctor of Philosophy in interdisciplinary studies, Doctor of Education, and Doctor of Psychology.

Union Institute & University graduate degree programs prepare graduates to effect change and serve their communities as leaders within the private and public sectors, education, and the social sciences and reflect the University's vision: to engage, enlighten, and empower highly motivated adults in their pursuit of a lifetime of learning and service.

UI&U offers master's programs through a variety of learning options, including online, low-residency, and hybrid course delivery.

UI&U's **Master of Arts** program offers opportunities for individualized learning, allowing learners to tailor their course of study to meet their unique personal and professional goals. Offerings include concentrations in creativity studies, health and wellness, history and culture, leadership, public policy and social issues, and literature and writing. The online format allows learners the flexibility to earn an advanced degree while managing professional and personal responsibilities, such as career and family.

UI&U's **Master of Education (M.Ed.)** program, which is offered online, prepares new leaders to better inform and advance the field of education. Many current learners and graduates are primary and secondary school teachers and administrators, nonprofit education staff members and executives, and those simply concerned with preparing the world's children with the best possible educational options. The M.Ed. program also prepares graduates for certification or licensure in teaching, administration, or counseling.

UI&U's **Master of Arts with a concentration in counseling psychology** program educates future psychologists and counselor practitioners to identify and treat psychological problems and issues in a variety of clinical, educational, and workplace settings. The program is designed specifically to offer the traditional courses and supervised internship experiences that are increasingly required by state and national agencies and credentialing bodies. Working with a team of faculty advisers who possess relevant practitioner experience, learners engage in critical inquiry, thoroughly examine and interact with literature, theory, and research, and pursue and share the results of applied research. With the exception of brief residencies held in Brattleboro, Vermont, learners work and study online or at a distance while completing their studies.

Union Institute & University's doctoral programs are rooted in UI&U's fundamental commitment to provide interdisciplinary, socially relevant studies in which learners critically consider their research within and beyond the classroom and then act upon that knowledge in the greater community. UI&U offers a rich academic environment with an emphasis on social justice and the integration of theory and practice, guiding learners to become agents of positive intellectual and social change. This exploration of the creative process provides learners with a foundation for generating new ideas and solutions to the issues they will encounter throughout their professional and civic lives.

UI&U's **Ph.D. in interdisciplinary studies** program has long been a hallmark of the University. With a focus on social justice and interdisciplinary studies, the Ph.D. program draws from established academic disciplines while developing new approaches and generating essential knowledge related to critical intellectual and social issues. Learners enrolled in this program choose from three distinct areas of concentration: ethical and creative leadership; public policy and social change; and humanities and culture. A specialization in Martin Luther King, Jr. studies is also offered. Faculty members are deeply grounded in their fields and are recognized, productive scholars in their respective areas of academic expertise. Their goal is to collaborate with learners and engage scholar-practitioners who utilize interdisciplinary approaches to acquire a deeply informed and integrated understanding of the practice of leadership. Studies are completed online, with brief academic residencies held bi-annually in Cincinnati, Ohio.

UI&U's **Doctor of Education (Ed.D.)** program offers specializations in educational leadership (Pre-K through 12) and higher education, both with an emphasis on ethics and social justice. The Ed.D. program is uniquely designed to align with the needs, experiences, and interests of mid-career professionals. Learners advance through the program in a small cohort of fellow scholar-practitioners. Seminars are delivered online, in Web-hosted meetings, as well as face-to-face during annual residencies in Cincinnati, Ohio. Learners benefit from the program's experienced faculty and a collaborative learning environment, as they develop the attitudes, knowledge, and skills needed to advance their careers.

UI&U's **Doctor of Psychology** program offers the Psy.D. degree with a concentration in clinical psychology. The program follows a distributed learning, scholar-practitioner model and offers a combination of online and low-residency learning, accessible to working adults with career, family, and community responsibilities. Learners meet in small cohorts monthly and attend semiannual academic meetings in Cincinnati, Ohio, and Brattleboro, Vermont. Learners are trained not only to assess and treat mental health problems but also to understand and treat problems within their sociopolitical context. These include issues related to poverty, violence, substance abuse, racism, homophobia, and other forms of oppression. Learners in the Psy.D. program also become deeply aware of the ethical issues involved in providing psychological services.

Research Facilities

Union Institute & University's library offers a wide range of academic services, including research and reference services, available to all members of the UI&U teaching and learning community through its Web site at http://www.myunion.edu/library. The library offers over 50,000 electronic, full-text periodical subscriptions via more than 230 online databases. Also offered is a growing collection of more than 171,095 e-books, accessible through the library's online catalog. In addition, the Dissertations and Theses Database offers over 1,200,000 online, full-text dissertations and theses from universities across the country. Throughout the year, the library offers database trials for learners to peruse and evaluate and provides access to Google Scholar to connect learners to the library's full-text resources.

UI&U librarians are also available for research support via online chat, on the phone or on-site at the Montpelier Center facility.

Financial Aid

A full range of federal and state financial aid programs, including grants and loans, are available to eligible UI&U learners. In addition, a growing number of scholarships are available. The UI&U Office of Financial Aid works with learners to educate, inform, and assist with financial support while they work toward a graduate degree at Union Institute & University. For more information, please contact UI&U Office of Financial Aid at finaid@myunion.edu or 800-486-3116 Ext. 2005 (toll free), or visit the Web site at http://www.myunion.edu/finaid.

Cost of Study

Tuition for UI&U master's and doctoral degree programs varies by program, ranging from $557 to $1078 per credit hour. Information regarding the most up-to-date tuition costs for each UI&U graduate program can be found on the UI&U Admissions Web site: http://www.myunion.edu/tuition, or contact the Office of Admissions at 513-487-1219.

Living and Housing Costs

UI&U graduate learners complete their studies through rigorous online, hybrid, or low-residency learning. During academic residencies or meetings, local housing is managed by the University in a number of dynamic geographic hubs, including Cincinnati, Ohio; Montpelier and Brattleboro, Vermont; and Miami, Florida.

Student Group

Currently, total enrollment at Union Institute & University is more than 2,000, with approximately 200 doctoral learners and 225 master's degree learners. The learner population is diverse—women compose 73 percent of enrolled graduate learners, and members of minority groups compose 29 percent.

Location

Union Institute & University's regional academic centers are conveniently located in Miami, Florida; Los Angeles and Sacramento, California; Montpelier and Brattleboro, Vermont; and Cincinnati, Ohio, the university's administrative headquarters. All academic centers are led by faculty and learner services staff members who are prepared to help learners create a path that meets their personal learning style and goals.

The University

Founded in 1964, Union Institute & University's mission is committed to educating generations of highly motivated adults who seek academic programs that engage, enlighten, and empower them in their pursuit of a lifetime of learning and service. Curricula dedicated to the University's four learning outcomes—communication, critical and creative thinking, ethical and social responsibility, and social and global perspectives—underscores Union's six graduate degree programs. Fulfilling critical leadership roles in education, nonprofit management, and public policy, the University's alumni draw upon their education to create change in their own lives and in the lives of others. In addition, Union's distance, online, and classroom learning options allow adults to pursue a degree while balancing family, community, and career obligations. To learn more about UI&U, visit http://www.myunion.edu.

Applying

Standard entry examinations such as the Graduate Record Examination (GRE) are not required when applying for UI&U's graduate degree programs. For additional information about the application process or to speak to an admissions counselor, prospective students should call 513-487-1219 or visit the UI&U Admissions Web site at http://www.myunion.edu/admissions.

Correspondence and Information

Office of Admissions
Union Institute & University
440 E. McMillan Street
Cincinnati, Ohio 45206

Phone: 513-487-1219
E-mail: admissions@myunion.edu
Web site: http://www.myunion.edu/admissions

THE FACULTY

Administrative Leadership
Roger Sublett, President; Ph.D., Tulane.

Richard Hansen, Provost; Ph.D., Denver.
Patricia Brewer, Associate Provost; Ed.D., Columbia.
Elizabeth Pruden, Associate Provost; Ph.D., Minnesota.
Larry Preston, Dean, Doctor of Philosophy in Interdisciplinary Studies Program; Ph.D., Missouri.
Toni Gregory, Associate Dean, Doctor of Philosophy in Interdisciplinary Studies Program; Ed.D., Cincinnati.
Nancy Boxill, Coordinator of MLK Studies, Doctor of Philosophy in Interdisciplinary Studies Program; Ph.D., Union (Ohio).
William Lax, Dean, Doctor of Psychology in Clinical Psychology Program; Ph.D., Fielding Institute.
Margarita O'Neill, Director of Clinical Training, Doctor of Psychology in Clinical Psychology Program; Ed.D., Massachusetts.
Arlene Sacks, Dean, Doctor of Education Program; Ed.D., West Virginia.
Brian Webb, Associate Dean, Master of Arts Online Program; D.Mus., Indiana.
Nicholas Young, Director, Master of Arts with a Concentration in Counseling Psychology Program; Ed.D, American International; Ph.D., Union (Ohio).

THE FACULTY
Master of Arts Program
Anna Blair, Ph.D., Union Institute.
Elden Golden, Ph.D., Louisville.
Judith McDaniel, Ph.D., Tufts.
Loree Miltich, Ph.D., Union Institute.
Woden Teachout, Ph.D., Harvard.
Asghar Zomorrodian, Ph.D., USC.

Master of Arts with a Concentration in Counseling Psychology Program
Dorothy Firman, Ed.D., Massachusetts Amherst.
Richard Judah, Ed.D., Penn State.
Christine Michael, Ph.D., Connecticut.
Scott Rice, Ph.D., Massachusetts Amherst.
Andy Vengrove, Ed.D, American International.

Master of Education Program
Jay Keehn, Master of Education Director; Ph.D., Barry.
Beverly Carter Remy, Ed.D., Nova Southeastern.
Susan Seigel, Ed.D., Massachusetts Amherst.
Ben Williams, Ph.D., Harvard.

Doctor of Philosophy in Interdisciplinary Studies Program
Shelley Armitage, Ph.D., New Mexico.
Nancy Boxill, Ph.D., Union Institute.
Marcel Kitissou, Ph.D., Syracuse.
Lois Melina, Ph.D., Gonzaga.
Karsten Piep, Ph.D., Miami (Ohio).
Andrea Scarpino, M.F.A., Ohio State.
Mary Ann Steger, Ph.D., Southern Illinois Carbondale.
Christopher Voparil, Ph.D., The New School for Social Research.

Doctor of Education Program
Constance Beutel, Ph.D., San Francisco.
Jim Caraway, Ph.D., Emory.
Jim Henderson, Ed.D., Rutgers.
Anu Mitra, Ph.D., Rochester.
Joseph Nolan, Ph.D., Texas Woman's.
Michael Raffanti, Ed.D., Fielding Graduate University.

Doctor of Psychology in Clinical Psychology Program
Lewis Mehl-Madrona, M.D./Ph.D., Psychological Studies Institute.
Joy McGhee, Psy.D., Wright State.
Jennifer Ossege, Psy.D., Xavier.
Jennifer Scott, Psy.D., Xavier.
Richard Sears, Psy.D., Wright State.

Union engages, enlightens, and empowers adult learners.

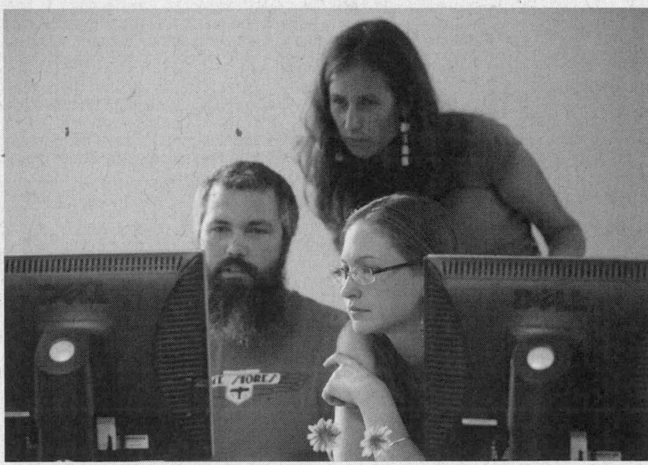

The graduate-level degree programs at UI&U are grounded in real-life applications and are designed exclusively for self-motivated adults.

UNIVERSITY OF CONNECTICUT

Graduate School

Programs of Study

The Graduate School of the University of Connecticut offers programs leading to the degrees of Master of Arts, Master of Science, Master of Business Administration, Master of Dental Science, Master of Engineering, Master of Fine Arts (offered in art and dramatic arts), Master of Music, Master of Professional Studies (offered in homeland security leadership, human resource management, and humanitarian services administration), Master of Public Administration, Master of Public Health, and Master of Social Work, as well as to the degrees of Doctor of Audiology, Doctor of Education (educational leadership), Doctor of Musical Arts, Doctor of Nursing Practice, Doctor of Physical Therapy, and Doctor of Philosophy.

Study leading to the degree of Master of Arts or Master of Science is offered in accounting; adult learning; agricultural and resource economics; allied health; animal science; anthropology; applied financial mathematics; applied genomics; applied microbial systems analysis; art history; biochemistry; biodiversity and conservation biology; biomedical engineering; cell biology; chemical engineering; chemistry; civil engineering; clinical and translational research; communication sciences; comparative literary and cultural studies; computer science and engineering; curriculum and instruction; dramatic arts; ecology and evolutionary biology; economics; educational administration; educational psychology; educational technology; electrical engineering; English; environmental engineering; financial risk management; French; genetics and genomics; geography; geological sciences; German; higher education and student affairs; history; human development and family studies; international studies; Italian; Judaic studies; kinesiology; linguistics; materials science; materials science and engineering; mathematics; mechanical engineering; medieval studies; microbiology; music; natural resources—land, water, and air; nursing; nutritional science; oceanography; pathobiology; pharmaceutical science; philosophy; physics; physiology and neurobiology; plant science; political science; polymer science; psychology; sociology; Spanish; special education; statistics; structural biology and biophysics; and survey research.

Study leading to the degree of Doctor of Philosophy is offered in adult learning; agricultural and resource economics; animal science; anthropology; biochemistry; biomedical engineering; biomedical science; business administration; cell biology; chemical engineering; chemistry; civil engineering; communication sciences; comparative literary and cultural studies; computer science and engineering; curriculum and instruction; ecology and evolutionary biology; economics; educational administration; educational psychology; electrical engineering; English; environmental engineering; French; genetics and genomics; geography; geological sciences; German; history; human development and family studies; Italian; kinesiology; linguistics; materials science; materials science and engineering; mathematics; mechanical engineering; medieval studies; microbiology; music; natural resources–land, water, and air; nursing; nutritional science; oceanography; pathobiology; pharmaceutical science; philosophy; physics; physiology and neurobiology; plant science; political science; polymer science; psychology; public health; social work; sociology; Spanish; special education; statistics; and structural biology and biophysics.

Research Facilities

The Homer Babbidge Library at Storrs provides a wide variety of study facilities, including individually assigned research studies, group studies, and areas designed for the use of computers, videos, and microtext. The building contains approximately 3 million volumes of the system's total of more than 4 million volumes, as well as microtext, maps, manuscripts, archives, recordings, and other materials. The library's book and journal holdings as well as many periodical indexes are accessible through HOMER, the online information system. A wide array of electronic resources is available in the reference area of the Babbidge Library. The Thomas J. Dodd Research Center is a fully equipped research facility and a major archive for historic papers. The University has several dozen centers and institutes that promote research in specialized areas of study.

Financial Aid

Available sources of aid include graduate assistantships for teaching and research, University predoctoral fellowships, doctoral dissertation fellowships, and aid in a variety of forms for students in specific programs.

Cost of Study

Course-related fees in 2011–12 for full-time students total $6065 per semester for in-state students and $14,219 per semester for out-of-state students. Fees for part-time study are prorated. Fees are subject to change without notice.

Living and Housing Costs

On-campus housing for graduate students is limited. In 2011–12, the basic rate for students living on campus is $3486 per semester. Information about other on-campus housing options is available online at http://www.reslife.uconn.edu. The fee for the comprehensive board plan is $2566 per semester. Other options are available. Fees are subject to change without notice.

Student Group

Approximately 7,000 students are enrolled in graduate degree programs. About 2,400 are working toward doctoral degrees.

Location

Most graduate degree programs offered by the University are located at the Storrs campus, which is 25 miles northeast of Hartford. Storrs is a scenic, agricultural area. Degree programs in the biomedical sciences and the marine sciences are offered at the University of Connecticut Health Center in Farmington (near Hartford) and at the Marine Sciences Institute at Avery Point (on Long Island Sound), respectively. The School of Social Work is located in West Hartford.

The University

The University of Connecticut grew out of the Storrs Agricultural School, which was founded in 1881 as a direct result of the gift of land, money, and buildings presented to the Connecticut General Assembly by Charles and Augustus Storrs of Mansfield. Master's degree study was offered by 1920. The Graduate School was established officially in 1939, and the University conferred its first Ph.D.'s a decade later.

Applying

Applicants should consult the academic department or program of their choice concerning application deadlines. Applicants are encouraged to apply online. Many programs have early closing dates. Application to some programs may require scores on one or more graduate admission tests, an interview or audition, or demonstrated proof of adequate facility in English for international applicants (the TOEFL is generally required for international applicants whose native language is not English). A complete summary of these requirements is available at http://www.grad.uconn.edu/.

Correspondence and Information

The Graduate School
Unit 1006
University of Connecticut
438 Whitney Road Extension
Storrs, Connecticut 06269-1006

Phone: 860-486-3617
E-mail: gradschool@uconn.edu
Web site: http://www.grad.uconn.edu/

FACULTY HEADS

Accounting: A. J. Rosman, Ph.D.
Adult Learning: C. D. Cobb, Ph.D.
Agricultural and Resource Economics: R. Lopez, Ph.D.
Allied Health: L. Silbart, Ph.D.
Animal Science: D. Fletcher, Ph.D.
Anthropology: S. O. McBrearty, Ph.D.
Applied Financial Mathematics: J. G. Bridgeman, M.A.
Applied Genomics: L. Strausbaugh, Ph.D.
Applied Microbial Systems Analysis: D. R. Benson, Ph.D.
Art: J. Thorpe, M.F.A.
Art History: J. Thorpe, M.F.A.
Biochemistry: D. R. Benson, Ph.D.
Biodiversity and Conservation Biology: K. Wells, Ph.D.
Biomedical Engineering: D. R. Peterson, Ph.D.
Biomedical Science: B. E. Kream, Ph.D.
Biophysics and Structural Biology: D. R. Benson, Ph.D.
Business Administration: K. Fox, J.D.
Cell Biology: D. R. Benson, Ph.D.
Chemical Engineering: C. B. Carter, Ph.D.
Chemistry: A. R. Howell, Ph.D.
Civil Engineering: A. C. Bagtzoglou, Ph.D.
Communication Science: C. A. Coehlo, Ph.D.
Comparative Literary and Cultural Studies: R. H. Chinchilla, Ph.D.
Computer Science and Engineering: R. A. Ammar, Ph.D.
Curriculum and Instruction: M. A. Doyle, Ph.D.
Dental Science: A. R. Hand, D.D.S.
Dramatic Arts: V. Cardinal, M.F.A.
Ecology and Evolutionary Biology: K. Wells, Ph.D.
Economics: M. Cosgel, Ph.D.
Educational Administration: C. D. Cobb, Ph.D.
Educational Psychology: H. Swaminathan, Ph.D.
Educational Technology: M. Young, Ph.D.
Electrical Engineering: R. Bansal, Ph.D.
Engineering: M. Choi, Ph.D.
English: W. S. Franklin, Ph.D.
Environmental Engineering: A. C. Bagtzoglou, Ph.D.
Financial Risk Management: R. D. Gopal, Ph.D.
French: R. H. Chinchilla, Ph.D.
Genetics: D. R. Benson, Ph.D.
Geography: J. P. Osleeb, Ph.D.
Geological Sciences: P. Visscher, Ph.D.
German: R. H. Chinchilla, Ph.D.
Higher Education and Student Affairs: S. Saunders, Ph.D.
History: S. A. Roe, Ph.D.
Human Development and Family Studies: R. M. Sabatelli, Ph.D.
International Studies: E. Mahan, Ph.D.
Italian: R. H. Chinchilla, Ph.D.
Judaic Studies: A. M. Dashefsky, Ph.D.
Kinesiology: C. M. Maresh, Ph.D.
Linguistics: W. Snyder, Ph.D.
Materials Science: H. L. Marcus, Ph.D.
Materials Science and Engineering: C. B. Carter, Ph.D.
Mathematics: J. L. Tollefson, Ph.D.
Mechanical Engineering: B. Cetegen, Ph.D.
Medieval Studies: T. J. Jambeck, Ph.D.
Microbiology: D. R. Benson, Ph.D.
Music: C. Jarjisian, D.M.A.
Natural Resources: J. C. Volin, Ph.D.
Nursing: R. M. Cusson, Ph.D.
Nutritional Science: S. Koo, Ph.D.
Oceanography: A. C. Bucklin, Ph.D.
Pathobiology: S. J. Geary, Ph.D.
Pharmaceutical Science: D. Kendall, Ph.D.
Philosophy: C. L. Elder, Ph.D.
Physical Therapy: C. R. Denegar, Ph.D.
Physics: D. S. Hamilton, Ph.D.
Physiology and Neurobiology: J. L. Renfro, Ph.D.
Plant Science: R. J. McAvoy, Ph.D.
Political Science: M. A. Boyer, Ph.D.
Polymer Science: D. H. Adamson, Ph.D.
Professional Studies: P. C. Diplock, Ph.D.
Psychology: J. A. Green, Ph.D.
Public Administration: A. K. Donahue, Ph.D.
Public Health (M.P.H. Program): D. Gregorio, Ph.D.
Public Health (Ph.D. Program): A. M. Ferris, Ph.D.
Social Work: S. Raheim, Ph.D.
Sociology: D. S. Glasberg, Ph.D.
Spanish: R. H. Chinchilla, Ph.D.
Special Education: H. Swaminathan, Ph.D.
Statistics: J. Glaz, Ph.D.
Structural Biology and Biophysics: D. R. Benson, Ph.D.
Survey Research: A. K. Donahue, Ph.D.

A study area in the Homer Babbidge Library on the Storrs campus.

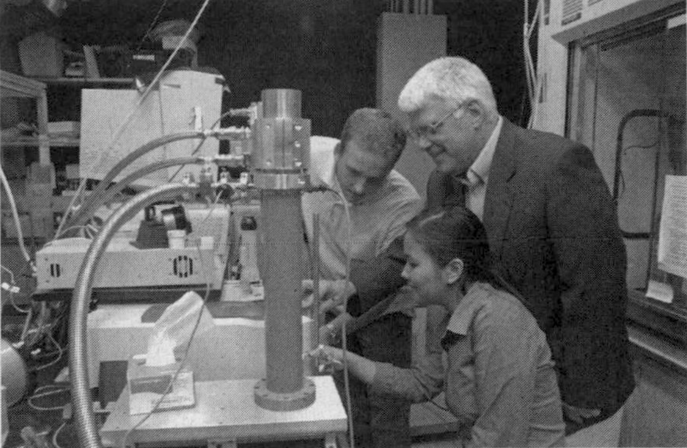

A faculty member works with graduate students in the lab.

Many new buildings on campus have been completed in recent years, including the Chemistry Building shown above.

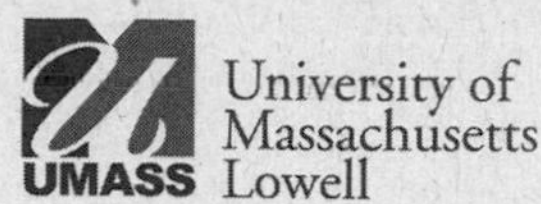

UNIVERSITY OF MASSACHUSETTS LOWELL

Graduate School

Programs of Study

The University of Massachusetts (UMass) Lowell offers more than 100 areas of graduate study in twenty doctoral degrees, over forty master's degrees, and more than seventy graduate certificate programs, which are regionally and nationally accredited. Lowell's internationally renowned research faculty members take a deep personal interest in the professional development of their students.

The Doctor of Philosophy (Ph.D.) is offered in biomedical engineering and biotechnology (intercampus), chemistry (with options in biochemistry, environmental studies, polymer science, and polymer science/plastics engineering, which is offered jointly with the Plastics Engineering Department), computer science (with options in bioinformatics and computational mathematics), criminal justice (with options in crime, criminals, and community; global perspectives on crime and justice; justice system and policy; technology and criminal justice; and victims, crime, and justice) marine sciences and technology (intercampus), nursing (health promotion option), physics (with options in applied mechanics, atmospheric sciences, applied physics, and energy engineering), and radiological sciences. Both the Doctor of Philosophy (Ph.D.) and the Doctor of Engineering (D.Eng.) are available in chemical engineering, civil and environmental engineering, computer engineering, electrical engineering, energy engineering (with options in nuclear or renewable/solar), mechanical engineering, and plastics engineering. The Doctor of Science (Sc.D.) is offered in work environment (with options in cleaner production and pollution prevention, epidemiology, occupational and environmental hygiene, occupational ergonomics and safety, and work environment policy). A Doctor of Physical Therapy (D.P.T.) is offered by the School of Health and Environment. The Doctor of Education (Ed.D.) is available in language arts and literacy, leadership in schooling, and mathematics and science education. The Education Specialist (Ed.S.) is offered in curriculum and instruction; administration, planning, and policy; and reading and language. The Master of Arts (M.A.) is offered in community and social psychology, criminal justice, economic and social development of regions, and peace and conflict studies.

The Master of Science (M.S.) is available in biological sciences (with an option in biotechnology, and Professional Science Master's [P.S.M.] options in applied biotechnology, environmental biotechnology, biosafety, and project management in life sciences), biomedical engineering and biotechnology (with a P.S.M. option), chemistry (with P.S.M. options in chemistry and polymer science, and pharmaceutical biochemistry), clinical laboratory sciences (with a P.S.M. option), computer science (with options in biochemical informatics and entrepreneurship), environmental studies (with concentrations in atmospheric science and environmental engineering sciences, and a P.S.M. option in atmospheric sciences), health informatics and policy (with options in health informatics, health policy, and health management), marine sciences and technology (an intercampus program with a P.S.M. option in coastal and ocean administration, science, and technology), mathematics (with options in applied and computational mathematics, mathematics for teachers, statistics and operations research, and an industrial mathematics P.S.M. option), nursing (with options in adult psychiatric/mental health, family health, and adult/gerontological nursing), physics (with areas of study in atomic physics, elementary particle physics, experimental and theoretical condensed-matter physics, experimental and theoretical nuclear physics, laser physics, optics, and photonics, or an option in optical sciences), radiological sciences and protection (with a P.S.M. option), and work environment (with options in cleaner production and pollution prevention, epidemiology, industrial hygiene, occupational ergonomics and safety, and work environment policy, and P.S.M. options in cleaner production and pollution prevention, environmental epidemiology, ergonomics and safety, and occupational and environmental hygiene).

The Master of Science in Engineering (M.S.Eng.) is offered in chemical engineering, civil engineering (with options in environmental and geoenvironmental, geotechnical, structural, and transportation), computer engineering, electrical engineering (with concentrations in information systems, optoelectronics, and power and energy engineering), energy engineering (nuclear and renewable/solar), mechanical engineering, and plastics engineering (with concentrations in elastomeric materials, materials design, medical, and processing materials). The Master of Education (M.Ed.) is offered in curriculum and instruction (a science education option is available online), educational administration, and reading and language. The Master of Music (M.M.) is available in music education (teaching) and sound recording technology. The College of Management offers an accredited Master of Business Administration (M.B.A.) (with options in accounting, finance, and information technology) which is available on-campus, online, or blended; and a Master of Science in innovation and technological entrepreneurship (MSITE) program.

UMass Lowell is among the national leaders in graduate certificate education. Graduate certificates are designed to provide knowledge and expertise vital to today's changing and complex needs in the workplace. In most cases, courses may be applied toward a master's degree program. Most certificates consist of four courses and 12 graduate credits. Graduate certificates are offered in a wide variety of areas including biomedical, health, and social sciences; computers, communications, and information systems; engineering; management; education; and environmental studies. A number of programs are also available online.

Research Facilities

UMass Lowell is a nationally ranked research university with more than $50 million in funded research being conducted each year. Research happens on many levels of the campus—in academic departments, through thirty-seven interdisciplinary research groups, by graduate and undergraduate students, and with corporate sponsorship and leading national research institutes. Researchers have projects funded by the National Science Foundation (NSF), National Institute on Occupational Health and Safety (NIOSH), Department of Defense, Department of Education, and many other federal and state granting agencies. Industrial-community relations are nurtured and enhanced through research collaborations, technology exchange, student internships, and advisory boards. Faculty members routinely interact with industry, business, community groups, and government agencies. Each spring UMass Lowell students showcase their innovative research and present posters at the Annual Student Research and Community Engagement Symposium.

The $70-million Emerging Technologies and Innovation Center (ETIC) is scheduled to open in fall 2012. The 84,000-square-foot facility is expected to be the hub of industry partnerships and new manufacturing technologies. The ETIC will provide core facilities for use in fundamental and translational research. The building design meets critical criteria for temperature, humidity, and vibration. It will house Class 100, Class 1,000, and Class 10,000 clean room spaces, wet lab and engineering lab space, and a plastics processing high bay. This research and academic facility is one of several new buildings on campus.

In addition to departmental lab facilities, the University has hundreds of workstations, PCs, and terminals connected to multiple servers via a state-of-the-art network infrastructure. Multimedia labs, distance learning classrooms, and online programs are available. UMass Lowell's electronic library includes more than 300 databases, more than 28,000 journals, and computer workstations and wireless systems. The library has consortium arrangements with other major libraries, and remote computer access is available. UMass Lowell is also a member of the Inter-University Consortium for Political and Social Research (ICPSR) with direct, free access to all of ICPSR's data resources and user support.

Financial Aid

Nearly 500 teaching and research assistantships (TAs/RAs) carrying stipends, tuition and fee waivers (full or partial), and partial health insurance waivers were awarded to qualified graduate students across all disciplines in 2010–11. Students interested in a teaching or research assistant position should contact the graduate coordinator or chair of the department to which they are applying. The Office of Financial Aid assists students through the Federal Direct, Perkins, and Stafford Student Loan programs. Low-interest student loans are also available for citizens of Massachusetts and Canada through the Massachusetts Educational Financing Authority (MEFA). The University also awards Dean's and Provost's scholarships and University fellowships to new students.

Cost of Study

In 2011–12, approximate tuition and fees for a 3-credit graduate course are $1784 for Massachusetts residents and $3300 for out-of-state students. New England Regional Tuition is available for some programs of study, in which qualified out-of-state students pay 150 percent of the Massachusetts resident tuition charges.

Living and Housing Costs

Graduate students can find reasonably priced furnished and unfurnished rooms and apartments in the greater Lowell area. The cost of living varies with the type of accommodations desired and the needs and resources of the individual. Apartments commonly require one month's security deposit.

Student Group

The fall 2010 total enrollment was 14,686, of whom 3,426 were graduate students and 12,101 were undergraduates. Of the graduate students enrolled approximately 50 percent were women and 450 were international students.

Student Outcomes

UMass Lowell awards a significant percentage of its total degrees at the graduate level. Response from both graduate student alumni and industry employers reveals high satisfaction with education received and level of preparedness and professional perspective. Graduate students are highly sought by major corporations, both as interns during the course of their studies and as full-time employees upon graduation.

Location

In the heart of the birthplace of America's Industrial Revolution, Lowell, Massachusetts, is 25 miles from Boston and home to the first urban national park in the U.S. The Merrimack River runs through this city of 105,000, which hosts professional baseball and hockey adjacent to the campus. Access to Boston is easy via car or commuter train. New Hampshire, Vermont, and Maine, as well as the shores and beaches of the Atlantic Ocean and Cape Cod, are short driving distances away.

The University

UMass Lowell is a comprehensive university with a national reputation in the fields of science, engineering, and technology. The University is committed to educating students for lifelong success in a diverse world and conducting research and outreach activities that sustain the economic, environmental, and social health of the region. The University offers more than 14,000 students over 120 degree choices, internships, programs, and doctoral studies in the colleges of Fine Arts, Humanities, and Social Sciences; Sciences; Engineering; and Management; the School of Health and Environment; and the Graduate School of Education. Graduate students have access to selected courses at other campuses through the UMass Graduate Studies Consortium.

For more than a century, the UMass Lowell has been educating students to work in the real world, solve real problems, and help real people. The University began as the Lowell Normal School, founded in 1894 to prepare students to become teachers, and the Lowell Textile School, founded in 1895 to train technicians and managers for the textile industry. Both institutions extended their offerings to meet the growing needs of the region and in 1975, Lowell State and Lowell Tech, as they were then known, merged to form the University of Lowell. In 1991, the campus became part of the five-campus University of Massachusetts system.

Applying

Applications (except for computer science and biological sciences) can be submitted at any time; however, early applications ensure that all materials are processed on time and that due consideration is given to those seeking assistantships and fellowship awards. GRE General Test, GMAT (for the M.B.A.), MTEL (for the Graduate School of Education), and TOEFL (for international students) scores; official transcripts; a statement of purpose; a $50 nonrefundable application fee; and three letters of reference are required. Some departments have early deadlines and additional requirements. Complete application packages with step-by-step instructions and course catalogs are available upon request. Online applications are recommended and are available on the Graduate Admissions Web site.

Correspondence and Information

Linda Southworth, Director, Graduate Admissions Office
University of Massachusetts Lowell
883 Broadway Street, Dugan Hall
Lowell, Massachusetts 01854-5130

Phone: 978-934-2390
800-656-GRAD (toll-free)
Fax: 978-934-4058
E-mail: graduate_admissions@uml.edu
Web site: http://www.uml.edu/grad

THE FACULTY

COLLEGE DEANS
E-mail format for faculty members is first name_last name@uml.edu.

Fine Arts, Humanities, and Social Sciences
Dr. Nina Coppens, Dean (ad interim), Durgin 112; 978-934-3832.

Education
Dr. Anita Greenwood, O'Leary Library 510; 978-934-4601.

Engineering
Dr. John Ting, Kitson 311; 978-934-2576.

Health and Environment
Dr. Shorty McKinney, Weed 104; 978-934-4510.

Intercampus Graduate School of Marine Sciences and Technology
Dr. Robert R. Gamache, Olney 302A; 978-934-3904.

Management
Dr. Kathryn Carter, Pasteur 305; 978-934-2741.

Sciences
Dr. Robert Tamarin, Olney 524; 978-934-3847.

GRADUATE PROGRAM COORDINATORS AND DEPARTMENT CHAIRS

Biological Sciences
Dr. Jerome Hojnacki, Coordinator, Olsen 515; 978-934-2870.
Dr. Juliette Rooney-Varga, Coordinator, Olsen 524; 978-934-4715.
Dr. Mark Hines, Chair, Olsen 517; 978-934-2867.

Biomedical Engineering and Biotechnology (intercampus)
Dr. Sanjeev Manohar, Director, Engineering 106; 978-934-3162.

Chemical Engineering
Dr. Francis Bonner, Coordinator, Engineering 306; 978-934-3154.
Dr. Alfred Donatelli, Chair, Engineering 104; 978-934-3171.

Chemistry/Polymer Science
Dr. David Ryan, Coordinator, Olney 318A; 978-934-3698.
Dr. James Whitten, Chair, Olney 315B; 978-934-3666.

Civil and Environmental Engineering
Dr. Chronis Stamatiadis, Coordinator, Pasteur 113; 978-934-2283.
Dr. Clifford Bruell, Chair, Engineering 105; 978-934-2284.

Clinical Laboratory and Nutritional Sciences
Dr. Alease Bruce, Coordinator, Weed 302; 978-934-4481.
Dr. Eugene Rogers, Chair, Weed 309A; 978-934-4478.

Computer Science
Dr. Cindy Chen, Coordinator, Olsen 205; 978-934-1968.
Dr. Jie Wang, Chair, Olsen 201; 978-934-3620.

Criminal Justice
Dr. Paul Tracy, Coordinator, Mahoney 203A; 978-934-4145.
Dr. Eve Buzawa, Chair, Mahoney 214; 978-934-4262.

Economic and Social Development of Regions
Dr. Monica Galizzi, Co-Director, Falmouth 302H, 978-934-2790.
Dr. Philip Moss, Co-Director, O'Leary 500N; 978-934-2787.

Education
Dr. Michaela Wyman-Colombo, Doctoral Coordinator, O'Leary 523; 978-934-4610.
Dr. Vera Ossen, Coordinator (all licensure programs), O'Leary 510; 978-934-4604.
Dr. Jay Simmons, Chair, O'Leary 518; 978-934-4615.

Electrical and Computer Engineering
Dr. Tenneti Rao, Coordinator (master's), Ball 307; 978-934-3323.
Dr. Anh Tran, Coordinator (master's), Ball 317, 978-924-3027.
Dr. Alkim Akyurtlu, Coordinator (doctoral), Ball 417, 978-934-3027.
Dr. Craig Armiento, Chair, Ball 301; 978-934-3395.

Energy Engineering (M.E.)
Dr. John Duffy, Coordinator (renewable/solar), Engineering 330A; 978-934-2968.
Dr. Gilbert Brown, Coordinator (nuclear), Engineering 220; 978-934-3166.

Environmental Studies
Dr. Kenneth Lee, Coordinator (environmental engineering sciences), Falmouth 107C; 978-934-2255.
Dr. Matthew Barlow, Coordinator (atmospheric sciences), Olney 302, 978-934-3908.
Dr. Nelson Eby, Chair (atmospheric sciences) Olney 302B; 978-934-3097.

Health Informatics and Policy
Dr. James Lee, Coordinator, Weed 300; 978-934-4522 (AJames_Lee@uml.edu).
Dr. Nicole Champagne, Chair, Weed 313H; 978-934-4132.

Management
Dr. Gary Mucica, Coordinator (M.B.A.), Pasteur 303; 978-934-2853.
Kathleen Rourke, Coordinator (M.B.A.), Pasteur 303; 978-934-2848.
Dr. Steven Tello, Coordinator (M.S. in Innovation and Technological Entrepreneurship), Pasteur 303; 978-934-4240.

Marine Sciences and Technology (intercampus)
Dr. Robert Gamache, Dean, Olney 302A; 978-934-3904.

Mathematical Sciences
Dr. Ravi Montenegro, Coordinator, Olney 428E; 978-934-2442.
Dr. Stephen Pennell, Chair, Olney 428M; 978-934-2710.

Mechanical Engineering
Dr. Majid Charmchi, Coordinator, Ball 224; 978-934-2969.
Dr. John McKelliget, Chair, Engineering 331; 978-934-2974.

Music
Dr. Gena Greher, Coordinator (music education), Durgin 326; 978-934-3893.
Dr. Alex Case, Coordinator (sound recording technology), Durgin 323; 978-934-3878.
Dr. John Shirley, Chair, Durgin 314; 978-934-3886.

Nursing
Dr. Susan Reece, Coordinator (M.S. and graduate certificate programs), O'Leary 540M; 978-934-4421.
Dr. Barbara Mawn, Coordinator (Ph.D.), O'Leary 535; 978-934-4485.
Dr. Susan Houde, Chair, O'Leary 540J; 978-934-4426.

Physical Therapy
Dr. Keith Hallbourg, Coordinator, Weed 200; 978-934-4402.
Dr. Sean Collins, Chair, Weed 202; 978-934-4375.

Physics
Dr. James Egan, Coordinator, Olney 136; 978-934-3780.
Dr. Robert Giles, Chair, Olney 114; 978-934-3780.

Plastics Engineering
Dr. Stephen McCarthy, Coordinator (master's program), Ball 207A; 978-934-3417.
Dr. Jan-Chan Huang, Coordinator (doctoral programs), Ball 213; 978-934-3428.
Dr. Robert Malloy, Chair, Ball 204; 978-934-3435.

Psychology
Dr. Andrew Hostetler, Coordinator, Mahoney 3, 978-934-3979.
Dr. Richard Siegel, Chair, Mahoney 104B; 978-934-3961.

Radiological Sciences (Physics)
Dr. Clayton French, Coordinator, Pinanski 207; 978-934-3286.

Work Environment
Dr. Bryan Buchholz, Coordinator, Kitson 204D; 978-934-3241.
Dr. David Kriebel, Chair, Kitson 202D; 978-934-3271.

Sailing on the Merrimack River.

Riverside walk adjacent to the two campuses.

UNIVERSITY OF NEW HAVEN

Graduate Studies

Programs of Study

The University of New Haven (UNH) offers Master of Arts degree programs in community psychology and industrial/organizational psychology. The Master of Business Administration program has eight available areas of concentration, including options in accounting, business policy and strategic leadership, finance, global marketing and e-commerce, human resource management, sports management, a fifth-year CPA exam track, and a track for prospective chartered financial analyst (CFA) candidates. Dual-degree programs allow students to earn both the M.B.A. and the Master of Science in Industrial Engineering or both the M.B.A. and the Master of Public Administration. An Executive M.B.A. degree program designed for experienced, upper-level executives and managers is also offered by the University.

The Master of Science degree is offered in the areas of cellular and molecular biology, computer science, criminal justice, education, electrical engineering, engineering and operations management, environmental engineering, environmental science, engineering management, fire science, forensic science, health-care administration, human nutrition, industrial engineering, labor relations, management of sports industries, mechanical engineering, national security and public safety, and taxation. The Master of Public Administration degree is also available.

The University also offers a Ph.D. program in criminal justice.

Research Facilities

The holdings of the Marvin K. Peterson Library include more than 244,000 volumes and 1,400 print journals and newspaper subscriptions; electronic access to more than 17,940 full-text journal and newspaper titles; U.S. government documents; and numerous corporate annual reports, pamphlet files, and microfilm as well as current and extensive back-issue files of periodicals. Interlibrary loan search and other resources are available through OCLC, First Search, LexisNexis, Dialog, Dow Jones News/Retrieval, and CD-ROM systems.

The UNH Center for Computing Services provides both administrative and academic computing support. Administrators, faculty members, and students have access to the latest in computer technology. Personal computers for student use are spread throughout the campus, with the largest concentration located in the Marvin K. Peterson Library. In addition, the Computer-Aided Engineering Center laboratory in the Tagliatela College of Engineering houses workstations plus micros connected by an Ethernet LAN. Graphics, printing and plotting devices, laser printing, and a wide variety of data files, software, and simulation packages are also available.

Financial Aid

Financial aid is available for graduate students through assistantships and loans. The University participates in Federal Stafford Student Loan programs. Teaching, research, or administrative assistantships are available to full-time students. Compensation includes $8 per hour as well as a 50 percent tuition reduction; students typically work 15–20 hours per week.

Cost of Study

Tuition for master's degree students for the 2011–12 academic year is $750 per graduate credit or $2250 per course for most graduate courses. The Graduate Student Council fee is $60 per year, and there is a $25 technology fee each term. All charges and fees are subject to change.

Living and Housing Costs

There is no on-campus housing for graduate students, but the Center for Graduate and Adult Student Services maintains an off-campus housing Web site with listings of apartments in the local area at a variety of costs, a forum for accepted students to find roommates, local maps, and information on local services.

Student Group

Many students are from Connecticut, but each year an increasing number come from other states and many other countries. The graduate student body of more than 1,700 ranges from recent college graduates to professionals with several years of experience in their fields. About 51 percent of the graduate students are women, approximately 20 percent are international students, and nearly 16 percent are members of minority groups. Graduates are employed in government service, teaching, private agencies, and business.

Location

The University of New Haven is located in south central Connecticut. Although the campus is located in West Haven, it is less than 3 miles from downtown New Haven and students can easily take advantage of the cultural offerings of the city. New Haven has rail, bus, and air service, and its location at the junction of two major interstate highways places the school within easy driving distance of New York, Boston, and Providence.

The University

The University of New Haven was founded in 1920 and is accredited as a general-purpose institution by the New England Association of Schools and Colleges. A number of graduate classes are held at several off-campus locations across the state as well as New Mexico. The Graduate School follows a trimester schedule with start dates in September, January, and April. Most graduate classes are held in the early evening to accommodate both part-time and full-time students.

Applying

Applicants must hold a baccalaureate degree from an accredited college or university. An applicant for admission to the Graduate School must submit the following before the initial registration: a formal application online (free) or a paper application (requires nonrefundable $75 application fee); two letters of recommendation; final official transcripts from all previous college work. In addition, a satisfactory TOEFL score (except for students whose native language is English) and certified financial support forms are required for all international students. In some programs, students may be required to take a specific standardized test as part of the application process. All correspondence and requests for materials should be directed to the Graduate Admissions Office. Descriptions of programs and procedures are available in the *Graduate Catalog*. Information about the University of New Haven is available on the Web site at http://www.newhaven.edu/grad.

Correspondence and Information

Graduate Admissions Office
University of New Haven
Echlin Hall, 2nd Floor
300 Boston Post Road
West Haven, Connecticut 06516

Phone: 203-932-7440
800-DIAL-UNH (toll-free)
Fax: 203-932-7137
E-mail: gradinfo@newhaven.edu
Web site: http://www.newhaven.edu/grad

FACULTY HEADS

The faculty consists of approximately 520 full- and part-time professors. The coordinators for the various graduate programs and the Associate Provost for Graduate Studies are listed below.

Graduate School: Ira Kleinfeld, Associate Provost for Graduate Studies, Research, and Faculty Development; Eng.Sc.D., Columbia.
Business Administration/Industrial Engineering (dual degree): Alexis N. Sommers, Ph.D., Purdue.
Business Administration/Public Administration (dual degree): Charles N. Coleman, M.P.A., West Virginia.
Cellular and Molecular Biology: Michael Rossi, Ph.D., Kentucky.
Community Psychology: Michael Morris, Ph.D., Boston College.
Computer Science: Barun Chandra, Ph.D., Chicago.
Criminal Justice (Ph.D.): Richard Ward, D.Crim., Berkeley.
Criminal Justice (M.S.): William Norton, Ph.D., Florida State.
Education: Nancy Niemi, Ph.D., Rochester.
Electrical Engineering: Bouzid Aliane, Ph.D., Polytechnic.
Engineering Management: Alexis N. Sommers, Ph.D., Purdue.
Environmental Engineering: Agamemnon D. Koutsospyros, Ph.D., Polytechnic.
Environmental Science: Roman N. Zajac, Ph.D., Connecticut.
Executive Master of Business Administration: Ben B. Judd, Ph.D., Texas at Arlington.
Fire Science: Sorin Illiescu, M.S., New Haven.
Forensic Science: Virginia M. Maxwell, D.Phil., Oxford.
Health-Care Administration: Charles N. Coleman, M.P.A., West Virginia.
Human Nutrition: Rosa Mo, Ed.D., Columbia.
Industrial Engineering: Alexis Sommers, Ph.D., Purdue.
Industrial/Organizational Psychology: Stuart Sidle, Ph.D., DePaul.
Labor Relations: Charles N. Coleman, M.P.A., West Virginia.
Management of Sports Industries: Gil B. Fried, J.D., Ohio State.
M.B.A./Business Administration: Charles N. Coleman, Coordinator; M.P.A., West Virginia.
Mechanical Engineering: Stephen M. Ross, Ph.D., Johns Hopkins.
National Security and Public Safety: William L. Tayofa, Ph.D., Maryland.
Public Administration: Charles N. Coleman, M.P.A., West Virginia.

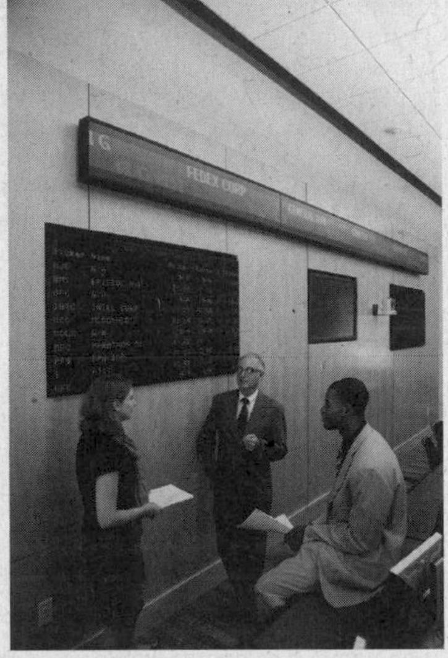

The Samuel S. Bergami, Jr. Center is a simulated Wall Street trading floor, complete with stock ticker and real-time data feeds, where College of Business students manage real and virtual porfolios.

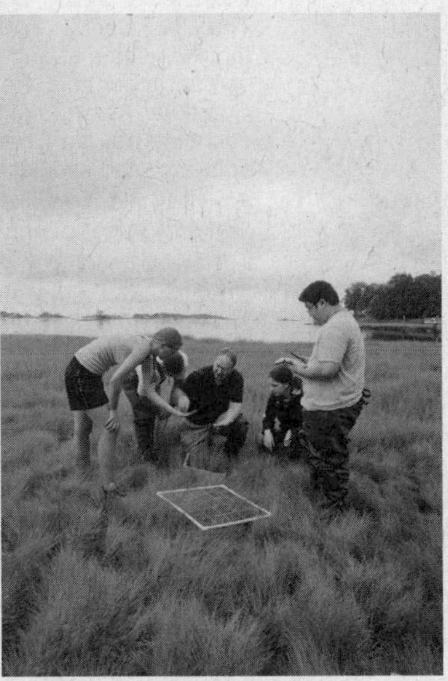

A professor and students in the Environmental Science program collect specimens along Long Island Sound to study the effects of pollutants on terrestrial and wetland ecology.

The Forensic Science Program, one of the finest in the world, supports extensive, well-equipped labs for hands-on work with modern equipment and instruments used in this profession.

UNIVERSITY OF OKLAHOMA

Graduate College

Programs of Study

The University of Oklahoma (OU) combines a mixture of academic excellence, varied social cultures, and a blend of scholarly and creative activities that offer exceptional opportunities for graduate study. Graduate education is offered in ninety-seven master's programs and fifty-five doctoral programs on the Norman campus. At the OU Health Sciences Center (OUHSC), located 19 miles away in Oklahoma City, graduate degrees are offered in twenty-nine master's programs and sixteen doctoral programs. In addition to the Doctor of Philosophy, OU confers the Doctor of Education, Doctor of Engineering, Doctor of Musical Arts, and Doctor of Public Health.

The University of Oklahoma also offers graduate programs at the Tulsa Graduate Research and Education Center, located approximately 120 miles northeast of the main campus in the city of Tulsa. On the Tulsa campus, OU offers graduate programs in architecture, urban studies, human relations, library and information studies, organization dynamics, public administration, social work, and telecomputing. Interdisciplinary degree programs are available at both the master's and doctoral levels on all three campuses.

Master's degree programs require a minimum of 30 semester hours of course work. Doctoral programs require a minimum of 90 semester hours of course work and are awarded for excellence in research scholarship. Doctoral students are also required to complete general written and oral examinations and defend the results of their dissertation research.

Research Facilities

OU is in the process of establishing a new research campus with a center for genomic and biogenetic research, a field in which OU is a national leader. Research and scholarly activity take place on the landscaped 567-acre main campus in Norman, which houses most of the University's academic colleges and research buildings.

OU provides an exceptional networking and computational environment for students, faculty, and staff members. All graduate students at the University have access to e-mail service, digital libraries, the Internet, a central help desk, campus software and licensing, and many other benefits to enhance their graduate experiences. The academic areas of the campus are part of the University intranet system that provides computer access in residence halls, classrooms, student computer labs, and University offices. The $50-million Sarkeys Energy Center has 200 teaching and research laboratories, as well as classrooms, offices, and the Youngblood Energy Library. There are central advanced analytical services, including the Electron Microprobe Library and Samuel Robert Noble Electron Microscopy Laboratory.

The Norman campus is home to Bizzell Memorial Library, the largest research library in the state, with more than 4.9 million volumes and 63,000 print and electronic serials subscriptions. Special collections include the internationally known History of Science Collections, Western History Collections, and Political Commercial Archives. There are also six specialized branch libraries. The Sam Noble Museum of Natural History opened in 2000. The 195,000-square-foot facility is one of the two largest university-based museums in the world. The museum is home to millions of artifacts, ranging from the world's largest apatosaurus to priceless Native American objects. The Fred Jones Jr. Museum of Art, Catlett Music Center, Donald W. Reynolds Performing Arts Center, and the Rupel L. Jones Theatre provide excellent facilities for graduate studies in the Weitenhoffer Family College of Fine Arts. In 2005, the Fred Jones Jr. Art Museum opened a new addition, designed by acclaimed architect Hugh Newell Jacobsen of Washington, D.C. Named in honor of Mary and Howard Lester of San Francisco, the wing added more than 34,000 square feet to the earlier 27,000-square-foot building and houses the Weitzenhoffer Collection, the single most important collection of French Impressionism ever given to an American public university. The University of Oklahoma Press and *World Literature Today* are two internationally recognized agencies for research and scholarship.

Immediately adjacent to the central campus in Norman is the south campus, site of the 271-acre University of Oklahoma Research Campus. Here, the Stephenson Research and Technology Center provides a home for the OU Supercomputing Center for Education and Research, for interdisciplinary programs in biosciences and bioengineering, and for other research initiatives. The National Weather Center houses the University's research programs in meteorology and the National Oceanic and Atmospheric Administration's (NOAA) weather, research and operations programs. One Partners Place fosters collaboration between research and business enterprises. Also located on the south campus are Andrew M. Coats Hall, housing the College of Law; the OU Foundation; Lloyd Noble Center and parking complex; and the Jimmie Austin University of Oklahoma Golf Course.

The University also has a 1,675-acre north campus, which includes the University Research Park, incubator firms, NOAA's National Severe Storms Laboratory, and the National Weather Service's advanced weather forecasting office.

OU's Health Sciences Center includes a 200-acre complex of educational, research, and health-care facilities operated by nineteen public and private entities along with an 11-acre College of Medicine campus in Tulsa. OUHSC is the recipient of an $8.7-million grant, which established the Oklahoma Center for Molecular Medicine. Other research and study units associated with the University include the Biological Station at Lake Texoma, the Earth Sciences Observatory at Leonard near Tulsa, the Aquatic Biology and Fisheries Research Center in Noble and Norman, the Oklahoma Climatological Survey, the Oklahoma Biological Survey, the Oklahoma Archeological Survey, and the Center for the Analysis and Prediction of Storms. The Oklahoma Geological Survey, a state agency responsible to the University of Oklahoma Board of Regents, is also housed on the Norman campus.

Financial Aid

Approximately 40 percent of all graduate students attending the University are employed by their departments as either teaching or research assistants. Salaries for these positions vary from unit to unit, but the University's starting rate in 2011–12 is $13,036.32, for a 0.50 FTA graduate assistant on a 12-month appointment. Tuition waivers and health insurance are available for students holding qualified graduate assistant positions. Numerous funding, scholarship, and fellowship opportunities are also available through the University, individual departments, and outside programs.

Cost of Study

Tuition and fees for Oklahoma residents are $310.55 per graduate credit hour for 2011–12; nonresident tuition and fees are $760.05 (nonresidents appointed as at least half-time graduate assistants pay the in-state rate). Additional fees are charged in support of academic programs and/or campus activities. These fees vary, depending on a particular student's major, class schedule, and campus of enrollment.

Living and Housing Costs

The University offers several on-campus apartment choices. Additionally, there are a large number of privately owned apartments, duplexes, and houses available in Norman, many of which are served by the local mass transit provider, the Cleveland Area Rapid Transit (CART) system, which is free for OU students.

Student Group

Nearly 25,000 students on the Norman campus and almost 4,000 at the Health Sciences Center enrolled for the 2009 spring semester. More than 3,500 of these students were enrolled in the Graduate College in Norman. Approximately one third of the graduate students at OU are enrolled in doctoral programs. One fifth of the overall student body comes from outside Oklahoma, with students from every state. In addition, international students representing almost eighty nations make up nearly 20 percent of the graduate student body.

Location

As part of the dynamic Southwest, Oklahoma benefits from both its rich historic heritage and the vital and modern growth of its metropolitan areas. Although by location a suburb of Oklahoma City, Norman is an independent community with a permanent population of more than 95,000. Norman residents enjoy extensive parks and recreation programs and a 10,000-acre lake and park area. *Money* magazine named Norman as the nation's sixth best place to live in the 2008 edition of its annual rankings.

The College

The Graduate College is the center of advanced study, research, and creative activity for the University. Faculty members and students share an obligation to achieve greater knowledge in their chosen fields and to present their achievements to the scholarly community. Students were first accepted at the University of Oklahoma in 1892. Graduate instruction was offered as early as 1899, and the first master's degree was conferred in 1900. The Graduate School was formally organized in 1909, and the first doctorate was awarded in 1929.

Applying

Application procedures vary depending on the student's academic background. There is a $40 application fee for U.S. citizens and permanent residents and a $90 application fee for international students. Applications for assistantships, fellowships, and other forms of financial aid should be directed to the academic units. Deadlines vary from department to department, but applications should generally be filed no later than January for students desiring admission in the fall term.

Correspondence and Information

Graduate College
University of Oklahoma
731 Elm Avenue, Room 100
Norman, Oklahoma 73019

Phone: 800-522-0772 (toll-free)
E-mail: gradinfo@ou.edu
Web site: http://gradweb.ou.edu/

AREAS OF INSTRUCTION

The graduate faculty consists of more than 600 active scholars in residence on the Norman campus and another 270 at the Health Sciences Center. In addition, the graduate faculty is supplemented by visiting scholars from other institutions and by specialists from government and industry. The names of the programs and the degrees offered are listed along with the telephone number. The area code for all numbers is 405 except for the nursing program, which has a toll-free number.

Norman Campus

Accounting (M.Ac.): phone: 325-4221; e-mail: fayres@ou.edu.
Accounting (Ph.D.): phone: 325-4221; e-mail: rlipe@ou.edu.
Aerospace and Mechanical Engineering (M.S., Ph.D.): phone: 325-1735; e-mail: rparthasarathy@ou.edu.
Anthropology (M.A., Ph.D.): phone: 325-2490; e-mail: svehik@ou.edu.
Architecture (M.Arch., M.L.A., M.R.C.P., M.S.C.A.): phone: 325-2444; e-mail: nharm@ou.edu.
Art (M.A., M.F.A.): phone: 325-2691; e-mail: hils@ou.edu.
Botany and Microbiology (M.S., Ph.D.): phone: 325-6281; e-mail: guno@ou.edu.
Business Administration (M.B.A., Ph.D.): phone: 325-2931; e-mail: rdauffen@ou.edu.
Chemical Engineering (M.S., Ph.D.): phone: 325-4366; e-mail: nollert@ou.edu.
Chemistry and Biochemistry (M.S., Ph.D.): phone: 325-2967; e-mail: grichteraddo@ou.edu.
Civil Engineering and Environmental Science (M.S., Ph.D.): phone: 325-4253; e-mail: gamiller@ou.edu.
Communication (M.A., Ph.D.): phone: 325-1571; e-mail: amyjj@ou.edu.
Computer Science (M.S., Ph.D.): phone: 325-0566; e-mail: ggruenwald@ou.edu.
Dance (M.F.A.): phone: 325-4051; e-mail: jlindberg@ou.edu.
Drama (M.A., M.F.A.): phone: 325-4021; e-mail: torr@ou.edu.
Economics (M.A., Ph.D.): phone: 325-2861; e-mail: aholmes@ou.edu.
Education (M.Ed., Ph.D., Ed.D.): phone: 325-5976; e-mail: gnoley@ou.edu.
Electrical and Computer Engineering (M.S., Ph.D.): phone: 325-4721; e-mail: sluss@ou.edu.
Engineering (M.S., Ph.D.): phone: 325-2621; e-mail: landers@ou.edu.
Engineering Physics (M.S., Ph.D.): phone: 325-3961; e-mail: msantos@ou.edu.
English (M.A., Ph.D.): phone: 325-6219; e-mail: dmair@ou.edu.
Geography (M.A., Ph.D.): phone: 325-5325; e-mail: fshelley@ou.edu.
Geology and Geophysics (M.S., Ph.D.): phone: 325-3253; e-mail: delmore@ou.edu.
Health and Exercise Sciences (M.S.): phone: 325-2717; e-mail: mgbemben@ou.edu.
History (M.A., Ph.D.): phone: 325-6058; e-mail: rgriswold@ou.edu.
History of Science (M.A., Ph.D.): phone: 325-2213; e-mail: slivesey@ou.edu.
Human Relations (M.H.R.): phone: 325-1756; e-mail: smmendoza@ou.edu.
Industrial Engineering (M.S., Ph.D.): phone: 325-3721; e-mail: rlshehab@ou.edu.
International Studies (M.A.): phone: 325-8893; e-mail: rhcox@ou.edu.
Journalism and Mass Communication (M.A., Ph.D.): phone: 325-5206; e-mail: dcraig@ou.edu.
Landscape Architecture (M.L.A.): phone: 325-2444; e-mail: schurch@ou.edu.
Liberal Studies (M.L.S.): phone: 325-1061; e-mail: tgabert@ou.edu.
Library and Information Studies (M.L.I.S.): phone: 325-3921; e-mail: klatrobe@ou.edu.
Mathematics (M.A., M.S., M.S./M.B.A., Ph.D.): phone: 325-3971; e-mail: pgoodey@ou.edu.
Meteorology (M.S., Ph.D.): phone: 325-6097; e-mail: fcarr@ou.edu.
Modern Languages (French, German, Spanish for M.A., Ph.D.): phone: 325-6181; e-mail: genova@ou.edu.
Music (M.Mus., D.M.A.): phone: 325-5344; e-mail: iwagner@ou.edu.
Music Education (M.Mus.Educ., Ph.D.): phone: 325-5344; e-mail: iwagner@ou.edu.
Natural Science (M.Nat.Sci.): phone: 325-1498; e-mail: eamarek@ou.edu.
Petroleum and Geological Engineering (M.S., Ph.D.): phone: 325-2921; e-mail: crai@ou.edu.
Philosophy (M.A., Ph.D.): phone: 325-6491; e-mail: wriggs@ou.edu.
Physics and Astronomy (M.S., Ph.D.): phone: 325-3961; e-mail: doezema@ou.edu.
Political Science (M.A., Ph.D.): phone: 325-5517; e-mail: mps@ou.edu.
Professional Meteorology (M.S.): phone: 325-6097; e-mail: fcarr@ou.edu.
Psychology (M.S., Ph.D.): phone: 325-4599; e-mail: ldeven@ou.edu.
Public Administration (M.P.A.): phone: 325-5517; e-mail: alfranklin@ou.edu.
Regional and City Planning (M.R.C.P.): phone: 325-2399; e-mail: cwarnken@ou.edu.
Social Work (M.S.W.): phone: 325-2821; e-mail: jimar@ou.edu.
Sociology (M.A., Ph.D.): phone: 325-1571; e-mail: cstjohn@ou.edu.
Zoology (M.S., Ph.D.): phone: 325-5271; e-mail: wmatthews@ou.edu.

Health Sciences Campus (e-mail: grad-college@ouhsc.edu)

Biochemistry and Molecular Biology (Ph.D.): phone: 271-2227.
Biological Psychology (M.S., Ph.D.): phone: 271-2011.
Biostatistics and Epidemiology (M.S., M.P.H., Ph.D., Dr.P.H.): phone: 271-2229.
Cell Biology (M.S., Ph.D.): phone: 271-2377.
Communication Sciences and Disorders (M.S., Ph.D.): phone: 271-4124.
Health Administration and Policy (M.H.A., M.P.H., M.P.A./M.P.H., M.P.H./M.B.A., M.P.H./J.D., M.P.H./M.D., Dr.P.H.): phone: 271-2114.
Health Promotion Sciences (M.S., M.P.H., Dr.P.H.): phone: 271-2017.
Microbiology and Immunology (M.S., Ph.D.): phone: 271-2133.
Neuroscience (M.S., Ph.D.): phone: 271-2406.
Nursing (M.S., M.S./M.B.A.): phone: 877-367-OURN (toll-free).
Nutritional Sciences (M.S.): phone: 271-2113.
Occupational and Environmental Health (M.S., M.P.H., M.S./J.D., Ph.D., Dr.P.H.): phone: 271-2070.
Orthodontics (M.S.): phone: 271-6087.
Pathology (Ph.D.): phone: 271-2693.
Periodontics (M.S.): phone: 271-6531.
Pharmaceutical Sciences (M.S., M.S./M.B.A., Ph.D.): phone: 271-3830.
Physiology (M.S., Ph.D.): phone: 271-2226.
Radiological Sciences (M.S., Ph.D.): phone: 271-5132.
Rehabilitation Sciences (M.S.): phone: 271-2131.

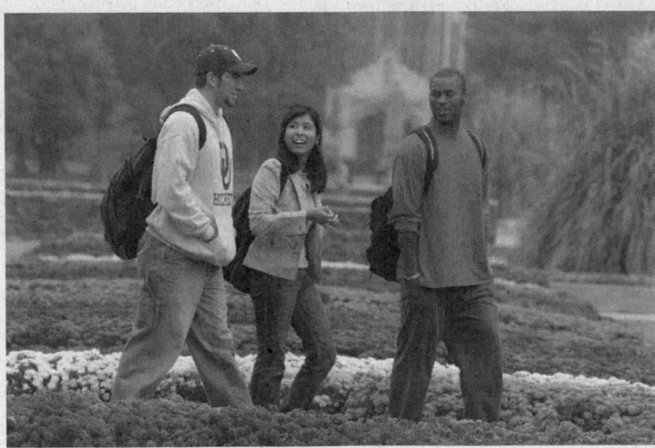

Students walk to class on the Norman campus.

UNIVERSITY OF SOUTH CAROLINA

The Graduate School

Programs of Study

The University of South Carolina is the state's flagship university with a comprehensive offering of degree programs including seventy-two doctoral programs, 134 master's programs, four specialist programs, and twenty certificate programs (a complete list can be found at http://gradschool.sc.edu/graduate_programs.asp). Doctoral degree specializations with significant enrollment are offered in anthropology, biological sciences, biomedical science, business administration, chemistry, communication sciences and disorders, comparative literature, education fields (counselor education, curriculum and instruction, educational administration, education psychology, language and literacy, and physical education), engineering (biomedical, chemical, civil, computer, electrical, mechanical, and nuclear), English, exercise science, geography, geology, history, linguistics, marine science, mass communications, mathematics, several music fields, nursing fields, pharmaceutical science, philosophy, physical therapy, physics, political science, psychology (clinical/community, experimental, and school) public health areas (biostatistics, environmental health sciences, epidemiology, health promotion and education, and health services policy and management), social work, sociology, and statistics.

Master's degrees are offered in all the above fields. Students can also earn master's degrees in accounting, art and theater areas, creative writing, criminology and criminal justice, earth resources management, genetic counseling, hospitality and sport management, human resources, international business, several language areas, library and information science, journalism, nurse anesthesia, professional science master's, public administration, rehabilitation counseling, retailing, and teaching areas.

Research Facilities

The University of South Carolina is one of only twenty-three public universities recognized by the Carnegie Foundation for very high research activity and curricular engagement, outreach, and partnerships. The University's Office of Research and Economic Development provides an extensive Web site to highlight the University of South Carolina's research resources, equipment and facilities (RREF) at http://www.sc.edu/rref/. Active research focus areas include behavioral sciences, bioinformatics, biomedical sciences, children and families, computing, engineering, environmental sciences, future fuels, health disparities, liberal arts, mathematics and statistics, nanotechnology, physical activity, physical sciences, and social sciences. The University's Thomas Cooper Library provides access to more than 7.5 million volumes, periodicals, microfilm entries, and manuscripts in the University system through the USCAN integrated information system. Significant research centers and institutes include the Baruch Institute for Marine Biology and Coastal Research, the Institute for Biological Research and Technology, the Center for Family in Society, the Southeast Manufacturing Technology Center, the Research Division of the Moore School of Business Administration, the Institute for International Studies, and the Institute for Southern Studies.

Financial Aid

Fellowships are available in many departments. Graduate research and teaching assistantships are available in most departments and provide competitive stipends and full or partial tuition remission. Information about fellowships and assistantships should be obtained from the department of interest.

Cost of Study

The University of South Carolina has one of the best tuition rates in the entire Southeastern region. Tuition and academic fees are based on a student's state residency, program of study, and number of credit hours. The University Bursar's Office provides information regarding tuitions and fees. Prospective students should review the University's current Fee Schedule for additional information at http://www.sc.edu/bursar/studentfees.shtml.

Living and Housing Costs

Graduate students normally live in off-campus housing, but there are limited housing opportunities on campus for married or single students. The Off-Campus Student Services Office assists students in locating off-campus housing. For complete information see the University's housing Web site at http://www.housing.sc.edu/.

Student Group

Graduate enrollment averages about 6,500. Approximately 37 percent of the graduate students were from out-of-state, representing every state, the District of Columbia, Puerto Rico, and over ninety other countries. The University of South Carolina has the highest percentage of African-American student enrollment of any flagship university in the nation. International students compose 29 percent of doctoral enrollment; the Office of International Student Services provides support for international students prior to arrival and throughout their study.

Student Outcomes

Research funding at the University of South Carolina reached a record $218.8 million in fiscal year 2010, providing graduate students with increased research opportunities. Doctoral and master's program graduates are nationally competitive for academic, research, and leadership positions in national and multinational corporations, public and private institutions, and government agencies, and are actively recruited on campus.

Location

The University is located in downtown Columbia near the Capitol and the state government complex. Columbia, with a population of about 745,000 residents within the metropolitan area, offers a wide range of cultural, sports, and entertainment attractions. Boasting an ideal climate with an average temperature of 65 degrees, the city is geographically located in the center of the state within a 1½ to 3 hours drive to the ocean and the mountains.

The University

The University was founded in 1801, the first state college to be supported by annual public appropriations. Some of the most striking architecture of the region can be found on the campus. In support of its research initiatives, the University has launched the first phase of its research campus, Innovista, a live, learn, and work enterprise that will eventually house 8 million square feet of research buildings, residences, and retail and restaurant space.

Applying

Applications must be submitted online (http://www.gradschool.sc.edu/apply.htm) and require a nonrefundable fee of $50. Application requirements and deadlines vary; please check the appropriate college, school, or department Web site (http://gradschool.sc.edu/graduate_programs.asp). Detailed admission information is given in the *Graduate Studies Bulletin available online at http://bulletin.sc.edu/index.php.*

Correspondence and Information

The Graduate School
University of South Carolina
901 Sumter Street
Byrnes, Suite 304
Columbia, South Carolina 29208

Phone: 803-777-4243
Fax: 803-777-2972
E-mail: gradapp@mailbox.sc.edu
Web site: http://www.gradschool.sc.edu/

DEANS OF COLLEGES AND HEADS OF DEPARTMENTS

Graduate School: Dr. Lacy Ford, Vice Provost and Professor of History.
Lacy Ford, Interim Dean.
Nancy P. Zimmerman, Associate Dean for Academic Affairs.
Dale Moore, Director of Graduate Admissions.

Moore School of Business: Hildy Teegen, Dean.

College of Education: Les Sternberg, Dean.
Department of Educational Leadership and Policies: Katherine Chaddock, Chair.
Department of Educational Studies: Robert Johnson, Chair.
Department of Instruction and Teacher Education: Diane Stephens, Chair.
Department of Physical Education: Karen French, Chair.

College of Engineering and Information Technology: Harry J. Ploehn, Interim Dean.
Department of Chemical Engineering: Mike Matthews, Chair.
Department of Civil and Environmental Engineering: David Waugh, Interim Chair.
Department of Computer Science and Engineering: Michael Huhns, Interim Chair.
Department of Electrical Engineering: Tangali S. Sudarshan, Chair.
Department of Mechanical Engineering: Jamil A. Khan, Chair.

School of the Environment: Madilyn M. Fletcher, Director.

College of Hospitality, Retail, and Sport Management: Brian L. Mihalik, Dean.
School of Hotel, Restaurant, and Tourism Management: Sandra Strick, Interim Chair.
Department of Retailing: Marianne Bickle, Chair.
Department of Sport and Entertainment Management: Andrew Gillentine, Chair.

College of Arts and Sciences: Mary Anne Fitzpatrick, Dean.
Department of Anthropology: Ann E. Kingsolver, Chair.
Department of Art: Brad Collins, Chair.
Department of Biology: Charles R. Lovell, Chair.
Department of Chemistry and Biochemistry: John H. Dawson, Chair.
Program in Comparative Literature: Marja Warehime, Director.
Department of Criminology and Criminal Justice: Shane R. Thye, Interim Chair.
Department of Earth and Ocean Sciences: Venkataraman Lakshmi, Chair.
Department of English Language and Literature: William E. Rivers, Chair.
Department of Geography: Gregory Carbone, Chair.
Department of History: Lacy K. Ford, Chair.
Department of Languages, Literatures, and Cultures: Marja Warehime, Chair.
Program in Linguistics: Robin Morris, Director.
Program in Marine Science: Claudia Benitez-Nelson, Director.
Department of Mathematics: Jerrold R. Griggs, Chair.
Department of Philosophy: Anne Bezuidenhout, Chair.
Department of Physics and Astronomy: Chaden Djalali, Chair.
Department of Political Science: Daniel R. Sabia, Chair.
Department of Psychology: John E. Richards, Interim Chair.
Department of Sociology: Lala Carr Steelman, Chair.
Department of Statistics: Don Edwards, Chair.
Department of Theatre, Speech, and Dance: Jim Hunter, Chair.
Program in Women's and Gender Studies: Drucilla K. Barker, Director.

Law School: Walter F. Pratt Jr., Dean.

College of Mass Communications and Information Studies: Charles Bierbauer, Dean.
School of Journalism and Mass Communications: Carol J. Pardun, Director.
School of Library and Information Science: Samantha K. Hastings, Director.

School of Medicine: Richard A. Hoppmann, Dean.

School of Music: Tayloe Harding, Dean

College of Nursing: Peggy Hewlett, Dean.

College of Pharmacy: Randall Rowen, Dean.

Arnold School of Public Health: G. Thomas Chandler, Dean.
Department of Communication Sciences and Disorders: Elaine Frank, Chair.
Department of Environmental Health Science: Dwayne E. Porter, Interim Chair.
Department of Epidemiology and Biostatistics: Robert McKeown, Chair.
Department of Exercise Science: J. Larry Durstine, Chair.
Department of Health Services Policy and Management: David Murday, Interim Chair.
Department of Health Promotion, Education, and Behavior: Edward Frongillo, Chair.

College of Social Work: Dennis Poole, Dean.

The University of South Carolina is committed to a policy of affirmative action that ensures equal opportunity in education and employment to all qualified persons regardless of race, sex, religion, creed, handicap, disability, veteran status, national origin, or ancestry.

WASHINGTON UNIVERSITY IN ST. LOUIS

Graduate School of Arts and Sciences

Programs of Study

The Graduate School of Arts and Sciences offers more than thirty programs leading to the doctorate (Ph.D.) and to the Master of Arts (A.M.). In addition, programs are offered leading to the Master of Arts in Education (M.A.Ed.), Master of Arts in Teaching (M.A.T.), Master of Fine Arts in Writing (M.F.A.W.), and Master in Music (M.M.).

Opportunities for combining a degree available through the Graduate School of Arts and Sciences with a degree from one of the University's professional schools (business, engineering, law, medicine) are also available.

Research Facilities

The Washington University community is served by a network of libraries designed to meet the instructional and research needs of faculty members, students, and staff members. Washington University libraries contain the largest collection of any private academic library system between the Mississippi River and California. John M. Olin Library, the central University library, and twelve school and departmental libraries house many important and unique collections and provide state-of-the-art computerized information retrieval. The combined holdings include more than 3 million books and bound periodicals, 18,000 current serial subscriptions, and access to thousands of electronic journals and databases. For more information, students can visit http://library.wustl.edu.

More than thirty centers and institutes provide a spectrum of research opportunities. They include the Center for Air Pollution Impact and Trend Analysis; Center for the Study of American Business; Center for American Indian Studies; Business, Law, and Economics Center; Arts and Sciences Computing Center; Institutes for Biomedical Computing; McDonnell Center for Cellular and Molecular Neurobiology; Construction Management Center; Carolyne Roehm Electronic Media Center; Center for Engineering Computing; Center for Genetics in Medicine; McDonnell Center for Studies of Higher Brain Function; Center for the History of Freedom; Office of International Studies; International Writers Center; Center for the Study of Islamic Societies and Civilizations; Management Center; Fred Gasche Laboratory for Microstructured Materials Technologies; Markey Center for Research in Molecular Biology of Human Disease; Center for Optimization and Semantic Control; Center for Plant Science and Biotechnology; Center for Political Economy; Center for the Study of Public Affairs; Center for Robotics and Automation; Social Work Research Development Center; McDonnell Center for Space Sciences; Center for the Application of Information Technology; and Urban Research and Design Center.

Financial Aid

The majority of full-time students receive financial support. Financial assistance in the form of scholarships, fellowships, and traineeships is offered annually on a competitive basis through the Graduate School from government, private, or endowed sources. Also available are scholarships, teaching assistantships, research assistantships, and, in applied social sciences, clinical internships; grants and fellowships in national competition; and loans. Specific information may be obtained from the departmental or administrative unit to which the student intends to apply.

Cost of Study

Tuition for the 2011–12 academic year for the Graduate School is $40,950. The cost per credit unit is $1706.

Living and Housing Costs

Many graduate students live in University-owned apartments, some with data connections and shuttle bus service. Listing information for these units as well as non-University housing is available through the University's Apartment Referral Service (http://offcampushousing.wustl.edu/). Rent ranges from $450 to $950 per month for one- to three-bedroom units, respectively.

Student Group

Of the more than 14,000 people attending Washington University, more than 5,000 are graduate students; approximately 2,000 of them are enrolled in the Graduate School of Arts and Sciences. Students come to Washington University from all fifty states and more than eighty international locations.

Location

Washington University has two campuses that lie at opposite ends of Forest Park (one of the largest municipal parks in the nation). The campuses are approximately 5 miles west of downtown St. Louis. The Danforth campus is the location of the Graduate School of Arts and Sciences and all other schools of the University except Medicine. The latter is located on the east, or medical, campus. The Division of Biology and Biomedical Sciences is also located on the medical campus. Free shuttle buses run between the campuses on a regular schedule.

The St. Louis area has nearly 2.4 million residents. The cost of living is affordable. The University's central location provides easy access to the zoo, museums, Science Center, Missouri Botanical Gardens, St. Louis Symphony, Opera Theatre, St. Louis Repertory Theatre, Black Repertory Theatre, Blues hockey, Rams football, and Cardinals baseball. Outdoor adventure beyond the city can be found in the Ozark Mountains and on the rivers of Missouri. Camping, hiking, floating, rock climbing, and spelunking are among the many possibilities within a few hours' drive of St. Louis.

The Graduate School

The Graduate School of Arts and Sciences is a charter member of both the Association of Graduate Schools and the Council of Graduate Schools. The School provides a physical and academic environment in which inquiry, intellectual growth, and discovery can thrive and flourish.

Applying

Prospective students may apply online. Applicants should check with the department or program to which they are applying, as application deadlines vary. Most programs require GRE scores. For international students whose native language is not English, most programs require an official copy of a TOEFL or TSE score.

Correspondence and Information

Graduate School of Arts and Sciences
Campus Box 1187
Washington University in St. Louis
One Brookings Drive
St. Louis, Missouri 63130-4899

Phone: 314-935-6880
Fax: 314-935-4887
E-mail: Graduate_Admissions@artsci.wustl.edu
Web site: http://graduateschool.wustl.edu

FACULTY HEADS, DEGREES OFFERED, AND DEPARTMENTAL INTERESTS

Anthropology (Ph.D.): Erik Trinkaus (trinkaus@artsci.wustl.edu). Sociocultural anthropology (including medical anthropology), archaeology, physical anthropology (including primate studies, paleontology, and human biology).

Art History and Archaeology (A.M., Ph.D.): John Klein (jrklein@wustl.edu). Ancient, medieval, Renaissance, early modern, European, modern and contemporary European and American, and Asian art history; classical archaeology.

Division of Biology and Biomedical Sciences (Ph.D.): Rebecca Riney (800-852-9074, toll-free; e-mail: DBBSPhDAdmissions@wusm.wustl.edu).

Biochemistry: John Cooper (DBBSPhDAdmissions@wusm.wustl.edu). Metabolic regulation, signal transduction, receptors, membrane channels and transporters, membrane structure and dynamics, membrane trafficking, cholesterol and lipid metabolism, nucleic acid-protein structure interactions and function, DNA replication and repair, recombination, transcription, translation, enzyme kinetics, cancer biology, cell cycle regulation, apoptosis, cell motility, cytoskeleton, cell division, extracellular matrix, vascular biology, aging, senescence, telomere biology, heat-shock proteins, prion proteins, gene expression, RNA editing and binding proteins, microbial pathogenesis, parasitology, virology, drug design and metabolism, plant natural products, photosynthesis and plant energy production, molecular imaging in cells and tissues, carbohydrate metabolism, proteases.

Computational and Molecular Biophysics: Daved Fremont (DBBSPhDAdmissions@wusm.wustl.edu). Protein and nucleic acid kinetics and thermodynamics, single-molecule enzymology, nanoscience, biomolecular folding, macromolecular structure determination, ion channels and lipid membranes, computational biophysics.

Computational and Systems Biology: Barak Cohen (DBBSPhDAdmissions@wusm.wustl.edu). Systems biology, genomics, sequence analysis, regulatory networks, synthetic biology, metagenomics, metabolomics, proteomics, single cell dynamics, high-throughput technology development, applied math and mathematical models of biological processes, computational biology, comparative genomics, personalized medicine, next generation sequencing and its applications, bioinformatics.

Developmental, Regenerative, and Stem Cell Biology: Kerry Kornfeld (DBBSPhDAdmissions@wusm.wustl.edu) and James Skeath (DBBSPhDAdmissions@wusm.wustl.edu). Development, stem cell biology, regenerative biology, cell biology, genetics, cell signaling, the biology of cancer, epigenetics, circadian rhythms, systems biology.

Evolution, Ecology, and Population Biology: James Cheverud (DBBSPhDAdmissions@wusm.wustl.edu). Theoretical, experimental population genetics; population, community ecology; phylogenetics, systematics, plant, animal evolution; primate evolution.

Human and Statistical Genetics: Anne Bowcock (DBBSPhDAdmissions@wusm.wustl.edu) and John Rice (DBBSPhDAdmissions@wusm.wustl.edu). Human genetics, statistical genetics, gene mapping, genetics, Mendelian disease, complex disease, mammalian genetics, systems biology, functional genomics.

Immunology: Kenneth Murphy (DBBSPhDAdmissions@wusm.wustl.edu). Molecular immunology, lineage development, autoimmunity, cancer immunotherapy, transcription factors.

Molecular Cell Biology: Phyllis Hanson (DBBSPhDAdmissions@wusm.wustl.edu) and Jason Weber (jweber@dom.wustl.edu). Cell adhesion, protein trafficking and organelle biogenesis, cell cycle, receptors, signal transduction, gene expression, metabolism, cytoskeleton and motility, membrane excitability, molecular basis of diseases.

Molecular Genetics and Genomics: Tim Schedl (DBBSPhDAdmissions@wusm.wustl.edu) and James Skeath (DBBSPhDAdmissions@wusm.wustl.edu). Genetics, comparative genomics, functional genomics, model organisms, epigenetics, genetics of human disease, development, cell biology, molecular biology, complex traits, bioinformatics, systems biology.

Molecular Microbiology and Microbial Pathogenesis: Tamara Doering (DBBSPhDAdmissions@wusm.wustl.edu). Molecular microbiology, microbial physiology, infectious disease, microbial pathogenesis, bacteriology, mycology, parasitology, virology, host defense.

Neurosciences: Paul Taghert (DBBSPhDAdmissions@wusm.wustl.edu). Neurobiology, neurology, functional imaging, behavior, cognition, computational neuroscience, electrophysiology, sensory systems, motor systems, neuroglia, neuronal development, learning, memory, language, synaptic plasticity, mind, consciousness, neurodegeneration, diseases of the nervous system, neuronal injury.

Plant Biology: Barbara Kunkel (DBBSPhDAdmissions@wusm.wustl.edu). Plant genetics, biochemistry, cell biology, development, molecular evolution, physiology, hormone signaling, response to environment, plant disease.

Business (Ph.D.): Anjan Thakor (phdinfo@olin.wustl.edu). Accounting, business economics, finance, marketing, organizational behavior, strategy, operations and manufacturing management.

Chemistry (Ph.D.): Barbara Tessmer (barbara22@wustl.edu). Bioinorganic, biological, bioorganic, biophysical, materials, nuclear, organic, organometallic, physical, polymer, radiochemistry, spectoroscopy, theoretical.

Classics (A.M.): Catherine Keane (classics@artsci.wustl.edu). Greek and Latin language; Greek and Roman literature, philosophy, history, and material culture.

Comparative Literature (Ph.D.): Lynne Tatlock (ltatlock@wustl.edu). World literature, literary theory, translation studies, global and multicultural theory, comparative drama, comparative arts, East/West comparisons, narrative theory, film.

Earth and Planetary Sciences (Ph.D.): Michael E. Wysession (epscinfo@levee.wustl.edu). Planetary sciences, geology, geobiology, geochemistry, geodynamics.

East Asian Languages and Cultures (A.M., J.D./A.M., Ph.D.): Robert Hegel (rhegel@artsci.wustl.edu). Chinese; Japanese; Chinese fiction, theater, poetry, modern literature; Japanese modern and classical fiction; translation theory; East Asian studies.

Economics (Ph.D.): Constantine Azariadis (azariadi@wustl.edu). Economic theory, industrial organization, political economy, public economics, macroeconomics, public finance, development economics.

Education (M.A.Ed., M.A.T., Ph.D.): Natalia Kolk (nakolk@wustl.edu). Teacher education, educational studies, urban education, policy studies, science and math education, literacy studies, learning sciences.

English and American Literature (Ph.D.): Vincent Sherry (vsherry@wustl.edu). African and African-American studies, American, Anglophone Caribbean literatures, British, contemporary literature, eighteenth-century, Irish literature, medieval, modernism, nineteenth-century British, postcolonial literature and theory, Renaissance, seventeenth-century, the long nineteenth-century, theory, twentieth century, women and gender studies, gender and sexuality.

Germanic Languages and Literatures (Ph.D.): Stephan K. Schindler (german@artsci.wustl.edu). Contemporary German literature, German literature and culture prior to 1700, literature and history, film studies, gender studies, German-European literary and cultural relations.

History (Ph.D.): Steve Miles (smiles@wustl.edu). African, American, civil rights history, China, gender, Japan, medieval Europe, early modern Britain, central Europe.

Jewish, Islamic, and Near Eastern Languages and Cultures (A.M.): Ahmet Karamustafa (akaramus@wustl.edu). Islamic and Near Eastern studies, Islamic history, Islamic intellectual traditions, Arabic language and literature, Persian language and literature, modern Middle East history. Pamela Barmash (pbarmash@wustl.edu). Jewish studies, Hebrew Bible, rabbinic literature, medieval Jewish history, modern Hebrew literature, modern Jewish history.

Mathematics (Ph.D.): David Wright (wright@math.wustl.edu). Affine algebraic geometry and polynomial automorphisms: geometry of affine n-space, properties that characterize polynomial rings, properties that characterize variables, the structure of polynomial automorphism groups, formal inverse, the Jacobian conjecture and related issues.

Movement Science (Ph.D.): Michael J. Mueller (muellerm@wustl.edu). Philosophy of human movement function and dysfunction, with special emphasis on bioenergetics, biomechanics, and biocontrol.

Music (M.M., A.M., Ph.D.): Robert Snarrenberg (rsnarren@artsci.wustl.edu). Piano, voice, composition, musicology, ethnomusicology, theory.

Philosophy (Ph.D.): Mark Rollins (mark@wustl.edu). Ethics, social and political philosophy, history of philosophy, philosophy of law, philosophy of science, philosophy of mind, philosophy of language, theory of knowledge, aesthetics.

Philosophy/Neuroscience/Psychology (Ph.D.): Kimberly Mount (pnp@wustl.edu). Philosophy of mind and language, with a special emphasis on the philosophical dimensions of psychology, neuroscience, and linguistics.

Physics (Ph.D.): Kenneth F. Kelton (kfk@wustl.edu). Experimental and theoretical condensed matter and materials physics, with a focus on structural studies of liquids, glasses, and complex periodic and aperiodic phases; nucleation processes; and the glass transition.

Political Economy and Public Policy (A.M.): Norman Schofield (schofield@wustl.edu). International political economy, public policy.

Political Science (Ph.D.): Jim Spriggs (jspriggs@wustl.edu). American politics, comparative politics, formal theory, international politics, law and courts, normative theory, political methodology.

Psychology (Ph.D.): Deanna Barch (dbarch@wustl.edu). Behavior/brain/cognition, clinical, development and aging, social/personality.

Rehabilitation and Participation Science (Ph.D.): Jack Engsberg (engsbergj@wusm.wustl.edu). Philosophy of rehabilitation and participation with special emphasis placed on neurorehabilitation, performance, and community participation.

Romance Languages and Literatures (Ph.D.): Harriet Stone (hastone@wustl.edu). French literature, Spanish and Latin American literature.

Social Work (Ph.D.): Renee Cunningham Williams (phdsw@wustl.edu). Mental health, social and economic development, addictions, aging, child welfare, civic service, disabilities, health, poverty and social policy, youth development and schools.

Speech and Hearing (Ph.D.): Beth Elliott (elliottb@wustl.edu). Speech and hearing sciences, clinical audiology, deaf education, speech and language, sensory neuroscience.

Statistics (A.M.): Steven Krantz (sk@wustl.edu). Mathematical statistics, biostatistics.

The Writing Program (M.F.A.W.): David Schuman (english@wustl.edu). Fiction writing, nonfiction writing, poetry writing.

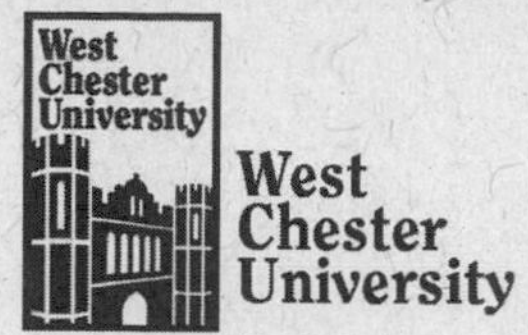

WEST CHESTER UNIVERSITY OF PENNSYLVANIA

Graduate Studies

Programs of Study

West Chester University of Pennsylvania offers graduate study leading to the M.A., M.B.A., M.Ed., M.M. (Master of Music), M.P.H., M.S., M.S.W., M.S.N., and M.P.A. degrees.

The Master of Arts is offered in communication studies, communicative disorders, English, French, geography and planning, geosciences, history, holocaust and genocide studies, mathematics, music history, philosophy, psychology (general, clinical, and industrial/organizational psychology), Spanish, and teaching English as a second language.

The Master of Business Administration is awarded in general business.

The Master of Education and/or certification is available in autism, early childhood education, elementary and secondary school counseling, applied studies in teaching and learning, reading, school health, secondary education, and special education. An online M.Ed.in special education is also offered.

The Master of Music is offered in music education, music theory or composition, music performance, and piano pedagogy.

The Master of Science is offered in applied statistics, biology, computer science, criminal justice, higher education counseling, and physical education.

The Master of Public Administration is awarded in three concentrations: human resource management, public administration, and nonprofit.

West Chester University also offers the Master of Public Health, the Master of Social Work, and the Master of Science in Nursing.

Research Facilities

The Francis Harvey Green Library houses more than 623,000 volumes, 7,700 print and electronic periodical subscriptions, and 72,500 audiovisual items. Its services include interlibrary loans, reference advice, computerized online literature searches, and an instructional materials center. The library's Web site provides continually updated access to a wide array of resources and services including PILOT, the library's catalog, and links to more than 180 specialized databases. The University makes Braille printers, translators, and speech synthesizers available to its visually impaired students. The Library houses a coffee café and a separate study lounge for graduate students.

The Merion Science Center houses a fully equipped observatory and planetarium and extensive, well-equipped laboratories. Boucher Hall has state-of-the-art science labs for electronics, mineral spectroscopy, optics, and liquid crystal studies as well as an animal facility and greenhouse.

Financial Aid

A limited number of graduate assistantships are available on a competitive basis. In 2010–11, each carried an annual stipend of $5000 plus remission of tuition. In addition, some summer assistantships are available. Frederick Douglass Graduate Assistantships are also available. Scholarships and awards are offered by individual departments as well. West Chester University also participates in the Federal Perkins Loan and the Federal Stafford Student Loan programs.

Cost of Study

The basic per-semester tuition for full-time in-state residents taking 9 to 15 credits in 2010–11 was $3483 plus a $691 general fee; part-time students were billed at a per-credit rate of $387 for tuition and a $65 general fee for fewer than 9 credits. Out-of-state students paid $5573 for 9 to 15 credits and the general fee; part-time students were billed at the per-credit rate of $619.

Living and Housing Costs

West Chester University offers limited on-campus housing for single graduate students. Choices include designated quiet and honors dormitories, as well as apartment living in a 4- or 5-person fully furnished unit, with each bedroom having either single or double occupancy. Current costs (subject to change) are $2405 (double) in the residence hall or $3040 (single) in the apartments.

Many meal plans are available to students and range in cost from $1088 to $1281 per semester.

The Office of Off-Campus and Commuter Services can provide assistance in identifying available off-campus housing. The office maintains listings and evaluations of apartments and rooms, many within walking distance of the campus.

Student Group

The student body at West Chester University numbers 14,492, of whom 2,258 are graduate students. The Graduate Student Association (GSA) represents graduate students and their interests. The School of Education sponsors an active chapter of Phi Delta Kappa, the international graduate honor society. African-American and Hispanic student unions are active at West Chester. In addition, graduate students are invited to participate in the activities of undergraduate honor societies in which they hold membership. These include Alpha Lambda Delta, Alpha Mu Gamma, Alpha Psi Omega, Gamma Theta Upsilon, Kappa Delta Pi, Pi Gamma Mu, Pi Kappa Delta, Pi Mu Epsilon, Sigma Alpha Iota, Psi Chi, Phi Alpha Theta, Phi Delta Kappa, Phi Epsilon Kappa, Phi Eta Sigma, Phi Kappa Delta, Phi Mu Alpha Sinfonia, and Sigma Delta Pi.

Location

The University is located in West Chester, a community in southeastern Pennsylvania strategically located at the center of the mid-Atlantic corridor. The seat of Chester County government for almost two centuries, West Chester retains much of its historical charm in its buildings and unspoiled countryside while offering the twenty-first-century advantages of a town in the heart of an expanding economic area. West Chester is just 25 miles west of Philadelphia and 17 miles north of Wilmington, Delaware.

Philadelphia is just an hour away, and travel to New York or Washington is possible in less than 3 hours.

The University

West Chester University is the largest of the fourteen institutions in the Pennsylvania State System of Higher Education and the fourth largest in the Philadelphia metropolitan area. Officially founded in 1871, the University traces its heritage to the West Chester Academy, which existed from 1812 to 1869. The University's quadrangle buildings, part of the original campus, are on the National Register of Historic Places, and its 385-acre campus features well-maintained facilities, including eight modern residence halls.

Applying

Applicants are encouraged to apply online at http://www.wcupa.edu/grad—click on Apply Now. Students should apply by April 15 for fall or October 15 for spring semester of entry. Students are required to submit official transcripts from all postsecondary institutions they have attended, two letters of recommendation, and scores on the General Test of the Graduate Record Examination (GRE), Graduate Management Admission Test (GMAT), or Miller Analogies Test (MAT).

Correspondence and Information

Lawrence J. Walsh Jr., M.A., Director of Graduate Enrollment
West Chester University
Office of Graduate Studies and Extended Education
102 West Rosedale Avenue
West Chester, Pennsylvania 19383
Phone: 610-436-2943
E-mail: gradstudy@wcupa.edu
Web site: http://www.wcupa.edu/grad

GRADUATE PROGRAM INFORMATION AND COORDINATORS

Listed below are West Chester University's graduate degree programs and the program coordinators. For information concerning a specific degree program, students should contact the graduate coordinator listed; for general admission information, they should contact the Office of Graduate Studies at gradstudy@wcupa.edu.

Administration (M.P.A.): Dr. Laurie Bernotsky (lbernotsky@wcupa.edu).
Applied Statistics (M.S.): Dr. Randall Reiger (rreiger@wcupa.edu).
Biology (M.S.): Dr. Sharon Began (sbegan@wcupa.edu).
Business (M.B.A.): Dr. Paul Christ (mba@wcupa.edu).
Communication Studies (M.A.): Dr. Denise Polk (dpolk@wcupa.edu).
Communicative Disorders (M.A.): Dr. Mareile Koenig (mkoenig@wcupa.edu).
Computer Science (M.S.): Dr. Afrand Agah (aagah@wcupa.edu).
Counselor Education (M.Ed., M.S., Specialist I certificate): Dr. Tina Alessandria (kalessandria@wcupa.edu).
Criminal Justice (M.S.): Dr. Mary Brewster (mbrewster@wcupa.edu).
Early Childhood Education: Dr. Catherine Prudhoe (cprudhoe@wcupa.edu).
Early and Middle Grades Education (M.Ed. and certification): Dr. Connie DiLucchio (cdilucchio@wcupa.edu).
English (M.A.): Dr. Carolyn Sorisio (csorisio@wcupa.edu).
Geography (M.A.): Dr. Joan Welch (jwelch@wcupa.edu).
Geosciences (M.A.): Dr. Martin Helmke (mhelmke@wcupa.edu).
Health (M.Ed. in school health): Dr. Bethann Cinelli (bcinelli@wcupa.edu).
Health (M.P.H.): Dr. Lynn Carson (lcarson@wcupa.edu).
History (M.A. in history): Dr. Tia Malkin-Fontecchio (tmalkin-fontecchio@wcupa.edu).
History (M.A. in holocaust and genocide studies): Dr. John Friedman (jfriedman@wcupa.edu).
Languages and Cultures (M.A. in French or Spanish): Dr. Rebecca Pauly (rpauly@wcupa.edu).
Mathematics (M.A.): Dr. Gail Gallitano (ggallitano@wcupa.edu).
Music (M.A. in music history and M.M. in music education, instrumental performance, keyboard performance, music theory and composition, and vocal/choral performance): Dr. Bryan Burton (Jburton3@wcupa.edu).
Nursing (M.S.N.): Dr. Ann Stowe (astowe@wcupa.edu).
Philosophy (M.A.): Dr. Matt Pierlott (mpierlott@wcupa.edu).
Physical Education (M.S. in physical education): Dr. Sheri Melton (smelton@wcupa.edu).
Psychology (M.A. in clinical, industrial/organizational, and general psychology): Dr. Vanessa Johnson (vjohnson@wcupa.edu).
Reading (M.Ed. and reading specialist certification): Dr. Kevin Flanigan (kflanigan@wcupa.edu).
Secondary Education (M.Ed.): Dr. Cynthia Haggard (chaggard@wcupa.edu).
Special Education (M.Ed. and certificate programs): Dr. Vicki McGinley, (vmcginley@wcupa.edu).
Social Work (M.S.W.): Dr. Ann Abbott (aabbott@wcupa.edu).
TESL (M.A. in teaching English as a second language): Dr. Charles Grove (cgrove@wcupa.edu).

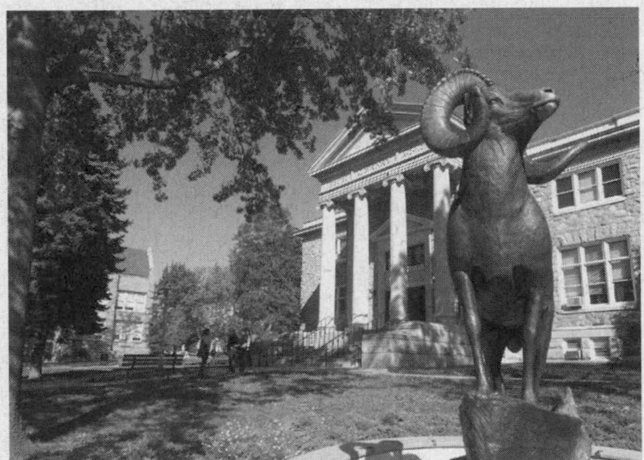

Ram mascot in front of Old Library.

Philips Memorial Hall.

WILLIAM PATERSON UNIVERSITY OF NEW JERSEY

Graduate Programs

Programs of Study

William Paterson University offers a wide range of degree programs, with additional certification and endorsement programs, in the University's five colleges: the College of the Arts and Communication, the Cotsakos College of Business, the College of Education, the College of Humanities and Social Sciences, and the College of Science and Health. Nine degrees are awarded: Master of Arts (M.A.), Master of Fine Arts (M.F.A.), Master of Science (M.S.), Master of Education (M.Ed.), Master of Business Administration (M.B.A.), Master of Arts in Teaching (M.A.T.), Master of Music (M.M.), Master of Science in Nursing (M.S.N.), and Doctor of Nursing Practice (D.N.P.). Degree requirements vary.

The M.A. is offered in clinical and counseling psychology, English (with concentrations in literature and writing), history, professional communication, public policy and international affairs, and applied sociology. The M.F.A. in art offers concentrations in fine arts, media arts, and design arts, with studio courses in ceramics, computer art and animation, textiles, furniture design, graphic design, painting, photography, printmaking, and sculpture; in addition, there is an M.F.A. in professional and creative writing. The M.S. is offered in biology, biotechnology, communication disorders (speech-language pathology), and exercise and sport studies. The M.Ed. is offered in professional counseling (with concentrations in mental health and school counseling), curriculum and learning (with concentrations in bilingual/English as a second language, early childhood, language arts, learning technologies, school library media, and teaching children mathematics), educational leadership, literacy (concentrations in language arts and reading), and special education (with specializations in advanced studies, developmental disability, and learning disability). The M.M. is offered in music, with concentrations in jazz studies, music education, and music management. The M.B.A. is offered with concentrations in accounting, entrepreneurship, finance, general business, marketing, and music management. The M.S.N. is offered in community-based nursing, with tracks in administration, advanced practice education, and nurse faculty scholar track. The M.A.T. is offered in teaching. The D.N.P. is in nursing practice.

The College of Education also offers teacher certification programs for college graduates who wish to obtain initial teaching certification in New Jersey, as well as endorsement programs for certified teachers who wish to obtain additional teaching certification.

Graduate nursing offers two school-nurse certification programs, a noninstructional track and an instructional track, which includes a teacher of health endorsement.

The University also offers two professional certificate programs: assessment and evaluation in research and skills certificate for sociology, and adult nurse practitioner certificate (post-master's).

Research Facilities

Biological science facilities are housed in the completely renovated Science Hall and newly constructed Science Hall West. They include a staffed laboratory-animal facility; behavior and neuroscience laboratories with spaces for animal surgery and behavioral and physiological research; honeybee colonies and observation hives; an advanced-microscopy suite (SEM, TEM, confocal, fluorescence); animal and plant cell-culture laboratories with CO2 incubators and laminar flow hoods; biotechnology laboratories fully equipped for DNA, RNA, and protein-biochemistry research; three large environmental growth chambers; a new five-bay research and collections greenhouse; and a dedicated field station for ecological studies. Nearby natural areas include a 1,000-acre preserve adjacent to campus.

Hobart Hall houses three broadcast-quality TV studios, two computer labs, a film studio, a presentation training room, an FCC-licensed FM radio station, an uplink and four downlink satellite dishes, a cable system, and digital editing workstations.

The Atrium is a state-of-the-art technology center on campus that holds more than 175 multimedia computers arranged in smart classrooms. The digital media center, which supports multimedia and Internet development, includes scanners, CD-ROM writers, digitizers, and related software tools. Similar digital media centers exist in Valley Road and the Science Building. There are 153 smart classrooms including forty computer labs across campus.

William Paterson University has a fiber-optic 10 gigabit Ethernet backbone interconnecting all faculty offices, classrooms, and laboratories.

The University is a member of NJEDge.Net, a nonprofit technology consortium of academic and research institutions in New Jersey.

In the University's Valley Road building, the Russ Berrie Institute Professional Sales Laboratory is fully equipped for videoconferencing and distance learning. In addition, the Financial Learning Center includes a ticker board, two wall boards that provide stock quotes and other data feeds, a 36-seat computer lab with dual screens for each student, and videoconferencing/long-distance learning facilities.

The David and Lorraine Cheng Library is open seven days a week when classes are in session and includes more than 360,000 volumes and more than 17,000 audiovisual items, with access to more than 50,000 electronic and print periodicals and journals. Approximately 100 databases serve the needs of students. Services include professional reference assistance (in person, by appointment, and chat), electronic reserves, interlibrary loan, group studies, and viewing facilities. Nonprint resources include software, DVDs, videocassettes, and streaming video. Wireless throughout, the library also has an Electronic Resource Center, a Group Tech Center, and a Presentation/Preview Room. The Graduate Research Center provides additional quiet space for graduate students.

Financial Aid

The University is participating in the Federal Direct Loan Program. This program consists of Federal Direct Stafford Student Loans (subsidized and unsubsidized) and the Federal Direct PLUS Loans (Graduate PLUS and Parent PLUS) program. Students must file the Free Application for Federal Student Aid (FAFSA) to determine their eligibility. The University makes a limited number of graduate assistantships available each year. Assistantships normally carry a stipend of $6000 and a waiver of tuition and fees. Graduate assistants must carry a minimum of 9 credits in each of the fall and spring semesters and work 20 hours per week in an assigned area. Graduate assistantships require a minimum grade point average of 3.0 and are awarded on the basis of availability and applicants' qualifications. Application forms are available in the Office of Graduate Studies. The University also participates in alternative/private loan programs. Information is available via the Alternative Student Loans link on http://www.wpunj.edu/finaid.

Cost of Study

In 2011–12, full-time graduate tuition and fees were $621 per credit for New Jersey residents and $964 per credit for out-of-state students. Tuition and fees are subject to change in accordance with policies established by the Board of Trustees.

Living and Housing Costs

On-campus housing is available for single graduate students. Housing options include suite-style, single, and double accommodations or apartment-style living offered in a grouping of 4 students to an apartment. Currently, on-campus housing costs range from $3090 to $4330 per semester, with meal plans available at an additional cost of $1000 to $2280 per semester. The University does not offer family student housing; however, off-campus housing is available in the areas surrounding the University.

Student Group

The University has more than 11,000 students, of whom 1,501 (13 percent) are graduate students. Eighty percent of the students enrolled in graduate programs pursue their studies on a part-time basis. The traditional service area of the University consists of New Jersey's northernmost counties.

Location

Set on a 370-acre wooded hilltop, the University commands a breathtaking view of the surrounding communities. Located 20 miles west of New York City, the campus is easily accessible from major highways that provide access to the cultural and educational resources available within the metropolitan area.

The University

Located on 370 wooded acres in suburban Wayne, New Jersey, William Paterson University provides a challenging, supportive, intellectual environment for more than 11,300 students enrolled in five academic colleges. Founded in 1855 and accredited by the Middle States Commission on Higher Education, William Paterson today offers more than 250 undergraduate and graduate academic programs, including a number of programs leading to endorsement for teacher certification and other professional licensing qualifications. Its advanced facilities provide students with a wide range of learning opportunities in its classrooms, laboratories, and studios, and throughout the campus, as well as at various off-campus locations. William Paterson's faculty members provide a valuable blend of accomplished scholarship and practical, applied experience. Its distinguished faculty includes 37 Fulbright Scholars and recipients of numerous other awards, grants, and fellowships. Students benefit from individualized attention from faculty mentors; small class sizes; and numerous research, internship, and clinical experiences. Financial aid, including a limited number of graduate assistantships, is available to qualified students.

Applying

To receive application information and materials, students should contact the Office of Graduate Admissions and Enrollment Services.

Correspondence and Information

Office of Graduate Admissions and Enrollment Services
William Paterson University of New Jersey
300 Pompton Road, Raubinger Room139
Wayne, New Jersey 07470-2103

Phone: 973-720-3641
973-720-2237
Fax: 973-720-2035
E-mail: graduate@wpunj.edu
Web site: http://www.wpunj.edu

GRADUATE PROGRAMS AND DIRECTORS

Doctor of Nursing Practice (D.N.P.): Professor Kem Louie (973-720-3215). The D.N.P. degree prepares advanced practice nurses and nurse administrators to be clinical scholars recognized for outstanding patient care outcomes and leadership in nursing practice and health-care organizations. The D.N.P. is the highest-level clinical degree in nursing as recognized by the American Association of Colleges of Nursing (AACN).

Art: Professor Thomas Uhlein (973-720-3289) and Professor Michael Rees. The M.F.A. program is designed as the professional degree for the fine artist, craftsperson, designer, or media artist or for those wishing to teach at the college or university level. Concentrations are available in fine arts, design arts, or media arts.

Bilingual/English as a Second Language: Professor Bruce Williams (973-720-3654).

Biology: Professor Pradeep Patnaik (973-720-3454). The M.S. in biology degree program offers students several areas of focus study, each a coherent course of study and research: physiology with an emphasis on neurobiology, ecology, and molecular biology with an emphasis on biotechnology, and general biology.

Biotechnology: Professor Pradeep Patnaik (973-720-3454). The M.S. in biotechnology program prepares students for a variety of opportunities in molecular biology, immunology, genetic engineering, and protein biochemistry.

Business Administration: Professor Frank Grippo (973-720-3118). The M.B.A. program is designed to provide students with both the background and perspective necessary for success in today's and tomorrow's business environments. Emphasis is placed on preparing students for the competitive global marketplace. Computer courses are designed to enhance students' skills by providing up-to-date software packages. The major areas of concentration are accounting, entrepreneurship, finance, management, marketing, music management, and general business.

Certification and Endorsement Programs: College of Education (973-720-3685). Certification programs are intended for graduates who wish to obtain initial teacher certification or endorsement (additional licenses) in the state of New Jersey.

Clinical and Counseling Psychology: Professor Bruce J. Diamond (973-720-3400). The M.A. program prepares students for the professional practice of psychological counseling, assessment, and mental-health research in nonschool settings.

Communication Disorders: Professor Nicole Magaldi (973-720-3353). This ASHA-accredited M.S. program provides students the training required to work as speech/language pathologists. As part of their course of study, students in the program gain valuable clinical experience working in the William Paterson Speech and Hearing Clinic, which offers clinical services in the diagnosis and treatment of speech and language disorders.

Creative and Professional Writing: Professor Phoebe Jackson (973-720-3704). This Master of Fine Arts program provides a supportive academic environment focused on the production of high-caliber writing. Designed to hone essential creative skills and nourish talent in poetry, fiction, memoir, literary biography, TV/film/theater scripts, cultural reviews, and more, the program's goal is to advance students' writing to a professionally competitive level.

Curriculum and Learning: Professor Rochelle Goldberg Kaplan (973-720-2598) and Professor Heejung An (973-720-2280). The M.Ed. program offers concentrations in bilingual/English as a second language, early childhood, learning technologies, middle school mathematics, high school mathematics, school library media, language arts, and teaching children mathematics.

Education Leadership: Professor Kevin Walsh (973-720-3136). The M.Ed. graduate program is designed for teachers who aspire to leadership positions in schools.

English: Professor Phoebe Jackson (973-720-3704). The M.A. in literature concentration: modern English and its background, major authors, early drama, and the novel; seventeenth- and eighteenth-century, romantic, Victorian, and modern British literature; nineteenth- and twentieth-century American literature; and related literature, including women's studies and film. The M.A. in writing concentration: creative writing, advanced critical writing, writing for the magazine market, fiction writing, poetry writing, book and magazine editing, teaching writing as process, journalism, and script writing for the media.

Exercise and Sport Studies: Professor Gordon Schmidt (973-720-2790). The M.S. program offers two concentrations: exercise physiology and sport pedagogy.

History: Professor George (Dewar) Macleod (973-720-3047). With an emphasis on global history, the curriculum of the M.A. program offers a wide range of courses that reflect changes in the discipline. Thematic courses, such as the history of crime, science, women, and sexuality complement the traditional menu of national histories.

Literacy: Professor Salika Lawrence (973-720-3088) and Professor Carrie Hong (973-720-2130). The M.Ed. program offers two major concentrations. The reading specialist concentration is designed for classroom teachers and reading professionals who are interested in extending their knowledge of teaching and learning. The language arts concentration focuses on the historical and developmental aspects of the English language as they occur in society in general and the elementary school environment in particular.

Music: Professor Timothy Newman (973-720-2373). The M.M. program is designed to help students achieve success in their music career as an arranger/composer, performer, educator, or manager. Areas of concentration include: music education, jazz studies (performance or arranging); and music management.

Nursing: Professor Kem Louie (973-720-3215). The M.S.N. program prepares students to function as advanced practice nurses (adult or family nurse practitioners), educators, or administrators in community-based settings, including home health-care. Through course work and clinical practice, the individual develops expertise in advanced health nursing care, leadership, and research skills.

Professional Communication: Professor Casey Lum (973-720-2342). The M.A. program is ideal for students and working professionals seeking success in communication fields, including public relations, management, integrated communication, corporate and strategic communication, news media, and professional writing.

* **Professional Counseling:** Professor Paula Danzinger (973-720-3085). The M.Ed. program consists of two separate concentrations: school counseling and mental-health counseling. This program is accredited by CACREP.

Public Policy and International Affairs: Professor Arnold Lewis (973-720-3873). The M.A. program provides the foundation for understanding how contemporary public policy crosses and supersedes national boundaries in an increasingly global environment of trade and information.

Applied Sociology: Professor Vincent Parrillo (973-720-3881). The M.A. in applied sociology emphasizes diagnostic skills and applied knowledge about diversity in the workplace and society, both of which are of great value in many occupations.

* **Special Education:** Professor Christopher Mulrine, M.Ed. with advanced studies (973-720-3123); Professor Peter Griswold, M.Ed. with learning disabilities (973-720-2118); Professor Jeanne D'Haem, M.Ed. with teacher of students with disabilities (973-720-2594).

* **Teaching:** Professor Julie Rosenthal (973-720-3087). The M.A.T. degree enables graduates to obtain elementary (K–5) teacher certification as well as elementary (K–5) teacher certification with 5–8 subject area endorsement.

**Teacher education programs are fully approved by the National Council of Accreditation of Teacher Education and meet the standards of the National Association of State Directors of Teacher Education and Certification.*

A view of the campus at William Paterson University of New Jersey.

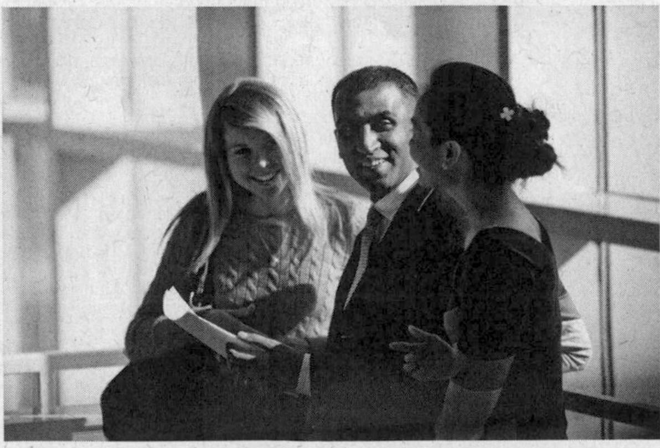

William Paterson University offers a wide range of degree programs

APPENDIXES

Institutional Changes Since the 2011 Edition

Following is an alphabetical listing of institutions that have recently closed, merged with other institutions, or changed their names or status. In the case of a name change, the former name appears first, followed by the new name.

Alliance Theological Seminary (Nyack, NY): now listed as a unit of Nyack College (Nyack, NY)

American InterContinental University (Houston, TX): name changed to American InterContinental University Houston

American InterContinental University Buckhead Campus (Atlanta, GA): closed

American InterContinental University Dunwoody Campus (Atlanta, GA): name changed to American InterContinental University Atlanta

American InterContinental University–London (London, United Kingdom): name changed to American InterContinental University London

Arkansas State University - Jonesboro (State University, AR): name changed to Arkansas State University

Bard Graduate Center for Studies in the Decorative Arts, Design, and Culture (New York, NY): name changed to Bard Graduate Center: Decorative Arts, Design History, Material Culture

Birmingham-Southern College (Birmingham, AL): no longer offers graduate degrees

California School of Podiatric Medicine at Samuel Merritt College (Oakland, CA): name changed to California School of Podiatric Medicine at Samuel Merritt University

Church of God Theological Seminary (Cleveland, TN): name changed to Pentecostal Theological Seminary

Clarke College (Dubuque, IA): name changed to Clarke University

College of Santa Fe (Santa Fe, NM): name changed to Santa Fe University of Art and Design and no longer offers graduate degrees

Dongguk Royal University (Los Angeles, CA): name changed to Dongguk University Los Angeles

Embry-Riddle Aeronautical University (Prescott, AZ): name changed to Embry-Riddle Aeronautical University–Prescott

Embry-Riddle Aeronautical University (Daytona Beach, FL): name changed to Embry-Riddle Aeronautical University–Daytona

Embry-Riddle Aeronautical University Worldwide (Daytona Beach, FL): name changed to Embry-Riddle Aeronautical University—Worldwide

Emily Carr Institute of Art & Design (Vancouver, BC, Canada): name changed to Emily Carr University of Art & Design

Emmanuel School of Religion (Johnson City, TN): name changed to Emmanuel Christian Seminary

Everest University (Clearwater, FL): no longer a campus of Everest University

Framingham State College (Framingham, MA): name changed to Framingham State University

Hannibal-LaGrange College (Hannibal, MO): name changed to Hannibal-LaGrange University

Hebrew Union College–Jewish Institute of Religion (Los Angeles, CA): merged into a single entry for Hebrew Union College–Jewish Institute of Religion (New York, NY) by request from the institution

Hebrew Union College–Jewish Institute of Religion (Cincinnati, OH): merged into a single entry for Hebrew Union College–Jewish Institute of Religion (New York, NY) by request from the institution

Jesuit School of Theology at Berkeley (Berkeley, CA): now listed as a unit of Santa Clara University (Santa Clara, CA)

Johnson Bible College (Knoxville, TN): name changed to Johnson University

Keller Graduate School of Management (Long Island City, NY): now listed as a unit of DeVry College of New York (Long Island City, NY)

Keller Graduate School of Management (New York, NY): now listed as a unit of DeVry University Manhattan Extension Site (New York, NY)

Lancaster Bible College & Graduate School (Lancaster, PA): name changed to Lancaster Bible College

Medical College of Georgia (Augusta, GA): name changed to Georgia Health Sciences University

Mennonite Brethren Biblical Seminary (Fresno, CA): name changed to Fresno Pacific Biblical Seminary and now a unit of Fresno Pacific University (Fresno, CA)

Meritus University (Fredericton, NB, Canada): closed

Mount Mercy College (Cedar Rapids, IA): name changed to Mount Mercy University

Mount Sinai School of Medicine of New York University (New York, NY): name changed to Mount Sinai School of Medicine

Northeastern Ohio Universities College of Medicine and Pharmacy (Rootstown, OH): name changed to Northeastern Ohio Universities Colleges of Medicine and Pharmacy

Polytechnic University of the Americas–Miami Campus (Miami, FL): name changed to Polytechnic University of Puerto Rico, Miami Campus

Polytechnic University of the Americas–Orlando Campus (Winter Park, FL): name changed to Polytechnic University of Puerto Rico, Orlando Campus

Salem State College (Salem, MA): name changed to Salem State University

Sherman College of Straight Chiropractic (Spartanburg, SC): name changed to Sherman College of Chiropractic

Union Theological Seminary and Presbyterian School of Christian Education (Richmond, VA): name changed to Union Presbyterian Seminary

University of Colorado at Boulder (Boulder, CO): name changed to University of Colorado Boulder

University of Phoenix–Western Washington Campus (Tukwila, WA): merged into a single entry for University of Phoenix–Washington Campus (Seattle, WA)

Vassar College (Poughkeepsie, NY): no longer offers graduate degrees

Western New England College (Springfield, MA): name changed to Western New England University

Western States Chiropractic College (Portland, OR): name changed to University of Western States

Westfield State College (Westfield, MA): name changed to Westfield State University

Westminster Choir College of Rider University (Princeton, NJ): name changed to Westminster Choir College and now a unit of Rider University (Lawrenceville, NJ)

West Suburban College of Nursing (Oak Park, IL): name changed to Resurrection University

Worcester State College (Worcester, MA): name changed to Worcester State University

Abbreviations Used in the Guides

The following list includes abbreviations of degree names used in the profiles in the 2012 edition of the guides. Because some degrees (e.g., Doctor of Education) can be abbreviated in more than one way (e.g., D.Ed. or Ed.D.), and because the abbreviations used in the guides reflect the preferences of the individual colleges and universities, the list may include two or more abbreviations for a single degree.

Degrees

Because some degrees (e.g., Doctor of Education) can be abbreviated in more than one way (e.g., D.Ed. or Ed.D.), and because the abbreviations used in the guides reflect the preferences of the individual colleges and universities, the list may include two or more abbreviations for a single degree.

A Mus D	Doctor of Musical Arts
AC	Advanced Certificate
AD	Artist's Diploma Doctor of Arts
ADP	Artist's Diploma
Adv C	Advanced Certificate
Adv M	Advanced Master
AGC	Advanced Graduate Certificate
AGSC	Advanced Graduate Specialist Certificate
ALM	Master of Liberal Arts
AM	Master of Arts
AMBA	Accelerated Master of Business Administration Aviation Master of Business Administration
AMRS	Master of Arts in Religious Studies
APC	Advanced Professional Certificate
APMPH	Advanced Professional Master of Public Health
App Sc	Applied Scientist
App Sc D	Doctor of Applied Science
Au D	Doctor of Audiology
B Th	Bachelor of Theology
CAES	Certificate of Advanced Educational Specialization
CAGS	Certificate of Advanced Graduate Studies
CAL	Certificate in Applied Linguistics
CALS	Certificate of Advanced Liberal Studies
CAMS	Certificate of Advanced Management Studies
CAPS	Certificate of Advanced Professional Studies
CAS	Certificate of Advanced Studies
CASPA	Certificate of Advanced Study in Public Administration
CASR	Certificate in Advanced Social Research
CATS	Certificate of Achievement in Theological Studies
CBHS	Certificate in Basic Health Sciences
CBS	Graduate Certificate in Biblical Studies
CCJA	Certificate in Criminal Justice Administration
CCSA	Certificate in Catholic School Administration
CCTS	Certificate in Clinical and Translational Science
CE	Civil Engineer
CEM	Certificate of Environmental Management
CET	Certificate in Educational Technologies
CGS	Certificate of Graduate Studies
Ch E	Chemical Engineer
CM	Certificate in Management
CMH	Certificate in Medical Humanities
CMM	Master of Church Ministries
CMS	Certificate in Ministerial Studies
CNM	Certificate in Nonprofit Management
CP	Certificate in Performance
CPASF	Certificate Program for Advanced Study in Finance
CPC	Certificate in Professional Counseling Certificate in Publication and Communication
CPH	Certificate in Public Health
CPM	Certificate in Public Management
CPS	Certificate of Professional Studies
CScD	Doctor of Clinical Science
CSD	Certificate in Spiritual Direction
CSS	Certificate of Special Studies
CTS	Certificate of Theological Studies
CURP	Certificate in Urban and Regional Planning
D Admin	Doctor of Administration
D Arch	Doctor of Architecture
D Com	Doctor of Commerce
D Couns	Doctor of Counseling
D Div	Doctor of Divinity
D Ed	Doctor of Education
D Ed Min	Doctor of Educational Ministry
D Eng	Doctor of Engineering
D Engr	Doctor of Engineering
D Ent	Doctor of Enterprise
D Env	Doctor of Environment
D Law	Doctor of Law
D Litt	Doctor of Letters
D Med Sc	Doctor of Medical Science
D Min	Doctor of Ministry
D Miss	Doctor of Missiology
D Mus	Doctor of Music
D Mus A	Doctor of Musical Arts
D Phil	Doctor of Philosophy
D Prof	Doctor of Professional Studies
D Ps	Doctor of Psychology
D Sc	Doctor of Science
D Sc D	Doctor of Science in Dentistry
D Sc IS	Doctor of Science in Information Systems
D Sc PA	Doctor of Science in Physician Assistant Studies
D Th	Doctor of Theology
D Th P	Doctor of Practical Theology
DA	Doctor of Accounting Doctor of Arts
DA Ed	Doctor of Arts in Education
DAH	Doctor of Arts in Humanities
DAOM	Doctorate in Acupuncture and Oriental Medicine
DAST	Diploma of Advanced Studies in Teaching
DBA	Doctor of Business Administration
DBH	Doctor of Behavioral Health
DBL	Doctor of Business Leadership
DBS	Doctor of Buddhist Studies
DC	Doctor of Chiropractic
DCC	Doctor of Computer Science
DCD	Doctor of Communications Design
DCL	Doctor of Civil Law Doctor of Comparative Law
DCM	Doctor of Church Music
DCN	Doctor of Clinical Nutrition
DCS	Doctor of Computer Science
DDN	Diplôme du Droit Notarial
DDS	Doctor of Dental Surgery
DE	Doctor of Education Doctor of Engineering
DED	Doctor of Economic Development
DEIT	Doctor of Educational Innovation and Technology
DEL	Doctor of Executive Leadership
DEM	Doctor of Educational Ministry
DEPD	Diplôme Études Spécialisées
DES	Doctor of Engineering Science
DESS	Diplôme Études Supérieures Spécialisées
DFA	Doctor of Fine Arts
DGP	Diploma in Graduate and Professional Studies
DH Ed	Doctor of Health Education
DH Sc	Doctor of Health Sciences
DHA	Doctor of Health Administration

DHCE	Doctor of Health Care Ethics
DHL	Doctor of Hebrew Letters Doctor of Hebrew Literature
DHS	Doctor of Health Science
DHSc	Doctor of Health Science
Dip CS	Diploma in Christian Studies
DIT	Doctor of Industrial Technology
DJ Ed	Doctor of Jewish Education
DJS	Doctor of Jewish Studies
DLS	Doctor of Liberal Studies
DM	Doctor of Management Doctor of Music
DMA	Doctor of Musical Arts
DMD	Doctor of Dental Medicine
DME	Doctor of Manufacturing Management Doctor of Music Education
DMEd	Doctor of Music Education
DMFT	Doctor of Marital and Family Therapy
DMH	Doctor of Medical Humanities
DML	Doctor of Modern Languages
DMP	Doctorate in Medical Physics
DMPNA	Doctor of Management Practice in Nurse Anesthesia
DN Sc	Doctor of Nursing Science
DNAP	Doctor of Nurse Anesthesia Practice
DNP	Doctor of Nursing Practice
DNS	Doctor of Nursing Science
DO	Doctor of Osteopathy
DOT	Doctor of Occupational Therapy
DPA	Doctor of Public Administration
DPC	Doctor of Pastoral Counseling
DPDS	Doctor of Planning and Development Studies
DPH	Doctor of Public Health
DPM	Doctor of Plant Medicine Doctor of Podiatric Medicine
DPPD	Doctor of Policy, Planning, and Development
DPS	Doctor of Professional Studies
DPT	Doctor of Physical Therapy
DPTSc	Doctor of Physical Therapy Science
Dr DES	Doctor of Design
Dr OT	Doctor of Occupational Therapy
Dr PH	Doctor of Public Health
Dr Sc PT	Doctor of Science in Physical Therapy
DRSc	Doctor of Regulatory Science
DS	Doctor of Science
DS Sc	Doctor of Social Science
DSJS	Doctor of Science in Jewish Studies
DSL	Doctor of Strategic Leadership
DSW	Doctor of Social Work
DTL	Doctor of Talmudic Law
DV Sc	Doctor of Veterinary Science
DVM	Doctor of Veterinary Medicine
DWS	Doctor of Worship Studies
EAA	Engineer in Aeronautics and Astronautics
ECS	Engineer in Computer Science
Ed D	Doctor of Education
Ed DCT	Doctor of Education in College Teaching
Ed L D	Doctor of Education Leadership
Ed M	Master of Education
Ed S	Specialist in Education
Ed Sp	Specialist in Education
EDB	Executive Doctorate in Business
EDM	Executive Doctorate in Management
EDSPC	Education Specialist
EE	Electrical Engineer
EJD	Executive Juris Doctor
EMBA	Executive Master of Business Administration
EMFA	Executive Master of Forensic Accounting
EMHA	Executive Master of Health Administration
EMIB	Executive Master of International Business
EML	Executive Master of Leadership
EMPA	Executive Master of Public Administration
EMPP	Executive Master's of Public Policy
EMS	Executive Master of Science
EMTM	Executive Master of Technology Management
Eng	Engineer
Eng Sc D	Doctor of Engineering Science
Engr	Engineer
Ex Doc	Executive Doctor of Pharmacy
Exec Ed D	Executive Doctor of Education
Exec MBA	Executive Master of Business Administration
Exec MPA	Executive Master of Public Administration
Exec MPH	Executive Master of Public Health
Exec MS	Executive Master of Science
G Dip	Graduate Diploma
GBC	Graduate Business Certificate
GCE	Graduate Certificate in Education
GDM	Graduate Diploma in Management
GDPA	Graduate Diploma in Public Administration
GDRE	Graduate Diploma in Religious Education
GEMBA	Global Executive Master of Business Administration
GEMPA	Gulf Executive Master of Public Administration
GM Acc	Graduate Master of Accountancy
GMBA	Global Master of Business Administration
GPD	Graduate Performance Diploma
GSS	Graduate Special Certificate for Students in Special Situations
IEMBA	International Executive Master of Business Administration
IM Acc	Integrated Master of Accountancy
IMA	Interdisciplinary Master of Arts
IMBA	International Master of Business Administration
IMES	International Master's in Environmental Studies
Ingeniero	Engineer
JCD	Doctor of Canon Law
JCL	Licentiate in Canon Law
JD	Juris Doctor
JSD	Doctor of Juridical Science Doctor of Jurisprudence Doctor of the Science of Law
JSM	Master of Science of Law
L Th	Licenciate in Theology
LL B	Bachelor of Laws
LL CM	Master of Laws in Comparative Law
LL D	Doctor of Laws
LL M	Master of Laws
LL M in Tax	Master of Laws in Taxation
LL M CL	Master of Laws (Common Law)
M Ac	Master of Accountancy Master of Accounting Master of Acupuncture
M Ac OM	Master of Acupuncture and Oriental Medicine
M Acc	Master of Accountancy Master of Accounting
M Acct	Master of Accountancy Master of Accounting
M Accy	Master of Accountancy
M Actg	Master of Accounting
M Acy	Master of Accountancy
M Ad	Master of Administration
M Ad Ed	Master of Adult Education
M Adm	Master of Administration
M Adm Mgt	Master of Administrative Management
M Admin	Master of Administration
M ADU	Master of Architectural Design and Urbanism
M Adv	Master of Advertising
M Aero E	Master of Aerospace Engineering
M AEST	Master of Applied Environmental Science and Technology
M Ag	Master of Agriculture
M Ag Ed	Master of Agricultural Education
M Agr	Master of Agriculture
M Anesth Ed	Master of Anesthesiology Education
M App Comp Sc	Master of Applied Computer Science

M App St	Master of Applied Statistics
M Appl Stat	Master of Applied Statistics
M Aq	Master of Aquaculture
M Arc	Master of Architecture
M Arch	Master of Architecture
M Arch I	Master of Architecture I
M Arch II	Master of Architecture II
M Arch E	Master of Architectural Engineering
M Arch H	Master of Architectural History
M Bioethics	Master in Bioethics
M Biomath	Master of Biomathematics
M Ch	Master of Chemistry
M Ch E	Master of Chemical Engineering
M Chem	Master of Chemistry
M Cl D	Master of Clinical Dentistry
M Cl Sc	Master of Clinical Science
M Comp	Master of Computing
M Comp E	Master of Computer Engineering
M Comp Sc	Master of Computer Science
M Coun	Master of Counseling
M Dent	Master of Dentistry
M Dent Sc	Master of Dental Sciences
M Des	Master of Design
M Des S	Master of Design Studies
M Div	Master of Divinity
M Ec	Master of Economics
M Econ	Master of Economics
M Ed	Master of Education
M Ed T	Master of Education in Teaching
M En	Master of Engineering Master of Environmental Science
M En S	Master of Environmental Sciences
M Eng	Master of Engineering
M Eng Mgt	Master of Engineering Management
M Engr	Master of Engineering
M Ent	Master of Enterprise
M Env	Master of Environment
M Env Des	Master of Environmental Design
M Env E	Master of Environmental Engineering
M Env Sc	Master of Environmental Science
M Fin	Master of Finance
M Geo E	Master of Geological Engineering
M Geoenv E	Master of Geoenvironmental Engineering
M Geog	Master of Geography
M Hum	Master of Humanities
M Hum Svcs	Master of Human Services
M IBD	Master of Integrated Building Delivery
M IDST	Master's in Interdisciplinary Studies
M Kin	Master of Kinesiology
M Land Arch	Master of Landscape Architecture
M Litt	Master of Letters
M Mat SE	Master of Material Science and Engineering
M Math	Master of Mathematics
M Mech E	Master of Mechanical Engineering
M Med Sc	Master of Medical Science
M Mgmt	Master of Management
M Mgt	Master of Management
M Min	Master of Ministries
M Mtl E	Master of Materials Engineering
M Mu	Master of Music
M Mus	Master of Music
M Mus Ed	Master of Music Education
M Music	Master of Music
M Nat Sci	Master of Natural Science
M Oc E	Master of Oceanographic Engineering
M Pet E	Master of Petroleum Engineering
M Pharm	Master of Pharmacy
M Phil	Master of Philosophy
M Phil F	Master of Philosophical Foundations
M Pl	Master of Planning
M Plan	Master of Planning
M Pol	Master of Political Science
M Pr Met	Master of Professional Meteorology
M Prob S	Master of Probability and Statistics
M Psych	Master of Psychology
M Pub	Master of Publishing
M Rel	Master of Religion
M S Ed	Master of Science Education
M Sc	Master of Science
M Sc A	Master of Science (Applied)
M Sc AHN	Master of Science in Applied Human Nutrition
M Sc BMC	Master of Science in Biomedical Communications
M Sc CS	Master of Science in Computer Science
M Sc E	Master of Science in Engineering
M Sc Eng	Master of Science in Engineering
M Sc Engr	Master of Science in Engineering
M Sc F	Master of Science in Forestry
M Sc FE	Master of Science in Forest Engineering
M Sc Geogr	Master of Science in Geography
M Sc N	Master of Science in Nursing
M Sc OT	Master of Science in Occupational Therapy
M Sc P	Master of Science in Planning
M Sc Pl	Master of Science in Planning
M Sc PT	Master of Science in Physical Therapy
M Sc T	Master of Science in Teaching
M SEM	Master of Sustainable Environmental Management
M Serv Soc	Master of Social Service
M Soc	Master of Sociology
M Sp Ed	Master of Special Education
M Stat	Master of Statistics
M Sys Sc	Master of Systems Science
M Tax	Master of Taxation
M Tech	Master of Technology
M Th	Master of Theology
M Tox	Master of Toxicology
M Trans E	Master of Transportation Engineering
M Urb	Master of Urban Planning
M Vet Sc	Master of Veterinary Science
MA	Master of Accounting Master of Administration Master of Arts
MA Missions	Master of Arts in Missions
MA Comm	Master of Arts in Communication
MA Ed	Master of Arts in Education
MA Ed Ad	Master of Arts in Educational Administration
MA Ext	Master of Agricultural Extension
MA Islamic	Master of Arts in Islamic Studies
MA Military Studies	Master of Arts in Military Studies
MA Min	Master of Arts in Ministry
MA Miss	Master of Arts in Missiology
MA Past St	Master of Arts in Pastoral Studies
MA Ph	Master of Arts in Philosophy
MA Psych	Master of Arts in Psychology
MA Sc	Master of Applied Science
MA Sp	Master of Arts (Spirituality)
MA Th	Master of Arts in Theology
MA-R	Master of Arts (Research)
MAA	Master of Administrative Arts Master of Applied Anthropology Master of Applied Arts Master of Arts in Administration
MAAA	Master of Arts in Arts Administration
MAAAP	Master of Arts Administration and Policy
MAAE	Master of Arts in Art Education
MAAT	Master of Arts in Applied Theology Master of Arts in Art Therapy
MAB	Master of Agribusiness
MABC	Master of Arts in Biblical Counseling Master of Arts in Business Communication
MABE	Master of Arts in Bible Exposition
MABL	Master of Arts in Biblical Languages

MABM	Master of Agribusiness Management
MABS	Master of Arts in Biblical Studies
MABT	Master of Arts in Bible Teaching
MAC	Master of Accountancy Master of Accounting Master of Arts in Communication Master of Arts in Counseling
MACC	Master of Arts in Christian Counseling Master of Arts in Clinical Counseling
MACCM	Master of Arts in Church and Community Ministry
MACCT	Master of Accounting
MACD	Master of Arts in Christian Doctrine
MACE	Master of Arts in Christian Education
MACFM	Master of Arts in Children's and Family Ministry
MACH	Master of Arts in Church History
MACI	Master of Arts in Curriculum and Instruction
MACIS	Master of Accounting and Information Systems
MACJ	Master of Arts in Criminal Justice
MACL	Master of Arts in Christian Leadership
MACM	Master of Arts in Christian Ministries Master of Arts in Christian Ministry Master of Arts in Church Music Master of Arts in Counseling Ministries
MACN	Master of Arts in Counseling
MACO	Master of Arts in Counseling
MAcOM	Master of Acupuncture and Oriental Medicine
MACP	Master of Arts in Counseling Psychology
MACS	Master of Arts in Catholic Studies
MACSE	Master of Arts in Christian School Education
MACT	Master of Arts in Christian Thought Master of Arts in Communications and Technology
MAD	Master in Educational Institution Administration Master of Art and Design
MADR	Master of Arts in Dispute Resolution
MADS	Master of Animal and Dairy Science Master of Applied Disability Studies
MAE	Master of Aerospace Engineering Master of Agricultural Economics Master of Agricultural Education Master of Architectural Engineering Master of Art Education Master of Arts in Education Master of Arts in English
MAEd	Master of Arts Education
MAEL	Master of Arts in Educational Leadership
MAEM	Master of Arts in Educational Ministries
MAEN	Master of Arts in English
MAEP	Master of Arts in Economic Policy
MAES	Master of Arts in Environmental Sciences
MAET	Master of Arts in English Teaching
MAF	Master of Arts in Finance
MAFE	Master of Arts in Financial Economics
MAFLL	Master of Arts in Foreign Language and Literature
MAFM	Master of Accounting and Financial Management
MAFS	Master of Arts in Family Studies
MAG	Master of Applied Geography
MAGU	Master of Urban Analysis and Management
MAH	Master of Arts in Humanities
MAHA	Master of Arts in Humanitarian Assistance Master of Arts in Humanitarian Studies
MAHCM	Master of Arts in Health Care Mission
MAHG	Master of American History and Government
MAHL	Master of Arts in Hebrew Letters
MAHN	Master of Applied Human Nutrition
MAHSR	Master of Applied Health Services Research
MAIA	Master of Arts in International Administration
MAIB	Master of Arts in International Business
MAICS	Master of Arts in Intercultural Studies
MAIDM	Master of Arts in Interior Design and Merchandising
MAIH	Master of Arts in Interdisciplinary Humanities
MAIOP	Master of Arts in Industrial/Organizational Psychology
MAIPCR	Master of Arts in International Peace and Conflict Management
MAIS	Master of Arts in Intercultural Studies Master of Arts in Interdisciplinary Studies Master of Arts in International Studies
MAIT	Master of Administration in Information Technology Master of Applied Information Technology
MAJ	Master of Arts in Journalism
MAJ Ed	Master of Arts in Jewish Education
MAJCS	Master of Arts in Jewish Communal Service
MAJE	Master of Arts in Jewish Education
MAJS	Master of Arts in Jewish Studies
MAL	Master in Agricultural Leadership
MALA	Master of Arts in Liberal Arts
MALD	Master of Arts in Law and Diplomacy
MALER	Master of Arts in Labor and Employment Relations
MALM	Master of Arts in Leadership Evangelical Mobilization
MALP	Master of Arts in Language Pedagogy
MALPS	Master of Arts in Liberal and Professional Studies
MALS	Master of Arts in Liberal Studies
MALT	Master of Arts in Learning and Teaching
MAM	Master of Acquisition Management Master of Agriculture and Management Master of Applied Mathematics Master of Arts in Management Master of Arts in Ministry Master of Arts Management Master of Avian Medicine
MAMB	Master of Applied Molecular Biology
MAMC	Master of Arts in Mass Communication Master of Arts in Ministry and Culture Master of Arts in Ministry for a Multicultural Church Master of Arts in Missional Christianity
MAME	Master of Arts in Missions/Evangelism
MAMFC	Master of Arts in Marriage and Family Counseling
MAMFCC	Master of Arts in Marriage, Family, and Child Counseling
MAMFT	Master of Arts in Marriage and Family Therapy
MAMHC	Master of Arts in Mental Health Counseling
MAMI	Master of Arts in Missions
MAMS	Master of Applied Mathematical Sciences Master of Arts in Ministerial Studies Master of Arts in Ministry and Spirituality
MAMT	Master of Arts in Mathematics Teaching
MAN	Master of Applied Nutrition
MANP	Master of Applied Natural Products
MANT	Master of Arts in New Testament
MAOL	Master of Arts in Organizational Leadership
MAOM	Master of Acupuncture and Oriental Medicine Master of Arts in Organizational Management
MAOT	Master of Arts in Old Testament
MAP	Master of Applied Psychology Master of Arts in Planning Master of Psychology Master of Public Administration
MAP Min	Master of Arts in Pastoral Ministry
MAPA	Master of Arts in Public Administration
MAPC	Master of Arts in Pastoral Counseling Master of Arts in Professional Counseling
MAPE	Master of Arts in Political Economy
MAPL	Master of Arts in Pastoral Leadership
MAPM	Master of Arts in Pastoral Ministry Master of Arts in Pastoral Music Master of Arts in Practical Ministry
MAPP	Master of Arts in Public Policy
MAPPS	Master of Arts in Asia Pacific Policy Studies
MAPS	Master of Arts in Pastoral Counseling/Spiritual Formation Master of Arts in Pastoral Studies Master of Arts in Public Service
MAPT	Master of Practical Theology
MAPW	Master of Arts in Professional Writing
MAR	Master of Arts in Religion
Mar Eng	Marine Engineer
MARC	Master of Arts in Rehabilitation Counseling
MARE	Master of Arts in Religious Education
MARL	Master of Arts in Religious Leadership

MARS Master of Arts in Religious Studies
MAS Master of Accounting Science
Master of Actuarial Science
Master of Administrative Science
Master of Advanced Study
Master of Aeronautical Science
Master of American Studies
Master of Applied Science
Master of Applied Statistics
Master of Archival Studies
MASA Master of Advanced Studies in Architecture
MASD Master of Arts in Spiritual Direction
MASE Master of Arts in Special Education
MASF Master of Arts in Spiritual Formation
MASJ Master of Arts in Systems of Justice
MASL Master of Arts in School Leadership
MASLA Master of Advanced Studies in Landscape Architecture
MASM Master of Aging Services Management
Master of Arts in Specialized Ministries
MASP Master of Applied Social Psychology
Master of Arts in School Psychology
MASPAA Master of Arts in Sports and Athletic Administration
MASS Master of Applied Social Science
Master of Arts in Social Science
MAST Master of Arts in Science Teaching
MASW Master of Aboriginal Social Work
MAT Master of Arts in Teaching
Master of Arts in Theology
Master of Athletic Training
Master's in Administration of Telecommunications
Mat E Materials Engineer
MATCM Master of Acupuncture and Traditional Chinese Medicine
MATDE Master of Arts in Theology, Development, and Evangelism
MATDR Master of Territorial Management and Regional Development
MATE Master of Arts for the Teaching of English
MATESL Master of Arts in Teaching English as a Second Language
MATESOL Master of Arts in Teaching English to Speakers of Other Languages
MATF Master of Arts in Teaching English as a Foreign Language/Intercultural Studies
MATFL Master of Arts in Teaching Foreign Language
MATH Master of Arts in Therapy
MATI Master of Administration of Information Technology
MATL Master of Arts in Teacher Leadership
Master of Arts in Teaching of Languages
Master of Arts in Transformational Leadership
MATM Master of Arts in Teaching of Mathematics
MATS Master of Arts in Theological Studies
Master of Arts in Transforming Spirituality
MATSL Master of Arts in Teaching a Second Language
MAUA Master of Arts in Urban Affairs
MAUD Master of Arts in Urban Design
MAURP Master of Arts in Urban and Regional Planning
MAWSHP Master of Arts in Worship
MAYM Master of Arts in Youth Ministry
MB Master of Bioinformatics
Master of Biology
MBA Master of Business Administration
MBA-AM Master of Business Administration in Aviation Management
MBA-EP Master of Business Administration–Experienced Professionals
MBAA Master of Business Administration in Aviation
MBAE Master of Biological and Agricultural Engineering
Master of Biosystems and Agricultural Engineering
MBAH Master of Business Administration in Health
MBAi Master of Business Administration–International
MBAICT Master of Business Administration in Information and Communication Technology
MBATM Master of Business Administration in Technology Management
MBC Master of Building Construction
MBE Master of Bilingual Education
Master of Bioengineering
Master of Bioethics
Master of Biological Engineering
Master of Biomedical Engineering
Master of Business and Engineering
Master of Business Economics
Master of Business Education
MBET Master of Business, Entrepreneurship and Technology
MBiotech Master of Biotechnology
MBIT Master of Business Information Technology
MBL Master of Business Law
Master of Business Leadership
MBLE Master in Business Logistics Engineering
MBMI Master of Biomedical Imaging and Signals
MBMSE Master of Business Management and Software Engineering
MBOE Master of Business Operational Excellence
MBS Master of Biblical Studies
Master of Biological Science
Master of Biomedical Sciences
Master of Bioscience
Master of Building Science
MBT Master of Biblical and Theological Studies
Master of Biomedical Technology
Master of Biotechnology
Master of Business Taxation
MC Master of Communication
Master of Counseling
Master of Cybersecurity
MC Ed Master of Continuing Education
MC Sc Master of Computer Science
MCA Master of Arts in Applied Criminology
Master of Commercial Aviation
MCAM Master of Computational and Applied Mathematics
MCC Master of Computer Science
MCCS Master of Crop and Soil Sciences
MCD Master of Communications Disorders
Master of Community Development
MCE Master in Electronic Commerce
Master of Christian Education
Master of Civil Engineering
Master of Control Engineering
MCEM Master of Construction Engineering Management
MCH Master of Chemical Engineering
MCHE Master of Chemical Engineering
MCIS Master of Communication and Information Studies
Master of Computer and Information Science
Master of Computer Information Systems
MCIT Master of Computer and Information Technology
MCJ Master of Criminal Justice
MCJA Master of Criminal Justice Administration
MCL Master in Communication Leadership
Master of Canon Law
Master of Comparative Law
MCM Master of Christian Ministry
Master of Church Music
Master of City Management
Master of Communication Management
Master of Community Medicine
Master of Construction Management
Master of Contract Management
Master of Corporate Media
MCMP Master of City and Metropolitan Planning
MCMS Master of Clinical Medical Science
MCN Master of Clinical Nutrition
MCP Master of City Planning
Master of Community Planning
Master of Counseling Psychology
Master of Cytopathology Practice
Master of Science in Quality Systems and Productivity
MCPC Master of Arts in Chaplaincy and Pastoral Care
MCPD Master of Community Planning and Development
MCR Master in Clinical Research
MCRP Master of City and Regional Planning
MCRS Master of City and Regional Studies

MCS	Master of Christian Studies Master of Clinical Science Master of Combined Sciences Master of Communication Studies Master of Computer Science Master of Consumer Science
MCSE	Master of Computer Science and Engineering
MCSL	Master of Catholic School Leadership
MCSM	Master of Construction Science/Management
MCST	Master of Science in Computer Science and Information Technology
MCTP	Master of Communication Technology and Policy
MCTS	Master of Clinical and Translational Science
MCVS	Master of Cardiovascular Science
MD	Doctor of Medicine
MDA	Master of Development Administration Master of Dietetic Administration
MDB	Master of Design-Build
MDE	Master of Developmental Economics Master of Distance Education Master of the Education of the Deaf
MDH	Master of Dental Hygiene
MDM	Master of Design Methods Master of Digital Media
MDP	Master of Development Practice
MDR	Master of Dispute Resolution
MDS	Master of Dental Surgery
ME	Master of Education Master of Engineering Master of Entrepreneurship Master of Evangelism
ME Sc	Master of Engineering Science
MEA	Master of Educational Administration Master of Engineering Administration
MEAP	Master of Environmental Administration and Planning
MEBT	Master in Electronic Business Technologies
MEC	Master of Electronic Commerce
MECE	Master of Electrical and Computer Engineering
Mech E	Mechanical Engineer
MED	Master of Education of the Deaf
MEDS	Master of Environmental Design Studies
MEE	Master in Education Master of Electrical Engineering Master of Energy Engineering Master of Environmental Engineering
MEEM	Master of Environmental Engineering and Management
MEENE	Master of Engineering in Environmental Engineering
MEEP	Master of Environmental and Energy Policy
MEERM	Master of Earth and Environmental Resource Management
MEH	Master in Humanistic Studies Master of Environmental Horticulture
MEHS	Master of Environmental Health and Safety
MEIM	Master of Entertainment Industry Management
MEL	Master of Educational Leadership Master of English Literature
MELP	Master of Environmental Law and Policy
MEM	Master of Ecosystem Management Master of Electricity Markets Master of Engineering Management Master of Environmental Management Master of Marketing
MEME	Master of Engineering in Manufacturing Engineering Master of Engineering in Mechanical Engineering
MENG	Master of Arts in English
MENVEGR	Master of Environmental Engineering
MEP	Master of Engineering Physics
MEPC	Master of Environmental Pollution Control
MEPD	Master of Education–Professional Development Master of Environmental Planning and Design
MER	Master of Employment Relations
MES	Master of Education and Science Master of Engineering Science Master of Environment and Sustainability Master of Environmental Science Master of Environmental Studies Master of Environmental Systems Master of Special Education
MESM	Master of Environmental Science and Management
MET	Master of Educational Technology Master of Engineering Technology Master of Entertainment Technology Master of Environmental Toxicology
Met E	Metallurgical Engineer
METM	Master of Engineering and Technology Management
MF	Master of Finance Master of Forestry
MFA	Master of Fine Arts
MFAM	Master in Food Animal Medicine
MFAS	Master of Fisheries and Aquatic Science
MFAW	Master of Fine Arts in Writing
MFC	Master of Forest Conservation
MFCS	Master of Family and Consumer Sciences
MFE	Master of Financial Economics Master of Financial Engineering Master of Forest Engineering
MFG	Master of Functional Genomics
MFHD	Master of Family and Human Development
MFM	Master of Financial Mathematics
MFMS	Master's in Food Microbiology and Safety
MFPE	Master of Food Process Engineering
MFR	Master of Forest Resources
MFRC	Master of Forest Resources and Conservation
MFS	Master of Food Science Master of Forensic Sciences Master of Forest Science Master of Forest Studies Master of French Studies
MFST	Master of Food Safety and Technology
MFT	Master of Family Therapy Master of Food Technology
MFWB	Master of Fishery and Wildlife Biology
MFWCB	Master of Fish, Wildlife and Conservation Biology
MFWS	Master of Fisheries and Wildlife Sciences
MFYCS	Master of Family, Youth and Community Sciences
MG	Master of Genetics
MGA	Master of Global Affairs Master of Governmental Administration
MGC	Master of Genetic Counseling
MGD	Master of Graphic Design
MGE	Master of Geotechnical Engineering
MGEM	Master of Global Entrepreneurship and Management
MGH	Master of Geriatric Health
MGIS	Master of Geographic Information Science Master of Geographic Information Systems
MGM	Master of Global Management
MGP	Master of Gestion de Projet
MGPS	Master of Global Policy Studies
MGREM	Master of Global Real Estate Management
MGS	Master of Gerontological Studies Master of Global Studies
MH	Master of Humanities
MH Ed	Master of Health Education
MH Sc	Master of Health Sciences
MHA	Master of Health Administration Master of Healthcare Administration Master of Hospital Administration Master of Hospitality Administration
MHA/MCRP	Master of Healthcare Administration/Master of City and Regional Planning
MHAD	Master of Health Administration
MHB	Master of Human Behavior
MHCA	Master of Health Care Administration

MHCI	Master of Human-Computer Interaction
MHCL	Master of Health Care Leadership
MHE	Master of Health Education Master of Human Ecology
MHE Ed	Master of Home Economics Education
MHEA	Master of Higher Education Administration
MHHS	Master of Health and Human Services
MHI	Master of Health Informatics Master of Healthcare Innovation
MHIIM	Master of Health Informatics and Information Management
MHIS	Master of Health Information Systems
MHK	Master of Human Kinetics
MHL	Master of Hebrew Literature
MHM	Master of Healthcare Management
MHMS	Master of Health Management Systems
MHP	Master of Health Physics Master of Heritage Preservation Master of Historic Preservation
MHPA	Master of Heath Policy and Administration
MHPE	Master of Health Professions Education
MHR	Master of Human Resources
MHRD	Master in Human Resource Development
MHRIR	Master of Human Resources and Industrial Relations
MHRLR	Master of Human Resources and Labor Relations
MHRM	Master of Human Resources Management
MHS	Master of Health Science Master of Health Sciences Master of Health Studies Master of Hispanic Studies Master of Human Services Master of Humanistic Studies
MHSA	Master of Health Services Administration
MHSM	Master of Health Systems Management
MI	Master of Instruction
MI Arch	Master of Interior Architecture
MI St	Master of Information Studies
MIA	Master of Interior Architecture Master of International Affairs
MIAA	Master of International Affairs and Administration
MIAM	Master of International Agribusiness Management
MIB	Master of International Business
MIBA	Master of International Business Administration
MICM	Master of International Construction Management
MID	Master of Industrial Design Master of Industrial Distribution Master of Interior Design Master of International Development
MIE	Master of Industrial Engineering
MIH	Master of Integrative Health
MIHTM	Master of International Hospitality and Tourism Management
MIJ	Master of International Journalism
MILR	Master of Industrial and Labor Relations
MiM	Master in Management
MIM	Master of Industrial Management Master of Information Management Master of International Management
MIMLAE	Master of International Management for Latin American Executives
MIMS	Master of Information Management and Systems Master of Integrated Manufacturing Systems
MIP	Master of Infrastructure Planning Master of Intellectual Property
MIPER	Master of International Political Economy of Resources
MIPP	Master of International Policy and Practice Master of International Public Policy
MIPS	Master of International Planning Studies
MIR	Master of Industrial Relations Master of International Relations
MIS	Master of Industrial Statistics Master of Information Science Master of Information Systems Master of Integrated Science Master of Interdisciplinary Studies Master of International Service Master of International Studies
MISE	Master of Industrial and Systems Engineering
MISKM	Master of Information Sciences and Knowledge Management
MISM	Master of Information Systems Management
MIT	Master in Teaching Master of Industrial Technology Master of Information Technology Master of Initial Teaching Master of International Trade Master of Internet Technology
MITA	Master of Information Technology Administration
MITM	Master of Information Technology and Management
MITO	Master of Industrial Technology and Operations
MJ	Master of Journalism Master of Jurisprudence
MJ Ed	Master of Jewish Education
MJA	Master of Justice Administration
MJM	Master of Justice Management
MJS	Master of Judicial Studies Master of Juridical Science
MKM	Master of Knowledge Management
ML	Master of Latin
ML Arch	Master of Landscape Architecture
MLA	Master of Landscape Architecture Master of Liberal Arts
MLAS	Master of Laboratory Animal Science Master of Liberal Arts and Sciences
MLAUD	Master of Landscape Architecture in Urban Development
MLD	Master of Leadership Development
MLE	Master of Applied Linguistics and Exegesis
MLER	Master of Labor and Employment Relations
MLHR	Master of Labor and Human Resources
MLI Sc	Master of Library and Information Science
MLIS	Master of Library and Information Science Master of Library and Information Studies
MLM	Master of Library Media
MLRHR	Master of Labor Relations and Human Resources
MLS	Master of Leadership Studies Master of Legal Studies Master of Liberal Studies Master of Library Science Master of Life Sciences
MLSP	Master of Law and Social Policy
MLT	Master of Language Technologies
MLTCA	Master of Long Term Care Administration
MM	Master of Management Master of Ministry Master of Missiology Master of Music
MM Ed	Master of Music Education
MM Sc	Master of Medical Science
MM St	Master of Museum Studies
MMA	Master of Marine Affairs Master of Media Arts Master of Musical Arts
MMAE	Master of Mechanical and Aerospace Engineering
MMAS	Master of Military Art and Science
MMB	Master of Microbial Biotechnology
MMBA	Managerial Master of Business Administration
MMC	Master of Manufacturing Competitiveness Master of Mass Communications Master of Music Conducting
MMCM	Master of Music in Church Music

MMCSS	Master of Mathematical Computational and Statistical Sciences
MME	Master of Manufacturing Engineering Master of Mathematics Education Master of Mathematics for Educators Master of Mechanical Engineering Master of Medical Engineering Master of Mining Engineering Master of Music Education
MMF	Master of Mathematical Finance
MMFT	Master of Marriage and Family Therapy
MMG	Master of Management
MMH	Master of Management in Hospitality Master of Medical Humanities
MMI	Master of Management of Innovation
MMIS	Master of Management Information Systems
MMM	Master of Manufacturing Management Master of Marine Management Master of Medical Management
MMME	Master of Metallurgical and Materials Engineering
MMP	Master of Management Practice Master of Marine Policy Master of Medical Physics Master of Music Performance
MMPA	Master of Management and Professional Accounting
MMQM	Master of Manufacturing Quality Management
MMR	Master of Marketing Research
MMRM	Master of Marine Resources Management
MMS	Master of Management Science Master of Management Studies Master of Manufacturing Systems Master of Marine Studies Master of Materials Science Master of Medical Science Master of Medieval Studies Master of Modern Studies
MMSE	Master of Manufacturing Systems Engineering
MMSM	Master of Music in Sacred Music
MMT	Master in Marketing Master of Management Master of Math for Teaching Master of Music Teaching Master of Music Therapy Master's in Marketing Technology
MMus	Master of Music
MN	Master of Nursing Master of Nutrition
MN NP	Master of Nursing in Nurse Practitioner
MNA	Master of Nonprofit Administration Master of Nurse Anesthesia
MNAL	Master of Nonprofit Administration and Leadership
MNAS	Master of Natural and Applied Science
MNCM	Master of Network and Communications Management
MNE	Master of Network Engineering Master of Nuclear Engineering
MNL	Master in International Business for Latin America
MNM	Master of Nonprofit Management
MNO	Master of Nonprofit Organization
MNPL	Master of Not-for-Profit Leadership
MNpS	Master of Nonprofit Studies
MNR	Master of Natural Resources
MNRES	Master of Natural Resources and Environmental Studies
MNRM	Master of Natural Resource Management
MNRS	Master of Natural Resource Stewardship
MNS	Master of Natural Science
MO	Master of Oceanography
MOD	Master of Organizational Development
MOGS	Master of Oil and Gas Studies
MOH	Master of Occupational Health
MOL	Master of Organizational Leadership
MOM	Master of Oriental Medicine
MOR	Master of Operations Research
MOT	Master of Occupational Therapy
MP	Master of Physiology Master of Planning
MP Ac	Master of Professional Accountancy
MP Acc	Master of Professional Accountancy Master of Professional Accounting Master of Public Accounting
MP Aff	Master of Public Affairs
MP Th	Master of Pastoral Theology
MPA	Master of Physician Assistant Master of Professional Accountancy Master of Professional Accounting Master of Public Administration Master of Public Affairs
MPAC	Master of Professional Accounting
MPAID	Master of Public Administration and International Development
MPAP	Master of Physician Assistant Practice Master of Public Affairs and Politics
MPAS	Master of Physician Assistant Science Master of Physician Assistant Studies
MPC	Master of Pastoral Counseling Master of Professional Communication Master of Professional Counseling
MPD	Master of Product Development Master of Public Diplomacy
MPDS	Master of Planning and Development Studies
MPE	Master of Physical Education Master of Power Engineering
MPEM	Master of Project Engineering and Management
MPH	Master of Public Health
MPH/MCRP	Master of Public Health/Mster of Community and Regional Planning
MPHE	Master of Public Health Education
MPHTM	Master of Public Health and Tropical Medicine
MPIA	Master in International Affairs Master of Public and International Affairs
MPM	Master of Pastoral Ministry Master of Pest Management Master of Policy Management Master of Practical Ministries Master of Project Management Master of Public Management
MPNA	Master of Public and Nonprofit Administration
MPO	Master of Prosthetics and Orthotics
MPOD	Master of Positive Organizational Development
MPP	Master of Public Policy
MPPA	Master of Public Policy Administration Master of Public Policy and Administration
MPPAL	Master of Public Policy, Administration and Law
MPPM	Master of Public and Private Management Master of Public Policy and Management
MPPPM	Master of Plant Protection and Pest Management
MPRTM	Master of Parks, Recreation, and Tourism Management
MPS	Master of Pastoral Studies Master of Perfusion Science Master of Planning Studies Master of Political Science Master of Preservation Studies Master of Prevention Science Master of Professional Studies Master of Public Service
MPSA	Master of Public Service Administration
MPSRE	Master of Professional Studies in Real Estate
MPT	Master of Pastoral Theology Master of Physical Therapy
MPVM	Master of Preventive Veterinary Medicine
MPW	Master of Professional Writing Master of Public Works
MQM	Master of Quality Management
MQS	Master of Quality Systems
MR	Master of Recreation Master of Retailing
MRA	Master in Research Administration
MRC	Master of Rehabilitation Counseling
MRCP	Master of Regional and City Planning Master of Regional and Community Planning
MRD	Master of Rural Development

MRE	Master of Real Estate Master of Religious Education
MRED	Master of Real Estate Development
MREM	Master of Resource and Environmental Management
MRLS	Master of Resources Law Studies
MRM	Master of Resources Management
MRP	Master of Regional Planning
MRS	Master of Religious Studies
MRSc	Master of Rehabilitation Science
MS	Master of Science
MS Cmp E	Master of Science in Computer Engineering
MS Kin	Master of Science in Kinesiology
MS Acct	Master of Science in Accounting
MS Accy	Master of Science in Accountancy
MS Aero E	Master of Science in Aerospace Engineering
MS Ag	Master of Science in Agriculture
MS Arch	Master of Science in Architecture
MS Arch St	Master of Science in Architectural Studies
MS Bio E	Master of Science in Bioengineering Master of Science in Biomedical Engineering
MS Bm E	Master of Science in Biomedical Engineering
MS Ch E	Master of Science in Chemical Engineering
MS Chem	Master of Science in Chemistry
MS Cp E	Master of Science in Computer Engineering
MS Eco	Master of Science in Economics
MS Econ	Master of Science in Economics
MS Ed	Master of Science in Education
MS El	Master of Science in Educational Leadership and Administration
MS En E	Master of Science in Environmental Engineering
MS Eng	Master of Science in Engineering
MS Engr	Master of Science in Engineering
MS Env E	Master of Science in Environmental Engineering
MS Exp Surg	Master of Science in Experimental Surgery
MS Int A	Master of Science in International Affairs
MS Mat E	Master of Science in Materials Engineering
MS Mat SE	Master of Science in Material Science and Engineering
MS Met E	Master of Science in Metallurgical Engineering
MS Mgt	Master of Science in Management
MS Min	Master of Science in Mining
MS Min E	Master of Science in Mining Engineering
MS Mt E	Master of Science in Materials Engineering
MS Otal	Master of Science in Otalrynology
MS Pet E	Master of Science in Petroleum Engineering
MS Phys	Master of Science in Physics
MS Poly	Master of Science in Polymers
MS Psy	Master of Science in Psychology
MS Pub P	Master of Science in Public Policy
MS Sc	Master of Science in Social Science
MS Sp Ed	Master of Science in Special Education
MS Stat	Master of Science in Statistics
MS Surg	Master of Science in Surgery
MS Tax	Master of Science in Taxation
MS Tc E	Master of Science in Telecommunications Engineering
MS-R	Master of Science (Research)
MSA	Master of School Administration Master of Science Administration Master of Science in Accountancy Master of Science in Accounting Master of Science in Administration Master of Science in Aeronautics Master of Science in Agriculture Master of Science in Anesthesia Master of Science in Architecture Master of Science in Aviation Master of Sports Administration
MSA Phy	Master of Science in Applied Physics
MSAA	Master of Science in Astronautics and Aeronautics
MSAAE	Master of Science in Aeronautical and Astronautical Engineering
MSABE	Master of Science in Agricultural and Biological Engineering
MSAC	Master of Science in Acupuncture
MSACC	Master of Science in Accounting
MSaCS	Master of Science in Applied Computer Science
MSAE	Master of Science in Aeronautical Engineering Master of Science in Aerospace Engineering Master of Science in Applied Economics Master of Science in Applied Engineering Master of Science in Architectural Engineering Master of Science in Art Education
MSAH	Master of Science in Allied Health
MSAL	Master of Sport Administration and Leadership
MSAM	Master of Science in Applied Mathematics
MSANR	Master of Science in Agriculture and Natural Resources Systems Management
MSAPM	Master of Security Analysis and Portfolio Management
MSAS	Master of Science in Applied Statistics Master of Science in Architectural Studies
MSAT	Master of Science in Accounting and Taxation Master of Science in Advanced Technology Master of Science in Athletic Training
MSB	Master of Science in Bible Master of Science in Business
MSBA	Master of Science in Business Administration Master of Science in Business Analysis
MSBAE	Master of Science in Biological and Agricultural Engineering Master of Science in Biosystems and Agricultural Engineering
MSBC	Master of Science in Building Construction
MSBE	Master of Science in Biological Engineering Master of Science in Biomedical Engineering
MSBENG	Master of Science in Bioengineering
MSBIT	Master of Science in Business Information Technology
MSBM	Master of Sport Business Management
MSBME	Master of Science in Biomedical Engineering
MSBMS	Master of Science in Basic Medical Science
MSBS	Master of Science in Biomedical Sciences
MSC	Master of Science in Commerce Master of Science in Communication Master of Science in Computers Master of Science in Counseling Master of Science in Criminology
MSCC	Master of Science in Christian Counseling Master of Science in Community Counseling
MSCD	Master of Science in Communication Disorders Master of Science in Community Development
MSCE	Master of Science in Civil Engineering Master of Science in Clinical Epidemiology Master of Science in Computer Engineering Master of Science in Continuing Education
MSCEE	Master of Science in Civil and Environmental Engineering
MSCF	Master of Science in Computational Finance
MSChE	Master of Science in Chemical Engineering
MSCI	Master of Science in Clinical Investigation Master of Science in Curriculum and Instruction
MSCIS	Master of Science in Computer and Information Systems Master of Science in Computer Information Science Master of Science in Computer Information Systems
MSCIT	Master of Science in Computer Information Technology
MSCJ	Master of Science in Criminal Justice
MSCJA	Master of Science in Criminal Justice Administration
MSCJPS	Master of Science in Criminal Justice and Public Safety
MSCJS	Master of Science in Crime and Justice Studies
MSCL	Master of Science in Collaborative Leadership
MSCLS	Master of Science in Clinical Laboratory Studies
MSCM	Master of Science in Church Management Master of Science in Conflict Management Master of Science in Construction Management
MScM	Master of Science in Management
MSCM	Master of Supply Chain Management
MSCNU	Master of Science in Clinical Nutrition

MSCP	Master of Science in Clinical Psychology Master of Science in Computer Engineering Master of Science in Counseling Psychology
MSCPE	Master of Science in Computer Engineering
MSCPharm	Master of Science in Pharmacy
MSCPI	Master in Strategic Planning for Critical Infrastructures
MSCR	Master of Science in Clinical Research
MSCRP	Master of Science in City and Regional Planning Master of Science in Community and Regional Planning
MSCS	Master of Science in Clinical Science Master of Science in Computer Science
MSCSD	Master of Science in Communication Sciences and Disorders
MSCSE	Master of Science in Computer Science and Engineering
MSCTE	Master of Science in Career and Technical Education
MSD	Master of Science in Dentistry Master of Science in Design Master of Science in Dietetics
MSDR	Master of Dispute Resolution
MSE	Master of Science Education Master of Science in Economics Master of Science in Education Master of Science in Engineering Master of Science in Engineering Management Master of Software Engineering Master of Special Education Master of Structural Engineering
MSECE	Master of Science in Electrical and Computer Engineering
MSED	Master of Sustainable Economic Development
MSEE	Master of Science in Electrical Engineering Master of Science in Environmental Engineering
MSEH	Master of Science in Environmental Health
MSEL	Master of Science in Educational Leadership
MSEM	Master of Science in Engineering Management Master of Science in Engineering Mechanics Master of Science in Environmental Management
MSENE	Master of Science in Environmental Engineering
MSEO	Master of Science in Electro-Optics
MSEP	Master of Science in Economic Policy
MSEPA	Master of Science in Economics and Policy Analysis
MSES	Master of Science in Embedded Software Engineering Master of Science in Engineering Science Master of Science in Environmental Science Master of Science in Environmental Studies
MSESM	Master of Science in Engineering Science and Mechanics
MSET	Master of Science in Educational Technology Master of Science in Engineering Technology
MSEV	Master of Science in Environmental Engineering
MSEVH	Master of Science in Environmental Health and Safety
MSF	Master of Science in Finance Master of Science in Forestry Master of Spiritual Formation
MSFA	Master of Science in Financial Analysis
MSFAM	Master of Science in Family Studies
MSFCS	Master of Science in Family and Consumer Science
MSFE	Master of Science in Financial Engineering
MSFOR	Master of Science in Forestry
MSFP	Master of Science in Financial Planning
MSFS	Master of Science in Financial Sciences Master of Science in Forensic Science
MSFSB	Master of Science in Financial Services and Banking
MSFT	Master of Science in Family Therapy
MSGC	Master of Science in Genetic Counseling
MSH	Master of Science in Health Master of Science in Hospice
MSHA	Master of Science in Health Administration
MSHCA	Master of Science in Health Care Administration
MSHCI	Master of Science in Human Computer Interaction
MSHCPM	Master of Science in Health Care Policy and Management
MSHE	Master of Science in Health Education
MSHES	Master of Science in Human Environmental Sciences
MSHFID	Master of Science in Human Factors in Information Design
MSHFS	Master of Science in Human Factors and Systems
MSHI	Master of Science in Health Informatics
MSHP	Master of Science in Health Professions Master of Science in Health Promotion
MSHR	Master of Science in Human Resources
MSHRL	Master of Science in Human Resource Leadership
MSHRM	Master of Science in Human Resource Management
MSHROD	Master of Science in Human Resources and Organizational Development
MSHS	Master of Science in Health Science Master of Science in Health Services Master of Science in Health Systems Master of Science in Homeland Security
MSHT	Master of Science in History of Technology
MSI	Master of Science in Information Master of Science in Instruction
MSIA	Master of Science in Industrial Administration Master of Science in Information Assurance and Computer Security
MSIB	Master of Science in International Business
MSIDM	Master of Science in Interior Design and Merchandising
MSIDT	Master of Science in Information Design and Technology
MSIE	Master of Science in Industrial Engineering Master of Science in International Economics
MSIEM	Master of Science in Information Engineering and Management
MSIID	Master of Science in Information and Instructional Design
MSIM	Master of Science in Information Management Master of Science in International Management
MSIMC	Master of Science in Integrated Marketing Communications
MSIR	Master of Science in Industrial Relations
MSIS	Master of Science in Information Science Master of Science in Information Systems Master of Science in Interdisciplinary Studies
MSISE	Master of Science in Infrastructure Systems Engineering
MSISM	Master of Science in Information Systems Management
MSISPM	Master of Science in Information Security Policy and Management
MSIST	Master of Science in Information Systems Technology
MSIT	Master of Science in Industrial Technology Master of Science in Information Technology Master of Science in Instructional Technology
MSITM	Master of Science in Information Technology Management
MSJ	Master of Science in Journalism Master of Science in Jurisprudence
MSJC	Master of Social Justice and Criminology
MSJE	Master of Science in Jewish Education
MSJFP	Master of Science in Juvenile Forensic Psychology
MSJJ	Master of Science in Juvenile Justice
MSJPS	Master of Science in Justice and Public Safety
MSJS	Master of Science in Jewish Studies
MSK	Master of Science in Kinesiology
MSL	Master of School Leadership Master of Science in Leadership Master of Science in Limnology Master of Strategic Leadership Master of Studies in Law
MSLA	Master of Science in Landscape Architecture Master of Science in Legal Administration
MSLD	Master of Science in Land Development
MSLFS	Master of Science in Life Sciences
MSLP	Master of Speech-Language Pathology
MSLS	Master of Science in Library Science
MSLSCM	Master of Science in Logistics and Supply Chain Management

MSLT Master of Second Language Teaching
MSM Master of Sacred Ministry
Master of Sacred Music
Master of School Mathematics
Master of Science in Management
Master of Science in Mathematics
Master of Science in Organization Management
Master of Security Management
MSMA Master of Science in Marketing Analysis
MSMAE Master of Science in Materials Engineering
MSMC Master of Science in Mass Communications
MSME Master of Science in Mathematics Education
Master of Science in Mechanical Engineering
MSMFE Master of Science in Manufacturing Engineering
MSMFT Master of Science in Marriage and Family Therapy
MSMIS Master of Science in Management Information Systems
MSMIT Master of Science in Management and Information Technology
MSMOT Master of Science in Management of Technology
MSMS Master of Science in Management Science
Master of Science in Medical Sciences
MSMSE Master of Science in Manufacturing Systems Engineering
Master of Science in Material Science and Engineering
Master of Science in Mathematics and Science Education
MSMT Master of Science in Management and Technology
Master of Science in Medical Technology
MSMus Master of Sacred Music
MSN Master of Science in Nursing
MSN-R Master of Science in Nursing (Research)
MSNA Master of Science in Nurse Anesthesia
MSNE Master of Science in Nuclear Engineering
MSNED Master of Science in Nurse Education
MSNM Master of Science in Nonprofit Management
MSNS Master of Science in Natural Science
Master of Science in Nutritional Science
MSOD Master of Science in Organizational Development
MSOEE Master of Science in Outdoor and Environmental Education
MSOES Master of Science in Occupational Ergonomics and Safety
MSOH Master of Science in Occupational Health
MSOL Master of Science in Organizational Leadership
MSOM Master of Science in Operations Management
Master of Science in Organization and Management
Master of Science in Oriental Medicine
MSOR Master of Science in Operations Research
MSOT Master of Science in Occupational Technology
Master of Science in Occupational Therapy
MSP Master of Science in Pharmacy
Master of Science in Planning
Master of Science in Psychology
Master of Speech Pathology
MSPA Master of Science in Physician Assistant
Master of Science in Professional Accountancy
MSPAS Master of Science in Physician Assistant Studies
MSPC Master of Science in Professional Communications
Master of Science in Professional Counseling
MSPE Master of Science in Petroleum Engineering
MSPG Master of Science in Psychology
MSPH Master of Science in Public Health
MSPH/M Ed Master of Science in Public Health/Master of Education
MSPH/MCRP Master of Science in Public Health/Msater of City and Regional Planning
MSPH/MSIS Master of Science in Public Health/Master of Science in Information Science
MSPH/MSLS Master of Science in Public Health/Master of Science in Library Science
MSPHR Master of Science in Pharmacy
MSPM Master of Science in Professional Management
Master of Science in Project Management
MSPNGE Master of Science in Petroleum and Natural Gas Engineering
MSPS Master of Science in Pharmaceutical Science
Master of Science in Political Science
Master of Science in Psychological Services
MSPT Master of Science in Physical Therapy
MSpVM Master of Specialized Veterinary Medicine
MSR Master of Science in Radiology
Master of Science in Reading
MSRA Master of Science in Recreation Administration
MSRC Master of Science in Resource Conservation
MSRE Master of Science in Real Estate
Master of Science in Religious Education
MSRED Master of Science in Real Estate Development
MSRLS Master of Science in Recreation and Leisure Studies
MSRMP Master of Science in Radiological Medical Physics
MSRS Master of Science in Rehabilitation Science
MSS Master of Science in Software
Master of Social Science
Master of Social Services
Master of Software Systems
Master of Sports Science
Master of Strategic Studies
MSSA Master of Science in Social Administration
MSSCP Master of Science in Science Content and Process
MSSD Master of Science in Sustainable Design
MSSE Master of Science in Software Engineering
Master of Science in Space Education
Master of Science in Special Education
MSSEM Master of Science in Systems and Engineering Management
MSSI Master of Science in Security Informatics
Master of Science in Strategic Intelligence
MSSL Master of Science in School Leadership
Master of Science in Strategic Leadership
MSSLP Master of Science in Speech-Language Pathology
MSSM Master of Science in Sports Medicine
MSSP Master of Science in Social Policy
MSSPA Master of Science in Student Personnel Administration
MSSS Master of Science in Safety Science
Master of Science in Systems Science
MSST Master of Science in Security Technologies
MSSW Master of Science in Social Work
MSSWE Master of Science in Software Engineering
MST Master of Science and Technology
Master of Science in Taxation
Master of Science in Teaching
Master of Science in Technology
Master of Science in Telecommunications
Master of Science Teaching
MSTC Master of Science in Technical Communication
Master of Science in Telecommunications
MSTCM Master of Science in Traditional Chinese Medicine
MSTE Master of Science in Telecommunications Engineering
Master of Science in Transportation Engineering
MSTM Master of Science in Technical Management
MSTOM Master of Science in Traditional Oriental Medicine
MSUD Master of Science in Urban Design
MSW Master of Social Work
MSWE Master of Software Engineering
MSWREE Master of Science in Water Resources and Environmental Engineering
MSX Master of Science in Exercise Science
MT Master of Taxation
Master of Teaching
Master of Technology
Master of Textiles
MTA Master of Tax Accounting
Master of Teaching Arts
Master of Tourism Administration
MTCM Master of Traditional Chinese Medicine
MTD Master of Training and Development
MTE Master in Educational Technology
MTESOL Master in Teaching English to Speakers of Other Languages
MTHM Master of Tourism and Hospitality Management
MTI Master of Information Technology

MTIM Master of Trust and Investment Management
MTL Master of Talmudic Law
MTM Master of Technology Management
Master of Telecommunications Management
Master of the Teaching of Mathematics
MTMH Master of Tropical Medicine and Hygiene
MTOM Master of Traditional Oriental Medicine
MTP Master of Transpersonal Psychology
MTPC Master of Technical and Professional Communication
MTR Master of Translational Research
MTS Master of Theological Studies
MTSC Master of Technical and Scientific Communication
MTSE Master of Telecommunications and Software Engineering
MTT Master in Technology Management
MTX Master of Taxation
MUA Master of Urban Affairs
MUD Master of Urban Design
MUEP Master of Urban and Environmental Planning
MUP Master of Urban Planning
MUPDD Master of Urban Planning, Design, and Development
MUPP Master of Urban Planning and Policy
MUPRED Master of Urban Planning and Real Estate Development
MURP Master of Urban and Regional Planning
Master of Urban and Rural Planning
MURPL Master of Urban and Regional Planning
MUS Master of Urban Studies
MVM Master of VLSI and Microelectronics
MVP Master of Voice Pedagogy
MVPH Master of Veterinary Public Health
MVS Master of Visual Studies
MWC Master of Wildlife Conservation
MWE Master in Welding Engineering
MWPS Master of Wood and Paper Science
MWR Master of Water Resources
MWS Master of Women's Studies
Master of Worship Studies
MZS Master of Zoological Science
Nav Arch Naval Architecture
Naval E Naval Engineer
ND Doctor of Naturopathic Medicine
NE Nuclear Engineer
Nuc E Nuclear Engineer
OD Doctor of Optometry
OTD Doctor of Occupational Therapy
PBME Professional Master of Biomedical Engineering
PD Professional Diploma
PGC Post-Graduate Certificate
PGD Postgraduate Diploma
Ph L Licentiate of Philosophy
Pharm D Doctor of Pharmacy
PhD Doctor of Philosophy
PhD Otal Doctor of Philosophy in Otalrynology
PhD Surg Doctor of Philosophy in Surgery
PhDEE Doctor of Philosophy in Electrical Engineering
PM Sc Professional Master of Science
PMBA Professional Master of Business Administration
PMC Post Master Certificate
PMD Post-Master's Diploma
PMS Professional Master of Science
Professional Master's
Post-Doctoral MS Post-Doctoral Master of Science
Post-MSN Certificate Post-Master of Science in Nursing Certificate
PPDPT Postprofessional Doctor of Physical Therapy
PSM Professional Master of Science
Professional Science Master's
Psy D Doctor of Psychology
Psy M Master of Psychology
Psy S Specialist in Psychology
Psya D Doctor of Psychoanalysis
Re Dir Director of Recreation
Rh D Doctor of Rehabilitation
S Psy S Specialist in Psychological Services
Sc D Doctor of Science
Sc M Master of Science
SCCT Specialist in Community College Teaching
ScDPT Doctor of Physical Therapy Science
SD Doctor of Science
Specialist Degree
SJD Doctor of Juridical Science
SLPD Doctor of Speech-Language Pathology
SM Master of Science
SM Arch S Master of Science in Architectural Studies
SM Vis S Master of Science in Visual Studies
SMBT Master of Science in Building Technology
SP Specialist Degree
Sp C Specialist in Counseling
Sp Ed Specialist in Education
Sp LIS Specialist in Library and Information Science
SPA Specialist in Arts
SPCM Special in Church Music
Spec Specialist's Certificate
Spec M Specialist in Music
SPEM Special in Educational Ministries
SPS School Psychology Specialist
Spt Specialist Degree
SPTH Special in Theology
SSP Specialist in School Psychology
STB Bachelor of Sacred Theology
STD Doctor of Sacred Theology
STL Licentiate of Sacred Theology
STM Master of Sacred Theology
TDPT Transitional Doctor of Physical Therapy
Th D Doctor of Theology
Th M Master of Theology
VMD Doctor of Veterinary Medicine
WEMBA Weekend Executive Master of Business Administration
XMA Executive Master of Arts
XMBA Executive Master of Business Administration

INDEXES

Profiles, Displays, and Close-Ups

Directories and Subject Areas

Following is an alphabetical listing of directories and subject areas. Also listed are cross-references for subject area names not used in the directory structure of the guides, for example, "Arabic (*see* Near and Middle Eastern Languages)."

Graduate Programs in the Humanities, Arts & Social Sciences

Addictions/Substance Abuse Counseling
Administration (*see* Arts Administration; Public Administration)
African-American Studies
African Languages and Literatures (*see* African Studies)
African Studies
Agribusiness (*see* Agricultural Economics and Agribusiness)
Agricultural Economics and Agribusiness
Alcohol Abuse Counseling (*see* Addictions/Substance Abuse Counseling)
American Indian/Native American Studies
American Studies
Anthropology
Applied Arts and Design—General
Applied Behavior Analysis
Applied Economics
Applied History (*see* Public History)
Applied Psychology
Applied Social Research
Arabic (*see* Near and Middle Eastern Languages)
Arab Studies (*see* Near and Middle Eastern Studies)
Archaeology
Architectural History
Architecture
Archives Administration (*see* Public History)
Area and Cultural Studies (*see* African-American Studies; African Studies; American Indian/Native American Studies; American Studies; Asian-American Studies; Asian Studies; Canadian Studies; Cultural Studies; East European and Russian Studies; Ethnic Studies; Folklore; Gender Studies; Hispanic Studies; Holocaust Studies; Jewish Studies; Latin American Studies; Near and Middle Eastern Studies; Northern Studies; Pacific Area/Pacific Rim Studies; Western European Studies; Women's Studies)
Art/Fine Arts
Art History
Arts Administration
Arts Journalism
Art Therapy
Asian-American Studies
Asian Languages
Asian Studies
Behavioral Sciences (*see* Psychology)
Bible Studies (*see* Religion; Theology)
Biological Anthropology
Black Studies (*see* African-American Studies)
Broadcasting (*see* Communication; Film, Television, and Video Production)
Broadcast Journalism
Building Science
Canadian Studies
Celtic Languages
Ceramics (*see* Art/Fine Arts)
Child and Family Studies
Child Development
Chinese
Chinese Studies (*see* Asian Languages; Asian Studies)
Christian Studies (*see* Missions and Missiology; Religion; Theology)
Cinema (*see* Film, Television, and Video Production)
City and Regional Planning (*see* Urban and Regional Planning)
Classical Languages and Literatures (*see* Classics)
Classics
Clinical Psychology
Clothing and Textiles
Cognitive Psychology (*see* Psychology—General; Cognitive Sciences)
Cognitive Sciences
Communication—General
Community Affairs (*see* Urban and Regional Planning; Urban Studies)
Community Planning (*see* Architecture; Environmental Design; Urban and Regional Planning; Urban Design; Urban Studies)
Community Psychology (*see* Social Psychology)
Comparative and Interdisciplinary Arts
Comparative Literature
Composition (*see* Music)
Computer Art and Design
Conflict Resolution and Mediation/Peace Studies
Consumer Economics
Corporate and Organizational Communication
Corrections (*see* Criminal Justice and Criminology)
Counseling (*see* Counseling Psychology; Pastoral Ministry and Counseling)
Counseling Psychology
Crafts (*see* Art/Fine Arts)
Creative Arts Therapies (*see* Art Therapy; Therapies—Dance, Drama, and Music)
Criminal Justice and Criminology
Cultural Anthropology
Cultural Studies
Dance
Decorative Arts
Demography and Population Studies
Design (*see* Applied Arts and Design; Architecture; Art/Fine Arts; Environmental Design; Graphic Design; Industrial Design; Interior Design; Textile Design; Urban Design)
Developmental Psychology
Diplomacy (*see* International Affairs)
Disability Studies
Drama Therapy (*see* Therapies—Dance, Drama, and Music)
Dramatic Arts (*see* Theater)
Drawing (*see* Art/Fine Arts)
Drug Abuse Counseling (*see* Addictions/Substance Abuse Counseling)
Drug and Alcohol Abuse Counseling (*see* Addictions/Substance Abuse Counseling)
East Asian Studies (*see* Asian Studies)
East European and Russian Studies
Economic Development
Economics
Educational Theater (*see* Theater; Therapies—Dance, Drama, and Music)
Emergency Management
English
Environmental Design
Ethics
Ethnic Studies
Ethnomusicology (*see* Music)
Experimental Psychology
Family and Consumer Sciences—General
Family Studies (*see* Child and Family Studies)
Family Therapy (*see* Child and Family Studies; Clinical Psychology; Counseling Psychology; Marriage and Family Therapy)
Filmmaking (*see* Film, Television, and Video Production)
Film Studies (*see* Film, Television, and Video Production)
Film, Television, and Video Production
Film, Television, and Video Theory and Criticism
Fine Arts (*see* Art/Fine Arts)
Folklore
Foreign Languages (*see* specific language)
Foreign Service (*see* International Affairs; International Development)
Forensic Psychology
Forensic Sciences
Forensics (*see* Speech and Interpersonal Communication)
French
Gender Studies
General Studies (*see* Liberal Studies)

Genetic Counseling
Geographic Information Systems
Geography
German
Gerontology
Graphic Design
Greek (*see* Classics)
Health Communication
Health Psychology
Hebrew (*see* Near and Middle Eastern Languages)
Hebrew Studies (*see* Jewish Studies)
Hispanic and Latin American Languages
Hispanic Studies
Historic Preservation
History
History of Art (*see* Art History)
History of Medicine
History of Science and Technology
Holocaust and Genocide Studies
Home Economics (*see* Family and Consumer Sciences—General)
Homeland Security
Household Economics, Sciences, and Management (*see* Family and Consumer Sciences—General)
Human Development
Humanities
Illustration
Industrial and Labor Relations
Industrial and Organizational Psychology
Industrial Design
Interdisciplinary Studies
Interior Design
International Affairs
International Development
International Economics
International Service (*see* International Affairs; International Development)
International Trade Policy
Internet and Interactive Multimedia
Interpersonal Communication (*see* Speech and Interpersonal Communication)
Interpretation (*see* Translation and Interpretation)
Islamic Studies (*see* Near and Middle Eastern Studies; Religion)
Italian
Japanese
Japanese Studies (*see* Asian Languages; Asian Studies; Japanese)
Jewelry (*see* Art/Fine Arts)
Jewish Studies
Journalism
Judaic Studies (*see* Jewish Studies; Religion)
Labor Relations (*see* Industrial and Labor Relations)
Landscape Architecture
Latin American Studies
Latin (*see* Classics)
Law Enforcement (*see* Criminal Justice and Criminology)
Liberal Studies
Lighting Design
Linguistics
Literature (*see* Classics; Comparative Literature; specific language)
Marriage and Family Therapy
Mass Communication
Media Studies
Medical Illustration
Medieval and Renaissance Studies
Metalsmithing (*see* Art/Fine Arts)
Middle Eastern Studies (*see* Near and Middle Eastern Studies)
Military and Defense Studies
Mineral Economics
Ministry (*see* Pastoral Ministry and Counseling; Theology)
Missions and Missiology
Motion Pictures (*see* Film, Television, and Video Production)
Museum Studies
Music
Musicology (*see* Music)
Music Therapy (*see* Therapies—Dance, Drama, and Music)
National Security
Native American Studies (*see* American Indian/Native American Studies)
Near and Middle Eastern Languages
Near and Middle Eastern Studies
Near Environment (*see* Family and Consumer Sciences)
Northern Studies
Organizational Psychology (*see* Industrial and Organizational Psychology)
Oriental Languages (*see* Asian Languages)
Oriental Studies (*see* Asian Studies)
Pacific Area/Pacific Rim Studies
Painting (*see* Art/Fine Arts)
Pastoral Ministry and Counseling
Philanthropic Studies
Philosophy
Photography
Playwriting (*see* Theater; Writing)
Policy Studies (*see* Public Policy)
Political Science
Population Studies (*see* Demography and Population Studies)
Portuguese
Printmaking (*see* Art/Fine Arts)
Product Design (*see* Industrial Design)
Psychoanalysis and Psychotherapy
Psychology—General
Public Administration
Public Affairs
Public History
Public Policy
Public Speaking (*see* Mass Communication; Rhetoric; Speech and Interpersonal Communication)
Publishing
Regional Planning (*see* Architecture; Urban and Regional Planning; Urban Design; Urban Studies)
Rehabilitation Counseling
Religion
Renaissance Studies (*see* Medieval and Renaissance Studies)
Rhetoric
Romance Languages
Romance Literatures (*see* Romance Languages)
Rural Planning and Studies
Rural Sociology
Russian
Scandinavian Languages
School Psychology
Sculpture (*see* Art/Fine Arts)
Security Administration (*see* Criminal Justice and Criminology)
Slavic Languages
Slavic Studies (*see* East European and Russian Studies; Slavic Languages)
Social Psychology
Social Sciences
Sociology
Southeast Asian Studies (*see* Asian Studies)
Soviet Studies (*see* East European and Russian Studies; Russian)
Spanish
Speech and Interpersonal Communication
Sport Psychology
Studio Art (*see* Art/Fine Arts)
Substance Abuse Counseling (*see* Addictions/Substance Abuse Counseling)
Survey Methodology
Sustainable Development
Technical Communication
Technical Writing
Telecommunications (*see* Film, Television, and Video Production)
Television (*see* Film, Television, and Video Production)
Textile Design
Textiles (*see* Clothing and Textiles; Textile Design)
Thanatology
Theater
Theater Arts (*see* Theater)
Theology
Therapies—Dance, Drama, and Music
Translation and Interpretation
Transpersonal and Humanistic Psychology
Urban and Regional Planning
Urban Design
Urban Planning (*see* Architecture; Urban and Regional Planning; Urban Design; Urban Studies)
Urban Studies

Video (*see* Film, Television, and Video Production)
Visual Arts (*see* Applied Arts and Design; Art/Fine Arts; Film, Television, and Video Production; Graphic Design; Illustration; Photography)
Western European Studies
Women's Studies
World Wide Web (*see* Internet and Interactive Multimedia)
Writing

Graduate Programs in the Biological Sciences

Anatomy
Animal Behavior
Bacteriology
Behavioral Sciences (*see* Biopsychology; Neuroscience; Zoology)
Biochemistry
Biological and Biomedical Sciences—General
Biological Chemistry (*see* Biochemistry)
Biological Oceanography (*see* Marine Biology)
Biophysics
Biopsychology
Botany
Breeding (*see* Botany; Plant Biology; Genetics)
Cancer Biology/Oncology
Cardiovascular Sciences
Cell Biology
Cellular Physiology (*see* Cell Biology; Physiology)
Computational Biology
Conservation (*see* Conservation Biology; Environmental Biology)
Conservation Biology
Crop Sciences (*see* Botany; Plant Biology)
Cytology (*see* Cell Biology)
Developmental Biology
Dietetics (*see* Nutrition)
Ecology
Embryology (*see* Developmental Biology)
Endocrinology (*see* Physiology)
Entomology
Environmental Biology
Evolutionary Biology
Foods (*see* Nutrition)
Genetics
Genomic Sciences
Histology (*see* Anatomy; Cell Biology)
Human Genetics
Immunology
Infectious Diseases
Laboratory Medicine (*see* Immunology; Microbiology; Pathology)
Life Sciences (*see* Biological and Biomedical Sciences)
Marine Biology
Medical Microbiology
Medical Sciences (*see* Biological and Biomedical Sciences)
Medical Science Training Programs (*see* Biological and Biomedical Sciences)
Microbiology
Molecular Biology
Molecular Biophysics
Molecular Genetics
Molecular Medicine
Molecular Pathogenesis
Molecular Pathology
Molecular Pharmacology
Molecular Physiology
Molecular Toxicology
Neural Sciences (*see* Biopsychology; Neurobiology; Neuroscience)
Neurobiology
Neuroendocrinology (*see* Biopsychology; Neurobiology; Neuroscience; Physiology)
Neuropharmacology (*see* Biopsychology; Neurobiology; Neuroscience; Pharmacology)
Neurophysiology (*see* Biopsychology; Neurobiology; Neuroscience; Physiology)
Neuroscience
Nutrition
Oncology (*see* Cancer Biology/Oncology)
Organismal Biology (*see* Biological and Biomedical Sciences; Zoology)
Parasitology
Pathobiology
Pathology
Pharmacology
Photobiology of Cells and Organelles (*see* Botany; Cell Biology; Plant Biology)
Physiological Optics (*see* Physiology)
Physiology
Plant Biology
Plant Molecular Biology
Plant Pathology
Plant Physiology
Pomology (*see* Botany; Plant Biology)
Psychobiology (*see* Biopsychology)
Psychopharmacology (*see* Biopsychology; Neuroscience; Pharmacology)
Radiation Biology
Reproductive Biology
Sociobiology (*see* Evolutionary Biology)
Structural Biology
Systems Biology
Teratology
Theoretical Biology (*see* Biological and Biomedical Sciences)
Therapeutics (*see* Pharmacology)
Toxicology
Translational Biology
Tropical Medicine (*see* Parasitology)
Virology
Wildlife Biology (*see* Zoology)
Zoology

Graduate Programs in the Physical Sciences, Mathematics, Agricultural Sciences, the Environment & Natural Resources

Acoustics
Agricultural Sciences
Agronomy and Soil Sciences
Analytical Chemistry
Animal Sciences
Applied Mathematics
Applied Physics
Applied Statistics
Aquaculture
Astronomy
Astrophysical Sciences (*see* Astrophysics; Atmospheric Sciences; Meteorology; Planetary and Space Sciences)
Astrophysics
Atmospheric Sciences
Biological Oceanography (*see* Marine Affairs; Marine Sciences; Oceanography)
Biomathematics
Biometry
Biostatistics
Chemical Physics
Chemistry
Computational Sciences
Condensed Matter Physics
Dairy Science (*see* Animal Sciences)
Earth Sciences (*see* Geosciences)
Environmental Management and Policy
Environmental Sciences
Environmental Studies (*see* Environmental Management and Policy)
Experimental Statistics (*see* Statistics)
Fish, Game, and Wildlife Management
Food Science and Technology
Forestry
General Science (*see* specific topics)
Geochemistry
Geodetic Sciences
Geological Engineering (*see* Geology)

Graduate Programs in Engineering & Applied Sciences

Robotics (*see* Artificial Intelligence/Robotics)
Safety Engineering
Software Engineering
Solid-State Sciences (*see* Materials Sciences)
Structural Engineering
Surveying Science and Engineering
Systems Analysis (*see* Systems Engineering)
Systems Engineering
Systems Science
Technology and Public Policy
Telecommunications
Telecommunications Management
Textile Sciences and Engineering
Textiles (*see* Textile Sciences and Engineering)
Transportation and Highway Engineering
Urban Systems Engineering (*see* Systems Engineering)
Waste Management (*see* Hazardous Materials Management)
Water Resources Engineering

Graduate Programs in Business, Education, Health, Information Studies, Law & Social Work

Accounting
Actuarial Science
Acupuncture and Oriental Medicine
Acute Care/Critical Care Nursing
Administration (*see* Business Administration and Management; Educational Administration; Health Services Management and Hospital Administration; Industrial and Manufacturing Management; Nursing and Healthcare Administration; Pharmaceutical Administration; Sports Management)
Adult Education
Adult Nursing
Advanced Practice Nursing (*see* Family Nurse Practitioner Studies)
Advertising and Public Relations
Agricultural Education
Alcohol Abuse Counseling (*see* Counselor Education)
Allied Health—General
Allied Health Professions (*see* Clinical Laboratory Sciences/Medical Technology; Clinical Research; Communication Disorders; Dental Hygiene; Emergency Medical Services; Occupational Therapy; Physical Therapy; Physician Assistant Studies; Rehabilitation Sciences)
Allopathic Medicine
Anesthesiologist Assistant Studies
Archival Management and Studies
Art Education
Athletics Administration (*see* Kinesiology and Movement Studies)
Athletic Training and Sports Medicine
Audiology (*see* Communication Disorders)
Aviation Management
Banking (*see* Finance and Banking)
Bioethics
Business Administration and Management—General
Business Education
Child-Care Nursing (*see* Maternal and Child/Neonatal Nursing)
Chiropractic
Clinical Laboratory Sciences/Medical Technology
Clinical Research
Communication Disorders
Community College Education
Community Health
Community Health Nursing
Computer Education
Continuing Education (*see* Adult Education)
Counseling (*see* Counselor Education)
Counselor Education
Curriculum and Instruction
Dental and Oral Surgery (*see* Oral and Dental Sciences)
Dental Assistant Studies (*see* Dental Hygiene)
Dental Hygiene
Dental Services (*see* Dental Hygiene)
Dentistry
Developmental Education
Distance Education Development
Drug Abuse Counseling (*see* Counselor Education)
Early Childhood Education
Educational Leadership and Administration
Educational Measurement and Evaluation
Educational Media/Instructional Technology
Educational Policy
Educational Psychology
Education—General
Education of the Blind (*see* Special Education)
Education of the Deaf (*see* Special Education)
Education of the Gifted
Education of the Hearing Impaired (*see* Special Education)
Education of the Learning Disabled (*see* Special Education)
Education of the Mentally Retarded (*see* Special Education)
Education of the Physically Handicapped (*see* Special Education)
Education of Students with Severe/Multiple Disabilities
Education of the Visually Handicapped (*see* Special Education)
Electronic Commerce
Elementary Education
Emergency Medical Services
English as a Second Language
English Education
Entertainment Management
Entrepreneurship
Environmental and Occupational Health
Environmental Education
Environmental Law
Epidemiology
Exercise and Sports Science
Exercise Physiology (*see* Kinesiology and Movement Studies)
Facilities and Entertainment Management
Family Nurse Practitioner Studies
Finance and Banking
Food Services Management (*see* Hospitality Management)
Foreign Languages Education
Forensic Nursing
Foundations and Philosophy of Education
Gerontological Nursing
Guidance and Counseling (*see* Counselor Education)
Health Education
Health Law
Health Physics/Radiological Health
Health Promotion
Health-Related Professions (*see* individual allied health professions)
Health Services Management and Hospital Administration
Health Services Research
Hearing Sciences (*see* Communication Disorders)
Higher Education
HIV/AIDS Nursing
Home Economics Education
Hospice Nursing
Hospital Administration (*see* Health Services Management and Hospital Administration)
Hospitality Management
Hotel Management (*see* Travel and Tourism)
Human Resources Development
Human Resources Management
Human Services
Industrial Administration (*see* Industrial and Manufacturing Management)
Industrial and Manufacturing Management
Industrial Education (*see* Vocational and Technical Education)
Industrial Hygiene
Information Studies
Instructional Technology (*see* Educational Media/Instructional Technology)
Insurance
Intellectual Property Law
International and Comparative Education
International Business
International Commerce (*see* International Business)
International Economics (*see* International Business)
International Health
International Trade (*see* International Business)
Investment and Securities (*see* Business Administration and Management; Finance and Banking; Investment Management)

Investment Management
Junior College Education (*see* Community College Education)
Kinesiology and Movement Studies
Laboratory Medicine (*see* Clinical Laboratory Sciences/Medical Technology)
Law
Legal and Justice Studies
Leisure Services (*see* Recreation and Park Management)
Leisure Studies
Library Science
Logistics
Management (*see* Business Administration and Management)
Management Information Systems
Management Strategy and Policy
Marketing
Marketing Research
Maternal and Child Health
Maternal and Child/Neonatal Nursing
Mathematics Education
Medical Imaging
Medical Nursing (*see* Medical/Surgical Nursing)
Medical Physics
Medical/Surgical Nursing
Medical Technology (*see* Clinical Laboratory Sciences/Medical Technology)
Medicinal and Pharmaceutical Chemistry
Medicinal Chemistry (*see* Medicinal and Pharmaceutical Chemistry)
Medicine (*see* Allopathic Medicine; Naturopathic Medicine; Osteopathic Medicine; Podiatric Medicine)
Middle School Education
Midwifery (*see* Nurse Midwifery)
Movement Studies (*see* Kinesiology and Movement Studies)
Multilingual and Multicultural Education
Museum Education
Music Education
Naturopathic Medicine
Nonprofit Management
Nuclear Medical Technology (*see* Clinical Laboratory Sciences/Medical Technology)
Nurse Anesthesia
Nurse Midwifery
Nurse Practitioner Studies (*see* Family Nurse Practitioner Studies)
Nursery School Education (*see* Early Childhood Education)
Nursing Administration (*see* Nursing and Healthcare Administration)
Nursing and Healthcare Administration
Nursing Education
Nursing—General
Nursing Informatics
Occupational Education (*see* Vocational and Technical Education)
Occupational Health (*see* Environmental and Occupational Health; Occupational Health Nursing)
Occupational Health Nursing
Occupational Therapy
Oncology Nursing
Optometry
Oral and Dental Sciences
Oral Biology (*see* Oral and Dental Sciences)
Oral Pathology (*see* Oral and Dental Sciences)
Organizational Behavior
Organizational Management
Oriental Medicine and Acupuncture (*see* Acupuncture and Oriental Medicine)
Orthodontics (*see* Oral and Dental Sciences)
Osteopathic Medicine
Parks Administration (*see* Recreation and Park Management)
Pediatric Nursing
Pedontics (*see* Oral and Dental Sciences)
Perfusion
Personnel (*see* Human Resources Development; Human Resources Management; Organizational Behavior; Organizational Management; Student Affairs)
Pharmaceutical Administration
Pharmaceutical Chemistry (*see* Medicinal and Pharmaceutical Chemistry)
Pharmaceutical Sciences
Pharmacy
Philosophy of Education (*see* Foundations and Philosophy of Education)
Physical Education
Physical Therapy
Physician Assistant Studies
Physiological Optics (*see* Vision Sciences)
Podiatric Medicine
Preventive Medicine (*see* Community Health and Public Health)
Project Management
Psychiatric Nursing
Public Health—General
Public Health Nursing (*see* Community Health Nursing)
Public Relations (*see* Advertising and Public Relations)
Quality Management
Quantitative Analysis
Radiological Health (*see* Health Physics/Radiological Health)
Reading Education
Real Estate
Recreation and Park Management
Recreation Therapy (*see* Recreation and Park Management)
Rehabilitation Sciences
Rehabilitation Therapy (*see* Physical Therapy)
Religious Education
Remedial Education (*see* Special Education)
Restaurant Administration (*see* Hospitality Management)
School Nursing
Science Education
Secondary Education
Social Sciences Education
Social Studies Education (*see* Social Sciences Education)
Social Work
Special Education
Speech-Language Pathology and Audiology (*see* Communication Disorders)
Sports Management
Sports Medicine (*see* Athletic Training and Sports Medicine)
Sports Psychology and Sociology (*see* Kinesiology and Movement Studies)
Student Affairs
Substance Abuse Counseling (*see* Counselor Education)
Supply Chain Management
Surgical Nursing (*see* Medical/Surgical Nursing)
Sustainability Management
Systems Management (*see* Management Information Systems)
Taxation
Teacher Education (*see* specific subject areas)
Teaching English as a Second Language (*see* English as a Second Language)
Technical Education (*see* Vocational and Technical Education)
Teratology (*see* Environmental and Occupational Health)
Therapeutics (*see* Pharmaceutical Sciences; Pharmacy)
Transcultural Nursing
Transportation Management
Travel and Tourism
Urban Education
Veterinary Medicine
Veterinary Sciences
Vision Sciences
Vocational and Technical Education
Vocational Counseling (*see* Counselor Education)
Women's Health Nursing

Special Advertising Section

Cell & Molecular Biology

Graduate School of Biomedical Sciences

University of Medicine & Dentistry of New Jersey
Stratford, NJ

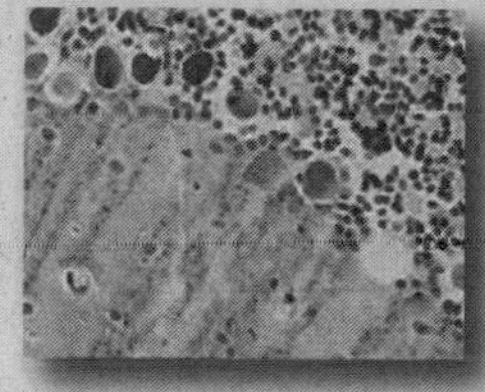

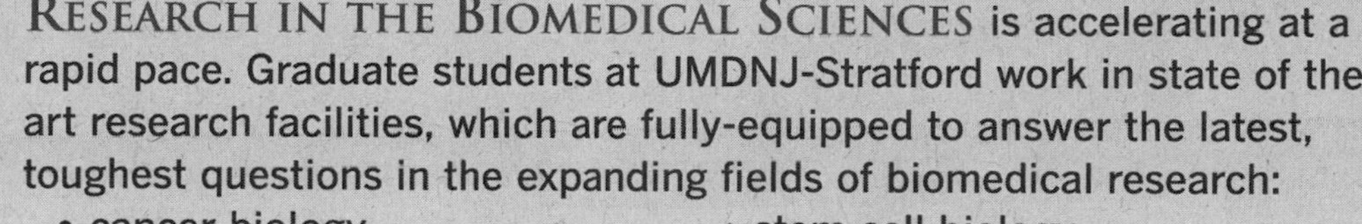

Research in the Biomedical Sciences is accelerating at a rapid pace. Graduate students at UMDNJ-Stratford work in state of the art research facilities, which are fully-equipped to answer the latest, toughest questions in the expanding fields of biomedical research:

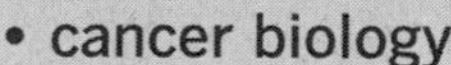

- cancer biology
- developmental genetics
- transcription mechanisms
- meiosis and fertility
- circadian rhythms
- stem cell biology
- microRNAs
- ribosome biogenesis
- models of human disease
- DNA repair and replication

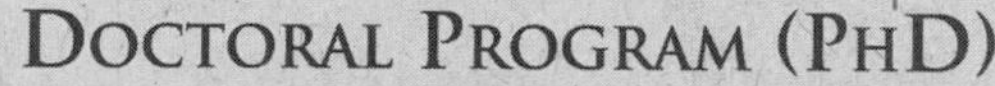

Doctoral Program (PhD)

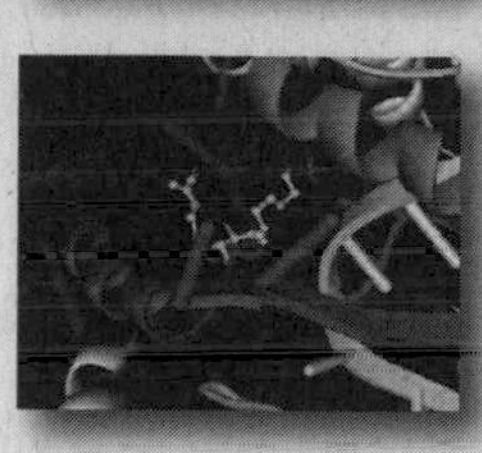

Curriculum Courses:

Core: Biochemistry, Molecular Biology of the Cell

Skills: Experimental Design, Critical Readings, Scientific Writing, Ethics

Focus: Genetics, Cancer, Cell Culture & Stem Cells, Bioinformatics

Immediate lab experience and within a year begin dissertation research

Competitive stipend and tuition waived

Masters Program (MBS or MS)

Master of Biomedical Science (non-thesis)

Master of Science in the Biomedical Sciences (thesis)

Master of Science in Molecular Pathology and Immunology (thesis)

Summer Undergraduate Research Experience

Hands-on research experience	No tuition
Competitive stipend	10 week program

Combined Degree Programs (with MPH or DO)

Search: GSBS Stratford
som.umdnj.edu/gsbstrat

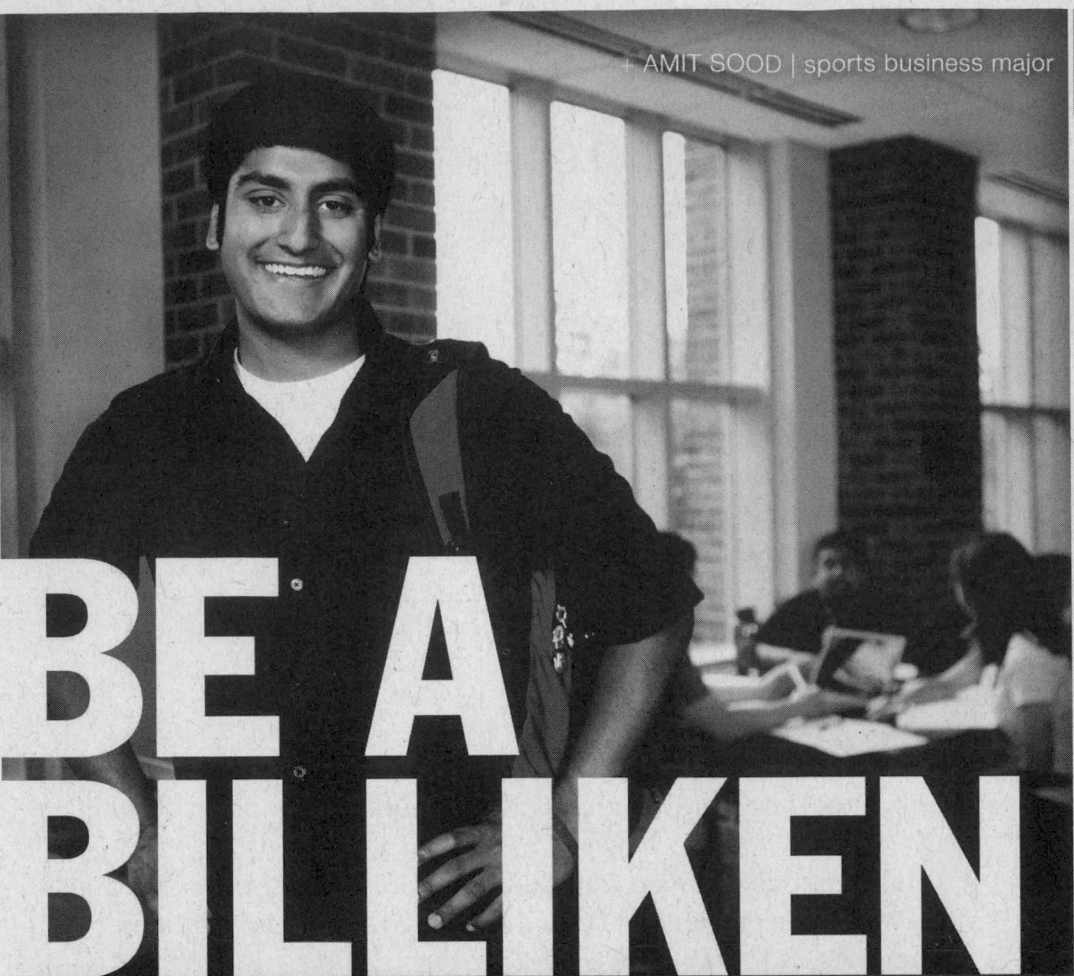

NOTES

NOTES